HARRAP'S SHORTER

DICTIONARY
English-French / French-English

DICTIONNAIRE
Anglais-Français / Français-Anglais

HARRAP'S SHORTER

DICTIONARY

English-French / French-English

HARRAP

HARRAP'S SHORTER

DICTIONNAIRE

Anglais-Français / Français-Anglais

HARRAP

This edition first published in 1996
by Chambers Harrap Publishers Ltd
43-45 Annandale Street, Edinburgh EH7 4AZ, UK

Dépôt Légal: février 1996

The previous edition of
Harrap's Shorter French and English Dictionary
was first published in 1991
Reprinted 1992 (twice)
Reprinted with supplement 1993 (twice), 1994, 1995 (twice)

Printed in new format 1987
Reprinted 1987 (three times), 1988, 1989, 1990

ISBN 0 245 60524 X (standard edition, UK)
ISBN 0 245 60572 X (thumb-indexed edition, UK)
ISBN 0 245 502963 (standard edition, France)

Library of Congress Cataloging in
Publication Data for this book is available
from The Library of Congress

Typeset in Great Britain at the University Press, Cambridge

Printed and bound in France by Partenaires

CONTRIBUTORS / COLLABORATEURS

Editor-in-Chief / Rédacteur en chef
Peter Terrell

Managing Editor / Coordination éditoriale
Katharine Coates

Editors / Rédacteurs
Timothy Gutteridge
Isabelle Elkaim
Stuart Fortey
Jane Goldie
Laurence Hautekeur
Nathalie Le Gall
Nadine Mongeard Morandi
Georges Pilard
Liam Rodger
Catherine Roux
Anna Stevenson

Other Contributors / Autres collaborateurs
Elisabeth Campbell
Sophie Marin
Dr Mary Rigby
Jean-Pierre Roudgé

Terminologists / Terminologues
Patricia Clarke
Michel Celemenski
Jean Gaillard
Céline Haddad
Claude Henri Perrin
Claudine Rebersat
M J Shields, MITI
Steve Steadman
Catherine Stringer

Proofreaders / Correcteurs
Elizabeth Cunningham
Susan Dunsmore
Jacqueline Gregan
Margaret Hill
Irene Lakhani
Ruth Rae
Sheilagh Wilson
Ann Williamson

Data Management / Informatique éditoriale
Ilona Morison
Lesley Cameron
Elaine McAdam

Administration / Administration
Alison Barr
Louise McGinnity

Keyboarders / Clavistes
Sarah Geere
Michelle Lochhead
Marian Shepherd
Isabelle Vitale

CONTENTS / TABLE DES MATIÈRES

PREFACE

For most of this century, Harrap's *Shorter Dictionary* has been the standard work of reference bridging the language gap between the English- and French-speaking communities. This new edition, the result of several years' work by a sizeable team of French and English lexicographers, brings the benefits of developments in linguistics and information technology to Harrap's widely acknowledged expertise and resources.

The needs of today's bilingual dictionary users - specialist translators, students and general readers - were carefully considered in establishing the objectives for the editorial team. These were to produce still better coverage of general usage and a significant enrichment of specialist vocabulary, so that the dictionary will provide the gateway to every aspect of written and spoken English and French.

Many thousands of additional entries have been introduced, reflecting the dynamic nature of language in a fast-changing multicultural world. Key areas of new vocabulary range from IT and finance to medicine, the media and marketing.

The breadth of vocabulary, the richness of idiom and the coverage of British and North American English and regional varieties of French will satisfy the most demanding users.

The systematic use of semantic signposts, in the form of source language indicators and collocators, ensures that the user will be guided to a translation of the correct sense or usage of a word or phrase. Ease of reference is enhanced by maximizing the number of entries presented as headwords.

The French and English languages will continue to evolve but this new edition of Harrap's *Shorter Dictionary* will provide comprehensive, reliable guidance for all those wishing to cross the bridge between them for many years to come.

Harrap, 1996

PRÉFACE

Depuis bien des années, le Harrap's *Shorter* est le plus couramment utilisé des dictionnaires français-anglais. Pour cette nouvelle édition, Harrap a mis à profit les progrès de la linguistique et de l'informatique afin de perfectionner son dictionnaire déjà reconnu pour sa qualité et la richesse de ses informations.

Les besoins de l'utilisateur d'aujourd'hui (traducteurs professionnels, étudiants, grand public) ont été soigneusement pris en considération avant que ne soient établis les objectifs de notre équipe de rédacteurs. Ainsi, il nous a été possible de réaliser un ouvrage encore plus riche, tant en vocabulaire de base que dans des domaines spécialisés, et qui traite de tous les aspects de la langue parlée comme de la langue écrite.

Plusieurs milliers de mots et d'expressions ont été ajoutés afin de refléter la langue toujours changeante d'un monde multiculturel sans cesse en mouvement. Ce vocabulaire a été sélectionné dans des domaines aussi divers que l'informatique, la finance, la médecine, les médias ou le marketing.

L'étendue du vocabulaire, la richesse de la langue, les anglicismes, les américanismes, les canadianismes et les exemples de français régional ne manqueront pas de satisfaire jusqu'aux utilisateurs les plus exigeants.

L'utilisation systématique d'indicateurs clairs en langue source, qu'ils soient synonymes ou collocateurs, permettra au lecteur d'identifier sans risque d'erreur la traduction du sens ou de l'usage recherché. L'ouvrage est enfin plus facile à consulter, grâce à l'accroissement du nombre d'expressions faisant désormais l'objet d'entrées à part entière.

Nul doute que le français et l'anglais continueront à changer mais il est certain que cette nouvelle édition du Harrap's *Shorter*, grâce à sa fiabilité et à son exhaustivité, guidera l'utilisateur dans ses recherches pendant de nombreuses années à venir.

Harrap, 1996

HOW TO USE THE DICTIONARY

Entry structure

1 Where a word can be used either as a noun/adjective or as a verb, each is given as a separate headword, for example:

book[1] *n*	**manger**[1] *nm*	**thin**[1] *adj*
book[2] *vt*	**manger**[2] *vi*	**thin**[2] *vi*

2 Roman numerals (**1, 2, 3** etc) are used to indicate a change of grammatical category, from noun to adjective, for example, or from transitive to intransitive verb.

3 Letters are used within each grammatical category to point to a change in sense, for example:

briefly *adv* **(a)** (*in a few words*) ... **(b)** (*for a short time*) ...

4 Within entries a comma is used to separate translations which have the same meaning or use. A semicolon between translations indicates a shift in meaning and is regularly accompanied by an indicator to explain this shift.

5 On the English-French side of the dictionary, a large number of commonly used compound words, whether hyphenated or written as two words, have been entered as headwords in alphabetical order. Other compounds are listed under the headword which is the compound's first element, for example:

adventure playground

On the French-English side of the dictionary, compound expressions have been allocated to compound blocks in cases where this improves ease of reference. The compound blocks are marked up with an arrow, for example:

▶ pacte

6 If a headword occurs within an entry in an example or a compound without any change to its form, it is represented by its initial letter only, for example:

spade *n* ...; **to call a s. a s.** ...

This also applies to compounds consisting of more than one word, for example:

terra firma *n* ...; **to be back on t. again** ...

If the form of the headword changes (other than for use with a capital letter) it is written in full:

spade *n* ...; **ace of spades** ...

If an English verb is used in an example in which the past participle has the same form as the infinitive, then the form in the example is not abbreviated, for example:

split: I've split my skirt ...

Indicating material

7 Indicators in italic print and in brackets are used to identify the sense of a word which is being translated, for example:

> **caner** *vi Arg* (*avoir peur*) to have the jitters; (*se dégonfler*) to chicken out: (*mourir*) to snuff it, to kick the bucket

8 Collocators in italic print and in brackets are used to show which type of word combinations are possible for a particular translation, for example:

> **unhealthy** *adj* (*person*) maladif; (*state of mind, influence*) malsain; (*air, place*) malsain. insalubre; (*engine*) détraqué
>
> **walk through** *vipo* (*one's exams etc*) réussir sans effort

9 Field labels in italic print are used to identify the area of usage for which a translation is being given. For example,

> **banquier** *nm Fin, Cartes* banker

shows that the translation of 'banquier' applies both in the financial and the card-playing sense.

10 Style labels are used to identify whether a word or expression is familiar, slang, old-fashioned, literary or vulgar etc, for example:

> **chier** *vi Vulg* to shit, to crap
> **spiffing** *adj Old-fashioned Br F* épatant
> **yucky** *adj F* dégoûtant
> **wondrous** *Arch, Lit* merveilleux

11 The label *Am* is used to refer to North American usage, i.e. Canada and the United States. The label *US* is used to refer to United States usage and spelling.

12 The words *or* and *ou* are used to separate interchangeable parts of a source language item or a translation, for example:

> **to stub one's toe on** *or* **against sth** se heurter *ou* se cogner le pied contre qch

(you can say either 'to stub one's toe on sth' or 'to stub one's toe against sth'; either 'se heurter le pied contre qch' or 'se cogner le pied contre qch')

13 Obliques are used to separate obviously different parts of a translation, for example:

> **the scent had gone cold** on avait perdu sa/leur/*etc* trace

14 Genders are given for French headwords (*nm* for masculine, *nf* for feminine). Where only *n* is given this means that the headword can be either masculine or feminine.

Pronunciation

15 The phonetics of headwords are given according to the symbols of the International Phonetic Alphabet. For English, received pronunciation (RP) has been taken as the norm. This is generally described as the English of Southern England, though it is perhaps more accurate to call it the English of the speaker who has no regional inflections. American pronunciation has been given alongside the British where there is a marked difference (**tomato** [tə'mɑːtəʊ, *Am* tə'meɪtəʊ]).

Pronunciation is not given for headwords that are composed of two separate words, whether hyphenated or not, provided that each of the parts of such headwords are separately entered in the dictionary with a pronunciation.

Where pronunciation shifts from one sound to another, as in a string of headwords like:

leading [ˈliːdɪŋ]
leading [ˈledɪŋ]
leading article [ˈliːdɪŋ]
leading lady

the pronunciation of a word can be checked by moving backwards in the headword list to the last pronunciation given (so here the pronunciation of 'leading' as in 'leading lady' is the same as in 'leading article').

Translations

16 Genders are not given for noun translations where the masculine and feminine forms make the gender obvious, for example:

dancer *n* danseur. -euse

Genders are not repeated for a word that occurs more than once within a category, but they are repeated across categories. The user should therefore look to the beginning of the category or entry if in doubt as to gender.

17 Feminine forms are given for adjectives which do not follow regular patterns, for example:

frais, *f* fraîche
ambigu, -uë

18 Where possible the dictionary gives translations which match the style level of the source language and so the style level is only given once – for the source language. For example:

bonce *n Br F* (*head*) boule *f*
bimbo *n Pej* minette *f*
chien-chien *nm F* doggie

19 Where a translation is not possible (usually because of cultural differences in educational and legal systems etc) an equals sign (=) is used to alert the user to the fact that what follows is not a translation but a definition intended to help them understand the concept.

A double swung dash (≈) indicates a cultural equivalent.

Phrasal verbs

20 A feature of this dictionary is the special treatment given to English phrasal verbs. These are given headword status and highlighted by a solid triangle. Phrasal verbs are analysed as follows:

▶ *vi* (verb, intransitive)

get off: he got off at Victoria Station
listen in: do you mind if I l. in while you talk?

▶ *vipo* (verb, intransitive with prepositional object)

These are intransitive verbs combined with a particle. Some of them can take an object and some of them must take an object:

join in: they all joined in the chorus
(object 'the chorus' can be omitted)

come across: where did you c. across that word?
(object 'that word' necessary)

Especially in the second type, the combination behaves like a transitive verb and can often form a passive:

a type of virus which had never been come across before

▶ *vtsep* (verb, transitive, separable)

The two parts of the verb may be separated:

dig up: they're digging the road up, they're digging up the road

A passive form is possible:

the road is being dug up again

If the object of the verb is a personal pronoun (or 'it') then the two parts of the verb must be separated:

look up: I'll l. him up when I'm in Paris

▶ *vtas* (verb, transitive, always separate)

get over with: she got her work over with as quickly as possible

tide over: can you lend me £5 to t. me over till Monday?

The object cannot come after the particle.

▶ *vtaspo* (verb, transitive, always separate, with prepositional object)

The particle must always be separate from the verb, and an object must be used both after the verb and after the particle:

keep from: to k. sth from sb

Grammar references

21 The dictionary contains a grammar of French, written in English, and a grammar of English, written in French.

The index to these grammar sections is provided by the dictionary text itself.

So, for example, if the user looks up 'past historic' or 'split infinitive' or 'country' or 'pronom personnel' in the dictionary, he will find, in addition to translations of these words, a reference (for example, [①**A26-38**; **B13-22**,6]) to the part of one or both of the grammar sections where more language information is given.

COMMENT UTILISER LE DICTIONNAIRE

Structure des articles

1 Lorsqu'un mot peut être utilisé en tant que nom/adjectif et en tant que verbe, il apparaît sous deux mots d'entrée différents. Par exemple:

book[1] *n*	**manger**[1] *nm*	**thin**[1] *adj*
book[2] *vt*	**manger**[2] *vi*	**thin**[2] *vi*

2 Des chiffres (**1**, **2**, **3** etc) sont utilisés pour indiquer un changement de catégorie grammaticale, de nom à adjectif par exemple, ou encore de verbe transitif à verbe intransitif.

3 Des lettres sont utilisées à l'intérieur de chaque catégorie grammaticale pour marquer un changement de sens. Par exemple:

briefly *adv* **(a)** (*in a few words*) ...; **(b)** (*for a short time*) ...

4 Au sein des articles, les virgules séparent les traductions ayant le même sens ou le même emploi. Un point virgule séparant deux traductions indique une nuance sémantique et est accompagné d'une indication expliquant cette nuance.

5 Du côté anglais, un grand nombre de mots composés d'usage courant, qu'ils s'écrivent en deux mots ou soient reliés par un trait d'union, ont été transformés en entrées à part entière et classés par ordre alphabétique. Le reste se trouve dans l'entrée qui compose leur premier élément. Par exemple:

adventure playground

Du côté français, afin de faciliter l'accès à l'information, on trouvera certains mots composés classés par ordre alphabétique dans ce qui constitue un bloc de composés, situé à la fin de l'entrée et reconnaissable à sa flèche liminaire. Par exemple:

▶ **pacte**

6 Si un mot d'entrée est repris au sein de l'article dans un exemple ou un groupe de mots sans que sa forme subisse aucun changement, il est représenté par son initiale. Par exemple:

spade *n* ...; **to call a s. a s.** ...

Ceci est également valable pour les mots composés (en deux mots ou reliés par un trait d'union). Par exemple:

terra firma *n* ...; **to be back on t. again** ...

Si sa forme subit un changement (autre que son emploi avec une majuscule), il est écrit en entier:

spade *n* ...; **ace of spades** ...

Si le participe passé d'un verbe anglais apparaît dans un exemple et que sa forme est identique à celle de l'infinitif, il n'est pas abrégé. Par exemple:

split: I've split my skirt ...

Indications guidant l'utilisateur

7 Les synonymes et explications en italique et entre parenthèses servent à déterminer le sens du mot traduit. Par exemple:

caner *vi Arg* (*avoir peur*) to have the jitters; (*se dégonfler*) to chicken out; (*mourir*) to snuff it, to kick the bucket.

8 Les exemples types d'emploi apparaissant en italique et entre parenthèses indiquent quels genres de combinaisons sont possibles avec une traduction particulière. Par exemple:

unhealthy *adj* (*person*) maladif; (*state of mind, influence*) malsain; (*air, place*) malsain, insalubre; (*engine*) détraqué

walk through *vipo* (*one's exams etc*) réussir sans effort

9 Les champs sémantiques figurant en italique servent à déterminer le domaine d'utilisation de la traduction donnée. Ainsi:

banquier *nm Fin, Cartes* banker

montre que la traduction de 'banquier' vaut à la fois pour le domaine financier et pour celui des jeux de cartes.

10 Les indications de niveaux de langue indiquent si un mot ou une expression sont familiers, argotiques, vieillis, littéraires ou vulgaires etc:

chier *vi Vulg* to shit, to crap
spiffing *adj Old-fashioned Br F* épatant
wondrous *Arch, Lit* merveilleux
yucky *adj F* dégoûtant

11 Le signe *Am* désigne un emploi nord-américain – c'est-à-dire du Canada et des États-Unis. Le signe US désigne un emploi et un usage spécifiques aux États-Unis.

12 On a eu recours aux mots *or* et *ou* pour séparer les éléments interchangeables d'une locution de la langue de départ ou d'une traduction. Par exemple:

to stub one's toe on *or* **against sth** se heurter *ou* se cogner le pied contre qch

(on peut dire ou bien 'to stub one's toe on sth' ou 'to stub one's toe against sth'; ou bien 'se heurter le pied contre qch' ou 'se cogner le pied contre qch')

13 On a utilisé une barre oblique pour séparer diverses possibilités de traduction, lorsque la différence entre elles apparaît d'elle-même. Par exemple:

the scent had gone cold on avait perdu sa/leur/*etc* trace

14 Les genres sont donnés pour les mots d'entrée français (*nm* pour masculin, *nf* pour féminin). Un mot suivi de *n* uniquement peut avoir les deux genres masculin et féminin.

Prononciation

15 La transcription phonétique des mots d'entrée utilise les symboles de l'alphabet phonétique international. Pour l'anglais, c'est la prononciation consacrée ("received pronunciation") qui a été prise comme norme. Celle-ci est traditionnellement définie comme l'anglais parlé dans le sud de l'Angleterre, bien qu'il soit peut-être plus exact de la décrire comme étant un anglais dépourvu de toute inflexion régionale. La prononciation américaine a été donnée parallèlement à celle d'usage en Grande-Bretagne lorsqu'il existe une différence marquée entre les deux (**tomato** [tə'mɑːtəʊ, *Am* tə'meɪtəʊ]).

La prononciation des mots d'entrée constitués de deux éléments (reliés ou non par un trait d'union) a été volontairement omise dans les cas où chacun des éléments se trouve déjà dans le dictionnaire avec sa transcription phonétique.

Dans les cas où il y a passage d'un son à un autre dans la prononciation de toute une série d'entrées, comme dans

leading ['li:dɪŋ]
leading ['ledɪŋ]
leading article ['li:dɪŋ]
leading lady

on trouvera la prononciation d'une entrée en se référant à l'entrée qui la précède immédiatement (ainsi la prononciation de **leading** dans **leading lady** est la même que dans **leading article**).

Traductions

16 Les genres ne sont pas donnés lorsque leur indication est rendue superflue par la présence des deux formes masculine et féminine. Par exemple:

dancer *n* danseur, -euse

Les genres ne sont pas répétés lorsqu'une traduction apparaît plus d'une fois dans une même catégorie. Ils sont cependant répétés de catégorie à catégorie. Ainsi un retour en début de catégorie ou d'article permet à l'utilisateur de s'assurer du genre des traductions.

17 Les formes féminines des adjectifs sont indiquées si elles ne suivent pas les modèles réguliers. Par exemple:

frais, *f* fraîche
ambigu,-uë

18 Chaque fois que cela est possible, le dictionnaire fournit des traductions qui correspondent au registre de la langue de départ. L'indication de registre n'apparaît donc qu'une fois – pour la langue de départ. Par exemple:

bimbo *n Pej* minette *f*
bonce *n Br F* (*head*) boule *f*
chien-chien *nm F* doggie

19 Si une traduction n'est pas possible (généralement en raison de différences culturelles au niveau du système éducatif ou du système juridique etc) un signe 'égal' (=) attire l'attention de l'utilisateur sur le fait que ce qui suit n'est pas une traduction mais une définition destinée à lui permettre de saisir un concept particulier.

Le signe '≈' introduit un équivalent culturel.

Verbes composés

20 Une des caractéristiques de ce dictionnaire est la façon dont il traite les verbes composés anglais. Ceux-ci ont en effet acquis le statut d'entrées, et sont mis en relief par des triangles pleins. Les verbes composés sont analysés de la façon suivante:

▶ *vi* (verbe intransitif)

get off: he got off at Victoria Station
il descendit à la gare Victoria
listen in: do you mind if I l. in while you talk?
ça vous dérange si j'écoute pendant que vous parlez?

▶ *vipo* (verbe intransitif à complémentation)

Il s'agit de verbes intransitifs associés à une particule qui peut ou doit être suivie d'un complément d'objet:

join in: they all joined in the chorus
(*le complément* 'the chorus' *peut être omis*)
ils se mirent tous à chanter (en chœur)

come across: where did you c. across that word?
(*le complément* 'that word' *est nécessaire*)
où avez-vous trouvé ce mot?

Dans le second cas en particulier, la combinaison verbe/préposition se comporte comme un verbe transitif, et peut généralement se mettre à la voix passive:

a type of virus which had never been come across before
un genre de virus qui n'avait jamais été rencontré auparavant

▶ *vtsep* (verbe transitif, séparable)

Les deux parties du verbe peuvent être séparées:

dig up: they're digging the road up, they're digging up the road
ils font des travaux sur la route

Il existe une forme passive:

the road is being dug up again
la route est de nouveau en travaux

Si le complément du verbe est un pronom personnel (ou bien 'it'), les deux parties du verbe doivent être séparées:

look up: I'll l. him up when I'm in Paris
je le contacterai quand je serai à Paris

▶ *vtas* (verbe transitif, toujours séparé)

get over with: she got her work over with as quickly as possible
elle a fini son travail aussi vite que possible

tide over: can you lend me £5 to t. me over till Monday?
pourrais-tu me prêter cinq livres pour me dépanner jusqu'à lundi?

Le complément d'objet ne peut pas suivre la particule.

▶ *vtaspo* (verbe transitif, toujours séparé, à complémentation)

La particule doit toujours être séparée du verbe, et le verbe et la particule doivent être suivis d'un complément d'objet:

keep from: to k. sth from sb

Section grammaticale

21 Le dictionnaire comporte une grammaire française écrite en anglais et une grammaire anglaise écrite en français.

Les renvois aux sections grammaticales correspondantes se trouvent dans le corps du texte.

Ainsi, si l'on regarde les mots 'past historic' ou 'split infinitive' ou 'country', ou encore 'pronom personnel' on verra, en plus de la traduction, un renvoi (par exemple, [①**A26-38**; **B13-22**,6]) à la ou aux section(s) grammaticale(s) concernée(s).

SYMBOLES PHONÉTIQUES DE L'ANGLAIS

ENGLISH PHONETIC SYMBOLS

Consonnes / Consonants

[b] but [bʌt]; tab [tæb]

[d] dab [dæb]; madder ['mædə*r*]; build [bɪld]

[dʒ] jam [dʒæm]; jail, gaol [dʒeɪl]; gem [dʒem]; gin [dʒɪn]; rage [reɪdʒ]; edge [edʒ]; badger ['bædʒə*r*]

[f] fat [fæt]; laugh [lɑ:f]; ruff, rough [rʌf]; elephant ['elɪfənt]

[g] go [gəʊ]; ghost [gəʊst]; guard [gɑ:d]; again [ə'gen]; egg [eg]; exist [eg'zɪst]; hungry ['hʌŋgrɪ]

[h] hat [hæt]; cohere [kəʊ'hɪə*r*]

[j] yam [jæm]; yet [jet]; youth [ju:θ]

[k] cat [kæt]; kitten ['kɪt(e)n]; choir, quire ['kwaɪə*r*]; cue, queue [kju:]; arctic ['ɑ:ktɪk]; pique [pi:k]; exercise ['eksəsaɪz]

[l] lad [læd]; all [ɔ:l]; table ['teɪb(ə)l]; chisel ['tʃɪz(ə)l]

[m] mat [mæt]; ram [ræm], prism ['prɪz(ə)m]

[n] no, know [nəʊ]; ban [bæn]; banner ['bænə*r*]; pancake ['pænkeɪk]; nab [næb]; gnat [næt]

[ŋ] bang [bæŋ]; sing [sɪŋ]; singer ['sɪŋə*r*]; anchor ['æŋkə*r*]; anger ['æŋgə*r*]; link [lɪŋk]

[p] pat [pæt]; top [tɒp]

[r] rat [ræt]; arise [ə'raɪz]; barring ['bɑ:rɪŋ]

[*r*] (*seulement prononcé en cas de liaison avec le mot suivant*) far [fɑ:*r*]; sailor ['seɪlə*r*]; finger ['fɪŋgə*r*]

[s] sat [sæt]; scene [si:n]; mouse [maʊs]; ice [aɪs]; psychology [saɪ'kɒlədʒɪ]

[ʃ] sham [ʃæm]; dish [dɪʃ]; sugar ['ʃʊgə*r*]; ocean ['əʊʃən]; nation ['neɪʃən]; machine [mə'ʃi:n]

[t] tap [tæp]; pat [pæt]; patter ['pætə*r*]; trap [træp]

[tʃ] chat [tʃæt]; search [sɜ:tʃ]; chisel ['tʃɪz(ə)l]; thatch [θætʃ]; rich [rɪtʃ]

[θ] thatch [θætʃ]; ether ['i:θə*r*]; faith [feɪθ]; breath [breθ]

[ð] that [ðæt]; there [ðeə*r*]; mother ['mʌðə*r*]; breathe [bri:ð]

[v] vat [væt]; avail [ə'veɪl]; rave [reɪv]

[w] wall [wɔ:l]; await [ə'weɪt]; quite [kwaɪt]; what [wɒt]; why [waɪ]

[z] zinc [zɪŋk]; buzz [bʌz]; houses ['haʊzɪz]; business ['bɪznɪs]

[ʒ] pleasure ['pleʒə*r*]; vision ['vɪʒən]; beige [beɪʒ]

[χ] loch [lɒχ] (*prononciation écossaise*)

Voyelles / Vowels

[æ] bat [bæt]; add [æd]

[ɑ:] art [ɑ:t]; ask [ɑ:sk]; car [kɑ:*r*]; father [fɑ:ðə*r*]

[e] bet [bet]; leopard ['lepəd]; menace ['menɪs]; said [sed]

[ɜ:] curl [kɜ:l]; herb [hɜ:b]; learn [lɜ:n]; myrrh [mɜ:*r*]

[ə] decency ['di:sənsɪ]; obey [ə'beɪ]; amend [ə'mend]; delicate ['delɪkət]

[i:] bee [bi:]; fever ['fi:və*r*]; see, sea [si:]; release [rɪ'li:s]

[ɪ] bit [bɪt]; added ['ædɪd]; drastic ['dræstɪk]; sieve [sɪv]

[ɒ] wad [wɒd]; wash [wɒʃ]; lot [lɒt]; what [wɒt]

[ɔ:] all [ɔ:l]; haul [hɔ:l]; saw [sɔ:]; caught, court [kɔ:t]; short [ʃɔ:t]; wart [wɔ:t]; thought [θɔ:t]

[ʊ] put [pʊt]; wool [wʊl]; wood, would [wʊd]; full [fʊl]

[u:] shoe [ʃu:]; prove [pru:v]; threw, through [θru:]; frugal ['fru:g(ə)l]; room [ru:m]

[ʌ] cut [kʌt]; sun, son [sʌn]; cover ['kʌvə*r*]; rough [rʌf]

Diphtongues / Diphthongs

[aɪ] aisle, isle [aɪl]; height [haɪt]; life [laɪf]; fly [flaɪ]; beside [bɪ'saɪd]

[aʊ] fowl, foul [faʊl]; house [haʊs]; cow [kaʊ]

[eə] bear, bare [beə*r*]; there, their [ðeə*r*]; airy ['eərɪ]

[eɪ] date [deɪt]; day [deɪ]; rain, rein, reign [reɪn]

[əʊ] low [ləʊ]; soap [səʊp]; rope [rəʊp]; road, rode, rowed [rəʊd]; sew, so, sow (*verb*) [səʊ]

[ɪə] beer, bier [bɪə*r*]; appear [ə'pɪə*r*]; really ['rɪəlɪ]

[ɔɪ] boil [bɔɪl]; toy [tɔɪ]; oyster ['ɔɪstə*r*]; loyal ['lɔɪəl]

[ʊə] poor [pʊə*r*]; sure [ʃʊə*r*]

FRENCH PHONETIC SYMBOLS

SYMBOLES PHONÉTIQUES DU FRANÇAIS

Consonants / Consonnes

[b] beau [bo]; abbé [abe]; robe [rɔb]

[d] donner [dɔne]; sud [syd]

[f] feu [fø]; bref [brɛf]; phrase [fraz]

[g] garde [gard]; guerre [gɛr]; second [səgɔ̃]; exister [ɛgziste]

[ʒ] gilet [ʒilɛ]; manger [mɑ̃ʒe]; âge [ɑʒ]

[k] camp [kɑ̃]; képi [kepi]; quatre [katr]; écho [eko]; taxer [takse]; accident [aksidɑ̃]

[l] lait [lɛ]; aile [ɛl]; facile [fasil]

[m] mon [mɔ̃]; flamme [flam]; prisme [prism]

[n] né [ne]; canne [kan]; automne [otɔn]

[ŋ] (*in words of foreign origin*) parking [parkiŋ]; smoking [smɔkiŋ]

[ɲ] campagne [kɑ̃paɲ]; gnaule [ɲol]

[p] pain [pɛ̃]; tape [tap]

[r] rare [rar]; arbre [arbr]; rhume [rym]

[s] sou [su]; rébus [rebys]; cire [sir]; scène [sɛn]; six [sis]

[ʃ] chose [ʃoz]; chercher [ʃɛrʃe]; schisme [ʃism]

[t] table [tabl]; nette [nɛt]; théâtre [teɑtr]

[v] voir [vwar]; vie [vi]; wagon [vagɔ̃]

[w] ouate [wat]; ouest [west]; noir [nwar]; (*also in words of foreign origin*) tramway [tramwɛ]; whist [wist]

[z] cousin [kuzɛ̃]; zéro [zero]; deuxième [døzjɛm]

[j] yacht [jɔt, jat]; piano [pjano]; ration [rasjɔ̃]; voyage [vwajaʒ]; travailler [travaje]; cahier [kaje]

[ɥ] muet [mɥɛ]; huit [ɥit]; luire [lɥir]; aiguille [egɥij]

Vowels / Voyelles

[a] chat [ʃa]; tache [taʃ]; toit [twa]; phare [far]

[ɑ] âge [ɑʒ]; âgé [ɑʒe]; tâche [tɑʃ]

[e] été [ete]; donner, donné [dɔne]; légal [legal]

[ə]* le [lə]; ce [sə]; entremets [ɑ̃trəmɛ]

[ø] feu [fø]; nœud [nø]; heureuse [ørøz]

[œ] seul [sœl]; œuf [œf]; sœur [sœr]; cueillir [kœjir]

[ɛ] elle [ɛl]; très [trɛ]; terre [tɛr]; rêve [rɛv]; père [pɛr]

[i] vite [vit]; signe [siɲ]; sortie [sɔrti]

[ɔ] donner [dɔne]; album [albɔm]; fort [fɔr]

[o] dos [do]; impôt [ɛ̃po]; chaud [ʃo]

[u] tout [tu]; goût [gu]; août [u]; cour [kur]

[y] cru [kry]; ciguë [sigy]; mur [myr]

[ɑ̃] enfant [ɑ̃fɑ̃]; temps [tɑ̃]; paon [pɑ̃]; centre [sɑ̃tr]; branche [brɑ̃ʃ]

[ɛ̃] vin [vɛ̃]; plein [plɛ̃]; thym [tɛ̃]; prince [prɛ̃s]; plainte [plɛ̃t]

[ɔ̃] mon [mɔ̃]; plomb [plɔ̃]; longe [lɔ̃ʒ]; comte [kɔ̃t]

[œ̃] un [œ̃]; lundi [lœ̃di]; humble [œ̃bl]

*The symbol (ə) (in brackets) indicates that the mute e is pronounced in careful speech but not in rapid speech.

Acknowledgment

The Publisher would like to acknowledge the contribution made by previous editorial teams; this new edition, which builds on their achievements, marks the latest stage in the long and distinguished history of this dictionary.

We would also like to thank Lexus and Gert Ronberg for the work originally carried out on *Grammaire anglaise*, and Lexus, Raymond Perrez, Noël Peacock and Sabine Citron for their original work on *French Grammar*.

Remerciements

Les éditions Harrap voudraient remercier les précédents rédacteurs pour leur contribution; cette nouvelle édition, qui a bénéficié de leur travail, marque une nouvelle étape dans la longue et remarquable histoire de ce dictionnaire.

Nous remercions également Lexus at Gert Ronberg pour leur travail sur la Grammaire anglaise, ainsi que Lexus, Raymond Perrez, Noël Peacock et Sabine Citron pour leur collaboration passée à French Grammar.

ENGLISH-FRENCH

ANGLAIS-FRANÇAIS

A, a[1] [eɪ] *n* **(a)** (*letter*) A, a *m*; **two a's** deux a; **the car's old, but it gets me from A to B** c'est une vieille voiture mais elle me permet de me déplacer; **the train is the best way of getting from A to B** le train c'est le meilleur moyen de se déplacer d'un endroit à un autre; **the roads are so crowded that it takes forever to get from A to B** les routes sont si encombrées que le moindre trajet prend une éternité; **the numbering system helps the user get from A to B** le système de numérotation permet à l'utilisateur de s'y retrouver; *Am* **to be A-OK** (*in health*) tenir la forme; **everything's A-OK** tout baigne dans l'huile; **an A to Z of ...** (*Indian cooking, rose growing, car maintenance*) un guide détaillé de ...; **an A to Z of London** un plan de Londres; **we've been through all the details from A to Z** nous avons étudié tous les détails un par un; **A1** ['eɪ'wʌn] de première qualité; **in A1 condition** (*car, house*) en parfait état; (*person*) en parfaite santé; **51A** (*house number*) 51 bis; **A-bomb** bombe *f* A; *Br Aut* **A-road** ≈ route *f* nationale; **A-side** (*of record*) face *f* A

(b) *Sch* (*grade*) **to get an A in French** avoir 17 en français; **an A minus/plus** 14/19; *Am Sch, Univ* **he got straight A's** (*top marks*) il a eu de très bonnes notes partout; *Eng Sch* **A-level** ≈ baccalauréat *m*, *F* bac *m*

(c) *Mus* la *m*; **in A flat** en la bémol

a[2], *before vowel sound* **an** [ə, ən; *stressed* eɪ, æn] *indef art* [ⓘA4,Aa; B4,B; A4-5,B-C] **(a)** un, une **a man** un homme; **an old man** un vieillard; **a hill** une colline; **a hotel** [əhəʊ'tel], *Old-fashioned* **an hotel** [ənəʊ'tel] un hôtel; **an hour** [ən'aʊər] une heure; **a unit** [ə'juːnɪt] une unité; **an uncle** [ən'ʌŋk(ə)l] un oncle; **an MP** [ən'em'piː] un député; **a man and (a) woman** un homme et une femme; **a wife and mother** (*same person*) une épouse et mère

(b) (*def art in Fr*) **to have a red nose** avoir le nez rouge; **I have a sore throat/back/knee** j'ai mal à la gorge/au dos/au genou; **to have a taste for sth** avoir le goût de qch; *Iron* **a fine excuse!** la belle excuse!; **a computer is a useful machine** (*generalizing*) les ordinateurs sont des machines bien utiles

(c) (*distributive*) **at thirty pence a kilo** à trente pence le kilo; **five francs a head** cinq francs par tête; **three times a week/a year** trois fois par semaine/par an; **fifty kilometres an hour** cinquante kilomètres à l'heure

(d) (**= a certain**) **I know a doctor who ...** je connais un médecin qui ...; **in a sense** dans un sens

(e) (**= the same**) **to come in two at a time** entrer deux par deux; **of a size** de la même grandeur *ou* taille

(f) (**= a single**) **I haven't understood a word** je n'ai pas compris un seul mot; **I couldn't see a thing** je n'y voyais rien du tout; **there wasn't a book to be found in the house** il n'y avait pas un seul livre dans la maison; **not a chance!** aucune chance!; **we haven't a hope of finishing in time** il n'y a aucun espoir pour que nous terminions à temps

(g) (*omitted in Fr*) **he is an Englishman/a father/a barrister** il est anglais/père/avocat

(h) to put an end to sth mettre fin à qch; **to make a fortune** faire fortune; **what a man!** quel homme!; **what a pity!** quel dommage!; **as a rule** en règle générale; **within a short time** en peu de temps

(i) (*before nouns in apposition*) **Caen, a large town in Normandy** Caen, ville importante de Normandie; **forty years a sailor and he still gets seasick!** il a beau être marin depuis quarante ans, il lui arrive toujours d'avoir le mal de mer

A3 ['eɪ'θriː] *n, adj* A3 *m*

A4 ['eɪ'fɔːr] *n, adj* A4 *m*; **an A4 sheet** une feuille A4; **A4 paper tray** bac de papier A4

AA [eɪ'eɪ] *n* **(a)** (*abbr* **anti-aircraft**) D. C. A. *f*; **AA fire/guns** tir *m*/canons *mpl* de D. C. A. **(b)** (*abbr* **Automobile Association**) = société *f* de dépannage pour les automobilistes, ≈ Touring Club *m* de France **(c)** (*abbr* **Alcoholics Anonymous**) A. A. *mpl*; **an AA meeting** une réunion des Alcooliques anonymes

AAA [eɪeɪ'eɪ] (*normally spoken: 3As*) *n* **(a)** *abbr* **Amateur Athletics Association (b)** *abbr* **American Automobile Association**

Aachen ['ɑːkən] *n* Aix-la-Chapelle

AB [eɪ'biː] *n* **(a)** *Naut* (*abbr* **able(-bodied) seaman**) matelot *m* de deuxième classe **(b)** *US* (*abbr* **Artium Baccalaureus**) = **B. A.**

ABA [eɪbiː'eɪ] *n* **(a)** *abbr* **Amateur Boxing Association (b)** *abbr* **American Bar Association**

aback [ə'bæk] *adv* **to be taken a.** en rester déconcerté *ou* interdit; **this remark rather took me a.** cette remarque m'a quelque peu décontenancé

abacus, *pl* **-ci, -cuses** ['æbəkəs, -saɪ, -kəsɪz] *n* **(a)** *Math* boulier *m* (compteur) **(b)** *Archit* abaque *m*, tailloir *m*

abaft [ə'bɑːft] *Naut* **1** *adv* sur l'arrière, vers l'arrière **2** *prep* **a. the mast** sur l'arrière du mât

abalone [æbə'ləʊnɪ] *n* (*shellfish*) ormeau *m*

abandon[1] [ə'bændən] *n* **with reckless a.** avec inconscience; *Hum* **with gay a.** avec une joyeuse désinvolture

abandon[2] *vt* **(a)** (*leave*) (*car, building, one's family*) abandonner; *Naut* **to a. ship** abandonner *ou* évacuer le navire; **to a. to the insurer** délaisser à l'assureur **(b)** (*give up*) (*plan, principle*) renoncer à, abandonner; *Comptr* (*file, routine*) abandonner; *Sp* **to a. play** (*temporarily*) interrompre la partie; (*permanently*) annuler la partie; **to a. all hope** abandonner tout espoir (**of doing sth** de faire qch); **to a. oneself to sth** s'abandonner à qch

abandoned [ə'bændənd] *adj* **(a)** (*car, settlement, outpost*) abandonné; **the building had an a. look** le bâtiment avait l'air abandonné **(b)** *Old-fashioned* (*unrestrained*) (*behaviour, woman*) dévergondé

abandonment [ə'bændənmənt] *n* abandon *m*

abase [ə'beɪs] *vt Lit, Arch* abaisser, humilier; **to a. oneself** s'abaisser, s'humilier

abasement [ə'beɪsmənt] *n Lit* humiliation *f*

abash [ə'bæʃ] *vt* (*usu in passive*) **to be** *or* **feel abashed at** *or* **by sth** rester tout interdit de qch

abate [ə'beɪt] *vi* (*of storm, fear, anger, pain*) se calmer, s'apaiser; (*of flood*) baisser; (*of noise*) diminuer; **the wind abated** le vent est tombé

abatement [ə'beɪtmənt] *n* diminution *f*, affaiblissement *m*; (*of storm*) apaisement *m*; (*of flood*) abaissement *m*

abattoir ['æbətwɑːr] *n* abattoir *m*

abbess ['æbɪs] *n* abbesse *f*

abbey ['æbɪ] *n* **(a)** abbaye *f* **(b) a.** (**church**) (eglise *f*) abbatiale *f*; **Westminster A.** l'abbaye *f* de Westminster

abbot ['æbət] *n* abbé *m*

abbreviate [ə'briːvɪeɪt] *vt* (*word, speech*) abréger; **abbreviated dialling** numérotation *f* abrégée

abbreviation [əbriːvɪ'eɪʃən] *n* (*of word*) abréviation *f*

ABC, abc [eɪbiː'siː] *n* **(a)** (*alphabet*) ABC *m*, abc *m*; **to know one's A.** connaître son alphabet *m* **(b)** *Fig* (*of an art, a science*) b a ba *m*; **it's as easy as A.** c'est facile comme bonjour

abdicate ['æbdɪkeɪt] **1** *vt* (*throne, one's responsibilities*) abdiquer; (*right, position*) renoncer à **2** *vi* abdiquer

abdication [æbdɪ'keɪʃən] *n* (*of throne*) abdication *f*; (*of right, responsibilities*) renonciation *f*

abdomen ['æbdəmən] *n* abdomen *m*; (*general area*) ventre *m*

abdominal [əb'dɒmɪn(ə)l] *adj* abdominal, -aux

abduct [əb'dʌkt] *vt Jur* enlever, kidnapper

abduction [əb'dʌkʃən] *n Jur* enlèvement *m*, rapt *m*, kidnapping *m*

abductor [əb'dʌktər] **1** *n* **(a)** *Jur* ravisseur, -euse, kidnappeur, -euse **(b)** *Anat* (muscle *m*) abducteur *m* **2** *adj Anat* (*muscle*) abducteur

abeam [ə'biːm] *adv Naut, Av* par le travers

abed [ə'bed] *adv Arch* au lit

aberrant [æ'berənt] *adj* aberrant, anormal

aberration [æbə'reɪʃən] *n* aberration *f*, déviation *f*; *Astron, Math, Opt etc* aberration; **a temporary a. on his part** (*in behaviour*) un écart de conduite de sa part; **mental a.** égarement *m* (de l'esprit), aberration, confusion *f* mentale; **in a moment of a.** dans un moment de folie

abet [əˈbet] *vt* (**-tt-**) (*crime*) encourager; **to a. sb in a crime** encourager *ou* pousser qn à un crime

abetting [əˈbetɪŋ] *n Jur* **(aiding and) a.** (*before or during a crime*) complicité *f*

abeyance [əˈbeɪəns] *n* (*of law*) suspension *f*; **the matter is still in a.** la question est toujours en suspens; *Jur* la question est toujours pendante; **law in a.** loi *f* inappliquée; **to fall into a.** tomber en désuétude; *Jur* **estate in a.** succession *f* vacante

abhor [əbˈhɔːr] *vt* (**-rr-**) abhorrer, avoir en horreur; **nature abhors a vacuum** la nature a horreur du vide

abhorrence [əbˈhɒrəns] *n* horreur *f* (**of** de); **his a. of flying** le fait qu'il a horreur de prendre l'avion; **to hold sth in a.** avoir qch en horreur; **such actions will be held in a. by all decent people** de tels actes seront odieux à tous les gens convenables

abhorrent [əbˈhɒrənt] *adj* odieux, répugnant (**to** à); **such things are a. to the rational mind** de telles choses répugnent à l'esprit rationnel

abide [əˈbaɪd] (*pt & pp* **abided**) **1** *vt* (*in neg phrases*) **I can't a. him** je ne peux pas le supporter *ou* le sentir; **I can't a. that sound/dishonesty** je ne supporte pas ce bruit/la malhonnêteté; **I can't a. it when you talk to me like that** je ne supporte pas que tu me parles comme ça **2** *vi* **(a)** *esp Lit* (*of thing*) demeurer; **those memories will a. with me as long as I live** ces souvenirs me resteront *ou* m'accompagneront jusqu'à ma mort **(b)** *Arch Lit* (*of person*) rester, demeurer (**with sb** avec qn)

► **abide by** *vipo* (*promise*) rester fidèle à, tenir; (*rule, decision, law*) se conformer à, se soumettre à, respecter; **I a. by my decision/what I said** je maintiens ma décision/ce que j'ai dit

abiding [əˈbaɪdɪŋ] *adj* permanent; (*impression*) durable; **an a. sense of gratitude** un sentiment de gratitude éternelle

ability [əˈbɪlɪtɪ] *n* **(a)** (*to do sth*) capacité *f*; (*skill*) habileté *f*, capacité, compétence *f*; **an a. to do sth** une capacité à faire qch; **a man of considerable a.** un homme très doué; **she shows artistic a.** elle manifeste des dons artistiques; **to do sth to the best of one's a.** faire qch de son mieux; **the needs and abilities of each student** les besoins et les aptitudes de chaque étudiant **(b)** *Jur* (*to inherit*) habilité *f*; (*to make a will*) capacité *f* légale

abject [ˈæbdʒekt] *adj* **(a)** (*miserable*) misérable; **a. poverty** misère *f* effroyable **(b)** (*despicable*) bas, vil, abject **(c)** (*servile*) (*apology, letter*) servile

abjectly [ˈæbdʒektlɪ] *adv* **(a)** (*miserably*) misérablement **(b)** (*despicably*) bassement, vilement, abjectement **(c)** (*to apologize*) servilement

abjure [əbˈdʒʊər] *vt* (*one's religion*) abjurer; (*one's faith*) renier

ablative [ˈæblətɪv] *Gram* **1** *n* ablatif *m*; **in the a.** à l'ablatif; **a. absolute** ablatif absolu **2** *adj* (*case*) ablatif

ablaze [əˈbleɪz] *adv, adj pred* en feu, en flammes; **to be a.** être en feu *ou* en flammes, flamber; **to set sth a.** embraser qch; **a. with light** resplendissant de lumière; **her eyes were a. with anger** ses yeux étaient enflammés de colère; **the speaker set the audience a. with enthusiasm for reform** l'orateur avait empli le public d'un enthousiasme ardent en faveur d'une réforme

able [ˈeɪb(ə)l] *adj* **(a)** (*person*) compétent, capable; **to be a. to do sth** (*know how to*) savoir faire qch, être capable de faire qch; (*be physically capable*) pouvoir faire qch; (*succeed in doing sth*) réussir à faire qch; **I shan't be a. to come** je ne pourrai pas venir; **someone else will be better a. to help you** quelqu'un d'autre sera plus à même de vous aider; **I'll do it if I'm a.** je le ferai si je le peux; *Naut* **a. seaman** matelot *m* de deuxième classe; **an a. piece of work** un travail compétent *ou* bien fait; **your a. assistance** votre aide efficace **(b)** *Jur* (*to bequeath, succeed*) apte, habile

able-bodied *adj* fort, robuste; *Mil* bon pour le service; *Naut* **a. seaman** matelot *m* de deuxième classe; **every a. person helped in the search** toute personne en état de le faire a participé aux recherches

ablution [əˈbluːʃən] *n* ablution *f*; *F Hum* **to perform one's ablutions** faire ses ablutions

ably [ˈeɪblɪ] *adv* avec compétence; **she performed a. in the 100 metres** elle s'est bien comportée dans le 100 mètres; **a. assisted by** efficacement assisté par

abnegation [æbnɪˈgeɪʃən] *n* (*of belief etc*) renoncement *m* (**of** à); **self-a.** abnégation *f*

abnormal [æbˈnɔːm(ə)l] *adj* anormal; **a. psychology** psychopathologie *f*

abnormality [æbnɔːˈmælɪtɪ] *n* **(a)** caractère *m* anormal, anormalité *f* **(b)** (*event etc*) anomalie *f*, aberration *f*

abnormally [æbˈnɔːm(ə)lɪ] *adv* anormalement; *Hum* **he was late but not a. late** il était en retard mais pas plus que d'habitude; **he was a. shy** il était d'une timidité maladive

aboard [əˈbɔːd] **1** *adv* à bord; **to go a.** monter à bord; **to take sth a.** embarquer qch; **all a.!** *Naut* embarquez!; *Rail etc* en voiture!; **welcome a.!** *Naut, Av* bienvenue à bord!; *Fig* bienvenue dans l'équipe! **2** *prep* (*train, bus, plane*) dans; *Naut* à bord de; **a. ship** à bord (du navire)

abode [əˈbəʊd] *n Lit* (*home*) demeure *f*; *F* **welcome to my humble a.** bienvenu dans mon petit chez-moi; *Jur* **place of a.** domicile *m*; **of no fixed a.** sans domicile fixe

abolish [əˈbɒlɪʃ] *vt* (*custom, committee etc*) abolir, supprimer; (*law*) abroger

abolition [æbəˈlɪʃən] *n* (*of custom, abuse*) abolition *f*, suppression *f*; (*of law*) abrogation *f*; **a. of slavery/the death penalty** abolition de l'esclavage/de la peine de mort

abominable [əˈbɒmɪnəb(ə)l] *adj* abominable; **the a. snowman** l'abominable homme *m* des neiges

abominably [əˈbɒmɪnəblɪ] *adv* (*to behave*) abominablement; **it's a. hot** il fait abominablement chaud

abominate [əˈbɒmɪneɪt] *vt* abominer, détester, avoir en abomination

abomination [əbɒmɪˈneɪʃən] *n* abomination *f*; **to hold in a.** avoir en abomination; *F* **this coffee's an a.** ce café est abominable

aboriginal, *Austr* **Aboriginal** [æbəˈrɪdʒɪn(ə)l] *adj* aborigène, indigène; *Austr* **A. art/customs/languages** art/coutumes/langues aborigène(s)

Aborigine [æbəˈrɪdʒɪnɪ] *n Austr* aborigène *mf* (d'Australie)

abort¹ [əˈbɔːt] *n* **(a)** *Mil, Av etc* mission *f* non accomplie; **launch a.** termination *f* prématurée d'un/du lancement **(b)** *Comptr* (*of program*) suspension *f* d'exécution, abandon *m*

abort² **1** *vi* **(a)** *Obst* (*of woman*) avorter; (*of foetus*) ne pas tenir; (*miscarry*) (*of woman*) faire une fausse couche **(b)** *Fig* (*of project*) avorter **2** *vt* **(a)** *Obst* (*woman*) faire avorter; **the foetus was aborted** la grossesse a été interrompue **(b)** *Fig* (*project*) faire avorter **(c)** *Comptr* (*program*) suspendre l'exécution de, abandonner

abortion [əˈbɔːʃən] *n* **(a)** *Obst* avortement *m*, interruption *f* de grossesse; **to have an a.** se faire avorter; **to perform an a.** faire un avortement; **a. clinic** clinique *f* où l'on pratique des avortements; **the a. debate** le débat sur l'avortement; **a. law** loi *f* sur l'avortement; **a. on demand** avortement libre **(b)** *Fig* (*of plan*) avortement *m* **(c)** *F* (*person, animal*) avorton *m*, monstre *m*

abortionist [əˈbɔːʃənɪst] *n Pej* avorteur, -euse

abortive [əˈbɔːtɪv] *adj* (*plan etc*) avorté, manqué; **a. attempt** vaine tentative; *Mil etc* **an a. attack** une attaque avortée; **an a. mission** une mission non accomplie

abound [əˈbaʊnd] *vi* abonder, foisonner; **to a. in** *or* **with sth** abonder en qch, regorger de qch; **the forest abounds with deer** la forêt regorge de daims

about [əˈbaʊt] **1** *prep* [①A64,2] **(a)** (*around*) autour de; **the hills (round) a. the town** les collines autour *ou* à l'entour de la ville; **the people a. us** les gens auprès de nous, les gens qui nous entourent; **look a. you** regarde autour de toi; **it's good to have a few new faces a. the place** c'est bien de voir de nouvelles têtes par ici; **keep your wits a. you** garde ta présence d'esprit; *Fml* **to have sth a. one's person** avoir qch sur soi

(b) (*in various parts of*) **to wander a. the town/the streets** se balader en ville/dans les rues

(c) (*characteristic of*) **there is something unusual a. him** il y a dans sa personne quelque chose de pas ordinaire; **she found something amusing a. the situation** elle a trouvé que la situation avait quelque chose d'amusant; **there's something a. a horse that ...** il y a chez le cheval un je ne sais quoi qui ...

(d) (*on the subject of*) sur, à propos de, au sujet de; **a book a. France** un livre sur la France; **to speak a. sth** parler de qch; **to argue a. sth** se disputer à propos de *ou* au sujet de qch; **to quarrel a. nothing** se quereller à propos de rien; **what are they talking a.?** de quoi parlent-ils?; **what are you talking a.? of course I remembered!** qu'est-ce que tu racontes? bien sûr que j'y ai pensé!; **what's it all a.?** de quoi s'agit-il?; **how** *or* **what a. a game of bridge/going to Paris?** si on faisait un bridge/allait à Paris?; **well, what a. it? shall we go?** alors, qu'est-ce qu'on fait? on y va?; **what a. my bath?** et mon bain?; **what a. us?** et nous, alors?; **what a. the children?** (*what's to be done with them?*) et les enfants?; **what a. money?** (*have you got enough?*) tu as de l'argent?; **you remember that book? – what a. it?** tu te souviens de ce livre? – et alors?

(e) (*active in, engaged in*) **to go a. one's work/business** vaquer à son travail/ses affaires; **while you are a. it** pendant que vous y êtes; **be quick a. it!** (*in irritation*) dépêchez-vous!; **you were long enough a. it!** ça vous aura pris assez de temps!

2 *adv* **(a)** (*in different directions*) de part et d'autre; **to stroll a.** se promener de-ci de-là *ou* de part et d'autre; **he looked a. to see if anyone was waiting for him** il a regardé autour de lui pour voir si quelqu'un l'attendait; **to follow sb a.** suivre qn partout; **to wave one's arms a.** agiter ses bras en tous sens; **there were clothes all a.** il y avait des vêtements un peu partout; **don't leave those papers lying a.** ne laissez pas traîner ces papiers

(b) (*in the general area*) là; **is Jack a.?** est-ce que Jack est là?; **he must be somewhere a.** il doit être quelque part (par là), il doit être dans les parages; **there was nobody a.** il n'y avait personne (de visible); **there's never a policeman a. when you need one** il n'y a jamais un seul agent de police dans les parages quand on en a besoin; **there weren't many people a.** il n'y avait pas grand monde

(c) (*active*) **to be up** *or* **out and a. again** (*after illness*) être de nouveau sur pied; **she's usually up** *or* **out and a. by 7 o'clock** elle est généralement debout à 7 heures; **to be a. early** être matinal; **there's a great deal of flu a. at present** il y a beaucoup de grippe actuellement

(d) (*in opposite direction, order*) **the other way a.** en sens inverse, dans le sens contraire; **to turn a.** faire demi-tour, se retourner; *Mil* **a. turn!**, *US* **a. face!** demi-tour!

(e) (*approximately*) environ; **there are a. thirty** il y en a environ trente, il y en a une trentaine; **she's a. my age** elle a à peu près mon âge; **it will cost a. a hundred francs** ça coûtera dans les cent francs; **a. one o'clock** vers une heure; **he's a. as tall as you** il est à peu près de ta taille; **you've got a. as much intelligence as a two-year-old!** tu es à peu près aussi futé qu'un gamin de deux ans!; **that's a. right** c'est à peu près ça *ou* cela; **it's a. time** il serait *ou* est temps; **I've had (just) a. enough of you!** je commence à en avoir assez de toi!

(f) [ⓘA50,g] (*ready, intending*) **to be a. to do sth** être sur le point de faire qch; **what were you a. to say?** qu'est-ce que vous alliez dire?; **he is a. to leave** il est sur le départ, il est sur le point de partir; *esp Am* **I'm not a. to pay 5,000 francs for that** je n'ai pas l'intention de payer cela 5000 francs; **he's not a. to change his ways just because of that** il n'y a pas de risque qu'il change ses manières de faire rien que pour ça

about-face, about-turn *n* demi-tour *m*; (*of opinion, in policy*) revirement *m*; **to do an a.** (*turn around*) faire demi-tour; (*change one's mind*) changer complètement d'avis *ou* d'opinion

above [əˈbʌv] **1** *prep* **(a)** [ⓘA64] au-dessus de; **the water reached a. their knees** l'eau leur montait jusqu'au-dessus des genoux; **a. sea level** au-dessus du niveau de la mer; **his voice was heard a. the shouting** on entendait sa voix par-dessus le tumulte; **temperature a. normal** température supérieure à *ou* au-dessus de la normale; **a. criticism** hors de l'atteinte de la critique; **that's a. me** (*beyond my understanding*) cela me dépasse; **they value friendship a. all else** ils placent l'amitié par-dessus tout; **a. all** surtout; **over and a. that** en plus de cela

(b) (*of person*) **to be a. suspicion** être au-dessus de tout soupçon; **I am a. doing that** je me respecte trop pour faire cela; **she's not a. telling the occasional lie** il lui arrive de mentir de temps en temps; **he thinks he's a. all that** il pense qu'il est au-dessus de tout ça; *F* **to get a. oneself** se donner des airs

(c) (*in rank*) **he is a. me (in rank)** il est mon supérieur (hiérarchique)

(d) (*of number*) **a. twenty** plus de vingt; **a. $100** plus de 100 dollars; **women aged 18 and a.** les femmes âgées de 18 ans et plus; **the temperature didn't rise a. 10°C** la température n'a pas dépassé 10°C

(e) (*upstream from*) **the Seine a. Paris** la Seine en amont de Paris

(f) (*north of*) **a. this latitude** au nord de cette latitude

2 *adv* **(a)** au-dessus; **the tenants (of the flat) a.** les locataires du dessus; *esp Lit* **the sky a. was clear** au-dessus de moi/nous/*etc* le ciel était clair; **a view from a.** une vue plongeante; **a policy imposed from a.** une politique imposée d'en haut

(b) (*in book, document etc*) ci-dessus; **the paragraph a.** le paragraphe ci-dessus; **as a.** comme ci-dessus

3 *adj* (*in book etc*) **the a. quotation** la citation ci-dessus

4 *n* **the a. is a quotation from Hamlet** le passage ci-dessus est une citation de Hamlet

aboveboard [əˈbʌvbɔːd] *adj* franc; *f* franche; **his conduct was completely a.** il a agi en tout bien (et) tout honneur

above-mentioned, above-named [əbʌvˈmenʃənd, -ˈneɪmd] *adj & n* susmentionné, -ée, susdit, -ite

above-the-line advertising *n* publicité *f* pure

abracadabra [æbrəkəˈdæbrə] *int* abracadabra

abrasion [əˈbreɪʒən] *n* **(a)** (*of surface*) (*by rope*) usure *f* par frottement; *Tech* abrasion *f* **(b)** (*on skin*) écorchure *f*, éraflure *f*

abrasive [əˈbreɪsɪv] **1** *adj* (*surface, substance*) abrasif; *Fig* (*person*) caustique **2** *n* abrasif *m*

abreast [əˈbrest] *adv* de front; **three/four a.** trois/quatre de front; **to march two a.** marcher par deux; **to march four a.** marcher par rangs de quatre; *Naut* **(in) line a.** en ligne de front; **to come a. of a car** arriver à la hauteur d'une voiture; **to keep a. of a science** suivre les progrès d'une science; **I try to keep a. of the latest theories** j'essaie de me tenir au courant des dernières théories

abridge [əˈbrɪdʒ] *vt* (*talk*) abréger; (*book, chapter*) raccourcir, abréger

abridged [əˈbrɪdʒd] *adj* (*version*) abrégé

abridg(e)ment [əˈbrɪdʒmənt] *n* **(a)** (*action*) abrégement *m* **(b)** (*result*) abrégé *m*, résumé *m*

abroad [əˈbrɔːd] *adv* **(a)** à l'étranger; **to live a.** vivre à l'étranger; **our colleagues from a.** nos collègues étrangers **(b)** (*in every direction*) de tous côtés; **the news got a.** la nouvelle s'est répandue; **when it got a. that ...** quand la nouvelle s'est répandue que ... **(c)** *Arch* (*outside*) **to venture a.** sortir (de la maison)

abrogate [ˈæbrəgeɪt] *vt Fml* (*law*) abroger

abrogation [æbrəˈgeɪʃən] *n Fml* (*of law*) abrogation *f*

abrupt [əˈbrʌpt] *adj* **(a)** (*person, manner, tone*) abrupt; (*style*) heurté, saccadé **(b)** (*sudden*) (*drop in sales*) brusque; (*departure*) brusque, précipité; (*change*) brutal; **the evening came to an a. end** la soirée s'acheva brusquement; **there was an a. change in the weather** le temps a changé brutalement **(c)** (*steep*) (*slope, incline*) abrupt, raide, escarpé; (*rise*) ardu, raide

abruptly [əˈbrʌptlɪ] *adv* **(a)** (*to interrupt, refuse, speak*) abruptement **(b)** (*to come to an end, decline*) brusquement **(c) to fall away a.** (*of cliff*) descendre à pic *ou* en pente raide

abruptness [əˈbrʌptnɪs] *n* **(a)** (*of person, manner*) brusquerie *f*, manières *fpl* abruptes; (*of style*) caractère *m* heurté *ou* saccadé **(b)** (*suddenness*) (*of departure*) précipitation *f* **(c)** (*of slope, incline*) raideur *f*

ABS [eɪbiːˈes] *n* (*abbr* **anti-lock braking system**) ABS *m*; **A. system** système *m* ABS

abscess [ˈæbses] *n* abcès *m*

abscond [əbˈskɒnd] *vi* **(a)** *Jur* (*run away*) s'enfuir; (*from prison*) s'enfuir, s'évader **(from** de); **to a. from justice** se soustraire à la justice **(b)** *F* (*make off*) décamper, filer

absconder [əbˈskɒndər] *n Jur* fugitif, -ive; (*prisoner*) évadé, -ée

absconding [əbˈskɒndɪŋ] *n Jur* évasion *f*, fuite *f*

▶ **abseil down** [ˈæbseɪl] *vi Sp* descendre en rappel

abseiling [ˈæbseɪlɪŋ] *n Sp* (*in mountaineering*) rappel *m*

absence [ˈæbsəns] *n* **(a)** absence *f* **(from** de); **during one of his absences abroad** lors d'un de ses voyages à l'étranger; **in the a. of the manager** en l'absence du directeur; *Prov* **a. makes the heart grow fonder** = l'éloignement renforce l'affection; *Jur* **sentenced in one's a.** condamné par contumace; *Admin* **leave of a.** congé *m*; *Mil etc* **a. without leave** absence illégale **(b)** (*lack*) absence *f*; **the a. of a tail in human beings** l'absence de queue chez l'être humain; **in the a. of definite information** faute de *ou* à défaut de renseignements précis **(c) a. of mind** distraction *f*

absent[1] [ˈæbsənt] *adj* **(a)** *Sch etc* absent **(from** de); **to a. friends!** (*toast*) à tous nos amis absents!; *Mil etc* **a. without leave** porté manquant **(b)** (*lacking*) absent **(c)** (*expression, look etc*) absent

absent[2] [æbˈsent] *vt* **to a. oneself** (*for a few moments*) s'absenter **(from** de); **to a. oneself from a meeting** (*not attend*) être absent à une réunion

absentee [æbsənˈtiː] *n* **(a)** absent, -ente; (*from roll call*) manquant, -ante; **a. landlord** propriétaire *mf* absentéiste **(b)** *Ind etc* (*regularly absent*) absentéiste *mf*

absenteeism [æbsənˈtiːɪz(ə)m] *n* absentéisme *m*

absently [ˈæbsəntlɪ] *adv* distraitement

absentminded [æbsəntˈmaɪndɪd] *adj* distrait

absentmindedly [æbsəntˈmaɪndɪdlɪ] *adv* (*to say, listen*) distraitement; **she a. left it on the train** elle l'a laissé dans le train par distraction

absentmindedness [æbsəntˈmaɪndɪdnɪs] *n* distraction *f*

absinth(e) [ˈæbsɪnθ] *n* absinthe *f*

absolute [ˈæbsəluːt] **1** *adj Gram, Math etc* absolu; **case of a. necessity** cas de nécessité absolue *ou* de force majeure; **it's an a. disgrace** c'est un véritable scandale; **he's an a. fool** c'est un parfait imbécile; **it would be a. madness** ce serait de la folie pure; *Mktg* **a. frequency** fréquence *f* absolue; *Pol* **a. majority** majorité *f* absolue; *Pol* **a. monarch** monarque *m*

absolu; **a. power** pouvoir *m* absolu; *Math* **a. value** valeur *f* absolue; **a. zero** zéro *m* absolu **2** *n Phil* **the a.** l'absolu *m*
absolutely [æbsəˈluːtlɪ] *adv* absolument; **you're a. right** vous avez absolument *ou* tout à fait raison; **that's ridiculous – a.** c'est ridicule – (oui,) tout à fait; **do you support him? – a. /a. not** vous le soutenez? – absolument/absolument pas; **I a. refuse** je refuse catégoriquement; **I a. insist that you attend the meeting** je tiens absolument à ce que vous soyez présent à la réunion; **it is a. forbidden** c'est absolument *ou* formellement interdit; *Gram* **verb used a.** verbe employé absolument
absolution [æbsəˈluːʃən] *n Rel* absolution *f*; **to give sb a.** donner l'absolution à qn
absolutism [ˈæbsəluːtɪz(ə)m] *n Pol* absolutisme *m*
absolve [əbˈzɒlv] *vt* (*person*) absoudre (**from, of** de); **she was absolved from** *or* **of all blame** il fut reconnu qu'elle n'était aucunement responsable; **he felt he had been absolved from** *or* **of blame** il s'estimait complètement innocenté
absorb [əbˈsɔːb, -ˈzɔːb] *vt* **(a)** (*liquid, heat etc*) absorber; (*shock, sound*) amortir; (*costs*) se charger de; (*loss*) essuyer; (*information*) enregistrer, assimiler; *Com* (*company*) racheter; **to a. a deficit** résorber un déficit; **to a. debts** éponger des dettes; **these units were absorbed into the new army** ces unités furent intégrées dans le nouveau corps d'armée **(b)** (*interest, occupy*) (*person*) absorber; **to be/become absorbed in sth** s'absorber dans qch; **to listen with absorbed interest** écouter avec un intérêt profond
absorbency [əbˈsɔːbənsɪ, -ˈzɔːb-] *n* capacité *f* d'absorption
absorbent [əbˈsɔːbənt, -ˈzɔːb-] *adj, n* absorbant *m*
absorber [əbˈsɔːbər, -ˈzɔːb-] *n Aut etc* (*of shock etc*) amortisseur *m*
absorbing [əbˈsɔːbɪŋ, -ˈzɔːb-] *adj* (*subject, article, discussion*) passionnant; (*work*) absorbant, prenant
absorption [əbˈsɔːpʃən, -ˈzɔːp-] *n* **(a)** (*of liquid*) absorption *f*; (*of sound, impact etc*) amortissement *m*; *Com* (*of company*) rachat *m* **(b)** (*interest*) absorption *f*; **her a. in the book was so great that ...** elle était tellement absorbée dans son livre que ...
abstain [əbˈsteɪn] *vi* **(a)** s'abstenir; **to a. from (doing) sth** s'abstenir de (faire) qch; **to a. from meat** s'abstenir de manger de la viande **(b)** *Pol* s'abstenir
abstainer [əbˈsteɪnər] *n* **(a)** (*from drink*) **to be a total a.** ne pas boire d'alcool; **he's become a total a.** il a complètement arrêté de boire **(b)** (*in vote*) abstentionniste *mf*
abstemious [əbˈstiːmɪəs] *adj* (*person*) sobre; (*diet, eating habits*) frugal; **you're being very a.!** tu t'es mis à la diète
abstemiously [əbˈstiːmɪəslɪ] *adv* sobrement; (*to eat*) frugalement
abstemiousness [əbˈstiːmɪəsnɪs] *n* sobriété *f*
abstention [əbˈstenʃən] *n* **(a)** abstention *f* (**from** de); **their a. from making any comment** le fait qu'ils se soient abstenus de tout commentaire **(b)** *Pol* (*in voting*) abstention *f*
abstinence [ˈæbstɪnəns] *n* abstinence *f* (**from** de); *Rel* **day of a.** jour *m* d'abstinence; **total a.** abstinence complète
abstract¹ [ˈæbstrækt] **1** *adj* **(a)** (*number, noun, art*) abstrait; **a. artist** abstrait *m* **(b)** (*obscure*) abstrait, abstrus **2** *n* **(a) the a.** l'abstrait *m*; **in the a.** dans l'abstrait **(b)** (*work of art*) œuvre *f* abstraite **(c)** (*summary*) résumé *m*, abrégé *m*
abstract² [æbˈstrækt] *vt* **(a)** *Fml* (*remove*) sortir, extraire (**sth from sth** qch de qch); *esp Hum* (*steal*) subtiliser (**sth from sb** qch à qn); *Ch* extraire (par distillation) **(b)** (*text*) résumer, abréger **(c)** *Phil* (*quality*) abstraire, faire abstraction de
abstracted [æbˈstræktɪd] *adj* distrait
abstractedly [æbˈstræktɪdlɪ] *adv* distraitement, d'un air distrait
abstraction [æbˈstrækʃən] *n* **(a)** *Fml* (*theft*) subtilisation *f*; *Ch, Ind* extraction *f* (par distillation) **(b)** (*abstract idea*) abstraction *f*, idée *f* abstraite **(c)** (*distraction*) distraction *f*; **in a moment of a.** dans un moment d'inattention **(d)** *Phil* abstraction *f*
abstractly [ˈæbstræktlɪ] *adv* abstraitement
abstruse [əbˈstruːs] *adj* abstrus
abstruseness [əbˈstruːsnɪs] *n* caractère *m* abstrus
absurd [əbˈsɜːd] **1** *adj* absurde **2** *n Phil* **the a.** l'absurde *m*
absurdity [əbˈsɜːdɪtɪ] *n* absurdité *f*; **the a. of paying people to ...** l'absurdité consistant à payer des gens pour ...
absurdly [əbˈsɜːdlɪ] *adv* absurdement; **rather a. I seem to have forgotten your name** c'est absurde mais je crois bien que j'ai oublié votre nom; *F* **she's a. rich** elle est ridiculement riche
ABTA [ˈæbtə] *n* (*abbr* **Association of British Travel Agents**) association *f* des agents de voyage britanniques
abundance [əˈbʌndəns] *n* **(a)** abondance *f*; **in a.** en abondance, à profusion; **they had an a. of musical talent** ils avaient un immense talent musical **(b)** *Biol etc* (*of species etc*) abondance *f* **(c)** *Cards* (*in solo whist*) abondance *f*
abundant [əˈbʌndənt] *adj* abondant (**in** en); (*in wheat etc*) fertile; **to be a. in natural resources** abonder en ressources naturelles; **there is a. evidence that ...** il y a de nombreuses preuves démontrant que ...
abundantly [əˈbʌndəntlɪ] *adv* **(a)** (*in abundance*) abondamment, en abondance **(b)** (*obvious*) largement; **they made their feelings a. clear** ils exprimèrent leurs sentiments tout à fait clairement; **I think that's a. clear** je pense que c'est limpide; **is that clear? – a.** c'est clair? – limpide
abuse¹ [əˈbjuːs] *n* **(a)** (*misuse*) abus *m* (**of** de); (*of facilities*) usage *m* abusif; (*of term etc*) emploi *m* abusif; *Jur* **a. of authority** abus d'autorité *ou* de pouvoir; *Parl* **a. of privilege** abus de droit; **a. of trust** abus de confiance; **alcohol a.** l'abus *ou* l'excès *m* d'alcool **(b)** (*insults*) injures *fpl*, insultes *fpl*; **term of a.** injure *f*; **to shower a. on sb** accabler qn d'injures **(c)** (*of child etc*) mauvais traitement *m*; **sexual a.** sévices *mpl* sexuels
abuse² [əˈbjuːz] *vt* **(a)** (*misuse*) (*one's authority, sb's trust, patience etc*) abuser de; (*one's power*) mésuser de, abuser de; **a much abused word** un mot employé abusivement **(b)** (*insult*) injurier, insulter **(c)** (*ill-treat*) maltraiter; (*sexually*) faire subir des sévices à; **abused child** (*sexually*) enfant *mf* victime de sévices
abusive [əˈbjuːsɪv] *adj* **(a)** (*use*) abusif **(b)** (*words*) injurieux; (*person*) grossier; **a. language** des grossièretés *fpl*; **he got** *or* **became a.** il devint grossier
abusively [əˈbjuːsɪvlɪ] *adv* (*to speak*) injurieusement; **an a. worded letter** une lettre aux termes injurieux
▶ **abut on, abut against** [əˈbʌt] *vipo* **(-tt-)** (*field, river etc*) confiner à; *Constr* (*partition*) s'appuyer *ou* buter contre; (*wall*) s'arc-bouter contre
abutment [əˈbʌtmənt] *n Archit, Constr* (*of defensive wall*) arc-boutant *m*, *pl* arcs-boutants; (*of wall*) contrefort *m*; (*of bridge*) butée *f*, culée *f*; (*of arch*) piédroit *m*
abysmal [əˈbɪzm(ə)l] *adj* **(a)** (*extreme*) (*stupidity, ignorance*) profond **(b)** *F* (*bad*) abominable, épouvantable
abysmally [əˈbɪzm(ə)lɪ] *adv* atrocement; **a. ignorant** d'une ignorance profonde; **the area is a. lacking in good restaurants** le quartier est absolument dépourvu de bons restaurants
abyss [əˈbɪs] *n Geog, Fig* abîme *m*, gouffre *m*; (*in ocean*) abysse *m*, zone *f* abyssale
abyssal [əˈbɪs(ə)l] *adj* (*depths*), *Geol* abyssal
Abyssinia [æbɪˈsɪnɪə] *n* Abyssinie *f*
Abyssinian [æbɪˈsɪnɪən] **1** *adj* abyssinien, abyssin; (*cat*) abyssin **2** *n* **(a)** Abyssinien, -ienne **(b)** *Ling* abyssinien *m*
AC [eɪˈsiː] *n* **(a)** *El* (*abbr* **alternating current**) CA *m* **(b)** *abbr* **air conditioning**
A/C, a/c *Com* (*abbr* **account**) c.
acacia [əˈkeɪʃə] *n Bot* acacia *m*; **false a.** faux acacia
academia [ækəˈdiːmɪə] *n Univ* milieu *m* universitaire
academic [ækəˈdemɪk] **1** *adj* **(a)** (*of school*) scolaire; (*of university*) universitaire; **the a. year** l'année scolaire/universitaire; **we aim for a. excellence** notre objectif est l'excellence de notre enseignement; **her a. achievements are impressive** elle a fait de brillantes études; **the first a. study of ...** la première étude faite par un universitaire de ...
(b) (*intellectual*) (*subjects*) d'enseignement général; (*person*) studieux, doué pour les études
(c) (*theoretical*) **a. discussion** discussion *f* abstraite; *Pej* **of purely a. interest** qui n'est intéressant qu'au point de vue théorique; **that's a. now** c'est hors de propos à présent, ça n'a plus d'importance; **I know this is a bit a., but why exactly ...?** je sais que ma question n'a qu'un intérêt théorique, mais pourquoi exactement ...?
(d) *Art* (*painting etc*) académique
2 *n* universitaire *mf*
academically [ækəˈdemɪklɪ] *adv* académiquement; **to be a. gifted** être doué intellectuellement; **she's not very a. inclined** elle n'est pas très douée pour les études; **the school doesn't have a tremendous reputation a.** l'école n'est pas fabuleusement cotée pour la qualité de son enseignement
academician [əkædəˈmɪʃən] *n* académicien, -ienne; *Br* **Royal A.** = membre *m* de l'Académie royale des Beaux-Arts
academicism [ækəˈdemɪsɪz(ə)m], **academism** [əˈkædəmɪz(ə)m] *n Art esp Pej* académisme *m*
academy [əˈkædəmɪ] *n* **(a)** académie *f*; *Br* **the Royal A. (of Arts)** = l'Académie royale des Beaux-Arts; **a. of music** conservatoire *m*; **fencing a.** salle *f* d'escrime; **military a.** école *f* militaire **(b)** (*school*) *Scot* ≈ lycée *m*; *Br, US* ≈ collège *m* (privé)
acanthus [əˈkænθəs] *n* **(a)** (*shrub*) acanthe *f* **(b)** *Archit* (feuille *f* d')acanthe *f*
accede [ækˈsiːd] *vi* **(a) to a. to the throne** monter sur le trône **(b)** *Fml* (*assent*) **to a. to** (*treaty*) donner son adhésion à; (*request, demand*) accéder à

accelerate [əkˈseləreɪt] **1** *vt* (*one's pace, progress*) accélérer; (*movement*) presser, accélérer; (*events*) précipiter **2** *vi Aut* accélérer; (*of motion etc*) s'accélérer
accelerated [əkˈseləreɪtɪd] *adj* (*motion etc*) accéléré; *Cin* **a. motion** accéléré *m*; *Acct* **a. depreciation** amortissement *m* dégressif
acceleration [əkseləˈreɪʃən] *n* accélération *f*; **negative a.** accélération retardatrice *ou* négative; *Aut* **the car has good a.** cette voiture a une bonne accélération; *Phys* **uniform a.** vitesse *f* uniformément accélérée; **a. lane** voie *f* d'accélération
accelerator [əkˈseləreɪtər] *n* **(a)** *Aut* **a. (pedal)** (pédale *f* d')accélérateur *m*; **to step on the a.** accélérer, *F* appuyer sur le champignon; *Aut* **a. heel point** point *m* talon **(b)** *Comptr, Phys* accélérateur *m*; *Comptr* **a. card** carte *f* accélératrice
accent[1] [ˈæksənt] *n* **(a)** (*pronunciation*) accent *m*; **to have a Liverpool a.** avoir l'accent de Liverpool; **to have a German a.** avoir un accent allemand; **she speaks French with/without an a.** elle parle français avec un/sans accent
(b) *Lit* **in broken accents** d'une voix brisée *ou* entrecoupée; **to speak in accents of doom** se montrer très pessimiste
(c) (*sign*) accent *m*; **acute/grave a.** accent aigu/grave
(d) (*stress*) accent *m*; **the a. is on the final syllable** l'accent est sur la dernière syllabe; *Fig* **we're putting the a. on efficiency** nous mettons l'accent sur l'efficacité; **fashion with the a. on youth** mode qui met l'accent sur la jeunesse
accent[2] [ækˈsent] *vt* (*syllable etc*) accentuer
accented [ækˈsentɪd] *adj* accentué; *Ling* accentuel; **a. character** caractère *m* accentué
accentuate [ækˈsentʃʊeɪt] *vt* (*detail etc*) accentuer, faire ressortir; (*contrast*) accuser; **to a. the need for sth** accentuer la nécessité de qch
accentuated [ækˈsentʃʊeɪtɪd] *adj* accentué; (*limp, stutter*) fortement marqué; *Mus* **the offbeat is a.** le temps faible est accentué
accentuation [æksentʃʊˈeɪʃən] *n* (*of vowel, detail etc*) accentuation *f*
accept [əkˈsept] **1** *vt* **(a)** (*take when offered*) (*gift, invitation, offer*) accepter; **please a. my apologies** je vous prie de bien vouloir accepter mes excuses; **the machine won't a. foreign coins** cette machine n'accepte pas la monnaie étrangère
(b) *Com* **to a. a bill** accepter un effet; **to a. (delivery of) goods** réceptionner des marchandises
(c) (*recognize as valid*) (*reasons*) admettre; (*treaty*) donner son adhésion à; **while we a. that this may be more expensive ...** tout en admettant que ceci puisse être plus cher ...; **I cannot a. that you knew nothing of this** je n'arrive pas à croire que vous n'avez rien su de ceci; **to a. responsibility for sth** prendre *ou* accepter la responsabilité de qch; **to a. no responsibility** décliner toute responsabilité; **it is generally accepted that ...** il est généralement admis que ...; **contrary to accepted opinion, ...** contrairement à l'idée communément admise, ...; **the accepted custom** (*socially approved*) l'usage *m* admis; **to be accepted** (*socially etc*) être accepté
(d) (*resign oneself to*) accepter; **she just accepts these hardships** elle accepte tout bonnement ces épreuves
2 *vi* accepter; **they offered me a contract and I accepted** ils m'ont proposé un contrat que j'ai accepté
acceptability [əkseptəˈbɪlɪtɪ] *n* acceptabilité *f*
acceptable [əkˈseptəb(ə)l] *adj* **(a)** (*admissible*) acceptable; **behaviour of this sort is not a.** un comportement de la sorte est inacceptable *ou* inadmissible; **I trust these terms will be a. to you** j'espère que ces conditions vous seront acceptables; **just about a.** juste passable **(b)** (*welcome, satisfactory*) bienvenu; **a most a. gift** un cadeau des plus bienvenus; **your cheque was most a.** votre chèque était fort apprécié
acceptance [əkˈseptəns] *n* **(a)** (*of gift, invitation, apology etc*) acceptation *f*; (*of candidate*) admission *f*; **to find a.** trouver créance; **to gain a.** (*of views, theory etc*) être accepté; **she's got two provisional acceptances** (*for university*) elle a été provisoirement admise dans deux universités
(b) *Com, Ind* (*of something ordered*) réception *f*; *Fin* **to present a bill for a.** présenter une traite à l'acceptation; *Fin* **a. bill** traite *f* contre acceptation; *Fin* **a. fee** commission *f* d'acceptation
(c) (*of one's fate, circumstances*) acceptation *f*; **his unquestioning a. of this explanation** le fait qu'il ait accepté cette explication sans sourciller
acceptance bank *or* **house** *n Banking* banque *f* d'escompte d'effets étrangers
acceptance speech *n* discours *m* de réception
acceptance test *or* **trial** *n* essai *m* de réception *ou* de recette
acceptation [æksepˈteɪʃən] *n Fml* acception *f*; **in the full a. of the word** dans toute l'acception du mot
accepting house [əkˈseptɪŋ] *n Banking* maison *f* d'acceptation
acceptor [əkˈseptər] *n Com, Ch etc* accepteur *m*
Access® [ˈækses] *n* carte *f* Eurocard Mastercard
access[1] [ˈækses] *n* **(a)** (*to person, place*) accès *m* (**to** à); **there is easy a. to the beach** on accède facilement à la plage; **to have a. to sth/sb** avoir accès à qch/auprès de qn; **to give sb a. to sth/sb** donner à qn accès à qch/auprès de qn; **the burglars gained a. through a window** les cambrioleurs sont passés *ou* entrés par une fenêtre; **we must not give terrorists a. to the media** nous ne devons pas donner l'accès aux médias aux terroristes; *Fml* **difficult of a.** d'un accès *ou* d'une approche difficile; *Comptr* **a. denied** (*DOS message*) accès refusé; *Aut* **a. only** accès interdit (sauf aux riverains); **her ex-husband has unlimited a. to the children** son ex-mari a un droit de visite illimitée auprès de ses enfants; *Comptr* **a. authorization code** code *m* d'autorisation d'accès; **a.-authorized person** personne *f* autorisée d'accès; *Mktg* **a. barrier** barrière *f* d'accès; **a. broadcasting** télévision *f* ouverte; *Comptr* **a. control** contrôle *m* d'accès; *Comptr* **a. level** (*in network*) niveau *m* d'accès; *TV etc* **a. prime-time** access *m* prime-time, période *f* précédant les heures de grande écoute
(b) (*of rage etc*) accès *m*; *often Iron* (*of enthusiasm, generosity*) élan *m*
access[2] *vt Comptr* (*data*) accéder à, avoir accès à
accessary [əkˈsesərɪ] *n* = **accessory 2(c)**
access code *n Comptr* code *m* d'accès
accessibility [əksesɪˈbɪlɪtɪ] *n* accessibilité *f*
accessible [əkˈsesəb(ə)l] *adj* (*place, novel, style etc*) accessible (**to** à); (*person*) (*easy to talk to*) abordable, facile à aborder; (*easy to have a meeting with etc*) accessible; **she has a very a. manner** elle est d'un abord très facile; **information a. to everyone** connaissances à la portée de tout le monde
accession [əkˈseʃən] *n* **(a)** (*to post, power etc*) accession *f* (**to** à); (*to throne*) avènement *m*, accession (**to** à) **(b)** (*to treaty*) accession *f*, adhésion *f* (**to** à); (*to demand*) accession **(c)** (*increase*) accroissement *m* (par addition); (*item, esp library book*) addition *f*; **accession(s) book** (*in library*) registre *m* des additions; **a. number** numéro *m* matricule
accessory [əkˈsesərɪ] **1** *adj* accessoire (**to** à); *Bot* **a. bud** *or* **shoot** prompt-bourgeon *m*, *pl* prompts-bourgeons **2** *n* **(a)** (*item*) accessoire *m*; **car/camera accessories** accessoires d'automobile/d'appareil-photo **(b)** (*clothing*) (*usu pl*) **accessories** accessoires *mpl* **(c)** *Jur* complice *mf*; **a. to a crime** complice d'un crime; **a. before the fact** complice par instigation *ou* par assistance; **a. after the fact** complice par aide après coup
access rights *npl* (*of divorced parents*) droits *mpl* de visite
access road *n Aut* route *f* d'accès
access time *n Comptr* temps *m* d'accès
accident [ˈæksɪdənt] *n* accident *m*; *Jur* cas *m* fortuit; **by a.** (*by chance*) par hasard, accidentellement; **I'm sorry, it was an a.** je suis désolé, c'était un accident; **an a. in the home/at work** un accident domestique/du travail; **to have an a.** (*in car, kitchen, F of child in pants etc*) avoir un accident; **car a.** accident de voiture; **road a.** accident de la route; **the victims of the a.** les victimes de l'accident, les accidentés *mpl*; *prov* **accidents will happen** on ne peut pas parer à tout; **it was an a. waiting to happen** c'est un accident qui devait arriver; **it's no a. that she made the film here** ce n'est pas par hasard si elle a tourné le film ici; **that was no a.** ce n'est pas le fait du hasard; **their last child was an a.** leur dernier enfant est un accident; **a. particulars form** déclaration *f* d'accident
accidental [æksɪˈdent(ə)l] **1** *adj* **(a)** (*chance*) accidentel, fortuit; **a. meeting** rencontre *f* fortuite; *Jur* **a. death** mort *f* accidentelle; **I gave him the a. impression that ...** sans le vouloir je lui ai donné l'impression que ... **(b)** (*incidental*) accessoire, subsidiaire **2** *n Mus* accident *m*, signe *m* accidentel
accidentally [æksɪˈdent(ə)lɪ] *adv* **(a)** (*by chance*) par hasard, accidentellement **(b)** (*not deliberately*) accidentellement, par mégarde; *Hum* **a. on purpose** comme par hasard, exprès
accident and emergency unit *n* (*in hospital*) service *m* des urgences, urgences *fpl*
accident blackspot *n* point *m* noir
accident insurance *n* assurance *f* accidents
accident-prone *adj* prédisposé aux accidents; **he is a.** il lui arrive toujours des malheurs
accident victim *n* victime *f* d'un/de l'accident
acclaim[1] [əˈkleɪm] *n* **to meet with great critical a.** être salué

par la critique; **the a. of his peers** la reconnaissance de ses pairs; **I had never anticipated such wild a.** je ne m'attendais pas à de telles louanges

acclaim[2] *vt* **(a)** acclamer; **to be acclaimed by the critics** être acclamé des critiques; **he was acclaimed as the new Caruso** il fut acclamé et proclamé le nouveau Caruso; **her acclaimed portrayal of Cleopatra** sa représentation acclamée de Cléopâtre **(b)** *(proclaim)* **Charlemagne was acclaimed emperor** Charlemagne fut acclamé *ou* proclamé empereur

acclamation [æklə'meɪʃən] *n* acclamation *f*; **carried by a.** adopté par acclamation

acclimate [ə'klaɪmeɪt, 'æklɪmeɪt] *vt Am* = **acclimatize**

acclimation [æklɪ'meɪʃən] *n Am* = **acclimatization**

acclimatization [əklaɪmətaɪ'zeɪʃən] *n* acclimatement *m* **(to** à); *Fig* acclimatation *f*

acclimatize [ə'klaɪmətaɪz] **1** *vt* acclimater; *(plant etc)* naturaliser; **to become acclimatized to a new environment** s'acclimater à un nouvel environnement; **to a. oneself to sth** s'acclimater à qch **2** *vi* s'acclimater

accolade ['ækəleɪd] *n* accolade *f*; **the ultimate a.** la consécration suprême

accommodate [ə'kɒmədeɪt] **1** *vt* **(a)** *(provide room for) (specific number of people)* loger, recevoir; **restaurant that can a. 50 people** restaurant qui peut recevoir *ou* servir 50 personnes **(b)** *(satisfy)* satisfaire; **we will try to a. you** nous essaierons de vous satisfaire; **to do sth to a. sb** faire qch pour arranger qn **(c)** *(provide)* **to a. sb with sth** donner *ou* fournir qch à qn; **to a. sb with a loan** faire un prêt à qn **(d)** *(reconcile) (one's tastes to sb else's)* accommoder; *(opinions, differences)* concilier; **to a. oneself to circumstances** s'adapter aux circonstances **2** *vi Physiol (of eye)* accommoder

accommodating [ə'kɒmədeɪtɪŋ] *adj* complaisant, obligeant

accommodation [əkɒmə'deɪʃən] *n* **(a)** [①A11,f,i] *(Am usu* **accommodations)** logement *m*; *(in hotel)* chambre(s) *f(pl)* (d'hôtel); **to look for a.** *(flat to rent)* chercher un logement; *(hotel room)* chercher une chambre (d'hôtel); **the huts were meant for short-term a.** les cabanes étaient destinées à servir de logement à court terme; **furnished/unfurnished a.** chambres garnies *ou* meublées/non meublées; **hotel a.** hébergement *m* en hôtel; **a. allowance** indemnité *f* de logement; **a. capacity** *(of hotel)* capacité *f* d'accueil; **a. department** service *m* hébergement; **a. industry** industrie *f* de l'hébergement; **a. only** logement sans restauration; **a. package** forfait *m* hébergement; **a. shortage** capacités *fpl* d'hébergement insuffisantes; **a. unit** unité *f* d'hébergement; **there is a. in this hotel for 50 people** cet hôtel peut loger 50 personnes

(b) *(adaptation)* ajustement *m*, adaptation *f* **(to** à); *Physiol (of eye)* accommodation *f*

(c) *esp Fml (of argument)* arrangement *m*; **to come to an a.** arriver à un compromis; **to come to an a. with one's creditors** parvenir à un arrangement avec ses créanciers

(d) *Fin (of money)* avance *f*, prêt *m*; **a. bill** traite *f* de complaisance

accommodation address *n* adresse *f* de convention

accommodation ladder *n Naut* échelle *f* de commandement *ou* de coupée

accompaniment [ə'kʌmpənɪmənt] *n* **(a)** *Mus* accompagnement *m* **(on the piano** au piano) **(b)** *Culin* accompagnement *m*

accompanist [ə'kʌmpənɪst] *n Mus* accompagnateur, -trice

accompany [ə'kʌmpənɪ] *vt* **(a)** accompagner; **to be accompanied by sb** être accompagné de qn; **she accompanied me to the door** elle m'a raccompagné jusqu'à la porte; **the hot weather is often accompanied by afternoon thunderstorms** la chaleur s'accompagne souvent d'orages dans l'après-midi; **fever accompanied by** *or* **with delirium** fièvre accompagnée de délire; **a meal accompanied with wine** un repas accompagné de vin; **accompanied baggage** bagages *mpl* accompagnés **(b)** *Mus* accompagner **(on the piano** au piano); **he accompanied himself on the guitar** il s'accompagna à la guitare

accomplice [ə'kɒmplɪs, -'kʌm-] *n* complice *mf*; **his accomplices in crime** les complices de ses crimes

accomplish [ə'kɒmplɪʃ, -'kʌm-] *vt (task)* accomplir, mener à bonne fin, venir à bout de; *(journey, crossing)* effectuer; **to a. one's object** atteindre son but

accomplished [ə'kɒmplɪʃt, -'kʌm-] *adj* **(a)** *(completed)* achevé; **a. fact** fait *m* accompli **(b)** *(dancer, pianist, performance etc)* accompli

accomplishment [ə'kɒmplɪʃmənt, -'kʌm-] *n* **(a)** *(of task etc)* accomplissement *m*; *(of project)* réalisation *f* **(b)** *(feat, achievement)* prouesse *f*, exploit *m*; **that's quite an a.** c'est un véritable exploit, c'est une véritable prouesse **(c)** *(talent)* talent *m*; **one of his many accomplishments** un de ses nombreux talents

accord[1] [ə'kɔːd] *n* **(a)** *(agreement)* accord *m*, consentement *m*; **with one a.** d'un commun accord; **this was in a. with their policy** ceci était en accord avec leur politique **(b)** *(pact)* accord *m*; **to reach an a.** parvenir à un accord **(c)** *(initiative)* **to do sth of one's own a.** faire qch de son plein gré; **the table seemed to be moving of its own a.** la table avait l'air de bouger toute seule

accord[2] **1** *vi* s'accorder, concorder **(with** avec); **this accords with her earlier statement** ceci concorde avec sa première déclaration **2** *vt Fml* accorder, concéder **(to** à); *(significance, status)* accorder; **a privilege/title accorded him by the crown** un privilège/un titre qui lui a été concédé par la couronne

accordance [ə'kɔːdəns] *n* accord *m*, conformité *f*; **in a. with** conformément à; **this is in a. with the rules** ceci est conforme au règlement; **his statement is not in a. with the facts** sa déclaration ne concorde pas avec les faits

according [ə'kɔːdɪŋ] *adv* **(a)** *(depending on)* **a. to how it is done** suivant la façon dont on le fait; **a. to whether one is rich or poor** selon qu'on est riche ou pauvre; **a. to which method you use** selon la méthode employée **(b)** *(in conformity with)* **a. to instructions** selon *ou* suivant *ou* d'après les ordres; **a. to age** par rang d'âge; **a. to plan** conformément au plan; **a. to our means** selon nos moyens **(c)** *(citing a source)* **a. to him** selon lui, d'après lui, à ce qu'il dit; **the Gospel a. to St Luke** l'Évangile selon saint Luc; **a. to what I've heard** d'après ce que j'ai entendu dire

accordingly [ə'kɔːdɪŋlɪ] *adv* **(a)** *(to act, dress etc)* en conséquence **(b)** *(therefore)* donc; **a., I wrote to him** je lui ai donc écrit, par conséquent je lui ai écrit

accordion [ə'kɔːdɪən] *n Mus* accordéon *m*; **piano a.** accordéon à touches; **a. player** accordéoniste *mf*; *Sewing etc* **a. pleats** plis *mpl* en accordéon

accordionist [ə'kɔːdɪənɪst] *n Mus* accordéoniste *mf*

accost [ə'kɒst] *vt (person)* accoster, aborder; *(of prostitute)* racoler

account[1] [ə'kaʊnt] *n* **(a)** *Fin, Com, Banking* compte *m*; **to open an a.** *(in bank)* ouvrir un compte; **to have an a. with Lloyds** avoir un compte à la Lloyds; **to have an a. with a shop/Marks & Spencer** avoir un compte dans un magasin/chez Marks & Spencer; **put it on** *or* **charge it to my a.** inscrivez-le *ou* mettez-le à mon compte; **to pay a sum on a.** payer une somme en acompte *ou* à compte *ou* à valoir; **to settle an a.** régler une note *ou* un compte; *Fig* **to settle accounts** régler ses comptes **(with sb** avec qn); **that should settle accounts with him** ça devrait régler mes comptes avec lui; **to keep (an) a. of sth** *(record)* tenir un compte de qch; **a. balance** *(status)* situation *f* de compte; *(after audit)* reliquat *m* de compte; **a. book** livre *m* de compte; *Banking* **a. charges** frais *mpl* de tenue de compte; **a. commission** commission *f* de compte; **a. credit** avoir *m* de compte; **a. fee** commission *f* de compte; **a. handling fee** commission *f* de tenue de compte; *Banking* **a. management charges** frais *mpl* de tenue de compte; *Banking etc* **a. manager** chargé *m* de compte; *Acct* **a. payable** compte créditeur, dette *f* fournisseur; *Banking* **a. position** situation *f* de compte; *Acct* **a. receivable** compte client, compte débiteur; **a. statement** relevé *m* de compte; **accounts payable** dettes *fpl* fournisseurs; **accounts payable book** *or* **ledger** livre *m* des créanciers; **accounts receivable** créances *fpl*, créances clients; **accounts receivable book** *or* **ledger** livre *m* des débiteurs

(b) *(in advertising, PR)* budget *m*, compte-client *m*, *pl* comptes-clients; **one of our major accounts** un de nos plus gros clients; **we lost the Guinness a.** nous avons perdu la clientèle de Guinness *ou* le budget Guinness; *Mktg* **a. handler** responsable *mf* des comptes-clients; **a. manager** responsable *mf* client, responsable des comptes-clients, directeur *m* de clientèle

(c) *St Exch* **the A.** la liquidation (mensuelle); **a. day** (jour *m* de) liquidation, (jour de) règlement *m*; **dealings for the a.** négociations *fpl* à terme

(d) *Fin, Com (of expenses)* état *m*, note *f*; *(of transactions)* exposé *m*

(e) *(advantage)* parti *m*; **to turn sth to a.** tirer parti *ou* avantage de qch, mettre qch à profit; **to turn sth to good a.** tirer un bon parti de qch

(f) to call sb to a. demander une explication *ou* des comptes à qn **(for sth** de qch); **to be brought to a.** devoir rendre des comptes; **to give a good a. of oneself** bien se comporter

(g) *(importance)* **of no a.** *(person, matter)* insignifiant, de peu d'importance; **to take sth into a., to take a. of sth** tenir compte de qch, faire entrer qch en ligne de compte; **taking**

everything into a. tout bien calculé; **to leave out of a., to take no a. of** ne pas tenir compte de; (*circumstance*) négliger

(h) (*because*) **on a. of sth** en raison de qch; (*esp in negative context*) à cause de qch; **I did it on your a.** je l'ai fait pour vous; **I did it on a. of you** (*reproaching*) je l'ai fait à cause de vous; **the road was closed on a. of the accident** la route était barrée à cause *ou* en raison de l'accident; **he can't play football on a. of his health** il ne peut pas jouer au football en raison de sa santé; **on no a., not on any a.** en aucun cas; **I don't want to talk to her on any a.** je ne veux lui parler en aucun cas *ou* sous aucun prétexte; **you're not on any a. to ...** tu ne dois en aucun cas *ou* sous aucun prétexte ...

(i) (*responsibility*) **to act on one's own a.** agir de sa propre initiative *ou* de soi-même; **to set up in business on one's own a.** s'établir à son compte

(j) (*report*) (*of events*) récit *m*; (*of facts, actual situation*) exposé *m*; (*in newspaper*) compte rendu *m*; **to give an a. of sth** faire le récit de qch; **an interesting a. of his travels** un récit intéressant de ses voyages; **his a. of the siege of Gerona** le récit qu'il fait/faisait du siège de Gérone; **his latest book contains an amusing a. of how he learned to drive** son dernier livre relate de façon amusante la manière dont il a appris à conduire; **her a. (of the events) was slightly different** son exposé des événements était légèrement différent; **on any a.** à tous points de vue; **by all accounts** au dire de tout le monde

account² *vt Fml* **to a. sb guilty** tenir qn pour coupable

▶ **account for** *vipo* (a) (*one's behaviour, expense*) (*explain*) rendre compte de; (*justify*) justifier; (*circumstance*) expliquer; **that accounts for his interest in baseball** voilà qui explique son intérêt pour le baseball; **I can't a. for it** je ne me l'explique pas; **five people have still not been accounted for** (*after accident etc*) cinq personnes n'ont toujours pas été retrouvées; **there is no accounting for taste** chacun son goût

(b) (*constitute*) constituer; **oil accounts for 10 per cent of exports** le pétrole constitue dix pour cent des exportations; **all my time is already accounted for** mon temps est *ou* je suis déjà complètement pris

(c) (*destroy*) (*plane*) abattre; (*submarine*) couler; (*troops*) tuer; *Fig* **he accounted for three batsmen** il a renversé le guichet de trois batteurs; **that accounts for him** (*striking sb off list etc*) son compte est réglé, à celui-là

accountability [əkaʊntə'bɪlɪtɪ] *n* responsabilité *f* (**to** envers); **local government a. is an important issue** la nécessité pour les municipalités de rendre compte de leurs actions est une question d'actualité

accountable [ə'kaʊntəb(ə)l] *adj* **to be a. to sb for sth** être responsable de qch envers qn; **to hold sb a.** tenir qn (pour) responsable (**for sth** de qch); **to be a. for a sum of money** être redevable d'une somme d'argent; **I am a. to no one** je n'ai de comptes à rendre à personne; **the police must be made more a. for their actions** la police doit rendre davantage compte de ses actions; **a. government/police force** gouvernement/police responsable; **a. marketing** mercatique *f* responsable

accountancy [ə'kaʊntənsɪ] *n Fin* comptabilité *f*, expertise *f* comptable, *F* compta *f*

accountant [ə'kaʊntənt] *n Fin* comptable *mf*; **chief a.** chef *m* de (la) comptabilité; **chartered a.,** *Am* **certified public a.** = expert *m* comptable

account card *n* (a) (*record of charges in hotel etc*) fiche *f* de compte *ou* de facture (b) (*for use in department store*) carte-clients *f*

account director *n Mktg* directeur *m* des comptes-clients

account executive *n Mktg* responsable *mf* des comptes-clients

account holder *n Banking* titulaire *mf* de compte

accounting [ə'kaʊntɪŋ] *n Fin* comptabilité *f*, *F* compta *f*; *Banking* **a. day** journée *f* comptable; **a. entry** écriture *f* comptable; **a. entry sheet** *or* **form** bordereau *m* de saisie; **a. method** méthode *f* de comptabilité, procédé *m ou* mode *m* comptable; **a. period** période *f* comptable; **a. policy** politique *f* comptable; **a. records** états *mpl* comptables; **a. system** système *m* comptable

accounting firm *n* cabinet *m* d'expertise comptable

accounting year *n* année *f* comptable

account number *n* numéro *m* de compte

accounts [ə'kaʊnts] *npl* (a) comptabilité *f*, comptes *mpl*; **to keep the a.** tenir les livres *mpl ou* les écritures *fpl ou* les comptes; **to enter sth in the a.** comptabiliser qch; **who does your a.?** qui est-ce qui fait votre comptabilité?; **a. clerk** aide-comptable *mf*; **a. ledger** grand livre *m* des comptes (b) **a. (department)** (service *m* de la) comptabilité *f*, *F* compta *f*

accounts software *n* logiciel *m* de comptabilité

accoutrements [ə'ku:trəmənts], *US* **accouterments** [ə'ku:təmənts] *npl* (*equipment*) équipement *m*; **all the a. of her profession** tout l'attirail *m* propre à sa profession

accredit [ə'kredɪt] *vt* (a) (*attribute*) attribuer (**to** à) (b) (*appoint, authorize*) (*ambassador*) accréditer (**to a government** auprès d'un gouvernement)

accreditation [əkredɪ'teɪʃən] *n* accréditation *f*

accredited [ə'kredɪtɪd] *adj* (*person*) accrédité, autorisé; **a. journalist** journaliste *mf* accrédité(e); **a. college** école *f* reconnue (par l'État)

accretion [ə'kri:ʃən] *n* accroissement *m*; (*of skills*) accumulation *f*; **an a. of fungus** une accumulation de moisissures

accrual [ə'kru:əl] *n Fin* accumulation *f*; *Acct* **accruals** (*accrued expenses*) charges *fpl* à payer; (*accrued income*) produits *mpl* à recevoir

accrue [ə'kru:] **1** *vi* (a) *Fin* (*of interest*) s'accumuler; **accrued interest** intérêt *m* couru, intérêts *mpl* échus (b) (*of moneys, land etc*) **to a. to sb** revenir à qn; **accrued dividends** dividendes *mpl* accrus; **accrued income** produit *m* à recevoir; **accruing interest** intérêts *mpl* à échoir **2** *vt* (*interest*) produire

accumulate [ə'kju:mjʊleɪt] **1** *vt* (*fortune etc*) accumuler, amasser; (*objects*) amonceler, entasser; (*heat, electricity etc*) emmagasiner; (*dust*) ramasser **2** *vi* s'accumuler

accumulated [ə'kju:mjʊleɪtɪd] *adj attrib* accumulé

accumulation [əkju:mjʊ'leɪʃən] *n* (a) (*act*) accumulation *f*; (*of objects*) amoncellement *m*, entassement *m*; (*of heat, electricity etc*) emmagasinage *m* (b) (*result*) (*of objects, sand etc*) amas *m*, tas *m*; (*of facts, evidence*) accumulation *f*

accumulative [ə'kju:mjʊlətɪv] *adj* qui s'accumule; *Fin* cumulatif

accumulator [ə'kju:mjʊleɪtər] *n* (a) *MecE, Constr, El* accumulateur *m* (b) *Horseracing* **a. (bet)** pari *m* avec report (c) (*person*) **he's an a. of useless gadgets** il accumule les gadgets inutiles

accuracy ['ækjʊrəsɪ] *n* (*of calculation, forecast*) exactitude *f*; (*of firearm, shot etc*) précision *f*; (*of report, statement etc*) justesse *f*; (*of translation*) fidélité *f*

accurate ['ækjʊrət] *adj* (*calculation, forecast*) correct, exact; (*firearm, shot, meter*) précis; (*report*) juste; (*translation, portrayal*) fidèle; **a. scales** balance *f* juste; **my typing is much more a.** ma frappe est beaucoup plus précise; **to be (strictly) a. ...** pour être tout à fait exact ...

accurately ['ækjʊrətlɪ] *adv* (*to calculate*) exactement; (*to measure, aim, report*) avec précision; (*to translate, portray*) fidèlement; (*to draw*) correctement; **very a. measured/predicted** calculé/prédit avec une grande précision; **he a. predicted that ...** il a justement prédit que ...

accurateness ['ækjʊrətnɪs] *n* exactitude *f*, précision *f*

accursed [ə'kɜ:sɪd] *adj Lit* maudit

accusation [ækjʊ'zeɪʃən] *n* accusation *f*; **to bring an a. against sb** porter *ou* déposer plainte contre qn; **an a. of bribery was made against him** on l'a accusé de corruption; **to make an a.** lancer une accusation; **he made some wild accusations about my having bugged his telephone** il m'a absurdement accusé d'avoir mis son téléphone sur écoute

accusative [ə'kju:zətɪv] *Gram* **1** *n* (cas *m*) accusatif *m*; **in the a.** à l'accusatif **2** *adj* (*case*) accusatif

accusatory [ə'kju:zətərɪ, ækjʊ'zeɪtərɪ] *adj* accusateur, -trice

accuse [ə'kju:z] *vt* accuser (**sb of sth** qn de qch; **of doing sth** de faire qch); **you stand accused** vous êtes inculpé; *Iron* **no one could a. her of being punctual** on ne peut pas l'accuser d'être ponctuelle

accused [ə'kju:zd] *n Jur* **the a.** l'inculpé, -ée; (*of offence*) le prévenu, la prévenue; (*of crime*) l'accusé, -ée

accuser [ə'kju:zər] *n* accusateur, -trice

accusing [ə'kju:zɪŋ] *adj attrib* (*look, finger etc*) accusateur, -trice; **she pointed an a. finger at him** elle dirigea vers lui un doigt accusateur; *Fig* elle l'a mis en cause

accusingly [ə'kju:zɪŋlɪ] *adv* (*to ask*) d'une manière accusatrice; (*to look, stare*) d'un air *ou* d'un œil accusateur

accustom [ə'kʌstəm] *vt* habituer, accoutumer (**sb to sth** qn à qch; **to do sth** à faire qch); **to a. oneself to** (*new job, country, climate etc*) s'habituer *ou* se faire *ou* s'accoutumer à; **to a. oneself to doing/being sth** s'habituer à faire/être qch

accustomed [ə'kʌstəmd] *adj* (a) **I am a. to getting up early** j'ai l'habitude de me lever de bonne heure; **they weren't a. to strangers/politeness** ils n'étaient pas habitués aux étrangers/à la politesse; **to get** *or* **grow a. to sth/to doing sth** s'habituer à qch/à faire qch; **her eyes had got a. to the dark** ses yeux s'étaient accoutumés à l'obscurité (b) (*habitual*) habituel, coutumier

AC/DC ['eɪsi:'di:si:] *n El* (*abbr* **alternating current/direct current**) CA/CC *m*; *Fig F* **to be A.** (*bisexual*) marcher à voile et à vapeur

ace [eɪs] **1** *n* **(a)** *Cards* as *m*; **a. of spades** as de pique; *F* **to have an a. up one's sleeve** avoir un atout en réserve **(b)** *Tennis* **(service) a.** ace *m* **(c)** *F* (*expert*) as *m*; **flying a.** as de l'aviation; *esp Am* **a. reporter** journaliste *mf* d'élite **(d) within an a. of sth** à deux doigts de qch **2** *adj Sl* (*very good*) extra

acerbic [ə'sɜːbɪk] *adj* (*fruit, taste*) aigre; *Fig* (*person, comment*) acerbe, mordant

acerbity [ə'sɜːbɪtɪ] *n* aigreur *f*, acerbité *f*

acetate ['æsɪteɪt] *n Ch* acétate *m*

acetic [æ'siːtɪk, -'set-] *adj Ch* (*acid etc*) acétique

acetone ['æsɪtəʊn] *n Ch* acétone *f*

acetylene [æ'setɪliːn] *n Ch* acétylène *m*; **a. lamp** lampe *f* à acétylène; **a. torch** torche *f* à acétylène; **a. welding** soudure *f* autogène

acetylsalicylic acid [æsɪtaɪlsælɪ'sɪlɪk] *n Pharm* acide *m* acétylsalicylique

ACH [eɪsiː'eɪtʃ] *n Banking* (*abbr* **automated clearing house**) chambre *f* de compensation automatisée

ache[1] [eɪk] *n* mal *m*, douleur *f*, *Spec* algie *f*; **stomach a.** mal de ventre; **to have (a) stomach a.** avoir mal au ventre; **she's always telling people about all her aches and pains** elle n'arrête pas de se plaindre de ses maux à tout le monde; **I've just got a few aches and pains, that's all** j'ai quelques douleurs, c'est tout; *Fig esp Lit* **I have an a. in my heart** j'ai de la peine

ache[2] *vi* **my head aches** j'ai mal à la tête; **it makes my head a.** cela me donne mal à la tête; **I'm aching all over** j'ai mal partout; *Fig* **it makes my heart a.** cela me serre le cœur; **he was aching to join in the fight** il brûlait de prendre part au combat

achieve [ə'tʃiːv] *vt* **(a)** (*accomplish*) (*aim, goal*) atteindre, arriver à; **to a. a great deal** (*in life*) accomplir beaucoup de choses; (*in task*) réussir à faire beaucoup de choses; **to a. very little** (*in life, task*) ne pas faire grand-chose; **to a. one's purpose** *or* **ends** parvenir *ou* en venir à ses fins; **to a. the impossible** réussir l'impossible; **to a. success** réussir; **we achieved what we set out to do** nous avons rempli nos objectifs; **I feel that we have achieved something** j'ai le sentiment que nous sommes arrivés à quelque chose; **he will never a. anything** il n'arrivera jamais à rien; **this policy achieved very little** cette politique n'a pas donné de grands résultats; **what will that a.?** (*of suggestion etc*) qu'est-ce que ça fera de plus?, pour en venir à quoi?; **achieved room rate** prix *m* total des chambres

(b) (*gain*) (*honour, notoriety*) acquérir; (*reputation*) se faire

achievement [ə'tʃiːvmənt] *n* **(a)** (*feat*) exploit *m*, haut fait *m*; **their real a. lay in ...** leur véritable prouesse résida dans ...; **getting him to talk about anything is quite an a.** arriver à le faire parler de quoi que ce soit relève vraiment d'un exploit; **a lasting a.** une réalisation durable; **her many achievements** ses nombreux succès **(b)** (*of a project etc*) accomplissement *m*, réalisation *f*, exécution *f*

achievement-orient(at)ed [ə'tʃiːvmənt'ɔːrɪent(eɪt)ɪd] *adj* **to be a.** mettre l'accent sur la réussite; *Pej* être obsédé par la réussite

achiever [ə'tʃiːvər] *n* homme *m*/femme *f* performant(e), battant, -ante

Achilles [ə'kɪliːz] *n* Achille *m*; **A. tendon** tendon *m* d'Achille; *Fig* **gambling is his A. heel** le jeu est son point faible

aching ['eɪkɪŋ] *adj* (*tooth, head etc*) qui vous/me/*etc* fait mal; (*leg, shoulder etc*) endolori; **to have an a. heart** avoir une peine de cœur; **her death left an a. void in his life** sa mort a laissé un vide douloureux dans sa vie

achromatic [ækrə'mætɪk] *adj Opt* achromatique

achy ['eɪkɪ] *adj* courbaturé; **I feel rather a.** j'ai mal un peu partout; **I have an a. feeling in my joints** mes jointures sont douloureuses

acid[1] ['æsɪd] *adj* **(a)** acide; **a. drop** (*sweet*) bonbon *m* acidulé **(b)** (*tone, reply*) acerbe

acid[2] *n* **(a)** acide *m*; **a. bath** bain *m* acide; **a. rain** pluies *fpl* acides; *Ch* **a. solution** solution *f* acide; **a. test** épreuve *f* à la pierre de touche; *Fig* épreuve décisive *ou* concluante, test *m* décisif; *Acct* **a. test ratio** ratio *m* de liquidité immédiate **(b)** *F* **(= LSD)** acide *m*

acidic [ə'sɪdɪk] *adj Ch* acide; *Fig* (*comment etc*) acerbe

acidify [ə'sɪdɪfaɪ] *vt* acidifier

acidity [ə'sɪdɪtɪ] *n* **(a)** *Ch* acidité *f*; *Med* aigreurs *fpl*; **excessive a. in the stomach** une acidité gastrique excessive **(b)** *Fig* (*of reply*) aigreur *f*

acidly ['æsɪdlɪ] *adv* aigrement

acidosis [æsɪ'dəʊsɪs] *n Med* acidose *f*

acidulous [ə'sɪdjʊləs] *adj* acidulé

ack-ack ['æk'æk] *n Old-fashioned, Mil* (*weapon*) artillerie *f* anti-aérienne; (*system*) ≈ Défense *f* contre avions, D.C.A. *f*; **a. fire** tir *m* anti-aérien

acknowledge [ək'nɒlɪdʒ] *vt* **(a)** (*recognize*) (*mistake, debt etc*) reconnaître; (*service*) reconnaître, se montrer reconnaissant de, exprimer sa reconnaissance de; *TV, Cin* (*in credits*) mentionner; **to a. sth as a fact** faire la constatation de qch; **acknowledged as the** *or* **to be the best Chinese restaurant in the city** reconnu comme le meilleur restaurant chinois de la ville; **to a. oneself beaten, to a. defeat** s'avouer *ou* se reconnaître vaincu; **she acknowledged my presence** elle m'a fait signe qu'elle m'avait vu; **he didn't even a. my presence** il m'a complètement ignoré; **she never acknowledges me** (*greets*) elle fait toujours comme si elle ne me voyait pas

(b) (*reply to*) (*courtesy, greeting etc*) répondre à; **to a. (receipt of) a letter** accuser réception d'une lettre; *Naut* **to a. a signal** faire l'aperçu

acknowledge character *n Comptr* (*in datacomms*) caractère *m* d'accusé de réception

acknowledged [ək'nɒlɪdʒd] *adj attrib* (*fact*) reconnu, avéré; (*expert etc*) qui fait autorité; **an a. thief** un voleur reconnu

acknowledg(e)ment [ək'nɒlɪdʒmənt] *n* **(a)** (*of mistake, service etc*) reconnaissance *f*; (*of fact*) constatation *f*; *Comptr* (*in datacomms*) accusé *m* de réception; **I waved/smiled at him, but received no a.** je lui ai fait signe/ai souri mais il ne m'a pas répondu; **in a. of** pour témoigner ma/sa/*etc* reconnaissance de; **acknowledgments** (*in book*) remerciements *mpl*; (*in credits*) mentions *fpl* (au générique), remerciements; **to quote an author without a.** citer un auteur sans mentionner son nom; **to give some a. to the fact that ...** reconnaître le fait que ...; **there's not enough a. of the debt he owes to Goldstein** il ne rend pas suffisamment hommage à Goldstein; **a. of debt** reconnaissance de dette

(b) (*of payment*) reçu *m*, quittance *f*; **a. (of receipt)** (*of letter*) accusé *m* de réception; **a. of reservation** confirmation *f* de réservation

acme ['ækmɪ] *n Lit* (*of perfection, politeness*) comble *m*

acne ['æknɪ] *n Med* acné *f*

acolyte ['ækəlaɪt] *n Rel* acolyte *m*; *Fig* disciple *m*

acorn ['eɪkɔːn] *n* gland *m* (de chêne)

acoustic [ə'kuːstɪk] *adj* acoustique; (*signal etc*) sonore; *Comptr* **a. coupler** coupleur *m* acoustique; *TV etc* **a. feedback** effet *m* Larsen, rétroaction *f* acoustique, bouclage *m* acoustique; **a. hood** capot *m* antibruit; *Mus* **a. guitar** guitare *f* acoustique; **a. tile** carreau *m* *ou* panneau *m* insonorisant; *Anat* **a. nerve** nerf *m* acoustique *ou* auditif

acoustically [ə'kuːstɪklɪ] *adv* acoustiquement

acoustics [ə'kuːstɪks] *n* (①**A10**,c) acoustique *f*; **the a. of the hall are good** cette salle a une bonne acoustique

acquaint [ə'kweɪnt] *vt* **(a)** *esp Fml* **to a. sb with sth** (*his duties, situation, fact*) mettre qn au courant de qch, informer qn de qch; **to a. sb with the controls** instruire qn sur le fonctionnement des commandes; **a stay in the jungle had acquainted him with these dangers** un séjour dans la jungle l'avait familiarisé avec ces dangers; **to a. oneself with the facts/the situation** se mettre au courant des faits/de la situation; **the doctor acquainted himself with her case history** le médecin s'est informé de ses antécédents médicaux

(b) to be acquainted with sb connaître qn; **to be acquainted with sth** connaître qch, être au fait *ou* au courant de qch; **to become** *or* **get acquainted** (*of two people*) faire connaissance; **to become** *or* **get acquainted with sb** faire *ou* lier connaissance avec qn; **we soon became** *or* **got acquainted** nous avons vite fait connaissance; **I got acquainted with him later** j'ai fait sa connaissance plus tard; **to become acquainted with the facts** prendre connaissance des faits

acquaintance [ə'kweɪntəns] *n* **(a)** (*person*) connaissance *f*; **he is an a. (of mine)** c'est quelqu'un que je connais; **a casual a. (of mine)** quelqu'un que je connais de loin; **to have a wide circle of acquaintances** avoir des relations très étendues **(b) a. with** (*person, fact, language*) connaissance *f* de; **to make sb's a.** faire la connaissance de qn; **during our brief a.** pendant la courte période où nous avons été en contact; **his apparent lack of a. with the facts** son ignorance apparente des faits

acquiesce [ækwɪ'es] *vi* acquiescer, donner son assentiment **(in, to à)**; **to a. in an arrangement** accepter un arrangement

acquiescence [ækwɪ'es(ə)ns] *n* assentiment *m*, consentement *m*, acquiescement *m* **(in, to à)**

acquiescent [ækwɪ'es(ə)nt] *adj* consentant

acquire [ə'kwaɪər] *vt* (*house, knowledge, experience etc*) acquérir; (*habit*) prendre, contracter; (*friend*) se faire;

(*overtones*) prendre; **to a. a taste for sth** prendre goût à qch; **gin/Proust is an acquired taste** le gin c'est quelque chose/ Proust est un auteur qu'on apprend à aimer; *Psy* **acquired characteristic** caractère *m* acquis; **he acquired a stoop** son dos s'est voûté; **to a. an accent** prendre un accent; **we seem to have acquired some friends** (*are being followed etc*) on dirait que nous avons de la compagnie; **we seem to have acquired a cat** il semble qu'on ait hérité d'un chat

Acquired Immune Deficiency Syndrome [ə'kwaɪəd] *n Med* Syndrome *m* d'immuno-déficience acquise

acquirement [ə'kwaɪəmənt] *n* acquisition *f* (**of** de)

acquisition [ækwɪ'zɪʃən] *n* (**a**) (*act*) acquisition *f* (**of** de); *Acct* **a. cost** coût *m* d'acquisition (**b**) (*object, person*) acquisition *f*; **she could be a useful a.** elle pourrait se révéler être une acquisition utile

acquisitive [ə'kwɪzɪtɪv] *adj* thésauriseur, -euse; **an a. nature** une nature avide

acquit [ə'kwɪt] *vt* (**-tt-**) (**a**) *Jur* (*person accused of a crime*) acquitter; **to a. sb of sth** (*mistake*) absoudre qn de; (*of charge*) décharger qn de qch (**b**) *Fin* (*debt*) acquitter, s'acquitter de, régler (**c**) **to a. oneself with distinction** s'en sortir très honorablement; **he acquitted himself well/badly** il s'en est bien/mal acquitté; **how did he a. himself?** comment s'en est-il sorti?

acquittal [ə'kwɪt(ə)l] *n* (**a**) *Jur* (*of defendant*) acquittement *m*, décharge *f*; (*of debt*) acquittement (**b**) (*of duty*) exécution *f*, accomplissement *m*

acre ['eɪkər] *n* acre *f* (= 0, 4 hectare); (*approx* =) arpent *m*, demi-hectare *m*; **vast acres** des terres *fpl* étendues; **acres of forest** des hectares *mpl* de forêts; *Fig F* **acres of ...** des tas de ...; **acres of room** énormément de place

acreage ['eɪkərɪdʒ] *n* superficie *f* (*en mesures agraires*)

acrid ['ækrɪd] *adj* (**a**) (*taste, smoke*) âcre (**b**) *Fig* (*style*) mordant; (*criticism*) acerbe

acrimonious [ækrɪ'məʊnɪəs] *adj* acrimonieux; (*person*) acariâtre; **the discussion was becoming a.** la discussion s'envenimait

acrimoniously [ækrɪ'məʊnɪəslɪ] *adv* avec acrimonie

acrimony ['ækrɪmənɪ], **acrimoniousness** [ækrɪ'məʊnɪəsnɪs] *n* acrimonie *f*; (*of tone, character*) aigreur *f*; **the tone of a. in his voice** l'aigreur qu'il y avait dans sa voix

acrobat ['ækrəbæt] *n* acrobate *mf*

acrobatic [ækrə'bætɪk] *adj* acrobatique; **a. feat** acrobatie *f*

acrobatics [ækrə'bætɪks] *n* [①A10,c] acrobatie *f*

acronym ['ækrənɪm] *n* sigle *m*

Acropolis [ə'krɒpəlɪs] *n* Acropole *f*

across [ə'krɒs] *adv, prep* (**a**) (*from one side to the other*) en travers (de); **line drawn a. the page** ligne tirée en travers de la page; **with his arms folded a. his chest** les bras croisés sur la poitrine; **they talked to each other a. the table** ils se parlaient de part et d'autre de la table; **there was no bridge a. the river** aucun pont n'enjambait la rivière; **to find a way a. the mountain** trouver un chemin pour traverser la montagne; **from a. the entire range** de toute la gamme

(**b**) (*of motion*) **to walk a. (a street)** traverser (une rue); **we helped him a. the road** nous l'avons aidé à traverser la rue; **a. country** à travers champs; **to swim a. a river** traverser une rivière à la nage; **to go a. a bridge** passer (sur) un pont, franchir un pont; **they got the barrel a. the river/road** ils ont fait passer le tonneau de l'autre côté de la rivière/rue; **is he a. the river/road yet?** est-ce qu'il a enfin traversé la rivière/la rue?; **she threw it a. the room/ courtyard** elle l'a balancé en travers de *ou* de l'autre côté de la pièce/de la cour; **we cut a. the park** nous avons coupé à travers le parc; **to get** *or* **come a.** (*of play*) passer la rampe; **to get sth a. to sb** (*make understand*) faire comprendre qch à qn; **he doesn't come a. as an aggressive person** il ne donne pas l'impression de quelqu'un d'agressif

(**c**) (*of distance*) **2 km a.** 2 km de large; **he is broad a. the shoulders** il est large d'épaules; **the distance a.** (*width*) la distance en largeur; (*of crossing*) la longueur de la traversée; **it's too far a.** c'est trop loin

(**d**) (*on the other side*) **a. the street** de l'autre côté de la rue; **the woman from a. the street** la femme d'en face; **there's a supermarket just a. the road from us/our house** il y a un supermarché juste en face/en face de notre maison; **just a. the border** de l'autre côté *ou* au-delà de la frontière; **from a. the sea** par-delà la mer

(**e**) (*in crossword*) horizontalement

across-the-board 1 *adj* général; **an a. wage increase** une augmentation générale des salaires; **a. cuts** réduction linéaire générale **2** *adv* (*to apply*) de façon générale

acrostic [ə'krɒstɪk] *n Liter* acrostiche *m*

acrylic [ə'krɪlɪk] **1** *adj* (*fibre, paint etc*) acrylique; **a. garment** vêtement en acrylique **2** *n* (**a**) (*resin*) résine *f* acrylique (**b**) (*material*) acrylique *m*, fibre *f* acrylique (**c**) (*garment*) vêtement *m* en acrylique (**d**) (*paint*) peinture *f* acrylique

act[1] [ækt] *n* (**a**) (*of justice, kindness etc*) acte *m*; (*deed*) action *f*; **a. of war** acte de guerre; *Rel* **a. of faith** acte de foi; **the Acts of the Apostles** les Actes des Apôtres; **an a. of folly** une folie; **an a. of despair** un acte désespéré; **the a. of a criminal/madman** l'action d'un criminel/fou; **to catch sb in the (very) a.** prendre qn sur le fait *ou* en flagrant délit; **she was caught in the a. of taking the money** on l'a surprise en train de voler l'argent

(**b**) (*in play*) acte *m*; **A. I, scene 1** Acte I, scène 1; **a one-a. play** une pièce en un acte

(**c**) (*in cabaret, circus etc*) numéro *m*; **circus a.** numéro de cirque; **to put on an a.** (*pretend*) jouer la comédie; **it's all an a.** (*pretence*) c'est du cinéma; *Fig* **to get in on the a.** se mettre dans le mouvement; *Fig* **to be/to let sb in on the a.** être/mettre qn dans le coup; *F* **to have one's a. together** (*professionally*) bien connaître son affaire; (*personally*) être un homme/une femme accompli(e), avoir sa vie bien en main; *F* **get your a. together!** (*professionally*) faites un effort!, *F* vous ne pourriez pas vous secouer, un peu!; (*personally*) prends ta vie en main!

(**d**) *Jur, Pol* loi *f*; **A. of Parliament** loi, décret *m*; **Companies A.** = loi sur les sociétés; **factory a.** législation *f* industrielle; **land a.** loi agraire

act[2] **1** *vt* (*play, character*) jouer; (*role*) jouer, tenir; **to a. Hamlet** jouer Hamlet; *Fig* **to a. the fool** faire l'imbécile; **to a. a part** jouer un rôle; *Fig* jouer la comédie, feindre; **to a. the part of an honest man** se conduire *ou* agir en honnête homme

2 *vi* (**a**) (*take action*) agir; **it is time to a.** il est temps d'agir; **to a. out of fear/greed/selfishness** agir sous l'emprise de la peur/par cupidité/par égoïsme; **I acted for the best** j'ai fait pour le mieux; **to a. for sb** agir au nom de qn; (*of lawyer*) représenter qn; **I'm acting for her** j'agis en son nom; **the police refused to a.** la police a refusé d'intervenir; **to a. as secretary** exercer les fonctions de secrétaire; **the stick acted as a tent pole** le bâton servit de montant pour la tente; **the smell acts as a warning to other animals** les autres animaux sont avertis par l'odeur; **the engine acts as a brake** le moteur fait fonction de frein; **to a. as a warning** servir d'avertissement; **to a. as a motivation** constituer une motivation

(**b**) (*behave*) se comporter, agir; **they a. as if nothing had happened** ils se comportent *ou* ils font comme si rien ne s'était passé; **he acts as if he were** *or F* **like he was the boss** il se comporte comme si c'était lui le patron; **stop acting like a child!, a. your age!** arrête de faire l'enfant!

(**c**) *Th, Cin* jouer; (*pretend*) jouer la comédie; **he can't a.** c'est un mauvais acteur; **I always wanted to a.** j'ai toujours voulu être acteur; **to a. in a film** tourner dans un film; **to a. stupid/all innocent** faire l'idiot/l'innocent

▶ **act on** *vipo* (**a**) (*affect*) influer sur, agir sur; (*of remedy etc*) agir sur; **acid acts on metal** l'acide agit sur le métal; *Med* **to a. on the brain/the bowels** exercer une action sur *ou* agir sur le cerveau/l'intestin; **the rumours acted on their fears** les rumeurs ont joué sur leurs craintes (**b**) (*respond to*) (*advice*) agir d'après, suivre; (*order*) exécuter; (*letter*) donner suite à; **acting on my lawyer's advice** conformément aux conseils de mon avocat; **the police acted on the information** la police a agi après avoir reçu l'information

▶ **act out** *vtsep* **to a. out a fantasy** vivre un fantasme; **local people a. out scenes from the town's history** les gens du coin jouent des scènes de l'histoire de leur ville; **she acts out our deepest fears** elle exprime nos peurs les plus profondes

▶ **act up** *vi F* (*of child*) se conduire mal; (*of machine*) marcher mal; **the car's acting up again** la voiture recommence à faire des siennes; **don't start acting up!** conduis-toi bien!; **my knee/back is acting up again** mon genou/dos recommence à me faire souffrir

▶ **act upon** *vipo* = **act on** ['æktɪŋ] **1** *adj attrib* (*temporary*) suppléant, intérimaire; **a. manager** directeur *m* intérimaire, gérant *m* provisoire **2** *n Th, Cin* (*of actor*) jeu *m*, interprétation *f*; (*profession*) métier *m* d'acteur; **she's done some a.** elle a fait du théâtre/du cinéma; **the a. is marvellous** le jeu des acteurs est merveilleux

action ['ækʃən] *n* (**a**) (*of person, remedy etc*) action *f*; (*single act*) action, acte *m*, fait *m*; *Br* **(industrial) a.** mouvement *m* de revendication; (*strike*) grève *f*; **the a. of water** (*on river bank etc*) le travail des eaux, l'action de l'eau; **we want a. not words** nous voulons des actes non des paroles; **to take a.** agir; (*intervene*) intervenir; *Br* (*go on strike*) se mettre en grève; **their quick a. prevented more deaths** leur action rapide a évité d'autres morts; **course** *or* **line of a.** ligne *f* de conduite; **a man of a.** un homme d'action; **sphere of a.** sphère *f* d'activité; *Br* **day of a.** journée *f* d'action; **to put a plan into a.** mettre un projet à exécution; **to come into a.** entrer en action *ou* en jeu; **in a.** (*of machine*) en marche; (*of sportsman*) à l'œuvre; *F* **she destroys interviewers, you should see her in a.** elle anéantit les interviewers, tu l'as vue à l'œuvre?; **out of a.** (*machine, vehicle etc*) hors de service, hors d'usage; (*person*) hors de combat; **to put a machine out of a.** détraquer une machine; **the flu put** *or* **kept him out of a. for a month** la grippe l'a mis hors de combat pendant un mois; **impulsive a.** action irréfléchie, coup *m* de tête; **she's not responsible for her actions** elle n'est pas responsable de ses actes; *Prov* **actions speak louder than words** les actes en disent plus long que les paroles; *Art* **a. painting** peinture *f* gestuelle

(b) *Th, Cin, TV, Liter* (*of play, novel etc*) action *f*; **the a. takes place in ...** l'action se passe à ...; *Cin* **a.!** on tourne!, action!

(c) (*movement*) (*of player*) action *f*; (*of horse*) allure *f*; **a song with actions** une chanson mimée

(d) *Tech* (*of watch, clock*) mécanisme *m*; (*of pump, lock*) jeu *m*

(e) *Jur* action *f*; **a. at law, legal a.** action en justice; (*trial etc*) procès *m*; **a. for libel** procès *ou* plainte *f* en diffamation; **a. for damages** action en dommages et intérêts; **to bring an a. against sb** intenter une action *ou* un procès à *ou* contre qn

(f) *Mil etc* combat *m*, engagement *m*; **naval a.** engagement naval, opération *f* navale; **to go into a.** entrer en action, engager le combat; **ready for a.** prêt à combattre; **to send troops into a.** faire intervenir *ou* faire donner des troupes; **to see a.** (*of soldier*) combattre; **to put a gun/plane/***etc* **out of a.** (*destroy*) mettre un canon/avion/*etc* hors de combat; (*disable*) mettre un canon/un avion/*etc* hors de service *ou F* de cause; **killed in a.** tué à l'ennemi; **as a result of enemy a.** à la suite de l'action ennemie; **a. programme** plan *m* d'action, plan de manœuvre; **a. stations!** tout le monde à son poste!; *Fig* vingt-deux!

(g) *F* (*excitement*) action *f*; **there's plenty of a. in the movie** il y a plein d'action dans ce film; **they were looking for some a.** (*nightlife etc*) ils cherchaient un peu d'animation; **where's the a. around here?** où est-ce que ça bouge par ici?

(h) *Sl* **they want a piece** *or* **slice of the a.** (*profits*) ils veulent une part du gâteau

actionable [ˈækʃənəb(ə)l] *adj Jur* (*remarks, action*) qui expose à des poursuites

action film *n* film *m* d'action

action movie *n* film *m* d'action

action-packed *adj* (*film, novel, match*) plein d'action; (*day, morning etc*) bien rempli

action replay *n* reprise *f*; (*in slow motion*) ralenti *m*

activate [ˈæktɪveɪt] *vt* **(a)** (*put into operation*) (*mechanism, alarm*) déclencher **(b)** *Ch* activer; **activated carbon** charbon actif *ou* activé **(c)** *Phys* rendre radioactif

activation [æktɪˈveɪʃən] *n* activation *f*; (*of alarm*) déclenchement *m*

active [ˈæktɪv] **1** *adj* **(a)** (*person*) actif; (*mind*) éveillé; (*imagination*) vif; **a. life** vie *f* active; **to be still a.** (*of elderly person*) être encore alerte *ou* actif; **to be/become a.** (*of volcano*) être/entrer en activité; **she's very a. in the party** elle est très active au sein du parti; **he was very a. in seeing that the measure was passed** il a contribué très activement à l'approbation de cette mesure; **to take an a. part in sth** prendre une part active *ou* effective à qch; **to take an a. dislike to sb** se prendre d'une vive aversion contre qn; *Mil* **on a. service** en service actif; **to see a. service** (*fight*) combattre; *Mil* **to be on the a. list** être sur l'annuaire de l'armée active; *Comptr* **a. file** fichier *m* actif; *Comptr* **a. matrix screen** écran *m* à matrice active; *Comptr* **a. program** programme *m* en cours d'exécution; *Comptr* **a. window** fenêtre *f* active *ou* activée

(b) *Gram* (*voice*) actif

2 *n* [①**A40,9**] *Gram* actif *m*, voix *f* active; **verb in the a.** (**voice**) verbe *m* à l'actif *ou* à la voix active

actively [ˈæktɪvlɪ] *adv* activement; **they were a. seeking peace** ils cherchaient activement à faire la paix; **to a. dislike sb** avoir une vive aversion pour qn

activist [ˈæktɪvɪst] *n Pol* activiste *mf*; **anti-nuclear/peace activists** activistes antinucléaires/en faveur de la paix

activity [ækˈtɪvɪtɪ] *n* activité *f*; **economic a.** activité économique; **his numerous activities leave him little leisure** ses nombreuses occupations lui laissent peu de loisirs; **activities** (*at holiday camp*) animation *f*

activity break *n* (courtes) vacances *fpl* actives

activity holiday *n* vacances *fpl* actives

act of God *n* an a. un cas de force majeure

actor [ˈæktər] *n Th* acteur *m*, comédien *m*; *Cin, Fig* acteur; **to be an a.** *Th* faire du théatre, être acteur *ou* comédien; *Cin* faire du cinéma, être acteur

actress [ˈæktrɪs] *n Th* actrice *f*, comédienne *f*; *Cin* actrice; **as the a. said to the bishop** *phrase humoristique à connotation sexuelle, donnée comme réponse ou bien dite par un locuteur lorsqu'il réalise que ce qu'il vient de dire peut être interpreté de manière humoristique, par ex.* I've never seen one this big before ... as the actress said to the bishop

actual [ˈæktʃʊəl] *adj* **(a)** (*concrete*) réel, véritable; (*case*) concret; **a. size** grandeur *f* réelle, vraie grandeur; **to give the a. figures** donner les chiffres mêmes; *F* **in a. fact** en fait; *Com* **a. cost** coût *m* définitif; **a. costs** coûts *mpl* constatés; **a. demand level** niveau *m* de demande réelle; **a. dollars** dollars *mpl* courants; **a. operating costs** coût *m* réel d'exploitation; **her a. words were ...** ce qu'elle a dit en fait, c'est ...; **this is the a. house where she was born** voici en fait la maison où elle est née; *Br F* **the a. managing director visited us today** le directeur général nous a rendu visite en personne aujourd'hui; *Br F* **it's your a. 24-carat gold** c'est de l'or à 24 carats, du vrai de vrai

(b) (*current*) actuel, présent; **the a. state of affairs** l'état de choses actuel

actuality [æktʃʊˈælɪtɪ] *n Fml* **(a)** (*reality*) réalité *f* **(b)** **play that lacks a.** pièce qui n'a aucun rapport avec la vie d'aujourd'hui

actually [ˈæktʃʊəlɪ] *adv* **(a)** (*really*) réellement, en fait, en réalité; **what a. happened?** que s'est-il passé au juste?; **what he a. means is ...** ce qu'il veut vraiment dire, c'est ...; **I didn't a. see it myself** en réalité, je ne l'ai pas vu de mes propres yeux; **the piano's just for decoration, no one a. plays it** le piano fait partie du décor, en fait personne n'en joue; **we haven't a. decided yet** on n'a pas encore vraiment décidé; **yes, but what will the government a. do?** oui, mais que va vraiment faire le gouvernement?

(b) (*even, surprisingly*) **he a. swore** il est (même) allé jusqu'à lâcher un juron; **she a. said good morning to me** à mon grand étonnement elle m'a dit bonjour; **he was a. on time for once** pour une fois il était à l'heure

(c) (*in fact*) en fait; **a., yes, I do mind, very much!** à vrai dire, oui, ça m'ennuie beaucoup!; **I'm not sure, a.** je n'en suis pas certain, en fait; **what do you do? – I'm a lawyer a.** que faites-vous? – je suis avocat; **a., I rather like it** à vrai dire, ça me plaît assez; **he's not a very nice person a.** il n'est pas très gentil à vrai dire

(d) *Fml* (*at this moment*) actuellement, à présent

actuarial [æktʃʊˈeərɪəl] *adj* actuariel

actuary [ˈæktʃʊərɪ] *n* actuaire *m*; **actuaries' tables** tables *fpl* de mortalité

actuate [ˈæktʃʊeɪt] *vt* **(a)** (*machine etc*) mettre en action, faire marcher **(b)** (*sb*) faire agir; **actuated by jealousy** poussé par la jalousie

actuation [æktʃʊˈeɪʃən] *n* (*of machine etc*) mise *f* en action

actuator *n* actionneur *m*

acuity [əˈkjuːɪtɪ] *n Fml* (*of mind, comment*) acuité *f*; **visual a.** acuité visuelle

acumen [ˈækjʊmən] *n* pénétration *f*, finesse *f* (d'esprit), perspicacité *f*; **he's got plenty of business a.** il a un très bon sens des affaires

acupressure [ˈækjʊpreʃər] *n Med* acupressing *m*

acupuncture [ˈækjʊpʌŋktʃər] *n Med* acupuncture *f*, acuponcture *f*

acupuncturist [ˈækjʊpʌŋktʃərɪst] *n Med* acupuncteur, -trice, acuponcteur, -trice

acute [əˈkjuːt] **1** *adj* **(a)** (*pain*) aigu, *f* aiguë, intense, vif; (*disease, crisis, shortage*) aigu; **a. remorse** remords cruels; **to become more a.** (*of anxiety etc*) s'aviver; **operation for a. appendicitis** opération à chaud pour l'appendicite; **to suffer a. embarrassment** être vivement embarrassé; **the problem was made more a.** le problème a été intensifié

(b) (*mind*) fin, perspicace; (*hearing, sense of smell*) fin; (*vision*) perçant; **an a. observer** un observateur pénétrant; **she has an a. awareness of their problems** elle a une perception pénétrante de leurs problèmes; **an a. businesswoman** une femme d'affaires avisée *ou* perspicace

(c) *Math* (*angle*) aigu, *f* aiguë

(d) *Gram* (*accent*) aigu, *f* aiguë

2 *n* accent *m* aigu

acute-angled *adj* à angle(s) aigu(s)

acutely [əˈkjuːtlɪ] *adv* **(a)** (*to feel*) vivement; **he felt the loss a.** il ressentit cette perte intensément; **we are a. aware** *or* **conscious of that** nous en sommes extrêmement conscients **(b)** (*with perspicacity*) finement, avec perspicacité

acuteness [ə'kju:tnɪs] *n* **(a)** (*of pain*) acuité *f*, intensité *f*; (*of remorse, emotion, attack of illness*) intensité **(b)** (*of mind*) pénétration *f*, perspicacité *f*; (*of hearing, judgement*) finesse *f*; (*of vision, sense of smell*) acuité *f*; **we need someone of your a.** nous avons besoin de quelqu'un qui possède votre perspicacité

AD [eɪ'di:] *adv* (*abbr* **anno Domini**) après Jésus-Christ; (*written form*) apr. J.-C.; **in 1066 AD** en 1066 apr. J.-C.

ad [æd] *n F* annonce *f*; *TV, Rad* pub *f*; **small ads** petites annonces; **an ad agency** une agence publicitaire; *TV* **while the ads are on** pendant la pub; **ad break** coupure *f* publicitaire

adage ['ædɪdʒ] *n* adage *m*

adagio [ə'dɑ:ʒɪəʊ, ə'dɑ:dʒ-] *adv, n Mus* adagio *m*

Adam ['ædəm] *n* Adam *m*; *Hum* **I don't know him from A.** je ne le connais ni d'Ève ni d'Adam; *Hum* **A.'s ale** de l'eau *f*, du château-la-pompe; **A.'s apple** pomme *f* d'Adam

adamant ['ædəmənt] *adj* inflexible, intransigeant; **he is a. on this point** sur ce point il ne transige pas; **she is a. that she saw him** elle affirme l'avoir vu et ne veut pas en démordre; **they are a. in their conviction** ils ne veulent pas en démordre

adamantly ['ædəməntlɪ] *adv* inflexiblement, d'une manière intransigeante; **they a. refused** ils refusèrent catégoriquement

adapt [ə'dæpt] **1** *vt* (*machine, vehicle etc*) adapter; **to a. a novel for the stage** adapter un roman à la scène; **text adapted from Cicero** texte d'après Cicéron; **to a. oneself to circumstances/new surroundings** s'adapter aux circonstances/à un nouvel environnement **2** *vi* (*of person, species*) s'adapter **(to** à); **failure to a.** incapacité *f* à s'adapter

adaptability [ədæptə'bɪlɪtɪ] *n* faculté *f* d'adaptation; **a. to the environment** adaptabilité *f* au milieu

adaptable [ə'dæptəb(ə)l] *adj* **(a)** (*adjustable*) adaptable, ajustable **(to** à) **(b)** (*person*) souple, qui s'adapte facilement; (*species*) qui s'adapte facilement

adaptation [ædæp'teɪʃən] *n* **(a)** adaptation *f* **(of sth to sth** de qch à qch); **a. for the stage** adaptation à la scène **(b)** (*novel, play*) adaptation *f* **(c)** *Biol* adaptation *f*, finalité *f*

adapted [ə'dæptɪd] *adj* (*novel etc*) adapté **(for the stage** à la scène); **a telephone a. for use by people with hearing difficulties** un téléphone adapté à l'usage des malentendants; **a. to sth** approprié à qch, fait pour qch

adapter, adaptor [ə'dæptər] *n* **(a)** *El* (*plug*) adaptateur *m*; (*with several sockets*) prise *f* multiple; *Comptr* **a. card** carte-adaptateur *f* **(b)** *MecE* (*connecting pipes*) raccord *m* **(c)** *Phot* (*for camera*) parquet *m* d'adaptation; **lens a.** bague *f* porte-objectif **(d)** (*for record*) centreur *m* **(e)** (*writer*) adaptateur, -trice

adaptive [ə'dæptɪv] *adj Biol* (*mechanism*) adaptif; *Aut* **a. engine controls** commandes *fpl* adaptatives moteur

ADC [eɪdi:'si:] *n Mil abbr* **aide-de-camp**

add [æd] **1** *vt* **(a)** ajouter **(to** à); **this book adds little to the debate** ce livre n'apporte pas grand-chose au débat; **have you anything you would like to a.?** aimeriez-vous ajouter quelque chose?; **it'll a. another hour to the journey** ça allongera le trajet d'une heure **(b)** *Math* additionner; **to a. six to eight** additionner six et huit, ajouter six à huit; **a. these numbers (together)** additionnez ces nombres, faites l'addition de ces nombres; *Math* **to a. a zero** apposer un zéro **2** *vi* (*perform addition*) faire des additions

▶ **add in** *vtsep* (*salt etc*) ajouter

▶ **add on** *vtsep* (*conservatory etc*) ajouter; **should we a. on something as a tip?** est-ce qu'il faut laisser un pourboire?

▶ **add to** *vipo* (*increase*) (*building*) faire une addition à, agrandir; (*difficulty, surprise etc*) augmenter, ajouter à; (*beauty of sth*) rehausser; (*crisis*) accentuer; **the news added to their despondency** cette nouvelle ajouta à leur abattement; **this will a. to the cost** ceci va venir s'ajouter au prix; **to a. to my misfortune** pour mettre le comble à mon malheur; **to a. to what we were saying yesterday ...** pour compléter ce que nous disions hier ...

▶ **add up 1** *vi* **(a)** (*calculate*) additionner; **that boy can't a. up** ce garçon ne sait pas additionner **(b)** (*give correct total*) faire le compte; **the accounts don't a. up** ces comptes ne tombent pas juste **(c)** (*make sense*) **the facts don't a. up** les faits ne riment à rien; **it just doesn't a. up!** ça ne rime à rien!; **it's beginning to a. up** ça devient plus clair **2** *vtsep* (*figures etc*) additionner; **when you a. it all up it was quite cheap** si on fait le total, c'était assez bon marché; **you've added this up wrong** tu t'es trompé dans l'addition

▶ **add up to** *vipo* **(a)** (*of figures*) s'élever à, se chiffrer à; **it adds up to £22** cela s'élève à 22 livres **(b)** (*amount to*) **is that all you've done? it doesn't a. up to much** est-ce que c'est tout ce que tu as fait? ça ne fait pas beaucoup; **it all adds up to an enjoyable day out** cela nous/vous/*etc* fait une agréable journée de sortie

add-back *n Acct* réintégration *f*

added ['ædɪd] *adj attrib* supplémentaire; **a. enjoyment was provided by a jazz band** un orchestre de jazz a aussi contribué à notre/leur/*etc* plaisir; **a. ingredients** (*on food package*) autres ingrédients; **no a. sugar** sans ajout de sucre; **no a. preservatives** sans conservateurs

added value *n* valeur *f* ajoutée

addendum, *pl* **-a** [ə'dendəm, -ə] *n* (*to book etc*) addenda *m inv*, addition *f*

adder ['ædər] *n* (*snake*) vipère *f*

addict¹ ['ædɪkt] *n* **(a)** *Med* intoxiqué, -ée; **(drug) a.** toxicomane *mf*; **heroin a.** héroïnomane *mf* **(b)** *F* (*of football, dance*) fana *mf*; **I'm a coffee a.** je suis accro au café; **I never miss an episode, I'm a complete a.** je ne rate jamais un épisode, je suis complètement accro

addict² [ə'dɪkt] *vt* (*used in passive*) **to be/become addicted to** (*alcohol, opium etc*) s'adonner à, *F* être/devenir accro à; (*a TV programme, aerobics*) ne pas pouvoir se passer de, *F* être/devenir accro à; **to become** *or* **get addicted to drugs/heroin** devenir toxicomane/héroïnomane; **you can easily get addicted to coffee** c'est facile de devenir accro au café

addiction [ə'dɪkʃən] *n* (*to drugs*) dépendance *f*; (*to chocolate, the cinema etc*) goût *m* immodéré **(to** pour); **a. to drugs** la dépendance envers la drogue, la toxicomanie; **my earlier a. to the Italian cinema** ma passion dévorante d'autrefois pour le cinéma italien; **coffee at 4. 00 had become something of an a. with her** elle ne pouvait plus se passer du café de 4 heures

addictive [ə'dɪktɪv] *adj Med* (*drug*) qui cause un phénomène de dépendance, *Spec* toxicomanogène; *Fig* **soap operas are very a.** on a du mal à se passer des feuilletons, on devient vite accro aux feuilletons; **it could become a.** on prend vite l'habitude

adding ['ædɪŋ] *n* addition *f*; **a. machine** machine *f* à calculer, calculatrice *f*

adding up *n* addition *f*

addition [ə'dɪʃən] *n* **(a)** [ⓘA71,7; B56,c,4] (*adding*) *Math* addition *f*; **the a. of three more musicians** l'adjonction *f* de trois musiciens supplémentaires; **in a.** en outre, de plus; **in a. to sth** en plus de qch; **in a. to that sum** en plus de cette somme; **in a. to these misfortunes** par surcroît de malheur; **to pay something in a.** payer un supplément

(b) (*something added*) addition *f*; (*to building*) extension *f*, rajout *m*; **additions to the staff** adjonction *f* de personnel; **he has just had an a. to his family** sa famille a grandi; **where is the latest a.?** (*baby*) où est le petit dernier/la petite dernière?; **an important a. to our collection** une nouvelle pièce de choix à notre collection; **she will be a valuable a. to the staff** sa contribution sera fort appréciable; **the east wing is an eighteenth-century a.** l'aile est a été ajoutée au dix-huitième siècle

additional [ə'dɪʃən(ə)l] *adj* supplémentaire; **70p for each a. 50 grams** (*in list of postal rates*) 70 pence par 50 grammes supplémentaires; **a. information can be found on page 28** se référer à la page 28 pour des informations complémentaires; **a. charge** supplément *m* de prix; **a. expenditure** surcroît *m* de dépenses; **a. expenses** dépenses *fpl* supplémentaires; *Fin, Com etc* **a. payment** supplément; **a. postage** surtaxe *f* (postale); **a. premium** surprime *f*; **a. security** contre-caution *f*; *Admin* **a. tax** impôt *m* additionnel; (*because of underpayment*) supplément d'imposition; **for** *or* **at no a. charge** sans supplément

additionally [ə'dɪʃən(ə)lɪ] *adv* en plus, en outre

additive ['ædɪtɪv] *n* additif *m*

addled ['æd(ə)ld] *adj* **(a)** *Old-fashioned* (*egg*) pourri, gâté **(b) an a. mind** un esprit confus

add-on **1** *n Comptr* produit *m* supplémentaire *ou* complémentaire, extension *f* **2** *adj attrib* additionel; *Comptr* **a. board** carte *f* d'extension; **a. fare** supplément *m*

address¹ [ə'dres, *Am* 'ædres] *n* **(a)** [ⓘA71,6] (*of person, letter*) adresse *f*; **what is your a.?** quelle est ton adresse?; **of no (known) a.** sans domicile connu; **home** *or* **private/business a.** adresse privée *ou* personnelle/de bureau; **a Glasgow a.** une adresse à Glasgow; **not known at this a.** (*on returned letter*) inconnu à cette adresse; **she no longer lives at that a.** elle n'habite plus à cette adresse; **a. and phone number** coordonnées *fpl*; *Comptr* **a. file** fichier *m* d'adresses; **a. line** ligne *f* d'adressage; **a. space** cadre-adresse *m*

(b) (*speech*) discours *m*, allocution *f*

(c) (*title*) **form of a.** titre *m*; **what's the correct form of a. for a bishop?** comment doit-on s'adresser à un évêque?

(d) *Comptr* adresse *f*

(e) *Fml, Arch* (*skill*) habileté *f*, doigté *m*; **she showed**

considerable a. in her handling of the situation elle fit preuve d'une grande habileté dans la façon dont elle traita l'affaire

(f) *Arch* **to pay one's addresses to a lady** faire la cour à une femme

address² *vt* (a) (*letter, postcard, parcel*) adresser (**to sb** à qn); **it's addressed to you** ça t'est adressé; **stamped addressed envelope** enveloppe *f* timbrée avec son adresse; **it's incorrectly addressed** l'adresse est incorrecte

(b) (*direct*) (*reproaches, criticism etc*) adresser (**to sb** à qn)

(c) (*speak to*) (*sb, crowd etc*) s'adresser à; **to a. sb** (*start to speak to*) adresser la parole à qn; **he addressed her as 'Your Majesty'** il l'a appelée 'Votre Majesté'; **to a. a meeting** prendre la parole à une réunion

(d) (*tackle*) (*question, problem etc*) aborder; *Fml* **to a. oneself to a task** entreprendre une tâche

(e) *Comptr* adresser, accéder à

(f) *Golf* (*ball*) viser

addressable [ə'dresəb(ə)l] *n Comptr* adressable; *Mktg* **a. audience** audience *f* utile; *Mktg* **a. market** marché *m* utile

address book *n* carnet *m* d'adresses

addressee [ædre'siː] *n* (*of telegram etc*) destinataire *mf*

addressing [ə'dresɪŋ] *n* adressage *m*

addressing machine *n* machine *f* à adresser

address label *n* étiquette *f* d'adresse

adduce [ə'djuːs] *vt Fml* (*reasons, evidence etc*) alléguer, apporter; (*authority*) invoquer, citer

adduct [ə'dʌkt] *vt Physiol* (*muscle etc*) déterminer l'adduction de

adduction [ə'dʌkʃən] *n Physiol* adduction *f*

adductor [ə'dʌktər] *n, adj Med* (*muscle*) adducteur *m*

adenoidal [ædɪ'nɔɪd(ə)l] *adj* adénoïde; (*voice*) nasillard

adenoids ['ædɪnɔɪdz] *npl Med* végétations *fpl* (adénoïdes)

adept 1 *adj* [ə'dept] expert, habile (**in sth** à qch; **at doing sth** à faire qch) **2** *n* ['ædept] expert, -erte (**in** en)

adequacy ['ædɪkwəsɪ] *n* (*of arrangements, skills etc*) caractère *m* adéquat; (*of person*) compétence *f*, capacité *f*; (*of theory*) adéquation *f*; **they had doubts as to the a. of the pay/ration** ils doutaient que la paye/ration soit suffisante; **they doubted her a. as a mother** ils doutaient de ses capacités de mère

adequate ['ædɪkwət] *adj* (*in quantity*) suffisant; (*appropriate, good enough*) adéquat; **the money we were given was more than a.** l'argent que l'on nous avait donné était plus que suffisant; **a. supply** (*of meat etc*) quantité suffisante; **room of a. size** pièce d'une grandeur raisonnable; **a. to the task** (*of tool*) approprié à la tâche; **a. training for the job** (*enough*) une formation suffisante pour le poste; (*right quality*) une formation adéquate pour le poste; **a. remuneration for the work carried out** rémunération proportionnée *ou* correspondant au travail accompli; **to be given a. warning** être suffisamment averti; **a. time to do sth** suffisamment de temps pour faire qch

adequately ['ædɪkwətlɪ] *adv* (*in quantity*) suffisamment; (*suitably*) convenablement

adhere [əd'hɪər] *vi* adhérer

▶ **adhere to** *vipo* (a) (*stick to*) adhérer à (b) (*rule etc*) observer; (*one's decision*) persister dans, s'en tenir à, maintenir; (*plan*) s'en tenir à, se conformer à; **to a. to a party** adhérer *ou* donner son adhésion à un parti; **I don't a. to that philosophy at all** je n'adhère pas du tout à cette philosophie

adherence [əd'hɪərəns] *n* (a) (*of label etc*) adhérence *f* (**to** à) (b) (*to party, position*) adhésion *f* (**to** à); (*to rule etc*) observation *f* (**to** de)

adherent [əd'hɪərənt] *n* (*of party, belief etc*) adhérent, -ente; (*of doctrine*) partisan, -ane

adhesion [əd'hiːʒən] *n* (a) (*of label, road wheels etc*) adhérence *f* (b) (*of person*) adhésion *f* (**to** à)

adhesive [əd'hiːsɪv] **1** *adj* (*tape etc*) adhésif; (*label*) gommé; *Med* **a. plaster**, *Am* **a. tape** sparadrap *m* **2** *n* colle *f*, adhésif *m*

adhesiveness [əd'hiːsɪvnɪs] *n* adhérence *f*

ad hoc ['æd'hɒk] *adv, adj* ad hoc; **a. committee** comité spécial *ou* ad hoc; **we prefer to decide things on an a. basis** nous préférons prendre des décisions à mesure que les circonstances l'exigent; **it's all a bit a.** tout est un peu improvisé

ad hominem [æd'hɒmɪnem] *adv, adj* ad hominem

adieu, *pl* **-s** *or* **-x** [ə'djuː, -z] *Arch Lit* **1** *int* adieu! **2** *n* **to bid sb a.** dire adieu à qn, faire ses adieux à qn

ad infinitum ['ædɪnfɪ'naɪtəm] *adv* à l'infini; *F* **he went on talking a.** il parlait à n'en plus finir; **and so on a.** et ainsi de suite ad infinitum

adipose ['ædɪpəʊs] *adj Biol* (*tissue*) adipeux

adjacent [ə'dʒeɪsənt] *adj* (*angle, plot of land*) adjacent, contigu, *f* -uë, attenant (**to** à); (*country*) limitrophe (**to** de); **a. rooms** pièces contiguës; **the two rooms are a.** les deux pièces sont contiguës; **in an a. street** dans une rue adjacente

adjectival [ædʒɪk'taɪv(ə)l] *adj Gram* adjectif, adjectival; **a. clause** proposition *f* adjective

adjectivally [ædʒɪk'taɪv(ə)lɪ] *adv* adjectivement; **present participle used a.** participe présent adjectivé

adjective ['ædʒɪktɪv] *adj, n* [①A17-21; B8-11] *Gram* adjectif *m*

adjoin [ə'dʒɔɪn] **1** *vt* (*place*) être contigu à, toucher à, attenir à; **our garden adjoins theirs** notre jardin est contigu au leur; **Kansas adjoins Colorado** le Kansas est un état limitrophe du Colorado **2** *vi* **the two houses a.** les deux maisons sont contiguës

adjoining [ə'dʒɔɪnɪŋ] *adj* contigu, *f* -uë; (*state, country*) limitrophe; **the a. room** la pièce voisine *ou* à côté; **a. rooms** pièces attenantes; (*bedrooms*) chambres attenantes; **garden a. mine** jardin attenant *ou* contigu au mien

adjourn [ə'dʒɜːn] **1** *vt* ajourner, différer, remettre, renvoyer (**for a week** à huitaine); **the trial was adjourned until the next day** le procès fut ajourné au lendemain; **the judge adjourned the hearing** le juge a suspendu l'audience **2** *vi* (a) (*of person*) (*close session*) lever la séance; (*interrupt session*) suspendre la séance; **to a. to the drawing room** (*after dinner etc*) passer au salon; **shall we a.?** (*after dinner etc*) on passe au salon? (b) (*of meeting etc*) (*be closed*) être levé; (*be interrupted*) être suspendu (**until** jusqu'à)

adjournment [ə'dʒɜːnmənt] *n* (*of trial etc*) ajournement *m*; (*of meeting, matter etc*) renvoi *m*, remise *f*; **a. for a week** remise à huitaine; *Jur* **an a.** une suspension d'audience

adjudge [ə'dʒʌdʒ] *vt* (a) **to a. sb guilty** déclarer qn coupable; **to a. sb the winner** déclarer qn vainqueur (b) (*prize, reward*) adjuger, décerner (**to sb** à qn); **to a. damages** adjuger *ou* accorder des dommages-intérêts

adjudicate [ə'dʒuːdɪkeɪt] **1** *vt* (*issue*) juger, décider; (*prize*) adjuger, décerner; *Jur* **to a. sb bankrupt** déclarer *ou* mettre qn en faillite **2** *vi* (a) (*act as referee*) arbitrer; **who is adjudicating?** (*in competition*) qui sont les membres du jury? (b) (*announce decision*) se prononcer (**on** sur)

adjudication [ədʒuːdɪ'keɪʃən] *n* jugement *m*, décision *f*, arrêt *m*; *Jur* **a. of bankruptcy** jugement déclaratif de faillite

adjudicator [ə'dʒuːdɪkeɪtər] *n* (a) (*in dispute*) arbitre *m* (b) (*in competition etc*) membre *m* du jury

adjunct ['ædʒʌŋkt] *n* (a) (*person*) adjoint, -ointe (**to** de), auxiliaire *mf* (b) (*thing*) accessoire *m* (**to** de) (c) *Gram* (*of verb etc*) complément *m*

adjust [ə'dʒʌst] **1** *vt* (a) (*scales, instrument, pressure, watch etc*) régler, ajuster; (*microscope, engine*) mettre au point; (*mechanism, brakes*) régler; (*valve*) tarer; *Naut* (*compass*) compenser, corriger; **to a. the sights of a rifle** ajuster le tir d'une arme à feu; **to a. the controls of a device** mettre au point le réglage d'un appareil; **to a. the picture on a television set** régler l'image d'un téléviseur; **she adjusted the seat belt to the correct length** elle régla la ceinture de sécurité à la bonne longueur; **the seat can be adjusted for height** la hauteur du siège est réglable

(b) (*reformulate*) ajuster; (*wages*) rajuster; (*in accounts*) régulariser; **the figures have been seasonally adjusted** les chiffres sont les données corrigées des variations saisonnières; **pensions have been adjusted upwards** les pensions ont été relevées; **the terms of the contract have been adjusted** les termes du contrat ont été modifiés; *Fin* **to a. prices** ajuster les prix; **to a. an average** (*in insurance*) répartir une avarie; **to a. a claim** (*of insurance company*) régler une demande d'indemnité

(c) (*one's hat, collar, tie*) arranger, rajuster; *Euph* **to a. one's clothing** (*do up flies*) remonter la braguette

(d) (*adapt*) (*one thing to another*) ajuster (**to** à); **to a. oneself to sth** s'adapter à qch; **his eyes adjusted themselves to the light** ses yeux s'accommodèrent à la lumière

2 *vi* (a) (*of person*) s'adapter (**to sth** à qch); **he found it difficult to a. after his wife died** il eut des difficultés à se faire à la mort de sa femme

(b) (*of device*) se régler, s'ajuster; **the seat adjusts for height** la hauteur du siège est réglable

adjustable [ə'dʒʌstəb(ə)l] *adj* ajustable, réglable; *Aut* **a. front seats** sièges *mpl* avant réglables; **fully a. seat** siège multi-positions; **the seat is a. for height** la hauteur du siège est réglable; *Br* **a. spanner** clef *f* anglaise, clef à molette

adjusted [ə'dʒʌstɪd] *adj Psy* (**well**) **a.** (bien) équilibré

adjuster [ə'dʒʌstər] *n* (a) *Fin* **average a.** dispacheur *m* (b) (*device*) appareil *m* de réglage; *Aut* (*on brake*) régleur *m*; **a. nut** écrou *m* de réglage; **a. screw** vis *f* de réglage

adjusting [ə'dʒʌstɪŋ] *n* (a) = **adjustment** (b) *Acct* **a. entry**

écriture *f* de régularisation; **a. screw** vis *f* de réglage *ou* de rappel

adjustment [ə'dʒʌstmənt] *n* **(a)** (*of scales, instrument, pressure, watch etc*) réglage *m*, ajustement *m*; (*of mechanism, brakes*) réglage; (*of microscope etc*) mise *f* au point; *Naut* (*of compass*) compensation *f*, correction *f*; **fine a.** réglage de précision; **out of a.** déréglé; **to make an a. to sth** régler qch, ajuster qch; **a slight a. improved the picture** une légère mise au point a amélioré l'image

(b) (*of figures, salaries*) réajustement *m*; (*of prices*) ajustement *m*; **no a. was made for seasonal variation** il n'y a pas eu de corrigé des variations saisonnières; **we had to make some adjustments to our plans** nous avons dû modifier quelque peu nos projets; **some adjustments had been made to the text** des modifications avaient été apportées au texte; **average a.** (*in insurance*) répartition *f* d'avarie, dispache *f*; *Acct* **a. account** compte *m* collectif

(c) (*adapting*) adaptation *f* (**to** à); **period of a.** période *f* d'adaptation

adjutant ['ædʒətənt] *n* **(a)** *Mil* (*rank*) capitaine *m*, adjudant *m* major; (*assistant*) officier *m* adjoint; **a. general** adjudant général **(b) a. (bird)** marabout *m* des Indes, *F* adjudant *m*

ad-lib[1] ['æd'lɪb] *adv* **to speak a.** improviser

ad-lib[2] *vti* (**-bb-**) improviser

ad-lib[3] **1** *n* improvisation *f* **2** *adj* improvisé; **most of his speech was a.** la plus grande partie de son discours était improvisée

ad-libbing [æd'lɪbɪŋ] *n* improvisation *f*

adman, ad-man, *pl* **-men** ['ædmæn, -men] *n F* publicitaire *m*

admass ['ædmæs] *n Br F* le grand public

admin ['ædmɪn] *n F* (*work*) travail *m* administratif; (*department*) administration *f*; **a. tasks** tâches *fpl* administratives; **are you sales or a.?** vous êtes au service des ventes ou à l'administration?

administer [əd'mɪnɪstə*r*] *vt* **(a)** (*manage*) (*territory, region*) administrer; (*business, property*) administrer, gérer; (*laws*) appliquer **(b)** (*give*) (*last sacraments, medication*) administrer (**to** à); (*reprimand*) faire, adresser (**to** à); **to a. justice** rendre la justice; *Jur* **to a. an** *or* **the oath to sb** faire prêter serment à qn, assermenter qn

administration [ədmɪnɪ'streɪʃən] *n* **(a)** (*of business, fortune etc*) administration *f*; **a. (department)** service *m* administratif; **business a.** gestion *f* administrative; *Acct* **a. costs** frais d'administration, frais de gestion; *Banking* **a. fee** frais de dossier **(b)** (*administrative work*) travail *m* administratif **(c)** (*of justice, sacraments, remedy*) administration *f*; (*of oath*) prestation *f*; *Jur* **letters of a.** lettres *fpl* d'administration **(d)** *esp US* **the A.** le gouvernement; **the Clinton A.** le gouvernement Clinton

administrative [əd'mɪnɪstrətɪv] *adj* administratif; (*error*) d'administration; **for a. convenience** pour faciliter le travail administratif; *Acct* **a. costs** coûts *mpl* administratifs; *Ind* **a. expenses** frais *mpl* d'administration; *Br* **the a. grade** (*in civil service*) les fonctionnaires *mpl* supérieurs; **a. headquarters** siège *m* administratif; **a. skills** compétences *fpl* administratives; **a. staff** personnel *m* administratif; **a. unit** unité *f* administrative; **a. work** travail *m* administratif

administratively [əd'mɪnɪstrətɪvlɪ] *adv* administrativement; **more convenient a.** plus commode d'un point de vue administratif

administrator [əd'mɪnɪstreɪtə*r*] *n* **(a)** administrateur, -trice **(b)** *Jur* (*of minor's property etc*) curateur *m*; (*of succession*) administrateur, -trice

admirable ['ædmərəb(ə)l] *adj* admirable

admirably ['ædmərəblɪ] *adv* admirablement; **she succeeded a.** elle a admirablement bien réussi

admiral ['ædmərəl] *n* **(a)** *Naut* amiral *m*; **a. of the fleet, fleet a.** vice-amiral *m* d'escadre **(b) red a.** (*butterfly*) vulcain *m*

admiralty ['ædmərəltɪ] *n Naut, Hist* amirauté *f*; **the A.** = le Ministère de la Marine; **First Lord of the A.** ≈ Ministre *m* de la Marine; **court of A.** = tribunal *m* maritime

Admiralty Board *n* = division *f* navale du ministère de la Défense

Admiralty Islands *npl Geog* îles *fpl* de l'Amirauté

admiration [ædmə'reɪʃən] *n* admiration *f* (**of, for** pour); **I have great a. for doctors** j'ai beaucoup d'admiration pour les médecins; **their roads are the a. of the world** leurs routes font l'admiration du monde entier

admire [əd'maɪə*r*] *vt* admirer; **I a. her as a leader** je l'admire en tant que dirigeante; **they a. him for sticking to his principles** ils l'admirent de s'en tenir à ses principes; **to a. oneself in a mirror** s'admirer dans une glace; **you can't help admiring his cheek!** on ne peut qu'admirer son culot!

admirer [əd'maɪərə*r*] *n* **(a)** admirateur, -trice; **I'm a great a. of people who speak their mind** j'admire énormément les gens qui disent ce qu'ils pensent **(b)** *Old-fashioned* (*suitor*) (*of woman*) soupirant *m*; *Hum* **is that a letter from one of your admirers?** est-ce que c'est une lettre de l'un de tes admirateurs?

admiring [əd'maɪrɪŋ] *adj* (*look, tone etc*) admiratif

admiringly [əd'maɪrɪŋlɪ] *adv* avec admiration

admissibility [ədmɪsɪ'bɪlɪtɪ] *n* (*of argument etc*) admissibilité *f*; *Jur* (*of appeal, testimony*) recevabilité *f*

admissible [əd'mɪsɪb(ə)l] *adj* **(a)** *Jur* (*appeal*) recevable **(b)** (*idea*) acceptable; (*behaviour, error*) admissible, acceptable

admission [əd'mɪʃən] *n* **(a)** (*to school*) admission *f*, accès *m*; (*to career*) accès; (*to museum, exhibition*) entrée *f*; **to gain a.** (*to a society*) se faire recevoir (**to** au sein de); (*to sb*) trouver accès (**to** auprès de); (*to college etc*) se faire admettre (**to** au sein de); **a. fee** droit *m* d'entrée; **a. free** entrée gratuite; **a. is by ticket only** entrée sur présentation d'un billet seulement

(b) (*price*) prix *m ou* droit *m* d'entrée; **a. £2** entrée 2 livres

(c) (*of argument, evidence*) admission *f*, acceptation *f*; *Jur* (*of allegation*) reconnaissance *f*; (*of crime*) confession *f*; (*of guilt*) aveu *m*; **by** *or* **on his own a.** de son propre aveu

(d) *Tech, Aut* (*of steam, gas etc*) admission *f*, adduction *f*, entrée *f*; (*of water*) injection *f*

admit [əd'mɪt] *vt* (**-tt-**) **(a)** (*person to place, air, light*) laisser entrer; (*to university, institution etc*) admettre; **children not admitted** les enfants ne sont pas admis; **a. one** (*on ticket*) entrée pour une personne; **he was admitted to hospital** il a été admis à l'hôpital

(b) (*truth, excuses*) admettre; (*fact*) consentir; (*principle, mistake*) reconnaître; **it must be admitted that …** il faut (bien) reconnaître que …; **to a. one's guilt** se reconnaître *ou* s'avouer coupable; **I a. (that) I was wrong** j'ai eu tort, j'en conviens *ou* je le reconnais; **it was hot, I must a.** je dois admettre qu'il a fait chaud; **I had to a. to myself that …** j'ai dû m'avouer à moi-même que …; **he admitted lying** il reconnut qu'il avait menti

▶ **admit of** *vipo Fml* (*allow of*) permettre, admettre; **the remark admits of several interpretations** cette remarque admet plusieurs interprétations; **his conduct admits of no excuse/explanation** sa conduite est sans excuse/est inexplicable

▶ **admit to** *vipo* (*confess*) (*sth*) admettre; **I must a. to having felt more than a little nervous** je dois avouer *ou* admettre que je me sentais assez nerveux

admittance [əd'mɪtəns] *n* **(a)** permission *f* d'entrer; (*to place, sb*) accès *m*; **to gain a. to a place** parvenir à entrer dans un lieu; **to refuse sb a.** refuser de laisser entrer qn; **no a.** entrée interdite, défense d'entrer **(b)** *El* admittance *f*

admittedly [əd'mɪtɪdlɪ] *adv* de l'aveu général; **a. he's right, but …** il faut reconnaître qu'il a raison, mais …; **they got there, two hours late a., but …** ils sont arrivés là-bas, avec deux heures de retard, j'en conviens, mais …; **the car's old a.** il faut reconnaître que la voiture est vieille; **although an a. problematic case, …** il s'agit d'un cas problématique, certes, mais …

admixture [əd'mɪkstʃə*r*] *n* **(a)** (*mixture*) mélange *m*; **there was an a. of sarcasm in his comments** il y avait une part de sarcasme dans ses remarques **(b)** *Pharm* (ad)mixtion *f*; **water with an a. of alcohol** eau additionnée d'alcool

admonish [əd'mɒnɪʃ] *vt* **(a)** (*reprimand*) admonester, reprendre, faire des remontrances à; **he admonished them for their cowardice** il leur a fait des remontrances pour leur manque de courage **(b)** *Fml* (*warn*) **to a. sb against sth** mettre qn en garde contre qch **(c)** *Fml* (*exhort*) **to a. sb to do sth** exhorter qn à faire qch

admonition [ædmə'nɪʃən] *n* **(a)** (*reprimand*) remontrance *f*, réprimande *f*; *Rel* admonition *f* **(b)** (*warning*) mise *f* en garde **(c)** (*exhortation*) exhortation *f* (**to** à)

ad nauseam [æd'nɔːsɪæm] *adv* à n'en plus finir

ado [ə'duː] *n* agitation *f*, bruit *m*, embarras *m*; **without (any) more a., without further a.** sans plus de façons *ou* de cérémonie *ou* d'embarras; **to make much a. about nothing** faire beaucoup de bruit pour rien

adobe [ə'dəubɪ] *n* (*house*) adobe *m*

adolescence [ædə'lesəns] *n* adolescence *f*

adolescent [ædə'lesənt] **1** *adj* adolescent; **in his a. years** quand il était adolescent; **stop being so a. about it!** ton attitude est vraiment trop puérile! **2** *n* adolescent, -ente

Adonis [ə'dəunɪs] *n Myth, Fig* Adonis *m*

adopt [ə'dɒpt] *vt* **(a)** (*child, custom*) adopter; **a stray cat adopted us** un chat abandonné nous a adoptés **(b)** (*guideline, plan, product*) adopter; (*career*) choisir, embrasser; (*measures, method*) adopter, instaurer; (*opinion*) se rallier à; (*advice*) suivre; *Pol* (*sb as a candidate*) sélectionner; **to a. a patronizing tone** prendre un ton protecteur; **don't you a. that attitude with me!** ne prends pas cette attitude avec moi! **(c)** *(minutes of meeting)* approuver

adopted [ə'dɒptɪd] *adj attrib (child, word)* adopté; **a. son** fils *m* adoptif; **my a. country** mon pays d'adoption

adoption [ə'dɒpʃən] *n* **(a)** *(of child, custom, country)* adoption *f*; **I am an American by a.** je suis américain d'adoption; **they have two children of their own and another by a.** ils ont deux enfants à eux et un enfant adopté; **have you considered a.?** *(adopting a child)* avez-vous songé à l'adoption?; *(having your child adopted)* avez-vous songé à le/la faire adopter? **(b)** *(of law, plan, product)* adoption *f*; *(of career)* choix *m*; *(of measures, method)* instauration *f*; *Pol (of sb as candidate)* sélection *f*

adoptive [ə'dɒptɪv] *adj (child, father)* adoptif

adorable [ə'dɔːrəb(ə)l] *adj* adorable

adorably [ə'dɔːrəblɪ] *adv* adorablement; **a. beautiful** beau à ravir

adoration [ædə'reɪʃən] *n* adoration *f*

adore [ə'dɔːr] *vt (person, god)* adorer; *F* **I a. those cakes** j'adore ces gâteaux-là; **don't you a. the way he smiles?** est-ce que tu ne trouves pas son sourire adorable?

adorer [ə'dɔːrər] *n* adorateur, -trice

adoring [ə'dɔːrɪŋ] *adj attrib (eyes, look)* plein d'adoration; *(expression)* d'adoration; **her a. grandfather** son grand-père qui l'adore/l'adorait

adoringly [ə'dɔːrɪŋlɪ] *adv* avec adoration

adorn [ə'dɔːn] *vt* orner, parer **(with** de**)**

adornment [ə'dɔːnmənt] *n* **(a)** *(act)* ornementation *f* **(b)** *(object)* ornement *m*, parure *f*; **without a.** sans ornements

adrenal [ə'driːn(ə)l] *Med* **1** *adj* surrénal; **a. gland** (glande *f ou* capsule *f*) surrénale *f* **2** *n* (glande *f ou* capsule *f*) surrénale *f*

adrenalin(e) [ə'drenəlɪn] *n* adrénaline *f*; *F* **it gets the a. going** ça fait monter l'adrénaline; *F* **he runs on a.** il marche à l'adrénaline; *F* **once the a. gets going** quand l'adrénaline commence à monter

Adriatic [eɪdrɪ'ætɪk] *adj, n* **the A. Sea, the A.** la mer Adriatique, l'Adriatique *f*

adrift [ə'drɪft] *adv, adj pred Naut* à la dérive; **to run** *or* **go a.** *(of ship)* aller à la dérive, dériver; **they were a. for days** ils dérivèrent pendant plusieurs jours; **to break a.** rompre ses amarres, partir à la dérive; **to turn a vessel a.** abandonner *ou* laisser aller un navire à la dérive; *Fig* **young people a. in the big city** des jeunes à la dérive dans la grande ville; *Fig* **to turn sb a.** abandonner qn; *Fig* **to cut oneself a. from sb** rompre avec qn; **to come a.** *(of rope etc)* se détacher, se défaire; *Fig (of plan etc)* tomber à l'eau

adroit [ə'drɔɪt] *adj* adroit, habile; **to be a. at doing sth** être habile à faire qch

adroitly [ə'drɔɪtlɪ] *adv* adroitement, habilement

adroitness [ə'drɔɪtnɪs] *n* adresse *f*, habileté *f* **(in doing** à faire**)**

adulation [ædjʊ'leɪʃən] *n* adulation *f*

adulatory [ædjʊ'leɪt(ə)rɪ] *adj* adulateur, -trice

adult ['ædʌlt, ə'dʌlt] *n* adulte *mf*; **a. education** enseignement *m* pour adultes; **an a. movie** un film pour adultes; **an a. lion** un lion adulte; **a. fare** tarif *m* adulte

adulterate [ə'dʌltəreɪt] *vt (substance, milk)* dénaturer; *(wine etc)* frelater; *(language)* corrompre

adulteration [ədʌltə'reɪʃən] *n (of medication)* dénaturation *f*; *(of drinks)* frelatage *m*; **a. of foodstuffs** fraude *f* alimentaire

adulterer [ə'dʌltərər], **adulteress** [ə'dʌltərɪs] *n* adultère *mf*

adulterous [ə'dʌltərəs] *adj* adultère

adulterously [ə'dʌltərəslɪ] *adv* par adultère; *(to live)* en état d'adultère; *(to lust)* dans une passion adultère

adultery [ə'dʌltərɪ] *n* adultère *m*; **numerous adulteries** nombreuses infidélités *fpl*; **to commit a.** commettre l'adultère

adulthood ['ædʌlthʊd] *n* âge *m* adulte; **to reach a.** devenir adulte, atteindre l'âge adulte

adumbrate ['ædʌmbreɪt] *vt Fml* esquisser

ad valorem [ædvæ'lɔːrem] *adj Com, Ind* **a. duty** droit *m* sur la valeur, droit ad valorem

advance[1] [əd'vɑːns] *n* **(a)** *(forward movement)* avance *f*; **with the a. of old age** avec l'âge; **a. towards sth** acheminement *m* vers qch; *Mil* **in their a. on the city** au cours de leur avance sur la ville; **in a.** *(to go)* en avant; *(to arrive)* en avance; **well/months in a.** largement/des mois à l'avance; **to know in a.** savoir à l'avance; **in a. of the others** avant les autres; **to be in a. of one's time** être en avance sur son temps, devancer son époque; **to pay in a.** payer d'avance; **to pay a sum in a.** *(part payment)* verser un acompte; *(total payment)* avancer un paiement; **thanking you in a.** *(in letter)* en vous remerciant à l'avance, avec mes remerciements anticipés; **a. booking** réservation *f* à l'avance; **a. booking charter** achat *m* de bloc-sièges; **a. notice** *or* **warning** préavis *m*; **a. payment** paiement *m* anticipé *ou* par anticipation; **a. reservation rack** *(in hotel)* planning *m* des réservations de type Whitney; **a. reservations office** bureau *m* des réservations; **a. warning triangle** triangle *m* de présignalisation

(b) *(progress) (of science etc)* progrès *m*, développement *m*, avancement *m*; **great advances in medicine** des progrès *ou* développements importants dans le domaine de la médecine; **some advances were made** on a fait des progrès

(c) *(sexual or business overture)* **to make advances to sb** faire une avance *ou* des avances à qn

(d) *Com, Fin (of funds)* avance *f*; **a. on a contract** avance *ou* acompte *m* sur un contrat; **an a. of £200 on his salary** une avance de 200 livres sur son salaire

(e) *(increase at auction)* **any a.?** qui dit mieux?; **any a. on a hundred?** cent, qui dit mieux?

advance[2] **1** *vt* **(a)** *(one's foot, Chess pawn, date of meeting etc)* avancer; *(troops)* faire avancer; **to a. the ignition** donner de l'avance à l'allumage

(b) *(science, knowledge etc)* faire progresser, faire avancer; *(growth, development etc)* accélérer; **this discovery has advanced our research by months** cette découverte nous fait gagner plusieurs mois de recherches

(c) *(idea, opinion, observation)* avancer, mettre en avant; *(pretext)* alléguer

(d) *Fin (money)* avancer **(to** à**)**; **sums advanced** avances *fpl*, provisions *fpl*

(e) *(counter on photocopier etc)* faire progresser; *(magnetic tape)* faire défiler; *(paper in printer)* faire avancer

(f) *(promote) (person)* élever, donner de l'avancement à

2 *vi* **(a)** *(move forward)* s'avancer **(towards** vers**)**; *(of troops)* se porter en avant; **to a. on a town/enemy positions/***etc* avancer sur une ville/des positions ennemies/*etc*; **the night is advancing** la nuit s'avance; **to a. two steps** *or* **paces** faire deux pas en avant

(b) *(progress) (in age, one's studies)* avancer; *Biol etc* évoluer; **the work is advancing** l'ouvrage avance *ou* progresse

(c) *(be promoted)* recevoir de l'avancement, monter (en grade)

(d) *Fin (of shares etc)* augmenter; **prices are advancing** les prix sont à la hausse

advance copy *n (of book)* exemplaire *m* de presse; *(for production checks)* exemplaire en avance

advanced [əd'vɑːnst] *adj* **(a)** *(studies, students, opinions, civilization)* avancé; *(economy)* développé; *(country)* développé, industrialisé; *(course)* supérieur; **she's very a. for two** elle est très avancée *ou* en avance pour une enfant de deux ans; **she's very a. for her age** elle est très en avance pour son âge; **to hold a. ideas** avoir des idées avancées; **a. mathematics** mathématiques *fpl* supérieures; **the night was far a.** il était tard dans la nuit; **he died at an a. age** il est mort très vieux

(b) *Tech (model, engine, reactor)* perfectionné; *(technique)* avancé; **a. gas-cooled reactor** réacteur *m* à gaz avancé; **a. passenger train** train *m* à grande vitesse, TGV *m*

(c) *Mil (post)* avancé

(d) a. check-in enregistrement *m* anticipé

advance guard *n Mil* avant-garde *f*

advancement [əd'vɑːnsmənt] *n* **(a)** *(of science)* avancement *m*, progrès *m*; **economic a.** essor *m* économique **(b)** *(of person)* avancement *m*, promotion *f*; **there is little scope for a.** il y a peu de possibilités d'avancement **(c)** *(of counter on photocopier etc)* progression *f*; *(of paper, tape)* avancement *m*, défilement *m*

advance party *n Mil* avant-garde *f*, détachement *m* d'avant-garde; *(scouts)* détachement précurseur

Advance Purchase Excursion *n* tarif *m* (aérien) spécial sujet à des restrictions de délai d'achat

advancing [əd'vɑːnsɪŋ] *adj, attrib (storm)* qui approche/approchait, qui s'avance/s'avançait; *(army)* qui avance/avançait

advantage[1] [əd'vɑːntɪdʒ] *n* **(a)** avantage *m*; **to have/gain the a. over sb** avoir/remporter l'avantage sur qn; **it has the a. of being cheap** ça a l'avantage d'être bon marché; **in this sport size is an a.** dans ce sport, c'est un avantage d'être grand; *Old-fashioned* **you have the a. of me** je n'ai pas l'honneur de vous connaître; **you will find it an a. to ...** vous aurez avantage à ...; **to take a. of sth** profiter de qch, tirer avantage *ou* profit de qch; **to take a. of the situation** profiter de l'occasion **(to do** pour faire**)**; **to take a. of an offer/opportunity** profiter d'une proposition/occasion; **they'll only take a.** *(of your generosity etc)* ils ne feront qu'en profiter; **that would be taking a.!** ce serait abuser!; **to take a. of sb** abuser de la crédulité *ou* de la bonne volonté de qn; *(sexually)* abuser de qn; **it is to their a. to keep quiet**

c'est dans leur intérêt de se taire; **that would be to your competitor's a.** cela avantagerait votre concurrent; **the recession/weather worked to their a.** la récession/le temps les a avantagés *ou* a travaillé pour eux; **to turn sth to a.** tirer parti de qch, mettre qch à profit; **to turn out to sb's a.** (*of event*) tourner à l'avantage de qn, profiter à qn; **to show sth off to a.** faire valoir qch, mettre qch en valeur

(**b**) *Tennis* avantage *m*; **a. Becker** avantage Becker

advantage[2] *vt* (*sb, sth*) avantager, favoriser

advantageous [ædvən'teɪdʒəs] *adj* avantageux (**to** pour)

advantageously [ædvən'teɪdʒəslɪ] *adv* avantageusement

advantage rule *n Sp* règle *f* de l'avantage; **to play the a.** laisser l'avantage, appliquer la règle de l'avantage; (*of players*) jouer l'avantage

Advent ['ædvənt] *n Rel* l'Avent *m*; **the Second A.** le second Avènement; **A. calendar** calendrier *m* de l'Avent; **A. Sunday** dimanche *m* de l'Avent; (*Church of Eng*) premier dimanche de l'Avent; **A. wreath** couronne *f* de l'Avent

advent ['ædvənt] *n* (*of spring, rainy season etc*) arrivée *f*; (*of era, computer age*) avènement *m*; (*of railways, the motorcar, computerization*) introduction *f*; **with the a. of McDonald as editor** avec l'arrivée de McDonald au poste de rédacteur en chef

Adventist ['ædvəntɪst] *n Rel* **Seventh-day A.** adventiste *mf* du septième jour

adventitious [ædven'tɪʃəs] *adj Fml* (*chance*) accidentel, fortuit; *Bot* (*roots*) adventif

adventure [əd'ventʃər] *n* aventure *f*; **after many adventures** après bien des péripéties; **the adventures of Tintin** les aventures de Tintin; **life of a.** vie *f* d'aventure, vie aventureuse; **where's your sense of a.?** où est ton sens de l'aventure?; **a. film** film *m* d'aventures; **a. holiday** circuit *m* aventure; **a. playground** aire *f* de jeux; **a. story** récit *m* d'adventures; (*novel*) roman *m* d'aventure(s)

adventurer [əd'ventʃərər] *n* (*explorer*) *Pej* aventurier *m*

adventuresome [əd'ventʃəsəm] *adj* (*person*) aventureux; *Pej* téméraire

adventuress [əd'ventʃərɪs] *n Pej* aventurière *f*

adventurous [əd'ventʃərəs] *adj* (*life, journey*) aventureux; (*person, child*) aventureux, hardi; **we had an a. trip** nous avons eu un voyage plein d'aventures; **be a., try the curry** sois un peu plus aventureux et essaie le curry

adventurously [əd'ventʃərəslɪ] *adv* aventureusement

adventurousness [əd'ventʃərəsnɪs] *n* hardiesse *f*, audace *f*; (*liking adventure*) esprit *m* d'aventure

adverb ['ædvɜːb] *n* (**①A21-25; B11-13**) *Gram* adverbe *m*

adverbial [əd'vɜːbɪəl] *adj Gram* adverbial; **a. phrase** locution *f* adverbiale

adverbially [əd'vɜːbɪəlɪ] *adv* adverbialement

adversary ['ædvəs(ə)rɪ] *n* adversaire *mf*

adverse ['ædvɜːs] *adj* (**a**) (*direction*) contraire, opposé; **a. wind** vent *m* contraire (**b**) (*hostile*) hostile (**to** à, envers); **a. fortune** fortune *f* adverse (**c**) (*comments, criticism*) défavorable; *Fin* (*balance*) déficitaire

adversely ['ædvɜːslɪ] *adv* **to influence sb a.** exercer une influence défavorable sur qn; **to report a.** faire un rapport défavorable (**on** sur); **a. affected** affecté

adversity [əd'vɜːsɪtɪ] *n* adversité *f*; **in a.** dans l'adversité

advert ['ædvɜːt] *n F* (**a**) (*publicity*) pub *f*, réclame *f*; **you're a walking a. for Benetton** tu as l'air tout droit sorti d'une pub pour Benetton (**b**) (*for job, accommodation etc*) annonce *f*

advertise ['ædvətaɪz] **1** *vt* (**a**) (*announce*) (*in newspaper*) (*event*) annoncer; (*job*) mettre une annonce pour; (*on poster*) (*sale etc*) afficher; **the job as advertised** le poste tel que décrit dans l'offre d'emploi; **house advertised for sale** (*in newspaper*) maison dont la mise en vente est annoncée; (*at estate agent's*) maison dont la mise en vente est affichée; **the job was advertised in the paper/in a shop window** il y avait une annonce pour cet emploi dans le journal/dans une vitrine

(**b**) (*do publicity for*) (*product, service*) faire de la réclame *ou* de la publicité pour; **as advertised** conforme à la spécification publicitaire; **as advertised on TV** vu à la télé

(**c**) *Fig* **you needn't a. the fact** vous n'avez pas besoin de le crier sur les toits; **you needn't a. your ignorance** ce n'est pas la peine d'étaler ton ignorance; **he didn't want to a. his presence** il ne voulait pas se faire remarquer

2 *vi* (*place advertisement*) insérer *ou* mettre une annonce; (*do publicity*) faire de la publicité *ou* réclame; **they a. on television** ils font de la publicité à la télévision; **it pays to a.** la publicité paie; **to a. for sb/sth** chercher qn/qch par voie d'annonce; **they advertised for an accountant/a nanny** ils ont passé une annonce pour trouver un comptable/une bonne d'enfants

advertised ['ædvətaɪzd] *adj attrib Rail etc* **the a. time of departure** l'heure *f* prévue pour le départ; **the a. programme** (*on TV*) le programme annoncé

advertisement [əd'vɜːtɪsmənt] *n* (**a**) (*publicity*) publicité *f*, réclame *f*, *F* pub *f*; *TV etc* spot *m* publicitaire; **an a. for toothpaste, a toothpaste a.** une publicité pour du dentifrice; **bad a.** contrepublicité *f*; *Fig* **you're not a good a. for your school** vous ne faites pas honneur à votre école (**b**) (*in newspaper*) annonce *f* (**for** pour); **to reply to** *or* **answer an a.** répondre à une annonce; **classified advertisements** petites annonces (**c**) (*on wall etc*) affiche *f*

advertiser ['ædvətaɪzər] *n* annonceur *m*

advertising ['ædvətaɪzɪŋ] *n* (*publicity, profession*) publicité *f*, *F* pub *f*; **she works in a.** elle travaille dans la publicité; **there is more a. than news** il y a plus de publicités que de nouvelles; **a. budget** budget *m* publicitaire; **a. concept** idée *f* publicitaire; **a. copy** texte *m* publicitaire; **a. department** service *m* de la publicité; **a. director** directeur *m* de la communication *ou* de la publicité, *F* dircom *m*; **a. executive** chef *m* de la publicité; **a. expenditure** dépenses *fpl* publicitaires; **a. gift** cadeau *m* publicitaire; **a. manager** directeur *m* de la communication *ou* de la publicité, *F* dircom *m*, chef de publicité; **a. market** marché *m* publicitaire; **a. medium** support *m* publicitaire; **a. message** message *m* publicitaire; **a. paper** journal *m* de petites annonces; **a. revenue** recettes *fpl* publicitaires; **a. sales agency** régie *f* publicitaire; **a. space** espace *m* publicitaire; **a. spot** spot *m* publicitaire; **a. standards** normes *fpl* publicitaires

advertising agency *n* agence *f* de publicité

advertising agent *n* agent *m* de publicité

advertising brochure *n* plaquette *f* publicitaire

advertising campaign *n* campagne *f* publicitaire *ou* de publicité

advertorial [ædvə'tɔːrɪəl] *n* publi-reportage *m*

advice [əd'vaɪs] *n* (**a**) conseil(s) *m(pl)*, avis *m*; **piece of a.** conseil; **that's good a.** c'est un bon conseil; **to ask** *or* **seek sb's a.** demander conseil à qn; **when I want your a. I'll ask for it!** quand j'aurai besoin de tes conseils, je saurai te les demander!; **to give sb a.** donner des conseils à qn; **to take sb's a.** suivre le conseil *ou* les conseils de qn; **take my a. and don't have anything to do with them** suis mon conseil et ne te mêle pas de leurs affaires; **if you take my a. you'll not have anything to do with them** suis mon conseil, ne te mêle pas de leurs affaires; **my a. (to you) would be to buy a new car** mon conseil serait que tu achètes une nouvelle voiture; **to take medical/legal a.** consulter un médecin/un avocat; **on sb's a.** sur l'avis *ou* le conseil de qn; **the magazine is a useful source of a.** le magazine est une source utile de conseils

(**b**) *Com* (*notice*) avis *m*; **as per a.** suivant avis; **until further a.** jusqu'à nouvel avis

advice column *n* courrier *m* du cœur; (*for practical advice*) rubrique *f* pratique

advice note *n Com* lettre *f ou* note *f* d'avis

advisability [ədvaɪzə'bɪlɪtɪ] *n* (*of course of action, policy*) bien-fondé *m*; **I'm wondering about the a. of this** je doute que ce soit à recommander

advisable [əd'vaɪzəb(ə)l] *adj pred* recommandé, judicieux; **it is a. to book early** il est recommandé de réserver à l'avance; **I'm going in my old car – is that a.?** j'y vais dans ma vieille voiture – est-ce que c'est bien prudent?; **it would be a. to …** il serait prudent de …; **it might be a. to …** peut-être conviendrait-il de …; **if you consider** *or* **think it a.** si bon vous semble

advise [əd'vaɪz] **1** *vt* (**a**) (*sb*) conseiller; (*caution*) recommander, conseiller; **to a. sb to do sth** conseiller à qn de faire qch; **I strongly a. you to …** je vous recommande instamment de …; **customers are advised to book early** il est recommandé *ou* conseillé aux clients de réserver à l'avance; **what do you a. me to do?** que me conseillez-vous?; **you'd be well advised to take an umbrella** vous feriez bien de prendre un parapluie; **they were well advised to go by air** ils ont bien fait de prendre l'avion; **they are advising taking a different route** ils conseillent de prendre un itinéraire différent

(**b**) *Fml* (*inform*) avertir, prévenir, instruire (**of** de); **to a. sb that …** avertir *ou* prévenir qn que …

2 *vi* (*of person*) être conseiller (**in, on** en)

▸ **advise against** *vipo* (*sth*) déconseiller; **to a. sb against sth** déconseiller qch à qn; **to a. sb against doing sth** déconseiller à qn de faire qch; **I would strongly a. against it** je le déconseille fortement

advisedly [əd'vaɪzɪdlɪ] *adv* (*to say sth*) en connaissance de cause; (*to use a word, an expression*) délibérément, de propos délibéré

adviser, advisor [əd'vaɪzər] *n* conseiller, -ère
advising bank [əd'vaɪzɪŋ] *n Fin* banque *f* notificatrice
advisory [əd'vaɪzərɪ] *adj* (*council, committee*) consultatif; **in an a. capacity** en tant que conseiller
advocacy ['ædvəkəsɪ] *n* (*of cause*) plaidoyer *m*
advocate¹ ['ædvəkət, -eɪt] *n* **(a)** *Scot Jur* avocat, -ate; **the Lord A.** = le Procureur général **(b)** (*supporter*) avocat, -ate; (*of cause, doctrine etc*) défenseur *m*; **the advocates of free trade** les partisans *mpl* du libre-échange; *Rel, Fig* **to be** *or* **play Devil's a.** se faire l'avocat du diable
advocate² ['ædvəkeɪt] *vt* (*sth*) plaider en faveur de; (*cause*) soutenir; (*use of sth, method of proceeding*) préconiser, conseiller; **she advocates leniency** elle préconise l'indulgence
adze, *US* **adz** [ædz] *n* (h)erminette *f*; (*of ice axe*) sape *f*
A & E [eɪən'di:] *n Med* (*abbr* **accident and emergency**) = service *m* des urgences; *F* urgences *fpl*
Aegean [ɪ'dʒi:ən] **1** *adj* **(a) the A. sea** la mer Égée **(b)** *Antiq* égéen, -enne **2** *n* **(a) the A.** la mer Égée **(b)** *Antiq* Égéen, -enne
aegis, *US* **egis** ['i:dʒɪs] *n* égide *f*; **under the a. of ...** sous l'égide de ...
aegrotat ['aɪgrəʊtæt] *n Br Univ* dispense *f* (d'examen) (*accordée pour cause de maladie*)
Aeneas [ɪ'ni:əs] *n* Énée *m*
Aeneid [ɪ'ni:ɪd] *n* Énéide *f*
aeolian [i:'əʊlɪən] *adj* éolien; *Mus* **a. harp** harpe *f* éolienne
aeon, *US* **eon** ['i:ən] *n* éternité *f*; **for aeons upon aeons** pendant des siècles *ou* des éternités; **aeons ago** il y a une éternité
aerate ['eəreɪt] *vt* **(a)** (*inject with air*) aérer **(b)** *Physiol* (*blood*) artérialiser **(c)** *Old-fashioned* (*water, mineral water*) gazéifier
aerated [eə'reɪtɪd] *adj* **(a)** (*with air*) aéré **(b)** *Old-fashioned* (*water*) gazeux **(c)** *F* (*excited, upset*) **to be/get a. about sth** être énervé/s'énerver à cause de qch
aeration [eə'reɪʃən] *n* **(a)** (*injecting with air*) aération *f* **(b)** *Physiol* (*of blood*) artérialisation *f*
aerial ['eərɪəl] **1** *adj* **(a)** aérien; **a. acrobatics** voltige *f* aérienne; **a. photography** photo(graphie) *f* aérienne; **a. walkway** passerelle *f*; **a. warfare** combat *m* aérien **(b)** *Bot* aérien; (*orchid etc*) aéricole; **a. root** racine *f* aérienne **2** *n Rad, TV* antenne *f*; **a. dish** antenne parabolique; **transmitting/receiving a.** antenne d'émission/réceptrice
aerie ['eərɪ, 'ɪərɪ] *n esp US* aire *f* (*d'un aigle*)
aerobatics [eərəʊ'bætɪks] *n* [①**A10**,c] *Av* acrobaties *fpl* aériennes, voltige *f* aérienne; **a. display** démonstration *f* aérienne
aerobics [eə'rəʊbɪks] *n* [①**A10**,c] aérobic *m*; **to do a.** faire de l'aérobic; **are you going to a. tonight?** est-ce que tu vas au cours d'aérobic ce soir?; **a. class/teacher** cours *m*/professeur *m* d'aérobic
aerodrome ['eərədrəʊm] *n* aérodrome *m*
aerodynamic [eərəʊdaɪ'næmɪk] *adj* aérodynamique; **a. drag** résistance *f* de l'air; **a. noise** bruit *m* aérodynamique; **a. shape** (*of car*) profil *m* *ou* forme *f* aérodynamique
aerodynamically [eərəʊdaɪ'næmɪklɪ] *adv* aérodynamiquement
aerodynamics [eərəʊdaɪ'næmɪks] *n* [①**A10**,c] **(a)** (*with sing verb*) (*science*) aérodynamique *f* **(b)** (*with pl verb*) (*quality*) aérodynamisme *m*
aero-engine ['eərəʊendʒɪn] *n* moteur *m* d'avion
aerofoil ['eərəʊfɔɪl], *Am* **airfoil** ['eəfɔɪl] *n Av* plan *m* à profil d'aile, surface *f* portante *ou* sustentrice; (*on car*) aileron *m*
aerogram ['eərəgræm] *n* aérogramme *m*; **a. form** aérogramme
aeromodeller, *US* **aeromodeler** ['eərəʊ'mɒdlər] *n* aéromodéliste *mf*
aeromodelling, *US* **aeromodeling** ['eərəʊ'mɒdlɪŋ] *n* aéromodélisme *m*
aeronaut ['eərənɔ:t] *n* aéronaute *mf*
aeronautic(al) [eərə'nɔ:tɪk, -ɪk(ə)l] *adj* aéronautique
aeronautics [eərə'nɔ:tɪks] *n* [①**A10**,c] aéronautique *f*
aeroplane ['eərəpleɪn] *n esp Br* avion *m*
aerosol ['eərəsɒl] *n* **(a) a. (can)** (bombe *f*) aérosol *m*; **a. spray** atomiseur *m* **(b)** (*substance*) **a. deodorant** déodorant *m* en atomiseur; **available in a. form** existe en atomiseur; **a. paint** peinture *f* aérosol
aerospace ['eərəspeɪs] *n Ind* aérospatiale *f*; **a. industries** industries *fpl* aérospatiales
aesthete, *US* **esthete** ['i:sθi:t] *n* esthète *mf*
aesthetic, *US* **esthetic** [i:s'θetɪk, ɪs-] *adj* esthétique; **in a. terms** en termes d'esthétique
aesthetically, *US* **esthetically** [i:s'θetɪklɪ, ɪs-] *adv* esthétiquement
aestheticism, *US* **estheticism** [i:s'θetɪsɪz(ə)m, ɪs-] *n* esthétisme *m*
aesthetics, *US* **esthetics** [i:s'θetɪks, ɪs-] *n* [①**A10**,c] esthétique *f*
aetiological, *US* **etiological** [i:tɪə'lɒdʒɪk(ə)l] *adj Med, Phil* étiologique
aetiology, *US* **etiology** [i:tɪ'ɒlədʒɪ] *n Med, Phil* étiologie *f*
afar [ə'fɑ:r] *adv usu Lit* **from a.** de loin
afear(e)d [ə'fɪəd] *adj Arch* effrayé, apeuré; **to be a. of sb/sth** être effrayé par *ou* avoir peur de qn/qch
affability [æfə'bɪlɪtɪ] *n* affabilité *f*, courtoisie *f* (**towards** envers, avec)
affable ['æfəb(ə)l] *adv* affable, courtois (**to** envers; **with** avec)
affably ['æfəblɪ] *adv* avec affabilité, avec courtoisie
affair [ə'feər] *n* **(a)** (*matter, concern*) affaire *f*; **the a. in hand** l'affaire qui nous occupe; **that's my a.! stick to your own affairs!** occupe-toi donc de tes affaires!; **what he does in private is his own a.** sa vie privée ne regarde que lui; **to put one's affairs in order** mettre de l'ordre dans ses affaires; **in the present state of affairs** dans l'état actuel des choses; *Iron* **that's a nice** *or* **fine state of affairs!** en voilà du propre!, c'est du joli!; **affairs of state** les affaires de l'État; **foreign affairs** les affaires étrangères; **our home affairs correspondent** notre spécialiste des affaires intérieures; *Arch* **a. of honour** affaire d'honneur, duel *m*; **the Watergate a.** l'affaire du Watergate

(b) (*sexual*) liaison *f*; **to have an a. with sb** avoir une liaison avec qn; **they're having an a.** ils ont une liaison; **an a. of the heart** une affaire de cœur

(c) (*event*) **the meal will be a lavish a.** le repas sera un véritable festin; **the festival was a dull a.** le festival était dépourvu d'intérêt; **it was one of those cheese and wine affairs** c'était une de ces soirées vin et fromage; **what kind of a. was it?** c'était comment?

(d) *F* (*thing*) **the cake's one of those fresh-cream affairs** c'est un de ces gâteaux à la crème fraîche; **the house is a three-storey a.** il s'agit d'une maison à trois étages; **this workbench is an ingenious a.** cet établi est vraiment ingénieux
affect¹ [ə'fekt] *vt* **(a)** (*have effect on*) (*person*) atteindre, toucher; (*organ etc*) affecter; (*decision*) influer sur; (*one's health*) altérer; (*smooth running, smooth traffic flow*) entraver; **roads have been seriously affected by the flooding** les routes ont été fortement touchées par l'inondation; **the economic crisis which is affecting the country at present** la crise économique qui frappe le pays en ce moment; **it affects me personally** cela me touche personnellement; **the strike didn't a. us** nous n'avons pas été touchés par la grève; **pensioners are not affected by this law** les retraités ne sont pas concernés par cette loi; **those most directly affected** les premiers intéressés; **how will this a. the traffic?** quelles seront les conséquences sur la circulation?

(b) (*move*) (*person*) affecter, toucher; **to be deeply affected by sth** être très affecté par qch
affect² *vt* **(a)** (*fake*) (*indifference, interest*) affecter, feindre, simuler; (*pain*) simuler; **to a. an accent** prendre un accent; **he affects to know a lot about ...** il prétend savoir beaucoup de choses sur ... **(b)** (*wear, use*) **he affects drab colours** il a un penchant pour les couleurs ternes
affect³ ['æfekt] *n Psy* affect *m*
affectation [æfek'teɪʃən] *n Pej* **(a)** (*of interest, indifference etc*) affectation *f*, simulation *f* **(b)** (*affectedness*) affectation *f*, manque *m* de naturel; **his working-class accent was clearly an a.** clairement, son accent prolétaire était affecté
affected¹ [ə'fektɪd] *adj* **(a)** *Med* atteint; **to be a. with a disease** être atteint d'une maladie; **the lung is a.** le poumon est atteint *ou* touché; **apply to the a. part** appliquer sur la partie malade **(b)** (*emotionally*) ému, touché
affected² *adj* **(a)** *Pej* (*artificial*) (*person*) affecté, maniéré; (*manners*) affecté, apprêté; (*style*) maniéré, recherché, apprêté **(b)** *Pej* (*indifference etc*) simulé
affectedly [ə'fektɪdlɪ] *adv* avec affectation, d'une manière affectée
affectedness [ə'fektɪdnɪs] *n* (*no pl*) affectation *f*, manque *m* de naturel
affecting [ə'fektɪŋ] *adj* (*sight, scene etc*) touchant, attendrissant
affection [ə'fekʃən] *n* **(a)** affection *f*, tendresse *f*; **to show sb a.** montrer de l'affection *ou* de la tendresse pour qn; **to feel a. for sb** avoir de l'affection *ou* de la tendresse pour qn; **a rare display of a.** une rare manifestation d'affection *ou* de tendresse; **to have an a. for sb** ressentir de l'affection pour qn; **I have a great deal of a. for you** j'ai beaucoup d'affection pour toi; **with much a.** (*in letter*) (bien) affectueusement; **he is held in great a.** il est très aimé; **to gain** *or* **win sb's a.** gagner l'affection de qn; **this town has a special place in my affections** j'aime tout particulièrement cette ville

(b) *Med* (*of chest, skin etc*) affection *f*
affectionate [ə'fekʃənət] *adj* affectueux (**towards** avec,

envers); **an a. hug** une étreinte affectueuse; *Old-fashioned* **your a. nephew** (*in letter*) votre dévoué neveu
affectionately [əˈfekʃənətlɪ] *adv* affectueusement; **yours a.** (*in letter*) bien affectueusement
affective [əˈfektɪv] *adj* affectif
affidavit [æfɪˈdeɪvɪt] *n Jur* déclaration *f* par écrit et sous serment; **to swear an a.** certifier sous serment une déclaration (écrite)
affiliate [əˈfɪlɪeɪt] **1** *vt* (*of society etc*) (*members etc*) s'affilier; **to a. oneself to** *or* **with a society** s'affilier à une société; **a. member** affilié *m* **2** *vi* **to a. to** *or* **with a society** s'affilier à une société; **affiliated company** société *f* affiliée **3** *n* (*person*) affilié, -ée; (*company*) filiale *f*
affiliation [əfɪlɪˈeɪʃən] *n* **(a)** (*to society*) affiliation *f*; **political affiliations** attaches *fpl* politiques **(b)** *Jur* procédure *f* en recherche de paternité; **a. order** assignation *f* d'enfant à un père putatif
affinity [əˈfɪnɪtɪ] *n* **(a)** (*liking, attraction*) affinité *f*; **to have an a. with sb/sth** avoir des affinités avec qn/qch; **there are many affinities between the two regions** les deux régions ont énormément de choses en commun **(b)** (*relationship*) lien *m* **(c)** *Math, Biol* affinité *f* (**with, to** avec; **between** entre); *Ch* **a. for a body** affinité pour un corps
affirm [əˈfɜːm] **1** *vt* **(a)** affirmer, soutenir (**that** que); **to a. sth to sb** affirmer qch à qn; **to a. one's intention to do sth** affirmer qu'on a l'intention de faire qch **(b)** *Jur* (*verdict*) confirmer, homologuer **2** *vi Jur* faire une affirmation *ou* déclaration solennelle
affirmation [æfəˈmeɪʃən] *n* **(a)** affirmation *f*, assertion *f* **(b)** *Jur* déclaration *f ou* affirmation *f* solennelle (*tenant lieu de serment*) **(c)** *Jur* (*of verdict*) confirmation *f*, homologation *f*
affirmative [əˈfɜːmətɪv] **1** *adj* (*answer*) affirmatif **2** *n* **to answer in the a.** répondre affirmativement *ou* par l'affirmative; **the answer is in the a.** la réponse est affirmative **3** *int* **a., captain** affirmatif, mon capitaine
affirmatively [əˈfɜːmətɪvlɪ] *adv* affirmativement
affix¹ [ˈæfɪks] *n Ling* affixe *m*
affix² [əˈfɪks] *vt* attacher (**to** à); (*seal, stamp, one's signature*) apposer (**to a document** à un document); **affixed to the wall** fixé au mur
afflict [əˈflɪkt] *vt* affliger; **to be afflicted with rheumatism** être affligé de rhumatismes; **he was afflicted by psoriasis** il souffrait de psoriasis; **she was afflicted by acute feelings of guilt** elle était accablée d'un fort sentiment de culpabilité; *Iron* **the family I'm afflicted with** la famille dont je suis affligé; *Fig* **the economic problems that a. the nation** les problèmes économiques qui accablent le pays
afflicted [əˈflɪktɪd] **1** *adj* affligé; (*parts, area*) (*by illness*) atteint **2** *npl* **the a.** les affligés *mpl*; **don't mock the a.** ne te moque pas de moi/lui/*etc*; **he can't help being stupid, don't mock the a.** ce n'est pas de sa faute s'il est bête, le pauvre
affliction [əˈflɪkʃən] *n* **(a)** (*suffering*) affliction *f*; **the afflictions of old age** les infirmités *fpl* de la vieillesse **(b)** *Fig* (*misfortune*) calamité *f*, revers *m*; **in her a.** dans sa détresse
affluence [ˈæfluəns] *n* (*wealth*) abondance *f*, richesse *f*; **to live in a.** vivre dans l'abondance
affluent [ˈæfluənt] *adj* (*wealthy*) riche; **a. society** société *f* d'abondance
affluently [ˈæfluəntlɪ] *adv* (*to live*) dans l'abondance
afford [əˈfɔːd] *vt* **(a)** (*usu with* **can**) (*financially*) avoir les moyens (**to do sth** de faire qch; **sth** d'acheter qch); **I can't a. it** mes moyens ne le permettent pas; **we can't a. a new car** nous ne pouvons pas nous offrir une nouvelle voiture; **we could easily a. another car** nous avons largement les moyens d'acheter une autre voiture; **I can a. to eat out twice a week** je peux me permettre d'aller au restaurant deux fois par semaine; **give what you can a.** donnez selon vos possibilités; **it's more than we can a.** c'est au-dessus de nos moyens; **an extravagance I could ill a.** une extravagance qui n'était guère dans mes moyens

(b) (*usu with* **can**) (*non-financial use*) **I can a. to wait** je peux attendre; **can you a. the time?** est-ce que vous avez le temps?; **I cannot a. to create a bad impression/not to go** je ne peux pas me permettre de faire une mauvaise impression/de ne pas y aller; **I can't a. not to** je n'ai pas vraiment le choix

(c) *Lit* (*give*) fournir, offrir; **to a. sb the opportunity to do sth** donner *ou* fournir à qn l'occasion de faire qch; **the trees afforded us very little shelter** les arbres ne nous fournissaient qu'un piètre abri; **it affords me great pleasure** cela me fait grand plaisir; **kind heaven a. him everlasting rest** que Dieu dans sa miséricorde lui donne le repos éternel
affordable [əˈfɔːdəb(ə)l] *adj* (*price, rent*) abordable; (*house, trip etc*) (d'un prix) abordable
afforest [əˈfɒrɪst] *vt* (*piece of land*) boiser
afforestation [əfɒrɪˈsteɪʃən] *n* boisement *m*
affray [əˈfreɪ] *n esp Jur* bagarre *f*, échauffourée *f*
affreightment [əˈfreɪtmənt] *n Com* affrètement *m*
affront¹ [əˈfrʌnt] *n* affront *m*, offense *f* (**to** à)
affront² *vt* offenser, faire (un) affront à; **he was affronted by the suggestion that he should help** il a été très vexé quand on lui a fait remarquer qu'il pourrait aider
Afghan [ˈæfgæn] **1** *adj* afghan; **A. hound** lévrier *m* afghan **2** *n* **(a)** Afghan, -ane **(b)** *Ling* afghan *m* **(c)** *Am* **a. (blanket)** couverture *f* de laine tricotée (au crochet)
Afghanistan [æfˈgænɪstɑːn] *n* Afghanistan *m*
aficionado [əfɪʃjəˈnɑːdəʊ] *n* aficionado *m*; **he's become quite an a.** c'est devenu un vrai aficionado
afield [əˈfiːld] *adv* **far/farther a.** très/plus loin; **she rarely ventures farther a. than the next village** elle s'aventure rarement au-delà du village voisin; **from as far a. as ...** de contrées aussi reculées que ...
afire [əˈfaɪər] *adv, adj pred Arch, Lit* en feu; *Fig* enflammé; **a. with enthusiasm** brûlant d'enthousiasme
aflame [əˈfleɪm] *adv, adj pred Lit* embrasé; **the trees were a. with colour** les arbres étaient flamboyants
AFL-CIO [eɪefelsiːaɪˈəʊ] *n abbr* **American Federation of Labor and Congress of Industrial Organizations**
afloat [əˈfləʊt] *adv, adj pred* **(a)** à flot, sur l'eau; **the biggest ship a.** le plus gros navire à flot; **to be a.** (*of ship*) être à flot; **to keep a ship a.** maintenir un navire à flot; **to keep a.** (*of person, boat*) flotter; *Fig* (*of company*) se maintenir à flot; *Fig* **to keep sb a. (financially)** renflouer qn; **to be a. in space** planer dans l'espace; **life a.** la vie en mer **(b)** (*flooded*) inondé; **the kitchen was a.** la cuisine était inondée
aflutter [əˈflʌtər] *adj* excité; **my heart was all a.** mon cœur battait la chamade; **to set sb's heart a.** faire battre le cœur de qn
AFM [eɪeˈfem] *n TV* (*abbr* **assistant floor manager**) régisseur *m* de plateau adjoint
afoot [əˈfʊt] *adv* **a plan is a. to ...** on projette de ..., on a formé un projet pour ...; **there's something a.** il se prépare *ou* se trame quelque chose; **there was trouble a.** des ennuis se préparaient
afore [əˈfɔːr] *adv, prep, conj Arch, Dial* = **before**
aforementioned [əˈfɔːmenʃənd] *adj attrib, n esp Jur* susmentionné, -ée, sus-dénommé, -ée
aforesaid [əˈfɔːsed] *adj attrib, n esp Jur* susdit, -ite
aforethought [əˈfɔːθɔːt] *adj esp Jur* **with malice a.** avec préméditation, avec intention criminelle; **I know it wasn't done with malice a.** (*non-legal context*) je sais que ce n'était pas intentionnel
a fortiori [ɑːfɔːtɪˈɔːrɪ] *adv* a fortiori
afoul [əˈfaʊl] *adv* **to run a. of the law** avoir des ennuis *ou* maille à partir avec la police; **he ran a. of the chairman's new policy** il s'est heurté à la nouvelle politique du président
afraid [əˈfreɪd] *adj pred* **(a)** (*scared*) pris de peur; **to be a. of sb/sth** avoir peur de qn/qch; **don't be a.** n'ayez pas peur, ne craignez rien; **he felt a.** il avait peur; **if you're not a. of hard work** si le travail intensif ne vous fait pas peur; **there's nothing to be a. of** il n'y a pas de raison d'avoir peur *ou* de quoi avoir peur; **that's (exactly) what I was a. of!** c'est bien ce que je craignais!; **he was a. to open his mouth** il n'osait pas dire un mot

(b) (*worried*) **to be a. that ...** avoir peur *ou* craindre que + *sub* ...; **I was a. you would ask me that question** je craignais *ou* j'avais peur que vous me posiez cette question; **I was a. that might happen** c'est bien ce que je craignais qu'il arrive; **I am a. he'll die** je crains qu'il ne meure

(c) (*regretful*) **I'm a. so/not** je crains que oui/non; **I'm a. she's out** je regrette mais elle est sortie; **I can't help you, I'm a.** je suis désolé, je crois que je ne peux rien faire pour vous; **I'm a. that's it, we've no more money** j'ai bien peur que ça y soit, cette fois, nous n'avons plus d'argent
afresh [əˈfreʃ] *adv* de nouveau, à nouveau; **to start sth a.** recommencer qch; **to look at a problem a.** jeter un nouveau regard sur un problème
Africa [ˈæfrɪkə] *n* Afrique *f*; **in A.** en Afrique
African [ˈæfrɪkən] **1** *adj* africain; **an A. American** un Afro-américain; **A. violet** (*plant*) saintpaulia *m*; **A. elephant** éléphant *m* d'Afrique **2** *n* Africain, -aine
Afrikaaner [æfrɪˈkɑːnər] **1** *adj* afrikaner, afrikaander **2** *n* Afrikaner *mf*, Afrikaander *mf*
Afrikaans [æfrɪˈkɑːns] *n Ling* afrikaans *m*
Afro [ˈæfrəʊ] **1** *adj* (*hairdo*) afro *inv* **2** *n* coiffure *f* afro
Afro-American **1** *adj* afro-américain **2** *n* Afro-américain, -aine
aft [ɑːft] *adv Naut, Av* sur *ou* à *ou* vers l'arrière; **to go a.** aller

à l'arrière; **a. of the mast** sur l'arrière du mât; **to have the wind dead a.** avoir le vent en poupe

after ['ɑːftər] **1** *adv* après; **to come a.** venir après *ou* à la suite; **he was ill for months a.** il en est resté malade pendant des mois; **soon/long a.** bientôt/longtemps après; **the night/the week a.** la nuit/la semaine d'après; **a year a.** un an après *ou* plus tard; **the day a.** le lendemain

2 *prep* **(a)** (*of place*) après; **to run a. sb** courir après qn; **close the door a. you** fermez la porte derrière vous; **I called a. him to …** je lui ai crié de …; *F* **to be a. sb/sth** (*searching for*) être en quête de qn/qch, chercher qn/qch; **the police are a. you** la police est à vos trousses; *F* **what's he a.?** (*what does he want?*) qu'est-ce qu'il a en tête *ou* derrière la tête?; (*what is he looking for?*) qu'est-ce qu'il cherche?; **are you a. my job?** est-ce que tu veux me prendre ma place?; **she's a. a full-time job** elle cherche un travail à temps plein; **they are a. some fun** ils veulent s'amuser

(b) (*of time*) après; **to reign a. sb** régner après qn; **a. three days** trois jours après *ou* plus tard; **a. dinner** après dîner; **a. this date** passé cette date; **a. all** (*all things considered*) après tout; (*in spite of everything*) finalement; **she's only young, a. all** elle est jeune, après tout; **so you went to the party a. all?** alors, finalement, vous êtes allés à la soirée?; **a. all we've done for you!** après tout ce que nous avons fait pour toi!; **the day a. the battle** le lendemain de la bataille; **the day a. tomorrow** après-demain; **it is a. five (o'clock)** il est cinq heures passées; *Am* **twenty a. four** quatre heures vingt; **one a. the other** l'un après l'autre, les uns après les autres; **a. dinner speech** discours *m* d'après-dîner; *Br* **a. hours drinking** = verres *mpl* servis après l'heure de fermeture légale des pubs; **a. tax** après imposition, après impôt

(c) he read page a. page il lut page sur page; **day a. day** jour après jour; **year a. year** une année après l'autre, tous les ans; **there was street a. street of apartment blocks** rue après rue, les immeubles se succédaient; **mile a. mile** mil(l)e après mil(l)e

(d) (*of order*) après; **a. you** (*going through door, at a meal etc*) après vous; **I put Milton a. Dante** je mets Milton au-dessous de Dante; **a. her, he is the best** après elle, c'est lui le meilleur

(e) (*of manner*) d'après; **landscape a. Turner** paysage d'après *ou* à la (manière de) Turner

(f) (*about*) **to ask** *or* **inquire a. sb** demander des nouvelles de qn; **Mrs. Smith asked a. you** Mme Smith a demandé de tes nouvelles

(g) (*Irish*) **to be a. doing sth** (*in the middle of*) être en train de faire qch; (*inclined to*) être disposé à faire qch

3 *conj* (*when subject changes*) après que + *ind ou F sub*; (*when subject stays the same*) après + *inf*; **I came a. he had gone** je suis venu après qu'il est *ou F* soit parti; **a. I had seen him I went out** après l'avoir vu, je suis sorti; **a. doing sth** après avoir fait qch

4 *adj* **(a)** (*yet to come*) à venir; **in a. years** plus tard (dans la vie)

(b) *Naut* arrière; **a. cabin** cabine *f* sur l'arrière; **a. hold** cale *f* arrière

afterbirth ['ɑːftəbɜːθ] *n Obst* placenta *m*

afterburner ['ɑːftəbɜːnər] *n* dispositif *m* de postcombustion

aftercare ['ɑːftəkeər] *n* (*after treatment*) postcure *f*; (*after giving birth*) soins *mpl* post-natals; (*after operation*) soins post-opératoires; (*of convalescent, delinquent etc*) surveillance *f*

afterdeck ['ɑːftədek] *n Naut* plage *f* arrière

aftereffect ['ɑːftərɪfekt] *n* (*of drug*) effet *m* secondaire; *Fig* (*of remark, coup etc*) répercussion *f*, contrecoup *m*; **I'm still feeling the aftereffects of last night's drinking** je ne me suis toujours pas remis de ce que j'ai bu hier soir

afterglow ['ɑːftəgləʊ] *n* **(a)** (*of the setting sun*) dernières lueurs *fpl*, derniers reflets *mpl*; *Fig* **he was basking in the warm a. of his triumph** il savourait le sentiment de volupté dans lequel son triomphe l'avait laissé **(b)** *Comptr* (*on screen*) rémanence *f*

afterlife ['ɑːftəlaɪf] *n* **(a)** *Rel* au-delà *m*, vie *f* après la mort; **we shall meet in the a.** nous nous retrouverons dans l'au-delà **(b)** (*later life*) **in a.** plus tard dans la vie

aftermath ['ɑːftəmæθ, -mɑːθ] *n* **(a)** (*of event*) suites *fpl*; **the a. of war** (*aftereffects*) les répercussions *fpl ou* le contrecoup de la guerre; (*period*) l'après-guerre *m*; **in the immediate a. of the accident** immédiatement après l'accident **(b)** *Agr* (*second mowing or crop*) regain *m*, arrière-foin *m*

aftermost ['ɑːftəməʊst] *adj Naut* le plus en arrière, le plus à l'arrière

afternoon [ɑːftə'nuːn] **1** *n* après-midi *mf inv*; **this a.** cet(te) après-midi; **in the a.** (pendant) l'après-midi; **early/late (on) this a.** en début/en fin d'après-midi; **on a sunny a.** par un(e) après-midi ensoleillé(e); **on Tuesday a.** mardi après-midi; **on the a. of Wednesday 22nd March** le mercredi 22 mars après-midi; **at 2 o'clock in the a.** à deux heures de l'après-midi; **good a.!**, *F* **a.!** (*hello*) bonjour!; (*goodbye*) au revoir!; **a. tea** goûter *m*, thé *m* (de cinq heures); **to work afternoons** travailler l'après-midi **2** *adv esp Am* **afternoons** (pendant) l'après-midi

afterpains ['ɑːftəpeɪnz] *npl Obst* tranchées *fpl*

afters ['ɑːftəz] *npl* (*with sing or pl verb*) *Br F* dessert *m*; **what's for a.?** qu'est-ce qu'il y a comme dessert?; **there was ice cream for a.** il y avait de la glace en dessert *ou* pour le dessert

after-sales ['ɑːftəseɪlz] *adj Com* après-vente *inv*; **a. (department)** service *m* après-vente; **a. marketing** mercatique *f ou* marketing *m* après-vente, MAV *f*; **a. service** service *m* après-vente

aftershave ['ɑːftəʃeɪv] **1** *adj* (*lotion*) après-rasage *inv* **2** *n* (lotion *f*) après-rasage *m*

aftershock ['ɑːftəʃɒk] *n* (*of earthquake*) réplique *f*

aftertaste ['ɑːftəteɪst] *n* arrière-goût *m*

afterthought ['ɑːftəθɔːt] *n* réflexion *f* après coup; **to be an a.** (*of sth added*) être un rajout de dernière minute; *F, Hum* **little Susie was an a.** la petite Susie est arrivée bien plus tard; **as an a.** après coup; **as an a., why not go twice?** après tout, pourquoi ne pas y aller deux fois?; **it's just an a., but why …?** ce n'est qu'une idée qui me vient maintenant, mais pourquoi …?

afterward ['ɑːftəwəd] *adv esp Am* = **afterwards**

afterwards ['ɑːftəwədz] *adv esp Br* après, ensuite; **a. they went home** ensuite *ou* après ils sont rentrés chez eux; **I regretted it a.** par la suite, je l'ai regretté; **a long time a.** longtemps après; **soon** *or* **shortly a.** peu de temps après

afterworld ['ɑːftəwɜːld] *n* au-delà *m inv*

again [ə'gen, *occ* ə'geɪn] *adv* **(a)** de nouveau, encore; **once a.** encore une fois, une fois de plus; **hello, it's me a.!** bonjour, c'est encore moi!; *F* **not you a.!** non, encore toi!; *F* **not spaghetti a.!** pas encore des spaghettis!; **don't do it a.!** ne recommencez pas!; **he never came back a.** il n'est plus jamais revenu; **never a.!** (*after bad experience*) plus jamais!; *Lit, Fml* **never a. will a king rule this land** plus jamais un roi ne régnera dans ce pays; **I'm not going to that shop a.** je ne remettrai jamais les pieds dans ce magasin; **a. and a., time and (time) a.** maintes et maintes fois; **I have told you so a. and a.** je vous l'ai dit vingt fois *ou* cent fois; **now and a.** de temps en temps, de temps à autre; **as much a.** deux fois autant; **half as much a.** moitié plus; **different a.** encore différent; **she was wearing something different a.** elle était encore habillée différemment; **to begin a.** recommencer; **to come a.** revenir; **I've seen him a.** je l'ai revu; **I hope I shall find it a.** j'espère bien le retrouver; *F* **what was your name a.?** rappelez-moi votre nom; **what was that a.?** (*could you say that again*) comment?

(b) (*rhetorical*) de plus, d'ailleurs, en outre; **a., I am not sure that …** d'ailleurs je ne suis pas sûr que …

(c) (*on the other hand*) **(then) a.** d'un autre côté; **then a., he may have forgotten** par ailleurs, il se peut qu'il ait oublié; **then a., others may disagree** d'un autre côté, certains peuvent ne pas être d'accord

against [ə'genst, *occ* ə'geɪnst] *prep* **(a)** (*in opposition to*) contre; **to fight a. sb** se battre contre qn; **to fight a. sth** (*against crime, cancer*) lutter contre qch; **to march a. the enemy** marcher à l'ennemi; **she was a. the idea** elle était opposée à l'idée; **to be a. abortion/nationalization** être contre l'avortement/la nationalisation; **to be a. sb** être contre qn, être opposé à qn; **what have you got a. him/going to Paris?** qu'est-ce que tu as contre lui/le fait d'aller à Paris?; **to have nothing a. sth** ne rien avoir contre qch; **the war set brother a. brother** la guerre a opposé des hommes à leurs frères; **a. my will** contre mon gré; **it was a. my instincts/principles** ça allait à l'encontre de mes instincts/principes; **to act a. the law** agir illégalement; **it's a. the law** c'est illégal *ou* contraire à la loi; **a. the rules** contraire au règlement; **conditions are a. us** les conditions nous sont défavorables; **there is no law a. it** il n'y a pas de loi qui s'y oppose; *Tex* **a. the nap** à rebrousse-poil; **it goes a. nature** c'est contre nature; **it was a race a. time** ça a été une véritable course contre la montre; **to be insured a. fire/theft** être assuré contre les incendies/le vol

(b) (*as protection from*) **to warn sb a. sb/sth** mettre qn en garde contre qn/qch; **protected a. the cold** protégé contre le froid; **a. this eventuality** pour parer à cette éventualité; **to vaccinate sb a. smallpox/malaria** vacciner qn contre la variole/la malaria

(c) (*in contact with*) **leaning a. the wall** appuyé contre le mur; **to place sth a. a wall** adosser qch à un mur; **he**

banged his head a. the wall il s'est cogné la tête contre le mur; **a cross is placed a. each name** (*beside*) une croix est placée à côté de chaque nom

(d) (*in comparison*) **three deaths this year (as) a. thirty in 1970** trois morts cette année contre trente en 1970; **a. this must be set their extreme youth** en contrepartie il faut tenir compte de leur extrême jeunesse; **to check sth a. a list** vérifier qch d'après une liste; **to rise/fall a. the dollar** augmenter/chuter par rapport au dollar

(e) (*in contrast to*) **to show up a. a background** se détacher sur un fond; **she was silhouetted a. the sky** sa silhouette se détachait sur le ciel; **the red stood out a. the grey** le rouge contrastait avec le gris; **a. the light** à contre-jour

(f) *Fin* en contrepartie de; **to issue a ticket a. payment of ...** remettre un ticket en contrepartie du paiement de ...

agape [ə'geɪp] *adv, adj* bouche bée; **to stand a.** rester bouche bée; **with mouth a.** bouche bée

agar(-agar) ['eɪgə('reɪge)r] *n* agar-agar *m*, gélose *f*

agaric ['ægərɪk] *n* (*toadstool*) agaric *m*; **fly a.** (amanite *f*) tue-mouches *m*, fausse oronge *f*

agate ['ægət] *n Miner* agate *f*; **an a. brooch** une broche en agate

agave ['ægeɪv, ə'geɪvɪ] *n* (*plant*) agave *m*

age[1] [eɪdʒ] *n* **(a)** âge *m*; **to be past middle a.** être sur le retour; **twenty years of a.** âgé de vingt ans; **what a. is she?, what's her a.?** quel âge a-t-elle?; **children of their own a.** des enfants de leur âge; **he's your a.** il a ton âge; **she's the same a. as me** *or* **as I am** elle a le même âge que moi; **they're the same a., they're of an a.** ils sont du même âge, ils ont le même âge; **when I was your a.** quand j'avais votre âge; **when you're my a.** quand vous aurez mon âge; **he doesn't look his a.** il ne fait pas son âge; *F* **act** *or* **be your a.!** ne fais pas l'enfant!; **at your a. you should know** à ton âge, tu devrais savoir; **at that a. children need a lot of attention** c'est un âge où les enfants demandent beaucoup d'attention; **15 is the worst a.** 15 ans est l'âge le plus difficile; **at the a. of 33** à l'âge de 33 ans; **I'm at an a. where I question things more** je suis arrivé à un âge où l'on se pose davantage de questions; **to be of an a. to marry** être en âge de se marier; **people of all ages** des gens de tout âge; **people over the a. of 50** les gens de plus de 50 ans; **a. mix** éventail *m* d'âges

(b) **(old) a.** vieillesse *f*; **wisdom comes with a.** la sagesse vient avec l'âge; **a. has not been kind to her** elle est marquée par l'âge; **the house is falling to pieces with a.** la maison tombe de vieillesse *ou* de vétusté; **a tree of great a.** un très vieil arbre; **the car's beginning to show its a.** la voiture commence à donner des signes de vieillesse; **you're showing your a.!** (*remembering things like that etc*) tu es d'un autre âge!; (*you've lost touch*) tu te fais vieux!; *Hum* **a. before beauty** c'est le privilège de l'âge

(c) (*adulthood*) **to be of a.** être majeur; **to come of a.** atteindre sa majorité; **coming of a.** entrée *f* en majorité; **a. of consent** = âge *m* légal auquel on peut se marier ou avoir des rapports sexuels; **to be under a.** *Jur* être mineur; (*not old enough to buy alcohol etc*) ne pas avoir l'âge

(d) (*era*) âge *m*, époque *f*, siècle *m*, ère *f*; **the a. we live in** notre siècle, le siècle où nous vivons; **in our a.** à notre époque; **in an earlier a. this wouldn't have been tolerated** il fut un temps où on n'aurait pas toléré cela; **she is the product of an earlier a.** elle est d'un autre temps; **in this a. of consumerism** en cette ère de consumérisme; **through the ages** à travers les âges *ou* les siècles; **the A. of Steam/the Dinosaurs** l'ère de la vapeur/des dinosaures

(e) *F* (*a long time*) **it's ages** *or* **an a. since I saw him, I haven't seen him for ages** il y a une éternité que je ne l'ai pas vu; **I've been waiting (for) ages** cela fait une éternité que j'attends; **you'll be here for ages yet** tu en as encore pour un bon bout de temps; **it takes them ages to get dressed** ils mettent *ou* ça leur prend une éternité pour s'habiller; **it's expensive, but it lasts for ages** c'est cher, mais ça dure très longtemps

age[2] (**aged** [eɪdʒd]; **ageing, aging** ['eɪdʒɪŋ]) **1** *vi* vieillir, prendre de l'âge; **to a. ten years** vieillir de dix ans; **he had aged beyond recognition** il avait tellement vieilli qu'on ne le reconnaissait plus **2** *vt* **(a)** (*of clothes etc*) vieillir; **the years had aged him** il avait beaucoup vieilli **(b)** *Ind etc* (*wine, whisky, wood*) vieillir

aged[1] ['eɪdʒɪd] **1** *adj* **(a)** *Lit* âgé, vieux; **an a. man** un vieillard **(b)** *Acct* **a. creditor** créancier *m* âgé; **a. debt** créance *f* âgée **2** *npl* **the a.** les personnes *fpl* âgées

aged[2] [eɪdʒd] *adj pred* **(a)** (*of the age of*) **a. twenty** âgé de vingt ans **(b)** (*older*) **I found him greatly a.** je l'ai trouvé bien vieilli

age group *n* tranche *f ou* classe *f* d'âge; **the 15-to-20 a.** le groupe *ou* la classe des 15-20 ans

ageing ['eɪdʒɪŋ] **1** *adj* **(a)** (*person, population*) vieillissant; (*industry*) déclinant; (*car*) qui prend/prenait de l'âge **(b)** (*making sb look older*) (*clothes*) qui vieillissent **2** *n* (*of person, wine etc*) vieillissement *m*; (*of person*) sénescence *f*

ageing process *n* processus *m* de vieillissement

ageism ['eɪdʒɪz(ə)m] *n* âgisme *m*

ageist ['eɪdʒɪst] *adj* (*policy etc*) âgiste, qui défavorise les personnes âgées; **or would that be a.?** ou est-ce que ce serait de la discrimination contre les personnes âgées?

ageless ['eɪdʒlɪs] *adj* **(a)** sans âge; (*young-looking*) toujours jeune **(b)** (*eternal*) éternel

age limit *n* limite *f* d'âge

agency ['eɪdʒənsɪ] *n* **(a)** *Com* agence *f*; **to have the sole a. for a firm** être le représentant exclusif d'une maison; **aid a.** association *f* d'aide aux pays en voie de développement; **news** *or* **press a.** agence de presse; **a. agreement** accord *m* de représentation; **a. contract** contrat *m* d'agence; **a. copy** (*from press agency*) dépêche *f* d'agence; **a. fee** frais *mpl* d'agence **(b)** (*action*) action *f*, opération *f*; **the a. of water** l'action de l'eau; **through sb's a.** par l'entremise *ou* l'intermédiaire de qn **(c)** *esp US* (*government department*) organisme *m* gouvernemental

agency agreement *n* accord *m* de représentation

agency work *n* travail *m* pour une agence

agenda [ə'dʒendə] *n* (*of meeting*) ordre *m* du jour, programme *m*; **question on the a.** question à l'ordre du jour; **what's on the a. for today?** qu'est-ce qu'il y a à l'ordre du jour?; *Fig* qu'est-ce qu'il y a de prévu aujourd'hui?; **to have a full a.** avoir un programme très chargé; *Fig* **drugs are back on the a.** la drogue revient à la une de l'actualité; **the problem of the homeless doesn't come very high on the government's a.** le problème des sans-abri ne figure pas parmi les priorités du gouvernement; **hidden a.** des projets *mpl* secrets

agent ['eɪdʒənt] *n* **(a)** *Com* agent *m*, représentant *m*; *Th, Cin, Publishing* agent; **a. for the firm of ...** représentant de la maison ...; **sole a.** agent exclusif; *Pol* **(election) a.** directeur *m* de campagne électorale; **a. middleman** agent intermédiaire **(b)** **(secret) a.** agent *m* secret; **double a.** agent double **(c)** (*instrument*) agent *m*; **to be the a. of sth** être le moteur *ou* la cause de qch; **the a. of change was the revolution** la révolution était le moteur du changement; **she was the a. of her own downfall** elle a été l'artisan de sa propre perte **(d)** (*chemical, therapeutic etc*) agent *m*

agent provocateur, *pl* **agents provocateurs** ['æʒɒnprɒvɒkæ'tɜːr] *n* (agent *m*) provocateur *m*

Age of Reason *n Hist* siècle *m* des lumières

age-old *adj attrib* (*custom etc*) séculaire

age ring *n* (*on tree*) cerne *m*

agglomerate[1] [ə'glɒmərət] **1** *adj Fml* aggloméré **2** *n Geol* agglomérat *m*

agglomerate[2] [ə'glɒməreɪt] **1** *vt* agglomérer **2** *vi* s'agglomérer

agglomeration [əglɒmə'reɪʃən] *n* agglomération *f*

agglutinate [ə'gluːtɪneɪt] *Physiol, Biol, Ling* **1** *vt* agglutiner **2** *vi* s'agglutiner

agglutination [əgluːtɪ'neɪʃən] *n* agglutination *f*

aggrandize [ə'grændaɪz] *vt* (*state*) agrandir; (*one's importance, role*) grossir, grandir

aggrandizement [ə'grændɪzmənt] *n* (*of state etc*) agrandissement *m*; **they're doing it purely for their own a.** ils ne font cela que pour se grandir aux yeux des autres

aggravate ['ægrəveɪt] *vt* **(a)** (*mistake, difficulty, situation*) aggraver; (*evil*) empirer; (*wound, quarrel*) envenimer; (*indignation, pain*) augmenter **(b)** *F* (*annoy, anger*) (*sb*) agacer, exaspérer

aggravating ['ægrəveɪtɪŋ] *adj* **(a)** (*circumstance*) aggravant **(b)** *F* (*exasperating*) exaspérant, agaçant; **I've had a very a. day** j'ai passé une journée atroce; **a. child** enfant insupportable; **it's very a.** c'est vraiment agaçant

aggravation [ægrə'veɪʃən] *n* **(a)** (*of situation, crime, illness*) aggravation *f*; (*of wound, quarrel*) envenimement *m* **(b)** *F* (*of person*) exaspération *f*, agacement *m*; **he does nothing but cause a.** il ne fait qu'embêter le monde; **I don't want to give** *or* **cause any more a.** je ne veux plus embêter qui que ce soit **(c)** *F* (*cause of aggravation*) circonstance *f* aggravante

aggregate[1] ['ægrɪgət] **1** *adj attrib* **(a)** collectif; *Econ* global; **for an a. period of three years** pendant trois ans en tout; **a. output** production *f* globale **(b)** *Bot, Geol* agrégé **2** *n* **(a)** (*total*) ensemble *m*, total *m*; **world aggregates** totaux mondiaux; **a complex a. of forces** un assemblage complexe de forces; **in the a.** dans l'ensemble; *esp Sp* **on a.** au total; **Milan won on a.** c'est Milan qui a totalisé le plus de points (**b**) *Phys* masse *f*, assemblage *m*, agrégation *f*; *Ch, Miner* agrégat *m* (**c**) *Constr* granulat *m*

aggregate[2] ['ægrɪgeɪt] **1** *vt* (**a**) *Phys* agréger (**b**) (*group together*) (*various categories*) rassembler, regrouper **2** *vi Phys* s'agréger

aggregation [ægrɪ'geɪʃən] *n* (**a**) *Phys* agrégation *f*, agglomération *f* (**b**) *Miner* agrégat *m*

aggression [ə'greʃən] *n* (**a**) (*attack*) agression *f*; **an act of a.** une agression; **war of a.** guerre *f* d'agression (**b**) (*aggressiveness*) agressivité *f*

aggressive [ə'gresɪv] *adj* (**a**) (*violent etc*) agressif (**towards** envers); *Psy* **a. impulse** impulsion *f* agressive (**b**) (*management, sales policy*) énergique, dynamique; (*chess player*) qui attaque

aggressively [ə'gresɪvlɪ] *adv* (**a**) (*to behave*) d'une manière agressive; (*to say*) d'un ton agressif; (*to look at*) d'un air agressif (**b**) (*to sell*) énergiquement, avec dynamisme; (*to push sth through*) avec vigueur, vigoureusement; **to play a.** avoir un jeu offensif

aggressiveness [ə'gresɪvnɪs] *n* (**a**) (*violent nature*) agressivité *f* (**b**) (*of management style, sales policy*) dynamisme *m*

aggressor [ə'gresər] *n* agresseur *m*; **a. nation** pays *m* agresseur

aggrieved [ə'griːvd] *adj* (*expression, tone*) vexé; **to be** *or* **feel a.** se sentir lésé (**at, by** de); *Jur* **the a. party** la partie lésée

aggro ['ægrəʊ] *n Br F* (**a**) (*hassle*) enquiquinement *m*; **it's not worth the a.** ça ne vaut pas le coup de s'enquiquiner; **there's a. with her all the time** on s'accroche tout le temps avec elle; **don't give me any more a.** arrête de m'enquiquiner; **can you do this for once without any a.?** est-ce que pour une fois tu pourrais faire ça sans m'embêter? (**b**) (*fighting*) bagarre(s) *f(pl)*, grabuge *m*; **to look for some a.** chercher la bagarre

aghast [ə'gɑːst] *adj* horrifié (**at** de); **to stand a.** en rester *ou* en être tout pantois; **they watched a. as …** horrifiés, ils regardaient …

agile ['ædʒaɪl] *adj* (*person, mind, limbs, movement*) agile

agilely ['ædʒaɪlɪ] *adv* (*to move, jump*) agilement, avec agilité; (*to argue*) adroitement

agility [ə'dʒɪlɪtɪ] *n* agilité *f*

aging ['eɪdʒɪŋ] *adj, n* = **ageing**

agio ['ædʒɪəʊ] *n Fin* (**a**) (*price*) agio *m* (**b**) (*business*) commerce *m* du change

agitate ['ædʒɪteɪt] **1** *vt* (*liquid, mind*) agiter **2** *vi* **to a. for/against sth** faire de l'agitation *ou* mener une campagne en faveur de/contre qch

agitated ['ædʒɪteɪtɪd] *adj* (*water, person*) agité; **now don't get a.!** allons, ne t'agite pas comme ça!

agitatedly ['ædʒɪteɪtɪdlɪ] *adv* (*to act*) de manière agitée; (*to say*) avec agitation, d'une voix agitée

agitation [ædʒɪ'teɪʃən] *n* (*of air, sea, person*) agitation *f*; *Pol* agitation, troubles *mpl*; **the a. for a change in the law** la campagne en faveur d'un changement de la loi; **in a state of a.** agité; **they arrived in a state of considerable a.** ils étaient fort agités quand ils sont arrivés

agitator ['ædʒɪteɪtər] *n* (**a**) (*person*) agitateur, -trice; (*for sth*) contestataire *mf* (**b**) (*machine*) agitateur *m*

agitprop ['ædʒɪtprɒp] *n Pol* agit-prop *f*

aglitter [ə'glɪtər] *adj pred* brillant; **her eyes were a. with mischief** ses yeux pétillaient de malice

aglow [ə'gləʊ] *adj pred* enflammé, embrasé; **the sky was a.** le ciel était embrasé; **to be a. with colour** briller de vives couleurs; *Fig* **face a. with delight** visage rayonnant de joie *ou* tout épanoui; *Fig* **a. with health** resplendissant de santé

AGM [eɪdʒiː'em] *n* (*abbr* **annual general meeting**) AGA *f*, AG *f*

agnostic [æg'nɒstɪk] *adj, n* agnostique *mf*

agnosticism [æg'nɒstɪsɪz(ə)m] *n* agnosticisme *m*

ago [ə'gəʊ] *adv* **ten years a.** il y a dix ans; **he arrived an hour a.** il est arrivé il y a une heure; (*in this place*) il est là depuis une heure; **a little while a., a short time a.** tout à l'heure; **long a.** il y a longtemps; **long, long a.** il y a très, très longtemps; **not long a.** il n'y a pas longtemps; **not so long a.** il n'y a pas si longtemps; **no longer a. than the last century** pas plus loin qu'au siècle dernier; **how long a. is it since …?** combien de temps y a-t-il que …?, depuis combien de temps …?; **as long a. as 1840** déjà en 1840, dès 1840; **I knew her long a.** je l'ai connue dans le temps; **that was years a.** ça fait des années de cela; **how long a. was that?** il y a combien de temps de cela?

agog [ə'gɒg] *adv, adj* **to be all a. (with excitement)** être agité *ou* en émoi (**about sth** à cause de qch); **everyone was a.** tout le monde était en émoi; **he was a. to hear the latest news** il brûlait d'impatience d'apprendre les dernières nouvelles; **she was a. at the news** elle était stupéfiée par cette nouvelle

agonize ['ægənaɪz] *vi* (**a**) (*worry*) se ronger les sangs, se tourmenter; **to a. over the smallest details** se tourmenter à propos du moindre détail; **you shouldn't a. so much about these decisions** tu ne devrais pas te ronger les sangs comme ça à propos de ces décisions (**b**) *Lit* (*suffer*) être au supplice *ou* au martyre

agonized ['ægənaɪzd] *adj* (*cry*) d'angoisse; **with an a. expression (on her face)** le visage déchiré par l'angoisse; **an a. look** un regard angoissé *ou* plein d'angoisse

agonizing ['ægənaɪzɪŋ] **1** *adj* (*pain, worry, death*) atroce; (*sight*) navrant, angoissant; (*situation, silence, wait*) angoissant; (*decision, choice, dilemma*) pénible **2** *n* angoisse *f*; **to come to a decision without any a. over the consequences** parvenir à une décision sans se tourmenter sur ses conséquences; **why all this a. about something that can't be helped?** pourquoi se tourmenter à propos de quelque chose qu'on ne peut pas changer?

agonizingly ['ægənaɪzɪŋlɪ] *adv* (*painful, difficult*) atrocement; **a. slow** d'une lenteur insupportable

agony ['ægənɪ] *n* (**a**) (*anguish*) angoisse *f*; **in an a. of fear** saisi d'une peur atroce; **to be in an a. of suspense** attendre avec angoisse; **to be in an a. of doubt** être en proie à un doute terrible; **the a. of homelessness** le calvaire des sans-abri; **the a. of watching a child die** la douleur insoutenable de voir mourir un enfant; **to suffer agonies, to be in a.** être au supplice *ou* au martyre; *F* **it's a. walking in these shoes** c'est un véritable supplice de marcher avec ces chaussures; *F* **to pile** *or* **put on the a.** forcer la dose; **it was a. to watch them lose** c'était atroce de les voir perdre (**b**) (**death**) **a.** agonie *f*

agony aunt *n Journ* = responsable *mf* de la rubrique courrier du cœur

agony column *n Journ F* courrier *m* du cœur

agoraphobia [æg(ə)rə'fəʊbɪə] *n Psy* agoraphobie *f*; **to have a.** souffrir d'agoraphobie

agoraphobic [æg(ə)rə'fəʊbɪk] *adj, n Psy* agoraphobe *mf*; **to be (an) a.** souffrir d'agoraphobie, être agoraphobe

agrarian [ə'greərɪən] **1** *adj* (*law, measure*) agraire; (*party*) agrarien **2** *n Pol* agrarien *m*

agree [ə'griː] **1** *vt* (**a**) (*reach agreement on*) (*price, conditions etc*) s'accorder *ou* se mettre d'accord sur; **to be agreed** (*date*) à convenir; (*price*) à débattre; **(are we) agreed?** (nous sommes) d'accord?; **unless otherwise agreed** sauf arrangement contraire; **to a. to do sth** se mettre d'accord pour faire qch; **as agreed** comme convenu

(**b**) (*concur*) **I a. that's expensive, but …** c'est cher, j'en conviens, mais …; **I a. that he was mistaken, but …** j'admets qu'il s'est trompé, mais …; **don't you a. that …?** ne croyez-vous pas que …?; **everyone agrees that he's the best singer** tout le monde s'accorde à dire que c'est le meilleur chanteur

(**c**) (*consent*) **to a. to do sth** accepter *ou* convenir de faire qch, consentir à faire qch; **to a. to differ** accepter ses différences (**on** *or* **about sth** sur qch); **everyone agrees that …** tout le monde accepte que …; **it is generally agreed that …** il est généralement admis que …; **he agreed to let us go home** il nous a permis de rentrer à la maison

2 *vi* (**a**) (*be of same opinion, concur*) être d'accord (**about** sur); (*after discussion*) se mettre d'accord (**about** sur); **I quite** *or* **entirely a.** je suis entièrement d'accord; **everyone agrees** tout le monde est d'accord; **I'm afraid I can't a.** (*with you, him etc*) j'ai bien peur de ne pas être du même avis; **I think it's too expensive and Peter agrees** je pense que c'est trop cher et Peter est d'accord avec moi *ou* est du même avis; **in the end she agreed** (*that it was too expensive*) elle a fini par l'admettre; **it's expensive, I a., but …** c'est cher, j'en conviens *ou* je suis d'accord, mais …; **I couldn't a. more!** tu l'as/elle l'a/*etc* bien dit!

(**b**) (*match*) (*of statements, totals, facts etc*) s'accorder, concorder; (*of ideas, opinions*) concorder, coïncider; *Gram* s'accorder

(**c**) (*accept*) consentir (**to** à); **she'll never a.** elle n'acceptera jamais *ou* ne sera jamais d'accord; **how did he get them to a.?** comment a-t-il fait pour qu'ils acceptent?; *Mktg* **to a. and counter** approuver et contre-argumenter

▶ **agree on** *vipo* (**a**) (*of people*) (*point*) être d'accord sur; (*after discussion*) se mettre d'accord sur; (*date*) se mettre d'accord sur, convenir de; **we a. on the need for research** nous concordons sur la nécessité de faire des recherches; *Jur* **conditions agreed on** conditions *fpl* acceptées d'un commun accord (**b**) (*of books, versions etc*) (*point*) s'accorder sur

▶ **agree to** *vipo* (*accept*) (*condition, proposal*) accepter; **to a. to sth being done** accepter que qch se fasse; **they have agreed to your visiting us** ils ont accepté que *ou* ils veulent bien que tu viennes nous voir

▶ **agree upon** *vipo* = **agree on**

▶ **agree with** *vipo* **(a)** (*be of same opinion as*) (*person*) être du même avis que, être d'accord avec; **he entirely agrees with you** il est entièrement d'accord avec vous, il est entièrement de votre avis; **they a. with each other** ils sont du même avis; *F* **I couldn't a. with you more!** tu l'as bien dit!; **to a. with a theory** accepter une théorie; **to a. with a decision** approuver une décision; *F* **I don't a. with all this violence on television** je n'approuve pas toute cette violence à la télé

(b) (*suit*) convenir à, réussir à; (*of food*) réussir à; **the climate doesn't a. with him** le climat ne lui convient pas *ou* ne lui réussit pas

(c) (*coincide with*) (*what person said*) concorder avec, être en accord avec; *Gram* **the verb agrees with the subject in number** le verbe s'accorde en nombre avec le sujet

agreeable [əˈgriːəb(ə)l] *adj* **(a)** (*pleasant*) agréable **(to** à); (*person*) aimable **(to** envers); **if that is a. to you** si cela vous convient **(b)** (*willing*) **to be a. to sth/to doing sth** consentir à qch/à faire qch, accepter qch/de faire qch; **I am (quite) a.** je veux bien

agreeably [əˈgriːəblɪ] *adv* agréablement

agreed [əˈgriːd] **1** *adj* (*price, time etc*) convenu; **a. statement** (*in the media*) déclaration *f* commune **2** *int* entendu!, soit!, d'accord!; **it was expensive, a., but …** c'était cher, soit *ou* d'accord, mais …

agreement [əˈgriːmənt] *n* **(a)** (*contract*) (*between people, countries*) accord *m* **(on, about** sur); **collective (wage) a.** convention *f* collective (des salaires); **to enter into** *or* **conclude an a. with sb** passer un accord *ou* un contrat avec qn; **to have an a. with sb** avoir conclu *ou* passé un accord avec qn; **to hold sb to an a.** faire respecter un accord à qn; **our a. was that …** nous avions convenu que …; **to come to an a.** tomber d'accord; **to come to** *or* **arrive at** *or* **reach an a. with sb** se mettre d'accord avec qn; (*compromise*) s'accommoder *ou* s'arranger avec qn; **to work out an a.** parvenir à un accord; *Com* **as per a.** comme (il a été) convenu; **by mutual a.** d'un commun accord; **marketing a.** accord de commercialisation

(b) the proposal met with unanimous a. la proposition a été reçue à l'unanimité; **to be in a. with sb** être d'accord avec qn; **to be in a. with a decision** approuver une décision; **there was a. on all sides that a change would be welcome** de toute part on convenait de l'opportunité d'un changement

(c) [①B8,4; B35-36,2] (*match*), *Gram* accord *m* **(with** avec); **to be in a. with** (*facts*) concorder avec; (*rules*) être conforme à, être en conformité avec; **a. of adjectives** accord des adjectifs

agribusiness [ˈægrɪbɪznɪs] *n* agro-alimentaire *m*

agrichemical [ægrɪˈkemɪk(ə)l] *n esp Am* = **agrochemical**

agricultural [ægrɪˈkʌltʃər(ə)l] *adj* (*product, machine, land, people etc*) agricole; **East Anglia is very a.** l'East Anglia est une région très agricole; **a. economy** économie *f* du secteur agricole; **a. engineer** ingénieur *m* agronome; **a. labourer** ouvrier *m* agricole; **a. tourism** tourisme *m* agricole; **a. worker** ouvrier *m* agricole

agricultural college *n* = institut *m* agronomique

agricultur(al)ist [ægrɪˈkʌltʃər(əl)ɪst] *n* agriculteur, -trice

agriculture [ˈægrɪkʌltʃər] *n* agriculture *f*

agritourism [ˈægrɪtʊərɪz(ə)m] *n* tourisme *m* agricole

agrochemical [ægrəʊˈkemɪk(ə)l] *n Agr* produit *m* agrochimique

agronomic [ægrəˈnɒmɪk] *adj* agronomique

agronomist [əˈgrɒnəmɪst] *n* agronome *mf*

agronomy [əˈgrɒnəmɪ] *n* agronomie *f*

aground [əˈgraʊnd] *adv Naut* échoué; **to run a.** (*of ship*) (s')échouer; *Fig* (*of policy, project etc*) échouer

ague [ˈeɪgjuː] *n Med, Arch* fièvre *f* (paludéenne) intermittente

ah [ɑː] *int* ah!, ha!; **ah, yes, now you come to mention it** euh, oui, maintenant que tu m'en parles

aha [əˈhɑː] *int* ah! ah!

ahead [əˈhed] *adv* **(a)** devant; **to send sb a.** envoyer qn en avant; **what lies a. for us?** qu'est-ce qui nous attend?, qu'est-ce que l'avenir nous réserve?; **to get a.** (*of person, car etc*) prendre de l'avance; *Fig* (*in career*) avancer (dans sa carrière); **to draw a.** (*of runner, cyclist etc*) décoller, prendre de l'avance; *Sp* **to be a. on points** avoir des points d'avance; **to be a. of sb** (*in space*) être en avant de qn; **to be a. of the bunch** mener le peloton; **to be a. of one's competitors** devancer ses concurrents; **to go on a.** prendre les devants; **to get a. of sb** dépasser qn; **to be two hours a. of sb** avoir deux heures d'avance sur qn; *Sch* **he is a. of his class** il est en avance sur sa classe; **to be a. of one's time** être en avance sur son temps; **to be a. of time** (*of person*) arriver/avoir fini/*etc* avant l'heure; **you've got your best years a. of you** vous avez vos meilleures années devant vous; **to look a.** (*in front*) regarder devant soi; (*to the future*) penser à l'avenir; **to plan a.** faire des projets; **you have to plan a. for a big wedding** il faut s'organiser à l'avance pour un grand mariage; **how far a. should one book?** combien de temps faut-il retenir d'avance?

(b) *Naut* **to be a.** être sur l'avant *ou* en avant (*du navire*); **the ship was right a.** le navire était droit devant; **to go a.** aller de l'avant; **full speed a.!** en avant toute!; **wind a.** vent debout; **line a.** en ligne de file, en colonne; **single line a.** ligne de file

ahem [əˈhem] *int* hum!

ahoy [əˈhɔɪ] *int Naut* **boat/ship a.!** oh(é) du canot/du navire!; **land a.!** terre!

AI [eɪˈaɪ] *n* **(a)** *Comptr* (*abbr* **artificial intelligence**) IA *f* **(b)** *Biol abbr* **artificial insemination (c)** *Pol abbr* **Amnesty International**

AID [eɪaɪˈdiː] *n* **(a)** *Biol* (*abbr* **artificial insemination by donor**) IAD *f* **(b)** *US Pol abbr* **Agency for International Development**

aid¹ [eɪd] *n* **(a)** (*help*) aide *f*, assistance *f*, secours *m*; (*to developing countries, for disaster relief*) aide; **with** *or* **by the a. of sb** avec l'aide de qn; **with** *or* **by the a. of sth** à l'aide de qch; **to go to sb's a.** aller *ou* se porter au secours de qn; **collection in a. of …** quête au profit de …; *F* **what's (all) this in a. of?** c'est en quel honneur?; *F* **what's all this wiring in a. of?** ça sert à quoi tous ces fils?; *F* **what's all this noise in a. of?** qu'est-ce que c'est que tout ce bruit?; **mutual a.** entraide *f*; **mutual-a. society** société *f* de secours mutuels *ou* d'assistance mutuelle; **medical a.** soins *mpl* médicaux

(b) (*device*) **beauty aids** produits *mpl* de beauté; **hearing** *or* **deaf a.** audiophone *m*; *Sch* **audio-visual aids** matériel *m* audio-visuel; **to act as an a. to international understanding** contribuer à la compréhension entre les nations

aid² *vt* (*person, company*) aider, venir en aide à; (*sb's recovery*) contribuer à; (*digestion*) faciliter; **to a. one another** s'aider les uns les autres, s'entraider; *Jur* **to a. and abet sb** être le complice de qn

AIDA [aɪˈiːdə] *Mktg* (*abbr* **attention-interest-desire-action**) AIDA

aide [eɪd] *n* aide *mf*, assistant, -ante; (*to president etc*) conseiller, -ère

aide-de-camp, *pl* **aides-de-camp** [ˈeɪddəˈkɒm] *n Mil* aide *m* de camp

aide-mémoire [ˈeɪdmemˈwɑːr] *n* aide-mémoire *m inv*

aiding [ˈeɪdɪŋ] *n Jur* **a. and abetting** complicité *f*

aid organization *n* organisme *m* d'aide

AIDS, Aids [eɪdz] *n Med* sida *m*; **A.-related** lié au sida; **A. sufferer** sidéen, -enne, malade atteint(e) du sida; **A. clinic** clinique *f* spécialisée dans le traitement du sida; **A. virus** virus *m* du sida

aikido [aɪˈkiːdəʊ] *n Sp* aïkido *m*

ail [eɪl] **1** *vt Arch* **what ails you?** qu'avez-vous? **2** *vi* être souffrant

aileron [ˈeɪlərɒn] *n Av* aileron *m*

ailing [ˈeɪlɪŋ] *adj* (*person*) souffrant; *Fig* (*company, economy*) en mauvaise passe; **the a. state of the economy/country** la mauvaise passe dans laquelle se trouve l'économie/le pays

ailment [ˈeɪlmənt] *n* mal *m*; **childish ailments** maladies *mpl* infantiles

aim¹ [eɪm] *n* **(a)** (*action*) action *f* de viser; **to miss one's a.** (*with firearm etc*) manquer la cible *ou* son coup; *Fig* frapper à faux; **to take a. at sb/sth** viser qn/qch; **to take a.** mettre en joue, viser; **he took careful a.** il visa avec soin; *Mil* **take a.!** en joue!; **her a. was good** elle visait bien **(b)** (*goal*) but *m*, dessein *m*, visées *fpl*; **his a. was to …** son but était de …, il avait pour but de …; **with the a. of doing sth** dans le but *ou* le dessein de faire qch

aim² **1** *vt* **(a)** (*stone*) lancer **(at** à); (*blow*) porter, allonger **(at** à)

(b) (*gun etc*) pointer **(at** sur); **to a. a gun at sb/sth** coucher qn/qch en joue avec un fusil, pointer un fusil sur qn; **to a. a camera** cadrer **(at** sur)

(c) (*remarks, TV programme*) destiner **(at** à); **to a. a criticism at sb** adresser une critique à qn; **these measures are aimed at reducing unemployment** ces mesures visent une réduction du chômage

2 *vi* **(a) to a. at sb/sth (with a gun/***etc***)** viser qn/qch, mettre *ou* coucher qn/qch en joue; **I aimed at the tyres** j'ai visé (dans) les pneus

(b) *Fig* **to a. at becoming sth, to a. to become sth** aspirer *ou* viser à devenir qch; **what are you aiming at?** (*what do you hope to do?*) quel but poursuivez-vous?; (*what do you mean?*) où voulez-vous en venir?; **to a. high** viser haut; *F* **I a. to go** (*intend*) j'ai l'intention d'y aller; **we're aiming for a 6 a. m. start** nous comptons partir à six heures du matin

aiming [ˈeɪmɪŋ] *n Mil* pointage *m*

aimless [ˈeɪmlɪs] *adj* sans but, sans objet; (*violence*) gratuite; **an a. sort of life** une vie désœuvrée; **a few a. remarks** quelques remarques en l'air

aimlessly ['eɪmlɪslɪ] *adv* sans but, sans objet; **to wander about a.** aller *ou* errer à l'aventure
aimlessness ['eɪmlɪsnɪs] *n* **the a. of their existence** leur existence sans but
ain't [eɪnt] *Arch, Sl* **(a) = am not, is not, are not,** *see* **be (b) = have not,** *see* **have**[2]
AIO [eɪaɪ'əʊ] *Mktg* (*abbr* **activities, interests and opinions**) AIO; **A. research** étude *f* AIO
air[1] [eər] *n* **(a)** air *m*; **a change of a. will do me good** un changement d'air me fera du bien; **we need a change of a.** nous avons besoin de changer d'air; **in the open a.** en plein air, au grand air, à ciel ouvert; **high up in the a.** très haut dans le ciel; **in the a.** en l'air, dans les airs; **to throw sth (up) in the a.** lancer qch en l'air; **to fly through the a.** voler *ou* voltiger en l'air; **war in the a.** guerre *f* aérienne; **a. injection** injection *f* d'air; **a. intake** prise *f* d'air
(b) *Fig* **I can't live on a.** je ne vis pas de l'air du temps; **to walk on a.** être aux anges; **to be in the a.** (*of rumour*) circuler; (*of idea*) être dans l'air; (*of project*) être encore vague; **everything's up in the a.** (*uncertain*) rien n'a été décidé pour l'instant; **the date is still up in the a.** la date n'a pas encore été fixée; **our plans are up in the a. again** et voilà nos projets qui retombent à l'eau; *F* **to go up in the a.** (*explode, Fig in anger*) exploser; **there's something in the a.** il y a quelque chose dans l'air; *F* **it's all hot a.** c'est du vent; **to melt** *or* **vanish into thin a.** s'évanouir, disparaître
(c) *Naut, Lit* (*wind*) brise *f*, vent *m*; **there was no a.** il n'y avait pas de vent
(d) *Mil, Av* (*attack, base, defence etc*) aérien; **by a.** par avion; **a. broker** courtier *m* de l'air; **a. carrier** transporteur *m* aérien; **a. inclusive tour** voyage *m* à forfait (par avion)
(e) *Rad, TV* **to be on the a.** (*of person*) être à l'antenne; (*of programme*) être diffusé; (*of station*) émettre; **we're going on the a. in two minutes** nous sommes à l'antenne dans deux minutes; **the station goes off the a. at midnight** les programmes finissent à minuit; **to put a play on the a.** mettre une pièce en ondes *ou* sur les ondes
(f) *Mus* air *m*
(g) (*look*) air *m*, mine *f*, apparence *f*; **he has an a. about him** il en impose; **to give oneself** *or* **to put on airs (and graces)** se donner des airs
air[2] **1** *vt* **(a)** (*room*) aérer, ventiler; (*clothing, bedding, duvet etc*) aérer, mettre à l'air **(b)** *Fig* (*one's opinions, differences*) exposer; (*one's knowledge*) faire parade de, faire étalage de; (*one's feelings*) donner libre cours à **(c)** *Rad, TV* (*programme*) passer, donner **2** *vi* **(a)** s'aérer **(b)** *US* (*of radio or TV programme*) passer
airbag ['eəbæg] *n* coussin *m* d'air, sac *m* gonflable
air bed *n* matelas *m* pneumatique
airborne ['eəbɔːn] *adj* **(a)** (*particles, seeds etc*) en suspension dans l'air; (*disease*) aéroporté **(b)** (*aircraft*) en vol; (*balloon*) en l'air; **to become a.** (*of aircraft*) décoller; **once we are a.** une fois que nous aurons décollé **(c)** *Mil* (*troops, unit*) aéroporté; **a. attack** attaque *f* exécutée par des troupes aéroportées, assaut *m* vertical **(d)** *Av* (*equipment, radar*) de bord
air brake *n* frein *m* pneumatique
airbrush ['eəbrʌʃ] *n Art etc* aérographe *m*, pistolet *m* vaporisateur
▶ **airbrush in** *vtsep Art, Phot* (*detail*) ajouter à l'aérographe
▶ **airbrush out** *vtsep Art, Phot* (*detail*) effacer à l'aérographe
airbrushing ['eəbrʌʃɪŋ] *n Art etc* peinture *f ou* retouchage *m* à l'aérographe
air-bubble *n* bulle *f* d'air
airburst ['eəbɜːst] *n* explosion *f* (*en plein ciel*)
airbus ['eəbʌs] *n* aérobus *m*, airbus *m*
air commodore *n* = général *m* de brigade aérienne
air compressor *n* compresseur *m* d'air
air-conditioned *adj* climatisé, à air conditionné
air-conditioning *n* climatisation *f*, *F* clim *f*
air-cooled ['eəkuːld] *adj* refroidi par air; *Aut* **a. engine** moteur *m* à refroidissement par air
air-cooling *n* refroidissement *m* par air
air cover *n* couverture *f* aérienne, protection *f* aérienne
aircraft ['eəkrɑːft] *n inv* avion *m*; **a. carrier** porte-avions *m inv*; **a. engineering** ingénierie *f* aéronautique; **a. factory** usine *f* d'aviation; **a. grounding** interdiction *f* de vol; **a. identification code** code *m* d'identification d'avion; **a. manufacturer** constructeur *m* d'avions, avionneur *m*
aircraftman, *pl* **-men** ['eəkrɑːftmən] *n Br* = soldat *m* de la Royal Air Force; **leading a.** = caporal *m* de la Royal Air Force
aircraftwoman, *pl* **-women** ['eəkrɑːftwʊmən, -wɪmɪn] *n Br* = femme *f* soldat de la Women's Royal Air Force; **leading a.** = femme *f* caporal de la Women's Royal Air Force
aircrew ['eəkruː] *n Av* équipage *m*
airdrome ['eədrəʊm] *n Am* aérodrome *m*
airdrop ['eədrɒp] *n Av* largage *m* (de charges)
air duct *n* conduite *f* d'air, amenée *f* d'air
Airedale ['eədeɪl] *n* (chien *m*) airedale *m*
airer ['eərər] *n* (*for clothes*) séchoir *m*
air fare *n* tarif *m* aérien
airfield ['eəfiːld] *n* champ *m ou* terrain *m* d'aviation, aérodrome *m*
air filter *n* filtre *m* à air
airflow ['eəfləʊ] *n* **(a)** *Tech* écoulement *m* d'air; **smooth/turbulent a.** écoulement régulier/turbulent; **a. meter** débitmètre *m* d'air **(b)** *US Aut* **a. body** carrosserie *f* aérodynamique
airfoil ['eəfɔɪl] *n Am* = **aerofoil**
Air Force *n* Armée *f* de l'air, Aviation *f*
airframe ['eəfreɪm] *n Av* cellule *f* d'avion, fuselage *m*
air freight[1] *n* fret *m* aérien; **send it by a.** envoyez-le par avion *ou* par air; **a. consignment note** récépissé *m* aérien; **a. consolidator** groupeur *m* de fret aérien; **a. container** conteneur-avion *m*, *pl* conteneurs-avions; **a. forwarding agent** groupeur *m* de fret aérien; **a. services** messageries *fpl* aériennes
air freight[2] *vt* expédier par fret aérien
air/fuel mixture *n* mélange *m* air/carburant
air gauge *n* micromètre *m* pneumatique
air gun *n* fusil *m* à air comprimé
airhead ['eəhed] *n esp Am Sl* tête de linotte *f*, tête en l'air *f*
airhole ['eəhəʊl] *n* trou *m* de ventilation *ou* d'aération
air hostess *n* hôtesse *f* de l'air
airily ['eərɪlɪ] *adv* avec désinvolture; (*to say*) d'un ton dégagé *ou* désinvolte
airiness ['eərɪnɪs] *n* **(a)** (*of building, flat*) caractère *m* spacieux **(b)** (*casualness*) désinvolture *f*
airing ['eərɪŋ] *n* **(a)** (*of room etc*) ventilation *f*, aération *f*; **give the room a good a.** aère bien la pièce **(b)** (*of clothes*) **give the clothes an a. outside** mets ces habits à l'air dehors; **a. cupboard** placard *m* chauffé où l'on fait sécher le linge **(c)** (*of new car etc*) présentation *f*; **they gave the project/the matter an a.** ils ont eu une première discussion à propos du projet/de la question; **to give one's grievances/feelings an a.** exposer ses griefs/ses sentiments **(d)** *Rad, TV* (*of programme*) diffusion *f*, transmission *f* **(e)** *Arch* (*walk*) (petite) promenade *f*; **to take an a.** prendre l'air
airless ['eəlɪs] *adj* **(a)** (*room, house etc*) privé d'air, qui sent le renfermé **(b)** *Tech* sans air **(c)** (*evening etc*) sans air, lourd
airlessness ['eəlɪsnɪs] *n* **(a)** (*of room*) manque *m* d'air *ou* d'aération **(b)** (*of weather*) lourdeur *f*
airlift[1] ['eəlɪft] *n Av* pont *m* aérien
airlift[2] *vt* (*supplies*) transporter par avion; **to a. in/out** (*supplies*) amener/emporter par avion; (*refugees*) amener/évacuer par avion
airline ['eəlaɪn] *n* **(a)** *Av* ligne *f ou* compagnie *f* aérienne, compagnie d'aviation; **a. club** club *m* de compagnie aérienne; **a. operator** compagnie aérienne; **a. passenger** passager *m* des compagnies aériennes; **a. ticket** billet *m* d'avion; **to be an a. pilot** être commandant de bord **(b)** (*of diver*) voie *f* d'air
airliner ['eəlaɪnər] *n* avion *m* de ligne
air link *n* liaison *f* aérienne
airlock ['eəlɒk] *n* **(a)** *Constr* (*of caisson*) écluse *f ou* sas *m* pneumatique *ou* à air; *Naut, Astronaut* sas **(b)** (*in pipe*) poche *f* d'air
airmail[1] ['eəmeɪl] **1** *adj* (*paper, envelope*) avion; **a. letter** aérogramme *m*; **a. edition** = édition *f* imprimée sur papier très fin; **a. paper** papier *m* avion; **a. sticker** étiquette *f* par avion **2** *adv* par avion **3** *n* (*service*) poste *f* aérienne, service *m* postal aérien; (*letters etc*) courrier *m* par avion; **by a.** par avion
airmail[2] *vt* (*letter etc*) envoyer par avion
airman, *pl* **-men** ['eəmən] *n* **(a)** aviateur *m* **(b)** *US Mil Av* **a. (basic)** = soldat *m* de la United States Air Force
air mile *n* mille *m* aérien; **to collect air miles** accumuler des Aéropoints
Air Ministry *n Hist* = Ministère *m* de l'Air
airpass ['eəpɑːs] *n* carte *f* d'abonnement de transport aérien
air passage *n Anat* conduit *m* aérifère
airplane ['eəpleɪn] *n esp Am* avion *m*
air plant *n* plante *f* aéricole, (plante) épiphyte *m*
airplay ['eəpleɪ] *n Rad* diffusion *f*; **to get** *or* **receive a.** (*of record etc*) passer sur les ondes
air pocket *n Av* trou *m* d'air; (*in pipe*) poche *f* d'air
airport ['eəpɔːt] *n Av* aéroport *m*; **London A.** l'aéroport de Londres; **a. of departure** aéroport de départ; **a. of destination** aéroport de destination; **a. advertising** publicité *f* dans les aéroports; **a. apron** aire *f* de stationnement (des

avions); **a. hotel** hôtel *m* d'aéroport; **a. landing tax** taxe *f* d'atterrissage; **a. lounge** hall *m* d'aéroport; **a. service charge** taxe d'aéroport; **a. shop** boutique *f* d'aéroport; **a. tax** taxe d'aéroport; **a. taxi** taxi *m* desservant l'aéroport

air power *n Mil* puissance *f* aérienne

air raid *n* raid *m* aérien; (*across border*) raid aérien, incursion *f* aérienne; **a. precautions** défense *f* passive; **a. warning** alerte *f* aérienne

air rifle *n* fusil *m* à air comprimé

air route *n* route *f* aérienne

airscrew ['eəskru:] *n Old-fashioned Av* hélice *f*

air-sea *adj* **a. rescue** sauvetage *m* aéro-maritime, sauvetage aérien en mer

air service *n* liaison *f* aérienne

airship ['eəʃɪp] *n* dirigeable *m*

air show *n* salon *m* aérien

airsick ['eəsɪk] *adj* **to be a.** avoir le mal de l'air; **to deal with a. passengers** s'occuper des passagers qui ont/avaient le mal de l'air

airsickness ['eəsɪknɪs] *n* mal *m* de l'air

airspace ['eəspeɪs] *n Av etc* espace *m* aérien

airspeed ['eəspi:d] *n Av* (*of plane*) vitesse *f*

airstream ['eəstri:m] *n* courant *m* d'air

airstrip ['eəstrɪp] *n Av* bande *f ou* piste *f* d'atterrissage

air supremacy *n* suprématie *f* aérienne

air temperature *n* température *f* ambiante

air terminal *n* aérogare *f*

air ticket *n* billet *m* d'avion

airtight ['eətaɪt] *adj* (*seal*) hermétique; (*container etc*) hermétique, étanche (à l'air)

airtime ['eətaɪm] *n Rad, TV* **(a)** (*length of programme*) temps *m* d'antenne **(b)** (*starting time*) heure *f* où commence l'émission; **five minutes to a.** on est à l'antenne dans cinq minutes

air-to-air *adj Mil* (*missile etc*) air-air *inv*

air-to-ground *adj Mil* (*missile etc*) air-sol *inv*, air-terre *inv*

air-to-surface *adj* (*missile etc*) *Mil* air-sol *inv*; *Naut* air-surface *inv*

air traffic *n* circulation *f* aérienne, trafic *m* aérien; **a. control** contrôle *m* aérien; **a. controller** contrôleur *m* aérien, aiguilleur *m* du ciel, contrôleur de trafic aérien

air transport *n* transport *m* aérien *ou* par avion

air travel *n* voyages *mpl* en avion; **a. organiser** organisateur *m* de voyages par avion

air valve *n* clapet *m* d'air

air vent *n* aérateur *m*, buse *f* de ventilation, diffuseur *m*; *Aut* (*on bonnet*) grille *f* d'entrée d'air

airwaves ['eəweɪvz] *npl Rad, TV* ondes *fpl*, ondes hertziennes; **the best DJ on the a.** le meilleur DJ sur les ondes *ou* ondes hertziennes

airway ['eəweɪ] *n* **(a)** *Av* (*route*) route *f ou* ligne *f ou* voie *f* aérienne; **a. marker** balise *f* d'entrée de piste **(b)** *Med* bronches *fpl* **(c)** *US Rad TV* chaîne *f*

air waybill *n* lettre *f* de transport aérien, connaissement *m* aérien

airwoman, *pl* **-women** ['eəwʊmən, -wɪmɪn] *n* aviatrice *f*

airworthiness ['eəwɜ:ðɪnɪs] *n Av* tenue *f* en l'air, navigabilité *f*; **certificate of a.** certificat *m* de navigabilité

airworthy ['eəwɜ:ðɪ] *adj* (*aircraft*) en état de prendre l'air, en bon état de vol *ou* de navigabilité; (*certified*) muni d'un certificat de navigabilité; **to be a.** tenir l'air

airy ['eərɪ] *adj* **(a)** (*room, house*) bien aéré **(b)** (*dress, material*) léger; **the cake was light and a.** le gâteau était très léger **(c)** (*person, attitude*) insouciant, désinvolte **(d)** (*promises*) vain, illusoire

airy-fairy *adj F* (*person, idea*) farfelu

aisle [aɪl] *n* **(a)** (*between seats*) passage *m*; (*in plane*) couloir *m*; (*in bus etc*) couloir central; (*at cinema etc*) allée *f*; (*in supermarket*) allée de circulation; *Th, F* **to have them rolling in the aisles** faire mourir de rire le public; **a. seat** (*in plane*) place *f* côté couloir **(b)** (*in church*) allée *f*; *Fig* **to walk up the a.** se marier (à l'église)

aitch [eɪtʃ] *n* (*letter*) h *m*; **to drop one's aitches** ne pas prononcer (correctement) les h

ajar [ə'dʒɑ:r] *adv, adj pred* (*door, window*) entrouvert, entrebâillé; **to swing a.** s'entrouvrir, s'entrebâiller

aka [eɪkeɪ'eɪ] *adv* (*abbr* **also known as**) alias

akimbo [ə'kɪmbəʊ] *adv* **with arms a.** les (deux) poings sur les hanches

akin [ə'kɪn] *adj* **a. to sb/sth** apparenté à qn/qch; **feeling a. to fear** sentiment voisin de la peur; **this is a. to treachery** cela s'apparente à de la traîtrise

alabaster ['æləbæstər, -bɑ:-] **1** *n* albâtre *m* **2** *adj attrib* **(a)** (*figurine, vase etc*) en albâtre **(b)** *Fig* (*complexion, hands etc*) d'albâtre

à la carte [ælə'kɑ:t] *adj, adv* à la carte

alacrity [ə'lækrɪtɪ] *n* empressement *m*, promptitude *f*; **he accepted with a.** il a accepté avec enthousiasme, il s'est empressé d'accepter

Aladdin [ə'lædɪn] *n* Aladin *m*; **the shop is an A.'s cave** (*full of wonderful things*) cette boutique est une véritable caverne d'Ali Baba

alarm[1] [ə'lɑ:m] *n* **(a)** (*signal*) alarme *f*, alerte *f*; **false a.** fausse alerte; **to raise** *or* **give the a.** donner l'éveil *ou* l'alerte *ou* l'alarme

(b) (*fright, anxiety*) alarme *f*, frayeur *f*; **there's no cause for a.** il n'y a aucune raison de s'alarmer; **he hid in a.** effrayé, il s'est caché

(c) (*warning device*) avertisseur *m*, alarme *f*; *Fig* **to set (the) a. bells ringing** déclencher l'alerte; (*give rise to suspicion*) mettre la puce à l'oreille de qn

(d) (*on clock*) sonnerie *f*; **a. (clock)** réveille-matin *m inv*, réveil *m*; **to wind up the a.** remonter la sonnerie; **to set the a. for six o'clock** mettre le réveil à six heures; **the a. went off at six o'clock** le réveil a sonné à six heures

(e) a. call (*by telephone*) réveil *m* par téléphone; (*in hotel*) appel *m* de réveil

(f) (*of bird etc*) cri *m* d'alarme

alarm[2] *vt* (*frighten*) effrayer; **to be alarmed at sth** s'alarmer *ou* s'effrayer de qch, être alarmé de qch; **don't be alarmed** ne vous effrayez pas; **there's no need to feel alarmed** inutile de s'alarmer; **the parents looked alarmed** les parents semblaient très inquiets

alarm clock *n* réveille-matin *m inv*, réveil *m*

alarming [ə'lɑ:mɪŋ] *adj* (*news etc*) alarmant, inquiétant

alarmingly [ə'lɑ:mɪŋlɪ] *adv* d'une manière alarmante *ou* très inquiétante; **the shots were coming a. close** les tirs se rapprochaient dangereusement; **to develop a. fast** se développer à une vitesse alarmante

alarmist [ə'lɑ:mɪst] *adj, n* alarmiste *mf*; **don't be such an a.** ne sois pas aussi alarmiste

alarm signal *n* signal *m* d'alarme

Alas *abbr* **Alaska**

alas [ə'læs] *int Lit, Fml* hélas!

Alaska [ə'læskə] *n* Alaska *m*; *Culin* **baked A.** omelette *f* norvégienne

alb [ælb] *n Rel* aube *f*

Albania [æl'beɪnɪə] *n* Albanie *f*

Albanian [æl'beɪnɪən] **1** *adj* albanais **2** *n* **(a)** Albanais, -aise **(b)** *Ling* albanais *m*

albatross ['ælbətrɒs] *n* (*bird*) albatros *m*; *Fig* **he was like an a. around her neck** c'était un poids qu'elle avait à traîner; **this issue has become an a. around the government's neck** ce problème est devenu un gros handicap pour le gouvernement

albeit [ɔ:l'bi:ɪt] *conj* quoique, bien que; **a brilliant, a. slipshod, writer** un écrivain brillant, bien que négligent

albinism ['ælbɪnɪz(ə)m] *n Biol* albinisme *m*

albino, *pl* **-os** [æl'bi:nəʊ, -əʊz] **1** *adj* (*person*) albinos; **a. rabbit** lapin *m* albinos *ou* russe **2** *n* albinos *mf*

Albion ['ælbɪən] *n Lit* (*England*) Albion *f*; **perfidious A.** la perfide Albion

album ['ælbəm] *n* **(a)** (*for photos, comic book*) album *m* **(b)** (*record*) album *m*

albumen ['ælbjʊmɪn, æl'bju:mɪn] *n* **(a)** (*in egg*) albumen *m* **(b)** (*in blood*) albumine *f*

albumin ['ælbjʊmɪn, æl'bju:mɪn] *n Ch* albumine *f*

alchemist ['ælkəmɪst] *n* alchimiste *m*

alchemy ['ælkəmɪ] *n* alchimie *f*

alcohol ['ælkəhɒl] *n* (*drink*), *Ch* alcool *m*; **I never touch a.** je ne bois jamais d'alcool; **a. content** teneur *f* en alcool, pourcentage *m* d'alcool; **low in a.** à faible teneur en alcool; **to have an a. problem** avoir un problème de boisson

alcoholic [ælkə'hɒlɪk] **1** *adj* alcoolique; **a. drink** boisson alcoolisée **2** *n* (*person*) alcoolique *mf*; *Med* éthylique *m*

Alcoholics Anonymous *n* Alcooliques *mpl* anonymes

alcoholism ['ælkəhɒlɪz(ə)m] *n* alcoolisme *m*

alcove ['ælkəʊv] *n* alcôve *f*; (*in wall*) niche *f*; **dining a.** coin *m* des repas, coin salle à manger

aldehyde ['ældɪhaɪd] *n Ch* aldéhyde *m*

alder ['ɔ:ldər] *n* (*tree*) aune *m*, aulne *m*

alderman, *pl* **-men** ['ɔ:ldəmən] *n Am* (*for city*) = conseiller *m* municipal; *Br* (*for county*) = conseiller général

Alderney ['ɔ:ldənɪ] *n* Aurigny *m*

ale [eɪl] *n* bière *f* anglaise (légère), ale *f*; **pale/brown a.** bière blonde/brune

Alec(k) ['ælɪk] *n F* **a smart A.** un(e) je-sais-tout; **I've had enough of his smart A. remarks** j'en ai assez de ses remarques désobligeantes; **who's the smart A. who forgot to switch it off?** quel est le malin qui a oublié de l'éteindre?

alehouse ['eɪlhaʊs] *n Arch* taverne *f*, cabaret *m*

alert¹ [ə'lɜːt] **1** *n* alerte *f*; **to be on the a.** être sur le qui-vive, être en état d'alerte; **police were on the a. for an escaped prisoner** la police était en état d'alerte à la suite de l'évasion d'un prisonnier; **to be on the a. against an attack** veiller en prévision d'une attaque; **the navy has been put on full a.** l'alerte générale a été déclarée dans la marine; **they're always on the a. for interesting stories** ils sont toujours à l'affût d'histoires intéressantes **2** *adj* **(a)** (*temporarily*) alerté, vigilant, éveillé; **to be a. to a danger** être conscient d'un danger **(b)** (*naturally*) actif, vif, preste; **a. mind** esprit *m* vif *ou* éveillé

alert² *vt* alerter; **troops have been alerted** les troupes sont en état d'alerte; **to a. sb to a danger** avertir qn d'un danger; **a noise alerted her to the presence of an intruder** un bruit l'avertit de la présence d'un intrus

alertness [ə'lɜːtnɪs] *n* **(a)** (*of sentry etc*) vigilance *f* **(b)** (*of mind*) vivacité *f*

Alexander the Great [ælɪg'zɑːndər] *n* Alexandre le Grand

Alexandria [ælɪg'zɑːndrɪə] *n* Alexandrie *f*

alexandrine [ælɪg'zɑːndraɪn] *adj, n Liter* alexandrin *m*

alfalfa [æl'fælfə] *n* (*plant*) luzerne *f*

alfresco [æl'freskəʊ] *adj, adv* en plein air; **a. meal** repas *m* en plein air

alga, *pl* **-ae** ['ælgə, 'ældʒiː] *n Bot* algue *f*

algal ['ælg(ə)l] *adj* des algues

algebra ['ældʒɪbrə] *n* algèbre *f*

algebraic(al) [ældʒɪ'breɪɪk, -ɪk(ə)l] *adj* (*sign, calculation etc*) algébrique

Algeria [æl'dʒɪərɪə] *n* Algérie *f*

Algerian [æl'dʒɪərɪən] **1** *adj* algérien **2** *n* Algérien, -ienne

Algiers [æl'dʒɪəz] *n* Alger *m*

ALGOL ['ælgɒl] *n Comptr* algol *m*

algorithm ['ælgərɪð(ə)m] *n* algorithme *m*

algorithmic [ælgə'rɪðmɪk] *n* algorithmique

alias ['eɪlɪəs] **1** *adv* alias **2** *n* (*pl* **aliases** ['eɪlɪəsɪz]) nom *m* d'emprunt, faux nom; *Comptr* alias *m*

alibi¹ ['ælɪbaɪ] *n Jur* alibi *m*; **to produce an a.** produire *ou* fournir un alibi; **to establish an a.** prouver *ou* établir son alibi; **they're using the economic crisis as an a. for their own incompetence** ils se servent de la crise économique pour déguiser leur propre incompétence

alibi² *vt* trouver un alibi pour

alien ['eɪlɪən] **1** *n* **(a)** *Jur* étranger, -ère (non naturalisé, -ée); **illegal a.** clandestin, -ine **(b)** (*from outer space*) extra-terrestre *mf* **2** *adj* **(a)** *Jur* étranger **(b)** (*from outer space*) extra-terrestre **(c)** *Fig* (*foreign*) (*land, territory, concept*) étranger; **a. to** contraire à; **an action entirely a. to her nature** une action entièrement contraire à sa nature; **such thoughts are a. to her** de telles pensées lui sont étrangères

alienable ['eɪlɪənəb(ə)l] *adj Jur* (*property*) aliénable

alienate ['eɪlɪəneɪt] *vt* **(a)** (*supporters, electorate, readers*) éloigner; **she has alienated many of her colleagues** elle s'est aliéné beaucoup de ses collègues; **to a. sb from his friends** détacher *ou* éloigner qn de ses amis; **to a. oneself from sb** se détacher *ou* s'éloigner de qn; **these young people feel alienated from society** ces jeunes gens se sentent en marge de la société; **to be** *or* **feel alienated by sb's manner** être rebuté par les manières de qn **(b)** *Jur* (*property etc*) aliéner **(c)** *Fin* (*money*) détourner

alienation [eɪlɪə'neɪʃən] *n* **(a)** désaffection *f* **(b)** *Jur* (*of property*) aliénation *f* **(c)** *Psy* **mental a.** aliénation *f* mentale; *Th* **a. effect** distanciation *f*

alight¹ [ə'laɪt] *adj pred* en feu; **to keep a flame/fire a.** maintenir une flamme/un feu; **to catch a.** prendre feu; **to set sth a.** mettre le feu à qch; *Fig* **his face was a. with joy** son visage resplendissait de joie

alight² *vi* **(a)** *Fml* (*from train, car etc*) descendre (**from** de) **(b)** (*of bird, eyes, glance*) se poser (**on** sur)

align [ə'laɪn] **1** *vt* **(a)** (*objects, soldiers etc*) aligner, mettre en ligne; (*paper in printer*) mettre bien droit; *Tech* (*axes*) faire coïncider; *Aut* (*wheels*) régler le parallélisme de; **to a. sth with sth** aligner qch avec qch; *Aut* **the wheels were badly aligned** les roues n'étaient pas centrées **(b)** *Fin* (*of country*) (*one's currency*) aligner (**on** sur) **(c) to a. oneself with sb** s'aligner sur qn; **they aligned themselves against the President/this policy** ils se sont ligués contre le président/cette politique **2** *vi* **(a)** s'aligner, se mettre en ligne; *Fig* **to a. with sb** s'aligner sur qn **(b)** (*of shafts etc*) coïncider

alignment [ə'laɪnmənt] *n* **(a)** alignement *m*; (*of railway etc*) tracé *m*; *Comptr* (*of characters, graphics*) alignement, cadrage *m*; *Aut* (*of wheels*) parallélisme *m*; **out of a.** désaligné; *Constr* hors d'œuvre; *Typ* sortant; **in a.** aligné; **to bring sth into a. with the new regulations** aligner qch sur la nouvelle réglementation; **this is not in a. with current practice** ceci n'est pas conforme à ce qui se pratique actuellement **(b)** *Fin* **a. of currencies** alignement *m* des monnaies

alike [ə'laɪk] **1** *adj pred* semblable, pareil; **they are very much a.** ils se ressemblent beaucoup; **no two are a.** il n'y en a pas deux de pareils; **you are all a.!** vous êtes tous les mêmes!; **they're very a. in dress/their tastes** leur façon de s'habiller/leurs goûts se ressemble(nt) beaucoup **2** *adv* (*to dress, treat etc*) de la même façon *ou* manière, pareillement, de même; **we don't think a.** nous ne sommes pas d'accord, nous n'avons pas le même point de vue; **every day, summer and winter a.** tous les jours, été comme hiver; **old and young a.** les vieux comme les jeunes; **the problem affects all of us a.** ce problème nous touche tous sans exception

aliment ['ælɪmənt] *n Scot Jur* = **alimony**

alimentary [ælɪ'mentərɪ] *adj Anat* **a. canal** tube *m* digestif

alimony ['ælɪmənɪ] *n Jur* pension *f* alimentaire

alive [ə'laɪv] *adj pred* **(a)** (*person, animal, plant*) **to be (still) a.** être (encore) vivant *ou* en vie, vivre (encore); **to keep sb a.** maintenir qn en vie; **to come a. again** (*after apparent death*) revenir à la vie; (*after real death*) ressusciter; **to stay a.** survivre; **to be burnt a.** être brûlé vif; **to be buried a.** être enterré vivant; **to be a. and well** bien se porter; **no one got out of the building a.** personne n'est sorti vivant de l'immeuble; **Mr Evans was last seen a. on 21st June** c'est le 21 juin qu'on a vu M. Evans vivant pour la dernière fois; *F* **to be a. and kicking** être plein de vie; **it feels good to be a.!** il fait bon vivre!; **dead or a.** mort ou vif; **when your father was a.** du vivant de votre père; **no one a.** personne au monde; **the oldest man a.** l'homme le plus vieux au monde

(b) (*memory, hope, custom*) **in parts of the country her memory/this custom is still very much a.** dans certaines régions, son souvenir/cette coutume est encore très vivant(e); **to keep sth a.** (*memory, custom*) garder *ou* entretenir qch; (*conversation*) entretenir qch, ne pas laisser languir qch; **to keep a religion a.** entretenir la pratique d'une religion

(c) (*aware*) **to be fully a. to sth** avoir pleinement conscience de qch; **I am a. to the fact that …** je n'ignore pas que …; **she's very a. to the latest developments in the industry** elle est très au courant des nouveaux développements dans le secteur; **she's very a. to the world around her** elle est très ouverte au monde qui l'entoure

(d) (*full of vitality*) vif, éveillé; **I've never felt so a.** je ne me suis jamais senti aussi plein de vie; **he came a. when someone mentioned food** il s'est réveillé quand quelqu'un a parlé de manger; **the evening came a. when the musicians arrived** la soirée s'est animée à l'arrivée des musiciens; **look a.!** remuez-vous (donc)!

(e) the cheese was a. with maggots le fromage grouillait de vers; **the street was a. with people** la rue fourmillait *ou* grouillait de monde

(f) *esp US El* **the wire was a.** le fil était sous tension

alkali ['ælkəlaɪ] *n Ch* alcali *m*; **a. metal** métal *m* alcalin

alkaline ['ælkəlaɪn] *adj Ch* alcalin

alkaloid ['ælkəlɔɪd] *adj, n Ch* alcaloïde *m*

all [ɔːl] [①**A36**,d; **B14**,B,1] **1** *adj* tout, *mpl* tous, *fpl* toutes; **a. France** toute la France; **a. men** tous les hommes; **a. the others** tous les autres; **a. four of them** tous les quatre; **to be a. things to a. men** être tout à tous; **to be a. heart** être plein de bonnes intentions; **he's a. man, isn't he?** quel homme, hein?; **a. day** toute la journée; **a. her life** toute sa vie; **(with) a. my love** (*at end of letter*) bien affectueusement; **the people/books had a. disappeared** les gens/les livres avaient tous disparus; **they are a. smokers** ce sont tous des fumeurs; **a. the way** (*of journey*) tout le long du chemin; (*of course of action*) jusqu'au bout; **he leaves the door open a. the time** il laisse tout le temps la porte ouverte; **people have been phoning a. the time you've been out** le téléphone n'a pas arrêté de sonner pendant que tu étais sorti; **I've been here a. the time** je n'ai pas bougé d'ici; **is that a. the luggage you're taking?** c'est tout ce que vous emportez comme bagages?; **for a. his wealth** en dépit de *ou* malgré sa fortune; **with a. speed** au plus vite, à toute vitesse; **by a. accounts they've had a most successful year** tout semble indiquer qu'ils ont eu une excellente année; **at a. hours** à toute heure; **in a. sorts of ways** de toutes les façons; **in a. honesty/sincerity** pour être honnête/sincère; **in a. frankness** en toute franchise; *Fml* **with a. due care (and attention)/dispatch** avec tout le soin requis/toute la promptitude requise; *Fml* **with a. due respect** avec tout le respect qui vous est dû; **what's a. that noise?** qu'est-ce que c'est que tout ce bruit?; **a. that's nonsense** tout ça, c'est des bêtises; **for a. that they say he's a genius, I think …** ils ont beau dire que c'est un génie, moi, je pense …; *F* **and a. that** et tout cela, et tout le reste; **you're not as ill as a. that** vous n'êtes pas aussi *ou* si malade que ça; **it's not a. that pleasant** ce n'est pas tellement agréable; **of a. the stupid things to say/do!** de toutes les idioties possibles!; **of a. times to phone!** il a bien choisi son heure pour téléphoner!; **you, of a. people, should know what I mean** toi au moins tu devrais savoir ce que je veux dire

2 *pron* **(a)** (*with pl*) tous, *f* toutes; **a. are agreed that ...** tous sont d'accord que ...; **a. of us** nous tous; **we a. love him** nous l'aimons tous; **a. of them are blue, they are a. blue** ils sont tous bleus, tous sont bleus; **a. together** tous à la fois, tous ensemble; **a. but he** *or* **him** tous sauf *ou* excepté lui; **a. and sundry** tous sans exception

(b) (*everything*) tout; **I want a. of it** je le veux en entier; **almost a.** presque tout; **I did a. I could** j'ai fait tout ce que j'ai pu; *Prov* **a. that glitters is not gold** tout ce qui brille n'est pas de l'or; *Iron Hum* **a. is forgiven** tout est pardonné; **I know it a.** (*of news etc*) je sais tout cela; (*of poem etc*) je le sais en entier; **best/worst of a., ...** le mieux/pire, c'est que ...; **most of a.** surtout, en particulier; **take it a.** prenez le tout; **in the middle of it a.** au milieu de tout cela; **for a. he may say** en dépit de ce qu'il dit, quoi qu'il en dise; **that's a.** c'est tout, voilà tout; **is that a.?** c'est tout?; *Iron* ce n'est que ça?; **if that's a.** si ce n'est que cela; **that's a. well and good** tout cela est bien joli; **a.'s well** tout va bien; **a.'s well that ends well** tout est bien qui finit bien; **I think that's about a.** je crois que c'est tout; **a. I said was 'good morning'** tout ce que j'ai dit a été 'bonjour'; **that's a. they ever do, complain** c'est tout ce qu'ils savent faire, se plaindre; **it was a. I could do not to laugh** j'avais le plus grand mal à ne pas rire; **when** *or* **after a.'s said and done** en fin de compte; *F* **he must be a. of sixty** il doit avoir au moins soixante ans; *F Iron* **it cost a. of £2** ça a coûté deux livres et pas moins

(c) once and for a. une fois pour toutes; **for a. I know** autant que je sache; **for a. I care** pour (tout) ce que cela me fait; **it's a. the same to me** ça m'est égal; **thirty men in a.** trente hommes en tout; **above a.** surtout; **most of a.** surtout, le plus; **when I was busiest of a.** au moment où j'étais le plus occupé

(d) *Sl* (*everything else*) **and a.** et (tout) le reste; **I know he's been very kind and a., but ...** je sais bien qu'il a été très gentil et tout, mais ...

(e) *Br Sl* (*nothing*) **damn** *or* **bugger** *or* **sod a.** rien du tout, que dalle; **I've done damn a. today** je n'ai rien fichu aujourd'hui

3 *adv* **(a)** (*entirely*) tout; **she is a. alone** elle est toute seule; **a. on one's own** tout seul; **to be (dressed) a. in black** être habillé(e) tout en noir *ou* tout de noir; **she is a. ears/impatience/smiles** elle est tout oreilles/impatience/sourires; **a. (a)round the room** dans toute la pièce; **I forgot a. about the meeting** j'ai complètement oublié qu'il y avait une réunion; **a. in one piece** tout d'une pièce; **are you still a. in one piece?** (*after accident*) est-ce que tu es encore en un seul morceau?; **she is a. for accepting this offer** elle est tout en faveur d'accepter cette offre; **my wife was a. for calling in a doctor** ma femme voulait à toute force *ou* à tout prix appeler un médecin; **I'm a. for it** je suis entièrement d'accord *ou* pour; **to be a. in favour of sth** être entièrement favorable à qch; **he's not a. bad** il n'est pas entièrement mauvais; **that's a. to the good!** tout va pour le mieux!; **a. the better/worse (for me)** tant mieux/pis (pour moi); **you will be a. the better for it** vous vous en trouverez (d'autant) mieux; **a. the harder** encore plus dur; **the time came a. too soon** l'heure n'arriva que trop tôt; **a. along** depuis le début; **a. at once** (*suddenly*) tout à coup, subitement; (*everything together*) tout d'un coup, tous à la fois; **a. of a sudden** tout à coup, soudain; **a. over** partout; **a. over the floor/pavement** partout par terre/sur le trottoir; *Fig* **the team was a. over the place** l'équipe faisait n'importe quoi; **she was a. over him at the party** elle n'a pas arrêté de lui tourner après à la soirée; **an a. girl band** un orchestre de femmes *ou* composé uniquement de femmes; **an a. new outfit** un ensemble tout neuf; **a. ready** fin prêt; **to be a. indignant about sth** être fou d'indignation à propos de qch; **it's a. mine!** c'est tout à moi!; *F* **to be a. in** être complètement crevé; *F* **he's gone a. red** il est devenu tout rouge; *F* **the dress was a. torn** la robe était toute déchirée; *F* **he's not a. there** il est un peu simplet; **to go a. out** ne pas s'épargner; **to go a. out to pass one's exams** faire son maximum pour réussir ses examens

(b) (*almost*) **a. but** presque; **it's a. but done** c'est pour ainsi dire fini, c'est presque fini *ou* fait

(c) (*in the slightest*) **at a.** du tout; **do you know him at a.?** est-ce que vous le connaissez (un peu)?; **I didn't speak at a.** je n'ai pas parlé du tout; **I'm not at a. astonished** je n'en suis aucunement étonné; **not at a.** pas du tout, *F* du tout; (*when thanked*) je vous en prie; **if he comes at a.** s'il vient; **it seemed to worry him very little, if at a.** ça n'a pas eu l'air de l'inquiéter le moins du monde; **if it is at a. cold** s'il fait un (tant soit) peu froid; **if it is at a. possible** si c'était possible; **why do it at a.?** pourquoi se donner la peine de le faire?

(d) (*altogether*) **in a.** en tout; **(taking it) a. in a.** à tout prendre

(e) (*in games*) *Fb etc* **five a.** cinq à cinq, cinq partout; *Tennis* **four (games) a.** quatre (jeux) partout; *Tennis* **fifteen a.** quinze à

4 *n* tout *m*, totalité *f*; **to stake one's a.** risquer le tout pour le tout; **I would give my a. to see her** je donnerais tout ce que j'ai pour la voir; **he was really giving his a. in the last aria** il a vraiment tout donné dans la dernière aria

all-absorbing *adj* absorbant, passionnant; **of a. interest** fascinant

Allah ['ælə] *n* Allah *m*

all-American *adj* cent pour cent américain

all-around *adj Am* (*athlete*) complet; (*man*) universel

allay [ə'leɪ] *vt* **(a)** (*storm, anger*) apaiser, calmer **(b)** (*fear*) calmer; (*suspicions*) endormir, dissiper **(c)** (*pain*) alléger, calmer, soulager; (*thirst, hunger, temperature*) apaiser

all-clear *n* (signal *m* de) fin *f* d'alerte; **to give the a.** *Mil* sonner la fin de l'alerte; (*for project etc*) donner le feu vert; **he gave us the a.** (*no-one was watching*) il nous a fait signe que la voie était libre

all-conquering *adj* (*love etc*) qui triomphe de tout

all-day *adj attrib* qui dure toute la journée

allegation [ælɪ'geɪʃən] *n* allégation *f*; **to make an a.** alléguer *ou* avancer quelque chose

allege [ə'ledʒ] *vt* alléguer, prétendre **(that** que**)**; **the words alleged to have been spoken by ...** les propos qui auraient été tenus par ...; **he was alleged to be dead** on le prétendait *ou* disait mort; **it is alleged that ...** on prétend que ...

alleged [ə'ledʒd] *adj attrib* (*attack, motive etc*) allégué; **the a. thief** le voleur présumé

allegedly [ə'ledʒɪdlɪ] *adv* prétendument; **a. he's the greatest violinist since Paganini** on dit de lui qu'il est le plus grand violoniste depuis Paganini

allegiance [ə'liːdʒəns] *n* fidélité *f*, obéissance *f* **(to** à**)**; **to owe a. to a party** devoir fidélité à un parti; **to renounce one's a. to a party** se détacher d'un parti; **to owe a. to a king** devoir fidélité et obéissance à un roi; **to take an oath of a.** prêter serment d'allégeance

allegorical [ælɪ'gɒrɪk(ə)l] *adj* allégorique

allegorically [ælɪ'gɒrɪklɪ] *adv* allégoriquement

allegory ['ælɪgərɪ] *n* allégorie *f*

allegretto [ælɪ'gretəʊ] *adv, n Mus* allegretto *m*

allegro [ə'legrəʊ, -'leɪ-] *adv, n Mus* allegro *m*

alleluia [ælɪ'luːjə] *int, n Rel* alléluia *m*

all-embracing *adj* (*love*) qui embrasse tout; (*category*) hétéroclite; **a. knowledge** vaste érudition *f*

allen key ['ælən] *n* clé *f* allen

allergen ['ælədʒen] *n Med* allergène *m*

allergic [ə'lɜːdʒɪk] *adj Med* allergique **(to** à**)**; *Fig* **I'm a. to him/rap music** il/le rap me hérisse

allergy ['ælədʒɪ] *n Med, Fig* allergie *f* **(to** à**)**

alleviate [ə'liːvɪeɪt] *vt* (*pain*) alléger, soulager; (*grief*) adoucir; (*thirst*) apaiser; (*problem*) alléger, modérer

alleviation [əliːvɪ'eɪʃən] *n* (*of pain*) allègement *m*, soulagement *m*; (*of grief*) adoucissement *m*; (*of thirst*) apaisement *m*; (*of problem*) allègement

all-expense tour *n* voyage *m* à forfait

alley ['ælɪ] *n* **(a)** (*narrow street*) ruelle *f*; **I wouldn't like to meet him in a dark a.!** je n'aimerais pas le rencontrer au coin d'un bois!; *F* **a. cat** chat *m* de gouttière **(b)** *Sp* **bowling a.** bowling *m*

alleyway ['ælɪweɪ] *n* (*street*) ruelle *f*

alliance [ə'laɪəns] *n* **(a)** alliance *f*; **to enter into an a.** s'allier **(with** avec**)**; **electoral a.** apparentement *m*, alliance électorale; **to make a political a. with a party** s'allier à un parti; **in a. with a German firm** en association avec une firme allemande **(b)** (*by marriage*) alliance *f*

allied ['ælaɪd] *adj* **(a)** allié **(to** à; **with** avec**)**; (*consideration, issue*) du même ordre, de la même nature; (*subjects, disciplines, sciences*) voisin; **the A. Powers** les Puissances *fpl* alliées; **closely a. industries** industries *fpl* connexes **(b)** *Biol, Med etc* du même ordre, de la même nature; *Biol* (*species*) voisin

alligator ['ælɪgeɪtər] *n* **(a)** (*animal*) alligator *m*; **a. clip** pince *f* alligator **(b)** (*skin*) crocodile *m*; **a. handbag** sac *m* en crocodile *ou F* en croco **(c)** *Am* **a. pear** (poire *f* d')avocat *m*

all-important *adj* capital; **speed is a.** la vitesse est capitale *ou* est de la plus grande importance

all-in **1** *adj* **(a)** *Com* **a. price** prix *m* tout compris, prix forfaitaire; **a. policy** police *f* tous risques; **a. tour** voyage *m* à

forfait **(b)** *Sp* **a. wrestling** lutte *f* libre, catch *m*; **a. wrestler** catcheur, -euse **2** *adv Com* tout compris; **the holiday costs £200 a.** les vacances coûtent 200 livres tous frais compris
all-inclusive *adj* (*price*) tout compris, forfaitaire; (*theory*) universel
alliteration [əlɪtə'reɪʃən] *n* allitération *f*
alliterative [ə'lɪtərətɪv, -reɪt-] *adj* allitératif
all-night *adj* (*party, session etc*) qui dure/qui va durer/qui a duré toute la nuit; **to maintain an a. vigil** veiller toute la nuit; *Admin etc* **a. service** permanence *f* de nuit; *Mil etc* **a. pass** permission *f* de la nuit
all-nighter [ɔːl'naɪtər] *n* **it turned into another a.** finalement, ça a encore duré toute la nuit
allocate ['æləkeɪt] *vt* (*sth to sb or sth*) allouer, assigner; **to a. duties** attribuer des fonctions **(to** à); **to a. a sum to sth** affecter *ou* assigner une somme à qch; **more money was allocated to defence** on a affecté plus d'argent à la défense; **in the time allocated** dans le temps *ou* les délais imparti(s); **you'll need to a. your time carefully** il va falloir que tu répartisses ton temps avec précaution; **allocated budget** allocation *f* budgétaire, budget *m* alloué
allocation [ælə'keɪʃən] *n* **(a)** (*action*) (*of sum of money*) allocation *f*, affectation *f*; (*of expenses, means etc*) répartition *f*; (*of capital*) affectation; (*of duties*) attribution *f*; *Fin* **a. to lowest tender** adjudication *f* au mieux-disant **(b)** (*share*) part *f* assignée *ou* allouée; (*money*) somme *f* assignée *ou* allouée; **my a.** la part/somme qui m'est assignée *ou* allouée
allograft ['æləʊgrɑːft] *n Med* allogreffe *f*
allopathy [æ'lɒpəθɪ] *n Med* allopathie *f*
all-or-none order *n St Exch* ordre *m* 'tout ou rien'
allot [ə'lɒt] *vt* **(-tt-) (a)** (*assign*) attribuer, assigner **(to sb** à qn); **to a. sth to a purpose** affecter *ou* destiner qch à un but; **in the allotted time** dans le temps imparti; **allotted budget** enveloppe *f* budgétaire **(b)** (*distribute*) (*tasks, seats*) répartir, distribuer; (*shares*) attribuer, répartir
allotment [ə'lɒtmənt] *n* **(a)** *Br* (*land*) jardin *m* (ouvrier) **(b)** (*distributing*) (*of rooms etc*) distribution *f*; (*of tasks*) partage *m*, répartition *f*; (*of property*) lotissement *m*; *Fin* **a. of shares** attribution *f ou* allotement *m* d'actions; *Fin* **letter of a.** (lettre *f* d')avis *m* de répartition **(c)** (*share*) portion *f*, part *f*; (*of airplane seats*) bloc-siège *m*
all-out *F* **1** *adj attrib* (*effort, resistance*) suprême, maximum; (*attack*) tous azimuts; (*strike, war*) total **2** *adv* **to go a.** y aller tous azimuts *ou* à fond; **to go a. for gold** y aller tous azimuts pour avoir la médaille d'or; **we're going a. for the end of the month** on fait le maximum pour y arriver avant la fin du mois
all-over *adj attrib* (*tan*) intégral; **with an a. pattern** dont le motif couvre toute la surface; **it gives a. relief** cela vous apportera un soulagement total
allow [ə'laʊ] *vt* **(a)** (*permit*) permettre; **to a. sb sth** permettre qch à qn; **to a. sb to do sth** permettre à qn de faire qch; **to a. sb home** laisser qn rentrer chez lui; **is he allowed sweets/help?** est-ce qu'il a le droit de manger des sucreries/de recevoir de l'aide?; **gambling is not allowed** les jeux d'argent sont interdits; **no conferring is allowed** il est interdit *ou* il n'est pas permis de se consulter; **she isn't allowed alcohol** elle n'a pas le droit de boire d'alcool; **to be allowed to compete** etre admis à concourir; **I am allowed to do it** on me permet *ou* il m'est permis de le faire; **a. me!** permettez(-moi)!; **a. me to ...** permettez-moi de ...; **passengers are not allowed on the bridge** la passerelle est interdite aux voyageurs; **as soon as circumstances a.** dès que les circonstances le permettront; **to a. oneself to be led/deceived/persuaded** se laisser mener/tromper/convaincre; **I will not a. you to be ill-treated** je ne vous laisserai pas maltraiter
(b) (*accept*) (*request, claim*) faire droit à; (*petition*) admettre; *Sp* (*penalty, goal*) accorder
(c) (*grant, allocate*) accorder; **to a. sb £5,000 a year** accorder *ou* allouer à qn une rente de 5 000 livres; **to a. a debtor time to pay** accorder un délai à un débiteur; **how much time/money are we allowed?** de combien de temps/d'argent disposons-nous?; **they haven't allowed enough time** ils n'ont pas laissé assez de temps; *Com, Fin* **to a. sb a discount** consentir *ou* accorder un escompte *ou* une remise à qn; **at the end of the six months allowed** à l'expiration du délai de six mois; **a. 20 minutes to get to the airport** comptez 20 minutes pour aller à l'aéroport
(d) (*admit*) admettre **(that** que)
(e) *Am F* (*maintain*) juger, opiner, affirmer **(that** que)
▶ **allow for** *vipo* tenir compte de; (*difficulties, delay etc*) prévoir; **after allowing for** (*discount, expenses etc*) déduction faite de; **to a. for some wastage** prévoir plus large; **a. two litres for wastage** comptez deux litres de pertes en plus; **to a. so much for carriage** compter tant pour le transport; **you must a. for his being ill** il faut tenir compte de ce qu'il est malade; **has that been allowed for in your figures?** en avez-vous tenu compte dans vos estimations?
▶ **allow in** *vtsep* laisser entrer; **no-one is allowed in** personne n'a le droit d'entrer
▶ **allow of** *vipo Fml* permettre, admettre; **the facts a. of only one interpretation** les faits n'admettent qu'une seule interprétation
▶ **allow out** *vtsep* **to a. sb out** permettre à qn de sortir; **no-one is allowed out after dark** personne n'a le droit de sortir après la tombée de la nuit; **some prisoners are allowed out at weekends** certains détenus ont la permission de sortir le weekend
allowable [ə'laʊəb(ə)l] *adj* **(a)** (*permissible*) admissible **(b)** *Com etc* (*expense*) déductible
allowance [ə'laʊəns] *n* **(a)** (*money given*) pension *f*; *Am* (*pocket money*) argent *m* de poche; **his parents stopped** *or* **cut off his a.** ses parents ont arrêté de lui verser de l'argent régulièrement; (*while he was living away from home*) ses parents ont arrêté sa pension
(b) *Admin etc* (*compensation*) allocation *f*; **cost-of-living a.** indemnité *f* de vie chère; *Br formerly* **family a.** allocations familiales; **supplementary allowances** majorations *fpl* de pension; *Fin* **personal a.** abattement *m* personnel (sur l'impôt); **entertainment a.** frais *mpl* de représentation; **travel** *or* **travelling a.** indemnité de déplacement; **allowances in kind** prestations *fpl* en nature
(c) (free) luggage a. (*on plane, coach etc*) bagages *mpl* en franchise; **there is an a. of one item of luggage per passenger** chaque passager a droit à un bagage; **what's the duty-free a.** qu'est-ce qu'on a droit de ramener hors taxe?; *Sp* **time a.** rendement *m* de temps; *Horseracing* **weight a.** décharge *f*
(d) *Com, Fin* (*discount*) remise *f*, rabais *m*; **to make an a. on an article** faire un rabais sur un article
(e) to make allowances *or* **an allowance for sth** tenir compte de qch; (*delays*) prévoir qch; **to make allowances for sb** avoir de l'indulgence pour qn; **some a. must be made for shrinkage** il faut tenir compte du rétrécissement
(f) *Tech* tolérance *f*
alloy[1] ['ælɔɪ] *n* alliage *m*; **a. steel** acier *m* allié; **a. wheel** jante *f* (en) alliage
alloy[2] [ə'lɔɪ] **1** *vt* (*metals*) allier **2** *vi* (*of metals*) s'allier (l'un avec l'autre)
alloyed [ə'lɔɪd] *adj* (*metal etc*) allié **(with** à, avec)
all-pervading, all-pervasive *adj* (*stench*) envahissant, qui se répand partout; (*fear, corruption, influence*) omniprésent
all-powerful *adj* tout-puissant, toute-puissante, *pl* tout-puissants, toutes-puissantes
all-purpose *adj* (*glue, cleaner*) universel; (*vehicle*) tous usages; (*building, room*) polyvalent
all right [ɔːl'raɪt] *adj usu pred* **everything's a.** tout va très bien; **it's a.** (*there's no need to worry*) tout va bien, ne vous inquiétez pas; (*to person apologizing*) je vous en prie!; **a.!** (*expressing agreement*) bien!, entendu!; *Am* (*expressing great enthusiasm*) génial!; **a., a., I'm coming** (*expressing irritation*) d'accord, d'accord, j'arrive; **are you a.?** (*are you well?*) est-ce que vous allez bien?; (*did you hurt yourself?*) vous ne vous êtes pas blessé?; *Iron* tu ne te sens pas bien?; **I'm a. again now** (*after being ill*) je suis tout à fait remis maintenant; **I'm a. until Monday** (*financially*) ça ira jusqu'à lundi; **are you a. for cash/cigarettes?** tu as assez de liquide/de cigarettes?; **it's a. for <u>you</u> to laugh!** ça vous va bien de rire!; **any more? – no, I'm a. thanks** tu en veux encore? – non, ça va merci; **I'm a. at algebra** en algèbre je me débrouille *ou* je ne me défends pas trop mal; **it was a.** (*film, party etc*) ce n'était pas mal; **he's/she's a.** (*a good sort*) c'est un bon type; *F* **to be a bit of a.** (*of woman*) être une jolie fille; (*of man*) être un beau mec
all-risks insurance *n* assurance *f* tous risques
all round *adv* **(a)** (*in general*) à tous points de vue **(b)** (*for everyone*) pour tout le monde; **give them a big hand a.** applaudissez-les tous bien fort
all-round *adj attrib* **(a)** (*athlete etc*) complet; (*education*) général; (*expert*) dans tous les domaines; **a. improvement** amélioration *f* générale *ou* sur toute la ligne **(b)** *Aut* **car with a. vision** voiture *f* à carrosserie panoramique
all-rounder [ɔːl'raʊndər] *n* homme *m* universel, femme *f* universelle; (*athlete*) athlète *m* complet, athlète *f* complète; *Sch* **a good a.** un élève complet, une élève complète; **she's quite an a.** elle est douée pour tout
allspice ['ɔːlspaɪs] *n Bot, Culin* poivre *m* de la Jamaïque

all-star *adj attrib Th etc* **an a. cast** une distribution prestigieuse; **a. performance** spectacle *m* à la distribution prestigieuse
all-terrain *adj Aut* tout-terrain
all-time *adj attrib F (record)* sans précédent, inouï; **a. high/low** record le plus élevé/bas; **the a. greats of rock music** les plus grands du rock; **one of the a. hits** un des plus grands succès
allude [əˈluːd] *vi* **to a. to sth/sb** (*of person*) faire allusion à qch/qn; (*of phrase*) avoir trait à *ou* se rapporter à qch/qn; **I am not alluding to anybody in particular** je ne vise personne
allure¹ [əˈlʊər] *n* attrait *m*; **it holds no a. for me** ça ne m'attire pas du tout
allure² *vt* attirer, séduire
alluring [əˈlʊərɪŋ] *adj* attrayant, attirant, séduisant
allusion [əˈluːʒən] *n* allusion *f*; **to make an a. to sth** faire allusion à qch; **in a. to sth** par allusion à qch
allusive [əˈluːsɪv] *adj* allusif
alluvial [əˈluːvɪəl] **1** *adj Geol (terrain)* alluvial; (*deposit*) alluvien; **a. plain** plaine *f* alluviale; **a. deposits** alluvions *fpl* **2** *n Austr* alluvions *fpl* aurifères
alluvium [əˈluːvɪəm] *n Geol* limon *m*
all-weather *adj Av etc (plane, landing strip)* tous temps; (*clothes, Sp pitch*) pour tous les temps
all-wheel drive *n* quatre roues *fpl* motrices
ally¹ [ˈælaɪ] *n (country, person etc)* allié, -ée; *Hist* **the Allies** les Alliés *mpl*; **to become allies** s'allier (ensemble), se coaliser
ally² [əˈlaɪ] *vt (sb, sth)* allier (**to** à; **with** avec); **the country has allied itself with its neighbour** le pays s'est allié à *ou* avec l'état voisin; **we must a. ourselves with other unions** nous devons nous allier à *ou* nous associer avec d'autres syndicats; **this newspaper is allied with another** ce journal est associé avec un autre
alma mater [ˈælməˈmeɪtər, -ˈmɑːtər] *n* = l'université *f* ou l'école *f* où l'on a fait ses études
almanac [ˈɔːlmənæk, ˈæl-] *n* almanach *m*
almighty [ɔːlˈmaɪtɪ] **1** *adj attrib (omnipotent)* tout-puissant, toute-puissante; *F (scandal etc)* monstrueux, terrible; *F* **an a. row** *or* **din** un fracas de tous les diables **2** *n* **the A.** le Tout-Puissant, le Très-Haut **3** *adv Am F* très; **he's a. stubborn** il est têtu comme une mule
almond [ˈɑːmənd] *n* amande *f*; **sweet/bitter a.** amande douce/amère; **ground almonds** amandes pilées; **a. oil** huile *f* d'amande; **a. essence** essence *f* d'amande; **a. paste** pâte *f* d'amandes; **a.(-shaped) eyes** yeux *mpl* en amande; **a. tree** amandier *m*; **a. grove** amandaie *f*
almoner [ˈɑːmənər, ˈæl-] *n* **(a)** *Br (in hospital)* assistant, -ante social(e) **(b)** *Hist (distributor of alms)* aumônier *m*
almost [ˈɔːlməʊst] *adv* presque; **a. blind** presque *ou* quasi aveugle; **a. nothing** presque rien; **it's a. six (o'clock)** il est presque six heures; **he a. fell/missed the bus** il a failli tomber/rater l'autobus; **we're a. there** nous sommes presque arrivés; **you're a. there** (*in answering question*) tu y es presque; **I a. didn't see you** j'ai failli ne pas vous voir
alms [ɑːmz] *npl* aumône *f*; **to give a. to sb** donner *ou* faire l'aumône à qn, faire la charité à qn; **a. box** tronc *m* (pour les pauvres)
almshouse [ˈɑːmzhaʊs] *n* hospice *m*
aloe [ˈæləʊ] *n* **(a)** (*plant*) aloès *m* **(b)** *Pharm* **aloes** aloès *mpl*; **bitter aloes** amer *m* d'aloès
aloft [əˈlɒft] *adv* **(a)** *Naut* dans la mâture **(b)** (*in sky*) en haut, en l'air
alone [əˈləʊn] *adj pred, adv* **(a)** (*in isolation*) seul; **he lives (all) a.** il vit (tout) seul; **I like being a.** j'aime la solitude *ou* être seul; **I want to speak to you a.** je voudrais vous parler seul à seul; **a. at last!** enfin seul(s)!; **he was left a. when his wife died** il s'est retrouvé seul quand sa femme est morte; **we are not a. in thinking that ...** nous ne sommes pas seuls à penser que ...; **you a. can help me** vous êtes le seul qui puissiez m'aider, vous seul pouvez m'aider; **he a. knows ...** lui seul sait ...; **I did it a.** je l'ai fait tout seul; *F* **to go it a.** faire cavalier seul; *Bible* **man does not live by bread a.** l'homme ne vit pas que de pain; **my salary a. isn't enough** mon salaire à lui seul *ou* mon seul salaire ne suffit pas; **his shoes a. must have cost what I earn in a week** rien que ses chaussures ont dû coûter ce que je gagne en une semaine; **with that charm which is his a.** avec ce charme qui lui est propre
(b) (*undisturbed*) **to let** *or* **leave sb a.** (*not touch, not disturb*) laisser qn tranquille *ou* en paix; (*not interfere with*) laisser qn faire; **leave me a.!** laissez-moi tranquille!, *F* fichez-moi la paix!; **leave her a. to get on with it** laisse-la se débrouiller toute seule; **to let** *or* **leave sth a.** (*not get involved*) ne pas se mêler de qch; **leave these things a.** (*don't touch*) ne touchez pas à tout ça; **a subject better left a.** un sujet qu'il vaut mieux ne pas aborder; **your work is all right, leave it a.** votre travail est bien, n'y touchez plus; **let a. ...** sans parler de ..., sans compter ...; **the soup wasn't even warm, let a. hot!** la soupe ne risquait pas d'être chaude, elle était à peine tiède!
along [əˈlɒŋ] **1** *prep* le long de; **to walk a. the shore** se promener le long de la plage, longer la plage; **to go a. a street** suivre une rue; **to look a. the street/corridor** regarder dans la rue/le couloir; **to sail a. the coast** longer *ou* suivre la côte; **to crawl a. the ground** ramper à la surface du sol; *Fig* **victorious all a. the line** victorieux sur toute la ligne; **all a. the street** tout le long de la rue; **trees a. the river** arbres qui bordent la rivière; **they live somewhere a. this street** ils habitent quelque part dans cette rue; **it's somewhere a. here** c'est quelque part dans cette direction *ou* par là; **somewhere a. the way** en route, en chemin
2 *adv* **to move a.** avancer; **move a. so I can sit down** (*in row of seats etc*) pousse-toi que je puisse m'asseoir; **to stride a.** avancer à grandes enjambées; **come a. with me** venez avec moi; *F* **come a. now!** (*be reasonable*) allons, sois raisonnable!; **he'll be a. in ten minutes** il va arriver dans dix minutes; **there'll be another one a. in a minute** (*of bus*) il en passera un autre dans une minute; **bring a tent a. (with you)** apportez une tente; **can I bring a friend a.?** est-ce que je peux amener un ami?; **a. with Mozart, Haydn is my favourite composer** avec Mozart, Haydn est mon compositeur favori; *Sl* **get a. (with you)!** (*go away*) allez!, filez!; (*expressing astonishment, disbelief*) allons donc!; *Am* **a. about four o'clock** vers quatre heures; *Am* **the afternoon was well a.** l'après-midi tirait à sa fin; **all a.** (*all the time*) depuis toujours; **I knew that all a.** je le savais dès *ou* depuis le commencement, je l'ai toujours su; **I said so all a.** c'est ce que j'ai toujours dit; **he was lying all a.** il n'a fait que mentir, il a menti du début à la fin
alongside [əlɒŋˈsaɪd] **1** *prep esp Naut (boat, quay)* accosté à, le long de; **to come a. (of) a ship** accoster *ou* aborder un navire; **the police car pulled up a. us** la voiture de police nous a accostés; **to walk a. sb** marcher côte à côte avec qn *ou* à côté de qn; **read these instructions a. the illustrations** lisez ces instructions en accompagnement des illustrations; **if you look at it a. his earlier work** si vous le comparez à ses travaux plus anciens; **a. what others have done** par rapport à ce que *ou* à côté de ce que d'autres ont fait
2 *adv Naut* **to come a.** accoster; **a police car pulled up a.** une voiture de police nous/les/*etc* a accostés
aloof [əˈluːf] **1** *adv* **to keep a.** se tenir à l'écart *ou* à distance (**from sth** de qch); **to stand a. from a cause** se tenir *ou* rester en dehors d'une cause **2** *adj (person, manner)* distant; (*emphasizing coldness*) froid et distant
aloofness [əˈluːfnɪs] *n* attitude *f* distante, réserve *f*
alopecia [æləʊˈpiːʃə] *n Med* alopécie *f*
aloud [əˈlaʊd] *adv* à haute voix, (tout) haut; **to read a.** lire à haute voix; **I was thinking a.** je pensais tout haut; **he says a. what others only dare to whisper** il dit tout haut ce que les autres pensent tout bas
alp [ælp] *n Geog* **(a)** (*pasture*) alpe *f*, pâturage *m* de montagne **(b)** **the Alps** les Alpes *fpl*
alpaca [ælˈpækə] *n* **(a)** (*animal*) alpaga *m* **(b)** *Tex* alpaga *m*; **a. wool** laine *f* d'alpaga; **a. coat/jacket** manteau *m*/veste *f* en alpaga *ou* d'alpaga
alpenhorn [ˈælpənhɔːn] *n Mus* cor *m* des Alpes
alpha [ˈælfə] *n* alpha *m*; *Br (mark)* A *m*; *Lit, Fig* **the a. and omega** l'alpha et l'oméga; *Phys* **a. rays** rayons *mpl* alpha
alphabet [ˈælfəbet] *n* alphabet *m*; **a. soup** soupe *f* aux petites pâtes en forme de lettres
alphabetic(al) [ælfəˈbetɪk, -ɪk(ə)l] *adj* alphabétique; **in a. order** par ordre *ou* dans l'ordre alphabétique; **a. filing** classement *m* par ordre alphabétique
alphabetically [ælfəˈbetɪklɪ] *adv* alphabétiquement, par ordre alphabétique
alphabetize [ˈælfəbətaɪz] *vt* classer par ordre alphabétique; **to a. sth on sth** trier qch par ordre alphabétique sur la base de qch
alphanumeric(al) [ælfənjuːˈmerɪk, -ɪk(ə)l] *adj* alphanumérique; **a. keyboard** *or* **keypad** clavier *m* alphanumérique; **a. filing** classement *m* alphanumérique
alphasort¹ [ˈælfəsɔːt] *n Comptr* tri *m* alphabétique; **to do an a. on sth** trier qch par ordre alphabétique
alphasort² *vt Comptr* trier par ordre alphabétique
alphatest¹ [ˈælfətest] *n Comptr* alpha-test *m*, *pl* alpha-tests, essai *m* préliminaire
alphatest² *vt Comptr* conduire les alpha-tests sur, conduire les essais préliminaires sur
alpine [ˈælpaɪn] **1** *n (plant)* plante *f* alpine *ou* alpestre **2** *adj*

(*skiing*) alpin; (*site, landscape, climate*) alpestre; (*plant*) alpin, alpestre; **a. range** chaîne *f* de montagnes alpine
alpinism ['ælpɪnɪz(ə)m] *n* alpinisme *m*
alpinist ['ælpɪnɪst] *n* alpiniste *mf*
already [ɔːl'redɪ] *adv* déjà; **ten o'clock a.!** déjà dix heures!; **you've eaten enough a.** tu as déjà assez mangé
alright [ɔːl'raɪt] *adj* = **all right**
Alsatian [æl'seɪʃən] **1** *adj* alsacien; (*wine*) d'Alsace **2** *n* **(a)** Alsacien, -ienne **(b)** *Br* (*dog*) berger *m* allemand
also ['ɔːlsəʊ] *adv* aussi; **he a. saw it, he saw it a.** (*didn't only hear it*) il l'a vu aussi; (*as well as other people*) lui aussi, il l'a vu, il l'a vu, lui aussi; *esp Am* **I study French a.** (*as well as other subjects*) j'étudie également le français; **not only ... but a. ...** non seulement ... mais encore ... *ou* mais aussi ...; **it's very efficient and a. very cheap** c'est très efficace et de plus, très bon marché; *Horseracing* **a. ran** non classés, ont couru aussi
also-ran *n Horseracing* concurrent *m* non classé; *F* (*unsuccessful person, thing*) non-valeur *f*
alt [ɔːlt] *n Comptr* **a. (key)** touche *f* alt
Alta *abbr* **Alberta**
altar ['ɔːltər] *n* autel *m*; **to lead sb to the a.** conduire qn à l'autel; *Fig* **they were sacrificed on the a. of the party's interests** ils ont été sacrifiés dans l'intérêt du parti; **high a.** maître-autel *m, pl* maîtres-autels; **a. cloth** nappe *f* d'autel; **a. rail(s)** cancel *m*; **a. screen** retable *m*
altar boy *n* enfant *m* de chœur
altarpiece ['ɔːltəpiːs] *n* retable *m*
alter ['ɔːltər] **1** *vt* **(a)** (*sth, sb*) changer; (*design, one's opinion etc*) modifier; (*garment etc*) faire des retouches à; **that alters the case/the situation** voilà qui change les choses/la situation; **that doesn't a. the fact that ...** cela ne change rien au fait que ...; **this has not altered our determination to ...** ceci n'a pas altéré notre détermination à ...; *Naut* **to a. course** changer de route **(b)** *Am Austr F* (*castrate*) châtrer **2** *vi* (*of person, situation*) changer; **her whole outlook has altered** elle a complètement changé d'horizon
alteration [ɔːltə'reɪʃən] *n* changement *m*, modification *f* **(to** apporté(e) à); (*to garment*) retouche *f* **(to** à); **subject to a.** (*programme, timetable etc*) susceptible de révisions, sauf modifications; **marginal alterations** (*written*) corrections *fpl* en marge
altercation [ɔːltə'keɪʃən] *n Fml* altercation *f*, querelle *f*; **to have an a.** se quereller
alter ego ['æltə'riːgəʊ] *n* alter ego *m*
alternate[1] [ɔːl'tɜːnət] **1** *adj* **(a)** alterné, alternant; **she comes on a. days** elle vient tous les deux jours *ou* un jour sur deux; **they come on a. days** (*one after the other*) ils viennent en alternance un jour sur deux; **on a. afternoons/Wednesdays** un après-midi/mercredi sur deux; **a. layers of stone and timber** couches alternées de pierre et de bois; **a. periods of calm and distress** des périodes de calme alternant avec des périodes d'angoisse; *Av etc* **a. route** parcours *m* de rechange; **a. airfield** aérodrome *m* de dégagement
(b) *Math, Bot* (*angle, leaf*) alterne
(c) *Liter* (*rhyme*) croisé
(d) *US* = **alternative**
2 *n esp Am* remplaçant, -ante
alternate[2] ['ɔːltəneɪt] **1** *vt* (*methods*) employer tour à tour *ou* alternativement; (*jackets etc*) mettre tour à tour *ou* alternativement; **... alternating the tomato and cucumber slices ...** en faisant alterner les rondelles de tomates et de concombre; *Agr* **to a. crops** alterner les récoltes
2 *vi* alterner **(with** avec); **he alternated with his friend on watches throughout the night** son ami et lui se sont relayés toute la nuit pour monter la garde; **they alternated between welcoming his help and resenting his intrusion** tantôt ils lui étaient reconnaissants de son aide, tantôt ils lui en voulaient de son intrusion; **rain and sunshine alternated all afternoon** la pluie et le soleil se sont succédés tout l'après-midi
alternately [ɔːl'tɜːnətlɪ] *adv* alternativement, tour à tour, en alternance; **boys and girls were seated a.** les garçons et les filles étaient assis en alternance; *Bot* **leaves placed a.** feuilles *fpl* alternes
alternating ['ɔːltəneɪtɪŋ] *adj* **(a)** alternant, alterné **(b)** *El* (*current*) alternatif; *Tech* (*movement*) alternatif, de va-et-vient
alternation [ɔːltə'neɪʃən] *n* alternance *f*
alternative [ɔːl'tɜːnətɪv] **1** *adj attrib* **(a)** (*plan, route, course of action*) alternatif; **a. proposal** contre-proposition *f*; **an a. site will have to be found** il faudra trouver un autre endroit; **we'll find you a. employment** nous vous emploierons à autre chose; **to make a. arrangements** s'arranger autrement
(b) (*not conventional*) parallèle, alternatif
2 *n* (*choice*) alternative *f*; **there is no a.** il n'y a pas d'alternative; **they were given the a. of a fine or a month's imprisonment** on leur a donné le choix entre une amende et un mois de prison; **the a. would be to ...** une autre solution serait de ...; **to have no a.** ne pas avoir le choix; **he had no a. but to obey** il n'a pu faire autrement que d'obéir; **there are alternatives to nuclear power** le nucléaire n'est pas la seule solution possible; **the a. was starvation** c'était ça ou mourir de faim
alternative comedy *n* comédie *f* alternative
alternatively [ɔːl'tɜːnətɪvlɪ] *adv* (*on the other hand*) ou bien; (*in a different way*) (*employed etc*) autrement; **a. we could go to the beach** ou bien nous pourrions aller à la plage; **he's probably in the library, a. you might try the squash courts** il est sûrement à la bibliothèque, sinon, vous pouvez essayer les courts de squash
alternative medicine *n* médecine *f* douce
alternative tourism *n* tourisme *m* vert
alternator ['ɔːltəneɪtər] *n El* alternateur *m*
although [ɔːl'ðəʊ] *conj* quoique, bien que + *sub*; **a. I am a father** tout père que je suis; **Paul, a. rich, was not mean** Paul, bien que riche, n'était pas avare; **a. not beautiful, she was attractive** sans être belle elle plaisait; **it's not possible ... although ...** (*considering, changing mind*) cela n'est pas possible ... à moins que ...
altimeter ['æltɪmiːtər] *n Av* altimètre *m*; **radio a.** radiosonde *f*
altitude ['æltɪtjuːd] *n* **(a)** altitude *f*; **at these altitudes** à cette altitude; **a. recorder** enregistreur *m* d'altitude; **a. sickness** mal *m* de l'altitude *ou* des montagnes **(b)** *Astron, Geom* (*of star, triangle*) hauteur *f*
alt key *n Comptr* touche *f* alt
alto ['æltəʊ] *n Mus* **(a) a. clef** clef *f* de troisième ligne; **to sing a.** chanter la partie alto **(b)** (*male voice*) haute-contre *f, pl* hautes-contre; (*female voice*) contralto *m*, alto *f*; **I'm an a.** je suis haute-contre/alto **(c)** (*viola*) alto *m* (à cordes); **a. trombone/saxophone** trombone *m*/saxophone *m* alto
altogether [ɔːltə'geðər] **1** *adv* **(a)** (*entirely*) entièrement, tout à fait; **to change sth a.** changer qch de fond en comble *ou* radicalement; **it's a. out of the question** c'est absolument impossible; **I was not a. pleased** ça ne me faisait pas exactement plaisir **(b)** (*in total*) en tout; **a. the bill came to £63** au total ça a fait 63 livres; **how much is that a.?** ça fait combien en tout?; **a., it was a memorable occasion** somme toute, ce fut un événement mémorable; **taking things a.** à tout prendre **2** *n F Hum* **in the a.** complètement nu, en tenue d'Adam/d'Ève
altruism ['æltruɪz(ə)m] *n* altruisme *m*
altruist ['æltruɪst] *n* altruiste *mf*
altruistic [æltru'ɪstɪk] *adj* altruiste
alum ['æləm] *n* alun *m*; *Phot* **a. bath** bain *m* aluné
alumina [ə'luːmɪnə] *n Miner* alumine *f*
aluminium [æljʊ'mɪnɪəm], *Am* **aluminum** [ə'luːmɪnəm] *n* aluminium *m*; **a. alloy** alliage *m* d'aluminium; **a. foil** papier *m* alu(minium); **a. oxide** alumine *f*; **a. saucepan** casserole *f* en aluminium
aluminize [ə'luːmɪnaɪz] *vt* **(a)** *Metal* combiner avec de l'aluminium; **aluminized steel** acier *m* à l'aluminium **(b)** *Tech* (*mirror*) aluminer **(c)** *Ch* aluminer; (*in dyeing*) aluner
aluminum [ə'luːmɪnəm] *n Am* = **aluminium**
alumna, *pl* **-ae** [ə'lʌmnə, -iː] *n esp Am* (*of school*) ancienne élève *f*; (*of university*) ancienne étudiante *f*
alumnus, *pl* **-i** [ə'lʌmnəs, -aɪ] *n esp Am* (*of school*) ancien élève *m*; (*of university*) ancien étudiant *m*; **a. association** association *f* des anciens
alveolus, *pl* **-li** [æl'vɪələs, -laɪ] *n Anat* alvéole *f* pulmonaire
always ['ɔːlwəz, -wɪz, *stressed* -weɪz] *adv* **(a)** [ⓘ**A23,32,ii**] (*all the time*) toujours; **nearly** *or* **almost a.** presque toujours; **the office is a. open** le bureau est toujours ouvert *ou* est ouvert en permanence; **he is a. complaining** il se plaint tout le temps, il n'arrête pas de se plaindre; **I'll a. remember you!** je ne t'oublierai jamais! **(b)** (*as alternative*) toujours; **I can a. try** je peux toujours *ou* quand même essayer; **there's a. the old age pension** il y a toujours la retraite
alyssum ['ælɪsəm] *n* alysse *f*
Alzheimer's (disease) ['æltshaɪməz] *n Med* maladie *f* d'Alzheimer
AM ['eɪ'em] *n* (*abbr* **amplitude modulation**) AM *f*
am[1] [æm] *see* **be**
am[2] ['eɪ'em] *adv* [ⓘ**A75,A,e; B58,A,e**] (*abbr* **ante meridiem**) avant midi; **five am** cinq heures du matin; **we're leaving at six – am or pm?** nous partons à six heures – du matin ou de l'après-midi?
amalgam [ə'mælgəm] *n Metal, Fig* amalgame *m*
amalgamate [ə'mælgəmeɪt] **1** *vt Metal* amalgamer; *Fig* (*ideas*) amalgamer; (*companies, industries, Fin shares etc*)

fusionner **2** *vi* (*of metals, ideas*) s'amalgamer; (*of companies*) fusionner

amalgamation [əmælgə'meɪʃən] *n* (*of metals*) amalgamation *f*; (*of two companies, Fin of shares*) fusionnement *m*; (*collection*) (*of evidence etc*) accumulation *f*

amaryllis [æmə'rɪlɪs] *n* (*plant*) amaryllis *f* (belle-dame)

amass [ə'mæs] *vt* (*wealth, objects, information etc*) amasser, accumuler

amateur ['æmətər, -tjʊər, æmə'tɜːr] *n* **(a)** (*non-professional*) amateur *m*, dilettante *m*; **he paints as an a.** il peint en amateur *ou* en dilettante; *Pej* **he's a real a.** ce n'est qu'un amateur, c'est un amateur; **a. painter/musician** peintre *m*/ musicien *m* amateur; **they did a rather a. job** ils ont fait du travail d'amateur **(b)** *Sp* amateur *m*; **a. championship** championnat *m* amateur; **a. sport** sport *m* d'amateur; *Horseracing* **a. rider** gentleman rider *m*

amateurish ['æmətərɪʃ, æmə'tɜːrɪʃ] *adj Pej* (*piece of work etc*) d'amateur; (*actor, singer etc*) amateur

amateurishly ['æmətərɪʃlɪ] *adv Pej* en amateur; (*presented, written*) avec amateurisme

amateurism ['æmətərɪz(ə)m] *n* **(a)** (*in arts*) dilettantisme *m*, *Pej* amateurisme *m* **(b)** *Sp* amateurisme *m*

amatory ['æmət(ə)rɪ] *adj Lit, Hum* (*sentiment, conquests*) amoureux; (*letter*) d'amour; (*intentions, ambitions*) galant; (*poem*) érotique

amaze [ə'meɪz] *vt* ébahir, stupéfier; **his courage amazed me** son courage m'a stupéfié; **I was amazed at** *or* **by the price** le prix m'a ébahi, j'étais très étonné par le *ou* du prix; **I was amazed to learn that** ça m'a ébahi *ou* stupéfié de l'apprendre; **it amazes me that he could have done such a thing** je suis stupéfait qu'il ait pu faire une telle chose; **you a. me sometimes** (*are exasperating*) tu es incroyable quelquefois; **you never cease to a. me** tu m'étonneras toujours; *Iron* **you a. me!** non, vraiment?; *Iron* **go on, a. me!** vas-y, surprends-moi!

amazement [ə'meɪzmənt] *n* stupéfaction *f*, stupeur *f*, grand étonnement *m*; **to listen in a.** écouter avec stupeur; **to our a.** à notre grand étonnement, à notre stupéfaction; **I heard with a. that ...** j'ai été stupéfait d'apprendre que ...

amazing [ə'meɪzɪŋ] *adj* stupéfiant, étonnant; (*dexterity*) prestigieux; **it's a.!** je n'en reviens pas!; **it's a. that no one was hurt** c'est étonnant que personne n'ait été blessé; **you've been a.** tu as été formidable

amazingly [ə'meɪzɪŋlɪ] *adv* étonnamment; **a. quickly** à une vitesse stupéfiante *ou* étonnante; **we were a. lucky** nous avons eu une chance formidable; **a., no one was hurt** c'est étonnant mais personne n'a été blessé; **he's doing a. well** (*in business*) il réussit à merveille; (*recovering quickly*) il se remet merveilleusement bien

Amazon ['æməz(ə)n] *n* **(a) the (river) A.** l'Amazone *f*; **the A. basin** le bassin amazonien **(b)** *Myth* Amazone *f*; *Fig* femme *f* forte et athlétique

Amazonian [æmə'zəʊnɪən] *adj* **(a)** *Geog* de l'Amazone, amazonien; **the A. rainforest** la forêt tropicale (humide) amazonienne **(b)** *Myth* d'Amazone; *Fig* (*woman*) fort et athlétique; *Fig* **I like the A. type** j'aime les femmes fortes et athlétiques

ambassador [æm'bæsədər] *n* (*diplomat*), *Fig* ambassadeur *m*, ambassadrice *f*; **the French A. to Japan** l'ambassadeur de France au Japon

ambassadorial [æmbæsə'dɔːrɪəl] *adj* (*duties etc*) d'ambassadeur

ambassadress [æm'bæsədrɪs] *n* (*diplomat*), *Fig* ambassadrice *f*

amber ['æmbər] **1** *n* (*colour, stone*) ambre *m*; **yellow a.** ambre jaune; **he crossed on a.** (*traffic light*) il a traversé à l'orange **2** *adj* **(a)** (*necklace*) d'ambre, en ambre; **a. varnish** vernis *m* au succin **(b) a.(-coloured)** ambré; **a. light** (*traffic light*) feu *m* orange

ambergris ['æmbəgriːs] *n* ambre *m* gris

ambidextrous [æmbɪ'dekstrəs] *adj* ambidextre

ambience, ambiance ['æmbɪəns] *n* ambiance *f*

ambient ['æmbɪənt] *adj Tech* (*temperature, noise, light etc*) ambiant; *TV etc* **a. sound** son *m* d'ambiance

ambiguity [æmbɪ'gjuːɪtɪ] *n* **(a)** (*ambiguousness*) ambiguïté *f* **(b)** (*instance*) équivoque *f*; **his speech was full of ambiguities** son discours a été très ambigu

ambiguous [æm'bɪgjʊəs] *adj* ambigu, *f* -uë, équivoque

ambiguously [æm'bɪgjʊəslɪ] *adv* d'une manière ambiguë *ou* équivoque; **an a. worded reply** une réponse formulée de façon ambiguë

ambiguousness [æm'bɪgjʊəsnɪs] *n* ambiguïté *f*

ambit ['æmbɪt] *n Fml* (*of law, investigations*) portée *f*; **that does not come within our a.** cela n'entre pas dans nos compétences

ambition [æm'bɪʃən] *n* ambition *f*; **the a. to succeed** l'ambition de réussir; **to have great ambitions** avoir de grandes ambitions *ou* de hautes visées; **it's my a. to..., my a. is to...** j'ambitionne de ...; **my parents had great ambitions for me** mes parents avaient de grands projets pour moi

ambitious [æm'bɪʃəs] *adj* (*person, project etc*) ambitieux; **to be a. to do sth** ambitionner de faire qch; **they're very a. for their children** ils sont très ambitieux en ce qui concerne leurs enfants

ambitiously [æm'bɪʃəslɪ] *adv* ambitieusement; **they planned a.** ils ont fait des projets ambitieux

ambitiousness [æm'bɪʃəsnɪs] *n* (*of project, design*) caractère *m* ambitieux; (*of person*) ambition *f*

ambivalence [æm'bɪvələns] *n* ambivalence *f*

ambivalent [æm'bɪvələnt] *adj* ambivalent

amble[1] ['æmb(ə)l] *n* (*of horse*) amble *m*; (*of person*) pas *m ou* allure *f* tranquille; **to walk at an a.** (*of horse*) aller l'amble, ambler

amble[2] *vi* (*of horse*) aller (à) l'amble, ambler; **to make a horse a.** mettre un cheval à l'amble; **he ambled up to us** (*of person*) il s'est avancé vers nous d'un pas tranquille; **I'll just a. down to the shops** je descends faire un tour dans les magasins; **he just ambles in at 10.15** il arrive à 10.15 les mains dans les poches *ou* en se baladant

▶ **amble along** *vi* (*of horse*) aller à l'amble; (*of person*) aller *ou* marcher d'un pas tranquille; (*without destination*) flâner

ambrosia [æm'brəʊzɪə] *n Myth* ambroisie *f*

ambrosial [æm'brəʊzɪəl] *adj* ambrosiaque

ambulance ['æmbjʊləns] *n* ambulance *f*; **a. plane** avion *m* sanitaire; *US Sl* **a. chaser** = avocat *m* qui encourage les accidentés à porter plainte; **a. post** poste *m* d'ambulance; **a. ship** navire *m* hôpital; **a. train** train *m* sanitaire

ambulance crew *n* ambulanciers *mpl*

ambulance man *n* ambulancier *m*

ambulance woman *n* ambulancière *f*

ambulant ['æmbjʊlənt] *adj Med* ambulatoire

ambulatory[1] ['æmbjʊlətərɪ] *adj* **(a)** ambulant, mobile **(b)** *Med* (*treatment, sick person*) ambulatoire

ambulatory[2] *n* promenoir *m*, préau *m*; *Archit* (*in church*) déambulatoire *m*

ambush[1] ['æmbʊʃ] *n* embuscade *f*, guet-apens *m*, *pl* guets-apens; **to lie in a.** se tenir en embuscade; *Fig* être à l'affût; **to lay** *or* **set an a. for sb** tendre une embuscade à qn; **troops lying in a.** troupes embusquées; **they were caught in an a.** ils sont tombés dans une embuscade *ou* un guet-apens

ambush[2] *vt* (*enemy*) attirer dans une embuscade; **to be ambushed** tomber dans une embuscade

ameba, amebic *US* = **amoeba, amoebic**

ameliorate [ə'miːlɪəreɪt] *Fml* **1** *vt* améliorer **2** *vi* s'améliorer

amelioration [əmiːlɪə'reɪʃən] *n Fml* amélioration *f*

amen ['ɑː'men, 'eɪ'men] *int Rel* amen, ainsi soit-il; *Fig* certes; **and we all say a. to that** c'est ce que nous souhaitons tous

amenable [ə'miːnəb(ə)l] *adj* (*subject*) sujet (**to** à); (*person*) (*to law, discipline*) soumis; (*to advice*) docile; (*child*) soumis, docile; **a. to reason** raisonnable, disposé à entendre raison; **to prove a. to a suggestion** se ranger à une suggestion; **the case is not a. to ordinary rules** ce cas n'est pas sujet aux règles ordinaires; **to be a. to treatment** (*of illness*) pouvoir être traité

amend [ə'mend] **1** *vt* (*change*) modifier, amender; *Pol* (*bill*) amender; (*correct*) rectifier, corriger; **amended invoice** facture *f* rectificative **2** *vi* s'amender

amendment [ə'mendmənt] *n* (*change*) modification *f*; *Pol* (*of bill*) amendement *m*; (*correction*) rectification *f*, correction *f*; (*of mistake*) redressement *m*, correction; *Pol* **to move an a.** proposer un amendement (**to a bill** à un projet de loi); *US* **the third A.** (*to the Constitution*) le troisième amendement

amends [ə'mendz] *npl* **to make a.** faire amende honorable; **nothing could make a. for what they had done** rien ne pouvait réparer ce qu'ils avaient fait; **to make a. to sb for sth** dédommager qn de qch

amenity [ə'miːnɪtɪ] *n* **(a)** (*usu pl*) **amenities** (*playparks, cinemas, shopping malls etc*) facilités *fpl*, aménagements *mpl*; (*at sports centre, campsite etc*) équipements *mpl*; **close to all amenities** (*in accommodation advertisement*) = proximité tous commerces **(b)** *Fml, Arch* (*of place*) agrément *m*

amenorrhoea [eɪmenə'rɪə] *n Med* aménorrhée *f*

America [ə'merɪkə] *n* **(a)** (*continent*) Amérique *f*; **North/ South A.** Amérique du Nord/Sud; **in A.** en Amérique; **the Americas** les Amériques **(b)** (*United States*) États-Unis *mpl* (d'Amérique)

American [ə'merɪkən] **1** *adj* **(a)** (*continental*) américain; **A. Indian** Indien, -enne d'Amérique, Amérindien, -ienne **(b)** (*of United States*) américain; **A. Automobile Association** = société *f* de dépannage pour les automobilistes, ≈ Touring

Club *m* de France; **A. breakfast** petit déjeuner *m* américain; **A. cloth** toile *f* cirée; *Ling* **A. English** américain *m*, anglais *m* américain; **A. football** football *m* américain; **A. organ** harmonium *m*; **A. service** service *m* à l'américaine *ou* à l'assiette **2** *n* **(a)** Américain, -aine; **Native A.** Amérindien, -ienne **(b)** *Ling* américain *m*

American Express® (card) *n* carte *f* American Express®

Americanism [ə'merɪkənɪz(ə)m] *n Ling* américanisme *m*

Americanize [ə'merɪkənaɪz] *vt* américaniser; **to become Americanized** s'américaniser

American Plan *n Am* pension *f* complète

American-style option *n St Exch* option *f* américaine

Amerind ['æmərɪnd], **Amerindian** [æmə'rɪndɪən] **1** *adj* amérindien **2** *n* Amérindien, -ienne

amethyst ['æmɪθɪst] *n* améthyste *f*

Amex® ['æmeks] *n* (*American Express*) carte *f* Amex®

amiability [eɪmɪə'bɪlɪtɪ] *n* amabilité *f* (**to** envers)

amiable ['eɪmɪəb(ə)l] *adj* aimable (**to** envers); **to be very a.** être très aimable *ou* d'une grande amabilité

amiably ['eɪmɪəblɪ] *adv* aimablement, avec amabilité

amicability [æmɪkə'bɪlɪtɪ] *n* nature *f ou* disposition *f* amicale; **the a. of his nature** sa nature amicale

amicable ['æmɪkəb(ə)l, ə'mɪk-] *adj* (*manner, relationship, chat etc*) amical; (*separation, agreement*) à l'amiable; *Jur* **a. settlement** arrangement *m* à l'amiable

amicably ['æmɪkəblɪ, ə'mɪk-] *adv* amicalement; (*to part*) bons amis; (*to divorce, settle issue*) à l'amiable; **to live a. together** vivre en harmonie

amid [ə'mɪd] *prep* au milieu de; **the news came a. revelations of corruption** la nouvelle survint en plein milieu *ou* au moment des révélations de corruption; **the meeting ended a. some confusion** la réunion s'est terminée dans une certaine confusion

amide ['æmaɪd] *n Ch* amide *m*

amidships [ə'mɪdʃɪps] *adv Naut* au milieu du navire; **cabin a.** cabine *f* par le travers; **to put the helm a.** mettre la barre droite; **helm a.!** barre à zéro!, zéro (la barre)!

amidst [ə'mɪdst] *prep* = **amid**

amino-acid [æ'mi:nəʊ'æsɪd] *n Ch* aminoacide *m*

amiss [ə'mɪs] *adv, adj pred* **(a)** (*badly*) **to take sth a.** prendre qch de travers, mal prendre qch; **he took it very much a.** il a très mal pris la chose **(b)** (*out of place*) malvenu; **a cup of coffee wouldn't come** *or* **go a.** une tasse de café serait bienvenue; **a few more women presenters on TV wouldn't go a.** ce ne serait pas un mal *ou* une mauvaise chose s'il y avait plus de présentateurs femmes à la télévision; **something is a.** il y a quelque chose qui ne va pas *ou F* qui cloche; **there was nothing a. when I last saw him** tout allait bien la dernière fois que je l'ai vu

amity ['æmɪtɪ] *n Fml* (*between countries*) amitié *f*, concorde *f*, bons rapports *mpl*; **to live in a. with sb** vivre en bonne intelligence avec qn

ammeter ['æmi:tər] *n El* ampèremètre *m*

ammo ['æməʊ] *n F* munitions *fpl*

ammonia [ə'məʊnɪə] *n Ch* ammoniac *m*, gaz *m* ammoniac

ammoniac [ə'məʊnɪæk] **1** *adj* ammoniac, -aque; **sal a.** sel *m* ammoniac **2** *n* (**gum**) **a.** gomme *f* ammoniaque

ammonite ['æmənaɪt] *n* (*fossil*) ammonite *f*

ammonium [ə'məʊnɪəm] *n Ch* ammonium *m*; **a. carbonate/sulphate** carbonate *m*/sulfate *m* d'ammonium

ammunition [æmjʊ'nɪʃən] *n Mil* munitions *fpl*; *Fig* **the scandal provided the opposition with useful a.** le scandale a procuré à l'opposition un bon moyen d'offensive; *Fig* **protesters used the report as a.** les manifestants ont utilisé le rapport comme argument; **blank a.** munitions à blanc; **dummy a.** fausses munitions; **live a.** munitions réelles *ou* pour tir réel; **a. box** coffre *m* à munitions; **a. depot** *or* **dump** dépôt *m* de munitions; **a. train** train *m* de munitions

amnesia [æm'ni:zɪə] *n Med* amnésie *f*; **to suffer from a.** être amnésique *ou* souffrir d'amnésie

amnesiac [æm'ni:zɪæk], **amnesic** [æm'ni:zɪk] *n, adj* amnésique *mf*

amnesty[1] ['æmnɪstɪ] *n* amnistie *f*

amnesty[2] *vt* amnistier

amniocentesis [æmnɪəʊsen'ti:sɪs] *n Med* amniocentèse *f*

amoeba, *US* **ameba,** *pl* **-as, -ae** [ə'mi:bə, -əz, -i:] *n Biol* amibe *f*

amoebic, *US* **amebic** [ə'mi:bɪk] *adj Med* amibien; **a. dysentery** dysenterie *f* amibienne

amok [ə'mʌk] *adv* **to run a.** (*of gunman*) faire des ravages; (*of rioters, editor, F children*) se déchaîner

among [ə'mʌŋ], **amongst** [ə'mʌŋst] *prep* parmi; **house standing a. trees** maison située au milieu des arbres *ou* entourée d'arbres; **to wander a. the ruins** errer parmi les ruines; **a. the crowd** au milieu de la foule, parmi la foule; **to live a. savages** vivre au milieu des sauvages; **we are a. friends** nous sommes entre amis; **a. ourselves** entre nous; **this expression is current a. young people** cette expression est courante chez les jeunes; **a. the guests were ...** au nombre des invités *ou* parmi les invités se trouvaient ...; **that cake won't go far a. twelve** ce gâteau ne donnera pas grand-chose, divisé entre douze personnes; **the orchestra is a. the finest in Europe** l'orchestre est l'un des meilleurs d'Europe; **not one a. them** pas un d'entre eux *ou* parmi eux; **a. other things he said that ...** il a dit entre autres que ...; **they quarrel a. themselves** ils se disputent entre eux

amoral [eɪ'mɒrəl] *adj* amoral, -aux

amorous ['æmərəs] *adj Lit, Hum* (*look, advances, adventures*) amoureux; **to be of an a. disposition** être romantique; **he became quite a.** il a commencé à me/lui/*etc* faire des avances

amorously ['æmərəslɪ] *adv* amoureusement

amorphous [ə'mɔ:fəs] *adj* **(a)** *Ch* amorphe **(b)** (*mass, lump*) amorphe; *Fig* (*opinions, project*) vague

amortization [əmɔ:tɪ'zeɪʃən] *n Com, Fin* (*of debt etc*) amortissement *m*

amortize [ə'mɔ:taɪz] *vt Com, Fin* (*debt*) amortir

amount [ə'maʊnt] *n* **(a)** *Com* (*sum of money*) somme *f*; (*total*) (*of bill etc*) montant *m*, total *m*; **please tender the exact a.** (*on bus etc*) on est prié de faire l'appoint; (**up**) **to the a. of ...** jusqu'à concurrence de ...; *Fin* **a. carried forward** report à nouveau; **no a. (of money) could make up for what I've lost** rien ne pourrait compenser ce que j'ai perdu; **a. due** montant dû, somme due; **a. exclusive of VAT** montant hors TVA

(b) (*quantity*) quantité *f*; **a massive a. of time/effort** un temps/des efforts énorme(s); **a certain a. of discomfort/comfort** un certain manque de confort/un certain confort; **the a. of work that an engine will do** la somme de travail que peut fournir une machine; **in small amounts** par petites quantités; **no a. of persuasion would make her stay** il n'y avait pas moyen de la persuader de rester; **a dwindling a. of funds** des fonds en quantité décroissante; **varying amounts of enthusiasm** des expressions d'enthousiasme inégales; *F* **he has any a. of money/friends/books** il a de l'argent/des amis/des livres tant et plus

► **amount to** *vipo* **(a)** (*of money etc*) s'élever à, se monter à; **transactions amounting to several million pounds** opérations qui se chiffrent par plusieurs millions de livres; **I don't know what my debts a. to** j'ignore le montant de mes dettes, j'ignore à combien se montent *ou* s'élèvent mes dettes

(b) (*be equivalent to*) équivaloir à, se réduire à, revenir à; **these conditions a. to a refusal** ces conditions équivalent à un refus; **it amounts to the same thing** cela revient au même; **all that amounts to very little/to nothing** tout cela se réduit à peu de chose/à rien; **he'll never a. to much/to anything** il ne fera jamais grand-chose/rien

amour [ə'mʊər] *n Lit, Arch* intrigue *f* amoureuse, liaison *f*

amp [æmp] *n* **(a)** *El* (*abbr* **ampere**) ampère *m*; **13-a. plug** fiche *f* de 13 ampères **(b)** *Mus Sl* (*abbr* **amplifier**) ampli *m*

ampere ['æmpeər] *n El* ampère *m*

ampersand ['æmpəsænd] *n Typ* esperluette *f*

amphetamine [æm'fetəmɪn] *n Pharm* amphétamine *f*; **to be on amphetamines** (*of drug addict*) prendre des amphétamines

amphibia [æm'fɪbɪə] *npl Zool* amphibiens *mpl*

amphibian [æm'fɪbɪən] **1** *adj* amphibie **2** *n* **(a)** *Zool* amphibie *m* **(b)** (*tank*) char *m* amphibie; (*vehicle*) voiture *f* amphibie

amphibious [æm'fɪbɪəs] *adj* (*animal, plane etc*) amphibie

amphitheatre, *US* **amphitheater** ['æmfɪθɪətər] *n Archit, Th etc* amphithéâtre *m*

amphora, *pl* **-ae** ['æmfərə, -i:] *n Antiq* amphore *f*

ample ['æmp(ə)l] *adj* **(a)** (*garment*) ample, large; (*bag, stomach, bosom*) gros; **man of a. proportions** homme corpulent

(b) (*plentiful*) abondant; **this will be a.** ceci sera amplement suffisant, ceci suffira amplement; **to have a. means** avoir de gros moyens; **there are a. supplies of fish this week** (*in shops*) il y a gros arrivages de poisson cette semaine; **a. proof** preuve *m* évidente; **the money we have is a. for our needs** nous avons largement assez d'argent pour subvenir à nos besoins; **to have a. time** avoir largement le temps (**to do** de faire); **you'll be given a. warning** vous serez averti longtemps à l'avance; **he was given a. opportunity to explain his actions** il a eu de nombreuses occasions d'expliquer ses actes; **you'll have a. opportunity to practise your backhand this summer** tu auras largement l'occasion de pratiquer ton revers cet été

amplification [æmplɪfɪ'keɪʃən] *n* **(a)** (*expansion*) augmentation *f*, extension *f*; **if I could say something in a. of ...** si je pouvais dire quelque chose pour développer ... **(b)** (*of power, current, volume etc*) amplification *f* **(c)** *Opt* (*using lens etc*) grossissement *m*

amplifier ['æmplɪfaɪər] *n* **(a)** (*for sound system*) amplificateur *m*, *F* ampli *m*; **a. circuit** circuit *m* d'amplification **(b)** *Phot* (lentille *f*) amplificatrice *f*

amplify ['æmplɪfaɪ] *vt* **(a)** (*expand*) (*essay, remarks etc*) développer; (*report etc*) ajouter des détails à **(b)** (*current, power, volume etc*) amplifier

amplitude ['æmplɪtju:d] *n Fml* (*of dimensions, resources etc*) ampleur *f*; (*of space*) étendue *f*; *Astron* (*of star*) amplitude *f*; *Phys* (*of oscillations, vibrations*) amplitude; *Phys* **magnetic a.** déclinaison *f* magnétique

amplitude modulation *n* modulation *f* d'amplitude

amply ['æmplɪ] *adv* amplement; **a. rewarded** largement récompensé; **a. proportioned** aux dimensions généreuses

ampoule ['æmpu:l] *n Med* (*for hypodermic injection*) ampoule *f*

amputate ['æmpjʊteɪt] **1** *vt* (*leg etc*) amputer; **his right leg was amputated** il a été amputé de la jambe droite **2** *vi* amputer

amputation [æmpjʊ'teɪʃən] *n* amputation *f*

amputee [æmpjʊ'ti:] *n* amputé, -ée

Amtrak ['æmtræk] *n* société *f* des chemins de fer interurbains des États-Unis

amuck [ə'mʌk] *adv* = **amok**

amulet ['æmjʊlet] *n* amulette *f*

amuse [ə'mju:z] *vt* amuser, divertir, faire rire; **it amused her to do it** ça l'a amusée de le faire; **is something amusing you?** quelque chose vous amuse?; **to a. oneself** s'occuper, passer le temps; **to a. oneself by** *or* **with doing sth** (*have fun*) s'amuser à faire qch *ou* en faisant qch; (*pass the time*) s'occuper en faisant qch; **to a. oneself with sth** s'amuser avec qch; **to keep sb amused** (*occupied*) occuper qn; (*entertained*) amuser qn

amused [ə'mju:zd] *adj* amusé; **a. smile** sourire amusé; **to be a. at** *or* **by sth** s'amuser de qch, trouver qch drôle; **she wasn't at all a.** elle n'a pas du tout trouvé ça drôle

amusedly [ə'mju:zɪdlɪ] *adv* d'un air amusé

amusement [ə'mju:zmənt] *n* **(a)** amusement *m*; **source of a.** source *f* d'amusement; **smile of a.** sourire amusé; **to the great a. of the children** au grand amusement des enfants; **much to everyone's a.** au grand amusement de la compagnie **(b)** (*occupation, pastime*) amusement *m*, divertissement *m*, distraction *f*; **we have few amusements here** nous avons peu de distractions ici; **it offered** *or* **provided little a. for them** cela ne les amusait guère; **place of a.** lieu *m* de divertissement

amusement arcade *n* galerie *f* de jeux

amusement park *n* parc *m* d'attractions

amusing [ə'mju:zɪŋ] *adj* (*person*) amusant, drôle; (*book, film*) amusant, drôle, divertissant; **what an a. woman/idea** quelle femme/quelle idée amusante

amusingly [ə'mju:zɪŋlɪ] *adv* d'une manière amusante; **a. worded** drôle, amusant

an *see* **a**[2]

anabaptist [ænə'bæptɪst] *adj, n Rel, Hist* anabaptiste *mf*

anabolic [ænə'bɒlɪk] *adj* **a. steroid** stéroïde *m* anabolisant

anachronism [ə'nækrənɪz(ə)m] *n* anachronisme *m*; **she's an a.** c'est un véritable anachronisme

anachronistic [ənækrə'nɪstɪk] *adj* anachronique

anaconda [ænə'kɒndə] *n* (*snake*) anaconda *m*

anaemia, *US* **anemia** [ə'ni:mɪə] *n* anémie *f*; **to suffer from a.** souffrir d'anémie, faire de l'anémie

anaemic, *US* **anemic** [ə'ni:mɪk] *adj Med* anémique; *Fig* faible, mou; **to become a.** s'anémier

anaesthesia, *US* **anesthesia** [ænəs'θi:zɪə] *n* anesthésie *f*; **general/local a.** anesthésie générale/locale; **spinal a.** anesthésie rachidienne

anaesthetic, *US* **anesthetic** [ænəs'θetɪk] **1** *n* anesthésique *m*, anesthésie *f*; **under a.** sous anesthésie; **under the a.** sous l'effet de l'anesthésie **2** *adj* anesthésique

anaesthetist, *US* **anesthetist** [ə'ni:sθətɪst] *n* anesthésiste *mf*

anaesthetize, *US* **anesthetize** [ə'ni:sθətaɪz] *vt Med, Fig* anesthésier

anagram ['ænəgræm] *n* anagramme *f*

anal ['eɪn(ə)l] *adj Anat* anal, -aux

analeptic [ænə'leptɪk] *n, adj Pharm* analeptique *m*

analgesia [ænəl'dʒi:zɪə] *n Med* analgésie *f*

analgesic [ænəl'dʒi:sɪk, -zɪk] *adj, n Med* analgésique *m*; *Pharm* antalgique *m*

analog ['ænəlɒg] **1** *adj Comptr* analogique; **a. computer** calculateur *m* analogique; **a. clock/watch** horloge *f*/montre *f* (à affichage) analogique **2** *n US* = **analogue**

analogical [ænə'lɒdʒɪk(ə)l] *adj* analogique

analogically [ænə'lɒdʒɪklɪ] *adv* analogiquement, par analogie; **a. speaking** analogiquement parlant

analogous [ə'næləgəs] *adj* analogue (**to, with** à)

analogously [ə'næləgəslɪ] *adv* d'une manière analogue

analogue, *US* **analog** ['ænəlɒg] *n* analogue *m*; **this is an a. of what happens on a national level** ceci est analogue à ce qui se passe au niveau national

analogy [ə'nælədʒɪ] *n* analogie *f* (**to, with** avec; **between** entre); **by a. with ...** par analogie avec ...; **to draw an a.** faire une analogie; **on the a. of ...** en comparant avec ...

analyse, *US* **analyze** ['ænəlaɪz] *vt* (*text, events*), *Ch, Math* analyser, faire l'analyse de; (*feelings, attitude*) analyser; *Gram* (*sentence*) faire l'analyse logique de; *Psy* (*sb*) psychanalyser

analysis, *pl* **-es** [ə'næləsɪs, -i:z] *n* (*of text*), *Ch, Phys* analyse *f*; *Gram* (*of sentence*) analyse logique; *Psy* psychanalyse *f*; **nothing abnormal showed up under a.** l'analyse n'a rien révélé d'anormal; **our a. is that ...** notre analyse démontre que ...; **to hold up under** *or* **withstand a.** résister à l'analyse; *Am Psy* **to be in a.** (*of patient*) être en analyse; **in the final** *or* **last a.** (*ultimately*) en fin de compte, au bout du compte

analyst ['ænəlɪst] *n* analyste *mf*; *Psy* (psych)analyste *mf*

analytic(al) [ænə'lɪtɪk, -ɪk(ə)l] *adj* analytique; **a. mind** esprit *m* d'analyse; **a. psychology** psychologie *f* introspective

analyze ['ænəlaɪz] *vt US* = **analyse**

analyzer ['ænəlaɪzər] *n Comptr* analyseur *m*

anarchic [æ'nɑ:kɪk] *adj* anarchique

anarchist ['ænəkɪst] *adj, n* anarchiste *mf*

anarchy ['ænəkɪ] *n* anarchie *f*

anastigmatic [ænəstɪg'mætɪk] *adj Opt* anastigmat(ique)

anastomosis [ənæstə'məʊsɪs] *n Med* anastomose *f*

anathema [ə'næθəmə] *n Rel, Fig* anathème *m*; **his name is a.** son nom est tabou; *Fig* **it's/he's a. to me** c'est ma bête noire; **such theories were pronounced a.** l'anathème a été jeté sur ces théories; **their ideas were a. to him** leurs idées l'horripilaient

anathematize [ə'næθəmətaɪz] *vt Arch, Fml* frapper d'anathème

anatomical [ænə'tɒmɪk(ə)l] *adj* anatomique; **a. specimen** pièce *f* d'anatomie, préparation *f* anatomique

anatomically [ænə'tɒmɪklɪ] *adv* anatomiquement

anatomist [ə'nætəmɪst] *n* anatomiste *mf*

anatomy [ə'nætəmɪ] *n* **(a)** (*of human, animal*) anatomie *f* **(b)** (*science*) anatomie *f*; (*textbook*) cours *m* d'anatomie; **human a.** anatomie humaine **(c)** *Fig* analyse *f*, anatomie *f*

ancestor ['ænsestər] *n* ancêtre *m*, *Lit* aïeul *m*, *pl* aïeux; **a. worship** culte *m* des ancêtres

ancestral [æn'sestr(ə)l] *adj* **(a)** ancestral, héréditaire, de famille; **it's an a. right** c'est un droit ancestral; **his a. home** la demeure de ses ancêtres **(b)** *Biol* ancestral, -aux

ancestress ['ænsestrɪs] *n* ancêtre *f*, *Lit* aïeule *f*

ancestry ['ænsestrɪ] *n* **(a)** (*descent*) ascendance *f*; **both families were of French a.** les deux familles étaient d'ascendance française; **this custom is of more recent a.** cette coutume est d'apparition plus récente **(b)** (*no pl*) (*ancestors*) ancêtres *mpl*, ascendants *mpl*, aïeux *mpl*

anchor[1] ['æŋkər] *n* **(a)** *Naut etc* ancre *f*; *Fig* planche *f* de salut; **to let go** *or* **to drop the a.** jeter *ou* mouiller l'ancre; **to weigh a.** lever l'ancre, appareiller; **to lie** *or* **ride at a.** être à l'ancre, mouiller; **at a.** au mouillage; **to slip the a.** filer (sa chaîne) par le bout; **to drag her a.** (*of ship*) chasser sur son ancre *ou* sur ses ancres; *Constr* **a. iron** *or* **tie** grappin *m*; *Constr* **a. plate/stay** plaque *f*/câble *m* d'ancrage **(b)** *TV* (*presenter*) présentateur *m* principal, présentatrice *f* principale

anchor[2] **1** *vt* **(a)** *Naut* (*ship*) ancrer, mouiller **(b)** (*fix firmly*) *Constr* affermir par des ancres; *Naut etc* (*mast etc*) hauban(n)er; *Fig* **to be anchored to the spot** (*by indecision, terror*) être cloué sur place **2** *vi Naut* jeter l'ancre, mouiller

anchorage ['æŋkərɪdʒ] *n* **(a)** *Naut* (*act, place*) mouillage *m*; **to leave the a.** dérader **(b)** *Naut* (*fee*) droits *mpl* d'ancrage *ou* de stationnement **(c)** *Constr* ancrage *m*; (*of tie beam*) point *m* d'attache; **a. point** (*of seatbelt*) point *m* d'ancrage

anchor buoy *n Naut* bouée *f* de mouillage *ou* d'ancre

anchored ['æŋkəd] *adj Naut* ancré, mouillé, à l'ancre; *Fig* **firmly a. faith** foi solidement ancrée

anchoring ['æŋkərɪŋ] *n Naut* ancrage *m*, mouillage *m*

anchorite ['æŋkəraɪt] *n Rel* anachorète *m*

anchorman, *pl* **-men** ['æŋkəmən] *n* **(a)** *Sp* (*of team*) dernier coureur *m* **(b)** *Rad, TV* présentateur *m* principal

anchorwoman, *pl* **-women** ['æŋkəwʊmən, -wɪmɪn] *n Rad, TV* présentatrice *f* principale

anchovy ['æntʃəvɪ, æn'tʃəʊvɪ] *n* (*fish*) anchois *m*; **a. butter/paste** beurre *m*/pâte *f* d'anchois

ancient [ˈeɪnʃənt] **1** *adj* ancien; (*monument*) historique; (*oak*) centenaire; *F* (*person*) très vieux, décrépit; *F* (*car, hat etc*) antique, antédiluvien; *F* **this car is getting pretty a.** cette voiture est une vraie antiquité; **the a. world** le monde antique **2** *npl* **the ancients** les anciens *mpl*
ancient history *n also Fig* histoire *f* ancienne
Ancient Rome *n* la Rome antique
ancillary [ænˈsɪlərɪ] *adj* subordonné **(to** à); (*assisting*) auxiliaire; **a. equipment** matériel *m* annexe *ou* d'appoint, accessoires *mpl*; **a. staff** (*in hospital*) personnel *m* hospitalier non médical; **a. (worker)** (*in hospital*) auxiliaire *mf* de service
and [ænd, *unstressed* ənd, ən, n] **1** *conj* **(a)** (*connecting words*) et; **a./or** et/ou; **a knife a. fork** un couteau et une fourchette; **my father a. mother are out** mon père et ma mère sont sortis; **four a. five make(s) nine** quatre plus cinq font neuf; **ham a. eggs** des œufs au jambon; **now a. then** de temps en temps; **he came without pencils a. paper** il est venu sans crayons ni papier; **he speaks English, a. very well too** il parle anglais et même très bien; **a. (what about) the invalids?** et les malades?; **the water was nice a. warm** l'eau était bien chaude; **good a. ready** fin prêt; **a. what if I am going?** et si j'y allais?
(b) (*connecting clauses*) et; **he could read a. write** il savait lire et écrire; **move (an inch) a. you're a dead man** un pas et tu es mort; *esp Br* **go a. look for it** allez le chercher; **come a. see me** venez me voir; **try a. help me** essaie de m'aider; **to look for sth a. not see it** chercher qch sans le voir; **I waited an hour a. he still hadn't turned up** j'ai attendu une heure et il n'était toujours pas là; **they started taking drugs, so I came home – a. a good thing too!** ils ont commencé à prendre de la drogue alors je suis rentré – tu as bien fait!
(c) (*with numerals*) **two hundred a. two** deux cent deux; **four a. a half** quatre et demi; **four a. three-quarters** quatre trois quarts; **an hour a. twenty minutes** une heure vingt minutes; *Old-fashioned* **five a. twenty** vingt-cinq; *Br Arch* **three shillings a. sixpence, three a. six** trois shillings six pence
(d) (*repetition*) et; **for miles a. miles** pendant des kilomètres et des kilomètres, sur des kilomètres; **better a. better** de mieux en mieux; **smaller a. smaller** de plus en plus petit; **I knocked a. knocked (again)** j'ai frappé tant et plus; **over a. over again** maintes et maintes fois
(e) (*contrast*) et; **there are doctors a. (there are) doctors** il y a médecins et médecins
(f) a. so on, a. so forth, a. so on a. so forth et ainsi de suite
2 *n Comptr* (*usu written* **AND) A. circuit/element** circuit *m*/élément *m* ET
Andalusia [ændəˈluːsɪə, -zɪə] *n* Andalousie *f*
andante [ænˈdæntɪ] *adv, n Mus* andante *m*
andantino [ændænˈtiːnəʊ] *adv, n Mus* andantino *m*
Andean [ˈændɪən] *adj* andin, des Andes
Andes [ˈændiːz] *npl* **the A.** les Andes *fpl*, la Cordillère des Andes
andiron [ˈændaɪən] *n* chenet *m*
Andorra [ænˈdɔːrə] *n* (république *f* d')Andorre *f*; **A. (City)** Andorre-la-Vieille
androgen [ˈændrədʒən] *n Biol* androgène *m*
androgynous [ænˈdrɒdʒɪnəs] *adj* androgyne
anecdotal [ænɪkˈdəʊt(ə)l] *adj* anecdotique
anecdote [ˈænɪkdəʊt] *n* anecdote *f*
anemia, anemic *US* = **anaemia, anaemic**
anemometer [ænɪˈmɒmɪtər] *n Met* anémomètre *m*
anemone [əˈnemənɪ] *n* (*flower*) anémone *f*
aneroid [ˈænərɔɪd] *adj Phys* (*barometer*) anéroïde
anesthesia, anesthetic *etc US* = **anaesthesia, anaesthetic** *etc*
anesthesiologist [ænəsθiːzɪˈɒlədʒɪst] *n Am Med* anesthésiste *mf*
aneurism, aneurysm [ˈænjʊrɪz(ə)m] *n Med* anévrisme *m*, anévrysme *m*
anew [əˈnjuː] *adv* **(a)** (*again*) de nouveau; **to begin a.** recommencer **(b)** (*from beginning*) à nouveau; **to create sth a.** créer qch à nouveau
angel [ˈeɪndʒ(ə)l] *n* **(a)** ange *m*; **the a. of death** l'ange de la mort; **fallen a.** ange déchu; *F* **you a.!, you're an a.!** tu es un ange *ou* un amour!; *F* **be an a.** sois gentil; **a. face** visage *m* d'ange *ou* angélique; *Culin* **a. cake, a. food (cake)** gâteau *m* de Savoie **(b)** *Th etc F* (*financial backer*) bailleur *m* de fonds **(c)** *Av F* écho *m* radar non identifié
angelfish [ˈeɪndʒəlfɪʃ] *n* ange *m* de mer, angelot *m*
angelic [ænˈdʒelɪk] *adj* angélique
angelica [ænˈdʒelɪkə] *n Bot, Culin etc* angélique *f*
angelically [ænˈdʒelɪklɪ] *adv* comme un ange
angelus [ˈændʒələs] *n Rel* angélus *m*
anger[1] [ˈæŋgər] *n* colère *f*; **in a fit** *or* **moment of a.** dans un accès de colère; **to speak in a.** parler sous le coup de la colère; **the cannon was never fired in a.** on ne s'est jamais servi de ce canon en temps de guerre
anger[2] *vt* mettre en colère, irriter; **he is easily angered** il se met facilement en colère, il est irascible; **to be slow to a.** ne pas se mettre facilement en colère; **these remarks have angered Christians** ces commentaires ont exaspéré la communauté chrétienne; **he is angered by suggestions that he took bribes** cela le met en colère qu'on suggère qu'il ait pu accepter des pots-de-vin
angina [ænˈdʒaɪnə] *n Med* **a. (pectoris)** angine *f* de poitrine; **to have a.** avoir une angine de poitrine
angiology [ændʒɪˈɒlədʒɪ] *n Med* angiologie *f*, angéiologie *f*
angioplasty [ˈændʒɪəplæstɪ] *n Med* angioplastie *f*
Angle [ˈæŋg(ə)l] *n Hist* Angle *mf*
angle[1] [ˈæŋg(ə)l] *n* **(a)** *Math, Fig* angle *m*; (*viewpoint*) point *m* de vue; (*of newspaper article etc*) perspective *f*; **at an a. of …** formant un angle de …; **at an a.** de biais; **the house stands at an a. to the street** la maison fait angle sur la rue; **from a different a.** sous un angle différent, sous un autre angle; **seen from this a.** vu sous cet angle; **to study a problem from every a.** *or* **all angles** étudier un problème sur toutes ses faces *ou* sous tous les angles; *Fig* **what's your a. on this?** qu'est-ce que vous pensez de ceci?; **a. of vision, visual** *or* **viewing a.** angle de vision, angle visuel; *Cin* **a. shot** prise *f* de vue oblique
(b) *Mil* angle *m*; **a. of deflection** angle de dérive; **a. of elevation** *or* **altitude** angle de hausse *ou* de tir positif; **a. of sight** angle de mire *ou* de visée
(c) *Av, Naut* **a. of attack** angle *m* d'attaque; **a. of incidence** angle d'incidence; **critical a. (of attack), stalling a.** angle critique; **a. of ascent** *or* **climb** (*of plane, projectile*) angle de montée; **a. of heel** *or* **list, listing a.** (*of ship*) angle de gîte
(d) *Constr* (*of room*) coin *m*, encoignure *f*, angle *m*; **a. of torque** angle de torsion; **cutting a.** angle de coupe; *Constr* **a. bar** *or* **iron** *or* **plate** cornière *f*, équerre *f*; *Carp* **a. brace** (*tool*) foret *m* à angle; **a. gauge** goniomètre *m*
(e) *El, Electron* angle *m*; **phase a.** angle de phase
angle[2] *vt* **(a)** (*set at angle*) (*light beam*) orienter, diriger **(on, to** sur); **to a. a lamp onto one's book** orienter *ou* diriger le faisceau de sa lampe sur son livre; *Tennis* **to a. a shot** envoyer la balle en diagonale **(b)** *usu Pej* (*report*) orienter; (*facts*) présenter d'une manière tendancieuse *ou* partiale; **it's angled towards the 16-18 age range** cela vise les 16-18 ans, c'est destiné aux 16-18 ans; **studies are angled towards exams** les études sont très axées sur les examens
angle[3] *vi* (*fish*) pêcher à la ligne
▶ **angle for** *vipo* (*fish*) pêcher; *Fig* (*compliments*) chercher; **to a. for promotion** chercher à être promu; **to a. for an invitation** chercher à se faire inviter
angle bracket *n* **(a)** *Constr* équerre *f* **(b)** *Typ* chevron *m*
angled [ˈæŋg(ə)ld] *adj* **(a) acute-a.** acutangle, aux angles aigus; *Sp* **a. shot** coup *m* en diagonale **(b)** (*report etc*) partial, tendancieux
Anglepoise® [ˈæŋg(ə)lpɔɪz] *n* **A.** ® **lamp** lampe *f* à bras articulé
angler [ˈæŋglər] *n* **(a)** (*person*) pêcheur, -euse (à la ligne) **(b) a. (fish)** baudroie *f*, crapaud *m* de mer
Anglican [ˈæŋglɪkən] *Rel* **1** *adj* anglican; **the A. Church** l'Église *f* anglicane **2** *n* Anglican, -ane
Anglicanism [ˈæŋglɪkənɪz(ə)m] *n Rel* anglicanisme *m*
anglicism [ˈæŋglɪsɪz(ə)m] *n* anglicisme *m*
Anglicist [ˈæŋglɪsɪst] *n* angliciste *mf*
anglicization [æŋglɪsaɪˈzeɪʃən] *n* anglicisation *f*
anglicize [ˈæŋglɪsaɪz] *vt* angliciser
angling [ˈæŋglɪŋ] *n* (*fishing*) pêche *f* à la ligne
Anglo [ˈæŋgləʊ] *n US* Américain, -aine d'ascendance européenne
Anglo-American 1 *adj* anglo-américain **2** *n* Anglo-Américain, -aine, *pl* Anglo-Américains, -aines
Anglo-Catholic *adj, n Rel* anglo-catholique *mf*, *pl* anglo-catholiques
Anglo-French 1 *adj* franco-britannique, *pl* franco-britanniques **2** *n Ling* anglo-normand *m*
Anglo-Indian 1 *adj* anglo-indien, *pl* anglo-indiens **2** *n* **(a)** (*person of mixed ancestry*) Eurasien, -ienne **(b)** (*Briton who has lived in India*) Anglo-Indien, -ienne
Anglo-Irish 1 *adj* anglo-irlandais **2** *npl* **the A.** les Anglo-Irlandais *mpl*
anglophile [ˈæŋgləʊfaɪl] *adj, n* anglophile *mf*
anglophobe [ˈæŋgləʊfəʊb] *adj, n* anglophobe *mf*
anglophobia [ˈæŋgləʊˈfəʊbɪə] *n* anglophobie *f*
Anglo-Saxon 1 *adj* anglo-saxon **2** *n* **(a)** (*person*) Anglo-Saxon, -onne, *pl* Anglo-Saxons, -onnes **(b)** *Ling* anglo-saxon *m*

Angola [æŋ'gəʊlə] *n* Angola *m*
angora [æŋ'gɔːrə] *n* **(a) a. (cat/rabbit)** (chat *m*/lapin *m*) angora *m*; **a. (goat)** chèvre *f* angora **(b)** *Tex* angora *m*; **a. wool** laine *f* angora; **a. jumper** pull *m* en angora
angostura [æŋgəs'tjʊərə] *n Pharm etc* angusture *f*; **a. bitters**® bitters *mpl* à base d'angusture
angrily ['æŋgrɪlɪ] *adv* (*to answer etc*) avec colère
angry ['æŋgrɪ] *adj* (*person*) en colère (**at sb** contre qn; **about sth** à cause de qch), fâché, irrité (**with** *or Am* **at sb about sth** contre qn de qch); (*voice*) irrité; (*speech, letter*) furieux, virulent; **he was a. at being kept waiting** il était irrité qu'on le fît attendre; **to be a. with oneself** (*for not doing better*) être mécontent de soi; (*for giving offence, causing pain etc*) s'en vouloir; **to get a.** se mettre en colère, se fâcher, s'irriter; **to get a. with sb** se fâcher *ou* se mettre en colère contre qn; **to make sb a.** exaspérer qn, mettre qn en colère; **it makes me very a. when I hear people say that** ça m'exaspère d'entendre dire ça; **a. words were exchanged** il y eut un échange assez virulent; **an a. young man** un contestataire; *Lit* **the a. sea** la mer courroucée *ou* en courroux; **a. sky** (*stormy*) ciel *m* orageux *ou* menaçant; *Med* **a. sore** plaie *f* irritée *ou* enflammée
angstrom ['æŋstrəm] *n Phys* angström *m*
anguish ['æŋgwɪʃ] *n* **(a)** (*great anxiety*) angoisse *f*, douleur *f*; **to be in a.** être dans l'angoisse *ou* angoissé, être au supplice; **to cause sb a.** mettre qn dans l'angoisse, angoisser qn **(b)** *Med* angoisse *f*
anguished ['æŋgwɪʃt] *adj* angoissé
angular ['æŋgjʊlər] *adj* **(a)** (*rock, face*) anguleux; (*body*) maigre, osseux **(b)** (*movement*) saccadé **(c)** *Math, Phys* (*velocity etc*) angulaire
anhydride [æn'haɪdraɪd] *n Ch* anhydride *m*
anhydrous [æn'haɪdrəs] *adj Ch* anhydre
aniline ['ænɪlaɪn] *n Ch* aniline *f*; **a. dye** colorant *m* azoïque
animal ['ænɪm(ə)l] [ⓘ**A26**,c,i] **1** *n* animal *m*, *pl* -aux; **to behave like an a.** se comporter comme un animal; *Fig* **he's an a.** c'est une brute; *Fig* **she's not a political a.** elle n'est pas portée sur la politique; *Fig* **that's an entirely different a.** c'est tout à fait autre chose; *F* **there ain't no such a.** ça n'existe pas; *Art* **a. painter** animalier *m* **2** *adj* (*fat, kingdom etc*) animal; **a. instinct/need** (*of person*) instinct *m*/besoin *m* animal
animalcule [ænɪ'mælkjuːl] *n* animalcule *m*
animal husbandry *n* élevage *m*
animal rights *npl* droits *mpl* des animaux; **a. activist** activiste *mf* pour la défense des droits des animaux
animate[1] ['ænɪmɪt] *adj* (*alive*) vivant, animé, doué de vie; **to become a.** s'animer
animate[2] ['ænɪmeɪt] *vt* (*sb, party, conversation*) animer
animated ['ænɪmeɪtɪd] *adj* (*discussion*) animé; **to become a.** (*of person, discussion*) s'animer; *Cin* **a. cartoon** dessin *m* animé; **a. film** film *m* d'animation
animatedly ['ænɪmeɪtɪdlɪ] *adv* (*to say*) d'un ton animé; (*to discuss, speak, gesture*) avec animation
animatic [ænɪ'mætɪk] *n* (*storyboard*) animatique *f*
animation [ænɪ'meɪʃən] *n* **(a)** (*of person*) animation *f*, entrain *m*; (*of style*) chaleur *f*; (*of orator*) feu *m*, véhémence *f* **(b)** (*act*) stimulation *f* **(c)** *Cin* animation *f*
animator ['ænɪmeɪtər] *n Cin* animateur, -trice
animism ['ænɪmɪz(ə)m] *n Phil* animisme *m*
animist ['ænɪmɪst] *adj, n Phil* animiste *mf*
animosity [ænɪ'mɒsɪtɪ] *n* animosité *f*; **to feel a. against** *or* **towards sb** ressentir de l'animosité contre qn; **there was considerable a. towards this idea** cette idée soulevait une grande hostilité
animus ['ænɪməs] *n Fml* **(a)** (*hostility*) animosité *f* **(b)** (*motive, stimulus*) stimulation *f*
anion ['ænaɪən] *n Phys, El* anion *m*
anise ['ænɪs] *n* (*plant*) anis *m*; **star a.** anis étoilé
aniseed ['ænɪsiːd] *n* (graine *f* d')anis *m*; **a. balls** bonbons *mpl* à l'anis; *Culin* **a. cake** gâteau *m* à l'anis
anisette [ænɪ'zet] *n* (*liqueur*) anisette *f*
ankle ['æŋk(ə)l] *n* cheville *f*; **a. bone** astragale *m*; **a. boot** chaussure *f* montante, bottine *f*, bottillon *m*; **a. chain** bracelet *m* de cheville; **a. joint** articulation *f* du pied; **a.-length dress** robe *f* qui descend jusqu'à la cheville; **a. sock** socquette *f*; **a. strap** (*on shoe*) bride *f*; **a. support** chevillière *f*; **to be a.-deep in water/mud** avoir de l'eau/de la boue jusqu'aux chevilles
anklet ['æŋklət] *n* **(a)** (*ornament*) bracelet *m*/anneau *m* de cheville **(b)** *Am* (*sock*) socquette *f*
ankylose ['æŋkɪləʊz] *Med* **1** *vt* ankyloser **2** *vi* s'ankyloser
ankylosis [æŋkɪ'ləʊsɪs] *n Med* ankylose *f*
annalist ['ænəlɪst] *n* annaliste *m*
annals ['æn(ə)lz] *npl* annales *fpl*
Anne [æn] *n* Anne *f*; *Hist* **A. of Austria** Anne d'Autriche
anneal [ə'niːl] *vt Tech* (*glass*) recuire, adoucir; (*metal*) détremper, recuire, adoucir
annealing [ə'niːlɪŋ] *n Tech* (*of glass*) recuit *m*, recuite *f*; *Metal* (*of metal*) adoucissement *m*, recuit, recuite; **box** *or* **close a.** recuit en vase clos; **a. furnace** four *m* à recuire
annex[1] ['æneks] *n US* = **annexe**
annex[2] [æ'neks] *vt* **(a)** (*take possession of*) (*province*) annexer **(b)** (*attach*) annexer (**sth to sth** qch à qch)
annexation [ænek'seɪʃən] *n* annexion *f* (**of** de)
annexe, *US* **annex** ['æneks] *n* **(a)** (*of building*) annexe *f* **(b)** (*to document*) annexe *f*
annihilate [ə'naɪəleɪt] *vt* (*fleet, army*) anéantir, réduire à néant; *F* **his opponent annihilated him** son adversaire l'a pulvérisé *ou* anéanti
annihilation [ənaɪə'leɪʃən] *n* **(a)** (*of fleet, people*) anéantissement *m* **(b)** *Nucl Phys* annihilation *f*; (*of electron and positron*) dématérialisation *f*
anniversary [ænɪ'vɜːs(ə)rɪ] *n* anniversaire *m*; **it's our wedding a.** c'est l'anniversaire de notre mariage; **on the a. of ...** le jour (de l')anniversaire de ...; **an a. dinner** un dîner d'anniversaire; **golden/silver/ruby (wedding) a.** noces *fpl* d'or/d'argent/de rubis
anno Domini ['ænəʊ'dɒmɪnaɪ, -niː] *adv* en l'an du Seigneur *ou* de grâce
annotate ['ænəteɪt] *vt* (*book etc*) annoter; **annotated draft** brouillon *m* annoté
annotation [ænə'teɪʃən] *n* annotation *f*
annotator ['ænəteɪtər] *n* annotateur, -trice
announce [ə'naʊns] *vt* annoncer; **the Prime Minister has announced his cabinet** le premier ministre a fait connaître *ou* a annoncé la composition de son cabinet; **to a. the birth/marriage/death of sb** faire part de la naissance/du mariage/du décès de qn
announcement [ə'naʊnsmənt] *n* annonce *f*; (*statement*) déclaration *f*; (*of birth, marriage etc*) faire-part *m inv*; *Journ* **a. of death** avis *m* de décès; **here is a passenger a.** avis voyageurs; **here is a staff a.** appel de service
announcer [ə'naʊnsər] *n* annonceur, -euse; *Rad, TV* speaker *m*, speakerine *f*; **a. booth** cabine *f* de présentation; **a. studio** studio *m* d'annonceur
annoy [ə'nɔɪ] *vt* (*person*) ennuyer, *F* embêter; (*stronger*) agacer, énerver; (*by going against sb's wishes etc*) contrarier; **you're really annoying me!** ce que tu peux m'embêter!; **is the light/noise annoying you?** est-ce que la lumière/le bruit t'ennuie *ou* te dérange?; **is this man annoying you?** est-ce que cet homme vous ennuie?
annoyance [ə'nɔɪəns] *n* énervement *m*, agacement *m*, *F* embêtement *m*; **look of a.** air *m* contrarié *ou* ennuyé; **much to his a.** à son grand déplaisir *ou* mécontentement; **source of a.** désagrément *m*, cause *f* d'ennuis; **petty annoyances** petits ennuis *mpl*, petites contrariétés *fpl*; **to cause a. to everyone** énerver tout le monde; (*by going against wishes etc*) contrarier tout le monde; **she failed to hide her a. at his words** elle n'a pas réussi à cacher l'énervement *ou* l'agacement que lui inspiraient ses paroles
annoyed [ə'nɔɪd] *adj* ennuyé, *F* embêté (**at, about** par, à cause de); (*stronger*) agacé, énervé (**at, about** par, à cause de); (*because sb has gone against one's wishes*) contrarié; **to be a. with sb/oneself** être en colère contre qn/soi-même; **to get a. with sb/sth** se mettre en colère *ou* s'énerver contre qn/qch; **promise you won't get a.** promets-moi que tu ne vas pas te mettre en colère *ou* t'énerver
annoying [ə'nɔɪɪŋ] *adj* ennuyeux, agaçant; (*habits*) agaçant; **the a. thing about it is that ...** ce qu'il y a d'ennuyeux là-dedans c'est que ...; **how a.!** que c'est ennuyeux *ou F* embêtant!
annoyingly [ə'nɔɪɪŋlɪ] *adv* (*irritatingly*) (*to behave*) d'une façon agaçante *ou* énervante; **a., he was late** il était en retard, ce qui était ennuyeux; **she's a. punctual** elle est agaçante à être aussi ponctuelle; **it's getting a. unreliable** il/elle devient de moins en moins fiable au point que c'en est agaçant; **he's so a. knowledgeable** il sait tellement de choses que c'en devient agaçant
annual ['ænjʊəl] **1** *adj* (*holiday, payment, report etc*) annuel; **he has an a. salary of £50,000** il gagne 50 000 livres par an; **a. accounts** bilan *m* annuel; **a. budget** budget *m* annuel; **a. contribution** (*to pension scheme etc*) cotisation *f* annuelle; *Acct* **a. depreciation** annuité *f* d'amortissement; **a. earnings** (*of company*) recette(s) *f*(*pl*) annuelle(s); **a. general meeting** assemblée *f* générale (annuelle); **a. guaranteed salary** salaire *m* annuel garanti; **a. income** revenu *m* annuel; *Fin* **a. instalment** annuité *f*; **a. profit** profit *m* annuel; **a. returns** déclarations *fpl* annuelles; **a. revenue** recette *f* annuelle; **a. ring** (*of tree*) couche *f* annuelle; **a. sales figures** chiffre *m*

d'affaires annuel; **a. spend** dépenses *fpl* annuelles; **a. turnover** chiffre *m* d'affaires annuel; *Acct* **a. writedown** annuité *f* d'amortissement
2 *n* (a) *Bot* plante *f* annuelle
(b) (*publication*) publication *f* annuelle; **(children's) a.** album *m* (annuel)
annually ['ænjʊəlɪ] *adv* (*in a year*) par an, annuellement; (*every year*) tous les ans
annual percentage rate *n* taux *m* effectif global
annuity [ə'nju:ɪtɪ] *n Fin* rente *f* (annuelle); **government a.** rente sur l'État; **perpetual a.** rente perpétuelle, rente en perpétuel; **life a.** rente viagère, pension *f* viagère; **to buy an a.** placer son argent en viager *ou* à fonds perdu; **to pay sb an a.** servir *ou* faire une rente à qn; **a. in redemption of debt** annuité *f*
annul [ə'nʌl] *vt* (**-ll-**) *Jur* (*contract*) annuler, résilier; (*bill*) annuler, casser; (*treaty*) dénoncer; (*marriage, will, agreement*) annuler, casser, déclarer nul; (*law*) abroger; (*decision*) infirmer
annular ['ænjʊlər] *adj* (*eclipse, finger*) annulaire
annulment [ə'nʌlmənt] *n Jur* (*of contract etc*) annulation *f*, résiliation *f*; (*of will, marriage, bill*) annulation, cassation *f*; (*of law*) abrogation *f*; (*of decree*) abolition *f*; **decree of a.** décret *m* abolitif
annunciation [ənʌnsɪ'eɪʃən] *n Rel* **the A.** l'Annonciation *f*
anode ['ænəʊd] *n El* anode *f*, électrode *f* positive
anodyne ['ænəʊdaɪn] 1 *n Med* calmant *m*, analgésique *m* 2 *adj* (a) *Med* antalgique, analgésique (b) (*remark, topic*) anodin
anoint [ə'nɔɪnt] *vt* oindre (**with** de); **to a. sb king/bishop** sacrer qn roi/évêque
anointing [ə'nɔɪntɪŋ] *n* onction *f*; (*of king etc*) sacre *m*
anomalous [ə'nɒmələs] *adj* anormal, irrégulier
anomaly [ə'nɒməlɪ] *n* anomalie *f*
anon[1] [ə'nɒn] *adv Arch, Hum* (a) (*later*) plus tard; **more of this a.** je reviendrai sur cela (b) (*soon*) tout à l'heure, bientôt; **see you a.** à bientôt; **I'll be with you a.** je vous rejoins tout de suite
anon[2] *adj abbr* **anonymous**
anonymity [ænə'nɪmɪtɪ] *n* anonymat *m*; **to preserve one's a.** garder l'anonymat, préserver son anonymat
anonymous [ə'nɒnɪməs] *adj* (a) (*gift, letter etc*) anonyme; **to remain a.** garder l'anonymat (b) (*building, face*) anonyme
anonymously [ə'nɒnɪməslɪ] *adv* anonymement; **to write a.** écrire sous (le couvert de) l'anonymat
anopheles mosquito [ə'nɒfɪli:z] *n* anophèle *m*
anorak ['ænəræk] *n* anorak *m*
anorexia [ænə'reksɪə] *n Med* anorexie *f*; **a. nervosa** anorexie mentale
anorexic [ænə'reksɪk] *adj, n Med* anorexique *mf*; **you look a.** tu n'as plus que la peau sur les os
another [ə'nʌðər] *adj, pron* [①A36-37,e; B14,B,1,b] (a) (*one more*) encore un(e); (*second*) un(e) autre, un(e) deuxième, un(e) second(e); **we're thinking of getting a. car** (*in addition to the one we have*) nous pensons acheter une deuxième voiture; **a. cup of tea** encore une tasse de thé; **a. fifty years** encore cinquante ans; **in a. ten years** dans dix ans (d'ici); **a. hour/20 miles and we'll be there** encore une heure/une vingtaine de mil(l)es et nous y serons; **I don't want to see a. fish as long as I live** je ne veux plus voir un seul poisson de toute ma vie; **without a. word** sans (un mot de) plus; **have a. (drink)!** encore un(e)?; **this is not just a. small car** ce n'est pas seulement une petite voiture parmi d'autres; **he is a. Picasso** c'est le nouveau Picasso; **the situation could become a. Vietnam** la situation pourrait tourner en un autre Vietnam
(b) (*different one*) un(e) autre; **we're thinking of getting a. car** (*to replace the car we have*) nous pensons acheter une nouvelle voiture *ou* changer de voiture; **take this cup away and bring me a. (one)** enlevez cette tasse et apportez-m'en une autre; **a. of the passengers** un autre passager; **that's (quite) a. matter** c'est (tout) autre chose; **science is one thing, art is a.** la science est une chose, l'art en est une autre; *Lit* **he loves a.** il en aime une autre; **she now has a. husband** elle a maintenant un nouveau mari; **a. athlete would have played safe** un autre athlète aurait joué la prudence; **a. time** une autre fois; **let's do it a. way** faisons autrement; *F* **tell me a.!** (*you're exaggerating*) ce n'est pas vrai!, à d'autres!; **one way or a.** d'une façon ou d'une autre; **taking one thing with a., we just manage** l'un dans l'autre, on arrive à joindre les deux bouts; **what with one thing and a., I forgot** avec tout ça j'ai oublié
(c) (*reciprocal*) **one a.** l'un l'autre; (*more than two people*) les uns les autres; **to help one a.** s'entraider; **love one a.** aimez-vous les uns les autres; **he and his wife adore one a.** lui et sa femme s'adorent; **they give one a. presents** ils se donnent des cadeaux

Ansaphone® ['ɑ:nsəfəʊn] *n Tel* répondeur(-)enregistreur *m*
ANSI ['ænsi:] *n Am* (*abbr* **American National Standards Institute**) = association *f* américaine de normalisation; **A. character** caractère *m* ANSI
answer[1] ['ɑ:nsər] *n* (a) [①B61,D] (*to question, letter*) réponse *f*; (*to criticism*) réponse, réplique *f*; **she made no a.** elle n'a pas répondu; **I knocked but there was no a.** j'ai frappé mais personne n'a répondu; *Tel* **there's no a.** ça ne répond pas; **he has an a. to everything** il a réponse à tout; **you think you know all the answers, don't you?** tu crois que tu sais tout, c'est ça?; **his only a. was to burst into tears** pour toute réponse il a fondu en larmes; **Scotland's a. to Pelé** le Pelé écossais; **they had no a. to this/this new scrum half** ils ne savaient pas quoi faire contre ça/ce nouveau demi de mêlée; **there's no a. to that!** comment répondre à ça!; **it's the a. to the government's prayers** c'est exactement ce dont le gouvernement avait besoin; **she's the a. to all his prayers** c'est la femme de ses rêves; *Fml* **in a. to your letter** en réponse à votre lettre; *Jur etc* **a. to a charge** réfutation *f* à une accusation; *Comptr* **a. mode** mode *m* réponse
(b) *Math, Fig* (*to problem*) solution *f*; **the a. is 624** la réponse est 624
answer[2] 1 *vt* (*person, question, letter*) répondre à; **what did he a.?** qu'a-t-il répondu?; **letters to be answered** courrier *m* en cours; **letters answered** lettres *fpl* auxquelles on a répondu; **the question is not easy to a.** c'est une question à laquelle il n'est pas facile de répondre; **to a. the bell/the telephone** répondre à un coup de sonnette/au téléphone; **to a. the door** (*go*) aller ouvrir; (*come*) venir ouvrir; **to a. a prayer** exaucer une prière; *Jur* **to a. a charge** répondre à *ou* réfuter une accusation; **to a. a description** répondre à un signalement; **to a. the helm** (*of ship*) obéir à la barre; **to a. a need** répondre à un besoin; **this should a. the purpose quite nicely** ceci fera très bien l'affaire; **it should a. the purposes of both students and translators** ce devrait être utile aux étudiants comme aux traducteurs; **that will a. my purpose** cela fera mon affaire
2 *vi* répondre; **it's not answering** (*phone*) ça ne répond pas
▶ **answer back** 1 *vi* (*be impertinent*) répondre; **don't a. back!** ne réponds pas! 2 *vtsep* (*be impertinent to*) répondre à
▶ **answer for** *vipo* répondre de; (*sb's integrity*) se porter garant de; **to a. for one's actions** prendre la responsabilité de ses propres actes; **to a. for one's crimes** payer pour ses crimes; **he/the motor car has a lot to a. for** il/la voiture est responsable de bien des problèmes
▶ **answer to** *vipo* (a) (*be accountable to*) être responsable envers, rendre compte à; **you'll have me to a. to** (*if you do that*) c'est à moi que vous devrez rendre des comptes; **to a. to sb for sth** être responsable de qch envers qn (b) (*correspond to*) (*description*) répondre à (c) **the dog answers to the name of Rover** le chien répond au nom de Rover
answerable ['ɑ:nsərəb(ə)l] *adj* (a) garant, responsable (**to sb for sth** de qch envers qn); **to be a. to an authority** relever d'une autorité; **he is a. to nobody** il n'a de comptes à rendre à personne (b) (*accusation*) réfutable
answerback ['ɑ:nsəbæk] *n Comptr* (*in datacomms*) réponse *f* en retour
answering ['ɑ:nsərɪŋ] *adj* **an a. cry** un cri jeté en réponse; *Tel* **a. machine** (*giving message*) répondeur *m* téléphonique; (*giving and taking message*) répondeur(-)enregistreur *m*; *Tel* **a. service** service *m* de répondeur téléphonique
answerphone ['ɑ:nsəfəʊn] *n Tel* répondeur(-)enregistreur *m*
answer tone *n* tonalité *f* de réponse
ant [ænt] *n* fourmi *f*; *Fig F* **to have ants in one's pants** ne pas tenir en place, avoir la bougeotte; **a. bear** tamanoir *m*; **a. colony** colonie *f* de fourmis; **a. hill** fourmilière *f*; **a. lion** fourmi-lion *m*
antacid [ænt'æsɪd] *adj, n Med* antiacide *m*
antagonism [æn'tægənɪz(ə)m] *n* hostilité *f* (**to, towards** envers); (*between two people*), *Physiol* antagonisme *m*
antagonist [æn'tægənɪst] *n* antagoniste *mf*, adversaire *mf*
antagonistic [æntægə'nɪstɪk] *adj* (*opposed*) opposé, contraire (**to** à); (*person, attitude*) hostile; (*parties*) antagonique; *Anat* (*muscle*) antagoniste
antagonize [æn'tægənaɪz] *vt* éveiller l'hostilité de; **to a. the public** ranger l'opinion contre soi; **don't a. him** ne te le mets pas à dos; **she only succeeded in antagonizing him further** elle n'a réussi qu'à le rendre encore plus hostile
Antarctic [æn'tɑ:ktɪk] 1 *adj* antarctique 2 *n* **the A.** l'Antarctique *m*
Antarctica [æn'tɑ:ktɪkə] *n* Antarctique *m*
ante[1] ['æntɪ] *n Cards* (*at poker*) première mise *f*; **to raise** *or* **up the a.** *Cards* lever la mise; *Fig* (*in dispute*) placer la barre plus haut
ante[2] *vi Cards* faire une mise
▶ **ante up** *vi US F* (*pay*) casquer

anteater ['æntiːtər] *n* fourmilier *m*; **great a.** tamanoir *m*; **scaly a.** pangolin *m*; **spiny a.** échidné *m*
antebellum [æntɪ'beləm] *adj US* d'avant la guerre Civile
antecedence [æntɪ'siːd(ə)ns] *n* **(a)** (*precedence*) antériorité *f* **(b)** (*priority*) priorité *f*
antecedent [æntɪ'siːd(ə)nt] **1** *adj* antérieur (**to** à) **2** *n* **(a)** [ⓘ**A32-33; B20-22,F**] *Gram, Math* antécédent *m* **(b) antecedents** (*of person*) (*past*) antécédents *mpl*; (*ancestors*) ancêtres *mpl*; (*of society etc*) origines *fpl*
antechamber ['æntɪtʃeɪmbər] *n* **(a)** (*room*) antichambre *f* **(b)** (*in engine*) préchambre *f*; **diesel engine with a.** moteur *m* diesel à chambre de précombustion
antedate [æntɪ'deɪt] *vt* (*precede*) précéder
antediluvian [æntɪdɪ'luːvɪən] *adj* antédiluvien
antelope ['æntɪləʊp] *n* (*pl* **antelopes, antelope**) antilope *f*
ante meridian [æntɪmə'rɪdɪən] *adv* [ⓘ**A75,A,e; B58,A,e**] *Fml* du matin
antenatal [æntɪ'neɪt(ə)l] *adj* prénatal, -als, anténatal, -als; **an a. clinic** un cours de préparation à l'accouchement
antenna [æn'tenə] *n* **(a)** (*pl* **-ae** [-iː]) (*of insect, crustacean*) antenne *f*; (*of mollusc*) tentacule *m*; (*of snail*) corne *f* **(b)** (*pl usu* **-as** [-əz]) *esp Am Rad, TV* antenne *f*
antepenultimate [æntɪpə'nʌltɪmət] *adj* antépénultième; **the a. syllable** l'antépénultième *f* (syllabe *f*)
anterior [æn'tɪərɪər] *adj* **(a)** antérieur, -eure (**to** à) **(b)** [ⓘ**A50,12,h; B29,8**] *Gram* **past a.** passé *m* antérieur **(c)** *Anat* (*muscle*) antérieur
anteroom ['æntɪruːm] *n* antichambre *f*, vestibule *m*
anthem ['ænθəm] *n Rel* motet *m*; *Lit* (*song of joy*) chant *m* d'allégresse; **national a.** hymne *m* national; **the party's a.** l'hymne du parti
anther ['ænθər] *n Bot* anthère *f*
anthologist [æn'θɒlədʒɪst] *n* anthologue *m*
anthology [æn'θɒlədʒɪ] *n* anthologie *f*
anthracite ['ænθrəsaɪt] *n Min* anthracite *m*
anthrax ['ænθræks] *n* charbon *m*, anthrax *m*
anthropoid ['ænθrəpɔɪd] **1** *n Zool* (*ape*) (singe *m*) anthropoïde *m* **2** *adj* **(a)** (*person*) (*apelike*) simiesque **(b)** (*ape*) (*resembling man*) anthropoïde
anthropological ['ænθrəpə'lɒdʒɪk(ə)l] *adj* anthropologique
anthropologist [ænθrə'pɒlədʒɪst] *n* anthropologue *mf*
anthropology [ænθrə'pɒlədʒɪ] *n* anthropologie *f*
anthropometry [ænθrə'pɒmɪtrɪ] *n* anthropométrie *f*
anthropomorphic [ænθrəpə'mɔːfɪk] *adj* anthropomorphe
anthropomorphism [ænθrəpə'mɔːfɪz(ə)m] *n* anthropomorphisme *m*
anthropomorphous [ænθrəpə'mɔːfəs] *adj* anthropomorphe
anthropophagous [ænθrə'pɒfəgəs] *adj* anthropophage
anthropophagy [ænθrə'pɒfədʒɪ] *n* anthropophagie *f*
anti ['æntɪ, *US* 'æntaɪ] **1** *prep* anti; **she was a. the idea** elle était contre cette idée; **he's a. everything** rien ne lui plaît; **she's a. anything which involves spending money** elle est contre tout ce qui entraîne des dépenses **2** *n* opposant, -ante
anti- ['æntɪ, *US* 'æntaɪ] *pref* anti-; **anti-American** anti(-)américain
anti-abortionist *n* adversaire *mf* de l'avortement
anti-aircraft *adj* (*gun, defence etc*) antiaérien
anti-apartheid *adj* anti(-)apartheid
antibacterial [æntɪbæk'tɪərɪəl] *adj Med* antibactérien
antiballistic [æntɪbə'lɪstɪk] *adj* antiballistique, antimissile; **a. missile** engin *m ou* fusée *f* antimissile
antibiotic [æntɪbaɪ'ɒtɪk] **1** *adj* antibiotique **2** *n* antibiotique *m*; **to be on antibiotics** être sous antibiotiques
antibody ['æntɪbɒdɪ] *n Physiol* anticorps *m*
anti-burst lock *n* serrure *f* renforcée
Antichrist ['æntɪkraɪst] *n* Antéchrist *m*
antichristian [æntɪ'krɪstʃən] *adj* antichrétien
anticipate [æn'tɪsɪpeɪt] **1** *vt* **(a)** (*expect*) (*possibility, reaction*) prévoir; (*difficulty, pleasure etc*) s'attendre à, envisager; **we don't a. any objections** nous n'envisageons pas d'objections; **we do not a. any delays** aucun retard n'est prévu; **to a. that ...** prévoir que ...; **to a. the worst** s'attendre au pire
(b) (*enjoy, count on in advance*) (*events*) anticiper sur; (*pleasure*) savourer d'avance; (*result, vote*) escompter; **to a. one's salary** anticiper sur son salaire; **anticipated profit** profit *m* espéré
(c) (*act in advance of*) (*person, sb's orders*) devancer, prévenir, aller au-devant de; **you must a. your opponent's moves/other drivers' intentions** il faut que vous anticipiez les mouvements de votre adversaire/les intentions des autres conducteurs; **her writing anticipated later developments in English fiction** son style présageait des développements futurs de la fiction anglaise; **don't a. me** (*in telling story*) attends la suite, laisse-moi finir
2 *vi* anticiper
anticipation [æntɪsɪ'peɪʃən] *n* **(a)** (*foresight*) prévision *f*; **in a. of trouble** en prévision de troubles; **thanking you in a.** en vous remerciant d'avance; **Brian showed great a.** (*in game*) Brian a très bien anticipé **(b)** (*expectation*) anticipation *f*; **they awaited his arrival with eager a.** ils l'attendaient avec beaucoup d'impatience
anticipatory pricing [æn'tɪsɪpeɪt(ə)rɪ] *n* fixation *f* des prix par anticipation
anticlerical [æntɪ'klerɪk(ə)l] *adj* anticlérical
anticlericalism [æntɪ'klerɪk(ə)lɪz(ə)m] *n* anticléricalisme *m*
anticlimax [æntɪ'klaɪmæks] *n* (*disappointment*) déception *f*; **the party itself was a bit of an a.** la soirée a été plutôt décevante; **after all the waiting the news almost felt like an a.** après toute cette attente la nouvelle n'a pas produit tout l'effet escompté
anticline ['æntɪklaɪn] *n* anticlinal *m*, -aux
anticlockwise [æntɪ'klɒkwaɪz] *adv, adj Br* **a., in an a. direction** dans le sens inverse des aiguilles d'une montre; **clockwise or a.?** dans le sens des aiguilles d'une montre ou l'inverse?
anticoagulant [æntɪkəʊ'ægjʊlənt] *adj, n Med* anticoagulant *m*
anticolonialism [æntɪkə'ləʊnɪəlɪz(ə)m] *n* anticolonialisme *m*
anticonstitutional [æntɪkɒnstɪ'tjuːʃən(ə)l] *adj* anticonstitutionnel
anti-corrosion guarantee *n* garantie *f* anti-corrosion
anti-corrosion primer *n* apprêt *m* anti-corrosion
antics ['æntɪks] *npl* bouffonneries *fpl*, singeries *fpl*; **he's up to his a. again** le voilà qui fait de nouveau des siennes
anticyclone [æntɪ'saɪkləʊn] *n* anticyclone *m*
anti-dazzle *adj* anti-aveuglant; (*headlights, rear view mirror*) anti-éblouissant
anti-democratic *adj* antidémocratique
antidepressant [æntɪdɪ'presənt] *adj, n Pharm* antidépresseur *m*
anti-dieselling valve [æntɪ'diːz(ə)lɪŋ] *n Aut* thermovalve *f*
anti-dive geometry *n Aut* géométrie *f* anti-plongée
antidote ['æntɪdəʊt] *n Med, Fig* antidote *m* (**to** contre), contrepoison *m* (**to** à)
anti-establishment *adj* anticonformiste
antifascism [æntɪ'fæʃɪz(ə)m] *n Pol* antifascisme *m*
antifascist [æntɪ'fæʃɪst] *adj, n* antifasciste *mf*
antifebrile [æntɪ'fiːbraɪl] *n, adj Pharm* antipyrétique *m*, fébrifuge *m*
antifreeze ['æntɪfriːz] *adj, n Aut* antigel *m*
antigen ['æntɪdʒen] *n Med* antigène *m*
anti-glare *adj* = **anti-dazzle**; **a. mirror** rétroviseur *m* jour/nuit; **a. screen** écran *m* antireflets
Antigua [æn'tiːgə] *n* Antigua *m*
anti-hero *n Liter* antihéros *m inv*
anti-heroine *n Liter* antihéroïne *f*
antihistamine [æntɪ'hɪstəmɪn] *adj, n Med* antihistaminique *m*
anti-icing **1** *n Aut* antigel *m*; *Av* antigivrant *m* **2** *adj* antigivre *inv*
anti-imperialist *n, adj* anti-impérialiste *mf*
anti-inflammatory *adj, n Med* anti-inflammatoire *m*
anti-inflationary *adj* (*measures, policy*) anti-inflationniste
anti-knock *adj, n Aut* antidétonant *m*
Antilles [æn'tɪliːz] *npl* **the A.** les Antilles *fpl*
anti-lock brakes *npl* anti-blocage *m* des freins
anti-lock braking system *n* système *m* anti-blocage des freins
antilogarithm [æntɪ'lɒgərɪðəm] *n Math* antilogarithme *m*
antimacassar [æntɪmə'kæsər] *n* têtière *f*
antimalarial [æntɪmə'leərɪəl] *n, adj Pharm* antipaludique *m*, antipaludéen *m*
antimatter ['æntɪmætər] *n* antimatière *f*
antimilitarism [æntɪ'mɪlɪtərɪz(ə)m] *n* antimilitarisme *m*
anti-missile *adj* antimissile
antimony [æn'tɪmənɪ] *n* antimoine *m*
antinazi [æntɪ'nɑːtsɪ] *adj, n Pol* antinazi, -ie
anti-nuclear *adj* antinucléaire
antiparticle ['æntɪpɑːtɪk(ə)l] *n Nucl Phys* antiparticule *f*
antipathetic(al) [æntɪpə'θetɪk, -ɪk(ə)l] *adj* **a. to** qui a de l'aversion pour
antipathy [æn'tɪpəθɪ] *n* antipathie *f*; **to feel a. for sb** avoir de l'antipathie pour *ou* contre qn
antipersonnel [æntɪpɜːsə'nel] *adj* (*bomb*) antipersonnel
antiperspirant [æntɪ'pɜːspɪrənt] *adj, n* déodorant *m*
antiphon ['æntɪfɒn] *n Rel* antienne *f*
anti-pinch sensor *n Aut* (*for windows*) détecteur *m ou* capteur *m* anti-pincement
antipodean [æntɪpə'diːən] *adj* **(a)** *Geog* des antipodes; **A. day** jour *m* méridien **(b)** *Br* (*from Australia and/or New Zealand*) d'Australie; de Nouvelle-Zélande; *Hum* **our a. cousins** nos cousins d'Australie/de Nouvelle-Zélande; **the kangaroo and other a. animals** le kangourou et les autres animaux australiens

antipodes [æn'tɪpədi:z] *npl Geog* **the a.** les antipodes *mpl*; **at the a.** aux antipodes; *Br* **the A.** l'Australie *f* et/ou la Nouvelle-Zélande
anti-pollution regulations *npl* réglementation *f* anti-pollution
antiproton [æntɪ'prəʊtɒn] *n Nucl Phys* antiproton *m*
antipyretic [æntɪpaɪ'retɪk] *n, adj Pharm* antipyrétique *m*, fébrifuge *m*
antiquarian [æntɪ'kweərɪən] **1** *adj* (*book*) ancien; **a. collection** collection *f* d'antiquités; **a. bookseller/bookshop** libraire *mf*/librairie *f* spécialisé(e) dans les éditions anciennes **2** *n* (*dealer*) antiquaire *mf*; (*collector*) amateur *m* d'antiquités; (*scholar*) historien, -ienne
antiquary ['æntɪkwərɪ] *n* (*collector*) amateur *m* d'antiquités; (*dealer*) antiquaire *mf*; (*scholar*) historien, -ienne
antiquated ['æntɪkweɪtɪd] *adj* (*outmoded*) (*method*) désuet, *f* -ète, suranné; (*car, tools*) vieillot; **an a. kitchen range** une cuisinière (à charbon) d'autrefois
antique [æn'ti:k] **1** *adj* antique, ancien; **a. furniture** meubles anciens; **she's got an a. gas cooker** sa cuisinière à gaz est une véritable antiquité **2** *n* (*ancient object, piece of furniture*) antiquité *f*; **be careful with that, it's an a.** fais attention, c'est ancien; *F* **that television's an a.** cette télévision est une antiquité
antique dealer *n* antiquaire *mf*
antique shop *n* magasin *m* d'antiquités
antiquity [æn'tɪkwɪtɪ] *n* **(a)** (*of custom*) ancienneté *f* **(b)** *Hist* (*Greek, Roman*) antiquité *f*; **the works of art of classical a.** les antiquités; **women in a.** la femme dans le monde ancien **(c) Roman antiquities** (*remains*) monuments *mpl* romains
anti-rabies *adj* antirabique
antiracism [æntɪ'reɪsɪz(ə)m] *n* antiracisme *m*
antiracist [æntɪ'reɪsɪst] *adj* antiraciste
antiraid precautions [æntɪ'reɪd] *n St Exch* barrières *fpl* antiraid
anti-roll bar *n Aut* barre *f* antiroulis
antirrhinum [æntɪ'raɪnəm] *n* (*plant*) muflier *m*
anti-run-on valve *n Aut* thermovalve *f*
anti-rust *adj, n* **a. (composition)** (enduit *m*) antirouille *m inv*; **a. treatment** traitement *m* antirouille
anti-Semite *n* antisémite *mf*
anti-Semitic *adj* antisémite
anti-Semitism [æntɪ'semɪtɪz(ə)m] *n* antisémitisme *m*
antisepsis [æntɪ'sepsɪs] *n Med* antisepsie *f*
antiseptic [æntɪ'septɪk] **1** *adj Med* antiseptique; *Fig* (*atmosphere*) aseptisé; (*person*) froid, peu amical **2** *n Med* antiseptique *m*
antiserum ['æntɪsɪərəm] *n Med* antisérum *m*
antislavery [æntɪ'sleɪvərɪ] *adj* antiesclavagiste
antisocial [æntɪ'səʊʃəl] *adj* **(a)** (*behaviour, element, vandalism*) asocial; (*bill, measure, policy*) antisocial **(b)** (*unsociable*) (*sort of person*) qui fait bande à part, sauvage; **he's being very a.** en ce moment il n'est pas très sociable; **I don't want to be a. but ...** (*I'd rather be alone*) désolé de faire bande à part mais ...; (*I have to leave, you have to leave*) je m'en voudrais de gâcher l'ambiance mais ...
antispasmodic [æntɪspæz'mɒdɪk] *n, adj Pharm* antispasmodique *m*
antistatic [æntɪ'stætɪk] *adj* antistatique
anti-submarine *adj* anti-sous-marin
anti-submarining ramp *n Aut* glissière *f* anti-plongée
anti-tank *adj Mil* antichar(s)
anti-terrorist *adj* antiterroriste
anti-theft *adj* (*lock*) antivol *inv*; **a. device** antivol *m inv*
antithesis, *pl* **-es** [æn'tɪθɪsɪs, -i:z] *n* **(a)** (*opposite*) antithèse *f*, opposé *m* **(of** de) **(b)** *Phil* (*in dialectic*) antithèse *f* **(between** entre; **to, of** de)
antithetical [æntɪ'θetɪk(ə)l] *adj* antithétique
antitoxin [æntɪ'tɒksɪn] *n Med* antitoxine *f*
anti-trust *adj US Econ* antitrust
antitussive [æntɪ'tʌsɪv] *n, adj Pharm* antitussif *m*
antivirus ['æntɪvaɪrəs] *n Comptr* antivirus *m*; **a. program** programme *m* antivirus
antivivisectionist [æntɪvɪvɪ'sekʃənɪst] *n* antivivisection(n)iste *mf*
antler ['æntlər] *n* (*of stag*) andouiller *m*; **the antlers** les bois *mpl*
antonym ['æntənɪm] *n* antonyme *m*
Antwerp ['æntwɜ:p] *n* Anvers *m*
anus ['eɪnəs] *n Anat* anus *m*
anvil ['ænvɪl] *n* (*of blacksmith, in ear*) enclume *f*
anxiety [æŋ'zaɪətɪ] *n* **(a)** (*worry, concern*) inquiétude *f*; **deep a.** anxiété *f*, angoisse *f*; **to cause sb great a.** donner de grandes inquiétudes *ou* bien des soucis à qn; **there is no cause for a.** il n'y a pas de quoi s'inquiéter; **to feel a.** s'inquiéter, être anxieux (**about** à propos de); **to be full of a.** être anxieux
(b) (*individual concern*) souci *m*; **the report failed to remove their anxieties** le rapport ne leur a pas ôté leurs inquiétudes
(c) (*desire*) désir *m*, souci *m* (**for sth** de qch); **a. to help sb/please sb** désir *ou* souci d'aider qn/de plaire à qn; **in her a. not to offend** dans son souci de n'offenser personne
(d) *Psy* anxiété *f*; **a. attack** crise *f* d'angoisse
anxious ['æŋkʃəs] *adj* **(a)** (*worried*) inquiet, *f* -ète, soucieux (**about** sur, de, au sujet de); **what are you so a. about?** pourquoi es-tu aussi inquiet *ou* soucieux?; **very** *or* **extremely a.** angoissé; **he was a. that all his work might come to nothing** il craignait que tout son travail n'ait servi à rien; **the a. faces of relatives** le visage angoissé des membres de la famille; **to be a. for sb/sb's safety** être inquiet *ou* s'inquiéter pour qn/la sécurité de qn; **I am a. about his health** sa santé me préoccupe, je m'inquiète de sa santé
(b) (*worrying*) inquiétant; **an a. moment** un moment d'anxiété; **it was an a. time for us** ça a été une période de grande inquiétude pour nous
(c) (*eager*) désireux; **to be a. to do sth** tenir à faire qch, être désireux de faire qch; **why are you so a. to go?** (*impatient*) pourquoi êtes-vous si impatient de partir?; (*eager*) pourquoi tenez-vous tant à y aller?
(d) *Psy* anxieux
anxiously ['æŋkʃəslɪ] *adv* **(a)** (*worriedly*) anxieusement, avec inquiétude, avec anxiété **(b)** (*with concern*) avec sollicitude **(c)** (*with impatience*) avec impatience
any ['enɪ] [①A34-35,a; B63-4,4; B4-5,C] **1** *adj* **(a)** (*some, one*) **have you a. milk/books?** avez-vous du lait/des livres?; **have you a. more milk?** avez-vous encore du lait?; **is there a. hope?** y a-t-il de l'espoir?; (*stressed*) y a-t-il aucun espoir?; **if you had a. sense (at all)** si tu avais ne serait-ce qu'un peu de bon sens
(b) (*in neg sentences or with implied negation*) **not a.** ne ... aucun; **he hasn't a. reason to complain** il n'a aucune raison de se plaindre; **he hasn't a. more money** il n'a plus d'argent; **without a. help** sans aucune aide; **she is forbidden to do a. work** tout travail lui est interdit; **it is difficult to find a. explanation for it** il est difficile d'y trouver une quelconque explication; **complaining won't do a. good** se plaindre n'avancera à rien
(c) (*no particular*) n'importe quel; **come a. day (you like)** venez n'importe quel jour; **a. man, woman or child** qui que ce soit, homme, femme, ou enfant; **a. doctor will tell you that** n'importe quel médecin vous le dira; **that may happen at a. time** cela peut arriver n'importe quand; **I expect him a. moment now** je l'attends d'un instant à l'autre; **take a. two cards** prenez deux cartes quelconques; *F* **a. old thing** n'importe quoi; *F* **a. old book** n'importe quel livre; **I don't want just a. (old) wine** je ne veux pas n'importe quel vin
(d) (*every*) **a. pupil who forgets his books will be punished** tout élève qui oubliera ses livres sera puni; **at a. rate, in a. case** en tout cas
2 *pron* **I haven't got a.** je n'en ai pas; **I haven't seen a.** je n'en ai pas vu; **have you a.?** en avez-vous?; **is there a. more?** y en a-t-il encore?; **I/you/*etc* needn't say a. more** pas besoin d'en dire davantage; **they won't take a. less** ils n'accepteront pas moins; **few, if a., can read** peu, si ce n'est aucun, savent lire; **he has no money and no prospect of a.** il est sans argent et sans l'espoir d'en avoir; **take a. of the bottles** prends n'importe laquelle des bouteilles; **a. of us** n'importe qui d'entre nous; **I don't think a. of the guests have arrived yet** je ne pense pas qu'aucun des invités soit encore arrivé; **there was no paper in a. of the boxes** il n'y avait de papier dans aucune des boîtes
3 *adv* **(a)** (*with comparative*) **I'm not a. better** je ne vais pas mieux; **I can't go a. further** je ne peux pas aller plus loin; **the weather couldn't be a. worse** le temps ne pourrait pas être pire *ou* plus mauvais; **I don't see him a. longer** *or* **more** je ne le vois plus; *F* **a. old how** n'importe comment; **I didn't do it a. more than you did** je ne l'ai pas fait plus que vous; **I don't like her a. more than you do** je ne l'aime pas plus que tu ne l'aimes
(b) *F* **that didn't help us a.** cela ne nous a été d'aucun secours; **her attitude didn't help a.** son attitude n'a rien arrangé
anybody ['enɪbɒdɪ], **anyone** ['enɪwʌn] *pron* (*no pl*) (*NOTE in examples where one of the forms is preferred the word has been printed in full*) **(a)** [①A34,12,a; B64,5] (*indeterminate*) quelqu'un; (*expecting answer 'no'*) personne; **can you see a. over there?** est-ce que vous voyez quelqu'un là-bas?; **does a. mind if I close the window?** est-ce que cela gêne quelqu'un si je ferme la fenêtre?; **would a. like some more cake?** est-ce que quelqu'un voudrait reprendre du gâteau?;

does a. dare to say so? y a-t-il personne qui ose le dire?; **he knows French if a. does** il sait le français comme pas un; **she'll know if a. does** si quelqu'un le sait, c'est bien elle

(**b**) (*in neg sentences*) [①A34,12,a; B64,5] **not a.** ne ... personne; **there isn't a. here** il n'y a personne ici; **there was hardly a.** il n'y avait presque personne; **don't speak to a.** ne parlez à personne, ne parlez pas à qui que ce soit

(**c**) (*no particular person*) n'importe qui, tout le monde; **a. will tell you so** le premier venu *ou* n'importe qui *ou* tout le monde vous le dira; **a. would think he was mad** on le croirait fou; **a. but me** tout autre que moi; **you're not just a.** tu n'es pas n'importe qui; **a. with any sense** quiconque a un peu de bon sens; **bring along a. you like** amenez qui vous voudrez; **I challenge a. to ...** je défie qui que ce soit de ...; **I haven't met a. else** je n'ai rencontré personne d'autre; *Sp* **it's a.'s match** n'importe qui peut gagner, n'importe qui peut remporter la victoire; **it's a.'s guess!** qui sait?; *Hum F* **one drink and he's a.'s** un verre et il est prêt à repartir avec n'importe qui

(**d**) *F* (*person with status*) **is he anybody?** est-ce que c'est quelqu'un d'important?; **he never will be anybody** il n'arrivera jamais à rien

anyhow ['enɪhaʊ] *adv* (**a**) = **anyway** (**b**) *F* (*carelessly*) **to do sth (all) a.** faire qch n'importe comment; **the clothes had been thrown on the bed just a.** les vêtements avaient été jetés n'importe comment *ou* en pagaille sur le lit

anyone *see* **anybody**

anyplace ['enɪpleɪs] *adv Am F* = **anywhere**

anything ['enɪθɪŋ] **1** *pron* [①A34-35,a; B64,5] (**a**) quelque chose; (*with implied negation*) rien; **can I do a. for you?** est-ce que je peux faire quelque chose pour vous (aider)?; **is there a. I can do (to help)?** puis-je faire quelque chose?; **have you a. to write with?** avez-vous de quoi écrire?; **is there a. more pleasant than ...?** est-il rien de plus agréable que ...?; **will there be a. else, madam?** (*in shop*) désirez-vous autre chose, madame?, et avec cela, madame?; **a. bigger than that won't go through a letterbox** quelque chose de plus volumineux que ça ne passera pas par une boîte aux lettres; **have you a. smaller?** (*in different size*) est-ce que vous avez la taille en-dessous?; (*money*) vous n'avez pas plus petit?; **if a. should happen to me** s'il m'arrivait quelque chose; **do you see a. of your friend?** voyez-vous quelquefois votre ami?; **is (there) a. the matter?** y a-t-il quelque chose qui ne marche pas?

(**b**) (*in neg sentences*) **not a.** ne ... rien; **he doesn't do a.** il ne fait rien; **I shan't give you a. at all** je ne vous donnerai rien du tout; **hardly a.** presque rien; **it doesn't mean a.** cela ne veut rien dire

(**c**) (*no matter what*) n'importe quoi, tout; **he eats a.** il mange de tout; **a. you like** tout ce que vous voudrez; **a. will do** n'importe quoi fera l'affaire; **I love a. French** j'aime tout ce qui est français; **he would do a. for me** il ferait tout *ou* n'importe quoi pour moi; **I would have given a. not to go** j'aurais tout donné *ou* j'aurais donné n'importe quoi pour ne pas y aller; **he's a. but mad** il est loin d'être fou; **he's not mad, a. but** il n'est pas fou, loin de là

(**d**) *F* (*adv phrase, intensive*) **as easy/funny/strong as a.** facile/drôle/fort comme tout; **to work like a.** travailler comme un fou; **it's raining like a.** il pleut à verse; **it's not that you were wrong or a.** ce n'est pas que vous ayez tort, quoi; **I don't want to cause a problem or a. but ...** je ne veux pas causer de problème quoi mais ...

2 *adv* **she doesn't look a. like her sister** elle ne ressemble pas du tout *ou* en rien à sa sœur; **is it a. like Chinese food?** est-ce que ça ressemble un peu à de la cuisine chinoise?; **it didn't cost a. like £500** (*less*) ça a coûté bien moins de 500 livres; **the weather wasn't a. like as bad as I'd expected** le temps a été loin d'être aussi mauvais que ce à quoi je m'étais attendu; **if the food's a. like as good as it was at the last party** si on mange ne serait-ce qu'aussi bien qu'à la soirée précédente

anyway ['enɪweɪ] *adv* en tout cas, de toute façon; **a. it's too late** en tout cas *ou* de toute façon il est trop tard; **a. you can always try** vous pouvez toujours essayer; **a., let's get back to what we were saying** enfin *ou* bon, revenons à ce que nous disions

anywhere ['enɪweər] *adv* [①B64,5] (**a**) (*no matter where*) n'importe où; **put it a.** mettez-le n'importe où; **I'd know him a.** je le reconnaîtrais entre mille; **it's miles from a.** c'est au bout du monde *ou* en plein bled; **a. else** n'importe où (ailleurs); **this could be a. in Europe** ce pourrait être n'importe où en Europe; **has he a. near finished?** est-ce qu'il a bientôt terminé?

(**b**) **not a.** nulle part; **I've never been a.** je ne suis jamais allé nulle part; **you won't find a better curry a.** vous ne trouverez de meilleur curry nulle part; **I can't find it a.** je ne le trouve nulle part; *Fig* **we're not getting a.** nous n'arrivons à rien, nous n'avançons pas

(**c**) (*somewhere*) quelque part; **can you see it a.?** est-ce que vous le voyez?; **have you found a. to live?** avez-vous trouvé à vous loger?

AOCB [eɪəʊsiː'biː] (*abbr* **any other competent business**) affaires diverses

aorta [eɪ'ɔːtə] *n Anat* aorte *f*

aortic [eɪ'ɔːtɪk] *adj Anat* aortique

apace [ə'peɪs] *adv Arch, Lit* vite, rapidement

Apache [ə'pætʃɪ] *n* Apache *mf*

apart [ə'pɑːt] *adv* (**a**) (*at a distance*) à l'écart; **to hold oneself** *or* **stand a.** se tenir à l'écart (**from** de); **the house was set a little way a. from the others** la maison était un peu à l'écart des autres; **the garage stands a. from the house** le garage est séparé de la maison

(**b**) (*separated*) **they are a mile a.** ils sont à un mil(l)e l'un de l'autre; **lines 10 centimetres a.** lignes espacées de 10 centimètres; **to stand with one's feet a.** se tenir les jambes écartées; **they consider themselves in a class a.** ils se considèrent au-dessus des autres; **place set a. for worship** endroit réservé au culte; **cities as far a. as New York and Tokyo** des villes aussi éloignées que New York et Tokyo; **children born two years a.** des enfants nés à deux ans d'intervalle; **the boys and girls were kept a.** on tenait séparés les garçons et les filles; **they're never a.** ils ne se séparent jamais; **they're living a.** (*because of circumstances*) ils n'habitent pas ensemble; (*because of divorce, split-up*) ils sont séparés, ils vivent séparément; **it is difficult to tell them a.** il est difficile de les distinguer l'un de l'autre; **this problem cannot be treated a.** c'est un problème qu'on ne peut pas considérer séparément

(**c**) (*to pieces*) **to take a machine a.** démonter *ou* désassembler une machine; **my dress is coming a. at the seams** ma robe est en train de se découdre; *F* **to take a room a.** fouiller une pièce à fond

(**d**) **a. from** à part, sauf; **a. from the fact that ...** indépendamment du fait que ..., outre (le fait) que ...; **a. from a few mistakes** à part *ou* sauf quelques erreurs; **a. from him there is nobody who can do it** à part lui personne ne peut le faire; **I don't know anyone a. from you** je ne connais personne à part toi

apartheid [ə'pɑːtaɪt, -eɪt] *n Pol* apartheid *m*

apartment [ə'pɑːtmənt] *n* (**a**) *Am* appartement *m*; **a. block** *or* **building** immeuble *m* d'habitation (**b**) (*room*) pièce *f*; **state apartments** grands appartements *mpl*, salons *mpl* d'apparat; **(furnished) apartments to let** chambres *fpl* (meublées) à louer; **a. hotel** résidence *f* hôtelière, résidence de tourisme

apathetic [æpə'θetɪk] *adj* apathique; **to be a. about sth** être indifférent à qch; **the response to the appeal has been a.** l'appel a été reçu dans l'apathie générale

apathetically [æpə'θetɪklɪ] *adv* avec apathie *ou* indifférence; **to smile a.** faire un sourire apathique

apathy ['æpəθɪ] *n* apathie *f*, indifférence *f*; **an air of a.** un air apathique; **their a. about the issue** leur indifférence à l'égard de ce problème

ape¹ [eɪp] *n* grand singe *m* (sans queue); **the higher apes** les primates *mpl*; *Fig* **he's a big a.** c'est une grande brute; *Sl* **to go a.** (*become angry*) piquer une crise (**over sth/sb** à propos de qch/qn); (*enthuse*) s'emballer (**over sth/sb** pour qch/qn)

ape² *vt* (*imitate*) singer

apelike ['eɪplaɪk] *adj* (*face, appearance, creature*) simiesque; (*noises*) de singe

Apennines (the) [ðiː'æpənaɪnz] *npl* les Apennins *mpl*

aperient [ə'pɪərɪənt] *adj, n Med* laxatif *m*

aperitif [əperɪ'tiːf] *n* apéritif *m*

aperture ['æpətʃər] *n* orifice *f*; (*of lens, diaphragm*) ouverture *f*

apeshit ['eɪpʃɪt] *adv Sl* **to go a.** (*get angry*) piquer une crise

APEX ['eɪpeks] *n* (*abbr* **advance purchase excursion**) APEX *m*; **A. fare** tarif *m* APEX

apex, *pl* **apexes, apices** ['eɪpeks, -ɪz, 'eɪpɪsiːz] *n* (*of triangle, building, mountain*) sommet *m*; *Fig* (*of career*) apogée *m*, sommet *m*; *Sl Hum* **to fall arse over a.** tomber les quatre fers en l'air

aphasia [ə'feɪzɪə] *n Med* aphasie *f*

aphasic [ə'feɪzɪk] *adj, n Med* aphasique *mf*

aphid ['eɪfɪd, 'æfɪd] *n* = **aphis**

aphis, *pl* **-ides** ['eɪfɪs, 'æfɪs, -ɪdiːz] *n* (*insect*) aphis *m*, puceron *m*

aphorism ['æfərɪz(ə)m] *n* aphorisme *m*

aphoristic [æfə'rɪstɪk] *adj* aphoristique

aphrodisiac [æfrəʊ'dɪzɪæk] *adj, n* aphrodisiaque *m*

apiarist ['eɪpɪərɪst] *n* apiculteur, -trice

apiary ['eɪpɪərɪ] *n* rucher *m*
apiculture ['eɪpɪkʌltʃər] *n* apiculture *f*
apiculturist [eɪpɪ'kʌltʃərɪst] *n* apiculteur, -trice
apiece [ə'pi:s] *adv* chacun; **to cost ten pounds a.** (*of things*) coûter dix livres (la) pièce; **he gave them five francs a.** (*to each of them*) il leur donna cinq francs chacun
aplenty [ə'plentɪ] *adv Am F* en abondance
aplomb [ə'plɒm] *n* aplomb *m*; **with great a.** avec un aplomb formidable
apnoea [æp'ni:ə] *n Med* apnée *f*
apocalypse [ə'pɒkəlɪps] *n Rel, Fig* apocalypse *f*; **the four horsemen of the A.** les quatre cavaliers *mpl* de l'Apocalypse
apocalyptic [əpɒkə'lɪptɪk] *adj* apocalyptique
Apocrypha (the) [ðiːə'pɒkrɪfə] *npl Bible* **(a)** les livres *mpl* deutérocanoniques **(b)** (*not in Protestant Bible*) les apocryphes *mpl*
apocryphal [ə'pɒkrɪfəl] *adj* apocryphe; **the story's a.** je doute que l'histoire soit vraie
apogee ['æpədʒi:] *n* (*of career, fame*) apogée *m*
apolitical [eɪpə'lɪtɪk(ə)l] *adj* apolitique
Apollo [ə'pɒləʊ] *n Myth* Apollon *m*
apologetic [əpɒlə'dʒetɪk] *adj* **(a)** (*tone*) d'excuse; (*voice, smile*) désolé, contrit; **to be very a.** se confondre en excuses; **she was quite a. about it** elle a fait beaucoup d'excuses; **he was most a. about the whole affair** il était vraiment désolé de toute cette histoire **(b)** (*book etc*) apologétique
apologetically [əpɒlə'dʒetɪklɪ] *adv* (*in regret*) pour s'excuser, en s'excusant; **she looked/smiled at me a.** elle me regarda/ sourit d'un air contrit
apologize [ə'pɒlədʒaɪz] *vi* s'excuser (**for sth** de qch); **to a. for doing sth** s'excuser d'avoir fait qch; **to a. to sb for sth** s'excuser de qch auprès de qn, faire *ou* présenter des *ou* ses excuses à qn pour qch; **I was wrong, I a.** j'ai eu tort, excusez-moi *ou* je m'excuse; **I a. for having kept you waiting** excusez-moi de vous avoir fait attendre; **I had to a. for you** *or* **your behaviour** j'ai dû demander qu'on excuse ta conduite; **it's him you should be apologizing to** c'est à lui qu'il faut demander pardon, c'est auprès de lui que tu dois t'excuser; **there's no need to a.** vous n'avez pas à vous excuser
apology [ə'pɒlədʒɪ] *n* **(a)** excuses *fpl*; **to make/offer an a.** faire/présenter des excuses; **to make/send one's apologies** faire/envoyer ses excuses; **I owe you an a.** je vous dois des excuses; **by way of an a. (for having ...)** pour s'excuser/ m'excuser/*etc* (d'avoir ...); **will you accept this gift by way of an a.?** accepterez-vous ce cadeau avec mes excuses?; **I got a very handsome a. from them** ils se sont gracieusement excusés; **did you get an a.?** est-ce qu'il s'est/ ils se sont/*etc* excusé(s)?; **letter of a.** lettre *f* d'excuses; *Fig* **an a. for a ...** un/une ... lamentable; **an a. for a dinner** un semblant de dîner
(b) *Lit* (*defence*) apologie *f*, justification *f* (**for** de)
apoplectic [æpə'plektɪk] *adj* (*person*) apoplectique; (*attack*) d'apoplexie; **to be a. (with rage)** s'étrangler de rage; **she was a. when I told her** elle a failli avoir une attaque quand je le lui ai dit
apoplexy ['æpəpleksɪ] *n Med* apoplexie *f*
apostasy [ə'pɒstəsɪ] *n* apostasie *f*
apostate [ə'pɒstət] *adj, n* apostat, -ate
apostatize [ə'pɒstətaɪz] *vi* apostasier
apostle [ə'pɒs(ə)l] *n* (*disciple*), *Fig* apôtre *m*; **the Apostles' Creed** le Symbole des Apôtres; **a. spoon** cuiller *f* avec figurine d'apôtre
apostolic(al) [æpəs'tɒlɪk, -ɪk(ə)l] *adj Rel* (*benediction etc*) apostolique; **a. succession** succession *f* apostolique
apostrophe [ə'pɒstrəfɪ] *n Gram* apostrophe *f*
apostrophize [ə'pɒstrəfaɪz] *vt Liter* apostropher
apothecary [ə'pɒθɪkərɪ] *n Arch* apothicaire *m*
apotheosis, *pl* **-oses** [əpɒθɪ'əʊsɪs, -'əʊsi:z] *n* apothéose *f*
appal, *US* **appall** [ə'pɔ:l] *vt* (*Br* **appals,** *US* **appalls**; *Br, US* **appalled, appalling**) consterner; (*stronger*) choquer, révolter; **to be appalled at** *or* **by sb's behaviour** être choqué par le comportement de qn; **it appals me to think that ...** je suis horrifié à la pensée que ...; **I'm appalled!** ça me scandalise!
Appalachian [æpə'leɪtʃɪən] *adj, n* **the A. Mountains, the Appalachians** les (monts *mpl*) Appalaches *mpl*
appalling [ə'pɔ:lɪŋ] *adj* (*behaviour, conditions, smell etc*) épouvantable, effroyable; **to make an a. row** faire un bruit de tous les diables
appallingly [ə'pɔ:lɪŋlɪ] *adv* **(a)** (*badly*) épouvantablement, effroyablement; (*to cook, play*) effroyablement mal; **he speaks French quite a.** son français est épouvantable *ou* effroyable; **he's a. badly behaved** il se tient tellement mal que c'en est consternant; **to treat sb a.** se conduire épouvantablement mal envers qn **(b)** (*very*) (*ugly, boring, rude etc*) effroyablement; **he's a. stupid** il est d'une stupidité effroyable *ou* extraordinaire
apparatchik [æpə'rɑ:tʃɪk] *n Pol F* apparatchik *m*
apparatus, *pl* **-uses** [æpə'reɪtəs, -əsɪz] *n* (*usu no pl*) appareil *m*, dispositif *m*; **breathing a.** appareil respiratoire; **a piece of a.** un appareil; *Fig* **the a. of the state** l'appareil de l'État; *Liter* **critical a., a. criticus** (*of text*) appareil *ou* apparat *m* critique; *Physiol* **the digestive a.** l'appareil digestif; **laboratory a.** appareils de laboratoire; **mental a.** cellules *fpl* grises; *Gym* **a. work** (gymnastique *f ou* exercices *mpl* aux) agrès *mpl*
apparel [ə'pærəl] *n Arch, Lit, Am* vêtement(s) *m(pl)*
apparent [ə'pærənt] *adj* **(a)** (*clear, obvious*) apparent, manifeste, évident; **to make sth a.** indiquer qch clairement; **his indifference was a.** son indifférence était manifeste; **the truth became a. to her** la vérité lui apparut; **it was a. to me that ...** pour moi il était évident que ...; **as will soon become a.** comme on le verra bientôt **(b)** (*seeming*) apparent; **with a. ease** avec une facilité apparente; **in spite of his a. indifference** malgré son air d'indifférence; *Econ* **a. consumption** consommation *f* apparente
apparently [ə'pærəntlɪ] *adv* apparemment; **a. not** il paraît que non; **he is a. going to Venice** il paraît qu'il va aller à Venise
apparition [æpə'rɪʃən] *n* (*ghost, vision, appearance*) apparition *f*
appeal[1] [ə'pi:l] *n* **(a)** (*call*) appel *m* (**for** à); **to make** *or* **issue an a. for help** lancer un appel au secours; **to make an a. to sb** (*for help, support, money*) lancer un appel auprès de qn; **the president's a. for calm** l'appel au calme du président; **to make an a. to sb's generosity** faire appel à la générosité de qn; **an a. for donations** une demande de contributions; **a charity a.** un appel de la part d'une œuvre de bienfaisance
(b) *Jur* appel *m* (**against** de); **without a.** sans appel; **notice of a.** intimation *f* (d'appel); **to lodge an a.** se pourvoir en appel; **acquitted on a.** acquitté en seconde instance; **Court of A.** cour *f* d'appel; **Supreme Court of A.** cour de cassation; **military a. court** conseil *m* de révision
(c) (*attraction*) attrait *m*, attraction *f*; **to have** *or* **hold little a. for sb** ne guère attirer qn; **to have great a.** (*of thing*) être très attrayant; (*of person*) avoir beaucoup de charme; **to have a narrow a.** (*of music, politician etc*) plaire à peu de gens; **their music has a wide a.** leur musique plaît à toutes sortes de gens; *Com* **sales a.** attraction commerciale
appeal[2] *vi* **(a)** (*make a plea*) **to a. (to sb) for help/money** demander de l'aide/de l'argent (à qn); **I a. to you to ...** je vous supplie de ...; **to a. to sb's generosity** faire appel à la générosité de qn
(b) (*attract, interest*) attirer; **this appealed to his imagination** cela parlait à son imagination; **the plan/idea appeals to me** ce projet/cette idée me plaît *ou* me sourit; **it doesn't a. to me** cela ne me dit rien; **the idea did not a. to him** l'idée ne l'enchantait guère *ou* ne lui disait rien; **to a. to the emotions/the senses** faire appel aux sentiments/aux sens; **styles that a. to the young** modes qui plaisent aux jeunes
(c) *Jur etc* interjeter appel; **to a. against a judgment** appeler d'un jugement; **to a. to another court** en appeler à un autre tribunal, introduire un recours devant un autre tribunal; **to a. against a decision** réclamer contre une décision; *Jur* faire opposition à une décision, faire appel (à un tribunal) d'une décision
Appeal Court *n* cour *f* d'appel
appealing [ə'pi:lɪŋ] *adj* **(a)** (*imploring*) (*look, tone*) suppliant **(b)** (*attractive*) (*personality, person, smile*) sympathique; (*idea, prospect*) séduisant, attrayant; **there's something very a. about him/puppies** il y a quelque chose de très attirant chez lui/les chiots
appealingly [ə'pi:lɪŋlɪ] *adv* **(a)** (*beseechingly*) (*to say*) d'un ton suppliant; (*to look*) d'un air suppliant **(b)** (*attractively*) de façon attrayante
appear [ə'pɪər] *vi* **(a)** (*come into view*) paraître, apparaître, se montrer; (*in accounts, on a list etc*) figurer; **a head appeared at the window** un visage a paru *ou* est apparu *ou* s'est montré à la fenêtre; **a huge lorry suddenly appeared out of the fog** un gros camion a surgi tout à coup du brouillard; **she appeared to him in a dream** elle lui est apparue en rêve; **she only appears at meal times** elle n'apparaît qu'au moment des repas; **where did you a. from?** d'où est-ce que tu sors?; **to a. from nowhere** sortir de nulle part
(b) *Jur* comparaître, paraître; **to a. before a court** comparaître devant un tribunal; **to fail to a.** faire défaut; **failure to a.** défaut *m* de comparution; **to a. for sb** représenter qn; (*of counsel*) plaider pour qn

(c) *Th, Cin* paraître; **to a. on the stage** (*make entrance*) entrer en scène; (*act*) faire du théâtre; **to a. on TV** passer à la télé; *Fig* **that was when I appeared on the scene** c'est à ce moment que je suis arrivé

(d) (*of book, newspaper etc*) paraître, sortir

(e) (*seem*) sembler, paraître; **he appeared to hesitate** il paraissait *ou* semblait hésiter, il avait l'air d'hésiter; **she appears to have a lot of friends** elle semble avoir beaucoup d'amis; **there appears to be a mistake** il semble(rait) qu'il y ait erreur; **it appears not** il semble que non; **it appears to us that the situation is worse** la situation nous semble pire; **to make it a. that ...** faire croire que ...; **to a. to be lost** avoir l'air d'être perdu; **to a. sad** paraître *ou* sembler triste, avoir l'air triste

(f) (*become apparent*) **it appeared later that ...** on a vu par la suite *ou* plus tard que ...; **as appears from these records** comme il ressort de ces pièces

appearance [ə'pɪərəns] *n* **(a)** (*arrival etc*) apparition *f*, arrivée *f*; **they were startled by the a. of a teacher** ils ont été surpris par l'arrivée d'un professeur; **with the a. of fast-food restaurants** avec l'apparition *ou* l'arrivée des fast-foods; **to put in an a.** passer; *Iron* faire acte de présence

(b) (*of actor*) entrée *f* en scène; *Sp* (*of athlete*) entrée sur le terrain de jeu; **first a. of Miss Kane** (*as an actress*) début *m* de Mlle Kane; **to make one's first a.** débuter, faire ses débuts; **her Olympic a.** sa participation aux Jeux Olympiques

(c) *Jur* (*in court*) comparution *f*

(d) (*of book, newspaper etc*) parution *f*

(e) (*looks, demeanour*) apparence *f*, aspect *m*, air *m*; **she had the a. of somebody who had not slept well** elle avait l'air de quelqu'un qui a mal dormi; **from his a. one would say ...** à son air *ou* son extérieur on dirait ...; **you should not judge by appearances** il ne faut pas juger selon les apparences; **his beard gave him the a. of a sailor** avec sa barbe il avait l'air d'un marin; **they gave every a. of being bored** ils ont donné tous les signes possibles de l'ennui; **an a. of gaiety** un air de gaieté; **it is like a mushroom in a.** ça ressemble à un champignon; **at first a.** à première vue; **it has all the appearances of a conspiracy** ça a toutes les apparences d'une conspiration; **appearances are against him** les apparences sont contre lui; **appearances can be deceptive** les apparences peuvent être trompeuses; **to all appearances** selon toute apparence, apparemment; **to keep up appearances** sauver les apparences

appease [ə'piːz] *vt* apaiser; *Pej* endormir; (*anger, hunger*) apaiser, assouvir

appeasement [ə'piːzmənt] *n* **(a)** (*of person*) apaisement *m*; **to aim at the a. of terrorists/one's enemies** chercher à endormir les terroristes/ses ennemis; **policy of a.** politique *f* de conciliation **(b)** (*of anger, hunger etc*) assouvissement *m*

appellant [ə'pelənt] *adj, n Jur* appelant, -ante

appellate [ə'pelət, -leɪt] *adj Jur* (*court*) d'appel

appellation [æpe'leɪʃən] *n Fml* appellation *f*, nom *m*

append [ə'pend] *vt* (*attach*) (*document*) joindre (**to** à); (*in writing*) (*one's signature*) apposer (**to** à); (*notes, comments*) ajouter; *Comptr* (*to database*) ajouter; **to a. a document to a file** annexer *ou* joindre un document à un dossier; *Comptr* **a. mode** mode *m* ajout

appendage [ə'pendɪdʒ] *n Anat, Biol* appendice *m*; **the concert was just an a. to the main events of the day** le concert n'était qu'un prolongement des principaux événements de la journée; **I will not be treated as a mere a. of my husband** je n'existe pas qu'en fonction de mon mari, j'existe aussi par moi-même

appendectomy [æpen'dektəmɪ], **appendicectomy** [æpendɪ'sektəmɪ] *n Surg* appendicectomie *f*

appendicitis [əpendɪ'saɪtɪs] *n Med* appendicite *f*

appendix, *pl* **-ixes, -ices** [ə'pendɪks, -ɪksɪz, -ɪsiːz] *n* (ⓘ**A14,9**) **(a)** *Anat* appendice *m*; **to have one's a. (taken) out** se faire enlever l'appendice; **have you had your a. out?** tu as encore ton appendice?; *Med* **grumbling a.** appendicite *f* chronique **(b)** (*of report etc*) annexe *f*; (*of book*) appendice *m*

appertain [æpə'teɪn] *vi Fml* **(a)** (*belong*) appartenir (**to** à); **lands appertaining to the Crown** terres *fpl* appartenant à *ou* dépendant de la Couronne **(b)** (*of duties, responsibilities*) incomber (**to** à)

appetite ['æpɪtaɪt] *n* **(a)** (*for food*) appétit *m* (**for** pour); **to have a good a.** avoir bon appétit; **to have a poor a.** ne pas avoir beaucoup d'appétit; **to have a big a.** avoir un gros *ou* solide appétit; **to have a small a.** avoir un petit appétit, avoir peu d'appétit; **to take away** *or* **spoil sb's a.** couper l'appétit *ou* la faim à qn; **to give sb an a.** donner de l'appétit à qn, mettre qn en appétit; **the walk gave him an a.** la marche lui a ouvert l'appétit; **loss of a.** manque *m* d'appétit; *Med* inappétence *f*

(b) *Fig* (*for knowledge*) soif *f*; (*for travel, Chinese music etc*) goût *m*; (*for doing sth*) envie *f*; **that whetted his a. for travel** cela a aiguisé son goût des voyages; **a. for revenge** soif *f* de vengeance; **she had an enormous a. for books** elle avait une immense soif de lecture, elle était avide de lecture; **to have little a. for a fight** être peu enclin à une querelle *ou* à se disputer; **sexual a.** appétit *m* sexuel

appetizer ['æpɪtaɪzər] *n Culin, Fig* amuse-gueule *m, pl* amuse-gueule(s)

appetizing ['æpɪtaɪzɪŋ] *adj* (*food, smell*) appétissant, alléchant; *Fig* **he doesn't look very a.** il n'est pas ragoûtant

appetizingly ['æpɪtaɪzɪŋlɪ] *adv* d'une façon appétissante

applaud [ə'plɔːd] **1** *vt* (*performer etc*) applaudir; *Fig* (*decision etc*) applaudir à; **to a. sb's efforts** applaudir aux efforts de qn **2** *vi* (*of audience etc*) applaudir

applause [ə'plɔːz] *n* applaudissements *mpl*; *Fig* (*approval*) approbation *f*; **to meet** *or* **be greeted with a.** (*of performance, decision etc*) être applaudi, soulever les applaudissements; **to win a.** (*of performance, decision etc*) être applaudi (**from** par, de)

apple ['æp(ə)l] *n* pomme *f*; **eating** *or* **dessert a.** pomme à couteau *ou* à dessert; **cooking a.** pomme à cuire; **baked a.** pomme cuite (au four); *Prov* **an a. a day keeps the doctor away** = mangez une pomme par jour et vous resterez en bonne santé; *Fig* **he's/it's/***etc* **the a. of his eye** il y tient comme à la prunelle de ses yeux; *F* **the Big A.** = la ville de New-York; **a. brandy** ≈ calvados *m*; **a. core** trognon *m* de pomme; **a. orchard** pommeraie *f*; *Am F* **a. polisher** lèche-bottes *m*; **a. sauce** compote *f* de pommes

applecart ['æp(ə)lkɑːt] *n Fig* **to upset the a.** tout chambouler

apple green *adj* (*colour*) vert pomme *inv*

applejack ['æp(ə)ldʒæk] *n esp Am* ≈ calvados *m*

apple juice *n* jus *m* de pomme

apple pie *n* (*without top crust*) tarte *f* aux pommes; (*with top crust*) tourte *f* aux pommes; **as American as a.** typiquement américain

apple-pie *adj F* **in a. order** admirablement rangé, parfaitement en ordre; *F* **a. bed** lit *m* en portefeuille

apple tart *n* tarte *f* aux pommes

apple tree *n* pommier *m*

appliance [ə'plaɪəns] *n* **(a)** (*machine*) appareil *m*; **mechanical a.** engin *m* mécanique; **electrical/household appliances** appareils électriques/ménagers **(b)** (*fire engine*) autopompe *f*, pompe *f* à incendie

applicable [ə'plɪkəb(ə)l, 'æplɪkəb(ə)l] *adj* applicable (**to** à); **not a.** (*on form*) sans rapport; **delete where not a.** rayer les mentions inutiles

applicant ['æplɪkənt] *n* **(a)** (*for job*) candidat, -ate (**for** à), postulant *m*; (*for loan, funding, patent*) demandeur *m* (**for** de); *Fin* **a. for shares** souscripteur *m* d'actions **(b)** *Jur* demandeur, -deresse, requérant, -ante

application [æplɪ'keɪʃən] *n* **(a)** (*putting on*) application *f* (**of sth to sth** de qch à *ou* sur qch); *Aut, MecE Fml* **a. of the brake** freinage *m*

(b) (*thing applied*) application *f*; (*of paint*) couche *f*, enduit *m*

(c) (*use*) (*of theory, principle, discovery etc*) application *f*; **practical applications of a process** applications d'un procédé

(d) (*assiduousness*) assiduité *f*, application *f*; **to show a lot of a.** faire preuve d'une grande application *ou* assiduité; **a. to a task** application à un travail

(e) (*for job, help, patent*) demande *f* (**for**, de); (*for job*) candidature *f*; **to submit an a.** (*for help*) faire une demande; (*for job*) présenter sa candidature; **to make an a. for sth** formuler une demande pour obtenir qch; **full details on a.** informations complètes sur demande; *Fin* **a. for shares** demande de titres en souscription; **to make a. for shares** souscrire (à) des actions

(f) *Comptr* application *f*; **a. program** program *m* d'application; **a. software** logiciel *m* d'application

application form *n* formulaire *m* de demande; *Univ etc* formulaire d'inscription; (*for job*) formulaire *ou* (*more detailed*) dossier *m* (de candidature)

applicator ['æplɪkeɪtər] *n* (*for glue, eyeshadow, tampon*) applicateur *m*

applied [ə'plaɪd] *adj* (*maths etc*) appliqué; (*sciences*) expérimental, -aux; **a. psychology** psychotechnique *f*

appliqué [æ'pliːkeɪ] *n Sewing* broderie-application *f*

apply [ə'plaɪ] **1** *vt* **(a)** (*put on*) (*paint, lotion, bandage*) appliquer (**to** sur); (*brake*) actionner; **to a. the brake** freiner; **to a. pressure** exercer une pression; **to a. pressure on sb** faire pression sur qn

(b) (*use*) (*system, theory, experience*) appliquer, mettre en application; **to a. one's mind to sth** s'appliquer à qch; **to a. oneself to one's work** travailler avec application

2 *vi* (a) **to a. to sb for sth** s'adresser *ou* recourir à qn pour obtenir qch; **to a. for a job** faire une demande d'emploi, poser sa candidature à un emploi, *Fml* solliciter *ou* postuler un emploi; **to a. for a grant** faire une demande de bourse; **a. within** s'adresser ici; *Fin* **to a. for shares** souscrire (à) des actions

(b) (*of law, rule, order*) s'appliquer (**to** à); **that applies to all of you!** (*what I've just said*) cela s'adresse à vous tous!

appoint [ə'pɔɪnt] *vt* (a) (*director, etc*) nommer; (*committee*) constituer, nommer; (*heir*) instituer; **to a. sb to a post** nommer *ou* désigner qn à un poste; **to a. sb to do sth** désigner qn pour faire qch; **to a. sb (to be) manager** nommer qn directeur; **newly appointed officials** fonctionnaires *mpl* entrants *ou* nouvellement nommés (b) *Fml* (*time, place*) fixer, désigner; (*day*) arrêter

appointed [ə'pɔɪntɪd] *adj* (a) (*official*) nommé; (*agent*) attitré (b) *Fml* (*agreed*) (*place, hour*) convenu, dit; **on the a. day** le jour convenu *ou* dit (c) **well a. house** maison bien montée *ou* bien agencée *ou* bien installée

appointee [əpɔɪn'tiː] *n* personne *f* nommée; **she was an a. of the President** elle avait été nommée par le Président

appointment [ə'pɔɪntmənt] *n* (a) (*meeting*) (*at doctor's etc*) rendez-vous *m*; (*for business*) rendez-vous, entrevue *f*; **to make an a. with sb** (*for oneself*) donner rendez-vous à qn; (*for sb else*) fixer un rendez-vous avec qn; **I've made an a. with the doctor for you** je t'ai pris un rendez-vous chez le docteur; **please telephone if you cannot make** *or* **keep your a.** veuillez téléphoner s'il vous est impossible de venir à votre rendez-vous; **she didn't keep our** *or* **the a.** elle n'est pas venue au rendez-vous; **I've got an a. with the doctor** j'ai rendez-vous chez le médecin; (*announcing arrival to receptionist*) j'ai rendez-vous avec le médecin; **to meet sb by a.** rencontrer qn sur rendez-vous; **by a. only** sur rendez-vous seulement; **have you got an a.?** avez-vous un rendez-vous?; *Admin* êtes-vous convoqué?; **appointments diary** carnet *m* de rendez-vous, agenda *m*

(b) (*of sb to job*) nomination *f*; *Admin* (*of sb for task*) désignation *f*; *Mil, Naut* (*of sb to unit, ship*) affectation *f*; **he is a popular a.** tout le monde est content de sa nomination *ou* qu'il ait été nommé; **by a. to His/Her Majesty** (*of company, shop etc*) fournisseur breveté *ou* attitré de Sa Majesté; *Journ* **appointments** offres *fpl* d'emploi

(c) *Fml* **appointments** (*of house*) aménagement *m*

apportion [ə'pɔːʃən] *vt* (*expenses, praise*) répartir; (*property*) lotir; **to a. sth to sb** assigner qch à qn; **to a. (out) a sum among several people** partager *ou* distribuer une somme entre plusieurs personnes; **to a. blame** répartir la responsabilité *ou* les responsabilités

apportionment [ɔ'pɔːʃənmənt] *n* (*of taxes, expenses etc*) répartition *f*, partage *m*; (*of rations etc*) allocation *f*; (*of shares, property*) distribution *f*; (*of blame*) répartition

apposite ['æpəzɪt] *adj* approprié (**to** à); (*remark*) (fait) à propos, pertinent; (*observation*) juste

apposition [æpə'zɪʃən] *n* (①**A5**,C,1b; **B4**,B,2,ii] *Gram, Bot etc* apposition *f*; **words in a.** mots apposés *ou* en apposition

appraisal [ə'preɪzəl] *n* (*of standards, personnel*) évaluation *f*; (*of object for insurance purposes etc*) estimation *f*, appréciation *f*; (*before auction*) prisée *f*; **to carry out an a.** conduire une expertise; *Ins* **official a.** (*of object*) expertise *f*; **self a.** autocritique *f*

appraise [ə'preɪz] *vt* estimer, évaluer (**at so much** à tant); (*situation*) évaluer; (*damage*) faire l'expertise de; **to a. the value of sth** estimer *ou* apprécier la valeur de qch; **with an appraising eye** d'un œil critique

appreciable [ə'priːʃɪəb(ə)l] *adj* (*difference, variation, amount, distance*) appréciable, notable; (*change, improvement*) sensible

appreciably [ə'priːʃɪəblɪ] *adv* (*changed, improved, better*) sensiblement

appreciate [ə'priːʃɪeɪt, -sɪeɪt] **1** *vt* (a) (*know the value of, attach importance to*) (*person, thing*) apprécier; **she was never appreciated at her true worth** elle n'a jamais été appréciée à sa juste valeur; **no one appreciates me** personne ne m'apprécie à ma juste valeur; **to a. the value of sb/sth** reconnaître la valeur de qn/qch

(b) (*be grateful for*) être reconnaissant de, être sensible à; **I greatly a. your kindness** je suis très sensible à votre gentillesse; **I a. your having done this** je vous suis reconnaissant d'avoir fait cela; **I a. it** j'en suis reconnaissant; *esp Am* (*thanks*) je vous en remercie

(c) (*grasp, understand*) comprendre, se rendre compte de; **I fully a. (the fact) that …** je me rends bien compte que …; **he doesn't a. his good fortune** il ne se rend pas compte à quel point il a de la chance; **while I a. your predicament …** tout en comprenant bien votre situation difficile …; **we a. the risks/difficulties involved** nous sommes conscients des risques que cela implique/des difficultés que cela comporte; **I hadn't appreciated you needed one** je ne savais pas que vous en aviez besoin d'un

2 *vi* (*of goods, investment etc*) prendre de la valeur; (*of value*) augmenter; (*of currency*) s'apprécier; **the franc has appreciated in terms of other currencies** le franc s'est apprécié par rapport aux autres monnaies

appreciation [əpriːʃɪ'eɪʃən, əpriːsɪ-] *n* (a) (*gratitude*) gratitude *f*, reconnaissance *f*; **as a sign of our a.** en témoignage de notre gratitude *ou* reconnaissance; **I should like to express my a. of your kindness** j'aimerais vous dire combien je suis sensible à votre gentillesse; **in a. of her years of loyal service** pour témoigner de ma/notre/leur/*etc* reconnaissance pour ses années de bons et loyaux services; **the audience showed its a. of the performance by cheering** le public a acclamé le spectacle

(b) (*understanding*) compréhension *f*; **she has no a. of what is involved** elle ne se rend pas compte de ce que ça implique

(c) *Fin* (*increase*) accroissement *m ou* hausse *f* de valeur; **a. of assets** plus-value *f* d'actif

(d) (*review*) critique *f*; **to write an a. of a new play** faire la critique d'une nouvelle pièce

(e) (*evaluation*) (*of object*) appréciation *f*, estimation *f*; **literary a.** explication *f* de texte; **musical a.** appréciation musicale; **a literary/wine a. society** une société d'amateurs de littérature/de vin

appreciative [ə'priːʃɪətɪv, -sɪətɪv] *adj* (a) (*grateful*) reconnaissant; **I'm very a. of all you've done for me** je vous suis reconnaissant de tout ce que vous avez fait pour moi; **she's a very a. sort of person** c'est une personne qui sait faire preuve de reconnaissance *ou* de gratitude; **in a few a. words** avec quelques mots de reconnaissance

(b) (*review, audience*) favorable; (*praising*) élogieux

(c) (*showing liking etc*) **I gave him the present, but he wasn't very a.** je lui ai donné le cadeau, mais il n'a pas beaucoup aimé; **to be a. of music** apprécier la musique

(d) (*showing understanding, awareness*) **to be a. of sth** comprendre l'importance de qch, être sensible à qch; **he was very a. of their problems** il s'est montré très sensible à leurs problèmes

appreciatively [ə'priːʃɪətɪvlɪ, -sɪətɪvlɪ] *adv* (a) (*gratefully*) avec reconnaissance

(b) (*showing understanding, praising*) (*to review etc*) en termes élogieux, favorablement; (*to listen*) avec appréciation; **they clapped a.** ils applaudirent pour montrer leur enthousiasme; **she smiled a. at his joke** elle a aimé l'histoire qui l'a fait sourire; **she smiled a.** (*approving of point made*) elle eut un sourire approbateur; **the performance was received a.** le spectacle a été bien *ou* favorablement reçu

(c) (*showing liking*) **excellent coffee, he said a.** excellent café, dit-il avec plaisir; **a superb brandy, she said a.** un cognac exceptionnel, dit-elle en connaisseuse

apprehend [æprɪ'hend] *vt* (a) *Jur* (*arrest*) appréhender (b) *Fml* (*understand*) (*facts*) comprendre; **as far as I a. it** si je comprends bien (c) *Arch, Lit* (*fear*) (*danger etc*) appréhender, craindre

apprehension [æprɪ'henʃən] *n* (a) (*fear*) appréhension *f*; **to give cause for a.** motiver des craintes (b) *Jur* (*arrest*) appréhension *f*, arrestation *f*

apprehensive [æprɪ'hensɪv] *adj* (*look, smile etc*) timide, craintif; **to be a. for sb/for sb's safety** craindre pour qn/pour la sûreté de qn; **to be a. about sth/doing sth** appréhender qch/de faire qch; **there's nothing to be a. about** il n'y a aucune raison de s'inquiéter; **I'm feeling a bit a.** j'appréhende

apprehensively [æprɪ'hensɪvlɪ] *adv* avec appréhension

apprentice[1] [ə'prentɪs] *n* apprenti, -ie; **carpenter's/plumber's a., a. carpenter/plumber** apprenti menuisier/plombier; **sorcerer's a.** apprenti sorcier

apprentice[2] *vt* **to a. sb to sb** placer *ou* mettre qn en apprentissage chez qn

apprenticed [ə'prentɪst] *adj* en apprentissage (**to sb** chez qn)

apprenticeship [ə'prentɪʃɪp] *n* apprentissage *m*; **to serve an a.** faire un apprentissage; *Fig* **to serve one's a.** faire ses débuts

apprise [ə'praɪz] *vt Fml* **to a. sb of sth** apprendre qch à qn, prévenir *ou* informer qn de qch; **we were not apprised of his arrival** nous n'avons pas été informés de son arrivée

appro ['æprəʊ] *n Com F* **on a.** à l'essai

approach[1] [ə'prəʊtʃ] *n* (a) (*coming*) (*of person*) approche *f*; (*of spring*) venue *f*; (*of night*) tombée *f*; (*of death*) approche(s); **I could hear his a.** je l'entendais s'approcher; *Av* **a. end of the runway** entrée *f* de piste, seuil *m* de la piste; *Av* **a. aids** moyens *mpl* d'approche

(b) (*method*) méthode *f*, démarche *f*; **let's try a different a.** essayons une autre méthode; **her a. to the problem** sa façon d'aborder le problème; **I don't like her a.** je n'aime pas sa façon de s'y prendre

(c) *Fig* (*to person*) avance *f*, ouverture *f*; (*for business purposes*) proposition *f*, ouverture; **to make an a. to sb** faire une proposition à qn

(d) (*point of entry*) voie *f* d'accès; **the a. to a town** les abords *mpl ou* les approches *fpl* d'une ville; **all approaches to the town have been sealed off** tous les abords de la ville ont été bouclés; **a. to a harbour** atterrage *m*, accès *m* d'un port

(e) (*approximation*) **a. to an apology/a smile** semblant *m* d'excuse/de sourire; **it is the nearest a. to perfection** c'est ce qui s'approche le plus de la perfection

approach² 1 *vi* approcher, s'approcher; *Golf* jouer le coup d'approche; **Christmas/spring is approaching** Noël/le printemps approche

2 *vt* (a) (*get nearer to*) approcher; (*place*) approcher de; **the town can only be approached from the north** on ne peut accéder à *ou* gagner la ville que par le nord; **I'm approaching forty-five** je vais sur mes quarante-cinq ans; **the wind was approaching gale force** le vent soufflait presque en tempête; **something approaching a feeling of relief** un sentiment proche du soulagement

(b) (*go up to*) (*sb*) s'approcher de, aborder, approcher; (*of company, group, team*) pressentir, faire des propositions *ou* des ouvertures à; **I was approached by a man in the street** j'ai été abordé par un homme dans la rue; **to a. sb on the subject of ...** approcher qn au sujet de ...; **to be easy/difficult to a.** avoir l'abord facile/difficile

(c) (*question*) aborder, s'attaquer à; **she approaches the issue from the angle of ...** elle aborde la question du point de vue de ...

approachable [ə'prəʊtʃəb(ə)l] *adj* (a) (*person*) d'un abord facile, abordable (b) (*building, place*) accessible

approaching [ə'prəʊtʃɪŋ] *adj* (*death*) prochain; (*storm*) qui arrive; **the a. war ...** la guerre qui approche/approchait ...; **the a. car** (*from opposite direction to one's own*) la voiture qui vient/venait en sens inverse

approach shot *n Golf* coup *m* d'approche

approbation [æprə'beɪʃən] *n* approbation *f*; **smile of a.** sourire *m* approbateur

appropriate¹ [ə'prəʊprɪət] *adj* (*suitable, fitting*) approprié (**to** à); (*word, expression*) juste; (*clothes*) convenable (**to** à); (*name, site*) bien choisi; (*music*) de circonstance; (*moment*) opportun; **to take a. action** prendre les mesures indiquées; **he could have chosen a more a. time and place** il aurait pu choisir un moment et un endroit plus appropriés (**to** pour); **it seemed a. that she should have died in a theatre** cela semblait être dans l'ordre des choses qu'elle soit morte dans un théâtre

appropriate² [ə'prəʊprɪeɪt] *vt* (a) (*take*) s'approprier, s'emparer de; (*keep for oneself*) s'attribuer, se destiner, se réserver; **to a. sb's ideas** s'approprier les idées de qn (b) (*set aside*) (*money, funds*) affecter, destiner (**for a purpose** à une destination)

appropriately [ə'prəʊprɪətlɪ] *adv* (*suitably*) de manière appropriée; (*properly*) convenablement, proprement; **a. dressed** en tenue convenable

appropriateness [ə'prəʊprɪətnɪs] *n* (*of behaviour*) correction *f*, bienséance *f*; (*of remarks*) justesse *f*, à-propos *m*

appropriation [əprəʊprɪ'eɪʃən] *n* (a) (*taking*) appropriation *f*, prise *f* de possession (**of** de) (b) (*setting aside*) (*of money for specific purpose*) application *f*, affectation *f* (c) *Fin* affectation *f* de fonds; (*of sum*) attribution *f*; *Pol* crédit *m* (budgétaire)

approval [ə'pruːv(ə)l] *n* (a) approbation *f*, assentiment *m*, *Fml* agrément *m*; (*of dealer, distributor*) agrément; **to meet with sb's a.** recevoir *ou* obtenir l'approbation de qn; **gesture** *or* **sign of a.** geste *m ou* signe *m* d'approbation; **to nod a.** approuver d'un signe de (la) tête (b) *Com* **on a.** à condition, à l'essai; **book sent on a.** livre envoyé à l'examen (c) (*of document, proposal*) ratification *f*, homologation *f*; **for (your) a.** (*of draft letter*) pour approbation

approve [ə'pruːv] 1 *vt* (*action*) approuver, sanctionner; (*decision, proposal*) ratifier, homologuer; (*contract, dealer, distributer*) agréer; **read and approved** lu et approuvé; **approved by the government** agréé par l'État 2 *vi* être d'accord; **I told her what I had done and she seemed to a.** je lui ai dit ce que j'avais fait et elle a eu l'air de m'approuver

▶ **approve of** *vipo* approuver; **I don't a. of your friends** tes amis ne me plaisent pas; **I don't a. of the plan** je ne suis pas d'accord avec ce projet; **she doesn't a. of them smoking** ça ne lui plaît pas qu'ils fument

approved [ə'pruːvd] *adj* approuvé, agréé; *Admin* (**officially**) **a.** homologué; **a. dealer** concessionnaire *m* agréé; **a. stallion** étalon *m* autorisé

approved school *n Br Formerly* maison *f* de redressement

approving [ə'pruːvɪŋ] *adj* (*look, smile*) approbateur, -trice

approvingly [ə'pruːvɪŋlɪ] *adv* (*to look*) d'un air approbateur; (*to say*) d'un ton approbateur; (*to react*) avec approbation

approx *abbr* **approximately**

approximate¹ [ə'prɒksɪmɪt] *adj* (a) [①B56,C,3] (*calculation etc*) approximatif, approché; **a. value** valeur *f* approximative (b) *Biol, Phys* rapproché, proche, voisin

approximate² [ə'prɒksɪmeɪt] 1 *vt* **to a. sth in size/cost** se rapprocher de qch par les dimensions/le prix 2 *vi* **to a. in size/cost to sth** se rapprocher de qch par les dimensions/le prix; **to a. to the truth** se rapprocher de la vérité

approximately [ə'prɒksɪmətlɪ] *adv* approximativement, à peu près; **five miles are a. eight kilometres** cinq mil(l)es valent à peu près huit kilomètres; **his income is a. £15,000** son revenu est d'environ quinze mille livres

approximation [əprɒksɪ'meɪʃən] *n* approximation *f*; **his statement was no more than an a. of the truth** sa déclaration n'était qu'un semblant de vérité

appurtenance [ə'pɜːtɪnəns] *n* (*usu pl*) **appurtenances** accessoires *mpl*; *Jur* **house with all its appurtenances** immeuble avec ses appartenances et dépendances

APR [eɪpiː'ɑːr] *n* (*abbr* **annual percentage rate**) TEG *m*

après-ski [æpreɪ'skiː] *n* distractions *fpl* après le ski

apricot ['eɪprɪkɒt] *n* (a) abricot *m*; **a. tree** abricotier *m*; **a. yogurt/ice-cream** yaourt *m*/glace *f* à l'abricot; **a. jam** confiture *f* d'abricots; **a. tart** tarte *f* aux abricots (b) (*colour*) abricot *m inv*; **a. dress** robe (couleur) abricot

April ['eɪprɪl] *n* [①A75-6,B-C; B58-9,B-C] avril *m*; **in A.** en avril, au mois d'avril; **A. showers** ≈ giboulées *fpl* de mars; **A. Fool's Day** le premier avril; **to make an A. fool of sb** faire un poisson d'avril à qn; **A. fool!** poisson d'avril!

a priori ['eɪpraɪ'ɔːraɪ, ɑːprɪ'ɔːrɪ] *adv, adj* a priori

apron ['eɪprən] *n* (a) (*clothing*) tablier *m*; *Fig* **to be tied to one's mother's a. strings** être pendu aux jupons de sa mère (b) *Th* **a. (stage)** avant-scène *f*, *pl* avant-scènes (c) *Av* aire *f* de manœuvre *ou* de stationnement; (*for plane maintenance and repair*) tablier *m*, aire en dur

apropos ['æprəpəʊ] 1 *adj* (*remark*) opportun, pertinent 2 *prep* **a. (of)** à propos de

apse [æps] *n* (*in church*) abside *f*

apt¹ [æpt] *adj* (a) (*word*) juste; (*expression*) heureux, qui convient; (*description*) parlant; **it is very a. that it should end in this way** il est tout à fait approprié que cela se termine de cette manière (b) **to be a. to do sth** (*of person, thing*) avoir tendance à faire qch (c) (*student etc*) intelligent, doué; **to be a. at languages** être doué en *ou* pour les langues

apt² *Am* (*abbr* **apartment**) appt

aptitude ['æptɪtjuːd] *n* aptitude *f* (**for** à, pour); **to show great a.** montrer de grandes dispositions; **to have an a. for science** avoir une aptitude pour la science, avoir des dispositions scientifiques; **to have no a. for French** n'avoir aucune facilité pour le français

aptitude test *n* test *m* d'aptitude, test d'intelligence pratique

aptly ['æptlɪ] *adv* (*to say, comment*) avec justesse, à propos; (*described*) justement; **a. chosen name** nom bien choisi

aptness ['æptnɪs] *n* (a) (*appropriateness*) (*of expression, quotation etc*) justesse *f*, à-propos *m* (b) (*tendency*) tendance *f* (**to do sth** à faire qch)

aqualung ['ækwəlʌŋ] *n* scaphandre *m* autonome

aquamarine [ækwəmə'riːn] 1 *n* (*gem*) aigue-marine *f*, *pl* aigues-marines 2 *adj* (*dress etc*) bleu vert *inv*

aquanaut ['ækwənɔːt] *n* aquanaute *mf*

aquaplane¹ ['ækwəpleɪn] *n Sp* aquaplane *m*

aquaplane² *vi Sp* faire de l'aquaplane; *Aut* faire de l'aquaplaning

aquaplaning ['ækwəpleɪnɪŋ] *n Sp* aquaplane *m*; *Aut* aquaplaning *m*, effet *m* d'hydroglisseur

aquarelle [ækwə'rel] *n Art* aquarelle *f*

aquarium, *pl* **-iums, -ia** [ə'kweərɪəm, -ɪəmz, -ɪə] *n* aquarium *m*

Aquarius [ə'kweərɪəs] *n Astron* le Verseau; **to be (an) A.** être (du) Verseau

aquatic [ə'kwætɪk] *adj* (*plant etc*) aquatique; **a. display** numéro *m* aquatique; **a. sports** sports *mpl* nautiques

aquatics [ə'kwætɪks] *npl* [①A10,c] sports *mpl* nautiques

aquatint ['ækwətɪnt] *n* aquatinte *f*

aqueduct ['ækwɪdʌkt] *n* aqueduc *m*

aqueous ['eɪkwɪəs] *adj* aqueux; **a. humour** (*in eye*) humeur *f* aqueuse; *Pharm* **a. solution** soluté *m*

aquilegia [ækwɪ'liːdʒɪə] *n* (*plant*) aquilégie *f*

aquiline ['ækwɪlaɪn] *adj* aquilin; **a. nose** nez *m* aquilin *ou* busqué *ou* en bec d'aigle

Arab [ˈærəb] [ⓘA20-21,d] **1** *adj* **(a)** arabe; **the A. world** le monde arabe; *Pol* **the A. League** la Ligue arabe **(b)** (*horse*) arabe **2** *n* **(a)** (*person*) Arabe *mf* **(b)** (*horse*) arabe *m*
arabesque [ærəˈbesk] **1** *adj Art* (*decoration*) de style arabe **2** *n* **(a)** (*usu pl*) *Art* arabesque *f* **(b)** (*in ballet*) arabesque *f*
Arabia [əˈreɪbɪə] *n* Arabie *f*
Arabian [əˈreɪbɪən] [ⓘA20-21,d] **1** *adj* arabe **the A. Gulf** le golfe Arabique; *Liter* **the A. Nights** les Mille et Une Nuits; **the A. Peninsula** la péninsule d'Arabie **2** *n* (*from Arabia*) Arabe *mf*
Arabic [ˈærəbɪk] [ⓘA20-21,d] **1** *adj* (*language, literature*) arabe; **A. numerals** chiffres *mpl* arabes; **A. scholar** arabisant, -ante **2** *n Ling* arabe *m*
Arabist [ˈærəbɪst] *n* arabisant, -ante
arable [ˈærəb(ə)l] *adj* (*land*) arable
arachnid [əˈræknɪd] *n Zool* arachnide *m*
Aramaic [ærəˈmeɪɪk] *adj, n Ling* araméen *m*
arbiter [ˈɑːbɪtər] *n* (*of fashion etc*) arbitre *m*; **a. of taste** arbitre des élégances
arbitrage [ˈɑːbɪtrɑːʒ] *n Fin, St Exch* arbitrage *m*
arbitrager [ˈɑːbɪtrɑːʒər] *n Fin, St Exch* arbitragiste *m*
arbitrarily [ˈɑːbɪtreərəlɪ] *adv* arbitrairement
arbitrariness [ˈɑːbɪtrərɪnɪs] *n* (*of decision etc*) caractère *m* arbitraire
arbitrary [ˈɑːbɪtrərɪ] *adj* (*decision etc*) arbitraire
arbitrate [ˈɑːbɪtreɪt] **1** *vt* (*dispute*) arbitrer, trancher **2** *vi* arbitrer **(between** entre)
arbitration [ɑːbɪˈtreɪʃən] *n* arbitrage *m*; **to go to a.** (*of union*) soumettre le différend à l'arbitrage; (*of dispute*) être soumis à l'arbitrage; **to refer a question to a.** soumettre une question à un arbitrage; **a. board** commission *f* d'arbitrage; **a. clause** clause *f* compromissoire; **a. committee** commission *f* d'arbitrage; **a. court** tribunal *m* arbitral; **a. ruling** décision *f* arbitrale; **a. tribunal** tribunal *m* arbitral
arbitrator [ˈɑːbɪtreɪtər] *n* médiateur, -trice; *Jur* arbitre *m*
arbor *n US* = **arbour**
arboreal [ɑːˈbɔːrɪəl] *adj* **(a)** (*relating to trees*) d'arbre(s) **(b)** (*living in trees*) (*animal*) arboricole; (*existence*) dans les arbres
arboriculture [ˈɑːbərɪkʌltʃər] *n* arboriculture *f*
arbour, *US* **arbor** [ˈɑːbər] *n* berceau *m* de verdure, charmille *f*; (*on trellis*) tonnelle *f*; **vine a.** treille *f*
arbutus [ɑːˈbjuːtəs] *n* (*shrub*) arbousier *m*
arc¹ [ɑːk] *n Math etc* (*of circle etc*) arc *m*; **to describe an a.** décrire un arc; *Mil* **a. of fire** (*of cannon etc*) champ *m* de tir; **a. lamp** *or* **light** lampe *f ou* projecteur *m* à arc
arc² *vi* (**arcing** [ˈɑːkɪŋ]; **arced** [ɑːkt]) *El* faire jaillir un arc, amorcer l'arc
arcade [ɑːˈkeɪd] *n* (*covered passageway*) passage *m* (couvert); (*for shopping*) galerie *f* (marchande)
Arcadia [ɑːˈkeɪdɪə] *n* Arcadie *f*
Arcadian [ɑːˈkeɪdɪən] **1** *adj* arcadien **2** *n* Arcadien, -ienne
arcane [ɑːˈkeɪn] **1** *adj* mystérieux, ésotérique; (*knowledge, practice, ritual*) secret **2** *n* **the a.** le mystérieux
arch¹ [ɑːtʃ] *n* **(a)** *Archit, Constr* voûte *f*, arc *m*; *Constr* (*of bridge, viaduct*) arche *f*; **a. of a vault** arceau *m* d'une voûte; **a. stone** voussoir *m* **(b)** *Anat* (*of foot*) cambrure *f*, voûte *f* plantaire; **to have fallen arches** avoir les pieds plats; **a. support** (*in shoes*) cambrure
arch² **1** *vt* (*one's back*) arquer, courber; **the cat arches its back** le chat fait le dos rond **2** *vi* former une voûte
arch³ *adj* (*mischievous*) espiègle, malicieux
arch⁴ **1** *adj* (*great*) grand; **a. enemy** adversaire *m ou* ennemi *m* numéro un; **a. traitor** traître *m* insigne, architraître *m* **2** *pref* archi-
archaeological, *US* **archeological** [ɑːkɪəˈlɒdʒɪk(ə)l] *adj* archéologique
archaeologically, *US* **archeologically** [ɑːkɪəˈlɒdʒɪklɪ] *adv* archéologiquement
archaeologist, *US* **archeologist** [ɑːkɪˈɒlədʒɪst] *n* archéologue *mf*
archaeology, *US* **archeology** [ɑːkɪˈɒlədʒɪ] *n* archéologie *f*
archaic [ɑːˈkeɪɪk] *adj* archaïque
archaism [ˈɑːkeɪɪz(ə)m] *n* archaïsme *m*
archangel [ˈɑːkeɪndʒ(ə)l] *n* archange *m*
archbishop [ɑːtʃˈbɪʃəp] *n* archevêque *m*; **a.'s palace** palais *m* archiépiscopal
archbishopric [ɑːtʃˈbɪʃəprɪk] *n* archevêché *m*
archdeacon [ɑːtʃˈdiːk(ə)n] *n* archidiacre *m*
archdiocese [ɑːtʃˈdaɪəsɪs, -siːz] *n* archidiocèse *m*, archevêché *m*
archduchess [ɑːtʃˈdʌtʃɪs] *n* archiduchesse *f*
archduchy [ɑːtʃˈdʌtʃɪ] *n* archiduché *m*
archduke [ɑːtʃˈdjuːk] *n* archiduc *m*
arched [ɑːtʃt] *adj Archit* (*roof*) voûté; **a. window** (*semicircular*) fenêtre cintrée; (*pointed*) fenêtre en arc brisé
archeological, archeologically *etc US* = **archaeological, archaeologically** *etc*
archer [ˈɑːtʃər] *n Mil, Sp* archer *m*
archery [ˈɑːtʃərɪ] *n* tir *m* à l'arc
archetypal [ɑːkɪˈtaɪp(ə)l] *adj* **the a. English village** l'archétype *m* du village anglais
archetype [ˈɑːkɪtaɪp] *n* archétype *m*
archiepiscopal [ɑːkɪɪˈpɪskəp(ə)l] *adj* archiépiscopal, -aux
Archimedes [ɑːkɪˈmiːdiːz] *n* Archimède *m*; *Phys* **Archimedes' principle** principe *m* d'Archimède; **Archimedes' screw** vis *f* d'Archimède
archipelago, *pl* **-o(e)s** [ɑːkɪˈpeləgəʊ, -əʊz] *n Geog* archipel *m*
architect [ˈɑːkɪtekt] *n also Fig* architecte *mf*; **naval a.** ingénieur *m* des constructions navales *ou* du génie maritime; **to be the a. of one's own downfall** être l'artisan de sa propre ruine
architectural [ɑːkɪˈtektʃər(ə)l] *adj* architectural
architecturally [ɑːkɪˈtektʃərəlɪ] *adv* du point de vue de l'architecture
architecture [ˈɑːkɪtektʃər] *n Constr, Comptr* architecture *f*
architrave [ˈɑːkɪtreɪv] *n Archit* architrave *f*
archive¹ [ˈɑːkaɪv] *n* (*usu pl*) **archives** archives *fpl*; **we'll be showing film from the archives** nous présenterons des extraits d'archives; *Comptr* **a. copy** copie *f* archivée; *Comptr* **archiving facility** fonction *f* d'archivage; **a. footage** extraits *mpl* d'archives; **a. librarian** archiviste *mf*; **a. material** matériel *m* d'archives
archive² *vt* mettre aux archives; *Comptr* archiver
archivist [ˈɑːkɪvɪst] *n* archiviste *mf*
archly [ˈɑːtʃlɪ] *adv* d'un air espiègle *ou* malicieux; (*to say*) d'un ton espiègle *ou* malicieux
archness [ˈɑːtʃnɪs] *n* espièglerie *f*, malice *f*
archway [ˈɑːtʃweɪ] *n* (*entry*) porte *f* cintrée, voûte *f* d'entrée
arctic [ˈɑːktɪk] **1** *adj* (*territory, circle, expedition etc*) arctique **2** *n* **the A.** l'Arctique *m*; **an expedition to the A.** une expédition dans l'Arctique
arc-weld *vt Tech* souder à l'arc (électrique)
arc-welding *n Tech* soudure *f* à l'arc
ardent [ˈɑːd(ə)nt] *adj* (*desire, love*) passionné, ardent; (*admirer, believer*) fervent
ardently [ˈɑːd(ə)ntlɪ] *adv* ardemment
ardour, *US* **ardor** [ˈɑːdər] *n* (*of passion, desire*) ardeur *f*; (*religious*) ferveur *f*
arduous [ˈɑːdjʊəs] *adj* (*path, task*) ardu, pénible
arduously [ˈɑːdjʊəslɪ] *adv* péniblement
arduousness [ˈɑːdjʊəsnɪs] *n* difficulté *f*
are *see* **be**
area [ˈeərɪə] *n* **(a)** (*of circle, field, room etc*) superficie *f*, aire *f*; (*of floor*) surface *f*; **the room has an a. of 24 square metres** *or* **is 24 square metres in a.** la pièce a une superficie de 24 mètres carrés, la superficie de la pièce est de 24 mètres carrés; **surface a.** surface *f*
(b) (*region*) territoire *m*, région *f*; (*of town*) zone *f*, quartier *m*; (*of lung, brain, diskette, surface*) zone; (*part of office, hall, playground etc*) espace *m*; (*of influence etc*) périmètre *m*; *Fig* (*of knowledge, research*) domaine *m*; **a. of competence** domaine de compétence; **a. of coverage** (*of satellite*) zone de couverture; **a. of expertise** domaine de compétence; **a. of operations** branche *f* d'activité; **residential a.** (*in town*) quartier résidentiel; **industrial/suburban a.** zone industrielle/suburbaine; **A. of Outstanding Natural Beauty** (*in tourism*) réserve *f* classée pour sa beauté naturelle; **houses were searched over a wide a.** on a fouillé les maisons sur un large périmètre; **cotton (growing)/mining a.** région du coton/minière; **customs a.** territoire douanier; **currency a.** zone monétaire; **the Manchester a.** la région de Manchester; **the Greater London a.** l'agglomération *f* londonienne, le grand Londres; **a. of agreement** terrain *m* d'entente; *Fig* **problem a.** domaine problématique; **growth a.** secteur *m* de croissance; *Mil etc* **forward a.** zone de l'avant, zone avancée; **prohibited** *or* **restricted a.** zone prohibée; *Comptr* **storage a.** zone de mémoire; *Aut* **parking a.** parking *m*; **service a.** (*on motorway*) relais *m* d'autoroute; **play a.** (*in park*) aire *f* de jeu; **dining a.** (*in living room*) coin *m* salle à manger; (*in kitchen*) coin-repas *m*
area bombing *n* bombardement *m* sur zone
area director *n* directeur *m* régional
area manager *n* (*of company*) gestionnaire *mf* de région *ou* de secteur, directeur, -trice régional(e)
area rug *n US* tapis *m*, *Can* carpette *f*
areaway [ˈeərɪəweɪ] *n Am* (*courtyard*) cour *f* d'entrée en sous sol; **a. steps** escalier *m* de service (*du sous-sol*)
areca [ˈærɪkə] *n Bot* **a. nut** noix *f* d'arec; **a. palm (tree)** aréquier *m*

arena, *pl* **-as** [ə'ri:nə, -əz] *n* (*bullring etc*) arène *f*; *Fig* (*economic, international etc*) scène *f*; *Fig* **the political a.** l'arène politique; *Fig* **to enter the a.** entrer dans l'arène
aren't [ɑ:nt] **(a)** = **are not,** *see* **be (b) a. I?** = **am I not?,** *see* **be**
Argentina [ɑ:dʒən'ti:nə] *n* Argentine *f*
Argentine ['ɑ:dʒəntaɪn] **1** *adj* argentin **2** *n* **(a) the A.** l'Argentine *f* **(b)** (*person*) Argentin, -ine
Argentinian [ɑ:dʒən'tɪnɪən] **1** *adj* argentin **2** *n* Argentin, -ine
argon ['ɑ:gɒn] *n Ch* argon *m*
Argonaut ['ɑ:gənɔ:t] *n* **(a)** *Myth* Argonaute *m* **(b) a.** (*mollusc*) voilier *m*, argonaute *m*
argot ['ɑ:gəʊ] *n* argot *m*
arguable ['ɑ:gjʊəb(ə)l] *adj* **(a)** (*open to discussion*) discutable, contestable; **that's a.** c'est discutable; **it is a. whether it would have made any difference** on peut se demander si cela aurait changé quelque chose **(b)** (*capable of being maintained*) (*theory*) défendable; **it is a. that they didn't need our help** il est possible de soutenir qu'ils aient pu se passer de notre aide
arguably ['ɑ:gjʊəblɪ] *adv* **it's a. the city's best restaurant** on peut dire que c'est le meilleur restaurant de la ville
argue ['ɑ:gju:] **1** *vt* **(a)** (*debate*) discuter; (*question*) débattre; **she argued the case well** elle a bien débattu la question; **he argued the case for lower taxes** il a plaidé en faveur d'une baisse des impôts
(b) (*put a case*) **to a. that ...** soutenir *ou* maintenir que ... + *ind*
(c) *Fig* (*of fact etc*) (*existence of ancient civilization etc*) témoigner de, révéler
2 *vi* **(a)** (*debate*) discuter (**with sb about sth** avec qn de qch); (*quarrel*) se disputer (**with sb about sth** avec qn à propos de qch); **I'm not going to a. about it** (*I refuse to discuss it*) je ne veux pas en discuter; **to a. about politics** discuter (de) politique; **those two are always arguing** ces deux-là sont toujours à se disputer; **he's always arguing** c'est un argumentateur; **don't a.!** pas de discussion!; **they're always arguing about whose turn it is to do the washing-up** ils sont toujours à se disputer pour savoir qui va faire la vaisselle
(b) (*put a case*) plaider; **all this argues in his favour** tout ceci plaide *ou* témoigne en sa faveur
▶ **argue against** *vipo* plaider contre
▶ **argue away 1** *vtsep* (*make disappear*) nier l'importance de **2** *vi* **they've been arguing away for hours** (*quarrelling*) ils se disputent depuis des heures; (*discussing*) ils discutent depuis des heures
▶ **argue for** *vipo* plaider pour *ou* en faveur de
▶ **argue out** *vtsep* (*settle by argument*) résoudre par le débat; **I'll leave you to a. it out between you** je vous laisse résoudre la question *ou* le problème entre vous
arguing ['ɑ:gju:ɪŋ] *n* argumentation *f*; **that's enough a.** assez discuté; *F* **and no a.!** pas de discussion!
argument ['ɑ:gjʊmənt] *n* **(a)** (*debate*) discussion *f*, débat *m*; (*quarrel*) dispute *f*; **to have an a. about sth** (*debate*) discuter de *ou* sur qch; (*quarrel*) se disputer à propos de qch; **I don't want to have an a. about it** je ne veux pas qu'on se dispute pour ça; **to get into an a.** se disputer (**with sb** avec qn; **about sth/sb** à propos de qch/qn); **to get the best of an a.** l'emporter dans une discussion; **to obey without a.** obéir sans discuter
(b) (*reasoning, case*) argument *m* (**for** en faveur de; **against** contre); **that is another a. for dismissing him** c'est une raison de plus pour le congédier; **to follow sb's (line of) a.** suivre le raisonnement de qn; **suppose for a.'s sake that** ... supposons à titre d'exemple que ... + *sub*
(c) *Lit* (*of work*) argument *m*
argumentative [ɑ:gjʊ'mentətɪv] *adj* (*person*) raisonneur, disposé à argumenter *ou* à disputailler; (*tone*) polémique, agressif; **don't be so a.** arrête de faire le raisonneur
Argy ['ɑ:dʒɪ] *n Br Offensive Sl* Argentin, -ine
argy-bargy ['ɑ:dʒɪ'bɑ:dʒɪ] *n Br F* chamailleries *fpl*
aria ['ɑ:rɪə] *n Mus* aria *f*
arid ['ærɪd] *adj* (*land, subject*) aride
aridity [ə'rɪdɪtɪ], **aridness** ['ærɪdnɪs] *n* aridité *f*
Aries ['eəri:z] *n Astrol* le Bélier; **to be (an) A.** être (du) Bélier
aright [ə'raɪt] *adv Arch, Lit* bien, juste; **to put** *or* **set things a.** redresser la situation
arise [ə'raɪz] *vi* (**arose** [ə'rəʊz]; **arisen** [ə'rɪz(ə)n]) **(a)** (*come about*) (*of situation, deficit*) se produire; (*of problem*) surgir, survenir, se présenter; (*of storm*) se lever; **if complications a.** s'il survient des complications; **if the need arises** si besoin est; **the question has not yet arisen** la question ne s'est pas encore posée; **should the occasion a.** le cas échéant
(b) (*result*) émaner, provenir, résulter (**from** de); **obligations that a. from a clause** obligations qui émanent d'une clause
(c) *Lit* (*of person*) s'élever; **a prophet arose** un prophète surgit *ou* se révéla; **a., Sir John!** (*in knighthood ceremony*) relevez-vous, Sir John; *Bible* **to a. from the dead** ressusciter (des morts)
aristocracy [ærɪs'tɒkrəsɪ] *n* (*nobility*) aristocratie *f*; *Fig* **the a. of the fashion world** le gratin de la mode
aristocrat ['ærɪstəkræt, ə'rɪs-] *n* aristocrate *mf*
aristocratic [ærɪstə'krætɪk] *adj* aristocratique
aristocratically [ærɪstə'krætɪklɪ] *adv* aristocratiquement
Aristotelian [ærɪstɒ'ti:lɪən] *adj Phil* aristotélicien
Aristotle ['ærɪstɒt(ə)l] *n* Aristote *m*
arithmetic [ə'rɪθmətɪk] *n* [①**A71**,7; **B56**,**C**,4] (*calculations*) calcul *m*; (*subject*) arithmétique *f*; **my a. is absolutely appalling** je suis nul en calcul; **your a. is spot on** tes calculs tombent pile; **it's a simple question of a.** les chiffres parlent d'eux-mêmes; **the a. is against a Labour victory** mathématiquement, les Travaillistes ont peu de chances de gagner; *Sch* **a. book** livre *m* d'arithmétique
arithmetic(al) [ærɪθ'metɪk, -ɪk(ə)l] *adj* arithmétique; **a. mistakes** *or* **errors** des erreurs *fpl* de calcul
arithmetically [ærɪθ'metɪklɪ] *adv* arithmétiquement
Ariz *abbr* **Arizona**
Ark *abbr* **Arkansas**
ark [ɑ:k] *n* **(a)** arche *f*; *F* **it looked like it had come out of the a.** il avait l'air vieux comme Hérode **(b)** *Jewish Rel* **the A. of the Covenant** l'Arche *f* d'alliance
arm¹ [ɑ:m] *n* **(a)** (*of person*) bras *m*; **upper a.** haut *m* du bras, arrière-bras *m inv*; **to carry a child in one's arms** porter un enfant dans ses bras; **to hold sb in one's arms** tenir qn dans ses bras; **to carry sth under one's a.** porter qch sous le bras; **to carry a basket over** *or* **on one's a.** porter un panier au bras; **with a girl on his a.** une fille à son bras; **to walk a. in a.** marcher bras dessus bras dessous; **give me your a.** donne-moi le *ou* ton bras; **to hold out one's arms** (*in front*) tendre les bras; (*to sides*) lever les bras; **to receive sb with open arms** recevoir qn à bras ouverts; **to keep sb at a.'s length** tenir qn à distance
(b) (*of dress etc*) manche *f*; (*of chair*) accoudoir *m*, bras *m*; (*of sea, river, lever*) bras; **(pick-up) a.** (*on record player*) bras de lecture; *Fig* **the secular a.** le bras séculier; *Fig* **the long a. of the law** l'autorité de la loi, *F* le représentant de la loi
(c) *Mil* (*branch*) arme *f*
arm² **1** *vt* **(a)** (*person, regiment, fortified place*) armer; **to a. oneself with an umbrella** s'armer *ou* se nantir d'un parapluie; *Lit* **to a. oneself with patience** s'armer de patience **(b)** (*bomb, rocket, torpedo, mine*) armer **2** *vi* s'armer, prendre les armes; **the country was arming for war** le pays s'armait pour la guerre
armada [ɑ:'mɑ:də] *n* **(a)** *Hist* **the (Spanish) A.** l'Invincible Armada *f* **(b)** (*any fleet of warships*) armada *f*
armadillo [ɑ:mə'dɪləʊ] *n* (*animal*) tatou *m*
Armageddon [ɑ:mə'ged(ə)n] *n Bible, Fig* Armageddon *m*
armament ['ɑ:məmənt] *n* (*weapons*) (*of ship, tank, plane*) artillerie *f*; **armaments** (*weapons*) armement *m*, armes *fpl*
armature ['ɑ:mətʃər] *n* **(a)** *Zool* armure *f* **(b)** *El* armature *f* **(c)** *Constr, Art* armature *f*
armband ['ɑ:mbænd] *n* brassard *m*; (*for swimmers*) manchon *m*; **black a.** brassard de deuil
armchair ['ɑ:mtʃeər] *n* fauteuil *m*; **a. strategist/traveller** stratège *m*/voyageur *m* en chambre
armed [ɑ:md] *adj* (*person, conflict, torpedo, fuse*) armé; **a. to the teeth/with a gun** armé jusqu'aux dents/d'un fusil; **to offer a. resistance** résister par les armes, se défendre les armes à la main; *Mil* **a. forces** forces *fpl* armées; **a. truce** suspension *f* d'armes; **a. warfare** conflit *m* armé
armed robbery *n* vol *m* à main armée
Armenia [ɑ:'mi:nɪə] *n* Arménie *f*
Armenian [ɑ:'mi:nɪən] **1** *adj* arménien **2** *n* **(a)** Arménien, -ienne **(b)** *Ling* arménien *m*
armful ['ɑ:mfʊl] *n* brassée *f*; **to bring armfuls of flowers** *or* **flowers by the a.** apporter des fleurs à pleins bras, apporter des brassées de fleurs
armhole ['ɑ:mhəʊl] *n Sewing* emmanchure *f*
armistice ['ɑ:mɪstɪs] *n* armistice *m*
Armistice day *n* l'anniversaire *m* de l'Armistice (de 1918)
armless ['ɑ:mlɪs] *adj* sans bras
armlet ['ɑ:mlɪt] *n* **(a)** (*bracelet*) bracelet *m* (*porté au-dessus du coude*) **(b)** (*armband*) brassard *m*
armor *etc US* = **armour** *etc*
armorial [ɑ:'mɔ:rɪəl] *adj* armorial, -aux; **a. bearings** armoiries *fpl*
armour¹, *US* **armor** [ɑ:mər] *n* (*no pl*) **(a)** *Naut* (*of ship*) cuirasse *f*, cuirassement *m*, blindage *m*; *Mil* (*of vehicle, tank etc*) blindage **(b)** *Mil* (*units, vehicles*) blindés *mpl* **(c)** *Hist* (*of*

knight etc) armure *f*; **suit of a.** armure complète; **in full a.** armé de pied en cap

armour², *US* **armor** *vt Naut* (*ship*) cuirasser; *Mil* (*train etc*) blinder

armoured, *US* **armored** [ˈɑːməd] *adj Naut* (*ship*) cuirassé; *Mil* (*vehicle, train*) blindé; **a. troops,** *US* **a. corps** blindés *mpl*; **a. car** *Mil* engin *m* blindé de reconnaissance; (*used by police*) voiture *f* blindée; (*for cash, gold etc*) fourgon *m* bancaire; **a. personnel carrier** véhicule *m* blindé de transport de troupes

armourer, *US* **armorer** [ˈɑːmərər] *n Ind, Mil, Naut* armurier *m*

armour-piercing, *US* **armor-piercing** *adj* (*shell*) perforant, de rupture

armour-plated, *US* **armor-plated** *adj Naut* cuirassé, blindé; *Mil* blindé

armour-plating, *US* **armor-plating** *n* blindage *m*

armoury, *US* **armory** [ˈɑːmərɪ] *n* **(a)** (*store room*) magasin *m* d'armes; (*in barracks*) armurerie *f*; (*in museum etc*) salle *f* d'armes **(b)** *US* (*factory*) fabrique *f* d'armes; (*workshop*) armurerie *f*

armpit [ˈɑːmpɪt] *n* aisselle *f*

armrest [ˈɑːmrest] *n* accoudoir *m*, appuie-bras *m inv*

arms [ɑːmz] *npl* **(a)** (*weapons*) armes *fpl*; **side a.** armes blanches; **small a.** armes portatives; **call to a.** appel *m* aux armes; **nation in a.** nation *f* en armes; **100,000 men under a.** 100 000 hommes sous les drapeaux; **to take up a.** prendre les armes, s'armer (**against** contre); **to rise up in a.** se dresser en armes (**against sb/sth** contre qn/qch); *Fig* **to be up in a. about sth** s'insurger contre qch; **a. manufacturer** armurier *m*, fabricant *m* d'armes **(b)** *Her* armoiries *fpl*, armes *fpl*

arms dealer *n* trafiquant *m* d'armes

arms embargo *n* embargo *m* sur les armes

arm's-length *adj Com* (*relationship*) impartial; (*price*) réaliste

arms limitation talks *npl* négociations *fpl* pour la limitation des armements

arms race *n* course *f* aux armements

arms trade *n* commerce *m* des armes *ou* d'armes

arms trader *n* trafiquant *m* d'armes

army [ˈɑːmɪ] *n* [ⓘA11,g,i] *Mil, Fig* (*of ants, civil servants etc*) armée *f*; (*of people*) foule *f*, multitude *f*; **he joined the A. not the Air Force** il est entré dans l'armée de terre et non pas dans l'armée de l'air; **to be in the a.** être dans l'armée, être militaire; **to go into** *or* **join the a.** (*volunteer*) s'engager, s'enrôler; (*be conscripted*) partir au régiment *ou* à l'armée; **there was enough food for an a.** il y avait assez de nourriture pour un régiment; **standing** *or* **regular a.** armée permanente *ou* active; **professional a.** armée de métier; **a. lorry** camion *m* militaire; **a. barracks** caserne *f*, baraquement *m* militaire; **an a. officer** un officier de l'armée de terre

army ant *n* fourmi *f* légionnaire

army corps *n* corps *m* d'armée

Army List *n* annuaire *m* militaire, cadres *mpl* de l'armée

arnica [ˈɑːnɪkə] *n Bot, Pharm* arnica *f*

aroma [əˈrəʊmə] *n* arôme *m*

aromatherapy [ərəʊməˈθerəpɪ] *n* aromathérapie *f*

aromatic [ærəʊˈmætɪk] **1** *adj* (*herb, tea, smell*) aromatique **2** *n* **(a)** aromate *m* **(b)** *Ch* **aromatics** carbures *mpl* aromatiques *ou* à noyau

around [əˈraʊnd] **1** *adv* **(a)** autour; **all a.** tout autour, de tous côtés; **the woods (all) a.** les bois d'alentour; **for miles a.** sur (un rayon de) plusieurs kilomètres, sur des kilomètres; **people came from miles a.** les gens sont venus de partout *ou* de très loin; **the trunk was over two metres a.** le tronc faisait plus de deux mètres de circonférence

(b) (*in different directions, places*) **to walk a.** marcher par-ci, par-là; **I try to get a. as much as I can** j'essaie de me déplacer le plus possible; **to run a.** courir dans tous les sens; **to throw things a.** jeter des choses dans tous les sens; **swivel it a. a little** fais-le pivoter un peu; **he's now able to get a. again** il est de nouveau sur pied; *F* **she's been a.** (*is mature*) elle n'est pas née d'hier; (*sexually*) elle a des kilomètres au compteur, elle a des heures de vol

(c) (*in existence, in the area etc*) **this product has been a. for a long time** ce produit existe *ou* est en circulation depuis longtemps; **I still see her a.** il m'arrive encore de la voir; **I haven't seen him a. for ages** ça fait longtemps que je ne l'ai vu dans les parages; **are you a. this weekend?** tu es là ce weekend?; **there aren't many good translators a.** les bons traducteurs ne courent pas les rues; **is he still a.?** (*in the area*) est-ce qu'il est encore dans les parages *ou* là?; (*alive*) est-ce qu'il est encore de ce monde?; **it's the best value a.** c'est ce qu'il y a de meilleur marché

(d) (*in circular motion*) **to turn a.** se retourner; **to spin** *or* **whirl** *or* **wheel a.** faire volte-face; **he was waving his arms a.** il gesticulait dans tous les sens

2 *prep* **(a)** autour de; **his arms were a. her neck** il avait les bras autour de son cou; **she had her family a. her** elle a été entourée de sa famille; **the people a. him** les gens qui l'entourent; **we walked a. the lake** nous avons fait le tour du lac en marchant; *Aut* **it's just a. the bend** c'est juste au prochain virage

(b) (*in different parts*) **to travel a. the country** parcourir le pays; **there were books all a. the room** il y avait des livres dans toute la pièce; **a. town** en ville

(c) (*in the region of*) environ; **at a. four o'clock** vers quatre heures, sur les quatre heures; **it cost a. £200** ça a coûté dans les 200 livres *ou* environ 200 livres

(d) (*near*) **somewhere a. here** quelque part par ici; **is there anywhere a. here I can sleep?** est-ce que je peux trouver où dormir par ici?

arousal [əˈraʊz(ə)l] *n* (*from sleep*) éveil *m*, réveil *m*; (*of interest, suspicion*) éveil; (*of anger*) soulèvement *m*; (*sexual*) excitation *f*

arouse [əˈraʊz] *vt* (*person*) (*wake*) réveiller, éveiller; (*stir up*) (*from laziness, torpor*) secouer; (*sexually*) exciter; (*feeling*) exciter, éveiller; (*passions*) soulever; (*jealousy*) piquer, éveiller, provoquer; (*curiosity*) éveiller, chatouiller; (*sb's suspicion, interest*) éveiller; (*pity, enthusiasm*) inspirer; **they aroused her from her sleep** ils l'ont réveillée; **the crowd was aroused** la foule était agitée; **once (their anger was) aroused, ...** une fois leur colère éveillée, ...

arpeggio [ɑːˈpedʒɪəʊ] *n Mus* arpège *m*

arr (*abbr* **arrives**) (*on timetables etc*) arrive

arrack [ˈærək] *n* (*drink*) arac(k) *m*

arraign [əˈreɪn] *vt* **(a)** *Jur* poursuivre en justice; **to a. sb before a court** traduire qn en justice *ou* devant un tribunal **(b)** *Lit* (*criticize*) (*declaration, action etc*) attaquer, critiquer violemment

arraignment [əˈreɪnmənt] *n Jur* **(a)** (*of person*) mise *f* en accusation *ou* en jugement **(b)** (*charges*) acte *m* d'accusation

arrange [əˈreɪndʒ] **1** *vt* **(a)** (*put in an order*) (*furniture etc*) disposer, arranger; (*flowers*) disposer; **the chairs were arranged in a circle** les chaises étaient disposées en cercle; **they arranged themselves around the room** ils se sont répartis dans la pièce

(b) (*organize*) (*wedding*) arranger; (*concert, meeting etc*) organiser; (*date, time*) fixer; **an arranged marriage** un mariage de convenance; **everything is arranged** tout est en ordre; **it was arranged that ...** il fut convenu que ...; **try to a. it** tâchez d'arranger la chose; **that can be arranged** cela peut s'arranger; **a. it among yourselves** arrangez cela entre vous, entendez-vous là-dessus; **the meeting arranged for tomorrow** la réunion prévue pour demain; **at the time arranged** à l'heure prévue; **I've got nothing arranged** je n'ai rien de prévu; **have you arranged what to do if ...?** as-tu pris tes dispositions pour le cas où ...?; **what have you arranged?** (*with him*) qu'est-ce que vous avez prévu?; **to a. one's affairs** mettre ses affaires en ordre

(c) *Mus* (*piece*) adapter, arranger (**for (the) piano** pour (le) piano)

2 *vi* (*organize*) **to a. to do sth** (*make preparations*) s'arranger *ou* prendre ses dispositions pour faire qch; (*with sb else*) convenir de faire qch; **to a. for sth to be done** s'arranger *ou* prendre des dispositions *ou* prendre des mesures pour que qch se fasse; **I had arranged to ...** j'avais prévu de ...; **we arranged to meet** nous avons prévu de nous rencontrer; **I think I'll a. to be out when he comes** je crois que je m'arrangerai pour être sorti quand il viendra; **can you a. to have it finished by Friday?** est-ce que vous pouvez vous arranger pour qu'il soit terminé vendredi?; **to a. to have sth delivered** faire le nécessaire pour que qch soit livré; **they arranged for a taxi to meet me** ils se sont arrangés pour qu'un taxi vienne me chercher

arrangement [əˈreɪndʒmənt] *n* **(a)** (*preparation*) disposition *f*, aménagement *m* (**of** de); **to make arrangements** prendre des dispositions *ou* des mesures, faire des préparatifs (**for sth/to do sth/for sth to be done** pour qch/pour faire qch/pour que qch se fasse); **to make arrangements for a journey** faire ses préparatifs pour un voyage; **I've made all the arrangements** j'ai tout arrangé

(b) (*agreement*) arrangement *m*, accord *m*; *Fin* (*with creditors*) accommodement *m*; *Jur* transaction *f*; *Com etc* **to make an a.** *or* **to come to an a. with sb** prendre un arrangement avec qn; **to come to an a. with one's creditors** parvenir à un accord avec ses créanciers; **the a. was that ...** (*I or you etc would do*) on avait prévu que ...; **price by a.** prix à débattre; **by prior a.** sur accord préalable (**c**) *Mus* arrangement *m*, adaptation *f* (**for (the) piano** pour piano)

arranger [ə'reɪndʒər] *n Mus* arrangeur, -euse

arrant ['ærənt] *adj attrib* (*rogue, fool*) fini; (*liar*) fieffé; **don't talk such a. rubbish** comment est-ce que tu peux dire des bêtises pareilles?; **this is a. folly** c'est de la folie pure

array¹ [ə'reɪ] *n* (**a**) (*display*) étalage *m*, collection *f*; **a bewildering a. of salads** un étalage de salades stupéfiant; **an imposing a. of tools** une imposante collection d'outils (**b**) *Mil* rangs *mpl*; **in close a.** en rangs serrés; **in battle a.** en ordre de bataille (**c**) *Math* (*of figures*) tableau *m*; *Comptr* matrice *f*, tableau (**d**) *Lit* (*fine clothing*) parure *f*, appareil *m*; **in rich a.** paré de ses plus beaux atours

array² *vt* (**a**) (*troops etc*) (*in battle formation*) disposer, déployer; **his medals were arrayed across his chest** ses médailles étaient étalées sur sa poitrine (**b**) *Lit* (*clothe*) revêtir, parer (**sb in sth** qn de qch)

arrears [ə'rɪəz] *npl* arriéré *m*, arrérages *mpl*; **I'm £100 in a.** j'ai cent livres d'arriérés; **rent a.** arriéré de loyer; **to be in a. with the rent, to let one's rent fall into a.** être en retard pour payer son loyer; **I'm a month in a.** j'ai (pris) un retard d'un mois, je suis en retard d'un mois; **to be getting into a. with the repayments** prendre du retard pour payer *ou* avec les versements; **work in a.** travail *m* en retard; **to be paid monthly in a.** être payé à la fin du mois; **to be in a. with one's correspondence** avoir du retard dans sa correspondance

arrest¹ [ə'rest] *n* (**a**) (*of wrongdoer*) arrestation *f*; *Mil, Naut* arrêts *mpl*; **to put sb/to be under a.** mettre qn/être en état d'arrestation; *Mil, Naut* mettre qn/être aux arrêts; **you're under a.!** vous êtes en état d'arrestation!; **a. warrant** mandat *m* d'arrêt; **several arrests were made** plusieurs personnes ont été arrêtées; **to make an a.** (*of police officer*) procéder à une arrestation; *Mil, Naut* **open a.** arrêts simples; *Mil, Naut* **close a.** arrêts forcés *ou* de rigueur (**b**) (*of movement, progress etc*) arrêt *m*, suspension *f* (**c**) *Jur* **a. of judgment** sursis *m* à l'exécution d'un jugement

arrest² *vt* (**a**) (*capture*) (*sb*) arrêter; *Scot, Naut* (*property, ship*) saisir; **the arresting officer** le policier qui a effectué/qui effectue l'arrestation (**b**) (*stop*) (*movement, progress of sb, sth*) arrêter; **arrested growth** (*of person*) arrêt *m* dans la croissance; (*of thing*) arrêt dans le développement (**c**) *Jur* **to a. judgment** suspendre l'exécution d'un jugement (**d**) (*attention*) retenir, arrêter, fixer

arrester [ə'restər] *n* (**a**) *Tech* intercepteur *m*, séparateur *m*; **spark a.** pare-étincelles *m inv* (**b**) *Av* **a. gear** (*on runway*) dispositif *m* d'arrêt; (*on carrier deck*) dispositif d'appontage

arresting [ə'restɪŋ] **1** *adj* (*spectacle etc*) frappant, qui retient l'attention **2** *n* (**a**) *Jur* arrestation *f* (**b**) *MecE etc* arrêt *m*; **a. device** dispositif *m* d'arrêt

arrhythmia [ə'rɪðmɪə] *n Med* arythmie *f*

arrival [ə'raɪv(ə)l] *n* (**a**) arrivée *f*; *Com* (*of goods*) arrivage *m*; *Naut* (*of ship*) entrée *f*; (*of passengers*) débarquement *m*; **port of a.** port *m* d'arrivée; **on a.** (*of sb, sth*) à l'arrivée; (*of passengers*) au débarquement; **arrivals and departures** arrivées et départs; **a. and departure list** feuille *f* des arrivées et des départs, feuille des mouvements; **to await a.** (*on letter*) ne pas faire suivre; **a. form** fichette *f* d'arrivée; **a. quay** quai *m* d'arrivée; **arrivals list** liste *f* des arrivées

(**b**) (*person*) arrivant, -ante; **a new a.** un nouveau venu, une nouvelle venue; (*baby*) un nouveau-né, une nouveau-née; (*book*) une dernière parution; **late arrivals** retardataires *mpl*

arrival lounge *n* salle *f* d'arrivée

arrival time *n* heure *f* d'arrivée

arrive [ə'raɪv] *vi* (**a**) arriver (**at** à; **in** dans); **she has just arrived** elle arrive à l'instant, elle vient d'arriver; **the baby arrived at 4.37 am** le bébé est né à 4h37 du matin; **he is expected to a. next week** on attend son arrivée pour la semaine prochaine; **as soon as he arrived** dès son arrivée; **to a. unexpectedly** survenir, arriver à l'improviste; **to a. at the age of sixty** atteindre *ou* parvenir à *ou* arriver à l'âge de soixante ans; **to a. at a decision** arriver à *ou* en venir à *ou* aboutir à une décision; **we arrived at a situation where** *or* **in which …** nous en sommes arrivés à *ou* nous avons abouti à une situation dans laquelle …; **to a. at a price** (*of seller*) calculer *ou* fixer un prix; (*of seller and buyer*) convenir d'un prix

(**b**) *F* (*achieve recognition*) (*of person*) réussir, arriver, faire son trou; **you know you've really arrived when …** on sait qu'on a vraiment réussi le jour où …; **that was before the telephone had really arrived** c'était avant l'avènement du téléphone; **notebook computers have arrived in a big way** on voit des notebooks partout maintenant

arrogance ['ærəgəns] *n* arrogance *f*

arrogant ['ærəgənt] *adj* arrogant

arrogantly ['ærəgəntlɪ] *adv* avec arrogance; **a. to assume that …** avoir l'arrogance d'assumer que …

arrogate ['ærəgeɪt] *vt Lit, Jur* (**a**) (*appropriate*) **to a. sth to oneself** s'arroger qch (**b**) (*attribute wrongly*) attribuer injustement (**to sb** à qn)

arrow¹ ['ærəʊ] *n* (**a**) (*missile*) flèche *f*; **to shoot** *or* **let fly an a.** lancer *ou* décocher une flèche; **to fly straight as an a.** voler droit comme une flèche; **as swift as an a.** vif comme l'éclair; *Archit* **a. slit** arch(i)ère *f* (**b**) (*indicating direction*) (*on sign etc*) flèche *f*; (*of surveyor*) fiche *f* (**c**) *Br F* **arrows** (*darts*) fléchettes *fpl*

arrow² *vt* marquer d'une flèche; (*route, direction*) flécher

▶ **arrow in** *vtsep* (*insertion*) marquer d'une flèche

arrowhead ['ærəʊhed] *n* (**a**) (*on missile*) tête *f ou* fer *m ou* pointe *f* de flèche (**b**) (*plant*) sagittaire *f*, flèche *f* d'eau

arrow key *n Comptr* touche *f* fléchée, touche de direction

arrowroot ['ærəʊru:t] *n* (**a**) (*plant*) marante *f* (**b**) *Culin* arrow-root *m*

arse¹ [ɑ:s] *n Br Vulg* (**a**) cul *m*; **a kick up the a.** un coup de pied dans le cul; **to talk out of one's a.** raconter des conneries; **a. over tit** *or* **tip** *or* **apex** cul par-dessus tête; **to go a. over tip** tomber à la renverse; **get your a. in gear!** remuez-vous le cul!; **get your a. in here right now!** rapplique tout de suite!, ramène ta fraise!; **get your a. over to the Town Hall!** va promener ton cul à la mairie!; **to get it in the a.** (*get into trouble*) s'en prendre plein le cul; **it's my a. that's on the line** c'est moi qui va en prendre plein le cul; **to make an a. of sth** saloper qch; **he doesn't know his a. from his elbow** il est complètement paumé; **to make an a. of oneself** se ridiculiser; **to do sth a.-backwards** faire qch à l'envers *ou* n'importe comment; **my a.!** (*no way, I don't believe you etc*) mon cul!

(**b**) (*idiot*) connard *m*, connasse *f*

arse² *vt Br Vulg* **I couldn't be arsed doing it myself** ça m'a fait chier de le faire moi-même

▶ **arse about** *or* **around** *vi Br Vulg* déconner

arsehole ['ɑ:shəʊl] *n Br Vulg* (**a**) *Anat* trou *m* du cul; *Fig* **the a. of the universe** (*ugly town etc*) le trou du cul du monde (**b**) *Fig* (*stupid person*) connard *m*, connasse *f*; (*nasty person*) salaud *m*, salope *f*; **don't be such an a.!** arrête de faire/dire des conneries!; (*nasty person*) ne fais pas le salaud!

arse-licker ['ɑ:slɪkər] *n Br Vulg* lèche-cul *mf inv*

arse-licking *n Br Vulg* **they're sick of his a.** ils en ont marre de ce lèche-cul

arsenal ['ɑ:sən(ə)l] *n* arsenal *m*, -aux

arsenic ['ɑ:s(ə)nɪk] *n* arsenic *m*

arson ['ɑ:s(ə)n] *n* incendie *m* criminel *ou* volontaire; **to commit a.** provoquer (volontairement) un incendie; **to be charged with a.** être accusé d'avoir provoqué un incendie; **police suspect a.** la police suspecte un incendie criminel

arsonist ['ɑ:sənɪst] *n* incendiaire *mf*

art¹ [ɑ:t] *n* (**a**) art *m*; **the (fine) arts** les beaux-arts *mpl*; **a. for a.'s sake** l'art pour l'art; **a. class(es)** cours *m* de dessin; **a. exhibition** exposition *f* d'art; **a. form** forme *f* d'art; **a. object** objet *m* d'art; **a. reviewer** critique *m* d'art

(**b**) *Univ* **arts** lettres *fpl*; **arts faculty, faculty of arts** faculté *f* de lettres (et sciences humaines); **arts student** étudiant, -ante en lettres (et sciences humaines)

(**c**) (*technique*) art *m*; **the a. of war** l'art militaire, l'art de la guerre; **it's an a. in itself** c'est tout un art; **there's an a. to doing that** c'est tout un art que de faire cela; **to get** *or* **have sth down to a fine a.** maîtriser qch jusque dans les moindres détails; **she's got time-saving down to a fine a.** elle est passée maître dans l'art de gagner du temps; **a dying a.** un art en voie de disparition; **the black arts** la magie noire

(**d**) *Pej* (*trick*) stratagème *m*, ruse *f*

art² *Arch, Bible* (*2nd pers sing pr of* **be**) **thou a. good** tu es bon

art desk *n* bureau *m* de dessin

art director *n* directeur *m* artistique

art editor *n* rédacteur *m* artistique

artefact ['ɑ:tɪfækt] *n* (**a**) *Archeol* objet *m* (fabriqué *ou* façonné) (**b**) (*side-effect*) conséquence *f*; **to be a mere a. of sth** être simplement la conséquence de qch, découler simplement de qch

arterial [ɑ:'tɪərɪəl] *adj Anat, Med etc* (*blood etc*) artériel; **a. road** grande voie *f* de communication

arteriole [ɑ:'tɪərɪəʊl] *n Anat* artériole *f*

arteriosclerosis [ɑ:'tɪərɪəʊsklə'rəʊsɪs] *n Med* artériosclérose *f*

artery ['ɑ:tərɪ] *n* (**a**) *Anat* artère *f* (**b**) (*road, river etc*) artère *f*; **main arteries** grandes voies *fpl* de communication, grandes artères

artesian [ɑ:'ti:zɪən, -'ti:ʒən] *adj* **a. well** puits *m* artésien

artful ['ɑ:tfʊl] *adj* (**a**) (*person*) rusé, astucieux, malin, *f* -igne; **a. as a monkey** malin comme un singe (**b**) (*solution, device*) ingénieux; **an a. dodge** un truc ingénieux

artfully [ˈɑːtfʊlɪ] *adv* ingénieusement
artfulness [ˈɑːtfʊlnɪs] *n* **(a)** (*of person*) habileté *f* (**in doing** à faire) **(b)** (*of thing, reply*) ingéniosité *f*
art gallery *n* galerie *f*
art-house cinema *n* cinéma *m* d'art et d'essai
arthritic [ɑːˈθrɪtɪk] *adj, n Med* arthritique *mf*
arthritis [ɑːˈθraɪtɪs] *n Med* arthrite *f*
arthropod [ˈɑːθrəpɒd] *n Zool* arthropode *m*
arthrosis [ɑːˈθrəʊsɪs] *n Med* arthrose *f*
Arthurian [ɑːˈθjʊərɪən] *adj Liter, Myth* (*cycle etc*) d'Arthur; (*novel*) arthurien
artic [ɑːˈtɪk] *n Br Sl* (*lorry*) semi-remorque *f, pl* semi-remorques
artichoke [ˈɑːtɪtʃəʊk] *n* **(globe) a.** artichaut *m*; *Culin* **a. hearts** cœurs *mpl* d'artichaut
article¹ [ˈɑːtɪk(ə)l] *n* **(a)** (*object*) objet *m*; **a. of clothing** vêtement *m*; **toilet articles** produits *mpl* de toilette **(b)** *Journ etc* (*in newspaper, magazine, encyclopaedia*) article *m* **(c)** *Com, Jur* (*in agreement, treaty*) article *m*, clause *f*; **articles of apprenticeship** contrat *m* d'apprentissage; *Jur* **articles of association** statuts *mpl* de société; **articles of war** *Mil* code *m* (de justice) militaire; *Naut* code de justice maritime; *Naut* **ship's articles** contrat d'engagement, conditions *fpl* d'embarquement; **a. of faith** article de foi **(d)** [①**A4-8; B3-5**] *Gram* **definite/indefinite a.** article *m* défini/indéfini
article² *vt Jur etc* **to a. sb to an attorney/an architect** placer qn (comme élève) chez un avoué/un architecte; **articled clerk** clerc *m* d'avoué lié par un contrat d'apprentissage
articulate¹ [ɑːˈtɪkjʊlət] *adj* **(a)** (*speech*) net, distinct; **to be a.** (*of person*) s'exprimer facilement *ou* avec facilité; **try to be more a.** essaie d'être plus clair; **the child gave a very a. account** l'enfant a fait un compte rendu très clair **(b)** *Zool* articulé
articulate² [ɑːˈtɪkjʊleɪt] **1** *vt* **(a)** (*pronounce clearly*) (*word etc*) articuler; **he doesn't a. his words** il n'articule pas **(b)** (*express clearly*) (*one's thoughts, idea*) exprimer clairement **2** *vi* **(a)** *Anat* s'articuler; **bone that articulates** *or* **is articulated with another** os qui s'articule *ou* est articulé avec un autre **(b)** (*in speaking*) articuler
articulated [ɑːˈtɪkjʊleɪtɪd] *adj* **(a)** *Aut* **a. vehicle** semi-remorque *f, pl* semi-remorques **(b)** *Anat, Ling etc* articulé
articulately [ɑːˈtɪkjʊlətlɪ] *adv* **(a)** (*to express oneself, argue*) clairement; **as you so a. put it** comme vous l'avez si bien exprimé **(b)** (*to speak*) distinctement
articulateness [ɑːˈtɪkjʊlətnɪs] *n* **(a)** (*of speaker*) facilité *f* d'expression; (*of writing, speech*) clarté *f* **(b)** (*clarity of sound*) articulation *f* nette, netteté *f* d'énonciation
articulation [ɑːtɪkjʊˈleɪʃən] *n* **(a)** *Biol, Ling etc* articulation *f* **(b)** (*of thought*) expression *f*; **you've heard his a. of the new theory** vous avez entendu sa présentation de la nouvelle théorie
artifact [ˈɑːtɪfækt] *n* = **artefact**
artifice [ˈɑːtɪfɪs] *n* **(a)** (*trick*) artifice *m*, ruse *f*, stratagème *m*; **a. of war** ruse *ou* artifice de guerre **(b)** (*skill*) habileté *f*, adresse *f*
artificial [ɑːtɪˈfɪʃəl] *adj* **(a)** (*conditions, light, distinction, situation*) artificiel; **a. fibres** fibres *fpl* synthétiques; *Astron etc* **a. horizon** horizon *m* artificiel; **a. limb** prothèse *f* orthopédique; **a. manure** engrais *mpl* chimiques; **a. respiration** respiration *f* artificielle; **to give sb a. respiration** faire la respiration artificielle à qn; **a. wood** similibois *m* **(b)** (*behaviour, person*) affecté; (*style*) factice, recherché; **she is very a.** elle manque de naturel
artificial insemination *n* insémination *f* artificielle; **a. by donor/husband** insémination artificielle avec sperme de donneur/du mari
artificial intelligence *n Comptr* intelligence *f* artificielle
artificiality [ɑːtɪfɪʃɪˈælɪtɪ] **(a)** (*of product etc*) nature *f* artificielle **(b)** (*of person, smile*) manque *m* de naturel; (*of behaviour, manner*) affectation *f*
artificially [ɑːtɪˈfɪʃəlɪ] *adv* artificiellement; **a. coloured** (*on packet etc*) contient un colorant artificiel; **to behave a.** avoir un comportement affecté, manquer de naturel
artillery [ɑːˈtɪlərɪ] *n* artillerie *f*; **heavy/light a.** artillerie lourde/légère; **to lay down an a. barrage** déployer un barrage d'artillerie; **a. fire** tir *m* d'artillerie; **a. regiment** régiment *m* d'artillerie; **a. shell** obus *m*
artilleryman, *pl* **-men** [ɑːˈtɪlərɪmən, -men] *n* artilleur *m*
artisan [ɑːtɪˈzæn] *n* artisan *m*
artist [ˈɑːtɪst] *n* (*actor, painter, singer*) artiste *mf*; **he is an a.** (*painter*) il est artiste, il est peintre; (*footballer etc*) c'est un véritable artiste
artiste [ɑːˈtiːst] *n Th, Cin, TV* artiste *mf*
artistic [ɑːˈtɪstɪk] *adj* (*style, taste, temperament, arrangement*) artistique; **she came from an a. family** elle venait d'une famille d'artistes; **she's the a. one in the family** c'est l'artiste de la famille; **I'm not at all a.** je n'ai aucune inclination artistique, je n'ai pas la fibre artistique; **a. adviser** conseiller *m* artistique
artistically [ɑːˈtɪstɪklɪ] *adv* avec art, artistiquement, artistement; **to be a. gifted/inclined** avoir des dons/la fibre artistique(s); **a. speaking** du point de vue artistique
artistic director *n* directeur *m* artistique
artistry [ˈɑːtɪstrɪ] *n* (*of painter, footballer*) art *m*; (*of painting, sb's game*) qualité *f* artistique; **his goal was sheer a.** son but, c'était l'art et le vrai
artless [ˈɑːtlɪs] *adj* **(a)** (*natural*) naturel, sans artifice **(b)** (*naive*) naïf, ingénu
artlessly [ˈɑːtlɪslɪ] *adv* **(a)** (*naturally*) naturellement, sans artifice **(b)** (*naively*) naïvement, ingénument
artlessness [ˈɑːtlɪsnɪs] *n* **(a)** (*naturalness*) naturel *m*, simplicité *f* **(b)** (*naivety*) naïveté *f*, ingénuité *f*
art nouveau [ɑːnuːˈvəʊ] *n* modern style *m*; **a. furniture** meuble *m* de style art nouveau
art package *n Comptr* logiciel *m* de dessin
arts and crafts *npl* artisanat *m* d'expression; *Sch* travaux *mpl* manuels
art school *n* école *f* des beaux-arts
arts festival *n* festival *m* culturel
arts programme *n* programme *m* culturel
art student *n* étudiant, -ante des beaux-arts
art teacher *n* professeur *m* de dessin
artwork [ˈɑːtwɜːk] *n Art* (*in book production*) (*illustrations*) illustrations *fpl*; (*layout*) mise *f* en page; (*made-up page for printing*) document *m* d'exécution; **to use sth as a.** utiliser qch dans la maquette
arty [ˈɑːtɪ] *adj F* (*person, style, job, furniture*) artistique; (*existence*) bohème; *Pej* (*person*) qui donne dans le genre artiste; (*furniture etc*) qui se veut artistique; **he's an a. type** c'est le genre artiste; **the a. set** le milieu artiste
arty-crafty *adj F Hum Pej* bohème
arty-farty [ɑːtɪˈfɑːtɪ] *adj F Pej* aux prétentions artistiques, soi-disant artistique; **it's a lot of a. rubbish** c'est un tas d'idioties prétendument artistiques
arum [ˈeərəm] *n Bot* arum *m*; **a. lily** calla *f*
Aryan [ˈeərɪən] *Ling etc* **1** *adj* aryen **2** *n* Aryen, -enne
as [əz, *stressed* æz] **1** *prep* (*manner, function, role, condition*) comme; **they rose as one man** ils se levèrent comme un seul homme; **to acknowledge sb as an expert/one's equal** reconnaître qn en tant qu'expert/comme son égal; **to consider sb as a friend** considérer qn comme un ami; **to treat sb as a stranger** traiter qn en étranger; **to treat sth as a joke** tourner qch à la plaisanterie; **to recognize sb as one's son** reconnaître qn comme son fils; **I intended it as a compliment** j'ai dit ça en bien; **she was often ill as a child** enfant elle était souvent malade, elle était souvent malade dans son enfance; **to use sth as a flag** se servir de qch comme drapeau *ou* en guise de drapeau; **to send sth as a present** envoyer qch comme cadeau; *Th* **Olivier as Hamlet** Olivier dans le rôle de Hamlet; **to act as interpreter** servir d'interprète; **I acted in my capacity as a magistrate** j'ai agi en ma qualité de magistrat; **to be dressed as a boy** être habillé en garçon; **as a very old friend of your father's** en tant que vieil ami de votre père; **the novel as social history** le roman comme histoire sociale; **my rights as a mother** mes droits de mère; **as one doctor to another** soit dit entre médecins; **as someone new to the place** en tant que nouveau venu; **as revenge for ...** pour se venger de ...

2 *conj* [①**A69-70,2; B55,B**] **(a)** (*time*) **as I was opening the door** au moment où *ou* comme j'ouvrais la porte; **he went out (just) as I came in** il est sorti au moment (même) où *ou* comme j'entrais; **as I spoke, I could see ...** tandis que je parlais, je voyais ...; **as you get older** en vieillissant; **he's probably trying to contact us as we sit here** il essaie probablement de nous contacter en ce moment même; **one day as I was sitting ...** un jour que j'étais assis ...; **she drew back as I advanced** à mesure que j'avançais, elle reculait; **it's the last one as you come from the station** c'est le dernier en venant de la gare; **as and when required** à discrétion; **as and when I want** à mon bon plaisir; **as (and when) is necessary** quand c'est nécessaire

(b) (*reason*) puisque, comme; **as he has now left** puisqu'il *ou* comme il est maintenant parti

(c) (*concessive*) **ignorant as he is** tout ignorant qu'il est; **late as it was** malgré l'heure tardive; **try as she might, she couldn't open it** elle avait beau essayer, elle n'arrivait pas à l'ouvrir; **hard as it may be to believe, ...** c'est peut-être difficile à croire, mais ...; **much as I like her** quelle que soit mon affection pour elle; **be that as it may** quoi qu'il en soit

(d) (*manner*) comme; **do as you like** faites comme vous voulez *ou* voudrez; **it happened as I told you** cela s'est passé comme je vous l'ai dit; **as Mrs Smith remarked ...** comme Mme Smith l'a fait remarquer ...; **covered with dust as he was, he didn't want to come in** couvert qu'il était de poussière, il ne voulait pas entrer; **as they say, ...** comme on dit, ...; **why should I do as he says?** pourquoi devrais-je faire ce qu'il dit?; **as often happens** comme il arrive souvent, ainsi qu'il arrive souvent; **leave it as it is** laissez-le tel quel, laissez-le tel qu'il est; **as it is, we must ...** les choses étant ainsi, il nous faut ...; **there are too many cars as it is** il y a déjà trop de voitures; **as it were** pour ainsi dire; *Mil, Gym* **as you were!** revenez!, au temps!; **as a man lives, so he dies** comme on a vécu, ainsi l'on meurt; **as is** tel quel; *F* **the Apollo theatre as was** (*it now has another name*) le théâtre de l'Apollo comme on l'appelait; (*it now has another function*) l'ancien théâtre de l'Apollo

(e) (*result, purpose*) **he is not so foolish as to believe it** il n'est pas assez stupide pour le croire; **put on your gloves so as to be ready** mettez vos gants pour être prêt *ou* de manière à être prêt

(f) mother is well, as are the children maman va bien, de même que les enfants; **beasts of prey, such as the lion or tiger** les bêtes fauves, telles que *ou* comme le lion ou le tigre; **he was a foreigner, as they noticed from his pronunciation** il était étranger, ce qui se remarquait à sa prononciation; **it's the same one as I was telling you about** c'est celui-là même dont je vous parlais

(g) *Eng Dial* **it was her as told me** c'est elle qui me l'a dit

(h) (*in comparisons*) (*also adv*) **as ... as ...** aussi ... que ...; **not as ... as ...** pas aussi *ou* si ... que ...; **you are as tall as he (is)** *or* **as him** vous êtes aussi grand que lui; **you are not as** *or* **not so tall as he (is)** *or* **as him** vous n'êtes pas aussi grand que lui; **I'm not as rich as I was** je ne suis pas aussi riche que je l'ai été; **is it as high as that?** est-ce si *ou* aussi haut que ça?; **I came down as fast as I could** je suis descendu aussi vite que possible; **I worked as hard as I could** j'ai travaillé autant que j'ai pu; **as many as you want** autant que tu veux; **he's not such a fool as he looks** il n'est pas si bête qu'il en a l'air; **a house twice as large (as this)** une maison deux fois plus grande (que celle-ci); **as white as a sheet** blanc comme un linge; **as recently as last week** pas plus tard que la semaine dernière; **as much for your sake as for mine** tant pour vous que pour moi; **she doesn't enjoy it as much as I do** elle n'aime pas ça autant que moi; **I don't know why I like her as much as I do** je ne sais pas pourquoi elle me plaît à ce point; **as soon/as much as possible** aussitôt/autant que possible; **we could go as high as 5,000, but no higher** nous pourrions monter jusqu'à 5000, mais pas au-delà

3 *adv* **(a)** (*form, manner, kind*) **as per advice** suivant avis; **as per invoice** selon facture; **as promised** comme promis; **as ordered** conformément à la commande; **as requested** comme il a été requis; **as advertised on TV** vu à la télé; **as recommended** comme il est recommandé; **the GR241, as recommended by leading experts** le GR241, modèle recommandé par les plus grands experts; **ready to use as delivered** livré prêt à fonctionner; **if used as intended** s'il est utilisé selon les recommandations; **we didn't arrive at lunch time as intended** nous ne sommes pas arrivés à l'heure du déjeuner, comme cela avait été notre intention; **as noted/discussed above** comme il est mentionné/démontré plus haut; **B as in Bombay** B comme Bombay

(b) (*switching or identifying topic*) **as for that, as to that, as regards that** quant à cela, pour cela; **as for you** quant à vous; **as for money, I can lend you some** pour ce qui est de l'argent, je peux t'en prêter; **to question sb as to his/her motives** interroger qn sur ses motifs

(c) as well aussi; **I don't want trouble from you as well** je ne veux pas que toi aussi tu me causes des problèmes; **as well as the rent there was the heating to consider** en plus du loyer, il fallait penser au chauffage; **you can't expect me to cook as well as do the dishes** tu ne peux pas me demander de faire la cuisine et la vaisselle en plus; **by day as well as by night** le jour comme la nuit, de jour comme de nuit

(d) as if comme si; **it was as if ...** on aurait dit que ...; **he winked as if** *or* **though to say ...** il fit un clin d'œil, comme pour dire ...; **we can't go on as if** *or* **though nothing had happened** nous ne pouvons pas continuer comme si de rien n'était; **it isn't as if** *or* **though I haven't tried** ce n'est pourtant pas manque d'avoir essayé; **it isn't as if** *or* **though it's difficult** ce n'est pourtant pas difficile; **he made as if** *or* **though to go** il a fait mine de partir; **he looked as if** *or* **though he was about to go out** on aurait dit qu'il était sur le point de sortir; **as if you didn't know!** comme si tu ne le savais pas!

asap [eɪeseɪ'piː, 'eɪzæp] *adv* (*abbr* **as soon as possible**) = le plus tôt possible, dans les plus brefs délais

asbestos [æs'bestəs] *n* amiante *m*, asbeste *m*; **a. dust** poudre *f* d'amiante

asbestosis [æsbes'təʊsɪs] *n Med* asbestose *f*

ascend [ə'send] **1** *vi Fml* monter **2** *vt* **(a)** (*ladder*) monter à; (*stairs*) monter, gravir; (*mountain*) gravir, faire l'ascension de; (*throne*) monter sur **(b)** (*river*) remonter

ascendancy, -ency [ə'sendənsɪ] *n Fml* ascendant *m* **(over sb** sur qn); **to gain (the) a. over sb** prendre de l'ascendant sur qn

ascendant, -ent [ə'sendənt] **1** *adj* **(a)** *Astrol, Math etc* ascendant; (*power, faction*) dominant; **a. star** astre *m* ascendant **(b)** *Bot* (*stalk*) montant **2** *n Astrol* ascendant *m*; **to be in the a.** être à l'ascendant; *Fig* avoir le dessus, s'affirmer; **his star is in the a.** son étoile est à l'ascendant; **his fortunes are once more in the a.** ses finances commencent à mieux se porter

ascender [ə'sendər] *n Typ* (*of character*) hampe *f* (montante), ascendante *f*

ascending [ə'sendɪŋ] *adj* **(a)** *Astron, Math etc* ascendant; *Met* (*current*) ascendant; **in a. order** en ordre croissant; **steeply a. path** sentier *m* raide; *Jur* **a. line** ascendance *f*, ligne *f* ascendante; *Mus* **a. scale** gamme *f* ascendante *ou* montante; **a. series** progression *f* croissante; *Comptr* **a. sort** tri *m* en ordre croissant **(b)** *Bot* (*stalk*) montant

ascension [ə'senʃən] *n* ascension *f*; **her a. to the throne** son élévation *f* sur le trône

Ascension Day *n Rel* jour *m ou* fête *f* de l'Ascension

Ascension Island *n* l'île *f* de l'Ascension

ascent [ə'sent] *n* **(a)** (*of mountain*) ascension *f*; **first a.** première *f* (ascension); **balloon a.** ascension en ballon; **to make an a.** faire une ascension; *Fig* **the a. of man** le progrès de l'humanité; **his a. to power** son ascension jusqu'au pouvoir **(b)** *Tech* (*of piston etc*) montée *f*, remontée *f* **(c)** (*slope*) montée *f*, pente *f* **(d)** *Jur* **line of a.** ascendance *f*

ascertain [æsə'teɪn] *vt* (*fact*) déterminer; (*truth about sth*) s'assurer de; **to a. sth from sb** s'informer de qch auprès de qn; **I ascertained from his report that ...** j'ai déduit de son rapport que ...; **are we to a. from this that ...?** devons-nous en déduire que ...?

ascertainable [æsə'teɪnəb(ə)l] *adj* (*information, fact*) qui peut être déterminé; (*truth*) vérifiable; **that's as much detail as is a. from this distance** c'est tout ce qu'on peut distinguer avec certitude à cette distance

ascertainment [æsə'teɪnmənt] *n Fml* (*of fact*) détermination *f*; (*of truth*) vérification *f*

ascetic [ə'setɪk] **1** *adj usu attrib* (*life etc*) ascétique; **a thin a. face** un maigre visage d'ascète **2** *n esp Rel* ascète *mf*; **he led the life of an a.** il menait une vie d'ascète, il vivait en ascète

ascetically [ə'setɪklɪ] *adv* ascétiquement; (*to live*) en ascète

asceticism [ə'setɪsɪz(ə)m] *n* ascétisme *m*

ASCII ['æskiː] *n Comptr* (*abbr* **American Standard Code for Information Interchange**) ASCII *m*; **ASCII code** code *m* ASCII; **ASCII file** fichier *m* ASCII

ascorbic [əs'kɔːbɪk] *adj Ch* (*acid etc*) ascorbique

ascribable [ə'skraɪbəb(ə)l] *adj pred* attribuable **(to** à); (*of sth negative*) imputable **(to** à); **certain parts of the text are easily a.** l'origine de certaines parties du texte est facile à déceler

ascribe [ə'skraɪb] *vt* attribuer **(to** à); (*sth negative*) imputer **(to** à)

ascription [ə'skrɪpʃən] *n Fml* attribution *f* **(of sth to sth** de qch à qch); (*of sth negative*) imputation *f* **(of sth to sth** de qch à qch)

asdic ['æzdɪk] *n Naut* asdic *m*

asepsis [eɪ'sepsɪs] *n Med* asepsie *f*

aseptic [eɪ'septɪk] *adj Med* aseptique; *Fig* (*smile, charm*) aseptisé

asexual [eɪ'seksjʊəl] *adj Biol, Fig* asexué; (*flower*) neutre; **a. reproduction** reproduction *f* asexuée

ash[1] [æʃ] *n* **a. (tree)** frêne *m*; **a. furniture** meubles *mpl* en *ou* de frêne

ash[2] **1** *n* **(a)** [①A10,f] (*from fire etc*) cendre(s) *f(pl)*; *Ind etc* escarbilles *fpl*; **cigar a.** cendre de cigare; **to drop a. on the carpet** laisser tomber des cendres sur la moquette; **to reduce** *or* **burn sth to ashes** réduire qch en cendres; **volcanic a.** cendres volcaniques; **a. cloud** (*above volcano*) nuée *f* de cendres; *Lit* **to rake over the ashes of the past** tisonner les cendres du passé; **to rise from the ashes** renaître de ses cendres; **ashes** (*of dead*) cendres; **ashes to ashes, dust to dust** (*from funeral service*) tu es poussière, et tu retourneras en poussière; **a. heap** crassier *m*; *Cr* **the**

Ashes = le trophée que les équipes anglaises et australiennes se disputent

(**b**) (*colour*) cendré *m*, gris cendré *m inv*

2 *adj* (*in colour*) gris cendré *inv*

ashamed [ə'ʃeɪmd] *adj usu pred* honteux, confus; **to be a. of sb/sth** avoir honte de qn/qch; **I am a. of you** vous me faites honte; **to feel a.** être honteux *ou* confus; **you make me feel a.** (*of myself, you*) vous me faites honte; **I am a. to say that ...** j'avoue à ma grande honte que ...; **a. though I am to admit it, I have never been there** j'ai honte de l'avouer, mais je n'y suis jamais allé; **I'm not a. to admit it** je l'admets sans honte; **you ought to be a. of yourself** vous devriez avoir honte; **there is nothing to be a. of** il n'y a pas de quoi avoir honte; **... he said with an a. look on his face** ... dit-il, l'air confus

ash-blond(e) **1** *adj* (*hair*) blond cendré *inv* **2** *n* (*person*) **she's an a.** elle a les cheveux blond cendré

ashcan ['æʃkæn] *n Am* boîte *f* à ordures, poubelle *f*

ashen ['æʃən] *adj* (*colour*) cendré; (*face*) pâle comme la mort; **his face turned a.** il devint blême, son visage blêmit

ashen-faced ['æʃən'feɪst] *adj* pâle comme la mort

ashlar ['æʃlər] *n Constr, Archit* (**a**) (*stone*) pierre *f* de taille (**b**) (*facing*) parements *mpl*, revêtement *m*

ashore [ə'ʃɔːr] *adv Naut* (**a**) (*on land*) à terre; **to go a.** aller *ou* descendre à terre, débarquer; **to set** *or* **put sb a.** débarquer qn (**b**) (*to the shore*) (*to swim etc*) jusqu'au rivage, jusqu'à la rive; **to be driven a.** (*of ship*) être jeté à la côte; **to run a.** (*of ship*) s'échouer, faire côte

ashpan ['æʃpæn] *n* (*for stove*) cendrier *m*

ashtray ['æʃtreɪ] *n* cendrier *m*

Ash Wednesday *n Rel* le mercredi des Cendres

ashy ['æʃɪ] *adj* (**a**) cendreux, couvert de cendres (**b**) (*in colour*) cendré, couleur de cendre

Asia ['eɪʒə] *n* Asie *f*; **A. Minor** Asie Mineure

Asian ['eɪʒən] **1** *adj* asiatique; (*Indian/Pakistani*) indien; pakistanais; *F* **A. babe** Indienne *f*/Pakistanaise *f*/Orientale *f* super belle; *Med* **A. flu** grippe *f* asiatique **2** *n* Asiatique *mf*; (*Indian/Pakistani*) Indien, -ienne; Pakistanais, -aise

Asiatic [eɪsɪ'ætɪk] **1** *adj* asiatique **2** *n* Asiatique *mf*

aside [ə'saɪd] **1** *adv* de côté, à l'écart, à part; **to pull a.** (*curtain etc*) écarter; **to lay** *or* **put sth a.** mettre qch de côté; **to put sth a. for sb** (*in shop*) mettre qch de côté pour qn; **stand a.!** écartez-vous!; **to turn a.** se détourner (**from** de); **I took** *or* **drew him a.** je le pris à part *ou* à l'écart *ou* en particulier; **(leaving) politics a., I think ...** si on laisse de côté la politique, je pense ...; **injuries to my vanity a., it hasn't caused me much trouble** à part quelques blessures d'amour-propre, ça ne m'a pas vraiment causé de problèmes; **joking a.** blague à part; *Th* **(words spoken) a.** (paroles dites) en aparté

2 *prep phrase esp Am* **a. from** à part; (*except for*) excepté, sauf; **a. from my own interest** mon propre intérêt à part; **a. from being frightened I was unhurt** j'en ai été quitte pour la peur

3 *n Th, Fig* aparté *m* (**to sb** avec qn); **(purely) as an a.** soit dit entre nous

asinine ['æsɪnaɪn] *adj* (**a**) (*stupid*) stupide, sot (**b**) (*like an ass*) asinien

ask [ɑːsk] (**asked** [ɑːskt]) **1** *vt* (**a**) demander; **to a. sb sth** demander qch à qn; **a. him his name/how old he is** demandez-lui son nom/son âge; **to a. the time** demander l'heure; **to a. (sb) the way** demander son chemin (à qn); **to a. (sb) a question** poser une question (à qn) (**about** sur); **it may be asked whether ...** on peut se demander si ...; **I've often asked myself whether ...** je me suis souvent demandé si ..., je me suis souvent posé la question de savoir si ...; *F* **if you a. me** à mon avis; *F* **I a. you!** je vous demande un peu!

(**b**) (*request*) demander; **to a. sb for sth** demander qch à qn; **to a. a favour of sb, to a. sb a favour** demander une faveur à qn; **if it isn't asking too much** si ce n'est pas trop vous demander; **to a. sb's permission to do sth** demander à qn la permission de faire qch; **to a. to do sth** demander à faire qch, demander la permission *ou* l'autorisation de faire qch; **to a. to be excused** s'excuser de partir; (*in class*) demander la permission de sortir; **to a. sb to do sth** demander à qn de faire qch; **a. him to wait/to come in** priez-le d'attendre/d'entrer

(**c**) (*charge*) **to a. 600 francs for sth** demander 600 francs pour *ou* de qch; **how much** *or* **what are you asking for it?** combien en voulez-vous?

(**d**) (*question*) (*person*) interroger (**about** sur); **he asked me all about my work** il m'a interrogé longuement sur mon travail

(**e**) (*invite*) inviter; **to a. sb to lunch** inviter qn à déjeuner; **I have asked him to come for the weekend** je l'ai invité à passer le week-end chez nous; **can I a. a friend along?** est-ce que je peux inviter un ami à se joindre à nous?

2 *vi* (**a**) (*inquire*) se renseigner (**about** sur); **if you don't mind me** *or* **my asking** si vous permettez que je vous le demande; **the police were asking about you** la police a posé des questions à votre sujet

(**b**) (*request*) **all you have to do is a.!** il n'y a qu'à demander!

▶ **ask after** *vipo* (*show concern for, ask for news of*) (*person, sb's health*) demander des nouvelles de

▶ **ask around** *vi* (*enquire*) demander autour de soi, se renseigner; **some odd people have been asking around after you** il y a des drôles de types qui te cherchent

▶ **ask back** *vtsep* (*invite to one's home*) inviter à la maison; (*invite again*) réinviter; **do you want to a. them back for a drink?** tu veux les inviter à boire un verre à la maison?

▶ **ask for** *vipo* (**a**) **to a. for sb** demander à voir qn; (*on the telephone*) demander à parler à qn; **to a. for sth** demander qch; **to a. for something to eat/to drink** demander (quelque chose) à manger/à boire; **to a. for more** en redemander; **to a. for sth back** (*that has been lent*) redemander qch; **when I want your opinion I'll a. for it** lorsque j'aurai besoin de ton avis, je te le demanderai; **to be asking for trouble** aller au-devant des ennuis; *F* **he's been asking for it!** il l'a bien cherché!, il ne l'a pas volé!; **that's asking for a cold** tu/il/*etc* cherche(s) vraiment à tomber malade!; *F* **you asked for that!** tu l'as cherché!

(**b**) *esp Scot* = **ask after**

▶ **ask in** *vtsep* (*invite in*) inviter à entrer; **I would a. you in for tea but ...** je vous inviterais bien à (entrer) prendre le thé mais ...

▶ **ask out** *vtsep* (*on a date etc*) inviter à sortir

▶ **ask round** *vtsep* (*invite to one's home*) inviter; **why don't we a. them round for dinner one night?** pourquoi ne pas les inviter à dîner un soir?

▶ **ask up** *vtsep* (*invite up*) inviter à monter; **they asked us up to their flat** ils nous ont invités à monter dans leur appartement *ou* chez eux

askance [ə'skæns, -ɑːns] *adv Fig* **to look a. at sb/sth** regarder qn/qch de travers *ou* avec méfiance; **she looked rather a. when I suggested Burger King** elle a fait un drôle d'air quand j'ai suggéré Burger King

askew [ə'skjuː] *adv* de biais, de travers; (*to put one's hat on*) de guingois; *Fig* **his calculations were slightly a.** il s'était un peu trompé dans ses calculs; **I don't want anything going a.** je tiens à ce que rien n'aille de travers

asking ['ɑːskɪŋ] *n* (**a**) **it's yours for the a.** il n'y a qu'à (le) demander; **it was theirs for the a.** ils n'ont eu qu'à demander (**b**) **a. price** prix *m* demandé

ask price *n St Exch* cours *m* offert, cours vendeur

aslant [ə'slɑːnt] **1** *adv* obliquement, de travers, de biais **2** *prep* en travers de

asleep [ə'sliːp] *adj pred* endormi; **to be a.** dormir; **to fall a.** s'endormir; **they lay a. on the floor** ils s'étaient endormis par terre; **to be fast** *or* **sound a.** être profondément endormi *ou* plongé dans le sommeil; **my foot is a.** j'ai le pied engourdi

ASLEF ['æzlef] *n Br abbr* **Associated Society of Locomotive Engineers and Firemen**

ASM [eɪe'sem] *n* (**a**) *Mil abbr* **air-to-surface missile** (**b**) *Th abbr* **assistant stage manager**

as-new *adj* comme neuf

asocial [eɪ'səʊʃəl] *adj* asocial, -aux

asp [æsp] *n* (*snake*) (vipère *f*) aspic *m*

asparagus [ə'spærəgəs] *n* (*no pl*) *Culin* asperges *fpl*; **a stick of a.** une asperge; **a. soup** soupe *f* aux asperges; **a. tips** pointes *fpl* d'asperges; *Bot* **a. fern** asparagus *m*

aspect ['æspekt] *n* (**a**) (*of problem, subject etc*) aspect *m*; **the worrying a. of the situation is ...** ce qu'il y a d'inquiétant dans cette situation c'est ...; **there were amusing aspects to the situation** la situation avait des côtés amusants (**b**) *Fml* (*appearance*) air *m*; **man of serious a.** homme à l'air sérieux (**c**) (*outlook*) (*of house etc*) exposition *f*, orientation *f*; **to have a northern a.** être exposé au nord; **flats with southern a.** appartements côté midi (**d**) *Astrol* (*of planets*) aspect *m* (**e**) [①**A39**,7] *Gram* aspect *m*

aspen ['æspən] *n* (*tree*) (peuplier *m*) tremble *m*; **a. leaf** feuille *f* de tremble

asperity [æ'sperɪtɪ] *n* (*of climate*) rigueur *f*, sévérité *f*; (*of character, voice*) aspérité *f*, rudesse *f*; (*of reproach*) âpreté *f*; (*of style*) aspérité

aspersion [ə'spɜːʃən] *n Fml, Hum* calomnie *f*; **to cast aspersions on sth/sb** calomnier qch/qn; **to cast aspersions on sb's honour** porter atteinte à l'honneur de qn

asphalt[1] ['æsfælt] *n Miner, Constr* asphalte *m*, bitume *m*; **a. roadway** chaussée *f* asphaltée

asphalt² *vt Constr* (*road etc*) asphalter, bitumer
asphalting ['æsfæltɪŋ] *n* asphaltage *m*, bitumage *m*
asphyxia [æs'fɪksɪə] *n* asphyxie *f*; **it led to a.** cela a provoqué l'asphyxie *ou* une asphyxie
asphyxiate [æs'fɪksɪeɪt] **1** *vt* asphyxier **2** *vi* mourir d'asphyxie
asphyxiation [æsfɪksɪ'eɪʃən] *n* asphyxie *f*
aspic ['æspɪk] *n Culin* gelée *f*; **eggs in a.** œufs *mpl* en gelée; **chicken/salmon in a.** aspic *m* de volaille/de saumon; *Fig* **preserved in a.** mis sous verre
aspidistra [æspɪ'dɪstrə] *n* (*plant*) aspidistra *m*
aspirant ['æspɪrənt] *n* candidat, -ate
aspirate¹ ['æspɪrət] *adj Ling* aspiré
aspirate² ['æspɪreɪt] *vt* (**a**) *Ling* (*vowel, h*) aspirer (**b**) *Tech* (*gas, liquid*) aspirer; **aspirating filter** filtre *m* à vide
aspiration [æspɪ'reɪʃən] *n* (**a**) *Ling, Med etc* aspiration *f* (**b**) (*ambition*) aspiration *f*; **to have aspirations to greater things/to become a doctor** aspirer à de grandes choses/à devenir médecin; **to have political aspirations** avoir des aspirations politiques; **to have presidential aspirations** aspirer à la présidence
aspirational group [æspɪ'reɪʃən(ə)l] *n Mktg* groupe *m* de référence
aspirator ['æspɪreɪtər] *n Phys, Med* aspirateur *m*
aspire [ə'spaɪər] *vi* aspirer; **to a. to** *or* **after sth** aspirer *ou* prétendre *ou* viser à qch, ambitionner qch; **to a. to do sth** aspirer à *ou* ambitionner de faire qch; **they aspired to greatness** ils aspiraient à la gloire
aspirin ['æsprɪn] *n* (*drug*) aspirine *f*; (*pill*) comprimé *m* d'aspirine
aspiring [ə'spaɪərɪŋ] *adj attrib* (*artiste etc*) en herbe; **to be an a. doctor/dancer** aspirer à devenir médecin/danseur
ass¹ [æs] *n* (**a**) (*animal*) âne *m*; **she a.** ânesse *f*; **a.'s milk** lait *m* d'ânesse; **wild a.** onagre *m* (**b**) (*idiot*) âne *m*, idiot, -ote; **don't be a silly a.** ne fais pas l'imbécile *ou* l'idiot; **to make an a. of oneself** se ridiculiser; (*make an exhibition of oneself*) se donner en spectacle
ass² *n Am Vulg* (*buttocks*) cul *m*; **she's got a great little a. on her** elle a un beau petit cul; **a nice piece of a.** (*woman*) un beau cul, une belle pépée; *see also* **arse**
ass³ *abbr* **assistant**
▶ **ass about** *or* **around** *vi Am Sl* déconner
assail [ə'seɪl] *vt Fml* (*enemy*) assaillir, attaquer; *Fig* **to a. sb with questions** accabler *ou* assaillir qn de questions; **assailed with doubts** saisi de doutes
assailant [ə'seɪlənt] *n* assaillant, -ante, agresseur *m*
assassin [ə'sæsɪn] *n* (*of head of state etc*) assassin *m*; *Hist* **Assassins** Assassins, Ismaïliens *mpl*
assassinate [ə'sæsɪneɪt] *vt* assassiner
assassination [əsæsɪ'neɪʃən] *n* assassinat *m*; **a. attempt** tentative *f* d'assassinat; **character a.** diffamation *f*
assault¹ [ə'sɔːlt] *n* (**a**) *Jur* tentative *f* de voie de fait; (*attempted rape*) tentative *f* de viol; (*rape*) viol *m*; **unprovoked a.** agression *f*; **a. and battery** voies *fpl* de fait, coups *mpl* et blessures *fpl*; **criminal a.** agression (**b**) *Mil* assaut *m*; *Fig* (*on government, person's beliefs etc*) attaque *f* (**on** contre); **to take** *or* **carry a town by a.** prendre une ville d'assaut; **to make an a. on sth** donner l'assaut à qch; *Fig* (*on problem, correspondence*) s'attaquer à qch
assault² *vt* (**a**) (*attack*) (*person*) agresser, attaquer; *Jur* se livrer à des voies de fait sur; (*sexually*) violenter; **to be assaulted** être victime d'une agression; (*sexually*) être victime d'un attentat à la pudeur (**b**) *Mil* (*town, position etc*) attaquer, assaillir, donner l'assaut à; *Fig* (*senses*) agresser
assault course *n Mil, Fig* parcours *m* du combattant
assault craft *n* engin *m* d'assaut
assay¹ [ə'seɪ] *n Metal* (*of precious metal, mineral*) essai *m*; *Ch* dosage *m*; *Admin* **a. office** bureau *m* de garantie des métaux précieux
assay² *vt* (**a**) *Metal* (*precious metal, mineral*) essayer, titrer, analyser; (*metal*) faire l'essai de; (*gold, silver*) coupeller (**b**) *Lit* (*attempt*) tenter
assaying [ə'seɪɪŋ] *n Metal* (*of mineral etc*) essai *m*, titrage *m*, analyse *f*; (*of gold, silver*) coupellation *f*
assemblage [ə'semblɪdʒ] *n* (**a**) *Tech* (*of pieces of woodwork etc*) assemblage *m* (**b**) (*of objects*) collection *f*; (*of individuals*) assortiment *m*
assemble [ə'semb(ə)l] **1** *vt* (**a**) (*people*) rassembler, réunir; (*documents, evidence*) réunir; (*insurgents etc*) ameuter; (*parliament*) convoquer; *Mil* (*troops*) rassembler; **he addressed the assembled schoolchildren** il s'est adressé à l'ensemble des élèves réunis (**b**) *Tech* (*in joinery*) assembler; (*machine*) ajuster, assembler, monter; (*watch etc*) habiller **2** *vi* (*of people*) s'assembler, se rassembler, se réunir; (*of insurgents etc*) s'ameuter
assembler [ə'semblər] *n Ind* monteur, -euse; *Comptr* assembleur *m*
assembly [ə'semblɪ] *n* (**a**) (*gathering*) réunion *f*; *Br Sch etc* rassemblement *m*; **place of a.** lieu *m* de réunion; *Jur* **unlawful a.** attroupement *m*; **right of a.** droit *m* à la liberté de réunion (**b**) *Pol etc* assemblée *f*; **the National A.** l'Assemblée nationale (**c**) *Ind etc* (*assembling*) montage *m*, assemblage *m*; **a. instructions** instructions *fpl* de montage *ou* d'assemblage (**d**) (*group of components*) assemblage *m*
assembly area *n Mil* zone *f* d'attente
assembly hall *n* (**a**) *Sch* = grande salle *f* où se réunissent les élèves le matin (**b**) *Ind* atelier *m* de montage
assembly language *n Comptr* langage *m* assembleur *ou* d'assemblage; **a. program** programme *m* en assembleur
assembly line *n* chaîne *f* de montage; **to work on the a.** travailler à la chaîne
assembly plant *n* usine *f* de montage
assembly rooms *npl* salle *f* des fêtes, salle de danse
assembly shop *n* salle *f* de montage
assent¹ [ə'sent] *n* assentiment *m*; *Jur* agrément *m*; **to withhold one's a. from a proposal** refuser son assentiment à une proposition; **he acted with the full a. of his colleagues** il a agi avec l'approbation totale de ses collègues; **to gain the a. of sb** *or* **sb's a.** obtenir l'assentiment de qn; **the royal a.** le consentement du souverain; **by common a.** du consentement de tous
assent² *vi* donner son assentiment (**to** à); **to a. to a bill** (*of sovereign*) sanctionner une loi
assert [ə'sɜːt] *vt* (**a**) (*one's rights, point of view etc*) faire valoir; **to a. oneself** s'imposer, se faire entendre; **you must a. your authority** il vous faut imposer votre autorité (**b**) (*declare*) (*one's innocence etc*) protester de; **to a. that …** affirmer *ou* prétendre *ou* soutenir que … + *ind*
assertion [ə'sɜːʃən] *n* (**a**) (*of right*) revendication *f* (**b**) (*claim*) assertion *f*, affirmation *f*; **her a. that she had never seen him was unconvincing** elle prétendait de façon peu convaincante qu'elle ne l'avait jamais vu
assertive [ə'sɜːtɪv] *adj* (*tone, person, manner etc*) assuré; **don't be too a.** ne te montre pas trop autoritaire; **he's not a. enough** il n'a pas assez d'autorité, il ne s'affirme pas assez
assertiveness [ə'sɜːtɪvnɪs] *n* assurance *f*; **a. training** cours *m* pour prendre de l'assurance
assess [ə'ses] *vt* (**a**) (*value of sth*) estimer; (*quality of product*) juger de; **to a. the damage** évaluer les dégâts; *Naut* évaluer l'avarie; *Jur* **to a. the damages** fixer les dommages et intérêts; *Admin* **to a. sb at so much** imposer *ou* taxer qn à tant; **to a. a property (for taxation)** évaluer une propriété; **if we a. this speech at its true worth** si nous estimons ce discours à sa juste valeur; **to a. the situation** évaluer la situation; **how do you a. the team's chances?** à votre avis, quelles sont les chances de l'équipe?, quelles chances accordez-vous à l'équipe?; **to a. the chances of sth happening** évaluer les chances que qch a de se produire
(**b**) *Admin* (*tax*) répartir, établir
(**c**) *Sch, Univ* évaluer; **students are continuously assessed** le niveau des étudiants est évalué par un contrôle continu
assessment [ə'sesmənt] *n* (**a**) (*of value of sth*) estimation *f*; (*for insurance or tax purposes*) évaluation *f*; *Jur* **a. of damages** fixation *f* de dommages et intérêts; *Sch* **continuous a.** contrôle *m* continu; **they gave their a. of the situation** ils ont donné leur avis sur la situation, ils ont dit ce qu'ils pensaient de la situation; **what is your a. of their chances?** à votre avis, quelles sont leurs chances?, quelles chances leur accordez-vous?
(**b**) *Admin* (*for tax*) (*of municipality, building*) imposition *f*; (*of taxpayer*) cotisation *f*; (*amount*) cote *f*, taxe *f* officielle; **basis of a.** assiette *f* des impôts; **notice of a.** avis *m* de contributions; **year of a.** année *f* d'imposition; **a. on landed property** cote foncière; **a. on income** impôt *m* sur le revenu
(**c**) *Admin* (*of tax*) répartition *f*, assiette *f*
assessor [ə'sesər] *n* (**a**) (*of tax*) répartiteur *m* (**b**) (*for insurance*) expert *m* (**c**) *Jur* assesseur *m*, juge *m* assesseur
asset ['æset] *n* (**a**) (*advantage*) avantage *m*, atout *m*; **she is a great a. to the firm** c'est un grand atout pour l'entreprise (**b**) *Fin etc* (*usu pl*) **assets** actif *m*, avoir(s) *m(pl)*; (*personal*) patrimoine *m*; *Jur* (*of inheritance, company*) masse *f*; (*on liquidation after bankruptcy*) masse active; **capital assets** actif immobilisé; **frozen assets** fonds *mpl* bloqués *ou* non liquides
asset management *n* gestion *f* de biens; (*of individual's wealth*) gestion de patrimoine
asset-strip *vt* démembrer
asset stripper *n* = personne *f* qui achète une société pour profiter de la réalisation de l'actif
asset-stripping *n* démembrement *m* (*suite au rachat d'une société*)

asseverate [ə'sevəreɪt] *vt Fml* (*one's innocence*) protester de; **to a. that …** affirmer (solennellement) que … + *ind*
asshole ['æshəʊl] *n US Vulg* **(a)** *Anat* trou *m* du cul **(b)** *Fig* (*idiot*) connard *m*, connasse *f*; (*nasty person*) fumier *m*, salaud *m*, salope *f*
assiduity [æsɪ'djuːɪtɪ] *n* assiduité *f* (**in doing sth** à faire qch)
assiduous [ə'sɪdjʊəs] *adj* assidu; **she was a. in her attention to detail** elle portait une attention assidue aux détails
assiduously [ə'sɪdjʊəslɪ] *adv* assidûment
assign¹ [ə'saɪn] *n Jur* légataire *mf*
assign² *vt* **(a)** (*allocate*) (*task, equipment, time, function*) assigner (**to** à); (*funds*) affecter (**to** à); **to a. sb to a task** assigner une tâche à qn; **they had been assigned to guard duty** on leur avait assigné la garde; **responsibilities haven't yet been assigned** les responsabilités n'ont pas encore été réparties *ou* assignées; **to a. sb to do sth** charger qn de faire qch **(b)** (*ascribe*) attribuer; **to a. a reason for sth** donner la raison de qch; **to a. a meaning to a word** attribuer un sens à un mot **(c)** *Jur* (*property*) céder, transférer; (*lawsuits, patent*) transmettre (**to sb** à qn)
assignation [æsɪg'neɪʃən] *n* **(a)** *Old-fashioned* (*meeting*) rendez-vous *m* secret; (*with lover*) rendez-vous galant; **to have an a. with sb** avoir un rendez-vous avec qn **(b)** *Jur* = **assignment** (*c*) **(c)** *Fml* (*allocation etc*) = **assignment (a)**
assignee [æsaɪ'niː] *n* cessionnaire *mf*
assignment [ə'saɪnmənt] *n* **(a)** (*of task, equipment, function*) assignation *f*; (*of funding*) affectation *f*, allocation *f*; (*of duties, responsibilities*) attribution *f*; (*sharing out*) répartition *f*; **a. of sb to a post** affectation de qn à un poste; *Mil* **he was on a. to headquarters** il était affecté au quartier général; *Acct* **a. of accounts receivable** *or* **of debts** transfert *m* de créances
(b) (*task*) *Sch etc* tâche *f* assignée; *Journ* (*of individual reporter*) reportage *m* assigné; **dangerous a.** tâche dangereuse; *Journ* **to be on a.** être en reportage
(c) *Jur etc* (*of property, debts etc*) cession *f*, transfert *m*; **deed of a.** acte *m* attributif, acte de transfert
assignment table *n Comptr* table *f* d'affectation
assimilate [ə'sɪmɪleɪt] **1** *vt* (*food, facts, immigrants etc*) assimiler **2** *vi* **(a)** (*become absorbed*) s'intégrer, être assimilé; (*of people*) s'intégrer **(b)** (*become similar*) **to a. to** *or* **with sth** s'assimiler à qch
assimilation [əsɪmɪ'leɪʃən] *n* (*of food, ideas, immigrants etc*) assimilation *f*
Assisi [ə'siːzɪ, ə'siːsɪ] *n* Assise *f*; **St. Francis of A.** saint François d'Assise
assist [ə'sɪst] **1** *vt* (*person*) aider, prêter son assistance à; (*in their work*) seconder, prêter (son) concours à; (*process*) faciliter; (*sth's growth, development*) contribuer à; **to a. sb in (doing) sth** aider qn à faire qch; **economic growth was assisted by lower interest rates** des taux d'intérêts plus faibles ont contribué à la croissance économique **2** *vi* **(a)** (*help*) aider **(b)** (*be present*) (*at ceremony etc*) assister (**at** à)
assistance [ə'sɪstəns] *n* aide *f*, secours *m*, assistance *f*; **to give sb a.** prêter son aide *ou* assistance à qn; (*in work, task*) prêter (son) concours à qn; **to come to sb's a.** venir en aide à qn; **with the a. of sth/sb** à l'aide de qch/avec l'aide de qn; **can I be of any** *or* **some a.?** puis-je être utile à quelque chose?, est-ce que je peux vous aider?; **to be of as much a. as one can** prêter toute l'assistance possible; **this theatre receives financial a. from the state** ce théâtre reçoit des subventions de l'État; *Br Admin Arch* **National A.** ≈ aide sociale
assistant [ə'sɪstənt] *n* **(a)** aide *mf*, adjoint, -ointe; **(shop) a.** vendeur, -euse; **laboratory a.** laborantin, -ine; **a. accountant** aide-comptable *mf*; **a. director** sous-directeur *m*; **a. editor** *TV* assistant monteur *m*; *Cin* monteur adjoint; *Journ* rédacteur *m* en chef adjoint; *TV* **a. floor manager** régisseur *m* de plateau adjoint; **a. housekeeper** (*in hotel*) aide-gouvernante *f*, assistante gouvernante *f*; **a. manager** sous-directeur, assistant *m* de direction; **a. lecturer,** *Am* **a. professor** ≈ maître *m* assistant; **a. producer** producteur *m* adjoint **(b)** *Sch* assistant, -ante; **French a.** assistant, -ante de français
assize [ə'saɪz] *n Jur* **(a)** (*usu pl*) **(court of) assizes, a. court** (cour *f* d')assises *fpl*; **to be brought before the assizes** être traduit en cour d'assises **(b)** *Scot* (*trial*) jugement *m* par jury; (*jury*) jury *m*
associate¹ [ə'səʊʃɪət, -sɪət] **1** *n* (*in business*) associé, -ée, partenaire *mf*; (*in criminal venture*) complice *mf*; (*of society of letters, science etc*) membre *m* correspondant, associé, -ée **2** *adj* associé; **a. director** réalisateur *m* associé; **a. producer** producteur *m* associé; *Am* **a. professor** ≈ professeur *m* de faculté; **a. membership** (*members*) membres *mpl* associés; (*participation*) adhésion *f* en tant que membre associé
associate² [ə'səʊʃɪeɪt, -sɪeɪt] **1** *vt* **(a)** (*mentally*) (*sb, sth*) associer (**with sb** avec qn; **with sth** à qch); **I don't a. the two things** pour moi, les deux choses sont indépendantes
(b) (*in partnership etc*) **to a. oneself** s'associer (**with sb** avec qn); **to be associated with sb in an undertaking** s'associer avec qn pour une entreprise; **to be associated with sth** (*with project, research etc*) participer à qch; (*with company etc*) avoir des liens avec qch, travailler avec qch; **we are not associated in any way with that company** nous n'avons absolument rien à faire *ou* voir avec cette société
2 *vi* **(a)** (*frequent*) **to a. with sb** fréquenter qn; **to a. with undesirable companions** avoir de mauvaises fréquentations
(b) (*join*) **to a. with sb in sth/doing sth** s'associer *ou* s'unir avec qn pour qch/pour faire qch
associate company *n* société *f* affiliée
associated [ə'səʊsɪeɪtɪd] *adj* associé
associated company *n* société *f* affiliée
association [əsəʊsɪ'eɪʃən] *n* **(a)** (*mental*) association *f*; **a. of ideas** association d'idées; **land full of historic associations** pays fertile en souvenirs historiques; **the name has unfortunate associations for her** ce nom lui évoque des pensées désagréables; **the associations of the name** ce qu'on associe à ce nom
(b) (*of people*) fréquentation *f* (**with sb** de qn); **through long a. with …** à force de fréquenter …; **in a. with …** associé à …; **to do sth in a. with sb** faire qch en association avec qn; **I have no a. with that company** je n'ai pas de liens avec cette compagnie; **it has only a tenuous a. with its original purpose** cela n'a plus qu'un rapport lointain avec l'idée de départ; **my a. with the company has now ended** ma collaboration avec cette compagnie est maintenant terminée
(c) (*organization*) association *f*, société *f*; (*of teachers etc*) amicale *f*; **to form an a.** constituer une société; **trade a.** association professionnelle; **Young Men's/Women's Christian A.** Union *f* chrétienne de jeunes gens/de jeunes femmes; *Jur* **deed of a.** acte *m* d'association
association football *n* football *m* association
association test *n* test *m* d'association
associative [ə'səʊsɪətɪv] *adj Psy* associatif, -ive
assonance ['æsənəns] *n Ling* assonance *f*
assorted [ə'sɔːtɪd] *adj* **(a)** (*sweets, screws etc*) assorti; (*colours*) varié; **an audience of a. academics and businessmen** un public très varié, composé d'universitaires et d'hommes d'affaires **(b)** (*matched*) assorti; **well a. couple** époux bien assortis
assortment [ə'sɔːtmənt] *n* (*of sweets, tools etc*) assortiment *m*; **I did it for an a. of reasons** je l'ai fait pour des raisons diverses; **quite an a. of people** des gens de toutes sortes
asst *abbr* **assistant**
assuage [ə'sweɪdʒ] *vt Lit* (*anger, hunger*) apaiser
assume [ə'sjuːm] *vt* **(a)** (*believe without proof*) présumer, supposer; **we can't a. anything** nous ne pouvons présumer de rien; **if we a. there will be no problems …** en supposant qu'il n'y aura aucun problème, …; **I a. that he will come** je présume qu'il viendra; **he was assumed to be rich** on le supposait riche; **in the absence of proof he must be assumed to be innocent** en l'absence de preuves, il doit être présumé innocent; **don't a. that people will like you because you are rich** ne crois pas que les gens t'aimeront parce que tu es riche; **let us a. that …** mettons *ou* supposons que …; **assuming that the story is true** en supposant *ou* en admettant que l'histoire soit vraie; **to a. the worst** mettre les choses au pis
(b) (*take over*) (*responsibility*) prendre sur soi, assumer; (*duty*) se charger de; (*power, command*) prendre; (*running of hotel, company etc*) prendre en main
(c) (*adopt*) (*right, title etc*) s'attribuer, s'arroger, s'approprier; (*name*) adopter, emprunter; *Jur* **to a. ownership** faire acte de propriétaire
(d) (*take on*) (*air, appearance, tone*) prendre, se donner; (*shape, character*) affecter, revêtir; (*of problem*) (*importance, vast proportions*) prendre; **his voice assumed a tone of authority** sa voix prit un ton autoritaire
(e) (*feign*) (*indifference*) feindre, simuler
assumed [ə'sjuːmd] *adj attrib* (*identity*) faux; (*cause of death, motive, rate of increase*) présumé; **with a. nonchalance** avec une nonchalance feinte; **a. name** nom *m* d'emprunt; (*of author*) pseudonyme *m*; **a. load** (*on bridge etc*) surcharge *f* hypothétique
assumption [ə'sʌmpʃən] *n* **(a)** (*supposition*) supposition *f*, hypothèse *f*; *Phil* postulat *m*; **it's a fair a. that …** on peut facilement supposer que …; **I am going on the a. that …** je me fonde sur l'hypothèse que …; **to work on the a. that …**

se fonder sur l'hypothèse que ...; **the assumptions on which society is based** les idées de base qui servent de fondement à la société

(**b**) (*of power, responsibility etc*) prise *f*; **a. of office** entrée *f* en fonctions; **his a. of the role of chairman** (*after nomination*) son entrée en fonctions en tant que président; (*without consent*) le fait qu'il s'arroge la fonction de président

(**c**) *Rel* (*of Virgin*) assomption *f*; **Feast of the A.** fête *f* de l'Assomption

assurance [ə'ʃʊərəns] *n* (**a**) (*promise*) promesse *f* (formelle); **I can give you an a. that ...** je peux vous assurer *ou* vous affirmer que ...; **he gave us any number of assurances that ...** il nous a assuré maintes et maintes fois que ...; **based on their a. that delivery would be within two days** en considération de leur promesse d'une livraison dans les deux jours

(**b**) (*affirmation*) affirmation *f*; **a. to the contrary** affirmation contraire

(**c**) (*confidence*) assurance *f*; **I have every a. that he will help us** j'ai la ferme assurance qu'il nous aidera

(**d**) (*self-confidence*) assurance *f*, confiance *f* en soi; **to lack a.** (*of person, answer*) manquer d'assurance; **to answer with a.** (*self-confidently*) répondre d'un ton assuré *ou* avec assurance

(**e**) *Br* (*insurance*) assurance *f*; **life a.** assurance sur la vie *f*, assurance-vie *f*, *pl* assurances-vie; **a. company** compagnie *f* d'assurances

assure [ə'ʃʊər] *vt* (**a**) (*sb*) assurer; **to a. sb of the truth of sth** assurer qn de la vérité de qch; **to a. sb of a fact** assurer *ou* affirmer un fait à qn; **he assures me that it is true** il me certifie que c'est vrai; **he assured me he was coming** il m'a assuré qu'il viendrait; **he will do it, I (can) a. you!** il le fera, je vous assure! (**b**) (*ensure*) (*peace, sb's happiness etc*) assurer (**c**) *Br* (*insure*) (*sb's life*) assurer; **to a. one's life** s'assurer (sur la vie)

assured [ə'ʃʊəd] **1** *adj* (**a**) (*certain*) (*success etc*) assuré; **they are a. of victory** ils sont certains de gagner; **she is a. a place in the finals** elle est certaine d'aller en finale; **you're a. of a warm welcome** on vous garantit un accueil chaleureux (**b**) (*self-confident*) (*person*) sûr de soi; (*manner, performance*) plein d'assurance, assuré (**c**) (*in insurance*) **the sum a.** la valeur assurée **2** *n* (*in insurance*) **the a.** l'assuré, -ée, *pl* les assurés, -ées

assuredly [ə'ʃʊərɪdlɪ] *adv Fml* assurément, sans aucun doute; **when she returns, as she a. will, ...** quand elle reviendra, ce qui ne laisse aucun doute, ...

Assyria [ə'sɪrɪə] *n Antiq* Assyrie *f*

Assyrian [ə'sɪrɪən] *Antiq* **1** *adj* assyrien **2** *n* (**a**) Assyrien, -ienne (**b**) *Ling* assyrien *m*

AST [eɪes'tiː] *n Am abbr* **Atlantic Standard Time**

aster ['æstər] *n* (*flower*) aster *m*; **China a.** aster de Chine, reine-marguerite *f*, *pl* reines-marguerites

asterisk[1] ['æst(ə)rɪsk] *n* astérisque *m*

asterisk[2] *vt* (*word etc*) marquer d'un astérisque

astern [ə'stɜːn] *Naut* **1** *adv* à l'arrière, sur l'arrière; **two guns a.** deux canons à l'arrière *ou* en poupe; **to go/come a.** (*of ship*) faire machine *ou* marche arrière; **full speed a.!** en arrière à toute vitesse!, en arrière toute!; **to make a boat fast a.** amarrer un canot derrière; **to fall** *or* **drop a.** (*of another ship*) rester en arrière; **ship right a.** navire droit derrière **2** *prep* **a. of a ship** derrière un navire, sur l'arrière d'un navire; **to pass a. of a ship** passer sur l'arrière d'un navire

asteroid ['æstərɔɪd] *n Astron* astéroïde *m*

asthma ['æsmə] *n* asthme *m*; **to have a.** avoir de l'asthme; **a. sufferer** asthmatique *mf*

asthmatic [æs'mætɪk] *adj, n* asthmatique *mf*

astigmatic [æstɪg'mætɪk] *adj, n Opt* astigmate *mf*

astigmatism [ə'stɪgmətɪz(ə)m] *n Opt* astigmatisme *m*

astir [ə'stɜːr] *adj pred Old-fashioned* (**a**) (*out of bed*) debout, levé (**b**) (*in motion*) animé; **the whole town was a.** toute la ville était en émoi

ASTMS ['æztems] *n Br abbr* **Association of Scientific, Technical and Managerial Staffs**

astonish [ə'stɒnɪʃ] *vt* stupéfier, étonner; **you a. me** vous m'étonnez; **it never fails to a. me that ...** ça m'étonnera toujours de voir que ...; **to be astonished at seeing sth** être étonné *ou* s'étonner de voir qch; **I was astonished at** *or* **by the price** j'ai été étonné du prix; **I am continually astonished by her audacity** son audace ne cesse de m'étonner; **I am astonished that ...** cela m'étonne que ... + *sub*; **she had an astonished look on her face** elle avait l'air étonné *ou* stupéfait

astonishing [ə'stɒnɪʃɪŋ] *adj* étonnant, surprenant; **it is a. to me that ...** je m'étonne que ... + *sub*

astonishingly [ə'stɒnɪʃɪŋlɪ] *adv* étonnamment; **a. enough, he arrived** chose étonnante, il est arrivé

astonishment [ə'stɒnɪʃmənt] *n* étonnement *m*, stupéfaction *f*; **look of a.** regard *m* étonné *ou* stupéfait; **I fell back in a.** j'ai failli en tomber à la renverse; **to my a.** à mon grand étonnement; **to everyone's a.** à la stupéfaction générale

astound [ə'staʊnd] *vt* abasourdir, frapper de stupeur, stupéfier; **I was astounded by it** j'en ai été stupéfait; **you a. me!** c'est stupéfiant!

astounding [ə'staʊndɪŋ] *adj* abasourdissant, renversant; **a., but true!** incroyable, mais vrai!

astrakhan [æstrə'kæn] *n* (*fur*) astrakan *m*; **a. coat** manteau *m* d'astrakan

astral ['æstrəl] *adj Astron* (*body etc*) astral; **a. projection** projection *f* astrale

astray [ə'streɪ] *adv, adj pred* (*lost*) égaré; (*morally*) dévoyé; **to go a.** (*of person, letter etc*) s'égarer; (*morally*) se dévoyer, se détourner du droit chemin; **my pen seems to have gone a.** j'ai égaré mon stylo; **to come a.** (*of hair*) se détacher; (*of wires*) se débrancher; **to lead sb a.** (*with false information*) égarer qn, induire qn en erreur; (*morally*) dévoyer qn, détourner qn du droit chemin

astride [ə'straɪd] **1** *adv Horseriding* à califourchon; **to ride a.** monter à califourchon **2** *prep* **to stand a. sth/sb** enjamber qch/qn; **to sit a. sth** être à cheval *ou* à califourchon sur qch

astringency [ə'strɪndʒənsɪ] *n* virulence *f*, acrimonie *f*

astringent [ə'strɪndʒənt] **1** *adj Med* astringent; *Fig* (*person, voice etc*) caustique **2** *n Med* astringent *m*

astringently [ə'strɪndʒəntlɪ] *adv* (*to say*) d'une voix péremptoire; **a. worded** virulent

astrologer [ə'strɒlədʒər] *n* astrologue *mf*

astrological [æstrə'lɒdʒɪk(ə)l] *adj* astrologique

astrology [ə'strɒlədʒɪ] *n* astrologie *f*

astronaut ['æstrənɔːt] *n* astronaute *mf*

astronautics [æstrə'nɔːtɪks] *n* [①**A10**,c] astronautique *f*

astronomer [ə'strɒnəmər] *n* astronome *mf*

astronomic(al) [æstrə'nɒmɪk, -ɪk(ə)l] *adj* (*year, unit etc*) astronomique; *Fig* **an a. price** un prix astronomique; **an a. failure/disaster** un échec/désastre de proportions astronomiques

astronomically [æstrə'nɒmɪklɪ] *adv* astronomiquement; *Fig* (*to increase*) de façon astronomique; **it's a. expensive** ça coûte les yeux de la tête

astronomy [ə'strɒnəmɪ] *n* astronomie *f*

astrophysicist [æstrəʊ'fɪzɪsɪst] *n* astrophysicien, -ienne

astrophysics [æstrəʊ'fɪzɪks] *n* [①**A10**,c] astrophysique *f*

astroturf ['æstrəʊtɜːf] *n* pelouse *f* artificielle

astute [ə'stjuːt] *adj* (*shrewd*) astucieux; (*person*) astucieux, malin, *f* maligne

astutely [ə'stjuːtlɪ] *adv* astucieusement, avec finesse; **she realised a. that ...** elle a eu la finesse de se rendre compte que ...

astuteness [ə'stjuːtnɪs] *n* astuce *f*, finesse *f*

asunder [ə'sʌndər] *adv Arch, Lit* (*to pieces*) **to tear sth a.** mettre qch en pièces; **the family had been torn a. by war** la famille avait été déchirée par la guerre; **to break a.** se casser en deux

asylum [ə'saɪləm] *n* (**a**) (*shelter*) (lieu *m* de) refuge *m*; (*in church etc*) asile *m* (inviolable); **to seek a.** chercher asile; **he was granted/refused a.** on lui a accordé/refusé l'asile; **the right to** *or* **of a.** le droit d'asile; **political a.** asile politique (**b**) *Arch* (*hospital etc*) hospice *m*; (*for lunatics*) asile *m* d'aliénés

asymmetric(al) [eɪsɪ'metrɪk, -ɪk(ə)l] *adj* asymétrique; **a charmingly a. room** une pièce dont l'asymétrie fait le charme

asymmetry [eɪ'sɪmɪtrɪ] *n* asymétrie *f*

asymptomatic [eɪsɪmptə'mætɪk] *adj Med* asymptomatique

asynchronous [eɪ'sɪŋkrənəs] *adj Comptr* asynchrone; **a. data transmission** transmission *f* de données asynchrone

at [æt, *unstressed* ət] *prep* [①**A65**; **B51**] (**a**) (*place*) à; **at the centre/the top** au centre/sommet; **at table/church/school/the station** à table/l'église/l'école/la gare; **at my side** à mes côtés, à côté de moi; **at hand** sous la main; **at Oxford** à Oxford; **at sea** en mer; **at home** à la maison, chez soi; **at my uncle's/the dentist's** chez mon oncle/le dentiste; **to sit at the window** être assis près de la fenêtre

(**b**) (*time*) **at six o'clock** à six heures; **at present** à présent; **at that time** (*period*) à cette époque, en ce temps-là; **at all times** tout le temps; **at the weekend** (pendant *ou* durant) le week-end; **at a time when ...** à un moment où ...; **two at a time** deux par deux, deux à la fois; **at the beginning of the year** au début de l'année; **at night** la nuit, le soir; **at (the age of) 20** à 20 ans

(**c**) (*price, speed, height etc*) **at two francs a pound** à deux francs la livre; **at 30 mph** à 30 mil(l)es l'heure; **at an**

altitude of 10,000 feet à une altitude de 10 000 pieds; **at 5 feet 2 inches he was too short** avec ses 5 pieds 2 pouces, il était trop petit; **at minus 13°** à moins 13°; **at a rate of 2 cm a year** à un rythme de 2 cm par an

(d) (*state, condition*) **to be at war/peace** être en guerre/paix; **she's not at her best in the morning** le matin, elle n'est pas au mieux de sa forme; **Skye is at its most beautiful in early June** c'est au début juin que Skye est la plus belle; **at all events** en tout cas; **we'll leave it at that for today** nous en resterons là pour aujourd'hui

(e) (*resulting from*) **at my request/invitation** sur ma demande/mon invitation; **at a word from her, he left the room** il a suffi qu'elle prononce un mot pour qu'il quitte la pièce

(f) (*skill*) **quick at repartee** prompt à la repartie; **to be good/bad at mathematics** être fort/faible en mathématiques; **to be good at games** être sportif; **she's very good at making people feel welcome** elle est très douée pour mettre les gens à l'aise

(g) (*direction*) **to look at sb/sth** regarder qn/qch; **to aim at sb** viser qn; **to throw sth at sb/sth** jeter qch sur qn/qch; **to laugh at sb** se moquer de qn; **to swear at sb** jurer contre qn; **to shout at sb** crier après *ou* contre qn; *F* **she is always (on) at him** elle est toujours après lui, elle lui casse tout le temps les pieds; *F* **he's been on at me to do it** il me casse les pieds pour que je le fasse; **at him!** (*to dog*) attaque!

(h) (*cause*) **to be surprised/delighted at sth** être étonné/enchanté de qch; **to be angry at sb** être fâché contre qn; **I'm very excited at the idea of going to Rome** je suis très content à l'idée d'aller à Rome

(i) (*activity*) **to be at work** être au travail; **to be hard at work on a project** travailler dur sur un projet; **school children at play** élèves en récréation; **he's at his beekeeping again** le revoilà à s'occuper de ses abeilles; **I've been at this all morning** je suis là-dessus depuis ce matin; **to keep sb at it** faire trimer qn; **keep at it!** continue!; **she's at it again!** voilà qu'elle recommence!, la voilà qui recommence!; **they're at it again!** (*arguing, having sex*) ils remettent ça!; **they're always at it over something** ils sont toujours à se disputer pour une chose ou pour une autre; **while we are at it** pendant que nous y sommes; **it's an old idea and a rather poor one at that!** cette idée est démodée, et d'ailleurs elle n'est pas très bonne!

(j) *F* **where are we at?** (*situation, in book etc*) où en sommes-nous?; **where's he at politically?** (*what are his views*) politiquement, il se situe où?; **Paris is where it's at!** c'est à Paris que ça se passe!; **that's not where I'm at** (*not my style*) ce n'est pas mon genre; **jazz is not really where I'm at** le jazz, ce n'est pas vraiment mon trip; **that's where I was at musically** c'est ce que j'écoutais (à l'époque)

atavism ['ætəvɪz(ə)m] *n* atavisme *m*

atavistic [ætə'vɪstɪk] *adj* atavique

ataxia [ə'tæksɪə], **ataxy** [ə'tæksɪ] *n Med* ataxie *f*; **locomotor a.** ataxie locomotrice progressive, tabes *m* dorsalis

ate *see* **eat**

atheism ['eɪθɪɪz(ə)m] *n* athéisme *m*

atheist ['eɪθɪɪst] *n* athée *mf*

atheistic(al) [eɪθɪ'ɪstɪk, -ɪk(ə)l] *adj* athée

Athenian [ə'θiːnɪən] **1** *adj* athénien, d'Athènes **2** *n* Athénien, -ienne

Athens ['æθənz] *n* Athènes *f*; **A. Convention** Convention *f* d'Athènes

athlete ['æθliːt] *n* athlète *mf*; *Med* **a.'s foot** pied *m* d'athlète, mycose *f*

athletic [æθ'letɪk] *adj* athlétique; **she's very a.** c'est une sportive; **an a.-looking young man** un jeune homme à l'allure sportive; **I don't do anything very a.** je ne fais pas beaucoup de sport

athletically [æθ'letɪklɪ] *adv* de façon athlétique

athletics [æθ'letɪks] *npl* (*usu with sing verb*) athlétisme *m*; **a. club** société *f* d'athlétisme

at-home *n* réception *f*; (*in evening*) soirée *f*

athwart [ə'θwɔːt] *Naut* **1** *adv* en travers, par le travers **2** *prep* en travers de

atishoo [ə'tɪʃuː] *int* (*sneeze*) atchoum!

Atlantic [ət'læntɪk] **1** *n* **the A. (Ocean)** l'(océan *m*) Atlantique *m* **2** *adj* (*coast etc*) atlantique; *Am* **A. Standard Time** = Temps *m* Universel **A. liner** transatlantique *m*

Atlantis [ət'læntɪs] *n Myth* Atlantide *f*

Atlas ['ætləs] *n* **(a)** *Myth* Atlas *m* **(b) the A. Mountains** l'Atlas *m*

atlas ['ætləs] *n* **(a)** (*book*) atlas *m* **(b)** *Anat* atlas *m* **(c)** *Archit* (*pl* **atlantes** [ət'læntiːz]) atlante *m*, télamon *m*

ATM [eɪtiː'em] *n Banking* (*abbr* **automated teller machine**) D. A. B. *m*

atmosphere ['ætməsfɪər] *n* (*of earth, air*), *Phys* atmosphère *f*; *Fig* atmosphère, ambiance *f*; *Fig* **there was a bit of an a. in the office** l'atmosphère était plutôt tendue au bureau; *Fig* **there was a great a.** il y avait une de ces ambiances; *Fig F* **I don't like atmospheres** je n'aime pas les mauvaises ambiances

atmospheric [ætməs'ferɪk] *adj* (*pressure, condition etc*) atmosphérique; *Fig* (*novel*) plein d'atmosphère; (*lighting, music*) qui met dans l'ambiance; **the music was very a.** la musique vous mettait complètement dans l'ambiance

atmospherics [ætməs'ferɪks] *npl Rad etc* (*interference*) (parasites *mpl*) atmosphériques *fpl*

ATOL [æ'tɒl] *n* (*abbr* **air travel organizer's licence**) licence *m* d'organisateur de voyages par avion

atoll ['ætɒl] *n Geog* atoll *m*

atom ['ætəm] *n Phys* atome *m*; *Fig* **not an a. of common sense** pas un grain de bon sens; **smashed to atoms** réduit en miettes *ou* en poudre; **a. bomb** bombe *f* atomique

atomic [ə'tɒmɪk] *adj* (*energy, war, weapon, explosion*) atomique, nucléaire; *Phys* (*weight, number etc*) atomique; **the a. age** l'ère *f ou* l'âge *m* atomique; **a. physicist** atomiste *mf*; **a. reactor** réacteur *m* nucléaire

atomization [ætəmaɪ'zeɪʃən] *n* (*of fuel*) atomisation *f*, pulvérisation *f*

atomize ['ætəmaɪz] *vt* (*matter*) atomiser; (*fuel*) atomiser, pulvériser; (*in spray, liquid*) vaporiser

atomized ['ætəmaɪzd] *adj* (*life, society*) fragmenté

atomizer ['ætəmaɪzər] *n* atomiseur *m*; **an a. spray** un atomiseur, un vaporisateur

atonal [eɪ'təʊn(ə)l] *adj Mus* atonal

▶ **atone for** [ə'təʊn] *vipo* (*sin, crime*) expier; (*mistake, behaviour*) racheter, réparer

atonement [ə'təʊnmənt] *n* (*for sin, crime*) expiation *f*; (*for mistake, behaviour*) réparation *f* (**for** de); **in a. for a wrong** en réparation d'un tort; *Rel* **to make a.** expier; *Jewish Rel* **Day of A.** Fête *f* du Grand Pardon

atop [ə'tɒp] *prep esp Lit* en haut de, au sommet de; **sitting a. a suitcase** assis sur une valise

atrium ['eɪtrɪəm] *n* **(a)** *Archit* atrium *m* **(b)** *Anat* oreillette *f*

atrocious [ə'trəʊʃəs] *adj* **(a)** *F* (*very bad*) (*pun, weather, journey etc*) atroce, exécrable; (*hat etc*) affreux; (*behaviour, manners, mess*) ignoble; (*injuries*) atroce; **his French is a.** son français est très mauvais; **his singing is a.** il chante atrocement *ou* affreusement mal **(b)** (*crime*) atroce; **a. act** atrocité *f*

atrociously [ə'trəʊʃəslɪ] *adv* **(a)** *F* (*very badly*) exécrablement; **a. bad** atroce, exécrable **(b)** (*cruelly*) atrocement

atrociousness [ə'trəʊʃəsnɪs] *n* **(a)** (*of crime*) atrocité *f* **(b)** *F* (*of pun, weather etc*) caractère *m* exécrable *ou* atroce; **we could scarcely believe the a. of the weather** nous avions peine à croire qu'il faisait un temps aussi exécrable *ou* atroce

atrocity [ə'trɒsɪtɪ] *n* **(a)** (*act*) atrocité *f* **(b)** (*of crime*) atrocité *f*

atrophied ['ætrəfɪd] *adj* atrophié

atrophy[1] ['ætrəfɪ] *n* atrophie *f*

atrophy[2] ['ætrəfɪ, -faɪ] **1** *vt* atrophier **2** *vi* s'atrophier

at-sign *n Typ* arrobas *m*

attaboy ['ætəbɔɪ] *int F* bravo!

attach [ə'tætʃ] **1** *vt* **(a)** (*join*) attacher, fixer (**to** à); (*two things*) attacher; (*document*) annexer, joindre; **the climbers were attached to each other by a rope** les alpinistes étaient reliés *ou* accrochés les uns aux autres par une corde; **the two pieces of paper weren't attached** (*to each other*) les deux feuilles de papier étaient indépendantes; (*enclosed*) les deux feuilles n'étaient pas jointes; **house with garage attached** maison avec garage attenant; **the kitten attached himself to her** (*followed her*) le chaton l'a adoptée

(b) (*assign*) (*importance*) prêter, attacher (**to** à); (*blame*) imputer (**to** à); **official attached to another department** fonctionnaire détaché à un autre service; **to be attached to a unit** être affecté à une unité

(c) *Jur* (*property, salary*) mettre une saisie-arrêt sur

2 *vi* **(a) to a. to** (*fix on to*) s'accrocher à; (*of appliance, shelves*) (*to wall*) se fixer à; (*of rope, hook*) être relié à

(b) no blame attaches to the crew l'équipage n'est nullement à blâmer

attaché [ə'tæʃeɪ] *n* attaché *m*; **military a.** attaché militaire; **a. case** attaché-case *m*, mallette *f*

attached [ə'tætʃt] *adj* **(a) to be a. to sb/sth** (*fond of*) être attaché à qn/qch; **she became very a. to the dog** elle s'est beaucoup attachée au chien **(b) the only woman not a.** (*not married*) la seule femme qui soit libre; **is he a. (to anyone) at the moment?** est-ce qu'il a quelqu'un en ce moment?

attachment [ə'tætʃmənt] *n* **(a)** (*for machine*) accessoire *m*; **lathe with drilling a.** tour avec accessoire pour foret

(b) (*act*) (*of object*) fixation *f* (**to** à); (*of document*) annexation *f* (**to** à)

(c) (*fastener*) attache *f*, lien *m*; **attachments of a muscle** attaches d'un muscle

(d) (*secondment*) rattachement *m*, stage *m*; **to serve an a. with the French army** faire un stage dans l'armée française; **to be on a. to a department** être détaché à un service

(e) (*fondness*) attachement *m* (**for sb** pour qn; **to sth** à qch), affection *f* (**for** pour); **to form an a. for sb** s'attacher à qn, se prendre d'affection pour qn; **because of his a. to the idea** à cause de l'attachement qu'il portait à cette idée

(f) *Jur* arrêt *m*, saisie *f*, saisie-arrêt *f*; **a. of real property** saisie immobilière

attack[1] [ə'tæk] *n* **(a)** *Mil, Sp* attaque *f*; **combined a.** attaque combinée; **to be/come under a. from sb** être attaqué par qn; **to launch an a.** lancer une attaque; **a. is the best form of defence** l'attaque est la meilleure forme de défense

(b) (*on person*) agression *f*, attaque *f* (**on** contre); *Pol* attentat *m*

(c) (*strong criticism*) attaque *f* (**on sb** contre qn; **on sth** de *ou* contre qch); **an a. on freedom of speech/on the right to strike** une atteinte à la liberté d'expression/au droit de grève

(d) *Med* (*of asthma etc*) attaque *f*, crise *f*; (*of fever*) poussée *f*; **a. of nerves** (*nervousness*) trac *m*; (*hysteria*) crise de nerfs; **to have an a. of the shakes** être pris de tremblements; **to have an a. of giddiness** être pris de vertiges; **an a. of self-doubt** une crise de doute

(e) *Mus* (*of note*) attaque *f*

attack[2] **1** *vt* **(a)** *Mil, Sp* attaquer; **to be attacked** subir une attaque, être attaqué; *Fig* **the government is attacking our rights** le gouvernement porte atteinte à nos droits **(b)** (*person*) (*in street etc*) agresser, attaquer **(c)** (*criticize*) (*person, project etc*) attaquer; (*abuse of sth etc*) s'attaquer à **(d)** (*set about with energy*) (*task, problem etc*) s'attaquer à **(e)** (*of disease*) (*person, organ etc*) s'attaquer à, atteindre; (*of rust*) (*metal*) attaquer, s'attaquer à, ronger; (*of fear, doubts*) assaillir **2** *vi* attaquer

attacker [ə'tækər] *n* attaquant, -ante, agresseur *m*, assaillant, -ante; *Sp* attaquant, -ante; **could you describe your a.?** pourriez-vous décrire votre agresseur?

attacking [ə'tækɪŋ] *adj* attaquant; (*game, play*) d'attaque

attagirl ['ætəgɜːl] *int F* bravo!

attain [ə'teɪn] **1** *vt* (*great age, one's ends, success etc*) atteindre, parvenir à, arriver à; (*high rank, position*) s'élever jusqu'à, parvenir à; (*knowledge*) acquérir; (*ambition*) réaliser; (*happiness*) atteindre; **to a. a reputation** se faire une réputation (**for** de) **2** *vi Fml* **to a. to perfection** atteindre la perfection; **to a. to power** arriver au pouvoir

attainable [ə'teɪnəb(ə)l] *adj* (*dream, ambition etc*) réalisable

attainment [ə'teɪnmənt] *n* **(a)** (*no pl*) (*achieving*) (*of goal, ambition*) réalisation *f*; (*of independence*) obtention *f*; (*of happiness*) conquête *f*; **for the a. of his purpose** pour atteindre ses fins, pour arriver à ses fins **(b)** (*skill, achievements*) (*usu pl*) **attainments** (*knowledge*) connaissance(s) *f(pl)*; (*skills*) talents *mpl*; **man of considerable attainments** homme qui a beaucoup d'instruction *ou* d'acquis; **her linguistic attainments** sa connaissance des langues

attempt[1] [ə'tempt] *n* **(a)** (*effort*) tentative *f*, essai *m*; **an a. at a smile** l'esquisse *f* d'un sourire; **was that an a. at an apology?** est-ce que c'était censé être une excuse?; **her feeble a. to justify herself** la piètre tentative qu'elle a faite pour se justifier; **without (making) any a. at concealment** sans chercher à se cacher; **they made no a. to help** ils n'ont pas essayé d'aider; **a. to escape** tentative d'évasion; **to make an a. at (doing) sth** *or* **to do sth** essayer *ou* tâcher de faire qch; **he made an a. at War and Peace** il a essayé de lire Guerre et paix; **to make an a. on a record** *or* **to beat a record** essayer de battre un record; **to make an a. on Everest** tenter l'ascension de l'Everest; **first a.** coup *m* d'essai, première tentative; **it wasn't bad for a first a.** ce n'était pas mal pour une première tentative *ou* un premier essai; **at the first a.** du premier coup; **at the fourth a.** à la quatrième tentative, au quatrième coup; **to make another a.** renouveler ses tentatives, revenir à la charge; **to give up the a.** y renoncer; **he died in the a.** il est mort en essayant

(b) (*attack*) attentat *m*; **a. on sb's life** attentat à la vie de qn; **to make an a. on sb's life** attenter à la vie de qn

attempt[2] *vt* **to a. to do sth** essayer *ou* tenter de faire qch, chercher à faire qch; **he attempted to get up** il essaya *ou* tenta de se lever; **he attempted a smile** il s'efforça de sourire; **to a. a piece of work** entreprendre un travail; **candidates must a. five questions** les candidats doivent traiter cinq questions; **to a. the impossible** tenter l'impossible; **attempted murder/theft** tentative *f* d'assassinat/de vol

attend [ə'tend] **1** *vi* **(a)** (*be present*) être présent; **two delegates did not a.** deux délégués étaient absents

(b) (*pay attention*) faire attention

(c) *Fml* (*serve*) **to a. on sb** servir qn, être au service de qn

2 *vt* **(a)** (*go to*) (*church, school, funeral*) aller à; (*be present at*) (*conference, meeting*) assister à; (*course*) suivre; **the lectures are well attended** les cours sont très suivis; **the celebrations were well attended** les cérémonies ont attiré beaucoup de monde

(b) (*of doctor*) (*sick person*) soigner, donner des soins à

(c) *Lit Fml* (*accompany*) accompagner; **success attended my efforts** mes efforts furent couronnés de succès; **it was attended by considerable publicity** cela s'est accompagné d'une vaste publicité

(d) *Fml* (*serve*) **we were attended by three waiters** nous étions servis par trois garçons; **to a. a prince** suivre *ou* accompagner un prince

▶ **attend to** *vipo* **(a)** (*deal with*) (*matter*) s'occuper de; (*one's business*) vaquer à; (*one's interests*) veiller à; (*one's health, appearance*) soigner; (*order*) exécuter; **I shall a. to it** je m'en occuperai, je m'en chargerai **(b)** (*customer etc*) s'occuper de; **are you being attended to?** est-ce qu'on s'occupe de vous? **(c)** (*pay attention to*) faire *ou* prêter attention à; **a. to what I'm saying** écoutez attentivement ce que je dis

attendance [ə'tendəns] *n* **(a)** (*presence*) (*at meeting*) présence *f*; **regular a.** assiduité *f*; **school a.** fréquentation *f* scolaire; **church attendances have fallen** le nombre de personnes qui vont à l'église a baissé; **his a. has been good/bad** il a été/il n'a pas été assidu; **poor a.** manque *m* d'assiduité; **a. register** registre *m* de présence

(b) (*people present*) assistance *f*; **there was a good a. at the meeting** il y avait une assistance nombreuse à la réunion; **there was a record a. at the final** la finale a attiré un nombre record de spectateurs; **the evening class had to be cancelled because of poor a.** le cours du soir a dû être annulé pour manque d'élèves

(c) to be in a. on (*of doctor*) (*sick person*) donner des soins à; (*of courtier*) (*king etc*) être de service auprès de; **with six bodyguards in a.** accompagné de six gardes du corps; **in close a.** à proximité

attendance allowance *n Br* = allocation *f* versée aux familles qui ont des handicapés à charge

attendance list *n* (*for meetings*) liste *f* de présence

attendance sheet *n* (*for meetings*) feuille *f* de présence

attendant [ə'tendənt] **1** *n* **(a)** (*official*) surveillant, -ante; (*in public lavatory, cloakroom etc*) préposé, -ée; (*in museum, car park etc*) gardien, -ienne; (*in theatre*) ouvreuse *f*; **(petrol-)pump a.** pompiste *mf*; **swimming pool a.** maître *m* nageur **(b)** (*usu pl*) **attendants** (*of king etc*) gens *mpl*, suite *f* **2** *adj Fml* **a. on sb/sth** qui accompagne qn/qch; **famine and its a. diseases** la famine et les maladies dont elle s'accompagne; *Jur* **a. circumstances** (*of crime etc*) circonstances *fpl* concomitantes

attending [ə'tendɪŋ] *adj Med* **the a. physician** le médecin traitant

attention [ə'tenʃən] *n* **(a)** attention *f* (**to** à); **a. to details** attention portée aux détails; **a. to truth** souci *m* de vérité; **to pay a. to sth** faire attention à qch; **to pay a.** *or* **give one's a. to sb** prêter attention à qn; **she didn't pay a. in class** elle n'a pas été attentive en cours; **to give sb/sth one's full a.** consacrer toute son attention à qn/qch; **you have my undivided a.** je suis tout à vous; **the report will receive our full a.** nous prêterons une attention toute particulière à ce rapport; **your a. please, ladies and gentlemen** mesdames et messieurs, votre attention s'il vous plaît; **particular a. should be given to posture** surveillez tout particulièrement votre attitude; *Admin, Com* **for the a. of Mr Green** à l'attention de M. Green; **to turn one's a. to sth** diriger son attention vers qch, porter son attention sur qch; **she constantly switched her a. between the two conversations** elle passait sans cesse d'une conversation à l'autre; **to call** *or* **attract** *or* **draw (sb's) a. to sth** attirer l'attention (de qn) sur qch, faire remarquer qch (à qn); **to draw a. to oneself** se faire remarquer; *Fml* **it has been brought to our a. that …** il a été porté à notre connaissance que …, on nous a fait savoir *ou* remarquer que …; **to catch sb's a.** attirer *ou* capter l'attention de qn; **to attract everybody's a.** fixer tous les regards; **to hold** *or* **engage sb's a.** retenir l'attention de qn; **to get a.** (*of application, plan etc*) être considéré; **the child doesn't get much a. at home** on ne s'occupe pas beaucoup de cet enfant chez lui; **he gets all the a.** il n'y en a que pour lui; **he just does it to get a.** il ne fait ça que pour se faire remarquer; **she likes being the centre of a.** elle aime être le centre du monde; (*at party*) elle aime se faire remarquer

(b) (*maintenance*) soins *mpl*, entretien *m*; **the engine needs** *or* **requires some a.** le moteur a besoin d'entretien *ou* d'être entretenu; **the batteries require daily/monthly a.** les accus exigent un entretien journalier/mensuel; **the bathroom looks as if it needs some a.** la salle de bains a besoin d'être un peu retapée

(c) *Old-fashioned* **attentions** (*acts of affection*) attentions *fpl*, prévenances *fpl*, empressement *m*; **he was always paying his wife little attentions** il était toujours plein d'attentions *ou* de prévenances pour sa femme; **to pay one's attentions to a lady** faire la cour à une dame

(d) *Mil* **a.!** garde-à-vous!; **to come to a.** se mettre au garde-à-vous; **to stand at a.** être *ou* se tenir au garde-à-vous

attention seeking *n* **it's just a.** il/elle ne cherche qu'à attirer l'attention sur lui/elle

attention span *n* capacité *f* de concentration; **a short/long a.** une faible/bonne capacité de concentration; **his a. is no longer than half an hour** il ne peut pas se concentrer pendant plus d'une demi-heure

attentive [ə'tentɪv] *adj* **(a)** (*pupil, listener, audience etc*) attentif (**to** à); (*in one's work*) soigneux (**to** de); **she is very a. to detail** elle porte une grande attention aux détails **(b)** (*anxious to please, considerate*) prévenant, empressé, attentionné; **to be very a. to sb** être très attentionné pour qn, être très empressé auprès de qn; **she was a. to his every need** elle était aux petits soins pour lui; *esp Fml* **thank you, most a.** merci, c'est très aimable à vous

attentively [ə'tentɪvlɪ] *adv* attentivement

attentiveness [ə'tentɪvnɪs] *n* **(a)** (*concentration*) attention *f* **(b)** (*anxiety to please*) prévenances *fpl*, empressement *m* (**to sb** auprès de qn); **to look after sb with a.** être plein de prévenances pour qn

attenuate [ə'tenjʊeɪt] **1** *vt* **(a)** (*seriousness of sth etc*) atténuer; **attenuating circumstances** circonstances *fpl* atténuantes **(b)** *Tech* (*gas etc*) raréfier **2** *vi Tech* s'atténuer, diminuer

attenuation [ətenjʊ'eɪʃən] *n* atténuation *f*

attenuator [ə'tenjʊeɪtər] *n TV etc* atténuateur *m*

attest [ə'test] **1** *vt* **(a)** (*affirm, prove*) (*fact*) attester; **to a. that …** attester que …; **the document attests the fact that …** le document atteste que …; *Agr* **attested herd** troupeau *m* tuberculiné **(b)** (*of witness*) (*sth*) affirmer sous serment; (*signature*) légaliser; **attested copy** copie *f* certifiée **(c)** *Jur* (*sb*) assermenter **2** *vi* **to a. to sth** (*be evidence of*) témoigner de qch; (*give evidence of*) attester qch

attestation [æte'steɪʃən] *n Jur* **(a)** (*of witness*) déposition *f*, témoignage *m* **(b)** (*of fact*) attestation *f* **(c)** (*of signature*) légalisation *f* **(d)** (*oath taking*) prestation *f* de serment

attic ['ætɪk] *n* grenier *m*; **a. room** mansarde *f*; **a. window** fenêtre *f* en mansarde; (*skylight*) lucarne *f*

Attica ['ætɪkə] *n Hist, Lit* Attique *f*

attire¹ [ə'taɪər] *n Fml* (*clothing*) tenue *f*

attire² *vt Arch, Lit* (*usu passive or reflexive*) vêtir, parer; **attired in black/silk** vêtu de noir/soie

attitude ['ætɪtju:d] *n* **(a)** (*of mind*) attitude *f*; **what's your a. to people who say that?** que pensez-vous des gens qui disent cela?; **what's your a. to abortion?** que pensez-vous de l'avortement?, quelle est votre attitude face à l'avortement?; **old-fashioned attitudes** des idées *fpl* démodées; **their a. is that …** leur point de vue est que …; **she takes the a. that …** elle considère que …; **his whole a. is 'I don't care'** tout lui est égal; **I don't like your a.** je n'aime pas ton attitude; **well, if that's your a.** très bien, si c'est comme ça que tu le prends; **she's got an a. problem** elle n'est pas du tout coopérative; *US F* **she's got a.** elle a du caractère; *F* **a car with a.** une voiture qui a du caractère

(b) (*pose*) attitude *f*, pose *f*; **to strike an a.** prendre une attitude dramatique, poser

(c) *Av etc* (*of plane, missile etc on its trajectory*) attitude *f*

attitude survey *n* enquête *f* d'attitudes

attn *abbr* **attention**

attorney [ə'tɜ:nɪ] *n Jur* **(a)** *Am* (*lawyer*) avocat *m*; *US* **District A.** ≈ procureur *m* de la République **(b)** (*legal agent*) procureur *m*, fondé *m* de pouvoir(s)

Attorney General *n Eng* = Procureur *m* général; *US* = Procureur général d'un État; *Can* = Ministre *m* de la Justice

attract [ə'trækt] *vt* (*of magnet, person, advert etc*) attirer (**to** à, vers); **he is not attracted to her** elle ne lui plaît pas, *F* elle ne lui dit rien; **I was sexually attracted to her** elle m'attirait physiquement; **what really attracts me to him is his sense of humour** ce qui me plaît chez lui c'est son sens de l'humour; **the prospect of a week in London doesn't a. me** ça ne me dit rien d'aller passer une semaine à Londres; **how does that a. you?** qu'est-ce que tu dis de ça?

attraction [ə'trækʃən] *n* **(a)** (*act, power*) attraction *f*, attirance *f* (**to** vers); **wealth has no a. for her** elle n'est pas attirée par la richesse; **the prospect holds little/no a. for me** cette perspective ne me dit pas grand-chose/rien du tout; **I can't** *or* **don't see the a. of it** je n'en vois pas l'intérêt; **his a. to her** son attirance pour elle

(b) (*thing, person*) attraction *f*; **the chief a.** (*at fair*) la grande attraction; (*in show etc*) le clou; **tourist a.** attraction pour touristes; **it's the main a. of the job** c'est ce que cet emploi a de plus attrayant

(c) (*of person*) (*usu pl*) **physical attractions** charmes *mpl* physiques; **that's one of my attractions** cela fait partie de mes charmes

attractive [ə'træktɪv] *adj* **(a)** (*person, offer, manner, prospect etc*) attrayant, attirant, séduisant; (*house, town, region*) beau, *f* belle; (*village*) coquet; (*price*) intéressant, attrayant, attractif; **do you find him a.?** il te plaît?, tu le trouves séduisant?; **in an a. shade of blue** dans une jolie teinte de bleu **(b)** (*magnet, properties*) attractif, attirant

attractively [ə'træktɪvlɪ] *adv* d'une manière attrayante *ou* séduisante; **a. bound in red leather** élégamment relié de cuir rouge; **a. priced** à un prix attrayant *ou* attractif; **an a. laid out garden** un jardin qui est un plaisir pour les yeux

attractiveness [ə'træktɪvnɪs] *n* attrait *m*; **the a. of their prices/offer** leurs prix attrayants/leur offre attrayante

attributable [ə'trɪbjʊtəb(ə)l] *adj* (*words, success, work of art*) attribuable (**to** à); (*crime, fault etc*) imputable (**to** à)

attribute¹ ['ætrɪbju:t] *n* **(a)** (*quality*) attribut *m* **(b)** [①**A17**,2-3] *Gram* épithète *f*

attribute² [ə'trɪbju:t] *vt* (*work of art, success etc*) attribuer (**to** à); (*quality, words*) prêter, attribuer (**to** à); (*mistake, error, crime etc*) imputer (**to** à)

attribution [ætrɪ'bju:ʃən] *n* (*of words, work of art etc*) attribution *f* (**to** à); (*of crime, fault etc*) imputation *f* (**to** à)

attributive [ə'trɪbjʊtɪv] *Gram* [①**A17**,2-3] **1** *adj* **a. adjective** épithète *f* **2** *n* épithète *f*

attributively [ə'trɪbjʊtɪvlɪ] *adv* [①**A17**,2-3] (*word used*) avec valeur d'épithète

attrition [ə'trɪʃən] *n* **(a)** (*wearing away*) usure *f* par le frottement; **policy of a.** politique *f* d'usure; **war of a.** guerre *f* d'usure **(b)** *Econ, Ind* attrition *f*, départs *mpl* volontaires

attune [ə'tju:n] *vt* accorder, harmoniser (**to** avec); **ear attuned to every sound** oreille exercée à saisir tous les sons; **to a. oneself** *or* **become attuned to sth** se faire à qch, s'accoutumer à qch

ATW [eɪti:'dʌb(ə)lju:] (*abbr* **around the world**) autour du monde

atypical [eɪ'tɪpɪk(ə)l] *adj* atypique

aubergine ['əʊbəʒi:n] *n Br Culin* aubergine *f*

auburn ['ɔ:bən] *adj* (*hair*) châtain roux, auburn *inv*

auction¹ ['ɔ:kʃən] *n* **(a)** *Com* **(sale by) a., a. sale** vente *f* aux enchères; (*for fish, vegetables etc*) (vente à la) criée *f*; **car a.** vente aux enchères de voitures; **to sell by a.** *or* **at a.** vendre aux enchères; (*fish etc*) vendre à la criée; **to put sth up for a.** mettre qch aux enchères; **the estate is up for a.** le domaine va être mis *ou* vendu aux enchères; **a. room** salle *f* des ventes; (*for fish, vegetables etc*) chambre *f* des criées **(b)** *Cards* enchère *f*; **a. bridge** bridge *m* aux enchères

auction² *vt* (*put up for auction*) mettre aux enchères; (*sell*) vendre aux enchères; (*foodstuffs, building by legal authority*) vendre à la criée

▶ **auction off** *vtsep* vendre aux enchères

auctioneer [ɔ:kʃə'nɪər] *n* commissaire-priseur *m*, *pl* commissaires-priseurs; (*at fish or vegetable market etc*) crieur, -euse

audacious [ɔ:'deɪʃəs] *adj* **(a)** (*daring*) (*attempt, neckline*) audacieux, hardi **(b)** (*insolent*) effronté, hardi

audaciously [ɔ:'deɪʃəslɪ] *adv* **(a)** (*bravely*) audacieusement, avec audace **(b)** (*insolently*) effrontément

audacity [ɔ:'dæsɪtɪ] *n* **(a)** (*bravery*) audace *f*, intrépidité *f*, hardiesse *f* **(b)** (*nerve*) audace *f*, effronterie *f*; **to have the a. to do sth** avoir l'audace de faire qch

audibility [ɔ:dɪ'bɪlɪtɪ] *n* perceptibilité *f*, audibilité *f*

audible ['ɔ:dɪb(ə)l] *adj* (*sound*) perceptible (à l'oreille); (*speech, voice*) audible; **he was scarcely a.** on l'entendait à peine; *Phys* **a. frequency** fréquence *f* audible

audibly ['ɔ:dɪblɪ] *adv* (*to speak*) de façon à être entendu; (*to yawn, purr*) bruyamment

audience ['ɔ:dɪəns] *n* **(a)** [①**A11**,g,i] (*spectators, listeners*) assistance *f*, assistants *mpl*; *Th* spectateurs *mpl*, auditoire *m*, public *m*; *Rad* auditeurs *mpl*; *TV* téléspectateurs *mpl*; *Mktg* (*for product, advertisement*) public *m*; **the whole a. applauded** toute la salle applaudit; **do we have any Americans in the a.?** y a-t-il des Américains dans la salle?; **to perform before a large a.** se produire devant un nombreux public; *Mktg* **a. exposure** exposition *f* au public; **a. mesurement** mesure *f* de l'audience; **a. participation** participation *f* de l'assistance; **a. research** étude *f* d'audience; **a. show** émission *f* en public; *Mktg* **a. size** audience *f* cumulée

(**b**) *Fml* (*with king, pope etc*) audience *f*; **to grant sb an a.** donner audience *ou* accorder une audience à qn; **to hold an a.** tenir une audience; **a. chamber** salle *f* d'audience

audio ['ɔːdɪəʊ] **1** *adj attrib* sonore; **a. cassette** cassette *f* (audio); **a. cassette recorder** magnétophone *m* à cassette; **a. CD** CD *m* audio; **a. (control) console** pupitre *m* son; **a. equipment** équipement *m* sonore; *TV etc* **a. feedback** effet *m* Larsen, bouclage *m*; *Rad etc* **a. frequency** audiofréquence *f*, fréquence *f* acoustique; **a. logo** logo *m* audio; **a. recording** enregistrement *m* audio, enregistrement son; **a. signal** signal *m* audio, signal son; **a. system** système *m* audio; **a. tape** bande *f* magnétique audio; **a. tape recorder** magnétophone *m* à bande; **a. track** piste *f* son **2** *n* son *m*

audioconference ['ɔːdɪəʊkɒnfərəns] *n* audioconférence *f*

audio library *n* sonothèque *f*, phonothèque *f*

audiometer ['ɔːdɪəʊmiːtər] *n Tech* audiomètre *m*

audiotyping ['ɔːdɪəʊtaɪpɪŋ] *n* audiotypie *f*

audiotypist ['ɔːdɪəʊtaɪpɪst] *n* audiotypiste *mf*

audiovisual [ɔːdɪəʊ'vɪzjʊəl] *adj* audiovisuel; **a. equipment** équipement *m* audiovisuel, matériel *m* audiovisuel; **a. archives** archives *fpl* audiovisuelles

audit[1] ['ɔːdɪt] *n Fin* audit *m* (comptable), vérification(s) *f(pl)* comptable(s), apurement *m*; *Admin* **A. office** ≈ Cour *f* des Comptes; *Econ* **internal a.** contrôle *m* interne

audit[2] *vt* (**a**) *Fin* (*accounts*) vérifier, apurer, examiner (**b**) *Am Univ* (*course*) assister en auditeur libre à

auditing ['ɔːdɪtɪŋ] *n* vérification *f* et certification *f* des écritures, apurement *m*

audition[1] [ɔː'dɪʃən] *n Th, Mus etc* audition *f*; **I've got an a.** je vais passer une audition; **she didn't even get an a.** elle n'a même pas obtenu d'audition

audition[2] *vti Th, Mus etc* auditionner (**for a part** pour un rôle)

auditor ['ɔːdɪtər] *n* (**a**) *Admin* vérificateur *m* des comptes (**b**) *Com, Fin* audit *m*, auditeur, -trice; (*of company*) commissaire *m* aux comptes; (*of insurance company*) censeur *m*; **firm of auditors** cabinet *m* d'audit, cabinet comptable (**c**) (*at conference, lecture etc*) auditeur, -trice; *Am Univ* auditeur, -trice libre

auditorium [ɔːdɪ'tɔːrɪəm] *n* auditorium *m*; (*of theatre, concert hall*) salle *f*; (*lecture theatre*) amphithéâtre *m*

auditors' report *n* rapport *m* des vérificateurs

auditory ['ɔːdɪtrɪ] *adj Anat* (*nerve etc*) auditif; **the a. organ** l'organe *m* de l'ouïe

audit trail *n* vérification *f* à rebours

AUEW [eɪjuːiː'dʌb(ə)ljuː] *n Br abbr* **Amalgamated Union of Engineering Workers**

Aug *abbr* **August**

Augean [ɔː'dʒiːən] *adj Myth* **the A. Stables** les écuries *fpl* d'Augias

auger ['ɔːgər] *n Carp* tarière *f*

aught [ɔːt] *n Arch, Lit* quelque chose *m*, quoi que ce soit; **for a. I know** (pour) autant que je sache

augment [ɔːg'ment] **1** *vt Fml* augmenter, accroître (**with, by** de); *Mus* **augmented interval** intervalle *m* augmenté; *Mktg* **augmented product** produit *m* augmenté **2** *vi Fml* augmenter, s'accroître

augmentation [ɔːgmen'teɪʃən] *n* (*of fortune etc*) augmentation *f*, accroissement *m*

augur[1] ['ɔːgər] *Lit* **1** *vt* augurer, présager, prédire; **it augurs no good** cela ne présage *ou* n'annonce rien de bon **2** *vi* **it augurs well/ill** c'est de bon/de mauvais augure (**for** pour); **it doesn't a. well for the future** cela ne présage *ou* n'annonce rien de bon

augur[2] *n Antiq, Lit* (*prophet*) augure *m*

augury ['ɔːgjʊrɪ] *n* (**a**) *Fml* (*sign*) augure *m*, présage *m* (**b**) (*practice*) science *f* des augures, science augurale

August ['ɔːgəst] *n* (①A75-6,B-C; B58-9,B-C) août *m*; **in A.** au mois d'août, en août; **(on) the first of A.** le premier août; **an A. evening** un soir d'août

august [ɔː'gʌst] *adj* (*assembly*) auguste; (*bearing, figure*) imposant, majestueux

Augustinian [ɔːgə'stɪnɪən] **1** *adj Rel, Hist* augustinien, de saint Augustin; **A. monk** *or* **friar** Augustin *m* **2** *n Rel* Augustin, -ine

Augustus [ɔː'gʌstəs] *n* Auguste *m*

auk [ɔːk] *n* (*bird*) alque *f*; **great a.** grand pingouin *m*

auld [ɔːld] *adj Scot* vieux; **a. lang syne** le temps jadis, le bon vieux temps

aunt [ɑːnt] *n* tante *f*; *Fig* **A. Sally** (*game*) ≈ jeu *m* de massacre; (*object, person*) objet *m* de dérision; (*argument*) argument *m* bidon

auntie, aunty ['ɑːntɪ] *n* (**a**) *F* tatie *f*, tata *f*, tantine *f*; **A. Julia** tatie *ou* tata Julia (**b**) *Br Sl* **Auntie** = la BBC

au pair[1] [əʊ'peər] **1** *n* (jeune fille *f*) au pair *f*; **she's working as an a.** elle travaille au pair **2** *adv* **she's staying with them a.** elle est chez eux au pair

au pair[2] *vi* travailler *ou* être au pair

aura ['ɔːrə] *n* (**a**) aura *f*; (*of place*) atmosphère *f*; **he's got an a. of ...** une aura de ... émane de lui (**b**) *Med* aura *f*; **epileptic a.** aura épileptique

aural ['ɔːrəl] *adj* auditif, sonore; **a. comprehension** compréhension *f* orale; **a. surgeon** *or* **specialist** auriste *m*; *Rad etc* **a. reception** réception *f* du son

aureola [ɔː'riːələ], **aureole** ['ɔːrɪəʊl] *n* (**a**) *Art* (*of saint*) auréole *f* (**b**) *Astron* (*of sun*) auréole *f*

auricle ['ɔːrɪk(ə)l] *n Anat* (**a**) (*of heart*) auricule *m* (**b**) (*external ear*) pavillon *m*

auricular [ɔː'rɪkjʊlər] *adj* (**a**) *Anat* auriculaire (**b**) *Rel* **a. confession** confession *f* auriculaire

aurochs ['ɔːrɒks] *n* (*animal*) aurochs *m*

Aurora [ɔː'rɔːrə] *n Myth* Aurore *f*

aurora [ɔː'rɔːrə] *n* aurore *f*; **a. borealis/australis** aurore boréale/australe

auscultate ['ɔːskəlteɪt] *vt Med* ausculter

auscultation [ɔːskəl'teɪʃən] *n Med* auscultation *f*

auspices ['ɔːspɪsɪz] *npl* auspices *mpl*; **favourable a.** d'heureux auspices; **under the a. of the United Nations** sous l'égide des Nations Unies

auspicious [ɔː'spɪʃəs] *adj* (*wind etc*) propice, favorable; (*sign*) de bon augure; (*age*) heureux, prospère; **an a. start to a career** des débuts prometteurs dans une carrière; **on this a. occasion** en ce jour mémorable

auspiciously [ɔː'spɪʃəslɪ] *adv* sous d'heureux auspices, favorablement; **to begin a.** bien commencer

auspiciousness [ɔː'spɪʃəsnɪs] *n* (*of beginning*) aspect *m* prometteur; **the a. of this omen** cet heureux auspice

Aussie ['ɒzɪ] *F* **1** *adj* australien **2** *n* (**a**) Australien, -ienne; **A. Land** Australie *f* (**b**) *Ling* anglais *m* australien

austere [ɒ'stɪər] *adj* (*life, style, person etc*) austère; (*home*) sans luxe, d'un goût sévère

austerely [ɒ'stɪəlɪ] *adv* austèrement, avec austérité; (*to live*) dans l'austérité, austèrement; (*furnished*) sans luxe, de façon dépouillée

austerity [ɒ'sterɪtɪ] *n* (*of life*) austérité *f*; (*of home furnishings*) dépouillement *m*; **a. measures** mesures *fpl* d'austérité

Australasia [ɒstrə'leɪʒə, -'leɪʃə] *n* Australasie *f*

Australasian [ɒstrə'leɪʒən, -'leɪʃən] **1** *adj* australasien **2** *n* Australasien, -ienne

Australia [ɒ'streɪlɪə] *n* Australie *f*

Australian [ɒ'streɪlɪən] **1** *adj* australien **2** *n* (**a**) Australien, -ienne (**b**) *Ling* anglais *m* australien

Austria ['ɒstrɪə] *n* Autriche *f*

Austria-Hungary *n Hist* Autriche-Hongrie *f*

Austrian ['ɒstrɪən] **1** *adj* autrichien **2** *n* Autrichien, -ienne

Austro-Hungarian ['ɒstrəʊhʌŋ'geərɪən] *adj Hist* austro-hongrois; **the A. Empire** l'empire d'Autriche-Hongrie

autarchy ['ɔːtɑːkɪ] *n* autarchie *f*

autarky ['ɔːtɑːkɪ] *n* autarcie *f*

authentic [ɔː'θentɪk] *adj* (*document, fact, story etc*) authentique

authentically [ɔː'θentɪklɪ] *adv* authentiquement

authenticate [ɔː'θentɪkeɪt] *vt* (**a**) (*prove genuine*), *Jur* authentifier (**b**) *Mil, Rad* (*correspondent*) identifier

authenticity [ɔːθen'tɪsɪtɪ] *n* authenticité *f*

author ['ɔːθər] *n* (*of book, plan etc*) auteur *m*; **to be an a.** être écrivain; *Lit* **to be the a. of one's own misfortunes** être l'artisan de ses malheurs

authoress [ɔːθə'res] *n Old-fashioned* femme *f* auteur, écrivain *m*

authoritarian [ɔːθɒrɪ'teərɪən] *adj, n* autoritaire *mf*

authoritative [ɔː'θɒrɪtətɪv] *adj* (**a**) (*character, tone*) autoritaire (**b**) (*statement, book, document etc*) qui fait autorité; **to have sth from an a. source** avoir qch de source autorisée *ou* de bonne source

authoritatively [ɔː'θɒrɪtətɪvlɪ] *adv* (**a**) (*commandingly*) autoritairement; (*to look*) d'un air autoritaire (**b**) **I can state a. that ...** je puis affirmer de source sûre que ...

authority [ɔː'θɒrɪtɪ] *n* (**a**) (*power*) autorité *f*; **those in a.** les autorités; **in a position of a.** en position d'autorité; **to be in** *or* **have** *or* **exercise a. over sb** (*officially*) avoir *ou* exercer une autorité sur qn; (*have power*) avoir de l'ascendant sur qn; **an air of a.** un air autoritaire

(**b**) (*authorization*) autorisation *f*, mandat *m*; **to have a. to act** avoir qualité pour agir; **to give sb a. to do sth** autoriser qn à faire qch; **they had the full a. of the law** ils ont agi avec la pleine autorité de la loi; **to act on sb's a.** agir sur l'autorité de qn; **to do sth on one's own a.** faire qch de sa propre autorité; **on what a./on whose a. did they search the house?** avec quelle autorisation/avec l'autorisation de qui ont-ils perquisitionné la maison?

(c) (*of person, book*) **to be an a.** être expert dans la matière; **to be an a. on sth** faire autorité en matière de qch; **to have sth on good a.** tenir *ou* savoir qch de bonne part *ou* de bonne source *ou* de source autorisée; **to quote sb as one's a.** se réclamer de qn; **to quote one's authorities** citer ses sources *ou* ses auteurs; **she spoke with a.** elle a parlé avec autorité

(d) *Admin* **the authorities** les autorités *fpl*; (*government*) l'administration *f*; **the health authorities** les services *mpl* de santé; **the military authorities** les autorités militaires

authorization [ɔːθəraɪ'zeɪʃən] *n* autorisation *f* (**to do sth** de faire qch); (*given to official*) pouvoir *m*, mandat *m*; **to give sb/to be given a. to do sth** donner à qn/recevoir l'autorisation de faire qch

authorize ['ɔːθəraɪz] *vt* (*sb, sth*) autoriser (**to do sth** à faire qch); **to be authorized to act on sb's behalf** avoir qualité pour agir au nom de qn; **to a. a payment** ordonnancer un paiement; **to a. a price** homologuer un prix

authorized ['ɔːθəraɪzd] *adj* autorisé; (*supplier etc*) agréé; *Mil etc* réglementaire; **a. to sign** habileté à signer; *Rel* **the A. Version** = la traduction anglaise de la Bible de 1611; **a. capital** capital *m* autorisé; *Admin* **a. charges** prix *mpl* homologués; **a. distributor** distributeur *m* agréé; **a. representative** (*of company*) agent *m* autorisé *ou* mandataire; **a. share capital** capital *m* autorisé; **a. signatory** signataire *m* autorisé *ou* accrédité

authorship ['ɔːθəʃɪp] *n* (*of book, plan etc*) paternité *f*; **to establish the a. of a book** identifier l'auteur d'un livre; **a manuscript of unknown a.** le manuscrit d'un auteur anonyme

autism ['ɔːtɪz(ə)m] *n Med* autisme *m*

autistic [ɔː'tɪstɪk] *Med* **1** *adj* autistique, autiste **2** *n* autiste *mf*

auto ['ɔːtəʊ] *n Am F* auto(mobile) *f*, voiture *f*; **a. accident** accident *m* de voiture

auto- ['ɔːtəʊ] *pref* auto-

auto-addresser ['ɔːtəʊədresər] *n* (*on laser printer*) adressage *m* automatique

auto-answer *n Comptr* (*in datacomms*) réponse *f* automatique

auto-antigen [ɔːtəʊ'æntɪdʒən] *n Med* auto-antigène *m*

autobank ['ɔːtəʊbæŋk] *n* distributeur *m* automatique de billets

autobiographical [ɔːtəʊbaɪə'græfɪk(ə)l], **autobiographic** [ɔːtəʊbaɪə'græfɪk] *adj* autobiographique

autobiography [ɔːtəʊbaɪ'ɒgrəfɪ] *n* autobiographie *f*

autocade ['ɔːtəʊkeɪd] *n US* cortège *m* de voitures

autocracy [ɔː'tɒkrəsɪ] *n* autocratie *f*

autocrat ['ɔːtəkræt] *n* autocrate *m*

autocratic(al) [ɔːtə'krætɪk, -ɪk(ə)l] *adj* (*government, policies*) autocratique; (*person*) autocrate; (*character*) absolu

autocratically [ɔːtə'krætɪklɪ] *adv* autocratiquement

autocue ['ɔːtəʊkjuː] *n TV* téléprompteur *m*

autodial ['ɔːtəʊdaɪəl] *n* numérotation *f* automatique

autodialler ['ɔːtəʊdaɪələr] *n* numéroteur *m* automatique

autodidact [ɔːtəʊ'daɪdækt] *n Fml* autodidacte *mf*

auto-dissolve *n TV, Cin* fondu *m* enchaîné automatique

autoexec. bat [ɔːtəʊeksek'bæt] *n Comptr* **a. (file)** fichier *m* autoexec. bat

autofocus ['ɔːtəʊfəʊkəs] *n* **camera with a.** appareil *m* autofocus

autogenous [ɔː'tɒdʒɪnəs] *adj Biol, Metal* autogène

autogiro [ɔːtəʊ'dʒaɪrəʊ] *n Av* autogyre *m*

autograft ['ɔːtəgrɑːft] *n Med* autogreffe *f*

autograph[1] ['ɔːtəgrɑːf, -græf] *n, adj* autographe *m*; **a. album** album *m* de signatures; **a. hunter** *or* **collector** collectionneur, -euse d'autographes

autograph[2] *vt* (*book, photo, programme etc*) signer, dédicacer

autogyro [ɔːtəʊ'dʒaɪrəʊ] = **autogiro**

auto-ignition *n* auto-allumage *m*

autoload ['ɔːtəʊləʊd] *vi Comptr* se charger automatiquement

automat ['ɔːtəmæt] *n Old-fashioned Am* cafétéria *f* à distributeurs automatiques

automatable ['ɔːtəmeɪtəb(ə)l] *adj* automatisable

automate ['ɔːtəmeɪt] *vt* automatiser

automated ['ɔːtəmeɪtɪd] *adj* automatisé; *Banking* **a. clearing house** chambre *f* de compensation automatisée; **a. reservation** réservation *f* télématique; **a. teller machine** distributeur *m* automatique de billets; **a. ticket** billet *m* informatisé; **a. withdrawal** retrait *m* automatique

automatic[1] [ɔːtə'mætɪk] *adj* (**a**) automatique; **fully a.** entièrement automatique; **a. backup** sauvegarde *f* automatique; **a. dialling** composition *f* automatique de numéros; **a. search** (*on cassette player*) recherche *f* automatique (de séquences musicales); **a. ticket distributor** distributeur *m* automatique de titres de transport; **a. ticket machine** billetterie *f* automatique; **a. time and date stamping machine** dateur *m* automatique (**b**) (*movement*) automatique, inconscient, machinal

automatic[2] *n* (**a**) *Aut* (voiture *f*) automatique *f*; **a Renault**® **a.** une Renault® (avec boîte de vitesses) automatique (**b**) (*pistol*) automatique *m*

automatically [ɔːtə'mætɪklɪ] *adv* (**a**) automatiquement; **a. renewable** renouvelable automatiquement (**b**) (*without thinking*) sans réfléchir, automatiquement

automatic pilot *n Av* pilotage *m* automatique; **to be** *or* **function on a.** (*of aircraft, Fig person*) être en pilotage automatique

automatic pistol *n* (pistolet *m*) automatique *m*

automatic transmission *n Aut* transmission *f* automatique

automation [ɔːtə'meɪʃən] *n* automatisation *f*

automatization [ɔːtɒmətaɪ'zeɪʃən] *n* automatisation *f*

automaton, *pl* **-ons, -a** [ɔː'tɒmətən, -ənz, -ə] *n* automate *m*

automobile ['ɔːtəməʊbiːl] *n Am* automobile *f*, voiture *f*; **a. club** club *m* automobile; **the a. industry** l'industrie *f* automobile; **a. manufacture** fabrication *f* d'automobiles; **a. workers** ouvriers *mpl* de l'industrie automobile

Automobile Association *n* = société *f* de dépannage pour les automobilistes, ≈ Touring Club *m* de France

automotive [ɔːtəʊ'məʊtɪv] *adj* (**a**) (*self-propelled*) automoteur, -trice (**b**) *Aut* automobile; **a. engineering** technique *f* automobile; **a. parts** pièces *fpl* d'automobile

autonomous [ɔː'tɒnəməs] *adj* autonome

autonomy [ɔː'tɒnəmɪ] *n* autonomie *f*

autopilot ['ɔːtəʊpaɪlət] *n Av* pilotage *m* automatique; **to be on a.** (*of aircraft, Fig person*) être en pilotage automatique

autopsy[1] ['ɔːtɒpsɪ, ɔː'tɒpsɪ] *n* autopsie *f*; **to carry out an a.** faire une autopsie; *Fig esp Pol* faire une analyse

autopsy[2] *vt* autopsier

auto-redial *n* re-numérotation *f* automatique

auto-refresh *n Comptr* autorafraîchissement *m*

autoreverse ['ɔːtəʊrɪvɜːs] *n* autoreverse *m*, inversion *f* automatique du sens de défilement

autosave ['ɔːtəʊseɪv] *n Comptr* sauvegarde *f* automatique

autosome ['ɔːtəsəʊm] *n* (*in genetics*) chromosome *m* somatique

autosuggestion [ɔːtəʊsə'dʒestʃən] *n Psy* autosuggestion *f*

autoswitch ['ɔːtəʊswɪtʃ] *n Comptr* commutateur *m* automatique

autumn ['ɔːtəm] *n* [①**A6-7**,d,v; **B4**,3,c] automne *m*; **in a.** en automne; **an a. evening** une soirée d'automne; **a. plants** plantes *fpl* automnales; **a. crocus** safran *m* cultivé; **a. leaves** feuilles *fpl* d'automne; **a. colours** couleurs *fpl* automnales *ou* de l'automne; *Lit* **he was in the a. of his years** il était à l'automne de sa vie

autumnal [ɔː'tʌmn(ə)l] *adj* automnal, d'automne; **a. equinox** équinoxe *m* d'automne; **a. shades** teintes *fpl* automnales; **there was an a. feeling in the air, it was a.** il y avait de l'automne dans l'air

auxiliary [ɔːg'zɪlɪərɪ, -zɪlərɪ] **1** *adj* [①**A38**,3; **B25-26**] (*staff, troops etc*) auxiliaire; (*machine etc*) auxiliaire, de secours; (*heating, lighting*) d'appoint; **a. driving lamps** feux *mpl* facultatifs; *Gram* **a. verb** verbe *m* auxiliaire **2** *n* [①**A38**,3; **B25-26**] auxiliaire *mf Gram* (verbe *m*) auxiliaire *m*; *Mil* **auxiliaries** (troupes *fpl*) auxiliaires *mpl*; **nursing a.** infirmier, -ière auxiliaire

AV [eɪ'viː] (**a**) (*abbr* **Authorized Version**) traduction *f* anglaise de la Bible de 1611 (**b**) (*abbr* **audiovisual**) audiovisuel

Av (*abbr* **avenue**) av.

avail[1] [ə'veɪl] *n* **of no a., without a.** sans effet; **to be of little a.** être peu utile *ou* peu avantageux; **to no a.** sans résultat; **to work to little** *or* **no a.** travailler sans (grand) résultat; **their efforts were all to no a.** leurs efforts n'ont produit aucun résultat

avail[2] *Lit* **1** *vt* **to a. oneself of sth** (*of guidebook, map*) se servir *ou* s'aider de qch; (*of offer*) profiter de qch; (*of right*) user *ou* faire usage de qch; (*of sb's services*) faire appel à qch; **to a. oneself of the opportunity to do sth** saisir l'occasion de faire qch **2** *vi* **nothing availed against the storm** contre la tempête nous ne pouvions/il ne pouvait/*etc* rien

availability [əveɪlə'bɪlɪtɪ] *n* (*of materials, people etc*) disponibilité *f*; **offer subject to a.** dans la limite des stocks disponibles; (*of tickets*) dans la limite des places disponibles

available [ə'veɪləb(ə)l] *adj* (*worker, room, theatre seat etc*) disponible; (*for interview etc*) libre; **they used the time a. to evacuate the area** ils ont utilisé le temps dont ils disposaient pour évacuer le secteur; **capital that can be made a.** capitaux *mpl* mobilisables; **a. for work** disponible; **when are you a. to start work?** à partir de quand pouvez-vous commencer à travailler?; **a. for delivery** livraison immédiate; *Com* **a. in all bookshops** en vente *ou* disponible chez tous les libraires; *Com* **also a. in white** existe également en blanc; **illegal drugs are readily a. in the town**

on se procure facilement de la drogue dans cette ville; **pocket calculators weren't a. then** les calculatrices de poche n'existaient pas à cette époque-là; **legal aid should be a. to everyone** l'assistance juridique devrait être accessible à tous; **I'm catching the first a. flight** je prends le premier avion; **they're not readily a.** il est difficile de s'en procurer; *Fin* **a. balance** solde *m* disponible; **a. bed capacity** capacité *f* d'accueil; **a. capital** capitaux *mpl* disponsibles; **a. funds** fonds *mpl* liquides *ou* disponibles, disponibilités *fpl*; *Phot* **a. light** lumière *f* naturelle; *Mktg* **a. market** marché *m* effectif; **a. means** moyens *mpl* disponibles; **to try every a. means** essayer tous les moyens possibles

aval [æ'væl] *n Banking* aval *m* bancaire

avalanche ['ævəlɑːntʃ] *n* (*of snow, Fig of congratulations, mail etc*) avalanche *f*; **an a. of tourists** une nuée de touristes

avalize ['ævəlaɪz] *vt Banking* avaliser

avant-garde [ævɒŋ'gɑːd] **1** *n* avant-garde *f* **2** *adj* d'avant-garde, avant-gardiste; **a. films** films *mpl* d'avant-garde

avarice ['ævərɪs] *n* cupidité *f*

avaricious [ævə'rɪʃəs] *adj* cupide

avariciously [ævə'rɪʃəslɪ] *adv* (*to behave*) cupidement

avast [ə'vɑːst] *int Old-fashioned Naut* tiens bon!, tenez bon!, baste!

Ave[1] ['ɑːvɪ] *n* **A. Maria** avé (Maria) *m inv*

Ave[2] (*abbr* **avenue**) av.

avenge [ə'vendʒ] *vt* (*person, crime*) venger; **to a. oneself for an insult/on sb** se venger d'une injure/de qn

avenger [ə'vendʒər] *n* vengeur *m*, vengeresse *f*

avenging [ə'vendʒɪŋ] *adj* (*angel etc*) vengeur, *f* vengeresse

avenue ['ævɪnjuː] *n* **(a)** allée *f*; (*with trees*) avenue *f*; *Fig* **to explore every a.** explorer toutes les voies; **this opens up another a. of investigation** ceci ouvre une nouvelle voie de recherche; **an a. to fame/wealth** un moyen de parvenir à la gloire/fortune **(b)** (*in street name*) avenue *f* **(c)** *esp US* (*wide street*) boulevard *m*

aver [ə'vɜːr] *vt* **(-rr-)** *Lit* déclarer, affirmer **(that** que**)**

average[1] ['ævərɪdʒ] **1** *n* **(a)** moyenne *f*; **on a.** en moyenne; **to work out the a.** établir la moyenne; **that gives an a. of 6** ça fait une moyenne de 6; **above (the) a.** au-dessus de la moyenne; **to spend an a. of £85 per week** dépenser en moyenne 85 livres par semaine; **a. unit cost** coût *m* moyen unitaire

(b) (*in marine insurance*) avarie(s) *f*(*pl*)

2 *adj* (*price, time, weight etc*) moyen; **the a. Englishman** l'Anglais *m* moyen; **of a. height** de taille moyenne; **the food is better than a.** la nourriture est au-dessus de la moyenne; **no better than a.** pas si bien que ça; **far from a.** exceptionnel; **in an a. week** dans une semaine ordinaire; **how was your day? – a.** comment s'est passée ta journée? – moyen; *F* **a very a. singer** un chanteur de qualité très moyenne

average[2] *vt* **(a)** (*amount to on average*) **to a. so much** atteindre une moyenne de tant; **sales a. a thousand copies a year** la vente moyenne *ou* la moyenne des ventes est de mille exemplaires par an; **to a. eight hours' work a day** travailler en moyenne huit heures par jour; **to a. 85 kph** rouler en moyenne à 85 km/h; **household spending averages £80 per week** les dépenses des ménages sont de *ou* atteignent les 80 livres par semaine en moyenne **(b)** (*calculate average of*) (*results, sales etc*) calculer *ou* faire la moyenne de

▶ **average out 1** *vtsep* (*calculate average of*) **I've averaged out how much I spend a week** j'ai calculé combien je dépense en moyenne par semaine **2** *vi* **how does it a. out per week?** combien ça fait en moyenne par semaine?; **it'll a. out over a month** sur un mois ça s'équilibrera

▶ **average out at** *vipo* (*amount to as an average*) équivaloir en moyenne à; **what does it a. out at?** ça fait combien en moyenne?

average adjuster *n Fin* dispacheur *m*, expert-répartiteur *m*

average adjustment *n Fin* dispache *f*

averse [ə'vɜːs] *adj* opposé **(to** à**)**; **to be a. to sth** (*to task, job*) répugner à qch; (*to criticism, change etc*) détester qch; **to be a. to doing sth** répugner à faire qch; **why are you so a. to the idea of helping?** pourquoi l'idée d'apporter ton aide te répugne-t-elle tant?; **he is not a. to a glass of beer** il prend volontiers un verre de bière

aversion [ə'vɜːʃən] *n* **(a)** (*feeling*) aversion *f*; **to feel** *or* **have an a. to sb** ressentir de l'aversion pour *ou* envers qn; **to feel** *or* **have a great a. to sth/to doing sth** avoir horreur *f* de qch/ de faire qch **(b)** (*thing*) objet *m* d'aversion; **my pet a.** ma bête noire

avert [ə'vɜːt] *vt* **(a)** (*eyes, one's gaze, thoughts*) détourner **(from** de**)** **(b)** (*suspicion, danger, misfortune*) écarter, éloigner, prévenir; (*catastrophe, accident, war*) éviter, parer à, conjurer; (*blow*) détourner

aviary ['eɪvɪərɪ] *n* volière *f*

aviation [eɪvɪ'eɪʃən] *n* aviation *f*; **a. history** histoire *f* de l'aviation

aviator ['eɪvɪeɪtər] *n Old-fashioned* aviateur, -trice

aviculture ['eɪvɪkʌltʃər] *n* aviculture *f*

avid ['ævɪd] *adj* passionné, fervent **(for** de**)**; **to be a. for sth** être avide de qch; **a. reader** lecteur, -trice passionné(e)

avidity [ə'vɪdɪtɪ] *n* avidité *f* **(for** de, pour**)**

avidly ['ævɪdlɪ] *adv* avidement, avec avidité

avionics [eɪvɪ'ɒnɪks] *n* [①A10,c] avionique *f*

avocado [ævə'kɑːdəʊ] *n* **a. (pear)** (*fruit*) avocat *m*; (*tree*) avocatier *m*

avoid [ə'vɔɪd] *vt* (*sb, sth*) éviter; (*punishment etc*) se soustraire à; (*sb's attentions, blow, difficulty*) esquiver; (*truth, fact*) nier; **you've been avoiding me** tu m'évites; **to a. doing sth** éviter de faire qch; **I could not a. speaking to him** je ne pouvais faire autrement que de lui parler; **to a. (paying) tax** échapper à *ou* se soustraire à l'impôt; **to a. sb like the plague** fuir qn comme la peste; **to a. sth like the plague** éviter qch à tout prix; **he avoided doing his homework until the last possible minute** il a reculé le moment de faire ses devoirs jusqu'à la dernière minute; **the comparison is hard to a.** la comparaison est difficile à éviter; **to a. sb's eye** fuir le regard de qn; **to a. the issue** éviter *ou* contourner le problème; *Pej* (*be devious*) esquiver la question

avoidable [ə'vɔɪdəb(ə)l] *adj* évitable

avoidance [ə'vɔɪdəns] *n* **a. of taxes** évasion *f* fiscale; **a. of payment** non-paiement *m*

avoirdupois [ævədə'pɔɪz] *n* **(a)** poids *m* du commerce; **ounce a.** once *f* avoirdupois **(b)** *Hum* (*stoutness*) excès *m* de poids, embonpoint *m*

avow [ə'vaʊ] *vt Fml* **(a)** (*declare*) **to a. oneself a socialist** se déclarer socialiste **(b)** (*admit*) (*mistake*) avouer, admettre; **to a. oneself beaten** s'avouer vaincu

avowal [ə'vaʊəl] *n* déclaration *f*

avowed [ə'vaʊd] *adj* (*enemy, believer etc*) déclaré; **a. atheist** athée *m* de son propre aveu

avowedly [ə'vaʊɪdlɪ] *adv* de son propre aveu

avuncular [ə'vʌŋkjʊlər] *adj* paternel

await [ə'weɪt] *vt Lit* (*sth, sb*) attendre; *Com* **awaiting your instructions** dans l'attente de vos instructions; **soldiers awaiting discharge** soldats en instance de libération; *Com* **parcel awaiting delivery** colis en souffrance; *Com* **awaiting collection** en souffrance; *Jur* **to be awaiting trial** être en instance de jugement

awake[1] [ə'weɪk] *adj pred* éveillé; **to stay a.** rester éveillé; **he lay a. for hours worrying** l'inquiétude l'a tenu éveillé pendant des heures; **I was a.** je ne dormais pas; **drink some coffee, and that will keep you a.** bois du café, ça te tiendra éveillé; **that noise is keeping me a.** ce bruit m'empêche de dormir; **to be a. to** (*aware of*) (*possibility*) avoir conscience de; (*danger, fact etc*) se rendre compte de, avoir conscience de; (*careful of*) (*one's interests*) veiller à

awake[2] (*pt* **awoke** [ə'wəʊk]; *pp* **awoken** [ə'wəʊkən]) **1** *vi* s'éveiller, se réveiller; **to a. from a deep sleep** se réveiller d'un profond sommeil; **I awoke to the sound of birds singing** à mon réveil j'ai entendu chanter les oiseaux; *Fig* **to a. to** (*danger, fact etc*) se rendre compte de, prendre conscience de; (*possibility*) prendre conscience de; **to a. from** (*illusion, dream etc*) revenir de; (*trance, unconsciousness*) sortir de **2** *vt* (*person, sb's remorse*) éveiller, réveiller; (*curiosity, suspicions, interest*) éveiller; (*hope, passion*) faire naître; *Fig* **to a. sb to sth** faire prendre conscience de qch à qn

awaken [ə'weɪk(ə)n] *vti* = **awake**[2]

awakening [ə'weɪk(ə)nɪŋ] *n* réveil *m*

award[1] [ə'wɔːd] *n* **(a)** (*for writer, actor etc*) prix *m*; *Mil etc* distinction *f* honorifique; *Sch etc* récompense *f*; **to make/be given an a.** décerner/recevoir un prix/une récompense; **the annual awards ceremony** la cérémonie annuelle de remise des prix; **the Oscar awards ceremony** la cérémonie de remise des Oscars **(b)** *Jur* (*money*) dommages-intérêts *mpl*; (*decision*) décision *f* (arbitrale), adjudication *f*; (*of contract*) adjudication *f*; **to make an a.** rendre un jugement (arbitral)

award[2] *vt* (*prize*) décerner, adjuger; (*medal*) décerner, remettre; (*contract*) adjuger; (*high office*) conférer; (*pay increase, grant, free kick*) accorder; **she was awarded first prize** on lui a décerné le premier prix; *Jur* **to a. sb a sum as damages** allouer *ou* attribuer une somme à qn à titre de dommages-intérêts

award-winning *adj* (*film, book etc*) primé; (*writer, actor*) à qui on a décerné un prix; **his a. performance** son interprétation qui lui a valu un prix

aware [ə'weər] *adj* **(a) to be a. of sth** (*fact*) avoir connaissance *ou* conscience de qch, être au courant de qch; **I wasn't a. of**

him je ne m'étais pas aperçu qu'il était là; **I am a. of all the circumstances** je connais tous les détails; **I am well** *or* **fully a. that ...** je n'ignore pas que ..., j'ai pleinement conscience que ...; **were you a. that your husband owed money?** saviez-vous que votre mari était endetté?; **not that I am a. of** pas que je sache; **as far as I'm a.** autant que je sache; **to become a. of** (*fact*) prendre connaissance de; **I became a. of a smell of burning/a presence** j'ai senti une odeur de brûlé/une présence

(**b**) (*well-informed*) **socially/environmentally a.** au courant *ou* informé des questions sociales/de l'environnement; **politically a.** politisé

awareness [əˈweənɪs] *n* (*of sth*) conscience *f*; **he has little a. of the situation** il n'a guère conscience de la situation; *Mktg* **a. study** étude *f* de notoriété

awash [əˈwɒʃ] *adj* (**a**) *Naut* (*of submarine etc*) à fleur d'eau; **rocks a. at high tide** roches couvertes d'eau à marée haute (**b**) (*flooded*) inondé; *Fig* **to be a. with money** crouler sous l'argent; **his desk was a. with complaints** son bureau croulait sous les lettres de réclamation

away [əˈweɪ] **1** *adv* (**a**) (*in opposite direction*) **to turn (one's face) a. from sth** détourner la tête de qch; **to look a.** détourner son regard; **the signpost pointed a. from the village** le bras du poteau indiquait une direction opposée à celle du village; **to go a.** partir, s'en aller; **to walk/drive a.** partir (à pied/en voiture); **to run/fly a.** s'enfuir/s'envoler

(**b**) (*at a distance*) **far a.** dans le lointain, au loin; **a. in the distance** tout au loin; **the town is five miles a.** la ville est à (une distance de) cinq mil(l)es; **it's less than five minutes' walk a.** c'est à moins de cinq minutes à pied; **the church was set a. from the road** l'église était située en retrait par rapport à la route; **to hold sth a. from sth** tenir qch éloigné *ou* loin de qch

(**c**) (*absent*) **a. from home** absent (de chez soi); **he is a.** (*from home, school etc*) il est absent; **she is a. on business** elle s'est absentée pour affaires; *Sp* **to play a.** jouer à l'extérieur

(**d**) (*disappearance*) **to melt a.** (*of snow*) fondre; **to boil a.** s'évaporer; **to fade** *or* **die a.** (*of sound*) s'éteindre; (*of protests*) se taire; **to fritter a.** (*one's money, time*) gaspiller; **put that knife a.!** range ce couteau!

(**e**) (*continuity*) **to work a.** travailler beaucoup *ou* (*stronger*) sans relâche; **he was coughing a.** il toussait beaucoup; **to laugh/hoot a.** ne pas s'arrêter de rire/klaxonner

(**f**) (*elliptical*) **a. with you!** (*don't be silly*) arrête!; *esp Arch, Lit* **a. with him!** emmenez-le!; *Arch, Lit* **we must a.** il nous faut partir

(**g**) (*in motion*) **and they're a.!** (*at beginning of race etc*) et ils sont partis!; *F* **a couple of drinks and he's a.** (*talking, doing sth*) deux verres et il est parti; *F* **well a.** (*progressing*) bien en train; (*drunk*) soûl

(**h**) (*without delay*) **to do sth right** *or* **straight a.** faire qch tout de suite *ou* sur-le-champ

(**i**) (*time*) **I knew him a. back in 1950** je l'ai connu dès 1950; **that was a. back** c'était il y a longtemps; **it's two weeks a.** c'est dans deux semaines; **Christmas is only two weeks a.** il n'y a que deux semaines jusqu'à Noël, nous ne sommes qu'à deux semaines de Noël

2 *adj Sp* **a. ground** terrain *m* adverse; **a. match** *or* **game** match *m* à l'extérieur; **a. team** équipe *f* visiteuse

AWB [eɪdʌb(ə)ljuːˈbiː] *n Com* (*abbr* **air waybill**) LTA *f*

awe[1] [ɔː] *n* (*fear*) crainte *f*; (*respect*) respect *m*, révérence *f*; **to strike sb with a.** (*of person*) imposer à qn un respect mêlé de crainte; (*of object, phenomenon*) faire une forte impression à qn; **to be in a. of sb/sth, to hold sb/sth in a.** (*fear*) craindre *ou* redouter qn/qch; (*respect*) avoir une crainte respectueuse de qn/qch

awe[2] *vt Fml* (*frighten*) remplir de crainte; (*make respect*) intimider, impressionner; **the children were awed by the cathedral/the tone of her voice** les enfants ont été terriblement impressionnés par la cathédrale/le ton de sa voix; **they were awed into silence** ils tombèrent dans un silence respectueux

aweigh [əˈweɪ] *adv Naut* **with anchor a.** l'ancre dérapée; **anchors a.!** levez l'ancre!

awe-inspiring *adj* imposant, impressionnant

awesome [ˈɔːsəm] *adj* (**a**) (*awe-inspiring*) (*height, strength*) imposant, impressionnant; (*responsibility, task*) imposant; (*prospect*) effrayant; **the a. silence of the desert** le silence imposant du désert (**b**) *US F* (*wonderful*) super

awe-struck, awe-stricken *adj* (*frightened*) terrifié; (*respectful*) intimidé, impressionné; **to be a. by sb/sth** être terriblement impressionné par qn/qch

awful [ˈɔːfʊl] **1** *adj* (**a**) horrible, effroyable; **to die an a. death** mourir d'une mort horrible; **that's the a. part of it** c'est cela le plus terrible; **an a. silence** un silence effroyable (**b**) *F* (*very bad*) horrible, affreux, abominable; **it's simply a.** c'est affreux *ou* horrible; **she's an a. woman** c'est une femme épouvantable; **what a. weather!** quel temps abominable!; **he's an a. fool** il est bien bête; **an a. lot of people** énormément de gens; **I don't care an a. lot** ça ne me fait pas grand-chose **2** *adv F* terriblement; **I'm a. glad to see you** je suis rudement content de vous voir; **an a. long time** terriblement longtemps

awfully [ˈɔːflɪ] *adv* (**a**) terriblement, effroyablement (**b**) *F* (*very*) énormément; **I'm a. sorry** je regrette infiniment *ou* énormément; **I'm a. glad** je suis rudement content; **a. funny** amusant *ou* drôle comme tout; *esp Old-fashioned* **thanks a.!** merci mille fois!; **he's an a. good player** il joue affreusement *ou* terriblement bien; *F Hum* **a. a.** *maniérisme utilisé pour décrire les manières et l'accent de la haute bourgeoisie britannique*; *par ex.* his family have several thousand acres in Hertfordshire, keep racehorses, are absolutely loaded and are terribly a. a.

awfulness [ˈɔːfʊlnɪs] *n* (**a**) (*of situation*) horreur *f* (**b**) *F* **the a. of the weather/this place** le temps/cet endroit abominable

awhile [əˈwaɪl] *adv Am, Lit* un moment, un peu

awkward [ˈɔːkwəd] *adj* (**a**) (*clumsy*) (*movement, person*) gauche, maladroit, balourd; (*sentence etc*) maladroit, gauche; **to be a. with one's hands** être inhabile de ses mains

(**b**) (*embarrassed*) embarrassé, gêné

(**c**) (*embarrassing*) embarrassant; **it would be a. if we met** une rencontre serait embarrassante; **an a. silence** un silence gêné; **to arrive at an a. moment** arriver mal à propos; **to ask a. questions** poser des questions embarrassantes

(**d**) (*difficult, not straightforward*) incommode, peu commode; (*tool*) peu maniable; (*bend*) difficile, dangereux; **the switch is in an a. place** l'interrupteur est situé à un endroit peu accessible; **their house is a. to get to** leur maison est d'un accès difficile; **I'm sorry to be a.** (*but that doesn't suit me*) je suis désolé d'être peu accommodant; **they're just trying to be a.** ils font ça pour compliquer les choses; **the a. age** l'âge *m* ingrat; *F* **he's an a. customer** c'est un type difficile, il n'est pas commode

awkwardly [ˈɔːkwədlɪ] *adv* (**a**) (*clumsily*) gauchement, maladroitement; **to put sth a.** mal tourner qch, dire qch d'une façon maladroite (**b**) (*showing embarrassment*) d'une manière embarrassée; (*to speak*) d'un ton embarrassé *ou* gêné (**c**) (*causing embarrassment*) d'une façon embarrassante (**d**) (*inconveniently*) **the lever is a. placed** le levier est mal placé; **their house is a. situated** leur maison est mal située

awkwardness [ˈɔːkwədnɪs] *n* (**a**) (*clumsiness*) gaucherie *f*, maladresse *f*; (*lack of grace*) balourdise *f* (**b**) (*embarrassment*) embarras *m*, gêne *f*; **a moment of a.** un moment de gêne (**c**) (*inconvenience*) (*of situation etc*) difficulté *f*, incommodité *f*

awl [ɔːl] *n* alêne *f*, poinçon *m*, perçoir *m*

awn [ɔːn] *n Bot* (*of barley etc*) barbe *f*

awning [ˈɔːnɪŋ] *n* (*of shop etc*) store *m*, banne *f*; (*of cart*) bâche *f*; (*of theatre, hotel etc*) marquise *f*; *Naut* tente *f*, tendelet *m*; (*on deck of boat*) cabane *f*; **a.** (**blind**) store à l'italienne; **rain a.** taud *m*, taude *f*; **a. deck** pont-abri *m*, *pl* ponts-abris

AWOL [ˈeɪwɒl] *adj Mil, F* (*abbr* **absent without leave**) **to go A.** s'absenter sans permission; **to be A.** être absent sans permission

awry [əˈraɪ] *adv, adj* de travers, de guingois; **to go all a.** (*of plans etc*) aller tout de travers; **services were thrown a. by the strike** les services ont été perturbés par la grève

axe[1], *US* **ax**, *pl* **axes** [æks, ˈæksɪz] *n* (**a**) hache *f*; **ice a.** piolet *m*; **a. head** fer *m* de hache; **a. handle** manche *m* de hache; *Fig* **to have an a. to grind** agir dans un but intéressé (**b**) *F* **to get the a.** (*of project etc*) être abandonné; (*of employee etc*) être mis à la porte; (*of department etc*) être supprimé; *Journ* **500 threatened with a.** 500 personnes menacées de chômage (**c**) *Mus Sl* (*instrument*) boîte *f*

axe[2], *US* **ax** *vt F* (*person, worker*) renvoyer, mettre à la porte; (*project*) abandonner (pour des raisons d'économie); (*job*) supprimer; **to a. public expenditure** tailler dans les dépenses publiques

axial [ˈæksɪəl] *adj Geom* axial

axil [ˈæksɪl] *n Bot* (*of leaf*) aisselle *f*

axiom [ˈæksɪəm] *n* axiome *m*

axiomatic [æksɪəˈmætɪk] *adj* (**a**) axiomatique (**b**) (*self-evident*) évident

axis, *pl* **axes** [ˈæksɪs, ˈæksiːz] *n* (**a**) *Geom, Geol etc* (*of sphere, plant, crystal*) axe *m*; **a. of the earth** axe de la terre; **a. of revolution** axe de révolution (**b**) *Anat* (*of neck*) axis *m* (**c**) *Hist* **the A.** l'Axe *m*

axle ['æks(ə)l] *n* (**a**) (*of vehicle*) **a.** (**tree**) essieu *m*; *Rail* **driving a.** essieu moteur; *Aut* **front/rear a.** essieu *ou* pont *m* avant/arrière; **a. box** boîte *f* de l'essieu; **a. shaft** arbre *m* d'essieu; **a. tramp** rebond *m* de l'essieu (**b**) (*of wheel*) tourillon *m*, arbre *m*, axe *m*

ay(e) [aɪ] **1** *int esp Scot* oui, mais oui; *Naut* **a. a., sir!** oui, commandant/lieutenant/*etc*! **2** *n* (*in voting*) **ayes and noes** voix *fpl* pour et contre; **the ayes have it** les voix pour l'emportent

azalea [ə'zeɪlɪə] *n* (*plant*) azalée *f*

AZERTY keyboard [ə'zɜːtɪ'kiːbɔːd] *n* clavier *m* AZERTY

azimuth ['æzɪməθ] *n Astron etc* azimut *m*

Azores (the) [ðiːə'zɔːz] *npl* les Açores *fpl*

AZT [eɪzed'tiː] *n Pharm* (*abbr* **azydothymidine**) AZT *m*

Aztec ['æztek] *Hist* **1** *adj* aztèque **2** *n* (**a**) Aztèque *mf* (**b**) *Ling* aztèque *m*

azure ['æʒər, 'eɪʒər] **1** *n Lit, Her* azur *m* **2** *adj* d'azur, azuré

B

B, b [biː] *n* **(a)** (*letter*) B, b *m*; **51B** (*street number*) 51 ter; *Mil* **B company** deuxième compagnie *f*; *Br* **B road** route *f* secondaire; **B side** (*of record*) face *f* B **(b)** *Mus* si *m*; **B flat** si bémol **(c)** *Sch* (*grade*) **I got a B in maths** j'ai eu 13 sur 20 en maths **(d)** *Med* **B-cells** lymphocytes *mpl* B.

b (*abbr* **born**) né

BA [biː'eɪ] *n Univ* (*abbr* **Bachelor of Arts**) **to have a BA in history** ≈ avoir une licence en histoire; **John Smith, BA** ≈ John Smith, licencié ès lettres/droit/*etc*

baa[1] [bɑː] *n* bêlement *m*; **b.!** bêê!; **b.-lamb** (*in children's language*) petit agneau *m*

baa[2] *vi* **(baaed, baa'd** [bɑːd]) bêler

baba ['bɑːbɑː] *n Culin* **rum b.** baba *m* au rhum

babble[1] ['bæb(ə)l] *n* **(a)** (*incoherence*) brouhaha *m*; **the b. of voices coming from downstairs** le brouhaha qui parvenait d'en bas; **his speech was full of the usual b. about…** son discours était le verbiage habituel sur… **(b)** (*of stream*) murmure *m*

babble[2] *vi* **(a)** (*tell secrets*) bavarder, jaser **(b)** (*chatter incoherently*) (*of baby*) babiller, gazouiller; (*of adult*) bafouiller **(c)** (*of stream*) murmurer, gazouiller

▶ **babble away, babble on** *vi* bavarder, papoter; **you were babbling away in your sleep last night** tu n'as pas arrêté de bredouiller des choses incompréhensibles dans ton sommeil cette nuit; **what are you babbling on about?** qu'est-ce que tu bafouilles encore?

babbler ['bæblər] *n* **(a)** (*who tells secrets*) bavard, -arde **(b)** (*incoherent talker*) **she's a b.** elle bafouille

babbling ['bæb(ə)lɪŋ] **1** *adj* **(a)** (*incoherent*) bafouilleur; **b. idiot** personne qui parle à tort et à travers; **I felt like a b. idiot** j'avais l'impression que je racontais n'importe quoi **(b)** (*stream*) murmurant **2** *n* = **babble**

babe [beɪb] *n* **(a)** *Lit* petit enfant *m*, bambin *m*; **a b. in arms** un bébé; *Fig* un naïf, une naïve; **his mother had died when he was still a b. in arms** il était encore au berceau quand sa mère mourut **(b)** *Am F* (*girl*) jolie fille *f*; **hi, b.!** salut, poupée!

Babel ['beɪb(ə)l] *n* **the Tower of B.** la Tour de Babel; *Fig* **b. of voices** brouhaha *m*

baboon [bə'buːn] *n* (*animal*) babouin *m*; *Fig* singe *m*

baby[1] ['beɪbɪ] *n* **(a)** bébé *m*; **when I was a b.** quand j'étais bébé; **a b. boy/girl** un petit garçon/une petite fille; **b. brother/sister** petit frère/petite sœur; **the b. of the family** le benjamin; **you're such a b.!** tu es un vrai bébé!; **don't be such a b.** arrête de faire le bébé; **I'm not a b.!** je ne suis plus un bébé!; **my b. pictures** (*of me*) des photos de moi, bébé; *Fig* **to throw the b. out with the bath water** jeter le bébé avec l'eau du bain; *Fig* **to leave sb holding the b.** refiler le bébé à qn; *Fig* **the dictionary is his b.** le dictionnaire est son bébé; **b. elephant/chimpanzee** bébé éléphant/chimpanzé; **b. carrots/aubergines** carottes *fpl*/aubergines *fpl* naines; **b. scales** pèse-bébé *m*, *pl* pèse-bébés; **b. talk** langage *m* enfantin; *Am* **b. tooth** dent *f* de lait

(b) *US F* (*girlfriend*) jeune fille *f*, nana *f*; (*boyfriend*) mec *m*; (*as form of address*) chéri, -ie; (*thing*) machin *m*; (*car*) bagnole *f*

baby[2] *vt* **(babied)** (*person*) *Pej* (*treat as baby*) materner; (*give love and attention to*) dorloter

baby boom *n* baby-boom *m*

baby boomer ['buːmə(r)] *n* enfant *mf* du baby-boom

baby buggy *n Am* landau *m*, voiture *f* d'enfant

baby carriage *n Am* landau *m*, voiture *f* d'enfant

baby-changing area *n* nurserie *f*, point-bébé *m*

baby-face *n* visage *m* poupin; **he's a real b.** il a le visage poupin

baby-faced ['beɪbɪfeɪst] *adj* au visage poupin

baby grand *n Mus* (piano *m*) demi-queue *m*

babyhood ['beɪbɪhʊd] *n* petite enfance *f*

babyish ['beɪbɪɪʃ] *adj Pej* de bébé

baby-listening microphone *n* babyphone *m*

baby-listening service *n* service *m* de surveillance à distance des bébés, service babyphone

Babylon ['bæbɪlən] *n Antiq* Babylone *f*

Babylonia [bæbɪ'ləʊnɪə] *n Antiq* Babylonie *f*

Babylonian [bæbɪ'ləʊnɪən] *Antiq* **1** *adj* babylonien **2** *n* Babylonien, -ienne

baby-minder *n* nourrice *f*

baby's breath *n* (*flower*) gypsophile *f*

baby seat *n* siège *m* auto bébé, siège enfant

baby-sit *vi* **(-sat, -sitting)** faire du baby-sitting, garder des/les enfants

baby-sitter *n* baby-sitter *mf*, *Can* gardienne *f*

baby-sitting *n* baby-sitting *m*, garde *f* d'enfants

baby snatcher ['snætʃə(r)] *n* kidnappeur, -euse; *Fig* (*man*) vieux barbon *m*; (*woman*) = femme *f* qui sort avec/épouse un garçon beaucoup plus jeune qu'elle

baby snatching ['snætʃɪŋ] *n* enlèvement *m ou* rapt *m* d'enfant, kidnapping *m*; *Fig* **I don't go in for b.** moi, je ne les prends pas au berceau

baby-walker *n* trotteur *m*

baccalaureate [bækə'lɔːrɪət] *n Univ US* ≈ licence *f*, *Can* baccalauréat *m*

baccara(t) ['bækərɑː] *n Cards* baccara *m*; **to play b.** jouer au baccara

bacchanal ['bækən(ə)l] *Lit* **1** *adj* bachique **2** *n* (*orgy*) bacchanale *f*, débauche *f* bachique

bacchanalia [bækə'neɪlɪə] *npl Lit* bacchanales *fpl*

bacchanalian [bækə'neɪlɪən] *adj Lit* bachique

baccy ['bækɪ] *n Old-fashioned F* tabac *m*

bachelor ['bætʃələr] *n* **(a)** célibataire *m*; **b. flat** garçonnière *f*; *Old-fashioned* **b. girl** célibataire *f*; **b. uncle** oncle *m* non marié **(b)** *Univ* ≈ licencié, -ée; **b.'s degree,** *F* **b.'s** = licence *f*; **to have a b.'s (degree) in French** = avoir une licence de français; **B. of Arts** ≈ licencié, -ée ès lettres; **B. of Laws** ≈ licencié, -ée en droit; **B. of Science** ≈ licencié, -ée ès sciences **(c)** *Hist* bachelier *m* (*aspirant à la chevalerie*); **knight b.** chevalier *m*

bachelorhood ['bætʃələhʊd], **bachelordom** ['bætʃələdəm] *n* célibat *m*, vie *f* de garçon

bacillary [bə'sɪlərɪ] *adj Biol* bacillaire

bacillus, *pl* **-i** [bə'sɪləs, -aɪ] *n Biol, Med* bacille *m*

back[1] [bæk] **1** *n* **(a)** (*of person, animal*) dos *m*; (*of chair etc*) dossier *m*; **mind your backs!** attention, s'il vous plaît!; **to be at the b. of sb** (*chase, harry*) poursuivre qn; **he had two policemen at his b.** il avait deux policiers à ses trousses; **with an army at his b.** (*supporting him*) soutenu par une armée; **to do sth behind sb's b.** faire qch dans le dos de qn; **he laughs at you behind your b.** il se moque de vous quand vous avez le dos tourné; **to talk about sb behind their b.** dire du mal de qn dans son dos; **to turn one's b. on sb** tourner le dos à qn; *Fig* abandonner qn; **when my b. was turned** quand j'avais le dos tourné; **to sit/stand with one's b. to sb** tourner le dos à qn; **to sit with one's b. to the engine** s'asseoir dans le sens contraire à la marche; **sitting with one's b. to the light** assis à contre-jour; **he was sitting with his b. to the wall** il était assis, dos au mur; *Fig* **our backs were to the wall** nous étions au pied du mur; **to be glad to see the b. of sb/sth** être content d'être débarrassé de qn/qch; **I saw him only from the b.** je ne l'ai vu que de dos; **to be on one's b.** (*lying down*) être étendu sur le dos; *F* (*ill*) être alité; *F* **I spent three months (flat) on my b.** j'ai passé trois mois au lit; *F* **the boss was on my b. all day** j'ai eu le patron sur le dos toute la journée; *F* **get off my b.!** fiche-moi la paix!; **to live off the backs of the poor/the Third World** vivre sur le dos des pauvres/du tiers-monde; **to put** *or* **get sb's b. up** mettre qn en colère; *Fig* **to put one's b. into it** s'y mettre énergiquement; **to have b. problems** avoir des problèmes de dos; **to break one's b.** se casser les reins; *F* **he won't break his b. working** il ne se casse pas au travail; **to break the b. of the work** faire le plus dur *ou* le plus gros du travail; **to break her b.** (*of ship*) se briser en deux, se casser; **b. pain** mal *m* de dos; **b. slapping** (*friendly behaviour*) démonstrations *fpl* d'amitié un peu exubérantes; (*congratulatory*) félicitations *fpl* un peu exubérantes

(b) (*reverse*) (*of knife, book, envelope, cheque etc*) dos *m*;

(*of fabric*) envers *m*; (*of page*) verso *m*; *Mus* (*of violin etc*) table *f* du fond; (*of medal*) revers *m*; (*of hand*) revers, dos; (*of house, clock, wardrobe etc*) arrière *m*; *also Fig* **to be at the b. of sth** être derrière qch; **outside agitators were at the b. of the trouble** des agitateurs extérieurs étaient à l'origine des troubles; *F* **I've parked the car round the b.** j'ai garé la voiture derrière; *F* **you'll feel the b. of my hand in a minute!** tu vas en prendre une!; **there was an advert on the b. of the bus** il y avait une publicité à l'arrière du bus; *Br F* **to have a face like the b. of a bus** être moche comme un pou; **carriage at the b. of the train** voiture en queue de *ou* du train; **the house has a garden at the b.** *or Am* **in b.** il y a un jardin derrière la maison; **the dress fastens at the b.** *or Am* **in b.** la robe s'agrafe dans le dos; **the worry was always there at the b. of his mind** ce souci lui trottait constamment dans la tête; **it was always there at the b. of his mind that ...** l'idée ne le quittait pas que ...; **it's something to keep at the b. of your mind** c'est quelque chose à ne pas oublier; **you have your sweater on b. to front** tu as mis ton pullover sens devant derrière *ou* à l'envers; *Fig* **she knows the system (inside out and) b. to front** elle connaît le système par cœur; **he knows London like the b. of his hand** il connaît Londres comme sa poche

(c) (*rear, furthest away part*) (*of cupboard, room, stage*) fond *m*; **b. of the mouth** arrière-bouche *f*; **b. of the throat** arrière-gorge *f*; **to sit in the b.** (*of car*) monter à l'arrière; **to sit at the b.** (*of bus*) s'asseoir à l'arrière; (*of church, hall etc*) s'asseoir dans le *ou* au fond; **at the b. of the book** à la fin du livre; *F* **the b. of beyond** le bout du monde; *F* **to live at the b. of beyond** habiter un trou perdu; **b. of the house** (*hotel services*) emplois *mpl* fonctionnels

(d) *Sp* arrière *m*; **(full) b.** arrière; **right/left b.** arrière droit/gauche; *Rugby* **the backs** les arrières; (*three quarters*) les trois quarts *mpl*

2 *adj* **(a)** (*part, wheel, axle etc*) arrière; (*door, garden etc*) de derrière; *Fig* **to put sth on the b. burner** remettre qch à plus tard; **b. entrance** entrée *f* située à l'arrière; **b. matter** (*in book*) annexes *fpl*; *Anat* **b. passage** rectum *m*; *Aut* **b. plate** (*for brakes*) plaque-support *f*; *Aut* **b. shelf** (*of car*) tablette *f* arrière; *Sp* **b. straight** (*on track*) ligne *f* opposée; **b. stretch** (*on race course*) ligne d'en face

(b) (*in opposite direction*) (*movement*) inverse; *Ling* **b. formation** dérivation *f* régressive; *Sp* **b. pass** passe *f* en arrière

(c) (*time*) **b. interest** arrérages *mpl*, intérêts *mpl* arriérés; **b. list** (*of publisher*) = liste *f* des titres disponibles et régulièrement réimprimés; *Com* **b. orders** commandes *fpl* en attente; **b. pay** rappel *m* de salaire; **b. rent** arriéré(s) *m(pl)* de loyer

(d) (*remote*) *Austr* **b. country** brousse *f*; **b. road** petite route *f*

3 *adv* **(a)** (*of place*) en arrière; **to step b. a pace** faire un pas en arrière; **he left him three miles b.** il l'a laissé à trois mil(l)es d'ici; **far b.** (*seated*) dans les derniers rangs; **house standing b. from the road** maison écartée du chemin *ou* en retrait; *Am* **b. of sth** derrière qch

(b) (*in return, retaliation*) **if somebody hits you, hit them b.** si quelqu'un te frappe, rends-lui ses coups; **if you kick me I'll kick you b.** si tu me donnes un coup de pied, je te le rendrai; **to get one's own b.** prendre sa revanche (**on sb** sur qn); **that's her way of getting b. at you** c'est sa façon de prendre sa revanche sur toi; **to call sb b.** (*shout, telephone*) rappeler qn

(c) [①**A23**,3,b] (*to original starting point*) **to come b.** revenir; **to arrive b.** rentrer; **to go b.** (*return*) retourner (**to** à); **to go** *or* **turn b.** (*retrace footsteps*) rebrousser chemin; **to make one's way b.** s'en retourner; **I'll be b. on Friday** je serai de retour vendredi; **I'll be b.** (*threat*) vous me reverrez; **I expect him b. tomorrow** j'attends son retour pour demain; **as soon as I am** *or* **get b.** dès mon retour; **he's just b. from a trip** il arrive de voyage; **she's b. at work** elle a repris son travail; **a few pages b.** quelques pages plus haut; **b. home** chez nous/lui/*etc*; **b. in Britain** en Grande-Bretagne

(d) (*of time*) **a few years b.** il y a (déjà) quelques années; **way b. in the Middle Ages** il y a bien longtemps au moyen âge; **as far b. as 1914** déjà en 1914, dès 1914; **b. in 1982** en 1982; **b. when I was young** quand j'étais jeune

back² **1** *vt* **(a)** (*support*) (*person*) soutenir, appuyer; (*in an argument*) donner raison à; *Com etc* (*person, project etc*) financer; *Fin* (*bill*) avaliser, endosser

(b) *Sp etc* (*gamble money on*) (*team*) parier *ou* miser sur; (*horse*) jouer, parier *ou* miser sur; **well-backed horse** cheval très coté; *Horseracing, Fig* **to b. a winner** parier *ou* miser sur le gagnant; *Horseracing, Fig* **to b. the wrong horse** parier *ou* miser sur le mauvais cheval

(c) (*move*) (*cart*) reculer; (*horse*) faire reculer; (*train*) refouler; **to b. one's car into the garage** entrer en marche arrière dans le garage; **to b. one's car into a lamppost/another car** rentrer dans un lampadaire/une autre voiture en reculant; *Naut* **to b. the oars, to b. water** ramer à rebours, déramer

(d) (*put backing on*) (*picture*) rentoiler

(e) *Mus* (*person*) accompagner

2 *vi* (*of horse*) reculer; *Aut etc* faire marche arrière, reculer; **to b. into sb** (*of person*) rentrer dans qn; *Aut* **to b. into the garage** entrer dans le garage en marche arrière; **I backed into my neighbour's car** je suis rentré dans la voiture de mon voisin en reculant; **to b. into the station** (*of train*) reculer dans la gare

▶ **back away** *vi* (*in fear*) reculer (**from** devant)

▶ **back down** *vi* **(a)** *Fig* (*in argument*) admettre qu'on est dans son tort; (*in conflict*) faire marche arrière **(b)** (*from ladder etc*) descendre à reculons

▶ **back off** *vi* **(a)** (*move away*) reculer **(b)** *Am Fig* = **back down (a)**

▶ **back on to** *vipo* (*of building*) **the colleges b. on to the river/garden** les collèges donnent sur la rivière/le jardin à l'arrière

▶ **back out 1** *vi* **(a)** (*of person etc*) sortir à reculons; *Aut* sortir en marche arrière **(b)** *Fig* (*withdraw*) retirer sa promesse, se dédire; (*of a responsibility*) se défiler; **to b. out of an undertaking** se dédire d'un engagement; **he's trying to b. out (of it)** il voudrait se dédire **2** *vtsep* (*car*) sortir en marche arrière

▶ **back up 1** *vtsep* **(a)** (*support*) (*person, story, version of events*) soutenir, appuyer; **to b. sb up in an argument** donner raison à qn **(b)** (*car etc*) faire reculer; *Am* **the accident has backed traffic up all the way to the service station** l'accident a créé un ralentissement jusqu'à la station-service **(c)** *Comptr* (*data, file*) sauvegarder **2** *vi* **(a)** (*of car*) reculer, faire marche arrière **(b)** *Comptr* sauvegarder **(c)** (*of drains*) être obstrué

backache [ˈbækeɪk] *n* mal *m* de dos; **to have b.** avoir mal au dos

backbench [ˈbækˈbentʃ] *n* **(a)** *Br Parl* (*usu pl*) **backbenches** = banc *m* des députés qui n'occupent pas de poste officiel dans le gouvernement ou dans l'opposition; **discontent on the backbenches** mécontentement parmi les députés de base; **she got b. support** elle a eu le soutien des députés de base; **b. MPs** = députés *mpl* qui n'occupent pas de poste officiel dans le gouvernement ou dans l'opposition **(b)** *Journ* équipe *f* de soutien; (*night desk*) équipe de nuit

backbencher [ˈbækˈbentʃər] *n Br Parl* député *m* de base (*qui n'occupe pas de poste officiel dans le gouvernement ou dans l'opposition*)

backbite [ˈbækbaɪt] **1** *vi* médire **2** *vt* (*person*) médire de

backbiting [ˈbækbaɪtɪŋ] *n* médisance *f*

backboard [ˈbækbɔːd] *n* (*in basketball*) panneau *m*

back boiler *n* = ballon *m* d'eau chaude situé derrière un foyer

backbone [ˈbækbəʊn] *n* (*of person, animal*) épine *f* dorsale, colonne *f* vertébrale; (*of fish*) grande arête *f*; *Fig* **English to the b.** anglais jusqu'au bout des ongles; **he's got no b.** il n'a rien dans le ventre *ou F* les tripes; **he hasn't got the b. to do it** il n'a pas les tripes pour le faire; **she is the b. of the movement** c'est elle qui mène le mouvement; **tourism is the b. of the economy** le tourisme est le pivot de l'économie

backbreaking [ˈbækbreɪkɪŋ] *adj* (*work etc*) éreintant

backburn¹ [ˈbækbɜːn] *n Austr* (*to control forest fire*) contre-feu *m*

backburn² *vi Austr* allumer un contre-feu

backchat [ˈbæktʃæt] *n Br F* (*impudence*) impertinence *f*; **none of your b.!** ne réponds pas!

backcloth [ˈbækklɒθ] *n Br* = **backdrop**

backcomb [ˈbækkəʊm] *vt* (*hair*) crêper

back copy *n Journ* (*of magazine, newspaper*) vieux numéro *m*, exemplaire *m* antérieur

backdate [ˈbækdeɪt] *vt* antidater; **increase backdated to July 1st** augmentation avec effet rétroactif au 1er juillet; **will it be backdated?** est-ce qu'il aura effet rétroactif?

back door *n* porte *f* arrière; (*of house*) porte *f* de derrière; *Fig* **to come in through** *or* **by the b.** (*get job through influential contacts*) être pistonné; **b. methods** méthodes *fpl* peu respectables; **she got the job through b. methods** elle a été pistonnée

backdrop [ˈbækdrɒp] *n* **(a)** *Th* toile *f* de fond; (*with perspective*) découverte *f* **(b)** *Fig* (*background*) toile *f* de fond, arrière-plan *m*, *pl* arrière-plans; **against a b. of continuing violence** avec, comme arrière-plan *ou* toile de fond, un climat de violence permanente

-backed ['bækt] *suff* **broad-b.** (*person*) qui a le dos large; **a high-b. chair** une chaise à haut dossier

backer ['bækər] *n* **(a)** *Horseracing* parieur, -euse **(b)** *Pol etc* partisan *m*; *Com* commanditaire *m*; *Fin* (*of bill*) donneur *m* d'aval; *Th etc* **we need a b.** il nous faut un mécène; **financial b.** bailleur, -euse de fonds

backfill¹ ['bækfɪl] *n Constr* (*of trench*) remplissage *m*

backfill² *Constr* **1** *vt* (*trench*) remplir **2** *vi* remplir

backfire¹ [bæk'faɪər] *n* **(a)** (*of engine*) retour *m* de flamme; (*noise*) pétarade *f* **(b)** *Am* (*to control forest fire*) contre-feu *m*

backfire² *vi* **(a)** *Aut* avoir des retours de flamme, pétarader, avoir un raté (d'allumage); *Fig* **the plan backfired on them** le projet leur est retombé sur le dos **(b)** *Am* (*to control forest fire*) allumer un contre-feu

backgammon ['bækgæmən] *n* backgammon *m*; **b. board** backgammon

background ['bækgraʊnd] *n* **(a)** (*position*) fond *m*, arrière-plan *m*, *pl* arrière-plans; **b. of mountains** fond de montagnes; **in the b.** dans le fond, à l'arrière-plan; *Comptr* en arrière-plan; **music was playing in the b.** il y avait de la musique en bruit de fond; **there's a lot of noise in the b.** il y a beaucoup de bruit de fond; **against a dark b.** sur (un) fond sombre; *Fig* **the protests took place against a b. of repression** les manifestations se sont inscrites dans un climat de *ou* sur fond de répression; **to keep (oneself)** *or* **to stay in the b.** s'effacer; *Fig* **she stays very much in the b.** elle reste dans l'ombre; **to push sb into the b.** mettre *ou* reléguer qn au second plan; (*outshine*) prendre le pas sur qn; *Fig* **to fade/melt into the b.** disparaître/se fondre dans l'arrière-plan; **he's rather faded into the b. since then** on n'entend plus tellement parler de lui depuis; **b. colour** couleur *f* de fond; *Comptr* **b. job** tâche *f* de fond; **b. light** éclairage *m* d'ambiance; *Comptr* **b. (mode) printing** impression *f* en arrière-plan; **b. noise** bruit *m* de fond; **b. radiation** radiations *fpl* de fond; *TV etc* **b. sound** fond *m* sonore; *Comptr* **b. task** tâche *f* d'arrière-plan

(b) (*social class*) origines *fpl*; (*education*) formation *f*; (*experience*) expérience *f*; (*to event*) contexte *m* historique **(to** de); (*to problem*) contexte **(to** de); **young man of good b.** garçon de bonne famille; **to come from a middle-class/deprived b.** venir d'un milieu bourgeois/défavorisé; **what's his professional b.?** quelle expérience professionnelle a-t-il?; **he's been given a b. briefing** on lui a fait un briefing sur l'historique de l'événement; **I need a bit more b. (information)** j'ai besoin de plus de données

background music *n* musique *f* d'ambiance *ou* de fond; *Th, Cin* fond *m* sonore

background reading *n* lectures *fpl* (*autour d'un sujet particulier*); **to do some b.** faire des lectures sur *ou* se documenter sur un sujet

backhand ['bækhænd] *n* **(a)** *Tennis* revers *m*; **her b. is weak** son revers manque de puissance **(b)** (*writing*) écriture *f* renversée *ou* penchée à gauche

backhanded [bæk'hændɪd] *adj usu attrib* (*blow*) de revers; *Fig* (*compliment*) équivoque

backhander ['bækhændər] *n F* **(a)** (*blow*) revers *m*; *Fig* (*attack*) attaque *f* indirecte **(b)** (*bribe*) pot-de-vin *m*

backing ['bækɪŋ] *n* **(a)** (*support*) (*for person*) soutien *m*, appui *m*; (*for picture*) entoilage *m*; **financial b.** (*for person, project etc*) financement *m*; *Fin* **b. of the currency** garantie *f* de la circulation **(b)** *Horseracing* (*bets*) paris *mpl* **(c)** (*movement*) (*of car, horse, cart*) recul *m* **(d)** (*providing with back*) (*of picture*) rentoilage *m* **(e)** *Mus* accompagnement *m*; **b. track** piste *f* de fond

back issue *n* (*of magazine, newspaper*) vieux numéro *m*

backlash ['bæklæʃ] *n* **(a)** *Fig* (*of event*) contrecoup *m*; (*political etc*) réaction *f*, retour *m* de manivelle **(against** contre) **(b)** *Aut* (*gearing*) jeu *m* entre-dents

backless ['bæklɪs] *adj* (*dress*) dos nu; (*seat etc*) sans dossier

backlit ['bæklɪt] *adj Comptr* (*screen*) rétro-éclairé

backlog ['bæklɒg] *n* (*of work*) retard *m*; *Com* **b. of orders** commandes non exécutées; **to have a b. of correspondence/work** avoir du retard dans son courrier/travail, avoir du courrier/travail en retard; **to clear a b.** se mettre à jour

back number *n* (*of magazine, newspaper*) vieux numéro *m*; *Fig* **she's a b.** elle est démodée

back office *n Banking* back-office *m*; **b. staff** personnels *mpl* de back-office

backpack¹ ['bækpæk] *n* sac *m* à dos

backpack² *vi* faire de la randonnée

backpacker ['bækpækər] *n* randonneur, -euse

backpacking ['bækpækɪŋ] *n* randonnée *f*; **to go b.** aller faire de la randonnée

back page *n* dernière page *f*

back-pedal *vi* (-ll-, *US* -l-) (*on bicycle*) rétropédaler; *Fig* faire marche arrière; **to b. on a promise** revenir sur une promesse

back-pedalling, *US* **-pedaling** ['bækped(ə)lɪŋ] *n* (*on bicycle*) rétropédalage *m*; *Fig* marche *f* arrière

back-pressure *n Aut* contre-pression *f*

back rest *n* (*of seat*) dossier *m*

back room *n* pièce *f* du fond; *Fig* **b. boy** personne *f* qui travaille dans la coulisse *ou* derrière la scène

backscratcher ['bækskrætʃər] *n* gratte-dos *m inv*

backscratching ['bækskrætʃɪŋ] *n Fig* échange *m* de faveurs

back seat *n* siège *m* arrière; *Fig* **to take a b.** (*of job, project*) passer au second plan; (*of person*) s'effacer

back-seat ['bæksiːt] *adj* **b. driver** personne *f* qui donne des conseils au conducteur; **I don't want any b. driving** je n'ai pas besoin de conseils pour conduire; **b. passenger** passager *m* arrière

backsheesh, backshish ['bækʃiːʃ] *n* bakchich *m*

back shift *n* (*people*) = équipe *f* du soir; **I hate the b.** je déteste être du soir; **to work** *or* **be on the b.** être (de l'équipe) du soir

backside [bæk'saɪd] *n F* derrière *m*, postérieur *m*

backsight ['bæksaɪt] *n* (*on rifle*) hausse *f*

back slang *n* = verlan *m*

backslash ['bækslæʃ] *n* barre *f* oblique inversée; **b. key** touche *f* barre oblique inversée

backslide ['bækslaɪd] *vi* **(backslid)** récidiver

backsliding ['bækslaɪdɪŋ] *n* récidive *f*

backspace¹ ['bækspeɪs] *n* **b. (key)** (*on keyboard*) espacement *m* arrière, touche *f* d'espacement arrière; **b. character** caractère *m* de retour arrière; **b. command** commande *f* de retour arrière

backspace² *vi* (*on keyboard*) revenir en arrière d'un caractère; **b. twice** revenir en arrière de deux caractères

backstage [bæk'steɪdʒ] **1** *adv Th* derrière la scène, en coulisse, dans les coulisses; *Fig* en coulisse; *Th* **to help b.** aider en coulisse(s) **2** *adj attrib Th* (*area, activity*) de derrière la scène; *Fig* en coulisses; **b. worker** personne *f* qui travaille dans les coulisses

backstairs [bæk'steəz] *n* (*for servants etc*) escalier *m* de service; (*hidden*) escalier dérobé; **b. influence** influence *f* (*exercée par un personnage apparemment sans pouvoir*); **b. gossip** commérages *mpl*

backstitch¹ ['bækstɪtʃ] *n Sewing* point *m* de piqûre

backstitch² *vi Sewing* coudre au point de piqûre

backstreet ['bækstriːt] *n* petite rue *f*; **he was brought up in the backstreets** il a été élevé dans les quartiers populaires; **b. abortion** avortement *m* clandestin; **b. abortionist** avorteur, -euse clandestin(e)

backstroke ['bækstrəʊk] *n* **(a)** *Swimming* dos *m* crawlé; **the 100 metres b.** le 100 mètres dos **(b)** *MecE* (*of piston etc*) course *f* arrière, course de retour

backtalk ['bæktɔːk] *n Am* = **backchat**

back-to-back [bæktə'bæk] **1** *adj* (*seats, people*) dos à dos; *Br* **a row of b. houses** une rangée de maisons adossées les unes aux autres; *Am Sp* **to play two games b.** jouer deux parties l'une à la suite de l'autre; *Fin* **b. credit** crédit *m* back to back **2** *n Br* (*house*) **a row of little back-to-backs** une rangée de petites maisons adossées les unes aux autres

backtrack ['bæktræk] *vi* revenir sur ses pas; *Fig* faire marche arrière; **to b. on a promise/decision** revenir sur une promesse/une décision

backup ['bækʌp] *n* (*support*) soutien *m*, appui *m*; *Mil etc* renfort *m*; *Med* soins *mpl* supplémentaires; **to ask for b.** (*of police etc*) demander des renforts; **we have a generator as b.** nous avons un générateur de secours; **b. car** voiture *f* de rechange; *Comptr* **b. copy/diskette/file** copie *f*/disquette *f*/ fichier *m* de sauvegarde; *Comptr* **b. system** (*for taking backups*) système *m* de sauvegarde; (*auxiliary system*) système de secours; **b. team** (*which provides support*) équipe *f* de soutien; (*which acts as replacement*) équipe de remplacement; **b. troops** troupes *fpl* de renfort

back-up *adj Am Aut* **b. lights** feux *mpl* de recul

backward ['bækwəd] **1** *adj* **(a)** *also Fig* (*movement, glance, step etc*) en arrière; **b. and forward motion** mouvement *m* de va-et-vient; *Econ* **b. integration** intégration *f* en amont; *Mktg* **b. invention** invention *f* en amont; (*simplification of product*) invention rétrograde; **b. pricing** rajustement *m* des prix

(b) (*child*) retardé, attardé; (*area, region*) moins développé; (*people*) attardé; **the b. state of the country** le retard dont souffre le pays; **to be b. in doing sth** être lent à faire qch; *Br F* **he isn't b. in coming forward** il n'a pas peur de se mettre en avant; **he isn't b. in coming forward with his ideas** il n'a pas peur de mettre ses idées en avant; **he**

isn't b. in coming forward to complain il n'est jamais le dernier à se plaindre

2 *adv* = backwards

backwardation [bækwə'deɪʃən] *n Fin* déport *m*

backwardness ['bækwədnɪs] *n* (*mental*) arriération *f* mentale, retard *m*; **b. in doing sth** hésitation *f* à faire qch

backwards ['bækwədz] *adv* (*to jump, lean*) en arrière; (*to go, walk*) à reculons; (*to fall*) à la renverse; (*to say, read sth*) à l'envers; **to look b.** jeter un coup d'œil en arrière; (*in time*) remonter dans le passé; **to flow b.** (*of water*) couler à contre-courant; *Fig* **to know sth b.** connaître qch parfaitement; *also Fig* **a step b.** un pas en arrière; **to walk b. and forwards** aller et venir; **movement b. and forwards** mouvement de va-et-vient; **to go b. and forwards** faire la navette (*entre deux endroits*)

backwash ['bækwɒʃ] *n* remous *m*; *Fig* conséquences *fpl* néfastes; **in the b. of the civil war** dans les remous qui ont suivi la guerre civile

backwater ['bækwɔːtər] *n* (*tributary*) bras *m* de décharge (*d'une rivière*); *Fig, often Pej* **to live in a b.** habiter un trou perdu; **a secluded b.** un coin tranquille

backwoods ['bækwʊdz] *npl esp Am* forêts *fpl* de l'intérieur; *Fig* **to live in the b.** habiter un trou perdu *ou* un bled

backwoodsman, *pl* **-men** [bæk'wʊdzmən] *n US F* (*uncouth man*) rustre *m*, rustaud *m*; *Br Pol* **Tory b.** = député *m* conservateur inconnu et souvent réactionnaire

back yard *n* (*of building*) arrière-cour *f*; *Am* (*garden*) jardin *m* de derrière; *Fig* **South America is the United States' b.** l'Amérique du Sud est à la porte des États-Unis; **the 'not-in-my-back-yard'** *or* **NIMBY syndrome** = attitude *f* de rejet vis à vis de la construction d'une centrale nucléaire *etc* dans sa commune

baclava [bə'klɑːvə] *n Culin* baklava *m*

bacon ['beɪkən] *n* bacon *m*; **b. and eggs** œufs *mpl* au bacon; **streaky b.** ≈ petit salé *m*; *Fig* **to save sb's b.** sauver la peau de qn; *Fig* **to bring home the b.** (*provide material support*) faire bouillir la marmite; (*be successful*) réussir

BACS [bæks] *n* (*abbr* **bankers' automated clearing services**) système *m* électronique de compensation de chèques; **to pay by B.** payer par virement électronique

bacteria [bæk'tɪərɪə] *npl* bactéries *fpl*; *F* **a b.** une bactérie

bacterial [bæk'tɪərɪəl] *adj* bactérien

bacteriological [bæktɪərɪə'lɒdʒɪk(ə)l] *adj* bactériologique; **b. warfare** guerre *f* bactériologique

bacteriologist [bæktɪərɪ'ɒlədʒɪst] *n* bactériologiste *mf*, bactériologue *mf*

bacteriology [bæktɪərɪ'ɒlədʒɪ] *n* bactériologie *f*

bacterium, *pl* **-ia** [bæk'tɪərɪəm, -ɪə] *n* bactérie *f*

Bactrian camel ['bæktrɪən] *n* chameau *m* (bactrien)

bad [bæd] **1** *adj* (**worse** [wɜːs]; **worst** [wɜːst]) **(a)** (*of poor quality*) mauvais, de mauvaise qualité; (*unfortunate, incorrect*) mauvais; **it's not b.** ce n'est pas mal; **the pay's not b.** ça ne paie pas mal; **things are not as b. as all that** ça ne va pas si mal que ça; *Br F* **it's not half b.** ce n'est pas mal du tout; **he's/she's not b. looking** il/elle n'est pas mal; **it was a b. buy** ce n'était pas un bon investissement; **b. debt** mauvaise créance, créance *f* douteuse; **b. translation** mauvaise traduction; **to go b.** (*of food*) se gâter, s'avarier; **to speak b. French** parler mal le français; **b. at maths** nul en maths; **he's b. at keeping a secret** il ne sait pas garder un secret; **he's b. at helping about the house** il n'aide pas souvent aux tâches ménagères; **to have a b. effect on sth** avoir un effet néfaste sur qch; **to be** *or* **have a b. influence on sb** avoir une mauvaise influence sur qn; **to get into b. habits** *or* **ways** prendre de mauvaises habitudes; **b. light stopped play** (*at cricket match*) la partie a été remise à cause d'un manque de lumière; **is this a b. time to ask for leave?** peut-être n'est-ce pas le moment de demander des congés?; **am I phoning at a b. time?** je vous dérange?; **to be in a b. way** (*of person*) aller mal; **he'll come to a b. end** il finira mal; **to have a b. name** avoir (une) mauvaise réputation; **it wouldn't be a b. thing** *or* **plan** *or* **idea to ...** cela ne serait pas une mauvaise idée de...; **things are going from b. to worse** les choses vont de mal en pis; **a b. apple** une pomme pourrie; *Fig* une brebis galeuse; *Fig* **one b. apple spoils the barrel** il ne faut qu'une brebis galeuse pour gâter un troupeau; *Fig* **there's b. blood/feeling between them** il y a du ressentiment *ou* de la rancune entre eux; *F* **he's always turning up like a b. penny** on n'arrive jamais à se débarrasser de lui; **don't worry, he'll turn up like a b. penny** ne t'en fais pas, tu sais bien qu'il revient toujours; *Comptr* **b. command** commande *f* erronée; *Comptr* **b. file name** nom *m* de fichier erroné; *Comptr* **b. sector** secteur *m* endommagé

(b) (*unpleasant, serious*) (*news, smell, mood etc*) mauvais; (*cold*) gros; (*headache*) violent; (*accident, mistake etc*) grave; **it's a b. business** c'est une mauvaise affaire; **is the pain b.?** est-ce que cela fait très mal?; **b. breath** mauvaise haleine; **b. weather** mauvais temps; *Naut* gros temps; *Fig* **she's b. news** elle ne te/lui/*etc* apportera que des ennuis; **to be on b. terms with sb** être mal *ou* en mauvais termes avec qn; **it's (really) too b.!, that's too b.!** c'est vraiment dommage!; *Old-fashioned* **it's too b. of him!** ce n'est vraiment pas bien de sa part!; **if you don't like it, that's just too b.** si cela ne te plaît pas, tant pis pour toi

(c) (*not healthy*) **to be b. for sb/sth** ne rien valoir à qn/ pour qch; **all that whisky is b. for him** tout ce whisky ne lui vaut rien; **smoking is b. for you** *or* **your health** c'est mauvais (à la santé) de fumer; **because of my b. leg** parce que ma jambe me fait souffrir; **I have a b. heart/back** j'ai le cœur/le dos fragile; **I'm not so b.** (*I'm well*) je ne vais pas trop mal; **how's business? – not so b.** comment vont les affaires? – pas trop mal

(d) (*wicked*) méchant; *F* **he's a b. lot** c'est un vaurien; **b. language** gros mots

2 *adv F* **that looks b.** (*of injury, accident etc*) ça a l'air grave; (*in eyes of other people*) c'est mal vu; (*augurs ill*) c'est mauvais signe; **to feel b. about sth** (*regret*) avoir du remords au sujet de qch; **I feel b. about firing him but I'll have to** cela m'embête d'avoir à le renvoyer, mais il faudra bien que je le fasse; **I feel b. about not having told him sooner** je m'en veux de ne pas lui avoir dit plus tôt; *F* **she was taken b. yesterday** (*became ill*) elle est tombée malade hier; *F* **to have it b.** (*be very much in love*) être mordu

3 *n* **to take the b. with the good** accepter la mauvaise fortune aussi bien que la bonne; *F* **to go to the b.** (*of person*) mal tourner; (*of business*) être en mauvaise passe; **to be 500 francs to the b.** en être de 500 francs (de sa poche); *F* **to be in b. with sb** être en mauvais termes avec qn

baddie, baddy ['bædɪ] *n F* méchant, -ante

bade *see* **bid**[2]

badge [bædʒ] *n* **(a)** (*metal, plastic*) badge *m*; *Mil, Sch* écusson *m*; (*to indicate membership of club*) insigne *m*; **b. of office** (*of mayor*) insigne **(b)** *Fig* symbole *m*, signe *m*

badger[1] ['bædʒər] *n* (*animal*) blaireau *m*; **b. baiting** déterrage *m* du blaireau

badger[2] *vt* (*person*) harceler; **to b. sb with sth/to do sth** harceler qn avec qch/pour qu'il fasse qch; **to b. sb into granting a favour, to b. a favour out of sb** obtenir une faveur de qn à force de harcèlement

badinage ['bædɪnɑːʒ] *n Fml, Lit* badinage *m*

badly ['bædlɪ] *adv* (**worse** [wɜːs]; **worst** [wɜːst]) **(a)** (*poorly*) (*informed, dressed, behave, explain sth etc*) mal; **to do b., to come off b.** mal réussir; **he did not b.** il ne s'en est pas trop mal tiré; **to be very b. off** (*financially*) être dans la gêne; *Fig* **I'm very b. off for clothes** je ne suis pas riche en vêtements; **to speak English b.** parler mal l'anglais; **he took it very b.** il a très mal pris la chose; **they get on b. (with each other)** ils ne s'entendent pas; **I get on b. with him** je ne m'entends pas bien avec lui

(b) (*seriously*) (*damaged, scratched*) très; **b. wounded** gravement *ou* grièvement blessé; **his arm was b. broken** il a eu une mauvaise fracture au bras; **he was b. disabled in the accident** il a été sérieusement handicapé dans l'accident; *Sp etc* **b. beaten** battu à plate(s) couture(s)

(c) (*greatly*) **to want sth b.** avoir très envie de qch; **if you want it b. enough you'll get it** quand on veut, on peut; **I need it b.** j'en ai bien *ou Fml* grand besoin; **he's b. in need of a haircut** il a bien besoin de se faire couper les cheveux

bad-mannered *adj* mal élevé

badminton ['bædmɪntən] *n* badminton *m*; **b. court/player** terrain *m*/joueur, -euse de badminton

bad-mouth *vt esp Am* (*person*) déblatérer sur, dire du mal de

badness ['bædnɪs] *n* **(a)** (*of cooking, writing etc*) mauvaise qualité *f* **(b)** (*of person*) méchanceté *f*

bad-tempered *adj* (*person*) grincheux; (*reply*) désagréable; **to be b.** (*temporarily*) être de mauvaise humeur; (*permanently*) avoir mauvais caractère

baffle[1] ['bæf(ə)l] *n* **(a)** *Tech* chicane *f*, déflecteur *m*; **b. plate** plaque-chicane *f*, *pl* plaques-chicanes **(b)** *Rad* **b. (board)** (*of loudspeaker*) écran *m*, baffle *m*

baffle[2] *vt* **(a)** (*mystify*) (*person*) laisser perplexe; **to b. the imagination** dépasser l'imagination; **it baffles the imagination why she agreed** Dieu sait pourquoi elle a accepté!; **mystery that has baffled all investigators** mystère qui a déjoué toutes les recherches; **the police admit they are baffled** la police admet qu'elle est perplexe; **I'm baffled as to why she said that** je ne comprends vraiment pas pourquoi elle a dit ça; **to b. definition** échapper à toute définition **(b)** *(foil)* *(plot, attempt)* déjouer

baffling [ˈbæf(ə)lɪŋ] *adj* *(behaviour)* déconcertant; *(mystery etc)* inexplicable

bag¹ [bæg] *n* **(a)** *(container)* sac *m*; *(handbag)* sac à main; **travel(ling) b.** sac de voyage; *Old-fashioned, Lit* **b. and baggage** avec armes et bagages; **to pack one's bags** faire ses bagages; *F* **we've bags of time** on a tout le temps; *F* **they've bags of money** ils sont pleins aux as; *F* **there's bags of room** la place ne manque pas; *esp Am Sl* **that's not my b.** *(I'm not good at it)* ce n'est pas mon fort; *(I'm not interested in it)* ce n'est pas mon genre; *F* **bags under the eyes** poches *fpl* sous les yeux; **to let it out of the b.** vendre la mèche; *F* **b. of bones** sac *m* *ou* tas *m* d'os

(b) *Br Sl Pej* *(woman)* **old b.** vieille toupie *f*

(c) *(in hunting)* **the b.** le tableau; **to make a good b.** faire un grand abattis de gibier; *Fig* *(of fighter pilot)* avoir un beau tableau de chasse; *F* **it's in the b.** l'affaire est dans le sac

(d) *Br Old-fashioned F* **bags** *(trousers)* pantalon *m*

bag² **(-gg-)** **1** *vt* **(a)** *F* *(take)* *(sth)* s'emparer de, mettre la main sur; *(best seats)* accaparer; *Br* **bags I go first!** c'est moi le premier!; *Br* **bags I sit in front!** c'est moi qui monte devant! **(b)** *(pack)* *(coal, potting compost)* mettre en sac; *(apples, sweets)* ensacher; *Am* *(purchases)* *(in supermarket)* emballer **(c)** *(kill)* *(game)* abattre, tuer; *Av F* *(enemy aircraft)* abattre **2** *vi* *(of garment)* bouffer, avoir trop d'ampleur; **trousers that b. at the knees** pantalon qui fait des poches aux genoux

bagatelle [bægəˈtel] *n* *(trifle)*, *Mus* bagatelle *f*

bagel [ˈbeɪg(ə)l] *n* *esp Am Culin* = petit pain *m* en forme de couronne, dans la cuisine traditionnelle juive, *Can* baguel *m*

baggage [ˈbægɪdʒ] *n* **(a)** *esp Am* bagages *mpl*; **one piece of b.** un bagage; **b. allowance** franchise *f* de bagages; *Rail* **b. car** fourgon *m* à bagages; **b. check** contrôle *m* des bagages; **b. claim** retrait *m* des bagages; **b. claim area** zone *f* de livraison des bagages; **b. claim sticker** étiquette *f* autocollante d'identification de bagage; **b. container** conteneur *m* à bagages; **b. conveyor belt** tapis *m* de livraison de bagages; **b. cover** *(insurance)* assurance *f* bagage(s); *(lid, hood)* cache-bagage *m*; **b. handler** bagagiste *m*; **b. lift** ascenseur *m* à bagages; **b. reclaim** retrait *m* des bagages; **b. room** consigne *f*; **b. tag** étiquette *f* *(pour bagages)*

(b) *Old-fashioned* *(girl)* coquine *f*

(c) *Mil* bagage *m*; **b. waggon** fourgon *m* à bagages

baggy [ˈbægɪ] *adj* *(sweater, trousers)* *(deliberately so)* ample, large; *(out of shape)* déformé

bag lady *n F* clocharde *f*

bagpipe(s) [ˈbægpaɪp, -s] *npl* cornemuse *f*; **b. player** joueur, -euse de cornemuse

bah [bɑː] *int* bah!

Bahama [bəˈhɑːmə] *n* **[ⓘA11,g,ii]** **the Bahamas, the B. Islands** les (îles *fpl*) Bahamas *fpl*, l'archipel *m* des Bahamas

bail¹ [beɪl] *n Jur* *(system)* cautionnement *m*; *(money)* caution *f*; **to go** *or* **stand b. for sb** se porter garant *ou* caution de qn, fournir une caution pour qn *(pour sa libération provisoire)*; **to grant sb b.** *(of judge)* libérer qn sous caution; **released on b.** libéré sous caution; **to be (out) on b.** être en liberté provisoire (sous caution); *F* **to jump b.** se dérober à la justice *(alors qu'on jouit de la liberté provisoire)*

bail² *vt Jur* *(person)* *(of judge)* libérer sous caution; *(of lawyer, family member etc)* se porter caution pour

bail³ *n Cr* **bails** barrettes *fpl*, bâtonnets *mpl*

bail⁴ *n Naut* *(bucket)* écope *f*

▶ **bail out** **1** *vtsep* **(a)** **to b. sb out** *Jur* se porter garant *ou* caution pour qn; *Fig* tirer qn d'affaire; *Fig* **to b. out a company** renflouer une entreprise **(b)** *(boat, water)* écoper, vider **2** *vi* écoper

bailer [ˈbeɪlər] *n Naut* *(bucket)* écope *f*

Bailey¹ [ˈbeɪlɪ] *n* **the Old B.** = le tribunal principal de Londres

Bailey² *n Mil* **B. bridge** pont *m* Bailey

bailiff [ˈbeɪlɪf] *n* **(a)** *Jur* huissier *m* **(b)** *(of estate, farm)* régisseur *m*; **water b.** garde-pêche *m*, *pl* gardes-pêche **(c)** *Br Hist* *(sovereign's representative)* bailli *m*

bailiwick [ˈbeɪlɪwɪk] *n Jur* baillage *m*; *Fig* *(territory)* territoire *m*; *Fig* **it's not my b.** *(field, area of expertise)* ce n'est pas mon rayon

bairn [beən] *n Scot* enfant *mf*

bait¹ [beɪt] *n* *(for fish)* amorce *f*, appât *m*; *Fig* appât, leurre *m*; **ground b.** amorce de fond; **to rise to** *or* **swallow** *or* **take the b.** *(of fish)*, *Fig* mordre à l'hameçon

bait² *vt* **(a)** *(tease)* *(animal)* harceler; *(person)* harceler, tourmenter **(b)** *(put bait on)* *(hook, trap etc)* amorcer **(with** avec); *(line)* mettre l'appât à

baiting [ˈbeɪtɪŋ] *n* **(a)** *(teasing)* *(of animals, person)* harcèlement *m*; *(of badger)* déterrage *m* **(b)** *(of hook, trap etc)* amorçage *m*

baize [beɪz] *n* feutre *m*; **green b.** tapis *m* de billard; **green b. door** porte *f* recouverte de feutre vert

bake [beɪk] **1** *vt Culin* (faire) cuire au four; *Tech* *(bricks, porcelain etc)* cuire; **to b. bread** faire cuire le pain; **earth baked by the sun** sol durci *ou* desséché par le soleil; *F* **I'm baked** je crève de chaleur, je cuis **2** *vi* *(of bread etc)* cuire; *(of person)* *(make cakes)* faire de la pâtisserie *ou* des gâteaux; *(make bread)* faire du pain; *F* **I'm baking** je crève de chaleur

baked [beɪkt] *adj* **b. beans** haricots *mpl* blancs à la tomate, *Can* fèves *fpl* au lard; **b. potato** pomme *f* de terre au four; **b. Alaska** omelette *f* norvégienne

baker [ˈbeɪkər] *n* boulanger, -ère; **b.'s (shop)** boulangerie *f*; **b.'s dozen** treize à la douzaine

bakery [ˈbeɪkərɪ] *n* boulangerie *f*

baking [ˈbeɪkɪŋ] **1** *adj F* **b. hot** *(food, container)* brûlant; *(day)* torride; **it's b. in here** on étouffe ici; **the b. streets** les rues écrasées de chaleur **2** *n* **(a)** *(of bread etc)* cuisson *f*; *(of bricks etc)* cuisson, cuite *f*; **I'll do a** *or* **some b. tomorrow** demain, je ferai de la pâtisserie **(b)** *(batch)* *(of bread)* fournée *f*; *(of bricks etc)* cuite *f*

baking powder *n* levure *f* chimique

baking sheet *n* plaque *f* (de four), tôle *f*

baking soda *n* bicarbonate *m* de soude

baking tin *n* *(for roast)* plat *m* à rôtir; *(for cake)* moule *m* à gâteau

baklava [bəˈklɑːvə] *n Culin* baklava *m*

baksheesh [ˈbækʃiːʃ] *n* bakchich *m*

Balaclava [bæləˈklɑːvə] *n* **B. (helmet)** passe-montagne *m*, *pl* passe-montagnes

balalaika [bæləˈlaɪkə] *n Mus* balalaïka *f*

balance¹ [ˈbæləns] *n* **(a)** *(steadiness)* équilibre *m*; **the b. of his mind** son équilibre mental; **while the b. of his mind was disturbed** alors qu'il n'était pas dans son état normal; **there's a good b. of funny and serious articles** il y a une proportion égale d'articles amusants et sérieux; **to keep** *or* **maintain one's b.** garder l'équilibre; **to lose one's b.** perdre l'équilibre; *Fig* **to catch sb off b.** prendre qn au dépourvu; **to throw sb off b.** faire perdre l'équilibre à qn; *Fig* déstabiliser qn; **to be off b.** être déséquilibré; **to put out of b.** *(scales, machine)* dérégler; *Fig* **to strike a b.** *(between two things)* trouver le juste milieu; *Pol* **the b. of power** l'équilibre des forces; *Pol* **the Liberals hold the b. of power** les Libéraux ont le pouvoir de faire pencher l'Assemblée d'un côté ou de l'autre; *Gym* **b. beam** poutre *f* (horizontale)

(b) *(remainder)* reste *m*; *Com, Fin* *(of account)* solde *m*; *Acct* balance *f*, bilan *m*; **credit/debit b.** solde créditeur/ débiteur; **b. carried forward** nouveau solde, report *m* à nouveau; **b. of trade** balance commerciale; **b. of payments** balance des paiements; **b. due** solde dû; *Fig* **on b.** tout bien considéré

(c) *Tech* *(for weighing)* balance *f*; *Astron* **the B.** la Balance; *Fig* **the b. of evidence** l'ensemble *m* des preuves; *Fig* **to swing the b. (in sb's favour)** faire pencher la balance (du côté de qn); *Fig* **to hang in the b.** être en jeu; **b. wheel** *(of watch)* balancier *m*; *(of clock)* roue *f* de rencontre

balance² **1** *vt* **(a)** *(object)* mettre *ou* maintenir en équilibre; *Aut Naut* équilibrer; *(counteract weight of)* faire contrepoids à; **to b. sth on one's head** mettre qch en équilibre sur sa tête; **women balancing pots on their heads** des femmes portant des pots sur la tête; **one thing balances another** une chose compense l'autre

(b) *Com, Fin* *(account)* balancer, solder, aligner; *(debt)* compenser; *(budget)* équilibrer; **to b. the books** balancer les livres

2 *vi* **(a)** *(of scales)* équilibrer; **the two things b.** les deux choses s'équilibrent

(b) *Com, Fin* *(of accounts)* s'équilibrer; **account that balances** compte *m* en balance; **I can't get the accounts to b.** je n'arrive pas à équilibrer les comptes

(c) *(of acrobat)* se maintenir en équilibre; **to b. on one foot** se tenir en équilibre sur un pied; **books balancing on the desk** des livres en équilibre sur le bureau

▶ **balance against** *vtaspo* **to b. one thing against another** comparer les avantages d'une chose par rapport à une autre; **you have to b. the advantages against the disadvantages** il faut peser le pour et le contre

▶ **balance out** **1** *vi* *(of figures)* correspondre **2** *vtsep* *(match)* *(sth)* compléter; **they b. each other out** *(because of their respective skills)* ils se complètent bien

balanced [ˈbælənst] *adj* **(a)** *(in weight)* équilibré, compensé; *Fig* *(judgement)* pondéré; *(report, account)* objectif; **to be well b.** *(of person)* être équilibré; **a (well-)b. diet** un régime (alimentaire) équilibré **(b)** *(in strength, value)* égal; *Fin* *(budget)* équilibré; **the two parties are pretty well b.** les deux parties sont à peu près égales

balancer shaft ['bælənsə(r)] *n Aut* arbre *m* d'équilibrage
balance sheet *n Acct* bilan *m* comptable; **b. consolidation** consolidation *f* de bilan; **b. item** poste *m* de bilan; **b. value** valeur *f* bilantielle
balancing ['bælənsɪŋ] *n* **(a)** mise *f* en équilibre; *Aut (of wheels)* équilibrage *m*; *Art (of elements in a painting)* balancement *m*; **b. pole** *(of tightrope walker)* contrepoids *m* **(b)** *Com, Fin* **b. of accounts** solde *m ou* alignement *m* des comptes **(c)** *(of two things)* ajustement *m*; *(of sth by sth)* compensation *f*
balancing act *n Th* tours *mpl* d'équilibre; *Fig* **a political b.** des acrobaties *fpl* politiques; **to do a b.** faire de l'équilibrisme; *Fig* **she's doing a b. between her job and her family** elle jongle avec son travail et sa famille
balcony ['bælkənɪ] *n* **(a)** *(on house)* balcon *m*; **on the b.** sur le balcon **(b)** *Th, Cin* balcon *m*; **we always sit in the b.** nous prenons toujours des places au balcon; **there are two b. seats left** il reste deux places au balcon
bald [bɔ:ld] *adj* **(a)** *(person)* chauve; *(tyre)* lisse; *Fig (hillside)* nu; **his b. head** son crâne chauve; **he is going b.** il commence à perdre ses cheveux *ou* à devenir chauve; *F* **b. as a coot** *or* **an egg** chauve comme un œuf *ou* une boule de billard; **b. patch** tonsure *f* **(b)** *Fig (style etc)* dépouillé, sec; **a b. statement of the facts** une simple exposition des faits
bald eagle *n* aigle *m* à tête blanche
balderdash ['bɔ:ldədæʃ] *Old-fashioned F* **1** *n* bêtises *fpl*, balivernes *fpl*; **to talk b.** dire des bêtises *ou* des balivernes; **the book is utter b.** le livre est complètement nul **2** *int* balivernes!
bald-headed *adj* chauve; *F Fig* **to go b. into** *or* **at sth** foncer tête baissée dans qch
balding ['bɔ:ldɪŋ] *adj* **a b. fifty-year old** un homme de cinquante ans avec une calvitie naissante; **he's b.** il commence à perdre ses cheveux, il devient chauve
baldly ['bɔ:ldlɪ] *adv Fig (to write)* d'un style dépouillé *ou* sec; *(to say)* sèchement; **b. worded** *(reply)* sec; *(statement)* bref; **to put it b.** pour parler clairement; **you didn't have to put it so b.!** tu n'avais pas besoin d'être aussi brutal!
baldness ['bɔ:ldnɪs] *n* **(a)** *(of person)* calvitie *f*; **premature b.** calvitie précoce **(b)** *Fig (of style etc)* sécheresse *f*
bale¹ [beɪl] *n Com (of goods)* balle *f*, ballot *m*; *(of hay, straw)* botte *f*; **b. of paper** ballot de dix rames de papier
bale² *vt (goods)* mettre en ballot; *(hay, straw)* botteler
bale³ *n Naut* = **bail⁴**
▶ **bale out 1** *vi Av* sauter en parachute d'un avion en perdition; **he baled out over the Atlantic** il s'est éjecté de l'avion au-dessus de l'Atlantique **2** *vtsep* = **bail out 1 (b)**
Balearic [bælɪ'ærɪk] *adj* **the B. Islands** les (îles *fpl*) Baléares *fpl*
baleen ['beɪli:n] *n (of whale)* fanon *m* de baleine
baleful ['beɪlfʊl] *adj Lit* sinistre, maléfique
balefully ['beɪlfʊlɪ] *adv* sinistrement
baler¹ ['beɪlər] *n* **(a)** *Agr (machine)* botteleuse *f* **(b)** *(person)* emballeur, -euse
baler² *n Naut (bucket)* écope *f*
baling ['beɪlɪŋ] *n (of goods)* mise *f* en balles, paquetage *m*; *Agr* **b. machine** botteleuse *f*
balk [bɔ:k] **1** *vt Fml (person's plans)* déjouer, contrarier; *(person)* contrarier **2** *vi (of horse)* refuser, (se) dérober; **to b. at a fence** refuser un obstacle; *Fig* **to b. at** *(difficulty, expense)* s'arrêter *ou* reculer *ou* hésiter devant
Balkan ['bɔ:lkən] **1** *adj* **the B. States** les États *mpl* balkaniques; **the B. Peninsula** la péninsule des Balkans **2** *npl* **the Balkans** *(region, mountains)* les Balkans *mpl*
balkanization [bɔ:lkənaɪ'zeɪʃən] *n* balkanisation *f*
Balkanize ['bɔ:lkənaɪz] *vt (country)* balkaniser
ball¹ [bɔ:l] *n* **(a)** *(for playing football, rugby, basketball etc, of child)* ballon *m*; *(for cricket, tennis, golf)* balle *f*; *(for croquet, bowling)* boule *f*; *(for billiards)* bille *f*; *(of wool, string)* pelote *f*; *Culin (of dough etc)* boulette *f*; **to wind wool into a b.** mettre de la laine en pelote; **to roll sth (up) into a b.** mettre qch en boule; **b. lightning** éclair *m* en boule; **b. of earth** motte *f*; **b. of fire** boule de feu; *Fig* **to be a b. of fire** déborder d'énergie; *Tennis* **to knock the b. about** faire des balles; *Fb* **to kick the b. about** s'amuser avec le ballon; *Cr* **no b.** balle nulle; **to play b.** jouer à la balle *ou* au ballon; *Am (baseball)* jouer au base-ball; *Fig* coopérer, jouer le jeu; *Fig* **to be on the b.** *(quick-witted)* avoir de la présence d'esprit; *(knowledgeable)* connaître son affaire; *Fig* **to keep one's eye on the b.** rester très vigilant; *Fig* **to keep the b. rolling** *(in conversation)* soutenir la conversation; *Fig* **to start** *or* **get the b. rolling** faire démarrer les choses, mettre les choses en route; *Fig* **the b. is in your court** c'est à vous de jouer; *Fig* **to have the b. at one's feet** avoir la partie belle
(b) b.(-and-socket) joint *Anat* articulation *f* à emboîtement *ou* à trois axes; *MecE* joint *m* à rotule, articulation *f* à genouillère; **b. race** piste *f* des billes, chemin *m* de roulement des billes; **b. ramp** plan *m* incliné, rampe *f*; **b. valve** soupape *f* à boulet
(c) *Vulg (testicle)* **balls** couilles *fpl*; *Fig (courage)* courage *m*; *(nonsense)* conneries *fpl*; **balls!** *(rubbish)* quelles conneries!; **to talk a lot** *or* **a load of balls** dire beaucoup de conneries; **balls to him!** qu'il aille se faire foutre!; *Fig* **they've got us by the balls** ils nous ont à leur merci; *Fig* **to have balls** *(courage)* avoir des couilles; **that type of thing takes balls** il faut avoir des couilles pour faire ce genre de truc
(d) *Anat (of foot)* plante *f*; *(of eye)* globe *m*; *(of thumb)* partie *f* charnue, gras *m*
ball² *vt* **to b. one's fist** serrer le poing
ball³ *vt US Vulg (have sex with)* **to b. sb** se faire qn
ball⁴ *n (dance)* bal *m*, *pl* bals; *F* **to have (oneself) a b.** s'éclater; **how was the party? – an absolute b.!** et la soirée, c'était comment? – génial!; **b. dress** *or* **gown** robe *f* de bal
▶ **ball up** *vtsep US Vulg* = **balls up**
▶ **balls up** *Br Vulg* **1** *vtsep* foutre la merde *ou* le merdier dans; **don't b. things up again!** ne recommence pas à foutre la merde! **2** *vi* merder
balls-up ['bɔ:lzʌp] *n Br Vulg* merdier *m*; **to make a (right) b. of sth** foutre la merde *ou* le merdier dans qch
ballad ['bæləd] *n* **(a)** *Mus* romance *f* **(b)** *Liter* ballade *f*
ballast¹ ['bæləst] *n* **(a)** *Naut, Av* lest *m*; **ship in b. (-trim)** navire *m* sur lest; **to take in b.** faire son lest; **to discharge b.** se délester, jeter du lest; **b. tank** *(of submarine)* ballast *m*; *Fig* **I'm carrying a bit too much b.** j'ai un peu de poids en excédent; *Fig* **to act** *or* **serve as b.** apporter un équilibre **(b)** *Constr* pierraille *f*, cailloutage *m*; *Rail* ballast *m*, empierrement *m*; **b. bed** *(of railway track)* coffre *m*, empierrement; *(of road)* encaissement *m*; *Rail* **b. truck** *or* **car** wagon *m* de terrassement
ballast² *vt* **(a)** *Naut, Av* lester **(b)** *Constr* empierrer, caillouter; *Rail* ballaster
ball bearing *n MecE* roulement *m* à billes
ball boy *n Tennis* ramasseur *m* de balles
ball cock *n* robinet *m ou* soupape *f* à flotteur
ballerina [bælə'ri:nə] *n* ballerine *f*
ballet ['bæleɪ, *esp Am* bæ'leɪ] *n* danse *f* classique, ballet *m*; **I'm going to the b. this evening** je vais voir un ballet *ou* un spectacle de danse classique ce soir; **the Bolshoi b.** le ballet Bolshoi; **b. dancer** danseur, -euse (de danse) classique *ou* de ballet; **b. lesson/school** cours *m*/école *f* de danse classique; **b. shoe** chausson *m* de danse
ball game *n (played with ball)* jeu *m* de ballon; **no ball games, ball games not allowed** *(notice)* ballons *mpl* interdits; *Am* **to go to the b.** aller au match de base-ball; *Fig* **that's a whole new b., that's a different ball game altogether** ça c'est une tout autre histoire
ball girl *n Tennis* ramasseuse *f* de balles
ballistic [bə'lɪstɪk] *adj* balistique; *F* **to go b.** piquer une crise, grimper aux rideaux; **b. missile** missile *m* balistique
ballistics [bə'lɪstɪks] *n* [①**A10,c**] balistique *f*
balloon¹ [bə'lu:n] *n* **(a)** *(toy)* ballon *m*; *Av* ballon (dirigeable), montgolfière *f*; *Fig* **when the b. goes up** quand il va y avoir du grabuge; *Fig* **to go down like a lead b.** *(of suggestion, joke)* tomber complètement à plat **(b) b. glass** (verre *m*) ballon *m*; *Ch* **b. flask** ballon **(c)** *(in cartoons, comic strips)* bulle *f*, phylactère *m*; *Psy* **b. test** test *m* de la bulle *ou* de frustration
balloon² *vi (of skirt, sail etc)* ballonner; *(of cheeks)* gonfler; **to b. (up)** *(of arm, leg etc)* enfler; **she ballooned out in the last months of her pregnancy** elle avait un ventre énorme durant les derniers mois de sa grossesse
ballooning [bə'lu:nɪŋ] *n* **(a)** *(sport)* ballon *m*, montgolfière *f*; **to go b.** faire du ballon *ou* de la montgolfière **(b)** *(of skirt, sail etc)* ballonnement *m*
balloonist [bə'lu:nɪst] *n* aérostier *m*
ballot¹ ['bælət] *n (process)* tour *m* de scrutin; *(vote)* scrutin *m*, vote *m*; **b. stuffing** fraude *f* électorale *(consistant à ajouter des bulletins dans les urnes)*; **to vote by b.** voter par (voie de) scrutin; **to put sth to the b.** soumettre qch à un vote; **second b.** deuxième tour de scrutin; **to cast one's b. for sb** voter pour qn
ballot² 1 *vt Pol (union members)* appeler à voter **2** *vi* **(a)** *Pol* voter par (voie de) scrutin; **to b. for/against sb** voter pour/contre qn **(b)** *Arch (draw lots)* tirer au sort; **to b. for a place** tirer une place au sort
ballot box *n* urne *f*; **to be defeated at the b.** être battu aux élections
balloting ['bælətɪŋ] *n* **(a)** *Pol* scrutin *m* **(b)** *Arch (drawing of lots)* tirage *m* au sort
ballot paper *n* bulletin *m* de vote
ballot rigging *n* fraude *f* électorale

ballpark ['bɔːlpɑːk] *n Am* terrain *m* de base-ball; *Fig* **b. figure** estimation *f*, approximation *f*; *Fig* **you're not even in the b.!** tu es loin du compte!; **are we in the same b.?** est-ce qu'on est sur la même longueur d'ondes?

ball peen hammer [piːn] *n* marteau *m* de carrossier

ballplayer ['bɔːlpleɪər] *n Am Sp* joueur *m* de base-ball

ballpoint ['bɔːlpɔɪnt] *n* **b. (pen)** stylo *m* (à) bille

ballroom ['bɔːlruːm] *n* salle *f* de bal, salle de danse; **b. dancing** danses *fpl* de salon; **b. dancing championship** championnat *m* de danses de salon; **to go b. dancing** aller danser

ballup ['bɔːlʌp] *n US Vulg* = **balls-up**

bally ['bælɪ] *adj Old-fashioned Br F* sacré, satané

ballyhoo[1] [bælɪ'huː] *n F Pej* **(a)** *(publicity)* battage *m* (publicitaire) **(b)** *(fuss)* blabla *m*; **to see through the b.** ne pas être dupe; **what's all the b. about?** pourquoi tout ce remue-ménage?

ballyhoo[2] *vt esp Am F (book, show)* faire du battage (publicitaire) pour promouvoir

balm [bɑːm] *n Pharm, Fig* baume *m*; **b. to the soul** baume au cœur

balminess ['bɑːmɪnɪs] *n* **(a)** *(mildness)* **the b. of the evening air** l'air embaumé du soir **(b)** *Br F* = **barminess**

Balmoral [bɑːl'mɒrəl] *n (shoe)* balmoral *m*

balmy ['bɑːmɪ] *adj* **(a)** *(air, weather)* doux; **the air was b. with the scent of roses** l'air était embaumé du parfum des roses **(b)** *Br F* = **barmy**

balneotherapy [bælnɪəʊ'θerəpɪ] *n* balnéothérapie *f*

baloney [bə'ləʊnɪ] **1** *n Am (sausage)* saucisse *f* bolognaise; *F* **it's all b.** *(nonsense)* c'est des bêtises; **the film/book is a load of b.** le film/livre est complètement nul; **the usual b. from the government** les boniments habituels du gouvernement; **don't give me that b.!** à d'autres! **2** *int* ne dites pas de bêtises!

balsa ['bɔːlsə] *n* **b. (wood)** balsa *m*; **b. wood raft** radeau *m* en bois de balsa

balsam ['bɔːlsəm] *n* **(a)** *(substance)* baume *m* **(b)** *(plant)* balsamine *f*; **b. fir** *(tree)* sapin *m* baumier

Baltic ['bɔːltɪk] **1** *n* **the B. (Sea)** la (mer) Baltique **2** *adj* balte, baltique; **B. port** port *m* balte; **B. States** pays *mpl* baltes

baluster ['bæləstər] *n* balustre *m*; **balusters** rampe *f* d'escalier

balustrade [bælə'streɪd] *n* balustrade *f*

bamboo [bæm'buː] *n* bambou *m*; **b. cane** bambou; **b. chair** chaise *f* en bambou; *Culin* **b. shoots** pousses *fpl* de bambou

Bamboo Curtain *n Pol* rideau *m* de bambou

bamboozle [bæm'buːz(ə)l] *vt F (person)* embobiner; **you've been bamboozled** tu t'es fait embobiner; **to b. sb out of sth** *(cheat)* refaire qn de qch; *(trick)* soutirer qch à qn; **to b. sb into doing sth** embobiner qn pour qu'il fasse qch

ban[1] [bæn] *n* interdiction *f*; *Hist (banishment)* ban *m*, bannissement *m*, proscription *f*; *Rel* interdit *m*; **atomic test b.** interdiction des essais nucléaires; **to put** *or* **impose a b. on sth** interdire qch; **to lift the b. on sth** lever l'interdiction qui porte sur qch; **is there a b. on smoking?** est-il interdit de fumer?

ban[2] *vt* **(-nn-)** *(sb, sth)* interdire; **b. the bomb!** non à la bombe atomique!; **to be banned from driving** se voir retirer son permis de conduire; **he should be banned for life** *(from driving)* on devrait lui retirer son permis de conduire à vie; **dogs have been banned from the beach** les chiens sont interdits sur la plage; **to be banned from a club** être exclu d'un club; **he's been banned from the restaurant/bar** il n'a plus le droit de rentrer dans ce restaurant/bar

banal [bə'næl] *adj* banal, ordinaire

banality [bə'nælɪtɪ] *n* banalité *f*

banana [bə'nɑːnə] *n* banane *f*; **b. (tree)** bananier *m*; *F* **to go bananas** *(become excited)* déjanter; *(become angry)* grimper aux rideaux; *F* **you're bananas!** *(crazy)* tu es cinglé!; *Fig F* **top b.** grand chef *m*; **b. plantation** bananeraie *f*

banana boat *n* bananier *m*

banana republic *n Pej* république *f* bananière

banana skin *n (of fruit), Fig* peau *f* de banane

banana split *n Culin* banana split *f inv*

bancassurance ['bæŋkəʃʊərəns] *n Banking* bancassurance *f*

band[1] [bænd] *n* **(a)** *(round hat)* ruban *m*; *(round cigar)* bague *f* **(b)** *(stripe)* *(of colour)* bande *f*, raie *f*; *Rad* **bands of the spectrum** bandes du spectre **(c)** *Rad* bande *f* de fréquence **(d)** *(range)* tranche *f*; **children in the 10-15 age b.** les enfants dans la tranche des 10-15 ans **(e)** *MecE etc* bande *f*, courroie *f*; **b. saw** scie *f* à ruban; *Ind* **b. conveyor** tapis *m* roulant **(f)** *Rel, Jur* **bands** *(on collar)* rabat *m* **(g)** *(wedding ring)* alliance *f*; **b. of gold** alliance en or

band[2] *n* **(a)** *Mus (jazz)* orchestre *m*, groupe *m*; *(rock music)* groupe; **to be** *or* **play in a b.** faire partie d'un orchestre/un groupe **(b)** *(group)* bande *f*, troupe *f*, *Pej* clique *f*

▶ **band together** *vi (unite)* se liguer **(to do** pour faire)

bandage[1] ['bændɪdʒ] *n Med* bandage *m*, bande *f*; *(blindfold)* bandeau *m*; **to have** *or* **wear a b. on one's arm, to have one's arm in a b.** avoir le bras bandé; **to put a b. on sb/sth** bander qn/qch

bandage[2] *vt (person, wound, leg)* bander, panser

▶ **bandage up** *vtsep (person)* bander, panser; **I'll b. this up for you** je vais te faire un bandage; **I bandaged her up with towels** je lui ai fait un bandage avec des serviettes de toilette

bandaging ['bændɪdʒɪŋ] *n* **(a)** *(bandages)* bandage *m*, pansement *m* **(b)** *(action)* pansement *m*

Band-Aid® ['bændeɪd] *n esp Am* sparadrap *m*; *Fig* **a b. solution/measure** une solution/une mesure d'attente *ou* provisoire

bandan(n)a [bæn'dænə] *n* bandana *m*

bandbox ['bændbɒks] *n Old-fashioned Fig* **she looks as if she's just stepped out of a b.** elle est tirée à quatre épingles

banded ['bændɪd] *adj* **(a)** *(striped)* rayé **(b)** *Com* **b. pack** lot *m*; **b. pack selling** vente *f* par lot

bandit ['bændɪt] *n* bandit *m*, brigand *m*

banditry ['bændɪtrɪ] *n* brigandage *m*

bandmaster ['bændmɑːstər] *n Mil etc* chef *m* de musique; *(of brass band)* chef de fanfare

bandoleer, bandolier [bændə'lɪər] *n* cartouchière *f* *(portée en bandoulière)*

bandsman, *pl* **-men** ['bændzmən] *n* *(in military band)* musicien *m*; *(in brass band)* fanfariste *m*

bandstand ['bændstænd] *n* kiosque *m* à musique

bandwagon ['bændwæg(ə)n] *n* char *m* des musiciens *(en tête de la cavalcade)*; *Fig* **to climb** *or* **jump on the b.** prendre le train en marche

bandwidth ['bændwɪdθ] *n Rad* largeur *f* de bande; *(of computer monitor)* bande *f* passante

bandy[1] ['bændɪ] *vt (witticisms, insults etc)* échanger; *(statistics)* se renvoyer; **they were bandying words** *(quarrelling)* ils se chamaillaient; **don't b. words with me, young man!** ne venez pas me faire la leçon, jeune homme!

bandy[2] *adj* aux jambes arquées; **b. legs** jambes arquées; **to be b., to have b. legs** avoir les jambes arquées

▶ **bandy about, bandy around** *vtsep* **her name was being bandied about as a possible candidate** son nom est revenu plusieurs fois parmi ceux des candidats possibles; **I don't like the papers bandying my name about** je n'aime pas que mon nom revienne à tout propos dans les journaux; **decentralization is a word the government bandies about a lot** la décentralisation est un mot que le gouvernement a souvent à la bouche

bandy-legged *adj* aux jambes arquées

bane [beɪn] *n Lit* plaie *f*; **she is the b. of pretentious authors** elle est la bête noire des auteurs prétentieux; *F* **he's the b. of my life** il m'empoisonne l'existence

baneful ['beɪnfʊl] *adj Lit* funeste; *(influence)* néfaste

banefully ['beɪnfʊlɪ] *adv* funestement

bang[1] [bæŋ] *n* **(a)** *(blow)* coup *m* (violent); **she got a bad b. on the head** elle a reçu un mauvais coup sur la tête

(b) *(noise)* *(of rifle etc)* détonation *f*; *(of door)* claquement *m*; **the door shut with a b.** la porte s'est refermée en claquant; **to shut the door with a b.** claquer la porte; **to shut the windows/cupboard with a b.** fermer les fenêtres/les portes du placard en les faisant claquer; **to go off with a b.** *(of firework)* détoner; *F Fig* **to go (off)** *or US* **over with a b.** être une réussite; **to end with a b.** finir en beauté

(c) *Am Sl (pleasure)* **to get a b. from doing sth** prendre son pied à faire qch; **she gets a real b. out of her grandchildren** elle retire beaucoup de plaisir de ses petits-enfants

(d) *Sl (of heroin)* shoot *m* d'héroïne

(e) *Vulg (sexual intercourse)* baise *f*

bang[2] **1** *vi* **(a)** *(make noise)* *(of door, shutter)* claquer, battre; *(of gun)* retentir; **the door banged shut** la porte s'est refermée en claquant; **to b. at** *or* **on the door** frapper à la porte à grands coups; **to b. on the table with one's fist** taper du poing sur la table **(b)** *Sl (of heroin addict)* se shooter **2** *vt* **(a)** *(strike)* frapper (violemment); **to b. one's head** se cogner la tête; *Fig* **to b. one's head against a brick wall** se taper la tête contre les murs; *Fig* **to b. a few heads together** taper du poing sur la table **(b)** *(make noise with)* *(door, window)* (faire) claquer **(c)** *Vulg (woman)* baiser

bang[3] **1** *int* pan!, v'lan!, boum!; *Br F* **b. went fifty pounds!** et vlan! cinquante livres se sont envolées; *Br F* **b. went my hopes of a quiet weekend** pour le week-end tranquille c'était râpé **2** *adv* **to go b.** éclater; **he crashed b. into the tree** il est rentré en plein dans l'arbre; *F* **to fall b. in the middle** tomber en plein milieu; *F* **b. on time** pile à l'heure; *F* **it's b. on** c'est au poil; *F* **b. up-to-date** *(equipment etc)* à la pointe de la technologie; (*reference book etc*) vraiment à jour; **to be b. up-to-date on sth** être vraiment à jour pour ce qui est de qch; *Br F* **to be caught b. to rights** être pris la main dans le sac

bang[4] *n* (*also* **bangs**) (*hair*) frange *f*; **to have bangs, to wear one's hair in a b.** avoir une frange

▶ **bang about, bang around** *vi* faire du potin

▶ **bang away** *vi* **(a)** (*with hammer*) donner des coups, taper; (*with gun*) tirer, donner des coups de feu; **to b. away at a typewriter/piano** taper sur un clavier de machine à écrire/ piano **(b)** (*criticize*) **they've been banging away at the government for months** cela fait des mois qu'ils s'acharnent sur le gouvernement **(c)** *F* (*have sex*) baiser

▶ **bang down** *vtsep* (*lid*) refermer violemment; **he banged the book down on the table** il a fait claquer le livre sur la table

▶ **bang into** *vipo* (*collide with*) (*sb, sth*) foncer dans

▶ **bang on** *vi Sl* **he's always banging on about it** il n'arrête pas de bassiner tout le monde avec ça; **if I have to listen to him banging on one more time about it** s'il se remet à me casser les oreilles avec ça

▶ **bang out** *vtsep* (*tune*) jouer tant bien que mal

▶ **bang up** *vtsep Br Sl* **(a)** (*imprison*) boucler; **to be banged up** être en taule **(b)** (*make pregnant*) (*usu passive*) **to get banged up** se faire mettre en cloque

banger ['bæŋər] *n Br* **(a)** *F* (*sausage*) saucisse *f*; **bangers and mash** purée *f* avec des saucisses **(b)** (*firework*) pétard *m* **(c)** *F* (*car*) **old b.** vieux tacot *m*, vieille guimbarde *f*

Bangladesh [bæŋglə'deʃ] *n* Bangladesh *m*

Bangladeshi [bæŋglə'deʃɪ] **1** *n* Bangladais, -aise **2** *adj* (*government, representative etc*) bangladais

bangle ['bæŋg(ə)l] *n* (*for wrist*) bracelet *m* rigide; (*for ankle*) anneau *m* attaché autour de la cheville

banish ['bænɪʃ] *vt* **(a)** (*exile*) (*person*) bannir, exiler, proscrire **(b)** *Fig* (*drive away*) (*fear, care, idea*) chasser; **to b. sth from one's thoughts** chasser qch de ses pensées; **you can b. all thoughts of a holiday** ce n'est plus la peine de compter sur des vacances

banishment ['bænɪʃmənt] *n* bannissement *m*, exil *m*; **to go into b.** partir pour l'exil; **to be sent into b.** être banni *ou* exilé

banisters ['bænɪstəz] *npl* rampe *f* (d'escalier); **to slide down the b.** glisser le long de la rampe d'escalier

banjo, *pl* **-os, -oes** ['bændʒəʊ, -əʊz] *n Mus* banjo *m*

banjoist ['bændʒəʊɪst] *n* joueur, -euse de banjo, banjoiste *mf*

bank[1] [bæŋk] *n* **(a)** (*of river, canal*) berge *f*, bord *m*, rive *f*; (*of lake*) bord, rive; **the banks of the Thames** les berges de la Tamise **(b)** (*on side of road etc*) talus *m*; (*manmade*) terrasse *f*, levée *f* de terre; *Constr* banquette *f*, remblai *m*; *Rail* rampe *f*; *Horseracing* banquette (irlandaise) **(c)** (*mass*) (*of fog, cloud, sand*) banc *m*; **banks of flowers** des multitudes de fleurs; *Geog* **the Banks of Newfoundland** le Banc de Terre-Neuve **(d)** *Av* inclinaison *f*; (*turn*) virage *m* incliné

bank[2] **1** *vt* **(a)** (*river*) contenir par des berges; *Constr* **to b. a road** surhausser *ou* relever un virage; **banked corner** virage relevé **(b)** (*mass, form*) **to be banked** (*of clouds, snow*) être tassé **2** *vi* (*of road*) être incliné; *Av* s'incliner sur l'aile; (*turn*) virer (sur l'aile)

bank[3] *n* **(a)** *Com, Fin* banque *f*; (*for coins*) tirelire *f*; **is there a b. nearby?** y a-t-il une banque par ici?; **could you tell me where the nearest Midland® b. is?** pouvez-vous me dire où se trouve la Midland® la plus proche?; **the B. of England/ France** la Banque d'Angleterre/de France; **b. accounting** comptabilité *f* bancaire; **b. advice note** avis *m* de la banque; **b. base rate** taux *m* de base bancaire; **b. borrowings** emprunts *mpl* bancaires, concours *m* bancaire; **b. branch code** code *m* guichet; **b. buying rate** taux *m* de change à l'achat; **b. cheque** chèque *m* bancaire; **b. commission** commission *f* bancaire; **b. credit** avoir *m* en banque, crédit *m* bancaire; **b. details** relevé *m* d'identité bancaire, RIB *m*; **b. discount rate** escompte *m* officiel; **b. draft** traite *f* bancaire; **b. guarantee** garantie *f* bancaire, caution *f* de banque; **b. interest** intérêt *m* bancaire; **b. ledger** livre *m ou* journal *m* de banque; **b. lending** concours *m* bancaire; **b. loan** prêt *m* bancaire; **b. money** monnaie *f* scripturale; **b. notification** avis *m* de la banque; **b. overdraft** découvert *m* bancaire; *Acct* **b. reconciliation** rapprochement *m* bancaire; **b. references** références *fpl* bancaires; **b. selling rate** taux *m* de change à la vente; **b. shares** valeurs *fpl* bancaires; **b. sort code** code *m* banque et code guichet; **b. transactions** transactions *fpl* bancaires; **b. transfer** virement *m* bancaire; **b. treasurer** trésorier *m* de banque

(b) (*in game*) banque *f* (*de celui qui tient le jeu*); **to break the b.** faire sauter la banque; *Fig* **it won't break the b.** (*of expenditure*) ça ne va pas me/nous/*etc* ruiner

(c) (*store*) (*for blood, sperm, information*) banque *f*

bank[4] **1** *vt* (*money*) mettre *ou* déposer en banque **2** *vi* **to b. with sb** avoir un compte en banque chez qn; **who do you b. with?** à quelle banque êtes-vous?; **do you b. with us?** avez-vous un compte chez nous?

bank[5] *n* **(a)** (*group, series*) (*of switches, dials, of cylinders*) rangée *f*; *Cin* (*of projectors*) rampe *f*; (*of speakers, transformers etc*) groupe *m*, batterie *f*; *Comptr* (*of chips*) banc *m* **(b)** *Naut* (*of rowers*) banc *m*; (*of oars*) rang *m*; (*of seats*) travée *f*

▶ **bank on** *vipo* (*sth*) compter sur; (*event*) miser sur; **to b. on success** escompter un succès; **I wouldn't b. on her being there** ça m'étonnerait qu'elle soit là; **don't b. on it** ne comptez pas là-dessus

▶ **bank up 1** *vtsep* (*earth etc*) remblayer, terrasser; (*fire*) remettre du bois/du charbon dans **2** *vi* (*of snow, clouds, mist etc*) s'entasser, s'accumuler

bankable ['bæŋkəb(ə)l] *adj Fin* bancable; *Fig* **to be b.** (*of film star etc*) être une valeur sûre; *Fig* **a b. idea** une idée qui vaut de l'or

bank account *n* compte *m* en banque

bank balance *n* solde *m* bancaire

bankbook ['bæŋkbʊk] *n* (*of account holder*) livret *m ou* carnet *m* de compte *ou* banque; (*for accounting*) journal *m ou* livre *m* de banque

bank card *n Br* carte *f* bancaire

bank charges *npl* frais *mpl ou* agios *mpl* bancaires

bank clerk *n* employé, -ée de banque

banker ['bæŋkər] *n* **(a)** *Fin* banquier *m*; **b.'s card** carte *f* bancaire; **b.'s draft** chèque *m* bancaire *ou* de banque; **b.'s order** ordre *m* de transfert permanent **(b)** (*in game*) banquier *m*, tailleur *m*; **to be b.** tenir la banque

bank holiday *n Br* fête *f* légale (*où les banques n'ouvrent pas*), *F* jour *m* férié

banking[1] ['bæŋkɪŋ] *n* **(a)** *Constr* remblayage *m*; (*of bend*) surhaussement *m*, relèvement *m* **(b)** *Av* inclinaison *f*; (*turning*) virage *m* incliné

banking[2] *n* **(a)** (*business*) affaires *fpl ou* opérations *fpl* de banque; **electronic b.** bancatique *f*; **b. centre** place *f* bancaire; **b. consortium** consortium *m* de banques; **b. hours** heures *fpl* d'ouverture de la banque; **b. law** droit *m* bancaire; **b. network** réseau *m* bancaire; **b. products** produits *mpl* bancaires; **b. regulator** régulateur *m* bancaire; **b. secrecy** secret *m* bancaire; **b. services** services *mpl* bancaires; **b. terms** conditions *fpl* de banque **(b)** (*profession*) profession *f* de banquier, la banque; **b. profession** métier *m* de banquier; **she's in b.** elle travaille dans la banque

bank manager *n* directeur, -trice de banque; **my b.** mon banquier

banknote ['bæŋknəʊt] *n* billet *m* de banque

bank rate *n* taux *m* bancaire

bank robber *n* cambrioleur, -euse, *F* casseur, -euse

bankroll ['bæŋkrəʊl] *vt Am F* (*person, project*) financer

bankrupt[1] ['bæŋkrʌpt] **1** *n* (*person*) failli, -ie; **fraudulent b.** banqueroutier, -ière **2** *adj* failli; **to go b.** (*of person, business*) faire faillite; (*fraudulently*) faire banqueroute; **to be b.** être en faillite; **to declare sb b.** déclarer *ou* mettre qn en faillite; *Fig* **to be morally b.** avoir perdu toute crédibilité

bankrupt[2] *vt* (*person*) mettre en faillite, *F* ruiner

bankruptcy ['bæŋkrəptsɪ] *n* faillite *f*; **fraudulent b.** banqueroute *f*; **to bring sb to the verge of b.** amener qn au bord de la ruine; **B. Court** = tribunal *m* de commerce; *Hum* **you'll have me in b. court!** tu veux ma ruine!; **b. proceedings** procédure *f* de faillite

bank statement *n* relevé *m* bancaire *ou* de compte, *Can* état *m* de compte

banner ['bænər] **1** *n* (*flag*) bannière *f*; **the Star-Spangled B.** la bannière étoilée; *Journ* **b. heading** *or* **headline** manchette *f* **2** *adj Am* (*year etc*) excellent

bannisters ['bænɪstəz] *npl* = **banisters**

banns [bænz] *npl* bans *mpl*; **to read** *or* **publish the b.** = (faire) publier les bans

banquet[1] ['bæŋkwɪt] *n* banquet *m*; **b. hall** salle *f* de banquet; **b. facilities** (*notice in hotel etc*) possibilité d'organiser des banquets

banquet[2] **1** *vt* (*person*) offrir un banquet à **2** *vi* banqueter

banqueting ['bæŋkwɪtɪŋ] *n* **b. manager** responsable *m* des banquets; **b. room** salle *f* de réception *ou* de banquet

banquette [bæŋ'ket] *n esp Am* (*seat*) banquette *f*

banshee [bæn'ʃiː] *n Myth* fée *f* de la mythologie irlandaise, qui hurle pour annoncer une mort imminente; **to wail like a b.** hurler comme un sauvage

bantam ['bæntəm] *n* **(a)** (*chicken*) = poulet *m* de petite taille **(b)** *Boxing* = **bantamweight**

bantamweight ['bæntəmweɪt] *n* poids *m* coq; **b. champion** champion *m* poids coq

banter ['bæntər] *n* (*jokes*) badinage *m*; (*teasing*) taquineries *fpl*

bantering ['bæntərɪŋ] *adj* (*tone etc*) taquin
Bantu ['bæntu:] **1** *adj* bantou **2** *n* **(a)** Bantou, -oue **(b)** *Ling* bantou *m*
banyan ['bænjən] *n* (*tree*) banian *m*
BAOR [bi:eɪəʊ'ɑ:r] *abbr* **British Army of the Rhine**
bap [bæp] *n Br Culin* petit pain *m* rond au lait
baptism ['bæptɪz(ə)m] *n* baptême *m*; *Fig* **b. of fire** baptême du feu
baptismal [bæp'tɪzm(ə)l] *adj* (*register*) baptistaire; (*name*) de baptême; **b. font** fonts *mpl* baptismaux
Baptist ['bæptɪst] **1** *n* **(a)** *Rel* baptiste *mf* **(b) (St.) John the B.** saint Jean-Baptiste **2** *adj* baptiste; **B. doctrine** doctrine *f* baptiste, baptisme *m*
baptist(e)ry ['bæptɪstrɪ] *n* baptistère *m*
baptize [bæp'taɪz] *vt* (*person, ship etc*) baptiser; **to be baptized a Catholic/(in the name of) John** être baptisé catholique/du nom de Jean
bar¹ [bɑ:r] *n* **(a)** (*of iron, gold etc*) barre *f*; (*of chocolate*) tablette *f*; (*smaller*) barre; (*of electric fire*) résistance *f*; (*of medal*) barrette *f*; (*in gym*) barre; **with b.** (*medal*) ≈ avec palme; **bars** (*of window, cage, prison*) barreaux *mpl*; **to be behind (prison) bars** être derrière les barreaux
(b) (*obstacle*) empêchement *m*, obstacle *m*; (*in river, harbour*) barre *f* (de sable), traverse *f*; **to be a b. to sth** faire obstacle à qch; **a colour b. anywhere is illegal** il est illégal de faire de la discrimination raciale où que ce soit
(c) (*ban*) **there is a b. on bringing drink into the club** il est interdit d'introduire de l'alcool au sein du club
(d) (*in court*) *Br* **the prisoner at the b.** l'accusé, -ée; *Fig* **to be judged at the b. of public opinion** être jugé par l'opinion publique
(e) *Jur* (*profession*) **the B.** l'Ordre *m* des avocats, le barreau; **to read for the B.** faire son droit; **to be called to the B.** être reçu au barreau, être reçu avocat
(f) (*pub*) bar *m*, café *m*, *F* bistro *m*; (*counter*) comptoir *m*, bar; *F* **he's always propping up the b.** c'est un vrai pilier de bar *ou* de bistro; **b. meal** repas *m* au bar; **b. staff** personnel *m* de bar
(g) (*line*) barre *f*; *Mus* mesure *f*; *Mus* **b. (line)** barre; *Mus* **double b.** double barre
(h) *Met* bar *m*
(i) *Comptr* (*menu bar*) barre *f*
bar² *vt* **(-rr-) (a)** (*obstruct*) (*the way*) barrer; **to b. sb.'s way** barrer la route à qn, être dans le chemin de qn; **he's been barred from the club** il a été exclu du club **(b)** (*forbid*) (*action*) défendre, prohiber, interdire; (*subject of conversation*) exclure; **to b. sb from doing sth** défendre à qn de faire qch; **she's been barred from playing** elle a été interdite de jeu **(c)** (*put bars on*) (*window*) mettre des barreaux à **(d)** *Old-fashioned* (*lock*) (*door etc*) barrer; **to b. the door against sb** barrer la porte à qn
bar³ *prep* (*except*) sauf, excepté, à l'exception de; **we've decided everything b. the time** nous avons tout prévu sauf l'heure; **we've finished all of them b. one** nous les avons tous terminé sauf un; **the finest/the quickest b. none** sans conteste le meilleur/le plus rapide; **it's all over b. the shouting** les jeux sont faits
barb [bɑ:b] *n* **(a)** (*on fish hook*) barbillon *m*, dardillon *m*; (*on arrow*) barbillon; (*of barbed wire*) picot *m* **(b)** (*on fish, animal*) barbillon *m*; *Bot* arête *f*; (*on feather*) barbe *f* **(c)** *Fig* (*gibe*) pique *f*, remarque *f* acerbe
Barbados [bɑ:'beɪdɒs] *n* Barbade *f*
barbarian [bɑ:'beərɪən] *adj, n* barbare *mf*
barbaric [bɑ:'bærɪk] *adj* barbare
barbarism ['bɑ:bərɪz(ə)m] *n* **(a)** (*of person, behaviour*) barbarie *f* **(b)** *Gram, Ling* barbarisme *m*
barbarity [bɑ:'bærɪtɪ] *n* **(a)** (*cruelty*) barbarie *f*, cruauté *f* **(b)** (*action*) acte *m* de barbarie, atrocité *f*
barbarize ['bɑ:bəraɪz] *vt* **to b. sb** faire de qn un monstre; **to b. the language** estropier la langue
barbarous ['bɑ:bərəs] *adj* barbare
barbarously ['bɑ:bərəslɪ] *adv* cruellement
Barbary ['bɑ:bərɪ] *n* **B. ape** magot *m*; **B. horse** cheval *m* barbe; **the B. States** la Barbarie, les États *mpl* barbaresques
barbecue¹ ['bɑ:bɪkju:] *n* (*fireplace, party*) barbecue *m*; **to cook sth on the b.** faire cuire qch au barbecue; **to have a b.** faire un barbecue; **b. sauce** sauce *f* barbecue
barbecue² *vt* (*meat*) (faire) griller au barbecue; **barbecued chicken** poulet rôti *ou* grillé au barbecue
barbed [bɑ:bd] *adj* **(a)** barbelé; **b. arrow** flèche *f* à barbelures **(b)** *Fig* (*comment etc*) acerbe **(c)** *Bot* hameçonné
barbed wire *n* (fil *m* de fer) barbelé *m*; **b.-wire fence** clôture *f* de barbelé; **b.-wire entanglements** barbelés *mpl*
barbel ['bɑ:b(ə)l] *n* **(a)** (*fish*) barbeau *m* (commun) **(b)** (*on fish*) barbillon *m*
barbell ['bɑ:bel] *n Gym* haltère *m*
barber ['bɑ:bər] *n* coiffeur *m* pour hommes, *Old-fashioned* barbier *m*; **I'm going to the b.'s** je vais chez le coiffeur
barbershop ['bɑ:bəʃɒp] *n Am* salon *m* de coiffure (*pour hommes*); *Mus* **b. harmony** chants *mpl* à quatre voix d'hommes; **b. quartet** = quatuor *m* chantant en harmonie
barbican ['bɑ:bɪkən] *n* (*fortification*) barbacane *f*
Barbie® ['bɑ:bi:] *n* **B. doll** (poupée *f*) Barbie *f*
barbie ['bɑ:bi:] *n Austr F* barbecue *m*
barbiturate [bɑ:'bɪtjʊreɪt] *n Ch* barbiturique *m*; **b. poisoning** intoxication *f* aux barbituriques
barbituric [bɑ:bɪ'tjʊ:rɪk] *adj* barbiturique
barcarol(l)e ['bɑ:kərəʊl] *n Mus* barcarolle *f*
Barcelona [bɑ:sɪ'ləʊnə] *n* Barcelone *f*
bar chart *n* histogramme *m*
bar code *n* code *m* à barres, code-barres *m*, *pl* codes-barres; **b. reader** lecteur *m* de code-barres
bard¹ [bɑ:d] *n* **(a)** *Arch* (*poet*) poète *m*; *Lit* **the B. (of Avon)** Shakespeare **(b)** (*Celtic*) barde *m*
bard² *n Culin* barde *f*
bard³ *vt Culin* barder
bar diagram *n* histogramme *m*
bardic ['bɑ:dɪk] *adj* (*poetry*) des bardes
bardolatry [bɑ:'dɒlətrɪ] *n Hum Pej* = admiration *f* sans bornes pour Shakespeare et ses œuvres
bare¹ [beər] *adj* **(a)** (*without covering, unadorned*) (*head, leg, chest, room etc*) nu; (*cupboard, shelf*) vide; (*tree*) dénudé, dépouillé; (*country*) nu, dénudé; *El* (*wire*) dénudé; **to strip a house b.** (*remove contents*) dévaliser une maison; **they stripped the car b.** (*removed wheels etc*) ils n'ont laissé que la carcasse de la voiture; **the wind stripped the tree b.** le vent a dénudé l'arbre; **the room was b. of furniture/pictures** la pièce ne comportait aucun meuble/tableau; **at this time of year, the garden is b. of flowers** à cette époque de l'année, le jardin n'a plus de fleurs; **to fight with b. hands** se battre à mains nues; **I'll kill him with my b. hands** je le tuerai de mes propres mains; **in one's b. feet** pieds nus; **to lie** *or* **sleep on the b. boards** coucher sur la dure; **the b. facts** les faits bruts; **the b. bones of the case are ...** les grandes lignes de cette affaire sont ...; **to lay b.** (*surface, mistakes, one's heart*) mettre à nu, exposer; (*secret, fraud*) dévoiler; (*foundations, roots etc*) déchausser
(b) *attrib* (*just sufficient*) **to earn a b. living** gagner tout juste *ou* à peine de quoi vivre; **the b. minimum** le strict minimum; **the b. necessities (of life)** le strict nécessaire; *Sch* **he got a b. pass** il a eu son examen en ayant juste la moyenne; **a b. pass isn't good enough in my father's eyes** pour mon père réussir un examen de justesse n'est pas suffisant; **b. majority** faible majorité *f*
bare² *vt* (*sth*) mettre à nu; **to b. one's head** se découvrir; **to b. one's teeth** montrer les dents; **to b. one's heart** *or* **soul** ouvrir son cœur, mettre son âme à nu
bareback ['beəbæk] **1** *adv* **to ride b.** monter (un cheval) à nu *ou* à cru **2** *adj* **b. rider** cavalier, -ière qui monte à cru
barefaced ['beəfeɪst] *adj attrib F Pej* (*lie, liar etc*) éhonté, effronté
barefoot(ed) ['beəfʊt, -ɪd] **1** *adj* aux pieds nus **2** *adv* nu-pieds, pieds nus; **she goes b.** elle marche pieds nus
barehanded [beə'hændɪd] **1** *adj* aux mains nues **2** *adv* les mains nues
bareheaded [beə'hedɪd] **1** *adj* à la tête nue **2** *adv* nu-tête, (la) tête nue
bare-legged 1 *adj* aux jambes nues **2** *adv* (les) jambes nues
barely ['beəlɪ] *adv* (*just*) à peine, tout juste; **I b. know her** je la connais à peine; **he can b. read and write** c'est tout juste s'il sait lire et écrire; **you've b. got here and you're leaving** tu viens à peine d'arriver et tu es déjà reparti; **a b. furnished room** (*lacking furniture*) une pièce avec très peu de meubles
bareness ['beənɪs] *n* **(a)** (*of room*) aspect *m* dépouillé; (*of hillside, wall*) nudité *f* **(b)** (*of style etc*) dépouillement *m*
barf [bɑ:f] *vi esp Am F* vomir; **b. bag** sac *m* pour vomir
bar fly *n Am F* pilier *m* de bar
bargain¹ ['bɑ:gɪn] *n* **(a)** (*deal*) marché *m*, affaire *f*; **a good/bad b.** une bonne/mauvaise affaire; **to make** *or* **strike a b. with sb** conclure *ou* faire un marché avec qn; **I'll make a b. with you** on fait un marché; **I thought we had a b.** je croyais qu'on s'était mis d'accord; **you haven't kept your side** *or* **part of the b.** vous n'avez pas respecté notre accord; **to drive a hard b.** ne pas faire de cadeaux; **it's a b.!** c'est entendu!; **into the b.** par-dessus le marché, en plus
(b) (*good buy*) occasion *f*, affaire *f*; **b. offer** offre *f* avantageuse, occasion; **b. package** offre spéciale; **b. price** prix *m* exceptionnel; **b. sale** soldes *mpl*; **b. store** magasin *m* bon marché
bargain² *vi* négocier **(with** avec); (*in market place*) marchander **(with** avec)

▶ **bargain away** *vtsep* brader
▶ **bargain for** *vipo* (*reaction, question*) s'attendre à, compter sur; **he got more than he bargained for** il ne s'attendait pas à cela; **you might get more than you bargained for** tu auras peut-être du fil à retordre; **I didn't b. for that** je ne m'attendais pas à cela, je ne comptais pas là-dessus
▶ **bargain on** *vipo* s'attendre à, compter sur; **I hadn't bargained on him being there** je ne m'attendais pas à ce qu'il soit là, je n'avais pas compté qu'il serait là
bargain basement *n* rayon *m* des soldes; *Fig* **at b. prices** à des prix très réduits
bargain break *n* séjour *m* discompté
bargain counter *n* rayon *m* des soldes
bargain hunter *n* chineur, -euse
bargain hunting *n* **to go b.** chiner
bargaining ['bɑːgɪnɪŋ] *n* (*in market etc*) marchandage *m*; *Ind* négociations *fpl*; **b. unit** unité *f* de négociation; **to be in a good b. position, to have a lot of b. power** être dans une bonne position pour négocier; **this has reduced their b. power** cela a affaibli leur position dans les négociations; **to use sb/sth as a b. chip** utiliser qn/qch comme monnaie d'échange
barge[1] [bɑːdʒ] *n* (*for transporting goods*) péniche *f*, barge *f*, chaland *m*; (*for living on*) péniche; (*ceremonial*) bateau *m* d'apparat
barge[2] *vt* (*goalkeeper, player*) écarter d'un coup d'épaule; **to b. sb out of the way** écarter qn d'un geste brusque; **there's a lot of barging going on** (*in race*) on joue beaucoup des épaules
▶ **barge in** *vi* **(a)** (*enter abruptly*) faire irruption **(b)** (*interrupt*) intervenir mal à propos; **don't keep barging in with questions** arrête de me/nous/*etc* interrompre avec tes questions
▶ **barge into** *vipo* **(a)** (*collide with*) (*person, lamppost etc*) rentrer dans; **you nearly barged into me!** tu as failli me rentrer dedans! **(b)** (*enter abruptly*) (*room*) faire irruption dans
▶ **barge through 1** *vipo* **to b. through a door** passer une porte en trombe; **to b. through a crowd** se forcer un passage à travers la foule **2** *vtsep* **just b. your way through** force le passage
bargee [bɑː'dʒiː], *Am* **bargeman** ['bɑːdʒmən] *n* marinier *m*
bargepole ['bɑːdʒpəʊl] *n* (*for propelling barge*) gaffe *f*; *Fig* **I wouldn't touch it with a b.** (*it's disgusting*) ça me dégoûterait d'y toucher; (*it's risky for me*) je ne veux rien avoir à faire avec ça; (*it's risky for you*) si j'étais vous je ne m'en mêlerais pas
bar graph *n* histogramme *m*
baritone ['bærɪtəʊn] *n Mus* (*voice, singer, instrument*) baryton *m*
barium ['beərɪəm] *n Ch* baryum *m*; *Med* **b. meal** (bouillie *f* de) sulfate *m* de baryum
bark[1] [bɑːk] *n* **(a)** (*of tree*) écorce *f*; **to strip the b. off a tree** écorcer un arbre **(b)** (*for tanning*) tan *m*
bark[2] *vt* (*tree*) écorcer; *Fig* **to b. one's shins** s'écorcher *ou* s'érafler les jambes (**on** sur)
bark[3] *n* (*of dog*) aboiement *m*; (*of fox*) glapissement *m*; *Fig* **his b. is worse than his bite** il aboie plus qu'il ne mord
bark[4] 1 *vi* (*of dog*) aboyer (**at** après, contre, à); (*of fox*) glapir; *Fig* (*of person*) crier (**at** sur); *Fig* **to be barking up the wrong tree** faire fausse route **2** *vt* (*sth*) (*of person*) dire en aboyant; **to b. an order** aboyer un ordre
bark[5] *n Naut* (*three-master*) trois-mâts *m*; *Lit* (*any boat*) barque *f*
▶ **bark out** *vtsep* (*sth*) aboyer
barkeep(er) ['bɑːkiːp, -ər] *n Am* barman *m*
barker[1] ['bɑːkər] *n* (*at fair*) aboyeur *m*
barker[2] *n* (*machine*) écorceuse *f*
barking ['bɑːkɪŋ] **1** *adj* **(a)** (*dog*) aboyeur; (*fox*) glapissant **(b)** *F* (*cough*) sec, *f* sèche **(c)** *Sl* **b. (mad)** complètement cinglé **2** *n* (*of dog*) aboiement *m*; (*of fox*) glapissement *m*
barley ['bɑːlɪ] *n* orge *f*; **b. sugar** sucre *m* d'orge; **b. water** sirop *m* d'orgeat
barleycorn ['bɑːlɪkɔːn] *n* grain *m* d'orge
barm [bɑːm] *n* (*of beer*) levure *f*; (*yeast*) levain *m*
barmaid ['bɑːmeɪd] *n Br* serveuse *f* (*dans un bar*), barmaid *f*
barman, *pl* **-men** ['bɑːmən] *n* barman *m*
barminess ['bɑːmɪnɪs] *n Br F* folie *f*
bar mitzvah [bɑː'mɪstvə] *n* bar-mitsva *f*
barmy ['bɑːmɪ] *adj Br F* (*crazy*) toqué, cinglé
barn [bɑːn] *n* grange *f*; (*for cows*) étable *f*; (*for horses*) écurie *f*; *F* **they live in an old b. of a house** ils habitent dans un vrai hangar; *Hum* **were you born in a b.?** on ne t'a jamais appris à fermer tes portes?; **he couldn't hit a b. door** (*he's a poor shot*) c'est un mauvais tireur; *TV* **b. door** (*on light*) volet *m* réglable
barnacle ['bɑːnək(ə)l] *n* (*mollusc*) bernacle *f*; **b. goose** (*bird*) bernacle, bernache *f* (nonnette)
barn dance *n* (*social event*) bal *m* folklorique
barney ['bɑːnɪ] *n Br F* (*argument*) prise *f* de bec, dispute *f*; **I had a bit of a b. with the bus driver** j'ai eu une prise de bec avec le conducteur du bus; *Hum* **I had a bit of a b. with a bus** (*of car driver*) j'ai eu un accrochage avec un bus; **we've had a b.** nous nous sommes disputés; **to get into a b. with sb** se disputer avec qn
barn owl *n* (chouette *f*) effraie *f*
barnstorm ['bɑːnstɔːm] *vi* **(a)** *Br Th* faire une tournée théâtrale **(b)** *Am Pol* faire une tournée électorale
barnstormer ['bɑːnstɔːmər] *n Am Pol* orateur électoral, oratrice électorale
barnyard ['bɑːnjɑːd] *n* basse-cour *f*, *pl* basses-cours; **b. humour** humour *m* au ras des pâquerettes
barometer [bə'rɒmɪtər] *n* (*instrument*), *Fig* baromètre *m*; **b. reading** hauteur *f* barométrique
barometric [bærə'metrɪk] *adj* (*pressure etc*) barométrique
baron ['bærən] *n* (*nobleman*) baron *m*; *Fig* **press/oil b.** magnat *m* de la presse/du pétrole; *Culin* **b. of beef** double aloyau *m*
baroness ['bærənes] *n* baronne *f*
baronet ['bærənet] *n* baronnet *m*
baronetcy ['bærənɪtsɪ] *n* dignité *f* de baronnet; **to be given a b.** être élevé au rang de baronnet
baronial [bə'rəʊnɪəl] *adj usu attrib* baronnial; **b. hall** demeure *f* seigneuriale
barony ['bærənɪ] *n* (*domain*) baronnie *f*
baroque [bə'rɒk] *adj, n Archit, Art, Mus* baroque *m*
barque [bɑːk] *n Naut* = **bark[5]**
barrack[1] ['bærək] *n* **(a)** *Mil* (*usu pl*) (*with sing or pl verb*) **barracks** caserne *f*, quartier *m*; **to be confined to barracks** être consigné; **b. square** cour *f* du quartier *ou* de caserne **(b)** *Pej F* (*house*) maison *f* grande et laide
barrack[2] *vt Mil* (*troops*) caserner
barrack[3] *vt Br F* (*jeer at*) (*person*) se moquer de
barracking ['bærəkɪŋ] *n Br F* mauvais accueil *m*; **to get** *or* **be given a b.** se faire malmener
barrackroom ['bærəkruːm] *n* chambrée *f*; **b. language** langage *m* de corps de garde *ou* de caserne; **b. lawyer** chicanier, -ière
barracuda [bærə'kjuːdə] *n* barracuda *m*, bécune *f*
barrage[1] ['bærɑːʒ] *n* (*dam*), *Mil* barrage *m*; *Fig* (*of questions, insults*) torrent *m*; *Br Mil* **b. balloon** ballon *m* de barrage *ou* de protection
barrage[2] *vt* **to b. sb with** (*questions, offers of help etc*) assaillir qn de
barred [bɑːd] *adj* (*locked*) (*door*) barré; (*with bars on*) (*window*) muni de barreaux
barrel[1] ['bær(ə)l] *n* **(a)** (*container*) (*for wine etc*) tonneau *m*, barrique *f*, fût *m*; (*for oil*) baril *m*; (*for herring etc*) caque *f*, baril; *F* **to have sb over a b.** avoir qn à sa merci; **they've got us over a b.** nous sommes coincés, nous sommes à leur merci

(b) *F* (*large amount*) grande quantité *f* (**of** de); **she's a b. of fun** *or* **laughs** c'est un sacré boute-en-train; **he's not exactly a b. of fun** *or* **laughs** il n'est pas franchement très marrant; **it wasn't a b. of laughs** (*interview, project*) ça n'a pas été une partie de plaisir; (*film, show*) ce n'était pas très rigolo

(c) (*cylinder, tube*) cylindre *m*, partie *f* cylindrique; (*of gun, lock, key*) canon *m*; (*of pump*) corps *m*, barillet *m*; (*of lock*) cylindre, barillet; (*of capstan, winch*) fusée *f*, mèche *f*, tambour *m*; *Mil* (*of artillery piece*) tube *m*; **b. organ** orgue *m* de Barbarie; *Av* **b. roll** tonneau *m*; *Archit* **b. vault** voûte *f* en berceau
barrel[2] *vt* mettre en fût
▶ **barrel along** *vi F* (*in car etc*) foncer
barren ['bær(ə)n] **1** *adj* (*land, Old-fashioned, Lit woman*) stérile; (*hillside*) sans végétation; *Fig* (*subject*) maigre; **the area is b. of interest for the art-lover** la région ne présente aucun intérêt pour les amateurs d'art; **he's going through a b. period** (*of author*) il n'a pas beaucoup d'inspiration ces temps-ci; **b. lands** lande(s) *f(pl)* **2** *npl Am* **barrens** lande(s) *f(pl)*
barrenness ['bærənnɪs] *n* stérilité *f*
barrette [bə'ret] *n esp Am* barrette *f*
barricade[1] ['bærɪkeɪd, bærɪ'keɪd] *n* barricade *f*
barricade[2] *vt* barricader
▶ **barricade in** *vtsep* (*person*) barricader dans une pièce *etc*; **they barricaded themselves in** ils se sont barricadés
▶ **barricade off** *vtsep* (*street*) barrer
barrier ['bærɪər] *n* barrière *f*; *Fig* barrière (**between** entre), obstacle *m* (**to**, à); **to break down the barriers** abattre les barrières; **language b.** barrière linguistique; **b. methods of contraception** méthodes de contraception locale; *Geog* **b. ice** banquise *f*

barrier cream *n* crème *f* protectrice des mains (*qui fait écran à la saleté et aux produits chimiques*)
barrier reef *n* récif-barrière *m*
barring [ˈbɑːrɪŋ] **1** *n* **(a)** (*of door etc*) barrage *m* **(b)** (*of action*) interdiction *f*; (*of person*) exclusion *f* **2** *prep* (*except*) excepté, sauf; **b. accidents** sauf accident, sauf imprévu; **b. a miracle** à moins d'un miracle
barrister [ˈbærɪstər] *n Br Jur* ≈ avocat, -ate
barrow[1] [ˈbærəʊ] *n* (*in garden etc*) brouette *f*; *esp Br* (*handcart*) voiture *f ou* charrette *f* à bras; *Rail* diable *m*; *Br* **b. boy** marchand *m* des quatre saisons
barrow[2] *n Archeol* tumulus *m*, tertre *m* (funéraire)
Bart *abbr* **baronet**
bartender [ˈbɑːtendər] *n Am* barman *m*
barter[1] [ˈbɑːtər] *n* troc *m*; **b. society** société *f* vivant du troc
barter[2] **1** *vt* troquer; **to b. sth for sth** troquer qch contre qch **2** *vi* faire du troc
Bartholomew [bɑːˈθɒləmjuː] *n Hist* **the Massacre of St. B.** le Massacre de la Saint-Barthélemy
basal [ˈbeɪsəl] *adj* basal
basalt [ˈbæsɔːlt] *n* basalte *m*
basaltic [bəˈsɔːltɪk] *adj* basaltique
bascule [ˈbæskjuːl] *n Constr* bascule *f*; **b. bridge** pont (-levis) *m* à bascule, *pl* ponts(-levis) à bascule
base[1] [beɪs] *n* **(a)** (*foundation*), *Fig* base *f*; (*of column, statue*) socle *m*; (*of machine tool etc*) sole *f*, embase *f*; *El* (*of lamp*) culot *m*; **b. coat** (*of paint*) première couche *f*; *Fin* **b. rate** taux *m* de base
(b) *Math, Ch etc* base *f*; *Ling* base, racine *f*
(c) *Mil etc* (*of operations, supplies*) base *f*; **b. camp** camp *m* de base; **Glasgow is a good b. from which to explore the Highlands** Glasgow est un point idéal pour partir à la découverte des Highlands; *TV, Rad* **b. station/studio** station *f*/studio *m* de base
(d) *Sp* (*in baseball, rounders*) base *f*; *Fig* **you won't even get to first b. with the chairman if you don't play golf** tu n'arriveras à rien avec le président si tu ne joues pas au golf; **he didn't even get to first b. with her** (*girlfriend*) il n'est parvenu à rien avec elle; **to be (way) off b.** (*mistaken*) être (complètement) à côté de la plaque; *Am F* (*crazy*) être fou *ou* cinglé; *Am F* **to touch b. with sb** contacter qn; **I just thought I would call and touch b.** je me suis dit que j'appellerais pour prendre des nouvelles
base[2] *vt* **(a)** (*found*) (*calculation, hope*) baser, fonder (**on** sur); (*novel, film*) baser (**on** sur); (*opinion*) asseoir, fonder (**on** sur); **what are your accusations based on?** sur quoi tes accusations sont-elles fondées?; **to b. oneself on sth** se baser sur qch **(b)** (*have as headquarters*) (*usu passive*) **to be based in Bath** être basé à Bath
base[3] *adj* **(a)** *Fml* (*ignoble*) (*man, accusations etc*) vil; (*reason*) bas, indigne; (*action*) ignoble, indigne **(b)** (*inferior*) **b. metals** métaux vils **(c)** (*counterfeit*) **b. coin(age)** fausse monnaie *f*
baseball [ˈbeɪsbɔːl] *n Sp* base-ball *m*; **b. player/game** joueur *m*/match *m* de base-ball
baseboard [ˈbeɪsbɔːd] *n Am* plinthe *f*; **b. heater** plinthe électrique
Basel [ˈbɑːz(ə)l] *n* Bâle *f*
baseless [ˈbeɪslɪs] *adj* sans base, sans fondement
baseline [ˈbeɪslaɪn] *n Tennis* ligne *f* de fond; *Art* ligne de fuite; *Com* **b. sales** ventes *fpl* de base
basely [ˈbeɪslɪ] *adv Fml* de façon ignoble
basement [ˈbeɪsmənt] *n* (*in house, shop*) sous-sol *m*; **in the b.** au sous-sol; **b. flat** (appartement *m* de) sous-sol *m*, *pl* sous-sols
baseness [ˈbeɪsnɪs] *n Fml* (*of action, accusation etc*) bassesse *f*
bash[1] [bæʃ] *n F* **(a)** (*blow*) coup *m*; (*with fist*) coup de poing, gnon *m*; *Br F* **to have a b. at sth** (*attempt*) essayer qch; **I'll have a b. at mending it** je vais essayer de le réparer **(b)** (*dent*) bosse *f*, gnon *m* **(c)** (*party*) fête *f*, soirée *f*
bash[2] *vt F* **to b. one's head** se cogner la tête
▶ **bash about, bash around** *vtsep Br F* (*beat*) (*person*) battre, maltraiter, rudoyer; (*handle roughly*) (*suitcase, toys etc*) maltraiter; **the parcel's been** *or* **got a bit bashed about** le colis a été un peu abîmé
▶ **bash down** *vtsep Br F* (*smash*) (*door*) enfoncer
▶ **bash in** *vtsep Br F* (*smash*) (*door*) enfoncer; **I'll b. your face in** je vais te défoncer la tête
▶ **bash into** *vipo Br F* (*person, object*) rentrer dans
▶ **bash on** *vi Br F* continuer
▶ **bash up** *vtsep Br F* (*person*) tabasser; (*car*) esquinter
bashful [ˈbæʃfʊl] *adj* **(a)** (*timid*) modeste, timide; **b. lover** amoureux *m* transi **(b)** (*modest*) modeste, pudique
bashfully [ˈbæʃfʊlɪ] *adv* **(a)** (*timidly*) modestement, timidement **(b)** (*modestly*) pudiquement
bashfulness [ˈbæʃfʊlnɪs] *n* **(a)** (*timidity*) modestie *f*, timidité *f* **(b)** (*modesty*) pudeur *f*
bashing [ˈbæʃɪŋ] *n F* volée *f* de coups, rossée *f*; *Mil, Sp etc* **to take** *or* **get a b.** prendre une raclée *ou* une peignée; **queer-/Paki-b.** persécution *f* des homosexuels/des Pakistanais; *Fig* **Margaret Thatcher-/Ronald Reagan-b.** acharnement contre Margaret Thatcher/Ronald Reagan
BASIC [ˈbeɪsɪk] *n Comptr* BASIC *m*
basic [ˈbeɪsɪk] **1** *adj* (*elementary*) (*understanding, vocabulary, agreement etc*) de base; (*fundamental*) (*principle etc*) fondamental; (*truth, problem*) premier; (*rudimentary*) (*furniture, accommodation, skills*) rudimentaire; **to learn some b. French** apprendre les bases du français; **my French is a bit b.** mon français est plutôt rudimentaire; **I've got the b. idea** je vois de quoi il s'agit en gros; **trust is b. to any human relationship** la confiance est la base des relations humaines; **these facts are b. to an understanding of the problem** ces faits sont essentiels pour comprendre le problème; *Am TV* **b. cable** câble *m* de base; **b. offer** offre *f* de base; **b. population** population-mère *f*
2 *npl* **basics** choses *fpl* essentielles, essentiel *m*; (*of a language, science etc*) bases *fpl*, rudiments *mpl*; **let's get down to basics** allons à l'essentiel; **to get back to basics** (*important things in life*) retourner aux choses essentielles; *Pol* **back to basics** *expression qui suggère un retour aux valeurs traditionnelles en matière d'éducation ou de moralité; lancée par les Conservateurs comme argument de renouveau politique au début des années 90, par ex.* the Prime Minister's 'back to basics' campaign in education has rebounded on him
basically [ˈbeɪsɪklɪ] *adv* (*different, sound, right etc*) fondamentalement; **b. I think you're right** au fond je pense que tu as raison; **I think it's b. a question of experience** je pense qu'en fait c'est une question d'expérience; **b. what he said was...** en gros, ce qu'il a dit c'est que...
basic commodity *n Econ* denrée *f* de base
basic cover *n* (*insurance*) assurance *f* de garantie de base
basic pay *n* salaire *m* de base
basic rate *n* tarif *m* de base
basic salary *n* salaire *m* de base, traitement *m* de base
basic wage *n* salaire *m* de base
basil [ˈbæz(ə)l] *n Bot, Culin* basilic *m*
basilica [bəˈzɪlɪkə] *n Archit* basilique *f*
basilisk [ˈbæzɪlɪsk] *n Myth* basilic *m*; *Fig Lit* **a b. stare** un regard assassin
basin [ˈbeɪs(ə)n] *n* **(a)** (*bowl*) (*for washing up etc*) bassine *f*, cuvette *f*; (*of fountain*) vasque *f*, coupe *f*; **(wash-)hand b.** lavabo *m* **(b)** (*of river*) bassin *m*; **the Paris B.** le Bassin parisien; **coal b.** bassin houiller **(c)** *Naut* (*for mooring*) bassin *m*; (*in canal, river*) garage *m*
basinful [ˈbeɪs(ə)nfʊl] *n* (*of soup*) plein bol *m*, bolée *f*; (*of water*) pleine cuvette *f*; *Sl* **to have had a b.** (*enough*) en avoir ras le bol, en avoir marre
basing fare [ˈbeɪsɪŋ] *n* tarif *m* de référence
basing point *n* (*for establishing air fares*) point *m* de référence
basis, *pl* **bases** [ˈbeɪsɪs, -iːz] *n* **(a)** (*of talks etc*) base *f*; (*of opinion etc*) fondement *m*; (*of tax*) assiette *f*; **on the b. of ...** sur la base de ...; **I will be taking part on an unofficial b.** je participerai à titre non officiel; **on the b. of what you told me** d'après ce que tu m'as dit; **the rumours have no b. in fact** ces rumeurs ne sont fondées sur aucun fait; *Acct* **b. for depreciation** base amortissable; **b. of calculations** base de calcul **(b)** *Math* matrice *f* de base
bask [bɑːsk] *vi* **to b. in the sun** se chauffer (au soleil), *F* lézarder; *Fig* **to b. in sb's favour** jouir de la faveur de qn; **basking shark** pèlerin *m*
basket [ˈbɑːskɪt] *n* (*with or without handles*) corbeille *f*; (*with handles*) panier *m*; (*carried on back*) hotte *f*; (*for coal etc*) banne *f*, manne *f*; (*plaited shopping basket*) cabas *m*, couffin *m*; (*for carrying baby*) couffin; (*in basketball*) panier; *Fig* **b. of currencies** panier de monnaies; *St Exch* **b. of shares** panier d'actions; *Br F Old-fashioned* **(you) silly b.!** espèce d'idiot!; *F* **b. case** (*person*) cinglé; **she's turning into a b. case** elle est en train de devenir folle *ou F* cinglée; **(economic) b. case** pays *m* invalide sur le plan économique; **b. chair** chaise *f* en rotin *ou* osier; **b. hilt** (*of sword*) (garde *f* en) coquille *f*; **b. making** vannerie *f*; **b. maker** vannier *m*
basketball [ˈbɑːskɪtbɔːl] *n* basket-ball *m*, *F* basket *m*; **b. player** basketteur, -euse
basketful [ˈbɑːskɪtfʊl] *n* plein panier *m*
basketry [ˈbɑːskɪtrɪ], **basketwork** [ˈbɑːskɪtwɜːk] *n* vannerie *f*
Basle [bɑːl] *n* Bâle
Basque [bɑːsk] **1** *adj* basque; **the B. Country** le Pays basque **2** *n* **(a)** Basque *mf* **(b)** *Ling* basque *m*
basque [bɑːsk] *n* (*bodice*) guêpière *f*; (*of jacket*) basque *f*
bas-relief [ˈbæsrɪliːf] *n* bas-relief *m*; **in b.** en bas-relief
bass[1] [bæs] *n* (*fish*) (*freshwater*) perche *f* commune; (*saltwater*) bar *m*; **striped b.** bar rayé

bass² [beɪs] **1** *n* (*voice, singer, instrument*) basse *f*; (*on amplifier*) basses; (*double bass*) contrebasse *f*; **he sings b.** il chante dans les basses; **deep b.** basse profonde **2** *adj attrib Mus* (*voice, part*) de basse; **b. clef** clef *f* de fa; **b. drum** grosse caisse *f*; **b. guitar** basse *f*; **b. tones** sons *mpl* graves
bass³ [bæs] *n* (*material*) tille *f*, filasse *f*
basset ['bæsɪt] *n* **b. (hound)** basset *m*
bassinet(te) [bæsɪ'net] *n Old-fashioned* **(a)** (*cradle*) moïse *m* **(b)** (*pram*) voiture *f* d'enfant
bassist ['beɪsɪst] *n Mus* contrebassiste *mf*
basso ['bæsəʊ] *n* **b. profundo** (voix *f* de) basse *f* profonde
bassoon [bə'suːn] *n Mus* basson *m*; **double b.** contrebasson *m*
bassoonist [bə'suːnɪst] *n Mus* basson *m*, bassoniste *mf*
bast [bæst] *n* = **bass³**
bastard ['bɑːstəd] **1** *n* **(a)** bâtard, -arde; *Jur* enfant *mf* naturel(le) **(b)** *Sl* (*person*) salaud *m*; **you b.!** espèce de salaud!; **you lucky b.!** sacré veinard(e)!; **the poor b.** le pauvre vieux; **a b. of a job** une saloperie de travail; **it's a b.** (*of work, problem*) c'est vachement difficile **2** *adj* (*child*) bâtard
bastardize ['bɑːstədaɪz] *vt* **(a)** (*debase*) corrompre **(b)** *Arch* (*child*) déclarer illégitime
bastardy ['bæstədɪ] *n Arch* bâtardise *f*
baste¹ [beɪst] *vt Sewing* bâtir, faufiler
baste² *vt Culin* (*roast*) arroser de sa graisse/de son jus
basting¹ ['beɪstɪŋ] *n Sewing* (*action*) faufilage *m*, faufilure *f*; (*stitching*) bâti *m*, faufilure; **b. thread** fil *m* à faufiler
basting² *n Culin* (*of roast*) arrosage *m*
bastion ['bæstɪən] *n* (*fortification*), *Fig* bastion *m*
bat¹ [bæt] *n Zool* chauve-souris *f*, *pl* chauves-souris; *Fig* **like a b. out of hell** comme un bolide; *F* **to have bats in the belfry** avoir une araignée au plafond
bat² *n* **(a)** (*for cricket, baseball etc*) batte *f*; (*for ping-pong*) raquette *f*; **he's a good b.** il manie bien la batte; *F* **to do sth off one's own b.** faire qch de sa propre initiative; *esp Am* **to do sth right off the b.** faire qch tout de suite; *esp Am* **to go to b. for sb** (*intercede for*) intervenir *ou* intercéder pour *ou* en faveur de qn **(b)** *Am* **to go on a b.** se soûler
bat³ *vi* (**-tt-**) (*use bat*) (*in cricket, baseball etc*) manier la batte; *Cr* (*be at wicket*) être au guichet
bat⁴ *vt* (*one's eyelids*) battre; *Fig* **he didn't b. an eyelid** il n'a pas sourcillé *ou* tiqué
batch [bætʃ] *n* (*of bread, F of people*) fournée *f*; (*of letters*) tas *m*, paquet *m*; (*of goods etc, Comptr of data*) lot *m*; (*of cement, concrete*) gâchée *f*; **in batches of 20** (*people*) par groupes de 20; (*of files etc*) par lots de 20
batch command *n Comptr* commande *f* séquentielle
batch file *n Comptr* fichier *m* séquentiel
batch processing *n Comptr* traitement *m* par lots
bated ['beɪtɪd] *adj* **with b. breath** (*to wait, watch*) en retenant son souffle
bath¹, *pl* **baths** [bɑːθ, bɑːðz] *n* **(a)** (*washing*) bain *m*; **to take** *or* **have a b.** prendre un bain; **to give a child a b.** baigner *ou* donner un bain à un enfant; *Old-fashioned Br* **(public) baths** (*for washing*) bains publics; (*for swimming*) piscine *f*; *Br* **the Order of the B.** l'Ordre *m* du Bain; **b. pearls** perles *fpl* de bain **(b)** (*tub*) baignoire *f*; **he's in the b.** il est dans son bain; **hip b., sitz b.** bain *m* de siège **(c)** (*bathroom*) salle *f* de bain(s) **(d)** *Phot etc* cuvette *f*; (*liquid*) bain *m*
bath² **1** *vt* baigner, donner un bain à **2** *vi* prendre un bain
bathe¹ [beɪð] *n Old-fashioned* bain *m* (de rivière/de mer), baignade *f*; **to go for a b.** (aller) se baigner
bathe² **1** *vt* (*wash*) *Med* (*wound*) laver; *Am* (*child*) baigner; **to b. one's face** se passer de l'eau sur le visage; **face bathed in tears** visage baigné de larmes; **bathed in perspiration** trempé de sueur, en nage; **bathed in light** baigné de lumière **2** *vi* **(a)** *Old-fashioned* (*swim*) se baigner, prendre un bain (de rivière/de mer) **(b)** *Am* (*have bath*) prendre un bain
bather ['beɪðər] *n Old-fashioned* baigneur, -euse
bathers [beɪðəs] *npl Austr F* (*swimming costume*) maillot *m*
bathing ['beɪðɪŋ] *n* **(a)** *esp Old-fashioned* (*swimming*) bains *mpl* (de rivière/de mer), baignade *f*; **b. is prohibited** la baignade est interdite, il est interdit de se baigner; **the water isn't warm enough for b.** l'eau n'est pas assez chaude pour se baigner; **b. cap** bonnet *m* de bain; **b. place** baignade **(b)** *Med* (*of wound etc*) lavage *m*
bathing costume *n* maillot *m* de bain
bathing suit *n* maillot *m* de bain
bathing trunks *npl* caleçon *m ou* slip *m* de bain
bath mat *n* descente *f ou* tapis *m* de bain
bathos ['beɪθɒs] *n Liter* chute *f* du sublime au ridicule
bath rail *n* barre *f* de soutien dans la baignoire
bathrobe ['bɑːθrəʊb] *n* peignoir *m*
bathroom ['bɑːθruːm] *n* salle *f* de bain(s); **to go to the b.** aller aux toilettes; **b. scales** pèse-personne *m*, *pl* pèse-personnes
bath salts *npl* sels *mpl* de bain
bath sheet *n* drap *m* de bain
bath towel *n* serviette *f* de bain
bathtub ['bɑːθtʌb] *n* baignoire *f*
bath water *n* eau *f* du bain; **my b.'s too hot** mon bain est trop chaud
batik ['bætɪk, bə'tiːk] *n* batik *m*; **b. skirt** jupe *f* en batik
batman, *pl* **-men** ['bætmən] *n Mil* ordonnance *mf*
baton ['bætən] *n* **(a)** (*of official*) bâton *m*; *Sp* (*in relay race*) témoin *m*; *Mus* (*of conductor*) baguette *f*, bâton; **orchestra under the b. of Jonathan Butcher** orchestre sous la direction de Jonathan Butcher; *Sp* **b. change** passage *m* de témoin; **b. mike** micro *m* tenu à la main **(b)** *Br* (*of policeman*) bâton *m*; **b. charge** charge *f* à la matraque; *Mil* **b. round** balle *f* en plastique
bats [bæts] *adj Br F* loufoque; **to be b. about sb/sth** être fou de qn/qch; **I'm not exactly b. about the idea** je ne raffole pas de cette idée
batsman, *pl* **-men** ['bætsmən] *n Cr* batteur *m*
battalion [bə'tæljən] *n Mil* **(a)** bataillon *m*; **b. commander** commandant *m* de bataillon; **tank b., armoured b.** bataillon de chars **(b)** *US* groupe *m* d'artillerie
batten¹ ['bæt(ə)n] *n Carp* (*for joint*) couvre-joint *m*, *pl* couvre-joints; (*lathe*) latte *f*, liteau *m*; (*in floor*) planche *f*
batten² *vt* **(a)** *Carp* latter, voliger **(b)** **to b. down the hatches** *Naut* condamner les panneaux; *Fig* se préparer à affronter la crise/la situation
▶ **batten on** *vipo* (*live off*) vivre aux crochets de
▶ **batten onto** *vipo* (*person*) mettre le grappin sur; (*idea*) se mettre dans la tête; **once he battens onto you** une fois qu'il vous a mis le grappin dessus
batter¹ ['bætər] *n Cr, Baseball* batteur *m*
batter² *n Culin* pâte *f* à frire; **pancake b.** pâte à crêpes
batter³ **1** *vt* **(a)** (*child, wife etc*) battre **(b)** *Mil* (*town*) bombarder **2** *vi* **to b. at** *or* **on a door** marteler une porte; **the waves battered against the coast** les vagues s'abattaient le long de la côte
▶ **batter down** *vtsep* (*door etc*) abattre, démolir; (*wall*) battre en brèche
▶ **batter in** *vtsep* (*door etc*) enfoncer; **the victim's skull was battered in** la victime a eu le crâne défoncé
battered ['bætəd] *adj* **(a)** (*face*) meurtri; **b. wives** femmes *fpl* battues; **b. child** *or* **baby** enfant *mf* maltraité(e), enfant martyr(e) **(b)** (*furniture, car, house etc*) délabré; (*hat, pan*) cabossé
battering ['bætərɪŋ] *n* (*of child, wife*) mauvais traitements *mpl*; **that's not the first b. he's given her** ce n'est pas la première fois qu'il la bat; *Fig* **his confidence took a b.** sa confiance en soi en a pris un coup; *Fig* **to give sb a b.** (*defeat*) mettre une raclée à qn; *Fig* **to take a b.** se prendre une raclée; **b. ram** bélier *m*
battery ['bæt(ə)rɪ] *n* **(a)** *El* (*for calculator, watch etc*) pile *f*; (*for car*) batterie *f*; **(storage) b.** accumulateur *m*, *F* accu *m*; **to be b. operated** *or* **powered** (*of radio, toy*) fonctionner sur piles; **batteries not included** (*notice in catalogue*) livré sans piles; **b. back-up** alimentation *f* de secours par batterie; **b. cable** câble *m* de batterie; **b. charger** chargeur *m* (de batterie); **b. compartment** compartiment *m* réservé à la batterie/aux piles; **b. life** durée *f* de vie de la batterie/des piles; **b. low warning light** voyant *m* de baisse (de tension) de la batterie/des piles
(b) *Mil* batterie *f*; *Fig* **a b. of criticism** un feu roulant de critiques
(c) (*set, group*) (*of furnaces, tests*) batterie *f*
(d) *Jur* voie *f* de fait
(e) (*for poultry*) batterie *f*
(f) *Sp* (*in baseball*) **the b.** le lanceur et le receveur
battery farming *n* élevage *m* en batterie(s)
battery hen *n* poule *f* de batterie
battery pack *n* boîtier *m* d'alimentation par pile
batting ['bætɪŋ] *n Cr etc* maniement *m* de la batte
battle¹ ['bæt(ə)l] *n Mil, Fig* bataille *f*, combat *m*; (*against poverty, disease etc*) lutte *f* (**against** contre); **to fight/win a b.** livrer/gagner une bataille; **killed in b.** tué au combat; **to do b. with sb** livrer bataille à qn; **to join b. with sb** entrer en lutte avec qn, livrer bataille à qn; *Fig* **that's half the b.** c'est déjà ça de gagné; **understanding the instructions is half the b.** quand on a compris les instructions la partie est déjà à moitié gagnée; **a b. of words** une altercation; **b. cry** cri *m* de guerre; **b. fleet** flotte *f* de ligne *ou* de combat; **b. royal** (*fight involving several people*) mêlée *f* générale, bagarre *f*; (*argument*) dispute *f* violente
battle² **1** *vi* se battre, lutter (**with sb for sth** contre qn pour qch); **to b. with** *or* **against a fire** combattre *ou* lutter contre un incendie **2** *vt* **to b. one's way through difficulties**

surmonter les difficultés; **I had to b. my way to the top** il a fallu que je me batte pour arriver au sommet

battle-axe *n* hache *f* d'armes; *Pej Fig* (*woman*) virago *f*, mégère *f*

battle cruiser *n Naut* croiseur *m* de combat

battledore ['bæt(ə)ldɔːr] *n Hist, Sp* raquette *f*; **to play at b. and shuttlecock** jouer au volant

battledress ['bæt(ə)ldres] *n Mil* tenue *f* de campagne

battlefield ['bæt(ə)lfiːld], **battleground** ['bæt(ə)lgraʊnd] *n Mil, Fig* champ *m* de bataille

battle-hardened *adj* aguerri

battlements ['bæt(ə)lmənts] *npl* parapet *m*, rempart *m*

Battle of Britain *n Hist* Bataille *f* d'Angleterre

battle-scarred ['bæt(ə)lskɑːd] *adj* (*town*) qui porte les traces de combats violents; (*soldier*) qui porte encore les traces de ses blessures; *Fig* (*politician*) qui en a vu de rudes

battleship ['bæt(ə)lʃɪp] *n Naut* cuirassé *m*; *Hist* bâtiment *m* de ligne

battle zone *n* zone *f* de bataille *ou* d'engagement

batty ['bætɪ] *adj F* toqué, timbré

batwing ['bætwɪŋ] *adj* en forme d'aile de chauve-souris; **b. sleeves** manches *fpl* chauve-souris

bauble ['bɔːb(ə)l] *n* babiole *f*, colifichet *m*

baud [bɔːd] *n Comptr* baud *m*; **at 2,400 b.** à (une vitesse de) 2 400 bauds; **b. rate** débit *m* en bauds

baulk [bɔːk] *n, vti* = **balk**

bauxite ['bɔːksaɪt] *n Miner* bauxite *f*

Bavaria [bə'veərɪə] *n* Bavière *f*

Bavarian [bə'veərɪən] **1** *adj* bavarois **2** *n* Bavarois, -oise

bawdiness ['bɔːdɪnɪs] *n* (*of conversation*) grivoiserie *f*; (*of humour, joke, poetry*) paillardise *f*, grivoiserie

bawdy ['bɔːdɪ] *adj* (*conversation*) grivois; (*humour, joke, poetry etc*) paillard, grivois

bawdyhouse ['bɔːdɪhaʊs] *n Arch* maison *f* de passe

bawl [bɔːl] **1** *vi* **(a)** (*shout*) hurler, brailler, *F* beugler; **to b. at sb** hurler après qn **(b)** *F* (*weep*) brailler **2** *vt* (*order*) gueuler

▶ **bawl out** *vtsep* **(a)** (*shout*) (*order*) gueuler **(b)** *F* (*scold*) engueuler

bawling ['bɔːlɪŋ] *n* **(a)** (*shouting*) hurlements *mpl*, braillements *mpl* **(b)** *F* (*weeping*) braillement(s) *m(pl)*; **stop that b.** arrête de brailler

bawling out *n F* (*reprimand*) engueulade *f*; **to give sb a b. out** engueuler qn; **to get a b. out** se faire engueuler

bay[1] [beɪ] *n* (*shrub*) **sweet b., b. laurel** laurier *m* commun, laurier des poètes; *Culin* **b. leaf** feuille *f* de laurier; **b. tree** laurier; **b. wreath** couronne *f* de laurier(s)

bay[2] *n Geog* baie *f*; (*small*) anse *f*; **Hudson B.** la Baie d'Hudson; **the B. of Biscay** le golfe de Gascogne

bay[3] *n* (*alcove*) enfoncement *m*, renfoncement *m*; **b. window** bow-window *m*, fenêtre *f* en saillie

bay[4] *n* **to keep** *or* **hold at b.** (*the enemy*) tenir en échec; (*assailant*) tenir en respect; (*creditors, persistent caller etc*) tenir tête à; *F* **I'm managing to keep my cold at b.** jusqu'ici j'ai réussi à combattre le rhume; **to bring a stag to b.** mettre un cerf aux abois, forcer *ou* acculer un cerf; **to be at b.** (*of stag*), *Fig* être aux abois

bay[5] *vi* (*of hound*) aboyer, donner de la voix; **to b. at the moon** hurler *ou* aboyer à la lune

bay[6] *adj, n* (*horse*) bai *m*

baying ['beɪɪŋ] *n* (*of hound*) aboiement *m*

bayonet[1] ['beɪənɪt] *n Mil* baïonnette *f*; **with fixed bayonets** baïonnette au canon; **b. charge** charge *f* à la baïonnette; *El* **b. holder** *or* **socket** (*of light fitting*) douille *f* à baïonnette; *MecE etc* **b. joint** joint *m* en baïonnette

bayonet[2] *vt* (**-t-**) (*sb*) passer à la baïonnette

bayou ['baɪuː] *n Geog US* bayou *m*

bazaar [bə'zɑːr] *n* **(a)** (*in Middle East*) bazar *m* **(b)** (*in aid of charity*) vente *f* de charité

bazooka [bə'zuːkə] *n Mil* bazooka *m*

B & B [biːən'biː] *n Br* (*abbr* **bed and breakfast**) bed and breakfast *m*

BBC [biːbiː'siː] *n* (*abbr* **British Broadcasting Corporation**) **what's on BBC/on BBC1?** qu'est-ce qu'il y sur la BBC/sur BBC 1?; **BBC English** anglais *m* BBC sans accent régional; **BBC programme** émission *f* de la BBC

BBS [biːbiː'es] *n Comptr* (*abbr* **bulletin board system**) serveur *m* télématique

BC [biː'siː] *abbr* **1** *adv* (**before Christ**) avant Jésus-Christ; **in (the year) 25 BC** en (l'an) 25 avant J.-C. **2** *n Geog* (**British Columbia**) C.-B. *f*

BCG [biːsiː'dʒiː] *n Med* (*abbr* **bacille Calmette-Guérin**) B. C. G. *m*

be [biː] (*pr ind* **am** [æm], **are** [ɑːr], **is** [ɪz], *pl* **are**; *past ind* **was** [wɒz], **were** [wɜːr], **was**, *pl* **were**; *pr sub* **be**; *past sub* **were**; *prp* **being** ['biːɪŋ]; *pp* **been** [biːn]; *imp* **be**; **I am, he is, she is, it is, we are, you are, they are** *can be shortened into* **I'm, he's, she's, it's, we're, you're, they're**; **is not, are not, was not, were not** *into* **isn't, aren't, wasn't, weren't**) [①**A54**,17,a; **B63**,3]

1 *vi* **(a)** [①**A52**,b,vi] (*specifying attribute*) être; **Mary is pretty** Marie est jolie; **the sky was blue** le ciel était bleu; **time is money** le temps, c'est de l'argent; **he's a bit odd, is Bob** c'est un drôle de garçon que Bob; **his father is a doctor** son père est médecin; **he is an Englishman** il est anglais, c'est un Anglais; **are they English?** sont-ils anglais?; **if I were you** à votre place, si j'étais vous; **as it is, we must go** les choses étant ce qu'elles sont, il nous faut partir; **unity is strength** l'union fait la force; **three and two are five** trois et deux font cinq; **money isn't everything** l'argent n'est pas tout dans la vie; **you be MacBeth and I'll be** ... tu seras MacBeth et moi je serai ...; (*kids playing*) tu étais MacBeth et moi j'étais ...

(b) (*specifying location, time, health, price*) **the books are on the table** les livres sont *ou* se trouvent sur la table; **I was at the meeting** j'ai assisté *ou* j'étais à la réunion; **where am I?** où suis-je?; **I don't know where I am** (*I am lost*) je ne sais pas où je suis; (*I have lost my place*) je ne sais pas où j'en suis; **where was I?** (*after digression when talking*) où en étais-je?; **you never know where you are with him** avec lui on ne sait jamais à quoi s'en tenir; **here I am** me voici; **ah, there you are!** ah, vous voilà!; **how are you?** comment allez-vous?, **I am better** je vais mieux; **how much is that?** combien cela coûte-t-il?, c'est combien?; **how far is it to London?** combien y a-t-il d'ici à Londres?; **when is the concert?** quand est-ce que le concert a lieu?; **today is the tenth, it is the tenth today** nous sommes (aujourd'hui) le dix (du mois); **tomorrow is Friday** demain, c'est vendredi; **it is six o'clock** il est six heures; **it is late** il est tard; **it is a fortnight since I saw him** il y a quinze jours que je ne l'ai pas vu; **it is my birthday tomorrow** demain, c'est mon anniversaire

(c) to be cold/hot (*of person*) avoir froid/chaud; (*of water etc*) être froid/chaud; **it is fine/cold** il fait beau (temps)/froid; **to be ashamed of sb/sth** avoir honte de qn/qch; **to be hungry/thirsty** avoir faim/soif; **to be right/wrong** avoir raison/tort; **my hands are cold** j'ai froid aux mains; **to be twenty (years old)** avoir vingt ans; **the wall is six metres high** le mur fait six mètres de haut; **he was so foolish as to do it** il a eu la sottise de le faire

(d) (*exist, remain*) **to be or not to be** être ou ne pas être; **business is not what it was** les affaires ne sont plus ce qu'elles étaient; **that may be** cela se peut; **to see things as they are** voir les choses comme elles sont; **be that as it may** quoi qu'il en soit; **let me be!** laissez-moi tranquille!; **there is, there are** (*impersonal*) il y a; **there is a man in the garden** il y a un homme dans le jardin; **what is there to see?** qu'est-ce qu'il y a à voir?; **there will be dancing** on dansera; **there were a dozen of us** nous étions une douzaine

(e) (*go, come*) **I have been to see David** j'ai été *ou* je suis allé voir David; **I have been to the museum** j'ai visité le musée, je suis allé au musée; **I have never been to Venice** je n'ai jamais été *ou* je ne suis jamais allé à Venise; **he was into the room like a flash** il est entré en trombe dans la pièce; **where have you been?** où étais-tu?; **has anyone been?** est-ce que quelqu'un est venu *ou* passé?; **has the postman been?** est-ce que le facteur est passé?; *Br Sl* **(now) you've been and gone and done it!** vous en avez fait une belle!; **be off (with you)!** va-t-en!

(f) (*with impers subject*) **it is easy to do it** il est facile de le faire; **it is right that ...** il est juste que + *sub*...; **it is said that ...** on dit que ...; **it is for you to decide** c'est à vous de décider; **what is it?** (*what do you want?*) que voulez-vous?; (*what is wrong?*) qu'est-ce qu'il y a?; **as it were** pour ainsi dire, en quelque sorte; *F* **what's it to be?** (*in pub, bar*) qu'est-ce que vous prenez?; (*make up your mind*) décidez donc!

2 *aux v* **(a)** [①**A48**,10,b; **A48**,11,c; **A49-50**,b-c; **A50**,e] (*forming continuous tenses*) **I am/was doing sth** je fais/faisais qch; (*be in the process of*) je suis/j'étais en train de faire qch; **they are always laughing** ils sont toujours à rire; **the house is being built** la maison est en construction; **I have been waiting for a long time** il y a longtemps que j'attends, j'attends depuis longtemps

(b) (*with a few intransitive verbs as aux of perfect*) **the sun is set** le soleil est couché; **the guests were all gone** les invités étaient tous partis

(c) [①**A40**,9; **A53**,16; **B36**,J] (*forming passive*) **he was killed** il a été tué; **she is respected by all** elle est respectée de tous; **he was always being laughed at** on se moquait toujours de lui; **she is to be pitied** elle est à plaindre; **what's to be done?** que faire?

(d) [①**A50**,f] (*denoting future*) **I am to see them tomorrow** je dois les voir demain; **he was never to see them again** il ne devait plus les revoir; **and in July 1962 when the government anounced there was to be an election ...** et en juillet 1962 quand le gouvernement annonça qu'il y aurait des élections ...; **there was to be an election next year but it's been cancelled** il devait y avoir des élections l'année prochaine mais elles ont été annulées; **am I to do it or not?** (*obligation*) est-ce qu'il faut que je le fasse ou non?

(e) **I am all for reform** je suis pour *ou* je suis partisan de la réforme; **I'm all for staying here** je ne demande qu'à rester ici; **what are you at?** que faites-vous?

(f) [①A46,8,b] (*in tag questions*) **so you're back, are you?** alors, vous voilà de retour?; **she is beautiful, isn't she?** elle est belle, n'est-ce pas?; **they're big, aren't they?** ils sont grands, n'est-ce pas?

(g) (*elliptical*) **John's very stupid – I know he is/no he isn't** John est un imbécile – je le sais bien/non, ce n'est pas un imbécile

(h) [①A40,9; C32,4] (*imperatives*) **be quiet!** tiens-toi tranquille!; **don't be ridiculous!** ne sois pas ridicule!

beach[1] [biːtʃ] *n* plage *f*; **to go to the b.** aller à la plage; *Fig* **you're not the only pebble on the b.** (*to boyfriend, girlfriend*) un(e) de perdu(e), dix de retrouvé(e)s; (*don't be selfish*) tu n'es pas tout seul au monde; **b. chair** chaise *f* longue; **b. hotel** hôtel *m* de plage; **b. tent** tente *f* de plage; **b. wear** vêtements *mpl* de plage

beach[2] *vt* (*ship*) (*run aground*) échouer; (*pull up on to beach*) tirer à sec; **to b. itself** (*of whale*) s'échouer; **a beached whale** une baleine échouée

beachball [ˈbiːtʃbɔːl] *n* ballon *m* de plage

beachball pointer *n Comptr* pointeur-balle *m*

beach buggy *n* buggy *m*

beachcomber [ˈbiːtʃkəʊmər] *n* (a) (*person*) personne *f* qui ramasse les objets échoués ou laissés sur la plage (b) (*wave*) vague *f* déferlante

beachhead [ˈbiːtʃhed] *n Mil* (*for landing*) tête *f* de pont

beach hut *n* cabine *f* (de bains *ou* de plage)

beacon [ˈbiːk(ə)n] *n* (a) *Naut, Av* (*lighthouse*) phare *m*; (*marking channel, runway*) balise *f*; (*light, signal*) feu *m*; (*at crossing*) signal *m* lumineux; *Fig* phare; **radar b.** balise radar, radar *m* de radionavigation; **b. light** feu de balisage (b) *Arch* (*fire*) feu *m* (*pour donner l'alarme*); (*location*) tour *f*/colline *f* où un feu est allumé pour donner l'alarme

bead[1] [biːd] *n* (a) (*of glass, enamel etc*) perle *f*; **(string of) beads** collier *m*; **b. curtain** rideau *m* de perles; **beads of dew** perles de rosée; **there were beads of perspiration on his forehead** la sueur perlait sur son front (b) (*for prayers*) grain *m*; **(string of) beads** chapelet *m*; **to tell one's beads** égrener *ou* dire son chapelet (c) (*on sparkling wine etc*) bulle *f* (d) *Archit, Carp* (*moulding*) baguette *f* (e) (*on gun*) guidon *m*, mire *f* (f) *Metal* cordon *m* de soudure (g) *Aut* (*on tyre*) bourrelet *m*; **b. apex** bord *m* de talon (de pneu); **b. wire** armature *m* de bourrelet

bead[2] **1** *vt* (a) couvrir *ou* orner de perles (b) *Archit, Carp* appliquer une baguette sur **2** *vi* (*of liquid*) perler

beaded [ˈbiːdɪd] *adj* (a) (*material*) perlé (b) *Archit, Carp* **b. strip** chapelet *m*

beading [ˈbiːdɪŋ] *n* (a) (*decoration*) garniture *f* de perles (b) *Archit, Carp* baguette *f* (c) (*of tyre*) talon *m*, bourrelet *m*

beadle [ˈbiːd(ə)l] *n* bedeau *m*

beady [ˈbiːdɪ] *adj* (*eyes*) petits et brillants; **a b.-eyed shopkeeper** un commerçant qui tient ses clients à l'œil dans sa boutique; *Br F* **I've got my b. eye on you** je t'ai à l'œil

beagle [ˈbiːg(ə)l] *n* beagle *m*, briquet *m*

beagling [ˈbiːglɪŋ] *n* chasse *f* au briquet

beak [biːk] *n* (a) (*of bird, tortoise, jug, vase etc*) bec *m*; *F Hum* (*of person*) tarin *m*, blair *m* (b) *Br Sl* (*judge*) juge *m*; (*headmaster*) dirlo *m*

beaked [biːkt] *adj* (*animal*) à bec; (*nose*) crochu; **b. whale** hyperodon *m*

beaker [ˈbiːkər] *n* (a) (*container*) gobelet *m*, timbale *f* (b) *Ch* vase *m* à bec

be-all and end-all *n F* (*aim*) but *m* suprême, fin *f* des fins; **it's not the b. if it doesn't work** ce n'est pas la fin du monde si ça ne marche pas; *Hum Pej* **he thinks he's the b.** il ne se prend pas pour n'importe qui; **she thinks her son's the b.** elle pense que son fils est une petite merveille

beam[1] [biːm] *n* (a) *Constr* poutre *f* (en bois), solive *f*, madrier *m*; (*small*) poutrelle *f*; **ceiling b.** doubleau *m*

(b) *Gym* **(balance) b.** poutre *f* horizontale

(c) (*width*) **(breadth of) b.** (*of ship*) largeur *f*; **broad in the b.** (*ship*) à larges baux; *F* (*person*) large de hanches

(d) (*of ship*) travers *m*; **on the port/starboard b.** par le travers bâbord/tribord

(e) (*of light, sun*) rayon *m*; (*of headlamp etc*) faisceau *m*; *Fig* (*smile*) grand *ou* large sourire *m*; **the headlights were on full b.** la voiture était en pleins phares; *Aut* **b. deflector** déflecteur *m* de faisceau, traverse *f*

(f) *El* faisceau *m*; **electronic/radar b.** faisceau électronique/radar; **radio b.** faisceau hertzien; *Av* **radio landing b.** axe balisé d'atterrissage; *F* **you're way off b.** (*mistaken*) tu es complètement à côté de la plaque; **the calculations are way off b.** les calculs sont archifaux

beam[2] **1** *vt* (a) *TV* (*pictures*) transmettre; *Telecom* (*message*) transmettre par ondes dirigées; *Av* **to be beamed in on Orly** (*of aircraft*) être dirigé sur Orly (b) *Fig* (*of person*) **she beamed her thanks** elle a fait un grand sourire en guise de remerciement **2** *vi* (*of sun*) rayonner; (*of person*) faire un grand sourire; **beaming with health** resplendissant de santé; **she beamed with pride** (*smiled*) elle a eu un sourire de fierté; **she is beaming with pride** (*radiating pride*) elle rayonne de fierté

beam-ends *npl* (*of ship*) baux *mpl*; **to be on her b.** (*of ship*) être sur le flanc; *Fig* **to be on one's b.** être *ou* se trouver à bout de ressources

beaming [ˈbiːmɪŋ] *adj* (*sun, face*) rayonnant, radieux; (*smile*) radieux

bean [biːn] *n* (a) (*vegetable*) haricot *m*; **broad b.** fève *f*; **French b.,** *Am* **string b.** haricot *m* vert, *Can* fève verte; **runner b.** haricot d'Espagne; *Br* **butter b.,** *Am* **Lima b.** haricot de Lima; **kidney b., haricot b.** haricot Soissons; **soya b.** graine *f* de soja; *Culin* **dried beans** haricots secs; *F* **to be full of beans** être en pleine forme; *F* **it isn't worth a b.** ça ne vaut pas un radis; *F* **he hasn't a b.** il n'a pas un radis; *Am F* **not to know beans about sth** savoir que dalle sur qch; *Am F* **she knows how many beans make five** elle n'est pas née d'hier, c'est un vieux renard; *Old-fashioned* **old b.** (*form of address*) mon vieux

(b) (*of coffee*) grain *m*; (*of cocoa*) graine *f*, fève *f*

(c) *Am Sl* (*head*) caboche *f*

beanbag [ˈbiːnbæg] *n* (a) (*bag*) balle *f* lestée (b) (*cushion, chair*) fauteuil *m* poire

bean curd *n Culin* pâte *f* de soja

beanery [ˈbiːnərɪ] *n US* = petit restaurant *m* pas cher

beanfeast [biːnfiːst], **beano** [ˈbiːnəʊ] *n Br F* (*festive occasion*) bombe *f*

beanpole [ˈbiːnpəʊl] *n* rame *f* pour haricots; *Fig* (*person*) échalas *m*, perche *f*

bean sprout *n* germe *m* de soja

beanstalk [ˈbiːnstɔːk] *n* tige *f* de haricot

bear[1] [beər] *n* (a) (*animal*), *Fig* ours *m*; **to be like a b. with a sore head** être d'une humeur massacrante; **the Great B. Lake** le grand lac de l'Ours; *Astron* **the Great/Little B.** la Grande/Petite Ourse; **she b.** ourse *f*; **b. hug** forte étreinte *f*; **to give sb a b. hug** serrer qn très fort dans ses bras (b) *St Exch* baissier *m*, joueur *m* à la baisse; **to go a b.** spéculer à la baisse; **to sell a b.** vendre à découvert; **b. spread** spread *m* baissier; **b. trading** spéculation *f* à la baisse

bear[2] **(-r-)** *St Exch* **1** *vt* **to b. the market** chercher à faire baisser les cours **2** *vi* spéculer à la baisse

bear[3] (*pt* **bore** [bɔːr]; *pp* **borne** [bɔːn]) **1** *vt* (a) (*burden, arms, name, date, signature*) porter; *Lit* **to b. gifts** apporter des cadeaux; **I still b. the scars** (*of attack etc*) j'en porte encore les cicatrices; *Fig* j'en garde encore les cicatrices; **to b. all the marks of sth** être caractéristique de qch; **the murder bore all the marks of a mafia killing** le meurtre avait tout d'un crime mafieux; **to b. sth in mind** (*remember*) se souvenir de qch; (*take into account*) tenir compte de qch; **b. us in mind if ever you want to sell it** pensez à nous si jamais vous décidez de le vendre; **it bears no relation/resemblance to ...** cela n'a aucun rapport/aucune ressemblance avec ...; **his account bears no relation to the truth** sa version n'a rien à voir avec ce qui s'est vraiment passé; **he bore himself with dignity** il est resté très digne; **to be borne backwards/along** être refoulé/emporté; **to b. the costs** supporter *ou* assumer les frais; **we will b. the costs** nous prendrons les frais en charge; **to b. the responsibility for sth** être responsable de qch; **I refuse to b. the responsibility for that** je décline toute responsabilité à ce sujet; **she bears a heavy responsibility** elle porte une lourde responsabilité; **to b. one's troubles with patience** supporter ses malheurs avec courage

(b) (*tolerate*) (*weight*) supporter, soutenir; (*suffering, consequences, pain*) supporter; **he can't b. being beaten** il ne supporte pas d'être battu; **he could b. it no longer** il ne pouvait plus tenir; **I can't b. this** je ne peux pas supporter ça; **his language does not b. repeating** il a été si grossier que je n'ose même pas répéter ce qu'il a dit; **I can't b. (the sight of) him** je ne peux pas le voir *ou* le souffrir *ou* le sentir; **I can't b. the idea of it** je ne peux pas en supporter l'idée; **it doesn't b. thinking about** l'idée en est insupportable (**c**) *Lit, Arch* (*give birth to*) (*see also* **born**) donner naissance à; **she has borne him three sons** elle lui a donné trois fils

(**d**) (*yield*) **to b. interest** porter intérêt; **to b. fruit** (*of tree*) donner des fruits; *Fig* (*of work etc*) porter ses fruits; **my enquiries bore fruit** mes recherches ont été couronnées de succès *ou* ont porté leurs fruits

2 *vi* (**a**) (*move, lie*) **to b. (to the) right/left** (*of person*) tourner à droite/à gauche, prendre à droite/à gauche; (*of road*) tourner à droite/à gauche

(**b**) **pressure has been brought to b.** on a exercé une pression sur lui/elle/*etc*

▶ **bear away** *vtsep* (*sth*) emporter

▶ **bear down 1** *vi* (*of woman in labour*) pousser **2** *vtsep Lit* (*usu passive*) **to be borne down by poverty** être accablé par la misère

▶ **bear down (up)on** *vipo* (*person, enemy, boat etc*) foncer sur

▶ **bear on** *vipo* (**a**) (*weigh*) **to bring all one's strength to b. on a lever** s'appuyer de toutes ses forces sur un levier; **to bring all one's energies to b. on sth** apporter *ou* consacrer toute son énergie à qch; **to bring one's mind to b. on sth** porter son attention sur qch; **to bring influence/pressure to b. on sb** exercer une influence/une pression sur qn; **it was gradually borne in on him that ...** peu à peu il s'est rendu compte que ... (**b**) (*be relevant to*) avoir un rapport avec; **I don't see how that bears on what I'm doing** je ne vois pas le rapport que ça a avec ce que je fais

▶ **bear out** *vtsep* (*confirm*) (*assertion*) confirmer; **to b. sb out, to b. out what sb has said** confirmer *ou* corroborer ce que qn a dit; **I feel—and I'm sure Peter will b. me out on this— ...** j'estime—et je suis sûr que Peter confirmera *ou* corroborera ce point—...

▶ **bear up** *vi* (**a**) (*of person*) **to b. up under misfortune** faire face au malheur; **she's bearing up remarkably well** elle tient drôlement bien le coup; **b. up!** tenez bon!, du courage!; *Br F* **how are you? – bearing up** comment ça va? *ou* ça va? – on fait aller (**b**) (*of results*) tenir

▶ **bear upon** *vipo* = **bear on**

▶ **bear with** *vipo* (**a**) (*tolerate*) (*sb's bad mood etc*) supporter (**b**) (*be patient with*) **if you'll b. with me I'll explain** si vous patientez un instant, je vais vous expliquer; **b. with me while I finish this** je termine ceci et je suis à vous; **I won't be a minute if you could b. with me** je suis à vous dans une minute

bearable ['beərəb(ə)l] *adj* supportable

bearably ['beərəblı] *adv* d'une façon supportable; **it was hot but b. so** il faisait chaud mais c'était supportable

bear-baiting ['beəbeıtıŋ] *n* combat *m* d'ours et de chiens

bear cub *n* ourson *m*

beard¹ [bıəd] *n* (*of man, animal, Bot of ear of barley etc*) barbe *f*; **to have a b.** porter la barbe; **to grow a b.** se laisser pousser la barbe; **a week's b.** une barbe de huit jours

beard² *vt* (*sb*) braver, défier; *Fig* **it was very brave of you to b. the lion in his den** c'est très courageux de ta part d'avoir été l'affronter

bearded ['bıədıd] *adj* (*man*) barbu; **b. lady** (*in circus*) femme *f* à barbe

-bearded ['bıədıd] *suff* **black-/white-b.** à la barbe noire/blanche

beardless ['bıədlıs] *adj* imberbe

bearer ['beərər] *n* (*of news, letter, cheque*) porteur *m*; (*of passport*) titulaire *mf*; **the bearers** (*at funeral*) les porteurs; *Fin* **b. bill** effet *m* au porteur; **b. bond/cheque** titre *m*/chèque *m* au porteur; **b. paper** papier *m* au porteur; **b. share** action *f* au porteur

bear garden *n* fosse *f* aux ours; *Fig* pétaudière *f*; *Fig* **to turn the place into a b.** mettre le désordre partout; *Fig* **the room was like a b.** la pièce était sens dessus dessous

bearing ['beərıŋ] **1** *adj* (*axle etc*) porteur; **b. wall** mur *m* d'appui; **b. surface** (*of beam*) surface *f* d'appui; (*of joist*) tablette *f*; *MecE* surface portante *ou* de portage

2 *n* (**a**) (*of arms*) port *m*

(**b**) (*deportment*) port *m*, maintien *m*, allure *f*; **because of her dignified b. throughout** parce qu'elle est restée digne jusqu'au bout

(**c**) *MecE* palier *m*; **self-lubricating b.** palier graisseur; **ball/roller/needle b.** roulement *m* à billes/à rouleaux/à aiguilles

(**d**) (*direction*) orientation *f*; (*in surveying*) gisement *m*, azimut *m*; *Naut, Av* relèvement *m*, position *f*; **true b.** (*in surveying*) azimut *ou* gisement géographique; *Naut, Av* relèvement vrai; **compass b.** relèvement au compas; **to take the ship's bearings** faire le point; *Naut* **to take one's bearings** s'orienter, se repérer; **to lose one's bearings** *Naut* perdre sa direction *ou* sa route; *Fig* ne plus s'y retrouver; **to get one's bearings** *Naut* retrouver sa direction *ou* sa route; *Fig* s'y retrouver

(**e**) (*connection*) rapport *m* (**on a question** avec une question); **it has no b. on the matter** (*of fact etc*) cela n'a aucun rapport avec l'affaire

-bearing ['beərıŋ] *suff* **fruit-b.** fructifère, qui porte des fruits; **interest-b. capital** capital qui rapporte; **silver-b.** argentifère; **wool-b.** lanifère

bearish ['beərıʃ] *adj* (**a**) *Fig* (*manners*) d'ours; (*person*) bourru (**b**) *St Exch* (*market*) à la baisse, baissier; **to be b.** spéculer à la baisse; **b. tendency** tendance *f* à la baisse

bear market *n* marché *m* à la baisse, marché baissier

bear pit *n* fosse *f* aux ours

bearskin ['beəskın] *n* (**a**) peau *f* d'ours; **b. rug** peau d'ours (**b**) *Mil* (*helmet*) bonnet *m* à poil

beast [bi:st] *n* (**a**) bête *f*; **wild b.** (*not domesticated*) bête sauvage; (*fierce*) bête féroce; *Lit* **the king of the beasts** le roi des animaux; **b. of prey** carnassier *m*; *Lit* **b. of burden** (*ass etc*), *Fig* bête de somme; *Bible* **the B.** l'Antéchrist *m*; **beasts** (*on farm*) bétail *m*, bestiaux *mpl*

(**b**) *Fig* (*brute*) brute *f*; *F* (*unkind person*) vache *f*, peau *f* de vache; **to sink to the level of a b.** s'avilir; **the little b.** le petit diable; **he's a perfect b.!** c'est une peau de vache!; **it was a b. of a day** (*bad weather*) il a fait un temps abominable *ou* un temps de chien; **I've had a b. of a day** (*full of problems*) j'ai eu une journée affreuse; **a b. of a job** (*task*) un travail pénible

beastliness ['bi:stlınıs] *n esp Old-fashioned* **the b. of his behaviour** sa conduite ignoble

beastly ['bi:stlı] *F* **1** *adj* (*person*) affreux; (*place, smell, taste*) dégoûtant; **a b. job** (*task*) un travail pénible; **what b. weather!** quel sale temps! **2** *adv* bigrement, vachement

beat¹ [bi:t] *n* (**a**) (*stroke, blow*) (*of heart, clock, drum*) battement *m*; *Mus* mesure *f*, temps *m*; **music with a strong b.** musique avec un fort rythme (**b**) *Br* (*of policeman*) ronde *f*; **policeman on the b.** agent qui fait sa ronde; *Fig F* **it's off my b. altogether** cela ne relève pas de ma compétence, ce n'est pas de mon ressort

beat² (*pt* **beat**; *pp* **beaten** ['bi:t(ə)n]) **1** *vt* (**a**) (*hit*) (*person, rug, eggs, wood for game birds etc*) battre; **to b. sb with a stick** donner des coups de bâton à qn; **to b. one's breast** se frapper la poitrine; **to b. a drum** battre du tambour; **the world is beating a path to her door** tout le monde se rue sur elle; *F* **b. it!** (*go away*) file!, fiche le camp!; *Am Sl* **to b. one's meat** se branler; **to b. its wings** (*of bird*) battre des ailes

(**b**) (*defeat, conquer*) (*enemy*) battre, vaincre; (*record*) battre; (*get ahead of*) battre, devancer; **to b. sb at chess** battre qn aux échecs; *F* **that beats me!** ça me dépasse!; *F* **it beats me why he did it** je ne pige vraiment pas pourquoi il a fait ça; *F* **that beats everything!** ça c'est le comble *ou* le bouquet!; *F* **you can't b. a good book** rien de tel qu'un bon livre; *F* **I got up early to b. the traffic** je me suis levé tôt pour éviter les embouteillages; *F* **he beat me to it** (*arrived, telephoned before me etc*) il m'a devancé; *Prov* **if you can't b. them, join them** mieux vaut s'allier aux gens que l'on ne peut pas vaincre

(**c**) *US Sl* (*cheat, get the better of*) rouler, refaire; **to b. the customs** frauder la douane

2 *vi* (**a**) (*of heart, rain*) battre; **the waves are beating against the shore** les vagues déferlent sur le rivage

(**b**) *Naut* **to b. to windward** louvoyer

(**c**) *Fig* **to b. about** *or Am* **around the bush** tourner autour du pot

beat³ *adj F* (**a**) **you've got me b.** (*defeated*) je m'avoue vaincu; (*unable to answer*) je sèche; **I think Leconte's got Sampras b.** je pense que Leconte a déjà battu Sampras; **this crossword's got me b.** je sèche sur ces mots croisés; **it's got** *or* **it has me b. why she did it** je ne comprends pas pourquoi elle a fait ça (**b**) (*very tired*) crevé; **dead b.** complètement crevé

▶ **beat back** *vtsep* (*people, enemy troops, flames*) repousser

▶ **beat down 1** *vtsep* (*door*) enfoncer; (*nettles, grass etc with stick*) rabattre; (*earth*) damer; *Fig* **to b. down the price of sth** (*by bargaining*) faire baisser le prix de qch; **to b. sb down** faire baisser le prix à qn **2** *vi* (*of rain*) tomber à verse; (*of sun*) taper; **the rain was beating down on the tin roof** la pluie s'abattait sur le toit en tôle; **the sun is beating down on our heads** le soleil nous tape sur la tête

▶ **beat in** *vtsep* (*door etc*) défoncer

▶ **beat off 1** *vtsep* (*person, assault*) repousser **2** *vi Am Vulg* (*masturbate*) se branler

▶ **beat out** *vtsep* (**a**) (*extinguish*) (*flames*) étouffer (**b**) (*flatten*) (*sheet metal*) battre, aplatir; (*gold etc*) marteler; (*bodywork*)

débosseler; **to beat out the dents in a car door** débosseler une porte de voiture **(c)** *Mus* **to b. out the rhythm,** *F* **to b. it out** marquer le rythme **(d)** *F* **I'll b. your brains out!** je vais te démolir!; *Fig* **to b. one's brains out** se creuser la tête *ou* la cervelle **(e) to b. the dust out of sth** battre qch pour en faire sortir la poussière

▶ **beat up 1** *vtsep* **(a)** *(person)* tabasser **(b)** *(eggs)* battre **(c)** *(game)* rabattre, traquer **2** *vi Naut* louvoyer *ou* gagner vers la terre

▶ **beat up on** *vipo esp Am F (hit)* battre, tabasser; **stop beating up on yourself** arrête de culpabiliser

beaten [ˈbiːt(ə)n] *adj* **(a)** *(gold, metal)* battu, martelé; **b. earth** terre *f* battue; *Fig* **off the b. track** *(house, to live)* à l'écart; **let's go somewhere a bit more off the b. track** sortons un peu des sentiers battus **(b)** *(enemy)* battu, vaincu

beater [ˈbiːtər] *n* **(a)** *(person)* batteur, -euse; *(in hunting)* rabatteur *m* **(b)** *(device) (for eggs)* fouet *m*

beatific [biːəˈtɪfɪk] *adj Lit (vision)* béatifique; *(smile)* béat

beatifically [biːəˈtɪfɪklɪ] *adv Lit* d'un air béat

beatification [biːætɪfɪˈkeɪʃən] *n Rel* béatification *f*

beatify [biːˈætɪfaɪ] *vt Rel* béatifier

beating [ˈbiːtɪŋ] **1** *adj (heart)* battant, palpitant; *(rain)* battant **2** *n* **(a)** *(of wings, heart etc)* battement *m*; *(of game)* rabattage *m*, rabat *m*; *(of wood for game)* traque *f* **(b)** *(thrashing)* raclée *f*, rossée *f*; **to give sb a b.** donner une raclée à qn, rosser qn **(c)** *(in match etc)* défaite *f*, *F* raclée *f*; **to get a good b.** être battu à plate(s) couture(s); *F* recevoir une bonne raclée **(d)** *Naut* louvoyage *m*

beatitude [biːˈætɪtjuːd] *n* béatitude *f*; *Bible* **the Beatitudes** les Béatitudes

beatnik [ˈbiːtnɪk] *n* beatnik *mf*

beat-up [ˈbiːtʌp] *adj F (car, chair etc)* déglingué

beau, *pl* **beaus, beaux** [bəʊ, bəʊz] *n* **(a)** *Arch (dandy)* élégant *m*, dandy *m* **(b)** *Arch, US (of young girl)* prétendant *m*, galant *m*

beaut [bjuːt] *F* **1** *n* **what a b.!** quelle merveille!; **what a b. of a car!** quelle voiture! **2** *adj Austr (meal)* délicieux; *(weather)* superbe; *(car)* génial

beautician [bjuːˈtɪʃən] *n* esthéticien, -ienne; *(make-up artist)* visagiste *mf*

beautiful [ˈbjuːtɪfʊl] *adj* **(a)** *(person, place, face etc)* (très) beau, (très) belle; **the b. people** le beau monde **(b)** *(dinner, weather etc)* magnifique

beautifully [ˈbjuːtɪfʊlɪ] *adv (intensifier)* admirablement, à merveille; **b. dressed** merveilleusement bien habillé

beautify [ˈbjuːtɪfaɪ] *vt* embellir

beauty [ˈbjuːtɪ] *n* **(a)** *(appearance)* beauté *f*; **the beauties of nature** les beautés de la nature; **that's the b. of it** c'est ça qu'il y a de bien; **b. aids** *or* **preparations** produits *mpl* de beauté; **b. sleep** sommeil *m* avant minuit *(considéré comme le plus réparateur)*; **b. treatment** soins *mpl* esthétiques

(b) *(person, object)* **she was a b. in her day** c'était une beauté dans son temps; **B. and the Beast** la Belle et la Bête; **Sleeping B.** la Belle au bois dormant; *F* **isn't it a b.?** *(of flower)* n'est-ce pas qu'elle est belle?; *(of car)* n'est-ce pas qu'elle est super?; *(of mistake)* elle est bonne celle-là!; *Sl* **he fetched him a b. on the chin** il lui a flanqué un coup magnifique *ou* formidable au menton; *F* **that black eye is a real b.** c'est un bel œil au beurre noir

beauty competition *n* concours *m* de beauté

beauty parlour *n* institut *m* de beauté

beauty queen *n* reine *f* d'un concours de beauté

beauty salon *n* institut *m* de beauté

beauty spot *n (place)* site *m ou* coin *m* pittoresque; *(on skin)* grain *m* de beauté; *(artificial)* mouche *f*

beaver [ˈbiːvər] *n* **(a)** *(animal, fur)* castor *m*; *F* **to work like a b.** travailler d'arrache-pied; **b. coat/jacket** manteau *m*/veste *f* de castor; **b. lamb (coat)** (manteau en) mouton *m* doré **(b)** *Am Vulg (female genitals)* chatte *f*

▶ **beaver away** *vi* travailler d'arrache-pied **(at** à)

becalmed [bɪˈkɑːmd] *adj (ship)* encalminé

became *see* **become**

because [bɪˈkɒz, -kəz] **1** *conj* parce que; **I eat b. I'm hungry** je mange parce que j'ai faim; **I was all the more astonished b. I had been told that ...** j'en fus d'autant plus étonné qu'on m'avait assuré que ...; **b. he dashed off a sonnet he thinks himself a poet** il se prend pour un poète simplement parce qu'il a torché un sonnet; **why? – just b.** pourquoi? – parce que **2** *prep phrase* **b. of sth** à cause de qch; **b. of his illness** à cause de *ou* en raison de sa maladie

béchamel [ˈbeʃəmel] *n Culin* **b. sauce** béchamel *f*, sauce *f* (à la) béchamel

beck¹ [bek] *n* **to have sb at one's b. and call** avoir qn à ses ordres *ou* à sa disposition; **to be at sb's b. and call** obéir aux moindres volontés de qn, être aux ordres de qn

beck² *n Dial* ruisseau *m* de montagne

beckon [ˈbek(ə)n] *vti* faire signe **(to sb** à qn); **to b. sb in** faire signe à qn d'entrer; *Fig* **the bright lights of the city beckoned** les lumières de la ville étaient une tentation; **I can't stay, work beckons** il faut que je m'en aille, j'ai du travail; **and fame beckoned** et les portes de la gloire lui étaient ouvertes; **to b. sb** appeler qn du doigt *ou* de la main

become [bɪˈkʌm] *(pt* **became** [bɪˈkeɪm]; *pp* **become) 1** *vi* **(a)** *(a priest, an adult, sb's enemy etc)* devenir; **to b. king/a doctor** devenir roi/médecin; **to b. old/thin** vieillir/maigrir; **to b. suspicious of sb** commencer à avoir des soupçons à propos de qn, devenir soupçonneux à l'égard de qn; **the murmurs became louder** les murmures se faisaient plus forts; **to b. accustomed/attached/interested** s'accoutumer/s'attacher/s'intéresser; **to b. known** *(of person)* commencer à être connu; **it will soon b. clear that ...** il sera bientôt évident que ...

(b) what has become of Tom? qu'est devenu Tom?; **what will b. of him?** que va-t-il devenir?; **I don't know what has become of her** je ne sais pas ce qu'elle est devenue

2 *vt esp Fml (sb) (of behaviour etc)* être digne de; *(of clothes, colour etc)* aller bien à

becoming [bɪˈkʌmɪŋ] *adj* **(a)** *(proper) (behaviour)* convenable, bienséant **(b)** *(colour, clothes)* seyant; **red is very b. to her** le rouge lui va très bien *ou* lui sied; **green looks very b. on you** le vert te va très bien; **you look very b. in that dress** cette robe te va très bien

becquerel [bek(ə)ˈrel] *n Phys* becquerel *m*

bed¹ [bed] *n* **(a)** lit *m*; **to be in b.** *(to rest)* être couché, être au lit; *(through illness)* être alité, garder le lit; **to keep sb in b.** garder qn au lit; **to read in b.** lire au lit; **to get out of b.** se lever; **to get out of b. on the wrong side** se lever du pied gauche; **I'm sorry to get you out of b.** je suis désolé de vous tirer du lit; *Hum* **I wouldn't kick her out of b.** si elle voulait de moi, je ne dirais pas non; **to go to b.** se coucher; *Journ* **the paper has gone to b.** le journal est bouclé; **I'm going home to b.** je vais rentrer me coucher; **to keep to one's b.** garder le lit; *F* **to go to b. with a man/woman** coucher avec un homme/une femme; **to put a child to b.** coucher un enfant, mettre un enfant au lit; **she always takes her teddy to b. with her** elle emmène toujours son ours au lit avec elle; **it's time for b.** c'est l'heure d'aller au lit *ou* d'aller se coucher; **to make the b.** faire le lit; *Fig* **you've made your b. and now you must lie in it** comme on fait son lit, on se couche; **we've got a spare b.** *(you can stay the night)* nous avons de quoi vous coucher; **to sleep in separate beds** faire lit à part; *Fig* **b. head** chevet *m*, tête *f* (de lit); **b. linen** draps *mpl* (et taies *fpl* d'oreiller *etc*); **b. occupancy** occupation *f* des lits; **b. sheet** drap *m*

(b) *(of river, sea)* lit *m*; *(of billiard table)* fond *m*; **filter b.** lit de filtrage; **place the roast on a b. of vegetables** placez le rôti sur un lit de légumes

(c) *(in garden) (for vegetables)* carré *m*; *(for flowers)* parterre *m*; **oyster b.** banc *m* d'huîtres; *(on oyster farm)* parc *m* à huîtres

(d) *Geol* assise *f*, couche *f*; *Miner* gisement *m*

(e) *Constr etc (of concrete)* assise *f*, lit *m*; *(of stone)* assise; *Rail* infrastructure *f*

(f) *MecE (of lathe)* banc *m*

bed² *vt* **(-dd-)** *(woman)* coucher avec

▶ **bed down 1** *vi (of animal)* se gîter; *F (of person)* se coucher **2** *vtsep (horses)* faire la litière à

▶ **bed out** *vtsep (plants)* repiquer

B Ed [biːˈed] *n Univ abbr* **Bachelor of Education**

bed and board *n* pension *f* complète

bed and breakfast *n (at hotel)* chambre *f* et petit déjeuner; *esp Br* **we stayed in a b.** nous avons dormi dans un bed and breakfast

bedbug [ˈbedbʌg] *n* punaise *f*

bedchamber [ˈbedtʃeɪmbər] *n Arch* chambre *f* à coucher

bedclothes [ˈbedkləʊðz] *npl* couvertures *fpl* et draps *mpl*; **to turn down the b.** ouvrir le lit

beddable [ˈbedəb(ə)l] *adj Hum* baisable

bedding [ˈbedɪŋ] *n* **(a) b. plants** plants *mpl* à repiquer **(b)** *(for bed)* literie *f* **(c)** *(for animals)* litière *f*

bedding out *n (of plants)* dépotage *m*, dépotement *m*

bedevil [bɪˈdev(ə)l] *vt* **(-ll-,** *US* **-l-) (a)** *(torment)* tourmenter **(b)** *(cause difficulties or problems for)* **industrial relations bedevilled by politics** rapports entre patrons et ouvriers empoisonnés par la politique; **the project is bedevilled by problems** le projet est en proie à de nombreux problèmes; **the strikes which had bedevilled the industry** les grèves qui avaient affligé l'industrie; **to be bedevilled by complaints** être assailli de réclamations

bedfellow [ˈbedfeləʊ] *n* compagnon *m*/compagne *f* de lit; *Fig*

they make strange bedfellows c'est une association inattendue, c'est un couple disparate
bed jacket *n* liseuse *f*
bedlam ['bedləm] *n* (a) *Fig* bazar *m*; **the meeting was absolute b.** la réunion était un véritable bazar (b) *Arch* (*asylum*) maison *f* de fous *ou* d'aliénés
bed-night *n* nuitée *f*
Bedouin ['bedʊɪn] 1 *adj* bédouin 2 *n* (*pl* **Bedouin**) Bédouin, -ine
bedpan ['bedpæn] *n* bassin *m*
bedpost ['bedpəʊst] *n* colonne *f* de lit
bedraggled [bɪ'dræg(ə)ld] *adj* (*muddy*) crotté, taché de boue; (*wet*) trempé; **you look a bit b.** tu es dans un piteux état
bedridden ['bedrɪd(ə)n] *adj* alité, cloué au lit; (*permanently*) grabataire
bedrock ['bedrɒk] *n Geol* roche *f* de fond; *Fig* (*of one's belief etc*) fondement *m*; *Fig* **to get down to b.** parler des choses sérieuses
bedroll ['bedrəʊl] *n US* matériel *m* de couchage
bedroom ['bedru:m] *n* chambre *f* (à coucher); **spare b.** chambre d'ami; **b. furniture/curtains** meubles *mpl*/rideaux *mpl* de chambre; **b. slippers** pantoufles *fpl*; *Th* **b. farce** comédie *f* légère, vaudeville *m*
-bedroom, -bedroomed ['bedru:m(d)] *suff* **a two/three-bedroom(ed) house** une maison à deux/trois chambres
Beds *abbr* **Bedfordshire**
bed settee *n* convertible *m*, canapé-lit *m*, *pl* canapés-lits
bedside ['bedsaɪd] *n* chevet *m*; **to have a good b. manner** (*of doctor*) être agréable avec les malades; **I didn't think much of his b. manner** je ne l'ai pas trouvé très agréable; **b. lamp** lampe *f* de chevet; **b. rug** descente *f* de lit; **b. table** table *f* de nuit *ou* de chevet
bedsit ['bedsɪt], **bed-sitter** ['bedsɪtər], **bed-sittingroom** [bed'sɪtɪŋru:m] *n Br* chambre *f* meublée
bedsock ['bedsɒk] *n* chausson *m* de nuit
bedsore ['bedsɔ:r] *n* escarre *f*
bedspace ['bedspeɪs] *n* (*in hotels etc*) capacité *f* d'accueil
bedspread ['bedspred] *n* dessus *m* de lit
bedstead ['bedsted] *n* châlit *m*, bois *m* de lit
bedtick ['bedtɪk] *n Am* (*bug*) punaise *f*
bedtime ['bedtaɪm] *n* heure *f* du coucher; **b.!** c'est l'heure d'aller au lit *ou* de se coucher!; **when is your b.?** à quelle heure vous couchez-vous?; **it's past your b.** vous devriez déjà être couché; **it's long past my b.** je devrais être couché depuis longtemps; **they were allowed to stay up past their b.** on leur a permis de se coucher plus tard que d'habitude; **to tell sb a b. story** raconter une histoire à qn avant qu'il ne s'endorme
bed-wetter ['bedwetər] *n* (*child*) enfant *mf* qui fait pipi au lit; **he's a b.** il fait pipi au lit
bed-wetting ['bedwetɪŋ] *n* énurésie *f* nocturne; **if b. is a problem for your child** si votre enfant fait pipi au lit
bee [bi:] *n* (a) abeille *f*; **bees' nest** nid *m* d'abeilles; **to keep bees** élever des abeilles; *Fig* **to be a busy b.** être très actif; *Fig* **to have a b. in one's bonnet** avoir une idée fixe; **he's got a b. in his bonnet about it** c'est pour lui une idée fixe; **he's got a b. in his bonnet about burglars** les cambrioleurs, c'est une idée fixe chez lui; *Br F* **she thinks she's the b.'s knees** elle ne se prend pas pour n'importe qui; **she thinks he's the b.'s knees** elle le trouve formidable; **b. balm** (*plant*) monarde *f* d'Amérique; **b. orchid** (*plant*) ophrys *f* abeille (b) *Am* (*meeting*) réunion *f* (*pour travaux en commun*); **spelling b.** concours *m* (oral) d'orthographe
Beeb [bi:b] *n F* **the B.** la BBC
beech [bi:tʃ] *n* (*tree*) hêtre *m*; **b. (wood)** (bois *m* de) hêtre; **b. furniture** meubles *mpl* en hêtre; **b. mast** faînes *fpl*
beechnut ['bi:tʃnʌt] *n* faîne *f*
bee-eater ['bi:i:tər] *n* (*bird*) guêpier *m* (d'Europe)
beef[1] [bi:f] *n* (a) (*no pl*) *Culin* bœuf *m*; **b. stew** ragoût *m* de bœuf, bœuf mode; *Fig* **to have plenty of b.** (*muscles*) avoir du muscle, être costaud; **give it some b.!** fais un petit effort!; **the team's a bit short of b.** l'équipe manque un peu de muscle; **b. cattle** bœufs de boucherie; **b. tea** bouillon *m* de bœuf; **b. tomato** = marmande *f*
(b) *US* (*animal*) (*pl* **beeves** [bi:vz]; **beefs** [bi:fs]) bœuf(s) *m*(*pl*) à l'engrais; **a b.** un bœuf, une vache; **b. farm** élevage *m* de bœufs; **b. farmer** éleveur *m* de bœufs
(c) *F* (*complaint*) (*pl* **beefs**) plainte *f*, grief *m*; **he enjoys a good b.** il aime ronchonner *ou* rouspéter; **what's your b.?** qu'est-ce que tu as à ronchonner?; **my main b. is that …** ce qui m'énerve le plus c'est que …
beef[2] *vi F* ronchonner, rouspéter
▶ **beef up** *vtsep F* (*text, character in play etc*) étoffer, donner plus de consistance à; (*army*) renforcer; **we need to b. up our coverage of Latin America** il faut que nous couvrions l'Amérique latine davantage
beefburger ['bi:fbɜ:gər] *n* hamburger *m*
beefcake ['bi:fkeɪk] *n F* beaux hommes *mpl* musclés
Beefeater ['bi:fi:tər] *n F* = hallebardier *m* de service à la Tour de Londres
beefing ['bi:fɪŋ] *n F* (*moaning*) ronchonnements *mpl*, rouspétances *fpl*
beefsteak ['bi:fsteɪk] *n Culin* bifteck *m*; **b. tomato** = marmande *f*
beefy ['bi:fɪ] *adj F* (a) (*muscular*) musclé, costaud (b) (*fleshy*) bien en chair
beehive ['bi:haɪv] *n* (a) (*for bees*) ruche *f* (b) (*hairstyle*) coiffure *f* toute en hauteur
beekeeper ['bi:ki:pər] *n* apiculteur, -trice
beekeeping ['bi:ki:pɪŋ] *n* apiculture *f*
beeline ['bi:laɪn] *n Fig* **to make a b. for sth** aller droit *ou* directement vers qch
Beelzebub [bɪ'elzɪbʌb] *n Bible* Belzébuth *m*
been *see* **be**
beep[1] [bi:p] *n* (*of satellite, computer, watch etc*) bip *m*, signal *m ou* bip sonore; *Aut* coup *m* de klaxon; *Aut* **to give the horn a b.** klaxonner; *Aut* **to give sb a b.** klaxonner qn
beep[2] 1 *vi* (*of satellite, computer, watch etc*) faire bip, émettre un signal *ou* bip sonore; (*of car driver*) klaxonner; **to b. at sb** klaxonner qn 2 *vt* (a) *Aut* **to b. the horn** klaxonner (b) (*person*) (*on pager*) appeler au récepteur d'appel; **I'm being beeped** (*of doctor etc*) on m'appelle
beeper ['bi:pər] *n* récepteur *m* d'appels
beeping ['bi:pɪŋ] *n* (*of satellite, computer, watch etc*) bip-bip *m*; **a sudden b. of car horns** des coups de klaxon brutaux
beer [bɪər] *n* bière *f*; **to go for a b.** aller boire une bière; **will you join me in a b.?** (*have one too*) est-ce que tu prends une bière aussi?; *Fig* **life's not all b. and skittles** la vie n'est pas qu'une partie de rigolade
beer barrel *n* tonneau *m* à bière
beer belly *n F* gros ventre *m* de buveur de bière
beer bottle *n* bouteille *f* de bière
beer cellar *n* (*bar*) brasserie *f*
beer garden *n* café *m* en plein air
beer glass *n* verre *m* à bière; (*with handle*) chope *f*
beer gut *n F* gros ventre *m* de buveur de bière
beer mat *n* sous-bock *m inv*
beer pump *n* pompe *f* à bière
beery ['bɪərɪ] *adj* (a) (*atmosphere etc*) qui sent la bière (b) **b. voice** voix *f* avinée
beeswax ['bi:zwæks] *n* cire *f* d'abeilles; **b. (polish)** cire d'abeilles
beet [bi:t] *n* (a) betterave *f*; **fodder b.** betterave fourragère; **b. sugar** sucre *m* de betterave; **b. industry** industrie *f* betteravière (b) *Am* = **beetroot**
beetle[1] ['bi:t(ə)l] *n* (*insect*) coléoptère *m*; *Aut F* (**Volkswagen**) **b.** coccinelle *f*
beetle[2] *n* (*for beating, pounding*) (*large*) masse *f* (*en bois*); (*small*) maillet *m*; (*for paving*) hie *f*, demoiselle *f*
beetle[3] *vi* (*of cliff*) surplomber
▶ **beetle along** *vi F* (*hurry along*) se dépêcher, se presser; **I must be beetling along now** il faut que je mette les bouts
▶ **beetle away, beetle off** *vi F* décamper
beetle-browed [bi:t(ə)l'braʊd] *adj* (*with overhanging eyebrows*) aux sourcils proéminents; (*with bushy eyebrows*) aux sourcils touffus
beetle-crusher ['bi:t(ə)lkrʌʃər] *n F* écrase-merde *m*, *pl* écrase-merdes
beetling ['bi:tlɪŋ] *adj* (*cliff, rock etc*) surplombant, en surplomb
beetroot ['bi:tru:t] 1 *n Bot, Culin* betterave *f* (potagère) 2 *adj* **b. (red)** rouge foncé; **he turned b.** il est devenu rouge comme une tomate
befall [bɪ'fɔ:l] *vt* (*conj like* **fall**; *used only in third person*) *Lit, Arch* (*person*) arriver à, survenir à
befit [bɪ'fɪt] *vt* (**-tt-**) *Lit* (*used only in third person*) convenir à; **as befits her position** comme il convient à son rang; **it does not b. a man to …** ce n'est pas le fait d'un homme de …
befitting [bɪ'fɪtɪŋ] *adj* convenable, seyant (**for sb/sth** à qn/qch), digne (**of sb** de qn); **with b. modesty/generosity** avec la modestie/générosité qui convient
before [bɪ'fɔ:r] 1 *adv* (a) (*of time*) auparavant, avant; **two days b.** deux jours avant *ou* auparavant, l'avant-veille *f*; **the day b.** la veille; **the year b.** l'année d'avant, un an auparavant; **she had come two years b.** elle était venue deux ans auparavant; **a moment b.** un instant plus tôt; **I have seen him b.** je l'ai déjà vu; **I have never seen him b.** je ne l'ai jamais vu (de ma vie); **we've met b.** nous nous sommes déjà rencontrés; **I've told you b.** je te l'ai déjà dit; **you should have told me so b.** vous auriez dû me le dire plus tôt; **she gave me the same advice as b.** elle m'a redonné le même conseil; **to go on as b.** faire comme avant

(b) (*of place*) devant; *Lit* **to go on b.** (*at front of procession*) marcher en tête; (*in advance*) partir devant; **this page and the one b.** cette page et la précédente

2 *prep* **(a)** (*of place*) devant; **b. my (very) eyes** sous mes (propres) yeux; **b. God and man** devant Dieu et les hommes; **to appear b. the judge** comparaître devant le juge; **that is the task b. us** c'est là la tâche qui nous incombe

(b) (*of time*) avant; **b. that, she was a teacher** auparavant *ou* avant ça, elle était professeur; **where did you go b. that?** où est-ce que vous êtes allé avant ça?; **b. long** avant longtemps, sous peu; **not b. Easter** pas avant Pâques; **it ought to have been done b. now** ce devrait déjà être fait; **to arrive an hour b. time** arriver avec une heure d'avance *ou* une heure à l'avance; *F* **it's not b. time, and not b. time** ce n'est pas trop tôt; **I got here b. you** je vous ai devancé, je suis arrivé avant vous; **you were b. me** (*in queue*) vous étiez avant moi; **the day b. the battle** la veille de la bataille; **two days b. Christmas** l'avant-veille de Noël; **b. answering/leaving** avant de répondre/partir; **b. tax** hors taxe, HT; (*income*) avant impôt

(c) (*of order*) **b. anything else I must have ...** il me faut avant tout ...; **death b. dishonour** plutôt la mort que le déshonneur; **ladies b. gentlemen** les dames d'abord; **this word should come b. that one** ce mot devrait être placé devant celui-là; **the welfare of the country comes b. everything** le bien de la patrie prime tout; **she puts family b. friends** pour elle, la famille est plus importante que les amis

3 *conj* **(a)** (*of time*) avant que (ne) + *sub*; **come and see me b. you leave** venez me voir avant de partir *ou* avant votre départ; **I saw him the day b. he died** je l'ai vu la veille de sa mort; **don't come in b. I call you** n'entrez pas avant que je vous appelle; **it was long b. he came** (*it happened before that*) c'était longtemps avant qu'il arrive; **how long will it be b. you hear?** quand est-ce que tu sauras?; *F* **b. you know where you are, b. I/he/***etc* **knew where I/he/***etc* **was** en moins de rien; **b. I forget, they expect you this evening** avant que je n'oublie, il faut que je te dise qu'ils comptent sur toi ce soir

(b) (*of order*) **I will die b. I yield** je préfère mourir plutôt que de céder

(c) (*or else*) avant que (ne) + *sub*; **get out b. I throw you out** sortez avant que je vous jette dehors; **tell me b. I die of curiosity** dis-le moi, je n'en peux plus de curiosité; **give it to her b. she cries** donne-le lui avant qu'elle ne se mette à pleurer

beforehand [bɪ'fɔːhænd] *adv* à l'avance, au préalable; **to come an hour b.** venir une heure à l'avance; **I must tell you b. that ...** il faut vous dire d'avance *ou* au préalable que ...; **if I come I'll let you know b.** si je viens je vous préviendrai; **we should make sure b.** nous ferions mieux de nous en assurer au préalable

befriend [bɪ'frend] *vt* (*make friends with*) se lier d'amitié avec; **I was befriended by a stray dog** un chien perdu s'est attaché à moi

befuddle [bɪ'fʌd(ə)l] *vt* **(a)** (*confuse*) embrouiller; **his mind is befuddled with drink** l'alcool lui a embrouillé l'esprit **(b)** (*make drunk*) griser; **befuddled (with drink)** éméché

beg [beg] **(-gg-) 1** *vi* (*for money*) mendier; (*plead*) supplier; **to sit up and b.** (*of dog*) faire le beau; **to b. for mercy** demander grâce; **I b. of you!** je vous en prie!; **these jobs are going begging** ce sont des emplois qui trouvent peu d'amateurs; **there's a piece of cake going begging** il reste un morceau de gâteau

2 *vt* **to b. sb to do sth** prier *ou* supplier qn de faire qch; **to b. a favour of sb** demander instamment un service à qn; **she begged to be sent back to school** elle supplia qu'on la renvoie à l'école; *Fml* **I b. to inform you that ...** j'ai l'honneur de vous faire savoir que ...; **I b. your pardon** je vous demande pardon; **to b. forgiveness** implorer le pardon; **I b. to differ** permettez-moi d'être d'un autre avis; *Fml* **to b. leave to do sth** demander la permission de faire qch; **to b. the question** (*evade the issue*) ne pas aborder la question; (*in logic*) faire une pétition de principe; **wanting to climb Mount Everest rather begs the question 'why'** on serait enclin à se demander pourquoi quelqu'un aurait envie d'escalader le Mont Everest

▶ **beg off** *vi* (*from a meeting, party etc*) demander à être excusé

beget [bɪ'get] *vt* (*pt* **begot** [bɪ'gɒt], *Bible* **begat** [bɪ'gæt]; *pp* **begotten** [bɪ'gɒt(ə)n]) **(a)** *Bible, Lit* engendrer; **Abraham begat Isaac** Abraham engendra Isaac; *Bible* **the only begotten Son of the Father** le Fils unique du Père **(b)** *Lit Fig* engendrer, causer

beggar¹ ['begər] *n* **(a)** (*in street*) mendiant, -ante; *Prov* **beggars can't be choosers** il ne faut pas être difficile quand on n'a pas le choix **(b)** *esp Br F* (*person*) **poor b.!** pauvre diable!; **lucky b.!** chançard!, veinard!; **you little b.!** petit coquin!, petit espiègle!

beggar² *vt* **(beggared** ['begəd]) **(a) to b. sb** réduire qn à la mendicité; **they are beggaring themselves doing it** en faisant cela ils vont tout droit à la ruine **(b)** *Fig* **to b. description** être indescriptible

beggarly ['begəlɪ] *adj* (*very poor*) minable, misérable; (*wage*) dérisoire, minable

beggar-my-neighbour *n Cards* bataille *f*

beggary ['begərɪ] *n* mendicité *f*

begging ['begɪŋ] *n* mendicité *f*; **to live by b.** vivre d'aumône; **b. bowl** sébile *f* (*de mendiant*); **b. letter** lettre *f* quémandant de l'argent

begin [bɪ'gɪn] *vti* (*pt* **began** [bɪ'gæn]; *pp* **begun** [bɪ'gʌn]) commencer; (*piece of work, new chapter*) commencer, entamer; **b. at the beginning** commencez par le commencement; **before winter begins** avant le début de l'hiver; **the day began well/badly** la journée commença bien/mal; **to b. to do sth, to b. doing sth** commencer à faire qch, se mettre à faire qch; **to b. to laugh/cry, to b. laughing/crying** se mettre à rire/à pleurer; **he soon began to complain** il ne tarda pas à se plaindre; **we began** *or* **we were beginning to get hungry** nous commencions à avoir faim; **it doesn't b. to compare with ...** cela est loin d'être comparable à ...; **I couldn't (even) b. to explain/describe it to you** c'est presque impossible à t'expliquer/de te le décrire; **to b. by doing sth** commencer par faire qch; **the play begins with a prologue** la pièce commence *ou* débute par un prologue; **to b. again** recommencer

▶ **begin with 1** *vi* **to b. with** (*in the first place*) premièrement, pour commencer; (*at first*) au départ **2** *vipo* commencer par; **what did you have to b. with?** (*in restaurant etc*) par quoi avez-vous commencé?

beginner [bɪ'gɪnər] *n* **(a)** (*novice*) débutant, -ante, novice *mf*; **English for beginners** anglais pour débutants; **b.'s class** cours *m* de débutants; **(it's just) b.'s luck** aux innocents les mains pleines; **she just had b.'s luck** elle n'y connaît rien, elle a simplement eu de la chance; **complete** *or* **absolute b.** grand débutant **(b)** *Th* **beginners please!** en scène!

beginning [bɪ'gɪnɪŋ] *n* (*of speech, career etc*) commencement *m*, début *m*; (*of the world etc*) origine *f*, naissance *f*; **in the b.** au commencement, au début; **from the b.** dès le commencement *ou* le début; **from b. to end** depuis le commencement jusqu'à la fin; **at the b. of the week** au début de la semaine; **at the b. of term** à la rentrée (des classes); **the first beginnings of civilization** l'aube *f* de la civilisation; **I have the beginnings of a cold** je couve un rhume, j'ai un début de rhume; **to make a b.** commencer, débuter; **the b. of the end** le début de la fin; **to have one's beginnings in sth** avoir qch pour origine

begone [bɪ'gɒn] *vi Arch, Lit* (*used as imp*) va-t'en!, allez-vous-en!

begonia [bɪ'gəʊnɪə] *n* bégonia *m*

begrudge [bɪ'grʌdʒ] *vt* **(a)** (*be unwilling to give*) donner à contrecœur; **you don't b. me the money do you?** tu ne me donnes pas cet argent à contrecœur, n'est-ce pas?; **they b. him his food** ils lui reprochent sa nourriture; **to b. doing sth** faire qch à contrecœur; **I b. spending so much money** c'est à contrecœur que je dépense une telle somme; **I b. the money I spent on that dress** je regrette d'avoir eu à payer autant pour cette robe; **he begrudged every moment spent away from his wife** chaque minute passée loin de sa femme lui était pénible

(b) (*be envious of*) **to b. sb sth** envier qch à qn; **I don't b. him his success** je ne lui en veux pas d'avoir réussi

beguile [bɪ'gaɪl] *vt Lit* **(a)** (*charm*) enjôler, séduire; **to b. sb with promises** bercer qn de promesses; **to b. sb into doing sth** séduire qn pour qu'il fasse qch **(b)** (*while away*) **to b. the time** faire passer le temps

beguiling [bɪ'gaɪlɪŋ] *adj* (*smile*) enjôleur, séduisant

begum ['beɪgəm] *n* bégum *f*

behalf [bɪ'hɑːf] *n* **on** *or Am* **in b. of sb** au nom de qn, de la part de qn; (*to sign*) au nom de qn, pour qn; **he is acting on my b.** il agit pour moi *ou* pour mon compte; **don't be uneasy on my b.** ne vous inquiétez pas à mon sujet; **speaking on my own b.** *or* **on b. of myself** en mon (propre) nom; **on b. of my husband and myself** de la part de mon mari et moi; **she accepted the award on his b.** elle a reçu le prix en son nom *ou* pour lui

behave [bɪ'heɪv] *vi* **(a)** se comporter, se conduire; (*well*) bien se comporter, bien se conduire; **to b. well/badly to(wards) sb** bien/mal agir *ou* se comporter envers qn; **what a way to b.!** quelles manières!; **to know how to b.** savoir vivre; **I'll**

teach him how to b.! je lui apprendrai la politesse!; **b. yourself!** (*to husband etc*) tiens-toi comme il faut *ou* bien!; (*to child*) sois sage!, tiens-toi comme il faut *ou* bien! **(b) to b. (itself)** (*of machine, clock etc*) marcher, fonctionner; **the television hasn't behaved properly since** la télévision ne marche pas bien depuis

-behaved [bɪ'heɪvd] *suff* **well-b.** sage, qui se conduit *ou* se tient bien; **badly-b.** qui se conduit *ou* se tient mal

behaviour, *US* **behavior** [bɪ'heɪvjər] *n* **(a)** (*of person*) comportement *m* **(towards** envers); (*of pupil*) conduite *f* **(to(wards) sb** avec *ou* envers qn); **good b.** bonne conduite; **to be on one's best b.** se tenir (particulièrement bien); *Psy* **b. pattern** type *m* de comportement **(b)** (*of machine, car*) fonctionnement *m*

behavioural, *US* **behavioral** [bɪ'heɪvjər(ə)l] *adj* de comportement; **b. analysis/study** étude *f* de comportement; **b. pattern** type *m* de comportement; **b. scientist** behavioriste *mf*

behaviourism, *US* **behaviorism** [bɪ'heɪvjərɪz(ə)m] *n Psy* behaviorisme *m*

behaviourist, *US* **behaviorist** [bɪ'heivjərist] *n, adj* behavioriste *mf*

behead [bɪ'hed] *vt* décapiter

beheading [bɪ'hedɪŋ] *n* décapitation *f*

behemoth [bɪ'hi:mɒθ] *n Lit* monstre *m*

behest [bɪ'hest] *n Lit* commandement *m*, ordre *m*; **at whose b.?** sur l'ordre de qui?

behind [bɪ'haɪnd] **1** *adv* derrière; **to attack sb from b.** attaquer qn par derrière; **to stay** *or* **remain b.** (*be at the back*) rester *ou* demeurer en arrière; (*not leave*) ne pas partir; **I'll stay b. and wait for them** je resterai derrière pour les attendre; **the teacher kept him b.** *or* **made him stay b.** le professeur l'a retenu *ou* l'a mis en retenue; **I left my umbrella b.** (*at home*) j'ai oublié mon parapluie à la maison; (*at sb else's home*) j'ai oublié mon parapluie (chez lui/eux/*etc*); **to be b. with** *or* **in one's work** être en retard dans son travail; **to be b. with the rent** être en retard pour payer son loyer; **to get** *or* **fall b. in one's work** prendre du retard dans son travail; *Sp* **they are only three points b.** ils ne sont qu'à trois points; **to follow close b.** suivre de très près

2 *prep* derrière; **he hid b. it** il s'est caché derrière; **look b. you** regardez derrière vous; **I'm right b. you** (*at your back*) je suis juste derrière toi; *Fig* (*I support you*) je suis avec toi; **to walk** *or* **follow close b. sb** suivre qn de près; *Fig* **he has the minister b. him** il a le ministre derrière *ou* avec lui, il est protégé par le ministre; *Fig* **to be b. sth** être derrière qch; **the reasons b. sth** les raisons de qch; **to be b. schedule** avoir du retard; **she's ten minutes b. the leaders** (*in race*) elle a dix minutes de retard sur le peloton de tête; *Fig* **to put sth b. one** ne plus penser à qch, oublier qch (volontairement); **let's put it all b. us** oublions tout cela, n'y pensons plus; **it's all b. me now** tout ça c'est du passé; **b. the times** (*country*) arriéré, attardé; **you're b. the times** (*old-fashioned*) tu n'es pas à la page; (*not aware of latest developments*) tu retardes d'un métro

3 *n F* (*buttocks*) derrière *m*; **to kick sb's b.** botter le derrière à qn; **get up off your b. and find yourself a job!** remue-toi un peu et trouve du boulot!

behindhand [bɪ'haɪndhænd] *adv* en retard; **to be b. with the rent/with one's work** être en retard pour payer le loyer/dans son travail; **I've got awfully b.** j'ai pris énormément de retard

behind-the-scenes *adj* en coulisse

behold [bɪ'həʊld] *vt* (*pt, pp* **beheld** [bɪ'held]) *Lit, Arch* voir; **b.!** voyez!

beholden [bɪ'həʊld(ə)n] *adj Fml* **to be b. to sb** être redevable à qn **(for** de)

beholder [bɪ'həʊldər] *n Prov* **beauty is in the eye of the b.** il n'y a point de laides amours

behove [bɪ'həʊv], *US* **behoove** [bɪ'hu:v] *vt impers Arch* incomber à; **it ill behoves her to criticize** ça lui va mal de critiquer

beige [beɪʒ] *adj, n* (*colour*) beige *m*

Beijing [beɪ'dʒɪŋ] *n* Beijng

being ['bi:ɪŋ] **1** *n* **(a)** (*existence*) existence *f*; **to come into b.** prendre forme, prendre naissance; **the company is still in b.** la société existe toujours; **my entire b. rebels at the idea** tout mon être se révolte à cette idée; **I loathe him with all my b.** je le hais de tout mon être **(b) (human) b.** être *m* humain; **human beings** le genre humain, les (êtres) humains *mpl*; **the Supreme B.** l'Être suprême; **a b. from another planet** un être venu d'une autre planète **2** *adj* **for the time b.** pour le moment

Beirut [beɪ'ru:t] *n* Beyrouth *m*

bejewelled, *US* **bejeweled** [bɪ'dʒu:əld] *adj* paré de bijoux

belabour, *US* **belabor** [bɪ'leɪbər] *vt* (*beat*) rouer de coups; **to b. sb with insults** accabler *ou* abreuver qn d'injures; *Fig* **to b. a point** insister lourdement sur un point

belated [bɪ'leɪtɪd] *adj* (*information, invitation etc*) tardif; (*guest, traveller etc*) en retard; **to wish you a b. happy birthday** pour te souhaiter un bon anniversaire avec un peu de retard

belatedly [bɪ'leɪtɪdlɪ] *adv Fml* en retard, avec du retard, tardivement; **he apologized, somewhat b., for his conduct** il s'est excusé de sa conduite, mais un peu tard

belay [bɪ'leɪ] *vt* **(a)** *Naut* (*line*) amarrer **(b)** (*mountaineer*) assurer

belaying [bɪ'leɪɪŋ] *n* **(a)** *Naut* amarrage *m*; **b. pin** *or* **cleat** cabillot *m*, taquet *m* **(b)** (*in mountaineering*) assurance *f*, assurage *m*

belch[1] [beltʃ] *n* (*of person*) éructation *f*, *F* rot *m*; **he gave a b.** il a fait un rot

belch[2] **1** *vi* éructer, *F* roter; **he belched all through the meal** il a roté pendant tout le repas **2** *vt Fig* **the house was belching smoke and flames** la maison crachait de la fumée et des flammes

▶ **belch forth, belch out 1** *vtsep* (*flames, smoke etc*) vomir, cracher **2** *vi* **smoke and flames were belching out of the house** la maison crachait de la fumée et des flammes

beleaguer [bɪ'li:gər] *vt* (*city*) assiéger; *Fig* critiquer; (*project, ideology etc*) s'attaquer à; **she was beleaguered by problems** elle croulait sous les problèmes

beleaguered [bɪ'li:gəd] *adj* (*city*) assiégé; *Fig* (*project, ideology*) très critiqué; (*government, politician*) assailli de toutes parts; (*parents, look, manner*) accablé

belfry ['belfrɪ] *n* beffroi *m*, clocher *m*

Belgian ['beldʒən] **1** *adj* belge; (*history, ambassador*) de Belgique **2** *n* Belge *mf*

Belgium ['beldʒəm] *n* Belgique *f*

belie [bɪ'laɪ] *vt* (*prp* **belying** [bɪ'laɪɪŋ]) (*image, feelings*) s'opposer à, être en contradiction avec; (*wealth*) être en contradiction avec; **his appearance belies it** il n'en a pas l'air; **his looks b. his age** il ne fait pas son âge

belief [bɪ'li:f] *n* **(a)** conviction *f*; *Rel* croyance *f*; **b. in ghosts** croyance aux revenants; **b. in God** croyance en Dieu; **she did it in the b. that ...** elle l'a fait en étant persuadée que ...; **it is beyond b.** c'est incroyable; **to the best of my b.** autant que je sache; **it is my b. that ...** je suis convaincu que ..., j'ai la conviction que ... **(b)** (*trust*) foi *f*, confiance *f* **(in** on)

believable [bɪ'li:vəb(ə)l] *adj* (*story, account*) croyable, crédible; (*character in novel, person*) crédible; **far from b.** pas du tout crédible

believe [bɪ'li:v] **1** *vt* [①**A46,9,a,iii**] (*person, news, rumour etc*) croire; **I b. that it is true** je crois que c'est vrai; **I b. (that) I am right** je crois avoir raison; **I b. him to be alive** je le crois vivant; **she is believed to be in Paris** on la croit à Paris; **the house was believed to be haunted** on croyait la maison hantée; **he believes himself to have been unfairly treated** il se croit (la) victime d'une injustice; **I b. not** (*I don't think so*) je crois que non; **I b. so** (*I think so*) je crois que oui; **I don't b. a word of it** je n'en crois rien *ou* pas un mot; **I don't know what to b.** je ne sais que croire; **I could scarcely** *or* **hardly b. my eyes** j'en croyais à peine mes yeux; **you can't b. everything you read in the papers** il ne faut pas croire tout ce qu'on lit dans les journaux; **to make sb b. that ...** faire croire à qn que ...; **I can well b. it** je suis prêt à le croire, je veux bien le croire; **b. it or not, he fell for her!** tu le croiras si tu veux, il s'est épris d'elle; **would you b. it!** vous vous rendez compte!; **if he is to be believed** à l'en croire, s'il faut l'en croire; **she's a smart one, b. me!** *or F* **b. you me!** c'est une maligne, crois-moi!; **I wouldn't have believed it of you** je n'aurais pas cru ça de toi; *F* **I don't b. it!** c'est pas vrai!; *F* **don't you b. it!** n'en croyez rien!

2 *vi* **to b. in (one) God** croire en (un seul) Dieu; **to b. in ghosts** croire aux revenants; **I b. in his innocence** je crois en son innocence; **to b. in sth** (*support*) être partisan de qch, être pour qch; **I don't b. in making promises** je ne fais jamais de promesses; **to b. in sb/oneself** croire en qn/soi; **I don't b. in doctors** je ne fais pas confiance aux médecins

believer [bɪ'li:vər] *n Rel* croyant, -ante; **to be a b. in sth** croire à qch; (*supporter of*) être partisan de qch, être pour qch; **I'm a great b. in newborn babies being breast-fed** je suis très en faveur de l'allaitement au sein pour les nouveau-nés

Belisha [bə'li:ʃə] *n Br formerly* **B. beacon** = sphère *f* orange lumineuse (indiquant un passage clouté)

belittle [bɪ'lɪt(ə)l] *vt* (*person*) rabaisser; (*person's merits, efforts*) déprécier, amoindrir; **to b. oneself** (*disparage*) se déprécier; (*demean*) se déconsidérer (*aux yeux de qn, auprès de qn*); **a belittling remark** une remarque désobligeante

bell[1] [bel] *n* **(a)** cloche *f*; (*small*) clochette *f*; (*on door*) sonnette *f*; (*on bicycle*) sonnette, timbre *m*; (*for cattle etc*) clochette, clarine *f*; (*for cat*) grelot *m*; *Br F* **to give sb a b.** (*telephone*) passer un coup de fil à qn; **electric b.** sonnerie *f* (électrique); **set of bells** (*in church*) sonnerie; **great b.** (*of a church*) bourdon *m*; **there's the b.** (*on door*) on sonne; (*in school*) la cloche sonne; **to ring the b.** (*on door*) sonner; (*handbell*) agiter la sonnette; *Fig* **that rings a b.** cela me rappelle *ou* me dit quelque chose; *Naut* **six bells** six coups (de cloche); *MecE* **b. crank lever** levier *m* coudé

(b) (*of flower*) calice *m*; (*of trumpet etc*) pavillon *m*; (*of blast furnace*) cône *m*, cloche *f*

bell[2] *vt Fig* **to b. the cat** attacher le grelot

bell[3] *n* (*cry*) (*of stag*) bramement *m*, brame *m*

bell[4] *vi* (*of stag*) bramer

▶ **bell out** *vi* (*of tube etc*) s'évaser

belladonna [belə'dɒnə] *n Bot, Pharm* belladone *f*

bell-bottomed ['belbɒtəmd] *adj* **b. trousers = bell-bottoms**

bell-bottoms ['belbɒtəmz] *npl* pantalon *m* (à) pattes d'éléphant

bellboy ['belbɔɪ] *n Am* groom *m*

bell buoy *n Naut* bouée *f* à cloche

bell captain *n Am* chef *m* chasseur

belle [bel] *n* beauté *f*; **the b. of the ball** la reine du bal

bellflower ['belflaʊər] *n* campanule *f*

bell heather *n* (*plant*) bruyère *f* cendrée

bellhop ['belhɒp] *n Am F* groom *m*

bellicose ['belɪkəʊs] *adj* belliqueux

bellicosity [belɪ'kɒsɪtɪ] *n* (*of speech, behaviour*) caractère *m* belliqueux, agressivité *f*; (*of person*) humeur *f* belliqueuse

-bellied [-'beliːd] *suff* **round-/swollen-/***etc* **b.** au ventre rond/enflé/*etc*

belligerence [be'lɪdʒərəns] *n* agressivité *f*

belligerent [be'lɪdʒərənt] **1** *adj* **(a)** (*aggressive*) (*person, tone of voice, attitude etc*) agressif, belliqueux **(b)** (*at war*) (*country*) belligérant **2** *n* belligérant, -ante

bell jar *n Ch* cloche *f*

bellow[1] ['beləʊ] *n* (*of bull*) beuglement *m*, mugissement *m*; (*of person*) braillement *m*

bellow[2] **1** *vi* (*of bull*) beugler, mugir; (*of person*) brailler; **to b. with pain** hurler de douleur; **to b. at sb** (*with rage*) brailler dans les oreilles de qn; **I bellowed at him but he was too far away to hear** j'ai crié dans sa direction mais il était trop loin pour m'entendre **2** *vt* (*order*) brailler; *F* (*song*) beugler

▶ **bellow out** *vtsep* = **bellow**[2] **2**

bellowing ['beləʊɪŋ] *n* (*of animal*) beuglement *m*, mugissement *m*; (*of person*) braillement *m*

bellows ['beləʊz] *npl* **(a)** [①**A10,e**] (*for fire*) **(pair of) b.** soufflet *m* **(b)** *Mus* (*of organ*) soufflerie *f*

bell pull *n* (*in room*) cordon *m* de sonnette; (*at door*) sonnette *f* (*qu'on tire*)

bell push *n* bouton *m* de sonnette

bell-ringer *n* carillonneur *m*

bell-ringing *n* (*sound*) carillonnement *m*; (*art*) art *m* du carillonnement

bell-shaped *adj* en forme de cloche

bell tent *n* tente *f* conique

bell tower *n* clocher *m*, campanile *m*

bellwether ['belweðər] *n* (*sheep*) mouton *m* qui mène le troupeau; *Fig* chef *m* de file

belly[1] ['belɪ] *n* **(a)** (*of person*) ventre *m*, *F* bedaine *f*; (*large*) panse *f*; (*of animal*) panse; *Culin* **b. of pork** poitrine *f* de porc; **to have an empty b.** avoir l'estomac vide; **to have a full b.** avoir le ventre plein; **his eyes are bigger than his b.** il a les yeux plus gros que le ventre; **to do a b. flop** (*of diver*) faire un plat; **b. laugh** gros rire *m*; *Fig F* **to go b. up** (*of company*) faire faillite **(b)** (*of plane, ship, jug etc*) ventre *m* **(c)** *Mus* (*of violin etc*) table *f* d'harmonie **(d)** *Naut* (*of sail*) creux *m*, renflement *m*

belly[2] *Naut* **1** *vt* (*of wind*) (*sail*) enfler, gonfler **2** *vi* (*of sail*) faire (le) sac, s'enfler, se gonfler

▶ **belly out** *vtsep, vi* = **belly**[2]

bellyache[1] ['belɪeɪk] *n F* mal *m* au ventre

bellyache[2] *vi F* ronchonner, rouspéter, râler; **he's always bellyaching about something** il faut toujours qu'il rouspète après qch

bellyacher ['belɪeɪkər] *n F* râleur, -euse; **to be a b.** être un râleur

bellyaching ['belɪeɪkɪŋ] *n F* rouspétance *f*, jérémiades *fpl*; **I don't want any b.** je n'accepterai aucune rouspétance; **your constant b. is driving me up the wall** tes jérémiades incessantes me fatiguent

bellybutton ['belɪbʌt(ə)n] *n F* nombril *m*

belly dance *n* danse *f* du ventre

belly dancer *n* danseuse *f* du ventre

belly-flop *vi F* (*of diver*) faire un plat

bellyful ['belɪfʊl] *n Fig F* **to have had a b.** en avoir ras le bol, en avoir marre; **I've had a** *or* **my b. of him** j'en ai marre *ou* plein le dos de lui

bellyland ['belɪlænd] *vi Av* atterrir sur le ventre

belly landing *n Av* atterrissage *m* sur le ventre

belong [bɪ'lɒŋ] *vi* **(a)** (*be property of*) **to b. to** appartenir à; **that book belongs to me** ce livre m'appartient *ou* est à moi; **to b. to the Crown** (*of land etc*) dépendre de la Couronne

(b) (*be connected to*) **what category do they b. to?** à quelle catégorie appartiennent-ils?; **to b. to a society** faire partie d'une société; **do you b. to this club?** êtes-vous membre de ce cercle?; **I b. here** (*come from*) je suis d'ici; (*feel at ease*) je me sens chez moi ici; **to feel that one doesn't b.** ne pas se sentir à sa place

(c) (*usually go*) **this is where the spoons b.** c'est ici qu'on range les cuillers; **where does this book b.?** où va *ou* se range ce livre?; **things that b. together** choses qui vont ensemble; **to put things back where they b.** remettre les choses à leur place

belonging [bɪ'lɒŋɪŋ] *n* **to feel** *or* **have a sense of b.** se sentir chez soi *ou* à sa place

belongings [bɪ'lɒŋɪŋz] *npl* affaires *fpl*

beloved **1** *adj* [bɪ'lʌvd] bien-aimé; **b. by all** aimé de tous; **the b. wife of ...** l'épouse bien-aimée de ... **2** *n* [bɪ'lʌvɪd] bien-aimé, -ée, chéri, -ie; **my b.** mon bien-aimé, ma bien-aimée; *Rel* **dearly b.** mes bien chers frères

below [bɪ'ləʊ] **1** *adv* en bas, (en-)dessous; **voices from b.** des voix qui venaient d'en bas; **the tenants (of the flat) b.** les locataires du dessous; **on the floor b.** à l'étage d'en-dessous; *F* **it's ten (degrees) b.** il fait moins dix; **here b.** (*on earth*) ici-bas; *Naut* **all hands b.!** tout le monde en bas!; **the passage quoted b.** (*immediately afterwards*) le passage cité ci-dessous; (*further on*) le passage cité plus loin *ou* ci-après

2 *prep* au-dessous de; **b. the knee** au-dessous du genou; **b. (the) average** au-dessous de la moyenne; **people b. the age of 65** les gens âgés de moins de 65 ans; *F* **I'm feeling a bit b. par** je ne suis pas dans mon assiette; **temperature b. normal** température inférieure à la normale; **ten degrees b. zero** dix degrés au-dessous de zéro; **b. sea level** au-dessous du niveau de la mer; **b. the surface** sous la surface; **b. the bridge** (*downstream*) en aval du pont

below-the-line *adj Mktg* **b. advertising** publicité *f* directe; **b. costs** coûts *mpl* hors-médias; **b. promotion** publicité *f* hors-médias

belt[1] [belt] *n* **(a)** (*round waist*) ceinture *f*; *Mil* ceinturon *m*; **to tighten one's b.** serrer sa ceinture; *Fig* se serrer la ceinture; *F* **I'm a b. and braces type** (*very cautious*) je suis du genre à penser que deux précautions valent mieux qu'une; **to be a brown/black b.** (*in judo*) être ceinture marron/noire; *Boxing* **to hold the b.** être le champion; *Boxing* **a blow beneath the b.** un coup bas; *Fig* **to hit sb beneath** *or* **below the b.** donner à qn un coup en traître *ou* un coup bas; **that was a bit beneath** *or* **below the b.** (*of joke, remark*) c'était un coup bas; *Fig* **to have sth under one's b.** (*move, project*) en avoir fini avec qch; (*driving licence, degree*) avoir qch en poche; **once you've got a few years' experience under your b.** une fois que tu as quelques années d'expérience à ton actif; **b. buckle** boucle *f* de ceinture

(b) *Tech* courroie *f* (*de transmission*); **b. drive** transmission *f* par courroie; **b. driven** entraîné par courroie

(c) (*area*) région *f*, zone *f*

(d) *F* (*blow*) (*with hand*) gifle *f*; (*with bat, stick*) coup *m*; **he gave the ball a terrific b.** il a tapé un grand coup dans la balle

belt[2] **1** *vt F* (*hit with belt*) donner des coups de ceinture à; (*hit with hand*) gifler; (*hit with bat, stick*) (*ball*) frapper dans, taper dans; (*person*) frapper; **less of your cheek or I'll b. you one!** ne sois pas insolent ou je t'en mets une! **2** *vi F* **to b. down the stairs** descendre l'escalier quatre à quatre; **she belted out of the house** elle est sortie de la maison en courant

▶ **belt along** *vi F* courir/aller/conduire à toute vitesse

▶ **belt out** *vtsep F* (*order etc*) vociférer, gueuler; (*song*) gueuler, brailler

▶ **belt up** *vi* **(a)** *Br Sl* se taire; **b. up!** ta gueule! **(b)** *Aut F* (*put on seatbelt*) attacher sa ceinture de sécurité

belt conveyor *n Constr etc* transporteur *m* à courroie *ou* à ruban *ou* à bande

belted ['beltɪd] *adj* ceinturé; **b. tyre** pneu *m* à ceinture

belting ['beltɪŋ] *n* **(a)** *Tech* (*belts*) courroie(s) *f(pl)*; (*material*) matériau *m* à courroies **(b)** *F* **to give sb a (good) b.** (*spanking*) donner une bonne fessée à qn; (*beating-up*) donner une bonne raclée à qn; (*in match, competition etc*) mettre la pâtée à qn

beltway [ˈbeltweɪ] *n US* périphérique *m*
belvedere [ˈbelvɪdɪər] *n Archit* belvédère *m*
bemoan [bɪˈməʊn] *vt* pleurer; **to b. the loss of sth** se lamenter de *ou* pleurer la perte de qch; **to b. one's fate** pleurer sur son sort; **she was bemoaning the fact that they had no money** elle se lamentait de ce qu'ils n'avaient pas d'argent
bemuse [bɪˈmjuːz] *vt Lit* (*confuse*) rendre perplexe, dérouter
bemused [bɪˈmjuːzd] *adj* perplexe
ben [ben] *n Scot Geog* sommet *m*, mont *m*; **B. Nevis** le Ben Nevis
bench [bentʃ] *n* (**a**) (*seat*) (*in park, garden*) banc *m*; (*upholstered*) banquette *f*; (*in lecture hall, amphitheatre*) gradin *m*; *Sp* banc (*pour les joueurs qui ne sont pas sur le terrain*); *Jur* (*for judge, magistrates*) siège *m*; *Aut* **b. seat** banquette; *Br Jur* **the B.** (*magistrates*) la magistrature; (*court*) la Cour; **to be on the B.** (*as a magistrate*) être magistrat; (*as a judge*) siéger au tribunal; **to retire from the B.** prendre sa retraite; *Sp* **to be on the b.** (*waiting to play*) être remplaçant; (*as punishment*) avoir été renvoyé du terrain
(**b**) *Tech* (*work table*) (*for carpenter*) établi *m*; (*for fitter*) banc *m*, marbre *m*; (*in greenhouse*) tablette *f*; **b. test** essai *m* au banc; *Ch etc* **laboratory b.** paillasse *f*
benchmark [ˈbentʃmɑːk] *n Comptr, Fig* référence *f*; (*in surveying*) repère *m* (de nivellement); **b. market** marché *m* de référence; *Comptr* **b. programme** programme *m* d'évaluation des performances; *Can Admin* **b. position** poste-repère *m*; **b. test** test *m* de performance
benchtest[1] [ˈbentʃtest] *n* banc *m* d'essai
benchtest[2] *vt* faire passer au banc d'essai
bend[1] [bend] *n Naut* (*knot*) nœud *m*
bend[2] *n* (**a**) (*curve*) courbure *f*; (*in road*) tournant *m*, virage *m*; (*in pipe*) coude *m*; (*in river*) courbe *f*; **bends for 3 kilometres** (*road sign*) virages sur 3 kilomètres; *Aut* **to take a b. at speed** prendre un virage à toute vitesse; *F* **to be round the b.** être fou *ou* cinglé; *F* **you're driving me** *or* **sending me round the b.** tu me rends dingue *ou* fou (**b**) *Med F* **the bends** maladie *f* des caissons; **to have the bends** souffrir de la maladie des caissons (**c**) (*action*) (*of body*) inclination *f*
bend[3] (*pt* **bent** [bent]; *pp* **bent**, *Arch* **bended**) **1** *vt* (*knee, arm etc*) plier; (*head*) baisser; (*of age*) (*the back*) courber; (*pipe, rail*) cambrer, cintrer; (*wood, iron*) (*into a specific shape*) cambrer, arquer; (*metal*) (*of strong man in circus*) tordre; (*bow, spring*) tendre, bander; *Phys* (*light*) réfracter; (*ray*) infléchir; *Fig* (*law, rule etc*) faire une entorse à; **to b. one's head over a book** pencher la tête sur un livre; **to b. sb to one's will** plier qn à sa volonté; **to b. a rod/a key** (**out of shape**) tordre une barre de fer/une clef; *Br F* **to b. the elbow** (*drink*) lever le coude; *Br F* **to b. sb's ear** casser les oreilles à qn; **thanks for letting me b. your ear** merci de m'avoir laissé m'épancher
2 *vi* (*of rod, branch etc*) plier, ployer; (*of branch, person*) se courber; (*of person*) se pencher; (*of road, river*) tourner; **to b. under the strain** (*of wood, iron*) arquer; (*of steel plate etc*) s'envoiler; (*of rod, wheel*) se voiler; **old man bending under a heavy load** vieillard courbé sous un pesant fardeau; *Fig* **to b.** (**to pressure**) céder (à la pression); *Fig Lit* **to b. to sb's will** se plier à la volonté de qn; *Fig* **to b. before the wind** plier
▶ **bend back 1** *vtsep* recourber; (*to original straight position*) détordre; (*to original bent position*) replier; (*light*) infléchir **2** *vi* (*of person*) se pencher en arrière; (*of light*) s'infléchir
▶ **bend down 1** *vtsep* (*branch*) courber, ployer; **the tree was bent down by the weight of the fruit** l'arbre penchait sous le poids des fruits **2** *vi* (*of person*) se courber, se baisser
▶ **bend forward** *vi* se pencher en avant
▶ **bend over 1** *vi* (*of person*) se pencher; *Fig* **to b. over backwards** se mettre en quatre (**to do** pour faire) **2** *vipo* **to b. over sb** se pencher sur qn **3** *vtsep* (*steel plate etc*) plier
bended [ˈbendɪd] *adj Lit* **on one's b. knees, on b. knee** (*ask for sth*) à genoux; **to go down on b. knee** *or* **knees** (*kneel down*) se mettre à genoux, s'agenouiller; *Fig* **to go down on one's b. knees to sb** (*beg*) supplier qn
bender [ˈbendər] *n Sl* (*drinking session*) soûlerie *f*; **to go on a b.** se soûler
bending [ˈbendɪŋ] *n* **too much b. is bad for the back** il est mauvais pour le dos de se pencher trop souvent; *Tech* **b. moment** moment *m* de flexion, moment fléchissant; *Tech* **b. strength** résistance *f* à la flexion; *Tech* **b. test** essai *m ou* épreuve *f* de ployage *ou* de flexion
beneath [bɪˈniːθ] **1** *adv* dessous, au-dessous; **from b.** de dessous **2** *prep* sous; **to marry b. one** faire une mésalliance; **she thinks everybody's b. her** elle s'imagine que tout le monde lui est inférieur; **b. contempt** parfaitement méprisable; **he would consider it b. him to complain** il considère qu'il serait indigne de lui de se plaindre; **to be b. sb's dignity** (*of behaviour etc*) ne pas être digne de qn; **the plank gave way b. me** la planche a cédé sous mon poids
Benedictine [benɪˈdɪktɪn] **1** *n* (**a**) *Rel* Bénédictin, -ine (**b**) (*also* [-tiːn]) (*liqueur*) Bénédictine *f* **2** *adj Rel* bénédictin
benediction [benɪˈdɪkʃən] *n* bénédiction *f*; (*at meals*) bénédicité *m*
benefaction [benɪˈfækʃən, ˈbenɪ-] *n Lit* (**a**) (*kindness*) bienfaisance *f* (**b**) (*act of kindness*) bienfait *m*; (*donation*) don *m* charitable
benefactor, -tress [ˈbenɪfæktər, -trɪs] *n* bienfaiteur, -trice
benefice [ˈbenɪfɪs] *n Rel, Hist* bénéfice *m*
beneficence [bɪˈnefɪs(ə)ns] *n Lit* (**a**) (*kindness*) bienfaisance *f* (**b**) (*act of charity*) œuvre *f* de bienfaisance
beneficent [bɪˈnefɪsənt] *adj Lit* bienfaisant
beneficial [benɪˈfɪʃəl] *adj* (**a**) (*doing good*) bon, bénéfique; **b. to** (*the health, business*) bon pour (**b**) *Jur* **b. owner** *or* **occupant** usufruitier, -ière
beneficiary [benɪˈfɪʃərɪ] *adj, n Jur* bénéficiaire *mf*, ayant droit *m*, *pl* ayants droit; (*of family allowance*) allocataire *mf*; *Fig* **the main beneficiaries of the new law will be working mothers** ce sont les mères qui travaillent qui bénéficieront le plus de la nouvelle loi
benefit[1] [ˈbenɪfɪt] *n* (**a**) (*advantage*) avantage *m*; **to derive b. from sth** profiter de qch, tirer profit de qch; **in order to derive full b. from the medicine** de façon à tirer tout le profit de ce médicament; **it's no b. to me, I get** *or* **gain no b. from it** je n'en retire aucun avantage; **a performance for the b. of the blind** une représentation au profit des aveugles; **for the b. of the others** à l'intention des autres; **that remark was for my b.** cette remarque était à mon intention *ou* m'était destinée; **I'm not doing this for my own b.** *or F* **for the b. of my health** je ne fais pas ça pour moi; **for the b. of one's health** dans l'intérêt de sa santé; **to give sb the b. of the doubt** accorder à qn le bénéfice du doute; **she hasn't had the b. of a university education** elle n'a pas eu la chance d'aller à l'université; **to offer sb the b. of one's experience** faire profiter qn de son expérience; **b. in kind** avantage en nature
(**b**) *Th* **b.** (**performance**) représentation *f* de bienfaisance; *Sp* **a b. match to raise money for the victims' families** un match organisé au bénéfice des familles des victimes
(**c**) *Br Admin* (*allowance*) indemnité *f*, allocation *f*; **social security benefits** prestations *fpl* sociales; **to be on b.** toucher l'aide sociale; **unemployment b.** allocation de chômage; **sickness b.** indemnité de maladie; **maternity b.** allocation de maternité; **housing b.** allocation logement; **child b.** = allocations familiales
benefit[2] **1** *vt* être avantageux à, profiter à; **a steady exchange rate benefits trade** un change stable est avantageux pour le commerce *ou* favorise le commerce; **who(m) does it b.?** qui en bénéficie?; **it will b. mankind** c'est l'humanité toute entière qui en profitera; **to b. the cause of disarmament** favoriser le désarmement **2** *vi* **to b. by** *or* **from sth** bénéficier de qch, profiter de qch, tirer avantage de qch; **you will b. by a holiday** un congé vous fera du bien; **who benefits most from his death?** à qui sa mort profite-t-elle le plus?; **to b. from a rise in prices** profiter *ou* tirer profit d'une hausse des prix
Benelux [ˈbenɪlʌks] *n Pol* Bénélux *m*; **the B. countries** les pays *mpl* du Bénélux
benevolence [bɪˈnevələns] *n* (**a**) (*kindness*) bienveillance *f*, bonté *f* (**b**) (*charitableness*) bienfaisance *f*
benevolent [bɪˈnevələnt] *adj* (**a**) (*kindly disposed*) bienveillant (**to** envers); *Hist* **b. despotism** despotisme *m* éclairé (**b**) (*charitable*) bienfaisant, charitable (**to** envers)
benevolent fund *n* fonds *m* de secours
benevolently [bɪˈnevələntlɪ] *adv* avec bienveillance
benevolent society *n* association *f* de bienfaisance; *Fig Hum* **I'm not a b.** je ne suis pas l'Armée du Salut
B. Eng *abbr* **Bachelor of Engineering**
Bengal [beŋˈgɔːl] *n* Bengale *m*
Bengali [beŋˈgɔːlɪ], **Bengalese** [beŋgəˈliːz] **1** *adj* bengali, bengalais **2** *n* (**a**) Bengali *mf inv*, Bengalais, -aise (**b**) *Ling* bengali *m*
benighted [bɪˈnaɪtɪd] *adj Lit* (*country etc*) plongé dans (les ténèbres de) l'ignorance
benign [bɪˈnaɪn] *adj* (*smile, look etc*) bienveillant; (*climate*) doux, *f* douce; *Med* **b. tumour** tumeur *f* bénigne
Benjamin [ˈbendʒəmɪn] *n Arch* **the B. of the family** le benjamin de la famille
benny [ˈbenɪ] *n Sl* (*drug*) (comprimé *m* de) benzédrine *f*
bent[1] [bent] *n* (*aptitude*) disposition *f* (**for** pour); **to have a natural b. for music** avoir des dispositions naturelles pour la musique; **she has a scientific b.** elle a l'esprit scientifique;

to follow one's b. (*inclination*) suivre son penchant *ou* son inclination
bent[2] *pt, pp see* **bend**[3]
bent[3] *adj* **(a)** (*branch*) courbé, plié; (*axle, lever*) coudé; (*back*) voûté; (*out of shape*) (*aerial, coathanger*) tordu; **to become b.** (*with age*) se voûter **(b)** *Sl* (*corrupt*) (*politician, police officer etc*) malhonnête, pourri **(c)** *Old-fashioned Sl* (*homosexual*) homosexuel, inverti **(d)** (*determined*) déterminé, résolu (**(up)on doing sth** à faire qch); **he is b. on seeing me** il veut absolument me voir; **the government is b. on eliminating dissent** le gouvernement est résolu à éliminer toute opposition
bentwood ['bentwʊd] *adj* (*chair*) en bois courbé
benumbed [bɪ'nʌmd] *adj Fml* engourdi
benzene ['benzi:n] *n Ch* benzène *m*
benzin(e) ['benzi:n, ben'zi:n] *n Ch, Ind* benzine *f*
benzodiazepine [benzəʊdaɪ'eɪzəpi:n] *n Pharm* benzodiazépine *f*
benzol ['benzɒl] *n Ch* benzol *m*
bequeath [bɪ'kwi:ð] *vt* léguer (**to** à)
bequest [bɪ'kwest] *n* legs *m*; **it was a b. from my grandmother** je l'ai hérité de ma grand-mère; **she made a b. of £2 000 to her favourite charity** elle a légué 2 000 livres à l'œuvre de bienfaisance qu'elle préférait
berate [bɪ'reɪt] *vt Fml* (*person*) réprimander; (*plan, intention*) condamner
Berber ['bɜ:bər] **1** *adj* berbère **2** *n* **(a)** Berbère *mf* **(b)** *Ling* berbère *m*
bereave [bɪ'ri:v] *vt* (*pt, pp usu* **bereft** [bɪ'reft]) **he has been bereaved** (*by a death*) il est en deuil
bereaved [bɪ'ri:vd] **1** *adj* en deuil; (*family, parents etc*) du défunt, de la défunte; **the entire nation feels b.** le pays tout entier est en deuil **2** *npl* **the b.** la famille du défunt/de la défunte
bereavement [bɪ'ri:vmənt] *n* deuil *m*; **owing to a recent b.** en raison d'un deuil récent; **she has suffered a b.** elle a été affligée par un deuil
bereft [bɪ'reft] *adj Fml* **to be b. of sth** être privé de qch; **b. of all hope** ayant perdu tout espoir; **to leave sb b. of speech** rendre qn muet; **she collapsed into a chair, her face b. of colour** elle s'effondra sur une chaise, le visage livide
beret ['bereɪ, 'berɪ] *n* béret *m*; *Mil* **the red berets** les bérets rouges, les parachutistes *mpl*
berg [bɜ:g] *n F* (*iceberg*) iceberg *m*
bergamot ['bɜ:gəmɒt] *n* (*plant*) bergamote *f*
beriberi ['berɪ'berɪ] *n Med* béribéri *m*
berk [bɜ:k] *n Br Sl* andouille *f*, con *m*, *f* conne; **to make a complete b. of oneself** se conduire comme une andouille *ou* un con; **to feel a right b.** se sentir con *ou f* conne
Berks [bɑ:ks] *abbr* **Berkshire**
Berlin [bɜ:'lɪn] *n* Berlin *m*; *Hist* **East/West B.** Berlin Est/Ouest; **the B. airlift** le pont aérien de Berlin; **the B. Wall** le mur de Berlin
Berliner [bɜ:'lɪnər] *n* Berlinois, -oise
berm(e) [bɜ:m] *n* **(a)** (*fortification*) berme *f* **(b)** (*path*) berme *f*, banquette *f*
Bermuda [bə'mju:də] *n* les Bermudes *fpl*; **B. Plan** tarif *m* chambre avec petit déjeuner anglais; *Naut* **B. rig** gréement *m* Marconi; **B. shorts**, *F* **bermudas** bermuda *m*; **B. Triangle** triangle *m* des Bermudes
Bern(e) [bɜ:n] *n* Berne *f*
Bernese [bɜ:'ni:z, 'bɜ:-] **1** *adj* bernois; **the B. Alps** l'Oberland bernois *m* **2** *n* Bernois, -oise
berried ['berɪd] *adj* **(a)** *Bot* à baies, couvert de baies **(b)** *Zool* (*lobster etc*) œuvé
berry[1] ['berɪ] *n* **(a)** (*fruit*) baie *f*; **to go b. picking** aller cueillir des baies **(b)** *Zool* (*of crustacean*) œuf *m*; **lobster in b.** homard œuvé
berry[2] *vi* **to go berrying** aller cueillir des baies
berserk [bə'zɜ:k] *adj F* fou furieux, *f* folle furieuse; **to go b.** devenir fou furieux; **to send sb b.** rendre qn fou furieux
berth[1] [bɜ:θ] *n* **(a)** *Naut, Rail* couchette *f*; *F* **I can give you a b. for the night** tu peux pieuter ici cette nuit si tu veux **(b)** *Naut* (*for ship*) poste *m* à quai; **she left her b. this morning** il est sorti du quai ce matin; **(anchoring) b.** poste *m* de mouillage *ou* d'amarrage **(c)** (*distance*) *Naut* **to give a ship a wide b.** éviter *ou* parer un navire, passer au large d'un navire; *Fig* **to give sb a wide b.** éviter qn **(d)** *F* (*job*) boulot *m*; **to find a soft** *or* **an easy b.** trouver un emploi pépère
berth[2] **1** *vt* (*ship*) (*of helmsman*) faire accoster le long du quai, amener *ou* amarrer à quai; (*of port official*) donner *ou* assigner un poste à; **where is she berthed?** à quel quai se trouve-t-il? **2** *vi* **(a)** (*of ship*) aborder à quai, se ranger à quai; **when do we b.?** quand accostons-nous? **(b) to b. forward/aft** (*of passengers, crew*) coucher à l'avant/à l'arrière
berthing ['bɜ:θɪŋ] *n* (*of ship*) abordage *m* à quai
beryl ['berɪl] *n Miner* béryl *m*
beryllium [be'rɪlɪəm] *n Ch* béryllium *m*
beseech [bɪ'si:tʃ] *vt* (*pt, pp* **besought** [bɪ'sɔ:t]) *Lit* implorer, supplier, conjurer (**sb to do sth** qn de faire qch); **help me, I b. you** aidez-moi, je vous en supplie *ou* conjure
beseeching [bɪ'si:tʃɪŋ] *adj* (*air, ton*) suppliant
beset [bɪ'set] (*pt, pp* **beset**; *prp* **besetting**) *vt Fml usu passive* (*of misfortunes, temptations etc*) assaillir; **beset with dangers/difficulties** environné *ou* entouré de dangers/de difficultés; **to be beset by doubts** être assailli de doutes *ou* par le doute
besetting [bɪ'setɪŋ] *adj attrib Fml* (*idea, thought etc*) obsédant; **it's his b. sin** c'est son péché mignon
beside [bɪ'saɪd] *prep* **(a)** (*place*) (*person*) à côté de, auprès de; (*object*) à côté de; **seated b. me** assis à côté de *ou* auprès de moi, assis à mes côtés; **a house b. the lake** une maison au bord du lac
(b) (*comparison*) à côté de; **b. him everyone else appears slow** à côté de lui, tous les autres paraissent lents; **I feel very underdressed b. you** par rapport à toi *ou* à côté de toi, je ne me sens pas assez habillée
(c) (*in addition to*) en dehors de; **other people b. ourselves** d'autres (personnes) que nous
(d) (*wide of*) **that is b. the point** *or* **question** cela n'a rien à voir (avec l'affaire en question); **whether you arrrived or not is b. the point** que tu sois arrivé ou non n'est pas le problème; **b. oneself (with joy/anger)** fou de joie/colère; **b. oneself with enthusiasm** débordant d'enthousiasme
besides [bɪ'saɪdz] **1** *adv* **(a)** (*in addition*) en outre, en plus; **many more b.** encore bien d'autres; **and many more people b.** et bien d'autres gens encore
(b) (*moreover*) d'ailleurs, du reste, (et) en outre
2 *prep* (*in addition to*) excepté, hormis; **ten of us, b. myself** (nous sommes/serons/*etc*) dix, sans me compter; **there are others b. him** il y en a d'autres que lui; **have you got it in anything b. black?** est-ce que vous l'avez dans d'autres couleurs qu'en noir?; **what else can you do b. type?** que savez-vous faire en dehors de *ou* à part taper à la machine?; **b. watching television, I did nothing all night** à part regarder la télévision, je n'ai rien fait de la soirée; **b. his grandmother, he was the only one with blue eyes** à part sa grand-mère, il était le seul de la famille à avoir les yeux bleus; **b. being an excellent singer, she also plays the violin** c'est une excellente chanteuse, et en plus elle joue du violon; **b. which, he was unwell** sans compter qu'il était indisposé
besiege [bɪ'si:dʒ] *vt* (*city*) assiéger; *Fig* (*building*) faire le siège de; (*person*) assaillir; **we have been besieged with requests to ...** nous avons été assaillis de demandes de ...; **the public besieged the tourist office with complaints** l'office du tourisme fut envahi par les plaintes du public
besmirch [bɪ'smɜ:tʃ] *vt Lit* salir, tacher; *Fig* (*sb's memory*) salir, entacher, ternir
besom ['bi:zəm] *n* **(a)** (*broom*) balai *m* (de jonc) **(b)** *Pej* (*woman*) bonne femme *f*
besotted [bɪ'sɒtɪd] *adj* **(a)** (*in love*) entiché (**with sb** de qn); **to be b. with sth** (*car, computer etc*) adorer qch; **she was b. with the idea of going to Mexico** l'idée d'aller au Mexique l'obsédait **(b)** (*with drink*) abruti
bespatter [bɪ'spætər] *vt* éclabousser; **bespattered with mud** tout couvert de boue
bespeak [bɪ'spi:k] *vt Fml* (*be sign of*) témoigner de
bespectacled [bɪ'spektək(ə)ld] *adj* qui porte des lunettes, à lunettes
bespoke [bɪ'spəʊk] *adj usu attrib esp Br* (*clothing*) (fait) sur mesure; **b. tailor/shoemaker** tailleur *m*/cordonnier *m* à façon
besprinkle [bɪ'sprɪŋk(ə)l] *vt* saupoudrer (**with** de)
Bess [bes] *n* (*dimin of* **Elizabeth**) *Eng Hist* **Good Queen B.** = la reine Elisabeth Ière d'Angleterre
best[1] [best] **1** *adj* (*superl of* **good**) **(a)** meilleur; **the b. man on earth** le meilleur homme du monde; **may the b. man win** que le meilleur gagne; **my b. dress** ma plus belle robe; **to be dressed in one's b. clothes** être sur son trente et un; **to be on one's b. behaviour** bien se conduire; **I am acting in your b. interests** j'agis au mieux de vos intérêts; **with the b. will in the world** avec la meilleure volonté du monde; **the b. part of the year** (*most of*) la plus grande partie de l'année; **I waited for the b. part of an hour** j'ai attendu presque une heure; **I'm b. at biology** (*it's my strongest subject*) la biologie, c'est mon point fort; (*better than others*) je suis le meilleur en biologie; **it is b. to ...** le mieux, c'est de ...; **the b. thing you can do** *or* **the b. course to take is to ...** ce qu'il y a de mieux à faire, c'est de ...; **it would be b. to ..., the b. plan**

would be to ... le mieux serait de ...; **to know what is b. for sb** savoir ce qui va *ou* convient le mieux à qn; **I only want what's b. for you** je ne veux que ce qu'il y a de mieux pour toi; **I thought it (would be) b. to stay** j'ai pensé qu'il valait mieux rester; *Br Culin* **b. end** (*of lamb*) = filet *m*; **b. end of neck** carré *m*; **the b. years of one's life** les meilleures années de sa vie; **to put one's b. foot forward** (*do one's best*) faire de son mieux; (*make an effort*) faire un petit effort; *F Hum* **it's the b. thing since sliced bread** c'est ce qu'on a inventé de mieux depuis le fil à couper le beurre

(**b**) **at b.** au mieux; **at b. he will get 2,000 votes** au mieux, il aura 2 000 voix; **your article is at b. unhelpful, at worst obstructive** au mieux, votre article n'apporte rien d'utile, au pire il constitue un obstacle

2 *n* (**a**) (*maximum, peak*) le meilleur, la meilleure; **this is the b. there is** voici ce qu'il y a de meilleur *ou* de mieux; **I am in the b. of health** je me porte à merveille, je suis en excellente santé; **to do sth to the b. of one's ability** faire qch de son mieux; **to the b. of my belief/knowledge** à ce que je crois/autant que je sache; **the b. of it is that ...** le plus beau de l'affaire, c'est que ...; **to have** *or* **get the b. of both worlds** gagner sur les deux tableaux; **he can sing with the b. (of them)** il chante comme un dieu *ou* divinement; **she's up there with the b. of them** elle peut rivaliser avec les meilleurs; **we are the b. of friends** nous sommes les meilleurs amis du monde; **he was undemonstrative at the b. of times** même dans ses meilleurs moments, il était peu démonstratif; **let's make it the b. of five** le premier qui remporte trois jeux *ou* parties sur cinq a gagné; *Br Sch Old-fashioned F* **six of the b.** une correction magistrale; **to be dressed in one's Sunday b.** porter ses habits du dimanche; **I keep it for b.** (*of dress, suit etc*) je le garde pour des occasions spéciales

(**b**) (*good wishes*) *F* **the b. of luck!** bonne chance!; *F* **all the b.** (*spoken*) toutes mes amitiés; (*written*) amitiés; *Am* **my brother sends his b.** mon frère vous dit bien des choses *ou* vous prie d'accepter toutes ses amitiés

(**c**) (*optimum performance*) **I did my b.** j'ai fait de mon mieux; **your b. wasn't good enough** tu as peut-être fait de ton mieux, mais ça n'a pas suffi; **to do one's b.** *or* **the b. one can to ...** faire de son mieux pour ...; **I did my b. to comfort her** je l'ai consolée du mieux que j'ai pu, j'ai fait de mon mieux pour la consoler; **he did his b. to smile** il s'efforça de sourire; **I am doing my (level) b.** *or* **the b. I can for you** je fais tout ce que je peux pour vous; **that's the b. I can offer** c'est ce que je peux vous offrir de mieux; **is that the b. you can do?** vous ne pouvez pas faire mieux?; **do the b. you can** (*given the circumstances*) arrangez-vous; (*in exam*) faites de votre mieux; **to bring out the b. in people** faire ressortir les bons côtés des gens; **to get the b. out of sb** tirer ce que qn a de mieux à donner; **to get the b. out of sth** tirer le meilleur parti de qch

(**d**) (*appearance, condition*) **to look one's b.** être *ou* paraître à son avantage; **to be at one's b.** être en grande forme *ou* au meilleur de sa forme; **I am not at my b. in the morning** je ne suis pas au mieux de ma forme le matin; **you haven't seen the house at its b.** tu n'as pas vu la maison sous son meilleur jour; **that is Dickens at his b.** voilà du meilleur Dickens

(**e**) (*advantage*) **to get** *or* **have the b. of it** *or* **of the bargain** faire une bonne affaire; **to have the b. of an argument** l'emporter dans une discussion; **to get the b. of sb in an argument** l'emporter sur qn dans une discussion

(**f**) (*compromise*) **to make the b. of sth** s'accommoder de qch; **you'll just have to make the b. of it** il faudra t'y faire; **to make the b. of things** *or* **a bad job** faire avec ce qu'on a, faire contre mauvaise fortune bon cœur

(**g**) (*result, outcome*) **to act for the b.** agir pour le mieux; **I did it for the b.** j'ai fait pour le mieux; **it's all for the b.** tout est pour le mieux; **I meant it for the b.** cela partait d'une bonne intention; **to hope for the b.** ne pas désespérer, avoir bon espoir; **we must hope for the b.** il faut être optimiste; **only the b. will do** ne fera l'affaire que ce qu'il y a de meilleur; **your parents only want the b. for you** tes parents ne veulent que ce qu'il y a de mieux pour toi

3 *adv* [①**A40**, **C**,**1**,**a**] (*superl of* **well**) **he does it b.** c'est lui qui le fait le mieux; **I comforted her as b. I could** je la consolai de mon mieux; **I got down as b. I could** je suis descendu comme j'ai pu; **you know b.** c'est vous (qui êtes) le mieux placé pour en juger; **mother knows b.** maman a raison; **he's b. able to decide** il est le plus à même de décider; **do as you think b.** faites comme bon vous semble(ra); **he had b. agree** il ferait mieux d'accepter; **the b. dressed man** l'homme le mieux habillé; **the b. kept secret of the war** le secret le mieux gardé de la guerre; **the b. known book** le livre le mieux *ou* le plus connu; **the b.-looking women** les femmes les plus jolies; **to come off b.** (*in argument, discussion*) l'emporter, avoir l'avantage, avoir le dessus; **I like beef b.** je préfère le bœuf; **what goes down b. with the public is ...** ce que le public préfère c'est ...; **these things are b. left to the police** il vaut mieux laisser à la police le soin de s'occuper de ces choses-là

best[2] *vt* (*in argument etc*) l'emporter sur, battre; **she is rarely bested in an argument** il est rare qu'elle soit battue *ou* qu'on l'emporte sur elle dans un débat

best before *adj* **b. date** (*for foodstuffs*) date *f* limite de consommation; (*for batteries, car oil etc*) date limite d'utilisation; **b. 25. 11. 94** à consommer/utiliser avant le 25. 11. 94

best boy *n TV, Cin* aide-électricien *m*, stagiaire *m*

bestial [ˈbestɪəl] *adj* bestial

bestiality [bestɪˈælɪtɪ] *n* bestialité *f*

bestially [ˈbestɪəlɪ] *adv* avec bestialité, bestialement

best-in-class *n Mktg* chef *m* de file

bestir [bɪˈstɜːr] *vt* (**-rr-**) *Fml* **to b. oneself** se démener, s'activer

best man *n* (*at wedding*) garçon *m* d'honneur (*qui garde les alliances, fait un discours etc*)

best-of-breed *n Mktg* nec *m* plus ultra

bestow [bɪˈstəʊ] *vt Lit* accorder, donner (**sth (up)on sb** qch à qn); **to b. a favour on sb** accorder une faveur à qn

bestowal [bɪˈstəʊəl] *n* octroi *m*

bestride [bɪˈstraɪd] *vt Fml* (*pt* **bestrode** [bɪˈstrəʊd]; *pp* **bestridden** [bɪˈstrɪd(ə)n]) (**a**) (*straddle*) être à cheval *ou* à califourchon sur (**b**) (*cross*) (*ditch etc*) enjamber

best seller *n* (*book, record*) best-seller *m*; **to be a b.** (*of book, record*) être un best-seller; (*of author, musician etc*) être un auteur/un musicien/*etc* à succès; **the month's best sellers** les meilleures ventes du mois; **this book is the year's b.** ce livre est le plus gros succès de l'année; **it's been on the b. list for months** il est au palmarès des meilleures ventes depuis des mois

best-selling *adj* (*book, author*) à succès; **this is our b. item** c'est l'article que nous vendons le mieux; **it's been on the b. list for months** il est au palmarès des ventes depuis des mois

bet[1] [bet] *n* pari *m* (**on** sur); **to win/lose a b.** gagner/perdre un pari; **to make** *or* **lay a b.** parier, faire un pari; *F* **your best b. would be to ...** ce que vous avez de mieux à faire, c'est de ...; **I'd take a b. on it** je serais prêt à le parier; *F* **it's my b.** *or* **my b. is that he'll come** je parie qu'il viendra; **all bets are off** les paris sont annulés

bet[2] (*pt* **bet**; *pp* **bet**, *occ* **betted**) **1** *vt* (*sum of money*) parier; **I'll b. you that ...** je vous parierais que ..., parions que ...; **to b. ten to one that ...** parier à dix contre un que ...; *F* **I'll b. you anything (you like) that ...** je te parie tout ce que tu veux que ..., j'en donnerais *ou* mettrais ma tête à couper que ...; *F* **I b. you don't!** chiche (que tu ne le feras pas)!; *F* **b. you I will!** chiche (que je le fais)!; *F* **you b. I will/you did/***etc***!** bien sûr que oui!; **you b. I won't/you didn't/***etc***!** bien sûr que non!

2 *vi* **to b. on a horse** miser sur *ou* jouer un cheval; **to b. with sb** parier avec qn; **to b. on sth** parier sur qch; **I never b. on a sure thing** ce serait un pari perdu d'avance; **do you want to b.?** (*as challenge*) tu paries?; **I b.!** (*expressing disbelief*) sûrement!; **you b.!** bien sûr

beta-blocker [ˈbiːtəblɒkər] *n* (*drug*) bêtabloquant *m*

Betamax cassette [ˈbiːtəmæks] *n* Betamax *f*

beta test[1] [ˈbiːtə] *n Comptr* bêta-test *m*, *pl* bêta-tests, essai *m* approfondi

beta test[2] *vt Comptr* conduire les bêta-tests sur, conduire les essais approfondis sur

beta testing *n Comptr* béta-tests *mpl*

betel [ˈbiːt(ə)l] *n* (*for chewing*), *Bot* bétel *m*; **b. nut** (noix *f* d')arec *m*; **b. (nut) palm** arec, aréquier *m*

Bethlehem [ˈbeθlɪhem, -lɪəm] *n* Bethléem *m ou f*

betide [bɪˈtaɪd] *vt Arch, Lit, Hum* (*used only in*) **woe b. him/you/***etc* malheur *ou* gare à lui/à toi/*etc*

betimes [bɪˈtaɪmz] *adv Arch* de bonne heure

betoken [bɪˈtəʊkən] *vt Fml* dénoter

betray [bɪˈtreɪ] *vt* (**a**) (*be disloyal to*) (*sb, one's country, faith etc*) trahir; **to b. sb's trust** trahir la confiance de qn (**b**) (*disclose*) (*secret, one's ignorance, emotion*) révéler, trahir

betrayal [bɪˈtreɪəl] *n* (**a**) (*disloyalty*) trahison *f* (**of** de); **b. of trust** abus *m* de confiance (**b**) (*disclosure*) (*of one's ignorance, secret etc*) révélation *f*

betrayer [bɪˈtreɪər] *n* (**a**) (*of country*) traître, -esse; **she attacked her b. with a knife** elle attaqua avec un couteau celui/celle qui l'avait trahie (**b**) (*of secret*) dénonciateur, -trice

betrothal [bɪˈtrəʊðəl] *n Fml* fiançailles *fpl*
betrothed [bɪˈtrəʊðd] *adj, n Fml, Arch* fiancé, -ée
better¹ [ˈbetər] **1** *adj* (*comp of* **good**) meilleur; **you will find no b. hotel** vous ne trouverez pas mieux comme hôtel; **he's a b. man than you** (*morally*) il est mieux que vous; **you're b. than I am** (*at maths etc*) vous êtes plus fort que moi; **to be b. at sth than sb** être meilleur à qch que qn; **fruit juice is b. for you than coffee** le jus de fruit est meilleur pour la santé que le café; **he is no b.** (*of patient*) il ne va pas mieux; **he is no b. than his brother** il ne vaut pas mieux que son frère; *Old-fashioned, Hum* **she's no b. than she should be** elle n'a rien d'une sainte; **to appeal to sb's b. feelings** faire appel aux bons sentiments de qn; **I had hoped for b. things** j'avais espéré mieux; **to get b.** (*of patient*) se remettre, se rétablir; (*at doing sth*) faire des progrès; (*of weather, situation etc*) s'améliorer; (*of wine etc*) se bonifier; **the weather is b.** il fait meilleur; **to be b.** (*in health*) aller *ou* se porter mieux; **I hope you will soon be b.** j'espère que vous serez bientôt rétabli; **is your cold any b.?** ton rhume va mieux?; **is your headache any b.?** tu as encore mal à la tête?; **is your foot any b.?** est-ce que tu as moins mal au pied?; **it's b. that way** c'est mieux comme ça; **it's b. to do without it** mieux vaut *ou* il vaut mieux s'en passer; **it would be b. for you to go** (*to that place*) il vaudrait mieux que vous y alliez; **that's b.** voilà qui est mieux; **it would be b. if you called me tomorrow** ce serait *ou* il vaudrait mieux que tu m'appelles demain; **nothing could be b., it couldn't be b.** cela ne peut pas être mieux, c'est on ne peut mieux; **b. luck next time!** tu feras mieux la prochaine fois!; **for the b. part of the day** pendant la plus grande partie de la journée; *Br F* **my b. half** ma (chère) moitié, ma légitime; (*man*) mon homme; *Br* **to go one b. than sb,** *Am* **to go sb one b.** (r)enchérir *ou* surenchérir *ou* faire une surenchère sur qn

2 *n* **(a) I expected b. of you** je m'attendais à mieux de ta part; **one's betters** (*socially*) ses supérieurs; (*more experienced*) ses aînés, ceux qui ont de l'expérience

(b) change for the b. changement *m* en bien; (*in state of health*) amélioration *f*; **he has changed for the b.** (*his character has improved*) il a changé à son avantage; **things are taking a turn for the b.** les choses prennent meilleure tournure; **to get the b. of sb** l'emporter sur qn, prendre le dessus sur qn; **to get the b. of** (*obstacle etc*) surmonter, vaincre; (*one's anger etc*) maîtriser; **his anger/shyness got the b. of him** sa colère/timidité a eu raison de lui; **to be (all) the b. for doing sth** se trouver mieux d'avoir fait qch; **I'm all the b. for seeing you** ça me fait du bien de te voir; **I'd feel all the b. for a holiday** je partirais volontiers en vacances; **you will be all the b. for it** vous vous en trouverez (d'autant) mieux; **I think all the b. of you for it** je vous en estime d'autant plus; **all the b.!** tant mieux!

3 *adv* [①**A40**,**C**,**1**,**a**] (*comp of* **well**) mieux; **so much the b.** tant mieux; **to take sb for b. or for worse** (*in marriage ceremony*) s'unir à qn pour le meilleur comme pour le pire; **b. and b.** de mieux en mieux; **I know that b. than you** je sais cela mieux que vous; **I am feeling b.** je me sens mieux; **you are looking b.** tu as meilleure mine; **to know sb b., to get to know sb b.** mieux connaître qn; **the more I know him the b. I like him** plus je le connais plus je l'aime; **I can understand it all the b. because ...** je le conçois d'autant mieux que ...; **you'd b. stay** il vaut mieux que vous restiez; **I'd b. begin by ...** je ferais bien de commencer par ...; **we'd b. be going back** il est temps de rebrousser chemin; **you'd b. not** il ne vaudrait mieux pas; **hadn't you b. phone first?** est-ce qu'il ne vaudrait pas mieux que tu appelles avant?; **to think b. of it** changer d'opinion, se raviser; **to think b. of sb for doing sth** estimer qn davantage d'avoir *ou* pour avoir fait qch; **that's b. still** (*what you have done*) c'est encore mieux; **b. still you could come tomorrow** mieux encore tu pourrais venir demain, ce qui serait mieux c'est que tu viennes demain; **b. dressed** mieux habillé; **b. known** plus connu; **b. looking** (*more attractive*) plus beau *ou* joli; **he's b. tempered than his brother** il est plus agréable que son frère; **I hope you're a bit b. tempered tomorrow!** j'espère que tu seras de meilleure humeur demain!; **to be b. off** (*wealthier*) être plus aisé; (*well situated*) se trouver dans de meilleures conditions; **he's b. off where he is** il est bien mieux où il est; **you're b. off without him** tu es bien mieux sans lui; **the children of b.-off parents** les enfants dont les parents sont aisés
better² *vt* **(a)** (*improve*) (*sth*) améliorer; **to b. oneself** améliorer sa condition **(b)** (*surpass*) (*exploit, piece of work*) surpasser; *Sp* (*time*) améliorer; **can you b. that?** pouvez-vous faire mieux que cela?
better³ *n* (*person who bets*) parieur, -euse
betterment [ˈbetəmənt] *n Fml* amélioration *f*
betting [ˈbetɪŋ] *n* (*bets*) paris *mpl*; (*price*) cote *f*; **the b. ran high** on a parié gros; **the b. is twenty to one** la cote est à vingt contre un; **the b. is that ...** il y a fort à parier que ...; **what's the b. he doesn't turn up?** combien tu paries qu'il ne viendra pas?; **if I were a b. man** si j'étais homme à parier; **b. book** carnet *m* de paris
betting shop *n* = bureau *m* du pari mutuel
betting slip *n* bulletin *m* de pari
bettor [ˈbetə(r)] *n* = **better³**
between [bɪˈtwiːn] **1** *prep* entre; **a table stood b. him and the door** une table le séparait de la porte; **to stand b. two opponents** s'interposer *ou* intervenir entre deux adversaires; **no one can come b. us** personne ne peut nous séparer; **to be b. life and death** être entre la vie et la mort; **to be something b. ... and ...** tenir autant de ... que de...; **b. eight and nine o'clock** entre huit et neuf heures; **b. now and Monday** d'ici (à) lundi; **b. twenty and thirty** de vingt à trente; **you must choose b. them** il faut choisir entre eux; **to distinguish b. A, B and C** distinguer entre A, B et C; **b. the two/the three of them** à eux deux/trois; **they scored 1 500 b. them** (*of two people*) ils ont marqué 1 500 à eux deux; (*of more than two people*) ils ont marqué 1 500 à eux tous; **we bought it b. us** nous l'avons acheté à nous deux/à nous trois/*etc*; **they shared the loot b. them** ils se sont partagé le butin; **b. ourselves ...** entre nous ...; **this is strictly b. ourselves** *or* **b. you and me** que cela reste entre nous; *F* **b. you (and) me and the gatepost** (soit dit) entre nous; **b. one thing and another ...** d'une chose à l'autre ...; **there's no love lost b. them** ils ne peuvent pas se souffrir *ou* se sentir

2 *adv* **(in) b.** entre les deux; (*in the intervening time*) dans l'intervalle
between-decks [bɪˈtwiːnˈdeks] *Naut* **1** *adv* dans l'entrepont **2** *n* entrepont *m*
betweentime(s) [bɪˈtwiːntaɪm(z)], **betweenwhile(s)** [bɪˈtwiːnwaɪl(z)] *adv* dans l'intervalle, entre-temps
betwixt [bɪˈtwɪkst] *adv F* **it's b. and between** c'est entre les deux
bevel¹ [ˈbev(ə)l] *n* biseau *m*; **b. cut** fausse coupe *f*; **b. edge** bord *m* biseauté *ou* en chanfrein; **b. gear** engrenage *m ou* pignon *m* conique; **b. rule** *or* **square** fausse équerre *f*
bevel² (**-ll-**, *US* **-l-**) **1** *vt* biseauter, chanfreiner, tailler en biseau **2** *vi* aller en biseau
bevelled, *US* **beveled** [ˈbevəld] *adj* (*edge*) biseauté, en biseau, en chanfrein
bevelling, *US* **beveling** [ˈbev(ə)lɪŋ] *n* biseautage *m*, chanfreinage *m*
beverage [ˈbevərɪdʒ] *n* boisson *f*; *Can* **b. room** bar *m*
bevy [ˈbevɪ] *n* **(a)** (*group*) bande *f*, troupe *f*; **b. of girls** bande de filles **(b)** (*of larks, quail*) volée *f*
bewail [bɪˈweɪl] *vt* pleurer; (*one's fate*) se lamenter sur
beware [bɪˈweər] *vi* (*used only in inf and imp*) (*of sb*) se méfier, *Lit* se défier (**of** de); (*of sth*) se méfier (**of** de), prendre garde (**of** à); **b.!** prenez garde!; **b. of pickpockets** attention aux pickpockets; **b. of the dog** (*sign*) ≈ chien méchant; **to b. of doing sth** se garder de faire qch
bewhiskered [bɪˈwɪskəd] *adj Lit, Hum* qui porte des rouflaquettes
bewilder [bɪˈwɪldər] *vt* **(a)** (*puzzle*) désorienter, dérouter **(b)** (*confuse*) ahurir, abasourdir
bewildered [bɪˈwɪldəd] *adj* **(a)** (*puzzled*) désorienté; (*air*) perplexe **(b)** (*confused*) ahuri, abasourdi
bewildering [bɪˈwɪldərɪŋ] *adj* **(a)** (*puzzling*) (*problem, question*) déroutant **(b)** (*confusing*) (*number, variety*) ahurissant
bewilderingly [bɪˈwɪldərɪŋlɪ] *adv* **the problem is b. complex** le problème est d'une complexité déroutante; **even more b., ...** chose encore plus ahurissante, ...; **b. varied/frequent** d'une variété/fréquence ahurissante
bewilderment [bɪˈwɪldəmənt] *n* **(a)** (*puzzlement*) perplexité *f* **(b)** (*confusion*) ahurissement *m*
bewitch [bɪˈwɪtʃ] *vt* ensorceler, jeter un sort sur; *Fig* captiver
bewitching [bɪˈwɪtʃɪŋ] *adj* ravissant
bey [beɪ] *n* bey *m*
beyond [bɪˈjɒnd] **1** *adv* au-delà, par-delà; **the next century and b.** le siècle à venir et au-delà

2 *prep* **(a)** (*of place*) au-delà de, par-delà; **the house is b. the church** la maison est au-delà de *ou* plus loin que l'église; **b. the seas** par-delà les *ou* au-delà des mers

(b) (*of time*) **b. a certain date** passé une certaine date

(c) (*surpassing*) **to live b. one's means** vivre au-dessus de ses moyens; **it's b. me** cela me dépasse, je n'y comprends rien; **it's b. me how they can do it** je ne comprends vraiment pas comment ils peuvent le faire; **circumstances b. our control** circonstances indépendantes de notre volonté; **what you're asking is b. my power** ce que vous demandez me dépasse *ou* dépasse mes attributions; **it's b. my power to save him** je ne peux rien pour le sauver; **b. reach** inaccessible, hors de portée; **b. my reach** hors de ma portée; **I'm b. caring what they do next** peu m'importe ce qu'ils feront ensuite; **frankly, I'm b. caring** franchement, ça m'est complètement égal, *F* franchement, j'en ai rien à fiche; **b. praise** au-dessus de tout éloge; **b. doubt** hors de doute, sans le moindre doute; **b. question** indiscutablement, incontestablement; **to be b. question** être indiscutable *ou* incontestable; **it is a fact b. doubt** *or* **question** c'est un fait avéré; **b. belief** incroyable, à ne pas y croire; *Fml* **b. measure** outre mesure, sans mesure; **that's (going) b. a joke** cela dépasse les bornes (de la simple plaisanterie); **b. repair** irréparable; **she is b. recovery** (*of sick person*) elle est perdue; **the agreement is b. saving** l'accord est à l'eau

(**d**) (*except*) **he has nothing b. his wages** il n'a rien que son salaire

3 *n* **the b.** l'au-delà *m*

bezel [ˈbezəl] *n* (**a**) (*of cut gem*) biseau *m*, bezel *m* (**b**) (*of ring*) chaton *m*

BF [biːˈef] *n Br Sl abbr* **bloody fool**

bhp [biːeɪtʃˈpiː] *n* (*abbr* **brake horsepower**) ch *mpl*, CV *mpl*

bi-annual [baɪˈænjʊəl] *adj* semestriel

bi-annually [baɪˈænjʊəlɪ] *adv* deux fois par an

bias¹ [ˈbaɪəs] *n* (**a**) préjugé *m*, parti *m* pris (**against** contre; **for** pour); **to be without b.** être sans parti pris; **the b. in his remarks was obvious** il était clair à ses remarques qu'il était de parti pris (**b**) *Sewing* biais *m*; **material cut on the b.** étoffe coupée en *ou* de biais; *Aut* **b. tyre** pneu *m* à structure diagonale

bias² *vt* (*pt, pp* **bias(s)ed**) rendre partial, influencer, prévenir (**towards, in favour of** en faveur de; **against** contre)

bias binding *n* (ruban *m* en) biais *m*

bias(s)ed [ˈbaɪəst] *adj* (**a**) (*person*) partial; **b. opinion** opinion *f* préconçue; **you're b. in her favour** tu as un parti pris pour elle (**b**) (*in statistics*) **b. sample** échantillon *m* biaisé *ou* avec erreur systématique; **b. error** erreur *f* systématique (**c**) (*bowling ball*) décentré

bib [bɪb] *n* (**a**) (*child's*) bavette *f*, bavoir *m* (**b**) (*of apron*) bavette *f*; *Old-fashioned F* **in one's best b. and tucker** sur son trente et un

bible [ˈbaɪb(ə)l] *n* bible *f*; **the B.** la Bible; *Fig* **this dictionary is his b.** il fait de ce dictionnaire sa bible; **B. class** groupe *m* de discussion religieuse; **B. stories** histoires *fpl* tirées de la Bible

Bible-bashing, Bible-thumping *n Pej* **B. preacher** évangéliste *m* zélé

Bible Belt *n* = États *mpl* du sud des États-Unis où les ultra-religieux sont très nombreux

biblical [ˈbɪblɪk(ə)l] *adj* biblique

bibliographer [bɪblɪˈɒgrəfər] *n* bibliographe *mf*

bibliographical [bɪblɪəˈgræfɪk(ə)l] *adj* bibliographique

bibliography [bɪblɪˈɒgrəfɪ] *n* bibliographie *f*

bibliophile [ˈbɪblɪəfaɪl] *n* bibliophile *mf*

bibulous [ˈbɪbjʊləs] *adj Fml, Hum* (*person*) qui s'adonne à la boisson; (*celebration*) bien arrosé

bicameral [baɪˈkæmərəl] *adj Pol* bicaméral; **b. system** bicaméralisme *m*, bicamérisme *m*

bicarb [baɪˈkɑːb] *n F* bicarbonate *m* de soude

bicarbonate [baɪˈkɑːbəneɪt] *n* (*of soda etc*) bicarbonate *m*

bicentenary [baɪsenˈtiːnərɪ], *US* **bicentennial** [baɪsenˈtenɪəl] *adj, n* bicentenaire *m*; **the b. celebrations** les cérémonies du bicentenaire

biceps [ˈbaɪseps] *n Anat* (muscle *m*) biceps *m*

bicker [ˈbɪkər] *vi* se chamailler, se quereller

bickering [ˈbɪkərɪŋ] *n* chamailleries *fpl*, querelles *fpl*

bickie [ˈbɪkɪ] *n Br F* biscuit *m*

bicolour(ed), *US* **bicolor(ed)** [baɪˈkʌlər, -ləd] *adj* bicolore

bicultural [baɪˈkʌltʃərəl] *adj esp Am* biculturel

bicycle¹ [ˈbaɪsɪk(ə)l] *n* bicyclette *f*, vélo *m*; **to go by b.** aller à *ou F* en bicyclette *ou* vélo; **to ride a b.** faire de la bicyclette *ou* du vélo; **to know how to ride a b.** savoir monter à bicyclette *ou* à vélo, savoir faire du vélo; **he was riding his b.** il était à bicyclette *ou* à vélo; **b. race** course *f* de bicyclette; *Fb* **b. kick** retourné *m* bicyclette; **b. club** club *m* de cyclistes

bicycle² *vi* (*for exercise*) faire de la bicyclette *ou* du vélo; (*travel*) aller à bicyclette *ou* à vélo (**to** à)

bicycle chain *n* chaîne *f* de vélo; (*for securing bike*) antivol *m inv*

bicycle clip *n* pince *f* à vélo

bicycle path *n* piste *f* cyclable

bicycle rack *n* râtelier *m* à bicyclettes

bicycle track *n* piste *f* cyclable

bid¹ [bɪd] *n* (**a**) (*offer*) (*at auction*) enchère *f*; **higher** *or* **further b.** offre *f* supérieure, surenchère *f*; **lowest/highest b.** enchère la plus basse/forte; **to make a b.** faire une offre, enchérir

(**b**) (*attempt*) tentative *f* (**for sth** de qch; **to do sth** pour faire qch); **to make a b. for sth** tenter d'obtenir qch; **to make a b. for power** (*legally*) viser le pouvoir; (*illegally*) tenter un coup d'état; **she failed in her b. to beat the record** elle a échoué dans sa tentative de battre le record

(**c**) *Cards* (*in bridge*) annonce *f*; (*in solo whist*) demande *f*; **b. of two diamonds** ouverture de deux carreaux; **no b.!** je passe!, parole!

(**d**) (*in takeover*) offre *f*; (*tender*) soumission *f*; **to make a b.** soumissionner; **to put a b. in on a flat** faire une offre pour un appartement; **b. bond** caution *f* de soumission

bid² *vti* (*pt* **bade** [bæd, beɪd], **bid**; *pp* **bidden** [bɪd(ə)n], **bid**) (**a**) (*pt, pp* **bid**) (*offer*) **to b. for sth** faire une offre pour qch; **what am I bid for this table?** qu'est-ce que vous m'offrez pour cette table?; **to b. ten pounds** faire une offre de dix livres

(**b**) *Cards* **to b. three diamonds** enchérir de trois carreaux

(**c**) (*in call for tenders*) faire une soumission (**on sth** pour qch)

(**d**) *Fml* (*greet*) **to b. sb welcome/good day** souhaiter la bienvenue/le bonjour à qn; **to b. sb goodbye** faire ses adieux à qn

(**e**) *Arch, Fml* (*seem probable*) **the weather bids fair to be fine** *or* **to improve** le temps s'annonce beau; **he bids fair to become ...** il promet de devenir ...

(**f**) *Arch, Lit* (*order*) commander, ordonner (**sb (to) do sth** à qn de faire qch); **to b. sb be silent** ordonner à qn de se taire, commander le silence à qn

▶ **bid up** *vtsep Fin* **to bid up the price of goods** enchérir sur le prix des marchandises

biddable [ˈbɪdəb(ə)l] *adj* (*child etc*) obéissant, docile

bidder [ˈbɪdər] *n* (*at sale*) enchérisseur *m*; (*at cards*) demandeur, -euse; **there were no bidders** il n'y a pas eu de preneurs; **the highest b.** le plus offrant

bidding [ˈbɪdɪŋ] *n* (**a**) (*at auction*) enchères *fpl*; **the b.** les enchères; **to start the b. at £5 000** commencer les enchères à 5 000 livres; **to open the b.** ouvrir les enchères; **the b. is against you** est-ce que vous voulez surenchérir? (**b**) *Fml* (*order*) **at sb's b.** sur l'ordre de qn; **to do sb's b.** exécuter les ordres de qn; **he needed no second b.** il n'a pas eu besoin qu'on lui répète cet ordre

bide [baɪd] *vt* (**bided**) **to b. one's time** attendre le bon moment

bidet [ˈbiːdeɪ] *n* bidet *m*

bidirectional [baɪdɪˈrekʃən(ə)l] *adj* bidirectionnel; **b. printing** impression *f* bidirectionnelle

bid price *n St Exch* cours *m* d'achat, cours *ou* prix *m* acheteur, cours demandé

biennial [baɪˈenɪəl] **1** *adj* (**a**) (*event*) biennal (**b**) (*plant*) bisannuel **2** *n Bot* plante *f* bisannuelle

biennially [baɪˈenɪəlɪ] *adv* tous les deux ans

bier [bɪər] *n* (*for coffin, body*) bière *f*

biff¹ [bɪf] **1** *n Sl* baffe *f* **2** *int* v'lan!, pan!

biff² *vt Sl* (*hit*) flanquer une baffe à

bifocal [baɪˈfəʊk(ə)l] *Opt* **1** *adj* bifocal, à double foyer **2** *npl* **bifocals** verres *mpl* bifocaux *ou* à double foyer

bifurcate [ˈbaɪfəkeɪt] *vi Fml* bifurquer

bifurcation [baɪfəˈkeɪʃən] *n Fml* bifurcation *f*

big [bɪg] **1** *adj* (**bigger** [ˈbɪgər]; **biggest** [ˈbɪgɪst]) (**a**) (*object*) (*large, tall*) grand; (*bulky*) gros; **b. hotel** grand hôtel; **b. drop in prices** forte baisse des prix; **to be doing a b. trade** faire de grosses affaires; *Sp* **b. field (of starters)** champ fourni; *F* **you've got a b. mouth** (*you let the secret out*) tu n'es pas capable de la fermer; **b. toe** gros orteil; *F* **a b. A** un A majuscule; *F* **the b. screen** le grand écran; **to give sb a b. hand** applaudir qn bien fort; **b. hair** belle crinière *f*

(**b**) (*serious, important*) (*problem, explosion, argument, difference*) gros; (*mistake*) grave; (*decision*) important; **this is our b. day** c'est le grand jour pour nous; **you've got a b. day ahead of you tomorrow** tu as une journée importante devant toi demain; **you want to look your best on the b. day** tu veux être la plus belle possible le grand jour; *F* **he had b. ideas** il voyait grand; **don't get any b. ideas about doing this yourself** ne crois pas que tu vas pouvoir faire ça tout seul; *F* **I've got b. plans for you** j'ai de grands projets pour toi; **b. budget film** super-production *f*; *F* **b. money** *or Am* **bucks** fric *m*; *F* **to earn b. money** gagner beaucoup d'argent; *F* **I'm talking b. money here** je te parle de beaucoup d'oseille; *F* **the b. (white) Chief, the b. Cheese, b. Daddy** le grand chef; **the b. names in the theatre world** les grands noms du théâtre; **she's a b. noise in publishing** c'est quelqu'un d'important dans le monde de l'édition; **they'll need to bring in the b. guns from New York on this one** il faudra qu'ils amènent les experts de New York sur ce coup-là; *Th, Cin* **the b. battle scene** la grande scène de bataille; **this is your b. scene** (*of main character*) la scène est à toi;

(*of minor character*) c'est ta scène; **b. business** les grands milieux d'affaires

(**c**) (*person*) (*tall*) grand et fort; (*fat*) gros; *F* (*important*) important; **you're a b. girl/boy now** tu es une grande fille/un grand garçon maintenant; **she's b. enough to look after herself** elle est assez grande pour se défendre; *F* **he's getting too b. for his boots** *or Am* **britches** il ne se sent plus; **my b. brother** mon frère aîné; (*in children's language*) mon grand frère; **to get big(ger)** (*taller*) grandir; (*fatter*) grossir; **you're the biggest fool of the lot!** c'est toi le plus bête de tous!; *Arch Lit* **to be b. with child** être sur le point d'enfanter; **a b. eater** un gros mangeur; **b. spender** personne qui dépense beaucoup d'argent; **he's a b. spender when it comes to clothes** il dépense beaucoup d'argent en vêtements; *Iron* **you know what he's like, the last of the b. spenders!** tu le connais, toujours à faire des frais!

(**d**) (*idioms*) **she goes for Frenchmen in a b. way** elle se pâme devant les Français; **he goes in for office memos in a b. way** il envoie des quantités de mémos; **we don't celebrate Christmas in a b. way** nous ne faisons pas tellement la fête à Noël; **you really do things in a b. way** tu ne fais pas les choses à moitié; **they've decided to get into exports in a b. way** ils ont décidé de se lancer à fond dans les exportations; *also Iron* **that was b. of you** c'était vraiment généreux de votre part; *F* **to be b. on sth** (*keen*) aimer beaucoup qch; **Walkmans® were b. last year** les Walkmans® ont bien marché l'année dernière

2 *adv F* **to talk b.** (*boast*) se vanter, faire l'important; **to think b.** voir grand; **to go over** *or* **down b.** avoir un succès fou; **the last song went down b. with the audience** la dernière chanson a fait un tabac auprès du public; **to make it b.** réussir

bigamist [ˈbɪgəmɪst] *n* bigame *mf*

bigamous [ˈbɪgəməs] *adj* bigame; **b. marriage** bigamie *f*; **to enter into a b. marriage** se rendre coupable de bigamie

bigamy [ˈbɪgəmɪ] *n* bigamie *f*; **to commit b.** être coupable de bigamie

Big Apple *n F* ville *f* de New-York

Big Bang *n Astron* big bang *m*; *Br Fin F* = déréglementation *f* de la bourse de Londres en octobre 1986

big bank *n* grande banque *f*, enseigne *f* bancaire

big-bellied [bɪgˈbelɪd] *adj* (*fat*) ventru, pansu; **she's b.** (*of pregnant woman*) elle a un gros ventre

Big Blue *n* (*IBM*) Big Blue *m*

big-boned [bɪgˈbəʊnd] *adj* fortement charpenté

Big Brother *n* tyran *m* paternaliste; (*government*) État *m* qui exerce un paternalisme autoritaire; *F* **B. is watching you** on t'a à l'œil

big cat *n* félin *m*

big end *n Aut* tête *f* de bielle

big game *n* (*animals*) grands fauves *mpl*; **b. hunter** chasseur *m* de grands fauves; **b. hunting** chasse *f* aux grands fauves

biggie [ˈbɪgɪ] *n F* **that's a b.** (*fish, car etc*) c'en est un(e) gros(se); **it's gonna be a b.** (*book, film, record*) il va faire un malheur; **there's a storm coming and it's a b.** il y a un orage qui se prépare, j'te dis pas

biggish [ˈbɪgɪʃ] *adj* (*tall, large*) assez grand; (*fat*) assez gros

bighead [ˈbɪghed] *n F* crâneur, -euse

bigheaded [bɪgˈhedɪd] *adj F* crâneur

bigheadedness [bɪgˈhedɪdnɪs] *n F* suffisance *f*, prétention *f*

big-hearted [bɪgˈhɑːtɪd] *adj* **to be b.** avoir du cœur; *also Iron* **in his usual b. way** le cœur sur la main, comme à son habitude

bight [baɪt] *n Geog* (*in coast-line*) renfoncement *m*; **the Great Australian B.** la Grande Baie Australienne, le Grand Golfe Australien *ou* de l'Australie

big match *n Sp* grand match *m*

bigness [ˈbɪgnɪs] *n* (*of person*) (*tallness*) grande taille *f*; (*fatness*) grosseur *f*; (*of thing*) grandes dimensions *fpl*; **his b. made him self-consciousness** il était complexé parce qu'il était si gros

bigot [ˈbɪgət] *n* sectaire *mf*, fanatique *mf*; (*religious*) fanatique, bigot *m*

bigoted [ˈbɪgətɪd] *adj* sectaire (**against** à l'égard de); **don't be so b.** ne sois pas si borné

bigotry [ˈbɪgətrɪ] *n* sectarisme *m*; (*religious*) bigoterie *f*

big shot *n F* gros bonnet *m*, grosse légume *f*, huile *f*; **he thinks he's a real b.** il croit qu'il est vraiment quelqu'un; **a big-shot lawyer from London** un crack du barreau de Londres

big time *n F* **to be in the b., to have made the b.** être en haut de l'échelle, être le dessus du panier, être arrivé; **to hit** *or* **make the b.** réussir; **once they've had a taste of the b.** une fois qu'ils ont goûté au succès

big-time *adj F* **a b. lawyer/executive** un avocat/cadre qui a réussi; **b. actor** acteur *m* de premier plan; **b. operator** gros trafiquant *m*

big top *n* chapiteau *m*

big wheel *n* (**a**) (*at fair*) grande roue *f* (**b**) *Am F* (*important person*) gros bonnet *m*, huile *f*

bigwig [ˈbɪgwɪg] *n F Hum, Pej* gros bonnet *m*, grosse légume *f*

bijou [ˈbiːʒuː] *n* **b. flat** *or* **residence** petit appartement *m* ravissant

bike[1] [baɪk] *n F* (*bicycle*) vélo *m*; (*motorbike*) moto *f*; *Br Sl* **on your b.!** (*go away*) tire-toi!; (*hurry up*) magne-toi!; (*I don't believe you, don't talk rubbish*) à d'autres!, tu charries!; **b. carrier** porte-vélo *m*

bike[2] *vi F* faire du vélo; (*on motorbike*) faire de la moto; **we biked there** nous y sommes allés à *ou* en vélo/moto

biker [ˈbaɪkər] *n* cycliste *mf*; (*on motor bike*), *Pej* motard *m*; (*courier*) coursier *m*

bikini [bɪˈkiːnɪ] *n* bikini *m*

bilabial [baɪˈleɪbɪəl] *adj, n Ling* (consonne *f*) bilabiale *f*

bilateral [baɪˈlætər(ə)l] *adj* bilatéral

bilaterally [baɪˈlætər(ə)lɪ] *adv* bilatéralement

bilberry [ˈbɪlbərɪ] *n* airelle *f*, myrtille *f*

bile [baɪl] *n Physiol* bile *f*; **b. duct** canal *m* biliaire; *Fig Fml* **to be full of b.** (*bad tempered*) être plein de hargne

bilestone [ˈbaɪlstəʊn] *n* calcul *m* biliaire

bilge [bɪldʒ] *n Naut* fond *m* de cale; **b. pump** pompe *f* de drain *ou* de cale; **b. (water)** eau *f* de cale; *F* **to talk a lot of b.** dire des bêtises; **b.!** sottises!

bilharzia [bɪlˈhɑːtsɪə] *n Med* (**a**) (*disease*) bilharziose *f* (**b**) (*parasite*) bilharzia *f*, bilharzie *f*

biliary [ˈbɪlɪərɪ] *adj Physiol* biliaire

bilingual [baɪˈlɪŋgwəl] *adj* bilingue; **b. secretary** secrétaire *mf* bilingue

bilingualism [baɪˈlɪŋgwəlɪz(ə)m] *n* bilinguisme *m*

bilious [ˈbɪlɪəs] *adj* (**a**) *Physiol* bilieux; **b. attack** crise *f* de foie; **he looks rather b.** on dirait qu'il va nous faire une crise de foie; *Fig* **b. yellow/green** jaunâtre/verdâtre (**b**) *Fig* (*bad-tempered*) colérique

biliousness [ˈbɪlɪəsnɪs] *n Med* affection *f* bilieuse; *Fig* hargne *f*

bilk [bɪlk] *vt Old-fashioned F* (*cheat*) avoir; **he bilked her (out) of all her money** il lui a extorqué tout son argent; **you've been bilked** tu t'es fait avoir

Bill [bɪl] *n Br F* **the (Old) B.** (*police*) les flics *mpl*, les poulets *mpl*

bill[1] [bɪl] *n* (**a**) (*of bird*) bec *m* (**b**) *Geog* bec *m*, promontoire *m*

bill[2] *vi* (*of birds*) se becqueter; *F* **to b. and coo** (*of couple*) se faire des mamours

bill[3] *n* (**a**) (*notice of payment due*) *Com* facture *f*; (*for gas, electricity*) facture, note *f*; (*in hotel*) note; *Br* (*in restaurant*) addition *f*; **can I/we have the b., please?** (*in restaurant*) l'addition, s'il vous plaît?; **put it on my b.** (*in hotel*) mettez-le sur ma note

(**b**) *Am* (*banknote*) billet *m* de banque; **five-dollar b.** billet de cinq dollars

(**c**) *Com, Fin* effet *m* (de commerce); **bills** valeurs *fpl*, papier *m* (bancable); **long(-dated)/short(-dated) bills** effets à longue/courte échéance; **b. of exchange** lettre *f* de change; **bills for collection** effets à l'encaissement; **bills for collection form** formulaire *m* d'encaissement; **b. made out to bearer** effet au porteur; **b. 'without protest'** traite *f* 'sans frais'; **bills of exchange statement** lettre *f* de change relevé, LCR *f*; **bills payable ledger** livre *m ou* journal *m* des effets à payer; **bills receivable ledger** livre *m ou* journal *m* des effets à recevoir

(**d**) *Th etc* (*poster*) affiche *f*; (*for political party*) affiche, placard *m*; **(stick) no bills!** défense d'afficher; **to head** *or* **top the b.** (*of actor*) être en tête d'affiche; *F* **that will fill** *or* **fit the b.** cela fera l'affaire

(**e**) (*list*) **b. of fare** carte *f* du jour, menu *m*; *Fig* **the doctor gave me a clean b. of health** le docteur m'a trouvé en parfaite santé; **the investigators gave the engine a clean b. of health** les enquêteurs ont conclu que le moteur était en parfait état; **b. of lading** connaissement *m*; *US Rail* feuille *f* d'expédition; **b. of entry** déclaration *f* d'entrée (en douane); **b. of sale** acte *m ou* contrat *m* de vente; *Constr* **b. of quantities** devis *m*

(**f**) *Pol* projet *m* de loi; (*private*) proposition *f* de loi; **to pass/reject a b.** adopter/repousser un projet de loi

bill[4] *vt* (**a**) (*invoice*) envoyer une facture à (**for** pour) (**b**) *Th, Fig* (*sb*) annoncer, afficher (**as** comme)

billboard [ˈbɪlbɔːd] *n esp Am* panneau *m ou* support *m* d'affichage; **b. advertising** publicité *f* sur panneaux

billet[1] [ˈbɪlɪt] *n* (**a**) *Mil* (*requisition*) billet *m* de logement (**b**) *Mil* (*accommodation*) (*in sb's house*) logement *m*; (*in town*) cantonnement *m*; (*of evacuee*) logement (**c**) *Old-fashioned Br F* (*job*) situation *f*

billet[2] (**-t-**) **1** *vt* (*troops, evacuee*) loger (**on sb** chez qn); **to b. troops on** *or* **in a town** cantonner des troupes dans une ville **2** *vi* loger (**with** chez)

billeting [ˈbɪlɪtɪŋ] *n* (*in private house*) logement *m* chez l'habitant; (*on town*) cantonnement *m*; **b. officer** officier *m* de cantonnement
billfold [ˈbɪlfəʊld] *n Am* (*wallet*) portefeuille *m*
billhook [ˈbɪlhʊk] *n* (*for pruning, chopping*) serpe *f*; (*small*) serpette *f*
billiard [ˈbɪljəd] *n* **(a)** (*usu pl with sing verb*) **billiards** (jeu *m* de) billard *m*; **to play billiards** jouer au billard; **to have** *or* **play a game of billiards** faire *ou* disputer une partie de billard; **bar billiards** billard russe; **b. ball** bille *f ou* boule *f* de billard; **b. cue** queue *f* de billard; **b. room** (salle *f* de) billard; **b. table** billard **(b)** *Am* (*shot*) carambolage *m*
billing [ˈbɪlɪŋ] *n* **(a)** *Th* affichage *m*; **to get top b.** (*of actor*) être en tête d'affiche **(b)** *Fin* facturation *f*; **b. machine** caisse *f* (enregistreuse); **b. office** bureau *m* de facturation
billion [ˈbɪljən] *n* [①A70,16,1] (*one thousand million*) milliard *m*; *Old-fashioned Br* (*one million million*) billion *m*
billionaire [bɪljəˈneər] *n* milliardaire *mf*
Bill of Rights *n Hist Br* = loi *f* de 1689 déterminant les droits du citoyen anglais; *US* = amendements *mpl* de 1791 à la Constitution de 1787
billow[1] [ˈbɪləʊ] *n Lit* (*large wave*) lame *f*; *Lit* **the billows** les flots *mpl*; **billows of smoke** nuages *mpl* de fumée
billow[2] *vi* (*of sea*) se soulever en vagues; (*of crowds, smoke etc*) ondoyer; **the sails billowed in the wind** les voiles se gonflaient au vent
billowy [ˈbɪləʊɪ] *adj* (*sea*) houleux
billposter [ˈbɪlpəʊstər], **billsticker** [ˈbɪlstɪkər] *n* afficheur *m*, colleur *m* d'affiches; **billposters will be prosecuted** ≈ défense d'afficher
billposting [ˈbɪlpəʊstɪŋ], **billsticking** [ˈbɪlstɪkɪŋ] *n* affichage *m*
billy, *pl* **billies** [ˈbɪlɪ, -z] *n* **(a)** *Austr, New Zealand* (*can*) gamelle *f*; **to boil the b.** faire du thé **(b) b. (club)** gourdin *m*; *Am* (*for police*) matraque *f*
billycan [ˈbɪlɪkæn] *n* = **billy (a)**
billy-goat *n* bouc *m*
billy-o(h) [ˈbɪlɪəʊ] *n Br Old-fashioned F* **it's raining like b.** il pleut à verse; **to run like b.** courir très vite *ou* à toutes jambes
bimbo [ˈbɪmbəʊ] *n Pej* minette *f*, jolie sotte *f*; **she's a real b.** elle n'a rien dans la tête
bimedia [ˈbaɪmiːdɪə] *adj* **to be a b. reporter** être journaliste à la radio et à la télévision
bimetallic [baɪmɪˈtælɪk] *adj* **(a)** *Econ* (*system*) bimétallique **(b)** *Tech* **b. strip** bilame *f*
bimetallism [baɪˈmetəlɪz(ə)m] *n Econ* bimétallisme *m*
bimonthly [baɪˈmʌnθlɪ] **1** *adj* **(a)** (*every two months*) bimestriel; **to appear on a b. basis** paraître tous les deux mois **(b)** (*twice a month*) bimensuel; **to appear on a b. basis** paraître deux fois par mois **2** *n* (*magazine*) (*every two months*) bimestriel *m*; (*twice monthly*) bimensuel *m* **3** *adv* **(a)** (*every two months*) tous les deux mois **(b)** (*twice a month*) deux fois par mois
bin[1] [bɪn] *n* coffre *m*, huche *f*, bac *m*; (*dustbin*) poubelle *f*; **wine b.** casier *m* à bouteilles, porte-bouteilles *m inv*; *Sl* **the b.** la maison de fous
bin[2] *vt F* (*throw in the bin*) mettre à la poubelle
binary [ˈbaɪnərɪ] **1** *adj Math etc* binaire; **b. code/number** code *m*/nombre *m* binaire; *Comptr* **b. search** recherche *f* binaire *ou* dichotomique; *Astron* **b. star** binaire *f*; *Mil* **b. weapon** arme *f* binaire; *Comptr* **b. word** mot *m* binaire **2** *n Astron* binaire *f*
bin bag *n* sac-poubelle *m*, *pl* sacs-poubelles
bind[1] [baɪnd] *n F* (*nuisance*) plaie *f*; **what an awful b.!** quelle plaie *ou* barbe!; **to be in a b.** (*difficult situation*) être dans une mauvaise passe; **I'm in a bit of a b.** j'ai un petit problème, je suis un peu coincé
bind[2] (*pt, pp* **bound** [baʊnd]) **1** *vt* **(a)** (*attach*) (*object*) attacher, lier (**to** à); (*sheaf of corn*) lier; (*prisoner*) attacher, ligoter; **to b. sb hand and foot** lier pieds et poings à qn; *Fig* **to be bound hand and foot** (*powerless*) avoir les mains liées; **they are bound together by a close friendship** ils sont liés d'une étroite amitié; **they are very much bound up with each other** (*of lovers*) ils sont très attachés l'un à l'autre; (*of friends*) ils sont très liés; **the present is bound up with the past** le présent est étroitement lié au passé; **to b. one's skis** fixer ses skis
(b) (*dress*) (*wound*) bander, panser
(c) (*cover*) (*book*) relier; **bound in boards** cartonné; **bound in cloth** relié toile
(d) (*cause to cohere*) (*sand etc*) lier, agglutiner, agglomérer; **stones bound together with cement** pierres liées avec du ciment; **b. the mixture with egg white** liez le mélange avec du blanc d'œuf
(e) *usu passive* (*of obligation, promise etc*) lier, engager; **to be bound to do sth** (*obliged*) être obligé *ou* tenu de faire qch; **to be bound by an oath** être lié par un serment; **to b. sb to pay a debt** astreindre *ou* obliger qn à payer une dette; **to b. oneself to do sth** s'engager à faire qch
(f) *Sewing* (*coat, hat*) border; (*buttonhole*) brider
2 *vi* (*of gravel etc*) se lier, s'agglomérer, s'agglutiner
▶ **bind over** *vtsep Jur* **to b. sb over to keep the peace** exiger de qn sous caution qu'il ne se livrera à aucune voie de fait; **to be bound over** être sommé d'observer une bonne conduite
▶ **bind up** *vtsep* **(a)** (*tie*) (*sheaf of corn*) lier **(b)** (*wound*) bander, panser
binder [ˈbaɪndər] *n* **(a)** (*for papers*) relieur *m* **(b)** (*of books*) relieur, -euse **(c)** *Agr* (*machine*) (*for sheaves of corn*) lieuse *f*; (*for hay*) botteleuse *f* **(d)** (*on sewing machine*) ourleur *m* **(e)** *Culin* (*for sauce*) liant *m*; *Constr* matériau *m* d'agrégation; (*for road surface*) liant, agglomérant *m*
bindery [ˈbaɪnd(ə)rɪ] *n* atelier *m* de reliure
binding [ˈbaɪndɪŋ] **1** *adj* **(a)** *Constr* (*agent*) agglomérant, agglutinant **(b)** (*contract etc*) obligatoire (**upon sb** pour qn), qui engage; **agreement b. (up)on sb** contrat *m* qui lie qn; **decision b. on all parties** décision *f* obligatoire pour tous **(c)** *Med* constipant **2** *n* **(a)** *Sp* (*on ski*) fixation *f*; **safety (release) bindings** fixations de sécurité **(b)** (*of book*) reliure *f* **(c)** *Constr* agglutination *f*, agrégation *f*; (*of road surface*) liant *m*, agglomérant *m*; **b. material** matière agglomérante *ou* d'agrégation **(d)** (*of dress etc*) bordure *f*, liséré *m*
bindweed [ˈbaɪndwiːd] *n* (*plant*) liseron *m*
bin end *n* (*of wine*) fin de série *f*
binge [bɪndʒ] *F* **1** *n* **to go on a b.** (*of drinking*) prendre une cuite; (*of eating*) se gaver; (*of shopping*) faire une razzia **2** *vi* (*drink a lot*) prendre une cuite; (*eat a lot*) s'en mettre plein la lampe, se gaver; **he binged on chocolate** il s'est gavé de chocolat
bingo [ˈbɪŋgəʊ] **1** *n* bingo *m*; *Br F* **to go to b.** aller jouer au bingo; **b. hall** salle *f* de bingo **2** *int* et voilà!
bin liner *n* petit sac-poubelle *m*
binman, *pl* **-men** [ˈbɪnmæn, -men] *n Br* éboueur *m*
binnacle [ˈbɪnək(ə)l] *n Naut* habitacle *m*
binocular [bɪˈnɒkjʊlər, baɪ-] *adj* (*vision etc*) binoculaire
binoculars [bɪˈnɒkjʊləz] *npl* [①A10,e] jumelles *fpl*; **to look at sth through b.** regarder qch avec des jumelles
binomial [baɪˈnəʊmɪəl] **1** *adj Math* (*factor etc*) binôme; **the b. theorem** le binôme de Newton, le théorème de Newton **2** *n* binôme *m*
bint [bɪnt] *n Br Sl Pej* (*woman*) grognasse *f*
biochemical [baɪəʊˈkemɪk(ə)l] *adj* biochimique; **b. oxygen demand** demande *f* biochimique en oxygène
biochemist [baɪəʊˈkemɪst] *n* biochimiste *mf*
biochemistry [baɪəʊˈkemɪstrɪ] *n* biochimie *f*
biodegradability [baɪəʊdɪgreɪdəˈbɪlɪtɪ] *n* biodégradabilité *f*
biodegradable [baɪəʊdɪˈgreɪdəb(ə)l] *adj* biodégradable
biodiversity [baɪəʊdaɪˈvɜːsɪtɪ] *n* biodiversité *f*
bioethics [baɪəʊˈeθɪks] *n* [①A10,c] bioéthique *f*; **b. debate** débat sur la bioéthique
biogenesis [baɪəʊˈdʒenɪsɪs] *n* biogenèse *f*
biographer [baɪˈɒgrəfər] *n* biographe *mf*
biographical [baɪəˈgræfɪk(ə)l] *adj* biographique; **b. novel** biographie *f* romancée
biography [baɪˈɒgrəfɪ] *n* biographie *f*
biological [baɪəˈlɒdʒɪk(ə)l] *adj* biologique; **b. clock** horloge *f* physiologique *ou* biologique; **my b. clock is running down** (*of woman*) je deviens trop vieille pour avoir un enfant; **b. control** (*of insects*) élimination *f* des insectes par des méthodes biologiques; **b. warfare** guerre *f* bactériologique
biologically [baɪəˈlɒdʒɪklɪ] *adv* biologiquement
biologist [baɪˈɒlədʒɪst] *n* biologiste *mf*
biology [baɪˈɒlədʒɪ] *n* biologie *f*
biomass [ˈbaɪəʊmæs] *n* biomasse *f*
biomaterial [baɪəʊməˈtɪərɪəl] *n* biomatériau *m*
biometrics [baɪəʊˈmetrɪks] *n* [①A10,c] biométrie *f*
bionic [baɪˈɒnɪk] *adj* bionique
bionics [baɪˈɒnɪks] *n* [①A10,c] bionique *f*
biophysics [baɪəʊˈfɪzɪks] *n* [①A10,c] biophysique *f*
biopsy [ˈbaɪɒpsɪ, baɪˈɒpsɪ] *n* biopsie *f*
biorhythm [ˈbaɪəʊrɪð(ə)m] *n* rythme *m* biologique, biorythme *m*
BIOS [ˈbaɪɒs] *n Comptr* (*abbr* **basic input/output system**) BIOS *m*
bioscope [ˈbaɪəskəʊp] *n Cin* **(a)** *Old-fashioned* (*projector*) bioscope *m* **(b)** (*in South Africa*) (*cinema*) cinéma *m*
biosphere [ˈbaɪəsfɪər] *n* biosphère *f*
biosynthesis [baɪəʊˈsɪnθɪsɪs] *n* biosynthèse *f*
biotechnology [baɪəʊtekˈnɒlədʒɪ], *F* **biotech** [ˈbaɪəʊtek] *n* biotechnologie *f*

biotope ['baɪətəʊp] *n Biol* biotope *m*
bipartisan [baɪpɑːtɪ'zæn] *adj Pol etc* bipartite, biparti
bipartite [baɪ'pɑːtaɪt] *adj* **(a)** *Biol* bipartite, biparti **(b)** *Jur* (*document*) rédigé en double **(c)** (*agreement*) bipartite, biparti
biped ['baɪped] *adj, n* bipède *m*
biplane ['baɪpleɪn] *n Av* (avion *m*) biplan *m*
bipolar [baɪ'pəʊlər] *adj El, Physiol etc* bipolaire
birch¹ [bɜːtʃ] *n* **(a)** (*tree*) bouleau *m*; **b. (wood)** (bois *m* de) bouleau **(b) b. (rod)** verge *f*; **to give sb the b.** donner le fouet à qn, fouetter qn
birch² *vt* donner le fouet à, fouetter
birching ['bɜːtʃɪŋ] *n* correction *f* (*au fouet*); **to give sb a b.** fouetter qn
bird [bɜːd] *n* **(a)** oiseau *m*; **(farmyard) b.** volaille *f*; **b. call** cri *m* d'oiseau; (*device*) appeau *m*, pipeau *m*; **b.'s nest** nid *m* d'oiseau; *Culin* **b.'s nest soup** soupe *f* aux nids d'hirondelles; **b. of passage** oiseau de passage; **I'm just a b. of passage** je ne suis que de passage; **b. of prey** oiseau de proie, rapace *m*; **b. of paradise** oiseau de paradis, paradisier *m*; **b. shot** cendrée *f*; **b. strike** collision *f* d'un avion avec un oiseau; *F* **a little b. told me** mon petit doigt me l'a dit; *Lit* **a b. of ill omen** un oiseau de mauvais augure; **to eat like a b.** avoir un appétit d'oiseau; *F* **to give sb the b.** huer *ou* siffler qn; *F* **to get the b.** être hué *ou* sifflé; *Prov* **a b. in the hand is worth two in the bush** un tiens vaut mieux que deux tu l'auras; *Fig* **the b. has flown** l'oiseau s'est envolé; *Prov* **birds of a feather flock together** qui se ressemble s'assemble; **you and your father are birds of a feather** toi et ton père, vous ne valez pas mieux l'un que l'autre, toi et ton père, je vous mets dans le même sac; *Euph* **it's time you talked to him about the birds and the bees** (*facts of life*) il serait temps de lui expliquer que les bébés ne naissent pas dans les choux; *F* **it's (strictly) for the birds** c'est de la roupie de sansonnet

(b) *Br Sl* (*woman*) nana *f*; **who's the b. in the corner?** qui est la fille au coin?

(c) *Br Sl* (*time in prison*) taule *f*, tôle *f*; **to do b.** faire de la taule

(d) *F* (*fellow*) type *m*, individu *m*; **he's a queer b.** c'est un drôle d'oiseau; **a home b.** un casanier, une casanière; *Fig* **night b.** noctambule *mf*

birdbath ['bɜːdbɑːθ] *n* vasque *f* pour les oiseaux
bird brain *n F Pej* tête *f* de linotte
bird-brained ['bɜːdbreɪnd] *adj F Pej* écervelé; **to be b.** avoir une cervelle d'oiseau *ou* de moineau
birdcage ['bɜːdkeɪdʒ] *n* cage *f* (à oiseaux); (*large*) volière *f*
birdcatcher ['bɜːdkætʃər] *n* oiseleur *m*
bird-dog *vt Am F* surveiller de près
bird fancier *n* personne *f* qui s'y connaît en oiseaux; (*breeder*) oiselier *m*
bird-house *n* (*aviary*) volière *f*
birdie ['bɜːdɪ] *n F* **(a)** *Golf* un coup de moins que la normale **(b)** (*in children's language*) gentil petit oiseau *m*; *Phot F* **watch the b.!** regarde le petit oiseau!
birdlike ['bɜːdlaɪk] *adj* (*appetite*) d'oiseau; **b. movements/ features** mouvements *mpl*/traits *mpl* semblables à ceux d'un oiseau
birdlime ['bɜːdlaɪm] *n* glu *f*
bird-nesting *n* **to go b.** = rechercher des nids pour y prendre les œufs
bird sanctuary *n* réserve *f* d'oiseaux *ou* ornithologique
birdseed ['bɜːdsiːd] *n* graines *fpl* pour oiseaux
bird's-eye ['bɜːdzaɪ] *n* **(a) b. view** vue *f* aérienne; *Phot* photographie *f* aérienne oblique; *Cin* (prise *f* de vue en) plongée *f*; *Fig* **b. view of the situation** vue d'ensemble de la situation **(b)** *Bot* véronique *f*; **b. mahogany** acajou *m* moucheté; **b. maple** érable *m* madré *ou* à broussin
bird table *n* (*in garden*) mangeoire *f* (*pour les oiseaux*)
bird-watcher *n* ornithologue *mf* amateur
bird-watching ['bɜːdwɒtʃɪŋ] *n* observation *f* des oiseaux (*dans leur milieu naturel*); **to go b.** aller observer les oiseaux
biretta [bɪ'retə] *n Cathol* barrette *f*
biro ® ['baɪrəʊ] *n Br* stylo *m* (à) bille
birth [bɜːθ] *n* **(a)** (*of child, nation, industry*) naissance *f*; *Fig* (*of idea etc*) genèse *f*; **date/place/country of b.** date *f*/lieu *m*/ pays *m* de naissance; **to give b. to a child** mettre un enfant au monde, donner naissance à un enfant; **she has given b. to a daughter** elle a donné naissance à une fille; **at b.** à la naissance; *Hum F* **he should have been drowned at b.!** on aurait dû le noyer à la naissance!; **will the father be present at the b.?** le père assistera-t-il à l'accouchement *ou* à la naissance?; **it was a difficult b.** cela a été un accouchement difficile; **Irish by b.** Irlandais de naissance; **from b.** (*be blind, deaf etc*) de naissance; (*be delicate*) dès *ou* depuis la naissance; **b. statistics** statistiques *fpl* de natalité

(b) (*of animal*) mise *f* bas; **to give b. to a litter** mettre bas une portée

birth certificate *n* (*original*) acte *m* de naissance; (*copy*) extrait *m* de naissance
birth control *n* contrôle *m ou* limitation *f* des naissances
birthday ['bɜːθdeɪ] *n* (*anniversary*) anniversaire *m*; (*day of birth*) jour *m* de naissance; **she was 42 on her last b.** elle a 42 ans; *F Hum* **to be in one's b. suit** être dans le *ou* en costume d'Adam/d'Ève, être dans le plus simple appareil; **b. card/cake/present/party** carte *f*/gâteau *m*/cadeau *m*/fête *f* d'anniversaire; **let me buy the b. girl a drink** laisse-moi te payer un verre pour ton anniversaire
Birthday Honours *npl Br* = distinctions *fpl* honorifiques accordées à l'occasion de l'anniversaire du souverain
birthing ['bɜːθɪŋ] *n esp Am Med* **b. room** salle *f* d'accouchement
birthmark ['bɜːθmɑːk] *n* tache *f* de naissance, envie *f*
birthplace ['bɜːθpleɪs] *n* lieu *m* de naissance; *Fig* (*of religion etc*) berceau *m*
birth rate *n* (taux *m* de) natalité *f*
birthright ['bɜːθraɪt] *n* (*something to which one is entitled*) droit *m* de naissance, droit du sang; (*of first-born*) droit *m* d'aînesse; (*inheritance*), *Fig* patrimoine *m*; *Fig* **clean air is everyone's b.** tout le monde a le droit de vivre dans un endroit non pollué
birthstone ['bɜːθstəʊn] *n Astrol etc* pierre *f* porte-bonheur, *pl* pierres porte-bonheur
biryani [bɪr'jɑːnɪ] *n* (*Indian dish*) biriani *m*
Biscay ['bɪskeɪ] *n* **the Bay of B.** le golfe de Gascogne
biscuit ['bɪskɪt] *n* **(a)** *Br* biscuit *m*; *Am* (*scone*) petit pain *m*; **ship's b.** biscuits de mer; **dog b.** biscuit pour chien; **b. barrel** boîte *f* à biscuits; **b. factory** biscuiterie *f*; *F* **that (really) takes the b.!** ça, c'est le bouquet! **(b)** *Cer* **b. ware** biscuit *m* **(c)** (*colour*) marron *m* clair
bisect [baɪ'sekt] **1** *vt Geom* (*line, angle*) couper *ou* diviser en deux parties égales **2** *vi* (*of road etc*) bifurquer
bisection [baɪ'sekʃən] *n Geom* bissection *f*
bisector [baɪ'sektər] *n Geom* bissectrice *f*, ligne *f* de bissection
bisexual [baɪ'seksjʊəl] **1** *adj* (*attracted to both sexes*) bisexuel; (*having characteristics of both sexes*) bisexué **2** *n* bisexuel *m*; **to be a b.** être bisexuel
bishop ['bɪʃəp] *n* **(a)** *Rel* évêque *m*; **b.'s palace** palais *m* épiscopal, évêché *m* **(b)** *Chess* fou *m*
bishopric ['bɪʃəprɪk] *n* (*office, diocese*) évêché *m*
bismuth ['bɪzməθ] *n Miner, Pharm* bismuth *m*
bison ['baɪsən] *n* bison *m*
bisque¹ [biːsk] *n Cer* biscuit *m*
bisque² *n Culin* (*lobster etc*) bisque *f*
bistre ['bɪstər] *adj, n* bistre *m*
bistro ['biːstrəʊ] *n* petit resto *m*
bisulphite [baɪ'sʌlfaɪt] *n Ch* bisulfite *m*; **sodium b.** bisulfite de sodium *ou* de soude
bit¹ [bɪt] *n* **(a)** (*on bridle*) mors *m*; **to champ at the b.** (*of horse*) mâcher son mors; (*of person*) ronger son frein; **to take the b. between one's teeth** (*of horse, person*) prendre le mors aux dents **(b)** (*for brace*) mèche *f*; (*for drill*) foret *m*
bit² *n* **(a)** (*piece*) (*of bread, cake etc*) morceau *m*; (*of paper, string, old carpet etc*) bout *m*; (*of straw etc*) brin *m*; **a b. of news** une nouvelle; **a b. of luck** une chance; **a (little) b. of hope** un petit brin d'espoir

(b) (*part*) partie *f*, morceau *m*; (*of book, film, report etc*) passage *m*; **to tear sth to bits** déchirer qch en morceaux; **smashed to bits** brisé (en mille morceaux); **to take sth to bits** démonter qch; **to come to bits** (*dismantle*) se démonter; (*break*) tomber en morceaux; *Fig* **to go to bits** (*of person*) s'effondrer, craquer; **in bits** en morceaux; **he has eaten every b.** il a tout mangé; **this is the difficult b.** c'est là où ça se complique; **made of bits and pieces** *or F* **bits and bobs** fait de bric et de broc; *F* **my bits and pieces** *or* **bobs** mes affaires

(c) (*little*) **a b.** un peu **(of** de); **a tiny** *or* **little b.** un tout petit peu; **I'm a b. late** je suis un peu en retard; **I'm a b. hungry** j'ai un peu faim, *F* j'ai un petit creux; **she's a b. of an artist** (*paints, draws*) elle est artiste à ses heures perdues; (*in way puts colours, textures together*) elle a un côté artiste; **it was a b. of a nuisance** c'était vraiment ennuyeux; **quite a b. of sun/rain/trouble** pas mal de soleil/de pluie/d'ennuis; **I've had quite a b. to drink** j'ai un peu trop bu; *F* **he's a b. of a lad** (*likes a good time*) il aime faire la bringue; (*runs after women*) c'est un coureur (de jupons); **we got a b. of a shock** ça nous a fait un choc; **to give you a b. of an idea** pour te donner une petite idée; **it was a b. too much of a coincidence** c'était un peu fort comme coïncidence; **b. by b.** peu à peu, petit à petit; **not a b. (of it)!** pas du tout!; **I don't**

care a b. cela m'est bien *ou* complètement égal; **it's not a b. of use** cela ne sert absolument à rien; **hold on** *or* **wait a b.!** attendez un peu *ou* un instant!; *F* **in a b.** dans quelques minutes; *F* **after a b.** quelques minutes après; **that takes a b. of doing** ça, c'est bien difficile; **a good b. older/colder** nettement plus âgé/froid; **every b. as good/interesting as** aussi bon/intéressant que; *F* **it's a b. much!** ça, c'est vraiment trop fort!; **we all had to do our b.** nous avons dû tous nous y mettre, nous avons dû tous y mettre du nôtre; **I did my b. too, you know** moi aussi j'ai fait ma part, tu sais; *F* **to make quite a b.** (*earn money*) gagner pas mal d'argent *ou* de fric; **to have a b. put away** avoir un petit pécule; **that must be worth quite a b.!** ça doit valoir pas mal d'argent; *F* **she's a nice b. of stuff** *or* **skirt** c'est un beau brin de fille; **he's a b. of all right** c'est un beau mec, il est pas mal

(**d**) *F* (*coin*) pièce *f*; *Br Arch* **threepenny b.** pièce de trois pence; *Am* **two bits** vingt-cinq cents

bit[3] *n Comptr* bit *m*; **bits per second** bits par seconde; **b. command** commande *f* binaire; **b. rate** débit *m* binaire

bit[4] *see* **bite**[2]

bitch[1] [bɪtʃ] *n* (**a**) (*dog*) chienne *f*; (*fox etc*) femelle *f*; **terrier b.** terrier *m* femelle (**b**) *Sl Pej* (*woman*) garce *f* (**c**) *Sl* **a b. of a job** un travail de chien; **life's a b.!** quelle *ou* cette chienne de vie!; **I've had a b. of a day!** j'ai eu une putain de journée!

bitch[2] *Sl* **1** *vi* (*complain*) rouspéter; **stop bitching about the weather** arrête de rouspéter après le temps; **bitching session** séance *f* de défoulement **2** *vt Am* (*job*) saloper; **he bitched up the whole business for us** il nous a tout bousillé

bitchy ['bɪtʃɪ] *adj Sl* (*woman*) garce, vache; (*remark etc*) vache; **that was a b. thing to do!** quelle vacherie!, quel sale coup!; **to be b.** (*of woman*) être garce *ou* vache; (*of man*) être vache

bite[1] [baɪt] *n* (**a**) (*of person*) coup *m* de dent; (*in dentistry*) articulé *m* dentaire; *esp Am Sl* **to put the b. on sb** (*extort money from*) gruger qn; (*borrow money from*) taper qn

(**b**) (*in fishing*) touche *f*; **I haven't had a b. all day** je n'ai pas eu une seule touche de toute la journée

(**c**) (*of dog etc*) morsure *f*; (*of insect*) piqûre *f*, morsure; **the dog had given him a playful b. on the arm** le chien lui avait mordu le bras en jouant

(**d**) *F* (*of food*) bouchée *f*, morceau *m*; **would you like a b. (to eat)?** voulez-vous manger quelque chose?; **I could do with a b. to eat** je mangerais bien quelque chose; **I haven't had a b. all day** je n'ai rien mangé de la journée; **come over for a b. of supper** viens manger un morceau à la maison ce soir; **can I have a b.?** (*of apple, chocolate bar*) je peux en avoir un peu?; **to take a (big) b. out of sth** mordre dans qch (à pleines dents); *Fig* **the repairs took a big b. out of our savings** les réparations ont fait un trou dans nos économies; *Fig* **you don't get two bites (at the cherry)** l'occasion ne se présente qu'une fois

(**e**) (*of sauce, wine*) piquant *m*; *Fig* **your speech needs more b.** ton discours manque de mordant

bite[2] (*pt* **bit** [bɪt]; *pp* **bitten** [bɪt(ə)n]) **1** *vt* (*of animal, person*) mordre, donner un coup de dent à; (*of insect*) piquer; **the dog bit him in the leg** le chien l'a mordu à la jambe; **to b. one's lips** se mordre les lèvres; **to b. one's nails** se ronger les ongles; *also Fig* **to b. one's tongue** se mordre la langue; **to b. the dust** mordre la poussière; *Prov* **once bitten twice shy** chat échaudé craint l'eau froide; *Fig* **to b. the bullet** serrer les dents; **let's b. the bullet and give him what he wants** faisons contre mauvaise fortune bon cœur et donnons-lui ce qu'il veut; **to get bitten** (*by dog*) se faire mordre; (*by insect*) se faire piquer; *F* **what's biting/bitten him?** quelle mouche l'a piqué?; *F* **he got bitten by the skiing/chess bug at the age of six** il se passionne pour le ski/les échecs depuis l'âge de six ans; *Fig* **to b. the hand that feeds you** cracher dans la soupe

2 *vi* (**a**) (*of fish*) mordre (à l'hameçon); (*of insect*) piquer; **does the dog b.?** est-ce que le chien mord?; **he bit into the apple** il a mordu dans la pomme; **are they** *or* **the fish biting (today)?** alors, ça mord?; *Fig* **don't worry, I don't b.!** n'ayez pas peur, je ne mords pas!; *Fig* **sanctions are beginning to b.** les sanctions commencent à se faire sentir

(**b**) (*of screw, file*) mordre (**on** sur); (*of tool*) mordre, s'engager; (*of anchor*) mordre, prendre fond; **screw that won't b.** vis qui foire

▶ **bite back** *vtsep* (*reply*) ravaler

▶ **bite off** *vtsep* enlever *ou* détacher d'un coup de dent(s); *F* **to b. sb's head off** rembarrer qn; *Fig* **to b. off more than one can chew** tenter quelque chose au-dessus de ses forces

biter ['baɪtər] *n* **it's a case of the b. bit** c'est l'arroseur arrosé

biting ['baɪtɪŋ] *adj* (*cold*) âpre, perçant; (*wind*) cinglant; (*style, wit, irony*) mordant, caustique

biting point *n Aut* (*of clutch*) point *m* d'attaque

bitmap ['bɪtmæp] *Comptr* **1** *n* bitmap *m* **2** *adj* pixélisé, bitmap; **b. font** fonte *f* pixélisée *ou* bitmap

bit-mapped ['bɪtmæpt] *adj Comptr* (*image*) pixélisé, bitmap; **b. font** police *f* pixélisée *ou* bitmap

bit part *n Th, Cin* rôle *m* de figurant

bit player *n Th, Cin* figurant, -ante

bit-slice processor *n Comptr* processeur *m* en tranches

bitten ['bɪtən] *see* **bite**[2]

bitter ['bɪtər] **1** *adj* (*taste, Fig person, tears, experience, disappointment*) amer; (*words*) acerbe; (*wind*) glacial; (*weather*) rigoureux; (*cold*) glacial, cinglant; (*enemy, hatred*) implacable; (*conflict, opposition, resistance*) âpre; (*tone*) aigre, âpre; **b. orange** orange *f* amère; **b. aloes** aloès *m* médicinal; **not being promoted was a b. pill for him to swallow** ça a été dur à avaler pour lui de ne pas être promu; **to feel** *or* **be b. about sth** ressentir de l'amertume à propos de qch; **she's very b. about it** elle en est très amère, *F* elle l'a pas digéré; *Fig* **to go on/resist to the b. end** aller/résister jusqu'au bout

2 *n* (**a**) *Br* (*beer*) bière *f* brune

(**b**) **bitters** bitter(s) *m(pl)*, amer(s) *m(pl)*

bitterly ['bɪtəlɪ] *adv* (*to say*) amèrement, avec amertume; (*to cry*) amèrement; (*to argue*) aigrement; **it was b. cold** il faisait un froid de loup *ou* de canard; **I've regretted it b. ever since** je n'ai cessé de le regretter amèrement; **b. disappointed** amèrement déçu; **to be b. opposed to sth** être farouchement opposé à qch

bittern ['bɪtən] *n* (*bird*) butor *m*

bitterness ['bɪtənɪs] *n* (*of drink, pain, person*) amertume *f*; (*of weather*) rigueur *f*; (*of weather, reproach*) âpreté *f*; (*of words, quarrel*) aigreur *f*, acrimonie *f*

bittersweet ['bɪtəswiːt] **1** *adj also Fig* doux-amer **2** *n* (*plant*) douce-amère *f*, *pl* douces-amères

bitty ['bɪtɪ] *adj F* (*book etc*) (d'un style) décousu

bitumen ['bɪtjʊmɪn] *n* (**a**) *Ch, Miner* bitume *m* (**b**) *Austr F* (*road*) route *f* goudronnée

bituminous [bɪ'tjuːmɪnəs] *adj* bitumineux; **b. coal** houille *f* grasse *ou* collante

bivalent [baɪ'veɪlənt] *adj Ch* bivalent

bivalve ['baɪvælv] *adj, n* (*mollusc*) bivalve *m*

bivouac[1] ['bɪvʊæk] *n* bivouac *m*

bivouac[2] *vi* (**bivouacked; bivouacking**) bivouaquer

biweekly [baɪ'wiːklɪ] **1** *adj* (**a**) (*every two weeks*) bimensuel (**b**) (*twice a week*) bihebdomadaire **2** *adv* (**a**) (*every two weeks*) tous les quinze jours (**b**) (*twice a week*) deux fois par semaine

bizarre [bɪ'zɑːr] *adj* bizarre

bizarrely [bɪ'zɑːlɪ] *adv* bizarrement

bizarreness [bɪ'zɑːnɪs] *n* bizarrerie *f*

B/L, b/l *Com* (*abbr* **bill of lading**) connt

blab[1] [blæb] *n* = **blabber**[1]

blab[2] (**-bb-**) *Pej F* **1** *vi* (**a**) (*betray secret*) vendre la mèche (**b**) (*prattle*) jaser, bavarder **2** *vt* (*secret*) divulguer, laisser échapper

▶ **blab out** *vtsep* = **blab**[2] **2**

blabber[1] ['blæbər] *n F* bavard, -arde, jaseur, -euse

blabber[2] *vi F* jacasser

blabbermouth ['blæbəmaʊθ] *n* grande langue *f*, bavard, -arde

Black [blæk] *n* Noir, Noire; **B.-on-B. violence** violence *f* des Noirs sur les Noirs

black[1] [blæk] **1** *adj* (**a**) (*colour*) (*coffee, dress, hair, Africa, music etc*) noir; (*cloud, sky etc*) sombre; **as b. as night** noir comme la nuit; **a b. man/woman** un Noir/une Noire; **b. with age** noirci par le temps; **it** *or* **the night was pitch b.** il faisait noir comme dans un four; **his hands were b.** il avait les mains toutes noires; *Fig* **to be in sb's b. books** être mal vu de qn; *Hum* **little b. book** (*of addresses*) carnet *m* d'adresses; (*of wrongdoers*) liste *f* noire; *Br Jur, Hist* **the b. cap** le bonnet noir (*que coiffait le juge en prononçant une condamnation à mort*); **b. flag** drapeau *m* noir; **b. swan** cygne *m* noir; **is it b. tie?** (*at dinner etc*) est-ce que la tenue habillée est de rigueur?

(**b**) *Fig* (*gloomy, sombre*) (*mood, thought*) noir; **to look as b. as thunder** avoir l'air furieux; **to give sb a b. look** jeter un regard noir à qn; **things are looking b.** les affaires prennent une mauvaise tournure; **to paint things blacker than they are** noircir la situation; **she's not as b. as she's painted** elle n'est pas si mauvaise qu'on le dit; **he's in one of his b. moods** il est dans un de ses mauvais jours; **it's a b. day for Britain** c'est un mauvais jour pour la Grande-Bretagne

(**c**) *Fig* (*sinister, malevolent*) malveillant; **b. hearted** malveillant

(**d**) *Fig* (*macabre*) (*joke, comedy*) macabre; **b. mass** messe *f* noire

(**e**) *Fig* (*illegal*) **b. economy** économie *f* souterraine

(**f**) *Old-fashioned Br F* **B. Maria** panier *m* à salade

2 *n* **(a)** noir *m*; **she always wears b.** elle porte toujours du noir, elle est toujours en noir; **to work in b. and white** (*of artist*) faire du dessin à l'encre *ou* au crayon noir; **I have his consent in b. and white** j'ai son consentement par écrit; **I should like to have it in b. and white** je voudrais avoir cela noir sur blanc; **she sees everything in b. and white** pour elle, c'est tout l'un ou tout l'autre; **she would swear that b. is white to help him** elle serait prête à tout pour l'aider; **he'll swear b. is white for the price of a couple of drinks** il est prêt à jurer n'importe quoi en échange d'un verre ou deux

(b) *Fin F* **to be in the b.** être en crédit; **to get back into the b.** sortir du rouge

(c) *Sp* **the b.** (*in roulette*) le noir; (*in snooker*) la bille *ou* boule noire

black² *vt* **(a)** (*blacken*) **to b. one's face** se noircir le visage; **to b. sb's eye** pocher l'œil à qn **(b)** *Ind* (*boycott*) mettre à l'index **(c)** (*polish*) (*shoes*) cirer

▶ **black out 1** *vi* (*faint*) perdre connaissance, s'évanouir; (*lose memory*) avoir un trou (de mémoire) **2** *vtsep* **(a)** (*house etc*) (*completely*) éteindre les lumières dans, faire le black-out dans; (*partially*) voiler *ou* masquer les lumières dans; *Th* **to b. out the stage** faire l'obscurité sur scène **(b)** *Rad, TV* **industrial action has blacked out this evening's programmes** un mouvement de grève a interrompu les programmes de la soirée **(c)** (*delete*) rayer (*d'un gros trait noir*)

▶ **black up** *vi Th* se maquiller la peau en noir, se noircir le visage

black-and-blue *adj* **to beat sb b.** rosser qn, couvrir qn de bleus; **to be b. all over** être couvert de bleus, être tuméfié

black and tan *n* (*drink*) = mélange *m* de bière et de porter

black-and-tan *adj* **b. terrier** chien *m* noir et feu *inv*

Black and Tans *npl* = police *f* auxiliaire envoyée en Irlande en 1921 pour combattre l'IRA

black-and-white *n* (*photograph*) photo *f* noir et blanc; **b. film/television** film *m*/télévision *f* (en) noir et blanc; **b. postcard** carte *f* en noir et blanc

black art *n* sciences *fpl* occultes

blackball ['blækbɔːl] *vt* blackbouler

blackballing ['blækbɔːlɪŋ] *n* blackboulage *m*

blackbeetle ['blækbiːt(ə)l] *n F* (*insect*) blatte *f*, cafard *m*, cancrelat *m*

black belt *n* (*in judo*) ceinture *f* noire

blackberry ['blækb(ə)rɪ] *n* mûre *f*; **b. bush** ronce *f ou* mûrier *m* des haies; **b. jam** confiture *f* de mûres; **b. tart** tarte *f* aux mûres

blackberrying ['blækberɪɪŋ] *n* **to go b.** aller cueillir des mûres, aller à la cueillette des mûres

blackbird ['blækbɜːd] *n* **(a)** merle *m* (noir) **(b)** *Am* (variété *f* d')étourneau *m*

blackboard ['blækbɔːd] *n* tableau *m* noir

black-bordered [blæk'bɔːdəd] *adj* à bordure noire

black box *n Av* boîte *f* noire

black bread *n* pain *m* de seigle

black bun *n Scot* = sorte *f* de pain au raisin

blackcock ['blækkɒk] *n* (*bird*) tétras *m* lyre, coq *m* des bouleaux

Black Country *n* = région *f* industrielle de l'Angleterre, autour de Birmingham

blackcurrant [blæk'kʌrənt] *n* (*bush, fruit*) cassis *m*

Black Death *n* Peste *f* Noire

blacken ['blæk(ə)n] **1** *vt* (*wall, Fig sb's reputation*) noircir; (*sky*) obscurcir; (*paper, glass*) (*with smoke*) enfumer; *Fig* **to b. sb's character** calomnier qn **2** *vi* noircir, devenir noir; *Fig* (*of face*) s'assombrir

blackening ['blæk(ə)nɪŋ] *n* noircissement *m*

black eye *n* œil *m* poché *ou F* au beurre noir; **to give sb a b.** pocher l'œil à qn

black-eyed ['blækaɪd] *adj* **b. pea** dolique *m*

blackfly ['blækflaɪ] *n F* (*insect*) mouche *f* noire

Black Forest *n* Forêt-Noire *f*; **B. gateau** forêt *f* noire

blackguard ['blægɑːd] *n Arch* fripouille *f*, canaille *f*

blackhead ['blækhed] *n* (*on face*) point *m* noir

black hole *n Astron* trou *m* noir

black ice *n Met* verglas *m*

blacking ['blækɪŋ] *n* **(a)** *Ind* (*of ship, company*) mise *f* à l'index **(b)** *Arch* (*for shoes*) cirage *m*

blackish ['blækɪʃ] *adj* noirâtre, tirant sur le noir

blackjack¹ ['blækdʒæk] *n Am* **(a)** (*weapon*) nerf *m* de bœuf **(b)** *Cards* vingt-et-un *m*

blackjack² *vt Am* frapper avec un nerf de bœuf

black knight *n St Exch* chevalier *m* noir

blacklead ['blækled] *vt Old-fashioned* (*stove etc*) passer à la mine de plomb

blackleg¹ ['blækleg] *n Ind F Pej* jaune *m*, briseur *m* de grève

blackleg² *vi* (-gg-) *Ind F Pej* briser une grève, être un briseur de grève

blacklist¹ ['blæklɪst] *n* liste *f* noire

blacklist² *vt* (*person, company etc*) inscrire *ou* mettre sur la liste noire

black magic *n* magie *f* noire

blackmail¹ ['blækmeɪl] *n* chantage *m*; **emotional b.** chantage aux sentiments

blackmail² *vt* soumettre à un chantage, *F* faire chanter; **to be blackmailed** être victime d'un chantage; **I'm being blackmailed for £5,000** je suis victime d'un chantage, on me réclame 5 000 livres; **to b. sb into resigning** faire chanter qn pour qu'il démissionne

blackmailer ['blækmeɪlər] *n* maître chanteur *m*, *pl* maîtres chanteurs

black mark *n* mauvais point *m*; **that earned him a b.** ça a été un mauvais point pour lui

black market *n* marché *m* noir; **to buy/sell on the b.** acheter/vendre au marché noir; **the b. in jeans** le marché noir du jean; **b. cigarettes/whisky** des cigarettes/du whisky au marché noir

black marketeer *n* profiteur *m* du marché noir

blackness ['blæknɪs] *n* (*of hair, sky etc*), *Fig* noirceur *f*

blackout ['blækaʊt] *n* **(a)** (*during war*) black-out *m inv*; *Fig* **to impose a news b.** interdire la divulgation d'une information; (*in general*) imposer le black-out sur l'information **(b)** *El* panne *f* d'électricité **(c)** *Th* obscurcissement *m* de la scène **(d)** (*loss of consciousness*) évanouissement *m*; (*memory lapse*) trou *m* de mémoire

black pudding *n* boudin *m* noir

Black Rod *n Br Parl* = huissier *m* de la Chambre des Lords

Black Sea *n* Mer *f* Noire

black sheep *n Fig* mouton *m* noir

Blackshirt ['blækʃɜːt] *n Pol* chemise *f* noire

blacksmith ['blæksmɪθ] *n* forgeron *m*; (*who shoes horses*) maréchal-ferrant *m*, *pl* maréchaux-ferrants

black spot *n Aut etc* point *m* noir

blackthorn ['blækθɔːn] *n* **(a)** (*shrub*) épine *f* noire, prunier *m* épineux, prunellier *m* **(b)** (*stick*) gourdin *m* (*en épines*)

blacktop ['blæktɒp] *n esp Am* **(a)** (*substance*) bitume *m* **(b)** (*road*) route *f* bitumée

black velvet *n* = mélange *m* de champagne et de stout

blackwater ['blækwɔːtər] *adj Med* **b. fever** hématurie *f*

black widow *n* (*spider*) veuve *f* noire

bladder ['blædər] *n* **(a)** (*for urine*) vessie *f*; **to have a full b.** avoir la vessie pleine **(b)** (*sac*) vésicule *f*; **air b.** (*of fish*) vésicule aérienne; (*of seaweed*) vésicule aérocyste **(c)** (*of ball*) vessie *f*

bladderwort ['blædəwɜːt] *n* (*plant*) utriculaire *f*

bladderwrack ['blædəræk] *n* (*seaweed*) goémon *m* jaune vésiculeux

blade [bleɪd] *n* **(a)** (*of knife, sword, skate*) lame *f*; (*of guillotine*) couperet *m*; (*of saw*) feuille *f*, lame **(b)** (*of propeller*) pale *f*; (*of oar*) pelle *f*, pale; (*of ventilator, turbine*) ailette *f*; (*of waterwheel*) aube *f*; (*of spade*) fer *m*; *Aut* (*of windscreen wiper*) balai *m*, raclette *f* **(c)** (*of grass*) brin *m* **(d)** *Arch* (*sword*) sabre *m*, épée *f* **(e)** *Arch, Hum* **a young b.** un jeune gaillard

bladed ['bleɪdɪd] *adj* à lame(s)/à pales; **three-b.** (*penknife*) à trois lames; (*propeller*) à trois pales

blah(-blah) ['blɑː(blɑː)] *n F* bla-bla *m inv*, baratin *m*; **the usual b.** le baratin habituel

blame¹ [bleɪm] *n* **(a)** (*reproof*) reproches *mpl*; **to deserve b.** mériter des reproches; **to be free from b.** être irréprochable

(b) (*responsibility*) responsabilité *f*, faute *f*; **to lay** *or* **put the b. (for sth) on sb, to lay the b. (for sth) at sb's door** rejeter *ou* faire retomber la responsabilité *ou* la faute (de qch) sur qn; **to bear** *or* **take the b.** endosser la responsabilité **(for sth** de qch); **why is it always me that gets the b.?** pourquoi est-ce que tout retombe toujours sur moi?; **I got the b. for breaking the window** c'est moi qu'on a accusé d'avoir cassé la fenêtre; **to shift the b. onto sb** rejeter la responsabilité sur qn; **where does the b. lie?** à qui la faute?; **the b. lies with her** c'est (de) sa faute

blame² *vt* (*person*) rendre responsable; **to b. sb for sth** reprocher qch à qn; (*hold responsible for*) rendre qn responsable de qch, attribuer à qn la responsabilité de qch; **he can't be blamed for the accident** on ne peut pas le rendre responsable de l'accident; **to b. sth on sb** rejeter la faute *ou* la responsabilité de qch sur qn; **the accident was blamed on the bad weather** on a dit que le mauvais temps était la cause de l'accident; **to b. sb for doing sth** reprocher à qn de faire *ou* d'avoir fait qch; **he can't be blamed for trying** on ne peut pas lui reprocher d'avoir essayé; **I have nothing to b. myself for** je n'ai rien à me reprocher; **I b. the**

parents pour moi, ce sont les parents qui sont responsables; **I b. myself** je me sens responsable, c'est (de) ma faute; **don't b. me!** ne me mets pas ça sur le dos!; **don't b. me if you're late** tu ne viendras pas dire que c'est de ma faute si tu es en retard; **I wouldn't b. you if you left me** si tu me quittais, je ne te le reprocherais pas; **I wouldn't b. you if you left him** je te comprendrais si tu le quittais; **she's leaving him and who can b. her?** elle le quitte et on la comprend bien; **to have only oneself to b., to have nobody to b. but oneself** n'avoir à s'en prendre qu'à soi-même; **he is to b.** c'est de sa faute; **she was in no way to b.** elle n'était en aucun cas responsable; **the bad weather was to b.** c'était à cause du mauvais temps

blamed [bleɪmd] *adj esp US Euph* sacré

blameless [ˈbleɪmlɪs] *adj* irréprochable, *Lit* irrépréhensible; **to lead a b. life** avoir une vie irréprochable; **none of us is b.** nous sommes tous responsables

blamelessly [ˈbleɪmlɪslɪ] *adv* de façon irréprochable

blameworthy [ˈbleɪmwɜːðɪ] *adj Fml* (*person*) coupable, blâmable; (*action, behaviour*) répréhensible

blanch [blɑːntʃ] **1** *vt* (*vegetables, almonds*) blanchir; **blanched almonds** amandes *fpl* émondées **2** *vi* (*of person*) blêmir, pâlir

blancmange [bləˈmɒnʒ] *n Culin* blanc-manger *m, pl* blancs-mangers

bland [blænd] *adj* **(a)** (*person, speech*) (*insipid*) insipide; (*suspiciously smooth*) doucereux, mielleux; (*smile*) de politesse **(b)** (*without flavour*) (*food, drink*) fade; *Fig* (*music, film*) insipide

blandish [ˈblændɪʃ] *vt* amadouer

blandishments [ˈblændɪʃmənts] *npl* cajoleries *fpl*; **to resist sb's b.** ne pas se laisser amadouer par qn

blandly [ˈblændlɪ] *adv* (*to reply, smile*) mielleusement

blank[1] [blæŋk] *adj* **(a)** (*empty, with nothing on it*) (*paper*) blanc, *f* blanche; (*page*) blanc, vierge; (*tape, cassette*) vierge; (*wall*) aveugle; (*cartridge*) à blanc; *Comptr* (*disk, screen*) vide; (*unformatted*) vierge; *Comptr* **the screen suddenly went b.** l'écran s'est soudain effacé; **to leave b.** (*part of form etc*) laisser blanc, ne pas remplir; **leave the other side of the paper b.** ne rien écrire sur l'envers de la feuille; *Cards* **to be b. in clubs** ne pas avoir de trèfles dans son jeu; *Com, Fin* **b. credit** crédit *m* en blanc; **b. space** blanc *m*, espace *m* vide; *Comptr* **b. unformatted disk** disquette *f* vierge

(b) (*vacant*) (*look*) vide, sans expression; **my mind went b.** je me suis senti la tête vide, j'ai eu un trou; **to look b.** avoir l'air complètement déconcerté *ou* ahuri; **a look of b. astonishment** un air ébahi

(c) (*absolute, complete*) (*impossibility, refusal*) absolu

blank[2] *n* **(a)** (*in document etc*) blanc *m*, vide *m*; *Am* (*for telegram etc*) formulaire *m*, formule *f*; *Mil* cartouche *f* à blanc; (*on target*) blanc; **to fire blanks** tirer à blanc; *Sl* **he's shooting blanks** (*not producing children*) son sperme n'est pas assez concentré; **to leave blanks** laisser des blancs; **his mind is a b.** (*he has lost his memory*) il ne se souvient de rien; **I'm sorry, my mind is a b.** je suis désolé, j'ai un trou; **the rest is a b.** après cela, c'est le vide; *Cards* **to have a b. in clubs** ne pas avoir de trèfles dans son jeu

(b) (*in dominoes*) blanc *m*; *Fig* **to draw a b.** (*be unsuccessful in search*) faire chou blanc; *Am* (*be unable to remember*) avoir un trou de mémoire

(c) (*metal disc*) (*in minting coins*) flan *m*; *Metal, MecE* flan, masselotte *f*, galette *f*

(d) *Typ* (*to replace swear word etc*) tiret *m*

blank cheque *n* chèque *m* en blanc; *Fig* carte *f* blanche; **to give sb a b. to do sth** donner carte blanche à qn pour faire qch

blank-endorse *vt Fin* endosser en blanc

blanket[1] [ˈblæŋkɪt] **1** *n* (*for bed, horse*) couverture *f*; *Fig* (*of fog, mist*) manteau *m*; (*of snow*) couche *f*; *Old-fashioned F* **he was born on the wrong side of the b.** c'est un enfant naturel **2** *adj attrib* (*general*) (*acceptance*) général, global; **b. contract** contrat *m* global; *Rad, TV* **b. coverage** (*of event*) reportage *m* (très) complet; **b. term** terme *m* général

blanket[2] *vt* **the mountain was blanketed in fog/snow** la montagne était couverte d'un manteau de brouillard/de neige

blanket bath *n Med* = toilette *f* d'un malade alité faite par une infirmière

blanket stitch *n Sewing* point *m* de languette

blanking [ˈblæŋkɪŋ] *n TV* suppression *f* de faisceau; (*erasing*) effacement *m*

blankly [ˈblæŋklɪ] *adv* (*to look at sb*) (*without expression*) sans expression, avec l'air de ne rien comprendre; (*in confusion*) d'un air déconcerté; **to stare b. into space** avoir le regard perdu dans le vide

blankness [ˈblæŋknɪs] *n* **(a)** (*of person*) air *m* confus *ou* décontenancé **(b)** (*of eyes, expression*) vacuité *f*

▶ **blank out 1** *vtsep* (*parts of text, tape etc*) effacer; **her face had been blanked out** (*on negative*) on avait effacé son visage; (*on print*) on avait caché son visage; **she's blanked out the memory** elle a effacé cet événement de sa mémoire **2** *vi* (*lose consciousness*) tomber dans les pommes

blank verse *n Liter* vers *mpl* blancs *ou* non rimés

blare[1] [bleər] *n* (*of trumpet*) beuglement(s) *m(pl)*; (*of radio*) braillement(s) *m(pl)*; **the b. of the brass band** le son éclatant de la fanfare; **the b. of car horns** le son discordant des klaxons de voiture

blare[2] *vi* (*of trumpet*) sonner; (*of car horn*) retentir; (*of radio*) beugler, *F* gueuler, brailler; **the band blared** le son de la fanfare retentit de façon discordante

▶ **blare away** *vi* (*of radio etc*) *F* gueuler

▶ **blare out 1** *vi* (*of trumpet*) sonner; (*of voice*) résonner (de façon discordante) **2** *vtsep* (*of loudspeaker, band*) faire retentir

Blarney [ˈblɑːnɪ] *n F* **to have kissed the B. Stone** avoir le don pour embobiner les gens

blarney[1] [ˈblɑːnɪ] *n* boniments *mpl*; **don't give me any of your b.** arrête tes boniments

blarney[2] *vt F* embobiner; **to b. sb into doing sth** faire faire qch à qn en l'embobinant; **to b. one's way out of trouble/into a job** se sortir d'embarras/obtenir un emploi grâce à son bagou(t)

blasé [ˈblɑːzeɪ] *adj* blasé

blaspheme [blæsˈfiːm] *vti* blasphémer

blasphemer [blæsˈfiːmər] *n* blasphémateur, -trice

blasphemous [ˈblæsfəməs] *adj* (*person*) blasphémateur, -trice; (*words etc*) blasphématoire

blasphemously [ˈblæsfəməslɪ] *adv* de façon blasphématoire; **to speak b.** blasphémer

blasphemy [ˈblæsfəmɪ] *n* blasphème *m*

blast[1] [blɑːst] *n* **(a)** (*gust of wind*) coup *m ou* rafale *f* de vent; **b. of heat** bouffée *f* de chaleur; **b. of steam** jet *m* de vapeur

(b) (*of whistle, siren*) coup *m*; **b. on the trumpet** sonnerie *f* de trompette; **to give a b. on the whistle** donner un coup de sifflet

(c) *Fig* **to be** *or* **be working at full b.** être en pleine activité, travailler à plein rendement; *F* **to turn the radio on full b.** faire gueuler *ou* brailler la radio

(d) (*shock wave*) (*from explosion etc*) souffle *m*; **a lot of people were killed by the b.** beaucoup de gens ont été tués par l'explosion

(e) (*explosion*) explosion *f*; **b. hole** *Min* pétard *m*, trou *m* de mine; *Mil* fourneau *m* de mine

(f) *Am F* (*thrill*) **to get a b. out of doing sth** prendre son pied en faisant qch

(g) *F* **a b. from the past** (*song*) un vieux tube; **that's a real b. from the past** (*fashion, behaviour etc*) c'est comme autrefois; (*brings back memories*) ça me ramène des années en arrière

blast[2] *int* mince (alors)!, zut (alors)!

blast[3] **1** *vt* **(a)** *Min* (*with dynamite etc*) faire sauter **(b)** (*of frost*) (*plant*) brûler, flétrir; (*of lightning*) (*tree etc*) foudroyer; *Fig* **to b. sb's hopes** anéantir les espoirs de qn **(c)** *F* **b. it!** zut alors!; **b. you/her!** je te/la maudis!; **b. this computer!** maudit ordinateur! **(d)** *F* (*criticize*) démolir **2** *vi* (*of brass instrument*) sonner; (*of radio etc*) hurler, brailler

▶ **blast away** *vi* **(a)** (*of radio etc*) hurler, brailler **(b)** (*with gun, rifle etc*) tirer en rafales

▶ **blast off** *vi* (*of rocket, missile*) décoller

blasted [ˈblɑːstɪd] *adj attrib* **(a)** (*heath*) désolé; (*oak*) foudroyé **(b)** *F* (*intensifier*) sacré; **you b. idiot!** espèce d'idiot!

blast furnace *n Metal* haut fourneau *m*

blasting [ˈblɑːstɪŋ] *n* **(a)** *Min* travail *m* aux explosifs; **beware of b.!** attention aux coups de mine! **(b)** *F* (*severe criticism*) critique *f* féroce *ou* violente; (*reprimand*) savon *m*; **her latest novel got a b. from reviewers** son dernier roman a été démoli par les critiques *ou* la critique

blastoderm [ˈblæstəʊdɜːm] *n Biol* blastoderme *m*

blastoff [ˈblɑːstɒf] *n* (*of rocket*) décollage *m*; **b. is at 2 o'clock** la fusée décollera à deux heures

blatancy [ˈbleɪtənsɪ] *n* (*of injustice, crime etc*) caractère *m* flagrant

blatant [ˈbleɪtənt] *adj* (*injustice*) criant; (*lie, prejudice, disregard*) flagrant, manifeste; **a b. liar** un fieffé menteur, un menteur éhonté; **don't be so b.** (*in your approach*) sois un peu plus diplomate; **it was a b. attempt to win him over** c'était une tentative évidente de s'assurer ses faveurs

blatantly [ˈbleɪtəntlɪ] *adv* (*to lie etc*) d'une manière flagrante; **it's b. obvious that ...** il est évident que ...; **yes, that's b. obvious** oui, évidemment

blather ['blæðər] *n, vi* = **blether**

blaze¹ [bleɪz] *n* **(a)** (*fire*) flamme(s) *f(pl)*, feu *m*; (*in fireplace*) flambée *f*; *Fig* (*of sun*) flamboiement *m*; (*of colours, diamonds etc*) éclat *m*; **many people died in the b.** beaucoup de gens ont péri dans les flammes; **in a b.** en feu, en flammes; *Fig* **b. of anger** éclat de colère; **in a b. of anger** enflammé de colère; **the street was a b. of light** la rue était tout illuminée; **the garden was a b. of colour** le jardin était resplendissant de couleur; **he married her in a b. of publicity** il l'a épousée sous le feu des médias; **the film was released in a b. of publicity** la sortie du film a été accompagnée d'une publicité monstre; **in a b. of glory** (*to die, retire, return*) plein de gloire
(b) *Old-fashioned F* **go to blazes!** allez au diable!; **what the blazes does he want/is he doing?** mais qu'est-ce qu'il veut/fait, bon sang?; **to work like blazes** travailler comme un forcené; **to run like blazes** courir comme un dératé

blaze² *vi* **(a)** (*of fire etc*) flamber; **they had left all the lights blazing** ils avaient laissé toutes les lumières allumées; **the house was blazing** (*on fire*) la maison flambait; **the house was blazing with lights** la maison était tout illuminée; **his eyes were blazing with anger/passion** ses yeux lançaient des éclairs de colère/passion **(b)** (*of sun, colours*) flamboyer

blaze³ *n* **(a)** (*on face of horse, ox*) marque *f* allongée blanche **(b)** (*on tree*) **b. (mark)** blanchis *m*, griffe *f*

blaze⁴ *vt* (*tree*) griffer, blanchir; **to b. a trail** tracer un chemin; *Fig* faire œuvre de pionnier, montrer la voie; (*in science etc*) poser des jalons

▶ **blaze away** *vi* **(a)** flamboyer **(b)** (*with gun*) = **blast away (b)**

▶ **blaze down** *vi* (*of sun*) taper; **the sun was blazing down on the beach** le soleil dardait ses rayons sur la plage

▶ **blaze up** *vi* (*of fire*) s'embraser, s'enflammer; *F* (*in anger*) (*of person*) s'emporter

blazer ['bleɪzər] *n* (*clothing*) blazer *m*

blazing ['bleɪzɪŋ] *adj usu attrib* **(a)** (*on fire*) en feu, enflammé; (*ship*) embrasé **(b)** *Fig* (*fire, sun*) ardent **(c)** *F* **a b. row** une dispute violente **(d)** *F pred* (*angry*) fou de rage; **he was b.** il fulminait, il était fou de rage

blazon¹ ['bleɪzən] *n Her* (*arms*) blason *m*

blazon² *vt* **(a)** *Fig* **his name was blazoned over the front pages of all the newspapers** son nom s'étalait en grosses lettres à la une de tous les journaux **(b)** *Her* blasonner

▶ **blazon abroad** *vtsep Fml* (*news*) annoncer à son de trompe

▶ **blazon out** *or* **forth** *vtsep Fml* annoncer *ou* proclamer à son de trompe

bldg *abbr* **building**

bleach¹ [bliːtʃ] *n* (*for hair*) décolorant *m*; **(household) b.** eau *f* de Javel

bleach² **1** *vt* (*clothes*) passer à l'eau de Javel; (*hair*) décolorer; **hair/sheets bleached by the sun** cheveux/draps décolorés par le soleil **2** *vi Tex etc* blanchir; *Ch etc* se décolorer; **do not b.** (*washing instruction*) javel interdite; **the colours had bleached out** les couleurs étaient passées

bleachers ['bliːtʃəz] *npl Am Sp* gradins *mpl*

bleaching ['bliːtʃɪŋ] *n Tex etc* blanchiment *m*; (*of hair*), *Ch* décoloration *f*; **b. agent** *Tex* produit *m* blanchissant; *Ch* décolorant *m*

bleak [bliːk] *adj* **(a)** (*weather*) morne, triste; (*terrain*) exposé au vent; (*wind*) froid **(b)** *Fig* (*future*) lugubre; (*smile*) pâle; **the prospects are b.** les perspectives sont peu encourageantes

bleakly ['bliːklɪ] *adv* (*to smile, stare*) d'un air affligé *ou* désolé; (*to reply, answer*) d'un ton affligé *ou* désolé

bleakness ['bliːknɪs] *n* (*of weather, landscape*) aspect *m* morne, tristesse *f*; *Fig* (*of future, room*) caractère *m* lugubre

blearily ['blɪərɪlɪ] *adv* (*to look at sb*) les yeux troubles

bleary ['blɪərɪ] *adj* (*eyes*) trouble

bleary-eyed [blɪərɪ'aɪd] *adj* aux yeux troubles; **to be b. with lack of sleep** avoir des petits yeux (à cause du manque de sommeil)

bleat¹ [bliːt] *n* (*of sheep*) bêlement *m*; *Fig* (*complaint*) plainte *f*

bleat² *vi* (*of sheep*) bêler; (*of ram*) blatérer; (*of goat, old man etc*) chevroter; *Fig* (*complain*) se plaindre; **what's he bleating about?** de quoi se plaint-il?

bleating ['bliːtɪŋ] **1** *adj* (*voice*) chevrotant **2** *n* (*of sheep*) bêlement *m*; *Fig* (*complaining*) plaintes *fpl*

bleed [bliːd] (*pt, pp* **bled** [bled]) **1** *vi* **(a)** saigner; **his nose is bleeding** il saigne du nez; **to b. to death** saigner à mort; *Iron* **my heart bleeds for you** tu me fends le cœur **(b)** (*of tree etc*) pleurer, perdre sa sève **(c)** (*of colour*) (*on washing*) couler **(d)** *MecE* **b. nipple** téton *m* de purge; **b. screw** vis *f* de purge; **b. valve** soupape *f ou* valve *f* de purge **2** *vt* **(a)** *Med* saigner; *F* **to b. sb white** *or* **dry** saigner qn à blanc **(b)** *MecE* (*brakes, pipes, radiator etc*) purger

bleeder ['bliːdər] *n* **(a)** *Br Sl Pej* salaud *m*; **poor b.** pauvre type *m*; **you lucky b.!** sacré veinard! **(b)** *MecE* dispositif *m* de drainage, purgeur *m*

bleeding ['bliːdɪŋ] **1** *adj* **(a)** saignant, qui saigne; *Lit* **with a b. heart** le cœur brisé; *Fig Pej* **b. heart** personne *f* au cœur tendre **(b)** *Br Sl* (*intensifier*) sacré; **you b. liar!** sacré menteur! **2** *n* **(a)** saignement *m*, hémorragie *f*; *Bot* écoulement *m* de sève; **b. from the nose** saignement de nez **(b)** *Med, Hist* (*blood-letting*) saignée *f* **(c)** *MecE* (*of brakes, radiator*) purge *f*

bleeding-heart [bliːdɪŋ'hɑːt] *adj* **b. liberals** = des libéraux *mpl* au cœur tendre

bleep¹ [bliːp] *n* (*of electronic device*) bip *m*

bleep² **1** *vi* (*of electronic device*) faire bip **2** *vt* (*with pager*) appeler au moyen d'un bip; **I'm being bleeped** on m'appelle

bleeper ['bliːpər] *n* bip *m*, récepteur *m* d'appel *ou* de poche, alphapage *m*

bleeping ['bliːpɪŋ] *n* (*of electronic device*) bip-bip *m*

blemish¹ ['blemɪʃ] *n* (*mark*) tache *f*; **there's not a b. on it** (*on piece of furniture etc*) il/elle n'a pas le moindre défaut; *Fig* **there's not a b. on her record** il n'y a rien à redire à ses états de service; **a reputation without b.** une réputation sans tache; **the case left her without a b. on her reputation** le procès se termina sans que sa réputation soit entachée

blemish² *vt* (*work of art etc*) abîmer, gâcher; *Fig* (*reputation etc*) entacher, ternir; **blemished fruit** fruits tachés

blench *vi* (*turn pale*) blêmir; **to b. with terror** pâlir de terreur

blend¹ [blend] *n* (*of teas, whiskies, tobaccos etc*) mélange *m*

blend² **1** *vt* (*teas, coffees, whiskies etc*) mélanger; **to b. sth with sth** mélanger qch à *ou* avec qch; **to b. one colour with another** (*mix*) mélanger une couleur avec une autre; (*harmonize*) allier *ou* marier deux couleurs; **to b. one colour into another** (*in painting*) fondre une couleur dans une autre
2 *vi* se mêler, se mélanger, se confondre **(into** en); (*of voices etc*) se marier harmonieusement; (*of colours, flavours*) s'allier, se marier; (*of ideas etc*) fusionner; **oil does not b. with water** l'huile ne se mélange pas à l'eau; **the colours b. well** les couleurs se marient bien *ou* vont bien ensemble; **the new building blends into the background** le nouveau bâtiment se fond dans son environnement; *Fig* **she tends to b. into the background** elle a tendance à se fondre dans les décors

▶ **blend in** **1** *vi* (*harmonize*) s'harmoniser, se marier **(with** avec); (*of person*) s'intégrer; **that new building doesn't b. in with its surroundings** ce nouveau bâtiment ne se marie pas bien *ou* ne va pas bien avec ce qui l'entoure **2** *vtsep* (*mix*) (*flour etc*) incorporer

blender ['blendər] *n* (*kitchen appliance*) mixer *m*, mixeur *m*

blending ['blendɪŋ] *n* (*of teas, tobaccos etc*) mélange *m*; (*of two characteristics*) alliance *f*; (*in winemaking*) coupage *m*

bless [bles] *vt* (*pt, pp* **blessed** [blest]; *pp Arch* **blest** [blest]) **(a)** (*of God, priest*) (*people*) bénir; (*bell*) consacrer, bénir; **I b. the day I learnt to swim** béni soit le jour où j'ai appris à nager; **God b. you!** que Dieu vous bénisse!; **b. you!** (*when sb sneezes*) à vos souhaits!; *F* **b. you for doing the washing-up** merci bien d'avoir fait la vaisselle; **Mary, b. her, has agreed to do it** Mary, Dieu soit loué, a accepté de le faire; **b. her (heart)!** quel ange!
(b) *usu passive* (*be fortunate in possessing*) **to be blessed with sth** jouir de qch, avoir le bonheur de posséder qch; **to be blessed with a cheerful disposition** être doté d'un heureux caractère; **they have been blessed with two fine children** ils ont deux enfants adorables; *Iron* **they are blessed with eight children** ils ont huit enfants sur les bras; *F* **he hasn't a penny to b. himself with** il n'a pas le sou
(c) (*glorify*) **to b. God** bénir *ou* adorer Dieu
(d) *Old-fashioned* (*expressing surprise*) **b. me!, (God) b. my soul!** mon Dieu!; **well, I'm blest!** par exemple!; **I'm blest if I know** que le diable m'emporte si je le sais

blessed ['blesɪd] *adj* **(a)** *Rel* (*Sacrament, Virgin etc*) saint; **the late king of b. memory** le feu roi, d'heureuse mémoire; *Bible* **b. are the poor in spirit** heureux les pauvres d'esprit **(b)** *F* (*intensifier*) **every b. day** tous les jours que Dieu fait; **the whole b. day** toute la sainte journée; **the whole b. lot** tout le bazar, tout le bataclan; **it's a b. nuisance having to …** quelle barbe d'avoir à …; **I can't see a b. thing** je n'y vois rien

blessedly ['blesɪdlɪ] *adv* parfaitement; **the speech was b. short** Dieu merci, le discours fut bref

blessedness ['blesɪdnɪs] *n* félicité *f*; *Rel* béatitude *f*

blessing ['blesɪŋ] *n* **(a)** (*divine sanction, favour*) bénédiction *f*; **to give** *or* **pronounce the b.** donner la bénédiction; **to ask** *or* **say a b.** (*at meal*) dire le bénédicité; **the blessings of God** les grâces *fpl* de Dieu; **to give a plan one's b.** donner sa bénédiction à un projet; **it's a b. no-one was hurt** c'est une bénédiction que personne n'ait été blessé
(b) (*benefit, advantage*) **the blessings of civilization** les bienfaits *mpl* de la civilisation; **it turned out to be a b. in**

disguise à la longue, j'ai/il a/*etc* pu m'en/s'en/*etc* féliciter; **losing my job was a b. in disguise** finalement, ça a été une bonne chose de perdre mon travail; **to count one's blessings** s'estimer heureux avec ce qu'on a; **count your blessings** ne te plains pas, estime-toi heureux

blest [blest] **1** *adj* bienheureux **2** *npl Rel Arch* **the B.** les bienheureux *mpl*, les saints *mpl* du Paradis

blether[1] ['bleðər] *n F* **(a)** (*nonsense*) paroles *fpl* en l'air, bêtises *fpl* **(b)** (*person*) = personne *f* qui parle à tort et à travers *ou* qui dit des bêtises

blether[2] *vi F* parler à tort et à travers, dire des bêtises; **blethering idiot** espèce *f* d'idiot

blight[1] [blaɪt] *n* **(a)** *Agr* (*on cereals*) rouille *f*; (*on potatoes*) brunissure *f*; (*on peaches etc*) cloque *f* **(b)** *Fig* influence *f* néfaste; **his arrival cast a b. over the company** son arrivée a jeté un froid sur l'assistance

blight[2] *vt Agr* (*wheat*) rouiller; (*of wind*) flétrir; *Fig* **to b. sb's hopes** anéantir les espoirs de qn; *Fig* **a marriage blighted by money problems** un mariage assombri par des problèmes d'argent

blighter ['blaɪtər] *n Old-fashioned Br F* **(a)** (*fellow*) individu *m*, type *m*; **poor b.** pauvre type; **(you) lucky b.!** veinard! **(b)** *Pej* (*despicable person*) salaud *m*; **the little b.** le petit coquin

Blighty ['blaɪtɪ] *n Br Mil, Hist F* (*Britain*) Grande-Bretagne *f*, le pays; (*wound*) = pendant la première guerre mondiale, une blessure suffisamment grave pour qu'elle nécessite un rapatriement en Grande-Bretagne

blimey ['blaɪmɪ] *int Br Sl* mince alors!

blimp [blɪmp] *n* **(a)** *Av* (petit) dirigeable *m* de reconnaissance **(b)** *Br Fig* (*reactionary*) réactionnaire *m* endurci; **a real Colonel B.** une vraie culotte de peau, un scro(n)gneugneu

blind[1] [blaɪnd] **1** *adj* **(a)** (*person, Fig obedience, faith, hatred*) aveugle; **b. from birth** aveugle de naissance; **b. in one eye** borgne; **a b. man/woman** un/une aveugle; **to be struck b.** être frappé de cécité; **I'm b. without my glasses** je ne vois rien sans mes lunettes; **he's as b. as a bat** il est myope comme une taupe; **to turn a b. eye on** *or* **to sth** fermer les yeux sur qch; **to be b. to sb's faults** ne pas voir les défauts de qn, être aveugle aux défauts de qn; *Prov* **love is b.** l'amour est aveugle; *Av* **b. flying** vol *m* sans visibilité, vol en P.S.V.; *F* **he didn't take a b. bit of notice** il n'a pas fait la moindre attention; *F* **in a b. stupor** (*drunk*) bourré; **b. test** test *m* aveugle

(b) (*bend*) masqué, sans visibilité

(c) (*without exit*) (*window, door*) feint, aveugle; **b. alley** impasse *f*, cul-de-sac *m*, *pl* culs-de-sac; *Fig* impasse; **b.-alley job** situation *f* sans avenir

2 *npl* **the b.** les aveugles *mpl*; **she goes to the b. school** elle est dans une école pour aveugles *ou* pour non-voyants

3 *adv* **to fire b.** tirer au jugé; *Av* **to fly b.** voler à l'aveuglette; *Culin* **bake b. for five minutes** cuire le fond de tarte cinq minutes; *F* **to go at a thing b.** se lancer à l'aveuglette dans une entreprise; **she swore b. that ...** elle a juré ses grands dieux que ...; **b. drunk** complètement ivre *ou* soûl

blind[2] *vt* (*person*) aveugler, rendre aveugle; (*temporarily*) (*of tears*) aveugler; (*dazzle*) aveugler, éblouir; **blinded ex-servicemen** aveugles *mpl* de guerre; **blinded by passion** aveuglé par la passion; **love blinded her to his faults** aveuglée par l'amour, elle n'a pas vu ses défauts; **to b. sb to the facts** cacher les faits à qn; *Fig* **don't b. me with science** pas la peine de m'éblouir avec ta science

blind[3] *n* **(a)** *Br* (*at window*) store *m*; *Aut* (*on radiator*) rideau *m*; **shop b.** (*over pavement*) banne *f* **(b)** *Fig* (*pretext*) prétexte *m*

blind date *n F* rendez-vous *m* arrangé, rencontre *f* arrangée (*avec qn qu'on ne connaît pas*); (*person*) inconnu(e) (*avec qui on a rendez-vous*); **I have a b.** j'ai rendez-vous avec un(e) inconnu(e); **I've fixed you up with a b.** je t'ai organisé une rencontre avec quelqu'un que tu ne connais pas

blinder ['blaɪndər] *n* **(a)** *Br Sl* **to go on a b.** (*get very drunk*) se bourrer (la gueule) **(b)** *Sp F* (*outstanding feat*) **he played a b. (of a game)** il a eu un jeu spectaculaire; **the first goal was a b.** le premier but a été spectaculaire **(c)** *Am* (*for horse*) œillère *f*

blindfold[1] ['blaɪndfəʊld] **1** *adj* les yeux bandés **2** *adv* (*to enter into an undertaking*) aveuglément; *Chess* (*to play*) sans voir l'échiquier; **I can do it b.** (*I am very familiar with the task*) je pourrais le faire les yeux fermés **3** *n* bandeau *m* sur les yeux; **they put a b. over my eyes** ils m'ont mis un bandeau sur les yeux

blindfold[2] *vt* **to b. sb** bander les yeux à *ou* de qn, couvrir les yeux de qn avec un bandeau; **to be blindfolded** avoir les yeux bandés, avoir un bandeau sur les yeux

blinding ['blaɪndɪŋ] **1** *adj* aveuglant; **b. headache** mal *m* de tête effroyable; **it was a b. revelation** ça a été une véritable révélation; **the b. intensity of his criticism** l'intensité affolante de ses critiques **2** *n* aveuglement *m*; (*by headlights, light etc*) éblouissement *m*

blindingly ['blaɪndɪŋlɪ] *adv* **it's b. obvious** c'est tout à fait évident, cela saute aux yeux **(that** que)

blindly ['blaɪndlɪ] *adv* **(a)** (*to look at sth, sb*) sans le/la/*etc* voir; (*to grope*) à l'aveuglette **(b)** *Fig* (*to obey*) aveuglément; (*to follow*) aveuglément, sans réfléchir

blind man's bluff *n* (*game*) colin-maillard *m*; **to play b.** jouer à colin-maillard

blindness ['blaɪndnɪs] *n* cécité *f*; *Fig* aveuglement *m*; **b. to the facts** refus *m* d'envisager *ou* de voir les faits

blind side *n Rugby* côté *m* fermé; *Aut* **he came up on my b.** il s'est approché dans mon angle mort

blind spot *n* (*on road*) angle *m* mort; *Anat* papille *f* optique; *Fig* (*of person*) point *m* faible, faiblesse *f*; **I have a b. where maths are concerned** (*don't understand them*) je n'y connais absolument rien en mathématiques

blindworm ['blaɪndwɜːm] *n* orvet *m*

blink[1] [blɪŋk] *n* **(a)** (*of eyes*) battement *m ou* clignement *m* de paupières **(b)** (*of light*) lueur *f* momentanée; *Comptr* **b. rate** (*of cursor*) vitesse *f* de clignotement **(c)** *Br Sl* **to be on the b.** (*of television set etc*) être en panne, faire des siennes

blink[2] **1** *vi* **(a)** (*of person*) battre *ou* cligner des paupières, clignoter; *Fig* **without blinking** (*calmly, without surprise*) sans sourciller; *Fig* **he was the first to b.** (*in confrontation*) c'est lui qui a cédé le premier; **to b. at sb/sth** regarder qn/qch en clignant des yeux; **she blinked at the sight in astonishment** elle regardait et n'en croyait pas ses yeux; *Fig* **to b. at the fact that ...** (*pretend not to see*) nier le fait que ...; *Fig* **to b. at the facts** fermer les yeux sur la vérité **(b)** (*of light, cursor*) clignoter **2** *vt* **to b. one's eyes** cligner des yeux

▶ **blink away** *vtsep* (*tears*) refouler d'un battement de paupières

blinker[1] ['blɪŋkər] *n* **(a)** (*for horse*), *Fig* œillère *f* **(b)** (*at airfield*) phare *m* à éclats; *Aut* clignotant *m*

blinker[2] *vt* (*horse*) mettre des œillères à; *Fig* **they are very blinkered, that's very blinkered thinking on their part** ils ont des œillères

blinking ['blɪŋkɪŋ] **1** *adj* **(a)** (*eyes*) qui clignotent **(b)** (*light*) clignotant, papillotant **(c)** *Old-fashioned Br F* **what a b. nuisance!** quelle barbe!; **b. idiot!** espèce d'idiot!; **a b. good meal** un repas sacrément bon; **I b. well <u>did</u> see her there** je l'y ai vue de mes propres yeux **2** *n* **(a)** (*of eyes*) clignotement *m* **(b)** (*of light*) papillotage *m*

blintz(e) [blɪnts] *n Am Culin* crêpe *f* fourrée (*au fromage, aux fruits etc*)

blip [blɪp] *n* (*of radar*) (*on screen*) spot *m*; (*noise*) top *m* d'écho; *Fig F* (*in statistics*) écart *m* momentané

bliss [blɪs] *n* grand bonheur *m*, béatitude *f*, **breakfast in bed, what b.!** le petit déjeuner au lit, quel bonheur!; **it was b. to plunge into the water** c'était un bonheur de plonger dans l'eau; **it's sheer b.!** c'est le bonheur total!; **isn't it b. not having your mother here!** quel bonheur de ne plus avoir ta mère ici, hein?

blissful ['blɪsfʊl] *adj* (*person*) (bien)heureux; (*holiday, weekend etc*) plein de bonheur; **we had a b. time in France** nous avons passé un merveilleux séjour en France; **... she said with a b. sigh** ... dit-elle en soupirant de bonheur; **he was in b. ignorance of what was happening** il n'avait pas la moindre idée de ce qui se passait; **I'd rather remain in b. ignorance** j'aime autant ne pas savoir

blissfully ['blɪsfʊlɪ] *adv* **... she said b.** ... dit-elle, au comble du bonheur; **he smiled b.** il eut un grand sourire de bonheur; **b. happy** au comble du bonheur; **to be b. ignorant of sth/unaware that ...** ne pas se douter le moins du monde de qch/que ...; **the house is b. quiet without the children** la maison est merveilleusement calme sans les enfants

blister[1] ['blɪstər] *n* **(a)** (*on skin*) ampoule *f*, cloque *f* **(b)** (*in paint*) cloque *f*, boursouflure *f*; (*in glass*) bulle *f*; *Metal* soufflure *f* **(c)** *Com* **b. pack** blister *m*

blister[2] **1** *vt* (*hand etc*) provoquer des ampoules sur **2** *vi* **(a)** (*of heel etc*) se couvrir d'ampoules **(b)** (*of paint*) cloquer

blistered ['blɪstəd] *adj* couvert d'ampoules

blistering ['blɪstərɪŋ] **1** *adj* (*sun, heat*) brûlant, ardent; *Fig* (*attack*) foudroyant; **she's setting a b. pace** elle mène un train d'enfer **2** *n* **(a)** (*on skin*) ampoules *fpl*; **b. is inevitable** la formation d'ampoules est inévitable **(b)** (*of paint*) cloquage *m*

blisteringly ['blɪstərɪŋlɪ] *adv* **it was a b. hot day** c'était une journée d'une chaleur étouffante; **it was b. hot** il faisait une chaleur étouffante

blithe [blaɪð] *adj* joyeux, allègre; (*irresponsible*) (*disregard, attitude, response etc*) désinvolte

blithely [ˈblaɪðlɪ] *adv* joyeusement, allègrement; (*irresponsibly*) avec désinvolture; **she b. ignored him** elle l'a ignoré avec une complète désinvolture; **he was b. unaware of the danger** il ne se doutait pas le moins du monde du danger qu'il courait
blithering [ˈblɪðərɪŋ] *adj F* sacré; **b. idiot!** espèce d'idiot!
BLitt [biːˈlɪt] *n* (*abbr* **Bachelor of Letters**) (*diploma*) licence *f* ès lettres; (*person*) licencié, -ée ès lettres
blitz¹ [blɪts] *n Mil* blitz *m*, bombardement *m* aérien; *Br Hist* **the B.** le Blitz; *Fig* **to have a b. on sth** s'attaquer à qch; *Fig* **the b. of holiday advertisements starts immediately after Christmas** dès que les fêtes sont finies, on est bombardé de publicité par les agences de voyage
blitz² *vt* bombarder; **the house was blitzed** la maison a été endommagée/détruite par un bombardement; *Fig F* **to b. sb with letters/complaints** bombarder qn de lettres/plaintes
blitzed [blɪtst] *adj Sl* (*drunk*) bourré
blizzard [ˈblɪzəd] *n* tempête *f* de neige; (*in North America*) blizzard *m*
bloat [bləʊt] **1** *vt* boursoufler, bouffir **2** *vi* bouffir
bloated [ˈbləʊtɪd] *adj* bouffi, boursouflé; *Fig* (*estimate, bill*) salé; **to feel b.** (*because of water retention, overeating*) se sentir ballonné *ou* gonflé; **he suffers from a b. ego** sa suffisance n'a pas de limites; **b. with pride** bouffi d'orgueil
bloater [ˈbləʊtər] *n* (*herring*) hareng *m* bouffi
blob [blɒb] *n* (*of colour*) tache *f*; (*of ink*) pâté *m*
bloc [blɒk] *n Pol etc* bloc *m*
block¹ [blɒk] *n* **(a)** (*slab*) (*of marble, paper etc*) bloc *m*; (*of wood*) tronçon *m*; (*of chocolate*) grosse tablette *f*; (*for chopping*) billot *m*; (*for getting on horse*) montoir *m*; (*for athletes*) bloc de départ; **like a b. of stone** (*transfixed*) immobile; (*unfeeling*) dur; (*not speaking*) silencieux, muet; *Am* **to be on the b.** (*up for auction*) être mis aux enchères; **blocks** (*for children*) (jeu *m* de) cubes *mpl*
(b) *esp Am* (*buildings between two streets*) pâté *m* de maisons; *Austr* (*plot of land*) lot *m*; **he lives two blocks from us** il habite à deux rues de nous; **it's two blocks north/south of here** c'est à deux rues d'ici vers le nord/sud; **we live on the same b.** nous habitons dans le même pâté de maisons; **to walk round the b.** faire le tour du pâté de maisons; *Br* **b. of flats** immeuble *m*; **b. association** association *f* de riverains
(c) (*obstruction*) **traffic b.** embouteillage *m*; **mental b.** blocage *m* psychologique; **I have a mental b. about computers** je fais un blocage psychologique avec les ordinateurs; *Fin* **to put a b. on an account** bloquer un compte
(d) *Sl* (*head*) caboche *f*; **I'll knock your b. off!** je vais te casser la gueule!
(e) (*of rooms*) contingent *m*; **to book a b. of four weeks** réserver quatre semaines consécutives; **b. of seats** bloc-sièges *m*; *Fin* **b. of shares** paquet *m* d'actions
(f) *Aut* (**engine**) **b.** bloc-moteur *m*, *pl* blocs-moteurs; **to put a car up on blocks** mettre une voiture sur cales
(g) *Comptr* bloc *m*; **b. copy** copie *f* de bloc; **b. marker** délimiteur *m* de bloc; **b. moving** déplacement *m* de bloc; **b. structure** (*of file*) structure *f* de bloc
(h) (*in engraving*) (*wood*) planche *f*, bois *m*; **to write sth in b. capitals** écrire qch en majuscules d'imprimerie
(i) *Tech* (*pulley*) poulie *f*; **b. and tackle** palan *m*
block² **1** *vt* **(a)** (*passage etc*) bloquer, obstruer; (*wheel*) bloquer, enrayer; (*flow of traffic*) entraver, gêner; (*progress*) arrêter; *Fin* (*cheque, account*) bloquer; **to b. sb's way** barrer le passage *ou* le chemin à qn; **to b. the view** cacher la vue; *Parl* **to b. a bill** faire obstruction à un projet de loi **(b)** *Sp* (*ball*) bloquer; *Fb etc* (*opponent*) gêner; **the goalkeeper blocked the shot** le gardien arrêta le tir; *Tennis* **she blocked the serve magnificently** elle fit un superbe retour de service **(c)** *Comptr* (*text*) bloquer **(d)** (*room*) retenir, bloquer **2** *vi* (*of actor*) prendre ses marques
▶ **block in** *vtsep esp Aut* (*sb*) empêcher de sortir, bloquer le passage à; **I'm blocked in** je suis coincé
▶ **block off** *vtsep* (*street*) barrer
▶ **block out** *vtsep* **(a)** (*prevent entry of*) empêcher d'entrer *ou* de passer; **those trees b. out all the sun** ces arbres empêchent le soleil de passer; **to b. out the memory of sth/sb** refouler le souvenir de qch/qn; **it's impossible to b. that music out** il est impossible d'ignorer cette musique **(b)** (*draft*) (*book, project*) ébaucher, esquisser
▶ **block up** *vtsep* **(a)** (*close*) (*hole*) boucher; (*door, window*) boucher, murer **(b)** (*clog*) (*pipe etc*) obstruer, engorger; (*sink*) boucher
blockade¹ [blɒˈkeɪd] *n Mil, Pol* blocus *m*; **to impose/break a b.** imposer/forcer un blocus; **to raise** *or* **lift a b.** lever un blocus; *Hist* **to run the b.** forcer le blocus; *Hist* **b. runner** forceur *m* de blocus
blockade² *vt* **(a)** (*town, port*) bloquer, faire le blocus de; (*fortified place*) faire le blocus de **(b)** *Am* (*flow of traffic*) bloquer; (*street*) encombrer
blockage [ˈblɒkɪdʒ] *n* (*of pipe, artery etc*) obstruction *f*; (*in street*) embouteillage *m*
block booking *n* (*of theatre tickets etc*) réservation *f ou* location *f* de groupe
blockbuster [ˈblɒkbʌstər] *n F* **his speech was a real b.** son discours a fait énormément d'effet; **this show will be a b.** ce spectacle aura un succès fou; **a b. of a film** un film à grand spectacle *ou* commercial; **a b. of a novel** un roman à succès
block diagram *n* schéma *m* fonctionnel; *Geog* bloc-diagramme *m*, *pl* blocs-diagrammes
blocked [blɒkt] *adj* (*account, cheque, market*) bloqué; **b. space** (*reserved*) espace *m* réservé
blocked up *adj* bouché; **my nose is b.** j'ai le nez bouché
blockhead [ˈblɒkhed] *n F* lourdaud *m*
blockhouse [ˈblɒkhaʊs] *n Mil* blockhaus *m*
blocking [ˈblɒkɪŋ] *n* **(a)** (*of street*) encombrement *m*, embouteillage *m*; (*of port*) blocus *m* **(b)** *El* (*of current*) blocage *m* **(c)** (*of book binding*) gaufrage *m*, frappe *f* **(d)** (*of actor, camera*) prise *f* des marques
block letter *n Typ* lettre *f* moulée; **to write sth in block letters** écrire qch en majuscules d'imprimerie
block-oriented [blɒˈkɔːrɪəntɪd] *adj Comptr* orienté bloc
block vote *n* vote *m* groupé (*où un délégué vote pour tous les membres de sa section*)
bloke [bləʊk] *n Br F* (*man*) type *m*
blond, *f* **blonde** [blɒnd] *adj, n* blond, *f* blonde
blood¹ [blʌd] *n* sang *m*; **to give b.** (*of donor*) donner du sang; **his b. will be on your hands** tu porteras la responsabilité de sa mort; *Fig* **his b. is up** il est furieux; **it makes my b. boil/run cold** cela me fait bouillir/me glace le sang; **to commit a crime in cold b.** commettre un crime de sang-froid; *Fig* **the committee needs new** *or* **fresh b.** le comité a besoin d'être rajeuni; **to shed** *or* **spill b.** verser le sang; *Fig* **it's not worth shedding** *or* **spilling b. over** inutile de se battre pour ça; *Fig* **to be out for b.** chercher à se venger; *Fig* **to be after** *or* **out for sb's b.** vouloir se venger de qn, en vouloir à qn; *Fig* **the boss is after your b.** le patron en a après toi; *prov* **it's like trying to get b. out of a stone** c'est comme si on se heurtait à un mur; **the theatre is in her b.** elle a le théâtre dans le sang; *Prov* **b. is thicker than water** la famille passe avant tout; **prince of the b.** prince *m* du sang; **warm the milk until it is at b. heat** chauffe le lait jusqu'à ce qu'il atteigne la température du corps; **b. horse** pur-sang *m inv*; **b. red** (*colour*) rouge sang *m inv*
blood² *vt* **(a)** (*first-time hunter*) initier (*en l'aspergeant du sang de la bête morte*); (*hounds*) donner le goût du sang à **(b)** *Fig esp Sp* initier
blood-and-thunder *adj* (*film, novel etc*) sensationnel, mélodramatique
blood bank *n* banque *f* du sang
blood bath *n* carnage *m*, massacre *m*
blood blister *n* pinçon *m*
blood brother *n* frère *m* de sang
blood cell *n* globule *m* sanguin
blood count *n* numération *f* globulaire
bloodcurdling [ˈblʌdkɜːdlɪŋ] *adj* (*story, scream*) à vous tourner les sangs, à (vous) figer le sang
blood donor *n* donneur, -euse de sang
blood doping *n Sp, Med* = transfusion *f* sanguine utilisée comme méthode de dopage
-blooded [ˈblʌdɪd] *suff* **hot-/cold-b.** à sang chaud/froid
blood group *n* groupe *m* sanguin; **what b. are you?** quel est votre groupe sanguin?
bloodhound [ˈblʌdhaʊnd] *n* (*dog, Fig detective*) limier *m*
bloodiness [ˈblʌdɪnɪs] *n* état *m* sanglant; (*of battle*) sauvagerie *f*
bloodless [ˈblʌdlɪs] *adj* **(a)** (*victory etc*) sans effusion de sang **(b)** (*pale*) exsangue, pâle **(c)** (*lifeless*) sans vitalité
bloodlessly [ˈblʌdlɪslɪ] *adv* sans effusion de sang
blood-letting *n* **(a)** (*violent feud, bloodshed*) effusion *f* de sang **(b)** *Med, Hist* saignée *f*
blood money *n* prix *m* du sang
blood orange *n* sanguine *f*
blood plasma *n* plasma *m* sanguin
blood poisoning *n* septicémie *f*, toxémie *f*
blood pressure *n* tension *f* (artérielle); **to have high b.** avoir beaucoup de tension *ou* une tension élevée; **to take** *or* **measure sb's b.** prendre la tension de qn
blood product *n Med* dérivé du sang *m*
blood pudding *n* boudin *m* noir
blood-red *adj* rouge sang *inv*
blood relation *n* parent, -ente par le sang
blood sample *n* prise *f* de sang

blood sausage *n* boudin *m* noir
blood serum *n* sérum *m* sanguin
bloodshed [ˈblʌdʃed] *n* **(a)** effusion *f* de sang; **without b.** sans verser de sang **(b)** *(slaughter)* carnage *m*
bloodshot [ˈblʌdʃɒt] *adj (eye)* injecté de sang; **to become b.** *(of eye)* s'injecter
blood sports *npl* chasse *f*
bloodstain [ˈblʌdsteɪn] *n* tache *f* de sang
bloodstained [ˈblʌdsteɪnd] *adj* taché *ou* souillé de sang, ensanglanté
bloodstock [ˈblʌdstɒk] *n* pur-sang *mpl*
bloodstone [ˈblʌdstəʊn] *n Miner* jaspe *m* sanguin
bloodstream [ˈblʌdstriːm] *n Physiol* sang *m*
bloodsucker [ˈblʌdsʌkər] *n Zool* sangsue *f*; *Fig F* sangsue, parasite *m*
bloodsucking [ˈblʌdsʌkɪŋ] *adj attrib Zool* hématophage; *Fig F* vampirique
blood test *n* examen *m ou* prise *f* de sang; **I'm having a b. tomorrow** on doit me faire une prise de sang demain
bloodthirsty [ˈblʌdθɜːstɪ] *adj (person)* sanguinaire; *(film, book)* très violent
bloody[1] [ˈblʌdɪ] **1** *adj* **(a)** *(stained with blood)* ensanglanté, taché de sang; *(revolution, battle etc)* sanglant; **he came home with a b. nose** il est rentré en saignant du nez; *Fig* **to give sb a b. nose** donner une raclée à qn

(b) *Br Sl (intensifier)* sacré; **a b. liar** un sacré menteur; **(you) b. fool!** espèce d'imbécile!; **b. hell!** merde, bon sang!; **he wouldn't even tell me his b. name!** il n'a même pas voulu me dire son foutu nom!; **politicians are all the b. same!** ces foutus hommes politiques sont tous les mêmes!

2 *adv Br Sl* **it's b. hot!** quelle putain de chaleur!; **he can b. well do it himself!** il n'a qu'à se démerder tout seul; **I b. well am going out** j'ai bien l'intention de sortir (et personne ne m'en empêchera); **I'm b. tired** je suis complètement crevé; **not b. likely!** il n'y a pas de danger!
bloody[2] *vt (pt, pp* **bloodied***) (one's hands etc)* ensanglanter, souiller de sang; *Fig* **to b. one's hands** se salir les mains
Bloody Mary *n* **(a)** *Hist* la reine Mary I (d'Angleterre) **(b)** *(drink)* = mélange *m* de vodka et de jus de tomate
bloody-minded *adj Br Sl* **he's just b.** c'est un mauvais coucheur; **don't be so b.** arrête d'emmerder le monde
bloody-mindedness [blʌdɪˈmaɪndɪdnɪs] *n Br Sl* **it's sheer b.** ce n'est rien que pour emmerder le monde; **the b. of the decision is unbelievable** la décision, prise uniquement pour emmerder le monde, est incroyable; **I admire her b.** j'admire la façon qu'elle a d'emmerder le monde
bloom[1] [bluːm] *n* **(a)** *(flower)* fleur *f*; **to come** *or* **burst into b.** fleurir; **flower in b.** fleur éclose; **the roses are in b.** les roses sont ouvertes; **in full b.** épanoui; *Lit* **in the b. of youth** à *ou* dans la fleur de l'âge; **the constant arguing soon took the b. off their marriage** les disputes perpétuelles firent rapidement perdre son charme à leur mariage **(b)** *(on grape, peach etc)* velouté *m*, pruine *f*, duvet *m*; *(of cheeks)* éclat *m*; *Ch* **cobalt/zinc b.** fleur *f* de cobalt/zinc
bloom[2] *vi (of plant)* fleurir, être en fleur; *Fig (of child)* être éclatant *ou* resplendissant de santé
bloomer [ˈbluːmər] *n Br F (mistake)* bourde *f*; *(in social circumstances)* gaffe *f*
bloomers [ˈbluːməz] *npl* culotte *f* bouffante *(de femme)*
blooming [ˈbluːmɪŋ] **1** *adj* **(a)** *(flower)* éclos; *Fig* florissant; **b. with health** resplendissant de santé **(b)** *Br F (intensifier)* **you b. idiot!** espèce d'idiot!; **it's a b. lie!** ça, pour un mensonge!; **the woman's a b. genius** cette femme, c'est vraiment un génie **2** *adv Br F* **I b. well will go!** et moi, je te dis que j'irai! **3** *n* floraison *f*, fleuraison *f*
blooper [ˈbluːpər] *n Am F* = **bloomer**
blossom[1] [ˈblɒs(ə)m] *n (of trees)* fleur *f*; **tree in b.** arbre *m* en fleur(s); **apple/cherry/orange b.** fleur de pommier/de cerisier/d'oranger; **to come into b.** fleurir
blossom[2] *vi (of tree)* fleurir; *Fig (of friendship, relationship)* s'épanouir; **she had blossomed into a charming young woman** elle était devenue une charmante jeune femme
▶ **blossom out** *vi* = **blossom**[2]
blossoming [ˈblɒsəmɪŋ] **1** *n* fleuraison *f*, floraison *f*; *Fig* épanouissement *m* **2** *adj* qui commence à fleurir; *Fig (friendship, partnership)* en herbe
blot[1] [blɒt] *n* tache *f*; *(of ink)* pâté *m*; *Fig* **a b. on sb's honour/reputation** une tache faite à l'honneur/la réputation de qn; *Fig* **to be a b. on the landscape** *(of building)* gâcher le paysage
blot[2] **(-tt-) 1** *vt* **(a)** *(stain)* tacher, souiller; *(with ink)* faire des pâtés sur; *Fig* **to b. one's copybook** ternir sa réputation; **to b. one's copybook with sb** descendre dans l'estime de qn **(b)** *(letter etc)* passer un buvard sur; *(lipstick)* passer un Kleenex® sur **2** *vi (of blotting paper)* boire l'encre
▶ **blot out** *vtsep (obliterate) (memory etc)* effacer; *(word)* rayer, barrer; *(of fog etc) (feature of landscape etc)* cacher, masquer
blotch[1] [blɒtʃ] *n* **(a)** *(of ink, paint)* tache *f*, éclaboussure *f* **(b)** *(on skin)* tache *f*, marbrure *f*
blotch[2] **1** *vt (skin)* couvrir de taches; **cold blotches the skin** le froid marbre la peau; **her face was blotched with tears** son visage portait des traces de larmes **2** *vi* **this pen blotches** ce stylo fuit
blotchy [ˈblɒtʃɪ] *adj* tacheté; *(complexion)* brouillé, couperosé
blotter [ˈblɒtər] *n* **(a)** *(for ink) (paper)* buvard *m*; *(desk pad)* sous-main *m inv*; *(with handle)* tampon *m* buvard **(b)** *Com Old-fashioned* brouillard *m*, main *f* courante
blotting [ˈblɒtɪŋ] *n* séchage *m* au papier buvard; **b. paper** (papier *m*) buvard *m*; **b. pad** (bloc *m*) buvard; *(large)* sous-main *m inv*
blotto [ˈblɒtəʊ] *adj Br Sl (drunk)* bourré
blouse [blaʊz] *n* **(a)** *(woman's)* chemisier *m*, corsage *m* **(b)** *Am (sailor's etc)* vareuse *f*
blow[1] [bləʊ] *n* **(a)** *(through mouth)* souffle *m*; **give your nose a good b.** *(to child)* mouche-toi bien **(b)** *(of whistle)* coup *m*
blow[2] *(pt* **blew** [bluː]; *pp* **blown** [bləʊn]) **1** *vi* **(a)** *(of wind)* souffler; **the wind's blowing from the west** le vent souffle de l'ouest; **it was blowing a gale** le vent soufflait en tempête; **the wind was blowing down the chimney** le vent s'engouffrait dans la cheminée; **my papers blew out of the window** mes papiers se sont envolés par la fenêtre; **the door blew open** le vent a ouvert la porte

(b) *(of person, animal)* souffler; *(of whale)* rejeter l'eau par les évents; *(of whistle)* retentir, se faire entendre; **to b. on one's fingers** souffler dans ses doigts; *F* **to b. into town** arriver en ville à l'improviste; **when did you b. into town?** quand est-ce que tu es arrivé?

(c) *Am F (boast)* se vanter

(d) *(of fuse)* sauter; *(of boiler etc)* exploser

(e) *F* **b.!** zut!

2 *vt* **(a) the wind is blowing the rain against the windows** le vent pousse la pluie contre les vitres; **to b. a ship ashore** *(of wind)* pousser un navire à la côte; **to be blown out to sea** être poussé au large; **he was nearly blown off his feet** *(by wind, explosion)* il a failli être emporté

(b) *(of person) (trumpet)* jouer de; **to b. a whistle** donner un coup de sifflet; **he blew the whistle** il donna un coup de sifflet; **to b. the dust off sth** souffler sur qch pour enlever la poussière; **to b. sb a kiss** envoyer un baiser à qn; **to b. one's nose** se moucher; **to b. the horn** sonner du cor; *Fig* **to b. one's own trumpet** chanter ses propres louanges, se faire mousser

(c) *(soap bubbles)* faire; *(glass)* souffler; *(egg)* vider

(d) *(horse etc)* essouffler

(e) *(fuse, gasket, safe)* faire sauter; *F* **the Grand Canyon blew my mind** quel pied le Grand Canyon!; *F* **the prices blew my mind** les prix m'ont affolé

(f) *F (ruin, spoil)* gâcher, bousiller; *(opportunity)* louper; **that's blown it!** ça a tout gâché *ou* bousillé, ça a tout fait louper

(g) *F (money)* claquer **(on** dans)

(h) *F* **b. the expense!** au diable l'avarice!; **I'll be blowed if ...** je veux bien être pendu si ...; **well, I'm blowed!** ça, par exemple!; **b. it!** zut!
blow[3] *n (with fist etc, Fig of fate)* coup *m*; **at the first b.** du premier coup; **at a (single) b.** d'un (seul) coup; **to strike a b.** asséner *ou* donner un coup; *Fig* **to strike a b. for/against sth** remporter une bataille en faveur de/contre qch; **to come to blows, to exchange blows** en venir aux coups *ou* aux mains; **to return b. for b.** rendre coup pour coup; **his death is a sad b. to his family** sa mort est un rude coup pour sa famille; **b. to sb's pride** atteinte *f* (faite) à l'amour-propre de qn
▶ **blow about 1** *vi (of leaves etc)* voler çà et là **2** *vtsep (sth)* agiter, faire voler; *(leaves etc)* disperser
▶ **blow away 1** *vtsep* **(a)** *(of wind etc)* emporter **(b)** *Am Sl (kill)* descendre, flinguer **2** *vi (of papers etc)* s'envoler; **his hat blew away in the wind** son chapeau s'est envolé à cause du vent; **all my cares have blown away** tous mes soucis se sont évanouis *ou* envolés
▶ **blow down 1** *vtsep (of wind) (fence etc)* abattre, renverser; *(tree)* abattre; *Old-fashioned F* **well b. me down!** c'est pas Dieu possible! **2** *vi (of fence etc)* s'abattre, se renverser; *(of tree)* s'abattre
▶ **blow in 1** *vtsep* **(a)** *(of explosion, wind etc) (window, door)* enfoncer **(b)** *(of person)* souffler; **b. some more air in** souffle un peu plus d'air dedans **2** *vi* **(a)** *(of window etc)* s'enfoncer **(b) the dust is blowing in** le vent fait entrer la poussière **(c)**

F (*of person*) arriver à l'improviste; **when did you b. in?** quand est-ce que tu es arrivé?

▶ **blow off 1** *vtsep* **(a)** (*of wind*) (*hat, slates*) emporter; **the wind blew the papers off my desk** le vent a fait s'envoler les papiers qui étaient sur mon bureau **(b)** (*of person*) (*dust etc*) enlever en soufflant dessus **(c)** (*with gun, explosives*) faire sauter; **the gunman threatened to b. their heads off** l'homme au pistolet a menacé de leur faire sauter la cervelle; **she got her hand blown off** sa main a été arrachée dans l'explosion **2** *vi* (*of hat etc*) s'envoler

▶ **blow out 1** *vtsep* **(a)** (*candle*) souffler **(b)** (*air*) chasser, expulser; (*one's cheeks*) gonfler; **to b. one's brains out** se faire sauter la cervelle; **to blow sb's brains out** faire sauter la cervelle à qn; **to b. itself out** (*of storm*) se dissiper, se calmer **2** *vi* **(a)** (*of candle*) s'éteindre **(b)** *Aut etc* (*of gasket*) sauter; (*of tyre*) éclater; *El* (*of fuse*) sauter

▶ **blow over 1** *vtsep* (*of wind*) (*table etc*) renverser **2** *vi* **(a)** (*fall down*) se renverser **(b)** (*come to an end*) (*of storm*) se calmer, se dissiper; *Fig* (*of argument*) se calmer; **the scandal soon blew over** le scandale a été vite oublié

▶ **blow up 1** *vi* (*of mine*) éclater, sauter; (*of boiler etc*) crever, exploser; *Fig* (*of person*) piquer une colère (**at sb** contre qn); **the argument blew up out of nowhere** la dispute a commencé sans raison; **to b. up into a crisis** (*of situation*) prendre les proportions d'une crise; **there's a gale blowing up** il se prépare une tempête; *Fig* **to b. up in sb's face** (*go wrong*) claquer dans les doigts de qn

2 *vtsep* **(a)** (*bomb, booby trapped car etc*) faire sauter, (faire) exploser; (*building*) faire sauter

(b) (*tyre, balloon etc*) gonfler

(c) *Phot* agrandir; **I'd like this photograph blown up** j'aimerais un agrandissement de cette photo

(d) *F* (*exaggerate*) (*incident etc*) exagérer; **you're blowing this up out of all proportion** tu en fais un drame

blowback ['bləʊbæk] *n Aut* retour *m* de flamme

blow-by *n Aut* fuite *f* de gaz

blow-by-blow *adj* (*account*) minutieux, détaillé

blowcock ['bləʊkɒk] *n* robinet *m* d'extraction *ou* de vidange

blowdart ['bləʊdɑːt] *n* petite flèche *f*

blow-dry¹ *n* (*at hairdresser's*) brushing *m*

blow-dry² *vt* (*one's hair*) sécher (avec un séchoir); **to b. sb's hair** faire un brushing à qn

blow-drying *n* **too much b. can damage your hair** à force d'être séchés au séchoir, les cheveux s'abîment

blower ['bləʊər] *n* **(a)** *Br F* (*telephone*) bigophone *m*; **on the b.** au bigophone; **to get on the b. to sb** passer un coup de fil à qn **(b)** (*in ventilation system*) turbine *f* de ventilation; (*supercharger*) soufflante *f*

blowfly, *pl* **-flies** ['bləʊflaɪ, -flaɪz] *n* mouche *f* de la viande, mouche bleue

blowgun ['bləʊgʌn] *n Am* (*for darts*) sarbacane *f*

blowhard ['bləʊhɑːd] *n F* (*boaster*) vantard, -arde, crâneur, -euse

blowhole ['bləʊhəʊl] *n* **(a)** *Zool* (*of whale*) évent *m* **(b)** (*in ice*) = trou *m* où un phoque *etc* vient respirer **(c)** (*in tunnel*) bouche *f* d'aération

blowing ['bləʊɪŋ] *n* **(a)** (*of wind*) souffle *m*; **he could hear the b. of the wind outside** il entendait le vent souffler dehors **(b)** (*of glass*) soufflage *m*

blow job *n Vulg* (*oral sex*) pipe *f*; **to give sb a b.** tailler une pipe à qn

blowlamp ['bləʊlæmp] *n* **(a)** (*for welding, brazing*) chalumeau *m*, lampe *f* à souder *ou* à braser **(b)** (*for removing paint*) brûloir *m*

blown [bləʊn] *adj* **(a)** (*person*) essoufflé, hors d'haleine **(b)** *El* **b. fuse** fusible *m* fondu, plomb *m* sauté

blowout ['bləʊaʊt] *n* **(a)** *Sl* (*large meal*) gueuleton *m*, grande bouffe *f*; **we had a b. last night** on a fait un gueuleton hier soir **(b)** *Aut etc* (*of tyre*) éclatement *m* **(c)** *Min etc* (*of gas, oil etc*) éruption *f* au cours d'un sondage

blowpipe ['bləʊpaɪp] *n* **(a)** (*for darts*) sarbacane *f* **(b)** *Ch, Metal* chalumeau *m*; (*of glassblower*) fêle *f*

blowtorch ['bləʊtɔːtʃ] *n Am* = **blowlamp**

blow-up ['bləʊʌp] *n F* **(a)** (*argument*) dispute *f*, bagarre *f*; (*tantrum*) accès *m* de fureur; **we had a b. last night** on s'est bagarrés *ou* disputés hier soir **(b)** *Phot* agrandissement *m*

blow-valve *n* (*on steam boiler*) reniflard *m*

blowy ['bləʊɪ] *adj* (*day, weather*) de (grand) vent

blowzy ['blaʊzɪ] *adj* (*woman*) négligé

blub [blʌb] *vi F* = **blubber²**

blubber¹ ['blʌbər] *n* (*of whale*) graisse *f*, lard *m*; *F* (*of person*) graisse

blubber² *vi F* chialer, pleurer comme un veau *ou* une madeleine (**over** sur)

blubbering ['blʌbərɪŋ] *n* larmoiements *mpl*

bludgeon¹ ['blʌdʒən] *n* gourdin *m*, matraque *f*

bludgeon² *vt* matraquer; **he was bludgeoned to death** il a été matraqué à mort; *Fig* **to b. sb into doing sth** forcer qn à faire qch par des méthodes brutales

blue¹ [bluː] **1** *adj* **(a)** (*dress, sky etc*) bleu; **to go** *or* **turn b.** (*of sky, litmus paper*) virer au bleu; (*of person*) (*because suffocating, near death*) devenir violacé *ou* bleu; **to go** *or* **turn b. with cold** devenir bleu de froid; **her face was b. with cold** elle avait le visage violacé par le froid *ou* bleu de froid; *F* **I've told you so until I'm b. in the face** je me tue à te le dire; *F* **she can complain until she's b. in the face** elle peut se plaindre autant qu'elle veut; *F* **to be in a b. funk** avoir une trouille bleue; *F* **to scream** *or* **yell b. murder** crier comme un putois, hurler comme un damné; **once in a b. moon** tous les trente-six du mois; *Med* **b. baby** enfant *mf* bleu(e); *Fig* **to take a b. pencil to sth** censurer qch

(b) *F* (*depressed*) triste, déprimé; **to feel b.** avoir le cafard

(c) *F* (*indecent*) (*joke*) grivois, paillard; **to tell b. jokes** en dire de vertes, en raconter des vertes et des pas mûres

(d) *Pol* conservateur, -trice

2 *n* **(a)** (*colour*) bleu *m*; *Fig* **a bolt from the b.** un événement imprévu; **her resignation was** *or* **came like a bolt from the b.** sa démission a été une véritable surprise; **he arrived out of the b.** il est arrivé à l'improviste; **his resignation came out of the b.** sa démission nous a pris par surprise; **you can't just fire him out of the b. like that** tu ne peux pas le renvoyer du jour au lendemain comme ça

(b) the blues *F* (*depression*) le cafard; *Mus* le blues; **to have (a fit of) the blues, to get the blues** avoir le cafard; **this kind of weather gives me the blues** ce temps me donne le cafard

(c) *Pol* conservateur, -trice; **a true b.** (*patriot*) un(e) patriote; *Pol* un conservateur, une conservatrice

(d) *Sp* **Oxford/Cambridge b.** membre *m* d'une équipe sportive de l'université d'Oxford/de Cambridge

(e) *Mil* **the Blues** *Br* la Cavalerie de la Maison du Souverain; *US Hist* l'armée *f* du Nord

blue² *vt Br F* **to b. one's money** claquer son argent (**on** dans); **don't tell me you've blued the lot!** ne me dis pas que tu as tout claqué!

Bluebeard ['bluːbɪəd] *n* Barbe-bleue *m*

bluebell ['bluːbel] *n* (*flower*) jacinthe *f* sauvage *ou* des bois; *Scot* (*harebell*) campanule *f*

blueberry ['bluːb(ə)rɪ] *n* (*shrub, fruit*) airelle *f*, myrtille *f*, *Can* bleuet *m*

bluebird ['bluːbɜːd] *n* rouge-gorge *m* bleu

blue-black *adj* (*hair, plumage*) noir aux reflets bleus; (*sky*) bleu (de) nuit; (*ink, coat*) bleu-noir *inv*

blue blood *n* sang *m* bleu

bluebottle ['bluːbɒt(ə)l] *n* **(a)** (*insect*) mouche *f* de la viande **(b)** *Old-fashioned Br F* (*policeman*) flic *m*

blue cheese *n* (fromage *m*) bleu *m*

blue chip *n St Exch* valeur *f* de père de famille *ou* de premier ordre

blue-chip *adj St Exch* **b. stocks** *or* **shares** valeurs *fpl* de père de famille *ou* de tout repos; **b. company** affaire *f* de premier ordre

blue-collar *adj* **b. worker** ouvrier *m*, travailleur *m* manuel, col *m* bleu; **b. union** syndicat *m* ouvrier

blue-eyed *adj* aux yeux bleus; *Br F* **his mother's b. boy** le chouchou de sa maman, le petit chéri de sa maman; **the boss's b. boy** le chouchou du patron

blue film *n* film *m* porno

bluegrass ['bluːgrɑːs, -æs] *n* **(a) the B. state** Kentucky *m* **(b)** *Mus* folklore *m* du Kentucky

blue movie *n* film *m* porno

blueness ['bluːnɪs] *n* bleu *m*

blue-pencil *vt Old-fashioned* (*article*) censurer

blueprint ['bluːprɪnt] *n* plan *m*, *Spec* épure *f*; *Fig* **a b. for success** une recette *ou* une garantie de succès

blue ribbon *n* (*first prize*) premier prix *m*

blue-ribbon *adj Am* **b. committee** comité *m* constitué par des personnalités; *Jur* **b. jury** jury *m* d'experts; *Sp* **b. event** épreuve *f* phare

blue rinse *n* (*for hair*) rinçage *m* colorant qui donne des reflets bleutés

bluestocking ['bluːstɒkɪŋ] *n Pej* (*woman*) bas-bleu *m*, *pl* bas-bleus

blue whale *n* baleine *f* bleue, rorqual *m* bleu

bluff¹ [blʌf] **1** *adj* **(a)** (*cliff, coast*) escarpé, à pic **(b)** (*person*) carré et sincère **2** *n* (*cliff*) cap *m ou* falaise *f* à pic, à-pic *m inv*

bluff² *n* **(a)** (*at poker*) bluff *m*; **to call sb's b.** (*at poker*) inviter qn à mettre cartes sur table; *Fig* prendre qn au mot **(b)** (*deception*) bluff *m*; **piece of b.** coup *m* de bluff

bluff³ 1 *vt Cards etc* bluffer; *Fig* **he bluffed her into agreeing**

il a bluffé pour le lui faire accepter **2** *vi* bluffer, faire du bluff; *Cards* bluffer

▶ **bluff out** *vtsep* (*use cleverness*) **to b. one's way out of a tricky situation** se tirer d'affaire par un coup de bluff; **we'll just have to b. it out** nous n'aurons qu'à bluffer

bluffer ['blʌfər] *n* bluffeur, -euse

blunder[1] ['blʌndər] *n* bévue *f*, *F* gaffe *f*

blunder[2] *vi* faire une bévue *ou F* une gaffe; **to b. along** avancer d'un pas maladroit; (*in task*) progresser tant bien que mal; **she was blundering about the room** elle avançait dans la pièce en se cognant contre tout ce qu'elle rencontrait; **to b. against** *or* **into sth** heurter qch, se heurter contre *ou* à qch; **to b. against** *or* **into sb** heurter qn; **she blundered into a situation she knew nothing about** elle s'est trouvée prise dans une situation dont elle ignorait tout; **he managed to b. through** il s'en est tiré tant bien que mal; **to b. on the truth/the solution** tomber sur la vérité/la solution par accident

blunderbuss ['blʌndəbʌs] *n Hist* tromblon *m*

blunderer ['blʌndərər] *n* gaffeur, -euse

blundering ['blʌndərɪŋ] **1** *adj* maladroit **2** *n* maladresse *f*

blunt[1] [blʌnt] *adj* **(a)** (*knife, cutting edge etc*) émoussé; (*pencil*) mal taillé; *Jur* (*instrument*) contondant **(b)** *Fig* (*person*) brusque, carré; (*question*) brusque; (*reply*) carré; (*fact*) brutal; (*refusal*) net, carré; **to be b.,...** pour parler franchement, ...

blunt[2] *vt* **(a)** (*knife etc*) émousser; (*pencil*) épointer **(b)** *Fig* (*sb's feelings, anger*) émousser

bluntly ['blʌntlɪ] *adv* (*to ask*) brusquement; (*to reply*) carrément, brutalement; **to put it b., ...** (pour parler) franchement, ...; **to speak b.** parler net *ou* carrément

bluntness ['blʌntnɪs] *n* **(a)** (*of knife, sword etc*) manque *m* de tranchant; **because of the b. of the pencil** parce que le crayon n'avait pas de pointe **(b)** *Fig* (*of person*) brusquerie *f*; (*of question, manner, attitude*) rudesse *f*; **b. of speech** francparler *m*, franchise *f*

blur[1] [blɜːr] *n* (*vague shape*) forme *f* confuse; *Phot* flou *m*; **without my glasses, everything is a b.** sans mes lunettes, je suis complètement dans le brouillard; **b. of tears** voile *m* de larmes; *Fig* **it's all a b. now** (*of past events*) ce n'est plus qu'un vague souvenir; **her memories were a b.** ses souvenirs étaient très vagues; **the first years of her marriage had gone by in a b.** les premières années de son mariage étaient passées à toute vitesse; **when travelling at such speeds, the countryside is little more than a b.** quand on avance à une telle vitesse, le paysage n'est qu'une suite de formes confuses

blur[2] (-rr-) **1** *vt* **(a)** (*make hazy*) brouiller, troubler; **eyes blurred with tears** yeux voilés *ou* brouillés de larmes; **the haze has blurred the outline of the mountain** la brume a estompé les contours de la montagne; **time had blurred the memory** le souvenir était devenu confus avec le temps **(b)** (*smear*) (*with ink etc*) barbouiller; *Typ* maculer, mâchurer **2** *vi* **(a)** (*become hazy*) **her memories had blurred with time** ses souvenirs s'étaient estompés avec le temps **(b)** (*smear*) (*of ink*) s'estomper

blurb [blɜːb] *n F* notice *f* publicitaire; (*on book*) promotion *f* (en quatrième de couverture); (*on front page of paper etc*) accroche *f*

blurred [blɜːd] *adj* (*photograph*) flou; (*contours*) indécis, flou, estompé; (*memories*) confus, vague; *Med* **b. vision** vue *f* trouble; **to have b. vision** voir trouble

blurring ['blɜːrɪŋ] *n Phot* flou *m*

▶ **blurt out** *vtsep* (*secret*) lâcher étourdiment, laisser échapper; **he's dead, she blurted out** il est mort, a-t-elle lâché

blush[1] [blʌʃ] *n* **(a)** (*of shyness, shame*) rougeur *f*; **a b. rose to her cheeks** le sang lui est monté au visage; **to hide one's blushes** baisser les yeux d'embarras; **to bring a b. to sb's cheeks** faire rougir qn; *Lit* **the first b. of dawn** les premières rougeurs de l'aube; **b. wine** vin *m* rosé très léger **(b)** *Fml* **at first b.** à l'abord, au premier abord

blush[2] *vi* (*of person*) rougir; **he blushed at the thought** il rougit à cette pensée; **to b. for** *or* **with shame** rougir de honte; **to b. crimson** devenir cramoisi; **to b. to the roots of one's hair** rougir jusqu'à la racine des cheveux; *Fig* **to b. to admit sth** rougir de devoir admettre qch

blusher ['blʌʃər] *n* (*for face*) blush *m*, fard *m* à joues

blushing ['blʌʃɪŋ] **1** *adj* (*person*) rougissant; **the b. bride** la mariée **2** *n* rougissement *m*

bluster[1] ['blʌstər] *n* (*of storm*) fureur *f*, fracas *m*; *Fig* **I wasn't impressed by his b.** ses grands cris ne m'impressionnaient pas; **his threats were no more than b.** ses menaces fulminantes n'étaient en fait que du vent

bluster[2] *vi* (*of wind*) souffler en rafales; *Fig* (*speak aggressively*) fanfaronner

▶ **bluster out** *vtsep* **to b. one's way out of a situation** se sortir d'une situation en fanfaronnant; **to b. it out** s'en sortir en fanfaronnant

blustering ['blʌstərɪŋ] **1** *adj* (*wind*) violent; *Fig* (*person, tone*) fanfaron **2** *n* fanfaronnade(s) *f(pl)*

blustery ['blʌst(ə)rɪ] *adj* (*wind*) violent; (*day*) de (grand) vent

blvd (*abbr* **boulevard**) boul, bd

BMA [biːem'eɪ] *n* (*abbr* **British Medical Association**) ≈ ordre *m* des médecins

B-movie *n* film *m* de série B; **he was a B. actor** c'était un acteur de série B

BO [biː'əʊ] *n F* (*abbr* **body odour**) = odeur *f* corporelle; **to have BO** sentir (la transpiration), sentir mauvais

boa ['bəʊə] *n* (*snake*) boa *m*; **b. constrictor** boa constricteur, constrictor *m*; **feather b.** (*scarf*) boa

boar [bɔːr] *n* (*animal*) verrat *m*; **wild b.** sanglier *m*; (*young*) marcassin *m*; **b. hunting** chasse *f* au sanglier; *Culin* **b.'s head** hure *f* de sanglier

board[1] [bɔːd] *n* **(a)** (*plank*) planche *f*; (*thick*) madrier *m*; (*for bread*) planche à (couper le) pain; (*for notices*) panneau *m* de publicité *ou* d'affichage; (*inscribed with information*) écriteau *m*; *Sch* **to write sth on the b.** écrire qch au tableau; *Old-fashioned, Hum Th* **the boards** les planches

(b) *Admin etc* conseil *m*, comité *m*, commission *f*; **b. (of directors)** (*of company*) conseil d'administration; **to be on the b.** (*of company*) faire partie *ou* être membre du conseil d'administration; **advisory b.** comité consultatif; **disciplinary b.** conseil de discipline; **medical b.** conseil de santé; **b. of examiners** jury *m* d'examen; **b. of trustees** (*of museum, school etc*) conseil de gestion

(c) (*table*) table *f*; (*food*) table, nourriture *f*; **full b.** pension *f* complète; *Fig* **to sweep the b.** faire table rase

(d) (*for draughts*) damier *m*; (*for chess*) échiquier *m*

(e) *Av, Naut* **on b.** à bord; **to take goods on b.** embarquer des marchandises; *Fig* **to take on b.** (*work, responsibility*) accepter; (*problem*) assumer; (*comments, information*) assimiler; **to go on b.** monter à bord, s'embarquer; *Fig* **to go by the b.** (*of plan, hopes etc*) être abandonné; (*of reputation*) être perdu; *Fig* **to let sth go by the b.** abandonner qch, laisser tomber qch

(f) (*in bookbinding*) (*cardboard*) carton *m*; **the boards** (*of book*) les plats *mpl*; **in paper boards** cartonné; **limp boards** cartonnage *m* souple

(g) *Am TV etc* console *f*

(h) *Comptr* (*in PC*) carte *f*; (*in mainframe*) panneau *m*; **on b.** installé

board[2] **1** *vt* **(a)** (*of passengers*) (*ship, plane*) aller *ou* monter à bord de; (*train, bus*) monter dans; *Naut* (*come alongside*) aborder, accoster; *Admin* (*ship*) (*for inspection*) arraisonner **(b)** (*book*) cartonner **2** *vi* **(a)** (*lodge*) être en pension; **I b. at Mrs Brown's** *or* **with Mrs Brown** je suis en pension chez Mme Brown; *Sch* **he'll start boarding when he's twelve** à douze ans, il ira en pension **(b)** *Av* **flight 123 is now boarding** l'embarquement a commencé pour le vol 123

▶ **board in** *vtsep* = **board up**

▶ **board out** *vtsep* (*children*) mettre en pension

▶ **board up** *vtsep* (*door, window*) condamner

board and lodging *n* pension *f* complète; **with b.** nourri et logé

boarder ['bɔːdər] *n* **(a)** (*lodger*) pensionnaire *mf*; *Sch* interne *mf*; **she takes in boarders** elle prend des pensionnaires **(b)** *Naut* abordeur *m*

board game *n* jeu *m* de société

boarding ['bɔːdɪŋ] *n* **(a)** *Naut, Av* embarquement *m*; *Naut* (*for inspection*) arraisonnement *m*; *Naut* (*by pirates, enemy*) abordage *m*; **flight 123 is now ready for b.** le vol 123 est maintenant prêt pour l'embarquement; *Av* **in preparation for b., please extinguish all cigarettes** veuillez éteindre vos cigarettes en vue de l'embarquement; *Av* **b. bridge** (pré-) passerelle *f*; *Av* **b. gate** porte *f* d'embarquement **(b)** *Sch* pensionnat *m*; **b. kennels** (*for dogs*) = chenil *m* où l'on peut faire garder les chiens pendant les vacances

boarding card *n Av* carte *f* d'embarquement

boarding house *n* pension *f* de famille

boarding party *n* (*for inspection*) détachement *m* de visite; (*of pirates etc*) détachement d'abordage

boarding pass *n Av* carte *f* d'embarquement

boarding school *n* pensionnat *m*; **he's being sent to b.** on l'envoie en pension

board meeting *n Com* réunion *f* du conseil d'administration

board of enquiry *n* commission *f* d'enquête

Board of Trade *n Admin Br* = Ministère *m* du Commerce; *US* = chambre *f* de commerce

boardroom ['bɔːdruːm] *n* salle *f* de réunion (*du conseil d'administration*); **there is uncertainty in boardrooms**

across the country l'incertitude règne au sein des conseils d'administration de toutes les entreprises du pays; **to be promoted to the b.** être promu au conseil d'administration
board test *n TV, Cin* animatique *f*
boardwalk ['bɔːdwɔːk] *n Am* = passage *m* ou trottoir *m* fait de planches de bois (au bord de la mer); **on the b.** sur les planches
boast¹ [bəʊst] *n* vantardise *f*; **it is their b. that ...** ils se vantent que ...; **it was her proud b. that she had read ...** elle se vantait d'avoir lu ...; **it turned out to be no more than an empty b.** finalement, ce n'était que des fanfaronnades
boast² **1** *vi* se vanter (**of** *or* **about sth** de qch); **without wishing to b., I ...** sans vouloir me vanter, je ...; **that's nothing to b. about** il n'y a pas de quoi se vanter **2** *vt* **(a) he boasted that he could beat me** il s'est vanté de pouvoir me battre **(b) the school boasts a fine library** l'école est fière de posséder une belle bibliothèque; **the entire town boasts just one pub** il n'y a qu'un seul pub dans toute la ville
boaster ['bəʊstər] *n* vantard, -arde, fanfaron, -onne
boastful ['bəʊstfʊl] *adj* vantard, fanfaron
boastfully ['bəʊstfʊlɪ] *adv* avec vantardise
boasting ['bəʊstɪŋ] *n* vantardise *f*
boat¹ [bəʊt] *n* **(a)** *Naut* bateau *m*; (*small*) canot *m*, embarcation *f*; **I came by b.** je suis venu en bateau *ou* par (le) bateau; *Fig* **we're all in the same b.** nous sommes tous dans le même cas *ou* logés à la même enseigne; **b. deck** pont *m* des embarcations; **b. drill** manœuvres *fpl* d'évacuation; **b. neck** (*on dress, jumper*) encolure *f* bateau; **b. stations!** à vos postes d'abandon! **(b)** (*for sauce, gravy*) saucière *f*
boat² *vi* se promener en bateau; (*in rowboat etc*) canoter, faire du canotage
boatbuilder ['bəʊtbɪldər] *n* constructeur *m* de bateaux
boater ['bəʊtər] *n* (*hat*) canotier *m*
boathook ['bəʊthʊk] *n* gaffe *f*
boathouse ['bəʊthaʊs] *n* hangar *m* à bateaux
boating ['bəʊtɪŋ] *n* canotage *m*; **to go b.** faire du canotage; **b. accident** accident *m* de bateau; **b. holiday** vacances *fpl* en bateau; **b. song** barcarolle *f*
boatload ['bəʊtləʊd] *n* (*of wood, cars, fruit etc*) cargaison *f*; **six boatloads of refugees** six bateaux pleins de réfugiés; **to arrive by the b.** arriver par bateaux entiers
boatman, *pl* **-men** ['bəʊtmən, -men] **(a)** (*operator*) passeur *m* **(b)** (*renter*) loueur *m* de canots
boat people *npl* boat people *mpl*
boat race *n* course *f* d'aviron
boatswain ['bəʊs(ə)n] *n Naut* maître *m* d'équipage, maître principal de manœuvre, bosco *m*
boat train *n* = train *m* assurant un service en correspondance avec une compagnie maritime
boatyard ['bəʊtjɑːd] *n* chantier *m* de construction pour canots et bateaux de plaisance
Bob [bɒb] *n F* **and B.'s your uncle!** et ça y est!, et voilà (le travail)!
bob¹ [bɒb] *n* **(a)** (*hairstyle*) (coupe *f* au) carré *m*; **to wear one's hair in a b.** avoir les cheveux coupés au carré; **to have a b.** avoir une coupe au carré, avoir un carré **(b)** *Sp* (*sleigh*) bob(sleigh) *m* **(c)** (*on pendulum*) lentille *f*; (*on plumb line*) plomb *m*; (*on end of kite tail*) poids *m*; (*on fishing line*) bouchon *m*
bob² *vt* (**-bb-**) **to have one's hair bobbed** se faire couper les cheveux au carré
bob³ **1** *vi* s'agiter; **bobbing for apples** = à Halloween, jeu consistant à essayer d'attraper avec les dents des pommes flottant dans une bassine d'eau; **to b. down** se baisser subitement; **to b. up** surgir brusquement; *Fig* réapparaître d'une façon inattendue; **to b. up and down** (*in one's seat*) s'agiter; **to b. up and down in the water** danser sur l'eau; **to b. under** (*of fisherman's float*) plonger **2** *vt* **to b. a curtsey** faire une petite révérence
bob⁴ *n* **(a)** (*sudden movement*) petit coup *m* **(b)** (*curtsey*) petite révérence *f*
bob⁵ *n inv Br Old-fashioned F* (*shilling*) shilling *m*; **that must cost a few b.** ça ne doit pas être donné; **he's not short of a b. or two** il n'est pas dans l'indigence, il a de quoi
bobbin ['bɒbɪn] *n* **(a)** *Tex* (*for shuttle*) bobine *f*; (*for lace*) fuseau *m*; **b. frame** bobinoir *m*; **b. winder** bobineuse *f* **(b)** *El* corps *m* de bobine
bobble ['bɒb(ə)l] *n F* (*on hat etc*) pompon *m*
bobby ['bɒbɪ] *n Old-fashioned Br F* (*policeman*) flic *m*; **we need more bobbies on the beat** il nous faut plus de policiers dans le quartier
bobby-dazzler ['bɒbɪ'dæzlər] *n Old-fashioned Br F* (*girl*) jolie fille *f*; **his new car's a b.** sa nouvelle voiture est vraiment extra
bobby pin *n Am* pince *f* (à cheveux)
bobby socks *npl* socquettes *fpl* (*de fillette*)
bobbysoxer ['bɒbɪsɒksər] *n Old-fashioned Am F* = jeune fille *f* portant socquettes et jupe ample, à la mode des années 50
bobcat ['bɒbkæt] *n Am* (*animal*) lynx *m* rufus
bobsled¹ ['bɒbsled], **bobsleigh¹** ['bɒbsleɪ] *n* bobsleigh *m*, *F* bob; **b. race** course *f* de bobsleigh
bobsled², bobsleigh² *vi* faire du bobsleigh *ou F* du bob
bobtail ['bɒbteɪl] *n* **(a)** (*of horse, dog*) queue *f* écourtée **(b)** (*dog*) bobtail *m*
bock [bɒk] *n* (*glass*) bock *m*; **b. (beer)** bière *f* brune (allemande)
bod [bɒd] *n* **(a)** *Br F* (*fellow*) type *m*; **any old b. can do it** n'importe quel péquenaud peut le faire **(b)** *F* (*body*) corps *m*; **what a great b. he's got!** il est vachement bien (foutu)!
bode [bəʊd] **1** *vi* **to b. well/ill** être de bon/de mauvais augure (**for** pour) **2** *vt Arch, Lit* présager
bodge [bɒdʒ] *vt F* (*piece of work*) bousiller, saboter; **to b. sth up** (*make temporary or unskilful repair*) rafistoler qch, faire une réparation de fortune sur qch
bodice ['bɒdɪs] *n* (*of dress*) corsage *m*
-bodied ['bɒdɪd] *suff* **a large-/slender-b. man** un homme au corps gros/svelte; **a full-b. wine** un vin robuste
bodily ['bɒdɪlɪ] **1** *adj* corporel, physique; **b. needs** besoins *mpl* matériels; **b. strength** force *f* physique; **to be in b. fear of sb** craindre d'être attaqué par qn **2** *adv* **(a)** (*forcibly*) **he was carried b. to the door** on l'a saisi (à bras-le-corps) et transporté jusqu'à la porte; **they hurled him b. through the window** ils le saisirent à bras-le-corps et le firent sortir par la fenêtre sans ménagement **(b)** (*as whole*) entièrement, en masse
bodkin ['bɒdkɪn] *n* (*for threading*) passe-lacet *m*, *pl* passe-lacets; (*for piercing*) poinçon *m*
body ['bɒdɪ] *n* **(a)** (*of person, animal*) corps *m*; (*dead body*) cadavre *m*, corps; *Fig* **to throw oneself b. and soul into sth** se jeter corps et âme dans qch; *Fig* **to have just enough to keep b. and soul together** avoir tout juste de quoi vivre; *F* **(it'll be) over my dead b.!** plutôt crever!; **if he comes into this house it'll be over my dead b.!** il faudra qu'il me passe sur le corps s'il veut rentrer dans cette maison!; **this obsession with the b. beautiful** cette obsession que tout le monde a d'avoir un corps parfait; *Fig* **b. blow** choc *m*; **to be a real b. blow to sb's hopes** être un véritable coup porté aux espoirs de qn; *Sp* **b. swerve** feinte *f*

(b) (*of wine*) corps *m*; (*of hair*) volume *m*; *Mus* **to give b. to the tone** nourrir le son

(c) (*group*) corps *m*; (*organization*) organisme *m*; (*of laws*) recueil *m*; (*of water*) étendue *f*; **large b. of people** foule *f* nombreuse, assistance *f* nombreuse; **there is a large b. of support for the policy** un grand nombre de personnes sont en faveur de cette politique; **b. of troops** troupe *f* armée; **the main b.** (*of employees, refugees etc*) la majeure partie; *Mil* le gros des troupes; **to come in a b.** venir en masse; *Old-fashioned* **learned b.** corps savant; **public b.** corporation *f*

(d) (*main part*) (*of document, building etc*) corps *m*; (*of church*) nef *f*; (*of musical instrument*) coffre *m*; (*of plane*) fuselage *m*; (*of pram*) nacelle *f*; *Jur* **the b. of evidence** l'ensemble *m* des preuves; *Typ* **b. setting** composition *f* (des caractères); *Typ* **b. size** taille *f* de corps

(e) *Aut* carrosserie *f*; **b. panel** panneau *m* de carrosserie; **b. part** pièce *f* de carrosserie; **b. platform** plate-forme *f*; **b. repair centre** atelier *m* (de réparation) de carrosserie; **b. roll** roulis *m* de la caisse, mouvement *m* de caisse; **b. style** style *m* de carrosserie

(f) *Phys etc* corps *m*; *Astron* **heavenly b.** corps céleste, astre *m*

(g) (*underwear*) body *m*
body bag *n* = sac *m* servant au transport de dépouilles mortelles
body builder *n* culturiste *mf*; *Aut* carrossier *m*
body building *n* culturisme *m*
bodycheck¹ ['bɒdɪtʃek] *n Sp* (*in ice hockey*) interception *f*; (*in wrestling*) coup *m* de bélier
bodycheck² *vt Sp* (*in ice hockey, football*) intercepter
body clock *n* horloge *f* interne
body corporate *n* personne *f* morale
body count *n* (*of corpses*) comptage *m* des morts; (*of those present*) comptage du nombre des présents; **to do** *or* **carry out a b.** compter les morts/les présents
bodyguard ['bɒdɪgɑːd] *n* **(a)** (*individual*) garde *m* du corps, *F* gorille *m* **(b)** (*no pl*) (*group*) gardes *mpl* du corps
body language *n* langage *m* du corps; **I could tell by his b.** je le savais d'après la façon dont il se tenait
bodylock ['bɒdɪlɒk] *n Aut* **b. seat restraint** blocage *m* de maintien du corps
body lotion *n* lait *m* pour le corps

body odour *n* odeur *f* corporelle
body politic *n* corps *m* politique
body popper *n* smurfer, -euse
body popping *n* smurf *m*
body scrub *n* produit *m* exfoliant pour le corps
bodyshell ['bɒdɪʃel] *n Aut* caisse *f*, coque *f*, carcasse *f*
body shop *n Aut* atelier *m* de carrosserie
body snatcher *n Hist* déterreur *m* de cadavres
body stocking *n* body *m*
body-surf *vi* body-surfer
body-surfer *n* body-surfe(u)r, -euse
body-surfing *n* body-surfing *m*
body warmer *n* petit gilet *m* chaud
bodywork ['bɒdɪwɜːk] *n Aut* **(a)** (*structure*) carrosserie *f* **(b)** (*repairs*) travail *m* de carrosserie
Boer [bʊər] **1** *adj* boer; **the B. War** la guerre des Boers **2** *n* Boer *mf*
boffin ['bɒfɪn] *n Br F, Hum* savant *m*
bog [bɒg] *n* **(a)** (*marsh*) marécage *m*; **peat b.** tourbière *f* **(b)** *Br F* (*lavatory*) chiottes *fpl*, gogs *mpl*, gogues *mpl*; **b. brush** brosse *f* à chiottes; **b. paper** PQ *m*; **b. roll** rouleau *m* de PQ; **b. seat** cuvette *f* des chiottes
▶ **bog down** *vtsep* (*usu passive*) **to get bogged down** (*of car etc*) s'embourber, s'enliser, s'enfoncer dans une fondrière; *F* (*of person, discussion etc*) s'enliser; **don't let's get bogged down in details** ne nous perdons pas dans les détails
bogey[1] ['bəʊgɪ] *n* **(a)** (*source of fear*) spectre *m*, hantise *f*; **unionization is the b. of the company** la syndicalisation est la hantise de la société **(b)** *F* (*source of bad luck*) chose *f* qui porte malheur; (*cause of worry*) bête *f* noire **(c)** *F* (*in nose*) crotte *f* de nez **(d)** *Golf* un coup au-dessus du par **(e)** (*spirit*) fantôme *m*, spectre *m* (*effrayant*); *Arch* (*devil*) diable *m*
bogey[2] *vt Golf* **to b. a hole** jouer un trou en un coup au-dessus du par
bogeyman, *pl* **-men** ['bəʊgɪmæn, -men] *n* **the b.** le croque-mitaine, le Père Fouettard; **the b. will get you** le Père Fouettard va venir te chercher
boggle ['bɒg(ə)l] **1** *vi* **(a) to b. at doing sth** rechigner à faire qch **(b) the mind boggles** ça laisse rêveur **2** *vt* **it boggles the mind** *or* **the imagination** ça laisse rêveur
boggy ['bɒgɪ] *adj* marécageux
bogie ['bəʊgɪ] *n Rail* bog(g)ie *m*
bog-ordinary, bog-standard *adj Br F* tout simple
bogus ['bəʊgəs] *adj* faux, *f* fausse; *Com* **b. company** société *f* fantôme; **he's completely b.** (*not genuine in feelings etc*) c'est un faux jeton
Bohemia [bəʊ'hiːmɪə] *n* **(a)** *Geog* Bohême *f* **(b)** (*unconventional life*) (vie *f* de) bohème *f*
Bohemian [bəʊ'hiːmɪən] **1** *adj* **(a)** *Geog* bohémien **(b)** *Fig* (*life etc*) de bohème **2** *n* **(a)** *Geog* Bohémien, -ienne **(b)** (*arty type*) bohème *mf*; (*gipsy*) bohémien, -ienne
boil[1] [bɔɪl] *n Med* furoncle *m*
boil[2] *n* **to come to the b.** (*of water etc*) commencer à bouillir, arriver à ébullition; *Fig F* (*athlete, performer*) parvenir au mieux de sa forme; **let the water come to a** *or* **the b.** attendre que l'eau arrive à ébullition; **the water is on the b.** l'eau bout; **to bring the water to the b.** amener l'eau à l'ébullition; *Fig* **their romance has gone off the b.** leur histoire tourne au ralenti, leur histoire ne marche plus très fort; **to go off the b.** (*of athlete, actor etc*) perdre son entrain
boil[3] **1** *vi* **(a)** (*of liquid*) bouillir; (*violently*) bouillonner; **to begin to b.** arriver à ébullition; *Culin* **allow to b. gently** laissez mijoter; **to let the kettle b. dry** laisser évaporer complètement l'eau de la bouilloire; **the kettle's boiling** la bouilloire siffle; **are the potatoes boiling?** est-ce que les pommes de terre bouillent?; *F* **to keep the pot boiling** (*bring in enough money*) faire bouillir la marmite; **it makes me** *or* **my blood b.!** ça me met hors de moi!; **to b. with rage** bouillir de colère; *F* **I'm boiling!** (*very hot*) je crève de chaleur *ou* de chaud!

(b) *Lit* (*of sea*) bouillonner

2 *vt* **(a)** (*liquid*) faire bouillir; *Culin* (*potatoes, vegetables, meat*) faire cuire à l'eau; (*sugar*) cuire; **to b. the kettle** (*by gas*) mettre la bouilloire sur le feu; (*by electricity*) brancher la bouilloire; **to b. an egg** faire cuire un œuf à la coque; *Hum* **he can't b. an egg** (*does not know how to cook*) il n'est même pas capable de faire cuire un œuf; *Sl* **go (and) b. your head!** va te faire cuire un œuf!

(b) (*in papermaking*) (*fibres*) décreuser

▶ **boil away** *vi* **(a)** continuer à bouillir **(b)** (*evaporate*) s'évaporer
▶ **boil down 1** *vtsep* (*solution*) réduire; (*syrup etc*) (faire) réduire; *Fig* (*article*) condenser **2** *vi* (*of sauce etc*) se réduire
▶ **boil down to** *vipo F* se ramener *ou* se résumer *ou* revenir à; **what her story boils down to is that ...** ce à quoi se résume son histoire, c'est que ...; **this is what it all boils down to** voilà à quoi cela revient *ou* se résume
▶ **boil over** *vi* **(a)** (*of liquid*) déborder, *F* se sauver; (*of pot*) déborder **(b)** *F* (*become angry*) exploser (de colère) **(c)** (*worsen*) empirer; **the dispute is in danger of boiling over into a strike** le conflit risque de virer à la grève
boiled [bɔɪld] *adj* bouilli; *Culin* cuit à l'eau; **b. egg** œuf *m* à la coque; **b. ham** jambon *m* blanc; **b. potatoes** pommes *fpl* de terre à l'eau *ou* à l'anglaise; *Br* **b. sweet** bonbon *m* à sucer
boiler ['bɔɪlər] *n* **(a)** chaudière *f*; *Culin* **double b.** bain-marie *m*, *pl* bains-marie; **b. maker** chaudronnier *m*; **b. room** salle *f* des chaudières; *Naut* chambre *f* de chauffe; **b. suit** bleu *m* de chauffe **(b)** *Culin* poule *f* (à la casserole)
boilerman, *pl* **-men** ['bɔɪləmən, -men] *n* chauffeur *m*
boiling ['bɔɪlɪŋ] **1** *adj* **(a)** (*water*) bouillant **(b)** *Lit* (*sea*) bouillonnant **2** *adv* **b. hot** bouillant; *F* **it's been a b. hot day** il a fait une chaleur à crever aujourd'hui; *F* **I'm b. hot** je crève de chaleur *ou* de chaud **3** *n* bouillonnement *m*, ébullition *f*
boiling point *n* point *m* d'ébullition; *Fig* **I reached b. when he said ...** j'ai failli sortir de mes gonds *ou* exploser quand il a dit ...
boiling-water reactor *n Nucl Phys* réacteur *m* à eau bouillante
boil-in-the-bag *adj Culin* (*rice etc*) en sachet de cuisson
boisterous ['bɔɪst(ə)rəs] *adj* (*person*) (*noisy*) bruyant, tapageur; (*unruly*) turbulent; (*wind*) violent; (*sea*) tumultueux; **b. spirits** gaieté *f* débordante *ou* tapageuse
boisterously ['bɔɪst(ə)rəslɪ] *adv* bruyamment
boisterousness ['bɔɪst(ə)rəsnɪs] *n* turbulence *f*, agitation *f*
bold [bəʊld] **1** *adj* **(a)** (*fearless, confident*) hardi; (*tone, look*) assuré, confiant; (*audacious*) (*move, plan, thinker*) audacieux; **to put on a b. front** *or* **face, to put a b. front** *or* **face on it** faire bonne figure

(b) (*impudent*) impudent, effronté; *Old-fashioned, Hum* **if I may be** *or* **make so b.** si je puis me permettre; **she made so b. as to ask what my salary was** elle a eu l'effronterie de me demander combien je gagnais; *F* **as b. as brass** (*to do sth*) avec un culot pas possible; **he's as b. as brass** il a un culot pas possible

(c) (*strong, distinctive*) (*style, brushstrokes*) nerveux, vigoureux; **b. colours** couleurs *fpl* vives; **b. features** traits *mpl* accusés

(d) *Typ* gras; **b. character** caractère *m* gras; **b. italics** caractères italiques gras; **b. print** caractères gras; **b. type** *or* **face** caractères gras

2 *n Typ* **in b.** en gras

boldly ['bəʊldlɪ] *adv* **(a)** (*confidently, fearlessly*) hardiment; (*audaciously*) audacieusement; **to state sth b.** affirmer qch avec assurance; **to deal with sth b.** (*subject, problem etc*) traiter qch de façon directe **(b)** (*impudently*) effrontément, avec impudence **(c)** *Art* avec vigueur
boldness ['bəʊldnɪs] *n* **(a)** (*fearlessness*) hardiesse *f*; (*audacity*) audace *f* **(b)** (*impudence*) effronterie *f*, impudence *f* **(c)** *Art* (*of style, brushstrokes*) nervosité *f*, vigueur *f*
bole [bəʊl] *n* (*of tree*) fût *m*, tronc *m*
bolero [bə'leərəʊ] *n* **(a)** (*dance, music*) boléro *m* **(b)** (*also* ['bɒlərəʊ]) (*jacket*) boléro *m*
boletus [bɒ'liːtəs] *n* (*fungus*) bolet *m*
Bolivia [bə'lɪvɪə] *n* Bolivie *f*
Bolivian [bə'lɪvɪən] **1** *adj* bolivien **2** *n* Bolivien, -ienne
boll [bəʊl] *n Bot* (*of cotton, linen*) capsule *f*; **b. weevil** anthonome *m* (*du cotonnier*)
bollard ['bɒlɑːd] *n* **(a)** *Naut* (*for mooring*) bitte *f* **(b)** *Br* (*in road*) borne *f*
bollocking ['bɒləkɪŋ] *n Sl* (*reprimand*) engueulade *f*; **he got a b. from the boss** il s'est fait engueuler par le patron
bollocks ['bɒləks] *npl Vulg* couilles *fpl*; **b.!** c'est des conneries!
▶ **bollocks up** *vtsep Vulg* bousiller
Bologna [bə'lɒnjə] *n* Bologne *f*
Bolognese [bɒlə'niːz, -eɪz] **1** *adj* bolognais **2** *n* Bolognais, -aise
boloney [bə'ləʊnɪ] *n* = baloney
Bolshevik ['bɒlʃəvɪk], **Bolshevist** ['bɒlʃəvɪst] *adj, n* bolchevik *mf*, bolcheviste *mf*
Bolshevism ['bɒlʃəvɪz(ə)m] *n* bolchevisme *m*
bolshie, bolshy ['bɒlʃɪ] *F* **1** *adj* **he's b.** c'est un mauvais coucheur; **he turned b.** il a commencé à râler; **she's in a b. mood** elle est de très mauvais poil; **she was a bit b. about going to school** elle a un peu rechigné pour aller à l'école **2** *n Old-fashioned Pol* rouge *mf*
bolster[1] ['bəʊlstər] *n* (*pillow*) traversin *m*
bolster[2] *vt* (*strengthen*) **to b. sb.'s confidence** redonner de la confiance à qn; **it bolstered his ego** ça a fait du bien à son amour propre; **to b. one's courage** se donner du courage

▶ **bolster up** *vtsep Fig* (*regime, government*) appuyer, soutenir; (*theory*) étayer; **he bolstered himself up with a few drinks** il a bu quelques verres pour se donner du courage; **bolstered up by recent successes** fort de ses récents succès; *Fin* **to b. up the pound** soutenir la livre

bolt¹ [bɒlt, bəʊlt] *n* (**a**) (*closing device*) (*for door etc*) verrou *m*; (*of lock*) pêne *m* (**b**) *MecE* (*for nut*) boulon *m* (**c**) *F* (*rush*) **to make a b. for it** décamper, déguerpir; **he tried to make a b. for it** il a essayé de se tailler; **she made a b. for the door** elle s'est précipitée vers la porte (**d**) *Met* **a b. of lightning** la foudre; *Fig* **it was** *or* **came like a b. from the blue** ce fut comme un coup de foudre (**e**) (*roll*) **a b. of cloth** une coupe de tissu (**f**) *Arch* (*of crossbow*) carreau *m*; *Fig* **he's shot his b.** (*is exhausted*) il est épuisé; (*of politician etc*) il a joué sa dernière carte

bolt² **1** *vt* (**a**) (*close*) (*door etc*) verrouiller (**b**) *MecE* (*join*) boulonner, cheviller; **to be bolted to the floor** être fixé au sol par des boulons (**c**) *F* (*eat quickly*) (*one's dinner etc*) avaler à toute vitesse, engloutir **2** *vi* (**a**) (*of door etc*) se verrouiller (**b**) (*of horse*) s'emballer, prendre le mors aux dents; *F* (*of person*) décamper, déguerpir (**c**) (*of plant*) monter en graine

bolt³ *adv* **b. upright** droit comme un piquet

▶ **bolt down** **1** *vipo* (*stairs, street*) dévaler **2** *vtsep* **to b. down one's food** *or* **a meal** manger avec un lance-pierres; **don't b. your food down** ne mange pas si vite

▶ **bolt in** **1** *vi* (*enter quickly*) entrer comme un bolide **2** *vtsep* (*lock in*) enfermer (au verrou)

▶ **bolt out** **1** *vi* (*leave quickly*) sortir comme un bolide; **they bolted out of the door** ils sont sortis comme des bolides **2** *vtsep* (*lock out*) enfermer dehors

bolt hole *n* (*of animal*) refuge *m*; *Mil* abri *m* de bombardement; *Fig* échappatoire *f*, refuge; *Fig* **to use sth as a b.** trouver refuge dans qch; *Fig* **to arrange a b. for oneself** se ménager une porte de sortie

bomb¹ [bɒm] *n Mil etc* bombe *f*; **the b.** (*atom bomb*) la bombe atomique; **to release** *or* **drop a b.** lâcher *ou* larguer une bombe; *F* **this room looks as if a b. had hit it** cette pièce est un véritable champ de bataille; *Br F* **to go like a b.** (*of car*) être une vraie fusée; (*of party*) être génial; (*of play, show etc*) casser la baraque, marcher très bien; *Am* **it's a b.** (*of musical, play etc*) c'est un fiasco *ou* un flop; *F* **it costs a b.** ça coûte les yeux de la tête; **b. attack** bombardement *m*; *Av* **b. bay** soute *f* à bombes; **b. crater** entonnoir *m*, cratère *m*; **b. hoax** fausse alerte *f* à la bombe; **b. threat** menace *f* d'attentat à la bombe

bomb² **1** *vt* (*town etc*) bombarder, lancer des bombes sur; *Sl* **to b. the hell** *or* **shit out of a place** pilonner un endroit **2** *vi Am* (*of play etc*) faire un flop

▶ **bomb along** *F* **1** *vi* (*of car, driver*) bomber **2** *vipo* **to b. along the road** bomber sur la route

▶ **bomb down** *vipo F* (*of car, driver*) **to b. down the road at 100 mph** foncer à 160 (km/h)

▶ **bomb off** *vi F* (*of car, driver*) partir comme un bolide *ou* en trombe

▶ **bomb out** *vtsep* **they have been bombed out of their homes** ils sont à la rue parce que leurs maisons ont été bombardées; **the whole street had been bombed out** toute la rue avait été détruite par les bombardements

bombard [bɒm'bɑːd] *vt Mil etc* bombarder; *Fig* **to b. sb with questions** bombarder qn de questions

bombardier [bɒmbə'dɪər] *n* (**a**) *Av* bombardier *m* (**b**) *Br Mil* brigadier *m*

bombardment [bɒm'bɑːdmənt] *n Mil* bombardement *m*

bombast ['bɒmbæst] *n* emphase *f*

bombastic [bɒm'bæstɪk] *adj* (*style*) ampoulé, emphatique

bombastically [bɒm'bæstɪklɪ] *adv* dans un style ampoulé *ou* emphatique

bombazine ['bɒmbəziːn] *n Tex* bombasin *m*

bomb disposal *n* déminage *m*; **b. expert** démineur *m*

bombe [bɒm] *n* (*ice-cream*) bombe *f* glacée

bombed out ['bɒmd] *adj Sl* (**a**) (*exhausted*) crevé, nase (**b**) (*very crowded*) plein à craquer (**c**) (*with work*) surchargé (**with** de) (**d**) (*drunk*) bourré; (*on drugs*) défoncé (**e**) (*without a chance*) **to be b.** n'avoir aucune chance

bomber ['bɒmər] *n* (**a**) (*aircraft*) bombardier *m* (**b**) (*person*) *Av* bombardier *m*; (*terrorist*) poseur, -euse de bombe(s); **b. jacket** bomber *m*

bombing ['bɒmɪŋ] *n* attentat *m* à la bombe; *Av* bombardement *m*; **b. campaign** campagne *f* d'attentats à la bombe; **b. raid** bombardement aérien; **b. run** course *f* de visée

bombproof ['bɒmpruːf] *adj* à l'épreuve des bombes; **b. shelter** abri *m* blindé

bomb scare *n* alerte *f* à la bombe

bombshell ['bɒmʃel] *n* (**a**) *Mil* obus *m*; *Fig* **the news came as a b. to us** cette nouvelle nous a fait l'effet d'une bombe; **to drop a b.** faire part d'une nouvelle qui fait l'effet d'une bombe (**b**) *F* (*attractive woman*) beauté *f*

bombsight ['bɒmsaɪt] *n Av* viseur *m ou* collimateur *m* de bombardement

bombsite ['bɒmsaɪt] *n* zone *f* bombardée; **to look like a b.** ressembler à un champ de bataille

bombthrower ['bɒmθrəʊər] *n* (**a**) (*device*) lance-bombes *m inv* (**b**) (*person*) lanceur, -euse de bombes

bona fide ['bəʊnə'faɪdɪ] **1** *adj* (*excuse, contract, reason, agreement*) valable; (*offer*) sérieux, sincère; (*agent*) agréé; (*charity*) vrai; **are you sure he was a b. salesman?** es-tu sûr que c'était vraiment un vendeur? **2** *n* **one's bona fides** [-faɪdɪz] sa bonne foi

bonanza [bə'nænzə] **1** *n Min* riche filon *m*; *Fig* aubaine *f*; **the tourist industry has had a bit of a b.** l'industrie touristique a fait de bonnes affaires; **to strike a b.** *Min* rencontrer un riche filon; *Fig* faire une affaire en or **2** *adj* **b. year** année *f* exceptionnelle

Bonapartist ['bəʊnəpɑːtɪst] *n, adj Hist* bonapartiste *mf*

bonbon ['bɒnbɒn] *n* bonbon *m*

bonce [bɒns] *n Br F* (*head*) caboche *f*

bond¹ [bɒnd] *n* (**a**) (*tie*) lien *m*; *Lit* **bonds** (*chains*) fers *mpl*, liens; *Fig* **the bonds of friendship/marriage** les liens de l'amitié/du mariage; **there is a very close b. between us** nous sommes très liés

(**b**) *Ch* liaison *f*; (*of glue*) adhérence *f*; *Constr etc* attache *f*

(**c**) (*commitment*) engagement *m*, contrat *m*; *Jur* obligation *f*; *Fml* **my word is my b.** (*you can trust me*) je vous donne ma parole d'honneur; (*I cannot back out*) j'ai donné ma parole d'honneur

(**d**) *Fin* bon *m*, obligation *f*; **registered b.** bon nominatif; **mortgage b.** titre *m* hypothécaire; **b. holder** détenteur *m* d'obligations; **b. issue** émission *f* d'obligations, emprunt *ou* émission obligataire; **to make a b. issue** émettre un emprunt; **b. market** marché *m* obligataire; **b. note** titre *m* d'obligation

(**e**) *Jur* (*for bail*) caution *f*

(**f**) *Com* (*warehouse*) dépôt *m*; **to be in b.** être à l'entrepôt *ou* en dépôt; **to take goods out of b.** dédouaner des marchandises

bond² *vt* (**a**) (*metals etc*) coller; *Constr* (*stones*) liaisonner (**b**) *Com* (*goods*) entreposer, mettre en dépôt *ou* à l'entrepôt (**c**) *Fig* **hardship had bonded them together** les privations qu'ils avaient endurées avaient créé un lien très fort entre eux

bondage ['bɒndɪdʒ] *n* (**a**) *Lit* (*slavery*) esclavage *m*, asservissement *m* (**b**) *Hist* (*serfdom*) servage *m* (**c**) (*sexual practice*) bondage *m*, = pratique *f* sexuelle où l'un des partenaires est attaché

bonded ['bɒndɪd] *adj* (**a**) *Constr* (*masonry*) en liaison (**b**) *Com* (*goods*) en dépôt, en entrepôt; **b. warehouse** entrepôt *m* en douane (**c**) *Fin* (*debt*) garanti par obligations

bonder ['bɒndər] *n Com* entrepositaire *m*

bonding ['bɒndɪŋ] *n* (**a**) *Constr* (*of stones*) liaison *f* (**b**) (*of metals*) collage *m*; **b. agent** (*adhesive*) agent *m* de collage *ou* d'adhésivité (**c**) *Com* (*of goods*) entreposage *m* (**d**) (*emotional attachment*) lien *m* affectif; **the b. process** la formation de liens affectifs; **male b.** la formation de liens affectifs entre hommes (**e**) **b. scheme** (*with tour operator*) agrément *m*

bondstone ['bɒndstəʊn] *n Constr* parpaing *m*

bone¹ [bəʊn] *n* (**a**) (*of human, animal*) os *m*; (*of fish*) arête *f*; **the handle was made from b.** le manche était en os; **to be as dry as a b.** *or* **b. dry** (*of earth*) être desséché; (*of well*) être à sec; (*of washing*) être complètement sec; *Old-fashioned* **he won't make old bones** il ne fera pas de vieux os; **chilled** *or* **frozen to the b.** gelé *ou* transi jusqu'à la moëlle; **to cut expenses to the b.** réduire les dépenses au minimum; **to work one's fingers to the b.** se tuer au travail; **to be b. idle** *or* **lazy** être paresseux comme une couleuvre; **I feel it in my bones** je le sens; **b. of contention** sujet *m* de dispute; *F* **to have a b. to pick with sb** avoir un compte à régler avec qn; **to make no bones about doing sth** ne pas hésiter à faire qch; **he made no bones about it** il y est allé carrément, il n'y est pas allé par quatre chemins; **she made no bones about her displeasure** elle n'a pas caché son mécontentement; **near** *or* **close to the b.** (*joke etc*) douteux, limite; **b. structure** ossature *f*

(**b**) (*of corset*) baleine *f*

(**c**) **bones** (*of the dead*) ossements *mpl*

bone² *vt* (**a**) (*meat*) désosser; (*fish*) ôter les arêtes de (**b**) (*corset*) garnir de baleines

▶ **bone up on** *vipo Sl* (*study*) potasser

bone china *n Cer* porcelaine *f* tendre

boned [bəʊnd] *adj* (**a**) (*meat*) désossé; (*fish*) sans arêtes (**b**) (*corset*) baleiné

bone-dry *adj* (*earth*) desséché; (*well*) à sec; (*washing*) complètement sec

bonehead ['bəʊnhed] *n F* (*stupid person*) idiot, -ote; (*stubborn person*) tête *f* de bois
boneless ['bəʊnlɪs] *adj* (*meat*) sans os; (*from which bones have been removed*) désossé; (*fish*) sans arêtes
bone marrow *n* moelle *f* osseuse
bone meal *n* (*fertiliser*) engrais *m* d'os (broyés)
boner ['bəʊnər] *n Am* **(a)** *F* (*mistake*) gaffe *f*; **I made a real b.** j'ai fait une de ces gaffes! **(b)** *Vulg* (*erection*) **to have a b.** avoir le gourdin *ou* la trique
boneshaker ['bəʊnʃeɪkər] *n F esp Hum* **(a)** (*car*) vieux clou *m*, vieille guimbarde *f* **(b)** *Arch* (*bicycle*) vélocipède *m*
bonfire ['bɒnfaɪər] *n* (*with fireworks*) feu *m* de joie; (*for burning leaves etc*) feu de jardin; **to make** *or* **build a b.** (*with wood, leaves etc*) faire un feu
Bonfire Night *n Br* = 5 novembre, célébration *f* de l'échec de la tentative de faire sauter le Parlement
bong [bɒŋ] *n* (*of bell, drum*) coup *m*
bongo ['bɒŋgəʊ] *n* bongo *m*; **a set of bongos** un bongo
bonhomie [bɒnɒ'miː] *n* bonhomie *f*
bonito [bə'niːtəʊ] *n* (*fish*) bonite *f*
bonk[1] [bɒŋk] *n Br F* **to have a b.** tirer un coup
bonk[2] **1** *vt* **(a)** *Br F* (*have sex with*) **to b. sb** se faire qn **(b)** *F* (*hit*) taper; **he got bonked on the head by a tennis ball** il s'est pris une balle de tennis sur la tête **2** *vi Br F Hum* (*have sex*) tirer un coup, s'envoyer en l'air (**with sb** avec qn)
bonkers ['bɒŋkəz] *adj Br Sl* cinglé; **it's driving me b.!** ça me rend dingue!
bonnet ['bɒnɪt] *n* **(a)** (*hat*) (*woman's, child's*) bonnet *m* **(b)** *Br Aut* capot *m*; **to have a look under the b.** jeter un coup d'œil sous le capot; **b. release** déverrouillage *m* du capot; **b. strut** tige *f* (de maintien) de capot, béquille *f* de capot
bonny ['bɒnɪ] *adj esp Scot* joli
bonsai ['bɒnsaɪ] *n* bonsaï *m*
bonus, *pl* **-uses** ['bəʊnəs, -əsɪz] *n* (*esp at work*) prime *f*; **to work on a b. system** travailler à la prime; **cost-of-living b.** indemnité *f* de vie chère *ou* de cherté de vie; *Com etc* **Christmas b.** gratification *f* de fin d'année; *Fig* **the hot weather was an unexpected b.** le beau temps fut vraiment bienvenu étant donné qu'on ne s'y attendait pas; **it's a real b. having a theatre close by** le fait qu'il y ait un théâtre tout près constitue vraiment un plus
bony ['bəʊnɪ] *adj* **(a)** (*person, body, face*) osseux; (*knees, shoulders*) anguleux; (*fingers, arms*) squelettique; (*meat*) plein d'os; (*fish*) plein d'arêtes **(b)** (*like bone*) osseux
boo[1] [buː] **1** *int* hou!; *F* **he wouldn't say b. to a goose** c'est un timide **2** *n* huée *f*; **her arrival was greeted with boos** elle s'est fait huer à son arrivée
boo[2] *vti* **to b. (at) sb** huer qn; **to be booed off the stage** quitter la scène au milieu des huées
boob[1] [buːb] *n F* **(a)** (*fool*) idiot, -ote, crétin *m*; *esp Am* **b. tube** (*television*) télé *f* **(b)** *Br* (*mistake*) gaffe *f* **(c)** (*breast*) nichon *m*; **b. tube** bustier *m*
boob[2] *vi Br F* faire une gaffe
boo-boo ['buːbuː] *n F* (*blunder*) gaffe *f*, bourde *f*
booby ['buːbɪ] *n* **(a)** *Old-fashioned* (*fool*) idiot, -ote, crétin *m*, nouille *f*; *US Sl* **b. hatch** (*mental hospital*) maison *f* de fous **(b)** (*bird*) fou *m*
booby prize *n* = prix *m* décerné par plaisanterie au dernier
booby trap *n* attrape-nigaud *m*, *pl* attrape-nigauds; *Mil* piège *m*; (*explosive device*) engin *m* piégé
booby-trap *vt* (*car etc*) piéger
boogie-woogie ['buːgɪ'wuːgɪ] *n Mus* boogie-woogie *m*
booing ['buːɪŋ] *n* huées *fpl*
book[1] [bʊk] *n* **(a)** (*for reading*) livre *m*; (*of opera*) livret *m*, libretto *m*; (*of songs, prayers etc*) recueil *m*; *Tel* annuaire *m*; *Tel* **I'm in the b.** (*listed in directory*) je suis dans l'annuaire; **a b. on** *or* **about gardening** un livre de jardinage; **old books** vieux bouquins *mpl*; (*antiquarian*) vieilles éditions *fpl*; **the b. trade** l'industrie *f* du livre, la librairie; **not published in b. form** inédit en librairie; **her articles have now been published in b. form** ses articles ont maintenant été publiés sous forme de livre; *Fig* **by** *or* **according to the b.** selon les règles; **to do things** *or* **go by the b.** suivre les règles; **to be a closed b. to sb** (*of subject*) être du chinois pour qn; **she's a closed b. to me** (*I don't understand her*) cette fille est un mystère pour moi; **she's an open b.** (*her feelings etc are obvious*) elle ne peut rien cacher, elle est transparente; **to read sb like an open b.** lire à livre ouvert dans la pensée de qn; **in my b.** d'après moi; **that doesn't suit my b.** ça ne me convient pas; *Old-fashioned* **the good B.** la Bible; **to swear on the B.** prêter serment sur la Bible

(b) (*for writing in*) *Com, Fin etc* registre *m*; *Sch* cahier *m*; **account b.** livre *m* de comptes; **to keep the books of a firm** tenir les comptes d'une entreprise; *Fig* **he's on our books** (*member of our club etc*) c'est un de nos membres; (*player in our team*) c'est un de nos joueurs; (*employee*) il est dans nos fichiers; **to be in sb's good books** être dans les petits papiers de qn, être bien vu par qn; **to be in sb's bad books** être mal vu par qn; **to bring sb to b. for sth** forcer qn à rendre compte de qch; *F* **to throw the b. at sb** accabler qn d'accusations; *Horseracing* **to make a b.** faire un pari; **we've opened a b. on how late he'll be** les paris sont ouverts sur le retard qu'il va avoir; *Acct* **b. of original entry** livre-journal *m*; *Com* **b. value** valeur *f* comptable

(c) b. of stamps/tickets carnet *m* de timbres/billets; **b. of matches** pochette *f* d'allumettes; **b. matches** allumettes *fpl* plates
book[2] **1** *vt* **(a)** *F* (*of policeman*) (*motorist*) dresser une contravention à; (*of referee*) (*player*) donner un avertissement à; **I was booked for speeding yesterday** hier j'ai eu une contravention pour excès de vitesse; **have you booked him?** (*in police station*) tu as pris tous ses renseignements?

(b) (*seat, room, table*) réserver, retenir; *Rail, Av* (*ticket, seat*) réserver; *Th etc* (*performer*) engager; **I've booked you on the next flight** je vous ai réservé une place sur le prochain vol; **fully booked** (*theatre, flight*) complet; **I'm booked for this evening** (*have engagement*) je suis pris ce soir

2 *vi Rail, Av, Th* réserver une place; (*in restaurant, hotel*) réserver; **to b. through to Nice** prendre tous les billets nécessaires pour Nice
▶ **book in 1** *vi* (*of hotel guest*) se faire inscrire sur le registre **2** *vtsep* (*of receptionist*) inscrire au registre
▶ **book into 1** *vipo* **to b. into a hotel** prendre une chambre d'hôtel **2** *vtaspo* **I've booked myself into the best hotel in town** (*in advance*) j'ai réservé une chambre dans le meilleur hôtel de la ville; (*on the spur of the moment*) j'ai pris une chambre dans le meilleur hôtel de la ville
▶ **book out 1** *vi* (*of hotel guest*) quitter un/l'hôtel **2** *vtsep* (*find other hotel for*) trouver un autre hôtel pour; **I booked them out at noon** (*they left*) ils ont réglé leur note à midi
▶ **book up 1** *vi* (*make reservations*) réserver; **have you booked up for your holiday?** est-ce que vous avez réservé pour vos vacances? **2** *vtsep* (*usu passive*) **the hotel is all booked up** l'hôtel est complet; **I'm booked up for this evening** (*have engagement*) je suis pris ce soir
bookable ['bʊkəb(ə)l] *adj Th etc* (*seat*) qui peut être réservé à l'avance
bookbinder ['bʊkbaɪndər] *n* relieur, -euse
bookbinding ['bʊkbaɪndɪŋ] *n* reliure *f*
bookcase ['bʊkkeɪs] *n* bibliothèque *f*
book club *n* club *m* du livre
book end *n* serre-livres *m inv*
book fair *n* salon *m* du livre; (*secondhand*) foire *f* aux livres
bookie ['bʊkɪ] *n Horseracing F* bookmaker *m*, book *m*
booking ['bʊkɪŋ] *n* **(a)** (*of order*) enregistrement *m*, inscription *f* **(b)** (*of room, seat etc*) réservation *f*; (*of seats, tickets*) location *f*; *Th etc* (*of performer*) engagement *m*; **to make a b.** (*for theatre, plane seat etc*) réserver une place; (*for restaurant*) réserver (une table); **do you have a b.?** (*to hotel guest*) avez-vous réservé?; **you have a b. in the name of Smith** (*to hotel clerk*) j'ai réservé au nom de Smith; **bookings diary** agenda *m* de réservation; **b. form** feuille *f ou* fiche *f* de réservation; **b. status** état *m* de la réservation
booking agency *n* agence *f* de réservation
booking clerk *n* employé, -ée chargé(e) des réservations
booking fee *n* frais *mpl* de réservation
booking office *n* bureau *m* des réservations
bookish ['bʊkɪʃ] *adj* **(a)** (*studious*) studieux **(b)** *Pej* (*person, style*) pédant
book-keeper *n Com* comptable *m*
book-keeping *n Com* comptabilité *f*
book-learning *n* érudition *f*, *Pej* savoir *m* livresque
booklet ['bʊklɪt] *n* (*pamphlet*) brochure *f*; (*small book*) plaquette *f*
booklover ['bʊklʌvər] *n* bibliophile *m*
bookmaker ['bʊkmeɪkər] *n Horseracing* bookmaker *m*
bookmark(er) ['bʊkmɑːk, -ər] *n* signet *m*
bookmobile ['bʊkməbiːl] *n Am* bibliobus *m*
bookplate ['bʊkpleɪt] *n* ex-libris *m inv*
bookrest ['bʊkrest] *n* lutrin *m*
book review *n* revue *f* littéraire; **b. page** (*in newspaper*) chronique *f* littéraire
bookseller ['bʊkselər] *n* libraire *mf*; **secondhand b.** bouquiniste *mf*
bookselling ['bʊkselɪŋ] *n* librairie *f*, commerce *m* du livre
bookshelf, *pl* **-shelves** ['bʊkʃelf, -ʃelvz] *n* rayon *m*, étagère *f*
bookshop ['bʊkʃɒp] *n* librairie *f*
bookstall ['bʊkstɔːl] *n* **(a)** (*selling second-hand books*) (*in aid of charity*) étalage *m* de livres d'occasion; (*for profit*) étalage

de bouquiniste **(b)** (*in station*) kiosque *m*, bibliothèque *f* de gare

bookstore ['bʊkstɔːr] *n Am* librairie *f*

book token *n* chèque-cadeau *m* pour des livres

bookworm ['bʊkwɜːm] *n* **(a)** (*person*) mordu, -ue de lecture **(b)** (*insect*) anobion *m*, ptine *m*

Boolean ['buːlɪən] *adj* booléen; **B. algebra** algèbre *f* booléenne; **B. function** fonction *f* booléenne; **B. operator** opérateur *m* booléen

boom¹ [buːm] *n* **(a)** (*at harbour mouth*) barrage *m* flottant, barre *f ou* estacade *f* flottante **(b)** *Naut* (*for jib*) bout-dehors *m*, *pl* bouts-dehors; **derrick b.** mât *m* de charge; **swinging b.** tangon *m* **(c)** (*of crane*) flèche *f*; *Cin, TV* (*for microphone*) perche *f*, *F* girafe *f*; **b. microphone** micro *m* sur perche

boom² *n* (*sound*) (*of cannon, thunder, waves*) grondement *m*; (*of wind*) mugissement *m*; (*of organ*) ronflement *m*; (*of bells*) bourdonnement *m*; *Aut* (*of engine*) ronflement, grondement; **the b. of his voice** les éclats *mpl* de sa voix

boom³ *vi* (*of thunder, waves*) gronder; (*of wind*) mugir; (*of guns*) gronder, tonner; (*of organ*) ronfler; (*of bells*) résonner sourdement; (*of voice*) retentir; **'stop!' he boomed** 'arrête!' dit-il de sa voix retentissante

boom⁴ *n Com, Fin etc* boom *m*; **b. town** (*growing*) ville *f* champignon; (*prosperous*) ville prospère

boom⁵ *vi* (*of trade, business etc*) être florissant

▶ **boom out 1** *vi* (*sound loudly*) résonner **2** *vtsep* (*utter loudly*) (*order*) hurler

boomerang¹ ['buːməræŋ] *n* (*for throwing*), *Fig* boomerang *m*

boomerang² *vi Fig* faire boomerang; **the joke boomeranged on him** la plaisanterie lui est retombée dessus

booming ['buːmɪŋ] *adj* (*wind*) mugissant; (*thunder*) retentissant; **b. voice** voix *f* retentissante

boon¹ [buːn] *n* **(a)** (*useful item*) avantage *m*; **I found it a great b.** cela m'a rendu grand service **(b)** *Arch Lit* (*favour*) faveur *f*

boon² *adj* **b. companion** ami, -ie très proche; **they're b. companions** ils sont inséparables

boondocks ['buːndɒks], **boonies** ['buːniːz] *npl Am F* (grande) banlieue *f*; **to live in the boonies** habiter à Perpète(-les-Oies)

boor [bɔːr] *n* rustre *m*, rustaud *m*

boorish ['bɔːrɪʃ] *adj* (*manners, behaviour, person*) rustre, grossier

boorishly ['bɔːrɪʃlɪ] *adv* grossièrement, de façon rustre

boorishness ['bɔːrɪʃnɪs] *n* grossièreté *f*

boost¹ [buːst] *n* **(a) to give a b. to** (*industry, production, exports, sales etc*) relancer; (*morale*) remonter; (*product*) faire du battage pour; *F* **to give sb a b.** (*morally*) regonfler qn; (*in finding a job*) donner un coup de pouce à qn; (*over a wall*) soulever qn; **to give sb.'s confidence a boost** redonner confiance à qn; **to give sb's morale a b.** remonter le moral à qn; **that win will have given her ego a b.** cette victoire aura regonflé son amour-propre **(b)** *El* survoltage *m*; *Av* surpression *f*

boost² *vt* **(a)** (*industry, production, exports etc*) relancer; (*recruitment, numbers etc*) augmenter; (*morale*) remonter; (*product*) faire du battage pour; *F* (*person*) (*morally*) regonfler; (*in finding job*) donner un coup de pouce à; **to b. sb's hopes/confidence** redonner de l'espoir/de la confiance à qn **(b)** (*speed, energy, pressure of sth*) augmenter; *El* survolter; (*engine*) suralimenter

booster ['buːstər] *n* **(a)** *El* survolteur *m* **(b)** (*of missile*) propulseur *m* auxiliaire de départ, booster *m*; **b. rocket** fusée *f* de démarrage **(c)** *Av* démarreur *m* auxiliaire, accélérateur *m* (de décollage) **(d)** (*supercharger*) compresseur *m*; (*on heater*) ventilateur *m*; (*for brakes*) servo-frein *m* **(e)** *Electron* suramplificateur *m*, booster *m* **(f)** *Ch* renforçateur *m* **(g)** *Med* **b. dose/injection** dose *f*/injection *f* de rappel, rappel *m*

booster cushion *n* (*in car*) réhausseur *m*

booster seat *n* (*in car*) (siège *m*) réhausseur *m*, siège de réhausse

booster station *n Telecomm* station *f* relais; *HydE* station auxiliaire de pompage

boot¹ [buːt] *n* **(a)** (*footwear*) botte *f*; (*short*) bottine *f*; (*for football, rugby*) chaussure *f*; **walking** *or* **climbing boots** chaussures de marche; **riding boots** bottes de cheval *ou* de cavalier; **... or you'll feel (the toe of) my b. up your backside** ... sinon tu vas recevoir un bon coup de pied au derrière; *F* **to put** *or* **stick the b. in** (*kick someone*) flanquer des coups de pied à; **they really put the b. in** (*kicked him*) ils l'ont vraiment défoncé à coups de pied; *Fig* **you really know how to put the b. in!** tu es vraiment doué pour enfoncer le couteau dans la plaie!; *Fig* **the b.'s on the other foot** les rôles sont renversés *ou* inversés; *Fig* **you can bet your boots that ...** je te fiche mon billet que ...; *Fig F* **to give sb (the order of) the b.** (*from job*) mettre *ou* flanquer qn à la porte; (*from relationship*) plaquer qn; *Fig* **to get the b.** (*from job*) être mis à la porte; (*from relationship*) se faire plaquer; *F* **as tough as old boots** (*meat*) dur comme de la semelle; (*plant*) très résistant; **to die with one's boots on** (*in battle*) mourir les bottes aux pieds; *Fig* rester fidèle au poste jusqu'à la mort

(b) *Br Aut* coffre *m*; **b. light** éclaireur *m* de coffre

(c) (*kick*) coup *m* de pied; **to give a ball a b.** donner un coup de pied dans un ballon; **he needs a b. up the backside** il a besoin d'un bon coup de pied au derrière

(d) *Comptr* **b. disk** disque *m*/disquette *f* de démarrage; **b. sector** secteur *m* d'initialisation; **b. track** piste *f* d'amorçage

boot² **1** *vt F* flanquer des coups de pied à; **to b. sb out** (*dismiss*) flanquer qn à la porte; **her parents booted her out of the house** ses parents l'ont mise à la porte **2** *vi* (*of computer*) s'amorcer

boot³ *n* (*only in the phrase*) **to b.** en sus, par-dessus le marché; **and a liar/a thief to b.** et par-dessus le marché c'est un menteur/un voleur

▶ **boot up** *Comptr* **1** *vi* (*of computer*) s'amorcer; (*of computer, person*) démarrer **2** *vtsep* (*computer*) amorcer, faire démarrer

bootable ['buːtəb(ə)l] *adj Comptr* amorçable

bootblack ['buːtblæk] *n* cireur *m* de chaussures

boot camp *n US Mil Sl* = camp *m* d'entraînement des nouvelles recrues

bootee [buː'tiː] *n* **(a)** (*short boot*) bottillon *m* **(b)** (*baby's*) chausson *m*

booth [buːð, buːθ] *n* (*at fair*) baraque *f*; *Am* (*at exhibition*) stand *m*; *Tel* cabine *f*; (*in restaurant*) alcôve *f*

bootjack ['buːtdʒæk] *n* tire-botte *m*, *pl* tire-bottes

bootlace ['buːtleɪs] *n* lacet *m* (de botte)

bootleg¹ ['buːtleg] *adj* (*whisky*) de contrebande; (*record, video*) pirate

bootleg² (-gg-) **1** *vt* (*alcohol*) (*produce*) produire illégalement; (*transport*) transporter illégalement; (*sell*) vendre illégalement; (*video, tape*) pirater **2** *vi* (*deal*) (*in alcoholic drinks*) trafiquer, faire de la contrebande; (*in videos, software etc*) faire du piratage

bootlegger ['buːtlegər] *n* (*of videos, software etc*) personne *f* qui se livre au piratage; *US Hist* (*of alcohol*) bootlegger *m*

bootlegging ['buːtlegɪŋ] *n* (*of videos, software*) piratage *m*; (*of alcohol*) contrebande *f*

bootlicker ['buːtlɪkər] *n F* lèche-bottes *mf inv*

bootlicking ['buːtlɪkɪŋ] *n F* lèche-bottes *m*; **b. is his speciality** il est spécialiste du lèche-bottes

bootloader ['buːtləʊdər] *n Comptr* chargeur-amorce *m*

bootmaker ['buːtmeɪkər] *n* bottier *m*

boot sale *n Br* ≈ brocante *f*

bootstrap ['buːtstræp] *n* **(a)** (*on boot*) languette *f*; *Fig* **to pull oneself up by one's bootstraps** se faire tout seul **(b)** *Comptr* amorce *f*, programme *m* d'amorcement; **b. loader** chargeur-amorce *m*, chargeur *m* initial; **b. routine** routine *f* d'amorçage

booty ['buːtɪ] *n* butin *m*

booze¹ [buːz] *vi F* boire, picoler; **he's gone out boozing** il est allé picoler

booze² *n F* boisson *f* (alcoolique); **there's no more b.** il n'y a plus rien à boire; **to go on the b.** se mettre à boire; **I'm (staying) off the b.** j'ai arrêté de boire

boozer ['buːzər] *n Sl* **(a)** (*drunkard*) poivrot, -ote **(b)** *Br* (*pub*) pub *m*; **down the b.** au pub

booze-up *n Br Sl* bringue *f*; **we're having a b. on Friday** on fait une bringue vendredi

boozily ['buːzɪlɪ] *adv F* **to look at sb b.** regarder qn à travers les vapeurs de l'alcool; **to say sth b.** dire qch d'une voix avinée

boozy ['buːzɪ] *adj F* (*breath, face*) vineux; (*voice*) aviné; (*look, manner*) d'ivrogne; **a b. evening** une soirée bien arrosée; **a b. old man** un vieil ivrogne

bop¹ [bɒp] *n* **(a)** *Mus* bop *m* **(b)** *F* (*at disco*) danse *f*; **to go for a b.** aller danser

bop² *vi F* (*at disco*) danser

bop³ *n F* (*blow*) léger coup *m*

bop⁴ *vt F* (*hit*) donner un léger coup à

bo-peep [bəʊ'piːp] *n F* cache-cache *m inv*

boracic [bə'ræsɪk] *adj Ch* (*acid*) borique; *Pharm* **b. ointment** pommade *f* boriquée

borage ['bɒrɪdʒ] *n Bot, Culin* bourrache *f*

borax ['bɔːræks] *n Ch etc* borax *m*

bordeaux [bɔː'dəʊ] *n* (*wine*) bordeaux *m*

border¹ ['bɔːdər] *n* **(a)** (*of rug, plate, picture*) bordure *f*

(b) (*edge*) (*of path*) bord *m*; **there were flowers along the b. of the path** il y avait des fleurs sur le bord du chemin

(c) (*between two countries*) frontière *f*; **to cross the b.** passer la frontière; **north of the B.** (*from viewpoint of England*) en Écosse; (*from viewpoint of Ireland*) en Irlande du nord; (*from viewpoint of the US*) au Canada; **south of the B.** (*from viewpoint of Scotland*) en Angleterre; (*from viewpoint of Northern Ireland*) en République d'Irlande; (*from viewpoint of Canada*) aux États-Unis; (*from viewpoint of the US*) au Mexique; **the Borders, the B. country** (*in Britain*) = les comtés *mpl* limitrophes de la frontière entre l'Écosse et l'Angleterre; **b. controls** contrôles *mpl* aux frontières; **b. crossing** passage *m* de frontière

(**d**) (*hem*) bordure *f*

(**e**) (*flowerbed*) plate-bande *f*, *pl* plates-bandes

border[2] *vt* (**a**) (*be adjacent to*) (*lake, garden*) border; (*country*) confiner à *ou* avec; **the countries that b. the Mediterranean** les pays qui sont en bordure de la Méditerranée (**b**) *Sewing* lisérer

▶ **border on** *vipo* (**a**) (*of territory*) (*another country*) confiner à; **the two countries b. on each other** les deux pays se touchent *ou* ont une frontière commune; **his estate borders on mine** ses terres touchent les miennes (**b**) (*be almost equivalent to*) (*madness, cruelty etc*) approcher de, être voisin de; **to b. on rudeness/a lie/the absurd** friser l'impolitesse/le mensonge/l'absurde; **he was bordering on sixty** il frisait la soixantaine; **emotion bordering on terror** émotion voisine de la terreur

borderer ['bɔːdərər] *n Br* habitant, -ante des comtés limitrophes de la frontière entre l'Écosse et l'Angleterre

border guard *n* garde-frontière *m*, *pl* gardes-frontière

bordering ['bɔːdərɪŋ] *adj* (*country*) contigu, *f* -uë, limitrophe

borderland ['bɔːdəlænd] *n* pays *m* frontalier *ou* limitrophe; *Fig* **the b. between sleeping and waking** l'état de demi-sommeil

borderline ['bɔːdəlaɪn] **1** *n* (*between two categories etc*) distinction *f*; (*between two countries*) frontière *f*; *Fig* **the b. between sanity and insanity** la limite entre le bon sens et la folie; **she's on the b.** c'est un cas limite **2** *adj* **a b. case** un cas limite; **it's b.** c'est un cas limite

border post *n* poste-frontière *m*, *pl* postes-frontières

border region *n* région *f* frontalière

border town *n* ville *f* frontière *ou* frontalière

bore[1] [bɔːr] *n* (**a**) (*person*) personne *f* ennuyeuse, *F* raseur, -euse; **what a (crashing) b. (he is)!** ce qu'il est barbant *ou* rasoir!; **he's a real b. on the subject of gardening** il est vraiment barbant quand il se met à parler de jardinage (**b**) (*thing*) chose *f* ennuyeuse; **the film was a bit of a b.** le film était un peu ennuyeux; **I know it's a b. but it's got to be done** je sais que ce n'est pas marrant mais il faut le faire; **what a b.!** quelle barbe!

bore[2] *vt* ennuyer, *F* raser, *F* barber; *F* **it/he bores me rigid** *or* **stiff** *or* **to death** *or* **to tears** ça/il m'ennuie à mourir; *F* **to b. the pants off sb** ennuyer qn à mourir; **I won't b. you with the details** je vous passe les détails

bore[3] *n* (**a**) (*diameter*) calibre *m*; (*of pipe etc*) alésage *m*; (*of firearm*) calibre (**b**) (*cylinder*) (*of firearm*) âme *f*; **smooth/rifled b.** âme lisse/rayée (**c**) *Min* (*hole*) trou *m* de sonde, sondage *m*, forage *m*

bore[4] **1** *vt* (*well*) foncer; (*hole*) forer, creuser; (*cylinder*) aléser **2** *vi* **to b. into wood** (*of insect*) creuser un trou *ou* une galerie dans le bois; **to b. through sth** percer qch; *Min* **to b. for water/minerals** faire un sondage *ou* sonder pour trouver de l'eau/des minéraux

bore[5] *n* (*wave*) mascaret *m*

bore[6] *pt see* **bear**[3]

Boreal ['bɔːrɪəl] *adj* (*forest*) boréal

bored [bɔːd] *adj* (*look, sigh etc*) d'ennui; (*person*) qui s'ennuie; **you look b.** tu as l'air de t'ennuyer; **to be** *or* **get b.** s'ennuyer; **I'm never b.** je ne m'ennuie jamais; **she is b. with him/it** elle en a assez de lui/elle en a assez; **he's a bit b. with his job** il s'ennuie un peu dans son travail; **I'm getting b. with this conversation** j'en ai assez de cette conversation; *F* **to be b. rigid** *or* **to tears** *or* **out of one's mind** s'ennuyer à mourir

boredom ['bɔːdəm] *n* ennui *m*

borehole ['bɔːhəʊl] *n Min* (*exploratory*) trou *m* de sonde, sondage *m*; (*for mine*) trou de mine

borer ['bɔːrər] *n* (*device*) (*for wood, metal*) foret *m*; *Min* (*of well*) sonde *f*

boric ['bɔːrɪk] *adj Ch* (*acid etc*) borique

boring[1] ['bɔːrɪŋ] *adj* (*tedious*) ennuyeux, *F* barbant, *F* rasant, *F* rasoir

boring[2] **1** *adj* (*insect*) térébrant **2** *n* (*of hole etc*) percement *m*; *MecE* forage *m*, perçage *m*; (*of cylinder*) alésage *m*; *Min* sondage *m*, forage

boring machine *n MecE* foreuse *f*, perceuse *f*

born [bɔːn] **1** (*pp of* **bear**[3] *used in formation of passive verb*) **to be b.** naître; **I was b. in London/in 1930** je suis né à Londres/en 1930; **my mother died when I was b.** ma mère est décédée en me mettant au monde; **Queen Victoria was still on the throne when I was b.** la reine Victoria régnait toujours quand je suis né; **the house where I was b.** ma maison natale; **he is French b.** il est français de naissance; **to be b. deaf/blind** être sourd/aveugle de naissance; **to be b. lucky** être né coiffé; *F* **do you think I was b. yesterday?** pour qui me prends-tu?; *F* **I wasn't b. yesterday** je ne suis pas né d'hier *ou* tombé de la dernière pluie; *Hum* **were you b. in a barn** *or* **a stable?** on ne t'a jamais appris à fermer tes portes?; *Fig* **it was a decision b. of necessity** cette décision était dictée par les circonstances; **... he said, with a cynicism b. of experience** ... dit-il avec le cynisme que lui conférait l'expérience

2 *adj* **a b. storyteller/linguist** un conteur/linguiste né; **she's a b. liar** elle ment comme elle respire; **a b. loser** un raté irrécupérable; **a Londoner b. and bred** un vrai Londonien de Londres; **in all my b. days** de toute ma vie

born-again *adj Rel, Hum* régénéré; **b. Christian** chrétien, -ienne régénéré(e); *Fig* **b. vegetarian** personne *f* devenue végétarienne (et qui essaye de convaincre les autres)

borne *see* **bear**[3]

Borneo ['bɔːnɪəʊ] *n* Bornéo *m*

borough ['bʌrə] *n Br* (**a**) (*town*) ville *f* (*avec municipalité*); **b. council** conseil *m* municipal (**b**) (*electoral district*) circonscription *f* électorale (urbaine)

borrow ['bɒrəʊ] **1** *vt* emprunter (**from** à); **to b. money from sb** emprunter de l'argent à qn, faire un emprunt à qn; **can I b. the car?** est-ce que je peux prendre la voiture?; **to b. an idea from sb** emprunter une idée à qn; **this word was borrowed from Latin** ce mot est un emprunt au latin **2** *vi* emprunter; **to b. from sb** (*money*) faire un emprunt à qn, emprunter de l'argent à qn

▶ **borrow against** *vipo Fin* emprunter sur

borrowed ['bɒrəʊd] *adj* **b. capital** capitaux *mpl* empruntés *ou* d'emprunt; **the doctors say he's living on b. time** (*close to death*) les médecins disent qu'il n'en a plus pour longtemps; **the company is living on b. time** les jours de l'entreprise sont comptés; **my grandfather is living on b. time** (*is very old*) mon grand-père a de la chance d'être encore en vie; **he'd been living on b. time since he was caught stealing from his employer** (*his job was in danger*) il était en sursis depuis qu'on l'avait pris à voler son employeur

borrower ['bɒrəʊər] *n* emprunteur, -euse

borrowing ['bɒrəʊɪŋ] *n* (*action, money*) emprunt *m*; **b. capacity** capacité *f* d'endettement, capacité à emprunter; **b. limit** maximum *m* d'emprunt, limite *f* d'endettement; **b. power** possibilité *f* d'emprunter; **b. rate** taux *m* d'emprunt; **b. requirement** besoins *mpl* d'emprunt

borsch [bɔːʃ] *n Culin* bortsch *m*

borstal ['bɔːst(ə)l] *n Br Admin* maison *f* de redressement (*pour jeunes délinquants âgés de 15 à 21 ans*); **b. boy** jeune délinquant *m*

borzoi ['bɔːzɔɪ] *n* (*dog*) lévrier *m* russe, barzoï *m*

bosh [bɒʃ] *Old-fashioned F* **1** *n* bêtises *fpl*, blagues *fpl* **2** *int* n'importe quoi!, sottises!

bos'n ['bəʊs(ə)n] *n* = **boatswain**

bosom ['bʊzəm] **1** *n* (*of woman*) seins *mpl*; *Old-fashioned, Lit* (*of person*) poitrine *f*; *Fig* **in the b. of one's family** au sein de sa famille; **in the b. of the Church** dans le giron de l'Église **2** *adj* **b. friend** ami *m* intime; **they are b. friends** ils sont grands amis

Bosnia ['bɒznɪə] *n* Bosnie *f*; **B.-Herzegovina** Bosnie-Herzégovine *f*

Bosnian ['bɒznɪən] **1** *n* Bosnieque *mf* **2** *adj* bosniaque

bosomy ['bʊzəmɪ] *adj* (*woman*) à la poitrine opulente; **she was a b. lady** elle avait une poitrine opulente

Bosp(h)orus (the) [ðə'bɒsfərəs, ðə'bɒspərəs] *n* le Bosphore

boss[1] *F* **1** *n* (*person in charge*) patron, -onne, chef *m*; *US* (*of political party*) chef; **the trade-union bosses** les gens *mpl* à la tête du syndicat; **show them who's (the) b.** montre-leur qui commande ici; **to be one's own b.** être son propre patron **2** *adj esp Am* (*excellent*) épatant, merveilleux

boss[2] [bɒs] *n* (**a**) (*knob*) protubérance *f*; *Archit, Metal, Zool etc* bosse *f*; (*on furniture*) capiton *m* (**b**) *MecE* mamelon *m*, portée *f*; *Av* (*of propeller*) moyeu *m*; *Aut* (*centre of steering wheel*) bossette *f*; **centre b.** (*of wheel, crank*) tourteau *m*

boss[3] *vt F* (*person*) donner des ordres à; *Fig* **to b. the show** faire la loi

▶ **boss about, boss around** *vtsep* donner des ordres à; **stop bossing me about!** j'en ai assez que tu me donnes des ordres!

boss-eyed *adj Br F* qui louche; **to be b.** avoir un œil qui dit merde à l'autre

bossily ['bɒsɪlɪ] *adv F* de façon autoritaire

bossiness ['bɒsɪnɪs] *n F* (*of person, manner*) façons *fpl* autoritaires

bossy ['bɒsɪ] *adj F* autoritaire; **don't be so b., don't be such a b. boots** arrête de jouer au petit chef

bosun ['bəʊs(ə)n] *n* = **boatswain**

botanical [bə'tænɪk(ə)l] *adj* botanique; **b. garden(s)** jardin *m* botanique

botanist ['bɒtənɪst] *n* botaniste *mf*

botanize ['bɒtənaɪz] *vi* herboriser

botany ['bɒtənɪ] *n* botanique *f*; **B. wool** laine *f* très fine (importée d'Australie)

botch¹ [bɒtʃ] *n F* travail *m* mal fait *ou* salopé; **you've made an awful b. of it** tu as complètement salopé le boulot; **to make a b. of an interview/speech** rater complètement un entretien/un discours; **she made a terrible b. of putting up the shelves** elle a mis les étagères n'importe comment

botch² *vt F* (*job*) saloper; (*interview, speech*) rater; **he botched the shelves** il a mis les étagères n'importe comment

▶ **botch up** *vtsep* (*job*) saloper; (*interview, speech*) rater

botched [bɒtʃt] *adj F* **a b. attempt at suicide** une tentative de suicide ratée; **his b. apology only made matters worse** ses excuses minables n'ont fait qu'empirer la situation; **a b. job** un travail de sagouin

botcher ['bɒtʃər] *n F* bousilleur *m*

botch-up *n* = **botch¹**

botel ['bəʊtel] *n* bateau-hôtel *m*, *pl* bateaux-hotels; (*on barge*) péniche-hôtel *f*, *pl* péniches-hôtels

both [bəʊθ] **1** *adj, pron* [①**A4**,**B**; **A37**,**g**] les deux, tous (les) deux, toutes (les) deux; **b. brothers, b. (of) the brothers** les deux frères; **b. (of them) are dead** ils sont morts tous (les) deux; **b. of us saw it** nous l'avons vu tous les deux; **he has two houses, b. of which are vacant** il a deux maisons, qui sont vides toutes les deux; **she kissed him on b. cheeks** elle l'a embrassé sur les deux joues; **to hold sth in b. hands** tenir qch à deux mains; **on b. sides** des deux côtés; **b. alike** l'un comme l'autre; **look b. ways** (*when crossing street*) regarde des deux côtés; **you can't have it b. ways** on ne peut pas avoir le beurre et l'argent du beurre; *Naut* **stop b. engines** stoppez partout

2 *adv* **b. you and I** vous et moi; **b. you and I know it's not that simple** vous savez comme moi que cela n'est pas aussi simple; **she is b. intelligent and beautiful** elle est à la fois intelligente et belle

bother¹ ['bɒðər] *n* **(a)** (*trouble*) ennui *m*; **to be having a bit** *or* **a spot of b.** avoir quelques ennuis (**with** avec); **it's such a b. having to take it back** c'est tellement embêtant d'avoir à le ramener; **to be in b. with the police** avoir des ennuis avec la police; **if it's not too much b.** si cela ne vous dérange pas trop; **I hope I haven't put you to a lot of b.** j'espère que je ne vous ai pas trop dérangé; **it's a lot of b. to go to** ça représente beaucoup de dérangement pour pas grand-chose; **I hate to be a b., but ...** je suis désolé de vous déranger, mais ...; **it's no b. at all** ça ne m'ennuie pas du tout; **it's not worth the b.** cela ne vaut pas la peine; **to go to the b. of doing sth** se donner la peine de faire qch

(b) *Br Sl* (*fighting*) bagarre *f*; **there was a bit of b. in the pub** il y a eu un peu de bagarre dans le pub

bother² **1** *vt* **(a)** (*annoy*) ennuyer; (*disturb*) déranger; (*be in the way of*) gêner; **does the light b. you?** est-ce que la lumière vous gêne *ou* dérange?; **my back's still bothering me** (*giving pain*) j'ai toujours des problèmes de dos; **his old wound bothers him in damp weather** sa vieille blessure le fait souffrir par temps humide; **I hate to b. you but ...** je suis désolé de vous déranger mais ...; **he didn't even b. to apologize** il n'a même pas pris la peine de s'excuser; **don't b. me!** laissez-moi tranquille!; **I can't be bothered (to do it)** ça ne me dit rien (de le faire); **b. (it)!** zut!; **b. the man!** qu'il aille au diable!

(b) (*worry*) inquiéter; **to be bothered about sth** s'inquiéter de qch, se faire du mauvais sang pour qch; **don't b. yourself** *or* **your head about me** ne vous inquiétez pas pour moi; *F* **I'm not bothered** cela m'est égal!

2 *vi* **(a)** (*take trouble*) s'occuper (**with** de); prendre *ou* se donner la peine (**to do sth** de faire qch); **don't b. to ring me up/to turn the lights off** ce n'est pas la peine de me téléphoner/d'éteindre la lumière; **don't b. with the dishes just now** ne t'embête pas à faire la vaisselle maintenant; **I'll call you next week — don't b.!** (*I can get on without you*) je t'appellerai la semaine prochaine — te fatigue pas!

(b) (*worry*) s'inquiéter (**about** de); **he doesn't b. about anything** il ne s'inquiète de rien

botheration [bɒðə'reɪʃən] *int Old-fashioned F* zut!

bothersome ['bɒðəsəm] *adj* gênant

bottle¹ ['bɒt(ə)l] *n* **(a)** bouteille *f*; (*small*) (*for perfume etc*) flacon *m*; (*wide-mouthed*) bocal *m*; (*for baby*) biberon *m*; *Med* urinal *m*, *F* pistolet *m*; **bring your own b.** (*on invitation*) chacun doit amener une bouteille; (*notice in restaurant*) = les clients peuvent apporter leur vin (*étant donné que le restaurant n'a pas de licence*); **he drank the whole b.** il a bu toute la bouteille; **brought up on the b.** (*baby*) élevé au biberon; *F* **to be fond of the b.** aimer la bouteille; *F* **to be on the b.** boire; *F* **to hit** *or* **take to the b.** commencer à picoler; *F* **he's been hitting the b. a lot recently** il picole beaucoup ces temps-ci; *Pej* **b. blonde** (*with dyed hair*) blonde *f* décolorée

(b) *Br Sl* (*courage, nerve*) cran *m*, culot *m*; **to have a lot of b.** avoir beaucoup de cran; **to lose one's b.** se dégonfler; (*permanently*) perdre son assurance

bottle² *vt* (*wine etc*) mettre en bouteilles; (*jam etc*) mettre en bocal; **autumn is the best time for bottling fruit** l'automne est la meilleure saison pour faire des conserves de fruits

▶ **bottle out** *vi Br Sl* (*be too frightened*) se dégonfler

▶ **bottle up** *vtsep* (*one's feelings*) étouffer; (*one's anger*) refouler, ravaler

bottle bank *n* dépôt *m* de verre

bottlebrush ['bɒt(ə)lbrʌʃ] *n* **(a)** (*for cleaning*) goupillon *m* **(b)** (*plant*) callistemon *m*

bottled ['bɒt(ə)ld] *adj* (*wine, beer, gas etc*) en bouteille(s); **b. fruit** fruits *mpl* en bocaux; **b. water** eau *f* minérale

bottle-fed *adj* nourri au biberon

bottle-feed *vt* (*baby, lamb etc*) nourrir au biberon

bottle-feeding *n* alimentation *f* au biberon

bottleful ['bɒt(ə)lfʊl] *n* **a b. of sth** une pleine bouteille de qch; **by the b.** à pleine bouteille

bottle green **1** *n* vert *m* bouteille **2** *adj* vert bouteille *inv*

bottleneck ['bɒt(ə)lnek] *n* **(a)** goulot *m* (de bouteille) **(b)** *Fig* (*in road*) rétrécissement *m* de la chaussée; (*traffic jam*) embouteillage *m*, bouchon *m*; (*in production etc*) goulet *m ou* goulot *m* d'étranglement **(c)** *Mus* (*guitar style*) bottleneck *m*

bottle opener *n* ouvre-bouteille(s) *m inv*, décapsuleur *m*

bottle party *n* = soirée *f* où chacun amène sa bouteille

bottle-washer *n* (*person*) laveur, -euse de bouteilles; (*machine*) rince-bouteilles *m inv*

bottling ['bɒt(ə)lɪŋ] *n* (*of wine etc*) mise *f* en bouteille(s); (*of fruit*) mise en bocaux

bottom ['bɒtəm] **1** *n* **(a)** *F* (*of person*) derrière *m*

(b) bottoms (*of pyjamas, tracksuit*) pantalon *m*, bas *m*

(c) (*of hill, stairs, page*) bas *m*; (*of well, box, sea*) fond *m*; **at the b. of the garden/of my bag** au fond du jardin/de mon sac; **he's at the b. of the class** il est le dernier de sa classe; **at the b. of the page** au *ou* en bas de la page; **to send a ship to the b.** envoyer un bâtiment par le fond; **to go to the b.** (*of ship*) couler; **to strike** *or* **touch b.** (*of ship*) toucher le fond; **to touch b.** (*of swimmer*), *Fig* toucher le fond; **from the b. of one's heart** du fond du cœur; **to get to the b. of sth** (*solve*) tirer qch au clair; **to get to the b. of things** aller au fond des choses; **to be at the b. of sth** (*be instigator*) être derrière qch, être l'instigateur de qch; (*be cause*) être la cause de qch; **at b.** au fond, dans le fond; **b. fishing** pêche *f* à la ligne de fond

(d) (*of chair*) siège *m*; *Naut* (*of ship*) carène *f*, fond *m*; **the b. of my glass/plate** (*inside*) le fond de mon verre/assiette; (*outside*) le dessous de mon verre/assiette; **to put sth b. up(wards)** mettre qch sens dessus dessous; **box with a false b.** boîte à double fond; **to knock the b. out of** (*box etc*) défoncer; *Fig* (*argument*) démolir; **the b. has fallen out of the market** le marché s'est effondré; *F* **bottoms up!** (*empty your glass*) cul sec!; (*cheers*) à votre santé!; *Billiards* **to put b. on a ball** faire de l'effet à revenir *ou* de l'effet rétrograde

(e) *Aut* (*gear*) première *f*

2 *adj* **b. half** partie *f* inférieure; **it's on the b. shelf** il se trouve sur l'étagère du bas; **the b. book in the pile** le livre qui est en bas de la pile; **b. end of the table** bout *m* de la table; **b. stair** (*going up*) première marche *f*; (*going down*) dernière marche; *MecE* **b. dead centre** point *m* mort bas; *Typ* **b. margin** marge *f* du bas; **b. price** prix *m* plancher; *Aut* **in b. gear** en première; *F* **you can bet your b. dollar that ...** vous pouvez être sûr que ...

▶ **bottom out** *vi* (*of inflation, unemployment, prices*) atteindre son niveau le plus bas; (*of recession*) atteindre son plancher

bottom drawer *n Br* (*trousseau*) trousseau *m*

bottomless ['bɒtəmlɪs] *adj* **(a)** (*well etc*) sans fond; *Fig* **b. pit** gouffre *m*; **it's like pouring money into a b. pit** c'est comme jeter de l'argent par les fenêtres; **he's a b. pit** (*always hungry*) c'est un crevard **(b)** (*resources, reserves*) inépuisable

bottom line *n* (*of balance sheet*) solde *m* final; *Fig* (*end result, outcome*) résultat *m*; **the b. is that he is unsuited to the job** le fait est qu'il n'est pas fait pour ce travail; **that's the b.** (*what matters*) c'est la seule chose qui compte; (*how things stand*) voilà où en sont les choses

bottommost ['bɒtəmməʊst] *adj attrib* (*shelf*) le plus bas, d'en bas; **the b. book in the pile** le livre qui se trouve tout en bas de la pile; *Lit* **the b. depths** le tréfonds
bottom-of-the-range 1 *n* modèle *m* de base **2** *adj* bas de gamme
botulism ['bɒtjʊlɪz(ə)m] *n Med* botulisme *m*
bouclé ['bu:kleɪ] *adj, n Tex* bouclé *m*; **b. wool** bouclette *f*; **b. sweater** pull *m* en bouclette
boudoir ['bu:dwɑ:r] *n Old-fashioned Lit* boudoir *m*
bouffant ['bu:fɒn] *adj* (*hair*) gonflant; (*sleeve, skirt*) bouffant
bougainvillea [bu:gən'vɪlɪə] *n* (*plant*) bougainvillée *f*
bough [baʊ] *n* (*of tree*) branche *f*, rameau *m*
bought *see* **buy**[2]
bouillon ['bu:jɒn] *n Culin* bouillon *m*, consommé *m*; *Am* **b. cube** cube *m* de bouillon *ou* de consommé; *Am* **b. cup** tasse *f* à bouillon *ou* à consommé
boulder ['bəʊldər] *n* (gros) bloc *m* de pierre
boulevard ['bu:ləvɑ:d] *n* **(a)** (*street*) boulevard *m* **(b)** *Am* (*on road*) terre-plein *m* (central), *pl* terre-pleins (centraux)
bounce[1] [baʊns] *n* **(a)** (*of ball*) rebond *m*; **you get a better b. on grass** cela rebondit mieux sur l'herbe; **to catch the ball on the b.** prendre la balle au bond; *Am F* **to get the b.** (*from job*) se faire virer; **she gave him the b.** (*from relationship*) elle l'a plaqué **(b)** *F* (*of person*) entrain *m*; **a shampoo to put the b. back in your hair** un shampooing qui redonnera de la vitalité à vos cheveux
bounce[2] **1** *vi* (*of ball*) rebondir; (*of breasts*) ballotter; **to b. (up and down) on a bed/trampoline** sauter sur un lit/trampoline; **the epaulettes bounced (up and down) on his shoulders** les épaulettes dansaient sur ses épaules; **to b. up and down** (*not sit still*) s'agiter; **to b. into/out of a room** (*of person*) entrer dans une/sortir d'une pièce en coup de vent *ou* en trombe; *F* **cheque that bounces** chèque *m* sans provision *ou F* en bois; *F* **the cheque bounced** le chèque a été refusé (parce qu'il était sans provision)
2 *vt* **(a)** (*ball*) faire rebondir; *Fig* **to b. a few ideas around** explorer quelques idées; **to b. a baby on one's knee** faire sauter un bébé sur ses genoux; *F* **to b. a cheque** (*of bank*) refuser un chèque sans provision
(b) *Am F* (*person*) (*from job, nightclub etc*) flanquer à la porte
▶ **bounce back** *vi* (*of ball*) rebondir; *Fig* (*of actor etc*) (*after failure*) faire son retour; (*from illness, disappointment*) se remettre
▶ **bounce off 1** *vtaspo* **to bounce a ball off a wall/off the ground** faire rebondir une balle contre un mur/sur le sol; *Fig* **to b. an idea off sb** soumettre une idée à qn (pour voir sa réaction) **2** *vipo* (*of ball, rain, bullets etc*) (*window, houses*) rebondir contre; (*roof, pavement*) rebondir sur; *Fig* **criticism bounces off him** (*does not penetrate*) les critiques ne l'atteignent pas
bouncer ['baʊnsər] *n* **(a)** *F* (*in nightclub etc*) videur *m* **(b)** *Sl* (*cheque*) chèque *m* sans provision *ou F* en bois **(c)** *Cr* balle *f* qui rebondit en hauteur
bouncing ['baʊnsɪŋ] *adj* (*ball*) rebondissant; *Fig* (*baby*) plein de vie et de santé
bouncy ['baʊnsɪ] *adj* **(a)** (*ball*) qui rebondit; (*hair*) plein de vigueur **(b)** *Fig* (*person*) plein d'entrain
bouncy castle *n* château *m* gonflable (*sur lequel les enfants s'amusent à sauter*)
bound[1] [baʊnd] *n* (*usu pl*) (*limit*) limite(s) *f(pl)*, bornes *fpl*; **out of bounds** interdit; *Mil etc* consigné; **to go beyond the bounds of reason** dépasser les bornes de la raison; **it is not beyond the bounds of possibility** c'est dans le domaine du possible; **my fury knew no bounds** je n'ai (pas) pu contenir ma fureur; **his ambition knows no bounds** son ambition ne connaît pas de bornes; **to keep within bounds** ne pas exagérer; **to keep one's imagination within (reasonable) bounds** mettre un frein à son imagination; **to keep one's spending within (reasonable) bounds** modérer *ou* limiter ses dépenses
bound[2] *n* (*jump*) bond *m*, saut *m*; **at one b.** d'un (seul) bond, d'un saut
bound[3] *vi* (*of person, dog*) bondir; (*of ball etc*) rebondir; **he bounded across the room to greet them** il a traversé la pièce d'un bond pour venir les saluer
bound[4] *adj* **(a)** *Naut* **ship b. for America** (*still in port*) navire en partance pour l'Amérique; (*under way*) navire en route pour l'Amérique; **a plane b. for Paris** un avion à destination de Paris; **the plane which was b. for Paris crashed** l'avion qui volait à destination de Paris s'est écrasé; **where are you b. for?** où allez-vous?
(b) (*sure*) **he's b. to come** il ne peut pas manquer de venir, il viendra sûrement; **it's b. to rain tomorrow** il pleuvra sûrement demain; **it's b. to happen** c'est fatal; *F* **he'll come, I'll be b.** il viendra, j'en suis sûr *ou* je vous le promets; *Am* **he's b. (and determined) to come and see you** il veut absolument venir vous voir
(c) *Com* **b. by contract** lié par contrat
(d) *Ling* **b. morpheme** morphème *m* lié
bound[5] *vt* (*usu passive*) (*area of town*) limiter, délimiter; (*country, region*) être limitrophe de; **France is bounded by Spain in the south** l'Espagne est limitrophe de la France au sud; **an area bounded by Smith Street on the west, James Avenue on the south** une zone délimitée par Smith Street à l'ouest et James Avenue au sud
bound[6] *pt, pp see* **bind**[2]
boundary ['baʊnd(ə)rɪ] *n* limite *f*; *Fig* (*between private and professional life etc*) frontière *f*; *Cr* **to hit** *or* **score a b.** envoyer la balle jusqu'aux limites du terrain; **the boundaries of human knowledge** les limites de la connaissance humaine; *Br* **b. change** (*of parliamentary constituency*) = modification *f* des limites d'une circonscription; **b. line** (*between properties*) limite *f*; *Fig* frontière *f*; *Sp* ligne *f* du jeu; **to form the b. line between two estates** marquer la limite entre deux domaines; **b. stone** borne *f*, pierre *f* de bornage
bounden ['baʊndən] *adj Lit* **b. duty** devoir *m* impérieux
bounder ['baʊndər] *n Old-fashioned F* goujat *m*
boundless ['baʊndlɪs] *adj* sans bornes, illimité
bounteous ['baʊntɪəs] *adj Lit* **(a)** (*harvest etc*) abondant **(b)** (*person*) libéral, généreux
bounteousness ['baʊntɪəsnɪs] *n Lit* **(a)** (*of harvest etc*) abondance *f* **(b)** (*of person*) bonté *f*, générosité *f*
bountiful ['baʊntɪfʊl] *adj Lit* **(a)** (*harvest, supply etc*) abondant **(b)** (*person*) généreux
bounty ['baʊntɪ] *n* **(a)** (*reward*) récompense *f*; *esp US* **b. hunter** chasseur *m* de primes **(b)** *Lit* (*of person*) bonté *f*, générosité *f*; **the b. from one's garden** les fruits *mpl ou* produits *mpl* de son jardin
bouquet *n* **(a)** [bəʊ'keɪ, bu:-] (*of flowers*) bouquet *m* (composé par un fleuriste); *TV* **b. of channels** bouquet de chaînes **(b)** [bu:'keɪ] (*of wine*) bouquet *m*
Bourbon ['bʊəb(ə)n] *n Hist* Bourbon *mf*; **B. biscuit** = biscuit *m* au chocolat fourré de crème
bourbon ['bɜ:b(ə)n] *n* (*whiskey*) bourbon *m*
bourdon ['bʊəd(ə)n] *n Mus* (*of organ, bagpipes*) bourdon *m*
bourgeois ['bʊəʒwɑ:] *adj, n usu Pej* bourgeois, -oise
bourgeoisie [bʊəʒwɑ:'zi:] *n usu Pej* bourgeoisie *f*
bout [baʊt] *n* **(a)** (*in boxing, wrestling*) combat *m* **(b)** (*brief attack*) (*of malaria, rheumatism, bronchitis etc*) accès *m*; (*of fever*) accès, poussée *f*; (*of coughing*) quinte *f*; (*of self-pity*) crise *f*; (*of depression, intense activity*) période *f*; **she had a bad b. of flu** elle a eu une mauvaise grippe; **a b. of drinking** une période d'excès de boisson
boutique [bu:'ti:k] *n* boutique *f* de mode; (*in department store*) boutique
bovine ['bəʊvaɪn] *adj Zool* bovin; *Fig Pej* (*person*) lourd; **b. expression** *or* **look** regard *m* bovin; **b. stupidity** lourdeur *f*; *Vet* **b. spongiform encephalopathy** encéphalite *f* bovine spongiforme
bovver ['bɒvər] *n Br Sl* (*hooliganism, rowdiness*) **to go out looking for b.** chercher la bagarre; **b. boots** rangers *mpl*; **b. boys** voyous *mpl*
bow[1] [bəʊ] *n* **(a)** (*of archer*) arc *m*; **to draw a b.** bander *ou* tendre un arc; *Fig* **to have more than one string to one's b.** avoir plus d'une corde à son arc; **b. legs** jambes *fpl* arquées *ou* torses; **b. window** fenêtre *f* en saillie, bow-window *m* **(b)** *Mus* (*for violin etc*) archet *m*; (*movement*) coup *m* d'archet **(c)** (*of ribbon*) nœud *m*; **b. tie** nœud papillon
bow[2] *Mus* **1** *vt* jouer (avec l'archet); **bowed instrument** instrument *m* à archet **2** *vi* jouer (de l'archet)
bow[3] [baʊ] *n* (*as greeting etc*) salut *m*; (*from waist*) révérence *f*; **to make a deep** *or* **low b. to sb** saluer qn bien bas; **to take a b.** (*of performer*) saluer; **to take one's final b.** (*retire from stage etc permanently*) faire ses adieux
bow[4] **1** *vi* **(a)** (*as greeting etc*) s'incliner (**to** devant); *Pej* **to b. and scrape** faire des salamalecs *ou* des courbettes **(b)** (*to sb's will, decision etc*) se soumettre (**to** à); **to b. to the inevitable** s'incliner devant les faits; **I bowed to her (greater) wisdom** je me suis incliné devant tant de sagesse **2** *vt* (*head*) incliner, baisser; (*knee*) fléchir; (*sb's back, shoulders*) courber, voûter; **to become bowed** se voûter
bow[5] *n* **(a)** *Naut* (*often pl*) avant *m*, étrave *f*, bossoir *m*; **on the port/starboard b.** par le bossoir bâbord/tribord; **to cross the bows of a ship** couper la route d'un navire; **b. rope** amarre *f* de bout *ou* de l'avant; **b. wave** lame *f* d'étrave **(b)** (*oarsman*) nageur *m* de tête *ou* de l'avant; **b. oar** aviron *m* de l'avant
▶ **bow down** [baʊ] **1** *vi* (*incline one's head*) s'incliner; **to b. down before sb** faire des courbettes devant qn; (*very deeply*) se prosterner devant qn; *Fig* **the teachers b. down before the headmaster** les professeurs s'écrasent devant le

directeur **2** *vtsep* (*of poverty etc*) accabler; **he is bowed down by care** il est accablé par les soucis

▸ **bow out** *vi F* (*leave job, relationship etc voluntarily*) tirer sa révérence

bowdlerize ['baʊdləraɪz] *vt* (*literary work*) expurger, couper; *Fig* **a bowdlerized version of the party** une version tronquée de la soirée

bowed [baʊd] *adj* **with b. head** la tête inclinée; (*with shame etc*) la tête baissée; **b. with age** courbé par le fardeau des ans

bowel ['baʊəl] *n Anat* intestin *m*; **bowels** intestins; **b. complaint** affection *f* intestinale; **b. movement** transit *m* intestinal; **have you had a b. movement today?** est-ce que vous êtes allé (à la selle) aujourd'hui?; *Lit* **the bowels of the earth** les entrailles *fpl* ou le sein de la terre

bower ['baʊər] *n* **(a)** (*in wood, garden*) berceau *m* de verdure, charmille *f*; (*made of trelliswork*) tonnelle *f* **(b)** *Poet, Arch* (*lady's boudoir*) appartement *m*, boudoir *m*

bowerbird ['baʊəbɜːd] *n* oiseau *m* à berceau

bowfronted [bəʊ'frʌntɪd] *adj* (*piece of furniture*) pansu; (*house*) à la façade arrondie

bowhead ['bəʊhed] *n* (*whale*) baleine *f* boréale

bowing¹ ['baʊɪŋ] *n* (*as greeting etc*) saluts *mpl*; *Pej* **b. and scraping** courbettes *fpl*, salamalecs *mpl*

bowing² ['bəʊɪŋ] *n Mus* coups *mpl* d'archet; **her wonderful b.** son jeu magnifique à l'archet

bowl¹ [bəʊl] *n* **(a)** (*for soup, cereal etc*) bol *m*; (*made of crystal etc*) coupe *f*; (*for washing hands, dishes*) cuvette *f*, bac *m* (d'évier); (*plastic*) bassine *f*; (*of toilet*) cuvette **(b)** (*of tobacco pipe*) fourneau *m*, godet *m*; (*of spoon*) cuilleron *m*; (*of stemmed glass*) coupe *f*; (*of scales*) plateau *m* **(c)** *Geog* cuvette *f*, bassin *m* **(d)** *US* (*for concerts etc*) amphithéâtre *m*

bowl² *n* [①A10,d] *Sp* boule *f*; **bowls** (*game*) (*on grass*) boules; (*in bowling alley*) bowling *m*; **to play (at) bowls** jouer aux boules/au bowling

bowl³ **1** *vt* **(a)** (*hoop*) faire rouler **(b)** *Sp* (*ball*) lancer, rouler **(c)** *Cr* (*ball*) lancer, servir; (*player*) renverser le guichet à **2** *vi* **(a)** (*play bowls*) (*on grass*) jouer aux boules; (*in bowling alley*) jouer au bowling **(b)** *Cr* lancer *ou* servir la balle; **well bowled!** bien lancé!

▸ **bowl along** *vi* (*in car, train*) rouler rapidement

▸ **bowl out** *vtsep Cr* renverser le guichet de

▸ **bowl over** *vtsep* **(a)** (*knock down*) (*skittles, person etc*) renverser **(b)** *F* (*astound*) époustoufler; **I was bowled over by her beauty** sa beauté m'a époustouflé, j'ai été époustouflé par sa beauté; **I was bowled over by winning first prize** j'ai été sidéré *ou* époustouflé de gagner le premier prix

bowlegged [bəʊ'legɪd] *adj* aux jambes arquées

bowler¹ ['bəʊlər] *n* **(a)** (*in bowls*) (*on grass*) joueur, -euse de boules, bouliste *mf*; (*in bowling alley*) joueur, -euse de bowling **(b)** *Cr* lanceur, -euse, serveur, -euse

bowler² *n* **b. (hat)** (chapeau *m*) melon *m*

bowlful ['bəʊlfʊl] *n* (*of milk, soup etc*) plein bol *m*; (*of washing up water*) cuvette *f*

bowline ['bəʊlɪn] *n Naut* **(a)** (*rope*) bouline *f* **(b)** (*knot*) nœud *m* de chaise *ou* d'agui

bowling ['bəʊlɪŋ] *n* **(a)** (*game*) (*on grass*) jeu *m* de boules; (*tenpin*) bowling *m* **(b)** (*action*) lancement *m* de la boule *ou* *Cr* de la balle; *Cr* **accurate b.** des lancers *mpl* de balle précis

bowling alley *n* (*building*) bowling *m*; (*single lane*) piste *f* de bowling

bowling green *n* terrain *m* de boules (*gazonné*)

bowman, *pl* **-men** ['bəʊmən] *n Hist* archer *m*

bowsaw ['bəʊsɔː] *n* (*tool*) scie *f* à archet *ou* à arc *ou* à chantourner

bowser ['baʊzər] *n Petr* camion-citerne *m*, *pl* camions-citernes

bowsprit ['bəʊsprɪt] *n Naut* beaupré *m*

bowstring ['bəʊstrɪŋ] *n* corde *f* d'arc

bow-wow ['baʊ'waʊ] **1** *int* oua-oua! **2** *n F* (*dog in children's language*) toutou *m*

box¹ [bɒks] *n* **(a)** **b. (tree)** buis *m* **(b)** (*wood*) (bois *m* de) buis *m*

box² *n* **(a)** (*container*) (*small*) boîte *f*; (*large*) coffre *m*, caisse *f*; *Gym* (*for vaulting*) plinth *m*; (*casing of computer*) boîte; **a b. of cigars/chocolates** une boîte de cigares/chocolats; **jewel b.** coffret *m* à bijoux; **safety deposit b.** coffre-fort *m*, *pl* coffres-forts; **Christmas b.** (*gratuity*) ≈ étrennes *fpl*; *Fig* **in a pine** *or* **wooden b.** (*coffin*) dans une cercueil

(b) (*shape*) **b. camera** appareil *m* compact; *US* **b. canyon** cañon *m* *ou* canyon *m* encaissé; **b. kite** cerf-volant *m* en forme de cube; *Sewing* **b. pleat** pli *m* creux *ou* rond; **b. spanner** *or* **wrench** clef *f* à douille; **b. spring** (*for mattress*) sommier *m* à ressorts

(c) (*postal*) **b. number 12** référence 12; **write to b. number 12** (*in newspaper advertisement*) écrire en rappelant la référence 12

(d) *Br F* **the b.** (*television*) la télé; **on the b.** à la télé

(e) (*enclosed space*) (*in stables*) stalle *f*; *Th* loge *f*; (*on ground floor*) baignoire *f*; *Tel* cabine *f* téléphonique; *Fb* (*for penalties*) surface *f* de réparation; **my flat is a bit of a b.** mon appartement est à peu près grand comme un mouchoir de poche

(f) *Tech* (*of axle, brake*) boîte *f*; (*of wheel*) moyeu *m*; (*of lock*) palâtre *m*, palastre *m*

(g) (*printed, drawn*) (*to fill in on form etc*) case *f*; (*boxed text*) pavé *m*, encadré *m*; (*frame around article*) cadre *m*; (*on screen*) boîte *f*, case; (*that can be drawn*) encadré; **to draw a b. round sth** encadrer qch

box³ *vt* (*goods*) mettre en carton

box⁴ *n* (*blow*) **b. (on the ear)** gifle *f*, claque *f*, taloche *f*; **to give sb a b. on the ear** gifler qn

box⁵ **1** *vt* **to b. sb's ears** gifler qn, *F* flanquer une gifle *ou* une claque *ou* une taloche à qn **2** *vi Sp* boxer, faire de la boxe; (*of two opponents*) combattre

▸ **box in** *vtsep* **(a)** (*surround*) (*person*) coincer; **the defence seem to have him boxed in** la défense semble l'avoir coincé **(b)** (*enclose*) (*bath, wash basin etc*) encastrer; **don't you feel boxed in in such a small room?** tu ne te sens pas un peu à l'étroit dans une pièce aussi petite?; **to be boxed in** (*by other cars*) être coincé par d'autres voitures

box-calf *n* (*leather*) box-calf *m*, *F* box *m*

boxcar ['bɒkskɑːr] *n Am Rail* wagon *m*, fourgon *m*

boxed [bɒkst] *adj* **(a)** *Com etc* en boîte; (*jewellery*) en écrin; **b. in** (*bath etc*) encastré; (*person*) (*surrounded*) coincé; (*confined*) à l'étroit **(b)** (*ad, article*) encadré; **b. article** encadré *m*

Boxer ['bɒksər] *n Hist* Boxer *m* (chinois); **the B. Rebellion** la révolte des Boxers

boxer ['bɒksər] *n* **(a)** (*fighter*) boxeur *m*; **b. shorts** (*underwear*) caleçon *m* **(b)** (*dog*) boxer *m*

boxer engine *n* moteur *m* à cylindres à plat, boxer *m*

box file *n* boîte-archive *f*, *pl* boîtes-archives

boxful ['bɒksfʊl] *n* (*small*) pleine boîte *f*; (*large*) plein coffre *m*, pleine caisse *f*

box girder *n* poutre *f* caisson

Boxing ['bɒksɪŋ] *n Br* **B. Day** = le lendemain de Noël

boxing ['bɒksɪŋ] *n Sp* boxe *f*; **he loves b.** il adore la boxe; **b. glove** gant *m* de boxe; **b. match** match *m* de boxe; **b. ring** ring *m*

box junction *n Br Aut* = zone *f* quadrillée en jaune située à une intersection

box office ['bɒksɒfɪs] **1** *n Th, Cin* bureau *m* de location; *Fig* (*profits*) box-office *m*; **the film did well at the b.** *or* **was good b.** le film a enregistré beaucoup d'entrées **2** *adj attrib* **a b. success/failure** un succès/échec au box-office; **she's always a big b. draw** *or* **attraction** elle est sûre de faire des entrées; *Cin* **b. receipts** recettes *fpl* en salles

box-pleated *adj* à plis creux *ou* ronds

boxroom ['bɒksruːm] *n* débarras *m*

boxwood ['bɒkswʊd] *n* (bois *m* de) buis *m*

boy [bɔɪ] *n* **(a)** garçon *m*; **boys will be boys** il faut bien que jeunesse se passe; **she ought to have been a b.** c'est un garçon manqué; **b. scout** scout *m*

(b) *Sch* élève *m*; **day b.** externe *m*

(c) *F* (*man*) **a new b.** (*in company*) un nouveau; **the race was won by a local b.** c'est un jeune de la région qui a gagné la course; **a nice old b.** un vieux monsieur sympathique; *Old-fashioned Br* **I say, old b.!** dis, mon vieux!; **one of the boys** un joyeux vivant; **he's having a night out with the boys** il est sorti avec ses copains; **come on boys!** allons-y les gars!; *Br F* **the boys in blue** (*police*) = la police; *Sl* **he threatened to send the boys round** il a menacé d'envoyer ses gars; *Sl* **the big boys** (*important men*) les grosses légumes *fpl*; *Fig* **to play with the big boys** jouer dans la cour des grands; *esp Am* **oh b.!** ben alors!, dis donc!; *esp Am* **b., am I glad to be home!** dis donc, qu'est-ce que je suis content d'être rentré à la maison!

(d) (*employee*) (*in Africa*) boy *m*; **office b.** garçon *m* de bureau

boycott¹ ['bɔɪkɒt] *n* boycott *m*, boycottage *m*; **to put under a b., to put a b. on** (*goods, company, event etc*) boycotter

boycott² *vt* (*person, company, event etc*) boycotter

boyfriend ['bɔɪfrend] *n* (*of girl, woman*) (petit) ami *m*, *Can F* chum *m*

boyhood ['bɔɪhʊd] *n* (*when very young*) enfance *f*, première jeunesse *f*; (*in teens*) adolescence *f*; **b. friends** amis *mpl* d'enfance

boyish ['bɔɪɪʃ] *adj* **(a)** (*hopes, enthusiasm*) d'enfant, enfantin **(b)** (*charm*) juvénile; (*tomboyish*) (*clothes, figure, face*) de garçon; **b. good looks** (*of man*) air *m* de beau gosse; (*of*

woman) air de joli garçon; **b. haircut** coupe *f* de cheveux à la garçonne **(c)** *(manners)* de garçon
boyishly [ˈbɔɪɪʃlɪ] *adv (to smile, laugh)* comme un enfant; *(tomboyishly)* comme un garçon
boyishness [ˈbɔɪɪʃnɪs] *n* manières *fpl* de garçon *ou* de jeune homme
boy-meets-girl *adj* **b. story** *(book, film)* banale histoire *f* d'amour
bozo [ˈbəʊzəʊ] *n Am Sl (stupid man)* débile *m*, abruti *m*
bps [biːpiːˈes] *n Comptr (abbr* **bits per second)** bps
BR [biːˈɑːr] *n (abbr* **British Rail)** = service *m* national des chemins de fer britannique
bra [brɑː] *n* soutien-gorge *m*, *pl* soutiens-gorge; **b. top** brassière *f*
brace[1] [breɪs] *n* **(a)** *Constr etc* étai *m*; **cross** *or* **diagonal b.** écharpe *f*, diagonale *f* **(b)** *Med (on teeth)* appareil *m* dentaire; *(on leg)* armature *f* orthopédique; *(on torso)* corset *m*; **neck b.** minerve *f* **(c)** *Br* **braces** *(for trousers)* bretelles *fpl* **(d)** *(pair) (of partridges, pheasants etc)* couple *m*; *(of pistols etc)* paire *f*; **two b. of partridges** deux couples de perdrix **(e)** *(drill)* **b. (and bit)** vilebrequin *m* (et sa mèche); *Aut* **wheel b.** vilebrequin (à roues)
brace[2] *vt* **(a)** *Constr etc (construction, wall, roof)* étayer; *Av (wing)* croisillonner
 (b) *(tense) (bow)* tendre, bander; **to b. (the skin of) a drum** tendre la peau d'un tambour, bander un tambour; **the passengers braced themselves for the impact** les passagers se raidirent avant le choc; **she braced herself between two rocks** elle s'arc-bouta entre deux rochers; **b. yourself!** *(hold tight)* tiens bon!; *(be brave)* courage!; **b. yourself for a shock** prépare-toi à recevoir un choc
 (c) *(strengthen) (body)* fortifier; *(nerves)* tonifier; **a whisky to b. myself** un whisky pour me donner du courage; **to b. oneself to do sth** rassembler ses forces pour faire qch, s'armer de courage pour faire qch
bracelet [ˈbreɪslɪt] *n* **(a)** *(jewellery)* bracelet *m*; **chain b.** gourmette *f*; **b. watch** montre-bracelet *f* pour femme, *pl* montres-bracelets **(b)** *F* **bracelets** *(handcuffs)* bracelets *mpl*; **put the bracelets on him** passe-lui les bracelets
bracer [ˈbreɪsər] *n F* (petit verre *m* de) remontant *m*
brachial [ˈbrækɪəl, ˈbreɪk-] *adj Anat* brachial
brachiopod [ˈbrækɪəpɒd] *n (mollusc)* brachiopode *m*
brachycephalic [brækɪsɪˈfælɪk] *adj* brachycéphale
bracing [ˈbreɪsɪŋ] **1** *adj (air, climate etc)* vivifiant, tonifiant; *Fig (effect)* stimulant **2** *n* **b. strut** jambe *f* de force
bracken [ˈbræk(ə)n] *n (plant)* fougère *f*
bracket[1] [ˈbrækɪt] *n* **(a)** *Constr, MecE (for fixing or supporting)* tasseau *m*, équerre *f*; *(for holding part)* support *m*; *(for lamp)* applique *f*; *Archit* corbeau *m*; **b. lamp** (lampe *f* d')applique **(b)** *Typ etc (square)* crochet *m*; *(round)* parenthèse *f*; *(connecting two lines)* accolade *f*; **in brackets** entre parenthèses/crochets/accolades **(c)** *Admin (level of income, tax)* tranche *f*; *(of salaries)* fourchette *f*; **the 15-to-20 age b.** le groupe *ou* la classe des 15 à 20 ans; **people in the upper income brackets** les gens dans les tranches de revenu les plus élevées; **what tax b. are you in?** dans quelle tranche d'imposition es-tu?
bracket[2] *vt* **(-t-)** **(a)** *(words etc)* mettre entre parenthèses; *(in square brackets)* mettre entre crochets; *(in a vertical list)* réunir par une accolade **(b)** *Fig (two ideas)* associer; *(two candidates)* placer ex aequo; **bracketed together** *(candidates)* classé ex aequo; **his name has often been bracketed with hers** son nom a souvent été associé au sien; **he didn't want to be bracketed (together) with them** il ne voulait pas qu'on les mette dans le même sac
bracketing [ˈbrækɪtɪŋ] *n (action)* mise *f* entre parenthèses; *(with square brackets)* mise entre crochets; *(in a vertical list)* réunion *f* par une accolade
brackish [ˈbrækɪʃ] *adj (water)* saumâtre
bract [brækt] *n Bot* bractée *f*
brad [bræd] *n (nail)* clou *m* de tapissier, semence *f*
bradawl [ˈbrædɔːl] *n (tool)* alêne *f* plate, poinçon *m*
bradycardia [brædɪˈkɑːdɪə] *n Med* bradycardie *f*
brae [breɪ] *n Scot* colline *f*
brag[1] [bræg] *n* **(a)** *(boast)* vantardise *f*, forfanterie *f* **(b)** *Cards* = sorte *f* de poker
brag[2] **1** *vi* **(-gg-)** *(boast)* se vanter **(of, about** de); **it's not something to b. about!** il n'y a pas de quoi s'en vanter!; **you've got nothing to b. about** tu n'as pas de quoi te vanter **2** *vt* **to b. that one has done sth** se vanter d'avoir fait qch; **he bragged that he would** win il s'est vanté de pouvoir gagner
braggadocio [brægəˈdəʊtʃɪəʊ] *n Lit* vantardise *f*
braggart [ˈbrægət] *n Old-fashioned* vantard, -arde, hâbleur, -euse
bragging [ˈbrægɪŋ] **1** *adj* vantard, hâbleur, -euse **2** *n* vantardise *f*, hâblerie *f*
Brahman [ˈbrɑːmən] *n* brahmane *mf*
Brahmanism [ˈbrɑːmənɪz(ə)m] *n* brahmanisme *m*
Brahmin [ˈbrɑːmɪn] *n* **(a)** *(in India)* brahmane *mf* **(b)** *US F (intellectual)* intellectuel, -elle; *(member of the upper classes)* membre *m* de la haute
braid[1] [breɪd] *n* **(a)** *esp Am (of hair)* tresse *f*, natte *f*; **she wears her hair in braids** elle porte *ou* se fait des nattes **(b)** *(on cushion, clothing etc)* galon *m*, passepoil *m*; **gold b.** *(on officer's uniform)* galon
braid[2] *vt* **(a)** *(straw)* tresser; *esp Am (hair)* tresser, natter **(b)** *(clothing)* galonner, soutacher; *(edge of chair etc)* passementer
braiding [ˈbreɪdɪŋ] *n* **(a)** *esp Am (of hair)* tressage *m*, nattage *m* **(b)** *(decoration) (on cushion, clothing)* galon *m*, passepoil *m*
Braille [breɪl] *n* Braille *m*; **to read B.** lire le Braille; **in B.** en Braille; **B. alphabet** alphabet *m* Braille
brain[1] [breɪn] *n* **(a)** *(organ)* cerveau *m*; *Culin* **brains** cervelle *f*; **to blow sb's brains out** faire sauter la cervelle à qn; **b. death** mort *f* cérébrale; **b. disease** maladie *f* cérébrale; *Old-fashioned* **b. fever** fièvre *f* cérébrale; **b. stem** pédoncule *m* cérébral; *F* **to have money on the b.** être obsédé par l'argent; *F* **to have a tune on the b.** avoir un air dans la tête; **my b. reeled when I thought of it** ça m'a donné le vertige d'y penser
 (b) *(intelligence)* **brains** intelligence *f*; **he has brains** *or* **a good b.** il est intelligent; **I haven't got the brains to become a doctor** je ne suis pas assez intelligent pour devenir médecin; **anyone with half a b.** n'importe qui d'un tant soit peu intelligent; **he's the brains of the family** c'est lui le plus intelligent de la famille; **she's the brains of the business** c'est elle le cerveau de l'entreprise; **use your brains** fais marcher ta cervelle
 (c) *F (intelligent person)* cerveau *m*; **to call in the best brains** faire appel à tous les talents; **she's a real b. at maths** c'est une tête en maths; *Br* **brains trust,** *Am* **b. trust** brain-trust *m*, *pl* brain-trusts; *F* **the b. drain** l'exode *m* *ou* la fuite des cerveaux
brain[2] *vt Sl (hit over head)* assommer; **I brained myself on the cupboard door** je me suis cogné contre la porte du placard
brainbox [ˈbreɪnbɒks] *n Sl* **(a)** *Old-fashioned (skull)* boîte *f* cranienne **(b)** *(intelligent person)* tête *f*; **she's a real b.** c'est une sacrée tête
brainchild [ˈbreɪntʃaɪld] *n F* trouvaille *f*
brain damage *n* lésions *fpl* cérébrales
brain dead *n* **to be b.** *(of accident victim)* être en coma dépassé; *Fig F (extremely stupid)* ne rien avoir dans la cervelle
brainless [ˈbreɪnlɪs] *adj F (stupid)* stupide; **he's a b. idiot** c'est un idiot sans pareil
brainpower [ˈbreɪnpaʊər] *n* intelligence *f*
brain scan *n* **she had a b.** on lui a fait un scanner du cerveau
brainstorm [ˈbreɪnstɔːm] *n* **(a)** *Br* **I must have had a b.** j'ai dû avoir un moment d'égarement **(b)** *Am F (brilliant idea)* idée *f* de génie
brainstorming [ˈbreɪnstɔːmɪŋ] *n* brainstorming *m*, remue-méninges *m*; **b. session** réunion *f* de remue-méninges; **we had a b. session** nous avons eu un brainstorming
brain surgeon *n* neurochirurgien, -ienne
brain surgery *n* neurochirurgie *f*
brain-teaser *n* casse-tête *m inv*
brain tumour *n* tumeur *m* au cerveau
brainwash [ˈbreɪnwɒʃ] *vt* faire un lavage de cerveau à; **to b. sb into doing sth** faire un lavage de cerveau à qn pour qu'il fasse qch; *Fig* **they've been brainwashed into believing that …** on leur a mis dans la tête que …; **I won't be brainwashed into buying things I don't need** je refuse de me laisser manipuler pour acheter des choses dont je n'ai pas besoin
brainwashing [ˈbreɪnwɒʃɪŋ] *n* lavage *m* de cerveau
brain wave *n Br F* idée *f* de génie, idée lumineuse
brainwork [ˈbreɪnwɜːk] *n* travail *m* intellectuel
brainy [ˈbreɪnɪ] *adj F (person)* intelligent; *(idea)* génial; **she's really b.** il y en a là-dedans; **I can't cope with b. stuff like that** c'est trop compliqué pour moi
braise [breɪz] *vt Culin* braiser, cuire à l'étouffée; **braised beef** bœuf *m* braisé; **braised chicken** poulet *m* en cocotte
braising [ˈbreɪzɪŋ] *n* cuisson *f* à l'étouffée; **b. beef** bœuf *m* à braiser
brake[1] [breɪk] *n (on car, train etc)* frein *m*; **to apply the brake(s)** *(in traffic)* freiner; **to put the b. on** *(after parking)* mettre *ou* serrer le frein; **to slam on the brakes** écraser la pédale de frein, *F* piler; **to release the brake(s)** desserrer le frein; *Fig* **to put a b.** *or* **the brakes on a project** donner un coup de frein à un projet; *Fig* **b. on growth** frein à

l'expansion; **b. adjuster spanner** clé *f* de réglage des freins; **b. fade** fading *m*

brake[2] *vi Aut* (*in traffic*) freiner; **to b. hard** freiner brusquement, écraser la pédale de frein, *F* piler

brake[3] *n* (*undergrowth*) fourré *m*, hallier *m*

brake[4] *n* (*vehicle*) = **break[3]**

brake block *n* patin *m* de frein

braked trailer ['breɪkt] *n* remorque *f* freinée

brake fluid *n* liquide *m* de freins

brake horsepower *n* puissance *f* au frein

brake lever *n* levier *m* de frein

brake light, brake lamp *n* feu *m* de stop

brakelight function ['breɪklaɪt] *n Am TV, Rad* signal *m* de fin de temps de parole

brake lining *n* garniture *f* de frein

brake pad *n* plaquette *f* de frein

brake pedal *n* pédale *f* de frein

brake shoe *n* patin *m ou* sabot *m* de frein

brakesman, *Am* **brakeman,** *pl* **-men** ['breɪk(s)mən] *n Rail etc* garde-frein(s) *m*, *pl* gardes-frein(s)

brake van *n Rail* wagon-frein *m*, *pl* wagons-freins; (*guard's van*) fourgon *m*

braking ['breɪkɪŋ] *n* (*in traffic*) freinage *m*; (*abrupt*) coup *m* de frein; **b. distance** distance *f* de freinage

bramble ['bræmb(ə)l] *n* **(a)** (*shrub*) ronce *f ou* mûrier *m* des haies; **brambles** (*thorns*) ronces **(b)** (*fruit*) mûre *f* (de ronce), mûre sauvage; **b. jelly** gelée *f* de mûres

brambly ['bræmblɪ] *adj* plein *ou* couvert de ronces

bran [bræn] *n* (*of oats, wheat*) son *m*; **b. flakes** son en flocons; **b. mash** (*animal feed*) son mouillé; *Br* **b. tub** = baquet *m* rempli de son ou de sciure dans lequel on plonge la main pour en retirer une surprise

branch[1] [brɑːntʃ] *n* **(a)** (*of tree*) branche *f*, rameau *m*; **the branches** le branchage, les branches **(b)** (*of road*) embranchement *m*; (*of river*) bras *m*; (*of candlestick, family, science, industry etc, of artery*) branche *f* **(c)** *Admin, Com* (*of shop*) succursale *f*; (*of company*) agence *f*, succursale; (*of bank*) agence, succursale, guichet *m*; **where's the nearest b. of C&A?** où se trouve le C&A le plus proche?; **b. manager** directeur *m* de succursale **(d)** *Mil* (*of armed forces*) division *f*; (*in administration*) branche *f* **(e)** *Comptr* branchement *m*

branch[2] *vi* **(a)** (*of road etc*) bifurquer; **at the point where the road branches** à l'endroit où la route bifurque **(b)** (*of tree*) faire des branches

▶ **branch off** *vi* (*of road, Fig in conversation etc*) bifurquer; *Fig* **then I branched off into quantum mechanics** puis j'ai bifurqué vers la mécanique quantique

▶ **branch out** *vi* (*of person, organization etc*) étendre ses activités, se diversifier; **to b. out into …** étendre ses activités à …; **I'm going to b. out on my own** je vais faire cavalier seul

branched [brɑːntʃt] *adj* **(a)** *Bot* branchu, rameux **(b)** (*candlestick*) à (plusieurs) branches

branchia, *pl* **-iae** ['bræŋkɪə, -ɪiː] *n* branchie *f*

branchiate ['bræŋkɪət] *adj Zool* branchié

branch line *n Rail* ligne *f* secondaire

branch office *n* (*of bank, company*) agence *f*, succursale *f*

brand[1] [brænd] *n* **(a)** *Com, Mktg* marque *f* (de fabrique); *Fig* **he has his own b. of humour** il a un humour un peu particulier; **a good b. of cigars** une bonne marque de cigares; **b. advertising** publicité *f* de marque *ou* sur la marque; **b. beliefs** croyances *fpl* vis-à-vis d'une marque; **b. competition** concurrence *f* entre marques; **b. concept** concept *m* de marque; **b. extension** extension *f* de la marque; **b. familiarity** connaissance *f* de la marque; **b. identifier** identificateur *m* de marque; **b. image** image *f* de marque; **b. imitation** imitation *f* de marque; **b. life-cycle** cycle *m* de vie de la marque; **b. loyalty** (*of consumer*) fidélité *f* à la marque; **creation of b. loyalty** fidélisation *f* à la marque; **b. manager** chef *m* de produit *ou* de marque; **b. mapping** carte *f* perceptuelle des marques, carte des positions de marques; **b. mark** emblème *m* de marque; **b. positioning** positionnement *m* de la marque; **b. preference** préférence *f* pour une marque; **b. sensitivity** sensibilité *f* aux marques; **b. switching** changement *m* de marque

(b) (*on cattle*) marque *f* au fer rouge; *Hist* (*on criminal*) flétrissure *f*, marque au fer rouge; (*branding iron*) fer *m* rouge; **the cattle have his b. on them** le bétail porte sa marque

(c) (*burning wood*) brandon *m*, tison *m*

brand[2] *vt* (*with branding iron*) (*person, animal, goods*) marquer au fer rouge; *Hist* (*criminal*) flétrir, marquer au fer rouge; (*slave*) marquer; **to b. sb (as) a liar/coward/***etc* coller à qn une étiquette de menteur/lâche/*etc*; *Fig* **to be branded on sb's memory** (*of sight, scene*) être gravé dans la mémoire de qn; **the experience branded them for life** l'expérience les a marqués à vie

brand awareness *n* renommée *f ou* mémorisation *f* de la marque, notoriété *f* de la marque

branded ['brændɪd] *adj* **(a)** (*cattle, criminal etc*) marqué au fer rouge **(b)** (*product*) de marque

branding ['brændɪŋ] *n* **(a)** (*of cattle*) marquage *m* au fer rouge; **b. iron** fer *m* à marquer **(b)** *Mktg* marquage *m*

brandish ['brændɪʃ] *vt* (*weapon etc*) brandir

brand leader *n* (*on market*) marque *f* dominante

brand-loyal *adj Mktg* fidèle à la marque

brand name *n* marque *f*

brand new *adj* tout neuf, flambant neuf

brandy ['brændɪ] *n* (*cognac*) cognac *m*; (*clear spirit*) eau-de-vie, *pl* eaux-de-vie; **b. and soda** = cognac à l'eau de seltz; *Br Culin* **b. butter** (*for Christmas pudding*) beurre *m* parfumé au cognac; **b. glass** verre *m* à cognac; **b. snap** (*biscuit*) = biscuit *m* au gingembre parfois fourré à la crème fraîche

brash [bræʃ] *adj* (*person*) (*impudent*) effronté, présomptueux, impudent; (*showing off*) exubérant; (*manner*) présomptueux; (*colour*) cru

brashly ['bræʃlɪ] *adv* (*with impudence*) effrontément, présomptueusement, impudemment; (*when showing off*) avec exubérance

brashness ['bræʃnɪs] *n* (*impudence*) effronterie *f*, impudence *f*; (*showing off*) exubérance *f*

brass [brɑːs] *n* **(a)** (*metal*) laiton *m*; *Fig* **to get down to b. tacks** en venir aux faits; *Br* **I haven't got a b. farthing** (*any money*) je n'ai pas un rond; *Br* **it's not worth a b. farthing** ça ne vaut pas un clou; *Mil F* **the top b.** les huiles *fpl*; *Br Sl* **it's a bit b. monkeys today** (*very cold*) on se les caille; **b. foundry** fonderie *f* de cuivre; *Mil F* **b. hat** officier *m* d'état-major; *Mus* **b. instrument** cuivre *m*; **b. plate** plaque *f* de cuivre; (*of doctor, lawyer etc*) plaque

(b) (*item*) (*in church*) plaque *f* tombale en cuivre; **brass(es)** (*household objects etc*) cuivres *mpl*; **to do** *or* **clean the b.** *or* **brasses** faire les cuivres; **the b.** (*in band, orchestra*) les cuivres

(c) *Br F* (*money*) argent *m*, galette *f*

(d) *Br F* (*cheek, nerve*) **b.** **(neck)** culot *m*; **to have the b. (neck) to do sth** avoir le culot de faire qch; **what a b. neck!** quel culot!; **to have a b. neck** avoir du culot, être culotté, *Can* avoir du front tout le tour de la tête

▶ **brass off** *vtsep Br F* (*usu passive*) **to be brassed off** en avoir marre, en avoir ras-le-bol; **I'm brassed off with waiting** j'en ai marre *ou* ras-le-bol d'attendre

brass band *n* fanfare *f*

brasserie ['bræsərɪ] *n* (*restaurant, bar*) brasserie *f*

brassica ['bræsɪkə] *n Bot* brassica *m*

brassie ['bræsɪ] *n Golf* brassie *m*

brassière ['bræzɪər, *US* brə'zɪə] *n* soutien-gorge *m*, *pl* soutiens-gorge

brassiness ['brɑːsɪnɪs] *n* **(a)** (*of piece of music*) sons *mpl* cuivrés **(b)** *F* (*insolence*) culot *m*

brass rubbing *n* décalquage *m* par frottement d'une plaque en cuivre

brassware ['brɑːsweər] *n* dinanderie *f*

brasswork ['brɑːswɜːk] *n* dinanderie *f*, chaudronnerie *f* d'art

brassy[1] ['brɑːsɪ] *n Golf* brassie *m*

brassy[2] *adj* **(a)** *Pej* (*yellow, blonde*) artificiel; (*cheap jewellery*) qui fait toc **(b)** (*sound*) cuivré **(c)** *Pej F* (*person*) effronté

brat [bræt] *n Pej* gamin, -ine, morveux, -euse

bravado [brə'vɑːdəʊ] *n* bravade *f*

brave[1] [breɪv] **1** *adj* courageux; **be b. for a little bit longer** courage, c'est presque fini; **as b. as a lion** courageux comme un lion; **to put a b. face on it** faire bonne contenance; **to make a b. effort to smile** s'efforcer bravement de sourire; **it was a b. effort nonetheless** néanmoins c'était un bel effort; *Fig* **a b. new world for small business** un paradis pour les petites entreprises **2** *n* (*Am Indian warrior*) brave *m*

brave[2] *vt* (*person*) braver, défier; (*danger etc*) braver, affronter

bravely ['breɪvlɪ] *adv* courageusement, vaillamment

bravery ['breɪvərɪ] *n* courage *m*, bravoure *f*; **she was decorated for b.** elle a été décorée pour son courage

bravo [brɑː'vəʊ] *int* bravo!

bravura [bræ'vʊːrə] *n Mus* morceau *m* de bravoure

brawl[1] [brɔːl] *n* rixe *f*, bagarre *f*; **drunken b.** querelle *f* d'ivrognes

brawl[2] *vi* (*of people*) se bagarrer

brawler ['brɔːlər] *n* bagarreur, -euse

brawling ['brɔːlɪŋ] *n* rixes *fpl*, bagarres *fpl*

brawn [brɔːn] *n* **(a)** *F* muscles *mpl*; **to have plenty of b.** avoir du biceps; **he's got more b. than brains** il a du muscle mais pas grand-chose dans la tête **(b)** *Br Culin* fromage *m* de tête

brawny ['brɔːnɪ] *adj* (*arm*) fort, musculeux; (*person*) musclé, bien bâti

bray¹ [breɪ] *n* (*of donkey*) braiment *m*
bray² *vi* (*of donkey*) braire
braze [breɪz] *vt Tech* (*using solder*) braser; (*using brass*) souder au laiton
brazen ['breɪz(ə)n] *adj* **(a)** (*shameless*) effronté, impudent; **b. lie** mensonge *m* éhonté; **I wish they weren't so b. about it** ils pourraient au moins faire ça discrètement; **a b. hussy** une effrontée **(b)** *Lit* (*made of brass*) (*vase, pot etc*) d'airain **(c)** *Mus* cuivré
▶ **brazen out** *vtsep* **to b. it out** s'en tirer par des fanfaronnades
brazen-faced ['breɪz(ə)nfeɪst] *adj* éffronté, impudent
brazenly ['breɪz(ə)nlɪ] *adv* effrontément, impudemment
brazier ['breɪzɪər] *n* brasero *m*
Brazil [brə'zɪl] *n* Brésil *m*
brazil [brə'zɪl] *n* **b. (nut)** noix *f* du Brésil
Brazilian [brə'zɪlɪən] **1** *adj* brésilien **2** *n* Brésilien, -ienne
breach¹ [briːtʃ] *n* **(a)** (*of regulations etc*) infraction *f*, contravention *f*; (*of law, professional secrecy etc*) violation *f* **(of** de); (*of discipline*) manquement *m* **(of** à); (*of contract*) rupture *f* **(of** de); **the company is in b. of the law** la société enfreint la législation; **the company is suing him for b. of contract** la société lui fait un procès pour rupture de contrat; **b. of faith** manquement à sa parole; **b. of trust** abus *m* de confiance; *Jur* (*by trustee etc*) violation d'un des devoirs d'un mandataire; **b. of good manners** manque *m* de savoir-vivre; **to commit a b. of etiquette** manquer au protocole; **b. of privilege** atteinte *f* portée aux privilèges; **b. of the peace** atteinte à l'ordre public; *Old-fashioned Jur* **b. of promise** rupture de promesse de mariage
(b) (*between two friends etc*) brouille *f*
(c) (*in wall, Mil in defences*) brèche *f*; *Fig* **they found a b. in his defences** ils ont trouvé sa faille; *Mil* **to stand in the b.** monter sur la brèche; **to make a b. in the enemy's lines** percer les lignes de l'ennemi; *Fig* **to step into the b.** se porter volontaire pour remplacer qn; **it was very good of you to step into the b.** c'est très aimable à vous de l'avoir remplacé(e)
breach² **1** *vt* **(a)** (*violate*) (*contract, agreement, treaty*) rompre **(b)** (*make hole in*) (*dam, wall*) ouvrir une brèche dans; *Mil* (*wall*) battre en brèche; (*enemy lines*) percer; **to b. the surface of the water** apparaître à la surface de l'eau; (*of rocks*) pointer à la surface de l'eau **2** *vi* (*of whale*) sauter au-dessus de la surface de l'eau
bread¹ [bred] *n* **(a)** pain *m*; **a loaf of b.** un pain; **b. and butter** pain beurré; **a slice of b. and butter** une tartine de beurre, une tartine beurrée; *Fig* **poetry doesn't earn you your b. and butter** la poésie ne nourrit pas son homme; *Fig* **the customers are our b. and butter** les clients sont notre gagne-pain; *Culin* **b. and butter pudding** pain perdu *m* (*cuit au four*); **to be on b. and water** être au pain (sec) et à l'eau; *Rel* **give us this day our daily b.** donne-nous aujourd'hui notre pain de ce jour; *Fig* **to earn one's (daily) b.** gagner sa vie *ou* son pain; *Fig* **to take the b. out of sb's mouth** enlever le pain de la bouche de qn; *Fig* **to put b. on the table** (*of person*) faire bouillir la marmite; **we want policies that will put b. on the table** nous voulons des politiques qui nous permettent de gagner notre pain; *Fig* **he knows which side his b. is buttered on** il sait où est son avantage *ou* son intérêt; *Fig* **b. and circuses** du pain et des jeux; **b. roll** petit pain *m*; **b. slicer** *or* **cutter** coupe-pain *m inv*
(b) *Old-fashioned esp Am Sl* (*money*) blé *m*, avoine *f*, galette *f*
bread² *vt* (*fish etc*) passer à la chapelure
bread-and-butter *adj F* **b. letter** (*to host*) lettre *f* de remerciements; **b. issues** problèmes *mpl* essentiels, questions *fpl* essentielles
breadbasket ['bredbɑːskɪt] *n* **(a)** corbeille *f* à pain; *esp Am Fig* **the b. of the world** la principale région productrice de céréales panifiables dans le monde **(b)** *Old-fashioned Sl* (*stomach*) estomac *m*, bedaine *f*
bread bin *n* (*horizontal*) boîte *f* à pain; (*vertical*) huche *f* à pain
breadboard ['bredbɔːd] *n* **(a)** planche *f* à pain **(b)** *Electron etc* montage *m* expérimental
breadcrumb¹ ['bredkrʌm] *n* miette *f* (de pain); *Culin* **breadcrumbs** chapelure *f*; **fried in breadcrumbs** pané; **to coat fish with breadcrumbs** passer du poisson à la chapelure
breadcrumb² *vt* (*fish etc*) passer à la chapelure
breaded ['bredɪd] *adj* pané
breadfruit ['bredfruːt] *n* (*fruit*) fruit *m* à pain; **b. tree** arbre *m* à pain
bread knife *n* couteau *m* à pain
breadline ['bredlaɪn] *n* = file *f* d'attente pour toucher des bons de pain ou recevoir de la nourriture gratuite; *Fig* **on the b.** indigent, sans ressources
bread pudding *n Culin* gâteau *m* de pain
bread sauce *n Culin* = sauce *f* faite avec du beurre, de la mie de pain et des oignons
breadth [bredθ] *n* **(a)** (*width*) largeur *f*; (*of material*) largeur, lé *m* **(b)** *Fig* (*of thought, mind, views etc*) largeur *f*; (*of style, sound*) ampleur *f*; **her b. of understanding** l'ampleur de ses connaissances
breadthwise ['bredθwaɪz], **breadthways** ['bredθweɪz] *adv* dans le sens de la largeur
breadwinner ['bredwɪnər] *n* soutien *m* de famille; **to be the b.** faire bouillir la marmite
break¹ [breɪk] *n* **(a)** (*fracture*) (*in limb*) fracture *f*; **b. in the voice** *Physiol* (*at puberty*) mue *f*; (*caused by emotion*) altération *f* de la voix; *Lit* **b. of day** point *m* du jour
(b) (*interruption*) (*in hedge, wall etc*) trouée *f*, percée *f*, brèche *f*; (*in clouds*) trouée; *El* (*in circuit*) rupture *f*; (*in series, line*) interruption *f*; *Typ* (*in word*) césure *f*; (*in pagination*) fin *f* de page; *Rad, TV* **(commercial) b.** page *f* de publicité; *Rad, TV* **b. (in transmission)** interruption; **b. in** *or* **of continuity** interruption, solution *f* de continuité; **b. in the journey** arrêt *m*; **b. in the weather** changement *m* du temps; **there will be a b. in the weather tomorrow** le temps va changer demain; **without a b.** sans s'arrêter; *Comptr* **b. character** caractère *m* d'interruption; *Comptr* **b. key** touche *f* d'interruption; *Typ* **b. line** (*of paragraph*) dernière ligne *f*; *El* **b. switch** disjoncteur *m*, interrupteur *m*
(c) (*breach*) (*between countries, spouses*) rupture *f*; (*between two friends*) brouille *f*; **b. with a tradition** rupture avec une tradition; **in a b. with tradition** en rupture avec la tradition; **to make a b. with the past** rompre avec son passé
(d) (*rest*), *Mus* pause *f*; *Sch* (*between classes*) récréation *f*; (*holiday*) vacances *fpl*; **an hour's b. for lunch** une heure de pause pour le déjeuner; **a weekend in the country makes a pleasant b.** un week-end à la campagne fait du bien; **a much needed b.** un repos indispensable; **give it a b.!** (*talk about something else*) change de disque!; **give me a b.** (*stop nagging*) fiche-moi la paix; (*I've heard that story/excuse before*) arrête ton char; **give work/tennis a b. for a while** tu devrais arrêter un peu de travailler/de jouer au tennis
(e) *F* (*escape*) évasion *f*; **to make a b. for it** s'évader; *Fig* **to make the b.** larguer les amarres
(f) *F* (*chance*) chance *f*; **a good/bad b.** une bonne/mauvaise chance; **this could be your big b.** ça pourrait être la chance de ta vie; **she's never had an even b. in her life** rien n'a jamais été facile dans sa vie; **we had a lucky b.** nous avons eu de la veine; **give him a b.** donne-lui une chance; (*he won't do it again*) donne-lui une seconde chance
(g) *Billiards etc* (*opening shot*) acquit *m*; (*series of shots*) série *f*, suite *f* (de coups gagnants); *Tennis* (*of opponent's service*) break *m*; **she had a b. of serve** (*lost her serve*) elle a perdu son service; (*won her opponent's serve*) elle a gagné le service de son adversaire; *Tennis* **to have two b. points** avoir deux balles de break
(h) *Mus* (*solo jazz passage*) solo *m*; (*pause*) break *m*
break² (*pt* **broke** [brəʊk]; *pp* **broken** ['brəʊk(ə)n]) **1** *vt* **(a)** (*fracture, shatter, sever*) (*glass*) casser, briser; (*egg, toy etc*) casser; (*window, ties of friendship etc*) briser; (*rope, Naut moorings etc*) rompre; (*stick*) casser, rompre; (*skin*) entamer; *Jur* (*seals*) (*illegally*) briser; (*legally*) lever; *El* (*current*) interrompre; (*circuit*) couper; *Av* (*sound barrier*) franchir; **to b. sth into pieces** mettre qch en morceaux; **to b. one's arm/neck** se casser le bras/le cou; **to b. a branch off a tree** détacher une branche d'un arbre; *Lit Arch* **to b. bread with sb** rompre le pain avec qn; *Constr* **to b. ground** donner les premiers coups de pioche; *Fig* **to b. (new** *or* **fresh) ground** faire œuvre de pionnier, innover; *Fig* **to b. the ice** rompre *ou* briser la glace; **to b. a ten pound note** entamer un billet de dix livres; **to get broken** se casser
(b) (*interrupt*) (*silence, fast etc*) rompre; *Typ* (*page*) couper; **to b. step** rompre le pas; **to b. ranks** rompre les rangs; **to b. the thread of a story** interrompre le fil d'une narration; **to b. one's journey** s'arrêter en route, faire une étape; *Naut* faire escale; *Av* **to b. one's journey in Singapore** faire (une) escale à Singapour
(c) (*weaken impact of*) (*fall, force of sth*) amortir; (*wind*) arrêter; (*current*) rompre; **to b. the force of a blow** amortir un coup
(d) (*overcome, destroy*) (*strike, person's resistance*) briser; (*person's pride*) abattre, dompter; (*person's health*) ruiner; (*alibi*) écarter; (*record*) battre; (*horse*) dresser, entraîner; (*bad habit*) corriger; **to b. sb into the work** rompre qn au travail; **to b. sb of a habit** corriger *ou* guérir qn d'une habitude; **to b. oneself of a habit** se corriger *ou* se défaire d'une habitude; **to b. sb** (*financially*) ruiner qn; (*of grief etc*) briser qn; **to b. the bank** (*when gambling*)

faire sauter la banque; *Hum* **one night out won't b. the bank** une sortie ne va pas me/vous/*etc* ruiner; *Tennis* **to b. one's opponent's service** gagner le service de son adversaire; **to b. sb's heart/spirit** briser le cœur à qn/le courage de qn

(e) (*fail to respect*) (*law, regulation, ceasefire*) enfreindre, ne pas observer; (*one's word, appointment etc*) manquer à; (*contract, agreement, treaty*) rompre; **to b. one's word to sb** manquer à sa parole envers qn; **to b. a promise** ne pas tenir sa promesse; **to b. gaol** s'évader de prison; **to b. cover** (*of animal*) débucher; *Mil, Sch* **to b. bounds** violer la consigne; **his insolence has broken all bounds** son insolence a passé les bornes

(f) (*reveal, disclose*) **to b. the news of sth to sb** apprendre qch à qn; **to b. a piece of bad news gently to sb** apprendre une mauvaise nouvelle doucement à qn

(g) *Physiol* **to b. wind** lâcher un vent

2 *vi* **(a)** (*fracture, shatter etc*) (*of glass*) se casser, se briser; (*of egg, toy etc*) se casser; (*of window*) se briser; (*of wood, rope*) se rompre; (*of limb*) se fracturer, se casser; (*of wave*) se briser, déferler; (*of heart*) se briser, se fendre; **my waters have just broken** (*of pregnant woman*) je suis en train de perdre les eaux; **to b. with sb/a tradition** rompre avec qn/ une tradition; **to b. in two/into pieces** se casser en deux/en morceaux; **the sea was breaking against the rocks** la mer se brisait sur les rochers

(b) (*collapse, give way*) (*of health*) s'altérer; **to b. under torture** s'effondrer sous la torture

(c) (*change*) (*of weather*) changer; (*of heatwave*) passer, prendre fin; (*of voice*) *Physiol* muer; (*with emotion*) se briser, s'étrangler

(d) (*start*) (*of storm*) éclater, se déchaîner; (*of news, scandal*) éclater; **we bring you the stories as they b.** nous transmettons les événements au fur et au mesure qu'ils arrivent; **day was beginning to b.** le jour commençait à se lever

(e) *Billiards* donner l'acquit

(f) *Boxing* (*move away from each other*) se séparer; **b.!** break!, stop!

(g) *Typ* (*in paginating*) faire une coupure de page

(h) **to b. free of one's bonds** briser ses liens

break³ *n* **(a)** (*carriage*) break *m* **(b)** *Aut* **shooting b.** break *m* (de chasse)

▶ **break away 1** *vtsep* détacher **(from** de) **2** *vi* **(a)** (*escape*) s'évader; *Sp* se détacher; **she broke away from the guards** elle a échappé à la surveillance de ses gardiens **(b)** (*cut ties with*) se dégager, se détacher **(from** de); (*of province*) (*from State*) se séparer; **when did you b. away from your family?** quand est-ce que tu as coupé les ponts avec ta famille?; *Pol* **to b. away from a party** abandonner un parti; **the year France broke away from NATO** l'année où la France a quitté l'OTAN **(c)** (*come off*) se détacher **(from** de)

▶ **break back** *vi Tennis* = gagner le service de son adversaire après avoir perdu son propre service

▶ **break down 1** *vtsep* **(a)** (*destroy*) (*door*) enfoncer; (*wall etc*) abattre, démolir

(b) (*overcome*) (*resistance*) briser; (*prejudice*) vaincre, surmonter; **to b. down all opposition** vaincre toute opposition

(c) (*separate into parts*) *Fin etc* (*account, figures*) décomposer, ventiler; (*statistics*) analyser; (*bill, estimate*) détailler; *Ch* (*substance*) décomposer; (*molecules*) dissocier; *Com* **to b. down bulk** ventiler un lot; **we need to b. the figures down a bit further** il faut que nous décomposions *ou* ventilions les chiffres un peu plus; **we can b. the problem down into three parts** le problème peut se décomposer en trois parties; **the story can be broken down into two parts** on peut diviser l'histoire en deux parties

2 *vi* **(a)** (*fail*) (*of health*) se détériorer, s'altérer; (*of car, train, machinery*) tomber en panne; (*of ship*) subir une avarie; **that's where your argument breaks down** c'est là que ton argument s'effondre *ou* ne tient plus debout

(b) (*collapse*) (*of negotiations*) échouer; (*of resistance*) s'effondrer; (*of person*) (*have nervous breakdown*) faire une dépression nerveuse; (*burst into tears*) éclater en sanglots, fondre en larmes; (*confess*) faire des aveux complets, passer aux aveux; **their marriage is breaking down** leur mariage se désagrège

(c) (*separate*) se décomposer **(into** en)

▶ **break even** *vi* (*financially*) (*of person, company*) rentrer dans ses frais

▶ **break in 1** *vtsep* **(a)** (*destroy*) (*door etc*) enfoncer

(b) (*accustom to being used*) (*horse*) dresser; (*pipe*) culotter; (*new shoes*) faire, briser; *Am* (*car*) roder; **to b. sb/ oneself in to sth** rompre qn/se rompre à qch; **I'm getting these shoes broken in at last** ces chaussures commencent enfin à se faire

2 *vi* **(a)** (*interrupt*) interrompre; **to b. in on sb/a conversation** interrompre qn/une conversation; **I really must b. in at this point** il faut vraiment que je vous interrompe ici

(b) (*enter premises*) (*of burglar*) s'introduire *ou* entrer *ou* pénétrer par effraction; **I'd lost my front-door key so I had to b. in** j'avais perdu la clé de ma porte d'entrée et donc j'ai dû forcer la porte; **the police broke in through a window** la police est entrée par la fenêtre

▶ **break into** *vipo* **(a)** (*house*) (*illegally*) entrer *ou* pénétrer par effraction dans; (*desk, safe*) forcer; **I had to b. into my flat through a window** j'ai dû forcer une fenêtre pour entrer chez moi; **they've been broken into three times** ils se sont fait cambrioler trois fois

(b) (*begin suddenly*) **to b. into laughter** éclater de rire; **to b. into a song** se mettre à chanter; **to b. into a trot/run/ sprint** se mettre au trot/à courir/à sprinter; **her face broke into a smile** son visage s'éclaira d'un sourire

(c) (*use part of*) (*stocks, large-denomination bank note, savings*) entamer

(d) (*interrupt*) (*conversation*) interrompre

▶ **break loose** *vi* (*from bonds*) se dégager; (*escape*) s'évader **(from** de); (*of ship*) partir à la dérive

▶ **break off 1** *vtsep* **(a)** (*remove*) casser, rompre, détacher **(from** de); **I've broken the handle off a cup** j'ai cassé l'anse d'une tasse

(b) (*end*) (*temporarily*) interrompre; (*permanently*) abandonner; (*negotiations*) rompre; **to b. off relations with** (*person*) cesser tout contact avec; (*country*) rompre les relations avec

(c) (*romantic relationship*) rompre; **to b. it off** rompre **(with sb** avec qn)

2 *vi* **(a)** (*become detached*) se casser net, se détacher net, se détacher **(from** de); **the handle broke off in my hand** l'anse m'est restée dans la main

(b) (*stop*) **to b. off for ten minutes** prendre dix minutes de pause; **to b. off for lunch** s'arrêter pour déjeuner; **shall we b. off for the rest of the day?** on s'arrête là pour aujourd'hui?

(c) (*stop talking*) s'interrompre, se taire; **to b. off in the middle of a speech** s'arrêter *ou* s'interrompre au milieu d'un discours

▶ **break open 1** *vtsep* (*door*) enfoncer; (*lock, safe, till*) forcer; *F* (*bottle of wine etc*) ouvrir, déboucher; **to b. a desk open** ouvrir un bureau en forçant la serrure, forcer un bureau **2** *vi* (*of box etc*) s'ouvrir

▶ **break out 1** *vi* **(a)** (*escape*) (*from prison etc*) s'échapper, s'évader **(of** de) **(b)** (*start*) (*of argument, war, riots*) éclater; (*of fire, epidemic*) se déclarer; **panic broke out in the cinema when …** ce fut la panique dans le cinéma lorsque … **(c)** (*develop*) **to b. out into a sweat** se mettre à transpirer; **to b. out in spots** (*of face etc*) se couvrir de boutons; **the baby is breaking out into a rash** le bébé est en train de faire une éruption; **to break out in a laugh** éclater de rire **2** *vipo* **(a)** *F* (*bottle of wine etc*) ouvrir, déboucher **(b)** *Am* (*prepare for use*) sortir; (*flag*) déployer

▶ **break through 1** *vipo* (*barrier, police cordon etc*) enfoncer; (*wall*) faire une brèche dans; *Av* (*sound barrier*) franchir; (*of sun*) (*clouds*) percer; **to b. through sb's reserve** vaincre la réserve de qn **2** *vi* (*of sun*) percer

▶ **break up 1** *vtsep* **(a)** (*reduce to pieces*) mettre *ou* briser en morceaux; (*building, ship etc*) démolir; (*property*) morceler; (*empire*) dissoudre; (*crowd, family*) disperser; *Com* (*conglomerate, trust*) scinder, diviser; (*company*) scinder; (*coalition*) rompre; *Ch* (*compound*) résoudre; *Agr* (*earth*) ameublir; **to b. a word up into syllables** décomposer un mot en syllabes

(b) (*bring to an end*) (*marriage*) détruire; (*meeting*) dissoudre; (*conference*) mettre fin à; **to b. up a fight** séparer des combattants; *F* **b. it up!** la paix!

2 *vi* **(a)** (*disintegrate*) (*of ship*) se briser; (*of empire*) se dissoudre; (*of road surface*) se désagréger; (*of thawing ice*) se briser; (*of crowd, group etc*) se disperser; (*of clouds*) se dissiper, se disperser; *Fig F* **I just broke up** (*with laughter*) j'ai été pris d'un fou rire

(b) (*end*) (*of party, celebration etc*) se terminer; *Sch* être en vacances; **the meeting broke up in disorder** la réunion s'est terminée dans la pagaille; *Sch* **we b. up on the 4th** nos vacances commencent le 4, nous sommes en vacances le 4; **the schools will be breaking up for summer soon** les écoles vont bientôt fermer pour l'été; **their marriage has broken up** ils se sont séparés

(c) (*end relationship*) rompre; **they're breaking up** … séparent

(d) (*of weather*) se gâter

breakable ['breɪkəb(ə)l] **1** *adj* cassable, fragile **2** *npl* **breakables** objets *mpl* fragiles
breakages ['breɪkɪdʒɪz] *npl* **have there been any b.?** (*was anything broken?*) est-ce qu'il y a eu de la casse?; **to pay for b.** payer la casse
breakaway ['breɪkəweɪ] *n* **(a)** sécession *f* **(from** de); **b. union/party** syndicat *m*/parti *m* dissident **(b)** *Fb* (*of winger etc*) échappée *f*
break-dance *vi* danser le smurf
break-dancer *n* danseur, -euse de smurf
break-dancing *n* smurf *m*
breakdown ['breɪkdaʊn] *n* **(a)** (*failure*) (*of efforts*) échec *m*; (*in negotiations, communications*) rupture *f*; (*of marriage*) échec *m*; (*of system*) écroulement *m*; (*of service*) arrêt *m* complet
(b) (*collapse*) (*of health*) délabrement *m*; **(nervous) breakdown** dépression *f* (nerveuse); **she's had a b.** (*and has not yet recovered*) elle fait une dépression; *Hum* **I'm going to have a b.** je vais craquer; **mental b.** dépression nerveuse
(c) *Aut, Rail etc* (*mechanical*) panne *f*; **I've had a b.** je suis tombé en panne; **b. and recovery service** service *m* de remorquage et de dépannage
(d) (*into component parts*) (*of statistics etc*) analyse *f*; (*of account, figures etc*) décomposition *f*, ventilation *f*; (*of bill, costs*) détail *m*; (*of population*) (*by class, age etc*) répartition *f*, classement *m*; (*of script*) pré-découpage *m*; (*for recording*) dépouillement *m*; *Banking* **b. of charges/interest** décompte *m* d'agios/d'intérêts; *TV, Cin* **b. sheet** (*artistic*) fiche *f* artistique; (*technical*) fiche technique
(e) *Ch* dissociation *f*
breakdown gang *n* équipe *f* de dépannage
breakdown service *n* service *m* de dépannage
breakdown truck *n* dépanneuse *f*, camion *m* de dépannage
breakdown van *n* dépanneuse *f*, camion *m* de dépannage
breaker ['breɪkər] *n* **(a)** **b.'s yard** (*for cars, boats etc*) chantier *m* de démolition **(b)** (*of horses*) dresseur, -euse **(c)** (*wave*) (vague *f*) déferlante *f* **(d)** *Aut* rupteur *m*
breakeven ['breɪkiːv(ə)n] **1** *adj attrib Fin* **b. analysis** analyse *f* du point mort; **b. point** seuil *m* de rentabilité; **b. prices** prix *mpl* permettant de rentrer dans ses frais **2** *n* seuil *m* de rentabilité; *Acct* point *m* mort; **to reach b.** atteindre le seuil de rentabilité
breakfast[1] ['brekfəst] *n* [①**A6**,d,iii] petit déjeuner *m*; **to have (one's) b.** déjeuner, prendre le *ou* son (petit) déjeuner; **while we were at b.** pendant que nous déjeunions; **what do you want for b.?** qu'est-ce que tu veux pour le petit déjeuner?; **b. buffet** buffet *m* du petit déjeuner; **b. chef** chef *m* de petit déjeuner; **b. cook** cafetier *m*; **b. cereals** céréales *fpl* (en flocons); **b. meeting** réunion *f* pendant le petit déjeuner; **b. tray** plateau *m* petit déjeuner
breakfast[2] *vi* déjeuner (le matin)
breakfast room *n* salle *f* de petit déjeuner
breakfast television *n* programmes *mpl* télévisés du matin, télévision *f* du matin
break-in *n* **(a)** (*by burglar etc*) effraction *f* **(b)** *MecE, Am Aut* rodage *m*
breaking ['breɪkɪŋ] *n* **(a)** (*of window etc*) bris *m*; (*of silence etc*) rupture *f*; (*of journey*) interruption *f*; *Av* (*of sound barrier*) franchissement *m*; *Jur* **b. and entering** (*into house*) entrée *f* par effraction; *Jur* **b. of seals** (*illegal*) bris *m* des scellés; (*legal*) levée *f* des scellés; **b. of new** *or* **fresh ground** *Agr* défrichage *m*; *Fig* (*in research, science etc*) œuvre *f* de pionnier
(b) (*disintegration*) (*of waves*) déferlement *m*; *Med* (*of bone etc*) fracture *f*; **b. of the voice** *Physiol* mue *f*; (*with emotion*) altération *f* de la voix; *MecE* **b. strain** tension *f* de rupture; **b. point** *MecE* point *m* de rupture; (*of resistance*) limite *f* critique; *Fig* (*of strength etc*) limite; **she has reached b. point** elle est au bout du rouleau, elle est à bout; **their marriage has reached b. point** leur mariage a atteint le point critique; **to try sb's patience to b. point** pousser à bout la patience de qn
(c) (*of horse*) dressage *m*
(d) (*of fall, force of sth*) amortissement *m*
(e) (*of strike, sb's heart*) action *f* de briser
(f) (*of law, treaty etc*) violation *f*; (*of promise*) rupture *f*
(g) *Com* **b. bulk** fractionnement *m* d'un lot
breakneck ['breɪknek] *adj* **b. speed** *or* **pace** vitesse *f* *ou* allure *f* folle
break-out *n* (*from prison etc*) évasion *f*
breakpoint ['breɪkpɔɪnt] *n* **(a)** *Typ* point *m* de césure **(b)** *Tennis* **two breakpoints** deux balles de break
breakthrough ['breɪkθruː] *n* **(a)** *Mil* (*of enemy lines*) percée *f* **(b)** (*technological etc achievement*) percée *f*; (*in negotiations*) progrès *m*; **their latest b. in computing technology** leur dernière découverte en technologie informatique; **to make a b.** (*discovery*) faire une percée; (*in negotiations*) progresser; **the b. came only after a week of deadlock** la situation ne s'est débloquée qu'après une semaine
break-up ['breɪkʌp] *n* **(a)** (*of empire, meeting*) dissolution *f*; (*of marriage etc*) échec *m*; (*of ship etc*) dislocation *f*; **they still saw one another after the b.** ils ont continué à se voir après leur séparation; **b. of a company** scission *f* d'une entreprise; *Acct* **b. value** valeur *f* d'inventaire, VI *f* **(b)** (*of ice*) débâcle *f*
breakwater ['breɪkwɔːtər] *n* **(a)** (*wall*) brise-lames *m inv*, môle *m*; (*jetty*) jetée *f* **(b)** (*of bridge*) éperon *m*
bream [briːm] *n* (*fish*) brème *f*; **sea b.** dorade *f*, brème de mer
breast[1] [brest] *n* **(a)** (*of woman*) sein *m*; **child at the b.** enfant au sein; **b. cancer** cancer *m* du sein; **b. pump** tire-lait *m inv* **(b)** (*chest*) (*of person, Culin of lamb*) poitrine *f*; (*of horse*) poitrail *m*; (*of bird*) gorge *f*; (*of shirt etc*) devant *m*; *Culin* (*of chicken*) blanc *m*; **to make a clean b. of it** tout avouer; **b. high** *or* **deep** (*water etc*) jusqu'à la poitrine; **b. pocket** poche *f* poitrine, *pl* poches poitrine; **inside b. pocket** poche poitrine intérieure, poche portefeuille
breast[2] *vt Lit* (*storm*) affronter; (*hill*) atteindre le sommet de; **to b. the waves** (*of swimmer*) fendre la lame; *Sp* **to b. the tape** être le premier à franchir la ligne d'arrivée
breastbone ['brestbəʊn] *n* (*of person, animal, bird*) sternum *m*
breastfeed ['brestfiːd] (*pt, pp* **-fed** [-fed]) **1** *vt* (*baby*) nourrir au sein, allaiter **2** *vi* allaiter
breastfeeding ['brestfiːdɪŋ] *n* allaitement *m* maternel
breastplate ['brestpleɪt] *n* (*armour*) cuirasse *f*
breaststroke ['bres(t)strəʊk] *n* (*in swimming*) brasse *f*; **I can only do** *or* **swim b.** je ne sais nager que la brasse
breastwork ['brestwɜːk] *n Mil* parapet *m*
breath [breθ] *n* (*smelt*) haleine *f*; (*breathed*) souffle *m*; **his b. smelt of onions** son haleine sentait l'oignon; **to have bad b.** avoir mauvaise haleine; **I felt his b. on my neck** j'ai senti son souffle dans mon cou; **to draw b.** respirer; **give me time to draw b.** donnez-moi le temps de souffler; **to draw** *or* **take a deep** *or* **long b.** respirer profondément *ou* à pleins poumons; **to pause for b.** (*when speaking*) s'arrêter pour reprendre sa respiration; **to draw one's last** *or* **dying b.** rendre le dernier soupir; **the b. of life** le souffle vital *ou* de la vie; *Fig* **music is the very b. of life to me** je ne pourrais pas vivre sans musique; **(all) in the same b.** tout d'une haleine; **he agreed and disagreed (all) in the same b.** il a dit qu'il était d'accord puis il est immédiatement revenu sur ce qu'il avait dit; **but in the next b. he said the opposite** mais quelques secondes plus tard il a dit le contraire; **they are not to be mentioned in the same b.** on ne saurait les comparer; **to hold one's b.** retenir son souffle; *F* **I wouldn't hold my b.!** je ne compterais pas trop là-dessus; **to gasp for b.** haleter; **to waste one's b.** perdre son temps en discours inutiles, perdre sa salive; **I'm wasting my b.** je perds mon temps, je me fatigue pour rien; **save your b.** ne te fatigue pas; **to be short of b.** être essoufflé, avoir la respiration coupée; **out of b.** à bout de souffle, hors d'haleine, essoufflé; **to get** *or* **run out of b.** s'essouffler; **to take sb's b. away** couper la respiration *ou* le souffle à qn; *Fig* couper le souffle à qn; **to get one's b. (back), to recover** *or* **catch one's b.** reprendre haleine; **under one's b.** (*to talk*) d'une voix très basse, à voix basse; (*to swear*) entre ses dents; **the first b. of spring** le premier souffle du printemps; **a b. of wind/of air** un souffle de vent/d'air; **to go out for a b. of (fresh) air** sortir prendre l'air; *Fig* **it's/she's like a b. of fresh air** c'est/elle est comme une bouffée d'air frais; **a b. of scandal** l'ombre *f* d'un scandale
breathalyse, *US* **breathalyze** ['breθəlaɪz] *vt* faire subir l'alcootest à; **he was breathalysed** on l'a fait souffler dans le ballon
breathalyser, *US* **breathalyzer** ['breθəlaɪzər] *n* **b. (test)** alcootest *m*
breathe [briːð] **1** *vi* **(a)** respirer; **to b. hard** haleter; **to b. heavily** (*noisily*) respirer bruyamment; (*with difficulty*) respirer péniblement; **you can't b. in here** (*it's too hot*) on ne peut pas respirer ici; **I feel as if I can't b.** je me sens oppressé; **I need room to b.** (*in relationship*) j'ai besoin d'espace, il faut que je respire; **to b. (easily) again** (*with relief*) respirer de nouveau; **to b. on one's fingers** souffler dans ses doigts; *F* **to b. down sb.'s neck** (*supervise*) être sur le dos de qn; (*look over their shoulder*) regarder par-dessus l'épaule de qn; *F* **he's breathing down my neck for this translation** il me casse les pieds à propos de cette traduction; *F* **the police are breathing down our necks** (*very close to arresting us*) la police nous talonne; *F* **there's a police car breathing down our necks** on a une voiture de police aux fesses
(b) (*of voice, instrument, wind*) soupirer, souffler doucement; **open the bottle to let the wine b.** ouvre la bouteille pour permettre au vin de respirer

2 *vt* **(a)** (*air*) respirer

(b) (*sigh*) exhaler, laisser échapper; (*prayer*) murmurer; **to b. a sigh of relief** pousser un soupir de soulagement; *Lit* **to b. one's last** rendre le dernier soupir, rendre l'âme; **don't b. a word (of it)**! n'en soufflez (pas un) mot!; **to b. fire** (*be very angry*) cracher des flammes; **to b. new life into sth** insuffler une force nouvelle à qch; **he was breathing whisky fumes all over me** il me soufflait des relents de whisky en pleine figure

(c) *Ling* (*sound, consonant*) aspirer

▶ **breathe in 1** *vtsep* (*smoke, fumes*) inhaler **2** *vi* inspirer

▶ **breathe out** *vi* expirer

breathed [bri:ðd] *adj Ling* (*unvoiced*) sourd, non voisé

breather ['bri:ðər] *n* **(a)** *F* (*rest*) pause *f*; **to give sb a b.** laisser souffler qn, laisser un moment de répit à qn; **to go out for a b.** aller respirer un peu d'air, sortir prendre l'air; **to take a b.** faire une pause **(b)** *F* (*person*) **heavy b.** (*on telephone*) = homme *m* qui donne des coups de téléphone anonymes **(c)** *Aut* **b. pipe** (tuyau *m* de) reniflard *m*; **b. port** orifice *m* de reniflard

breathing ['bri:ðɪŋ] *n* (*of person*) respiration *f*; **heavy b.** (*noisy*) respiration bruyante; (*difficult*) respiration pénible; **b. apparatus** (*for fireman, miner etc*) masque *f* à oxygène; (*for diver*) scaphandre *m*; **b. space** (*respite*) répit *m*; *Fig* **I need some b. space** (*in relationship*) j'ai besoin de respirer *ou* d'espace

breathless ['breθlɪs] *adj* **(a)** (*person*) (*out of breath*) à bout de souffle, hors d'haleine, essoufflé; **b. with running** essoufflé d'avoir couru; **he was b. with excitement** l'exultation lui avait coupé le souffle **(b)** (*very fast*) (*chase, speed*) fou **(c)** *Fig* **to have sb b.** (*of film etc*) tenir qn en haleine; **b. silence** *or* **hush** silence *m* absolu; **b. suspense** suspense *m* total; **b. calm** calme *m* plat

breathlessly ['breθlɪslɪ] *adv* **(a)** (*out of breath*) tout essoufflé **(b)** (*to wait, listen*) en retenant son souffle

breathlessness ['breθlɪsnɪs] *n* essoufflement *m*; (*of patient*) manque *m* de souffle, oppression *f*

breathtaking ['breθteɪkɪŋ] *adj* (*beauty, imagination, audacity etc*) à vous couper le souffle; **with a b. lack of tact** avec un manque de tact incroyable; **it's b.** (*view*) c'est à vous couper le souffle; (*stupidity etc*) c'est édifiant

breathtakingly ['breθteɪkɪŋlɪ] *adv* (*beautiful*) extraordinairement; (*stupid, tactless etc*) incroyablement

breath test *n* alcootest *m*; **he failed the b.** l'alcootest a révélé un taux d'alcoolémie illégal, *F* il s'est fait prendre à l'alcootest

breath-test *vt* faire subir l'alcootest à

breathy ['breθɪ] *adj* **(a) b. voice** voix *f* haletante **(b)** *Mus* (*voice*) qui manque d'attaque

breech [bri:tʃ] *n* **(a)** *Obst* **b. (delivery** *or* **birth)** (accouchement *m* par le) siège *m*; **b. presentation** présentation *f* par le siège **(b)** (*of firearm*) culasse *f*, tonnerre *m*; **b. action** *or* **mechanism** mécanisme *m* de culasse

breeches ['brɪtʃɪz] *npl* (*knee-length*) haut-de-chausses *mpl*, culotte *f*; (*full-length*) pantalon *m*; **knee b.** culotte; *Naut* **b. buoy** bouée *f* culotte

breed[1] [bri:d] *n* (*of people, animals*) race *f*; *Fig* **she is one of the new b. of executives** elle fait partie de la nouvelle race *ou* génération de cadres; **a new b. of modems** une nouvelle génération de modems; **thatchers are a dying b.** les couvreurs de toits en chaume sont une race en voie de disparition

breed[2] (*pt, pp* **bred** [bred]) **1** *vt* **(a)** (*give birth to*) (*children, offspring*) produire, procréer; *Fig* engendrer, donner naissance à; **dirt breeds disease** la saleté entraîne des maladies; **all these rumours are breeding insecurity** toutes ces rumeurs engendrent l'insécurité

(b) (*raise*) (*cattle, rabbits etc*) élever; **they're specially bred for racing** ils sont élevés spécialement pour la course; **to be town/country bred** (*of person*) avoir été élevé à la ville/à la campagne; *Prov* **what's bred in the bone will come out in the flesh** bon chien chasse de race

2 *vi* **(a)** (*of animals*) se multiplier, se reproduire; (*of people*) se reproduire

(b) (*of animal breeder*) faire de l'élevage

breeder ['bri:dər] *n* **(a)** (*animal*) reproducteur, -trice; *Nucl Phys* **b. reactor** surgénérateur *m*, *F* couveuse *f* **(b)** (*person*) (*of animals*) éleveur, -euse; **poultry b.** aviculteur, -trice

breeding ['bri:dɪŋ] *n* **(a)** (*reproduction*) reproduction *f*, multiplication *f* **(b)** (*raising*) (*of domestic animals etc*) élevage *m*; **animal kept for b. purposes** (animal *m*) reproducteur *m*; **sheep b.** élevage des moutons **(c)** (*education*) (*of child etc*) éducation *f*; **(good) b.** bonne éducation, bonnes manières *fpl*, savoir-vivre *m*; **to lack b.** manquer de savoir-vivre *ou* d'éducation

breeding ground *n* = lieu *m* de reproduction de certains animaux; *Fig* foyer *m*, terrain *m* propice; **b. of anarchists** foyer d'anarchistes; **b. of crime/violence** terrain propice au crime/à la violence; **damp areas are a b. for germs** les zones humides sont des foyers de microbes *ou* constituent un terrain propice aux microbes

breeding stock *n* animaux *mpl* élevés en vue de la reproduction

breeze[1] [bri:z] *n* (*wind*) brise *f*; **gentle** *or* **light b.** petite *ou* légère brise; *Naut* **strong** *or* **stiff b.** vent *m* frais; **fresh b.** bonne brise; *Am F* **it was a b.** (*easy*) c'était simple comme bonjour, c'était un jeu d'enfant

breeze[2] *n* **b. block** *or* **brick** parpaing *m*

▶ **breeze in** *vi* (*quickly*) entrer en coup de vent; (*casually*) entrer d'une façon désinvolte

▶ **breeze out** *vi* (*quickly*) sortir en coup de vent; (*casually*) sortir d'une façon désinvolte

▶ **breeze through 1** *vi* (*pass exam with ease*) réussir les doigts dans le nez **2** *vipo* (*exam*) réussir les doigts dans le nez; **to b. through life** se laisser vivre

breezeway ['bri:zweɪ] *n US* passage *m* couvert (*souvent entre la maison et le garage*)

breezily ['bri:zɪlɪ] *adv* (*in lively fashion*) avec verve; (*casually*) avec désinvolture

breezy ['bri:zɪ] *adj* **(a)** (*day, place etc*) venteux **(b)** *F* (*pleasant*) jovial; (*casual*) désinvolte; (*speech*) plein de verve

Bremen ['breɪmən] *n* Brême

Bren [bren] *n Mil* **B. (gun)** fusil-mitrailleur *m*; **B. carrier** chenillette *f* porte-fusil-mitrailleur, *pl* chenillettes porte-fusil(s)-mitrailleur(s)

brent [brent] *n* **b. (goose)** bernache *f* cravant

brethren ['breðrɪn] *npl esp Rel* frères *mpl*; **my dearly beloved b.** mes très chers frères

Breton ['bretɒn] **1** *adj* breton **2** *n* **(a)** Breton, -onne **(b)** *Ling* breton *m*

breve [bri:v] *n* **(a)** (*accent*) brève *f* **(b)** *Mus* double ronde *f*; **b. rest** double pause *f*

breviary ['bri:vɪərɪ] *n Rel* bréviaire *m*

brevity ['brevɪtɪ] *n* **(a)** (*of style*) brièveté *f*, concision *f*; (*of expression*) laconisme *m*; *Prov* **b. is the soul of wit** le secret d'un bon mot d'esprit réside dans sa concision **(b)** (*of life etc*) brièveté *f*, courte durée *f*

brew[1] [bru:] *n* **(a)** (*of beer*) cuvée *f*; **home b.** bière *f*/cidre *m* de ménage; *Fig* **the book is a heady b. of ...** le livre est un mélange formidable de ... **(b)** *F* (*tea*) thé *m*

brew[2] **1** *vt* **(a)** (*beer*) brasser; **home brewed** (*beer, cider*) de ménage, (fait à la) maison **(b)** (*tea*) faire (infuser) **2** *vi* (*of tea*) infuser; *Met, Fig* **there's a storm brewing** il y a de l'orage dans l'air; *Fig* **there's something brewing** il se trame quelque chose, il y a quelque chose qui se prépare; **there's trouble brewing** il va y avoir du grabuge

▶ **brew up** *vi Br F* faire du thé

brewer ['bru:ər] *n* brasseur *m*; **b.'s yeast** levure *f* de bière

brewery ['bru:ərɪ] *n* brasserie *f*

brewing ['bru:ɪŋ] *n* **(a)** (*of beer*) brassage *m*; **the b. industry** la brasserie **(b)** (*of tea*) infusion *f*

brew-up *n Br F* **to have a b.** faire du thé

briar[1] ['braɪər] *n* **(a)** (*shrub*) bruyère *f* **(b)** (*pipe*) bruyère *f*

briar[2] *n* = **brier**[1]

briarroot ['braɪəru:t], **briarwood** ['braɪəwʊd] *n* racine *f* de bruyère

bribable ['braɪbəb(ə)l] *adj* corruptible

bribe[1] [braɪb] *n* pot-de-vin *m*, *pl* pots-de-vin; **to take bribes** toucher des pots-de-vin

bribe[2] *vt* soudoyer, acheter, *F* graisser la patte à; **to b. sb into silence** acheter le silence de qn; **to b. sb into doing sth** soudoyer *ou* acheter *ou F* graisser la patte à qn pour qu'il/elle fasse qch; *Fig* **I bribed her with some chocolate to go to bed** je lui ai donné du chocolat pour qu'elle aille se coucher

bribery ['braɪbərɪ] *n* corruption *f*; **open/not open to b.** corruptible/incorruptible; **b. and corruption** corruption; *Hum* **that's b. and corruption!** c'est une tentative de corruption!

bribing ['braɪbɪŋ] *n* corruption *f*, *F* graissage *m* de patte; *Jur* (*of witnesses*) subornation *f*

bric-a-brac ['brɪkəbræk] *n* (*no pl*) bric-à-brac *m*

brick[1] [brɪk] *n* **(a)** brique *f*; **air b.** brique perforée; *Fig* **to invest in bricks and mortar** investir dans la pierre; *Prov* **you cannot make bricks without straw** on ne peut pas faire de miracles; *F* **to come down on sb like a ton of bricks** tomber sur le dos à qn; *Fig* **to drop a b.** faire une bourde *ou* une gaffe; **box of (building) bricks** (*toys*) jeu *m* de cubes *ou* de construction; **b. kiln** four *m* à briques; **b. red** rouge brique *m inv*; **he went b. red** il est devenu tout rouge; **b. wall** mur *m* en briques; *Fig* **to come up against a b. wall** se heurter à un obstacle infranchissable; **to knock one's head against a b.**

wall se démener en pure perte; **it's like knocking your head against a b. wall** c'est peine perdue; **it's like talking to a b. wall** (*he or she etc won't listen*) c'est comme parler à un mur *ou* à un sourd

(**b**) *Old-fashioned Br F* **he's a b.** c'est un chic type

(**c**) (*of ice-cream*) pain *m*; (*of tea*) bloc *m*

▶ **brick up** *or* **in** *vtsep* (*window, doorway etc*) murer

brickbat [ˈbrɪkbæt] *n Fig* **she got a lot of brickbats for her performance** son interprétation lui a valu beaucoup de critiques; **the government has been receiving more brickbats than bouquets** le gouvernement a été plus critiqué qu'applaudi

brickfield [ˈbrɪkfiːld] *n* briqueterie *f*

bricklayer [ˈbrɪkleɪər], *Br F* **brickie** [ˈbrɪkɪ] *n* maçon *m*

bricklaying [ˈbrɪkleɪɪŋ] *n* briquetage *m*

brickmaker [ˈbrɪkmeɪkər] *n* briquetier *m*

brickwork [ˈbrɪkwɜːk] *n* briquetage *m*, maçonnerie *f* de brique

brickworks [ˈbrɪkwɜːks] *n* (*place*) briqueterie *f*

brickyard [ˈbrɪkjɑːd] *n* briqueterie *f*

bridal [ˈbraɪd(ə)l] *adj attrib* nuptial, de noce(s); **b. veil** voile *m* de mariée; **the b. party** les mariés *mpl*, leurs témoins et leurs parents; **b. suite** (*in hotel*) suite *f* nuptiale

bride [braɪd] *n* (*about to be married*) future mariée *f*; (*married*) jeune mariée; **the b. and (bride)groom** (*about to be married*) les futurs époux *mpl*; (*married*) les jeunes mariés *mpl*; **with his young b.** avec sa jeune épouse; **his b. of four months** la femme avec qui il est/était marié depuis quatre mois

bridegroom [ˈbraɪdgruːm] *n* (*about to be married*) futur marié *m*; (*married*) jeune marié

bridesmaid [ˈbraɪdzmeɪd] *n* demoiselle *f* d'honneur

bride-to-be *n* future mariée *f*

bridge[1] [brɪdʒ] *n* (**a**) (*across river etc*) pont *m*; *Fig* **we'll cross that b. when we get** *or* **come to it** chaque chose en son temps; **b. building** construction *f* de ponts; *Fig* réconciliation *f* (**b**) (*in wrestling*) pont *m*; **to make a b.** ponter (**c**) (*in billiards etc*) chevalet *m* (**d**) (*on ship*) passerelle *f* (**e**) (*of nose*) arête *f*; (*of violin*) chevalet *m*; (*of spectacles*) arcade *f* (**f**) (*on teeth*) bridge *m*

bridge[2] *vt* (*river etc*) construire un pont sur; **to b. a gap** relier les bords d'une brèche; *Fig* (*in knowledge etc*) combler une lacune; (*of snack*) boucher un trou; **to b. the gap between two groups** réduire l'écart qui existe entre deux groupes; *Com* **to b. the gap** (*esp for supplies*) faire la soudure

bridge[3] *n Cards* bridge *m*; **to play b.** jouer au bridge; **game of b.** (partie *f* de) bridge; **b. partner** partenaire *mf* au bridge; **b. player** bridgeur, -euse, joueur, -euse de bridge; *Br Culin* **b. roll** petit pain *m* (au lait)

bridgehead [ˈbrɪdʒhed] *n Mil, Fig* tête *f* de pont

bridgework [ˈbrɪdʒwɜːk] *n esp Am* (*on teeth*) bridge *m*

bridging [ˈbrɪdʒɪŋ] *n* (**a**) *Constr* **the b. of the river took several months** la construction du pont sur la rivière a pris plusieurs mois; **b. party** équipe *f* de pontonniers (**b**) *Fig* (*of gap*) comblement *m* (**c**) *El, Electron* shuntage *m*; *El, Electron* **b. connection** montage *m* en pont; *Constr, Carp* **b. piece** entretoise *f*; *Cin* **b. title** titre *m* de liaison

bridging loan *n Fin* prêt *m* relais, crédit *m* relais

bridle[1] [ˈbraɪd(ə)l] *n* (*for horse*) bride *f*; *Fig* (*restraint*) frein *m*; **b. bit** mors *m* de bride; **b. path** piste *f* cavalière

bridle[2] **1** *vt* (*horse*) brider; *Fig* (*one's passions*) maîtriser, mettre un frein à; **to b. one's tongue** tenir sa langue **2** *vi* (*of horse*) redresser la tête; *Fig* (*of person*) s'indigner, se scandaliser; *Fig* **she bridled at the implication** elle s'est indignée en entendant l'insinuation

brief[1] [briːf] **1** *adj* (*letter, interval etc*) court; (*pause*) petit; (*discussion, explanation etc*) bref, succinct, concis; (*account, report*) sommaire, bref; (*stay etc*) bref, de courte durée; **we exchanged a few b. words** nous avons échangé quelques mots; **give me a b. idea of what happened** donne-moi une petite idée de ce qui s'est passé; **I caught a b. glimpse of her** je n'ai fait que l'entrevoir; **a very b. pair of shorts** un short très court; **for a b. period** pendant peu de temps, pendant une courte période; **in b.** en bref; **to be b., …** (*in short*) bref, …; **please be b.** soyez bref s'il vous plaît

2 *npl* **briefs** (*for man, woman*) slip *m*; **bikini briefs** slip *m* de bikini

brief[2] *n* (**a**) *Jur* dossier *m*; *US* **b. (of argument)** conclusions *fpl* (*présentées à la cour avant l'audience*); **to take a b.** accepter un dossier; **to hold a b.** être chargé d'un dossier; **to hold a b. for sb** représenter qn en justice; **to hold a watching b. for sb** veiller (en justice) aux intérêts de qn; *Fig* **I don't hold any** *or* **I hold no b. for him** ce n'est pas mon affaire de plaider sa cause; *Fig* **I hold no b. for this policy** je n'adhère absolument pas à cette politique (**b**) (*instructions*) (*of committee etc*), *Pol* mission *f* (**c**) *Br Sl* (*lawyer*) avocat *m*

brief[3] *vt* (**a**) *Eng Jur* (*lawyer*) confier une cause à (**b**) *Av, Com etc* (*inform*) donner des informations à (**about** sur), faire l'exposé à (**about** de); (*instruct*) donner *ou* fournir des instructions *ou* des directives à; **have you been briefed?** (*brought up to date*) est-ce que vous avez été mis au courant?; (*given instructions*) est-ce qu'on vous a donné vos instructions?; **was the Prime Minister briefed?** est-ce que le Premier Ministre a été renseigné sur la question?

briefcase [ˈbriːfkeɪs] *n* serviette *f*; (*for carrying under arm*) porte-documents *m inv*

briefing [ˈbriːfɪŋ] *n* (**a**) *Eng Jur* **b. of a barrister** ≈ constitution *f* d'avoué (**b**) (*orders*) (*for mission*) instructions *fpl*, directives *fpl*; (*meeting*) réunion *f* d'information, *F* briefing *m*; *Av* briefing; **they gave me a final b.** ils m'ont donné les dernières directives; **b. room** salle *f* de réunion

briefly [ˈbriːflɪ] *adv* (**a**) (*in a few words*) brièvement, en peu de mots, en bref (**b**) (*for a short time*) (*to work, stay*) brièvement; (*to pause, smile etc*) un court instant; **we spoke b. on the telephone** nous avons échangé quelques mots au téléphone

briefness [ˈbriːfnɪs] *n* (*of time, visit*) brièveté *f*; (*of speech*) concision *f*

brier[1] [ˈbraɪər] *n* (**a**) (*wild rose*) églantier *m*; **wild b.** églantier commun, rosier *m* sauvage; **sweet b.** églantier odorant; **b. rose** églantine *f* (**b**) **briers** (*thorny bushes*) ronces *fpl*

brier[2] *n* = **briar**[1]

brierroot [ˈbraɪəruːt], **brierwood** [ˈbraɪəwʊd] *n* = **briarroot, briarwood**

Brig [brɪg] *n Mil abbr* **Brigadier**

brig [brɪg] *n Naut* (**a**) (*ship*) brick *m* (**b**) *esp US* (*prison*) prison *f*, cellule *f* (*à bord d'un navire*)

brigade [brɪˈgeɪd] *n Mil* brigade *f*; *Fig Hum Pej* (*group of people*) bande *f*; **infantry b.** régiment *m* d'infanterie; *US* **artillery b.** brigade d'artillerie; *Fig* **one of the old b.** un vieux de la vieille

brigadier [brɪgəˈdɪər] *n Mil* **b. (general)** général *m* de brigade

brigand [ˈbrɪgənd] *n Old-fashioned* brigand *m*, bandit *m*

brigandage [ˈbrɪgəndɪdʒ] *n Old-fashioned* brigandage *m*

bright [braɪt] **1** *adj* (**a**) (*star, metal, gem etc*) brillant; (*sun*) éclatant; (*fire, light etc*) vif, *f* vive; (*day, weather, sound*) clair; (*colour*) vif, éclatant; **b. eyes** yeux *mpl* brillants *ou* lumineux; *Met* **it'll be brighter tomorrow** le temps sera plus clair demain; *Met* **b. intervals** éclaircies *fpl*; *Met* **to become brighter** s'éclaircir; **b. red** (*colour*) rouge *m* vif; **b. red socks** des chaussettes rouge vif; **to go b. red** (*blush*) devenir tout rouge *ou* rouge comme une tomate; **b. future** avenir *m* brillant *ou* qui promet; **the company's future looks b.** cette société est très prometteuse; **it was the only b. spot in the day** c'était la seule chose positive de la journée; **the only b. spot in the play was her acting** son jeu était le seul intérêt de la pièce; **brighter days** (*happier*) des jours plus heureux; **the unemployment situation is looking a bit brighter** la situation de l'emploi commence à s'améliorer; **to look on the b. side (of things)** prendre les choses du bon côté; *Fig* **the b. lights** (*big city*) la ville; **as soon as he could, he headed for the b. lights of the city** dès qu'il a pu, il est allé s'installer en ville

(**b**) (*cheerful, lively*) vif, animé, sémillant; (*face, smile*) gai

(**c**) (*clever*) intelligent; **a b. idea** une idée lumineuse; **she's a real b. spark** c'est une vraie lumière; *Iron* **some b. spark has locked the door** il y a un gros malin qui a fermé la porte à clef; **he's not very b.** ce n'est pas une lumière, il n'est pas très futé *ou* malin; *Iron* **that's b.!** c'est vraiment intelligent

2 *adv* **to get up/leave b. and early** se lever/partir de bonne heure

3 *npl US Aut* **brights** pleins phares *mpl*; **put the brights on** mets en (pleins) phares

brighten [ˈbraɪt(ə)n] **1** *vt* (*colour*) aviver; *Fig* (*room, person*) égayer **2** *vi* (*of person, face*) s'épanouir; (*of eyes*) s'allumer, briller; (*of weather*) s'éclaircir; (*of future*) s'éclaircir, devenir moins sombre; (*of prospects*) s'améliorer; **their mood brightened** ils se sont déridés

▶ **brighten up** *vtsep, vi* = **brighten**

brightening [ˈbraɪt(ə)nɪŋ] *n* (**a**) (*of sky, weather*) éclaircissement *m*; *Fig* **there was a momentary b. of her mood** elle s'est égayée un moment (**b**) (*of colours*) avivage *m*

bright-eyed *adj* aux yeux brillants; *Fig* (*eager*) enthousiaste; *F* **b. and bushy-tailed** (*eager*) très enthousiaste; (*alert*) en pleine forme

brightly [ˈbraɪtlɪ] *adv* (**a**) (*coloured, to sparkle*) vivement; **the sun was shining b.** le soleil était éclatant; **to burn b.** (*of fire*) être vif; **b. lit** (*street, shop window etc*) bien éclairé; **b. polished** reluisant (**b**) (*to say*) gaiement, gaîment

brightness [ˈbraɪtnɪs] *n* (*of sun, light, sound*) éclat *m*; (*of lighting*) intensité *f*; (*of surface*) luminosité *f*; (*of day, sound,*

room) clarté *f*; (*of colour*) vivacité *f*; (*of child etc*) intelligence *f*; (*of steel*) brillant *m*, éclat; *TV* **b. (control)** (dispositif *m* de réglage de la) luminosité
brill¹ [brɪl] *n* (*fish*) barbue *f*
brill² *adj Br F* (*abbr* **brilliant**) super *inv*
brilliance [ˈbrɪljəns], **brilliancy** [ˈbriljənsɪ] *n* **(a)** (*of sun*) éclat *m*; (*of shine*) brillant *m*, lustre *m*; (*of sound*) netteté *f*; *Opt etc* luminance *f* **(b)** (*intelligence*) (*of person*) intelligence *f* remarquable; (*of mind, style, acting etc*) génie *m*; (*of plan, scheme*) ingéniosité *f*; (*skill*) (*of surgeon etc*) habileté *f* remarquable
brilliant¹ [ˈbrɪljənt] *adj* **(a)** (*lighting*) intense, brillant; (*sun*) brillant, éclatant; (*smile*) radieux **(b)** (*painter, scientist, actor etc*) excellent, brillant; (*speech*) remarquable; (*future, career*) brillant; (*idea*) lumineux; (*success*) éclatant; **she was b. in her last film** elle était formidable dans son dernier film; **you were b.!** tu étais formidable *ou* magnifique!; **he's not b.** il n'est pas brillant; *F* **I'm not feeling too b.** (*I feel ill*) je ne suis pas dans mon assiette
brilliant² *n* (*diamond, cut*) brillant *m*
brilliantine [ˈbrɪljəntiːn] *n* (*for hair*) brillantine *f*
brilliantly [ˈbrɪljəntlɪ] *adv* **(a)** (*coloured*) vivement; **the sun was shining b.** le soleil était éclatant; **b. lit** très bien éclairé **(b)** (*performed, played*) brillamment; **b. intelligent** d'une intelligence brillante; *Mus* **to play b.** jouer avec brio
brim¹ [brɪm] *n* (*of glass, hat etc*) bord *m*; **to fill a glass to the b.** remplir un verre à ras bord
brim² *vi* **(-mm-) eyes brimming with tears** yeux noyés de larmes; **to be brimming with ideas** (*of person*) déborder d'idées
▶ **brim over** *vi* déborder, regorger (**with sth** de qch); *Fig* **brimming over with health/life/ideas** débordant de santé/de vie/d'idées
brimful [ˈbrɪmfʊl] *adj* (*glass etc*) plein jusqu'au bord; **to fill a glass b.** remplir un verre à ras bord; *Fig* **b. of health/of life/of ideas** débordant de santé/de vie/d'idées
brimless [ˈbrɪmlɪs] *adj* (*chapeau*) sans bord(s)
-brimmed [brɪmd] *suff* **broad/narrow-b.** à larges bords/à bords étroits
brimstone [ˈbrɪmstəʊn] *n* **(a)** *Arch* (*sulphur*) soufre *m* (brut) **(b) b. (butterfly)** citron *m*
brindled [ˈbrɪnd(ə)ld] *adj* moucheté, tacheté
brine [braɪn] *n* **(a)** *Culin* saumure *f*; **tuna in b.** thon mariné **(b)** (*seawater*) eau *f* de mer; *Lit* **the b.** (*the sea*) la mer, l'océan *m*
bring [brɪŋ] *vt* (*pt, pp* **brought** [brɔːt]) **(a)** (*lead, carry*) (*person, animal*) amener; (*object, letter, news etc*) apporter; **b. your friend** amenez votre ami; **she brought a lot of luggage (with her)** elle a apporté beaucoup de bagages; **what brings you to London?** qu'est-ce qui vous amène à Londres?; **to b. sth onto the market** introduire qch sur le marché; **to b. a child into the world** mettre un enfant au monde; *Jur* **to b. before a court** (*person*) faire comparaître devant un tribunal; (*case*) soumettre *ou* déférer à un tribunal; *Jur* **to b. an action** introduire une action en justice; *Jur* **to b. an action against sb** intenter un procès contre *ou* à qn; *Jur* **to b. an accusation** *or* **a charge against sb** porter une accusation contre qn

(b) (*lead to, cause*) **to b. sb (good) luck/bad luck** porter bonheur/malheur à qn; **the announcement brought an angry reaction** la nouvelle a suscité la colère; **production has been brought to a standstill** la production a été paralysée; **to b. new hope to sb** redonner de l'espoir à qn; **you've brought it on yourself** vous l'avez cherché; **to b. tears to sb's eyes** faire venir les larmes aux yeux de qn; **to b. discord into a family** semer la discorde dans une famille; **it has brought me great happiness** cela m'a apporté un grand bonheur

(c) (*cause to come to a particular condition*) **to b. sb to his senses** ramener qn à la raison; **to b. sb into the conversation** (*involve*) mêler qn à la conversation; **to b. sb's name into the conversation** mentionner le nom de qn dans la conversation; **to b. water to the boil** faire bouillir de l'eau; **to b. sth into question** mettre qch en question; **to b. sth into disrepute** discréditer qch; **to b. sth to sb's attention** attirer l'attention de qn sur qch; **to b. sth to mind** rappeler qch; **to b. to light** (*old artefacts, manuscripts etc*) déterrer; (*crime, secret*) révéler; **to b. sth to an end** mettre fin à qch; **to b. sth to a successful conclusion** faire aboutir qch; **to b. oneself to do sth** se résoudre *ou* se décider à faire qch; **he cannot b. himself to speak about it** il lui est trop pénible d'en parler

(d) (*be sold for*) **the house won't b. very much** la maison ne rapportera pas beaucoup
▶ **bring about** *vtsep* **(a)** (*cause*) amener, causer, occasionner; (*reconciliation*) amener; (*person's downfall*) entraîner; (*accident etc*) provoquer, causer; (*change*) provoquer **(b)** *Naut* (*boat*) retourner, faire virer
▶ **bring along** *vtsep* (*person*) amener; (*object*) apporter
▶ **bring away** *vtsep* (*carry*) (*object*) rapporter; (*memories, impressions*) garder; **I brought away a lot of happy memories from my stay** j'ai gardé de mon séjour le souvenir de beaucoup de moments heureux
▶ **bring back** *vtsep* **(a)** (*carry*) (*object*) rapporter; (*lead*) (*person*) ramener; **crying won't b. him back** pleurer ne le fera pas revenir; *Jur* **to b. a case back before the court** ressaisir le tribunal d'un dossier

(b) (*of letter, song etc*) (*memories*) rappeler; **it brings back my childhood to me** cela me rappelle mon enfance

(c) (*restore*) (*freedom, discipline, monarchy etc*) rétablir; (*confidence*) ramener; **the electors will decide whether the government should be brought back** les électeurs décideront si le gouvernement doit être maintenu; **a couple of days in bed will b. him back to normal** quelques jours au lit le remettront d'aplomb; **to b. sb back to health** rendre la santé à qn; **to b. sb back to life** ramener qn à la vie
▶ **bring down** *vtsep* **(a)** (*destroy*) (*tree, game bird, plane, wall etc*) abattre; *F* **her performance brought the house down** son interprétation lui a valu des applaudissements à tout rompre; *F* **the audience brought the house down** les spectateurs ont applaudi à tout rompre

(b) (*cause to fall*) (*adversary*) terrasser; (*government*) faire tomber

(c) (*lead, carry*) (*person*) faire descendre; (*object*) descendre (**from** de); **what brings you down to the fourth floor?** qu'est-ce qui t'amène au quatrième étage?

(d) (*reduce*) (*price, costs, temperature*) faire baisser; (*currency*) déprécier, avilir; (*birthrate, inflation, unemployment, swelling*) réduire

(e) (*land*) (*plane*) faire atterrir

(f) (*cause to appear*) (*esp a person in authority*) attirer; **stop making so much noise or you'll b. the headmaster down on us** ne fais pas tant de bruit, tu vas attirer l'attention du proviseur sur nous
▶ **bring forth** *vtsep* **(a)** *Arch, Lit* (*young*) mettre au monde; (*of animal*) mettre bas; (*of plant*) (*fruit*) produire **(b)** *Fig* (*idea*) faire naître; (*suggestion*) donner lieu à; (*condemnation, objections*) provoquer; (*of research, investigations*) générer
▶ **bring forward** *vtsep* **(a)** (*carry, lead*) (*chair etc*) avancer; (*person*) amener, faire avancer, faire approcher; (*witness, evidence*) produire, présenter; (*argument*) avancer, présenter **(b)** (*in time*) (*meeting etc*) avancer **(c)** *Com* (*sum of money*) reporter; **brought forward** report *m*
▶ **bring in** *vtsep* **(a)** (*lead, carry*) (*person*) introduire, faire entrer; (*object*) rentrer; **b. him in** faites-le entrer; **to b. in the harvest** rentrer la moisson; **to b. sb in for questioning** emmener qn au poste de police pour l'interroger

(b) (*introduce*) (*fashion etc*) introduire, lancer; (*bill*) déposer, présenter; **to b. in new measures** instaurer des mesures; **new legislation will be brought in next year** une nouvelle loi prendra effet l'an prochain

(c) (*involve*) (*person*) faire intervenir, faire appel à; **the company is bringing consultants in** la société fait appel à des experts-conseils

(d) (*earn*) **to b. in interest** rapporter, porter intérêt; **investment that brings in 10%** placement qui rapporte 10%; **this land brings her in an income of £5,000** cette terre lui procure un revenu de 5 000 livres; **how much money is he bringing in?** (*earning*) combien est-ce qu'il gagne?

(e) *Jur* **to b. in a verdict** rendre un verdict

(f) to b. in the New Year (*celebrate it*) fêter le nouvel an
▶ **bring off** *vtsep* **(a)** (*person*) (*from ship*) débarquer; **the injured men will be brought off by helicopter** les blessés seront évacués en hélicoptère **(b)** (*complete successfully*) réussir; **they brought it off** ils ont réussi **(c)** *Vulg* (*bring to orgasm*) **to b. sb/oneself off** branler qn/se branler
▶ **bring on** *vtsep* **(a)** (*cause to appear*) (*illness, asthma attack*) causer, provoquer; *Hum* **what brought this on?** (*why are you offering to help with dishes etc*) qu'est-ce que tu me caches? **(b)** (*of sun etc*) (*plants*) faire pousser; (*of teacher, trainer*) (*person*) faire faire des progrès à **(c)** *Th* (*person, animal*) amener sur la scène; (*object*) apporter sur la scène; **please b. on our next contestant** faites entrer le concurrent suivant **(d) I brought it on myself** (*it was my own fault*) c'est entièrement de ma faute
▶ **bring out** *vtsep* **(a)** (*extract, lead*) (*object*) sortir; (*person*) faire sortir; *Fig* **to b. sb out (of his/her shell)** (*make less shy*) faire sortir qn de sa réserve **(b)** (*cause to appear*) (*meaning of sth*) révéler, faire ressortir; (*colour, detail etc*) faire ressortir; (*publish*) (*book*) publier, sortir; **to b. out the best/the worst in sb** faire ressortir les qualités/les défauts

de qn; **the sun has brought out the roses** le soleil a fait s'épanouir les roses; **strawberries b. her out in a rash** les fraises lui donnent de l'urticaire
▶ **bring over** *vtsep* (*lead, carry*) (*person*) amener, faire venir; (*object*) amener, apporter
▶ **bring round** *vtsep* **(a)** (*lead, carry*) (*person*) amener; (*object*) amener, apporter; **b. her round to meet us some time** amène-la un jour, qu'on puisse faire sa connaissance **(b)** (*restore to consciousness*) faire reprendre connaissance à, ranimer **(c)** (*restore to good mood*) rendre sa bonne humeur à **(d)** (*persuade*) convertir **(to an opinion** à une opinion) **(e)** (*steer*) (*conversation*) (r)amener **(to a subject** sur un sujet) **(f)** *Naut* (*ship*) faire virer
▶ **bring through** *vtas* (*cure with success*) guérir; (*lead with success*) conduire à la réussite; **his faith, which had brought him through the crisis** sa foi, qui l'avait aidé à surmonter la crise; **she brought all of us through the exam** grâce à elle, nous avons tous réussi l'examen
▶ **bring to** *vtsep* (*restore to consciousness*) faire reprendre connaissance à, ranimer
▶ **bring together** *vtsep* (*people*) réunir; (*put in touch with each other*) mettre en contact; (*documents*) rassembler, réunir; **he brought them together again** (*for meeting*) il les a réunis; (*after quarrel*) il les a réconciliés; *Jur* **to b. the parties together** mettre les parties en présence
▶ **bring up** *vtsep* **(a)** (*carry, lead upstairs*) (*object*) monter; (*person*) faire monter; (*carry, lead forward*) (*object*) approcher; (*troops*) faire avancer; (*reinforcements, fresh supplies etc*) faire venir; **to be brought up before the magistrate** comparaître devant le tribunal; **to b. sth/sb up to professional standard** élever qch/qn à un niveau professionnel

(b) (*vomit*) vomir; **to b. up one's food** vomir

(c) (*rear*) (*children*) élever; **I was brought up to be polite** on m'a appris la politesse; **well/badly brought up child** enfant bien/mal élevé; **to b. sb up the hard way** élever qn à la dure

(d) (*mention*) (*question*) soulever, mettre sur le tapis; **to b. sth up against sb** reprocher qch à qn

(e) (*stop*) **to be brought up short by a roadblock/an accident** (*of car*) s'arrêter brusquement à cause d'un barrage routier/d'un accident; **to be brought up short by sb's indifference** (*when talking*) être choqué par l'indifférence de qn

bringing-up ['brɪŋɪŋ'ʌp] *n* (*of child*) éducation *f*

bring-and-buy *adj Br* **b. sale** vente *f* de charité

brink [brɪŋk] *n* (*of precipice, river*) bord *m*; *Fig* **to be on the b. of** (*tears, war, success, starvation etc*) être au bord de; (*discovery*) être à la veille de; (*death*) être à deux doigts de; (*ruin*) être au bord *ou* à deux doigts de; *Fig* **I was on the b. of telling him/of doing it** j'étais à deux doigts de le lui dire/de le faire; *Fig* **to be on the b. of extinction** (*of animal*) être en voie de disparition; *Fig* **to stand shivering on the b.** hésiter à faire le plongeon

brinkmanship ['brɪŋkmənʃɪp] *n esp Pol* politique *f* de la corde raide; **he's a master in the art of b.** c'est un maître dans l'art de savoir jusqu'où il peut aller *ou Iron* jusqu'où il peut aller trop loin

briny ['braɪnɪ] **1** *adj* saumâtre **2** *n Lit, Hum* **the b.** la grande bleue

briquette [brɪ'ket] *n* (*of coal*) briquette *f*

brisk [brɪsk] *adj* **(a)** (*person, attitude, tone*) vif; (*to the point of curtness*) sec **(b)** (*movement*) vif; *Com* (*business, trade*) actif; (*demand*) fort; **at a b. pace** à vive allure; **to take a b. walk** aller se promener d'un bon pas; **business is b.** les affaires marchent bien; **to do a b. trade** (*of shop*) marcher à plein rendement; (*of street seller*) faire de bonnes affaires; **we're doing a b. trade in this particular item** cet article se vend très bien **(c)** (*air*) vivifiant; (*morning, wind, weather etc*) frais

brisket ['brɪskɪt] *n Culin* poitrine *f*

briskly ['brɪsklɪ] *adv* **(a)** (*to say*) d'un ton vif; (*to the point of curtness*) sèchement **(b)** (*to move*) vivement; **to step out b.** marcher d'un bon pas; **to sell b.** bien se vendre

briskness ['brɪsknɪs] *n* **(a)** (*of person, voice*) vivacité *f*; (*to the point of curtness*) brusquerie *f*; **the b. with which she goes about her job** l'extrême diligence avec laquelle elle fait son travail **(b)** (*of movement*) vivacité *f*; (*of business, trading*) dynamisme *m* **(c)** (*of air etc*) fraîcheur *f*

bristle¹ ['brɪs(ə)l] *n* **(a)** (*of pig, caterpillar, badger*) soie *f*; (*of brush*) soie, poil *m*; (*of beard*) poil raide; **his face was covered with bristles** il avait une barbe de trois jours **(b)** *Bot* soie *f*, poil *m*

bristle² *vi* (*of animal, hair etc*) se hérisser; *Fig* **to b. (with anger)** se hérisser **(at** à)
▶ **bristle with** *vipo* grouiller de; **the room was bristling with security men** la pièce grouillait d'agents de sécurité; **situation bristling with difficulties** situation hérissée de difficultés; **bristling with machine guns** (*fort, trench*) hérissé de mitrailleuses; **soldiers bristling with weapons** des soldats bardés d'armes

bristly ['brɪslɪ] *adj* **(a)** (*face*) couvert de poils raides; (*animal*) couvert de soies; (*moustache*) hérissé **(b)** *Bot* poilu, garni de soies

Bristol ['brɪst(ə)l] *n* **B. board** carton *m* Bristol, bristol *m*; *Naut, Fig* **(shipshape and) B. fashion** en bon ordre

bristols ['brɪst(ə)lz] *npl Old-fashioned Br Sl* (*breasts*) nichons *mpl*

Brit [brɪt] *n F* (*abbr* **Briton**) Britannique *mf*, Anglais, -aise, *Pej* rosbif *mf*

Britain ['brɪt(ə)n] *n* Grande-Bretagne *f*

Britannia [brɪ'tænɪə] *n* = nom *m* symbolique de la Grande-Bretagne

Britannic [brɪ'tænɪk] *adj* **His/Her B. Majesty** Sa Majesté britannique

Briticism ['brɪtɪsɪz(ə)m] *n Ling* anglicisme *m*

British ['brɪtɪʃ] [①**A20**,d] **1** *adj* britannique, de la Grande-Bretagne; **the B. consul** le consul de Grande-Bretagne; **B. goods** produits *mpl ou* marchandises *fpl* britanniques; **B. English** anglais *m* britannique **2** *npl* **the B.** les Britanniques *mpl*, *F* les Anglais *mpl*

British Columbia *n* Colombie *f* britannique

Britisher ['brɪtɪʃər] *n Am* Britannique *mf*, *F* Anglais, -aise

British Isles *npl* **the B.** les îles *fpl* Britanniques

British Standards Institution *n* = association *f* britannique de normalisation

British Summer Time *n* = heure *f* d'été en Grande-Bretagne

British thermal unit *n* = 1055,06 joules *mpl*

Briton ['brɪt(ə)n] *n* **(a)** [①**A20**,d] Britannique *mf*, *F* Anglais, -aise **(b)** *Hist* (*Celt*) Breton, -onne (*de la Grande-Bretagne*)

Brittany ['brɪtənɪ] *n* Bretagne *f*

brittle ['brɪt(ə)l] **1** *adj* fragile, cassant; *Fig* (*laugh*) un peu forcé; **to suffer from b. bones** avoir les os fragiles; *Fig* **in a b. voice** d'une voix crispée; **there is still a slightly b. air about the new coalition** la nouvelle coalition donne toujours une légère impression de fragilité; **a b. and rather unconvincing defence** une défense faible et peu convaincante **2** *n* = bonbon *m* croquant à base de mélasse et de noix

brittleness ['brɪt(ə)lnɪs] *n* (*of bones*) fragilité *f*; *Fig* **the b. of her voice** sa voix crispée; **the b. of his humour** son humour caustique

broach¹ [brəʊtʃ] *n* (*for tapping cask*) perçoir *m*

broach² *vt* (*cask*) percer; *Fig* (*question etc*) aborder; **I broached with your mother the subject of your leaving school** j'ai abordé la question de ton départ de l'école avec ta mère

broad [brɔːd] **1** *adj* **(a)** (*wide*) large; **the road is 15 metres b.** la route a 15 mètres de large *ou* de largeur; **to make sth broader** élargir qch; **a b. smile** un large sourire; **to have a b. back** avoir une forte carrure; *Fig* avoir bon dos; **it was already b. daylight** il faisait déjà grand jour; **in b. daylight** en plein jour; *Fig* au grand jour, devant tout le monde; *Fig* **it's as b. as it's long** cela revient au même, c'est tout un, c'est bonnet blanc et blanc bonnet; **b. views** *or* **ideas** *or* **outlook** idées *fpl* larges; **to have b. tastes in literature** avoir des goûts éclectiques en littérature; *Fig* **the party is a b. church** le parti rassemble de nombreux courants différents; *Am Sp* **b. jump** saut *m* en longueur; *Ling* **b. vowel** voyelle *f* large

(b) (*general*) (*rule, implications*) général; (*distinction*) sommaire; **b. outline** (*of project etc*) aperçu *m*; **term used in its broadest sense** terme employé dans un sens (très) large; **the project has b. support** le projet bénéficie d'un large soutien; **to be in b. agreement** être d'accord dans les grandes lignes

(c) (*accent*) prononcé; **to speak b. Scots/Yorkshire** parler avec un accent écossais/du Yorkshire prononcé; **b. humour** humour *m* de mauvais goût *ou* peu délicat; **b. joke** grosse plaisanterie *f*

2 *n* **(a) the b. of the back** le milieu du dos

(b) *Br* **the Broads** la région des lacs du Norfolk

(c) *esp US Sl* (*woman*) gonzesse *f*

broad bean *n* fève *f*

broad-brimmed *adj* (*hat*) à large bord

broadcast¹ ['brɔːdkɑːst] (*pt, pp* **broadcast**) **1** *vt* **(a)** (*programme etc*) *Rad* transmettre, (radio)diffuser; *TV* transmettre, diffuser; **the match will be broadcast live** le match sera diffusé en direct **(b)** *Agr* (*seed*) semer à la volée; *Fig* (*news*) répandre; **don't b. it!** ne le crie pas sur les toits! **2** *vi* **(a)** (*of person*) (*on radio*) parler/chanter/*etc* à la radio; (*on* *television*) passer à la télévision **(b)** (*of radio or TV authority*) émettre

broadcast² **1** *n Rad, TV* émission *f*; **simultaneous/recorded/live/outside b.** émission simultanée/en différé/en direct/hors studio; **b. antenna** antenne *f* d'émission; **b. journalism** *Rad* presse *f* électronique *ou* parlée, journalisme *m* de radiodiffusion; *TV* journalisme de télévision; *TV etc* **b. master** copie *f* antenne; **b. network** réseau *m* de transmission; **b. satellite** satellite *m* de télédiffusion **2** *adj* **(a)** *Rad* (radio)diffusé; *TV* télévisé **(b)** *Agr* semé à la volée; **b. sowing** semis *m* à la volée **3** *adv Agr* **to sow b.** semer à la volée

broadcaster ['brɔːdkɑːstər] *n* (*reporter*) *Rad* reporter *m* radio; *TV* reporter de la télévision; (*who gives talks, speaks*) personne *f* qui fait de la radio/la télévision; *Rad, TV* **independent b.** (*station*) station *f* de radio/chaîne *f* de télévision privée

broadcasting ['brɔːdkɑːstɪŋ] *n* **(a)** *Rad* radiodiffusion *f*; *TV* diffusion *f*; **she works in b.** *Rad* elle fait de la radio; *TV* elle fait de la télévision; **(television) b.** télévision *f*; **news b.** *Rad* reportage *m* (radio); *TV* téléreportage *m*, reportage (télévisé); **music/children's b.** émissions *fpl* musicales/pour les enfants; **this is the end of today's b.** voici la fin de nos émissions pour aujourd'hui; **b. centre** centre *m* de diffusion; **b. company** *TV* société *f* de télédiffusion; *Rad* société *f* de radiodiffusion; *Br* **B. House** = siège *m* de la BBC; **b. network** réseau *m* de diffusion; **b. rights** droits *mpl* de diffusion *ou* d'antenne; **b. station** station *f* émettrice

(b) *Agr* semis *m* à la volée

broadcloth ['brɔːdklɒθ] *n Tex* **(a)** (*for men's clothing*) drap *m* fin **(b)** *Am* (*poplin*) popeline *f*

broaden ['brɔːd(ə)n] **1** *vt* élargir; **to b. sb's outlook** *or* **horizons** élargir l'horizon de qn; **travel broadens the mind** les voyages ouvrent de nouveaux horizons **2** *vi* s'élargir

▶ **broaden out** *vi* (*of river, road, valley*) s'élargir

broad-leaved *adj* (*tree*) à larges feuilles, *Spéc* latifolié

broadloom ['brɔːdluːm] *n* **b. (carpet)** moquette *f* grande largeur

broadly ['brɔːdlɪ] *adv* **(a)** (*widely*) largement; **smiling b.** avec un large sourire **(b)** (*generally*) généralement; **b. speaking** généralement parlant, d'une façon générale; **to b. agree** être d'accord sur les grandes lignes **(c)** (*to speak*) avec un accent prononcé

broad-minded *adj* tolérant; **to be b.** avoir l'esprit large, être tolérant, être large d'esprit; **she takes a b. attitude to that kind of thing** elle est très tolérante pour ce genre de choses

broad-mindedness [brɔːd'maɪndɪdnɪs] *n* largeur *f* d'esprit, tolérance *f*

broadness ['brɔːdnɪs] *n* **(a)** (*width*) largeur *f* **(b)** (*of accent*) **because of the b. of his Yorkshire accent** à cause de son accent du Yorkshire à couper au couteau

broadsheet ['brɔːdʃiːt] *n* **(a)** (*newspaper*) journal *m* grand format (*de qualité*); **b. format** plein format *m*; **the b. press** les journaux grand format **(b)** (*pamphlet*) feuille *f* imprimée

broad-shouldered [brɔːd'ʃəʊldəd] *adj* large d'épaules, aux larges épaules

broadside ['brɔːdsaɪd] *n Naut* **(a)** (*of ship*) flanc *m*, travers *m*; **collision b. on** abordage *m* par le travers **(b)** (*from guns*) bordée *f*; *Fig* (*attack*) attaque *f* virulente; **to fire a b.** *Naut* tirer une bordée; *Fig* lancer une attaque virulente **(at** contre)

broad-spectrum *adj* (*antibiotic*) au spectre d'action très large

broadways, broadwise ['brɔːdweɪz, -waɪz] *adv* dans le sens de la largeur

brocade¹ [brə'keɪd] *n Tex* brocart *m*; **b. curtains/skirt** rideaux/jupe en brocart

brocade² *vt Tex* brocher; **brocaded gown** robe de brocart

broccoli ['brɒkəlɪ] *n* brocoli *m*; **eat your b.** mange tes brocolis

brochure ['brəʊʃjʊər, -ʃər] *n* brochure *f*; (*folding*) dépliant *m*

brogue¹ [brəʊg] *n* (*shoe*) chaussure *f* de marche *ou* de golf

brogue² *n* (*accent*) accent *m*

broil [brɔɪl] **1** *vt Am Culin* (*under grill*) passer au gril; (*over fire*) griller, (faire) cuire sur le gril **2** *vi F* **we were broiling (hot)** on grillait; **a broiling hot day** un jour où il fait une chaleur à crever

broiler ['brɔɪlər] *n* **(a)** *Am* (*grill*) gril *m*, rôtissoire *f*; **put it under the b.** passez-le au gril **(b) b. (fowl)** poulet *m* (à rôtir); **b. house** éleveuse *f* **(c)** *F* **it's a real b. (of a day)** on crève de chaleur

broke [brəʊk] **1** *pt see* **break² 2** *adj F* fauché, à sec; **to go b.** (*of company*) faire faillite; **to be (stony** *or* **dead) b.** être sans le sou, être fauché, être à sec; *Sl* **to go for b.** jouer le tout pour le tout

broken ['brəʊk(ə)n] **1** *pp see* **break²**

2 *adj* **(a)** (*limb, egg, stick, toy etc*) cassé; (*glass, window*) cassé, brisé; (*friendship*) brisé; (*rope, Naut moorings etc*) rompu; (*stones*) (con)cassé; *Com* **b. lots** articles *mpl* dépareillés

(b) (*terrain*) accidenté; (*shoreline*) découpé; (*outline*) irrégulier; **b. white line** (*on road*) ligne *f* discontinue

(c) (*sleep*) interrompu; (*words*) entrecoupé; **we had rather a b. night** nous avons été réveillés plusieurs fois pendant la nuit; **voice b. with sobs** voix entrecoupée de sanglots; **in a b. voice** d'une voix brisée; **to speak b. English** parler un mauvais anglais

(d) (*marriage, heart*) brisé; (*promise*) violé; **b. health** mauvaise santé *f*; **b. home** foyer *m ou* famille *f* désuni(e); **a b. man** (*financially*) un homme ruiné; (*by grief etc*) un homme brisé

broken-down *adj* (*car etc*) en panne; (*mechanism*) détraqué; (*house, furniture*) délabré; (*horse*) fourbu; **a b. old man** un vieil homme usé

brokenhearted [brəʊk(ə)n'hɑːtɪd] *adj* au cœur brisé; **to die b.** mourir de douleur *ou* de chagrin

brokenly ['brəʊk(ə)nlɪ] *adv* (*to speak*) de façon entrecoupée

broken-winded *adj Vet* (*horse*) poussif

broker¹ ['brəʊkər] *n* **(a)** *Com* (*for insurance etc*) courtier *m*; **insurance b.** courtier d'assurances; **wine b.** négociant *m* en vins **(b)** *St Exch* agent *m* de change; **outside b.** courtier *m* libre

broker² *vt Fig* **to b. an agreement** négocier un accord en tant qu'intermédiaire

brokerage ['brəʊkərɪdʒ] *n Fin* **(a)** (*fee*) (frais *mpl* de) courtage *m* **(b) b. house** (*business*) maison *f* de courtage

broking ['brəʊkɪŋ] *n Fin* (*profession*) courtage *m*

brolly ['brɒlɪ] *n Br F* (*umbrella*) pépin *m*, pébroc *m*

bromeliad [brəʊ'miːlɪæd] *n Bot* broméliacée *f*

bromide ['brəʊmaɪd] *n* **(a)** *Ch, Typ* bromure *m*; **potassium b.** bromure de potassium; *Phot* **b. (paper)** papier *m* au gélatinobromure (d'argent) **(b)** *Fig* (*platitude*) banalité *f*

bronchial ['brɒŋkɪəl] *adj Anat, Med* (*artery, asthma etc*) bronchique; **the b. tubes** les bronches *fpl*; *Med* **b. pneumonia** broncho-pneumonie *f*

bronchiole ['brɒŋkɪəʊl] *n Anat* bronchiole *f*

bronchitic [brɒŋ'kɪtɪk] *adj, n Med* bronchitique *mf*

bronchitis [brɒŋ'kaɪtɪs] *n Med* bronchite *f*; **she has b.** elle a une bronchite

bronchopneumonia [brɒŋkəʊnjuː'məʊnɪə] *n Med* broncho-pneumonie *f*

bronchus, *pl* **bronchi** ['brɒŋkəs, -kiː] *n Med* bronche *f*

bronco ['brɒŋkəʊ] *n* cheval *m* sauvage *ou* non dressé dans l'ouest américain

broncobuster ['brɒŋkəʊbʌstər] *n Am* dresseur *m* de chevaux

brontosaurus [brɒntə'sɔːrəs] *n* brontosaure *m*

bronze¹ [brɒnz] **1** *n* **(a)** (*metal*) bronze *m*; **the B. Age** l'âge *m* de bronze **(b)** *Art* (*object*) (objet *m* en) bronze *m* **(c)** *Sp etc F* (*medal*) médaille *f* de bronze **2** *adj* **(a)** (*statue*) de *ou* en bronze; *Sp etc* **b. medal** médaille *f* de bronze **(b)** (*colour*) (couleur) bronze *inv*

bronze² *vt* bronzer

bronzed [brɒnzd] *adj* (*skin*) bronzé

bronzing ['brɒnzɪŋ] *n* bronzage *m*

brooch [brəʊtʃ] *n* broche *f*

brood¹ [bruːd] *n* **(a)** (*of chicks*) couvée *f*, nichée *f*; **b. hen** (poule *f*) couveuse *f*; *also Fig* **b. mare** (jument *f*) poulinière *f*; **b. cell** (*in beehive*) cellule *f* d'incubation **(b)** *Fig* (*children*) enfants *mpl*, *Pej* marmaille *f*; **a member of the McGowan b.** un membre de la progéniture des McGowan **(c)** *Fig Pej* (*of scoundrels etc*) race *f*, engeance *f*

brood² *vi* (*of hen*) couver; *Fig* broyer du noir; **to b. about** *or* **on** *or* **over** (*the past, mistakes*) remâcher; (*idea*) ruminer; **there's no point in brooding over what might have happened** ça ne sert à rien de ruminer en imaginant ce qui aurait pu se passer; **she's brooding about the exam** (*which she has sat*) elle repense à son examen; (*which she will sit*) elle n'arrête pas de penser à son examen; **stop brooding about what he said** arrête de ruminer ce qu'il a dit; **to b. about things** ruminer; *Lit* **night brooded over the castle** les ténèbres enveloppaient le château

brooder ['bruːdər] *n* **(a)** (*hen*) (poule *f*) couveuse *f* **(b)** (*enclosure*) couveuse *f* (artificielle) **(c)** *Fig* (*person*) **he's such a b.** il est toujours à ruminer

broody ['bruːdɪ] *adj* (*hen*) couveuse *f*, qui demande à couver; *Fig* (*person*) songeur, pensif; **to feel b.** (*of woman*) être en mal d'enfant

brook¹ [brʊk] *n* ruisseau *m*; **b. trout** saumon *m* de fontaine

brook² *vt Lit* (*used only in neg sentences*) tolérer, supporter; **the matter brooks no delay** l'affaire n'admet aucun retard; **he will b. no insolence** il ne supporte pas d'impertinence; **I will b. no refusal** je ne tolérerai pas que tu/il/*etc* refuse(s)

broom [bruːm] *n* (a) (*shrub*) genêt *m* (à balai) (b) (*for sweeping*) balai *m*; *Fig* **new b.** = personne *f* nouvellement arrivée qui veut remanier l'organisation de l'entreprise; *Prov* **a new b. sweeps clean** = de nouveaux dirigeants mettent en œuvre de nouvelles méthodes
broomstick ['bruːmstɪk] *n* manche *m* à balai
Bros [brɒs] *Com* (*abbr* **Brothers**) **Thomas B.** maison *f* Thomas frères
broth [brɒθ] *n Culin* (*clear*) bouillon *m*; (*with vegetables etc*) potage *m*; **Scotch b.** soupe *f* (de mouton) avec orge et légumes
brothel ['brɒθ(ə)l] *n* maison *f* (close *ou* de prostitution), *F* bordel *m*; **b. keeper** tenancier, -ière de bordel; *Br F* **b. creepers** chaussures *fpl* à semelles de crêpe
brother ['brʌðər] **1** *n* (a) (*sibling*) frère *m*; **older b.** frère aîné; **younger b.** (frère) cadet *m*; *Com* **Thomas Brothers** maison *f* Thomas frères (b) *Rel* (*in community*) frère *m*; **B. John** Frère John (c) (*fellow member*) (*in guild*) confrère *m*; *Black American Sl* frère *m*; **brothers!** (*at union meeting etc*) camarades!; **brothers in arms** frères d'armes; **b. officers** officiers *mpl* de la même brigade *ou Mil* du même régiment; **his b. officers** les autres officiers de sa brigade *ou Mil* de son régiment **2** *int esp Am F* bon sang!
brotherhood *n* (a) (*relationship*) fraternité *f*; **the b. of man** la fraternité des hommes (b) (*organization*) fraternité *f*; (*religious*) confrérie *f* (c) *esp US* (*trade union*) syndicat *m* ouvrier
brother-in-law *n* (*pl* **brothers-in-law**) beau-frère *m*, *pl* beaux-frères
brotherliness ['brʌðəlɪnɪs] *n* (*of relation*) amour *m* fraternel
brotherly ['brʌðəlɪ] *adj* (*love etc*) fraternel
brought [brɔːt] *see* **bring**
brouhaha ['bruːhɑːhɑː] *n* brouhaha *m*
brow [braʊ] *n* (a) *Anat* front *m*; **to knit one's brows** froncer les sourcils (b) (*of hill*) sommet *m*; **the b. of a hill** (*on road*) le haut d'une côte
browbeat ['braʊbiːt] *vt* intimider; **to b. sb into doing sth** intimider qn pour qu'il fasse qch
browbeaten ['braʊbiːt(ə)n] *adj* persécuté
browbeating ['braʊbiːtɪŋ] *n* intimidation *f*
brown¹ [braʊn] **1** *adj* (a) (*coat, shoes*) marron *inv*; (*hair*) brun, châtain; (*eyes*) brun, marron; **light b. hair** cheveux châtain clair; **to be b.** (*tanned*) être hâlé *ou* bronzé; **to be as b. as a berry** (*tanned*) être tout bronzé *ou* noir; **b. ale** = bière *f* brune; **b. paper** papier *m* d'emballage, papier kraft; **b. paper bag** sac *m* en papier kraft (b) *Com* **b. goods** produits *mpl* électroménagers tel que télévisions, magnétoscopes etc **2** *n* brun *m*, marron *m*
brown² **1** *vt* (a) (*of sun*) brunir, bronzer; **face browned by the sun** visage bruni *ou* hâlé par le soleil (b) *Culin* (*fish, meat etc*) faire dorer, faire rissoler; (*butter, sauce*) faire roussir; (*almonds*) praliner **2** *vi* (a) (*in sun*) brunir (b) *Culin* dorer, rissoler
brown-bag¹ *vti Am F* **to b. (it)** = apporter son déjeuner (sur son lieu de travail)
brown-bag² *adj Am* **b. seminar** séminaire *m* où les participants apportent leur déjeuner
brown-bagger [braʊn'bægər] *n Am F* = personne *f* qui apporte son déjeuner sur son lieu de travail
brown bear *n* ours *m* brun
brown bread *n* pain *m* bis
browned-off [braʊn'dɒf] *adj esp Br F* **to be b.** en avoir marre *ou* ras le bol; **I'm b. with always having to do the dishes** j'en ai marre de devoir toujours faire la vaisselle; **he's very b. with you** il en a vraiment marre de toi
brown-eyed *adj* aux yeux bruns *ou* marrons
brown-haired *adj* aux cheveux bruns *ou* châtains
brownie ['braʊnɪ] *n* (a) (*elf*) lutin *m* (bienfaisant), farfadet *m* (b) **B.** (*guide*) =jeannette *f*; *Fig* **to win** *or* **get b. points** se faire bien voir (c) *Am Culin* = petit gâteau *m* au chocolat et aux noisettes
Browning ['braʊnɪŋ] *n* (*gun*) browning *m*
browning ['braʊnɪŋ] *n* (a) (*by sun*) brunissement *m*, bronzage *m* (b) *Culin* (*of almonds*) pralinage *m*; **the b. of the meat is important** c'est important de faire rissoler la viande (c) *Br Culin* (*substance*) colorant *m* brun (pour les sauces)
brownish ['braʊnɪʃ] *adj* brunâtre
brown-nose *Am Sl* **1** *vi* faire du lèche-cul **2** *vt* faire du lèche-cul à
brown-noser ['braʊnnəʊzər] *n Am Sl* lèche-cul *mf*
brownout ['braʊnaʊt] *n US El* baisse *f* de tension
Brown Owl *n* (*in Brownies*) cheftaine *f*
brown owl *n* (*bird*) chat-huant *m*, *pl* chats-huants
brown rice *n* riz *m* complet
Brownshirt ['braʊnʃɜːt] *n Hist* Chemise *f* brune
brown sugar *n* sucre *m* brun, cassonade *f*
brown trout *n* truite *f* saumonée
browse [braʊz] *vi* (a) (*of animal*) brouter, paître; **to b. on leaves** brouter des feuilles; *Fig* **I'm just browsing, thank you** (*in shop*) je regarde, merci (b) *Comptr* se promener
browse mode *n Comptr* mode *m* survol
▶ **browse through** *vipo* (a) *Fig* **to b. through a book/magazine** feuilleter un livre/un magazine; **to b. through sb's books/records** jeter un coup d'œil aux livres/disques de qn (b) *Comptr* se promener dans, survoler
brucellosis [bruːsɪ'ləʊsɪs] *n Med, Vet* brucellose *f*
bruise¹ [bruːz] *n* bleu *m*, contusion *f*, *Spec* ecchymose *f*; (*on fruit*) meurtrissure *f*, talure *f*; **she just has cuts and bruises** (*of accident victim*) elle n'a que quelques égratignures
bruise² **1** *vt* (a) (*part of body*) meurtrir; (*fruit*) meurtrir, taler; **to b. one's arm** se faire un bleu au bras, se meurtrir le bras; **you've bruised my arm!** tu m'as fait un bleu au bras!; *Fig* **to b. sb's pride** blesser l'amour propre de qn (b) (*crush*) (*substance*) broyer, écraser, concasser **2** *vi* (*of person*) se faire des bleus; (*of fruit etc*) s'abîmer; **he bruises easily** il se fait des bleus très facilement; *Fig* il est très sensible
bruised [bruːzd] *adj* meurtri; *Fig* (*pride*) blessé; **badly b.** couvert de bleus
bruiser ['bruːzər] *n F* (*boxer*) boxeur *m*; (*bully*) cogneur *m*; *F* **their baby's a real b.!** (*big*) leur bébé est vraiment costaud
bruising ['bruːzɪŋ] **1** *n* (a) (*on skin*) bleus *mpl*, meurtrissures *fpl*, contusions *fpl*, *Spec* ecchymoses *fpl*; (*on fruit*) meurtrissures, talures *fpl*; *Fig* **to take a b.** (*of ego, self-confidence etc*) en prendre un coup (b) (*of substance*) broyage *m*, écrasement *m*, concassage *m* **2** *adj Fig* (*hurtful to emotions, self-confidence etc*) douloureux
brumbie, brumby ['brʌmbɪ] *n Austr F* cheval *m* sauvage *ou* non dressé
brunch [brʌntʃ] *n F* brunch *m*
brunette [bruː'net] *n* brune *f*; **she's a b.** elle est brune
brunt [brʌnt] *n* (*of blow etc*) choc *m*; **the car took the b. of it** c'est la voiture qui a tout pris; *Fig* **the b. of his argument** le point principal de sa thèse; **to bear the b. of** (*attack, storm etc*) soutenir le plus fort de; (*sb's anger*) soutenir le poids de; **to bear the b. of the expense** supporter la plus grande partie des frais
brush¹ [brʌʃ] *n* (a) (*undergrowth*) broussailles *fpl*; *US, Austr etc* (*backwoods*) brousse *f*; **b. fire** incendie *m* de forêt
(b) (*for hair, clothes etc*) brosse *f*; (*for sweeping*) balai *m*; (*with dustpan*) balayette *f*; (*for paint, paste*) pinceau *m*; **flat b.** queue-de-morue *f*, *pl* queues-de-morue; **paste b.** pinceau à colle; **to paint with a full b.** (*of artist*) peindre dans la pâte
(c) (*tail*) (*of fox*) queue *f*
(d) *El* balai *m*; **(contact) b.** frotteur *m*; **b. holder** porte-balai(s) *m inv*
(e) **to give sth a b.** (*clothes*) donner un coup de brosse à qch; (*floor*) donner un coup de balai à qch; **to give one's hair a b.** se donner un coup de brosse; **to give one's teeth a b.** se brosser les dents
(f) (*encounter*) (*with enemy*) rencontre *f*, échauffourée *f*; *F* (*with boss*) prise *f* de bec; *F* **to have a b. with the police** avoir des ennuis avec la police; *Fig* **to have a b. with death** frôler la mort
(g) (*light stroke*) effleurement *m*; **she felt the b. of his lips on her neck** elle a senti ses lèvres lui effleurer le cou
brush² *vt* (a) (*clothes, carpet*) brosser; **to b. one's hair** se brosser les cheveux; **to b. one's teeth** se brosser *ou* se laver les dents; **to b. sth clean** nettoyer qch avec une brosse *ou* à la brosse (b) (*touch in passing*) (*surface*) effleurer, raser, frôler (c) *Tex* (*wool, nylon*) gratter
▶ **brush against** *vipo* frôler, effleurer
▶ **brush aside** *vtsep* (*person, difficulty*) écarter; (*objection, problem*) mépriser
▶ **brush away** *vtsep* (a) (*remove*) (*from clothes*) enlever d'un coup de brosse; (*from floor*) enlever d'un coup de balai; (*tears*) essuyer; **b. the leaves away from the path** balaye les feuilles qui sont sur le chemin (b) (*treat as unimportant*) (*person, difficulty*) écarter; **to b. away criticism** mépriser les critiques
▶ **brush down** *vtsep* (*person*) donner un coup de brosse à; (*horse*) brosser
▶ **brush off** **1** *vtsep* (a) (*remove*) (*from clothes*) enlever d'un coup de brosse; (*from floor*) enlever d'un coup de balai; **b. those flies off** chasse ces mouches (b) *F* (*reject*) envoyer promener; **he never brushes anyone off** il n'envoie jamais les gens promener; **to b. off pleas for help** rejeter des demandes d'aide **2** *vi* (*of dirt etc*) s'enlever à la brosse
▶ **brush over** **1** *vtaspo* **b. the varnish over the surface** badigeonner la surface de vernis **2** *vipo* **to b. over an issue** (*not treat in detail*) effleurer une question; (*ignore*) ignorer une question

▶ **brush past** *vipo* passer tout près de; **but he just brushed past me** mais il est passé à côté de moi sans s'arrêter
▶ **brush up** *vtsep* **(a)** (*collect*) (*crumbs etc*) ramasser (avec une brosse) **(b)** *F* (*subject*) (*improve knowledge of*) se remettre à; (*for exam etc*) réviser; **to b. up one's French** (*improve*) se remettre au français, remettre son français à niveau
brushdown ['brʌʃdaʊn] *n* **to give sb a b.** donner un coup de brosse à qn; **to give a horse a b.** brosser *ou* panser un cheval
brushed [brʌʃt] *adj Tex* (*wool, nylon*) gratté
brushing ['brʌʃɪŋ] *n* (*of hair, carpet etc*) brossage *m*; (*of floor*) balayage *m*
brushoff ['brʌʃɒf] *n F* **to give sb the b.** envoyer promener qn
brush-up *n* coup *m* de brosse
brushwood ['brʌʃwʊd] *n* **(a)** (*undergrowth*) broussailles *fpl* **(b)** (*worthless wood*) mort-bois *m*; (*for fire etc*) menu bois *m*; (*twigs*) brindilles *fpl*
brushwork ['brʌʃwɜːk] *n Art* (*of artist*) touche *f*
brusque [bruːsk] *adj* (*manner*) brusque, rude; (*tone*) rude, bourru
brusquely ['bruːsklɪ] *adv* (*to behave*) de façon brusque, avec rudesse; (*to answer*) avec rudesse
brusqueness ['bruːsknɪs] *n* brusquerie *f*, rudesse *f*; (*of tone*) rudesse
Brussels ['brʌs(ə)lz] *n* Bruxelles; **B. sprouts** choux *mpl* de Bruxelles
brutal ['bruːt(ə)l] *adj* brutal; **the b. truth** la vérité toute nue
brutality [bruː'tælɪtɪ] *n* brutalité *f*; *Jur* sévices *mpl* (**to** envers)
brutalize ['bruːtəlaɪz] *vt* **(a)** (*make brutal*) rendre brutal **(b)** (*ill-treat*) brutaliser, maltraiter
brutally ['bruːtəlɪ] *adv* brutalement; **to be b. frank** *or* **honest with sb** être d'une franchise brutale avec qn
brute [bruːt] **1** *n* (*animal*) bête *f*, brute *f*; *Fig* (*person*) brute; **you b.!** espèce de brute!; *F* **a b. of a job** un travail pénible **2** *adj* **b. beast** bête *f*, brute *f*; *Fig* **b. strength** *or* **force** force *f* brutale; **by b. force** par la force; **you'll have to use b. force** il faudra user de la manière forte
brutish ['bruːtɪʃ] *adj* bestial; *Fig* (*stupid*) abruti; (*violent*) brutal
brutishly ['bruːtɪʃlɪ] *adv* comme une brute
bryony ['braɪənɪ] *n* (*plant*) bryone *f* couleuvrée
BSc [biːes'siː] *n Univ* (*abbr* **Bachelor of Science**) **to have a BSc** être licencié *m* en sciences; **John Smith, BSc** ≈ John Smith, licencié ès sciences
BSE [biːes'iː] *n* (*abbr* **bovine spongiform encephalopathy**) EBS *f*
BSI [biːes'aɪ] *n abbr* **British Standards Institution**
BST [biːes'tiː] *n abbr* **British Summer Time**
BT [biː'tiː] *n abbr* **British Telecom**
bubble¹ ['bʌb(ə)l] *n* (*of air, soap, gas etc*) bulle *f*; (*in glass*) soufflure *f*, bulle; *Metal* boursouflure *f*; **to blow bubbles** faire des bulles de savon; *Fig* **to burst sb's b.** détruire les illusions de qn; **the economic b.** l'illusion d'un miracle économique
bubble² *vi* (*of boiling liquid etc*) bouillonner; *Ch, Ind* (*of gas through liquid*) barboter; (*of liquid poured*) faire glouglou, glouglouter
▶ **bubble over** *vi* (*of soup, milk*) (bouillonner et) déborder; (*of champagne*) (mousser et) déborder; *Fig* **to b. over with vitality/with high spirits** déborder de vie/de gaieté; **to b. over with joy** pétiller de joie; **he was bubbling over with laughter** il ne se retenait pas de rire
bubble and squeak *n Br Culin F* = friture *f* de pommes de terres et de choux
bubble bath *n* bain *m* moussant
bubble car *n* œuf *m* de Pâques, = voiture *f* dont l'habitacle est en forme de bulle
bubble gum *n* bubble-gum *m*
bubble-jet printer *n* imprimante *f* à bulles
bubble memory *n Comptr* mémoire *f* à bulles
bubble pack *n Com* (*for pills etc*) plaquette *f*; (*for large item*) emballage *m* coque
bubble wrap *n* film *m* de protection à bulles
bubbling ['bʌb(ə)lɪŋ] **1** *adj* bouillonnant **2** *n* bouillonnement *m*; *Ch, Ind* barbotage *m*; (*in paintwork*) boursouflures *fpl*
bubbly ['bʌblɪ] **1** *adj* plein de bulles; *Fig* (*person*) pétillant, plein d'entrain; (*personality*) plein de vitalité **2** *n F* (*champagne*) champagne *m*; (*sparkling wine*) vin *m* mousseux
bubonic [bjuː'bɒnɪk] *adj Med* **b. plague** peste *f* bubonique
buccal ['bʌk(ə)l] *adj Anat* buccal
buccaneer¹ [bʌkə'nɪər] *n* boucanier *m*
buccaneer² *vi* faire le boucanier
buck¹ [bʌk] *n* **(a)** (*male deer*) daim *m*, chevreuil *m* (mâle) **(b)** (*male reindeer, chamois etc*) mâle *m*; **b. rabbit** lapin *m* (mâle) **(c)** *esp US Pej* (*young black*) (jeune) Noir *m*; (*American Indian*) (jeune) Indien *m* (d'Amérique); **b.'s fizz** = cocktail *m* fait à partir de champagne et de jus d'orange **(d)** *Am F* (*dollar*) dollar *m*; **to make a fast** *or* **quick b.** faire du fric **(e)** (*sawhorse*) chèvre *f* (*de sciage*); *Gym* cheval-d'arçons *m*, *pl* chevaux-d'arçons *ou* cheval-d'arçons **(f)** (*jump*) (*of horse*) saut *m* de mouton
buck² **1** *vi* **(a)** (*of horse*) faire le saut de mouton; (*of aircraft*) se cabrer **(b)** *Am* (*of person*) résister, regimber; **to b. against** *or* **at sth** résister à qch **2** *vt* **(a)** (*of horse*) **to b. sb (off)** désarçonner qn **(b)** *Fig* **he bucked the odds by being chosen yet again** contre toute attente, il a encore été choisi; **you can't b. the odds** tu ne peux pas forcer le destin; **you can't b. the system** on ne peut rien faire contre l'ordre établi; **to b. a trend** aller à l'encontre d'une tendance; **to b. the question** ne pas répondre à la question
buck³ *n Fig* **to pass the b.** (*shift blame*) rejeter la responsabilité sur quelqu'un d'autre; (*make sb else decide*) laisser la décision à quelqu'un d'autre; *F* **the b. stops here** (*with me*) en fin de compte c'est moi qui en suis responsable *ou* c'est moi le responsable; (*with you*) en fin de compte, c'est toi qui en es responsable *ou* c'est toi le responsable
▶ **buck for** *vipo Am F* (*strive to achieve*) chercher à obtenir
▶ **buck up** *Old-fashioned F* **1** *vtsep* (*of person*) remonter le moral à; **this whisky will b. you up** ce whisky vous remontera; **getting that job has really bucked her up** ça lui a remonté le moral d'obtenir cet emploi; **to b. one's ideas up** se ressaisir, se prendre en mains **2** *vi* (*become more cheerful*) reprendre courage; (*hurry*) se grouiller, se remuer; **b. up!** (*be cheerful*) courage!; (*hurry*) remue-toi!, grouille-toi!
buckaroo ['bʌkəruː] *n US* cow-boy *m*
bucked [bʌkt] *adj Old-fashioned F* enchanté; **I was really b. to hear the news** ça m'a fait vraiment plaisir d'apprendre la nouvelle
bucket¹ ['bʌkɪt] *n* **(a)** seau *m*; **a b. of water** un seau d'eau; *Br F* **it's coming down in** *or* **raining buckets** il pleut à verse *ou* à seaux; *F* **to cry** *or* **weep buckets** pleurer à chaudes larmes; *Sl* **to kick the b.** casser sa pipe; **b. chain** = chaîne *f* de personnes qui se passent des seaux d'eau pour éteindre un incendie **(b)** *Min, Ind* baluchon *m*, baquet *m*; (*of crane*) benne *f*; (*of water wheel*) auget *m*, auge *f*; (*of dredger*) godet *m*, louchet *m*; **b. dredger** drague *f* à godets; **b. elevator** élévateur *m* à godets; *Aut* **b. seat** baquet; **b. wheel** roue *f* à augets
bucket² *vi Br F* **(a)** (*move jerkily*) cahoter; **the car bucketed down the street** la voiture avançait en cahotant dans la rue **(b)** (*rain heavily*) pleuvoir à verse *ou* à seaux
▶ **bucket along** *vi Br F* (*of car etc*) aller à une vitesse folle
▶ **bucket down** *vi Br F* pleuvoir à verse *ou* à seaux
bucketful ['bʌkɪtfʊl] *n* (*pl* **bucketsful** *or* **bucketfuls**) plein seau *m*
bucket shop *n esp Br F* **(a)** (*travel agent's*) agence *f* de voyages de discompte **(b)** *St Exch* courtier *m* marron
bucking ['bʌkɪŋ] *n* (*of horse*) sauts *mpl* de mouton
buckle¹ ['bʌk(ə)l] *n* **(a)** (*fastener*) (*for strap, belt etc*) boucle *f* **(b)** (*deformation*) (*of wheel etc*) gauchissement *m*, voile *m*
buckle² **1** *vt* **(a)** (*fasten*) (*suitcase, belt etc*) boucler; (*safety belt*) attacher; **to b. sth to sth** attacher qch à qch (à l'aide d'une boucle) **(b)** (*deform*) (*metal*) gauchir; (*wheel*) voiler; (*accumulator plate*) tordre **2** *vi* (*of wheel*) se voiler; (*of metal*) gauchir; *Fig* (*under attack*) céder; (*under criticism*) se décomposer; **the bridge buckled under the weight of traffic** le pont s'est déformé sous le poids des véhicules; **his knees buckled** ses jambes cédèrent sous lui; *Fig* **I'm buckling at the knees** (*exhausted*) je suis sur les rotules
▶ **buckle down** *vi* (*set to work*) s'y mettre; **to b. down to a task** se mettre *ou* s'atteler à un travail; **isn't it time you buckled down to your homework?** il serait peut-être temps de faire tes devoirs, non?; **he buckled down and finished cleaning the car** il s'est armé de courage et a fini de nettoyer la voiture
▶ **buckle on** *vtsep* (*belt, sword*) attacher; (*armour*) revêtir, mettre
▶ **buckle to** *vi* = **buckle down**
▶ **buckle up** **1** *vi* **(a)** *Aut* attacher sa ceinture de sécurité **(b)** = **buckle² 2**; **2** *vtsep* = **buckle² 1(a)**
buckled ['bʌk(ə)ld] *adj* **(a)** (*fastened*) (*belt*) bouclé **(b)** (*deformed*) (*metal*) déformé, gauchi; (*wheel*) voilé; (*accumulator plate*) tordu
buckling ['bʌk(ə)lɪŋ] *n* (*of metal etc*) déformation *f*, gauchissement *m*; (*of wheel, sheet iron*) voilure *f*
buckram ['bʌkrəm] *n Tex* bougran *m*
Bucks [bʌks] *abbr* **Buckinghamshire**
bucksaw ['bʌksɔː] *n* (*tool*) scie *f* à bûches

buckshee [bʌk'ʃi:] *adj, adv Br F* gratis *inv*; **we got in b.** on est entré gratis *ou* sans payer
buckshot ['bʌkʃɒt] *n (ammunition)* chevrotine *f*
buckskin ['bʌkskɪn] *n* peau *f* de daim; **b. breeches, buckskins** culotte *f* de peau (de daim)
buck tooth ['bʌktu:θ] *n* **to have buck teeth** avoir des dents de lapin
bucktoothed ['bʌktu:θt] *adj (person)* aux dents de lapin; **he gave a b. grin** il a souri en montrant ses dents de lapin
buckwheat ['bʌkwi:t] *n Agr* sarrasin *m*
bucolic [bju:'kɒlɪk] **1** *adj (life, poetry, poet)* bucolique **2** *npl Liter* **bucolics** *(poems)* bucoliques *fpl*
bud¹ [bʌd] *n (on shrub, tree)* bourgeon *m*; *(of flower)* bouton *m*; **to be in b.** *(of tree)* bourgeonner
bud² *int Am F* **hey, b.**! hep, vous là-bas!; *(à un ami)* salut mon pote *ou* mon vieux!
bud³ **(-dd-)** *vi (of shrub, tree)* bourgeonner; *(of flower)* être en bouton(s)
Buddha ['bʊdə] *n* Bouddha *m*
Buddhism ['bʊdɪz(ə)m] *n* bouddhisme *m*
Buddhist ['bʊdɪst] **1** *n* bouddhiste *mf* **2** *adj (priest, doctrine)* bouddhiste; *(art, temple)* bouddhique
budding ['bʌdɪŋ] **1** *adj (shrub, tree)* bourgeonnant; *(flower)* en bouton; *Fig (artist, lawyer, genius etc)* en herbe; *(passion, talent)* naissant **2** *n (of plant, tree)* bourgeonnement *m*
buddleia ['bʌdlɪə] *n* buddleia *m*
buddy ['bʌdɪ] *n F* copain *m*, copine *f*, pote *m*; **hey b., what are you doing in my car?** eh mec, qu'est-ce que tu fais dans ma bagnole?; *esp Am* **b. movie** film *m* qui raconte les histoires de deux copains
buddy-buddy *adj esp Am (close, friendly)* copain, *f* copine **(with** avec); **those two are very b.** ils sont très copain-copain
budge [bʌdʒ] **1** *vi* **(a)** *(move)* bouger; **if you (so much as) b.** si vous faites le moindre mouvement; **the door won't b.** la porte est bloquée **(b)** *(give way)* céder, reculer; **to refuse to b.** refuser de céder **2** *vt* **(a)** *(change mind of)* **I couldn't b. him** il est resté inébranlable **(b)** *(move)* bouger; *Fig* **I won't b. an inch** je ne reculerai pas d'un centimètre
► **budge up, budge along** *vi* se pousser
budgerigar ['bʌdʒərɪgɑ:r] *n* perruche *f*
budget¹ ['bʌdʒɪt] **1** *n Fin etc* budget *m*; *(allocated ceiling)* enveloppe *f* budgétaire; **we are within b.** *(at the moment)* nous n'avons pas dépassé le budget; **the museum was finished within b.** le musée a été fini sans dépasser le budget; **it was finished well below** *or* **within b.** c'est revenu bien moins cher que prévu; **the project is already well over b.** on a déjà largement dépassé le budget qui était alloué pour le projet; *F* **I'm on a b. this month** je fais des économies ce mois-ci; **family/household b.** budget familial/du ménage; *Can* **to bring down the b.** présenter le budget; *Parl* **to pass the b.** voter le budget
2 *adj* **(a)** *(inexpensive)* économique, bon marché; **b. brand/fare** marque *f*/tarif *m* économique; **b. holiday** des vacances *fpl* économiques *ou* pas chères; **b. meals** repas *mpl* bon marché; **b. prices** prix *mpl* raisonnables *ou* avantageux; **b. rate** tarif *m* économique
(b) *Fin (relating to budgets)* budgétaire; **b. deficit** déficit *m* budgétaire; **b. estimates** prévisions *fpl* budgétaires; **b. forecast** prévisions *fpl* budgétaires; **b. surplus** excédent *m* budgétaire
budget² **1** *vi* prévoir ses dépenses **2** *vt (time, money)* gérer
► **budget for** *vipo (allow for in accounts)* porter *ou* inscrire au budget; *(expense)* prévoir, *Spec* budgétiser; **we didn't b. for all these car repair bills** nous n'avions pas prévu toutes ces dépenses pour la réparation de la voiture; **I'm budgeting for my holidays** je surveille mes dépenses pour pouvoir partir en vacances
budget account *n (in store)* = compte *m* permanent; *(in bank)* compte crédit *(pour régler les factures de la vie courante)*
budgetary ['bʌdʒɪtərɪ] *adj Fin etc* budgétaire
budgeting ['bʌdʒɪtɪŋ] *n* budgétisation *f*
budget speech *n Can, Br* = discours *m* à l'occasion de la présentation du budget au parlement
budgie ['bʌdʒɪ] *n F (bird)* perruche *f*
buff¹ [bʌf] **1** *n* **(a)** *(shine)* **to give sth a b.** faire briller qch; *Metal* **b. stick** polissoir *m* **(b)** *(colour)* couleur *f* chamois **(c)** *F* **in the b.** tout nu **(d)** *(fan)* enthousiaste *mf*; **he's a film b.** c'est un cinéphile; **she's a history b.** elle est passionnée d'histoire; **computer b.** mordu, -ue *ou* passionné, -ée d'informatique **2** *adj (coloured)* de couleur chamois; *(envelope)* (en) kraft
buff² *vt (car, shoes)* lustrer; *Metal (metal etc)* polir; **to b. one's nails** se polir les ongles
► **buff up** *vtsep (car, shoes)* lustrer, faire briller
buffalo, *pl* **-oes** *or inv* ['bʌfələʊ, -əʊz] *n* **(a)** buffle *m*; **water b.** karbau *m*; **young b.** bufflon *m* **(b)** *US (bison)* bison *m*
buffer¹ ['bʌfər] *n Rail (at end of train)* tampon *m*; *(at end of line)* butoir *m*, heurtoir *m*; *El, Electron* (circuit *m*) tampon; *Comptr* tampon, mémoire *f* intermédiaire; *Fig* **to run into the buffers** tomber à l'eau; *F* **to act as a b.** *(between people)* faire tampon; *Mil* **recoil b.** frein *m*, amortisseur *m* de recul; *TV, Cin* **b. frame** cadre *m* de sécurité; *Comptr* **b. memory** mémoire *f* tampon; *Rad* **b. stage** étage *m* tampon *ou* intermédiaire
buffer² *n Br F* **old b.** vieux *m*; *(fool)* vieille ganache *f*, vieux bonze *m*
buffer³ *n (for polishing)* polissoir *m*
buffering ['bʌfərɪŋ] *n Comptr (storage)* stockage *m* en mémoire tampon; *(use)* utilisation *f* de mémoire tampon
buffer state *n Pol* état *m* tampon
buffer stock *n Com* stocks *m* de sécurité, stock stratégique
buffer zone *n Pol* zone *f* tampon
buffet¹ ['bʌfɪt] *n (with fist)* coup *m*; *(slap)* gifle *f*
buffet² *vt (person)* bourrer de coups de poing; **buffeted by the waves/the wind** *(ship)* battu *ou* ballotté par les vagues/secoué par le vent; *Fig* **to be buffeted by events** être ballotté par les événements
buffet³ *n* **(a)** ['bʌfɪt] *(piece of furniture)* buffet *m* **(b)** ['bʊfeɪ] *(meal, counter)* buffet *m*; **cold b.** *(on menu)* viandes *fpl* froides, assiette *f* anglaise; *(meal)* buffet froid; *Rail* **b. car** voiture-buffet, *pl* voitures-buffets, wagon-restaurant *m*, *pl* wagons-restaurants; **b. lunch/supper** buffet; *Rail* **b. service** service *m* de restauration
buffeting ['bʌfɪtɪŋ] *n* succession *f* de coups *ou* de chocs; *(by waves)* ballottement *m*; *(by wind)* secousses *fpl*; **the ship took a b. in the storm** le navire a été violemment ballotté par la tempête; *Fig* **she's taken quite a b. in the past couple of months** elle a beaucoup enduré au cours de ces derniers mois
buffing ['bʌfɪŋ] *n Metal etc* polissage *m*; **b. wheel** meule *f* à polir
buffoon [bə'fu:n] *n* bouffon *m*; **to act** *or* **play the b.** faire le pitre
buffoonery [bə'fu:nərɪ] *n* bouffonneries *fpl*
bug¹ [bʌg] *n* **(a)** *(insect)* **(bed) b.** punaise *f* (des lits) **(b)** *esp Am (any insect)* insecte *m* **(c)** *Med F* virus *m*, microbe *m*; **to catch a b.** attraper un microbe; **there's a b. going round** il y a un virus qui traîne; **she's got a stomach b. of some kind** elle a des ennuis gastriques; *Fig* **to have** *or* **have been bitten by the skiing b.** avoir la passion *ou* la folie du ski; *Fig* **the travel b.** la passion des voyages **(d)** *Comptr* bogue *f* **(e)** *(concealed listening device)* micro *m* caché; **to plant a b.** cacher un micro
bug² *vt* **(a)** *(room)* cacher des micros dans; *(telephone) (with hidden microphone)* cacher un micro dans; *(tap)* brancher sur table d'écoute; *(conversation)* enregistrer *(de façon clandestine)* **(b)** *F (annoy) (of thing, person)* taper sur les nerfs à, embêter, *Vulg* emmerder; **stop bugging me about it** arrête de m'embêter *ou Vulg* m'emmerder avec ça; **it really bugs me to think of her having all that money** ça m'énerve vraiment de savoir qu'elle a tout cet argent; **he's been bugging me to buy it** il n'arrête pas de m'embêter pour que je l'achète
bugaboo ['bʌgəbu:] *n esp Am Fig* = **bugbear**
bugbear ['bʌgbeər] *n F (goblin)* croquemitaine *m*; *Fig (cause of fear)* épouvantail *m*; **maths is my b.** les maths c'est mon cauchemar; **inflation is the government's chief b.** l'inflation est le grand cauchemar du gouvernement
bug-eyed *adj F* aux yeux exorbités; **to go b. at sth** ouvrir de grands yeux ébahis devant qch
bug-free *adj* **(a)** *Comptr (program)* exempt d'erreurs *ou* de bogues **(b)** *(room) (without listening devices)* sans micros clandestins; *(having no insects)* d'où les insectes ont été chassés
bugger¹ ['bʌgər] *n* **(a)** *Sl (despicable person)* salaud *m*; **silly b.!** espèce d'idiot!; **poor b.** pauvre type; **a b. of a job** un travail pénible; **this recipe's a real b. to make** cette recette est vachement compliquée; **she knows b. all about it** elle n'y connaît foutrement rien; **he doesn't care** *or* **give a b.** il s'en fout complètement **(b)** *Jur (pederast)* pédéraste *m*
bugger² *vt* **(a)** *Sl* **b. (it)!** merde!; **I'll be buggered if I'm going to pay for it!** pas question que je paye!; **that's really buggered it!** *(spoilt things)* ça a tout gâché; *(broken it)* ça l'a complètement bousillé **(b)** *Jur* sodomiser
► **bugger about, bugger around** *Sl* **1** *vi* déconner; **to b. about** *or* **around with one's car** s'amuser avec sa voiture; **stop buggering about with my computer** arrête de tripoter mon ordinateur **2** *vtsep (person)* emmerder, faire chier

▶ **bugger off** *vi Sl* se casser, foutre le camp; **b. off!** (*go away*) fous le camp!; (*leave me alone*) fous-moi la paix!

▶ **bugger up** *vtsep Sl* (*spoil*) (*plan, holiday etc*) foutre en l'air; (*machine, TV etc*) bousiller; **having to work overtime buggered up my weekend** ça m'a foutu mon week-end en l'air de devoir faire des heures supplémentaires; **you've buggered the whole thing up** tu as tout foutu en l'air

buggered ['bʌgəd] *adj pred Sl* **to be b.** (*exhausted*) être crevé; (*broken*) être foutu

buggery ['bʌgərɪ] *n* **(a)** *Jur* sodomie *f* **(b)** *Sl* **to run like b.** courir ventre à terre; **my plans have been shot to b.** ça a foutu mes projets en l'air

bugging ['bʌgɪŋ] *n* (*of room*) installation *f* de micros (*pour espionner*); (*of telephone*) mise *f* sur table d'écoute; **b. device** micro *m* pour écoute clandestine

buggy[1] ['bʌgɪ] *n* **(a)** (*carriage*) boghei *m*, buggy *m*; **(beach) b.** buggy; **(moon) b.** jeep *f* lunaire **(b)** *Am* (*for baby*) landau *m*; *Br* (*pushchair*) poussette *f*

buggy[2] *adj Comptr* plein de bogues

bughouse ['bʌghaʊs] *US Sl* **1** *n* (*for the insane*) maison *f* de fous **2** *adj* (*insane*) fou, *f* folle

bugle[1] ['bju:g(ə)l] *n Mil* clairon *m*; **b. call** coup *m ou* sonnerie *f* de clairon

bugle[2] *n* (*plant*) bugle *f*

bugler ['bju:glər] *n* (sonneur *m* de) clairon *m*

bugless ['bʌglɪs] *adj Comptr* sans bogues

bug-ridden *adj Comptr* plein de bogues

build[1] [bɪld] *n* (*of person*) carrure *f*; **man of powerful b.** homme à forte carrure; **of slight b.** fluet

build[2] (*pt, pp* **built** [bɪlt]) **1** *vt* (*house etc*) construire, bâtir; (*ship, bridge, road etc*) construire; (*temple*) édifier; (*nest*) faire; **the walls were built of granite** les murs étaient (construits *ou* bâtis) en granit; **the house is being built** la maison est en construction; **to b. one's hopes on sth** fonder *ou* baser ses espoirs sur qch **2** *vi* **(a)** *Constr* construire, bâtir; **to b. on a piece of land** bâtir un terrain; *Fig* **to b. on sand** bâtir sur le sable; **to b. on one's success** mettre à profit sa réussite; **to b. on an opportunity** profiter d'une occasion **(b)** (*increase*) (*of pressure, Fig of excitement, tension*) augmenter

▶ **build in** *vtsep* (*incorporate*) intégrer, incorporer; *Constr* (*wardrobe, beam etc*) encastrer; **to b. in safety features** intégrer des dispositifs de sécurité

▶ **build into** *vtaspo* **to b. sth into a product** incorporer qch dans un produit

▶ **build on** *vtsep* (*add to existing structure*) (*porch etc*) ajouter; **we've built on a garage** nous avons ajouté un garage; **the stables are built on to the house** les écuries sont attenantes à la maison

▶ **build up 1** *vtsep* **(a)** (*increase*) (*demand*) développer; *Mil etc* (*reserves*) constituer; (*forces, reinforcements etc*) mettre sur pied; (*one's strength*) reprendre; **don't b. your hopes up** ne te fais pas trop d'illusions

(b) (*create*) (*theory, system*) bâtir, échafauder, construire; (*business*) développer; (*reputation*) se faire; (*collection, library*) constituer; **to b. up custom** *or* **a clientele** (*of company*) se faire *ou* se constituer une clientèle; **his father built the company up from nothing** son père a créé la société à partir de rien; *Med etc* **to b. up an immunity** développer une immunité

(c) (*strengthen*) **the children need vitamins to b. them up** les enfants ont besoin de vitamines pour reprendre des forces

(d) (*usu passive*) **this area has been very much built up** on a beaucoup construit par ici

(e) (*publicize*) (*film, book, actor etc*) dire du bien de; **the film wasn't as good as it had been built up to be** le film n'était pas aussi bon qu'on le prétendait

(f) (*wall*) (*make higher*) rehausser; (*rebuild*) réparer

2 *vi* (*of pressure*) s'accumuler, augmenter; (*of tension*) augmenter, monter; (*of traffic*) devenir dense; (*of snow, clouds*) s'amonceler; (*of hurricane, storm*) se préparer

builder ['bɪldər] *n Constr* entrepreneur *m* en bâtiment; (*of ships etc*) constructeur *m*; *Fig* (*of empire etc*) créateur *m*, fondateur *m*

building ['bɪldɪŋ] *n* **(a)** (*house, factory etc*) bâtiment *m*, immeuble *m*; (*large*) édifice *m*; **public b.** édifice public **(b)** (*action*) construction *f*; **the b. trade** le bâtiment; *Fig* **the b. of better relations** l'établissement *m* de meilleures relations; **b. materials** matériaux *mpl* de construction; **b. slip** (*for ship*) cale *f* de construction

building block *n* (*toy*) cube *m*

building contractor *n* entrepreneur *m* de bâtiment

building plot *n* terrain *m* à bâtir

building site *n* (*vacant land*) terrain *m* à bâtir; (*where work is going on*) chantier *m* (de construction)

building society *n Br* = société *f* de crédit immobilier; **b. account** plan *m* d'épargne logement

building worker *n* ouvrier *m* du bâtiment

build-up *n* **(a)** (*of pressure*) accumulation *f*, augmentation *f*; (*of tension*) augmentation; **the b. of traffic on the motorway** la formation de bouchons sur l'autoroute; **traffic b.** bouchon *m*

(b) (*of system etc*) élaboration *f*, développement *m*

(c) *Mil* (*of forces, reinforcements etc*) mise *f* sur pied; (*of reserves of troops, supplies etc*) constitution *f*; **there has been a b. of troops along the border** on a envoyé du renfort aux troupes le long de la frontière

(d) (*publicity*) battage *m* (publicitaire); **her latest book is getting a lot of b.** on fait beaucoup de battage autour de son dernier livre; **despite the big b., the film didn't do well** en dépit du battage dont il a fait l'objet, le film n'a pas bien marché

(e) (*preparatory period*) **the b. to the match** la période d'avant le match; **in the b. to the election, there will be ...** pendant la période qui précédera les élections, il y aura ...

built [bɪlt] *adj* bâti; **British b.** de construction britannique; **a powerfully b. man** un homme à forte carrure *ou* charpente; **b. attraction** (*in tourism*) centre *m* d'intérêt 'non-naturel'

built-in *adj* (*wardrobe, bath, beam*) encastré; **b. obsolescence** (*in machine*) obsolescence *f* programmée; *Fig* **a b. resistance to ...** une opposition viscérale à ...

built-up *adj* (*beam*) composé, rapporté; (*shoulders of suit*) rehaussé; **b. shoes** chaussures *fpl* à semelles compensées; **b. area** agglomération *f* (urbaine)

bulb [bʌlb] *n* **(a)** (*tulip etc*) bulbe *m*, oignon *m* **(b)** *El* ampoule *f* **(c)** *Phys* (*of thermometer*) réservoir *m*; *Ch* (*flask*) ballon *m*; *Culin* (*of baster*) poire *f* **(d)** *Anat* bulbe *m*

bulbous ['bʌlbəs] *adj* bulbeux; **b. nose** gros nez *m*

Bulgaria [bʌl'geərɪə] *n* Bulgarie *f*

Bulgarian [bʌl'geərɪən] **1** *adj* bulgare **2** *n* **(a)** Bulgare *mf* **(b)** *Ling* bulgare *m*

bulge[1] [bʌldʒ] *n* (*in wall, ceiling*) bombement *m*, renflement *m*; (*on face, body, caused by a growth etc*) protubérance *f*; (*in tyre*) hernie *f*; *Mil* (*of front*) saillant *m*; *Econ F* (*increase*) poussée *f*; **this dress shows all my bulges** cette robe révèle toutes mes rondeurs; **the gun made a b. in his pocket** le révolver faisait une protubérance dans sa poche

bulge[2] *vi* **to b. (out)** bomber, ballonner; (*stick out*) faire saillie; (*of wall, ceiling etc*) faire ventre; **his eyes were bulging** il avait les yeux exorbités; **sack bulging with potatoes** sac bourré de pommes de terre; **I knew from the way his pocket bulged** j'ai su à la protubérance que formait sa poche

bulging ['bʌldʒɪŋ] **1** *adj* (*forehead, wall, ceiling*) bombé; (*stomach*) ballonné; (*eyes*) protubérant; (*cheeks*) bouffi; (*bag, wallet etc*) bourré, plein à craquer **2** *n* (*of wall etc*) bombement *m*, renflement *m*; (*of stomach*) ballonnement *m*

bulimia [bju:'lɪmɪə, bʊ'l-] *n Med* boulimie *f*

bulk[1] [bʌlk] *n* **(a)** (*size*) masse *f*, volume *m*; (*of parcel*) encombrement *m* **(b) the b.** (*greater part*) (*of people*) la masse, la plupart; (*of army*) le gros; (*of one's property, work, money etc*) la plus grosse partie **(c)** *Comptr* (*of information*) volume *m*, masse *f* **(d)** *Com etc* **to buy in b.** acheter en gros *ou* par grosses quantités; **to sell in b.** vendre en gros; **b. buying** achat *m* en gros; **b. cargo** cargaison *f* en vrac; *Naut* **b. carrier** (*of crude oil etc*) navire *m* pour le transport en vrac, vraquier *m*; **b. discount** remise *f* quantitative; **b. order** grosse commande *f*; **b. rate** (*for sending letters*) affranchissement *m* à forfait

bulk[2] **1** *vi Fig* **to b. large** occuper une place importante **(in sb's eyes** aux yeux de qn) **2** *vt* **to b. sth out** étoffer qch

bulkhead ['bʌlkhed] *n* (*on ship etc*) cloison *f*

bulkiness ['bʌlkɪnɪs] *n* **(a)** volume *m* excessif; (*of parcel*) encombrement *m* **(b)** (*of sweater*) épaisseur *f*

bulky ['bʌlkɪ] *adj* **(a)** (*parcel etc*) volumineux, encombrant; (*book*) épais **(b)** (*sweater*) gros, épais

bull[1] [bʊl] **1** *n* **(a)** taureau *m*; *Astron* **the B.** le Taureau; *Fig* **to take the b. by the horns** prendre le taureau par les cornes; **like a b. in a china shop** comme un éléphant dans un magasin de porcelaine; **to go at sth like a b. at a gate** foncer tête baissée *ou* la tête la première dans qch; **b. calf** jeune taureau, taurillon *m*

(b) (*male*) (*elephant, whale etc*) mâle *m*; **b. elephant** éléphant *m* mâle

(c) *Br Mil Sl* (*polishing*) fourbissage *m*

(d) *Sl* (*nonsense*) conneries *fpl*; **he talks a lot of b.** il raconte beaucoup de conneries

(e) *St Exch* spéculateur *m* à la hausse, haussier *m*; **b. spread** spread *m* haussier; **b. trading** spéculation *f* à la hausse; **b. transaction** opération *f* à la hausse

(f) (*of target*) mouche *f*, mille *m*; **he got six bulls** il a fait mouche six fois, il a mis six fois dans le mille

(g) (*dog*) bouledogue *m*; **b. bitch/pup** chienne *f*/chiot *m* de bouledogue; **b. terrier** bull-terrier *m*, *pl* bull-terriers; **b. mastiff** molosse *m*

2 *int Sl* foutaise!, quelle(s) connerie(s)!

bull² *St Exch* **1** *vt* **to b. the market** chercher à faire monter les cours **2** *vi* spéculer à la hausse

bull³ *n Rel* bulle *f*; **papal b.** bulle du pape

bulldog ['bʊldɒg] *n* bouledogue *m*; *Fig* (*tenacious person*) personne *f* très tenace; *Br Univ* (*official*) appariteur *m* du censeur (*aux universités d'Oxford et de Cambridge*)

bulldog clip *n* pince *f* à dessin, attache *m* de bureau

bulldoze ['bʊldəʊz] *vt* (*land*) dégager *ou* déblayer au bulldozer; (*house etc*) démolir au bulldozer; *Fig* **to b. sb into doing sth** forcer qn à faire qch; **I was bulldozed into it** on m'a forcé à le faire; **to b. sth through a committee** forcer une commission à adopter qch

bulldozer ['bʊldəʊzər] *n Constr* bulldozer *m*

bulldyke ['bʊldaɪk] *n Sl* lesbienne *f* à l'allure masculine

bullet ['bʊlɪt] *n* (*from rifle, revolver*) balle *f*; *F* **to stop a b.** recevoir une balle; **b. hole** trou *m* de balle; *Typ* **b. point** gros point *m*; **b. train** (*in Japan*) = train *m* à grande vitesse; **b. wound** blessure *f* par balle

bullet-headed *adj* **(a)** à tête ronde **(b)** *US Fig* (*obstinate*) entêté, têtu

bulletin ['bʊlɪtɪn] *n* bulletin *m*, communiqué *m*; **b. services** services *mpl* télématiques

bulletin board *n* tableau *m* d'affichage; *Comptr* serveur *m* télématique

bulletproof ['bʊlɪtpru:f] *adj* (*glass, car*) à l'épreuve des balles; **b. vest** gilet *m* pare-balles

bullfight ['bʊlfaɪt] *n* course *f* de taureaux, corrida *f*

bullfighter ['bʊlfaɪtər] *n* matador *m*, toréador *m*

bullfighting ['bʊlfaɪtɪŋ] *n* courses *fpl* de taureaux; (*as art*) tauromachie *f*

bullfinch ['bʊlfɪntʃ] *n* (*bird*) bouvreuil *m*

bullfrog ['bʊlfrɒg] *n* grenouille *f* taureau

bull-headed *adj F* **(a)** (*impetuous*) d'une impétuosité de taureau; **to go at sth b.** foncer la tête la première dans qch **(b)** (*obstinate*) entêté, têtu

bullhorn ['bʊlhɔ:n] *n Am* porte-voix *m inv*

bullion ['bʊljən] *n inv* (*gold*) or *m* en barres *ou* en lingot(s); (*silver*) argent *m* en lingot(s); *Fin* métal *m*; **b. van** fourgon *m* bancaire

bullish ['bʊlɪʃ] **(a)** *St Exch* (*market, trend*) à la hausse, haussier; **to be b.** spéculer à la hausse **(b)** *Fig* (*optimistic*) optimiste (**about sth** au sujet de qch, à propos de qch)

bull market *n St Exch* marché *m* haussier, marché orienté à la hausse

bull-necked ['bʊlnekt] *adj* au cou de taureau

bullock ['bʊlək] *n* bœuf *m*; **young b.** bouvillon *m*; **b. cart** char *m* à bœufs

bullpen ['bʊlpen] *n US* (*in police station*) = grande cellule *f* commune

bullring ['bʊlrɪŋ] *n* arène *f*

bull's-eye ['bʊlzaɪ] *n* **(a)** (*of target*) mouche *f*, mille *m*; **to hit the** *or* **get a b.** (*in archery*) faire mouche, mettre dans le mille; (*at darts*) mettre dans le mille; *Fig* **to hit the b.** (*of remark*) faire mouche **(b)** (*in glass*) boudine *f*; **b. panes** carreaux *mpl* à boudines *ou* en culs-de-bouteille **(c)** (*sweet*) gros bonbon *m* à la menthe

bullshit¹ ['bʊlʃɪt] *Vulg* **1** *n* foutaise *f*; **he's a real b. artist** (*talks a lot of nonsense*) il ne dit que des conneries; (*can impress people*) c'est un vrai baratineur **2** *int* foutaise!

bullshit² *Vulg* **1** *vi* dire des conneries **2** *vt* **to b. one's way into a job** obtenir un emploi grâce à son culot; **to b. one's way through an exam** réussir à un examen à force de baratin; **to b. sb into doing sth** baratiner qn pour qu'il fasse qch; **he bullshitted her into believing he would marry her** avec son baratin, il lui a fait croire qu'il l'épouserait

bullshitter ['bʊlʃɪtər] *n Vulg* (*smooth talker*) baratineur, -euse; **he's a b.** (*talks nonsense*) il dit des conneries

bully¹ ['bʊlɪ] *n* tyran *m*; *Sch* petit tyran (*qui fait subir des brimades à ses camarades*); **don't be such a b.** ne sois pas si tyrannique

bully² *vt* (*wife, employee*) brimer; (*classmates, little sister etc*) brimer, persécuter; **to b. sb into doing sth** faire faire qch à qn à force de menaces *ou* d'intimidations; **to b. sb into submission** faire céder qn à force de menaces

bully³ *int Old-fashioned F* **b. for you!** (*what luck*) vous avez de la chance!; (*well done*) bravo!

▶ **bully off** *vi* (*in hockey*) engager (le jeu)

bully beef *n F* bœuf *m* de conserve, *F* singe *m*

bullyboy ['bʊlɪbɔɪ] *n* voyou *m*, dur *m*; **b. tactics** tactiques *fpl* de voyou

bullying ['bʊlɪɪŋ] **1** *adj* brutal, -aux **2** *n* brimades *fpl*

bully-off *n* (*in hockey*) engagement *m* (du jeu)

bulrush ['bʊlrʌʃ] *n* (*plant*) jonc *m* des marais

bulwark ['bʊlwɜ:k] *n* **(a)** (*fortification*); *Fig* rempart *m* **(b)** *Naut* **bulwarks** bastingage *m*

bum¹ [bʌm] *n Br F* (*bottom*) derrière *m*; **b. bag** banane *f*

bum² *esp Am Sl* **1** *adj* moche, minable; **b. advice** des conseils *mpl* minables; **b. check** chèque *m* en bois; **b. rap** (*false charge*) accusation *f* inventée de toutes pièces; (*unfair punishment*) punition *f* injuste; **b. steer** tuyau *m* bidon

2 *n* **(a)** (*worthless person*) fainéant, -ante; (*tramp*) clochard, -arde, trimardeur *m*; **to give sb the b.'s rush** (*from relationship, meeting*) virer qn avec perte et fracas; **to give a suggestion/an idea the b.'s rush** ne tenir aucun compte d'une suggestion/idée

(b) to be on the b. (*live off other people*) vivre aux crochets des autres; (*travel round country*) vagabonder

bum³ (-mm-) **1** *vi Am Sl* (*beg*) vivre aux crochets des autres, vivre en parasite **2** *vt Sl* **to b. a cigarette from** *or* **off sb** taper une cigarette à qn; **to b. a ride** (*from stranger*) faire de l'auto-stop; **I managed to b. a ride from a lorry driver** je me suis fait prendre en auto-stop par un routier; **do you mind if I b. a ride to the station?** ça t'ennuierait de me déposer à la gare?

▶ **bum around** *Sl* **1** *vi* glander, glandouiller; (*travel*) vadrouiller **2** *vipo* **to b. around Europe/Paris** vadrouiller en Europe/à Paris

▶ **bum around with** *vipo Sl* traîner avec

bumble ['bʌmb(ə)l] *vi* (*be inefficient*) s'agiter et ne rien faire d'efficace

bumblebee ['bʌmb(ə)lbi:] *n* bourdon *m*

bumbler ['bʌmb(ə)lər] *n F* **an old b.** un vieux maladroit

bumbling ['bʌmb(ə)lɪŋ] *adj* **b. fool** *or* **idiot** andouille *f*

bumboat ['bʌmbəʊt] *n Naut* canot *m* d'approvisionnement

bumf [bʌmf] *n* **(a)** *F* (*useless paper*) paperasse *f* **(b)** *Sl* (*lavatory paper*) papier *m* cul

bumfreezer ['bʌmfri:zər] *n Br Sl* = veste *f* qui arrive au ras des fesses

bumhole ['bʌmhəʊl] *n Sl* trou *m* de balle

bummer ['bʌmər] *n Sl* (*something worthless*) fiasco *m*; **the film's a b.** ce film est nul; **I didn't get the job — what a b.!** je n'ai pas eu le boulot — c'est con!; **it's a real b. when you find out ...** ça en fiche un coup quand on découvre que ...

bump¹ [bʌmp] *n* **(a)** (*collision*) choc *m*, heurt *m*; (*jolt*) secousse *f*, cahot *f*; (*by boat in bumping race*) heurt; **the boat hit the jetty with a b.** le bateau a cogné contre la jetée; **to sit down with a b.** s'asseoir brusquement; *Aut* **b. steer** réversibilité *f* de direction

(b) (*lump*) (*in path, road surface etc*) bosse *f*; (*on head*) (*as result of being hit*) bosse; (*in phrenology*) protubérance *f*, *F* bosse; *Hum* **she patted her b.** (*unborn baby*) elle a tapoté son ventre; **she's had a b. on the head** elle s'est cogné la tête; *Aut* **to hit a b.** passer sur une bosse

(c) *F* **bumps and grinds** (*of stripper*) déhanchements *mpl*

(d) *Av* (*air current*) trou *m* d'air

bump² **1** *vt* **(a)** (*hit*) cogner, frapper; (*boat in front in bumping race*) heurter; **to b. one's head on** *or* **against sth** se cogner la tête contre qch **(b)** *Av F* **to be bumped (from a flight)** perdre sa place sur un vol (*pour cause de sur-réservation*) **2** *vi F* **to b. and grind** (*of stripper*) se déhancher

bump³ *adv, int* pan!, boum!; *F* **things that go b. in the night** des bruits étranges dans la nuit

▶ **bump along** *vi* (*in cart etc*) cahoter

▶ **bump into** *vipo* **(a)** (*collide with*) (*of person*) se cogner *ou* se heurter *ou* buter contre; (*of vehicle*) heurter **(b)** (*meet*) rencontrer par hasard

▶ **bump off** *vtsep F* (*kill*) supprimer, *F* faire la peau à

▶ **bump up** *vtsep F* (*prices*) gonfler (d'une façon exagérée)

bumper ['bʌmpər] **1** *n* **(a)** *Br Aut* pare-chocs *m inv*, bouclier *m*, pare-chocs bouclier; **front/rear b.** pare-chocs avant/arrière; **the cars were b. to b.** les voitures étaient pare-chocs contre pare-chocs; **b. apron** tablier *m* de pare-chocs; **b. guard** butoir *m* de pare-chocs; **b. skirt** jupe *f* de pare-chocs **(b)** (*large measure of alcoholic drink*) rasade *f* **2** *adj* **b. crop** *or* **harvest** récolte *f* magnifique *ou* exceptionnelle; **it's been a b. year for tourism** ça a été une année exceptionnelle pour le tourisme

bumpety-bump ['bʌmpɪtɪ'bʌmp] *adv F* en cahotant; **my heart went b.** mon cœur a battu à tout rompre

bumph [bʌmf] *n* = **bumf**

bumping ['bʌmpɪŋ] *n* **(a)** (*collision*) heurt(s) *m(pl)*, choc(s) *m(pl)*; (*jolting*) cahotement *m*; **b. race** course-poursuite *f*, *pl* courses-poursuites (*dans laquelle chaque bateau doit* *rattraper le précédent et de son avant en heurter l'arrière)* **(b)** *(refusing transport because of overbooking)* bumping *m*, refus *m* d'embarquer suite à sur-réservation

bumpkin ['bʌmpkɪn] *n* **(country) b.** rustre *m*, rustaud *m*

bump-start¹ *n Aut* démarrage *m* poussé; **to give sb a b.** pousser la voiture de qn pour la faire démarrer

bump-start² *vt Aut* **to b. a car** pousser une voiture pour la faire démarrer

bumptious ['bʌmpʃəs] *adj* orgueilleux, suffisant

bumpy ['bʌmpɪ] *adj* **(a)** *(road etc)* cahoteux, défoncé; **we had a b. flight** nous avons été secoués dans l'avion; *Fig* **we've got a b. road ahead of us** nous avons une période difficile devant nous; *Fig* **to give sb a b. ride** faire passer un mauvais moment à qn; **the proposals were given a b. ride** les propositions ont rencontré une vive opposition **(b)** *(forehead etc)* couvert de bosses

bun [bʌn] *n* **(a)** *Culin* petit pain *m* au lait; *Fig F* **to have a b. in the oven** avoir un polichinelle dans le tiroir; *Old-fashioned F* **b. fight** *(tea party)* réunion *f* pour le thé **(b)** *(in hair)* chignon *m*; **she wears her hair in a b.** elle se fait un chignon **(c)** *Am Sl* **buns** *(man's buttocks)* miches *fpl*; **a nice pair of buns** un beau cul, de belles miches

bunch¹ [bʌntʃ] *n* **(a)** *(of flowers)* bouquet *m*; *(of radishes, carrots etc)* botte *f*; *(of grapes)* grappe *f*; *(of herbs)* touffe *f*; *(of feathers)* houppe *f*; *(of keys)* trousseau *m*; *(of bananas)* régime *m*; **to wear one's hair in bunches** porter des couettes

(b) *(of people)* groupe *m*; *US* *(of livestock)* troupeau *m*; **he's the best** *or* **the pick of the b.** c'est lui le meilleur (de la bande); **they're quite an intelligent b.** c'est un groupe plutôt intelligent; **the b. (of people) I work with** les gens avec qui je travaille; **what a stupid b.!** ce qu'ils peuvent être bêtes!; **they seem like a pretty nice b. of people** ils ont l'air très sympa; *Sp* **the b.** le peloton; *Am F* **thanks a b.** merci beaucoup; *F* **a whole b. of stuff** *or* **things** plein de trucs, tout un tas de choses; *Br Sl* **a b. of fives** un coup de poing

bunch² *vt* *(flowers etc)* mettre en bouquet; *(radishes etc)* mettre en bottes

▶ **bunch together 1** *vi* *(of people)* se serrer **2** *vtsep* *(books etc on shelf)* serrer; **to be bunched together** *(of runners, horses etc)* être serrés

▶ **bunch up 1** *vt* **(a)** *(dress)* retrousser **(b)** *(books etc on shelf)* serrer; **to be bunched up** *(of runners, horses etc)* être serrés **2** *vi* *(of material)* se retrousser

bundle¹ ['bʌnd(ə)l] *n* tas *m*; *(secured, fastened in some way)* *(of washing etc)* paquet *m*, ballot *m*; *(of goods)* ballot; *(of asparagus etc)* botte *f*; *(of canes, wires etc)* faisceau *m*; *(of banknotes, papers)* liasse *f*; *(of wood)* fagot *m*; *Am F* **to make a b.** *(lot of money)* faire son beurre; *Am F* **thanks a b.** merci beaucoup; *Am F* **to go a b. on sth/sb** *(like)* être fou de qch/qn; *F* **she's a b. of nerves** c'est un paquet de nerfs; *F* **my driving test wasn't exactly a b. of fun** passer mon permis de conduire n'a pas vraiment été une partie de plaisir; *Hum* **they came with their b. of joy** *(new baby)* ils sont venus avec leur bambin

bundle² *vt* **(a)** *(make bundle of)* faire un paquet de; *(documents)* mettre en liasses; *(straw)* mettre en bottes; **she bundled the baby in a blanket** elle a enveloppé le bébé dans une couverture; *Mktg, Com* **to b. sth with sth** offrir qch en plus de qch; *Mktg, Com* **to come bundled with sth** être livré avec qch **(b)** *(put, lead hastily)* **to b. papers into a drawer** fourrer des papiers dans un tiroir; **to b. sb into a car** embarquer qn dans une voiture; **he bundled me down the stairs** il m'a fait descendre les escaliers en toute hâte

▶ **bundle off** *vtsep* **(a)** *(send hastily)* envoyer à la hâte *ou* sans attendre; **the baby was bundled off to hospital** le bébé a été envoyé à l'hôpital sans attendre; **they bundled me off the train** ils m'ont fait descendre du train en toute hâte **(b)** *Pej* *(get rid of)* se débarrasser de (sans cérémonie); **his father bundled him off to boarding school** son père l'a expédié en pension

▶ **bundle out** *vtsep* faire sortir sans cérémonie *ou* ménagement

▶ **bundle up 1** *vtsep* **(a)** *(make parcel of)* = **bundle²** *(a)* **(b)** *(collect)* *(one's things etc)* rassembler **2** *vi* *(wear warm clothes)* s'emmitoufler

bundling selling ['bʌndlɪŋ] *n* vente *f* par lots

bung¹ [bʌŋ] *n* **(a)** *(for cask)* bonde *f*, bondon *m* **(b)** *Br Sl* *(money given)* bakchich *m*

bung² *vt* **(a)** *(opening)* boucher **(b)** *Br F* *(put)* mettre, fourrer; **b. it in a drawer** fourre-le dans un tiroir; **b. it over** *(throw it)* balance-le; **I bunged him a tenner** je lui ai filé un billet de dix livres; **they bunged him in prison** ils l'ont jeté en prison

▶ **bung up** *vtsep F* *(block)* *(drain)* boucher; **I'm** *or* **my nose is all bunged up** j'ai le nez complètement bouché

bungalow ['bʌŋgələʊ] *n* pavillon *m*; *(in India)* bungalow *m*

bungee ['bʌndʒiː] *n* **b. (cord)** tendeur *m*; **b. jump/jumping** saut *m* à l'élastique

bunghole ['bʌŋhəʊl] *n* *(in cask)* bonde *f*

bungle¹ ['bʌŋg(ə)l] *n* gâchis *m*, ratage *m*, *F* bousillage *m*; **to make a b. of sth** gâcher *ou F* cochonner *ou F* saloper qch

bungle² **1** *vt* *(piece of work)* gâcher, *F* cochonner, *F* saloper; *(hold-up, operation, escape attempt)* rater **2** *vi* s'y prendre maladroitement; **someone has bungled** quelqu'un a fait une bourde

bungler ['bʌŋglər] *n* incapable *mf*, bon *m* à rien, bonne *f* à rien

bungling ['bʌŋglɪŋ] **1** *adj* **b. idiot** incapable *mf*, bon *m* à rien, bonne *f* à rien **2** *n* gâchis *m*, *F* bousillage *m*; **your b. has cost us the contract** tes bourdes nous ont fait perdre le contrat

bunion ['bʌnjən] *n Med* oignon *m*

bunk¹ [bʌŋk] *n* **(a)** *Naut, Rail etc* couchette *f*; **b. beds** lits *mpl* superposés **(b)** *Old-fashioned F* *(sleeping place)* logement *m*; **I can give you a b. for the night** je peux te loger pour la nuit

bunk² *vi Naut* coucher **(forward** à l'avant)

bunk³ *n Br F* **to do a b.** déguerpir, décamper

bunk⁴ *n Old-fashioned F* *(nonsense)* bêtises *fpl*

▶ **bunk down** *vi F* **(a)** *(go to bed)* aller se coucher **(b)** *(sleep)* passer la nuit **(with friends** chez des amis)

▶ **bunk off 1** *vi F* **(a)** *(leave without permission)* *(from work)* partir avant l'heure sans en avoir l'autorisation; *(from school)* faire l'école buissonnière **(b)** *(leave hurriedly)* filer **2** *vipo* **to b. off school** faire l'école buissonnière

bunker¹ ['bʌŋkər] *n* **(a)** *(in home)* *(for coal)* coffre *m* à charbon; *Naut* *(for coal, oil etc)* soute *f*; *(for oil)* réservoir *m*; *Com* **b. adjustment factor** ajustement *m* fret **(b)** *Golf* banquette *f*, bunker *m* **(c)** *Mil* blockhaus *m*; **nuclear b.** abri *m* antiatomique

bunker² **1** *vt* **(a)** *Naut* *(fuel)* mettre en soute **(b)** *Golf* **to be bunkered** se trouver dans le sable **2** *vi Naut* se ravitailler en charbon

bunkhouse ['bʌŋkhaʊs] *n Am* *(for lumberjacks etc)* baraquement *m* pourvu de couchettes

bunkum ['bʌnkəm] *n F* foutaise(s) *f(pl)*, âneries *fpl*

bunny ['bʌnɪ] *n F* **(a)** *(in children's language)* **b. (rabbit)** Jeannot lapin *m*, petit lapin **(b)** **b. (girl)** = employée *f* de boîte de nuit Playboy (habillée en lapin)

Bunsen ['bʌns(ə)n] *n Ch etc* **B. burner** bec *m* Bunsen

bunting¹ ['bʌntɪŋ] *n* *(bird)* bruant *m*

bunting² *n* *(flags)* drapeaux *mpl*, fanions *mpl*; **decorated with b.** pavoisé

buoy¹ [bɔɪ] *n Naut* bouée *f*

buoy² *vt Naut* *(channel)* baliser; *(wreck)* marquer

▶ **buoy up** *vtsep Naut* *(object)* faire flotter; *Fig* *(person, currency)* soutenir, maintenir; *Fig* **buoyed up with new hope** animé *ou* soutenu par un nouvel espoir

buoyancy ['bɔɪənsɪ] *n* **(a)** *Naut, Av etc* *(of object)* flottabilité *f*; **centre of b.** centre *m* de poussée; **b. bag/tank** ballonnet *m*/réservoir *m* de flottabilité **(b)** *Fig* entrain *m*, allant *m*; *St Exch* dynamisme *m*; *Com* *(of market)* fermeté *f*; *(of prices, currency)* stabilité *f*; **she has great b.** elle a un ressort incroyable

buoyant ['bɔɪənt] *adj* **(a)** *Naut, Av etc* qui flotte; **salt water is more b. than fresh** l'eau salée porte mieux que l'eau douce **(b)** *Fig* *(person)* qui a du ressort; *Com* *(market)* soutenu, ferme; *(prices)* stable; **to be in a b. mood** être plein d'entrain; **a b. step** un pas élastique

buoyantly ['bɔɪəntlɪ] *adv* avec entrain

BUPA ['buːpə] *n* *(abbr* **British United Provident Association)** = service *m* de santé privé

bur [bɜːr] *n* = **burr¹ (a)**

Burberry® ['bɜːbərɪ] *n* **(a)** *(raincoat)* imperméable *m* (de la marque Burberry, Burberry *m* **(b)** *(garment)* vêtement *m* de la marque Burberry

burble ['bɜːb(ə)l] *vi* *(of stream)* murmurer; *Fig* *(of baby)* gazouiller; *(of person)* murmurer (des sons inarticulés); *F Pej* *(talk nonsense)* débiter des inepties

▶ **burble away, burble on** *vi F Pej* débiter des inepties

burbot ['bɜːbət] *n* *(fish)* lotte *f*, barbot *m*, barbot(t)e *f*

burden¹ ['bɜːd(ə)n] *n* **(a)** fardeau *m*, charge *f*; **b. of taxation** poids *m* de la fiscalité *ou* des impôts; *Jur* **b. of proof** charge de la preuve; **the b. of proof rests with him** c'est à lui qu'il incombe d'apporter des preuves; **I'm a b. to you** je suis un fardeau pour toi; **to make sb's life a b.** rendre la vie dure à qn **(b)** *Fml* *(theme, gist)* *(of speech, complaint, argument)* substance *f*; *Old-fashioned* *(of song)* refrain *m* **(c)** *Naut* *(of ship)* charge *f*, contenance *f*

burden² *vt* accabler **(sb with sth** qn de qch); **to b. one's memory with useless facts** se charger *ou* s'encombrer la mémoire de faits inutiles; **I'm sorry to b. you with my worries** je suis désolé de vous accabler avec mes soucis; **a**

donkey burdened with wood un âne chargé d'un fardeau de bois; **she is burdened with a retarded child** elle a un enfant handicapé à sa charge
burdensome ['bɜːd(ə)nsəm] *adj Fml* lourd
burdock ['bɜːdɒk] *n (weed)* bardane *f*, glouteron *m*
bureaucracy [bjʊə'rɒkrəsɪ] *n Pej* bureaucratie *f*
bureaucrat ['bjʊərəkræt] *n Pej* bureaucrate *m*
bureaucratic [bjʊərə'krætɪk] *adj Pej* bureaucratique
bureau, *pl* **-eaux** ['bjʊərəʊ, -əʊz] *n* **(a)** *(furniture)* bureau *m*; *(with roll top)* secrétaire *m*; *US (chest of drawers)* commode *f* **(b)** *US (government department)* bureau *m*, service *m*
burette, *US* **buret** [bjʊ'ret] *n Ch* burette *f*, éprouvette *f* graduée
burg [bɜːg] *n Am F (village)* bled *m*; *(town)* ville *f*; **there's nothing happening in this b.** il ne se passe rien dans ce coin *ou* bled
burgeon ['bɜːdʒən] *vi Lit* fleurir
burgeoning ['bɜːdʒənɪŋ] *adj Lit, Fml (industry, population etc)* en expansion; **a b. talent** un talent en herbe; **the b. movement for independence** le mouvement naissant pour l'indépendance
burger ['bɜːgər] *n F* hamburger *m*
burgess ['bɜːdʒɪs] *n* **(a)** *Hist (in England)* citoyen *m* **(b)** *Eng Hist (MP)* député *m (représentant une ville)* **(c)** *US* = conseiller *m* municipal
burgher ['bɜːgər] *n Arch, Hum (citizen)* citoyen *m*
burglar ['bɜːglər] *n* cambrioleur *m*; **b. alarm** alarme *f* anti-vol; **b. proof** inviolable
burglarize ['bɜːgləraɪz] *vt Am* cambrioler
burglary ['bɜːglərɪ] *n* cambriolage *m*; *(breaking and entering)* vol *m* avec effraction
burgle ['bɜːg(ə)l] *vt* cambrioler; **it's the third time they've been burgled** c'est la troisième fois qu'ils se sont faits cambrioler
Burgundian [bɜː'gʌndɪən] **1** *adj* bourguignon **2** *n* Bourguignon, -onne
Burgundy ['bɜːgəndɪ] *n* **(a)** *Geog* Bourgogne *f* **(b)** *(wine)* bourgogne *m*, vin *m* de Bourgogne **(c)** *(colour)* bordeaux *m*
burial ['berɪəl] *n* enterrement *m*, inhumation *f*; *Fig* **the b. of sb's hopes** la fin des espoirs de qn; **b. ground** cimetière *m*; **b. mound** tumulus *m*; **b. place** (lieu *m* de) sépulture *f*; *(for radioactive substances)* dépôt *m* souterrain; **b. service** office *m* des morts
burin ['bjʊərɪn] *n (for engraving)* burin *m*
burk [bɜːk] *n Br Sl* **you (great) b.!** espèce d'idiot!
burlap ['bɜːlæp] *n Tex* toile *f* d'emballage
burlesque¹ [bɜː'lesk] **1** *adj* burlesque **2** *n* **(a)** *(satire)* burlesque *m*; *(caricature)* parodie *f* **(b)** *US Th* revue *f* vulgaire
burlesque² *vt* parodier, tourner en ridicule
burliness ['bɜːlɪnɪs] *n* **(a)** *(person's build)* forte *ou* solide charpente *f* **(b)** *Am (brusqueness)* brusquerie *f*
burly ['bɜːlɪ] *adj* **(a)** *(well built)* bien bâti, *F* costaud **(b)** *Am (brusque)* brusque, bourru
Burma ['bɜːmə] *n* Birmanie *f*
Burmese [bɜː'miːz] **1** *adj* birman; **B. cat** chat *m* birman ganté **2** *n* **(a)** Birman, -ane **(b)** *Ling* birman *m*
burn¹ [bɜːn] *n* **(a)** *Med etc* brûlure *f*; **the child suffered severe burns** l'enfant a subi de graves brûlures **(b)** *Astronaut* allumage *m*; *(of rocket)* poussée *f*; *Fig F* **I was doing a slow b.** la moutarde me montait au nez
burn² *(pt, pp* **burnt** [bɜːnt], *occ* **burned) 1** *vt* **(a)** *(sth, sb)* brûler; **to b. coal/oil/gas** *(of boiler)* marcher au charbon/au mazout/au gaz; *Fig* **to b. one's boats** *or* **one's bridges** brûler ses vaisseaux; **to b. sth to ashes** réduire qch en cendres; **to b. sth to a cinder** *or* **a crisp** carboniser qch; *Old-fashioned F* **to be burnt** *(of police informer)* être grillé; **to be burnt alive, to be burnt to death** être brûlé vif; **the house was burned to the ground** la maison a été complètement brûlée; **to b. one's fingers** se brûler les doigts; *Fig* **he got his fingers burnt, he burnt his fingers over it** il s'est fait échauder (dans cette affaire); **to b. a hole in sth with a cigarette/the iron** faire un trou dans qch avec une cigarette/le fer à repasser; *Fig* **money burns a hole in his pocket** l'argent lui brûle les doigts; *Fig* **to have money to b.** avoir de l'argent à ne plus savoir quoi en faire; **acids b. into metal** les acides rongent le métal; **mustard burns the tongue** la moutarde pique *ou* brûle la langue; **I burned my tongue** je me suis brûlé la langue
(b) *Ind (bricks, charcoal)* cuire; *(rubber)* vulcaniser, cuire
2 *vi* **(a)** *(of house, forest, fire, wood)* brûler; *Culin (of meat, toast etc)* brûler; *(of sauce, milk etc)* attacher; *(of wound, eyes)* brûler, piquer; **the smell of burning rubber** l'odeur de caoutchouc brûlé; **to b. low** *(of fire)* baisser; *Fig* **to b. with** *(impatience, passion, desire)* brûler de; *(anger, hatred)* bouillonner de; **his cheeks were burning with shame** il avait les joues rouges de honte
(b) *(of mixture in engine)* exploser
burn³ *n Scot (stream)* ruisseau *m*
▶ **burn down 1** *vtsep (town, house etc)* brûler, incendier **2** *vi* **(a)** *(of building etc)* être détruit par le feu *ou* par un incendie **(b)** *(of fire)* baisser
▶ **burn in** *vtsep Comptr* roder
▶ **burn off** *vtsep* **(a)** *(remove by burning) (bracken, gas)* brûler; *(paint)* décaper au chalumeau; *(rust etc)* enlever au feu **(b)** *(consume, use up) (calories)* brûler; **to b. off some energy** se dépenser
▶ **burn out 1** *vtsep Aut etc (brake linings or pads)* brûler; *El (coil)* brûler, court-circuiter; *(lamp)* griller; **the house was burnt out** le feu a complètement détruit l'intérieur de la maison; **to b. itself out** *(of fire)* s'éteindre; *Fig* **it'll b. itself out** *(of love affair)* une passion comme ça ne dure pas; *Fig* **to b. oneself out** s'épuiser (par excès de travail), se vider **2** *vi (of fire, oil lamp)* s'éteindre; *(of candle)* s'éteindre, brûler jusqu'au bout; *(of light bulb)* griller
▶ **burn up 1** *vtsep* **(a)** *(consume)* brûler (entièrement), consumer; **to b. up energy** se dépenser; *F* **to b. up the miles** *or* **the motorway** avaler les kilomètres **(b)** *(of sun) (leaves etc)* griller, flétrir; *F (make angry)* mettre en pétard **2** *vi* **(a)** *F (get angry)* se mettre en pétard; **to b. up inside** bouillir intérieurement **(b)** *(of rocket)* brûler, se consumer; *(of person with high temperature)* être brûlant; **the pavement was burning up** le trottoir était brûlant
burner ['bɜːnər] *n (on stove)* brûleur *m*, feu *m*; *(in gas or acetylene lamp)* bec *m*
burn-in *n Comptr (of machine)* rodage *m*
burning ['bɜːnɪŋ] **1** *adj (fever, thirst, desire etc)* brûlant, ardent; *(coal)* embrasé, allumé, ardent; *(town, house)* incendié, enflammé, en feu; *(heat)* brûlant, torride; *(sun, Fig question)* brûlant; *F* **I'm b. (hot)** je crève de chaleur; **b. bush** *Bible* buisson *m* ardent; *(shrub)* fraxinelle *f* **2** *n (of house etc)* incendie *m*; *Ch* combustion *f*; *Hist* **b. (at the stake)** supplice *m* du bûcher; **there's a smell of b.** ça sent le brûlé; **b. sensation** *(heat)* sensation *f* de chaleur (excessive); *(discomfort)* sensation de brûlure; *(pain)* douleur *f* cuisante
burnish¹ ['bɜːnɪʃ] *n (on metal)* bruni *m*, poli *m*
burnish² *vt (metal)* brunir, polir; *Phot (print)* satiner; *Lit* **her hair was like burnished gold** elle avait les cheveux d'un or cuivré
burnisher ['bɜːnɪʃər] *n Metal* **(a)** *(person)* brunisseur, -euse **(b)** *(instrument)* brunissoir *m*, polissoir *m*
burnishing ['bɜːnɪʃɪŋ] *n* brunissage *m*, polissage *m*
burnous(e) [bɜː'nuːs] *n* burnous *m*
burnout ['bɜːnaʊt] *n Fig* saturation *f*, épuisement *m*
burnt [bɜːnt] *adj* **(a)** *(person, object)* brûlé; *(smell, taste)* de brûlé, de roussi; **to be b. beyond recognition** être carbonisé; *Prov* **a b. child dreads** *or* **fears the fire** chat échaudé craint l'eau froide; *Culin* **b. almonds** amandes *fpl* grillées; **b. sugar** caramel *m* **(b)** *(earth, clay)* cuit
burnt offering *n Rel* holocauste *m*; *Hum (meat)* viande *f* brûlée *ou* calcinée; *(dish)* plat *m* brûlé
burnt out *adj (volcano)* éteint; *(house, car etc)* carbonisé; *MecE (bearings)* grippé; *El (coil, light bulb)* grillé; *Fig* **b. case** homme *m*/femme *f* qui est au bout du rouleau
burp¹ [bɜːp] *n* éructation *f*, *F* rot *m*
burp² **1** *vi* éructer, *F* roter **2** *vt (baby)* faire roter
burr¹ [bɜːr] *n* **(a)** *Bot (of burdock etc)* teigne *f*; *Fig* **to stick to sb like a b.** se cramponner *ou* s'accrocher à qn **(b)** *(on metal)* bavure *f*, barbe *f*; **to take the burrs off metal** ébarber le métal **(c) b. walnut** ronce *f* de noyer
burr² *n* **(a)** *Ling* grasseyement *m*; **to speak with a b.** grasseyer **(b)** *(of machine)* ronflement *m*
burr³ **1** *vt* **to b. one's r's** grasseyer **2** *vi (of machine etc)* ronfler
burro ['bʊrəʊ] *n US* âne *m*
burrow¹ ['bʌrəʊ] *n* terrier *m*
burrow² **1** *vi (dig) (of rabbit, dog etc)* creuser (la terre); *Fig* **to b. into the archives** fouiller dans les archives; **to b. in one's pocket/bag** fourrager dans sa poche/son sac **2** *vt (hole)* creuser; **to b. one's way underground** creuser (un chemin) sous terre; **to b. the ground** *(of rabbits)* creuser *ou* fouir la terre
burrowing ['bʌrəʊɪŋ] *adj (animal)* fouisseur; *(insect)* fossoyeur, mineur
bursar ['bɜːsər] *n Sch (official in charge of finance)* économe *mf*, intendant, -ante
bursary ['bɜːsərɪ] *n* **(a)** *(office)* économat *m*, intendance *f* **(b)** *esp Scot (grant)* bourse *f* (d'études); **b. student** boursier, -ière
bursitis [bɜː'saɪtɪs] *n Med* bursite *f*; **I have b. in my shoulder** j'ai une bursite à l'épaule

burst¹ [bɜːst] *n* **(a)** (*of bomb, boiler etc*) éclatement *m*, explosion *f* **(b)** (*of flame*) jaillissement *m*, jet *m*; (*of gunfire, machine gun*) rafale *f*; (*of laughter*) éclat *m*; (*of anger*) explosion *f*; (*of eloquence*) élan *m*; (*of applause*) salve *f*; (*of activity*) poussée *f*; (*of enthusiasm*) accès *m*; *Sp* **b. of speed** accélération *f*; **to put on a b. of speed** faire une accélération; *Sp* **final b.** sprint *m*; **b. advertising** matraquage *m* publicitaire; *Comptr* **b. mode** mode *m* continu

burst² (*pt, pp* **burst**) **1** *vi* (*of boiler, bomb etc*) éclater, exploser; (*of dam*) éclater, céder; (*of abscess, blister*) crever, percer; (*of bubble*) crever; (*of storm, paper bag*) éclater; *Hum* **he'll b. if he eats any more** il va éclater s'il mange davantage; *F* **to be bursting (for the toilet)** avoir terriblement envie d'aller aux toilettes; **we've got a burst pipe** (*in house*) nous avons un tuyau qui a éclaté; *Fig* **her heart was ready to b.** (*with sorrow*) elle avait le cœur brisé; (*with happiness*) elle débordait de joie; **to be bursting at the seams** (*of dress etc*) se découdre; *Fig* (*of building etc*) être plein à craquer; **to be bursting with pride** crever d'orgueil; **to be bursting with health** déborder de santé; **to be bursting with impatience** bouillir d'impatience; **I was bursting to tell him so** je mourais d'envie de le lui dire; **a cry burst from his lips** un cri s'échappa de ses lèvres; *Lit* **to b. upon sb's sight** se présenter aux yeux de qn; *Lit* **to b. upon sb's ears** (*of sound*) parvenir brusquement aux oreilles de qn

2 *vt* (*balloon, tyre, paper bag*) faire éclater; (*boiler*) faire éclater *ou* exploser; *Lit* (*one's bonds*) rompre; **to b. a blood vessel** se rompre un vaisseau sanguin; *Fig* **he nearly b. a blood vessel when I told him** il a failli attraper un coup de sang quand je le lui ai dit; **to b. its banks** (*of river*) sortir de son lit

▶ **burst in 1** *vtsep* (*door*) enfoncer **2** *vi* (*of person*) faire irruption, entrer en trombe; **to b. in on sb** faire irruption chez qn/dans le bureau de qn; **to b. in on a conversation** interrompre brusquement une conversation

▶ **burst into** *vipo* **(a)** (*enter noisily*) **to b. into a room** faire irruption dans une pièce **(b)** (*suddenly start*) **to b. into flame(s)** s'enflammer brusquement; **to b. into song** entonner une chanson; **to b. into blossom** (*of tree*) commencer à fleurir; **to b. into laughter/tears** éclater de rire/fondre en larmes

▶ **burst open 1** *vtsep* (*door*) (*open suddenly*) ouvrir brusquement; (*smash open*) enfoncer, briser; (*cover, lock*) faire sauter **2** *vi* (*of door*) s'ouvrir brusquement

▶ **burst out 1** *vt* (*say suddenly*) s'écrier; **to b. out laughing/crying** éclater de rire/fondre en larmes **2** *vi* (*leave noisily*) **to b. out of a room** sortir précipitamment d'une pièce

▶ **burst through** *vipo* (*police cordon*) enfoncer; **to come bursting through the door** (*open it suddenly*) entrer précipitamment; (*smash it*) enfoncer la porte; **the sun burst through the clouds** le soleil creva les nuages

bursting [ˈbɜːstɪŋ] *n* (*of bomb, tyre etc*) éclatement *m*, explosion *f*; (*of dam*) rupture *f*

burton [ˈbɜːt(ə)n] *n Br Sl* **to have gone for a b.** (*be dead*) être mort; (*of hopes, plans etc*) être tombé à l'eau; (*be broken*) (*of plate etc*) être cassé; (*of iron, television etc*) être foutu; (*be lost*) (*of ball etc*) être perdu pour de bon; **there's another plate gone for a b.!** voilà une autre assiette de cassée!

bury [ˈberɪ] *vt* (*pt, pp* **buried**) **(a)** (*body*) enterrer, inhumer, ensevelir; (*at sea*) immerger; (*object*) enterrer, enfouir; **to b. sb alive** enterrer qn vivant; **to b. itself** (*of animal*) se terrer, s'enfouir; **buried treasure** trésor *m* enterré *ou* enfoui; *El* **buried cable** câble *m* souterrain

(b) (*of snow, landslide*) (*town, house*) ensevelir; **I found the letter buried under my papers** j'ai trouvé la lettre enfouie sous mes papiers; **to b. oneself in the country** s'enterrer à la campagne; **to b. oneself in one's work** se plonger *ou* s'absorber dans son travail; **to b. one's face in one's hands** se cacher la figure dans les mains; *Fig* **to b. one's head in the sand** pratiquer la politique de l'autruche; **she always has her head buried in a book** elle est toujours plongée dans un livre; **to be buried in thought** être absorbé dans ses pensées

burying [ˈberɪɪŋ] *adj* (*insect*) **b. beetle** nécrophore *m*

bus¹, *pl* **buses**, *US* **busses** [bʌs, ˈbʌsɪz] *n* **(a)** bus *m*, autobus *m*; (*on long-distance services*) car *m*; **by b.** en bus; **to miss the b.** manquer *ou* rater le bus; *Fig F* manquer le coche; *F* **old b.** (*car*) vieille bagnole *f*; (*aircraft*) coucou *m*; **b. advertising** publicité *f* sur/dans les autobus; **have you got enough money for your b. fare?** est-ce que tu as assez d'argent pour le bus?; **b. route/stop/ticket** trajet *m*/arrêt *m*/ticket *m* de bus; **are you on a b. route?** est-ce qu'il y a un bus qui passe près de chez toi? **(b)** *Comptr, Electron* bus *m*; **b. controller** contrôleur *m* de bus; *Comptr* **b. structure** structure *f* de bus

bus² **1** *vi* voyager en autobus **2** *vt* (*sb, sth*) transporter en autobus/en car; **the children are bus(s)ed to school** les enfants sont emmenés à l'école en autobus; **are you bus(s)ing it?** tu y vas en autobus?

busbar [ˈbʌzbɑːr] *n Electron* bus *m*

bus board *n Comptr* carte *f* bus

bus boy *n Am* aide-serveur *m*, *pl* aides-serveurs

busby [ˈbʌzbɪ] *n Mil* bonnet *m* de hussard

bus conductor *n* receveur *m* d'autobus

bus conductress *n* receveuse *f* d'autobus

bus depot *n* dépôt *m* d'autobus; (*long-distance bus station*) gare *f* routière

bus driver *n* conducteur, -trice d'autobus, chauffeur *m* de bus; (*long distance*) chauffeur de car

bush¹ [bʊʃ] *n* **(a)** buisson *m*; **a great b. of red hair** une grosse tignasse rousse **(b)** (*in Africa, Austr*) **the b.** la brousse; **to take to the b.**, *Austr* **to go b.** prendre la brousse; **b. hat** chapeau *m* de brousse; *Av* **b. pilot** pilote *m* de ligne opérant dans une région peu habitée *ou* dans la brousse *ou Can* dans le Grand Nord; **b. shirt, b. jacket** = saharienne *f*

bush² *n MecE* bague *f*, douille *f*, manchon *m*; (*between bearing and shaft*) coussinet *m*

bush³ *vt MecE* baguer, manchonner; (*bearing*) mettre un coussinet à

bushbaby [ˈbʊʃbeɪbɪ] *n* galago *m*

bushed [bʊʃt] *adj F* **(a)** (*exhausted*) fatigué, éreinté **(b)** *Can* (*confused*) rendu déséquilibré par un isolement prolongé **(c)** *Austr* (*lost*) perdu *ou* égaré dans la brousse; *Fig* (*bewildered*) désorienté

bushel [ˈbʊʃəl] *n* **(a)** (*unit of measurement*) boisseau *m* (= approx 36 litres); *Fig* **to hide one's light under a b.** cacher son talent **(b)** *US F* (*great amount*) grande quantité *f*

bushfire [ˈbʊʃfaɪər] *n* feu *m* de brousse

bushing¹ [ˈbʊʃɪŋ] *n MecE* (*sleeve*) bague *f*, bague *f* de culbuteur; (*between bearing and shaft*) coussinet *m*

Bushman, *pl* **-men** [ˈbʊʃmən] (*in S. Africa*) **1** *adj* boschiman **2** *n* **(a)** Boschiman, -ane **(b)** *Ling* boschiman *m*

bushman, *pl* **-men** [ˈbʊʃmən] *n* broussard *m* (*en Australie*)

bush telegraph *n F* téléphone *m* arabe

bushwhacker [ˈbʊʃwækər] *n* **(a)** *Am* = personne *f* qui vit dans des régions boisées et reculées; *Austr* broussard *m* **(b)** *Am* (*guerrilla*) guérillero *m*

bushy [ˈbʊʃɪ] *adj* **(a)** (*country, eyebrows*) broussailleux; (*beard*) fourni; (*hair*) touffu, embroussaillé **(b)** (*shrub*) épais, touffu

busily [ˈbɪzɪlɪ] *adv* (*to prepare*) activement; (*to search*) d'un air affairé

business [ˈbɪznɪs] *n* **(a)** (*affair, matter*) affaire *f*; **it's a bad** *or* **sad** *or* **sorry b.** c'est une bien triste affaire; **it's a bad** *or* **sad** *or* **sorry b. when you can't trust your own brother** c'est triste quand on ne peut même pas faire confiance à son propre frère; **I'm sick of the whole b.** j'en ai assez de toute cette affaire; **it's quite a b. finding a plumber** ce n'est pas une petite affaire que de trouver un plombier; **it was a real b. persuading him to come** j'ai/nous avons/*etc* eu beaucoup de mal à le persuader de venir; **what's your b. (with him)?** que (lui) voulez-vous?; **it's/it's not my b. to ...** c'est/ce n'est pas à moi de ...; **it's not your b., it's none of your b.** cela ne vous regarde pas, ce n'est pas votre affaire; **you have no b. (being) in here** vous n'avez rien à faire ici; **you had no b. telling her** ce n'était pas à toi de le lui dire; **what b. is it of yours where she spent the night?** qu'est-ce que ça peut te faire où elle a passé la nuit?; **mind your own b.** occupez-vous de ce qui vous regarde *ou* de vos affaires; **I mind my own b.** je m'occupe de mes affaires; **I was just walking along, minding my own b., when ...** je marchais tranquillement dans la rue quand ...; **to go about one's b.** vaquer à ses occupations; *esp Fml* **I sent him about his b.** (*sent him away*) je l'ai envoyé promener; **to make it one's b. to do sth** prendre sur soi de faire qch; **... or I'll make it my b.** ... ou je vais m'en occuper personnellement; **let's get down to b.!** au travail!; **can we get down to b.?** est-ce qu'on peut commencer?, est-ce qu'on peut se mettre au travail?; **we got through a lot of b.** nous avons abattu de la besogne; **to mean b.** être sérieux; **the b. before a meeting** l'ordre *m* du jour; **(any) other b.** (*on agenda*) questions *fpl* diverses; **can we turn to the b. of who's going to be responsible?** est-ce que nous pouvons discuter de la question de qui sera responsable?; *F* **she can sing like nobody's b.** (*does it very well*) elle chante très bien; *F* **they're working like nobody's b.** (*very hard*) ils travaillent très dur; *Euph* **has the dog done its b.?** est-ce que le chien a fait ses besoins?

(b) (*dealings*) affaires *fpl*; (*commerce*) commerce *m*; **somebody in the antiques/restaurant b.** quelqu'un qui est dans les antiquités/la restauration; **to go into** *or* **to set up in b. as a grocer** s'établir épicier, ouvrir une épicerie; **to be in/**

go into b. on one's own *or* **for oneself** être/s'établir *ou* s'installer à son compte; **she's in b.** elle est dans les affaires; **the shop has been in b. for twenty years** le magasin existe depuis vingt ans; **they've been in b. together for twenty years** ils sont associés depuis vingt ans; *Fig* **now we're in b.** maintenant nous pouvons y aller; *Fig* **it looks as if we're back in b.** on dirait que les choses reprennent pour nous; **to go out of b.** fermer; **supermarkets have put many small shops out of b.** les supermarchés ont obligé beaucoup de petits magasins à fermer; **I've got some b. to discuss with him** il faut que je discute affaires avec lui; **they've put a lot of b. our way** ils nous ont donné beaucoup de travail; **to go to London on b.** aller à Londres pour affaires; **a profitable piece of b.** une affaire rentable *ou* qui rapporte; **to lose b.** perdre de la clientèle; **to do b. with sb** faire des affaires avec qn; **shop that does good b.** commerce qui marche bien; **it's good/bad for b.** c'est bon/mauvais pour les affaires; **how's b.?** comment vont les affaires?; **b. is b.** les affaires sont les affaires; **b. as usual** (*sign*) ouvert; **it's b. as usual in the town despite the floods** la vie continue dans la ville malgré les inondations; **this shop will be open for b. from tomorrow** ce magasin ouvrira demain; **hours of b.** (*sign*) heures d'ouverture; **to mix b. with pleasure** joindre l'utile à l'agréable; **you shouldn't mix b. with pleasure** il ne faut pas mélanger le travail et les loisirs; **b. before pleasure** le travail avant tout; **b. is slow** les affaires ne vont pas; **she has a good head for b.** elle a le sens des affaires; **to talk b.** parler affaires; **the tourist trade is big b.** le tourisme est une industrie qui rapporte beaucoup d'argent; **looking for b.?** (*said by prostitute*) tu viens, chéri?; **b. administration** gestion *f* commerciale; **b. assignment** mission *f* commerciale; **b. associate** associé, -ée; **b. buyer** acheteur *m* industriel; **b. career** carrière *f* dans les affaires; **b. centre** centre *m* d'affaires; **b. computer** ordinateur *m* de bureau; **b. concern** exploitation *f* commerciale; **b. cycle** cycle *m* économique, temps *m* de cycle; *F* **b. end** (*of knife, hatchet*) côté *m ou* extrémité *f* coupant(e) *ou* tranchant(e); (*of gun*) canon *m*; **b. enterprise** entreprise *f* commerciale; **b. environment** environnement *m* commercial; **b. ethics** déontologie *f* professionnelle; **b. expansion** extension *f* du commerce; **b. expenses** frais *mpl* professionnels; **b. experience: with b. experience** rompu aux affaires; **b. failure** défaillance *f* d'entreprise; **b. fare** tarif *m* affaires; **b. gift** cadeau *m* promotionnel; **b. hotel** hôtel *m* d'affaires; **b. house agency** (*travel agency*) agence *f* spécialisée dans le tourisme d'affaires; **b. management** gestion *f* d'entreprise *ou* des sociétés, direction *f* des entreprises; (*study*) économie *f* d'entreprise; **b. market** marché *m* industriel *ou* des entreprises; **b. meeting** rendez-vous *m* d'affaires; *Mktg* **b. mission** mission *f* d'activité *ou* de l'entreprise; *Journ, Rad, TV* **b. news** chronique *f* économique; **b. portfolio** portefeuille *m* d'activités; **b. premises** locaux *mpl* commerciaux; **b. relations** relations *fpl* d'affaires, relations commerciales; *Econ* **b. sector** secteur *m* tertiaire, secteur d'affaires; **b. services** services *mpl* du secteur tertiaire, services aux entreprises; **b. strategy** stratégie *f* d'entreprise; *Comptr* **b. systems** logiciels *mpl* de bureautique; **b. tourism** tourisme *m* d'affaires; **b. trend** courant *m* d'affaires

(**c**) (*company, firm*) affaire *f*, entreprise *f*; (*shop*) commerce *m*; **to run a b.** gérer une entreprise; **to carry on a b.** avoir une affaire/un commerce; **b. for sale** commerce à vendre; **a farm is a b. like any other** une ferme est une entreprise comme les autres

(**d**) (*trade*) métier *m*; **what's his line of b.?, what b. is he in?** qu'est-ce qu'il fait (comme métier)?; **I'm not in this b. for the good of my health** je ne fais pas ce métier pour le plaisir; **I'm not in the b. of solving your problems** ce n'est pas à moi de résoudre tes problèmes; **the best in the b.** le meilleur de tous

(**e**) *Th* jeux *mpl* de scène

business account *n Fin* compte *m* professionnel

business address *n* (*of firm*) adresse *f* commerciale; **write to me at my b.** écrivez-moi à mon travail

business card *n* carte *f* (de visite)

business class *n* (*in aircraft*) classe *f* affaires; **to travel b.** voyager en classe affaires

business correspondent *n Rad, TV* correspondant *m* financier

business hours *npl* (*of shop*) heures *fpl* d'ouverture; (*of employee*) heures de travail

business letter *n* lettre *f* commerciale

businesslike [ˈbɪznɪslaɪk] *adj* (*person, manner*) sérieux; (*attitude, appearance*) professionnel; (*transaction*) régulier, sérieux

business lunch *n* déjeuner *m* d'affaires

businessman, *pl* **-men** [ˈbɪznɪsmən] *n* homme *m* d'affaires; **big b.** homme d'affaires important

business manager *n* directeur *m* commercial

business park *n* parc *m* d'activités

business plan *n* plan *m* d'activité, projet *m* d'entreprise, programme *m* de financement et de gestion

business reply envelope *n* enveloppe-réponse *f*, *pl* enveloppes-réponses

business school *n* école *f* de commerce

business studies *npl* études *fpl* commerciales

business suit *n* costume *m*

business travel *n* voyages *mpl* d'affaires; **b. department** implant *m*

business traveller *n* personne *f* qui voyage pour affaires

business trip *n* voyage *m* d'affaires; **to go on a b.** voyager pour affaires

businesswoman, *pl* **-women** [ˈbɪznɪswʊmən, -wɪmɪn] *n* femme *f* d'affaires; **she's a good b.** elle s'y connait en affaires

busing [ˈbʌsɪŋ] *n* = **bussing**

busk [bʌsk] *vi esp Br* chanter/jouer d'un instrument dans les rues/le métro

busker [ˈbʌskər] *n esp Br* musicien, -ienne ambulant(e)

bus lane *n* couloir *m ou* voie *f* reservé(e) aux autobus

bus mailing *n Mktg* publipostage *m* groupé, multipostage *m*

busman, *pl* **-men** [ˈbʌsmən] *n F* **to take a b.'s holiday** faire la même chose pendant ses loisirs que pendant son travail; **that's a bit of a b.'s holiday** vous appelez ça des vacances!

bus phoning *n Mktg* télévente *f* groupée

bus shelter *n* abribus *m*

bussing [ˈbʌsɪŋ] *n* (*of schoolchildren etc*) transport *m* par autobus (*surtout dans le cadre de la politique de déségrégation aux États-Unis*)

bus station *n* gare *f* routière

bust¹ [bʌst] *n* (**a**) *Anat* (*of woman*) poitrine *f*; **what (size) b. are you?** combien est-ce que vous faites de tour de poitrine?; **what b. is this dress?** combien cette robe fait-elle de tour de poitrine?; **to be small/big in the b.** avoir une petite/grosse poitrine; **it's too tight round the b.** c'est trop serré à la poitrine; **b. measurement** tour *m* de poitrine (**b**) (*by sculptor*) buste *m*

bust² *adj F* (*iron, radio etc*) foutu; **if it ain't b. don't fix it** le mieux est l'ennemi du bien; **to go b.** faire faillite

bust³ *vt F* (**a**) (*break*) casser; (*balloon etc*) crever; *Am* **to b. sb's nose** donner un coup de poing à qn sur le nez; *Am Vulg* **to b. one's ass doing sth** se crever le cul à faire qch (**b**) (*arrest*) (*thief etc*) coffrer; (*gang of traffickers*) démanteler; **he was busted for armed robbery** il s'est fait coffrer pour vol à main armée; **you're busted** tu es fait (**c**) (*raid*) (*bar etc*) faire une descente dans (**d**) *Am esp Mil* (*reduce in rank*) rétrograder; **he's been busted to private** il a été rétrogradé au rang de simple soldat (**e**) *Am* (*wild horses*) dresser

bust⁴ *n F* (*by police*) (*of thief etc*) arrestation *f*; (*raid*) descente *f*; (*search*) perquisition *f*

▶ **bust out** *vi F* s'échapper

▶ **bust up** *F* **1** *vtsep* (**a**) (*marriage, friendship etc*) casser; **to b. up a meeting** interrompre une réunion (**b**) (*damage, destroy*) (*bar, flat*) saccager **2** *vi* (*of spouses, lovers*) casser; **their marriage has bust up** ils ont cassé

bustard [ˈbʌstəd] *n* (*bird*) outarde *f*

buster [ˈbʌstər] *n Am F* (*child*) (petit) garçon *m*; (*man*) homme *m*, type *m*; **hi, b.!** (*as address*) salut, mon pote!; **now listen, b. …** écoute, mec …

bustle¹ [ˈbʌs(ə)l] *n* (*activity*) agitation *f*; **the b. in the streets** l'animation *f* des rues

bustle² **1** *vi* **to b. (about)** s'activer, s'affairer; **the streets are bustling with people** les rues grouillent de monde **2** *vt* **to b. sb out of the house** faire sortir qn précipitamment

bustle³ *n* (*of skirt*) tournure *f*

bustling [ˈbʌs(ə)lɪŋ] *adj* (*person*) très actif; (*street*) animé; **the b. crowds of shoppers** la foule animée des gens qui font leurs courses

bust-up *n F* (**a**) (*of marriage, relationship*) échec *m*; **their b. was quite a shock to me** leur séparation m'a fait un choc (**b**) (*quarrel*) engueulade *f*; **to have a b.** se brouiller (**c**) (*brawl*) bagarre *f*

busty [ˈbʌstɪ] *adj F* (*woman*) à la poitrine plantureuse

busy¹ [ˈbɪzɪ] *adj* (**busier, busiest**) (**a**) (*person*) occupé; **not now—I'm b.** pas maintenant—je suis occupé; **you have been b.!** tu as bien travaillé!; **my work keeps me b. all morning** mon travail m'occupe toute la matinée; **to keep (oneself) b.** s'occuper; **to be b. with sth** être occupé à qch; **to be b. doing sth** être occupé à faire qch; **I suppose it's time I got b.** il est temps que je m'y mette; *F* **get b.!** grouille-toi!; **b. Lizzie** (*plant*) impatiente *f*

(**b**) (*day etc*) chargé; *Rail* (*line*) à grand trafic; **it's a b. road** c'est une route à grande circulation; **the roads were very b. this morning** il y avait beaucoup de circulation sur les routes ce matin; **the train was very b.** il y avait beaucoup de monde dans le train; **b. street** (*full of people*) rue *f* animée *ou* passante; (*full of shoppers*) rue très commerçante; **the hotel industry is at its busiest in August** l'industrie hôtelière est au plus haut de son activité au mois d'août; **we're not b. at the moment** (*of business etc*) nous travaillons au ralenti en ce moment; **this is a b. time of year for us** (*of business etc*) nous travaillons beaucoup à cette période de l'année; **this is a b. time of year for gardeners** c'est une période de l'année où il y a beaucoup à faire pour les jardiniers

(**c**) *esp Am Tel* occupé; **the line is b.** la ligne est occupée; **b. signal** *or* **tone** tonalité *f* occupé; **I keep getting the b. signal** ça sonne toujours occupé

busy² *vt* **to b. oneself with sth** s'occuper à qch; **to b. oneself (with) doing the housework/ironing the shirts** s'occuper en faisant le ménage/en repassant les chemises; **I can always find something to b. myself with** je trouve toujours à m'occuper; **to b. oneself with other people's problems** s'occuper des problèmes des autres

busybody ['bɪzɪbɒdɪ] *n* curieux, -euse, indiscret, -ète; **he's an awful b.** il se mêle des affaires de tout le monde

but [bʌt] **1** *conj* (**a**) (*coordinating*) mais; **he is small b. strong** il est petit mais fort; **b. I tell you I saw it!** (mais) puisque je vous dis que je l'ai vu!; **he does nothing b. complain** il n'arrête pas de se plaindre

(**b**) [①A70,c] (*subordinating*) **I can't go out for a minute b. something happens** je ne peux pas sortir une minute sans qu'il se passe quelque chose; *Arch, Lit* **I cannot b. believe that ...** il m'est impossible de ne pas croire que ...; **what could I do b. invite him?** que pouvais-je faire d'autre que de l'inviter?

(**c**) (*intensive*) **not just once b. twice** pas une fois, mais deux; **nobody, b. nobody** personne, mais absolument personne

2 *adv esp Lit* **had I b. known!** si j'avais su!; **one can b. try** on peut toujours essayer; **it seems b. yesterday** c'est comme si c'était hier; **it seems b. yesterday that she was here** on dirait qu'hier encore elle était ici; **if I could b. see him!** si seulement je pouvais le voir!; **he's b. a boy** ce n'est qu'un garçon

3 *prep* (**a**) (*except*) **any day b. tomorrow** n'importe quel jour excepté *ou* sauf demain; *Arch, Lit* **all b. he** *or* **him** tous excepté *ou* sauf lui; *Arch, Lit* **none b. he** personne d'autre que lui; **nobody b. me could have done something so stupid** il n'y a que moi pour faire quelque chose d'aussi stupide; **nobody b. me knew about it** personne d'autre que moi n'était au courant; **anyone b. me** tout autre que moi; **I wish the prize had been won by anyone b. him** j'aurais voulu que n'importe qui d'autre que lui remporte le prix; **anything b. that** tout plutôt que cela; **he's anything b. a hero** c'est loin d'être un héros; **he is anything b. happy** il n'est pas du tout heureux; **is she lazy? – anything b.!** est-ce qu'elle est paresseuse? – bien au contraire!; **it's nothing b. laziness** ce n'est que de la paresse; **there is nothing for it b. to obey** il n'y a qu'à obéir

(**b**) **the last b. one** l'avant-dernier; **the next house b. one** la deuxième maison (à partir d'ici)

(**c**) **b. for** sans; **b. for the rain I should have gone out** s'il n'avait pas plu je serais sorti; **he wouldn't have left b. for me** (*it was my fault for being there*) il serait resté si je n'avais pas été là; (*it was for my sake*) il ne serait pas parti si ça n'avait pas été pour moi; **b. for you I would have been killed** (*if you hadn't been there*) si vous n'aviez pas été là, j'aurais été tué

4 *n* **there is a b.** il y a un mais; **I don't want any buts!** il n'y a pas de mais; **you're coming to dinner at our place and I don't want any buts** tu viens dîner chez nous, et je ne veux pas de discussions

butane ['bju:teɪn] *n Ch* butane *m*

butch [bʊtʃ] *adj F* (*man, woman*) très masculin; (*haircut, clothes*) de mec

butcher¹ ['bʊtʃər] *n* (**a**) (*for meat*) boucher, -ère; **to go to the b.'s** aller chez le boucher; **b.'s block** billot *m* de boucher; **b.'s boy** garçon *m* boucher; **b.'s shop/trade** boucherie *f* (**b**) *Pej* (*killer*) boucher *m* (**c**) *F* (*surgeon*) boucher *m*, charcutier *m*

butcher² *vt* (**a**) (*animal*) (*kill for meat*) abattre; (*cut up*) dépecer (**b**) *Pej* (*kill*) (*sb*) massacrer; *F* **he butchered that song** il a massacré cette chanson (**c**) *F* (*of surgeon*) (*patient*) charcuter

butcher's ['bʊtʃəz] *n Br Sl* **to have a b. at sth/sb** viser *ou* mater qch/qn; **let's have a b. at the photos then** laisse-moi voir les photos

butchery ['bʊtʃərɪ] *n* (**a**) (*trade*) boucherie *f* (**b**) *Pej* (*bloodshed*) boucherie *f*, massacre *m*

butler ['bʌtlər] *n* maître *m* d'hôtel; **b.'s pantry** office *f*

butt¹ [bʌt] *n* (**a**) (*cask*) barrique *f*, futaille *f* (**b**) (*for rainwater*) tonneau *m*

butt² *n* (**a**) (*of cigar etc*) mégot *m* (**b**) *Am F* (*of person*) derrière *m*; **get off your b. and do something!** remue-toi le cul et fais quelque chose! (**c**) **b.** (**end**) (*of tool*) gros bout *m*; (*of fishing rod*) gros brin *m*; (*of rifle*) crosse *f*; *Fig* **the b. end of the conversation** la fin de la conversation (**d**) *Billiards* (*of cue*) masse *f*, talon *m* (**e**) *Carp* **b.** (**end**) about *m*; **b. hinge** charnière *f*; **b. joint** joint *m* bout à bout; *Metal* **b. welding** soudure *f* bout à bout

butt³ *n* (**a**) *Mil* (*mound*) butte *f* (de tir); **the butts** le champ de tir (**b**) (*target, Fig of humour, joke*) cible *f*

butt⁴ *n* (*with head*) coup *m* de tête *ou F* de boule; (*of ram etc*) coup de tête

butt⁵ *vt* (*of person*) donner un coup de tête *ou F* de boule à; (*of ram etc*) donner un coup de tête à

▶ **butt in** *vi* interrompre la conversation; **if I could just b. in here** permettez-moi d'intervenir

▶ **butt into** *vipo* **to b. into the conversation** interrompre la conversation

▶ **butt out** *vi esp Am F* **b. out!** ne t'en mêle pas!; **I decided to b. out** j'ai décidé de rester en dehors de ça

butter¹ ['bʌtər] *n* beurre *m*; *Fig* **b. wouldn't melt in her mouth** on lui donnerait le bon Dieu sans confession; **b. dish** beurrier *m*; **b. knife** couteau *m* à beurre

butter² *vt* (**a**) (*bread*) beurrer (**b**) *Culin* (*vegetables etc*) mettre du beurre dans

▶ **butter up** *vtsep F* passer de la pommade à

butterball ['bʌtəbɔ:l] *n US F* (*plump person*) personne *f* boulotte

butter bean *n* haricot *m* blanc

butter cream *n* crème *m* au beurre

buttercup ['bʌtəkʌp] *n* renoncule *f* des champs, *F* bouton *m* d'or

butterfat ['bʌtəfæt] *n* (*of milk*) matière *f* grasse

butterfingered ['bʌtəfɪŋgəd] *adj F* maladroit, empoté; **to be b.** tout laisser tomber

butterfingers ['bʌtəfɪŋgəz] *n F* maladroit, -oite, empoté, -ée (*qui laisse tout tomber*); **b.!** espèce de maladroit!

butterfly ['bʌtəflaɪ] *n* (**a**) (*insect*) papillon *m* (diurne); *Fig* (*person*) papillon; *F* **to have butterflies (in one's stomach)** avoir l'estomac noué, avoir le trac; **b. net** filet *m* à papillons; *Tech* **b. nut** écrou *m* à oreilles *ou* à ailettes, écrou ailé, (écrou) papillon; *St Exch* **b. spread** spread *m* papillon; **b. valve** vanne *f ou* volet *m* papillon (**b**) *Swimming* **b.** (**stroke**) (nage *f ou* brasse *f*) papillon *m*

buttermilk ['bʌtəmɪlk] *n* babeurre *m*

butter mountain *n EC* montagne *f* de beurre

butterscotch ['bʌtəskɒtʃ] *n* caramel *m* (dur) au beurre

buttery¹ ['bʌtərɪ] *n* (*esp in some English universities*) office *f*, dépense *f*, restaurant *m*; **b. hatch** passe-plats *m inv*

buttery² *adj* (*taste*) de beurre; **with a b. texture** avec la consistance du beurre; **b. fingers** doigts pleins de beurre

butting ['bʌtɪŋ] *n* (*by person*) coups *mpl* de tête; (*by ram, goat*) coups de corne; **he was disqualified for b.** il a été disqualifié pour avoir donné un/des coup(s) de tête

buttock ['bʌtək] *n* fesse *f*; **the buttocks** les fesses, le derrière; **cross b.** (*in wrestling*) ceinture *f* arrière *ou* à rebours, tour *m* de hanche

button¹ ['bʌtən] *n* (**a**) (*on dress etc*) bouton *m*; **as bright as a b.** (*child*) vif, éveillé; *Am* **she's as cute as a b.** elle est trognon; *F* **it's not worth a b.** ça ne vaut pas un clou; *F* **I don't care a b.** je m'en fiche pas mal; **a b. nose** un petit nez; **chocolate buttons** (*sweets*) pastilles *fpl* de chocolat; *Br Old-fashioned* **buttons** (*page boy*) groom *m* (**b**) (*for doorbell etc*) bouton *m*; *Comptr* (*on mouse*) bouton; (*for menu selection*) case *f*; *F* **to be right on the b.** (*of answer*) tomber pile; *F* **you've hit it right on the b.** tu as mis en plein dans le mille (**c**) *Am* (*badge*) badge *m* (**d**) (*of foil*) bouton *m*, mouche *f*

button² **1** *vt* (**a**) (*garment*) boutonner; *F* **b. your lip** *or* **it, keep your lip buttoned** ferme-la, la ferme, boucle-la (**b**) *Fencing* (*foil*) moucheter **2** *vi* (*of garment*) se boutonner; **a dress that buttons at the back/side** une robe qui se boutonne par derrière/sur le côté

▶ **button up** *vtsep* (**a**) (*fasten*) boutonner; **buttoned up** (*person*) boutonné jusqu'au menton (**b**) *Fig* **we've got the deal all buttoned up** l'affaire est dans le sac

button apathy *n TV* passivité *f* du téléspectateur

button-down *adj* (*collar*) à pointes boutonnées; **b. shirt** chemise *f* à col boutonné

buttoned-up [bʌtən'dʌp] *adj F* (*taciturn*) constipé

buttonhole¹ ['bʌtənhəʊl] *n* (**a**) (*in garment*) boutonnière *f*; **b. stitch** point *m* de boutonnière (**b**) *Surg* boutonnière *f*, petite incision *f* (**c**) (*flower*) (fleur *f* portée à la) boutonnière *f*

buttonhole² *vt F* **to b. sb** coincer qn
button mushroom *n* petit champignon *m* de couche
button-through *n, adj* **b. (dress)** robe *f* chemisier; **b. (skirt)** jupe *f* boutonnée jusqu'en bas
buttress¹ ['bʌtrɪs] *n Archit* contrefort *m*; *Fig* pilier *m*, *Lit* étai *m*
buttress² *vt Constr* arc-bouter, étayer; *Fig* étayer
butty ['bʌtɪ] *n Eng Dial* sandwich *m*
buxom ['bʌksəm] *adj* (*full-bosomed*) à forte poitrine; (*plump*) bien en chair, aux formes rebondies *ou* plantureuses
buy¹ [baɪ] *n* achat *m*; **a good/bad b.** un bon/mauvais achat, une bonne/mauvaise affaire
buy² (*pt, pp* **bought** [bɔːt]) **1** *vt* **(a)** acheter (**from** à); (*company*) racheter; **to b. sb sth** acheter qch à qn; **to b. sth for sb** acheter qch pour qn; **to b. sth cheap** acheter qch (à) bon marché; **money can't b. you love/health/happiness** l'amour/la santé/le bonheur ne s'achète pas; **a dearly bought advantage** un avantage chèrement payé; *F* **he's bought it** (*is dead*) il a passé l'arme à gauche; *Fig* **to b. time** gagner du temps
(b) *Pej* (*bribe*) (*witness etc*) acheter
(c) *F* (*believe*) gober, croire; **I won't b. that!** tu ne me feras pas gober *ou* croire ça!; **I'll b. that!** (*believe it*) je te/le/*etc* crois; (*that's good, I agree*) d'accord
2 *vi* acheter; *Fin* **to b. spot** acheter au comptant; **to b. forward** acheter à terme
▶ **buy back** *vtsep* (*house etc*) racheter (**from** à)
▶ **buy in** *vtsep* (*supplies etc*) s'approvisionner en
▶ **buy into** *vipo* (*purchase share in*) (*business*) acheter une part de
▶ **buy off** *vtsep F* acheter; **she refused to be bought off** elle refusa de se laisser acheter
▶ **buy out** *vtsep* **(a)** *Com* (*partner etc*) (r)acheter la part de, désintéresser; **he was bought out for £50,000** on lui a (r)acheté sa part pour 50 000 livres **(b)** *Mil* racheter; **to b. oneself out** racheter son contrat avec l'armée
▶ **buy up** *vtsep* (*surplus grain, wine etc*) acheter; (*in anticipation of shortages*) rafler; *F* **you must have bought up the entire store** tu as dû dévaliser tout le magasin
buyback ['baɪbæk] *n* rachat *m*; **b. arrangement** accord *m* de reprise; **b. right** droit *m* de rachat
buyer ['baɪər] *n* **(a)** (*consumer*) acheteur, -euse; **buyer's market** marché *m* demandeur *ou* d'acheteurs; *Fin* **b. credit** crédit-acheteur *m*; **b. credit guarantee** garantie *f* de crédit-acheteur **(b)** (*for shop*) acheteur, -euse, responsable *mf* des achats; **head b.** acheteur *m* principal
buyer-readiness *n Mktg* prédisposition *f* à l'achat
buying ['baɪɪŋ] *n* **b. and selling** l'achat *m* et la vente; *Mktg* **b. behaviour** comportement *m* d'achat; **b. centre** (*buyer group*) centrale *f* d'achat; **b. (department)** service *m* (des) achats; **b. group** centrale *f* d'achat; **b. office** centrale *f ou* bureau *m* d'achat; **b. power** pouvoir *m* d'achat; **b. ring** groupement *m* d'achat
buy order *n St Exch* injonction *m* à l'achat
buy-out *n Com* (*of company*) rachat *m*; (*of partner*) désintéressement *m*
buzz¹ [bʌz] *n* **(a)** (*of insect, Fig of conversation*) bourdonnement *m*; (*of plane*) vrombissement *m*; *Rad* ronflement *m*; **to give sb a b.** *Tel F* donner un coup de fil à qn; *Sl* (*thrill*) faire planer qn; *Sl* **being recognized gives him a b.** ça le fait planer d'être reconnu; *Sl* **there's nothing quite like the b. you get from skiing** rien ne vaut le frisson qu'on ressent en skiant; *Sl* **she gets a real b. out of those grandchildren of hers** elle retire énormément de plaisir de ses petits-enfants **(b)** (*rumour, gossip*) rumeur *f*; **the b. is that he's been fired** on murmure qu'il a été renvoyé
buzz² **1** *vi* (*of insect, ears*) bourdonner; (*of aircraft*) vrombir; **the whole town was buzzing with excitement** la ville était en pleine agitation; **she is buzzing with ideas** elle a plein d'idées; **her head was buzzing with ideas** elle avait la tête bourdonnante d'idées **2** *vt F* **(a)** *Av* (*plane, ship*) frôler; (*building, town*) raser **(b)** (*call*) (*on telephone*) donner un coup de fil à; (*on intercom*) appeler (à l'interphone)
▶ **buzz about, buzz around** *vi* (*of bees, flies*) voler en bourdonnant; *F* (*of person*) s'activer; **I like to hear the bees buzzing about** j'aime entendre le bourdonnement des abeilles
▶ **buzz off** *vi Br F* décamper; **b. off!** allez, file *ou* décampe!
buzzard ['bʌzəd] *n* buse *f*, busard *m*
buzzer ['bʌzər] *n* (*device*) sonnette *f*; (*sound*) sonnerie *f*; **there's the b.** (*on machine*) ça sonne; (*at door*) on sonne
buzzing ['bʌzɪŋ] *n* (*of insect, Med of ears*) bourdonnement *m*; **a b. noise** un bourdonnement
buzz word *n* mot *m* en vogue
by¹ [baɪ] **1** *prep* [①A66] **(a)** (*agent*) par; **to be punished by sb** être puni par qn; **to be loved by sb** être aimé de qn; **made by hand** fait à la main; **to have a child by sb** avoir un enfant de qn; **she has a daughter by her first marriage/husband** elle a une fille de son premier mariage/mari; *Lit* **to die by one's own hand** mourir de ses propres mains; **he took me by the arm/hand** il m'a pris par le bras/la main; **to live by one's work** vivre de son travail; **what do you mean by that?** qu'entendez-vous par là?; **by force** de force; **by way of a joke** par plaisanterie; **by chance** par hasard; **by heart** par cœur
(b) (*near*) (*sb*) (au)près de, à côté de; (*sth*) près de, à côté de; (*in compass reading*) quart; **sitting by the fire** assis près du feu; **by the side of the road** au bord de la route; **by the sea** au bord de la mer; **north by east** nord quart nord-est
(c) (*via*) par; **to go by the same road** aller par la même route; **by land and sea** par terre et par mer; **by land/sea** par (voie de) terre/mer
(d) (*means of transport*) **to travel by rail** voyager en *ou* par le chemin de fer; **to come by car/motorcycle** venir en voiture/à motocyclette
(e) (*past*) **he walked by the churchyard** il est passé devant le cimetière; **she drove by me** elle m'a dépassé (*en voiture*)
(f) (*time: at or before*) **he will be here by three o'clock** il sera ici avant *ou* pour trois heures; **you will hear from us by Monday** vous aurez de nos nouvelles d'ici lundi; **he ought to be here by now** *or* **by this time** il devrait être déjà ici; **I'll be gone by the time (that) you have finished** quand vous aurez fini, je serai parti; **you'll have it by tomorrow** vous l'aurez pour demain; **they were tired by the end of the day** ils étaient fatigués à la fin de la journée; **by 1970** (*talking about the past*) en 1970; **by 2025** (*talking about the future*) d'ici (à) 2025
(g) (*during*) **by day** de jour, le jour; **by night** de nuit, la nuit; **by daylight** au jour, à la lumière du jour
(h) **by oneself** (tout) seul; **to do sth (all) by oneself** faire qch (tout) seul
(i) (+ *doing sth*) **to earn one's living by teaching** gagner sa vie en enseignant; **I shall gain/lose by (doing) it** j'y gagnerai/j'y perdrai; **to begin/end by laughing** commencer/finir par rire; **we shall lose nothing by waiting** nous n'avons rien à perdre en attendant
(j) (*according to*) **to call sb by his name** appeler qn par son nom; **cheerful by nature** gai par nature, d'un naturel gai; **by my watch** à ma montre; **to set one's watch by the time signal** régler sa montre sur le signal horaire; **to judge sb by appearances** juger qn sur les apparences; **I can tell by your face** on le voit à votre visage; **he's a plumber by trade** il est plombier de son métier; **I know him by name/sight** je le connais de nom/vue
(k) (*with numbers, measurements etc*) **to divide by three** diviser par trois; **three metres by two** trois mètres sur deux; **to sell sth by the pound/dozen** vendre qch à la livre/douzaine; **to rent a house by the year** louer une maison à l'année; **by degrees** par degrés; **by turns** chacun son tour, tour à tour; **they did it by turns** ils l'ont fait chacun leur tour; **he was happy and sad by turns** il était tour à tour heureux et triste; **one by one** un à un; **to come in by twos** *or* **two by two** entrer deux par deux; **little by little** peu à peu, petit à petit; **day by day** jour par jour, de jour en jour
(l) (*to the extent of*) de; **longer by two metres** plus long de deux mètres; **by far** de loin; **they overcharged me by ten per cent** ils m'ont compté dix pour cent en trop
(m) (*in oaths*) **by God** au nom de Dieu; **to swear by all one holds sacred** jurer par tout ce qu'on a de plus sacré
(n) *Mil* **by the right, quick march!** ≈ en avant, marche!
(o) (*with regard to*) **to do one's duty by sb** faire son devoir envers qn; *F* **it's all right by me!** ça (me) va!, d'accord!; *F* **if that's okay by you** si ça te va, si tu es d'accord
2 *adv* **(a)** (*near*) près; **close by** tout près, ici près, tout à côté; **by and large** dans l'ensemble
(b) (*aside*) **to lay** *or* **set** *or* **put sth by** mettre qch de côté; **to put** *or* **lay money by** mettre de l'argent de côté
(c) **to go** *or* **pass by** (*elapse*) passer; **time goes by** le temps passe; **to come** *or* **stop by** (*to see sb, fetch sth*) passer
(d) **by and by** (*soon*) bientôt, tantôt; (*in the immediate future*) tout à l'heure; **by the by(e), by the way** à propos
bye¹ [baɪ] *n* **(a)** *Cr* balle *f* passée **(b)** *Sp* **to have a b.** (*of player*) être exempt (*d'une épreuve, d'un match, dans un tournoi*) **(c)** **by the b. ...** à propos ...
bye² *int F* au revoir!, salut!; **b. for now!** à bientôt!
bye-bye *F* **1** *int* salut!, au revoir! **2** *n* (*in children's language*) **to go to b., to go bye-byes** aller faire dodo
bye-law *n* = **bylaw**
by-election *n Pol* élection *f* partielle

bygone [ˈbaɪgɒn] **1** *adj* passé, ancien, d'autrefois; **in b. days** autrefois, dans l'ancien temps **2** *npl* **to let bygones be bygones** oublier le passé

bylaw [ˈbaɪlɔː] *n* arrêté *m* municipal; *Am Jur* **bylaws** (*of company*) statuts *mpl* de société

by-line *n* **(a)** *Journ* signature *f*; **a report under the b. of Mary Jones** un reportage signé Mary Jones **(b)** *Sp* limites *fpl* du terrain

BYO [biːwaɪˈəʊ] *n Austr* (*abbr* **bring your own**) = restaurant *m* qui ne sert pas d'alcool et où l'on peut apporter sa boisson

BYOB [biːwaɪəʊˈbiː] *adj F abbr* **bring your own bottle**

bypass¹ [ˈbaɪpɑːs] *n* **(a)** *Aut* route *f* de contournement; **temporary b.** déviation *f* **(b)** *Med* pontage *m*; **she's had a b., she's had b. surgery** on lui a fait un pontage **(c)** *Tech* (conduit *m* de) dérivation *f*; *Aut* **b. filter** filtre *m* en dérivation; **b. valve** soupape *f ou* clapet *m* de dérivation, clapet by-pass **(d)** *El* dérivation *f*

bypass² *vt* **(a)** (*town etc*) (*of motorist*) contourner, éviter; (*of road*) contourner; *Fig* (*middleman etc*) court-circuiter **(b)** *Tech* (*steam etc*) amener en dérivation **(c)** *El* mettre hors circuit

by-play *n Th etc* (*action*) jeu *m* accessoire, jeu de second plan; (*speech*) aparté *m* mimé, jeu muet

by-product *n Ind* sous-produit *m*, *pl* sous-produits, dérivé *m*; *Fig* effet *m* secondaire

byre [ˈbaɪər] *n esp Scot* étable *f* à vaches

byroad [ˈbaɪrəʊd] *n* petite route *f*

bystander [ˈbaɪstændər] *n* spectateur, -trice

byte [baɪt] *n Comptr* **(eight-bit) b.** octet *m*

byway [ˈbaɪweɪ] *n* petite route *f*; *Fig* **byways of history** à-côtés *mpl* de l'histoire

byword [ˈbaɪwɜːd] *n Arch* proverbe *m*, dicton *m*; *Fig* **to have become a b.** être devenu proverbial; **she is a b. for punctuality** elle est l'exemple même de la ponctualité; **she has become a b. for punctuality** sa ponctualité est devenue proverbiale

Byzantine [bɪˈzæntaɪn, baɪ-] **1** *adj Hist, Fig* byzantin; **the B. Empire** l'Empire *m* byzantin **2** *n Hist* Byzantin, -ine

Byzantium [bɪˈzæntɪəm, baɪ-] *n Antiq* Byzance *f*

C

C¹, c [siː] *n* **(a)** *(letter)* C, c *m*; **two c's** deux c; *US F* **C note** billet *m* de cent dollars; *Obst F* **C-section** césarienne *f* **(b)** *Mus* do *m*, ut *m* **(c)** *Sch (grade)* **to get a C in maths** avoir 10 en maths
C² *(abbr* **centigrade***)* C.
c, ca *(abbr* **circa***)* env.
C4 *abbr* **Channel Four**
CA [siːˈeɪ] *n Br, Fin abbr* **chartered accountant**
C/A, c/a *Banking (abbr* **current** *or* **cheque** *or Am* **checking account***)* C/C *m*, CCB *m*
CAA [siːeɪˈeɪ] *n Br Av, Admin (abbr* **Civil Aviation Authority***)* = organisme *m* de réglementation de l'aviation civile
CAB *abbr* **Citizens' Advice Bureau**
cab [kæb] *n* **(a)** *(taxi)* taxi *m*; *Arch (horse-drawn)* fiacre *m*; **to call** *or* **hail a c.** appeler *ou* héler un taxi; **by c.** en taxi; **hansom c.** cab *m* **(b)** *(of truck, train, crane etc)* cabine *f*; **driver's c.** cabine *ou* poste *m* de conduite
cabal [kəˈbæl] *n esp Pol, usu Pej* **(a)** *(plot)* cabale *f* **(b)** *(group)* coterie *f*
cabana [kəˈbænə] *n (room by beach/swimming pool)* cabine *f* de bain
cabaret [ˈkæbəreɪ] *n* **(a)** **c. (show)** *(in nightclub)* spectacle *m* de music-hall *ou* de cabaret; **she's in c.** c'est une artiste de cabaret; **c. act/artist** numéro *m*/artiste *mf* de cabaret **(b)** *(nightclub, restaurant)* cabaret *m*
cabbage [ˈkæbɪdʒ] *n* **(a)** chou *m*, *pl* choux; **red c.** chou rouge; **c. white** *(butterfly)* piéride *f* du chou; **c. lettuce** laitue *f* pommée; **c. palm** *(tree)* palmiste *m*; **c. rose** rose *f* chou, *pl* roses chou **(b)** *Med F (person)* légume *m*; **the accident left him a c.** l'accident en a fait un légume, il est à l'état végétatif depuis l'accident
cab(b)alistic [kæbəˈlɪstɪk] *adj* cabalistique
cabbie, cabby [ˈkæbɪ] *n F* chauffeur *m* de taxi
cab driver *n* chauffeur *m* de taxi
caber [ˈkeɪbər] *n Scot Sp* **tossing the c.** = concours *m* de lancement d'un tronc d'arbre *(dans les jeux des Highlands)*
cabin [ˈkæbɪn] *n* **(a)** *(hut)* cabane *f*, case *f*; *Br Rail (signal box)* poste *m ou* cabine *f* d'aiguillage **(b)** *Naut* cabine *f*; *(on barge etc)* cabane *f*; *Av* cabine, habitacle *m*; *Av* **c. attendant** *(male)* steward *m*; *(female)* hôtesse *f* de l'air; *Av* **c. baggage** bagages *mpl* à main; *Old-fashioned Naut* **c. boy** mousse *m*; *Av* **c. crew** équipage *m*; *Naut* **c. cruiser** yacht *m* de croisière (à moteur); **c. trunk** malle *f* de cabine; **c. staff** personnel *m* de cabine, membres *mpl* de l'équipage; **c. steward** steward *m* **(c)** *Aut (of passenger car)* habitacle *m*; *(of lorry)* cabine *f*
cabinet [ˈkæbɪnɪt] *n* **(a)** *(piece of furniture)* meuble *m* à tiroirs; *(for TV)* meuble télé; *(for video)* meuble vidéo; *(for stereo system)* meuble hi-fi; **filing c.** classeur *m*; *(for index cards)* fichier *m*; **bathroom c.** armoire *f* de toilette *ou* de salle de bains; **medicine c.** armoire à pharmacie **(b)** *Pol* cabinet *m*, ministère *m*; **to form a c.** former un cabinet *ou* un ministère; **c. meeting** conseil *m* des ministres **(c)** *Arch (room)* cabinet *m*
cabinet-maker *n* ébéniste *mf*
cabinet-making *n* ébénisterie *f*
cabinet minister *n* ministre *m* (d'État), membre *m* du cabinet (ministériel)
cabinet reshuffle *n* remaniement *m* ministériel
cable¹ [ˈkeɪb(ə)l] *n* **(a)** *Naut* câble *m*; **c.('s) length** *(measure)* encâblure *f*

(b) *El* câble *m*; **to lay a c.** poser un câble; **overhead/underground/submarine c.** câble aérien/souterrain/sous-marin; **twin c.** câble à deux conducteurs; *Aut* **c. terminal** cosse *f*

(c) *Telecom* câble *m*, câblogramme *m*; **c. address** adresse *f* télégraphique; **c. transfer** *(of money)* virement *m* télégraphique

(d) *TV* **c. (television)** (télévision *f* par) câble *m*; **c. broadcasting** télédiffusion *f* par câble; **c. company** câblo-diffuseur *m*, câblo-opérateur *m*, câblo-distributeur *m*; **c. distribution** câblo-distribution *f*, distribution *f* par câble; **c. network** réseau *m* câblé

(e) *Knitting* torsade *f*
cable² *Telecom* **1** *vt (message)* câbler; **to c. sb** câbler à qn, envoyer un câble à qn; **to c. sth to sb** câbler qch à qn **2** *vi* câbler; **to c. to sb** envoyer un câble à qn

cable car *n* funiculaire *m*; *(overhead)* téléphérique *m*
cabled [ˈkeɪb(ə)ld] *adj* câblé; **c. network** réseau *m* câblé
cablegram [ˈkeɪb(ə)lgræm] *n Telecom* câblogramme *m*
cableless [ˈkeɪb(ə)lɪs] *adj* sans câble
cable needle *n Knitting* aiguille *f* à torsades
Cable News Network *n TV* réseau *m* d'information américain par câble et satellite
cable railway *n* funiculaire *m*
cable release *n Phot* déclencheur *m*
cable ship *n* câblier *m*
cable stitch *n Knitting* point *m* de torsades
cableway [ˈkeɪb(ə)lweɪ] *n* téléphérique *m*
cabling [ˈkeɪb(ə)lɪŋ] *n El etc (cables)* câbles *mpl*, câblage *m*
cabman, *pl* **-men** [ˈkæbmən] *n* chauffeur *m* de taxi
caboodle [kəˈbuːd(ə)l] *n F* **the whole (kit and) c.** tout le bazar *ou* bataclan
caboose [kəˈbuːs] *n* **(a)** *Am Rail (of goods train)* fourgon *m* de queue **(b)** *US Sl (jail)* tôle *f*, taule *f* **(c)** *Can (for loggers etc)* baraquement *m* mobile **(d)** *Naut (kitchen)* cuisine *f*, coquerie *f*
cabotage [kæbəˈtɑːdʒ] *n Av, Naut* cabotage *m*; **c. fare** tarif *m* de cabotage; **c. route** itinéraire *m* de cabotage
cab rank *n* station *f* de taxis
CAC 40 index [kæk] *n St Exch* indice *m* CAC 40
cacao [kəˈkɑːəʊ, kəˈkeɪəʊ] *n Bot* **(a)** **c. (bean)** (graine *f* de *ou* fève *f* de) cacao *m*; **c. pod** cabosse *f* **(b)** **c. (tree)** cacaotier *m*, cacaoyer *m*
cache¹ [kæʃ] *n* **(a)** *(arms, drugs etc that have been hidden)* objets *mpl* cachés; **a c. of guns/drugs** une cache d'armes/de drogues; **the c. had a value of …** les armes/drogues/*etc* cachées là avaient une valeur de … **(b)** *(hiding place)* cache *f* **(c)** *Comptr* **c. (memory)** antémémoire *f*, mémoire-cache *f*
cache² *vt* **(a)** *(hide)* cacher **(b)** *Comptr (data)* mettre en antémémoire *ou* en mémoire-cache
cachet [ˈkæʃeɪ] *n Pharm, Fig* cachet *m*; *Mktg* label *m*; *Fig* **to have a certain c.** avoir un certain cachet
cack-handed [kækˈhændɪd] *adj F (clumsy)* maladroit
cackle¹ [ˈkæk(ə)l] *n* **(a)** *(of hen)* caquet *m* **(b)** *Fig F (talking)* caquet *m*, jacassement *m*; *(laughter)* gloussement(s) *m(pl)*; **cut the c.!** la ferme!
cackle² *vi* **(a)** *(of hen)* caqueter; *(of goose)* cacarder **(b)** *Fig F (talk)* caqueter, jacasser; *(laugh)* glousser
cacophonous [kəˈkɒfənəs] *adj* cacophonique
cacophony [kəˈkɒfənɪ] *n* cacophonie *f*
cactus, *pl* **-ti** [ˈkæktəs, -tiː, -taɪ] *n* cactus *m*
CAD *n* **(a)** [kæd] *Comptr (abbr* **computer-assisted design***)* CAO *f* **(b)** [siːeɪˈdiː] *Com* **(cash against documents)** comptant *m* contre documents
cad [kæd] *n Old-fashioned Br* mufle *m*, goujat *m*
cadaver [kəˈdævər] *n esp US Med* cadavre *m*
cadaverous [kəˈdævərəs] *adj* **(a)** *(pale) (complexion etc)* cadavéreux, cadavérique **(b)** *(haggard) (appearance, face)* cadavérique
CAD/CAM [ˈkædkæm] *n Comptr (abbr* **computer-assisted design/computer-assisted manufacture***)* CFAO *f*
caddie¹ [ˈkædɪ] *n Golf* caddie *m*; **c. car(t)** chariot *m* (pour crosses de golf)
caddie² *vi Golf* **to c. for sb** servir de caddie à qn
caddish [ˈkædɪʃ] *adj Old-fashioned Br (behaviour)* de mufle; *(person)* mufle; **a c. thing to do** une preuve de muflerie
caddy¹ [ˈkædɪ] *n* **(tea) c.** boîte *f* à thé
caddy² *n, vi* = **caddie**
cadence [ˈkeɪdəns] *n* cadence *f*, rythme *m*; *Mus* cadence
cadenza [kəˈdenzə] *n Mus* cadence *f*
cadet [kəˈdet] *n Mil etc* élève *m* d'une école militaire, élève officier; *Sch* élève de la préparation militaire; **c. corps** peloton *m* de préparation militaire
cadge [kædʒ] *F, often Pej* **1** *vt* mendier, quémander **(from, off** à); *(money, cigarette)* taxer, taper **(from, off** à); **can I c. a lift?** ça ne t'ennuierait pas de me déposer? **2** *vi* mendier
cadger [ˈkædʒər] *n F Pej* quémandeur, -euse; *(of cigarette, money)* tapeur, -euse
Cadiz [kəˈdɪz] *n* Cadix *m ou f*

cadmium ['kædmɪəm] *n Miner* cadmium *m*
cadre [kɑːdər] *n Mil, Pol* cadre *m*
CAE [siːeɪ'iː] *n Comptr* (*abbr* **computer-aided engineering**) ingénierie *f* assistée par ordinateur
caecum, *pl* **-a,** *US* **cecum,** *pl* **-a** ['siːkəm, -ə] *n Anat* cæcum *m*
Caesar ['siːzər] *n* César *m*; **Julius C.** Jules César
Caesarean, Caesarian [sɪ'zeərɪən] **1** *n* **(a)** *Obst* césarienne *f*; **it was a C.** (*of delivery*) on lui a fait une césarienne; **to be a C.** (*of baby*) être né par césarienne; **she has to have a C.** il va falloir lui faire une césarienne; **the baby was born by C.** l'enfant est né par césarienne **(b)** *Hist* Césarien, -ienne **2** *adj Obst* **C. section** césarienne *f*
caesura [sɪ'zjʊərə] *n Liter* césure *f*
café ['kæfeɪ] *n* ≈ café-restaurant *m, pl* cafés-restaurants; (*in France*) café *m*
cafeteria [kæfɪ'tɪərɪə] *n* (*in large store*) cafétéria *f*; (*for employees*) cantine *f* en self-service
caff [kæf] *n Br Sl* ≈ café-restaurant *m, pl* cafés-restaurants
caffeine ['kæfiːn] *n* caféine *f*; **c. free** (*without caffeine*) sans caféine; (*decaffeinated*) décaféiné
caftan ['kæftæn] *n* caf(e)tan *m*
cage[1] [keɪdʒ] *n* **(a)** (*for birds, animals etc*) cage *f*; **c. bird** oiseau *m* de volière **(b)** (*of lift*) cabine *f* **(c)** *Min* cage *f* d'extraction
cage[2] *vt* (*bird etc*) mettre en cage; **caged animal** animal en cage; **I feel caged in** je me sens enfermé
cagey ['keɪdʒɪ] *adj F* (*careful*) prudent, circonspect; (*not frank*) cachottier; **to be c. about one's age** ne pas vouloir avouer son âge, rester vague concernant son âge
cagily ['keɪdʒɪlɪ] *adv* (*carefully*) très prudemment; **to answer c.** (*deliberately vaguely*) donner une réponse vague
caginess ['keɪdʒɪnɪs] *n* (*carefulness*) prudence *f*; (*deliberate vagueness*) vague *m*; **there was a certain c. in her replies** elle évitait de répondre en restant dans le vague
cagoule [kə'guːl] *n* anorak *m* léger et long (avec capuche)
cahoots [kə'huːts] *npl F* **to be in c. (with sb)** être de mèche (avec qn)
caiman ['keɪmən] *n* caïman *m*
Cain [keɪn] *n Bible* Caïn *m*; *F* **to raise C.** (*make noise*) faire un bruit *ou* un fracas de tous les diables; (*make scene*) faire une scène monumentale
cairn [keən] *n* **(a)** (*of stones*) cairn *m*, tumulus *m* de pierres **(b)** (*dog*) **c. (terrier)** terrier *m* cairn
cairngorm [keən'gɔːm] *n* (*gem*) pierre *f* de cairngorm
Cairo ['kaɪrəʊ] *n* Le Caire
caisson ['keɪs(ə)n] *n* **(a)** *Constr* (*for working underwater*) caisson *m*; *Med* **c. disease** maladie *f* des caissons **(b)** *Naut* (*in dry dock*) bateau-porte *m, pl* bateaux-portes **(c)** *Mil* (*for ammunition*) caisson *m*
cajole [kə'dʒəʊl] *vt* enjôler; **to c. sb into/out of doing sth** persuader/dissuader qn de faire qch
cajolery [kə'dʒəʊlərɪ] *n* cajolerie(s) *f(pl)*
Cajun ['keɪdʒən] **1** *adj* (*language, music, recipe*) cajun *inv* **2** *n* **(a)** (*person*) Cajun *mf* **(b)** *Ling* cajun *m*
cake[1] [keɪk] *n* **(a)** *Culin* gâteau *m*; (*small*) pâtisserie *f*; **(small) cakes** (petits) gâteaux, pâtisseries; **fruit c.** cake *m*; *Iron F* **that takes the c.!** ça c'est le comble *ou* le bouquet!; *F Fig* **it's a piece of c.** c'est simple comme bonjour, c'est du gâteau!; *F* **they're going** *or* **selling like hot cakes** ça se vend comme des petits pains; *Prov* **you can't have your c. and eat it** on ne peut pas avoir le beurre et l'argent du beurre; **a great c. of mud** un gros paquet de boue **(b)** *Old-fashioned* (*of soap*) pain *m*; (*of chocolate, paint*) tablette *f*
cake[2] *vi* (*solidify*) former une croûte; (*of mud*) sécher; (*of blood etc*) coaguler
caked [keɪkt] *adj* (*mud*) séché; (*blood*) coagulé; **c. with mud/blood** couvert de boue/sang séché(e)
cake mix *n* préparation *f* pour gâteau
cake shop *n* pâtisserie *f*
cake stand *n* présentoir *m* à gâteaux
cake tin *n* moule *m* à gâteau
cakewalk ['keɪkwɔːk] *n* (*dance*) cake-walk *m*; *Am Fig F* **it was a c.** (*very easy*) c'était du gâteau
CAL [kæl] *n Comptr* (*abbr* **computer-aided learning**) EAO *m*
Cal *abbr* **California**
calabash ['kæləbæʃ] *n* **(a) c. (gourd)** calebasse *f*, gourde *f*; **c. tree** calebassier *m* **(b)** (*bottle*) calebasse *f*, gourde *f*
calaboose ['kæləbuːs] *n US Sl* (*prison*) taule *f*, tôle *f*; **ten days in the c.** dix jours de taule *ou* tôle
calamine ['kæləmaɪn] *n* calamine *f*; **c. lotion** lotion *f* calmante à la calamine
calamitous [kə'læmɪtəs] *adj* désastreux
calamity [kə'læmɪtɪ] *n* désastre *m*, calamité *f*; *F* **C. Jane** Miss Catastrophe *f*
calcareous [kæl'keərɪəs] *adj Geol etc* calcaire
calceolaria [kælsɪə'leərɪə] *n* (*plant*) calcéolaire *f*
calcification [kælsɪfɪ'keɪʃən] *n* calcification *f*
calcify ['kælsɪfaɪ] *Ch etc* **1** *vt* calcifier **2** *vi* se calcifier
calcium ['kælsɪəm] *n Ch* calcium *m*; **c. deficiency** déficience *f* en calcium; **c. carbide/chloride** carbure *m*/chlorure *m* de calcium
calculable ['kælkjʊləb(ə)l] *adj* calculable
calculate ['kælkjʊleɪt] **1** *vt* **(a)** (*sum, figure, amount, distance*) calculer **(b)** (*intend*) **calculated to do sth** fait pour faire qch; **the remark was calculated to shock** la remarque était délibérément choquante **(c)** *Am F* (*think*) croire, supposer **(that** que) **2** *vi esp Am* (*rely*) **to c. on sth/on doing sth** compter sur qch/compter faire qch
calculated ['kælkjʊleɪtɪd] *adj* (*insolence etc*) délibéré, calculé; (*crime*) prémédité; **words c. to reassure us** paroles propres à nous rassurer; *Comptr* **c. field** champ *m* calculé; **c. risk** risque *m* calculé
calculating ['kælkjʊleɪtɪŋ] **1** *adj* (*person*) calculateur, -trice; **this was not the action of a c. murderer** ce n'était pas un meurtre prémédité **2** *n* calcul *m*; (*estimate*) estimation *f*; **c. machine** machine *f* à calculer
calculation [kælkjʊ'leɪʃən] *n* calcul *m*; **to make a c.** effectuer un calcul; **to upset sb's calculations** bouleverser les calculs de qn
calculator ['kælkjʊleɪtər] *n* **(a)** (*machine*) calculatrice *f*, machine *f* à calculer; (*pocket*) calculatrice, calculette *f* **(b)** (*person*) calculateur, -trice
calculus ['kælkjʊləs] *n Math, Med* calcul *m*
Calcutta [kæl'kʌtə] *n* Calcutta *m ou f*
Caledonia [kælɪ'dəʊnɪə] *n Lit, Antiq* (*Scotland*) Calédonie *f*
Caledonian [kælɪ'dəʊnɪən] *Lit, Antiq* **1** *adj* calédonien **2** *n* Calédonien, -ienne
calendar ['kælɪndər] *n* (*of dates*), *Rel* calendrier *m*; (*of institution, university etc*) annuaire *m*; *Jur* (*list of cases*) rôle *m* des causes; (*in criminal law*) rôle des assises; *US* (*of Congress*) ordre *m* du jour; **I'll check my c.** je vais vérifier mon agenda; **c. of (forthcoming) events** calendrier des manifestations; **the club has a full c. this month** le club a un calendrier chargé ce mois-ci; **an important date in the publishing c.** une date importante dans le calendrier de l'édition; **c. month** mois *m* civil; **c. year** année *f* civile
calender[1] ['kælɪndər] *n Tech* calandre *f*
calender[2] *vt Tech* calandrer
calendered ['kælɪndəd] *adj* (*paper*) calandré, satiné
calends ['kælɪndz] *npl Antiq* calendes *fpl*
calf[1], *pl* **calves** [kɑːf, kɑːvz] *n* **(a)** (*animal*) veau *m*; **cow in** *or* **with c.** vache *f* pleine; **buffalo c.** buffletin *m*; **elephant c.** éléphanteau *m*; **sea c.** phoque *m* commun; **whale c.** baleineau *m*; *F* **c. love** les premières amours *fpl*; *F* **it was just c. love** c'était un amour de jeunesse **(b)** (*leather*) veau *m*; **c. binding** (*of book*) reliure *f* en veau *ou* en vélin **(c)** (*broken off from iceberg*) glaçon *m*
calf,[2] *pl* **calves** *n* (*of leg*) mollet *m*; **c-length boots** demi-bottes *fpl*
calfskin ['kɑːfskɪn] *n* (cuir *m* de) veau *m*; **c. wallet** portefeuille *m* en veau
caliber ['kælɪbər] *n US* = **calibre**
calibrate ['kælɪbreɪt] *vt Tech* (*measuring instrument etc*) étalonner; (*bore*) calibrer; (*thermometer*) graduer; *Mil* (*piece of artillery*) vérifier le calibre de
calibration [kælɪ'breɪʃən] *n* (*of measuring instrument*) étalonnage *m*; (*of bore*) calibrage *m*
calibre, *US* **caliber** ['kælɪbər] *n* (*of firearm, Fig of person*) calibre *m*; **a man of your c.** un homme de votre calibre *ou* envergure; **a very high c. translator** un traducteur de très grande envergure
calico ['kælɪkəʊ] **1** *n Tex* calicot *m*; **printed c.,** *US* **c.** calicot imprimé, indienne *f* **2** *adj* **(a)** *Tex* de calicot **(b)** *US* (*cow*) tacheté; (*cat*) moucheté
California [kælɪ'fɔːnɪə] *n* Californie *f*
Californian [kælɪ'fɔːnɪən] **1** *adj* californien **2** *n* Californien, -ienne
caliper ['kælɪpər] *n* **(a)** *Aut* étrier *m* (de frein à disque) **(b)** = **calliper**
caliph ['keɪlɪf] *n* calife *m*
caliphate ['keɪlɪfɪt] *n* califat *m*
calisthenics [kælɪs'θenɪks] *n* [①**A10**,c] *esp US* gymnastique *f* rythmique
calk[1] [kɔːk] *vt Art etc* décalquer
calk[2] *vt* (*ship*) calfater, étouper
call[1] [kɔːl] *n* **(a)** (*shout*) appel *m*, cri *m*; (*of bird*) cri; **to give sb a c.** appeler qn
(b) (*summons*) (*of person*) convocation *f*; (*of bugle*) sonnerie *f*; **c. for help** appel *m* au secours; **the President's c. for calm** l'appel au calme lancé par le Président; **to come**

at/answer sb's c. venir/répondre à l'appel de qn; **on c.** (*doctor*) de garde; (*interpreter, engineer etc*) disponible à tout moment; **to be within c.** être à portée de voix; **to give sb a c.** (*waken*) réveiller qn; *Euph* **to obey** *or* **answer a c. of nature** satisfaire un besoin naturel; **c. for tenders** appel d'offres; **c. sheet** (*in hotel etc*) feuille *f* des réveils

(**c**) *Rel* vocation *f*; **he felt a c. (to the ministry)** il se sentait une vocation religieuse

(**d**) *Tel* **(telephone) c.** coup *m* de téléphone *ou F* de fil, *Fml* appel *m* téléphonique; **to make a c.** passer un coup de téléphone *ou F* de fil; **to give sb a c.** téléphoner à qn, appeler qn (au téléphone), *F* passer un coup de fil à qn; **you have a c. from Canada** on vous appelle du Canada; **you had a c. from Pam** Pam t'a appelé; **there was a c. for you** il y a eu un coup de téléphone *ou* un appel pour toi; **he's on a c.** il est en ligne; **will you accept the c.?** (*when charges are reversed*) est-ce que vous prenez *ou* acceptez l'appel?; **to put a c. through** passer la communication; **to return sb's c.** rappeler qn; **local c.** appel local

(**e**) (*visit*) visite *f*; *Com* (*of representative*) passage *m*; **to pay** *or* **make a c. on sb** rendre visite à qn; *Euph* **to pay a c.** (*go to toilet*) aller se laver les mains

(**f**) (*demand*) demande *f*; **there's not much c. for ...** il n'y a pas une forte demande de ...; **there's not much c. for them** ce n'est pas un article très demandé

(**g**) (*need*) besoin *m*; **there's no c. for rudeness!** pas besoin *ou* ce n'est pas la peine d'être impoli!

(**h**) *Cards* (*at bridge*) appel *m*; (*at solo whist, boston*) demande *f*; **c. for trumps** invite *f* d'atout; **a c. of three diamonds** une annonce de trois carreaux

(**i**) *Tennis, Cr* (*of umpire*) décision *f*

(**j**) *Fin* (*for money*) demande *f*, appel *m* de fonds *ou* de versement; **c. for capital** appel de fonds; **payable at c.** remboursable sur demande *ou* à vue; **money at** *or* **on c., c. money** prêts *mpl* au jour le jour, argent *m* à court terme; *Banking* **c. deposit** dépôt *m* à vue; *St Exch* **c. (option)** call *m*

call² **1** *vt* (**a**) (*attract attention of*) (*person*) appeler; **come quickly, he called** venez vite, a-t-il crié

(**b**) (*say out loud*) **to c. sb's name** appeler qn; **to c. the banns** publier les bans; **to c. a halt** faire halte; **to c. the roll** faire l'appel

(**c**) (*summon*) (*person, fire brigade, lift*) appeler; (*meeting*) convoquer; *Jur* (*case*) appeler; **to c. sb's attention to sth** attirer l'attention de qn sur qch; **to c. a strike** appeler à la grève; **to c. the doctor** faire venir le médecin, appeler le médecin; **I was called to the manager's office** j'ai été appelé dans le bureau du directeur; **c. me at six o'clock** (*wake me*) réveillez-moi à six heures; **to be called away on an emergency** être appelé en urgence; **she's been called away, her mother is ill** elle a dû s'absenter parce que sa mère est malade

(**d**) *Tel* (*person*) téléphoner à, appeler; (*taxi*) appeler; **I called her house** j'ai téléphoné chez elle; **I got the impression it was a case of 'don't c. us, we'll c. you'** j'ai eu l'impression que ça voulait dire 'on vous écrira'

(**e**) (*name*) appeler; **he is called Martin** (*that is his name*) il s'appelle Martin; (*by other people*) on l'appelle Martin; **c. me by my Christian** *or* **first name** appelez-moi par mon prénom; **to c. sb after sb** appeler qn comme qn; **she's called Margaret, after her grandmother** elle s'appelle Margaret, comme sa grand-mère; **to c. oneself a colonel** s'attribuer le titre de colonel; **c. yourself a carpenter!** et tu te prétends menuisier!; **and they c. themselves socialists!** et ils se disent socialistes!; **do you c. that clean?** c'est ce que tu appelles propre?; **to c. sb names** injurier qn, invectiver qn; **to c. sb a liar/a thief** traiter qn de menteur/de voleur; **we'll c. it three** mettons trois; **I c. that a dirty trick** voilà ce que j'appelle un sale tour

(**f**) *Cards* (*two diamonds etc*) appeler, déclarer; **to c. spades** déclarer pique

(**g**) (*call on*) **to c. a guarantee** faire jouer une garantie

2 *vi* (**a**) (*to attract attention*) **to c. to sb** appeler qn; **the bird was calling to its mother** l'oiseau appelait sa mère

(**b**) (*summon*) **duty calls** le devoir m'appelle

(**c**) (*visit, come to door etc*) passer; **has anyone called?** est-ce que quelqu'un est passé?; **I called at your house** je suis passé chez vous; **I must c. at the grocer's** il faut que je passe chez l'épicier; **to c. again** repasser; **the train calls at every station** le train s'arrête à toutes les gares; *Naut* **to c. at a port** (*of ship*) faire escale à un port

(**d**) *Tel* appeler; **who's calling, please?, may I ask who's calling?** c'est de la part de qui, s'il vous plaît?; **to c. again** rappeler

(**e**) *Cards* appeler (l'atout); (*at poker*) forcer l'adversaire à déclarer son jeu

▶ **call back** **1** *vtsep* (*person*) (*summon again*), *Tel* rappeler; *Th* (*with applause*) rappeler sur scène; **to c. sb back from vacation** demander à qn de rentrer de vacances **2** *vi* (**a**) (*return*) repasser; **I'll c. back for it** je repasserai le prendre *ou* le chercher (**b**) *Tel* rappeler

▶ **call by** *vi* = **call round 1** (**a**)

▶ **call down** **1** *vtsep* **they called her down from upstairs** ils lui ont demandé de descendre; **to c. down God's wrath upon sb** appeler la colère de Dieu sur qn **2** *vi* **I called down after him** je l'ai appelé du haut de l'escalier/de la fenêtre/*etc*

▶ **call for** *vipo* (**a**) (*summon*) (*person*) appeler, faire venir; (*sth*) faire apporter; (*drink etc*) commander; **to c. for help** crier au secours, appeler à l'aide

(**b**) (*collect*) (*sb, sth*) venir prendre, venir chercher; **to be called for** (*by messenger*) à remettre au messager; (*on envelope*) poste restante; *Rail* en gare

(**c**) (*request, demand*) (*explanation, apology*) demander, exiger; **the opposition were calling for his resignation** l'opposition exigeait sa démission; **some union members are calling for industrial action** certains syndicalistes appellent à la grève; **the police are calling for tougher penalties** la police réclame des sanctions plus fermes; **to c. for volunteers** demander des volontaires

(**d**) (*require*) (*attention, reform*) demander, réclamer, exiger; **situation that calls for tactful handling** situation qui demande à être gérée avec tact; **this calls for a celebration/a drink!** il faut fêter/arroser ça!; **that sort of behaviour isn't called for** on se passe bien de ce genre de comportement; **that wasn't called for** ça n'était vraiment pas nécessaire

▶ **call in** **1** *vtsep* (**a**) (*person*) (*into building, office etc*) faire entrer; **c. Miss Smith in, please** faites entrer Mlle Smith, s'il vous plaît; **she called the children in** (*back into the house*) elle a fait rentrer les enfants

(**b**) (*withdraw from circulation*) (*coin, book*) retirer de la circulation; (*of manufacturer*) (*defective product*) rappeler; **to c. in one's money** faire rentrer ses fonds; **to c. in a loan** (*of bank*) demander le remboursement d'un prêt

(**c**) (*specialist, army*) (*for advice, help*) faire appel à

2 *vi* (**a**) (*visit*) rendre visite; **to c. in at sb's house/at the grocer's** passer chez qn/chez l'épicier; **to c. in to see sb** aller/venir voir qn; **I'll c. in on my way home** je passerai en rentrant chez moi

(**b**) (*by telephone*) passer un coup de téléphone *ou F* de fil; **nurses called in and offered to help** des infirmières ont téléphoné pour offrir leur aide; **to c. in sick** téléphoner pour prévenir qu'on est malade

▶ **call off** *vtsep* (**a**) (*cancel*) (*appointment, strike, match, holiday*) annuler; (*deal*) rompre, annuler; **they were going to get married, but they called it off** ils étaient sur le point de se marier mais ils ont tout annulé; **she called it off** elle a rompu (**b**) (*tell to come away*) (*dog*) rappeler

▶ **call on** *vipo* (**a**) (*request*) **to c. on sb for sth** demander instamment qch à qn, réclamer qch à qn; **to c. on sb to do sth** demander instamment à qn de faire qch, prier instamment qn de faire qch; **I c. on the government to act** je demande instamment au gouvernement d'agir; **I now c. on Mr Stewart** (*to speak*) la parole est à M. Stewart; **the limited resources the police can c. on** les ressources limitées que la police peut mettre en œuvre; **to call on the experts/sb's services** faire appel aux *ou* avoir recours aux experts/services de qn

(**b**) (*person*) (*visit*) rendre visite à; (*drop in on*) passer voir

(**c**) (*name of God*) invoquer

▶ **call out** **1** *vtsep* (**a**) (*summon*) (*person*) faire sortir, prier de sortir; (*fire brigade*) appeler; **to c. out workers (on strike)** donner l'ordre de grève à des ouvriers (**b**) (*shout*) crier; **she called out the winning number** elle a annoncé le numéro gagnant **2** *vi* (**a**) (*shout out*) appeler; **to c. out in anger/pain** crier de colère/douleur; **to c. out for sth** appeler pour demander qch (**b**) **to c. out for** (*urgently require*) nécessiter de façon urgente; **it's calling out for it!** c'est urgent de le faire!; *F* **this room is calling out for red velvet curtains** il faut à tout prix des rideaux de velours rouge dans cette pièce

▶ **call round** **1** *vi* (**a**) (*in person*) passer; **c. round when you're in the area** passez nous/me/*etc* voir quand vous serez dans la région (**b**) (*on telephone*) passer une série de coups de fil; **c. round and see if any of the local shops have any** téléphonez pour savoir si les boutiques du coin en ont **2** *vipo* (*on phone*) **I've called round all her friends** j'ai appelé tous ses amis

▶ **call up** **1** *vtsep* (**a**) (*summon*) (*person*) faire monter; *Mil etc* (*reinforcements*) appeler (**b**) (*evoke*) (*spirit*) invoquer; (*memory*) évoquer (**c**) *Tel* (*person*) téléphoner à, appeler (au téléphone) (**d**) *Mil, Naut* (*reservist*) mobiliser; (*for military *service*) appeler; **to be called up** être mobilisé/appelé **(e)** *Fin* **called-up capital** capital *m* appelé **(f)** *Comptr* (*help screen etc*) appeler **2** *vi* **I called up after him** je l'ai appelé du bas de l'escalier/l'échelle/*etc*

callable [ˈkɔːləb(ə)l] *adj Fin* (*loan*) remboursable avant échéance; **c. loan** crédit *m* révocable

callbox [ˈkɔːlbɒks] *n* cabine *f* téléphonique

callboy [ˈkɔːlbɔɪ] *n Th etc* avertisseur *m*

call button *n* bouton d'appel

caller [ˈkɔːlər] *n* **(a)** (*visitor*) visiteur, -euse; **to be a frequent c. at sb's house** aller souvent chez qn **(b)** *Tel* personne *f* qui appelle (au téléphone); *Comptr* appelant *m*; **did the c. say anything?** est-ce qu'il/elle a dit quelque chose?; **the vast majority of callers just need someone to talk to** la plupart des gens qui nous appellent ont juste besoin de parler; **one minute please, c.** un instant s'il vous plaît, monsieur/madame **(c)** (*in bingo hall*) celui/celle qui annonce les numéros gagnants

call forwarding *n Tel* redirection *f* d'appel; **c. device** dispositif *m* de redirection d'appel

call girl *n* call-girl *f*

call holding *n Tel* mise *f* en attente d'appels

calligrapher [kəˈlɪgrəfər] *n* calligraphe *mf*

calligraphy [kəˈlɪgrəfɪ] *n* calligraphie *f*

calling [ˈkɔːlɪŋ] *n* **(a)** (*shouting*) appel *m*; **the stallholders' c. of their wares** les cris des marchands qui vantent leurs marchandises **(b)** (*of meeting etc*) convocation *f* **(c)** (*vocation*) vocation *f* **(for** pour); **I felt no/a c. for a religious life** je n'avais pas/j'avais la vocation **(d)** (*profession*) profession *f*, métier *m*

calling card *n Am* carte *f* de visite

calling in *n Fin* (*of debt*) demande *f* de remboursement immédiat

calling off *n* **(a)** (*cancellation*) (*of appointment, match, holidays*) annulation *f*; (*of deal*) rupture *f*; **the c. of the strike** l'annulation de l'ordre de grève **(b)** (*of dog, guards etc*) rappel *m*

calling up *n* **(a)** (*of memory*) évocation *f* **(b)** (*by telephone*) appel *m* au téléphone **(c)** *Mil, Naut* appel *m* (sous les drapeaux)

calliper [ˈkælɪpər] *n* **(a)** *Tech* **c. compasses, (pair of) callipers** compas *m* de calibre *ou* à calibrer **(b)** *Med* **c. (splint)** attelle-étrier *f*, *pl* attelles-étriers

callisthenics [kælɪsˈθenɪks] *n* [①A10,c] gymnastique *f* rythmique

call key *n Telecom* touche *f* d'appel

call letters *npl Am Rad, Naut* indicatif *m* d'appel

call option *n St Exch* option *f* d'achat

callosity [kæˈlɒsɪtɪ] *n Fml* callosité *f*

callous [ˈkæləs] *adj* (*person*) dur, sans cœur; (*treatment, behaviour*) dur, brutal; (*remark*) dur; **to be c. to sb** être dur avec qn; **the c. way in which the government has reacted** la dureté de la réaction du gouvernement; **to show a c. indifference to sth** montrer une indifférence totale pour qch

calloused [ˈkæləst] *adj* (*skin, feet, hands*) calleux

callously [ˈkæləslɪ] *adv* durement

callousness [ˈkæləsnɪs] *n* (*of person*) dureté *f*, insensibilité *f*, manque *m* de cœur; (*of treatment, behaviour*) dureté

callout [ˈkɔːlaʊt] *n* (*by maintenance man*) dépannage *m*; **c. charge** (frais *mpl* de) déplacement *m*; **c. maintenance insurance** assurance *f* maintenance visite

callow [ˈkæləʊ] *adj* (*youth*) sans expérience

callowness [ˈkæləʊnɪs] *n* manque *m* d'expérience

call sign *n Rad, Naut* indicatif *m* d'appel

call-up *n Mil* appel *m* (sous les drapeaux); **c. papers** fascicule *m* de mobilisation; **to receive one's c. papers** être appelé sous les drapeaux

callus [ˈkæləs] *n* (*on skin*) cal *m*, *pl* cals, durillon *m*

calm¹ [kɑːm] **1** *n* (*peace*), *Naut* calme *m*; (*person*) tranquillité *f*, sérénité *f*; **the government appealed for c.** le gouvernement appela au calme; *Naut* **flat c.** calme plat; **period of c.** accalmie *f*; *Naut, Fig* **the c. before the storm** le calme avant la tempête **2** *adj* (*peaceful*) calme, tranquille; (*person*) calme, posé; (*sea*) calme; (*day*) sans vent; **to remain** *or* **keep c.** rester calme; **to grow calmer** se calmer

calm² *vt* (*anger, people, storm of protest etc*) calmer, apaiser; (*pain*) calmer, atténuer; **this will c. your nerves** *or* **you** cela vous calmera; **c. yourself** calmez-vous!

▶ **calm down 1** *vi* (*of person, storm*) se calmer; (*of sea, wind*) calmir, se calmer; **things have calmed down** (*after crisis, busy spell etc*) les choses se sont calmées **2** *vtsep* (*person*) calmer

calming [ˈkɑːmɪŋ] **1** *adj* (*effect etc*) tranquillisant, calmant **2** *n* (*of waves, anger etc*) apaisement *m*; (*of pain*) atténuation *f*

calmly [ˈkɑːmlɪ] *adv* calmement; **she c. shot him** elle lui tira dessus sans sourciller; **he just c. wrote out a cheque for £50,000** il a fait un chèque de 50 000 livres sans cérémonie

calmness [ˈkɑːmnɪs] *n* (*of person*) tranquillité *f*, calme *m*; (*of sea*) calme

caloric [kəˈlɒrɪk] *adj Phys* calorique

calorie [ˈkælərɪ] *n Phys* calorie *f*; **to be low/high in calories** (*of food*) être pauvre/riche en calories; **low-c. diet, c. controlled diet** régime *m* hypocalorique *ou* basses calories *ou* faible en calories; **calories per serving** nombre *m* de calories par portion; *F* **to watch** *or* **count the calories** surveiller sa ligne

calorific [kæləˈrɪfɪk] *adj Phys* calorifique; **c. value** pouvoir *m ou* apport *m* calorifique

calumniate [kəˈlʌmnɪeɪt] *vt Fml* calomnier

calumny [ˈkæləmnɪ] *n* calomnie *f*

Calvary [ˈkælvərɪ] *n* **(a)** **(Mount) C.** le Calvaire **(b)** *Fig* **c.** calvaire *m*

calve [kɑːv] *vi* (*of cow*) vêler

calving [ˈkɑːvɪŋ] *n* (*of cow*) vêlage *m*, vêlement *m*; **at c. time** pendant le vêlement

Calvinism [ˈkælvɪnɪz(ə)m] *n Rel, Hist* calvinisme *m*

Calvinist [ˈkælvɪnɪst] *n, adj Rel, Hist* calviniste *mf*

calypso [kəˈlɪpsəʊ] *n Mus* calypso *m*

calyx, *pl* **-yxes, -yces** [ˈkeɪlɪks, -ɪksiːz, -ɪsiːz] *n Bot* calice *m*

CAM [kæm] *n Comptr* (*abbr* **computer-assisted manufacture**) FAO *f*

cam [kæm] *n Tech etc* came *f*; *Aut* **c. follower** poussoir *m*

camber¹ [ˈkæmbər] *n* (*of road*) bombement *m*; (*of beam*) cambrure *f*; *Naut* (*of deck*) tonture *f*; *Aut* (*of wheel*) carrossage *m*; *Av* (*of wing*) flèche *f*

camber² **1** *vt* (*road surface*) bomber; (*beam*) cambrer **2** *vi* (*of road*) bomber; (*of beam*) cambrer

Cambodia [kæmˈbəʊdɪə] *n* Cambodge *m*

Cambodian [kæmˈbəʊdɪən] **1** *adj* cambodgien **2** *n* **(a)** Cambodgien, -ienne **(b)** *Ling* cambodgien *m*

cambric [ˈkæmbrɪk, ˈkeɪm-] *n Tex* batiste *f*

Cambs [kæmz] *abbr* **Cambridgeshire**

camcorder [ˈkæmkɔːdər] *n Phot* caméscope *m*

camel [ˈkæməl] *n* **(a)** (*animal*) chameau *m*; **she c.** chamelle *f*; **c. driver** chamelier *m*; *Mil* **c. corps** compagnies *fpl* de méharistes **(b)** (*colour*) chameau *m inv*

camelhair [ˈkæməlheər] *n* poil *m* de chameau; **c. brush** (*for watercolour painting*) pinceau *m* en petit-gris; **c. coat** manteau *m* en poil de chameau

camellia [kəˈmiːlɪə] *n* camélia *m*

cameo [ˈkæmɪəʊ] *n* **(a)** (*gem*) camée *m*; **c. (brooch)** camée **(b)** *Th, Cin* **c. (role** *or* **part)** brève apparition *f* (*joué par un acteur connu*)

camera [ˈkæmərə] *n* **(a)** *Phot* appareil-photo *m*, *pl* appareils-photos; *TV, Cin* caméra *f*; **I'm no good with a c.** je ne suis pas doué pour prendre des photos; *TV, Cin* **in front of the c.** devant les caméras; *TV* **on c.** à l'écran; **film c.** caméra *f*; **c. angle** angle *m* de prise de vue; **c. assistant** assistant opérateur *m*; **c. blocking** (*rehearsal*) prise *f* de repères; **c. crew** équipe *f* de prise de vue, équipe caméra; **c. cue** signal *m* caméra; **c. head** tête *f* de caméra; *TV, Cin* **c. matte** cache *m* de caméra; **c. operator** cadreur *m*, opérateur *m* de prise de vue; **c. platform** plateforme *f* de prise de vue; **c. script** liste *f* des mouvements de caméra; **c. test** essai *m* (de) caméra; **c. tower** échafaudage *m* pour caméra, tour *f*; **c. tube** tube *m* image *ou* analyseur, tube de caméra; **c. unit** unité *f* de tournage

(b) *Jur* **in c.** à huis clos; **the trial was held in c.** le procès a eu lieu à huis clos

cameraman, *pl* **-men** [ˈkæmərəmən] *n Cin, TV* cameraman *m*, *pl* cameramen; **assistant c.** opérateur *m*

camera obscura [ɒbˈskjʊərə] *n Opt* chambre *f* noire

camera-ready copy *n Typ* épreuves *fpl* bonnes à filmer

camera-shy *adj* **he is c.** il n'aime pas être pris en photo; (*doesn't like being filmed*) il n'aime pas être filmé

camerawork [ˈkæmərəwɜːk] *n* photographie *f*; *TV, Cin* prise(s) *f(pl)* de vues, photographie; (*document*) document *m* d'exécution

Cameroon [kæməˈruːn] *n* **the Republic of C.** la République fédérale du Cameroun

camiknickers [ˈkæmɪnɪkəz] *npl* sous-vêtement *m* féminin comprenant une culotte et une chemise

camisole [ˈkæmɪsəʊl] *n* caraco *m*

camomile [ˈkæməmaɪl] *n Bot, Culin* camomille *f*; **c. tea** (tisane *f* de) camomille

camouflage¹ [ˈkæməflɑːʒ] *n Mil etc, Fig* camouflage *m*; *Mil* **c. painting/net(ting)** peinture *f*/filet *m* de camouflage

camouflage² *vt Mil etc* camoufler; *Fig* (*one's intentions etc*) dissimuler

camp¹ [kæmp] **1** *n* camp *m*, campement *m*; **to break c.** lever le camp; *Fig* **to go over to the other c.** passer dans l'autre camp; *Fig* **to have a foot in both camps** manger à deux râteliers; **gipsy c.** camp *ou* campement de gitans; **(holiday) c.** camp de vacances; (*for children*) ≈ colonie *f* de vacances **2** *adj F* **(a)** (*affected*) affecté; (*suggesting homosexuality*) efféminé **(b)** (*kitsch*) (*decor*) kitsch

camp[2] **1** *vi* camper **2** *vt F* **to c. it up** forcer la dose

▶ **camp out** *vi* camper

campaign[1] [kæm'peɪn] *n* campagne *f*; **on c.** en campagne; **to lead** *or* **conduct a c. against sb** mener (une) campagne contre qn; **advertising c.** campagne publicitaire; *Mil* **c. medal** médaille *f* commémorative

campaign[2] *vi Mil* faire (une)/des campagne(s); *Pol* faire campagne; **she campaigned on an anti-drug platform** elle a axé sa campagne sur la lutte contre la drogue; **they campaigned for his release** ils ont mené une campagne pour sa libération; **campaigning journalism** journalisme *m* militant

campaigner [kæm'peɪnər] *n* (*activist*) militant, -ante; **old c.** *Mil* vieux soldat *m*, vieux troupier *m*; *Fig* vétéran *m*

campanologist [kæmpə'nɒlədʒɪst] *n* carillonneur *m*

campanology [kæmpə'nɒlədʒɪ] *n* art *m* du carillon

campanula [kæm'pænjʊlə] *n* (*flower*) campanule *f*

camp bed *n* lit *m* de camp

camp chair *n* pliant *m*, chaise *f* pliante

camper ['kæmpər] *n* (*person*) campeur, -euse; (*vehicle*) camping-car *m*, *pl* camping-cars

campfire ['kæmpfaɪər] *n* feu *m* de camp

camp follower *n Mil* (*prostitute*) prostituée *f* (*qui suit les soldats dans leurs déplacements*); (*civilian*) civil *m* qui accompagne une armée; *Fig* compagnon *m* de route

camphor ['kæmfər] *n* camphre *m*; **c. oil** essence *f* de camphre; **c. tree** camphrier *m*

camphorated ['kæmfəreɪtɪd] *adj* (*oil etc*) camphré

camping ['kæmpɪŋ] *n* camping *m*; **to go c.** faire du camping; **c. ground** terrain *m* de camping; **c. holiday** vacances *fpl* (en) camping; **c. site** (terrain *m* de) camping; **c. equipment** *or* **gear** matériel *m ou* équipement *m* de camping; **c. stove** réchaud *m* de camping

camping-caravanning *n* campage-caravanage *m*, camping-caravaning *m*

campion ['kæmpɪən] *n* (*plant*) lychnide *f*, lychnis *m*; **white c.** compagnon *m* blanc

camp site *n* camp *m*; (*specially designed*) (terrain *m* de) camping *m*

camp stool *n* pliant *m*, chaise *f* pliante

campus ['kæmpəs] *n* campus *m* (universitaire); **they live on c.** (*of students*) ils vivent sur le campus

camshaft ['kæmʃɑːft] *n* arbre *m* à came(s); **c. drive** entraînement *m* d'arbre à cames; **c. timing gear** pignon *m* de calage d'arbre à cames

can[1] [kæn] *n* **(a)** (*for drink, esp Am food*) boîte *f* **(b)** (*for petrol, oil, water etc*) bidon *m*; (*for milk, film*) boîte *f*; *F Fig* **to carry the c.** payer les pots cassés; *F* **I'm not carrying the c. for you** je ne vais pas payer les pots cassés pour toi; *F* **in the c.** (*of film*) en boîte; *Fig* (*of deal etc*) dans la poche; *F Fig* **c. of worms** problème *m* insoluble; *F Fig* **don't let's open up that c. of worms** ne nous occupons pas de ce problème pour le moment; *Am* **trash** *or* **garbage c.** poubelle *f*; **watering c.** arrosoir *m* **(c)** *F* **cans** (*earphones*) casque *m* **(d)** *Sl* (*prison*) taule *f*, tôle *f* **(e)** *Am Sl* (*lavatory*) **the c.** les chiottes *fpl*

can[2] *vt* **(-nn-)** **(a)** (*put in cans*) (*meat etc*) mettre en boîte *ou* en conserve; **canned fruit** fruits en conserve *ou* en boîte; *Am Sl* **c. it!** (*shut up!*) la ferme! **(b)** *US Sl* (*dismiss*) (*person*) virer

can[3] (*stressed* [kæn], *unstressed* [k(ə)n]) *modal aux v* [①A57,c; B37,K,2] (*pr* **can**; *neg* **cannot** ['kænɒt], *US* **can not** ['kæn'nɒt]; *pt, cond* **could** [kʊd]; *no inf, prp, pp; defective parts are supplied from* **to be able to**; **cannot** *and* **could not** *are often contracted into* **can't** [kɑːnt], **couldn't** ['kʊdnt]) **(a)** (*be able to*) pouvoir; **I c. do it** je peux le faire; **we cannot** *or US* **c. not possibly do it** nous ne pouvons absolument pas le faire; **I will come as soon/as often as I c.** je viendrai aussitôt/aussi souvent que possible; **he will do what he c.** il fera ce qu'il pourra; **I will help you all I c., I will do all I c. to help you** je vous aiderai de mon mieux, je ferai tout mon possible pour vous aider; **I can't very well accept** il m'est difficile d'accepter; *F* **I'd like it finished by tomorrow — c. do!** j'aimerais que ce soit fini demain — aucun problème!; *F* **no c. do** c'est impossible; **(it) can't be helped!** tant pis!, on n'y peut rien!; **it can't be done** il est impossible de le faire; **how could he say that?** comment a-t-il pu dire cela?; **how c. you say that?** comment peux-tu dire une chose pareille?; **what c. it be?** qu'est-ce que cela peut bien être?; **c. it be true?** serait-ce vrai?; **(it) could be** c'est possible; **I never <u>could</u> understand maths** je n'ai jamais été capable de comprendre les maths; **what <u>can</u> he want?** qu'est-ce qu'il peut bien me/nous/*etc* vouloir?; **how <u>could</u> you!** comment avez-vous pu faire une chose pareille?; **he could not have been kinder** il n'aurait pu être plus aimable

(b) (*know how to*) savoir; **I c. swim** je sais nager; **a man who c. cook** un homme qui sait faire la cuisine; **she c. play the violin** elle sait jouer du violon

(c) (*indicating possibility*) **you don't know how hot it c. get** vous ne savez pas à quel point il peut faire chaud; **the crossing c. be rough** il arrive que la traversée soit mauvaise; **adult animals c. grow to 20 feet** l'animal adulte peut mesurer jusqu'à 6 mètres; **you <u>can't</u> be serious!** tu plaisantes!

(d) (*indicating permissibility*) pouvoir; **when c. I move in?** quand est-ce que je peux emménager?; **could you be quiet please?** pourriez-vous vous taire, s'il vous plaît?; **c. I ask you something?** est-ce que je peux vous demander quelque chose?; **you can't smoke in here** il est défendu de fumer ici

(e) (*asking help*) pouvoir; **c. you help me?** peux-tu m'aider?; (*asking more politely*) pourrais-tu m'aider?; **could you get me some water?** pourriez-vous m'apporter de l'eau?

(f) (*making suggestion*) pouvoir; **we could always telephone** nous pourrions toujours téléphoner; **you could go to the beach** tu pourrais aller à la plage; **I c. help if you like** je peux t'aider si tu veux

(g) (*with 'see', 'hear' etc: not translated*) **I c. see nothing** je ne vois rien; **c. you see that hill?** est-ce que tu vois cette colline?; **I could hear them talking** je les entendais parler; **I c. see you don't believe me** je vois bien que vous ne me croyez pas; **how c. you tell?** comment le savez-vous?

(h) (*in conditional*) **he could have done it** il aurait pu le faire; **I could not have asked for anything better** je n'aurais pas désiré mieux; **I could weep/could have wept** j'ai/j'avais envie de pleurer; **I could have smacked his face!** je l'aurais giflé!; **you could have warned me!** tu aurais pu me prévenir!

(i) (*elliptically*) **I cannot but believe him** je suis bien forcé de le croire; **you c. but try** vous pouvez toujours essayer

Canada ['kænədə] *n* Canada *m*; **in C.** au Canada; **C. Day** la fête du Canada; **C. goose** bernache *f* du Canada

Canadian [kə'neɪdɪən] **1** *adj* canadien; *Ling* **C. French/English** français *m*/anglais *m* du Canada **2** *n* Canadien, -ienne

Canadianism [kə'neɪdɪənɪz(ə)m] *n* canadianisme *m*

canal [kə'næl] *n* **(a)** (*waterway*) canal *m*, -aux; **ship c.** canal maritime; **c. boat** *or* **barge** péniche *f*; *Geog* **the C. zone** la zone du Canal de Panama **(b)** *Anat etc* canal *m*; **auditory c.** conduit *m* auditif

canalization [kænəlaɪ'zeɪʃən] *n* canalisation *f*

canalize ['kænəlaɪz] *vt* (*river etc*), *Fig* canaliser; **to c. one's efforts/energy into sth** canaliser ses efforts/son énergie dans qch

canapé ['kænəpeɪ] *n Culin* canapé *m*

canard ['kænɑːd, kə'nɑːd] *n Lit* canard *m*, fausse nouvelle *f*

Canary [kə'neərɪ] *n* **the C. Islands, the Canaries** les îles *fpl* Canaries

canary [kə'neərɪ] *n* (*bird*) serin *m*, canari *m*; **c. seed** (grains *mpl* de) millet *m*; **c. yellow** jaune *m* canari

canasta [kə'næstə] *n Cards* canasta *f*

cancan ['kænkæn] *n* cancan *m*; **c. dancer** danseuse *f* de cancan

cancel ['kæns(ə)l] **(-ll-,** *US* **-l-)** **1** *vt* **(a)** (*meeting, reservation, message, cheque, debt*) annuler; (*order*) *Com* annuler; *Mil* lever; (*deal, contract*) annuler, résilier; (*train*) supprimer; (*stamp*) oblitérer; **to c. each other** (*of two book-keeping entries*) s'annuler; **500, no c. that, 350 ...** 500, ou plutôt, 350 ... **(b)** *Math* (*factors in fraction*) éliminer **2** *vi* (*having made booking*) se décommander

▶ **cancel out** *vtsep Math* (*term*) annuler; **to c. each other out** s'annuler; **inflation cancelled out the increase in salary** l'inflation a annulé la hausse des salaires

cancel button *n Comptr* case *f* 'annuler'

cancellation [kænsə'leɪʃən] *n* annulation *f*; *Com* (*of order, sale, contract*) annulation, résiliation *f*; (*of stamp*) oblitération *f*; **there have been several cancellations** (*in restaurant, hotel*) il y a plusieurs réservations qui ont été annulées; **c. charge** *or* **fee** frais *mpl* d'annulation; **c. clause** clause *f* d'annulation *ou* de résiliation; **c. form** bon *m ou* bulletin *m* d'annulation; **c. holiday** = vacances *fpl* annulées et soldées

cancer ['kænsər] *n* **(a)** *Med* cancer *m*; **to have c.** avoir un *ou* le cancer; **c. of the lung/skin, lung/skin c.** cancer du poumon/de la peau; **c. of the pancreas** cancer du pancréas; *Fig* **we must remove the c. of militarism** il faut enrayer le cancer du militarisme; **c. patient** cancéreux, -euse; **c. specialist** cancérologue *mf*; **c. research** cancérologie *f* **(b)** *Astron* **C.** le Cancer; **to be (a) C.** être (du) Cancer **(c)** *Geog* **the Tropic of C.** le tropique du Cancer

cancer-causing ['kænsəkɔːzɪŋ] *adj* (*substance etc*) cancérigène
cancerous ['kæns(ə)rəs] *adj* cancéreux
candelabra, *pl* **-as** [kændɪ'lɑːbrə, -əz], **candelabrum,** *pl* **-a** [kændɪ'lɑːbrəm, -ə] *n* candélabre *m*
candid ['kændɪd] *adj* franc, *f* franche, sincère; **c. camera** caméra *f* invisible *ou* cachée
candida ['kændɪdə] *n Med* candidose *f*
candidacy ['kændɪdəsɪ] *n* candidature *f*
candidate ['kændɪdeɪt] *n* (*for job, office*) candidat, -ate (**for** à); **to stand as c. for sth** se présenter comme candidat à qch, poser sa candidature à qch; **presidential c.** candidat aux élections présidentielles; **successful candidates will have** ... les candidats retenus auront ...
candidature ['kændɪdətʃər] *n Br* candidature *f*
candidiasis ['kændɪdɪ'eɪsɪs] *n Med* muguet *m*, candidose *f*
candidly ['kændɪdlɪ] *adv* franchement, sincèrement
candidness ['kændɪdnɪs] *n* franchise *f*, sincérité *f*
candied ['kændɪd] *adj Culin* glacé, confit (au sucre); **c. peel** zeste *m* confit
candle¹ ['kænd(ə)l] *n* bougie *f*, *Old-fashioned* chandelle *f*; (*lit in church*) cierge *m*; **c. power** intensité *f* lumineuse; *Fig* **to burn the c. at both ends** brûler la chandelle par les deux bouts; *Fig* **he can't hold a c. to you** il ne vous arrive pas à la cheville; **c. grease** suif *m*
candlelight ['kænd(ə)llaɪt] *n* lumière *f* de bougie; **by c.** à la chandelle, à la bougie
candle-lit *adj* (*room*) éclairé à la bougie; (*meal*) aux chandelles
Candlemas ['kænd(ə)lməs] *n Rel* Chandeleur *f*
candlestick ['kænd(ə)lstɪk] *n* (*tall*) chandelier *m*; (*low*) bougeoir *m*
candlewick ['kænd(ə)lwɪk] *n* **(a)** *Tex* candlewick *m*, chenille *f* de coton; **c. bedspread/dressing gown** dessus *m* de lit/robe *f* de chambre en chenille de coton **(b)** (*of candle*) mèche *f* de bougie *ou* de chandelle
candour, *US* **candor** ['kændər] *n* franchise *f*, sincérité *f*
candy¹ ['kændɪ] *n Culin* **(a)** (**sugar**) **c.** sucre *m* candi; **stick of** (**sugar**) **c.** sucre d'orge; **c. apple** pomme *f* d'amour **(b)** *Am* (*sweet*) bonbon *m*; (*sweets*) bonbons; *F* **it's like taking c. from a baby** c'est simple comme bonjour; **c. store** confiserie *f*
candy² **1** *vt* (*sugar*) faire candir; (*fruit*) glacer **2** *vi* (*of sugar*) se candir, se cristalliser
candyfloss ['kændɪflɒs] *n Br Culin* barbe *f* à papa
candy-striped *adj Tex* à raies (de deux couleurs)
candy-striper ['kændɪstraɪpər] *n US Med F* = bénévole *mf*
cane¹ [keɪn] *n* **(a)** *Bot* (*of bamboo*) (canne *f* de) bambou *m*; (*of rattan*) rotin *m*; (*of raspberry bush*) tige *f*; **c. chair/furniture** siège *m*/meubles *mpl* en rotin; **c.-seated chair** chaise *f* cannée; **c. sugar** sucre *m* de canne **(b)** (*walking stick*) canne *f* **(c)** (*for punishment*) verge *f*, baguette *f*, badine *f*; **to get the c.** recevoir des coups de verge *ou* de baguette
cane² *vt* **(a)** (*person, pupil*) (*beat*) donner des coups de verge *ou* de baguette à **(b)** *Sl* (*defeat*) démolir **(c)** (*chair*) canner
canine ['keɪnaɪn, 'kæ-] **1** *adj, attrib* de chien; (*race, species*) canin; **c. devotion** dévotion *f* de chien; **c. tooth** canine *f* **2** *n* **(a)** (*tooth*) canine *f* **(b) canines** (*animals*) canidés *mpl*
caning ['keɪnɪŋ] *n* **(a)** (*punishment*) coups *mpl* de verge *ou* de baguette (*comme châtiment corporel*) **(b)** *Sl* **to get a c.** (*be defeated*) se faire démolir **(c)** (*in furniture*) cannage *m*
canister ['kænɪstər] *n* boîte *f* (en fer blanc)
canker ['kæŋkər] *n* **(a)** *Med, Fig* chancre *m* **(b)** *Vet* (*in horse's hoof*) crapaud *m*; (*of dog etc*) gale *f* de l'oreille **(c)** *Bot* chancre *m*; (*in wood*) nécrose *f*
cankerworm ['kæŋkəwɜːm] *n* ver *m* rongeur (des plantes)
cannabis ['kænəbɪs] *n* cannabis *m*; **c. resin** résine *f* de cannabis
canned [kænd] *adj* **(a)** *TV, Cin* (*laughter, applause*) préenregistré; **c. music** musique *f* de supermarché **(b)** *Sl* (*drunk*) soûl, beurré; **to get c.** se soûler, se beurrer
cannelloni [kænɪ'ləʊnɪ] *n* cannelloni *mpl*
cannery ['kænərɪ] *n* conserverie *f*
cannibal ['kænɪb(ə)l] *n, adj* cannibale *mf*
cannibalism ['kænɪbəlɪz(ə)m] *n* cannibalisme *m*
cannibalization [kænɪbəlaɪ'zeɪʃ(ə)n] *n Mktg, Aut* cannibalisation *f*
cannibalize ['kænɪbəlaɪz] *vt Tech, Aut etc* (*machine etc*) récupérer des pièces en bon état sur, cannibaliser; **cannibalized income** revenu *m* cannibalisé
cannily ['kænɪlɪ] *adv esp Scot* (*cautiously*) prudemment, avec circonspection; (*cleverly*) avec ruse
canning ['kænɪŋ] *n* (*of food*) mise *f* en conserve; **c. factory** conserverie *f*; **c. industry** industrie *f* de conserves alimentaires
cannon¹ ['kænən] *n* **(a)** (*usu inv*) *Mil* canon *m*; *Am Fig* **he's a loose c.** on ne sait pas trop ce qu'il va faire; **c. shot** (*ball*) boulet *m* de canon; (*act, noise*) coup *m* de canon; **c. fodder** chair *f* à canon **(b)** *Billiards* carambolage *m*; **c. off the cushion** bricole *f*
cannon² *vi Billiards* faire un carambolage, caramboler; **to c. off the cushion** (*of player*) jouer la bricole
▶ **cannon into** *vipo* se heurter à
cannonade¹ [kænə'neɪd] *n Old-fashioned Mil* canonnade *f*
cannonball ['kænənbɔːl] *n Mil, Fig* boulet *m* de canon; *Tennis* **c. serve** service *m* boulet de canon
cannot ['kænɒt] *see* **can³**
cannula ['kænələ] *n Med* canule *f*
canny ['kænɪ] *adj esp Scot* (*cautious*) prudent, circonspect; (*aware*) avisé; (*clever*) rusé; (*thrifty*) économe; **c. answer** réponse *f* de Normand
canoe¹ [kə'nuː] *n* canoë *m*; (**dugout**) **c.** pirogue *f*; *Fig* **to paddle one's own c.** mener seul sa barque
canoe² *vi* (*pp, pt* **canoed**; *prp* **canoeing**) faire du canoë; **to c. up the river** remonter la rivière en canoë
canoeing [kə'nuːɪŋ] *n* canoë *m*; **to go c.** faire du canoë; **c. holiday** vacances *fpl* organisées pour faire du canoë; **c. trip** voyage *m* en canoë
canoeist [kə'nuːɪst] *n* canoéiste *mf*
canon¹ ['kænən] *n* **(a)** *Rel* (*of mass etc*) canon *m*; **c. law** droit *m* canon **(b)** *Lit* (*rule*) canon *m* **(c)** *Liter* (*of author*) œuvre *f*; **the literary c.** les classiques *mpl* **(d)** *Mus* canon *m*
canon² *n Rel* (*priest*) chanoine *m*
canonical [kə'nɒnɪk(ə)l] **1** *adj* **(a)** *Rel* (*right, epistle, residence etc*) canonique; *Fig* (*accepted*) autorisé, accepté; **c. hours** *Cathol* heures *fpl* canoniales; *Church of Eng* heures pendant lesquelles il est permis de célébrer les mariages; **c. dress** vêtements *mpl* sacerdotaux **(b)** *Mus* (*passage*) en canon **2** *npl* **canonicals** vêtements *mpl* sacerdotaux
canonization [kænənaɪ'zeɪʃən] *n Rel* canonisation *f*
canonize ['kænənaɪz] *vt Rel* canoniser
canoodle [kə'nuːd(ə)l] *vi esp Hum* se faire des mamours
can opener *n* ouvre-boîte(s) *m*, *pl* ouvre-boîtes
canopy ['kænəpɪ] *n* (*over throne*) dais *m*; (*over bed*) baldaquin *m*; (*over fireplace*) hotte *f*; (*over doorway*) auvent *m*, marquise *f*; (*of parachute*) calotte *f*, voilure *f*; *Av* (*of cockpit*) verrière *f*; *Archit* (*of roof, over window*) gable *m*, gâble *m*; *Rel* (*above altar etc*) ciel *m*; *Fig* **c. of leaves** voûte *f* de feuillage *ou* de verdure
cant¹ [kænt] *n* **(a)** (*of thieves, beggars*) argot *m* **(b)** (*hypocritical talk*) langage *m* hypocrite; **c. phrase** cliché *m*
cant² *vi* **(a)** (*talk hypocritically*) faire l'hypocrite **(b)** (*of thieves, beggars etc*) parler en argot
cant³ *n* **(a)** *Carp, Constr etc* (*slope*) inclinaison *f*, dévers *m*; *Rail* (*of outer rail*) surélévation *f*, dévers; **to give sth a c.** incliner qch; **to have a c.** pencher **(b)** *Archit, Carp* (*edge*) chanfrein *m*, biseau *m*
cant⁴ **1** *vt* **(a)** (*turn over*) renverser, retourner; *Naut* (*boat for repair*) chavirer **(b)** (*tilt*) (*beam, pillar*) dévoyer, incliner; (*barrel*) incliner, pencher; *Rail* (*outer rail*) surhausser **(c)** *Carp etc* (*edge*) biseauter, écorner **2** *vi* **(a)** *Carp, Constr etc* s'incliner **(b)** (*tilt*) se trouver incliné, pencher
can't [kɑːnt] (*abbr* **cannot**) *see* **can³**
Cantab ['kæntæb] (*abbr* **Cantabrigiensis**) de l'Université de Cambridge
cantaloup(e) ['kæntəluːp] *n* (*melon*) cantaloup *m*
cantankerous [kæn'tæŋk(ə)rəs] *adj* (*bad-tempered*) revêche, acariâtre; (*irritable*) querelleur, -euse
cantata [kæn'tɑːtə] *n Mus* cantate *f*
canteen [kæn'tiːn] *n* **(a)** (*in school, factory etc*) cantine *f* **(b)** *Mil* (*shop*) magasin *m* à l'usage des soldats; (*water bottle*) bidon *m*; (*mess tin*) gamelle *f* **(c)** **c. of cutlery** ménagère *f*
canter¹ ['kæntər] *n Horseriding* petit galop *m*; *Fig* **let's have a quick c. through tomorrow's agenda** revoyons rapidement l'emploi du temps de demain
canter² **1** *vi Horseriding* aller au petit galop; *Fig* **to c. through a speech** (*do quickly*) expédier un discours; **to c. through an exam** (*do easily*) réussir un examen haut la main **2** *vt* (*horse*) faire aller au petit galop
Canterbury ['kæntəb(ə)rɪ] *n* Canterbury *m*; *Hist* Cantorbéry *m*; **C. bell(s)** (*flower*) campanule *f*
canticle ['kæntɪk(ə)l] *n* cantique *m*
cantilever ['kæntɪliːvər] *n Archit* encorbellement *m*; *Av* cantilever *m*; *Constr etc* **c. beam** poutre *f* en porte-à-faux; **c. bridge** pont *m* cantilever
canto ['kæntəʊ] *n Liter* (*of poem*) chant *m*
canton ['kæntɒn] *n* canton *m*
cantonal ['kæntən(ə)l] *adj* cantonal
Cantonese [kæntə'niːz] **1** *adj* cantonais **2** *n* **(a)** Cantonais, -aise **(b)** *Ling* cantonais *m*
cantonization [kæntənaɪ'zeɪʃən] *n* morcellement *m*
cantonment [kæn'tuːnmənt] *n* cantonnement *m*

cantor ['kæntɔːr] *n Rel* chantre *m*
Canuck [kə'nʌk, kə'nʊk] *n Pej* Canadien, -ienne français(e)
canula ['kænələ] *n Med* canule *f*
canvas ['kænvəs] *n* (**a**) *Tex* (grosse) toile *f*; (*for tapestry*) canevas *m*; *Mil etc* **under c.** sous la tente; **c. bucket** seau *m* en toile; **c. shoes** chaussures *fpl* de toile (**b**) *Art* (*material, painting*) toile *f* (**c**) *Boxing* tapis *m* (**d**) (*sails*) voile(s) *f(pl)*; **under c.** sous voiles
canvass[1] ['kænvəs] *n* = **canvassing**
canvass[2] **1** *vt* (**a**) *Pol, Com* (*solicit*) (*votes, orders*) solliciter; **to c. sb** (*for vote*) solliciter la voix de qn (*en faisant du porte-à-porte*); (*for custom*) solliciter la clientèle de qn; (*for support in job application etc*) solliciter l'appui de qn; *Com* **to c. a client** démarcher un client; *Pol* **to c. a district** faire une tournée électorale dans une région
(**b**) (*debate, discuss*) discuter
(**c**) (*get opinion of*) sonder; **to c. opinions** sonder l'opinion (on à propos de)
(**d**) *US Pol* (*inspect*) (*votes*) pointer, vérifier
2 *vi* (**a**) *Pol* faire campagne, faire une tournée électorale; **candidates were out canvassing today** les candidats ont fait une tournée électorale aujourd'hui; **I'm canvassing on behalf of the Labour Party** je fais campagne pour le parti travailliste
(**b**) *Com* faire du démarchage; **to c. for customers** prospecter un quartier/une région en y recherchant la clientèle
canvasser ['kænvəsər] *n Pol* = personne *f* qui sollicite les voix des électeurs en faisant du porte-à-porte; *Com* prospecteur, -trice; (*door-to-door*) représentant, -ante, démarcheur, -euse; **no canvassers** (*notice on door*) démarchage interdit
canvassing ['kænvəsɪŋ] *n Pol* (*of votes*) démarchage *m* électoral; *Com* (*of orders*) démarchage; (*for support in job application etc*) sollicitation *f* d'appui
canyon ['kænjən] *n Geog* canyon *m*, cañon *m*
CAP [siːeɪ'piː] *n EC* (*abbr* **Common Agricultural Policy**) PAC *f*
cap[1] [kæp] *n* (**a**) (*headgear*) bonnet *m*; (*with peak*) casquette *f*; (*of university graduate, jockey*) toque *f*; **swimming c.** bonnet de bain; *Sp* **to win one's c.** être sélectionné dans l'équipe nationale; *Univ* **in c. and gown** en costume d'apparat; *Fig* **to come/go c. in hand** se présenter chapeau bas *ou* humblement (**to sb** devant qn); *Fig* **if the c. fits(, wear it)!** qui se sent morveux se mouche!; *Fig* **to put on one's thinking c.** réfléchir, méditer la question; *Old-fashioned F* **to set one's c. at sb** jeter son dévolu sur qn
(**b**) (*cover*) (*of pen, tyre valve*) capuchon *m*; (*of pump*) calotte *m*; (*of bottle*) capsule *f*; *Phot* (*for lens*) capuchon, bouchon *m*; *Tech* (*protective*) chapeau *m*; (*of bearing, valve*) chapeau, couvercle *m*; (*for tooth*) couche *f* d'émail; *F* (**Dutch**) **c.** (*contraceptive*) diaphragme *m* (contraceptif)
(**c**) (*upper part*) (*of column*) chapiteau *m*; (*of mushroom*) chapeau *m*
(**d**) (*for toy gun*) amorce *f*, capsule *f*; **percussion c.** amorce
(**e**) *Orn* (*of bird*) capuchon *m*
(**f**) (*spending limit*) plafond *m*
cap[2] *vt* (**-pp-**) (**a**) (*cover*) recouvrir (**sth with sth** qch de qch); (*bottle*) capsuler; **the mountain was capped with snow** le sommet de la montagne était recouvert de neige; **to c. a tooth** mettre une couche d'émail sur une dent
(**b**) (*surpass, do better than*) surpasser; **to c. a quotation** renchérir sur une citation; **that caps everything** *or* **the lot** *or* **it all!** ça c'est le comble! *ou* le bouquet!; **c. that!** tu n'es pas cap de faire mieux!
(**c**) *Scot, New Zealand Sch* (*candidate*) conférer un diplôme à
(**d**) *Sp* **to be capped for England** être sélectionné dans l'équipe d'Angleterre
(**e**) *Admin* (*impose limit on*) (*spending*) limiter; (*borough etc*) limiter les dépenses de
cap[3] *n Typ F* majuscule *f*; **put in small caps** à imprimer en petites capitales
capability [keɪpə'bɪlɪtɪ] *n* capacité *f* (**to do sth** de faire qch); **we have the military c. to ...** nous avons les capacités militaires de ...; **to have outstanding/limited capabilities** (*of person*) être très doué/avoir des moyens limités
capable ['keɪpəb(ə)l] *adj* (**a**) capable (**of sth** de qch; **of doing sth** de faire qch); **to show what one is c. of** montrer ce dont on est capable; **c. of love** capable d'aimer; **the machine is c. of producing 300 items a minute** cette machine a une capacité de production de 300 pièces à la minute; **she's not c. of lying** elle est incapable de mentir; **that man's c. of anything** cet homme est capable de tout (**b**) (*competent*) capable, compétent; **the business is in c. hands** l'affaire est entre de bonnes mains (**c**) *Fml* **c. of improvement** susceptible d'amélioration *ou* d'être amélioré
capably ['keɪpəblɪ] *adv* avec compétence, d'une manière compétente
capacious [kə'peɪʃəs] *adj* vaste, spacieux; (*clothing*) ample
capacitance [kə'pæsɪtəns] *n El* capacité *f*
capacitate [kə'pæsɪteɪt] *vt Jur* donner pouvoir *ou* qualité à (**to act** pour agir)
capacitor [kə'pæsɪtər] *n El* condensateur *m*
capacity [kə'pæsɪtɪ] *n* (**a**) (*of cylinder, tank, hotel, theatre, train, stadium etc*) capacité *f*; (*of barrel, drum, cask*) contenance *f*; **there was a c. crowd at the match** le stade était plein *ou* bondé pour le match; **we played to c. audiences** on a fait salle comble; **there was a c. audience at the theatre** le théâtre était comble; **the stadium has a c. of 50 000** le stade peut accueillir 50 000 personnes; *Th, Sp etc* **to play to c.** jouer à guichets fermés; *F* **he has a remarkable c. for alcohol/beer** il peut absorber des quantités extraordinaires d'alcool/de bière; **c. occupancy** (*of hotel etc*) occupation *f* maximale; **c. utilization** rentabilisation *f*
(**b**) *Ind etc* (*output*) rendement *m*; **to work at (full) c.** travailler à plein rendement; **production c.** capacité *f* de production
(**c**) *El* capacité *f*
(**d**) (*aptitude*) **c. for work** capacité *f* de travail; **he has no c. for love** il est incapable d'aimer; **to be beyond sb's c.** dépasser les compétences de qn; **to be within sb's c.** être dans les possibilités de qn; **to the utmost of my c.** dans la mesure de mes moyens
(**e**) *Jur* **to have c. /no c. to act** avoir/ne pas avoir capacité pour agir
(**f**) (*position*) **in the c. of ...** en qualité de ...; **to act in one's official c.** agir dans le cadre de ses fonctions; **in my c. as chairwoman** en ma qualité de présidente
caparison[1] [kə'pærɪs(ə)n] *n Hist* caparaçon *m*
caparison[2] *vt Hist* caparaçonner
cape[1] [keɪp] *n* (*cloak*) pèlerine *f*, cape *f*; (*small*) collet *m*; (*of priest*) camail *m*, *pl* camails
cape[2] *n Geog* cap *m*, promontoire *m*; **the C. (of Good Hope)** le Cap (de Bonne-Espérance); **C. Town** le Cap; **C. Coloured** métis, -isse (d'Afrique du Sud)
caper[1] ['keɪpər] *n* (**a**) *Bot, Culin* (*bud*) câpre *f* (**b**) (*plant*) câprier *m*
caper[2] *n* (**a**) (*movement*) cabriole *f*, gambade *f*; **to cut a c.** faire des cabrioles (**b**) (*prank*) farce *f*, *F* bonne rigolade *f*; **I've had enough of his capers** j'en ai assez de ses bêtises; **what a c.!** (*fuss*) quel cirque! (**c**) *Sl* (*robbery*) hold-up *m inv*
caper[3] *vi* **to c. (about)** faire des cabrioles, cabrioler, gambader
capercaillie, capercailzie [kæpə'keɪlɪ] *n* (*bird*) grand tétras *m*, (grand) coq *m* de bruyère
capful ['kæpfʊl] *n* (*of liquid, disinfectant etc*) plein bouchon *m*
capillary [kə'pɪlərɪ] **1** *adj* (*tube, pressure etc*) capillaire; *Anat* **the c. vessels** les vaisseaux *mpl* capillaires **2** *npl Anat* **the capillaries** les capillaires *mpl*
capital[1] ['kæpɪt(ə)l] *adj* (**a**) (*principal*) capital; **c. letter** (lettre *f*) capitale *f*, (lettre) majuscule *f*; **a c. A** un A majuscule; *F* **he's lazy with a c. L** c'est un paresseux avec un grand P; **c. city** capitale *f* (**b**) *Jur* **c. crime** *or* **offence** crime *m* capital *ou* puni de mort (**c**) (*important*) capital; **c. error** erreur *f* fatale; **of c. importance** d'une importance capitale (**d**) *Old-fashioned Br F* (*excellent*) excellent
capital[2] *n* (**a**) *Typ* capitale *f*, majuscule *f*
(**b**) (*city*) capitale *f*
(**c**) *Fin* capital *m*, capitaux *mpl*, fonds *mpl*; (*assets*) avoir *m*; **to live on one's c.** vivre sur son capital; *Fig* **to make c. out of sth** profiter *ou* tirer parti de qch; *Fig* **they're trying to make political c. out of the scandal** ils essaient de récupérer ce scandale; **c. equipment** biens *mpl* d'équipement; **c. goods** moyens *mpl* de production; *Banking* **c. budget** budget *m* des investissements; **c. contribution** apport *m* en capital, dotation *f* en capital, apport de capitaux; *Acct* **c. employed** capital *m* engagé; **c. expenditure** dépenses *fpl* en capital *ou* en immobilisations; **c. injection** injection *f* de capital, injection de capitaux; *Acct* **c. items** biens *mpl* capitaux; **c. levy** impôt *m* sur le capital; **c. loss** moins-value *f*; **c. market** marché *m* des capitaux; **c. share** part *f* sociale; **c. transfer** transfert *m* de capitaux; **c. transfer tax** taxe *f* sur le transfert de capitaux; **c. turnover** rotation *f* des capitaux
capital[3] *n Archit* chapiteau *m*
capital assets *npl* actif *m* immobilisé
capital gain *n* plus-value *f* (en capital); **to make a capital gain on sth** réaliser une plus-value sur qch; **capital gains tax** impôt *m* sur les plus-values (en capital)
capital-intensive *adj* (*industry etc*) qui nécessite un investissement important
capital investment *n* investissement *m* de capitaux

capitalism [ˈkæpɪtəlɪz(ə)m] *n* capitalisme *m*
capitalist [ˈkæpɪtəlɪst] *n* capitaliste *mf*
capitalist(ic) [ˈkæpɪtəlɪst, -ˈlɪstɪk] *adj (system, society etc)* capitaliste
capitalization [kæpɪtəlaɪˈzeɪʃən] *n* **(a)** *Fin (of interest etc)* capitalisation *f* **(b)** *Typ* emploi *m* des majuscules; *(putting into caps)* mise *f* en majuscules
capitalize [ˈkæpɪtəlaɪz] *vt* **(a)** *Fin (income etc)* capitaliser **(b)** *Typ (word) (first letter)* écrire avec une majuscule; *(entire word)* écrire en majuscules
▶ **capitalize (up)on** *vipo Fig (sth)* tourner à son avantage
capital punishment *n* peine *f* capitale
capital tax *n Fin* impôt *m* sur le capital
capitation [kæpɪˈteɪʃən] *n Econ* capitation *f*; *Admin* **c. grant** allocation *f* par tête
Capitol (the) [ðəˈkæpɪtɒl] *n (of Rome, Washington etc)* le Capitole
capitulate [kəˈpɪtjʊleɪt] *vi* capituler **(to** devant**)**
capitulation [kəpɪtjʊˈleɪʃən] *n (surrender)* capitulation *f*
capon [ˈkeɪpən] *n Culin* chapon *m*
cappuccino [kæpʊˈtʃiːnəʊ] *n* cappucino *m*
caprice [kəˈpriːs] *n* **(a)** *(whim)* caprice *m* **(b)** *Mus* caprice *m*
capricious [kəˈprɪʃəs] *adj* capricieux
capriciously [kəˈprɪʃəslɪ] *adv* capricieusement
Capricorn [ˈkæprɪkɔːn] *n* **(a)** *Astron* Capricorne *m*; **to be (a) C.** être (du) Capricorne **(b)** *Geog* **the Tropic of C.** le tropique du Capricorne
caps [kæps] *npl (abbr* **capital letters***)* majuscules *fpl*, capitales *fpl*; *Comptr* **c. lock** blocage *m* majuscule; *Comptr* **c. lock key** touche *f* de verrouillage des majuscules
capsicum [ˈkæpsɪkəm] *n* **(a)** *Culin (hot)* piment *m*; *(mild)* poivron *m* **(b)** *(plant)* piment *m*; *(mild)* poivron *m*
capsize [kæpˈsaɪz] **1** *vi (of boat)* chavirer; **we capsized** nous avons chaviré **2** *vt (boat)* faire chavirer
capstan [ˈkæpst(ə)n] *n* **(a)** *Naut etc* cabestan *m* **(b)** *Tech (of lathe)* revolver *m*; **c. lathe** tour *f* à revolver
capsular [ˈkæpsjʊlər] *adj Biol etc* capsulaire
capsule [ˈkæpsjuːl] *n* capsule *f*; *Med (of drug)* gélule *f*; **space c.** capsule spatiale
Capt *n abbr* **Captain**
captain¹ [ˈkæptɪn] *n* **(a)** *Naut, Sp* capitaine *m*; *Av* commandant *m* de bord; *(in fire brigade)* capitaine; *(of quiz team etc)* leader *m*; *(in Girl Guides)* chef(e)taine *f*; *US (in restaurant)* maître *m* d'hôtel; *Br* **c. of the school, school c.** = élève *mf* délégué(e) qui a certaines responsabilités et représente son établissement au cours de cérémonies officielles; *Fig* **captains of industry** capitaines d'industrie
(b) *(officer, rank)* capitaine *m*; *Naut* capitaine de vaisseau; *(US police)* = officier *m* de police responsable d'un quartier; **c. of the fleet** capitaine de pavillon; **C. James Brown** *(in title)* le capitaine James Brown; **yes, c.!** oui, mon capitaine!
captain² *vt Sp (team)* être capitaine de; *(expedition etc)* conduire, mener; *Sp* **he captained the side in the World Cup** c'était lui le capitaine de l'équipe pour la Coupe du Monde
captaincy [ˈkæptɪnsɪ] *n* **(a)** *Mil, Naut* grade *m* de capitaine; **to take over the c. of the ship** prendre le commandement du vaisseau **(b)** *Sp* fonction *f* de capitaine; **under** *or* **during his c.** quand il était capitaine
caption¹ [ˈkæpʃən] *n (of cartoon, photograph, illustration)* légende *f*; *Cin (in silent film)* sous-titre *m*, *pl* sous-titres; *TV, Cin* **c. generator** générateur *m* de caractères
caption² *vt (illustration)* légender, écrire la légende de; *(film, television programme)* sous-titrer
captious [ˈkæpʃəs] *adj Fml (reasoning)* captieux; *(person)* pointilleux, chicaneur
captivate [ˈkæptɪveɪt] *vt (of story, story-teller)* captiver; *(of smile, charm etc)* séduire
captivating [ˈkæptɪveɪtɪŋ] *adj (person, smile)* séduisant; *(personality)* captivant, fascinant; *(smile)* enchanteur
captivation [kæptɪˈveɪʃən] *n* fascination *f*
captive [ˈkæptɪv] **1** *adj* captif; **he was taken c.** il a été fait prisonnier; *Mktg* **c. audience** audience *f* captive; **he had a c. audience** le public était forcé de l'écouter; **c. market** clientèle *f* captive, marché *m* captif; *Mktg* **c.-product pricing** fixation *f* du prix des produits liés; **c. state** état *m* de captivité **2** *n* captif, -ive, prisonnier, -ière
captivity [kæpˈtɪvɪtɪ] *n* captivité *f*; **animals in c.** animaux en captivité
captor [ˈkæptər] *n* ravisseur, -euse
capture¹ [ˈkæptjər] *n* **(a)** *(of ship, criminal, animal etc)* capture *f* **(b)** *Comptr (of data)* saisie *f* **(c)** *(thing or person taken)* prise *f*
capture² *vt (ship, criminal, animal etc)* capturer; *(town)* prendre, s'emparer de **(from** sur**)**; *(sb's attention, imagination)* captiver; *(of artist, painting) (sb's likeness)* saisir; *(of film, book, director etc) (atmosphere)* rendre; *Comptr (data)* saisir; **to c. the moment** *(of photographer, photograph)* saisir l'instant; **to c. sb/sth (on film)** immortaliser qn/qch (sur la pellicule); *Com* **to c. a market** accaparer un marché
Capuchin [ˈkæpʊʃɪn] *n Rel* capucin, -ine
capuchin [ˈkæpʊʃɪn] *n (monkey)* capucin *m*
car [kɑːr] *n* **(a)** *Aut* **(motor) c.** voiture *f*, automobile *f*; **to go by c.** aller en voiture; **c. ferry** car-ferry *m*, ferry(-boat) *m*; **c. hire** location *f* de voitures; **c. hire company** société *f* de location de voitures; **c. industry/manufacturer** industrie *f*/ constructeur *m* automobile; **c. insurance** assurance *f* auto; **c. radio** autoradio *m*; **c. rental** location *f* de voitures; **c. theft** vols *mpl* de voiture **(b)** *Am Rail* voiture *f*, wagon *m*; **buffet** *or* **refreshment c.** voiture-bar *f*, *pl* voitures-bars **(c)** *(cabin) (of balloon)* nacelle *f*; *Am (of lift)* cabine *f*
carafe [kəˈræf, -ˈrɑːf] *n* carafe *f*; *(small)* carafon *m*
caramel [ˈkærəməl] *n* **(a)** *Culin* caramel *m*; **c. cream, cream c.** crème *f* caramel; **c. custard** crème (renversée) au caramel **(b)** *(sweet)* caramel *m* **(c)** *(colour)* (couleur *f*) caramel *m inv*
caramelize [ˈkærəməlaɪz] *Culin* **1** *vt* caraméliser **2** *vi* se caraméliser
carapace [ˈkærəpeɪs] *n Zool* carapace *f*
carat [ˈkærət] *n* **(a)** *(for gold)* carat *m* (de fin); **eighteen-c. gold** or *m* à dix-huit carats **(b)** *(for diamonds)* **metric c.** carat *m* (de 200 milligrammes)
caravan [ˈkærəvæn] *n* **(a)** *Br (pulled by car)* caravane *f*; **c. park** terrain *m* de caravaning; **c. site** camping *m* (pour caravanes); **c. holiday** vacances *fpl* en caravane **(b)** *(horse-drawn) (of gypsy, fair people)* roulotte *f* **(c)** *(in desert)* caravane *f*; **to travel in c.** voyager en convoi; **c. route** piste *f* caravanière
caravanette [kærəvæˈnet] *n* camping-car *m*, *pl* camping-cars
caravan(n)ing [ˈkærəvænɪŋ] *n* caravaning *m*; **to go c., to go on a c. holiday** faire du caravaning
caravanserai [kærəˈvænsəraɪ] *n* caravansérail *m*
caraway [ˈkærəweɪ] *n (plant)* carvi *m*, cumin *m* des prés; **c. seeds** graines *fpl* de carvi
carb [kɑːb] *n Aut F* carburateur *m*
carbide [ˈkɑːbaɪd] *n Ch, Ind* carbure *m*
carbine [ˈkɑːbaɪn] *n Mil* **(a)** *Hist* carabine *f* **(b)** *US (automatic)* mitraillette *f*
carbohydrate [kɑːbəʊˈhaɪdreɪt] *n* **(a)** *Ch* hydrate *m* de carbone **(b)** *(in food)* **carbohydrates** glucides *mpl*
carbolic [kɑːˈbɒlɪk] *adj Ch* phénique; **c. acid** acide *m* phénique, phénol *m*; **c. soap** = savon *m* de Marseille
car bomb *n* voiture *f* piégée
carbon [ˈkɑːbən] *n Ch* carbone *m*; **c. (paper)** (papier *m*) carbone; **c. (copy)** *(of letter etc)* double *m ou* copie *f ou* exemplaire *m* (au carbone); *Fig* **she is a c. copy of her mother** c'est une copie conforme de sa mère; **c. (-14) dating** *(in archaeology)* datation *f* au carbone 14; *Aut* **c. deposit** calaminage *m*; **c. fibre** fibre *f* de carbone; *Aut* **c. filter** filtre *m* au charbon; *Comptr* **c. ribbon** ruban *m* de carbone; **c. electrode** électrode *f* de charbon; **c. steel** acier *m* enrichi en carbone
carbonaceous [kɑːbəˈneɪʃəs] *adj Ch* carboné; *Geol* carbonifère
carbonate [ˈkɑːbəneɪt] *n Ch* carbonate *m*
carbonated [ˈkɑːbəneɪtɪd] *adj* gazéifié, gazeux; **c. water** eau *f* gazeuse
carbon dioxide *n* gaz *m* carbonique
carbonic [kɑːˈbɒnɪk] *adj Ch* carbonique
Carboniferous [kɑːbəˈnɪfərəs] *adj, n Geol* carbonifère *m*
carboniferous [kɑːbəˈnɪfərəs] *adj* carbonifère
carbonization [kɑːbənaɪˈzeɪʃən] *n (of wood etc)* carbonisation *f*; *Aut etc* encrassement *m*, calaminage *m*
carbonize [ˈkɑːbənaɪz] **1** *vt Ch* carboniser; *Ind (wood etc)* carboniser, charbonner **2** *vi Aut etc* s'encrasser, se calaminer
carbon monoxide *n* oxyde *m* de carbone
car-boot sale *n Br* = vente *f* à la brocante où les vendeurs exposent leurs marchandises à l'arrière de leur voiture
carborundum [kɑːbəˈrʌndəm] *n* carborundum *m*
carboy [ˈkɑːbɔɪ] *n* bonbonne *f*
carbuncle [ˈkɑːbʌŋk(ə)l] *n* **(a)** *Med* furoncle *m* **(b)** *(gem)* escarboucle *f*
carburation [kɑːbjʊˈreɪʃən] *n* carburation *f*
carburettor, *US* **carburetor** [kɑːbjʊˈretər] *n Aut* carburateur *m*; **c. damper** amortisseur *m* de commande sur carburateur
carcass [ˈkɑːkəs] *n* **(a)** *(of animal)* cadavre *m*, carcasse *f* **(b)** *(of house, ship)* charpente *f* **(c)** *F Pej (of person) (corpse)* macchabée *m*; *F Hum (body)* carcasse *f*; **move** *or* **shift your c.!** pousse-toi de là!
carcinogen [kɑːˈsɪnədʒen] *n Med* substance *f* cancérigène
carcinogenic [kɑːsɪnəʊˈdʒenɪk] *adj Med* cancérigène, carcinogène

carcinoma [kɑːsɪˈnəʊmə] *n Med* carcinome *m*

card¹ [kɑːd] *n* **(a)** *Cards* **(playing) c.** carte *f* (à jouer); **to play cards** jouer aux cartes; **to win at cards** gagner aux cartes; **to play one's cards well** bien jouer ses cartes; *Fig* **to play one's cards right** bien se débrouiller, bien mener sa barque; **play your cards right and you could get promoted** si tu te débrouilles bien, tu peux avoir une promotion; *Fig* **to play one's last c.** jouer son va-tout; *Fig* **to hold all the (winning** *or* **best) cards** avoir tous les atouts dans son jeu *ou* en main; *Fig* **to keep one's cards close to one's chest** cacher son jeu; *Cards, Fig* **to put one's cards on the table** mettre cartes sur table; *Fig* **to have a c. up one's sleeve** avoir un atout dans son jeu; *Fig* **it is on** *or Am* **in the cards that …** il est bien possible que …, il se pourrait fort bien que …; **I don't think that's on the cards** je ne pense pas que ce soit possible; *Fig* **to throw in the** *or* **one's cards** abandonner; *Old-fashioned F* **he's a (real) c.** *or* **quite a c.** c'est un original

(b) (*with printed information*) carte *f*; (*postcard*) carte (postale); *Golf* carte du parcours; *Sp* (*list of races*) programme *m* des courses; **here's my c.** voici ma carte; *Br F* **to get** *or* **be given one's cards** être renvoyé; **birthday/ Christmas c.** carte d'anniversaire/de Noël

(c) (*for card index*) fiche *f*

(d) (*for holding wool, buttons*) carte *f*

(e) (*cardboard*) carton *m*

(f) *Comptr* carte *f*; **c. slot** emplacement *m* pour carte

(g) (*plastic*) carte *f*; **c. reader** lecteur *m* de cartes; **banker's c., cheque c.** carte (d'identité) bancaire; **smart c.** carte à puce

card² *n Tex* (*tool*) carde *f*, peigne *m*

card³ *vt Tex* (*wool etc*) carder, peigner

cardamom [ˈkɑːdəməm] *n* cardamome *m*

cardan joint [ˈkɑːdən] *n Aut* joint *m* de cardans

cardboard [ˈkɑːdbɔːd] *n* carton *m*; (*thin*) bristol *m*; **c. box** carton *m*, boîte *f* en carton; **c. city** quartier *m* où les sans-abris vivent dans des cartons; **c. cutout** personnage *m* découpé dans du carton; *Fig* **c. characters** (*in play, novel etc*) personnages *mpl* sans aucune profondeur

card-carrying *adj* **c. member** adhérent, -ente **(of** à)

card catalogue *n* fichier *m*

card file *n* fichier *m*

card game *n* (*type*) jeu *m* de cartes; (*occasion*) partie *f* de cartes

cardiac [ˈkɑːdɪæk] *adj Anat, Med* cardiaque; **c. arrest** arrêt *m* cardiaque *ou* du cœur; **he suffered c. arrest** il a eu un arrêt cardiaque; **c. massage** massage *m* cardiaque

cardigan [ˈkɑːdɪgən] *n* cardigan *m*, gilet *m*

cardinal [ˈkɑːdɪn(ə)l] **1** *adj* **(a)** [ⓘA70,16,1; B56,A] (*importance, significance*) capital; **c. numbers** nombres *mpl* cardinaux; **c. error** erreur *f* fondamentale; **the four c. points (of the compass)** les quatre points *mpl* cardinaux; **c. virtues** vertus *fpl* cardinales **(b)** (*colour*) pourpre, rouge cardinal *inv* **2** *n Rel* cardinal *m*, -aux

card index *n* fichier *m*; **c. box** boîte *f* à fiches, fichier; **c. filing cabinet** fichier; **c. system** fichier

carding [ˈkɑːdɪŋ] *n Tex* cardage *m*, peignage *m*; **c. machine** cardeuse *f*

cardiogram [ˈkɑːdɪəʊgræm] *n Med* cardiogramme *m*

cardiograph [ˈkɑːdɪəʊgrɑːf] *n Med* cardiographe *m*

cardiologist [kɑːdɪˈɒlədʒɪst] *n Med* cardiologue *mf*

cardiology [kɑːdɪˈɒlədʒɪ] *n Med* cardiologie *f*

cardiovascular [kɑːdɪəʊˈvæskjʊlər] *adj Med* (*disease*) cardio-vasculaire, *pl* cardio-vasculaires

card key *n* (*for hotel room etc*) carte-clé *f*

card-operated lock *n* (*in hotel etc*) serrure *f* à carte perforée

cardphone [ˈkɑːdfəʊn] *n Tel* publiphone *m ou* téléphone *m* à carte

card player *n* joueur -euse de cartes

cardsharp(er) [ˈkɑːdʃɑːp, -ər] *n* tricheur, -euse professionnel(le)

card table *n* table *f* de jeux

card trick *n* tour *m* de cartes

card vote *n Br Pol* vote *m* où des délégués votent à main lévée

cardy [ˈkɑːdɪ] *n F* = **cardigan**

care¹ [keər] *n* **(a)** (*worry*) souci *m*, inquiétude *f*; **to be full of cares** avoir beaucoup de soucis; **to be free of** *or* **from c.** être insouciant; **a life of c.** une vie pleine de soucis; **she doesn't have a c. in the world** elle n'a aucun souci; **cares of State** responsabilités *fpl* d'État

(b) (*attention*) soin(s) *m(pl)*, attention *f*; **constant c.** soins continuels *ou* assidus; **to do sth with great c.** faire qch avec beaucoup de soin; **to put a lot of c. into sth** apporter beaucoup de soin à qch; **to put a lot of c. into doing sth** mettre beaucoup de soin à faire qch; **to drive without due c.** conduire de façon imprudente; **with c.** (*on parcel etc*) fragile; **they didn't receive the proper c. in hospital** ils n'ont pas reçu les soins appropriés à l'hôpital; **to take c. of** (*invalid, child, customer, problem etc*) s'occuper de; **he doesn't take c. of his bicycle** il ne prend pas soin de son vélo; **to take good c. of sb/sth** prendre bien soin de qn/qch; **to take c. of oneself** savoir se débrouiller tout seul; (*healthwise*) prendre soin de sa santé; **take c. of yourself** (*look after yourself*) soignez-vous bien; **to take c. of one's health** ménager sa santé; **to take c. of itself** s'arranger tout seul *ou* de soi-même; **this should take c. of that stain** cela devrait venir à bout de cette tache; **to take c. to do sth** avoir (bien) soin *ou* prendre (bien) garde de faire qch; **take c. when you cross the road** fais attention en traversant la rue; **take c.!** (*look out!*) faites attention!, prenez garde!; **cheerio, take c.** au revoir

(c) (*looking after*) (*of teeth, hair etc*) soin(s) *m(pl)*; (*of machine, shoes, clothes etc*) entretien *m*; **c. label** (*on clothes*) conseils *mpl* d'entretien; **c. parcel** (*for famine relief etc*) colis *m* d'aide humanitaire; *Br Admin* **c. in the community** soins *mpl* au niveau local; *Br Admin* **children in c.** enfants confiés aux services sociaux; **to be in/go into c.** (*of child*) être/être confié à l'Assistance publique; **to put a child in c.** confier un enfant à l'Assistance publique; **to put sb/sth in sb's c.** confier qn/qch à qn; **to be in** *or* **under sb's c.** être sous la responsabilité de qn; **to be under a doctor's c.** se faire soigner par un médecin; **write to me c. of Mrs Smith** *or* **c/o Mrs Smith** *or US* **in c. of Mrs Smith** écrivez-moi aux bons soins de Mme Smith *ou* chez Mme Smith

care² **1** *vi* (*be concerned*) se soucier, se préoccuper **(about** de); **people who c.** des gens compatissants; **no one seems to c.** tout le monde s'en moque; **no one seems to c. about the environment/the elderly** personne ne semble se préoccuper *ou* se soucier de l'environnement/des personnes âgées; **of course we c. about you!** mais bien sûr qu'on t'aime; **that's all he cares about** il n'y a que cela qui l'intéresse; **who cares?** qu'est-ce que ça peut faire?; **do you really c.?** (*how I am, what my feelings are etc*) est-ce que ça t'intéresse vraiment?; **she just doesn't c.** elle s'en moque complètement, *F* elle n'en a rien à faire; **for all I c.** pour ce que ça me fait; **I don't c.!** ça m'est égal!, je m'en fiche!; **as if I cared!, I couldn't c. less** je m'en fiche éperdument, je m'en fous; **couldn't-c.-less attitude** je-m'en-foutisme *m*

2 *vt* **(a)** (*mind*) **I don't c. what he says** peu m'importe ce qu'il dit; **what do I c.?** qu'est-ce que ça peut bien me faire?; **I don't c. whether he likes it or not** que cela lui plaise ou non, ça m'est parfaitement égal

(b) (*like*) **would you c. to come with me?** voulez-vous m'accompagner?, aimeriez-vous m'accompagner?; **if you c. to join us** si vous voulez vous joindre à nous

▶ **care for** *vipo* **(a)** (*tend*) (*patients, children*) soigner; **to look well cared for** (*of animal, child, hair etc*) avoir l'air soigné *ou* une apparence soignée; (*of car, garden etc*) avoir l'air bien entretenu **(b)** (*like*) **I don't c. for this music** je n'aime pas tellement cette musique; **he doesn't c. for her** elle ne lui plaît pas; **would you c. for some tea?** voulez-vous du thé? **(c)** (*love*) (*person*) aimer, tenir à

careen [kəˈriːn] **1** *vt Naut* **(a)** (*make keel over*) (*boat*) abattre *ou* mettre en carène **(b)** (*clean*) caréner **2** *vi* **(a)** *Naut* (*of ship*) se coucher **(b)** *Am* (*of car etc*) pencher sur le côté

careening [kəˈriːnɪŋ] *n Naut* (*cleaning*) carénage *m*

career¹ [kəˈrɪər] *n* (*working life, profession*) carrière *f*; **his dancing c.** sa carrière de danseur; **a job with c. prospects** un emploi qui offre des perspectives; **it's a good/bad c. move** c'est bon/mauvais pour ta/sa/*etc* carrière

career² *vi* **to c. (along)** aller à toute vitesse; **to c. into a lorry** (*of vehicle*) foncer dans un camion; **the car careered off the road** la voiture a quitté la route à vive allure

career break *n* interruption *f* de carrière

career diplomat *n* diplomate *m* de carrière

careerist [kəˈrɪərɪst] *n usu Pej* carriériste *mf*

careers officer *n* conseiller, -ère d'orientation

careers service *n* service *m* d'orientation professionnelle

career woman *n* = femme *f* qui poursuit une carrière

carefree [ˈkeəfriː] *adj* sans souci

careful [ˈkeəfʊl] *adj* **(a)** (*taking pains*) soigneux **(of** de), attentif **(of** à); **a c. worker** un travailleur méticuleux; **c. speakers would avoid this usage** les gens qui parlent correctement éviteraient cet usage; **to be c. of** (*appearance*) être soucieux de; **be c. of his feelings** ne heurte pas ses sentiments; **to be c. with one's money** regarder à la dépense; **to be c. to do sth** avoir soin de faire qch, veiller à faire qch; **she was c. not to mention this** elle a fait bien attention de ne pas mentionner cela; **(be) c.!** faites attention!; **be c. you don't fall** *or* **not to fall** faites attention de ne pas tomber; **be c. what you say** faites attention à ce que vous dites; **we are very c. (about) who we employ** nous faisons très attention quand nous engageons quelqu'un; **c. consideration of a question** examen *m* attentif *ou* approfondi d'une question

(**b**) (*prudent*) prudent, circonspect; **you can't be too c. these days** de nos jours, on n'est jamais trop prudent; **a c. answer** une réponse bien pesée *ou* réfléchie; **a c. driver** un conducteur prudent

carefully ['keəfʊlɪ] *adv* (**a**) (*painstakingly*) soigneusement, avec soin; (*to choose*) avec soin; (*to listen*) attentivement; **a c. worded document** un document aux termes choisis avec soin (**b**) (*to drive, approach sb*) prudemment

carefulness ['keəfʊlnɪs] *n* (**a**) (*taking pains*) soin *m*, attention *f* (**b**) (*prudence*) prudence *f*

careless ['keəlɪs] *adj* (**a**) (*negligent*) négligent; (*work*) négligé; (*error, moment*) d'inattention; **accused of c. driving** accusé d'imprudence au volant; **to be c. about one's appearance** être négligé de sa personne; **she's very c. about her things** elle n'est pas soigneuse avec ses affaires (**b**) (*unconcerned*) insouciant, peu soucieux (**of, about** de); *Fml* **to be c. of sb's feelings** manquer de délicatesse avec qn; **a c. remark** une observation inconsidérée *ou* irréfléchie; **with a c. wave of her hand** en faisant un léger geste de la main

carelessly ['keəlɪslɪ] *adv* (**a**) (*negligently*) négligemment, sans soin (**b**) (*casually*) avec insouciance; **he threw the towel c. over his shoulder** il balança nonchalamment la serviette sur son épaule

carelessness ['keəlɪsnɪs] *n* (**a**) (*negligence*) négligence *f* (**b**) *esp Lit* (*lack of concern*) insouciance *f*, inattention *f*

carer ['keərər] *n* aide *mf* à domicile

caress¹ [kə'res] *n* caresse *f*

caress² *vt* caresser

caret ['kærət] *n Typ* signe *m* d'insertion

caretaker ['keəteɪkər] *n* (*of building, school*) concierge *mf*, gardien, -ienne; (*of museum etc*) gardien, -ienne; *Pol* **c. government** gouvernement *m* intérimaire

careworn ['keəwɔːn] *adj* (*face etc*) rongé *ou* usé par les soucis

cargo, *pl* **-oes** ['kɑːgəʊ, -əʊz] *n Naut, Av* cargaison *f*, chargement *m*; **full c.** plein chargement; **general** *or* **mixed c.** cargaison mixte; **c. afloat** cargaison flottante; **c. boat** *or* **ship** *or* **vessel** cargo *m*; **c. floor** (*of truck*) plancher *m* de chargement; **c. insurance** assurance *f* sur facultés; **c. list** bordereau *m* de chargement; **c. plane** avion-cargo *m*, *pl* avions-cargos; *Naut, Av* **c. space** espace *m* cargo

Caribbean [kærɪ'biːən, *US* kə'rɪbɪən] *adj, n* **the C. (Sea)** la Mer des Caraïbes *ou* des Antilles; **the C. (islands)** les Antilles *fpl*

caribou ['kærɪbuː] *n* caribou *m*, *pl* -ous

caricature¹ ['kærɪkətjʊər] *n* caricature *f*

caricature² *vt* caricaturer

caricaturist [kærɪkə'tjuːrɪst] *n* caricaturiste *mf*

caries ['keəriːz] *n Med* carie *f*

carillon [kə'rɪljən] *n Mus* carillon *m*

caring ['keərɪŋ] *adj* (*society*) humain; **she's a c. person** c'est une personne très humaine *ou* généreuse; **a c. family atmosphere** une atmosphère familiale chaleureuse; **the c. professions** = les professions *fpl* médicales et para-médicales

carless ['kɑːlɪs] *adj* sans voiture

carload ['kɑːləʊd] *n* (**a**) *Aut* pleine voiture *f*; **a c. of people/ furniture** une voiture pleine de passagers/de meubles; **to arrive by the c.** arriver par voitures entières (**b**) *Am Rail* plein wagon *m*

Carmelite ['kɑːməlaɪt] *n* **C. (nun)** carmélite *f*

carmine ['kɑːmaɪn] **1** *n* carmin *m* **2** *adj* carmin *inv*

carnage ['kɑːnɪdʒ] *n* carnage *m*

carnal ['kɑːn(ə)l] *adj* charnel; **c. sins** péchés *mpl* de la chair; **c. knowledge** connaissance *f* charnelle; **to have c. knowledge of sb** *Lit, Bible* connaître qn; *Jur* avoir des relations sexuelles avec qn

carnation¹ [kɑː'neɪʃən] *n, adj* (*colour*) incarnat *m*

carnation² *n* (*flower*) œillet *m*

carnet ['kɑːneɪ] *n Com* (*customs pass*) carnet *m* de passage en douanes

carnival ['kɑːnɪv(ə)l] *n* (**a**) (*festive occasion*) carnaval *m*, -als, fête *f*; **during C.** pendant le Carnaval; **a c. atmosphere** une ambiance de fête *ou* de carnaval (**b**) (*funfair*) fête *f* foraine (**c**) *Rel* (*before Lent*) carnaval *m*, -als

carnivora [kɑː'nɪvərə] *npl Zool* carnivores *mpl*

carnivore ['kɑːnɪvɔːr] *n* (*animal*) carnivore *m*

carnivorous [kɑː'nɪv(ə)rəs] *adj* (**a**) (*animal*) carnivore, carnassier (**b**) (*person, plant*) carnivore

carob ['kærəb] *n* (**a**) (*tree*) caroubier *m* (**b**) *Culin* caroube *m*

carol¹ ['kær(ə)l] *n* chant *m*, chanson *f*; **(Christmas) c.** (chant de) Noël *m*; **c. singer** chanteur, -euse (de chants de Noël); **to go c. singing** aller chanter des chants de Noël

carol² (**-ll-**, *US* **-l-**) **1** *vi* (**a**) (*sing carols*) chanter des chants de Noël (**b**) *Lit* (*sing*) chanter (joyeusement); (*of lark*) chanter **2** *vt* chanter joyeusement; **I'll be with you in a minute, she carolled** je suis à vous dans un instant, lança-t-elle gaiement

Carolina [kærə'laɪnə] *n* Caroline *f*; **South/North C.** Caroline du Sud/du Nord; **the Carolinas** la Caroline du Sud et la Caroline du Nord

Carolingian [kærə'lɪndʒɪən] *Hist* **1** *adj* carolingien **2** *n* Carolingien, -ienne

carom ['kærəm] *n Am Billiards* carambolage *m*

carotid [kə'rɒtɪd] *Anat, Med* **1** *adj* **c. artery** artère *f* carotide **2** *n* (artère *f*) carotide *f*

carousal [kə'raʊz(ə)l] *n Old-fashioned, Hum* beuverie *f*

carouse [kə'raʊz] *vi Old-fashioned, Hum* faire la fête *ou F* la bombe

carousel [kærə'sel] = **carrousel**

carp¹ [kɑːp] *n inv* (*fish*) carpe *f*

carp² *vi* se plaindre; **to c. about sb/sth** se plaindre de qn/qch

carpal ['kɑːp(ə)l] **1** *adj* carpien **2** *n* carpe *m*

car park *n Br* parc *m* de stationnement, parking *m*

Carpathian [kɑː'peɪθɪən] *adj, n* **the C. Mountains, the Carpathians** les (Monts *mpl*) Carpates *mpl*

carpel ['kɑːp(ə)l] *n Bot* carpelle *m*, carpophylle *m*

carpenter¹ ['kɑːpɪntər] *n* charpentier *m*, menuisier *m* en bâtiments; (*making smaller objects*) menuisier

carpenter² *vt* charpenter

carpentry ['kɑːpɪntrɪ] *n Constr* charpenterie *f*; (*for smaller items*) menuiserie *f*; **that's a nice piece of c.** (*chair, table, etc*) c'est un beau travail de menuiserie

carpet¹ ['kɑːpɪt] *n* (**a**) tapis *m*; (*fitted, in car*) moquette *f*; **to lay a c.** poser un tapis/une moquette; *Fig* **to sweep sth under the c.** enterrer qch; *Fig* **to be on the c.** (*of question*) être sur le tapis; (*of person*) être sur la sellette; *Fig* **to have** *or* **put sb on the c.** réprimander qn (**b**) *Fig* (*of flowers, leaves etc*) tapis *m*

carpet² *vt* (**a**) (*floor*) recouvrir d'un tapis; (*with fitted carpet*) recouvrir d'une moquette; (*room*) moquetter; **all the rooms are carpeted** il y a de la moquette dans toutes les pièces; *Fig* **the pond was carpeted with weed** le bassin était tapissé d'algues (**b**) *F* (*person*) réprimander

carpetbagger ['kɑːpɪtbægər] *n* (**a**) *esp US Pol F* candidat étranger/candidate étrangère à la circonscription (**b**) *US Hist* profiteur, -euse venue(e) d'un état nordiste (*après la guerre de sécession*)

carpet bombing *n Mil* bombardement *m* intensif

carpeting ['kɑːpɪtɪŋ] *n* (**a**) (*laying of carpet*) pose *f* de(s) tapis/de(s) moquette(s) (**of** dans) (**b**) (*carpets*) moquette *f* (**c**) *F* (*severe reprimand*) réprimande *f*; **to give sb a c.** passer un savon à qn

carpet slippers *npl* pantoufles *fpl*

carpet-sweeper *n* balai *m* mécanique

carpet tack *n* fixe-tapis *m inv*

carpet tile *n* dalle *f* (de moquette)

car phone *n* téléphone *m* de voiture

carping ['kɑːpɪŋ] **1** *adj* (*person*) très critique, pointilleux; (*criticism*) malveillant **2** *n* critiques *fpl*

carport ['kɑːpɔːt] *n Aut* auvent *m* pour voitures

carpus ['kɑːpəs] *n Med* carpe *m*

carriage ['kærɪdʒ] *n* (**a**) (*vehicle*) voiture *f*; (*together with horses and driver*) équipage *m*; **open/closed c.** voiture découverte/fermée; **c. and pair** voiture à deux chevaux; **invalid c.** voiture d'infirme; **c. entrance** porte *f* cochère; *esp Am* **the c. trade** la clientèle haut de gamme

(**b**) *Br Rail* voiture *f*, wagon *m*

(**c**) *Tech* (*of lathe, typewriter etc*) chariot *m*; **c. release arm** (*on typewriter*) levier *m* de dégagement du chariot; *Mil* **gun c.** affût *m*

(**d**) (*transport*) transport *m*; *Com* (*cost*) (frais *mpl* de) port *m*; **c. forward** (en) port dû, port avancé; **c. free** franc de port, franco; **c. insurance paid** port payé, assurance comprise; **c. paid** (en) port payé

(**e**) (*bearing*) (*of person*) port *m*, maintien *m*

carriage clock *n* = horloge *f* à boîtier rectangulaire muni d'une poignée

carriage return *n* (*on keyboard*) retour *m* de chariot

carriageway ['kærɪdʒweɪ] *n Br Aut* chaussée *f*

carrier ['kærɪər] *n* (**a**) *Med etc* (*of disease, germs etc*) porteur, -euse (**b**) *Com* (*company*) transporteur *m*; *Jur* voiturier *m* (**c**) (*container*) (*on bicycle etc*) (*basket*) panier *m*; (*behind the saddle*) porte-bagages *m inv*; (*for homing pigeon etc*) cartouche *f*; **c. (bag)** sac *m* (*en papier, en plastique*) (**d**) *Ind* (*mechanism*) transporteur *m* (**e**) **(aircraft) c.** porte-avions *m inv* (**f**) *Telecom* (fréquence *f*) porteuse *f*; **c. tone** tonalité *f*

carrier-based ['kærɪə'beɪst] *adj Av, Naut* embarqué

carrier pigeon *n* pigeon *m* voyageur

carrion ['kærɪən] *n* (*no pl*) charogne *f*; **c. crow** corneille *f* noire, corbine *f*

carrot ['kærət] *n* carotte *f*; *Fig* **a pay rise is the c. management is holding out to the unions** le patronat tente d'amadouer les syndicats en promettant une hausse des salaires; **the c. and the stick** la carotte et le bâton; *F* **carrots, c. top** (*hair*) cheveux *mpl* roux *ou* carotte; (*person*) rouquin *m*, poil *m* de carotte
carroty ['kærətɪ] *adj F* (*person, hair*) roux, *f* rousse
carrousel [kærə'sel] *n* **(a)** (*for slides*) magasin *m* **(b)** (*at airport*) carrousel *m* (pour bagages) **(c)** *Am* (*at fairground*) chevaux *mpl* de bois, manège *m*
carry ['kærɪ] **(carried) 1** *vt* **(a)** (*of person, wind*) (*burden, bag, child, scent etc*) porter; (*goods, passengers etc*) transporter; *Med* (*disease*) véhiculer; (*of wires etc*) (*sound etc*) conduire, transmettre; (*of pipes*) (*water etc*) amener, transporter; (*revolver, watch etc*) (*on one's person*) porter (sur soi); **I don't c. much money about** *or* **on me** je n'ai jamais beaucoup d'argent sur moi; **the current carried the raft out to sea** le courant a emporté le radeau au large; **rats c. diseases** les rats sont porteurs de maladies; **a memory that he will c. with him to the grave** un souvenir qu'il n'oubliera jamais; **the bus carried us to our destination** l'autobus nous a conduits jusqu'à notre destination; **we were carrying livestock** (*of ship*) nous avions du bétail à bord; **to c. sth in one's head** avoir qch en mémoire; *Fig* **the other team members have to c. him** les autres membres de l'équipe doivent le porter; **he's being carried by the other members of the team** il se repose sur les autres membres de l'équipe; **his strong constitution carried him through his illness** sa forte constitution lui a permis de surmonter sa maladie; **to c. a child** (*be pregnant*) porter un enfant, être enceinte; **I can't c. a tune** je suis incapable de chanter sans faire de fausses notes

(b) (*involve*) **to c. (no) conviction** (ne pas) être convaincant; **to c. a guarantee** être garanti; **to c. a fine/penalty** être passible d'amende/d'une peine; **to c. a risk** comporter un risque; **to c. responsibility** comporter des responsabilités; **to c. weight/authority** (*of person, opinion*) avoir du poids/de l'autorité; **to c. significance (for sb/sth)** avoir de l'importance (pour qn/qch); **to c. interest** (*of money*) porter intérêt

(c) (*take, lead, extend*) **to c. an argument to its logical conclusion** aller au bout d'un raisonnement; **to c. sth too far** pousser qch trop loin; **to c. the battle** *or* **fight into the enemy's camp** *Mil* faire du territoire ennemi le lieu du conflit; *Fig* attaquer l'ennemi sur son propre terrain

(d) (*capture, win*) (*fortress*) enlever; (*position*) emporter d'assaut; **to c. all before one** (*be successful*) remporter tous les prix; (*win support, approval*) vaincre toutes les résistances, triompher sur toute la ligne; *Hum* **she carries all before her** (*has large bosom*) il y a du monde au balcon; **to c. the day** l'emporter; **to c. several states** l'emporter dans plusieurs états; **to c. one's point** établir la validité de son argument

(e) (*proposal*) (*pass*) adopter; (*secure passage of*) faire adopter *ou* passer; **the bill was carried** le projet a été adopté

(f) *Com* (*keep in stock*) (*article*) faire, vendre, avoir; (*goods*) avoir en magasin *ou* en dépôt; **to c. an advertisement/article** (*of newspaper etc*) comporter une publicité/un article; **do you c. bathroom accessories?** (*to sales assistant*) est-ce que vous vendez des accessoires pour salles de bain?

(g) (*hold*) **to c. oneself well/badly** se tenir bien/mal; **to c. one's head high** porter la tête haute

(h) *Archit, Constr* (*beam, vault*) porter, supporter

(i) *Math* **c. two** je retiens deux, on retient deux

2 *vi* **(a)** (*of sound, gun etc*) porter; **her voice carries well** elle a une voix qui porte bien

(b) *Sl* (*possess drugs*) avoir de la drogue sur soi; **he was arrested for carrying** il a été arrêté parce qu'il avait de la drogue sur lui

▶ **carry along** *vtsep* (*sb, sth*) emporter, entraîner; (*of stream etc*) (*mud etc*) charrier
▶ **carry away** *vtsep* **(a)** (*take*) (*object*) emporter, enlever; (*person*) entraîner, emmener **(b)** (*make excited, over-enthusiastic*) **he let his enthusiasm c. him away** il s'est laissé emporter par son enthousiasme; **I got carried away** je me suis emballé; **don't get carried away!** ne te laisse pas emporter!; *Iron F* ne t'emballe pas!
▶ **carry back** *vtsep* **(a)** (*bring*) (*object*) rapporter; (*person*) ramener **(b)** (*take*) (*object*) reporter; (*person*) remmener; **that carries me back to my youth** cela me ramène à l'époque de ma jeunesse
▶ **carry down** *vtsep* **(a)** (*from upstairs etc*) (*sb, sth*) descendre **(b)** (*usu passive*) (*tradition*) transmettre
▶ **carry forward** *vtsep Acct* **to c. an item forward** reporter un article; **carried forward** report, à reporter; **carried forward from the previous year** report de l'exercice précédent; **carried forward to the next year** report à l'exercice suivant
▶ **carry off** *vtsep* **(a)** (*bring, take*) (*object*) emporter; (*person*) emmener **(b)** (*win*) (*prize*) remporter **(c)** (*be successful in*) (*sth unusual*) faire passer, faire accepter; **to c. it off** réussir le coup; **they managed to c. the robbery off** ils ont mené à bien le cambriolage; **it's a difficult role and he didn't quite c. it off** c'est un rôle difficile, et il n'a pas su se montrer à la hauteur **(d)** *Old-fashioned* (*of disease*) emporter
▶ **carry on 1** *vtsep* (*task*) poursuivre, continuer; (*tradition*) continuer; (*business, trade*) exercer; (*correspondence*) entretenir; **they were carrying on a conversation** ils étaient en train de parler

2 *vi* **(a)** (*continue*) continuer; **to c. on doing sth** continuer à faire qch; **just c. on with what you were doing** continuez ce que vous étiez en train de faire; **c. on!** continuez!; *Mil* **c. on, sergeant!** vous pouvez disposer, sergeant; **I shall c. on to the end** j'irai jusqu'au bout; **will you be able to c. on during my absence?** (*assume responsibility*) pourras-tu prendre les choses en main pendant mon absence?

(b) *F* (*behave*) se comporter; **I don't like the way she carries on** je n'aime pas ses façons; **from the way he carries on anyone'd think that ...** vu la façon dont il se comporte, on croirait vraiment que ...

(c) *F* (*behave badly*) faire des scènes, s'emporter; **don't c. on like that!** ne vous emballez pas comme ça!

(d) *F* (*have an affair*) avoir une liaison (**with** avec)

▶ **carry out** *vtsep* **(a)** (*bring, take*) (*object*) porter dehors/hors de la salle/*etc*; (*person*) transporter dehors **(b)** (*do, execute*) (*plan, threat, decision*) mettre à exécution; (*experiment*) effectuer; (*instructions, order*) exécuter; (*idea, Com order etc*) donner suite à; (*wish*) satisfaire à; (*responsibilities*) assumer; (*job*) mener à bonne fin; (*task, duty*) s'acquitter de; **the police carried out a search** la police a effectué une perquisition; **to c. out a procedure** suivre une procédure
▶ **carry over 1** *vtsep* (*take, bring*) transporter de l'autre côté; *Com, Math* (*figure, sum*) reporter; (*practice, tradition*) continuer; **to c. over one's holiday entitlement/tax allowance to the next year** reporter ses congés/son abattement fiscal sur l'année suivante; **that will have to be carried over to the next meeting** il faudra poursuivre ce point lors de la prochaine réunion **2** *vi* (*of effect, implications*) avoir des répercussions (**into** sur); **the right carries over to future owners** les futurs propriétaires conservent ce droit
▶ **carry through** *vtsep* **(a)** (*complete*) (*undertaking*) mener à bien *ou* à bonne fin *ou* à bon terme; (*task*) exécuter **(b) his strong constitution carried him through** sa forte constitution lui a permis de s'en sortir
▶ **carry up** *vtsep* monter
carryall ['kærɪɔːl] *n* (sac *m*) fourre-tout *m inv*
carrycot ['kærɪkɒt] *n* porte-bébé *m inv*
carrying ['kærɪɪŋ] *adj* **(a) c. axle** (*of locomotive*) essieu *m* porteur **(b) c. capacity** (*of vehicle*) charge *f* utile; (*of tourist attraction*) capacité *f* d'accueil
carrying forward *n Acct* report *m*
carrying-on *n F* (*foolish behaviour*) **carrying(s)-on** (*of child*) cirque *m*; (*of unfaithful spouse, lover*) écart *m* de conduite
carry-on[1] *n F* cinéma *m*; **what a c. just to buy a ticket!** quelle histoire *ou* quel cinéma rien que pour acheter un billet!
carry-on[2] *adj* (*luggage*) à main
carry-out *Scot, Am* **1** *n* (*meal*) repas *m* à emporter; (*restaurant*) restaurant *m* qui fait des plats à emporter; (*alcohol*) = alcool *m* acheté (surtout) dans un pub pour être consommé à l'extérieur **2** *adj attrib* (*meal, food*) à emporter; **c. menu** liste *f* des plats à emporter
carryover ['kærɪəʊvər] *n* **it's a c. from my childhood** (*habit, tradition*) c'est une habitude qui vient de mon enfance; (*fear, phobia*) c'est une peur qui vient de mon enfance
carsick ['kɑːsɪk] *adj* **to be/get c.** avoir mal au cœur en voiture
carsickness ['kɑːsɪknɪs] *n* mal *m* de la route; **c. pills** comprimés *mpl* contre le mal de la route
cart[1] [kɑːt] *n* (*abbr* **cartridge**) cartouche *f*, cassette *f*; **c. tape** bande *f* magnétique en cartouche
cart[2] *n* charrette *f* (*à deux roues*); (*small*) carriole *f*; (*with four wheels*) chariot *m*; *Fig* **to put the c. before the horse** mettre la charrue avant les bœufs; **c. track** chemin *m* charretier, chemin de terre
cart[3] *vt* **(a)** *F* (*carry*) trimballer **(b)** (*transport by cart*) charrier, voiturer
▶ **cart about, cart around** *vtsep F* (*parcels etc*) trimbal(l)er
▶ **cart away, cart off** *vtsep F* (*rubbish etc*) enlever, emporter; (*person*) emmener; **he was carted away** *or* **off to prison** ils sont venus le chercher pour l'emmener en prison

cartage ['kɑːtɪdʒ] *n* **(a)** (*transport*) (*in cart*) charroi *m*, charriage *m*; (*in lorry*) camionnage *m* **(b)** (*cost*) (*by cart*) (coût *m* de) charriage *m*; (*by lorry*) (coût *m* de) camionnage *m*

cartel [kɑː'tel] *n Com* cartel *m*; **oil/steel c.** cartel du pétrole/de l'acier; **to form a c.** former un cartel; **c. laws** lois *fpl* anti-trust

carter ['kɑːtər] *n* charretier *m*

Cartesian [kɑː'tiːzɪən] *adj, n Phil* cartésien

carthorse ['kɑːthɔːs] *n* cheval *m* d'attelage

Carthusian [kɑː'θjuːzɪən] **1** *adj* **(a)** *Rel* chartreux **(b)** *Br Sch* de l'école de Charterhouse **2** *n* **(a)** *Rel* chartreux, -euse **(b)** *Br Sch* élève *m*/ancien élève de l'école de Charterhouse

cartilage ['kɑːtɪlɪdʒ] *n* cartilage *m*

cartload ['kɑːtləʊd] *n* charretée *f*, voiturée *f* **(of** de); (*transported in tip cart*) tombereau *m*

cartographer [kɑː'tɒgrəfər] *n* cartographe *mf*

cartographic(al) [kɑːtə'græfɪk, -ɪk(ə)l] *adj* cartographique

cartography [kɑː'tɒgrəfɪ] *n* cartographie *f*

cartomancy ['kɑːtəmænsɪ] *n* cartomancie *f*

carton ['kɑːtən] *n* **(a)** (*box*) (boîte *f* en) carton *m* **(b)** (*container*) (*for yoghurt, cream etc*) pot *m*; (*for milk, orange juice etc*) brick *m*; **a c. of cigarettes** une cartouche de cigarettes

cartoon [kɑː'tuːn] *n* **(a)** (*in newspaper etc*) dessin *m* humoristique *ou* satirique; *Cin* dessin animé; **c. character** personnage *m* de bande dessinée/de dessin animé; **strip c., c. strip** bande *f* dessinée, BD *f* **(b)** (*caricature*) caricature *f* **(c)** *Art* (*sketch*) carton *m*

cartoonist [kɑː'tuːnɪst] *n* **(a)** (*in newspaper etc*) dessinateur, -trice de dessins humoristiques *ou* satiriques **(b)** (*caricaturist*) caricaturiste *m*

cartridge ['kɑːtrɪdʒ] *n* **(a)** *Mil* (*for firearm*) cartouche *f*; **c. clip** chargeur *m*; **c. belt** (*for soldier*) cartouchière *f*; (*for machine gun*) bande-chargeur *f* souple *ou* articulée, *pl* bandes-chargeurs **(b)** (*container, unit*) (*of film, ink, fuse etc*) cartouche *f*; (*on record-player*) cellule *f* de lecture; (*for tape recorder*) cassette *f*; **c. pen** stylo *m* (à plume) à cartouche; **c. tape** bande *f* magnétique en cartouche **(c)** *Ind, Art* **c. paper** papier *m* à cartouches, papier-cartouche *m*

cartwheel ['kɑːtwiːl] *n* roue *f* de charrette; *Gym* **to turn cartwheels** faire la roue; **to do a c.** faire une roue

cartwright ['kɑːtraɪt] *n* charron *m*

carve [kɑːv] **1** *vt* **(a)** (*wood, stone*) sculpter; (*design, name on marble etc*) graver, ciseler; **to c. a statue in** *or* **out of marble** sculpter une statue dans le marbre; **carved lion** lion sculpté; *Fig* **carved in stone** *or* **tablets of stone** (*instructions, orders etc*) auquel on doit obéir à la lettre; **her recommendations are not carved in stone** il n'est pas nécessaire d'obéir à la lettre à ses recommandations **(b)** (*meat, poultry*) découper **2** *vi* **(a)** (*sculpt*) sculpter **(in** dans) **(b)** (*of material*) **wood that carves well/badly** bois qui se prête bien/mal à la sculpture **(c)** (*at meal*) découper

▶ **carve out** *vtsep* (*cut out*) (*piece of wood etc*) tailler, découper; (*sculpt*) (*statue etc*) sculpter; *Fig* **the company carved out a niche in the market** la société s'est taillé une place sur le marché; **to c. out a career for oneself** se faire une carrière

▶ **carve up** *vtsep* **(a)** (*cut*) (*meat, poultry*) découper; *Fig F* **to c. sb up** (*disfigure*) défigurer qn; *Fig* **Europeans carved up the continent (among themselves)** les Européens se sont partagé le continent **(b)** *Aut F* (*overtake dangerously*) faire une queue de poisson à; **did you see how that idiot carved me up?** tu as vu la queue de poisson que m'a faite cet imbécile?

carver ['kɑːvər] *n* **(a)** (*sculptor*) sculpteur *m* **(b)** (*knife*) couteau *m* à découper **(c)** *Br* (*chair*) fauteuil *m* de table (*qu'occupe le chef de famille*)

carvery ['kɑːvərɪ] *n* grill *m*

carving ['kɑːvɪŋ] *n* **(a)** *Art* (*technique, object*) sculpture *f*; (*on wood, metal*) gravure *f*; (*on metal, stone*) ciselure *f*; **wood c.** sculpture sur bois **(b)** (*of meat*) découpage *m*; **c. knife/fork** couteau *m*/fourchette *f* à découper; **c. set** service *m* à découper; **c. table** table *f* à découper

carwash ['kɑːwɒʃ] *n Aut* lave-auto *m*, *pl* lave-autos

caryatid [kærɪ'ætɪd] *n Archit* cariatide *f*

cascade[1] [kæs'keɪd] *n* (*waterfall*), *Fig* cascade *f*

cascade[2] *vi* (*of water etc, Fig of balloons, hair*) tomber en cascade; **the tins came cascading down** les boîtes de conserve sont tombées les unes après les autres

CASE [keɪs] *n Comptr* (*abbr* **computer-aided software engineering**) ingénierie *f* des systèmes assistée par ordinateur

case[1] [keɪs] *n* **(a)** (*instance, situation*) cas *m*; **a c. in point** un cas d'espèce; **to put the c. clearly** exposer clairement le cas *ou* la situation; **if that's the c.** dans ce cas-là, *Fml* s'il en est ainsi; **should that be the c.** le cas échéant; **it's a c. of now or never** il s'agit de saisir l'occasion *ou* de faire vite; **in c. of emergency/accident/need** en cas d'urgence/d'accident/de besoin; **in c. he isn't there** au cas *ou* dans le cas où il n'y serait pas; **just in c.** à titre de précaution, *F* au cas où; **just in c. it rains I'll take an umbrella** je prends un parapluie, juste au cas où il pleuvrait; **I'll take an umbrella, just in c.** je prends un parapluie au cas où; **in any c.** (*at any rate*) en tout cas; (*besides*) de toute façon; **in that c.** dans ce cas; **in such a c., in such cases** en pareil cas, en pareille circonstance; **in these cases it's best to wait** dans de telles circonstances, il vaut mieux attendre; **in his c.** dans son cas; **let's take the c. of Mrs. Smith** prenons le cas de Mme Smith; **or not, as the c. may be** ou non, suivant le cas; **in most cases** dans la plupart des cas; **it appears to be a c. of mistaken identity** il semble y avoir erreur sur la personne; **if it's a c. of not having enough money** si c'est une question d'argent

(b) *Med* (*of jaundice, scarlet fever etc*) cas *m*; (*patient*) malade *mf*; **heart c.** cardiaque *mf*; *F* **he's a c.** (*odd*) c'est un drôle de type

(c) *Jur etc* affaire *f*; **famous cases** causes *fpl ou* affaires célèbres; **the police are working on the c.** la police enquête sur cette affaire; **the c. will be heard on January 5th** l'audience aura lieu le 5 janvier; **to state the c.** faire l'exposé des faits; *Fig* **to state or put one's c.** plaider sa cause; **to put the c. for the defence** présenter la défense du prévenu; **the c. for the Crown** (*in criminal trial*) l'accusation *f*; **there is no c. against you** vous êtes hors de cause; **the judge ruled that there was no c. to answer** le juge a rendu un non-lieu; *Fig* **the c. for sb/sth** les arguments *mpl* en faveur de qn/qch; **to put up a strong c. for sb** (*defend*) prendre le parti de qn, défendre qn; (*recommend*) recommander qn très chaudement; **divorce c.** procès *m* en divorce

(d) *Gram* cas *m*; **c. ending** désinence *f*

case[2] *n* **(a)** (*large*) **(packing) c.** caisse *f*, boîte *f* (d'emballage); **c. of wine** caisse de vin

(b) (*for specific object*) (*for spectacles, cigarettes, musical instrument etc*) étui *m*; (*for jewellery*) coffret *m*, écrin *m*; (*for pencils, geometry etc instruments*) trousse *f*; **(display** *or* **glass) c.** vitrine *f*; **record c.** mallette *f* porte-disques; **dressing c.** nécessaire *m ou* trousse de toilette; **card c.** porte-cartes *m inv*

(c) (*suitcase*) valise *f*; (*briefcase*) porte-documents *m inv*

(d) (*outer part*) (*of piano*) coffre *m*, caisse *f*; (*of organ*) buffet *m*; (*of clock*) caisse; (*of watch etc*) boîtier *m*; (*of lock*) palastre *m*, coffre; (*of cartridge*) douille *f*, étui *m*; (*of engine cylinder*) chemise *f*, enveloppe *f*; (*of turbine*) bâche *f*; *Aut* (*of differential etc*) carter *m*

(e) (*in bookbinding*) couverture *f*

(f) *Typ* casse *f*; **lower c.** bas *m* de casse; **lower-c. letter** minuscule *f*; **upper c.** haut *m* de casse; **upper-c. letter** (lettre *f*) majuscule *f*, (lettre) capitale *f*

case[3] *vt* **(a)** (*put in box*) (*goods*) mettre en caisse(s) **(b)** (*put outer layer on*) envelopper **(with** de); (*boiler, cylinder*) chemiser; (*turbine*) bâcher **(c)** (*in bookbinding*) (*book*) cartonner **(d)** *Sl* **to c. the joint** (*before burglary*) examiner les lieux

casebook ['keɪsbʊk] *n* **(a)** *Jur* recueil *m* de jurisprudence **(b)** *Med* dossier *m* médical

cased [keɪst] *adj* (*edition*) cartonné

case-harden *vt Metal* (*steel*) tremper *ou* durcir à la surface

case-hardened *adj Metal* trempé à la surface; *F* (*person*) endurci

case-hardening *n Metal* (*of steel*) cémentation *f*

case history *n* antécédents *mpl*; **to take sb's c.** prendre les antécédents de qn

casein ['keɪsiːn] *n Ch, Ind* caséine *f*

case law *n* droit *m* jurisprudentiel

case load *n* (nombre *m* de) dossiers *mpl* (*d'une assistante sociale, un médecin etc*)

casement ['keɪsmənt] *n* (*frame*) châssis *m* de fenêtre à deux battants; **c. window** fenêtre *f* à deux battants, croisée *f*

case study *n* étude *f* de cas

casework ['keɪswɜːk] *n Med* traitement *m* individuel; (*social work*) assistance *f* individuelle

caseworker ['keɪswɜːkər] *n* assistant, -ante social(e)

cash[1] [kæʃ] *n* (*no pl*) (*coins, banknotes*) argent *m*, liquide *m*; (*in commerce*) liquide, espèces *fpl*; *F* (*money*) argent, *F* fric *m*; **I haven't got any c.** (*no money*) je n'ai pas d'argent; (*no change*) je n'ai pas de monnaie; *F* **I'm short of c.** je suis à sec; **that's an awful lot of c.** c'est beaucoup d'argent *ou F* de fric; **to pay (in) c.** payer comptant; (*money not cheque*) payer en liquide *ou* en espèces; **will that be c. or shall I charge it to your account?** (*not credit*) vous payez comptant ou est-ce que je le mets sur votre compte?; (*money not cheque*) vous payez en liquide ou est-ce que je le mets sur votre compte?; **c. (purchases) only** (*notice at checkout*) paiements en liquide seulement; *Com* **c. against documents** comptant contre documents; *Acct* **c. at bank** avoir *m* en banque; **c. on delivery** paiement à la livraison; **c. in hand** fonds *mpl ou* espèces *mpl ou* argent *m* en caisse; **it's all c. in hand in this sort of work** dans cette branche, tout se paye de la main à la main; *Acct* **c. in till** encaisse *f*; *Acct* **c. on hand** argent *m* en caisse; *Com* **c. with order** paiement *m* à la commande, envoi *m* contre paiement; *Com* **c. balance** (*status*) situation *f* de caisse; (*amount remaining*) solde *m* actif, solde de caisse; *Mktg* **c. cow** (*product*) vache *f* à lait; *Acct* **c. contribution** apport *m* en numéraire; *Agr* **c. crop** culture *f* commerciale; *Com* **c. deal** marché *m* au comptant; *Fin* **c. deposit** versement *m* d'espèces, dépôt *m* d'espèces; **c. discount, discount for c.** escompte *m* de caisse; *Acct* **c. expenditure** dépenses *fpl* de caisse; *Fin* **c. incentive** stimulation *f* financière; *Acct* **c. ledger** journal *m* de caisse; **c. management** gestion *f* de la trésorerie; *Acct* **c. order** ordre *m* au comptant; *Acct* **c. outflow** sorties *fpl* de trésorerie; *Acct* **c. overs** excédent *m* de caisse; **c. payment** paiement *m* (au) comptant, paiement en espèces; *Banking* **c. point** distributeur *m ou* guichet *m* automatique, terminal *m* monétique; *Acct* **c. position** situation *f* de caisse; **c. price** prix *m* au comptant; *Com* **c. purchase** achat *m* au comptant, achat contre espèces; *Acct* **c. ratio** ratio *m* de trésorerie; *Com* **c. rebate** remboursement *m*; *Acct* **c. receipt** reçu *m* pour paiement en espèces, reçu d'espèces; *Acct* **c. received** (*balance sheet item*) entrée *f* d'argent; **c. reduction** = réduction *f* accordée si on paie en liquide; *Acct* **c. report (form)** situation *f* de caisse; **c. reserves** réserves *fpl* en espèces; *St Exch* **c. settlement** liquidation *f* en espèces; *Fin* **c. shortage** insuffisance *f* de trésorerie; *Acct* **c. statement** état *m ou* bordereau *m ou* relevé *m* de caisse; *Acct* **c. surplus** restant *m* en caisse; **c. transaction** transaction *f ou* opération *f* au comptant; *Mktg* **c. trap** poids *m* mort; *Acct* **c. unders** manque *m* de caisse; *Acct* **c. voucher** pièce *f* de caisse, PC *f*; **c. withdrawals** retraits *mpl* d'espèces

cash[2] *vt* (*cheque, postal order etc*) toucher, encaisser; **to c. a cheque for sb** verser à qn le montant d'un chèque

▶ **cash in** *vtsep Fin* (*exchange for money*) **to c. in savings stamps** se faire rembourser des timbres-épargne; *Sl* **to c. in one's chips** *or* **checks** (*die*) casser sa pipe

▶ **cash in on** *vipo F* (*derive benefit from*) profiter de, tirer profit de

▶ **cash up** *vi Br* faire les comptes

cashable ['kæʃ(ə)bl] *adj* (*bill etc*) encaissable

cash and carry *n* magasin *m* de demi-gros

cash book *n* livre *m ou* journal *m* de caisse

cash box *n* caisse *f*

cash card *n* carte *f* de retrait

cash desk *n* caisse *f*

cash dispenser *n* distributeur *m* automatique (de billets), terminal *m* monétique, *Can* guichet *m* automatique

cashew [kæ'ʃuː] *n* **c. (nut tree)** acajou *m* à pommes, anacardier *m*; **c. (nut)** (noix *f* de) cajou *m*

cashflow ['kæʃfləʊ] *n Fin* cash-flow *m*, trésorerie *f*; *Acct* (*in cashflow statement*) marge *f* brute d'autofinancement; *F* **I've got a c. problem** j'ai des problèmes d'argent; **c. forecast** prévision *f* de trésorerie; **c. management** gestion *f* de trésorerie; *Acct* **c. statement** état *m* des mouvements de la trésorerie

cashier[1] [kæ'ʃɪər] *n* caissier, -ière; *US* **c.'s check** chèque *m* de banque; **c.'s desk** comptoir-caisse *m*; **c.'s office** bureau *m* du caissier

cashier[2] *vt Mil, Naut* (*dismiss*) casser

cashless ['kæʃlɪs] *adj* **the c. society** la société où l'argent liquide n'est plus utilisé; **c. transaction** transaction *f* sans argent

cash machine *n* point *m* d'argent, distributeur *m* automatique (de billets), *Can* guichet *m* automatique

cashmere ['kæʃmɪər] *n Tex* cachemire *m*; **c. shawl** (châle *m* de) cachemire; **c. sweater** pull *m* en cachemire

cash point *n* caisse *f*; *Banking* point *m* d'argent, distributeur *m* de billets

cash register *n* caisse *f* enregistreuse

casing ['keɪsɪŋ] *n* **(a)** (*process*) (*of goods*) encaissage *m*, mise *f* en caisses; (*of book*) cartonnage *m*; (*of mine shaft etc*) tubage *m*, cuvelage *m* **(b)** (*outer layer*) (*of pump etc*) enveloppe *f*, garniture *f*; (*of cylinder*) blindage *m*, chemise *f*; (*of turbine*) huche *f*, bâche *f* fermée; (*of machine*) cage *f*, coquille *f*; *Constr* (*for reinforced concrete*) coffrage *m*; *Aut* (*of differential*) carter *m*; (*of clutch*) boîte *f*, caisse *f*, carter; **tyre c.** enveloppe *f* (extérieure) de pneu

casino [kə'siːnəʊ] *n* casino *m*

cask [kɑːsk] *n* fût *m*, tonneau *m*; *Com* **wine in the c.** vin en fût

casket ['kɑːskɪt] *n* **(a)** (*for jewellery*) coffret *m*, cassette *f*; (*for money*) cassette **(b)** *esp Am* (*coffin*) cercueil *m* **(c)** (*for ashes*) urne *f*

CASM ['kæz(ə)m] *n Comptr* (*abbr* **computer-aided sales and marketing**) vente *f* et marketing assistés par ordinateur

Caspian ['kæspɪən] *adj* caspien; **the C. Sea** la mer Caspienne

Cassandra [kə'sændrə] *n Myth* Cassandre *f*; *Fig* oiseau *m* de malheur

cassata [kə'sɑːtə] *n Culin* cassate *f*

cassava [kə'sɑːvə] *n Bot* cassave *f*, manioc *m*; **c. (flour)** farine *f* de cassave, manioc

casserole[1] ['kæsərəʊl] *n Culin* **(a)** *Br* (*pan*) cocotte *f* **(b)** (*food*) ragoût *m* en cocotte; **beef c.** ragoût de bœuf

casserole[2] *vt* (*meat etc*) cuire à la cocotte

cassette [kə'set] *n* **(a)** (*audio, video etc*) cassette *f*; *Comptr* **c. drive** lecteur *m* de cassettes; **c. machine** magnétophone *m*; **c. player** lecteur *m* de cassette; (*without radio*) magnétophone *m* à cassettes; **c. recorder** enregistreur *m* de cassette **(b)** *Phot* chargeur *m*

cassock ['kæsək] *n Rel* soutane *f*

cassowary ['kæsəweərɪ] *n* (*bird*) casoar *m*

cast[1] [kɑːst] *n* **(a)** *Th, Cin, TV* distribution *f*; **the members of the c.** la distribution; **members of the c. include …** parmi les comédiens il y a …; *esp Rad* **other parts were played by members of the c.** les autres rôles étaient tenus par les comédiens déjà nommés; **you were in the c. of …** vous avez joué dans …; *Th* **to have a c. of three** être joué par trois acteurs; *Cin Hum* **a c. of thousands** des milliers d'acteurs

(b) (*of dice, net*) coup *m*; (*in fishing*) (*of line, fly, net*) lancer *m*

(c) *Med* plâtre *m*; *Art, Metal etc* (*mould*) moule *m* en creux; (*item*) pièce *f* moulée; (*of plaster*) plâtre; **plaster c.** *Art* moulage *m* au plâtre; *Med* plâtre; **to take a c. of sth** mouler qch; **the dentist took a c. of my teeth** le dentiste a fait un moulage en plâtre de mes dents; **they took a c. of the footprints** ils ont relevé les empreintes de pas; **to have one's arm in a c.** avoir le bras dans le plâtre

(d) (*squint*) **to have a c. in one's eye** avoir une coquetterie dans l'œil

(e) *Lit* **a man of his c.** un homme de sa trempe; **c. of mind** mentalité *f*

(f) (*of earthworm*) déjections *fpl*

(g) (*skin of insect, snake*) dépouille *f*

(h) (*regurgitated food*) pelote *f* régurgitée (*par les hiboux, les faucons*)

cast[2] (*pt, pp* **cast**) **1** *vt* **(a)** (*shadow*) porter, projeter; *Fml* (*stone etc*) jeter, lancer; (*net, line*) lancer; *Fml* **she cast her eyes over the letter** elle a parcouru la lettre; *Naut* **to c. anchor** jeter l'ancre; **to c. doubt on sth** jeter le doute sur qch; **this cast doubt on his ability** cela jeta un doute sur ses capacités; **to c. its skin** (*of reptile*) muer; **to c. a shoe** (*of horse*) perdre un fer; **to c. a spell over sb** ensorceler qn, envoûter qn

(b) *Pol etc* **to c. a vote, to c. one's vote** voter (**for** pour); **the numbers of votes cast for …** le nombre de voix pour …

(c) *Th, Cin, TV* (*play, film*) distribuer les rôles de; **to c. sb for a part** attribuer un rôle à qn; **she was cast as** *or* **in the role of Desdemona** on lui a donné le rôle de Desdémone; *Fig* **to c. sb in the role of the villain** donner à qn le rôle du méchant

(d) (*horoscope*) faire

(e) *Art, Metal etc* (*metal*) fondre; (*cylinder etc*) mouler, couler; (*medal*) sabler; (*statue*) couler; **the statue had been cast in bronze** la statue avait été coulée dans le bronze; **cast in one piece** coulé en bloc

2 *vi* lancer; **to c. for fish** pêcher au lancer

cast[3] *adj Art, Metal* coulé, fondu; **c. steel** fonte *f* d'acier, acier *m* fondu; *Cer* **c. ware** pièces *fpl* coulées

▶ **cast about, cast around** *vi* chercher; **to c. around for sth** chercher qch

▶ **cast aside** *vtsep* jeter sur le côté; *Fig* (*wife, friends, doubts*) abandonner, se défaire de; **to c. aside one's fears** oublier ses craintes; **to c. aside one's former life** changer de vie; **are you going to c. all this aside for a foolish dream?** est-ce que tu vas renoncer à tout ça pour une chimère?

▶ **cast away** *vtsep Naut* **to be cast away** faire naufrage

▶ **cast back** *vtsep* **to c. one's mind back** revenir en arrière; **to c. one's mind back to sth** se rappeler qch; **c. your mind back a year** souvenez-vous de *ou* rappelez-vous l'année dernière

▶ **cast down** *vtsep* **(a)** (*eyes*) baisser; (*weapons*) déposer **(b)** *Lit* **to be cast down** (*dejected*) être abattu *ou* découragé *ou* déprimé

▶ **cast off 1** *vtsep* **(a)** (*reject*) (*person*) rejeter **(b)** (*clothes*)

enlever, se dépouiller de; (*bonds etc*) se défaire de, se libérer de; *Fig* (*shyness etc*) se débarrasser de (**c**) *Knitting* (*stitches*) arrêter (**d**) *Naut* (*moorings*) larguer **2** *vi* (**a**) *Naut* (*of ship*) larguer les amarres (**b**) *Knitting* arrêter les mailles

▶ **cast on** *Knitting* **1** *vtsep* (*stitches*) monter **2** *vi* monter les mailles

▶ **cast out** *vtsep* (**a**) (*reject*) (*person*) rejeter (**b**) (*exorcise*) (*evil spirits*) chasser, exorciser

▶ **cast up** *vtsep* (**a**) **to c. sth up to sb** (*as reproach*) reprocher qch à qn (**b**) (*of sea*) rejeter

castanets [kæstəˈnets] *npl* (**pair of**) **c.** (paire *f* de) castagnettes *fpl*

castaway [ˈkɑːstəweɪ] *n* naufragé, -ée

caste [kɑːst] *n* caste *f*; **high/low-c.** de haute/basse caste; *Fig* **to lose c.** se discréditer

casteless [ˈkɑːstlɪs] *adj* sans caste

castellated [ˈkæstɪleɪtɪd] *adj Archit* crénelé; (*with turrets*) à tourelles

caster [ˈkɑːstər] *n* (**a**) *Metal etc* (*machine*) fondeuse *f* (**b**) (*for sugar, cocoa*) saupoudroir *m*; *Culin* **c. sugar** sucre *m* semoule, sucre en poudre

caster action *n Aut* (*of steering*) effet *m* de chasse

castigate [ˈkæstɪgeɪt] *vt* (**a**) *Old-fashioned* (*punish*) (*person*) châtier, corriger (**b**) *Fml* (*criticize*) (*person, book etc*) critiquer sévèrement, étriller

castigation [kæstɪˈgeɪʃən] *n* (**a**) *Old-fashioned* (*punishment*) châtiment *m*, correction *f* (**b**) *Fml* (*criticism*) critique *f* sévère

Castile [kæˈstiːl] *n* Castille *f*; **New C.** Nouvelle-Castille

Castilian [kæsˈtɪlɪən] **1** *adj* castillan **2** *n* (**a**) (*person*) Castillan, -ane (**b**) *Ling* castillan *m*

casting [ˈkɑːstɪŋ] **1** *adj* **c. vote** (*given to chairperson etc when votes are divided equally*) voix *f* prépondérante; **the chairman has the c. vote** la voix du président est prépondérante

2 *n* (**a**) (*in fishing*) lancer *m*; **c. net** épervier *m*

(**b**) *Art, Metal etc* (*process*) moulage *m*, fonte *f*; (*individual item*) pièce *f* coulée, pièce de fonte; **heavy castings** grosses pièces; **die c.** (*item*) pièce moulée sous pression; **sand c.** (*process*) coulée *f* en sable

(**c**) *Th, Cin* distribution *f* des rôles, casting *m*; *F* **she got the part through the c. couch** elle a eu le rôle parce qu'elle a couché avec le metteur en scène

casting director *n* directeur *m* de casting

casting off *n Knitting* arrêt *m* (de mailles)

casting on *n Knitting* montage *m* (de mailles)

cast iron *n* fonte *f*; **c. block** bloc *m* en fonte; *Fig* **c. alibi** alibi *m* irréfutable; *Fig* **c. guarantee** garantie *f* en béton

castle[1] [ˈkɑːs(ə)l] *n* (**a**) château *m*; (*fortress*) château fort; *Fig* **to build castles in the air** *or* **in Spain** bâtir des châteaux en Espagne (**b**) *Chess* tour *f*

castle[2] *vi Chess* roquer

castling [ˈkɑːs(ə)lɪŋ] *n Chess* roque *f*

cast-off 1 *n* (**a**) (*item of clothing*) **I used to wear my brother's cast-offs** je portais les vieilles nippes *fpl* de mon frère

(**b**) *Fig* (*person*) laissé-pour-compte *m*, laissée-pour-compte *f*; **one of society's cast-offs** un laissé-pour-compte de la société; **the manager had built a team from other clubs' cast-offs** le directeur sportif avait formé une équipe avec les joueurs dont les autres équipes ne voulaient pas; **I'm not going out with one of his cast-offs** je ne veux pas sortir avec une copine dont il ne veut plus

2 *adj* **c. clothing** vêtements *mpl* dont on ne veut plus

castor [ˈkɑːstər] *n* (*on chair, bed etc*) roulette *f*; **the desk is on castors** le bureau est sur roulettes

castor oil *n Pharm* huile *f* de ricin

castrate [kæsˈtreɪt] *vt* (*animal, man*) châtrer, castrer; *Fig* (*text etc*) mutiler, expurger

castration [kæsˈtreɪʃən] *n* (*of animal, man*) castration *f*; *Fig* (*of text etc*) mutilation *f*, expurgation *f*

castrato, *pl* **-ti** [kæˈstrɑːtəʊ, -tɪ] *n Mus* castrat *m*

casual [ˈkæʒjʊ(ə)l] **1** *adj* (**a**) (*remark*) en passant, désinvolte; (*glance*) au hasard; **it was just a c. remark** j'ai/il a/*etc* dit ça en passant; **to engage in c. conversation** parler de choses et d'autres *ou* de la pluie et du beau temps; **to throw out a c. suggestion** suggérer quelque chose en passant; **to the c. observer** pour un observateur non-averti; **c. sex** (*one-off*) relations *fpl* sexuelles sans lendemain; (*on-going*) relations sexuelles sans engagement

(**b**) (*relaxed*) (*person, manner, approach*) décontracté; **they were very c. about the danger** ils ne se sont pas souciés du danger

(**c**) (*not serious, not taking sth seriously*) insouciant; **your attitude's too c.** tu es trop insouciant; **I found the police very c. about the whole situation** j'ai trouvé que la police a manqué de sérieux dans cette affaire

(**d**) (*jacket etc*) décontracté, *F* décontract; **c. clothes,** (**clothes for**) **c. wear** tenue *f* sport *inv ou* décontracté *ou F* décontract

(**e**) (*in work*) **c. employment** (*temporary*) emploi *m* temporaire; (*without social benefits*) = emploi précaire sans avantages sociaux; **c. worker** (*temporary*) employé, -ée *ou* travailleur *m* temporaire; (*without social benefits*) = employé, -ée qui ne bénéficie d'aucun avantage social

(**f**) (*encounter*) fortuit, accidentel

2 *npl* (**a**) **casuals** (*shoes*) mocassins *mpl*

(**b**) (**football**) **casuals** hooligans *mpl*

casual labour *n* main-d'œuvre *f* occasionnelle *ou* temporaire

casually [ˈkæʒjʊ(ə)lɪ] *adv* (**a**) (*to remark, suggest*) en passant (**b**) (*to walk, do sth*) avec décontraction; **she told him, quite c., that she had …** elle lui a dit, tout tranquillement, qu'elle avait … (**c**) (*not seriously enough*) (*to treat sth*) avec trop de décontraction; **they're treating this far too c.** il y a un manque de sérieux (**d**) **to dress c.** s'habiller décontracté *ou F* décontract; **you're much too c. dressed to …** tu es habillé de façon bien trop décontractée pour … (**e**) (*to meet*) par hasard

casualness [ˈkæʒjʊ(ə)lnɪs] *n* (**a**) (*of remark*) désinvolture *f* (**b**) (*of style of dress, approach*) décontraction *f* (**c**) (*lack of seriousness*) manque *m* de sérieux

casualty [ˈkæʒjʊəltɪ] *n* (*victim*) (*in accident, fire, earthquake etc*) victime *f*; (*in war*) blessé, -ée; (*in road accident*) blessé, -ée, accidenté, -ée; **to be a c. of sth** être la victime de qch; **there were no casualties** il n'y a pas eu de victimes; *Mil* **casualties** pertes *fpl*; *Fig* **the party had many casualties in the last election** le parti a perdu beaucoup de députés aux dernières élections; **freedom of speech was one of the first casualties** la liberté d'expression a été une des premières choses à disparaître; **these children are the casualties of the divorce rate** ces enfants sont les victimes du divorce; *Mil* **c. list** *or* **return** état *m* des pertes; *Med* **c.** (**department**) (*of hospital*) service *m* des urgences; *Med* **she was taken to c.** elle a été emmenée aux urgences

casuist [ˈkæzjʊɪst] *n* casuiste *m*

casuistry [ˈkæzjʊɪstrɪ] *n* casuistique *f*

CAT [kæt] *n Med* (*abbr* **computerized axial tomography**) **CAT scan** tomographie *f*

cat [kæt] *n* (**a**) (*male*) chat *m*; (*female*) chatte *f*; **tom c.** matou *m*; **ginger** *or F* **marmalade c.** chat roux tigré; **wild c.** chat sauvage; **the big cats** (*lions, tigers etc*) les grands félins; **it smelled of cats** ça sentait le pipi de chat; *F* **that looks like something the c.'s brought in** ça, c'est dégoûtant; *F* **you look like something the c.'s brought in** tu es dans un état lamentable; **to quarrel like c. and dog** s'entendre comme chien et chat; *F* **c. got your tongue?** tu as perdu ta langue?; *F* **he thinks he's the c.'s whiskers** il se croit sorti de la cuisse de Jupiter; *Fig* **to see which way the c. jumps** voir d'où vient le vent; **to play a c.-and-mouse game with sb** jouer au chat et à la souris avec qn; *Prov* **when the c.'s away the mice will play** quand le chat n'est pas là, les souris dansent; *Prov* **a c. may look at a king** = un chien regarde bien un évêque; *F* **to be like a c. on hot bricks** *or* **on a hit tin roof** ne pas tenir en place; *F* **to let the c. out of the bag** vendre la mèche; *F* **to put** *or* **set the c. among the pigeons** mettre le loup dans la bergerie; *F* **there's no** *or* **there isn't enough room to swing a c.** on ne peut pas se tourner; **c. show** exposition *f* féline

(**b**) *Pej* (*woman, girl*) sale vache *f*

(**c**) *US Sl* (*man*) type *m*, individu *m*

(**d**) **c.** (**-o'-nine-tails**) (*whip*) chat *m* à neuf queues

cataclysm [ˈkætəklɪz(ə)m] *n* cataclysme *m*

cataclysmic [kætəˈklɪzmɪk] *adj* cataclysmique

catacombs [ˈkætəkuːmz] *npl* catacombes *fpl*

catafalque [ˈkætəfælk] *n* catafalque *m*

Catalan [ˈkætəlæn] **1** *adj* catalan **2** *n* (**a**) (*person*) Catalan, -ane (**b**) *Ling* catalan *m*

catalepsy [ˈkætəlepsɪ] *n Med* catalepsie *f*

cataleptic [kætəˈleptɪk] *adj, n Med* cataleptique *mf*

catalogue[1], *US* **catalog** [ˈkætəlɒg] *n* (**a**) *Com* (*book*) catalogue *m*; **c. selling** vente *f* par catalogue (**b**) (*list*) (*of books, works etc*) catalogue *m*; *Fig* **the holiday was a c. of disasters** les vacances ont été une suite de catastrophes; **subject c.** catalogue thématique

catalogue[2], *US* **catalog** *vt* cataloguer

catalogue number *n* référence *f*; (*for library book*) référence bibliographique

cataloguing, *US* **cataloging** [ˈkætəlɒgɪŋ] *n* catalogage *m*

Catalonia [kætəˈləʊnɪə] *n* Catalogne *f*

catalysis [kəˈtælɪsɪs] *n Ch* catalyse *f*

catalyst [ˈkætəlɪst] *n Ch, Fig* catalyseur *m*

catalytic [kætəˈlɪtɪk] *adj Ch* catalytique; *Fig* catalyseur; *Aut* **c. converter** pot *m* catalytique, catalyseur *m*, pot à catalyseur

catamaran [kætəmə'ræn] *n Naut* catamaran *m*
cataplasm ['kætəplæz(ə)m] *n Med* cataplasme *m*
catapult¹ ['kætəpʌlt] *n* (a) *Br* (*for stones etc*) fronde *f* (b) (*on aircraft carrier*) catapulte *f*
catapult² 1 *vt* (*sb, sth*) catapulter, projeter; (*plane*) catapulter; **he catapulted the stone over the wall** il a lancé la pierre par-dessus le mur; *Fig* **these reforms catapulted the country into the 20th century** ces réformes ont propulsé le pays dans le vingtième siècle; **to c. sb to stardom** (*of film etc*) propulser qn vers la célébrité 2 *vi* entrer en trombe (**into a room** dans une pièce)
cataract ['kætərækt] *n* (*in river*), *Med* cataracte *f*
catarrh [kə'tɑːr] *n Med* catarrhe *m*; **bronchial c.** bronchite *f*
catarrhal [kə'tɑːr(ə)l] *adj* (*cough, person*) catarrheux
catastrophe [kə'tæstrəfɪ] *n* catastrophe *f*; **to head for/end in c.** aller vers la/se terminer en catastrophe
catastrophic [kætə'strɒfɪk] *adj* (*effect etc*) catastrophique
catastrophically [kætə'strɒfɪklɪ] *adv* d'une façon catastrophique
catatonia [kætə'təʊnɪə] *n Med* catatonie *f*
catatonic [kætə'tɒnɪk] *n, adj Med* catatonique *mf*
cat burglar *n F* monte-en-l'air *m inv*
catcall¹ ['kætkɔːl] *n Th etc* sifflet *m* de mécontentement; **there were catcalls from the audience** le public a sifflé en signe de mécontentement
catcall² 1 *vt* (*actor*) siffler 2 *vi* (*of audience*) siffler (en signe de mécontentement)
catch¹ [kætʃ] *n* (a) (*of ball etc*) prise *f* au vol; **that was a good c.** bien joué!; **to make an easy/a difficult c.** attraper une balle facile/difficile; **to play c.** (*of children*) jouer au ballon
(b) (*in fishing*) pêche *f*; **to have a good c.** faire (une) bonne pêche; **the day's c.** la pêche de la journée
(c) (*person as marriage partner*) parti *m*; **he's/she's no great c.** ce n'est pas un bon parti
(d) (*fastening*) (*on door etc*) loquet *m*, loqueteau *m*; (*of window*) loqueteau; (*to permit dismantling, opening etc*) crochet *m*; (*to limit movement of mechanism, drawer etc*) taquet *m*
(e) (*disadvantage*) **there's a c. in it** il y a un truc; **that's** *or* **there's the c.** voilà le hic; *Sch etc* **c. question** colle *f*; *Fig* **c. 22 situation** cercle *m* vicieux
(f) **with a c. in one's voice** la voix pleine d'émotion
(g) *Mus* canon *m*
(h) (*in rowing*) attaque *f*
catch² (*pt, pp* **caught** [kɔːt]) 1 *vt* (a) (*ball etc*) attraper, saisir; (*fish, thief etc*) attraper, prendre; **c.!** (*when throwing sth to sb*) attrape!; **well caught!** bien joué!; *Fb* le beau blocage!; (*said by sports coach etc*) excellente réception de la balle!; *Naut* **to c. the wind** (*of sail etc*) prendre le vent; **I caught him as he fell** je l'ai retenu *ou* attrapé au moment où il tombait; **I caught him by the hand** je l'ai attrapé par la main; **to c. sb in the act** *or* **red-handed** prendre qn sur le fait *ou* la main dans le sac; **don't get caught!** ne te fais pas prendre!; **you'll be in trouble if your mother catches you** gare à toi si ta mère t'attrape; **caught you!** je t'y prends!; **to c. sb doing sth** prendre *ou* surprendre qn en train de faire qch; *F* **you won't c. me doing that again** on ne m'y reprendra plus; **to be caught in a storm** être surpris par un orage; **you might c. her if you run** vous pouvez la rattraper si vous courez; **you're unlikely to c. her at home** je ne pense pas que tu la trouveras chez elle; **you caught me just as I was going into a meeting** tu m'as parlé au moment où j'allais en réunion; **we caught him in a good mood** il était de bonne humeur quand nous l'avons vu; **to c. sb napping** prendre qn au dépourvu; *F* **c. you later!** on se voit plus tard!
(b) (*not miss*) (*train etc*) attraper, prendre; *F* (*manage to see*) (*film*) voir; *F* (*manage to hear*) (*radio programme*) écouter; *F* **c. this outstanding singer next month** ne manquez pas ce chanteur étonnant le mois prochain
(c) (*perceive*) (*sounds*) saisir, percevoir; **to c. a glimpse of sth, to c. sight of sth** apercevoir qch; **I caught a few words** j'ai entendu *ou* j'ai saisi quelques mots; **I didn't c. what you were saying** je n'ai pas entendu ce que vous disiez; **I caught a hint of bitterness** (*in what she said*) j'ai senti un peu d'amertume dans ses paroles; **the author has caught the mood of the time** l'auteur a su rendre l'ambiance de l'époque
(d) (*make impression on*) (*sb's attention*) attirer; **to c. sb's eye** attirer l'attention de qn; **nothing in the shop caught my fancy** je n'ai rien trouvé qui me plaisait dans la boutique; **their story caught the imagination of the public** leur histoire a passionné le public *ou* retenu l'attention du public
(e) (*entangle*) **I caught my dress on a nail** j'ai fait un accroc à ma robe avec un clou; **he caught his foot on a root and fell** il s'est pris le pied dans une racine et il est tombé; **don't c. your fingers in the door!** ne te coince pas les doigts dans la porte!; **there's something caught in the door** il y a quelque chose de coincé dans la porte
(f) (*contract*) (*illness*) attraper; *Fig* (*habit*) prendre; **to c. (a) cold** s'enrhumer, attraper un rhume; **I caught this cold from you** c'est toi qui m'a passé ce rhume; **to c. fire** *or* **light** prendre feu
(g) (*of blow, object*) **the punch caught me in the chest** j'ai reçu le coup de poing en plein dans la poitrine; **the stone caught her on the arm** elle a reçu la pierre sur le bras; *Boxing* **he caught him with a left to the chin** il lui a porté un gauche au menton; *F* **you'll c. it!** tu vas dérouiller!
(h) **to c. the sun** (*of person*) prendre des couleurs; **the sun caught her hair/the drops of dew** le soleil brilla dans ses cheveux/les perles de rosée; **my bedroom catches the sun** le soleil donne dans ma chambre; **the garden really catches the sun in the afternoon** le jardin est très ensoleillé l'après-midi
(i) *F* (*fool*) attraper, avoir; **you won't c. me!** ça ne prend pas (avec moi)!
2 *vi* (a) attraper; (**here**) **c.!** tiens, attrape!; **I'm hopeless at catching** (*ball etc*) je n'arrive jamais à rien attraper
(b) (*of gears*) s'enclencher
(c) (*of fire*) prendre, s'allumer
(d) (*become entangled*) (*in door, machinery etc*) se prendre; (*on thorn, nail etc*) s'accrocher; **my fingers caught in the drawer** je me suis coincé les doigts dans le tiroir
(e) *US* **to c. on fire** prendre feu
▶ **catch at** *vipo* (*grab at*) essayer de saisir; (*hold on to*) s'accrocher à; **to c. at an opportunity** saisir une opportunité
▶ **catch on** *vi* (a) (*of fashion etc*) réussir, avoir du succès; (*of tune*) accrocher; **the game never caught on in Europe** ce jeu n'a jamais pris en Europe *ou* eu de succès en Europe (b) *F* (*understand*) saisir, piger; **he still hasn't caught on** il n'y est toujours pas; **to c. on quickly** comprendre vite
▶ **catch out** *vtsep* (*trap*) (*by difficult question*) prendre, piéger; (*of circumstances*) surprendre; **the police caught her out when they asked her ...** la police l'a piégée en lui demandant ...; **to c. sb out in a lie** prendre *ou* surprendre qn à mentir; **a lot of investors got caught out when the stock market collapsed** beaucoup d'investisseurs se sont fait piéger quand la bourse s'est effondrée; **we got caught out by the rain** nous avons été surpris par la pluie
▶ **catch up** 1 *vi* (*close gap, get closer*) rattraper; **to c. up with sb** rattraper qn; **we caught up with them at the lights** nous les avons rattrapés au feu rouge; **the runners behind are catching up** les coureurs qui sont derrière se rapprochent; **to c. up on** *or* **with one's work/sleep** rattraper du travail/du sommeil en retard; *F* **it will c. up with you (one of these days)** ça va te retomber sur le nez
2 *vtsep* (a) (*reach*) (*person, car in front etc*) rattraper
(b) (*entangle*) **I got caught up in a discussion** j'ai été entraîné dans une discussion; **she got really caught up in the electoral campaign** elle s'est laissé complètement absorber par la campagne électorale; **they were caught up in a traffic jam for hours** ils ont été bloqués dans un embouteillage pendant des heures; **to be caught up in a wave of enthusiasm** être entraîné dans un mouvement d'enthousiasme
(c) (*snatch up*) (*object*) saisir; (*baby, child*) prendre au bras
catch-all *n F* fourre-tout *m inv*; **c. category/clause** catégorie *f*/clause *f* fourre-tout
catch-as-catch-can *n* (*wrestling*) catch *m*, lutte *f* libre
catch crop *n Agr* culture *f* dérobée
catcher ['kætʃər] *n* (a) attrapeur, -euse; **rat c.** (*person, dog*) preneur *m* de rats (b) *Baseball* attrapeur *m*, receveur *m*; **c.'s mitt** gant *m* de baseball
catching ['kætʃɪŋ] 1 *adj* (*disease, habit etc*) contagieux; (*laughter, enthusiasm*) communicatif 2 *n* (a) (*of ball*) réception *f* (b) (*of toothed wheel*) engrenure *f*; (*of gearing*) enclenchement *m*
catchline ['kætʃlaɪn] *n* accroche *f*; (*identification for story*) intitulé *m*
catchment ['kætʃmənt] *n* (*of water*) captation *f*, captage *m*; **c. area** *or* **basin** bassin *m* hydrographique; **c. area** (*of airport, school*) zone *f* desservie
catchpenny ['kætʃpenɪ] *adj* (*book, ornaments*) raccoleur; **c. scheme** *or* **show** attrape-nigaud *m*, *pl* attrape-nigaud(s)
catchphrase ['kætʃfreɪz] *n* (*of comedian*) formule *f* (comique); (*political*) slogan *m*; (*in advertising*) accroche *f*
catchword ['kætʃwɜːd] *n* (a) *Pol* slogan *m* (b) *Th* (*cue*) réplique *f*
catchy ['kætʃɪ] *adj* (*tune*) entraînant, facile à retenir; (*slogan*) facile à retenir

catechism [ˈkætəkɪz(ə)m] *n* catéchisme *m*
catechist [ˈkætəkɪst] *n* catéchiste *mf*
catechize [ˈkætəkaɪz] *vt* **(a)** *Rel* catéchiser **(b)** *Fig* (*question*) interroger, questionner
categoric(al) [kætɪˈgɒrɪk, -ɪk(ə)l] *adj* catégorique; *Phil* **categorical imperative** impératif *m* catégorique
categorically [kætɪˈgɒrɪklɪ] *adv* (*to answer, refuse etc*) catégoriquement
categorization [kætɪgəraɪˈzeɪʃ(ə)n] *n* catégorisation *f*
categorize [ˈkætɪgəraɪz] *vt* classer par catégories; **I don't like being categorized** je n'aime pas qu'on me colle une étiquette
category [ˈkætɪgərɪ] *n* catégorie *f*; *Mktg* **c. leader** chef *m* de file dans sa catégorie
cater [ˈkeɪtər] *vt* **to c. a party** fournir le repas d'une soirée; **we're having the meal catered** nous faisons fournir le repas
▶ **cater for** *vipo* **(a)** (*provide with food*) (*people, function etc*) fournir les repas à, préparer les repas pour **(b)** (*provide with special requirement*) **parties catered for** (*notice in hotel etc*) = banquets, noces; **hotel that caters for English visitors** hôtel qui s'adresse surtout à la clientèle anglaise; **the hotel doesn't c. for children** l'hôtel ne prévoit pas d'aménagements pour les enfants; **to c. for all tastes** satisfaire tous les goûts; **I hadn't catered for that** (*allowed for*) je n'avais pas prévu ça
▶ **cater to** *vipo* (*needs*) satisfaire à
cater-corner(ed) *adj, adv Am* diamètralement opposé
caterer [ˈkeɪtərər] *n Com* traiteur *m*
catering [ˈkeɪtərɪŋ] *n* restauration *f*; *Av* service *m* traiteur; **who did the c. at your wedding?** qui a préparé le repas/le buffet à votre mariage?; **c. company** société *f* de restauration; **c. contract** contrat *m* de restauration; **c. industry** industrie *f* de la restauration; **c. manager** chef *m* ou responsable *mf* de la restauration; **c. staff** personnel *m* de restauration
caterpillar [ˈkætəpɪlər] *n* **(a)** chenille *f* **(b)** *Tech* **c. (tread** *or* **track)** chenille *f*; **c. tractor** tracteur *m* à chenilles
caterwaul [ˈkætəwɔːl] *vi* **(a)** (*of cat*) feuler **(b)** *Fig* (*of person*) hurler
caterwauling [ˈkætəwɔːlɪŋ] *n* **(a)** (*of cats*) feulements *mpl* **(b)** *Fig* (*of person*) hurlements *mpl*
catfish [ˈkætfɪʃ] *n* **(a)** silure *m*, poisson-chat *m*, *pl* poissons-chats **(b)** (*wolffish*) blennie *f*
cat flap *n* chatière *f*
catgut [ˈkætgʌt] *n* **(a)** *Mus* corde *f* de boyau; **c. strings** (*for violin*) cordes en boyau de chat **(b)** *Med* catgut *m*
catharsis [kəˈθɑːsɪs] *n* catharsis *f*
cathartic [kəˈθɑːtɪk] *adj* cathartique
cathedral [kəˈθiːdrəl] *n* cathédrale *f*; **c. town** ville *f* épiscopale, évêché *m*
Catherine [ˈkæθrɪn] *n Hist* **C. the Great** la Grande Catherine
Catherine wheel *n* (*firework*) soleil *m*
catheter [ˈkæθɪtər] *n Med* cathéter *m*; **indwelling c.** sonde *f* intérieure *ou* à demeure; **he has to have a c.** il faut qu'on lui pose un cathéter
cathode [ˈkæθəʊd] *n El* cathode *f*; **photo(electric) c.** cathode photoélectrique; **c. beam/ray/screen** faisceau *m*/rayon *m*/écran *m* cathodique; **c. ray tube** tube *m* à rayons cathodiques, tube cathodique; *Comptr* **c. ray tube monitor** moniteur *m* à tube cathodique
Catholic [ˈkæθlɪk] *Rel* **1** *adj* catholique **2** *n* catholique *mf*; **she has become a C.** elle est devenue catholique
catholic [ˈkæθlɪk] *adj* (*wide-ranging*) éclectique; (*broad-minded*) à l'esprit large; (*universal*) universel; **to be c. in one's tastes** avoir des goûts éclectiques
Catholicism [kəˈθɒlɪsɪz(ə)m] *n Rel* catholicisme *m*
cathouse [ˈkæthaʊs] *n Am Sl* (*brothel*) bordel *m*
catkin [ˈkætkɪn] *n Bot* chaton *m*
catlick [ˈkætlɪk] *n F* **to give oneself** *or* **have a c.** se laver le bout du nez, faire une toilette de chat
cat litter *n* litière *f* pour chat
catmint [ˈkætmɪnt] *n* (*plant*) cataire *f*, herbe *f* aux chats
catnap¹ [ˈkætnæp] *n F* petite sieste *f*, somme *m*; **to take** *or* **have a c.** faire une petite sieste
catnap² *vi F* faire une petite sieste *ou* un somme
catnip [ˈkætnɪp] *n* (*plant*) cataire *f*, herbe *f* aux chats
cat's cradle *n* (*game*) = jeu *m* qui consiste à faire des figures avec une ficelle
cat's eyes *n Aut* catadioptres *mpl*, cataphotes® *mpl*, yeux *mpl* de chat
catspaw, cat's-paw [ˈkætspɔː] *n Old-fashioned* **to be sb's c.** être le pigeon de qn; **to be made a c. of** être dupé
catsuit [ˈkætsuːt] *n* combinaison *f*
catsup [ˈkætsəp] *n US* = **ketchup**
cattery [ˈkætərɪ] *n* pension *f* pour chats
cattiness [ˈkætɪnɪs] *n F* vacherie *f*, rosserie *f*
cattle [ˈkæt(ə)l] *n* [ⓘA11,f,ii] (*no pl*) bétail *m*, bestiaux *mpl*; **horned c.** bêtes *fpl* à cornes, bovins *mpl*; **we were herded onto trucks like c.** on nous a entassés dans des camions comme du bétail; **c. breeding** élevage *m* du bétail; **c. crossing** passage *m* de troupeaux; **c. market** (*for animals*), *Fig* marché *m* aux bestiaux; *Rail* **c. truck** *or Am* **car** wagon *m* à bétail *ou* bestiaux
cattle-cake *n* tourteau *m*
cattle-grid *n* = grille *f* placée sur un fossé pour empêcher le passage du bétail
cattleman, *pl* **-men** [ˈkæt(ə)lmən] *n Am* bouvier *m*
catty [ˈkætɪ] *adj F* **(a)** (*esp woman*) vache, rosse; **c. remark** vacherie *f*, rosserie *f* **(b) there's a c. smell** ça sent le pipi de chat
catty-corner(ed) *adj, adv Am* diamétralement opposé
catwalk [ˈkætwɔːk] *n* passerelle *f*; *Naut* coursive *f*; (*for fashion models*) passerelle *f* de défilé de mode; **on the c.** (*model*) sur la passerelle du défilé
Caucasian [kɔːˈkeɪʒən, -ˈkeɪzɪən] **1** *adj* **(a)** *Geog, Ling* caucasien **(b)** (*in ethnology*) caucasien **2** *n* Caucasien, -ienne; (*white person*) blanc *m*, blanche *f*
Caucasus (the) [ðəˈkɔːkəsəs] *n* le Caucase
caucus [ˈkɔːkəs] *n esp Pol* **(a)** (*group*) bloc *m* **(b)** (*meeting*) réunion *f* du bloc
caudal [ˈkɔːd(ə)l] *adj Zool* caudal; **c. fin** (nageoire *f*) caudale *f*
caught *see* **catch²**
caul [kɔːl] *n* coiffe *f* (*de nouveau-né*); **born with a c.** né coiffé
cauldron [ˈkɔːldrən] *n* chaudron *m*
cauli [ˈkɒlɪ] *n Br F* chou-fleur *m*, *pl* choux-fleurs
cauliflower [ˈkɒlɪflaʊər] *n* chou-fleur *m*, *pl* choux-fleurs; *Culin* **c. cheese** chou-fleur au gratin, gratin *m* de chou-fleur; *Boxing etc* **c. ear** oreille *f* en chou-fleur
caulk [kɔːk] *vt* (*boat*) calfater, étouper
caulking [ˈkɔːkɪŋ] *n* calfatage *m*; **c. iron** calfait *m*, burin *m*
causal [ˈkɔːz(ə)l] *adj* causal
causality [kɔːˈzælɪtɪ] *n* causalité *f*; **what's the c.?** quelles sont les causes?
causally [ˈkɔːzəlɪ] *adv* **to be c. connected** avoir un rapport de cause à effet
causation [kɔːˈzeɪʃən] *n* causalité *f*
causative [ˈkɔːzətɪv] *adj Gram* (*verb*) causatif
cause¹ [kɔːz] *n* **(a)** (*origin*) cause *f*; **c. and effect** la cause et l'effet; **to be the c. of an accident** être la cause d'un accident
(b) (*reason*) raison *f*, motif *m*, sujet *m*; **I have c. to be thankful** j'ai lieu d'être reconnaissant; **you've no c. to be indignant** vous n'avez pas lieu d'être indigné, vous n'avez pas de quoi être indigné; **to have good c. for doing sth** avoir de bonnes raisons pour faire qch; **to give c. for complaint** susciter des plaintes; **his condition is giving c. for concern** son état est inquiétant; **and with good c.** et pour cause; **without c.** sans raison
(c) (*purpose etc*) cause *f*; **to win sb over to one's c.** gagner qn à sa cause; **to make common c.** faire cause commune **(with** avec**)**; **in the c. of justice** pour (la cause de) la justice; **to work for a good c.** travailler pour une bonne cause; **it's for a good c.** c'est pour une bonne cause; *F* **it's all in a good c.** ce n'est pas du temps perdu
(d) *Jur* cause *f*; **to plead sb's c.** plaider la cause de qn
cause² *vt* (*misfortune, delay etc*) causer, occasionner; (*accident*) provoquer, causer; (*mirth, quarrel, surprise*) provoquer; **to c. a fire** provoquer un incendie; **to c. grief** causer du chagrin; **to c. trouble** (*disturbance*) semer la perturbation; (*problems*) causer des ennuis; **to c. a sensation** faire sensation; **all the worry you've caused us** toute l'inquiétude que tu nous as causée; **to c. sb/sth to do sth** faire faire qch à qn/qch; **a dog caused him to swerve** un chien lui a fait faire une embardée; **to c. sb to be punished** faire punir qn; **to c. sth to be done** faire faire qch; **something caused him to change his mind** quelque chose l'a fait changer d'avis
causeway [ˈkɔːzweɪ] *n* (*over marshy area*) chaussée *f*
caustic [ˈkɔːstɪk] **1** *adj* (*substance*) caustique; *Fig* (*humour, joke etc*) caustique, décapant; **c. soda** soude *f* caustique **2** *n Ch, Med* caustique *m*
cauterization [kɔːtəraɪˈzeɪʃən] *n Med* cautérisation *f*
cauterize [ˈkɔːtəraɪz] *vt Med* cautériser
caution¹ [ˈkɔːʃən] *n* **(a)** (*prudence*) prudence *f*, précautions *fpl*; **with great c.** avec beaucoup de prudence *ou* de précautions; **c. is advised** on conseille la prudence **(b)** (*warning*) avis *m*, avertissement *m*; **c.! steep gradient/pressurized container** attention! descente rapide/récipient sous pression **(c)** *Jur, Sp etc* (*reprimand*) réprimande *f*; **he has been let off with a c.** il s'en est tiré avec une

réprimande; **to be given a c.** se faire réprimander **(d)** *Old-fashioned F* (*amusing person*) numéro *m*, phénomène *m*
caution² *vt* **(a)** (*warn*) avertir, mettre en garde; *Sp* (*player, boxer*) mettre en garde; **to c. sb against sth** mettre qn en garde contre qch; **to c. sb against doing sth** déconseiller à qn de faire qch **(b)** *Jur* **to c. a suspect** = prévenir un suspect que tout ce qu'il dira pourra être utilisé contre lui lors du procès **(c)** *Jur* (*reprimand*) réprimander
cautious [ˈkɔːʃəs] *adj* circonspect; (*driver, remark*) prudent; **to be c. in doing sth** faire qch avec prudence *ou* précaution; **c. optimism** optimisme *m* prudent; **to play a c. game** jouer serré
cautiously [ˈkɔːʃəslɪ] *adv* (*to proceed*) avec prudence *ou* précaution; (*to drive*) prudemment; **to be c. optimistic** faire preuve d'un optimisme prudent
cautiousness [ˈkɔːʃəsnɪs] *n* (*of driver, remark etc*) prudence *f*
cavalcade [kævəlˈkeɪd] *n* cortège *m*; (*on horseback*) cavalcade *f*
Cavalier [kævəˈlɪər] *n Eng Hist* royaliste *m*; **the Cavaliers and Roundheads** les Cavaliers *mpl* et les Têtes *fpl* rondes
cavalier [kævəˈlɪər] *adj* (*attitude etc*) cavalier, désinvolte; **with a c. air** avec désinvolture
cavalry [ˈkævəlrɪ] *n* cavalerie *f*; **c. officer** officier *m* de cavalerie
cavalryman, *pl* **-men** [ˈkævəlrɪmən] *n Mil* cavalier *m*, soldat *m* de cavalerie
cave¹ [keɪv] *n* caverne *f*, grotte *f*; **c. art** art *m* rupestre; **c. dweller** (*troglodyte*) troglodyte *mf*; (*in prehistoric times*) homme *m* des cavernes; **c. dwelling** maison *f* troglodyte; **c. paintings** peintures *fpl* rupestres
cave² *vi Sp* faire de la spéléologie
cave³ [ˈkeɪvɪ, ˈkɑːveɪ] *int Br Sch Arch F* attention!, pet!
▶ **cave in** *vi* **(a)** (*of ground, structure etc*) céder, s'affaisser, s'effondrer **(b)** *F* (*of person, government*) céder, s'avouer vaincu; (*of team, defence*) s'effondrer
caveat [ˈkævɪæt] *n* **(a)** *Fml* mise *f* en garde **(against** contre**)** **(b)** *Jur* opposition *f* **(to** à**)**
cave-in *n* (*of ground, structure etc*) affaissement *m*, effondrement *m*; *F* (*of person, government*) capitulation *f*
caveman, *pl* **-men** [ˈkeɪvmæn, -men] *n* (*prehistoric man*) homme *m* des cavernes; *Fig Hum* primitif *m*
caver [ˈkeɪvər] *n* spéléologue *mf*
cavern [ˈkævən, -ɜːn] *n* caverne *f*
cavernous [ˈkævənəs] *adj* (*room etc*) immense et vide; (*yawn*) à se décrocher la mâchoire; **a monster with a c. mouth** un monstre à la gueule immense
caviar(e) [ˈkævɪɑːr] *n* caviar *m*; *prov* **(it's) c. to the general** c'est donner de la confiture aux cochons
cavil [ˈkævɪl] *vi* **(-ll-,** *US* **-l-)** *Fml* chicaner, ergoter **(at** *or* **about sth** sur qch**)**
caving [ˈkeɪvɪŋ] *n Sp* spéléologie *f*
cavity [ˈkævɪtɪ] *n* cavité *f*, creux *m*; *Med* (*abdominal, thoracic*) cavité; **(dental)** c. cavité dentaire; *Constr* **c. wall** mur *m* double; **c. wall insulation** isolation *f* des murs doubles
cavort [kəˈvɔːt] *vi* faire des cabrioles; *Fig* **to spend the summer cavorting around Europe** parcourir l'Europe pendant l'été
cavy [ˈkeɪvɪ] *n* (*animal*) cobaye *m*, cochon *m* d'Inde
caw¹ [kɔː] *vi* (*of crow etc*) croasser
caw² *n* (*of crow etc*) croassement *m*
cawing [ˈkɔːɪŋ] *n* (*of crow etc*) croassement *m*
cayenne [keɪˈen] *n* **c. (pepper)** (poivre *m* de) cayenne *m*
cayman [ˈkeɪmən] *n* (*animal*) caïman *m*
Cayman Islands *npl* îles *fpl* Caïmans
CB [siːˈbiː] *n* (*abbr* **Citizen's Band**) CB *f*
CBC [siːbiːˈsiː] *n TV, Rad* (*abbr* **Canadian Broadcasting Corporation**) (societé *f*) Radio-Canada *f*
CBE [siːbiːˈiː] *n abbr* **Commander of the Order of the British Empire**
CBI [siːbiːˈaɪ] *n Br* (*abbr* **Confederation of British Industry**) = patronat *m* britannique
CBS [siːbiːˈes] *n abbr* **Columbia Broadcasting System**
CC [siːˈsiː] *n abbr* **County Council**
cc [siːˈsi] **1** *n* **(a)** (*on memorandum*) (*abbr* **carbon copy**) copie **(b)** (*abbr* **cubic centimetres**) cm³ **2** *vt* envoyer une copie à
CCTV [siːsiːtiːˈviː] *n* (*abbr* **closed circuit television**) télévision *f* en circuit fermé
CD [siːˈdiː] *n* **(a)** (*abbr* **compact disc**) CD *m*; **on CD** sur CD; **CD player** lecteur *m* laser; **CD stacker** meuble *m* à CD **(b)** *Admin* (*abbr* **Corps Diplomatique**) CD *m*; **a car with CD plates** une voiture avec des plaques du Corps Diplomatique
CDI [siːdiːˈaɪ] *n Comptr* (*abbr* **interactive compact disc**) CD-I *m*
Cdr *n Mil abbr* **Commander**
Cdre *n Naut abbr* **Commodore**
CD-ROM [siːdiːˈrɒm] *n Comptr* (*abbr* **compact disc-read only memory**) CD-ROM *m*; **available on C.** existe en CD-ROM; **C. drive** lecteur *m* de CD-Rom, lecteur de disque optique; **C. newspaper** journal *m* sur CD-Rom
CDT [siːdiːˈtiː] *n* (*abbr* **Central Daylight Time**) = heure *f* d'été du centre des États-Unis
CDV [siːdiːˈviː] *n* (*abbr* **compact disc video**) vidéodisque *m*
cease¹ [siːs] *n Fml* **without c.** sans cesse
cease² **1** *vi* cesser; **hostilities have ceased** les hostilités ont cessé; **they have ceased to exist** ils n'existent plus; **it never ceases to amaze me that …** cela m'étonne toujours que …; **without ceasing** sans arrêt; **we will not c. from campaigning for her release** nous ne cesserons pas de nous battre pour sa libération **2** *vt* cesser; **to c. doing sth** cesser de faire qch; *Mil* **to c. fire** cesser le feu; *Com* **to c. trading** cesser ses activités, cesser toute activité commerciale
cease-fire *n* cessez-le-feu *m inv*
ceaseless [ˈsiːslɪs] *adj* incessant, continuel
ceaselessly [ˈsiːslɪslɪ] *adv* sans cesse, continuellement
cecum [ˈsiːkəm] *n US* = **caecum**
cedar [ˈsiːdər] *n Bot* **c. (tree)** cèdre *m*; **c. of Lebanon** cèdre du Liban; **c. panelling** lambris *mpl* en cèdre; *Am* **c. closet** (*for protecting clothes etc against moths*) placard *m* en cèdre
cede [siːd] *vt Jur* (*property, province, debt*) céder **(to** à**)**; **to c. a point** (*in argument*) concéder un point
cedilla [sɪˈdɪlə] *n Ling* cédille *f*
Ceefax® [ˈsiːfæks] *n TV* service *m* de télétexte de la BBC
ceiling [ˈsiːlɪŋ] *n* **(a)** (*of room etc*) plafond *m*; **c. light** plafonnier *m*; **c. tile** dalle *f* pour plafond; *F* **to hit the c.** (*become angry*) sauter les plombs **(b)** *Econ etc* plafond *m*; *Fin* **to have a c. of** être plafonné à; **to reach a c.** (*of prices etc*) plafonner; **c. price** prix *m* plafond **(c)** *Av* plafond *m*; **to fly at the c.** plafonner **(d)** *Met* plafond *m* (nuageux)
celadon [ˈselədɒn] *n* (*porcelain*) céladon *m*; **c. green** (vert *m*) céladon
celandine [ˈseləndaɪn] *n* (*flower*) **greater c.** chélidoine *f*, grande éclaire *f*; **lesser c.** ficaire *f*, petite éclaire
celeb [səˈleb] *n F* célébrité *f*
celebrant [ˈselɪbrənt] *n Rel* célébrant *m*, officiant *m*
celebrate [ˈselɪbreɪt] **1** *vt* **(a)** (*mark with festivity*) (*event*) fêter, célébrer; **the city is celebrating the anniversary of its founding** la ville fête l'anniversaire de sa fondation; **to c. sb's birthday** fêter l'anniversaire de qn; **let's open a bottle of wine to c. the occasion** ouvrons une bouteille de vin pour fêter ça **(b)** *Rel* (*mass, wedding, feast*) célébrer **2** *vi* faire la fête; **let's c. with a new car/a weekend in Paris** achetons une nouvelle voiture/allons passer un week-end à Paris pour fêter ça; **will you be celebrating tonight?** tu vas arroser ça ce soir?; **let's c. with some champagne** on va arroser ça au champagne
celebrated [ˈselɪbreɪtɪd] *adj* célèbre **(for sth** par qch**)**
celebration [selɪˈbreɪʃən] *n* **(a)** (*party, drink etc*) fête *f*, festivités *fpl*; **the Independance Day celebrations** les festivités à l'occasion de l'anniversaire de l'Indépendance; **this calls for a c.!** il faut fêter ça!, ça s'arrose!; **a party in c. of sth** une fête pour célébrer qch **(b)** *Rel* (*of communion, feast*) célébration *f*
celebrity [sɪˈlebrɪtɪ] *n* **(a)** (*person*) célébrité *f*; **c. football match** = match *m* de football dans lequel une des équipes est composée de célébrités; **c. magazine** magazine *m* people **(b)** (*fame*) célébrité *f*, renommée *f*
celeriac [sɪˈlerɪæk] *n* céleri-rave *m*, *pl* céleris-raves
celerity [sɪˈlerɪtɪ] *n Fml* célérité *f*
celery [ˈselərɪ] *n* céleri *m*; **head of c.** pied *m* de céleri; **stick of c.** branche *f* de céleri; **c. soup** soupe *f* au céleri
celestial [sɪˈlestɪəl] *adj* céleste
celiac [ˈsiːlɪæk] *adj, n US* = **coeliac**
celibacy [ˈselɪbəsɪ] *n* (*sexual abstinence*) abstinence *f* sexuelle, chasteté *f*; (*not being married*) célibat *m*; *Rel* **to take a vow of c.** faire vœu de chasteté
celibate [ˈselɪbət] **1** *adj* (*person*) (*chaste*) qui n'a pas de rapports sexuels, chaste; (*unmarried*) célibataire; (*life*) (*by choice*) de chasteté; (*forced*) sans rapports sexuels **2** *n* personne *f* qui n'a pas de rapports sexuels
cell [sel] *n* **(a)** (*in prison*) cellule *f*; **they spent a night in the cells** ils ont passé la nuit en cellule **(b)** (*of monk, hermit*) cellule *f* **(c)** (*in beehive*) cellule *f*, alvéole *m* **(d)** *El, Electron etc* (*of battery*) cellule *f*; **dry c.** pile *f* sèche; **wet c.** pile à liquide; **photoelectric/photovoltaic c.** cellule photoélectrique/photovoltaïque; **solar c.** pile solaire, photopile *f* **(e)** *Biol* cellule *f*; **c. wall** paroi *f* cellulaire; **blood c.** globule *m*; **cancer c.** cellule cancéreuse **(f)** *Pol* **communist c.** cellule *f* communiste **(g)** *Comptr* (*on spreadsheet*) cellule *f*
cellar [ˈselər] *n* cave *f*; (*for wine, provisions also*) cellier *m*; (*of wine merchant*) chai *m*; **to keep a good c.** avoir une bonne cave

cellarman, *pl* **-men** ['seləmən] *n* sommelier *m*
cellist ['tʃelɪst] *n Mus* violoncelliste *mf*
cello ['tʃeləʊ] *n Mus* violoncelle *m*; **c. concerto** concerto *m* pour violoncelle
cellular ['seljʊlər] *adj Biol (structure etc)* cellulaire; *Tex* **c. blanket** couverture *f* alvéolaire; **c. board** *(cardboard)* carton *m* ondulé; *Electron* **c. logic** logique *f* cellulaire; *Telecom* **c. phone** téléphone *m* cellulaire, radio téléphone *m*
cellulite ['seljʊlaɪt] *n* cellulite *f*
celluloid ['seljʊlɔɪd] *n (no pl)* celluloïd(e) *m*; *Cin* **on c.** sur la pellicule; **c. epic** film *m* à grand spectacle, épopée *f* cinématographique
cellulose ['seljʊləʊs] **1** *adj* celluleux **2** *n* cellulose *f*
Celsius ['selsɪəs] *adj* **C. thermometer** thermomètre *m* de Celsius; **ten degrees C.** dix degrés Celsius
Celt [kelt] *n* Celte *mf*
Celtic ['keltɪk] *Ling* **1** *adj* celtique, celte **2** *n (ancient)* celtique *m*; *(modern)* langues *fpl* celtiques *ou* celtes
cement¹ [sɪ'ment] *n* **(a)** *Constr* ciment *m*; **Portland c.** ciment de Portland; **quick-setting c.** ciment à prise rapide; **c. mixer** bétonnière *f*; **c. path** allée *f* en ciment; **c. powder** poudre *f* à ciment **(b)** *(for tooth)* amalgame *m* **(c)** *(glue)* colle *f*
cement² *vt* **(a)** *(join) (stones, bricks, Fig friendship)* cimenter **(b)** *(in dentistry)* obturer
cementation [siːmen'teɪʃən] *n* cimentation *f*
cemetery ['semətrɪ] *n* cimetière *m*
cenotaph ['senətɑːf] *n* cénotaphe *m*
censer ['sensər] *n Rel* encensoir *m*
censor¹ ['sensər] *n* **(a)** *Admin, Mil* censeur *m*; **the film c.** la censure cinématographique; *Mil, Cin etc* **to get past the c.** échapper à la censure; *TV, Rad* **c. bleep** bip *m* de censure **(b)** *Antiq* censeur *m*
censor² *vt* **(a)** *(ban) (book, film, article etc)* interdire, censurer; *(scene)* supprimer, couper; *(line, word)* supprimer **(b)** *(cut parts of) (film, article, newspaper)* censurer; *(play, book, scenario)* censurer, expurger
censoring ['sensərɪŋ] *n* censure *f*
censorious [sen'sɔːrɪəs] *adj Fml* sévère **(of** vis-à-vis de)
censorship ['sensəʃɪp] *n* censure *f*; **there is no longer any c. of his films** ses films ne sont plus censurés; **c. laws** censure
censurable ['senʃərəb(ə)l] *adj Fml* censurable, blâmable
censure¹ ['senʃər] *n Fml* critiques *fpl*; *Jur* réprimande *f*; **he deserves c.** il mérite des reproches; *Pol* **vote of c.** motion *f* de censure
censure² *vt Fml* blâmer, critiquer
census ['sensəs] *n* recensement *m*; **to take a c.** faire un recensement; **c. of population** recensement de la population; *US* **C. Bureau** Bureau *m* des statistiques; **c. return** formulaire *m* de recensement; **c. taker** agent *m* recenseur
cent [sent] *n (coin, sum)* cent *m*; *F (smallest amount of money)* sou *m*; **to pay to the last c.** payer jusqu'au dernier sou
centaur ['sentɔːr] *n Myth* centaure *m*
centenarian [sentɪ'neərɪən] **1** *n (person)* centenaire *mf* **2** *adj* centenaire
centenary [sen'tiːnərɪ] **1** *n* (anniversaire *m*) centenaire *m*; **c. celebrations** célébrations *fpl* du centenaire **2** *adj* centenaire
centennial [sen'tenɪəl] **1** *adj* centenaire **2** *n Am* = **centenary 1**
center, centerboard *etc US* = **centre, centreboard** *etc*
centering ['sent(ə)rɪŋ] *n Typ* centrage *m*
centigrade ['sentɪgreɪd] *adj* centigrade; **c. thermometer** thermomètre *m* centigrade; **ten degrees c.** dix degrés centigrades
centigramme, *US* **centigram** ['sentɪgræm] *n* centigramme *m*
centilitre, *US* **centiliter** ['sentɪliːtər] *n* centilitre *m*
centimetre, *US* **centimeter** ['sentɪmiːtər] *n* centimètre *m*; **square/cubic c.** centimètre carré/cube
centipede ['sentɪpiːd] *n* mille-pattes *m inv*, *Spec* scolopendre *f*
central ['sentr(ə)l] **1** *adj* **(a)** *(in location)* central, -aux; **in a c. position** situé au centre; **the office is very c.** *(in town)* le bureau est situé en plein centre; *Fin* **c. account** compte *m* centralisateur; **c. bank** banque *f* centrale; *Com* **c. buyer** acheteur *m* principal; *Com* **c. buying group** centrale *f* d'achat(s); **c. point** centre *m*; *Com* **c. purchasing department** centrale *f* d'achat; *Com* **c. purchasing group** centrale *f* d'achat(s); **c. reservations office** centrale *f* de réservation; **c. reservations** réservations *fpl* centralisées
(b) *(in importance)* central; **the c. character** le personnage central; **c. to the debate is the question of safety** la question de la sécurité se situe au cœur du débat; **of c. importance** d'une importance capitale
2 *n Am Old-fashioned Tel* central *m* (téléphonique)
Central America *n* Amérique *f* centrale
central government *n* gouvernement *m* central
central heating *n* chauffage *m* central; **does the flat have c.?** est-ce qu'il y a le chauffage central dans l'appartement?
centralize ['sentrəlaɪz] *vt* centraliser
centralized ['sentrəlaɪzd] *adj (power, planning etc)* centralisé; *Comptr* **c. data capture** saisie *f* centralisée; **c. management** gestion *f* intégrée; **c. purchasing** achats *mpl* centralisés; *Comptr* **c. storage** mémoire *f* centrale
central locking *n Aut* verrouillage *m* central *ou* centralisé, fermeture *f* centralisée, condamnation *f* centralisée des portes
centrally ['sentrəlɪ] *adv* centralement; **c. situated** situé dans le centre, central; **c. heated** avec chauffage central; **the flat is c. heated** l'appartement a le chauffage central
central nervous system *n* système *m* nerveux central
central processing unit *n Comptr* unité *f* centrale (de traitement), processeur *m* central
central reservation *n Br Aut* terre-plein *m* (central), *pl* terre-pleins (centraux)
Central Standard Time *n Am* heure *f* normale du Centre
centre¹, *US* **center** ['sentər] *n* **(a)** *(of circle, earth, town etc)* centre *m*; *(of table etc)* milieu *m*; *(of wheel)* corps *m*, centre; *Med (of infection)* foyer *m*; **in the c.** au centre, au milieu; **the great urban centres** les grandes agglomérations *fpl* urbaines; **commercial/industrial c.** centre commercial/industriel; **civic/community c.** centre civique/social; **shopping c.** centre commercial; **sports c.** centre sportif; *Phys* **c. of gravity** centre de gravité; *Journ* **c. page** page *f* centrale; *Journ* **c. spread** pages centrales; **c. of attraction** *Phys* centre d'attraction *ou* de gravitation; *Fig* centre d'attraction
(b) *Pol* centre *m*; **the c. party** le parti du centre; **to be left/right of c.** être du centre gauche/droit
(c) *Sp (player)* centre *m*; *Fb, Hockey* **c. forward** avant-centre *m*, *pl* avant(s)-centres; **c. half** demi *m*
(d) *MecE etc (of lathe)* pointe *f*; **out of c.** décentré; **c. punch** pointeau *m* (de marquage); **ten centimetres c. to c.** dix centimètres centre à centre
centre², *US* **center** *vt* **(a)** *Tech (wheel, sth on lathe etc)* centrer; **to c. a line** *(when keying)* centrer une ligne **(b)** *Cin, Phot (image)* centrer, cadrer **(c)** *Fb etc (ball etc)* centrer
▶ **centre on, centre round 1** *vipo* être centré *ou* axé sur **2** *vtsep (usu passive)* **to be centred on sb/sth** se concentrer sur qn/qch
centreboard, *US* **centerboard** ['sentəbɔːd] *n Naut* dérive *f*
centrefold, *US* **centerfold** ['sentəfəʊld] *n (in magazine, newspaper)* double page *f* centrale détachable; *(nude picture)* photo *f* de pin-up; **to do a c.** *(nude picture)* poser comme pin-up; **c. girl** = pin-up *f*
centrepiece, *US* **centerpiece** ['sentəpiːs] *n (on table)* décoration *f* centrale d'une table; *Fig* pièce *f* de résistance
centre-point steering *n Aut* direction *f* à point milieu
centrifugal [sentrɪ'fjʊg(ə)l] *adj (force, pump etc)* centrifuge
centrifuge¹ ['sentrɪfjuːdʒ] *vt (liquid)* centrifuger
centrifuge² *n* centrifugeur *m*, centrifugeuse *f*
centring, *US* **centering** ['sent(ə)rɪŋ] *n (of sth on lathe, of text etc)* centrage *m*; **c. tool** centreur *m*
centripetal [sen'trɪpɪtəl] *adj (force etc)* centripète
centrist ['sentrɪst] *Pol* **1** *n* centriste *mf* **2** *adj* centriste
Centronics cable [sen'trɒnɪks] *n* câble *m* Centronics
Centronics printer *n* imprimante *f* Centronics
centuries-old ['sentʃərɪzəʊld] *adj* vieux/*f* vieille de plusieurs siècles
century ['sentʃərɪ] *n* **(a)** siècle *m*; **in the nineteenth c.** au dix-neuvième siècle; **the wedding of the c.** le mariage du siècle; **trees centuries old** arbres séculaires *ou* centenaires **(b)** *Cr (one hundred runs)* centaine *f*, série *f* de cent
century note *n Am Sl (hundred dollar bill)* billet *m* de cent dollars
CEO [siːiː'əʊ] *n Com (abbr* **chief executive officer**) = directeur *m* général; **President and CEO** = président-directeur général, P. D. G. *m*
cephalic [se'fælɪk] *adj (vein, index etc)* céphalique
ceramic [sə'ræmɪk] **1** *adj* céramique; **c. hob** *(on cooker)* plaque *f* vitro-céramique **2** *npl* **ceramics** céramique *f*
cereal ['sɪərɪəl] *n* céréale *f*; **(breakfast) cereals** céréales; **c. crops** céréales
cerebellum [serɪ'beləm] *n Anat* cervelet *m*
cerebral ['serɪbrəl, *Am* sə'riːbrəl] *adj* **(a)** *Anat* cérébral; **c. death** mort *f* cérébrale; **c. hemisphere** hémisphère *m* cérébral; **c. palsy** paralysie *f* cérébrale **(b)** *(intellectual)* cérébral
cerebrospinal fluid [serebrəʊ'spaɪn(ə)l] *n Med* liquide *m* céphalo-rachidéen
cerebrum ['serɪbrəm] *n Anat* cerveau *m*
ceremonial [serɪ'məʊnɪəl] **1** *adj* de cérémonie **2** *n* cérémonial *m*
ceremonially [serɪ'məʊnɪəlɪ] *adv* en grande cérémonie
ceremonious [serɪ'məʊnɪəs] *adj* cérémonieux

ceremoniously [serɪ'məʊnɪəslɪ] *adv* cérémonieusement, avec cérémonie

ceremony ['serɪmənɪ] *n* cérémonie *f*; **the marriage c.** la cérémonie du mariage; **with c.** avec cérémonie, cérémonieusement; **without c.** sans cérémonies; **we don't stand on c.** nous ne faisons pas de cérémonies

cert [sɜːt] *n F (certainty)* **a dead c.** une certitude (absolue); *Horseracing* un gagnant sûr; **he's a dead c. for the job** à tous les coups, il a le poste; **if one thing's a c. it's that ...** s'il y a une chose qui est sûre c'est que ...

certain ['sɜːt(ə)n] *adj* **(a)** *(sure) (success, failure etc)* certain, assuré; *(cure, solution)* infaillible; **they face c. death/ dismissal** leur mort/renvoi est assuré(e); **it's absolutely c.** c'est sûr et certain; **there is c. to be some opposition to the bill** il est sûr que la loi rencontrera une opposition; **he is c. to come** il viendra à coup sûr; **to my c. knowledge, they are ...** je sais pertinemment qu'ils sont ...; **in the c. belief that he was right** convaincu qu'il avait raison; **I am almost c.** j'en suis presque sûr; **I am c. that he will come** je suis certain *ou* sûr qu'il viendra; **to know sth for c.** tenir qch pour certain, être bien sûr de qch; **I can't say for c.** je ne peux pas vous dire de façon certaine; **you'll have it tomorrow for c.** vous l'aurez demain sans faute; **to make c. that ...** *(find out, ensure)* s'assurer que ...; **I'd better make c.** je ferais mieux de m'en assurer; **to make c. of sth** *(find out)* s'assurer de qch; *(make sure to get sth)* s'assurer qch; **I made c. of the date** je me suis assuré de la date; **to make c. of a seat** s'assurer une place; **don't worry, I made c. of that!** ne t'inquiète pas, j'ai pris toutes les dispositions!
 (b) *(particular)* certain; **women of a c. age** les femmes d'un certain âge; **a c. person** une certaine personne; **c. people** (de) certaines gens, certains *mpl*; **a c. Mr Thomas** un certain M. Thomas; **he used to write to me on a c. day** il m'écrivait à jour fixe

certainly ['sɜːtənlɪ] *adv (definitely)* certainement; *(admittedly)* certes; **she c. knows her facts** elle sait parfaitement de quoi elle parle; **you shall c. have it tomorrow** vous l'aurez demain sans faute; **it c. won't be ready tomorrow** ça ne serait jamais prêt pour demain; **may I? – c.!** *or* **you c. may!** vous permettez? – je vous en prie! *ou* certainement!; **will you tell him? – c. not!** tu vas lui dire? – certainement pas!; **did you tell him? – c. not!** tu lui as dit? – bien sûr que non!

certainty ['sɜːtəntɪ] *n* **(a)** *(sureness) (of future event)* certitude *f*; **there is no c. that we will win** il n'est absolument pas certain que nous gagnions **(b)** *(thing)* **I know it for a c.** je le sais parfaitement; **we now know for a c. that he was here last night** nous avons maintenant la preuve qu'il était là hier soir; **it's a dead c.** c'est une certitude absolue **(c)** *(conviction)* certitude *f*, conviction *f*; **she said it with some c.** elle a dit cela avec une certaine conviction

certifiable ['sɜːtɪfaɪəb(ə)l] *adj* **(a)** *(insane) (person)* dont l'état nécessite l'internement psychiatrique; *F* **he's c.** il est fou à lier **(b)** *(document, fact etc)* que l'on peut certifier

certificate [sə'tɪfɪkət] *n* **(a)** certificat *m*; **birth/marriage/ death c.** certificat de naissance/mariage/décès; *Fin etc* **bearer c.** titre *m* au porteur; **(government) savings c.** bon *m* d'épargne; *Aut* **test c.** = certificat de contrôle technique; *Av* **c. of airworthiness** certificat de navigabilité; *Banking* **c. of deposit** certificat de dépôt; *Acct* **c. of dishonour** certificat de non-paiement; *Com* **c. of incorporation** certificat d'enregistrement de société; **c. of insurance** attestation *f* d'assurance; *Com* **c. of origin** certificat d'origine; **c. of quality** certificat de qualité; *Fin* **c. of transfer** acte *m* de cession; *Com* **c. of value** certificat de valeur
 (b) *(professional, educational)* diplôme *m*; **teaching/ nursing c.** diplôme d'enseignement/d'infirmière; **coaching/ first aid c.** brevet *m* d'entraîneur/de secourisme; *Naut* **master's c.** brevet de capitaine

certificated [sə'tɪfɪkeɪtɪd] *adj* diplômé

Certificate of Secondary Education *n Eng Sch Formerly* = BEPC *m*

certification [sɜtɪfɪ'keɪʃən] *n* certification *f*, authentification *f*; *(of product)* homologation *f*

certified ['sɜːtɪfaɪd] *adj* **(a)** *(having certificate)* diplômé; *US Sch* **c. teacher** instituteur, -trice diplomé(e); *US Com* **c. public accountant** expert *m* comptable **(b)** *(guaranteed)* **c. by a notary** notarié; **c. accounts** comptes *mpl* approuvés; **c. cheque** chèque *m* certifié; **c. copy** copie *f* certifiée conforme, copie authentique; *Com* **c. invoice** facture *f* certifiée; *US* **c. letter** lettre *f* recommandée **(c)** *(declared insane)* dont l'état nécessite l'internement psychiatrique

certify ['sɜːtɪfaɪ] **1** *vt* **(a)** *(confirm)* certifier, attester; *(death)* constater; **to c. that sth is true** certifier que qch est vrai; **this is to c. that A. Gooch has ...** *(on certificate)* ce document certifie que A. Gooch a ...; **to c. sb insane** *(of doctor)* déclarer que l'état de santé de qn nécessite l'internement psychiatrique; *F* **you ought to be certified** tu es complètement fou **(b)** *(guarantee) (document)* authentifier, homologuer, légaliser; *Acct* **to c. the books** viser les livres de commerce **2** *vi* **to c. to sth** attester qch

certitude ['sɜːtɪtjuːd] *n* certitude *f*

cervical ['sɜːvɪk(ə)l, sɜː'vaɪk(ə)l] *adj Anat* **(a)** *(pertaining to cervix)* du col de l'utérus; **c. cancer** cancer *m* du col de l'utérus; **c. smear** frottis *m* vaginal **(b)** *(of the neck)* cervical; **c. collar** minerve *f*; **c. vertebra** vertèbre *f* cervicale

cervix, *pl* **-vices** ['sɜːvɪks, -vɪsiːz] *n Anat* **(a) c. (uteri)** col *m* de l'utérus **(b)** *(neck)* cou *m*

cessation [se'seɪʃən] *n* cessation *f*, arrêt *m*

cession ['seʃən] *n (of territory)* cession *f*; *Jur (to creditors)* cession de biens

cesspit ['sespɪt] *n* = **cesspool**

cesspool ['sespuːl] *n (for sewage)* fosse *f* d'aisances; *Fig* cloaque *m*; **the district is a c. of drug-dealing and prostitution** le quartier est un cloaque où règnent le trafic de drogue et la prostitution

Ceylon [sɪ'lɒn] *n Hist* Ceylan *m*

C&F [siːænd'ef] *Com (abbr* **cost and freight)** C et F

cf [siː'ef] *(abbr* **confer)** cf

CFC [siːef'siː] *n (abbr* **chlorofluorocarbon)** CFC *m inv*

cg *(abbr* **centigram)** cg

CH [siː'eɪtʃ] *(abbr* **central heating)** c. c., ch. c.

ch *(abbr* **chapter)** chapitre *m*

Chad [tʃæd] *n* Tchad *m*

chafe [tʃeɪf] **1** *vt* **(a)** *(make worn) (rope, collar)* user; *(make sore) (skin)* irriter; **the boots chafed her ankles** les bottes lui blessaient les chevilles; **apply to chafed skin** *(of lotion etc)* appliquer sur la peau irritée **(b)** *Fig (annoy)* irriter, agacer **(c)** *(warm) (sb's limbs etc)* frictionner **2** *vi* **(a)** *(of skin)* être irrité; **his skin chafed under the coarse material** sa peau était irritée à cause du tissu rugueux **(b)** *Fig (of person)* **to c. at** *or* **under sth** s'énerver contre qch, s'irriter de *ou* contre qch; **to c. under restraint** ronger son frein

chafed [tʃeɪft] *adj (rope, shirt)* usé; *(skin)* irrité

chaff¹ [tʃɑːf] *n* **(a)** *Agr (husks)* balle *f*; *Fig* **the bulk of his collected poems is mere c.** la plupart de ses poèmes ne valent pas grand-chose **(b)** *Electron* ruban *m* métallique antiradar

chaff² *vt (tease)* taquiner

chaffinch ['tʃæfɪntʃ] *n (bird)* pinson *m*

chafing ['tʃeɪfɪŋ] *n* **(a)** *(of skin)* irritation *f* **(b)** *(warming) (of limbs)* friction *f*

chafing dish *n Old-fashioned Culin* réchaud *m* de table

chagrin¹ ['ʃægrɪn] *n Fml* dépit *m*; **much to my c.** à mon grand dépit

chagrin² *vt esp Lit* dépiter; **to be chagrined at sth** être contrarié par qch

chain¹ [tʃeɪn] *n* **(a)** chaîne *f*; *(small) (for medallion etc)* chaînette *f*; **to put a dog on a c.** attacher un chien à une chaîne; **prisoner in chains** prisonnier enchaîné; *Fig* **to break** *or* **burst one's chains** rompre ses chaînes; *Fig* **to have nothing to lose but one's chains** n'avoir rien d'autre à perdre que ses chaînes; **to form a c.** *(to pass buckets of water etc)* former *ou* faire la chaîne; **to pull the c.** *(in WC)* tirer la chasse d'eau; **a c. of events** un enchaînement de faits; *Naut* **anchor c.** chaîne d'ancrage; **bicycle c.** chaîne de bicyclette; *Aut* **(snow) chains** chaînes
 (b) *Geog (of mountains)* chaîne *f*
 (c) *Com (of stores, restaurants)* chaîne *f*; **fast food c.** chaîne de restauration rapide
 (d) *Phys, Ch etc* chaîne *f*
 (e) *Arch (measurement)* = 20,12 m; **surveyor's c., measuring c.** chaîne *f* d'arpenteur *ou* d'arpentage

chain² *vt (door etc)* fermer avec une chaîne; **to c. sb** enchaîner qn **(to sth/sb** à qch/qn); **to c. sth to sth** attacher qch à qch avec une chaîne/des chaînes; **she chained herself to the railings** elle s'est enchaînée à la grille; *Fig* **chained to one's desk** rivé à son bureau; *Fig* **she is chained to the kitchen sink** elle ne sort pas de sa cuisine

▸ **chain down** *vtsep (cargo on ship)* attacher avec des chaînes; *(person)* enchaîner; *Fig* **to be chained down by one's work** être esclave de son travail

▸ **chain up** *vtsep (dog)* attacher à une chaîne; *(person)* enchaîner; *(bike, gate)* mettre une chaîne à; **I left it chained up** j'ai mis le cadenas

chain armour *n* mailles *fpl*; *(suit)* cotte *f* de mailles

chain drive *n Aut* entraînement *m* par chaîne

chain gang *n* chaîne *f* de forçats

chain guard *n (on bicycle etc)* carter *m*

chain guide *n Aut* guide *m* chaîne

chaining [ˈtʃeɪnɪŋ] *n Comptr* chaînage *m*
chain letter *n* chaîne *f*
chain link *n* chaînon *m ou* maillon *m* de chaîne
chain mail *n* mailles *fpl*; (*suit*) cotte *f* de mailles
chain reaction *n Phys, Ch, Fig* réaction *f* en chaîne
chain saw *n* tronçonneuse *f*
chain-smoke 1 *vt* **he chains-smokes untipped cigarettes** il fume des cigarettes sans filtre du matin au soir; **he was chain-smoking Gitanes** il fumait Gitane sur Gitane **2** *vi* fumer cigarette sur cigarette
chain-smoker *n* personne *f* qui fume cigarette sur cigarette
chain stitch *n Sewing* point *m* de chaînette
chain store *n* magasin *m* à succursales (multiples); (*individual store*) succursale *f*
chain tensioner *n Aut* tendeur *m* de chaîne
chair[1] [tʃeər] *n* **(a)** chaise *f*; (*armchair*) fauteuil *m*; **folding c.** chaise pliante, pliant *m*; **easy c.** fauteuil; **invalid c.**, *Old-fashioned* **Bath c.** voiture *f* de malade, fauteuil roulant; **c. attendant** (*in park etc*) loueur, -euse de chaises, chaisier, -ière **(b)** *Univ* (*of professor*) chaire *f* **(c)** (*in meeting*) fauteuil *m* de président; (*chairperson*) président, -ente; **to be in the c.** présider (la séance) **(d)** *US F* **the c.** (*electric chair*) la chaise électrique; **to go to the c.** passer sur *ou* à la chaise électrique
chair[2] *vt* **(a)** (*preside over*) (*meeting*) présider **(b)** (*person*) (*after victory etc*) porter en triomphe
chairback [ˈtʃeəbæk] *n* dossier *m* de chaise
chairlift [ˈtʃeəlɪft] *n Ski* télésiège *m*
chairman, *pl* **-men** [ˈtʃeəmən] *n* président, -ente; *Com* (*of company*) président-directeur *m* général; **c. and managing director** président-directeur *m* général, P. D. G. *m*; **c. of the board** Président du conseil; **to act as c.** présider (la séance); **Mr C.** Monsieur le Président; **Madam C.** Madame la Présidente
chairmanship [ˈtʃeəmənʃɪp] *n* présidence *f*; **under the c. of Mr Stevens** sous la présidence de M. Stevens
chairperson [ˈtʃeəpɜːsən] *n* président, -ente
chairwoman, *pl* **-women** [ˈtʃeəwʊmən, -wɪmɪn] *n* présidente *f*
chalet [ˈʃæleɪ] *n* chalet *m*; **c. park** parc *m* résidentiel de loisirs
chalice [ˈtʃælɪs] *n* **(a)** *Rel* calice *m* **(b)** *Arch, Lit* coupe *f*
chalk[1] [tʃɔːk] *n* (*for writing etc*), *Geol, Billiards* craie *f*; **they are as different as c. and cheese** c'est le jour et la nuit; *Br F* **not by a long c.** pas du tout; *Br F* **by a long c.** de beaucoup; **c. hills/cliffs** collines/falaises crayeuses; **a set of coloured chalks** un assortiment de craies de couleur; *Sewing* **French c.** craie de tailleur; **c. drawing** dessin *m* à la craie; **c. line** (*drawn*) trait *m* à la craie; *Carp etc* (*string*) cordeau *m*; (*made by string*) ligne *f* faite au cordeau
chalk[2] *vt* (*mark*) marquer à la craie; (*write*) écrire (à la craie); *Carp etc* **to c. a line** tringler une ligne; *Billiards* **to c. one's cue** mettre de la craie sur sa queue de billard
▸ **chalk up** *vtsep* **(a)** (*write*) écrire à la craie **(b) c. it up** (*give credit in shop*) mettez-le sur mon ardoise **(c)** (*put down to*) **you'll just have to c. it up to experience** maintenant, tu sauras; **they chalked their defeat up to lack of practice** ils ont mis leur défaite sur le compte du manque d'entraînement **(d)** (*achieve*) (*victory, success, points*) remporter
chalkdust [ˈtʃɔːkdʌst] *n* poussière *f* de craie
chalkpit [ˈtʃɔːkpɪt] *n* carrière *f* de craie, crayère *f*
chalky [ˈtʃɔːkɪ] *adj* **(a)** (*terrain, soil*) crayeux; (*deposit*) calcique **(b)** (*colour*) pâle, terreux; (*texture, taste*) plâtreux; **c. white** (*complexion, houses*) blanc, *f* blanche; (*because of illness, shock etc*) pâle comme un linge
challenge[1] [ˈtʃælɪndʒ] *n* **(a)** défi *m*; *Sp* défi, challenge *m*; *Mil* (*by sentry*) interpellation *f*; **to throw down** *or* **issue a c.** lancer un défi; **to accept** *or* **take up a c.** relever un défi; *Pol* **a c. to his leadership** une tentative pour le supplanter à la tête du parti; **to enjoy a c.** aimer les défis; **I find the work a real c.** ce travail est une vraie gageure pour moi; **environmental problems are the major c. for our generation** les problèmes d'environnement constituent la principale gageure *ou* le principal défi pour notre génération **(b)** *Jur* (*of jury member*) récusation *f*
challenge[2] *vt* **(a) to c. sb** (*to a fight*) provoquer qn; **to c. sb to do sth** défier qn de faire qch; **to c. sb to single combat** provoquer qn en combat singulier; **to c. sb to a game of chess/to a game of tennis** proposer une partie d'échecs/de tennis à qn; (*with serious intent to beat them*) défier qn aux échecs/au tennis

(b) (*statement etc*) protester contre, disputer; (*sb's word*) mettre en question *ou* en doute *ou* en cause; (*sb's qualifications, account, figures*) contester; **their position was challenged by younger artists** leur position a été remise en question par des artistes plus jeunes; **to c. sb's right to do sth** contester à qn le droit de faire qch

(c) (*stimulate*) **you need a job that will c. you** il te faut un travail stimulant

(d) *Mil* (*of sentry*) interpeller

(e) *Jur* (*member of jury*) récuser
challenge cup *n Sp* coupe-challenge *f*, *pl* coupes-challenge
challenge match *n Sp* challenge *m*
challenger [ˈtʃælɪndʒər] *n* (*to a fight*) provocateur, -trice; *Sp* challengeur *m*; *Mktg* challengeur, prétendant *m*
challenging [ˈtʃælɪndʒɪŋ] *adj* **(a)** (*look, remark etc*) provocateur, -trice; (*air*) de défi **(b)** (*job*) stimulant
chamber [ˈtʃeɪmbər] *n* **(a)** *Pol* (*upper, lower*) Chambre *f* **(b)** *Jur* **chambers** (*of barrister, judge*) cabinet *m*; **in chambers** en chambre du conseil; **to hear a case in chambers** juger une cause en référé **(c)** *Metal* (*of furnace*) laboratoire *m*; *Phys* (*for ionization, expansion*) chambre *f*; (*of revolver*) chambre; **air c.** (*in pump*) chambre à air **(d)** *Anat* ventricule *m* **(e)** *Arch, Lit* (*room*) salle *f*; *Lit* **(bed-)c.** chambre *f* (à coucher); **council c.** salle du conseil
chamberlain [ˈtʃeɪmbəlɪn] *n* chambellan *m*
chambermaid [ˈtʃeɪmbəmeɪd] *n* (*in hotel*) femme *f* de chambre
chamber music *n* musique *f* de chambre
Chamber of Commerce *n* chambre *f* de commerce
Chamber of Commerce and Industry *n* chambre *f* de commerce et d'industrie
chamber orchestra *n* orchestre *m* de chambre
chamber pot *n* pot *m* de chambre
chameleon [kəˈmiːlɪən] *n* (*animal*), *Fig* caméléon *m*
chamfer[1] [ˈtʃæmfər] *n Carp etc* biseau *m*, chanfrein *m*
chamfer[2] *vt Carp etc* (*beam etc*) biseauter, chanfreiner; (*cut grooves in*) (*column etc*) canneler
chammy [ˈʃæmɪ] *n F* = **chamois (b)**
chamois *n* **(a)** [ˈʃæmwɑː] (*deer*) chamois *m* **(b)** [ˈʃæmɪ] **c. (leather)** (*for washing car*) chamois *m*, peau *f* de chamois; **c. jacket** veste en peau de chamois
champ[1] [tʃæmp] *n Sp F* champion, -ionne
champ[2] 1 *vt* (*of horse etc*) (*fodder*) mâcher bruyamment; (*bit*) ronger, mâcher, mâchonner **2** *vi Fig F* **to c. at the bit** (*of person*) ronger son frein
champagne [ʃæmˈpeɪn] **1** *n* (*drink, colour*) champagne *m*; **c. glass** (*tall*) flûte *f* à champagne; (*broad*) coupe *f* à champagne; **c. flute** flute à champagne; **c. reception** réception *f* avec champagne; **there'll be a c. reception** on servira le champagne **2** *adj* **c. (-coloured)** champagne *inv*
champers [ˈʃæmpəz] *n F* (*champagne*) champ *m*
champion[1] [ˈtʃæmpɪən] **1** *n* **(a)** *Sp* champion, -ionne; **world c.** champion, -ionne du monde; **a c. footballer** un champion du football **(b)** (*of cause*) champion, -ionne **2** *adj Br Dial* formidable
champion[2] *vt* (*cause*) se faire le champion de; (*person*) soutenir
championship [ˈtʃæmpɪənʃɪp] *n* **(a)** *Sp etc* championnat *m*; **c. match** match *m* de championnat **(b)** (*of cause*) défense *f*
chance[1] [tʃɑːns] **1** *n* **(a)** (*luck*) hasard *m*, chance *f*; **by c.** par hasard; **somebody I met by c.** quelqu'un que j'ai rencontré par hasard; **do you by any c. know his address?** est-ce que par hasard tu connaîtrais son adresse?; **to leave nothing to c.** ne rien laisser au hasard; **to leave everything to c.** s'en remettre entièrement au hasard; *F* **to have an eye to** *or* **for the main c.** chercher à tirer profit de toutes les occasions; *F* **c. would be a fine thing!** ah, si seulement je pouvais!

(b) (*opportunity*) occasion *f*; **now's your c.** c'est maintenant qu'il faut y aller; **it's your last c.** c'est ta dernière chance; **it's a c. in a million** c'est une occasion qui ne se présentera pas deux fois; **I had a c. to work in the States** j'ai eu l'occasion de travailler aux États-Unis; **I go to the theatre when I get the c.** je vais au théâtre quand j'en ai l'occasion; **can you translate this for me when you get a c.?** est-ce que tu pourras me traduire ça quand tu auras le temps?; **there are no second chances, there is no second c.** tu n'as pas droit à l'erreur; **to give sb a c.** (*in job*) mettre qn à l'essai; (*to do better*) donner une chance à qn; **give me another c.** donne-moi une autre chance; **you didn't give me a c.!** (*to tell you*) tu ne m'en as pas laissé le temps!; *F* **given half a c. she'd play tennis every day** si elle pouvait elle jouerait au tennis tous les jours

(c) (*possibility*) **to have** *or* **stand a c.** (*of succeeding*) avoir des chances de succès; **he never had a c., the truck was coming straight at him** il n'avait aucune chance de s'en sortir, le camion est arrivé droit sur lui; **she stands a good c. of being chosen** elle a de bonnes chances d'être choisie; **he hasn't the slightest c.** *or F* **a c. in hell of succeeding** il n'a pas la moindre chance de réussir; **they have an even** *or* **a fifty-fifty c. of winning** ils ont une chance sur deux *ou* cinquante pour cent de chances de gagner; **there's little/no/**

a good c. of that happening il y a peu de chance/aucune chance/de bonnes chances que cela se produise; *F* **do you think they'll win? – no c.!** est-ce que tu crois qu'ils vont gagner? – il n'y a pas de chance!; *F* **can I stay the night? – no c.!** est-ce que je peux passer la nuit ici? – pas question!; **(the) chances are (that) he'll forget** il y a fort à parier qu'il oubliera

(**d**) (*risk*) risque *m*; **she takes too many chances** elle prend trop de risques; **to take a c.** courir un risque; **he took a c. on them not finding out** il a pris le risque en espérant qu'ils ne le découvrent pas; **I'll have to take a c. on that** j'en prends le risque; **I'm taking no chances** je ne veux pas prendre de risques; **to take a sporting c.** tenter le coup; **to take one's chances** tenter sa chance

2 *adj attrib* **c. customer** client *m* imprévu; **c. discovery** découverte *f* accidentelle *ou* fortuite; **c. meeting** rencontre *f* fortuite

chance² **1** *vi Lit* (*happen*) **to c. to do sth** faire qch par hasard; **only when she chanced to visit him was the body discovered** c'est en passant chez lui par hasard qu'elle a découvert le corps **2** *vt* (*risk*) risquer; *F* **to c. it** *or* **one's luck** *or* **one's arm** risquer *ou* tenter le coup; **to c. doing sth** prendre le risque de faire qch

▶ **chance on, chance upon** *vipo* (*find by accident*) tomber (par hasard) sur

chancel [ˈtʃɑːns(ə)l] *n Rel Archit* chœur *m*; **c. screen** jubé *m*

chancellery [ˈtʃɑːnsələrɪ] *n* chancellerie *f*

chancellor [ˈtʃɑːnsələr] *n* (**a**) *Univ, Rel* chancelier *m* (**b**) *Pol* **C.** chancelier *m Br Pol* **C. (of the Exchequer)** Chancelier de l'Échiquier, = Ministre *m* des Finances; *Br Jur* **the Lord (High) C.** le Grand Chancelier, = le Ministre de la Justice

chancer [ˈtʃɑːnsər] *n Br Sl* (*opportunist*) filou *m*; **he's a real c.** il n'en rate pas une

chancery [ˈtʃɑːnsərɪ] *n* (**a**) *Jur Br* **(Court of) C.** cour *f* de la chancellerie; *US* **(court of) c.** cour d'équité (**b**) (*of embassy*) chancellerie *f*

chancre [ˈʃæŋkər] *n Med* chancre *m*

chancy [ˈtʃɑːnsɪ] *adj F* risqué

chandelier [ʃændəˈlɪər] *n* lustre *m*

chandler [ˈtʃɑːndlər] *n Com* **ship('s) c.** fournisseur *m* de navires; **corn c.** marchand *m* de blé *ou* de grains

change¹ [tʃeɪndʒ] *n* (**a**) (*alteration*) (*of air, job etc*) changement *m*; (*in expression, voice*) altération *f*; (*modification*) modification *f*; **c. of address** changement de domicile *ou* d'adresse; **to have a c. of opinion** *or* **of heart** changer d'avis; **c. for the better/worse** (*of health etc*) amélioration *f*/détérioration *f*; **there's been a c. in the weather** il y a eu un changement de temps; **there's been a c. in the law** la loi a été modifiée; **sudden c. of fortune** revirement de fortune; **there is no/little c. in the situation** il n'y a pas/il y a peu de changement dans la situation; **there are going to be some changes in this office!** il va y avoir du nouveau *ou* du changement dans ce bureau!; **some changes were made to the train timetable** il y a eu des changements *ou* des modifications dans les horaires de train; **you need a c.** tu as besoin de changer d'air; **the c. will do you good** le changement te fera du bien; *Prov* **a c. is as good as a rest** changer de décor fait autant de bien que partir en vacances; **this trip will be** *or* **make a bit of a c. for you** ce voyage vous changera un peu; **you must find it a bit of a c. living in the country** vous devez trouver un drôle de changement à vivre à la campagne; **he was early for a c.** pour une fois il était en avance; **why don't you wash the dishes for a c.?** si tu faisais la vaisselle, pour une fois?; **it** *or* **that makes a c.** ça change un peu; **yes, it makes a (nice) c., doesn't it?** oui, ça change (un peu) (de l'ordinaire) n'est-ce pas?; **it was a c. from the old system** ça changeait du système précédent; **the c. of life,** *F* **the c.** (*of woman*) le retour d'âge; *F* **to go through the c.** (*of woman*) traverser la ménopause; *Mus* **chord c.** changement d'accord; *Th* **scene c.** changement de décor; **c. of clothes** vêtements *mpl* de rechange

(**b**) (*money*) monnaie *f*; **small** *or* **loose c.** petite *ou* menue monnaie; **to get c.** faire de la monnaie; **to get c. for £5** faire la monnaie de 5 livres; **have you got c. for a £10 note?** est-ce que tu as de la monnaie sur un billet de 10 livres?; **keep the c.** gardez la monnaie; **the machine doesn't give c.** cet appareil ne rend pas la monnaie; *F* **you won't get much c. out of £100** (*if you buy that*) il ne va pas te rester grand-chose sur tes 100 livres; *F* **he won't get much c. out of me** il en sera pour ses frais avec moi

(**c**) (*in bell-ringing*) **to ring the changes** carillonner avec variations *ou* avec permutations; *Fig* **to ring the changes on** (*subject*) ressasser, rabâcher, broder des variations sur; (*menu, programme etc*) varier, introduire des changements dans

change² **1** *vt* (**a**) (*alter*) (*one's plans, lifestyle etc*) changer, modifier; **to c. water into wine** changer l'eau en vin; **you can't c. a dictatorship into a democracy overnight** on ne transforme pas une dictature en démocratie en une nuit; **the witch changed him into a frog** la sorcière l'a transformé en crapaud; **to c. one's ways** *or* **habits** changer (ses habitudes); **to c. one's mind** *or* **opinion** changer d'avis; **to c. the subject** changer de sujet; **don't c. the subject!** ne détourne pas la conversation!; **to c. colour** changer de couleur

(**b**) (*replace*) (*sheets*) changer; **to c. one's clothes** se changer; **to c. one's dress/one's shoes** changer de robe/de chaussures; **to c. the baby** changer le bébé; *Aut* **to c. a tyre** changer *ou* remplacer un pneu; *Aut* **to c. the oil** faire la *ou* une vidange; *Aut* **to c. gear** changer de vitesse; **to c. channels** (*on TV*) changer de chaîne; **to c. trains/one's seat** changer de train/de place; **I've changed doctors** j'ai changé de médecin

(**c**) (*exchange*) **to c. one thing for another** changer une chose pour *ou* contre une autre; **to c. places** *or* **seats with sb** changer de place avec qn; *Fig* **I wouldn't (like to) c. places with him** je ne changerais pas avec lui; *Fig* **to c. sides** changer de camp, virer de bord; *Mil* **to c. the guard** relever la garde

(**d**) (*money*) changer; **to c. a note into coins** faire de la monnaie sur un billet; **to c. dollars into francs** changer des dollars contre des francs *ou* en francs; **they won't c. pounds** ils ne changeront pas des livres

2 *vi* (**a**) (*alter*) changer; (*of moon*) changer de quartier; (*of luck, wind*) tourner; **she's changed since I last saw her** elle a changé depuis la dernière fois que je l'ai vue; **some things never c.** certaines choses ne changent jamais; **to c. for the better** changer en mieux, s'améliorer; (*of weather*) tourner au beau; **the situation has changed for the worse** la situation a changé en mal; **to c. beyond recognition** être méconnaissable; **to c. into sth** (*by magic, through biological transformation*) se transformer en qch; **he changed into a psychopath** il est devenu psychopathe; **the country had changed from dictatorship to democracy overnight** en une nuit, le pays était passé de la dictature à la démocratie; **the lights changed from green to amber** les feux sont passés du vert à l'orange; **to c. from one system to another** passer d'un système à un autre

(**b**) (*put on other clothes*) se changer; **to c. into another dress** changer de robe; **to c. into trousers** se mettre en pantalon; **to c. into something more comfortable/less formal** mettre un vêtement plus confortable/moins habillé; **to c. out of a wet shirt** enlever *ou* quitter une chemise mouillée

(**c**) *Rail, Air etc* (*of passenger*) changer; **we had to c. twice** nous avons eu deux correspondances; (*in underground*) nous avons eu deux changements; **all c.!** tout le monde descend!

(**d**) (*of sentries, shifts*) se relever

▶ **change down** *vi Aut* (*use lower gear*) rétrograder; **to c. down (in)to second** passer en seconde

▶ **change over** *vi* (**a**) (*convert*) **the UK changed over to decimal currency in 1971** le Royaume-Uni est passé à la monnaie décimale en 1971; **we c. over next year** on passe au nouveau système l'an prochain

(**b**) (*switch*) **let's c. over** (*exchange places etc*) on change?; (*exchange jobs, roles etc*) on échange?; *TV* **to c. over (to another channel)** passer sur une autre chaîne; *TV* **c. over for the news** change de chaîne pour regarder les informations; *TV* **why don't you c. over to ITV?** et si on mettait ITV?

(**c**) *Sp* (*change ends*) changer de côté; (*in relay race*) passer le témoin

▶ **change up** *vi Aut* (*use higher gear*) passer à la vitesse supérieure; **to c. up (in)to third** passer en troisième

changeability [tʃeɪndʒəˈbɪlɪtɪ], **changeableness** [ˈtʃeɪndʒəb(ə)lnɪs] *n* (*of weather etc*) variabilité *f*; (*of moods*) changements *mpl*

changeable [ˈtʃeɪndʒəb(ə)l] *adj* changeant; (*weather*) variable, instable; (*wind*) inégal; **c. character** caractère *m* changeant *ou* instable

changeless [ˈtʃeɪndʒlɪs] *adj* (*rituals, landscape*) immuable

changeling [ˈtʃeɪndʒlɪŋ] *n* = enfant *mf* que des fées ont substitué(e) contre un(e) autre

change machine *n* changeur *m* de monnaie

changeover [ˈtʃeɪndʒəʊvər] *n* (**a**) (*to new system*) changement *m*, passage *m* (**b**) (*after election etc*) relève *f* (**c**) *Sp* changement *m* de côté; (*in relay race*) passage *m* du témoin

changing [ˈtʃeɪndʒɪŋ] **1** *adj* (*nature, world, mood*) changeant **2** *n* changement *m*; **the c. of the guard** la relève de la garde; *Aut* **c. down** (*of gears*) rétrogradage *m*; *Sp etc* **c. room** vestiaire *m*

channel¹ [ˈtʃæn(ə)l] *n* **(a)** (*of river*) lit *m*; (*waterway*) chenal *m*; **the (English) C.** la Manche; **on the other side of the C.** outre-Manche; **C. port** port *m* sur la Manche
(b) (*of distribution*) canal *m*, circuit *m*; (*for complaint, inquiry etc*) voie *f*; **to go through (official) channels** suivre la filière *ou* la voie hiérarchique; **through diplomatic channels** par voie diplomatique; **channels of communication** canaux de communication; **there were still channels of communication open** la communication n'était pas totalement interrompue; **channels of communication are still open** (*between us*) nous sommes toujours en relation, le dialogue continue; *Mktg* **c. management** gestion *f* du circuit de distribution; *Mktg* **c. of distribution** circuit *ou* canal de distribution
(c) *TV* chaîne *f*; *Rad* station *f*
(d) *El, Electron etc* voie *f*; (*on stereo*) sortie *f*
(e) (*for irrigation*) canal *f*
(f) (*groove*) (*in wood*) rainure *f*; (*on column*) cannelure *f*
channel² *vt* **(-ll-**, *US* **-l-) (a)** (*direct*) (*effort, energy, information*) canaliser **(towards** vers; **into** dans); (*resources, aid etc*) acheminer; **she channelled all her energy into charity work** elle a investi toute son énergie dans des œuvres de bienfaisance **(b)** (*cut channels in*) (*ground*) creuser des rigoles dans
Channel Four *n TV* chaîne *f* de télévision britannique privée
channel hop *vi TV* zapper
Channel Islands (the) *npl* les îles *fpl* Anglo-Normandes
Channel Tunnel (the) *n* le tunnel sous la Manche
chant¹ [tʃɑːnt] *n* **(a)** (*of demonstrators*) slogans *mpl* (scandés); **the c. went up ...** on commença à scander ... **(b)** *Mus, Rel* chant *m*; **Gregorian c.** chant grégorien
chant² **1** *vt* **(a)** (*slogans, name etc*) scander **(b)** *Rel* psalmodier **2** *vi* **(a)** (*of demonstrators, crowd etc*) scander des slogans **(b)** *Rel* psalmodier
chantey [ˈʃæntɪ] *n US* chanson *f* de marin
chanting [ˈtʃɑːntɪŋ] **1** *adj* (*voice etc*) monotone, traînant **2** *n* **(a)** (*of demonstrators*) slogans *mpl* (scandés) **(b)** *Rel* chants *mpl*, psalmodie *f*
chantry [ˈtʃɑːntrɪ] *n Rel Arch* chantrerie *f*, chanterie *f*
chaos [ˈkeɪɒs] *n* chaos *m*; (*in filing system, sb's life*) pagaille *f*, *très F* bordel *m*; **it'll be c. if you try to introduce these changes** ça va être la pagaille si tu fais ces changements; **the country is in a state of c.** le pays est dans un état de confusion totale; *Journ* **c. on roads as bus drivers strike** la grève des chauffeurs de bus entraîne le chaos sur les routes; **it was c. in the post office** c'était la pagaille au bureau de poste; **it's just c.!** c'est la confusion totale!; **c. theory** théorie *f* du chaos
chaotic [keɪˈɒtɪk] *adj* chaotique; (*office, filing system*) en désordre; **in a c. state** en pagaille; **a c. love life** une vie amoureuse chaotique
chaotically [keɪˈɒtɪklɪ] *adv* en pagaille; **clothes all c. piled into one drawer** des vêtements tous mis en pagaille dans un tiroir; **a c. disorganized life** une vie totalement chaotique
chap¹ [tʃæp] *n F* (*man*) type *m*, mec *m*; **a good c.** un type bien; **an odd c.** un drôle de type; **be a good c.** sois sympa; *Old-fashioned* **I say, old c.!** dis, mon vieux!
chap² *n* (*on skin*) gerçure *f*, crevasse *f*
chap³ **(-pp-)** **1** *vt* (*skin*) gercer; **chapped lips** lèvres gercées **2** *vi* se gercer
chapel [ˈtʃæp(ə)l] *n* **(a)** (*of school etc*) chapelle *f*; (*private*) oratoire *m*; (*in cathedral etc*) chapelle latérale; **c. of rest** = chapelle ardente **(b)** *Rel* (*protestant*) temple *m*; *Scot Cathol* **to go to c.** aller à la messe **(c)** (*of print union, NUJ*) branche *f* syndicale (*dans l'industrie du livre et de l'édition*); **Father/Mother of C.** président/présidente de la branche syndicale
chaperone¹ [ˈʃæpərəʊn] *n* (*for young girl*), *Hum* chaperon *m*; **to act as c.** servir de chaperon; **the foreign journalists had a c.** les journalistes étrangers étaient accompagnés partout où ils allaient
chaperone² *vt* (*girl, young woman*) chaperonner
chaplain [ˈtʃæplɪn] *n Rel* aumônier *m*
chaplaincy [ˈtʃæplɪnsɪ] *n* aumônerie *f*
chappie [ˈtʃæpɪ] *n F* (*man*) type *m*, gus *m*; (*little boy, baby*) petit gars *m*
Chaps [tʃæps] *n Banking* (*abbr* **clearing house automated payment system)** Sit *m*
chapter [ˈtʃæptər] *n* **(a)** (*of book*), *Fig* chapitre *m*; *Fig* **to give c. and verse for sth** citer les références exactes de qch; **a new c. in East-West relations** un nouveau chapitre dans les relations est-ouest; **what a c. of accidents!** quelle série noire! **(b)** *Rel* (*of canons, monks*) chapitre *m*; **c. house** salle *f* capitulaire **(c)** (*of society etc*) groupe *m*; **a Hell's Angel c.** une bande de Hell's Angels
char¹ [tʃɑːr] **(-rr-)** **1** *vt* (*wood, bones*) carboniser, réduire en cendres; **the charred remains of a building** les restes carbonisés d'un bâtiment **2** *vi* se carboniser
char² *n Br Sl* (*tea*) thé *m*
char³ *n Br F* (*charlady*) femme *f* de ménage
char⁴ *vi Br F* (*work as charlady*) faire des ménages
char⁵ *n* (*fish*) omble *m* (chevalier)
charabanc [ˈʃærəbæŋ] *n Br Hist* char *m* à bancs; *Hum* (*sightseeing coach*) car *m* de touristes
character [ˈkærɪktər] *n* **(a)** *Liter, Th etc* personnage *m*; **a c. straight out of a novel** un vrai personnage de roman
(b) (*distinctive quality*) (*of person, race, book etc*) caractère *m*; **her face is full of c.** son visage a beaucoup de caractère; **to have c.** avoir du caractère; **this region has a c. of its own** cette région a un caractère particulier; **books of this c.** les livres de ce genre; **his behaviour/remark was in/out of character** la façon dont il s'est conduit/la remarque qu'il a faite lui correspond bien/ne lui correspond pas
(c) (*moral qualities*) caractère *m*; (*reputation*) réputation *f*; **man of (strong) c.** homme de caractère *ou* de volonté; **to be lacking in c.** manquer de caractère; *Fml* **a person of good c.** une personne honorable; **a place of very dubious c.** un endroit mal famé; **a c. reference** des références *fpl*
(d) (*person*) **a suspicious c.** un individu suspect *ou* louche; **he's quite a c.!** (*odd, remarkable*) c'est un sacré numéro!, c'est un personnage!
(e) *Comptr, Typ* caractère *m*; **in Greek characters** en caractères grecs; **special/binary c.** caractère spécial/binaire; **characters per inch** caractères par pouce; **characters per second** caractères par seconde; **c. code** code *m* de caractère; **c. generator** générateur *m* de caractères; **c. insert** insertion *f* de caractère; **c. recognition** reconnaissance *f* de caractères; **c. smoothing** lissage *m* de caractères; **c. space** espace *m*; **c. spacing** espacement *m* des caractères
character actor *n* acteur *m* de genre
character assassination *n* calomnie *f*, diffamation *f*
character-forming, -building *adj* qui forme le caractère; **it's c.** ça forme le caractère
characteristic [kærɪktəˈrɪstɪk] **1** *adj* (*sign, taste etc*) caractéristique; **this attitude is c. of him** cette attitude lui correspond bien, c'est bien de lui **2** *n* **(a)** caractéristique *f*, trait *m* caractéristique **(b)** *Math* (*of logarithm*) caractéristique *f*
characteristically [kærɪktəˈrɪstɪklɪ] *adv* de façon caractéristique; **he was c. blunt/evasive** comme à son habitude, il a été abrupt/vague
characterization [kærɪktəraɪˈzeɪʃən] *n* caractérisation *f*
characterize [ˈkærɪktəraɪz] *vt* **(a)** (*of writer*) (*person*) caractériser; (*century etc*) dépeindre **(b)** (*be characteristic of*) être caractéristique de, caractériser; **the long pauses that c. his speech** les longs silences qui caractérisent son discours
characterless [ˈkærɪktəlɪs] *adj* sans caractère
character licensing *n Mktg* cession *f* de licence sur un personnage
character part *n* rôle *m* de composition
character set *n Comptr* jeu *m* de caractères
character sketch *n* portrait *m* littéraire
character witness *n* = témoin *m* attestant de l'honorabilité de l'accusé
charade [ʃəˈrɑːd] *n* **(a)** (*farce*) mascarade *f* **(b)** (*game*) **to play charades** jouer aux charades *fpl* mimées
charcoal [ˈtʃɑːkəʊl] *n* **(a)** charbon *m* de bois; **c. filter** filtre *m* à charbon **(b)** *Art* fusain *m*; **c. drawing** (dessin *m* au) fusain
charcoal-broiled [ˈtʃɑːkəʊlˈbrɔɪld] *adj* (*steak etc*) grillé au charbon de bois
charcoal-burner *n* **(a)** (*person*) charbonnier *m* **(b)** (*stove*) réchaud *m* à charbon de bois
chard [tʃɑːd] *n Bot, Culin* **Swiss c.** bette *f*, blette *f*
charge¹ [tʃɑːdʒ] *n* **(a)** (*cost*) frais *mpl*, prix *m*; *Admin* droits *mpl*; *Jur* privilège *m*, droit *m*; (*to an account*) imputation *f*; **list of charges** tarif *m*; **scale of charges** barème *m* des prix; **no c. for admission** (*in museum etc*) entrée gratuite; **there is no extra c. for installation** l'installation est comprise dans le prix; **to make a c. for sth** faire payer qch; **free of c.** gratis, (à titre) gratuit, à titre gracieux; *Com, Banking* exempt de frais, sans frais; *esp Am* **will that be cash or c.?** vous payez comptant ou vous le portez à votre compte?; **service c.** prestation *f* de service; **extra c.** supplément *m* (de prix); **bank charges** frais bancaires, agios *mpl*; **minimum c.** (*in taxi*) prise *f* en charge; (*in café, restaurant*) = prix minimum à payer; *Banking* **c. over business assets** nantissement *m* de fonds de commerce
(b) (*accusation*) accusation *f*; *Jur* chef *m* d'accusation, acte *m* d'accusation; (*by public prosecutor*) réquisitoire *m*; **to bring** *or* **lay a c. against sb** porter une accusation *ou* porter plainte contre qn; **on a c. of having ...** accusé d'avoir

…; **what's the c.?** de quoi est-il/suis-je/*etc* accusé?; **he denies the c.** il nie les accusations

(c) (*responsibility*) garde *f*, soin *m*; **to place sth in sb's c.** confier qch à qn *ou* à la garde de qn *ou* aux mains de qn; **to have c. of sth** avoir la garde de qch; **to take c. of sth/sb** se charger de qch/qn; **I'll take c. while the director is sick** je m'occupe de tout pendant que le directeur est malade; **to be in c. of** piloter; **Jane is in c. of sales** Jane est chargée *ou* responsable des ventes; **he is in overall c. of the project** il est responsable du projet dans son ensemble; **he was put in c. of 100 men** on a mis 100 hommes sous sa responsabilité; **who is in c.?** qui est le responsable?; **look, I'm in c. here!** regarde, c'est moi le patron ici!; **I want to speak to the person in c.** je veux parler au responsable *ou* à la personne responsable; **who was in c. of the vehicle?** (*driving*) qui était au volant?; *Jur* **to take sb in c.** arrêter qn

(d) (*person, thing entrusted*) = personne *f*/chose *f* confiée à la garde de qn; **the nanny is out for a walk with her charges** la nourrice est partie se promener avec les enfants qu'elle garde *ou* dont elle a la charge

(e) *Mil* charge *f*, attaque *f*; **to sound the c.** sonner la charge

(f) *Tech* (*of cartridge, bomb etc*), *El* charge *f*; *Fig* **the word has an emotional c.** le mot a une charge affective

charge[2] **1** *vt* **(a)** (*price*) faire payer; *Com, Fin* (*account*) charger (**with** de); **he charged me £15** il m'a fait payer 15 livres; *F* **they charged me a fortune for this haircut** j'ai payé une fortune pour me faire couper les cheveux; **how much do you c. for an hour?** combien prenez-vous de l'heure?; *Tel* **calls charged for** conversations *fpl* taxées; **to c. the postage to the customer** faire payer les frais d'envoi au client; **commission charged by the bank** commission prélevée par la banque; **c. it to my account/the bill** mettez-le sur mon compte/la note

(b) (*accuse*) accuser (**with sth** de qch; **with doing** de faire *ou* d'avoir fait); *Jur* inculper (**with a crime** d'un crime); *US* **to c. that …** alléguer que …

(c) (*entrust, order*) **to c. sb to do sth** ordonner à qn de faire qch; **to c. sb with a task** confier une tâche à qn

(d) (*of troops, forwards, bull etc*) charger

(e) *El* (*electrical conductor, battery etc*) (re)charger (**with** de); *Fig* **a highly charged atmosphere** une atmosphère très tendue; **charged with emotion** chargé d'émotion

2 *vi* **(a)** *Mil* charger, faire une charge; (*of animal*) charger; *F* (*run heavily*) (*of person*) se précipiter, foncer; *Mil* **c!** chargez!; **he charged in** il s'est précipité dans la maison/la pièce/*etc*; **the crowd charged across the square** la foule s'est ruée à travers la place; **stop charging around, you kids, this is a living room!** arrêtez de courir dans tous les sens, les enfants, ici c'est un salon!

(b) (*require payment*) faire payer (**for sth** qch); **do you c. for delivery?** est-ce qu'il y a des frais de livraison?

(c) (*of battery*) se (re)charger

▶ **charge down** *vtsep Rugby* (*ball*) contrer

▶ **charge up 1** *vtsep* **(a)** (*in shop etc*) **to c. sth up to sb's account** mettre qch sur le compte de qn; **could you c. it up?** pourriez-vous le mettre sur mon compte? **(b)** (*battery*) (re)charger **2** *vi* (*of battery*) se (re)charger

chargeable ['tʃɑːdʒəb(ə)l] *adj* **(a)** *Jur* (*person*) **we would be c. with fraud** on nous accuserait de fraude; **a c. offence** un délit **(b)** *Com etc* (*to an account*) imputable; **to be c. to sb** (*payable by*) être à la charge de qn, être pris en charge par qn; **is it c.?** est-ce qu'il y a des frais?; **a small fee is c. for delivery and installation** il y a quelques frais de livraison et d'installation; **who is it c. to?** c'est à la charge de qui?; **could you make that c. to …?** est-ce que vous pourriez facturer …?; **is this a c. expense?** est-ce que c'est frais facturable?; **c. distance** (*in taxi*) distance *f* tarifaire; *Com* **c. weight** poids *m* de taxation

charge account *n* compte *m* clients

charge card *n Br* carte *f* de crédit; (*for use in store*) carte de paiement

charge-cooled ['tʃɑːdʒkuːld] *adj Aut* (*engine*) suralimenté refroidi

chargé d'affaires ['ʃɑːʒeɪdæ'feər] *n* chargé *m* d'affaires

charge hand *n Br* chef *m* d'équipe

charge nurse *n Br* infirmier en chef

charger ['tʃɑːdʒər] *n* **(a)** *El* (*for battery*) chargeur *m* **(b)** (*horse*) cheval *m* de bataille, destrier *m*

charge sheet *n Br* (*in police station*) cahier *m* des délits et écrous

charily ['tʃeərɪlɪ] *adv* (*cautiously*) avec précaution, avec prudence

chariot ['tʃærɪət] *n* char *m*

charioteer [tʃærɪə'tɪər] *n* conducteur *m* de char

charisma [kə'rɪzmə] *n* charisme *m*; **to have c.** avoir du charisme

charismatic [kærɪz'mætɪk] *adj* charismatique

charitable ['tʃærɪtəb(ə)l] *adj* **(a)** (*person, action*) charitable; **c. donation** don *m* à une œuvre de bienfaisance; *Fig* **the critics were not c.** les critiques n'ont pas été très tendres *ou* bienveillants **(b)** (*organization*) caritatif, de bienfaisance, de charité; (*work*) de bienfaisance, de charité; **c. society** organisation *f* caritative; **c. status** statut *m* d'organisation caritative; *Jur* **c. trust** société *f* à but non lucratif

charitably ['tʃærɪtəblɪ] *adv* avec charité

charity ['tʃærɪtɪ] *n* **(a)** (*money, food*) charité *f*, aumônes *fpl*; **to live on c.** vivre d'aumônes; **I don't want your c.** je ne veux pas que tu me fasses la charité; **c. ball** bal *m* de bienfaisance; *Br* **Charity Commissioners** = conseil *m* chargé de superviser les activités des organisations caritatives; **c. organization** organisation *f* caritative; **c. run** course *f* à pied au profit d'une œuvre de bienfaisance; **c. shop** magasin *m* d'articles d'occasion dont les profits vont à une organisation caritative; **c. work** travail *m* bénévole pour une organisation caritative

(b) (*organization*) organisation *f* caritative; **registered c.** œuvre *f* reconnue d'utilité publique; **we're not a c.!** nous ne sommes pas des philanthropes *ou* une organisation de bienfaisance!

(c) (*kindness*) charité *f*; **out of c.** par charité; *Prov* **c. begins at home** charité bien ordonnée commence par soi-même

charlady ['tʃɑːleɪdɪ] *n Br* femme *f* de ménage

charlatan ['ʃɑːlət(ə)n] *n* charlatan *m*

charleston ['tʃɑːlstən] *n* (*dance*) charleston *m*

Charley, Charlie ['tʃɑːlɪ] *n Br F* **I felt a right** *or* **a proper C.** j'ai vraiment eu l'air bête

charley horse *n Am F* **to have a c.** avoir des crampes

Charlie Chaplin ['tʃæplɪn] *n Cin* Charlot

charlotte ['ʃɑːlət] *n Culin* **apple c.** charlotte *f* aux pommes

charm[1] [tʃɑːm] *n* **(a)** (*attractiveness*) charme *m*, agrément *m*; (*of youth etc*) charme, attrait *m*; **a film of great c.** un film plein de charme; **the village has a quiet c.** le village a un charme tranquille; **to be devoid of c.** manquer de charme; *F* **to turn on the c.** faire du charme; **(physical) charms** (*of person*) charmes, attraits; **the c. of this system is that it's so easy to use** ce qu'il y a de bien avec ce système, c'est qu'il est facile à utiliser; *Iron* **what c. school did you go to?** oh, comme tu parles bien!

(b) (*spell*) charme *m* (**against** contre), sortilège *m*, sort *m*, enchantement *m*; **to be under a c.** être envoûté; *F* **it worked like a c.** ça a marché à merveille

(c) (*talisman*) amulette *f*, fétiche *m*; **(lucky) c.** porte-bonheur *m inv*

charm[2] *vt* (*person*) (*delight*) charmer, enchanter; (*snake*) charmer; **she charmed them into signing** elle a obtenu leur signature à force de charme; **he leads a charmed life** c'est un veinard

charm bracelet *n* bracelet *m* porte-bonheur

charmer ['tʃɑːmər] *n* charmeur, -euse; **he's quite a c.** c'est un charmeur; **snake c.** charmeur, -euse de serpents

charming ['tʃɑːmɪŋ] *adj* (*person, child, village, story*), *Iron* charmant; **Prince C.** le Prince Charmant

charmingly ['tʃɑːmɪŋlɪ] *adv* d'une façon charmante

charnel ['tʃɑːn(ə)l] *n* **c. house** (*for bones*) ossuaire *m*; (*for corpses*) charnier *m*

charring ['tʃɑːrɪŋ] *n* carbonisation *f*

chart[1] [tʃɑːt] *n* **(a)** *Math etc* (*graph*) graphique *m*; (*diagram*) diagramme *m*; (*table*) tableau *m*; *Med* **temperature c.** feuille *f* de température; *Com* **colour c.** nuancier *m*; *Acct* **c. of accounts** plan *m* comptable général **(b)** *Mus* **(pop) charts** hit-parade *m*; **c. topper** numéro *m* un; **it's number one in** *or* **it's top of the charts** c'est le numéro un au hit-parade **(c)** *Naut, Av* (*for navigation*) carte *f*; **c. room** cabine *f* des cartes

chart[2] **1** *vt* **(a)** *Naut* (*sea etc*) hydrographier, faire l'hydrographie de; (*rock etc*) porter sur une carte **(b)** (*patient's temperature etc*) porter sur la feuille; (*plot graph of*) (*series of readings etc*) établir le graphique de; *Fig* **the book charts the rise of the labour movement** ce livre retrace la montée du mouvement travailliste **2** *vi Mus F* (*of record*) être classé; **it charted at 16** il a été classé 16ème

charter[1] ['tʃɑːtər] *n* **(a)** *Hist, Jur* (*of town, university etc*) charte *f*; (*of company*) statuts *mpl*; *Pol* **the Atlantic C.** la Charte de l'Atlantique **(b)** (*of plane, ship, bus*) affrètement *m*; **on c.** (*to company*) affrété

charter[2] *vt* **(a)** (*hire*) (*ship, plane*) affréter, noliser; (*ship*) prendre à fret; (*coach*) affréter **(b)** (*company etc*) accorder une charte à

chartered ['tʃɑːtəd] *adj* **(a)** (*ship, plane*) affrété, nolisé; (*coach*) affrété **(b)** (*company, bank*) privilégié; *Br* **c. accountant** expert *m* comptable; *Br* **c. surveyor** = géomètre *mf* expert
charterer ['tʃɑːtərər] *n Naut, Av* affréteur *m*
charter flight *n* vol *m* charter, vol nolisé; (*at reduced rate*) charter *m*
chartering ['tʃɑːtərɪŋ] *n* (*of plane, ship, coach*) affrètement *m*; (*of plane, boat*) nolisation *f*; (*at reduced rates*) charterisation *f*; **c. broker** courtier *m* d'affrètement
charter plane *n* charter *m*; (*for passengers, cargo*) avion *m* affrété *ou* nolisé; (*very small, for passengers*) avion-taxi *m*, *pl* avions-taxis
charwoman, *pl* **-women** ['tʃɑːwʊmən, -wɪmɪn] *n Br* femme *f* de ménage
chary ['tʃeərɪ] *adj* (*cautious*) prudent, circonspect; **to be c. of doing sth** hésiter à faire qch; **to be c. of praise** (*sparing with it*) être avare de compliments
chase¹ [tʃeɪs] *n* **(a)** (*pursuit*) chasse *f*, poursuite *f*; **to give c. to sb** donner la chasse à qn; **in c. of sb** à la poursuite de qn; **a car c.** une poursuite en voitures; **paper c.** rallye-paper *m*, *pl* rallye-papers **(b)** *Horseracing* steeple *m* **(c) the c.** (*hunting*) la chasse à courre
chase² **1** *vt* **(a)** (*pursue*) (*thief, enemy etc*) poursuivre, donner la chasse à; (*hunt*) (*deer*) chasser; **to c. a dog away** chasser un chien; **to c. sb out of the house** chasser qn de la maison **(b)** *F* (*court*) (*man, woman*) courir après **2** *vi* **I've been chasing around all day** j'ai couru toute la journée; **the kids were chasing all over the house** les gosses passaient leur temps à courir partout dans la maison
chase³ *vt* **(a)** (*engrave*) (*gold, silver*) ciseler; **chased work** ouvrage *m* ciselé **(b)** (*emboss*) (*metal*) repousser; **chased silver** argent *m* repoussé
▶ **chase after** *vipo F* (*man, woman*) courir après; (*car, animal etc*) être à la poursuite de, poursuivre; **we've been all over town chasing after that spare part** nous avons dû faire tout le tour de la ville pour trouver cette pièce détachée
▶ **chase away** *vtsep* chasser
▶ **chase up** *vtsep* **(a)** (*insistently contact or try to contact*) relancer; **I'll c. them up about those files** je vais leur réclamer ces fichiers; **to c. up a debtor** relancer un débiteur **(b)** (*payment*) réclamer; **I'll c. the matter up for you** je vais tenter d'activer les choses pour vous
chaser ['tʃeɪsər] *n F* **(a)** (*drink*) (*after beer*) = verre *m* d'alcool que l'on prend après un verre de bière; (*after whisky*) = verre de bière etc que l'on prend après un whisky **(b) woman c.** coureur *m* de jupons
chasing ['tʃeɪsɪŋ] *n* **(a)** (*engraving*) (*of gold, silver*) ciselage *m*, ciselure *f* **(b)** (*embossing*) (*of metal*) repoussage *m*
chasm ['kæz(ə)m] *n* (*abyss*) abysse *m*, abîme *m*, gouffre *m* béant; *Fig* (*between two people*) abîme; **the c. between their political viewpoints** l'abîme qui sépare leurs opinions politiques
chassis ['ʃæsɪ] *n Aut, Av etc, Sl* (*of woman*) châssis *m*; **c. number** numéro *m* de châssis
chassisless construction ['ʃæsɪlɪs] *n Aut* carrosserie *f* autoporteuse
chaste [tʃeɪst] *adj* **(a)** (*sexually*) chaste **(b)** *Lit* (*speech, taste, style*) sobre, simple
chastely ['tʃeɪstlɪ] *adv* **(a)** (*in sexual sense*) chastement **(b)** *Lit* (*soberly*) sobrement
chasten ['tʃeɪs(ə)n] *vt esp Lit* (*of providence, suffering etc*) (*person*) éprouver; (*humble*) rabattre la présomption *ou* l'orgueil de; (*subdue*) assagir; **he was in a chastened mood** il était abattu; **my son returned from Bangladesh chastened by what he had seen** le voyage de mon fils au Bangladesh, et ce qu'il y a vu, lui a mis du plomb dans la tête
chasteness ['tʃeɪstnɪs] *n* (*sexual*) chasteté *f*
chastening ['tʃeɪs(ə)nɪŋ] *adj* salutaire; **it had a c. effect on her** ça l'a assagie
chastise [tʃæs'taɪz] *vt* **(a)** (*reprimand, criticize*) réprimander **(b)** *Old-fashioned, Fml* (*punish*) châtier; (*beat*) (*child*) corriger
chastisement [tʃæs'taɪzmənt] *n Old-fashioned, Fml* (*punishment*) châtiment *m*; (*beating*) (*of child*) correction *f*
chastity ['tʃæstɪtɪ] *n* (*sexual*) chasteté *f*; **to take a vow of c.** faire vœu de chasteté; **c. belt** ceinture *f* de chasteté
chasuble ['tʃæzjʊb(ə)l] *n Rel* chasuble *f*
chat¹ [tʃæt] *n* petite conversation *f*, causette *f*; **to have a c. with sb** bavarder avec qn; (*about a problem, their work performance etc*) dire un mot à qn; **it's time we had a little c.** il est temps que nous ayons une petite discussion; **the c. at work is all about cars** au travail, on ne discute que de voitures
chat² *vi* (**-tt-**) causer, bavarder; **to c. with sb** bavarder avec qn, faire la causette avec qn; **to c. about one thing and another** parler de choses et d'autres
▶ **chat up** *vtsep F* (*talk flirtatiously to*) baratiner, draguer; *Fig* **to c. up a client** baratiner un client
chat show *n TV* talk-show *m*, *pl* talk-shows
chattel ['tʃæt(ə)l] *n Jur* bien *m* meuble, bien mobilier; **chattels** biens *mpl*; **goods and chattels** biens et effets *mpl*
chatter¹ ['tʃætər] *n* (*of people*) bavardage *m*; (*of birds*) caquet(age) *m*, jacasserie *f*; (*of monkeys*) babil *m*; (*of teeth*) claquement *m*; (*of machine-gun*) martèlement *m*
chatter² *vi* (*of person*) bavarder, jaser; (*of birds*) caqueter, jacasser; (*of monkeys*) babiller; (*of teeth*) claquer; **my teeth were chattering** je claquais des dents
chatterbox ['tʃætəbɒks] *n F* grand(e) bavard(e), moulin *m* à paroles
chatterer ['tʃætərər] *n* = **chatterbox**
chattering ['tʃætərɪŋ] *n* (*of people*) bavardage *m*; (*of birds*) caquetage *m*; (*of monkeys*) babil *m*; (*of teeth*) claquement *m*; (*of machine-gun*) martèlement *m*; *Pej* **the c. classes** les intellectuels *mpl* qui s'écoutent parler (*terme journalistique appliqué, dès le début des années 80, à une poignée de personnes qui pensent que leurs opinions ont de l'importance mais qui ne représentent guère l'opinion de la majorité*
chatty ['tʃætɪ] *adj* (*person*) bavard; (*letter*) plein de bavardages; (*article etc*) écrit sur le ton de la conversation; **Mr Smith was very c.** *or* **in a very c. mood today** M. Smith était très bavard aujourd'hui; **the interview with the President was rather too c.** il y avait un peu trop de bavardage dans l'entretien avec le Président
chat-up line *n F* **that's his standard c.** c'est son baratin habituel
chauffeur¹ ['ʃəʊfər] *n Aut* chauffeur *m* (*employé par un particulier*); **c.-driven** (*car*) avec chauffeur
chauffeur² *vt* (*person*) accompagner, conduire; (*car*) conduire; **we were chauffeured to the airport** on nous a conduits à l'aéroport
chauvinism ['ʃəʊvɪnɪz(ə)m] *n Pej* **(a)** (*patriotism*) chauvinisme *m* **(b) (male) c.** machisme *m*
chauvinist ['ʃəʊvɪnɪst] *Pej* **1** *n* **(a)** (*patriot*) chauvin, -ine **(b)** *F* **(male) c.** macho *m*, machiste *m* **2** *adj* **(a)** (*patriotic*) chauvin **(b)** *F* **(male) c.** macho, machiste; **male c. pig** phallocrate *m*
chauvinistic [ʃəʊvɪ'nɪstɪk] *adj Pej* **(a)** (*patriotic*) chauvin **(b)** *F* (*of male chauvinist*) macho, machiste
cheap [tʃiːp] **1** *adj* **(a)** (*inexpensive*) bon marché *inv*, pas cher; **it's c. to run** (*car*) elle est économique à l'entretien; **a cheaper model** un modèle moins cher *ou* meilleur marché; **it works out cheaper to take a whole bottle** cela revient moins cher de prendre la bouteille entière; **the cheapest** le meilleur marché, le moins cher; *F* **he's very c.** (*shopkeeper*) il n'est pas cher; **to do sth on the c.** (*at little cost*) faire qch à peu de frais; (*meanly*) faire qch chichement; **it's c. at the price** c'est une affaire; **c. and cheerful** sans prétentions; **c. fare/rate** tarif *m*/taux *m* réduit
(b) *Pej* (*of little worth*) de peu de valeur; (*emotion*) superficiel; **life is c. there** la vie a peu de valeur là-bas; **it's c. and nasty** c'est de la camelote; **a c. remark** une remarque facile; **that was a c. thing to do** ça n'était pas bien de faire ça; *F* **to feel c.** avoir honte; *F* **to make oneself c.** s'abaisser
(c) *Am Pej* (*mean*) pingre
2 *adv* **to go c.** se vendre bon marché; **he got off c.** il s'en est tiré à bon compte
cheap day return *n* aller-retour *m* à tarif réduit valable une journée
cheapen ['tʃiːp(ə)n] *vt* **(a)** (*degrade*) (*sth*) diminuer la valeur de; **to c. oneself** s'abaisser **(b)** (*lower price of*) (ra)baisser *ou* faire baisser le prix de
cheapjack ['tʃiːpdʒæk] *Pej F* **1** *n* camelot *m* **2** *adj* (*solution*) facile; (*remark*) facile, mesquin; **c. goods** de la camelote
cheaply ['tʃiːplɪ] *adv* (*to buy*) (à) bon marché, à bas prix; (*to do sth, to travel*) à peu de frais; **to eat out c.** manger dehors pour pas cher; **the room was c. furnished** (*at little cost*) la pièce avait été meublée à moindre frais; (*nastily*) le mobilier de la pièce était de mauvaise qualité
cheapness ['tʃiːpnɪs] *n* **(a)** (*low price*) bas prix *m* **(b)** *Pej* (*low worth*) peu *m* de valeur, mauvaise qualité *f*; (*of remark*) bassesse *f*
cheapo ['tʃiːpəʊ] *F* **1** *adj* (*inexpensive*) bon marché, pas cher **2** *n* **it's a real c.** c'est un truc pas cher
cheapskate ['tʃiːpskeɪt] *Pej F* **1** *n* radin, -ine **2** *adj* (*remark*) facile, mesquin
cheat¹ [tʃiːt] *n* **(a)** (*at games*) tricheur, -euse **(b)** (*dishonest person*) escroc *m* **(c)** (*deception*) triche *f*
cheat² **1** *vt* **(a)** (*at games*) tricher **(b)** (*be dishonest to*) tromper, *F* rouler; (*defraud*) frauder; **I felt cheated** je me suis senti dupé; **to c. sb out of sth** escroquer qch à qn; **to**

cheat sb into doing sth faire faire qch à qn en le trompant; **I feel as if I've been cheated of my chance to represent my country** (*because of injury, illness*) j'ai l'impression d'avoir été privé de la possibilité de représenter mon pays **2** *vi* **(a)** (*at games*) tricher **(b)** (*be dishonest*) tricher, frauder

▶ **cheat on** *vipo* **(a)** (*be unfaithful to*) (*wife, husband*) tromper **(b)** (*be dishonest about*) (*expenses*) tricher sur

cheating [ˈtʃiːtɪŋ] *n* **(a)** (*dishonesty*) tromperie *f* **(b)** (*in games*) tricherie *f*, *F* triche *f*; **that's c.!** c'est de la triche!

check¹ [tʃek] *n* **(a)** (*inspection*) contrôle *m*, vérification *f*; (*of accounts etc*) vérification; **to keep a c. on sth** contrôler qch; **to run a c. on sb/sth** enquêter sur qn/vérifier qch; **c. list** liste *f* de contrôle; *Av* check-list *f*, *pl* check-lists

(b) *Am* **c. (mark)** (*tick*) coche *f*; **there's a c. mark against his name** son nom a été coché

(c) *Am* (*bill in restaurant etc*) addition *f*, note *f*

(d) *Am* (*for deposited item*) billet *m*, ticket *m*; *Rail etc* **luggage c.** bulletin *m* de bagages *ou* d'enregistrement; **cloakroom c.** bulletin de consigne

(e) *US* (*gambling chip*) jeton *m*

(f) *Am Fin* = **cheque**

(g) (*restraint*) frein *m*; **to keep** *or* **hold the enemy in c.** tenir l'ennemi en échec; **to keep one's feelings in c.** se contraindre, se contenir; *Pol* **a system of checks and balances** un système reposant sur l'équilibre des pouvoirs; **there is no effective c. on presidential power** il n'y a pas de limitation réelle du pouvoir du président

(h) (*reversal*) revers *m*; **her plans had suffered a c.** ses projets avaient été contrariés

(i) *Chess* échec *m*; **c.!** échec au roi!

check² **1** *vt* **(a)** (*verify, examine*) (*account, pressure etc*) vérifier; (*against the original*) (*document*) compulser sur l'original; *Typ* (*proofs*) (*go over*) réviser; (*compare*) comparer; **I'll c. the arrival time/when they're supposed to arrive** je vérifierai l'heure d'arrivée/quand ils sont censés arriver; **to c. the names on a list** (*mark off*) pointer les noms sur une liste; (*by calling out*) faire l'appel des noms sur une liste; **to c. sth against sth** comparer qch à qch; **c. these names against the ones on the list** vérifie que ces noms sont les mêmes que ceux de la liste; *Sch* **c. your work before handing it in** relisez votre travail avant de le rendre; *Com* **to c. the books** pointer les écritures; **checked and double checked** vérifié et revérifié; **to c. that ...** vérifier *ou* s'assurer que ... + *ind*

(b) (*officially inspect*) (*tickets*) contrôler

(c) *Am* (*hand in*) (*baggage*) (faire) enregistrer; (*at restaurant etc*) (*hat, raincoat*) mettre au vestiaire; (*take in*) (*baggage*) enregistrer; (*hat, raincoat*) prendre; **checked baggage** bagages *mpl* enregistrés

(d) *Am* (*mark with tick*) cocher; **c. the appropriate box** cocher la case appropriée

(e) (*halt*) faire échec à, arrêter net; (*crisis, price rise*) enrayer; (*attack*) arrêter; **to c. inflation** juguler l'inflation

(f) (*restrain*) (*tears, anger*) refouler, retenir; (*passion, emotion*) réprimer, refréner

(g) *Chess* (*king*) mettre en échec, faire échec à

(h) *Scot* (*reprimand*) réprimander

2 *vi* **(a)** (*verify*) vérifier; **they usually have vacancies, but it's a good idea to c.** d'ordinaire, ils ont de la place, mais il vaut mieux s'en assurer *ou* vérifier; **we checked with the university** nous avons vérifié auprès de l'université; **you'd better c. with her** vous feriez mieux de lui demander

(b) (*halt*) hésiter, s'arrêter (**at**, devant)

(c) (*match*) **that checks with what we were told** cela confirme ce qu'on nous a dit; *US* **c.!** (*confirming data etc*) d'accord!

check³ *n Tex* carreau *m*; **c. material/shirt** tissu *m*/chemise *f* à carreaux

▶ **check in** **1** *vi* **(a)** (*at hotel*) remplir la fiche d'entrée *ou* le registre; **have you checked in yet?** (*not said by receptionist*) est-ce que tu es passé à l'hôtel?

(b) (*at airport*) se faire enregistrer

2 *vtsep* **(a)** (*of receptionist*) enregistrer l'arrivée de; **I checked them in myself** c'est moi-même qui les ai accueillis

(b) (*make reservation for*) faire une réservation pour; **they checked the actress into a four-star hotel** ils ont fait une réservation pour l'actrice dans un hôtel quatre étoiles; **I've checked myself into a hotel for the night** je suis descendu dans un hôtel pour la nuit

(c) (*at airport etc*) (*baggage*) enregistrer

▶ **check off** *vtsep* **(a) to c. sth off (against sth)** vérifier qch (avec qch); *Com* **to c. off goods** recenser des marchandises **(b)** *Am* (*name etc*) cocher

▶ **check on** *vipo* (*information etc*) vérifier, recouper; **to c. on sb** (*for security reasons etc*) enquêter sur qn, prendre des renseignements sur qn

▶ **check out** **1** *vi* **(a)** (*leave hotel*) quitter l'hôtel; *F Euph* (*die*) caner **(b)** *F* (*of story, statement*) tenir debout; **it doesn't c. out** ça ne tient pas debout, ça ne marche pas **2** *vtsep* **(a)** (*investigate*) (*information etc*) vérifier, recouper; (*person*) (*for security reasons etc*) enquêter sur; *esp Am F* **there's a new night-club we could c. out** il y a une nouvelle boîte que nous pourrions essayer; *F* **c. it out!** regarde un peu ça!, *F* vise un peu ça!; **c. it out in your local store** allez voir dans votre magasin **(b)** (*of hotel receptionist*) **to c. sb out** encaisser la note de qn (*avant son départ*)

▶ **check over** *vtsep* (*look over*) vérifier

▶ **check through** *vtsep* **(a)** (*examine*) (*baggage etc*) contrôler, examiner **(b)** (*send by plane*) faire envoyer (par avion); **I'd like my luggage checked through to Los Angeles** je voudrais faire envoyer directement mes bagages à Los Angeles

▶ **check up** *vi* (*make sure*) vérifier

▶ **check up on** *vipo* = **check on**

check bit *n Comptr* bit *m* de contrôle

checkbook [ˈtʃekbʊk] *n Am* = **chequebook**

check box *n Comptr* case *f* de pointage, case d'option

check byte *n Comptr* octet *m* de contrôle

check-control *n Aut* appareil *m* de signalisation des défauts

checked [tʃekt] *adj* (*material etc*) à carreaux, quadrillé

checker¹ [ˈtʃekər] *n* (*person*) contrôleur, -euse; *Comptr* **grammar/spelling c.** correcteur grammatical/orthographique

checker² *vt Am* = **chequer**

checkerboard [ˈtʃekəbɔːd] *n Am* damier *m*

checkered [ˈtʃekəd] *adj Am* = **chequered**

checkers [ˈtʃekəz] *npl* [①A10,d] *Am* jeu *m* de dames

check-in *n Av* **(a)** (*of passengers*) enregistrement *m*; **c. time** heure *f* d'enregistrement **(b) c. (desk)** guichet *m ou* comptoir *m* d'enregistrement

checking [ˈtʃekɪŋ] *n* **(a)** (*verification, examination*) contrôle *m*, vérification *f*; (*more detailed*) pointage *m* **(b)** *Am Fin* **c. account** compte *m* courant, compte chèque

checklist [ˈtʃeklɪst] *n* liste *f* récapitulative

checkmark [ˈtʃekmɑːk] *n Am* coche *f*

checkmate¹ [ˈtʃekmeɪt] *n Chess* échec *m* et mat; *Fig* **it was c.** (*we won*) ce fut une victoire; (*we lost*) ce fut un échec

checkmate² *vt Chess* (*king*) faire échec et mat à; *Fig* faire échec à; (*sb's plans*) contrecarrer, déjouer

checkout [ˈtʃekaʊt] *n* **(a)** (*in supermarket*) **c. (point** *or* **desk)** caisse *f*; **c. girl** caissière *f*; **c. display** devant *m* de caisse, nez *m* de caisse; **c. display item** article *m* de caisse **(b)** (*in hotel*) **c. time** heure *f* de départ; (*when room has to be vacated*) heure limite d'occupation des chambres; **c. time is 12 noon** les clients doivent libérer la chambre avant midi

checkpoint [ˈtʃekpɔɪnt] *n* contrôle *m*

check question *n Mktg* question *f* de contrôle, question filtre

checkroom [ˈtʃekruːm] *n Am* vestiaire *m*; **c. ticket** ticket *m* de vestiaire

checksum [ˈtʃeksʌm] *n Comptr* somme *f* de contrôle

checkup [ˈtʃekʌp] *n* **(a)** *Med* examen *m* médical (complet), bilan *m* de santé, check-up *m*; **to give sb a c.** faire le bilan de santé de qn; **to have a c.** se faire faire un check-up; **it's just a c.** c'est juste une visite de routine **(b)** (*inspection*) vérification *f*, inspection *f*; (*of machinery*) révision *f*

cheddar [ˈtʃedər] *n* (fromage *m* de) cheddar *m*

cheek¹ [tʃiːk] *n* **(a)** *Anat* joue *f*; **to dance c. to c.** danser joue contre joue; *Fig* **c. by jowl with sb** coude à coude avec qn; *Fig* **to turn the other c.** tendre l'autre joue **(b)** *F* (*buttock*) fesse *f* **(c)** *Br F* (*impudence*) toupet *m*, culot *m*; **he's got a c.!** il est culotté *ou* gonflé!; **that's enough of your c.!** j'en ai assez de cette impertinence!; **the c. (of it)!, some c.!** quel culot *ou* toupet!

cheek² *vt Br F* dire des impertinences à, faire l'insolent avec

cheekbone [ˈtʃiːkbəʊn] *n* pommette *f*, *Spec* os *m* malaire; **high/prominent cheekbones** pommettes hautes/saillantes

cheekily [ˈtʃiːkɪlɪ] *adv Br F* (*to do sth*) d'une manière impertinente *ou* effrontée; (*to say*) d'un air impertinent *ou* effronté

cheekiness [ˈtʃiːkɪnɪs] *n Br F* effronterie *f*

cheeky [ˈtʃiːkɪ] *adj Br F* effronté, impertinent; **don't be c.!** pas d'impertinence!; **a c. little wine** un bon petit pinard

cheep¹ [tʃiːp] *n* (*of bird*) piaulement *m*; *F* **you can't get a c. out of her** elle ne dit jamais mot

cheep² *vi* (*of bird*) piauler

cheer¹ [tʃɪər] *n* **(a)** (*shout*) hourra *m*; **cheers** acclamations *fpl*, bravos *mpl*; **to give three cheers** pousser trois hourras; **three cheers for Mary!** un ban pour Mary!, vive Mary! **(b)** *F* **cheers!** (*toast*) (à votre) santé!; *Br* (*at parting*) à bientôt!; *Br* (*thanks*) merci! **(c)** *Lit* (*good spirits*) bonne disposition *f* (d'esprit); **be of good c.!** prenez courage!; **we were of good c.** nous étions de bonne humeur

cheer² 1 *vt* **(a)** (*shout for*) acclamer **(b)** (*encourage, make happier*) remonter le moral à **2** *vi* (*shout*) pousser des hourras *ou* des acclamations

▶ **cheer on** *vtsep* (*support*) encourager

▶ **cheer up 1** *vi* (*become more cheerful*) s'égayer, devenir plus gai; **the weather's cheered up** le temps s'est arrangé; **c. up!** courage! **2** *vtsep* **(a)** (*make more cheerful*) réjouir, remonter le moral à **(b)** (*make brighter*) (*room etc*) égayer

cheerful ['tʃɪəfʊl] *adj* (*person*) gai, de bonne humeur; (*face*) souriant, riant; (*room*) gai, d'aspect agréable; (*conversation, music etc*) joyeux; (*news etc*) encourageant; **that's a c. thought!** ça c'est encourageant!; *Iron* comme vous êtes optimiste!; **you're (very) c. this morning** tu es de bonne humeur ce matin

cheerfully ['tʃɪəfʊlɪ] *adv* **(a)** (*happily*) gaiement, avec entrain, allègrement **(b)** (*willingly*) de bon cœur, volontiers **(c)** (*without compunction*) sans remords; **she would c. leave the work for the others** elle laisserait sans remords le travail aux autres; **I could quite c. strangle him** je l'étranglerais volontiers

cheerfulness ['tʃɪəfʊlnɪs] *n* (*of person*) gaieté *f*, bonne humeur *f*; (*of room*) aspect *m* agréable

cheerily ['tʃɪərɪlɪ] *adv* gaiement, avec gaieté

cheering ['tʃɪərɪŋ] **1** *n* acclamations *fpl*, bravos *mpl* **2** *adj* (*sight, display*) réjouissant; (*piece of news, conversation*) qui remonte le moral

cheerio [tʃɪərɪ'əʊ] *int Br F* (*at parting*) au revoir; (*in drinking a toast*) à la vôtre/tienne!; **it's c. 1994** bye-bye 1994

cheerleader ['tʃɪəli:dər] *n Am* = meneur, -euse de ban (*surtout dans les matches de football*)

cheerless ['tʃɪəlɪs] *adj* morne, triste, sombre

cheery ['tʃɪərɪ] *adj* (*person, smile, wave, colour*) joyeux, gai

cheese [tʃi:z] *n* **(a)** fromage *m*; **blue c.** (fromage) bleu *m*; **cream c.** fromage frais; **cottage c.** fromage blanc (*salé et grenu*); **cauliflower/macaroni c.** chou-fleur *m*/macaronis *mpl* au gratin; **toasted c.** toast *m* au fromage; *Phot F* **(say) c.!** souriez!; **c. sandwich/omelette** sandwich *m*/omelette *f* au fromage; **the c. industry** l'industrie *f* fromagère; **c. biscuit** (*for cheese*) biscuit *m* salé; (*cheese-flavoured*) biscuit au fromage; **c. mite** mite *f* du fromage; **c. straws** allumettes *f* au fromage **(b)** (*individual piece of cheese*) (*pl* **cheeses**) **a c.** un fromage (entier), une meule (de fromage)

▶ **cheese off** *vtsep* (*usu passive*) *Br F* **to be/get cheesed (off)** en avoir marre (**with** de); **it cheeses me off** ça m'embête

cheeseboard ['tʃi:zbɔ:d] *n* **(a)** (*for cutting cheese*) plateau *m* à fromage **(b)** (*as part of meal*) plateau *m* de fromages; **a selection from our** *or* **the c.** (*in restaurant etc*) une sélection de fromages

cheeseburger ['tʃi:zbɜ:gər] *n Culin* cheeseburger *m*

cheesecake ['tʃi:zkeɪk] *n* **(a)** *Culin* cheesecake *m* **(b)** (*no pl*) *F* (*photos, women*) pin-up *fpl*

cheesecloth ['tʃi:zklɒθ] *n* (*for cheese*) gaze *f*, étamine *f*; *Tex* crépon *m*

cheese grater *n* râpe *f* à fromage

cheese maker *n* fromager, -ère

cheese manufacturer *n* fromager, -ère

cheeseparing ['tʃi:zpeərɪŋ] **1** *adj* parcimonieux **2** *n* économies *fpl* de bouts de chandelle

cheesy ['tʃi:zɪ] *adj* **(a)** (*in taste*) qui a un goût de fromage; (*in smell*) qui sent le fromage **(b)** *Am F* (*poor quality*) moche **(c)** *F* **a c. grin** un large sourire

cheetah ['tʃi:tə] *n* guépard *m*

chef [ʃef] *n* chef *m* (de cuisine)

chemical ['kemɪk(ə)l] **1** *adj* chimique; **c. company** compagnie *f* de produits chimiques; **c. dependency** toxicodépendance *f* **2** *n* produit *m* chimique

chemical engineer *n* ingénieur *m* chimiste

chemical engineering *n* génie *m* chimique

chemically ['kemɪk(ə)lɪ] *adv* chimiquement

chemical warfare *n* guerre *f* chimique

chemical weapons *npl* armes *fpl* chimiques

chemist ['kemɪst] *n* **(a)** *esp Br Com* pharmacien, -ienne; **c.'s (shop)** pharmacie *f* **(b)** (*scientist*) chimiste *mf*

chemistry ['kemɪstrɪ] *n* chimie *f*; **organic/inorganic c.** chimie organique/minérale; **industrial c.** chimie industrielle; *Fig* **there was a certain c. between the members of the band** il y avait une certaine affinité entre les musiciens; *Fig* **the c.'s right/wrong** ça passe bien/mal (entre nous/eux/*etc*); *Fig* **the c.'s missing** le courant ne passe pas, on n'a pas d'atomes crochus; **c. set** panoplie *f* de chimiste

chemotherapy [ki:mə'θerəpɪ], *F* **chemo** ['ki:məʊ] *n Med* chimiothérapie *f*; **to have c.** suivre un traitement de chimiothérapie

cheque, *Am* **check** [tʃek] *n Fin* chèque *m*; **who should I make the c. out to?** à quel ordre dois-je faire *ou* écrire le chèque?; **will you take a c.?** est-ce que vous acceptez les chèques?; **c. for ten pounds** chèque de dix livres; **c. made out to bearer** chèque au porteur; **c. without cover** chèque sans provision; *F* **dud c.** chèque en bois; **c. number** numéro *m* de chèque

chequebook, *Am* **checkbook** ['tʃekbʊk] *n* carnet *m* de chèques, chéquier *m*; *Pej* **c. journalism** journalisme *m* mercantile (*qui consiste à offrir des sommes importantes afin d'obtenir l'exclusivité d'un récit, d'un témoignage etc*); **c. stub** souche *f* de chéquier

cheque (guarantee) card *n Br* carte *f* bancaire (*sans laquelle un chéquier n'est pas valable*)

chequer, *Am* **checker** ['tʃekər] *vt* (*variegate with colour*) diaprer, bigarrer

chequered, *Am* **checkered** ['tʃekəd] *adj* **(a)** (*pattern*) quadrillé, à carreaux; (*two colours only*) en damier **(b)** (*variegated*) diapré, bigarré; *Fig* (*life*) plein de vicissitudes; **she's had a somewhat c. career** (*varied*) elle a fait toutes sortes de métiers; (*ups and downs*) elle a eu une carrière en dents de scie; **this text has had a fairly c. history** ce texte a eu une histoire assez compliquée

cherish ['tʃerɪʃ] *vt* **(a)** (*hope*) bercer, caresser; (*past, occasion, memory, possessions, gift*) chérir; (*idea, opinion*) nourrir, entretenir; **to c. illusions** se nourrir d'illusions; **his most cherished hopes** ses espérances les plus chères **(b)** (*love*) (*person*) chérir

cheroot [ʃə'ru:t] *n* petit cigare *m*

cherry ['tʃerɪ] **1** *n* **(a)** (*fruit*) cerise *f*; **wild c.** merise *f*; **c. brandy** cherry-brandy *m*, *F* cherry *m*; *F* **you don't get two bites at the c.** il n'y a pas de deuxième chance; *prov* **life is just a bowl of cherries** il faut voir la vie en rose; **c. tart** tarte *f* aux cerises; **c. stone** noyau *m* de cerise; **c. tomato** tomate *f* cerise **(b) c. (tree)** cerisier *m*; **wild c. (tree)** merisier *m*; **c. orchard** cerisaie *f* **(c) c.-red** rouge *m* cerise **(d)** *Sl* (*virginity*) **to lose one's c.** perdre sa fleur **2** *adj* **c. (-red)** cerise *inv*

cherry-pick *vt* **to c. the best** sélectionner ce qu'il y a de meilleur

cherub, *pl* **cherubs,** *Bible* **cherubim** ['tʃerəb, -z, -əbɪm] *n Bible* chérubin *m*; *Art* angelot *m*, ange *m* joufflu; *Fig* **a little c.** (*child*) un petit ange

cherubic [tʃɪ'ru:bɪk] *adj Bible, Art* de chérubin; *Fig* (*smile, face etc*) d'ange

chervil ['tʃɜ:vɪl] *n Bot, Culin* cerfeuil *m*

Ches *abbr* **Cheshire**

Cheshire ['tʃeʃər] *n* **C. cheese** fromage *m* de Chester, chester *m*; **to grin like a C. cat** sourire jusqu'aux oreilles

chess [tʃes] *n* échecs *mpl*; **a c. game, a game of c.** une partie d'échecs; **to play c.** jouer aux échecs; **c. player** joueur, -euse d'échecs

chessboard ['tʃesbɔ:d] *n* échiquier *m*

chessman, *pl* **-men** ['tʃesmən], **chesspiece** ['tʃespi:s] *n* pièce *f* (du jeu d'échecs)

chest [tʃest] *n* **(a)** *Anat* poitrine *f*; (*of horse*) poitrail *m*; *Fig* **to get it off one's c.** dire ce qu'on a sur le cœur; **c. pains** douleurs *mpl* dans la poitrine; **c. size** tour *m* de poitrine; **what c. size are you?** quel est votre tour de poitrine? **(b)** (*box*) coffre *m*, caisse *f*; **c. of drawers** commode *f*; **tea c.** caisse à thé; **medicine c.** (coffret *m* de) pharmacie *f*

chest cold *n* rhume *m* de poitrine

chesterfield ['tʃestəfi:ld] *n* (*sofa*) canapé *m* capitonné

chest expander *n* extenseur *m*

chest infection *n* infection *f* des voies respiratoires

chestnut ['tʃesnʌt] **1** *n* **(a)** **(sweet** *or* **Spanish) c.** châtaigne *f*; (*when cooked*) marron *m*; **c. puree** purée *f* de marrons; **(horse) c.** marron (d'Inde); *F* **an old c.** (*joke*) une plaisanterie usée; *Fig* **to pull sb's chestnuts out of the fire** tirer les marrons du feu à qn **(b) (sweet) c. (tree)** châtaignier *m*; **(horse) c. (tree)** marronnier *m* (d'Inde) **(c)** (*wood*) châtaignier *m* **(d)** (*colour*) châtain *m* **(e)** (*horse*) alezan *m* **2** *adj* **(a)** (*hair*) châtain **(b)** (*horse*) alezan

chesty ['tʃestɪ] *adj F* **to be c.** être bronchitique; **a c. cough** une toux de poitrine

cheval glass [ʃə'væl] *n* psyché *f*

chevron ['ʃevrən] *n Her, Mil* chevron *m*

chew¹ [tʃu:] *n* **(a)** (*action*) **to have a c. at sth** mâchonner qch **(b)** (*tobacco*) chique *f*; (*sweet*) bonbon *m*

chew² *vt* (*food*) mâcher, mastiquer; (*tobacco*) chiquer; (*cigar, end of pen etc*) mâchonner; **the rats had chewed through the rope** les rats avaient coupé la corde en la rongeant; **to c. one's nails** se ronger les ongles; **to c. the cud** (*of cow*) ruminer; *F* **to c. the rag** *or* **the fat** (*chat*) discuter le coup; (*complain*) ronchonner, râler

▶ **chew on** *vipo* **(a)** (*gnaw*) mâchouiller, ronger; **he chewed on his pipe** il mâchouillait sa pipe **(b)** *F* (*consider*) réfléchir

sur; **how much longer do you need to c. on it?** combien te faut-il encore de temps pour réfléchir à la question?
▶ **chew out** *vtsep Am F (reprimand)* engueuler
▶ **chew over** *vtsep F (think over)* réfléchir à; *(discuss)* discuter de
▶ **chew up** *vtsep (damage by chewing)* abîmer à force de mâchonner; *Fig (damage) (bank card, tape etc)* endommager; **the dog has chewed up the newspaper** le chien a mangé le journal; **his arm had been badly chewed up by the machinery** son bras avait été déchiqueté par la machine
chewing ['tʃu:ɪŋ] *n* mastication *f*, mâchement *m*, mâchonnement *m*; **c. tobacco** tabac *m* à chiquer
chewing gum *n* chewing-gum *m*; **a piece of c.** un chewing
chewy ['tʃu:ɪ] *adj* **(a)** *Pej (meat etc)* difficile à mâcher **(b)** *(sweet)* mou, *f* molle, tendre
chiaroscuro [kɪɑ:rə'skʊərəʊ] *n Art* clair-obscur *m*
chic [ʃi:k, ʃɪk] **1** *adj* élégant, chic **2** *n* chic *m*
chicane [ʃɪ'keɪn] *n Aut, Sp, Cards* chicane *f*
chicanery [ʃɪ'keɪnərɪ] *n* chicanerie *f*, chicane *f*
chicano [tʃɪ'kænəʊ] *n US* citoyen, -enne d'origine mexicaine
chichi ['ʃi:ʃi:] *F* **1** *adj* prétentieux **2** *n* prétention *f*
chick [tʃɪk] *n* **(a)** *(young bird)* oiselet *m*, poussin *m*; *Fig (child)* poussin **(b)** *esp US F (young woman)* fille *f*, nana *f*
chickadee [tʃɪkə'di:] *n Am (bird)* mésange *f* (à tête noire)
chicken ['tʃɪkɪn] **1** *n* **(a)** *(bird)* poulet *m*; *Prov* **don't count your chickens before they are hatched** il ne faut pas vendre la peau de l'ours avant de l'avoir tué; *Am* **prairie c.** tétras *m* cupidon, cupidon *m* des prairies, *Can* poule *f* des prairies; **c. breast** blanc *m* de poulet; **c. liver** foie *m* de volaille; **c. sandwich** sandwich *m* au poulet **(b)** *F (coward)* lâche *mf*, froussard, -arde **(c)** *Am F (young person)* mineur, -eure, gamin, -ine; **she's no (spring) c.** elle n'est plus de la première jeunesse **2** *adj F (cowardly)* lâche, froussard
▶ **chicken out** *vi F* se dégonfler; **she chickened out of going** elle s'est dégonflée; **she chickened out of her dental appointment** elle avait rendez-vous chez le dentiste mais elle s'est dégonflée
chicken farm *n* élevage *m* de poulets, élevage avicole
chicken farmer *n* aviculteur *m*
chickenfeed ['tʃɪkɪnfi:d] *n* nourriture *f* pour les volailles; *Fig* **it's c.** c'est de la gnognote; **£2,000 is c.** 2 000 livres, c'est pas grand chose
chicken hawk *n Am, Sl* pédophile *m*
chickenhearted [tʃɪkɪn'hɑ:tɪd], **chickenlivered** [tʃɪkɪn'lɪvəd] *adj Old-fashioned F* poltron, froussard
chickenpox ['tʃɪkɪnpɒks] *n Med* varicelle *f*; **to have c.** avoir la varicelle
chicken run *n* enclos *m (d'un poulailler)*
chicken wire *n* grillage *m*
chickpea ['tʃɪkpi:] *n* pois *m* chiche
chickweed ['tʃɪkwi:d] *n (plant)* mouron *m* des oiseaux, morgeline *f*
chicory ['tʃɪkərɪ] *n* **(a)** *(plant)* endive *f* **(b) (ground) c.** chicorée *f* (en poudre)
chide [tʃaɪd] *vt Arch, Lit (pt* **chided** ['tʃaɪdɪd] *or* **chid** [tʃɪd]; *pp* **chided** *or* **chidden** ['tʃɪd(e)n]) réprimander, gronder
chief [tʃi:f] **1** *n (pl* **chiefs**) *(of tribe, gang)* chef *m*; *Mil* **c. of staff** chef d'état-major; *Am* **fire/police c.** chef des pompiers/de la police; *F* **the c.** *(boss)* le patron; *Fig F* **he's the big white c.** c'est lui le grand patron; **in c.** en chef; *Mil, Naut* **commander-in-c.** commandant *m* en chef; **editor in c.** rédacteur *m* en chef; *prov* **too many chiefs and not enough Indians** trop de gens qui donnent des ordres et pas assez pour les exécuter
2 *adj (most important)* principal; *(in rank)* (en) chef; **my c. assistant** mon principal collaborateur; **the c. reason for doing sth** la raison majeure *ou* principale pour faire qch; **c. photographer** *(on newspaper)* photographe *m* en chef; **c. reporter** grand reporter *m*
Chief Executive *n US Pol* chef *m* de l'Exécutif, Président *m* des États-Unis
chief executive officer *n (of company)* président-directeur *m* général
Chief Inspector *n Br (of police)* inspecteur *m* principal
Chief Justice (of the United States) *n US* président *m* de la Cour suprême
chiefly ['tʃi:flɪ] *adv* principalement, surtout
chieftain ['tʃi:ftən] *n (of clan)* chef *m*
chiffon ['ʃɪfɒn] *n* mousseline *f* de soie
chignon ['ʃi:njɒn] *n* chignon *m*
chihuahua [tʃɪ'wɑ:wɑ:] *n* chihuahua *m*
chilblain ['tʃɪlbleɪn] *n Med* engelure *f*; **to have chilblains** avoir des engelures
child, *pl* **children** [tʃaɪld, 'tʃɪldrən] *n* enfant *mf*; **to treat sb like a c.** traiter qn en enfant; **I'm not a c.!** je ne suis pas un enfant!; *Old-fashioned* **come here, c.!** viens ici, (mon/ma) petit(e)!; **the c. in all of us** l'enfant qui est en chacun de nous; **ever since I was a c.** depuis mon enfance; *Old-fashioned* **I have known him from a c.** *(when he was a child)* je l'ai connu enfant; *(when I was a child)* je le connais depuis mon enfance; **it's c.'s play** *(easy)* c'est un jeu d'enfant; **our children's children** les enfants de nos enfants; **children's shoes/clothes** chaussures/vêtements pour enfants; **children's literature** littérature enfantine *ou* pour enfants; *Bible* **the children of Israel** les enfants d'Israël; *Aut* **c. booster cushion** réhausseur *m*; *Aut* **c. booster seat** siège *m* réhausseur; **c. bride** femme *f* enfant; **I was his c. bride** j'étais une enfant quand il m'a épousée; *Aut* **c. restraint** dispositif *m* de retenue pour enfant, ceinture *f* pour enfant; *Aut* **c. seat** siège *m* enfant; **children's area** *n (in restaurant etc)* coin *m* enfants
child abuse *n* mauvais traitements *mpl* à enfant; *(sexual)* sévices *mpl* sexuels infligés à un enfant
child abuser *n* personne *f* coupable de mauvais traitements à enfant; *(sexual)* personne coupable de sévices sexuels infligés à un enfant
child-bearing *n* maternité *f*; **after 20 years of c.** après 20 ans de maternités successives; **of c. age** en âge d'avoir des enfants; **past c. (age)** *(woman)* trop âgée pour avoir des enfants; **to have c. hips** avoir les hanches larges
child benefit *n Br Admin* ≈ allocation *f* familiale
childbirth ['tʃaɪldbɜ:θ] *n* accouchement *m*; **to die in c.** mourir en couches
child-friendly *adj (area, city)* aménagé pour les enfants; *(furniture, house)* pas dangereux pour les enfants
childhood ['tʃaɪldhʊd] *n* enfance *f*; **to be in one's second c.** être retombé en enfance; **c. memory** souvenir *m* d'enfance; **c. sweetheart** amour *m* d'enfance
childish ['tʃaɪldɪʃ] *adj* **(a)** *Pej (person, behaviour, remarks)* puéril; **don't be so c.** ne faites pas l'enfant, ne soyez pas aussi puéril **(b)** *(of children, childlike) (laughter, curiosity, innocence)* enfantin; *(ailment)* infantile; *(question)* naïf; **c. games** jeux enfantins *ou* d'enfant
childishness ['tʃaɪldɪʃnɪs] *n Pej* enfantillage *m*, puérilité *f*
child labour *n* travail *m* des enfants
childless ['tʃaɪldlɪs] *adj* sans enfant(s); *(marriage)* stérile; **she died c.** elle est morte sans enfants
childlike ['tʃaɪldlaɪk] *adj* enfantin; *(question)* naïf, *f* naïve; *(smile)* d'enfant; **he was c. in his curiosity** il avait une curiosité enfantine *ou* d'enfant
child lock *n Aut* sécurité-enfants *f*; **I put the c. on** j'ai mis la sécurité
child-minder *n* gardienne *f* d'enfants
child-minding ['tʃaɪldmaɪndɪŋ] *n* garde *f* d'enfants
childproof ['tʃaɪldpru:f] *adj (lock etc)* ne pouvant pas être ouvert par les enfants, de sécurité; *(not breakable)* ne pouvant être cassé par les enfants
children *see* **child**
child welfare *n* protection *f* de l'enfance
Chile ['tʃɪlɪ] *n* Chili *m*
Chilean ['tʃɪlɪən] **1** *adj* chilien **2** *n* Chilien, -ienne
chili ['tʃɪlɪ] *n esp Am* = **chilli**
chill¹ [tʃɪl] *n* **(a)** *Med* coup *m* de froid; **to catch a c.** prendre froid; **c. of fear** frisson *m* de peur; **his laugh sent a c. down my spine** son rire m'a fait froid dans le dos **(b)** *(of water, marble etc)* froideur *f*, fraîcheur *f*; **there's a c. in the air** le fond de l'air est frais; **to take the c. off** *(water)* (faire) tiédir; *(wine)* chambrer; *Fig* **to cast a c. over the company** jeter un froid sur l'assemblée
chill² *adj* froid, glacé; *(wind)* froid
chill³ **1** *vt* **(a)** *(of wind) (person, air)* refroidir, glacer; **chilled to the bone** gelé jusqu'aux os; *Fig* **chilled with fear** transi de peur **(b)** *(put in fridge) (wine, melon, dessert etc)* mettre au frais; *Ind* **chilled meat** viande réfrigérée *ou* frigorifiée; **chilled products** produits frigorifiés; **best served chilled** *(on label)* servir glacé *ou* très frais **2** *vi* refroidir
chilli ['tʃɪlɪ] *n Culin* **c. (pepper)** piment *m* (rouge); **c. con carne** chili *m* con carne; **c. powder** poudre *m* de piment; **c. sauce** sauce *f* aux piments
chilliness ['tʃɪlɪnɪs] *n (of air)* froid *m*, froideur *f*; *Fig (of person, welcome)* froideur
chilling ['tʃɪlɪŋ] *adj (wind, welcome)* glacial, -als; *(story, events)* qui donne la chair de poule
chilly ['tʃɪlɪ] *adj* **(a)** *(cold) (weather etc)* frais, *f* fraîche; **to feel c.** *(of person)* avoir froid; **it's** *or* **it feels c. this morning** il fait frais *ou F* frisquet ce matin **(b)** *(person) (feels the cold a lot)* frileux **(c)** *Fig (person, manner, welcome)* froid; *(politeness)* glacial
chime¹ [tʃaɪm] *n* **c. (of bells)** carillon *m*; **the chimes of St. Mary's** le carillon de St. Mary; **to ring the chimes** carillonner; **(door) chimes** carillon de porte

chime² **1** *vi* (*of clock, bells*) carillonner **2** *vt* **(a)** (*bells*) sonner en carillon **(b)** (*of clock*) (*the hour*) sonner

▶ **chime in** *vi F* **(a)** (*intervene*) placer son mot, intervenir; **they all chimed in at once** ils sont tous intervenus en même temps **(b)** (*agree*) **his story chimes in with what we already know** sa version correspond à ce que nous savons déjà

chimera [kaɪ'mɪərə, kɪ-] *n Myth, Lit Fig* chimère *f*; *Fig* **to pursue a c.** poursuivre des chimères

chiming ['tʃaɪmɪŋ] **1** *adj* carillonnant; (*clock*) à carillon **2** *n* carillonnement *m*, carillon *m*

chimney ['tʃɪmnɪ] *n* **(a)** (*of house, factory*) cheminée *f*; *F* **to smoke like a c.** (*of person*) fumer comme un sapeur; **c. breast** manteau *m* de (la) cheminée; **c. corner** coin *m* du feu; **c. stack** (*of house*) tuyau *m* de cheminée; (*of factory*) cheminée (d'usine); **c. sweep** ramoneur *m* **(b)** (*in mountaineering*) cheminée *f*

chimneypiece ['tʃɪmnɪpiːs] *n esp Br* (manteau *m* de) cheminée *f*

chimneypot ['tʃɪmnɪpɒt] *n* mitre *f*

chimpanzee [tʃɪmpæn'ziː, *US* tʃɪm'pænziː] *F* **chimp** [tʃɪmp] *n* chimpanzé *m*

chin [tʃɪn] *n* menton *m*; *Fig* **to keep one's c. up** tenir bon, tenir le coup; *Fig* **to take sth on the c.** encaisser qch sans broncher; **she took the news on the c.** elle a écouté la nouvelle sans broncher; **c. strap** (*on helmet*) jugulaire *f*

China ['tʃaɪnə] *n* Chine *f*; **the C. Sea** la mer de Chine; **C. tea** thé *m* de Chine

china ['tʃaɪnə] *n* **(a)** (*no pl*) (*material*) porcelaine *f*; (*plates etc*) vaisselle *f* (de porcelaine); **made of c.** en porcelaine; **c. clay** kaolin *m*; **c. doll** poupée *f* en porcelaine; **c. plate** assiette *f* en porcelaine **(b)** *Br Sl* (*friend*) pote *m*; **my old c.!** mon vieux!

Chinagraph® ['tʃaɪnəgrɑːf] *n* (*pencil*) crayon *m* gras

Chinaman, *pl* **-men** ['tʃaɪnəmən] *n Old-fashioned* Chinois *m*

Chinatown ['tʃaɪnətaʊn] *n* quartier *m* chinois; **in C.** dans le quartier chinois

chinaware ['tʃaɪnəweər] *n* porcelaine *f*

chinchilla [tʃɪn'tʃɪlə] *n* (*rodent, fur*) chinchilla *m*; **c. coat/jacket** manteau/veste en chinchilla

chin-chin *int F* (*as a toast*) santé!, à la vôtre/la tienne!

chine [tʃaɪn] *n Anat, Culin* échine *f*

Chinese [tʃaɪ'niːz] **1** *adj* chinois; **the C. Ambassador** l'ambassadeur *m* de Chine; *Culin* **C. cabbage** *or* **leaves** chou *m* chinois; **C. checkers** dames *fpl* chinoises; **C. gooseberry** kiwi *m*; **C. lantern** lanterne *f* vénitienne; **C. white** blanc *m* de Chine **2** *n* **(a)** Chinois, -oise **(b)** *Ling* chinois *m* **(c)** *F* (*food*) **I feel like a c. tonight** j'ai envie de manger chinois ce soir

Chink [tʃɪŋk] *n Offensive Sl* (*Chinese*) Chinetoque *mf*

chink¹ [tʃɪŋk] *n* (*gap*) (*in wall etc*) fente *f*, crevasse *f*, lézarde *f*; (*in door*) entrebâillement *m*; *Fig* **to have a c. in one's armour** avoir une faiblesse; **the c. in sb's armour** le talon d'Achille de qn

chink² *n* (*sound*) tintement *m*

chink³ **1** *vt* (*money*) faire sonner *ou* tinter; (*glasses etc*) faire tinter **2** *vi* sonner (sec)

Chinky ['tʃɪŋkɪ] *n Offensive F* **(a)** (*restaurant*) (restaurant *m*) chinois *m*; (*meal*) repas *m* chinois **(b)** (*person*) Chinetoque *mf*

chinless ['tʃɪnlɪs] *adj* au menton fuyant; *Br F* **c. wonder** *terme normalement appliqué à un (jeune) homme de la haute bourgeoisie ou de l'aristocratie dont ni la physionomie ni la personnalité ne font marque; un menton fuyant est censé être un des traits marquants de cette classe sociale; par ex.* Cynthia will be bringing her new boyfriend – no doubt a c. wonder she met at a fox hunt

chino ['tʃiːnəʊ] *n Tex* chino *m*; **chinos** (*trousers*) chinos *mpl*; **a pair of chinos** une paire de chinos

chintz [tʃɪnts] *n Tex* chintz *m*, perse *f*, indienne *f*; **c. curtains** rideaux de chintz

chinwag ['tʃɪnwæg] *n Br F* causette *f*; **to have a c.** tailler une bavette (**with** avec)

chip¹ [tʃɪp] *n* **(a)** (*small piece*) (*of wood*) éclat *m*, copeau *m*; (*of marble*) écaille *f*, éclat; (*of chocolate*) pépite *f*; **diamond chips** semence *f* de diamants; *Fig* **he's a c. off the old block** c'est son père tout craché; *Fig* **to have a c. on one's shoulder** être aigri, en vouloir à tout le monde; **get rid of that c. on your shoulder** cessez d'en vouloir à tout le monde
(b) (*piece missing*) (*in plate*) ébréchure *f*; (*in knife blade*) brèche *f*; **this cup has a c.** cette tasse est ébréchée
(c) *Br Culin* (*usu pl*) (*Am = French fries*) **chips** frites *fpl*
(d) *Am Culin* (*Br = crisps*) **chips** (pommes *fpl*) chips *mpl*
(e) *Cards etc* jeton *m*; *Fig* **when the chips are down** aux moments critiques; *Fig F* **he's had his chips** il est cuit *ou* fichu
(f) *Comptr* (**silicon**) **c.** puce *f*; **c. manufacturer** fabricant *m* de pastilles de silicium; **c. technology** technologie *f* des puces
(g) *Sp* (*shot*) pichenette *f*

chip² (-pp-) **1** *vt* **(a)** (*cut at*) tailler **(b)** (*damage*) (*knife, plate*) ébrécher; (*furniture*) écorner; (*enamel*) écailler; (*tooth*) casser **(c)** *Sp* (*ball*) prendre en dessous, donner une pichenette à; **he chipped the ball over the net** d'une pichenette, il a envoyé la balle au-dessus du filet **2** *vi* (*of stone, china*) s'ébrécher

chip away **1** *vtsep* (*plaster etc*) décaper, enlever petit à petit **2** *vi* (*of plaster*) s'écailler

chip away at *vipo* **to c. away at the old paintwork** enlever la vieille peinture petit à petit; **to c. away at sb's authority** grignoter l'autorité de qn; **just keep chipping away at him until he changes his mind** continuez à le travailler au corps jusqu'à ce qu'il change d'avis

▶ **chip in** **1** *vi* **(a)** *F* (*contribute*) (*in collection*) participer; (*in discussion*) intervenir; *Pej* (*interrupt*) s'emmêler, mettre son grain de sel; **they chipped in to buy her a present** ils ont tous participé à l'achat de son cadeau; **if everyone chips in with an idea** si chacun proposait une idée **(b)** *Cards* miser **2** *vtsep F* (*contribute*) donner; **everyone chipped in £5** tout le monde a donné 5 livres

▶ **chip off** **1** *vi* (*fall off, break off*) (*of paint etc*) s'écailler **2** *vtsep* (*break off*) enlever **somebody had chipped the nose off the statue** quelqu'un avait cassé le nez de la statue; **to c. a piece off a plate** ébrécher une assiette

chip basket *n Br* panier *m* de friteuse

chipboard ['tʃɪpbɔːd] *n Carp* aggloméré *m*; **a piece of c.** un panneau d'aggloméré

chip cutter *n Br* coupe-frites *m inv*

chipmunk ['tʃɪpmʌŋk] *n* tamia *m* rayé, écureuil *m* rayé, *Can* suisse *m* rayé *ou* barré

chipolata [tʃɪpə'lɑːtə] *n esp Br Culin* **c.** (**sausage**) chipolata *f*

chip pan *n Br* friteuse *f*

chipped [tʃɪpt] *adj* **(a)** (*knife, plate*) ébréché; (*enamel*) écaillé; (*tooth*) cassé **(b)** *Culin Am* **c. beef** = bœuf *m* séché ou fumé coupé en tranches fines; *Br* **c. potatoes** pommes *fpl* (de terre) frites

chipper ['tʃɪpər] *adj F* (*person*) gai, vif

chippings ['tʃɪpɪŋz] *npl* (*of stone, marble*) éclats *mpl*; (**wood**) **c.** copeaux *mpl* (de bois); **loose c.** (*road sign*) gravillons *mpl*, *Can* gravelle *f*

chippy ['tʃɪpɪ] *n Br F* **(a)** (*fish and chip shop*) friterie *f* **(b)** *Old-fashioned* (*carpenter*) charpentier *m*

chipset [tʃɪpset] *n Comptr* ensemble *m* de puces

chip shop *n Br* friterie *f*

chiromancer ['kaɪərəʊmænsər] *n* chiromancien, -ienne

chiromancy ['kaɪərəʊmænsɪ] *n* chiromancie *f*

chiropodist [kɪ'rɒpədɪst] *n Med* pédicure *mf*

chiropody [kɪ'rɒpədɪ] *n Med* pédicurie *f*

chiropractic [kaɪrə'præktɪk] *n Med* chiropraxie *f*

chiropractor ['kaɪrəpræktər] *n Med* chiropracteur *m*

chirp¹ [tʃɜːp] *n* (*of birds*) pépiement *m*, gazouillement *m*, gazouillis *m*; (*of chick*) piaulement *m*; (*of grasshopper*) chant *m*

chirp² *vti* **(a)** (*of bird*) pépier, gazouiller; (*of chick*) piauler; (*of grasshopper*) chanter **(b)** (*of person*) babiller

chirpily ['tʃɜːpɪlɪ] *adv F* gaiement

chirpiness ['tʃɜːpɪnɪs] *n F* humeur *f* joyeuse

chirpy ['tʃɜːpɪ] *adj F* d'humeur joyeuse

chirrup¹ ['tʃɪrəp] *n* = **chirp¹**

chirrup² *vti* = **chirp²**

chisel¹ ['tʃɪz(ə)l] *n* ciseau *m*, burin *m*; **wood c.** ciseau à bois; **hollow c.** gouge *f*; **cold c.** ciseau à froid, burin

chisel² *vt* (-ll-, *US* -l-) **(a)** (*wood, stone*) ciseler; (*metal*) buriner, ciseler; **to c. sth off** enlever qch au burin **(b)** *Sl* (*cheat*) rouler; **to c. sb out of sth** rouler qn de qch

chiselled ['tʃɪz(ə)ld] *adj* **delicately c. features** visage délicatement ciselé

chiseller ['tʃɪz(ə)lər] *n Sl* (*swindler*) escroc *m*

chit¹ [tʃɪt] *n Old-fashioned F* (*child*) mioche *mf*, gosse *mf*, gamin, -ine; (*girl*) jeune fille *f ou* femme *f*

chit² *n* (*note*) petit mot *m*, billet *m*; (*for money owed*) note *f*

chitchat ['tʃɪttʃæt] *n F* bavardage *m*, papotage *m*

chitterlings, chitlings, chitlins ['tʃɪtəlɪŋz, 'tʃɪtlɪŋz, 'tʃɪtlɪns] *npl Old-fashioned Culin* = tripes *fpl*

chivalrous ['ʃɪvəlrəs] *adj* courtois; *Hist* (*worthy of a knight*) chevaleresque

chivalrously ['ʃɪvəlrəslɪ] *adv* courtoisement; *Hist* chevaleresquement

chivalry ['ʃɪvəlrɪ] *n* **(a)** (*of medieval knight*) chevalerie *f*; **in the days of c.** aux temps de la chevalerie **(b)** (*courteous behaviour*) courtoisie *f*; *esp Hum* **it's nice to see c. is not dead** ça fait plaisir de voir que la galanterie n'a pas entièrement disparu

chives [tʃaɪvz] *npl* ciboulette *f*, civette *f*

chiv(v)y ['tʃɪvɪ] *vt Br F* (*pester*) harceler; **to c. sb into doing**

sth harceler qn jusqu'à ce qu'il fasse qch; **you'll have to c. them along** il faudra que tu les presses un peu; **go and c. them along** va leur dire de se dépêcher

chlamydia [klə'mɪdɪə] *n Med* chlamydia *f*

chloral ['klɔːr(ə)l] *n Ch* chloral *m*

chlorate ['klɔːreɪt] *n Ch* chlorate *m*

chloric ['klɔːrɪk] *adj Ch* (*acid etc*) chlorique

chloride ['klɔːraɪd] *n Ch* chlorure *m*; **c. of silver** chlorure d'argent

chlorinate ['klɒrɪneɪt] *vt* (*water*) chlo(ru)rer

chlorination [klɒrɪ'neɪʃən] *n* chloration *f*; **c. plant** (*equipment*) appareil *m* de chloration; **c. plant** *or* **works** usine *f* de chloration

chlorine ['klɔːriːn] *n Ch* chlore *m*

chlorite ['klɔːraɪt] *n* (**a**) *Ch* chlorite *m* (**b**) *Miner* chlorite *f*

chlorofluorocarbon [klɒrə'flʊərəʊkɑːbən] *n* chlorofluorocarbone *m*

chloroform[1] ['klɒrəfɔːm] *n* chloroforme *m*

chloroform[2] *vt* chloroformer

chlorophyl(l) ['klɒrəfɪl] *n Ch, Bot* chlorophylle *f*

chloroquine ['klɔːrəʊkwiːn] *n Med* chloroquine *f*

choc [tʃɒk] *n F* **a box of chocs** une boîte de chocolats

chocaholic [tʃɒkə'hɒlɪk] *n F* accro *mf* du chocolat

choc-ice ['tʃɒkaɪs] *n* = esquimau *m* au chocolat

chock[1] [tʃɒk] *n* (*under car wheel, door etc*) cale *f*; *Av* **to remove the chocks** enlever les cales; **chocks away!** enlevez les cales!

chock[2] *vt* (**a**) (*barrel, wheel, door*) caler (**b**) (*in engineering etc*) (*part*) coincer

chock-a-block *adj F* plein à craquer, bourré (**with** de)

chock-full *adj F* bourré (**of** de)

chocolate ['tʃɒklət] **1** *n* (*also drink*) chocolat *m*; **c. bar, bar of c.** tablette *f* de chocolat; **white c.** chocolat blanc; **cooking c.** chocolat à cuire; **drinking c.** (*drink*) chocolat; (*powder*) chocolat en poudre; **hot c.** chocolat chaud; **a c.** un chocolat; **c. biscuit/ice cream/cake** biscuit/glace/gâteau au chocolat; **c. chip cookies** biscuits aux pépites de chocolat *ou Can* brisures de chocolat; **c. factory** chocolaterie *f* **2** *adj* (**a**) (*coloured*) **c. (brown)** chocolat *inv* (**b**) (*made of chocolate*) en chocolat; (*chocolate-flavoured*) au chocolat, chocolaté

choice[1] [tʃɔɪs] *n* (**a**) (*act of choosing*) choix *m*; **to make** *or* **take one's c.** faire son choix, choisir; **a difficult/easy c.** un choix difficile/facile; **by** *or* **out of c.** par choix; **to do sth of one's own c.** faire qch volontairement

(**b**) (*thing chosen*) choix *m*; **the red wine was her c.** c'est elle qui avait choisi le vin rouge; **Spain would be my c.** je choisirais l'Espagne

(**c**) (*alternative*) choix *m*; **to have the c. of two evils** avoir le choix entre deux maux; **what c. did she have?** (*rhetorical*) qu'est-ce qu'elle pouvait faire d'autre?; **you have no c. in the matter** vous n'avez pas le choix

(**d**) (*selection*) assortiment *m*, choix *m*; **available in a c. of colours** disponible en plusieurs couleurs; **there isn't much c.** il n'y a pas grand choix; **to have a wide c.** avoir amplement de quoi choisir; *Mktg* **c. set** ensemble *m* de considérations, éventail *m* de choix

choice[2] *adj* (**a**) (*well chosen*) bien choisi; **in a few c. sentences** en quelques phrases bien choisies; *Hum* **she used some c. language** elle a juré comme un charretier (**b**) (*of good quality*) (*article*) de choix; (*wine*) fin

choir ['kwaɪər] *n* (**a**) [ⓘA11,g,i] *Mus* chœur *m*, chorale *f*; **male voice c.** chœur *ou* chorale d'hommes; **c. practice** répétition *f* chorale; *Rel* **c. school** maîtrise *f*, manécanterie *f* (**b**) *Archit* (*of church*) chœur *m*; **c. stall** stalle *f*; **c. screen** jubé *m*

choirboy ['kwaɪəbɔɪ] *n Rel* jeune choriste *m*, petit chanteur *m*

choirmaster ['kwaɪəmɑːstər] *n Rel* maître *m* de chapelle *ou* de chœur

choke[1] [tʃəʊk] *n* (**a**) *Aut* starter *m*; (*on carburettor*) buse *f*; **to pull out the c.** mettre le starter; **you've given it too much c.** tu as mis trop de starter; **c. cable** câble *m* de starter (**b**) (*in voice*) étranglement *m* (**c**) **c. chain** (*for dog*) collier *m* étrangleur (**d**) (*of artichoke*) foin *m* (**e**) *El* **c. (coil)** bobine *f* d'impédance, self *f*

choke[2] **1** *vt* (**a**) (*strangle*) étouffer, suffoquer; (*of weeds*) (*flowers*) étouffer; **voice choked with sobs** voix entrecoupée par les sanglots (**b**) (*block*) (*pipe etc*) obstruer, boucher (**with** de); **the streets were choked with traffic** les rues étaient congestionnées **2** *vi* (**a**) (*become stifled*) étouffer; **I choked on a bone** je me suis étranglé avec un os; **he was choking with anger** il suffoquait de colère; **to c. with laughter** s'étrangler de rire (**b**) *Sl* (*die*) clamser

▶ **choke back** *vtsep* (*suppress*) (*tears, words, anger*) refouler, ravaler

▶ **choke up** *vtsep* (*block*) boucher, obstruer; **the drain is all choked up with leaves** la bouche d'égout est complètement obstruée par les feuilles; **she was all choked up** (*upset*) elle était bouleversée *ou* toute émue

choked [tʃəʊkt] *adj Br F* (*disappointed*) déçu; (*annoyed*) ennuyé

choker ['tʃəʊkər] *n* (*necklace*) collier *m* de chien

choking ['tʃəʊkɪŋ] **1** *adj* étouffant, suffocant; **he made a c. sound** il a fait un bruit comme quelqu'un qui s'étouffe **2** *n* étouffement *m*, suffocation *f*

cholera ['kɒlərə] *n* choléra *m*; **to have c.** avoir le choléra

choleric ['kɒlərɪk, kə'lerɪk] *adj Fml* colérique, coléreux

cholesterol [kɒ'lestərɒl] *n Med* cholestérol *m*; **c. level** taux *m* de cholestérol; **with a high/low c. content** riche/pauvre en cholestérol

chomp[1] [tʃɒmp] *vti* mâcher bruyamment

chomp[2] *n* mâchonnement *m* bruyant

choo-choo ['tʃuːtʃuː] *n Br F* (*in children's language*) petit train *m*; **the train goes c.** le train fait tchou-tchou

chook [tʃuːk] *n Austr F* (*chicken*) poulet *m*

choose [tʃuːz] (*pt* **chose** [tʃəʊz]; *pp* **chosen** ['tʃəʊz(ə)n]) **1** *vt* choisir; **there is nothing to c. between them** l'un vaut l'autre, ils se valent; **I didn't c. to go there** je n'ai pas choisi d'y aller; **since you chose not to accept** puisque vous avez décidé de ne pas accepter; **well if you will c. to ignore my advice** bon, si tu préfères ne pas tenir compte de mes conseils **2** *vi* choisir; **c. for yourself** je vous laisse le choix; **to pick and c.** se montrer difficile, faire le/la difficile; **I'll do as I c.** je ferai comme il me plaît *ou* comme bon me semble; **to c. from** *or* **between several people** choisir entre *ou* parmi plusieurs personnes

chooser ['tʃuːz(ə)r] *n Comptr* sélecteur *m*

choosing ['tʃuːzɪŋ] *n* choix *m*; **it was none of my c.** ce n'est pas moi qui l'ai choisi; **the circumstances were not of his c.** les circonstances n'étaient pas de son fait

choosy ['tʃuːzɪ] *adj F* difficile; **I'm not c.** (*at this moment*) ça m'est égal; (*in general*) je ne suis pas difficile; **don't be so c.** ne fais pas le difficile; **he isn't too c. who he does business with** il n'est pas très difficile quant aux gens avec lesquels il traite

chop[1] [tʃɒp] *n* (**a**) (*blow*) (*with axe etc*) coup *m*; *F* **to get the c.** (*of person*) se faire saquer, être mis à la porte; (*of project*) être annulé; (*of chapter, part of text, film etc*) être supprimé (**b**) *Culin* (*pork, lamb*) côtelette *f* (**c**) (*in karate etc*) coup *m* porté avec le tranchant de la main; *Tennis* **c. (stroke)** volée *f* coupée-arrêtée

chop[2] (**-pp-**) **1** *vt* (**a**) (*wood*) couper, fendre; (*meat, vegetables etc*) couper en morceaux; **to c. sth in(to) pieces** couper qch en morceaux; **to c. sth finely** hacher qch menu; **to c. logic** couper les cheveux en quatre (**b**) *Tennis* (*ball*) couper **2** *vi F* **c., c.!** vite, vite!

chop[3] *vi* **to c. and change** changer sans cesse; **he's always chopping and changing** (*changing his mind*) il change d'opinion à tout bout de champ; (*changing policy/ approach*) il change de politique/méthode tout le temps

▶ **chop at** *vipo* (*sth*) (*with axe, knife etc*) donner des coups à; (*aim blow at*) tenter de porter un coup à

▶ **chop down** *vtsep* (*tree etc*) abattre

▶ **chop off** *vtsep* trancher, couper; **to c. sb's head off** trancher la tête à qn

▶ **chop up** *vtsep* couper en morceaux, hacher

chophouse ['tʃɒphaʊs] *n* grill *m*

chopper ['tʃɒpər] *n* (**a**) (*tool*) couperet *m*, hachoir *m* (**b**) (*person*) (*of wood*) fendeur, -euse (**c**) *F* (*helicopter*) hélicoptère *m* (**d**) (*motorcycle*) chopper *m*; (*bicycle*) vélo *m* cross (**e**) *Vulg* (*penis*) bite *f*

choppers ['tʃɒpəz] *npl F* (*false teeth*) râtelier *m*; (*teeth*) ratiches *fpl*

chopping ['tʃɒpɪŋ] *n* (*of wood*) coupe *f*; **c. block** billot *m*; **c. board** planche *f* à hacher, hachoir *m*; **c. knife** couperet *m*, hachoir

choppy ['tʃɒpɪ] *adj* (*sea, lake*) agité

chops [tʃɒps] *npl F* bajoues *fpl*; **he had a smile all over his fat c.** un large sourire lui couvrait la tronche; **to lick one's c.** se lécher les babines

chopsticks ['tʃɒpstɪks] *npl* baguettes *fpl*

chop suey ['suːɪ] *n* chop suey *m*

choral ['kɔːr(ə)l] *adj Mus* choral, -als; **c. society** chorale *f*; **c. symphony** symphonie *f* avec chœur

choral(e) [kə'rɑːl] *n Mus* (**a**) (*hymn*) choral *m*, *pl* -als (**b**) *US* (*choir*) chorale *f*

chord[1] [kɔːd] *n Mus* accord *m*; **a c. sequence** une suite d'accords; **c. progression** progression *f* harmonique

chord[2] *n* (**a**) (*of harp*) corde *f*; *Fig* **to strike a c., to strike the right c.** faire vibrer la corde sensible; **his words struck a c. with the audience** ses paroles ont trouvé un écho auprès du public (**b**) *Math* (*of arc*) corde *f*

chore [tʃɔːr] *n* **(a)** (*usu pl*) **chores** (*in household*) travaux *mpl* ménagers; **the daily chores** les travaux quotidiens; **to do the chores** faire le ménage **(b)** (*unwelcome task*) corvée *f*
choreograph ['kɒrɪəgrɑːf] *vt* (*ballet, show*) faire la chorégraphie de
choreographer [kɒrɪ'ɒgrəfər] *n* chorégraphe *mf*
choreographic [kɒrɪə'græfɪk] *adj* chorégraphique
choreography [kɒrɪ'ɒgrəfɪ] *n* chorégraphie *f*
chorister ['kɒrɪstər] *n* choriste *mf*
chortle[1] ['tʃɔːt(ə)l] *n F* gloussement *m* (de joie); **she gave a c.** elle a gloussé, elle a poussé un gloussement de joie
chortle[2] **1** *vi F* glousser (de joie), pousser un gloussement de joie **2** *vt* **oh, no, he chortled** ah non, dit-il dans un gloussement
chorus[1] *pl* **-uses** ['kɔːrəs, -əsɪz] *n* **(a)** (*of song*) refrain *m*; **to join in the c.** (*of several people*) chanter le refrain en chœur; (*of one person*) se joindre aux autres pour le refrain **(b)** [①A11,g,i] (*group of singers, actors*) chœur *m*; **in the c.** (*of musical*) dans les chœurs **(c) to sing in c.** chanter en chœur; **no!, they shouted in c.** non!, se sont-ils exclamés en chœur; **c. of praise** concert *m* de louanges; **a c. of criticism** une avalanche de critiques; **they greeted him with a c. of cheers** ils l'accueillirent avec des hourras
chorus[2] *vt* **(-s-)** dire en chœur; (*song*) chanter en chœur; **yes please!, they chorused** oui s'il vous plaît, ont-ils répondu en chœur
chorus girl *n* girl *f*
chorusmaster ['kɔːrəsmɑːstər] *n* maître *m* de chant
chosen ['tʃəʊz(ə)n] **1** *pp see* **choose 2** *adj* choisi; **the c. people** les élus *mpl*; **the c. few** les heureux élus **3** *npl* **the c.** les élus *mpl*
chough [tʃʌf] *n* (*bird*) crave *m* à bec rouge
chou(x) [ʃuː] *n Culin* **c. pastry** pâte *f* à choux
chow [tʃaʊ] *n* **(a)** (*dog*) chow-chow *m* **(b)** *F* (*food*) boustifaille *f*; **c. time** l'heure *f* du repas
▶ **chow down** *vi Am F* bouffer
chow-chow *n* (*dog*) chow-chow *m*
chowder ['tʃaʊdər] *n Am Culin* = soupe *f* de poissons/fruits de mer
Christ [kraɪst] **1** *n* Christ *m*, Jésus-Christ *m*; **the C. Child** l'Enfant Jésus *m* **2** *int F* bon Dieu!; **C. Almighty!** nom de Dieu!
christen ['krɪs(ə)n] *vt* **(a)** (*person, ship*) baptiser; (*nickname*) surnommer; **to c. a child George** baptiser un enfant Georges **(b)** (*use for first time*) étrenner
Christendom ['krɪs(ə)ndəm] *n* chrétienté *f*; **throughout C.** dans toute la chrétienté; **he's the biggest fool in C.** c'est l'homme le plus bête du monde
christening ['krɪs(ə)nɪŋ] *n* baptême *m*; **c. ceremony** cérémonie *f* du *ou* de baptême; **c. robe** (*for baby*) robe *f* de baptême
Christian ['krɪstʃən] *Rel* **1** *n* chrétien, -ienne; **to be a C.** être chrétien **2** *adj* **(a)** chrétien; **C. burial** sépulture *f* en terre sainte; **C. charity** charité *f* chrétienne; **the C. era** l'ère *f* chrétienne **(b)** (*good, kind*) chrétien, de chrétien; **that wasn't very C. of you** ce n'était pas très aimable de ta part; **that's not a very C. attitude** ce n'est pas une attitude très chrétienne
Christianity [krɪstɪ'ænɪtɪ] *n* christianisme *m*; **in a spirit of C.** en chrétien
Christianize ['krɪstʃənaɪz] *vt* christianiser, convertir au christianisme
Christian name *n* prénom *m*
Christian Scientist *n* scientiste *mf* chrétien, -ienne
Christmas ['krɪsməs] *n* Noël *m*; **at C.** à (la) Noël; **to spend C. at home** passer Noël chez soi; **Merry** *or* **Happy C.!** joyeux Noël!; **Father C.** le père Noël; **C. dinner/present** repas *m*/ cadeau *m* de Noël; **C. box** étrennes *fpl*; **C. cake** gâteau *m* de Noël (*aux fruits secs*); **C. stocking** ≈ soulier *m ou* sabot *m* de Noël
Christmas card *n* carte *f* de Noël
Christmas carol *n* (chant *m* de) noël *m*
Christmas Day *n* jour *m* de Noël; **on C.** le jour de Noël
Christmas Eve *n* veille *f* de Noël
Christmas pudding *n* pudding *m* de Noël, plum-pudding *m*
Christmas rose *n Bot* rose *f* de Noël
Christmassy ['krɪsməsɪ] *adj F* typique de Noël; **to be in a C. mood** être dans l'ambiance de Noël; **not in a C. mood** pas d'humeur à supporter Noël; **it all looks so C.** c'est tout décoré pour Noël
Christmastide ['krɪsməstaɪd] *n Old-fashioned* période *f* de Noël; **at C.** à la Noël
Christmas tree *n* sapin *m* de Noël
Christopher Columbus ['krɪstəfər] *n* Christophe Colomb
chromatic [krəʊ'mætɪk] *adj Mus, Phys* chromatique
chromatography [krəʊmə'tɒgrəfɪ] *n* chromatographie *f*
chrome [krəʊm] *n* **(a) c. (steel)** acier *m* chromé *ou* au chrome; **c. nickel** nickel-chrome *m*; **c. tape** bande *f* magnétique chromée **(b)** *Art* **c. yellow** jaune *m* de chrome
chromium ['krəʊmɪəm] *n Ch* chrome *m*; **c. plating** chromage *m*; **c.-plated** chromé
chromosome ['krəʊməsəʊm] *n Biol* chromosome *m*; **X-c.** chromosome X
chronic ['krɒnɪk] *adj* **(a)** *Med, Fig* chronique; **to suffer from c. ill health** être de santé fragile; **c. invalid** invalide *mf* chronique; *Fig* **a c. drunkard/liar** un buveur/menteur invétéré; **c. unemployment** chômage *m* chronique **(b)** *Br F* (*very bad*) atroce; **their singing was c.** ils chantaient atrocement mal; **my back was hurting something c.** j'avais un mal de dos chronique
chronically ['krɒnɪklɪ] *adv* chroniquement
chronicity [krɒ'nɪsɪtɪ] *n Med* chronicité *f*
chronicle[1] ['krɒnɪk(ə)l] *n* chronique *f*; *Fig* **a c. of disasters** une suite de catastrophes; *Bible* **(the book of) Chronicles** les Chroniques
chronicle[2] *vt* **to c. events** faire la chronique d'événements
chronicler ['krɒnɪklər] *n* chroniqueur *m*
chronological [krɒnə'lɒdʒɪk(ə)l] *adj* (*order etc*) chronologique; **c. filing** classement *m* par ordre chronologique
chronologically [krɒnə'lɒdʒɪklɪ] *adv* chronologiquement, par ordre chronologique
chronology [krə'nɒlədʒɪ] *n* chronologie *f*
chronometer [krə'nɒmɪtər] *n* chronomètre *m*
chronometry [krə'nɒmɪtrɪ] *n* chronométrie *f*
chrysalid ['krɪsəlɪd], **chrysalis,** *pl* **chrysalises** ['krɪsəlɪs, 'krɪsəlɪsɪz] *n Ent* chrysalide *f*
chrysanthemum [krɪ'sænθəməm] *n* chrysanthème *m*
chub [tʃʌb] *n* (*fish*) chevesne *m*, meunier *m*
chubbiness ['tʃʌbɪnɪs] *n* (*of person*) apparence *f* potelée
chubby ['tʃʌbɪ] **1** *adj* (*person*) potelé, boulot, dodu, grassouillet; (*hands*) potelé; (*face*) joufflu; (*cheeks*) rebondi; **c.-cheeked** aux joues rebondies **2** *n* **come on, c.!** allez, gros dodu!
chuck[1] [tʃʌk] *vt* **(a)** *F* (*throw*) (*stone etc*) balancer; **c. me that hammer** balance-moi le marteau; **to c. one's money about** *or* **around** gaspiller son argent **(b)** *F* (*finish with*) (*job*) lâcher, laisser tomber; (*girlfriend, boyfriend*) plaquer **(c)** *F* (*throw away*) balancer, foutre en l'air **(d)** *Br F* **c. it!** (*stop it!*) arrête! **(e) to c. sb under the chin** donner une petite tape à qn sous le menton
chuck[2] *n* **(a)** *F* **to give sb the c.** (*from job*) virer *ou* sa(c)quer qn; (*from relationship*) plaquer qn **(b)** (*under the chin*) petite tape *f*
chuck[3] *n Tech* (*for lathe, drill*) mandrin *m*
▶ **chuck away** *vtsep F* balancer, flanquer *ou* foutre en l'air; **that's just chucking money away** ça c'est flanquer l'argent par les fenêtres
▶ **chuck in** *vtsep F* (*finish with*) (*job*) lâcher, laisser tomber; (*person*) plaquer, virer; **he chucked it all in and bought a farm** il a tout plaqué pour acheter une ferme; **to c. one's hand in** *Cards* jeter ses cartes sur la table; *Fig* (*admit defeat*) s'avouer vaincu
▶ **chuck off** *vtsep F* virer; **he was chucked off the team** il s'est fait virer de l'équipe
▶ **chuck on** *vtsep F* (*clothes, aftershave*) mettre
▶ **chuck out** *vtsep F* **(a)** (*throw away*) jeter **(b)** (*from pub, house etc*) flanquer à la porte, vider; *Br* **chucking-out time** l'heure *f* de la fermeture (des pubs)
▶ **chuck up** *F* **1** *vtsep* (*finish with*) (*job*) lâcher, laisser tomber; **she chucked everything up and became a nurse** elle a tout plaqué pour devenir infirmière **2** *vi esp Am* (*vomit*) vomir, rendre
chucker-out ['tʃʌkə'raʊt] *n Br F* (*in disco etc*) videur *m*
chuckle[1] ['tʃʌk(ə)l] *n* rire *m* étouffé, petit rire; **to give a c.** lâcher un petit rire
chuckle[2] *vi* rire tout bas *ou* en soi-même **(at, over** de**)**
chuck wagon *n Am F* = cantine *f* ambulante dans une exploitation agricole
chuff [tʃʌf] *vi* (*of train*) haleter
chuffed [tʃʌft] *adj Br F* tout content **(about** de**)**; **dead c. with his present** super content de son cadeau; **I'm really c. with myself** je suis tout content de moi
chug[1] [tʃʌg] *n* (*of steam engine*) souffle *m*
chug[2] *vi* **(-gg-)** (*of steam engine*) souffler, haleter
▶ **chug along** *vi F* (*move slowly*) avancer doucement; **the guy in front was chugging along at 30 km/h** le type devant moi se traînait à 30 à l'heure
chum [tʃʌm] *n F* camarade *mf*, copain *m*, copine *f*
▶ **chum up with** *vipo* **(-mm-)** *F* copiner avec
chummy ['tʃʌmɪ] *adj F* (bon) copain, *f* (bonne) copine; **she's**

quite c. with the boss elle est assez copine avec le patron; **he's a c. sort of bloke** c'est un type sympa (et sociable); **he's a bit too c. for my liking** il est un peu trop familier à mon goût

chump [tʃʌmp] *n* **(a)** *F (foolish person)* idiot, -ote **(b)** *Culin* **c. chop** côtelette *f* d'agneau (*coupée dans le gigot*) **(c)** *F (head)* **off one's c.** timbré, maboul

chunder ['tʃʌndər] *vi esp Austr Sl (vomit)* dégueuler

chunk [tʃʌŋk] *n* (*of bread, cheese etc*) gros morceau *m*; (*of bread*) quignon *m*; (*of wood*) tronçon *m*

chunky ['tʃʌŋkɪ] *adj F* **(a)** (*person*) trapu **(b)** (*pullover*) gros; (*glass*) solide

Chunnel ['tʃʌn(ə)l] *n F* **the C.** le tunnel sous la Manche, l'Eurotunnel

▶ **chunter away** ['tʃʌntər] *vi F* papoter; **he's still chuntering away about it** il continue son baratin; **with those two chuntering away in the background** avec ces deux-là qui papotent/papotaient dans le fond

church [tʃɜːtʃ] *n* [①A6,d,i] **(a)** (*building*) église *f*; (*French Protestant*) temple *m*; **to go to c.** aller à l'église; (*of Catholic*) aller à l'église *ou* à la messe; (*of French Protestant*) aller au temple; **I saw her in c. on Sunday** je l'ai vue à l'église dimanche; **c. service** office *m*, culte *m*; **c. wedding** mariage *m* religieux

(b) (*institution*) **the Anglican C.** l'Église anglicane; **to go into the C.** (*take orders*) entrer dans les ordres; **to leave the C.** quitter l'église; **High C.** = section *f* de l'Église anglicane qui se rapproche du catholicisme en matière de rituel; **Low C.** = section de l'Église anglicane qui se distingue par la simplicité du rituel; **the (Roman) Catholic C.** l'Église catholique

Church Fathers *npl* Pères *mpl* de l'Église

churchgoer ['tʃɜːtʃgəʊər] *n Rel* pratiquant, -ante; **an occasional c.** une personne qui va à l'église de temps en temps

churchgoing ['tʃɜːtʃgəʊɪŋ] *Rel* **1** *adj* pratiquant; **the c. public** les gens qui vont à l'église **2** *n* fréquentation *f* des églises; **c. is not regarded as an essential part of ...** aller à l'église n'est pas considéré comme une part essentielle de ...

church hall *n* salle *f* paroissiale

Churchillian [tʃɜː'tʃɪljən] *adj* churchillien

churchman, *pl* **-men** ['tʃɜːtʃmən] *n Rel* **(a)** (*clergyman*) homme *m* d'église **(b)** (*member of a church*) membre *m* d'une église

Church of England *n* Église *f* anglicane

churchwarden [tʃɜːtʃ'wɔːd(ə)n] *n* **(a)** *Rel* marguillier *m*, bedeau *m* **(b)** **c. (pipe)** longue pipe *f* (*en terre*), pipe hollandaise

churchwoman, *pl* **-women** ['tʃɜːtʃwʊmən, -wɪmɪn] *n Rel* **(a)** (*clergywoman*) femme *f* d'église **(b)** (*member of a church*) femme *f* membre d'une église

churchy ['tʃɜːtʃɪ] *adj F* calotin, bondieusard

churchyard ['tʃɜːtʃjɑːd] *n* (*graveyard*) cimetière *m*; (*grounds*) enclos *m* d'église

churl [tʃɜːl] *n* rustre *m*

churlish ['tʃɜːlɪʃ] *adj* (*rude*) grossier; (*surly*) (*behaviour, person*) revêche; **it would be c. to refuse** ce serait mal élevé de refuser

churlishly ['tʃɜːlɪʃlɪ] *adv* (*rudely*) avec grossièreté; (*in a surly way*) de façon revêche

churlishness ['tʃɜːlɪʃnɪs] *n* (*rudeness*) grossièreté *f*; (*surliness*) attitude *f* revêche; **he agreed, but with his usual c.** il accepta, revêche comme à l'ordinaire

churn¹ [tʃɜːn] *n* **(a)** *Agr* (*for butter*) baratte *f* **(b)** *Agr* (*for milk*) bidon *m* à lait **(c)** *Mktg* perte *f* de clients passés à la concurrence

churn² **1** *vt* (*milk, cream*) baratter; (*butter*) battre; **to c. water** (*of propellor etc*) faire des remous **2** *vi* (*of sea*) bouillonner; *Fig* **my stomach's churning** (*with nerves, excitement*) j'ai l'estomac noué

▶ **churn out** *vtsep F* (*produce in large numbers*) (*books etc*) produire en série, *F* pondre en série; (*objects*) produire en série

▶ **churn up** *vtsep* (*mud*) remuer; **to c. up water** faire bouillonner l'eau; *Fig* **I felt all churned up** (*nervous*) j'étais tout retourné; (*excited*) j'étais tout excité

churning ['tʃɜːnɪŋ] *n* (*of cream*) barattage *m*

chute [ʃuːt] *n* **(a)** (*for parcels etc*) glissière *f*; (*for coal*) déversoir *m*; (**rubbish** *or Am* **garbage**) **c.** vide-ordures *m inv* **(b)** *Sp* (*for sleds*) piste *f*; (*in swimming pool, playground*) toboggan *m* **(c)** (*waterfall*) chute *f* d'eau **(d)** *F* (*parachute*) parachute *m*

chutney ['tʃʌtnɪ] *n Culin* chutney *m*

chutzpah ['hʊtspə] *n* culot *m*

chyme [kaɪm] *n Med* chyme *m*

CIA [siːaɪ'eɪ] *n US Admin* (*abbr* **Central Intelligence Agency**) CIA *f*

ciborium, *pl* **-ia** [sɪ'bɔːrɪəm, -ɪə] *n Rel* (*vessel*) ciboire *m*

cicada [sɪ'kɑːdə, -'keɪdə] *n* (*insect*) cigale *f*

cicatrice ['sɪkətrɪs], **cicatrix** ['sɪkətrɪks] *n Fml* cicatrice *f*

Cicero ['sɪsərəʊ] *n* Cicéron *m*

cicerone [sɪsə'rəʊnɪ] *n Old-fashioned* cicérone *m*

CID [siːaɪ'diː] *n Br Admin* (*abbr* **Criminal Investigation Department**) ≈ P. J. *f*; **Joanna Smith, CID** Joanna Smith, de la P. J.

cider ['saɪdər] *n* **(a)** *Br* (*alcoholic drink*) cidre *m*; **c. apples** pommes *fpl* à cidre **(b)** *Am* (*apple juice*) jus *m* de pommes; **hard c.** cidre *m*

cider press *n* pressoir *m* à cidre

cider vinegar *n* vinaigre *m* de cidre

cif ['siːaɪef] *Com* (*abbr* **cost, insurance and freight**) CAF *m*

cigar [sɪ'gɑːr] *n* cigare *m*; **c. butt** mégot *m* de cigare; **c. case** étui *m* à cigares; **c. cutter** coupe-cigares *m inv*; **c. holder** fume-cigare *m*, *pl* fume-cigare(s); **c. lighter** (*in car*) allume-cigare(s) *m*; **c.-shaped** en forme de cigare

cigarette, *occ US* **cigaret** [sɪgə'ret] *n* cigarette *f*; **c. advertising** publicité *f* pour les cigarettes; **c. ash** cendre *f* de cigarette; **c. butt** mégot *m* de cigarette; **c. card** image *f* offerte avec un paquet de cigarettes; **c. case** étui *m* à cigarettes, porte-cigarettes *m inv*; **c. end** bout *m* de cigarette, mégot *m*; **c. holder** fume-cigarette *m*, *pl* fume-cigarettes; **c. packet** paquet *m* de cigarettes; **c. smoke** fumée *f* de cigarette; **c. smoker** fumeur, -euse (de cigarettes)

cigarette lighter *n* briquet *m*; (*in car*) allume-cigare(s) *m*

cigarette machine *n* (*vending machine*) distributeur *m* automatique de cigarettes; (*for rolling cigarettes*) rouleuse *f*

cigarette paper *n* papier *m* à cigarettes

ciggie ['sɪgɪ] *n Br F* tige *f*, clope *f*

CIM waybill [siːaɪ'em] *n Com* lettre *f* de voiture CIM

C(-)in(-)C [siːɪn'siː] *n Mil, Naut* (*abbr* **Commander in Chief**) commandant *m* en chef

cinch [sɪntʃ] *n* **(a)** *F* (*something very easy*) **it's a c.** c'est simple comme bonjour, c'est un jeu d'enfant **(b)** *F* (*certainty*) certitude *f*; **it's a c.** c'est certain *ou* couru **(c)** *Am* (*for horse*) sangle *f*, sous-ventrière *f*, *pl* sous-ventrières

cinder ['sɪndər] *n* cendre *f*; **burnt to a c.** (*meat, toast etc*) complètement carbonisé; *Am* **c. block** parpaing *m*; *Sp* **c. track** (piste *f*) cendrée *f*

Cinderella [sɪndə'relə] *n Liter* Cendrillon *f*; *Fig* **poetry has always been the C. of the arts** la poésie a toujours été le parent pauvre des arts

Cinders ['sɪndəz] *n F* Cendrillon *f*

cine ['sɪnɪ] *pref Br Cin* **c. camera** caméra *f*; **c. film** film *m*; **c. projector** projecteur *m* de cinéma

cinema ['sɪnəmə] *n* **(a)** (*art*) cinéma *m*; **French c.** le cinéma français; *TV* **c. channel** chaîne *f* de cinéma **(b)** *Br* (*place*) cinéma *m*; **to go to the c.** aller au cinéma; **c. advertising** publicité *f* au cinéma

cinemagoer ['sɪnəməgəʊər] *n* cinéphile *mf*; **he's not much of a c.** ce n'est pas un grand amateur de cinéma

cinema-going **1** *n* fréquentation *f* des salles de cinéma **2** *adj* **the c. public** les cinéphiles *mfpl*

cinematic [sɪnə'mætɪk] *adj* cinématique

cinematograph [sɪnə'mætəgræf] *n Br Old-fashioned* cinématographe *m*

cinematographer [sɪnəmə'tɒgrəfər] *n* directeur *m* de la photographie, chef opérateur *m*

cinematography [sɪnəmə'tɒgrəfɪ] *n* **(a)** (*technique*) cinématographie *f* **(b)** (*camerawork*) prises *fpl* de vue

cineraria [sɪnə'reərɪə] *n* (*plant*) cinéraire *f*

cinnabar ['sɪnəbɑːr] *n Miner* cinabre *m*

cinnamon ['sɪnəmən] **1** *n* **(a)** *Culin* cannelle *f*; **c. stick** bâton *m* de cannelle **(b)** *Bot* **c. (tree)** cannelier *m* **2** *adj* (*colour*) cannelle *inv*

cinq(ue)foil ['sɪŋkfɔɪl] *n* **(a)** (*plant*) potentille *f* rampante, quintefeuille *f* **(b)** *Archit* quintefeuille *m*

cipher¹ ['saɪfər] *n* **(a)** (*secret writing*) chiffre *m*, code *m*; (*message*) message *m* chiffré *ou* codé; **to write a message in c.** chiffrer un message; **c. clerk** chiffreur, -euse **(b)** (*monogram*) chiffre *m* **(c)** *Math* zéro *m*; *Fig* **he's a mere c.** c'est un zéro *ou* une nullité

cipher² *vt* (*message*) chiffrer

circa ['sɜːkə] *prep* (*of time*) aux alentours de; (*of amount*) environ

circadian [sɜː'keɪdɪən] *adj* circadien

circle¹ ['sɜːk(ə)l] *n* **(a)** *Math etc* cercle *m*; **to draw a c.** tracer un cercle; **to stand in a c.** (*of people*) se tenir en cercle; **the chairs were arranged in a c.** les chaises étaient disposées en cercle; *Fig* **to go round in circles** tourner en rond; **to have circles under one's eyes** avoir les yeux cernés, avoir des cernes sous les yeux; **Arctic/Antarctic C.** cercle (polaire) arctique/antarctique; *Gym* **to do a c. (on the horizontal bar)** faire le (grand) soleil; *Archeol* **stone c.** cercle de pierres

(b) (*movement*) (*of planet*) révolution *f*, orbite *f*; **to come full c.** (*of planet*) compléter son orbite; (*of argument, person walking*) revenir à son point de départ; (*of fashion, history*) revenir au même point

(c) *Th* **first c.** (premier) balcon *m*, corbeille *f*; **upper c.** deuxième balcon

(d) (*group*) cercle *m*, groupe *m*; **a c. of friends** un cercle d'amis; **the family c.** le cercle familial; **in certain circles** dans certains milieux; **in theatrical circles** dans le monde du théâtre; **the inner c.** (*of friends*) le cercle intime

circle[2] **1** *vt* **(a)** (*go round*) tourner autour de, faire le tour de **(b)** (*surround*) entourer (**with** de) **2** *vi* (*of plane, tiger around prey*) tourner; (*of birds*) tourner, tournoyer; **to c. round sth** tourner/tournoyer autour de qch; **the planes are circling overhead** les avions décrivent des cercles au-dessus de nos têtes; *Fig* **she circled round the issue** elle tournait autour du pot

circlet ['sɜːklɪt] *n* bandeau *m*

circlip ['sɜːklɪp] *n MecE* circlip *m*; **c. pliers** pince *f* à circlip

circuit ['sɜːkɪt] *n* **(a)** *El* circuit *m*; **in/out of c.** en/hors de circuit **(b)** (*journey, movement around*) (*of sun*) révolution *f*; (*of assizes judge*) tournée *f*; **to make one c. of the track** faire un tour de circuit; **to make a c. of the estate** faire le tour du domaine; **to make a wide c.** faire un grand détour; **to go on c.** (*of judge*) aller en tournée **(c)** (*route, places visited*) (*of assizes judge*) circonscription *f* de tournée, ressort *m*; (*series of venues etc*) circuit *m*; **the hottest act on the club c.** le meilleur numéro du circuit **(d)** *Sp* (*motor racing*) circuit *m*, parcours *m*

circuit board *n Comptr* plaquette *f*, carte *f* de circuits

circuit breaker *n* coupe-circuit *m inv*, disjoncteur *m*

circuit judge *n Jur* juge *m* itinérant

circuitous [sə'kjuːɪtəs] *adj* (*route*) détourné, indirect; (*reasoning*) long et compliqué; **by c. means** par des moyens détournés *ou* indirects

circuitously [sə'kjuːɪtəslɪ] *adv* (*to reach destination etc*) par le chemin le plus long; (*to reason etc*) avec beaucoup de circonvolutions; **the path winds c. to the summit** le chemin monte en lacets jusqu'au sommet

circuitry ['sɜːkɪtrɪ] *n* (*no pl*) *Electron* circuits *mpl*; **the c. on this board is really simple** le montage de cette plaquette est vraiment simple

circuit training *n Sp* programme *m* d'exercices en salle

circular ['sɜːkjʊlər] **1** *adj* (*movement, argument*) circulaire **2** *n* (lettre *f*) circulaire *f*; (*publicity material*) prospectus *m*; *Br Journ* **Court c.** rubrique *f* de la Cour (*décrivant les engagements de la famille royale*)

circularity [sɜːkjʊ'lærɪtɪ] *n* circularité *f*

circularize ['sɜːkjʊləraɪz] *vt* (*customers etc*) envoyer une/des circulaire(s) *ou* un/des prospectus à

circular saw *n* scie *f* circulaire

circulate ['sɜːkjʊleɪt] **1** *vi* (*of rumour, person at party, money*) circuler **2** *vt* **(a)** (*air, wine etc*) faire circuler **(b)** (*money*) mettre en circulation; (*news*) répandre, faire circuler

circulating ['sɜːkjʊleɪtɪŋ] *adj* circulant; *Acct* **c. assets** actif *m* circulant; **c. library** bibliothèque *f* ambulante *ou* mobile

circulation [sɜːkjʊ'leɪʃən] *n* **(a)** (*of air, liquid, news*) circulation *f*; **to put a book into c.** mettre un livre en circulation; **for private c.** (*in publishing*) hors commerce; **the memo was for internal c. only** c'était une note de service à usage interne uniquement; **newspaper with a large c.** journal à grand tirage; *Journ* **a c. of 500,000** un tirage de 500 000 exemplaires; *Journ* **c. figures** chiffres *mpl* de diffusion

(b) *Physiol* (*of blood etc*) circulation *f*; **to have poor** *or* **bad c.** avoir une mauvaise circulation; **to restore the c. in one's legs** se dégourdir les jambes

(c) (*of currency*) circulation *f* (de la monnaie); **to put forged notes into c.** mettre de faux billets en circulation; **notes in c.** billets en circulation; **to be in c.** être en circulation; *Fig* **to be in/out of c.** (*of person*) être/ne plus être dans le circuit; **to withdraw sth from c.** retirer qch de la circulation

circulatory [sɜːkjʊ'leɪt(ə)rɪ, 'sɜːkjʊlət(ə)rɪ] *adj Anat etc* circulatoire, de (la) circulation

circumcise ['sɜːkəmsaɪz] *vt* (*boy*) circoncire; (*girls*) exciser

circumcision [sɜːkəm'sɪʒən] *n* circoncision *f*; **female c.** excision *f*; *Rel* **the C.** la (fête de la) Circoncision

circumference [sə'kʌmfərəns] *n* circonférence *f*; **to be thirty metres in c.** avoir trente mètres de circonférence

circumflex ['sɜːkəmfleks] **1** *n Gram* accent *m* circonflexe **2** *adj* circonflexe

circumlocution [sɜːkəmlə'kjuːʃən] *n* circonlocution *f*, périphrase *f*; **without c.** sans ambages

circumlocutory [sɜːkəmlə'kjuːt(ə)rɪ] *adj* périphrastique

circumnavigate [sɜːkəm'nævɪgeɪt] *vt* faire le tour de (*par la mer*)

circumnavigation [sɜːkəmnævɪ'geɪʃən] *n* circumnavigation *f*

circumscribe ['sɜːkəmskraɪb] *vt* **(a)** (*limit*) (*powers, field of operations*) limiter, restreindre **(b)** *Math* (*circle etc*) circonscrire

circumscribed ['sɜːkəmskraɪbd] *adj* **(a)** (*limited*) restreint, limité **(b)** *Math* (*circle etc*) circonscrit

circumscription [sɜːkəm'skrɪpʃən] *n* **(a)** (*limitation*) restriction *f*, limitation *f* **(b)** *Math* circonscription *f*

circumspect ['sɜːkəmspekt] *adj* (*person, conduct*) circonspect, avisé, prudent; (*speech etc*) mesuré

circumspection [sɜːkəm'spekʃən] *n* circonspection *f*

circumspectly ['sɜːkəmspektlɪ] *adv* avec circonspection

circumstance ['sɜːkəmstəns] *n* **(a)** (*situation*) (*usu pl*) **circumstances** circonstances *fpl*; **in** *or* **under the circumstances** dans ces circonstances, en de telles circonstances; **in** *or* **under no circumstances** en aucun cas, sous aucun prétexte; **it depends on the circumstances** cela dépend des circonstances, *F* c'est selon; **he was the victim of c.** *or* **circumstances** il a été la victime des circonstances; **due to circumstances beyond our control** en raison de circonstances indépendantes de notre volonté; **by force of circumstances** par la force des choses

(b) (*financial situation*) **in easy circumstances** à l'aise; **if his circumstances allowed** si ses moyens le permettaient

(c) **with pomp and c.** en grande cérémonie, en grand apparat

circumstantial [sɜːkəm'stænʃəl] *adj* **(a)** (*indirect*) *Jur* **c. evidence** preuves *fpl* indirectes; **it's all a bit c.** il n'y a rien de concret **(b)** (*detailed*) détaillé, circonstancié

circumstantiate [sɜːkəm'stænʃɪeɪt] *vt Fml* (*report*) donner des détails circonstanciés sur

circumvent [sɜːkəm'vent] *vt* circonvenir; **to c. the law** contourner la loi

circumvention [sɜːkəm'venʃən] *n* (*of law etc*) contournement *m*

circus, *pl* **-uses** ['sɜːkəs, -əsɪz] *n* (*show, troupe*), *Antiq, Fig* cirque *m*; **to join a c.** entrer dans un cirque; *Av* **flying c.** parade *f* aérienne itinéraire; **travelling c.** cirque forain; **c. act** numéro *m* de cirque

cirrhosis [sɪ'rəʊsɪs] *n Med* cirrhose *f*; **c. of the liver** cirrhose du foie; **to have c.** avoir une cirrhose

cirrus, *pl* **-ri** ['sɪrəs, -raɪ] *n Met* cirrus *m*

cisalpine [sɪs'ælpaɪn] *adj* cisalpin; *Hist* **C. Gaul** la Gaule cisalpine

cissy ['sɪsɪ] *n, adj F Pej* = **sissy**

Cistercian [sɪ'stɜːʃən] *adj, n Rel* cistercien, -ienne; **the C. Order** l'ordre *m* de Cîteaux

cistern ['sɪstən] *n* (*in attic*) réservoir *m* d'eau; (*in lavatory*) réservoir de chasse d'eau; (*underground*) citerne *f*; (*of pump*) réservoir

citadel ['sɪtədəl, -del] *n* citadelle *f*

citation [saɪ'teɪʃən] *n* **(a)** (*from author*) citation *f* **(b)** *Mil* citation *f*; (*à l'ordre du jour*) **(c)** *Jur* (*summons*) citation *f* à comparaître

cite [saɪt] *vt* **(a)** (*quote*) (*passage, author, example*) citer **(b)** *Mil* (*soldier for heroism*) citer **(c)** *Jur* **to c. sb before a court** citer qn devant un tribunal

citizen ['sɪtɪzən] *n* **(a)** (*of nation*) citoyen, -enne; (*of city, town*) habitant, -ante; **c. of the world** citoyen du monde; **a private c.** un simple particulier **(b)** *Am* (*as opposed to army, navy*) civil *m*

citizen army *n* armée *f* de citoyens

citizen rights *npl* droits *mpl* civiques

citizenry ['sɪtɪzənrɪ] *n* ensemble *m* des habitants

Citizens' Advice Bureau *n Br* = service *m* gratuit d'aide juridique

citizen's arrest *n* = arrestation *f* effectuée par un individu en vertu du droit commun

citizens' band (radio) *n* (radio *f* de la) citizen band *f*

citizenship ['sɪtɪzənʃɪp] *n* (*of nation*) citoyenneté *f*; (*of city, town*) droit *m* de cité *ou* de bourgeoisie; **to be granted full c. of a country** se voir accorder la citoyenneté d'un pays; **good c.** civisme *m*

citrate ['sɪtreɪt] *n Ch* citrate *m*

citric ['sɪtrɪk] *adj Ch* (*acid etc*) citrique

citron ['sɪtrən] *n* (*fruit*) cédrat *m*; **c. (tree)** cédratier *m*

citronelle [sɪtrə'nel] *n* (*plant*) citronnelle *f*

citrus fruit ['sɪtrəs] *n* agrume *m*

City ['sɪtɪ] *n Br* **the C.** (*district*) la Cité de Londres; (*financial world*) le monde de la finance; *Journ* **C. pages** pages *fpl* financières

city ['sɪtɪ] *n* [①B6,3,e] (grande) ville *f*, *Lit* cité *f*; *Br* **cathedral c.** ville épiscopale, évêché *m*; **the Holy C.** la Ville sainte; **the Celestial C.** la Cité céleste; **the Eternal C.** la Ville éternelle; **the C. of Manchester** la ville de Manchester; **c. break** (*holiday*) court séjour *m* en ville; **c. children** enfants des (grandes) villes; **c. life** la vie citadine; **c. streets** rues *fpl* des grandes villes; *Journ* **c. editor** *Br* rédacteur, -trice de la rubrique financière; *Am* rédacteur, -trice de la chronique du jour; **c. fathers** édiles *mpl*
city centre *n* centre-ville *m*; **c. traffic/shops** circulation/ boutiques du centre-ville
city hall *n Am* hôtel *m* de ville; *Fig* **you can't win against c.** on ne peut pas gagner contre la bureaucratie
city ledger *n Acct* (*in hotels, business*) débiteurs *mpl* divers
city-state *n* état-cité *m*, *pl* états-cités
city terminal *n* (*of airline*) terminal *m* urbain
civet ['sɪvɪt] *n* (*animal, scent*) civette *f*
civic ['sɪvɪk] *adj* (*duty, pride etc*) civique; **the c. authorities** les autorités *fpl* municipales; **c. buildings** bâtiments *mpl* municipaux; *Br* **c. centre** centre *m* civique *ou* social; **c. rights** droits *mpl* civils
civics ['sɪvɪks] *n* [①A10,c] *Sch* instruction *f* civique
civies ['sɪvɪz] *npl F* vêtements *mpl* civils
civil ['sɪv(ə)l] *adj* **(a)** (*rights, marriage, year etc*) civil; *Jur* **c. action** *or* **proceedings** action *f* civile; **c. aircraft** appareil *m* de l'aviation civile; **c. air transport** transport *m* aérien civil; **c. airline** compagnie *f* d'aviation civile; **c. aviation** aviation *f* civile; **c. commotion** agitation *f* sociale; **c. defence** protection *f* civile **(b)** (*polite*) poli, *Vieilli* civil; **he was very c. to me/to them** il s'est montré très aimable; **keep a c. tongue in your head!** soyez plus poli!; **that's very c. of you** c'est bien aimable (de votre part)
civil engineer *n* ingénieur *m* des travaux publics
civil engineering *n* génie *m* civil
civilian [sɪ'vɪljən] **1** *n* civil, -ile **2** *adj* civil; **c. clothes** tenue *f* civile; **in c. life** dans le civil
civility [sɪ'vɪlɪtɪ] *n* courtoisie *f*, politesse *f*; **exchange of civilities** échange *m* d'amabilités
civilization [sɪvɪlaɪ'zeɪʃən] *n* civilisation *f*; *F* **it's miles from c.** c'est à des kilomètres de toute civilisation
civilize ['sɪvɪlaɪz] *vt* civiliser
civilized ['sɪvɪlaɪzd] *adj* (*life, people*) civilisé; **the little girl is really quite c.** la petite fille est très bien élevée; **they have real coffee in their office — very c.** ils ont du vrai café dans leur bureau — la classe!; **their divorce was a very c. affair** ils ont divorcé comme des gens civilisés; **let's be c. about this** restons civilisés; **can't you eat in a c. manner?** tu ne peux pas manger convenablement?
civilizing ['sɪvɪlaɪzɪŋ] *adj* **the c. influence of ...** l'influence civilisatrice de ...; **the new teacher has had a c. influence on them** le nouveau professeur semble les avoir calmés
civil law *n* (*law*) code *m* civil; (*subject*) droit *m* civil; (*Roman law*) droit romain
Civil List *n Br Admin* liste *f* civile (*budget de la famille royale*); **C. pension** pension *f* sur les fonds de la Couronne
civil rights *npl Jur* droits *mpl* civils; **c. activist/lawyer** activiste *mf*/avocat *m* cherchant à protéger les droits civils; **c. movement** mouvement *m* des droits civils
civil servant *n* fonctionnaire *mf*
civil service *n* administration *f* (civile), fonction *f* publique; **to be in the c.** être fonctionnaire *ou* dans l'administration *ou* dans la fonction publique
civil war *n* guerre *f* civile
civvies ['sɪvɪz] *npl F* vêtements *mpl* civils
civvy ['sɪvɪ] *adj F* **to get back to c. street** rentrer dans le civil; **on c. street** dans le civil
cl (*abbr* **centilitre**) cl.
clack¹ [klæk] *n* (*sound*) bruit *m* sec, claquement *m*; **click-c.** clic-clac *m*
clack² *vi* (*make sound*) cliqueter
clacking ['klækiŋ] *n* (*noise*) claquement *m*
clad¹ [klæd] *pt, pp see* **clothe**
clad² *vt* (**-dd-**) *Tech* (*wall, metal plate etc*) revêtir (**with** de)
cladding ['klædɪŋ] *n Tech* revêtement *m*
claim¹ [kleɪm] *n* **(a)** (*demand*) (*for damages, compensation etc*) revendication *f*, réclamation *f*; **to make** *or* **put in a c. for damages** demander une indemnité, réclamer des dommages-intérêts; **to put in a c.** (*in insurance*) demander à être indemnisé; **pay claim** revendications *fpl* salariales; **claims book** livre *m* des réclamations; **claims cover** garantie *f* de recours; **c. form** formulaire *m* de demande d'indemnité
(b) (*right*) droit *m* (**to sth** à qch); **legal c. to sth** titre *m* juridique à qch; **to put in a c.** faire valoir ses droits; **to have a c. to sth** avoir droit à qch; **what is her c. to the throne?** quel est son titre à la couronne?; **they have no c. to the land** ils n'ont aucun droit sur le terrain; **to lay c. to** (*property etc*) prétendre à, revendiquer son droit à; (*skills*) s'attribuer; *Fig* **to have a c. on sb** avoir prise sur qn; *Fig* **I have many claims on my time** je suis très pris; **his only c. to fame** la seule chose notable qu'il ait faite
(c) (*assertion*) déclaration *f*; **she makes no c. to being original** elle ne prétend pas être originale; **exaggerated claims have been made for this medicine** on a exagéré l'efficacité de ce médicament
(d) *Min* concession *f* (minière)
claim² **1** *vt* **(a)** (*demand as a right*) (*right, territory*) revendiquer; (*respect, attention*) exiger, demander; **to c. sth from sb** réclamer qch à qn; **to c. damages** réclamer des dommages et intérêts; **to c. a privilege** prétendre à un privilège; **have you claimed your allowance?** est-ce que tu as réclamé ton allocation?; **to c. the right to do sth** revendiquer le droit de faire qch; **to c. responsibility for an attack** (*of terrorist*) revendiquer un attentat
(b) (*assert*) **to c. that ...** prétendre *ou* affirmer que ... + *ind*; **he claims knowledge of their plans** il prétend *ou* affirme qu'il connait leurs projets; **to c. acquaintance with sb** prétendre connaître qn; **he claims to be an expert** il se prétend expert; **I don't c. to be an expert** je ne prétends pas être un expert
(c) (*collect, take*) (*baggage*) récupérer; (*lost property*) réclamer; **has anyone arrived to c. her?** (*lost child*) est-ce que quelqu'un est venu la chercher?; **the sea claims many victims** la mer fait de nombreuses victimes
2 *vi* (*in insurance*) demander à être indemnisé
▶ **claim back** *vtsep* (*expenses, cost*) se faire rembourser
claimant ['kleɪmənt] *n* (*for social security, insurance etc*) demandeur, -eresse; (*to throne*) prétendant, -ante; **rightful c.** ayant droit *m*, *pl* ayants droit
claims adjuster *n* répartiteur *m*
clairvoyance [kleə'vɔɪəns] *n* **(a)** (*second sight*) voyance *f*, don *m* de seconde vue **(b)** (*shrewdness*) clairvoyance *f*
clairvoyant [kleə'vɔɪənt] **1** *adj* **(a)** doué de seconde vue **(b)** (*shrewd*) clairvoyant **2** *n* voyant, -ante, extra-lucide *mf*, *pl* extra-lucides
clam [klæm] *n* palourde *f*, clam *m*; **to shut up like a c.** refuser de dire quoi que ce soit; *Am* **c. chowder** soupe *f* aux palourdes
▶ **clam up** *vi* (**-mm-**) *F* se taire; **don't c. up on me** parle-moi
clambake ['klæmbeɪk] *n Am* (*picnic*) = pique-nique *m* où l'on mange des fruits de mer; *F* (*noisy gathering*) grande réunion *f* tapageuse
clamber¹ ['klæmbər] *n* **it was quite a c.** c'était une sacrée grimpette
clamber² *vi* escalader; **to c. up a wall** escalader un mur; **he clambered over the pile of bricks** il a escaladé le tas de briques; **they clambered out of the car** ils se sont extirpés de la voiture
clamminess ['klæmɪnɪs] *n* (*of skin*) moiteur *f* froide; (*of air*) humidité *f* froide
clammy ['klæmɪ] *adj* (*hands, skin*) moite; (*atmosphere*) froid et humide
clamor ['klæmər] *n, vi US* = **clamour**
clamorous ['klæmərəs] *adj esp Lit* bruyant; (*crowd*) vociférant
clamorously ['klæmərəslɪ] *adv esp Lit* bruyamment
clamour¹ ['klæmər] *n* **(a)** (*noise*) clameur *f*, cris *mpl*, vociférations *fpl* **(b)** (*protest*) tollé *m*; **there was a great c.** ça a été un tollé général
clamour² *vi* vociférer, crier; **to c. for sth** réclamer *ou* demander qch à grands cris
clamp¹ [klæmp] *n* crampon *m*, presse *f*; (*of vice*) mordache *f*; (*for wire*) pince *f*; *Surg* clamp *m*; *Aut* (**wheel**) **c.** sabot *m* de Denver
clamp² *vt* **(a)** (*fasten*) cramponner; (*precision instrument*) bloquer; *Surg* clamper; **to c. two pieces of wood together** cramponner deux morceaux de bois **(b)** (*car*) mettre un sabot à
clamp³ *n Agr* (*for potatoes*) silo *m* (temporaire)
clamp⁴ *vt Agr* (*potatoes*) mettre en silo
▶ **clamp down 1** *vtsep* fixer par un crampon **2** *vi F* (*become stricter*) sévir (**on sb/sth** contre qn/qch); **the police are clamping down on illegal parking** la police sévit contre *ou* devient plus sévère avec les automobilistes en stationnement interdit
clampdown ['klæmpdaʊn] *n* renforcement *m* des mesures (de répression) (**on** contre); **as a result of the c.** suite au mesures de répression
clamping ['klæmpɪŋ] *n* (*of cars*) immobilisation *f* des voitures au moyen de sabots de Denver
clan [klæn] *n* (*of tribe*) *Scot* clan *m*; *Fig* bande *f*, clique *f*; **the**

head of the c. le chef de *ou* du clan; *Fig* **gathering of the clans** réunion *f* d'adhérents *ou* de partisans; **c. name** nom *m* du clan; **c. tartan** couleurs *fpl* du clan

clandestine [klænˈdestɪn] *adj* clandestin

clandestinely [klænˈdestɪnlɪ] *adv* clandestinement

clang[1] [klæŋ] *n* son *m ou* bruit *m* métallique

clang[2] **1** *vi* retentir, résonner, rendre un son métallique; **the gate clanged shut** le portail s'est refermé avec un bruit métallique **2** *vt* (*bell etc*) faire résonner; **she clanged the gate shut** elle ferma le portail bruyamment

clanger [ˈklæŋər] *n Br F* bourde *f*; **to drop a c.** faire une gaffe *ou* une boulette, gaffer

clank[1] [klæŋk] *n* (*of chains etc*) bruit *m* métallique

clank[2] *vi* (*of chain, bucket*) rendre un bruit métallique

clannish [ˈklænɪʃ] *adj Pej* (*person*) qui a l'esprit de clan; (*group*) fermé

clansman, *pl* **-men, clanswoman,** *pl* **-women** [ˈklænzmən, -mən, -wʊmən, -wɪmɪn] *n* = membre *m* d'un clan

clap[1] [klæp] *n* (*with hands*) **to give sb a c.** applaudir qn; **to give sb a big c.** applaudir qn bien fort; **she got a c. for that** on l'a applaudie pour ça; **to give sb a c. on the back** donner une tape sur le dos de qn; **a c. of thunder** un coup de tonnerre

clap[2] (**-pp-**) **1** *vt* (**a**) **to c. one's hands** battre des mains; **to c. a performer** applaudir un artiste; **to c. sb on the back** donner à qn une tape sur le dos (**b**) (*put*) mettre, *F* coller; **to c. sb in irons** mettre qn aux fers; **to c. sb in prison** fourrer qn en prison; *F* **to c. eyes on sb/sth** voir qn/qch; *F* **I've never clapped eyes on her before** je ne l'ai jamais vue de ma vie **2** *vi* (*of person, audience etc*) applaudir

clap[3] *n Sl* (*gonorrhoea*) chaude-pisse *f*; **he's got a dose of the c.** il a la chaude-pisse; **to give sb the c.** passer la chaude-pisse à qn

► **clap on** *vtsep* **he clapped his hat on** il a enfoncé son chapeau sur la tête; *Naut* **to c. on more sail** augmenter de toile

clapboard [ˈklæpbɔːd] *n Am Constr* planche *f* à clin; **c. (house)** maison *f* à clins

Clapham [ˈklæpəm] *n Br* **the man on the C. omnibus** le citoyen lambda; **it's like C. Junction in here** c'est un vrai moulin ici

clapometer [klæˈpɒmɪtər] *n TV etc* applaudimètre *m*

clapped out [klæpt] *adj Br F* (*person*) crevé, éreinté; (*car, television etc*) pourri

clapper [ˈklæpər] *n* (**a**) (*of bell*) battant *m*; **c. valve** (soupape *f* à) clapet *m* (**b**) *Agr* (*for scaring birds*) moulin *m* à claquet; *Br F* **like the clappers** (*to work*) comme un enragé; (*to run*) comme un dératé; (*to drive*) comme un fou

clapperboard [ˈklæpəbɔːd] *n TV, Cin* clap *m*, claquette *f*

clapping [ˈklæpɪŋ] *n* (*applause*) applaudissements *mpl*

claptrap [ˈklæptræp] *n* (**a**) *F* sottises *mpl*; **to talk c.** raconter des histoires; **what c.!** quel tissu d'âneries *ou* de sottises! (**b**) *TV, Cin* (*clapperboard*) clap *m*

claque [klæk] *n Th* claque *f*

claret [ˈklærət] **1** *n* (**a**) (*wine*) bordeaux *m* rouge (**b**) (*colour*) bordeaux *m inv* **2** *adj* **c. (-coloured)** bordeaux *inv*

clarification [klærɪfɪˈkeɪʃən] *n* (**a**) (*further explanation*) clarification *f*; (*of question etc*) éclaircissement *m*, élucidation *f*; **to ask for c.** demander des éclaircissements (**b**) (*of butter, stock*) clarification *f*; (*of wine*) collage *m*

clarify [ˈklærɪfaɪ] **1** *vt* (**a**) (*thinking*) clarifier; (*mind, views, opinions*) éclaircir; (*question*) élucider (**b**) (*butter, stock*) clarifier; (*wine*) coller **2** *vi* (*of liquid, one's thoughts*) se clarifier, s'éclaircir

clarinet [klærɪˈnet] *n* clarinette *f*

clarinettist [klærɪˈnetɪst] *n* clarinettiste *mf*

clarion [ˈklærɪən] *n Lit* clairon *m*; *Fig* **the speech was a c. call to ...** le discours était un appel à ...

clarity [ˈklærɪtɪ] *n* clarté *f*

clash[1] [klæʃ] *n* (**a**) (*noise*) fracas *m*; (*of swords etc*) cliquetis *m*; (*of cymbals*) son *m* assourdissant

(**b**) (*conflict*) (*of colours, styles*) discordance *f*; (*of opinions*) conflit *m*, choc *m*; (*of doctrines*) opposition *f*; (*between people*) affrontement *m*; (*between mobs*) échauffourée *f*; **a c. of interests** un conflit d'intérêts; **we had a slight c. of opinions** nous avons eu un léger désaccord; **clashes on the border** des affrontements à la frontière; **there was a c. (between them) over the methods to be used** il y a eu un conflit entre eux quant aux méthodes à utiliser; **c. of personalities, personality c.** incompatibilité *f* de caractères

clash[2] **1** *vi* (**a**) (*of cymbals*) résonner (bruyamment); (*of swords etc*) s'entrechoquer

(**b**) (*come into conflict*) entrer en conflit, s'affronter; **police clashed with protestors** il y a eu des heurts entre la police et les manifestants; **they clashed over how to solve the problem** ils sont entrés en conflit quant à la manière de résoudre le problème; **their personalities c.** leurs personnalités se heurtent, il y a incompatibilité entre leurs caractères

(**c**) (*of colours*) jurer, détonner; (*of evidence, explanations etc*) ne pas correspondre; (*of literary styles*) être discordant; (*of events, appointments*) tomber le même jour/la même heure **2** *vt* (*cymbals*) faire résonner

clashing[1] [ˈklæʃɪŋ] *adj* (**a**) (*sound*) bruyant, retentissant (**b**) (*opinions*) opposé; (*colours, styles*) discordant

clasp[1] [klɑːsp] *n* (**a**) (*fastener*) (*on brooch, medal etc*) agrafe *f*; (*on book, necklace, handbag*) fermoir *m*; **c. knife** canif *m* (**b**) (*grip*) étreinte *f*

clasp[2] *vt* (**a**) (*fasten*) (*bracelet etc*) fermer (**b**) (*grip*) (*in hand*) serrer; (*in arms*) (*person*) étreindre, enlacer; (*object*) prendre dans ses bras; **to be clasped in each other's arms** se tenir étroitement enlacés; **to c. sb's hand** serrer la main à qn; **to c. one's hands** joindre les mains; **to c. one's knees** entourer ses genoux de ses bras

class[1] [klɑːs] *n* (**a**) (*in social hierarchy*) classe *f*; **c. distinctions** distinctions *fpl* entre les classes; **c. prejudice** préjugés *mpl* sociaux; **c. struggle** lutte *f* des classes; **c. traitor** personne *f* qui renie ses origines sociales; **c. war** lutte *f* des classes

(**b**) *F* (*quality*) classe *f*; **to have c.** avoir de la classe; **that's what I call c. furniture** ça, c'est que j'appelle des meubles classes

(**c**) [①A11,g,i] *Sch* (*lesson*) cours *m*; (*group of pupils*) classe *f*; **the French c.** le cours de français; **evening c.** cours du soir; **day release classes** scolarité *f* à temps partiel; **in c.** en classe

(**d**) *US Sch* (*students in year*) promotion *f*; **the c. of '89** la promotion 1989

(**e**) (*category*) catégorie *f*, classe *f*; *Rail, Av, Naut, Biol* classe; **to be in a c. of one's own, to be in a c. by oneself** (*of person, thing*) être unique, être de loin le/la meilleur(e); *Iron* être imbattable; **what c. are you travelling?** en quelle classe est-ce que vous voyagez?; *Br Univ* **what c. (of) degree did you get?** quelle mention est-ce que tu as eu (à ton diplôme)?; **of Olympic c.** digne de participer aux Jeux Olympiques

class[2] *vt* classer; **to c. sb/sth with ...** assimiler qn/qch à ...; **classed first** classé premier

class action *n Am* recours *m* collectif

class-conscious *adj* conscient des différences de classe

class-consciousness *n* conscience *f* des différences de classe

classic [ˈklæsɪk] **1** *adj* classique; **c. records of the sixties** des classiques de la musique des années soixante; *F* **a c. example** un exemple classique *ou* typique; *Horseracing* **c. race** course *f* classique **2** *n* (*book etc*) classique *m*; *Horseracing* classique *f*; **a c. of romantic poetry** un classique de la poésie romantique; **classics** (*usu with sing verb*) (*subject*) les langues *fpl* classiques, les humanités *fpl*; **a classics degree** une licence en latin et (en) grec

classical [ˈklæsɪk(ə)l] *adj* (**a**) (*civilization etc*) de l'antiquité; **c. Greece** la Grèce antique; **the c. world** le monde de l'antiquité; **in c. times** dans l'antiquité; **c. scholar** humaniste *mf* (**b**) *Mus, Art, Liter etc* classique

classically [ˈklæsɪk(ə)lɪ] *adv* classiquement; **c. trained** (*pianist etc*) ayant reçu une formation classique

classicism [ˈklæsɪsɪz(ə)m] *n* (**a**) *Art, Liter, Archit etc* classicisme *m* (**b**) *Ling* tour *m ou* locution *f* emprunté(e) aux langues classiques

classicist [ˈklæsɪsɪst] *n* humaniste *mf*; (*advocate of classical studies*) partisan, -ane des études classiques

classification [klæsɪfɪˈkeɪʃən] *n* (**a**) (*action*) (*of plants, animals*) classification *f*; (*of papers, competitors, books etc*) classement *m* (**b**) (*category*) classification *f*, classe *f*

classified [ˈklæsɪfaɪd] *adj* (**a**) (*arranged*) classé; *Journ* **c. advertisements** petites annonces *fpl*; *Sp* **c. results** résultats *mpl* et classements *mpl* (**b**) (*secret*) (*document, information*) confidentiel

classifieds [ˈklæsɪfaɪdz] *npl Journ* **the c.** les petites annonces *fpl*

classifier [ˈklæsɪfaɪər] *n* (*person*) classificateur, -trice

classify [ˈklæsɪfaɪ] *vt* (**a**) classer; **their music is classified as jazz** leur musique est classée comme étant du jazz (**b**) (*make secret*) (*document etc*) classer confidentiel

classless [ˈklɑːslɪs] *adj* (*society*) sans classes; (*accent*) neutre

classmate [ˈklɑːsmeɪt] *n* (**a**) *Sch* (*in same class*) camarade *mf* de classe (**b**) *Am Univ* (*in same year*) camarade *mf* de promotion

classroom [ˈklɑːsruːm] *n Sch* (salle *f* de) classe *f*

classy [ˈklɑːsɪ] *adj F* (*person*) qui a de la classe, classieux; (*restaurant*) chic *inv*; (*car, hotel*) de luxe

clatter[1] [ˈklætər] *n* bruit *m*, vacarme *m*, fracas *m*; (*of typewriters*) claquement *m*; (*of machine*) ferraillement *m*; **the c. of dishes** les bruits de vaisselle

clatter² **1** *vi* faire du bruit; **we could hear him clattering about in the attic** on l'entendait qui faisait un bruit de tous les diables dans le grenier; **the old cart clattered by** le vieux chariot est passé en faisant du bruit; **to come clattering down** dégringoler avec fracas **2** *vt* faire résonner; **don't c. your spoons!** ne faites pas de bruit avec vos cuillers!

Claudius [ˈklɔːdɪəs] *n Hist* Claude *m*

clause [klɔːz] *n* **(a)** *Jur (of treaty, law)* clause *f*, article *m*; *(of will)* disposition *f*; **c. of a/the contract** clause contractuelle **(b)** [①A3; B1,1] *Gram* proposition *f*

claused bill [klɔːzd] *n Com* connaissement *m* clausé

claustrophobia [klɔːstrəˈfəʊbɪə, klɒs-] *n* claustrophobie *f*

claustrophobic [klɔːstrəˈfəʊbɪk, klɒs-] *adj (person)* claustrophobe; **this room feels quite c.** cette pièce donne une impression de claustrophobie; **I feel c.** j'ai un sentiment de claustrophobie

clavichord [ˈklævɪkɔːd] *n Mus* clavicorde *m*

clavicle [ˈklævɪk(ə)l] *n Anat* clavicule *f*

claw¹ [klɔː] *n* **(a)** *(of cat etc)* griffe *f*; *(of bird of prey)* serre *f*; *(of lobster)* pince *f*; **to sharpen its claws** *(of cat)* se faire les griffes; **to show its/one's claws** *(of cat), Fig* sortir ses griffes; **to draw in its/one's claws** *(of cat), Fig* rentrer ses griffes, faire patte de velours; **c.-footed** *(table etc)* à pied de griffon; *Fig* **to get one's claws into sb** *(trap)* mettre le grappin sur qn; **she's got her claws in me** *(dislikes me)* elle a une dent contre moi; **c. marks** griffures *fpl* **(b)** *Tech (of hammer)* panne *f* fendue

claw² **1** *vt (scratch)* griffer, donner un coup de griffe à; *Fig* **to c. one's way to the top** arriver au sommet par tous les moyens **2** *vi* **to c. at sth** *(of cat)* saisir qch avec ses griffes, s'accrocher à qch; *(grip)* s'accrocher à qch, agripper qch; *(try to grip)* essayer de s'accrocher à qch *ou* d'agripper qch; **she clawed at my face** *(scratched me)* elle a essayé de me griffer au visage

▶ **claw back** *vtsep* **(a)** *Fin (expenditure)* récupérer **(b)** *(regain)* regagner péniblement; **she clawed her way back to a prominent position** à force de persévérance, elle a réussi à regagner une position influente

clawback [ˈklɔːbæk] *n Fin* récupération *f*

claw hammer *n* marteau *m* à panne fendue

clay [kleɪ] *n* argile *f*, (terre-)glaise *f*; **(modelling) c.** pâte *f* à modeler; *Lit* **idol with feet of c.** idole aux pieds d'argile; *Lit* **mortal c.** le corps humain; **c. pit** glaisière *f*; **c. soil** sol *m* argileux *ou* glaiseux; *Tennis* **to play on c.** jouer sur terre battue; *Tennis* **to be good on c.** jouer bien sur la terre battue

clay court *n Tennis* court *m* en terre battue; **to be a good c. player** jouer bien sur la terre battue

clayey [ˈkleɪɪ] *adj (soil)* argileux, glaiseux

claymore [ˈkleɪmɔːr] *n Scot Hist* = sabre *m* écossais à deux tranchants

clay pigeon *n Sp* pigeon *m* d'argile; **c. shooting** ball-trap *m*

clay pipe *n* pipe *f* de *ou* en terre

clean¹ [kliːn] **1** *adj* **(a)** propre, net; *(clothes)* propre; *(water)* pur, propre; *(sheet of paper)* blanc, *f* blanche; *(break)* franc, net; *(wound)* pas infecté; *(joke)* décent; **to keep sth c.** tenir qch propre; *F* **keep it c.!** *(the joke, story etc)* pas de grossièretés!; *F* **he's c.** *(off drugs)* il n'y touche plus; *(unarmed)* il n'est pas armé; *(no electronic bugs)* il n'a pas de micro; **good c. fun** jeu *m* innocent; **to make a c. break** *(in relationship)* en finir une bonne fois pour toutes; *Fig* **to show sb a c. pair of heels** *(run away)* s'enfuir devant qn; **he's showing the other runners a c. pair of heels** il a pris une belle avance sur les autres concurrents; **to make a c. copy of sth** mettre qch au net; **he made a c. sweep of the medals/prizes** il a raflé toutes les médailles/tous les prix; **c. (driving) licence** permis *m* de conduire vierge; *Com* **c. on board** net de réserves à bord; **c. bill** *Fin* effet *m* libre; *Com* connaissement *m* net; **the doctor gave him a c. bill of health** le docteur l'a trouvé en parfaite santé; **c. living** vie *f* saine; *Typ* **c. proof** *(with few corrections)* épreuve *f* peu chargée; *(final)* épreuve pour bon à tirer

(b) *(sharp, well-defined)* **c. (out)lines** contours *mpl* nets; **car with c. lines** voiture aux lignes élégantes

(c) *Sp F (honest) (player, boxer)* fair-play *inv*, qui joue franc jeu

2 *adv F (completely)* **I c. forgot** j'ai complètement oublié; **they got c. away** ils se sont échappés sans laisser de traces; **we're c. out of sugar** nous n'avons plus de sucre du tout; **to cut c. through sth** couper *ou* traverser qch de part en part; **to come c.** avouer, dire toute la vérité

clean² *n* nettoyage *m*; **to give sth a c.** nettoyer qch

clean³ **1** *vt (floor, house etc, Med sore, ulcer)* nettoyer; *Culin (fish, poultry)* vider; *(boiler)* décrasser; **to c. one's teeth** se laver les dents; **to c. one's nails** se nettoyer *ou* se curer les ongles; **to c. the mud off one's shoes** enlever la boue de ses chaussures; **to c. one's plate** *(eat everything on it)* finir son assiette; *Am* **to c. house** faire le ménage **2** *vi* **(a)** *(do the cleaning)* faire le ménage **(b)** *(of pan, floor etc)* se nettoyer **(c)** *(of cleaning product, detergent)* nettoyer

▶ **clean out** *vtsep* **(a)** *(cupboard etc)* nettoyer; *(furnace, boiler)* curer, décrasser; *(ditch)* vidanger **(b)** *F (leave without money)* nettoyer, laisser sans un rond; **they cleaned out the safe** ils ont vidé le coffre; **cleaned out** *(penniless)* nettoyé (à sec), fauché **(c)** *(buy, take all of)* **to c. a shop out of sugar** dévaliser un magasin de son stock de sucre

▶ **clean up** **1** *vtsep* **(a)** *(dirt etc)* enlever; *(room etc)* nettoyer; *(make less polluting) (engine)* dépolluer; *Fig (television)* assainir; **to c. oneself up** se débarbouiller; *Fig* **to c. up a town** *(get rid of enemy, gangsters etc)* nettoyer une ville; **to c. up one's act** *(of lewd comedian)* rendre son spectacle moins choquant; *(of corrupt or inefficient organization)* faire le ménage; *(of unsatisfactory employee, pupil)* s'améliorer

(b) *Am Sl (obtain)* **to c. up a thousand dollars** gagner *ou* ramasser mille dollars

2 *vi* **(a)** *(in room, building etc)* nettoyer; *(wash oneself)* se débarbouiller

(b) *(put back in order)* nettoyer, ranger, remettre tout en ordre; **he expects us to c. up after him** il compte sur nous pour nettoyer après lui

(c) *(repair damage)* réparer les dégâts

(d) *F (make a lot of money)* ramasser une fortune

clean-cut *adj (lines)* d'une grande netteté; *(man)* à l'apparence très soignée

cleaner [ˈkliːnər] *n* **(a)** *(person)* employé, -ée du service de nettoyage; *(in home)* personne *f* qui fait le ménage; *(woman)* femme *f* de ménage; **(dry) c.** teinturier, -ière; **to take sth to the c.'s** donner qch à nettoyer *ou* au nettoyage; *F* **to take sb to the c.'s** *(cheat)* nettoyer qn, plumer qn; *(defeat)* battre qn à plates coutures **(b)** *(device, machine)* **(vacuum) c.** aspirateur *m*; **pipe c.** cure-pipe *m*, *pl* cure-pipes **(c)** *(product)* produit *m* nettoyant *ou* pour nettoyer; *(for clothes)* détachant *m*

cleaning *n* [ˈkliːnɪŋ] nettoyage *m*; *(in household)* ménage *m*; *(of boiler)* décrassage *m*; *Culin (of fish)* vidage *m*; **c. fluid** liquide *m* de nettoyage; **c. staff** personnel *m* de nettoyage; **(household) c. materials** produits *mpl* d'entretien; **c. woman** *or* **lady** *(in home, office)* femme *f* de ménage

cleaning up *n (of room, Fig of neighbourhood)* nettoyage *m*; *(of exhaust gases)* dépollution *f*

clean-limbed [kliːnˈlɪmd] *adj* bien proportionné

cleanliness [ˈklenlɪnɪs] *n* propreté *f*; **c. of habit** habitudes *fpl* de propreté; *Prov* **c. is next to godliness** la propreté du corps s'apparente à la pureté de l'âme

clean-living *adj (person)* réglé, qui mène une vie réglée

cleanly¹ [ˈkliːnlɪ] *adv* proprement, nettement; **to break c.** se casser net

cleanly² [ˈklenlɪ] *adj (person)* propre (par habitude); **c. habits** habitudes *fpl* de propreté

cleanness [ˈkliːnnɪs] *n (of habits, language, apartment etc)* propreté *f*; *(of water)* pureté *f*; *(of lines)* netteté *f*, pureté

clean-out *n* nettoyage *m*; **to give a room a c.** nettoyer une pièce

clean room *n Med* pièce *f* aseptisée; *Comptr* chambre *f* blanche

clean-room clothing *n Comptr* vêtements *mpl* de salle blanche

cleanse [klenz] *vt (face)* démaquiller; *(wound)* nettoyer; *(blood)* purifier; *(air)* épurer; *Arch, Lit (heart, soul)* purifier

cleanser [ˈklenzər] *n (for skin)* démaquillant *m*

clean-shaven *adj (man, face)* glabre

cleansing [ˈklenzɪŋ] *n (of woman's face)* démaquillage *m*; *(of blood, soul)* purification *f*; **c. cream/milk** *or* **lotion** *(for skin)* crème *f*/lait *m* de démaquillage; **c. pads** disques *mpl* démaquillants

cleansing department *n Br Admin* service *m* du nettoyage

cleanup [ˈkliːnʌp] *n (of room, Fig town)* nettoyage *m*; **to give sth a c.** nettoyer qch

clear¹ [klɪər] **1** *adj* **(a)** *(sky, complexion, eye, sound etc)* clair; *(weather)* clair, dégagé; *(water)* clair, limpide; **on a c. day** par temps clair; *TV* **the picture was very c.** l'image était très nette; **to have c. skin** avoir la peau nette; **a c. conscience** une conscience tranquille; **my conscience is c.** j'ai la conscience tranquille; **c. voice** voix *f* claire *ou* nette

(b) *(unmistakeable, manifest)* clair, net; *(sign)* évident; **a c. case of bribery** un cas manifeste de corruption; **the meaning of the sentence was c.** le sens de la phrase était clair; **to make one's meaning** *or* **oneself c.** se faire comprendre; **have I made myself c.?** est-ce que je me suis bien fait comprendre?; **to make it c. to sb that …** bien faire comprendre à qn que ...; **she made it quite c. that ...** elle lui/nous/*etc* a bien fait comprendre que ...; **the letter doesn't make it c. when they will arrive** la lettre n'indique pas clairement quand ils vont arriver; **I want to be quite c. on this point** je tiens à ce qu'il n'y ait aucun malentendu sur ce point; **is that c.?** (*do you understand?*) c'est clair?; **it is c. that ...** il est clair *ou* évident que ...; **it was not c. who had won** on ne savait pas exactement qui avait gagné; **it is not yet c. whether ...** on ne sait pas encore si ...; **as c. as daylight** *or* **crystal** clair comme le jour *ou* comme de l'eau de roche

(c) (*not confused*) (*description, explanation, argument, style*) clair, net; (*reasoning*) lucide, clair; (*instructions*) clair; **c. thinker/mind** esprit *m* lucide; **c. thinking is essential** la clarté de pensée est essentielle; **to keep a c. head** garder les idées claires

(d) (*certain*) **to be c. about sth** être certain de qch; **are you c. about what you have to do?** es-tu sûr de ce que tu as à faire?; **there's something I'm not c. about** il reste quelque chose dont je ne suis pas sûr; **I wasn't c. what she meant** je n'étais pas sûr de ce qu'elle voulait dire

(e) (*unqualified*) **c. profit** bénéfice *m* net; **a c. ten thousand pounds a year** un revenu net de dix mille livres; **c. majority** majorité *f* absolue; *Sp* **c. winner** vainqueur *m* incontesté; **there wasn't a c. winner** on ne pouvait pas dire qui l'avait emporté; *Jur* **three c. days** trois jours francs

(f) (*unobstructed, free*) libre; (*view etc*) dégagé; **his latest X-rays are c.** ses dernières radios ne montrent rien d'anormal; **to be c. of sth** (*rid of*) être débarrassé de qch; **he was c. of all signs of the disease** il ne montrait aucun symptôme de la maladie; **we were c. of the last checkpoint** nous avions passé le dernier poste de contrôle; **the sea is c. of ice** la mer est libre; **the exhaust pipe is 30 cm c. of the ground** le tuyau d'échappement est à 30 cm du sol; *Av* **you are c. to take off** vous êtes autorisé à *ou* vous pouvez décoller; **all c.!** (*there's no traffic, no-one is watching*) vous pouvez y aller, la voie est libre; *Mil* fin d'alerte

2 *adv* **we could hear them c. across the valley** on les entendait de l'autre bout de la vallée; **to jump five centimetres c. of the bar** franchir la barre avec cinq centimètres de reste; **to hang c. of the ground** être suspendu de manière à ne pas toucher le sol; **to stand c.** s'écarter (**of** de); **stand c. of the doors!** attention aux portes!; *Rail* = attention au départ!; **to keep** *or* **steer c. of sth** éviter qch; *Naut* **to steer c. of a rock** passer au large d'un écueil; **they pulled him c. of the wreckage** ils l'ont dégagé de l'épave; **she was thrown c. of the car** elle a été éjéctée de la voiture; **to get c. of sb** échapper à qn; **to get c.** s'échapper; *Sp* **to punch the ball c.** écarter le ballon d'un coup de poing

3 *n* **(a)** (*of person*) **to be in the c.** (*free from suspicion*) être libre de tout soupçon; (*free from debt*) ne pas avoir de dettes; (*out of danger*) être hors de danger

(b) *Mil etc* **despatch sent in c.** (*not coded*) dépêche *f* en clair

clear² **1** *vt* **(a)** (*free of obstacles*) (*road, area, entrance*) dégager; (*room etc*) débarrasser, désencombrer; (*forest*) défricher; (*streets, room*) (*of people*) faire évacuer; (*pipe*) déboucher; *Jur* **to c. the court** faire évacuer la salle; **to c. one's conscience** décharger sa conscience; **to c. one's throat** se racler la gorge; **he cleared a space on the floor** il a dégagé un espace sur le sol; **they cleared 20 acres of forest** ils ont défriché 8 hectares de forêt; **to c. a way** *or* **a passage for sb** frayer un passage à qn; *Fig* **to c. the way for sth** ouvrir la voie pour qch; **to c. a way for oneself** se frayer un passage; **to c. the table** (*after meal*) débarrasser la table; **to c. one's desk** (*tidy*) débarrasser son bureau; (*complete pending tasks*) régler les affaires en suspens; *Naut* **to c. the decks for action** faire le branle-bas de combat; *Fig* **to c. the decks** déblayer le terrain; *Comptr* **to c. the screen** vider l'écran; **the rain had cleared the streets** la pluie avait vidé les rues; **to c. slums** assainir des taudis; *Mil* **to c. an area of mines** déminer un terrain; **fresh air clears the head** un peu d'air frais vous éclaircit les idées; *Com* **to c. goods** (*in sale etc*) solder *ou* liquider des marchandises; *Rail* **to c. the line** dégager la voie; (*after an accident*) déblayer la voie

(b) (*exonerate*) disculper, innocenter; **he was cleared of all blame** il a été entièrement disculpé; **to c. oneself** se justifier; **to c. one's/sb's name** se disculper/disculper qn

(c) (*make less dense*) (*fog etc*) dissiper; **to c. the air** (*of thunderstorm*) rafraîchir l'air; (*of discussion etc*) mettre les choses au point

(d) (*remove*) **to c. sth from** *or* **off sth** enlever qch de qch; **c. all this out of here** débarrassez-moi de tout cela

(e) (*empty*) **to c. the postbox** lever le courrier; *Med* **to c. the bowels** purger les intestins

(f) (*go past, over etc without touching*) **to c. a barrier (by 10 centimetres)** franchir une barrière (avec 10 centimètres de reste); **to c. a ditch** sauter *ou* franchir un fossé; *Naut* **to c. the harbour** sortir du port, quitter le port; **the ship just cleared the bottom** le bateau a évité le fond de justesse

(g) (*make a profit of*) **to c. 10%** faire un bénéfice net de 10%; **I cleared a hundred pounds** j'ai touché cent livres net

(h) *Banking* (*cheque*) compenser, virer

(i) *Admin* (*authorize*) (*ship*) expédier; (*goods through customs*) dédouaner; **to c. customs** être dédouané; **cleared through customs** dédouané; **to c. sb** (*for security purposes*) attribuer à qn un certificat de sécurité; **he's been cleared** l'enquête de sécurité a été favorable; **to c. sth with sb** (*obtain permission for*) obtenir de qn la permission de faire qch; **I'll need to c. it with the boss** il faut que j'obtienne la permission du patron; **to c. an article for publication** (*ask for authorization*) demander l'autorisation de publier un article; (*authorize*) autoriser la publication d'un article; **the plane was cleared for take-off** l'avion a été autorisé à décoller, l'avion a reçu l'autorisation de décoller

(j) *Fin* (*debt*) acquitter; (*mortgage*) purger; (*account*) solder; **to c. one's property of debt** purger son bien de dettes

(k) (*free from impurities*) (*liquid*) clarifier; (*blood*) purifier

(l) *Sp* (*ball*) dégager; **to c. the ball with one's head** écarter le ballon d'un coup de tête

2 *vi* **(a)** (*of the weather*) s'éclaircir; (*of mist*) se dissiper; (*of sky*) se dégager; **her face cleared** sa visage se détendit

(b) (*of cheque*) être viré

(c) (*of liquid*) se clarifier

(d) *Sp* (*of goalkeeper, full-back*) dégager; **he cleared off the line with his head** il a écarté le ballon de la ligne des buts d'un coup de tête

▶ **clear away** **1** *vtsep* (*remove*) enlever, ôter; (*obstacle*) écarter; (*one's things*) ranger **2** *vi* (*of mist*) se dissiper

▶ **clear off** **1** *vtsep* (*remove*) retirer, enlever **2** *vi Br F* (*leave*) filer, déguerpir, se tirer; **my wife cleared off** ma femme s'est tirée; **c. off!** tire-toi!, casse-toi!, dégage! **3** *vipo* dégager de; **he told them to c. off his land** il leur a dit de dégager de sa propriété

▶ **clear out** **1** *vtsep* (*empty*) (*cupboard*) vider; (*garage, shed*) débarrasser; *F* (*leave without money*) nettoyer **2** *vi Br F* (*leave building, room etc*) filer, déguerpir; (*leave home*) (*of spouse etc*) se tirer; **c. out!** filez!, dehors!

▶ **clear up** **1** *vtsep* **(a)** (*tidy*) (*room*) (re)mettre en ordre; (*one's things*) ranger; **we had to c. up the mess** (*after party*) il a fallu tout ranger *ou* nettoyer; *Fig* il a fallu tout arranger **(b)** (*misunderstanding*) dissiper; (*mystery, doubt, problem*) éclaircir; (*difficulty*) résoudre; **to c. up a matter** tirer une affaire au clair **(c)** (*cure*) guérir **2** *vi* **(a)** (*of weather*) se (re)mettre au beau **(b)** (*of rash, headache etc*) disparaître **(c)** (*tidy up*) ranger; (*after flood, earthquake, bombing etc*) déblayer

clearance ['klɪərəns] *n* **(a)** (**slum**) **c.** assainissement *m* des taudis

(b) (*of land*) défrichement *m*; *Hist* **the (Highland) Clearances** l'expulsion *f* des habitants des Highlands aux XVIIIème et XIXème siècles pour faire paître les moutons

(c) *Banking* (*of a cheque*) compensation *f*

(d) (*authorization*) autorisation *f*; (*by customs*) dédouanage *m*, dédouanement *m*; **we got c. to inspect the documents** nous avons eu l'autorisation d'examiner les documents; *Av* **(flight) c.** autorisation de vol; *Admin, Mil* **(security) c.** autorisation

(e) *Tech* (*space*) espace *m* (libre); (*of piston etc*) jeu *m*; *Constr* (*under bridge, doorway etc*) hauteur *f* libre

(f) *Fb* dégagement *m*

(g) *Med* (*of kidneys*) clairance *f*

clearance sale *n Com* liquidation *f*

clear-cut *adj* (*outline, feature*) net; (*opinion*) bien défini, tranché, net; (*order*) précis; (*division, dividing line*) net; **it's not quite as c. as that** ce n'est pas aussi simple que ça

clear-headed [klɪə'hedɪd] *adj* lucide

clearing ['klɪərɪŋ] *n* **(a)** (*unblocking, freeing of obstacles*) (*of track*) dégagement *m*, déblaiement *m*; (*of ground*) défrichement *m*; (*of ditches*) curage *m*

(b) (*removal*) (*of rubbish*) enlèvement *m*

(c) (*emptying*) (*of room*) évacuation *f*; *Mil* **c. station** (*for wounded*) centre *m* de triage *ou* d'évacuation

(d) *Fin* (*of debts*) acquittement *m*

(e) *Banking* compensation *f*, clearing *m*; **c. account** compte *m* de compensation; *St Exch* **c. member** adhérent-compensateur *m*, membre *m* de compensation; **c. price** cours *m* de compensation; **c. system** système *m* de compensation

(f) (*in forest*) clairière *f*

clearing bank *n* banque *f* compensatrice, banque de compensation *f ou* de clearing *m*

clearing house *n* (**a**) *Banking* chambre *f* de compensation, comptoir *m* général de virement, clearing (house) *m* (**b**) *Br Univ* = organisme *m* de tri des demandes d'entrée à l'université

clearing up *n* (*of house etc*) remise *f* en ordre; (*after earthquake, flood, bombing etc*) déblaiement *m*; **c. operations have started** les opérations de déblaiement ont commencé

clearly [ˈklɪəlɪ] *adv* (**a**) (*to see*) clair; (*to explain, write, speak*) clairement, d'une manière claire; (*to hear*) distinctement; (*to distinguish*) clairement, nettement; **you're not thinking very c.** tu raisonnes de travers; **c. legible** bien lisible; **is that c. understood?** c'est bien compris?
(**b**) (*obviously, plainly*) évidemment; **he is c. wrong** il est évident qu'il a tort; **they are c. different** il est évident qu'ils sont différents; **c., this can't be right** c'est faux, il n'y a aucun doute là-dessus; **c., we'll have to pay** nous devrons payer, c'est certain; **this is c. unacceptable** c'est tout à fait inacceptable; **c. not** manifestement pas

clearness [ˈklɪənɪs] *n* (**a**) (*of water, atmosphere etc*) clarté *f*, limpidité *f* (**b**) (*of image*) netteté *f* (**c**) (*of ideas, explanations*) clarté *f*

clearout [ˈklɪəraʊt] *n* **this room needs a good c.** cette pièce a besoin d'un bon nettoyage par le vide; **to have a c.** faire le nettoyage par le vide; **to give the cupboards a c.** faire le nettoyage par le vide dans les placards; *Fig* **the party has had a c.** le parti s'est débarrassé de quelques-uns de ses membres

clear-sighted *adj* (**a**) (*having good judgement*) lucide, clairvoyant (**b**) (*having good sight*) qui a une bonne vue

clear-sightedness [klɪəˈsaɪtɪdnɪs] *n* (*good judgement*) lucidité *f*, clairvoyance *f*

clear-up *n* (*of room etc*) remise *f* en ordre; **this place needs a good c.** cet endroit a bien besoin d'être remis en ordre; **c. rate (for crimes)** pourcentage *m* d'affaires élucidées par la police

clearway [ˈklɪəweɪ] *n Br Aut* grande route *f* à stationnement interdit

cleat [kliːt] *n esp Naut* taquet *m* (*de tournage*)

cleavage [ˈkliːvɪdʒ] *n* (**a**) (*of woman*) décolleté *m*; **what a c.!** quel décolleté!; **it fell down her c.** c'est tombé dans son décolleté; **to show a lot of c.** (*of woman*) avoir un décolleté plongeant; (*of dress*) être très décolleté (**b**) (*split*) (*in party*) clivage *m* (**c**) (*splitting*) *Tech* fendage *m*; *Geol, Ch* clivage *m*; *Biol* division *f*

cleave [kliːv] (*pt* **cleaved, cleft** [kleft], *Lit* **clove** [kləʊv]; *pp* **cleaved, cleft,** *Lit* **cloven** [ˈkləʊv(ə)n]) **1** *vt Lit* (*wood, waters*) fendre **2** *vi* (**a**) *Lit* **to c. (asunder)** se fendre, se feuilleter (**b**) (*of crystals*) se cliver

▶ **cleave to** *vipo* (*pt, pp* **cleaved**) *Lit* (*person, party, principle*) être fidèle à

cleaver [ˈkliːvər] *n* fendoir *m*; (*for meat*) couperet *m*; (*for wood*) merlin *m*

clef [klef] *n Mus* clef *f*; **bass c.** clef de fa; **C c.** clef d'ut

cleft [kleft] **1** *n* fente *f*, fissure *f*, crevasse *f* **2** *adj* fendu; **c. stick** bâton *m* fourchu; *Fig* **to be in a c. stick** se trouver dans une impasse; *Med* **c. palate** palais *m* fendu

clematis [ˈklemətɪs, kləˈmeɪtɪs] *n* clématite *f*

clemency, *pl* **-cies** [ˈklemənsɪ, -sɪz] *n* (**a**) (*mercy*) clémence *f*, indulgence *f* (**to** envers); **to show c.** faire preuve de clémence (**b**) (*of weather*) douceur *f*

clement [ˈklemənt] *adj Fml* (**a**) (*person*) clément, indulgent (**to** envers, pour) (**b**) (*weather*) doux, clément

clementine [ˈkleməntiːn, -aɪn] *n* clémentine *f*

clench [klen(t)ʃ] **1** *vt* (*teeth, fist*) serrer; **between clenched teeth** (*to say*) les dents serrées; **to c. sth in one's hand** serrer qch dans la main **2** *vi* (*of teeth, hands*) se serrer

Cleopatra [klɪəˈpætrə] *n Antiq* Cléopâtre *f*; **C.'s needle** l'Obélisque *m* de Cléopâtre

clerestory [ˈklɪəstɔːrɪ] *n Archit* claire-voie *f*, *pl* claires-voies

clergy [ˈklɜːdʒɪ] *n* [①**A11**,f,ii] (*no pl*) *Rel* clergé *m*

clergyman, *pl* **-men** [ˈklɜːdʒɪmən] *n Rel* ecclésiastique *m*; (*protestant*) pasteur *m*; (*catholic*) prêtre *m*

clergywoman, *pl* **-women** [ˈklɜːdʒɪwʊmən, -wɪmɪn] *n Rel* femme *f* pasteur

cleric [ˈklerɪk] *n Rel* ecclésiastique *m*

clerical [ˈklerɪk(ə)l] *adj* (**a**) (*work*) d'écritures, de bureau; (*staff*) de bureau; **c. assistant** employé, -ée de bureau; **c. error** faute *f* de copiste, erreur *f*; (*in something written*) faute d'écriture; (*in book-keeping*) erreur d'écritures (**b**) *Rel* clérical; (*dress*) ecclésiastique

clericalism [ˈklerɪk(ə)lɪz(ə)m] *n Rel* cléricalisme *m*

clerk¹ [klɑːk, *US* klɜːrk] *n* (**a**) (*in office*) employé, -ée de bureau; (*of solicitor*) clerc *m*; **bank c.** employé, -ée de banque; **filing c.,** *US* **file c.** employé, -ée au classement; **records c.** archiviste *mf*; **shipping c.** expéditionnaire *mf*, employé, -ée de l'expédition; *Jur* **c. of the court** greffier *m* (du tribunal); *Constr* **c. of (the) works** conducteur *m* des travaux; *Sp* **c. of the course** commissaire *m* de piste (**b**) *Am* (*in shop*) vendeur, -euse (**c**) *Am* (*receptionist*) réceptionniste *mf* (**d**) *Rel* **c. (in holy orders)** ecclésiastique *m*

clerk² *vi Am* (**a**) (*work in office*) travailler comme employé, -ée de bureau (**b**) (*in shop*) travailler comme vendeur, -euse (**c**) *US Pol d'u Jur* **to c. for a senator/a judge** être assistant d'un sénateur/d'un juge

clever [ˈklevər] *adj* (**a**) (*intelligent*) intelligent; (*plan, gadget*) ingénieux, astucieux; *Sch* **c. at mathematics** fort en mathématiques; **he was too c. for us** il s'est montré plus malin que nous; *Pej* **he's/she's too c. by half** il/elle est bien trop malin/maligne; **don't get c. with me** ne fais pas le malin avec moi; *F* **a c. Dick** un petit malin (**b**) (*skilful*) habile, adroit; **to be c. with one's hands** être adroit *ou* habile de ses mains; **c. at doing sth** habile à faire qch; *F* **to play it c.** jouer serré

cleverly [ˈklevəlɪ] *adv* (**a**) (*intelligently*) avec intelligence, intelligemment; (*planned*) ingénieusement; **the dog had c. worked out how to …** le chien avait astucieusement découvert comment … (**b**) (*skilfully*) habilement, adroitement

cleverness [ˈklevənɪs] *n* (**a**) (*intelligence*) intelligence *f*; (*of invention etc*) ingéniosité *f* (**b**) (*with hands*) adresse *f*, dextérité *f*

cliché [ˈkliːʃeɪ] *n* cliché *m*

clichéd [ˈkliːʃeɪd] *adj* rebattu; **that's very c.** c'est un cliché

cliché-ridden *adj* bourré *ou* truffé de clichés

click¹ [klɪk] *n* (*sound*) bruit *m* sec, déclic *m*, clic *m*; (*of camera*) déclic; *Comptr* (*of keys, mouse*) clic; (*with tongue*) claquement *m* de langue; *Ling* clic; **he gave a c. of the tongue** il fit claquer sa langue; *Fig F* **something went c.** il y a eu comme un déclic, et puis ça a été le déclic

click² **1** *vi* (**a**) (*make a sound*) faire un petit bruit sec; *Comptr* (*with mouse*) cliquer; **she clicked along the pavement in her high heels** ses hauts talons faisaient de petits bruits secs sur le trottoir; **cameras were clicking** on entendait le déclic des appareils; **to c. together** (*of two parts*) s'emboîter (avec un bruit sec); **to c. shut** (*of door etc*) se refermer avec un bruit sec
(**b**) *Fig* (*become clear*) faire tilt; **now it's clicked** (*of one thing*) ça a fait tilt; (*of something more complicated*) tout s'est mis en place; **it'll c. if you work at it** tu finiras par comprendre si tu t'y mets
(**c**) *F* (*of two people*) **we clicked right away** nous nous sommes entendus à merveille tout de suite/dès le début; **to c. with the public** (*of play, film*) avoir du succès auprès du public
2 *vt* **to c. one's heels** (*when saluting*) (faire) claquer les talons; **to c. one's tongue** claquer la langue

▶ **click away** *vi* (*take photos*) prendre sans cesse des photos; **the photographers were clicking away furiously** les photographes s'en donnaient à cœur joie

▶ **click on 1** *vi Br F* (*understand*) piger **2** *vipo Comptr* cliquer, cliquer sur

clicking [ˈklɪkɪŋ] *n* (*noise*) cliquetis *m*

click language *n* langue *f* à clics

client [ˈklaɪənt] *n Com* (*of shop, lawyer etc*) client, -ente; **c. file** dossier *m* client, fichier *m* client; **c. list** liste *f* de clients; *Pej* **c. state/government** état *m*/gouvernement *m* à la solde d'un autre

clientele [kliːɒnˈtel] *n* (*of shop, lawyer etc*) clientèle *f*

client-server database *n Comptr* base *f* de données client-serveur

cliff [klɪf] *n* falaise *f*; (*in mountains*) à-pic *m*, *pl* à-pics

cliffhanger [ˈklɪfhæŋər] *n* (*film, novel etc*) film *m*/roman *m*/*etc* à suspense; (*situation*) situation *f* qui vous tient en haleine; **it was a real c.** ça m'a/nous a/*etc* tenu en haleine jusqu'à la fin; **a real c. of an ending** un finale qui vous tient en haleine; **the election/race was a c.** le résultat de l'élection/de la course est resté incertain jusqu'à la dernière minute

climacteric [klaɪˈmæktərɪk] *n* climatère *m*

climactic [klaɪˈmæktɪk] *adj* (*scene*) qui constitue le paroxysme; **the c. moment of the film** le paroxysme du film

climate [ˈklaɪmət] *n Met, Fig* climat *m*; *Aut* **c. control system** climatiseur *m*

climatic [klaɪˈmætɪk] *adj* climatique

climatologist [klaɪməˈtɒlədʒɪst] *n* climatologue *mf*

climatology [klaɪməˈtɒlədʒɪ] *n* climatologie *f*

climax¹ [ˈklaɪmæks] *n* (**a**) (*highest point*) paroxysme *m*; (*of play, piece of music etc*) point *m* culminant; (*of career*) apogée *f*, point culminant; **the c. of the festivities** l'apogée des réjouissances; **to reach a c.** (*of music*) atteindre son point culminant; **to work up to a c.** (*in rhetoric*) procéder par gradation (ascendante); *Th etc* corser l'action; **as a c. to**

the entertainment ... comme bouquet de la fête ... **(b)** (*sexual*) orgasme *m*

climax² *vi* **(a)** (*reach climax*) atteindre son paroxysme *ou* point culminant; **to c. in a firework display** finir en beauté par un feu d'artifice **(b)** (*have an orgasm*) jouir

climb¹ [klaɪm] *n* (*of rock face*) montée *f*, ascension *f*; (*of mountain*) ascension, course *f*; (*steep slope*) (*of road etc*) côte *f*, montée; *Fig* ascension; *Sp, Aut* **hill c.** course de côte; **to go for a c.** faire de l'escalade; *Av* **rate of c.** vitesse *f* ascensionnelle *ou* de montée; **a short c. takes you to the village** une petite montée vous mène au village

climb² **1** *vi* **(a)** grimper; **to c. on(to) the roof** monter *ou* grimper sur le toit; **to c. over the wall** escalader le mur; **to c. out of a hole** se hisser hors d'un trou; **to c. into bed** grimper dans son lit; *Fig* **to c. to power** gravir tous les échelons qui mènent au pouvoir; **to c. (socially** *or* **in the world)** s'élever (au-dessus de sa condition)

(b) *Sp* (*go mountain climbing*) faire de l'alpinisme; (*go rock climbing*) faire de la varappe

(c) (*rise*) (*of road*) monter; (*of prices*) monter, augmenter, *F* grimper

(d) *Av* prendre de l'altitude, monter; **the plane climbed 200 feet** l'avion a pris 60 mètres d'altitude

2 *vt* (*tree*) grimper à *ou* dans; (*ladder*) monter *ou* grimper à; (*cliff, mountain*) escalader

▸ **climb down** **1** *vi* **(a)** (*descend*) descendre; **to c. down out of a tree** descendre d'un arbre **(b)** *Fig* (*in negotiations etc*) reculer **2** *vipo* descendre

▸ **climb up** *vipo* = **climb² 2**

climb-down *n Fig* reculade *f*

climber ['klaɪmər] *n* **(a)** (*of mountain*) alpiniste *mf*; (*of rock face*) varappeur, -euse; (*leopard, koala etc*) grimpeur, -euse; *Fig Pej* **(social) c.** arriviste *mf* **(b)** *Bot* plante *f* grimpante

climbing ['klaɪmɪŋ] **1** *adj* (*plant*) grimpant; (*animal*) grimpeur **2** *n* escalade *f*; *Sp* alpinisme *m*; **(rock) c.** varappe *f*; *Pej* **social c.** arrivisme *m*

climbing frame *n* (*for children*) cage *f* à poules

climbing irons *npl* (*for mountaineer*) grappins *mpl*; (*on boots*) crampons *mpl*; (*for climbing trees, poles*) étriers *mpl*

climbing wall *n Sp* mur *m* d'escalade *ou* de varappe

clime [klaɪm] *n Lit* (*climate*) climat *m*; **they have gone to sunnier** *or* **warmer climes** ils sont partis sous des cieux plus cléments; **in these climes** sous ces climats

clinch¹ [klɪntʃ] *n* **(a)** *F* (*embrace*) étreinte *f*; **to go into a c.** (*of lovers*) s'étreindre **(b)** *Boxing* clinch *m*; **to break a c.** briser un corps à corps; **to go into a c.** se prendre corps à corps

clinch² **1** *vt* (*settle*) (*deal*) conclure, clore; (*argument*) confirmer; **that clinches it!** c'est terminé!; **that was what clinched it for me** c'est ce qui m'a décidé **2** *vi* **(a)** *Boxing* en venir aux prises, se prendre corps à corps **(b)** *F* (*of lovers*) s'étreindre

clincher ['klɪntʃər] *n F* **(a)** (*argument*) argument *m* irréfutable; **that was the c. for me** (*that realization, experience etc*) c'est ce qui m'a décidé **(b)** *Sp* but *m*/point *m* décisif

cling¹ [klɪŋ] *vi* (*pt, pp* **clung** [klʌŋ]) (*of child*) s'accrocher, se cramponner (**to sth/sb** à qch/qn); *Fig Pej* coller (**to sb** qn); (*of plant*) (*to wall*) s'accrocher (**to** à); **to c. to the figure** (*of garment*) mouler le corps; **he clung to the rope for dear life** il s'agrippa à la corde de toutes ses forces; **the two children were clinging to each other** les deux enfants étaient serrés l'un contre l'autre; *Fig* **to c. (on) to one's children/wife/ideas** s'accrocher à ses enfants/sa femme/ses idées; **to c. to an opinion** persister dans une opinion; **to c. to a hope** se raccrocher à un espoir

cling² *n* **c. (peach)** pavie *f*

clingfilm ['klɪŋfɪlm] *n Br* film *m* alimentaire

clinging ['klɪŋɪŋ] *adj* (*plant*) qui s'accroche; (*garment*) collant, qui colle; (*material*) qui moule le corps; (*perfume*) tenace; *F* (*person*) collant; (*parent, boyfriend etc*) possessif; **c. vine** (*plant*) vigne *f* grimpante; *Am Fig F* (*person*) pot *m* de colle

clingy ['klɪŋɪ] *adj Pej* collant; **she's so c.** (*child*) elle est toujours dans mes jupes; **he's the c. type** c'est le genre collant

clinic ['klɪnɪk] *n Med* **(a)** (*for outpatients*) dispensaire *m*, centre *m* médical **(b)** *Br* (*nursing home*) clinique *f*

clinical ['klɪnɪk(ə)l] *adj* **(a)** *Med* clinique; (*thermometer*) médical; **c. psychology** psychologie *f* clinique **(b)** *Fig* (*analysis, approach*) froid

clinically ['klɪnɪklɪ] *adv* **(a)** *Med* cliniquement; **c. dead** cliniquement mort **(b)** *Fig* (*coldly, in detached way*) froidement

clinician [klɪ'nɪʃ(ə)n] *n* clinicien, -ienne

clink¹ [klɪŋk] *n* (*sound*) tintement *m*

clink² **1** *vi* (*of glasses etc*) tinter **2** *vt* faire tinter; **to c. glasses** choquer les verres, trinquer

clink³ *n Br Sl* (*prison*) taule *f*, tôle *f*; **to be in (the) c.** être en taule *ou* tôle

clinker ['klɪŋkər] *n* **(a)** *Constr* (*for tiling*) brique *f* hollandaise; (*vitrified*) brique vitrifiée, brique à four **(b)** (*cinders*) (*of forge etc*) mâchefer *m*

clinker-built *adj Naut* bordé à clin(s)

clip¹ [klɪp] *n* **(a)** (*for attaching, holding*) pince *f*; (*brooch*) clip *m*; (*hair ornament*) barrette *f*; **(paper) c.** trombone *m*; **bicycle** *or* **trouser c.** pince à pantalon, pince-pantalon *m inv*; *TV, Rad* **c. mike** micro *m* cravate **(b)** *El* (*of wire, cable*) cosse *f*

clip² *vt* (-pp-) **to c. (together)** (*papers*) attacher (avec un trombone); **to c. one document to another** attacher un document à un autre; **to c. a brooch on a blouse** accrocher une broche à un chemisier; **to c. a microphone to sb's tie** attacher *ou* fixer un micro à la cravate de qn

clip³ *n* **(a)** (*cut*) (*of dog etc*) tondage *m*; **to give a hedge a c.** couper *ou* tailler une haie; **to give one's nails a c.** se couper les ongles **(b)** *F* (*blow*) **c. (on the ear)** taloche *f* **(c)** *Cin* (*of film, programme etc*) extrait *m* **(d)** *US* (*from newspaper*) coupure *f*

clip⁴ *vt* **(a)** (*cut*) (*dog, lawn*) tondre; (*hedge*) couper, tailler; (*metal plate*) couper, cisailler; **to c. the wings of a bird** rogner les ailes à un oiseau; *Fig* **to c. sb's wings** rogner les ailes à qn; **to c. ten seconds off a record** améliorer un record de dix secondes **(b)** *Rail etc* (*ticket*) poinçonner **(c)** (*hit*) *Tennis* **to c. the line** (*of ball*) mordre la ligne; *F* **to c. sb's ear** flanquer une taloche à qn; **I just clipped the wall** j'ai effleuré le mur

▸ **clip on** **1** *vtsep* attacher **2** *vi* s'attacher

clip art *n Comptr* clipart *m*

clipboard ['klɪpbɔːd] *n* planchette *f* porte-papiers; *Comptr* presse-papiers *m*, bloc-notes *m*; *Comptr* **c. file** fichier *m* presse-papiers

clip-clop ['klɪpklɒp] *n* = bruit *m* de sabots; **the horse went c. down the street** on entendit le bruit des sabots du cheval qui descendait la rue

clip joint *n Am Sl* = boîte *f* de nuit/restaurant *m* où l'on se fait escroquer

clip-on **1** *adj* qui s'attache avec une pince; **c. earring** clip *m*; **c. tie** cravate *f* à système; **c. microphone** micro-cravate *m* **2** *n* (*earring*) clip *m*

clipped [klɪpt] *adj* (*pronunciation, speech*) saccadé

clipper ['klɪpər] *n Naut* clipper *m*; *Av* **c. class** classe *f* affaires

clippers ['klɪpəz] *npl* (*for the hair etc*) tondeuse *f*; **(hedge) c.** taille-buissons *m inv*; **(nail) c.** coupe-ongles *m inv*

clippie ['klɪpɪ] *n Old-fashioned Br F* receveuse *f* (d'autobus)

clipping ['klɪpɪŋ] *n* **(a)** (*from newspaper*) coupure *f* de presse **(b) clippings** (*from nail*) rognures *fpl*; (*from hair*) mèches *fpl* (*de cheveux coupés*); (*from hedge*) bouts *mpl* de branches

clique [kliːk] *n Pej* coterie *f*, clique *f*

cliqu(e)y ['kliːkɪ], **cliquish** ['kliːkɪʃ] *adj F* qui a l'esprit de clique

clitoral ['klɪtərəl] *adj* clitoridien

clitoridectomy [klɪtərɪ'dektəmɪ] *n* clitoridectomie *f*

clitoris ['klɪtərɪs] *n* clitoris *m*

cloak¹ [kləʊk] *n* (grande) cape *f*; *Fig Lit* **under the c. of night** sous le couvert de la nuit

cloak² *vt* couvrir *ou* revêtir d'une (grande) cape; *Fig* **cloaked in mystery** enveloppé de mystère

cloak-and-dagger *adj* (*film, novel*) de cape et d'épée; **it was all very c.** c'était très mystérieux; **what's all this c. stuff about?** qu'est-ce que c'est que tout ce mystère?

cloakroom ['kləʊkruːm] *n* (*for coats etc*) vestiaire *m*; *Br* (*lavatory*) toilettes *fpl*; *Br* **ladies' c.** (*lavatory*) toilettes des dames; **c. attendant** préposé, -ée au vestiaire; *Br* (*in lavatory*) préposé, -ée aux cabinets de toilette, *F* dame *f* pipi, *pl* dames pipi

clobber¹ ['klɒbər] *n Br F* **(a)** (*clothes*) frusques *fpl*, fringues *fpl* **(b)** (*belongings*) bazar *m*, fourbi *m*

clobber² *vt Br F* (*hit*) tabasser; (*defeat heavily*) flanquer une raclée à

clobbering ['klɒbərɪŋ] *n Br F* **to get a c.** (*be beaten up*) prendre une dérouillée *ou* une raclée; (*be heavily defeated*) se prendre une pâtée; **to give sb a c.** (*beat up*) tabasser qn, flanquer une raclée à qn; (*defeat*) flanquer une raclée à qn

cloche [klɒʃ] *n* cloche *f*

clock¹ [klɒk] *n* **(a)** horloge *f*; (*small*) pendule *f*; *F* **to watch the c.** (*of employee*) avoir les yeux rivés sur l'horloge, ne penser qu'à l'heure de la sortie; **I don't pay you to come in here and watch the c.** je ne vous paie pas pour que vous passiez votre temps à ne rien faire; **a full hour by the c.** une bonne heure d'horloge; **to work round the c.** travailler vingt-quatre heures sur vingt-quatre; **a race against the c.** une course contre la montre; **to beat the c.** arriver/finir avant l'heure; **to put** *or* **turn the clocks back** (*in autumn*) retarder les pendules; *Fig* **to put the c. back** revenir en arrière, *Pej* régresser; **the measures will turn the c. back to Victorian times** les mesures nous feront retourner à l'époque victorienne; *Aut* **dashboard c.** pendule de tableau de bord (**b**) *Aut* (*milometer*) compteur *m*; (*in taxi*) compteur horokilométrique, taximètre *m*; **15 000 miles on the c.** 15 000 mil(l)es au compteur

(**c**) *Comptr* horloge *f*; **c. rate** fréquence *f* d'horloge; **c. speed** fréquence *f* d'horloge; **c. speed doubler** doubleur *m* de fréquence (d'horloge)

clock[2] *vt F* (**a**) *Sp etc* (*measure speed of*) (*runner etc*) chronométrer (**b**) (*reach speed*) faire; *Aut* **to c. ninety** faire du 150 chrono; **the fastest time he's clocked this year** son meilleur temps cette année (**c**) *Br Sl* (*see*) repérer

▶ **clock in 1** *vi* (**a**) *Sp* (*have a time of*) **for the 100 metres she clocked in at nine seconds** elle a fait neuf secondes aux 100 mètres; **the last of the marathon runners clocked in at six hours** le dernier marathonien a effectué le parcours en six heures (**b**) *Ind* (*record arrival at work*) pointer (en arrivant); **you clocked in 10 minutes late** vous avez pointé avec 10 minutes de retard **2** *vtsep Ind* **to c. sb in** pointer pour qn

▶ **clock off** *Ind* **1** *vi* (*record departure from work*) pointer (en partant) **2** *vtsep* **to c. sb off** pointer pour qn

▶ **clock on** *vi, vtsep* = **clock in 1(b), 2**

▶ **clock out** *vi, vtsep* = **clock off**

▶ **clock up** *vtsep* (*achieve*) (parvenir à) atteindre; **she has clocked up 700 kilometres in two days** elle a fait 700 kilomètres en deux jours

clock-doubled ['klɒkdʌb(ə)ld] *adj Comptr* à fréquence d'horloge doublée

clock golf *n* golf *m* miniature

clocking in ['klɒkɪŋ] *n Ind* pointage *m* à l'arrivée; **c. card** fiche *f* de pointage

clocking off *n Ind* pointage *m* à la sortie

clocking on *n Ind* = **clocking in**

clocking out *n Ind* = **clocking off**

clocklike ['klɒklaɪk] *adj* (*regularity*) d'horloge

clockmaker ['klɒkmeɪkər] *n* horloger, -ère

clock-watcher ['klɒkwɒtʃər] *n F* employé, -ée qui ne pense qu'à l'heure de sortie, tire-au-flanc *m inv*

clockwise ['klɒkwaɪz] *adv, adj* dans le sens des aiguilles d'une montre

clockwork ['klɒkwɜːk] **1** *n* mouvement *m* d'horloge; (*in toy etc*) mécanisme *m* à ressort; **as regular as c.** réglé comme du papier à musique; **everything's going like c.** tout va *ou* marche comme sur des roulettes; **the hotel runs like c.** l'hôtel marche sans problème **2** *adj* (*toy*) mécanique; (*mechanism*) qui se remonte; **everything is done with c. precision** tout est réglé comme du papier à musique; *Sl* **as queer as a c. orange** (*homosexual*) pédé comme un phoque

clod [klɒd] *n* (**a**) (*of earth*) motte *f* (**b**) *F* (*stupid person*) lourdaud *m*; **you great c.!** espèce de lourdaud!

clodhopper ['klɒdhɒpər] *n F* (**a**) (*person*) lourdaud *m* (**b**) **clodhoppers** (*shoes*) (grosses) godasses *fpl*

clog[1] [klɒg] *n* (*shoe*) gros brodequin *m* à semelle de bois; (**wooden**) **c.** sabot *m*; *F* **to pop one's clogs** (*die*) casser sa pipe; **c. dance** sabotière *f*

clog[2] (-gg-) **1** *vt* (**a**) (*block*) (*artery, pipe etc*) boucher, obstruer; (*firearm, machine*) encrasser; (*filter*) boucher, encrasser; **our boots got clogged with mud** nos bottes se sont crottées dans la boue (**b**) (*prevent from moving*) (*animal*) entraver; *Fig* (*enterprise etc*) entraver, gêner **2** *vi* (*of artery, pipe etc*) se boucher, s'obstruer; (*of firearm, machine*) s'encrasser; (*of filter*) se boucher, s'encrasser

▶ **clog up** *vtsep, vi* = **clog**[2] **1 (a), 2**

cloister[1] ['klɔɪstər] *n* (**a**) *Archit* (*usu pl*) **cloisters** (*of convent, church etc*) cloître *m* (**b**) *Rel* (*monastery*) monastère *m*

cloister[2] *vt* cloîtrer

cloistered ['klɔɪstəd] *adj* (**a**) (*life*) de cloître, cloîtré; *Fig* **a c. childhood** une enfance protégée; **to lead a very c. life** mener une vie très protégée (**b**) *Archit* entouré d'un cloître

clone[1] [kləʊn] *n Bot, Biol, Comptr etc* clone *m*; **a Gazza/Princess Di c.** un sosie de Gazza/Lady Di

clone[2] *vt Bot, Biol, Comptr* cloner

cloner ['kləʊnər] *n Mktg* cloneur *m*

cloning ['kləʊnɪŋ] *n Bot, Biol, Comptr* clonage *m*

close[1] [kləʊs] **1** *adj* (**a**) (*in distance, time*) proche; (*to each other*) rapproché; (*ties*) étroit; **we must be c. now** nous devons être près maintenant; **our office is c. to the town hall** notre bureau est près de la mairie; **he was c.** (*of person guessing*) il brûlait; **to be c. to tears** être au bord des larmes; **to be (very) c. to victory** être (tout) près de la victoire; *Mil* **c. combat** corps à corps *m*; *Mus* **c. harmony** tessiture *f* limitée; **c. intervals** intervalles *mpl* rapprochés; **c. proximity** proximité *f* immédiate; **I saw him at c. quarters** je l'ai vu de près; **to fire at c. range** tirer à bout portant; *Mktg* **c. substitute** substitut *m* rapproché

(**b**) (*in relationship*) proche; **to be c. to sb** être proche de qn; **he and his brother are very c.** lui et son frère sont très proches; **Italian is c. to French** l'italien est proche du français; **to be in c. contact** être en contact étroit; **a c. friend** un ami intime; **a c. relative** un parent proche, un proche

(**c**) (*careful*) (*attention*) soutenu; (*observer*) attentif; (*study*) minutieux; **on closer examination** en y regardant de plus près; **after c. consideration** après mûre réflexion; **to keep (a) c. watch on sb/sth** surveiller qn/qch de près; **a c. copy of sth** une bonne imitation de qch

(**d**) (*secret*) intime; **to keep sth a c. secret** garder le secret absolu sur qch; **to keep sth c.** (*be secretive*) ne rien dire de qch; **to play a c. game** jouer serré

(**e**) (*weather*) lourd; **it's c. in here** (*stuffy*) on étouffe ici; **it's c. today** il fait lourd aujourd'hui

(**f**) (*dense*) serré, dense; (*thicket, woods*) épais, touffu; **c. grain** (*of metal, stone, wood etc*) grain *m* serré *ou* fin; *Mil* **in c. order** *or* **ranks** en rangs serrés; **c. texture** (*of metal, stone etc*) (con)texture *f* serrée, tissu *m* serré

(**g**) (*contest*) serré; **c. election** élection *f* vivement contestée; *Sp* **c. finish** arrivée *f* serrée; **c. match** match *m* serré; **a c. shave** un rasage de près; *Fig* **that was a c. shave** *or* **thing** *or* **call** nous l'avons/ils l'ont/*etc* échappé belle, *F* c'était moins une *ou* cinq

(**h**) **c. season** (*in hunting*) chasse *f* fermée; *Fishing* pêche *f* fermée; (*in sport*) trêve *f*

(**i**) *Ling* **c. vowel** voyelle *f* fermée

(**j**) *F* **to be c. with money** être près de ses sous

2 *adv* (*near*) près, de près; **to be** *or* **follow c. behind sb** suivre qn de près; **to stand c. against a wall** se coller contre un mur; **houses c. together** maisons serrées les unes contre les autres; **to sit/stand c. together** etre/se tenir serrés; **to keep c.** rester tout près; **it keeps c. to the original** cela reste proche de l'original; **c. to** *or* **by sb/sth** (tout) près de *ou* à proximité de qn/qch; **to keep c. to sb** se tenir tout près de qn; **he lives c. to here** il habite tout près *ou* à deux pas (d'ici); **to come** *or* **draw c./closer to sb** s'approcher/se rapprocher de qn; **it's brought us closer** ça nous a rapprochés; **put it closer to the door** mets-le plus près de la porte; **c. to the ground** au ras *ou* près du sol; **to cut c.** (*hair*) couper ras; **to keep c. to the text** rester près du texte; **she came c. to losing her job** elle a failli perdre son emploi; **to come c. to death** frôler la mort; **to come c. to the world record** frôler le record du monde; **c. at hand, c. by** tout près, tout contre; **c. on nine (o'clock)** tout près de neuf heures; **to be c. on fifty** (*age*) friser la cinquantaine

close[2] *n* (**a**) *Br* (*street*) impasse *f*, cul-de-sac *m*, *pl* culs-de-sac (**b**) (*of cathedral*) enceinte *f*

close[3] [kləʊz] *n* (*end*) fin *f*, conclusion *f*; (*of year*) fin; (*of meeting, session*) clôture *f*, levée *f*; *St Exch* **at c. of business** à la *ou* en clôture; *Lit* **at c. of day** à la tombée du jour; *Cr* **at c. of play** à la fin de la journée; **to draw to a c.** tirer à sa fin

close[4] **1** *vt* (**a**) (*door, eyes, book, shop etc*) fermer; (*road*) barrer; **a road closed to motor traffic** une route interdite à la circulation automobile; **cold closes the pores** le froid resserre les pores; *Fig* **to c. ranks** serrer les rangs, faire bloc; **the party closed ranks around its leader** le parti a fait bloc autour de son leader

(**b**) (*bring to an end*) (*matter*) conclure, terminer; (*meeting, session*) lever, clore; (*debate*) fermer; (*account*) fermer, clôturer; **to declare the discussion closed** prononcer la clôture des débats

(**c**) (*shut down*) (*factory, shop, railway line etc*) fermer (définitivement)

(**d**) (*finalize*) (*sale*) conclure; (*deal*) arrêter

(**e**) *Acct* **to c. the books** régler les livres; **to c. an account** arrêter un compte

2 *vi* (**a**) (*of door etc*) (se) fermer; (*of wound, hole etc*) se refermer; **the theatre will c. for a month** le théâtre fermera pendant un mois; **theatres c. on Good Friday** les théâtres font relâche le vendredi saint

(**b**) (*end*) finir, se terminer; **I must c. now** (*in letter writing*) je dois te quitter; **I will c. with a story** pour terminer, je vais vous raconter une histoire

(**c**) (*shut down*) (*of factory, shop, railway line etc*) fermer (définitivement)

(**d**) *St Exch* clôturer; **the shares closed at £1.57** les actions ont clôturé à 1,57 £

▶ **close down 1** *vtsep* (*factory etc*) fermer (définitivement) **2** *vi* (**a**) (*of factory, shop etc*) fermer (définitivement), fermer ses portes; (*of shopkeeper*) fermer boutique (**b**) *Rad, TV* terminer ses émissions

▶ **close in 1** *vi* (**a**) (*approach*) (*of night*) tomber; **the police/his creditors are closing in** l'étau de la police/de ses créanciers se resserre (**b**) (*get shorter*) (*of days*) raccourcir **2** *vtsep* (*enclose*) (*land etc*) clôturer

▶ **close in on** *vipo* (*person*) encercler, cerner; **darkness closed in on us** la nuit nous enveloppa
▶ **close off** *vtsep* fermer; (*road*) barrer; *Acct* **to c. off an account** arrêter un compte
▶ **close out** *vtsep St Exch* **to c. a position** boucler *ou* clore *ou* fermer une position
▶ **close round** *vipo* (*person*) cerner, se presser autour de
▶ **close up 1** *vi* **(a)** (*of aperture*) s'obturer; (*of wound, hole etc*) se refermer **(b)** (*of people*) se serrer, se tasser; *Mil etc* **c. up!** serrez (les rangs)! **(c)** (*of shopkeeper*) fermer **2** *vtsep* **(a)** (*seal*) (*opening etc*) boucher, obturer **(b)** (*shop, house*) fermer **(c)** *Typ* (*characters*) rapprocher; *Mil etc* (*ranks*) serrer; **the car accelerated to c. up the gap** la voiture accéléra pour réduire l'écart
▶ **close with** *vipo* **(a)** *Com* **to c. with sb** conclure un/le marché avec qn **(b)** (*in fighting*) **to c. with sb** se battre avec qn

close box *n Comptr* case *f* de fermeture
close-cropped ['kləʊs'krɒpt] *adj* (*hair*) coupé ras; (*grass*) rasé, tondu ras
closed [kləʊzd] *adj* (*door, electrical circuit etc*) fermé; **c.** (*notice*) *Th* relâche; (*on shop*) fermé; **behind c. doors** (*of official meeting etc*) à huis clos; **with eyes c.** les yeux fermés; **to have a c. mind** être hermétique aux idées des autres *ou* aux idées nouvelles; **it remains a c. book to me** je n'y comprends rien; **road c.** (*notice*) rue barrée; **c. question** question *f* fermée; **c. season** (*in hunting*) période *f* d'interdiction, fermeture *f* de la chasse; *TV, Cin* **c. set** plateau *m* fermé; *Ind* **c. shop** atelier *m*/chantier *m*/*etc* qui n'admet pas de travailleurs non syndiqués; **c.-shop policy** exclusivité *f* syndicale; *Comptr* **c. user group** groupe *m* fermé d'utilisateurs
closed-circuit television *n* télévision *f* à *ou* en circuit fermé
close-down *n* **(a)** (*of factory etc*) fermeture *f* **(b)** *TV, Rad* fin *f* des émissions
close-fisted [kləʊs'fɪstɪd] *adj* avare, pingre
close-fitting *adj* (*dress etc*) bien ajusté
close-knit *adj* (*community etc*) étroitement lié, très uni
closely ['kləʊslɪ] *adv* **(a)** (*to examine, watch*) de près, attentivement; (*to listen*) attentivement; (*to resemble*) beaucoup; (*followed, observed*) de près; (*connected, guarded, related*) étroitement; **c. cut** tondu ras; **c. contested** vivement contesté **(b)** (*densely*) **a c. planted forest** une forêt très dense; **c. packed** (*people*) entassé; **c. packed in a box** serré dans une boîte; **two c. written pages** deux pages d'une écriture serrée; **a c. printed book** un livre imprimé très petit; **a c. reasoned argument** une argumentation très détaillée
closeness ['kləʊsnɪs] *n* **(a)** (*nearness*) proximité *f* **(to** de) **(b)** (*of relationship, contact etc*) intimité *f* **(to sb** avec qn) **(c)** (*of description*) exactitude *f*; (*of translation*) fidélité *f*, exactitude **(d)** (*stuffiness*) manque *m* d'air **(e)** (*of weather*) lourdeur *f* **(f)** (*reserve, secretiveness*) (*of person*) réserve *f*, caractère *m* réservé **(g)** (*meanness*) avarice *f*, pingrerie *f*
close-range *adj Mil* **c. weapon** arme *f* à courte portée
close-run *adj* (*election, race*) serré; **we won in the end, but it was a c. thing** on a fini par gagner, mais il s'en est fallu d'un cheveu; **he may not be as boring as Thomas but it's a c. thing** il n'est peut-être pas aussi ennuyeux que Thomas, mais presque
close-set *adj* (*eyes*) rapproché
close-shaven *adj* rasé de près
closet¹ ['klɒzɪt] **1** *n* **(a)** *esp Am* (*cupboard*) placard *m*, armoire *f*; *F* **to come out of the c.** (*of homosexual*) se déclarer homosexuel, révéler (publiquement) qu'on est homosexuel; *F* **many economists are coming out of the c. as Keynesians** beaucoup d'économistes se révèlent keynésiens; *F* **many Country music fans are now coming out of the c.** bien des fans de country avouent maintenant leur passion
(b) *Arch* (*room*) cabinet *m* de travail, bureau *m*
(c) *Old-fashioned* **(water) c.** waters *mpl*, cabinets *mpl*
2 *adj* (*secret*) (*discussions etc*) confidentiel; **c. homosexual/communist** homosexuel, -elle/communiste *mf* qui n'ose pas s'avouer
closet² *vt* **(-t-) to be closeted with sb** être enfermé avec qn
close-up ['kləʊsʌp] *n Cin, TV* gros plan *m*, plan serré; **in c.** en gros plan; *Fig* **the programme gives us a c. of life in prison** l'émission nous donne une vision en gros plan de la vie carcérale
closing ['kləʊzɪŋ] **1** *adj* (*final*) dernier, final, -als *ou* -aux; **the c. bid** la dernière enchère; **c. headlines** rappel *m* des titres; *St Exch* **c. prices** cours *mpl* de clôture; *St Exch* **c. trade** transaction *f* de clôture; **c. speech** discours *m* de fin de séance *ou* de clôture; **c. remarks** remarques *fpl* en guise de conclusion (*à la fin d'une conférence etc*)
2 *n* **(a)** (*shutting*) (*of shops, factory, theatre etc*) fermeture *f* **(b)** (*ending*) (*of bank account*) fermeture *f*; (*of meeting, session*) levée *f*; (*of conference*) clôture *f*
(c) *Fin, Admin* (*of account*) arrêté *m*, règlement *m*; *St Exch* **c. (out) of a position** clôture *f* d'une position
closing date *n* date *f* limite; **the c. for applications for the course is ...** le registre des inscriptions sera clos le ...
closing down *n* (*of factory*) fermeture *f* (définitive); **c. sale** (*sign in shop window*) liquidation *f* totale avant fermeture définitive
closing off *n* **(a)** *Acct* (*of accounts*) arrêt *m* **(b)** *Comptr* (*of bad sector*) fermeture *f*
closing time *n* heure *f* de fermeture
closure ['kləʊʒər] *n* **(a)** (*of factory etc*) fermeture *f* (définitive); *St Exch* **c. by repurchase** clôture *f* par rachat **(b)** *Parl* clôture *f*; **to move the c.** voter la clôture
clot¹ [klɒt] *n* **(a)** (*of blood*) caillot *m* **(b)** *Br F* (*stupid person*) patate *f*, andouille *f*
clot² **(-tt-) 1** *vi* (*of blood*) (se) coaguler **2** *vt* (*cream*) caillebotter; (*blood*) coaguler
cloth, *pl* **cloths** [klɒθ, klɒθs] *n* **(a)** (*material*) étoffe *f*; (*linen, cotton*) toile *f*; **c. of gold** drap *m* d'or; **c. binding** reliure *f* en toile; *Br* **c. cap image** *expression qui dénote le côté ouvrier des origines ou des attitudes de qn*; **the Labour Party wants to get rid of its c. cap image** les travaillistes veulent se débarrasser de leur image 'prolo'; *Br F* **hey, c. ears, didn't you hear me?** espèce de sourdingue, tu n'as pas entendu ce que j'ai dit? **(b)** (*individual piece*) linge *m*; (*for cleaning*) chiffon *m*; (*tablecloth*) nappe *f*; *Th* toile *f* (de décor) **(c)** *Rel F* **the c.** (*the clergy*) le clergé; **a man of the c.** un membre du clergé
cloth-bound *adj* relié toile
clothe [kləʊð] *vt* (*pt, pp* **clad** [klæd] *or* **clothed** [kləʊðd]) (*dress*) vêtir, habiller **(in, with** de); **three children to feed and c.** trois enfants à nourrir et à habiller; **warmly/lightly clad** chaudement/légèrement vêtu
cloth-eared *adj Br F* (*deaf*) dur de la feuille
clothes [kləʊðz] *npl* vêtements *mpl*, habits *mpl*; **in one's best c.** (tout) endimanché; **to put on/take off one's c.** s'habiller/se déshabiller; **to go to bed with one's c. on** *or* **in one's c.** se coucher tout habillé; **with no c. on** (tout) nu; **dirty c.** (*washing*) linge *m* sale
clothes basket *n* panier *m* à linge
clothes brush *n* brosse *f* à habits
clothes closet *n Am* penderie *f*
clothes hanger *n* cintre *m*
clothes hook *n* patère *f*
clotheshorse ['kləʊðzhɔːs] *n* séchoir *m* (à linge); *esp Am Fig F* **she's a c.** à part les fringues, rien ne l'intéresse
clothesline ['kləʊðzlaɪn] *n* corde *f* à linge
clothes peg *n* pince *f* à linge
clothespin ['kləʊðzpɪn] *n esp Am* pince *f* à linge
clothes pole *n* **(a)** poteau *m* de corde à linge **(b)** *Scot, US* (*prop*) perche *f* de corde à linge
clothes prop *n* perche *f* de corde à linge
clothier ['kləʊðɪər] *n Com* **(a)** (*clothes seller*) marchand, -ande de confections **(b)** (*cloth seller*) marchand, -ande de drap; (*cloth maker*) fabricant, -ante de drap
clothing ['kləʊðɪŋ] *n* (*no pl*) (*clothes*) habillement *m*, vêtements *mpl*; **warm c.** vêtements chauds; **articles of c.** vêtements; **the c. trade** l'industrie *f* du vêtement
clothing allowance *n* indemnité *f* vestimentaire
clotted ['klɒtɪd] *adj Br Culin* **c. cream** = crème *f* très épaisse
clotting ['klɒtɪŋ] *n* (*of blood*) coagulation *f*
cloud¹ [klaʊd] *n* **(a)** *Met* nuage *m*, *Lit* nuée *f*; *Fig* **to have one's head in the clouds** être dans les nuages *ou* dans la lune; *F* **to be on c. nine** être aux anges; *Prov* **every c. has a silver lining** à quelque chose malheur est bon; *Fig* **to be under a c.** (*suspected*) être *ou* faire l'objet de soupçons; (*out of favour*) être en défaveur; **he left the firm under a c.** il a quitté la société dans une atmosphère de scandale étouffé; **this was not enough to remove the c. of suspicion hanging over him** cela ne suffit pas à faire oublier la méfiance à son égard **(b)** (*of smoke, dust*) nuage *m*, voile *m* **(c)** (*swarm*) (*of locusts etc*) nuée *f*
cloud² **1** *vt* (*liquid*) troubler, rendre trouble; (*mirror*) ternir; (*by breathing on it*) embuer; (*sb's happiness*) troubler; (*reputation*) ternir; **a clouded sky** un ciel plein de nuages; **eyes clouded with tears** yeux voilés de larmes; **to c. the issue** embrouiller la question **2** *vi* (*of sky*) se couvrir *ou* se voiler (de nuages)
▶ **cloud over** *vi* (*of sky*) se couvrir *ou* se voiler (de nuages); *Fig* (*of face*) s'assombrir; **it clouded over in the afternoon** ça s'est couvert dans l'après-midi
▶ **cloud up 1** *vi* **it's clouding up** ça se couvre; **the mirror had**

clouded up le miroir s'était couvert de buée **2** *vtsep* (*windows*) embuer
cloud bank *n* banc *m* de nuages
cloudburst ['klaudbɜ:st] *n* trombe(s) *f(pl)* d'eau, averse *f* violente
cloud chamber *n Nucl* chambre *f* de détente *ou* d'ionisation
cloud-cuckoo-land *n* **you're living in c. if you think ...** tu te fais des idées *ou* tu rêves doucement *ou Can* tu rêves en couleurs si tu penses que ...; **that's c.** il rêve/tu rêves/*etc*
clouded ['klaudɪd] *adj* (*sky*) couvert (de nuages); (*liquid*) trouble; **to become c.** (*of sky*) se couvrir; (*of mind*) s'obscurcir
cloudiness ['klaudɪnɪs] *n* **(a)** (*of sky*) aspect *m* nuageux **(b)** (*of liquid*) turbidité *f*
cloudless ['klaudlɪs] *adj* (*sky*) sans nuages
cloudy ['klaudɪ] *adj* **(a)** (*weather*) couvert; (*sky*) nuageux; **it's c.** le temps est couvert; **a c. day** un jour nuageux **(b)** (*liquid*) trouble; *Med* (*urine*) chargé
clout[1] [klaut] *n* **(a)** *F* (*influence*) influence *f*; (*power*) poids *m*; **to have (plenty of) c.** (*be powerful*) être puissant; (*be influential*) avoir de l'influence *ou* le bras long **(b)** *F* (*blow*) coup *m*, taloche *f*; **he gave himself a c. on the ...** il s'est donné un coup sur le ... **(c)** *Br Old-fashioned, Dial* (*cloth*) chiffon *m*
clout[2] *vt F* flanquer une taloche à
clove[1] [kləuv] *n Bot, Culin* **c. of garlic** gousse *f* d'ail
clove[2] *n* **(a)** *Bot, Culin* clou *m* de girofle; **oil of cloves** essence *f* de girofle; **c. tree** giroflier *m* **(b)** (*flower*) **c. pink** œillet-giroflée *m*, *pl* œillets-giroflées, œillet *m* des fleuristes
clove[3] *pt see* **cleave**
clove hitch *n* (*knot*) demi-clef *f*, *pl* demi-clefs
cloven ['kləuv(ə)n] *adj* **c. foot** *or* **hoof** (*of ruminant, devil*) pied *m* fourchu
cloven-footed, -hoofed ['kləuv(ə)n'futɪd, -'hu:ft] *adj Zool* au pied fourchu
clover ['kləuvər] *n* (*plant*) trèfle *m*; **c. leaf** feuille *f* de trèfle; *F* **to be** *or* **live in c.** être *ou* vivre comme un coq en pâte
cloverleaf, *pl* **-leafs, -leaves** ['kləuvəli:f, -li:fs, -li:vz] *n* **c. (intersection)** croisement *m ou* carrefour *m* en trèfle
clown[1] [klaun] *n* (*in circus*), *Fig* clown *m*; *Th* bouffon *m*; **to act the c.** faire le clown; **to make a c. of oneself** se ridiculiser
clown[2] *vi* = **clown about**
▶ **clown about, clown around** *vi* faire le clown *ou* le pitre
clowning ['klaunɪŋ] *n Th, Fig* bouffonneries *fpl*, pitreries *fpl*
clownish ['klaunɪʃ] *adj* clownesque
cloy [klɔɪ] *vi Lit* **delights that never c.** plaisirs dont on ne se lasse pas
cloying ['klɔɪɪŋ] *adj* (*cake, taste etc*), *Fig* écœurant
club[1] [klʌb] *n* **(a)** (*political, literary, gentlemen's etc*) club *m*, cercle *m*; (*sporting*) club; **football/tennis/yacht c.** club de football/tennis/yachting; **I've got a cold — join the c.!** j'ai un rhume — on est deux!; *F* **to be in the (pudding) c.** (*pregnant*) avoir un polichinelle dans le tiroir; **c. chair** club; **c. tie** cravate *f* aux couleurs d'une association sportive **(b)** (*nightclub*) boîte *f* de nuit; **the London c. scene** les milieux nocturnes londoniens **(c)** (*weapon etc*) massue *f*, gourdin *m*; *Golf* club *m*, crosse *f*; *Gym* **(Indian) c.** massue de gymnastique **(d)** *Cards* trèfle *m*; **ace of clubs** as *m* de trèfle
club[2] *vt* **(-bb-)** (*hit*) frapper avec une massue *ou* avec un gourdin; **to c. sb to death** tuer qn à coups de gourdin
▶ **club together** *vi* se cotiser, mettre son argent en commun; **to c. together to buy sth** se cotiser pour acheter qch
clubbable ['klʌbəb(ə)l] *adj Old-fashioned* sociable
clubber ['klʌbər] *n F* fêtard *m*, adepte *mf* des boîtes de nuit
clubbing ['klʌbɪŋ] *n F* **to go c.** aller en boîte
club class *n* (*on plane*) classe *f* affaires
club foot *n Med* pied *m* bot
clubfooted ['klʌbfutɪd] *adj Med* qui a un pied bot
clubhouse ['klʌbhaus] *n Golf, Tennis etc* pavillon *m*
clubland ['klʌblənd] *n* **(a)** (*area of gentlemen's clubs*) = quartier *m* des alentours de Saint James où se trouvent la plupart des clubs sélects de Londres **(b)** (*nightclub area*) = quartier *m* des boîtes de nuit
club sandwich *n esp Am Culin* sandwich *m* club
cluck[1] [klʌk] *n* (*of hens*) gloussement *m*
cluck[2] *vi* (*of hen*) glousser; (*of person*) faire claquer sa langue
clucking ['klʌkɪŋ] *n* (*of hens, Fig of scandalized person*) gloussement *m*
clue [klu:] *n* **(a)** indication *f*, indice *m*; (*to crime*) indice; **to get** *or* **find the c. to sth** trouver *ou* découvrir la clef de qch; **her hat provides a c. to her profession** on devine sa profession à son chapeau; **to give sb a c.** donner un indice à qn, mettre qn sur la voie *ou* sur la piste; *F* **I haven't got a c.** je n'en sais absolument rien, je n'en ai pas la moindre idée; *F* **he hasn't got a c. what he's doing** il fait n'importe quoi; *F* **when it comes to physics I haven't got a c.** je ne pige rien à la physique **(b)** (*in crossword*) définition *f*; **what's the c. to 13 down?** quelle est la définition du 13 vertical?
▶ **clue in** *vtsep F* (*inform*) renseigner, mettre au courant *ou* au parfum
▶ **clue up** *vtsep F* (*usu passive*) **I'm not very clued up on astrophysics** je ne suis pas très calé en astrophysique
clueless ['klu:lɪs] *adj F* **he's quite c.** il ne sait rien de rien
clump[1] [klʌmp] *n* **(a)** (*cluster*) (*of trees*) groupe *m*, bouquet *m*; (*of bushes, flowers*) massif *m* **(b)** (*lump*) (*of earth*) motte *f* **(c)** (*sound*) bruit *m* de pas lourd(s); **the c. of his footsteps** le bruit lourd de ses pas
clump[2] **1** *vi* **(a)** (*group*) se grouper en masse compacte **(b) to c. (about** *or* **around)** (*of person*) marcher lourdement; **with the neighbours clumping about upstairs** avec les voisins qui font du potin en haut **2** *vt* grouper en masse compacte; (*bushes, flowers*) planter en massif
clumsily ['klʌmzɪlɪ] *adv* **(a)** (*to move*) maladroitement, gauchement **(b)** (*drawn*) grossièrement; **c. built** mal bâti **(c)** (*to break bad news etc*) maladroitement, gauchement, sans tact
clumsiness ['klʌmzɪnɪs] *n* **(a)** (*of person, movement etc*) maladresse *f*, gaucherie *f* **(b)** (*of shape*) grossièreté *f*, lourdeur *f*; (*of sentence*) lourdeur, maladresse *f* **(c)** (*lack of tact*) manque *m* de tact, maladresse *f*
clumsy ['klʌmzɪ] *adj* **(a)** (*person, movement etc*) maladroit, gauche; **these boots are really c.** ce sont de vrais godillots, ces bottes **(b)** (*heavy*) (*phrase*) maladroit, gauche; (*shape*) lourd, disgracieux; **c. forgery** contre-façon *f* grossière **(c)** (*tactless*) (*person, excuse, remark*) maladroit, gauche
clung *pt, pp see* **cling**[1]
clunk [klʌŋk] *n* bruit *m* sourd
cluster[1] ['klʌstər] *n* (*of flowers, cherries*) bouquet *m*; (*of grapes*) grappe *f*; (*of stars*) amas *m*; (*of people, islands, houses, diamonds*) groupe *m*; *Comptr* cluster *m*, bloc *m* (d'information sur disque); (*of terminals*) grappe (de terminaux); *Mktg* **c. analysis** analyse *f* par segments; *Mil* **c. bomb** bombe *f* à fragmentation; *Mktg* **c. sampling** sondage *m* aréolaire *ou* par grappes *ou* par zones
cluster[2] *vi* **to c. round sb/sth** (*of people*) se grouper *ou* se rassembler autour de qn/qch; **to c. together** (*of particles etc*) se conglomérer
clutch[1] [klʌtʃ] *n* **(a)** *Aut etc* embrayage *m*; **to let in the c.** embrayer; **to release** *or* **let out the c.** débrayer; **c. bell housing** cloche *f* d'embrayage; **c. cone** cône *m* d'embrayage; **c. disc/plate** disque *m*/plateau *m* d'embrayage; **c. fluid** fluide *m* d'embrayage; **c. housing** carter *m* d'embrayage; **c. pedal** pédale *f* d'embrayage *ou* de débrayage; **c. slip** patinage *m* de l'embrayage; **c. start** démarrage *m* à l'embrayage
(b) (*action*) prise *f*, étreinte *f*; **to make a c. at sth** essayer de saisir qch; **c. bag,** *Am* **c. purse** pochette *f*
(c) (*claw*) (*of animal*) griffe *f*; (*of bird of prey*) serre *f*; **to fall into sb's clutches** tomber sous la patte *ou* la griffe *ou* entre les griffes de qn; **to escape from sb's clutches** se tirer des pattes *ou* des griffes de qn
clutch[2] **1** *vt* saisir; **to c. sth with both hands** saisir qch à deux mains; **to c. hold of sth** s'agripper *ou* se cramponner à qch **2** *vi* **to c. at sth** tenter de s'agripper *ou* se cramponner à qch; *Fig* **to c. at straws** se raccrocher à n'importe quoi
clutch[3] *n* (*of eggs, chicks*) couvée *f*
clutter[1] ['klʌtər] *n* encombrement *m*, désordre *m*, *F* pagaille *f*, *F* pagaïe; (*of furniture etc*) entassement *m*; **the Victorians loved c.** les Victoriens adoraient accumuler des objets dans leurs maisons; **among the c. on her desk** au milieu du désordre *ou F* de la pagaille qu'il y a sur son bureau; **everything's in a c.** tout est en désordre *ou F* en pagaille *ou* pagaïe
clutter[2] *vt* (*room, desk*) encombrer (**with** de); **to c. one's mind with useless facts** s'encombrer la mémoire de faits inutiles
▶ **clutter up** *vtsep* = **clutter**[2]
cluttered ['klʌtəd] *adj* encombré (**with** de); **the c. appearance of the room** l'impression d'encombrement qui se dégageait de la pièce
cm (*abbr* **centimetre**) cm
CMOS ['si:mɒs] *n Comptr* (*abbr* **complementary metal oxide silicon**) CMOS
CMR waybill [si:em'ɑ:] *n Com* lettre *f* de voiture CMR
CND [si:en'di:] *n Br* (*abbr* **Campaign for Nuclear Disarmament**) = campagne *f* pour le désarmement nucléaire
CNN [si:en'en] *n TV* (*abbr* **Cable News Network**) réseau *m* d'information américain diffusé par câble et satellite
CO [si:'əu] *n Mil abbr* **(a) Commanding Officer (b) conscientious objector**

Co, co [kəʊ] *n Com* (*abbr* **company**) Cie; *Fig* **Jane and co** Jane et compagnie

c/o (*abbr* **care of**) aux bons soins de, chez

coach¹ [kəʊtʃ] *n* **(a)** *Br* (*motor vehicle*) car *m*; *Am Av* **c. class** classe *f* économie; *Am Av* **c. fare** tarif *m* économie; **coach shuttle** autocar *m* navette; **c. tour** circuit *m* (touristique) en car, voyage *m* en autocar; (*excursion*) excursion *f* en car; **c. tour operator** autocariste *m*; **c. trip** excursion *f* en car **(b)** *Rail* voiture *f*, wagon *m* **(c)** (*trainer*) *Sp* entraîneur *m*, *F* coach *m*; *Sch* répétiteur, -trice **(d)** (*horse-drawn*) carrosse *m*; *Hist* **(stage) c.** diligence *m*; **c. and four** carrosse à quatre chevaux

coach² *vt Sch* donner des leçons particulières à; *Sp* (*person, team*) entraîner; **to c. sb in French** donner des leçons particulières en français à qn; *Th* **to c. sb for a part** faire répéter son rôle à qn; **the police coached the witness** la police a préparé le témoin à la déclaration; **he had been carefully coached in what to say** on lui avait bien expliqué quoi dire

coachbuilder [ˈkəʊtʃbɪldər] *n Aut* carrossier *m*

coach house *n* remise *f*

coaching [ˈkəʊtʃɪŋ] *n* **(a)** *Sp* entraînement *m*; *Sch* leçons *fpl* particulières **(b)** *Hist* **c. inn** relais *m*

coachman, *pl* **-men** [ˈkəʊtʃmən] *n* cocher *m*

coach party *n* groupe *m* voyageant en autocar; **we have three coach parties coming tomorrow** il y a trois cars qui arrivent demain; **the coach parties visiting the castle** les cars de touristes qui visitent le château

coach station *n* gare *f* routière

coachwork [ˈkəʊtʃwɜːk] *n Aut* carrosserie *f*

coagulant [kəʊˈægjʊlənt] *n* coagulant *m*

coagulate [kəʊˈægjʊleɪt] **1** *vt* coaguler **2** *vi* (se) coaguler

coagulation [kəʊægjʊˈleɪʃən] *n* coagulation *f*

coal¹ [kəʊl] *n* charbon *m*; (*ore*) houille *f*; **a piece** *or* **lump of c.** un morceau de charbon; **the c. (mining) industry** l'industrie *f* minière *ou* houillère; *Fig* **to carry coals to Newcastle** porter de l'eau à la rivière; *Fig* **to haul sb over the coals** réprimander qn vertement; **live coals** braise *f*, charbons *mpl* ardents; **c. bunker** coffre *m* à charbon; *Naut* soute *f* à charbon; **c. cellar** cave *f* à charbon; *Min* **c. cutter** (*person*) haveur *m*; (*machine*) haveuse *f*; **c. scuttle** seau *m* à charbon, charbonnière *f*; **c. shovel** pelle *f* à charbon; **c. strike** grève *f* des mineurs

coal² *Naut* **1** *vt* (*ship*) approvisionner en charbon; **to c. ship** charbonner **2** *vi* charbonner

coal-black *adj* noir comme du charbon

coalesce [kəʊəˈles] *vi* (*of parties, movements*) s'unir, fusionner; *Ch* se combiner

coalescence [kəʊəˈlesəns] *n* union *f*, fusion *f*

coalface [ˈkəʊlfeɪs] *n Min* front *m* de taille

coalfield [ˈkəʊlfiːld] *n Min* bassin *m* houiller

coal-fired [kəʊlˈfaɪəd] *adj* (alimenté) au charbon

coal gas *n* gaz *m* de houille

coalition [kəʊəˈlɪʃən] *n* coalition *f*; *Pol* **to form a c.** former une coalition, se coaliser; **a c. government** une coalition gouvernementale

coalman, *pl* **-men** [ˈkəʊlmən] *n* (petit) marchand *m* de charbon, charbonnier *m*

coal merchant *n* négociant *m* en charbon, marchand *m* de charbon

coal mine *n* mine *f* de charbon *ou* de houille, houillère *f*

coal miner *n* mineur *m*

coal mining *n* exploitation *f* du charbon *ou* de la houille

coalshed [ˈkəʊlʃed] *n* hangar *m* à charbon

coal tar *n* goudron *m* de houille

coal-tar soap *n* savon *m* au coaltar

coaltit [ˈkəʊltɪt] *n* (*bird*) mésange *f* noire

coarse [kɔːs] *adj* **(a)** (*vulgar*) grossier, vulgaire; (*language, joke*) grossier

(b) (*material*) gros, grossier; (*skin*) épais et rugueux; **the c. weave of the material** le tissage grossier de l'étoffe; **c. cut marmalade** marmelade *f* avec des écorces d'orange; **c. features** traits *mpl* grossiers *ou* lourds; *Phot* **c. grain** gros grain *m*; **c. hair** cheveux *mpl* rêches; **c. salt** gros sel *m*; **c. sandpaper** papier de verre *m* épais; **c. red wine** du gros rouge; **this is a fairly c. wine** ce vin n'est pas très fin

(c) c. fish poissons *mpl* d'eau douce (*sauf truites et saumons*); **c. fishing** pêche *f* à la ligne

coarsely [ˈkɔːslɪ] *adv* **(a)** (*vulgarly*) grossièrement, vulgairement **(b)** (*ground*) grossièrement; (*chopped etc*) gros

coarsen [ˈkɔːs(ə)n] **1** *vt* rendre (plus) grossier **2** *vi* devenir (plus) grossier

coarseness [ˈkɔːsnɪs] *n* **(a)** (*vulgarity*) grossièreté *f*, vulgarité *f* **(b)** (*roughness*) (*of skin, hair*) rudesse *f*; (*of material*) texture *f* grossière

coast¹ [kəʊst] *n* (*of sea*) côte *f*, rivage *m*; (*extensive*) littoral *m*; *Br* **the c.** (*seaside*) la côte; **from c. to c.** d'un bout à l'autre du pays; **the country's Caribbean c.** la côte caraïbe du pays; **two miles off the c. of France** *or* **the French c.** à deux mil(l)es de la côte française; **the country has no sea c.** le pays n'est bordé par aucune mer; **we took the c. road** nous avons pris la route qui longe la mer; *Fig F* **the c. is clear** le champ *ou* la voie est libre

coast² *vi* (*on bicycle, in car etc*) avancer en roue libre; (*downhill*) descendre en roue libre; (*on sledge*) descendre en luge; *Fig* **he coasted home** (*in race*) il a gagné sans effort; **she coasted through her exams** elle a passé ses examens sans difficulté *ou F* les doigts dans le nez; *Fig* **you're coasting** (*not working hard*) tu te la coules douce

coastal [ˈkəʊst(ə)l] *adj* côtier; **c. defence** défense *f* côtière; **c. navigation** navigation *f* côtière, cabotage *m*; **c. resort** station *f* balnéaire; **c. waters** eaux *fpl* territoriales

coaster [ˈkəʊstər] *n* **(a)** *Naut* (*ship*) cabotier *m*, caboteur *m* **(b)** (*for wine bottle or carafe*) dessous *m* de bouteille/de carafe; (*for glass*) dessous de verre

coastguard [ˈkəʊstgɑːd] *n* **(a)** (*no pl*) (*force*) garde-côtes *mpl*; **he's in the c.** il est garde-côte; **a c. official** un garde-côte; **c. vessel** *or* **cutter** garde-côte *m*, *pl* garde-côtes **(b)** (*also* **coastguard(s)man** [kəʊstˈgɑːd(z)mən]) garde-côte *m*, *pl* garde-côtes

coasting [ˈkəʊstɪŋ] *n Naut* navigation *f* côtière; **c. vessel** caboteur *m*

coastline [ˈkəʊstlaɪn] *n* littoral *m*

coat¹ [kəʊt] *n* **(a)** (*short*) veste *f*; (*long*) manteau *m*; (*for men*) manteau, pardessus *m*; *esp Am* (*of man's suit*) veston *m*; **morning c.** jaquette *f*; **car c.** manteau trois quarts; **lab c.** blouse *f* blanche; *Hist* **c. of mail** cotte *f* de mailles **(b)** *Her* **c. of arms** armes *fpl*, armoiries *fpl*, écusson *m* **(c)** (*of dog, horse*) robe *f*; (*of big cat*) pelage *m* **(d)** (*of snow etc*) manteau *m*, couche *f* **(e)** (*of paint, varnish, tar etc*) couche *f*, application *f*

coat² *vt* (*with paint, tar etc*) enduire, couvrir; (*with chocolate etc*) enrober; (*cable*) revêtir, armer **(with** de**)**; (*paper*) coucher; **to c. with sugar** enrober de sucre; (*pill*) dragéifier; (*almonds*) recouvrir de sucre; **to c. sth with dust** couvrir qch de poussière

coated [ˈkəʊtɪd] *adj* (*with dust, mud*) (re)couvert **(with** de**)**; (*with sugar, chocolate*) enrobé **(with** de**)**; (*tongue*) chargé, pâteux; (*paper*) couché

coat hanger *n* cintre *m*

coat hook *n* patère *f*

coating [ˈkəʊtɪŋ] *n* (*of paint, varnish etc*) couche *f*; (*of chocolate*) couche, enrobage *m*

coat rack *n* portemanteau *m*

coat-tails [ˈkəʊtˈteɪlz] *npl* basques *fpl ou* pan *m* d'un habit; (*of tail coat*) queue-de-pie *f*; *esp Pol* **to ride on sb's c.** se faire élire dans le sillage de qn

co-author¹ *n* coauteur *m*

co-author² *vt* (*book*) écrire en collaboration; **a book co-authored by Marsh and Brown** un livre écrit conjointement par Marsh et Brown

coax [kəʊks] *vt* (*person*) enjôler; **to c. sb into doing sth** amener qn à faire qch en l'enjôlant *ou* par les cajoleries; **to c. sth out of sb** obtenir qch de qn en l'enjôlant *ou* par les cajoleries

coaxial [kəʊˈæksɪəl] *adj El* (*cable etc*) coaxial

coaxing [ˈkəʊksɪŋ] **1** *adj* (*tone etc*) cajoleur, enjôleur **2** *n* cajoleries *fpl*; **he took a lot of c.** il s'est bien fait tirer l'oreille; **no amount of c. would get him to agree** malgré les efforts pour l'enjôler, on n'a pas réussi à le faire accepter

cob [kɒb] *n* **(a)** (*horse*) cob *m* **(b) c. (swan)** cygne *m* mâle **(c)** (*hazelnut*) aveline *f*, grosse noisette *f* **(d) (corn) c.** (*with grain*) épi *m* de maïs; (*without grain*) rafle *f*; *Culin* **corn on the c.** maïs *m* en épi **(e)** *Br* (*type of loaf*) pain *m* rond, miche *f* de pain

cobalt [ˈkəʊbɔːlt] *n Ch* cobalt *m*; **c. bloom** fleur *f* de cobalt; **c. blue** bleu *m* de cobalt; **c. bomb** bombe *f* au cobalt

cobber [ˈkɒbə] *n Austr F* copain *m*, pote *m*

cobble¹ [ˈkɒb(ə)l] *n* (*of roadway*) pavé *m*

cobble² *vt* (*road etc*) paver

cobble³ *vt Old-fashioned Br* (*shoes*) réparer

▶ **cobble together** *vtsep* (*make hastily, get together*) (*bookcase, newspaper article, team etc*) bricoler

cobbled [ˈkɒb(ə)ld] *adj* (*path, street*) pavé

cobbler [ˈkɒblər] *n* **(a)** *Br* (*shoe repairer*) cordonnier *m*; (*maker of shoes*) bottier *m* **(b)** *Am Culin* = dessert *m* chaud à base de fruits recouvert d'une génoise

cobblers [ˈkɒbləz] **1** *npl Br Sl* **(a)** (*rubbish*) conneries *fpl*; **that's c.** c'est des conneries tout ça **(b)** *Vulg* (*testicles*) couilles *fpl* **2** *int Br Sl* quelles foutaises!

cobblestone ['kɒb(ə)lstəʊn] *n* (*on roadway*) pavé *m*
cobloaf ['kɒbləʊf] *n Br* pain *m* rond, miche *f* de pain
cobnut ['kɒbnʌt] *n* aveline *f*, grosse noisette *f*
COBOL ['kəʊbɒl] *n Comptr* (*abbr* **Common Business-Oriented Language**) Cobol *m*
cobra ['kəʊbrə] *n* cobra *m*
cobweb ['kɒbweb] *n* (*web*) toile *f* d'araignée; (*thread*) fil *m* d'araignée; *Fig* **to go for a walk to blow away the cobwebs** prendre l'air pour se rafraîchir les idées; *Fig* **to brush the cobwebs off sth** ressortir qch
coca ['kəʊkə] *n Bot* coca *m or f*; *Pharm* coca *f*
cocaine [kə'keɪn] *n* cocaïne *f*; **c. addict** *or* **user** cocaïnomane *mf*
coccyx ['kɒksɪks] *n Anat* coccyx *m*, rachis *m* coccygien
cochineal ['kɒtʃɪniːl] *n* cochenille *f*
cock[1] [kɒk] *n* **(a)** (*male fowl*) coq *m*; **fighting c.** coq de combat; *Fig* **c. of the walk** *or* **of the roost** coq de village; **at university he was the c. of the walk** à l'université, c'était un vrai petit coq (de village); **c. bird** oiseau *m* mâle; **c. canary** serin *m*; **c. lobster** homard *m* mâle; **c. pheasant** coq faisan *m*; **c. sparrow** moineau *m* mâle
(b) *Vulg* (*penis*) bit(t)e *f*
(c) *Tech etc* (*in plumbing*) robinet *m*
(d) (*on firearm*) chien *m*; **at full c.** au cran de l'armé; *Fig* **to go off at half c.** rater; (*of person*) démarrer au quart de tour
(e) *Br Sl* (*form of address*) **wotcher c.!** salut, mon vieux!
cock[2] *vt* **(a) to c. one's eye at sb/sth** donner un coup d'œil à qn/qch; **to c. one's hat** (*put on one side*) mettre son chapeau de côté **(b)** (*of horse, dog*) **to c. (up) its ears** dresser les oreilles **(c)** (*gun*) armer
▶ **cock up** *Br Sl* **1** *vtsep* bousiller **2** *vi* merder
cockade [kɒ'keɪd] *n* cocarde *f*
cock-a-doodle-doo ['kɒkəduːd(ə)l'duː] *int* cocorico!
cock-a-hoop *adj, adv* (en) jubilant; (*having done sth*) triomphant; **all c.** fier comme Artaban
cock-a-leekie [kɒkə'liːkɪ] *n Scot Culin* **c. (soup)** = bouillon *m* de volaille aux poireaux et à l'avoine
cock-and-bull *F* **1** *adj* **c. story** histoire *f* abracadabrante **2** *n* balivernes *fpl*
cockatoo [kɒkə'tuː] *n* cacatoès *m*
cockchafer ['kɒktʃeɪfər] *n* (*beetle*) hanneton *m*
cockcrow ['kɒkkrəʊ] *n* chant *m* du coq; **to rise at c.** se lever au (premier) chant du coq *ou* à l'aube
cocked [kɒkt] *adj* **c. hat** chapeau *m* à cornes; *F* **to knock sb into a c. hat** (*defeat*) battre qn à plate(s) couture(s), démolir qn; (*be better than*) dépasser qn de très loin, *F* enfoncer qn; **as for cooking, she knocks me into a c. hat** pour ce qui est de la cuisine, je ne lui arrive pas à la cheville
cocker ['kɒkər] *n* **c. (spaniel)** cocker *m*
cockerel ['kɒk(ə)r(ə)l] *n* jeune coq *m*, coquelet *m*
cockeyed ['kɒkaɪd] *adj F* **(a)** (*absurd*) farfelu; (*story*) qui ne tient pas debout **(b)** (*person*) qui a un œil qui dit zut à l'autre
cockfight ['kɒkfaɪt] *n* combat *m* de coqs
cockfighting ['kɒkfaɪtɪŋ] *n* combats *mpl* de coqs
cockiness ['kɒkɪnɪs] *n* assurance *f* excessive; **because of his c.** parce qu'il était trop sûr de lui
cockle ['kɒk(ə)l] *n* (*mollusc*) coque *f*, fausse praire *f*; *Fig* **that will warm the cockles of your heart** voilà qui vous réchauffera le cœur
cockleshell ['kɒk(ə)lʃel] *n* **(a)** (*boat*) coquille *f* de noix **(b)** (*of mollusc*) coquille *f* de coque
Cockney ['kɒknɪ] **1** *adj* cockney **2** *n* **(a)** (*person*) Cockney *mf* (*des quartiers de l'est de Londres*) **(b)** (*dialect*) cockney *m*
cockpit ['kɒkpɪt] *n* **(a)** (*of plane*) poste *m* de pilotage, cockpit *m*; (*of racing car*) cockpit **(b)** (*in cockfighting*) arène *f* de combats de coqs
cockroach ['kɒkrəʊtʃ] *n* (*insect*) blatte *f*, cafard *m*
cockscomb ['kɒkskəʊm] *n* (*on bird*) crête *f* de coq
cocksure ['kɒk'ʃʊər] *adj* trop sûr de soi
cocktail ['kɒkteɪl] *n* (*drink*), *Fig* cocktail *m*; **c. bar** bar *m* (*plus chic*); **c. cabinet** bar (à cocktails); **c. dress** robe *f* de cocktail; **c. lounge** bar (*plus chic*); **c. mixer** *or* **shaker** shaker *m*; **c. party** cocktail; **c. sausage** petite saucisse *f* de cocktail; **c. stick** pique *f*
cockup ['kɒkʌp] *n Br Sl* connerie *f*, cagade *f*; **the mission was a complete c.** la mission a complètement merdé *ou* foiré; **to make a c. of sth** (*exam, interview, speech, relationship*) foutre qch en l'air
cocky ['kɒkɪ] *adj F* trop sûr de soi, culotté; **don't get c.!** ne prends pas tes airs supérieurs
cocoa ['kəʊkəʊ] *n* (*powder, drink*) cacao *m*; **c. bean** graine *f ou* fève *f* de cacao; **c. butter** beurre *m* de cacao
coconut ['kəʊkənʌt] *n* (noix *f* de) coco *m*; **c. fibre** fibre *f* de coco, coir *m*; **c. matting** natte *f* en fibres de coco; **c. milk/butter** lait *m*/beurre *m* de coco; **c. oil** huile *f* de coprah, huile de coco; **c. palm** *or* **tree** cocotier *m*; **c. shy** jeu *m* de massacre (*où l'on essaie d'abattre des noix de coco*)
cocoon[1] [kə'kuːn] *n* (*of silkworm etc*) cocon *m*
cocoon[2] *vt* envelopper (**in** dans); *Fig* **workers in the public sector have been cocooned from unemployment** les travailleurs du secteur public ont été protégés du chômage
cocooning [kə'kuːnɪŋ] *n* cocooning *m*
COD, cod [siːəʊ'diː] *Com* (*abbr* **cash** *or Am* **collect on delivery**) contre remboursement, paiement à la livraison
cod [kɒd] *n* (*fish*) morue *f*; **fresh c.** morue fraîche, cabillaud *m*; **dried c.** morue sèche, merluche *f*; **c.'s roe** œufs *mpl* de morue
coda ['kəʊdə] *n Mus* coda *f*
coddle ['kɒd(ə)l] *vt* **(a)** (*spoil*) choyer, dorloter; **to c. oneself** se dorloter **(b)** *Culin* (*eggs*) à peine faire cuire; **coddled eggs** des œufs *mpl* à peine cuits
code[1] [kəʊd] *n* **(a)** *Telecom, Comptr* code *m*; *Telecom* **(dialling) c.** indicatif *f*; **the terrorist used a c. word** le terroriste a utilisé un code; *Comptr* **computer c.** code machine; **c. translation** transcodage *m*
(b) (*secret writing*) code *m*, chiffre *m*; **to write a message in c.** coder *ou* chiffrer un message; **the letter was in c.** la lettre était codée; **c. book** (*for encoding*) code *ou* carnet *m* de chiffrement; (*for decoding*) code *ou* carnet de déchiffrement; **c. letter** lettre *f* code; **c. message** message *m* codé *ou* chiffré; **c. name** nom *m* de code
(c) (*rules etc*) code *m*; **c. of conduct** déontologie *f*, code de conduite; **c. of criminal procedure** code d'instruction criminelle; **c. of honour** code *ou* règles *fpl* de l'honneur; **c. of practice** règlements *mpl* et usages, déontologie
code[2] *vt* **(a)** (*message etc*) coder, mettre en code *ou* en chiffre **(b)** *Comptr* coder
▶ **code up** *vtsep Typ* (*text*) insérer les codes dans
coded ['kəʊdɪd] *adj* **(a)** (*message etc*) codé, chiffré **(b)** *Comptr* codé; **c. signal** (*video etc*) signal *m* codé; *Aut* **c. engine immobilizer** antidémarrage *m* codé, ADC *m*
co-defendant *n Jur* coaccusé, -ée; (*in civil law*) codéfendeur, -eresse
codeine ['kəʊdiːn] *n Pharm* codéine *f*
coder ['kəʊdər] *n* (*device*) codeur *m*
codex, *pl* **-ices** ['kəʊdeks, -ɪsiːz] *n* manuscrit *m* (ancien)
codger ['kɒdʒər] *n Br F* **an old c.** un vieux bonhomme
codicil ['kɒdɪsɪl] *n Jur* (*of will*) codicille *m*
codification [kəʊdɪfɪ'keɪʃən] *n* codification *f*
codify ['kəʊdɪfaɪ] *vt* (*laws etc*) codifier
coding ['kəʊdɪŋ] *n* **(a)** (*putting into code*) codification *f*, codage *m* **(b)** *Comptr* (*providing codes*) codage *m*; (*system of codes*) codes *mpl*; **c. error** erreur *f* de codage
co-director *n* codirecteur, -trice
cod-liver oil *n* huile *f* de foie de morue
codpiece ['kɒdpiːs] *n* braguette *f*
co-driver *n Sp* copilote *mf*
codswallop ['kɒdzwɒləp] *n Br Sl* foutaises *fpl*; **it's a load of (old) c.** c'est un tas de foutaises
co-ed ['kəʊ'ed] *F* **1** *adj* (*school*) mixte; **to go c.** (*of school*) devenir mixte **2** *n* **(a)** *Br* (*school*) école *f* mixte **(b)** *US* (*pupil*) élève *f* d'une école mixte
coeducation ['kəʊedjʊ'keɪʃən] *n* enseignement *m* mixte
coeducational ['kəʊedjʊ'keɪʃənəl] *adj* mixte
coefficient [kəʊɪ'fɪʃənt] *n Math, Phys* coefficient *m*
coelacanth ['siːləkænθ] *n* cœlacanthe *m*
coeliac, *US* **celiac** ['siːlɪæk] **1** *adj* cœliaque; **c. disease** maladie *f* cœliaque **2** *n Am Med F* = personne *f* atteinte de maladie cœliaque
coerce [kəʊ'ɜːs] *vt* forcer, contraindre (**sb into doing sth** qn à faire qch)
coercion [kəʊ'ɜːʃən] *n* coercition *f*, contrainte *f*; *Jur* coaction *f*; **to act under c.** agir sous la coercition; **to use c. to obtain a confession** utiliser la contrainte pour obtenir une confession
coexist [kəʊɪg'zɪst] *vi* coexister (**with** avec)
coexistence ['kəʊɪg'zɪstəns] *n* coexistence *f* (**with** avec); *Pol* **peaceful c.** coexistence pacifique
coexistent ['kəʊɪg'zɪstənt] *adj* coexistant (**with** avec)
C of E [siːə'viː] *adj Rel* (*abbr* **Church of England**) anglican
coffee ['kɒfɪ] **1** *n* **(a)** café *m*; **two coffees, please!** deux cafés, s'il vous plaît!; **black c.** café noir; *Br* **white c.,** *Am* **c. with milk** café crème, crème *m*; **c. break** pause-café *f*, *pl* pauses-café; **c. cream** (*chocolate*) chocolat *m* fourré au café; **c. cup** tasse *f* à café; **c. grounds** marc *m* de café; **c. pot** cafetière *f*; **c. spoon** cuillère *f* à café; (*small*) cuillère à moka **(b)** **c.(-colour)** (*dark*) café *m inv*; (*light*) café au lait *inv* **2** *adj* (*dark*) café *inv*; (*light*) café au lait *inv*
coffee bar *n* café *m*
coffee bean *n* grain *m* de café
coffee-coloured *adj* (*dark*) café *inv*; (*light*) café au lait *inv*

coffee grinder *n* moulin *m* à café
coffee machine *n* (*drinks dispenser*) machine *f* à café; (*in home*) cafetière *f* (électrique)
coffee mill *n* moulin *m* à café
coffee shop *n* café *m*
coffee table *n* table *f* basse
coffee-table *adj* **c. book** livre *m* de grand format abondamment illustré (*surtout décoratif*)
coffee tree *n* caféier *m*
coffer¹ [ˈkɒfər] *n* **(a)** (*chest*) coffre *m*; *Fig* **the coffers** (*of country, organization etc*) les caisses *fpl*; *Fig* **to swell the State coffers** renflouer les caisses de l'État **(b)** *Archit* (*of ceiling*) caisson *m* **(c)** (*in dam, lock etc*) chambre *f*, bassin *m*, sas *m* **(d)** = **cofferdam**
coffer² *vt* **(a)** *Min, Constr* (*well*) coffrer **(b)** (*ceiling*) diviser en caissons; **coffered ceiling** plafond *m* à caissons
cofferdam [ˈkɒfədæm] *n HydE* coffre *m*, batardeau *m*, caisson *m* hydraulique
coffering [ˈkɒfərɪŋ] *n Min etc* coffrage *m*
coffin [ˈkɒfɪn] *n* **(a)** cercueil *m*, bière *f*; *F* **that's another nail in his c.** (*he's closer to death*) c'est (pour lui) un pas de plus vers la tombe; (*he's closer to defeat, disaster etc*) c'est un autre coup funeste pour lui; *Sl* **c. nail** (*cigarette*) clope *m or f* **(b)** (*of horseshoe*) cavité *f* du sabot
cofounder [kəʊˈfaʊndər] *n* cofondateur, -trice
cog [kɒg] *n* **(a)** (*of cogwheel*) dent *f*; **the cogs** la denture; *Fig* **I'm only a c. in the machinery** je ne suis qu'un rouage de la machine; **c. rail** crémaillère *f*; **c. railway** *or US* **railroad** chemin *m* de fer à crémaillère **(b)** (*wheel*) pignon *m*, roue *f* dentée
cogency [ˈkəʊdʒənsɪ] *n* force *f*, puissance *f*
cogent [ˈkəʊdʒənt] *adj* (*argument*) convaincant; (*reason*) valable, convaincant
cogently [ˈkəʊdʒəntlɪ] *adv* avec force, puissamment
cogitate [ˈkɒdʒɪteɪt] *Fml* **1** *vi* méditer, réfléchir (**on, over** sur) **2** *vt* (*plan etc*) méditer, imaginer
cogitation [kɒdʒɪˈteɪʃən] *n* réflexion *f* (**on, over** sur)
cognac [ˈkɒnjæk] *n* cognac *m*
cognate [ˈkɒgneɪt] **1** *n* **(a)** *Ling* mot *m* de même origine **(b)** *Jur* cognat *m* **2** *adj Fml* apparenté; *Ling* de même origine
cognition [kɒgˈnɪʃən] *n* cognition *f*, connaissance *f*
cognitive [ˈkɒgnɪtɪv] *adj* cognitif
cognizance [ˈkɒgnɪzəns, ˈkɒnɪzəns] *n* **(a)** *Fml* (*knowledge*) connaissance *f*; **to take c. of sth** prendre connaissance de qch **(b)** *Jur* (*of a court*) compétence *f*; **within** *or* **under the c. of a court** de la compétence *ou* du ressort d'une cour
cognizant [ˈkɒgnɪzənt, ˈkɒnɪzənt] *adj* **(a)** *Fml* ayant connaissance (**of** de); **to be c. of a fact** être instruit *ou* avoir connaissance d'un fait **(b)** *Jur* **court c. of an offence** tribunal *m* compétent pour juger un délit
cognoscenti [kɒnjəʊˈʃentɪ, kɒgnə-] *npl* connaisseurs, -euses, spécialistes *mf*
cogwheel [ˈkɒgwiːl] *n* roue *f* à dents *ou* dentée, roue d'engrenage
cohabit [kəʊˈhæbɪt] *vi* vivre maritalement (**with** avec)
cohabitation [kəʊhæbɪˈteɪʃən] *n* vie *f* maritale, union *f* libre (**with** avec)
cohabitee [kəʊhæbɪˈtiː] *n* compagnon *m*, compagne *f*
cohere [kəʊˈhɪər] *vi* (*of whole, of parts*) tenir ensemble; (*of argument, style*) se suivre (logiquement), être cohérent; **they don't c. as a team** ils ne forment pas une équipe unie
coherence [kəʊˈhɪərəns] *n* (*of argument, style*) suite *f* (logique), cohérence *f*
coherent [kəʊˈhɪərənt] *adj* (*whole*) cohérent; (*plan, speech, thinker etc*) cohérent, logique; (*argument*) qui se tient, logique; *F* **the man wasn't c.** il racontait n'importe quoi, il était incohérent
coherently [kəʊˈhɪərəntlɪ] *adv* d'une manière cohérente, avec cohérence
cohesion [kəʊˈhiːʒən] *n* cohésion *f*
cohesive [kəʊˈhiːsɪv] *adj* cohésif; *Phys* (*force*) de cohésion
cohort [ˈkəʊhɔːt] *n Antiq, Mil* cohorte *f*; *Fig* **he was there with his cohorts** il était là avec toute une armée de suiveurs; **a c. of lawyers** une armée d'avocats
coiffure [kwɑːˈfjʊər] *n* coiffure *f*
coil¹ [kɔɪl] *n* **(a)** (*of rope*) rouleau *m*; (*of wire*) rouleau, torque *f* **(b)** (*single loop*) (*of rope*) pli *m*, repli *m*; (*of snake*) anneau *m* **(c)** (*in hairdressing*) rouleau *m* (de cheveux), chignon *m* **(d)** *Med* (*contraceptive*) stérilet *m* **(e)** *El* bobine *f*; *Aut* **c. ignition system** circuit *m* d'allumage par bobine
coil² **1** *vt* (en)rouler; *El* (*wire*) bobiner; **to c. sth around sth** enrouler qch autour de qch; **to c. itself up** (*of snake*) s'enrouler, se lover **2** *vi* serpenter; (*of snake*) se lover
coiled [kɔɪld] *adj* (en)roulé; (*spring*) en spirale; (*snake*) lové; *Fig* **like a c. spring** tendu, prêt à l'action
coin¹ [kɔɪn] *n* **(a)** pièce *f* de monnaie; **a 10p c.** une pièce de 10 pence **(b)** (*no pl*) (*currency*) monnaie *f*; *Fig* **to pay sb back in their own c.** rendre à qn la monnaie de sa pièce
coin² *vt* **(a) to c. money** frapper de la monnaie; *Fig F* **he's simply coining money** *or* **coining it** il fait des affaires en or **(b)** (*invent*) (*new word*) inventer, créer; **to c. a phrase** inventer une formule; *Iron* **…, to c. a phrase …,** pour employer le cliché habituel
coinage [ˈkɔɪnɪdʒ] *n* **(a)** (*coins*) monnaie(s) *f(pl)*, *Spec* numéraire *m* **(b)** (*coining*) (*of money*) frappe *f* **(c)** (*invention*) **the word is a recent c.** c'est un mot nouveau, c'est un néologisme **(d)** (*currency*) (*of country*) système *m* monétaire
coincide [kəʊɪnˈsaɪd] *vi* **(a)** (*in space, time*) coïncider (**with** avec) **(b)** (*agree*) (*of interests, opinions etc*) coïncider, s'accorder (**with** avec)
coincidence [kəʊˈɪnsɪdəns] *n* coïncidence *f*; **what a c.!** quelle coïncidence!; **it is no c. that …** ce n'est pas une coïncidence si …
coincidental [kəʊɪnsɪˈdent(ə)l] *adj* **it was more than merely c. that …** ce n'était pas une coïncidence si …; **this had the c. effect of …** par coïncidence, cela a eu le résultat de …; **any similarity with … is purely c.** toute ressemblance avec … ne serait que pure coïncidence
coincidentally [kəʊɪnsɪˈdentlɪ] *adv* par (pure) coïncidence
coiner [ˈkɔɪnər] *n* (*of word, expression*) inventeur, -trice
coin-op *n F* laverie *f* automatique
coin-operated [ˈkɔɪnɒpəreɪtɪd] *adj* automatique; **c. laundry** laverie *f* automatique
co-insurance *n* coassurance *f*
co-insurer *n* coassureur *m*
coitus [ˈkəʊɪtəs, ˈkɔɪ-] *n Fml* coït *m*; **c. interruptus** coït interrompu
Coke® [kəʊk] *n F* Coca® *m*
coke¹ *n* (*fuel*) coke *m*; **c. oven** four *m* à coke
coke² **1** *vt* (*coal*) cokéfier, convertir en coke **2** *vi* (*of coal*) se cokéfier, se convertir en coke
coke³ *n F* (*cocaine*) neige *f*, blanche *f*, coke *f*
coking [ˈkəʊkɪŋ] **1** *adj* (*coal*) cokéfiable **2** *n* cokéfaction *f*, coké(i)fication *f*
Col *abbr* **(a)** (**Colonel**) Col **(b) Colombia (c) Colorado**
col¹ [kɒl] *n Geog* col *m*
col² (*abbr* **column**) col
COLA [ˈkəʊlə] *n Am Admin* (*abbr* **cost of living** *Can* **allowance** *or US* **adjustment**) *Can* IVC *f*, indemnité *f* de vie chère
colander [ˈkʌləndər, ˈkɒl-] *n* passoire *f*
cold¹ [kəʊld] **1** *adj* **(a)** (*weather, bath, meal, engine etc*) froid; **c. drink** boisson *f* fraîche; **it's c.** (*icecream, food, object etc*) c'est froid; (*weather*) il fait froid; **to get** *or* **grow c.** se refroidir; *Met* **it's getting c.** le temps se refroidit, il commence à faire froid; *Met* **it's getting colder** la température baisse; **to be** *or* **feel c.** (*of person*) avoir froid; **the c. tap** le robinet d'eau froide; *F* **out c.** sans connaissance, inanimé; **to knock sb out c.** étendre qn raide; *esp Am* **you'll knock them c.!** (*with your performance*) tu vas faire un tabac; **you're c.** (*in game*) tu gèles; **my hands are c.** j'ai les mains froides, j'ai froid aux mains; **my feet are as c. as ice** j'ai les pieds glacés; *Fig* **to have c. feet** avoir la frousse; **c. buffet** buffet *m* froid; **c. meats,** *Am* **c. cuts** assiette *f* anglaise; **the scent had gone c.** (*in hunting*), *Fig* on avait perdu sa/leur/*etc* trace; *Met* **c. snap** coup *m* de froid; *Aut, Comptr* **c. start** démarrage *m* à froid; *Aut* **c. start protection** protection *f* de démarrage à froid

(b) *Fig* (*person, manner, welcome etc*) froid; **to be c. with sb** se montrer froid avec qn; **to give sb the c. shoulder** tourner le dos à qn, snober qn; *F* **that leaves me c.** cela me laisse froid; *F* **he's a c. fish** c'est un pisse-froid

2 *adv* **(a)** *Am F* **to turn sb down c.** envoyer promener qn

(b) (*without preparation*) à froid; *Surg* **to operate c.** opérer à froid
cold² *n* **(a)** (*of the weather etc*) froid *m*; **I feel the c.** je suis très frileux; *Fig* **to leave sb out in the c.** laisser qn à l'écart; **to be left out in the c.** rester sur le carreau; *Fig* **to come in from the c.** rentrer en faveur *ou* en grâce **(b)** *Med* (**common**) **c.** rhume *m*; **to have a c.** être enrhumé, avoir un rhume; **a bad** *or* **heavy c.** un gros rhume; **c. in the head, head c.** rhume de cerveau; **c. on the chest, chest c.** rhume de poitrine; **to catch (a) c.** s'enrhumer, attraper un rhume; **c. remedy** remède *m* contre le rhume
cold-blooded [ˈkəʊldˈblʌdɪd] *adj* **(a)** (*animal*) à sang froid; **reptiles are c.** les reptiles sont des animaux à sang froid **(b)** *Fig* (*unemotional*) froid, insensible; (*murderer etc*) sans pitié; (*murder etc*) (commis) de sang-froid
cold-bloodedly [ˈkəʊldˈblʌdɪdlɪ] *adv* (*unemotionally*) froidement; (*to murder*) de sang-froid, froidement
cold-bloodedness [ˈkəʊldˈblʌdɪdnɪs] *n* froideur *f*, insensibilité *f*

cold call *n Com* visite *f* à froid; (*on phone*) appel *m* à froid
cold calling *n Com* visites *fpl* à froid; (*on phone*) appels *mpl* à froid
cold chisel *Tech* ciseau *m* à froid, burin *m*
cold cream *n* cold-cream *m*
cold front *n Met* front *m* froid
cold-hearted [kəʊld'hɑːtɪd] *adj* (*person*) froid, insensible; (*words*) dur; (*action*) impitoyable; **that was a c. thing to do/say** c'était faire preuve d'insensibilité que de faire/dire ça
coldly ['kəʊldlɪ] *adv* froidement; (*to look at sb, sth*) avec froideur
coldness ['kəʊldnɪs] *n* **(a)** (*of climate etc*) froideur *f* **(b)** *Fig* (*of welcome, person etc*) froideur *f*; **there is a c. between them** il y a un froid entre eux
cold-pressed ['kəʊldpresd] *adj* embouti à froid; (*olive oil*) pressé à froid
cold-rivet *vt MecE* riveter à froid
cold riveting *n* rivure *f* à froid
cold selling *n* vente *f* à froid
cold-shoulder *vt* (*sb*) tourner le dos à, snober, se montrer très froid avec; **the party continues to be cold-shouldered by the electorate** le parti est toujours boudé par les électeurs
cold sore *n* herpès *m*
cold storage *n Com* conservation *f* par le froid; **to keep in c.** mettre dans une chambre frigorifique; *Fig* **to put in c.** mettre en veilleuse; **c. dock** dock *m* frigorifique
cold store *n* chambre *f* froide *ou* frigorifique; (*warehouse*) entrepôt *m* frigorifique
cold turkey *n Sl* (*withdrawal from drugs*) **to go through c.** être en manque; *Sl* **to quit smoking c.** arrêter de fumer du jour au lendemain
cold war *n Pol* guerre *f* froide
cold warrior *n Pol* partisan, -ane de la guerre froide
coleslaw ['kəʊlslɔː] *n Culin* salade *f* de chou vert à la mayonnaise
colic ['kɒlɪk] *n Med, Vet* colique *f*
coliform bacteria ['kɒlɪfɔːm] *npl* colibacilles *mpl*
colitis [kə'laɪtɪs] *n Med* colite *f*
collaborate [kə'læbəreɪt] *vi* (*in work*), *Pej* collaborer (**with** avec, **on** à)
collaboration [kəlæbə'reɪʃən] *n* (*in work*), *Pej* collaboration *f*; **in c. with** en collaboration avec
collaborator [kə'læbəreɪtər] *n* (*in work*), *Pej* collaborateur, -trice
collage ['kɒlɑːʒ] *n Art* collage *m*
collagen ['kɒlədʒən] *n* collagène *m*
collapse[1] [kə'læps] *n* **(a)** (*of building*) effondrement *m*, écroulement *m*; (*of land*) éboulement *m*; *Fig* (*of hopes, moral values, market, economy*) effondrement; (*of country, institution*) effondrement, débâcle *f*; (*of prices*) effondrement, chute *f* subite; (*of the franc etc*) effondrement, *F* dégringolade *f* **(b)** *Med* (*of lungs*) collapsus *m*; **she's had a c.** elle a perdu connaissance
collapse[2] **1** *vi* **(a)** (*of building, institution etc*) s'écrouler, s'effondrer; (*of screen, bookshelf etc*) s'écrouler; (*of resistance, support, prices, economy*) s'effondrer; (*of bridge, axle etc*) s'effondrer, s'affaisser
 (b) (*of person*) s'effondrer, s'affaisser subitement; **I collapsed from the heat** je me suis évanoui tellement il faisait chaud; **he collapsed into an armchair** il s'effondra dans un fauteuil; **I feel like I'm about to c.** j'ai l'impression que je vais m'effondrer; *Med* **her lung has collapsed** elle a eu *ou* fait un collapsus pulmonaire
 (c) (*be collapsible*) se (re)plier
 2 *vt* **(a)** (*table etc*) plier
 (b) (*merge*) (*paragraphs, entries*) mettre ensemble, fusionner
collapsed lung [kə'læpst] *n Med* collapsus *m* pulmonaire
collapsible [kə'læpsəb(ə)l] *adj* (*chair, boat etc*) pliant, repliable; (*handle etc*) rabattable; *Aut* (*steering column*) rétractile, rétractable; *Aut* **c. hood** capote *f* pliante *ou* rabattable
collar[1] ['kɒlər] *n* **(a)** (*of shirt etc*) col *m*; (*for dog*) collier *m*; **to seize** *or* **grab sb by the c.** prendre *ou* saisir qn au collet; *Fig* **to get hot under the c.** (*angry*) se mettre *ou* *F* se ficher en rogne; (*embarrassed*) se sentir gêné; **detachable c.** faux col **(b)** *MecE* bague *f*; (*of pipe*) collet *m* **(c)** *Zool* (*marking*) (*on bird, animal*) collier *m*
collar[2] *vt* (*seize by the collar*) saisir *ou* prendre au collet; *Fig, F* (*catch*) pincer
collarbone ['kɒləbəʊn] *n* clavicule *f*
collate [kə'leɪt] *vt* **(a)** (*assemble*) (*documents, data*) rassembler; *Comptr* (*documents*) interclasser; (*in bookbinding*) (*sheets*) assembler, collationner **(b)** (*compare*) (*text*) collationner (**with** avec)
collateral [kə'lætər(ə)l] **1** *n Fin* nantissement *m*; **what can you provide as c.?** qu'est-ce que vous pouvez fournir en nantissement? **2** *adj* **(a)** (*cause etc*) accessoire, subsidiaire **(b)** *Com, Jur* **c. security** garantie *f* additionnelle, nantissement *m* subsidiaire; *Fin* **c. loans** crédits *mpl* sur nantissement **(c)** (*branch, family, artery*) collatéral
collateralize [kə'lætərəlaɪz] *vt Banking* garantir
collation [kə'leɪʃən] *n* **(a)** (*assembling*) (*of documents, data*) rassemblement *m*; (*in bookbinding*) (*of sheets*) assemblage *m*, collationnement *m* **(b)** (*comparing*) (*of texts*) collation *f* **(c)** *Old-fashioned, Fml Culin* collation *f*
collator [kə'leɪtər] *n* (*on photocopier*) interclasseuse *f*
colleague ['kɒliːg] *n* collègue *mf*; (*doctor, lawyer*) confrère *m*, consœur *f*
collect[1] ['kɒlekt] *n Rel* (*prayer*) collecte *f*
collect[2] [kə'lekt] **1** *vt* **(a)** (*as pastime*) (*stamps, books etc*) collectionner, faire collection de; **she has collected more than 2,000 records** elle a une collection de plus de 2 000 disques
 (b) (*gather*) (*crowd, one's belongings, material*) rassembler; (*friends, documents*) réunir; (*data, news*) recueillir; (*of post office*) (*letters*) faire la levée de; *Mil* (*wounded*) ramasser; **he had collected six parking fines** il avait ramassé six P. V.; **he collects parking fines** il collectionne les P. V.; **that tray is there to c. the drips** ce plateau sert à recueillir les gouttes
 (c) *Fig* (*one's thoughts, strength*) rassembler; **to c. oneself** se reprendre, se calmer
 (d) (*pick*) (*flowers*) cueillir; (*mushrooms*) ramasser
 (e) *Fin* (*salary*) toucher; (*debt*) recouvrer; **to c. taxes** percevoir *ou* lever des impôts
 (f) (*recover, call for*) (*luggage, ticket, car*) aller chercher, aller prendre; (*goods*) enlever; **I'll c. you at midday** je passerai vous prendre à midi
 2 *vi* **(a)** (*of people*) s'assembler, se rassembler, se réunir; (*of things*) s'amasser
 (b) (*gather money*) faire la quête, quêter (**for** pour)
collect[3] *adj, adv Am* en port dû; **to send a telegram c.** envoyer un télégramme en port dû; *Tel* **to call (sb) c.** appeler (qn) en PCV, *Can* faire un appel à frais virés (à qn)
collectable [kə'lektəb(ə)l] **1** *adj* **(a)** (*sought-after*) prisé par les collectionneurs **(b)** (*debt*) recouvrable **2** *n* objet *m* de collection
collect call *n Am Tel* appel *m* en PCV, *Can* appel à frais virés
collected [kə'lektɪd] *adj* **(a)** (*assembled*) réuni; **the c. works of Jane Austen** les œuvres complètes de Jane Austen **(b)** (*calm*) plein de sang-froid; **to remain calm and c.** garder son sang-froid
collectible [kə'lektəb(ə)l] *adj, n* = **collectable**
collecting [kə'lektɪŋ] *n* **he does a lot of c. for the blind** il quête beaucoup *ou* il fait de nombreuses quêtes pour les aveugles
collection [kə'lekʃən] *n* **(a)** (*of stamps, butterflies etc*) collection *f*; (*of songs, poems*) recueil *m*; **spring c.** (*in fashion industry*) collection de printemps
 (b) (*act of collecting*) (*of sum of money, debts*) recouvrement *m*; (*of taxes*) perception *f*; (*of water, electric current*) captage *m*; (*of data*) collecte *f*; **c. times are 8. 45 and 17. 30** (*from letterbox*) les levées sont à 8h45 et 17h30; *Com* **c. charge** *ou* **fee** commission *f* de paiement *ou* d'encaissement; **c. (department)** service *m* de recouvrement; **c. and delivery** enlèvement *m* et livraison; **c. of customs duties** perception *f* douanière; **c. of taxes** levée *f* des impôts
 (c) (*group, accumulation*) (*of people*) assemblée *f*, rassemblement *m*; (*of things*) amas *m*; (*ordered*) assemblage *m*; **a c. of rubbish had built up outside the door** des ordures s'étaient amassées devant la porte
 (d) (*in church*) quête *f*; (*for charity etc*) collecte *f*, quête; **to take up a c.** faire la quête
 (e) *Fin* (*of bill*) encaissement *m*; **to send sth for c.** envoyer qch à l'encaissement
 (f) (*picking up*) (*of foods*) enlèvement *m*; **your watch will be ready for c. tomorrow** votre montre sera prête demain
 (g) (*removal*) (*of garbage*) ramassage *m*
collection box *n* (*in church, of fund-raiser*) tronc *m*
collection plate *n* plat *m* de quête, ≈ corbeille *f*
collective [kə'lektɪv] **1** *adj* collectif; *Ind* **c. agreement** convention *f* collective; **c. bargaining** négociation *f* afin d'établir une convention collective; **c. farm** ferme *f* collective; *Gram* [①**A11**,**g**; **B8**,**9**] **c. noun** nom *m* collectif; *Jur* **c. ownership** propriété *f* collective; (*of building*) copropriété *f*; *Mktg* **c. promotion** communication *f* collective **2** *n* **(a)** *Gram* collectif *m* **(b)** (*farm etc*) coopérative *f*
collectively [kə'lektɪvlɪ] *adv* collectivement; **c. owned** mis en commun; **c. owned building** immeuble *m* en copropriété
collectivism [kə'lektɪvɪz(ə)m] *n* collectivisme *m*

collectivist [kəˈlektɪvɪst] *adj, n* collectiviste *mf*
collectivity [kɒlekˈtɪvɪtɪ] *n* collectivité *f*
collectivization [kəlektɪvaɪˈzeɪʃən] *n* collectivisation *f*
collectivize [kəˈlektɪvaɪz] *vt* collectiviser
collector [kəˈlektər] *n* **(a)** (*of paintings, stamps etc*) collectionneur, -euse; **c.'s item** pièce *f* de collection **(b)** (*for charity*) quêteur, -euse; **c. of taxes** percepteur *m* **(c)** *MecE etc* (*for oil, steam etc*) collecteur *m*; (*of overflow*) récepteur *m*
collect picture *n Journ* photo *f* d'un défunt recueillie par un journaliste auprès de ses proches
colleen [ˈkɒliːn] *n* (*in Ireland*) jeune fille *f*
college [ˈkɒlɪdʒ] **1** *n* **(a)** [①A6,d,i] (*of further or higher education*) établissement *m* d'enseignement supérieur; (*technical*) IUT *m*, collège *m* technique; **to go to c., to be at c.** (*be a student there*) faire des études supérieures; **I've got to go off to c. now** il faut que j'aille en cours maintenant; **c. of art** école *f* des beaux-arts; **c. of education** = école *f* normale; **c. of music** conservatoire *m* (de musique); **agricultural c.** = institut *m* agronomique; **military/navy c.** école militaire/navale; **technical c.** collège technique
(b) (*part of British university*) collège *m* (*comme ceux d'Oxford*); **the c. team** l'équipe du collège; **he played rugby for his c.** il a joué au rugby pour son collège *ou* dans l'équipe de son collège
(c) *Rel* collège *m*; **the C. of Cardinals** le Collège des cardinaux, le Sacré Collège
(d) *Pol* **electoral c.** collège *m* électoral
2 *adj attrib* **c. education** études *fpl* supérieures; **c. student** étudiant, -ante
collegiate [kəˈliːdʒɪət] *adj* (*system*) des collèges; (*life*) dans un collège/les collèges; (*university*) organisé en collèges; **c. church** collégiale *f*
collide [kəˈlaɪd] *vi* (*of vehicles etc*) se heurter, se tamponner, entrer en collision; **to c. with** (*of vehicle*) heurter, tamponner, entrer en collision avec; (*ship*) aborder; **to c. with sb** (*of person*) se heurter à *ou* contre qn; *Fig* **the two countries have collided over the issue of human rights** les deux pays se sont heurtés sur la question des droits de l'homme
collie [ˈkɒlɪ] *n* (*dog*) colley *m*, chien *m* de berger écossais
collier [ˈkɒlɪər] *n* **(a)** (*ship*) (navire *m*) charbonnier *m* **(b)** *Min* (*person*) mineur *m* (*de charbon*)
colliery [ˈkɒlɪərɪ] *n Min* houillère *f*, mine *f* de charbon
collision [kəˈlɪʒən] *n* **(a)** collision *f*; (*of ships*) abordage *m*, collision; *Fig* (*of interests etc*) conflit *m*; **to come into c. with sth** (*with moving object*) entrer en collision avec qch; (*with stationary object*) rentrer dans qch; (*of ship*) aborder qch; *Naut* **to be on a c. course** être sur un cap de collision; *Fig* **they are on a c. course** ils vont se rentrer dedans; **to be on a c. course with sb** avoir toutes les chances de rentrer en conflit avec qn; *Fig* **to avoid a c. with sb** éviter les heurts avec qn **(b)** *Nucl Phys* (*of particles*) choc *m*, collision *f*
collision damage waiver *n Aut* suppression *f* de franchise pour les dommages causés aux véhicules
colloid [ˈkɒlɔɪd] *n* colloïde *m*
colloquial [kəˈləʊkwɪəl] *adj* familier, parlé
colloquialism [kəˈləʊkwɪəlɪz(ə)m] *n* expression *f* familière
colloquially [kəˈləʊkwɪəlɪ] *adv* familièrement, en style familier; **known c. as ...** communément appelé ...
collude [kəˈluːd] *vi* être de connivence (**with sb** avec qn)
collusion [kəˈluːʒən] *n* collusion *f*; **to act in c. with sb** agir de connivence avec qn; **to do sth in c. with sb** faire qch de connivence avec qn; **to be in c. with sb** être d'intelligence *ou* de connivence avec qn
collywobbles [ˈkɒlɪwɒb(ə)lz] *npl F* **to have the c.** (*an upset stomach*) avoir mal au ventre; (*be nervous*) avoir la frousse; **he gives me the c.** il me fiche la frousse
Colo *abbr* **Colorado**
Colombia [kəˈlʌmbɪə] *n* Colombie *f*
Colombian [kəˈlʌmbɪən] **1** *adj* colombien **2** *n* Colombien, -ienne
colon[1] [ˈkəʊlən] *n Anat* côlon *m*
colon[2] *n* (*punctuation mark*) deux-points *mpl*
colonel [ˈkɜːn(ə)l] *n Mil, US Av* colonel *m*
colonial [kəˈləʊnɪəl] **1** *adj* colonial; *US Archit etc* (*style*) du dix-huitième siècle, colonial; **in c. times** au *ou* du temps des colonies **2** *n* colonial, -iale
colonialism [kəˈləʊnɪəlɪz(ə)m] *n* colonialisme *m*
colonialist [kəˈləʊnɪəlɪst] *adj, n* colonialiste *mf*
colonic [kəˈlɒnɪk] *adj* du côlon; **c. irrigation** lavement *m*
colonist [ˈkɒlənɪst] *n* colon *m*
colonization [kɒlənaɪˈzeɪʃən] *n* colonisation *f*
colonize [ˈkɒlənaɪz] *vt* coloniser
colonizer [ˈkɒlənaɪzər] *n* colonisateur, -trice
colonnade [kɒləˈneɪd] *n Archit* colonnade *f*
colony [ˈkɒlənɪ] *n* (*also of animals, writers*) colonie *f*; **to live in the colonies** vivre aux colonies; *Hist* **the Colonies** les Colonies; **the English c. in Paris** la colonie anglaise de Paris
colophon [ˈkɒləfən] *n Typ* (*of publisher, printer*) logo *m*
color, color-blind *etc US* = **colour, colour-blind** *etc*
Colorado [kɒləˈrɑːdəʊ] *n* Colorado *m*; **C. beetle** doryphore *m*
coloration [kʌləˈreɪʃən] *n* coloration *f*, coloris *m*
coloratura [kɒlərəˈtʊərə] *n Mus* chant *m* agrémenté de fioritures; **c. aria** air *m* de colorature; **c. (soprano)** (soprano *f*) colorature *f*
colossal [kəˈlɒs(ə)l] *adj* colossal
colossus, *pl* **-i, -uses** [kəˈlɒsəs, -aɪ, -əsɪz] *n* colosse *m*; **the C. of Rhodes** le colosse de Rhodes
colostomy [kəˈlɒstəmɪ] *n Surg* colostomie *f*; **to have a c.** subir une colostomie; **c. bag** poche *f*
colour[1], *US* **color** [ˈkʌlər] *n* [①A7,d,ix; **B10**,D,1] **(a)** couleur *f*; **what c. is it?** de quelle couleur est-ce?; **it's the c. of a ripe cherry** ça a *ou* c'est de la couleur d'une cerise mûre; **a dark grey c.** une couleur gris foncé; **it's a sort of greenish c.** c'est d'une couleur un peu verdâtre; **local c.** couleur locale; **the political c. of a journal** la couleur politique d'un journal; **to give** *or* **lend c. to a story** rendre une histoire plus vivante; *Fig* **I've still to see the c. of his money** je n'ai pas encore vu la couleur de son argent; **c. balance** équilibre *m* des couleurs; **c. chart** nuancier *m*; *Comptr* **c. graphics** graphisme *m* en couleur; **c. magazine** magazine *m* en couleur; *Comptr* **c. monitor** moniteur *m* couleur; **c. photography/television** photographie *f*/télévision *f* en couleur(s); **c. photocopying** photocopie *f* en couleurs; *Typ, Phot* **c. positive** positif *m* (en) couleur; **c. print** reproduction *f* en couleurs; *Comptr* **c. printer** imprimante *f* couleur; *Typ* **c. printing** impression *f* couleur; *Comptr* **c. screen** écran *m* couleur; **c. separation** séparation *f* des couleurs, séparation quadrichromique
(b) *Art etc* (*tones*) coloris *m*; **light colours** coloris clairs; **c. value** valeur *f* chromatique
(c) (*pigment*) matière *f* colorante, couleur *f*; **box of colours** boîte de couleurs
(d) (*complexion*) teint *m*, couleurs *fpl*; **she had a lot of c. in her cheeks** ses joues avaient de belles couleurs; **to lose c.** perdre ses couleurs; **a week in the country will bring the c. (back) to her cheeks** une semaine à la campagne, et elle reprendra des couleurs; **indignation brought the c. to his cheeks** l'indignation colorait ses joues; *Br* **to be off c.** ne pas être dans son assiette; *Fig* **the joke was a bit off c.** la plaisanterie était d'un goût douteux
(e) (*race*) couleur *f*; **to discriminate against sb on the basis of c.** faire de la discrimination contre qn en fonction de sa couleur de peau; **the c. problem** les problèmes *mpl* raciaux
(f) **colours** (*insignia etc*) (*of party*) couleurs *fpl*; *Naut* pavillon *m*, couleurs; *Mil* **the (regimental) colours** le fanion du régiment; **to serve with the colours** servir sous les drapeaux; **with colours flying** (à) enseignes déployées; *Fig* **to pass with flying colours** (*in exam*) être reçu brillamment *ou* haut la main; **to sail under false colours** naviguer sous un faux pavillon; *Fig* **to show oneself in one's true colours** se révéler tel que l'on est; **to see sb in his/her true colours** voir qn sous son vrai jour; *Fig* **to nail one's colours to the mast** afficher ses opinions
(g) *Sp, Horseracing* **colours** (*of jockey, team*) couleurs *fpl*; *Sp, Sch* **to get one's colours** recevoir une haute distinction sportive
colour[2], *US* **color** **1** *vt* **(a)** colorer; (*card, drawing*) colorier; (*etching*) enluminer; **to c. sth blue** colorer *ou* colorier qch en bleu **(b)** (*description*) (*exaggerate*) exagérer; (*enliven*) rendre plus vivant; (*with false details*) enjoliver **(c)** (*bias, distort*) (*fact, view of reality, judgement*) influencer; (*stronger*) déformer **2** *vi* (*of person*) (*become embarrassed*) rougir
▶ **colour in** *vtsep* (*add colour to black and white illustration*) colorier; (*film, photo*) coloriser
colour bar *n* discrimination *f ou* ségrégation *f* raciale
colour bearer *n* porte-drapeau *m*
colour-blind *adj* daltonien
colour blindness *n* daltonisme *m*
colour-coded *adj* repéré par des couleurs; **everything is c.** on classe tout par un système de couleurs
colour-coding *n* système *m* de classement par couleurs; **what's their c.?** de quelle couleur sont-elles dans le classement?
Coloured, *US* **Colored** [ˈkʌləd] *n* **(Cape) C.** (*in South Africa*) métis, -isse
coloured *adj* **(a)** coloré; (*drawing*) colorié; (*shirt*) de couleur; **gaily c. butterfly** papillon multicolore; **brightly c. clothing** des vêtements aux couleurs vives; *Fig* **highly c. narrative** récit *m* coloré **(b)** (*person etc*) de couleur

coloureds, *US* **coloreds** ['kʌlədz] *npl* **(a)** (*clothes*) couleurs *fpl*; **separate whites and c.** (*washing instructions*) lavez les couleurs et le blanc séparément **(b)** (*people*) gens *mpl* de couleur
colourful, *US* **colorful** ['kʌləfʊl] *adj* (*sky etc*) coloré; (*style*) coloré, pittoresque; **a c. character** un original; **c. language** langage *m* coloré
colouring, *US* **coloring** ['kʌlərɪŋ] *n* **(a)** (*act*) coloration *f*; (*of children's pictures*) coloriage *m*; **c. book** livre *m* de coloriage **(b)** (*shade*) (*of painting, style*) coloris *m* **(c)** (*complexion*) (*of person*) teint *m*
colouring-in *n* coloriage *m*; **c. book** livre *m* de coloriage
colourist, *US* **colorist** ['kʌlərɪst] *n Art* **as a c., he ...** pour le maniement des couleurs, il ...
colourless, *US* **colorless** ['kʌləlɪs] *adj* **(a)** (*clear*) sans couleur, incolore **(b)** (*pale*) terne, incolore; (*face*) blême; (*complexion*) pâle, délavé; (*light*) pâle, falot **(c)** *Fig* (*dull*) (*style*) insipide, fade; (*voice*) terne; (*person*) sans caractère
colourlessness, *US* **colorlessness** ['kʌləlɪsnɪs] *n* **(a)** absence *f* de couleur; (*of complexion*) pâleur *f* **(b)** *Fig* (*of style*) fadeur *f*; (*of person*) manque *m* de personnalité
colour line *n* discrimination *f ou* ségrégation *f* raciale; **to cross the c.** faire fi de la ségrégation raciale
colour party *n* garde *f* du drapeau
colour scheme *n* (*of room, decor*) couleurs *fpl*, coloris *mpl*; (*of plane, vehicle*) couleurs
colour sergeant *n* sergent chef *m* (*de la garde du drapeau*)
colour supplement *n Journ* supplément *m* en couleurs
colourway ['kʌləweɪ] *n* coloris *m*
colt [kəʊlt] *n* (*horse*) poulain *m*, jeune cheval *m* mâle
coltish ['kəʊltɪʃ] *adj* **(a)** (*immature*) sans expérience **(b)** (*playful*) folâtre
coltsfoot ['kəʊltsfʊt] *n* (*plant*) pas-d'âne *m*
Columbia [kə'lʌmbɪə] *n* **British C.** Colombie-britannique *f*; **(District of) C.** (District *m* fédéral de) Columbia *f*
Columbine ['kɒləmbaɪn] *n Th* Colombine *f*
columbine ['kɒləmbaɪn] *n* (*plant*) ancolie *f*
Columbus [kə'lʌmbəs] *n* **(Christopher) C.** Christophe Colomb
column ['kɒləm] *n* **(a)** (*of building, smoke, figures etc*) colonne *f*; **putting into columns** colonnage *m*; *Av* **control c.** levier *m* de commande; *Aut* **c. change** levier *m* de vitesses sur colonne de direction
(b) *Mil, Naut* (*formation*) colonne *f*; **to march in c. /in two columns** marcher en colonne/en deux colonnes; **supply/ relief c.** colonne de ravitaillement/de secours
(c) *Journ* colonne *f*; (*feature*) rubrique *f*; **six c. page** page de six colonnes; **sports c.** rubrique *ou* chronique *f* sportive; **it got a lot of c. inches** (*of story*) on lui a consacré beaucoup d'espace dans le journal; **c. centimetre** (*for advertisement*) centimètre-colonne *m*; **c. inch** ≈ centimètre-colonne *m*; **c. space** colonnage *m*
(d) *Comptr, Typ* **c. mode** mode *m* colonne; **c. header** en-tête *m* de colonnes; **c. printing** impression *f* en colonnes; **c. spacing** espacement *m* des colonnes
columnist ['kɒləmɪst, -əmnɪst] *n Journ* chroniqueur, -euse, courriériste *mf*; **sports c.** chroniqueur sportif, chroniqueuse sportive
colza ['kɒlzə] *n* (*plant*) colza *m*; **c. oil** huile *f* de colza
COM [kɒm] *n Comptr* (*abbr* **Computer Output Microfilm**) **C. unit** unité *f* d'impression sur microfilm; **C. plotter** traceur *m* C. O. M. ; **C. printer** imprimante *f* sur microfilm
coma ['kəʊmə] *n Med* coma *m*; **to go into/be in a c.** entrer/ être dans le coma
co-management *n* cogérance *f*
comatose ['kəʊmətəʊs] *adj Med* comateux; (*person*) dans le coma; *Fig* (*state*) comateux
comb¹ [kəʊm] *n* **(a)** (*for hair, wool etc*) peigne *m*; (*for horse*) étrille *f*; **to run a c. through one's hair, to give one's hair a c.** se donner un coup de peigne **(b)** (*of cock*) crête *f* **(c)** (*honeycomb*) rayon *m*; **honey in the c.** miel *m* en rayon
comb² *vt* **(a)** (*sb's hair*) peigner; **to c. one's hair** se peigner; **to c. down a horse** étriller un cheval **(b)** *Tex etc* (*wool etc*) peigner, carder; **combed cotton** coton peigné **(c)** (*search thoroughly*) (*area, town etc*) ratisser, passer au peigne fin **(for sb** pour (re)trouver qn); **she combed the book for references to the crisis** elle a passé le livre au peigne fin *ou* au crible pour trouver des références à la crise
▶ **comb out** *vtsep* **(a)** (*hair*) peigner; (*untangle*) démêler; **to c. the knots out of one's hair** démêler ses cheveux **(b)** (*wool*) peigner **(c)** (*remove*) (*fleas*) retirer avec un peigne
combat¹ ['kɒmbæt] *n* combat *m*; **in c.** au combat; **single c.** combat singulier; **camouflaged c. clothing** tenue *f* léopard; **c. dress** tenue *f* de combat; *US* **c. fatigue** psychose *f* traumatique (du combattant); **c. jacket** veste *f* de tenue de combat; (*green canvas*) veste de treillis; **c. mission** mission *f* de combat; **women are now used in a c. role** on envoie maintenant les femmes dans des situations de combat; **c. troops** troupes *fpl* de combat; **c. zone** zone *f* de combat
combat² (-t-) **1** *vt* (*disease, prejudice, crime*) lutter contre, combattre **2** *vi* combattre (**against** contre)
combatant ['kɒmbətənt] *adj, n* combattant, -ante
combative ['kɒmbətɪv] *adj* combatif
combination [kɒmbɪ'neɪʃən] *n* **(a)** combinaison *f*; (*of circumstances*) concours *m*; *Ch* combiné *m*, combinaison; **nitrogen in c. with oxygen** l'azote combiné avec l'oxygène; **an interesting c. of flavours** un mélange intéressant de parfums; **c. rate** (*in advertising*) couplage *m*, tarif *m* couplage **(b)** (*of people, workers etc*) association *f*; **to enter into a c. with ...** s'associer avec ... **(c)** (*for lock*) combinaison *f*; **c. lock** serrure *f* à combinaisons *ou* à code **(d)** *Old-fashioned Br* (*clothing*) **(pair of) combinations** combinaison-culotte *f*, *pl* combinaisons-culottes
combination spanner *n* clé *f* mixte
combine¹ ['kɒmbaɪn] *n* **(a)** *Com, Fin* cartel *m* **(b)** *Agr* **c. (harvester)** moissonneuse-batteuse *f*, *pl* moissonneuses-batteuses
combine² [kəm'baɪn] **1** *vt* combiner (**with** à); (*qualities etc*) allier (**with** à); **to c. forces** joindre ses forces (**with** à); **to c. strength of body with strength of mind** allier la force du corps à celle de l'âme; **to c. business with pleasure** joindre l'utile à l'agréable; **the play combines drama and music** la pièce allie intrigue et musique **2** *vi* (*of people*) s'unir, s'associer, s'allier; (*aggressively*) se liguer (**against** contre); (*of workers*) se syndiquer; *Pol* (*of parties*) s'allier; (*merge*) fusionner; *Ch* (*of elements*) se combiner; **everything combined to give me this impression** tout concourait à me donner cette impression
combined [kəm'baɪnd] *adj* (*efforts*) réuni; **the c. sound of a pneumatic drill and the traffic** le bruit d'un marteau piqueur additionné à celui de la circulation; *Mil* **c. force** force *f* mixte; **c. fleets** flottes *fpl* combinées; *Mil etc* **c. operation** opération *f* combinée *ou* interarmées; *Com* **c. transport bill of lading** connaissement *m* de transport combiné; **c. transport company** entrepreneur *m* de transport combiné, ETC *m*
combining [kəm'baɪnɪŋ] *n* combinaison *f*; *Gram* **c. form** affixe *m*
combo ['kɒmbəʊ] *n Mus* petite formation *f* musicale; *Comptr* **c. box** équipement *m* de jonction
combust [kəm'bʌst] *vi* brûler
combustible [kəm'bʌstɪb(ə)l] **1** *adj* combustible **2** *n* matière *f* inflammable; (*fuel*) combustible *m*
combustion [kəm'bʌstʃən] *n* combustion *f*; **c. chamber** chambre *f* de combustion; **c. gases** gaz *m* de combustion
come¹ [kʌm] *vi* (*pt* **came** [keɪm]; *pp* **come**) **(a)** venir; (*arrive*) venir, arriver (**to** à, **from** de); **to c. from France/Edinburgh** venir de France/d'Édimbourg; **here c. the children** voici les enfants qui arrivent; **here he comes!** le voilà qui arrive!; **I'm coming with you** je viens avec vous, je vous accompagne; **she comes this way every week** elle vient par ici chaque semaine; **what way do you usually c.?** par où passes-tu d'habitude?; **they don't c. here often** ils ne viennent pas souvent ici; **we're coming to a crossroads** nous arrivons à un croisement; **c. here!** venez ici!, *F* arrive ici!; (*to dog*) au pied!; **coming!** j'arrive!; **ok ok, I'm coming!** d'accord, je viens!; **(are you) coming?** (*with me, us etc*) tu viens?; **c. and see/do** viens voir/faire; **to c. for sb/sth** venir chercher qn/ qch; **to c. to sb for advice** venir demander conseil à qn; **you've come to the wrong person** vous vous adressez à la mauvaise personne; **you've come to the wrong place** vous vous êtes trompé de chemin, vous faites fausse route; **if you're looking for sun, you've come to the wrong place** si c'est le soleil que vous cherchez, il ne fallait pas venir ici; **to c. to the end of sth** arriver à la fin de qch; **I was coming to the end of my stay** j'arrivais à la fin de mon séjour; **when you come to the last coat of paint ...** quand tu en seras à la dernière couche de peinture ...; **to c. to the throne** monter sur le trône; **a crisis is coming** une crise se prépare; **the fireworks c. next** le feu d'artifice est après; **what comes after the performance?** qu'est-ce qu'il y a après la représentation?; **what are things coming to (when ...)?** où allons-nous (si ...)?; **letters came pouring in** ce fut une avalanche de lettres; **he has come a long way** il vient de loin; *Fig* il a fait du chemin; **computers have come a long way** les ordinateurs ont beaucoup évolué; *Fig* **they saw you coming (a mile off)** ils t'ont vu venir (de loin); **to c. and go** aller et venir; **the idea came to me that ...** il m'est venu à l'esprit que ...; **suddenly it came to me** (*I remembered*) tout d'un coup, je m'en suis souvenu; (*I had idea*) tout d'un coup, j'ai eu une idée; **the idea came to me one morning** l'idée

m'est venue à l'esprit un matin; **a smile came to her lips** un sourire parut sur ses lèvres *ou* lui vint aux lèvres; **c. now!, c., c.!** allons!, voyons!; *F* **she's as obstinate/intelligent as they c.** il n'y a pas plus têtue/intelligente qu'elle; *F* **he had it coming to him** il n'a eu que ce qu'il méritait; *Fig* **I don't know whether I'm coming or going** je perds la tête *ou F* les pédales; **c. summer (and) we'll all meet again** quand viendra l'été, on se retrouvera tous; **she'll be ten c. January** elle aura dix ans en janvier; **I've got £500 coming to me** je vais (bientôt) toucher 500 livres; **we mustn't let a small disagreement c. between us** nous n'allons pas nous disputer à cause d'un petit malentendu; **a woman came between them** ils se sont disputés à cause d'une femme; **she won't let anything c. between her and her work** son travail passe avant tout

(b) (*happen*) **we must take things as they c.** il faut prendre les choses comme elles viennent; **c. what may, we'll get it finished** quoi qu'il arrive, nous finirons; **how did the door c. to be open?** comment se fait-il que la porte soit ouverte?; *F* **how c.?** pourquoi?; (*how*) comment se fait-il?; **now that I c. to think of it** maintenant que j'y pense

(c) (*originate*) venir; **word that comes from Latin** mot qui vient du latin; **that's surprising coming from him** cela étonne de sa part, venant de lui, c'est étonnant; **to c. from** *or* **of a good family** être issu *ou* venir d'une bonne famille

(d) (*be*) **that comes easy/natural(ly) to him** cela lui est facile/naturel, ça lui vient facilement/naturellement; **it came as a shock/a relief to me** cela a été un choc/un soulagement pour moi; **gold watches don't c. cheap** les montres en or ne sont pas données; **that doesn't c. within my duties** cela ne rentre pas dans mes fonctions

(e) (*become*) **to c. undone/untied/loose** (*of tie, knot, bootlaces etc*) se dénouer/se délacer/se défaire

(f) in the years/days to c. dans les années/les jours à venir; **that will not be for some time to c.** cela va prendre un peu de temps

(g) (*of teeth*) sortir

(h) *F* **that's coming it a bit strong** ça, c'est un peu fort; **don't c. the big boss with me** ne prends pas ce ton autoritaire avec moi; **don't c. it with me** (*don't pretend*) à moi, on ne me la fait pas!; (*as threat*) arrête!; **don't even think about coming it with me!** ne joue pas à ça avec moi!

(i) *F* (*reach orgasm*) jouir; (*ejaculate*) prendre son pied, décharger

come² *n F* (*semen*) sperme *m*, *Vulg* foutre *m*

▶ **come about** *vi* **(a)** (*of event, occurrence etc*) arriver, se passer, se produire; **it came about that …** il arriva *ou* il advint que … **(b)** (*of ship*) virer de bord; (*of wind*) tourner

▶ **come across 1** *vipo* (*find*) (*person*) rencontrer par hasard, tomber sur; (*object*) trouver par hasard, tomber sur **2** *vi* **(a)** (*make an impression*) **to c. across well/badly** (*at interview*) faire une bonne/mauvaise impression, bien/mal passer; (*on TV*) bien/mal passer; **they c. across as nice people** ils ont l'air gentils; **the story doesn't c. across so well on the screen** l'histoire ne rend pas très bien à l'écran; **how did her story c. across?** quelle impression est-ce que son histoire t'a faite *ou* laissée? **(b)** *F* (*pay up*) payer ce que l'on doit

▶ **come across with** *vipo F* (*supply*) (*money*) cracher

▶ **come after 1** *vipo* **(a)** (*chase*) poursuivre **(b)** (*follow*) venir *ou* être après, suivre; **n comes after k in the alphabet** le n vient après le k dans l'alphabet; **what comes after the dancing?** qu'est-ce qu'il y a après la danse? **2** *vi* (*follow*) suivre, venir après

▶ **come along** *vi* **(a) c. along!** (*hurry*) allons-y!; (*come here*) allons, viens par ici! **(b)** (*make progress*) **how's the work coming along?** comment ça avance, le travail?; **the preparations are coming along fine** les préparatifs avancent bien **(c)** (*arrive*) arriver; **everything was peaceful until he came along** tout était calme avant qu'il n'arrive; **these things c. along when you least expect them** ces choses-là arrivent quand on s'y attend le moins **(d)** (*come as well*) **the children came along** les enfants sont venus avec moi/nous *ou* aussi; **would you like to c. along?** tu voudrais venir?

▶ **come apart** *vi* (*fall to pieces*) tomber en morceaux; *Fig* (*of person*) craquer; (*of plans etc*) aller à la catastrophe; **to c. apart at the seams** (*of garment*) se défaire aux coutures

▶ **come at** *vipo* **(a)** (*attack*) attaquer; **criticisms/jibes were coming at me from all sides** des critiques/quolibets arrivaient sur moi de tous côtés **(b)** (*approach*) **to c. at a problem from a different angle** aborder un problème sous un angle différent

▶ **come away** *vi* **(a)** (*leave*) partir, s'éloigner; **why not c. away with us to Paris for the weekend?** pourquoi ne pas venir avec nous à Paris ce week-end?; **c. away from that cat** éloigne-toi de ce chat **(b)** (*become detached*) se détacher; (*when glued*) se décoller, se détacher; (*when nailed*) se déclouer, se détacher; **the handle came away in his hand** l'anse lui est restée dans la main

▶ **come back** *vi* **(a)** (*return*) revenir; **to c. back (home)** rentrer; **it's all coming back to me** cela me revient (à la *ou* en mémoire); **her name will c. back to me later** son nom me reviendra plus tard; **to c. back to what I was saying …** pour en revenir à ce que je disais … **(b)** (*of fashion*) revenir; (*of long skirts etc*) revenir (à la mode) **(c)** (*from losing position etc*) revenir; **to c. back from a defeat/setback** revenir après une défaite/un échec **(d)** *F* (*retort*) répliquer, riposter

▶ **come by 1** *vipo* (*acquire*) **how did you c. by this camera/those bruises?** comment as-tu fait pour avoir cet appareil-photo/ces bleus?; **how did she c. by all that money?** comment s'est-elle procuré tout cet argent?; **how did you c. by your fortune?** d'où vient ta fortune?; **how did you c. by your Nordic looks?** d'où vient que tu as l'air nordique? **2** *vi* (*go past, visit*) passer

▶ **come down 1** *vi* **(a)** (*descend*) (*from ladder, stairs*) descendre; (*from mountain etc*) descendre, faire la descente; (*of plane*) (*crash*) s'écraser; (*land*) atterrir; (*of rain*) tomber; **to c. down to breakfast** descendre déjeuner *ou* prendre le petit déjeuner; **the plane came down in the sea** (*crashed*) l'avion est tombé en mer; (*landed*) l'avion a amerri; **hemlines are coming down this year** les jupes rallongent cette année; *Fig* **to c. down (in the world)** déchoir; *Fig* **to c. down to earth** descendre des nues

(b) (*decrease*) (*of temperature, prices*) baisser; **he'll c. down a few pounds if you bargain** il baissera son prix de quelques livres si tu marchandes

(c) (*decide*) se décider; **to c. down in favour of sb/sth** se décider en faveur de qn/qch; **to c. down on sb's side** décider en faveur de qn

(d) (*reach*) **her hair came down to her waist** les cheveux lui tombaient *ou* descendaient jusqu'à la taille; **the curtains should c. right down to the floor** les rideaux devraient tomber jusqu'au sol

(e) (*be an inheritance*) être laissé en héritage *ou* légué (**to sb** à qn, **from** par); (*of tale, tradition*) être transmis (**from** par); **the necklace came down to her from her great-aunt** elle tient ce collier de sa grand-tante; **the tales that have come down to us** les contes qui nous sont parvenus

(f) (*collapse*) (*of tree etc*) s'abattre; (*of structure*) s'écrouler

(g) (*be removed*) être défait *ou* décroché; **that wallpaper will have to c. down** il va falloir enlever ce papier peint; **the Christmas decorations are coming down today** aujourd'hui, on enlève les décorations de Noël; **that disgusting poster is coming down now!** enlève-moi tout de suite cet affreux poster!; **the tree will have to c. down** (*be felled*) il faut abattre cet arbre; **these houses are coming down soon** on va bientôt démolir ces maisons

(h) (*be a question of*) **to c. down to** se résumer *ou* se réduire à; **the whole difficulty comes down to this question** toute la difficulté se réduit à cette question; **it all comes down to money** ce n'est qu'une question d'argent

(i) *Am F* (*to happen*) se préparer

2 *vipo* (*stairs, street*) descendre

▶ **come down on** *vipo F* (*criticize, punish*) tomber sur le dos de; **one mistake and he'll c. down on you like a ton of bricks** si tu fais la moindre erreur, il te tombera sur le dos; **she came down on me for not having told her about it earlier** elle m'est tombée dessus parce que je ne lui en avais pas parlé plus tôt

▶ **come down with** *vipo* (*succumb to*) (*cold, flu etc*) attraper

▶ **come forward** *vi* (*present oneself*) se proposer; **no one has come forward with any alternative ideas** personne n'a rien proposé d'autre; **the police have appealed for witnesses to c. forward** la police a demandé aux témoins de se faire connaître; **to c. forward as a candidate** poser sa candidature, se porter candidat; *Hum* **he's not backward in coming forward** il ne se gêne pas

▶ **come in** *vi* **(a)** (*enter*) entrer; **to c. in again** rentrer; **c. in!** entrez!; (*on radio*) répondez!; *Br F* **Mrs Brown comes in twice a week** (*to clean*) Madame Brown vient (faire le ménage) deux fois par semaine; **Mr Jones isn't coming in today** (*to office etc*) M. Jones n'est pas là aujourd'hui; *Cin, Fig* **this is where we came in** on a déjà vu ça

(b) (*of tide*) monter; (*of ship*) arriver; *Pol* (*of party*) arriver *ou* parvenir au pouvoir; *Cr* (*of batsman*) venir prendre son tour au guichet; **we don't have much money coming in** il n'y a pas beaucoup d'argent qui rentre; *Sp* **to c. in first/second** arriver premier/second; **this fashion is coming in**

again cette mode revient *ou* reprend; **reports of a coup are coming in** on nous annonce qu'il y a eu un coup d'état

(c) (*have a role*) (*in matter*) avoir un rôle à jouer; **and where do I c. in?** et moi, quel sera mon rôle?; **that's where I c. in** (*to help*) voilà où je peux vous aider, voilà où j'interviens; **to c. in useful (to sb/for sth/for doing sth)** servir (à qn/à qch/à *ou* pour faire qch); **extra money always comes in useful** *or* **handy** il est toujours utile d'avoir de l'argent en plus

(d) (*join an enterprise etc*) **to c. in with sb** s'associer à qn; **they were the founder members, the others didn't c. in till later** ce sont les membres fondateurs, les autres ne s'y sont associés que plus tard

▶ **come in for** *vipo* **to c. in for praise** être félicité; **to c. in for criticism** être critiqué, être en butte aux critiques; **the government came in for a lot of criticism over its handling of the crisis** le gouvernement a été très critiqué pour la façon dont il gère la crise; **to c. in for a share of sth** avoir part à qch

▶ **come in on** *vipo* (*be given a part in*) prendre part à; **they let him c. in on the deal** ils l'ont laissé prendre part à l'affaire

▶ **come into** *vipo* **(a)** (*enter*) (*room*) entrer dans; **to c. into the world** venir au monde; **to c. into power** (*of party, person etc*) arriver *ou* parvenir au pouvoir; **to c. into force** *or* **effect** (*of law, ruling etc*) entrer en vigueur; **when does the law c. into force** *or* **effect?** quand la loi prend-elle effet *ou* entre-t-elle en vigueur?; **to c. into possession of sth** entrer en possession de qch; **how did this painting c. into your possession?** comment êtes-vous entré en possession de ce tableau?; **to c. into sb's mind** (*of idea*) venir à l'esprit de qn

(b) (*inherit*) (*money, property etc*) hériter (de); (*inheritance*) entrer en possession de, recueillir; *F* **to c. into some money** (*inherit it*) hériter d'un magot; (*win it*) gagner le gros lot

(c) (*be involved in*) **luck doesn't c. into it** la chance n'a rien à voir là-dedans

▶ **come of** *vipo* **(a)** (*result from*) **what will c. of it?** qu'en adviendra-t-il?, qu'en résultera-t-il?; **no good will c. of it** cela tournera mal; **that's what comes of being too ambitious** voilà ce qui arrive quand on est trop ambitieux **(b) to c. of age** (*reach legal status*) atteindre la *ou* sa majorité

▶ **come off 1** *vi* **(a)** (*become detached*) (*of button etc*) se détacher, sauter; (*of paint, stain etc*) s'enlever, partir; (*become unstuck*) se décoller; **does this bit c. off?** est-ce que ça s'enlève?; **the colour came off on my dress** la couleur a déteint sur ma robe; **the chain has come off** (*of bicycle*) la chaîne a sauté; **the top of the pen had come off** le bouchon du stylo avait sauté

(b) (*fall from horse, motorbike etc*) tomber

(c) (*take place*) (*of meeting etc*) avoir lieu

(d) (*succeed*) réussir, aboutir; **did it c. off all right?** ça s'est bien passé?; **my little trip abroad didn't c. off** mon petit voyage à l'étranger est tombé à l'eau; **the experiment came off** l'expérience a réussi

(e) (*acquit oneself*) **to c. off badly** mal s'en tirer; **you'll c. off worst** tu auras le dessous

(f) *Sl* (*reach orgasm*) jouir

2 *vipo* **(a)** (*climb down from, leave*) (*wall, ladder etc*) descendre de; **to c. off a ship/plane** débarquer d'un navire/d'un avion; **I've just come off the night shift** (*finished work*) je viens de quitter l'équipe de nuit; (*finished working nights*) je viens de finir le travail de nuit

(b) (*fall from*) (*horse, motorbike etc*) tomber de

(c) (*become detached from*) **the handle has come off the knife** le manche s'est détaché du couteau

(d) (*be removed from*) **that stain will never c. off the carpet** cette tache sur le tapis ne partira jamais

(e) *F* **c. off it!** arrête ton baratin!; **c. off it, he's not 21!** arrête de dire n'importe quoi, il n'a pas 21 ans!

▶ **come on** *vi* **(a) c. on!** (*with motion, encouraging, challenging*) vas-y!, allez!; *F* (*expressing incredulity*) tu rigoles!; **c. on, hurry!** allez, dépêche-toi; **c. on, let's have a game!** allons! faisons une partie!; **c. on Scotland!** allez l'Écosse!

(b) (*make progress*) (*of plants etc*) se développer; (*of people*) faire des progrès; **Jackie's French is really coming on** le français de Jackie s'améliore vraiment; **Jackie is really coming on with her French** Jackie fait de gros progrès en français; **how's the work coming on?** est-ce que le travail avance?; **the building work is coming on fine** la construction avance bien

(c) (*start*) (*of winter etc*) venir, arriver; (*of night*) tomber; (*of symptoms*) apparaître; **I feel a cold coming on** je sens que je suis en train de m'enrhumer; **I have a sore throat coming on** je commence à avoir mal à la gorge

(d) *Th* (*appear*) entrer en scène; *Sp* (*on to field*) (r)entrer

(e) (*be shown*) (*of film etc*) passer; **the play/film is coming on next week** on va donner la pièce/le film va passer la semaine prochaine; **when does that programme c. on?** quand passe cette émission?; **the film's coming on** le film va commencer

(f) *esp US F* **to come on to sb** (*make sexual overtures to*) draguer qn

▶ **come out** *vi* **(a)** (*from room, prison, hospital etc*) sortir; **to c. out of a place/a room** sortir d'un lieu/d'une pièce

(b) (*become detached*) partir; (*of screw*) se dévisser; (*of tooth*) tomber; (*of page*) se détacher; **my filling has come out** j'ai perdu mon plombage

(c) *esp Br Ind* **to c. out (on strike)** se mettre en grève

(d) (*emerge*) **to c. out of an affair badly/well** mal/bien se tirer d'une affaire; **they came out of the business looking rather foolish** à la suite de cette affaire, ils avaient l'air plutôt ridicule; *Sch* **to c. out first/second** sortir premier/second, être reçu premier/second

(e) (*appear*) (*of sun, stars*) paraître; (*of buds*) éclore; (*of pimple*) sortir; (*of rash*) apparaître; **to c. out in a rash** (*of person*) se couvrir de boutons, avoir une éruption

(f) (*become known*) (*of the truth*) être découvert; (*of election, sports results etc*) être révélé *ou* communiqué; **as soon as the news came out ...** dès qu'on a su la nouvelle ...; **it came out that ...** il s'avéra que ..., il se trouva que ...

(g) (*be published, issued*) (*of book, journal*) paraître, sortir; (*of record, film*) sortir

(h) (*of photo*) **he always comes out well** il est toujours bien sur les photos; **these photos have come out well** ces photos sont bien sorties

(i) (*be removed*) (*of stain*) s'enlever; (*of colour, dye*) déteindre; **when do your stitches c. out?** quand est-ce qu'on t'enlève les points?

(j) *Math* (*be solved*) **I can't get this sum to c. out** je n'y arrive pas, la somme ne tombe pas juste; **it won't c. out** ça ne marche pas; **to c. out at ...** (*of total etc*) être de ..., se monter à ...; (*of average*) être de ...; **it comes out at ...** le résultat est de ...; *Fig* **everything will c. out (all) right in the end** tout finira par s'arranger

(k) *Br* (*of debutante*) débuter, faire son entrée dans le monde

(l) *F* (*as gay or lesbian*) se déclarer homosexuel

(m) (*decide*) **to c. out strongly** se prononcer avec vigueur **(for** pour, **against** contre); **we've come out against the idea of moving** nous avons renoncé à déménager; **the committee came out in her favour** le comité s'est décidé en sa faveur

▶ **come out with** *vipo* (*say*) sortir, dire; (*remark*) sortir, faire; **I'm always wondering what he'll c. out with next** je me demande toujours ce qu'il va sortir; **she finally came out with what was bothering her** elle a fini par dire ce qui la tracassait

▶ **come over 1** *vi* **(a)** (*travel, walk etc across*) traverser; **a lot of Americans came over during the war** de nombreux Américains sont venus (en Europe) pendant la guerre; **friends are coming over from Canada** des amis arrivent du Canada; **some friends are coming over** (*who live not far away*) des amis viennent me/nous/*etc* voir; **c. over tomorrow** passe demain; **he came over and spoke to me** il est venu me parler

(b) (*change allegiance*) **to c. over to sb's side** passer dans le camp de qn *ou* du côté de qn; **to c. over to sb's way of thinking** se rallier à l'opinion de qn

(c) (*make impression*) **how did she c. over?** quelle impression vous a-t-elle faite?; **he doesn't c. over well on television** il ne passe pas bien à la télévision, il n'est pas très médiatique; **her voice comes over well** sa voix passe *ou* rend bien; **he comes over as (being) rather pompous** il a l'air (d'être) assez solennel

(d) *F* (*suddenly become*) **to c. over (all) funny** être pris d'un malaise

2 *vipo* (*affect*) (*of mood etc*) (*person*) envahir, gagner; **a change has come over him** il a bien changé; **what's come over you?** qu'est-ce qui te prend?

▶ **come round** *vi* **(a)** (*travel*) faire le tour; **the road is blocked, I had to c. round by the village** la route est bloquée, j'ai dû faire un détour par le village

(b) (*visit*) **c. round and see me one day** venez me voir un de ces jours

(c) (*arrive*) **the weekend will soon c. round** ce sera bientôt le week-end; **birthdays seem to c. round more**

often after you're 40 les anniversaires semblent revenir plus souvent quand on a dépassé la quarantaine

(**d**) (*regain consciousness*) reprendre connaissance, revenir à soi

(**e**) (*change one's mind*) changer d'avis; **to c. round to sb's way of thinking** se convertir à l'opinion de qn; **they soon came round to the idea** ils se sont faits à cette idée; **he's come round** il a cédé

(**f**) *Naut* (*of ship*) venir dans le vent; (*of wind*) remonter

▶ **come through 1** *vi* (**a**) (*penetrate*) (*of tooth*) percer; (*of water*) pénétrer

(**b**) (*survive*) **he came through without a scratch** il s'en est tiré indemne

(**c**) (*arrive*) (*of message etc*) arriver, parvenir; **my visa is taking a long time to c. through** mon visa met du temps à arriver *ou* à me parvenir

2 *vipo* (**a**) (*penetrate*) **water is coming through the roof** l'eau s'infiltre par le toit; **the nail has come through the wood** le clou a traversé le bois

(**b**) (*survive*) survivre à; **he came through the war without a scratch** il a survécu à la guerre sans une égratignure; **I'm sure you will c. through this crisis** je suis sûr que tu te sortiras de cette crise; **she came through her exams with flying colours** elle a réussi brillamment (à) ses examens

▶ **come to 1** *vi* (**a**) = **come round** (**d**)

(**b**) *Naut* (*of ship*) lofer, venir dans le vent

2 *vipo* (**a**) (*amount to*) s'élever à; **the bill came to $80** la note s'éleva à 80 dollars; **how much does it c. to?** combien cela fait-il?; **the plan never came to anything** le projet n'a abouti à rien; **that nephew of yours will never c. to anything** ton neveu n'arrivera jamais à rien

(**b**) (*be a question of*) **when it comes to ...** en ce qui concerne ...; **when it comes to music I haven't got a clue** je ne m'y connais absolument pas en musique; **c. to that, what are you doing here?** au fait, qu'est-ce que vous faites ici?; **if it comes to that ...** à ce compte-là ...; **it comes to this/that ...** cela revient à ceci que ...; **let's hope it won't c. to that** espérons que nous n'en arrivions pas là; **when it comes to buying a car, find yourself a reputable dealer** si vous voulez acheter une voiture, adressez-vous à un concessionnaire de bonne réputation

(**c**) (*get as far as*) en venir à; **I wish she'd c. to the point** si seulement elle en venait au fait; **if it comes to a fight, we outnumber them** si on en vient à se battre, nous sommes plus nombreux qu'eux; **it's really come to something when ...** si ce n'est pas malheureux que ...; **what is the world coming to?** où est-ce qu'on va!

▶ **come together** *vi* (**a**) (*gather*) s'assembler, se réunir; (*of troops*) opérer une jonction (**b**) (*meet*) se rencontrer; **the two roads c. together at this point** les deux routes se rejoignent à cet endroit

▶ **come up 1** *vi* (**a**) (*by stairs, on ladder, up a hill etc*) monter; **would you like to c. up for tea?** (*to my room etc*) vous voulez monter prendre un thé?; **a man came up from the office downstairs** un homme est monté du bureau d'en-dessous; **to c. up after a dive** revenir à la surface après un plongeon

(**b**) *Br* **to c. up to town** venir en ville

(**c**) (*approach*) **a man came up (to me) and started talking** un homme est venu vers moi *ou* s'est approché de moi et a commencé à me parler; **a police car came up alongside ours** une voiture de police s'est mise à la hauteur de la nôtre; **it's coming up to 10 o'clock** il est presque 10 heures; *Tennis* **to c. up to the net** monter au filet

(**d**) (*appear*) apparaître; (*of plant*) sortir de terre, pousser; (*of sun*) se lever; **some words came up on the screen** quelques mots sont apparus sur l'écran; *Naut* **to c. up on the horizon** (*of land etc*) paraître à l'horizon; **there's a cabaret act coming up (next)** il y a un numéro de cabaret tout de suite après; **there are some interesting films coming up on television** il y a quelques films intéressants qui vont passer à la télévision; **one coffee, coming up** (*in café*) un café, oui m'sieur/m'dame!

(**e**) (*arise*) (*of opportunity, question etc*) se présenter; (*of problem etc*) survenir, surgir; **to deal with problems as they c. up** traiter les problèmes au fur et à mesure; **have any vacancies come up recently?** est-ce que des postes se sont libérés récemment?; **I'll let you know if anything comes up** (*if I find further information*) s'il y a du nouveau, je vous tiendrai au courant; (*anything that is suitable*) je vous tiendrai au courant si je vois quelque chose qui vous convienne; **call me if something comes up that you can't handle** appelle-moi s'il y a quelque chose qui te pose problème; *Jur* **to c. up before the Court** comparaître (devant le tribunal); **the case comes up (for trial) tomorrow** la cause sera entendue demain; **two houses in our street are coming up for sale soon** dans notre rue, deux maisons seront bientôt à vendre; **the question has never yet come up** cette question n'a encore jamais été soulevée; **the subject came up twice in the conversation** le sujet est revenu deux fois dans la conversation; **your name came up twice** on a mentionné votre nom deux fois

(**f**) (*shine, look clean*) **the sideboard came up beautifully** le buffet a retrouvé toute sa splendeur

2 *vipo* (*stairs*) monter; (*street*) remonter

▶ **come up against** *vipo* (**a**) (*encounter*) se heurter à; **the reformers came up against some pretty strong opposition** les réformateurs se sont heurtés à une opposition plutôt violente; **who does she c. up against in the next round?** qui doit-elle affronter dans la prochaine manche? (**b**) (*hit, come into contact with*) rencontrer; **his hand came up against something cold** sa main rencontra quelque chose de froid; **the tunnellers came up against solid rock** les ouvriers qui creusaient le tunnel se sont retrouvés face à un mur de roche dure

▶ **come upon** *vipo* (*find*) (*person, object*) tomber sur

▶ **come up to** *vipo* (**a**) (*reach*) (*sth*) atteindre; **the water came up to my knees** l'eau m'arrivait jusqu'aux genoux; **I only c. up to her shoulder** je ne lui arrive qu'aux épaules; **we're coming up to the halfway mark** nous atteindrons bientôt la moitié (**b**) (*equal*) égaler; **to c. up to sb's expectations** répondre à l'attente de qn; **to c. up to standard** être au niveau

▶ **come up with** *vipo* (*produce*) (*solution, money*) trouver; (*idea, theory*) proposer; (*suggestion*) faire; **unless someone comes up with a better idea** à moins que quelqu'un ait une meilleure idée

comeback [ˈkʌmbæk] *n* (**a**) (*return*) retour *m* (en vogue); (*of politician*) retour au pouvoir; (*of actor*) retour à la scène/à l'écran, come-back *m inv*; (*of sports person*) retour, come-back; **to make a c.** faire un come-back; **70's fashions are making a c.** la mode des années 70 revient (**b**) *F* (*reply*) réplique *f* (**c**) (*justification for complaint*) **to have no c.** n'avoir aucun recours

Comecon [ˈkɒmɪkɒn] *n* (*abbr* **Council for Mutual Economic Aid**) COMECON *m*

comedian [kəˈmiːdɪən] *n* (*in variety show etc*) (*man*) comique *m*; (*female*) actrice *f* comique; *Fig* (*amusing person*) comédien, -ienne; (*practical joker*) farceur, -euse

comedienne [kəmiːdɪˈen] *n* actrice *f* comique

comedown [ˈkʌmdaʊn] *n F* (*loss of status*) déchéance *f*; **isn't that a bit of a c. for you?** c'est un peu la dégringolade pour toi, non?

comedy [ˈkɒmɪdɪ] *n* (**a**) (*genre*) comédie *f*, genre *m* comique; **c. of manners** comédie de mœurs; **c. actor/actress** acteur/actrice de comédie (**b**) (*play, film*) comédie *f*; *TV* **(situation) c.** comédie de situation, sitcom *m ou f*; *Fig* **it was a c. of errors from start to finish** ce fut une farce grotesque du début à la fin; *Fig* **we weren't taken in by her little c.** sa petite comédie n'a pas pris

come-hither *adj F* (*look*) aguichant

comely [ˈkʌmlɪ] *adj Lit* (*person*) avenant

come-on *n F* incitation *f*; **it was a c. to get buyers interested** c'était pour attirer les clients; **to give sb the c.** (*sexually*) faire du gringue à qn

comer [ˈkʌmər] *n* **open to all comers** ouvert à tous; **I'm ready to take on all comers** je suis prêt à me battre avec n'importe qui

comestible [kəˈmestɪb(ə)l] **1** *adj esp Am* comestible **2** *npl Old-fashioned, Fml* **comestibles** comestibles *mpl*

comet [ˈkɒmɪt] *n Astron* comète *f*

come-to-bed *adj* **c. eyes** regard *m* aguichant *ou* suggestif

comeuppance [kʌmˈʌpəns] *n F* **he got his c.** il n'a eu que ce qu'il mérite

comfort[1] [ˈkʌmfət] *n* (**a**) (*ease*) confort *m*; **to live in c.** être aisé; **the boots are fur-lined for extra c.** les bottes sont fourrées pour plus de confort; **to do sth in the c. of one's own home** faire qch confortablement chez soi; *US* **c. station** toilettes *fpl*

(**b**) **comforts** commodités *fpl*; **tobacco was one of the soldiers' few comforts** le tabac était l'un des seuls plaisirs des soldats

(**c**) (*consolation*) réconfort *m*, consolation *f*; **to give sb c.** réconforter qn; **to take c. from** *or* **in sth** trouver du réconfort *ou* de la consolation dans qch; **that's cold c.** c'est là une piètre consolation; **to get too close for c.** (*of ship, truck*) devenir trop dangereux; **the deadline's getting a bit too close for c.** la date limite est un peu trop proche à mon goût; **it was a great c. to him** ça lui a été d'un grand réconfort, ça l'a beaucoup soulagé; **some c. you are/that is!**

tu parles d'une consolation!; **there was little c. in the news that the strike would continue** la nouvelle selon laquelle la grève allait continuer était peu réconfortante

comfort[2] *vt* (*console*) réconforter, consoler; (*of beverage etc*) réconforter; **they comforted the wounded** ils ont réconforté les blessés; **it comforted him to know she had had a decent burial** ça l'a réconforté de savoir qu'elle avait eu un enterrement décent

comfortable ['kʌmfətəb(ə)l] *adj* **(a)** (*bed, armchair, hotel, garment etc*) confortable; (*warmth, sensation*) agréable, doux, *f* douce; **you will be more c. in this armchair** vous serez mieux dans ce fauteuil; **to make oneself c.** se mettre à son aise; **to be c.** (*of person*) être à l'aise *ou* à son aise; **to feel c.** se sentir bien *ou* à son aise; **I wouldn't feel c. accepting that money** ça me mettrait mal à l'aise d'accepter cet argent; **he couldn't get c. in bed** il ne savait pas comment se mettre dans le lit pour être à l'aise; **she makes people feel c.** elle met les gens à l'aise

(b) (*not in pain*) **to be c.** ne pas souffrir; **he had a c. night** il a passé une bonne nuit

(c) (*substantial*) (*majority, lead, income*) confortable; **to be in c. circumstances** mener une vie aisée; **two hours will give you a c. margin** en deux heures, tu auras largement le temps

comfortably ['kʌmftəblɪ] *adv* **(a)** (*to sit etc*) confortablement; (*warm etc*) agréablement **(b)** (*in financial, material sense*) **to be c. off** être à l'aise; **to live c.** être à l'aise, vivre dans l'aisance **(c)** (*without difficulty*) (*to win*) facilement; **we can get there c. in an hour** une heure suffira amplement pour y aller

comforter ['kʌmfətər] *n* **(a)** (*person*) consolateur, -trice **(b)** *US* (*quilt*) édredon *m* **(c)** *Br Old-fashioned* (*scarf*) cache-nez *m inv* **(d)** (*baby's dummy*) tétine *f*, sucette *f*

comforting ['kʌmfətɪŋ] *adj* réconfortant; **c. words** paroles réconfortantes

comfortless ['kʌmfətlɪs] *adj* (*room etc*) sans confort, peu confortable; (*prospect, thought*) décourageant; **he was left alone and c.** il s'est retrouvé seul et sans réconfort

comfy ['kʌmfɪ] *adj F* = **comfortable (a)**

comic ['kɒmɪk] **1** *adj* (*song etc*) comique; **c. opera** opéra-comique *m*, *pl* opéras-comique; **to provide some c. relief** décrisper l'atmosphère **2** *n* **(a)** (*performer*) (*man*) comique *m*; (*woman*) actrice *f* comique **(b) c. (book)** bande *f* dessinée, BD *f* **(c)** *Am F* (*in newspaper*) **comics** (page *f* des) bandes *fpl* dessinées

comical ['kɒmɪk(ə)l] *adj* comique, drôle; **what a c. idea!** quelle drôle d'idée!

comically ['kɒmɪklɪ] *adv* de façon comique; **they tried, c., to distract her attention** ils essayaient de détourner son attention et c'était comique

comic strip *n* bande *f* dessinée, BD *f*

coming ['kʌmɪŋ] **1** *adj* (*year, week*) qui vient; (*trials, difficulties, elections*) à venir; (*storm*) qui approche; **c. generations** les générations *fpl* futures **2** *n* (*of person*) venue *f*, arrivée *f*; (*of night*) approche *f*; (*of the Messiah*) avènement *m*, venue; *Rel* **the second C.** le second avènement; **comings and goings** allées *fpl* et venues

comma ['kɒmə] *n* virgule *f*; **inverted commas** guillemets *mpl*; **to put a word in inverted commas** mettre un mot entre guillemets; *Comptr* **c.-separated values format** format *m* valeurs séparées par des virgules

command[1] [kə'mɑːnd] *n* **(a)** (*order*) ordre *m*, commandement *m*; **to give a c.** donner un ordre; **to do sth at sb's c.** faire qch sur les ordres de qn; **to be at sb's c.** être aux ordres de qn; **word of c.** commandement; **c. economy** économie *f* planifiée; *Br Th* **c. performance** représentation *f* commandée par le souverain

(b) *Mil* (*authority*) (*of army, expedition*) commandement *m* (**of** de, **over** sur); (*of fort, town etc*) gouvernement *m*; **he was given (the) c. of a division/fleet** on lui a confié le commandement d'une division/d'une flotte; **to be in c. of a battalion** avoir le commandement d'un bataillon, commander un bataillon; **to be in c. of a pass** (*hold it*) commander un défilé; **c. of the seas** maîtrise *f* des mers; *Fig* **c. over oneself** maîtrise de soi; **who is in c.?** qui est-ce qui commande?; **to be first/second in c.** commander en premier/en second; **under (the) c. of ...** sous le commandement de ...; **c. module** (*of spacecraft*) = partie *f* avant d'un vaisseau spatial

(c) *Mil* (*troops*) **to be responsible for one's c.** être responsable de ses troupes; **it was my first c.** c'était la première fois que j'étais au commandement; **they were my first c.** c'est la première section que j'ai commandée; **bomber/fighter c.** aviation *f* de bombardement/de chasse

(d) *Mil* (*area*) **Scottish/Northern c.** région *f* militaire d'Écosse/du Nord; **air/naval c.** région aérienne/maritime

(e) (*knowledge*) (*of language*) connaissance *f*, maîtrise *f*; **to have a c. of several languages** parler plusieurs langues couramment; **she has a good c. of English** *or* **of the English language** elle a une bonne maîtrise de l'anglais

(f) *Comptr* commande *f*; (*from menu options also*) article *m*; **c. button** case *f* de commande; **c. code** code *m* de commande; **c. file** fichier *m* de commande; **c. line** ligne *f* de commande; **c. sequence** séquence *f* de commandes

command[2] **1** *vt* **(a)** (*order*) ordonner, commander (**sth** qch; **sb to do sth** à qn de faire qch); **he did what** *or* **as I commanded him** il a fait ce que je lui ai demandé; **do as I c.!** fais ce que je te demande!; *esp Lit* **we are yours to c.** nous sommes à vos ordres

(b) *Mil* (*be in command of*) (*ship, regiment*) commander

(c) (*have at one's disposal*) avoir à sa disposition; **all the skill he could c.** toute l'habileté qu'il possédait

(d) (*inspire*) (*respect, admiration*) inspirer; (*attention*) forcer; **to c. a high price** se vendre très cher

(e) (*of fort etc*) (*town, entry to pass*) dominer; **window that commands a view over the valley** fenêtre qui donne sur la vallée

2 *vi* commander

commandant [kɒmən'dænt] *n Mil* (*of camp etc*) commandant *m*

commandeer [kɒmən'dɪər] *vt Mil* réquisitionner; *Fig* **the boss commandeered our photocopier** le patron a fait main basse sur notre photocopieuse

commander [kə'mɑːndər] *n Mil* (*of army, company etc*) commandant *m*; (*of section*) chef *m*; *Av* chef de bord; *Naut* capitaine *m* de frégate; **one of the great commanders of history** un des grands chefs de l'histoire

commander-in-chief *n* commandant *m* en chef

commanding [kə'mɑːndɪŋ] *adj* **(a)** *Mil* **c. officer** officier *m* commandant, chef *m* de corps; **who is your c. officer?** qui est votre chef de corps? **(b)** (*tone*) d'autorité, de commandement; (*air*) imposant; (*beauty*) majestueux **(c)** (*position, height*) dominant; (*lead*) considérable

command language *n Comptr* langage *m* de commande

commandment [kə'mɑːndmənt] *n Rel* commandement *m*; **the Ten Commandments** les Dix Commandements; **to keep the commandments** observer les commandements

commando [kə'mɑːndəʊ] *n Mil* commando *m*

command-orientated [kə'mɑːndɔːrɪənteɪtɪd] *adj Comptr* (*program*) orienté commande

commemorate [kə'meməreɪt] *vt* (*person, person's memory*) commémorer

commemoration [kəmemə'reɪʃən] *n* commémoration *f*; **in c. of sb/sth** en commémoration de qn/qch

commemorative [kə'memərətɪv] *adj* commémoratif (**of** de); **c. issue of a stamp** émission *f* d'un timbre commémoratif

commence [kə'mens] *vti US, Br Fml* commencer; **he commenced speaking** il commença à parler

commencement [kə'mensmənt] *n* **(a)** *US, Br Fml* commencement *m*, début *m* **(b)** *US Univ* remise *f* des diplômes; **c. day** jour *m* de la remise des diplômes

commend [kə'mend] *vt* **(a)** (*praise*) (*person*) faire l'éloge de, louer; **to c. sb for bravery** faire l'éloge de la bravoure de qn

(b) (*recommend*) (*sth*) recommander; **a course of action that did not c. itself to me** une façon de faire que je ne pouvais pas approuver; **the train journey has little to c. it** je ne vous recommande pas le voyage en train; **the hotel has little to c. it apart from the cooking** il n'y a pas grand chose de bien à dire sur cet hôtel à part la cuisine

(c) *Lit* (*entrust*) **to c. sth to sb's care** recommander *ou* confier qch aux soins de qn; **to c. one's soul to God** recommander son âme à Dieu

(d) *Arch, Fml* (*remember*) **c. me to Dr Smith** rappelez-moi au bon souvenir du Docteur Smith

commendable [kə'mendəb(ə)l] *adj* louable; (*action*) digne d'éloges; **with c. promptness** avec une rapidité digne d'éloges

commendably [kə'mendəblɪ] *adv* d'une manière louable

commendation [kɒmen'deɪʃən] *n* (*praise*) éloge *m* (**of** de); (*award in competition*) mention *f* spéciale; **worthy of c.** digne d'éloges

commensurable [kə'mensərəb(ə)l, -ʃər-] *adj* **(a)** *Math* commensurable (**with, to** avec) **(b)** = **commensurate (b)**

commensurate [kə'mensərət, -ʃər-] *adj* **(a)** (*of same proportions*) coétendu (**with** à) **(b)** (*proportionate*) proportionnel (**to, with** à); **the salary offered will be c. with experience** le salaire sera proportionnel à l'expérience; **there was no post c. with his abilities** aucun poste ne correspondait à ses compétences; **of c. value** d'une valeur équivalente

comment[1] ['kɒment] *n* observation *f*, commentaire *m*; **to**

make a c. on sth faire des observations sur qch; **no c.** sans commentaire; **to refrain from c.** s'abstenir de faire des commentaires; **c. card** fiche *f* d'observations

comment[2] **1** *vt* **to c. that ...** (faire) remarquer *ou* (faire) observer que ... +*ind* **2** *vi* **(a)** faire un/des commentaire(s); **I'd rather not c.** je préfère m'abstenir de tout commentaire; **to c. on sth** faire des observations *ou* des commentaires sur qch; **nobody commented on it** personne n'a fait de commentaire à ce sujet **(b)** *Liter* **to c. on a text** commenter un texte

commentary ['kɒmənt(ə)rɪ] *n* **(a)** *TV, Rad* commentaire *m*; **with c. by Terry Davis** commenté par Terry Davis; **c. booth** cabine *f* du commentateur **(b)** *Liter* (*on text etc*) commentaire *m*

commentate ['kɒmənteɪt] *vi TV, Rad* faire le commentaire; **to c. on an event** faire le commentaire d'un *ou* commenter un événement

commentator ['kɒmənteɪtər] *n* **(a)** *TV, Rad* commentateur, -trice; **(sports) c.** commentateur sportif, commentatrice sportive **(b)** *Liter* (*on text*) commentateur, -trice

commerce ['kɒmɜːs] *n* **(a)** (*trade*) commerce *m*; **Chamber of C.** Chambre *f* de commerce **(b)** *Fml* (*social relations*) relations *fpl*, rapports *mpl* (**between** entre)

commercial [kə'mɜːʃəl] **1** *adj* **(a)** commercial; (*port, tribunal etc*) de commerce; (*vehicule*) utilitaire; (*value*) marchand; **a course in c. French** un cours de français commercial; **c. radio/television** radio/télévision commerciale **(b)** *also Pej* (*profit-orientated*) (*mind*) mercantile, commercial; (*record, music, channel*) commercial; (*film*) (*mainstream*) grand public *inv*; **his films are terribly c.** ses films sont vraiment commerciaux **2** *n Rad, TV* publicité *f*, pub *f*, spot *m* publicitaire

commercial artist *n* graphiste *mf*

commercial attaché *n* attaché *m* commercial

commercial bank *n* banque *f* de commerce

commercial bill *n* effet *m* de commerce

commercialism [kə'mɜːʃəlɪz(ə)m] *n* esprit *m* commercial; *Pej* (*obsession with profit*) mercantilisme *m*

commercialization [kəmɜːʃəlaɪ'zeɪʃən] *n also Pej* commercialisation *f*

commercialize [kə'mɜːʃəlaɪz] *vt Pej* commercialiser

commercial law *n* droit *m* commercial

commercially [kə'mɜːʃəlɪ] *adv* commercialement

commercial paper *n Fin* billet *m* de trésorerie

commercial traveller *n Old-fashioned* voyageur *m* de commerce

commie ['kɒmɪ] *n, adj F Pej* (*communist*) coco *mf*, communiste *mf*

commis chef *n* commis *m*, commis cuisinier, commis de cuisine

commiserate [kə'mɪzəreɪt] *vi* **to c. with sb** compatir avec qn

commiseration [kəmɪzə'reɪʃən] *n* commisération *f*, compassion *f* (**with** pour); **commiserations are in order, I think** (*for you*) j'avoue que vous n'avez pas de chance

commissariat [kɒmɪ'seərɪət] *n Mil* (*department*) Commissariat *m* de l'armée de terre, *Old-fashioned* intendance *f*

commissary ['kɒmɪsərɪ] *n US Mil* (*store*) dépôt *m* de vivres; (*officer*) officier *m* d'intendance

Commission [kə'mɪʃən] *n EC* Commission *f*

commission[1] [kə'mɪʃən] *n* **(a)** *Com* (*payment*) commission *f*; (*on exchange*) commission de change; **sale on c.** vente *f* à la commission; **three per cent c.** trois pour cent de commission; **c. agent** représentant *m* à la commission, agent *m* commissionnaire; *Horseracing* bookmaker *m*; *Acct* **c. note** note *f* de commission; *Com* **c. only** rémunération *f* à la commission

(b) *Com etc* (*order*) commande *f*, mission *f*; **work done on c.** travail fait sur commande; **to carry out a c.** s'acquitter d'une commande

(c) (*investigating body*) commission *f*; **fact-finding c.** commission d'enquête

(d) *Naut etc* (*of ship*) armement *m*; **to put a ship into c.** armer un navire; **in c.** (*ship*) en commission; (*plane, factory*) en service; **out of c.** (*ship*) désarmé; (*car, machine*) hors service; **you'll be out of c. for six weeks** vous serez obligé de suspendre vos activités pendant six semaines

(e) *Mil* = brevet *m* (d'officier); **to resign one's c.** démissionner, donner sa démission; **to get a** *or* **one's c.** être nommé officier

(f) (*of a crime*) perpétration *f*

commission[2] *vt* **(a)** (*order*) (*person*) commissionner (**to do sth** pour faire qch); (*book, painting*) commander; **to c. an artist to paint a portrait** commander un portrait à un artiste; **to be commissioned to do sth** être chargé de faire qch **(b)** (*appoint*) préposer *ou* déléguer à une fonction; *Mil* (*officer*) nommer à un commandement; *Mil* **to be commissioned** être nommé officier **(c)** *Naut etc* (*ship*) armer; (*plane, factory*) mettre en service

commissionaire [kəmɪʃə'neər] *n* (*at hotel*) chasseur *m*, groom *m*; (*at cinema*) portier *m*

commissioned [kə'mɪʃənd] *adj* **(a)** *Naut* (*ship*) armé **(b)** *Mil* **c. officer** officier *m*

commissioner [kə'mɪʃənər] *n* commissaire *m*; (*member of a commission*) membre *m* d'une/de la commission; (*delegate*) délégué *m* d'une/de la commission; **c. of police** = préfet *m* de police; *Jur* **c. for oaths** = officier *m* habilité à recevoir les déclarations sous serment

commissioning [kə'mɪʃənɪŋ] *n* **(a)** *Mil* (*of officer*) nomination *f* à un commandement **(b)** *Naut etc* (*of ship*) armement *m*; (*of new power plant etc*) mise *f* en service *ou* en exploitation

commissioning editor *n* (*in publishing*) directeur, -trice éditorial(e)

commis waiter ['kɒmɪ] *n* commis *m*

commit [kə'mɪt] *vt* **(-tt-) (a)** (*carry out*) (*crime*) commettre; **to c. suicide** se suicider

(b) (*promise*) **to c. oneself** s'engager; **to c. oneself to sth/doing sth** s'engager à qch/faire qch; **without committing myself** sans m'engager; **to c. sth to sth** (*funds to project etc*) engager qch dans qch; **he had committed 2,000 troops to the defence of the village** il avait assigné 2 000 soldats à la défense du village

(c) (*entrust*) confier, remettre (**sb/sth to sb's care** qn/qch aux soins *ou* à la garde de qn); **to c. sb's body to the earth/the deep** porter un corps en terre/confier un corps aux flots; **to c. one's soul to God** rendre son âme à Dieu; **to c. sth to writing** coucher qch par écrit; **to c. sth to memory** apprendre qch par cœur

(d) (*confine*) **she has been committed** (*to mental institution*) on l'a fait interner; **to c. sb (to prison)** envoyer qn en prison

(e) *Jur* **to c. sb for trial** mettre qn en accusation; (*send to assizes*) renvoyer qn aux assises

(f) *Pol* (*bill*) renvoyer à une commission

commitment [kə'mɪtmənt] *n* **(a)** (*obligation*) engagement *m*; **family commitments** obligations *fpl* familiales; **I cannot do it because of other commitments** d'autres obligations m'empêchent de le faire; **there are no teaching commitments attached to this job** ce poste ne comporte pas d'heures d'enseignement obligatoires; **my teaching commitments this term** les heures d'enseignement que je dois assurer ce trimestre; **without any c. on your part** sans aucun engagement de votre part

(b) (*to a political party, union etc*) engagement *m* (**to** pour); **his commitment to the proposed reform of the tax system** son soutien pour la réforme du système fiscal qui a été proposée; **so many men avoid c. in relationships** il y a tellement d'hommes qui refusent de s'investir dans les relations amoureuses; **I found her lacking in c.** je trouvais qu'elle ne s'investissait pas assez; **to make a c.** s'engager; **c. fee** (*paid to bank*) commission *f* d'engagement

(c) *Jur* emprisonnement *m*

(d) (*act of entrusting*) (*of document to notary etc*) dépôt *m*

committal [kə'mɪt(ə)l] *n* **(a)** *Jur* emprisonnement *m*, mise *f* en prison; (*of insane person*) internement *m* dans un hôpital psychiatrique; **c. for trial** détention *f* préventive; **c. order** ordre *m* d'internement; **c. proceedings** mise *f* en accusation (*afin de décider si une affaire doit être renvoyée devant la Crown Court*) **(b)** (*of corpse*) mise *f* en terre; **the c. of a body to the ground/the deep** la mise en terre/l'immersion *f* d'un mort

committed [kə'mɪtɪd] *adj* engagé (**to** dans); **a c. socialist** un socialiste engagé; **he didn't seem very c.** son engagement ne semblait pas être très ferme; **to be c. to an idea** être attaché à une idée

committee [kə'mɪtɪ] *n* [①**A11**,g,i] comité *m*, commission *f*; *Parl* commission; **to be** *or* **sit on a c.** être membre *ou* faire partie d'un comité *ou* d'une commission; **in c.** en commission; **standing c.** commission permanente; *Br Parl* **C. of Ways and Means** = Commission du budget; **c. meeting** réunion *f* de comité; **c. member** membre *m* du comité *ou* de la commission; *Br Parl* **c. stage** = stade *m* de discussion d'un projet de loi par une commission

committeeman [kə'mɪtɪmən, -mæn] *n esp US* homme *m* membre d'un/de plusieurs comité(s)

committeeperson [kə'mɪtɪpɜːsən] *n esp US* membre *m* d'un/de plusieurs comité(s)

committeewoman [kə'mɪtɪwʊmən] *n esp US* femme *f* membre d'un/de plusieurs comité(s)

commode [kə'məʊd] *n* **(a)** (*with drawers*) commode *f* **(b)** (*toilet*) chaise *f* percée

commodious [kə'məʊdɪəs] *adj* spacieux

commodity [kə'mɒdɪtɪ] *n Econ etc* marchandise *f*, produit *m*;

primary *or* **basic c.** produit de base; *St Exch* **c. dealer** courtier *m* en matières premières; **c. market** marché *m* des matières premières

commodore ['kɒmədɔːr] *n Naut* chef *m* de division; (*of convoy*) chef de convoi; (*in Merchant Navy*) capitaine *m* le plus ancien; (*of yacht club*) président *m*

common¹ ['kɒmən] *adj* **(a)** (*frequent*) ordinaire, courant; **mixed marriages are c. here** les mariages mixtes sont courants ici; **c. name** (*of plant*) nom *m* vulgaire; **in c. use** d'usage courant; **it is c. (practice) to ...** il est courant de ...; **it is c. knowledge** tout le monde le sait; **the agreement is c. knowledge** l'accord est connu de tous; **c. or garden cabbage** chou *m* commun; *Hum* **I'm just a c. or garden journalist** je ne suis qu'un journaliste ordinaire *ou* un journaliste parmi tant d'autres; **you may think this just a c. or garden wristwatch but ...** tu as peut-être l'impression que c'est une montre ordinaire *ou* comme les autres mais ...; **the c. cold** le rhume; **c. decency** les convenances *fpl* (sociales)

(b) (*shared*) commun; **he was, by c. consent ...** il était, de l'avis de tous, ...; **by c. consent, it has been decided to ...** d'un commun accord, on a décidé de ...; **c. interest group** groupe *m* d'intérêt commun; **we have c. interests** nous avons des intérêts communs; **to make c. cause with sb** s'allier à qn; *Fig* **there is no c. ground between them** il n'y a pas de terrain d'entente entre eux; *Jur* **c. land** champs *mpl* communs; *Av* **c. rated fare** tarif *m* commun; *Av* **c. rated points** destinations pour lesquelles les tarifs sont identiques à partir d'un même point de départ; **c. staircase** escalier *m* commun; **c. wall** mur *m* commun *ou* mitoyen

(c) (*average*) **the c. people** les gens *mpl* du peuple *ou* ordinaires; **the c. man** l'homme *m* du peuple; **he lacks the c. touch** il ne sait pas parler aux gens; **c. salt** sel *m* ordinaire; **he's nothing but a c. criminal** ce n'est qu'un vulgaire criminel; **c. prostitute** vulgaire prostituée *f*; **c. thief** vulgaire voleur *m*

(d) *Pej* (*vulgar*) (*person, manners, language, style, joke*) vulgaire; (*accent*) populaire; **he's rather a c. little man** il est plutôt commun

common² *n* **(a) to have sth in c. with sb/sth** avoir qch en commun avec qn/qch; **they have nothing in c.** ils n'ont rien en commun **(b)** (*land*) terrain *m* communal; **the village c.** les terrains communaux, les communaux *mpl* **(c)** *Jur* **(right of) c.** droit *m* de (vaine) pâture

Common Agricultural Policy *n EC* politique *f* agricole commune

common carrier *n* (*of goods*) transporteur *m* public, entreprise *f* de transport public

common denominator *n* dénominateur *m* commun

common divisor *n Math* facteur *m* commun

commoner ['kɒmənər] *n* **(a)** (*not noble*) roturier, -ière **(b)** *Jur* usager, -ère du droit de vaine pâture **(c)** *Univ* (*at Oxford*) étudiant, -ante ordinaire (*qui ne reçoit pas de bourse*)

common factor *n Math* facteur *m* commun

common law *n* droit *m* coutumier

common-law *adj Jur* **c. husband/wife** concubin *m*/concubine *f*; **c. marriage** concubinage *m*, union *f* libre; **the children of c. marriages** les enfants issus d'unions libres

commonly ['kɒmənlɪ] *adv* **(a)** (*frequently*) communément, ordinairement; **what is c. known as ...** ce qu'en langage courant on appelle ... **(b)** *Pej* (*vulgarly*) vulgairement, de façon vulgaire

Common Market *n* Marché *m* commun

commonness ['kɒmənnɪs] *n* **(a)** (*frequency*) fréquence *f* **(b)** *Pej* (*vulgarity*) vulgarité *f*

common noun [①A8,3,A,2] *n Gram* nom *m* commun

common ownership *n* copropriété *f*

commonplace ['kɒmənpleɪs] **1** *n* (*platitude*) lieu *m* commun, banalité *f*, platitude *f*; **it is a c. that ...** c'est un lieu commun de dire que ...; *Old-fashioned* **c. book** recueil *m* de pensées **2** *adj* banal, -als; **such operations are becoming c.** de telles opérations deviennent de plus en plus banales

common room *n Sch* (*for pupils*) salle *f* commune; (*for teachers*) salle des professeurs; *Br Univ* **junior c.** = salle de repos à l'usage des étudiants; **senior c.** = salle de repos à l'usage des professeurs

commons ['kɒmənz] *npl* **(a)** (*people*) **the c.** le peuple; **the (House of) C.** la Chambre des Communes **(b)** *Old-fashioned* (*food*) **to be on short c.** faire maigre chère

common sense *n* bon sens *m*, sens commun; **she has a great deal of c.** elle a beaucoup de bon sens; **it's only c. to ...** ça tombe sous le sens de ...; **a c. approach/solution** une approche/solution dictée par le bon sens

common stock *n Am St Exch* actions *fpl* ordinaires

common time *n Mus* mesure *f* à quatre temps

commonweal ['kɒmənwiːl] *n Lit* bien *m* commun

commonwealth ['kɒmənwelθ] *n* **(a) the British C. (of Nations)** le Commonwealth; **C. country** pays *m* du Commonwealth **(b)** (*state*) **the C.** (*in British history*) le Commonwealth; **the C. of Australia** le Commonwealth d'Australie; **the C. of Massachusetts/Pennsylvania** l'état *m* du Massachusetts/de Pennsylvanie

commotion [kə'məʊʃən] *n* (*noise*) agitation *f*, commotion *f*; **in a state of c.** en émoi; **to create a c.** faire du bruit; **what's all the c. about?** pourquoi toute cette agitation?

comms package [kɒmz] *n Comptr* logiciel *m* de communication

comms port *n Comptr* port *m* de communication

communal ['kɒmjʊn(ə)l] *adj* (*shared*) (*bathroom, garden etc*) commun; **c. life** la vie commune *ou* communautaire; *Jur* **c. estate** communauté *f* (conjugale); **c. property** biens *mpl* en commun *ou* en copropriété; **c. violence** violence *f* entre communautés

communally [kə'mjuːnəlɪ] *adv* en commun; **c. owned** en copropriété

commune¹ ['kɒmjuːn] *n* **(a)** (*of hippies etc*) communauté *f*; *Hist* **the Paris C.** la Commune (de Paris) **(b)** *Admin* (*in France, Belgium, Italy etc*) commune *f*

commune² [kə'mjuːn] *vi* **(a)** *Lit* communiquer (**with sb** avec qn); **to c. with nature** être en communion avec la nature **(b)** *US Rel* communier

communicable [kə'mjuːnɪkəb(ə)l] *adj* (*disease*) transmissible; (*idea*) communicable

communicant [kə'mjuːnɪkənt] *n Rel* communiant, -ante

communicate [kə'mjuːnɪkeɪt] **1** *vi* **(a)** communiquer; **to c. with sb** communiquer avec qn; **to c. by letter** communiquer par lettre; **he finds it difficult to c.** il a du mal à communiquer; **we can't seem to c.** on ne se comprend pas; **we've stopped communicating** on a cessé de communiquer, on ne se parle plus; **to c. well/badly** avoir de grandes qualités relationnelles/manquer de qualités relationnelles

(b) (*connect*) (*of rooms*) communiquer; **rooms that c. with one another** chambres qui communiquent

(c) *Rel* communier, recevoir la communion

2 *vt* (*news etc*) communiquer, faire parvenir; (*illness*) passer; (*emotion, heat etc*) communiquer

communicating [kə'mjuːnɪkeɪtɪŋ] *adj* (*room*) communicant; **c. door** = porte *f* de communication entre deux pièces

communication [kəmjuːnɪ'keɪʃən] *n* **(a)** (*contact*) **to be in c. with ...** être en relation avec ...; **to be in close c. with one another** être en relation constante; **we haven't had any c. for six months** nous ne sommes plus en relation(s) depuis six mois; **to break off all c. with sb** rompre toutes relations avec qn; **communications between the two have broken down** ils ne sont plus en relation; **line of c.** lien *m*; *Mil* ligne *f* de communication

(b) (*message etc*) communication *f*; **no official c. of his death has yet been received** on n'a encore reçu aucune communication officielle de sa mort

(c) (*of information, feeling etc*) communication *f* (**to sb** à qn); **c. gap** manque *m* de communication; **c. problem** problème *m* de communication; **c. skills** (*of person*) qualités *fpl* relationnelles; **means of c.** moyens *mpl* de communication

(d) *Mil* **communications** (*system*) transmissions *fpl*, liaison(s) *f(pl)*; **radio c.** liaison (par) radio; **c. trench** boyau *m*

communication cord *n Br Rail* corde *f* de signal d'alarme

communications conglomerate *n* groupe *m* multimédia

communications director *n* directeur *m* de la communication, dircom *m*

communications-intensive *adj* utilisant intensivement les moyens de communication

communications link *n* liaison *f* de communications

communications manager *n* directeur *m* de la communication, dircom *m*

communications satellite *n* satellite *m* de communications

communications sector *n* secteur *m* des communications

communications software *n Comptr* logiciel *m* de communication

communicative [kə'mjuːnɪkətɪv] *adj* communicatif; (*skills*) en matière de communication; **she's not very c.** elle n'est pas très communicative

communion [kə'mjuːnjən] *n* **(a)** *Rel* **(Holy) C.** sainte communion *f*; **to administer Holy C. to sb** administrer la sainte communion à qn; **to take (Holy) C.** communier; **the c. of saints** la communion des saints; **c. wine** (*in Protestant church*) vin *m* de communion; *Cathol* vin de messe; **c. cup** calice *m* **(b)** *Lit* communication *f* (**with sb** avec qn)

communiqué [kə'mjuːnɪkeɪ] *n* communiqué *m*

communism ['kɒmjʊnɪz(ə)m] *n* communisme *m*

communist [ˈkɒmjʊnɪst] *adj, n* communiste *mf*
Community [kəˈmjuːnɪtɪ] *adj EC* communautaire; **C. law** droit *m* communautaire
community [kəˈmjuːnɪtɪ] *n* **(a)** (*group*) communauté *f*; **c. policing** surveillance *f* d'une ville par îlots; **c. radio** radio *f* communautaire; **c. singing** = chansons *fpl* populaires reprises en chœur par l'assistance; **c. spirit** esprit *m* de communauté
(b) (*village etc*) communauté *f*; **a small mining c.** une petite communauté minière; **a c. of 2,000** une communauté de 2 000 habitants
(c) *Rel* communauté *f* (religieuse)
(d) (*public*) **the c.** le public; **harmful to the c.** nuisible à la communauté
(e) (*something shared*) (*of possessions, interests etc*) communauté *f*; (*of tastes*) communauté, identité *f*; **there's no c. of values between them** il n'y a pas de communauté de valeurs entre eux
community care *n Br Admin* = soins *mpl* au niveau local
community centre *n* centre *m* social
Community charge *n Br formerly* = impôt *m* local
community chest *n US* fonds *m* de secours
community service *n* travail *m* d'intérêt général, TIG *m*
commutable [kəˈmjuːtəb(ə)l] *adj* **(a)** *Jur* (*sentence*) commuable **(b)** (*interchangeable*) permutable, interchangeable
commutation [kɒmjʊˈteɪʃən] *n* commutation *f*; *Jur* **c. of sentence** commutation de peine; *US Rail* **c. ticket** carte *f* d'abonnement
commutator [ˈkɒmjʊteɪtər] *n El* commutateur *m*
commute¹ [kəˈmjuːt] *n Am* trajet *m* (*entre travail et domicile*); **it's an easy c.** c'est un trajet commode
commute² **1** *vi* faire la navette entre sa résidence et son travail; **I c. here every day** je fais le trajet tous les jours; **to c. by train/car** se rendre à son travail en train/voiture **2** *vt* **(a)** (*exchange*) échanger (**for, into** pour, contre); **to c. an annuity into** *or* **for a lump sum** racheter une rente par un versement global **(b)** *Jur* **to c. a penalty into** *or* **for another** commuer une peine en une autre **(c)** (*interchange*) interchanger **(d)** *Metal* transformer
commuter [kəˈmjuːtər] *n* (*from suburbs*) banlieusard, -arde (*qui fait la navette entre sa résidence et son travail*), *Belg* navetteur, -euse; **I've been a c. for fifteen years** ça fait quinze ans que je fais la navette (entre chez moi et le travail); **the problems caused by c. traffic** les problèmes provoqués par l'utilisation de la voiture pour se rendre au travail; **c. traffic is very heavy this evening** la circulation en direction de la banlieue est très dense ce soir; **c. airline** compagnie *f* d'aviation court-courrier; **c. belt** (grande) banlieue *f*; *Rail* **c. line** ligne *f* de banlieue; **c. plane** commuter *m*; **c. train** train *m* de banlieue
commuterland [kəˈmjuːtəlænd] *n* = grande banlieue *f* considérée comme un pays à part, où l'on ne fait rien d'autre que dormir
commuting [kəˈmjuːtɪŋ] *n* **tired with c.** las de faire le trajet entre son domicile et son travail
comp [kɒmp] *n* **(a)** *Typ* (*compositor*) metteur *m* (en pages) **(b)** (*ticket*) exonéré *m*
compact¹ [kɒmˈpækt, ˈkɒmpækt] *adj* **(a)** (*dense, closely packed*) (*snow, ground etc*) compact; (*style*) concis **(b)** (*small*) (*apartment, kitchen etc*) petit mais fonctionnel; (*telephone, computer, camera etc*) compact; *Am* (*car*) petit et économique; (*person*) trapu; **to have a c. build** être trapu
compact² [ˈkɒmpækt] *n* **(a)** (*for powder*) (*in handbag*) poudrier *m* **(b)** *Am Aut* voiture *f* petite et économique
compact³ [kəmˈpækt] *vt* rendre compact; (*snow*) tasser; *Constr* compacter
compact⁴ [ˈkɒmpækt] *n Fml* (*agreement*) convention *f*, accord *m*
compact disc *n* disque *m* compact; **c. player** lecteur *m* de disques compacts; **c. video** vidéodisque *m*
compacting [kəmˈpæktɪŋ] *n Comptr* compression *f*
compactly [kəmˈpæktlɪ] *adv* d'une manière compacte
compactness [kəmˈpæktnɪs] *n* **(a)** (*of earth, snow, muscles*) dureté *f*; (*of style*) concision *f* **(b)** (*smallness*) (*of computer, design, camera etc*) compacité *f*; **the c. of the kitchen** la cuisine petite mais fonctionnelle
Companies Act [ˈkʌmpənɪz] *n Jur* Loi *f* sur les sociétés
Companies House *n Br Com* institut *m* où sont enregistrées toutes les informations concernant les entreprises du pays
companion¹ [kəmˈpænjən] *n* **(a)** (*male*) compagnon *m*; (*female*) compagne *f*; (**lady**) **c.** dame *f* de compagnie; **c. in arms** compagnon d'armes; **a drinking/travelling c.** un compagnon de boisson/voyage; **c. fare** (*for additional person*) tarif *m* par personne supplémentaire; **C. to English Literature** (*title of book*) guide *m* de la littérature anglaise **(b)** (*other of a pair*) (*of book etc*) pendant *m* (**of** à)
companion² *n Naut* **c.** (**hatch**) capot *m* (*de descente*); **c. ladder** échelle *f* de commandement
companionable [kəmˈpænjənəb(ə)l] *adj* sociable
companionship [kəmˈpænjənʃɪp] *n* compagnie *f*; (*comradeship*) camaraderie *f*; **the dog provides c. for her** le chien lui fait de la compagnie *ou* lui tient compagnie
companionway [kəmˈpænjənweɪ] *n Naut* escalier *m* des cabines
company [ˈkʌmpənɪ] *n* **(a)** (*companionship*) compagnie *f*; **in sb's c.** en compagnie de qn; **I like his c.** j'aime sa compagnie, j'aime être avec lui; **to keep sb c.** tenir compagnie à qn; **he's very good c.** c'est un compagnon agréable, il est de bonne compagnie; **it's nice to have c.** c'est agréable d'avoir de la compagnie; **she needs the c. of children of her own age** elle a besoin d'être avec des enfants de son âge; **to be fond of one's own c.** aimer être seul; *Prov* **two's c., three's a crowd** = vous seriez/nous serions/*etc* mieux tous les deux; **to part c. with sb** (*split up*) se séparer de qn; (*disagree*) ne plus être d'accord avec qn
(b) (*acquaintances*) compagnie *f*, société *f*; **I don't like the c. he keeps** je n'aime pas ses fréquentations; **to get into bad c.** faire de mauvaises fréquentations
(c) (*people present*) assemblée *f*, personnes *fpl* présentes; **to do sth in c.** faire qch en public; **present c. excepted** à part les personnes ici présentes; **the most intelligent of the c. were in agreement** les plus intelligentes des personnes présentes étaient d'accord
(d) (*guests*) invités *mpl*; **are you expecting c.?** vous attendez de la visite?; *F* **we've got c.!** (*there's someone else here, we're being followed*) nous avons de la compagnie
(e) [①**A11**,g,i] *Com, Ind* entreprise *f*, société *f*; **insurance c.** compagnie *f* d'assurances; (**the firm of**) **Thomas and C.** (la maison) Thomas et Cie; **c. car** (*for working*) voiture *f* de fonction; (*for senior executives*) voiture de société; **c. savings scheme** plan *m* d'épargne d'entreprise, PEE *m*; **on** *or* **in c. time** (*to make telephone call etc*) pendant les heures de travail
(f) *Th* compagnie *f*
(g) *Naut* **the ship's c.** l'équipage *m* (*au complet, y compris les officiers*)
(h) *Mil* compagnie *f*; **c. officer** officier *m* de compagnie
(i) (*of girl guides*) compagnie *f*
(j) (*guild*) corporation *f* de marchands
company director *n* chef *m* d'entreprise
company law *n* droit *m* des sociétés
company lawyer *n* avocat, -ate d'une entreprise *ou* société
company policy *n* politique *f* de la maison *ou* de la société; **it isn't c.** ce n'est pas la politique de la maison *ou* de la société
company secretary *n* secrétaire *m* général
comparability [kɒmpərəˈbɪlɪtɪ] *n* comparabilité *f*
comparable [ˈkɒmpərəb(ə)l] *adj* comparable (**with** avec, **to** à)
comparative [kəmˈpærətɪv] **1** *adj* **(a)** (*comparing*) comparatif; *Gram* **c. adverb** adverbe *m* de comparaison *ou* comparatif; *Mktg* **c. advertising** publicité *f* comparative; *Gram* **the c. degree** le comparatif; **c. grammar/philology** grammaire *f*/philologie *f* comparée; **c. methodology** méthodologie *f* comparative; **c. rating scale** échelle *f* d'évaluation comparative; **a c. study** une étude comparative; *Mktg* **c. test** test *m* comparatif **(b)** (*relative*) (*cost, comfort, wealth etc*) relatif; **he's a c. stranger to me** je ne le connais pratiquement pas **2** *n* [①**A18-19**,4; **A22**,c; **B10-11**,E; **B12-13**,F] *Gram* comparatif *m*; **in the c.** au comparatif
comparatively [kəmˈpærɪtɪvlɪ] *adv* **(a)** (*in comparison*) comparativement, par comparaison **(b)** (*relatively*) (*easy, expensive etc*) relativement
compare¹ [kəmˈpeər] *n Lit* **beyond c.** sans comparaison; **beauty without c.** beauté sans pareille
compare² **1** *vt* (*facts, ideas*) comparer; **to c. sth to sth** (*liken*) comparer qch à qch; (*contrast*) comparer qch avec qch; **to c. sth with sth** (*contrast*) comparer qch avec qch; **compared with** *or* **to …** en comparaison de …, à côté de …, par rapport à …; **compared with last year's figures** par rapport aux chiffres de l'année dernière; **to c. notes** (*exchange impressions*) échanger ses impressions
2 *vi* être comparable (**with** à); **he can't c. with you** on ne peut pas le comparer à vous; **nothing compares to you** tu es unique; **other kinds of washing powder just can't c.** les autres marques de lessive ne sont pas à la hauteur de celle-ci; **to c. favourably with sth** ne le céder en rien à qch; **the French car compares well with the Italian one** la voiture française supporte la comparaison avec l'italienne
comparison [kəmˈpærɪs(ə)n] *n* comparaison *f*; **to make** *or* **draw a c. between sth and sth** faire la comparaison de qch avec qch; **in** *or* **by c.** en comparaison; **in c. with …** comparé

à ...; **without c., beyond all c.** sans comparaison; **there is no c.** il n'y a pas de comparaison; **to stand** *or* **bear c.** supporter la comparaison; **that's a rather unfair c.** ce n'est pas très juste de me/le/*etc* comparer à lui/elle/*etc*; *Gram* **degrees of c.** degrés *mpl* de comparaison; *Mktg* **c. advertising** publicité *f* comparative; *Mktg* **c. shopping** achats *mpl* comparatifs

compartment [kəm'pɑːtmənt] *n* **(a)** *Rail* compartiment *m*; **sleeping c.** compartiment lit (*dans un wagon-lit*) **(b)** (*of a drawer etc*) case *f*, compartiment *m*

compartmentalize [kɒmpɑːt'ment(ə)laɪz] *vt* compartimenter

compass ['kʌmpəs] *n* **(a)** (*in surveying*), *Naut etc* (*with moving needle*) boussole *f*; (*with moving card*) compas *m*; **c. bearing** position *f* au compas; *Naut* **to take a c. bearing** prendre un relèvement au compas; **c. card** rose *f* des vents; *Naut* **c. dial** rose des vents; **c. error** erreur *f ou* déviation *f* du compas

(b) *Geom* **(pair of) compasses** compas *m*

(c) *Fml* (*scope*) (*of knowledge, powers*) étendue *f*; (*of inquiry, reforms*) cadre *m*; (*of time*) espace *m*; (*of mind*) portée *f*; *Mus* (*of voice*) étendue, diapason *m*, registre *m*; **to be beyond the c. of the human mind** dépasser les limites de l'entendement humain

compassion [kəm'pæʃən] *n* compassion *f*, pitié *f*; **to arouse c.** faire pitié, exciter la compassion; **to show c.** montrer de la compassion; **you have no c.** tu n'as pas de pitié

compassionate [kəm'pæʃənət] *adj* compatissant **(to** à; **towards** pour); **on c. grounds** pour raisons familiales; **c. leave** congé *m* exceptionnel (*en cas de décès d'un proche etc*)

compassionately [kəm'pæʃənətlɪ] *adv* avec compassion

compatibility [kəmpætə'bɪlɪtɪ] *n* (*of people*), *Comptr* compatibilité *f*

compatible [kəm'pætəb(ə)l] *adj* (*person*), *Comptr* compatible **(with** avec); **IBM-c.** compatible IBM

compatibly [kəm'pætəblɪ] *adv* d'une manière compatible **(with** avec)

compatriot [kəm'pætrɪət, -'peɪ-] *n* compatriote *mf*

compel [kəm'pel] *vt* **(-ll-)** contraindre, forcer, obliger **(to do sth** à faire qch); **to be compelled to do sth** être contraint *ou* obligé de faire qch; **don't feel compelled to do it** ne vous sentez pas obligé de le faire; **to c. sb's admiration/respect** forcer l'admiration/le respect de qn

compelling [kəm'pelɪŋ] *adj* (*force, curiosity, urge, desire etc*) irrésistible; (*film, performance*) captivant; **her book makes c. reading** son livre est captivant *ou* prenant; **a c. speaker** un orateur qui subjugue *ou* captive son auditoire

compellingly [kəm'pelɪŋlɪ] *adv* irrésistiblement

compendium, *pl* **-ums** [kəm'pendɪəm, -z] *n* (*summary*) abrégé *m*, précis *m*, compendium *m*; **c. of laws** recueil *m* des lois; *Br* **c. of games** malle *f* de jeux

compensable [kəm'pensəb(ə)l] *adj* indemnisable; *Acct* **c. loss** perte *f* indemnisable

compensate ['kɒmpənseɪt] **1** *vt* **(a)** (*make amends for/to*) dédommager, indemniser **(for** de) **(b)** *Tech* (*pendulum etc*) compenser; **to c. one another** (*of factors etc*) se compenser **2** *vi* **(a) to c. for sth** compenser qch; **experience may c. for lack of qualifications** l'expérience peut compenser le manque de qualifications **(b)** *Psy* compenser

compensated ['kɒmpənseɪtɪd] *adj El etc* compensé

compensating ['kɒmpənseɪtɪŋ] *adj* compensateur; **c. errors** erreurs *fpl* qui se compensent

compensation [kɒmpən'seɪʃən] *n* compensation *f*; (*for loss, injury, damage*) dédommagement *m*, indemnisation *f*; **all of the victims will receive c.** toutes les victimes recevront une indemnité; **in c.** à titre compensatoire *ou* de compensation *ou* de dédommagement; **c. for loss of custom** indemnité *f* de clientèle; **c. for wrongful dismissal** indemnité de rupture abusive; **c. in lieu of notice** indemnité compensatrice de préavis; *Com* **c. plan** mode *m* de rémunération

compensator arm ['kɒmpenseɪtər] *n MecE* bras *m* compensateur

compensator valve *n MecE* valve *f* de compensation

compensatory [kɒmpən'seɪt(ə)rɪ] *adj* compensatoire

compère[1] ['kɒmpeər] *n Th, TV etc* animateur *m*, présentateur, -trice

compère[2] *vt Th, TV etc* (*programme*) présenter, animer

compete [kəm'piːt] *vi* rivaliser **(with sb** avec qn, **for sth** pour qch); *Com* (*of one company*) faire de la concurrence **(with** à); (*of two companies*) se faire concurrence; **we can't c.** (*are not competitive*) nous ne sommes pas concurrentiels; **children here aren't encouraged to c.** ici, les enfants ne sont pas encouragés à la compétition; **the player had competed for every point** le joueur s'était battu sur chaque point; **to c. with one another** se faire concurrence; *Sp* **to c. against sb** concourir avec qn; **France is competing against several countries for the contract** la France est en compétition avec plusieurs autres pays pour décrocher ce contrat; **to c. for a prize** concourir pour un prix; **to c. with sb for a prize** disputer un prix à qn; **her cooking can't c. with yours** sa cuisine ne peut pas rivaliser avec la tienne

competence ['kɒmpɪtəns] *n* **(a)** (*ability*) compétences *fpl*, capacités *fpl* **(in** *or* **for sth** en qch, **in doing** pour faire) **(b)** *Fml* (*scope of functions*) (*of civil servant*) attributions *fpl*; *Jur* compétence *f*; **to be within/beyond the c. of a court** être/ne pas être de la compétence *ou* du ressort d'un tribunal

competency ['kɒmpɪtənsɪ] *n* = **competence**

competent ['kɒmpɪtənt] *adj* **(a)** (*able*) (*doctor, worker etc*) compétent, capable; **a c. piece of work** du bon travail; **c. to do sth** capable de faire qch; (*qualified*) apte à faire qch, qualifié pour faire qch; **he's quite c. at French** il a un bon niveau de français; **c. knowledge of English** bonne connaissance *f* de l'anglais **(b)** *Jur* (*tribunal*) compétent; **c. to inherit** habilité à succéder

competently ['kɒmpɪtəntlɪ] *adv* avec compétence

competition [kɒmpɪ'tɪʃən] *n* **(a)** (*rivalry*) rivalité *f*, concurrence *f*; **to be in c.** être en compétition; **to enter into c. with sb** concurrencer *ou* faire concurrence à qn; **there was a lot of c. for the job** il y avait beaucoup de concurrence pour cette place

(b) (*contest*) concours *m*; *Sp* compétition *f* (sportive); **a poetry c.** un concours de poésie; **to win a prize in open c.** remporter un prix dans un concours ouvert à tous; **to take part in competitions** faire de la compétition; **that's him out of the c.** le voilà hors compétition; **c. car** voiture *f* de compétition

(c) *Com, Econ* concurrence *f*; **free c.** libre concurrence

(d) the c. (*rivals*) *Com* la concurrence; *Sp* les concurrents *ou* adversaires; (*for a job*) les autres candidats; **you're up against some tough c.** (*in race*) vous êtes en face d'adversaires de taille; (*for job, university*) la concurrence est rude; **the company has to stay ahead of the c.** l'entreprise doit rester plus compétitive que les autres

competitive [kəm'petɪtɪv] *adj* **(a)** (*person*) qui a l'esprit de compétition, qui aime la compétition; (*atmosphere, environment*) de compétition; **a c. school/society** une école/ société où l'on met l'accent sur la compétition; **he's so c.** il a un esprit de compétition tellement développé; **c. spirit** esprit *m* de compétition; **c. examination** concours *m*; **c. sports** sports *mpl* de compétition

(b) *Com, Econ* (*price*) concurrentiel, compétitif; (*product*) concurrent; (*firm, company, industry*) compétitif; **to offer c. terms** proposer des prix très compétitifs; **in a c. marketplace** dans un marché de concurrence; **industry must get more c.** l'industrie doit devenir plus compétitive; **c. awareness** sensibilité *f* compétitive; **c. discounting** remise *f* compétitive; **c. edge** avance *f* sur la concurrence; **c. position** position *f* concurrentielle; *Mktg* **c. positioning** positionnement *m* concurrentiel; *Mktg* **c. scope** domaine *m ou* champ *m* concurrentiel; **c. strategy** stratégie *f* concurrentielle

competitively [kəm'petɪtɪvlɪ] *adv* **(a)** dans un esprit de compétition **(b)** *Com, Econ* **c. priced** à un prix concurrentiel *ou* compétitif

competitiveness [kəm'petɪtɪvnɪs] *n* **(a)** compétitivité *f* **(b)** *Com, Econ* (*of product*) concurrence *f*; (*of firm, company*) compétitivité *f*

competitor [kəm'petɪtər] *n Sp, Com* concurrent, -ente

compilation [kɒmpɪ'leɪʃən] *n* **(a)** (*activity*) compilation *f* **(b)** (*list*) compilation *f*; **c. album** (*record*) (album *m* de) compilation

compile [kəm'paɪl] *vt* compiler

compiler [kəm'paɪlər] *n* (*of dictionary etc*) compilateur, -trice, rédacteur, -trice; *Comptr* compilateur

complacency [kəm'pleɪsənsɪ] *n* contentement *m* de soi; **there is no room for c.** il n'y a pas de quoi faire de l'auto-satisfaction; **this is no time for c.** ce n'est pas le moment de faire de l'auto-satisfaction

complacent [kəm'pleɪsənt] *adj* (*person*) content de soi; (*look, remark*) très satisfait; **to be c. about sth** faire de l'auto-satisfaction à propos de qch; **we shouldn't become c. about unemployment just because of a few successes** nous ne devrions pas accepter le chômage sous prétexte que nous avons marqué quelques points

complacently [kəm'pleɪsəntlɪ] *adv* (*to smile, reply*) d'un air suffisant; **some of our managers have been sitting c. behind their desks** certains de nos dirigeants se sont un peu trop reposés sur leurs lauriers

complain [kəm'pleɪn] *vi* **(a)** se plaindre **(about** de, **to** à); (*officially*) se plaindre **(to** auprès de); **he's always complaining** il se plaint toujours; **to c. that ...** se plaindre que *ou* de ce que ... + *ind*; **don't come complaining to me about it** tu ne viendras pas te plaindre à moi; **I can't c.** je n'ai pas à me plaindre **(b)** (*of sore throat, headaches etc*) se plaindre (**of** de)

complainant [kəm'pleɪnənt] *n Jur* plaignant, -ante

complaint [kəm'pleɪnt] *n* **(a)** (*grievance*) plainte *f*; **I have no cause** *or* **grounds for c.** je n'ai aucun motif de plainte; **do you have any complaints about the company?** est-ce que vous avez à vous plaindre de l'entreprise?; **her latest c. was that ...** la dernière chose dont elle s'est plainte a été que ...; **I've got no c. against you** je n'ai rien à te reprocher **(b)** (*official*) plainte *f*, réclamation *f*; **to lodge** *or* **make a c. against sb** porter plainte contre qn **(c)** (*illness*) maladie *f*; **liver c.** maladie *ou* affection *f* du foie

complaints book *n* cahier *m* de réclamations

complaints office *n* bureau *m* *ou* service *m* des réclamations

complaisance [kəm'pleɪzəns] *n Fml* complaisance *f*

complaisant [kəm'pleɪz(ə)nt] *adj Fml* complaisant

complement¹ ['kɒmplɪmənt] *n* **(a)** (*of bus etc*) (*passengers*) charge *f* complète; *Naut* (*crew etc*) effectif *m*; *Naut* **full c.** effectif complet; **have we got a full c.?** (*in office, team etc*) est-ce que nous sommes au complet? **(b)** *Math* (*of verb, angle etc*) complément *m*; *Gram* complément; (*following 'to be', 'to seem' etc*) attribut *m*

complement² *vt* compléter; (*of wine, sauce etc*) mettre en valeur; **they c. each other well** (*of two people*) ils se complètent parfaitement

complementary [kɒmplɪ'ment(ə)rɪ] *adj* (*angle, colour*) complémentaire; *Comptr* **c. MOS** MOS *m* complémentaire

complete¹ [kəm'pliːt] *adj* **(a)** complet, *f* complète, entier; (*surprise, failure*) total; **I need a c. break from teaching** j'ai besoin de vraies vacances où je ne penserai plus du tout à mes cours; **is the pack c.?** (*of cards*) le jeu est-il complet?; *Com* **c. with battery** livré avec pile; **my happiness is c.** mon bonheur est total, rien ne manque à mon bonheur; **a visit to Brussels would not be c. without a meal here** la visite de Bruxelles ne serait pas complète sans un repas ici; **to give a c. account** donner tous les détails; **a c. (and utter) failure** un échec total; **the operation has been a c. success** l'opération a pleinement réussi; **she is a c. fool** elle est complètement idiote; **he's a c. stranger** c'est un total inconnu

(b) (*finished*) terminé, achevé

complete² *vt* **(a)** (*finish*) (*job, task*) achever, terminer; (*training, apprenticeship*) accomplir **(b)** (*find missing parts of*) (*collection, number, tea service*) compléter **(c)** (*fill in*) (*form, questionnaire*) remplir

completely [kəm'pliːtlɪ] *adv* complètement, totalement; **I c. understand your frustration** je comprends tout à fait ta frustration

completeness [kəm'pliːtnɪs] *n* sentiment *m* d'accomplissement; **there's a c. to it** (*to novel, film etc*) il a un caractère abouti; **they added a final volume for c.** ils ont ajouté un dernier volume pour que l'ensemble soit complet

completion [kəm'pliːʃən] *n* (*of work*) achèvement *m*; **in the process of c.** en (cours d')achèvement; **near c.** près d'être achevé; **to reach c.** (*of project etc*) s'achever; **occupation on c. (of contract)** (*of property*) prise *f* de possession des lieux à la signature du contrat; **c. date** (*for building, repair work*) date *f* d'achèvement; **c. guarantee** caution *f* de bonne fin

complex ['kɒmpleks] **1** *adj* (*question, phrase*) complexe; *Math* **c. number** nombre *m* complexe **2** *n* **(a)** (*building(s)*) complexe *m*; **industrial c.** complexe industriel; **shopping c.** centre *m* commercial **(b)** *Psy* complexe *m*; *F* **he has a c. about his teeth** il fait un complexe à cause de *ou* pour ses dents; *F* **you'll give her a c.** tu vas lui donner un complexe

complexion [kəm'plekʃən] *n* **(a)** teint *m*; **to have a dark/fair c.** avoir le teint mat/clair; **to have a good** *or* **clear c.** avoir une belle peau **(b)** *Fig* nature *f*, caractère *m*; **that puts a new** *or* **a different c. on it** voilà qui change la situation

complexity [kəm'pleksɪtɪ] *n* complexité *f*

compliance [kəm'plaɪəns] *n* acquiescement *m* (**with** à); **in c. with your wishes** conformément à vos désirs; *Com* **c. test** test *m* de conformité

compliant [kəm'plaɪənt] *adj* **(a)** complaisant, accommodant **(b)** *Pej* (*submissive*) servile

complicate ['kɒmplɪkeɪt] *vt* compliquer (**with** de); **that complicates matters** cela complique les choses

complicated ['kɒmplɪkeɪtɪd] *adj* compliqué; **to become c.** (*of situation etc*) se compliquer

complication [kɒmplɪ'keɪʃən] *n* complication *f*; *Med* **if no complications set in** s'il ne survient pas de complications; **you're always creating complications!** tu compliques toujours les choses!

complicity [kəm'plɪsɪtɪ] *n* complicité *f* (**in** à)

compliment¹ ['kɒmplɪmənt] *n* **(a)** compliment *m*; **to pay a c. to sb, to pay sb a c.** faire *ou* adresser un compliment à qn; **to return the c.** retourner le compliment; **my compliments to the chef** mes compliments au chef; **with the compliments of the chef** avec les compliments du chef; **compliments of the season** meilleurs vœux de fin d'année; **with compliments** avec nos compliments

(b) *Old-fashioned* (*greetings*) **to pay one's compliments to sb** faire une visite (de politesse) à qn; **to present** *or* **send one's compliments to sb** se rappeler au bon souvenir de qn

compliment² *vt* complimenter, féliciter, faire des compliments à; **to c. sb on sth/on doing sth** féliciter qn de qch/d'avoir fait qch; **she complimented him on his English/haircut** elle l'a félicité *ou* elle lui a fait des compliments pour son anglais/sa coupe de cheveux

complimentary [kɒmplɪ'ment(ə)rɪ] *adj* **(a)** flatteur (**about** à l'égard de); **they weren't very c. about my paintings** ils ne se sont pas montrés très flatteurs à l'égard de mes tableaux; **c. remarks** compliments *mpl*, félicitations *fpl* **(b)** (*free*) gratuit, gracieux; **c. ticket** billet *m* de faveur; **c. copy** (*of book*) exemplaire *m* envoyé à titre gracieux

compliments slip *n* papillon *m* présentant les compliments de la société

comply [kəm'plaɪ] *vi* **to c. with** (*code, specifications, rule etc*) se conformer à; (*contract*) respecter; (*law*) se soumettre à; (*request*) accepter; (*wish*) satisfaire; (*order*) obéir à; **we asked them to move on but they did not c.** nous leur avons demandé de circuler mais ils n'ont pas obéi

component [kəm'pəʊnənt] **1** *adj* **c. part** pièce *f* détachée; (*of theory*) composante *f* **2** *n Ind, Phys, Ch* composant *m*; *Fig* (*of program, education, system etc*) élément *m*

comport [kəm'pɔːt] *Fml* **1** *vt* **to c. oneself** se comporter **2** *vi* concorder (**with** avec)

comportment [kəm'pɔːtment] *n* *Fml* conduite *f*, comportement *m*

compose [kəm'pəʊz] **1** *vt* **(a)** (*poem, symphony etc*), *Typ* composer **(b)** (*constitute*) composer, constituer; **to be composed of sth** se composer *ou* être composé *ou* constitué de qch **(c)** *Art* (*people in painting*) composer **(d)** (*calm*) (*mind*) calmer, tranquilliser; **to c. one's thoughts** mettre de l'ordre dans ses pensées; **she composed her features into a smile** elle réussit à esquisser un sourire; **c. yourself!** calmez-vous! **(e)** *Fml* (*settle*) (*difference*) régler **2** *vi Mus* composer

composed [kəm'pəʊzd] *adj* (*calm*) calme

composer [kəm'pəʊzər] *n Mus* compositeur, -trice

composing [kəm'pəʊzɪŋ] *n Mus, Typ etc* composition *f*; *Typ* **c. room** (salle *f* de) composition

composite ['kɒmpəzɪt] **1** *adj Bot* (*flower*) composé; *Cin* **c. shot** impression *f* combinée **2** *n* composé *m*; *Bot* composée *f*; *Pol* = motion *f* composite; **my main character is a c. of several people** mon personnage principal est un mélange de plusieurs personnes

composition [kɒmpə'zɪʃən] *n* **(a)** (*of symphony, poem etc*) composition *f*; **a sonata of his own c.** une sonate de sa composition **(b)** (*piece of music*) composition *f* **(c)** (*constitution*) (*of air, water, committee etc*) composition *f* **(d)** *Art* (*distribution of elements*) composition *f* **(e)** (*mixture*) mélange *m*, composé *m* **(f)** *Sch* (*essay*) dissertation *f*, rédaction *f*; *Old-fashioned* **prose c.** thème *m* **(g)** *Com* (*settlement*) (*with creditors*) arrangement *m*, accommodement *m*; (*on bankruptcy*) concordat *m* préventif; **to make a c.** composer

compositor [kəm'pɒzɪtər] *n Typ* compositeur *m*, metteur *m* (en pages)

compos mentis ['kɒmpɒs'mentɪs] *adj Jur* sain d'esprit; **to be c.** (*not drunk, not half asleep*) être en possession de toutes ses facultés; **I'm not c. yet** je suis encore à moitié endormi

compost¹ ['kɒmpɒst] *n* (*for garden*) compost *m*, terreau *m*; **c. heap** tas *m* de compost

compost² *vt* (*vegetable matter*) faire du compost à partir de

composure [kəm'pəʊʒər] *n* calme *m*, sang-froid *m*; **to regain** *or* **recover one's c.** retrouver son sang-froid, se calmer

compote ['kɒmpɒt] *n Culin* compote *f*

compound¹ ['kɒmpaʊnd] [ⓘA14,12] **1** *adj* composé, combiné; *Gram* (*word, noun*) composé; *Mus* (*time*) composé; *Surg* (*fracture*) compliqué; *Math* (*number*) complexe; **c. entry** (*in bookkeeping*) article *m* composé; **c. eye** (*of insect*) œil *m* composé; *Math* **c. fraction** fraction *f* composée; *Fin* **c. interest** intérêts *mpl* composés **2** *n* (*combination*) *Ch* (corps *m*) composé *m*; *Tech* composition *f*, mastic *m*; *Gram* mot *m* composé; **chemical c.** composé chimique

compound² [kəm'paʊnd] **1** *vt* **(a)** (*worsen*) (*problem etc*) aggraver **(b)** *Ch, Pharm* (*elements*) combiner; (*drug*) préparer **(c)** (*settle*) (*difference*) régler, arranger; **to c. a debt** faire une transaction pour le règlement d'une dette **2** *vi*

(a) *Fml* s'arranger, composer (**with sb** avec qn) (b) *Com* (*with one's creditors*) arriver à un concordat
compound³ [ˈkɒmpaʊnd] *n* (a) (*of palace etc*) enceinte *f*; (*of prison*) cour *f* (b) (*in South Africa*) (*for miners*) quartier *m* des noirs; (*for livestock*) parc *m* à bétail
comprehend [kɒmprɪˈhend] *vt* (*understand, include*) comprendre
comprehensible [kɒmprɪˈhensəb(ə)l] *adj* compréhensible, intelligible
comprehensibly [kɒmprɪˈhensəblɪ] *adv* d'une manière compréhensible *ou* intelligible
comprehension [kɒmprɪˈhenʃən] *n* entendement *m*; (*of text etc*) compréhension *f*; *Sch* **c. (test)** test *m* de compréhension; **a reading/listening c.** un exercice de compréhension écrite/orale; **it is above** *or* **beyond my c.** cela dépasse mon entendement
comprehensive [kɒmprɪˈhensɪv] **1** *adj* (*wide-ranging*) (*answer, introduction, coverage, list etc*) complet; (*study, view*) d'ensemble; (*defeat, victory*) écrasant; **c. insurance** assurance *f* tous-risques; **c. knowledge** vastes connaissances *fpl*; **c. policy** (*in insurance*) police *f* tous risques, police multirisque; *Br Sch* **c. school** = école *f* publique d'enseignement secondaire; **c. site insurance** assurance *f* tous-risques chantiers **2** *n Br Sch* = école *f* publique d'enseignement secondaire
comprehensively [kɒmprɪˈhensɪvlɪ] *adv* de façon complète; **c. beaten** *or* **defeated** battu à plate(s) couture(s)
comprehensiveness [kɒmprɪˈhensɪvnɪs] *n* (*of answer, treatment of subject*) caractère *m* complet
compress¹ [ˈkɒmpres] *n Med* compresse *f*
compress² [kəmˈpres] **1** *vt* (a) (*gas, air, spring*) comprimer; (*of compressor*) (*air etc*) refouler; **to c. one's lips** serrer *ou* pincer les lèvres (b) (*speech, detail etc*) condenser; **to c. 3,000 years of history into a 45 minute video** condenser 3 000 ans d'histoire en une vidéo de 45 minutes **2** *vi Tech* (*of gas, spring etc*) se comprimer
compressed [kəmˈprest] *adj* (*air etc*) comprimé; (*style*) condensé; **c. lips** lèvres *fpl* serrées *ou* pincées
compression [kəmˈpreʃən] *n* (a) (*of gas, spring etc*) compression *f*; **c. chamber/period/pump** chambre *f*/période *f*/pompe *f* de compression; *Aut* **c. ignition** allumage *m* par compression; **c. stroke** (*in engine*) (temps *m* de) compression; **c. ratio** (*of engine*) rapport *m* volumétrique, taux *m* de compression (b) (*of thought, style etc*) concentration *f*
compressive [kəmˈpresɪv] *adj* compressif, de compression; **c. strain** déformation *f* occasionnée par la compression; **c. strength** résistance *f* à la compression; **c. stress** effort *m* de compression
compressor [kəmˈpresər] *n* (*of gas, air etc*) compresseur *m*; *Comptr* **c. program** programme *m* de compression
comprise [kəmˈpraɪz] *vt* être composé de, comprendre; **the flat is comprised of** *or* **comprises three rooms** l'appartement comprend trois pièces; **a meal comprising meat and vegetables** un repas composé de viande avec des légumes
compromise¹ [ˈkɒmprəmaɪz] *n* compromis *m*; **to agree to a c.** accepter un compromis; **to make** *or* **reach** *or* **arrive at a c.** faire *ou* parvenir à un compromis (**with sb** avec qn); **policy of no c.** politique *f* intransigeante; **there must be no c.** il ne faut pas faire de compromis
compromise² **1** *vt* (*person, one's principles*) compromettre; **to c. oneself with sb** se compromettre avec qn **2** *vi* transiger, composer (**with sb** avec qn); **if he agrees to c.** s'il accepte un compromis; **let's c.** faisons un compromis, transigeons
compromising [ˈkɒmprəmaɪzɪŋ] *adj* (*situation etc*) compromettant
comptroller [kənˈtrəʊlər] *n Admin* contrôleur *m*; (*of accounts*) vérificateur *m*
compulsion [kəmˈpʌlʃən] *n* (a) (*obligation*) contrainte *f*; **under c.** sous la contrainte; **to be under c. to do sth** être astreint à faire qch; **there's no c. to do it** il n'y a pas d'obligation à le faire (b) *Psy* (*urge*) compulsion *f*; **to feel a c. to do sth** avoir une envie irrésistible de faire qch
compulsive [kəmˈpʌlsɪv] *adj Psy* (*behaviour*) compulsif; (*smoker, gambler, liar*) invétéré; **I am a c. eater** je suis boulimique; **c. eating is a sign of stress** la boulimie est un signe de stress; **I found it c. reading/viewing** j'ai trouvé que c'était absolument captivant *ou* prenant
compulsively [kəmˈpʌlsɪvlɪ] *adv* **to smoke/lie/talk c.** ne pas pouvoir s'empêcher de fumer/de mentir/de parler; **to eat c.** être boulimique; **it's c. readable/watchable** c'est passionnant
compulsorily [kəmˈpʌlsərɪlɪ] *adv* obligatoirement; *Admin* **to be retired c.** être mis à la retraite d'office
compulsory [kəmˈpʌlsərɪ] *adj* (a) (*attendance, wear, subject*) obligatoire; **c. liquidation** liquidation *f* forcée; **c. school attendance** présence *f* obligatoire à l'école; **military service/Latin is c.** le service militaire/le latin est obligatoire; *Jur* **c. purchase order** ordre *m* d'expropriation; **c. redundancy** licenciement *m* sec; **c. retirement** retraite *f* d'office; *Jur* **c. sale** adjudication *f* forcée; **c. schooling** scolarisation *f* obligatoire (b) (*coercive*) coercitif; **c. powers** pouvoirs *mpl* coercitifs
compunction [kəmˈpʌŋkʃən] *n* remords *m*, scrupule *m*; **without c.** sans remords *ou* scrupules
computation [kɒmpjʊˈteɪʃən] *n Fml* calcul *m*; **to make a c. of** faire le calcul de, calculer
computational [kɒmpjʊˈteɪʃən(ə)l] *adj Comptr* de calcul; **c. linguistics** linguistique *f* informatique *ou* computationnelle
compute [kəmˈpjuːt] **1** *vt* calculer **2** *vi* faire des calculs; *F* **it doesn't c.** ce n'est pas logique
computer [kəmˈpjuːtər] *n* ordinateur *m*; **she's in computers** elle est dans l'informatique; **to have sth on c.** avoir qch sur ordinateur; **analog/digital c.** calculateur *m* analogique/numérique; **the c. age** l'ère *f* des ordinateurs *ou* de l'informatique; **to go on a c. course** suivre un cours d'informatique; **c. animation** animation *f* par ordinateur; **c. art** dessin *m* par ordinateur; *Am* **c. camp** colonie *f* de vacances centrée sur l'informatique; **c. centre** centre *m* informatique, infocentre *m*; **c. code** code *m* d'ordinateur; **c. dealer** revendeur *m* informatique; **c. diagram** diagramme *m* réalisé par *ou* sur ordinateur; *F* **c. freak** (*enthusiast*) dingue *mf* d'informatique; **c. generation** génération *f* d'ordinateur; **c. genius** génie *m* de l'informatique; **c. hardware** matériel *m* informatique; **c. instruction** instruction *f* machine; **c. keyboard** clavier *m* d'ordinateur; **c. link-up** liaison *f* informatique; **c. manager** directeur *m* informatique; **c. manufacturer** constructeur *m* informatique; **c. marketing workstation** station *f* de travail informatisée de gestion mercatique; **c. model** modèle *m* réalisé par *ou* sur ordinateur; **c. modelling** réalisation *f* de modèles sur ordinateur; **c. network** réseau *m* informatique *ou* d'ordinateurs; **c. operator** opérateur, -trice (sur ordinateur); **c. output** sortie *f* d'ordinateur; **c. printout** impression *f*; (*continuous*) listing *m*, listage *m*; **c. revolution** révolution *f* informatique; **c. room** salle *f* des ordinateurs; **c. simulation** simulation *f* par ordinateur; **c. supplier** fournisseur *m* informatique; **c. system** système *m* informatique; **c. terminal** terminal *m* informatique
computer-aided [kəmpjuːtərˈeɪdɪd] *adj* assisté par ordinateur; **c. design** conception *f* assistée par ordinateur; **c. engineering** ingénierie *f* assistée par ordinateur; **c. instruction** enseignement *m* assisté par ordinateur; **c. learning** enseignement *m* assisté par ordinateur; **c. manufacturing** fabrication *f* assistée par ordinateur; **c. sales and marketing** vente *f* et marketing assistés par ordinateur
computer analyst *n* analyste *mf* programmeur
computer-assisted [kəmpjuːtərəˈsɪstɪd] *adj* assisté par ordinateur; **c. interviewing** entretien *m* assisté par ordinateur
computer-controlled *adj* contrôlé par ordinateur; **c. lock** serrure *f* électronique
computer crime *n* fraude *f* informatique, criminalité *f* informatique
computer dating *n* = rencontres *fpl* organisées par ordinateur
computer-enhanced [kəmpjuːtərənˈhɑːnst] *adj* (*graphics etc*) amélioré par ordinateur
computer expert *n* informaticien, -ienne
computer fraud *n* fraude *f* informatique
computer game *n* jeu *m* informatique *ou* électronique
computer graphics *n* [①A10,c] graphiques *mpl*; (*technique*) infographie *f*
computer hacker *n* pirate *mf* informatique
computerizable [kəmpjuːtəˈraɪzəb(ə)l] *adj* informatisable
computerization [kəmpjuːtəraɪˈzeɪʃən] *n* (*of organization, records etc*) informatisation *f*
computerize [kəmˈpjuːtəraɪz] *vt* (*organization, filing system etc*) informatiser
computerized [kəmˈpjuːtəraɪzd] *adj* informatisé; **c. accounts** compatabilité *f* informatisée; **c. banking** informatique *f* bancaire; **c. key** clé *f* magnétique; **c. data** données *fpl* informatiques; **c. typesetting** composition *f* par ordinateur
computer language *n* langage *m* machine
computer literacy *n* connaissances *fpl* en informatique
computer literate *adj* **to be c.** avoir des connaissances en informatique
computer processing *n* traitement *m* sur ordinateur
computer program *n* programme *f* machine
computer programmer *n* programmeur, -euse
computer programming *n* programmation *f*

computer science *n* informatique *f*
computer scientist *n* informaticien, -ienne
computer-to-computer *adj* (*transmission*) d'ordinateur à ordinateur
computer translation *n* traduction *f* par ordinateur
computer-typeset *vti* composer sur ordinateur
computer typesetting *n* composition *f* informatisée
computer virus *n* virus *m* informatique
computing [kəm'pju:tɪŋ] *n* (**a**) (*calculating*) calcul *m*; **c. machine** machine *f* à calcul; **c. power** puissance *f* de calcul (**b**) (*science*) informatique *f*
comrade ['kɒmreɪd, -rəd] *n* camarade *mf*, compagnon *m*; *Pol* camarade; **C. Jones** le/la camarade Jones; *Mil, Fig* **comrades in arms** compagnons d'armes
comradeship ['kɒmreɪdʃɪp, -rəd-] *n* camaraderie *f*
comsat ['kɒmsæt] *n Astronaut* satellite *m* de communication
Con *Pol abbr* **Conservative**
con[1] [kɒn] *n F* **c. (trick)** arnaque *f*, escroquerie *f*; **what a c.!** quelle arnaque!; **c. man** *or* **artist** arnaqueur *m*, escroc *m*; **c. woman** arnaqueuse *f*
con[2] *vt* (**-nn-**) *F* (*trick*) arnaquer, escroquer; **I've been conned** je me suis fait arnaquer; **they were conned out of £500** ils se sont fait arnaquer de cinq cents livres; **to c. sb into doing sth** persuader qn de faire qch par la ruse
con[3] *n* **the pros and cons** le pour et le contre
con[4] *n Sl* (*convict*) taulard *m*, tôlard *m*; **an ex-c.** un ancien taulard
con[5] *vt* (**-nn-**) *Old-fashioned* (*study*) consulter
concatenated [kɒn'kætəneɪtɪd] *adj Comptr* concaténé
concatenation [kɒnkætə'neɪʃən] *n Comptr* enchaînement *m*
concave ['kɒnkeɪv] *adj* concave, incurvé
concavity [kɒn'kævɪtɪ] *n* concavité *f*
conceal [kən'si:l] *vt* (*object, intentions, truth etc*) cacher, dissimuler; (*thoughts*) cacher, voiler; **to c. oneself** se cacher; **to c. one's intentions** cacher *ou* déguiser ses intentions *ou* son jeu; **to c. sth from sb** (*hide, not tell*) cacher qch à qn
concealed [kən'si:ld] *adj* caché; (*bend*) masqué; (*lighting*) indirect; *Aut* **danger! c. entrance** (*notice*) danger! sortie de véhicules; **c. microphone** micro *m* caché
concealment [kən'si:lmənt] *n* dissimulation *f*; **to keep sb in c.** cacher qn; **place of c.** cachette *f*; *Fin* **c. of assets** dissimulation d'actif
concede [kən'si:d] *vt* (*privilege etc, Sp corner etc*) concéder; *Pol, Sp etc* **to c. defeat** s'avouer vaincu; **to c. that one is wrong** reconnaître qu'on a tort
conceit [kən'si:t] *n* (**a**) (*vanity*) vanité *f*, suffisance *f*; **eaten up with c.** pétri *ou* pourri de vanité (**b**) *Liter* métaphore *f* astucieuse
conceited [kən'si:tɪd] *adj* suffisant, vaniteux; **I don't want to sound c. but ...** je ne veux pas avoir l'air prétentieux mais ...; **he is unbearably c.** il est d'une suffisance insupportable
conceitedly [kən'si:tɪdlɪ] *adv* avec suffisance, avec vanité; **he c. imagined that ...** il a eu la prétention d'imaginer que ...
conceivable [kən'si:vəb(ə)l] *adj* concevable, imaginable; **it is c.** cela se conçoit; **it is c. that ...** il est concevable que ... + *sub*; **by every c. means** par tous les moyens possibles et imaginables; **what c. reason could I have?** quelle raison pourrais-je bien avoir?
conceivably [kən'si:vəblɪ] *adv* **she could c. have done it, it's c. possible that she did it** il n'est pas exclu qu'elle l'ait fait; **I don't see how it's c. possible** ce n'est pas concevable; **this is c. the best/worst ...** c'est peut-être le meilleur/pire ...; **is he capable of it? — c.** en est-il capable? — c'est fort possible
conceive [kən'si:v] **1** *vt* (**a**) (*form*) (*plan*) concevoir; **to c. a dislike for sb** prendre qn en aversion (**b**) (*imagine*) **I cannot c. why ...** je n'arrive pas à imaginer pourquoi ...; **it is difficult to c. how ...** il est difficile de concevoir *ou* d'imaginer comment ... (**c**) (*child*) concevoir; **to be conceived** (*of child*) être conçu **2** *vi* (*become pregnant*) concevoir
▶ **conceive of** *vipo* imaginer; **I can c. of him having done it** je peux très bien imaginer qu'il l'ait fait
concentrate[1] ['kɒnsəntreɪt] *n* (*of tomatoes, orange juice etc*) concentré *m*; (*mineral*) minerai *m* concentré; **made from c.** (*orange juice etc*) fait à base de concentré
concentrate[2] **1** *vt* (*troops, attention, efforts*) concentrer (**on** sur); **the presence of danger helped to c. our minds** la présence du danger nous a aidés à nous concentrer; **with concentrated fury** avec une fureur intense; **industry is concentrated in the south** l'industrie est concentrée dans le sud **2** *vi* (**a**) (*mentally*) se concentrer; **to c. on sth** se concentrer sur qch; **to c. on doing sth** s'appliquer à faire qch (**b**) (*specialize*) **to c. on sth** se concentrer sur qch (**c**) (*group*) se concentrer, être groupé; **the population tends to c. in cities** la population tend à se concentrer dans les villes
concentration [kɒnsən'treɪʃən] *n* (**a**) (*mental*) concentration *f*, application *f*; **to lose one's c.** se déconcentrer; **the work requires c.** le travail demande de la concentration; **c. span** concentration
(**b**) (*specializing*) spécialisation *f*; **in view of their recent c. on other areas of the market** étant donné qu'ils se sont récemment concentrés sur d'autres secteurs du marché
(**c**) (*grouping*) (*of troops etc*) concentration *f*; **there was a c. of cases of food poisoning in the area** il y a eu plusieurs cas d'intoxication alimentaire dans le quartier; **c. of effort** convergence *f* des efforts; *Ch* **(degree of) c.** (*of acid etc*) titre *m*; **the large urban concentrations** les grandes agglomérations *fpl* urbaines
concentration camp *n* camp *m* de concentration
concentric [kən'sentrɪk] *adj Geom* concentrique
concept ['kɒnsept] *n* concept *m*; **this is a difficult c. for children** c'est un concept difficile à comprendre pour les enfants
concept car *n* concept-car *m*
conception [kən'sepʃən] *n* (**a**) (*action*) (*of child, idea etc*) conception *f* (**b**) (*idea*) conception *f*, idée *f*; **to have a clear c. of sth** se représenter clairement qch par la pensée; **he has no c. of how long the work takes** il ne se rend absolument pas compte du temps que prend le travail
concept-testing *n Mktg* tests *mpl* de concept
conceptual [kən'septjʊəl] *adj* conceptuel
conceptualize [kən'septjʊəlaɪz] *vti* conceptualiser
concern[1] [kən'sɜ:n] *n* (**a**) (*interest*) intérêt *m* (**in** dans); **it's no c. of mine/yours** cela ne me/vous regarde pas; **this is a matter of public c.** c'est une question d'intérêt général
(**b**) (*worry, compassion*) inquiétude *f*, souci *m*; (*stronger*) anxiété *f*; **to show c.** se montrer inquiet; **there is growing c. for her safety** on est de plus en plus inquiet à son sujet *ou* sur son sort; **there is growing c. that ...** on craint de plus en plus que ...; **my only c. has been to ensure that ...** ma seule préoccupation a été de m'assurer que ...; **there is no cause for c.** il n'y a pas de raison de s'inquiéter; **to express c. about sth** exprimer de l'inquiétude au sujet de qch; **thank you for your c.** tu es gentil de m'avoir posé la question/de me l'avoir proposé/*etc*
(**c**) *Com, Ind* entreprise *f*; **a large publishing c.** une grande maison d'édition
concern[2] *vt* (**a**) (*apply to, affect*) (*person, matter*) concerner, toucher; (*be the business of*) (*person*) regarder, être l'affaire de; **matters that c. the public** choses qui intéressent le public; **to whom it may c.** à qui de droit; **to c. oneself with** *or* **about sth** s'intéresser à qch, s'occuper de qch; **don't c. yourself with that for the moment** ne t'occupe pas de cela pour l'instant; **where work is/children are concerned** en ce qui concerne le travail/les enfants, pour ce qui est du travail/des enfants; **to be concerned with sth** s'occuper de qch; **the parties/people concerned** les intéressés *mpl*; *Com etc* **the department concerned** le service compétent; **as far as I am concerned** en ce qui me concerne, quant à moi; **as far as this question is concerned** en ce qui concerne cette question, pour ce qui est de cette question
(**b**) (*be about*) traiter de; **the book is concerned with politics** ce livre traite de politique; **it concerns your mother** c'est au sujet de votre mère
(**c**) (*usu passive*) (*worry*) **to be concerned about sb/sth** s'inquiéter *ou* être inquiet de qn/qch; **I am concerned for his health** son état de santé m'inquiète
concerned [kən'sɜ:nd] *adj* (*smile, look*) inquiet, soucieux; **we feel very c. about this** cela nous préoccupe au plus haut point, cela nous inquiète beaucoup; **he didn't seem at all c.** il n'avait pas du tout l'air inquiet *ou* de s'inquiéter
concerning [kən'sɜ:nɪŋ] *prep* concernant, au sujet de, à l'égard de; **information c. the crime** des informations au sujet du *ou* concernant le délit
concert[1] ['kɒnsət] *n* (**a**) *Mus* concert *m*; **Bob Dylan in c.** Bob Dylan en concert; **to give a c.** donner un concert; **c. grand** piano *m* de concert; **c. performer** concertiste *mf*; *St Exch* **c. party** action *f* de concert; **c. tour** tournée *f*; **c. pitch** diapason *m* (**b**) *Fml* (*association*) concert *m*; **to act in c. (with sb)** agir de concert (avec qn)
concert[2] [kən'sɜ:t] *vt* (*measures etc*) concerter
concerted [kən'sɜ:tɪd] *adj* (*plan, effort etc*) concerté; **c. action** action *f* concertée *ou* d'ensemble
concertgoer ['kɒnsətgəʊər] *n* amateur, -trice de concerts
concert hall *n* salle *f* de concert
concertina[1] [kɒnsə'ti:nə] *n Mus* concertina *m*
concertina[2] *vi* (**concertinaed** [-nəd]) (*of car etc in collision*) se plier en accordéon
concertmaster ['kɒnsətmɑ:stər] *n Am* (*of orchestra*) premier violon *m*
concerto [kən'tʃɜ:təʊ] *n Mus* concerto *m*; **piano/violin c.** concerto pour piano/violon

concert pianist *n* pianiste *mf* de concert
concession [kən'seʃən] *n* **(a)** (*allowance*) concession *f*; **to make concessions** faire des concessions; **the only c. the film makes to reality is ...** la seule concession que le film fasse à la réalité est ... **(b)** *Com* concession *f*; **c. close** (*in selling*) conclusion *f* par concession **(c)** *Min* **(mining) c.** concession *f* minière **(d)** *Br* (*reduction*) tarif *m* réduit; **price: £4.50 (concessions £3)** prix des billets: 4.50 livres (tarif réduit 3 livres)
concessionary [kən'seʃən(ə)rɪ] *Com* **1** *adj* (*company etc*) concessionnaire; *Br* (*fare, rate etc*) réduit **2** *n* = **concession(u)aire**
concession(n)aire [kənseʃə'neər] *n Com* concessionnaire *mf*
concession ticket *n Br* (*for theatre, cinema*) billet *m* à prix réduit
conch [kɒŋk, kɒn(t)ʃ] *n* (*mollusc*) conque *f*
conchie, conchy ['kɒntʃɪ] *n Old-fashioned F* (*abbr* **conscientious objector**) objecteur *m* de conscience
concierge [kɒnsɪ'eəʒ] *n* (*in hotel*) concierge *mf*; **c.'s desk** comptoir *m* du concierge
conciliate [kən'sɪlɪeɪt] **1** *vt* **(a)** (*win over*) apaiser; **she refused to be conciliated** elle refusait la conciliation **(b)** (*reconcile*) (*theories, beliefs*) concilier, réconcilier **2** *vi Fml* **to c. between two people/countries** réconcilier deux peuples/pays
conciliation [kənsɪlɪ'eɪʃən] *n* conciliation *f*; **c. board, c. service** (*in industrial dispute*) conseil *m* d'arbitrage, = conseil des prud'hommes
conciliator [kən'sɪlɪeɪtər] *n* conciliateur, -trice; (*in industrial dispute*) médiateur, -trice
conciliatory [kən'sɪlɪət(ə)rɪ] *adj* conciliant; (*spirit*) de conciliation; *Jur* conciliatoire
concise [kən'saɪs] *adj* concis; (*style*) concis, dense; (*dictionary*) abrégé
concisely [kən'saɪslɪ] *adv* brièvement, avec concision
conciseness [kən'saɪsnɪs], **concision** [kən'sɪʒən] *n* concision *f*; **to aim at c.** (*in one's style*) essayer d'être concis
conclave ['kɒnkleɪv] *n* **(a)** (*meeting*) conseil *m*, réunion *f*; **to be in c. with sb** tenir conseil avec qn **(b)** *Cathol* conclave *m*
conclude [kən'klu:d] **1** *vt* **(a)** (*finish*) (*speech, book, programme*) conclure, finir, achever; (*session*) clôturer; (*meal*) terminer **(b)** (*infer*) conclure; **from this I c. that ...** de ceci je conclus que ... **(c)** (*sign etc*) (*peace, treaty*) conclure; (*deal, contract*) arranger, régler **2** *vi* **(a)** (*of play, evening, book etc*) s'achever, se terminer **(with** avec) **(b)** (*at end of speech etc*) conclure; **to c. ...** en conclusion ..., pour conclure ...
concluding [kən'klu:dɪŋ] *adj* (*chapter, episode*) dernier; (*concert*) de clôture; **the c. word** le mot de la fin; **c. remarks** remarques *fpl* pour conclure
conclusion [kən'klu:ʒən] *n* **(a)** (*inference*) conclusion *f*; **to draw a c. from sth** tirer une conclusion de qch; **draw your own conclusions** tirez vos propres conclusions; **to come to** *or* **reach the c. that ...** conclure que ... + *ind*, (en) arriver à la conclusion que ... + *ind*; **without coming to any c.** sans arriver à une conclusion; **you're jumping to conclusions** tu tires une conclusion hâtive; **don't jump to conclusions!** réfléchis avant de conclure!; **he jumped to the wrong c.** il a tiré une conclusion erronée
(b) (*end*) (*of essay, film*) conclusion *f*; (*of session*) clôture *f*; **in c.** pour conclure, en conclusion; **to bring a matter to a successful c.** mener une affaire à bonne fin
(c) (*signing etc*) (*of treaty etc*) conclusion *f*
conclusive [kən'klu:sɪv] *adj* (*argument*) concluant, décisif; (*test*) probant
conclusively [kən'klu:sɪvlɪ] *adv* (*to argue, show*) de façon concluante
concoct [kən'kɒkt] *vt* **(a)** (*make*) (*cocktail*) préparer; (*dish*) concocter **(b)** (*think up*) (*plan*) imaginer, élaborer, concocter; (*plot*) machiner
concoction [kən'kɒkʃən] *n* **(a)** (*action*) (*of food etc*) confection *f* **(b)** (*drink, dish etc*) mélange *m*, concoction *f* **(c)** (*of plan*) élaboration *f*; (*of plot*) machination *f*; **a c. of lies** un tissu de mensonges
concomitant [kən'kɒmɪtənt] *Fml* **1** *adj* concomitant **(with** de) **2** *n* **the concomitants of old age/marriage** ce qui va de pair avec la vieillesse/le mariage
concord ['kɒŋkɔ:d] *n* **(a)** *Fml* (*between people*) entente *f*, harmonie *f*; *Lit* **to live in c.** vivre en harmonie **(with** avec) **(b)** *Gram* concordance *f* **(c)** *Mus* accord *m* consonant
concordance [kən'kɔ:dəns] *n* **(a)** *Fml* accord *m*, concordance *f* **(with** avec); **to be in c. with ...** être en accord avec ... **(b)** *Mus* consonance *f* **(c)** *Liter* (*of Bible*) index *m*, concordance *f*
concordant [kən'kɔ:dənt] *adj* **(a)** en accord, concordant **(with** avec) **(b)** *Mus* consonant
concordat [kɒn'kɔ:dæt] *n* concordat *m*
Concorde ['kɒnkɔ:d] *n Av* Concorde *m*
concourse ['kɒnkɔ:s] *n* **(a)** (*of railway station*) hall *m* **(b)** *Fml* (*gathering place*) lieu *m* de rassemblement **(c)** *Fml* (*crowd*) foule *f*, rassemblement *m*
concrete[1] ['kɒnkri:t] **1** *n Constr* béton *m*; **reinforced c.** béton *m* armé; **c. mixer** bétonnière *f*; *Fig* **c. jungle** forêt *f* de béton **2** *adj* (*example, term, noun*) concret; (*suggestion, proposal*) concret, pratique; **c. music** musique *f* concrète; **c. poem** calligramme *m*
concrete[2] *vt Constr* (*wall etc*) bétonner
▶ **concrete over** *vtsep* (*garden, field etc*) bétonner
concreting ['kɒnkri:tɪŋ] *n Constr* bétonnage *m*
concretion [kən'kri:ʃən] *n Med, Geol etc* concrétion *f*
concubinage [kɒn'kju:bɪnɪdʒ] *n* concubinage *m*
concubine ['kɒŋkjʊbaɪn] *n* concubine *f*
concur [kən'kɜ:r] *vi* **(-rr-)** **(a)** (*agree*) (*of person*) être d'accord **(with sb/sth** avec qn/qch), être du même avis **(with sb** que qn); **to c. with sb's views/opinions/conclusions** partager le point de vue/l'opinion/les conclusions de qn; **he proposed a different approach and she concurred** il a proposé une approche différente et elle a approuvé **(b)** (*of findings, results of experiment*) concorder **(with** avec) **(c)** *Fml* (*of events*) coïncider; **to c. in a result** concourir à un résultat
concurrence [kən'kʌrəns] *n* (*agreement*) accord *m*; (*assent*) assentiment *m*, consentement *m* **(in** à); *Fml* **c. of events** concours *m* de circonstances
concurrent [kən'kʌrənt] *adj* **(a)** (*in time*) simultané; *Math* concourant; *Jur* **two c. sentences** deux peines *fpl* confondues; *Fml* **c. cause** cause *f* contribuante **(b)** (*in agreement*) (*views etc*) qui concordent
concurrently [kən'kʌrəntlɪ] *adv* simultanément **(with** avec); *Jur* **the two sentences to run c.** avec confusion des deux peines
concuss [kən'kʌs] *vt* commotionner; **she was badly concussed in the accident** elle a subi de graves commotions lors de l'accident
concussion [kən'kʌʃən] *n* commotion *f* cérébrale; **suffering from c.** souffrant de commotion cérébrale
condemn [kən'dem] *vt* **(a)** (*sentence*) condamner; **to c. sb to death** condamner qn à mort; **to be condemned to sth/to do sth** être condamné à qch/à faire qch; **she was condemned to a life of poverty** elle était condamnée à vivre dans la pauvreté **(b)** (*declare unsafe*) condamner; **this meat has been condemned** cette viande a été jugée impropre à la consommation **(c)** (*censure*) (*person, policy, abuse etc*) condamner; **she condemned the remarks as pure prejudice** elle a condamné les remarques comme étant de purs préjugés
condemnation [kɒndem'neɪʃən] *n* **(a)** (*of prisoner*) condamnation *f* **(b)** (*of building*) condamnation *f* **(c)** (*censure*) condamnation *f*
condemned [kən'demd] *adj* **(a)** **c. man** condamné *m*; **c. cell** cellule *f* des condamnés **(b)** (*building*) condamné; (*meat*) jugé impropre à la consommation
condensation [kɒnden'seɪʃən] *n* (*of gas, liquid, text etc*) condensation *f*; (*on windows*) buée *f*
condense [kən'dens] **1** *vt* (*gas, liquid, text etc*) condenser; **to c. a chapter into a single paragraph** condenser un chapitre en un seul paragraphe **2** *vi* se condenser
condensed [kən'denst] *adj* **(a)** (*milk*) concentré, condensé **(b)** *Comptr* **c. mode** mode *m* condensé; **c. print** impression *f* condensée
condenser [kən'densər] *n El* condensateur *m*; (*for condensing liquids*) condenseur *m*; **c. microphone** microphone *m* électrostatique
condensing [kən'densɪŋ] *n* condensation *f*
condescend [kɒndɪ'send] *vi* **(a)** (*agree, accept with reluctance*) condescendre **(to do sth** à faire qch), daigner **(to do sth** faire qch) **(b)** (*be condescending*) se montrer condescendant **(to sb** envers qn)
condescending [kɒndɪ'sendɪŋ] *adj* condescendant
condescendingly [kɒndɪ'sendɪŋlɪ] *adv* d'une manière condescendante, avec condescendance
condescension [kɒndɪ'senʃən] *n* condescendance *f* **(to** envers, pour)
condiment ['kɒndɪmənt] *n* condiment *m*; **c. set** service *m* à condiments
condition[1] [kən'dɪʃən] *n* **(a)** (*state*) état *m*; **in good c.** en bon état; **in bad c., in a poor c.** en mauvais état; **you're in no c. to drive** (*you're ill, tired, drunk*) tu n'es pas en état de conduire; **in your c.** (*to pregnant woman*) dans ton état; **to keep oneself in c.** se maintenir en forme; **I'm out of c.** je n'ai pas la condition physique; **he's in excellent c.** sa condition physique est excellente
(b) (*circumstance*) (*usu pl*) condition *f*; **working conditions** (*in factory etc*) conditions de travail; **normal operating conditions** (*of machine*) régime *m* de fonctionnement normal; **weather conditions** conditions météorologiques; **road** *or*

driving conditions état *m* des routes; **drive with particular care as conditions on the roads are hazardous** soyez prudents sur les routes: le mauvais temps rend la circulation très dangereuse; **the human c.** la condition humaine

(**c**) (*term*) condition *f*; **to impose conditions on sb** (im)poser des conditions à qn; **conditions of sale/carriage** conditions de vente/transport; **conditions of a contract** stipulations *fpl ou* termes *mpl* d'un contrat; **on c. that …** à (la) condition que … + *sub*; **you can borrow the book, on one c.** tu peux emprunter le livre, à une condition; **it was a c. of the lease that …** l'une des stipulations du bail était que …; **under these conditions** dans ces conditions

(**d**) *Med* (*of heart, liver etc*) maladie *f*, affection *f*; **to have a heart c.** avoir une maladie du cœur

condition[2] *vt* (**a**) *Psy* (*subject*) conditionner (**to do** à faire); **a conditioned reflex** un réflexe conditionné (**b**) **to c. one's hair** utiliser de l'après-shampooing (**c**) (*subject to a condition*) (*usu pass*) déterminer; **to be conditioned by** dépendre de

conditional [kən'dɪʃən(ə)l] **1** *adj* (*offer, agreement, Gram tense*) conditionnel; **c. on sth** dépendant de qch; **my promise was c.** j'ai promis sous certaines conditions; **c. acceptance** acceptation *f* sous réserve; **c. acceptance of an offer** acceptation *f* provisoire d'une offre; **c. access television** télévision *f* à accès conditionnel **2** *n* [①**A50-1,13; B31-32,3**] *Gram* conditionnel *m*; **in the c.** (*verb*) au conditionnel

conditionally [kən'dɪʃən(ə)lɪ] *adv* de façon conditionnelle

conditioner [kən'dɪʃənər] *n* **air c.** climatiseur *m*; (**fabric**) **c.** adoucissant *m*; (**hair**) **c.** après-shampoing *m*, démêlant *m*

conditioning [kən'dɪʃənɪŋ] *n Psy* conditionnement *m*

condo ['kɒndəʊ] *n Am F* = **condominium (b)**

condole [kən'dəʊl] *vi Fml* **to c. with sb** faire *ou* exprimer ses condoléances à qn

condolence [kən'dəʊləns] *n* **condolences** condoléances *fpl*; **to offer sb one's condolences** présenter ses condoléances à qn; **a letter of c.** une lettre de condoléances

condom ['kɒndəm] *n* préservatif *m*

condominium [kɒndə'mɪnɪəm] *n* (**a**) (*shared sovereignty*) condominium *m*; **the territory was made a c.** le territoire fut placé sous un régime de condominium (**b**) *Am* (*building*) immeuble *m* en copropriété; (*apartment*) appartement *m* dans un immeuble en copropriété; (*ownership*) copropriété *f*

condone [kən'dəʊn] *vt* trouver des excuses pour, excuser; **I am not condoning the crime** je ne cherche pas à excuser le crime

condor ['kɒndɔːr] *n* condor *m*

conduce [kən'djuːs] *vi Fml* (*of action or thing*) contribuer (**to** à)

conducive [kən'djuːsɪv] *adj* **c. to sth** favorable à qch; **this weather is not c. to work** ce temps n'incite pas au travail

conduct[1] ['kɒndʌkt] *n* (**a**) (*behaviour*) conduite *f* (**towards sb** à l'égard de *ou* avec *ou* envers qn) (**b**) (*management*) conduite *f*, gestion *f*; **the lawyer's c. of the case** la manière dont l'avocat a mené l'affaire

conduct[2] [kən'dʌkt] **1** *vt* (**a**) (*manage, direct*) (*business, operations, orchestra, religious service*) diriger; (*carry out*) (*campaign, survey*) mener; (*experiment*) effectuer; *Jur* **to c. one's own case** plaider soi-même sa cause; **to c. the traffic** faire la circulation

(**b**) **to c. oneself** se comporter, se conduire

(**c**) (*lead*) **to c. sb round a building/factory/museum** faire visiter un bâtiment/une usine/un musée à qn; **conducted tours** visites *fpl* guidées; **to give sb a conducted tour** faire faire une visite guidée à qn

(**d**) *El, Phys* (*heat, electricity*) conduire, être conducteur de

2 *vi Mus* diriger; (*work as conductor*) être chef d'orchestre; **who's conducting?** qui est le chef d'orchestre?, qui dirige?

conducting [kən'dʌktɪŋ] *n Mus* direction *f* d'orchestre

conduction [kən'dʌkʃən] *n Phys, El* conduction *f*

conductive [kən'dʌktɪv] *adj Phys, El* conducteur, -trice

conductivity [kɒndʌk'tɪvɪtɪ] *n Phys, El* conductivité *f*

conductor [kən'dʌktər] *n* (**a**) *Br* (*on bus*) receveur *m*; *Am Rail* chef *m* de train (**b**) *Mus* chef *m* d'orchestre (**c**) *Phys, El* (*of electricity etc*) conducteur *m*; **c. wire** fil *m* conducteur; *Rail* **c. rail** rail *m* conducteur *ou* sous tension

conductress [kən'dʌktrɪs] *n Br* (*on bus*) receveuse *f*

conduit ['kɒndjʊɪt] *n* **c.** (**pipe**) conduit *m*, tuyau *m*; (*in machine*) tuyau de communication; *El* tube *m*

condyle ['kɒndɪl] *n Med* condyle *m*

cone [kəʊn] *n* (*of light, volcano, retina etc*) cône *m*; (*of pine*) pomme *f* de pin, cône; (*for ice cream*) cornet *m*; (**traffic**) **c.** cône *ou* balise *f* de signalisation; *Aut* **c. clutch** embrayage *m* à cônes

▶ **cone off** *vtsep* **to c. off two lanes of a motorway** fermer la circulation sur deux voies d'une autoroute (*avec des cônes de signalisation*)

cone-bearing *adj* conifère

cone-shaped ['kəʊnʃeɪpt] *adj* en forme de cône, conique

coney ['kəʊnɪ] *n Old-fashioned* lapin *m*; **c.** (**skin**) peau *f* de lapin

confab ['kɒnfæb] *n F* (*conversation*) colloque *m*; **to have a c.** (**about sth**) (*discuss*) discuter (de qch), se consulter (sur qch)

confection [kən'fekʃən] *n* (**a**) *esp Am Culin* (*cake, sweet*) friandise *f* (**b**) *Fml* (*act*) confection *f*

confectioner [kən'fekʃənər] *n* (*selling sweets*) confiseur, -euse; (*making, selling cakes*) pâtissier, -ière; **c.'s** (**shop**) confiserie *f*; **J. Smith bakers & confectioners** boulangerie-pâtisserie J. Smith; **c.'s custard** crème *f* pâtissière; *Am* **c.'s sugar** sucre *m* glace

confectionery [kən'fekʃən(ə)rɪ] *n* (*sweets*) confiserie *f*

confederacy [kən'fed(ə)rəsɪ] *n* (*alliance*) confédération *f*; *US Hist* **the C.** les États *mpl* Confédérés

confederate[1] [kən'fed(ə)rət] **1** *adj* confédéré; *US Hist* **the C. States** les États *mpl* Confédérés **2** *n* confédéré *m*; (*in crime*) complice *mf*

confederate[2] [kən'fedəreɪt] **1** *vt* (*states*) confédérer; **to c. oneself with …** se liguer avec … **2** *vi* (*join*) se confédérer (**with** avec); (*conspire*) conspirer (**with** avec, **against** contre)

confederation [kənfedə'reɪʃən] *n* confédération *f*

Confederation of British Industry *n* ≈ Conseil *m* national du patronat français

confer [kən'fɜːr] (**-rr-**) **1** *vt* (*title, rank, powers*) conférer (**on** à); (*degree, diploma*) remettre (**on** à) **2** *vi* se consulter (**with** avec, **on, about** sur); **contestants are not allowed to c.** les concurrents n'ont pas le droit de se consulter

conference ['kɒnfərəns] *n* (**a**) conférence *f*; **press** *or* **news c.** conférence de presse; **to be in c.** (*with several people*) être en conférence (**with** avec); (*with one or two people*) être en réunion; **round-table c.** table *f* ronde; **we hope to get management to the c. table** nous espérons réunir la direction en table ronde; *Tel* **c. call** téléconférence *f*; **c. room** salle *f* de conférence

(**b**) (*of professional association etc*) congrès *m*; **at a c.** à un congrès; *Pol* **Party C.** congrès annuel du parti; **c. centre** centre *m* de conférences; **c. coordinator** responsable *mf* des congrès; **c. delegate** congressiste *mf*; **c. organizer** organisateur *m* de conférences *ou* de congrès; **c. pack** = dossier offert aux conférenciers avec informations générales sur la conférence, petits cadeaux etc

conference line *n Naut, Com* ligne *f* maritime de conférence

conference ship *n* navire *m* de conférence

conferment [kən'fɜːmənt] *n* (*of rank, powers*) attibution *f*; (*of title, diploma*) remise *f*

confess [kən'fes] **1** *vi* (**a**) (*of criminal*) avouer, faire des aveux; **to c. to a crime** avouer un crime

(**b**) (*admit*) **to c. to sth** avouer qch; **to c. to doing** *or* **having done sth** avouer avoir fait qch; **I c. to not liking her** j'avoue que je ne l'aime pas; **to c. to a liking for …** avouer avoir un penchant *ou* un faible pour …

(**c**) *Rel* se confesser (**to sb** à qn, auprès de qn)

2 *vt* (**a**) (*admit*) (*fault*) avouer, confesser; **to c. that …** avouer *ou* confesser que … + *ind*; **I must c. that …** je dois avouer que …, je dois reconnaître que …; **I was wrong, I c.** j'admets que j'ai eu tort; **I don't understand either, I must c.** je dois avouer que je ne comprends pas non plus; **medical experts c. themselves helpless** les médecins s'avouent impuissants

(**b**) *Rel* (*of sinner*) (*sins*) confesser, se confesser de; (*of priest*) (*penitent*) confesser; **to c. oneself** se confesser (**to sb** à qn, auprès de qn)

confession [kən'feʃən] *n* (**a**) aveu *m*, confession *f*; **to make a full c.** faire des aveux complets; **I have a c. to make** j'ai un aveu à faire; **on their own c.** de leur propre aveu; **that would be a c. of failure** cela reviendrait à s'avouer vaincu (**b**) *Rel* confession *f*; **to go to c.** aller se confesser; **to hear sb's c.** (*of priest*) entendre la confession de qn, entendre qn en confession, confesser qn; **c. of faith** confession de foi; **the seal of c.** le secret de la confession *ou* du confessionnal

confessional [kən'feʃən(ə)l] **1** *adj* confessionnel **2** *n Rel* confessionnal *m*

confessor [kən'fesər] *n Rel* (*priest*) confesseur *m*; (*sinner*) personne *f* qui se confesse; *Hist* **Edward the C.** Édouard le Confesseur

confetti [kən'fetɪ] *npl* [①**A13,7**] confettis *mpl*

confidant, *f* **confidante** [kɒnfɪ'dænt] *n* confident, -ente

confide [kən'faɪd] *vt* (*secret*) confier (**to sb** à qn); **she confided to me that …** elle m'a confié que …; **to c. sth to sb's care** confier qch à la garde de qn

▶ **confide in** *vipo* se confier à

confidence ['kɒnfɪdəns] *n* **(a)** (*trust*) confiance *f* **(in** en); **to place** *or* **put one's c. in sb/sth** placer *ou* mettre sa confiance en qn/qch, faire confiance à qn/qch; **have a bit more c.!** (*in me*) fais-moi un peu plus confiance; **to win sb's c.** gagner la confiance de qn; **to have every c. in sb** faire entièrement confiance à qn, avoir toute confiance en qn; **I have every c. that …** je ne doute pas un instant que …; **she has no c. in her own ability** elle n'a aucune confiance en elle; **with complete c.** en toute confiance; **vote of c.** vote *m* de confiance; *Pol* **motion of no c.** motion *f* de censure; **c. trick** escroquerie *f*, abus *m* de confiance; **c. trickster** escroc *m*

(b) (*certainty*) **because of their c. that it would work** parce qu'ils étaient sûrs que ça marcherait

(c) (*self-assurance*) assurance *f*, confiance *f* en soi; **full of c.** (*person*) plein d'assurance *ou* de confiance en soi; (*performance*) plein d'assurance; (*letter, article*) qui dénote une grande assurance; **with c.** (*to act etc*) avec assurance

(d) in c. confidentiellement, en confidence; **remarks made in c.** des remarques formulées confidentiellement; **to take sb into one's c.** se confier à qn; **to be in sb's c.** partager les secrets de qn

(e) (*secret*) confidence *f*; **to exchange confidences** échanger des confidences

confident ['kɒnfɪdənt] *adj* sûr **(of** de); (*self-assured*) sûr de soi, assuré; (*remark, performance*) plein d'assurance; **are you feeling c.?** tu te sens sûr de toi?; **we are c. that it will work** nous sommes sûrs *ou* persuadés que ça marchera; **I'm c. about this translation** je suis sûr que cette traduction est bonne; **c. of success** sûr de réussir; **be c.!** aie confiance en toi!; **c. hope** ferme espoir *m*

confidential [kɒnfɪ'denʃəl] *adj* **(a)** (*information, report, tone etc*) confidentiel; **keep it c.** n'en parlez à personne **(b)** (*attached to one person*) (*position*) de confiance; (*secretary*) particulier; **c. agent** homme *m* de confiance

confidentiality [kɒnfɪdenʃɪ'ælɪtɪ] *n* (*of information, report*) caractère *m* confidentiel, confidentialité *f*

confidentially [kɒnfɪ'denʃəlɪ] *adv* (*to tell sb sth*) confidentiellement, en confidence; **c., I don't trust him** entre nous, je ne lui fais pas confiance

confidently ['kɒnfɪdəntlɪ] *adv* (*with trust*) avec confiance, en toute confiance; (*with self-assurance*) avec assurance

confiding [kən'faɪdɪŋ] *adj* confiant

config. sys (file) [kɒnfɪg'sɪs] *n Comptr* fichier *m* config. sys

configurable [kən'fɪgjʊrəb(ə)l] *adj Comptr* configurable, paramétrable

configuration [kənfɪgjʊ'reɪʃən] *n* (*shape*) configuration *f*; *Comptr* configuration, paramétrage *m*

configure [kən'fɪgər] *vt Comptr* configurer, paramétrer

confine [kən'faɪn] *vt* **(a)** (*in prison etc*) enfermer; **to be confined to one's room** (être obligé de) garder la chambre; **confined to bed** alité; *Mil* **confined to barracks** consigné; **confined space** espace restreint **(b)** (*limit*) **to c. oneself to sth/to doing sth** se borner *ou* se limiter *ou* s'en tenir à qch/à faire qch; **let us c. ourselves to the question of …** tenons-nous en à la question de …; **c. your answer to the matter in hand** limitez votre réponse au sujet qui nous occupe **(c)** *Old-fashioned Obst* **to be confined** accoucher

confinement [kən'faɪnmənt] *n* **(a)** (*in prison*) emprisonnement *m* **(b)** (*limitation*) limitation *f*, restriction *f* **(to** à) **(c)** *Old-fashioned Obst* couches *fpl*, accouchement *m*

confines ['kɒnfaɪnz] *npl Lit* (*of a place etc*) confins *mpl*; **within the c. of this subject** dans les limites de ce sujet; **within/beyond the c. of human knowledge** dans/au delà des limites de la connaissance humaine

confirm [kən'fɜːm] **1** *vt* **(a)** (*corroborate*) (*news, suspicions*) confirmer, corroborer; (*reservation*) confirmer; *Av* **flight confirmed** vol confirmé; **to be confirmed** (*notice*) (*concert, film etc*) à confirmer; **to c. that …** confirmer que … + *ind*

(b) (*reinforce*) (*power*) raffermir, consolider; (*person's reputation, position*) consolider; **to c. sth as sth** confirmer qch comme étant qch; **to c. sb's fears** confirmer les craintes de qn

(c) (*approve, validate*) (*treaty, result*) confirmer; (*nomination*) approuver; (*decision*) entériner; (*election*) valider

(d) *Rel* confirmer, donner la confirmation à; **to be confirmed** recevoir la confirmation

2 *vi* confirmer; **please c. in writing** veuillez confirmer par écrit

confirmation [kɒnfə'meɪʃən] *n* **(a)** (*of news, doubts, reservation etc*) confirmation *f*; **there has been no c. of the rumour** la rumeur n'a pas été confirmée; **in c. of** en confirmation de; *Com* **c. of receipt** accusé *m* de réception **(b)** (*reinforcement*) (*of person's authority*) raffermissement *m*, consolidation *f* **(c)** (*validation*) (*of treaty, result*) confirmation *f*; (*of nomination*) approbation *f*; (*of decision*) entérinement *m*; (*of election*) validation *f*; **in c. of …** (*booking*) pour confirmer …; **she wrote in c. of her acceptance** elle a écrit pour confirmer qu'elle acceptait **(d)** *Rel* confirmation *f*

confirmed [kən'fɜːmd] *adj* **(a)** (*habit, liar, womanizer etc*) invétéré; (*drunkard*) incorrigible, invétéré; **c. bachelor** célibataire *m* endurci **(b) c. seat** place *f* confirmée **(c)** *Fin* **c. credit** crédit *m* confirmé; **c. irrevocable letter of credit** lettre *f* de crédit irrévocable confirmé

confirming bank *n* banque *f* confirmatrice

confirming house *n Banking* organisme *m* confirmateur

confiscate ['kɒnfɪskeɪt] *vt* confisquer **(from sb** à qn)

confiscation [kɒnfɪs'keɪʃən] *n* confiscation *f*

confiscatory [kɒnfɪs'keɪtərɪ] *adj* (*power*) de confiscation

conflagration [kɒnflə'greɪʃən] *n Fml* (*fire*), *Fig* conflagration *f*

conflate [kən'fleɪt] *vt* (*issues, reports*) amalgamer

conflation [kən'fleɪʃən] *n* fusion *f*

conflict[1] ['kɒnflɪkt] *n* (*between people, of feelings etc*) conflit *m*; **c. of interests** conflit d'intérêts; **a c. of interest situation** une situation présentant un conflit d'intérêts; **to come into/to be in c.** entrer/être en conflit **(with** avec); **this was in c. with her principles** c'était en conflit *ou* en contradiction avec ses principes

conflict[2] [kən'flɪkt] *vi* être en conflit *ou* en désaccord **(with sth** avec qch); **this conflicts with his earlier statement** ceci est en contradiction avec sa déclaration précédente; **duties that c. with each other** charges incompatibles; **it conflicts with another appointment** j'ai/elle a/*etc* un autre rendez-vous à cette heure

conflicting [kən'flɪktɪŋ] *adj* (*opinions*) opposé; (*advice, evidence*) contradictoire; **c. interests** des intérêts *mpl* qui s'opposent

confluence ['kɒnflʊəns] *n Geog* (*place*) confluent *m*; (*action*) (*of two rivers, glaciers*) confluence *f*

conform [kən'fɔːm] **1** *vi* se conformer **(to** *or* **with sth** à qch); **to c. to a standard** (*of equipment*) être conforme à *ou* répondre à une norme; **to c. to the law** obéir aux lois; **to c. (in shape) to another part** être identique à une autre pièce; **this conforms with what we were told/we expected** ceci est conforme à ce que l'on nous avait dit/nos attentes; **to c. to fashion** suivre la mode **2** *vt* conformer **(sth to sth** qch à qch)

conformism [kən'fɔːmɪz(ə)m] *n* conformisme *m*

conformist [kən'fɔːmɪst] *adj, n* conformiste *mf*

conformity [kən'fɔːmɪtɪ] *n* conformité *f* **(to, with** à); **in c. with …** conformément à …; **their action was in c. with the law** ce qu'ils ont fait était en conformité avec la loi

confound [kən'faʊnd] *vt* **(a)** (*confuse, surprise*) confondre; **they were confounded by this news** cette nouvelle les a consternés; **he confounded his critics** il a fait mentir les gens qui le critiquaient **(b)** (*bring to nothing*) (*sb's plans etc*) renverser; (*hopes*) réduire à néant **(c)** *Lit* (*put in confusion*) mettre la confusion dans; **to c. sth with sth** confondre qch avec qch **(d)** *Old-fashioned F* (*curse*) **c. him!** la peste soit de lui!; **c. it!** la barbe!

confounded [kən'faʊndɪd] *adj Old-fashioned F* sacré; **you c. idiot!** espèce d'idiot!

confraternity [kɒnfrə'tɜːnɪtɪ] *n* association *f*

confront [kən'frʌnt] *vt* (*enemy, danger, problem, situation*) affronter, faire face à; **to c. the issue** faire face au problème; **to c. sb with** (*witness etc*) confronter qn avec; (*sth*) mettre qn en face de; **she confronted him with his responsibilities** elle l'a mis face à ses responsabilités; **a difficult situation confronts them** ils doivent faire face à une situation difficile; **to be confronted by** (*sb, sth*) être en face de, se trouver en présence de; **to be confronted by** *or* **with a difficulty** se trouver face à une difficulté

confrontation [kɒnfrʌn'teɪʃən] *n* **(a)** (*of two people, armies etc*) affrontement *m* **(with** avec) **(b)** (*bringing into contact*) (*of witnesses etc*) confrontation *f*

confrontational [kɒnfrʌn'teɪʃən(ə)l] *adj* (*situation*) d'affrontement; (*policy*) de confrontation; (*management style*) agressif; **he's quite c.** il aime la confrontation

Confucian [kən'fjuːʃən] *adj Phil* confucéen, confucianiste

confuse [kən'fjuːz] *vt* **(a)** (*bewilder*) (*person*) embrouiller; (*animal*) troubler; **to get confused** s'embrouiller, s'y perdre **(b)** (*put into disorder*) **to c. the issue, to c. things** *or* **matters** compliquer les choses **(c)** (*mix up*) (*dates, names etc*) confondre; **he always confuses the two** il confond toujours les deux; **to c. sth/sb with** *or* **and sth/sb** confondre qch/qn avec qch/qn

confused [kən'fjuːzd] *adj* **(a)** (*person*) (*because not understanding sth*) embrouillé; (*not knowing what to do*) perdu; (*after blow on head, anaesthetic etc*) sonné, groggy;

(*mind*) troublé; **to get c.** (*of person*) s'embrouiller; **I'm c.** (*don't understand*) je suis perdu, je n'y comprends rien; **I'm still a little c. as to why he did it** je ne comprends toujours pas très bien pourquoi il a fait cela; **the old lady's a bit c.** (*mentally*) la vieille dame ne sait plus trop où elle en est *ou* est un peu perdue **(b)** (*disordered*) (*mass, speech, logic, reasoning*) confus

confusedly [kən'fju:zɪdlɪ] *adv* confusément

confusing [kən'fju:zɪŋ] *adj* (*unclear, causing lack of understanding*) embrouillé, confus; **it's very c.** on s'y perd; **it's too c. for the user** l'utilisateur s'y perdra; **I hope my explanation wasn't too c.** j'espère que mon explication ne vous a pas trop embrouillé; **there's a c. number of different makes** il y a tant de marques différentes qu'on s'y perd

confusingly [kən'fju:zɪŋlɪ] *adv* (*unclearly, causing lack of understanding*) de manière embrouillée, confusément; **c., they both had the same name** ils avaient le même nom, ce qui provoquait souvent des confusions

confusion [kən'fju:ʒən] *n* **(a)** (*bewilderment*) confusion *f*; *Med* confusion *f* mentale; **in his c. he forgot his hat** dans sa confusion il a oublié son chapeau; **to add to the c. …** pour ajouter à la confusion …; **this news added to her c.** cette nouvelle a ajouté à sa confusion; **there's still some c. about the exact number killed** on ne connaît toujours pas le nombre de victimes; **it will only lead to c.** ce ne va faire qu'embrouiller les choses
(b) (*disorder*) confusion *f*, désordre *m*; **everything was in c.** tout était en désordre, tout était pêle-mêle; **to spread c. everywhere** jeter partout le désordre *ou* la confusion
(c) (*mixing up*) **c. of sth with** *or* **and sth** confusion *f* de qch avec qch
(d) (*embarrassment*) confusion *f*; **to be covered in c.** être rempli de confusion

confute [kən'fju:t] *vt Fml* (*disprove*) (*argument, person*) réfuter

conga[1] ['kɒŋgə] *n* conga *f*

conga[2] *vi* danser la conga

congeal [kən'dʒi:l] **1** *vi* (*of fat, oil*) se figer; (*of blood*) se coaguler, se figer **2** *vt* (*blood*) faire coaguler; (*oil*) faire figer

congenial [kən'dʒi:nɪəl] *adj* (*person, character*) sympathique, aimable; (*work*) agréable (**to** à); **I find his company c.** je le trouve d'une compagnie agréable; **an evening spent in c. company** une soirée passée en compagnie de gens sympathiques

congenital [kən'dʒenɪt(ə)l] *adj* (*defect, idiot etc*) congénital

congenitally [kən'dʒenɪtlɪ] *adv* congénitalement; **to be c. insane** souffrir de folie congénitale

conger ['kɒŋgər] *n* **c. (eel)** congre *m*

congest [kən'dʒest] *vt* **(a)** (*traffic, roads etc*) encombrer, embouteiller **(b)** *Med* (*with blood, mucus*) congestionner

congested [kən'dʒestɪd] *adj* **(a)** (*street, road, airport etc*) encombré; (*room*) (*with furniture*) encombré; (*with people*) plein; **the c. state of the roads** l'encombrement *m* des routes; **the traffic gets c. at …** il y a des encombrements à … **(b)** *Med* (*lungs*) congestionné; **I'm feeling really congested** j'ai les bronches très prises

congestion [kən'dʒestʃən] *n* **(a)** (*of traffic etc*) encombrements *mpl*; (*actual instance*) embouteillage *m*; **the new road will relieve the c. in the town** la nouvelle route va décongestionner la ville **(b)** *Med* congestion *f*

conglomerate[1] [kən'glɒmərət] *n Econ* conglomérat *m*; *Geol* conglomérat, aggloméré *m*

conglomerate[2] [kən'glɒməreɪt] *vi Geol, Ind* s'agglomérer

conglomeration [kənglɒmə'reɪʃən] *n* conglomération *f*; (*of rocks etc*) agrégat *m*; *Fig* **a c. of ideas** un mélange d'idées

Congo ['kɒŋgəʊ] *n* **the (River) C.** le Congo; **the C.** (*state*) le Congo

congrats [kən'græts] *npl Br F* = **congratulations**

congratulate [kən'grætjʊleɪt] *vt* (*person*) féliciter (**on** de); **I c. you** je vous félicite, (je vous fais) mes compliments; **to c. oneself on sth/on having done sth** se féliciter de qch/ d'avoir fait qch; **they are to be congratulated** ils méritent d'être félicités

congratulations [kəngrætjʊ'leɪʃənz] *npl* félicitations *fpl*; **give her my c.** transmets-lui mes félicitations, félicite-la de ma part; **c.!** félicitations!; **c. on passing your exams** félicitations pour tes examens; **warmest c. on your promotion!** (*on card*) toutes nos félicitations pour votre promotion; **c. are in order, I hear** au fait, félicitations!

congratulatory [kən'grætjʊleɪtərɪ] *adj* (*letter etc*) de félicitation(s)

congregate ['kɒŋgrɪgeɪt] *vi* se rassembler, s'assembler

congregation [kɒŋgrɪ'geɪʃən] *n* **(a)** (*in church*) assemblée *f* des fidèles, assistance *f*; **I'm not a member of your c.** je ne fais pas partie de votre paroisse, je ne viens pas à l'église ici **(b)** (*group, action of grouping*) rassemblement *m* **(c)** *Univ* (*at Oxford, Cambridge*) (*of Professors etc*) assemblée *f* générale

congregational [kɒŋgrɪ'geɪʃən(ə)l] *adj Rel* en assemblée; **c. worship** culte *m* public; **the C. Church** l'Église *f* congrégationaliste

Congress ['kɒŋgres] *n US Pol* Congrès *m*

congress ['kɒŋgres] *n* **(a)** (*conference*) congrès *m* **(b)** *Fml* (*sexual*) rapports *mpl* sexuels

Congressional [kən'greʃən(ə)l] *adj US Pol* (*committee, election*) du Congrès

Congressman, -woman, *pl* **-men, -women** ['kɒŋgresmən, -wʊmən, -mən, -wɪmɪn] *n US Pol* membre *m* du Congrès

congruence ['kɒŋgrʊəns] *n* **(a)** *Fml* adéquation *f* (**with** avec) **(b)** *Geom* congruence *f* (**with** à)

congruent ['kɒŋgrʊənt] *adj* **(a)** *Fml* conforme (**with** à) **(b)** *Geom* (*triangle*) congruent

congruity [kɒŋ'gru:ɪtɪ] *n Fml* = **congruence (a)**

congruous ['kɒŋgrʊəs] *adj Fml* = **congruent (a)**

conic ['kɒnɪk] *adj Geom* conique

conical ['kɒnɪk(ə)l] *adj* conique; **a c. paper hat** un chapeau pointu en papier; **c. projection** (*in mapmaking*) projection *f* conique

conifer ['kɒnɪfər] *n* conifère *m*

coniferous [kə'nɪfərəs] *adj* conifère; (*forest*) de conifères

conjectural [kən'dʒektʃər(ə)l] *adj* conjectural

conjecture[1] [kən'dʒektʃər] *n* conjecture *f*; **to hazard a c.** risquer une hypothèse *ou* une supposition; **it's a matter of c.** cela relève de l'hypothèse *ou* de la conjecture; **it's sheer c.** ce ne sont que des suppositions

conjecture[2] *vti* faire des conjectures, supposer

conjoin [kən'dʒɔɪn] *vt Fml* unir, réunir

conjoint [kɒn'dʒɔɪnt] *adj Fml* conjoint, associé

conjointly [kɒn'dʒɔɪntlɪ] *adv Fml* conjointement, ensemble

conjugal ['kɒndʒʊg(ə)l] *adj* conjugal

conjugate ['kɒndʒʊgeɪt] **1** *vt Gram* (*verb*) conjuguer **2** *vi Gram, Biol* se conjuguer

conjugation [kɒndʒʊ'geɪʃən] *n* [①**B22-23**] *Gram, Biol* conjugaison *f*

conjunction [kən'dʒʌŋkʃən] *n* **(a)** conjonction *f*; **in c. with sb** conjointement avec qn; **these factors, in c. with others, were responsible for …** ces facteurs combinés à d'autres furent responsables de …; *Astron* **planets in c.** planètes en conjonction; **c. tickets** billets *mpl* complémentaires **(b)** [①**A68–70; B55**] *Gram* conjonction *f*

conjunctive [kən'dʒʌŋktɪv] *adj* (*tissue etc*) conjonctif

conjunctivitis [kəndʒʌŋktɪ'vaɪtɪs] *n Med* conjonctivite *f*; **to have c.** avoir de la conjonctivite

conjure ['kʌndʒər] **1** *vi* faire des tours de passe-passe *ou* de prestidigitation; *Fig* **a name to c. with** un nom qui fait rêver **2** *vt* **(a)** (*produce*) **they conjured a bottle of wine out of nowhere** *or* **thin air** ils ont fait apparaître une bouteille de vin comme par enchantement **(b)** [kən'dʒʊər] *Fml* (*entreat*) conjurer (**sb to do sth** qn de faire qch)

▶ **conjure up** *vtsep* **(a)** (*call to mind*) (*images, memories*) évoquer **(b)** (*call up*) (*spirit etc*) faire apparaître **(c)** (*produce*) **they conjured up some armchairs** ils ont déniché des fauteuils d'on ne sait où; **she conjured up an incredible meal out of almost nothing** elle a réussi à préparer un repas fantastique avec presque rien; **I'll c. something up** (*to eat*) je vais me débrouiller pour préparer quelque chose avec ce que j'ai; **I can't just c. extra staff up out of thin air!** je ne peux pas sortir du personnel supplémentaire de mon chapeau!

conjurer, conjuror ['kʌndʒərər] *n* prestidigitateur *m*, illusionniste *mf*

conjuring ['kʌndʒərɪŋ] *n* prestidigitation *f*; **c. trick** tour *m* de passe-passe *ou* de prestidigitation

conk[1] [kɒŋk] *n Br Sl* (*nose*) blair *m*, pif *m*

conk[2] *vt Sl* (*hit*) foutre un gnon à

▶ **conk out** *vi F* **(a)** (*of machine, television etc*) tomber en panne **(b)** (*lose consciousness*) tomber dans les pommes **(c)** (*go to sleep*) s'endormir, s'écrouler **(d)** *US* (*die*) clamser, clamecer

conker ['kɒŋkər] *n Br F* marron *m* (d'Inde); **conkers** = jeu *m* de marrons qui se joue à deux et consistant à détruire le marron de l'adversaire

Conn *abbr* **Connecticut**

connect[1] [kə'nekt] **1** *vt* **(a)** (*join*) (*sth*) relier, rattacher (**to** à); *MecE etc* (*two shafts*) embrayer; (*pipes*) joindre; *El* (*circuits*) interconnecter; (*wires*) connecter; **a road connects the two cities, the two cities are connected by a road** une route relie les deux villes, les deux villes sont reliées par une route; **a corridor connects the room to the library** il y a un couloir qui relie la pièce à la bibliothèque; **we were connected with the studio by radio** nous étions en liaison radio avec le studio; **the telephone/electricity hasn't been connected** le téléphone/l'électricité n'a pas été branché(e); **c. this wire to the other terminal** connectez ce fil à l'autre borne

(b) *Tel* mettre en ligne *ou* en communication (**with** avec); **will you c. me with reservations, please?** est-ce que vous pouvez me passer votre service des réservations?; **to c. two subscribers** mettre deux abonnés en communication

(c) (*link, associate*) associer (**sb/sth with sb/sth** qn/qch avec qn/à qch); **there is nothing to c. the two crimes** il n'y a aucun lien entre les deux crimes; **at first I didn't c. the name with the face** au début je n'ai pas fait le lien *ou* le rapprochement entre le nom et le visage; **to be connected with …** (*of person*) avoir des relations *ou* un lien avec …; (*of thing*) se rattacher *ou* se rapporter à …; **the questions were connected with another subject** les questions étaient relatives *ou* se rapportaient à un autre sujet; **to be connected with** *or* **to a family** (*be related to*) avoir un lien de parenté avec une famille

2 *vi* (a) (*of wires*) être reliés (**with** à); (*of roads*) se rejoindre; (*of rooms*) communiquer (**with** avec); **this road connects with the motorway** cette route rejoint l'autoroute; **the tunnels don't c.** les deux tunnels ne sont pas reliés *ou* ne communiquent pas

(b) **to c. with a train/a flight** (*of train, plane*) assurer la correspondance avec un train/un vol; (*of person*) prendre la correspondance

(c) *F* (*of blow*) atteindre son but; (*of boxer*) frapper *ou* atteindre son adversaire; (*of tennis player, cricketer, racket, bat*) frapper la balle

connect² *n Comptr* connexion *f*; **c. time** durée *f* (d'établissement) de la connexion

▶ **connect up** *vtsep* (*pipes*) raccorder; (*wires*) connecter

connected [kə'nektɪd] *adj* (*linked*) (*facts, events etc*) connexe, lié; **to be well c.** (*of person*) avoir des relations

connecting [kə'nektɪŋ] *adj* (*cable, wire*) de connexion; **c. door** porte *f* de communication; **c. flight/train** correspondance *f*; **c. piece** pièce *f* de raccordement; **c. pipe** tuyau *m* de raccordement *ou* de jonction; *Aut* **c. rod** bielle *f*, biellette *f*; **c. rooms** (*in hotel*) pièces *fpl* communicantes; **c. time** (*for travel*) temps *m* de correspondance

connection [kə'nekʃən] *n* (a) (*link, association*) rapport *m*, lien *m* (**between** entre, **with** avec); **I didn't make the c.** je n'ai pas fait le rapprochement; **in c. with …** à propos de …; **in this c.** à ce propos, à cet égard

(b) (*personal relationship*) relations *fpl*, rapports *mpl*; **I have broken off all c. with him** j'ai cessé toutes relations avec lui; **to establish a business c. with a firm** établir des relations commerciales avec une entreprise

(c) (*acquaintance*) relation *f*; **she has important connections** elle a des relations en haut lieu; **I have some useful connections within the police** j'ai des relations très utiles dans la police

(d) (*family relationship*) parenté *f*; **to form a c. by marriage with a good family** s'allier à *ou* avec une bonne famille; **there's no c. with the Yorkshire Smythes** il n'y a pas de lien de parenté avec les Smythe du Yorkshire; **my family has Scottish connections** il y a des Écossais dans ma famille

(e) *MecE etc* connexion *f*; (*of pipes, wires etc*) assemblage *m*, raccordement *m*; (*of machine parts*) accouplement *m*, engrenage *m*; *El* raccordement, connexion, branchement *m*; *Comptr* connexion, liaison *f*; *Tel* communication *f*; *El* **the c. is loose** il y a un faux contact; *Tel* **we had a very bad c.** la communication était très mauvaise

(f) *El* (*connecting device*) **earth** *or* *US* **ground c.** prise *f* de terre

(g) (*in journey*) (*train, plane, boat etc*) correspondance *f*; **I missed my c.** j'ai manqué *ou* raté ma correspondance

connective [kə'nektɪv] **1** *adj Biol* **c. tissue** tissu *m* conjonctif **2** *n Gram* conjonction *f* de coordination

connectivity [kɒnek'tɪvɪtɪ] *n Comptr* connectivité *f*

connector [kə'nektər] *n El* connecteur *m*; *MecE etc* raccord *m*; **c. kit** kit *m* de connexion

connexion [kə'nekʃən] *n* = **connection**

conning tower ['kɒnɪŋ] *n* (*of submarine*) kiosque *m*

conniptions [kə'nɪpʃənz] *n Am F* **to have c.** piquer une crise (**about sth** à propos de qch)

connivance [kə'naɪvəns] *n* connivence *f*; **c. at** *or* **in a crime** complicité *f* dans un crime; **to be in c. with sb** être de connivence avec qn

connive [kə'naɪv] *vi* (*scheme, plot*) être de connivence (**with** avec, **to do** pour faire); **to c. at** (*abuse, irregularity etc*) se rendre complice de

conniving [kə'naɪvɪŋ] *adj attrib* malhonnête; **you c. bastard!** espèce de pourri!

connoisseur [kɒnə'sɜːr] *n* connaisseur, -euse (**of** en); **to be a c. of sth** s'y connaître en qch, être un connaisseur en matière de qch

connotation [kɒnə'teɪʃən] *n* (*of term*) connotation *f*

connote [kɒ'nəʊt] *vt Fml* (*of word*) (*notion, idea*) suggérer, comporter; **the word connotes courage** le mot suggère une idée de courage

connubial [kə'njuːbɪəl] *adj Fml* conjugal

conquer ['kɒŋkər] *vt* (*country, world, sb's heart*) conquérir; (*difficulty, one's shyness, fears*) vaincre, surmonter; (*inflation, illness*) vaincre; **Everest was conquered in 1953** l'Everest été conquis en 1953

conquering ['kɒŋkərɪŋ] *adj* (*army, hero*) conquérant, victorieux

conqueror ['kɒŋkərər] *n* (a) (*of country*) conquérant *m*; *Hist* (**William**) **the C.** Guillaume le Conquérant (b) (*victor*) vainqueur *m*

conquest ['kɒŋkwest] *n* (*victory, prize*), *Fig* conquête *f*; *Hist* **the (Norman) C.** la conquête de l'Angleterre; *Fig* **his many conquests** ses nombreuses conquêtes; *Fig* **to make a c. of sb** faire la conquête de qn

conrod ['kɒnrɒd] *n Aut* bielle *f*

Cons *Pol abbr* **Conservative**

consanguinity [kɒnsæŋ'gwɪnɪtɪ] *n Fml* consanguinité *f*

conscience ['kɒnʃəns] *n* conscience *f*; **to have a clear** *or* **an easy c.** avoir la conscience tranquille; **to have a guilty** *or* **bad c.** avoir mauvaise conscience; **to have sth on one's c.** avoir qch sur la conscience; **it's on my c.** (*what I did*) je l'ai sur la conscience; **it's on my c. that I left him alone** je l'ai laissé tout seul et j'ai mauvaise conscience; **I can't sleep with that on my c.** je ne peux pas dormir avec ça sur la conscience; **he had no c. about abandoning them to their fate** il n'avait aucun scrupule à les abandonner à leur sort; **a matter of c.** une affaire de conscience; **freedom of c.** liberté *f* de conscience; **one cannot in all c. believe that …** on ne peut pas raisonnablement croire que …; **c. clause** clause *f* de conscience; **c. money** somme *f* restituée par remords de conscience

conscience-stricken *adj* pris de remords

conscientious [kɒnʃɪ'enʃəs] *adj* (*worker, work*) consciencieux; **to be c. about timekeeping** être très ponctuel

conscientiously [kɒnʃɪ'enʃəslɪ] *adv* (*to work*) consciencieusement

conscientiousness [kɒnʃɪ'enʃəsnɪs] *n* minutie *f*, conscience *f*

conscientious objection *n* objection *f* de conscience

conscientious objector *n* objecteur *m* de conscience

conscious ['kɒnʃəs] **1** *adj* (a) *Med* **to be c.** être conscient; **to become c.** reprendre connaissance; **he's not c. yet** il n'a pas encore repris connaissance; *Hum* (*he's still in bed*) il n'a pas encore fait surface

(b) (*aware*) conscient; **to be c. of sth** avoir conscience de qch, être conscient de qch; **to become c. of sth** s'apercevoir de qch; **I wasn't c. of having annoyed you** je ne m'étais pas rendu compte que je t'avais énervé; **to be c. that …** être conscient du fait que …

(c) (*intentional*) conscient; **it was not a c. decision** ce n'était pas une décision prise de façon consciente; **it required a c. effort to …** il fallait se forcer pour …

(d) *Phil, Psy* conscient; **the c. mind** la conscience; **to have a c. dislike of sb** éprouver une aversion consciente pour qn

2 *n Phil, Psy* **the c.** le conscient

-conscious *suff* **fashion-c.** qui suit de près la mode; **clothes-c.** qui s'habille avec soin; **health-c.** qui se préoccupe de sa santé; **safety-c.** soucieux de sécurité

consciously ['kɒnʃəslɪ] *adv* consciemment; (*deliberately*) sciemment

consciousness ['kɒnʃəsnɪs] *n* (a) *Med* conscience *f*, connaissance *f*; **to lose c.** perdre connaissance *ou* conscience; **to regain c.** reprendre connaissance, revenir à soi (b) (*awareness*) conscience *f* (**of** de); **the organization aims to raise people's c. of these problems** l'organisme a pour objet de sensibiliser les gens à ces problèmes; **c. raising** sensibilisation *f* (c) *Phil, Psy* conscience *f*

conscript¹ ['kɒnskrɪpt] *n Mil* conscrit *m*; **c. army** armée *f* de conscrits

conscript² [kən'skrɪpt] *vt Mil* enrôler, appeler (sous les drapeaux); **to be conscripted** être appelé (sous les drapeaux); *Fig* **I've been conscripted to do the dishes** on m'a enrôlé pour faire la vaisselle

conscription [kən'skrɪpʃən] *n Mil* conscription *f*

consecrate ['kɒnsɪkreɪt] *vt* (a) *Rel* (*church, communion bread*) consacrer; (*king, bishop*) sacrer (b) (*dedicate*) consacrer; **to c. one's life to sth** consacrer sa vie à qch, se vouer à qch; **the day was consecrated to the memory of the country's dead** la journée a été dédiée à la mémoire des morts du pays

consecrated ['kɒnsɪkreɪtɪd] *adj Rel* (*church, bread*) consacré; **in c. ground** en terre sainte *ou* bénite

consecration [kɒnsɪ'kreɪʃən] *n* (a) (*of church, communion bread*) consécration *f*; (*of king, bishop*) sacre *m* (b) (*dedication*) **the c. of her life to helping the poor** le fait de consacrer sa vie à aider les pauvres

consecutive [kən'sekjʊtɪv] *adj* consécutif; **on three c. days** trois jours de suite, trois jours consécutifs

consecutively [kən'sekjʊtɪvlɪ] *adv* **two days c.** deux jours de suite, deux jours consécutifs; **to deal with problems c.** traiter les problèmes l'un après l'autre

consensual [kən'sensjʊel] *adj* consensuel

consensus [kən'sensəs] *n* (*of opinion, evidence etc*) consensus *m*; **to reach a c.** arriver à un consensus; **a c. was beginning to emerge** un consensus commençait à apparaître; **the c. was that the new road was unnecessary** l'opinion générale était que la nouvelle route n'était pas nécessaire; **what is the c. of opinion?** quelle est l'opinion générale?; **c. management** gestion *f* par consensus; **c. politics** politique *f* de consensus

consent¹ [kən'sent] *n* consentement *m*, accord *m*, assentiment *m*; **to give/withhold one's c. to sth** donner/ne pas donner son consentement à qch; **I'll never give my c.** je n'y consentirai jamais, je ne donnerai jamais mon accord; **do I have your c.?** est-ce que j'ai votre accord?; **by common c.** de l'aveu de tout le monde; **by mutual c.** de gré à gré; (*divorce*) par consentement mutuel; *Jur* **age of c.** âge *m* nubile

consent² *vi* **to c. to sth/to do sth** consentir à qch/à faire qch; **I c.** j'y consens

consenting [kən'sentɪŋ] *adj Jur* (*adult*) consentant; *Hum* **she is a c. adult, after all** elle est majeure et vaccinée après tout

consequence ['kɒnsɪkwəns] *n* **(a)** (*result*) conséquence *f*, suites *fpl*; **the c. is that ...** il en résulte *ou* il s'ensuit que ...; **in c., as a c.** par conséquent; **in c. of ...** par suite de ...; **this decision had dire consequences for the region** cette décision a eu des conséquences terribles pour la région; **unforeseen consequences** conséquences imprévues; **to take the consequences** accepter les conséquences

(b) (*importance*) importance *f*; **it is of no c.** cela n'a pas d'importance, cela ne fait rien; **it is of some c. to me** ça a de l'importance pour moi; **he is of no c.** il ne compte pas; **a woman of c.** une femme avec qui il faut compter

(c) *Br* **consequences** (*game*) (jeu *m* des) petits papiers *mpl*

consequent ['kɒnsɪkwənt] *adj* **(a)** (*resulting*) résultant; **c. upon sth** qui est la conséquence de qch, qui résulte de qch; **a glut and the c. drop in prices** un surplus et la baisse des prix qui en résulte **(b)** (*in logic*) conséquent

consequential [kɒnsɪ'kwenʃəl] *adj* (*resulting*) conséquent, consécutif (**to** à); *Jur* **c. damages** dommages *mpl* indirects; **c. effects** (*of action*) répercussions *fpl*

consequently ['kɒnsɪkwəntlɪ] *adv, conj* par conséquent, donc

conservancy [kən'sɜːvənsɪ] *n Br* (*for protection of forest, river etc*) commission *f* de conservation

conservation [kɒnsə'veɪʃən] *n* **(a)** conservation *f*; **c. of energy** économies *fpl* d'énergie **(b)** (*of environment*) protection *f* de l'environnement; **c. area** zone *f* protégée, réserve *f* naturelle; **c. expert** expert *m* de la protection de l'environnement

conservationist [kɒnsə'veɪʃənɪst] *n* partisan, -ane de la protection de l'environnement

conservatism [kən'sɜːvətɪz(ə)m] *n* conservatisme *m*

conservative [kən'sɜːvətɪv] **1** *adj* **(a)** conservateur, -trice; (*evaluation*) prudent; **at a c. estimate** au minimum, au bas mot **(b)** *Pol* conservateur, -trice; **the C. Party** le parti conservateur **2** *n Pol* conservateur, -trice; **the Conservatives** les conservateurs

conservatively [kən'sɜːvətɪvlɪ] *adv* (*to dress*) de façon classique; **it was c. estimated at £5,000** selon des estimations prudentes, cela devrait coûter 5 000 livres

conservatoire [kən'sɜːvətwɑːr] *n Mus* conservatoire *m*

conservatory [kən'sɜːvətrɪ] *n* **(a)** (*attached to house*) véranda *f* **(b)** = **conservatoire**

conserve¹ ['kɒnsɜːv] *n Culin* (*jam*) confiture *f*

conserve² [kən'sɜːv] *vt* (*ancient monument etc*) conserver, préserver; **to c. water/energy** faire des économies d'eau/d'énergie; **they had to c. their water supplies to get across the desert** il a fallu qu'ils économisent l'eau pour pouvoir traverser le désert

consider [kən'sɪdər] *vt* **(a)** (*reflect on, think over*) (*matter*) considérer; (*facts, proposal, offer*) étudier; **I'll c. it** j'y réfléchirai; **he was considering whether to go out when ...** il se demandait s'il allait sortir quand ...; **have you considered (buying) a larger model?** est-ce que vous avez envisagé d'acheter un modèle plus grand?; **the jury retired to c. its verdict** le jury se retira pour délibérer; **to c. sb for a job** envisager de donner un poste à qn

(b) (*take into account*) (*sb's feelings*) avoir égard à; (*expense*) regarder à; (*possibility*) envisager; **she never considers anybody but herself** elle ne fait jamais attention aux autres; **when you c. that ...** quand on pense *ou* songe que ...; **c. the cost!** pensez au coût!; **you ought to have considered my feelings** tu aurais dû penser à moi; **all things considered** tout bien considéré, tout compte fait

(c) (*regard*) considérer; **I c. him a friend** je le considère comme un ami; **c. it done** considérez cela comme fait; **c. yourself dismissed** tenez-vous pour congédié; **to c. oneself happy** s'estimer heureux; **I c. it my duty to ...** j'estime qu'il est de mon devoir de ...; **I would c. it an honour** ce serait pour moi un honneur; **we c. it likely that ...** nous estimons qu'il est probable que ...

considerable [kən'sɪdərəb(ə)l] *adj* **(a)** (*great*) grand; (*part, portion*) bon; (*difference*) sensible; **a c. number of ...** un nombre considérable de ...; **the new car attracted c. attention** la nouvelle voiture a fait l'objet d'une attention considérable; **she only found the house after c. difficulty** elle n'a trouvé la maison qu'avec beaucoup de difficulté **(b)** (*worthy of attention*) digne d'attention; (*person*) notable, important

considerably [kən'sɪdərəblɪ] *adv* considérablement

considerate [kən'sɪdərət] *adj* prévenant, plein d'égards (**towards, to** pour, envers); **it's very c. of you** c'est très aimable de votre part, c'est très gentil de ta part; **try to be more c.** essaie d'être un peu plus prévenant

considerately [kən'sɪdərətlɪ] *adv* avec considération, avec prévenance

consideration [kənsɪdə'reɪʃən] *n* **(a)** (*deliberation*) **under c.** (*question, candidate etc*) à l'étude; **to give c. to a question** mettre une question à l'étude; **I'll give it some c.** j'y penserai; **after due c.** après mûre réflexion; **to take sth into c.** prendre qch en considération, tenir compte de qch, prendre qch en ligne de compte; **taking all things into c.** tout bien considéré; **taking her age into c.** si l'on tient compte de son âge; **to leave sth out of c.** ne pas tenir compte de qch; *Mktg* **c. set** ensemble *m* de considérations

(b) (*factor*) facteur *m*; **there is another c.** il y a autre chose dont il faut tenir compte; **money is always the first c.** la question d'argent vient toujours en premier; **on no c.** à aucun prix; **money is no c.** l'argent n'entre pas en ligne de compte

(c) (*regard*) considération *f*; **to have no c. for anyone** n'avoir de considération pour personne; **show some c.!** fais preuve d'un peu de considération!; **out of c. for sb** par égard pour qn; **to treat sb with c.** traiter qn avec considération

(d) (*payment*) compensation *f*, rémunération *f*; *Com etc* **for a c.** moyennant paiement; **he'll do it for a c.** il le fera si vous le payez; **in c. of your services** en récompense de vos services

considered [kən'sɪdəd] *adj* **(a)** (*thought out*) **it is my c. opinion that ...** après mûre réflexion je pense que ...; **is that your c. opinion?** est-ce ainsi que vous voyez les choses? **(b)** (*thought of*) **to be highly** *or* **well c.** être très estimé

considering [kən'sɪdərɪŋ] **1** *prep* étant donné, vu; **c. his age/the circumstances** étant donné *ou* vu son âge/les circonstances **2** *conj* étant donné que, vu que; **c. (that) he is so young** étant donné *ou* vu qu'il est si jeune **3** *adv F* après tout, malgré tout; **it's not so bad, c.** ce n'est pas si mauvais après tout *ou* malgré tout

consign [kən'saɪn] *vt* **(a)** (*entrust*) confier, remettre (**sth to sb's care** qch à qn); **to c. a body to the grave** livrer un corps à la tombe **(b)** *Com* (*goods*) expédier (**to sb** à qn)

consignee [kɒnsaɪ'niː] *n* destinataire *mf*, réceptionnaire *mf*; *Com* (*of goods on consignment*) consignataire *mf*

consignment [kən'saɪnmənt] *n Com* **(a)** (*goods*) livraison *f*; (*incoming*) arrivage *m*, livraison **(b)** (*act*) (*of goods*) envoi *m*, expédition *f*; *Com* **on c.** en consignation; **to send sb goods on c.** livrer à qn une marchandise en dépôt permanent; **c. note** avis *m ou* bon *m* d'expédition; *Rail* récépissé *m*

consignor [kən'saɪnər] *n Com* expéditeur, -trice

▶ **consist in** [kən'sɪst] *vipo* consister en; **to c. in doing sth** consister à faire qch

▶ **consist of** *vipo* consister en, se composer de; **her inheritance consisted of a house** son héritage consistait en une maison

consistency [kən'sɪstənsɪ] *n* **(a)** (*of liquid etc*) consistance *f*; **to be the c. of sth** avoir la consistance de qch **(b)** (*internal logic*) cohérence *f*; (*in ideas*) logique *f*; **to lack c.** (*of statements, views etc*) manquer de suite *ou* de cohérence **(c)** (*staying the same*) (*of quality of work, ideas*) constance *f*; (*of athlete, performances*) régularité *f*; **c. check** contrôle *m* d'uniformité **(d)** (*compatibility*) (*of result with theory*) concordance *f*

consistent [kən'sɪstənt] *adj* **(a)** (*having internal logic*) (*reasoning, behaviour, person*) conséquent, cohérent, logique; **she was c. in her choice of partners** elle a toujours fait preuve de cohérence dans le choix de ses partenaires

(b) (*staying the same*) (*quality of work, ideas*) constant; (*refusal, failure*) persistant; (*athlete, performer*) régulier;

because of her c. denial of the accusation du fait qu'elle a toujours nié être coupable
(c) (*compatible*) compatible (**with** avec); **the results are c. with the theory** les résultats concordent avec la théorie; **this action is not c. with his character** cette action n'est pas en harmonie avec son caractère; **her behaviour is c. with a diagnosis of ...** son comportement est caractéristique d'un diagnostic de ...

consistently [kən'sɪstəntlɪ] *adv* (a) (*with logic*) de manière cohérente *ou* conséquente (b) (*with regularity*) (*to play, perform, work*) avec régularité; (*to fail, maintain*) constamment; **she has c. denied the accusation** elle a toujours nié cette accusation; **he has been c. better than the others** il a constamment été meilleur que les autres

consistory [kən'sɪstərɪ] *n Rel* (*pontifical*) consistoire *m*; **C. Court** tribunal *m* ecclésiastique

consolation [kɒnsə'leɪʃən] *n* consolation *f*; **words of c.** paroles *fpl* consolatrices; **that's one c.** c'est déjà une consolation; **if it's any c.** si ça peut te consoler; **it wasn't much c. to reflect that tomorrow was her birthday** c'était une piètre consolation de penser que son anniversaire était le lendemain; **c. prize** prix *m* de consolation

console[1] [kən'səʊl] *vt* consoler (**for** de); **c. yourself with the thought that it's Friday tomorrow** console-toi en pensant que demain c'est vendredi

console[2] ['kɒnsəʊl] *n* (a) (*of organ*), *El* console *f*; *Av* tableau *m* de bord; *Comptr* pupitre *m* de commande (b) *Rad, TV* (*cabinet*) meuble *m* pour radio/télévision (c) **c. table** (table *f*) console *f*

consolidate [kən'sɒlɪdeɪt] **1** *vt* (*foundations*) consolider, renforcer; *Mil* (*position*) raffermir; *Fig* (*position, lead*) conforter; *Com* grouper; *Fin* (*debt*) consolider; **to c. one's power** asseoir son pouvoir; **the company has consolidated its position as the market leader** la société a conforté sa position de leader sur le marché **2** *vi* se consolider

consolidated [kən'sɒlɪdeɪtɪd] *adj* consolidé; *Com* groupé; *Acct* **c. accounts** comptes *mpl* consolidés; *Fin* **c. debt** dette *f* consolidée; *Acct* **c. entry** écriture *f* de consolidation; **c. subsidiary** filiale *f* consolidée

consolidation [kənsɒlɪ'deɪʃən] *n* (a) (*of foundations, power etc*) consolidation *f*, renforcement *m*; (*of public opinion*) raffermissement *m* (b) *Fin* (*of national debt*) consolidation *f*; (*of shares*) regroupement *m*; *Jur* (*of laws*) unification *f* (c) *Com* (*combining bookings*) groupage *m*; **c. for export** groupement *m* à l'export

consolidator [kən'sɒlɪdeɪtər] *n Com* groupeur *m*

consoling [kən'səʊlɪŋ] *adj* consolateur, -trice

consols ['kɒnsɒlz, kən'sɒlz] *npl Br Fin* (fonds *mpl*) consolidés *mpl*

consonance ['kɒnsənəns] *n* (a) *Mus, Ling* consonance *f* (b) *Fml* (*of ideas etc*) accord *m*, conformité *f*

consonant ['kɒnsənənt] **1** *n Ling* consonne *f* **2** *adj Fml* **c. with** en accord avec, conforme à

consort ['kɒnsɔːt] *n* (*spouse*) (*of ruler etc*) époux, -ouse; **prince c.** prince *m* consort

▶ **consort with** [kən'sɔːt] *vipo* frayer avec, fréquenter

consortium [kən'sɔːtɪəm] *n Com, Fin* consortium *m*

conspicuous [kən'spɪkjʊəs] *adj* (a) (*easily visible*) bien visible, apparent, manifeste; (*monument, landmark*) bien visible; (*uniform etc*) voyant; **in a c. position** bien en évidence; **to be c. by one's absence** (*of person, quality*) briller par son absence (b) (*striking*) (*bravery, intelligence*) remarquable, frappant; **c. gallantry** acte *m* de bravoure insigne; **to make oneself c.** se faire remarquer (**by, through** par); **c. consumption** consommation *f* ostentatoire

conspicuously [kən'spɪkjʊəslɪ] *adv* (a) (*visibly*) visiblement, manifestement; **to be c. absent** briller par son absence (b) (*remarkably*) remarquablement; (*dressed*) de façon (un peu) ostentatoire

conspicuousness [kən'spɪkjʊəsnɪs] *n* (a) (*visibility*) caractère *m* bien visible; (*of uniform etc*) caractère voyant (b) (*striking nature*) (*of action*) caractère *m* insigne *ou* remarquable

conspiracy [kən'spɪrəsɪ] *n* conspiration *f*, conjuration *f*, complot *m*; *Jur* association *f* de malfaiteurs; **c. of silence** conspiration du silence; **c. to obtain documents illegally** conspiration pour obtenir des documents de façon illégale; **there's a c. against me** il y a un complot contre moi; **it's a c.** c'est un complot; **c. theorist** partisan *m* de la théorie de complot; **c. theory** explication *f* d'événements mystérieux se fondant sur une hypothèse de complot

conspirator [kən'spɪrətər] *n* conspirateur, -trice

conspiratorial [kənspɪrə'tɔːrɪəl] *adj* (*air*) de conspirateur; **she gave me a c. wink** elle m'a jeté un coup d'œil complice

conspire [kən'spaɪər] *vi* (a) (*of person*) conspirer (**against** contre, **with** avec); **to c. to do sth** comploter de faire qch (b) (*of events etc*) concourir, contribuer; **everything conspired to make him late** tout a contribué à le mettre en retard; **circumstances conspired against me** les circonstances se sont liguées contre moi

constable ['kʌnstəb(ə)l, 'kɒn-] *n Br* (*in police*) agent *m* de police; (*rural*) gendarme *m*; **good evening, c.** bonsoir, monsieur l'agent; **special c.** = supplétif *m*; **chief c.** = commissaire *m* (central) de police

constabulary [kən'stæbjʊlərɪ] *n* (*no pl*) *Br* police *f*; **the Kent C.** la Gendarmerie du Kent

constancy ['kɒnstənsɪ] *n* (*of character, temperature*) constance *f*; (*of friend*) fidélité *f*; (*of wind etc*) régularité *f*

constant ['kɒnstənt] **1** *adj* (a) (*unchanging*) (*temperature, price, pressure*) constant; (*friend*) fidèle; **to remain c.** (*of temperature, price*) rester constant (b) (*unceasing*) (*attention*) continuel; (*doubts, questions, complaining*) incessant; (*care*) continuel, assidu, soutenu; **through c. repetition** à force de répéter; **there was c. pressure for reform** il y avait une pression continuelle pour qu'une réforme soit mise en œuvre; **a c. stream of insults** un flot d'injures ininterrompu **2** *n Math, Phys* constante *f*; **time c.** constante de temps

constant-choke carburettor *n Aut* carburateur *m* à orifice constante

constantly ['kɒnstəntlɪ] *adv* constamment, continuellement

constant-velocity joint *n Aut* joint *m* de cardan, joint homocinétique

constellation [kɒnstə'leɪʃən] *n* constellation *f*

consternation [kɒnstə'neɪʃən] *n* consternation *f*; **a look of c.** un air consterné; **they looked at each other in c.** ils se regardaient atterrés; **to our c.** à notre consternation

constipate ['kɒnstɪpeɪt] *vt Med* constiper

constipated ['kɒnstɪpeɪtɪd] *adj Med, Fig* constipé; *Fig* **his rather c. prose style** son style plutôt empesé *ou* guindé

constipation [kɒnstɪ'peɪʃən] *n Med* constipation *f*

constituency [kən'stɪtjʊənsɪ] *n Pol* (a) (*voters*) électeurs *mpl* (*d'une circonscription*) (b) (*district*) circonscription *f* électorale; *Br* **the c. party** la section locale du parti

constituent [kən'stɪtjʊənt] **1** *adj* constitutif; *Pol* **c. assembly** assemblée *f* constituante **2** *n* (a) *Pol* (*of MP*) électeur, -trice (b) (*part*) élément *m* constitutif, composant *m*; *Ling* constituant *m*

constitute ['kɒnstɪtjuːt] *vt* (a) (*make up, form*) constituer; (*sb's happiness etc*) faire; **to c. a threat to ...** constituer une menace pour ...; **the countries that c. the EC** les pays qui constituent la CE; **factors that c. an offence** éléments constitutifs d'un délit; **that, to me, constitutes happiness** pour moi, c'est ça le bonheur (b) *Fml* (*appoint*) **to c. sb arbitrator** constituer qn arbitre

constitution [kɒnstɪ'tjuːʃən] *n* (a) *Pol* (*of state, organization*) constitution *f* (b) (*of person*) constitution *f*; **to have a strong/an iron c.** avoir une bonne constitution/une santé de fer (c) (*composition*) constitution *f*, composition *f*

constitutional [kɒnstɪ'tjuːʃən(ə)l] **1** *adj* (a) *Pol etc* (*monarchy, regime, reform*) constitutionnel; **the president's actions are not c.** les actions du président sont anticonstitutionnelles (b) *Med* (*disorder*) diathésique **2** *n* (*short walk*) (petite) promenade *f*

constitutionally [kɒnstɪ'tjuːʃən(ə)lɪ] *adv* (a) *Pol etc* constitutionnellement (b) (*by nature*) **c. lazy** paresseux de nature *ou* par nature

constitutive [kən'stɪtjuːtɪv] *adj* constitutif

constrain [kən'streɪn] *vt* (a) (*compel*) (*person*) contraindre, forcer (**to do** à *ou* de faire); **to find oneself constrained to do sth** se voir contraint de faire qch (b) (*restrict movement of*) (*of clothing etc*) gêner; (*of person*) contenir; **she did not feel constrained by the conventions of her time** elle ne se sentait pas obligée d'obéir aux conventions sociales de son époque

constrained [kən'streɪnd] *adj* (*air*) contraint, gêné; (*voice*) forcé; (*smile*) contraint

constraint [kən'streɪnt] *n* (a) (*compulsion, restriction*) contrainte *f*; *Jur etc* coercition *f*; **to do sth under c.** faire qch sous la contrainte (b) (*of manner*) gêne *f*, contrainte *f* (c) (*self-control*) retenue *f*; **to speak about sth without c.** parler librement de qch

constrict [kən'strɪkt] **1** *vt* (*opening*) resserrer, rétrécir; (*of clothing*) (*movements*) entraver **2** *vi* se resserrer

constricted [kən'strɪktɪd] *adj* (*opening, passage*) étroit

constriction [kən'strɪkʃən] *n* resserrement *m*, rétrécissement *m*; *Med* constriction *f*

constrictor [kən'strɪktər] *n Anat* (muscle *m*) constricteur *m*; **boa c.** boa *m* constricteur

construct[1] [kən'strʌkt] *vt* (*building, machine, novel*) construire; **well/badly constructed** (*phrase, play*) bien/mal agencé *ou* construit

construct[2] ['kɒnstrʌkt] *n Phil* (*idea*) concept *m*

construction [kən'strʌkʃən] *n* **(a)** (*of building, ship, machine etc*) construction *f*; **under c.** en (cours de) construction; **the c. industry** le bâtiment; **c. set** jeu *m* de construction; **c. site** chantier *m* (de construction); **c. workers** ouvriers *mpl* du bâtiment **(b)** (*thing constructed*) construction *f* **(c)** *Gram* construction *f* **(d)** (*interpretation*) (*of action etc*) interprétation *f*; **to put a good/bad c. on sb's words/actions** interpréter en bien/en mal les paroles/actions de qn; **to put another c. on sth** interpréter qch d'une autre façon

constructional [kən'strʌkʃən(ə)l] *adj* (*defect etc*) de construction; **c. engineering** construction *f* mécanique

constructive [kən'strʌktɪv] *adj* (*positive*) constructif; (*mind*) créateur; **c. criticism** critique *f* constructive; **c. dismissal** conduite *f* d'un employeur cherchant à provoquer la démission d'un employé

constructively [kən'strʌktɪvlɪ] *adv* (*to criticize*) d'une manière constructive

constructor [kən'strʌktər] *n* constructeur, -trice

construe [kən'stru:] *vt* (*interpret*) (*sb's words*) interpréter; **the phrase can be construed to mean two things** on peut interpréter l'expression de deux manières différentes

consul ['kɒns(ə)l] *n* (*diplomat*) consul *m*; **c. general** consul général

consular ['kɒnsjʊlər] *adj* consulaire; *Com* **c. fees** frais *mpl* consulaires; *Com* **c. invoice** facture *f* consulaire

consulate ['kɒnsjʊlət] *n* (*office*) consulat *m*; **c. general** consulat général

consult[1] [kən'sʌlt] *n F* = **consultation**

consult[2] **1** *vt* (*doctor, dictionary etc*) consulter **(on, about** sur) **2** *vi* consulter (**with sb** qn); **to c. together** se consulter

consultancy [kən'sʌltənsɪ] *n* **(a)** (*service*) conseil *m*; **to do c. work** être consultant; **c. fees** frais *mpl* de conseil; **c. (firm)** cabinet-conseil *m* **(b)** *Br Med* (*post*) **to be appointed to a c.** être nommé chef de service

consultant [kən'sʌltənt] *n* **(a)** *Com, Ind etc* consultant, -ante; **engineering c.** ingénieur *m* conseil; **beauty c.** esthéticien, -ienne; (*for face*) visagiste *mf*; **financial c.** conseiller *m* financier **(b)** *Br Med* médecin *m*/chirurgien *m* spécialiste; (*in hospital hierarchy*) chef *m* de service

consultation [kɒnsəl'teɪʃən] *n* (*of person, dictionary etc*), *Jur* consultation *f*; (*as a group*) délibération *f*; **in c. with sb** en consultation avec qn; **to hold a c.** délibérer, conférer; **can I have a c.?** (*ask your advice*) est-ce que je peux vous demander (un) conseil?

consultative [kən'sʌltətɪv] *adj* (*committee*) consultatif; **to play a c. role** avoir un rôle de consultant *ou* de conseil

consulting [kən'sʌltɪŋ] **1** *adj* (*doctor*) consultant; (*engineer*) conseil; **c. service** (service *m* de) conseil *m* **2** *n Med* **c. room** cabinet *m* de consultation

consumable [kən'sju:məb(ə)l] **1** *n* produit *m ou* article *m ou* bien *m* de consommation; *Comptr* **computer consumables** petit matériel *m* informatique **2** *adj* consommable

consume [kən'sju:m] *vt* (*food, drink, fuel etc*) consommer; (*exhaust*) épuiser; (*of fire*) (*building etc*) consumer, dévorer; **the discussion consumed many hours** la discussion a pris de nombreuses heures; **to be consumed with** (*desire*) brûler de; (*jealousy, envy, curiosity*) être en proie à

consumer [kən'sju:mər] *n* consommateur, -trice; **gas/electricity consumers** abonnés *mpl* au gaz/à l'électricité; **the c. society** la société de consommation; **c. advocate** défenseur *m* des intérêts des consommateurs; **c. credit** crédit *m* à la consommation; **c. durables** biens *mpl* de consommation durables; **c. nondurables** biens *ou* produits *mpl* de grande consommation; **c. resistance** résistance *f ou* réticence *f* des consommateurs

consumer goods *npl* biens *mpl* de consommation, produits *mpl* de grande consommation

consumerism [kən'sju:mərɪz(ə)m] *n* consumérisme *m*

consumer magazine *n* magazine *m* pour les consommateurs

consumer protection *n* défense *f* des consommateurs; **c. agency** bureau *m* d'accueil des consommateurs

consumer/user survey *n* étude *f* auprès des consommateurs finaux

consummate[1] ['kɒnsəmɪt] *adj* (*art*) consommé, achevé; (*liar*) fieffé; (*snob, hypocrite*) parfait; (*linguist, cook, musician etc*) de premier ordre; **she was c. in the art of concealing her feelings** elle était maître dans l'art de cacher ses sentiments; **to be a c. master of one's craft** connaître à fond son métier

consummate[2] ['kɒnsəmeɪt] *vt* (*marriage, relationship*) consommer

consummation [kɒnsə'meɪʃən] *n* **(a)** (*of marriage, relationship*) consommation *f* **(b)** (*of ambition, career*) aboutissement *m*

consumption [kən'sʌmpʃən] *n* **(a)** (*of goods, heat, coal, petrol etc*) consommation *f*; **unfit for human c.** impropre à la consommation; *Econ* **home c.** consommation intérieure; *Fig* **the president's remarks were strictly for domestic c.** les remarques du président ne s'adressaient qu'à son pays **(b)** *Old-fashioned Med* consomption *f*, phtisie *f*

consumptive [kən'sʌmptɪv] *adj, n Old-fashioned Med* phtisique *mf*

cont **(a)** *abbr* **contents** **(b)** (*abbr* **continued**) suite

contact[1] ['kɒntækt] *n* **(a)** (*act of touching*) contact *m*; **to come into c. with** entrer en contact avec, toucher; **the substance must not come into c. with the air** la substance ne doit pas être exposée à l'air; **point of c.** (*of two curves etc*) point *m* de contact; *Phot* **c. print** planche *f* contact; **c. sport** sport *m* de contact

(b) (*between people*) rapport *m*, contact *m*; **to be in/to come into c. with sb** être/entrer en contact *ou* en rapport avec qn; **are you still in c.?** (*of two people*) est-ce que vous êtes toujours en contact?; **the two leaders are in close c.** les deux dirigeants sont en contact étroit; **he didn't get in c. (with me/them/*etc*)** il n'est pas entré en contact (avec moi/eux/*etc*), il ne m'a/les a/*etc* pas contacté(s); **to put sb in c. with sb** mettre qn en rapport avec qn; **she hadn't come into c. with poverty** elle ne s'était pas trouvée au contact de la pauvreté; **anyone who has come into c. with the sick man** quiconque s'est trouvé au contact du malade; **to make c. with sb** (*by radio etc*) contacter qn, prendre contact avec qn; **after three days they made c. with civilization** après trois jours ils ont pris contact avec la civilisation; **to make eye c. with sb** rencontrer le regard de qn; **we made eye c.** nos regards se sont croisés; *Mil* **to establish c. with the enemy** prendre contact avec l'ennemi

(c) *Opt* verre *m ou* lentille *f* de contact; **to wear contacts** porter des lentilles de contact

(d) *Med* personne *f* ayant approché un malade contagieux; **sexual c.** partenaire *mf* sexuel(le)

(e) (*acquaintance etc*) relation *f*; **I have a c. who may be able to help you** je connais quelqu'un qui pourrait vous aider; **who's our c. in Paris?** qui est notre contact à Paris?

(f) *El etc* (*state, part*) contact *m*; **c. breaker** dispositif *m* de rupture, (inter)rupteur *m*; *Aut* **c. breaker plate** plateau *m* porte-rupteur; **c. breaker points** contacts rupteur

contact[2] *vt* se mettre en contact *ou* en rapport *ou* en relation avec, *F* contacter; **I can be contacted at this address** on peut me contacter à cette adresse

contactable [kɒn'tæktəb(ə)l] *adj* joignable

contact lens *n* verre *m ou* lentille *f* de contact; **to wear c. lenses** porter des lentilles de contact

contagion [kən'teɪdʒən] *n Lit, Fig* contagion *f*

contagious [kən'teɪdʒəs] *adj* (*disease*) contagieux; *Fig* (*laughter*) communicatif, contagieux

contagiousness [kən'teɪdʒəsnɪs] *n* contagiosité *f*; *Fig* **the c. of laughter** la contagion du rire

contain [kən'teɪn] *vt* **(a)** (*hold*) contenir **(b)** (*include*) (*of book, medicine etc*) contenir; **the ore contains a high percentage of iron** le minerai a une forte teneur en fer; **the document contains a reference to ...** le document contient une référence à ... **(c)** (*control*) (*rage, emotion, inflation*) contenir, maîtriser; *Mil* (*enemy*) contenir; (*epidemic, spread of an idea*) circonscrire; **he was unable to c. his laughter** il ne pouvait pas s'empêcher de rire; **I could no longer c. myself** je ne pouvais plus me contenir davantage

container [kən'teɪnər] *n* **(a)** récipient *m* **(b)** (*for transport*) conteneur *m*; **c. depot** entrepôt *m* de conteneurs, dépôt *m* pour conteneurs; **c. lorry** *or* **truck** camion *m* adapté au transport des conteneurs; **c. port** port *m* pour conteneurs; *Mktg* **c. premium** prime *f* contenant; **c. ship** navire *m* porte-conteneurs, porte-conteneurs *m*; **c. terminal** terminal *m* à conteneurs

containerization [kənteɪnəraɪ'zeɪʃən] *n* conteneurisation *f*; (*of port*) conversion *f* à la conteneurisation

containerize [kən'teɪnəraɪz] *vt* mettre en conteneur, conteneuriser; (*port*) convertir à la conteneurisation

containerized freight *n* fret *m* par conteneur

containment [kən'teɪnmənt] *n* **(a)** (*of disease, ideology*) action *f* de circonscrire; **a policy of c.** une politique d'endiguement **(b)** *Nucl Phys* confinement *m*

contaminate [kən'tæmɪneɪt] *vt* contaminer; **contaminated air** air *m* vicié; *Fig* **he has been contaminated by contact with political activists** il a été contaminé au contact d'activistes

contamination [kəntæmɪ'neɪʃən] *n* (*bacterial, radioactive etc*) contamination *f*

contango, *pl* **-oes** [kən'tæŋgəʊ, -əʊz] *n Br St Exch* report *m*; (*percentage*) taux *m* du report

contd (*abbr* **continued**) suite; **c. on p14** suite à la page 14; **to be c.** à suivre

contemplate ['kɒntempleɪt] **1** *vt* **(a)** (*look at*) contempler **(b)** (*think about, consider*) (*the universe, the past, one's life*) réfléchir à, méditer sur **(c)** (*envisage*) envisager; **to c. doing sth** envisager de *ou* songer à faire qch; **it's too awful to c.** c'est insupportable rien que d'y penser; **to c. suicide** songer au suicide; **that was never contemplated** il n'a jamais été question de cela **2** *vi* se recueillir, méditer

contemplation [kɒntem'pleɪʃən] *n* **(a)** (*of painting, shop window etc*) contemplation *f* **(b)** (*thinking about*) **they sat in silent c. of ...** ils méditaient en silence sur ... **(c)** (*meditation*) contemplation *f*

contemplative [kən'templətɪv] *adj Rel* (*life, order*) contemplatif

contemporaneous [kəntempə'reɪnɪəs] *adj* contemporain (**with** de)

contemporaneously [kəntempə'reɪnɪəslɪ] *adv* **c. with ...** à la même période *ou* époque que ...

contemporary [kən'temp(ə)rərɪ] **1** *adj* **(a)** (*of same time*) contemporain (**with** de) **(b)** (*present day*) contemporain, actuel, moderne; **c. events** événements *mpl* actuels **2** *n* **our contemporaries** nos contemporains *mpl*; **she and I are contemporaries** elle et moi sommes de la même génération; **a c. of mine at school** quelqu'un qui était dans la même année que moi à l'école

contempt [kən'tempt] *n* mépris *m*, dédain *m*; **to hold sb/sth in c.** mépriser qn/qch; **to treat sb/sth with c.** traiter qn/qch avec dédain *ou* mépris; **it is/he is beneath c.** c'est/il est tout ce qu'il y a de plus méprisable; **her c. for the law/our opinions** son mépris de la loi/nos opinions; **I have nothing but c. for him** je n'éprouve que du mépris pour lui; *Jur* **c. of court** outrage *m* au tribunal, offense *f* à la cour

contemptible [kən'temptəb(ə)l] *adj* méprisable

contemptibly [kən'temptɪblɪ] *adv* (*to say, to look at*) avec mépris; **a c. small amount** une quantité dérisoirement faible

contemptuous [kən'temptjʊəs] *adj* (*air, person*) méprisant; (*gesture, word*) de mépris, méprisant; **to be c. of sth** mépriser qch

contemptuously [kən'temptʊəslɪ] *adv* avec mépris, avec dédain

contend [kən'tend] **1** *vi* (*struggle*) affronter, lutter (**with, against** contre); (*argue*) se disputer (**with** avec, **about** sur); **the difficulties I have to c. with** les difficultés aux prises desquelles je suis; **they still had the perimeter fence to c. with** il leur restait encore à régler le problème de la clôture d'enceinte; **I have a lot to c. with** je dois faire face à beaucoup de problèmes; **several candidates were contending for the job** plusieurs candidats étaient en compétition pour le poste **2** *vt* (*maintain, argue*) **to c. that ...** prétendre *ou* soutenir que...

contender [kən'tendər] *n* concurrent, -ente; (*in election*) candidat, -ate; *Sp etc* (*for title*) challenger *m* (**for sth** de qch)

contending [kən'tendɪŋ] *adj* **the c. parties** les concurrents *mpl*; **the c. armies** les armées *fpl* opposées

content[1] ['kɒntent] *n* [①A10,f] **(a)** *Ch, Miner etc* teneur *f*; **gold/moisture c.** teneur en or/humidité; **high protein/fibre/fat c.** haute teneur en protéines/fibres/lipides; **peanut butter has a high protein c.** le beurre de cacahuètes est riche en protéines **(b)** (*of book, film etc*) fond *m*; **there is more emphasis on style than on c.** une plus grande importance est accordée au style qu'au fond

content[2] [kən'tent] *n* = **contentment**

content[3] *adj* content, satisfait (**with** de); **they were poor but c.** ils étaient pauvres mais heureux; **to be c. with sth** se contenter de qch; **he's quite c. to stay at home** il ne demande pas mieux que de rester à la maison; **she's never c. to just watch a film, she has to make comments** il ne lui suffit pas de regarder un film, il faut qu'elle fasse des commentaires; **not c. with having ruined our evening, he came round next day** non content d'avoir gâché notre soirée, il revint le lendemain

content[4] *vt* contenter, satisfaire; **to c. oneself with (doing) sth** se contenter de (faire) qch

contented [kən'tentɪd] *adj* content, satisfait (**with** de); (*smile*) de satisfaction; **he's a very c. baby** il est toujours content, ce bébé

contentedly [kən'tentɪdlɪ] *adv* avec contentement; **to live c.** vivre heureux

contentedness [kən'tentɪdnɪs] *n* contentement *m*

contention [kən'tenʃən] *n* **(a)** (*struggle*) lutte *f*; (*argument*) dispute *f* **(b)** (*competition*) **to be in c.** être en compétition (**for sth** pour qch); **the teams in c.** les équipes concurrentes *ou* rivales **(c)** (*opinion*) affirmation *f*; **my c. is that ...** je soutiens que ...

contentious [kən'tenʃəs] *adj* **(a)** (*issue etc*) controversé **(b)** (*person, mood*) querelleur

contentment [kən'tentmənt] *n* contentement *m*; **a smile of c.** un sourire de satisfaction

contents ['kɒntents] *npl* [①A10,f] (*of box, drawer, house etc*) contenu *m*; **(table of) c.** (*of book*) table *f* des matières; **c. list** liste *f* du contenu

contest[1] ['kɒntest] *n* **(a)** (*competition*) concours *m*; *Sp* compétition *f*; *Boxing etc* combat *m*; *Pol* **presidential c.** élection *f* présidentielle; *Fig* **there's simply no c.** il n'y a aucune comparaison; **beauty c.** concours de beauté **(b)** (*struggle*) combat *m*, lutte *f* (**with** avec, contre, **between** entre) **(c)** *US Jur* **no c.** pas de témoins à charge

contest[2] [kən'test] *vt* **(a)** (*call into question*) (*right, ability, will, inheritance*) contester; **to c. sb's right to do sth** contester à qn le droit de faire qch; *Fin* **contested debt** créance *f* litigieuse **(b)** *Pol* (*seat in Parliament*) se porter candidat pour; **to c. an election** disputer *ou* se présenter à une élection; *Sp* **to c. a race** participer à une course; *Pol* **a hotly contested seat** un siège très disputé

contestant [kən'testənt] *n* concurrent, -ente; (*in boxing, wrestling etc*) combattant *m*

contestation [kɒntes'teɪʃən] *n Fml* (*of right etc*) contestation *f*

context ['kɒntekst] *n* contexte *m*; **in this c.** (*regard*) à ce propos; **in/out of c.** en/hors contexte; **she was quoted out of c.** on a cité ses paroles hors de leur contexte; **in the c. of** dans le contexte de; **to put sth into c.** replacer qch dans son contexte

context-dependent *adj* **to be c.** dépendre du contexte

context-sensitive *adj Comptr* (*spellchecker*) contextuel

contextual [kən'tekstjʊəl] *adj* contextuel

contextualize [kən'tekstjʊəlaɪz] *vt* (*historical event, film etc*) placer dans son contexte; (*word, expression*) contextualiser, donner dans un contexte

contextually [kən'tekstjʊəlɪ] *adv* (*to examine*) dans son contexte; **to be c. dependent** dépendre du contexte

contiguous [kən'tɪgjʊəs] *adj Fml* contigu, -uë (**to** à, avec)

continence ['kɒntɪnəns] *n* **(a)** *Physiol* (*control of bladder, bowel*) continence *f* **(b)** *Fml* (*sexual*) chasteté *f*

continent[1] ['kɒntɪnənt] *n Geog* continent *m*; *Br* **the C.** l'Europe *f* continentale; *Br* **on the C.** en Europe (continentale)

continent[2] *adj* **(a)** (*in control of bladder, bowel*) continent **(b)** *Fml* (*sexually*) chaste

continental [kɒntɪ'nent(ə)l] **1** *adj* **(a)** *Geog* continental; **c. drift** dérive *f* des continents; **c. shelf** plate-forme *f* continentale **(b)** *Br* (*European*) de l'Europe continentale; **c. breakfast** = petit déjeuner *m* se composant de croissants et de pain; *Am* **C. plan** (*at hotel*) tarif *m* chambre avec petit déjeuner continental; **c. quilt** couette *f*, *Swiss* duvet *m* **2** *n Br* (*European*) continental, -ale, habitant, -ante de l'Europe (continentale)

contingency [kən'tɪndʒənsɪ] *n* **(a)** (*unexpected event*) éventualité *f*; **to provide for every c.** parer à toute éventualité; **contingencies** (*item on balance sheet*) frais divers; **prepared for all contingencies** préparé à toutes les éventualités; **to allow for contingencies** parer aux imprévus; **c. fund** caisse *f* *ou* fonds *m* de prévoyance; **c. plan** plan *m* d'urgence **(b)** *Fml* (*uncertainty*) (*of events*) contingence *f*

contingent [kən'tɪndʒənt] **1** *adj* **(a)** (*conditional*) conditionnel; **c. on sth** sous réserve de qch; **to be c. (up)on sth** (*of event*) dépendre de qch; *St Exch* **c. order** ordre *m* conditionnel **(b)** *Phil* contingent **2** *n Mil etc* contingent *m*; **a c. of holidaymakers** un contingent de vacanciers

continual [kən'tɪnjʊəl] *adj* continuel, incessant

continually [kən'tɪnjʊəlɪ] *adv* continuellement, sans cesse

continuance [kən'tɪnjʊəns] *n* **(a)** (*continuation*) continuation *f*; **the c. of these abuses is a scandal** il est scandaleux que ces abus puissent continuer **(b)** *esp US Jur* ajournement *m*

continuation [kəntɪnjʊ'eɪʃən] *n* **(a)** (*action*) (*of work, project etc*) continuation *f*; (*of road*) prolongement *m* **(b)** (*result*) (*of wall, road etc*) prolongement *m*; (*of novel*) suite *f*; **to be a c. of ...** faire suite à ... **(c)** *St Exch* report *m*

continue [kən'tɪnju:] **1** *vt* **(a)** (*work, activity etc*) continuer, poursuivre; (*straight line*) prolonger; (*journey*) poursuivre; (*conversation*) continuer; (*after interruption*) reprendre; (*species, tradition*) perpétuer; **to c. one's studies** poursuivre ses études; (*later in life*) reprendre ses études; **to c. to do sth** *or* **doing sth** continuer à *ou* de faire qch; **after lunch we continued working** après le déjeuner nous avons repris notre travail; *Journ* **to be continued** à suivre; **continued on page 30** suite à la page 30

(b) *Jur* (*trial*) ajourner

2 *vi* **(a)** continuer; (*of line*) se prolonger; **the situation cannot c.** la situation ne peut pas durer; **the situation continued into the 1960s** la situation s'est prolongée jusque dans le courant des années 1960; **to c. in office** garder sa charge; (*of political party*) rester au pouvoir; **she will c. as director until December** elle gardera les fonctions de directrice jusqu'en décembre; **his bad luck continues** ses malheurs se poursuivent; **to c. on one's way** continuer son chemin; **they continued to Rome** ils ont poursuivi leur chemin jusqu'à Rome

(**b**) (*resume talking*) continuer; **'and then', he continued** 'et puis', continua-t-il

continued [kən'tɪnju:d] *adj* (*effort, interest*) soutenu

continuing [kən'tɪnju:ɪŋ] *adj* continu; (*interest*) soutenu; **the c. story of a small American town** (*TV serial etc*) l'histoire *f* d'une petite ville américaine

continuing education *n* formation *f* permanente *ou* continue; **c. class** cours *mpl* de formation permanente *ou* continue

continuity [kɒntɪ'nju:ɪtɪ] *n* (**a**) continuité *f*; **to ensure c.** assurer la continuité (**between** entre) (**b**) *Cin, TV* continuité *f*; *TV, Rad* **c. announcement** annonce *f* de continuité; *TV, Rad* **c. announcer** speaker, -erine (de transition); **c. girl** scripte *f*, secrétaire *f* de plateau

continuous [kən'tɪnjʊəs] *adj* (**a**) continu; **c. succession** (*of visits etc*) suite *f* ininterrompue; **c. assessment** contrôle *m* continu; *Mktg* **c. innovation** innovation *f* continue; *Comptr* **c. mode** mode *m* continu; *Comptr* **c. paper** *or* **stationery** papier *m* (en) continu; *Cin* **c. performance** cinéma *m* permanent (**b**) [①A48-50; B28,F] *Gram* progressif

continuously [kən'tɪnjʊəslɪ] *adv* continuellement, continûment, sans interruption; *Aut* **c. variable transmission** transmission *f* à variateur continu *ou* à variation continue

contort [kən'tɔ:t] **1** *vt* (*features etc*) tordre; **face contorted by pain** visage tordu par la douleur **2** *vi* **his face contorted with rage/pain** il grimaçait de rage/de douleur

contortion [kən'tɔ:ʃən] *n* (*of features etc*) crispation *f*; (*of body*) contorsion *f*; *Fig* **he went through all sorts of contortions to justify this decision** il a fait des pieds et des mains pour justifier la décision

contortionist [kən'tɔ:ʃənɪst] *n* contorsionniste *mf*; **a c. act** un numéro de contorsionnisme; **you have to be a c. to get into this car!** il faut faire toute une gymnastique *ou* tout un tas de contorsions pour monter dans cette voiture

contour ['kɒntʊər] *n* (*of object*) contour *m*; (*of terrain*) profil *m*; **c. (line)** (*on map*) courbe *f* de niveau, courbe hypsométrique; **the contours of the hill** les contours de la colline; **c. map** carte *f* en courbes de niveau

Contra ['kɒntrə] *n Pol* Contra *m*

contra ['kɒntrə] **1** *prep* contre **2** *adj attrib Acct* **c. account** compte *m* de contrepartie; **c. entry** écriture *f* inverse, contre-passation *f*

contraband ['kɒntrəbænd] *n* contrebande *f*; **c. goods** marchandises *fpl* de contrebande

contrabass ['kɒntrəbeɪs] *n Mus* contrebasse *f*

contrabassoon [kɒntrəbə'su:n] *n Mus* contrebasson *m*

contraception [kɒntrə'sepʃən] *n* contraception *f*; **method of c.** méthode *f* contraceptive *ou* de contraception

contraceptive [kɒntrə'septɪv] *Med* **1** *n* contraceptif *m* **2** *adj* **c. advice** conseils *mpl* sur la contraception; **c. device** contraceptif *m*; **c. method** méthode *f* contraceptive *ou* de contraception; **c. pill** pilule *f* contraceptive; **c. sponge** éponge *f* contraceptive

contract[1] ['kɒntrækt] *n* (**a**) contrat *m*; (*of sale*) acte *m* de vente; **marriage c.** contrat de mariage; **to bind oneself by c.** s'engager par contrat; **to break one's c.** rompre son contrat; **that isn't in my c.** ce n'est pas dans mon contrat; **to be under c.** être sous contrat (**to** avec); **to enter into a c.** (*of person*) passer (un) contrat (**with** avec); **they were given a c. to build the new road** ils se sont vu attribuer le contrat pour construire la nouvelle route; **to put work out to c.** faire effectuer un travail en sous-traitance; **to tender for a c.** soumissionner à une adjudication; **conditions of c.** (*in tender*) cahier *m* des charges; **breach of c.** rupture *f* de contrat; **you are in breach of c.** vous violez *ou* vous ne respectez pas votre contrat; *St Exch* **c. note** avis *m* d'exécution, avis d'opération sur titre; **c. staff** personnel *m* en contrat à durée déterminée *ou* en CDD; (*in public sector*) contractuels *mpl*; **c. work** travail *m* en sous-traitant; *Sl* **there was a c. out on him** (*he was to be murdered*) un tueur à gages avait été engagé pour le tuer

(**b**) *Cards* **c. bridge** bridge *m* contrat

contract[2] [kən'trækt] **1** *vt* (**a**) (*obligation, illness*) contracter; (*habit*) prendre; **to c. debts** s'endetter (**b**) *Com* **to c. to do sth** s'engager (par contrat) à faire qch; **she has contracted to make two films** elle a signé un contrat pour faire deux films **2** *vi Com* **to c. for a supply of sth** s'engager à fournir qch; **to c. for work** entreprendre des travaux à forfait

contract[3] **1** *vt* (*muscles*) contracter; (*features*) crisper; *Physiol* (*tissues*) resserrer; *Ling* **to c. 'shall not' into 'shan't'** contracter 'shall not' en 'shan't' **2** *vi* (*of metal, muscle etc*) se contracter; (*of opening, material*) rétrécir; **the pupil contracts in bright light** la pupille se contracte à la lumière intense; [①A63,23] *Ling* **'cannot' contracts into 'can't'** 'cannot' se contracte en 'can't'

▶ **contract in** *vi Br* (*into insurance scheme*) souscrire; *Hist* (*of worker*) s'inscrire au syndicat

▶ **contract out 1** *vi Br* (*out of insurance policy, pension plan*) arrêter de souscrire (**of** à); (*of hospital*) se retirer du service public; *Hist* (*of union member*) cesser de payer sa cotisation au syndicat **2** *vtsep Com* (*work*) donner en sous-traitance (**to** à)

contract-awarding party ['kɒntrækəwɔ:dɪŋ] *n* adjudicateur *m*

contracting [kən'træktɪŋ] *adj* **c. parties** contractants *mpl*; **c. company** (*party to a contract*) contractant; (*sub-contractor*) sous-traitant *m*

contraction [kən'trækʃən] *n* (**a**) (*of metal, pupil etc*) contraction *f*; (*of muscle*) contraction, contracture *f*; (*of material*) rétrécissement *m*; *Physiol* (*of tissues*) resserrement *m*; *Obst* **contractions have begun** les contractions ont commencé (**b**) *Ling* (*of two words*) contraction *f*; (*word*) mot *m* contracté (**c**) *Fml* **c. of debts** endettement *m*

contract killer *n* tueur, -euse à gages

contract killing *n* **it looks like a c.** ça ressemble au travail d'un tueur à gages

contract law *n* droit *m* des contrats

contractor [kən'træktər] *n* (**a**) (*firm of builders*) entrepreneur *m* (en bâtiment); (*building worker*) ouvrier *m* en bâtiment; **the contractors haven't finished yet** les ouvriers n'ont pas encore fini (**b**) (*company, supplier*) **haulage c.** entreprise *f* de transports; **arms c.** fournisseur *m* d'armement (**c**) (*party to a contract*) entrepreneur *m*

contractual [kən'træktjʊəl] *adj* (*agreement, obligations etc*) contractuel; **on the present c. basis** selon les stipulations actuelles du contrat; *Acct* **c. allowance** indemnité *f* conventionnelle; **c. cover** (*in insurance*) garantie *f* conventionnelle; **c. date** date *f* contractuelle; **c. guarantee** garantie *f* contractuelle; **c. liability** responsabilité *f* contractuelle; **c. price** prix *m* contractuel

contractually [kən'træktjʊəlɪ] *adv* (*bound, obliged*) par contrat; (*stipulated*) dans le contrat; **I'm c. forbidden to ...** le contrat m'interdit de ...

contradict [kɒntrə'dɪkt] *vt* (*person*) contredire; (*rumour*) démentir; **to c. oneself** se contredire; **the statements of the witnesses c. each other** les dépositions des témoins se contredisent

contradiction [kɒntrə'dɪkʃən] *n* contradiction *f*; **this was a c. of what they had previously said** c'était un démenti de ce qu'ils avaient dit auparavant; **in c. with** en contradiction avec; **it's a c. in terms** c'est parfaitement contradictoire, c'est une contradiction dans les termes; **he's full of contradictions** il est plein de contradictions

contradictory [kɒntrə'dɪktərɪ] *adj* (**a**) (*statement etc*) contradictoire (**to** à) (**b**) *F* (*person*) raisonneur; **don't be so c.** ne sois pas aussi raisonneur

contradistinction ['kɒntrədɪs'tɪŋkʃən] *n Fml* **in c. to ...** contrairement à ...

contra(-)flow *n Br Aut* contre-courant *m*; **c. system** système *m* de circulation à contre-sens

contraindication ['kɒntrəɪndɪ'keɪʃən] *n Med* contre-indication *f*, *pl* contre-indications

contralto [kən'træltəʊ] *Mus* **1** *n* contralto *m* **2** *adj* de contralto

contraption [kən'træpʃən] *n F* machin *m*, engin *m*, truc *m*

contrapuntal [kɒntrə'pʌnt(ə)l] *adj Mus* (*piece, accompaniment etc*) en contrepoint

contrarily [kən'treərɪlɪ] *adv* de façon contrariante

contrariness [kən'treərɪnɪs] *n* esprit *m* de contradiction

contrariwise ['kɒntrərɪwaɪz] *adv* (**a**) (*on the other hand*) au contraire (**b**) (*in the opposite direction*) dans le sens opposé (**c**) [kən'treərɪwaɪz] (*perversely*) par esprit de contradiction

contrary ['kɒntrərɪ] **1** *n* contraire *m*; **on the c.** au contraire; **unless you hear to the c.** sauf avis contraire

2 *adj* (**a**) (*opposite*) contraire (**to** à); (*interests etc*) opposé (**to** à); **c. to nature** contre nature; **c. to reason** contraire à la raison; **c. to the terms of the contract** contraire aux termes du contrat

(**b**) (*unfavourable*) **c. winds** vents *mpl* contraires

(**c**) [kən'treərɪ] *F* (*person*) contrariant, qui a l'esprit de contradiction; (*remark*) formulé par esprit de contradiction

3 *adv* contrairement (**to** à); **to act c. to instructions** contrevenir aux ordres reçus; **c. to my expectations** contre mon attente; **c. to what I was told** contrairement à ce qu'on m'a dit

contrast[1] ['kɒntrɑ:st] *n* (*difference*), *TV, Phot, Art* contraste *m* (**between** entre); **in c. with** *or* **to sth/sb** par contraste avec qch/qn; **by c. the president was almost optimistic** par contraste, le président était presque optimiste; **to form a c.**

to ... faire contraste avec ...; **as a c. to ...** comme contraste à ...; **c. control (button)** (bouton *m* de) réglage *m* du contraste

contrast² [kən'trɑːst] **1** *vt* faire contraster, mettre en contraste (**with** avec); **it was impossible not to c. her attitude with her brother's** c'était impossible de ne pas comparer son attitude à celle de son frère **2** *vi* contraster (**with** avec); **to c. strongly** trancher (**with** sur)

contrasting [kən'trɑːstɪŋ] *adj* (*colours*) contrasté; (*opinion, attitude, temperament*) opposé; **the c. yellow on the wall opposite** le jaune qui fait contraste sur le mur d'en face

contrasty ['kɒntrɑːstɪ] *adj Phot* contrasté

contravene [kɒntrə'viːn] *vt* (*law etc*) transgresser, enfreindre; (*rule*) enfreindre, être en contravention avec

contravention [kɒntrə'venʃən] *n* (*of law*) infraction *f*; **to act in c. of the law** enfreindre la loi

contribute [kən'trɪbjuːt] **1** *vt* donner; (*money*) donner, verser; **to c. one's time** donner de son temps; **to c. one's share** payer sa part; **she contributed $50,000 to the cause** elle a versé 50 000 dollars au profit de la cause; **he didn't c. anything to the discussion** il n'a rien apporté à la discussion; **to c. an article to a newspaper** écrire un article pour un journal

2 *vi* (**a**) contribuer; **if everyone contributes we'll be able to get a bigger present** si tout le monde participe, nous pourrons acheter un cadeau plus important; **he rarely contributes to discussions** il contribue rarement aux discussions; **to c. to a charity** contribuer à une bonne œuvre; **to c. to a newspaper** collaborer à un journal; **to c. to the success** contribuer au succès; **everything contributed to make him happy** tout contribuait à le rendre heureux

(**b**) (*to pension scheme etc*) cotiser (**to** à)

contribution [kɒntrɪ'bjuːʃən] *n* (**a**) contribution *f*; (*to meal, present etc*) contribution, participation *f*; **I've already made a c.** (*to sb collecting for charity*) j'ai déjà donné; **contributions welcome** (*to charity*) toutes les contributions sont les bienvenues; **their c. to the carnival was a brass band** leur participation au carnaval s'est concrétisée par une fanfare; *Acct* **c. in kind** apport *m* en nature; *Acct* **c. (margin)** marge *f* sur les coûts variables (**b**) *Journ* (*article*) article *m* (**c**) (*to pension plan, NIC etc*) cotisation *f*

contributor [kən'trɪbjʊtə(r)] *n* (**a**) (*to charity*) donateur, -trice; **the contributors to the meal/the present** les personnes *fpl* qui ont contribué au repas/au cadeau (**b**) *Journ* collaborateur, -trice (**to a paper** d'un journal)

contributory [kən'trɪbjʊtərɪ] *adj* (*cause, factor etc*) concourant; **to be a c. factor in sth** contribuer à qch; **the weather may have had a c. effect, but ...** le temps a peut-être joué un rôle mais ...; *Jur* **c. negligence** (*on part of accident victim*) manque *m* de précautions

contrite [kən'traɪt, 'kɒntraɪt] *adj* contrit

contritely [kən'traɪtlɪ] *adv* d'un air contrit, avec contrition

contrition [kən'trɪʃən] *n* contrition *f*, pénitence *f*

contrivance [kən'traɪvəns] *n* (**a**) (*device*) appareil *m*, dispositif *m*, engin *m* (**b**) *esp Fml* (*invention*) (*of scheme, plan*) invention *f*; **I was fairly sure the scheme was of George's c.** j'étais presque certain que c'était un stratagème de George (**c**) (*inventiveness*) ingéniosité *f* (**d**) *Pej* (*scheme*) stratagème *m*

contrive [kən'traɪv] *vt* (*device etc*) inventer, concevoir; **to c. to do sth** trouver le moyen de faire qch; **she contrived to get herself mentioned in the article** elle a réussi à faire en sorte qu'on parle d'elle dans l'article

contrived [kən'traɪvd] *adj* forcé, qui manque de naturel

control¹ [kən'trəʊl] *n* (**a**) (*power*) contrôle *m*; (*over oneself*) maîtrise *f*; **to take c.** prendre le contrôle (**of** de); **to have c. over sth/sb** avoir le contrôle de qch/qn; **the state has no c. over the media** l'état n'a aucun contrôle sur les médias; **she has no c. over the children** elle n'a aucune autorité sur les enfants; **to be in c. of sth/sb** avoir le contrôle de qch/qn; **the government is now firmly back in c.** le gouvernement a maintenant fermement repris le contrôle; **to have c. of a business** être à la tête d'une entreprise, diriger une entreprise; **things/the situation had got out of c.** les choses étaient/la situation était devenue(s) incontrôlable(s); **the children/horses were out of c.** les enfants/les chevaux étaient incontrôlables; **she soon had the horse under c.** elle est vite parvenue à maîtriser le cheval; **to keep one's feelings under c.** contrôler *ou* maîtriser ses émotions; **everything is under c.** (*organized, in hand*) tout est en bonne voie; (*there's no need to panic*) tout va bien; **to bring under c.** (*fire etc*) maîtriser; (*illness*) enrayer; **circumstances beyond our c.** circonstances indépendantes de notre volonté; **these things are beyond our c.** ces choses-là ne dépendent pas de notre volonté; **to lose c. (of oneself)** ne plus être maître de soi; **to regain c. of oneself** se ressaisir; **to exercise strict c. over sth** exercer un contrôle strict sur qch; **to exercise strict c. over sb** tenir la bride serrée à qn

(**b**) *Econ etc* (*of exchange rates, rents*) contrôle *m*; **to impose controls on rents/prices** contrôler les loyers/prix; **new government controls on financial practices** nouvelles réglementations *fpl* gouvernementales sur les pratiques financières

(**c**) (*used in experiment*) témoin *m*

(**d**) (*action*) (*of mechanism*) commande *f*; (*of power, volume*) réglage *m*; **to lose c. of one's car** perdre le contrôle de sa voiture; **the driver/pilot lost c.** le conducteur/pilote a perdu le contrôle; **the truck went out of c.** le chauffeur a perdu le contrôle de son camion; **the ship was out of c.** le navire n'était plus manœuvrable; **temperature c.** régulation *f* thermique; **automatic c.** réglage automatique; **dual c.** double commande; **remote c.** télécommande *f*, commande à distance

(**e**) *Tech* (*device*) (organe *m* de) commande *f*; **the controls** les commandes; **to be at the controls** être aux commandes; *Av* **flying controls** commandes de vol; *Rad etc* **volume c.** bouton *m* de (réglage de) volume; **c. lever/mechanism** levier *m*/appareil *m* de commande; *Comptr* **c. bit** bit *m* de contrôle; *Aut* **c. box** régulateur *m* de charge; *Aut* **c. rod** (*steering*) tige *f* de cremaillère; (*gearbox*) réglette *f*; *TV* **c. room** (cabine *f* de) régie *f*; *Comptr* **c. unit** unité *f* de commande, contrôleur *m*; *Aut* **c. valve** valve *f* modulatrice

control² *vt* (**a**) (*be in charge of, direct*) (*business, production*) diriger; (*of troops*) (*area etc*) contrôler; (*action of machine*) commander; **to c. the traffic** réglementer la circulation

(**b**) (*master, restrain*) (*horse*) maîtriser; (*child, pupils, class*) avoir de l'autorité sur, tenir; (*one's passions*) dompter; (*one's reactions etc*) contrôler, maîtriser; (*one's tears*) retenir; (*price increases, inflation*) contenir, enrayer; *Med* (*diabetes etc*) équilibrer; (*vehicle*) maîtriser, garder le contrôle de; **to c. oneself** se contrôler, se maîtriser; **to try to c. oneself** faire un effort sur soi-même; **he can't c. his pupils** il ne tient pas ses élèves, il manque d'autorité sur ses élèves; **couldn't you c. that child a little better?** tu ne crois pas que tu pourrais avoir un peu plus d'autorité sur cet enfant?

(**c**) (*check*) (*quality etc*) contrôler

control bus *n Comptr* bus *m* de contrôle

control character *n Comptr* caractère *m* de contrôle

control code *n Comptr* code *m* de contrôle

control column *n Av* levier *m* de commande

control experiment *n* expérience *f* de contrôle

control freak *n F* personne *f* qui veut tout contrôler

control gear *n* appareils *mpl ou* organes *mpl* de commande

control group *n* (*in experiment*) groupe *m* témoin

control key *n Comptr* touche *f* contrôle

control knob *n Comptr* molette *f* de réglage

controllable [kən'trəʊləb(ə)l] *adj* (*speed, heat, brightness*) réglable; (*economic growth, inflation, mechanism*) qui peut être contrôlé; (*moods*) maîtrisable; **it's c. by the user** cela peut être réglé par l'utilisateur; **if you find that the class is just not c.** si vous trouvez que la classe est vraiment intenable; **the spread of the disease is c.** la progression de la maladie peut être maîtrisée *ou* enrayée; **the more easily c. aspects of the project** les aspects du projet les plus faciles à contrôler

controlled [kən'trəʊld] *adj* (*person*) qui sait se maîtriser *ou* se contrôler; (*market*) réglementé; (*experiment*) contrôlé; *Med* (*diabetes etc*) équilibré; **to remain c.** (*of person*) garder son sang froid; **the transition to democracy must take place in a c. manner** le passage à la démocratie doit se faire dans l'ordre; *Journ* **c. circulation magazine** revue *f* à diffusion restreinte; *Mil* **c. explosion** (*of car bomb etc*) explosion *f* contrôlée; **c. parking zone** zone *f* de stationnement réglementé; **c. test marketing** mercatique *f* test dirigée

controller [kən'trəʊlə(r)] *n* (*person*) contrôleur, -euse; *Fin, Comptr* contrôleur; (*of TV channel*) directeur *m* d'antenne; *Av* **flight c.** contrôleur de vol; *Comptr* **disk c.** contrôleur de disques; *Comptr* **c. card** carte *f* contrôleur

controlling [kən'trəʊlɪŋ] *adj* (*power*) dirigeant; *Fin, Com* **c. factor** facteur *m* déterminant; **c. interest** *or* **share** *or* **stake** (*in company*) participation *f* majoritaire

control market *n Mktg* marché *m* témoin

control panel *n Comptr etc* pupitre *m ou* tableau *m* de commande, panneau *m* de contrôle, tableau de bord; *TV, Cin* tableau de commande

control point *n Sp, Aut* contrôle *m*

control program *n Comptr* programme *m* de contrôle

control tower *n Av* tour *f* de contrôle

controversial [kɒntrə'vɜːʃəl] *adj* controversé; **he's trying to be c.** il cherche la controverse; **I only said that to be c.** je n'ai dit cela que pour provoquer la controverse

controversy [ˈkɒntrəvɜːsɪ, kənˈtrɒvəsɪ] *n* controverse *f*; **to avoid c.** éviter la controverse; **to court c.** inviter à la controverse; **to be the subject of c.** être sujet à controverse; **the decision was surrounded by c.** la décision a soulevé beaucoup de controverses

contumacious [kɒntjʊˈmeɪʃəs] *adj Fml* désobéissant

contumacy [ˈkɒntjʊməsɪ, kɒnˈtjuː-] *n* **(a)** *Jur* contumace *f* **(b)** *Fml* (*disobedience*) désobéissance *f*

contumely [ˈkɒntjuːmlɪ] *n Fml* (*scorn*) mépris *m*

contusion [kənˈtjuːʒən] *n Med* contusion *f*

conundrum [kəˈnʌndrəm] *n* **(a)** (*riddle*) devinette *f* **(b)** (*mystery*) énigme *f*

conurbation [kɒnɜːˈbeɪʃən] *n* conurbation *f*

convalesce [kɒnvəˈles] *vi Med* se remettre (d'une maladie); (*be resting*) être en convalescence

convalescence [kɒnvəˈlesəns] *n Med* convalescence *f*

convalescent [kɒnvəˈlesənt] *Med* **1** *n* convalescent, -ente; **c. home** maison *f* de convalescence **2** *adj* convalescent

convection [kənˈvekʃən] *n Phys, El* convection *f*; **c. drier** séchoir *m* à convection; **c. drying** séchage *m* par convection; **c. heater** convecteur *m*, radiateur *m* à convection

convector [kənˈvektər] *n* (*heater*) convecteur *m*, radiateur *m* à convection

convene [kənˈviːn] **1** *vt* (*meeting*) convoquer **2** *vi* se réunir

convener [kənˈviːnər] *n* **(a)** *Br* (*of trade union*) délégué, -ée *mf* (syndical(e)) **(b) he was the c. of the meeting** c'est lui qui a demandé la réunion

convenience [kənˈviːnɪəns] *n* **(a)** commodité *f*; **at your c.** quand cela vous conviendra; *Com* **at your earliest c.** dans les meilleurs délais; **at your own c.** à votre convenance; **for c. I use tinned fruit** j'utilise des fruits en conserves pour des raisons de commodité; **a bus service is provided for our customers' c.** un service d'autobus est à la disposition de nos clients; **marriage of c.** mariage *m* de convenance; *Naut* **flag of c.** pavillon *m* de complaisance **(b)** (*installation*) **(public) c.** w.c. *mpl* (publics), toilettes *fpl*; **the rooms are fitted with all modern conveniences** les chambres ont tout (le) confort moderne

convenience brand *n Com* marque *f* pratique

convenience foods *npl Com* aliments *mpl* tout prêts

convenience shopping *n* achats *mpl* de dépannage

convenience store *n* magasin *m* de quartier qui reste ouvert tard le soir, *Can* dépanneur *m*

convenient [kənˈviːnɪənt] *adj* commode, pratique; (*time*) opportun; **if it is c. for you** si cela vous convient, si vous n'y voyez pas d'inconvénient; **2 o'clock isn't very c. (for me)** 14 heures ne m'arrange pas; **a c. place to stop** un endroit commode pour s'arrêter; **to find a c. opportunity to do sth** trouver l'occasion de faire qch; **we climbed through a c. hole in the fence** un trou bien situé nous a permis de traverser la clôture; **the ticket collector wasn't there — how very c.!** le contrôleur n'était pas là — ça tombait très bien!; **the flat is very c. for the shops** l'appartement est bien situé pour les commerces

conveniently [kənˈviːnɪəntlɪ] *adv* commodément; (*to arrive*) opportunément, à propos; **the house is c. situated near the town centre** la maison est située près du centre-ville, ce qui est bien pratique; *Iron* **someone had c. forgotten to lock the door** (*accidentally*) quelqu'un avait oublié de fermer la porte, ce qui était bien pratique; (*deliberately*) comme par hasard, quelqu'un avait oublié de fermer la porte

convenor [kənˈviːnər] *n* = **convener**

convent [ˈkɒnvənt] *n Rel* couvent *m*; **to enter a c.** entrer au couvent; **she went to c. school** elle est allée à l'école chez les sœurs

convention [kənˈvenʃən] *n* **(a)** (*conference*) assemblée *f*, convention *f*, congrès *m*; *US Pol* convention; **medical c.** congrès médical; **c. centre** palais *m* des congrès

(b) (*agreement*) accord *m*; (*international*) convention *f* **(on** relative à)

(c) (*established practice*) usage *m*; *Mus, Th etc* convention *f*; **the c. is that …** la convention veut que …; **there is a c. that Ministers do not answer such questions** l'usage est que les ministres ne répondent pas à ce genre de questions; **to be a slave to c.** être l'esclave des usages

(d) (*custom*) (*usu pl*) **conventions** convenances *fpl*; **to observe the conventions** respecter les convenances; **social conventions** conventions *fpl* sociales

conventional [kənˈvenʃən(ə)l] *adj* **(a)** (*normal*) (*person, upbringing*) conventionnel, *Pej* sans originalité; (*beauty, good looks*) classique; **c. propriety** les convenances *fpl* **(b)** (*established, traditional*) (*method*) classique, traditionnel; **the c. wisdom is that …** la sagesse populaire veut que …; *Constr* **c. material** matériau *m* traditionnel; *Mil* **c. warfare/weapon** guerre *f*/arme *f* conventionnelle

conventionality [kənvenʃəˈnælɪtɪ] *n* (*of person, upbringing*) caractère *m* conventionnel *ou* ordinaire

conventionally [kənˈvenʃən(ə)lɪ] *adv* **(a)** (*in accepted fashion*) conventionnellement, *Pej* sans originalité; **she's not c. beautiful** elle n'est pas d'une beauté classique **(b)** (*traditionally*) d'une manière classique

conventioneer [kənvenʃəˈnɪər] *n Am* congressiste *mf*

converge [kənˈvɜːdʒ] **1** *vi* **(a)** *Opt, Phys* converger **(on** vers) **(b)** (*of people*) se diriger **(on** vers); **over a hundred had converged on the town** plus de cent s'étaient rassemblés dans la ville; **three armies were converging on Paris** trois armées convergeaient sur Paris **2** *vt* (*light beams etc*) faire converger

convergence [kənˈvɜːdʒəns] *n* (*of lines, opinions*) convergence *f*; *Math* focalisation *f*

convergent [kənˈvɜːdʒənt] *adj* convergent; *Opt* **c. lens** lentille *f* convexe *ou* convergente

conversant [kənˈvɜːsənt] *adj* **to be c. with sth** (*with French grammar, the law etc*) s'y connaître en qch; (*with type of engine etc*) connaître qch; (*with recent developments etc*) être au courant de qch

conversation [kɒnvəˈseɪʃən] *n* **(a)** conversation *f*; **to hold** *or* **have a c. with sb** avoir une conversation avec qn; **to get into c. (with sb)** entamer une conversation (avec qn); **to change the c.** changer de conversation; (*because one is embarrassed*) détourner la conversation; **she was just making c.** elle parlait par politesse; **from my c. with him I got the impression that …** lorsque je me suis entretenu avec lui, j'ai eu l'impression que …; **his c. was very dull** sa conversation était sans aucun intérêt; **I'm not good at (making) c.** je ne suis pas très doué pour faire la conversation; **c. piece** objet *m* qui suscite des commentaires; **the vase is quite a c. piece** le vase alimente bien des conversations; **c. skills** l'art *m* de la conversation; *F* **c. stopper** *or* **killer** remarque *f*/sujet *m* qui arrête net les conversations; *F* **that was a c. stopper** cela a arrêté net la conversation

(b) *Comptr* dialogue *m*; **c. mode** mode *m* conversationnel *ou* dialogue

conversational [kɒnvəˈseɪʃən(ə)l] *adj* **(a)** de la conversation; **in a c. tone** sur le ton de la conversation; **c. style** style *m* familier **(b)** *Comptr* (*mode*) dialogue

conversationalist [kɒnvəˈseɪʃənəlɪst] *n* **to be a c.** (*like talking*) aimer la conversation; (*be a good talker*) bien parler; **I'm not much of a c.** je ne suis pas brillant causeur

conversationally [kɒnvəˈseɪʃən(ə)lɪ] *adv* sur le ton de la conversation

converse¹ [kənˈvɜːs] *vi Fml* converser **(on, about** sur), deviser **(on, about** de)

converse² [ˈkɒnvɜːs] **1** *adj* (*results, theory etc*) contraire; *Math* réciproque **2** *n* inverse *m*, contraire *m*; (*in logic*) proposition *f* converse; *Math* proposition réciproque

conversely [ˈkɒnvɜːslɪ, kənˈvɜːslɪ] *adv* réciproquement, inversement

conversion [kənˈvɜːʃən] *n* **(a)** *Rel, Fig* conversion *f* **(to** à)

(b) (*adaptation, alteration*) conversion *f* **(of sth into sth** de qch en qch); **the c. of a house into flats** l'aménagement *m ou* la transformation d'une maison en appartements; **c. of securities** conversion de titres; *Fin* **c. loan/order/right** emprunt *m*/ordre *m*/droit *m* de conversion; *Fin* **c. of loan stock** conversion d'un emprunt; *Comptr* **c. program** programme *m* de conversion; *Fin* **c. rate** taux *m* de conversion; *Comptr* **c. software** logiciel *m* de conversion; **c. table** (*of measurements etc*) table *f ou* tableau *m* de conversion; *Comptr* **c. utility** utilitaire *m* de conversion

(c) *Rugby, US Fb* transformation *f*

(d) *Jur* **improper c. of funds** détournement *m* de fonds

convert¹ [ˈkɒnvɜːt] *n Rel, Fig* converti, -ie; **to become a c. to sth** se convertir à qch; **to make a c. of sb** convertir qn; **she's made another c.** elle a encore converti quelqu'un

convert² [kənˈvɜːt] **1** *vt* **(a)** *Rel, Fig* convertir **(to** à); **to be converted to Christianity** se convertir au christianisme; *Fig* **she converted them to her way of thinking** elle les a amenés à voir les choses à sa manière; *Fig* **you're preaching to the converted** tu prêches un converti

(b) (*alter, adapt*) transformer, convertir **(sth into sth** qch en qch); **the car has been converted to run on unleaded petrol** la voiture a été modifiée pour rouler à l'essence sans plomb; **her studio was a converted barn** son studio était une grange aménagée; **to c. miles into kilometres** convertir les mil(l)es en kilomètres; *Fin* **to c. loan stock/securities** convertir un emprunt/des valeurs; *Fin* **converted share** action *f* convertie

(c) *Rugby* **to c. a try** transformer un essai

(d) *Jur* **to c. funds to another purpose** affecter des fonds à un autre usage; **to c. funds to one's own use** détourner des fonds

2 *vi* **(a)** *Rel* se convertir **(to** à); *Fig* **she converted to a belief in capitalism** elle s'est mise à croire au capitalisme

(b) *(of settee etc)* se transformer **(into a bed** en lit); **we've converted to electricity** nous sommes passés à l'électricité

converter [kən'vɜːtər] *n (person), Metal, El, Rad, Comptr* convertisseur *m*; **steel c., Bessemer c.** convertisseur Bessemer; *Aut* **c. clutch** convertisseur-embrayage *m*

convertibility [kənvɜːtə'bɪlɪtɪ] *n* convertibilité *f*

convertible [kən'vɜːtəb(ə)l] **1** *adj* **(a)** *(thing)* convertible **(into** en); *(settee etc)* transformable **(b)** *Aut* décapotable **(c)** *Fin (loan, security)* convertible; **c. currency** monnaie *f ou* devise *f* convertible; **c. loan stock** emprunt *m* obligataire convertible; **c. money of account** monnaie *f* de compte convertible **2** *n Aut* (voiture *f*) décapotable *f*

convex ['kɒnveks] *adj* **(a)** *Phys* convexe **(b)** *(road (surface))* bombé

convexity [kən'veksɪtɪ] *n Phys* convexité *f*

convey [kən'veɪ] *vt* **(a)** *(communicate) (order)* transmettre, donner; *(one's thoughts, news)* transmettre, communiquer **(to** à); **please c. my good wishes to the young couple** veuillez transmettre tous mes vœux aux jeunes époux; **to c. one's meaning** communiquer sa pensée; **his writing conveys the mood of the country** sa manière d'écrire évoque l'atmosphère du pays; **does that name c. anything to you?** est-ce que ce nom vous dit quelque chose? **(b)** *(transport)* transporter; *(person)* transporter, (a)mener; *(of air) (sound, smell)* transmettre **(c)** *Jur* faire cession de, transférer, céder **(to** à)

conveyance [kən'veɪəns] *n* **(a)** *(transportation) (of goods)* transport *m* **(b)** *Old-fashioned, Fml (vehicle)* véhicule *m*, voiture *f*; **public c.** véhicule de transport(s) en commun **(c)** *Jur (of property)* transfert *m*, cession *f*, disposition *f*; *(document)* acte *m* translatif de propriété, acte de cession

conveyancing [kən'veɪənsɪŋ] *n Jur* **(a)** *(procedure)* procédure *f* translative de propriété **(b)** *(drawing up documents)* rédaction *f* des actes de cession *ou* des actes translatifs de propriété

conveyor [kən'veɪər] *n* **(a)** *Ind* (appareil *m*) transporteur *m*; *Min* convoyeur *m*; *(belt)* convoyeur, tapis *m* roulant; **bucket c.** transporteur à godets **(b)** *Fml (person) (of letter, parcel)* porteur, -euse

conveyor belt *n* convoyeur *m*, tapis *m* roulant

convict¹ ['kɒnvɪkt] *n (convicted person)* détenu, -ue; *Old-fashioned (prisoner)* forçat *m*, bagnard *m*; **former c.** repris *m* de justice

convict² [kən'vɪkt] *vt* **to c. sb (of a crime)** déclarer qn coupable (d'un crime); **he was convicted** il fut reconnu coupable; **you stand convicted by your own words** vos propres paroles vous condamnent

conviction [kən'vɪkʃən] *n* **(a)** *Jur* condamnation *f*; **previous convictions** condamnations antérieures; **c. for murder** condamnation pour meurtre **(b)** *(belief)* conviction *f*; **to act from c.** agir par conviction; **to have the courage of one's convictions** avoir le courage de ses opinions; **to carry c.** *(of voice, manner)* être convaincant; **to lack c.** *(of person, voice, manner)* manquer de conviction

convince [kən'vɪns] *vt* convaincre, persuader **(of** de, **that …** que …); **to allow oneself to be convinced** se laisser convaincre; **you'll never c. me of that** tu ne me feras jamais croire cela

convinced [kən'vɪnsd] *adj* convaincu; **to be c. (that) …** être convaincu que … + *ind*; **I'm not c.** je ne suis pas convaincu

convincing [kən'vɪnsɪŋ] *adj (argument, theory, performance etc)* convaincant; *(victory)* décisif; **she wasn't very c. as Juliet** elle n'était pas convaincante dans le rôle de Juliette; **the battle-scenes were very c.** les scènes de bataille étaient très réalistes

convincingly [kən'vɪnsɪŋlɪ] *adv* d'une manière convaincante; *(to win)* d'une manière décisive

convivial [kən'vɪvɪəl] *adj (person)* bon vivant; *(atmosphere)* convivial, joyeux; **to have a c. evening** passer une soirée conviviale

conviviality [kənvɪvɪ'ælɪtɪ] *n* convivialité *f*, esprit *m* de société

convocation [kɒnvə'keɪʃən] *n* **(a)** *(of meeting)* convocation *f* **(b)** *(meeting)* assemblée *f*; *Br Rel* assemblée, synode *m*

convoke [kən'vəʊk] *vt Fml (meeting)* convoquer

convoluted ['kɒnvəluːtɪd] *adj* **(a)** *(complicated)* compliqué, *F* emberlificoté **(b)** *Biol* convoluté

convolution [kɒnvə'luːʃən] *n* **(a)** *(complication) (of argument etc)* méandre *f* **(b)** *(twist)* circonvolution *f*; *Anat* **cerebral convolutions** circonvolutions cérébrales

convolvulus, *pl* **-uses** [kən'vɒlvjʊləs, -əsɪz] *n* volubilis *m*, belle-de-jour *f*, *pl* belles-de-jour

convoy¹ ['kɒnvɔɪ] *n Mil, Naut, Aut* convoi *m*; **ship under *or* in c.** bâtiment *m* convoyé *ou* en convoi; **to drive in c.** *(of lorries)* rouler en convoi; *(of private cars)* se suivre; **to be on c. duty** *(of ship)* assurer un convoi

convoy² *vt Mil, Naut, Aut* convoyer, escorter

convulse [kən'vʌls] **1** *vt* **(a)** *(of sobs, spasms etc) (person)* secouer; *Fig (disrupt) (sb's life)* bouleverser; **to be convulsed with laughter/pain** se tordre de rire/douleur; **scene that convulses the audience** scène qui fait tordre de rire toute la salle **(b)** *Med (muscle)* convulsionner **2** *vi (of person)* avoir des convulsions; *(of face, body etc)* se contracter

convulsion [kən'vʌlʃən] *n Med (usu pl)* **convulsions** convulsions *fpl*; *F* **to be in convulsions** *(laughing)* se tordre de rire; *Fig* **political convulsions** bouleversements *mpl* politiques

convulsive [kən'vʌlsɪv] *adj (movement etc)* convulsif; *(transition)* brutal; **the most c. years in the country's history** les années les plus agitées dans l'histoire du pays

convulsively [kən'vʌlsɪvlɪ] *adv* convulsivement

coo¹ [kuː] *int Br Sl* tiens!, ça alors!

coo² **1** *vi (of dove)* roucouler; *(of baby)* gazouiller; **the neighbours came to c. over the baby** les voisins sont venus s'extasier sur le bébé **2** *vt (of person)* dire (d'un ton attendri); *(greeting, endearment etc)* murmurer, susurrer; **what a beautiful baby, he cooed** quel beau bébé, s'est-il extasié

coo³ *n (of dove)* roucoulement *m*

cooing ['kuːɪŋ] *n (of dove)* roucoulement *m*; *(of baby)* gazouillement *m*; *(of person)* mots *mpl* attendris

cook¹ [kʊk] *n* cuisinier, -ère; *Naut* coq *m*; **to be a good/bad c.** être bon/mauvais cuisinier; **head c.** chef *m* (de cuisine); *Fig* **chief *or* head c. and bottlewasher** factotum *m*; *Prov* **too many cooks spoil the broth** on ne parvient jamais à rien quand tout le monde met son grain de sel

cook² **1** *vt (meal)* faire, préparer; *(meat etc)* (faire) cuire; **half-cooked** demi-cuit, à moitié cuit; **the meat should be cooked all the way through** la viande doit être bien cuite; *Fig F* **to c. the accounts *or* the books** falsifier *ou* truquer les comptes **2** *vi (of food)* cuire; *(of person)* faire la cuisine, cuisiner; **can you c.?** est-ce que tu sais faire la cuisine?; *Fig F* **what's cooking?** *(happening)* qu'est-ce qui se passe?

► **cook up** *vtsep F (fabricate) (excuse etc)* inventer, imaginer

cookbook ['kʊkbʊk] *n* livre *m* de cuisine

cook-chill *adj* cuisiné (et réfrigéré)

cooked [kʊkt] *adj* cuit; **c. breakfast** petit déjeuner *m* à l'anglaise

cooker ['kʊkər] *n* **(a)** *(stove)* cuisinière *f*; **gas/electric c.** cuisinière à gaz/électrique; **pressure c.** cocotte-minute® *f* **(b)** *Br F (apple)* pomme *f* à cuire

cookery ['kʊkərɪ] *n* cuisine *f*; **c. book/classes** livre *m*/leçons *fpl* de cuisine; *TV, Rad* **c. programme** émission *f* sur la cuisine

cookhouse ['kʊkhaʊs] *n* cuisine *f*

cookie ['kʊkɪ] *n* **(a)** *Am (sweet biscuit)* biscuit *m*; *F* **that's the way the c. crumbles!** c'est la vie (que veux-tu)! **(b)** *esp Am F (person)* **a tough c.** un dur à cuire; **a smart c.** un petit malin

cooking ['kʊkɪŋ] *n* **(a)** *(process)* cuisson *f*; **method of c.** cuisson **(b)** *(style, activity)* cuisine *f*; **plain *or* home c.** cuisine bourgeoise; **my mother's c.** la cuisine de ma mère; **do you like c.?** est-ce que tu aimes faire la cuisine?; **to do the c.** faire la cuisine; **c. time** temps *m* de cuisson; **c. utensils** batterie *f* de cuisine **(c)** *F (falsification)* **c. of the books *or* accounts** falsification *f* des comptes

cooking apple *n* pomme *f* à cuire

cooking chocolate *n* chocolat *m* à cuire

cooking fat *n* matière *f* grasse pour la cuisine

cooking foil *n* papier *m* d'aluminium

cooking oil *n* huile *f* de cuisine

cool¹ [kuːl] **1** *adj* **(a)** *(wind, weather etc)* frais, *f* fraîche; *(drink)* frais, rafraîchissant; *(coffee, bathwater etc)* tiède; **it's c.** *(weather)* il fait frais; **it's getting c.** *(weather)* le temps se rafraîchit; *Com etc* **keep in a c. place** tenir au frais

(b) *(calm)* calme; **to keep c., calm and collected** rester calme, garder son sang-froid; **keep c.!** du calme!; **to keep a c. head** garder la tête froide, garder son sang-froid

(c) *(unfriendly) (person, reception etc)* froid

(d) *F (unruffled)* sans gêne; **I call that c.!** ça, c'est du toupet!; **well, you're a c. customer!** eh bien, vous avez du culot *ou* du toupet!

(e) *F (of money)* **I lost a c. thousand** j'ai perdu mille livres bien comptées

(f) *F (elegant)* super *inv*; **you look c. in that jacket** tu es super avec cette veste; **he thinks he's so c.** il se croit vraiment super

(g) *esp Am Sl (acceptable)* sympa *inv*, cool *inv*; **my sister's**

c. ma sœur est sympa *ou* cool; **it's not c. to smoke** ce n'est pas cool de fumer; **is it c. to smoke dope here?** (*will anyone object?*) est-ce que c'est OK de fumer de l'herbe ici?

2 *n* **(a)** fraîcheur *f*; **in the c. of the evening** dans la fraîcheur du soir

(b) *F* (*calm*) **to keep/lose one's c.** garder/perdre son sang-froid

3 *adv F* **to play it c.** (*act calm*) jouer décontracté; (*be calm*) être décontracté

cool[2] **1** *vt* (*water, air*) rafraîchir, refroidir; **to c. sb's ardour** refroidir l'ardeur de qn; *F* **c. it!** calme-toi!, on se calme!; **to c. one's heels** poireauter, faire le pied de grue; **he was put in jail overnight to c. his heels** on l'a gardé au poste pour la nuit histoire de le calmer **2** *vi* (*of liquid*) se rafraîchir, (se) refroidir; *Fig* (*of friendship etc*) se refroidir; **his anger soon cooled** sa colère a vite passé

▶ **cool down 1** *vi* **(a)** (*of person*) (*become calm*) s'apaiser, se calmer; **we'll talk about it when you've cooled down** nous en parlerons quand tu te seras calmé; **he still hasn't cooled down** il ne s'est pas encore calmé, il n'a pas encore décoléré **(b)** (*of weather*) se rafraîchir; (*of liquid*) (se) refroidir, se rafraîchir; *Fig* **things have cooled down between them** les relations se sont refroidies entre eux **2** *vtsep* **(a)** (*make calm*) calmer, apaiser **(b)** (*of cold drink*) rafraîchir

▶ **cool off** *vi* (*of person*) (*by going for a swim etc*) se rafraîchir; (*of food*) refroidir; *Fig* (*of affection, enthusiasm*) se refroidir; (*of angry person*) se calmer

coolant ['ku:lənt] *n Tech* liquide *m* de refroidissement; **c. inlet/outlet** arrivée *f*/sortie *f* de liquide de refroidissement

cooler ['ku:lər] *n* **(a)** *Am* (*refrigerator*) réfrigérateur *m* **(b)** *Tech* (appareil *m*) refroidisseur *m* **(c)** *Sl* (*prison*) taule *f*, tôle *f*

cool-headed ['ku:l'hedɪd] *adj* (*person*) calme, imperturbable

coolie ['ku:lɪ] *n* coolie *m*

cooling ['ku:lɪŋ] **1** *adj* (*breeze, drink*) rafraîchissant; *Ind etc* réfrigérant **2** *n* (*of temperature etc*) refroidissement *m*; **there had been a c. in their relationship** leurs relations s'étaient refroidies; *Tech* **c. jacket** chemise *f* d'eau; *Fig* **c. off period** période *f* de réflexion

cooling fan *n* ventilateur *m* de refroidissement

cooling fin *n Aut* ailette *f* de refroidissement

cooling system *n* système *m* de refroidissement; *Aut* circuit *m* de refroidissement

cooling tower *n Ind* tour *f* de réfrigération, refroidisseur *m*

cooling water *n Aut, Nucl Phys* eau *f* de refroidissement

coolly ['ku:lɪ] *adv* **(a)** (*calmly*) (*to act*) avec calme; **she walked c. out of the room** elle a calmement quitté la pièce **(b)** *F* (*impudently*) effrontément **(c)** (*to welcome*) froidement

coolness ['ku:lnɪs] *n* **(a)** (*of air*) fraîcheur *f* **(b)** (*calm*) calme *m*, sang-froid *m* **(c)** (*of reception*) froideur *f*

coon [ku:n] *n* **(a)** *US F* (*raccoon*) raton *m* laveur **(b)** *Offensive Sl* (*Negro*) nègre *m*, négresse *f*

coonskin ['ku:nskɪn] *n US F* peau *f* de raton laveur

coop [ku:p] *n* (**hen** *or* **chicken**) **c.** cage *f* à poules, poulailler *m*; *Fig* **to fly the c.** prendre la fuite, filer

▶ **coop up** *vtsep* (*usu passive*) **to c. sb up** tenir qn enfermé; **we were cooped up for hours in a tiny room** nous sommes restés enfermés pendant des heures dans une pièce minuscule; **to feel cooped up** se sentir à l'étroit

co(-)op ['kəʊɒp] *n* coopérative *f*

cooper ['ku:pər] *n* tonnelier *m*

cooperage ['ku:pərɪdʒ] *n* tonnellerie *f*

co(-)operate [kəʊ'ɒpəreɪt] *vi* coopérer (**with sb in sth** avec qn à qch); **the two governments are co-operating in the drug war** les deux gouvernements coopèrent dans la lutte contre la drogue; **if you c. your sentence may be reduced** si vous coopérez, votre peine pourra être réduite

co(-)operation [kəʊɒpə'reɪʃən] *n* coopération *f*; **your c. would be appreciated** nous vous serions reconnaissants de votre coopération

co(-)operative [kəʊ'ɒp(ə)rətɪv] **1** *adj* **(a)** *Com* coopératif; **c. credit society** coopérative *f* de crédit; **c. advertising** publicité *f* coopérative *ou* associée; **c. dairy** coopérative *f* laitière; **c. exporting** exportation *f* collective; *Com* **c. group** coopérative *f* (de consommateurs); **c. selling** vente *f* en coopération; **c. society** société *f* coopérative **(b)** (*person, attitude*) coopératif; **to be c.** se montrer coopératif **2** *n Com* (*agricultural, viticultural etc*) coopérative *f*

co(-)opt [kəʊ'ɒpt] *vt* **(a)** (*onto committee*) coopter (**onto** à) **(b)** *F* (*commandeer*) réquisitionner; **I've been co-opted to help with the spring cleaning** j'ai été réquisitionné pour le nettoyage de printemps

co(-)ordinate[1] [kəʊ'ɔ:dɪnət] **1** *adj Gram* **c. clauses** propositions *fpl* coordonnées **2** *n Math, Astron etc* coordonnée *f*

co(-)ordinate[2] [kəʊ'ɔ:dɪneɪt] *vt* coordonner (**with** à, avec)

coordinated [kəʊ'ɔ:dɪneɪtɪd] *adj* (*physically, in movements*) coordonné; **you look very c. for a change** pour une fois tu portes des couleurs qui vont bien ensemble *ou* qui ne jurent pas; **to give sth a more c. appearance** donner à qch une apparence plus harmonieuse

co(-)ordinates *npl* (*clothes*) coordonnés *mpl*

co(-)ordinating [kəʊ'ɔ:dɪneɪtɪŋ] *adj* **(a)** coordinateur, -trice **(b)** [①A68,1; B55,A] *Gram* **c. conjunction** conjonction *f* de coordination

co(-)ordination [kəʊɔ:dɪ'neɪʃən] *n* coordination *f*; **you need good c. to play tennis** il faut avoir une bonne coordination pour jouer au tennis

co(-)ordinator [kəʊ'ɔ:dɪneɪtər] *n* coordinateur, -trice

coot [ku:t] *n* **(a)** (*bird*) (**common** *or* **bald**) **c.** foulque *f* (macroule), *Can* foulque noire **(b)** *Old-fashioned F* (*fool*) idiot, -ote

co-owner ['kəʊ'əʊnər] *n* (*of building etc*) copropriétaire *mf*

co-ownership ['kəʊ'əʊnəʃɪp] *n* copropriété *f*

cop[1] [kɒp] *n* **(a)** *F* (*policeman*) flic *m*; **speed c.** motard *m*; **to play cops and robbers** jouer aux gendarmes et aux voleurs; **c. shop** (*police station*) poste *m* de police; *TV* **c. show** série *f* policière **(b)** *Br Sl* (*arrest*) **it's a fair c.!** je suis fait **(c)** *Br Sl* **it's not much c.** (*not very good*) ça ne vaut pas grand-chose

cop[2] *vt Sl* (*catch*) (*person*) attraper, pincer; **c. this!** (*listen*) écoute-moi ça!; (*look*) regarde-moi ça!; **to get copped** (*by police etc*) se faire pincer; *Br* **to c. it** (*be caught and punished*) se faire pincer; (*get injured*) être blessé; (*die*) clamser; **to c. hold of sth** attraper qch; *Jur* **to c. a plea** plaider coupable (*pour éviter une charge plus grave*)

▶ **cop out** *vi Sl* (*avoid responsibility*) se défiler; (*choose easy solution*) choisir la solution de facilité

co-partner ['kəʊ'pɑ:tnər] *n* coparticipant *m*, coassocié *m*

co-partnership ['kəʊ'pɑ:tnəʃɪp] *n* coparticipation *f*

cope[1] [kəʊp] *n Rel* chape *f*

cope[2] *vt Constr* (*wall*) chaperonner, mettre un couronnement à

cope[3] *vi* se débrouiller, s'en tirer, s'en sortir; **to c. with** (*situation, danger, job, debt*) faire face à; (*difficulty*) venir à bout de; (*troublemaker*) se charger de; (*look after*) (*children*) s'occuper de; (*put up with*) (*children, noise etc*) supporter; **to be able to c. with a job** être à la hauteur d'une tâche; **I can't c. with her when she gets angry** je ne sais pas comment la prendre quand elle se met en colère; **the engine couldn't c. with the extra weight** le moteur n'était pas assez puissant pour supporter cette charge supplémentaire; **I just can't c.** je n'y arrive plus; **that's all right, thanks, I can c.** ça va, merci, j'y arriverai; **I'll c. with it** je m'en chargerai; **I'll c.** je me débrouillerai; **he seems to be coping** il a l'air de se débrouiller *ou* de s'en sortir

Copenhagen [kəʊpən'heɪg(ə)n] *n* Copenhague *f*

copiable ['kɒpɪəb(ə)l] *adj Comptr* copiable

copier ['kɒpɪər] *n* **(a)** (*person*) copiste *mf* **(b)** *Pej* (*imitator*) imitateur, -trice **(c)** (*device*) duplicateur *m*, copieur *m*; (*photocopying machine*) (photo)copieuse *f*

copilot ['kəʊpaɪlət] *n Av* copilote *m*

coping ['kəʊpɪŋ] *n Constr* (*of wall etc*) chaperon *m*; **c. stone** pierre *f* de couronnement

copious ['kəʊpɪəs] *adj* copieux, abondant; **c. notes** des notes *fpl* abondantes; **c. amounts** (*of beer etc*) de grandes quantités *fpl*

copiously ['kəʊpɪəslɪ] *adv* abondamment

co-plaintiff ['kəʊ'pleɪntɪf] *n Jur* codemandeur, -eresse

cop-out *n Sl* **(a)** (*act*) solution *f* de facilité; **that's a bit of a c.** c'est la solution de facilité **(b)** *Am* (*person*) personne *f* qui se défile

copper[1] ['kɒpər] **1** *n* **(a)** (*metal*) cuivre *m* (rouge); **c. wire** fil *m* de cuivre **(b)** *Br F* (*coin*) sou *m*; **coppers** petite monnaie *f*; **to give a beggar a few coppers** donner quelques sous à un mendiant **(c)** *Br* (*for washing*) cuve *f* à lessive **2** *adj* **c.(-coloured)** cuivré; *Bot* **c. beech** hêtre *m* rouge *ou* pourpre

copper[2] *n F* (*policeman*) flic *m*

copper[3] *vt* (*in metalwork*) cuivrer

copper-bottomed ['kɒpəbɒtəmd] *adj* (*pot, saucepan etc*) à fond en cuivre; *Fig* (*guarantee*) sûr

copperhead ['kɒpəhed] *n* (*snake*) trigonocéphale *m*

copperplate ['kɒpəpleɪt] *n* **(a)** **c. (writing)** écriture *f* moulée; **written in c.** calligraphié **(b)** (*in engraving*) taille-douce *f*; **c. engraving** chalcographie *f*

coppersmith ['kɒpəsmɪθ] *n* chaudronnier *m*

copperware ['kɒpəweər] *n* ustensiles *mpl* en cuivre

coppery ['kɒpərɪ] *adj* (*colour*) cuivré

coppice ['kɒpɪs] *n* taillis *m*, hallier *m*

copra ['kɒprə] *n Com* copra(h) *m*

co-presenter ['kəʊprɪzentər] *n* coprésentateur *m*

co-processor [kəʊ'prəʊsesər] *n Comptr* coprocesseur *m*; **maths c.** coprocesseur arithmétique

coproduction [kəʊprə'dʌkʃən] *n Cin etc* coproduction *f*

copse [kɒps] *n* taillis *m*
copter ['kɒptər] *n Av F* hélico *m*
Coptic ['kɒptɪk] **1** *adj* coptique, copte **2** *n Ling* copte *m*
copula ['kɒpjʊlə] *n Gram etc* copule *f*
copulate ['kɒpjʊleɪt] *vi* copuler, s'accoupler (**with** avec)
copulation [kɒpjʊ'leɪʃən] *n Physiol* copulation *f*, coït *m*
copulative ['kɒpjʊlətɪv] *adj Gram etc* copulatif; *Physiol, Anat* copulateur, -trice
copy[1] ['kɒpɪ] *n* **(a)** (*reproduction*) copie *f*; (*of statue etc*) reproduction *f*, copie; **this picture is only a c.** ce tableau n'est qu'une copie
(b) (*of handwritten letter, text*) copie *f*; (*of typewritten letter etc*) double *m*; **rough c.** brouillon *m*; **fair c.** copie (au net); **certified c.** copie authentique; **true c.** copie conforme
(c) (*of book*) exemplaire *m*; (*of newspaper*) numéro *m*; **500 copies of the book were printed** le livre a été tiré à 500 exemplaires
(d) *Typ* (*written material for printing*) manuscrit *m*, copie *f*; *Journ* copie; **this would make good c.** voilà un bon sujet d'article; *Journ* **he wrote some brilliant c.** il a écrit d'excellents articles *ou F* papiers; *Journ* **c. deadline** tombée *f*, dernière heure *f*; *Journ* **c. taster** premier lecteur *m*; *Mktg* **c. testing** pré-tests *mpl* publicitaires
(e) *Comptr* **c. and paste** copier-coller *m*; **c. block** copie *f* de bloc; **c. command** commande *f* de copie; **c. disk** disquette *f* de copie; **c. protection** protection *f* contre la copie
copy[2] **1** *vt* **(a)** (*work of art, drawing etc*) copier, imiter **(b)** (*model oneself on*) copier; (*sb's walk*) copier, imiter; *Art, Liter, Mus* (*sb's style*) copier, pasticher **(c)** (*write out*) (*letter etc*) (re)copier **(d)** *Sch* (*in order to cheat*) copier (**from sb** sur qn, **from sth** dans qch) **(e)** *Comptr* copier **(f)** (*send copy to*) envoyer une copie à; **to c. sb with sth** faire parvenir une copie de qch à qn **2** *vi Sch* copier (**from another pupil** sur un autre élève)
▶ **copy out** *vtsep* recopier; **to c. out a passage from a book** transcrire *ou* recopier un passage d'un livre
copybook ['kɒpɪbʊk] *n* cahier *m* d'écriture; *Fig* **to blot one's c.** ternir sa réputation (**with sb** auprès de qn); **he really blotted his copybook when he suggested that …** il a fait une vraie bourde lorsqu'il a proposé que …; **a c. example** un exemple classique
copycat ['kɒpɪkæt] *n F* copieur, -euse; **they're just copycats** ce ne sont que des copieurs
copycat crime *n* crime *m* inspiré par un autre
copy check *n Comptr* contrôle *m* par duplication
copy-edit *Typ* **1** *vi* corriger les épreuves **2** *vt* (*proofs*) corriger
copy-editing *n Typ* correction *f* d'épreuves
copy editor *n Typ* correcteur, -trice d'épreuves
copy-holder *n* (*for keyboarder*) porte-copies *m*, bras *m* porte-copies
copying ['kɒpɪɪŋ] *n* (*imitation*) imitation *f*; *Sch* (*cheating*) copiage *m*; **c. machine** duplicateur *m*; (*photocopier*) photocopieuse *f*; *Comptr* **c. program** programme *m* de copie
copyist ['kɒpɪɪst] *n* copiste *mf*
copy-protect *vt Comptr* protéger contre la copie
copy-protected *adj Comptr* protégé contre la copie
copyreader ['kɒpɪriːdər] *n* secrétaire *mf* de rédaction, correcteur *m*
copyright[1] ['kɒpɪraɪt] **1** *n* droit *m* d'auteur, copyright *m*; **it's still subject to c.** c'est toujours soumis au droit d'auteur; **breach** *or* **infringement of c.** violation *f* du droit d'auteur; **to hold the c. on sth** avoir le droit d'auteur sur qch; **it's his c.** c'est lui qui détient les droits d'auteur; **out of c.** (tombé) dans le domaine public; **c. notice** mention *f* de réserve **2** *adj* (*book*) qui est protégé par des droits d'auteur; (*article*) dont le droit de reproduction est réservé; **c. (in all countries)** tous droits de reproduction et de traduction réservés (pour tous pays); **c. library** bibliothèque *f* de dépôt légal
copyright[2] *vt* (*book*) réserver les droits de
copytaker ['kɒpɪteɪkər] *n Journ* opérateur *m*
copy typist *n* dactylographe *mf*
copywriter ['kɒpɪraɪtər] *n* rédacteur, -trice publicitaire
coquetry ['kəʊkɪtrɪ, 'kɒk-] *n esp Lit* coquetterie *f*
coquette [kəʊ'ket, kɒk-] *n esp Lit* coquette *f*
coquettish [kə'ketɪʃ, kɒk-] *adj* **(a)** (*woman*) flirteuse **(b)** (*smile etc*) aguichant
cor[1] [kɔːr] *n Mus* **c. anglais** cor *m* anglais
cor[2] *int Eng Sl* ça alors!
coracle ['kɒrək(ə)l] *n* (*boat*) coracle *m*
coral ['kɒr(ə)l] **1** *adj* **(a)** (*island*) de corail, corallien; (*necklace*) de corail; **c. reef** récif *m* corallien; **c. red** rouge *m* corail; **c. red paint** peinture rouge corail **(b)** (*colour*) de corail **2** *n* **(a)** corail *m*, -aux **(b)** (*colour*) corail *m*
Coral Sea *n* mer *f* de Corail
coral snake *n* serpent *m* corail
corbel ['kɔːb(ə)l] *n Archit* corbeau *m*, console *f*
cord [kɔːd] *n* **(a)** (*string*) grosse ficelle *f*; (*for curtains*) cordon *m*; (*of pyjama trousers*) cordon, ficelle; (*of dressing gown*) ceinture *f* **(b)** *Anat* (**umbilical**) **c.** cordon *m* (ombilical) **(c)** *Tex* (*corduroy*) velours *m* côtelé; **c. jacket** veston *m* en *ou* de velours côtelé; **cords** (*trousers*) pantalon *m* en *ou* de velours côtelé **(d)** *US El* cordon *m*, fil *m*
cordage ['kɔːdɪdʒ] *n Naut* cordage *m*
corded ['kɔːdɪd] *adj Tex* côtelé, à côtes
cordial ['kɔːdɪəl] **1** *adj* cordial **2** *n* (*drink*) cordial *m*, sirop *m*
cordiality [kɔːdɪ'ælɪtɪ] *n* cordialité *f*; *Fml* **exchange of cordialities** échange *m* de cordialités
cordially ['kɔːdɪəlɪ] *adv* cordialement; *Am* **c. yours** (*at end of letter*) bien cordialement
cordite ['kɔːdaɪt] *n* cordite *f*
cordless ['kɔːdlɪs] *adj* sans fil; *Comptr* **c. mouse** souris *f* sans fil; **c. telephone** téléphone *m* sans fil
cordon ['kɔːd(ə)n] *n* **(a)** (*of troops, ships etc*) cordon *m*; **police c.** cordon de police **(b) c. (tree)** cordon *m*
▶ **cordon off** *vtsep* (*close*) (*road*) barrer; (*area etc*) boucler; **the street was cordoned off by the police** (*they ordered it closed*) la police a barré la rue; (*they acted as a barrier*) on a isolé la rue par un cordon de police
cordon bleu ['kɔːrdɒn'blɜː] **1** *n* (*cookery, chef*) cordon(-)bleu *m* **2** *adj* **her cooking was up to c. standard** sa cuisine était digne d'un cordon(-)bleu
corduroy ['kɔːdərɔɪ] *n Tex* velours *m* côtelé; **c. trousers, corduroys** pantalon *m* en *ou* de velours côtelé; **c. road** chemin *m* de rondins
core[1] [kɔːr] *n* **(a)** (*of mass*) centre *m*, partie *f* centrale; (*of wood, argument*) cœur *m*; (*of apple etc*) trognon *m*; *Fig* **hard c.** noyau *m* dur; **selfish to the c.** d'un égoïsme foncier; *F* **he's rotten to the c.** il est pourri jusqu'à la moelle; **it shocked us to the c.** cela nous a complètement bouleversés; **the c. issue** la question centrale; **c. business** activité *f* centrale; **c. competence** principale compétence *f*; *Sch* **c. curriculum** tronc *m* commun; **c. market** marché *m* principal *ou* de référence; **c. message** (*in advertising*) message *m* principal; **c. time** *or* **hours** (*in flexitime scheme*) plage *f* fixe; **c. values** valeurs *fpl* principales; *Ling* **c. vocabulary** vocabulaire *m* de base
(b) *Geol etc* noyau *m*; (*of the earth*) nifé *m*, nife *m*; *Min* **c. sample** carotte *f*, témoin *m*, échantillon *m* carotté
(c) *Tech* (*of cable*) mèche *f*; *El* (*of electromagnet*) noyau *m*; *Nucl* (*of nuclear reactor*) cœur *m*; **c. hole** (*in engine block*) trou *m* de coulée *ou* d'usinage; *Comptr* **c. memory** mémoire *f* à tores (magnétiques); (*main memory*) mémoire centrale; *Aut* **c. plug** obturateur *m* de trou de coulée *ou* de trou d'usinage
core[2] *vt* (*apple etc*) enlever le cœur de, évider
coreligionist [kəʊrɪ'lɪdʒ(ə)nɪst] *n* coreligionnaire *mf*
corer ['kɔːrər] *n* **(apple) c.** vide-pomme *m*, *pl* vide-pommes
co-respondent [kəʊrɪ'spɒndənt] *n Jur* (*in adultery*) complice *mf*
Corfu [kɔː'fuː] *n* Corfou *f*
corgi ['kɔːgɪ] *n* corgi *m*
coriander [kɒrɪ'ændər] *n Bot, Culin* coriandre *f*; **c. (seeds)** graines *fpl* de coriandre
Corinthian [kə'rɪnθɪən] **1** *adj* **(a)** *Geog* corinthien **(b)** *Archit* (*column etc*) corinthien **2** *n Geog* Corinthien, -ienne
cork[1] [kɔːk] *n* **(a)** (*material*) liège *m*; **c. oak** chêne-liège *m*, *pl* chênes-lièges; **c. sole/mat** semelle/tapis de *ou* en liège **(b)** (*stopper*) bouchon *m* de liège; *Br F* **put a c. in it!** (*shut up*) la ferme!; **c. charge** (*in restaurant*) droit *m* de bouchon
cork[2] *vt* **(a)** (*bottle*) boucher **(b)** (*blacken*) **to c. one's face** se noircir le visage avec un bouchon brûlé
▶ **cork up** *vtsep* **the genie had been corked up in the bottle for years** le génie avait été enfermé dans la bouteille pendant des années; *Fig* **to c. up one's feelings** refouler ses émotions
corkage ['kɔːkɪdʒ] *n* (*in restaurant*) droit *m* de bouchon
corked [kɔːkt] *adj* (*wine*) bouchonné, qui sent le bouchon; **the wine tasted c.** le vin était bouchonné
corker ['kɔːkər] *n Sl* **(a)** (*thing, action*) chose *f*/action *f* qui vous en bouche un coin; **that was a c. of a goal** c'était un super but; **that joke was a c.** elle était super cette blague!; **a c. of a lie** un énorme mensonge **(b)** *Old-fashioned* (*man*) type *m* épatant; (*pretty woman*) canon *m*; **when it comes to telling lies he's a c.** comme menteur il se pose là
corking ['kɔːkɪŋ] *adj Old-fashioned Br Sl* (*wonderful*) épatant, fameux
corkscrew[1] ['kɔːkskruː] *n* tire-bouchon *m*, *pl* tire-bouchons; **c. curl** (*in hair*) anglaise *f*
corkscrew[2] *vi* **to c. (up/down)** (*of staircase*) monter/descendre en colimaçon; **the plane corkscrewed into the sea** l'avion est descendu en vrille et s'est écrasé dans la mer

cork-tipped ['kɔ:ktɪpt] *adj* (*cigarette*) à bout de liège
corkwood ['kɔ:kwʊd] *n* liège *m*
corm [kɔ:m] *n Bot* bulbe *m* (solide)
cormorant ['kɔ:mərənt] *n* (*bird*) cormoran *m*
corn¹ [kɔ:n] *n* **(a)** (*no pl*) *Br* (*wheat*) blé(s) *m(pl)*; **winter c.** semis *m* d'hiver; **c. bunting** (*bird*) (bruant *m*) proyer *m*; **c. chandler** *or* **merchant** marchand *m* de blé *ou* de grains; **c. salad** mâche *f*
(b) *esp Am* **(Indian) c.** maïs *m*; **c. belt** plaines *fpl* du centre des Etats-Unis (*où est cultivé le maïs*); **c. oil** huile *f* de maïs; **c. silk** barbe *f*; **c. whiskey** whisky *m* de maïs
(c) (*seed*) grain *m* (*de plante céréalière*)
(d) *F* (*sentimentality*) mièvrerie *f*; (*lack of originality*) banalité *f*; **that film was pure c.** ce film était d'une mièvrerie affligeante; **his routine was pure c.** (*of comedian*) son spectacle manquait totalement d'originalité
corn² *n Med* (*on toe etc*) cor *m*; **c. plaster** pansement *m* coricide; *Fig F* **to tread on sb's corns** froisser qn
corn bread *n* pain *m* de farine de maïs
corncob ['kɔ:nkɒb] *n* épi *m* de maïs; **c. (pipe)** pipe *f* en épi de maïs
corncockle ['kɔ:nkɒk(ə)l] *n* (*plant*) nielle *f* des blés
corncrake ['kɔ:nkreɪk] *n* (*bird*) râle *m* des genêts
corn dolly *n* poupée *f* fabriquée avec des épis de blé
cornea ['kɔ:nɪə] *n Anat* (*of eye*) cornée *f*
corneal ['kɔ:nɪəl] *adj Anat* cornéen; *Med* **c. graft** greffe *f* de la cornée
corned [kɔ:nd] *adj Culin* **c. beef** corned beef *m*, *Mil F* singe *m*
cornelian [kɔ:'ni:lɪən] *n* (*gem*) cornaline *f*
corner¹ ['kɔ:nər] *n* **(a)** (*of page, screen*) coin *m*; **to turn down the c. of a page** corner une page; **bottom left-hand c.** (*of page, photograph etc*) coin en bas à gauche; *Constr* **c. post** poteau *m* d'angle
(b) (*of room etc*) coin *m*; **the four corners of the earth** les quatre coins du monde; **to search every c. of the house** chercher dans tous les coins et recoins de la maison; **to put a child in the c.** mettre un enfant au coin; *Fig* **to drive sb into a c.** acculer qn, mettre qn au pied du mur; *Fig* **driven into a c.** acculé, au pied du mur; *Fig* **to be in a tight c.** être dans une mauvaise passe; *Fig* **to paint oneself into a c.** se mettre dans une impasse; **c. cupboard** armoire de coin
(c) (*on street*) coin *m*, angle *m*; **situated at** *or* **on the c.** situé au coin *ou* à l'angle; **the house on the c.** la maison qui fait l'angle, la maison au coin; **you'll find the grocer's round the c.** vous trouverez l'épicerie en tournant le coin; **it's just round the c.** c'est au coin de la rue; *Fig* **spring is just around the c.** ce sera bientôt le printemps; **with the elections just round the c.** avec les élections qui approchent; **another rise in mortgage rates is just round the c.** une autre augmentation des taux de prêt se prépare; **you never know what's around the c.** on ne sait jamais ce qui peut se produire; **to hang around street corners** traîner dans les rues; **to turn the c.** tourner le coin; *Fig* (*of economy, company*) passer le moment critique; (*of sick person*) commencer à se rétablir; **c. site** emplacement *m* en coin
(d) (*bend in road*) tournant *m*; *Aut* virage *m*; *Aut* **to take a c.** prendre un virage; **to cut a c. (close)** couper un virage; *Fig* **to cut corners** (*economize excessively*) faire des économies exagérées; (*not follow rules*) contourner les règlements; **if you cut corners now you'll just have more work to do later on** si tu fais les choses trop vite maintenant, tu auras plus à faire plus tard; **we had to cut a few corners to get the job finished on time** il nous a fallu simplifier un peu les choses pour finir ce travail à temps
(e) *Fb* **c. (kick)** corner *m*; **to take a c.** faire un corner; **c. flag** *or* **post** piquet *m* de coin
(f) (*of lips*) commissure *f*; **to look out of the c. of one's eye** regarder du coin de l'œil
(g) a little c. of Normandy un petit coin de Normandie; **they had created a little c. of France in Edinburgh** ils avaient recréé un petit coin de France à Edimbourg
corner² **1** *vt* **(a)** (*drive into a corner*) acculer, coincer; *Fig* coincer, mettre au pied du mur; **we've got him cornered** (*criminal etc*) nous l'avons coincé **(b)** *Com* (*market*) accaparer, *Belg* s'accaparer **(in** de) **2** *vi Aut* prendre un virage; **the car corners well** cette voiture prend bien les virages
cornered ['kɔ:nəd] *adj* (*driven into a corner*) acculé, coincé; *Fig* coincé, au pied du mur; **you've got me c.** là, tu m'as coincé
cornering ['kɔ:nərɪŋ] *n* **(a)** *Com* (*of market*) accaparement *m* **(b)** *Aut* **the car is good at c.** la voiture prend bien les virages; **c. ability** comportement *m* en virage *ou* en courbe; **c. stability** stabilité *f* en courbe
corner shop *n* magasin *m* de quartier, *Can* dépanneur *m*
cornerstone ['kɔ:nəstəʊn] *n Constr*, *Fig* pierre *f* angulaire
cornet ['kɔ:nɪt, *Am* kɔ:'net] *n* **(a)** *Mus* (*instrument*) cornet *m* à pistons; (*player*) cornettiste *mf* **(b)** (*of paper*) cornet *m* (en papier) **(c)** *Br* **(ice-cream) c.** cornet *m* de glace
cornet(t)ist [kɔ:'netɪst] *n Mus* cornettiste *mf*
Corn Exchange *n* halle *f* aux blés
cornfield ['kɔ:nfi:ld] *n* champ *m Br* de blé *ou Am* de maïs
cornflakes ['kɔ:nfleɪks] *npl Culin* flocons *mpl* de maïs, cornflakes *mpl*
cornflour ['kɔ:nflaʊər] *n Br* farine *f* de maïs
cornflower ['kɔ:nflaʊər] *n* (*plant*) bleuet *m*, barbeau *m*; **c. blue** bleu barbeau *inv*
cornice ['kɔ:nɪs] *n* (*of wardrobe, snow*), *Archit* corniche *f*
Cornish ['kɔ:nɪʃ] **1** *adj Geog* cornouaillais; *Br Culin* **C. pasty** = chausson *m* à la viande **2** *n Ling* cornique *m*
Cornishman, -woman, *pl* **-men, -women** ['kɔ:nɪʃmən, -wʊmən, -mən, -wɪmɪn] *n* Cornouaillais, -aise
corn meal *n* farine *f* de maïs
corn on the cob *n* maïs *m* en épi
corn poppy *n* coquelicot *m*
cornstarch ['kɔ:nstɑ:tʃ] *n Am Culin* farine *f* de maïs
cornucopia, *pl* **-as** [kɔ:njʊ'kəʊpɪə, -əz] *n Myth*; *Fig* corne *f* d'abondance
Cornwall ['kɔ:nw(ə)l] *n* Cornouailles *f*
corny ['kɔ:nɪ] *adj F* (*poor*) (*joke*) nul; (*sentimental*) (*story, film, novel*) tarte; **don't be so c.** ne sois pas aussi tarte
corolla [kə'rɒlə] *n Bot* corolle *f*
corollary [kə'rɒlərɪ] *n* corollaire *m* **(of** à)
corona, *pl* **-ae** [kə'rəʊnə, -ɪ] *n Astron, Bot, El* couronne *f*; *El* **c. discharge** effluve *f* électrique; *El* **c. shielding** dispositif *m* anti-effluves
coronary ['kɒrən(ə)rɪ] *Med* **1** *adj* coronarien; **c. artery** artère *f* coronaire; **c. thrombosis** infarctus *m* du myocarde **2** *n* **to have a c.** avoir un infarctus (du myocarde); *F* **I just about had a c. when I saw the bill** j'ai failli avoir une attaque quand j'ai vu l'addition
coronation [kɒrə'neɪʃən] *n* couronnement *m*; **c. mug** tasse *f* commémorative du couronnement
coroner ['kɒrənər] *n Jur* coroner *m* (= *officier civil chargé d'instruire, assisté d'un jury, en cas de mort violente ou subite*); **c.'s inquest** enquête *f* du coroner
coronet ['kɒrənɪt] *n* (petite) couronne *f*; (*lady's*) diadème *m*
corp, Corp **(a)** *Com* (*abbr* **corporation**) Cie **(b)** *Mil abbr* **corporal**
corporal¹ ['kɔ:pər(ə)l] *adj* corporel; **c. punishment** châtiment *m* corporel
corporal² *n Mil* (*in infantry*) caporal *m*; (*in cavalry, artillery*) brigadier *m*; *Av* caporal-chef *m*
corporate ['kɔ:p(ə)rət] *adj* **(a)** *Com* corporatif, de société, d'entreprise; **I mean 'we' in the c. sense** par 'nous' j'entends la société; *Am* **c. apartments** appartements *mpl* destinés au personnel d'une société; **c. banking** banque *f* d'entreprise; **c. budget** budget *m* de l'entreprise; **c. culture** culture *f* d'entreprise; **c. image** image *f* de marque de l'entreprise; **the company cares about its c. image** la société se préoccupe de son image; **our c. image demands that ...** notre image en tant que société exige que ...; **to be a good c. citizen** (*of company*) avoir le sens des responsabilités civiques; **c. literature** brochures *fpl* décrivant une société; **c. lending** crédit *m* aux entreprises; **c. member** (*of association*) société-membre *f*; **c. name** raison *f* sociale; *St Exch* **c. raider** attaquant *m*; **c. strategy** stratégie *f* de l'entreprise
(b) (*forming a single body*) constitué (en corps), formant (un) corps; *Jur* **body c., c. body** corps *m* constitué, corporation *f*; (*considered as an individual*) personne *f* morale
(c) (*of a group of people*) de corporation, de corps; **c. feeling** esprit *m* de corps
corporate law *n* droit *m* des sociétés
corporate lawyer *n* juriste *mf* spécialisé(e) dans le droit des sociétés
corporation [kɔ:pə'reɪʃən] *n* **(a)** *Com Am* société *f*, compagnie *f*; *Br* **public c.** entreprise *f* publique; *Br* **c. tax** impôt *m* sur les sociétés, IS *m* **(b)** *Br* **municipal c.** (*council*) conseil *m* municipal, municipalité *f* **(c)** *Jur* personne *f* morale **(d)** *Old-fashioned F* (*paunch*) bedaine *f*, bedon *m*
corporeal [kɔ:'pɔ:rɪəl] *adj* corporel, matériel
corps [kɔ:r, *pl* kɔ:z] *n inv* corps *m*; *Mil* corps d'armée; **the diplomatic c.** le corps diplomatique; **tank c.** blindés *mpl*
corpse¹ [kɔ:ps] *n* cadavre *m*
corpse² *vi Th* (*of actor*) avoir le fou rire sur scène
corpulence ['kɔ:pjʊləns] *n* corpulence *f*
corpulent ['kɔ:pjʊlənt] *adj* corpulent
corpus ['kɔ:pəs] *n* **(a)** (*of writings*) corpus *m* **(b)** *Jur* **c. delicti** corps *m* du délit **(c)** *Cathol* **C. Christi** la Fête-Dieu
corpuscle ['kɔ:pʌs(ə)l] *n Biol* corpuscule *m*; **red/white blood corpuscles** globules *mpl* rouges/blancs

corral¹ [kɒ'rɑːl] *n* corral *m*, *pl* -als
corral² *vt* (*livestock, horses etc*) renfermer dans un corral; *Fig* (*demonstrators*) isoler; **to c. sb into doing sth** amener qn à faire qch
correct¹ [kə'rekt] *vt* **(a)** (*translation, homework, proofs*) corriger **(b)** (*rectify*) (*error, imbalance, oversteer*) rectifier, corriger; (*instrument setting*) modifier; **to c. a misunderstanding** dissiper un malentendu; **to c. a squint** (*of glasses*) corriger un strabisme
(c) (*put right*) (*person*) reprendre, corriger; **he had the nerve to c. my grammar/English/pronunciation** il a eu le culot de corriger *ou* de me reprendre sur ma grammaire/ mon anglais/ma prononciation; **I said it was 2 o'clock but someone corrected me** j'ai dit qu'il était 2 heures mais quelqu'un m'a corrigé; **to c. oneself** se reprendre; **c. me if I'm wrong, but ...** reprenez-moi si je me trompe, mais ...; **I stand corrected** j'avais tort
(d) *Old-fashioned* (*punish*) (*guilty person*) punir, infliger une correction à
correct² *adj* **(a)** (*exact*) correct, exact, juste; **the c. time** l'heure exacte; **c. to a millimetre** exact à un millimètre près; **am I c.?** je ne me trompe pas?; **his prediction proved c.** sa prédiction s'est vérifiée; **you must be Mr Jones — that's c.** vous devez être M. Jones — c'est exact; **if my memory is c.** si j'ai bonne mémoire; **figures c. at time of going to press** chiffres exacts au moment de la publication
(b) (*appropriate*) (*behaviour*) convenable, correct; (*person*) convenable, comme il faut; **it's the c. thing to send a letter of thanks** la politesse veut que l'on envoie une lettre de remerciements; **it's the c. thing to do** c'est ce qu'il convient de faire; **as is only c.** comme il se doit, comme il convient
correcting fluid [kə'rektɪŋ] *n* correcteur *m* liquide
correction [kə'rekʃən] *n* **(a)** (*of proofs, homework*), *MecE* correction *f*; (*statement in newspaper*) mise *f* au point, rectificatif *m*; **to make corrections to a text** apporter des corrections à un texte; **subject to c.** sous toutes réserves **(b)** *Old-fashioned* (*punishment*) correction *f*, punition *f*; *Arch* **house of c.** maison *f* de correction *ou* de redressement
correction fluid *n* correcteur *m* liquide, liquide *m* correcteur
corrective [kə'rektɪv] **1** *n* rectificatif *m*, correctif *m* **2** *adj* correctif; (*lens*) correcteur, -trice; **c. make-up** maquillage *m* correcteur
correctly [kə'rektlɪ] *adv* **(a)** (*to answer, report, predict*) correctement; **or (to put it) more c.** ou pour mieux dire **(b)** (*to behave*) correctement
correctness [kə'rektnɪs] *n* **(a)** (*of description, answer*) exactitude *f*, justesse *f* **(b)** (*of dress, behaviour*) correction *f*
correlate ['kɒrɪleɪt] **1** *vi* correspondre **(with** à), être en corrélation **(with** avec) **2** *vt* corréler, mettre en corrélation **(with** avec); **poverty and ill-health are closely correlated** il y a une corrélation étroite entre la pauvreté et la maladie
correlation [kɒrɪ'leɪʃən] *n* corrélation *f* **(with** avec, **between** entre)
correlative [kɒ'relətɪv] **1** *adj* corrélatif **2** *n* corrélatif *m*
correspond [kɒrɪs'pɒnd] *vi* **(a)** (*conform*) correspondre, être conforme **(with, to** à); **to c. with** *or* **to reality** correspondre à la réalité **(b)** (*be equivalent*) correspondre **(to** à), être l'équivalent **(to** de), équivaloir **(to** à); **the gendarmes roughly c. to our motorway police** les gendarmes sont à peu près l'équivalent de notre 'motorway police' **(c)** (*write letters*) correspondre **(with** avec); **they corresponded for many years** ils ont correspondu *ou* ils se sont écrit pendant des années
correspondence [kɒrɪs'pɒndəns] *n* **(a)** (*relationship*) correspondance *f* **(with, to** avec), rapport *m* **(with, to** entre) **(b)** (*letter writing*) correspondance *f*; **to be in c. with sb** être en correspondance avec qn, correspondre avec qn; **they kept up a c. for many years** ils sont restés en correspondance pendant des années; **to do one's c.** faire sa correspondance **(c)** (*mail*) courrier *m*; **I don't get much c.** je ne reçois pas beaucoup de courrier
correspondence column *n Journ* courrier *m* des lecteurs
correspondence course *n* cours *m* par correspondance
correspondence tray *n* bac *m* à correspondance
correspondent [kɒrɪs'pɒndənt] *n* correspondant, -ante; *Journ* **our London c.** notre correspondant à Londres; **parliamentary c.** *Journ* rédacteur, -trice parlementaire; *TV* correspondant, -ante parlementaire; **special c.** envoyé *m* spécial
correspondent bank account *n* compte *m* de correspondant
corresponding [kɒrɪ'spɒndɪŋ] *adj* correspondant **(to** à); **as compared with the c. period last year** par rapport à la même période l'année dernière; **c. member** (*of society, club*) membre *m* correspondant
correspondingly [kɒrɪ'spɒndɪŋlɪ] *adv* (*to react, respond, adjust*) en conséquence; (*as a consequence*) donc, par conséquent; **prices are c. more expensive** les prix sont proportionnellement plus élevés
corridor ['kɒrɪdɔːr] *n* couloir *m*, corridor *m*; *Pol* (*of land*) corridor; *Av* **(air)** **c.** couloir aérien; *Hist* **the Polish C.** le couloir de Dantzig; *Fig* **the corridors of power** les hautes sphères *fpl* du pouvoir; **c. train** train *m* à couloir
corroborate [kə'rɒbəreɪt] *vt* (*evidence, confession*) corroborer, confirmer
corroboration [kərɒbə'reɪʃən] *n* corroboration *f*, confirmation *f*; **in c. of ...** à l'appui de ...
corroborative [kə'rɒb(ə)rətɪv] *adj* (*evidence, statement*) qui confirme *ou* corrobore
corrode [kə'rəʊd] **1** *vt* (*metal*) corroder, attaquer; *Fig* (*society, optimism*) désagréger **2** *vi* se corroder
corroded [kə'rəʊdɪd] *adj* corrodé, attaqué; **badly c. metal** métal très corrodé *ou* attaqué
corrosion [kə'rəʊʒən] *n* corrosion *f*
corrosion-resistant *adj* anti-corrosion
corrosive [kə'rəʊsɪv] *adj, n* corrosif *m*, corrodant *m*
corrugated ['kɒrʊgeɪtɪd] *adj* **c. cardboard** carton *m* ondulé; **c. iron** tôle *f* ondulée; **c. iron roof** toit *m* en tôle ondulée
corrupt¹ [kə'rʌpt] *adj* **(a)** (*dishonest*) (*official, politician*) corrompu **(b)** (*depraved*) corrompu, dépravé; **c. morals** immoralité *f* **(c)** *Comptr* (*disk, file*) corrompu, altéré, endommagé; **to go c.** s'endommager **(d)** *Liter* (*text*) corrompu, altéré
corrupt² *vt* **(a)** (*deprave*) (*youth*) corrompre; **to c. sb's morals** dépraver qn; **to be corrupted by power** être corrompu par le pouvoir **(b)** *Comptr* corrompre, altérer, endommager **(c)** *Liter* (*text etc*) corrompre, altérer
corruptible [kə'rʌptəb(ə)l] *adj* corruptible
corrupting [kə'rʌptɪŋ] *adj* dépravant, corrupteur, -trice; **c. influence** influence *f* corruptrice
corruption [kə'rʌpʃən] *n* **(a)** (*giving and taking bribes*) corruption *f*; **bribery and c.** corruption **(b)** (*act of making depraved*) corruption *f*, dépravation *f* **(c)** *Comptr* corruption *f*, altération *f*, dommage *m* **(d)** *Liter* (*of text*) corruption *f*, altération *f*
corruptive [kə'rʌptɪv] *adj* corrupteur, -trice
corruptly [kə'rʌptlɪ] *adv* d'une manière corrompue
corsage [kɔː'sɑːʒ] *n* **(a)** fleur *f* (*portée au corsage, à la taille ou au poignet*) **(b)** (*bodice of dress*) corsage *m*
corsair ['kɔːseər] *n Hist* (*pirate, ship*) corsaire *m*
corset ['kɔːsɪt] *n* corset *m*; **orthopaedic** *or* **surgical c.** corset orthopédique
Corsica ['kɔːsɪkə] *n* Corse *f*
Corsican ['kɔːsɪkən] **1** *adj* corse **2** *n* (*person*) Corse *mf*; *Ling* corse *m*
cortège [kɔː'teʒ] *n* cortège *m*; **funeral c.** convoi *m ou* cortège funèbre
cortex, *pl* **-ices** ['kɔːteks, -ɪsiːz] *n Bot, Anat* cortex *m*
corticosteroids [kɔːtɪkəʊ'sterɔɪdz] *npl Med* corticoïdes *mpl*
cortisone ['kɔːtɪzəʊn] *n Biol, Ch, Med* cortisone *f*
corundum [kə'rʌndəm] *n Miner* corindon *m*
coruscate ['kɒrəskeɪt] *vi Lit* scintiller
coruscating ['kɒrəskeɪtɪŋ] *adj Lit* **c. wit** esprit *m* scintillant
corvette [kɔː'vet] *n Naut* corvette *f*
cos¹ [kɒz] *n Math* (*abbr* **cosine**) cosinus *m*
cos² *conj F* = **because**
cos³ [kɒs] *n Br* **c. (lettuce)** (laitue *f*) romaine *f*
cosh¹ [kɒʃ] *n Br* matraque *f*
cosh² *vt Br* assommer, matraquer
cosignatory ['kəʊ'sɪgnətərɪ] *n* cosignataire *mf* **(to** de)
cosily ['kəʊzɪlɪ] *adv* (*warmly*) confortablement, douillettement; **c. wrapped up** bien emmitouflé
cosine ['kəʊsaɪn] *n Math* cosinus *m*
cosiness ['kəʊzɪnɪs] *n* **(a)** (*of armchair, room*) confort *m* **(b)** *Fig* (*of arrangement*) caractère *m* combinard
cosmetic [kɒz'metɪk] **1** *n* cosmétique *m*; **cosmetics** produits *mpl* de beauté, cosmétiques *mpl*; **the cosmetics industry/ counter** l'industrie *f*/le rayon des cosmétiques *ou* des produits de beauté **2** *adj* **(a)** cosmétique **(b)** (*superficial*) superficiel; **the policy change is c. rather than real** le changement de politique est plutôt un changement de forme que de fond; **the alterations they made to the translation are purely c.** les changements qu'ils ont apportés à la traduction sont très superficiels
cosmetician [kɒzmɪ'tɪʃən] *n* esthéticien, -ienne
cosmetic surgery *n* chirurgie *f* esthétique; **to have c.** se faire faire une opération de chirurgie esthétique
cosmic ['kɒzmɪk] *adj* (*ray, dust*) cosmique; *Fig* gigantesque
cosmology [kɒz'mɒlədʒɪ] *n* cosmologie *f*
cosmonaut ['kɒzmənɔːt] *n* cosmonaute *mf*

cosmopolitan [kɒzmə'pɒlɪt(ə)n] **1** *n* cosmopolite *mf* **2** *adj* (*city etc*) cosmopolite
cosmos ['kɒzmɒs] *n* cosmos *m*
Cossack ['kɒsæk] **1** *adj* cosaque **2** *n* Cosaque *m*
cosset ['kɒsɪt] *vt* dorloter, choyer
cossie ['kɒzɪ] *n Austr F* maillot *m* de bain
cost[1] [kɒst] *n* **(a)** (*price*) coût *m*, frais *mpl*; *Jur* **costs** frais d'instance, dépens *mpl*; *Jur* **they were ordered to pay costs** ils ont été condamnés aux dépens; **at little/great c.** à peu de/à grands frais; **to sell at c.** vendre au prix coûtant; **for the c. of a room in a hotel you could ...** pour le prix d'une chambre à l'hôtel, vous pourriez ...; **c., insurance and freight** coût, assurance, fret; **c. and freight** coût et fret; *Mktg* **c. per thousand** coût pour mille contacts, CPM *m*; *Acct* **c. of money** loyer *m* de l'argent; *Acct* **c. of sales** coût *m* de revient des produits vendus; **c. analysis** analyse *f* des coûts; **c. assessment** évaluation *f* du coût; **c. budget** budget *m* des charges; *Acct* **c. centre** centre *m* d'analyse; **c. conscious** (*company, person*) qui fait attention aux dépenses; *Com* **c. curve** courbe *f* (de l'évolution) des coûts, courbe de coût; *Com* **c. equation** équation *f* de coût; **c. escalation clause** clause *f* d'indexation; **c. factor** facteur *m* coût; *Acct* **c. overrun** dépassement *m* de coût
(b) (*in Fig phrases*) **to count the cost(s) of sth** calculer le coût de qch; **at any c., at all costs** à tout prix, à n'importe quel prix, coûte que coûte; **I learnt it to my c.** je l'ai appris à mes dépens; **as I know to my c.** comme je l'ai appris à mes dépens; **at the c. of one's life** au prix de sa vie; **the c. in human life** (*of disaster etc*) le prix en vies humaines
cost[2] *vt* **(a)** (*pt, pp* **cost**) coûter; **it costs $25** ça coûte 25 dollars; **it cost me £30 a night to stay here** ça m'a coûté 30 livres par nuit ici; **how much does it c.?** combien cela coûte-t-il?; **it costs nothing to join the library** l'inscription à la bibliothèque est gratuite; **that will c. him a great deal of money/trouble** cela lui coûtera beaucoup d'argent/de peine; **to c. a fortune** *or* **the earth** coûter une fortune, coûter les yeux de la tête; *Br F* **if you go by air it'll c. you** si tu y vas par avion, tu vas le sentir passer; **the attempt cost him his life** cette tentative lui a coûté la vie; **it must have cost her something to admit that** il a dû lui en coûter de l'avouer
(b) (*pt, pp* **costed**) *Com, Ind* (*estimate cost of*) (*article*) établir le prix de revient de; (*job*) évaluer le coût de; **how much was it costed at?** (*of work*) à combien est-ce que le coût a été évalué?
▶ **cost out** *vtsep* = **cost**[2] **(b)**
cost accounting *n* comptabilité *f* analytique
co-star[1] ['kəʊstɑːr] *n Cin* acteur *m*/actrice *f* qui partage la vedette avec un(e) autre
co-star[2] *vi Cin* partager la vedette (**with** avec); **co-starring ...** avec ...
Costa Rica ['kɒstə'riːkə] *n* Costa Rica *m*
Costa Rican ['kɒstə'riːkən] **1** *adj* costaricien **2** *n* Costaricien, -ienne
cost-benefit analysis *n Fin* analyse *f* coûts-bénéfices
cost/benefit ratio *n Fin* rapport *m* coût/profit
cost-competitive *adj* (*product*) à prix compétitif; **we're not c.** nos prix ne sont pas compétitifs
cost-cutting ['kɒstkʌtɪŋ] **1** *n* réduction *f* des frais *ou* des dépenses **2** *adj* **c. measures** mesures *fpl* visant à réduire les frais *ou* les dépenses
cost-effective *adj* rentable; **the project must be made c.** il faut rentabiliser le projet
cost-effectiveness *n Com* rentabilité *f*
coster(monger) ['kɒstər, 'kɒstəmʌŋgər] *n Old-fashioned Br* marchand, -ande des quatre saisons
costing ['kɒstɪŋ] *n Ind, Com* (*of article*) établissement *m* du prix de revient; (*of job*) évaluation *f* du coût
costive ['kɒstɪv] *adj Med* constipé
costliness ['kɒstlɪnɪs] *n* cherté *f*; *Fig* **the c. of an error** les conséquences *fpl* d'une erreur
costly ['kɒstlɪ] *adj* cher, coûteux, onéreux; *Fig* **it was a c. mistake** c'est une erreur qui a coûté cher
cost of living *n* coût *m* de la vie; **cost-of-living allowance** *or US* **adjustment** indemnité *f* de vie chère; **cost-of-living index** indice *m* du coût de la vie
cost-plus *adj Fin* à coût majoré; **c. pricing** fixation *f* du prix en fonction du coût
cost price *n Ind, Com* prix *m* coûtant, prix de revient; **to sell at below c.** vendre à perte
cost-push inflation *n* inflation *f* par les coûts
cost-reduce *vt Com* réduire le coût de
costume ['kɒstjʊm] *n* **(a)** costume *m*; **national c.** costume national; *Br* (**bathing** *or* **swimming**) **c.** maillot *m* de bain; *Th* **costume(s) department** service *m* des costumes; **c. designer** créateur *m* de costumes; *Cin, TV, Th* **c. drama** film *m*/pièce *f* historique; **c. jewellery** bijoux *mpl* fantaisie; *esp Am* **c. party** bal *m* costumé **(b)** *Old-fashioned* (*woman's suit*) tailleur *m*
costum(i)er [kɒs'tjʊmər, -ɪər] *n* costumier, -ière
cosy ['kəʊzɪ] **1** *adj* **(a)** (*room, pub*) confortable, douillet; **to feel** *or* **be c.** (*of person in room*) être confortablement *ou* douillettement installé; (*in coat, blankets etc*) être bien emmitouflé; **it's c. here** quel nid douillet
(b) *Fig* **a c. little job** (*undemanding*) un travail pépère; **a c. little arrangement** une bonne petite combine; **at university it's all very c.** à l'université, c'est pépère; **the c. relationship between government and the employers** les relations très privilégiées entre le gouvernement et le patronat; **it's all a bit too c. for my liking** (*of relationship between union and management etc*) c'est un peu trop copain-copain à mon goût
2 *n* (**egg**) **c.** couvre-œuf *m*, *pl* couvre-œufs; (**tea**) **c.** couvre-théière *m*, *pl* couvre-théières
▶ **cosy up to** *vipo* (*ingratiate oneself with*) se mettre dans les petits papiers de
cot [kɒt] *n* (*for child*) lit *m* d'enfant; *esp Am* (*folding bed*) petit lit *m* (pliant); (*camp bed*) lit de camp; *Naut* cadre *m* à l'anglaise
cotangent ['kəʊ'tændʒ(ə)nt] *n Math* cotangente *f*
cot death *n Med* mort *f* subite du nourrisson
cotel ['kɒtel] *n Am* auberge *f* de jeunesse
coterie ['kəʊtərɪ] *n* coterie *f*
cottage ['kɒtɪdʒ] *n* **(a)** petite maison *f* (à la campagne), cottage *m*; *Am* (*for holidays*) petite maison de vacances, *Can* chalet *m*; (**thatched**) **c.** chaumière *f*; *Br* **c. hospital** hôpital *m* de médecine générale en zone rurale; *Br* **c. flat** = appartement *m* situé dans un pavillon; *Culin* **c. loaf** ≈ double miche *f*, ≈ calotte *f* bretonne **(b)** *Br Sl* (*for homosexuals*) = toilettes *fpl* publiques utilisées comme lieu de rencontre par les homosexuels
cottage cheese *n* = fromage *m* blanc
cottage industry *n* industrie *f* artisanale, artisanat *m*; *Fig* (*small scale*) industrie familiale; *Fig F* **we're not a c. here** nous ne sommes pas des rigolos ici
cottage pie *n Br Culin* hachis *m* parmentier
cottager ['kɒtɪdʒər] *n* **(a)** *Br* (*in countryside*) habitant, -ante d'un cottage **(b)** *Am* (*in holiday resort*) propriétaire *mf*/locataire *mf* d'une petite maison de vacances *ou Can* d'un chalet
cottaging ['kɒtɪdʒɪŋ] *n Br Sl* relations *fpl* homosexuelles dans des toilettes publiques
cotter ['kɒtər] *n MecE* **c.** (**pin**) goupille *f* fendue
cotton ['kɒt(ə)n] *n* **(a)** (*crop*) coton *m*; **to pick c.** cueillir le coton; *US* **c. belt** région *f* du coton (*dans le sud des Etats-Unis*); **c. field** champ *m* de coton; **c. grass** (*plant*) linaigrette *f*, lin *m* des marais; **c. growing** culture *f* du coton **(b)** (*cloth*) (toile *f* de) coton *m*; **c. goods** cotonnades *fpl*; **c. shirt/sheet** chemise/drap en coton; **c. yarn** coton filé, fil *m* de coton **(c)** (*for sewing*) fil *m* à coudre
▶ **cotton on** *vi F* (*understand*) piger; **to c. on to sth** piger qch
▶ **cotton to** *vipo Am F* **(a)** (*take a liking to*) se prendre d'amitié pour **(b)** (*approve of*) (*person*) avoir à la bonne; (*behaviour, suggestion*) voir d'un bon œil; **I don't c. to that kind of behaviour** je n'approuve pas ce genre de comportement
cotton bush *n* cotonnier *m*
cotton candy *n Am Culin* barbe *f* à papa
cotton mill *n* filature *f* de coton
cotton picker *n* ramasseur, -euse de coton
cotton-picking ['kɒt(ə)n'pɪkɪŋ] *adj Am F* (*intensifier*) sacré; **that's a c. lie!** ce n'est qu'un mensonge!; **get your c. hands off me!** enlève tes sales pattes!
cotton plant *n* cotonnier *m*
cotton plantation *n* plantation *f* de coton
cottonseed ['kɒt(ə)nsiːd] *n* graine *f* de coton; **c. oil** huile *f* de coton
cottontail ['kɒt(ə)nteɪl] *n US* lapin *m* (de garenne)
cotton wool *n Br* ouate *f*, coton *m* hydrophile; **my legs feel like c.** j'ai les jambes en coton; *Fig* **to wrap sb in c.** mettre qn dans du coton
cotyledon [kɒtɪ'liːd(ə)n] *n Bot* cotylédon *m*
couch[1] [kaʊtʃ] *n* divan *m*; *Fig* **to be on the c.** (*in psychoanalysis*) être en analyse
couch[2] *vt* (*express*) (*phrase, comment*) formuler, rédiger; **the complaint was couched in very polite language** la plainte avait été formulée très poliment
couchette [kʊ'ʃet] *n Rail, Naut* couchette *f*; *Rail* **c. car** voiture-couchette *f*
couch grass *n* (*weed*) chiendent *m*
couch potato *n F* mollasson, -onne (*toujours affalé devant la télévision*), téléphage *m*; **he's a real c.** il est très télé

cougar ['ku:gər] *n* (*animal*) puma *m*
cough¹ [kɒf] *n* toux *f*; **I've got a c.** je tousse; **he gave a c. to warn me** il toussota pour m'avertir; **he cleared his throat with a c.** il toussota pour s'éclaircir la voix *ou F* la gorge; **dry c.** toux sèche
cough² *vi* (*of person, animal, F engine*) tousser; (*to warn sb*) toussoter
▶ **cough up 1** *vtsep* **(a)** (*produce by coughing*) cracher (en toussant), expectorer; **to c. up phlegm/blood** cracher des glaires/du sang **(b)** *F* (*pay*) sortir; **I had to c. up £50 for the meal** j'ai dû sortir 50 livres pour le repas **2** *vi F* (*pay*) casquer, cracher, raquer; **come on, c. up!** (*money owed me*) allez! file-moi mon argent!; (*pay your share*) allez! allonge!
cough drop *n* pastille *f* contre *ou* pour la toux
coughing ['kɒfɪŋ] *n* toux *f*; **fit of c., c. fit** quinte *f* de toux; **your c. woke me up** tu m'as réveillé en toussant
cough lozenge *n* pastille *f* contre *ou* pour la toux
cough mixture *n* sirop *m* contre *ou* pour la toux
cough sweet *n* pastille *f* contre *ou* pour la toux
cough syrup *n* sirop *m* contre *ou* pour la toux
could *see* **can³**
couldn't-care-less ['kʊd(ə)ntkeə'les] *adj* **c. attitude** laisser-aller *m*, *F* je-m'en-fichisme *m*, je-m'en-foutisme *m*
coulomb ['ku:lɒmb] *n El* coulomb *m*, ampère-seconde *m*
council ['kaʊnsəl] *n* **(a)** *Admin* conseil *m*; **(city) c.** (*people*) conseil municipal; (*government*) municipalité *f*; *Br* **the c. sent a repairman** la municipalité a envoyé un réparateur; *Br* **to be on the c.** être au conseil municipal; *Mil, Fig* **to hold a c. of war** tenir un conseil de guerre; *Br* **c. estate** cité *f* de H.L.M.; *Br* **c. house/flat** = habitation *f* à loyer modéré, H.L.M. *f*; **c. meeting** réunion *f* du conseil municipal; **c. offices** bureaux *mpl* de la municipalité **(b)** *Rel* concile *m*
councillor ['kaʊnsɪlər] *n* conseiller *m*, membre *m* du conseil; **C. John Smith** M. John Smith, membre du conseil
Council of Europe *n* Conseil *m* de l'Europe
counsel¹ ['kaʊns(ə)l] *n* **(a)** *Fml* (*advice*) conseil *m*, avis *m*; **to take c. with sb** consulter qn **(about** sur, au sujet de)
(b) to keep one's (own) c. (*about one's plans, intentions*) garder ses projets pour soi; (*about one's opinions*) garder son opinion pour soi
(c) (*no pl*) *Br Jur* (*in court*) avocat *m*; (*adviser*) conseil *m* juridique; **to be represented by c.** être représenté par un avocat; **to take the advice of c.** suivre les conseils d'un avocat; **c. for the defence** défenseur *m*; (*in criminal law*) avocat de la défense; **c. for the prosecution** procureur *m*; **King's/Queen's c.** conseiller *m* du Roi/de la Reine, conseiller de la Couronne
counsel² *vt* **(-ll-,** *US* **-l-)** (*patience, prudence*) conseiller; **to c. sb to do sth** conseiller à qn de faire qch
counselling [kaʊns(ə)lɪŋ] *n* (*activity, profession*) activité *f* de conseil; (*advice*) conseils *mpl*; **he needs (professional) c.** (*psychological*) il a besoin d'un soutien psychologique; **to offer c. for alcoholics/people suffering from AIDS** offrir un soutien psychologique et moral aux alcooliques/aux malades du SIDA
counsellor, *US* **counselor** ['kaʊns(ə)lər] *n* **(a)** (*diplomatic*) conseiller *m* d'ambassade **(b)** (*social, psychological*) conseiller, -ère **(c)** *US Jur* avocat, -ate
count¹ [kaʊnt] *n* **(a)** (*act of counting*) compte *m*, comptage *m*; (*of votes*) dépouillement *m*; (*of people*) dénombrement *m*, comptage; **to keep c.** tenir le compte **(of** de); **to lose c.** perdre le compte; **I've lost c. of how many times I've asked you to ...** je ne sais pas combien de fois je t'ai demandé de ...; **we'll have to do another c.** il faudra qu'on recompte; **a quick c. revealed that half were car owners** un comptage rapide a révélé que la moitié étaient propriétaires de voitures; **at the last c.** au dernier comptage
(b) (*total, result of count*) compte *m*, total *m*; **what was the c.?** quel était le total?; **this is short of the c.** cela ne fait pas le compte
(c) *Boxing* compte *m* (de dix secondes); **to take the c.** rester au tapis pour le compte, être knock-out; *Boxing, Fig* **to be out for the c.** être K-O.
(d) *Jur* chef *m* d'accusation; **not guilty on the first c.** non coupable au premier chef; *Fig* **I'm angry with them on both counts** je suis fâché avec eux pour les deux raisons; **to fail on a number of counts** (*of project etc*) échouer à plusieurs égards
count² 1 *vt* **(a)** (*enumerate*) (*people, vehicles, animals etc*) dénombrer, compter; (*money*) compter; **to c. the votes** (*at election*) dépouiller le scrutin; **I counted three wrecked cars** j'ai compté trois voitures démolies; **to c. sheep** (*in order to go to sleep*) compter les moutons
(b) (*include*) compter; **counting the dog there were four of us** nous étions quatre en comptant le chien; **without** *or* **not counting ...** sans compter ...
(c) (*consider*) compter **(as** comme); **I don't c. him as a friend** je ne le considère pas comme un ami; **to c. sb among one's friends** compter qn parmi ses amis; **to be counted as a member** compter parmi les membres; **I c. it (as) one of my triumphs** je considère cela comme un de mes triomphes; **c. yourself lucky you weren't killed** estime-toi heureux de n'avoir pas été tué
2 *vi* **(a)** compter; **to c. on one's fingers** compter sur ses doigts; **to c. (up) to 100** compter jusqu'à 100; **to c. from 1 to 100** compter de 1 à 100; **counting from tomorrow** à compter de demain
(b) (*be considered*) compter **(among** parmi); **he counts among my best friends** il compte parmi mes meilleurs amis; **two children c. as one adult** deux enfants comptent comme un adulte; **he's under five so he doesn't c.** il a moins de cinq ans, donc il ne compte pas; **marks in this exam c. towards your degree** les notes de cet examen comptent pour votre licence
(c) (*be of importance*) compter; **I don't c. around here** je ne compte pas ici; **every vote counts** chaque voix compte; **every minute counts** il n'y a pas une minute à perdre; **experience counts for more than qualifications** l'expérience compte plus que les diplômes; **doesn't that c. for anything?** est-ce que ça ne compte pas, ça?
count³ *n* (*nobleman*) comte *m*
▶ **count against** *vipo* jouer contre
▶ **count down** *vi Astronaut, Fig* compter à rebours
▶ **count in** *vtsep* (*include*) compter; **c. me in!** je suis de la partie, *F* je suis partant
▶ **count on** *vipo* **(a)** (*depend on*) compter sur; **we're counting on you to give a speech** nous comptons sur vous pour faire un discours; **you can always c. on him to be late** tu peux compter sur lui pour être en retard, tu peux être sûr qu'il sera en retard; **I wouldn't c. on the train arriving on time** je ne compterais pas sur le fait que le train soit à l'heure; **can we c. on your vote?** pouvons-nous compter sur votre voix? **(b)** (*expect*) compter; **I didn't c. on seeing you** je ne comptais pas te voir
▶ **count out** *vtsep* **(a)** (*add up*) (*money*) compter; **he counted me out twenty £1 coins** il m'a compté vingt pièces de 1 livre **(b)** (*exclude*) ne pas compter; **he's teetotal, so you can c. him out** il ne boit pas, donc ne le compte pas; **no thanks, c. me out!** non merci, ne comptez pas sur moi **(c)** *Boxing* **to be counted out** rester au tapis pour le compte, être (mis) knock-out
▶ **count up** *vtsep* (*add up*) compter
countable ['kaʊntəb(ə)l] *adj* [ⓘA9–11,3] *Gram* **c. noun** nom *m* dénombrable *ou* comptable
countdown ['kaʊntdaʊn] *n* (*for rocket launch*) compte *m* à rebours; *Fig* **the c. to Christmas has begun** on commence à compter les jours qui nous séparent de Noël
countenance¹ ['kaʊntɪnəns] *n esp Lit* **(a)** (*face*) (expression *f* du) visage *m*, mine *f*; **to lose c.** se décontenancer, perdre contenance; **to be out of c.** avoir perdu contenance, être décontenancé **(b)** (*support*) **to give** *or* **lend c. to sb/sth** apporter son appui *ou* son soutien à qn/qch, appuyer qn/qch
countenance² *vt* approuver, appuyer; **she wouldn't c. borrowing money** elle n'approuverait pas le fait d'emprunter de l'argent
counter¹ ['kaʊntər] *n* **(a)** (*in shop*) comptoir *m*; (*in supermarket*) rayon *m*; (*in bank etc*) guichet *m*; **payable over the c.** payable au guichet; **you can get these drugs over the c.** on peut acheter ces médicaments sans ordonnance, ces médicaments sont en vente libre; *Fin* **to buy shares over the c.** acheter des actions sur le marché hors cote; **sold over the c.** (*not pre-packaged*) vendu au détail; **to sell under the c.** vendre sous le manteau; *Banking* **c. services** services *mpl* de caisse; *Banking* **c. transactions** opérations *fpl* de caisse
(b) (*token in games*) (*square*) fiche *f*; (*round*) jeton *m*; **the hostage was being used as a bargaining c.** l'otage a été utilisé comme monnaie d'échange
(c) *Comptr etc* (*device*) compteur *m*
counter² 1 *n Fencing, Boxing* contre *m* **2** *adj* **(a)** contraire, opposé **(to** à) **(b)** (*in compounds*) contre-; **c. declaration** contre-déclaration *f*; **c. reaction** contre-réaction *f* **3** *adv* en sens inverse; **to act c. to one's orders** agir contrairement aux ordres (que l'on a) reçus; **to run c. to sth** aller à l'encontre de qch
counter³ 1 *vt* (*sb, sth*) aller à l'encontre de; (*sb's intentions*) contrecarrer; (*accusation, criticism*) répondre à; **measures have been taken to c. the threat of the disease** des mesures ont été prises pour lutter contre la menace que représente la maladie; *Boxing* **to c. a blow** contrer un coup; (*ward off*) parer un coup; **to c. that ...** riposter *ou* rétorquer

que ... + *ind* 2 *vi* riposter, contre-attaquer; *Boxing, Fencing* contrer; (*ward off*) parer

counteract [kaʊntəˈrækt] *vt* (*act against*) contrecarrer; (*neutralize*) (*influence, effects of drug*) neutraliser

counter-appraisal *n Am Com* contre-expertise *f*

counterattack[1] [ˈkaʊntərətæk] *n Mil, Fig* contre-attaque *f, pl* contre-attaques

counterattack[2] *vti Mil, Fig* contre-attaquer

counterattraction [ˈkaʊntərəˈtrækʃən] *n* attraction *f* concurrente; (*on TV*) émission *f* concurrente

counterbalance[1] [ˈkaʊntəbæləns] *n* contrepoids *m*

counterbalance[2] [kaʊntəˈbæləns] *vt* contrebalancer, faire contrepoids à

counterblast [ˈkaʊntəblɑːst] *n* contre-attaque *f, pl* contre-attaques

countercharge [ˈkaʊntətʃɑːdʒ] *n Jur* contre-accusation *f, pl* contre-accusations, contre-plainte *f, pl* contre-plaintes

countercheck [ˈkaʊntətʃek] *vt* vérifier (une seconde fois)

counterclaim[1] [ˈkaʊntəkleɪm] *n Jur etc* demande *f* reconventionnelle

counterclaim[2] *vi Jur* faire une demande reconventionnelle (*en dommages-intérêts*)

counterclockwise [kaʊntəˈklɒkwaɪz] *adv, adj esp Am* en sens inverse des aiguilles d'une montre

counterculture [ˈkaʊntəkʌltʃər] *n* contre-culture *f, pl* contre-cultures

counterespionage [kaʊntəˈrespɪənɑːʒ] *n* contre-espionnage *m*

counterfeit[1] [ˈkaʊntəfɪt] **1** *adj* faux; (*emotions*) feint; **a c. (bank)note** un faux billet; **c. money** de faux billets **2** *n* contrefaçon *f*, faux *m*; **the note was a c.** le billet était un faux

counterfeit[2] *vt* (*money etc*) contrefaire

counterfeiter [ˈkaʊntəfɪtər] *n* faussoire *mf*; (*of money*) faux monnayeur *m*

counterfoil [ˈkaʊntəfɔɪl] *n Br* (*of cheque, receipt*) souche *f*, talon *m*; **c. book** carnet *m* à souches

counter-guarantee *n St Exch* contre-garantie *f*

counter hand *n Br* vendeur, -euse

counter indication *n Med* contre-indication *f*

counterinsurgency [ˈkaʊntəɪnsɜːdʒənsɪ] *n* contre-insurrection *f*

counterintelligence [ˈkaʊntərɪnˈtelɪdʒəns] *n* contre-espionnage *m*

counterintuitive [ˈkaʊntəɪntjuːɪtɪv] *adj* qui va contre l'intuition

countermand [ˈkaʊntəmɑːnd] *vt* (*order*) annuler

countermarketing [ˈkaʊntəmɑːkətɪŋ] *n* contremercatique *f*, contremarketing *m*

countermeasure [ˈkaʊntəmeʒər] *n* contre-mesure *f, pl* contre-mesures

countermove [ˈkaʊntəmuːv] *n* contre *m*

counteroffensive [ˈkaʊntərəˈfensɪv] *n Mil* contre-offensive *f, pl* contre-offensives

counter-offer *n* contre-offre *f*

counterorder [ˈkaʊntərɔːdər] *n* contrordre *m*

counterpane [ˈkaʊntəpeɪn] *n* couvre-lit *m, pl* couvre-lits; (*quilted*) courtepointe *f*

counterpart [ˈkaʊntəpɑːt] *n* **(a)** (*person*) homologue *mf* **(b)** (*corresponding system*) équivalent *m*; (*of pair of works of art*) pendant *m*; (*piece that corresponds*) pièce *f* qui va de pair

counterparty risk [ˈkaʊntəpɑːtɪ] *n Banking* risque *m* de contrepartie

counterplot [ˈkaʊntəplɒt] *n* contre-ruse *f, pl* contre-ruses

counterpoint [ˈkaʊntəpɔɪnt] *n Mus* contrepoint *m*

counterpoise[1] [ˈkaʊntəpɔɪz] *n also Fig* contrepoids *m*; **in c.** en équilibre; **his sense of organization served as a c. to ...** son sens de l'organisation contrebalançait ...

counterpoise[2] *vt* contrebalancer, faire contrepoids à

counterproductive [ˈkaʊntəprəˈdʌktɪv] *adj* qui a des effets contraires; **that would be c.** cela irait à l'encontre du but recherché

counterproposal [ˈkaʊntəprəˈpəʊz(ə)l] *n* contre-proposition *f, pl* contre-propositions

counterpurchase [ˈkaʊntəpɜːtʃɪs] *n* contre-achat *m*

Counter-Reformation *n Rel, Hist* **the C.** la Contre-Réforme

counter-revolution *n Pol* contre-révolution *f, pl* contre-révolutions

counter-revolutionary *Pol* **1** *n* contre-révolutionnaire *mf, pl* contre-révolutionnaires **2** *adj* contre-révolutionnaire

countersegmentation [ˈkaʊntəsegmenteɪʃən] *n Mktg* contre-segmentation *f*, stratégie *f* d'indifférenciation

countershaft [ˈkaʊntəʃɑːft] *n Aut* (*layshaft*) arbre *m* intermédiaire

countersign [ˈkaʊntəsaɪn] *vt* (*order etc*) contresigner, signer en second, viser

countersignature [ˈkaʊntəˈsɪgnətjər] *n* contreseing *m*

countersink[1] [ˈkaʊntəsɪŋk] *n* **(a)** (*tool*) **c. bit** fraise *f* **(b)** (*for head of screw*) noyure *f*; (*of hole*) fraisure *f*

countersink[2] *vt* (*pt, pp* **countersunk**) *Carp, MecE etc* (*head of screw*) fraiser, noyer

counter staff *n(pl)* vendeurs, -euses

counterstroke [ˈkaʊntəstrəʊk] *n Mil, Fig* contre-offensive *f, pl* contre-offensives

countersunk [ˈkaʊntəsʌnk] *adj* (*screw*) fraisé, noyé

countertenor [ˈkaʊntətenər] *n Mus* (*person*) haute-contre *m, pl* hautes-contre, contre-ténor *m, pl* contre-ténors

counterterrorism [ˈkaʊntəˈterərɪz(ə)m] *n* contre-terrorisme *m*

counter-terrorist *adj* contre-terroriste

countertrade [ˈkaʊntətreɪd] *n* commerce *m* d'échange, troc *m*

countervailing [kaʊntəˈveɪlɪŋ] *adj attrib Fml* compensatoire

countervaluation [ˈkaʊntəvæljʊeɪʃən] *n* contre-expertise *f*

counterweight [ˈkaʊntəweɪt] *n* contrepoids *m*

countess [ˈkaʊntɪs] *n* comtesse *f*

counting [ˈkaʊntɪŋ] *n* compte *m*; (*of vote*) dépouillement *m*; (*of people*) compte, dénombrement *m*

countless [ˈkaʊntlɪs] *adj* innombrable, sans nombre

count noun *n* [①A9–11,3] nom *m* dénombrable *ou* comptable

countrified [ˈkʌntrɪfaɪd] *adj* aux allures campagnardes; **it's very c. here** c'est comme la campagne ici

country [ˈkʌntrɪ] *n* **(a)** [①A27,c,iii] (*political entity*) pays *m*; **in this c.** dans ce pays; **the Prime Minister isn't in the c.** le premier ministre est à l'étranger; **to die for/love one's c.** mourir pour/aimer sa patrie; *esp Br Pol* **to go to the c.** (*call election*) se présenter aux souffrages des électeurs; **c. of destination** pays *m* de destination; *Comptr* **c. keyboard** clavier *m* national; *Mktg* **c. version** (*of a product*) version *f* nationale

(b) (*opposed to town*) campagne *f*; **in the c.** à la campagne; **c. gentleman** gentilhomme *m* campagnard; **c. inn** auberge *f* rurale *ou* de campagne; **c. life** vie *f* à la campagne; **c. park** parc *m* naturel *ou* de loisirs

(c) (*opposed to capital*) province *f*; **a quiet little c. town** une petite ville tranquille de province; **c. cousin** cousin, -ine de province; **c. seat** manoir *m*

(d) (*region*) pays *m*, région *f*; **rough c.** terrain *m* accidenté; **open c.** rase campagne *f*; **flat c.** pays *ou* terrain plat; **wheat-growing c.** région à blé; **this is Proust c.** c'est le pays de Proust

country and western music *n* country *f ou m inv*

country bumpkin *n Hum* cul-terreux *m, pl* culs-terreux

country club *n* = club *m* sportif *ou* de loisirs situé à la campagne

country code *n* = règles *fpl* à suivre lorsque l'on se trouve à la campagne telles que ne pas laisser de papiers gras, refermer les portails etc

country dancing *n* danse *f* folklorique

countryfolk [ˈkʌntrɪfəʊk] *npl* gens *mpl* de la campagne

country house *n* manoir *m*; **c. hotel** relais-château *m*, auberge *f*

countryman, *pl* **-men** [ˈkʌntrɪmən, -men] *n* **(a)** (*not living in town*) campagnard *m* **(b)** **(fellow) c.** compatriote *m*

countryside [ˈkʌntrɪsaɪd] *n* campagne *f*; **beautiful c.** beau paysage *m*; **there's some beautiful c. around Bath** il y a de beaux paysages autour de Bath; **the voters in the c.** les électeurs des régions rurales

country-specific *adj Comptr* (*keyboard*) particulier à un pays

countrystyle [ˈkʌntrɪstaɪl] *adj* **c. cooking** cuisine *f* campagnarde

countrywoman, *pl* **-women** [ˈkʌntrɪwʊmən, -wɪmɪn] *n* **(a)** (*not living in town*) campagnarde *f* **(b)** **(fellow) c.** compatriote *f*

county [ˈkaʊntɪ] **1** *n* **(a)** comté *m*; *Br* **the c. of Kent** le comté du Kent; *US* **New York C.** le comté de New York; *Br* **c. society** l'aristocratie et la haute bourgeoisie du comté; *Br* **c. town** chef-lieu *m* de comté, *pl* chefs-lieux **(b)** (*population*) habitants *mpl* du comté **2** *adj* (*rural upper class*) **the c. set** la noblesse campagnarde; **she's very c.** elle fait très femme de la noblesse campagnarde

county council *n Br* = conseil *m* général

county councillor *n Br* = conseiller *m* général

county cricket *n Cr* = grands matchs *mpl* qui opposent les équipes de différents comtés

county line *n US* frontière *f* délimitant un comté

coup [kuː] *n* coup *m* (audacieux); *Pol* **c. (d'état)** coup d'État; **to bring off a c.** réussir un joli coup

coupé [kuːpeɪ] *n Aut* coupé *m*

couple[1] [ˈkʌp(ə)l] *n* **(a)** **a c.** quelques-uns, *f* quelques-unes; **a c. of** (*a few*) quelques; **a c. of seconds** deux secondes; *F* **to have a c.** (*of drinks*) prendre un verre ou deux **(b)** (*two people, dancers*) couple *m*; **the married c.** les (deux) époux *mpl*; **the newly married c.** les nouveaux *ou* jeunes mariés;

they make a lovely c. ils font un beau couple; **a married c.** un couple marié
couple² **1** *vt* **(a)** (*bring together*) (*oxen*) (ac)coupler; (*male and female*) accoupler; (*names, ideas etc*) associer; **common sense coupled with intelligence** le bon sens allié à l'intelligence; **the course couples theory with practical work** le cours allie la théorie à la pratique **(b)** (*two engines, batteries*) accoupler; *Rail* **to c. (up) a carriage** atteler *ou* accrocher un wagon **2** *vi* (*of male and female*) s'accoupler
coupler ['kʌplər] *n Comptr* coupleur *m*
couplet ['kʌplɪt] *n Liter* distique *m*; **rhyming couplets** distiques qui riment
coupling ['kʌp(ə)lɪŋ] *n* **(a)** (*bringing together*) accouplement *m*; (*of ideas, names*) association *f* **(b)** *Rail* (*of carriages*) attelage *m*; (*of batteries*) couplage *m*; *Aut* **c. bar** barre *f* d'accouplement **(c)** (*static device*) raccord *m*, joint *m*; *Rail* attelage *m*; (*device for transmitting motion*) accouplement *m*, embrayage *m*
coupon ['ku:pɒn] *n* (*to be filled in*) coupon *m*; (*exchangeable voucher*) bon *m*; *Br Admin* **petrol c.** bon *m* d'essence; *Br Sp* **football** *or* **pools c.** = formulaire *m* de concours de pronostics de football; **c. offer** offre *f* de bon de réduction
courage ['kʌrɪdʒ] *n* courage *m*; **to have the c. to do sth** avoir le courage de faire qch; **to take one's c. in both hands** prendre son courage à deux mains; **to restore sb's c.** redonner du courage à qn
courageous [kə'reɪdʒəs] *adj* courageux
courageously [kə'reɪdʒəslɪ] *adv* courageusement, avec courage
courgette [kʊə'ʒet] *n Br* courgette *f*
courier ['kʊrɪər] *n* **(a)** (*messenger*) messager *m*; *Com* coursier *m*; **to send sth/to arrive by c.** envoyer qch/arriver par coursier; **(motorcycle) c.** messager/coursier en moto; **she was a c. for drug dealers** elle servait de messager à des trafiquants de drogue **(b)** (*in tourism*) accompagnateur, -trice
course¹ [kɔ:s] *n* **(a)** (*process*) (*of river, time, business, events etc*) cours *m*; (*of illness*) évolution *f*; **in the c. of conversation/the evening** au cours de la conversation/de la soirée; **in the c. of time** (*gradually*) à la longue; (*eventually*) finalement; **the building is in the c. of completion** le bâtiment est en cours d'achèvement; **to be in the c. of doing sth** être en train de faire qch; **in the ordinary** *or* **normal c. of things** *or* **events** normalement; **in due c.** en temps utile; **to let nature take its c.** laisser la nature faire les choses; **let things take** *or* **run their c.** laisser les choses se faire *ou* suivre leur cours; **it's best to let the fever run its c.** il vaut mieux laisser la fièvre évoluer normalement; **that is a matter of c.** cela va sans dire; **as a matter of c.** tout naturellement, automatiquement; **blood tests are carried out as a matter of c.** des examens sanguins sont effectués automatiquement
(b) of c. bien sûr, bien entendu, naturellement; **of c. not!** bien sûr que non!; **of c. she was angry!** bien sûr qu'elle était fâchée!; **he forgot, of c.** bien entendu, il a oublié
(c) (*route*) route *f*, direction *f*; **to keep one's c.** ne pas dévier de sa route; *Naut* maintenir son cap; **to change (one's) c.** changer de direction; *Naut* changer le cap; *Naut, Fig* **to be on c.** suivre le cap fixé; **to be driven off c.** (*of ship*) être dévié de son cap, dévier de son cap
(d) c. (of action) ligne *f* de conduite; **to take a c. of action** adopter une ligne de conduite; **it is the only c. open to me** c'est la seule chose que je puisse faire; **there is no other c. open to us** nous n'avons pas d'autre solution; **the best c. would be to ...** la meilleure chose à faire *ou* le mieux serait de ...; **his best c. would be to ...** le mieux pour lui serait de ...; **the right c.** la bonne voie
(e) *Sch, Univ* cours *m*; **to give a c. of lectures** donner une série de cours; **to take** *or* **follow** *or* **do a c. (in sth)** suivre un cours (de qch); **a degree c.** un cours de licence; **he has published a French c.** il a publié une méthode de français
(f) *Med* **c. (of treatment)** traitement *m*; **a c. of injections** une série de piqûres
(g) (*of meal*) plat *m*; **first c.** entrée *f*; **four-c. dinner** dîner *m* de quatre plats
(h) *Sp etc* (*for races*) parcours *m*; (*for motor-racing*) circuit *m*; **(golf) c.** terrain *m* de golf, golf *m*; **to finish the c.** finir la course; *Fig* finir
(i) *Constr* (*of bricks*) assise *f*
course² **1** *vi* **(a)** (*of liquids*) ruisseler; **the blood coursed through her veins** le sang courait dans ses veines; **tears were coursing down my face** j'avais le visage ruisselant de larmes **(b)** (*in hunting*) courir le lièvre **2** *vt* (*hare*) courir
courseware ['kɔ:sweər] *n Comptr* didacticiel *m*
coursing ['kɔ:sɪŋ] *n* **(a)** (*hunting*) chasse *f* à courre au lièvre **(b)** (*racing hounds*) = concours *m* de vitesse entre lévriers lâchés sur un lièvre en champ clos
court¹ [kɔ:t] *n* **(a)** [①A6,d,i] *Jur* cour *f*, tribunal *m*; (*courtroom*) auditoire *m* de tribunal; **civil/criminal c.** tribunal civil/criminel; *Br* **county c.** tribunal de grande instance; **International C. of Justice** Cour internationale de justice; **to go to c.** aller en justice; **to take sb to c.** faire un procès à qn; **are you prepared to say that in c.?** est-ce que vous seriez prêt à le jurer devant le tribunal?; **in open c.** en plein tribunal; **case before the c.** affaire *f* en cause; **to come before the c.** (*of person*) comparaître devant le tribunal; (*of case*) être jugé; **to settle a case out of c.** arranger une affaire à l'amiable; **we've decided to settle out of c.** nous avons décidé d'arranger ça à l'amiable; **tell the c. what you saw** veuillez dire à la cour ce que vous avez vu; **sale by order of the c.** vente *f* judiciaire; **this is a matter for the courts, not the government** c'est à la justice d'en décider, pas au gouvernement; **c. appearance** (*of accused*) convocation *f* au tribunal; **c. reporter** chroniqueur *m* judiciaire; **c. ruling** décision *f* de justice
(b) (*for tennis, squash etc*) court *m*; **tennis c.** court (de tennis), tennis *m*; **grass c.** court sur gazon; **hard c.** court en dur; **he was on c. for three hours** il a été sur le court pendant trois heures
(c) (*royal etc*) cour *f*; **to pay c. to the king** faire sa cour au roi; **to hold c.** (*of celebrity etc*) s'entretenir avec toute une cour d'admirateurs; *Journ* **c. correspondent** correspondant *m* à la cour royale
(d) (*courtyard*) cour *f*; (*in names of blocks of flats*) = résidence *f*; (*in names of palaces*) château *m*, palais *m*
(e) *Old-fashioned* **to pay c. to a woman** faire la cour à une femme
court² **1** *vt* **(a)** (*seek*) (*sb's friendship*) (re)chercher, solliciter; (*sb's favour*) briguer; (*failure*) aller au-devant de; (*death*) braver; **to c. popularity** chercher à se faire bien voir **(with** auprès de); **to c. disaster** aller à la catastrophe; **to c. the electorate** chercher à gagner les voix des électeurs **(b)** *Old-fashioned* (*seek in marriage*) (*woman*) courtiser, faire la cour à; **they had been courting one another for nearly a year** ils se fréquentaient depuis presque un an **2** *vi Old-fashioned* **to be courting** (*of individual*) fréquenter; (*of couple*) se fréquenter; **courting couple** couple *m* d'amoureux
court card *n Cards* figure *f*
court case *n* affaire *f*
court circular *n Journ* = rubrique *f* décrivant les engagements officiels des membres de la famille royale
courteous ['kɜ:tɪəs] *adj* courtois, poli **(to, towards** envers)
courteously ['kɜ:tɪəslɪ] *adv* courtoisement, poliment
courtesan [kɔ:tɪ'zæn] *n* courtisane *f*
courtesy ['kɜ:təsɪ] *n* courtoisie *f*, politesse *f*; **common c.** la politesse la plus élémentaire; **he didn't have the c. to reply to my letter** il n'a pas eu la politesse de répondre à ma lettre; **by c. of ...** avec la gracieuse permission de ...; **exchange of courtesies** échange *m* de politesses; **c. call** visite *f* de politesse; **to pay sb a c. call** faire une visite de politesse à qn; **c. bus** navette *f* gratuite; **c. car** voiture *f* gratuite; (*from garage*) véhicule *m* de remplacement; *Aut* **c. light** plafonnier *m*; *Aut* **c. mirror** miroir *m* de courtoisie; **c. title** titre *m* de courtoisie
courthouse ['kɔ:thaʊs] *n esp Am* palais *m* de justice, tribunal *m*
courtier ['kɔ:tɪər] *n* courtisan *m*
courtly ['kɔ:tlɪ] *adj* (*polite*) courtois, d'une politesse raffinée; **c. love** l'amour *m* courtois
court martial, *pl* **courts martial** *n Mil* cour *f* martiale
court-martial *vt* **(-ll-,** *US* **-l-)** (*soldier*) faire passer en cour martiale; **to be court-martialled** passer en cour martiale
court of appeal *n* cour *m* d'appel
court of inquiry *n* commission *f* d'enquête
court of law *n* tribunal *m*; **would you be prepared to say that in a c.?** est-ce que vous seriez prêt à le jurer devant le tribunal?
court-ordered *adj* (*sale*) judiciaire
courtroom ['kɔ:tru:m] *n Jur* salle *f* d'audience; (*people*) auditoire *m* d'un/du tribunal; **his c. performances** ses performances *fpl* devant la cour; **c. drama** drame *m* judiciaire
courtship ['kɔ:tʃɪp] *n* (*of woman*) cour *f*; **their c. was a stormy affair** ils se sont beaucoup disputés au temps où il lui faisait la cour; *Zool* **c. display** parade *f* nuptiale
court shoe *n* escarpin *m*
court tennis *n US* jeu *m* de paume
courtyard ['kɔ:tjɑ:d] *n* (*of house etc*) cour *f*
couscous ['ku:sku:s] *n* couscous *m*
co-user ['kəʊju:zər] *n Comptr* co-utilisateur *m*
cousin ['kʌz(ə)n] *n* cousin, -ine; **first c., full c.** cousin, -ine germain(e); **second c.** cousin, -ine issu(e) de germains; *Fig*

our American cousins nos cousins américains; **a distant c. of the sparrow** un cousin éloigné du moineau

couth [ku:θ] *adj Br Hum* **he's not very c.** il n'est pas très raffiné

couture [ku:'tʊər] *n* **(haute) c.** haute couture *f*

couturier, *f* -ière [ku:'tjʊərɪeɪ, -ɪeər] *n* (grand) couturier *m*, (grande) couturière *f*; (*head of company*) directeur, -trice d'une maison de haute couture

covalent [kəʊ'veɪlənt] *adj Ch* covalent

cove¹ [kəʊv] *n Geog* anse *f*, petite baie *f*

cove² *n Old-fashioned Br F* (*fellow*) type *m*; **a queer c.** un drôle de pistolet

coven ['kʌv(ə)n] *n* bande *f ou* réunion *f* de sorcières

covenant¹ ['kʌvənənt] *n* **(a)** *Jur* convention *f*, contrat *m* **(b)** *Pol* pacte *m*, traité *m* **(c)** *Bible* (*of Jews*) alliance *f*

covenant² *Jur* **1** *vt* promettre par contrat; **to c. to do sth** convenir de faire qch; **to c. money** s'engager par contrat à payer une somme d'argent **2** *vi* **to c. with sb for sth** convenir (par contrat) de qch avec qn

Coventry ['kɒvəntrɪ] *n Br F* **to send sb to C.** mettre qn en quarantaine

cover¹ ['kʌvər] *n* **(a)** (*lid*) (*for pot etc*) couvercle *m*

(b) (*soft covering*) (*bedspread*) couvre-lit *m*, *pl* couvre-lits; (*for umbrella*) fourreau *m*; (*for car, boat, furniture, computer*) housse *f*; **covers** (*on bed*) couvertures *fpl*; *Met* **cloud c.** couverture nuageuse

(c) (*of book, magazine*) couverture *f*; (*in bookbinding*) plats *mpl*; **to read a book from c. to c.** lire un livre d'un bout à l'autre; **(front) c.** couverture; **hard/soft covers** couverture rigide/souple; **c. page** (*of newspaper etc*) (page *f* de) couverture

(d) (*envelope*) **under plain/separate c.** sous pli ordinaire/séparé

(e) (*shelter from weather*) abri *m*; **to take c.** (*from the rain etc*) se mettre à l'abri; **the rocks gave us some c.** les rochers nous ont fourni un abri; **to be under c.** être à couvert *ou* à l'abri

(f) *Mil etc* (*from gunfire etc*) couvert *m*, abri *m*; (*firing*) tir *m* de couverture *ou* de protection; **under c.** à couvert, à l'abri; **to take c.** se mettre à couvert, s'abriter; **to give sb c.** (*of aircraft, artillery etc*) couvrir qn; **the rocks provided c. for snipers** les rochers ont fourni des abris pour les tireurs isolés; **without c.** à découvert; **air/radar c.** couverture *f* aérienne/radar

(g) (*in hunting*) couvert *m*, fourré *m*, gîte *m*, *Old-fashioned* remise *f*; **to take c.** se remiser; **to break c.** (*of game*) débusquer; *Fig* (*of person*) sortir de sa retraite

(h) (*something that conceals*) voile *m*, masque *m*; (*for spy, police officer etc*) couverture *f*; **under the c. of** (*friendship etc*) sous le couvert *ou* le masque de; **under (the) c. of darkness** sous le couvert de la nuit; **to go under c.** (*of police officer etc*) adopter une identité d'emprunt (*pour les besoins d'une enquête*); **to blow sb's c.** (*in espionage, undercover police work*) démasquer qn

(i) (*in insurance*) couverture *f*, provision *f*; **with/without c.** avec couverture/à découvert; **full c.** garantie *f* totale; **c. clause** clause *f* de garantie

(j) (*in restaurant*) couvert *m*

cover² **1** *vt* **(a)** (*person, object*) couvrir **(with, in** de); **covered in** *or* **with snow** couvert de neige *ou* par la neige; **to c. one's head** se couvrir (la tête); **to c. one's ears** (*so as not to hear*) se boucher les oreilles; **writing covered the page** la page était couverte d'écriture; **the scarf covered her mouth** l'écharpe lui couvrait la bouche; **to be well covered** (*warmly dressed*) être bien couvert; *F* (*plump, fat*) être bien en chair; **to c. oneself with glory** se couvrir de gloire; **to c. sb with ridicule** couvrir qn de ridicule; **covered with shame** couvert de honte

(b) (*in order to protect*) recouvrir **(with** de); (*in bookbinding*) (*book*) couvrir; **a wire covered with plastic** un fil électrique recouvert de plastique

(c) (*hide*) (*one's anxiety, confusion etc*) couvrir, dissimuler; **to c. one's tracks** brouiller les pistes

(d) *Mil etc* (*protect*) protéger; (*person*) couvrir; **I've got you covered** (*I have a gun aimed at you*) j'ai mon fusil/revolver braqué sur toi

(e) (*deal with, take into account*) couvrir; **the course covers the first half of the century** le cours couvre la première moitié du siècle; **to c. all eventualites** parer à toute éventualité; **that's not covered** ce n'est pas traité; **it's covered in some detail** c'est traité en détail

(f) (*travel*) (*a distance*) couvrir, parcourir; **we covered 100 kilometres before breakfast** nous avons fait cent kilomètres avant le petit déjeuner; **to c. a lot of ground** (*travel great distance*) faire beaucoup de chemin; (*search etc over a wide area*) parcourir un champ très vaste; *Fig* (*of book, author etc*) couvrir de nombreux domaines; (*of meeting etc*) traiter bien des problèmes

(g) (*in insurance*) (*risk*) couvrir; *Fin* **to be covered** (*of creditor*) être couvert; **we're not covered for** *or* **against theft** nous ne sommes pas couverts contre le vol; **to c. oneself** se couvrir **(against a risk** d'un risque); *Fig* **the president covered himself by saying that ...** le président s'est couvert en disant que ...

(h) (*of money*) (*expenses, cost etc*) couvrir; **£100 won't c. the cost of a new carpet** 100 livres ne couvriront pas le coût d'une moquette neuve; **to c. a deficit** combler un déficit; *Acct* **to c. a loss** couvrir un déficit; **to c. an overdraft** couvrir un découvert; **will that c. it?** est-ce que ça suffira?

(i) *Journ, TV, Rad* (*sports event etc*) couvrir

(j) (*in breeding*) (*female*) couvrir, saillir

(k) *Mus* **to c. a song** faire une reprise d'une chanson

(l) *Sp* (*mark*) (*player*) marquer

2 *vi* **paint that covers well** peinture qui couvre bien *ou* bien couvrante

▶ **cover for** *vipo* (*replace*) remplacer; (*provide excuses for*) couvrir; **I refuse to c. for you with the boss** je refuse de te couvrir auprès du patron

▶ **cover in** *vtsep* (*fill in*) (*trench*) remplir

▶ **cover up 1** *vtsep* **(a)** (*conceal*) recouvrir; (*truth, illegal act*) dissimuler **(b)** (*with blanket etc*) couvrir, recouvrir; **keep the baby covered up** garde le bébé bien couvert; **they covered up the bodies** ils ont recouvert les corps; **that dress is a bit too low — c. yourself up a bit** cette robe est trop décolletée — couvre-toi un peu **2** *vi* (*conceal the truth*) cacher la vérité; **the government has been accused of covering up** on a accusé le gouvernement de vouloir étouffer l'affaire; **to c. up for sb** protéger qn; **architects and builders are covering up for each other** les architectes et les entrepreneurs se protègent les uns les autres

coverage ['kʌvərɪdʒ] *n* **(a)** *Journ etc* couverture *f* (médiatique); **some people objected to XTV's c. of these events** certaines personnes ont protesté contre la manière dont XTV a traité ces événements; *TV* **there was no c. of the match** on n'a pas retransmis ce match; **the c. given to the elections was biased** le compte-rendu des élections était partial; **the book gives good c. of the coup** le livre décrit bien la façon dont le coup d'État s'est déroulé; **sports get too much c. on TV** la télé consacre trop de temps au sport **(b)** (*in insurance*) couverture *f*, provision *f*

coverall(s) ['kʌvərɔ:l, -z] *n(pl) Am* bleu(s) *m(pl)* (de travail)

cover charge *n* **(a)** (*in restaurant*) couvert *m* **(b)** (*of newspaper*) prix *m*

covered ['kʌvəd] *adj* **(a)** (*market, way etc*) couvert; **c. wagon** charrette *f* à bâche **(b)** (*by insurance policy*) (*risk*) couvert; (*person*) assuré; *St Exch* **c. (short) position** position *f* (courte) couverte

cover girl *n* cover-girl *f*, *pl* cover-girls

covering ['kʌvərɪŋ] **1** *adj* **(a)** (*letter, document, note*) d'accompagnement **(b)** *Mil* (*forces, troupes*) de couverture; **c. fire** tir *m* de soutien *ou* de protection **2** *n* **(a)** (*protective*) (*for floor*) revêtement *m*; (*for plants, object in trailer*) bâche *f*; (*on furniture*) housse *f* **(b)** (*of snow, dust, chocolate*) couche *f*

coverlet ['kʌvəlɪt] *n* dessus-de-lit *m inv*

cover-line *n Journ* titraille *f*, titre *m* de rappel

cover note *n* (*in insurance*) attestation *f* provisoire d'assurance

cover sheet *n* (*to fax etc*) page *f* de garde

cover story *n Journ* sujet *m* qui fait la couverture *ou* la une

covert¹ ['kʌvət] *adj* (*threat etc*) caché, voilé; (*action etc*) secret, clandestin

covert² *n* (*in hunting*) couvert *m*, fourré *m*

covertly ['kʌvətlɪ] *adv* secrètement

cover-up *n* (*of irregularity etc*) dissimulation *f*; **the president denied there had been a c.** le président a nié qu'on ait tenté d'étouffer l'affaire; **in a c. attempt that went wrong** dans une tentative ratée pour étouffer l'affaire

cover version *n Mus* reprise *f*

covet ['kʌvɪt] *vt* **(-t-)** convoiter; **a highly coveted prize** un prix très convoité

covetous ['kʌvɪtəs] *adj* (*person*) avide **(of** de); (*gaze*) de convoitise; **to be c. of sb's property** convoiter les biens d'autrui

covetously ['kʌvɪtəslɪ] *adv* avec convoitise

covetousness ['kʌvɪtəsnɪs] *n* (*greed*) cupidité *f*, avidité *f*; (*for particular thing*) convoitise *f*

covey ['kʌvɪ] *n* (*of partridges etc*) compagnie *f*, vol *m*

cow¹ [kaʊ] *n* **(a)** vache *f*; *Fig F* **till the cows come home** (*to wait*) jusqu'à la Saint-Glinglin; (*to argue, talk*) à n'en plus finir; **c. parsley** (*plant*) cerfeuil *m* sauvage **(b)** *Pej F* (*woman*) peau *f* de vache; **old c.** vieille bique *f*, vieux chameau *m*; **silly**

c. espèce *f* d'idiote **(c)** (*of seal etc*) femelle *f*; **c. elephant** éléphant *m* femelle, éléphante *f*

cow² *vt* intimider; **to look cowed** avoir l'air d'un chien battu; **to c. sb into submission** intimider qn jusqu'à ce qu'il/elle se soumette

coward ['kaʊəd] *n* lâche *mf*, poltron, -onne; **I'm a terrible c. in the dark** j'ai très peur du noir; **he's a moral c.** c'est un lâche, il n'a pas le courage de ses opinions

cowardice ['kaʊədɪs], **cowardliness** ['kaʊədlɪnəs] *n* lâcheté *f*, poltronnerie *f*; **moral c.** lâcheté

cowardly ['kaʊədlɪ] *adj* lâche

cowbell ['kaʊbel] *n* clochette *f* (*pour bétail*)

cowboy ['kaʊbɔɪ] *n* **(a)** cowboy *m*; **to play cowboys and indians** jouer aux cowboys et aux indiens; **c. film** film *m* de cowboys **(b)** *Br F Pej* (*careless or dishonest workman*) fumiste *m*; **a bunch of cowboys, a c. outfit** des petits rigolos *mpl*; **what c. did this plumbing?** quel est le petit rigolo qui s'est occupé de la plomberie?

cowcatcher ['kaʊkætʃər] *n US Rail* chasse-pierres *m inv*

cower ['kaʊər] *vi* se tapir (à terre); **to c. before sb** (*show fear*) trembler devant qn

cowhand ['kaʊhæd] *n* vacher *m*

cowherd ['kaʊhɜːd] *n* vacher *m*, bouvier *m*

cowhide ['kaʊhaɪd] *n* peau *f ou* cuir *m* de vache

cowl [kaʊl] *n* **(a)** *Rel* (*hood*) capuchon *m*; (*habit*) habit *m* à capuchon; **c. neck** (*on sweater*) col *m* cagoule *ou* boule **(b)** (*on chimney*) capuchon *m*, abat-vent *m inv*; *Av, Naut* (*on engine, funnel*) capot *m*

cowled [kaʊld] *adj* (en)capuchonné

cowlick ['kaʊlɪk] *n F* épi *m* (*de cheveux*)

cowling ['kaʊlɪŋ] *n* (*on chimney*) capuchonnement *m*; *Av* (*on engine*) capot *m*; *Aut* capot de ventilateur

cowman, *pl* **-men** ['kaʊmən] *n* vacher *m*; *US* (*rancher*) propriétaire *m* d'un ranch

co-worker ['kəʊ'wɜːkər] *n* collègue *mf*

cowpat ['kaʊpæt] *n* bouse *f* de vache

cowpoke ['kaʊpəʊk] *n US F* cowboy *m*

cowpox ['kaʊpɒks] *n Vet* cowpox *m*, vaccine *f*

cowpuncher ['kaʊpʌntʃər] *n US F* cowboy *m*

cowrie, cowry ['kaʊrɪ] *n* (*mollusc*) porcelaine *f*; (*shell*) cauri *m*

cowshed ['kaʊʃed] *n* étable *f*

cowslip ['kaʊslɪp] *n* coucou *m*, primevère *f* commune

cox¹ [kɒks] *n Sp* (*in rowing*) barreur, -euse

cox² *vti Sp* (*in rowing*) gouverner, barrer

coxless four ['kɒkslɪs] *n* quatre *m* sans barreur

coxswain ['kɒks(ə)n] *n* barreur, -euse

coy [kɔɪ] *adj* (*shy*) timide; *Pej* (*affectedly shy*) qui fait la sainte-nitouche; (*seductive*) qui fait des mines; **a c. look** un air de sainte-nitouche; **to go all c.** (*of child*), *Pej* faire le/la timide; **with a c. little smile** avec un petit sourire séducteur; **why be so c. about accepting?** pourquoi faire semblant d'hésiter?; **he was rather c. about the price** il était plutôt évasif quant au prix; **the rather c. treatment of the sex scenes** la façon un peu mièvre dont sont traitées les scènes de sexe

coyly ['kɔɪlɪ] *adv* timidement; *Pej* en faisant le/la timide; **to reply c.** (*evasively*) faire une réponse évasive

coyness ['kɔɪnɪs] *n* (*shyness*) timidité *f*; *Pej* (*affected shyness*) fausse timidité; **... he said, with a certain c.** (*evasively and vaguely*) ... dit-il, restant dans le vague

coyote [kɔɪ'jəʊtɪ] *n* coyote *m*

coypu ['kɔɪpuː] *n* coypou *m*, ragondin *m*

coziness ['kəʊzɪnɪs] *n US* = **cosiness**

cozy ['kəʊzɪ] *adj US* = **cosy 1**

cp (*abbr* **compare**) comparer

cpi [siːpiː'aɪ] *Comptr* (*abbr* **characters per inch**) cpp

Cpl *Mil abbr* **Corporal**

CP/M [siːpiː'em] *n Comptr* (*abbr* **control program/monitor**) CP/M *m*

cps [siːpiː'es] *Comptr* (*abbr* **characters per second**) cps

CPU [siːpiː'juː] *n Comptr* (*abbr* **central processing unit**) unité *f* centrale

CR [siː'ɑːr] *Comptr* (*abbr* **carriage return**) retour *m* chariot

crab¹ [kræb] *n* **(a)** (*crustacean*) crabe *m*; *Culin* **c. paste** pâté *m* de crabe; **c. pot** casier *m* à crabes **(b)** *Med* **c. (louse)** morpion *m*; **to have crabs** avoir des morpions **(c)** *Astron* **the C.** (*constellation*) le Cancer; (*nebula*) le Crabe

crab² *vi esp US F* ronchonner (**about** contre)

crab apple *n* pomme *f* sauvage; **c. tree** pommier *m* sauvage

crabbed ['kræbɪd] *adj* **(a)** (*writing*) en pattes de mouche **(b)** (*grumpy*) maussade, grincheux

crabby ['kræbɪ] *adj* maussade, grincheux

crack¹ [kræk] **1** *n* **(a)** (*split*) fente *f*, fissure *f*; (*in skin, wood*) gerçure *f*; *Med* (*in skin*) crevasse *f*; (*in wall, ground*) crevasse, lézarde *f*; (*in varnish, enamel*) craquelure *f*; (*in glass, pottery, bell etc*) fêlure *f*; *Fig* **cracks were beginning to appear in the coalition** la coalition commençait à se fissurer

(b) (*of door etc*) entrebâillement *m*; **open the window a c.** ouvrez la fenêtre un petit peu; *Fig* **at the c. of dawn** à la pointe du jour

(c) (*sound*) (*of branches, ice etc*) craquement *m*; (*of whip*) claquement *m*; (*of rifle*) détonation *f*, claquement sec; *Fig F* **to get a fair c. of the whip** avoir toutes ses chances; *F* **to give sb a fair c. of the whip** donner toutes ses chances à qn

(d) *Fig F* (*attempt*) **to have a c. at sth** s'essayer à qch; **I'll have a c. (at it)** je vais tenter le coup; **to give sb** *or* **let sb have a c. at sth** laisser qn essayer de faire qch

(e) *F* (*blow*) **c. on the head** coup *m* sec sur la tête

(f) *F* (*gibe*) plaisanterie *f*; **to make a c.** faire une plaisanterie, lancer une vanne; **a cheap c. about short people** une plaisanterie facile sur les gens de petite taille; **nasty c.** plaisanterie acerbe *ou* acérée

(g) *Sl* (*drug*) crack *m*; **c. house** = établissement *m* où a lieu le trafic de crack

(h) *Br Dial* **there was some good c.** on s'est bien marré

2 *adj F* d'élite; *Sp* **c. player** as *m*, crack *m*; **c. regiment** régiment *m* d'élite; **c. shot** tireur *m* d'élite, fin tireur

crack² *int* crac!, clac!

crack³ **1** *vt* **(a)** (*damage, break etc*) (*glass, plate, bone, tooth*) fêler; (*lip*) gercer; (*wall, earth*) lézarder, crevasser; (*stone etc*) fendre; (*varnish, paint, plastic*) fendiller, craqueler

(b) (*make sound with*) (*whip*) faire claquer; (*one's fingers*) faire craquer

(c) *F* (*hit*) **to c. sb over the head** assommer qn; **he cracked his head against the wall** il s'est cogné au mur

(d) (*solve*) (*problem*) résoudre; (*code*) décrypter; **I think I've cracked it** je crois que j'y suis arrivé

(e) (*break open*) (*safe*) percer; (*nut*) (*with nutcrackers*) casser; *F* **to c. a bottle of wine (with sb)** boire une bouteille de vin (avec qn)

(f) (*make*) **to c. a joke** raconter une blague; **it's not the sort of thing you can c. jokes about** ce n'est pas le genre de choses sur lequel on peut plaisanter; **where are you going, the North Pole?, he cracked** où est-ce que tu vas, au Pôle Nord?, a-t-il plaisanté

(g) *Ind* (*heavy oil*) fractionner

2 *vi* **(a)** (*become cracked*) (*of glass, plate, bone etc*) se fêler; (*of wall*) se lézarder; (*of skin, lips*) se gercer; (*of paint, varnish*) se fendiller, se craqueler

(b) (*of voice*) se casser; (*at puberty*) muer

(c) (*of person*) (*under pressure*) craquer; (*of resistance*) lâcher; *Hum* **the boss has finally cracked** (*gone mad*) le patron a fini par craquer

(d) (*make sound*) craquer; (*of whip*) claquer; **a rifle cracked** un coup de fusil a claqué

▶ **crack down** *vi* sévir

▶ **crack down on** *vipo* (*become stricter about*) prendre des mesures plus sévères *ou* énergiques contre; (*punish*) (*drunk driving etc*) sévir contre

▶ **crack up 1** *vi* **(a)** (*break*) se briser en morceaux; **the ice is cracking up** la glace se brise **(b)** *F* (*of person*) (*have nervous breakdown*) craquer; (*of marriage, organization*) aller à la ruine **(c)** *F* (*be helpless with laughter*) s'écrouler (de rire) **2** *vtsep* **(a)** *F* (*cause to be helpless with laughter*) **it really cracked me up when I heard about it** je me suis vraiment écroulé de rire quand j'ai entendu parler de ça **(b)** *F* (*praise*) **it's not all it's cracked up to be** ce n'est pas tout ce qu'on en dit

crackbrained ['krækbreɪnd] *adj F* (*person*) fêlé, complètement dingue; (*idea, plan etc*) complètement dingue

crackdown ['krækdaʊn] *n* mesures *fpl* énergiques (**on sth** contre qch); **the government c. on reporting** les restrictions *fpl* gouvernementales concernant les reportages

cracked [krækt] *adj F* (*crazy*) dingue, cinglé

cracker ['krækər] *n* **(a)** (*biscuit*) biscuit *m* salé, cracker *m* **(b)** *Br F* (*excellent thing*) merveille *f*; (*pretty woman*) canon *m*; **the first goal was an absolute c.** le premier but était une pure merveille; **she's an absolute c.** elle est canon; **it's a c. of a joke!** cette histoire est à se tordre! **(c)** (*firework*) pétard *m*; (*at Christmas*) diablotin *m*; **to pull a c.** faire éclater un diablotin **(d)** (*for nuts*) casse-noisette(s) *m inv*, casse-noix *m inv* **(e)** *US Sl* (*poor white*) blanc *m* pauvre (*du sud des États-Unis*)

cracker barrel *n Am* boîte *f* à biscuits

cracker-barrel *adj US F* (*wisdom, philosophy etc*) populaire

crackers ['krækəz] *adj usu pred Br F* **he's c.** il est cinglé; **to go c.** perdre la boule

crackhead ['krækhed] *n Sl* (*drug addict*) drogué *m* au crack, consommateur, -trice de crack

cracking [ˈkrækɪŋ] *F* **1** *adj* excellent, épatant; **to be in c. (good) form** être en super forme, avoir la pêche; **at a c. pace** à fond de train **2** *adv* **to get c.** s'y mettre; **they got c. with their work** ils se sont mis au travail; **get c.!** grouille-toi! **3** *n* **(a)** (*sound*) craquement *m*; (*of whip*) claquement *m* **(b)** (*of paint*) craquelure *f*, craquelage *m* **(c)** *Ind* (*of oil*) fractionnement *m*, craquage *m*

crackle¹ [ˈkræk(ə)l] *n* **(a)** (*sound*) (*of dry leaves, twigs*) craquement *m*; (*of shots*) crépitement *m*, crépitation *f*; (*of something frying*) grésillement *m*; (*of fire*) crépitement, pétillement *m*; *Rad* crachotement *m*, crachements *mpl*; *Tel* **there's a bit of a c. on the line** il y a de la friture sur la ligne **(b)** (*finish*) (*of paint, porcelain*) craquelure *f*; *Cer* **c. finish** craquelage *m*

crackle² *vi* (*of dry leaves, twigs etc*) craquer; (*of shots*) crépiter; (*of something frying*) grésiller; (*of fire*) crépiter, pétiller; *Rad* crachoter

crackleware [ˈkræk(ə)lweər] *n Cer* craquelé *m*

crackling¹ [ˈkræklɪŋ] **1** *adj* pétillant, crépitant **2** *n* **(a)** *Br Culin* (*of roast pork*) = peau *f* de porc grillée **(b)** *Old-fashioned Br Sl* **a nice bit of c.** (*woman*) une belle pépée

crackpot [ˈkrækpɒt] *F* **1** *n* fêlé, -ée, cinglé, -ée; **he's a c.** il est fêlé *ou* cinglé **2** *adj* (*idea, scheme*) dingue

crackup [ˈkrækʌp] *n* **(a)** *F* (*nervous breakdown*) dépression *f* nerveuse **(b)** (*of system*) débâcle *f*; (*of civilization*) effondrement *m*

cradle¹ [ˈkreɪd(ə)l] *n* **(a)** (*of child, Fig of civilization*) berceau *m*; **from the c.** dès le berceau; **from the c. to the grave** du berceau à la tombe; *Med* **to have c. cap** (*of baby*) avoir des croûtes de lait; *F* **he's/she's a c. snatcher** il/elle les prend au berceau *ou* au biberon **(b)** *Ind etc* (*of machine etc*) berceau *m*, cadre *m*; (*for window cleaner*) nacelle *f*; *Constr, Min* pont *m* volant; (*for painter*) sellette *f* **(c)** *Med* (*over bed*) cerceau *m*, arceau *m* **(d)** *Tel* (*for receiver*) support *m*

cradle² *vt* **(a)** (*in cradle*) (*baby*) mettre *ou* coucher dans un berceau; *Fig* **cradled in luxury** bercé dans le luxe; **the village was cradled in a valley** le village était blotti au fond d'une vallée **(b)** (*in one's arms*) (*person*) bercer; (*object*) tenir délicatement; **to c. a child in one's arms** bercer un enfant dans ses bras; **he cradled the rifle in his arms** il serrait le fusil contre lui

cradlesong [ˈkreɪd(ə)lsɒŋ] *n Mus* berceuse *f*

craft [krɑːft] *n* **(a)** (*art*) art *m*; (*occupation*) métier *m* (manuel); (*professional skill*) (*of teacher etc*) métier; *Sch* travaux *mpl* manuels; **the c. of weaving** l'art du tissage; **painter who is master of his c.** peintre qui maîtrise parfaitement son art; **c. centre** centre *m* d'artisanat; *Sch* **c. class/teacher** cours *m*/ professeur *m* de travaux manuels **(b)** (*skill*) habileté *f*, adresse *f*; *Pej* (*cunning*) ruse *f* **(c)** *Naut* (*pl* **craft**) embarcation *f*, petit navire *m*; **small c.** canots *mpl*, petits bateaux *mpl*

craftily [ˈkrɑːftɪlɪ] *adv* (*cleverly*) astucieusement, ingénieusement, *Pej* avec ruse *ou* roublardise

craftiness [ˈkrɑːftɪnɪs] *n* ingéniosité *f*, *Pej* ruse *f*, roublardise *f*

craftsman, *pl* **-men** [ˈkrɑːftsmən] *n* **(a)** (*artisan*) artisan *m* **(b)** (*artist*) artiste *m*; **this is the work of a real c.** c'est l'œuvre de quelqu'un qui s'y connaît

craftsmanship [ˈkrɑːftsmənʃɪp] *n* (*skill*) habileté *f* (manuelle); (*knowledge, experience*) (connaissance *f* du) métier *m*; **a wonderful piece of c.** un chef-d'œuvre extraordinaire; **think of the c. that has gone into making this table!** songe à l'habileté qu'il a fallu pour faire cette table!

craftswoman, *pl* **-women** [ˈkrɑːftswʊmən, -wɪmɪn] *n* artiste *f*

craftwork [ˈkrɑːftwɜːk] *n* artisanat *m*

crafty [ˈkrɑːftɪ] *adj* astucieux, ingénieux, malin, *f* maligne; *Pej* rusé, roublard; **you c. old thing!** espèce de vieux renard!

crag [kræg] *n* rocher *m ou* flanc *m* de montagne escarpé, rocher à pic; **overhanging c.** rocher en surplomb

craggy [ˈkrægɪ] *adj* **(a)** (*rocky*) rocailleux **(b)** (*face*) anguleux, taillé à coups de serpe

cram [kræm] **(-mm-) 1** *vt* **(a)** (*force*) fourrer, entasser (**sth into sth** qch dans qch); **they crammed 60 people into the bus** ils ont entassé 60 personnes dans le bus; **to c. food into one's mouth** se fourrer la nourriture dans la bouche, se gaver de nourriture, *F* s'empiffrer

(b) (*fill*) bourrer (**sth with sth** qch de qch); **to c. sb with food** bourrer *ou* gaver qn de nourriture; **cupboards crammed with linen** armoires bourrées de linge; **at school they crammed our heads with facts** à l'école, ils nous ont bourré le crâne (d'informations)

(c) *Sch* (*candidate for exam*) faire bachoter; **to c. maths** (*of student*) potasser ferme les maths

(d) *Agr* (*poultry*) appâter, gaver

2 *vi* **(a)** (*enter*) s'entasser; **we all crammed into the car** nous nous sommes tous entassés dans la voiture

(b) *Sch F* potasser, se bourrer le crâne; **to c. for an exam** bachoter

▶ **cram in 1** *vtsep* (*force in*) fourrer, entasser; **you certainly crammed a lot in in two weeks** (*did a lot*) vous avez fait des tas de choses en deux semaines **2** *vi* (*enter*) s'entasser; **100 people crammed in** 100 personnes se *ou* s'y sont entassées

cram-full *adj* (*train, room etc*) bondé; **the streets were c. of people** les rues grouillaient de monde

crammer [ˈkræmər] *n Sch F* (*school*) boîte *f* à bac

cramming [ˈkræmɪŋ] *n Sch F* (*for an exam*) bachotage *m*, bourrage *m* de crâne

cramp¹ [kræmp] *n*, *Am* **cramps** [kræmps] *npl Med* crampe *f*; **to have (an attack of) c.** être pris d'une crampe, avoir une crampe; **to get c.** (*frequently*) avoir des crampes; *Am* **to have cramps** (*period pains*) avoir des maux de ventre

cramp² *n Carp* serre-joints *m*; *Constr etc* **c. (iron)** crampon *m*

cramp³ *vt* **(a)** (*hinder*) (*movements*) gêner; **to be cramped up in a small space** être à l'étroit; *F* **to c. sb's style** priver qn de ses moyens **(b)** *Constr* (*stones etc*) cramponner, agrafer; *Carp etc* serrer (*au serre-joint*)

cramped [kræmpt] *adj* (*room*) exigu, *f* exiguë; (*writing*) serré; **it's very c. in this office** on est très à l'étroit dans ce bureau; **to live/work in c. conditions** vivre/travailler dans un espace restreint; **to be c. for space** être *ou* se sentir à l'étroit

crampon [ˈkræmpɒn] *n* crampon *m* à glace

cranberry [ˈkrænbərɪ] *n* canneberge *f*; *Culin* **c. sauce** sauce *f* à la canneberge; **c. juice** jus *m* de canneberge

crane¹ [kreɪn] *n* **(a)** *MecE etc* grue *f*; *Cin* grue (de prise de vue); **c. driver** *or* **operator** conducteur *m* de grue, grutier *m* **(b)** (*bird*) grue *f*; **c. fly** tipule *f*

crane² **1** *vt* (*one's neck*) tendre, allonger **2** *vi* **to c. forward** tendre *ou* allonger le cou

crane's-bill, cranesbill [ˈkreɪnzbɪl] *n* bec-de-grue *m*, *pl* becs-de-grue, géranium *m*

cranial [ˈkreɪnɪəl] *adj Anat* (*nerve etc*) crânien; (*fracture*) du crâne

craniology [kreɪnɪˈɒlədʒɪ] *n* craniologie *f*

cranium, *pl* **-ia** [ˈkreɪnɪəm, -ɪə] *n Anat* crâne *m*

crank¹ [kræŋk] *n MecE, Aut* manivelle *f*; (*crankpin*) maneton *m*

crank² *vt* (*engine*) démarrer, lancer; (*with cranking handle*) faire démarrer à la manivelle

crank³ *n F* **(a)** (*eccentric*) excentrique *mf*; **a health food/ religious c.** un dingue des aliments naturels/de religion **(b)** *Am* (*bad-tempered person*) grincheux, -euse

▶ **crank out** *vtsep F* produire laborieusement

▶ **crank up** *vtsep* (*engine*) lancer *ou* faire partir à la manivelle; *Fig F* (*person in morning*) mettre en route

crankcase [ˈkræŋkkeɪs] *n Aut* carter *m*

crankiness [ˈkræŋkɪnɪs] *n F* **(a)** (*eccentricity*) excentricité *f*; (*whimsicality*) humeur *f* capricieuse **(b)** *Am* (*bad temper*) humeur *f* difficile

cranking handle [ˈkræŋkɪŋ] *n Aut* manivelle *f*

cranking speed *n Aut* vitesse *f* du démarreur, régime *m* de démarrage

cranking torque *n Aut* couple *m* de démarrage

crankpin [ˈkræŋkpɪn] *n Aut* maneton *m*

crankshaft [ˈkræŋkʃɑːft] *n Aut* vilebrequin *m*; **c. sensor** capteur *m* sur vilbrequin

cranky [ˈkræŋkɪ] *adj F* **(a)** (*eccentric*) excentrique; (*whimsical*) capricieux **(b)** *Am* (*bad-tempered*) grincheux

cranny [ˈkrænɪ] *n* (*crack*) fente *f*, lézarde *f*

crap¹ [kræp] **1** *n Sl* **(a)** (*excrement*) merde *f*; *Vulg* **to have** *or* **take a c.** chier

(b) *Fig* (*worthless thing(s)*) camelote *f*, saloperie *f*; (*nonsense*) foutaise(s) *f(pl)*, connerie(s) *f(pl)*; (*dirty, disgusting substance*) saloperie; **he's listening to that classical c. again** il est encore en train d'écouter ces conneries classiques; **he eats nothing but c.** il ne bouffe que des saloperies; **you don't believe all that c. about witches, do you?** tu ne crois quand même pas à toutes ces conneries sur les sorcières, hein?; **that's c.!, she never said that!** c'est de la connerie!, elle n'a jamais dit ça!; **what a load of c.!** quelles conneries!

2 *adj Sl* (*bad*) merdique; (*stupid*) con; **these books are c.** ces bouquins, c'est de la connerie *ou* de la merde

crap² *n Am* = **craps**; **c. game** jeu *m* de dés, craps *m*

crap³ *vi Vulg* chier; **he was so scared he was crapping himself** il avait tellement peur qu'il s'en chiait dessus

▶ **crap out of** *vipo Sl* (*lose one's nerve about*) **he crapped out of telling her she was fired** il aurait dû lui dire qu'on voulait la virer, mais il s'est défilé; **to c. out of sth** se défiler devant qch; **you can't c. out of it this time** tu ne peux pas te défiler cette fois-ci

crape [kreɪp] *n* **(a)** *Tex* (*for people in mourning*) crêpe *m* noir (de deuil) **(b)** *Med* **c. bandage** bande *f* Velpeau®

crapper ['kræpər] *n Sl* **(a)** (*lavatory*) chiottes *fpl* **(b)** (*coward*) trouillard *m*

crappy ['kræpɪ] *adj Sl* **(a)** (*dirty*) cradingue, crade **(b)** (*bad, stupid*) = **crap¹ 2**

craps [kræps] *npl* (*often with sing verb*) *Am* jeu *m* de dés, craps *m*; **to shoot c.** jouer aux dés

crapshooter ['kræpʃu:tər] *n Am* joueur, -euse de dés

crapulous ['kræpjʊləs], **crapulent** ['kræpjʊlənt] *adj Lit* intempérant

crash¹ [kræʃ] **1** *n* **(a)** (*noise*) fracas *m*; **there was a c. as the vase hit the ground** il y a eu un fracas quand le vase est tombé par terre; **the c. of thunder** le fracas du tonnerre; **there was a c. of thunder** il y eut un violent coup de tonnerre; **to fall with a c.** tomber avec fracas

(b) (*accident*) accident *m*; **car/train/plane c.** accident de voiture/ferroviaire/d'avion; **we were in a c.** (*car accident*) nous avons eu un accident de voiture; **this car has been in a c.** cette voiture a eu un accident; **the force of the c.** la force de l'impact; *Aut* **c. energy absorbing zone** zone *f* d'absorption de l'énergie de choc; *Aut* **c. sensor** détecteur *m* de collision *ou* de choc

(c) *Fig* (*disaster*) catastrophe *f*, débâcle *f*; **(financial) c.** débâcle financière, krach *m*; *Fin Hist* **the Wall Street C.** le krach de Wall Street

(d) (*of computer*) panne *f*

2 *int* patatras!; **c. went the vase** le vase tomba avec un grand fracas; **he drove c. into the wall** il est allé s'écraser contre le mur

crash² **1** *vi* **(a)** (*make sound*) retentir; (*of waves*) s'écraser; **the thunder crashed** (*once*) il y eut un violent coup de tonnerre; (*repeatedly*) le tonnerre retentit

(b) (*move*) **to c. (down)** tomber avec fracas; **the bottle crashed against the wall** la bouteille s'est écrasée contre le mur; **the bookcase came crashing down** la bibliothèque s'est écroulée avec fracas; **the vase crashed to the ground** le vase s'est écrasé par terre avec fracas; **the mast came crashing down** le mât s'abattit; **to c. through sth** passer à travers *ou* traverser qch avec fracas

(c) *Aut, Rail* entrer en collision; *Av* s'écraser au sol; **the two cars crashed head on** les deux voitures se sont tamponnées de front; **to c. into a tree** s'écraser contre un arbre, rentrer dans un arbre; **to c. into sb** rentrer dans qn; **I crashed into him/her** je lui suis rentré dedans

(d) (*of business*) faire faillite; *St Exch* s'effondrer

(e) (*of network, system etc*) sauter; (*of computer*) tomber en panne

(f) *Sl* (*sleep*) roupiller, pioncer; (*go to sleep*) se mettre à roupiller; **can I c. at your place tonight?** je peux pioncer chez toi ce soir?; **he crashed on the floor** il a roupillé par terre

2 *vt* **(a)** *Av* (*plane*) écraser au sol; *Aut* **to c. one's car** (*accidentally*) avoir un accident avec sa voiture; (*deliberately*) démolir sa voiture

(b) *Comptr* faire tomber en panne

(c) (*make noise with*) **to c. the gears** faire grincer la boîte de vitesses; **he crashed the books down on the table** il a posé les livres sur la table avec fracas

(d) *F* **to c. a party** aller à une réception sans être invité

crash³ *adj* **c. course** cours *m* accéléré *ou* intensif; **c. diet** régime *m* choc; *Admin* **c. programme** programme *m* choc *ou* d'urgence

▶ **crash out** *vi Sl* **(a)** (*go to sleep*) s'endormir; (*suddenly, when drunk etc*) s'écrouler; **he was crashed out on the sofa** il roupillait sur le divan **(b)** (*spend night, sleep*) pioncer

crash barrier *n Aut* glissière *f*

crash dive *n Naut* (*of submarine*) plongée *f* raide

crash-dive *Naut* **1** *vt* (*submarine*) faire plonger raide **2** *vi* plonger raide

crash helmet *n* casque *m* protecteur

crashing ['kræʃɪŋ] *adj F* **a c. bore** (*person*) une personne assommante; (*task*) une besogne assommante; (*party*) une soirée assommante; **to be a c. bore** être assommant

crashingly ['kræʃɪŋlɪ] *adv F* **c. boring** mortellement ennuyeux, ennuyeux à mourir

crash-land *Av* **1** *vi* atterrir brutalement **2** *vt* (*plane, helicopter*) faire atterrir brutalement

crash landing *n Av* atterrissage *m* en catastrophe

crash pad *n Sl* (*place to stay*) piaule *f* (*pour quelques jours*)

crash-test *vt* **to c. a car** tester une voiture en situation d'accident

crashworthiness ['kræʃwɜ:ðɪnɪs] *n* (*of vehicle, helicopter*) résistance *f* aux chocs

crass [krɑ:s] *adj* grossier; **c. ignorance** ignorance *f* crasse; **c. stupidity** immense stupidité *f*

crassly ['krɑ:slɪ] *adv* (*to behave, say*) avec grossièreté; **he's so c. stupid** il est d'une stupidité effarante

crassness ['krɑ:snɪs] *n* grossièreté *f*

crate¹ [kreɪt] *n* **(a)** (*for wine, whisky etc*) caisse *f*; (*for apples, oranges etc*) cageot *m*; (*for glass, china*) harasse *f*; (*for bottles*) casier *m* **(b)** *F* (*car*) caisse *f*; *Old-fashioned* (*aircraft*) coucou *m*

crate² *vt* (*goods*) mettre dans une caisse/des caisses

crater¹ ['kreɪtər] *n Geol* (*of volcano, moon*) cratère *m*; (*shell hole*) entonnoir *m*, cratère; **the explosion had left a c. 20 feet wide** l'explosion avait laissé un cratère de 6 mètres de large; **c. lake** lac *m* de cratère

crater² *vt* creuser; **a street cratered by shellfire** une rue défoncée par des éclats d'obus; **cratered face** visage *m* crevassé

cravat [krə'væt] *n* foulard *m*

crave [kreɪv] **1** *vt* **(a)** (*long for, need*) (*sth*) désirer ardemment, réclamer; **child that craves affection** enfant qui a un grand besoin d'affection; **she craves tobacco** elle a une envie furieuse de fumer **(b)** *Lit* (*beg*) **to c. sb's pardon** demander pardon à qn; **to c. indulgence** solliciter l'indulgence **2** *vi* **to c. for sth** désirer ardemment qch, réclamer qch

craven ['kreɪv(ə)n] *adj Lit* lâche

cravenly ['kreɪv(ə)nlɪ] *adv Lit* avec lâcheté, lâchement

craving ['kreɪvɪŋ] *n* désir *m* ardent, appétit *m* insatiable **(for** de); **c. for alcohol** passion *f* de l'alcool; (*need*) besoin *m* d'alcool; **I have a c. for chocolate** (*at this moment*) j'ai une envie furieuse de chocolat; (*in general*) j'ai la passion du chocolat; **pregnant women get strange cravings** les femmes enceintes ont souvent d'étranges envies

craw [krɔ:] *n* (*of bird*) jabot *m*; *Fig* **it sticks in my c.** ça me reste en travers de la gorge

crawfish ['krɔ:fɪʃ] *n esp US* = **crayfish**

crawl¹ [krɔ:l] *n* **(a)** (*action*) **the baby went for a c. along the floor** le bébé a rampé sur le sol **(b)** (*slow pace*) **to go along at a c.** (*on foot, in vehicle*) avancer très lentement; **the traffic had slowed to a c.** la circulation avait ralenti et on roulait au pas **(c)** *Swimming* crawl *m*; **to do the c.** nager le crawl, crawler **(d)** *TV* (*roller captions*) générique *m* sur déroulant

crawl² *vi* **(a)** (*of person*) (*on belly*) ramper, se traîner; (*on hands and knees*) marcher à quatre pattes; (*of snake, worm*) ramper; **to c. on one's hands and knees** aller à quatre pattes; **she was crawling about on the carpet** elle était à quatre pattes sur la moquette; **to c. into a hole** (*of reptile etc*) se glisser dans un trou; (*of person*) se traîner jusque dans un trou; **to c. to the door** aller jusqu'à la porte en rampant/à quatre pattes

(b) (*move slowly*) avancer lentement; *Aut F* faire du surplace

(c) (*be infested*) **to be crawling with vermin** grouiller de vermine; *F* **the streets were crawling with troops** les rues fourmillaient *ou* grouillaient de militaires; **to make sb's skin c.** donner un frisson de dégoût à qn

(d) *F* (*be obsequious*) **to c. to sb** s'aplatir devant qn, lécher les bottes à qn; **I refuse to c.** je refuse de m'aplatir

(e) *Swimming* crawler, nager le crawl

crawler ['krɔ:lər] *n F* (*obsequious person*) lèche-botte *m*, *pl* lèche-bottes

crawler lane *n Aut* voie *f* pour véhicules lents

crawlers *npl* (*baby's overalls*) grenouillère *f*

crawling ['krɔ:lɪŋ] **1** *adj* **(a)** (*baby*) qui marche à quatre pattes; **he's just got to the c. stage** il commence à marcher à quatre pattes; *Fig* **compared with the Japanese, we're still at the c. stage** comparés aux Japonais, nous en sommes encore aux balbutiements **(b)** (*infested*) grouillant **(with** de) **(c)** *F* (*obsequious*) lèche-bottes **2** *n F* (*obsequiousness*) **that's just c.** c'est du lèche-botte

crayfish ['kreɪfɪʃ] *n* **(freshwater) c.** écrevisse *f*; **(sea) c.** langouste *f*

crayon¹ ['kreɪɒn, -ən] *n Art* (*pencil*) crayon *m* de couleur; (*pastel*) crayon *m* pastel; (*wax*) crayon *m* de cire

crayon² *vt Art* **(a)** (*draw*) dessiner au crayon/au pastel/au crayon de cire **(b)** (*colour in*) (*sketch*) colorier

craze¹ [kreɪz] *n* manie *f* **(for sth** de qch); (*fad*) engouement *m*; **it's all the c.** ça fait fureur; **this is the latest dance c.** c'est la dernière danse à la mode

craze² **1** *vt* **(a)** *Lit* (*drive insane*) rendre fou **(b)** *Cer* (*porcelain*) craqueler **2** *vi Cer* se craqueler

crazed [kreɪzd] *adj* **(a)** (*with grief*) fou, *f* folle **(with** de); (*with fear*) affolé **(with** par) **(b)** *Cer* craquelé

-crazed [kreɪzd] *suff* rendu fou par; **drug/power-c.** rendu fou par la drogue/le pouvoir; **he was half-c. with grief** la douleur l'avait rendu à moitié fou

crazily ['kreɪzɪlɪ] *adv* **(a)** follement; (*to behave*) bizarrement; **c., they ...** ce qui est complètement fou, ils ... **(b)** (*to lean*) bizarrement

craziness ['kreɪzɪnɪs] *n* (*of person*) folie *f*, démence *f*

crazy ['kreɪzɪ] **1** *adj* **(a)** (*person*) fou, *f* folle, *F* dingue; **c. with**

fear fou de terreur; **to go c.** devenir fou (**with anger** de colère); **to drive** *or* **send sb c.** rendre qn fou; **you're c.**! vous êtes fou!; **but that's c., we've only just arrived**! mais c'est dingue, nous venons juste d'arriver!; **to be c. about** *or* **over sb/sth** être fou de qn/qch; **like c.** comme un enragé (**b**) (*odd*) (*dress, building, angle etc*) bizarre (**c**) *esp Am Sl* (*very good*) fou, *f* folle, dément **2** *n esp Am Sl* (*person*) original, -ale

crazy bone *n US Anat* petit juif *m*

crazy golf *n* mini-golf *m*

crazy house *n esp Am Sl* asile *f ou* maison *f* de fous

crazy paving *n* = dallage *m* irrégulier en pierres plates

CRC [siːɑːˈsiː] *n Typ* (*abbr* **camera-ready copy**) épreuves *fpl* bonnes à filmer

CRE [siːɑːˈriː] *n Br Admin* (*abbr* **Commission for Racial Equality**) = commission *f* pour l'égalité raciale

creak[1] [kriːk] *n* (*of hinge*) grincement *m*; (*of floor, chair, new shoes etc*) craquement *m*; **to give a c.** grincer/craquer

creak[2] *vi* (*of hinge*) grincer; (*of floor, chair, shoes*) craquer; *Fig* (*of plot etc*) être boiteux; **the chair creaked under his weight** la chaise a craqué sous son poids

creaking [ˈkriːkɪŋ] **1** *adj* (*hinge*) qui grince; (*timber, shoes*) qui craque **2** *n* (*of hinge*) grincement *m*; (*of timber, shoes*) craquement *m*

creaky [ˈkriːkɪ] *adj* (*hinge*) qui grince; (*timber, shoe*) qui craque; *Fig* (*dialogue, plot etc*) boiteux

cream[1] [kriːm] **1** *n* (**a**) (*of milk*) crème *f*; (*used in cakes etc*) crème (fraîche); **single/double c.** crème fluide *ou* fleurette/épaisse; **strawberries and c.** fraises *fpl* à la crème; **c. bun** = petit pain *m* au lait servi avec de la crème chantilly; **c. cake** gâteau *m* à la crème; **c. jug** pot *m* à crème; **c. sherry** sherry *m* doux

(**b**) *Fig* **the c.** (*best part etc*) la crème, le dessus du panier; **they're the c. of the crop** (*of students, job applicants etc*) c'est le dessus du panier, c'est la crème; **the c. of society** la crème de la société

(**c**) (*filling for chocolate*) fondant *m*; (*individual chocolate*) boule *f* de crème

(**d**) (*soup*) **c. of tomato/asparagus soup** crème *f* de tomates/d'asperges

(**e**) (*sauce*) **c. of horseradish** épaisse sauce *f* au raifort

(**f**) (*lotion etc*) crème *f* (*de toilette, de beauté*); **shoe c.** crème pour chaussures

(**g**) **c. of tartar** crème *f* de tartre

(**h**) (*colour*) crème *f*

2 *adj* **c. (-coloured)** crème *inv*

cream[2] **1** *vt* (**a**) (*remove cream from*) (*milk*) écrémer (**b**) (*add cream to*) (*coffee etc*) ajouter de la crème à (**c**) (*beat*) (*butter*) battre en crème; **to c. potatoes** réduire les pommes de terre en purée; **c. the butter and sugar** (*in recipe*) battre le beurre et le sucre jusqu'à ce qu'ils forment un mélange mousseux *ou* crémeux (**d**) *Am F* (*person*) (*beat up*) casser la figure à; (*defeat*) battre à plate couture, mettre la pâtée à (**e**) *Vulg Sl* **to c. one's jeans** (*ejaculate in*) juter dans son froc; (*of woman*) mouiller **2** *vi Vulg Sl* (*ejaculate*) décharger

▶ **cream off** *vtsep* (*remove*) écrémer; **to c. off the best part of sth** écrémer *ou* prélever la meilleure partie de qch; **the universities c. off the best students** les universités écrèment toujours les meilleurs étudiants

cream cheese *n* fromage *m* frais

cream cracker *n Br* cracker *m*

creamed [kriːmd] *adj Culin* (*chicken etc*) à la crème; **c. potatoes** pommes *fpl* de terre en purée

creamer [ˈkriːmər] *n* (**a**) *Am* (*jug*) pot *m* à crème (**b**) (*for coffee*) succédané *m* (*de lait*) (**c**) (*machine*) écrémeuse *f*

creamery [ˈkriːmərɪ] *n* laiterie *f*; (*shop*) crémerie *f*; **c. butter** beurre *m* laitier

cream puff *n* chou *m* à la crème

cream tea *n Br* = repas *m* se composant de thé et de scones servis avec de la crème et de la confiture

creamy [ˈkriːmɪ] *adj* (*containing cream, resembling cream*) crémeux; **rich c. sauce** sauce *f* onctueuse

crease[1] [kriːs] *n* (**a**) (*made on purpose*) pli *m*; (*accidental*) faux pli *m*; **to remove the creases from sth** enlever les faux plis de qch; **to put a c. in a pair of trousers** faire le pli d'un pantalon (**b**) *Cr* (**batting**) **c.** ligne *f* du batteur

crease[2] **1** *vt* (**a**) (*on purpose*) plisser, faire des plis à; (*accidentally*) froisser, chiffonner; (*with iron*) faire un/des faux pli(s) à; **well-creased trousers** pantalon avec un pli impeccable; **to c. one's brow** froncer les sourcils (**b**) (*of bullet*) (*scalp etc*) érafler **2** *vi* (**a**) (*become creased*) se froisser (**b**) *Br F* = **crease up 1**

▶ **crease up** *Br F* **1** *vi* (*laugh uncontrollably*) se tordre (de rire) **2** *vtsep* (*make laugh uncontrollably*) faire rire à se tordre

crease-resistant *adj* infroissable

create [krɪˈeɪt] **1** *vt* (*world, peer, jobs, role, difficulties etc*) créer; (*impression*) faire, produire; **she created a studio out of a shed** elle a créé un studio à partir d'une cabane; **if opportunities do not exist you must c. them** si les occasions n'existent pas, il faut les créer; **to c. a scene** (*fuss*) faire une scène; *Jur* **to c. a disturbance** troubler l'ordre public **2** *vi* (**a**) (*be creative*) créer (**b**) *Br F* (*make a scene*) faire du tapage, faire une scène (**about** à propos de)

creation [krɪˈeɪʃən] *n* (**a**) (*action*) (*of the world, a title etc*) création *f*; **job c.** création d'emplois (**b**) (*product*) création *f*; **the latest creations** (*fashions*) les dernières créations (**c**) (*universe*) création *f*; *Rel* **the C.** la Création

creative [krɪˈeɪtɪv] *adj* (*professional artist, designer etc*) créateur, -trice; (*activity, child, amateur artist etc*) créatif; **I don't do anything c.** je ne fais rien de créatif; *Hum* **c. accounting** comptabilité *f* créative; **c. drive** impulsion *f* créatrice; **c. brief** (*in advertising*) plan *m* de travail créatif, PTC *m*; **c. copy strategy** (*in advertising*) copie *f* stratégie créative; **c. director** directeur *m* de la création; **c. team** équipe *f* de création; **c. writing** création *f* littéraire; **c. writing workshop** atelier *m* d'écriture

creatively [krɪˈeɪtɪvlɪ] *adv* avec créativité; **more c.** avec plus de créativité, de façon plus créative

creativeness [krɪˈeɪtɪvnɪs], **creativity** [kriəˈtɪvɪtɪ] *n* créativité *f*

creator [krɪˈeɪtər] *n* (*of a fashion, role etc*) créateur, -trice; *Rel* **the C.** le Créateur

creature [ˈkriːtʃər] *n* (**a**) (*living being*) créature *f*, être *m* (vivant); **creatures from outer space** extra-terrestres *mpl* (**b**) (*animal*) animal *m*, bête *f* (**c**) (*person*) **poor c.**! le/la pauvre!; **c. comforts** confort *m* matériel; **to like one's c. comforts** aimer ses aises; *Pej* **c. of the government** créature *f* du gouvernement; **man is the c. of circumstances** l'homme dépend des circonstances; **I am a c. of habit** je suis un homme/une femme d'habitude

crèche [kreɪʃ, kreʃ] *n* (**a**) *Br* (*for children*) crèche *f*; **c. facilities** crèche (**b**) *Rel* crèche *f*

cred [kred] *n F see* **street cred(ibility)**

credence [ˈkriːdəns] *n* croyance *f*, foi *f*; **to give** *or* **attach c. to sth** ajouter foi à qch; **letters of c.** lettres *fpl* de créance

credentials [krɪˈdenʃəlz] *npl* (**a**) (*proof of identity*) pièces *fpl* justificatives d'identité; (*of a diplomat etc*) lettres *fpl* de créance (**b**) (*proof of ability*) références *fpl*; **what are your c.?** quelles sont vos références?; *Fig* **a film director with excellent c.** un metteur en scène aux excellents antécédents

credibility [kredɪˈbɪlɪtɪ] *n* (*of person, policy*) crédibilité *f*; **the government has lost c. in the eyes of** *or* **with the public** le gouvernement a perdu sa crédibilité aux yeux du public; **the president's actions gave him some c.** les actions du président lui ont conféré une certaine crédibilité; **c. gap** manque *m* de crédibilité

credible [ˈkredɪb(ə)l] *adj* crédible; **it is hardly c. that ...** il est difficile à croire que ... + *sub*

credibly [ˈkredɪblɪ] *adv* de façon crédible

credit[1] [ˈkredɪt] *n* (**a**) *Com, Fin* crédit *m*; (*in an account*) avoir *m*; **to be in c.** avoir de l'argent sur son compte; (*of account*) être créditeur; **my account is still in c.** j'ai toujours de l'argent sur mon compte, *esp Spec* mon compte est toujours créditeur; **to get back into c.** rembourser un découvert; (*of account*) redevenir créditeur; **to give sb c.** faire crédit à qn; **we do not give c.** (*of shop*) la maison ne fait pas crédit; **to sell on c.** vendre à crédit; **to live on c.** vivre à crédit; **to enter a sum to sb's c.** porter une somme au crédit *ou* à l'actif de qn, créditer qn d'une somme; **his c. is good** *Fin* il a une bonne réputation de solvabilité; *Fig* (*he is trusted*) on lui fait toute confiance; *Fig* **he still has c. with the trade unions** les syndicats lui font encore confiance; **c. advice** avis *m* de crédit; **c. balance** solde *m* créditeur; *Am* **c. line, line of c.** ligne *f* de crédit; **c. squeeze** restriction *f ou* resserrement *m* du crédit

(**b**) (*belief*) croyance *f*; **to give c. to** *or* **place c. in a rumour** ajouter *ou* accorder foi à un bruit; **facts that lend c. to a rumour** faits qui accréditent une rumeur; **to gain c.** (*of theory etc*) être accepté

(**c**) (*merit*) mérite *m*, honneur *m*; **to give sb c. for sth** reconnaître le mérite de qn dans qch; **you'll have to give him c. for that** il faudra bien que tu reconnaisses son mérite là-dedans; **I gave him c. for more sense** je lui supposais plus de jugement; **she's shrewder than most people give her c. for** elle est plus perspicace que la plupart des gens ne le pensent; **give me c. for <u>some</u> common sense!** fais-moi l'honneur de croire que j'ai un peu de bon sens!; **to take the c. for an action** s'attribuer le mérite d'une action; **they took the c., but she did all the work** ils se sont attribué le mérite, mais c'est elle qui a fait tout le travail; **I can't claim much of the c. for the project's success** je ne peux pas m'attribuer grand mérite pour la réussite du projet; **most of the c. should go to the actors** c'est aux acteurs que devrait revenir le plus grand mérite; **c. where c.'s due** il faut rendre à César ce qui lui appartient; **OK, but c. where c.'s due, it was he who ...** d'accord mais il faut bien reconnaître que c'est lui qui ...; **with c.** honorablement; *Sch* (*in an examination*) avec mention assez bien; **it must be said to her c. that ...** il faut porter à son crédit que ...; **the team have three wins to their c.** l'équipe compte trois victoires à son actif; **it does him c.** cela lui fait (grand) honneur; **your children do you c.** *or* **are a c. to you** vos enfants vous font honneur; **she is a c. to the school** elle fait honneur à l'école; **on the c. side, it must be said he was honest enough to own up** il faut dire en sa faveur qu'il a eu l'honnêteté d'avouer

(**d**) *Cin, TV* **credits** générique *m*; **to give sb a c.** (*in a book*) mentionner le nom de qn dans le liste des collaborateurs

(**e**) *Univ* unité *f* de valeur

credit[2] *vt* (**a**) *Com, Fin* **to c. sb/an account with a sum** créditer qn/un compte d'une somme; **to c. a sum to an account** porter une somme au crédit d'un compte (**b**) (*attribute*) attribuer, prêter (**sb with a quality** une qualité à qn); **to c. sb with superior intelligence** créditer qn d'une intelligence supérieure; **I credited you with more sense** je vous croyais *ou* supposais plus de jugement; **to be credited with having done sth** passer pour avoir fait qch (**c**) (*believe*) croire; **I wouldn't have credited it** je ne l'aurais pas cru possible; **you wouldn't c. it!, would you c. it!** tu te rends compte?

creditable ['kredɪtəb(ə)l] *adj* (*action*) estimable, digne d'éloges

creditably ['kredɪtəblɪ] *adv* honorablement, avec honneur

credit account *n Banking* compte *m* créditeur; (*with department store*) compte

credit agency *n* institution *f* de crédit

credit bank *n* banque *f* de crédit

credit card *n* carte *f* de crédit; **c. machine** pressographe *m*; **c. reader** lecteur *m* de cartes; **c. terminal** terminal *m* électronique de paiement, TEP *m*; **c. voucher** note *f* de débit

credit note *n* note *f* de crédit

creditor ['kredɪtər] *n* créancier, -ière; **c. account** compte *m* créditeur; **creditors' meeting** réunion *f* des créanciers; *Econ* **c. nation** nation *f* créditrice

credit rating *n* degré *m* de solvabilité; *Com, Fin* notation *f*; **c. agency** agence *f* de notation

credit risk *n* risque *m* de crédit; **to be a good/bad c.** représenter un risque peu important/important

creditworthiness ['kredɪtwɜːðɪnɪs] *n* solvabilité *f*

creditworthy ['kredɪtwɜːðɪ] *adj* solvable

credo, *pl* **-os** ['kriːdəʊ, 'kreɪ-, -əʊz] *n* credo *m inv*

credulity [krɪ'djuːlɪtɪ] *n* crédulité *f*; **his story stretched c.** son histoire était vraiment difficile à croire

credulous ['kredjʊləs] *adj* crédule

creed [kriːd] *n* (**a**) *Rel* credo *m inv*; **the (Apostles') C.** le Credo (**b**) (*beliefs*) croyance *f*, foi *f*; **political c.** credo *m ou* profession *f* de foi politique

creek [kriːk] *n esp Br* (*small bay*) crique *f*, anse *f*; *Am, Austr, New Zealand* (*stream*) ruisseau *m*, petit cours *m* d'eau; *F* **to be up the c. (without a paddle)** (*of person*) être dans le pétrin; (*of holiday, project etc*) être à l'eau

creel [kriːl] *n* panier *m* de pêche

creep[1] [kriːp] *n* (**a**) *Sl* (*person*) (*disgusting*) personnage *m* répugnant, salopard *m*, saligaud *m*; (*obsequious*) lèche-bottes *m inv*, lèche-cul *m inv*; **that c. she's married to** son salopard de mari (**b**) *F* **the creeps** la chair de poule; **to get the creeps** avoir la chair de poule; **to give sb the creeps** (*scare*) donner la chair de poule à qn; (*annoy*) horripiler qn (**c**) *Aut* rampage *m*

creep[2] *vi* (*pt, pp* **crept** [krept]) (**a**) (*of insect, animal*) ramper; (*of person*) se glisser; **to c. into bed** se glisser dans son lit; **he crept into the room** il entra furtivement *ou* à pas de loup dans la chambre; *Fig* **a moralizing tone has crept into her writing** un ton moralisateur s'est insidieusement glissé dans ses écrits; **a feeling of uneasiness crept over me** un sentiment de gêne commençait à me gagner; **to make sb's flesh c.** donner la chair de poule à qn

(**b**) *F* (*be obsequious*) ramper (*devant les grands*); **she's always creeping to the teacher** elle est toujours en train de ramper devant le professeur

(**c**) (*of plant*) ramper; (*upwards*) grimper

▶ **creep along** *vi* (*stealthily*) s'avancer furtivement, marcher à pas de loup; (*move slowly, in car etc*) se traîner

▶ **creep away** *vi* s'éloigner à pas de loup

▶ **creep by** *vi* passer furtivement; **time** *or* **the hours crept slowly by** les heures passaient lentement

▶ **creep up** *vi* (**a**) (*approach stealthily*) approcher furtivement (**to** de); **she crept up behind me** elle est arrivée derrière moi tout doucement (**b**) (*of inflation, prices etc*) monter petit à petit; **the speedometer crept up to 120** l'aiguille de l'indicateur de vitesse est montée tout doucement jusqu'à 120

▶ **creep up on** *vipo* surprendre, prendre par surprise; **don't c. up on me like that!** ne m'arrive pas comme ça dessus sans prévenir!; **old age has crept up on me** j'ai vieilli sans m'en rendre compte

creeper ['kriːpər] *n* (**a**) (*plant*) plante *f* rampante; (*climbing*) plante grimpante (**b**) **creepers** (*shoes*) chaussures *fpl* à semelles de crêpe; *US* (*crampons*) crampons *mpl* à verglas (**c**) *Am* **creepers** (*child's garment*) barboteuse *f*

creeping ['kriːpɪŋ] **1** *adj* (**a**) (*animal*) rampant; *Med* **c. paralysis** paralysie *f* progressive (**b**) *F* (*obsequious*) servile, rampant (**c**) (*plant*) rampant; (*upwards*) grimpant **2** *n F* (*obsequiousness*) servilité *f*

creepy ['kriːpɪ] *adj F* (**a**) (*film, story, person*) qui donne la chair de poule; **it was c.** c'était à vous donner la chair de poule; **a c. old house** une vieille maison sinistre (**b**) **I could feel something c. on my leg** je sentais quelque chose qui rampait sur ma jambe

creepy-crawly ['kriːpɪ'krɔːlɪ] *F* **1** *n* insecte *m* rampant, bestiole *f* rampante **2** *adj* **c. feeling** (sensation *f* de) fourmillement *m*

cremate [krɪ'meɪt] *vt* (*dead person*) incinérer

cremation [krɪ'meɪʃən] *n* incinération *f*, crémation *f*

crematorium, *pl* **-ia** [kremə'tɔːrɪəm, -ɪə] *n* crématorium *m*

crematory ['kriːmətɔːrɪ] *n Am* crématorium *m*

crenellated, *US* **crenelated** ['krenəleɪtɪd] *adj* (*wall etc*) crénelé

Creole ['kriːəʊl] **1** *n* Créole *mf*; *US* (*in Louisiana*) = descendant, -ante des colons français ou espagnols de la Louisiane **2** *adj* créole; *US* (*in Louisiana*) = qui descend des colons français ou espagnols de la Louisiane

creole ['kriːəʊl] *Ling* **1** *n* créole *m* **2** *adj* créole

creosote[1] ['krɪəsəʊt] *n* créosote *f*

creosote[2] *vt* (*wood*) créosoter

crêpe [kreɪp, krep] *n* (**a**) *Tex* crêpe *m*; **c. de Chine** crêpe de Chine; **c. bandage** bande *f* Velpeau®; **c. skirt** jupe *f* en crêpe (**b**) **c. (rubber)** crêpe *m*; **c.(-rubber) soles** semelles *fpl* (de) crêpe (**c**) **c. paper** papier *m* crépon (**d**) *Culin* crêpe *f*

crept *see* **creep**[2]

Cres (*abbr* **Crescent**) rue (*en croissant*)

crescendo [krɪ'ʃendəʊ] **1** *n Mus, Fig* crescendo *m inv*; **to build up to a c.** aller crescendo; *Fig* **to reach a c.** atteindre son paroxysme **2** *adv Mus* crescendo

crescent ['kresənt] **1** *n* (*shape*) croissant *m*; (*street*) rue *f* en croissant **2** *adj* **c.(-shaped)** en forme de croissant *ou* de demi-lune; **the c. moon** le croissant de la lune

cress [kres] *n* cresson *m*

crest[1] [krest] *n* (*of chicken, reptile*) crête *f*; (*of bird*) huppe *f*; (*of peacock*) aigrette *f*; *Anat* (*of bone*) crête, arête *f*; (*of helmet*) cimier *m*, crête; (*of hill, wave*) crête, sommet *m*; (*of roof*) faîte *m*; (*coat of arms*) armoiries *fpl*; (*insignia*) écusson *m*; *Fig* **to be on the c. of a wave** être à son meilleur niveau; **she rode to power on the c. of a wave of popular enthusiasm** elle a été portée au pouvoir par l'enthousiasme populaire

crest[2] *vt* (*wave, hill*) arriver au sommet de

crested ['krestɪd] *adj* (**a**) (*animal*) à crête; (*with feathered crest*) à huppe, huppé; **white-c. waves** moutons *mpl*, vagues *fpl* aux crêtes blanches (**b**) (*helmet*) orné d'un cimier; (*plumed*) panaché (**c**) *Her* (*coat of arms*) armorié; (*insignia*) orné d'un écusson

crestfallen ['krestfɔːl(ə)n] *adj* (*person*) abattu, découragé; (*look*) déconfit, abattu, découragé

cretaceous [krɪ'teɪʃəs] **1** *adj* crétacé **2** *n* **the C.** le crétacé

Cretan ['kriːt(ə)n] **1** *adj* crétois **2** *n* Crétois, -oise

Crete [kriːt] *n* Crète *f*

cretin ['kretɪn] *n Pej, Old-fashioned Med* crétin, -ine

cretinism ['kretɪnɪz(ə)m] *n Old-fashioned Med* crétinisme *m*

cretinous ['kretɪnəs] *adj Pej, Old-fashioned Med* crétin

cretonne [kre'tɒn, 'kretɒn] *n Tex* cretonne *f*

Creutzfeldt-Jakob disease ['krɔɪtsfelt'jaːkɒp] *n Med* maladie *f* de Creutzfeldt-Jakob

crevasse [krɪ'væs] *n* crevasse *f* (glaciaire)

crevice ['krevɪs] *n* fente *f*; (*in wall*) lézarde *f*; (*in rock*) crevasse *f*, fissure *f*

crew[1] [kruː] *n* [①**A11,g,iii**] (**a**) (*of ship, plane*) équipage *m*; (*in rowing*) équipe *f*; (*gang, team*) équipe; **ambulance/camera c.** équipe d'ambulanciers/de cameramen; *Av* **ground c.** personnel *m* au sol; *Ind* **maintenance c.** équipe d'entretien; **c. member** membre *m* d'un équipage/d'une équipe (**b**) *F* (*group of people*) bande *f*, troupe *f*; **sorry c.** triste engeance *f*; **they're a good c. to work with** c'est une bonne équipe avec qui travailler

crew² **1** *vt* (*ship*) armer d'un équipage; (*plane*) fournir un équipage à; **yacht that can't be crewed by less than six** yacht qui exige un équipage de six au moins; *Naut* **crewed charter** location *m* de bateau avec équipage **2** *vi* **to c. for sb** servir d'équipier à qn
crew cut *n* (*hairstyle*) cheveux *mpl* (coupés) en brosse, brosse *f*
crew neck *n* (*of sweater*) col *m* ras du cou; (*sweater*) pull *m* ras du cou
crib¹ [krɪb] *n* **(a)** (*cradle*) berceau *m*; *Am* (*cot*) lit *m* d'enfant; *Rel* (*in Nativity*) crèche *f* **(b)** *Agr* (*for feeding animals*) mangeoire *f*, râtelier *m* **(c)** *Br F* (*plagiarism*) plagiat *m*; *Sch* anti-sèche *f*; (*translation*) traduction *f* (*employée subrepticement*)
crib² *vt* (-bb-) **1** *vt* (*passage from a book*) reproduire, copier; *Sch* **to c. an exercise from sb** pomper un exercice sur qn **2** *vi Sch* pomper; **to c. from an author** plagier un auteur
cribbage ['krɪbɪdʒ] *n Cards* cribbage *m*
crib death *n Am* mort *f* subite du nourrisson
crick¹ [krɪk] *n* **c. in the back** tour *m* de reins; **c. in the neck** torticolis *m*
crick² *vt* **to c. one's neck** attraper un torticolis; **to c. one's back** se faire un tour de reins
cricket¹ ['krɪkɪt] *n* (*insect*) grillon *m*
cricket² *n Sp* cricket *m*; **to play c.** jouer au cricket; *Old-fashioned Br Fig* **that's not c.** cela n'est pas de jeu, cela ne se fait pas; **c. ball** balle *f* de cricket; **c. bat** batte *f* de cricket; **c. field** *or* **pitch** terrain *m* de cricket
cricketer ['krɪkɪtər] *n* joueur, -euse de cricket
crier ['kraɪər] *n* **town c.** crieur *m* public *ou* municipal
crikey ['kraɪkɪ] *int Br Sl* mince alors!
crime [kraɪm] *n* (*act*) crime *m*; *Jur* (*minor offence*) délit *m*; (*phenomenon*) criminalité *f*; **to commit a c.** commettre un crime/un délit; **a c. against nature/humanity** un crime contre nature/l'humanité; *Jur* **a c. of passion** un crime passionnel; *Fig* **it's a c. to cut down this tree** c'est un crime d'abattre cet arbre; *Fig* **it's not a c. to ...** ce n'est pas un crime de ...; **to make a study of c.** étudier la criminalité; **c. reporter** chroniqueur, -euse judiciaire
Crimea (the) [ðəkraɪ'mɪə] *n* la Crimée
Crimean [kraɪ'mɪən] *adj* de Crimée; *Hist* **the C. War** la guerre de Crimée
crime figures *n* chiffres *mpl* de la criminalité
crime rate *n* taux *m* de (la) criminalité
crime series *n* série policière *f*
crime story *n* (*novel*) roman *m* noir; (*detective novel*) roman policier
crime wave *n* vague *f* de criminalité
crime writer *n* (*novelist*) auteur *m* de romans noirs; (*of detective novels*) auteur de romans policiers
criminal ['krɪmɪn(ə)l] **1** *n* criminel, -elle **2** *adj Jur* criminel; *Fig* **it would be c. to cut down these trees** ce serait un crime d'abattre ces arbres; **c. act** action *f* criminelle; **to take c. proceedings against sb** poursuivre qn en justice; **c. case** affaire *f* criminelle; **to bring a c. action against sb** intenter une action en justice contre qn; *Jur* **c. conversation** adultère *m*; **c. suit** action criminelle, procès criminel
criminal court *n* cour *f* pénale
Criminal Investigation Department *n Br* = Police *f* Judiciaire
criminalization [krɪmɪnəlaɪ'zeɪʃən] *n* criminalisation *f*
criminalize ['krɪmɪnəlaɪz] *vt* criminaliser
criminal law *n* droit *m* pénal *ou* criminel
criminal lawyer *n* avocat *m* au pénal
criminally ['krɪmɪn(ə)lɪ] *adv* criminellement; **to be c. insane** être dément; (*of man*) être un fou dangereux; **the c. insane** les fous dangereux; **this is c. negligent** c'est une négligence criminelle; **it's c. wasteful** c'est un crime de gaspiller comme ça
criminal negligence *n* négligence *f* coupable *ou* criminelle
criminal offence *n* délit *m*; (*serious*) crime *m*
criminal record *n* casier *m* judiciaire
criminologist [krɪmɪ'nɒlədʒɪst] *n* criminologue *mf*
criminology [krɪmɪ'nɒlədʒɪ] *n* criminologie *f*
crimp¹ [krɪmp] *n* (*in hair*) frisure *f*; (*in sheet*) pli *m*
crimp² *vt* (*hair*) crêper; (*pastry*) gaufrer; (*material*) plisser, crêper
Crimplene® ['krɪmpliːn] *n* = synthétique *m* infroissable semblable au crêpe de Chine
crimson¹ ['krɪmz(ə)n] *adj, n* cramoisi *m*; **to blush c.** devenir cramoisi; **c. with rage** rouge de colère
cringe [krɪndʒ] *vi* **(a)** (*flinch*) avoir un mouvement de recul; **the dog cringed in the corner** le chien se blottit dans le coin; **he stayed cringing in the background** il se fit tout petit **(b)** (*be servile*) s'humilier, ramper, s'aplatir (**before sb** devant qn) **(c)** *F* (*be embarrassed*) avoir envie de rentrer sous terre; **her singing makes me c.** quand elle chante, ça me donne envie de rentrer sous terre; **it makes you c.** c'est très pénible **(d)** (*be disgusted*) avoir un sentiment de dégoût
cringe-making *adj Br F* qui donne envie de rentrer sous terre
cringing ['krɪndʒɪŋ] *adj* **(a)** (*afraid*) craintif **(b)** (*servile*) servile, obséquieux
crinkle¹ ['krɪŋk(ə)l] *n* pli *m*, ride *f*
crinkle² **1** *vt* (*paper*) froisser, chiffonner; **to c. one's nose** froncer le nez **2** *vi* se froisser; (*of apples*) se rider; **his nose crinkled at the smell** l'odeur lui fit froncer le nez
crinkle-cut *adj* (*crisps, chips*) dentelé
crinkly ['krɪŋklɪ] *adj* (*skin*) ridé; (*paper*) froissé, chiffonné; **my fingers have gone all c.** la peau de mes doigts est toute fripée
crinoline ['krɪn(ə)lɪn] *n* crinoline *f*
cripes [kraɪps] *int Old-fashioned Br Sl* mince alors!
cripple¹ ['krɪp(ə)l] *n* estropié, -ée, infirme *mf*, invalide *mf*; *Fig* **emotional c.** handicapé, -ée sur le plan affectif
cripple² *vt* **(a)** (*person*) estropier; **those who were crippled in the war** les mutilés *mpl* de guerre **(b)** *Fig* (*machine*) empêcher de fonctionner; (*ship*) désemparer; (*tank*) mettre hors de combat; (*industry, system*) paralyser
crippled ['krɪp(ə)ld] *adj* **(a)** (*person*) estropié, infirme; **c. with rheumatism** perclus de rhumatismes; **a c. arm** un bras malade **(b)** *Fig* (*ship*) désemparé; (*tank*) hors de combat; **the country is c. with debt** le pays est paralysé par les dettes
crippling ['krɪplɪŋ] *adj* **(a)** (*illness*) qui rend infirme **(b)** *Fig* (*taxation, strike etc*) paralysant; **the c. effect of the blockade** l'effet *m* paralysant du blocus
crisis, *pl* **-es** ['kraɪsɪs, -iːz] *n* (*in business, one's personal life etc*) crise *f*; **in c.** en pleine crise; **things are coming to a c.** la situation devient critique; **to go through a c.** traverser une crise; **a minor family c.** un petit problème familial; **c. management** gestion *f* de crises; **c. point** point *m* critique; **to reach c. point** atteindre un point critique
crisp¹ [krɪsp] **1** *adj* (*biscuit, pastry etc*) croquant, croustillant; (*apple, lettuce*) croquant, craquant; (*bacon*) croustillant; (*air*) vif; (*style*) vif et précis; (*tone*) tranchant; **the snow was c. underfoot** la neige craquait sous mes/nos/*etc* pas; **a c. five pound note** un billet de 5 livres tout neuf; **a c. white shirt** (*appearance*) une chemise blanche impeccable; (*texture*) une chemise blanche fraîchement lavée **2** *n* **(a)** **cooked to a c.** rôti à point pour croquer sous la dent; **burnt to a c.** carbonisé **(b)** *Br* **(potato) crisps** (pommes *fpl*) chips *fpl*; **one c.** une chips
crisp² *vt* (*meat etc*) donner du croustillant *ou* du croquant à
crispbread ['krɪspbred] *n* = pain *m* suédois
crisper ['krɪspər] *n* (*in refrigerator*) bac *m* à légumes
crisply ['krɪsplɪ] *adv* (*to speak*) d'un ton tranchant; (*to write*) d'un style vif et précis
crispness ['krɪspnɪs] *n* (*of biscuit, pastry etc*) croustillant *m*, croquant *m*; (*of apple, lettuce*) craquant *m*; (*of bacon*) croustillant; (*of snow*) dureté *f*; (*of air*) fraîcheur *f*; (*of style*) vivacité *f* et précision *f*; **to lose its c.** (*of fabric etc*) perdre sa raideur
crispy ['krɪspɪ] *adj* **c. bacon** bacon *m* croustillant
criss-cross¹ ['krɪskrɒs] **1** *adj* (*pattern etc*) entrecroisé **2** *n* entrecroisement *m*
criss-cross² **1** *vt* (*threads etc*) entrecroiser; **a brow criss-crossed with wrinkles** un front craquelé de rides; **a network of streets criss-crosses the town** un réseau de rues parcourt la ville dans tous les sens **2** *vi* s'entrecroiser
crit [krɪt] *n F* (*criticism*) critique *f*; **lit c.** critique littéraire
criterion, *pl* **-ia** [kraɪ'tɪərɪən, -ɪə] *n* critère *m*; **what criteria do you apply** *or* **what are your criteria when selecting candidates?** sur quels critères vous fondez-vous *ou* quels sont vos critères lorsque vous sélectionnez des candidats?
critic ['krɪtɪk] *n* (*in general*) critiqueur *m*; (*of other people's behaviour*) censeur *m*; *Cin, Liter etc* critique *m*; **she has her critics** il y en a qui la critiquent; **there are few critics of the policy** peu de gens critiquent la politique; **music/drama/literary c.** critique musical/dramatique/littéraire; **film c.** critique de cinéma
critical ['krɪtɪk(ə)l] *adj* **(a)** critique; **a c. audience** un public exigeant; **to be c. of sb/sth** (*of person*) se montrer *ou* être critique à l'égard de qn/qch; (*of report, article etc*) être critique à l'égard de qn/qch; **stop being so c.** arrête de critiquer

(b) *Cin, Liter etc* (*essay, study*) critique; **c. success** film *m*/ *etc* acclamé par les critiques; **the film received c. acclaim** le film a été salué unanimement par les critiques, le film a fait l'unanimité de la critique

(c) (*decisive*) (*situation, moment, age etc*) critique; *Med*

she is in a c. condition elle est dans un état critique; **she is going through a c. time** elle subit *ou* traverse une crise en ce moment; **the next few days will be c.** les prochains jours seront décisifs; *Opt* **c. angle** angle *m* limite *ou* critique

critically ['krɪtɪklɪ] *adv* **(a)** (*to consider sth*) en critique; (*to look at sth*) d'un œil critique **(b)** (*acclaimed etc*) par les critiques **(c)** *Med* **c. ill** dangereusement malade; **the c. ill** les grands malades *mpl*

critical mass *n Nucl Phys* masse *f* critique

critical path analysis *n* analyse *f* du chemin critique

critical path method *n* méthode *f* du chemin critique

criticism ['krɪtɪsɪz(ə)m] *n* **(a)** (*action, act of criticizing*) critique *f*; **it wasn't meant as a c.** ce n'était pas une critique; **to lay oneself open to c.** s'exposer à la critique; **the report contained strong c. of this department** le rapport contenait de graves critiques de ce service **(b)** *Cin, Liter etc* critique *f*; **to write a c. of a book** écrire la critique d'un livre

criticize ['krɪtɪsaɪz] **1** *vt* **(a)** (*express disapproval of*) (*person, behaviour etc*) critiquer; **to c. sb for sth** critiquer qn pour qch; **to c. sb for doing sth** critiquer qn d'avoir fait qch; **they have been criticized for not trying** on leur a reproché de ne pas avoir essayé; **his report has been criticized for being too …** on a reproché à son rapport d'être trop …; **to c. sth severely** se répandre en critiques sur qch **(b)** (*film, book etc*) critiquer, faire la critique de **2** *vi* critiquer; **stop criticizing** arrête de critiquer *ou* de faire des critiques

critique [krɪ'ti:k] *n* critique *f*; (*of book etc*) article *m* critique

critter ['krɪtər] *n US Dial* = **creature**

CRN [si:ɑ:r'en] *n Com* (*abbr* **customs registered number**) numéro *m* d'enregistrement douanier

croak¹ [krəʊk] *n* (*of frog*) coassement *m*; (*of raven*) croassement *m*; **…, he said in a c.** …, dit-il d'une voix rauque

croak² **1** *vi* **(a)** (*of frog*) coasser; (*of raven*) croasser; (*of person*) parler d'une voix rauque **(b)** *Sl* (*die*) crever, claquer **2** *vt* (*words, warning etc*) proférer d'une voix rauque; **I'm not well, she croaked** ça ne va pas, dit-elle d'une voix rauque

croaking ['krəʊkɪŋ] *n* (*of frog*) coassement *m*; (*of raven*) croassement *m*

croaky ['krəʊkɪ] *adj* (*voice*) rauque, enroué

Croat ['krəʊæt] **1** *adj* croate **2** *n* **(a)** Croate *mf* **(b)** *Ling* croate *m*

Croatia [krəʊ'eɪʃə] *n* Croatie *f*

Croatian [krəʊ'eɪʃən] **1** *adj* croate **2** *n* **(a)** Croate *mf* **(b)** *Ling* croate *m*

crochet¹ ['krəʊʃeɪ, -ʃɪ] *n* (travail *m* au) crochet *m*; **c. hook** crochet; **c. work** ouvrage *m ou* travail au crochet

crochet² **(crocheted** ['krəʊʃeɪd, -ʃɪd]**)** **1** *vt* (*shawl, tablecloth etc*) faire au crochet; **crocheted sweater** pull au crochet **2** *vi* faire du crochet

crocheting ['krəʊʃeɪɪŋ, -ʃɪ-] *n* (travail *m* au) crochet *m*

crock¹ [krɒk] *n* **(a)** (*pot*) pot *m* de terre; (*jug*) cruche *f*; *Vulg* **it's a c. of shit** (*nonsense*) c'est un tas de conneries **(b)** (*in gardening*) tesson *m* (*pour couvrir le trou d'un pot de fleurs*)

crock² *n F* **old c.** (*person*) vieux bonhomme *m* fini, croulant *m*; (*car*) vieux clou *m*, vieille bagnole *f*

crockery ['krɒkərɪ] *n* (*no pl*) (*tableware*) vaisselle *f* de table *ou* de cuisine

crocodile ['krɒkədaɪl] *n* **(a)** (*animal*) crocodile *m*; *El* **c. clip** pince *f* crocodile; **c. tears** larmes *fpl* de crocodile **(b)** **c. (skin)** peau *f* de crocodile, *F* croco *m*; **c. handbag** sac *m* à main en crocodile *ou F* en croco **(c)** *Br F* (*line of pupils*) élèves marchant en colonne deux par deux

crocus, *pl* **-uses** ['krəʊkəs, -əsɪz] *n* crocus *m*

croft [krɒft] *n esp Scot* petite ferme *f*

crofter ['krɒftər] *n esp Scot* petit fermier *m*

Crohn's disease [krəʊnz] *n Med* maladie *f* de Crohn

crone [krəʊn] *n Pej* **old c.** vieille bique *f*

crony ['krəʊnɪ] *n* copain *m*, copine *f*

cronyism ['krəʊnɪɪzəm] *n Pej* copinage *m*

crook¹ [krʊk] *n* **(a)** *F* (*criminal, rogue*) escroc *m* **(b)** (*of shepherd*) houlette *f*; (*of bishop*) crosse *f* **(c)** (*curve*) **in the c. of her arm** dans le creux de son bras

crook² *vt* courber, recourber; (*arm*) plier; **to c. one's finger** recourber son doigt

crook³ *adj Austr F* **(a)** (*ill*) malade; (*furious*) furieux; **to go c.** piquer une rage (**at sb** contre qn); **to feel a bit c.** ne pas se sentir dans son assiette **(b)** (*broken down*) (*machinery etc*) en panne **(c)** (*poor*) (*thing, place etc*) moche

crooked ['krʊkɪd] *adj* **(a)** *F* (*lawyer, salesman etc*) véreux; **c. means** moyens *mpl* douteux **(b)** (*not straight*) courbe; (*limb, tree*) déjeté; (*nose*) crochu; (*leg*) tors; **the painting was c.** le tableau était de travers; **his hat was on c.** son chapeau était de travers; **a c. smile** un sourire forcé **(c)** [krʊkt] (*with a hooked end*) **c. stick** bâton *m* recourbé

crookedly ['krʊkɪdlɪ] *adv* **(a)** *F* (*to deal*) malhonnêtement **(b)** (*to hang*) de travers

crookedness ['krʊkɪdnɪs] *n* **(a)** *F* (*dishonesty*) malhonnêteté *f* **(b)** (*of outlines etc*) irrégularité *f*; (*of smile*) fausseté *f*

croon [kru:n] **1** *vt* **(a)** (*song*) chantonner, fredonner **(b)** (*say*) dire d'une voix charmeuse **2** *vi* chantonner

crooner ['kru:nər] *n* (*singer*) chanteur, -euse de charme, crooner *m*

crop¹ [krɒp] *n* **(a)** *Agr* (*of cereals*) récolte *f*, moisson *f*; (*of fruit, potatoes etc*) récolte; **a poor/good c.** une mauvaise/bonne récolte; **to harvest the crops** faire la récolte *ou* la moisson; *Fig* **a fine c. of hair** une belle chevelure; **this year's c. of films** les films de cette année **(b)** (*haircut*) coupe *f* (de cheveux); **to give sb a close c.** couper ras les cheveux de qn **(c)** (*handle of whip*) manche *m*; **(riding) c.** cravache *f*; **hunting c.** stick *m* de chasse **(d)** (*of bird etc*) jabot *m*

crop² **(-pp-)** **1** *vt* **(a)** (*cut*) (*animal's ears, tail*) écourter, couper; (*hair*) couper ras; *Comptr* (*graphic*) rogner; (*photograph*) couper **(b)** (*of cattle*) (*grass*) brouter **(c)** *Agr* (*potatoes etc*) cultiver; **to c. land with corn** mettre une terre en blé **2** *vi* (*of land*) donner une récolte; **to c. well** donner une bonne récolte

▶ **crop up** *vi* (*arise*) se présenter, surgir; **her name cropped up in the conversation** son nom a surgi dans la conversation; **did anything c. up while I was away?** est-ce qu'il s'est passé quelque chose pendant mon absence?; **something has cropped up** (*I'll be late etc*) j'ai un empêchement

cropper ['krɒpər] *n* **(a)** *F* **to come a c.** (*fall*) faire une chute, *F* se prendre *ou* se ramasser une pelle; *Fig* (*fail*) se planter; **to come a c. over sth** se casser les dents sur qch **(b)** *Agr* (*person*) cultivateur, -trice **(c)** (*plant*) **good/bad c.** plante *f* qui donne de bonnes/de mauvaises récoltes *ou* qui donne bien/mal

cropping ['krɒpɪŋ] *n Comptr* (*of graphics*) rognage *m*, recadrage *m*

crop rotation *n* alternance *f* des cultures

croquet ['krəʊkeɪ, -kɪ] *n Sp* croquet *m*; **to play c.** jouer au croquet; **c. mallet** maillet *m*; **c. player** joueur, -euse de croquet

croquette [krɒ'ket] *n Culin* croquette *f*; **potato c.** croquette de pomme de terre

crosier ['krəʊzɪər] *n Rel* crosse *f* (*d'évêque*)

cross¹ [krɒs] *n* **(a)** (*sign, shape*) croix *f*; *Fig* **everyone has their c. to bear** chacun a sa croix à porter; *Rel* **to make the sign of the c.** faire le signe de (la) croix; **market c.** croix de la place du marché; **St Andrew's c.** croix de Saint-André; **Military C.** Croix de Guerre; **to sign with a c.** signer d'une croix

(b) (*of animals*) croisement *m* (**between … and …** entre … et …); (*of plants*) hybride *m*; *Fig* **to be a c. between sth and sth** être un mélange de qch et de qch; **it's a c. between a car and a van** c'est un compromis entre une voiture et une camionnette

(c) *Boxing* cross *m*, coup *m* croisé

cross² **1** *vt* **(a)** (*form into the shape of a cross*) (*two sticks etc*) croiser; **to c. one's legs/arms** (se) croiser les jambes/les bras; **to c. one's eyes** loucher, faire exprès de loucher; *Fig* **to c. swords** croiser le fer (**with** avec); **let's keep our fingers crossed** croisons les doigts; **I've got my fingers crossed for you** je croise les doigts pour toi; *Rel* **to c. oneself** faire le signe de croix, se signer; *F* **c. my heart (and hope to die)** croix de bois croix de fer (si je mens, je vais en enfer); *Fig* **we must have got our wires crossed** nous avons dû mal nous comprendre; *prov* **c. my palm with silver** (*said by fortune-teller*) une petite pièce, s'il vous plaît

(b) (*go across*) (*sea, river*) traverser, passer; (*street etc*) traverser; (*frontier*) traverser, franchir; (*threshold*) franchir; (*bridge*) passer (sur), traverser; **the bridge that crosses the river** le pont qui traverse *ou* enjambe la rivière; **to c. sb's path** se trouver sur le chemin de qn; *Br Pol* **to c. the floor (of the House)** changer de parti (politique); *Naut* **to c. the line** passer l'équateur; **to c. sb's mind** (*of thought*) traverser l'esprit de qn, venir à l'esprit *ou* à l'idée de qn; **didn't it c. your mind that she might have been lying?** est-ce qu'il ne t'est pas venu à l'idée qu'elle ait pu mentir?

(c) (*oppose*) (*person, person's plans*) contrarier, contrecarrer; (*go against*) (*person*) s'opposer à; **to be crossed in love** avoir une déception amoureuse

(d) (*in writing*) (*cheque*) barrer; **to c. one's t's** mettre les barres à ses t

(e) (*in breeding etc*) croiser; *Fig* (*two styles*) mélanger, marier

2 *vi* **(a)** (*of roads, letters etc*) se croiser; (*of lines*) se croiser, s'entrecroiser

(b) (*go across*) traverser; **to c. from Dover to Calais** faire la traversée de Douvres à Calais; **look before you c.** regarde avant de traverser

cross³ *adj* **(a)** (*angry*) fâché; **he looks c.** il a l'air fâché; **to get c.** se fâcher (**with** contre, **about** de); **Mummy's very c. with you!** Maman est très fâchée!; **don't be c. with me** il ne faut pas m'en vouloir; **to be c. with oneself** s'en vouloir; **you never hear a c. word from her** avec elle, on n'entend jamais un mot plus haut que l'autre; **we've never had a c. word** nous ne nous sommes jamais disputés **(b)** (*transverse*) transversal

▶ **cross off** *vtsep* (*remove*) (*name*) rayer, barrer; **to c. a name off a list** rayer un nom d'une liste

▶ **cross out** *vtsep* (*word, phrase etc*) biffer, barrer, rayer

▶ **cross over 1** *vipo* (*street*) traverser **2** *vi* (*go across street, sea, frontier etc*) traverser; **they crossed over to Cherbourg in their yacht** ils ont fait la traversée jusqu'à Cherbourg dans leur yacht

crossbar ['krɒsbɑːr] *n* (barre *f* de) traverse *f*, entretoise *f*; (*on man's bike*) barre; *Fb, Rugby etc* barre transversale

crossbeam ['krɒsbiːm] *n Constr* sommier *m*, traverse *f*; (*on piles*) chapeau *m*; *Gym* portique *m*

cross-bencher ['krɒsbentʃər] *n Br Parl* (député *m*) non-inscrit *m*

crossbill ['krɒsbɪl] *n* (*bird*) bec-croisé *m*, *pl* becs-croisés

crossbones ['krɒsbəʊnz] *npl* **skull and c.** tête *f* de mort (*du pavillon des pirates*)

cross-border *adj* transfrontières, transfrontalier

crossbow ['krɒsbəʊ] *n* arbalète *f*

crossbred ['krɒsbred] *adj* (*animal*) croisé; (*plant*) hybride

crossbreed¹ ['krɒsbriːd] *n* croisement *m*; (*person*) métis *m*, métisse *f*

crossbreed² [krɒs'briːd] *vt* (*pt, pp* **crossbred**) croiser; (*humans*) métisser; (*plants*) hybrider

cross-Channel *adj* (*ferry*) trans-Manche

crosscheck¹ ['krɒs'tʃek] *n* vérification *f* par recoupement

crosscheck² *vt* vérifier par recoupement; **I crosschecked my list against yours** j'ai vérifié que ma liste et la vôtre sont identiques, j'ai vérifié qu'il n'y a pas de disparités entre ma liste et la vôtre

cross-compiler *n Comptr* compilateur *m* croisé

cross-country 1 *adj* (*walk*) à travers champs; (*vehicle*) tout-terrain; *Sp* **c. running** cross *m*; **c. runner** coureur, -euse de fond, crossman *m*, *pl* crossmen, crosswoman *f*, *pl* crosswomen; **c. skiing** ski *m* de fond **2** *n Sp* **(a)** (*race, racing*) cross *m* **(b)** (*skiing*) ski *m* de fond

cross-cultural *adj* interculturel

cross-currency swap *n St Exch* crédit *m* croisé

cross-current *n* (*in air, water*) contre-courant *m*, *pl* contre-courants

crosscut ['krɒskʌt] *n* coupe *f* en travers; **c. saw** scie *f* passe-partout; **c. file** lime *f* à taille croisée

cross-dressing *n* travestisme *m*

crossed [krɒst] *adj Tel* **we seem to have a c. line** il y a des interférences sur la ligne; *Fin* **c. cheque** chèque *m* barré; **the regimental badge is two c. rifles** le badge du régiment représente deux fusils croisés

cross-examination *n Jur* contre-interrogatoire *m*, *pl* contre-interrogatoires; *Fig* interrogatoire *m* serré

cross-examine *vt Jur* soumettre à un contre-interrogatoire; *Fig* soumettre à un interrogatoire serré

cross-eyed ['krɒsaɪd] *adj* qui louche; **to be c.** loucher

cross-fertilization *n* hybridation *f*, pollinisation *f* croisée; *Fig* échanges *mpl*

cross-fertilize 1 *vt Bot* hybrider; *Fig* (*ideas*) échanger **2** *vi Bot* s'hybrider; *Fig* (*of teams, people at conference etc*) échanger des idées

crossfire ['krɒsfaɪər] *n Mil* feu *m* croisé; **to be caught in the c.** *Mil* être pris dans le feu croisé; *Fig* (*in argument*) être pris entre deux feux

cross-flow radiator *n Aut* radiateur *m* à flux transversal

cross-grained ['krɒsgreɪnd] *adj* **(a)** (*wood*) aux fibres irrégulières, à fibres torses **(b)** *Fig* (*person*) difficile, acariâtre

crosshair pointer ['krɒsheər] *n Comptr* pointeur-croix *m*

cross hairs *npl* (*on gunsight*) mire *f*, réticule *m*

crosshatch ['krɒshætʃ] *vt* (*in drawing*) hachurer en croisillons

crosshatching ['krɒshætʃɪŋ] *n* (système *m* de) hachures *fpl* croisées *ou* en croisillons

cross-headed ['krɒs'hedɪd] *adj Tech* (*screw, screwdriver*) cruciforme

cross hedge *n St Exch* couverture *f* croisée

cross-holding *n Fin* participation *f* croisée

cross-impact analysis *n Mktg* analyse *f* d'interférence

crossing ['krɒsɪŋ] *n* **(a)** (*of sea*) traversée *f*; (*of river, the Alps*) traversée, passage *m*; *Mil* (*of river*) franchissement *m*; **we had a fine** *or* **good c.** nous avons eu *ou* fait une belle traversée; **a sea c.** une traversée maritime **(b)** (*in street*) passage *m* pour piétons, passage clouté **(c)** (*of roads*) croisement *m*, intersection *f*, carrefour *m*; *Rail* **level** *or Am* **grade c.** passage *m* à niveau

cross-legged [krɒs'leg(ɪ)d] **1** *adj* **in a c. position** les jambes croisées **2** *adv* les jambes croisées; **to sit c.** être assis en tailleur

crossly ['krɒslɪ] *adv* (*with annoyance*) avec mauvaise humeur; (*angrily*) d'un air/d'un ton fâché

cross-member *n Aut* traverse *f*

crossover ['krɒsəʊvər] **1** *n* **(a)** croisement *m*; *Rail* voie *f* de croisement **(b)** *Mus* = chanteur, -euse qui est passé(e) d'un style de musique à un autre **2** *adj Mus* (*music*) qui associe deux styles; (*singer*) = qui est passé d'un style de musique à un autre

crosspatch ['krɒspætʃ] *n F* ronchon, -onne

crosspiece ['krɒspiːs] *n* (barre *f* de) traverse *f*

cross-ply tyre *n Aut* pneu *m* à structure diagonale

cross-pricing *n* fixation *f* de prix croisés

cross-purposes ['krɒs'pɜːpəsɪz] *n* **to be (talking) at c.** ne pas parler de la même chose

cross-question *vt* = **cross-examine**

cross-refer *vt* (**-rr-**) renvoyer; **the reader is cross-referred to page 332** il y a un renvoi à la page 332

cross-reference¹ *n* renvoi *m*; *Comptr* **c. table** table *f* de références

cross-reference² *vt* (*book*) établir les renvois de; **to c. X to Y** renvoyer de X à Y; **it's cross-referenced** (*to another article*) il y a un renvoi à un autre article

crossroad ['krɒsrəʊd] *n Am* (*across a road*) route *f* qui en coupe une autre; (*between main roads*) route secondaire, route départementale

crossroads ['krɒsrəʊdz] *n* (*with sing verb*) carrefour *m*, croisement *m*; *Fig* **the city is at the c. of Europe** la ville est au carrefour de l'Europe; *Fig* **we are now at the c.** (*decisive moment*) c'est l'heure des décisions irrévocables

cross section *n* coupe *f ou* section *f* transversale; **in c.** en coupe transversale; *Fig* **a c. of life** une tranche de vie; *Fig* **a c. of the population** un groupe représentatif de la population

cross-stitch *n Sewing* point *m* de croix

cross street *n Am* rue *f* transversale

crosstalk ['krɒstɔːk] *n* **(a)** *Br* série *f* de répliques du tac au tac **(b)** *Telecom* diaphonie *f*

cross-town *adj Am* (*bus, trolley*) qui traverse la ville

crosswalk ['krɒswɔːk] *n Am* passage *m* clouté, passage pour piétons

crossway ['krɒsweɪ] *n Am* = **crossroad**

crosswind ['krɒswɪnd] *n* vent *m* de travers

crosswise ['krɒswaɪz] *adv* (*at right angles*) à angle droit; (*diagonally*) en travers

crossword ['krɒswɜːd] *n* **c. (puzzle)** mots *mpl* croisés

crotch [krɒtʃ] *n* (*of person*) entrejambe *m*; (*of trousers*) entrejambe, *Spec* fourche *f*

crotchet ['krɒtʃɪt] *n Mus* noire *f*

crotchety ['krɒtʃətɪ] *adj* (*person*) grognon; (*mood*) difficile, acariâtre

croton ['krəʊt(ə)n] *n* (*plant*) croton *m*

crouch¹ [kraʊtʃ] *n* accroupissement *m*

crouch² *vi* (*of animal*) se tapir; (*of person*) s'accroupir; **the tiger was crouching for a spring** le tigre, tapi, était sur le point de sauter

▶ **crouch down** *vi* = **crouch²**

croup¹ [kruːp] *n* (*of horse*) croupe *f*

croup² *n Med* croup *m*; **to have c.** avoir le croup

croupier ['kruːpɪər] *n* croupier *m*

crow¹ [krəʊ] *n* (*bird*) corneille *f*; *Am Fig* **to eat c.** s'humilier (*en reconnaissant qu'on s'est trompé*); **c.'s nest** nid *m* de corneille; *Naut* nid *m* de pie; **as the c. flies** à vol d'oiseau

crow² *n* (*of cock*) chant *m* du coq, *F* cocorico *m*; *Fig* **he let out a c. of triumph** il a crié victoire, *F* il a poussé un cocorico, il a fait cocorico

crow³ *vi* **(a)** (*of cock*) chanter; *Fig* chanter victoire, *F* faire cocorico (**about** à propos de) **(b)** (*of baby*) gazouiller

crowbar ['krəʊbɑːr] *n* pince *f* (à levier)

crowd¹ [kraʊd] *n* [①A11,g,i] **(a)** (*large number of people*) foule *f*; (*in building*) foule, affluence *f*; **to come in a c.** *or* **in crowds** venir en foule; **to draw a c.** attirer la foule; **that's what happens when you get a c. of boys together** c'est ce qui se produit quand tout un groupe de garçons se trouve rassemblé; **there wasn't much of a c. at the game** il n'y avait pas grand monde au match; **there was quite a c. in the square** il y avait pas mal de monde dans le square; *Fig* **the c.** la foule; **to stand out from the c.** se distinguer (de la foule); *Fig* **to follow the c.** suivre le mouvement; *Th, Cin* **the c.** les figurants *mpl*; *Th, Cin* **to be a c. puller** attirer les foules; **c. scene** scène *f* de masses

(b) *F* (*group*) bande *f*, clique *f*; **they're a good c.** ce sont de braves types; **they stick to their own c.** ils font bande à part

crowd² **1** *vt* **(a)** (*force in, on*) (*people, objects*) entasser; (*fill*) remplir, bourrer **(with** de); **they crowded 10,000 people into the square** ils ont entassé 10 000 personnes sur la place; **too many books had been crowded onto the shelf** on avait entassé trop de livres sur l'étagère; **crowded together** pressés *ou* serrés l'un contre l'autre; **we are too crowded here** on est trop serrés ici; **the tourists crowding the streets** les touristes qui se pressaient dans les rues; **the hall was crowded with people** la salle était bondée

(b) (*come too close to*) *Sp* (*competitor*) tasser; (*another car*) serrer; *US* (*debtor*) importuner; **don't c. me!** (*don't pressure me*) ne me pousse pas!; **to be crowded off the pavement** être forcé de quitter le trottoir

2 *vi* **to c. (together)** se serrer; **they all crowded into the room** ils se sont tous entassés dans la pièce; **to c. round sb** se presser autour de qn; **they all crowded round** ils se sont tous amassés

▶ **crowd in on** *vipo* assaillir; **memories c. in on me here** ici, des souvenirs m'assaillent en foule

▶ **crowd out** *vtsep* (*force out*) (*person, object*) ne pas laisser de place à; **to c. sb out of a deal/a market** exclure qn d'une affaire/d'un marché

crowded ['kraʊdɪd] *adj* (*train, cinema, restaurant etc*) bondé; (*street*) (*with people*) bondé; (*with cars*) encombré; (*day*) chargé; **they lived in a room c. with furniture** ils vivaient dans une pièce encombrée de meubles; **it's a bit c. in here** il y a un peu trop de monde ici; **the c. events of that day** les nombreux événements de cette journée

crowfoot ['krəʊfʊt] *n* (*pl usu* **crowfoots**) (*plant*) renoncule *f* (âcre)

crowing ['krəʊɪŋ] *n* (*of cock*) chant *m*; *Fig* fanfaronnades *fpl*

crown¹ [kraʊn] *n* **(a)** (*of monarch, martyr, made of flowers etc*) couronne *f*; **c. of thorns** couronne d'épines; **to wear the c.** porter la couronne

(b) *Pol* **the C.** *or* **c.** la Couronne (*symbole de l'État monarchique*)

(c) (*of tooth, natural artificial*) couronne *f*

(d) (*coin*) couronne *f*

(e) (*highest part*) (*of vault*) clef *f*; (*of bridge, road*) bombement *m*; (*of hill*) crête *f*; (*of roof*) faîte *m*; **the c. (of the head)** le sommet de la tête; **c. wheel** *or* **gear** *MecE* roue *f* dentée sur une surface latérale; *Aut* couronne *f* (de pont); *Br Com* **c. cap** capsule *f* (métallique) de bouteille

(f) (*of hat*) fond *m*

crown² *vt* **(a)** (*person, person's head*) couronner **(with** de); **to c. sb king** couronner qn roi; **they crowned her head with a garland of flowers** ils lui ont couronné la tête d'une guirlande de fleurs; **the crowned heads of Europe** les têtes *fpl* couronnées d'Europe; *Br F* **I'll c. you!** (*hit you*) je vais te flanquer un de ces coups sur la tête!

(b) *Fig* (*person's happiness*) combler, couronner; (*person's efforts*) récompenser; *Br F* **to c. it all** pour comble de malheur

(c) (*be at summit of*) couronner; **the woods that c. the hill** les bois qui couronnent la colline

(d) (*in dentistry*) (*tooth*) couronner

(e) (*at draughts*) **to be crowned** aller à dame

crown colony *n* colonie *f* de la Couronne

Crown corporation *n Can* société *f* d'État

crown court *n* = tribunal *m* de grande instance

crown estates *npl* terres *fpl* domaniales *ou* appartenant à la Couronne

crowning ['kraʊnɪŋ] **1** *adj* (*ambition, achievement*) suprême; **c. glory** (*of career*) couronnement *m*; (*hair*) chevelure *f*; **the red hair that was her c. glory** la belle crinière rousse qui faisait l'admiration de tout le monde; **the c. moment** l'apothéose *f* **2** *n* (*of monarch etc*) couronnement *m*

crown jewels *npl* joyaux *mpl* de la Couronne

crown lands *npl* terres *fpl* domaniales *ou* appartenant à la Couronne

crown prince *n* prince *m* héritier

Crown rating system *n* (*for hotels*) système *m* de classement (des hôtels britanniques)

crown witness *n Jur* témoin *m* à charge

crow's(-)foot, *pl* **-feet** ['krəʊzfʊt, -fiːt] *n* patte *f* d'oie

crozier ['krəʊzɪər] *n Rel* (*of bishop*) crosse *f*

CRT [siːɑː'tiː] *n* **(a)** (*abbr* **cathode ray tube**) tube *m* cathodique **(b)** *Comptr* (*abbr* **carriage return**) retour *m* chariot

crucial ['kruːʃ(ə)l] *adj* **(a)** (*point etc*) crucial, -aux, décisif, critique; **the c. test** l'épreuve *f* décisive; **to be c. to sth** être crucial pour qch **(b)** *Sl* (*excellent*) d'enfer, supergénial

crucible ['kruːsɪb(ə)l] *n Metal, Ch, Ind, Fig* creuset *m*; *Fig* **their friendship was forged in the c. of war** leur amitié fut forgée pendant les temps difficiles de la guerre

crucifix ['kruːsɪfɪks] *n* crucifix *m*, christ *m*; (*at roadside*) calvaire *m*

crucifixion [kruːsɪ'fɪkʃən] *n* crucifixion *f*, crucifiement *m*

cruciform ['kruːsɪfɔːm] *adj* cruciforme

crucify ['kruːsɪfaɪ] *vt* **(a)** (*person*) crucifier; **Christ Crucified** le Crucifié **(b)** *Sl* (*person*) (*defeat*) flanquer *ou* mettre la pâtée à; (*criticize*) descendre en flammes; **we were crucified** (*in match*) ils nous ont mis la pâtée

crud [krʌd] *n Sl* (*dirt*) saletés *fpl*; (*nonsense*) bêtises *fpl*

cruddy ['krʌdɪ] *adj Sl* (*very bad*) merdique

crude [kruːd] **1** *adj* **(a)** (*unsophisticated, unrefined*) (*method, idea, style etc*) grossier; (*tool etc*) grossier, primitif; **a c. statement of the facts** un exposé brutal des faits **(b)** (*vulgar*) (*language, joke*) grossier, cru; (*manners*) grossier **2** *n Petr* pétrole *m* brut

crudely ['kruːdlɪ] *adv* **(a)** (*in an unrefined, unsophisticated manner*) d'une manière grossière, grossièrement; **a c. constructed canoe** un canoë construit sommairement; **to put it c.** (*bluntly*) pour être tout à fait franc **(b)** (*vulgarly*) crûment, grossièrement

crudeness ['kruːdnɪs], **crudity** ['kruːdɪtɪ] *n* **(a)** (*lack of refinement*) (*of style*) nature *f* grossière; (*of tool etc*) caractère *m* grossier *ou* primitif **(b)** (*vulgarity*) (*of expression etc*) crudité *f*; (*of manners etc*) grossièreté *f*

crude oil *n* pétrole *m* brut

cruel ['krʊəl] *adj* (*person, joke, treatment, winter*) cruel; **to be c. to sb** être cruel envers qn; **a c. blow** un coup dur; *Prov* **you have to be c. to be kind** qui aime bien châtie bien

cruelly ['krʊəlɪ] *adv* cruellement

cruelty ['krʊəltɪ] *n* cruauté *f* **(to** envers); *Jur* sévices *mpl* **(to sb** envers qn); **an act of c.** une cruauté

cruet ['krʊɪt] *n Culin* **c. (stand)** service *m* à condiments

Cruft's [krʌfts] *n* = très importante exposition *f* canine qui se tient à Londres

cruise¹ [kruːz] *n* **(a)** *Naut* croisière *f*; **(pleasure) c.** croisière; **to go on a c.** partir en croisière **(b)** *Mil* **c.(-type) missile** missile *m* de croisière

cruise² **1** *vi* **(a)** *Naut* (*of yacht, liner*) croiser, être en croisière; (*of passenger*) être en croisière

(b) (*of taxi, car*) marauder, être en maraude; **he was cruising up and down the high street** il montait et redescendait la rue principale; **we went cruising around the streets in search of …** nous avons roulé dans les rues à la recherche de …; *F* **you're cruising for a bruising** tu vas droit vers les ennuis

(c) *Av, Aut etc* (*maintain constant speed*) aller à une vitesse de croisière; **we were cruising at 60** nous allions à une vitesse de croisière de 60

(d) *Sl* (*look for sexual partner*) draguer

2 *vt* **(a)** (*of ship*) croiser dans; (*of ship's passenger*) être en croisière dans

(b) *Sl* **he was out cruising the streets** il se baladait en voiture

(c) *Sl* **to c. the bars** draguer dans les bars

cruise control *n Aut* commande *f* de vitesse de croisière

cruiser ['kruːzər] *n* **(a)** *Naut* **(battle) c.** croiseur *m*; **(cabin) c.** yacht *m* de croisière (*à moteur*) **(b)** = **cruiserweight**

cruiserweight ['kruːzəweɪt] *n Br Boxing* poids *m* mi-lourd

cruise ship *n* bateau *m* de croisière

cruising ['kruːzɪŋ] *n* **(a)** *Naut* croisière(s) *f(pl)*; **c. holiday** croisière **(b)** *Av* **c. range** autonomie *f* à vitesse de croisière; **c. speed/altitude** vitesse *f*/altitude *f* de croisière

crumb¹ [krʌm] *n* **(a)** (*small piece*) (*of bread*) miette *f*; (*opposed to crust*) mie *f* (de pain); *Fig* **they make the profit and we get the crumbs from their table** ils réalisent les bénéfices et nous récupérons les miettes; **c. of comfort** brin *m* de consolation; **crumbs of news** fragments *mpl* d'information **(b)** *F* (*contemptible person*) minable *mf*

crumb² *vt Culin* (*cutlet, fish*) paner, couvrir de chapelure

crumble¹ ['krʌmb(ə)l] **1** *vi* (*of stone, earth etc*) s'effriter; (*of bread, pastry*) s'émietter; *Fig* (*of empire, opposition, resistance, prices*) s'effondrer; **everything is crumbling to dust** tout tombe en poussière; **her world was crumbling (to pieces) around her** tout son univers s'effondrait autour d'elle **2** *vt* (*bread*) émietter; (*stone*) désagréger

crumble² *n Br Culin* **apple/rhubarb c.** = dessert *m* aux pommes/à la rhubarbe recouvert de pâte sablée

crumbling ['krʌmblɪŋ] **1** *adj* (*stone, earth*) qui s'effrite; (*wall etc*) qui s'écroule, croulant; *Fig* (*empire, opposition, resistance*) qui s'effondre **2** *n* (*of stone, earth*) effritement *m*; *Fig* (*of empire, opposition, resistance, prices etc*) effondrement *m*

crumbly ['krʌmblɪ] *adj* (*cake, bread*) friable, qui s'émiette (trop); (*cheese*) qui s'émiette; (*stone, brick*) friable, qui se désagrège

crumbs [krʌmz] *int Br F* ça alors!, zut!

crummy ['krʌmɪ] *adj F* (*film, job, idea etc*) minable; **what a c. joint!** quel endroit minable!; **to feel c.** (*ill*) ne pas se sentir dans son assiette; (*unhappy, upset*) ne pas se sentir fier (**about doing** d'avoir fait)

crump [krʌmp] *n* (*of shells*) détonation *f* assourdie

crumpet ['krʌmpɪt] *n* (**a**) *Culin* = petite galette *f* ronde et spongieuse (*que l'on sert avec du beurre, de la confiture etc*) (**b**) (*no pl*) *Br Sl* (*women*) nanas *fpl*; **a nice bit of c.** une belle nana; *Hum* (*man*) un beau gars *ou* garçon *ou* type; *Hum* **he's the thinking woman's bit of c.** il est le chéri des femmes intelligentes

crumple ['krʌmp(ə)l] **1** *vt* (*material, dress etc*) froisser, friper, chiffonner; **to c. paper** chiffonner *ou* froisser du papier; (*make into a ball*) faire une boule avec du papier; **to get crumpled** se froisser *ou* friper **2** *vi* (*of fabric*) se friper, se froisser, se chiffonner; (*of leaves, parchment*) se ratatiner; (*of mudguard, car*) se plier; (*of face*) se décomposer; *Fig* (*of opposition*) s'effondrer; **he crumpled as the bullet hit him** il s'est écroulé au moment où la balle l'a atteint; *Aut* **c. zone** zone *f* de déformation

▶ **crumple up 1** *vtsep* (*screw up into a ball*) (*paper*) faire une boule avec **2** *vi* (*of person*) s'écrouler; (*of car*) se plier

crumpled ['krʌmp(ə)ld] *adj* (*paper*) froissé, chiffonné; (*skirt etc*) froissé, fripé, chiffonné; (*car*) à la tôle froissée; (*car wing*) froissé

crunch[1] [krʌntʃ] *n* (**a**) (*sound*) craquement *m*; (*of snow, gravel etc*) crissement *m* (**b**) *Fig* (*critical moment*) **when it comes to the c.** au moment critique *ou* crucial; **when it came to the c. he let them down** il les a laissés tomber au moment critique *ou* crucial; **if it comes to the c. we can sell the car** au pire nous pourrons vendre la voiture

crunch[2] **1** *vt* (*with teeth*) croquer; *Comptr* (*numbers, data*) traiter à grande vitesse **2** *vi* craquer, crisser; **the hard snow crunched underfoot** la neige durcie crissait sous les pieds; **they crunched through the snow** ils avançaient dans la neige qui crissait sous leurs pas; **he was crunching on an apple** il croquait dans une pomme

▶ **crunch up** *vtsep* (*crush*) broyer; **the car had been crunched up** la voiture avait été broyée

crunching ['krʌntʃɪŋ] *n* = **crunch[1] (a)**

crunchy ['krʌntʃɪ] *adj* (*food*) croquant, croustillant; (*snow*) qui craque (sous les pas)

crupper ['krʌpər] *n* (**a**) (*part of harness*) croupière *f*, culière *f* (**b**) *Anat* (*of horse*) croupe *f*

crusade[1] [kruː'seɪd] *n Hist, Fig* croisade *f*; **to go on a c.** partir en croisade; **a one-man c. against drug-dealing** une croisade contre la drogue menée par un seul homme; **to start a c.** lancer une croisade (**against** contre)

crusade[2] *vi* (**a**) *Hist* partir en croisade (**b**) *Fig* mener une campagne (**against** contre, **for** pour); **she spent her life crusading against injustice/for women's rights** elle a passé sa vie à se battre contre l'injustice/pour les droits de la femme

crusader [kruː'seɪdər] *n* (**a**) *Hist* croisé *m*; **c. castle** château *m* de croisé (**b**) *Fig* champion, -ionne (**for sth** de qch); **a c. against injustice** un champion de la lutte contre l'injustice

crush[1] [krʌʃ] *n* (**a**) (*crowd*) foule *f*; **there was a terrible c.** il y a eu une terrible bousculade; **two people were injured in the c.** deux personnes ont été blessées dans la bousculade; *Th* **c. bar** bar *m* des spectateurs; **c. barrier** barrière *f* de sécurité (**b**) *Br* (*drink*) **orange c.** orangeade *f*; **lemon c.** citronnade *f* (**c**) *F* (*infatuation*) béguin *m*; **to have a c. on sb** avoir le *ou* un béguin pour qn, en pincer pour qn

crush[2] **1** *vt* (**a**) (*person, object*) écraser; (*grapes etc*) exprimer le jus de; (*of boa constrictor*) (*victim*) comprimer; (*dress*) froisser; (*ice*) piler; *Min etc* (*ore*) broyer, concasser; **crushed together** (*people*) entassés, serrés; **we were nearly crushed to death** on a failli être écrasés; **he crushed the clothes into the suitcase** il a tassé les vêtements dans la valise

(**b**) (*destroy*) (*enemy*) écraser; (*revolt*) étouffer, écraser; **to c. sb's hopes** réduire les espoirs de qn à néant; **this remark crushed her** (*humiliated her*) cette remarque l'a profondément humilié

2 *vi* (*in order to get into a place*) se presser en foule, se bousculer

crushing ['krʌʃɪŋ] **1** *adj* (*news, defeat etc*) écrasant; (*reply, remark etc*) cinglant, humiliant; **to be dealt a c. blow** (*of army, hopes etc*) en prendre un sacré coup; **to treat sb with c. contempt** écraser qn de son mépris **2** *n* (*of grapes*) pressage *m*; (*of ore*) broyage *m*, concassage *m*; (*of rebellion, uprising*) écrasement *m*; (*of hopes*) anéantissement *m*

crust [krʌst] *n* (**a**) (*of bread, pie*) croûte *f*; **there was not a c. to eat in the house** il ne restait absolument rien à manger dans la maison; *F* **we manage to earn a c.** nous arrivons à gagner notre croûte (**b**) (*of the earth, of ice etc*) croûte *f* (**c**) (*of wine*) dépôt *m* (**d**) (*on wound*) croûte *f*

▶ **crust over** *vi* (*become covered with a crust*) se couvrir d'une croûte; (*of wound etc*) former une croûte

crustacean [krʌs'teɪʃən] **1** *adj* crustacéen **2** *n* crustacé *m*

crusted ['krʌstɪd] *adj* **to be c. with ice** être couvert d'une croûte de glace

crusty ['krʌstɪ] *adj* (**a**) *Culin* (*bread, roll*) croustillant (**b**) (*person*) bourru

crutch [krʌtʃ] *n* (**a**) (*support*) béquille *f*; *Fig* soutien *m*; *Fig* **a c. to lean on** un soutien; **to go about** *or* **walk on crutches** marcher avec des béquilles (**b**) = **crotch**

crux, *pl* **cruxes** [krʌks, 'krʌksɪz] *n* (*of discussion etc*) cœur *m*; **the c. of the matter** le nœud de la question

cry[1] [kraɪ] *n* (**a**) (*call*) (*of person, animal*) cri *m*; **to give** *or* **utter a c.** pousser un cri; **a c. of pain** un cri de douleur; *also Fig* **a c. for help** un appel au secours; **there were cries of 'down with the king!'** on criait 'à bas le roi!'; **their c. was 'one man, one vote'** leur slogan était 'un homme, une voix'; **to be in full c.** (*of hounds etc*), *Fig* être lancé dans une poursuite acharnée (**after** de); **it's a far c. from what they promised us** cela n'a rien à voir avec ce qu'ils nous avaient promis; **it's still a far c. from what I asked for** cela reste loin de ce que j'avais demandé

(**b**) (*weeping*) **to have a c.** pleurer; **to have a good c.** pleurer un bon coup

cry[2] (*pt, pp* **cried** [kraɪd]) **1** *vi* (**a**) (*weep*) pleurer; **big girls don't c.** les grandes filles ne pleurent pas, on ne pleure pas quand on est une grande fille; **to c. over sth** pleurer *ou* verser des larmes sur qch; **to c. for joy** pleurer de joie; **I laughed until I cried** j'ai ri aux larmes

(**b**) (*shout, call*) crier, pousser un cri/des cris; **to c. aloud** pousser de grands cris; **to c. for help** crier au secours, appeler à l'aide; **to c. for mercy** demander grâce

2 *vt* (**a**) (*exclaim*) (*name etc*) crier; **that's not true!, he cried** ce n'est pas vrai!, s'écria-t-il; *Old-fashioned* **to c. one's wares** vendre sa marchandise à la criée

(**b**) **to c. one's eyes** *or* **one's heart out** pleurer à chaudes larmes; **she cried herself to sleep** elle s'est endormie en pleurant

▶ **cry down** *vtsep* (*person, thing*) décrier, dénigrer

▶ **cry off** *vi* (*cancel acceptance of invitation*) se décommander

▶ **cry out 1** *vi* (*shout*) pousser des cris; *F* **for crying out loud!** nom de nom!, mais bon sang! **2** *vtsep* (*name etc*) crier; **stop!, she cried out** arrêtez!, s'écria-t-elle

▶ **cry out for** *vipo* (**a**) (*shout out for*) réclamer à grands cris (**b**) *Fig* (*need desperately*) avoir désespérément besoin de; **that wall is crying out for a coat of paint** ce mur a besoin d'un bon coup de peinture

▶ **cry up** *vipo* (**a**) (*publicize, praise*) (*book, film*) vanter (**b**) (*exaggerate*) **to c. up one's opponent's chances** exagérer la force de son adversaire

crybaby ['kraɪbeɪbɪ] *n F* pleurnicheur, -euse

crying ['kraɪɪŋ] **1** *adj* (*need etc*) urgent; **it's a c. shame that ...** il est scandaleux que ... + *sub* **2** *n* (**a**) (*weeping*) pleurs *mpl* (**b**) (*shouting, calling*) cris *mpl*

cryogenics [kraɪə'dʒenɪks] *n* (*with sing verb*) cryogénie *f*

cryonics [kraɪ'ɒnɪks] *n* (*with sing verb*) cryoconservation *f*

cryosurgery [kraɪəʊ'sɜːdʒərɪ] *n* cryochirurgie *f*

crypt [krɪpt] *n* (*in church*) crypte *f*

cryptic ['krɪptɪk] *adj* (*message, silence, smile, look*) mystérieux, énigmatique; (*remark*) sibyllin; **he was very c. about his future plans** il a été très mystérieux sur ses projets d'avenir; **c. crossword** = mots *mpl* croisés dont les définitions sont pour ainsi dire codées

cryptically ['krɪptɪklɪ] *adv* mystérieusement; (*to speak*) à mots couverts; **the book ends c.** le livre se termine de façon énigmatique *ou* sur une énigme

crypto- ['krɪptəʊ] *pref* crypto-; **c.-communist** cryptocommuniste

cryptogram ['krɪptəgræm] *n* cryptogramme *m*

cryptographer [krɪp'tɒgrəfər] *n* cryptographe *mf*

crystal ['krɪst(ə)l] **1** *n* (**a**) *Ch, Miner* cristal *m*; **salt crystals** cristaux de sel; **in c. form** sous forme cristalline (**b**) **c. (glass)** cristal *m*; **as clear as c.** clair comme le jour *ou* comme de l'eau de roche; **c. factory** cristallerie *f* (**c**) (*on watch*) verre *m* de montre (**d**) *Electron etc* cristal *m*; *Rad* **c. set** récepteur *m* à cristal *ou* à galène **2** *adj* (*clear*) limpide, cristallin

crystal ball *n* boule *f* de cristal

crystal-clear *adj* limpide, cristallin; *Fig* (*argument*) clair comme le jour *ou* de l'eau de roche; **it's all c. to me now** ça me paraît clair comme de l'eau de roche maintenant; **to make sth c.** rendre qch bien clair

crystal gazing ['geɪzɪŋ] *n* divination *f* par la boule de cristal

crystalline ['krɪstəlaɪn] *adj* cristallin; *Anat* **c. lens** (*of the eye*) cristallin *m*

crystallization [krɪstəlaɪ'zeɪʃən] *n* cristallisation *f*

crystallize ['krɪstəlaɪz] *Ch, Fig* **1** *vt* cristalliser; **crystallized fruits** fruits *mpl* confits **2** *vi* se cristalliser

crystallography [krɪstə'lɒgrəfɪ] *n* cristallographie *f*

CS ['si:'es] *n* **CS gas** gaz *m* lacrymogène

CSE [si:es'i:] *n Br Sch formerly* (*abbr* **Certificate of Secondary Education**) = diplôme *m* sanctionnant la fin des études du premier cycle dans l'enseignement secondaire

CST [si:es'ti:] *n Am* (*abbr* **Central Standard Time**) heure *f* normale du Centre

CSV [si:es'vi:] *npl abbr Comptr* (**comma-separated values**) valeurs *fpl* séparées par des virgules

cub [kʌb] *n* **(a)** (*of fox*) renardeau *m*; (*of bear*) ourson *m*; (*of lion*) lionceau *m*; (*of wolf*) louveteau *m*; *Fig* **that impertinent young c.!** cette espèce de blanc-bec!; *Journ* **c. reporter** journaliste *mf* en herbe **(b) C.** (**scout**) louveteau *m*; **he goes to Cubs on Fridays** il va à la réunion des louveteaux le vendredi

Cuba ['kju:bə] *n* Cuba *m*; **in C.** à Cuba

Cuban ['kju:bən] **1** *adj* cubain; **C. heel** (*on shoe*) talon *m* en biseau, *Can* talon cubain **2** *n* Cubain, -aine

cubbyhole ['kʌbɪhəʊl] *n* (*room*) cagibi *m*; (*cupboard*) placard *m*

cube¹ [kju:b] *n* **(a)** *Math, Geom* cube *m*; **27 is the c. of three** 27 est le cube de trois; **c. root** racine *f* cubique **(b)** (*piece*) (*of bread, meat etc*) dé *m*; (*of sugar*) morceau *m*; **cut the meat into cubes** coupez la viande en dés

cube² *vt* **(a)** *Math* élever au cube; **27 cubed** 27 au cube **(b)** (*meat etc*) couper en dés

cubic ['kju:bɪk] *adj* **(a)** *Math* **c. capacity** volume *m*, cube *m*; (*of engine*) cylindrée *f*; **c. metre** mètre *m* cube; **c. measurement** cubage *m*; **c. measures** mesures *fpl* de volume **(b)** (*cube-shaped*) cubique

cubicle ['kju:bɪk(ə)l] *n* (*in swimming pool*) cabine *f*; (*for trying on clothes*) cabine d'essayage; (*in dormitory*) box *m*; (*of public toilet*) WC *m*(*pl*); **his office was little more than a c.** son bureau n'était pas plus grand qu'un box

cubism ['kju:bɪz(ə)m] *n Art* cubisme *m*

cubist ['kju:bɪst] *adj, n Art* cubiste *mf*

cuckold¹ ['kʌkəld] *n esp Lit* cocu *m*

cuckold² *vt esp Lit* cocufier, faire cocu

cuckoo¹ ['kʊku:] **1** *n* (*bird*) coucou *m*; **c. clock** coucou; *Bot* **c. spit** crachat *m* de coucou **2** *adj F* (*mad*) dingue; **to go c.** devenir dingue, perdre la boule **3** *int* coucou!

cucumber ['kju:kʌmbər] *n* concombre *m*; *Fig* **to be (as) cool as a c.** (*in a crisis etc*) être d'un calme imperturbable; **..., she said, cool as a c.** ... dit-elle avec un calme imperturbable; (*without showing any remorse*) ... dit-elle comme si de rien n'était; **c. sandwich** sandwich *m* au concombre; *Zool* **sea c.** concombre de mer

cud [kʌd] *n* (*of ruminant*) bol *m* alimentaire; **to chew the c.** (*of cow etc*) ruminer; *Fig* (*of person*) ruminer une idée, méditer

cuddle¹ ['kʌd(ə)l] *n* câlin *m*; **to give sb a c.** faire un câlin à qn

cuddle² **1** *vt* (*person*) serrer dans ses bras, câliner; **to c. one another** se faire des câlins; **children need lots of cuddling** les enfants ont besoin d'être beaucoup câlinés **2** *vi* (*of two people*) se faire des câlins, se câliner; **two young people kissing and cuddling** deux jeunes gens en train de s'embrasser et de se faire des câlins

▶ **cuddle up** *vi* (*lie, sit etc closely*) se pelotonner; **they cuddled up to each other for warmth** ils se sont pelotonnés *ou* blottis l'un contre l'autre pour se tenir chaud; **c. up if you're cold** (*to me*) pelotonne-toi si tu as froid; (*to each other*) serrez-vous *ou* pelotonnez-vous l'un contre l'autre si vous avez froid; **to c. up to sb** se blottir *ou* se pelotonner contre qn

cuddly ['kʌdlɪ] *adj* (*teddybear etc*) tout doux, *f* toute douce; (*child, animal etc*) mignon à croquer; *Hum* (*plump*) dodu; **I wasn't exactly what you would call a c. child** je n'étais pas le genre d'enfant à qui on a envie de faire des câlins; **a c. toy** une peluche

cudgel¹ ['kʌdʒ(ə)l] *n* gourdin *m*, trique *f*; *Fig* **to take up the cudgels on sb's behalf** prendre fait et cause pour qn

cudgel² *vt* (**-ll-**, *US* **-l-**) (*person*) donner des coups de bâton à; *Fig F* **to c. one's brains** se creuser les méninges *ou* la cervelle

cue¹ [kju:] *n* signal *m*, top *m*; *Th* (*verbal*) réplique *f*; *Mus* (*for instrument*) indication *f* de rentrée; **to miss one's c.** *Th* manquer la réplique; *TV, Cin etc* rater le signal; *Th, Fig* **to give sb his c.** donner la réplique à qn; *Fig* **he nodded, that was my c. to make the coffee** il a hoché la tête pour me faire signe de faire le café; **I suppose that's my c. to leave?** je dois comprendre que c'est le moment que je parte?; *Fig* **to take one's c. from sb** prendre exemple sur qn; *Fig* **(right) on c.** au bon moment; *TV* **c. card** carton *m* aide-mémoire

cue² *vt* donner le signal à; *Th* (*verbally*) donner la réplique à; **c. and cut!** moteur! et coupez!

cue³ *n* (*in billiards, snooker, pool*) queue *f*; **c. ball** boule *f* blanche; **c. rack** porte-queues *m inv*

▶ **cue in** *vtsep* **(a)** donner le signal à; *Th* (*verbally*) donner la réplique à **(b)** *esp Am* (*inform*) (*person*) mettre à la page

cuff¹ [kʌf] *n* **(a)** (*of shirt*) poignet *m*; (*that takes cuff links*) manchette *f*; (*of coat sleeve*) parement *m*; **double c.** poignet mousquetaire; *F* **off the c.** (*discours etc*) impromptu; *F* **to do sth off the c.** faire qch au pied levé; *F* **I can't tell you off the c.** je ne peux pas te le dire comme ça *ou* tout de suite **(b)** *Am* (*of trousers*) revers *m* de pantalon **(c)** *F* **cuffs** = **handcuffs**

cuff² *n* (*blow*) taloche *f*, calotte *f*; **he gave me a c. on the head** il m'a mis une taloche sur la tête

cuff³ *vt* **(a)** (*hit*) (*person*) talocher, calotter **(b)** *F* (*put handcuffs on*) mettre les menottes à

cuff links *npl* boutons *mpl* de manchette

cuisine [kwɪ'zi:n] *n* cuisine *f*

cul-de-sac ['kʌldəsæk] (*pl* **culs-de-sac, cul-de-sacs**) *n* cul-de-sac *m*, *pl* culs-de-sac, impasse *f*; *Fig* impasse

culinary ['kʌlɪnərɪ] *adj* (*skill, delight, purpose*) culinaire; (*implement*) de cuisine; (*herb*) pour la cuisine; **the c. art** l'art *m* culinaire

cull¹ [kʌl] *n* **(a)** (*killing*) (*of deer, wild boar*) battue *f*; (*of seals*) abattage *m* **(b)** (*animal*) (*before killing*) bête *f* à abattre; (*after killing*) bête abattue

cull² *vt* **(a)** (*reduce by killing*) (*herd of deer, seal colony*) réduire la taille de; (*kill*) (*deer, seals*) abattre **(b)** (*choose*) choisir (**from** dans); **the poems have been culled from her early work** les poèmes ont été choisis parmi ses premières œuvres; **information culled from various sources** des renseignements pris à differentes sources

culminate ['kʌlmɪneɪt] *vi* **to c. in sth** (*undesirable*) se terminer en *ou* par qch; (*desirable*) aboutir à qch; **the protests culminated in a battle with the police** ces manifestations se sont terminées par un affrontement avec la police; **the excavations culminated in the discovery of a temple** les fouilles ont abouti à la découverte d'un temple

culminating ['kʌlmɪneɪtɪŋ] *adj* (*point, moment*) culminant

culmination [kʌlmɪ'neɪʃən] *n* (*of events etc*) point *m* culminant, sommet *m*

culottes [ku:'lɒts] *npl* (*garment*) jupe-culotte *f*, *pl* jupes-culottes

culpability [kʌlpə'bɪlɪtɪ] *n Fml* culpabilité *f*

culpable ['kʌlpəb(ə)l] *adj Fml, Jur* (*negligence etc*) coupable

culprit ['kʌlprɪt] *n* (*guilty person*), *Fig* coupable *mf*, responsable *mf*; (*event*) cause *f*; **I'm the c.** c'est moi le coupable; **poor housing is the main c.** ce sont les mauvaises conditions de logement qui sont principalement responsables

cult [kʌlt] *n* **(a)** *Rel, Fig* (*worship*) culte *m* (**of** de); **to make a c. of sth** avoir un culte pour qch; **a personality c., a c. of personality** un culte de la personnalité; **c. figure** idole *f*; **the film/band has a c. following** c'est un film-/groupe-culte; **c. movie** film-culte *m* **(b)** (*sect*) secte *f*

cultivate ['kʌltɪveɪt] *vt* **(a)** (*earth, field, vegetables etc*) cultiver **(b)** *Biol* (*bacillus*) faire une culture de **(c)** (*develop*) (*an art*) cultiver; (*friends, person's friendship, reputation, accent*) cultiver; (*approach, manner*) adopter

cultivated ['kʌltɪveɪtɪd] *adj* **(a)** *Agr* (*land, plant*) cultivé **(b)** (*educated*) (*voice, manner*) qui témoigne d'une bonne éducation; (*mind*) cultivé

cultivation [kʌltɪ'veɪʃən] *n* culture *f*; **a field under c.** un champ cultivé

cultivator ['kʌltɪveɪtər] *n Agr* **(a)** (*machine*) (*for farm*) cultivateur *m*; (*for garden*) motoculteur *m* **(b)** (*person*) cultivateur, -trice

cultural ['kʌltʃər(ə)l] *adj* (*institute, development, attaché etc*) culturel; **c. event** manifestation *f* culturelle; **c. exchange** échange *m* culturel; **c. heritage** patrimoine *m* culturel

culture¹ ['kʌltʃər] *n* **(a)** (*artistic activity*) culture *f* **(b)** (*society*) culture *f*; **in Polynesian cultures** dans les cultures polynésiennes **(c)** (*refinement*) culture *f*; **he lacks c.** il n'a aucune culture **(d)** *Biol* culture *f*; **c. medium** bouillon *m* *ou* milieu *m* de culture

culture² *vt Biol* (*bacillus*) faire une culture de

cultured ['kʌltʃəd] *adj* **(a)** (*educated*) cultivé **(b)** (*pearl*) de culture

culture shock *n* choc *m* culturel

culture vulture *n F* = grand amateur *m*/grande amatrice *f* de culture

culvert ['kʌlvət] *n Constr* canal *m*, -aux souterrain; (*for cable*) conduit *m* souterrain

cum¹ [kʌm] *prep* **spare room c. study** chambre-bureau *f*; **a translation c. rewrite** tout autant une réécriture qu'une traduction; *St Exch* **c. dividend** coupon *m* attaché

cum² *n Sl* = **come²**

cumbersome ['kʌmbəsəm] *adj* (*clothing, luggage*) encombrant, gênant; (*system*) lourd, pesant; (*sentence*) lourd

cumin ['kʌmɪn, 'kju:-] *n Bot, Culin* cumin *m*

cummerbund ['kʌməbʌnd] *n* ceinture *f* de smoking

cumulative ['kju:mjʊlətɪv] *adj* cumulatif; *Com etc* (*error*) cumulé; **c. balance** solde *m* cumulé; *Jur* **c. evidence** accumulation *f* de témoignages; *Fin* **c. interest** intérêts *mpl* cumulatifs; **c. total** cumul *m*

cumulatively [ˈkjuːmjʊlətɪvlɪ] *adv* de façon cumulée
cumulonimbus [ˈkjuːmjʊləʊˈnɪmbəs] *n Met* cumulo-nimbus *m inv*
cumulus, *pl* **-li** [ˈkjuːmjʊləs, -laɪ] *n Met* cumulus *m*
cuneiform [kjʊˈneɪɪfɔːm] **1** *n* écriture *f* cunéiforme **2** *adj* cunéiforme
cunnilingus [kʌnɪˈlɪŋgəs] *n* cunnilingus *m*
cunning¹ [ˈkʌnɪŋ] *n* **(a)** *(deviousness)* ruse *f*, roublardise *f* **(b)** *(ingenuity)* astuce *f*, ingéniosité *f*
cunning² *adj* **(a)** *(devious)* rusé, roublard; *(look)* sournois; **c. as a fox** rusé comme un renard **(b)** *(ingenious)* *(device etc)* ingénieux, astucieux
cunningly [ˈkʌnɪŋlɪ] *adv* **(a)** *(deviously)* avec ruse **(b)** *(ingeniously)* ingénieusement, astucieusement
cunt [kʌnt] *n Vulg* **(a)** *(vagina)* con *m*, chatte *f* **(b)** *(woman, women)* **he was out looking for c.** il cherchait une femme à baiser **(c)** *(unpleasant person)* salaud *m*, salope *f*
cup¹ [kʌp] *n* **(a)** tasse *f*; *(metal)* gobelet *m*, timbale *f*; *(paper, plastic)* gobelet; **coffee/tea c.** tasse à café/à thé; **c. of coffee/of tea** tasse de café/de thé; *Fig F* **that's just my c. of tea** c'est tout à fait le genre de choses que j'aime; **science-fiction is not my c. of tea** la science-fiction n'est pas ma tasse de thé; **that's not everyone's c. of tea** tout le monde n'aime pas; **they're not my c. of tea** *(of people)* ils ne sont pas mon genre; *Culin* **cider/fruit c.** boisson *f* glacée au cidre/avec des fruits; **c. holder** *(in car etc)* support *m* de tasse
(b) *(measurement)* tasse *f*; **two cups of flour** deux tasses de farine
(c) *Sp* coupe *f*; **to win a c.** remporter *ou* gagner une coupe; **the Davis C.** la coupe Davis; **c. winners** vainqueurs *mpl* de coupe
(d) *Lit (goblet)* coupe *f*; *Rel* calice *m (du saint Sacrement)*; *Fig* **my c. runneth over** je déborde de joie; *Old-fashioned* **to be in one's cups** être gris
(e) *(of flower)* calice *f*; *(of bra, swimming costume)* bonnet *m*; **what size c. do you take?** *(in bra etc)* quelle profondeur de bonnet est-ce que vous mettez?
cup² *vt* **(-pp-) with one's chin cupped in one's hand** le menton dans le creux de la main; **to c. one's hand behind one's ear** mettre sa main en cornet; **to c. one's hands round one's mouth** mettre les mains en porte-voix; **she scooped up the water with her cupped hands** elle a recueilli l'eau dans ses mains jointes
cup-and-ball *adj MecE* **c. joint** joint *m* à rotule
cupbearer [ˈkʌpbeərər] *n* échanson *m*
cupboard [ˈkʌbəd] *n* placard *m*; **store c.** placard *ou* armoire *f* à provisions; *Fig* **c. love** amour *m* intéressé
cupcake [ˈkʌpkeɪk] *n Culin* petit gâteau *m (dans une caissette en papier)*
cup final *n* finale *f* de coupe
cupful [ˈkʌpfʊl] *n* tasse **(of** de**)**; **add two cupfuls of milk** ajouter deux tasses de lait
Cupid [ˈkjuːpɪd] *n* Cupidon *m*; *Art etc* Cupidon, Amour *m*
cupidity [kjuːˈpɪdɪtɪ] *n Fml* cupidité *f*
cupola [ˈkjuːpələ] *n Archit* coupole *f*, dôme *m*; *Naut (gun turret)* coupole; **c. (furnace)** cubilot *m*
cuppa [ˈkʌpə] *n Br F* tasse *f* de thé
cupping glass [ˈkʌpɪŋ] *n Med* ventouse *f*
cupric [ˈkjuːprɪk] *adj Ch (acid)* cuprique
cup-shaped [ˈkʌpʃeɪpt] *adj Bot* cupulaire
cup tie *n Fb* match *m* éliminatoire de coupe
cur [kɜːr] *n Lit* **(a)** *(dog)* sale cabot *m* **(b)** *(despicable man)* homme *m* méprisable, mufle *m*
curable [ˈkjʊərəb(ə)l] *adj Med, Fig* guérissable
curacy [ˈkjʊərəsɪ] *n Rel* vicariat *m*
curare [kjʊəˈrɑːrɪ] *n* curare *m*
curate [ˈkjʊərət] *n Rel* vicaire *m*; **c. in charge** desservant *m*; *Fig* **his latest book/film is a bit of a c.'s egg** il y a du bon et du mauvais dans son dernier livre/film
curative [ˈkjʊərətɪv] *adj (powers, effect, medicine)* curatif
curator [kjʊəˈreɪtər] *n (of museum, gallery)* conservateur *m*
curb¹ [kɜːb] *n* **(a)** *(check)* frein *m*; **to put a c. on sb's enthusiasm** mettre un frein à l'enthousiasme de qn; **to put a c. on one's passions** refréner ses passions, mettre un frein à ses passions **(b)** *Horseriding* **c. (chain)** gourmette *f*; **c. bit** mors *m* à gourmette **(c)** *Am (of pavement etc)* bordure *f*, rebord *m*
curb² *vt* **(a)** *(one's anger)* réprimer, refréner; *(one's passions)* maîtriser, brider; *(impatience, enthusiasm, tendency)* modérer; *(inflation etc)* freiner; **you must learn to c. your tongue!** tu dois apprendre à tenir ta langue! **(b)** *(horse)* mettre la gourmette à
curbstone [ˈkɜːbstəʊn] *n Am (of pavement)* pierre *f* de rebord
curd [kɜːd] *n* (lait *m*) caillé *m*; **curds and whey** lait caillé sucré
curdle [ˈkɜːd(ə)l] **1** *vi (of milk)* se cailler; *Fig* **my blood curdled** mon sang s'est glacé *ou* figé **2** *vt (milk)* cailler; *Fig (blood)* glacer, figer; *F* **he had a face that would c. milk** il avait une tête de gardien de prison
cure¹ [kjʊər] *n* **(a)** *(remedy)*, *Fig* remède *m* **(for** contre**)**; **there is no known c. for the condition** on ne connaît pas encore de remède pour cette maladie; **rest c.** cure *f* de repos; **to take a c.** faire une cure; **beyond** *or* **past c.** *(person)* incurable; *(situation)* irrémédiable; **the c. is worse than the disease** le remède est pire que le mal **(b)** *Rel* **c. of souls** cure *f ou* charge *f* d'âmes
cure² *vt* **(a)** *(person) (of illness)* guérir **(of** de**)**; *(of bad habit)* guérir, corriger; **this experience cured him of his infatuation** cette expérience l'a guéri de son engouement; *Prov* **what can't be cured must be endured** il faut savoir prendre son mal en patience **(b)** *(prepare) (food) (by salting)* saler; *(by smoking)* fumer; *(by drying)* faire sécher; *(hides)* saler
cure-all *n* panacée *f*
curettage [kjʊəˈretɪdʒ] *n Med* curet(t)age *m*
curfew [ˈkɜːfjuː] *n* couvre-feu *m*; **to ring the c. (bell)** sonner le couvre-feu; *esp Am Fig* **to be under c.** *(of teenager)* devoir rentrer à une heure précise
curing [ˈkjʊərɪŋ] *n (preparation) (by salting)* salaison *f*; *(by smoking) (of meat)* fumage *m*; *(of herring)* saurissage *m*; *(by drying)* séchage *m*
curio [ˈkjʊərɪəʊ] *n* curiosité *f*, bibelot *m*
curiosity [kjʊərɪˈɒsɪtɪ] *n* **(a)** curiosité *f*; **out of** *or* **from c.** par curiosité; **I was dying of c.** je mourais de curiosité; *Prov* **c. killed the cat** = la curiosité est un vilain défaut **(b)** *(object)* curiosité *f*, bibelot *m*
curious [ˈkjʊərɪəs] *adj* **(a)** *(inquisitive)* curieux, *Pej* indiscret, -ète; **to be c. to see/know** être curieux de voir/savoir; **they didn't seem at all c. as to** *or* **about how it had happened** ils n'avaient pas du tout l'air curieux de savoir comment cela s'était produit **(b)** *(strange) (way, circumstances)* curieux, singulier; **the two of them made a c. sight** ils formaient un étrange tableau tous les deux; **a c. looking object** un objet bizarre
curiously [ˈkjʊərɪəslɪ] *adv* **(a)** *(inquisitively)* avec curiosité, *Pej* indiscrètement **(b)** *(strangely)* curieusement, singulièrement; **c. enough ...** chose curieuse *ou* singulière ...
curl¹ [kɜːl] *n* **(a)** *(of hair)* boucle *f*; *(of smoke)* spirale *f*; **in curls** *(hair)* bouclé, frisé; **to fall in curls** *(of hair)* tomber en boucles **(b)** *(action)* action *f* de se recourber; **with a c. of the lip** avec une moue dédaigneuse
curl² **1** *vt (hair) (loosely)* boucler; *(tightly)* friser; **to c. one's lip** faire une moue dédaigneuse; **to c. sth round sth** enrouler qch autour de qch; **to c. oneself into a ball** *(of animal, person)* se rouler en boule **2** *vi* **(a)** *(of hair)* boucler; *(of paper)* rebiquer; *(of smoke)* s'élever en spirales; *(of waves)* onduler, déferler; *(of lip)* se relever avec dédain; *Fig* **stories that make your hair c.** histoires qui font dresser les cheveux; **his language would make your hair c.** il jure comme un charretier; *Fig* **it made my toes c.** *(with embarrassment)* c'était vraiment pénible; **to c. round sth** *(of plant etc)* s'enrouler autour de qch **(b)** *Sp* jouer au curling
▶ **curl up** **1** *vi* **(a)** *(lie, sit comfortably)* se blottir, se pelotonner; **I like to c. up in bed with a good book** j'aime me blottir au lit avec un bon livre; **to sleep curled up** dormir en chien de fusil; **curled up in bed** pelotonné dans son lit
(b) *(form a curl)* se rouler en boule, se recroqueviller; **hedgehogs c. up into a ball for protection** les hérissons se roulent en boule pour se protéger
(c) *(of leaves, paper etc)* rebiquer
(d) *Fig F (be embarrassed)* être extêmement gêné; **I wanted to c. up and die** je ne savais plus où me mettre
2 *vtsep (form into a curl)* **to c. oneself up** se rouler en boule, se recroqueviller; **to c. itself up** *(of cat etc)* se rouler en boule
curler [ˈkɜːlər] *n* **(a)** *(for hair)* bigoudi *m*; **in her curlers** avec ses bigoudis sur la tête, en bigoudis **(b)** *Sp* joueur, -euse de curling
curlew [ˈkɜːljuː] *n (bird)* courlis *m*
curlicue [ˈkɜːlɪkjuː] *n* trait *m* de plume en parafe
curliness [ˈkɜːlɪnɪs] *n (of hair) (loose)* boucles *fpl*; *(tight)* frisure *f*
curling [ˈkɜːlɪŋ] *n* **(a)** **c. irons** *or* **tongs** fer *m* à friser **(b)** *Sp* curling *m*; **c. stone** pierre *f ou* galet *m* de curling
curly [ˈkɜːlɪ] **1** *adj (hair) (loosely)* bouclé; *(tightly)* frisé; *(long piece of paper etc)* en spirale; *(lettuce)* frisé; **the dried leaves had gone c.** les feuilles séchées s'étaient recroquevillées **2** *n F* **(a) to have sb by the short and curlies** pouvoir faire ce qu'on veut de qn; **they've got us by the short and curlies** ils nous tiennent **(b)** *(person with curly hair)* **hi there, c.** salut, le/la frisé(e)

curly bracket *n Typ* accolade *f*
curly-headed, -haired ['kɜːlɪhedɪd, -heəd] *adj* (*with loose curls*) à la tête bouclée, aux cheveux bouclés; (*with tight curls*) aux cheveux frisés
currant ['kʌrənt] *n* **(a)** (*dried grape*) raisin *m* de Corinthe, raisin sec; **c. bun** petit pain *m* aux raisins **(b)** (*soft fruit*) groseille *f*; **c. bush** groseillier *m*
currency ['kʌrənsɪ] *n* **(a)** *Fin* (*unit*) (*of a country*) unité *f* monétaire, monnaie *f*, devise *f*; (*specie*) numéraire *m*; **foreign c.** devise étrangère; **to buy foreign c.** acheter des devises étrangères; **hard/soft c.** devise forte/faible; **the world's major currencies** les principales monnaies du monde; **to buy c.** acheter des devises; *Com* **c. adjustment bunker adjustment factor** ajustement *m* fret-devise; **c. adjustment factor** correctif *m* d'ajustement monétaire; **c. conversion** conversion *f* de monnaies; **c. fluctuation** mouvement *m* des devises; *St Exch* **c. swap** échange *m* de devises; **c. transfer** transfert *m* de devises
(b) (*circulation*) (*of ideas*) circulation *f*, cours *m*; **to give c. to a rumour** (*of person, newspaper etc*) faire courir un bruit; **to gain c.** (*of news*) s'accréditer; (*of expression, habit*) devenir de plus en plus courant; (*of ideas*) se répandre; **the expression is common c.** l'expression est monnaie courante; **this view had some c. at one time** cette opinion était accréditée à un moment donné
currency dealer *n* cambiste *m*
currency market *n* marché *m* monétaire
currency speculation *n* spéculation *f* sur les devises
currency speculator *n* spéculateur *m* sur devises
currency unit *n* unité *f* monétaire
current[1] ['kʌrənt] *adj* **(a)** (*existing, present*) (*feeling, tendency, situation*) actuel; **the c. theory is that ...** la théorie actuelle est que ...; **which is still c.** qui est toujours d'actualité; **c. issue** (*of magazine*) dernier numéro *m*; **c. month** mois *m* en cours; **the c. treasurer** le trésorier actuel (de l'association)
(b) *Fin* **c. assets** actif *m* circulant, actif réalisable et disponible; *Fin* **c. earnings** revenus *mpl* actuels; **c. expenditure** dépenses *fpl* courantes; *Acct* **c. financial** *or Am* **fiscal year** exercice *m* en cours; **c. income** (*in accounts*) produits *mpl* courants; (*actual earnings*) revenu *m* actuel; *Acct* **c. liabilities** passif *m* exigible *ou* circulant, dettes *fpl* à court terme; **c. price** prix *m* courant; *St Exch* cours *m* instantané; *Acct* **c. ratio** coefficient *m* de liquidité; **c. value** valeur *f* actuelle; **c. net value** valeur *f* actuelle nette, VAN *f*
(c) (*accepted, used*) courant, admis, reçu; **to be c.** avoir cours; **in c. use** d'usage courant; **the word is in c. use** le mot s'emploie couramment
current[2] *n* **(a)** (*of river, tide etc*) courant *m*; *Met* **air c.** courant d'air; *Fig* **the c. of opinion is against him** il y a un courant d'opinion contre lui; **to drift on the c.** se laisser aller au fil de l'eau, se laisser porter par le courant; *Fig* **to go with the c.** suivre le courant; **to swim against the c.** nager contre le courant *ou* à contre-courant; *Fig* **to go** *or* **swim against the c.** aller à contre-courant **(b)** *El* courant *m*; *Comptr* **c. smoother** régulateur *m* de tension
current account *n Br Banking* compte *m* courant, compte chèque; **c. with the post office** compte courant postal
current affairs *npl* actualités *fpl*; *TV, Rad* **c. programme** programme *m* d'actualités
currently ['kʌrəntlɪ] *adv* (*at present*) actuellement, en ce moment; **she is c. appearing in Othello** elle apparaît en ce moment dans Othello; **c. showing** (*at cinema*) à l'affiche
curriculum, *pl* **-a** [kə'rɪkjʊləm, -ə] *n Sch* programme *m* (d'enseignement); **on the c.** au programme; **c. meeting** réunion *f* de mise au point du programme
curriculum vitae ['viːtaɪ] *n esp Br* curriculum vitae *m*
curry[1] ['kʌrɪ] *n Culin* (*spices, dish*) curry *m*, cari *m*; **beef/chicken/vegetable c.** bœuf *m*/poulet *m*/légumes *mpl* au curry, cari de bœuf/poulet/légumes; **c. powder** curry, cari
curry[2] *vt Culin* (*chicken etc*) apprêter au cari *ou* au curry; **curried chicken** poulet *m* au curry, cari *m* de poulet
curry[3] *vt* **(a)** *Pej* **to c. favour with sb** s'insinuer dans les bonnes grâces de qn **(b)** (*groom*) (*horse*) étriller
currycomb ['kʌrɪkəʊm] *n* étrille *f*
curse[1] [kɜːs] *n* **(a)** (*evil spell*) malédiction *f*, mauvais sort *m*; **to put a c. on sb** jeter un sort à qn; **a c. on ...!** maudit soit ...!; *Fig* **I feel as if I'm under a c.** j'ai l'impression qu'on m'a jeté un sort **(b)** *Old-fashioned* (*swearword*) imprécation *f*, juron *m*; **to let out a c.** lâcher un juron; *Hum* **curses!** diantre! **(c)** (*scourge*) fléau *m*; **rabbits are a c. here** ici les lapins sont un fléau; *Old-fashioned F* **to have the c.** (*be menstruating*) avoir ses règles
curse[2] **1** *vt* (*person, object*) maudire; **he is cursed with a violent temper** il est affligé d'un mauvais caractère; **c. it!** le diable l'emporte!; **he cursed his luck** il a maudit son sort; **you'll c. the day you came here** tu maudiras le jour où tu es venu ici **2** *vi* (*swear*) jurer; **to c. and swear** jurer comme un charretier; **to c. at sb** injurier qn
cursed *adj* **(a)** [kɜːst] (*under a curse*) maudit **(b)** ['kɜːsɪd] *F* (*annoying*) sacré, satané; **it's a c. nuisance** c'est bigrement embêtant
cursing ['kɜːsɪŋ] *n* jurons *mpl*
cursive ['kɜːsɪv] **1** *adj* cursif; **c. handwriting** écriture *f* cursive **2** *n* écriture *f* cursive
cursor ['kɜːsər] *n* (*on slide rule*), *Comptr* curseur *m*; *Comptr* **move the c. to the right/left** déplacez le curseur vers la droite/gauche; **the word where the c. is** le mot pointé; **c. blink rate** vitesse *f* de clignotement du curseur; **c. control** contrôle *m* du curseur; **c. key** touche *f* de curseur; **c. movement** déplacement *m* du curseur; **c. position** position *f* du curseur
cursorily ['kɜːsərɪlɪ] *adv* (*to examine, look at*) superficiellement
cursoriness ['kɜːsərɪnɪs] *n* caractère *m* sommaire
cursory ['kɜːsərɪ] *adj* (*glance, examination, remarks*) superficiel
curt [kɜːt] *adj* (*manner*) brusque; (*tone, person*) cassant; (*reply, command*) sec, *f* sèche
curtail [kɜː'teɪl] *vt* **(a)** (*shorten*) (*visit*) abréger, écourter **(b)** (*limit*) (*person's freedom, privileges, spending*) réduire, restreindre; (*person's authority, powers*) diminuer
curtailment [kɜː'teɪlmənt] *n* (*of freedom, privileges, spending etc*) réduction *f*, restriction *f*; (*of authority, powers*) diminution *f*
curtain[1] ['kɜːt(ə)n] *n* **(a)** *Br* (*on window etc*) rideau *m*; **to draw the curtains** (*open*) ouvrir les rideaux; (*close*) tirer *ou* fermer les rideaux; **c. ring** anneau *m* de rideau; **c. rail** *or* **rod** tringle *f* à rideau; **c. hook** crochet *m* de rideau; **c. material** tissu *m* de rideau; **c. wall** (*of castle*) mur *m* d'enceinte; *Constr* enceinte *f* **(b)** *Th* rideau *m*; **safety c.** rideau de fer; *Fig F* **it's curtains for him** il est fichu
curtain[2] *vt* (*alcove etc*) garnir de rideaux
▶ **curtain off** *vtsep* (*conceal*) (*part of room*) séparer par un rideau
curtain call *n* rappel *m*; **to take a c.** être rappelé; **to take three c. calls** être rappelé trois fois
curtain-raiser ['kɜːt(ə)nreɪzər] *n Th* (*play*) lever *m* de rideau; *Fig* préambule *m*
curtainsider ['kɜːt(ə)nsaɪdər] *n Aut* camion *m* bâché
curtly ['kɜːtlɪ] *adv* (*to say*) brusquement, d'un ton cassant; **a c. worded letter** une lettre au ton sec
curtness ['kɜːtnɪs] *n* (*of manner, words*) brusquerie *f*; (*of person*) ton *m* cassant; (*of letter*) ton sec
curts(e)y[1] ['kɜːtsɪ] *n* révérence *f*; **to make a c. to sb** faire une révérence à qn
curts(e)y[2] *vi* (*of woman, girl*) faire une révérence **(to** à**)**
curvaceous [kɜː'veɪʃəs] *adj* (*woman*) qui a de jolies formes, *F* bien roulée; **c. figure** silhouette *f* de vamp
curvature ['kɜːvətʃər] *n* (*of the earth etc*) sphéricité *f*; *Phys, Opt* (*of space*) courbure *f*; *Med* **c. of the spine** courbure (de la colonne) vertébrale
curve[1] [kɜːv] *n* courbe *f*; (*in road*) tournant *m*, virage *m*; **the c. of the bay** la courbe de la baie; **curves** (*of woman*) rondeurs *fpl*, formes *fpl*; *US Fig* **to throw sb a c. (ball)** (*give unpleasant surprise to*) prendre qn par surprise; (*mislead*) induire qn en erreur; *Comptr* **c. smoothing** lissage *m* de courbes
curve[2] **1** *vi* se courber; **the road curves round the castle** la route fait le tour du château; **to c. down(wards)/up(wards)** monter/descendre en courbe **2** *vt* courber, recourber; (*pipe, surface etc*) cintrer
curved [kɜːvd] *adj* (*intentionally bent*) courbe; (*bent out of shape*) courbé, cintré; (*nose*) busqué
curvilinear [kɜːvɪ'lɪnɪər] *adj* curviligne
curvy ['kɜːvɪ] *adj* **(a)** (*curved*) courbé, cintré **(b)** *F* (*woman*) qui a des formes
cushion[1] ['kʊʃən] *n* **(a)** coussin *m*; **the mattresses acted as a c. when he fell** les matelas ont amorti sa chute; *Fig* **the annual increase in salary acts as a c. against inflation** l'augmentation annuelle des salaires amortit les effets de l'inflation **(b)** *Billiards, Snooker, Pool* bande *f*; **off the c.** par la bande **(c)** *Tech* (*of air etc*) coussin *m*
cushion[2] *vt* (*reduce effect of*) (*blow, impact, fall etc*) amortir; **they have been cushioned against unemployment** ils ont été protégés contre le chômage
cushioning ['kʊʃənɪŋ] *n MecE* matelassage *m*; **as a c. against inflation** pour amortir les effets de l'inflation
cushy ['kʊʃɪ] *adj F* (*life etc*) pépère, peinard; **c. job** *or* **number** boulot *m* peinard
cusp [kʌsp] *n* **(a)** *Astron* (*of moon*) corne *f* **(b)** *Math* (*of curve*) sommet *m* **(c)** (*of tooth*) cuspide *f*
cuspidor ['kʌspɪdɔːr] *n Am* crachoir *m*
cuss [kʌs] *n F* **(a)** (*swear word*) juron *m*; **it isn't worth a**

(tinker's) c. ça ne vaut pas un clou **(b)** (*person*) individu *m*, type *m*; **an awkward c.** un mauvais coucheur; **a stubborn c.** une tête de lard

cussed ['kʌsɪd] *adj F* (*annoying*) sacré, satané; (*stubborn*) entêté; **it's a c. nuisance** c'est bigrement embêtant

cussedness ['kʌsɪdnɪs] *n F* entêtement *m*; **out of sheer c.** par esprit de contradiction

custard ['kʌstəd] *n Culin* crème *f* anglaise; **baked c.** crème cuite au four; **c. apple** (*fruit*) anone *f* réticulée; **c. cream (biscuit)** biscuit *m* fourré à la crème; **c. pie** tarte *f* à la crème; **c. powder** préparation *f* instantanée pour crème anglaise; **c. tart** flan *m*

custodial [kʌ'stəʊdɪəl] *adj Jur* **c. sentence** peine *f* de détention

custodian [kʌs'təʊdɪən] *n* gardien, -ienne; (*of museum etc*) conservateur, -trice; **the police are the custodians of law and order** la police est la garante de l'ordre public

custody ['kʌstədɪ] *n* **(a)** (*guardianship*) (*of children etc*) garde *f*; **the court awarded c. (of the children) to the father** le tribunal a confié la garde des enfants au père; **to have c. of sb/sth** avoir la garde de qn/qch; **in safe c.** sous bonne garde **(b)** *Jur* détention *f*; **to take sb into c.** arrêter qn; **to be in c.** être en détention préventive

custom ['kʌstəm] **1** *n* **(a)** (*practice*) coutume *f*, usage *m*; (*of individual*) habitude *f*; **according to c.** selon l'usage; **it is the c. of the country** c'est la coutume du pays; **it is their c. to fast on that day** leur coutume veut qu'ils jeûnent ce jour-là; **it was a c. with him to ..., it was his c. to ...** il avait l'habitude de ...; **the manners and customs** (*of a country*) les us *mpl* et coutumes

(b) *Jur* (*of a country*) droit *m* coutumier, coutume *f*

(c) *Com* (*of a company, shop*) clientèle *f*; **to lose sb's c.** perdre la clientèle de qn; **I'll take my c. elsewhere** je vais aller voir ailleurs, *F* je vais changer de crémerie

2 *adj* **c. car** voiture *f* customisée, custom *m*

customarily ['kʌstəmərɪlɪ] *adv* habituellement, d'habitude; (*normally*) ordinairement

customary ['kʌstəm(ə)rɪ] *adj* **(a)** habituel, d'usage; **at the c. hour** à l'heure habituelle; **it is c. to ...** il est d'usage de ..., c'est la coutume de ...; **as is c.** comme il est d'usage; **her c. politeness** sa politesse habituelle *ou* coutumière **(b)** *Jur* **c. law** droit *m* coutumier; **c. right** droit d'usage

custom-built *adj* fait *ou* fabriqué sur commande; *Aut* **c. body** carrosserie *f* customisée

customer ['kʌstəmər] *n* **(a)** (*of shop etc*) client, -ente; **regular c.** (*of restaurant etc*) habitué, -ée; *prov* **the c. is always right** le client a toujours raison, le client est roi; *Mktg* **c.-acceptance test** test *m* d'acceptabilité auprès des consommateurs; **c. credit** crédit *m* client; **c. service (department)** service *m* clientèle; *Mktg* **c.-size specialist** entreprise *f* spécialisée en fonction du volume d'achat; **c.-support service** service *m* à la clientèle **(b)** *F* (*person*) individu *m*, type *m*; **an awkward c.** un type pas commode; **a queer c.** un drôle de type; **an ugly c.** un sale type

customization [kʌstəmaɪ'zeɪʃən] *n* personnalisation *f*

customize ['kʌstəmaɪz] *vt* (*vehicle*) customiser; (*kitchen, computer etc*) personnaliser; **customized marketing** mercatique *f* sur mesure, marketing *m* 'à la carte'; *Comptr* **c. option** option *f* 'personnaliser'

custom-made *adj* (*car etc*) fait *ou* fabriqué sur commande; (*clothes etc*) fait sur mesure

customs ['kʌstəmz] *n Admin* douane *f*; **to go through (the) c.** passer la douane; **c. agent** commissionnaire *mf* en douane; **c. allowance** tolérance *f ou* franchise *f* douanière; **c. barriers** barrières *fpl* douanières; **c. broker** agréé *m* en douane; **c. clearance** dédouanement *m*; **c. clearance area** aire *f* de dédouanement; **c. clearance authorization** autorisation *f* de dédouanement; **c. control** contrôle *m* douanier; **c. declaration** déclaration *f* de *ou* en douane; **c. drawback** ristourne *f* de droits de douane; **c. duties** droits *mpl* de douane; **c. examination** contrôle *m* douanier; **c. formalities** formalités *fpl* douanières; **c. house** bureau *m* de douane; **c. inspector** inspecteur *m* des douanes; **c. invoice** facture *f* douanière; **c. manifest** manifeste *m* de douane; **c. nomenclature** nomenclature *f* douanière, nomenclature générale des produits; **c. office** bureau *m* de douane; **c. officer** douanier, -ière, préposé, -ée de la douane; **c. papers** dossier *m* de douane; **c. permit** permis *m* de douane; **c. procedure** procédure *f* douanière; **c. receipt** acquit *m* de douane; **c. regulations** réglementation *f* douanière; **c. system** régime *m ou* système *m* douanier; **c. tariff** tarif *m* douanier; **c. union** union *f* douanière; **c. value** valeur *f* en douane

Customs and Excise department *n Br* régie *f* des impôts indirects

cut[1] [kʌt] *n* **(a)** (*in an object*) entaille *f*; *Com etc* (*in price, spending*) réduction *f*; *Cin, TV* (*in film etc*) coupure *f*; **to make a clean c.** trancher net; **power** *or* **electricity c.** coupure *f* de courant; *Cin* **the sudden c. from the battlefield to the dinner scene** la coupure brutale entre le champ de bataille et la scène du dîner; **to make a c. in a text** faire une coupure dans un texte; **a two-hundred word c.** une réduction de deux cents mots; **wage cuts** réductions de salaires; **to take a c. in one's wages** accepter une réduction de salaire; **everyone has agreed to take a c. in their wages** tout le monde a accepté de voir son salaire réduit

(b) (*blow*) (*with knife, sword*) coup *m*; *Cr, Tennis* coup tranchant; **c. with a whip** coup de fouet; *Fig* **the unkindest c. of all** le coup le plus dur; **she revels in the c. and thrust of debate** elle prend plaisir aux joutes oratoires

(c) (*of machine tool*) passe *f*; **(saw) c.** trait *m* de scie

(d) (*wound*) coupure *f*; (*gash*) balafre *f*; *Surg* incision *f*; **c. across the cheek** balafre à la joue

(e) (*style*) (*of garment, hair*) coupe *f*; (*of jewel*) taille *f*

(f) (*meat*) **c. off the joint** tranche *f* de rôti; **prime c.** morceau *m* de (premier) choix; **cheap cuts** bas morceaux

(g) *Fig F* (*portion*) commission *f*, *F* gratte *f*; **he gets his c.** il a sa part

(h) **short c.** raccourci *m*; *Fig* solution *f* de facilité; **to take a short c.** couper au plus court, prendre (par) un raccourci; *Fig* utiliser la solution de facilité

(i) *Cards* coupe *f*

(j) *F* **to be a c. above sb/sth** être un cran au-dessus de qn/qch

(k) (*of tobacco*) **I prefer a finer/coarser c. of tobacco** je préfère le tabac plus fin/grossier

cut[2] (*pt, pp* **cut**, *prp* **cutting**) **1** *vt* **(a)** couper; (*in slices*) trancher; (*rope*) couper, sectionner; (*hay*) faucher; **to c. the grass** (*with mower*) tondre le gazon; (*with shears*) couper le gazon; **to c. one's finger** se couper le doigt; **to c. one's nails** se couper les ongles; **to c. one's throat** se trancher la gorge; **to c. sb's throat** trancher la gorge de qn; **to have one's hair cut** se faire couper les cheveux; *Fig* **this remark cut him to the quick** cette parole l'a piqué au vif

(b) (*separate*) **to c. sth in two** *or* **in half** couper qch en deux; **to c. a slice of cake** couper une tranche de gâteau; **to c. to pieces** (*object*) couper en morceaux; (*army*) tailler en pièces; **to c. one's way through the wood** se frayer un chemin à travers le bois; **to c. a dog loose** libérer un chien en coupant sa laisse; **to c. a horse loose** libérer un cheval en coupant sa longe; *Fig* **to c. oneself loose from sth** se libérer de qch

(c) (*shorten, reduce*) (*film, scene, text etc*) couper; (*speech*) abréger, raccourcir; (*numbers, spending*) réduire; (*production*) diminuer; **the film was cut to 100 minutes** le film a été ramené à 100 minutes; **prices/wages have been cut by 10%** les prix/salaires ont été réduits de 10%; **this cuts their journey time by 20 minutes** cela réduit la durée de leur trajet de 20 minutes; **it helps to c. costs** cela permet de réduire les frais; **to c. a speech/a visit short** écourter un discours/une visite; **to c. sb short** couper la parole à qn; **to c. a long story short ...** bref ...; *F* **c. it short!** soyez bref!; *Fig* **it's cutting it** *or* **things fine** cela va faire juste

(d) (*omit, remove*) supprimer; **this scene was later cut** cette scène a été supprimée par la suite; *Sl* **c. the crap!** arrête tes conneries!

(e) (*edit*) (*film*) monter

(f) *Tech etc* (*stone, glass etc*) couper, tailler; (*canal*) percer, creuser; (*characters on metal or stone*) tailler, ciseler; (*garment*) tailler, couper; *Mus* (*record*) graver; *Fig* **to c. one's coat according to one's cloth** faire avec ce que l'on a

(g) **to c. a tooth** (*of child*) percer une dent; *Fig* **to c. one's teeth on sth** (*of lawyer etc*) se faire les dents sur qch

(h) *Cards* **to c. the cards** (*in general*) couper les cartes; (*to decide who deals etc*) tirer une carte pour savoir qui fera la donne/*etc*

(i) *Cr, Tennis* (*ball*) couper

(j) *El etc* (*turn off*) couper

(k) **to c. sb (dead)** (*ignore*) faire semblant de ne pas voir qn, ignorer qn complètement

(l) *Sch F* (*class*) sécher

(m) **to c. an elegant/a noble/a romantic figure** être très élégant/noble/romantique

2 *vi* **(a)** (*of knife, person*) couper; **those scissors don't c. very well** ces ciseaux ne coupent pas très bien; **cloth that cuts easily** tissu qui se coupe facilement; **that wind cuts like a knife** le vent te transperce; **to c. into a cake** entamer un gâteau; **to c. into the bark** inciser l'écorce; *Lit* **to c. through the waves** fendre les eaux; **that's an argument that cuts both ways** c'est un argument à double tranchant; *US* **to c. loose** (*free oneself*) s'émanciper; (*escape*) s'évader; *F* **to c. and run** filer (en vitesse), décamper, se sauver (**b**) *Cin, TV, Th* (*change scene*) **the action cuts to the street** l'action passe à la rue; *Cin* **c.**! coupez!

(**c**) *Cards* couper

cut[3] *adj* (**a**) (*crystal, diamond*) taillé; **a c. glass jug** une cruche en cristal taillé; *Br Fig* **a c. glass accent** un accent bourgeois; **well/elegantly c. suit** complet bien coupé/de coupe élégante; **c. and dried** (*opinions*) tout fait; **everything was c. and dried** (*decided*) tout était déjà décidé; **it's not as c. and dried as that** ce n'est pas aussi simple que ça (**b**) (*reduced, shortened*) réduit; **the c. version of the film** la version raccourcie du film

▶ **cut across** *vipo* (*playing field, forest etc*) couper à travers; *Fig* **concern for the environment cuts across party lines** les préoccupations écologiques transcendent les clivages politiques

▶ **cut along** *vi Old-fashioned Br F* filer

▶ **cut away** *vtsep* (*remove*) couper, ôter; **they had to c. away the wreckage to reach the victim** ils ont dû découper l'épave pour atteindre la victime; **c. away the fat** ôtez le gras

▶ **cut back 1** *vtsep* (**a**) (*prune*) (*rosebush, undergrowth etc*) tailler; (*tree*) élaguer (**b**) (*reduce*) (*prices*) baisser; (*production etc*) diminuer; **arms spending has been cut right back** les dépenses d'armement ont été nettement réduites **2** *vi* (**a**) (*financially*) économiser, réduire les dépenses (**b**) (*go back*) s'en retourner, rebrousser chemin (**c**) *Cin* (*of action*) revenir en arrière; **we c. back to the scene in the kitchen** nous revenons à la scène de la cuisine

▶ **cut back on** *vipo* (*financially*) économiser sur; (*time*) réduire; **we've already cut back on production** nous avons déjà diminué la production; **you'll have to c. back on the cakes** il faudra que vous mangiez moins de gâteaux; **to c. back on one's smoking** fumer moins

▶ **cut down 1** *vtsep* (**a**) (*fell*) (*tree*) couper, abattre; (*wheat*) couper

(**b**) (*kill*) abattre; *Lit* **to be cut down in one's prime** être fauché à la fleur de l'âge

(**c**) (*shorten, reduce*) (*speech etc*) abréger; (*book for publication*) raccourcir; (*spending*) couper, réduire; **to c. sth down to about 150,000 words** réduire qch à environ 150 000 mots; **we've been asked to c. down the amount of time we devote to sports** on nous a demandé de consacrer moins de temps au sport; **to c. trousers down** (*to make shorts*) transformer un pantalon en short

(**d**) (*cut through ropes*) **to c. down a hanged man** couper la corde d'un pendu; **the parachutist had to be cut down from the tree** pour décrocher le parachutiste de l'arbre il a fallu couper les cordes de son parachute

2 *vi* (*make reductions*) réduire; **I drink too much coffee so I'm trying to c. down** je bois trop de café, alors j'essaie de réduire

▶ **cut down on** *vipo* **we had to c. down on expenditure** nous avons dû réduire nos dépenses; **to c. down on the amount of time spent doing sth** passer moins de temps à faire qch; **try to c. down on the swearing** essayez de jurer un peu moins

▶ **cut in 1** *vi* (**a**) (*interrupt conversation*) intervenir dans la conversation; *Tel* interrompre la conversation; **she cut in (on me)** elle m'a coupé la parole; **you're wrong, she cut in** tu as tort, interrompit-elle

(**b**) *Aut* faire une queue de poisson; **he cut in in front of me** il m'a fait une queue de poisson

(**c**) (*at a dance*) **mind if I c. in?** vous permettez que je vous emprunte votre partenaire?

(**d**) *Tech* (*of mechanism, safety device*) entrer en action

2 *vtsep F* (*include in a deal*) **to c. sb in (on the deal)** donner à qn sa part du gâteau; **we could c. him in for £5,000** nous pourrions lui filer 5 000 livres

▶ **cut into** *vipo* (**a**) (*interrupt*) **to c. into a conversation** intervenir dans *ou* interrompre brusquement la conversation (**b**) (*use*) **to c. into one's savings** entamer ses économies; **this work cuts into my free time** ce travail empiète sur mes heures de loisir (**c**) (*hurt*) blesser; **the rope was cutting into his arm/skin** la corde lui blessait le bras/lui entaillait la peau; **the string is cutting into me** le cordon me coupe la chair

▶ **cut off** *vtsep* (**a**) (*remove by cutting*) (*piece*) couper, découper; **pages with the corners cut off** pages dont les coins ont été coupés; **to c. off 3cm of a shelf** couper 3cm à une étagère; **he's had all his hair cut off** il s'est fait couper les cheveux tout court; **to c. off sb's head** trancher la tête à qn; *Lit* **to be cut off in one's prime** être emporté *ou* fauché à la fleur de l'âge

(**b**) (*isolate*) (*personne*) couper (du monde); **to c. off the enemy** couper la ligne de retraite de l'ennemi; **to c. off sb's retreat** couper la retraite à qn; **to be cut off** (*by snow, floods*) (*of person, village etc*) se trouver isolé; **the village is cut off from the outside world by snow** le village est coupé du monde par la neige; **I feel cut off** je me sens coupé du monde; **to c. oneself off from the world** se retirer du monde; **she cut herself off from her family** elle s'est coupée de sa famille

(**c**) *Tel* (*person*) couper; **he's been cut off** (*during conversation*) il a été coupé; (*disconnected*) on lui a coupé le téléphone

(**d**) (*electricity, steam, ignition*) couper; **to c. off sb's water/supplies** couper *ou* supprimer l'eau/les vivres à qn; **it cut off the supply of blood to the brain** cela a stoppé l'irrigation du cerveau

(**e**) (*disinherit*) (*person*) déshériter; **the old man cut his son off without a penny** le vieillard n'a pas laissé un sou à son fils

▶ **cut out 1** *vtsep* (**a**) (*remove by cutting*) couper, enlever; *Surg* (*tumour etc*) enlever; **to c. a picture out of a magazine** découper une photo dans un magazine

(**b**) (*shape by cutting*) (*pictures*) découper; (*garment*) couper, tailler; (*neckline*) échancrer; **to c. a statue out of wood** tailler une statue dans le bois; *Fig* **to be cut out for sth** être fait pour qch, avoir des dispositions pour qch; **he's not cut out to be a leader** il n'a pas l'étoffe d'un dirigeant; **he's not cut out for it** il n'est pas fait pour cela; *Fig* **I've really got my work cut out** j'ai du pain sur la planche; **she's got her work cut out (for her) with those four kids** elle a de quoi faire avec ces quatre gamins

(**c**) (*eliminate*) supprimer, éliminer; **to c. out luxuries** se passer du luxe; **to c. out smoking** arrêter de fumer; **I wish he'd c. out the jokes** j'aimerais bien qu'il arrête ses plaisanteries; *F* **c. it out!** ça suffit maintenant!, ça va comme ça!; **the new building cuts out a lot of the light** le nouveau bâtiment coupe une bonne partie de la lumière

(**d**) (*oust*) **to c. sb out of a deal** évincer qn dans une affaire; **his father cut them out of his will** son père les a déshérités

2 *vi* (*stop*) (*of engine*) caler; (*of machine*) s'arrêter; (*of pilot light*) s'éteindre

▶ **cut through** *vipo* (**a**) (*rope*) couper; *Fig* **to c. through red tape** éviter la paperasserie (**b**) (*take as a short cut*) **to c. through the park** couper par le parc

▶ **cut up 1** *vtsep* (**a**) (*chop up*) (*wood, meat*) couper, débiter; (*chicken etc*) découper, dépecer; (*vegetables etc*) hacher, émincer; (*body*) couper en morceaux; **to c. sth up into small pieces** couper qch en petits morceaux (**b**) *F* (*usu passive*) (*upset*) **to be very cut up** être profondément affecté *ou* affligé (**about sth** par qch) **2** *vi Br F* **to c. up rough** (*physically*) devenir violent; (*verbally*) monter sur ses ergots

cut and paste *Comptr* **1** *vt* faire un couper-coller sur **2** *vi* faire un couper-coller

cut-and-paste *n Comptr* couper-coller *m*

cutaneous [kjuːˈteɪnɪəs] *adj* cutané

cutaway [ˈkʌtəweɪ] *n* (**a**) **c. (coat)** jaquette *f* (**b**) *Tech* (*drawing*) vue *f* en coupe; **c. model** maquette *f* en coupe

cutback [ˈkʌtbæk] *n* (*in production, budget*) réduction *f*, dégonflement *m*

cute [kjuːt] *adj F* (**a**) (*attractive*) mignon; **what a c. little kitten** quel mignon petit chaton (**b**) (*clever*) malin, *f* maligne; (*idea*) original; **don't get c. with me!** ne fais pas le malin avec moi!

cuteness [ˈkjuːtnɪs] *n F* (**a**) (*attractiveness*) charme *m* (**b**) (*cleverness*) finesse *f*

cuticle [ˈkjuːtɪk(ə)l] *n Anat, Bot* cuticule *f*; **c. pen** repousse-peaux *m inv*

cutie(-pie) [ˈkjuːtɪ(paɪ)] *n F* (**a**) (*baby, child*) mignon, -onne; (*girl, woman*) beauté *f* (**b**) (*shrewd person*) malin *m*, maligne *f*

cutlass [ˈkʌtləs] *n Naut* sabre *m* d'abordage

cutler [ˈkʌtlər] *n* coutelier, -ière

cutlery [ˈkʌtlərɪ] *n* (*knives, forks etc*) couverts *mpl*; *Com, Ind* coutellerie *f* (et argenterie *f* de table); **c. drawer** tiroir *m* à couverts

cutlet [ˈkʌtlɪt] *n Culin* (**a**) (*of lamb, veal*) côtelette *f* (**b**) (*croquette*) (*of chicken etc*) croquette *f*

cutoff [ˈkʌtɒf] *n* (**a**) *US* (*short cut*) raccourci *m* (**b**) *Electron* déconnexion *f*, mise *f* hors de contact, mise hors circuit (**c**) **c. point** limite *f*; **we've taken a score of 370 as the c. point in deciding who to interview** (*no less than*) les candidats doivent avoir au minimum 370 points pour pouvoir passer l'entretien; **the c. point for remedial lessons is 150** (*no more than*) seuls les élèves qui obtiennent 150 points ou en deçà pourront bénéficier de cours de rattrapage; **c. date** date *f* limite (**d**) **cutoffs** (*shorts*) = jean *m* transformé en short

cutout [ˈkʌtaʊt] *n* (**a**) **a cardboard c. of Humphrey Bogart** une

silhouette en carton de Humphrey Bogart **(b)** *El* coupe-circuit *m inv*, disjoncteur *m*; *Aut* **c. device** dispositif *m* de coupure; *Aut* **c. valve** conjoncteur-disjoncteur *m*, disjoncteur *m*
cut-price, *Am* **cut-rate** *adj Com (goods)* à prix réduit; *(as special offer)* bradé; **at cut-price rates** à un tarif réduit; **c. shop** solderie *f*
cut sheet feed *n Comptr* dispositif *m* d'alimentation feuille à feuille; *(act)* alimentation *f* feuille à feuille
cutter [ˈkʌtər] *n* **(a)** *(person) (of garments)* coupeur, -euse; *(of stone, diamonds)* tailleur *m* **(b)** *(tool, device)* lame *f*, couteau *m*; **rotary c.** roue *f* à couteaux; **coal c.** haveuse *f* **(c)** *Naut* canot *m (d'un bâtiment de guerre)*
cutthroat [ˈkʌtθrəʊt] **1** *n* assassin *m*; *Cards* **c. (bridge)** bridge *m* à trois; *Br* **c. (razor)** coupe-choux *m inv*, rasoir *m* à main **2** *adj* **c. competition** concurrence *f* acharnée *ou* sans pitié; **it's a c. business** la concurrence est acharnée
cutting [ˈkʌtɪŋ] **1** *adj* **(a) c. edge** arête *f* tranchante, tranchant *m*; *Fig* **to be at the c. edge (of technology)** être à la pointe
(b) *(wind)* cinglant
(c) *(remark etc)* mordant, blessant; *(criticism)* incisif; **she was rather c. about them** elle a dit des choses un peu dures sur eux
2 *n* **(a)** *MecE* **c. action** cisaillement *m*; **c. angle** angle *m* de coupe; **c. tool** outil *m* tranchant
(b) *TV, Cin (film editing)* montage *m*; **c. copy** copie *f* de montage *ou* de travail; **c. point** point *m* de coupe
(c) *(piece cut off) (of plant)* bouture *f*; *(of vine)* sarment *m*; **to grow a plant from a c.** faire pousser une plante à partir d'une bouture; **to take a c.** faire une bouture; **(newspaper) c.** coupure *f* de journal; **cuttings** *(of wood, metal etc)* rognures *fpl*, recoupes *fpl*; *(of carpet)* chutes *fpl*; *Journ* **cuttings file** fichier *m* de coupures; *Journ* **cuttings library** archives *fpl* de coupures de presse
(d) (railway) c. (voie *f* en) déblai *m*
cutting back *n (of tree)* élagage *m*; *(of production, budget)* réduction *f*
cuttingly [ˈkʌtɪŋlɪ] *adv (to say)* d'un ton caustique; **c. brief** bref et caustique
cutting room *n Cin* salle *f* de montage; **my best scenes ended up on the c. floor** mes meilleures scènes ont été coupées
cuttlebone [ˈkʌt(ə)lbəʊn] *n* os *m* de seiche
cuttlefish [ˈkʌt(ə)lfɪʃ] *n* seiche *f*
CV [siːˈviː] *n (abbr* **curriculum vitae)** CV *m*
CV joint *n Aut (abbr* **constant velocity joint)** joint *m* de cardan
cwo [siːdʌb(ə)ljuːˈəʊ] *Com (abbr* **cash with order)** envoi contre paiement
cwt *abbr* **hundredweight**
cyan [ˈsaɪən] *n* cyan *m*
cyanide [ˈsaɪənaɪd] *n Ch* cyanure *m*; **potassium c.** cyanure de potassium
cyanosis [saɪəˈnəʊsɪs] *n Med* cyanose *f*
cyber [ˈsaɪbər] *n Comptr* cyber *m*
cybernetic [saɪbəˈnetɪk] *adj* cybernétique
cybernetics [saɪbəˈnetɪks] *n* [①**A10**,c] *(with sing verb)* cybernétique *f*
cyberspace [ˈsaɪbəspeɪs] *n* cyber(e)space *m*
cyclamen [ˈsɪkləmən] *n Bot* cyclamen *m*
cycle[1] [ˈsaɪk(ə)l] *n* **(a)** *(pattern) (of movements etc)* cycle *m*; *Aut* **four-stroke c.** cycle à quatre temps; *Astron* **lunar c.** cycle lunaire; **trade c.** cycle économique **(b)** *(bicycle)* bicyclette *f*, vélo *m*; **c. lane** piste *f* cyclable; **c. path** piste *f ou* bande *f* cyclable; **c. racing** courses *fpl* cyclistes; **c. racing track** vélodrome *m*; **c. shop** magasin *m* de cycles; **c. track** piste *f* cyclable **(c)** *Am* = **motorcycle**
cycle[2] *vi* faire de la bicyclette *ou* du vélo; **to c. to/from school** aller à/revenir de l'école à bicyclette *ou* à vélo
cycler [ˈsaɪklər] *n US* cycliste *mf*
cyclic(al) [ˈsɪklɪk, -ɪk(ə)l] *adj (movement etc)* cyclique; **c. unemployment** chômage *m* conjoncturel
cycling [ˈsaɪklɪŋ] *n* cyclisme *m*; **c. club** club *m* de cyclisme; **c. holidays** cyclotourisme *m*; **c. track** piste *f* cyclable; **c. shorts** short *m* de cycliste
cyclist [ˈsaɪklɪst] *n* cycliste *mf*
cyclone [ˈsaɪkləʊn] *n Met* cyclone *m*
cyclonic [saɪˈklɒnɪk] *adj* cyclonique, cyclonal
cyclorama [saɪkləʊˈrɑːmə] *n* cyclorama *m*; **c. light** éclairage *m* de cyclorama
cyclostyle [ˈsaɪkləʊstaɪl] *vt Old-fashioned* polycopier
cyclotron [ˈsaɪklətrɒn] *n Nucl Phys* cyclotron *m*
cygnet [ˈsɪgnɪt] *n (bird)* jeune cygne *m*
cylinder [ˈsɪlɪndər] *n* **(a)** *Geom* cylindre *m*
(b) *Tech, Comptr etc* cylindre *m*; *(of pump, revolver)* barillet *m*; **to be firing on all cylinders** *(of engine)* tourner rond; *Fig (company)* fonctionner à plein régime; *(of person)* être en pleine forme; **four/eight-c. engine** moteur *m* à quatre/huit cylindres; **the engine isn't firing on all cylinders** le moteur boite; *Fig* **he's only firing on three cylinders, he's not firing on all cylinders** il n'est pas tout à fait dans son assiette; *Aut* **c. bank** rangée *f* de cylindres; **c. block** bloc-cylindres *m*, *pl* blocs-cylindres; **c. bore** alésage *m* de cylindre; **c. head** culasse *f*, calotte *f*; **c. head gasket** joint *m* de culasse; **c. wall** paroi *f* des cylindres
cylindrical [sɪˈlɪndrɪk(ə)l] *adj* cylindrique
cymbal [ˈsɪmb(ə)l] *n Mus* cymbale *f*
cynic [ˈsɪnɪk] *n* cynique *mf*; *Antiq, Phil* cynique *m*
cynical [ˈsɪnɪk(ə)l] *adj* cynique
cynically [ˈsɪnɪklɪ] *adv* cyniquement
cynicism [ˈsɪnɪsɪz(ə)m] *n* cynisme *m*
cypher [ˈsaɪfər] *n, vt* = **cipher**
cypress [ˈsaɪprəs] *n (tree)* cyprès *m*
Cypriot [ˈsɪprɪət] **1** *adj* chypriote **2** *n* Chypriote *mf*
Cyprus [ˈsaɪprəs] *n* Chypre *f*
Cyrillic [sɪˈrɪlɪk] **1** *adj* cyrillique **2** *n* **in C.** en caractères cyrilliques
cyst [sɪst] *n* **(a)** *Biol, Anat* sac *m* **(b)** *Med* kyste *m*
cystic fibrosis [ˈsɪstɪk] *n Med* mucoviscidose *f*
cystitis [sɪsˈtaɪtɪs] *n Med* cystite *f*; **to have c.** avoir une cystite
cytological [saɪtəˈlɒdʒɪk(ə)l] *adj Med* cytologique
cytology [saɪˈtɒlədʒɪ] *n Biol* cytologie *f*
czar [zɑːr] *n* = **tsar**
czarevitch [ˈzɑːrəvɪtʃ] *n* = **tsarevitch**
czarina [zɑːˈriːnə] *n* = **tsarina**
czarist [ˈzɑːrɪst] *adj, n* = **tsarist**
Czech [tʃek] **1** *adj* tchèque **2** *n* **(a)** Tchèque *mf* **(b)** *Ling* tchèque *m*
Czechoslovak [tʃekəʊˈsləʊvæk], **Czechoslovakian** [-ˈvækɪən] **1** *adj* tchécoslovaque **2** *n* Tchécoslovaque *mf*
Czechoslovakia [tʃekəʊsləˈvækɪə] *n* Tchécoslovaquie *f*
Czech Republic *n* République *f* tchèque

D

D, d [diː] *n* **(a)** (*letter*) D, d *m*; *Mil etc* **D day** le jour J; *Br Pol* **D notice** = avis *m* envoyé aux journaux par le gouvernement pour leur interdire de publier un article **(b)** *Mus* ré *m*
D *US Pol abbr* **Democrat**
d **(a)** (*abbr* **deceased**) m. **(b)** *Br Hist* (*abbr* **denarius**) pence
DA [diːˈeɪ] *n US Jur abbr* **district attorney**
dab[1] [dæb] *n* **(a)** (*touch*) petit coup *m*; **a d. with a cloth** un petit coup de chiffon **(b)** (*portion*) (*of ink, paint*) tache *f*; (*of butter*) petit morceau *m*; (*of colour*) touche *f*; (*of perfume*) goutte *f*; (*of glue*) point *m*; **a few dabs of mustard** un peu de moutarde; **just give it a d. of paint** mets-y un coup de peinture **(c)** *Br Old-fashioned F* **dabs** (*fingerprints*) empreintes *fpl* digitales
dab[2] *vt* (**-bb-**) (*touch*) donner un petit coup à; (*with pad etc*) tamponner; (*daub*) tapoter; **she dabbed the lump on her forehead with a wet facecloth** elle a tamponné la bosse qu'elle avait sur le front avec un linge humide; **to d. one's eyes (with a handkerchief)** se tamponner les yeux; **to d. paint on sth** donner un coup de peinture à qch
dab[3] *n* (*fish*) limande *f*
dab[4] *adj F* **to be a d. hand at (doing) sth** être doué pour (faire) qch
▶ **dab off** *vtsep* ôter en tamponnant
▶ **dab on** *vtsep* (*paint, antiseptic etc*) appliquer
dabble [ˈdæb(ə)l] **1** *vt* (*one's hands etc in water*) tremper; **she dabbled her feet in the brook** elle se trempa les pieds dans le ruisseau **2** *vi F* **to d. on the Stock Exchange** boursicoter; **to d. in politics** faire un peu de politique; **to d. in art/music** être un peu artiste/musicien; **to d. in black magic** toucher à la magie noire
dabbler [ˈdæblər] *n often Pej* (*amateur*) amateur *m*; **d. on the Stock Exchange** boursicoteur *m*
dace [deɪs] *n* (*fish*) vandoise *f*, dard *m*
dacha [ˈdætʃa] *n* dacha *f*
dachshund [ˈdækshʊnd] *n* (*dog*) teckel *m*
dactyl [ˈdæktɪl] *n Liter* dactyle *m*
dad [dæd] *n F* papa *m*
Dada [ˈdɑːdɑː] *n Art, Liter* dada *m*, dadaïsme *m*
Dadaism [ˈdɑːdɑːɪz(ə)m] *n Art, Liter* dadaïsme *m*
daddy [ˈdædɪ] *n F* papa *m*
daddy-longlegs [ˈdædɪˈlɒŋlegz] *n F* (*insect*) cousin *m*
dado [ˈdeɪdəʊ] *n Archit* **(a)** (*of pedestal*) dé *m* **(b)** (*of wall*) lambris *m* (d'appui)
daemon [ˈdiːmən] *n Arch, Lit* démon *m*
daff [dæf] *n Br F* = **daffodil 1**
daffodil [ˈdæfədɪl] **1** *n* (*flower*) jonquille *f* **2** *adj* **d. (yellow)** jonquille *inv*
daffy [ˈdæfɪ] *adj F* (*person*) timbré, toqué; (*idea, notion*) débile
daft [dɑːft] *adj Br F* (*person*) timbré, toqué; (*remark, idea, plan etc*) débile; **to act d.** faire l'idiot; **to go d.** devenir cinglé; (*become angry*) devenir fou de rage; **don't be d.!** ne sois pas bête!; **don't talk d.!** ne dis pas de bêtises!; **to be d. about sb/sth** être fou de qn/qch
daftie [ˈdɑːftɪ] *n Br F, Dial* toqué, -ée
daftness [ˈdɑːftnɪs] *n Br F* stupidité *f*
dagger [ˈdægər] *n* **(a)** poignard *m*, *Lit* dague *f*, *Fig* **to be at daggers drawn** être à couteaux tirés (**with** avec); **to look daggers at sb** foudroyer qn du regard **(b)** *Typ* croix *f*
dago [ˈdeɪgəʊ] *n Offensive Sl* métèque *m*
dahlia [ˈdeɪlɪə] *n* (*flower*) dahlia *m*
Dáil [dɑːl] *n* = Chambre *f* des députés de la République d'Irlande
daily [ˈdeɪlɪ] **1** *adj attrib* quotidien; **on a d. basis** (*paid, employed, calculated*) à la journée; (*used*) tous les jours, de façon quotidienne; *Admin* **d. allowance** indemnité *f* journalière; *Acct* **d. balance interest calculation** méthode *f* à échelles *ou* par échelles; **to earn one's d. bread** gagner son pain quotidien; *Rel* **give us this day our d. bread** donne-nous aujourd'hui notre pain de ce jour; *Gym F* **d. dozen** gymnastique *f* quotidienne; *F* **the d. grind** métro *m* boulot dodo; **I've had enough of the d. grind** j'en ai assez du métro boulot dodo; *Br* **d. help** *or* **woman** femme *f* de ménage; **d. paper** (journal *m*) quotidien *m*; **d. press** presse *f* quotidienne; **d. report** rapport *m* journalier; **d. takings** recette *f* journalière; *Fin* **d. trading report** rapport *m* de situation journalière; **d. visitors** visiteurs *mpl* journaliers
2 *adv* (*to phone, visit, happen*) tous les jours; **twice d.** deux fois par jour; **news of their defeat is awaited d.** on s'attend à apprendre leur défaite d'un jour à l'autre
3 *n* **(a)** *Journ* quotidien *m*
(b) *Br F* (*for housework*) femme *f* de ménage
(c) *TV, Cin* **dailies** rushes *mpl*
daintily [ˈdeɪntɪlɪ] *adv* délicatement
daintiness [ˈdeɪntɪnɪs] *n* (*of movement, way of working etc*) délicatesse *f*; (*of taste*) raffinement *m*
dainty [ˈdeɪntɪ] *adj* **(a)** (*dish, food*) fin; (*morsel*) de choix **(b)** (*person*) (*in manners*) délicat; (*in build*) menu; **short d. steps** petits pas délicats **(c)** (*choosy*) délicat, difficile; **these animals are d. feeders** ces animaux sont délicats sur la nourriture **(d)** (*delicate*) (*porcelain, ornament*) fin, délicat
dairy [ˈdeərɪ] *n* **(a)** (*on farm*) laiterie *f*; **d. butter** beurre *m* laitier; **d. cow** vache *f* laitière; **d. farm** ferme *f* laitière; **d. farming** élevage *m* de vaches laitières; **d. herd** (troupeau *m* de) vaches laitières; **d. ice cream** glace *f* à la crème; **d. produce** produits *mpl* laitiers **(b)** (*shop*) crémerie *f*
dairymaid [ˈdeərɪmeɪd] *n* fille *f* de laiterie
dairyman, *pl* **-men** [ˈdeərɪmən] *n* **(a)** (*on farm*) employé *m* de laiterie **(b)** (*who sells dairy products*) laitier *m*
dais [ˈdeɪɪs] *n* estrade *f*
daisy [ˈdeɪzɪ] *n* (*flower*) pâquerette *f*; (*bigger*) marguerite *f*; **as fresh as a d.** frais/*f* fraîche comme une rose; *Sl* **he's pushing up the daisies** il mange les pissenlits par les racines; **d. chain** guirlande *f* de pâquerettes; *Comptr* **d. chaining** connexion *f* en boucle
daisy-chain *vt Comptr* connecter en boucle
daisy wheel *n* (*on printer*) marguerite *f*; **d. printer** imprimante *f* à marguerite
Dak *abbr* **Dakota**
Dalai Lama [ˈdælaɪˈlɑːmə] *n* Dalaï-lama *m*
dale [deɪl] *n* vallée *f*; (*smaller*) vallon *m*
dalliance [ˈdælɪəns] *n Lit* badinage *m*
dally [ˈdælɪ] *vi* **(a)** *Old-fashioned* (*trifle*) folâtrer (**with sb** avec qn); **to d. with an idea** caresser une idée **(b)** (*dawdle*) lambiner, traînasser; **to d. over sth** s'attarder à qch
Dalmatian [dælˈmeɪʃən] *adj, n* **D. (dog)** dalmatien *m*
dam[1] [dæm] *n HydE* (*of reservoir*) barrage *m*; (*of canal*) digue *f*; **storage d.** barrage-réservoir *m*
dam[2] *vt* (**-mm-**) **to d. (up)** (*valley*) construire un barrage en aval de; (*river, lake*) endiguer; (*gutter*) obstruer; *Fig* (*one's feelings etc*) contenir
dam[3] *n Agr, Lit* mère *f*
damage[1] [ˈdæmɪdʒ] *n* **(a)** (*physical*) dégâts *mpl*; (*to engine, ship etc*) avarie(s) *f(pl)*; **to pay for the d.** payer les dégâts; **smoking can cause serious d. to your health** le tabac nuit gravement à la santé; *Br F* **what's the d.?** (*how much do I owe?*) ça fait combien?; **there's no great d. done** il n'y a pas trop de mal; **d. to property** dommage *m* matériel; **d. report** déclaration *f* de sinistre, constat *m* de dommages
(b) (*harm*) préjudice *m*; **to cause sb d.** porter préjudice à qn; **the d. is done** le mal est fait; **to do d. to a cause** faire du tort à une cause; **d. control** *or* **limitation** fait *m* de limiter les dégâts; **we have to do some d. limitation** il faut limiter les dégâts; **d. suffered** préjudice *m* subi
(c) *Jur* **damages** dommages-intérêts *mpl*, intérêts *mpl* compensatoires; **to be liable for damages** être tenu au versement de dommages-intérêts; **to be awarded damages of £5,000** *or* **£5,000 in damages** obtenir 5000 livres de dommages-intérêts
damage[2] *vt* **(a)** (*physically*) (*engine, machine*) endommager; (*goods*) avarier; (*furniture*) endommager, abîmer; **the storm damaged a lot of trees** de nombreux arbres ont été endommagés par la tempête; *Com* **damaged in transit** abîmé en cours de route; **damaged goods** marchandises *fpl* avariées **(b)** (*harm*) (*chances*) compromettre; (*person*) faire du tort à; (*sb's interests*) léser; (*sb's reputation*) porter atteinte à, ternir

damaging ['dæmɪdʒɪŋ] *adj* (*revelation, scandal, remark etc*) préjudiciable; **it's a d. blow to his re-election prospects/career** cela compromet sérieusement ses chances d'être réélu/sa carrière

Damascus [də'mɑːskəs] *n* Damas *m*; *Fig* **a conversion on the road to D.** une conversion subite

damask ['dæməsk] *n* (**a**) *Tex* damas *m*; **d. silk** soie *f* damassée (**b**) *Metal* **d. steel** acier *m* damassé (**c**) **d. rose** rose *f* de Damas (**d**) **d. (colour)** rose foncé *m inv*

dame [deɪm] *n* (**a**) *Am F* (*woman*) femme *f*; *Br* (*in pantomime*) vieille femme comique (*dont le rôle est joué par un homme*) (**b**) *Br* (*title*) = titre *m* honorifique donné à certaines femmes en signe de distinction

dammit ['dæmɪt] *int F* nom de Dieu; **it was as near as d.** il était moins une

damn[1] [dæm] *n F* **I don't give** *or* **care a d.** je m'en fiche éperdument, je n'en ai rien à fiche; **he doesn't give a d. about anything** il se fiche de tout; **it's not worth a d.** ça ne vaut rien

damn[2] *vt* (**a**) (*book, play etc*) (*criticize severely*) éreinter; (*condemn*) condamner; **to d. sb/sth with faint praise** faire de tièdes éloges de qn/qch, louer qn/qch avec si peu d'ardeur que cela revient à condamner; **you're damned if you do and damned if you don't** quoique tu fasses tu es perdant (**b**) *Rel* damner; *F* **well I'll be damned!** ça alors!; **I'm** *or* **I'll be damned if I'll do it** si tu crois que je vais le faire!; **d. the expense/the consequences** au diable l'avarice/tant pis pour les conséquences; **d. (it)!** zut!; **d. you!** va te faire fiche!; **d. and blast (it)!** sacré nom d'un chien!

damn[3] *F* **1** *adj* = **damned 1(b) 2** *adv* (**a**) **he's doing d. all** il n'en fout pas une (rame); **she knows d. all about it** elle y connaît que dal(l)e; **there's d. all in the fridge** il y a que dal(l)e dans le frigo; **it's got d. all to do with you** ça n'a absolument rien à voir avec toi; **what can you see? – d. all!** tu vois quelque chose? – que dalle! (**b**) = **damned 3**

damnable ['dæmnəb(ə)l] *adj* (**a**) *Rel* damnable (**b**) *F* (*detestable*) maudit

damnably ['dæmnəblɪ] *adv Old-fashioned F* (*difficult, expensive, rude etc*) diablement, rudement

damnation [dæm'neɪʃən] **1** *n Rel* damnation *f*; **eternal d.** la peine du dam **2** *int F* **d.!** enfer et damnation!

damned [dæmd] **1** *adj* (**a**) *Rel* damné
(**b**) *F* (*intensifier*) **you d. fool!** espèce d'idiot!; **you have to be a d. fool to do that!** il faut être un sacré abruti pour faire ça!; **he's a d. nuisance!** ce qu'il peut être casse-pieds!; **well I'm d.!** elle est bien bonne celle-là!; **it's one d. thing after another** tout va de travers
2 *npl Rel* **the d.** les damnés *mpl*; **to suffer the tortures of the d.** souffrir comme un damné
3 *adv F* rudement, vachement; **it's d. hot** il fait rudement chaud; **I should d. well hope so** ah, ben j'espère bien!; **you can do what you d. well like!** fais ce que tu veux, je m'en fiche!; **you know d. well what I mean** tu sais très bien ce que je veux dire; **they're d. good players** ils jouent vachement bien

damnedest ['dæmdest] *n F* **if that isn't the d. thing!** c'est vraiment bizarre!, c'est incroyable!; **to do one's d.** faire tout son possible

damnfool ['dæm'fuːl] *adj attrib F* idiot

damning ['dæmɪŋ] *adj* (*fact, evidence etc*) accablant; (*admission*) préjudiciable; **he was pretty d. about the film** il a été très critique vis-à-vis du film

Damocles ['dæməkliːz] *n* **the sword of D.** l'épée *f* de Damoclès

damp[1] [dæmp] **1** *n* (*of air*) humidité *f*; (*of skin*) moiteur *f*; **d. mark** tache *f* d'humidité **2** *adj* (*cloth, house, heat etc*) humide; (*skin*) moite; **his hands are always d.** il a toujours les mains moites; *Fig* **to be a d. squib** faire l'effet d'un pétard mouillé

damp[2] *vt* (*diminish*) (*fire, sound*) étouffer; (*shocks*) amortir; **to d. down a furnace** boucher un haut fourneau

dampcourse ['dæmpkɔːs] *n Constr* isolant *m* contre l'humidité

dampen ['dæmp(ə)n] *vt* (**a**) (*wet*) (*cloth*) humecter (**b**) (*diminish*) (*enthusiasm*) refroidir; **to d. sb's spirits** décourager qn; **that dampened his ardour** cela a freiné son ardeur

damper ['dæmpər] *n* (**a**) (*on enthusiasm etc*) douche *f* froide; **to act as a d. on sb's spirits** saper le moral de qn; **the news put rather a d. on the celebrations/the company** la nouvelle a jeté un froid sur les réjouissances/la compagnie (**b**) *Mus* (*of piano, sound*) étouffoir *m*; **d. pedal** pédale *f* forte (**c**) *Tech* (*of hearth, chimney, furnace*) registre *m*; (*of stove pipe*) soupape *f* de réglage *ou* à papillon; *Aut* amortisseur *m*, damper *m*; *El* amortisseur *m*; *Rad* sourdine *f*

damping ['dæmpɪŋ] *n Aut* amortissement *m*; **d. slipper** patin *m* amortisseur

dampish ['dæmpɪʃ] *adj* un peu humide

dampness ['dæmpnɪs] *n* humidité *f*; (*of skin*) moiteur *f*

damp-proof *adj* hydrofuge; **d. course** isolant *m* contre l'humidité

damp-proofing *n* isolation *f* contre l'humidité

damsel ['dæmz(ə)l] *n* (**a**) *Arch, Lit* demoiselle *f*; *Hum* **a d. in distress** une belle éplorée; **to do the d. in distress act** jouer les belles éplorées (**b**) (*insect*) **d. fly** demoiselle *f*

damson ['dæmz(ə)n] *n* prune *f* de Damas; **d. tree** prunier *m* de Damas

dance[1] [dɑːns] *n* (**a**) (*art form, steps*) danse *f*; *Mus* (air *m* de) danse; **will you have a d. with me?** voulez-vous danser?; *Fig F* **to lead sb a (merry) d.** donner du fil à retordre à qn; **d. band** orchestre *m* de musique de danse; **d. floor** piste *f* de danse; **d. hall** salle *f* de danse; **d. music** (*generally*) musique *f* pour danser; (*in nightclubs etc*) dance (music) *f* (**b**) (*ball*) (*for teenagers*) soirée *f*; (*for older people*) soirée dansante; (*formal*) bal *m*, *pl* bals; **her parents are giving a d. for her birthday** ses parents organisent un bal pour son anniversaire

dance[2] **1** *vi* danser; **are you dancing?** vous dansez?; **to d. with sb** danser avec qn; **to d. for joy** danser de joie; **to d. about** gambader; **they danced down the road with glee** ils descendaient la rue en dansant de joie **2** *vt* (*waltz etc*) danser; **he danced the last dance with Claudia** il a fait la dernière danse avec Claudia; *esp Lit* **to d. attendance on sb** faire l'empressé auprès de qn

dancer ['dɑːnsər] *n* danseur, -euse

dancing ['dɑːnsɪŋ] **1** *adj attrib* (*bear*) dansant; *Fig* **her d. eyes** son regard vif; **d. dervish** derviche *m* tourneur **2** *n* danse *f*; **to go d.** aller danser; **d. girl** danseuse *f* (de revue); **d. partner** partenaire *mf*; **d. school** école *f* de danse; **d. shoes** chaussures *fpl* de danse

dandelion ['dændɪlaɪən] *n* (*weed*) pissenlit *m*; **d. clock** fleur *f* de pissenlit fanée

dander ['dændər] *n F* **to get sb's/one's d. up** mettre qn/se mettre en colère

dandified ['dændɪfaɪd] *adj Pej* (*dress, manner etc*) de dandy; **he had become rather d. in his dress** il s'habillait de plus en plus comme un dandy

dandle ['dænd(ə)l] *vt* (*child*) (*on knees*) faire sauter; (*in arms*) bercer

dandruff ['dændrəf] *n* (*of scalp*) pellicules *fpl*; **he has very bad d.** il a beaucoup de pellicules; **d. shampoo** shampooing *m* contre les pellicules *ou* anti-pelliculaire

dandy ['dændɪ] **1** *n Old-fashioned usu Pej* dandy *m*, élégant *m* **2** *adj Am F* épatant, chouette; **everything's just (fine and) d.** tout marche à merveille; **that's all fine and d., but …** c'est très joli tout ça, mais …

Dane [deɪn] *n* [①**A20**,d] Danois, -oise

dang [dæŋ] *int, adj, adv Old-fashioned Euph* = **damn**

danger ['deɪndʒər] *n* danger *m*; **out of d.** hors de danger; **to keep out of d.** rester à l'abri du danger; **d. keep out** (*on sign*) danger; **to be in d. of doing sth** risquer de faire qch, courir le risque *ou* être en danger de faire qch; **in d. of (losing) his life** en danger de mort; **to put sb/sth in d.** mettre qn/qch en danger; **there is some d. that …** il y a un risque que … + *sub*; **there is some d. that the engine will explode** *or* **of the engine exploding** le moteur risque d'exploser; **there is no d. that …** il n'y a pas de danger que … + *sub*; **there's no danger that he'll forget** *or* **of his forgetting** il ne risque pas d'oublier, il n'y a pas de danger qu'il oublie; **he's a d. to society** c'est un danger public; *Med* **to be on the d. list** être dans un état critique; *Med* **to be off the d. list** être hors de danger; *Ind etc* **d. money** prime *f* de risque; *Fig* **d. sign** signal *m* d'alarme; *Rail etc* **d. signal** signal d'arrêt

dangerous ['deɪndʒərəs] *adj* (**a**) dangereux; (*illness*) grave; **you are (treading) on d. ground** vous vous engagez sur un terrain dangereux; **d. driving** conduite *f* dangereuse; **d. goods** marchandises *fpl* dangereuses (**b**) (*example, maxim*) pernicieux

dangerously ['deɪndʒərəslɪ] *adv* dangereusement; **d. ill** gravement malade; **he came d. close to accusing me of lying** il m'a presque traité de menteur; **he came d. close to falling** il a failli tomber; **his energy was at a d. low ebb** ses forces avaient dangereusement diminué

dangle ['dæŋg(ə)l] **1** *vi* pendiller; **with one's legs dangling** les jambes ballantes; **you can't keep him dangling like that** (*in state of uncertainty*) il ne faut pas le laisser dans l'incertitude **2** *vt* (*object*) balancer; **to d. one's fingers/feet in the water** tremper les doigts/pieds dans l'eau; *Fig* **to d. sth in front of sb** faire miroiter qch à qn

Danish ['deɪnɪʃ] **1** *adj* [①A20,d] danois; (*ambassador*) du Danemark; **D. blue (cheese)** bleu *m* du Danemark; **D. (pastry)** = sorte de chausson fourré aux fruits **2** *n Ling* danois *m*

dank [dæŋk] *adj* (*weather, dungeon*) humide (et froid)

Dantean ['dæntɪən, dæn'ti:ən], **Dantesque** [dæn'tesk] *adj* dantesque

Danube (the) [ðə'dænju:b] *n* le Danube

dapper ['dæpər] *adj* (*man, suit*) coquet; (*beard*) soigné

dapple¹ ['dæp(ə)l] *n* (**a**) (*on horse's coat*) tache *f* de couleur (**b**) (*horse*) pommelé *m*

dapple² *vt* tacheter; **a wall dappled with sunlight** un mur tacheté de lumière

dapple-grey *n* (*horse*) gris *m* pommelé

Darby and Joan ['dɑ:bɪ] *n* = Philémon et Baucis; **D. club** club *m* du troisième âge

dare¹ ['deər] [①A59,19; A40,C,1,a; B33,2,b,i] **1** *modal aux* (*third sg pr* **dare**; *pt* **dared**; *no pp*; **d. not** *often contracted to* **daren't**) oser; **I d. not** *or* **daren't speak to him** je n'ose pas lui parler; **don't you d. touch him!** ne touche pas un cheveu de sa tête!; **don't you d. (do that)!** ne t'avise pas de faire ça!; **how d. you!** comment oses-tu!, quelle audace!; **I d. say that ...** je suppose que ...; **I d. say** sans doute, c'est bien possible; **your opponent, d. I say it, has never been beaten** votre adversaire, si je puis me permettre de vous le faire remarquer, n'a jamais été battu

2 *vt* (*third sg pr* **dares**; *pt, pp* **dared**) (**a**) oser; **to d. to do sth** oser faire qch; **to d. to be different** avoir le courage d'être différent, oser être différent; **let him do it if he dare(s)!** qu'il le fasse s'il l'ose!

(**b**) (*challenge*) **to d. sb to do sth** défier qn de faire qch; **I d. you!** fais-le si tu oses!, chiche!

(**c**) *Fml* (*danger, death etc*) braver

dare² *n* défi *m*; **to do sth for** *or* **as a d.** faire qch pour relever un défi

daredevil ['deədev(ə)l] **1** *n* casse-cou *m inv* **2** *adj* (*pilot, driver*) casse-cou *inv*; (*escape, exploits*) audacieux

daring ['deərɪŋ] **1** *adj* (*person*) audacieux, hardi; (*attempt, attack, escape etc*) audacieux; (*dress, film, writer*) provocant **2** *n* audace *f*

daringly ['deərɪŋlɪ] *adv* de manière audacieuse; **a d. low dress** une robe au décolleté audacieux; **to be d. different** (*of person*) avoir le courage d'être différent, oser être différent; **this is a d. different film** avec ce film, le metteur en scène ose être différent

dark¹ [dɑ:k] *adj* (**a**) (*without light*) sombre, obscur; **it's d.** (*outside*) il fait nuit, il fait noir; (*inside*) il fait sombre; **it's getting** *or* **growing d.** il commence à faire sombre *ou* à faire nuit; **everything suddenly went d.** soudain ce fut le noir complet; **d. glasses** lunettes *fpl* noires *ou* de soleil; **the d. side of the moon** la face cachée de la lune

(**b**) (*colour*) foncé, sombre; **d. blue dresses** robes *fpl* bleu foncé

(**c**) (*eyes*) foncé; **to be d.** (*of white person*) être mat (de peau); (*of black person*) être très noir, avoir la peau très foncée; **she has d. hair** elle est brune

(**d**) (*unhappy*) (*thought etc*) triste; (*future, days*) sombre; (*angry*) (*look*) sombre, noir; **to look on the d. side of things** voir tout en noir; **to mutter d. threats** marmonner des menaces; **to harbour d. designs** nourrir de noirs desseins; **d. powers** puissances occultes

(**e**) (*secret*) mystérieux, secret, -ète; **to keep sth d.** tenir qch secret; *Fig* **a d. horse** (*unknown competitor*) un concurrent inconnu; (*unexpected competitor*) un concurrent que l'on ne croyait pas dangereux; **he's a d. horse** (*a stranger*) on ne sait rien de lui; (*gave nothing away*) il a bien caché son jeu

(**f**) *Hist* **the D. Ages** le haut moyen âge; *Fig* **we're still in the D. Ages** nous en sommes encore au moyen âge; *Hist* **the D. Continent** le Continent noir, l'Afrique *f*; *Hum* **they live in darkest Somerset** ils habitent au fin fond du Somerset

dark² *n* ténèbres *fpl*, obscurité *f*; **the child is afraid of the d.** l'enfant a peur du noir; **after d.** à la tombée de la nuit; **until d.** jusqu'à ce qu'il fasse nuit; **in the d.** dans le noir; *Fig* **to be (kept) in the d.** être (laissé) dans l'ignorance; **we kept her in the d. about it** on ne lui en a rien dit

darken ['dɑ:k(ə)n] **1** *vt* (*room, sky, Fig future etc*) assombrir; (*colour*) foncer; *Fig Lit* **her life had been darkened by her son's death** la mort de son fils l'avait plongée dans la nuit; *Old-fashioned, Hum* **never d. my door again!** ne remettez plus les pieds chez moi! **2** *vi* (*of sky, thoughts*) s'assombrir; (*of colour*) se foncer, s'assombrir; (*of skin*) brunir; **his face** *or* **brow darkened** il *ou* son visage s'assombrit

darkening ['dɑ:k(ə)nɪŋ] **1** *adj* (*sky, Fig face*) qui s'assombrit; **he looked up at the d. sky** il regarda le ciel qui s'assombrissait **2** *n* (*of sky, painting*) assombrissement *m*

dark-eyed *adj* aux yeux foncés

dark-haired *adj* aux cheveux foncés

darkie ['dɑ:kɪ] *n Old-fashioned Offensive Sl* moricaud, -aude

darkish ['dɑ:kɪʃ] *adj* un peu sombre

darkly ['dɑ:klɪ] *adv* (**a**) (*dimly, not clearly*) obscurément; **the house loomed d. in the fog** la maison se dessinait, sombre dans le brouillard (**b**) (*to look at sb, to say*) d'un air sombre; **she contemplated the future d.** elle avait une sombre vision de l'avenir

darkness ['dɑ:knɪs] *n* (**a**) obscurité *f*; **d. had fallen** il faisait sombre; **the room was in complete d.** il faisait tout à fait noir dans la pièce; **the house/village was in d.** (*no lights were on*) la maison/le village était dans l'obscurité (**b**) (*of colour*) teinte *f* foncée; (*of skin*) (*caused by weather*) hâle *m*; (*of white person*) teint *m* mat; (*of black person*) peau *f* très noire (**c**) *Arch* (*ignorance*) ignorance *f*

darkroom ['dɑ:kru:m] *n Phot* chambre *f* noire

dark-skinned *adj* à la peau mate

darky ['dɑ:kɪ] *n* = **darkie**

darling ['dɑ:lɪŋ] *n* chéri, -ie; **(my) d.!** (*to male*) mon chéri!, mon chou!; (*to female*) ma chérie!, mon chou!; **she's a little d.** c'est un petit amour; **be a d. and get it for me** tu serais un amour si tu allais me le chercher; **a d. little place** un petit endroit charmant; **he's his mother's d.** c'est le chouchou de sa maman; **the d. of the people** l'idole *f* du peuple; **to be the d. of the court/media/public** être la coqueluche de la cour/des média/du public

darn¹ [dɑ:n] *n* (*in stocking etc*) reprise *f*

darn² *vt* (*stocking etc*) repriser

darn³ *vti F* **d. (it)!** zut!; **d. this car!** satanée voiture!; **d. him!** qu'il aille au diable!; **d. your father and his ideas!** ah ton père et ses satanées idées!

darn⁴, darned [dɑ:nd] *adj F* sacré; **it's a d. nuisance** c'est vachement embêtant

darning ['dɑ:nɪŋ] *n* reprise *f*; **d. egg/wool/needle** œuf *m* /laine *f* /aiguille *f* à repriser

dart¹ [dɑ:t] *n* (**a**) (*weapon*) flèche *f* courte; **paper d.** avion *m* en papier (**b**) [①A10,d] (*in games*) fléchette *f*; **darts** (*game*) fléchettes; **do you want a game of darts?** tu veux faire une partie de fléchettes? (**c**) *Sewing* pince *f* (**d**) (*movement*) mouvement *m* soudain; **to make a sudden d.** foncer, se précipiter (**for, towards** sur, vers)

dart² **1** *vt* (*look*) lancer; (*tongue*) darder **2** *vi* se précipiter, foncer (**at sb/sth** sur qn/qch); **to d. in/out** entrer/sortir comme une flèche; **he darted across the road** il a traversé la rue comme une flèche; **her eyes darted from one face in the crowd to another** son regard passait rapidement d'un visage à l'autre dans la foule

dartboard ['dɑ:tbɔ:d] *n* cible *f* (*de jeu de fléchettes*)

dash¹ [dæʃ] *n* (**a**) (*drop*) goutte *f*; (*of cognac etc*) larme *f*; (*of lemon juice, vinegar*) filet *m*, goutte; **add a d. of lemon** ajoutez-y un filet de citron; **d. of colour** (*in painting*) touche *f* de couleur; *Fig* **a d. of humour/cynicism** un rien d'humour/de cynisme

(**b**) (*of pen, in Morse alphabet*) trait *m*; *Typ* tiret *m*

(**c**) (*run*) course *f* à toute vitesse; *US Sp* sprint *m*; **to make a d. forward** s'élancer en avant; **a quick d. across to Paris** un petit saut à Paris; **to make a d. at sth** se précipiter sur qch; **to make a d. at sb** foncer sur qn; **to make a d. for it** saisir l'occasion de s'enfuir

(**d**) (*style*) élan *m*, entrain *m*; *Old-fashioned* **to cut a d.** faire de l'épate

(**e**) *Aut F* (*dashboard*) tableau *m* de bord

dash² **1** *vt* (**a**) (*throw*) heurter violemment; **to d. sth to the ground** jeter qch par terre; **the ship was dashed against a rock** le navire a été jeté sur un écueil; **to d. sth to pieces** fracasser qch

(**b**) *Fig* (*destroy*) (*sb's hopes*) détruire; (*enthusiasm*) refroidir; **to d. sb's spirits** abattre le courage de qn; **he saw his hopes dashed** il a vu tomber à l'eau ses espérances

(**c**) (*rush*) **to d. sb to hospital** emmener qn à l'hôpital en urgence

(**d**) *F* **d. (it)!** zut!

2 *vi* **to come dashing in** entrer comme un bolide, entrer en trombe; **to d. up to sb** se précipiter vers qn; **to d. up/down the stairs** monter/descendre l'escalier quatre à quatre; **to d. into the room** entrer précipitamment *ou* en coup de vent dans la salle; **I'm just going to d. home and ...** je vais faire un saut chez moi et ...; **to d. across the road** traverser la route en courant; **I've been dashing around like a mad thing all day** j'ai couru toute la journée; *F* **I must d.** il faut que je file

▶ **dash away** *vi* partir comme une flèche, filer à toute vitesse

▶ **dash off** **1** *vi* (*leave quickly*) partir comme une flèche, filer à toute vitesse **2** *vtsep* (*make or do quickly*) faire en vitesse; (*letter*) écrire en vitesse

▸ **dash out** *vi* sortir à toute vitesse; **she dashed out into the road** elle s'est précipitée sur la route; **I forgot my briefcase when I dashed out of the house** je suis sorti de chez moi à toute vitesse et j'ai oublié ma mallette; **I'll d. out to the garden/the shop for some parsley** je vais faire un saut au jardin/au magasin chercher du persil

dashboard ['dæʃbɔːd] *n Aut* tableau *m* de bord

dashed [dæʃt] *Old-fashioned Br F* **1** *adj* sacré; **what a d. nuisance!** quel empoisonnement! **2** *adv* vachement; **it's d. hot** il fait vachement chaud

dashing ['dæʃɪŋ] *adj* (*person*) fringant; (*coat, jacket etc*) élégant; **to cut a d. figure** avoir fière allure; **a d. young man** un beau jeune homme

dashingly ['dæʃɪŋlɪ] *adv* avec élégance; **d. handsome** d'une beauté sublime

dashpot ['dæʃpɒt] *n Aut* dash-pot *m*

dastardly ['dæstədlɪ] *adj Old-fashioned, Lit* **(a)** (*person*) lâche **(b)** (*crime, plan, intentions*) infâme, ignoble

DAT [diːeɪ'tiː] *n* (*abbr* **digital audio tape**) cassette *f* numérique; **DAT recorder** magnétophone *m* numérique

data ['deɪtə, 'dɑːtə] *n* [①A9,b,i] informations *fpl*; *Comptr* données *fpl*; **an item of d.** une information; **what little d. we do have suggests that …** le peu d'informations que nous avons semble montrer que …; **d. analysis** analyse *f* de données; **d. block** bloc *m* de données; **d. buffer** mémoire *f* tampon; **d. bus** bus *m* de données; **d. capture** saisie *f* de données; **d. carrier** support *m* de données; **d. collection** recueil *m ou* collecte *f* de données; **d. communications** communication *f ou* transmission *f* de données, télématique *f*; **d. compression** compression *f* de données; **d. conversion** conversion *f* de données; **d. decryption** déchiffrement *m* de données; **d. encryption** chiffrement *m* de données; **d. entry** entrée *f* de données; **d. entry form** fiche *f* d'imputation; **d. flow** flux *m* de données; **d. format** format *m* des données; **d. gathering** collecte *f* de données; **d. integrity** intégrité *f* des données; **d. loss** perte *f* de données; **d. management** gestion *f* de données; **d. manipulation** manipulation *f* de données; **d. memory** mémoire *f* (pour les données); **d. path** chemin *m* d'accès aux données; **d. pattern** modèle *m* de données; **d. pen** crayon *m* électronique; **d. privacy** confidentialité *f* des données *ou* de l'information; **d. processor** machine *f* de traitement de l'information, processeur *m* de données; **d. reader** lecteur *m* de données; **d. reading system** système *m* de lecture de données; **d. security** sécurité *f* des données; **d. storage** stockage *m* de données; **d. stream** flot *m* de données; **d. switch** commutateur *m* de données; **d. systems technology** technologie *f* informatique; **d. terminal** terminal *m* de traitement de données; **d. transfer** transfert *m ou* transmission *f* de données; **d. transfer protocol** protocole *m* de transfert de données; **d. transfer rate** taux *m* de transfert de données; **d. type** type *m* de données

data bank *n* banque *f* de données

database[1] ['deɪtəbeɪs] *n* base *f* de données; **to have/put sth in a d.** avoir/mettre qch dans une base de données; **d. file** fichier *m* de base de données; **d. management** gestion *f* de base(s) de données

database[2] *vt* intégrer dans une base de données

datacomms ['deɪtəkɒms, 'dɑːtəkɒms] *n Comptr* communication *f ou* transmission *f* de données, télématique *f*; **d. linkup** liaison *f* télématique; **d. network** réseau *m* de communication de données; **d. software** logiciel *m* de communication

data processing *n Comptr* (*science*) informatique *f*; (*handling*) traitement *m* de l'information

data protection act *n* ≈ loi *f* informatique et libertés

dataset ['deɪtəset, 'dɑːtəset] *n Comptr* ensemble *m* de données

date[1] [deɪt] *n* (*fruit*) datte *f*; **d. palm** dattier *m*

date[2] *n* **(a)** [①A75,B; B58,B] date *f*; (*on coins, books etc*) millésime *m*; **d. of birth** date de naissance; **d. of departure** date de départ; **d. of dispatch** date d'envoi *ou* d'expédition; **d. of issue** date d'émission; **what's the d. (today)?** le combien sommes-nous aujourd'hui?; **to fix a d. for sth** prendre date *ou* fixer une date pour qch; **shall we fix a d. now?** est-ce que nous prenons date *ou* fixons une date maintenant?; **have you set a d. yet?** (*for wedding*) est-ce que vous avez déjà décidé de la date du mariage?; **I'm not free on that d.** je ne suis pas libre à cette date; **(on) what dates are you free?** à quelles dates êtes-vous libre?; **to be up to d.** (*with work, reading*) être à jour (**with** dans); (*with what's happening*) être au courant (**with** de); (*in fashion*) être à la page; **to bring one's diary up to d.** mettre à jour son journal; **my assistant will bring you up to d.** mon assistant vous mettra au courant; **to d.** à ce jour

(b) *Com, Fin* terme *m*, échéance *f*; **d. of maturity, due d.** (date *f* d')échéance

(c) *F* (*appointment*) rendez-vous *m inv*; (*boyfriend, girlfriend*) ami, -ie; **to make a d.** fixer un rendez-vous; **I have a d. tonight** j'ai un rendez-vous ce soir; (*with boyfriend etc*) je sors avec quelqu'un ce soir; *Am* **I don't have a d. for the prom** je n'ai pas de cavalier/de cavalière pour le bal de fin d'année; **where's your d.?** où est la personne qui t'accompagne?; **my d. didn't show up** on m'a posé un lapin

date[3] **1** *vt* **(a)** (*letter, work of art etc*) dater; (*bottle of wine etc*) millésimer; (*with machine*) (*ticket*) composter; **the letter is dated the 12th** la lettre est datée du 12; **your letter dated …** votre lettre en date du …; **to d. back** antidater; **his clothes d. him** ses vêtements démodés montrent qu'il n'est pas jeune; **that dates you** (*shows how old you are*) ça montre ton âge

(b) *esp Am F* (*sb*) sortir avec, fréquenter; **they're dating each other** ils sortent ensemble

2 *vi* **(a)** (*originate*) dater (**from** de), remonter (**from** à); **church dating from** *or* **back to the 13th century** église qui remonte au *ou* qui date du XIIIe siècle; **friendship dating back to the days of their youth** amitié qui remonte à leur jeunesse

(b) (*go out of fashion*) se démoder; **his style is beginning to d.** son style commence à dater

(c) *F* (*of couple*) sortir ensemble, se fréquenter

dated ['deɪtɪd] *adj* **(a)** démodé; **his style is rather d.** son style commence à dater **(b)** *Fin* **long-/short-d.** à longue/courte échéance

dateless ['deɪtlɪs] *adj* **(a)** (*timeless*) (*dress, style etc*) intemporel **(b)** (*not dated*) (*document, letter*) non daté

dateline ['deɪtlaɪn] *n Journ* (*of report etc*) date *f* et lieu de rédaction

date line *n Geog* **(international) d.** ligne *f* de changement de date (*le méridien 180°*); **to cross the (international) d.** passer la ligne de changement de date

date rape *n* viol *m* commis par l'homme avec lequel une femme vient de sortir

date stamp *n* timbre *m* à date, tampon *m ou* timbre dateur

date-stamp *vt* composter

date-stamping *n* compostage *m*

dating[1] ['deɪtɪŋ] *n* **(a)** (*of document etc*) datation *f*, datage *m*; (*of ticket*) (*with machine*) compostage *m* **(b)** *Archeol etc* datation *f*

dating[2] *n* **d. agency** agence *f* matrimoniale

dative ['deɪtɪv] *adj, n Gram* **d. (case)** datif *m*; **in the d.** au datif

datum ['deɪtəm] *n* [①A9,b,i] (*pl* **data**) *Fml* donnée *f*; **d. point** (*in robotics*) point *m* de référence

daub[1] [dɔːb] *n* **(a)** *Pej* (*picture*) croûte *f*, barbouillage *m* **(b)** *Constr* torchis *m*

daub[2] *vt* **(a)** *Art, Pej* (*painting, canvas*) barbouiller **(b)** (*smear*) barbouiller (**with** de)

daughter ['dɔːtər] *n* fille *f*

daughterboard ['dɔːtəbɔːd] *n Comptr* carte *f* fille

daughter-in-law *n* belle-fille *f*, *pl* belles-filles, bru *f*

daunt [dɔːnt] *vt* (*sb*) intimider; *Fml, Hum* **nothing daunted** intrépide(ment)

daunting [dɔːntɪŋ] *adj* (*task etc*) impressionnant, intimidant

dauntless ['dɔːntlɪs] *adj* intrépide

dauntlessly ['dɔːntlɪslɪ] *adv* intrépidement

davenport ['dævənpɔːt] *n Am* canapé(-lit) *m*

davit ['dævɪt] *n Naut* bossoir *m* d'embarcation

Davy ['deɪvɪ] *n Naut F* **to go to D. Jones's locker** (*drown*) boire à la grande tasse; **he's in D. Jones's locker** il a bu à la grande tasse

dawdle ['dɔːd(ə)l] *vi* traînasser, lambiner

▸ **dawdle away** *vtsep* **to d. the time away** passer le temps; (*waste*) perdre son temps

dawdler ['dɔːdlər] *n* traînard, -arde, lambin, -ine

dawdling ['dɔːdlɪŋ] **1** *n* lambineries *fpl*, traînasseries *fpl* **2** *adj* traînard

dawn[1] [dɔːn] *n* aube *f*, aurore *f*; *Fig* (*of life, civilization, new age*) aube; **at d.** à l'aube; **at the crack of d.** à la pointe du jour; **from d. to dusk** du lever au coucher du soleil; **until d.** jusqu'à l'aube, jusqu'au petit jour; **the d. chorus** le chant des oiseaux à l'aube; *St Exch* **d. raider** raider *m*

dawn[2] *vi* (*of day, morning*) se lever; *Fig* (commencer à) paraître; **day is dawning** le jour point *ou* se lève; *Fig* **when the truth dawned on him** quand il a compris la vérité; *Fig* **it dawned on me that …** j'ai commencé à me rendre compte que …; **another thought dawned on him** une autre pensée lui est venue à l'esprit

dawning ['dɔːnɪŋ] **1** *adj* (*day*) naissant **2** *n* aube *f*

day [deɪ] *n* **(a)** [①A75,B,1,b; B58,B,1,b] (*calendar unit*) jour *m*; **d. of the month** quantième *m* du mois; **what d. (of the week) is it (today)?** quel jour (de la semaine) sommes-nous?; **on this (d.) of all days!** justement aujourd'hui!; **of all (the) days to**

choose for a conference! quelle idée d'avoir choisi de faire une conférence justement aujourd'hui!; **to take/get a d. off** prendre/obtenir un jour de congé; *Jur etc* **ten clear days' notice** préavis *m* de dix jours francs; *Com* **d. of grace** jour de grâce; *Com* **days of grace** délai *m* de grâce

(b) [①B58,B,3](*referring to duration*) journée *f*; **it's been a sunny/rainy d.** il a fait une journée de soleil/pluie; **on wet days we stay in** les jours où il pleut nous restons à la maison; **all d. (long)** toute la journée; **what sort of d. have you had?** tu as passé une bonne journée?; **to work/to be paid by the d.** travailler/être payé à la journée; **it's all in a d.'s work** ça fait partie de la routine; **eight-hour d.** journée de huit heures; **in the course of the d.** dans la journée; **at the end of the d.** à la fin de la journée; *Fig* en fin de compte, au bout du compte; **to carry** *or* **win the d.** gagner la journée *ou* la bataille; *Lit* **d. is done** le jour s'achève; **d. rate** tarif *m* journalier

(c) (*time, frequency*) **the d. before/after he came** la veille/le lendemain de son arrivée; **two days previously** *or* **before** deux jours avant; **two days before/after his wedding** l'avant-veille *f*/le surlendemain de son mariage; **the d. before yesterday/after tomorrow** avant-hier/après-demain; **the d. before yesterday was Sunday** il y a deux jours c'était dimanche; **two days later** deux jours après *ou* plus tard, le surlendemain; **I met him one d.** je l'ai rencontré un jour; **one d., some d., one of these days** (*future*) un jour (ou l'autre), un de ces jours; **the baby's due any d. now** le bébé va naître d'un jour à l'autre; **the other d.** l'autre jour; **a year ago to the d.** il y a un an jour pour jour; **I remember it to this (very) d.** je m'en souviens encore aujourd'hui; **until the d. I die, until my dying d.** jusqu'à ma mort; *F* **from d. one** dès le début; **from that d. on(wards)** depuis ce jour; **from this d. forth** dorénavant, à compter de ce jour; **once/twice a d.** une/deux fois par jour; **every other d.** tous les deux jours, un jour sur deux; **d. after d., d. in d. out** jour après jour; **d. by d.** jour après jour; **from d. to d.** de jour en jour, d'un jour à l'autre; **to live from d. to d.** vivre au jour le jour; **d.-old** (*chicks, baby*) d'un jour; (*bread*) de la veille; *Mktg* **d.-after recall** mémorisation *f* un jour après; *Mktg* **d.-after recall test** test *m* du lendemain; *Fin* **d. bill** effet *m* à date fixe; **d. tour** excursion *f* d'une journée; *St Exch* **d. trade** opération *f* de journée; **d. visitor** excursionniste *mf*

(d) (*as distinguished from night*) **to work d. and night** travailler nuit et jour; **to travel by d.** voyager de jour; **d. bed** lit *m* de repos; *Th, F Hum* **don't give up the d. job** je ne crois pas que tu es prêt pour une carrière professionnelle; **d. labourer** journalier *m*, ouvrier *m* à la journée; **d. pupil** externe *mf*; *Ind* **to be on days** (*of worker*) être de jour; *Met* **d. temperature** température *f* diurne

(e) (*dawn*) jour *m*; **before d.** avant le jour; **at break of d.** au point du jour; **they were waiting for d. to break** ils attendaient que le jour pointe

(f) (*idioms*) *F* **he's sixty if he's a d.** il a soixante ans bien sonnés; **he doesn't look a d. older than 40/you** il n'a pas l'air d'avoir plus de 40 ans/d'être plus vieux que toi; **he doesn't look a d. older than when I last saw him** il n'a pas vieilli d'un poil depuis la dernière fois que je l'ai vu; **you've made my d.!** c'est la meilleure nouvelle de la journée; **it's not my d.!** c'est pas mon jour; *Fig* **let's call it a d.** (*finish work*) ça suffit pour aujourd'hui; (*end relationship*) finissons-en; *F* **let's make a d. of it!** allons faire la fête!; *F* **that'll be the d.!** j'aimerais voir ça!; **to pass the time of d. with sb** échanger quelques paroles de politesse avec qn

(g) (*anniversary, celebration*) fête *f*; **Mother's/Father's D.** la fête des Mères/des Pères; **Saint David's D.** la Saint-David, = la fête nationale galloise; **All Saints' D.** la Toussaint; **All Souls' D.** le Jour des Morts; **Christmas D.** le jour de Noël; **to name the d.** (*of wedding*) fixer le jour du mariage; *Rel* **the D. of Judgement** le jour du jugement

(h) (*time*) **the good old days** le bon vieux temps; **in the days of ...** au *ou* du temps de ...; **in my young days** au *ou* du temps de ma jeunesse; **in those days** en ce temps-là, à cette époque, alors; **these days** de notre temps; **in this d. and age** de nos jours; **those were the days** c'était la belle vie (alors); **in his d.** (*when he was young*) en son temps; (*when he was alive*) de son vivant; **she was a great actress in her d.** c'était une grande actrice à son époque; **he ended his days in poverty** il a fini ses jours pauvre; **in days to come** à l'avenir; **to have had its d.** (*of theory, fashion etc*) être démodé; (*of car, TV*) avoir fait son temps; **to have seen better days** (*of person*) avoir connu des jours meilleurs; (*of car, shoes*) avoir fait son temps; *F* (*of food*) avoir perdu de sa fraîcheur

daybook ['deɪbʊk] *n Com* journal *m*, -aux; *Acct* livre *m* de main-courante, main *f* courante, brouillard *m*

dayboy ['deɪbɔɪ] *n Sch* externe *m*

daybreak ['deɪbreɪk] *n* point *m* du jour, lever *m* du jour; **at d.** au lever du jour, au point du jour

daycare ['deɪkeər] *n* **the children go to d.** les enfants vont à la garderie; **d. centre** (*for children*) garderie *f*; **d. facilities** service *m* de garderie

daydream¹ ['deɪdriːm] *n* rêverie *f*

daydream² *vi* rêvasser; **to d. about the future** rêver à l'avenir

daydreaming ['deɪdriːmɪŋ] *n* rêverie *f*, rêvasserie *f*; **d. will get you nowhere** les rêveries ne te mèneront nulle part

day for night *n Cin etc* nuit *f* américaine

daygirl ['deɪgɜːl] *n Sch* externe *f*

daylight ['deɪlaɪt] *n* **(a)** jour *m*, lumière *f* du jour; **d. hours** heures durant lesquelles il fait jour; **it was still d.** il faisait encore jour; **there were still two hours of d. left** il ferait jour pendant deux heures encore; *Fig* **to put d. between oneself and sb** distancer qn; *Fig* **to (begin to) see d.** (*come to the end of a task*) entrevoir la fin; (*understand*) (commencer à) voir clair **(b)** (*dawn*) aube *f*, point *m* du jour; **before d.** avant l'aube **(c)** *F* **to beat the living daylights out of sb** rosser qn, tabasser qn; **to scare** *or* **frighten the living daylights out of sb** flanquer la trouille *ou* une peur bleue à qn

daylight-saving *n* **d. time** heure *f* avancée d'été

daylong ['deɪlɒŋ] *adj* d'une journée

day nurse *n Med* infirmier, -ière qui est de service de jour

day nursery *n* crèche *f*

day release *n* formation *f* continue en alternance

day return *n Rail etc* (billet *m* d')aller *m* et retour valable pour la journée

day school *n* externat *m*

day shift *n Ind* équipe *f* de jour; **to be on d.** (*of worker*) être de jour

daytime ['deɪtaɪm] *n* jour *m*, journée *f*; **in the d.** pendant la journée, de jour; **d. TV/classes** émissions *fpl* télévisées/cours *mpl* pendant la journée

day-to-day *adj* (*task*) courant, quotidien; (*worry, concern*) quotidien; **d. management of a company** administration courante d'une entreprise; **on a d. basis** au jour le jour

day trip *n* excursion *f ou* voyage *m* d'une journée

day tripper *n* excursionniste *mf*

daze¹ [deɪz] *n* **(a)** (*caused by drug, blow*) étourdissement *m*; **to be in a d.** être étourdi; (*stronger*) être hébété **(b)** (*caused by news*) ahurissement *m*; **to be in a d.** être hébété *ou* ahuri; **he was left in a d. by the news** la nouvelle l'a hébété *ou* ahuri

daze² *vt* **(a)** (*of drug, blow*) étourdir; (*stronger*) hébéter **(b)** (*bewilder*) abasourdir, ahurir

dazed [deɪzd] *adj* **(a)** (*by blow, lack of sleep*) tout étourdi, hébété **(b)** (*bewildered*) abasourdi, sidéré, hébété; **she had a d. look on her face, she looked d.** elle avait l'air abasourdi, elle paraissait abasourdie

dazzle¹ ['dæz(ə)l] *n* (*of headlights*) lueur *f* éblouissante *ou* aveuglante; *Fig* éclat *m*

dazzle² *vt* éblouir, aveugler; *Fig* éblouir; **dazzled with** *or* **by the light** aveuglé par la lumière; *Fig* **she was quite dazzled by him** il l'a complètement éblouie

dazzling ['dæzlɪŋ] *adj* (*light*) aveuglant, éblouissant; (*beauty, performance*) éblouissant; (*success*) éclatant

dazzlingly ['dæzlɪŋlɪ] *adv* **d. bright** éblouissant, aveuglant; **d. beautiful** d'une beauté éblouissante

dB (*abbr* **decibel**) dB

DBMS [diːbiːem'es] *n Comptr* (*abbr* **database management system**) SGBD *m*

DBS [diːbiː'es] *n Telecom abbr* **direct broadcasting satellite**

DC [diː'siː] *n* **(a)** *El abbr* **direct current (b)** *Am F* (*abbr* **District of Columbia**) = Washington

D & C [diːən'siː] *n Med* (*abbr* **dilatation and curettage**) dilatation *f* et curetage *m*

DD [diː'diː] *n Univ abbr* **Doctor of Divinity**

DDE [diːdiː'iː] *n Comptr* (*abbr* **dynamic data exchange**) DDE *m*

DDT [diːdiː'tiː] *n Ch* DDT *m*

DEA [diːiː'eɪ] *n US abbr* **Drug Enforcement Agency**

deacon ['diːkən] *n Rel* diacre *m*

deaconess ['diːkənɪs] *n Rel* diaconesse *f*

deactivate [diː'æktɪveɪt] *vt* désactiver

deactivation [diːæktɪ'veɪʃən] *n* désactivation *f*

dead [ded] **1** *adj* **(a)** (*person, tree, flower*) mort; **he is d.** il est mort *ou* décédé; **the d. man/woman** le mort/la morte; *F* **over my d. body!** moi vivant, jamais!; **it'll be over my d. body!** il faudra me tuer d'abord!; **to step into a d. man's shoes** être promu à la suite du décès de son supérieur; *Prov* **d. men tell no tales** les morts ne parlent pas; *Fig* **d. man** (*empty bottle*) cadavre *m*; **d. man's fingers** (*coral*) alcyon *m*; **d. man's handle** (*on train controls*) manette *f*, homme *m* mort; **to shoot sb d.** tuer qn net (d'un coup de revolver); *F* **d.**

as a doornail, d. as mutton mort et bien mort; **d. and gone, d. and buried** mort et enterré; **half d. with fright** à moitié mort de peur; **d. or alive** mort ou vif; **more d. than alive** plus mort que vif; **to leave sb for d.** laisser qn pour mort; *Fig* **I wouldn't be seen d. wearing it** je ne porterais ça pour rien au monde; *Fig* **I wouldn't be seen d. there** je n'irais pour rien au monde; *F* **to be d. from the neck up** être idiot; *F* **you're a d. man** tu es un homme mort; *F* **if Dad finds out, you're d.** *or* **a d. duck** si Papa l'apprend, gare à toi!; **the plan's a d. duck** c'est un plan foireux

(b) (*lacking sensitivity*) (*finger*) mort, engourdi; **to go d.** (*of limb*) s'engourdir; **to be d. to the world** (*asleep*) être profondément endormi; (*in drunken stupor*) être complètement hébété; **d. to all sense of honour** insensible à tout sentiment d'honneur

(c) (*lacking power, energy, activity, validity etc*) (*fire*) mort; (*voice, eyes*) éteint; (*colour*) terne; (*sound*) mat; *El* (*wire*) hors *ou* sans tension; (*battery*) épuisé; (*town*) mort; **this place is d. in winter** cet endroit est mort l'hiver; *Tel* **the phone is** *or* **has gone d.** il n'y a pas de tonalité; **the line is** *or* **has gone d.** la ligne a été coupée; *Mil* **d. angle** angle *m* mort; *Fb* **d. ball** ballon *m* mort; **d. end** (*street etc*) cul-de-sac *m, pl* culs-de-sac, impasse *f*; (*of pipe*) bout *m* aveugle; **d.-end job** emploi *m* sans avenir; *Fig* **to reach** *or* **come to a d. end** arriver à une impasse; **the d. hand of tradition** le poids de la tradition; **d. language** langue *f* morte; **to become a d. letter** (*of regulation*) tomber en désuétude; **d. letters** lettres *fpl* de rebut; **d.-letter office** bureau *m* des rebuts; **d. load** *or* **weight** *Constr* poids *m* mort; *Aut* poids utile; *Fig* **he's a d. weight** c'est un poids mort; **d. season** morte-saison *f, pl* mortes-saisons; **d. water** eau *f* stagnante; *Naut* remous *m* de sillage

(d) (*absolute, total*) *Naut* **d. calm** calme *m* plat; **d. centre** (*of piston*) point *m* mort; (*of lathe*) centre *m* fixe; **to fall into a d. faint** tomber en pâmoison, s'évanouir; *Sp* **d. heat** arrivée *f* ex-æquo; **it was a d. heat** il y a eu une arrivée ex-æquo; **d. level** niveau *m* parfait; **d. loss** perte *f* sèche; *F* (*person*) propre *mf* à rien; **this is a bit of a d. loss** (*party, meeting*) on perd notre temps ici; *Naut* **by d. reckoning** à l'estime; *F* **d. ringer** sosie *m* (**for** de); **they're d. ringers** ils se ressemblent comme deux gouttes d'eau; *F* **to make a d. set at sb** chercher à tout prix à mettre le grappin sur qn; *F* **to make a d. set at sth** vouloir obtenir qch à tout prix; **d. silence** silence *m* de mort; **d. stop** arrêt *m* complet

2 *npl* (*deceased*) **the d.** les morts *mpl*; **to rise from the d.** ressusciter des morts; **d. march** marche *f* funèbre

3 *n* (*depths*) **at d. of night** au plus profond de la nuit; **in the d. of winter** au plus fort de l'hiver

4 *adv* **(a)** *F* (*very*) **d. easy/simple** facile/simple comme tout; **d. clever/interesting** super *ou* vachement intelligent/intéressant; **d. stupid** bête comme ses pieds; **d. boring** vraiment rasoir

(b) (*completely*) absolument; **to be d. (set) against sth** être absolument opposé à qch; **with the tide running d. against us** avec le courant en plein contre nous; **d. ahead (of sb)** droit devant (qn); *Naut* **wind d. ahead** vent droit debout; *F* **d. beat** crevé; *F* **d. broke** fauché; **d. certain** sûr et certain, absolument certain; **d. drunk** ivre mort; **d. on the hour/half-past six** à l'heure/six heures et demi tapante(s); **he was d. right** il avait absolument raison; **d. slow** aussi lentement que possible; (*road sign*) au pas; *Hum* **he has two speeds — d. slow and stop** il a deux vitesses — la première et le point mort; **d. smooth surface** surface parfaitement plane; **d. sure** absolument certain, sûr et certain; **d. tired** mort de fatigue; **to be d. wrong** avoir complètement tort, se tromper du tout au tout; **to stop d.** s'arrêter net

dead-and-alive *adj* mort, triste; **a d. hole** un trou perdu, *Sl* un bled

deadbeat ['dedbiːt] *n esp Am F Pej* (*lazy person*) feignant, -ante

deaden ['ded(ə)n] *vt* (*blow*) amortir; (*pain*) endormir; (*sound*) assourdir, étouffer; (*senses*) émousser; (*feeling*) étouffer; **they had become deadened to ...** ils étaient devenus insensibles à ...

deadening ['ded(ə)nɪŋ] **1** *n* (*of blow*) amortissement *m*; (*of noise, sound*) assourdissement *m* **2** *adj* (*conformity, task*) engourdissant

deadhead¹ ['dedhed] *n F* **(a)** *esp Am* (*dullard*) nullité *f* **(b)** *Am* (*person with free ticket*) *Th* personne *f* en possession d'un billet de faveur; *Rail* personne en possession d'un titre de transport gratuit **(c) d. flight** parcours *m* à vide

deadhead² *vt* **to d. flowers** (*in garden*) enlever les fleurs fanées

deadline ['dedlaɪn] *n* (*day*) date *f* limite; (*time*) heure *f* limite; (*of journalist*) délai *m* de remise; **to work to a d.** travailler en fonction d'une date/heure limite; **the d. for returning your essays** la date limite *ou* la dernière limite pour rendre vos dissertations; **to meet a d.** respecter un délai

deadliness ['dedlɪnɪs] *n* **(a)** (*of poison etc*) nature *f* mortelle; *Fig* (*of wit, repartee*) mordant *m*, causticité *f* **(b)** *F* (*boredom*) ennui *m* mortel; **the utter d. of her style is difficult to describe** son style est tellement ennuyeux qu'on a peine à le décrire

deadlock¹ ['dedlɒk] *n* **(a)** impasse *f*; *Comptr* interblocage *m*, impasse; **to reach d.** arriver à une impasse; **to break the d.** sortir de l'impasse **(b)** *Tech* serrure *f* à pêne dormant; *Aut* serrure passive

deadlock² *vt* **talks are deadlocked** les discussions ont atteint une impasse, les discussions en sont au point mort

deadly ['dedlɪ] **1** *adj* **(a)** (*mortal*) (*poison, blow, enemy etc*) mortel; (*weapon*) meurtrier; (*hatred*) implacable, mortel; (*combat*) à mort; *Fig* (*pallor, silence etc*) de mort; (*wit, satire*) mordant, caustique; *also Fig* **to d. effect** de façon dévastatrice; **the seven d. sins** les sept péchés *mpl* capitaux; **d. nightshade** (*plant*) belladone *f* **(b)** *F* (*boring*) mortel, rasant **2** *adv* **(a)** (*pale*) comme un linge; *F* **d. dull** rasant; **d. boring** mortellement ennuyeux **(b)** (*completely*) **d. accurate** extrêmement précis; **to be d. serious** être tout à fait sérieux; **to speak in d. earnest** être absolument sincère

deadpan ['dedpæn] *adj* (*face*) impassible, figé; (*humour*) de pince-sans-rire

Dead Sea *n Geog* **the D.** la Mer Morte

deadweight ['dedweɪt] *n Com* port *m* en lourd; **d. tonnage** (*of ship*) tonnage *m* port en lourd

deadwood ['dedwʊd] *n Fig* (*person*) personne *f* improductive; (*thing*) chose *f* inutile; **there is too much d. in this office** il y a trop de gens payés à ne rien faire dans ce bureau

deaf [def] **1** *adj* sourd; **to go d.** devenir sourd; **d. in one ear** sourd d'une oreille; **d. and dumb** sourd-muet, *f* sourde-muette; **d. as a (door)post** sourd comme un pot; *Prov* **there are none so d. as those that will not hear** il n'y a pire sourd que celui qui ne veut (pas) entendre; *Fig* **d. to entreaties** sourd aux supplications; **to turn a d. ear to** (*person*) refuser d'écouter; (*pleas*) rester sourd à; **to fall on d. ears** ne pas être entendu **2** *npl* **the d.** les sourds *mpl*

deaf-aid *n* appareil *m* acoustique

deafen ['def(ə)n] *vt* (*sb*) assourdir, rendre sourd; **you're deafening me** vous me cassez les oreilles

deafening ['def(ə)nɪŋ] *adj* (*noise*) assourdissant

deaf-mute *n* sourd-muet, *f* sourde-muette, *pl* sourds-muets, sourdes-muettes

deafness ['defnɪs] *n* surdité *f*; *Fig* **their d. to any appeal** le fait qu'ils sont restés sourds à tout appel

deal¹ [diːl] *n* **a good d.** (*a lot*) beaucoup; **I have a great/good d. to do** j'ai beaucoup de/bien des choses à faire; **there's a great d. of truth in that** il y a beaucoup de vrai là-dedans; **a good d. of my time** une bonne partie de mon temps; **I think a great d. of him** je l'estime beaucoup; **not a great d.** pas énormément

deal² *n* **(a)** *Cards* donne *f*; **whose d. is it?** à qui de donner?; **your d.!** à vous la donne!

(b) *Com etc* affaire *f*, marché *m*; **d. on the Stock Exchange** coup *m* de Bourse; **big d.** grosse affaire; *F Iron* la belle affaire!; **it's no big d.** (*no problem*) c'est pas un problème; **don't make such a big d. out of it!** c'est pas la peine d'en faire tout un plat; **cash d.** transaction *f* au comptant; *Mktg* **d. prone** susceptible de réagir aux offres spéciales; *US Hist* **the New D.** le New Deal; **package d.** contrat *m* global; **to do a d.** conclure une affaire *ou* un marché (**with sb** avec qn); **it's a d.!** d'accord!, entendu!; *Pol* **d. between parties** accord *m* entre partis; **to give sb a fair d.** offrir un bon prix à qn; *Fig* offrir un traitement équitable à qn

deal³ (*pt, pp* **dealt** [delt]) **1** *vt* **(a)** (*cards*) donner, distribuer **(b) to d. sb a blow** porter un coup à qn; **the news dealt a serious blow to her hopes of winning** la nouvelle a sérieusement entamé ses chances de gagner **(c)** *F* (*drugs*) dealer **2** *vi* **(a)** (*trade*) **to d. in leather/in options** faire le commerce des cuirs/des primes **(b)** (*in drugs*) dealer **(c)** *Cards* faire la donne, donner, *F* faire

▶ **deal in** *vtsep* **to d. sb in** *Cards* donner *ou* distribuer des cartes à qn, servir qn; *Fig* (*in criminal activity*) inclure qn dans l'affaire; *Fig* **d. me in!** je suis partant!

▶ **deal out** *vtsep* (*supplies*) distribuer (**to, among** entre); (*cards*) donner, distribuer; **to d. out justice** rendre la justice; **to d. out criticism** critiquer à tour de bras

▶ **deal with** *vipo* **(a)** (*do business with*) (*sb*) avoir affaire à *ou* avec; *Com* traiter *ou* négocier avec; (*get supplies from*) (*grocer etc*) se fournir chez; **man easy/difficult to d. with** homme commode/peu commode **(b)** (*be about*) (*subject*) traiter de **(c)** (*handle*) (*person, problem, situation*) s'occuper de; *Com* (*order*) donner suite à; **I know how to d. with him** je sais m'y prendre avec lui; **I'll d. with this** je m'en occupe

dealer ['di:lər] *n* **(a)** *Cards* donneur, -euse **(b)** *Com* négociant *m* **(in** en); (*supplier*) fournisseur *m* **(in** de); *St Exch* marchand *m* de titres; *Aut etc* concessionnaire *m*, distributeur *m*; (*in drugs*) dealer *m*, trafiquant, -ante; *Mktg* **d. brand** marque *f* de revendeur; *Mktg* **d. test** test *m* auprès des distributeurs

dealership ['di:ləʃɪp] *n Aut* concession *f*

dealing ['di:lɪŋ] *n St Exch* transactions *fpl*; (*in drugs*) vente *f*; *St Exch* **d. room** salle *f* de marchés

dealing out *n* (*of supplies*) distribution *f*; (*of cards*) distribution, donne *f*

dealings ['di:lɪŋz] *npl* relations *fpl*, rapports *mpl*; *Pej* tractations *fpl* **(with** avec); *Com* transactions *fpl*; **to have d. with sb** avoir des rapports avec qn; *Com* faire *ou* traiter des affaires avec qn

dean [di:n] *n Rel, Univ* doyen *m*

deanery ['di:nərɪ] *n Rel* résidence *f* du doyen

dear [dɪər] **1** *adj* **(a)** (*loved*) cher, chère **(to** à); **he is d. to me** il m'est cher; **a d. friend of mine** un de mes chers amis; **my dearest wish is that** ... mon vœu le plus cher est que ...; **a place d. to the hearts of** ... un endroit qui est cher à ...; *Old-fashioned* **my d. chap** *or* **fellow,** ... mon cher ami, ...; **all that I hold d.** tout ce qui m'est cher; **what a d. little child!** quel amour d'enfant!; **a d. little house** une petite maison coquette; *F* **to run for d. life** courir aussi vite que possible

(b) (*in letter*) **D. Sir** Monsieur; **D. Madam** Madame; **D. Sir or Madam** Monsieur, Madame; **D. Mr Thomas** Cher Monsieur; **D. John Smith** Cher Monsieur Smith; **D. Alice** (Ma) chère Alice; **D. Alan and Avril** chers Alan et Avril; *esp Am F* **a d. John letter** une lettre de rupture

(c) (*costly*) cher, coûteux; **to get** *or* **become dearer** augmenter; **don't get the d./dearest ones!** ne prends pas les chers/plus chers!

2 *n* (*friend*) cher *m*, chère *f*; (*darling*) chéri, -ie; **you poor d.** mon/ma pauvre; **my d.** (*adult friend*) cher ami, *f* chère amie; (*darling*) mon chéri, *f* ma chérie; (*child*) mon petit chou; *F* **old d.** grand-mère *f*; **you're a d.!** tu es un amour!; **be a d. and** ... sois gentil/gentille et ...

3 *adv* (*to buy, sell, pay*) cher; *Fig* **he sold his life d.** il vendit chèrement sa vie

4 *int* **d. d.!, d. me!** mon Dieu, mon Dieu!; **(d.) oh d.!** (*what have I done*) oh là là!; (*that's a pity*) hélas!; **oh d. no!** (oh) que non!

dearie ['dɪərɪ] *F* **1** *n* mon (petit) chéri, *f* ma (petite) chérie **2** *int* **d. me!** mon Dieu!

dearly ['dɪəlɪ] *adv* **(a)** (*very much*) **I love him d.** je l'aime tendrement *ou* de tout mon cœur; **he d. loves to play jokes on people** il trouve tout son plaisir à jouer des tours aux gens; **I would d. like to meet her** je souhaite de tout mon cœur la rencontrer **(b)** *Fml* (*at great cost*) cher; **their success was d. won** leur victoire leur a coûté cher; **you shall pay d. for this** cela vous coûtera cher

dearness ['dɪənɪs] *n* **(a)** (*expensiveness*) (*of foodstuffs etc*) cherté *f*; **the d. of the prices** les prix élevés **(b)** (*lovableness*) **her d. to me** l'affection *ou* l'attachement que j'ai pour elle

dearth [dɜ:θ] *n Fml* (*of supplies, books etc*) disette *f*, pénurie *f*; (*of ideas, information*) pénurie, pauvreté *f*

death [deθ] *n* **(a)** (*end of life*) mort *f*; *Jur, Admin* décès *m*; *Journ* **deaths** nécrologie *f*; **deaths column** rubrique *f* nécrologique; **six food-poisoning deaths have been reported** on a signalé six décès par intoxication alimentaire; **there has been a d. in the family** il y a eu un décès dans la famille; **to die a violent d.** mourir de mort violente; **he died an easy d.** il n'a pas souffert; **at (the time of) his d.** à sa mort; **until d.** pour la vie; **till d. us do part** (*in marriage ceremony*) jusqu'à ce que la mort nous sépare; **a fight to the d.** une lutte à mort; **he fell to his d.** il a fait une chute mortelle; **to send sb to his/her d.** envoyer qn à la mort; **to be at d.'s door** *or* **on the verge of d.** être sur le point de mourir; **to drink/smoke oneself to d.** se tuer à force de boire/fumer; **to stab sb to d.** tuer qn à coups de couteau; **to work sb to d.** tuer qn à force de surmenage; **to be burnt to d.** (*accidentally*) périr dans les flammes; (*as form of martyrdom*) périr sur le bûcher; **to starve sb to d.** faire mourir qn de faim; **to beat sb to d.** battre qn à mort; **one false move could mean d.** (*for trapeze artist etc*) un faux mouvement pourrait entraîner la mort; **d. to traitors!** à mort les traîtres!; **d. adder** (*snake*) acanthopis *m*; *Fin* **d. benefit** capital *m* décès; **d. cap** (*toadstool*) amanite *f* phalloïde; *Lit* **d. knell** glas *m*; *Fig* **to sound the d. knell** sonner le glas **(for** de); **d. mask** masque *m* mortuaire; **d. rate** taux *m* de mortalité; *Am Aut* **d. seat** place *f* du mort; **d. throes** agonie *f*, affres *fpl* de la mort; **it was agonizing to watch her d. throes** c'était atroce de la voir à l'agonie; *Fig* **the project was in its d. throes** le projet était à ses dernières heures; **d. toll** bilan *m*

(b) (*execution*) **to put sb to d.** mettre qn à mort, exécuter qn; **condemned to d., under sentence of d.** condamné à mort; **d. camp** camp *m* de la mort; **d. cell** cellule *f* de condamné à mort; **d. squad** escadron *m* de la mort; **d. warrant** ordre *m* d'exécution; *Fig* **you've just signed your own d. warrant** tu viens de signer ton arrêt de mort

(c) *F* (*indicating exaggeration*) **to be sick to d. of sth** en avoir marre de qch; **you'll catch your d. (of cold)** vous allez attraper la crève; **that play has been done to d.** cette pièce a été beaucoup trop jouée; **he'll be the d. of me (yet)** il me fera mourir; **that car will be the d. of her** elle va se tuer avec cette voiture; **it would be the d. of him** ce serait sa mort; **to look like d. (warmed up)** ressembler à un mort

(d) *Fig* (*end*) **the d. of one's hopes/plans** la fin de ses espoirs/projets; **to be in at the d.** assister au dénouement

deathbed ['deθbed] *n* lit *m* de mort; **d. confession** confession faite sur le lit de mort

deathblow ['deθbləʊ] *n* coup *m* mortel *ou* fatal; *Fig* **marriage was** *or* **dealt a d. to her career** le mariage a porté un coup mortel à sa carrière

death certificate *n* extrait *m* d'acte de décès

death duties *npl Br Old-fashioned* droits *mpl* de succession

deathless ['deθlɪs] *adj Lit* impérissable, immortel; *Hum Iron* **d. prose** prose *f* immortelle

deathlike ['deθlaɪk] *adj* (*pallor etc*) de mort

deathly ['deθlɪ] **1** *adj* (*pallor*) de mort, cadavérique; (*calm*) sépulcral; **d. silence** silence *m* de mort **2** *adv* comme la mort; **d. pale** d'une pâleur mortelle, mortellement pâle

death penalty *n* peine *f* de mort

death rattle *n* râle *m* de la mort

death row *n US* = quartier *m* d'une prison où les condamnés attendent leur exécution

death's-head ['deθshed] *n* tête *f* de mort; **d. moth** (sphinx *m*) atropos *m*

death taxes *npl US* droits *mpl* de succession

deathtrap ['deθtræp] *n* (*place*) endroit *m* dangereux; (*vehicle*) véhicule *m* dangereux; **the house is a d.** cette maison est dangereuse

Death Valley *n US Geog* la Vallée de la Mort

deathwatch ['deθwɒtʃ] *n* **d. beetle** vrillette *f*, *F* horloge *f* de la mort

death wish *n Psy* pulsion *f* de mort; *Fig* **to have a d.** (*of government etc*) courir à sa perte

deb [deb] *n Br F* débutante *f*; **d.'s delight** beau parti *m*

debacle [deɪ'bɑ:k(ə)l] *n* débâcle *f*

debag [di:'bæg] *vt* (**-gg-**) *Old-fashioned Br F* (*sb*) déculotter

debar [di:'bɑ:r] *vt* (**-rr-**) **to d. sb from sth** exclure qn de qch, interdire qch à qn; **to d. sb from doing sth** interdire à qn de faire qch; **to be debarred from membership of sth** se voir refuser l'adhésion à qch

debase [dɪ'beɪs] *vt* **(a)** (*degrade*) (*sb*) avilir, dégrader; (*one's style*) rabaisser **(b)** (*make less valuable*) (*metal*) altérer; (*currency*) déprécier

debasement [dɪ'beɪsmənt] *n* **(a)** (*of sb*) avilissement *m* **(b)** (*of currency*) dépréciation *f*

debatable [dɪ'beɪtəb(ə)l] *adj* contestable, discutable; **it's d. whether he is to blame or she is** il est difficile de dire si c'est lui ou elle qui est à blâmer

debate¹ [dɪ'beɪt] *n* discussion *f*; (*esp formal, parliamentary*) débat *m*; **after much d.** après bien des discussions; **there has been some d. over the effectiveness of the treatment** l'efficacité du traitement a été mise en doute; **he was a tough opponent in d.** c'était un rude adversaire dans les débats; **the issue has been in** *or* **under d. for some time** cette question est débattue depuis un certain temps

debate² **1** *vt* (*question etc*) débattre, discuter, agiter; (*subject*) mettre en discussion; **a much/fiercely debated question** une question fort controversée/vivement débattue; **we don't have time to d. the issue now** on n'a plus le temps de discuter le problème; **I was debating (with myself** *or* **in my mind) whether to go or not** je délibérais si j'irais ou non **2** *vi* discuter **(with sb on sth** avec qn sur qch); (*take part in a debate*) prendre part à un débat; **she frequently debated for her university** elle prenait souvent part à des débats pour son université

debater [dɪ'beɪtər] *n* spécialiste *mf* des débats

debating [dɪ'beɪtɪŋ] *n* **d. society** société *f* de débats contradictoires; **she took up d. at university** elle a pris part à des débats formels à l'université

debauch¹ [dɪ'bɔ:tʃ] *n* débauche *f*; **it degenerated into a drunken d.** ça a tourné à l'ivrognerie

debauch² *vt Fml, Old-fashioned* (*sb*) débaucher; (*taste*) corrompre

debauched [dɪ'bɔːtʃt] *adj* (*person*) débauché; (*morals, tastes*) corrompu; (*life*) de débauche
debauchee [dɪbɔː'tʃiː] *n Arch* débauché, -ée
debauchery [dɪ'bɔːtʃərɪ] *n* débauche *f*; **drunken d.** ivrognerie *f*; **his numberless debaucheries** ses innombrables descentes dans la débauche
debenture [dɪ'bentʃər] **1** *n Fin* obligation *f*; **d. bond** titre *m* d'obligation, emprunt *m* obligataire; **d. stock** obligations *fpl* sans garantie; **d. holder** obligataire *mf* **2** *adj* obligataire
debilitate [dɪ'bɪlɪteɪt] *vt* débiliter
debilitating [dɪ'bɪlɪteɪtɪŋ] *adj* (*climate, heat*) débilitant; (*illness*) affaiblissant; **it had a d. effect on her concentration** cela a provoqué une baisse de sa concentration
debility [dɪ'bɪlɪtɪ] *n Med* débilité *f*, asthénie *f*
debit¹ ['debɪt] *n Fin* débit *m*; **to the d. of** au débit de; **d. and credit** doit *m* et avoir *m*; **to enter sth on the d. side of an account** porter qch au débit d'un compte; **d. account** compte *m* débiteur; **d. advice** avis *m* de débit *ou* de prélèvement; **d. balance** solde *m* débiteur *ou* déficitaire; **d. balance of an account** position *f* débitrice d'un compte; **d. card** carte *f* de débit; **d. column** colonne *f* débitrice; **d. entry** article *m* au débit; **d. interest** intérêts *mpl* débiteurs; **d. item** poste *m* débiteur; **d. note** facture *f ou* note *f* de débit; **d. side** (*of account*) débit; *Fig* **on the d. side** sur le plan négatif
debit² *vt Fin* (*account*) débiter; **to d. sb with a sum** porter une somme au débit de qn, débiter qn d'une somme; **to d. an amount to an account** porter un montant au débit d'un compte, débiter un compte d'un montant; **has this cheque been debited to my account?** est-ce que ce chèque a été débité de mon compte?
debonair [debə'neər] *adj* (*person*) d'une élégance nonchalante; (*smile, charm*) nonchalant; **you look very d.** tu es vraiment élégant
debouch [dɪ'baʊtʃ] *vi Geog, Mil* déboucher (**into** dans)
debrief [diː'briːf] *vt Mil, Av etc* (*pilot etc*) faire faire un compte-rendu (de fin de mission) à; **to be debriefed** faire rapport
debriefing [diː'briːfɪŋ] *n* rapport *m* (de fin de mission), debriefing *m*
debris ['debriː] *n* débris *mpl*; *Fig* (*after party*) détritus *mpl*; *Fig* **to salvage something from the d. of one's marriage** sauver quelque chose des restes de son mariage
debt [det] *n* dette *f*; (*to be recovered*) créance *f*; **bad d.** mauvaise créance; **to be in d.** être endetté, avoir des dettes; **to be £12,000 in d.** avoir 12 000 livres de dettes; **to be in d. to sb** être en dette envers qn; **to repay a d.** régler une dette; **to be out of d.** n'avoir plus de dettes, être quitte; **to get** *or* **run into d.** s'endetter, faire des dettes; *F* **to be up to the** *or* **one's ears in d.** être criblé de dettes; *Fig* **I shall always be in your d.** je vous serai toujours redevable; **to owe sb a(n immense) d. of gratitude** être (très) endetté envers qn; **d. of honour** dette d'honneur; **d. capacity** capacité *f* d'endettement; **d. chasing letter** lettre *f* de poursuite, lettre de relance des impayés; *St Exch* **d. equity swap** échange *m* de créances contre actifs; *Fin* **d. financing** financement *m* par endettement; *Fin* **d. instrument** titre *m* de créance; **d. rescheduling** rééchelonnement *m* des dettes; **d. servicing** service *m* de la dette; **d. swap** échange *m* de créances
debt collection *n* recouvrement *m* de créances; **d. agency** agence *f* de recouvrement de créances
debt collector *n* agent *m* de recouvrement
debtor ['detər] *n* débiteur, -trice; **d. nations** pays *mpl* débiteurs
debug [diː'bʌg] *vt* **(a)** (*remove faults in*) *Comptr* (*program*) déboguer; (*prototype etc*) éliminer les erreurs de; (*machine*) dépanner; *Comptr* **d. facility** option *f* de débogage, programme *m* débogueur **(b)** (*remove microphones from*) (*room*) débarrasser des microphones clandestins
debugger [diː'bʌgər] *n Comptr* (programme *m*) débogueur *m*
debugging [diː'bʌgɪŋ] *n Comptr* débogage *m*
debunk [diː'bʌŋk] *vt F* (*sb*) déboulonner, ridiculiser; (*theory*) discréditer; **to d. a myth** détruire un mythe
début¹ ['deɪbjuː] *n* début *m*; (*in society*) entrée *f* dans le monde; **to make one's d.** (*of actor etc*) débuter, faire ses débuts (**as** dans le rôle de)
début² *vi esp Am* débuter; **she début'd** ['deɪbjuːd] **in the role of …** elle a fait ses débuts *ou* a débuté dans le rôle de …
débutante ['debjʊtɑːnt, -tænt] *n Br* débutante *f*
decade ['dekeɪd] *n* **(a)** (*ten years*) décennie *f*; *Fr Hist* (*of republican calendar*) décade; **a few decades ago** il y a quelques dizaines d'années **(b)** *Rel* (*of rosary*) dizaine *f* **(c)** *Comptr* décade *f*
decadence ['dekədəns] *n* **(a)** (*of society etc*) décadence *f* **(b)** *Liter, Art* décadentisme *m*
decadent ['dekədənt] **1** *adj* décadent; **to become d.** tomber dans la décadence; *Hum* **how d.!** quelle décadence! **2** *n Liter, Art* décadent *m*
decaf ['diːkæf] *n F* déca *m*
decaffeinate [diː'kæfineɪt] *vt* décaféiner
decagram(me) ['dekəgræm] *n* décagramme *m*
decal [dɪ'kæl, 'diːkæl] *n Am F* décalcomanie *f*
decalcification [diːkælsɪfɪ'keɪʃən] *n* décalcification *f*
decalcify [diː'kælsɪfaɪ] *vt* (*bones etc*) décalcifier
Decalogue ['dekəlɒg] *n Bible* Décalogue *m*
decamp [diː'kæmp] *vi Mil* lever le camp; *F* (*leave*) aller s'installer ailleurs; (*leave suddenly, secretively etc*) décamper, filer, ficher le camp; **to d. to another room** aller s'installer dans une autre pièce
decant [dɪ'kænt] *vt* (*liquid*) transvaser; (*bottle of wine*) décanter dans une carafe/*etc*; *F* (*move, transfer*) (*people to a different district etc*) transférer
decanter [dɪ'kæntər] *n* (*for wine etc*) carafe *f*
decapitate [dɪ'kæpɪteɪt] *vt* décapiter
decapitation [dɪkæpɪ'teɪʃən] *n* décapitation *f*
decapod ['dekəpɒd] *n* (*crustacean*) décapode *m*
decarbonize [diː'kɑːbənaɪz] *vt* **(a)** *Metal* (*steel etc*) décarburer, décarboniser **(b)** *Aut* (*cylinder head*) décalaminer
decathlete [dɪ'kæθliːt] *n Sp* décathlonien, -ienne
decathlon [dɪ'kæθlɒn] *n Sp* décathlon *m*
decay¹ [dɪ'keɪ] *n* **(a)** (*rot*) (*of wood etc*) pourriture *f*, corruption *f*, décomposition *f*; (*of teeth*) carie *f*; *Phys* **d. time** période *f* d'extinction **(b)** (*decline*) (*of family, country etc*) décadence *f*, déchéance *f*; (*of beauty etc*) déclin *m*; (*of faculties*) dégradation *f*; (*of building*) délabrement *m*; **moral d.** déchéance morale; **to fall into d.** (*of house*) tomber en ruine, se délabrer; (*of state*) tomber en décadence; **in a state of d.** (*tooth*) carié; (*body*) en état de décomposition; (*building*) délabré
decay² **1** *vi* **(a)** (*rot*) (*of meat, fruit*) se gâter, pourrir; (*of timber*) pourrir; (*of teeth*) se carier **(b)** (*decline*) (*of nation, family*) tomber en décadence; (*of building*) tomber en ruine, se délabrer; (*of empire*) décliner; (*of beauty*) (se) passer, se flétrir **2** *vt* (*teeth*) carier
decayed [dɪ'keɪd] *adj* **(a)** (*civilization*) en ruines; (*building, part of town*) délabré **(b)** (*wood, fruit, flesh*) pourri; (*tooth*) carié
decaying [dɪ'keɪɪŋ] *adj* **(a)** (*in decline*) (*empire, civilization*) sur le déclin; (*building, part of town*) qui se délabre; **his d. fortunes** ses richesses qui s'amenuisent **(b)** (*rotting*) pourrissant; (*teeth*) en train de former des caries
decease¹ [dɪ'siːs] *n Jur, Admin* décès *m*
decease² *vi Jur, Admin* décéder
deceased [dɪ'siːst] **1** *adj* décédé; **son of Robert Martin, d.** fils de feu M. Robert Martin **2** *n* **the d.** le défunt/la défunte/les défunt(e)s
deceit [dɪ'siːt] *n* **(a)** (*action*) supercherie *f*, tromperie *f*; *Jur* fraude *f*; **to practice d. on sb** user de tromperie *ou* de fourberie envers qn **(b) = deceitfulness**
deceitful [dɪ'siːtfʊl] *adj* trompeur, -euse, fourbe; **to be d.** (*of person*) être faux; **it was very d. of her** c'était très faux de sa part
deceitfully [dɪ'siːtfʊlɪ] *adv* avec duplicité; **to obtain sth d.** obtenir qch en usant de duplicité; **the message was d. worded** le message avait été rédigé de manière à tromper; **d., she omitted to mention the fact** par duplicité, elle s'est gardée de mentionner ce fait
deceitfulness [dɪ'siːtfʊlnɪs] *n* fausseté *f*, duplicité *f*
deceive [dɪ'siːv] **1** *vt* (*sb*) tromper, abuser; (*one's wife, husband*) tromper; (*sb's hopes*) tromper, décevoir; **don't be deceived** ne vous y fiez pas; **to be deceived by appearances** se laisser tromper par les apparences; **to d. oneself** s'abuser, se méprendre; **don't d. yourself that it will be easy** ne croyez pas que ce sera facile; **to d. sb into thinking sth** faire croire qch à qn; **they deceived the electorate into voting for them by promising tax cuts** ils ont persuadé les électeurs de voter pour eux en promettant de diminuer les impôts; **I thought my eyes were deceiving me** je ne pouvais pas en croire mes yeux
2 *vi* tromper; **it was not done with intent to d.** cela n'a pas été fait dans l'intention de tromper
deceiver [dɪ'siːvər] *n* trompeur, -euse
decelerate [diː'seləreɪt] *vi* ralentir
deceleration [diːselə'reɪʃən] *n* ralentissement *m*, décélération *f*; **d. lane** voie *f* de décélération
December [dɪ'sembər] *n* [①**A75-C**,B-C; **B58-59**,B-C] décembre *m*; **in D.** en décembre, au mois de décembre; **(on) the third of D.** le trois décembre
decency ['diːsənsɪ] *n* **(a)** (*of dress etc*) décence *f* **(b)** (*convention*) bienséance *f*, convenances *fpl*; **common d.** les

convenances (sociales); **he didn't even have the (common) d. to let us know** il n'a pas eu la bienséance élémentaire de nous informer; **the decencies** les convenances; **to observe the decencies** observer les convenances

decent ['di:sənt] *adj* **(a)** (*suitable*) bienséant, convenable; (*respectable*) décent, honnête; *F* **are you d.?** est-ce que tu es visible?; *Old-fashioned* **to do the d. thing** (*do what is required*) faire le nécessaire; (*marry sb*) faire son devoir (*et épouser la femme qu'on a mise enceinte*); *Mil* (*commit suicide*) faire la seule chose possible dans les circonstances

(b) (*acceptable*) passable; **this wine is quite d.** ce vin est très buvable *ou* se laisse boire; **the flat is quite a d. size** l'appartement est d'une taille raisonnable; **I earn a d. wage** je gagne un salaire décent; **wait until you have a d. amount of money** attends d'avoir suffisamment d'argent

(c) *F* (*kind*) **a d. (sort of) chap** un bon type; **it's very d. of you** c'est très gentil de votre part

decently ['di:səntlɪ] *adv* **(a)** (*respectably*) décemment, convenablement; **I can't d. ...** décemment je ne peux pas ... **(b)** *F* (*acceptably well*) pas trop mal; **he pays quite d.** il ne paie pas mal **(c)** (*honourably*) de façon correcte, correctement; **he's treated me really d.** il m'a traité de façon vraiment correcte

decentralization [di:sentrəlaɪ'zeɪʃən] *n* décentralisation *f*

decentralize [di:'sentrəlaɪz] *vt* décentraliser; *Comptr* **decentralized processing** traitement *m* décentralisé

decent-sized *adj* (*house etc*) de bonnes dimensions

deception [dɪ'sepʃən] *n* tromperie *f*, supercherie *f*; **to obtain sth by d.** obtenir qch en usant de tromperie *ou* de supercherie; **thanks to their d. of the enemy** parce qu'ils étaient parvenus à tromper l'ennemi

deceptive [dɪ'septɪv] *adj* (*thing, appearance*) trompeur, -euse; **he** *or* **his manner is very d.** on ne peut jamais deviner ce qu'il va faire/dire

deceptively [dɪ'septɪvlɪ] *adv* **d. worded/written** trompeur; **he has a d. quiet manner** il a un air tranquille (bien) trompeur; **it looks d. simple** *or* **easy** ce n'est pas aussi simple *ou* facile que ça en a l'air; **the mountains seem d. close** les montagnes paraissent plus proches qu'elles ne le sont en réalité; **the chair is d. light** en dépit de sa légèreté, la chaise est très robuste

deceptiveness [dɪ'septɪvnɪs] *n* (*of sth*) caractère *m* trompeur

decibel ['desɪbel] *n Phys* décibel *m*; **d. level** niveau *m* en décibels

decide [dɪ'saɪd] **1** *vt* (*question*) trancher; (*result of match, sb's fate, career etc*) décider de; **nothing has been** *or* **is decided yet** il n'y a encore rien de décidé; **that decided me** cela me décida (**to do** à faire); **to d. to do sth** se décider *ou* se résoudre à faire qch, décider *ou* résoudre de faire qch; **it was decided to wait for his reply** on a décidé d'attendre sa réponse

2 *vi* **have you decided?** êtes-vous décidé?; **you d.** décide, toi; **to d. on** (*plan of action*) arrêter; (*work procedure*) déterminer; (*day*) fixer; **have you decided on a date/a name?** vous êtes-vous décidés sur une date/un nom?; **I've decided on Greece for my holiday** j'ai décidé d'aller passer mes vacances en Grèce; **to d. on doing sth** décider de faire qch; **to d. against sth** (*give verdict*) se prononcer contre qch; **we've decided against a holiday this year** nous avons décidé de ne pas prendre de vacances cette année

decided [dɪ'saɪdɪd] *adj* **(a)** (*tone*) résolu; (*refusal*) catégorique, net; (*opinion*) ferme; **they are quite d. about it** ils sont tout à fait décidés **(b)** (*distinct*) (*difference*) marqué, prononcé; (*change*) sensible; (*success*) incontestable; (*preference*) net; **it's a d. improvement** c'est nettement mieux

decidedly [dɪ'saɪdɪdlɪ] *adv* **(a)** (*to answer, say*) d'un ton résolu **(b)** (*distinctly*) décidément

decider [dɪ'saɪdər] *n* (*factor*) facteur *m* décisif; *Sp* (*goal*) but *m* décisif; (*point*) point *m* décisif; **the d.** (*game, match*) la belle

deciding [dɪ'saɪdɪŋ] *adj* (*factor, vote*) décisif; *Sp* **the d. game/set/match** la belle; **the chairman has the d. vote** la voix du président est décisive *ou* prépondérante

deciduous [dɪ'sɪdjʊəs] *adj Bot* à feuilles caduques; *Zool* (*antlers etc*) caduc

decilitre, *US* **deciliter** ['desɪli:tər] *n* décilitre *m*

decimal ['desɪm(ə)l] [①A71,2,b; B56,C,2] **1** *adj* (*fraction, system, coinage etc*) décimal; **d. coding** codification *f* décimale; **d. place** décimale *f*, chiffre *m* après la virgule; *Comptr* position *f* décimale; **correct to five d. places** exact jusqu'à la cinquième décimale; *Math* **d. point** virgule *f* (décimale); *F* **to go d.** adopter le système décimal **2** *n* fraction *f* décimale

decimalization [desɪməlaɪ'zeɪʃən] *n* décimalisation *f*

decimate ['desɪmeɪt] *vt* (*of disease etc*) (*population etc*) décimer

decimation [desɪ'meɪʃən] *n* décimation *f*

decimetre, *US* **decimeter** ['desɪmi:tər] *n* (*unit of measurement*) décimètre *m*

decipher [dɪ'saɪfər] *vt* (*hieroglyphs, difficult handwriting*) déchiffrer; (*coded message*) déchiffrer, décoder

decipherable [dɪ'saɪf(ə)rəb(ə)l] *adj* déchiffrable; **easily d.** facile à déchiffrer

decision [dɪ'sɪʒən] *n* **(a)** (*of question, to do sth*) décision *f*; (*on question*) vote *m*; **to give a d.** se prononcer; **to make a d.** prendre une décision; **the judge's d. is final** (*in competition etc*) la décision du juge est irrévocable; **to come to** *or* **arrive at** *or* **reach a d.** arriver à une décision (**about** quant à, touchant); **d. by arbitration** décision *f* arbitrale; **d. model** modèle *m* décisionnel *ou* déterministe *ou* de décision; **d. theory** théorie *f* de la décision **(b)** (*resolution*) résolution *f*, fermeté *f*; **..., he said with d.** ..., dit-il fermement

decision-maker *n* décideur *m*

decision-making *n* prise *f* de décisions; **d. tool** outil *m* d'aide à la décision; *Com* **d. unit** unité *f* de prise de décision

decision-tree analysis *n* analyse *f* d'un modèle de décision en arborescence

decisive [dɪ'saɪsɪv] *adj* **(a)** (*question, battle, proof etc*) décisif; (*experiment etc*) concluant **(b)** (*manner, tone, person etc*) décidé; (*approach*) tranché

decisively [dɪ'saɪsɪvlɪ] *adv* **(a)** (*conclusively*) d'une façon décisive **(b)** (*resolutely*) (*to act*) de façon décidée; (*to say*) d'un ton décidé

decisiveness [dɪ'saɪsɪvnɪs] *n* **(a)** (*of battle, question*) caractère *m* décisif; (*of experiment*) caractère concluant **(b)** = **decision (b)**

deck[1] [dek] *n* **(a)** *Naut* pont *m*; **on d.** sur le pont; **below deck(s)** dans l'entrepont; **after d.** pont arrière; **lower/upper d.** pont inférieur/supérieur; **to come/go on d.** monter sur le pont; **to clear the decks (for action)** faire le branle-bas de combat; *Fig* se préparer à agir; *F* **to hit the d.** (*to avoid injury*) tomber à plat ventre; (*get out of bed*) se lever; **hit the d.!** (*fall to the ground*) tout le monde à plat ventre!; (*get out of bed*) debout!; *also Fig* **all hands on d.!** tous sur le pont!; **d. cargo** *or* **load** pontée *f*

(b) (*of vehicle*) plate-forme *f*, *pl* plates-formes; **top d.** (*of bus*) impériale *f*

(c) *Constr* tablier *m*; (*of bridge*) plancher *m*; *Am* (*terrace*) terrasse *f*

(d) *esp Am* **d. of cards** jeu *m* de cartes; *F* **not to have** *or* **not to play with a full d.** (*not be very bright*) avoir quelques cases de vides

(e) (*for records etc*) platine *f*; **cassette d.** platine à cassette; **tape d.** platine à bande magnétique

(f) *US Aut* (*space behind back seat*) coffre *m*; (*cover of space*) plage *f* arrière

deck[2] *vt* **(a)** (*decorate*) parer, orner (**sth with sth** qch de qch); **to d. oneself out** s'endimancher; **I decked myself out in my Sunday best** je me suis paré de mes plus beaux habits; **they were decked out in their best clothes** ils étaient sur leur trente et un **(b)** *Naut* (*ship*) ponter **(c)** *esp Am F* (*knock to ground*) (*sb*) flanquer par terre

deck chair *n* transat *m*

deck hand *n* matelot *m* de pont

deckhouse ['dekhaʊs] *n Naut* rouf *m*

deckle ['dek(ə)l] *n* (*frame*) (*in papermaking*) cadre *m* volant, rebord *m*; **d. edge** (*of paper*) barbes *fpl*

deckle-edged *adj* (*paper*) à barbes

deck officer *n* officier *m* de pont

declaim [dɪ'kleɪm] *Fml* **1** *vi* déclamer (**against** contre) **2** *vt* (*verse etc*) déclamer

declamation [deklə'meɪʃən] *n* déclamation *f*

declamatory [dɪ'klæmətərɪ, -trɪ] *adj* (*style etc*) déclamatoire

declaration [deklə'reɪʃən] *n* **(a)** (*of love, faith, war etc*) déclaration *f*; **d. of income** déclaration de revenu; **d. of value** déclaration de valeur **(b)** *Cards* annonce *f*

Declaration of Independence *n US Hist* Déclaration *f* d'Indépendance

declare [dɪ'kleər] **1** *vt* **(a)** (*formally announce*) déclarer (**sth to sb** qch à qn); **to d. a change of policy** annoncer un changement de politique; **to d. war** déclarer la guerre (**on, against** à); **the two countries have declared war** (*on each other*) les deux pays se sont déclaré la guerre; **to d. a moratorium** décréter un moratoire; **to d. a strike** proclamer la grève; **she was declared the winner** elle a été déclarée vainqueur; *Fin* **to d. a dividend of ten per cent** déclarer un dividende de dix pour cent; **to d. sb guilty/innocent** déclarer qn coupable/innocent; **to d. sb bankrupt** prononcer la faillite de qn; **to d. a business bankrupt** déclarer une entreprise en faillite

(b) (*make public*) *Cards* (*trumps, suit*) appeler; *Fig* **to d. one's hand** avouer ses intentions; **to d. oneself** prendre parti; (*of lover*) se déclarer, faire sa déclaration; **have you**

anything to d.? (*at customs*) avez-vous quelque chose à déclarer?; **to d. an interest** déclarer un intérêt; **to d. itself** (*of disease*) se déclarer

2 *vi Cr* fermer son jeu (avant la chute des dix guichets); *Cards* annoncer son jeu; *Old-fashioned* **well I d.!** ciel!, ça alors!; **to d. for/against sth** déclarer pour/contre qch

declared [dɪ'kleəd] *adj* avoué, déclaré

declassification [di:klæsɪfɪ'keɪʃən] *n* (*of information, document*) levée *f* du sceau du secret (**of** portant sur)

declassify [di:'klæsɪfaɪ] *vt* (*secret document etc*) lever le sceau du secret qui porte sur

declension [dɪ'klenʃən] *n Gram* déclinaison *f*

declinable [dɪ'klaɪnəb(ə)l] *adj Gram* déclinable

declination [deklɪ'neɪʃən] *n* (**a**) *Astron* déclinaison *f* (**b**) *Am* (*refusal*) refus *m* courtois et formel

decline¹ [dɪ'klaɪn] *n* (*of day, empire*) déclin *m*; (*in price, number, enthusiasm*) baisse *f*; (*of business*) ralentissement *m*; **sales have shown a rapid d. over the last six months** on a observé une forte chute des ventes au cours des six derniers mois; **to go into a d.** (*of health, patient*) décliner; (*of company shares, economy*) chuter; **to be on the d.** (*of crime, birth rate*) être sur le déclin, décliner, être en baisse; (*of prices*) être en baisse, être en diminution; (*of patient*) décliner

decline² **1** *vt* (**a**) (*refuse*) (*honour, invitation*) décliner; (*sb's help*) repousser; **to d. to do sth** refuser de faire qch (**b**) *Gram* (*noun etc*) décliner **2** *vi* (**a**) (*refuse*) refuser (**b**) (*go down, come to end*) (*of sun*) décliner; (*of day*) décliner, tirer à sa fin; (*of health, influence etc*) décliner, baisser; *Com* (*of prices, business*) être en baisse; **to d. in importance** perdre de l'importance

declining [dɪ'klaɪnɪŋ] *adj* (**a**) (*sun*) couchant; *Lit* **in one's d. years** au déclin de la vie; **she spent her d. years in a nursing home** elle a passé la fin de ses jours dans une maison de retraite (**b**) *Econ* (*industry*) déclinant, sur le déclin; (*market*) en baisse; **d. demand** demande *f* déclinante; **d. sales** ventes *fpl* en baisse

declivity [dɪ'klɪvɪtɪ] *n Fml* déclivité *f*, pente *f*

declutch [di:'klʌtʃ] *vi Aut* débrayer

decoction [dɪ'kɒkʃən] *n Fml Tech* décoction *f*

decode [di:'kəʊd] *vt* (*message*) déchiffrer, décoder, transcrire en clair; *Comptr* décoder; *Fig* déchiffrer; **decoded message** message transcrit en clair

decoder [di:'kəʊdər] *n* (*person, machine*) décodeur *m*, déchiffreur *m*; *Comptr, TV* décodeur

decoding [di:'kəʊdɪŋ] *n* (*of message*) déchiffrement *m*, décodage *m*, transcription *f* en clair; *Comptr* décodage

decoke¹ [di:'kəʊk] *n Aut F* **the car needs a d.** la voiture a besoin d'un décalaminage *ou* d'être décalaminée; **d. machine** machine *f* de décalaminage

decoke² *vt Aut F* décalaminer

décolletage [deɪkɒl'tɑ:ʒ] *n* décolleté *m*

décolleté [deɪ'kɒlteɪ] **1** *adj* (*dress, woman*) décolleté **2** *n* décolleté *m*

decolonization [di:kɒlənaɪ'zeɪʃən] *n* décolonisation *f*

decolonize [di:'kɒlənaɪz] *vt* décoloniser

decommission [di:kə'mɪʃən] *vt* (*nuclear reactor, plant*) mettre hors service

decommissioning [di:kə'mɪʃənɪŋ] *n* (*of nuclear reactor, plant*) mise *f* hors service

decompose [di:kəm'pəʊz] **1** *vi* (*of organic matter*) se décomposer, entrer en décomposition **2** *vt* (*matter, compound, light etc*) décomposer

decomposition [di:kɒmpə'zɪʃən] *n* décomposition *f*

decompress [di:kəm'pres] *vt Tech* (*gas etc*) décomprimer; *Med* (*diver*) faire séjourner dans une chambre de décompression; *Comptr* décompresser

decompression [di:kəm'preʃən] *n Tech* décompression *f*; **d. chamber** chambre *f* de décompression; *Med* **d. sickness** *or* **illness** (*suffered by divers*) maladie *f* des caissons; *Comptr* **d. software** logiciel *m* de décompression

decompressor [di:kəm'presər] *n Comptr* logiciel *m* de décompression

decongestant [di:kən'dʒestənt] *adj, n Med* décongestionnant *m*

decongestion [di:kən'dʒestʃən] *n Med* décongestion *f*

deconsecrate [di:'kɒnsəkreɪt] *vt Rel* (*church*) désaffecter

deconsignment [di:kən'saɪnmənt] *n Com* déconsignation *f*

decontaminate [di:kən'tæmɪneɪt] *vt* décontaminer

decontamination [di:kəntæmɪ'neɪʃən] *n* décontamination *f*; **d. measures** mesures *fpl* de décontamination

decontrol¹ [di:kən'trəʊl] *vt* **to d. prices** mettre fin au contrôle des prix; **to d. trade** libérer le commerce du contrôle gouvernemental

decontrol² *n* (*of prices etc*) libération *f*

décor, decor ['deɪkɔ:r] *n Th etc* décor *m*; *F* **he's part of the d.** (*has been here for a long time*) il fait partie des meubles

decorate ['dekəreɪt] *vt* (**a**) (*room, streets*) décorer, orner (**with sth** de qch); (*cake, Christmas tree*) décorer (**b**) (*paint and wallpaper etc*) (*room*) peindre et tapisser, décorer (**c**) (*person*) (*with medal*) décorer, remettre une décoration à; **she was decorated for bravery** elle a été décorée pour son courage

decorating ['dekəreɪtɪŋ] *n* décoration *f*; **to do the d.** (*in flat, house*) faire les travaux (de décoration)

decoration [dekə'reɪʃən] *n* (**a**) (*of room, cake, Christmas tree etc*) décoration *f*; **decorations** (*in town for festival etc*) décorations (**b**) (*with paint and wallpaper etc*) (*of room*) peinture *f* et pose *f* de la tapisserie, décoration *f*; **we did all the d. ourselves** nous avons fait tous les travaux nous-mêmes (**c**) (*with medal*) remise *f* d'une décoration (**of sb** à qn); (*medal*) décoration, médaille *f*

decorative ['dek(ə)rətɪv] *adj* (*art, ornament, F woman*) décoratif; **the house is in excellent d. order** la décoration de la maison est en excellent état

decoratively ['dek(ə)rətɪvlɪ] *adv* décorativement

decorator ['dekəreɪtər] *n* décorateur *m*; *Br* (**painter and**) **d.** peintre *m* décorateur; *Br* **we're having the decorators in next week** les peintres viennent la semaine prochaine

decorous ['dekərəs] *adj* bienséant, convenable

decorously ['dekərəslɪ] *adv* avec bienséance, convenablement

decorticate [di:'kɔ:tɪkeɪt] *vt Fml* décortiquer

decorum [dɪ'kɔ:rəm] *n* décorum *m*, bienséance *f*; **a breach of d.** une inconvenance; **to have no sense of d.** ne pas avoir le sens du décorum; **her sense of d.** son sens des convenances *ou* du décorum; **to behave with d.** se comporter comme il faut

decouple [dɪ'kʌp(ə)l] *vt El* découpler

decoupling [dɪ'kʌplɪŋ] *n El* découplage *m*

decoy¹ ['di:kɔɪ] *n* (**a**) (*in hunting*) appât *m*, leurre *m*; **d.** (**bird**) moquette *f*, (oiseau *m*) appelant *m* (**b**) *Fig* (*person*) appât *m*; (*phone call*) piège *m*; **police d.** (*to trick criminal*) policier *m* en civil

decoy² [dɪ'kɔɪ] *vt* (*birds, sb*) leurrer; **to d. sb into a trap** attirer qn dans un piège; **to d. sb into doing sth** leurrer qn pour qu'il fasse qch; **the phone call decoyed her away from the office** le coup de téléphone était un piège pour la faire sortir du bureau

decrease¹ ['di:kri:s] *n* (*in unemployment, crime, population*) diminution *f*; (*in prices, strength, value, number*) diminution, baisse *f*; (*in political power*) affaiblissement *m*; **to be on the d.** (*of crime etc*) baisser; **d. in speed** ralentissement *m*; **d. in stocks** (*profit and loss item*) déstockage *m* de production

decrease² [dɪ'kri:s] **1** *vi* (*of population, unemployment, crime, inflation*) diminuer, baisser, décroître; (*of value, strength, prices, output*) diminuer, baisser; (*of power*) s'affaiblir; *Knitting* diminuer, faire une/des diminution(s) **2** *vt* diminuer, réduire; (*prices*) (*of government*) baisser; (*of economic forces*) faire baisser; *Knitting* **d. three stitches** diminuer de trois mailles, faire trois diminutions; **to d. the pain** faire diminuer la douleur

decreasing [dɪ'kri:sɪŋ] *adj* (*number, population, value, strength*) décroissant; (*prices, unemployment, crime, output*) en baisse; (*influence, importance*) déclinant, en déclin; **in d. order of importance** par ordre d'importance décroissante; *Acct* **d. rate** taux *m* dégressif

decreasingly [dɪ'kri:sɪŋlɪ] *adv* de moins en moins

decree¹ [dɪ'kri:] *n* (**a**) *Admin* décret *m*, arrêté *m*; **to issue a d.** promulguer un décret; **to rule by d.** régner par décret (**b**) *Rel* décret *m* (**c**) *Jur* décision *f*, arrêt *m*, jugement *m*; **d. nisi** ['naɪsaɪ] (*in divorce case*) jugement *m* provisoire; **d. absolute** jugement irrévocable

decree² *vt* (*order*) décréter, ordonner; *Jur* arrêter (**that** que); **fate decreed that ...** le sort avait voulu que ...; **the film was decreed a threat to public morals** on a décrété que le film était une menace pour la morale publique

decrepit [dɪ'krepɪt] *adj* (**a**) (*person*) décrépit (**b**) (*car, house, furniture etc*) délabré

decrepitude [dɪ'krepɪtju:d] *n Fml* (**a**) (*of person*) décrépitude *f* (**b**) (*of car, house etc*) délabrement *m*

decriminalization [di:krɪmɪnəlaɪ'zeɪʃən] *n Jur* (*of drug possession*) dépénalisation *f*

decriminalize [di:'krɪmɪnəlaɪz] *vt Jur* (*possession of drugs*) dépénaliser

decry [dɪ'kraɪ] *vt Fml* décrier, dénigrer; **the union has decried the suggested increase as an insult** le syndicat a qualifié l'augmentation proposée d'insulte; **his intervention has been decried as worsening the problem** on l'a accusé, en intervenant, d'avoir aggravé le problème

decrypt [diːˈkrɪpt] *vt Comptr* déchiffrer

decryption [diːˈkrɪpʃən] *n Comptr* déchiffrement *m*

dedicate [ˈdedɪkeɪt] *vt* **(a)** *(assign) (church)* dédier, consacrer; **to d. oneself** *or* **one's life to sb** se consacrer à qn, consacrer sa vie à qn; **to d. oneself** *or* **one's life to sth** se vouer à qch, se consacrer à qch **(b)** *(book, record)* dédicacer **(to** à)

dedicated [ˈdedɪkeɪtɪd] *adj* **(a)** *(to one's profession)* consciencieux; *(doctor, nurse, teacher)* dévoué; *(socialist, supporter)* convaincu; **to be d. to one's job** être dévoué à son travail; **she was d. to the cause** elle se consacrait à cette cause; **d. to the cause of freedom** engagé dans la lutte pour la liberté **(b)** *Comptr (terminal)* spécialisé; **d. circuit** circuit *m* dédié; *Telecom* **d. line** liaison *f* spécialisée; **d. word processor** machine *f* servant uniquement au traitement de texte

dedication [dedɪˈkeɪʃən] *n* **(a)** *(of church)* consécration *f*; *Am (of building)* inauguration *f* **(b)** *(of book)* dédicace *f*; **to write a d. in a book** dédicacer un livre; **to read out the dedications** *(of disc jockey)* lire les dédicaces **(c)** *(devotion) (to a cause)* attachement *m*, dévouement *m* **(to** à); *(to country, company)* dévouement; **a life of d.** une vie de dévouement; **to work with d.** travailler avec dévouement; **I admire your d. (to your work)** j'admire ton dévouement (à ton travail); **to work with great d. for the cause of freedom** travailler avec dévouement pour la liberté

deduce [dɪˈdjuːs] *vt* déduire **(from** de); **I d. therefore that you will not be there** j'en conclus donc que vous ne serez pas là

deduct [dɪˈdʌkt] *vt* déduire **(from** de); *(from a bill, price)* décompter; **to d. £50/10% from the price** rabattre 50 livres/ 10% sur le prix; **to d. a commission** prélever une commission; **to be deducted** à déduire; **tax is deducted at source** l'impôt est retenu *ou* prélevé à la source

deductibility [dɪdʌktɪˈbɪlɪtɪ] *n* déductibilité *f*

deductible [dɪˈdʌktɪb(ə)l] *adj* déductible

deduction [dɪˈdʌkʃən] *n* **(a)** *(subtraction)* déduction *f* **(from a quantity** sur une quantité); *(from pay)* retenue *f*, prélèvement *m*; **d. of a sum** décompte *m* d'une somme; *Fin* **d. at source** retenue *f* à la source; **d. of tax at source** retenue *f* salariale à la source; **after deductions, I'm left with a salary of …** une fois les prélèvements *ou* les retenues décompté(e)s, il me reste un salaire de … **(b)** *(conclusion)* déduction *f* **(from** de); **by a process of d.** par déduction; **there is only one d. that can be made** on ne peut déduire qu'une seule chose

deductive [dɪˈdʌktɪv] *adj (reasoning)* déductif, par déduction

deed[1] [diːd] *n* **(a)** *(action)* action *f*, acte *m*; **to do one's good d. for the day** faire sa bonne action *ou* sa B. A. quotidienne; *Lit* **d. of valour** haut fait *m* **(b)** *Jur (document)* acte *m* notarié; *Jur* **d. of acknowledgment** acte récognitif; **d. of covenant** = document *m* par lequel on s'engage à verser une certaine somme à quelqu'un ou à un organisme; **d. of sale** acte de vente; *Jur* **d. of transfer** acte de cession; **mortgage d.** acte hypothécaire; **to change one's name by d. poll** changer légalement son nom; **the deeds to the house** les titres *mpl* de propriété de la maison; **d. box** coffre *m* à documents

deed[2] *vt esp Am Jur (transfer by deed)* transférer par un acte

deejay [ˈdiːdʒeɪ] *n Mus F* disc-jockey *m*, *pl* disc-jockeys

deem [diːm] *vt Arch, Lit* **I do not d. it necessary/proper to …** je ne juge pas *ou* ne crois pas *ou* ne considère pas nécessaire/convenable de …; **it is deemed necessary/ proper to …** on juge *ou* croit nécessaire/convenable de …; **if it is deemed necessary** si c'est jugé nécessaire; **I d. it a great honour** je considère cela comme un grand honneur; **he was deemed (to be) the winner** il a été considéré comme étant le vainqueur

deep [diːp] **1** *adj* **(a)** *(water, wound, sleep, despair etc, Tennis serve, Fig thinker)* profond; *(shelf)* large, profond; **to be ten metres d.** avoir dix mètres de profondeur, avoir une profondeur de dix mètres; **to take a d. breath** respirer profondément; *Fig* respirer un grand coup; **to be in d. water** *(in serious difficulties)* être dans de sales draps, être en mauvaise posture; **I think we're getting into d. water here** je crois que nous sommes en train de nous engager sur un terrain dangereux; *F* **you're in d. trouble, my lad** tu as de sérieux problèmes, mon gars; **d. in debt** criblé de dettes; **he got deeper and deeper in debt** il s'est endetté de plus en plus; **d. in thought** plongé dans ses pensées; **to inflict a d. wound** *(of weapon)* pénétrer très profondément; **two/four d.** sur deux/quatre rangs; **his d. learning** ses connaissances profondes; **in deepest sympathy** *(on card)* avec toute ma sympathie; **d. concern** sincère *ou* vive préoccupation; *Journ* **d. throat** *(anonymous source)* corbeau *m*; **the D. South** *(of the United States)* le sud profond; *Hum* **in deepest Yorkshire** au fin fond du Yorkshire

(b) *(colour)* foncé, sombre; *(sound)* grave; **d. blue** bleu foncé; **in a d. voice** d'une voix profonde

(c) *F (not readily understandable)* **he's a d. one** il est plutôt mystérieux

2 *adv* profondément; **the harpoon sank d. into the flesh** le harpon a pénétré très profondément dans la chair; **to walk d. into the forest** pénétrer profondément dans la forêt; **to look d. into sb's eyes** pénétrer qn du regard; **to work d. into the night** travailler tard dans la nuit; *F* **we're in too d. to pull out now** nous sommes trop impliqués pour faire marche arrière maintenant; *Fml* **to drink d.** boire à longs traits; **d.-lying causes** causes profondes; **d. down he's very kind** au fond il est très gentil; **to run d.** être profond

3 *n Lit* **the d.** l'océan *m*; **to commit a body to the d.** immerger un mort

deep-dish *adj Am Culin* **d. pie** tourte *f*

deepen [ˈdiːp(ə)n] **1** *vt* **(a)** *(well etc)* approfondir, creuser; *(love, hatred, resentment etc)* rendre plus intense, accroître; **that only deepened his conviction** cela n'a fait que le conforter dans sa conviction **(b)** *(colour)* foncer; *(sound)* rendre plus grave **2** *vi* **(a)** *(of river, silence etc)* devenir plus profond; *(of conviction, belief)* augmenter; *(of mystery)* s'épaissir **(b)** *(of colour)* devenir plus foncé; *(of sound, voice)* devenir plus grave; *(of shadows)* s'épaissir

deep end *n (of swimming pool)* côté *m* le plus profond, grand bain *m*; *Fig* **to go off the d.** *(get angry)* s'emporter; *(panic)* s'affoler; *Fig* **to be thrown in at the d.** subir le baptême du feu; *Fig* **I decided to jump in at the d.** j'ai décidé de prendre le taureau par les cornes

deep-fat frying *n* cuisson *f* en bain de friture

deep-freeze[1] *vt (food)* congeler, surgeler

deep-freeze[2] *n* congélateur *m*; *Fig* **to put sth in the d.** mettre qch au frigidaire

deep-frozen *adj* surgelé

deep-fry *vt (fish etc)* faire cuire dans la friture

deep-fryer *n* friteuse *f*

deep-laid *adj (plan, scheme)* habilement comploté

deeply [ˈdiːplɪ] *adv* profondément; **to sigh d.** pousser un profond soupir; **they gazed d. into each other's eyes** leurs regards étaient plongés dans les yeux l'un de l'autre; *Fig* **to go d. into sth** pénétrer *ou* entrer profondément dans qch, approfondir qch; **she can't have looked into it very d.** elle n'a pas dû s'en occuper très sérieusement; **to fall d. in love with sb** tomber profondément amoureux de qn; **to care d. about sb** être profondément attaché à qn; **I care d. about your happiness/this country's future** ton bonheur/l'avenir de ce pays est très important pour moi; **d. interesting** fort intéressant; **d. offended** gravement offensé; **to be d. insulting** être très insultant

deepness [ˈdiːpnɪs] *n (of voice etc)* profondeur *f*; *Mus (of sound)* gravité *f*

deep-pan *adj Culin* **d. pizza** pizza *f* à pâte épaisse

deep-rooted *adj (tree)* profondément enraciné, aux racines profondes; *(affection, prejudice, dislike, antagonism etc)* profond; *(habit)* ancré

deep-sea *adj (plant, animal)* pélagique; **d. diver** plongeur *m* sous-marin; **d. fishery** *or* **fishing** pêche *f* hauturière; **d. fisherman** pêcheur *m* en haute mer

deep-seated [ˈdiːpˈsiːtɪd] *adj (aversion)* profond, bien enraciné; *(affection, prejudice, conviction etc)* profond

deep-set *adj (eyes)* enfoncé

deer [dɪər] *n inv* cerf *m*; **d. park** chasse *f* gardée pour le cerf

deerhound [ˈdɪəhaʊnd] *n (dog)* lévrier *m* d'Écosse

deerskin [ˈdɪəskɪn] *n* peau *f* de daim; *Com* daim *m*; **d. gloves** gants *mpl* en daim

deerstalker [ˈdɪəstɔːkər] *n* **(a)** *(hunter)* chasseur *m* (de cerf) à l'approche **(b)** *(hat)* chapeau *m* de chasse (à la Sherlock Holmes)

deerstalking [ˈdɪəstɔːkɪŋ] *n* chasse *f* (au cerf) à l'approche

de-escalate [diːˈeskəleɪt] **1** *vt (tension, bombing)* diminuer; *(crisis)* désamorcer **2** *vi (of tension)* diminuer; **the crisis shows no sign of de-escalating** la situation de crise ne semble pas se détendre

de-escalation [diːeskəˈleɪʃən] *n (of arms sales)* diminution *f*; *(of crisis, tension)* détente *f*

deface [dɪˈfeɪs] *vt (statue)* dégrader; *(poster, walls)* barbouiller; *(book) (of child)* gribouiller; *(to express dissatisfaction with contents)* noircir

de facto [ˈdeɪfæktəʊ] *adj, adv Lit, Jur* de facto; *Jur* **d. and de jure** de droit et de fait; *Jur* **d. possession** possession *f* de fait

defamation [defəˈmeɪʃən] *n* diffamation *f*; **that's d. of character** c'est de la diffamation; **to sue for d. of character** engager des poursuites en diffamation, faire un procès en diffamation; **to sue sb for d. of character** poursuivre qn en diffamation

defamatory [dɪˈfæmət(ə)rɪ] *adj* (*remark etc*) diffamatoire, diffamant

defame [dɪˈfeɪm] *vt* (*sb*) diffamer

default[1] [dɪˈfɔːlt] *n* **(a)** *Jur* (*failure to appear in court*) défaut *m*, non-comparution *f*; (*in criminal law*) contumace *f*; **judgment by d.** jugement *m* par contumace; **by d.** (*if not otherwise specified*) implicitement; *Tech* par défaut; *Comptr* **d. drive/font** lecteur *m*/police *f* par défaut; *Comptr* **d. setting** configuration *f* par défaut; *Comptr* **which is the d.?** quelle est la configuration/police/*etc* par défaut?; *Sp* **match won by d.** match gagné par forfait; **the machine sets itself to 1 by d.** la machine se réglera sur 1 par défaut

(b) *Com* défaut *m*, défaillance *f*; **d. in paying** défaut de paiement; *Fin* **d. interest** intérêts *mpl* moratoires; *Fig* **in d. of ...** à défaut de ..., faute de ...

(c) *Tennis* disqualification *f*

default[2] **1** *vi* **(a)** *Jur* (*fail to appear in court*) ne pas comparaître; (*in criminal law*) être en état de contumace **(b)** (*fail to pay*) **to d. on alimony payments** manquer aux versements de pension alimentaire; *St Exch* manquer à ses engagements **(c)** *Comptr* **to d. to sth** sélectionner qch par défaut **2** *vt Tennis* (*sb*) disqualifier

defaulter [dɪˈfɔːltər] *n* **(a)** *Jur* défaillant, -ante; (*in criminal law*) contumace *mf* **(b)** (*debtor*) débiteur *m* défaillant; **d. on a fine** personne *f* qui ne paie pas une amende **(c)** *Mil, Naut* retardataire *m*, réfractaire *m*; (*undergoing punishment*) consigné *m*

defaulting [dɪˈfɔːltɪŋ] *adj Jur* défaillant

defeasance [dɪˈfiːzəns] *n Banking, Jur* defeasance *m*

defeat[1] [dɪˈfiːt] *n* **(a)** (*of army, team, government*) défaite *f*; **to suffer a d.** essuyer une défaite; **..., he said with an air of d.** ..., dit-il d'un air de vaincu; **to admit d.** s'avouer vaincu **(b)** (*of plan*) échec *m*, renversement *m*; *Parl* (*of measure*) rejet *m*

defeat[2] *vt* **(a)** (*army, opponent*) battre, vaincre; (*government*) mettre en minorité; **they were defeated by their own lack of preparation** ils ont été battus *ou* vaincus à cause de leur manque de préparation; **it defeats me** (*I don't understand*) cela me dépasse **(b)** (*plan, attempt to do sth*) déjouer, faire échouer; (*hope*) frustrer; (*of meeting*) (*proposal*) rejeter; *Parl* (*measure*) faire échouer, rejeter; **to d. the ends of justice** contrarier la justice; **to d. one's own ends** aller à l'encontre de ses propres intentions; **that does rather d. the object of the exercise** cela va plutôt à l'encontre du but de l'opération

defeatism [dɪˈfiːtɪz(ə)m] *n* défaitisme *m*; **an air/mood of d.** un air/une atmosphère défaitiste *ou* de défaite

defeatist [dɪˈfiːtɪst] *adj, n* défaitiste *mf*

defecate [ˈdefəkeɪt] *vi Fml* déféquer

defecation [defəˈkeɪʃən] *n Fml* défécation *f*

defect[1] [ˈdiːfekt] *n* (*in construction, physical*) défaut *m*; *Com* vice *m*; (*mental*) déficience *f*

defect[2] [dɪˈfekt] *vi Mil, Pol* passer à l'ennemi; *Fig Pol* (*of MP*) passer dans le camp adverse; *Pol* **to d. to the West** passer à l'ouest; **she defected from the USSR in 1963** elle a quitté l'URSS en 1963; *Fig Pol* **to d. from the party** abandonner le parti; *Fig Pol* **to d. to the government** passer dans le camp du gouvernement; *Fig Com* **she's defected to our main competitor** elle est passée chez notre concurrent principal

defection [dɪˈfekʃən] *n Mil, Pol* défection *f*; **there have been a number of defections to the West** un certain nombre de gens sont passés à l'ouest

defective [dɪˈfektɪv] *adj* **(a)** (*machine*) défectueux; (*theory*) imparfait; (*memory*) infidèle; (*brakes*) en mauvais état; (*reasoning*) défectueux, mauvais; (*hearing, method*) mauvais; **to be d. in sth** manquer de qch; *Ind* **d. part** pièce *f* défectueuse **(b)** *Gram* (*verb etc*) défectif

defector [dɪˈfektər] *n Mil, Pol etc* transfuge *mf*

defence, *US* **defense** [dɪˈfens] *n* **(a)** (*action*) défense *f*; **to put up a stubborn d.** se défendre avec obstination; **I carry a knife for d.** je porte un couteau pour me défendre; **he killed the man in d. of his wife** il a tué l'homme pour défendre sa femme; **to come to sb's d.** venir à la défense de qn

(b) (*means*) **defences** (*of country*) moyens *mpl* de défense; **Holland's defences against the flood waters** les défenses *fpl* dont dispose la Hollande contre les inondations; **the body's natural defences** les défenses naturelles du corps; *Sp* **the d.** les défenseurs *mpl*; **seaward defences** (*of port*) ouvrages *mpl* de défense face à la mer; **d. electronics** électronique *f* de défense; **d. mechanism** (*of body*) système *m* immunitaire; (*of subconscious*) mécanisme *m* de défense; **d. spending** dépenses *fpl* pour la défense

(c) (*argument*) défense *f*, justification *f*; *Jur* défense; **to speak in d. of sb** défendre qn; **I must say, in my own d., that ...** je dois dire pour ma propre défense que ...; **d. counsel** défenseur *m*; (*in civil law*) avocat *m* de la défense; **to appear for the d.** (*of barrister*) représenter la défense; **d. witness** témoin *m* à décharge; **to conduct one's own d.** défendre soi-même sa cause

defenceless, *US* **defenseless** [dɪˈfenslɪs] *adj* sans défense

defend [dɪˈfend] **1** *vt* **(a)** (*person, border, country etc, Sp title*) défendre **(from, against** contre) **(b)** (*opinion*) défendre, justifier; **to d. one's actions** justifier ses actions **(c)** *Jur* (*defendant*) défendre **2** *vi* **(a)** *Jur* assumer *ou* soutenir la défense **(b)** *Sp* défendre

defendant [dɪˈfendənt] *n Jur* défendeur, -eresse; (*on appeal*) intimé, -ée; (*in criminal case*) accusé, -ée

defender [dɪˈfendər] *n* défenseur *m*; **D. of the Faith** défenseur de la foi

defending [dɪˈfendɪŋ] *adj* **(a)** *Sp* **d. champion** champion, -ionne en titre **(b)** *Jur* **d. counsel** défenseur *m*

defense *US* = **defence**

defensible [dɪˈfensəb(ə)l] *adj* (*cause*), *Mil* défendable; (*position, point of view*) tenable; (*opinion, behaviour*) défendable, justifiable; **the town was easily d.** la ville était facile à défendre

defensive [dɪˈfensɪv] **1** *adj* défensif, de défense; **don't be so d.!** ne te mets pas sur la défensive comme ça!; **to get d.** se montrer défensif **(about** au sujet de), se mettre sur la défensive; *Mil etc* **d. action** action *f* défensive; **d. position** position *f* de défense **2** *n* défensive *f*; **to be/go on the d.** se tenir/se mettre sur la défensive

defensively [dɪˈfensɪvlɪ] *adv* (*to say*) d'un ton défensif; (*to react*) d'une manière défensive

defensiveness [dɪˈfensɪvnɪs] *n* **when she reacted/spoke with such d.** quand elle a réagi/parlé d'une manière aussi défensive; **her d. in the face of criticism** la façon qu'elle a de se mettre sur la défensive quand on la critique

defer [dɪˈfɜːr] (**-rr-**) **1** *vt* **(a)** (*delay, postpone*) (*question, case*) différer, ajourner, remettre; (*meeting, decision*) remettre, reporter; (*payment*) reculer, renvoyer; (*verdict*) suspendre; **to d. sth to a later date** remettre *ou* reporter qch à plus tard; **to d. doing sth** différer de faire qch **(b)** *Mil etc* (*sb*) mettre en sursis (d'appel); **to d. sb on medical grounds** réformer qn **2** *vi* (*yield*) (*to sb's opinion*) se ranger **(to** à); (*to sb's wishes*) se soumettre **(to** à); (*to sb's knowledge*) s'en remettre **(to** à)

deference [ˈdefərəns] *n* déférence *f*; **to pay** *or* **show d. to sb, to treat sb with d.** témoigner de la déférence à *ou* envers qn; **out of** *or* **in d. to ...** par déférence pour ..., par égard pour ...

deferential [defəˈrenʃəl] *adj* (*air, tone*) de déférence, respectueux; (*behaviour*) respectueux; (*person*) déférent, respectueux; **to be d. to sb** se montrer plein de déférence *ou* de respect pour *ou* envers qn, se montrer respectueux envers qn

deferentially [defəˈrenʃəlɪ] *adv* (*to speak, look at*) avec déférence, avec respect; (*to behave*) avec déférence, respectueusement

deferment [dɪˈfɜːmənt] *n* **(a)** (*of case*) ajournement *m*, remise *f*; (*of payment*) renvoi *m* **(b)** *Mil etc* (*for health reasons*) réforme *f*; **to apply for d. (of call up)** faire une demande de sursis (d'appel)

deferral [dɪˈfɜːrəl] *n* = **deferment**

deferred [dɪˈfɜːd] *adj* (*share etc*) différé; *Fin* **d. depreciation** amortissements *mpl* différés; **d. payment** (*postponed*) paiement *m* différé; (*in instalments*) paiement par versements échelonnés; *Jur* **d. sentence** = jugement *m* dont le prononcé est suspendu

defiance [dɪˈfaɪəns] *n* défi *m*; **a gesture of d.** un geste de défi; **in d. of** (*the law, an order*) au mépris de

defiant [dɪˈfaɪənt] *adj* (*gesture, look, remark*) de défi, provocant; (*person*) audacieux, *Pej* irrevérencieux

defiantly [dɪˈfaɪəntlɪ] *adv* (*to say*) d'un ton provocant; (*to look at*) d'un air provocant *ou* de défi

defibrillation [dɪfɪbrɪˈleɪʃən] *n Med* défibrillation *f*

defibrillator [dɪˈfɪbrɪleɪtər] *n Med* défibrillateur *m*

deficiency [dɪˈfɪʃənsɪ] *n* **(a)** (*lack*) manque *m*, insuffisance *f* **(of** de); *Med* (*of minerals, vitamins*) carence *f* **(in, of** de); (*of function, organ*) déficience *f*; **d. disease** maladie *f* de carence **(b)** (*flaw, defect*) défaut *m*, imperfection *f* **(c)** (*deficit*) manquant *m*, déficit *m*; *Com* découvert *m*; *Pol* déficit budgétaire

deficient [dɪˈfɪʃənt] *adj* (*faulty*) défectueux; (*lacking*) insuffisant, incomplet; **to be d. in sth** manquer de qch

deficit [ˈdefɪsɪt] *n Fin, Com* déficit *m*; **to be in d.** être en déficit; **budget d.** budget déficitaire; **to make up the d.** combler le déficit

defile[1] [ˈdiːfaɪl] *n* (*pass*) défilé *m*

defile[2] [dɪˈfaɪl] *vi Mil etc* (*of troops etc*) défiler

defile[3] *vt* (*memory of sb, sth*) salir; (*sacred place, tomb*) profaner; (*painting, poster*) (*with racist etc remarks*) vandaliser; **they've defiled my home** (*entered uninvited*) ils ont violé l'intimité de ma maison; **I feel defiled** (*after rape*) je me sens souillé

defilement [dɪ'faɪlmənt] *n* (*of sacred place, tomb*) profanation *f*; (*of sb's memory*) (*action*) fait *m* de salir; (*result*) souillure *f*

definable [dɪ'faɪnəb(ə)l] *adj* définissable; **the border is not easily d.** la frontière n'est pas facile à déterminer

define [dɪ'faɪn] *vt* **(a)** (*word, object*) définir **(b)** (*specify*) (*difference*) définir; (*one's attitude, position etc*) préciser; (*objectives etc*) formuler; (*scope, extent of sth*) déterminer; (*powers*) délimiter; **to d. what it means to be French** définir ce qu'être français signifie; **well-defined limits** limites bien déterminées **(c) well-defined outlines** contours nettement dessinés *ou* dégagés

definite ['defɪnɪt] *adj* **(a)** (*distinct*) (*views, opinions*) bien arrêté; (*shape*) défini, bien déterminé; (*taste*) bien déterminé; **I can't put my finger on anything d.** je n'arrive pas à mettre le doigt sur quoi que ce soit de précis; **it shows a d. lack of …** cela montre un manque évident de …; **it's a d. advantage being a woman** c'est décidément un avantage d'être une femme; **there has been a d. improvement in her condition/work** il y a eu une amélioration certaine de son état/travail

(b) (*sure, certain*) (*date*) définitif, certain; (*response*) précis, catégorique; *Com* (*order*) ferme; **it's not d. yet** ce n'est pas encore définitif *ou* sûr; **at a d. time** à une heure déterminée; **and that's d.!** et c'est sûr!; **she is very d. about it** elle est tout à fait sûre de cela; **I'm d. it was him** je suis certain *ou* sûr que c'était lui; **he's d. about getting married** il est décidé à se marier

(c) [①A6-8;B3-4,2]*Gram* (*article*) défini; **past d.** passé *m* défini

definitely ['defɪnɪtlɪ] *adv* **(a)** (*distinctly*) (*improved, superior*) nettement; (*to need, lack sth*) décidément

(b) (*without doubt, certainly*) à coup sûr, sans aucun doute; **the meeting will d. be held next Monday** la réunion aura bien lieu lundi prochain; **he is d. mad/the man I saw** il n'y a pas de doute qu'il est fou/que c'est l'homme que j'ai vu, il est fou/c'est l'homme que j'ai vu, c'est sûr *ou* certain; **she's d. innocent** elle est innocente, c'est sûr *ou* certain; **are you going? – d.!** est-ce que vous y allez? – absolument!; **I'll d. be there** j'y serai à coup sûr; **I'll almost d. be there** j'y serai presque certainement, il est presque certain que j'y serai; **d. not!** certainement pas!; **I'll d. call you** je te téléphonerai sans faute; **that's d. my last offer** cette fois-ci, c'est ma dernière offre

(c) (*clearly, without ambiguity*) **he told me very d. that he didn't want to come** il m'a dit très clairement qu'il ne voulait pas venir

definition [defɪ'nɪʃən] *n* **(a)** (*meaning*) (*of word*) définition *f*; **by d.** par définition; **to give a d. of sth** donner une définition de qch, définir qch **(b)** (*specifying*) (*of powers, border etc*) délimitation *f*; (*of objectives*) formulation *f* **(c)** (*of image*) *Opt* netteté *f*; *TV* définition *f*

definitive [dɪ'fɪnɪtɪv] *adj* (*verdict, result*) définitif; (*authoritative*) (*biography, edition*) qui fait autorité; (*production of play*) inégalable; **she was, for me, the d. Juliet** pour moi, c'était <u>la</u> Juliette

definitively [dɪ'fɪnɪtɪvlɪ] *adv* définitivement

deflate [diː'fleɪt] **1** *vt* **(a)** (*ball, tyre*) dégonfler; *Fig* (*sb*) remettre à sa place; **to d. sb's ego** porter un coup à l'orgueil de qn; **he looked quite deflated** (*had lost his self-esteem*) il était penaud; **I felt rather deflated** (*disappointed*) j'étais assez déçu

(b) *Fin, Econ* **to d. the currency** provoquer la déflation de la monnaie; **to d. the economy** pratiquer une politique déflationniste; **to d. prices** faire baisser les prix

2 *vi* **(a)** (*of tyre etc*) se dégonfler

(b) *Fin, Econ* provoquer la déflation de la monnaie; **since the government started deflating** depuis que le gouvernement pratique une politique déflationniste

deflation [diː'fleɪʃən] *n* **(a)** (*of ball, tyre*) dégonflement *m*; *Fig* (*of person*) fait *m* de se dégonfler; **… which resulted in the d. of his ego** … ce qui l'a complètement abattu **(b)** *Fin, Econ* déflation *f*

deflationary [diː'fleɪʃən(ə)rɪ] *adj Econ* déflationniste

deflect [dɪ'flekt] **1** *vt* (*ball, bullet*) (faire) dévier; (*light*) défléchir; (*sound*) renvoyer; *Fig* (*sb*) détourner (**from** de); **to d. criticism** détourner la critique; **the government will not be deflected from its aims** le gouvernement ne se laissera pas détourner de ses objectifs; **to be deflected** (*of projectile*) dériver; **the ball was deflected into the net** le ballon a rebondi dans le filet **2** *vi* (*of projectile*) dévier; (*of light*) être défléchi; **the ball deflected off the post** le ballon a rebondi contre le poteau

deflection [dɪ'flekʃən] *n* (*of light*) déflexion *f*; (*of compass needle*) déviation *f*; (*of projectile*) déviation, détournement *m*; (*of criticism*) détournement; *El, Electron* (*of voltmeter etc*) déviation, déflexion; **it was a lucky d. off the post** heureusement la balle a été déviée par le montant du but; **he scored from a d. off the post** il a marqué un but après que le ballon ait rebondi contre le poteau

deflector [dɪ'flektər] *n Tech* déflecteur *m*; **sound d.** abat-son *m inv*

deflexion [dɪ'flekʃən] *n* = **deflection**

defloration [deflə'reɪʃən] *n Arch, Lit* (*of virgin*) défloration *f*

deflower [diː'flaʊər] *vt Arch, Lit* (*virgin*) déflorer

deflowering [diː'flaʊərɪŋ] *n Arch, Lit* (*of virgin*) défloration *f*

defocus [diː'fəʊkəs] *vi* passer au flou

defoliant [diː'fəʊlɪənt] *n* défoliant *m*

defoliate [diː'fəʊlɪeɪt] *vt* (*trees etc*) défeuiller

defoliation [diːfəʊlɪ'eɪʃən] *n* défoliation *f*

deforest [diː'fɒrɪst] *vt* (*region*) déboiser

deforestation [diːfɒrɪ'steɪʃən] *n* (*of region*) déboisement *m*

deform [dɪ'fɔːm] *vt* déformer

deformation [diːfɔː'meɪʃən] *n* (*of bone etc*) déformation *f*

deformed [dɪ'fɔːmd] *adj* (*person*) malformé; (*limb*) difforme, malformé; **the baby was born d.** le bébé est né avec une malformation

deformity [dɪ'fɔːmɪtɪ] *n* (*of body*) difformité *f*

defragment [diːfræg'ment] *vt Comptr* défragmenter

defragmentation [diːfrægmen'teɪʃən] *n Comptr* défragmentation *f*

defragmenter [diːfræg'mentər] *n Comptr* défragmenteur *m*

defraud [dɪ'frɔːd] **1** *vt* (*taxman*) frauder; (*bank, employer*) escroquer; **to d. sb of sth** escroquer qch à qn, frustrer qn de qch **2** *vi Jur* **conspiracy to d.** entente *f* délictueuse dans le but de frauder

defrauder [dɪ'frɔːdər] *n* fraudeur, -euse

defray [dɪ'freɪ] *vt* **to d. sb's expenses** rembourser les frais de qn, défrayer qn; **to d. the cost of sth** couvrir les frais de qch

defrayal [dɪ'freɪəl] *n* **d. of expenses** remboursement *m* des frais

defrock [diː'frɒk] *vt Rel* (*priest*) défroquer

defrost [diː'frɒst] **1** *vt* **(a)** (*refrigerator*) dégivrer **(b)** (*meat etc*) décongeler **2** *vi* **(a)** (*of refrigerator*) dégivrer **(b)** (*of meat*) se décongeler

defroster [diː'frɒstər] *n Aut* dégivreur *m*

deft [deft] *adj* adroit, habile

deftly ['deftlɪ] *adv* adroitement, habilement

deftness ['deftnɪs] *n* adresse *f*, habileté *f*, dextérité *f*

defunct [dɪ'fʌŋkt] *adj* (*person*) défunt, décédé; *Fig* (*industry*) défunt; (*project, practice, law*) révolu; (*company*) dissous, *f* dissoute

defuse [diː'fjuːz] *vt* (*bomb, Fig crisis*) désamorcer

defy [dɪ'faɪ] *vt* (*sb, the elements*) défier, braver; (*order, law*) braver; **to d. description** échapper à toute description, défier toute description; **I d. him to prove it** je le défie de le prouver

degeneracy [dɪ'dʒenərəsɪ] *n* dégénérescence *f*

degenerate¹ [dɪ'dʒen(ə)rət] *adj, n* dégénéré, -ée

degenerate² [dɪ'dʒenəreɪt] *vi* dégénérer (**from** de; **into** en); **the discussion degenerated into a fight** la discussion a dégénéré en bagarre

degeneration [dɪdʒenə'reɪʃən] *n* dégénérescence *f*; *Med* **fatty d.** dégénérescence graisseuse

degenerative [dɪ'dʒenərətɪv] *adj Med* (*disease*) dégénératif, -ive; **she has a d. heart condition** elle a des troubles cardiaques qui s'aggravent

degradation [degrə'deɪʃən] *n* **(a)** avilissement *m*, dégradation *f*; **to live a life of d.** vivre dans la dégradation **(b)** *Phys* dégradation *f*; *Geol* désagrégation *f* **(c)** *Mil* dégradation *f*

degrade [dɪ'greɪd] *vt* **(a)** (*sb*) avilir, dégrader; **I won't d. myself by answering that** je ne m'abaisserai pas à répondre à ça **(b)** *Phys* (*energy*) dégrader; *Geol* (*rocks*) désagréger **(c)** *Mil* (*officer*) dégrader, casser

degrading [dɪ'greɪdɪŋ] *adj* (*experience*) avilissant, dégradant

degree [dɪ'griː] *n* **(a)** (*extent*) degré *m*; **to some** *or* **a (certain) d.** à un certain degré, (jusqu')à un certain point; **she's right to a d.** elle a raison jusqu'à un certain point *ou* dans une certaine mesure; **to** *or* **in a high d.** éminemment; **in the highest d.** au plus haut *ou* au dernier degré; **to such a d. that …** à tel point que …; **by degrees** petit à petit, graduellement; **to feel a d. of optimism** ressentir un certain optimisme; *Jur* **marriage within the prohibited** *or* **forbidden degrees** mariage entre parents ou alliés au degré prohibé

(b) *Phys, Geog, Met etc* degré *m*; *Met* **it's 25 degrees** il fait 25 degrés; **we can expect temperatures of 15 to 20 degrees** nous pouvons nous attendre à des températures de 15 à 20 degrés; **degrees Fahrenheit/Celsius** degrés

Fahrenheit/Celsius; **ten degrees of frost/below zero** dix degrés au-dessous de zéro; *Geom* **angle of 30 degrees, 30-d. angle** angle *m* de 30 degrés; *Math* **equation of the second/third d.** équation *f* du second/troisième degré; *Phys* **d. of humidity** titre *m* d'eau *ou* d'humidité; *Gram* **d. of comparison** degré de comparaison

(c) *Univ* diplôme *m* (universitaire); **to take** *or* **do a d.** passer un diplôme (**in** en); **when did you do** *or* **take your d.?** quand as-tu eu ton diplôme?

-degree [də'gri:] *suff* **first/second/***etc***-d. burn** brûlure *f* du premier/deuxième/*etc* degré; *US* **first/second-d. murder** meurtre *m* avec/sans préméditation

dehire [di:'haɪər] *vt US Euph* (*sb*) remercier

dehumanize [di:'hju:mənaɪz] *vt* déshumaniser; **it was a dehumanizing experience** c'était une expérience déshumanisante

dehumidification [di:hju:mɪdɪfɪ'keɪʃən] *n* déshumidification *f*

dehumidifier [di:hju:'mɪdɪfaɪər] *n* déshumidificateur *m*

dehumidify [di:hju:'mɪdɪfaɪ] *vt* déshumidifier

dehydrate [di:haɪ'dreɪt] **1** *vt* déshydrater; **to become dehydrated** se déshydrater **2** *vi* (*of person*) se déshydrater

dehydrated [di:haɪ'dreɪtɪd] *adj* (*person, foodstuffs*) déshydraté; (*milk, eggs*) en poudre

dehydration [di:haɪ'dreɪʃən] *n* déshydratation *f*

dehydrator [di:haɪ'dreɪtər] *n* déshydrateur *m*

de-ice [di:'aɪs] *vt Aut, Av* dégivrer

de-icer [di:'aɪsər] *n Aut, Av* dégivreur *m*

de-icing [di:'aɪsɪŋ] *n Aut, Av* dégivrage *m*

deification [di:ɪfɪ'keɪʃən, deɪ-] *n* déification *f*

deify ['di:ɪfaɪ, 'deɪ-] *vt* déifier

deign [deɪn] *vt* **to d. to do sth** condescendre à faire qch, daigner faire qch

deindex [di:'ɪndeks] *vt Fin* (*salaries*) désindexer par rapport au coût de la vie

deindustrialization [di:ɪndʌstrɪəlaɪ'zeɪʃən] *n* désindustrialisation *f*

deinstall [di:ɪn'stɔ:l] *vt Comptr* désinstaller

deinstallation [di:ɪnstə'leɪʃən] *n Comptr* désinstallation *f*

deinstaller [di:ɪn'stɔ:lər] *n Comptr* désinstallateur *m*

deionized water [di:'aɪənaɪzd] *n* eau *f* déminéralisée

deism ['di:ɪz(ə)m, 'deɪ-] *n* déisme *m*

deity ['di:ɪtɪ, 'deɪ-] *n* (a) (*god*) dieu *m*, déesse *f*, déité *f*, divinité *f*; *Rel* **the D.** la Divinité, Dieu *m* (b) (*divinity*) (*of Christ etc*) divinité *f*

déjà vu ['deɪʒæ'vu:] *n* **I had a feeling of d.** j'ai eu une impression de déjà vu

deject [dɪ'dʒekt] *vt* (*sb*) abattre, décourager

dejected [dɪ'dʒektɪd] *adj* abattu, découragé; **to become d.** se décourager

dejectedly [dɪ'dʒektɪdlɪ] *adv* d'un air abattu *ou* découragé

dejection [dɪ'dʒekʃən] *n* découragement *m*

de jure ['di:'dʒʊərɪ] *adv Lit, Jur* de jure

dekko ['dekəʊ] *n Br Sl* coup *m* d'œil; **let's have a d.** fais/faites voir; **to take a d.** jeter un (coup d')œil (**at** sur)

Del *abbr* **Delaware**

delay[1] [dɪ'leɪ] *n* retard *m*; **d. in delivery** retard à la livraison; **without d.** sans retard *ou* délai; **without (any) further d.** sans plus tarder; **after much d.** après un long moment; **an hour's d.** une heure de retard; **all flights are subject to d.** tous les vols ont du retard; **delays of four hours can be expected** on peut s'attendre à des retards de quatre heures; **the road works caused traffic delays** les travaux ont retardé la circulation

delay[2] **1** *vt* (a) (*postpone*) (*one's departure*) retarder, remettre; (*payment*) différer, arriérer; **she delayed leaving until the last possible moment** elle a repoussé *ou* retardé son départ jusqu'au dernier moment; **I delayed writing to you until I knew the exact date** j'ai attendu de savoir la date exacte pour t'écrire

(b) (*hold up*) (*sb*) retenir, retarder; (*progress, traffic*) entraver, retarder; **they've been delayed by fog** ils ont été retardés par le brouillard; **she's suffering from delayed shock** elle souffre d'un choc après coup *ou* a posteriori

2 *vi* tarder (**in doing sth** à faire qch); *Mil* **delaying action** action *f* retardatrice; **don't d., book your holiday now** ne tardez pas, réservez vos vacances maintenant; **stop delaying and come to a decision!** arrête de remettre à plus tard ta décision!

delayed-action [dɪ'leɪd-] *adj* (*fuse, shutter*) à retardement

delayed cut-off *n* (*of courtesy light etc*) extinction *f* retardée

del credere [del'kreɪdərɪ] *n Com* ducroire *m*; **d. agent** commissionnaire *m* ducroire; **d. clause** clause *f* ducroire

delectable [dɪ'lektəb(ə)l] *adj* délectable, délicieux

delectation [di:lek'teɪʃən] *n Fml* délectation *f*

delegate[1] ['delɪgət] *n* délégué, -ée; **a d. to a conference** un membre d'une conférence; **a d. conference** une conférence de délégués syndicaux

delegate[2] ['delɪgeɪt] **1** *vt* (a) (*appoint*) (*sb*) déléguer (**to do sth** pour faire qch) (b) (*powers*) déléguer **2** *vi* déléguer; **she's not very good at delegating** elle ne sait pas déléguer

delegation [delɪ'geɪʃən] *n* (*act, representatives*) délégation *f*; **d. of power** délégation de pouvoir; **to send a d.** envoyer une délégation

delete[1] [dɪ'li:t] **1** *vt* (*erase*) effacer (**from** de); (*cross out*) rayer; *Comptr* effacer, supprimer; **d. where applicable, d. as appropriate** (*on form*) rayer les mentions inutiles **2** *vi Comptr* effacer

delete[2] *n Comptr* **d. (key)** touche *f* d'effacement; **d. character** caractère *m* d'effacement; **d. command** commande *f* d'effacement

deleterious [delɪ'tɪərɪəs] *adj Fml* (*to health*) nuisible, délétère

deleting [dɪ'li:tɪŋ] *n* effacement *m*

deletion [dɪ'li:ʃən] *n* (a) (*action*) (*of word, paragraph etc*) suppression *f*, effacement *m* (b) (*passage/word deleted*) passage *m*/mot *m* effacé *ou* supprimé; **without deletions or additions** sans ratures ni surcharges

delft [delft] *n Cer* faïence *f* de Delft; **d. blue** bleu *m* de faïence

deli ['delɪ] *n F* = **delicatessen**

deliberate[1] [dɪ'lɪb(ə)rət] *adj* (a) (*intentional*) (*mistake, lie, rudeness*) délibéré, intentionnel, voulu; (*insolence*) calculé; (*insult*) prémédité; **it was quite d.!** c'était voulu, c'était fait exprès!; **it wasn't d.** ce n'était pas voulu (b) (*unhurried*) (*person*) circonspect, avisé; (*movement etc*) mesuré; (*voice*) posé; **she has a very d. way of working** elle travaille de manière très réglée

deliberate[2] [dɪ'lɪbəreɪt] **1** *vi* (*of individual*) délibérer, réfléchir (**on** sur); (*of people, committee etc*) débattre, délibérer, réfléchir (**on** sur); **to d. over** *or* **on a question** délibérer d'une question; **they deliberated whether or not to let him go** ils délibéraient de le laisser partir ou non **2** *vt* (*question*) délibérer de

deliberately [dɪ'lɪb(ə)rətlɪ] *adv* (a) (*intentionally*) intentionnellement, exprès, à dessein; **I d. didn't invite her** c'est intentionnellement que je ne l'ai pas invitée (b) (*unhurriedly*) avec mesure; **he paused d.** il fit une pause calculée

deliberation [dɪlɪbə'reɪʃən] *n* (a) (*thought, discussion*) délibération *f*; **after due d.** après mûre délibération; **the deliberations of an assembly** les débats *mpl* d'une assemblée (b) (*lack of haste*) mesure *f*; **with d.** (*to say sth*) posément; (*to do sth*) de façon réfléchie; (*to walk*) d'un pas mesuré; (*to act*) avec circonspection

deliberative [dɪ'lɪbərətɪv] *adj* (*function*) délibératif; (*assembly*) délibérant

delicacy ['delɪkəsɪ] *n* (a) (*fineness*) (*of embroidery, carving, fingers, features*) délicatesse *f* (b) (*sensitivity*) (*of instrument, mechanism*) sensibilité *f*; (*tactfulness*) délicatesse *f*, tact *m*; **she showed great d. of feeling** elle a fait preuve d'une grande délicatesse *ou* sensibilité; **negotiations of the utmost d.** négociations très délicates (c) (*gentleness, lightness*) (*of touch*) légèreté *f* (d) (*fragility*) (*of health, fabric*) fragilité *f* (e) (*subtlety*) (*of colour, flavours*) délicatesse *f* (f) (*food*) mets *m* délicat

delicate ['delɪkət] **1** *adj* (a) (*fine*) (*embroidery, carving, fingers*) délicat; (*feature*) fin, délicat

(b) (*sensitive*) (*mechanism, matter, situation etc*) délicat; (*question*) épineux; (*feelings*) sensible; (*person*) (*over-refined, easily shocked*) précieux; (*tactful*) délicat, sensible; **it's a matter that needs d. handling** c'est une affaire qui doit être traitée avec délicatesse; **we're at a very d. stage in our negotiations** nous en sommes à une étape très délicate de nos négociations; **to tread on d. ground** toucher à des questions délicates

(c) (*gentle, light*) (*touch*) délicat

(d) (*fragile*) (*person, glass*) délicat; (*health, fabric*) fragile, délicat

(e) (*subtle*) (*colour, flavour*) délicat

2 *npl* **delicates** linge *m* délicat

delicately ['delɪkətlɪ] *adv* (a) (*finely*) (*carved, embroidered etc*) délicatement, finement (b) (*sensitively*) (*to handle question, approach a subject etc*) avec délicatesse; **the mechanism is very d. balanced** le réglage du mécanisme est très sensible (c) (*gently, lightly*) (*to put sth down, pick sth up etc*) délicatement (d) (*with subtlety*) (*coloured*) délicatement; **d. flavoured** aux saveurs délicates

delicateness ['delɪkətnɪs] *n* = **delicacy (a), (b), (c), (d), (e)**

delicatessen [delɪkə'tesən] *n* (a) (*shop*) épicerie *f* fine, traiteur *m* (b) (*food*) plats *mpl* cuisinés

delicious [dɪ'lɪʃəs] *adj* délicieux, exquis

deliciously [dɪ'lɪʃəslɪ] *adv* délicieusement

delight¹ [dɪ'laɪt] *n* (**a**) (*source of pleasure*) délice *m*; **the film is a d.** le film est un délice; **he is a d. to work with** c'est un plaisir de travailler avec lui; **it is such a d. to …** c'est si bon de …; **a d. to the eye** un bonheur pour les yeux; **to be sb's d.** faire le bonheur de qn; **the delights of the countryside** les délices *fpl* de la campagne

(**b**) (*pleasure*) plaisir *m*; **much to the d. of …, to the great d. of …** au grand plaisir de …, à la grande joie de …; **to take d. in (doing) sth** prendre grand plaisir à faire qch; **I take no d. in telling you this, but …** ce n'est pas de gaieté de cœur que je dois vous annoncer que …

delight² *vt* (*sb*) enchanter, ravir; **to d. the ear/the eye** charmer les oreilles/enchanter la vue

▶ **delight in** *vipo* (*sth*) se délecter de, aimer beaucoup; **to d. in doing sth** se délecter à *ou* aimer beaucoup faire qch; **he delights in the new baby** il est aux anges devant le bébé; **he delights in being a father** il est ravi d'être père

delighted [dɪ'laɪtɪd] *adj* ravi, enchanté (**with** de); **I'm d. to make your acquaintance** je suis ravi *ou* enchanté de faire votre connaissance; **I am d. for you** je suis ravi pour vous; **I'd be d. to!** j'en serais ravi!

delightedly [dɪ'laɪtɪdlɪ] *adv* avec ravissement

delightful [dɪ'laɪtfʊl] *adj* (*person, smile*) délicieux, ravissant, charmant; (*meal*) délicieux, exquis; (*place*) ravissant, charmant; (*weekend, evening, sense of humour*) délicieux; **a d. child** un enfant charmant; **they have a d. home** ils ont une maison ravissante

delightfully [dɪ'laɪtfʊlɪ] *adv* délicieusement; **he sings d.** il chante à ravir

delimit [diː'lɪmɪt] *vt* délimiter

delimitation [dɪlɪmɪ'teɪʃən] *n* délimitation *f*

delimiter [diː'lɪmɪtər] *n Comptr* délimiteur *m*

delineate [dɪ'lɪnɪeɪt] *vt* (**a**) (*draw*) (*triangle etc*) tracer; *Fml* (*sb's features*) dessiner; (*profile*) délinéer (**b**) (*describe*) (*plan, proposal*) présenter en détails; (*character in novel*) faire le portrait de

delineation [dɪlɪnɪ'eɪʃən] *n* (**a**) (*drawing*) (*of triangle etc*) dessin *m*, tracé *m* (**b**) (*description*) (*of plan, proposal etc*) présentation *f* en détails; (*of character in novel*) portrait *m*

delinquency [dɪ'lɪŋkwənsɪ] *n* (**a**) *Jur* délinquance *f* (**b**) *Fin* défaillance *f*, défaut *m* de paiement

delinquent [dɪ'lɪŋkwənt] **1** *n* (**a**) *Jur* délinquant, -ante (**b**) *Fin* défaillant, -ante **2** *adj* (**a**) *Jur* (*behaviour etc*) délinquant (**b**) *Fin* (*person*) défaillant; (*taxes*) impayé; **d. account** compte *m* en souffrance

delirious [dɪ'lɪrɪəs] *adj Med* en délire, délirant; *Fig* en délire; *Med* **to be d.** délirer; *Fig* **to be d. with joy** délirer de joie, être délirant de joie; *Fig* **I'm d.** je suis ravi; *Fig* **I'm d. at** *or* **about the prospect** cette perspective me rend fou de joie; *Fig* **she's d. about being pregnant** elle est ravie d'être enceinte; *Fig* **I'm not exactly d. about the prospect** la perspective ne m'enchante guère; *Med* **d. state** état *m* délirant

deliriously [dɪ'lɪrɪəslɪ] *adv* **to talk d.** délirer; *Fig* **to cheer d.** applaudir frénétiquement *ou* avec frénésie; **d. happy** délirant de joie

delirium [dɪ'lɪrɪəm] *n Med* délire *m*; **to be in a d.** être en plein délire; *Fig Lit* **to be in a d. of joy** être transporté de joie; *Med* **d. tremens** delirium *m* tremens

deliver [dɪ'lɪvər] **1** *vt* (**a**) (*parcel, telegram etc*) remettre (**to** à); (*letters*) distribuer (**to** à); (*goods*) livrer (**to** à); **do you want your newspaper (to be) delivered?** est-ce que vous voulez qu'on vous livre votre journal?, est-ce que vous voulez que votre journal vous soit livré?; **do you have your milk delivered?** est-ce que vous vous faites livrer votre lait?, est-ce qu'on vous livre votre lait?; **to d. a message** faire une commission; **to d. sth to sb's house** *Com* livrer qch au domicile de qn; (*non-commercial*) porter qch chez qn; *Com* **delivered free** livraison franco; *Com* **d. to domicile** livrer à domicile; **to d. the goods** livrer les marchandises; *Fig* remplir ses engagements; (*of new product etc*) tenir ses promesses

(**b**) *Obst* **to d. a child** mettre un enfant au monde; *Old-fashioned* **to d. a woman (of a child)** accoucher une femme; *Old-fashioned* **to be delivered of a child** accoucher d'un enfant

(**c**) (*blow*) porter, donner; (*ball etc*) lancer; *Fb* **to d. a pass** faire une passe

(**d**) (*speech*) faire, prononcer; (*lecture*) faire; *Jur* (*verdict*) prononcer, rendre

(**e**) (*provide*) (*service*) assurer; (*of machine, dynamo etc*) (*power*) débiter, fournir; *Aut* (*hp*) développer; *Fin* **to d. a profit** rapporter *ou* faire un profit; *Fin* **to d. shares** délivrer des valeurs

(**f**) *Fml* (*rescue*) (*sb*) délivrer (**from his enemies** de ses ennemis); **to d. sb from death** sauver qn de la mort; *Rel* **d. us from evil** délivre-nous du mal

2 *vi* (*of supplier*) livrer; *Fig* (*of new product supplier*) tenir ses promesses; **it/he just doesn't d.** il n'est pas à la hauteur

▶ **deliver up** *vtsep* (*surrender*) (*town*) restituer, rendre (**to** à); (*hostage, prisoner*) remettre, livrer (**to** à)

deliverance [dɪ'lɪv(ə)rəns] *n Fml* (*rescue*) délivrance *f* (**from** de)

delivered [dɪ'lɪvəd] *adj Com* **d. at domicile** rendu à domicile; **d. at frontier** rendu à la frontière; **d. free at domicile** livré franco domicile; **d. free on board** rendu franco bord

deliverer [dɪ'lɪvərər] *n* (**a**) *Fml* (*saviour*) libérateur, -trice, sauveur *m* (**b**) (*of goods*) livreur *m*

delivery [dɪ'lɪv(ə)rɪ] *n* (**a**) (*of parcel, goods etc*) livraison *f*; (*of letter*) remise *f*; (*of mail*) distribution *f*; **to take d. of sth** prendre livraison de qch; **charge for d.** (frais *mpl* de) port *m*; **parcels awaiting d.** colis *mpl* en souffrance; **free d.** livraison franco; **to pay on d.** payer à *ou* sur livraison; **d. address** adresse *f* de livraison; **d. charges** frais *mpl* de livraison; **d. conditions** conditions *fpl* de livraison; **d. date** date *f* de livraison; **d. deadline** terme *m* de livraison; *Com* **d. duty paid/unpaid** rendu, droits acquittés/non acquittés; **d. girl** livreuse *f*; **d. man/boy** livreur *m*; *Com* **d. note** bon *m ou* bordereau *m ou* bulletin *m* de livraison; **d. point** lieu *m* de livraison; **d. schedule** planning *m* de livraison; **d. time** délai *m* de livraison; **d. van** camion *m* de livraison; (*smaller*) camionnette *f* de livraison; (*smaller still*) voiture *f* de livraison

(**b**) *Obst* (*of woman*) accouchement *m*; **it was an easy d.** l'accouchement a été facile

(**c**) (*of speech*) prononciation *f*; (*of speaker*) diction *f*; **to have a good d.** avoir un bon débit

(**d**) *Sp* (*of ball*) lancement *m*, envoi *m*; (*of player*) manière *f* de lancer (la balle); *Mil* (*of rocket etc*) lancement

(**e**) (*of water, power etc*) débit *m*; (*of pump*) refoulement *m*

(**f**) (*of prisoner*) reddition *f*; *Jur* (*of property*) tradition *f*; (*of bequest etc*) délivrance *f* (**to** à); **for d.** (*of stocks*) au comptant

dell [del] *n* vallon *m*

delouse [diː'laʊs] *vt* (*sth*) ôter les poux de; (*sb*) épouiller, ôter les poux de

delphinium [del'fɪnɪəm] *n* (*flower*) pied-d'alouette *m*, *pl* pieds-d'alouette

delta ['deltə] *n* (**a**) (*in Greek alphabet*) delta *m inv* (**b**) (*of river*) delta *m*, *pl* deltas; *Av* **d. wing** aile *f* (en) delta

delude [dɪ'luːd] *vt* (*sb*) tromper, induire en erreur; **to d. oneself** se faire des illusions; **he deluded himself/me into thinking she would agree** il s'est persuadé/il m'a persuadé qu'elle accepterait

deluded [dɪ'luːdɪd] *adj* qui se fait des illusions

deluge¹ ['deljuːdʒ] *n* (**a**) (*flood*) déluge *m*; **a d. of rain** une pluie diluvienne (**b**) *Fig* (*of words*) déluge *m*; (*of letters, questions etc*) avalanche *f*

deluge² *vt* (*flood*), *Fig* inonder (**with** de)

delusion [dɪ'luːʒən] *n* illusion *f*; *Psy* fantasme *m*; (*bordering on insanity*) délire *m*; **to be under a d.** se faire des illusions, s'abuser; **to suffer from delusions** être sujet à des hallucinations; *Psy* **delusions of grandeur** folie *f* des grandeurs; *Hum* **you're suffering from delusions of grandeur!** tu te fais des illusions!

de luxe [dɪ'lʌks] *adj* de luxe; (*apartment*) (de) grand standing; **d. room** chambre *f* catégorie 'luxe'

delve [delv] *vi* fouiller; **to d. in(to) one's pocket** fouiller dans sa poche; **to d. into** (*the past*) remonter dans, fouiller dans; (*person's past*) fouiller dans; (*records, archives*) explorer

Dem [dem] *US Pol abbr* **Democrat**

demagnetize [diː'mægnɪtaɪz] *vt* démagnétiser

demagogic [demə'gɒgɪk] *adj* démagogique

demagogue ['deməgɒg] *n* démagogue *m*

demand¹ [dɪ'mɑːnd] *n* (**a**) (*request*) demande *f*, réclamation *f*; **d. for payment** demande de paiement; **final d. (notice)** dernier rappel *m*; **payable on d.** payable sur demande; *Fin* **d. deposit** remise *f ou* dépôt *m* à vue; *Banking* **d. deposit account** compte *m* à vue; **d. note** avertissement *m*

(**b**) *Econ* demande *f*; **to be in (great) d.** être (très) demandé *ou* recherché; **to be much in d. as …** (*of person*) être très demandé en tant que …; **there's not much d. for it** ce n'est pas très demandé, ce n'est pas très recherché; **d. analysis** analyse *f* de la demande; *Mktg* **d. curve** courbe *f* (d'évolution) de la demande; *Mktg* **d. driver** dynamisant *m* de la demande; **d. forecasting** prévision *f* de la demande

(**c**) **demands** (*of workers, kidnappers*) exigences *fpl*; (*of a situation, job etc*) nécessités *fpl*, exigences *fpl*; **to give in to sb's demands** céder aux exigences de qn; **you make too many demands on her** tu exiges trop d'elle; **to make great demands on sb's patience** exiger de qn beaucoup de patience; **I have many demands on my time** je suis très pris; **with all of these demands on your time, how do you manage to ...** tu es tellement pris, comment fais-tu pour ...

demand² *vt* **(a)** *(sth)* réclamer (**of, from** à); **to d. payment from sb** sommer qn de payer; **they're demanding payment** ils réclament le paiement; **to d. an apology/explanation** exiger des excuses/une explication; **I d. to speak to the manager** j'exige de parler au directeur; **to d. to know whether ...** insister pour savoir si ...; **to d. that ...** exiger que ... + *sub* **(b)** *(of situation, job etc)* demander, exiger; **the matter demands great care** l'affaire exige *ou* réclame beaucoup de soin

demanding [dɪˈmɑːndɪŋ] *adj (person)* exigeant; *(job)* exigeant, astreignant; *(task)* astreignant; **being a physiotherapist is physically d.** être kinésithérapeute est physiquement astreignant; **children are at their most d. between the ages of two and four** les enfants demandent le plus d'attention entre deux et quatre ans

demand-led *adj Econ* tiré par la demande

demand-pull inflation *n Econ* inflation *f* par la demande

demarcation [diːmɑːˈkeɪʃən] *n* démarcation *f*, délimitation *f*; **d. line** ligne *f* de démarcation; *Ind* **d. dispute** conflit *m* sur la répartition des tâches

demarket [ˈdiːmɑːkɪt] *vt* retirer du marché

demarketing [diːˈmɑːkɪtɪŋ] *n* démarketing *m*

demean [dɪˈmiːn] *vt* **to d. oneself** s'abaisser, s'avilir; **it was very demeaning having to ...** c'était très avilissant de devoir ...; **to d. one's office** rabaisser sa charge

demeanour, *US* **demeanor** [dɪˈmiːnər] *n (behaviour)* comportement *m*, attitude *f*, conduite *f*; *(bearing, mien)* air *m*

demented [dɪˈmentɪd] *adj* fou, *f* folle; *Med* dément; **to become d.** tomber en démence; **to be d. with grief/anger/worry** être fou de douleur/de colère/d'inquiétude; *Fig* **like one d.** *(to scream etc)* comme un fou

dementia [dɪˈmenʃɪə] *n Med* démence *f*

demerara [deməˈreərə] *n* **d. (sugar)** = cassonade *f*

demerit [diːˈmerɪt] *n* **(a)** *Fml (fault)* démérite *m*, tort *m* **(b)** *Am Sch* blâme *m*

demesne [dəˈmeɪn] *n* **(a)** *Jur (possession)* possession *f* **(b)** *Fml Hist (land)* domaine *m*

demigod [ˈdemɪɡɒd] *n* demi-dieu *m*, *pl* demi-dieux

demijohn [ˈdemɪdʒɒn] *n Ind etc* dame-jeanne *f*, *pl* dames-jeannes, bonbonne *f*

demilitarization [diːmɪlɪt(ə)raɪˈzeɪʃən] *n* démilitarisation *f*

demilitarize [diːˈmɪlɪtəraɪz] *vt* démilitariser

demi-pension [dəmɪˈpɑ̃sjɔ̃] *n* demi-pension *f*

demise [dɪˈmaɪz] *n Admin (of sb)* décès *m*, mort *f*; *Fig (of newspaper, empire etc)* disparition *f*; **this meant the d. of our hopes** cela a mis fin à nos espoirs

demisemiquaver [ˈdemɪsemɪkweɪvər] *n Mus* triple croche *f*

demist [diːˈmɪst] *vt* désembuer

demister [diːˈmɪstər] *n Aut* (dispositif *m*) antibuée *m*, désembueur *m*

demisting [dɪˈmɪstɪŋ] *n Aut* désembuage *m*

demo [ˈdeməʊ] *n F* **(a)** *(protest)* manif *f* **(b)** *TV, Mus (of singer etc)* disque *m*/cassette *f*/vidéo *f* de démonstration; **d. tape** bande *f* démo; *Comptr* **d. disk** disquette *f* de démonstration *ou* d'évaluation

demob¹ [diːˈmɒb] *vt* **(-bb-)** *Old-fashioned Br Mil F* démobiliser

demob² *n Old-fashioned Br Mil F* démobilisation *f*

demobilization [diːməʊbɪlaɪˈzeɪʃən] *n Mil* démobilisation *f*

demobilize [diːˈməʊbɪlaɪz] *vti Mil* démobiliser

democracy [dɪˈmɒkrəsɪ] *n* démocratie *f*; **people's d.** démocratie populaire

democrat [ˈdeməkræt] *n* démocrate *mf*; *US Pol* **the Democrats** le parti démocrate

democratic [deməˈkrætɪk] *adj* démocratique; *US Pol* **D. Party** parti *m* démocrate

democratically [deməˈkrætɪklɪ] *adv (elected etc)* démocratiquement

democratize [dɪˈmɒkrətaɪz] **1** *vt* démocratiser **2** *vi* se démocratiser

demodulation [diːmɒdjʊˈleɪʃən] *n Electron (of signal etc)* démodulation *f*

demodulator [diːˈmɒdjʊleɪtər] *n Comptr* démodulateur *m*

demographer [dɪˈmɒɡrəfər] *n* démographe *mf*

demographic [deməʊˈɡræfɪk] *adj* démographique; **d. trends** tendances *fpl* démographiques

demographics [deməʊˈɡræfɪks] *n* **[①A10,c]** statistiques *fpl* démographiques; **the d. show that ...** selon les statistiques démographiques ...

demography [dɪˈmɒɡrəfɪ] *n* démographie *f*

demolish [dɪˈmɒlɪʃ] *vt (building, wall, argument)* démolir; *F (cake, meal etc)* dévorer; *Fig* **to d. sb** *(in argument)* démolir qn; *(in competition, fight)* mettre la pâtée à qn

demolition [deməˈlɪʃən, diː-] *n* démolition *f*; **d. contractor** démolisseur *m*; *Sp* **d. derby** = course *f* de voitures dans laquelle celles-ci sont délibérement détruites; **d. squad** équipe *f* de démolition; **d. work** travail *m* de démolition

demon [ˈdiːmən] *n* démon *m*, diable *m*; **the D. drink** le démon de l'alcool; *Fig* **that child's a little d.** cet enfant est un petit démon; *Fig* **he's a d. for work** c'est un monstre de travail; *Fig* **she's a d. for punctuality** elle insiste énormément sur la ponctualité

demonetize [dɪˈmʌnɪtaɪz] *vt Fin (currency)* démonétiser

demoniac [dɪˈməʊnɪæk] *adj, n* démoniaque *mf*

demoniacal [diːməˈnaɪək(ə)l] *adj* démoniaque

demonic [dɪˈmɒnɪk] *adj (cruelty, rage)* démoniaque; **d. possession** possession *f* diabolique

demonology [diːməˈnɒlədʒɪ] *n* démonologie *f*

demonstrable [dɪˈmɒnstrəb(ə)l, ˈdemən-] *adj (fact)* démontrable; **that is d. nonsense** c'est clairement absurde

demonstrably [dɪˈmɒnstrəblɪ, ˈdemən-] *adv* **d. true/false statement** affirmation *f* visiblement *ou* manifestement vraie/fausse; **that's d. false** c'est faux de toute évidence; **that is d. not the case** de toute évidence *ou* manifestement ce n'est pas le cas

demonstrate [ˈdemənstreɪt] **1** *vt* **(a)** *(prove) (truth)* démontrer; **that just demonstrates how stupid he is** ça ne fait que démontrer à quel point il est stupide **(b)** *(show, explain) (machine, alarm system etc)* donner une démonstration pratique du fonctionnement de; *(one's skills, use of sth)* faire une démonstration de; **to d. how sth works** montrer comment qch fonctionne **2** *vi Pol etc* manifester, faire une manifestation (**against** contre; **for, in favour of** pour, en faveur de)

demonstration [demənˈstreɪʃən] *n* **(a)** *(of truth)* démonstration *f* **(b)** *(of machine, alarm system)* démonstration *f* pratique; **to give sb a d. of one's skills** faire une démonstration de ses talents à qn; **would you like a d.?** est-ce que vous voulez que je vous fasse une démonstration?; **a d. of affection** une manifestation *ou* un témoignage d'affection; **a d. of power** une démonstration de force; *Sch* **d. (class/lecture)** (séance *f* de) démonstration; **d. car** voiture *f* de démonstration **(c)** *(political etc)* manifestation *f*; **to hold** *or* **stage a d.** manifester

demonstrative [dɪˈmɒnstrətɪv] *adj* **(a)** *(person)* démonstratif **(b)** *(argument etc)* démonstratif **(c)** **[①A30,9; B13-14,A]** *Gram (adjectif etc)* démonstratif

demonstrator [ˈdemənstreɪtər] *n* **(a)** *(of machine etc)* démonstrateur, -trice; *Sch* **science d.** préparateur, -trice en science **(b)** *US (car)* voiture *f* de démonstration **(c)** *(political etc)* manifestant, -ante

demoralization [dɪmɒrəlaɪˈzeɪʃən] *n* démoralisation *f*

demoralize [dɪˈmɒrəlaɪz] *vt* démoraliser

demoralizing [dɪˈmɒrəlaɪzɪŋ] *adj* démoralisant

demote [dɪˈməʊt] *vt (person)* rétrograder; *Mil* **he's been demoted to private** il a été rétrogradé au grade de simple soldat; **she's been demoted to assistant manager** elle a été rétrogradée au poste de directeur-adjoint

demotic [dɪˈmɒtɪk] *adj Fml* populaire, du peuple; *Ling (Greek)* démotique

demotion [dɪˈməʊʃən] *n* rétrogradation *f*

demotivation [diːməʊtɪˈveɪʃən] *n* démotivation *f*

demur¹ [dɪˈmɜːr] *n Fml* objection *f*; **without d.** sans faire d'objection

demur² *vi* **(-rr-)** **(a)** *Fml* soulever des objections (**at, to** contre) **(b)** *Jur* opposer une exception

demure [dɪˈmjʊər] *adj* modeste, réservé; *Pej* d'une modestie affectée

demurely [dɪˈmjʊəlɪ] *adv* d'un air modeste *ou* réservé; *Pej* avec une modestie affectée

demureness [dɪˈmjʊənɪs] *n* modestie *f*, réserve *f*; *Pej* modestie affectée

demurrage [dɪˈmʌrɪdʒ] *n Com* surestarie *f*

demystify [diːˈmɪstɪfaɪ] *vt* démystifier

demythologize [diːmɪˈθɒlədʒaɪz] *vt* démythifier

den [den] *n* **(a)** *(of wild animal)* tanière *f*, antre *m*; *Fig (of criminals, brigands)* nid *m*, repaire *m*; *Fig* **d. of thieves** repaire de voleurs; **gambling d.** maison *f* de jeu; **d. of iniquity** lieu *m* de débauche *ou* de perdition **(b)** *esp Am (in home)* petit salon *m* familial

denationalization [diːnæʃənəlaɪˈzeɪʃən] *n* dénationalisation *f*

denationalize [diːˈnæʃənəlaɪz] *vt* dénationaliser

denature [diːˈneɪtʃər] *vt (product)* dénaturer

dengue [ˈdeŋɡɪ] *n Med* **d. (fever)** dengue *f*

denial [dɪˈnaɪəl] *n* **(a)** *(of right, request)* refus *m*; **d. of justice** déni *m* de justice **(b)** *(of truth of sth, guilt)* démenti *m*; **absolute** *or* **flat d.** dénégation *f* absolue *ou* catégorique; **to issue a d.** publier un démenti **(c)** *Bible* **Peter's d. of Christ** le reniement de Pierre

denier ['denɪər] *n Tex* (*of hosiery*) denier *m*; **a 30-d. stocking** un bas 30 deniers

denigrate ['denɪgreɪt] *vt Lit* dénigrer

denim ['denɪm] *n* **(a)** (*fabric*) (toile *f* de) jean *m*; **d. skirt** jupe *f* en jean **(b) denims** (*overalls*) bleus *mpl* (de travail); (*jeans*) jean *m*

denizen ['denɪzən] *n Lit, Hum* habitant, -ante, hôte *mf*; **denizens of the deep** hôtes *ou* habitants des profondeurs

Denmark ['denmɑːk] *n* Danemark *m*

denominate [dɪ'nɒmɪneɪt] *vt* **(a)** *Fml* (*name*) dénommer **(b)** *Fin* libeller; **denominated in dollars** libellé en dollars

denomination [dɪnɒmɪ'neɪʃən] *n* **(a)** *Rel* culte *m*, confession *f* **(b)** *Fin* valeur *f*; (*of share, of banknote*) coupure *f*; **in denominations of** en coupures de; **coins of all denominations** pièces *fpl* de toutes valeurs; **(notes of) small denominations** petites coupures **(c)** *Fml* (*name*) dénomination *f*

denominational [dɪnɒmɪ'neɪʃən(ə)l] *adj* confessionnel

denominator [dɪ'nɒmɪneɪtər] *n Math* dénominateur *m*; *also Fig* **lowest common d.** plus petit dénominateur commun; *also Fig* **to have a common d.** avoir un dénominateur commun

denotation [diːnəʊ'teɪʃən] *n* (*indication*) indication *f*; (*meaning*) signification *f*

denote [dɪ'nəʊt] *vt* **(a)** (*indicate*) dénoter, montrer, indiquer (**sth** qch; **that** que) **(b)** (*mean*) signifier; *Ling* dénoter

denouement [deɪ'nuːmɒn] *n* (*of play, situation*) dénouement *m*

denounce [dɪ'naʊns] *vt* **(a)** (*inform against*) (*criminal, crime*) dénoncer; **to d. sb to the authorities** signaler qn à la justice; **to d. sb as an impostor** taxer qn d'imposture **(b)** (*protest about*) (*abuse, government action, drug-taking etc*) dénoncer, s'élever contre; (*modern art etc*) condamner; **they have been denounced as nothing more than murderers** ils ont été accusés de n'être rien de moins que des assassins **(c)** (*declare termination of*) (*treaty*) dénoncer

dense [dens] *adj* **(a)** *Phys* (*body, metal etc*) dense **(b)** (*smoke, fog etc*) épais, *f* -aisse; (*crowd*) compact; (*population*) nombreux; (*text, argument*) dense **(c)** *F* (*stupid*) stupide, bête

densely ['denslɪ] *adv* **d. wooded country** pays couvert de forêts épaisses; **d. populated region** région très peuplée; **to be d. packed together** être serrés les uns contre les autres; **d. written** écrit dans un style dense

denseness ['densnɪs] *n* **(a)** (*of fog*) épaisseur *f*; (*of text, writing*) densité *f*; **in spite of the d. of the crowd** bien que la foule fût si compacte **(b)** *F* (*of person*) stupidité *f*

density ['densɪtɪ] *n* **(a)** *Phys, Ch, El etc* densité *f*; *Tech* masse *f* volumique; *Nucl Phys* **ion/neutron d.** densité ionique/neutronique **(b)** (*of population, traffic*) densité *f*; **d. chart** (*in hotel*) feuille *f* d'occupation journalière

dent¹ [dent] *n* (*in saucepan etc*) bosse *f*; (*in ground*) trou *m*; (*in pillow, cushion*) creux *m*; **there's a d. in the car** la voiture a une bosse; *Fig* **to make a d. in one's fortune** faire une brèche à sa fortune; *Fig* **to make** *or* **put a d. in sb's self-confidence** entamer la confiance en soi *ou* l'assurance de qn; *Fig* **to make** *or* **put a d. in one's savings/budget** faire un trou dans ses économies/son budget

dent² *vt* bosseler, cabosser; *Fig* **to d. sb's self-confidence** entamer la confiance en soi *ou* l'assurance de qn; **my self-confidence has been dented** mon assurance en a pris un coup

dental ['dent(ə)l] *adj* **(a)** *Med* dentaire; **d. appointment** rendez-vous *m* chez le dentiste; **d. care** soins *mpl* dentaires; **d. floss** soie *f* dentaire; **d. hygiene** hygiène *f* dentaire; **your d. hygiene is poor** vous avez une mauvaise hygiène dentaire; **d. hygienist** spécialiste *mf* de l'hygiène dentaire; **d. nurse** assistant, -ante dentaire; **d. practice** *or* **surgery** *or Am* **office** cabinet *m* dentaire; **d. surgeon** chirurgien *m* dentiste **(b)** *Ling* dental, -aux; **d. consonant** (consonne *f*) dentale *f*

dented ['dentɪd] *adj* bosselé, cabossé

dentifrice ['dentɪfrɪs] *n Old-fashioned* dentifrice *m*

dentine ['dentiːn] *n* dentine *f*

dentist ['dentɪst] *n* dentiste *mf*; **to go to the d.'s** aller chez le dentiste; *F* **the d.'s chair** le fauteuil du dentiste

dentistry ['dentɪstrɪ] *n* dentisterie *f*

dentition [den'tɪʃən] *n* dentition *f*

dentures ['dentʃəz] *npl* dentier *m*, prothèse *f* dentaire; **to wear d.** porter un dentier

denude [dɪ'njuːd] *vt* (*sth*) dénuder, dépouiller; **a landscape denuded of trees** un paysage sans arbres

denunciation [dɪnʌnsɪ'eɪʃən] *n* **(a)** (*of accomplice etc*) dénonciation *f* **(b)** (*condemnation*) (*of person, abuse, modern art etc*) condamnation *f* **(c)** (*of treaty*) dénonciation *f*

Denver ['denvər] *n Aut F* **D. boot** sabot *m* de Denver

deny [dɪ'naɪ] *vt* **(a)** (*fact, truth*) nier, refuser d'admettre; (*report*) démentir; (*accusation*) repousser; (*statement*) opposer un démenti à; **the accused denies the charge** l'accusé nie; **to d. having done sth** nier avoir fait qch; **there is no denying the fact** c'est un fait indéniable; **there's no denying that ...** on ne saurait nier que ...; **to d. all knowledge of sth** nier avoir connaissance de qch

(b) (*sb, one's faith*) renier

(c) (*request etc*) refuser; **to d. sb sth** *or* **sth to sb** refuser qch à qn; **to have one's request denied** se voir refuser sa demande; **to be denied access to sth/sb** se voir refuser l'accès à qch/qn; **to d. oneself sth** se priver de qch; **to d. oneself for one's children** se priver pour ses enfants

deodorant [diː'əʊdərənt] *n* (*for body*) déodorant *m*; (*for room*) désodorisant *m*; **d. spray** déodorant/désodorisant en bombe

deodorize [diː'əʊdəraɪz] *vt* désodoriser

deontology [diːɒn'tɒlədʒɪ] *n Phil* déontologie *f*

deoxidize [diː'ɒksɪdaɪz] *vt Ch, Ind* désoxyder

deoxyribonucleic [diː'ɒksɪraɪbəʊnjuː'kleɪɪk] *adj* **d. acid** acide *m* désoxyribonucléique

dep (*abbr* **departure/departs**) dép

depart [dɪ'pɑːt] **1** *vi* **(a)** *Fml* (*leave*) partir; **they departed for Canada from Portsmouth** ils sont partis pour le Canada depuis Portsmouth; **departing from** en partance de; **the train departing from platform four** le train au départ quai numéro quatre **(b)** (*differ, deviate*) **to d. from** (*version of events*) différer de, s'écarter de; (*custom*) abandonner; (*subject*) sortir de, s'écarter de; (*truth*) manquer à; **to d. from sb's wishes** ne pas respecter la volonté de qn **2** *vt Lit* **to d. this life** *or* **earth** quitter cette vie *ou* ce monde

departed [dɪ'pɑːtɪd] **1** *adj* **(a)** (*glory etc*) passé, évanoui **(b)** (*dead*) mort, défunt, décédé **2** *n* **the d.** le mort/la morte/les mort(e)s

department [dɪ'pɑːtmənt] *n* **(a)** (*in company, organization*) département *m*, service *m*; (*in shop*) rayon *m*; *Univ* département, U. F. R. *f* (= unité de formation et de recherche); **the French d.** (*at school*) = la section de français; **personnel/accounts d.** service du personnel/de la comptabilité; **d. store** grand magasin *m*; *Fig* **that's not (really) my d.** ce n'est pas mon rayon

(b) (*of government*) ministère *m*; *Br* **D. of Education and Science** = Ministère de l'Éducation; **D. of Trade and Industry** ministère du Commerce et de l'Industrie; **D. of Transport**, *Am* **D. of Transportation** ministère des Transports

(c) *Geog* (*in France*) département *m*

departmental [diːpɑːt'ment(ə)l] *adj* départemental; **d. head** chef *m* de service; *Univ* chef du département; **d. manager** chef *m* de service; **d. meeting** réunion *f* de service

departure [dɪ'pɑːtʃər] *n* **(a)** (*from place*) (*of person, train etc*) départ *m*; *Av* **there's only one d. a day for Montreal** il n'y a qu'un départ par jour pour Montréal; *Fml* **to take one's d.** prendre congé; **her unexpected d. from politics** son départ inattendu de la scène politique; **d. date** date *f* de départ; **d. gate** (*in an airport*) porte *f* (départ); **d. list** liste *f* des départs; *Av* **d. lounge** salle *f* de départ; **d. quay** quai *m* de départ; **d. tax** taxe *f* de départ; **d. time** heure *f* de départ; **departures book** (*in hotel*) registre *m* des départs

(b) *Fig* déviation *f* (**from a principle** d'un principe); (*from general rule*) exception *f*; (*from truth*) manquement *m* (**from** à); **d. from normal procedure** dérogation *f* à la procédure habituelle; **this type of holiday is something of a d. for him** ce type de vacances représente un grand changement pour lui; **a d. from his usual habits** une action contraire à ses habitudes; **politics is a new d. for her** la politique constitue un nouveau départ pour elle

depend [dɪ'pend] *vi* dépendre (**on** de); **that depends, it all depends** ça dépend; **that depends entirely on you** cela ne tient qu'à vous; **it depends on the weather** ça dépend du temps; **it depends on how much money I have** ça dépend de combien d'argent j'ai; **depending on whether ...** suivant que ...; **it depends on whether she accepts** ça dépend si elle accepte

▶ **depend on** *vipo* (*rely on*) (*person*) compter sur, faire confiance à; (*car, alarm system, weather etc*) compter sur; **we need somebody who can be depended on to be discreet** il nous faut quelqu'un sur la discrétion de qui on puisse compter; **he can be depended on not to become discouraged** on peut être sûr qu'il ne se découragera pas; *Iron* **you can d. on him to be late** on peut être sûr qu'il arrive en retard; **you can never d. on what he says** on ne peut pas se fier à ce qu'il dit; **you can d. on it** tu peux compter dessus; **to d. on imports from abroad** être tributaire de l'étranger; **to d. financially/emotionally on sb** dépendre de quelqu'un financièrement/sur le plan affectif

dependability [dɪpendə'bɪlɪtɪ] *n* (*of person*) sérieux *m*; (*of information*) véracité *f*; (*of machine*) fiabilité *f*; **I'm still not convinced of his d.** je ne suis pas encore convaincu de son sérieux *ou* qu'on peut compter sur lui

dependable [dɪ'pendəb(ə)l] *adj* (*person*) digne de confiance, sur qui l'on peut compter; (*information*) sûr; (*machine*) d'un fonctionnement sûr, fiable; **he is not d.** on ne peut pas compter sur lui; **to be a d. source of income** fournir un revenu régulier

dependance [dɪ'pendəns] *n Am* = **dependence**

dependant [dɪ'pendənt] *n* personne *f* à charge; **dependants** (*family members*) charges *fpl* de famille

dependence [dɪ'pendəns] *n* **(a)** (*reliance*) dépendance *f* (**on** de) **(b)** (*trust*) confiance *f* (**on** en) **(c)** *Med* (état *m* de) dépendance *f* (**on heroin** à l'égard de l'héroïne)

dependency [dɪ'pendənsɪ] *n* **(a)** *esp Am* = **dependence (b)** (*territory*) (*of country*) dépendance *f*

dependent [dɪ'pendənt] *adj* **(a)** dépendant (**on** de); *Jur* relevant (**on** de); **to be d. on** (*sb, sth*) dépendre de; (*financially*) (*sb*) dépendre (financièrement) de; **institution d. on voluntary contributions** institution soutenue par des contributions bénévoles; **two d. children** deux enfants à charge **(b)** *Med* **to be d. on heroin/drugs** être héroïnomane/toxicomane; **to be d. on insulin** être insulinodépendant **(c)** *Gram* (*clause*) subordonné

depict [dɪ'pɪkt] *vt* dépeindre, représenter

depiction [dɪ'pɪkʃən] *n* peinture *f*, description *f*

depilatory [dɪ'pɪlət(ə)rɪ] *adj, n* dépilatoire *m*

deplane [diː'pleɪn] *vi US* descendre d'avion, débarquer

deplete [dɪ'pliːt] *vt* réduire; **stocks are very depleted** les stocks sont très bas

depletion [dɪ'pliːʃən] *n* réduction *f*

deplorable [dɪ'plɔːrəb(ə)l] *adj* déplorable, lamentable

deplorably [dɪ'plɔːrəblɪ] *adv* déplorablement, lamentablement

deplore [dɪ'plɔːr] *vt* déplorer, regretter vivement; **to d. the fact that** déplorer le fait que

deploy [dɪ'plɔɪ] **1** *vt* (*troops, resources, Fig argument*) déployer; **I think your talents would be better deployed elsewhere** je pense que vos talents seraient mieux utilisés ailleurs **2** *vi* se déployer

deployment [dɪ'plɔɪmənt] *n Mil, Fig* déploiement *m*

depolarization [diːpəʊləraɪ'zeɪʃən] *n Opt, El* dépolarisation *f*

depolarize [diː'pəʊləraɪz] *vt Opt, El* dépolariser

deponent [dɪ'pəʊnənt] **1** *n* **(a)** *Gram* verbe *m* déponent **(b)** *Jur* témoin *m* déposant **2** *adj Gram* (*verb*) déponent

depopulate [diː'pɒpjʊleɪt] *vt* (*country*) dépeupler; **to become depopulated** se dépeupler

depopulation [diːpɒpjʊ'leɪʃən] *n* (*of country*) dépopulation *f*, dépeuplement *m*; **rural d.** dépeuplement des campagnes

deport [dɪ'pɔːt] *vt* (*foreigner*) expulser; (*political prisoner etc*) déporter

deportation [diːpɒ'teɪʃən] *n* (*of foreigner*) expulsion *f*; (*of political prisoner etc*) déportation *f*; **d. order** arrêté *m* d'expulsion

deportee [diːpɔː'tiː] *n* (*foreigner*) expulsé, -ée; (*political prisoner etc*) déporté, -ée

deportment [dɪ'pɔːtmənt] *n* tenue *f*, maintien *m*

depose [dɪ'pəʊz] **1** *vt* **(a)** (*monarch*) déposer, détrôner; *Fig* (*champion, head of party*) détrôner, destituer **(b)** *Jur* (*testify*) déposer, attester (**that** que) **2** *vi Jur* faire une déposition

deposit[1] [dɪ'pɒzɪt] *n* **(a)** *Banking* dépôt *m*; **to make a d.** déposer de l'argent; **to make a d. of £500** déposer 500 livres en banque; **bank d.** dépôt bancaire *ou* en banque; **on d.** en dépôt; *Br* **d. account** compte *m* livret, compte de dépôt *ou* d'épargne; **d. bank** banque *f* de dépôt; **d. book** livret *m* de dépôts; **d. money** monnaie *f* scripturale

(b) *Com* (*first payment*) acompte *m*; (*not returnable*) arrhes *fpl*; (*returnable*) caution *f*; (*on bottle*) consigne *f*; **d. receipt** récépissé *m* de dépôt; **to pay** *or* **put down a d. on sth** verser un acompte/des arrhes sur qch; *Br Pol* **to lose one's d.** (*of candidate*) = perdre sa caution

(c) (*of minerals*) gisement *m*, couche *f*

(d) (*material*) dépôt(s) *m(pl)*, précipité *m*; **alluvial deposits** alluvions *fpl*

(e) (*coating*) (*of wine etc*) dépôt *m*; *Tech* apport *m*; **d. of silver** précipité *m* d'argent

deposit[2] *vt* **(a)** (*money in bank*) déposer; (*document*) (*with a bank*) mettre en dépôt (**with** dans); (*with a solicitor etc*) confier (**with** à); *Fin* **to d. as security** nantir, gager; *Fin* **to d. security** déposer une caution **(b)** (*put down*) déposer, poser (**sth on sth** qch sur qch) **(c)** (*of liquid*) (*sediment*) déposer; **the flood waters deposited a layer of mud** les inondations ont laissé un dépôt de boue

deposition[1] [diːpə'zɪʃən] *n* **(a)** (*of monarch*) déposition *f* **(b)** *Jur* déposition *f*, témoignage *m*

deposition[2] *vt Mktg* (*product*) dépositionner

depositor [dɪ'pɒzɪtər] *n Banking* déposant, -ante

depository [dɪ'pɒzɪt(ə)rɪ] *n* dépôt *m*, magasin *m*, entrepôt *m*; **furniture d.** garde-meubles *m inv*

depot ['depəʊ] *n* **(a)** *Mil* dépôt *m*; *Com etc* dépôt, entrepôt *m*; **goods d.** dépôt de marchandises; **supply/ammunition d.** dépôt de ravitaillement/munitions **(b)** *US* (*station*) **(railroad) d.** gare *f* (de chemin de fer); **bus d.** gare routière; **freight d.** gare des marchandises

depravation [deprə'veɪʃən] *n* dépravation *f*

deprave [dɪ'preɪv] *vt* dépraver, corrompre

depraved [dɪ'preɪvd] *adj* (*person, taste*) dépravé, corrompu

depravity [dɪ'prævɪtɪ] *n* dépravation *f*, perversion *f*

deprecate ['deprɪkeɪt] *vt* (*action*) désapprouver; **stop deprecating yourself** arrêtez de vous dévaloriser

deprecating ['deprɪkeɪtɪŋ] *adj* **(a)** (*disapproving*) désapprobateur, -trice **(b)** (*apologetic*) modeste

deprecatingly ['deprɪkeɪtɪŋlɪ] *adv* **(a)** (*disapprovingly*) avec désapprobation **(b)** (*apologetically*) avec modestie, modestement

deprecatory ['deprɪkeɪtərɪ] *adj* **(a)** (*modest*) (*smile etc*) de modestie; (*remark*) modeste **(b)** (*disapproving*) désapprobateur, -trice; **to be d. about sth/sb** désapprouver qch/qn

depreciate [dɪ'priːʃɪeɪt] **1** *vt* **(a)** *Com* (*value of sth*) déprécier, rabaisser; *Fin* (*currency*) dévaloriser, déprécier; *Com, Ind* (*property, equipment etc*) amortir **(b)** (*denigrate*) dénigrer, déprécier **2** *vi* (*of property etc*) se déprécier, diminuer de valeur; (*of prices, shares etc*) baisser; (*of equipment*) se dévaluer, s'avilir; **the tractor depreciated by £200** la valeur du tracteur a baissé de 200 livres

depreciated [dɪ'priːʃɪeɪtɪd] *adj Acct* amorti; **d. currency** monnaie *f* dépréciée

depreciation [dɪpriːʃɪ'eɪʃən] *n* **(a)** (*of money, Ind equipment etc*) dépréciation *f*; *Fin* (*of currency*) dépréciation, dévalorisation *f*; (*amount*) moins-value *f*; *Acct* **d. period** période *f* d'amortissement; *Acct* **d. rate** taux *m* d'amortissement; *Acct* **d. schedule** tableau *m ou* plan *m* d'amortissement **(b)** (*denigration*) dénigrement *m*, dépréciation *f*

depreciatory [dɪ'priːʃɪət(ə)rɪ] *adj* (*remark etc*) de dénigrement, critique

depredation [deprɪ'deɪʃən] *n* (*usu pl*) (*of war*) déprédation(s) *f(pl)*; (*by soldiers, looters etc*) pillage *m*

depress [dɪ'pres] *vt* **(a)** (*sadden, dishearten*) (*person*) déprimer, décourager **(b)** *Tech* (*press down*) (a)baisser; *Aut etc* (*pedal*) appuyer sur **(c)** (*cause to fall*) (*trade*) faire languir; (*price of sth*) faire baisser

depressant [dɪ'presənt] *n Med* (*drug*) calmant *m*

depressed [dɪ'prest] *adj* **(a)** (*person*) déprimé; **to feel d.** être déprimé, *F* avoir le cafard; **the winter makes me feel depressed** l'hiver me déprime **(b)** *Com* (*market*) languissant, déprimé; **d. area** région touchée par la crise; **one of the most d. sectors of the economy** un des secteurs économiques les plus touchés par la crise; **the economy has been in a d. state for nearly three years** l'économie est dans un état de marasme depuis bientôt trois ans

depressing [dɪ'presɪŋ] *adj* **(a)** (*gloomy*) déprimant; (*countryside*) triste; **the unemployment figures make for d. reading** les chiffres du chômage sont plutôt déprimants **(b)** *Com* **to have a d. effect on the economy** déprimer l'économie

depressingly [dɪ'presɪŋlɪ] *adv* d'une manière déprimante

depression [dɪ'preʃən] *n* **(a)** (*of person*) dépression *f*; *Med* **state of d.** état dépressif; *Med* **to suffer (from) acute d.** être en pleine dépression **(b)** *Com* (*in business, region of country*) crise *f*; (*in industry*) crise, marasme *m*; **economic d.** dépression *f* économique; *Hist* **the (Great) D.** la crise de 29 **(c)** *Tech* (*pressing down*) (*of sth*) abaissement *m*; *Aut* (*of pedal*) enfoncement *m*; *Mil* **angle of d.** angle *m* de dépression **(d)** *Met* dépression *f* **(e)** (*sunken area*) (*in ground*) dépression *f*, enfoncement *m*, creux *m*

depressive [dɪ'presɪv] **1** *adj* **(a)** *Psy* (*tendencies, person*) dépressif **(b)** *Com* **to have a d. effect on the economy** déprimer l'économie **2** *n Psy* dépressif, -ive

depressor [dɪ'presər] *n Med* (*for tongue*) abaisse-langue *m inv*

depressurize [diː'preʃəraɪz] *Av* **1** *vt* dépressuriser **2** *vi* se dépressuriser

deprivation [deprɪ'veɪʃən] *n* **(a)** (*hardship*) privation *f*; **to suffer deprivations** souffrir de privations; **emotional d.** carence *f* affective **(b)** (*removal*) (*of rights, freedom etc*) privation *f*; (*of job, duties*) destitution *f*

deprive [dɪ'praɪv] *vt* **to d. sb of sth** priver qn de qch, enlever qch à qn; **to d. oneself** se priver; **I won't d. you of the pleasure of telling him about it** je ne te priverai pas du plaisir de le lui dire; **to d. sb of office** déposséder qn de sa charge

deprived [dɪ'praɪvd] *adj* (*child*) déshérité; **she had a d. childhood** elle a eu une enfance défavorisée

dept *n abbr* **department**
depth [depθ] *n* **(a)** (*of river, thought etc*) profondeur *f*; (*of love, feelings, passion*) profondeur, intensité *f*; **in d.** en profondeur; (*to study sth*) à fond; **a study in d. of …** une étude approfondie *ou* très poussée de …; **at a d. of 50 feet** par 50 pieds de fond; **to dive to a d. of 50 feet** descendre *ou* plonger à 50 pieds de fond; **I hadn't realised the d. of her feelings** je ne m'étais pas rendu compte de la profondeur de ses sentiments; *also Fig* **to go** *or* **get out of one's d.** perdre pied; **to be out of one's d.** (*of swimmer*) ne plus avoir pied; *Fig* avoir perdu pied, ne plus être sur son terrain; **I think she's a bit out of her d. in the new job** je crois qu'elle est un peu dépassée dans son nouveau travail; *MecE* **d. of cut** (*of machine-tool*) profondeur de passe *ou* de coupe; *Opt* **d. of field/focus** profondeur de champ/de foyer; *Naut* **d. charge** grenade *f* sous-marine; *Naut* **d. finder** sondeur *m*; *Aut* **d. indicator** (*for tyres*) témoin *m* indicateur d'usure
(b) (*of sound*) gravité *f*; (*of colour*) vigueur *f*, intensité *f*
(c) (*of forest etc*) fond *m*; (*of night*) milieu *m*; **in the depths of winter** en plein hiver; **the depths** (*of ocean etc*) les profondeurs *fpl*; (*of ignorance etc*) les ténèbres *fpl*; **in the depths of despair** dans le plus profond désespoir; **the lowest depths** (*of shame etc*) le dernier degré
(d) *Tech* (*of piston etc*) hauteur *f*; (*of layer*) épaisseur *f*
(e) *Mktg* (*of product, range*) profondeur *f*
(f) *Typ* (*of text*) encombrement *m*
deputation [depjʊ'teɪʃən] *n* **(a)** (*representatives*) députation *f* **(b)** (*action*) (*of sb*) députation *f*, délégation *f*
depute¹ [dɪ'pjuːt] *vt* **(a)** (*sb*) députer, déléguer (**to do sth** pour faire qch) **(b)** (*powers*) déléguer (**to** à)
depute² ['depjuːt] *n Scot* = **deputy**
deputize ['depjʊtaɪz] *vi* **to d. for sb** remplacer qn, faire l'intérim de qn, suppléer qn
deputy ['depjʊtɪ] *n* (*second-in-command*) adjoint, -ointe; (*temporary replacement*) remplaçant, -ante; **to act as d. for sb** suppléer *ou* remplacer qn; **d. director** directeur *m* adjoint; *Journ* **d. editor** rédacteur *m* en chef adjoint; **d. governor** sous-gouverneur *m*; *Sch* **d. head** directeur adjoint; **d. judge** juge suppléant; **d. manager** sous-directeur *m*, directeur *m* adjoint; **d. managing director** directeur *m* général adjoint; *Can Admin* **D. Minister** Sous-Ministre *m*; **D. Prime Minister** vice-Premier-Ministre *m*
DEQ [diːiː'kjuː] *Com* (*abbr* **delivered ex quay**) DEQ
derail [dɪ'reɪl] **1** *vt* (*train*) faire dérailler; *Fig* (*project, negotiations*) faire avorter; **to be derailed** (*train*) dérailler; *Fig* avorter; **the discussions were derailed by their insistence on …** les pourparlers ont avorté parce qu'ils ont insisté sur … **2** *vi* dérailler
derailment [dɪ'reɪlmənt] *n* (*of train*) déraillement *m*; *Fig* (*of plans, negotiations etc*) échec *m*; **in spite of the d. of talks by their insistence on …** bien que les pourparlers aient avorté suite à leur insistance sur …
derange [dɪ'reɪndʒ] *vt* (*person*) déranger; **she has been quite deranged by the experience** cette expérience l'a profondément dérangée
deranged [dɪ'reɪndʒd] *adj* dérangé; **he** *or* **his mind is deranged** il est dérangé, c'est un esprit dérangé
derangement [dɪ'reɪndʒmənt] *n Med* aliénation *f* mentale
Derby *n* **(a)** *Br* ['dɑːbɪ] *Horseracing* **the D.** le derby d'Epsom; **donkey D.** course *f* d'ânes; *Fb* **local d.** derby **(b)** *US* **d.** ['dɜːbɪ] (*hat*) chapeau *m* melon
deregulate [diː'regjʊleɪt] *vt Com* (*industry, air transport, bus services*) déréglementer; (*prices*) libérer
deregulation [diːregjʊ'leɪʃən] *n Com* (*of industry, air transport, bus services*) déréglementation *f*; (*of prices*) libération *f*; **d. of trade** libération *f* des échanges commerciaux
derelict ['derəlɪkt] **1** *adj* **(a)** (*car*) abandonné; (*house*) abandonné, (tombé) en ruines **(b)** *Fml* **to be d. (in one's duty)** être négligent de son devoir **2** *n* (*person*) épave *f* humaine
dereliction [derɪ'lɪkʃən] *n* **(a) d. of duty** négligence *m* dans le service **(b)** (*abandonment*) abandon *m*
derestricted [diːrɪ'strɪktɪd] *adj* (*road*) sans limitation de vitesse
derestriction sign [diːrɪ'strɪkʃən] *n Aut* fin *f* de limitation de vitesse
deride [dɪ'raɪd] *vt* (*person*) se moquer de, railler; (*sth*) tourner en dérision
derision [dɪ'rɪʒən] *n* dérision *f*; **object of d.** objet *m* de dérision
derisive [dɪ'raɪsɪv] *adj* moqueur
derisively [dɪ'raɪsɪvlɪ] *adv* (*to look at*) d'un air moqueur *ou* de dérision; (*to say*) d'un ton de dérision
derisory [dɪ'raɪsərɪ] *adj* **(a)** (*offer*) dérisoire **(b)** = **derisive**
derivation [derɪ'veɪʃən] *n* **(a)** dérivation *f*; **d. of a word from Latin** dérivation d'un mot du latin; **what is the d. of …?** quelle est l'origine de …? **(b)** *Math* (*of function*) dérivation *f*
derivative [dɪ'rɪvətɪv] **1** *adj Gram* (*word*) dérivé; *Pej* **his work is very d.** (*of author*) il n'a pas encore trouvé son style propre, il emprunte beaucoup aux autres; **I find his paintings rather d.** je trouve que ses peintures ne sont pas très originales **2** *n Gram, Ch, Ind* dérivé *m*; *Math* dérivée *f*; *St Exch* produit *m* dérivé; **petroleum d.** dérivé du pétrole; **to be a d. of sth** être un dérivé de qch
derive [dɪ'raɪv] *vt* (*origin, income, profit*) tirer (**from** de); (*pleasure*) prendre (**from** à); (*satisfaction*) trouver, tirer; (*ideas*) trouver, puiser; **to be derived from** dériver de, (pro)venir de; **income derived from an investment** revenu provenant d'un placement; *Ch* **to d. one compound from another** dériver un composé d'un autre; **word derived from Latin** mot qui vient du latin; *Mktg* **derived demand** demande *f* dérivée
▶ **derive from** *vipo* dériver de, (pro)venir de
dermatitis [dɜːmə'taɪtɪs] *n* dermite *f*, dermatite *f*
dermatologist [dɜːmə'tɒlədʒɪst] *n* dermatologue *mf*, dermatologiste *mf*
dermatology [dɜːmə'tɒlədʒɪ] *n* dermatologie *f*
derogate ['derəgeɪt] *vi Fml* déroger (**from** à)
derogation [derə'geɪʃən] *n Fml* **(a)** dérogation *f* (**of a law** à une loi) **(b) d. from a right** atteinte *f* portée à un droit
derogatory [dɪ'rɒgət(ə)rɪ] *adj* (*disrespectful*) (*meaning of word*) péjoratif; **d. remark** remarque *f* désobligeante; **to be d. to sb** se montrer désobligeant envers qn
derrick ['derɪk] *n* **(a)** *Petr* derrick *m*, tour *f* de forage **(b)** *Naut* (*crane*) mât *m* de charge
derring-do ['derɪŋ'duː] *n Arch* bravoure *f*; **deeds of d.** hauts faits *mpl*
derv [dɜːv] *n Br Aut* gazole *m*
dervish ['dɜːvɪʃ] *n* derviche *m*; **whirling** *or* **dancing d.** derviche tourneur
DES [diːiː'es] *Com* (*abbr* **delivered ex ship**) DES
desalinate [diː'sælɪneɪt] *vt* dessaler
desalination [diːsælɪ'neɪʃən] *n* (*of seawater*) dessalement *m*, dessalaison *f*; **d. plant** usine *f* de dessalement
descale [diː'skeɪl] *vt* (*kettle etc*) détartrer
descant ['deskænt] *n Mus* déchant *m*
descend [dɪ'send] **1** *vi* descendre; (*of rain*) tomber; **as darkness descended** pendant que l'obscurité descendait; **a feeling of sadness descended upon him** un sentiment de tristesse s'empara de lui; **an air of gloom descended on the whole house** un sentiment de tristesse envahit la maison; **to d. on** (*attack*) (*group of people*) s'abattre *ou* tomber *ou* faire une descente sur; (*village, town*) faire une descente sur; *Fig* **to d. on sb** (*intrude on*) (*without warning*) arriver chez qn à l'improviste; (*be unwelcome*) s'imposer chez qn; **to d. to sb's level/to doing sth** s'abaisser au niveau de qn/(jusqu')à faire qch; **to d.** *or* **be descended from sb** descendre de qn; **to d. from sb to sb** (*of property*) passer de qn à qn
2 *vt* (*hill, stairs*) descendre
descendant [dɪ'sendənt] *n* descendant, -ante
descender [dɪ'sendər] *n Typ* (*of character*) descendante *f*, jambage *m*
descending [dɪ'sendɪŋ] *n* **(a)** (*scale etc*) descendant; *Math* (*progression*) décroissant; **in d. order** en ordre décroissant; *Comptr* **d. sort** tri *m* en ordre décroissant **(b)** (*movement*) de descente
descent [dɪ'sent] *n* **(a)** (*of mountaineer, plane etc*) descente *f* **(b)** (*path, road etc*) descente *f*, pente *f* **(c)** (*origins*) descendance *f*; **to trace one's d. back to …** faire remonter sa famille à …; **to be of Norman d.** descendre des Normands **(d)** *Fig* (*attack, intrusion*) irruption *f* (**on** dans, sur) **(e)** *Jur* (*of property*) transmission *f* par droit de succession *ou* par héritage
descramble [diː'skræmb(ə)l] *vt Comptr* (*message*) déchiffrer
descrambler [diː'skræmblər] *n* (*for telephone*) déchiffreur *m*; *TV* désembrouilleur *m*
describe [dɪs'kraɪb] *vt* **(a)** (*sb, sth*) décrire; (*person wanted by police*) donner le signalement de; *Com* (*goods etc*) désigner; **can you d. the man?** pouvez-vous décrire cet homme?; **she described him as being tall and …** d'après sa description, il était grand et …; **the book describes how they escaped** le livre décrit la façon dont ils se sont évadés; **to d. sb/sth as stupid/as intelligent** qualifier qn/qch de stupide/d'intelligent; *Pej* **to d. oneself as an actor** se présenter comme acteur, se dire acteur **(b)** (*draw*) (*circle, line*) décrire; (*triangle*) tracer
description [dɪs'krɪpʃən] *n* **(a)** (*of sb, sth*) description *f*; (*for police purposes, on passport*) signalement *m*; *Com* (*of goods*) désignation *f*; **to be beyond d.** être indescriptible; **to give a**

d. of sb/sth décrire qn/qch; **to answer (to)** *or* **fit the d.** répondre au signalement **(b)** (*sort, kind*) sorte *f*, espèce *f*; **people of this d.** les gens *mpl* de cette espèce; **people of all descriptions** les gens de toutes sortes

descriptive [dɪs'krɪptɪv] *adj* descriptif

descriptor [dɪ'skrɪptər] *n Comptr* descripteur *m*

descry [dɪs'kraɪ] *vt Lit* discerner

desecrate ['desɪkreɪt] *vt* profaner, souiller

desecration [desɪ'kreɪʃən] *n* profanation *f*

desegregate [diː'segrɪgeɪt] *vt* (*country, school etc*) mettre fin à la ségrégation raciale dans; **desegregated school** école où la ségrégation raciale n'est plus pratiquée

desegregation [diːsegrɪ'geɪʃən] *n* déségrégation *f*

deselect [diːsɪ'lekt] *vt Br* ne pas resélectionner (*comme candidat à une élection*)

desensitize [diː'sensɪtaɪz] *vt Phot, Med etc* désensibiliser

desert[1] ['dezət] **1** *n* désert *m*; **the Sahara D.** le désert du Sahara; **d. boots** bottines *fpl* lacées; **d. island** île *f* déserte; **d. rat** (*animal*) gerboise *f*; *Mil F* (*in World War II*) militaire *m* britannique qui a fait la campagne de l'Afrique du Nord **2** *adj* (*region, flora etc*) désertique

desert[2] [dɪ'zɜːt] **1** *vt* (*place*) déserter, quitter; (*sb*) abandonner; *Mil* **to d. one's post** déserter *ou* abandonner son poste; *Pol* **to d. one's party** tourner casaque; **to d. sb** (*of courage*) abandonner qn; **her sense of humour has deserted her** elle a perdu son sens de l'humour **2** *vi Mil* déserter; **to d. from the army** déserter l'armée; **to d. to the enemy** passer à l'ennemi

deserted [dɪ'zɜːtɪd] *adj* (*person*) abandonné; (*place*) désert; **the streets were d.** les rues étaient désertes

deserter [dɪ'zɜːtər] *n Mil* déserteur *m*; **to be shot as a d.** être fusillé pour désertion

desertification [dɪzɜːtɪfɪ'keɪʃən] *n* (*of land*) désertification *f*

desertion [dɪ'zɜːʃən] *n* **(a)** (*of sb*) abandon *m*, délaissement *m*; *Jur* abandon du domicile conjugal; **he divorced her for d.** il a demandé le divorce parce qu'elle avait abandonné le domicile conjugal **(b)** *Mil* désertion *f*

deserts [dɪ'zɜːts] *npl* mérites *mpl*, dû *m*; **he has got his (just) deserts** il n'a que ce qu'il mérite

deserve [dɪ'zɜːv] *vt* (*sth*) mériter; (*praise*) être digne de; **the idea deserves serious consideration** cette idée mérite qu'on y réfléchisse sérieusement; **she thoroughly deserves it!** elle ne l'a pas volé!; **she deserves better** elle mérite mieux que ça; **he deserves to be punished** il mérite qu'on le punisse; **he deserved to win** (*and did*) il méritait de gagner; (*but did not*) il aurait mérité de gagner

deserved [dɪ'zɜːvd] *adj* (bien) mérité

deservedly [dɪ'zɜːvɪdlɪ] *adv* justement, à juste titre

deserving [dɪ'zɜːvɪŋ] *adj* (*person*) méritant, de mérite; (*action, cause*) méritoire; *Br Old-fashioned, Hum* **the d. poor** les pauvres méritants; **to be d. of** (*sympathy, recognition*) mériter; (*praise, respect*) être digne de

desiccate ['desɪkeɪt] *vt* dessécher; **desiccated coconut** noix *f* de coco déshydratée

desiderata [dɪzɪdə'rɑːtə] *npl Lit* desiderata *mpl*

design[1] [dɪ'zaɪn] *n* **(a)** (*intention*) dessein *m*, intention *f*; **by d.** à dessein, volontairement; **to have designs on sb/sth** avoir des desseins *ou* visées sur qn/qch

(b) (*pattern*) (*on sweater, carpet etc*) motif *m*, dessin *m*

(c) (*plan*) (*of novel etc*) plan *m*; (*for painting etc*) grandes lignes *fpl*, ébauche *f*; *Ind* (*for machine*) étude *f*, avant-projet *m*; (*of car, flat, house etc*) design *m*; **to study d.** étudier le design; **the sofa was made to** *or* **is of her own d.** le canapé a été fabriqué sur mesure pour elle; **industrial d.** esthétique *f* industrielle; **d. engineer** ingénieur *m* d'études; **d. office/department** bureau *m*/service *m* d'études; **d. stage** phase *f* de conception; **d. team** équipe *f* des concepteurs

(d) (*arrangement of parts*) (*in machine etc*) dessin *m*; **machine of faulty d.** machine de construction défectueuse; *Com* **our latest d.** notre dernier modèle; **d. centre** centre *m* d'exposition (de modèles)

design[2] *vt* **(a)** (*intend*) destiner **(for** à**)**; **machine designed for a special purpose** machine conçue pour un but spécial; **a speech designed to inspire confidence** un discours fait pour inspirer la confiance **(b)** (*project*) préparer **(c)** (*by drawing etc*) (*building, plane, kitchen etc*) concevoir; (*dress, hat etc*) créer; (*syllabus etc*) mettre au point

designate[1] ['dezɪgnət] *adj* désigné

designate[2] ['dezɪgneɪt] *vt* (*person*) désigner, nommer **(to an office** à une fonction**)**; (*funds*) destiner; **to d. sb as one's successor** désigner qn comme son successeur; **the town is a designated special development area** la ville a été désignée *ou* classée zone de développement; **this area has been designated a no-smoking zone** cette zone est destinée aux non-fumeurs; *Av* **designated carrier** = compagnie *f* aérienne désignée dans un accord bilatéral pour assurer les liaisons entre deux pays

designation [dezɪg'neɪʃən] *n* **(a)** (*of successor*) désignation *f*, nomination *f*; (*of funds*) désignation; **d. to a post** nomination à un emploi; **because of the d. of this building as a no-smoking zone** parce que le bâtiment est décrété zone non-fumeur **(b)** (*title, name*) désignation *f*, nom *m*

designedly [dɪ'zaɪnɪdlɪ] *adv* à dessein, exprès

designer [dɪ'zaɪnər] *n* **(a)** (*of project*) auteur *m*, inventeur, -trice **(b)** *Art, Ind* dessinateur, -trice; (*of clothes*) styliste *mf*, créateur, -trice; *Th, Cin* décorateur, -trice; **d. jeans/bedlinen/jewellery** jean *m*/literie *f*/bijoux *mpl* de marque; **d. drugs** drogues *fpl* de synthèse; **d. goods** produits *mpl* de marque; **d. label** griffe *f* de grande marque; *Hum* **d. stubble** barbe *f* de trois jours

designing [dɪ'zaɪnɪŋ] *adj Pej* (*scheming*) intrigant

desirability [dɪzaɪərə'bɪlɪtɪ] *n* **(a)** caractère *m* désirable *ou* souhaitable; **she referred to the d. of change/improvement** elle a fait référence au fait que des changements/améliorations étaient désirables *ou* souhaitables **(b)** (*sexual*) attrait *m*

desirable [dɪ'zaɪərəb(ə)l] *adj* **(a)** (*worth having*) souhaitable; (*change, improvement*) désirable; **a knowledge of French is d.** (*in job advert*) connaissance du français souhaitée; *Com* **d. property** (*house*) belle maison *f*; (*flat*) bel appartement *m* **(b)** (*sexually*) attrayant, désirable

desire[1] [dɪ'zaɪər] *n* **(a)** désir *m*, souhait *m* **(for** de**)**; **to have a d. for sth** désirer qch; **to have one's heart's d.** obtenir ce que l'on désire le plus (au monde); **to have a d. to do sth** avoir le désir *ou* avoir envie de faire qch; **to express the** *or* **a d.** exprimer le désir **(that** que; **to do** de faire**)**; **I feel no d. to …** je n'ai aucune envie de … **(b)** (*sexual*) désir *m*

desire[2] *vt* **(a)** (*sth*) désirer, avoir envie de; **to d. to do sth** désirer faire qch; **what he desired most was to …** ce qu'il désirait le plus au monde, c'était de …; **it is to be desired that …** il est souhaitable que … + *sub*; **it leaves much** *or* **a lot to be desired** cela laisse beaucoup à désirer; **it leaves nothing to be desired** cela ne laisse rien à redire; *Lit* **to d. sth of sb** (*request*) demander qch à qn; (*want*) désirer qch de qn; **to d. sb to do sth** (*make request*) prier qn de faire qch; **it was clear that she desired him to leave** il était clair qu'elle voulait qu'il parte; **I d. nothing of you but your friendship** je ne désire rien d'autre de vous que votre amitié

(b) (*sexually*) désirer

desirous [dɪ'zaɪərəs] *adj Fml* désireux **(of** de**)**

desist [dɪ'zɪst] *vi Lit* cesser **(from doing** de faire**)**

desk [desk] *n* **(a)** (*in office, of teacher*) bureau *m*; (*for writing at*) secrétaire *m*; (*pupil's*) pupitre *m*; **to have a d. job** avoir un travail de bureau; **I couldn't stand being stuck behind a d. all day** je ne pourrais pas supporter de rester assis à un bureau toute la journée; **reading d.** pupitre; *Rel* lutrin *m*; *Comptr etc* **control d.** pupitre de commande; **d. diary** agenda *m* de bureau; **d. lamp** *or* **light** lampe *f* de bureau; **d. microphone** micro *m* de table; **d. pad** bloc *m* de bureau; **d. research** recherche *f ou* étude *f* documentaire

(b) (*in shop*) caisse *f*; (*in hotel*) réception *f*; **please leave your keys at the d.** (*in hotel*) prière de laisser les clefs à la réception; **pay at the d.** (*in shop*) payez à la caisse; *Am* **d. clerk** (*in hotel*) réceptionniste *mf*, réceptionnaire *mf*

(c) *Journ* (*office*) **the news/sports d.** le service des informations/des sports; *Br* **Latin America d.** direction *f* des affaires latino-américaines

deskill [diː'skɪl] *vt* (*process, job*) automatiser; (*workforce*) déqualifier

deskman ['deskmæn] *n Journ* deskman *m*

desktop ['desktɒp] *n* **on my d.** sur mon bureau; **d. (computer)** ordinateur *m* de bureau *ou* de table; *Comptr* **d. (model)** modèle *m* de table; **d. calculator** calculatrice *f*; **d. publishing** publication *f* assistée par ordinateur, microédition *f*, *Can* éditique *f*; *Comptr* **d. publishing package** logiciel *m* de mise en page

desolate[1] ['desələt] *adj* **(a)** (*house*) abandonné; (*place*) désert, vide; (*future, prospect*) sombre **(b)** (*person, look*) affligé; (*cry*) de désolation

desolate[2] ['desəleɪt] *vt* **(a)** (*region etc*) (*of invaders, natural catastrophe*) ravager; (*of epidemic*) ravager, dépeupler; (*of recession, unemployment*) dévaster **(b)** (*sb*) accabler, affliger

desolately ['desələtlɪ] *adv* (*to say*) d'un ton désolé; (*to look at*) d'un air désolé

desolation [desə'leɪʃən] *n* **(a)** (*of defeated country etc*) désolation *f*, dévastation *f* **(b)** (*of landscape etc*) désolation *f* **(c)** (*of person*) désolation *f*, chagrin *m*

despair[1] [dɪ'speər] *n* désespoir *m*; **... she said in d.** ..., dit-elle, désespérée; **to be in d.** être au désespoir; **to be in d. over** *or* **about sth** être désespéré par qch; **in d., she took the children and left** désespérée *ou* par désespoir, elle prit les enfants et partit; **to do sth out of d.** faire qch par désespoir; **to drive sb to d.** réduire qn au désespoir, désespérer qn; **child who is the d. of his parents** enfant qui fait le désespoir de ses parents

despair[2] *vi* (se) désespérer, perdre espoir; **I d. of you** tu me désespères; **don't d.** ne désespère pas; **to d. of doing sth** désespérer de faire qch; **I d. of her ever speaking French well** je désespère de la voir enfin parler français correctement; *Fml* **they d. of his life** ils craignent pour sa vie

despairing [dɪ'speərɪŋ] *adj* désespéré

despairingly [dɪ'speərɪŋlɪ] *adv* désespérément, avec désespoir

despatch [dɪ'spætʃ] *n, vt* = **dispatch**

desperado [despə'rɑːdəʊ] *n* desperado *m*, hors-la-loi *m*

desperate ['desp(ə)rət] *adj* **(a)** (*very serious*) (*condition*) désespéré; **they are in d. need of food** ils ont désespérément besoin de nourriture
(b) (*characterized by despair*) (*struggle, remedy, attempt*) désespéré; (*resistance, fight, defence*) acharné; **refugees d. to save their children besieged the consulate** tenant désespérément à sauver leurs enfants, les réfugiés assiégèrent le consulat; **a d. man** un désespéré; **to do something d.** faire un malheur; **she made a d. attempt to save him** elle a tenté désespérément de lui sauver la vie; **to be d. for money/a job** avoir un besoin désespéré d'argent/de travail; **I'm d., it's d.** c'est urgent; *F* **I'm d. for a cup of tea** je meurs d'envie de boire une tasse de thé

desperately ['desp(ə)rətlɪ] *adv* **(a)** (*with despair*) (*to fight, plead etc*) désespérément **(b)** (*extremely*) extrêmement; (*in love*) éperdument; **to be d. in love with sb** aimer qn à la folie; **d. ill** gravement malade; **to be d. sorry** être navré

desperation [despə'reɪʃən] *n* désespoir *m*; **to drive sb to d.** pousser qn à bout, réduire qn au désespoir; **in d.** en désespoir de cause; **out of d.** par désespoir; **an act of d.** un acte de désespoir

despicable [dɪ'spɪkəb(ə)l] *adj* méprisable

despicably [dɪ'spɪkəblɪ] *adv* bassement

despise [dɪ'spaɪz] *vt* (*person, attitude, cowardice etc*) mépriser; (*offer, proposal*) dédaigner; **these things are not to be despised** cela n'est pas à dédaigner

despite [dɪ'spaɪt] *prep* en dépit de, malgré; **d. what she says** quoi qu'elle dise; **I did it d. myself** je l'ai fait malgré moi

despoil [dɪ'spɔɪl] *vt Fml* dépouiller, piller, spolier

despondency [dɪ'spɒndənsɪ] *n* découragement *m*, abattement *m*

despondent [dɪ'spɒndənt] *adj* découragé, abattu; **to become d.** se laisser abattre; **try not to be too d. about losing** ne te laisse pas trop abattre *ou* décourager par cette défaite

despondently [dɪ'spɒndəntlɪ] *adv* d'un air découragé *ou* abattu; (*to say*) d'un ton découragé *ou* abattu

despot ['despɒt] *n* despote *m*

despotic [dɪ'spɒtɪk] *adj also Fig* despotique

despotically [dɪ'spɒtɪklɪ] *adv also Fig* despotiquement

despotism ['despətɪz(ə)m] *n* despotisme *m*

des res ['dez'rez] *n F* (*house*) jolie petite maison *f*; (*flat*) joli petit appartement *m*

dessert [dɪ'zɜːt] *n* dessert *m*; **what did you have for d.?** qu'est-ce que tu as eu comme dessert?; **d. apple** pomme *f* à couteau; **d. knife/plate** couteau *m*/assiette *f* à dessert; **d. spoon** cuillère *f* à dessert; **d. trolley** chariot *m* de desserts; **d. wine** vin *m* de liqueur

dessertspoon [dɪ'zɜːtspuːn] *n* cuillère *f* (à dessert)

destabilization [diːsteɪbəlaɪ'zeɪʃən] *n* (*of government, economy*) déstabilisation *f*

destabilize [diː'steɪbəlaɪz] *vt* (*government, economy*) déstabiliser

destination [destɪ'neɪʃən] *n* **(a)** destination *f*; **to reach one's d.** arriver à sa destination **(b)** *Comptr* **d. disk** disque *m*/disquette *f* cible, disque/disquette de destination; **d. drive** lecteur *m* de destination; **d. file** fichier *m* de destination

destine ['destɪn] *vt* (*sb, sth*) destiner (**for** à; **to a calling** à une carrière)

destined ['destɪnd] *adj* **(a)** (*meant*) destiné; **he was d. for the Church** il était destiné à l'église; **d. to do sth** destiné à faire qch; **she is d. to be successful** elle est destinée au succès; **he was d. never to see her again** il ne devait plus la revoir; **the marriage wasn't d. to last** leur mariage ne devait pas durer **(b)** (*of plane etc*) **d. for** à destination de

destiny ['destɪnɪ] *n* destin *m*, sort *m*; **such was his d.** tel fut son destin

destitute ['destɪtjuːt] **1** *adj* **(a)** (*needy*) indigent, sans ressources; **to be utterly d.** être dans la misère **(b)** *Fml* (*lacking*) dépourvu, dénué (**of** de) **2** *npl* **the d.** les indigents *mpl*

destitution [destɪ'tjuːʃən] *n* (*extreme poverty*) indigence *f*, misère *f*

destock ['diː'stɒk] *vt* (*goods*) déstocker

destocking ['diː'stɒkɪŋ] *n* déstockage *m*

destroy [dɪ'strɔɪ] *vt* **(a)** (*demolish, wreck*) (*building, marriage, character of a place, letter etc*) détruire; (*sb's hopes, happiness, chances of doing sth*) anéantir; (*faith in sb*) détruire, anéantir; (*life, career*) gâcher; (*theory*) démentir; (*of failure, guilt etc*) (*person*) détruire, ravager; **to d. one's health** se détruire la santé; **to d. oneself with guilt** être ravagé par un sentiment de culpabilité **(b)** (*kill*) (*animal*) tuer, abattre; (*dog*) piquer

destroyer [dɪ'strɔɪər] *n* **(a)** *Naut* contre-torpilleur *m*, destroyer *m* **(b)** (*person or event causing destruction*) destructeur, -trice

destruct [dɪ'strʌkt] *vi* s'autodétruire; **d. button/mechanism** bouton *m*/mécanisme *m* de destruction

destructible [dɪ'strʌktɪb(ə)l] *adj* destructible

destruction [dɪ'strʌkʃən] *n* **(a)** (*of building*) destruction *f*, anéantissement *m*; (*of hopes, happiness, chances*) anéantissement **(b)** (*damage*) ravages *mpl*; **the d. caused by the fire/storm** les ravages du feu/de la tempête; **the army left a trail of d. in its wake** l'armée a tout détruit sur son passage; **the trail of d. left by soldiers on exercise** les dommages laissés par les soldats en exercice

destructive [dɪ'strʌktɪv] *adj* destructeur, -trice; **d. child** enfant qui détruit tout; **d. criticism** critique *f* négative *ou* non constructive; *Comptr* **d. read** lecture *f* destructive

destructively [dɪ'strʌktɪvlɪ] *adv* d'une manière destructrice

destructiveness [dɪ'strʌktɪvnɪs] *n* (*of explosive etc*) effet *m* destructeur *ou* destructif, pouvoir *m* destructeur *ou* destructif; (*of child etc*) penchant *m* à détruire, tendance *f* destructrice

desuetude [dɪ'sjuːɪtjuːd] *n Lit* désuétude *f*; **to fall into d.** tomber en désuétude

desultorily ['desəltrɪlɪ] *adv* (*to converse*) d'une manière décousue

desultory ['desəlt(ə)rɪ] *adj* (*conversation*) décousu, sans suite; (*attempt*) peu convaincant; (*manner*) désinvolte

detach [dɪ'tætʃ] **1** *vt* **(a)** détacher; (*carriages*) dételer; (*trailer*) décrocher; (*stamp etc*) décoller; **to d. sth from sth** détacher *ou* séparer qch de qch; **she managed to d. herself from the rest of the group** elle a réussi à s'éloigner du reste du groupe; **it took me a quarter of an hour to d. myself from him** ça m'a pris un quart d'heure pour me débarrasser de lui; **if you can bear to d. yourself from her** si tu pouvais t'arracher à elle **(b)** *Mil, Naut* (*troops, ship etc*) détacher **2** *vi* (*of handle etc*) se détacher

detachable [dɪ'tætʃəb(ə)l] *adj* amovible

detached [dɪ'tætʃt] *adj* **(a)** (*separate*) détaché, séparé (**from** de); **to become d.** (*of stamp, Med retina*) se décoller; (*of price tag, carriage*) se détacher; (*of trailer*) se décrocher; **to become d. from the rest of the group** se détacher accidentellement du reste du groupe; **d. house** maison *f* séparée; *Med* **d. retina** rétine *f* décollée **(b)** *Mil* (*officer*) en affectation spéciale **(c)** (*objective*) (*view, person*) objectif; (*disinterested*) (*person*) désintéressé; (*manner*) désinvolte; (*air*) détaché, indifférent; **you have to be d. in this job** il faut savoir garder ses distances dans ce travail

detachment [dɪ'tætʃmənt] *n* **(a)** (*separation*) action *f* de détacher, séparation *f* (**from** de); (*of carriages*) dételage *m*; (*of stamp, Med of retina*) décollement *m* **(b)** *Mil* détachement *m*; **on d.** détaché **(c)** (*objectivity, lack of involvement*) distance *f*, détachement *m* (**from** envers); (*lack of interest*) désintérêt *m*; (*of priest*) (*from worldly matters*) détachement (**from** envers); **I admire your d.** j'admire ton détachement; **with an air of d.** avec un air distancié *ou* détaché

detail[1] ['diːteɪl] *n* **(a)** détail *m*; **down to the last d.** jusqu'au moindre détail; **I'll remember every single d. of this day** je me souviendrai de cette journée dans les moindres détails; **the d. of the carving** le détail *ou* les détails de la sculpture; **to pay attention to d.** faire attention aux détails; **to go** *or* **enter into d.** *or* **(the) details** entrer dans *ou* donner tous les détails; **in d.** en détail; **in greater d.** plus en détail; **in every d.** dans le moindre détail; **in the fullest d.** dans le plus grand détail; **points** *or* **questions of d.** questions de détail; **minor details** petits détails (sans importance); **that's just a minor d.** ça n'a pas d'importance; **I can't give you any details** je ne peux vous donner aucune précision; **I'll send you the details of the property** je vous enverrai les informations concernant la propriété; **for further details please contact ...** pour plus de renseignements, veuillez contacter ...

(b) *Mil* (*duty*) extrait *m* de l'ordre du jour; **details** l'ordre *m* du jour

(c) *Mil* (*group of soldiers*) détachement *m*

detail[2] *vt* (a) (*describe*) exposer en détail (b) *Mil etc* **to d. sb for a duty** désigner qn pour un service, affecter qn à un service

detailed [ˈdiːteɪld] *adj* (*description*) détaillé; (*account*) détaillé, circonstancié; (*work*) minutieux; **to give a d. account of sth** raconter qch en détail

detailing [ˈdiːteɪlɪŋ] *n Art etc* (*details*) détail *m*

detain [dɪˈteɪn] *vt* (*sb*) (*in prison*) détenir; (*in hospital*) garder; (*hold back*) retenir, arrêter; (*prevent from leaving*) empêcher de partir; *Sch* (*pupil*) consigner; **this question need not d. us** cette question ne nous retiendra pas; **police have detained a man for questioning** la police a mis un homme en garde à vue; **I won't d. you for long** je ne vous garderai *ou* retiendrai pas longtemps; **I'm afraid I've been detained** (*when cancelling appointment*) je suis désolé, je suis retenu; **I'm sorry I'm late, I got detained** je suis désolé d'être en retard, j'ai été retenu

detainee [diːteɪˈniː] *n* détenu, -ue

detect [dɪˈtekt] *vt* (a) (*notice*) (*of person*) (*sound, change*) percevoir; (*movement*) apercevoir; (*of alarm system etc*) détecter; **to d. a note of irony in sb's voice** déceler une nuance d'ironie dans la voix de qn (b) (*find*) (*pulse*) sentir; (*source of a problem, missile*) détecter; (*weakness*) déceler

detectable [dɪˈtektəb(ə)l] *adj* perceptible, discernable

detection [dɪˈtekʃən] *n* (a) (*discovery*) découverte *f*; **to escape d.** (*of mistake, burglar etc*) passer inaperçu (b) (*location, finding*) (*of mines, planes etc*) détection *f* (c) (*by detective*) travail *m* de détective

detective [dɪˈtektɪv] *n* (*police officer*) agent *m* de la police judiciaire; (*private investigator*) détective *m* (privé); **d. film** film *m* policier; **d. story** roman *m* policier

detector [dɪˈtektər] *n* (*device*) détecteur *m*; **sound d.** détecteur par le son; *TV* **d. van** = voiture-radar *f* utilisée en Grande-Bretagne pour détecter les téléviseurs non déclarés

détente [deɪˈtɒnt] *n Pol* détente *f*

detention [dɪˈtenʃən] *n* (a) *Jur* (*in prison*) détention *f*; **d. without trial** détention arbitraire; *Mil* **six weeks' d.** six semaines de prison; *Mil* **d. barracks** locaux *mpl* disciplinaires; *Jur* **d. order** ordre *m* de détention (b) *Sch* retenue *f*; **to give a pupil d.** consigner un élève; **to be in d.** être consigné *ou* en retenue (c) *Naut* (*of ship*) arrêt *m*

detention centre *n Jur* (*for young persons*) maison *f* de redressement

deter [dɪˈtɜːr] *vt* (**-rr-**) (*sb*) décourager; (*enemy*) dissuader (**from doing sth** de faire qch); **why should that d. you from going?** pourquoi est-ce que ça t'empêche d'y aller?

detergent [dɪˈtɜːdʒənt] **1** *n* détergent *m*, lessive *f*; **d. additive** additif *m* détergent; **d. oil** huile *f* détergente **2** *adj* détersif

deteriorate [dɪˈtɪərɪəreɪt] *vi* (*of relations, weather, economy, building*) se détériorer; (*of health, product*) se détériorer, s'altérer; (*of work, situation*) se dégrader; **her condition has deteriorated** (*of patient*) son état s'est aggravé; **the house has been allowed to d.** on a laissé la maison se détériorer; **to d. even further** (*of situation, work, condition, weather etc*) encore empirer; (*of building*) se détériorer encore davantage

deterioration [dɪtɪərɪəˈreɪʃən] *n* (*of relations, weather, economy, building*) détérioration *f*; (*of health, product*) détérioration, altération *f*; **despite the continuing d. of the situation** bien que la situation continue à empirer; **d. in quality** baisse *f* de qualité

determinant [dɪˈtɜːmɪnənt] *n* facteur *m* déterminant

determination [dɪtɜːmɪˈneɪʃən] *n* (a) (*resoluteness*) détermination *f*, résolution *f*; **air of d.** air résolu *ou* décidé *ou* déterminé (b) (*establishment*) (*of date, position of planet*) détermination *f* (c) *Jur* (*decision, finding*) décision *f* (d) *Jur* (*termination*) (*of contract etc*) résolution *f*, résiliation *f*

determine [dɪˈtɜːmɪn] **1** *vt* (a) (*resolve*) se décider, se déterminer, se résoudre (**to do** à faire)

(b) (*establish*) (*nature, size of sth*) déterminer; (*date, price*) déterminer, fixer; (*border*) délimiter; **once I've determined the cost** (*found out*) une fois que je saurai le prix

(c) (*question etc*) décider, résoudre; (*point of dispute*) régler; **the magistrate determined that they were guilty** le magistrat les a déclarés coupables; **to d. sb's fate** décider du sort de qn; **this set will d. the outcome of the match** cette manche va déterminer le résultat du match

(d) *Jur* (*terminate*) (*contract, lease*) résoudre, résilier

2 *vi* (a) (*of person*) se décider, se déterminer, se résoudre (**on doing** à faire)

(b) *Jur* (*of contract*) être nul

determined [dɪˈtɜːmɪnd] *adj* (*person, attempt*) déterminé; (*effort*) résolu; **I'm d. that this year I'll learn how to ride a horse** je suis décidé *ou* résolu à apprendre à monter à cheval cette année; **I'm d. that he'll go to university** je suis déterminé *ou* décidé à ce qu'il aille à l'université; **with a d. air** d'un air déterminé *ou* résolu

determiner [dɪˈtɜːmɪnər] *n* [ⓘA32,11,b] *Gram* déterminant *m*

determining [dɪˈtɜːmɪnɪŋ] *adj* (*factor*) déterminant

deterrence [dɪˈterəns] *n* dissuasion *f*

deterrent [dɪˈterənt] **1** *n* (a) **to act as** *or* **be a d.** (*of penalty etc*) exercer un effet dissuasif (**to crime** contre le crime) (b) (*weapon*) arme *f* de dissuasion **2** *adj* (*effect*) (*of nuclear bomb, policy*) dissuasif

detest [dɪˈtest] *vt* détester, *Fml* abhorrer; **I d. having to wait** je déteste attendre

detestable [dɪˈtestəb(ə)l] *adj* détestable

detestably [dɪˈtestəblɪ] *adv* détestablement

detestation [diːtesˈteɪʃən] *n Fml* (a) (*hatred*) haine *f* (b) (*object of hatred*) chose *f* détestable, abomination *f*; **that's my particular d.** c'est ma bête noire

dethrone [dɪˈθrəʊn] *vt* détrôner

dethronement [dɪˈθrəʊnmənt] *n* détrônement *m*

detonate [ˈdetəneɪt] **1** *vt* (*explosive*) faire détoner; (*bomb*) faire exploser; (*mine*) faire sauter **2** *vi* détoner

detonation [detəˈneɪʃən] *n* détonation *f*, explosion *f*

detonator [ˈdetəneɪtər] *n* (a) (*for explosive*) détonateur *m*, amorce *f*; **percussion d.** détonateur à percussion (b) *Rail* (*fog signal*) détonateur *m*

detour[1] [ˈdiːtʊər] *n* détour *m*; (*on sign*) déviation *f*; **to make a d.** faire un détour; **he took us on an elaborate d.** il nous a fait faire un détour très compliqué

detour[2] **1** *vi* faire un détour **2** *vt* (*traffic*) dévier

detoxification [diːtɒksɪfɪˈkeɪʃən], *F* **detox** [ˈdiːtɒks] *n* désintoxication *f*, sevrage *m*; **d. centre** (*for addicts*) centre *m* de désintoxication; **to take part in a d. programme** suivre une cure de désintoxication

▶ **detract from** *vipo* (*sb's pleasure, beauty of sth*) diminuer, porter atteinte à; (*sb's worth, achievements*) déprécier; **it rather detracted from my enjoyment of the film** cela m'a quelque peu empêché d'apprécier le film

detractor [dɪˈtræktər] *n* détracteur, -trice

detrain [diːˈtreɪn] **1** *vt* (*troops*) débarquer (du train) **2** *vi Mil* (*of troops*) débarquer *ou* descendre (du train); *Am* (*of passengers*) descendre du train

detriment [ˈdetrɪmənt] *n* détriment *m*, préjudice *m*; **to the d. of ...** au détriment de ...; **without d. to ...** sans porter préjudice à ...

detrimental [detrɪˈment(ə)l] *adj* nuisible, préjudiciable (**to** à); **to have a d. effect on** (*health, chances etc*) nuire à; (*paintwork, tyres, skin*) être mauvais pour; **to have a d. effect on sb** (*of treatment, stress etc*) être mauvais pour qn; **it would be d. to my interests** cela desservirait mes intérêts; **smoking is d. to your health** fumer est mauvais pour la santé

detritus [dɪˈtraɪtəs] *n Geol* débris *mpl* de roches

de trop [dəˈtrəʊ] *adj pred* de trop

deuce[1] [djuːs] *n* (a) (*of dice, dominoes, cards*) deux *m* (b) *Tennis* égalité *f*, quarante à, quarante partout; **to be at d.** être à égalité; **there were 16 deuces** il y a eu 16 égalités

deuce[2] *n Old-fashioned F* **what the d. does he mean?** que diable veut-il dire?; **what the d.!** bon sang!; **there's the d. of a difference** il y a une sacrée différence

deuced [ˈdjuːsɪd, -uːst] *Old-fashioned Br F* **1** *adj* sacré **2** *adv* sacrément

devaluation [diːvæljʊˈeɪʃən] *n Econ* dévaluation *f*

devalue [diːˈvæljuː] *vt Econ* dévaluer; *Fig* (*person, achievements, efforts*) dévaloriser

devastate [ˈdevəsteɪt] *vt* (*crops, village*) dévaster, ravager; *Fig* (*of news*) (*person*) terrasser; (*hopes*) anéantir, briser; **I was devastated when I found out he'd been lying to me** ça m'a terrassé quand j'ai appris qu'il m'avait menti

devastating [ˈdevəsteɪtɪŋ] *adj* (*storm, effect, accuracy etc*) dévastateur, -trice, ravageur, -euse; (*argument, news, admission etc*) accablant, dévastateur, écrasant; (*criticism, attack*) cinglant; (*discovery*) dévastateur; (*charm, beauty etc*) irrésistible; (*shock etc*) foudroyant

devastatingly [ˈdevəsteɪtɪŋlɪ] *adv* (*handsome, funny*) terriblement, irrésistiblement; **d. beautiful** d'une beauté irrésistible; **d. accurate fire** tir(s) *m(pl)* d'une précision dévastatrice

devastation [devəsˈteɪʃən] *n* dévastation *f*, ravages *mpl*; **a scene of utter d.** un spectacle de dévastation complète

develop [dɪˈveləp] (**-p-** [dɪˈveləpt]) **1** *vt* (a) (*expand*) (*skills, theme etc*) développer; (*theory, argument*) développer, exposer; (*thought*) développer, élargir; **to d. one's muscles** développer ses muscles, se muscler

(b) *Econ* *(region)* mettre en valeur, développer; *Tech* *(new design, model etc)* mettre au point, réaliser; *Constr* *(site)* aménager; **to d. sth into sth** transformer qch en qch; **less developed countries** pays *mpl* moins développés; **developed countries** pays développés

(c) *(acquire)* *(infection, bad habit, mannerism)* contracter; *(cold, flu)* attraper; *(symptoms)* manifester; **to d. a temperature** *or* **a fever** (se mettre à) avoir *ou* faire de la température; **he has developed cancer/Parkinson's disease** il est atteint de cancer/de la maladie de Parkinson; **to d. a dislike/taste** *or* **liking for sth** se mettre à détester/aimer *ou* apprécier qch; **to d. a tendency to do sth** prendre l'habitude de faire qch; **the machine has developed a fault** la machine s'est mise à mal fonctionner; **to d. a stoop** se voûter; **when did she d. the rash?** quand l'éruption s'est-elle déclenchée?; **I've developed a rash on my chest** j'ai fait une éruption sur la poitrine

(d) *Phot* *(film)* développer

(e) *Math* *(surface, function)* développer

(f) *Phys etc* *(heat)* engendrer

2 *vi* **(a)** *(of body, the faculties etc)* se développer; **she has developed into a fine-looking young woman/a gifted pianist** elle est devenue une ravissante jeune femme/une pianiste douée

(b) *Econ* *(of country, region)* se développer; **to d. into** devenir

(c) *(become apparent)* se manifester, se révéler; *(of argument, crisis)* se produire; *(of fever)* se déclarer; **to d. into sth** devenir qch; *(bronchitis, riot)* se transformer en

developer [dɪ'veləpər] *n* **(a)** *Econ* promoteur *m* **(b)** *Sch* **late d.** enfant *mf* qui se développe tard **(c)** *Phot* *(chemical)* (agent *m*) révélateur *m*; *(for laser printer)* développeuse *f*; **d. kit** *(for laser printer)* kit *m* développeur

developing [dɪ'veləpɪŋ] **1** *adj* *(business)* en expansion; *(region)* qui se développe, en expansion; *(country)* en voie de développement; *(crisis)* en cours; **a d. interest in ...** un intérêt grandissant pour ...; **the d. situation in Bosnia** la situation jour après jour en Bosnie **2** *n* **(a)** = **development** **(b)** *Phot* développement *m*; **d. bath** (bain *m*) révélateur *m*; **d. tray** cuvette *f*

development [dɪ'veləpmənt] *n* **(a)** *(growth, expansion)* *(of body, faculties, concept, Mus of theme)* développement *m*; *(of subject)* développement, amplification *f*; *(of idea)* élargissement *m*

(b) *Econ* *(of region etc)* développement *m*, mise *f* en valeur; *(of area, land)* aménagement *m*, construction *f*; *(of Third World country)* développement; *Tech* *(of new design etc)* réalisation *f*, mise au point; **d. assistance** crédits *mpl* de développement; **d. costs** coûts *mpl* de développement; **d. stage** *(of a product etc)* phase *f* de développement

(c) *(progress, change)* développement *m*; *(of events etc)* déroulement *m*; *(of events, thought)* évolution *f*; **to await further developments** attendre la suite des événements; **a surprising d. in the situation** un développement étonnant de la situation; **the latest developments in the former Soviet Union** les derniers événements survenus dans l'ex-Union Soviétique; **the latest developments in medical research** les dernières découvertes médicales

(d) *Phot* développement *m*

(e) *Math* *(of surface, function)* développement *m*; *(of spiral)* développée *f*

development area *n Br Admin* zone *f ou* région *f* à développer

development capital *n* capital-développement *m*

development grant *n* subvention *f* pour le développement

deviant ['diːvɪənt] *adj, n Psy* déviant, -ante

deviate ['diːvɪeɪt] *vi* *(from instructions, plans, intentions etc)* s'écarter **(from** de); *(from a path, course of action, line)* dévier **(from** de)

deviation [diːvɪ'eɪʃən] *n* *(from norm, principles, standard procedure)* écart *m* **(from** par rapport à); *(of magnetic needle, from path, course of action, line)* déviation *f* **(from** de)

deviationism [diːvɪ'eɪʃənɪz(ə)m] *n Pol* déviationnisme *m*

deviationist [diːvɪ'eɪʃənɪst] *adj, n Pol* déviationniste *mf*

device [dɪ'vaɪs] *n* **(a)** *(fitting, part of a machine etc)* dispositif *m*; *(machine, gadget)* appareil *m*, dispositif; *Comptr* *(peripheral)* unité *f* périphérique, périphérique *m*; **locking d.** système *m* de verrouillage; **safety d.** dispositif de sécurité; **explosive/nuclear d.** engin *m* explosif/nucléaire; *Comptr* **d. driver** pilote *m* de périphérique **(b)** *(plan)* stratagème *m*, procédé *m*; **to leave sb to their own devices** *(alone)* laisser qn s'occuper comme bon lui semble; *(without help)* laisser qn se débrouiller **(c)** *Lit* *(on shield, flag etc)* emblème *m*, devise *f*

devil[1] ['dev(ə)l] *n* **(a)** *(evil being)* diable *m*, démon *m*; **the D.** le Diable

(b) *(person)* diable *m*; **he's a bit of a d.** *(awkward to deal with)* il est un peu enquiquineur; *(not always honest)* il est un peu malhonnête; *(not always reliable)* on ne peut pas compter sur lui; **poor d.!** pauvre diable!; **the silly d.!** quelle espèce d'idiot!; **you little d.!** petit diable!; *(annoyed)* petit garnement!; *(to little girl)* petite diablesse!; *(annoyed)* petite peste!

(c) *(in phrases)* **d.'s advocate** avocat *m* du diable; **to play d.'s advocate** se faire l'avocat du diable; **to be (caught) between the d. and the deep (blue) sea** être pris entre deux feux; **talk of the d.!** quand on parle du loup (on en voit la queue); **to have the d.'s own luck, to have the luck of the d.** avoir une veine de cocu; *Old-fashioned* **d. take it!** que le diable l'emporte!; *F* **go to the d.!** allez au diable!; **to play the d. with sth** mettre la confusion dans qch; **to give the d. his due ...** pour être honnête, il faut admettre que ...; *F* **there'll be the d. to pay** ça va barder; **(and) d. take the hindmost** sauve qui peut; *Prov* **the d. looks after his own** il y en a qui ont de la chance; *Prov* **better the d. you know than the d. you don't** mieux vaut ce qu'on connaît que ce qu'on ne connaît pas; *Prov* **the d. finds work for idle hands to do** l'oisiveté est la mère de tous les vices

(d) *F* *(as intensifier)* **what the d. are you doing?** que diable faites-vous là?; **how the d. ...?** comment diable ...?; **like the d.** *(to work)* avec acharnement; **to have the d. of a job** *or* **the d.'s own job (to do sth)** avoir un mal de chien *ou* un mal de tous les diables (à *ou* pour faire qch); **he's got the d. of a temper** il a un fichu caractère

devil[2] **(-ll-,** *US* **-l-) 1** *vi Br F* **to d. for sb** *(lawyer etc)* servir de nègre à **2** *vt Culin* *(meat)* faire griller et poivrer fortement; **devilled eggs** œufs durs à la diable

devilfish ['dev(ə)lfɪʃ] *n* **(a)** *(fish)* raie *f* manta **(b)** *(octopus)* pieuvre *f*

devilish ['dev(ə)lɪʃ] **1** *adj also Fig* diabolique **2** *adv Old-fashioned F* rudement

devilishly ['dev(ə)lɪʃlɪ] *adv* diaboliquement; **d. clever/cruel** d'une habileté/cruauté diabolique

devil-may-care *adj* insouciant, *F* je-m'en-foutiste; **d. spirit** *(reckless)* esprit *m* téméraire; *(carefree)* esprit insouciant

devilment ['dev(ə)lmənt], **devilry** ['dev(ə)lrɪ] *n* **(a)** *(mischief)* malice *f*, diablerie *f*, espièglerie *f*; **to do sth out of** *or* **for sheer d.** faire qch par pure malice *ou* espièglerie; **a piece of d.** une diablerie, une espièglerie; **what d. is he up to now?** qu'est-ce qu'il nous prépare comme sottise? **(b)** *(wickedness)* méchanceté *f*

devil's food cake *n Am Culin* = gâteau *m* au chocolat

devious ['diːvɪəs] *adj* *(person)* retors; *(mind)* retors, tortueux; *(way, means, route)* détourné, tortueux; *(scheme)* tortueux; **that was a bit d. of you** c'était un peu sournois de ta part

deviously ['diːvɪəslɪ] *adv* *(to achieve sth)* d'une façon détournée *ou* tortueuse, par des voies détournées *ou* tortueuses; *(to act, behave)* d'une façon tortueuse; **d. worded** rédigé d'une façon tortueuse

deviousness ['diːvɪəsnɪs] *n* *(devious behaviour)* détours *mpl*; *(of person)* caractère *m* retors; *(of scheme, mind)* caractère tortueux; **the increasing d. of their attempts** leurs efforts de plus en plus tortueux

devise[1] [dɪ'vaɪz] *n Jur* legs *m* (immobilier)

devise[2] *vt* **(a)** *(plan)* combiner, imaginer; *(solution, excuse, gadget)* inventer, imaginer; *(explanation, punishment, means of escape)* imaginer; *(plot)* tramer **(b)** *Jur* *(real estate)* léguer

devising [dɪ'vaɪsɪŋ] *n* **a scheme of his own d.** un plan qu'il avait imaginé lui-même

devitalize [diː'vaɪtəlaɪz] *vt* *(economy, country)* affaiblir

devoid [dɪ'vɔɪd] *adj pred* dénué, dépourvu **(of** de)

devolution [diːvə'luːʃən] *n* **(a)** *(of power, authority to individual)* délégation *f*, transmission *f*; *Pol* décentralisation *f* (administrative) **(b)** *Jur* dévolution *f*, transmission *f* par succession

devolve [dɪ'vɒlv] *vt* *(functions, powers)* déléguer, transmettre **(to sb** à qn)

▸ **devolve on, devolve to** *vipo Fml* **(a)** *(of responsibility, duty etc)* *(sb)* revenir à, incomber à **(b)** *Jur* *(of property)* *(sb)* être dévolu à

devote [dɪ'vəʊt] *vt* *(money, efforts)* consacrer **(to** à); *(time)* consacrer, accorder **(to** à); *(attention)* accorder **(to** à); **review specially devoted to history** revue entièrement consacrée à l'histoire; **to d. oneself to** *(occupation)* se vouer à, se consacrer à; *(study)* s'adonner à, se livrer à; **to d. oneself to sb/a cause** se dévouer à qn/une cause

devoted [dɪ'vəʊtɪd] *adj* *(father, daughter, service, care etc)* dévoué **(to** à); *(follower, fan)* adorateur, -trice; *(couple)* uni; **they are d. to each other** ils sont dévoués l'un à l'autre

devotedly [dɪ'vəʊtɪdlɪ] *adv* avec dévouement
devotee [devəʊ'tiː] *n* (*of person*) partisan, -ane; (*of sport*) passionné, -ée; (*of method*) adepte *mf*; (*of theory*) défenseur *m*; (*of god*) adorateur, -trice; **a d. of Haydn** un fervent *ou* un grand amateur de Haydn; **a d. of classical music** un passionné de musique classique
devotion [dɪ'vəʊʃən] *n* **(a)** (*to a god*) dévotion *f* **(to** à**)** **(b)** (*prayers*) **devotions** dévotions *fpl*, prières *fpl* **(c)** (*to friend, family*) dévotion *f*, attachement *m* **(to** à**)**; (*to leader of party, boss, cause*) dévouement *m* **(to sb** à *ou* pour qn; **to sth** à qch); **d. to duty** dévouement; **d. to work** assiduité *f ou* ardeur *f* au travail
devotional [dɪ'vəʊʃən(ə)l] *adj Rel* (*book, articles etc*) de dévotion, de piété; (*writings, literature*) religieux
devour [dɪ'vaʊər] *vt* dévorer; *Fig* **to d. sb with one's eyes** dévorer qn des yeux; *Fig* **to d. a book** dévorer un livre; *Fig* **to be devoured by jealousy/hatred** être dévoré par la jalousie/la haine
devouring [dɪ'vaʊərɪŋ] *adj attrib Fig* (*passion*) dévorant; (*enthusiasm*) débordant
devout [dɪ'vaʊt] *adj* **(a)** (*person*) dévot, pieux; **a d. Catholic/Muslim** un catholique/musulman fervent **(b)** (*wish etc*) fervent, sincère; **it is my d. wish that …** c'est mon vœu le plus sincère que …
devoutly [dɪ'vaʊtlɪ] *adv* **(a)** (*to pray*) avec dévotion; (*to live*) dans la dévotion **(b)** (*to wish, hope*) sincèrement; **it is d. to be wished that …** il faut sincèrement espérer que …
devoutness [dɪ'vaʊtnɪs] *n* dévotion *f*, piété *f*
dew [djuː] *n* **(morning) d.** rosée *f*; **evening d.** serein *m*; *Tech* **d. point** point *m* de rosée *ou* de condensation
dewclaw ['djuːklɔː] *n Zool* (*of dog etc*) ergot *m*
dewdrop ['djuːdrɒp] *n* goutte *f* de rosée
dewlap ['djuːlæp] *n* (*of cow*) fanon *m*; (*of person*) (*under chin*) plis *mpl* sous le menton, chairs *fpl* flasques sous le menton
dewy ['djuːɪ] *adj* couvert *ou* humide de rosée; *Fig* **d. complexion** teint *m* frais
dewy-eyed *adj* **(a)** (*look*) humide; **she gets all d. about her husband/France** elle est tout émue quand elle parle de son mari/la France **(b)** (*naive*) (*person*) naïf, -ve, ingénu; (*optimism, enthusiasm*) naïf; **don't act the d. innocent with me** ne fais pas l'ingénu avec moi
dexterity [deks'terɪtɪ] *n* (*mental*) dextérité *f*, doigté *m*; (*physical*) habileté *f*, adresse *f*; **manual d.** habileté manuelle
dext(e)rous ['dekstrəs] *adj* adroit, habile **(in doing sth** à faire qch**)**
dext(e)rously ['dekstrəslɪ] *adv* adroitement, avec dextérité
dextrin ['dekstrɪn] *n Ch, Ind* dextrine *f*
dextrose ['dekstrəʊs] *n Ch* dextrose *m*
DFC [diːef'siː] *n Br abbr* **Distinguished Flying Cross**
DFM [diːe'fem] *n Br abbr* **Distinguished Flying Medal**
DG [diː'dʒiː] *n Admin abbr* **Director General**
DH [diː'eɪtʃ] *n Br Admin* (*abbr* **Department of Health**) = Ministère *m* de la Santé
dhoti ['dəʊtɪ] *n* dhoti *m*
dhow [daʊ] *n* petit bateau *m* arabe à une voile
DHSS [diːeɪtʃe'ses] *n Br Admin formerly* (*abbr* **Department of Health and Social Security**) = Ministère *m* de la Santé
diabetes [daɪə'biːtiːz] *n Med* diabète *m*; **to have d.** avoir du diabète; **d. mellitus** diabète pancréatique
diabetic [daɪə'betɪk] *Med* **1** *n* diabétique *mf* **2** *adj* diabétique; **to be in a d. coma** faire un *ou* être en coma diabétique; **d. biscuits/jam** biscuits/confiture pour diabétiques
diabolic [daɪə'bɒlɪk] *adj* (*cruelty etc*) diabolique, atroce; (*plot*) infernal; (*laugh*) satanique
diabolical [daɪə'bɒlɪk(ə)l] *adj Br F* **(a)** (*very bad*) épouvantable, atroce; **it's d.!** (*of price*) c'est scandaleux!; **this wine tastes d.** ce vin est infect **(b)** (*intensifier*) **what a d. liberty** quel culot!
diabolically [daɪə'bɒlɪklɪ] *adv* **(a)** diaboliquement, de façon diabolique **(b)** *Br F* (*very badly*) de façon épouvantable; **it's d. expensive** c'est vachement cher
diacritic [daɪə'krɪtɪk] *Gram* **1** *n* (signe *m*) diacritique *m* **2** *adj* (*sign*) diacritique
diacritical [daɪə'krɪtɪk(ə)l] *adj* (*sign*) diacritique
diadem ['daɪədem] *n* diadème *m*
diaeresis, *US* **dieresis**, *pl* **-eses** [daɪ'erəsɪs, -əsiːz] *n Gram* tréma *m*
diagnose ['daɪəgnəʊz] *vt* (*illness*) diagnostiquer, faire le diagnostic de; (*engine problem etc*) diagnostiquer; **the doctor has diagnosed pneumonia** le médecin a diagnostiqué une pneumonie; **she has been diagnosed as a schizophrenic** d'après le diagnostic, elle est schizophrène; **the book attempts to d. the causes of the crisis** le livre tente de faire le diagnostic de la crise
diagnosis, *pl* **-ses** [daɪəg'nəʊsɪs, -siːz] *n Med, Fig* diagnostic *m*; **to make** *or* **give a d.** faire un diagnostic; **d. is not her strong point** le diagnostic n'est pas son point fort
diagnostic [daɪəg'nɒstɪk] **1** *adj* diagnostique; *Com* **d. audit** audit *m* de diagnostic; *Aut* **d. bay** station *f* diagnostic; *Comptr* **d. disk/program** disquette *f*/programme *m* de diagnostic; *Med* **d. kit** trousse *f* diagnostique; *Med, Comptr, Sch* **d. test** test *m* de diagnostic; **d. skill/ability** talent *m*/capacité *f* à diagnostiquer **2** *n* diagnostic *m*
diagnostician [daɪəgnɒ'stɪʃən] *n* diagnostiqueur *m*; **she's an excellent d.** elle fait de très bons diagnostics
diagnostics [daɪəg'nɒstɪks] *n* (①A10,c) *Med* diagnostique *f*
diagonal [daɪ'ægən(ə)l] **1** *adj* diagonal; *Constr* (*beam etc*) en écharpe; **d. ply** (*of tyre*) pli *m* diagonal **2** *n* diagonale *f*
diagonally [daɪ'ægən(ə)lɪ] *adv* diagonalement, en diagonale; **d. opposite sth** diamétralement opposé à qch
diagonal-ply tyre *n* pneu *m* à carcasse diagonale
diagram ['daɪəgræm] *n* diagramme *m*, schéma *m*; *Geom* figure *f*; *Phys etc* (*of temperature etc*) graphique *m*, courbe *f*; *MecE* (*of engine etc*) diagramme, caractéristique *f*; **to make a d. of sth** faire un schéma de qch, schématiser qch; *Fig* **do I need to draw you a d.?** est-ce que je dois te faire un dessin?
diagrammatic [daɪəgrə'mætɪk] *adj* schématique
dial[1] ['daɪəl] *n* (*of clock, scientific instrument*) cadran *m*; *Tel* cadran (d'appel); *Rad F* **don't touch that d.** (*announcement*) restez avec nous; **d. gauge** *or* **indicator** comparateur *m*; *Tel* **d. phone** téléphone *m* à cadran; *Am Tel* **d. tone** tonalité *f*
dial[2] (**-ll-**, *US* **-l-**) *Tel* **1** *vt* (*number*) composer, faire; **to d.** *Br* **999** *or* *US* **911** = appeler Police Secours; **d.-a-recipe/-horoscope** recette/horoscope par téléphone **2** *vi* composer *ou* faire le numéro
dialect ['daɪəlekt] *n* dialecte *m*; **provincial d.** patois *m*
dialectic(al) [daɪə'lektɪk, -ɪk(ə)l] *adj Phil* dialectique; **dialectical materialism** matérialisme *m* dialectique
dialectic(s) [daɪə'lektɪk, -s] *n(pl) Phil* dialectique *f*
dialler ['daɪələr] *n* composeur *m* de numéros
dialling, *US* **dialing** ['daɪəlɪŋ] *n Tel* composition *f* du numéro, numérotation *f*; **d. code** indicatif *m*; *Br* **d. tone** tonalité *f*; **I can't get a d. tone** je n'arrive pas à avoir la tonalité
dialogue, *US* **dialog** ['daɪəlɒg] *n* dialogue *m*; *Pol* **to enter into a d.** entamer le dialogue **(with sb** avec qn**)**; *Comptr* **d. box** boîte *f* de dialogue; *TV, Cin* **d. looping** doublage *m* du dialogue (en boucle); *Comptr* **d. mode** mode *m* dialogue; *Comptr* **d. screen** écran *m* de dialogue; *Cin etc* **d. writer** dialoguiste *mf*
dial-up line *n Telecom* ligne *f* commutée
dial-up modem *n* modem *m* réseau commuté
dialyse ['daɪəlaɪz] *vt Ch* dialyser
dialysis, *pl* **-es** [daɪ'ælɪsɪs, -iːz] *n Ch, Med* dialyse *f*; **she's in d.** elle est sous dialyse; **to have d. (treatment)** être sous dialyse; **d. machine** dialyseur *m*
diamanté [daɪə'mænteɪ, dɪə-] *n* broderie *f* diamantée
diameter [daɪ'æmɪtər] *n* diamètre *m*; **the wheel is 60 cm in d.** la roue a 60 cm de diamètre; **internal d.** (*of tube*) calibre *m*; (*of cylinder etc*) alésage *m*
diametric(al) [daɪə'metrɪk, -ɪk(ə)l] *adj* **in d. opposition** (*opinion etc*) diamétralement opposé **(to** à**)**
diametrically [daɪə'metrɪklɪ] *adv* **d. opposed** (*opinion etc*) diamétralement opposé **(to sth** à qch**)**
diamond ['daɪəmənd] *n* **(a)** (*gem*) diamant *m*; *Tech* **(cutting) d.** diamant de vitrier; **industrial d.** diamant industriel; **rough/cut d.** diamant brut/taillé; *Fig* **he's a rough d.** ses manières frustes cachent beaucoup de qualités; **d. cutter** (*person*) tailleur *m* de diamants; **d. cutting** taille *f* du diamant; **d. drill** foreuse *f* à pointe de diamant; **d. merchant** diamantaire *m*; **d. mine** mine *f* de diamants; **d. necklace/ring** collier *m*/bague *f* de diamants **(b)** (*shape*) losange *m*; **d. pattern** dessin *m* en losanges **(c)** *Cards* carreau *m*; **the six of diamonds** le six de carreau **(d)** *Baseball* terrain *m* de base-ball
diamond jubilee *n* (*of monarch, company*) soixantième anniversaire *m*
diamond-shaped *adj* en losange
diamond wedding *n* noces *fpl* de diamant
diapason [daɪə'peɪsən] *n Mus* **(a)** (*of organ*) principaux jeux *mpl* de fond **(b)** (*tuning fork*) diapason *m*
diaper ['daɪəpər] *n Am* (*for baby*) couche *f*, lange *m*
diaphanous [daɪ'æfənəs] *adj* diaphane
diaphragm ['daɪəfræm] *n* **(a)** *Anat* diaphragme *m* **(b)** (*membrane*) diaphragme *m*, membrane *f*; *Phot* diaphragme **(c)** (*contraceptive*) diaphragme *m* (contraceptif)
diarist ['daɪərɪst] *n* auteur *m* d'un journal (intime), diariste *mf*
diarrhoea, *US* **diarrhea** [daɪə'rɪə] *n Med* diarrhée *f*; **to have d.** avoir la diarrhée
diary ['daɪərɪ] *n* **(a)** (*recording events*) journal *m* (intime); **to keep a d.** tenir un journal (intime) **(b)** (*for appointments*) agenda *m*; (*showing a week at a time*) semainier *m*; **desk d.**

(*loose leaf*) bloc *m* calendrier; (*bound*) agenda **(c)** *Journ* **d. column** billet *m*, rubrique *f* d'échos; **d. job** reportage *m* prévisible

Diaspora (the) [ðədaɪ'æspərə] *n Jewish Rel* la Diaspora

diastole [daɪ'æstəlɪ] *n Med* diastole *f*

diatom ['daɪətəm] *n Biol* diatomée *f*

diatonic scale [daɪə'tɒnɪk] *n Mus* gamme *f* diatonique

diatribe ['daɪətraɪb] *n* diatribe *f* (**against** contre)

dibble[1] ['dɪb(ə)l], **dibber** ['dɪbər] *n* (*for bulbs etc*) plantoir *m*

dibble[2] **1** *vt* (*seeds*) semer au plantoir; (*plants*) repiquer au plantoir **2** *vi* semer/repiquer au plantoir

dibs [dɪbz] *npl* (*game*) osselets *m*

dice[1] [daɪs] *n inv* (*pl of* **die**) **(a)** [①**A10**,d; **A13**,3,c] (*in game*) dé *m*; **to throw the d.** lancer le(s) dé(s); *Am Fig F* **no d.** pas question **(b)** *Culin* cube *m*

dice[2] **1** *vi* jouer aux dés; **to d. with death** risquer sa vie **2** *vt Culin* (*vegetables etc*) couper en cubes

dicey ['daɪsɪ] *adj esp Br F* (*uncertain*) hasardeux; (*dangerous*) risqué

dichotomous question [daɪ'kɒtəməs] *n* question *f* fermée à choix unique

dichotomy [daɪ'kɒtəmɪ] *n* dichotomie *f*

dick [dɪk] *n F* **(a)** *esp US* (*detective*) détective *m*, flic *m* **(b)** *Vulg* (*penis*) bitte *f*, queue *f*

dickens ['dɪkɪnz] *n F* **what the d. are you doing?** que diable fais-tu?; **the** *or* **a d. of a row** un bruit de tous les diables; **we had the** *or* **a d. of a time getting here** on a eu un mal fou pour arriver ici

Dickensian [dɪ'kenzɪən] *adj* (*scene, Christmas etc*) à la Dickens; (*conditions*) qui sort d'un roman de Dickens

dicker ['dɪkər] *vi Am F* marchander; **to d. for sth** marchander qch

dickhead ['dɪkhed] *n Br Sl* (*idiot*) tête *f* de nœud

dicky[1] ['dɪkɪ] *n F* **(a)** (*in children's language*) **d. (bird)** (petit) oiseau *m*, zoziau *m*; *Br* **did you hear anything? – not a d. bird** est-ce que tu as entendu? – non, rien du tout; *Br* **they haven't heard a d. bird from her** elle n'a pas fait signe de vie; *Br* **not a d. bird to anyone about this** pas un mot de tout ça à quiconque **(b)** (*of shirt*) faux plastron *m*; *Br* **d. (bow)** nœud *m* papillon **(c)** *Br Old-fashioned Aut* (*seat*) spider *m*

dicky[2] *adj Br F* (*defective*) défectueux; (*heart*) malade, qui flanche; **to feel d.** se sentir tout chose

Dictaphone® ['dɪktəfəʊn] *n* Dictaphone® *m*

dictate[1] ['dɪkteɪt] *n* ordre *m*; **to follow the dictates of one's conscience** écouter sa conscience; **the dictates of fashion** les exigences de la mode

dictate[2] [dɪk'teɪt] **1** *vt* **(a)** (*letter, passage*) dicter **(b)** (*conditions of peace etc*) dicter **(c)** (*determine*) déterminer; (*of circumstances*) imposer, demander; **the size of the harvest will be dictated by the weather** l'importance de la moisson dépendra du temps **2** *vi* **(a)** (*lay down law*) faire la loi; **I won't be dictated to** on ne me donne pas d'ordres **(b)** (*to secretary etc*) dicter

dictating [dɪk'teɪtɪŋ] *n* **d. machine** machine *f* à dicter

dictation [dɪk'teɪʃən] *n* dictée *f*; **to take d. from sb** écrire sous la dictée de qn; **to give d.** dicter; **d. speed** vitesse *f* de dictée; *Sch* **to do d.** faire la dictée

dictator [dɪk'teɪtər] *n Pol, Fig* dictateur *m*

dictatorial [dɪktə'tɔːrɪəl] *adj* **(a)** (*power*) dictatorial **(b)** (*tone*) impérieux, autoritaire; (*person*) autoritaire

dictatorially [dɪktə'tɔːrɪəlɪ] *adv* **(a)** (*to govern*) de façon dictatoriale **(b)** (*to say*) impérieusement, autoritairement; **to be d. inclined** avoir des tendances dictatoriales

dictatorship [dɪk'teɪtəʃɪp] *n* dictature *f*

diction ['dɪkʃən] *n* **(a)** (*pronunciation*) diction *f* **(b)** (*choice of words*) style *m*

dictionary ['dɪkʃən(ə)rɪ] *n* dictionnaire *m* (**of** de); **English-French d.** dictionnaire anglais-français; **d. of quotations** dictionnaire de citations

dictum, *pl* **-ums, -a** ['dɪktəm, -əmz, -ə] *n* **(a)** (*statement*) affirmation *f*, dire *m* **(b)** (*saying*) maxime *f*, dicton *m*

did [dɪd] *see* **do[1]**

didactic [dɪ'dæktɪk] *adj* didactique

didactically [dɪ'dæktɪklɪ] *adv* didactiquement

diddle ['dɪd(ə)l] *vt F* (*sb*) duper, refaire, rouler; **he diddled me out of £500** il m'a refait *ou* roulé de 500 livres; **you've been diddled** tu t'es fait avoir *ou* rouler; **they diddled me into selling the house** ils ont réussi à m'embobiner et à me faire vendre la maison

diddler ['dɪdlər] *n F* escroqueur, -euse

didn't ['dɪd(ə)nt] = **did not**, *see* **do[1]**

die[1] [daɪ] *n* **(a)** [①**A13**,3,c] (*pl* **dice**) (*for playing, gambling*) dé *m*; *Fig* **the d. is cast** le sort est jeté, les dés sont jetés **(b)** (*pl* **dies** [daɪz]) *Metal* (*mould*) matrice *f*; **stamping** *or* **embossing d.** matrice *ou* machine *f* à estamper; **screw-cutting d.** mère *f* (de filet de vis); **d. plate** (*for tickets*) plaque *f* d'imprimante de billets; **d. sinker** graveur *m* d'étampes *ou* de matrices **(c)** *Metal* (*tool*) poinçonneuse *f* (à main)

die[2] (*pt, pp* **died** [daɪd]; *prp* **dying** ['daɪɪŋ]) **1** *vi* **(a)** mourir; **to be dying** être en train de mourir; **to d. of cancer** mourir d'un cancer; **to d. of grief/starvation** mourir de chagrin/faim; **he died yesterday** il est mort hier; **to d. in one's sleep** mourir pendant son sommeil; **to d. rich/a millionaire** mourir riche/millionnaire; **they died like heroes** ils sont morts en héros; **to d. from** *or* **of a wound** mourir des suites d'une blessure; **to d. in bed** mourir dans son lit; **to d. by one's own hand** se suicider, se donner la mort; *F* **never say d.!** (*don't give up*) il ne faut jamais désespérer; (*stay cheerful*) courage!, tenez bon!; *F* **I thought I would d. of boredom/of curiosity** j'ai cru mourir d'ennui/de curiosité; *F* **I nearly died laughing/of shame** j'étais mort de rire/de honte; *F* **we were dying of cold** nous mourions de froid; *F* **to be dying to do sth** brûler *ou* mourir d'envie de faire qch; *F* **I'm dying for a drink/cigarette** je meurs de soif/d'envie de fumer une cigarette

(b) (*of engine*) caler; (*of TV picture*) disparaître; (*of lights*) s'éteindre; (*of battery*) se mettre à plat; (*of love, passion, hopes, enthusiasm*) mourir; **old superstitions d. hard** les vieilles superstitions ont la vie dure; **the engine died (on me/us/***etc***)** le moteur a calé; *Lit* **day is dying** le jour s'en va; **their love died** leur amour s'est éteint; **his secret died with him** il a emporté son secret dans le tombeau

2 *vt* **to d. a natural death** (*not be murdered*) mourir de mort naturelle; (*of old age*) mourir de sa belle mort; (*of fashion etc*) passer de mode; **to d. a violent death** mourir de mort violente; **to d. a hero's death** mourir héroïquement *ou* en héros; *Fig* **to d. the death** (*of play*) faire un four; (*be embarrassed*) être mortellement embarrassé; **to d. a thousand deaths** souffrir mille morts

▶ **die away** *vi* (*of sound*) s'affaiblir; (*of voice*) s'éteindre; (*of wind*) tomber; *Mus* **to let the sound d. away** éteindre le son

▶ **die back** *vi* (*of plant*) (se) faner

▶ **die down** *vi* (*of fire etc*) baisser; (*of wind*) tomber; (*of sound*) s'éteindre; (*of excitement, storm, scandal*) se calmer; (*of applause*) mourir

▶ **die off** *vi* mourir; **they're dying off like flies** ils meurent les uns après les autres *ou* comme des mouches

▶ **die out** *vi* (*of family etc*) s'éteindre; (*of species*) disparaître

die casting *n* moulage *m* en coquille

die-hard **1** *n* réactionnaire *mf*; *Pol* ultra-conservateur *m* **2** *adj attrib* pur et dur; **d. policy** politique *f* réactionnaire; **his d. resistance to change** sa résistance obstinée au changement

dieresis [daɪ'erəsɪs] *n US* = **diaeresis**

diesel ['diːz(ə)l] **1** *adj* (*engine, train*) diesel; **d. oil** *or* **fuel** gazole *m*, diesel *m*, gasoil *m*; **d. emissions test** contrôle *m* des émissions de moteurs diesel; *Aut* **d. injection** injection *f* diesel; *Aut* **d. knock** cognement *m* (du moteur) diesel **2** *n* (*vehicle*) diesel *m*; (*oil, fuel*) gazole *m*, diesel, gasoil *m*

diesel-electric *adj* diesel-électrique, *pl* diesel-électriques

dieselling ['diːz(ə)lɪŋ] *n Aut* auto-allumage *m*

die stamping *n* matriçage *m*

diet[1] ['daɪət] *n* **(a)** (*what is eaten*) alimentation *f*; **their d. consists mainly of fish** leur nourriture se compose essentiellement de poisson; **to survive on a d. of fresh fruit and vegetables** survivre en se nourrissant de fruits et de légumes frais **(b)** *Med* régime *m*; (*to lose weight*) régime, diète *f*; **to be/go on a d.** être/se mettre au régime; **to put sb on a d.** mettre qn au régime; **d. pills** pastilles *fpl* amaigrissantes; **d. foods** (*for people with special requirements*) aliments *mpl* diététiques; **d. drink** boisson *f* à basses calories

diet[2] *vi* être au régime; **he needs to d.** il faut qu'il se mette au régime

diet[3] *n Pol* diète *f*

dietary ['daɪət(ə)rɪ] **1** *adj* alimentaire; **d. fibre** fibres *fpl* (alimentaires) **2** *n Fml* (*of patient, prison etc*) régime *m* (alimentaire)

dietetic [daɪə'tetɪk] *adj* diététique

dietetics [daɪə'tetɪks] *n* [①**A10**,c] diététique *f*

dietician, dietitian [daɪə'tɪʃən] *n* diététicien, -ienne

differ ['dɪfər] *vi* **(a)** (*be different*) différer (**from** de), être différent (**from** de); **to d. in size/shape/colour** être de tailles/de formes/de couleurs différentes; **to d. in price** différer de prix; **how do the two species d.?** en quoi est-ce que les deux espèces diffèrent?, qu'est-ce qui différencie les deux espèces?

(b) (*disagree*) être d'opinion différente *ou* d'avis différent; **I beg to d.** permettez-moi d'être d'un autre avis; **to agree to d.** garder chacun son opinion; **let's agree to d.** acceptons de dépasser nos différences; **that's where we d.** c'est sur ce point que nous sommes en désaccord; **I d. with her about** *or* **on** *or* **over the diagnosis** je ne suis pas d'accord avec elle sur le diagnostic

difference [ˈdɪf(ə)rəns] *n* **(a)** différence *f*, écart *m* **(between** entre); *(between two numbers etc)* différence; **d. in age/in altitude** différence d'âge/d'altitude; **d. in temperature** écart de température; **differences in price** écarts de prix; **there's a d. of two years between me and my brother** il y a une différence d'âge de deux ans entre mon frère et moi; **a world of d.** une différence énorme; **the d. in you is amazing** c'est incroyable à quel point tu as changé; **to notice a (big) d. in sb** remarquer que qn a (énormément) changé; **I don't quite see the d.** je ne saisis pas la nuance; **she doesn't make any d. between the children** *(of parent, teacher etc)* elle ne fait pas de distinction entre les enfants; **it doesn't make any d.** cela ne fait aucune différence; **it makes no d. (to me)** cela ne (me) fait rien, cela m'est parfaitement égal; **to make a d.** *(improve society)* faire avancer les choses; **the new colour scheme makes a big** *or* **all the d.** les nouvelles couleurs font toute la différence; **that makes all the d.** voilà qui change complètement les choses; **he's a businessman, but with a d.** c'est bien un homme d'affaires, mais pas comme les autres; **to split the d.** *(price, fee etc)* couper la poire en deux; **to pay** *or* **settle the d.** *(price, fee etc)* payer *ou* régler la différence; *Hum* **it's the same d.!** cela revient au même

(b) *(disagreement)* désaccord *m*, différend *m* **(about sth** au sujet de qch); **d. of opinion** différence *f* d'opinion, désaccord; **to have a d. of opinion with sb** se disputer avec qn; **to settle a d.** *(of two people)* régler un différend, se mettre d'accord; **we have our differences** nous ne sommes pas toujours d'accord

different [ˈdɪf(ə)rənt] *adj* **(a)** différent **(from,** *Am also* **than** de); **she feels a d. person** elle ne se sent plus la même; **that dress makes you look d.** cette robe vous change; **I do it in a d. way** je m'y prends tout autrement; **that's quite a d. matter** ça c'est une autre affaire

(b) *(various)* divers; **d. colours** couleurs diverses *ou* variées; **d. kinds of …** diverses *ou* différentes espèces de …; **at d. times** à différentes *ou* diverses reprises; **I talked to d. people about it** j'en ai parlé à plusieurs personnes; **d. people say d. things** les avis diffèrent

(c) *(unusual)* hors de l'ordinaire; **he just wants to be d.** tout ce qu'il veut c'est être différent, *Pej* il cherche à se faire remarquer; **it's certainly d.** c'est original

differential [dɪfəˈrenʃəl] **1** *adj* différentiel; *Math* **d. calculus** calcul *m* différentiel; *Aut etc* **d. gear** engrenage *m* différentiel; *Com* **d. pricing** établissement *m* des prix différentiels, tarification *f* différentielle **2** *n Math* différentielle *f*; *Aut* différentiel *m*; *(in prices, salaries)* écart *m*; **weight d.** différence *f* de poids; **wage** *or* **pay differentials** hiérarchie *f* salariale

differentially [dɪfəˈrenʃəlɪ] *adv (to pay)* à des taux différentiels

differentiate [dɪfəˈrenʃɪeɪt] **1** *vt also Math* différencier **(sth from sth** qch de qch) **2** *vi* **(a)** *(distinguish)* faire la différence **(between two things** entre deux choses) **(b)** *(discriminate)* **to d. between male and female employees** traiter les employés hommes différemment des employées femmes

differentiation [dɪfərenʃɪˈeɪʃən] *n* différenciation *f*

differently [ˈdɪf(ə)rəntlɪ] *adv* différemment

difficult [ˈdɪfɪkəlt] *adj* **(a)** *(task, problem etc)* difficile; **she's at a d. age** elle est à l'âge ingrat; **this question is d. to answer** il est difficile de répondre à cette question; **I find it d.** *or* **it is d. for me to …** j'ai de la peine à …, j'ai du mal à …; **it is d. to believe that …** on a peine à croire que … + *sub*; **why do you have to make life d. for people?** quel besoin as-tu de compliquer la vie aux gens?; **it makes life d. not knowing how long they'll be staying for** cela n'arrange pas les choses de ne pas savoir combien de temps ils vont rester; **he seems to have a habit of making things d. for himself** il semble avoir le chic pour se compliquer les choses; **she's very d. to talk to** il est très difficile de lui parler

(b) *(person)* difficile; **he's d. to get on with** il n'est pas commode; **don't be so d.!** ne fais pas le/la difficile!; **you're just being d.** tu fais le/la difficile; **why do you have to be d. about everything?** pourquoi faut-il que tout soit aussi compliqué avec toi?

difficulty [ˈdɪfɪkəltɪ] *n* **(a)** difficulté *f*; **to have d. in doing sth** avoir du mal *ou* des difficultés à faire qch; **to have d. (in) breathing** avoir du mal à respirer; **with d.** avec difficulté, avec du mal; **without much d.** sans grande difficulté

(b) *(obstacle, problem)* difficulté *f*; **the d. is to …** ce qui est difficile, c'est de …; **I see no d. about it** je n'y vois pas d'inconvénient; **the real d. is how to keep both sides happy** le plus difficile c'est de satisfaire les deux parties; **there will be no d. about that** cela ne fera pas de difficultés; **to raise** *or* **make difficulties** soulever des objections; **there's the d.!** voilà la difficulté!; **to run into a d.** rencontrer une difficulté; **to be in d.** *or* **difficulties** *(of swimmer)* être en difficulté; *Fig (of company, marriage)* connaître des difficultés; **ship in difficulties** navire *m* en difficulté; **financial difficulties** embarras *m* pécuniaire; **to get into difficulties** se mettre dans un mauvais pas; **to get out of one's difficulties** se tirer d'affaire

diffidence [ˈdɪfɪdəns] *n* manque *m* de confiance en soi, manque d'assurance

diffident [ˈdɪfɪdənt] *adj (person)* qui manque d'assurance *ou* de confiance en soi; *(smile)* timide; *(manner, air)* peu assuré; **to be d. about doing sth** hésiter à faire qch; **to be d. about one's abilities** se montrer modeste en ce qui concerne ses propres capacités

diffidently [dɪfɪdəntlɪ] *adv (to smile)* timidement, d'un air peu assuré; *(to express oneself, say sth)* sur un ton peu assuré

diffract [dɪˈfrækt] *vt Opt (light)* diffracter

diffraction [dɪˈfrækʃən] *n Opt (of light)* diffraction *f*

diffuse[1] [dɪˈfjuːs] *adj (light, style etc)* diffus; *(sense of unease)* indéfini

diffuse[2] [dɪˈfjuːz] **1** *vt (light)* diffuser, répandre; *Fml (news etc)* répandre **2** *vi (of light, gas etc)* se diffuser; *Fml (of knowledge)* se répandre

diffused [dɪˈfjuːzd] *adj* **d. lighting** éclairage *m* tamisé

diffuseness [dɪˈfjuːsnɪs] *n (of style)* prolixité *f*, caractère *m* diffus

diffuser [dɪˈfjuːzər] *n (for hairdryer, light)* diffuseur *m*; *TV, Cin (on a light)* (écran *m*) diffuseur *m*

diffusion [dɪˈfjuːʒən] *n (of liquid, style, news etc)* diffusion *f*; *(of ideas)* rayonnement *m*; *Phys (of rays)* dispersion *f*

diffusive [dɪˈfjuːsɪv] *adj* **(a)** *(property, characteristic)* diffusif **(b)** *(style)* diffus, prolixe

dig[1] [dɪg] *n* **(a)** *(in garden etc)* coup *m* de bêche; *Archeol* fouille *f*; **give the ground a good d.** retournez bien le sol; *Archeol* **to go on a d.** faire des fouilles; **a d. in the ribs** un coup de coude dans les côtes **(b)** *(remark)* remarque *f* désobligeante **(at sb** à qn); **to get a d. in at sb, to have a d. at sb** lancer une remarque désobligeante à qn; **that's a d. at you** cette remarque t'est destinée

dig[2] *(pt, pp* **dug** [dʌg]; *prp* **digging** [ˈdɪgɪŋ]) **1** *vt* **(a)** *(hole, grave, well etc)* creuser; *(soil, garden)* bêcher; *Fig* **to d. one's own grave** creuser sa propre tombe

(b) *(thrust)* enfoncer **(in** dans); **to d. sb in the ribs** donner un coup de coude à qn

(c) *Old-fashioned Sl (understand) (sth)* comprendre, piger; *(like)* bien aimer; **she really digs you** *(likes you)* elle en pince vraiment pour toi; **I d. that** *(like it)* ça me plaît *ou* me botte, j'aime bien ça

2 *vi (of workmen, dog etc)* creuser; *(of gardener)* bêcher; *Archeol* faire des fouilles; **to d. for gold** faire des fouilles pour trouver de l'or; **the dog was digging for its bone** le chien creusait pour trouver son os

▶ **dig in 1** *vtsep (compost etc)* enterrer; *Fig* **to d. one's heels** *or* **toes in** s'entêter; **she dug her heels in over the question** elle s'est montrée très intransigeante sur la question; **to d. oneself in** *F* s'incruster; *Mil* s'établir dans des tranchées **2** *vi* **(a)** *Mil (by digging trenches)* s'établir **(b)** *F (eat)* manger; *(start eating)* attaquer

▶ **dig into 1** *vipo* **(a)** *F (eat) (pie, tart etc)* manger **(b)** *(search) (sb's past, files)* fouiller dans **(c)** *(press into)* **my rucksack's digging into my back** mon sac à dos me blesse dans le dos **2** *vtaspo* enterrer dans; **to d. compost into the garden** enterrer du compost dans le jardin

▶ **dig out** *vtsep* **(a)** *(remove) (bullet, splinter etc)* extraire; *(person from ruins, snow drift etc)* dégager **(b)** *F (find) (address, person etc)* dénicher

▶ **dig over** *vtsep* retourner

▶ **dig up** *vtsep (plant etc)* déraciner; *(treasure)* mettre à jour; *(road)* piocher; *(body)* déterrer, exhumer; *F (find)* dénicher

digest [ˈdaɪdʒest] *n* condensé *m*, *F* digest *m*

digest[2] [dɪˈdʒest, daɪ-] *vt Physiol (food)* digérer; *Fig (insult)* digérer; *(reading matter)* digérer, assimiler

digestible [dɪˈdʒestəb(ə)l, daɪ-] *adj* digestible; **easily d.** digeste

digestion [dɪˈdʒestʃən, daɪ-] *n Physiol* digestion *f*; *Fig (of what one has read)* digestion, assimilation *f*; **to have a good d.** ne pas avoir de problèmes de digestion; **a glass of wine helps the digestion** un verre de vin facilite la digestion *ou* aide à digérer

digestive [dɪˈdʒestɪv, daɪ-] **1** *adj* digestif; **d. system** système *m* digestif; **d. tract** tube *m* digestif; **d. troubles** troubles *mpl* digestifs *ou* de digestion **2** *n* **(a)** *Pharm etc* digestif *m* **(b)** *Br* **d. (biscuit)** = sorte de sablé

Digger [ˈdɪgər] *n F (Australian)* Australien *m*; *(New Zealander)* Néo-Zélandais *m*

digger [ˈdɪgər] *n* **(a)** *Constr* **(mechanical) d.** excavateur *m* **(b)** (*person*) (*with spade*) personne *f* qui bêche; (*for gold etc*) chercheur *m* **(c) d. (wasp)** guêpe *f* fouisseuse

digging [ˈdɪgɪŋ] *n* (*of soil*) bêchage *m*, labour *m* à la bêche; (*of well, ditches etc*) creusement *m*; *Archeol* fouilles *fpl*

digit [ˈdɪdʒɪt] *n* **(a)** *Math* chiffre *m* (arabe); **double d. inflation** taux *m* d'inflation à deux chiffres; *Comptr* **d. selector** sélecteur *m* d'indice **(b)** (*on hand*) doigt *m*; (*on foot*) orteil *m*; *Br Hum* **extract the d.!** grouille-toi!

digital [ˈdɪdʒɪt(ə)l] *adj* **(a)** *Comptr, Telecom* numérique; **d. analog(ue) converter** convertisseur *m* analogique numérique; **d. audio broadcasting** diffusion *f* audio numérique; **d. audio cassette player** lecteur *m* de cassettes audionumériques; **d. audio tape** cassette *f* audionumérique; **d. clock** horloge *f* à affichage numérique; **d. computer** ordinateur *m*; **d. display** affichage *m* numérique; **d. frequency display** affichage digital des fréquences; **d. readout** affichage digital; **d. recording** (*of music*) enregistrement *m* numérique; **d. signal** signal *m* numérique; **d. sound** son *m* numérique; **d. video** vidéo *f* numérique; **d. watch** montre *f* à affichage numérique
(b) *Anat* digital

digitalis [dɪdʒɪˈteɪlɪs] *n* **(a)** *Bot* digitale *f* **(b)** *Pharm* digitaline *f*

digitalization [dɪdʒɪtəlaɪˈzeɪʃən] *n* numérisation *f*

digitalize [ˈdɪdʒɪtəlaɪz] *vt* numériser

digitize [ˈdɪdʒɪtaɪz] *vt Comptr* (*data*) convertir en numérique, numériser

digitizer [ˈdɪdʒɪtaɪzər] *n Comptr* numériseur *m*

diglossia [daɪˈglɒsɪə] *n Ling* diglossie *f*

dignified [ˈdɪgnɪfaɪd] *adj* (*person*) digne, plein de dignité; (*air, silence*) digne; **to have a d. manner** avoir de la dignité dans ses manières

dignify [ˈdɪgnɪfaɪ] *vt* (*sth*) donner de la dignité à; **to d. sb with the name of ...** honorer qn du nom de ...; **I won't d. that remark with a response** je ne m'abaisserai pas à répondre à cette remarque

dignitary [ˈdɪgnɪt(ə)rɪ] *n* dignitaire *m*

dignity [ˈdɪgnɪtɪ] *n* dignité *f*; **a woman of great d.** une femme d'une grande dignité; **to be** *or* **stand on one's d.** se retrancher derrière sa dignité; **to consider sth beneath one's d.** considérer que qch est en-dessous de soi; **it was beneath my d. even to respond** je me serais abaissé à seulement répondre; **the d. of labour** la dignité du travail

digress [daɪˈgres] *vi* faire une digression/des digressions; **to d. from a subject** s'écarter d'un sujet; **I'd like to d. for a moment** j'aimerais faire une parenthèse

digression [daɪˈgreʃən] *n* digression *f*; **by way of a d.** par parenthèse

digs [dɪgz] *npl Br F* (*lodgings*) logement *m*; **to live in d.** loger en meublé; **where are your d.?** où est-ce que tu crèches?

dihedral [daɪˈhiːdrəl] **1** *n* dièdre *m* **2** *adj* (*angle*) dièdre

dike [daɪk] *n, vt* = **dyke**

dilapidated [dɪˈlæpɪdeɪtɪd] *adj* (*building, car etc*) délabré, dans un état de délabrement; *Hum* (*hat, suit*) dépenaillé

dilapidation [dɪlæpɪˈdeɪʃən] *n* (*of building, car etc*) délabrement *m*, dégradation *f*; **in a state of d.** dans un état de délabrement

dilate [daɪˈleɪt] **1** *vt* dilater **2** *vi* (*of eyes etc*) se dilater
▶ **dilate on** *vipo Fml* (*subject*) s'étendre sur

dilation [daɪˈleɪʃən] *n* dilatation *f*; *Med* **d. and curettage** dilatation et curetage *m*

dilatoriness [ˈdɪlət(ə)rɪnɪs] *n* lenteur *f* (à agir)

dilatory [ˈdɪlət(ə)rɪ] *adj Fml* (*person*) lent (à agir); (*action*) tardif; (*answer*) dilatoire; **to be d. in doing sth** tarder à faire qch

dildo [ˈdɪldəʊ] *n* **(a)** (*device*) godemiché *m* **(b)** *Sl* (*stupid person*) abruti, -ie

dilemma [daɪˈlemə] *n* embarras *m*; (*in logic*) dilemme *m*; **to be in a d.** être bien embarrassé; **you place** *or* **put me in a d.** tu me mets dans l'embarras; **to be in a d. over a decision** être pris dans un dilemme au sujet d'une décision; **she's in a bit of a d. over whether to tell him or not** elle ne sait pas trop si elle doit le lui dire ou non; **to be on the horns of a d.** être pris dans un dilemme

dilettante, *pl* **-ti** [dɪlɪˈtɑːntɪ] **1** *n* dilettante *m* **2** *adj* **in a d. manner** (*to do sth*) en dilettante

dilettantism [dɪlɪˈtɑːntɪz(ə)m] *n* dilettantisme *m*

diligence [ˈdɪlɪdʒ(ə)ns] *n* assiduité *f*, application *f*, zèle *m*

diligent [ˈdɪlɪdʒ(ə)nt] *adj* (*student, work*) assidu, appliqué; (*employee*) consciencieux, zélé; (*inquiries, search*) consciencieux, minutieux

diligently [ˈdɪlɪdʒ(ə)ntlɪ] *adv* (*to study*) avec assiduité, assidûment; (*to work*) consciencieusement, avec zèle

dill [dɪl] *n* (*herb*) aneth *m*

dilly-dally [ˈdɪlɪˈdælɪ] *vi* (**dilly-dallied**) *F* **(a)** (*loiter*) traîner, traînasser, lambiner **(b)** (*vacillate*) hésiter, tergiverser; **to d. about whether to do sth** se tâter pour savoir si on fait qch

dilute¹ [daɪˈluːt, dɪ-] *adj* (*acid etc*) dilué, étendu

dilute² *vt* **(a)** (*orange juice, acid*) diluer (**with** avec); (*sauce*) allonger (**with** de); **to d. wine with water** couper du vin avec de l'eau; **d. to taste** (*written on bottle*) diluer à votre convenance; **to become diluted** se diluer **(b)** *Fig* (*theory etc*) édulcorer; **diluted radicalism** radicalisme *m* à l'eau de rose

dilution [daɪˈluːʃən, dɪ-] *n* dilution *f*; *Fig* (*of theory*) édulcoration *f*; *Fin* **d. of capital** dilution de capital

dim¹ [dɪm] *adj* (**dimmer, dimmest**) (*light*) faible, pâle; (*eyesight*) faible, trouble; (*forest, room, lighting*) sombre; (*outline, memory*) vague, faible, estompé; *F* (*chances, prospects*) faible, mince; (*person*) bête; **to grow d.** (*of light, faculties*) baisser; (*of recollection*) s'effacer; (*of eyesight*) se troubler; (*of outline*) s'effacer, s'estomper; *F* **to take a d. view of sth** avoir une piètre opinion de qch, désapprouver qch

dim² (**-mm-**) **1** *vt* (*light*) atténuer, réduire; (*sight*) obscurcir; (*memory, intelligence*) troubler; (*beauty, surface of a mirror*) ternir; *Fig* (*sb's glory*) éclipser; **to d. the lights** baisser les lumières; *Am Aut* **to d. one's headlights** se mettre en code; **dimmed headlights** phares *mpl* code **2** *vi* (*of light*) baisser; (*of eyes*) s'obscurcir; (*of outline*) s'effacer, s'estomper

dimbo [ˈdɪmbəʊ] *n F* ballot *m*, nigaud *m*

dim-dip *n Aut* veilleuses-codes *fpl*

dime [daɪm] *n Am* dime *f* (= un dixième de dollar); **it's not worth a d.** ça ne vaut pas un clou; *Fig* **they're a d. a dozen** il y en a à la pelle; **arts graduates are a d. a dozen** des licenciés ès lettres, il y en a à la pelle, les licenciés ès lettres courent les rues; **d. store** magasin *m* bon marché

dimension [daɪˈmenʃən, dɪ-] *n* [①B56-7,D,1] dimension *f*; **what are the dimensions of the room?** quelles sont les dimensions de la pièce?; **of large dimensions** de grandes dimensions; **the fourth d.** la quatrième dimension; *Fig* **there's another d. to the problem** le problème a une autre dimension

dimensional [daɪˈmenʃən(ə)l, dɪ-] *adj* dimensionnel

-dimensional *suff* **two/three-d.** à deux/trois dimensions

diminish [dɪˈmɪnɪʃ] **1** *vt* (*power, enthusiasm*) diminuer, réduire; (*sound, light*) diminuer, baisser; (*reputation*) diminuer, affaiblir; **to d. the importance of sth** diminuer l'importance de qch **2** *vi* (*of power, enthusiasm, reputation*) diminuer, s'affaiblir; (*of sound, light*) diminuer, s'atténuer, baisser

diminished [dɪˈmɪnɪʃt] *adj* (*power, reputation*) diminué, affaibli; (*light*) atténué; *Mus* (*interval*) diminué; **he's greatly d.** (*physically*) il est très diminué; *Jur* **d. responsibility** responsabilité diminuée

diminishing [dɪˈmɪnɪʃɪŋ] *adj* (*light, power etc*) décroissant, qui diminue; (*value*) à la baisse; (*popularity*) en baisse; *Econ, Fig* **law of d. returns** loi *f* des rendements non-proportionnels *ou* décroissants

diminuendo [dɪmɪnjʊˈendəʊ] *n Mus* diminuendo *m*

diminution [dɪmɪˈnjuːʃən] *n* diminution *f*, réduction *f* (**in** de)

diminutive [dɪˈmɪnjʊtɪv] **1** *n Gram* diminutif *m* **2** *adj* **(a)** (*tiny*) tout petit, minuscule **(b)** *Gram* diminutif

dimly [ˈdɪmlɪ] *adv* (*to see*) indistinctement; (*to sense, remember*) vaguement; **d. lit room** pièce mal éclairée

dimmed [dɪmd] *adj Comptr* (*command*) en grisé, estompé; **d. icon** icône *f* estompée

dimmer [ˈdɪmər] *n* **d. (switch)** *El* interrupteur *m* à gradation de lumière; *Cin* obscurateur *m* de salle; *Am Aut* **dimmers** (*headlights*) (phares *mpl*) codes *mpl*; (*parking lights*) feux *mpl* de position; **d. bulb** ampoule *f* veilleuse

dimness [ˈdɪmnɪs] *n* (*of lighting, sight*) faiblesse *f*; (*of room*) obscurité *f*; (*of memory*) imprécision *f*, vague *m*; *F* (*of person*) stupidité *f*, bêtise *f*

dimple¹ [ˈdɪmp(ə)l] *n* **(a)** (*on cheek, chin*) fossette *f* **(b)** (*on surface of water*) ride *f*

dimple² **1** *vt* **(a)** (*of smile*) (*sb's cheeks*) creuser des fossettes dans **(b)** (*of wind*) (*surface of water*) rider **2** *vi* **(a)** (*of cheeks*) se creuser de fossettes **(b)** (*of water*) onduler

dimpled [ˈdɪmp(ə)ld] *adj* (*cheeks*) à fossettes

dimwit [ˈdɪmwɪt] *n F* idiot, -ote; **you d.!** imbécile!

dimwitted [dɪmˈwɪtɪd] *adj F* idiot, bête

din [dɪn] *n* tapage *m*, vacarme *m*, boucan *m*; **the d. of the traffic** le vacarme *ou* le boucan que fait/faisait/*etc* la circulation; **to make** *or* **kick up a d.** faire du tapage *ou* du boucan *ou* du vacarme
▶ **din into** *vtaspo* **to d. sth into sb** enfoncer qch dans le crâne à qn; **to d. manners/the rules of the road into sb** inculquer les bonnes manières/le code de la route à qn

dinar [ˈdiːnɑːr] *n* (*monetary unit*) dinar *m*

dine [daɪn] *vi* dîner

▶ **dine in** *vi* (*of hotel guest*) dîner à l'hôtel
▶ **dine off** *vipo* **(a)** (*use*) (*porcelain, silver*) manger dans **(b)** (*eat*) manger au dîner
▶ **dine on** *vipo* (*eat*) manger au dîner
▶ **dine out** *vi* (*in restaurant*) dîner en ville *ou* dans un restaurant; (*of hotel guest*) dîner dehors; (*at friends' home*) dîner chez des amis; **you'll be dining out on that for years** ça te fera une bonne histoire à raconter pendant des années
diner ['daɪnər] *n* **(a)** (*person*) dîneur, -euse; **the restaurant serves two hundred diners every evening** ce restaurant sert deux cents repas chaque soir; **there were only a few late diners left in the restaurant** il n'y avait plus que quelques clients attardés dans le restaurant **(b)** *Am* (*restaurant*) petit restaurant; *Rail* wagon-restaurant *m*, *pl* wagons-restaurants
dinette [daɪ'net] *n* coin-repas *m*
ding-a-ling ['dɪŋə'lɪŋ] *n F* **(a)** (*of bell, phone*) sonnerie *f*; **to go d.** sonner, faire ding-ding-ding **(b)** *US* (*penis*) quéquette *f*, zizi *m*; (*idiot*) andouille *f*
dingbat ['dɪŋbæt] *n Am, Austr F* crétin *m*; **don't be such a d.!** quel crétin tu fais!
ding-dong ['dɪŋ'dɒŋ] **1** *n* **(a)** (*of bells*) tintement *m*, sonnerie *f*; (*of doorbell*) sonnerie; **to go d.** faire ding-ding-dong **(b)** *F* (*fight*) bagarre *f* **2** *adj F* **to have a d. argument** (*of two people*) se disputer violemment; **d. match** partie *f* vivement disputée
dinghy ['dɪŋ(g)ɪ] *n* dinghy *m*, *pl* dinghies; **(ship's) d.** youyou *m*; **sailing d.** dinghy à voile; **rubber** *or* **inflatable d.** canot *m* pneumatique
dinginess ['dɪndʒɪnɪs] *n* (*dirtiness*) aspect *m* miteux; (*darkness*) aspect sombre
dingo ['dɪŋgəʊ] *n* (*animal*) dingo *m*
dingy ['dɪndʒɪ] *adj* (*room, furniture etc*) défraîchi; (*colour*) terne; (*hotel*) miteux
dining ['daɪnɪŋ] *n Rail* **d. car** wagon-restaurant *m*, *pl* wagons-restaurants; *Sch etc* **d. hall** réfectoire *m*; **d. room** salle *f* à manger; **d.(-room) table** table *f* de salle à manger
dink [dɪŋk] *n Hum* (*abbr* **double income, no kids**) = couple *m* sans enfants, qui touche deux salaires
dinkum ['dɪŋkəm] *adj Austr F* (*person*) sincère; (*object*) authentique; **fair d.** vrai de vrai
dinky ['dɪŋkɪ] **1** *adj Br F* (*dainty*) mignon **2** *n Hum* (*abbr* **double income, no kids yet**) membre *m* d'un couple à deux revenues qui n'a pas encore d'enfant
dinner ['dɪnər] *n* [①A6,d,iii] **(a)** (*evening meal*) dîner *m*, *Can, Belg, Suisse* souper *m*; **what's for d.?** qu'y a-t-il au dîner?; **(it's) d. time!** à table!; **to go out to d.** (*in restaurant*) dîner en ville *ou* dans un restaurant; (*at friends' home*) dîner chez des amis; **to invite sb to d.** (*in restaurant*) inviter qn à dîner au restaurant; (*in one's home*) inviter qn à dîner; **at** *or* **during d.** au *ou* pendant le dîner; **to give the dog his d.** donner à manger au chien; **public d.** banquet *m*; *Mil* **regimental d.** repas *m* de corps; *Mktg* **d. marketing** mercatique *f* qui consiste à inviter les clients à dîner; **to discuss sth at the d. table** parler de qch autour d'un repas; **when was the last time we all sat down at the d. table together?** à quand remonte la dernière fois où nous nous sommes assis ensemble autour de la table de la salle à manger?
(b) *F* (*midday meal*) déjeuner *m*, *Can* dîner *m*
dinner-dance *n* dîner-dansant *m*, *pl* dîners-dansants
dinner hour *n Sch* heure *f* du déjeuner
dinner jacket *n Br* smoking *m*
dinner lady *n Br Sch* = femme *f* de service dans une cantine scolaire
dinner party *n* dîner *m*; **to give a d.** donner un dîner; **to have** *or* **give a d. for sb** organiser un dîner pour qn
dinner service *n* service *m* de table
dinner set *n* service *m* de table
dinner time *n* heure *f* du dîner; *F* (*midday*) heure du déjeuner
dinner trolley *n* chariot *m* à repas
dinnerware ['dɪnərweər] *n* vaisselle *f*
dinosaur ['daɪnəsɔːr] *n* dinosaure *m*
dint [dɪnt] *n Fml* **by d. of (doing) sth** à force de (faire) qch; **it was by d. of her efforts that …** c'est grâce à ses efforts que …
diocese ['daɪəsɪs] *n Rel* diocèse *m*
diode ['daɪəʊd] *n Electron* (lampe *f*) diode *f*
dioptre, *US* **diopter** [daɪ'ɒptər] *n Opt* dioptrie *f*
dioxide [daɪ'ɒksaɪd] *n Ch* dioxyde *m*, bioxyde *m*
dioxin [daɪ'ɒksɪn] *n Ch* dioxine *f*
Dip *abbr* diploma
dip¹ [dɪp] *n* **(a)** (*in ground*) inclinaison *f*, dépression *f*; (*in road*) caniveau *m*; (*in prices etc*) baisse *f* **(b)** (*swim*) baignade *f*; **I'm going for a d.** je vais faire un petit tour dans l'eau **(c)** *Culin* = sauce dans laquelle on trempe les crudités etc **(d)** *Agr* **(sheep) d.** bain *m* parasiticide (pour moutons) **(e)** *Naut* (*with flag*) salut *m* **(f)** *Sl* (*pickpocket*) pickpocket *m*
dip² **(-pp-) 1** *vt* **(a)** (*insert, put*) (*hands etc*) plonger **(into** dans); *Ind* (*metal*) immerger, décaper; *Agr* **to d. sheep** baigner les moutons
(b) (*lower*) baisser subitement; *Br Aut* **to d. one's headlights** se mettre en code; *Naut* **to d. a flag** (faire) marquer un pavillon
2 *vi* **(a)** (*in water etc*) plonger; **her head dipped below the surface** sa tête disparut sous l'eau
(b) (*of ground*) descendre, être incliné; (*of prices, temperature etc*) baisser; (*of scale*) pencher; **the road dips sharply** la route descend brusquement; **the sun dipped below the horizon** le soleil est descendu derrière l'horizon
▶ **dip into** *vipo* **(a)** (*use part of*) (*one's capital*) prendre dans; **I'm always dipping into my pocket** je suis toujours à débourser **(b)** (*read or study parts of*) (*book*) feuilleter; (*subject*) effleurer
Dip Ed ['dɪp'ed] *n* (*abbr* **Diploma in Education**) ≈ CAPES *m* (Certificat d'aptitude au professorat de l'enseignement secondaire)
diphtheria [dɪf'θɪərɪə] *n Med* diphtérie *f*; **to have d.** être atteint de la diphtérie
diphthong ['dɪfθɒŋ] *n Ling* diphtongue *f*
diploid ['dɪplɔɪd] *adj Biol* diploïde
diploma [dɪ'pləʊmə] *n* diplôme *m* **(in** de, en); **to sit a d.** passer l'examen d'obtention d'un diplôme; **d. course** cours *m* conduisant à un diplôme
diplomacy [dɪ'pləʊməsɪ] *n* **(a)** *Pol* diplomatie *f* **(b)** (*tactfulness*) diplomatie *f*, tact *m*; **to attain one's ends by d.** user d'adresse pour atteindre son but
diplomat ['dɪpləmæt] *n* diplomate *mf*
diplomatic [dɪplə'mætɪk] *adj* **(a)** *Pol* diplomatique; **d. bag** *or US* **pouch** valise *f* diplomatique **(b)** (*tactful*) politique, diplomatique; **d. answer** réponse *f* politique; **you should have been more d.** tu aurais dû être plus diplomate; **he knows how to be d.** il sait être diplomate *ou* agir avec diplomatie
diplomatically [dɪplə'mætɪklɪ] *adv* diplomatiquement
diplomatic corps *n* corps *m* diplomatique
diplomatic immunity *n* immunité *f* diplomatique
diplomatic service *n* service *m* diplomatique, diplomatie *f*; **to enter the d.** entrer dans la diplomatie *ou F* dans la carrière
diplomatist [dɪ'pləʊmətɪst] *n* diplomate *mf*
dipole ['daɪpəʊl] *n El* dipôle *m*
dipped [dɪpt] *adj* (*sloping*) incliné; *Br Aut* **d. headlights** codes *mpl*, feux *mpl* de croisement
dipper ['dɪpər] *n* **(a)** (*bird*) cincle *m* plongeur **(b)** *Am Astron* **the Great** *or* **Big D.** la Grande Ourse; **the big d.** (*at fairground*) le grand huit **(c)** *Br Aut* **d. (switch)** basculeur *m* de phares **(d)** (*ladle*) cuillère *f* à pot, louche *f*
dipping ['dɪpɪŋ] *n* **(a)** (*plunging*) plongée *f*, immersion *f*; *Metal* décapage *m*; *Agr* (*of sheep*) baignage *m* **(b)** *Br Aut* (*of headlights*) mise *f* en code
dippy ['dɪpɪ] *adj Old-fashioned F* toqué
dipso ['dɪpsəʊ] *n Sl* (*drinker*) poivrot, -ote
dipsomania [dɪpsə'meɪnɪə] *n* dipsomanie *f*
dipsomaniac [dɪpsə'meɪnɪæk] *n* dipsomane *mf*
dipstick ['dɪpstɪk] *n* **(a)** *Aut* jauge *f* (de niveau) d'huile; *Med* (*for urine test etc*) bandelette *f* réactive **(b)** *F* (*idiot*) abruti, -ie
DIP switch ['dɪpswɪtʃ] *n Comptr* interrupteur *m* DIP
dip switch ['dɪpswɪtʃ] *n Br Aut* **d. switch** basculeur *m* de phares, interrupteur *m* de feux de croisement
dir *abbr* **(a)** *Admin* **director (b)** *Comptr* **directory**
dire ['daɪər] *adj* **(a)** (*foreboding*) lugubre; **d. necessity** dure nécessité; **to be in d. need of sth** avoir un besoin urgent de qch; **to be in d. straits** être dans une très mauvaise passe **(b)** *F* (*bad*) (*meal, book etc*) épouvantable
direct¹ [dɪ'rekt, daɪ-] *vt* **(a)** (*send, aim*) (*letter, remarks etc*) adresser **(to sb** à qn); (*light*) diriger **(at sth** sur qch); (*funds*) consacrer **(at sth** à qch); **to d. sb's attention to sth** appeler *ou* attirer l'attention de qn sur qch; **accusation directed against sb** accusation visant *ou* qui vise qn; **to d. one's steps towards …** diriger ses pas *ou* se diriger vers …; **can you d. me to the station?** pouvez-vous m'indiquer le chemin de la gare?; **to d. one's efforts at doing sth** consacrer ses efforts à faire qch
(b) (*manage*) (*company, the economy*) diriger, mener, gérer; (*army, one's affairs*) conduire; **to d. traffic** régler la circulation
(c) *Th* (*play*) mettre en scène; *TV, Cin, Rad* réaliser; (*actors etc*) diriger; **directed by: …** *Th* mise *f* en scène …; *TV, Cin,*

Rad réalisation *f*: ...; **who directed it?** (*the play*) qui est le metteur en scène?; (*the film*) de qui est la mise en scène?, de qui est ce film?

(**d**) (*instruct*) (*sb*) ordonner à, dire à (**to do** de faire); **as directed** (*as ordered*) conformément aux ordres; (*as instructed*) selon les instructions; *Jur* **to d. the jury** (*of judge*) instruire le jury (sur un point de droit)

direct² **1** *adj* (**a**) (*straight, immediate*) (*route, control, influence etc*) direct; (*cause*) immédiat; **to be a d. descendant of sb** descendre de qn en ligne directe; **d. advertising** publicité *f* directe; **d. air link** liaison *f* aérienne directe; **d. banking** banque *f* à distance; **d.-comparison advertising** publicité *f* comparative directe; **d. competition** concurrence *f* directe; *Av* **d. flight** vol *m* direct; *Aut* **d. gear** prise *f* directe; *Mil etc* **d. hit** coup *m* au but; **d. investment** investissement *m* direct; **d. mail** (*advertising*) publipostage *m*, publicité *f* directe; **d. mail advertising** publicité directe *ou* par publipostage; **d. marketing** mercatique *f* directe, mercatique de contact, mercatique relationnelle; *Comptr* **d. memory access** accès *m* direct à la mémoire; **d. response advert** publicité à réponse directe; **d. response television** télévision *f* à réponse directe; *Pol* **d. rule** administration *f* centrale; **d. sale** vente *f* directe; **d. selling** vente directe; *Econ* **d. tax** impôt *m* direct; **d. taxation** contributions *fpl* directes

(**b**) (*blunt*) direct; (*refusal*) catégorique; **in d. contradiction** en contradiction directe

2 *adv* (*to go*) directement, tout droit; **to travel d. from London to Edinburgh** prendre un train/un vol/*etc* direct de Londres à Edimbourg; **to dispatch goods d. to sb** expédier des marchandises directement à qn; *Rad, TV* **the concert will be broadcast d. from Paris** ce concert sera transmis en direct de Paris

direct broadcast satellite *n Telecom* satellite *m* de télédiffusion directe

direct current *n El* courant *m* continu

direct debit *n Br Banking* prélèvement *m* automatique; **to pay by d.** payer par prélèvement automatique; **d. advice** avis *m* de prélèvement

direct dialling *n Tel* automatique *m*

direct-dial number *n Tel* numéro *m* direct

direct-dial telephone *n* ligne *f* téléphonique directe, téléphone *m* direct

direction [dɪ'rekʃən, daɪ-] *n* (**a**) (*management*) (*of company etc*) direction *f*, administration *f*; (*of traffic*) réglementation *f*; *Th* mise *f* en scène; *TV, Cin, Rad* réalisation *f*; **under the d. of** ... (*of orchestra*) sous la direction de ...; (*of company*) dirigé par ...

(**b**) (*way*) direction *f*, sens *m*; **in the d. of ...** dans la direction de ..., en direction de ...; *Aut* **d. of travel** sens *m* de la marche; **I'm going in your d.** je vais dans la même direction que toi; **we were going in the d. of Paris** nous nous dirigions vers Paris; **in every d.** dans tous les sens; **in all directions** en tous sens, dans tous les sens; **you are not looking in the right d.** vous ne regardez pas dans la bonne direction *ou* du bon côté; *Fig* **a step in the right d.** un pas dans la bonne direction; **in the opposite d.** en sens inverse; **in which d.?** de quel côté?; **to have a good/bad sense of d.** avoir un bon/mauvais sens de l'orientation; **to lose one's sense of d.** perdre le sens de l'orientation; **to lack d.** (*in life*) ne pas avoir de but; (*of novel, play*) ne mener nulle part; **change of d.** changement *m* de direction; *Av, Naut* changement de cap; *Fig* **improvements in many directions** améliorations sous bien des rapports; *Electron* **d. finder** radiogoniomètre *m*; *Aut* **d. sign** panneau *m* de signalisation

(**c**) **directions** (*instructions*) instructions *fpl*; **directions (for use)** notice *f* (explicative), mode *m* d'emploi; **you have been given the wrong directions** on vous a mal renseigné; **to give sb directions to a place** indiquer à qn comment aller à un endroit; **to ask for directions** (*to a place*) demander son chemin; *Th* **stage directions** indications *fpl* scéniques; *Jur* **d. to the jury** = exposé *m* de la loi fait par le juge au jury

directional [dɪ'rekʃən(ə)l, daɪ-] *adj* directionnel; *Electron* **d. aerial** *or* **antenna** antenne *f* directionnelle *ou* directive; *TV, Cin* **d. cut** montage *m* directionnel; *Aut* **d. indicator** indicateur *m* (de changement) de direction

directive [dɪ'rektɪv, daɪ-] *n Mil etc* directive *f*; **to issue a d.** donner une directive

directly [dɪ'rektlɪ, daɪ-] **1** *adv* (**a**) (*to go*) directement; (*to be descended from sb*) en ligne directe; **I'm flying d. from Glasgow** j'ai un vol direct au départ de Glasgow; **I am not d. concerned** je ne suis pas directement concerné; **d. opposite the church** juste en face de l'église; **to come d. to the point** aller droit au fait; **her views are d. opposite to my own** ses vues sont diamétralement opposées aux miennes

(**b**) (*bluntly*) (*to answer, speak*) franchement; (*to attack, criticize*) directement

(**c**) (*soon*) tout à l'heure; **I'm coming d.** je viens tout de suite

2 *conj* aussitôt que, dès que; **I'll come d. I've finished** je viendrai dès que j'aurai fini

directness [dɪ'rektnɪs, daɪ-] *n* (*of answer etc*) franchise *f*; (*of criticism, questions*) caractère *m* direct; **his d. of speech** son franc-parler

direct object *n* [①B49-50,2] *Gram* complément *m* d'objet direct

director [dɪ'rektər, daɪ-] *n* (*of company etc*) directeur, -trice; (*board member*) administrateur *m*; *Th* metteur *m* en scène; *TV, Cin, Rad* réalisateur, -trice; *Cathol* directeur de conscience; **d. of music** *Rel* maître *m* de chapelle; *Mil etc* chef *m* de musique; *Cin* **d. of photography** directeur, -trice de la photographie; *TV, Rad* **d. of programmes** directeur, -trice des programmes; *Jur* **d. of public prosecutions** = chef *m* de parquet; **d. of studies** *Univ* directeur, -trice de travaux *ou* d'études; *Sch* personne *f* chargée de l'organisation du programme d'études; **d.'s chair** régisseur *m*; *Fin* **d.'s fees** (*for attending meetings*) jetons *mpl* de présence; *Acct* **d.'s loan account** compte *m* courant d'administrateur

directorate [dɪ'rektər(e)ɪt, daɪ-] *n* conseil *m* d'administration

directorship [dɪ'rektəʃɪp, daɪ-] *n* (**a**) (*position*) poste *m ou* fonctions *fpl* de directeur; **she holds directorships in several companies** elle fait partie du conseil d'administration de plusieurs entreprises (**b**) (*term of office*) **during my d.** (*in past*) pendant que j'étais directeur; (*in present*) depuis que je suis directeur

directory [dɪ'rektərɪ, daɪ-] *n Tel* annuaire *m*; (*in France*) = bottin *m*; (*of addresses*) répertoire *m* d'adresses; *Comptr* répertoire; **street d.** guide *m* des rues; **commercial d.** annuaire du commerce; *Tel* **d. enquiries** renseignements *mpl*; *Comptr* **d. path** arborescence *f*; *Comptr* **d. structure** structure *f* arborescente, arborescence, structure du répertoire

direct speech *n* [①A73,v,iii] *Gram* discours *m* direct

dirge [dɜːdʒ] *n* hymne *m ou* chant *m* funèbre

dirigible ['dɪrɪdʒɪb(ə)l] *n, adj Fml* (*balloon*) dirigeable *m*

dirk [dɜːk] *n Scot* poignard *m*

dirt [dɜːt] *n* (**a**) saleté *f*; (*earth*) terre *f*; (*mud*) boue *f*; (*on unwashed object, hands etc*) crasse *f*; (*excrement*) crotte *f*; (*in machine, solution etc*) corps *mpl* étrangers, saletés; **hands ingrained with d.** mains encrassées; **covered in d.** crasseux, couvert de crasse; **to show the d.** (*of material*) être salissant; *Fig* **to treat sb like d.** traiter qn comme le dernier des derniers; *Am F* **to be d. poor** être vachement pauvre; *Am* **d. farmer/farming** exploitant *m*/exploitation *f* agricole; **d. road** chemin *m* en *ou* de terre (battue); **d. track** chemin en *ou* de terre (battue); *Sp* piste *f* en cendrée; **d.-track racing** courses *fpl* (motocyclistes) sur cendrée; *Am Sl* **to do sb d.** (*treat meanly*) faire un sale coup à qn

(**b**) *F* (*obscenities*) cochonneries *fpl*; **to talk d.** dire des obscénités, raconter des cochonneries

(**c**) (*gossip*) ragot *m*; **to dig the d. on sb** chercher à salir qn

dirt-cheap *F* **1** *adj* vraiment pas cher; **that's d.** c'est donné **2** *adv* pour trois fois rien; **I got it d.** je l'ai eu pour trois fois rien

dirtily ['dɜːtɪlɪ] *adv* (**a**) (*to eat*) salement (**b**) (*crudely*) grossièrement (**c**) (*to play, fight*) déloyalement

dirtiness ['dɜːtɪnɪs] *n* saleté *f*

dirty¹ ['dɜːtɪ] **1** *adj* (**a**) sale; (*with mud*) crotté; (*valve, piston etc*) encrassé; **to get d.** (*of child, clothes etc*) se salir; **to get one's hands d.** se salir les mains; **d. clothes** *or* **laundry** *or* **washing** linge *m* sale; *Typ* **d. copy** manuscrit *m* brouillé *ou* peu clair; **d. dishes** vaisselle *f* sale; *Ind etc* **d. money** indemnité *f* de salissure, *F* argent *m* sale; **d. weather** sale temps *m*; *Naut* gros temps; **d. job** sale boulot *m*

(**b**) (*sexually*) cochon; (*story etc*) cochon, sale; (*book, film*) pornographique; **d. joke** blague *f* cochonne *ou* obscène; **you've got a d. mind** tu as l'esprit mal tourné, tu as l'esprit entre le nombril et les genoux; *F* **d. old man** vieux cochon *m*; **to tell d. stories** raconter des cochonneries *ou* des obscénités; **d. weekend** week-end *m* coquin; **d. word** gros mot *m*; *Fig* **competitiveness is a d. word nowadays** le mot 'compétition' est tabou de nos jours

(**c**) (*nasty*) **it's a d. business** c'est une sale affaire; **d. look** (*angry*) sale coup *m* d'œil; **to give sb a d. look** regarder qn d'un sale œil

(**d**) *Com* (*bill of lading*) clausé

2 *n Br F* **to do the d. on sb** jouer un sale tour *ou* coup à qn

3 *adv* (**a**) *F* (*intensive*) **a d. great lorry** un énorme camion

(**b**) **to talk d.** (*swearing*) dire des gros mots; (*sexually*) dire des trucs cochons

dirty² **1** *vt* (*one's clothes etc*) salir; **to d. one's hands** se salir les mains; *Fig* **to d. one's reputation** entacher *ou* salir sa réputation **2** *vi* se salir, se souiller; **to d. easily** (*of material, car etc*) se salir facilement, être salissant
dirty trick *n* sale tour *m*; **to play a d. on sb** jouer un sale tour *ou* un sale coup à qn; *Pol* **dirty tricks campaign** campagne *f* de diffamation; (*in business*) procédés *mpl* malhonnêtes; **dirty tricks department** bureau *m* des diffamations
dirty work *n* sale boulot *m*; *Fig F* **to do sb's d.** faire le sale boulot pour qn
dis [dɪs] *vt* (**-ss-**) *Am Sl* (*show disrespect to*) manquer de respect à
disability [dɪsə'bɪlɪtɪ] *n* **(a)** (*infirmity*) infirmité *f*; *Admin* invalidité *f*; (*work-related*) incapacité *f* de travail; *Fig* (*handicap*) handicap *m*; **d. allowance/pension** pension *f* d'invalidité **(b)** *Jur* incapacité *f* légale, inhabilité *f* (**to do** à faire)
disable [dɪ'seɪb(ə)l] *vt Mil* (*person*) mettre hors de combat; (*maim*) estropier; (*ship*) désemparer; (*machine*) mettre hors de service; (*function, feature*) désactiver
disabled [dɪ'seɪb(ə)ld] **1** *adj* (*infirm*) infirme, handicapé; (*as result of accident etc*) handicapé, estropié; (*ship*) désemparé; **d. ex-serviceman** mutilé *m* de guerre **2** *npl* **the d.** (*people*) les handicapés; **facilities for the d.** aménagements *mpl* pour les handicapés; **d. access** facilité *f* d'accès pour personnes handicapées
disablement [dɪ'seɪb(ə)lmənt] *n* **(a)** (*physical handicap*) invalidité *f*; *Admin* **degree of d.** coefficient *m* d'invalidité **(b)** (*action*) *Mil* mise *f* hors de combat; (*of machine*) mise hors service
disabuse [dɪsə'bjuːz] *vt* détromper; **to d. sb of sth** (*of idea*) détromper qn de qch; (*of illusion*) faire perdre qch à qn
disadvantage¹ [dɪsəd'vɑːntɪdʒ] *n* désavantage *m*, inconvénient *m*; **the d. of the plan is that ...** l'inconvénient de ce projet est que ...; **to be at a d.** être désavantagé (**owing to sth** par qch); **to put sb at a d.** désavantager qn
disadvantage² *vt* désavantager
disadvantaged [dɪsəd'vɑːntɪdʒd] **1** *adj* défavorisé **2** *npl* **the d.** les défavorisés *mpl*; **the educationally d.** les personnes *fpl* défavorisées en matière d'éducation
disadvantageous [dɪsædvən'teɪdʒəs] *adj* désavantageux (**to** pour), défavorable (**to** à)
disaffected [dɪsə'fektɪd] *adj* (*supporters, troops etc*) mécontent (**with** de)
disaffection [dɪsə'fekʃən] *n* mécontentement *m*, insatisfaction *f*; **d. among the troops is growing** le mécontentement grandit au sein des troupes
disagree [dɪsə'griː] *vi* **(a)** (*of person*) ne pas être d'accord (**with** avec); (*quarrel*) se disputer, se brouiller (**with** avec); **to d. with sb** ne pas être du même avis que qn, ne pas être d'accord avec qn; **I d.** je ne suis pas de cet avis; **I can't say I d. with her** (*in opinion etc*) je ne peux pas dire que je ne suis pas de son avis; (*as regards an action*) je ne peux pas dire que je la désapprouve
(b) (*not correspond*) (*of accounts, figures*) ne pas concorder
(c) (*be unsuitable*) ne pas convenir (**with** à); **red wine disagrees with me** je ne supporte pas le vin rouge; **the climate disagrees with him** le climat ne lui convient pas *ou* ne lui va pas; **hard work disagrees with me** je ne suis pas fait pour les gros labeurs; **children d. with me** les enfants et moi, ça fait deux
disagreeable [dɪsə'griːəb(ə)l] *adj* (*person, job, smell*) désagréable; (*remark*) désobligeant; **he was very d. to her** il s'est montré très désagréable envers elle; **to make a d. impression on sb** faire une impression défavorable sur qn
disagreeableness [dɪsə'griːəb(ə)lnɪs] *n* (*of situation*) caractère *m* désagréable; (*of person*) mauvaise humeur *f*; (*of remark*) désobligeance *f* (**to** envers)
disagreeably [dɪsə'grɪːəblɪ] *adv* désagréablement; **to behave d. to(wards) sb** se montrer désagréable envers qn
disagreement [dɪsə'griːmənt] *n* **(a)** (*of figures*) différence *f* (**between** entre) **(b)** (*failure to agree*) désaccord *m* (**with sb about sth** avec qn sur qch), conflit *m* d'opinions; **we are in d.** nous sommes en désaccord; **to be in d. with sb** ne pas partager l'avis de qn, être en désaccord avec qn **(c)** (*quarrel*) brouille *f*, différend *m*; **to have a d. with sb** se disputer avec qn
disallow [dɪsə'laʊ] *vt* **(a)** (*reject*) (*hypothesis etc*) ne pas admettre, ne pas reconnaître; *Jur* (*testimony*) rejeter **(b)** *Fb etc* (*goal, try*) annuler
disappear [dɪsə'pɪər] *vi* disparaître (**from a place** d'un endroit); **to d. in** *or* **into the crowd** se perdre dans la foule; **since she disappeared** depuis sa disparition
disappearance [dɪsə'pɪərəns] *n* disparition *f*
disappearing [dɪsə'pɪərɪŋ] *adj* (*race, species*) en voie de disparition; **where's that d. programme changer?** où est-ce que la télécommande a encore été se cacher?; **to do a d. act** (*of conjurer*) (*make sb/sth disappear*) faire disparaître quelqu'un/quelque chose; (*make self disappear*) disparaître; *Fig F* (*sneak away*) s'esquiver, s'éclipser; *F* **the scissors have done a d. act** les ciseaux ont disparu; **he's done his famous d. act again** il s'est encore éclipsé
disappoint [dɪsə'pɔɪnt] *vt* (*person*) décevoir; (*after promising*) manquer de parole à; (*person's hopes*) tromper
disappointed [dɪsə'pɔɪntɪd] *adj* (*person*) déçu; (*candidate*) refusé; **d. customers** clients insatisfaits; **we were all d. that you couldn't come** nous avons tous été très déçus que tu ne puisses pas venir; **he was d. at** *or* **about not being invited** il a été déçu de ne pas être invité; **I am d. in** *or* **with you** tu m'as déçu; **I was d. with it** cela m'a déçu; **he was bitterly d.** il a eu une grande déception; **to be d. in love** avoir des chagrins d'amour
disappointing [dɪsə'pɔɪntɪŋ] *adj* décevant; **how d.!** quelle déception!
disappointingly [dɪsə'pɔɪntɪŋlɪ] *adv* **the unemployment figures are still d. high** il est décevant de constater que les chiffres du chômage restent élevés
disappointment [dɪsə'pɔɪntmənt] *n* déception *f*; **it was a bit of a d.** (*of film, holiday etc*) c'était un peu décevant; **bitter d.** vive contrariété *f*; **to suffer many disappointments** essuyer bien des déboires; **you've been a great d. to your parents** tu as beaucoup déçu tes parents; **to their great d., she did not come** à leur grande déception, elle n'est pas venue; **book early to avoid d.** réservez bien à l'avance pour ne pas être déçu
disapprobation [dɪsæprəʊ'beɪʃən] *n Fml* désapprobation *f* (**of** à l'égard de)
disapproval [dɪsə'pruːv(ə)l] *n* désapprobation *f* (**of** de); **look of d.** regard désapprobateur; **to look at sb with d.** regarder qn avec désapprobation; **much to our d.** bien que nous n'approuvions pas
disapprove [dɪsə'pruːv] *vi* **I d.** je ne suis pas d'accord; (*stronger, in principle*) je désapprouve; **to d. of sth** désapprouver qch; **to d. of sth being done** désapprouver que l'on fasse qch; **she disapproves of her son-in-law** son gendre n'est pas à son goût; **your mother disapproves of me** ta mère ne m'aime pas
disapproving [dɪsə'pruːvɪŋ] *adj* (*look, tone etc*) désapprobateur, -trice; **he was a stern, rather d. man** c'était un homme sévère, qui portait sur toutes choses un œil désapprobateur
disapprovingly [dɪsə'pruːvɪŋlɪ] *adv* (*to look*) d'un air désapprobateur; (*to say*) d'un ton désapprobateur
disarm [dɪs'ɑːm] **1** *vt* (*prisoner, country etc*) désarmer; (*bomb etc*) désamorcer; *Fig* **her frankness quite disarmed us** sa franchise nous a complètement désarmés **2** *vi* désarmer
disarmament [dɪs'ɑːməmənt] *n* désarmement *m*
disarming [dɪs'ɑːmɪŋ] *adj* (*smile, honesty etc*) désarmant
disarmingly [dɪs'ɑːmɪŋlɪ] *adv* **he was d. frank** il montrait une franchise désarmante; **to smile d.** sourire de façon désarmante
disarrange [dɪsə'reɪndʒ] *vt Fml* déranger, mettre en désordre; **to d. sb's plans** déranger *ou* bouleverser les projets de qn
disarrangement [dɪsə'reɪndʒmənt] *n* dérangement *m*
disarray [dɪsə'reɪ] *n* désordre *m*; **in complete d.** (*of person*) en plein désarroi; (*of objects, room, life*) en désordre; (*of troops*) en déroute; **the news threw the company into complete d.** cette nouvelle a semé la panique dans l'entreprise
disassemble [dɪsə'semb(ə)l] *vt* démonter
disassembler [dɪsə'semblər] *n Comptr* désassembleur *m*
disassociate [dɪsə'səʊʃɪeɪt] *vt* = **dissociate**
disassociation [dɪsəsəʊsɪ'eɪʃən] *n* = **dissociation**
disaster [dɪ'zɑːstər] *n also Fig F* désastre *m*; (*by shipwreck, fire, earthquake etc*) sinistre *m*; *F* (*person*) catastrophe *f*; **our journey was a series of disasters** notre voyage n'a été qu'une suite de malheurs; **they were near the summit when d. struck** ils avaient presque atteint le sommet quand la catastrophe a eu lieu; **he is heading for d.** il court à sa perte; **it would be a d.!** ce serait le désastre!; **to finish** *or* **end in d.** tourner à la tragédie; *Fig* **the party was an absolute d.** la soirée a été un vrai désastre; **air/railway d.** catastrophe aérienne/ferroviaire; **financial d.** désastre financier; **d. movie** film-catastrophe *m*, *pl* films-catastrophes
disaster area *n* région *f* sinistrée; **to declare a town a d.** déclarer une ville zone sinistrée; *F* **he's a bit of a d.** (*breaks things, causes problems*) c'est une catastrophe ambulante; (*has a lot of personal problems*) il a toujours plein de problèmes
disaster fund *n* fonds *m* de secours
disastrous [dɪ'zɑːstrəs] *adj* désastreux; **just how d. would that be?** est-ce que ce serait vraiment une catastrophe?

disastrously [dɪ'zɑːstrəslɪ] *adv* désastreusement; **the performance went d. wrong** la représentation a tourné au désastre; **the estimates were d. inaccurate** l'inexactitude des prévisions s'est révélée désastreuse; **his attitude was d. complacent** son attitude complaisante a eu des effets désastreux; **d. bad** désastreux; **d. optimistic** terriblement optimiste

disavow [dɪsə'vaʊ] *vt Fml* désavouer, renier

disavowal [dɪsə'vaʊəl] *n Fml* désaveu *m*

disband [dɪs'bænd] **1** *vt (troops etc)* licencier; *(committee etc)* dissoudre **2** *vi (of troops)* se débander; *(on instructions)* être licencié; *(of committee etc)* être dissout

disbar [dɪs'bɑːr] *vt* **(-rr-)** *Jur (lawyer)* rayer du barreau *ou* du tableau de l'ordre

disbarment [dɪs'bɑːmənt] *n Jur (of lawyer)* radiation *f* du tableau de l'ordre *ou* de la liste du barreau

disbelief [dɪsbɪ'liːf] *n* incrédulité *f* **(in sth** à l'égard de qch); **she looked at him in d.** elle l'a regardé, incrédule

disbelieve [dɪsbɪ'liːv] **1** *vt (sb, sth)* ne pas croire **2** *vi Fml* **to d. in sb/sth** ne pas croire à qn/qch

disbeliever [dɪsbɪ'liːvər] *n esp Rel* incrédule *mf*

disbelieving [dɪsbɪ'liːvɪŋ] *adj (look)* incrédule

disbud [dɪs'bʌd] *vt Bot (fruit tree)* ébourgeonner

disburse [dɪs'bɜːs] *vt Fml (money)* débourser

disbursement [dɪs'bɜːsmənt] *n* **(a)** *(paying out)* déboursement *m*; *Fin* **d. voucher** bon *m* de décaissement **(b)** *(money)* débours *m*

disc, *US* **disk** [dɪsk] *n* **(a)** *(record)* disque *m*; **d. jockey** disc-jockey *m*, *pl* disc-jockeys

(b) *Comptr* = **disk**

(c) *(of moon etc)* disque *m*; *Tech* disque, plateau *m*; *(made of cardboard etc)* rondelle *f*; *Mil etc* **identity** *or* **identification d.** plaque *f* d'identité; *Aut* **parking d.** disque de stationnement; *Aut* **(tax) d.** vignette *f*; *Aut* **d. brakes** freins *mpl* à disque; *Phot* **d. camera** appareil *m* photo à disque; *Aut* **d. clutch** embrayage *m* monodisque; **d. film** disque; *Agr* **d. harrow** pulvériseur *m*; *Agr* **d. plough** charrue *f* à disques; *MecE* **d. valve** clapet *m* disque; **d. wheel** roue *f* pleine *ou* à voile plein

(d) *Anat* disque *m*; **intervertebral d.** disque intervertébral; *Med* **slipped d.** hernie *f* discale; **to slip a d.** se faire une hernie discale

discard[1] ['dɪskɑːd] *n* **(a)** *Cards (action, card) (at cribbage)* écart *m*; *(at bridge)* défausse *f* **(b)** *Ind (rejected part)* pièce *f* de rebut

discard[2] [dɪs'kɑːd] **1** *vt* **(a)** *(object)* se débarrasser de; *(person, project)* abandonner; *(item of clothing, old car etc)* mettre au rebut; **one of her discarded lovers** un de ses amants abandonnés; **his discarded coat still lay on the sofa** son manteau était toujours sur le canapé, tel qu'il l'y avait jeté **(b)** *Cards (at cribbage) (card)* écarter; *(at bridge etc) (colour)* se défausser de **2** *vi Cards (at bridge)* se défausser

discern [dɪ'sɜːn] *vt (sth, sb)* distinguer, discerner, percevoir; **to d. a distant object** discerner *ou* reconnaître un objet dans le lointain

discernible [dɪ'sɜːnɪb(ə)l] *adj* perceptible

discernibly [dɪ'sɜːnɪblɪ] *adv* perceptiblement

discerning [dɪ'sɜːnɪŋ] *adj (person)* éclairé, plein de discernement; *(intelligence)* pénétrant; *(taste)* délicat; **with a d. eye** d'un œil averti; **a house/car for the d. buyer** une maison/voiture pour l'acheteur avisé; **for the d. reader** pour le lecteur averti

discernment [dɪ'sɜːnmənt] *n (judgement)* discernement *m*, jugement *m*

discharge[1] ['dɪstʃɑːdʒ] *n* **(a)** *(release) Med (of patient)* renvoi *m*; *Jur (of prisoner)* mise *f* en liberté, libération *f*; *(of the accused)* acquittement *m*; *Fin (of bankrupt)* réhabilitation *f*; **to apply for one's d.** *(of bankrupt)* demander sa réhabilitation

(b) *(dismissal) (of employee)* renvoi *m*; *(of servant)* congé *m*; *Mil (after active service)* démobilisation *f*; *Mil, Naut (for unfitness)* réforme *f*; *Mil, Naut* **to take one's d.** prendre son congé

(c) *(firing) (of firearm, artillery)* décharge *f*

(d) *(emission) (of water etc)* décharge *f*, évacuation *f*; *(of gas)* décharge, dégagement *m*; *(of steam)* échappement *m*; *(from pump)* débit *m*; *El (of electricity, battery)* décharge; *Med (of blood)* perte *f*; *(of pus)* écoulement *m*; *(vaginal)* pertes *fpl*; *Ind (water from factory etc)* eaux *fpl* usées; *MecE* **d. nozzle** buse *f* de sortie

(e) *(performance, fulfilment) (of duty)* accomplissement *m*; *(of debt)* paiement *m*; **in the d. of his duties** dans l'exercice de ses fonctions

(f) *(unloading) (of ship, cargo)* déchargement *m*

discharge[2] [dis'tʃɑːdʒ] **1** *vt* **(a)** *(release) (patient)* renvoyer; *(prisoner)* libérer, mettre en liberté; *(the accused)* acquitter; *Jur (bankrupt)* réhabiliter, décharger; *(debtor)* libérer; **he was discharged from hospital yesterday** il est sorti de l'hôpital hier; **to d. oneself from hospital** signer sa propre décharge; *Jur* **to d. the jury** congédier les jurés; *Fin* **discharged bankrupt** failli *m* réhabilité; **to d. sb from an obligation** décharger *ou* acquitter qn d'une obligation

(b) *(dismiss) (employee)* congédier, renvoyer; *(workman)* débaucher; *(civil servant)* destituer; *(troops)* licencier; *(soldier)* congédier, donner son congé à, désenrôler; *Mil, Naut (for unfitness) (enlisted man)* réformer; **to be discharged from the force** être congédié

(c) *(firearm)* décharger, faire partir; *(missile)* lancer; *El (battery etc)* décharger

(d) *(emit) (steam)* dégager; *(of chemical reaction) (gas)* dégager; *(of gland) (hormones)* sécréter; *(of reservoir etc) (water)* déverser; *(of pump)* débiter; **to d. pus** *(of abscess)* suppurer; **river that discharges its water into a lake** rivière qui déverse ses eaux dans un lac

(e) *(perform, fulfil) (one's duties)* accomplir, s'acquitter de; *Fin (debt)* liquider, solder; *(fine)* payer; *(account, obligation)* apurer

(f) *(unload) (ship, tank etc)* décharger; *(cargo)* décharger, débarquer; *(of vehicle) (passengers)* déposer

2 *vi* **(a)** *(of gun)* partir, se décharger

(b) *Med (of abscess, wound)* suppurer

(c) *(of river)* se jeter, déboucher **(into a lake** dans un lac)

(d) *El (of battery)* se décharger

discharge pipe *n* tuyau *m* de décharge *ou* de débit

discharge pump *n* pompe *f* d'extraction *ou* d'épuisement

disciple [dɪ'saɪp(ə)l] *n Rel, Fig* disciple *m*

disciplinarian [dɪsɪplɪ'neərɪən] *n* partisan, -ane d'une forte discipline; **he is a strict d.** il est strict en matière de discipline

disciplinary ['dɪsɪplɪnərɪ] *adj (measures, committee)* disciplinaire; *(problems)* de discipline; **to take d. action** *(of an employer)* prendre des mesures disciplinaires

discipline[1] ['dɪsɪplɪn] *n* **(a)** discipline *f*; **iron d.** discipline de fer; **to keep d.** *(of teacher)* maintenir la discipline **(b)** *(branch of learning)* discipline *f*

discipline[2] *vt* **(a)** *(pupils, troops)* discipliner; *(punish)* punir; **to d. oneself** se discipliner **(b)** *(character)* former

disciplined ['dɪsɪplɪnd] *adj* discipliné; *(showing self-control)* contrôlé

disclaim [dɪs'kleɪm] *vt* **(a)** *(deny) (knowledge, responsibility)* nier **(b)** *(reject) (person's authority)* démentir, renier **(c)** *Jur (right etc)* se désister de, renoncer à

disclaimer [dɪs'kleɪmər] *n* **(a)** *(denial)* démenti *m*; *(of responsibility)* dénégation *f*; **to issue a d.** publier un démenti; **d. of authorship** désaveu *m* **(b)** *Jur* désistement *m*, renonciation *f* **(of a right** à un droit)

disclose [dɪs'kləʊz] *vt* **(a)** *(make known) (secret, information etc)* divulguer, révéler; **to d. that ...** révéler que ... **(b)** *(show)* révéler

disclosure [dɪs'kləʊʒər] *n* **(a)** *(of one's thoughts etc)* révélation *f*; *(of secret)* divulgation *f*, révélation; *Fin* **d. threshold** seuil *m* d'annonce obligatoire **(b)** *(fact disclosed)* révélation *f* **(c)** *(of truth, fact)* mise *f* à jour

disco ['dɪskəʊ] *n F (place)* discothèque *f*; *(event)* soirée *f* disco; **we're having a d. at the party** il y aura une animation disco à la soirée; **d. dancer** danseur, -euse de disco; **d. dancing** disco *m*; **d. music** musique *f* disco, disco

discolour, *US* **discolor** [dɪs'kʌlər] **1** *vt (fabric etc)* ternir, délaver; **to become discoloured** se décolorer; *(of fabric)* se ternir; **discoloured by tobacco** jauni par le tabac **2** *vi (of fabric)* se ternir

discolo(u)ration, *US* **discoloration** [dɪskʌlə'reɪʃən] *n (of fabric)* ternissure *f*; *(of teeth)* jaunissement *m*

discombobulate [dɪskəm'bɒbjʊleɪt] *vt Am F* déconcerter, confondre

discomfit [dɪs'kʌmfɪt] *vt Fml (confuse)* déconcerter

discomfiture [dɪs'kʌmfɪtʃər] *n Fml (confusion)* embarras *m*, trouble *m*; **he showed signs of d.** il avait l'air embarrassé; **much to his d.** à son grand embarras

discomfort [dɪs'kʌmfət] *n* **(a)** *(lack of comfort)* inconfort *m* **(b)** *(pain)* malaise *m*, gêne *f*; **to be in some d.** *(of patient)* éprouver une sensation de gêne; **to cause (sb) d.** *(of stitches, wound etc)* gêner (qn)

discomposure [dɪskəm'pəʊʒər] *n Fml* trouble *m*, agitation *f*; *(of mind)* perturbation *f*

disconcert [dɪskən'sɜːt] *vt* déconcerter, troubler; **I don't want to d. you, but ...** je ne veux pas vous alarmer, mais ...

disconcerting [dɪskən'sɜːtɪŋ] *adj (news, attitude, habit etc)* déconcertant, troublant

disconcertingly [dɪskən'sɜːtɪŋlɪ] *adv* d'une manière

déconcertante; **they were d. eager to see him go** la hâte qu'ils avaient de le voir partir était déconcertante

disconnect [dɪskə'nekt] *vt* **(a)** *(gas, water supply, electricity, phone)* couper; *Tel* **I've been disconnected** *(I cannot continue the call)* on a coupé la communication; *(because I haven't paid the bill)* ils m'ont coupé le téléphone *ou* la ligne; **to get the telephone disconnected** faire débrancher le téléphone **(b)** *(separate)* disjoindre, séparer, détacher **(sth from sth** qch de qch); *(carriages)* décrocher; *(machine etc)* débrayer, désembrayer; *El (battery, kettle etc)* déconnecter, débrancher; **to d. a waterpipe from the main supply** isoler un tuyau d'eau de l'arrivée

disconnected [dɪskə'nektɪd] *adj* **(a)** *El* débranché; *MecE* débrayé **(b)** *(style etc) (lacking flow)* décousu; *(deliberately staccato)* entrecoupé **(c)** *(separate)* détaché, isolé

disconnection, disconnexion [dɪskə'nekʃən] *n* **(a)** *(action) (of phone, gas, water, in phone call)* coupure *f*; *(of battery, kettle)* débranchement *m* **(b)** *(of carriage)* décrochage *m*; *(of part of machine)* démontage *m* **(c)** *(state)* séparation *f* **(between** entre)

disconsolate [dɪs'kɒnsələt] *adj (person)* tout triste, inconsolable; *(sigh, look, face)* accablé

disconsolately [dɪs'kɒnsələtlɪ] *adv* tristement, désespérément

discontent [dɪskən'tent] *n* mécontentement *m*

discontented [dɪskən'tentɪd] *adj* mécontent **(with** de)

discontinue [dɪskən'tɪnju:] *vt* **(a)** *(service)* interrompre; *(practice)* abandonner; *(one's subscription)* résilier; *Com* **that item has been discontinued** cet article n'est plus suivi; *Com* **discontinued** *(on label)* fin de série; *Com* **discontinued line** fin de série **(b)** *Jur (trial)* abandonner

discontinuity [dɪskɒntɪ'nju:ɪtɪ] *n also Math* discontinuité *f*

discontinuous [dɪskən'tɪnjʊəs] *adj (with interruptions), Ling* discontinu; *(intermittent)* intermittent

discord ['dɪskɔ:d] *n* **(a)** *(disagreement)* discorde *f*; **there was some d. over it** cela a été la source d'un certain désaccord, cela été un sujet de discorde; **industrial/civil d.** dissensions *fpl* ouvrières/sociales **(b)** *Mus* dissonance *f*

discordance [dɪs'kɔ:dəns] *n* **(a)** *(of opinions etc)* discordance *f* **(b)** *(of sounds)* discordance *f*

discordant [dɪs'kɔ:dənt] *adj* **(a) d. opinions** opinions opposées *ou* discordantes; **a d. atmosphere** une atmosphère de discorde **(b)** *(sound)* discordant; *(voice)* discordant, criard **(c)** *Mus* dissonant

discotheque ['dɪskətek] *n* discothèque *f*

discount[1] ['dɪskaʊnt] *n* **(a)** *Com* remise *f*, rabais *m*; **to sell sth at a d.** vendre qch au rabais; **cash d.** escompte *m* de caisse; **trade d.** remise d'usage; **to allow a d. of 10%** consentir un rabais de 10%; **d. for early payment** escompte *m* de règlement; **d. coach card** carte *f* de réduction sur les lignes d'autocars; **d. price** prix *m* réduit; **d. rate** taux *m* d'escompte; **d. tariff** tarif *m* réduit; **d. ticket agency** agence *f* spécialisée dans la vente de billets bradés; **d. travel card** carte *f* de réduction pour les transports; **d. voucher** bon *m* de réduction

(b) *Fin* escompte *m*; **d. bank** banque *f* d'escompte; **d. house** comptoir *m* d'escompte; **discounts and allowances** remise, rabais, ristourne, RRR; **to be at a d.** *(of shares)* être en perte, se trouver en moins-value; *Fig (of politeness etc)* être en défaveur

discount[2] [dɪs'kaʊnt, 'dɪskaʊnt] *vt* **(a)** *Fin* escompter; *(bill)* prendre à l'escompte **(b)** *(not consider) (sb, sth)* ne pas tenir compte de; *(ignore) (sb's advice, warning)* faire peu de cas de; *(fact, importance of sth)* négliger; **you must d. half of what he says** il faut rabattre la moitié de ce qu'il dit; **police have discounted the possibility of suicide** la police a écarté la thèse du suicide

discountable [dɪs'kaʊntəb(ə)l] *adj Fin* escomptable

discounted bill [dɪs'kaʊntɪd] *n Fin* effet *m* escompté

discounted cashflow *n Acct* valeur *f* actualisée nette

discounted rate *n Fin* taux *m* d'escompte

discounting [dɪs'kaʊntɪŋ] *n* remise *f*; *Fin* **d. of a bill** escompte *m* commercial

discount store *n* magasin *m* de demi-gros, magasin minimarge

discourage [dɪs'kʌrɪdʒ] *vt* **(a)** *(cause to lose heart)* décourager, abattre; **to become discouraged** se décourager; **don't get discouraged** ne te décourage pas **(b)** *(put difficulties in the way of) (project, suitor etc)* décourager; **to d. sb from (doing) sth** décourager qn de (faire) qch; **they were discouraged from going by the weather/the price** le temps/prix les a dissuadés d'y aller; **we (actively) d. smoking** nous essayons de dissuader les gens de fumer; **you should d. it** tu devrais l'en/les en dissuader

discouragement [dɪs'kʌrɪdʒmənt] *n* **(a)** *(state)* découragement *m* **(b)** *(act of discouraging)* dissuasion *f*; **their d. of the use of this drug** le fait qu'ils déconseillent l'utilisation de ce médicament **(c)** *(something that discourages)* source *f* de découragement; **I hope this won't be a d. to you** j'espère que ceci ne te découragera pas; **to act as a d.** avoir un effet dissuasif

discouraging [dɪs'kʌrɪdʒɪŋ] *adj* décourageant; **he was very d. about my chances** il n'était pas du tout encourageant quant à mes chances

discourse ['dɪskɔ:s] *n* **(a)** *Lit (conversation)* conversation *f*, entretien *m*; *Ling* discours *m*; **d. analysis** analyse *f* du discours **(b)** *Lit (dissertation)* dissertation *f* **(on** sur)

▸ **discourse on, discourse upon** *vipo Lit* **(a)** *(speak of)* discourir sur **(b)** *(discuss)* parler de, s'entretenir de

discourteous [dɪs'kɜ:tɪəs] *adj* discourtois, impoli

discourteously [dɪs'kɜ:tɪəslɪ] *adv* impoliment, d'une façon impolie

discourtesy [dɪs'kɜ:təsɪ] *n* incivilité *f*, impolitesse *f*

discover [dɪ'skʌvər] *vt (the truth, a planet, the cause of a disease, actor etc)* découvrir; **we have discovered a good gardener** nous avons déniché un bon jardinier; **I discovered too late that ...** je me suis rendu compte trop tard que ...

discoverer [dɪs'kʌvərər] *n* découvreur *m*; **the d. of America** celui qui a découvert l'Amérique

discovery [dɪ'skʌvərɪ] *n* découverte *f*; *(thing found by chance)* trouvaille *f*; **he's quite a d.** *(of new actor, soccer player etc)* c'est une vraie révélation; **voyage of d.** voyage *m* d'exploration; **to make a d.** faire une découverte

discredit[1] [dɪs'kredɪt] *n* **(a)** *(doubt)* **to throw d. on a statement** mettre une affirmation en doute **(b)** *(dishonour)* **to be a d. to one's family** être une honte pour sa famille; **it does you no d. to admit you were mistaken** il n'y a aucune honte à admettre que tu t'es trompé; **much to their d.** ce qui ne leur faisait pas du tout honneur; **to bring d. on sb/sth** jeter le discrédit sur qn/qch, discréditer qn/qch; **to bring sth into d.** discréditer qch; **to bring d. on oneself** se discréditer

discredit[2] *vt* **(a)** *(rumour) (not believe)* ne pas croire; *(not trust)* mettre en doute; **such theories/methods have long been discredited** ces théories/méthodes sont discréditées depuis longtemps **(b)** *(lower in esteem) (person, opinion)* discréditer; **his conduct has discredited him with the public** sa conduite lui a fait perdre la considération du public

discreditable [dɪs'kredɪtəb(ə)l] *adj* peu digne, peu honorable; **conduct d. to a barrister** conduite *f* indigne d'un avocat; **there's nothing d. about being poor** il n'y a pas de honte à être pauvre

discreet [dɪ'skri:t] *adj* discret, -ète **(about** sur); **can you trust him to be d.?** peut-on compter sur sa discrétion?; **to maintain a d. silence** observer un silence discret; **a d. smile** un petit sourire contenu

discreetly [dɪs'kri:tlɪ] *adv* discrètement, avec discrétion; *(to dress, be situated)* discrètement

discrepancy [dɪ'skrepənsɪ] *n* désaccord *m* **(between** entre); *(between accounts)* différence *f*; *(between statements)* divergence *f*; *(between styles, source text and target text)* décalage *m*; **there is a d. between the two stories** les deux récits ne cadrent pas; *Fin* **there is a d. in the accounts** les comptes ne concordent pas

discrete [dɪs'kri:t] *adj Math etc* discret, -ète

discretion [dɪ'skreʃən] *n* **(a)** *(liberty of action)* discrétion *f*; **I shall use my own d.** je ferai comme je jugerai à propos; **to leave sth to sb's d.** laisser qch à la discrétion de qn; **at the manager's d.** comme le directeur le décidera; **at your d.** comme vous jugerez bon, comme vous voudrez; *Jur* **fine at** *or* **left to the d. of the judge** amende laissée à l'appréciation du juge **(b)** *(good sense)* jugement *m*, prudence *f*; **the age of d.** l'âge *m* de raison; *Prov* **d. is the better part of valour** prudence est mère de sûreté **(c)** *(tact)* discrétion *f*, réserve *f*; **he is the soul of d.** il est la discrétion même

discretionary [dɪ'skreʃən(ə)rɪ] *adj Jur* discrétionnaire; *Banking* **d. account** compte *m* sous mandat de gestion; *St Exch* **d. order** ordre *m* environ

discriminate [dɪ'skrɪmɪneɪt] **1** *vi* **to d. between one thing and another** distinguer une chose d'une autre, établir une distinction entre une chose et une autre; **to d. in favour of sb** favoriser qn **2** *vt* distinguer **(from** de, d'avec)

▸ **discriminate against** *vipo* faire de la discrimination envers; **to be (sexually/racially) discriminated against** être victime de discrimination (sexuelle/raciale)

discriminating [dɪ'skrɪmɪneɪtɪŋ] *adj* **(a)** *(person)* plein de discernement, capable de juger; *(buyer)* avisé, averti; *(audience, eye)* averti; *(ear, judgement)* fin **(b)** *Admin (duty, tariff)* différentiel

discrimination [dɪskrɪmɪ'neɪʃən] *n* **(a)** *(unfair treatment)* discrimination *f*; **without d.** sans distinction; **race** *or* **racial/**

sexual/religious d. discrimination raciale/sexuelle/religieuse (**b**) (*in matters of taste*) jugement *m*, discernement *m* (**c**) (*of differences etc*) discrimination *f*, discernement *m* (**between … and …** entre … et …)

discriminatory [dɪ'skrɪmɪnət(ə)rɪ] *adj Pej* (*law etc*) discriminatoire; **d. pricing** tarification *f* discriminatoire

discursive [dɪ'skɜːsɪv] *adj* (*style etc*) discursif

discus ['dɪskəs] *n Sp* disque *m*; **d. thrower** lanceur, -euse de disque; **the d.** (*event*) le lancer du disque

discuss [dɪ'skʌs] *vt* (*problem etc*) discuter, débattre; (*matter, question*) délibérer de; (*of book*) (*subject*) traiter de; **to d. a price** discuter *ou* débattre un prix; **I know they were discussing me** je sais qu'on parlait de moi; **I refuse to d. it** je refuse d'en parler; **have you discussed it with your parents?** est-ce que tu en as discuté avec tes parents?; **we were discussing what to do about the problem** nous discutions de ce qui devrait être fait pour résoudre le problème; **d.** (*in exam questions*) discutez

discussion [dɪ'skʌʃən] *n* discussion *f*; **a subject for d.** un sujet de discussion; **question under d.** question en discussion; **after much d. of sth** après avoir longtemps discuté qch; **the matter is not up for d.** le sujet n'est pas ouvert à la discussion; **d. programme** *TV, Rad* table *f* ronde; *TV* débat *m* télévisé; **d. table** table ronde

disdain¹ [dɪs'deɪn] *n* dédain *m* (**of** de)

disdain² *vt* (*sb, sth*) dédaigner; **to d. to do sth** dédaigner de faire qch

disdainful [dɪs'deɪnfʊl] *adj* dédaigneux (**of** de)

disdainfully [dɪs'deɪnfʊlɪ] *adv* dédaigneusement

disease [dɪ'ziːz] *n* maladie *f*; **to die of a d.** mourir d'une maladie; **skin d.** maladie de la peau

diseased [dɪ'ziːzd] *adj also Fig* malade

disembark [dɪsem'bɑːk] *vti* débarquer (**from** de)

disembarkation [dɪsembɑː'keɪʃən] *n* débarquement *m*

disembodied [dɪsɪm'bɒdɪd] *adj usu attrib* (*spirit*) désincarné

disembowel [dɪsɪm'baʊəl] *vt* éventrer, éviscérer

disenchant [dɪsɪn'tʃɑːnt] *vt* désillusionner; **a disenchanting experience/encounter** une expérience/rencontre décevante

disenchanted [dɪsɪn'tʃɑːntɪd] *adj* désillusionné; **she's d. with her job** son travail la déçoit beaucoup, elle n'a plus d'illusions quant à son travail

disenchantment [dɪsɪn'tʃɑːntmənt] *n* désillusion *f*

disencumber [dɪsɪn'kʌmbər] *vt Fml* **to d. oneself of sth** (*of coat etc*) se débarrasser de qch; (*of one's responsibilities, burdens*) s'affranchir de qch

disenfranchise [dɪsɪn'fræntʃaɪz] *vt* (*person*) priver du droit électoral *ou* de ses droits civiques; (*borough*) priver de ses droits de représentation

disenfranchisement [dɪsɪn'fræntʃɪzmənt] *n* (*of person*) déchéance *f* de ses droits civiques; (*of borough*) déchéance de ses droits de représentation

disengage [dɪsɪn'geɪdʒ] **1** *vt* dégager, débarrasser (**sb/sth from sth** qn/qch de qch); *MecE* (*cogwheel*) désengrener; (*part, component*) débrayer, désembrayer; **to d. oneself from sb's embrace** se dégager de l'étreinte de qn; **to d. oneself from the struggle** se retirer de la lutte **2** *vi* (*of person*) se dégager; *MecE* (*of catch etc*) se déclencher, se défaire; *Mil* (*of troops*) se retirer

disengaged [dɪsɪn'geɪdʒd] *adj MecE* débrayé

disengagement [dɪsɪn'geɪdʒmənt] *n* (**a**) (*of person*) détachement *m* (**from** de); *MecE* (*of part, component*) débrayage *m* (**b**) *Pol, Mil* désengagement *m*

disentangle [dɪsɪn'tæŋg(ə)l] *vt* débarrasser (**sb/sth from sth** qn/qch de qch); (*piece of string*) débrouiller, démêler; (*plot, mystery*) dénouer; **to d. itself** (*of rope etc*) se démêler; **to d. oneself from sth** se libérer *ou* se dégager de qch; *Fig* (*from scandal etc*) se sortir de qch

disequilibrium [dɪsiːkwɪ'lɪbrɪəm] *n* déséquilibre *m*

disestablish [dɪsɪ'stæblɪʃ] *vt* (*the Church*) séparer de l'État

disestablishment [dɪsɪ'stæblɪʃmənt] *n* **d. of the Church** séparation *f* de l'Église et de l'État

disfavour, *US* **disfavor** [dɪs'feɪvər] *n* défaveur *f*; **to regard** *or* **view** *or* **look on sth with d.** être défavorable à qch; **to fall into d.** tomber en disgrâce; **to fall into d. with sb** perdre le soutien *ou* les faveurs de qn; **to be in d. with sb** être en disgrâce auprès de qn; **at the risk of incurring sb's d.** au risque de déplaire à qn

disfigure [dɪs'fɪgər] *vt* (*person, statue etc*) défigurer; (*of buildings etc*) (*landscape*) gâter, enlaidir; **a disfiguring disease** une maladie qui défigure

disfigured [dɪs'fɪgəd] *adj* (*person, statue etc*) défiguré; (*landscape*) enlaidi

disfigurement [dɪs'fɪgəmənt] *n* (*of person, statue*) défiguration *f*; (*of landscape*) enlaidissement *m*

disfranchise [dɪs'fræntʃaɪz] *vt* = **disenfranchise**

disgorge [dɪs'gɔːdʒ] **1** *vt* (*smoke, information*) dégorger; (*food*) rendre **2** *vi* **river that disgorges into …** rivière qui se déverse dans …

disgrace¹ [dɪs'greɪs] *n* (**a**) (*disfavour*) disgrâce *f*, défaveur *f*; **to be in d.** (*out of favour*) être en disgrâce; (*of child*) être en pénitence; **she is in d. with the party** elle n'est pas en faveur auprès du parti

(**b**) (*shame*) honte *f*, déshonneur *m*; **there is no d. in doing that** il n'y a pas de honte à faire cela; **to bring d. on one's family** déshonorer sa famille; **to be a d. to one's family** être la honte de sa famille, faire honte à sa famille; **it's a d.!** c'est une honte *ou* un scandale!; **you're a d.** tu me fais honte!; **house prices are a d.** c'est une honte de vendre les maisons si cher; **the state of their house is a d.!** leur maison est dans un état honteux!

disgrace² *vt* (**a**) (*esp in passive*) **to be disgraced** (*out of favour*) être disgrâcié (**for** pour) (**b**) (*shame*) (*person*) déshonorer, faire déshonneur à; **to d. oneself** se couvrir de honte; **you disgraced me in front of all those people** tu m'as couvert de honte devant tous ces gens

disgraceful [dɪs'greɪsfʊl] *adj* honteux, infâme; **it's d.** c'est scandaleux *ou* honteux

disgracefully [dɪs'greɪsfʊlɪ] *adv* honteusement; (*late, rude, expensive*) scandaleusement

disgruntled [dɪs'grʌnt(ə)ld] *adj* (*discontented*) mécontent (**at** de); (*sulky*) maussade; **what are you looking so d. about?** pourquoi cet air mécontent?, pourquoi est-ce que tu fais la tête?

disguise¹ [dɪs'gaɪz] *n* (*costume*) déguisement *m*; **put this on as a d.** déguise-toi avec ça; **in d.** déguisé; **in the d. of a policeman** déguisé en agent de police

disguise² *vt* (**a**) (*change appearance of*) (*person*) déguiser, travestir; (*the truth, one's thoughts, feelings*) déguiser; (*one's voice, writing*) déguiser, contrefaire; **to d. oneself as a clown** se déguiser en clown; **there is no disguising the fact that …** il faut avouer que … (**b**) (*hide*) (*one's feelings, motives*) cacher, dissimuler; (*smell*) masquer; **to d. one's disappointment** cacher sa déception

disgust¹ [dɪs'gʌst] *n* (**a**) (*physical*) dégoût *m* (**at, for, towards** pour) (**b**) (*moral*) écœurement *m*, dégoût *m*; **that kind of attitude fills me with d.** ce genre d'attitude me dégoûte *ou* m'écœure; **she turned away from him in d.** dégoûtée *ou* écœurée, elle s'est détournée de lui; **much to my d.** à mon grand dégoût

disgust² *vt* (**a**) (*physically*) dégoûter, donner la nausée à (**b**) (*morally*) écœurer, dégoûter; **to be disgusted at** *or* **with** *or* **by sb/sth** être écœuré par qn/de qch; **he is disgusted that …** cela l'écœure *ou* le dégoûte que … + *sub*; **I feel disgusted with myself for not having protested** je me dégoûte de ne pas avoir protesté

disgusting [dɪs'gʌstɪŋ] *adj* (*sight, smell, prospect, behaviour, carpet*) dégoûtant, écœurant, répugnant, *F* dégueulasse; (*bad quality*) (*music, souvenirs*) épouvantable; (*salary*) (*very low*) ridicule; (*very high*) écœurant; **it's d.!** c'est dégoûtant *ou F* dégueulasse!

disgustingly [dɪs'gʌstɪŋlɪ] *adv* (**a**) **d. dirty** d'une saleté répugnante; **d. sweet/bad** épouvantablement sucré/mauvais; **d. rich/underpaid** scandaleusement riche/sous-payé; **a joke in d. bad taste** une blague d'un mauvais goût détestable (**b**) *F* **d. good-looking/well-read** beau/instruit comme c'est pas permis; **you look d. fit** vous avez l'air vachement en forme; **he makes it look d. easy** on dirait que c'est facile comme tout quand il le fait

dish¹ [dɪʃ] *n* (**a**) (*for food*) plat *m*; (*earthenware casserole*) terrine *f*; **vegetable d.** légumier *m*; **butter d.** beurrier *m*; **to wash** *or* **do the dishes** faire la vaisselle; **a d. of strawberries** un plat de fraises (**b**) (*food*) plat *m*, mets *m*; **it's not a d. I often make** ce n'est pas une recette *ou* un plat que je prépare souvent (**c**) *TV etc* **d.** (**antenna**) antenne *f* parabolique (**d**) *Old-fashioned F* (*female*) belle fille *f*; (*male*) beau mec *m*; **she's/he's a real d.** ce qu'elle est belle/ce qu'il est beau (**e**) (*container*) récipient *m*; *Phot* cuvette *f*

dish² *vt F* (**a**) **to d. sb's chances** gâcher les chances de qn (**b**) **to d. the dirt on sb** faire des révélations sur qn

▶ **dish out** *vtsep F* (*meat etc*) servir; (*give*) (*sweets, money*) distribuer; **to d. out punishment to** (*of boxer*) assener des coups à; (*of schoolmaster*) punir; **to d. out advice** prodiguer des conseils; **he is really dishing it out** (*of boxer*) il en assène; **she can really d. it out** (*be very critical*) quand elle s'y met, c'est une vraie langue de vipère

▶ **dish up 1** *vtsep* (*course, meal*) servir; *Fig F* (*of programme planners etc*) proposer, sortir **2** *vi Culin* servir; **shall I d. up?** je peux servir?, je sers?

disharmonious [dɪshɑː'məʊnɪəs] *adj* (*sound*) dissonant; (*relationship*) qui manque d'harmonie, peu harmonieux

disharmony [dɪsˈhɑːmənɪ] *n* **(a)** (*disagreement*) désaccord *m*, discorde *f*, manque *m* d'harmonie **(b)** (*of sound*) dissonance *f*
dishcloth [ˈdɪʃklɒθ] *n* (*for washing*) lavette *f*; (*for drying*) torchon *m* à (essuyer la) vaisselle
dishearten [dɪsˈhɑːt(ə)n] *vt* (*person*) décourager, abattre; **to become disheartened** perdre courage, se décourager
disheartening [dɪsˈhɑːt(ə)nɪŋ] *adj* décourageant
dishearteningly [dɪsˈhɑːt(ə)nɪŋlɪ] *adv* de façon décourageante; **d. brief** d'une brièveté décourageante; **d. few people turned up** peu de monde est venu, ce qui était décourageant
dished [dɪʃt] *adj Tech* concave
dishevelled [dɪˈʃev(ə)ld] *adj* (*person*) échevelé, dépeigné; **his d. appearance** son air échevelé; **d. hair** cheveux ébouriffés
dishmop [ˈdɪʃmɒp] *n* lavette *f* (à vaisselle)
dishonest [dɪsˈɒnɪst] *adj* malhonnête
dishonestly [dɪsˈɒnɪstlɪ] *adv* malhonnêtement
dishonesty [dɪsˈɒnɪstɪ] *n* malhonnêteté *f*; **an act of d.** un acte malhonnête, une malhonnêteté
dishonour¹, *US* **dishonor** [dɪsˈɒnər] *n* **(a)** (*shame, source of shame*) déshonneur *m*; **to bring d. on one's family** déshonorer sa famille; **to his eternal d.** à son grand déshonneur **(b)** *Fin* (*of cheque*) non-paiement *m*, refus *m* de paiement; (*of bill*) non-acceptation *f*
dishonour,², *US* **dishonor** *vt* **(a)** (*shame*) (*one's family*) déshonorer **(b)** (*promise, agreement*) ne pas respecter; *Fin* (*bill*) ne pas accepter, refuser de payer; **dishonoured cheque** chèque impayé
dishonourable, *US* **dishonorable** [dɪsˈɒnərəb(ə)l] *adj* (*person*) sans honneur; (*action, conduct*) honteux, indigne; **there's nothing d. about losing** perdre n'a rien de honteux; *Mil* **to receive a d. discharge** être renvoyé de l'armée pour manquement à l'honneur
dishonourably, *US* **dishonorably** [dɪsˈɒnərəblɪ] *adv* de façon déshonorante; *Mil* **to be d. discharged** être renvoyé de l'armée pour manquement à l'honneur
dishpan [ˈdɪʃpæn] *n esp Am* cuvette *f*, bassine *f*; **d. hands** mains abîmées à force de faire la vaisselle
dishrag [ˈdɪʃræg] *n* lavette *f*
dishtowel [ˈdɪʃtaʊ(ə)l] *n* torchon *m* à (essuyer la) vaisselle
dishwasher [ˈdɪʃwɒʃər] *n* **(a)** (*person*) plongeur, -euse **(b)** (*machine*) lave-vaisselle *m inv*, *Can* laveuse *f* à vaisselle; **d. safe** (*glass, plate etc*) garanti lave-vaisselle
dishwashing liquid [ˈdɪʃwɒʃɪŋ] *n Am* produit *m* à vaisselle
dishwater [ˈdɪʃwɔːtər] *n* **(a)** eau *f* de vaisselle **(b)** *Fig F* (*tasteless soup, coffee etc*) lavasse *f*
dishy [ˈdɪʃɪ] *adj Br F* séduisant, sexy; **he's/she's very d.** ce qu'il est beau/ce qu'elle est belle
disillusion [dɪsɪˈluːʒən] **1** *vt* désillusionner **2** *n* = **disillusionment**
disillusioned [dɪsɪˈluːʒənd] *adj* désillusionné, désenchanté; **I'm very d. with her** elle me déçoit beaucoup; **to become d.** perdre ses illusions
disillusionment [dɪsɪˈluːʒənmənt] *n* désillusionnement *m*, désenchantement *m*
disincentive [dɪsɪnˈsentɪv] *n Econ etc* facteur *m* décourageant; **heavy taxation is a d. to expansion** les taxes élevées découragent toute expansion; **to act as a d. to sth** avoir un effet dissuasif sur qch
disinclination [dɪsɪŋklɪˈneɪʃən] *n* **because of his d. to ...** parce qu'il est/était peu enclin à ...; **to have** *or* **show a d. to do sth** montrer peu d'empressement *ou* être peu enclin à faire qch
disinclined [dɪsɪnˈklaɪnd] *adj* peu disposé, peu enclin (**to do sth** à faire qch)
disinfect [dɪsɪnˈfekt] *vt* désinfecter
disinfectant [dɪsɪnˈfektənt] *n* désinfectant *m*
disinfection [dɪsɪnˈfekʃən] *n* désinfection *f*; **d. of the wound is vital** il est vital de désinfecter la plaie
disinflation [dɪsɪnˈfleɪʃən] *n Econ* désinflation *f*, déflation *f*
disinformation [dɪsɪnfəˈmeɪʃən] *n* désinformation *f*; **d. campaign** campagne *f* de désinformation
disingenuous [dɪsɪnˈdʒenjʊəs] *adj* (*person*) qui manque de franchise, peu sincère; **it was utterly d. of her to pretend that ...** ce n'était pas du tout honnête de sa part de prétendre que ...
disingenuously [dɪsɪnˈdʒenjʊəslɪ] *adv* peu franchement; **d. worded** formulé en termes peu sincères
disingenuousness [dɪsɪnˈdʒenjʊəsnɪs] *n* manque *m* de franchise
disinherit [dɪsɪnˈherɪt] *vt* (*one's son*) déshériter
disintegrate [dɪsˈɪntɪgreɪt] **1** *vi* (*of stone etc*) se désagréger, se désintégrer, s'effriter; (*of exploding plane, crashing train etc*) se désintégrer; (*of calm, confidence*) s'effriter; (*of health*) se dégrader, s'effriter; *Nucl Phys* se désintégrer; **her family was disintegrating around her** sa famille se désagrégeait autour d'elle **2** *vt* désagréger
disintegration [dɪsɪntɪˈgreɪʃən] *n* (*of stone etc*) désagrégation *f*, désintégration *f*, effritement *m*; (*of health*) dégradation *f*; (*of organization, family*) désagrégation; *Nucl Phys* désintégration
disinter [dɪsɪnˈtɜːr] *vt* (**-rr-**) (*corpse, antiques*) déterrer, exhumer; *Fig* (*scandal*) déterrer; **to d. sth from the archives** aller repêcher qch dans les archives
disinterest [dɪsˈɪnt(ə)rɪst] *n* = **disinterestedness**
disinterested [dɪsˈɪnt(ə)rɪstɪd] *adj* **(a)** (*unbiassed*) désintéressé **(b)** (*indifferent*) indifférent (**in** à); **she was completely d. in what had happened to her son** ce qui était arrivé à son fils lui était complètement indifférent
disinterestedness [dɪsˈɪnt(ə)rɪstɪdnɪs] *n* **(a)** (*lack of bias*) désintéressement *m* **(b)** (*indifference*) indifférence *f* (**in** à)
disintermediation [dɪsɪntəmiːdɪˈeɪʃən] *n* désintermédiation *f*
disinterment [dɪsɪnˈtɜːmənt] *n* déterrement *m*, exhumation *f*
disinvest [dɪsɪnˈvest] *vti* désinvestir (**from, in** de)
disinvestment [dɪsɪnˈvestmənt] *n* (*from a country*) désinvestissement *m*
disjointed [dɪsˈdʒɔɪntɪd] *adj* (*speech*) sans suite, incohérent; (*style*) haché, décousu; (*movements, delivery of speech*) entrecoupé
disk [dɪsk] *n* **(a)** *Comptr* disque *m*; (*floppy*) disquette *f*; **to get sth on d.** enregistrer qch sur disque/disquette; **d. access time** temps *m* d'accès disque; **d. box** boîte *f* à disquettes; **d. capacity** capacité *f* de disque/disquette; **d. controller** contrôleur *m* de disque; **d. controller card** carte *f* contrôleur de disque; **d. drive** unité *f* de disque/disquette, lecteur *m* de disque/disquette; **d. file** fichier *m* disque; **d. mailer** pochette *f* d'expédition de disquette; **d. memory** mémoire *f* à disque; **d. operating system** système *m* d'exploitation de disques; **d. space** espace *m* disque
(b) *US* = **disc**
disk-based [ˈdɪskbeɪst] *adj Comptr* conçu pour disque; (*for floppy*) conçu pour disquettes
diskcopy [ˈdɪskkɒpɪ] *n Comptr* copie *f* de disquette
diskette [dɪsˈket] *n Comptr* disquette *f*; **d. box** boîte *f* à disquettes
diskless [ˈdɪsklɪs] *adj Comptr* sans disque, sans unité de disque; **d. workstation** station *f* de travail sans unité de disque
dislike¹ [dɪsˈlaɪk] *n* aversion *f* (**of, for** pour); **they have the same likes and dislikes** ils ont les mêmes goûts et dégoûts; **to have a d. of sth** ne pas aimer qch; **to take a d. to** *or* **conceive a d. for sb** prendre qn en grippe; **to take a d. to** *or* **conceive a d. for sth** prendre qch en horreur
dislike² *vt* ne pas aimer; **I don't d. him** il ne me déplaît pas; **to d. doing sth** détester *ou* ne pas aimer faire qch; **to get oneself disliked** se rendre antipathique
dislocate [ˈdɪsləkeɪt] *vt* **(a)** *Med* (*shoulder, knee*) luxer, démettre, disloquer; **to d. one's jaw** se décrocher la mâchoire **(b)** (*business*) désorganiser; (*plan*) bouleverser
dislocation [dɪsləˈkeɪʃən] *n* **(a)** *Med* (*of shoulder, knee*) luxation *f*, déboîtement *m*, dislocation *f*; (*of jaw*) déboîtement *m* **(b)** (*of business*) désorganisation *f*; (*of plan etc*) bouleversement *m*
dislodge [dɪsˈlɒdʒ] *vt* (*enemy troops*) déloger, débusquer (**from** de); (*brick etc*) détacher; (*sth stuck*) dégager; **several bricks had become dislodged** plusieurs briques s'étaient détachées; **now he's been made manager nobody is ever going to d. him** maintenant qu'il a été nommé au poste de directeur, personne ne l'en fera jamais sortir; *Fig* **nothing would d. him from his position on arms control** rien ne pouvait ébranler sa conviction sur le contrôle des armements
disloyal [dɪsˈlɔɪəl] *adj* (*to one's king, friendship*) infidèle (**to** à); (*behaviour*) déloyal (**to** envers)
disloyalty [dɪsˈlɔɪəltɪ] *n* déloyauté *f*
dismal [ˈdɪzməl] *adj* (*face, person*) lugubre, sombre, triste; (*countryside, future*) morne; (*failure, performance*) lamentable; (*weather*) maussade; **my prospects look d.** mes chances sont maigres; *Hum* **the d. science** = l'économie *f*
dismally [ˈdɪzməlɪ] *adv* (*to say*) tristement; (*to fail, perform*) lamentablement
dismantle [dɪsˈmænt(ə)l] *vt* (*machine, rifle etc*) démonter; (*fortress, network*) démanteler
dismast [dɪsˈmɑːst] *vt Naut* (*ship*) démâter
dismay¹ [dɪsˈmeɪ] *n* consternation *f*; **in d.** consterné, atterré; **to my d.** à ma grande consternation; **to be filled with d.** être consterné *ou* atterré
dismay² *vt* consterner; **we were dismayed at** *or* **by the news** cette nouvelle nous jeta dans la consternation; **the dismaying news** la nouvelle accablante *ou* consternante
dismember [dɪsˈmembər] *vt also Fig* démembrer
dismemberment [dɪsˈmembəmənt] *n* démembrement *m*

dismiss [dɪsˈmɪs] *vt* **(a)** *(cease employing)* *(employee, servant)* congédier, renvoyer, licencier; *(civil servant)* révoquer; *Mil* **to d. sb from the service** *(career member)* rayer qn des cadres de l'armée; *(on military service)* réformer qn
(b) *(send away)* *(person)* congédier, donner la permission de se retirer à; *(door-to-door salesman etc)* congédier, éconduire; *(meeting)* dissoudre; *Mil* **to d. a parade** faire rompre les rangs (aux troupes); *Mil* **d.!** rompez (les rangs)!; *Cr* **dismissed for ten** *(of batsman)* mis hors jeu quand il n'a marqué que dix points; **you are dismissed** vous pouvez vous retirer
(c) *(cease or refuse to consider)* *(topic of conversation etc)* quitter, abandonner; *(threat, rumours)* ne pas tenir compte de; *(danger)* mépriser; *(theory, explanation)* rejeter; **to d. sth from one's mind** chasser *ou* éloigner qch de ses pensées; **the incident was dismissed as a mere schoolboy prank** on n'a vu dans cet incident qu'une simple farce d'écolier; **she is dismissed as an intellectual lightweight** on la considère comme une non-valeur sur le plan intellectuel
(d) *(reject)* *(proposal)* écarter; *Jur* *(request, appeal)* rejeter; **to d. a case** *(of judge)* rendre une fin de non-recevoir; **to d. a charge** rendre une ordonnance de non-lieu

dismissal [dɪsˈmɪs(ə)l] *n* **(a)** *(of employee)* congédiement *m*, renvoi *m*, licenciement *m*; *(of civil servant)* révocation *f*; **unfair d.** licenciement non justifié; **d. with/without notice** licenciement avec/sans préavis **(b)** *(of danger)* mépris *m*; *(of theory, explanation)* rejet *m* **(c)** *Jur* *(of case)* fin *f* de non-recevoir; *(of request, appeal)* rejet *m*

dismissive [dɪsˈmɪsɪv] *adj* *(laugh, person)* méprisant, dédaigneux; *(gesture)* de rejet; **to be d. about** *or* **of sth** *(of danger)* mépriser qch; *(of proposal)* ne pas accorder la moindre valeur à qch; **he was d. about** *or* **of my chances of winning** il pensait que je n'avais pas la moindre chance de gagner; **you shouldn't be so d. about the proposal** tu ne devrais pas condamner la proposition aussi vite

dismissively [dɪsˈmɪsɪvlɪ] *adv* *(to reply, comment etc)* dédaigneusement

dismount [dɪsˈmaʊnt] **1** *vi* *(from horse, bicycle)* descendre **2** *vt* **(a)** *(rider)* démonter, désarçonner **(b)** *(cannon, machine)* démonter

disobedience [dɪsəˈbiːdɪəns] *n* désobéissance *f* **(to sb** à qn); **civil d.** résistance *f* passive

disobedient [dɪsəˈbiːdɪənt] *adj* *(dog, child)* désobéissant; **to be d. to sb** désobéir à qn; **that was very d. of you** c'était très désobéissant de ta part

disobey [dɪsəˈbeɪ] *vt* *(person, order)* désobéir à; *(order, the law)* enfreindre

disobliging [dɪsəˈblaɪdʒɪŋ] *adj* désobligeant **(to** envers)

disobligingly [dɪsəˈblaɪdʒɪŋlɪ] *adv* avec désobligeance; **someone had very d. left the doors locked** quelqu'un avait eu l'extrême désobligeance de laisser les portes verrouillées

disorder[1] [dɪsˈɔːdər] *n* **(a)** *(confusion)* désordre *m*; **in d.** en désordre; **in a terrible state of d.** terriblement en désordre; **to throw sth into d.** *(room etc)* mettre du désordre dans qch; *(plans)* bouleverser qch; **they fled in d.** ils se sont enfuis en débandade **(b)** *(unrest)* désordre *m*, trouble *m*; **serious disorders have broken out** de graves désordres ont éclaté **(c)** *Med* trouble(s) *m(pl)*; **heart d.** troubles cardiaques; **nervous d.** troubles nerveux, affection *f* nerveuse; **personality d.** trouble caractériel *ou* de la personnalité

disorder[2] *vt* déranger, mettre en désordre; **the crisis had disordered his thoughts** la crise avait mis de la confusion dans ses idées

disordered [dɪsˈɔːdəd] *adj* *(room, existence)* désordonné; *(mind)* malade; *(stomach)* dérangé

disorderliness [dɪsˈɔːdəlɪnɪs] *n* **(a)** *(untidiness)* désordre *m*; **the d. of the room** le désordre dans lequel se trouvait la pièce; **the d. of their life** leur vie désordonnée **(b)** *(of mob)* turbulence *f*

disorderly [dɪsˈɔːdəlɪ] *adj* **(a)** *(untidy)* *(person, work etc)* désordonné; *(room etc)* en désordre **(b)** *(unruly)* *(mob etc)* turbulent, tumultueux; *(person, behaviour)* désordonné, déréglé; **to lead a d. life** mener une vie désordonnée *ou* déréglée; *Jur* **d. conduct** conduite *f* portant atteinte à l'ordre public; *Jur* **to charge sb with being drunk and d.** inculper qn pour ivresse et atteinte à l'ordre public; *Jur* **d. house** *(brothel)* maison *f* de débauche; *(gaming house)* maison de jeu

disorganization [dɪsɔːgənaɪˈzeɪʃən] *n* désorganisation *f*

disorganize [dɪsˈɔːgənaɪz] *vt* désorganiser; **to become disorganized** se désorganiser

disorganized [dɪsˈɔːgənaɪzd] *adj* *(person)* désorganisé; *(room)* désordonné; *(memories, ideas)* confus, désordonné

disorientate [dɪsˈɔːrɪənteɪt], **disorient** [dɪsˈɔːrɪənt] *vt* désorienter; **to be disorient(at)ed** être désorienté; **with disorient(at)ing speed** à une vitesse hallucinante

disorientation [dɪsɔːrɪənˈteɪʃən] *n* désorientation *f*

disown [dɪsˈəʊn] *vt* *(novel, painting)* désavouer; *(person)* renier; **to d. a child** *(deny paternity)* désavouer (la paternité d')un enfant; **if you go out looking like that I'll d. you!** si tu sors habillé comme ça, je ne te connais plus!

disparage [dɪˈspærɪdʒ] *vt* *(sb, sth)* déprécier, décrier, dénigrer

disparagement [dɪˈspærɪdʒmənt] *n* dénigrement *m*, dépréciation *f*

disparaging [dɪˈspærɪdʒɪŋ] *adj* *(term)* de dénigrement; **d. remark** remarque désobligeante; **he was extremely d. about the whole idea** il s'est montré extrêmement méprisant à l'égard de cette idée

disparagingly [dɪˈspærɪdʒɪŋlɪ] *adv* *(to say)* d'un ton méprisant; *(to look at)* d'un air méprisant; **to speak d. of sb** parler de qn en termes de mépris, faire des remarques désobligeantes à l'égard de qn

disparate [ˈdɪspərɪt] *adj Fml* disparate

disparity [dɪˈspærɪtɪ] *n* *(of wealth, status etc)* disparité *f*, écart *m* **(of** entre); *(between ideas, opinions)* différence *f* **(between** entre); *(between accounts, stories)* contradiction *f* **(between** entre); **d. of age** différence d'âge; **the d. in their ages** la différence d'âge entre eux

dispassionate [dɪsˈpæʃənət] *adj* **(a)** *(calm)* sans passion, dépassionné, calme **(b)** *(impartial)* impartial; **to take a d. view of things** juger impartialement les choses

dispassionately [dɪsˈpæʃənətlɪ] *adv* **(a)** *(calmly)* sans passion **(b)** *(impartially)* sans parti pris, impartialement

dispatch[1] [dɪˈspætʃ] *n* **(a)** *(sending)* *(of object)* expédition *f*, envoi *m*; **d. (department)** expéditions *fpl*; *Com* **d. note** bulletin *m ou* bordereau *m* d'expédition **(b)** *Old-fashioned* *(speed)* promptitude *f*; **with (all due) d.** promptement **(c)** *(message)* *(diplomatic etc)* dépêche *f*; **d. box** *Admin etc* boîte *f* à documents; *Br Parl* tribune *f*; **d. case** serviette *f* (en cuir); *Mil* **d. rider** estafette *f*; *Com, Mil etc* **to be mentioned in dispatches** être cité à l'ordre (du jour) **(d)** *(finishing off)* *(of a piece of business)* expédition *f* **(e)** *(execution)* *(of condemned man)* exécution *f*

dispatch[2] *vt* **(a)** *(send)* *(messenger, squadron)* dépêcher; *(letter)* expédier; **to d. an order** envoyer une commande **(b) to d. a piece of business/a job** expédier une affaire/un travail **(c)** *F* *(eat up)* *(meal)* expédier **(d)** *(kill)* *(animal)* achever; *(person)* expédier dans l'autre monde

dispatcher [dɪˈspætʃər] *n* **(a)** *Com etc* expéditeur, -trice **(b)** *Rail, Av etc* régulateur *m*, contrôleur *m*

dispel [dɪˈspel] *vt* **(-ll-)** *(doubt, clouds, fear)* chasser, dissiper; **to d. sb's illusions** faire perdre ses illusions à qn

dispensable [dɪˈspensəb(ə)l] *adj* dont on peut se passer; **nobody here is d.** il n'y a personne ici dont on peut se passer, il n'y a personne en trop ici; **I felt I had become d.** j'avais l'impression qu'on pouvait se passer de moi

dispensary [dɪˈspensərɪ] *n* **(a)** *(of pharmacy)* officine *f* **(b)** *(in hospital)* pharmacie *f*

dispensation [dɪspenˈseɪʃən] *n* **(a)** *Jur, Rel* *(exemption)* **d. from sth** dispense *f* de qch; **d. from fasting** dispense du jeûne **(b)** *Fml* *(distributing)* *(of prizes, alms)* distribution *f*; *(of justice)* administration *f*, exercice *m* **(c)** *(of Providence)* décret *m*, arrêt *m* **(d)** *(organization, way of running things)* système *m*; **under the present d.** dans le système actuel

dispense [dɪˈspens] *vt* **(a)** *(administer)* *(justice)* administrer, rendre; **to d. charity** faire la charité; **to d. advice** donner des conseils **(b)** *(of vending machine etc)* *(chocolate, condoms)* distribuer; *(change)* donner **(c)** *Pharm* *(medication, prescription)* préparer; *Br* **dispensing chemist** pharmacien *m* diplômé; **dispensing optician** = opticien, -ienne ne pouvant fournir que des montures de lunettes (et non pas des verres) **(d)** *(exempt)* *(person)* dispenser, exempter **(from doing** de faire); *Rel* **to d. sb from fasting** dispenser qn du jeûne

▶ **dispense with** *vipo* se passer de; **let's d. with the formalities** passons-nous des formalités; *Euph* **we've dispensed with her services** *(dismissed her)* nous nous sommes passés de ses services; **to d. with the need for sth** rendre qch superflu

dispenser [dɪˈspensər] *n* **(a)** *Pharm* pharmacien, -ienne **(b)** *(machine)* *(for cigarettes, sweets etc)* distributeur *m* **(c)** *Rel* *(of alms)* dispensateur, -trice, distributeur, -trice

dispensing machine [dɪˈspensɪŋ] *n* distributeur *m*

dispersal [dɪˈspɜːs(ə)l] *n* dispersion *f*

dispersant [dɪˈspɜːsənt] *n* dispersant *m*

disperse [dɪˈspɜːs] **1** *vt* **(a)** *(scatter)* *(crowd, seeds etc)* disperser, éparpiller; *(clouds)* dissiper, chasser; *Med* *(tumour)* résoudre, dissoudre; *(of prism etc)* *(light)* disperser; *(knowledge, information)* faire circuler **(b)** *(arrange)* *(troops etc)* disperser **2** *vi* *(of crowd, troops etc)* se disperser, s'éparpiller; *(of light)* se disperser; *(of darkness, clouds)* se dissiper

dispersing agent [dɪ'spɜːsɪŋ] *n* agent *m* dispersant
dispersion [dɪ'spɜːʃən] *n* **(a)** *(of light)* dispersion *f* **(b)** *Rel* **the D.** la Diaspora
dispirit [dɪ'spɪrɪt] *vt (person)* décourager, abattre
dispirited [dɪ'spɪrɪtɪd] *adj* découragé, abattu, démoralisé
dispiritedly [dɪ'spɪrɪtɪdlɪ] *adv (to say)* d'un ton découragé *ou* abattu; *(to look)* d'un air découragé *ou* abattu; *(to play, do sth)* sans enthousiasme
dispiriting [dɪ'spɪrɪtɪŋ] *adj* décourageant, démoralisant
dispiritingly [dɪ'spɪrɪtɪŋlɪ] *adv* de façon décourageante *ou* démoralisante; **their reply was d. unenthusiastic** le manque d'enthousiasme de leur réponse était décourageant *ou* démoralisant; **d., no-one had come to meet them** personne n'était venu à leur rencontre, ce qui les démoralisait
displace [dɪs'pleɪs] *vt* **(a)** *(shift) (sth)* déplacer; **weight of water displaced by a body** poids de l'eau déplacée par un corps; *Pol* **displaced persons** personnes déplacées; *Med* **to d. a bone** se déplacer un os **(b)** *(supplant)* remplacer **(by** par); *(person)* évincer; *(in sb's affections)* supplanter
displacement [dɪs'pleɪsmənt] *n* **(a)** *(of water, people)* déplacement *m*; *Naut (of ship)* déplacement; **ship of 5 000 tons d.** navire d'un déplacement de 5 000 tonnes; *Aut* **d. volume** cylindrée *f* **(b)** *(substitution)* **d. of A by B** remplacement *m* de A par B **(c)** *Psy* déplacement *m*; **d. activity** activité *f* de déplacement
displacer unit [dɪs'pleɪsər] *n Aut* amortisseur *m* à déplacement de fluide
display¹ [dɪ'spleɪ] *n* **(a)** *Com (of merchandise)* étalage *m*, exposition *f*; **for d. only** *(on product)* en démonstration uniquement; **on d. is merchandise from all over the world** des produits du monde entier sont exposés; **d. furniture** mobilier *m* de présentation; **d. pack** présentoir *m*, paquet *m* de présentation; **d. space** surface *f* d'exposition; **d. staff** étalagistes *mpl*; **d. window** vitrine *f*, étalage *m*
(b) *(show)* **the treasures are on d. in the museum** les trésors sont exposés dans le musée; **you'll have a fine d. of flowers** vous aurez un beau déploiement de fleurs
(c) *Fig (of feelings, opinions etc)* affichage *m*, étalage *m*; *(of affection)* étalage; *(of strength, skill, incompetence)* démonstration *f*; *(of luxury)* étalage; **to be fond of d.** aimer l'ostentation
(d) *(event) (of paintings etc)* exposition *f*; *(of regional dances, handicraft)* démonstration *f*
(e) *Typ* lignes *fpl* en vedette; **d. ad(vertisement)** pavé *m ou* placard *m* publicitaire
(f) *Comptr etc (screen)* écran *m*; *(screen, display unit)* afficheur *m*; *(text appearing)* affichage *m*; **d. area** surface *f ou* zone *f* d'affichage; **d. driver** pilote *m* d'affichage; *Aut* **d. panel** cadran *m* de bord; *TV etc* **d. screen** écran *m* de visualisation
(g) *(of bird)* parade *f*
display² **1** *vt* **(a)** *(put on show) (merchandise)* étaler, exposer; *(notice)* afficher; **to d. prices** afficher les prix **(b)** *(exhibit) (ignorance, bad manners)* afficher, étaler; *(talent, irritation, interest)* manifester; *(courage, tact)* faire preuve de **(c)** *Typ (line)* mettre en vedette **(d)** *Comptr etc* afficher, visualiser **2** *vi (of bird)* parader
display area *n Comptr* surface *f* d'affichage, zone *f* d'affichage; *(in store etc)* espace *m* d'exposition
display cabinet *n* vitrine *f* (d'exposition)
display case *n (with glass)* vitrine *f* (d'exposition); *(pack)* présentoir *m*
display copy *n (of book etc)* exemplaire *m* de démonstration
display rack *n* présentoir *m*
display shelf *n* présentoir *m*
display stand *n* présentoir *m*
display unit *n* présentoir *m*; *Comptr* unité *f* de visualisation; *(on car dashboard etc)* unité *f* d'affichage
displease [dɪs'pliːz] *vt (person)* fâcher, contrarier; **to be displeased at** *or* **with sb/sth** être mécontent de qn/de qch; *(stronger)* être fâché contre qn/de qch
displeasing [dɪs'pliːzɪŋ] *adj* déplaisant, désagréable **(to** à)
displeasure [dɪs'pleʒər] *n* mécontentement *m*, déplaisir *m*; **much to my/his/***etc* **d.** à mon/son/*etc* grand déplaisir; **to incur sb's d.** s'attirer le mécontentement de qn
disport [dɪ'spɔːt] *vti Old-fashioned, Hum* **to d. (oneself)** s'amuser, s'ébattre
disposable [dɪ'spəʊzəb(ə)l] **1** *adj* **(a)** *(towel, lighter etc)* jetable, à jeter; *(bottle)* non consigné; **d.** *Br* **nappy** *or Am* **diaper** couche *f* jetable; **d. wrapping** emballage *m* perdu **(b)** *(funds, income etc)* disponible **2** *n F (nappy)* couche *f* jetable
disposal [dɪ'spəʊz(ə)l] *n* **(a)** *(getting rid of)* mise *f* au rebut; *(of rubbish etc)* enlèvement *m*; **(refuse) d. plant** dépotoir *m*; **waste d.** traitement *m* des ordures; **waste d. unit** broyeur *m* d'ordures; **for the d. of the body, they …** pour se débarrasser du corps, ils …
(b) *(availability)* **to be at sb's d.** être à la disposition de qn; **I am entirely at your d.** je suis à votre entière disposition; **to put sth at sb's d.** mettre qch à la disposition de qn; **to have a sum of money at one's d.** disposer d'une somme; **to have a boat at one's d.** avoir un bateau à sa disposition; **with the limited means at our d.** avec les moyens limités qui sont à notre disposition
(c) *(of goods, property)* aliénation *f*; **for d.** à vendre; **d. of assets** cession *f* d'actifs; **d. of stocks** écoulement *m* de stocks; **I will decide on the d. of my property** *(who my heirs will be)* c'est moi qui prendrai les dispositions testamentaires relatives à ma propriété
(d) *Fml (arrangement)* disposition *f*
dispose [dɪ'spəʊz] **1** *vt* **(a)** *(make willing)* disposer, porter **(sb to (do) sth** qn à (faire) qch); **I am not disposed to help him** je ne suis pas disposé à l'aider **(b)** *Fml (arrange) (objects)* disposer, arranger; *(troops)* disposer, placer; **they had disposed themselves around the room** ils s'étaient répartis dans la pièce **2** *vi Prov* **man proposes, God disposes** l'homme propose et Dieu dispose
▶ **dispose of** *vipo* **(a)** *(get rid of) (sth, sb)* se débarrasser de; *(sth)* mettre au rebut **(b)** *Com (merchandise)* écouler; *(item)* vendre; *(a business, lease)* céder **(c)** *(settle) (matter)* régler **(d)** *F (eat) (food)* liquider; *(kill) (person)* liquider; *(beat) (opponent)* mettre la pâtée à **(e)** *Fml (use) (one's time)* employer **(f)** *Fml (have at one's disposal)* disposer de
disposed [dɪ'spəʊzd] *adj* **d. to sth** enclin *ou* porté à qch; **d. to do sth** porté à faire qch
-disposed *suff* **well/ill-d.** bien/mal intentionné **(to, towards** envers, pour)
disposition [dɪspə'zɪʃən] *n* **(a)** *(temperament)* nature *f*, humeur *f*; **child of a pleasant d.** enfant d'un bon naturel; **she is of** *or* **has a kindly d.** c'est une bonne nature **(b)** *Fml (arrangement) (of furniture)* disposition *f*, arrangement *m*; *(of troops)* disposition **(c)** *Jur* disposition *f* testamentaire **(d)** *(inclination)* désir *m*, intention *f* **(to do sth** de faire qch); *(tendency)* tendance *f*, inclination *f* **(to sth** à qch; **to do sth** à faire qch)
dispossess [dɪspə'zes] *vt (person)* déposséder; *(of house, land)* exproprier; **to d. sb of sth** déposséder *ou Jur* dessaisir qn de qch
dispossession [dɪspə'zeʃən] *n* dépossession *f*; *Jur* dessaisissement *m*; *(of house, land)* expropriation *f*
disproportion [dɪsprə'pɔːʃən] *n* disproportion *f*
disproportionate [dɪsprə'pɔːʃənət] *adj* disproportionné **(to** à)
disproportionately [dɪsprə'pɔːʃənətlɪ] *adv* d'une façon disproportionnée; **d. long/expensive** d'une longueur/d'un prix disproportionné(e)
disprove [dɪs'pruːv] *vt (pp* **disproved,** *Jur* **disproven** [dɪs'prəʊv(ə)n]) *(statement, hypothesis etc)* réfuter
disputable [dɪ'spjuːtəb(ə)l] *adj* contestable, discutable
disputant [dɪ'spjuːtənt, 'dɪspjʊtənt] *n* **(a)** *Fml* personne *f* participant à un débat **(b)** *US Jur* partie *f* en litige
disputation [dɪspjʊ'teɪʃən] *n Fml* **(a)** *(debate)* discussion *f* **(b)** *(argument)* controverse *f*, débat *m*
dispute¹ ['dɪspjʊt, dɪ'spjuːt] *n* **(a)** *(debate)* contestation *f*, controverse *f*; **the matter in d.** l'affaire contestée *ou* en contestation; **the fact is beyond d.** le fait est incontestable; **there's some d. about their true intentions** il y a un doute quant à leurs véritables intentions; **it's open to d.** c'est contestable **(b)** *(argument)* querelle *f*, dispute *f* **(as to** relative à); **to settle a d.** régler une querelle; **industrial d.** conflit *m* du travail; **wages** *or* **pay d.** conflit salarial; **to be in d.** être en conflit **(with** avec)
dispute² [dɪ'spjuːt] **1** *vi* se disputer, se quereller **2** *vt (subject)* discuter; *(statement etc)* contester; **to d. (the possession of) sth with sb** disputer qch à qn; **I'm not disputing that** je ne conteste pas cela, je ne dis pas le contraire
disqualification [dɪskwɒlɪfɪ'keɪʃən] *n* **(a)** *(from competition)* disqualification *f* **(b)** *(disqualifying factor)* cause *f* d'incapacité **(for** à) **(c)** *Jur* inhabilité *f* **(to act** à agir); **a year's d. (from driving)** un retrait de permis d'un an
disqualify [dɪs'kwɒlɪfaɪ] *vt Sp (player)* disqualifier; *(from military service)* rendre inapte à; **he was disqualified (from the competition) for failing to turn up on time** il a été éliminé *ou* exclu (de la compétition) pour ne s'être pas présenté à l'heure; **her youth disqualifies her from participating** son jeune âge ne l'autorise pas à participer; **it automatically disqualifies you from standing for election/ disqualifies you for the job** ceci vous met automatiquement dans l'incapacité de vous présenter aux élections/d'accéder à ce poste; **being a woman doesn't d. me from expressing an opinion** le fait que je suis une femme ne m'interdit pas de

donner mon avis; **to d. sb from driving** retirer son permis de conduire à qn; **she was fined for driving while disqualified** on lui a mis une amende pour avoir conduit alors qu'on lui avait retiré son permis; *Jur* **disqualified from making a will** inhabile à tester

disquiet¹ [dɪs'kwaɪət] *n Lit* inquiétude *f*

disquiet² *vt Lit* inquiéter, troubler

disquieting [dɪs'kwaɪətɪŋ] *adj* (*news, development etc*) inquiétant, troublant

disregard¹ [dɪsrɪ'gɑːd] *n* (*for facts, one's own safety*) mépris *m* (**of, for** de); (*of the law, convention*) inobservation *f*; **to show complete d. for the feelings of others** ne pas du tout prendre les sentiments des autres en considération; **with a complete d. for his own safety he ...** au mépris total du danger qu'il courait, il ...

disregard² *vt* (*sb, warning, fact*) ne tenir aucun compte de; (*regulations, laws of gravity*) mépriser; (*an order*) enfreindre; *Mil* (*orders*) manquer à; **I'll d. what you've just said** je ne tiendrai pas compte de ce que vous venez de dire

disremember [dɪsrɪ'membər] *vt US* ne pas se souvenir de

disrepair [dɪsrɪ'peər] *n* (*no pl*) délabrement *m*; **to fall into d.** (*of building*) tomber en ruine, se délabrer; **the building is in d.** le bâtiment est délabré

disreputable [dɪs'repjʊtəb(ə)l] *adj* **(a)** (*action, methods*) déshonorant, peu honorable; (*life*) peu honorable **(b)** (*person*) de mauvaise réputation; (*neighbourhood, pub*) mal famé; **to look d.** avoir l'air louche; (*untidy*) être peu soigné; **she has some d. friends** elle a des amis pas très fréquentables

disreputably [dɪs'repjʊtəblɪ] *adv* honteusement, d'une façon peu honorable

disrepute [dɪsrɪ'pjuːt] *n* **to bring sb into d.** ruiner la réputation de qn; **to bring the law/game into d.** discréditer la loi/le sport; **to fall into d.** tomber en discrédit; **to be in d.** être en défaveur (**with, among** auprès de)

disrespect [dɪsrɪ'spekt] *n* irrévérence *f*, irrespect *m*, manque *m* de respect (**for** envers); **to treat sb/sth with d.** manquer de respect à qn/pour qch; **I mean no d.** je ne veux pas paraître irrespectueux; **no d., but isn't that a bit daft?** sans vouloir vous manquer de respect *ou* sauf votre respect, n'est-ce pas un peu idiot?

disrespectful [dɪsrɪ'spektfʊl] *adj* irrespectueux, irrévérencieux; **to be d. to sb** manquer de respect à qn

disrespectfully [dɪsrɪ'spektfʊlɪ] *adv* (*to speak of sb, behave*) d'une manière irrespectueuse *ou* irrévérencieuse

disrobe [dɪs'rəʊb] **1** *vt* (*judge, priest*) aider à se dévêtir de sa robe **2** *vi* (*take off robe*) se dévêtir de sa robe; *Fml, Hum* (*undress*) se déshabiller

disrupt [dɪs'rʌpt] *vt* (*administration, plan etc*) désorganiser; (*railway, bus service, traffic*) perturber; (*meeting*) (*of power failure etc*) interrompre; (*of hecklers etc*) perturber; (*life, routine*) (*seriously*) bouleverser; (*less seriously*) déranger

disruption [dɪs'rʌpʃən] *n* (*of railway, bus service, traffic*) perturbation *f*; (*of meeting*) (*by power failure etc*) interruption *f*; (*by hecklers etc*) perturbation; (*of life, routine*) (*major*) bouleversement *m*; (*minor*) dérangement *m*; **there were several disruptions to the meeting** la réunion a été perturbée/interrompue à plusieurs reprises; **all the disruptions to everyday life caused by the earthquake** tous les bouleversements de la vie quotidienne provoqués par le tremblement de terre; **we apologize to viewers for the d. to this evening's programmes** nous prions aux téléspectateurs de bien vouloir nous excuser pour les changements intervenus dans la programmation ce soir

disruptive [dɪs'rʌptɪv] *adj* (*element*) perturbateur; (*pupil*) turbulent; **she has** *or* **is a d. influence on the class** c'est un élément perturbateur dans la classe; **d. strike** grève *f* paralysante

dissatisfaction [dɪssætɪs'fækʃən] *n* insatisfaction *f*, mécontentement *m* (**with** de)

dissatisfied [dɪs'sætɪsfaɪd] *adj* mécontent, insatisfait (**with** de); **I am very d. with the service I received** je suis très mécontent *ou* je ne suis pas du tout satisfait du service que j'ai reçu; **the meal/explanation left me d.** le repas/ l'explication m'a laissé sur ma faim

dissect [dɪ'sekt, daɪ-] *vt also Fig* disséquer

dissecting [dɪ'sektɪŋ, daɪ-] *adj attrib* (*table, room*) de dissection; **d. knife** scalpel *m*

dissection [dɪ'sekʃən, daɪ-] *n also Fig* dissection *f*

dissemble [dɪ'semb(ə)l] *Fml* **1** *vt* (*one's feelings, intentions etc*) dissimuler, cacher **2** *vi* dissimuler

disseminate [dɪ'semɪneɪt] **1** *vt* (*opinions etc*) disséminer, propager, répandre; (*information*) diffuser **2** *vi* (*of ideas etc*) se propager, se répandre

disseminated [dɪ'semɪneɪtɪd] *adj Med* **d. sclerosis** sclérose *f* en plaques

dissemination [dɪsemɪ'neɪʃən] *n* (*of opinions, beliefs*) dissémination *f*, propagation *f*; (*of information*) diffusion *f*

dissension [dɪ'senʃən] *n* dissension *f*; **to sow d.** semer la dissension *ou* le désaccord

dissent¹ [dɪ'sent] *n* **(a)** (*opposition*) dissensions *fpl*; **d. within the party** dissensions au sein du parti; **d. from the party line** désaccord *m* par rapport à la politique du parti; **to express one's d. from sth** exprimer son désaccord par rapport à qch; **voices of d.** voix discordantes **(b)** *Rel, Hist* dissidence *f*

dissent² *vi* **(a)** différer (**from sb about sth** de qn sur qch); **to d. from a report** avoir une opinion contraire à celle exprimée dans un rapport; **I'd like to d. from the idea** j'aimerais exprimer mon désaccord par rapport à cette idée **(b)** *Rel, Hist* être dissident

dissenter [dɪ'sentər] *n* **(a)** dissident, -ente **(b)** *Rel, Hist* personne *f* qui n'appartient pas à l'Église anglicane

dissenting [dɪ'sentɪŋ] *adj attrib* (*opinion, voice*) dissident

dissertation [dɪsə'teɪʃən] *n Univ* mémoire *m*, *Am* thèse *f*; *Fig* (*long explanation etc*) exposé *m*

disservice [dɪs'sɜːvɪs] *n* mauvais service *m*; **to do sb a d.** rendre un mauvais service à qn; **to do oneself a d.** se faire du tort

dissidence ['dɪsɪdəns] *n Pol* dissidence *f*; (*disagreement*) désaccord *m*, divergence *f*

dissident ['dɪsɪdənt] *adj, n Pol* dissident, -ente

dissimilar [dɪ'sɪmɪlər] *adj* dissemblable (**to** à, de); **they are not d.** ils se ressemblent; **a proposal not at all d. to your own** une proposition qui ne diffère pas énormément de la vôtre

dissimilarity [dɪsɪmɪ'lærɪtɪ] *n* dissemblance *f*, dissimilarité *f* (**to** de; **between** entre)

dissimulate [dɪ'sɪmjʊleɪt] *Fml* **1** *vt* dissimuler **2** *vi* dissimuler, feindre

dissimulation [dɪsɪmjʊ'leɪʃən] *n Fml* dissimulation *f*

dissipate ['dɪsɪpeɪt] **1** *vt* (*clouds, heat, fears, suspicions etc*) dissiper; (*fortune, one's energy*) gaspiller, dissiper **2** *vi* (*of cloud, heat, fears suspicions etc*) se dissiper; *Phys* (*of energy*) se dégrader

dissipated ['dɪsɪpeɪtɪd] *adj* (*life*) dissipé; (*person*) débauché; **to be d.** (*of person*) vivre dans la dissipation *ou* la débauche

dissipation [dɪsɪ'peɪʃən] *n* **(a)** (*of person*) vie *f* dissipée *ou* désordonnée **(b)** *Fml* (*of fog, one's assets*) dissipation *f*; (*of fortune*) gaspillage *m*, dissipation

dissociate [dɪ'səʊsɪeɪt] **1** *vt* **(a)** dissocier (**from** de); **the two functions have become dissociated** ces deux fonctions se sont dissociées; **to d. oneself from sb/a policy** se désolidariser de qn/d'une politique **(b)** *Ch* (*compound etc*) dissocier **2** *vi Ch* se dissocier

dissociation [dɪsəʊsɪ'eɪʃən] *n* dissociation *f*

dissolute ['dɪsəluːt] *adj* (*person*) dissolu, débauché; (*conduct*) licencieux; (*life*) dissolu, déréglé; **to lead a d. life** vivre dans la débauche, mener une vie dissolue

dissoluteness ['dɪsəluːtnɪs] *n* débauche *f*, dissolution *f*

dissolution [dɪsə'luːʃən] *n* (*of parliament, marriage etc*) dissolution *f*

dissolve¹ [dɪ'zɒlv] *n Cin, TV* fondu *m* enchaîné

dissolve² **1** *vt* (*sugar*) (faire) dissoudre, faire fondre; (*cloud, illusion*) dissiper; (*marriage, partnership, Parliament*) dissoudre **2** *vi* **(a)** (*of sugar, metal in acid*) se dissoudre, fondre; (*of cloud, illusion*) se dissiper; (*of crowd*) se disperser; (*of Parliament, opposition*) se dissoudre; *Fig* **to d. into tears** fondre en larmes; *Fig* **to d. into thin air** partir *ou* s'en aller en fumée **(b)** *Cin, TV* faire un fondu enchaîné

dissonance ['dɪsənəns] *n Mus* dissonance *f*; *Fig* (*of views*) discordance *f*

dissonant ['dɪsənənt] *adj Mus* dissonant; *Fig* (*voice, opinion*) discordant

dissuade [dɪ'sweɪd] *vt* **to d. sb from doing sth** dissuader qn de faire qch; **to d. sb from a particular course of action** dissuader qn de suivre une certaine ligne de conduite

dissuasion [dɪ'sweɪʒən] *n* dissuasion *f* (**from** de); **no amount of d. would have convinced him to stay** rien n'aurait pu le persuader de rester

distaff ['dɪstɑːf] *n* quenouille *f*; *Fig* **on the d. side** (*of family*) du côté maternel

distance¹ ['dɪstəns] *n* **(a)** [①**B57**;D,1,b] distance *f*; **at a d. of ...** à une distance de ...; **within five minutes' walking d.** à cinq minutes de marche; **a short d. away** tout près, à deux pas; **some d. away** assez loin; **it is quite a d. (away)** (*of house etc*) ce n'est pas tout près; **to see sth from a d.** voir qch de loin; **to see sth in the d.** voir qch au loin; **in the middle d.** au second plan; *Mil* **within striking d.** (*of target*) à portée de fusil/de canon/*etc*; (*of own forces*) à portée de l'ennemi **(b)** (*between two places*) distance *f*; (*between two things*) distance, intervalle *m*; (*in time*) intervalle; **to go part of the d. on foot** faire une partie du trajet à pied; **to keep sb at a d.** tenir qn à distance; **at this d. in time** à cet intervalle de temps; *Aut* **d. table** tableau *m* des distances entre les villes

(**c**) *Sp* parcours *m*; (*of boxing match*) durée *f*; **long-/medium-d. race/runner** course *f*/coureur *m* de fond/de demi-fond; *Sp, Boxing, Fig* **to go** *or* **last** *or* **stay the d.** tenir la distance; **the fight went the d.** le combat est allé jusqu'à la limite

(**d**) (*reserve*) réserve *f*, air *m* distant; **to keep one's d., to keep at a d.** (*from other people*) se tenir sur la réserve, garder ses distances; (*from sth dangerous, infectious*) garder ses distances, ne pas s'approcher; **to keep sb at a d.** se tenir sur la réserve avec qn, garder la distance avec qn

distance[2] *vt* (*competitor*) distancer; *Fig* **to d. oneself from sb/sth** prendre ses distances à l'égard de qn/par rapport à qch

distance banking *n* banque *f* à distance

distance education *n* enseignement *m* à distance *ou* par correspondance

distance learning *n* enseignement *m* à distance *ou* par correspondance; **to do a course by d.** suivre un cours par correspondance

distant ['dɪstənt] **1** *adj* (**a**) (*place, object, relation*) éloigné; (*country, memory, resemblance*) lointain; (*in time*) éloigné, lointain; **d. look** regard perdu dans le vague; *Rail* **d. signal** signal *m* à distance; **in the d. future** dans un avenir lointain; **in the not too d. future** dans un futur relativement proche; **in the (dim and) d. past** dans le temps, il y a bien longtemps

(**b**) (*reserved*) (*person, manner*) réservé, distant; **to be d. with sb** se montrer réservé *ou* distant avec qn

2 *adv* **three miles d.** à trois mil(l)es de distance; **not far d. from ...** à peu de distance de ...

distantly ['dɪstəntlɪ] *adv* (**a**) (*in the distance*) au loin; **he could d. hear ...** il entendait ... au loin; **d. related** d'une parenté éloignée; **to be d. related to sb** avoir un lien de parenté éloigné avec qn (**b**) (*to treat sb*) d'un air réservé, avec réserve

distaste [dɪs'teɪst] *n* dégoût *m* (**for** de), répugnance *f* (**for** pour); **she was unable to hide her d. for his attitude** il lui était impossible de cacher le dégoût que lui inspirait son attitude; **if you could only overcome your initial d. for opera** si seulement tu parvenais à surmonter ta répugnance pour l'opéra

distasteful [dɪs'teɪstfʊl] *adj* (*task, thought etc*) désagréable, déplaisant; (*joke*) de mauvais goût

distastefulness [dɪs'teɪstfʊlnɪs] *n* (*of task, thought etc*) caractère *m* désagréable *ou* répugnant; (*of joke*) mauvais *m* goût

distemper[1] [dɪ'stempər] *n Vet* maladie *f* des jeunes chiens

distemper[2] *n Art etc* détrempe *f*

distemper[3] *vt* (*wall*) badigeonner en couleur; *Art* (*painting, wall*) peindre

distend [dɪ'stend] **1** *vt* (*cheeks*) gonfler; (*nostrils*) dilater; (*stomach*) distendre, ballonner **2** *vi* (*of cheeks*) se gonfler; (*of nostrils*) se dilater; (*of stomach*) se ballonner, se distendre

distension [dɪ'stenʃən] *n* dilatation *f*, distension *f*

distich ['dɪstɪk] *n Liter* (*couplet*) distique *m*

distil, *US* **distill** [dɪ'stɪl] (**-ll-**) *Ch, Ind* **1** *vt* (*water etc*) distiller **2** *vi* (*of liquid, secretion etc*) distiller (**from** de)

▶ **distil off, distil out** *vtsep Ch, Ind* chasser par la distillation

distillate ['dɪstɪleɪt] *n Ch, Ind* distillat *m*

distillation [dɪstɪ'leɪʃən] *n* (**a**) *Ch, Ind* (*process*) distillation *f* (**b**) (*result*) *Ch, Ind* produit *m* de la distillation; *Fig* (*of ideas, theories*) condensé *m*

distilled water [dɪ'stɪld] *n* eau *f* distillée

distiller [dɪ'stɪlər] *n Ind* distillateur *m*

distillery [dɪ'stɪlərɪ] *n Ind* distillerie *f*

distinct [dɪ'stɪŋkt] *adj* (**a**) (*different*) distinct, différent (**from** de); **to keep two things d.** faire la distinction entre deux choses; **women, as d. from men** les femmes, par opposition aux hommes (**b**) (*clear*) distinct; (*difference*) net, clair; (*memory*) clair, net, précis; (*order*) formel, précis; (*promise*) formel; (*preference*) marqué; (*impression*) net; **to have a d. memory of sth** se souvenir clairement de qch; **the coast becomes more d.** la côte se précise

distinction [dɪ'stɪŋkʃən] *n* (**a**) (*difference*) distinction *f* (**between** entre); **to make** *or* **draw a d. between two things** faire une distinction entre deux choses; **without d. of age** sans distinction d'âge; **class d.** distinction de classes (**b**) (*honour*) distinction *f*; **academic distinctions** distinctions académiques (**c**) (*excellence*) distinction *f*; *Univ* mention *f*; **to gain d.** se distinguer; **man of d.** homme distingué; *Univ* **with d.** (*thesis etc*) avec mention

distinctive [dɪ'stɪŋktɪv] *adj* (*feature, style*) distinctif; **to be d. of sth** être caractéristique de qch

distinctively [dɪ'stɪŋktɪvlɪ] *adv* de manière distinctive *ou* caractéristique

distinctly [dɪ'stɪŋktlɪ] *adv* (**a**) (*clearly*) (*to speak, hear, see*) distinctement, clairement; **I d. remember telling you** je me rappelle clairement te l'avoir dit; **I told him d.** je le lui ai dit expressément (**b**) (*definitely*) décidément; **she is d. better** elle va sensiblement mieux; **by now the weather was d. cold** à présent il faisait vraiment froid

distinctness [dɪ'stɪŋktnɪs] *n* (**a**) (*clearness*) clarté *f*, netteté *f* (**b**) (*separate nature*) spécificité *f*; **not to lose sight of the d. of these two issues** ne pas perdre de vue le fait que ces deux questions sont distinctes

distinguish [dɪ'stɪŋgwɪʃ] **1** *vt* (**a**) (*recognize*) (*object, sound*) distinguer, discerner; **I could not d. him among the crowd** je n'ai pu le distinguer dans la foule (**b**) (*characterize, differentiate*) distinguer, différencier (**from** de); **reason distinguishes man from the other animals** la raison sépare l'homme des autres animaux; **to d. oneself by ...** se distinguer par ... **2** *vi* **to d. between two things** faire la distinction entre deux choses

distinguishable [dɪ'stɪŋgwɪʃəb(ə)l] *adj* (**a**) (*recognizable*) reconnaissable; (*sound, difference*) perceptible; (*improvement*) sensible; **the coast was hardly d.** c'est à peine si l'on distinguait la côte (**b**) (*that can be differentiated*) que l'on peut distinguer, qui se distingue (**from** de); **the two ideas are barely d.** les deux idées diffèrent à peine

distinguished [dɪ'stɪŋgwɪʃt] *adj* (*air, appearance*) distingué; (*author etc*) de distinction; (*performance*) brillant; **to look d.** avoir l'air distingué

distinguishing mark [dɪ'stiŋgwɪʃɪŋ] *n* signe *m* distinctif

distort [dɪ'stɔːt] **1** *vt* (**a**) (*physically*) (*metal*) déformer; (*features, face*) décomposer, déformer; (*limbs*) distordre; (*surface*) fausser, déjeter (**b**) *Fig* (*the truth*) déformer; (*facts, words*) fausser, dénaturer; **to d. the meaning of a text** dénaturer un texte (**c**) *Electron, Rad* (*reception etc*) déformer **2** *vi* (*of metal, wood*) se déformer, se fausser

distorted [dɪ'stɔːtɪd] *adj* (**a**) (*physically*) tordu, déformé; (*features, face*) déformé; **face d. by rage** visage convulsé de fureur (**b**) *Fig* (*version, account of event*) déformé, faussé

distorting [dɪ'stɔːtɪŋ] *adj* déformant; *Fig* **those changes had a d. effect on the inflation index** ces changements ont faussé l'indice de l'inflation; **d. mirror** glace *f* déformante

distortion [dɪ'stɔːʃən] *n* (**a**) (*physical*) distorsion *f*; (*of features*) altération *f*; (*of body*) contorsion *f* (**b**) *Fig* (*of text*) altération *f*; (*of facts, truth*) déformation *f* (**c**) *Electron, Rad, Opt* (*of transmission*) distorsion *f*, déformation *f*; (*of sound*) distorsion sonore; (*of magnetic field*) déviation *f*; *MecE* (*of part*) distorsion

distract [dɪ'strækt] *vt* (**a**) (*mind, attention*) distraire, détourner (**from** de); **stop distracting me!** arrête de me distraire!; **I don't want to d. you if you're working** je ne veux pas te déranger si tu travailles; **see if you can d. him from his problems** essaie de le distraire de ses problèmes (**b**) (*trouble*) préoccuper

distracted [dɪ'stræktɪd] *adj* préoccupé; (*look*) absent

distractedly [dɪ'stræktɪdlɪ] *adv* (*to pace about, look about*) d'un air préoccupé; (*to answer*) distraitement

distracting [dɪ'stræktɪŋ] *adj* qui distrait l'attention; **I find noise d. when I'm working** le bruit me dérange quand je travaille; **she has a d. influence on him** elle le distrait

distraction [dɪ'strækʃən] *n* (**a**) (*interruption*) (*when working etc*) distraction *f*; **I could do without the d. of you asking me that every five minutes** ça m'aiderait si tu ne me dérangeais pas pour me demander ça toutes les cinq minutes (**b**) (*amusement*) distraction *f*, divertissement *m*; **he's seeking d.** il cherche à se distraire (**c**) **to drive sb to d.** rendre qn fou/*f* folle, faire perdre la tête à qn; **to love sb to d.** aimer qn éperdument *ou* à la folie

distrain [dɪ'streɪn] *vi Jur* **to d. upon sb** contraindre qn par saisie de biens; **to d. upon a debtor** exécuter une saisie sur un débiteur

distraint [dɪ'streɪnt] *n Jur* saisie *f*, (saisie-)exécution *f*, *pl* (saisies-)exécutions

distraught [dɪ'strɔːt] *adj* angoissé; **he is d. over his wife's illness** la maladie de sa femme l'angoisse; **d. with grief/anger** fou/*f* folle de douleur/colère

distress[1] [dɪ'stres] *n* (**a**) (*mental suffering*) angoisse *f*; (*physical suffering*) douleur *f*; **to be in a state of great d.** (*unhappy*) être désespéré; (*anxious*) être fou d'angoisse; **to cause sb d.** (*unhappiness*) faire de la peine à qn; (*anxiety*) alarmer qn (**b**) (*difficulty*) détresse *f*, embarras *m*; *Naut* **ship in d.** navire en détresse; **d. signal** signal *m* de détresse; *US Com* **d. merchandise** marchandise *f* liquidée *ou* sacrifiée *ou*

bradée **(c)** *Jur* *(action)* saisie *f*; *(goods)* biens saisis; **d. warrant** mandat *m* de saisie
distress² *vt* **(a)** *(sb)* affliger, angoisser, faire de la peine à **(b)** *(piece of furniture)* vieillir
distressed [dɪ'strest] *adj* **(a)** *(suffering)* affligé, désespéré; **to be d. about sth** *(unhappy)* être affligé par qch; *(anxious)* être angoissé par qch **(b)** *(in difficulty)* dans la détresse **(c)** *(piece of furniture)* vieilli **(d)** *Jur* saisi
distressing [dɪ'stresɪŋ] *adj* affligeant, pénible
distribute [dɪ'strɪbju:t] *vt* **(a)** *(give out)* *(alms, prizes, leaflets)* distribuer; *(property)* répartir, partager; *Com* *(be distributor of)* distribuer; *(books, newspapers)* distribuer, diffuser; *Fin* *(dividend)* répartir **(b)** *(spread out)* *(over a surface etc)* disperser, répartir; **evenly distributed load** charge uniformément répartie
distributed database [dɪ'strɪbju:tɪd] *n* *Comptr* base *f* de données répartie
distribution [dɪstrɪ'bju:ʃən] *n* **(a)** *(giving out)*, *Com* distribution *f*; *(of books, newspapers)* distribution, diffusion *f*; *El etc* **d. (switch)board** tableau *m* de distribution; **d. centre** centre *m* de distribution; **d. chain** chaîne *f* de distribution; **d. contract** contrat *m* de distribution; **d. depot** dépôt *m* de distributeur; **d. market** marché *m* de la distribution; **d. method** mode *m* de distribution; **d. of profits** distribution *ou* répartition *f* des bénéfices; **d. outlet** point *m* de distribution
(b) *(of population, manpower etc)* répartition *f*; *(of property)* répartition, partage *m*; **d. of wealth** distribution *f* des richesses
distribution box *n El* boîte *f* de dérivation *ou* de jonction
distribution channel *n Com* circuit *m* de distribution
distribution network *n Com* réseau *m* de distribution
distribution rights *npl Cin* *(to a film)* droits *mpl* de distribution
distributive [dɪ'strɪbjʊtɪv] *adj, n Gram* distributif *m*
distributor [dɪ'strɪbjʊtər] *n* **(a)** *(person)* distributeur, -trice; *(of particular make of car etc)* concessionnaire *m*; **d. brand** marque *f* de distributeur; **d. discount** remise *f* au distributeur; *Mktg* **d. panel** panel *m* de distributeurs; *Com* **d.'s margin** marge *f* du distributeur **(b)** *El, Aut etc* *(device)* distributeur *m*; *El* **d. box** boîte *f* de dérivation *ou* de jonction; *Aut* **d. cap** tête *f* d'allumeur *ou* de distribution
distributorship [dɪ'strɪbjʊtəʃɪp] *n Com* **to have the d. for ...** distribuer ...
district ['dɪstrɪkt] *n* **(a)** *(of country)* région *f*, territoire *m*; *Admin* district *m*, secteur *m*; **electoral d.**, *US* **congressional d.** circonscription *f* électorale; **mining d.** région minière; **postal d.** secteur *m* postal; **urban d.** district urbain **(b)** *(of town)* quartier *m*; *Admin* *(of city)* = arrondissement *m*
district attorney *n US Jur* ≈ procureur *m* de la République
district council *n Br Admin* conseil *m* municipal
district court *n US Jur* = tribunal *m* d'instance
district manager *n Com etc* directeur *m* régional
district nurse *n Br Med* infirmière *f* visiteuse
distrust¹ [dɪs'trʌst] *n* méfiance *f*, défiance *f* **(of** de); **to have a d. of sth** se méfier *ou* se défier de qch
distrust² *vt* se méfier de, se défier de; **to d. one's own eyes** ne pas en croire ses propres yeux
distrustful [dɪs'trʌstfʊl] *adj* méfiant, défiant **(of** de**)**; **he was d. of his own capabilities** il ne croyait pas à *ou* manquait de foi en ses propres capacités; **to be d. of a policy/sb's intentions** ne pas se fier à une politique/à qn
disturb [dɪ'stɜ:b] *vt* **(a)** *(interrupt)* *(person)* déranger; *(criminal)* surprendre; *(sb's rest etc)* troubler; *Phys* *(magnetic field)* perturber; **to d. the peace** troubler l'ordre public; **do not d.** ne pas déranger **(b)** *(disarrange)* *(papers, room)* déranger; *(surface, ground)* agiter, remuer **(c)** *(worry)* *(sb)* inquiéter, troubler; *Jur* *(interfere with the rights of)* inquiéter *ou* troubler dans la jouissance d'un droit; **I am disturbed by his apparent indifference** l'indifférence qu'il montre m'inquiète *ou* me trouble
disturbance [dɪ'stɜ:bəns] *n* **(a)** *(interruption)* dérangement *m* **(b)** *(disarrangement)* trouble *m*; **atmospheric d.** perturbation *f* atmosphérique; **emotional disturbances** troubles émotifs **(c)** *(noise)* bruit *m*, tumulte *m*; *(fight)* bagarre *f*; *(riot)* émeute *f*; **political disturbances** troubles *mpl* politiques; **to cause** *or* **create a d.** troubler l'ordre public; *(at meeting etc)* semer la confusion; **it will cause major disturbances to traffic** cela perturbera énormément la circulation **(d)** *Jur* *(interference with rights)* trouble *m* de jouissance
disturbed [dɪ'stɜ:bd] *adj* **(a)** *(night, sleep etc)* agité **(b)** *(mentally, emotionally)* *(at a particular time)* perturbé; *(as a characteristic)* qui souffre de troubles du comportement; *Psy* **d. behaviour** troubles *mpl* du comportement
disturbing [dɪ'stɜ:bɪŋ] *adj* *(news, development etc)* inquiétant, troublant; *(stronger)* perturbant, dérangeant
disunite [dɪsjʊ'naɪt] *vt* *(family etc)* désunir, jeter la désunion dans; *(party)* diviser
disunited [dɪsjʊ'naɪtɪd] *adj* *(family)* désuni; *(party)* divisé
disunity [dɪs'ju:nɪtɪ] *n* désunion *f*
disuse [dɪs'ju:s] *n* *(of term etc)* désuétude *f*; *(of machine etc)* abandon *m*, mise *f* au rancart; **to fall into d.** *(of word, custom)* tomber en désuétude
disused [dɪs'ju:zd] *adj* *(machine)* mis au rancart; *(public building)* désaffecté; *(mine, well, railway line)* abandonné
disyllabic [dɪsɪ'læbɪk] *adj* dissyllabe, dissyllabique
ditch¹ [dɪtʃ] *n* fossé *m*; *(between fields)* douve *f*; *Av Sl* *(sea)* baille *f*; **drainage d.** rigole *f* d'écoulement
ditch² **1** *vt F* *(get rid of)* *(object)* jeter, se débarrasser de; *(car, project etc)* abandonner; *(inconvenient person)* se débarrasser de; *(boyfriend, girlfriend)* plaquer; *(friend)* laisser tomber **2** *vi Av* faire un amerrissage forcé
ditcher ['dɪtʃər] *n* personne *f* qui creuse des fossés
ditching ['dɪtʃɪŋ] *n Av* amerrissage *m* forcé
ditchwater ['dɪtʃwɔ:tər] *n* *(of ditch)* eaux *fpl* stagnantes; *F* **as dull as d.** ennuyeux comme la pluie *ou* un jour de pluie
dither¹ ['dɪðər] *n F* **to be all of a** *or* **in a d.** ne plus savoir où donner de la tête, paniquer
dither² *vi F* hésiter; **stop dithering!** décide-toi!; **she was dithering over whether to come or not** elle n'arrivait pas à décider si elle viendrait ou pas
ditherer ['dɪðərər] *n F* indécis, -ise; **don't be such a d.!** allez, décide-toi!
dithery ['dɪðərɪ] *adj F* indécis
ditto ['dɪtəʊ] *adv* idem, de même; *Com* dito; *F* **I'm hungry – d.** j'ai faim – moi aussi *ou* moi pareil *ou* moi de même
ditty ['dɪtɪ] *n F* chanson *f*, chansonnette *f*
diuretic [daɪjʊ'retɪk] *adj, n Med* diurétique *m*
diurnal [daɪ'ɜ:n(ə)l] **1** *adj Astron, Biol* diurne **2** *n Rel* diurnal *m, -aux*
div [dɪv] *n Br F* *(idiot)* abruti, -ie
diva ['di:və] *n Mus* diva *f*
divan [dɪ'væn] *n* divan *m*; **d. base** sommier *m*; **d. bed** divan-lit *m, pl* divans-lits
dive¹ [daɪv] *n* **(a)** *Swimming* plongeon *m*; *Naut* *(of submarine, deep-sea diver)* plongée *f*; *Aut* *(on braking)* plongée (au freinage); *Swimming* **high d.** plongeon de haut vol; *Av* **vertical d., nose d.** piqué *m*; *Av* **to go into a d.** faire un piqué; *Av* **to pull out of a d.** effectuer un rétablissement; **he made a d. for the shelter** il s'est précipité vers l'abri; **the goalie made a d. for the ball** le goal a plongé pour attraper le ballon; **to take a d.** *(of boxer)* se coucher; *(of salary, exchange rate)* plonger, chuter **(b)** *F Pej* *(place)* bouge *m*
dive² *vi* *(pt* **dived**, *US F* **dove** [dəʊv]; *pp* **dived)** plonger **(into** dans); *(of submarine)* plonger, effectuer une plongée; *(of aircraft)* piquer, descendre en piqué; **to d. (for the ball)** *(of goalkeeper)* plonger pour attraper le ballon; **to d. for pearls** pêcher des perles; *Av* **to d. down on an enemy** piquer de haut sur un ennemi; **to d. into one's pocket** plonger la main dans sa poche; **to d. into a doorway for shelter** se précipiter dans une entrée pour s'abriter; *F* **they all dived into the pub** ils se sont précipités dans le pub
► **dive in** *vi* **(a)** *(into water)* plonger **(b)** *F* *(start eating)* attaquer **(c)** *F* *(start doing sth)* s'y mettre; *(do sth without preparation)* se jeter à l'eau
dive-bomb *vt Av* attaquer en piqué
dive bomber *n Av* bombardier *m* en piqué
dive bombing *n Av* bombardement *m* en piqué
diver ['daɪvər] *n* **(a)** plongeur, -euse; *(in deep sea)* scaphandrier *m* **(b)** *Orn* *(bird)* plongeon *m*, plongeur *m*
diverge [daɪ'vɜ:dʒ] **1** *vi* *(of rays, lines etc)* diverger, s'écarter; *(of roads)* s'écarter; *(of opinions, persons)* diverger; *Fig* **our paths diverged** nos chemins se sont séparés **2** *vt* *(rays etc)* faire diverger
divergence [daɪ'vɜ:dʒəns] *n* divergence *f*
divergent [daɪ'vɜ:dʒənt], **diverging** [daɪ'vɜ:dʒɪŋ] *adj* divergent; **we take d. views on certain points** nos opinions divergent *ou* diffèrent sur certains points
diverging beam [daɪ'vɜ:dʒɪŋ] *n Aut* faisceau *m* divergent
divers ['daɪvəz] *adj Arch* *(several)* divers, plusieurs
diverse [daɪ'vɜ:s] *adj* **(a)** *(different)* divers, différent; **they are very d. in their approach** ils ont une approche très différente **(b)** *(varied)* divers, varié
diversely [daɪ'vɜ:slɪ] *adv* diversement
diversification [daɪvɜ:sɪfɪ'keɪʃən] *n* **(a)** *(of company etc)* diversification *f* **(b)** *(of tastes etc)* diversification *f*
diversify [daɪ'vɜ:sɪfaɪ] **1** *vi* *(of company etc)* se diversifier; **to d. into furniture** se diversifier et commencer à fabriquer *ou* produire/vendre/*etc* des meubles; **to d. into software/banking** se diversifier en pénétrant le secteur du logiciel/le secteur bancaire **2** *vt* diversifier

diversion [daɪ'vɜːʃən] *n* **(a)** (*of traffic etc*) déviation *f*; (*of plane, funds*) détournement *m*; *El* dérivation *f*; **to create** *or* **make a d.** (*to distract attention*) faire diversion **(b)** (*amusement*) distraction *f*, divertissement *m*; **to seek d. from sth** chercher à se distraire de qch **(c)** *Mil* diversion *f*

diversionary [daɪ'vɜːʃən(ə)rɪ] *adj* **(a)** (*activity*) destiné à faire diversion **(b)** *Mil* (*manœuvre*) de diversion

diversity [daɪ'vɜːsɪtɪ] *n* diversité *f*, variété *f*

divert [daɪ'vɜːt] *vt* **(a)** (*river, traffic*) détourner, dériver; (*blow*) parer, écarter; (*criticism*) parer; (*attention, conversation, sb from course of action, funds*) détourner **(from** de); *El* (*current*) dévier; *Naut* dérouter; *Av* (*plane, flight*) détourner; **I managed to d. his attention from the problem** j'ai réussi à détourner son attention de ce problème **(b)** (*amuse*) divertir, amuser; **to d. oneself by doing sth** faire qch pour se distraire

diverting [daɪ'vɜːtɪŋ] *adj* divertissant, amusant

divest [daɪ'vest] *vt* **(a)** *Fml* (*sb*) priver, dénuer **(of** de); **to d. oneself of** (*one's coat*) enlever; (*one's authority*) se dévêtir de; (*a duty*) se désinvestir de; (*right*) renoncer à **(b)** *Jur* (*sb*) déposséder **(of** de)

divestment [daɪ'vestmənt] *n Fin* **d. of assets** scission *f* d'actifs

divide¹ [dɪ'vaɪd] *n Geog* ligne *f* de partage des eaux; *Fig* (*racial, political, emotional etc*) fossé *m*; **the North-South d.** le fossé entre le nord et le sud

divide² **1** *vt* **(a)** (*split*) (*inheritance etc*) diviser; (*kingdom*) démembrer; (*land*) morceler; (*meat etc*) détailler; (*family*) mettre le désaccord dans, désunir; (*party*) diviser, scinder; **to d. sth in two** couper *ou* diviser qch en deux; **to d. sth into parts** diviser qch en parties

(b) (*distribute*) partager, répartir **(among** entre); (*spending, one's time, resources*) répartir; **to d. proportionally** répartir au prorata; **to d. profits among shareholders** répartir les bénéfices entre les actionnaires; **we d. the work among us** nous nous partageons le travail

(c) *Math* diviser

(d) (*separate*) séparer **(from** de); **the mountains that d. France from Spain** les montagnes qui séparent la France d'avec l'Espagne

2 *vi* **(a)** se diviser, se partager **(into** en); (*of political party*) se scinder, se diviser; (*of road*) bifurquer

(b) *Pol* (*of House*) aller aux voix

(c) *Math* **twelve divides by three** douze est divisible par trois; **they're learning to d.** ils apprennent à faire des divisions

▸ **divide off** *vtsep* séparer

▸ **divide out** *vtsep* (*distribute*) partager, répartir **(among** entre)

▸ **divide up** *vtsep* partager; **they divided the area/work up between them** ils se sont partagés le secteur/travail

divided [dɪ'vaɪdɪd] *adj* **(a)** (*territory etc*) divisé; (*attention*) distrait; **we are d. on this issue** nous sommes partagés sur ce sujet; **opinions are d.** les avis sont partagés; **house/family d. against itself** maison/famille désunie; **a (political) party d. against itself** un parti divisé; *Am* **d. highway** = autoroute *f* à deux chaussées (séparées par un rail); **d. skirt** jupe-culotte *f*, *pl* jupes-culottes **(b)** (*work*) partagé **(c)** (*scale, thermometer etc*) gradué

dividend ['dɪvɪdend] *n Math, Fin* dividende *m*; *Fin* **d. on shares** dividende d'actions; *Fig* **to pay dividends** (*of action etc*) porter des fruits; *Fin* **d. share** action *f* de jouissance

divider [dɪ'vaɪdər] *n* (*in room*) cloison *f* de séparation; (*for files*) intercalaire *m*

dividers [dɪ'vaɪdəz] *npl* (*instrument*) compas *m* à pointes sèches

dividing [dɪ'vaɪdɪŋ] *adj El* **d. box** boîte *f* de dérivation; **d. line** ligne *f* de démarcation; *Fig* séparation *f*, distinction *f*; **she has crossed the d. line between merely being a good athlete and being an athlete of international class** elle est passée de l'autre côté de la barrière qui sépare les bons athlètes des athlètes de classe internationale; **d. wall** mur *m* de séparation, cloison *f*

divination [dɪvɪ'neɪʃən] *n* divination *f*

divine¹ [dɪ'vaɪn] **1** *adj* (*judgement, worship etc*), *Fig* divin; **to attend d. service** aller à l'église; *Hist* **the d. right of kings** la monarchie de droit divin; *Fig F* **you look d. in that dress** vous êtes divine *ou* adorable dans cette robe; *also Fig* **d. inspiration** inspiration *f* divine **2** *n* théologien *m*

divine² *vt* **(a)** (*the future, sb's intentions*) deviner **(b)** (*water*) découvrir, détecter

divinely [dɪ'vaɪnlɪ] *adv also Fig* divinement; **she was looking d. beautiful** elle était divine

diviner [dɪ'vaɪnər] *n* devin *m*, devineresse *f*; **(water) d.** radiesthésiste *mf*, sourcier *m*

diving ['daɪvɪŋ] *n* (*underwater*) plongée *f* (sous-marine); (*from diving board*) plongeon(s) *m(pl)*; **d. bell** cloche *f* à plongeurs; *Swimming* **d. board** plongeoir *m*; *Naut* **d. rudder** (*of submarine*) gouvernail *m* de profondeur; **d. suit** tenue *f* de plongée

divining [dɪ'vaɪnɪŋ] *n* divination *f*; **(water) d.** radiesthésie *f*; **d. rod** baguette *f* divinatoire *ou* de sourcier

divinity [dɪ'vɪnɪtɪ] *n* **(a)** (*divine nature, god*) divinité *f*; **the D.** la Divinité **(b)** (*subject*) théologie *f*; *Univ* **Doctor of D.** docteur *m* en théologie **(c)** *Sch* instruction *f* religieuse

divisible [dɪ'vɪzɪb(ə)l] *adj* divisible **(by** par)

division [dɪ'vɪʒən] *n* **(a)** (*splitting*) division *f*, partage *m* **(into** en); (*of party*) scission *f*; (*of land*) morcellement *m*; (*of scale etc*) graduation *f*; (*distribution*) (*of profit etc*) répartition *f*, partage *m*; **d. of labour** division *f* du travail; **d. of votes** partage *m* de voix

(b) (*discord*) division *f*, désunion *f*; **to sow d.** semer la zizanie *ou* la discorde

(c) [ⒾA71,7; B56,C,4] *Math* division *f*; **long d.** = division décomposée en ses différentes étapes; **d. sign** signe *m* de division

(d) *Parl* vote *m*; **to come to a d.** voter; **without a d.** sans avoir à voter; *Br* **d. bell** = signal *m* sonore qui avertit les députés qu'ils vont être appelés à voter; *Br* **d. lobby** = pièces *fpl* dans lesquelles se rendent les députés selon qu'ils ont voté oui ou non

(e) (*section*), *Fb, Mil* division *f*; *Biol* groupe *m*, classe *f*; *Jur* (*of court*) section *f*, *esp US Rail* section de ligne; (*of scale, thermometer etc*) degré *m*; *Pol* **parliamentary d.** (*area*) circonscription *f* électorale

(f) *Constr etc* cloison *f*, séparation *f*

divisional [dɪ'vɪʒən(ə)l] *adj* de la division; **d. account** compte *m* divisionnaire; **d. director** directeur *m* de division

divisive [dɪ'vaɪsɪv] *adj* qui divise, qui crée des divisions

divisor [dɪ'vaɪzər] *n Math* diviseur *m*

divorce¹ [dɪ'vɔːs] *n* **(a)** *Jur* divorce *m*; **I want a d.** je veux divorcer; **to get a d.** divorcer; **to ask for a d.** demander le divorce; **d. case** cas *m* de divorce; **d., proceedings** action *f* en divorce; **to specialize in d. (cases)** (*of lawyer*) se spécialiser dans les cas de divorce; **to sue for (a) d.**, *US* **to file a petition for d.** demander le divorce; **their marriage ended in d.** ils ont divorcé; **one in three marriages ends in d.** un couple sur trois divorce **(b)** *Fig* divorce *m*, séparation *f* **(between sth and sth** de qch et de qch)

divorce² **1** *vt* **(a)** *Jur* (*of judge*) (*two people*) prononcer le divorce de; **to get divorced from sb, to d. sb** divorcer d'avec qn; **she is divorced from him** elle est divorcée d'avec lui **(b)** *Fig* **you cannot d. form from content** on ne peut pas séparer le fond et la forme **2** *vi* (*of husband and wife*) divorcer

divorced [dɪ'vɔːst] *adj* divorcé; *Fig* **d. from reality** (*life, idea*) chimérique; **passage d. from the context** passage isolé du contexte; **d. from commonsense** dénué de bon sens

divorcee [dɪvɔː'siː] *n* (*man*) divorcé *m*; (*woman*) divorcée *f*

divot ['dɪvət] *n* motte *f* de terre

divulge [daɪ'vʌldʒ] *vt* divulguer; **to d. sb's whereabouts** divulguer l'endroit où se trouve qn

divvy ['dɪvɪ] *n Br F* **(a)** *Fin* dividende *m* **(b)** (*idiot*) abruti, -ie; **stop being such a d.** arrête tes bêtises

▸ **divvy up** *vtsep F* partager

dixie, dixy ['dɪksɪ] *n esp Mil F* gamelle *f*

dixieland ['dɪksɪlænd] *n Mus* **d. (jazz)** dixieland *m*

DIY [diːaɪ'waɪ] *Br* (*abbr* **do-it-yourself**) **1** *n* bricolage *m* **2** *adj attrib* de bricolage; **a D. expert** un spécialiste du bricolage

dizzily ['dɪzɪlɪ] *adv* **(a)** (*to stagger etc*) pris de vertige **(b)** (*to rise*) (*of cliffs, share prices etc*) vertigineusement **(c)** *Fig* (*to behave, laugh*) étourdiment

dizziness ['dɪzɪnɪs] *n* étourdissement *m*, vertige(s) *m(pl)*, malaise *m*; **fit of d.** éblouissement *m*

dizzy ['dɪzɪ] *adj* **(a)** *Med* pris de vertige; **to feel d.** avoir le vertige; **to make sb d.** donner le vertige à qn; **d. with desire/fear** fou/*f* folle de désir/peur; **d. spell** éblouissement *m*, malaise *m* **(b)** *Fig* (*height, speed etc*) vertigineux **(c)** *Fig* (*scatterbrained*) écervelé; **d. blonde** blonde évaporée

DJ [diː'dʒeɪ] *n* **(a)** *abbr* **disc jockey** **(b)** *F abbr* **dinner jacket**

D Lit(t) [diː'lɪt] *n abbr* **Doctor of Letters**

DNA [diːe'neɪ] *n Ch* (*abbr* **deoxyribonucleic acid**) ADN *m*

do¹ [duː] (**he does** [dʌz]; *pt* **did** [dɪd]; *pr sub sg, pl* **do**; *pp* **done** [dʌn]; *in the aux use* **don't** [dəʊnt], **didn't** ['dɪd(ə)nt] *are common for* **do not, did not**; **doesn't** ['dʌz(ə)nt] for **does not**) **1** *aux* **(a)** [ⒾA45,8,a,i; A46,9,a; A47,c,i] (*usual form in questions and negative statements except with* **have**, *but see* **have, be,** *and modal verbs; also in negative commands*) **did you see him?** l'avez-vous vu?; **we do not know** nous ne le savons pas; **do not speak!** ne parlez pas!; **don't do it!** n'en faites rien!; **don't be afraid** n'ayez pas peur; **do you mind?** ça ne vous fait rien?; *Iron* vous permettez?

(b) [①A55,c,i] *(used for emphasis)* **he did go** il y est bien allé; **I do believe he is a thief** je crois vraiment que c'est un voleur; **it doesn't matter – it does (matter)!** ça ne fait rien – si, ça fait quelque chose!; **why don't you work? – I do (work)!** pourquoi ne travaillez-vous pas? – mais si, je travaille!; **do you remember him? – do I remember him** *or* **do I!** vous souvenez-vous de lui? – si je m'en souviens!; **do sit down** asseyez-vous donc!; **yes, people did live there** oui, des gens ont vécu là; **I don't like coffee, but I do like tea** je n'aime pas le café, mais j'aime bien le thé; **rarely does it happen that …** il arrive rarement que …

(c) [①A55,c,ii] *(replacing vi)* **they work in the fields as their fathers did** ils travaillent aux champs comme le faisaient leurs pères; **he writes better than I do** il écrit mieux que moi; **they have always existed and still do** ils ont toujours existé et existent encore; **if you want to speak to him, do it now** si vous désirez lui parler, faites-le maintenant

(d) *(replacing vt and taking its construction)* **he envies me as much as I do him** il me porte autant d'envie que je lui en porte

(e) *(replacing vt and object)* **if you understood the question as well as I do** si vous compreniez la question aussi bien que moi

(f) [①A46,8,b] *(in replies, tag questions etc)* **may I open these letters? – (please) do** puis-je ouvrir ces lettres? – je vous en prie!; **did you see him? – I did** l'avez-vous vu? – oui(, je l'ai vu); **do you like her? – no I don't** tu l'aimes bien? – non(, je ne l'aime pas); **you don't like it – yes I do** vous ne l'aimez pas – mais si; **you like him, don't you?** vous l'aimez bien, n'est-ce pas?; **she lives here, doesn't she?** elle habite ici, n'est-ce pas?; **that does you good, doesn't it?** ça fait du bien, hein?; **he doesn't believe that, does he?** il ne croit pas ça, hein?; **you like Paris? so do I** vous aimez Paris? moi aussi

(g) *Jur* **charged that he did on the 15th of August utter threats** accusé d'avoir proféré des menaces le 15 août

2 *vt* **(a)** *(carry out, complete) (good deed, one's duty, housework, calculation etc)* faire; *Math (problem)* résoudre; **she's doing medicine** *(studying it)* elle fait médecine; **to do the interpreting** faire l'interprète; **to do ten years (in prison)** faire dix ans de prison; **the car was doing sixty** la voiture faisait du soixante

(b) [①A45,8,a,i; A46,9,a; A47,c,i] *(with reference to general activity)* **what do you do (for a living)?** qu'est-ce que vous faites (dans la vie)?; **what are you doing?** qu'est-ce que vous faites?; **it gives me something to do** cela me donne de l'occupation; **don't do it again!** ne recommencez pas!; **don't!** ne faites pas ça!; **do as you're told** fais ce qu'on te dit; **what is to be done?** que faire?; **it can't be done** cela n'est pas possible, c'est impossible; **there's nothing to be done** il n'y a rien à faire; **it's as good as done** c'est une affaire faite; **she did nothing but cry** elle n'a fait que pleurer; **I don't know what to do** je ne sais que faire, je ne sais pas quoi faire; **what can I do for you?** que puis-je faire pour vous?; **what are you going to do about it?** que proposez-vous de faire?; **what would he do without you?** que deviendrait-il sans vous?; **it was all I could do to lift it** c'est à peine si j'ai pu le soulever; **it was all I could do not to laugh** j'ai eu du mal à ne pas rire; *F* **that's done it!** ça y est!

(c) *(with reference to behaviour, conduct)* **to do right/wrong** bien/mal faire; **to do right/wrong by sb** bien/mal agir envers qn; **you would do well to …** vous feriez bien de …; **well done!** très bien!, bravo!; **it isn't done** *(is not the practice)* cela ne se fait pas; **it is quite commonly done** c'est de pratique courante

(d) *(arrange, fix)* **to do sb's/one's hair** coiffer qn/se coiffer; **to do one's teeth** se brosser les dents; **he does repairs** il fait des réparations; **she's doing the flowers for the wedding** c'est elle qui s'occupe des fleurs pour le mariage

(e) *F (look around) (town, museum)* visiter, faire

(f) *Th (Hamlet etc)* faire

(g) *F (with reference to crime, dishonest conduct)* **to do sb** *(cheat)* refaire qn, faire qn; *(beat up)* casser la figure à qn, mettre une raclée à qn; **he got done last night** *(arrested)* il s'est fait ramasser la nuit dernière; **I've been done!** *(cheated)* j'ai été roulé!, on m'a eu!; **they did three other houses in the neighbourhood** *(burgled them)* ils sont passés dans trois autres maisons dans le quartier

(h) *F (use)* **to do drugs** se droguer; **I don't do drugs** je ne me drogue pas, je ne prends pas de drogues

(i) *Sl* **let's do lunch** il faudra qu'on déjeune ensemble un de ces jours

(j) *F (provide, serve, help) Old-fashioned* **they do you very well at this hotel** on est très bien servi dans cet hôtel; *Com* **we can do you this article at …** nous pouvons vous faire cet article à …; **that dress/hairstyle does something/nothing for you** cette robe/coiffure t'arrange *ou* te met en valeur/ne t'arrange pas *ou* ne te met pas du tout en valeur; **this music doesn't do anything for me** cette musique ne me dit rien, je n'aime pas cette musique

(k) *(in perfect tenses and past participle)* **to have done** *(finished)* avoir fini; *Lit* **day is done** la journée tire à sa fin; **have you done shouting?** as-tu fini de crier?; **done!** *(after a bargain made)* entendu!, marché conclu!; **to be done** *(of meat, vegetable)* être prêt *ou* cuit; **meat well done** viande bien cuite; **done to a turn** cuit à point

3 *vi* **(a) how do you do?** *(on first introduction)* enchanté (de faire votre connaissance); **to be doing well** *(of patient)* être sur la voie de la guérison; *(in business)* être en bonne voie, faire de bonnes affaires; *(of business)* bien aller, réussir; *(of plant)* bien pousser; **that young man will do well** c'est un garçon qui réussira; **he did brilliantly** il a réussi brillamment; **to do very well** *or* **nicely for oneself** *(prosper)* s'en tirer pas mal du tout

(b) *(serve, suffice)* **that will do** *(is satisfactory)* c'est bien (comme cela), c'est bon; *(stop it)* ça suffit, c'est assez; **tea will do** *(if you haven't got coffee)* du thé fera l'affaire; **this room will do for the office** cette pièce ira bien pour le bureau; **will this one do?** ceci fera l'affaire?; **that will never do** cela n'ira jamais, ça n'ira pas du tout; **to make do with what one has** s'arranger avec ce qu'on a; **we'll just have to make do** il faudra faire avec; **that will do me** cela fera mon affaire; **it would never do for them to see me** il ne faudrait pas qu'ils me voient

(c) *(happen)* **there's nothing doing** *(business is bad)* les affaires vont mal; **there's never anything doing at this time of year** il ne se passe jamais rien à cette période de l'année; **nothing doing!** *(I, she etc won't)* rien à faire!, ça ne prend pas!

do² *n* **(a) the do's and don'ts** ce qu'il faut faire et ce qu'il ne faut pas faire; **the do's and don'ts of society** ce qui se fait et ce qui ne se fait pas dans le monde; *F* **come on, fair do's!** *(I want my share)* dis donc, donne-moi ma part!; *(be fair)* dis donc, sois juste! **(b)** *F (party etc)* réception *f* **(c)** *Old-fashioned F (state of affairs)* **it's a poor do!** c'est triste!

do³ [dəʊ] *n Mus (fixed)* do *m*, ut *m*; *Scot F* **to be up to high do** être dans tous ses états

▶ **do away with** *vipo* **(a)** *(abolish) (custom)* abolir, abandonner; *(death penalty, monarchy)* abolir; *(practice, paperwork, homework)* supprimer; **we've done away with the typists** *(got rid of them)* nous nous sommes défait des dactylos; *F* **they should do away with school** ils devraient supprimer l'école **(b)** *F (kill)* supprimer; **she has threatened to do away with herself** elle a menacé de se supprimer

▶ **do by** *vipo F (treat)* **to do well** *or* **right/badly** *or* **wrong by sb** bien/mal agir *ou* se conduire envers qn; **she did very well by her granddaughter at Christmas** *(gave her lots of gifts)* elle a gâté sa petite-fille à Noël; **he has been hard done by** il a été traité durement; **he'll feel very hard done by if you don't at least send him a birthday card** il se sentira vraiment blessé si tu ne lui envoies même pas de carte d'anniversaire; *prov* **do as you would be done by** ne fais pas aux autres ce que tu ne voudrais pas qu'ils te fassent

▶ **do down** *vtsep* **(a)** *(swindle)* estamper **(b)** *(say bad things about)* dire du mal de; **to do oneself down** se rabaisser; **there's always someone ready to do you down** il y a toujours des gens prêts à dire du mal des autres

▶ **do for** *F* **1** *vipo* **(a)** *(murder)* tuer, faire son affaire à; **he's done for** *(will be killed)* c'est un homme mort; *(is ruined)* il est fini *ou F* fichu; **if he keeps on treating her this way, she'll do for him** s'il continue à la traiter de cette façon, elle va le descendre

(b) *(exhaust)* épuiser; **it was that last hill that did for me** c'est la dernière colline qui m'a épuisé

(c) *(clean house for)* faire *ou* tenir le ménage de; **who does for you?** qui fait votre ménage?

2 *vtaspo (charge with, convict of)* **to do sb for sth** *(murder, shoplifting)* condamner qn pour qch; **they'll do you for double-parking** ils vont te mettre une amende si tu restes garé en double file; *Hum* **she'll get done for child-molesting if she goes out with him** on va l'accuser de les prendre au berceau si elle sort avec lui

▶ **do in** *vtsep F* **(a)** *(murder)* descendre, faire son affaire à; **somebody on our street was done in last night** quelqu'un de notre rue a été descendu cette nuit **(b)** *(exhaust)* crever; **I'm absolutely done in** je suis crevé *ou* vanné **(c)** *(injure, damage) (of shoes etc) (toes etc)* faire mal à; **to do one's back/knee in** se niquer le dos/genou; *Sl* **that girl really does my head in** *(annoys me)* cette fille, elle me prend la tête

▶ **do out** *vtsep* **(a)** (*clean*) (*the kitchen, a room*) faire, nettoyer; (*drawer, cupboard*) ranger **(b)** (*decorate*) (*room*) faire (**in** en); (*woodwork*) peindre (**in** en)

▶ **do out of** *vtaspo F* (*cheat*) **to do sb out of sth** soutirer *ou* carotter qch à qn; (*money*) refaire *ou* escroquer qn de qch; **to do sb out of a job** (*of person*) prendre le travail de qn; **all this automation is doing people out of jobs** toute cette automatisation supprime des emplois; **the new structure did him out of his job** la nouvelle structure lui a fait perdre son travail; **you've done me out of a possible job** tu m'as fait perdre un emploi; **she's been done out of her share of the money** elle s'est fait escroquer de sa part de l'argent

▶ **do over** *vtsep* **(a)** *Am* (*redecorate*) (*house*) refaire la décoration de **(b)** *Br F* (*beat up*) (*sb*) casser la figure à, mettre une raclée à **(c)** *F* (*search*) (*flat etc*) retourner; **their place really got done over while they were away** (*burgled*) on a tout retourné chez eux pendant qu'ils étaient partis **(d)** *Am* (*repeat*) (*homework*) refaire

▶ **do up 1** *vi* (*of clothes*) s'agrafer **2** *vtsep* **(a)** (*fasten*) (*jacket, skirt, button, zip*) fermer; (*laces*) faire; (*hair*) relever **(b)** (*wrap*) (*parcel*) faire; (*objects*) emballer, empaqueter **(c)** (*improve appearance of*) remettre à neuf; (*room, inside of house etc*) décorer; *F* **to do oneself up** se faire beau/belle; **to be done up to the nines** être sur son trente et un

▶ **do with** *vipo* **(a) what did you do with my umbrella?** qu'avez-vous fait de mon parapluie?; **she didn't know what to do with herself** (*to keep busy*) elle ne savait que faire *ou* à quoi s'occuper; (*for joy*) elle ne se tenait pas de joie; (*for awkwardness*) elle était gênée, elle ne savait plus où se mettre; **I can't do a thing with my hair** je n'arrive pas à me coiffer; **I'll see if Bob can do anything with the car** je vais voir si Bob peut faire quelque chose à la voiture; **I can't do a thing with him** (*child*) je ne sais plus quoi faire

(b) (*need*) (*usually formed with* **could**) **I could do with a cup of tea** je prendrais bien une tasse de thé; **we can do with your help** vous n'êtes pas de trop; **you could do with a haircut** une coupe de cheveux ne te ferait pas de mal; **the house could do with a lick of paint** la maison aurait bien besoin d'un coup de pinceau; **we could do with something like that for the spare room** ce serait bien si on avait quelque chose comme ça pour la chambre d'ami

(c) (*be connected with*) **she's something to do with insurance** elle est dans les assurances; **it has to do with your mother, I'm afraid** j'ai bien peur que ça concerne ta mère; **I want nothing to do with him** je ne veux pas avoir affaire à lui; **to have nothing to do with sth** (*not be involved in or responsible for*) n'être pour rien dans qch, n'avoir rien à voir avec qch; (*not be connected with*) n'avoir rien à faire avec qch; **you should have nothing to do with it** (*don't get involved*) tu ne devrais pas t'en mêler; **I had nothing to do with it** je n'y suis pour rien; **it's nothing to do with the colour of your skin** cela n'a rien à voir avec la couleur de la peau; **it's nothing to do with you** vous n'avez rien à voir là-dedans

(d) (*finish*) **to have done with sth** en avoir fini avec qch; **I've done with trying to help people** j'en ai fini d'aider les gens; **let's have done with it!** finissons-en!; **to have done with sb** (*terminated relationship with lover, girlfriend etc*) avoir rompu avec qn; (*with friend*) en avoir fini avec qn; **I haven't done with him yet!** (*haven't finished scolding him*) je n'en ai pas encore fini avec lui!; **that's all over and done with!** c'est fini, tout ça!

(e) *F* (*finish using*) (*newspaper, scissors etc*) finir avec; **once you've done with it** quand tu auras fini

(f) *F* (*with negative*) (*not like*) **I can't be doing with getting up early** je ne peux pas me faire à me lever tôt; **I can't be doing with television** je n'aime pas la télévision; **I can't be doing with her** je ne l'aime pas

▶ **do without** *vipo* (*manage without*) (*sth*) se passer de; **to do without food** se passer de nourriture; *F* **I could do without him** je me passerais bien de lui; **we can do without the sarcasm** on n'a pas besoin de ces sarcasmes; **you could do without the heavy eye make-up** tu serais mieux avec moins de maquillage sur les yeux; **you'll just have to do without** il faudra s'en passer

DOA [diːəʊ'eɪ] *adj Med* (*abbr* **dead on arrival**) **to be D.** être mort avant son arrivée à l'hôpital

doc [dɒk] *n* (*abbr* **doctor**) **(a)** *F* toubib *m*; **thanks d.** merci docteur **(b) D. Martens**® (*shoes*) Doc Martens® *fpl*, *F* Docs

docile ['dəʊsaɪl] *adj* docile

docility [dəʊ'sɪlɪtɪ] *n* docilité *f*

dock¹ [dɒk] *n* **(a)** *Naut* (*of port*) bassin *m*; **to go into d.** entrer au bassin; **the docks** les docks *mpl*; *F* **in d.** (*of car, plane*) en réparation; **floating d.** dock flottant, chantier *m* à flot; **d. strike** grève *f* des dockers; **d.-warehouse** dock *m* entrepôt **(b)** *Th* **scene d.** remise *f* à décors

dock² 1 *vt* **(a)** *Naut* (*ship*) faire entrer au bassin *ou* à quai; (*for repairs*) faire entrer en cale sèche; (*on canal, river*) (*barge etc*) garer **(b)** (*two spacecraft*) arrimer **2** *vi* **(a)** (*of ship*) entrer *ou* arriver au port *ou* aux docks *ou* à quai; (*for repair*) entrer en cale sèche; **when do we d.?** quand arrivons-nous à quai?; **we'll be docking at New York** nous entrerons à quai à New York **(b)** (*of two spacecraft*) s'arrimer

dock³ *n Jur* banc *m* des accusés *ou* des prévenus; **prisoner in the d. Murphy** accusé Murphy

dock⁴ *vt* **(a)** (*sb's pay*) diminuer; **to d. two pounds from sb's wages** supprimer deux livres du salaire de qn **(b) to d. a horse('s tail)/a dog('s tail)** couper la queue à un cheval/un chien

dock⁵ *n* (*weed*) patience *f*

docker ['dɒkər] *n Br* docker *m*, débardeur *m*; **dockers' strike** grève *f* des dockers

docket¹ ['dɒkɪt] *n* **(a)** (*piece of paper*) (*accompanying parcel, file*) bordereau *m* **(b)** *Jur* (*summary*) registre *m* des jugements rendus; *US* (*list of cases*) rôle *m* des causes **(c)** *Br* (*customs document*) récépissé *m* de douane

docket² *vt* **(a)** *Jur* (*decision*) enregistrer; *US* (*case*) porter sur le rôle des causes **(b)** (*file, merchandise*) étiqueter

docking ['dɒkɪŋ] *n* **(a)** *Naut* mise *f* au bassin; (*for repairs*) radoub *m* **(b)** (*of two spacecraft*) arrimage *m*; **d. manoeuvre** manœuvre *f* d'abordage

docking station *n Comptr* (*for notebook*) station *f* d'accueil

dockland ['dɒklænd] *n* quartiers *mpl* des docks

dockyard ['dɒkjɑːd] *n* chantier *m* naval *ou* de constructions navales; **naval d.** arsenal *m* maritime

doctor¹ ['dɒktər] *n* **(a)** *Med* médecin *m*, docteur *m*; **to go to the d.('s)** aller chez le docteur; **the d. will see you now** le docteur va vous recevoir maintenant; **good morning d.** bonjour docteur; *Br F* **to be under the d. for sth** être suivi par le docteur pour qch; **I would like to see D. Brown** j'aimerais voir le Docteur Brown; **I am a d.** je suis médecin; **woman d.** femme *f* médecin; **family d.** médecin de famille; **ship's d.** médecin de bord; **army d.** médecin militaire; *Br* **National Health (Service) d.** = médecin conventionné; *F Fig* **that's just what the d. ordered** c'est exactement ce qu'il me fallait

(b) *Univ* docteur *m*; **D. of Divinity/Law/Medicine** docteur en théologie/droit/médecine; **D. of Literature/Science** docteur ès lettres/sciences; *Rel* **Doctors of the Church** docteurs de l'Église; **d.'s degree** doctorat *m*

doctor² *vt* **(a)** *Pej F* (*falsify, adulterate*) (*text*) falsifier; (*accounts, evidence*) falsifier, fausser; (*dice, cards*) piper; (*wine etc*) frelater **(b)** (*drug*) *Horseracing* (*horse*) doper; **to d. sb's drink** mettre de la drogue dans le verre de qn (*à son insu*) **(c)** *Old-fashioned* (*patient*) soigner **(d)** *Vet F* (*cat etc*) châtrer

doctoral ['dɒktər(ə)l] *adj* (*thesis, research etc*) de doctorat; (*robes*) de docteur

doctorate ['dɒktərɪt] *n Univ* doctorat *m*; **to have a d. in history** avoir un doctorat en histoire

doctoring ['dɒktərɪŋ] *n* **(a)** *Pej F* (*of text etc*) falsification *f* **(b)** (*of horse*) doping *m* **(c)** *Med F* (*profession*) profession *f* de médecin **(d)** (*care*) soins *mpl* (**of sb** donnés à qn) **(e)** *Vet* (*of cat etc*) castration *f*

doctrinaire [dɒktrɪ'neər] *adj Pej* doctrinaire

doctrinal [dɒk'traɪn(ə)l] *adj* doctrinal

doctrine ['dɒktrɪn] *n* doctrine *f*

docudrama ['dɒkjʊdrɑːmə] *n TV* docudrame *m*

document¹ ['dɒkjʊmənt] *n* document *m*; **legal d.** acte *m* authentique; *Com* **documents against acceptance/payment** documents *mpl* contre acceptation/paiement; *Jur* **documents relating to a case** dossier *m* d'une affaire; *Jur* **to draw up a d.** rédiger un acte; *Jur* **d. of title** acte *m* de propriété; **d. case** porte-documents *m inv*; **d. collator** unité *f* de classement de documents; **d. cover** pochette *f*; *Comptr* **d. file** fichier *m* document; **d. handling** manipulation *f* de documents; **d. holder** (*for keyboarder*) bras *m* porte-copies; *Comptr* **d. reader** lecteur *m* de documents

document² *vt* documenter; **the film documents the lives of the long-term unemployed** le film montre en détail la vie des chômeurs de longue durée; **well-documented book** livre bien documenté; **the first documented case of ...** le premier cas établi de ...

documentary [dɒkjʊ'ment(ə)rɪ] **1** *adj* (*evidence, film*) documentaire; (*proof*) littéral; *Com* **d. bill** traite *f* documentaire; *Com* **d. charges** frais *mpl* de crédit documentaire; *Com* **d. credit** crédit *m* documentaire; *Com* **d. credit application** demande *f* d'ouverture de crédit documentaire; *Com* **d. credit department** service *m* des crédits documentaires; **d. evidence** pièces *fpl* justificatives; **d. interview** interview-document *f*; *Com* **d. letter of credit**

lettre *f* de crédit documentaire; *Com* **d. remittance** remise *f* documentaire **2** *n Cin, TV* documentaire *m*

documentation [dɒkjʊmen'teɪʃən] *n* documentation *f*

dodder ['dɒdər] *vi* (*walk*) marcher d'un pas branlant; *Hum* **I'm doddering along** je vais mon petit bonhomme de chemin; **he's beginning to d. a bit** (*mentally*) il commence à devenir un peu gâteux

dodderer ['dɒdərər] *n Pej* croulant, -ante

doddering ['dɒdərɪŋ] *adj* **(a)** (*walk*) branlant **(b)** *Pej* (*person*) gaga *inv*, gâteux; **a d. old fool** un vieux gâteux

doddery ['dɒdərɪ] *adj F* (*shaky*) branlant, tremblotant; **I still feel a bit d. (on my feet)** (*after illness*) je ne me sens pas encore d'aplomb; *Pej* **a d. old fool** un vieux croulant

doddle ['dɒd(ə)l] *n Br F* **it's a d.** (*easy*) c'est simple comme bonjour

dodge[1] [dɒdʒ] *n* **(a)** (*to avoid sth*) saut *m* de côté; **she made a d. to the left** elle a fait un saut vers la gauche **(b)** *F usu Pej* (*trick*) truc *m*, combine *f*; **he's up to all the dodges** il connaît toutes les combines; **tax d.** combine pour payer moins d'impôts

dodge[2] **1** *vi* se jeter de côté; *Boxing, Fb* esquiver; **to d. behind a tree** se glisser prestement derrière un arbre **2** *vt* **(a)** (*blow*) esquiver; (*person*) éviter; (*police, search party*) échapper à, se dérober à **(b)** *F Pej* (*difficulty*) esquiver, éluder; (*question*) éluder, escamoter; **to d. doing one's duty** se dérober à son devoir; **to d. doing the housework/buying one's round** se défiler pour ne pas faire le ménage/payer sa tournée; **to d. military service** couper au service militaire; **stop dodging the issue** arrête d'éluder le problème

dodgem® ['dɒdʒəm] *adj, n Br* **d. cars, dodgems** autos *fpl* tamponneuses; **to have a ride** *or* **a go on the dodgems** faire un tour d'autos tamponneuses

dodger ['dɒdʒər] *n F* (*shirker*) tire-au-flanc *m inv*; *Old-fashioned* **an artful d.** un fin matois; **fare d.** voyageur, -euse sans billet; **they're after tax dodgers** ils cherchent à coincer ceux qui fraudent le fisc

dodgy ['dɒdʒɪ] *adj Br F* **(a)** (*situation*) délicat; (*translation, contract, meat*) douteux; (*knee, back*) fragile; **to be a bit d.** (*not work properly*) ne pas marcher très bien; **his heart's a bit d.** il a le cœur fragile; **my stomach's been a bit d. for the past day or two** j'ai l'estomac un peu patraque ces jours-ci; **the ceiling looks a bit d.** le plafond n'a pas l'air en très bon état, le plafond a l'air un peu suspect **(b)** (*person*) louche

dodo, *pl* **-oes, -os** ['dəʊdəʊ, -z] *n* **(a)** (*bird*) dronte *m*, dodo *m*; *Fig* **(as) dead as a d.** mort et enterré **(b)** *F* (*fool*) andouille *f* **(c)** *Mktg* poids *m* mort, produit *m* dodo

DOE [diːəʊ'iː] *n Br Admin* (*abbr* **Department of the Environment**) = ministère *m* de l'Environnement

doe [dəʊ] *n* **(a)** (*deer*) biche *f*; (*of fallow deer*) daine *f*; **d.-eyed** aux yeux de biche **(b)** (*of rabbit*) lapine *f*; (*of wild rabbit, hare*) hase *f*

doer ['duːər] *n* (*dynamic person*) personne *f* dynamique; **she's a d.** c'est une femme très active; **we need a d. rather than a talker** c'est un homme d'action qu'il nous faut plutôt qu'un orateur

doeskin ['dəʊskɪn] *n* peau *f* de daim; **d. glove** gant en peau de daim

doesn't ['dʌz(ə)nt] = **does not**, *see* **do[1]**

doff [dɒf] *vt Lit, Hum* (*one's hat*) enlever, ôter; **to d. one's cap/hat to sb** se découvrir devant qn

dog[1] [dɒg] *n* **(a)** (*animal*) chien *m*; **beware of the d.** (*sign*) (attention) chien méchant; **to set the dogs on sb** lancer les chiens sur qn; **sporting d.** chien de chasse; *Br Sp F* **the dogs** les courses *fpl* de lévriers; **d. biscuit** biscuit *m* pour chien; **d. licence** permis *m* requis pour la possession d'un chien; *Swimming* **d. paddle** nage *f* à la chien; **d. rose** (*flower*) églantine *f*, rose *f* sauvage; (*bush*) églantier *m*, rosier *m* sauvage

(b) *Zool* (*of certain animals*) mâle *m*; **d. fox** renard *m* mâle

(c) *Old-fashioned* (*person*) **you lucky d.!** veinard! *m*; **sly d.** fin renard *m*; **gay d.** coureur *m* (de jupons); **dirty d.** salaud *m*, sale type *m*

(d) *Am Sl* (*failed film, party etc*) fiasco *m*; *Pej* (*ugly woman*) cageot *m*; **dogs** (*feet*) panards *mpl*

(e) *Mktg* (*product*) poids *m* mort, gouffre *m* financier

(f) *Tech* (*pawl*) cliquet *m*

(g) (*idioms*) **to die like a d.** mourir comme un chien; **to treat sb like a d.** traiter qn comme un chien; **to follow sb about like a d.** suivre qn comme un petit chien; *Fig* **he's a d. in the manger** il fait l'empêcheur de tourner en rond; **to lead a d.'s life** mener une vie de chien; **to lead sb a d.'s life** faire mener une vie de chien à qn; **it's a d.'s life being a teacher** c'est une vie de chien que d'être professeur; *Prov* **you can't teach an old d. new tricks** = on ne peut pas apprendre un nouveau métier/etc à quelqu'un qui a dépassé un certain âge; *Prov* **every d. has his day** à chacun vient sa chance; *Prov* **give a d. a bad name (and hang him)** qui veut noyer son chien l'accuse de la rage; *F* **what a d.'s breakfast** *or* **dinner!** quel gâchis!; (*of text*) quel torchon!; *F* **to make a d.'s breakfast** *or* **dinner of sth** gâcher qch; *Br F* **to be dressed up like a d.'s dinner** être habillé comme un clown; *esp Am* **to put on the d.** (*put on airs and graces*) prendre des grands airs; (*spend a lot of money*) faire des frais; *F* **he doesn't stand a d.'s chance** il n'a pas la moindre chance; *F* **I'm going to see a man about a d.** = si on te demande, tu diras que tu ne sais pas; **it's a case of d. eat d.** c'est un cas où les loups se mangent entre eux; **it's a d.-eat-d. world** c'est un monde où les loups se mangent entre eux, c'est une jungle; **to go to the dogs** (*of business, country*) aller à la ruine; **he's really gone to the dogs** c'est la déchéance totale pour lui; **this restaurant has gone to the dogs since he took over** ce restaurant ne vaut plus rien du tout depuis qu'il l'a racheté

dog[2] *vt* (**-gg-** [dɒgd]) (*person*) suivre à la trace; **to d. sb's footsteps** marcher sur les talons de qn; **he is dogged by misfortune** il est poursuivi par la malchance; **she has been dogged by injury for the last year** elle a eu blessure sur blessure au cours de l'année passée

dog breeder *n* éleveur, -euse de chiens

dog breeding *n* élevage *m* de chiens

dogcart ['dɒgkɑːt] *n* (*vehicle*) dog-cart *m*, *pl* dog-carts

dog-catcher *n* = employé *m* municipal qui est chargé d'attraper les chiens errants

dog clutch *n Aut* embrayage *m* à crabot, crabot *m*

dog collar *n* collier *m* de chien; *F* (*of vicar*) faux col *m*

dog days *npl* **d. (of summer)** canicule *f*

doge [dəʊdʒ] *n Hist* doge *m*

dog-eared *adj* (*book*) aux pages cornées; (*page*) corné; **I'm afraid your book got a bit d.** je crois bien que les pages de ton livre se sont un peu cornées

dog-end *n F* mégot *m*

dogfight ['dɒgfaɪt] *n* combat *m* de chiens; *Mil, Av* combat aérien; *Fig* (*brawl*) bagarre *f*

dogfish ['dɒgfɪʃ] *n* chien *m* de mer, roussette *f*

dogfood ['dɒgfuːd] *n* pâtée *f* (pour chiens)

dogged ['dɒgɪd] *adj* (*person*) résolu, tenace; (*research, refusal, pursuit*) tenace; (*attachment*) fidèle

doggedly ['dɒgɪdlɪ] *adv* avec ténacité, résolument; **to work d.** travailler sans relâche; **to be d. intent on doing sth** avoir la ferme intention de faire qch

doggedness ['dɒgɪdnɪs] *n* ténacité *f*

doggerel ['dɒgərəl] *n* **d. (verse)** (*silly and comical*) poésie *f* burlesque; (*worthless, mediocre*) vers *mpl* de mirliton

doggie ['dɒgɪ] *n F* toutou *m*, chienchien *m*; **d. bag** = petit sac fourni par certains restaurants pour emporter les restes; **to do it d. fashion** (*sex*) faire l'amour en levrette; **d. paddle** nage *f* à la chien

doggo ['dɒgəʊ] *adv Br F* **to lie d.** se tenir coi

doggone ['dɒgɒn] *adj US F* sacré; **d. it!** zut!, nom d'un chien!

doggy ['dɒgɪ] **1** *adj* **(a)** (*smell etc*) de chien **(b)** *F* (*person*) qui adore les chiens **2** *n F* = **doggie**

dog handler *n Mil etc* maître-chien *m*, *pl* maîtres-chiens

doghouse ['dɒghaʊs] *n esp Am* chenil *m*; *Fig* **to be in the d.** être en défaveur *ou* en disgrâce; **you're in the d. with Mum** tu n'es pas en odeur de sainteté avec Maman

dog Latin *n F* latin *m* de cuisine

dogleg[1] ['dɒgleg] *n* (*in pipe, road etc*) coude *m*

dogleg[2] *vi* (*of pipe, road*) former un angle

doglike ['dɒglaɪk] *adj* (*devotion*) de chien

dogma, *pl* **-as** ['dɒgmə, -əz] *n* dogme *m*

dogmatic [dɒg'mætɪk] *adj* dogmatique

dogmatically [dɒg'mætɪklɪ] *adv* dogmatiquement; (*to say*) d'un ton dogmatique

dogmatism ['dɒgmətɪz(ə)m] *n* (*of opinion, person etc*) dogmatisme *m*

dogmatist ['dɒgmətɪst] *n* dogmatique *mf*

dogmeat ['dɒgmiːt] *n* viande *f* pour chiens

do-gooder ['duː'gʊdər] *n F Pej* âme *f* charitable, faiseur, -euse de bonnes œuvres

dog-paddle *vi* nager comme un chien

dog racing *n* courses *fpl* de lévriers

dogsbody ['dɒgzbɒdɪ] *n F* factotum *m*; **she's the general d.** c'est la bonne à tout faire

dog show *n* exposition *f* canine

dogsled ['dɒgsled] *n* luge *f* tirée par des chiens

Dog Star *n Astron* Sirius *m*

dog's-tooth ['dɒgztuːθ] *n* = **dogtooth**

dog tag *n US* (*of dog, F soldier*) plaque *f* d'identité

dog-tired *adj F* claqué, crevé, mort de fatigue

dogtooth ['dɒgtuːθ] *n* (*tooth*) canine *f*; *Tex* **d. check** pied *m* de poule; *Bot* **d. violet** érythrone *m*, dent-de-chien *f*

dogtrot ['dɒgtrɒt] *n* petit trot *m*; **to go somewhere at a d.** aller quelque part au petit trot
dogwatch ['dɒgwɒtʃ] *n Naut* petit quart *m*
dogwood ['dɒgwʊd] *n Bot* cornouiller *m*
doh [dəʊ] *n Mus* = do[3]
doily ['dɔɪlɪ] *n* **(a)** (*underneath plate etc*) petit napperon *m* **(b)** (*on plate*) dessus *m* d'assiette
doing ['du:ɪŋ] *n* **talking is one thing, d. is another** c'est bien beau de parler, encore faudrait-il agir; **that takes some d.** ça ne se fait pas en un tour de main; **this is his d.** c'est son ouvrage; **all this is your d.** c'est vous qui êtes la cause de tout cela; **it was none of my d.** ce n'est pas moi qui suis responsable; *F* **to give sb a d. (over)** casser la figure à qn, mettre une raclée à qn
doings ['du:ɪŋz] *npl* **(a)** (*of person*) ce qu'on fait, *Pej* agissements *mpl*; **to be informed of sb's d.** être au courant des faits et gestes de qn **(b)** *F* (*events*) événements *mpl*; **there have been great d. at their house** il y a eu bien du mouvement chez eux **(c)** *Br F* (*gadget etc*) machin *m*, truc *m*
doing up *n* (*renovation*) remise *f* à neuf
do-it-yourself *n* bricolage *m*; **d. enthusiast** passionné *m* de bricolage; **d. kit** panoplie *f* de construction; **d. shop** *or* **store** magasin *m* de bricolage
do-it-yourselfer [du:ɪtjə'selfər] *n* bricoleur, -euse
dol (*abbr* **dollar**) dol(l)
Dolby® ['dɒlbɪ] *n* Dolby® *m*; **D. system** système *m* Dolby® stéréo
doldrums (the) [ðə'dɒldrəmz] *npl Naut* la zone calme; *Fig* le cafard, les idées *fpl* noires; **to be in the d.** (*of person*) avoir le moral à zéro, être au trente-sixième dessous; (*of business, market*) être dans le marasme
dole [dəʊl] *n Br F* **d. (money)** indemnité *f* de chômage; **to be on the d.** être au chômage; **to go on the d.** s'inscrire au chômage; **d. queues are lengthening** le nombre des chômeurs s'accroît
▶ **dole out** *vtsep F* (*money, food, clothing*) distribuer; **I'm tired of doling out sympathy to everyone** j'en ai assez de réconforter tout le monde
doleful ['dəʊlfʊl] *adj* (*expression, look, song*) lugubre; (*cry*) plaintif; (*person*) triste, affligé
dolefully ['dəʊlfʊlɪ] *adv* tristement
doll [dɒl] *n* **(a)** (*for child*) poupée *f*; (*of ventriloquist*) marionnette *f*; **baby d.** baigneur *m*; **to play with a d.** jouer à la poupée; **d.'s house** maison *f* de poupée; *Fig* jolie petite maisonnette *f* **(b)** *F* (*woman*) poupée *f*; (*pretty woman*) belle poupée **(c)** *Am F* (*kind person*) amour *m*
▶ **doll up** *vtsep F* (*sb*) bichonner; **to d. oneself up** (*of woman*) se pomponner; (*of man*) se faire beau; **to be all dolled up** être sur son trente et un; **they've dolled their house up** ils ont retapé leur maison
dollar ['dɒlər] *n* dollar *m*; **dollars in real terms** dollars *mpl* constants; *Econ* **d. area** zone *f* dollar; **d. sign** signe *m* dollar
dollop ['dɒləp] *n F* (*of butter*) gros morceau *m*; (*of cream, mashed potato*) bonne cuillerée *f*; (*of mud*) tas *m*; **a good d. of cream** une bonne cuillerée de crème
dolly[1] ['dɒlɪ] *n* **(a)** *F* (*for child*) poupée *f* **(b)** *Br F* (*young woman*) **d.(-bird)** poupée *f* **(c)** *TV, Cin* travelling *m*, chariot *m*; **d. operator** machiniste *m* caméra **(d)** (*for clothes*) agitateur *m*; **d. tub** (*for laundry*) baquet *m* à lessive
dolly[2] *vi TV, Cin* faire un travelling
dolman ['dɒlmən] *n* **d. sleeve** (*on sweater etc*) manche *f* chauve-souris
dolmen ['dɒlmen] *n Archeol* dolmen *m*
dolomite ['dɒləmaɪt] *n Miner* dolomite *f*; *Geol* (*rock*) dolomie *f*
Dolomites (the) [ðə'dɒləmaɪts] *npl* les Dolomites *fpl*
dolphin ['dɒlfɪn] *n* (*mammal*) dauphin *m*
dolphinarium [dɒlfɪ'neərɪəm] *n* aquarium *m* pour dauphins
dolt [dəʊlt] *n* sot *m*, nigaud *m*, gourde *f*
doltish ['dəʊltɪʃ] *adj* sot, bête
domain [də'meɪn] *n* **(a)** (*property*), *Fig* domaine *m*; *Fig* **that is outside my d.** ce n'est pas mon domaine **(b)** *Math, Phys* (*of function*) domaine *m*
dome [dəʊm] *n* **(a)** *Archit* dôme *m*, coupole *f*; *Can* **d. fastener** bouton-pression *m*, pression *mf* **(b)** *Fig* (*of sky*) dôme *m*, voûte *f*; (*of hill*) dôme; (*of skull*) calotte *f*; *F* (*head*) tête *f* **(c)** *Metal* (*of furnace*) dôme *m*, voûte *f*
domed [dəʊmd] *adj* **(a)** (*building*) à dôme, à coupole **(b)** (*shaped like a dome*) en forme de dôme; (*skull*) ovoïde
Domesday ['du:mzdeɪ] *n Hist* **D. Book** = (livre *m* du) cadastre *m* de l'Angleterre (*établi en 1086 par Guillaume le Conquérant*)
domestic [də'mestɪk] **1** *adj* **(a)** (*misfortune, problem*) domestique; (*fuel*) de ménage; **she does d. work** (*to earn a living*) elle fait des ménages; **to be in d. service** être employé(e) de maison; **d. animal** animal *m* domestique; **d. appliances** appareils *mpl* ménagers; **newlyweds living in d. bliss** des jeunes mariés au comble du bonheur; **d. duties** *or* **tasks** travaux *mpl* ménagers; *Old-fashioned* **d. economy** économie *f* domestique; **d. life** vie *f* de famille; *Br Sch* **d. science** enseignement *m* ménager; **d. servant** domestique *mf*; **d. virtues** talents *mpl* de femme/d'homme d'intérieur
(b) (*trade, dissent, flight etc*) intérieur; (*economy, production, currency*) national; **d. airline** ligne *f* intérieure; **d. excursionist** excursionniste *mf* (dans son propre pays); *US* **d. mail** correspondance *f* à destination de l'intérieur; **d. market** marché *m* intérieur; **d. products** denrées *fpl* du pays; *Av* **d. route** ligne *f* intérieure; **d. sales** ventes *fpl* domestiques; **d. tourism** tourisme *m* national; **d. tourist** touriste *m* national; **d. travel** voyages *mpl* domestiques; **d. visitor** touriste *m* national
(c) (*person*) casanier
2 *n* domestique *mf*
domestically [də'mestɪk(ə)lɪ] *adv* à l'intérieur du pays
domesticate [də'mestɪkeɪt] *vt* **(a)** (*tame*) (*animal*) domestiquer, apprivoiser **(b)** (*naturalize*) (*animal, plant*) acclimater **(c) to be domesticated** (*of person*) être casanier, aimer la vie d'intérieur; **to become domesticated** prendre goût à la vie d'intérieur; **her husband is quite domesticated** son mari fait sa part des travaux ménagers
domesticity [dəʊme'stɪsɪtɪ] *n* **(a)** (*liking for home*) attachement *m* au foyer **(b)** (*home life*) vie *f* de famille; **the cosy d. of their life** leur petite vie tranquille
domicile[1] ['dɒmɪsaɪl] *n Com, Jur, Fin* domicile *m*
domicile[2] *vt* **(a)** *Fml* (*usu passive*) (*person*) **domiciled at Leeds** domicilié *ou* demeurant à Leeds **(b)** *Com* domicilier; *Fin* **domiciled bill** effet *m* domicilié; **bills domiciled in France** traites *fpl* payables en France; *Fin* **to d. acceptances** domicilier des acceptations
domiciliary [dɒmɪ'sɪlɪərɪ] *adj Fml* (*visit etc*) domiciliaire; (*assistance*) à domicile
domiciliation [dɒmɪsɪlɪ'eɪʃən] *n Fin* domiciliation *f*; **d. papers** dossier *m* de domiciliation
dominance ['dɒmɪnəns] *n* (*of disease, gene etc*) dominance *f*; (*of race, political party*) prédominance *f*; **Liverpool's d. of English football** la suprématie exercée par Liverpool sur le football anglais
dominant ['dɒmɪnənt] **1** *adj* (*character, gene, force etc*) dominant; (*person*) dominateur, -trice **2** *n Mus* dominante *f*; **d. chord** accord *m* de dominante; **d. seventh** septième *f* de dominante
dominantly ['dɒmɪnəntlɪ] *adv* d'une manière dominante
dominate ['dɒmɪneɪt] *vt* **(a)** (*person, a people*) dominer (sur); **to d. a match/game** (*of player, team*) dominer un match/un jeu; **to be dominated by sb** subir la loi de qn; **man dominated by ambition** homme en proie à l'ambition; **the wedding dominated his thoughts to the exclusion of everything else** le mariage prédominait sur toute autre chose dans ses pensées **(b)** (*of mountain etc*) (*landscape*) dominer; **the fortress dominates the town** la forteresse domine *ou* commande la ville
dominating ['dɒmɪneɪtɪŋ] *adj* (*feature, colour etc*) dominant; (*personality*) dominateur, -trice
domination [dɒmɪ'neɪʃən] *n* domination *f* **(over** sur); **to be under sb's d.** être dominé par qn; **Liverpool's d. of English football** la suprématie exercée par Liverpool sur le football anglais
domineer [dɒmɪ'nɪər] *vi* se montrer autoritaire
▶ **domineer over** *vipo* tyranniser
domineering [dɒmɪ'nɪərɪŋ] *adj* (*person, character etc*) dominateur, -trice, autoritaire
dominical [də'mɪnɪk(ə)l] *adj Rel* dominical
Dominican[1] [də'mɪnɪkən] *adj, n Rel* dominicain, -aine
Dominican[2] *Geog* **1** *adj* dominicain; **the D. Republic** la République Dominicaine **2** *n* Dominicain, -aine
dominion [də'mɪnjən] *n* **(a)** (*rule*) autorité *f*, empire *m*; **to have** *or* **hold d. over ...** exercer son empire *ou* dominer sur ... **(b)** (*land*) dominion *m*
domino, *pl* **-oes** ['dɒmɪnəʊ, -əʊz] *n* **(a)** [①A10,d] (*in game*) domino *m*; **dominoes** (*game*) (*usu with sing verb*) (jeu *m* de) dominos; **to play dominoes** jouer aux dominos; *Pol, Fig* **d. effect** effet *m* d'entraînement; *Pol, Fig* **the d. theory** la théorie des dominos **(b)** (*mask*) domino *m*
don[1] [dɒn] *n* **(a)** *Br Univ* professeur *m* (d'université) (*surtout à Oxford et Cambridge*) **(b)** (*Spanish title*) Don *m*
don[2] *vt* (**-nn-**) *Fml* (*uniform, clothes*) revêtir, endosser; (*hat*) mettre, coiffer
donate [dəʊ'neɪt] **1** *vt* faire un don de; *Med* **to d. blood** donner du *ou* son sang; **how much did you d.?** combien est-ce que tu as donné?; **to d. time** faire don de son temps **2** *vi* faire un don

donation [dəʊ'neɪʃən] *n* donation *f*, don *m*; **all donations are tax-deductible** tous les dons sont déductibles des impôts; **to make a d. to a charity** faire un don *ou* une donation à une œuvre de bienfaisance

donator [dəʊ'neɪtər] *n* donateur, -trice

done *see* **do¹**

doner kebab ['dɒnə, 'dəʊnə] *n* chiche-kebab *m*

dongle ['dɒŋg(ə)l] *n Comptr* fiche *f* gigogne, clé *f* gigogne

donkey ['dɒŋkɪ] *n* (**a**) (*animal*) âne *m*, *F* baudet *m*; (*female*) ânesse *f*; *F* **he would talk the hind legs off a d.** il est bavard comme une pie; *F* **it happened d.'s years ago** ça s'est passé il y a des années; *F* **I haven't seen him for d.'s years** je ne l'ai pas vu depuis une éternité; *Naut* **d. boiler** chaudière *f* auxiliaire; *Tech* **d. engine** petit-cheval *m*, *pl* petits-chevaux; *Clothing* **d. jacket** grosse veste *f*; **d. race** course *f* d'ânes (**b**) *Fig* (*idiot*) âne *m*, imbécile *mf*

donkey-work *n* (*drudgery*) travail *m* pénible

donnish ['dɒnɪʃ] *adj* (*person, air, tone*) intellectuel, -elle, *Pej* pédant; **he's a bit d.** il a un petit air professoral

donor ['dəʊnər] *n* (**a**) *Med* (*of blood, organ etc*) donneur, -euse; **d. card** carte *f* de donneur (**b**) (*to charity etc*) donateur, -trice

don't *see* **do¹**

don't know *n Pol F* (*voter*) indécis, -ise

donut ['dəʊnʌt] *n esp Am Culin* beignet *m*, *Can* beigne *m*

doodah ['du:dɑ:] *n F* truc *m*, machin *m*

doodle¹ ['du:d(ə)l] *n F* gribouillis *m*, griffonnage *m*

doodle² **1** *vt* griffonner *ou* gribouiller (distraitement) **2** *vi* griffonner *ou* gribouiller distraitement; *Fig* (*on piano*) pianoter

doodlebug ['du:d(ə)lbʌg] *n Br Hist F* bombe *f* volante

doolally [du:'lælɪ] *adj Sl* (*crazy, confused*) timbré

doom¹ [du:m] *n* destin *m* (funeste), sort *m* (malheureux); **an air/a feeling of d.** un air/sentiment funeste; *Lit* **he met his d.** il trouva la mort; *Fig* **to be full of** *or* **all d. and gloom** (*of person, forecast etc*) être pessimiste; **the situation's not all d. and gloom** la situation n'est pas aussi sombre qu'il y paraît

doom² *vt* condamner (**to** à); **doomed** (*town*) condamné; (*person*) perdu; (*ship, aircraft*) marqué par le destin; **an attempt doomed to failure** une tentative condamnée à l'insuccès *ou* vouée à l'échec

doom-laden *adj* (*forecast, words etc*) funeste, lugubre

Doomsday ['du:mzdeɪ] *n* **D. Book** *see* **Domesday**

doomsday ['du:mzdeɪ] *n* le (jour du) jugement dernier; *F* **till d.** indéfiniment; **to put off sth till d.** renvoyer qch aux calendes grecques

door [dɔ:r] *n* (*of house, refrigerator etc*) porte *f*; (*of train, car etc*) portière *f*, porte; (*of wardrobe*) porte, battant *m*; **two doors away** deux portes plus loin; **the house next d.** la maison à côté; **I live next d.** j'habite à côté; **the journey takes twenty-five minutes d. to d.** le voyage prend vingt-cinq minutes de porte à porte; **will you answer the d.?** tu peux aller ouvrir (la porte)?; **it was Bob who answered the d. (to me)** c'est Bob qui m'a ouvert (la porte); **to show sb the d.** éconduire *ou* congédier qn; **to show sb to the d.** conduire qn à la porte, reconduire qn; **out of doors** dehors, en plein air; **to shut the d. in sb's face** fermer la porte au nez de qn; *Fig* **doors kept being closed in our faces** tout le monde nous a fermé la porte au nez; **to leave the d. open to** *or* **for negotiations** laisser la porte ouverte à des négociations; **to close** *or* **shut the d. on any discussion** rendre impossible toute discussion; **behind closed doors** (*discussions etc*) entre quatre murs, à huis-clos; **to meet behind closed doors** se rencontrer à huis-clos; **to lay a charge at sb's d.** imputer qch à qn; **to put one's foot in the d.** mettre le pied dans l'embrasure de la porte; **the foot in the d. technique** (*of salesman*) = la vente (en porte-à-porte) forcée; **d. attendant** portier *m*; *Aut* **d. bin** vide-poche *f*; **d. chain** chaîne *f* de sûreté; **d. curtain** portière *f*; **d. handle** poignée *f ou* bouton *m* de porte; **d. knocker** marteau *m* de porte, heurtoir *m*; *Aut* **d. mirror** rétroviseur *m* extérieur; *Aut* **d. pocket** vide-poche *m*

doorbell ['dɔ:bel] *n* sonnette *f*; **to ring the d.** sonner à la porte

do-or-die *adj* (*effort, attempt etc*) acharné; **this d. attitude** cette attitude de détermination inébranlable

doorframe ['dɔ:freɪm] *n* chambranle *m ou* châssis *m* de porte

doorjamb ['dɔ:dʒæm] *n* montant *m* de porte

doorkeeper ['dɔ:ki:pər] *n* portier *m*, concierge *mf*

doorknob ['dɔ:nɒb] *n* poignée *f* (ronde) de porte

doorman, *pl* **-men** ['dɔ:mən] *n* portier *m*

doormat ['dɔ:mæt] *n* (**a**) (*for door*) paillasson *m* (**b**) *Fig* (*person*) lavette *f*, chiffe *f* molle; **don't be such a d.** ne te laisse pas marcher sur les pieds comme ça; **to treat sb like a d.** traiter qn comme une chose insignifiante

doornail ['dɔ:neɪl] *n F* **(as) dead as a d.** mort et bien mort

doorpost ['dɔ:pəʊst] *n* montant *m* de porte

doorstep¹ ['dɔ:step] *n* (**a**) seuil *m*, pas *m* (de la porte); **don't leave him standing on the d.** ne le laisse pas sur le pas de la porte; *Fig* **there are shops and a library on your d.** tu as des boutiques et une bibliothèque à ta porte (**b**) *Br F* (*slice of bread*) grosse tranche *f* de pain

doorstep² *vi* (*of canvasser*) faire du porte-à-porte

doorstepping ['dɔ:stepɪŋ] *n Journ F* = technique des journalistes qui importunent les gens à leur domicile

doorstop ['dɔ:stɒp] *n* (*fixed*) butoir *m*; (*wedge*) cale-porte *m*, *pl* cale-portes

door-to-door *adj* **d. canvassing/selling** porte-à-porte *m*; **to do d. canvassing/selling, to canvas/sell d.** faire du porte-à-porte; **to be a d. salesman** être V. R. P., faire du porte-à-porte

doorway ['dɔ:weɪ] *n* (baie *f* de) porte *f*; (*frame*) encadrement *m* de la porte; **in the d.** dans l'embrasure de la porte

dope¹ [dəʊp] *n* (**a**) (*drugs*) drogue *f*; *Sp* doping *m*, stimulant *m*; **d. test** test *m* antidopage *ou* antidoping; **to fail/take a d. test** être déclaré positif à/subir un test antidopage *ou* antidoping (**b**) *F* (*idiot*) crétin, -ine; **what a d.!** quelle nouille!, quel andouille! (**c**) *Old-fashioned Sl* (*information*) rencard *m*, tuyau *m*; **to give sb the d. on sth** rencarder qn sur qch (**d**) *Av, Aut* (*varnish*) enduit *m* (**e**) (*in petrol*) additif *m*, dopant *m*; (*for explosives*) absorbant *m*

dope² *vt* (**a**) (*drug*) (*person, horse*) (*to prevent from winning*) droguer; (*to increase chances*) doper; (*drink*) verser une drogue dans (**b**) *Av, Aut* (*varnish*) enduire (**c**) *Aut* **doped fuel** carburant dopé *ou* additionné d'anti-détonant

dopehead ['dəʊphed] *n Sl* (*drug user*) camé, -ée

dopey ['dəʊpɪ] *adj F* (**a**) (*drugged*) drogué; (*from sleep*) endormi (**b**) (*stupid*) stupide; **what a d. thing to say** que c'était stupide de dire une chose pareille

doping ['dəʊpɪŋ] *n* (**a**) (*to incapacitate*) administration *f* d'un narcotique (**of** à); (*to increase chances of winning*) dopage *m*, doping *m* (**b**) *Av, Aut* (*varnishing*) enduisage *m* (**c**) *Petr* (*of fuel*) dopage *m*

Doppler effect ['dɒplər] *n Phys* effet *m* Doppler

Doric ['dɒrɪk] *adj, n Archit* dorique *m*; *Ling* écossais *m*

dork [dɔ:k] *n F* (*idiot*) abruti, -ie

dorm [dɔ:m] *n Sch F* dortoir *m*

dormant ['dɔ:mənt] *adj* (**a**) (*passion etc*) assoupi, endormi; (*conflict*) latent; **to lie d.** être en sommeil; *Banking* **d. account** compte *m* sans mouvement (**b**) (*plant, bud*) dormant (**c**) (*volcano*) en repos

dormer (window) ['dɔ:mər] *n* fenêtre *f* en mansarde

dormitory ['dɔ:mɪt(ə)rɪ] *n* (**a**) dortoir *m*; **d. town** cité-dortoir *f*, *pl* cités-dortoirs (**b**) *Am Univ* (*residence*) maison *f ou* foyer *m* d'étudiants

dormouse, *pl* **-mice** ['dɔ:maʊs, -maɪs] *n Zool* loir *m*

dorsal ['dɔ:s(ə)l] *adj* dorsal; *Anat* (*towards back of body*) postérieur; **d. fin** (*of fish*) nageoire *f* dorsale

dory ['dɔ:rɪ] *n* (**a**) (*fish*) **(John) D.** dorée *f*, saint-pierre *m inv* (**b**) *Am* (*boat*) doris *m*

DOS [dɒs] *n Comptr* (*abbr* **disk operating system**) DOS *m*; **DOS command** commande *f* du DOS; **DOS prompt** indicatif *m* (du) DOS, invite *f* du DOS; **DOS switch** clé *f ou* paramètre *m* du DOS

dosage ['dəʊsɪdʒ] *n* (*of medicine*) dosage *m*, posologie *f*

dose¹ [dəʊs] *n* (**a**) *Med, Nucl Phys* dose *f*; **she's bearable in small doses** elle est supportable à petites doses; *F* **to get through sth like a d. of salts** faire qch en deux temps trois mouvements *ou* en deux coups de cuillère à pot; **that curry went through me like a d. of salts** ce curry est passé tout droit (**b**) *F* (*bout*) (*of flu etc*) attaque *f* (**c**) *Sl* (*venereal disease*) vérole *f*

dose² *vt* (**a**) (*person*) administrer un médicament à; **to d. oneself with quinine** se bourrer de quinine (**b**) (*medicine*) doser

▶ **dose up** *vt F* bourrer (**with** de)

dosh [dɒʃ] *n Br Sl* (*money*) fric *m*

doss¹ [dɒs] *n Br Sl* (**a**) (*bed*) lit *m*, pieu *m*; **I'm looking for a d. for tonight** je cherche un endroit où dormir ce soir (**b**) (*sleep*) somme *m*, roupillon *m*; **to have a d.** faire un somme (**c**) **it was a real d.** (*easy*) c'était de la tarte *ou* du gâteau

doss² *vi Br Sl* (*sleep*) pieuter; (*in doss house*) coucher à l'asile de nuit

▶ **doss around** *vi Br Sl* (*hang around*) se la couler douce

▶ **doss down** *vi Br Sl* (*sleep*) se coucher, se pieuter; **do you mind dossing down on the floor?** est-ce que ça t'embête de coucher par terre?; **I need somewhere to d. down for the night** j'ai besoin d'un endroit où coucher cette nuit

dosser ['dɒsər] *n Br Sl* (**a**) (*person*) clochard, -arde (**b**) (*place*) asile *m* de nuit

doss-house *n Br Sl* asile *m* de nuit

dossier ['dɒsɪeɪ, -ɪər] *n* dossier *m*; **to keep a d. on sb** avoir un dossier sur qn

dot[1] [dɒt] *n* (*in dotted line, over the letter i etc*) point *m*; *Mus* point d'augmentation; **'i' with two dots** 'i' surmonté de deux points; **dots and dashes** (*morse code*) points et traits; *F* **on the d.** (*to arrive*) à l'heure tapante; **on the d. of three o'clock, at three o'clock on the d.** à trois heures pile; *F* **since the year d.** depuis des siècles; *F* **that was in the year d.** c'était il y a une éternité; *F* **but she left early, d. d. d.** mais elle est partie de bonne heure, si vous voyez ce que je veux dire; *Comptr* **d. command** commande *f* avec point; *Comptr* **d. prompt** repère *m* de saisie de commandes

dot[2] *vt* (-tt-) **(a)** (*an i*) mettre un point sur; *Fig* **to d. one's i's (and cross one's t's)** mettre les points sur les i **(b)** (*surface*) marquer de points; (*drawing*) pointiller; **dotted with flowers/***etc* (*of surface etc*) parsemé de fleurs/*etc*; **his shirt was dotted with flecks of tomato sauce** sa chemise était tachetée de sauce tomate; **the islands are dotted all round the coast** les îles sont éparpillées tout autour de la côte **(c)** *Mus* (*note*) pointer **(d)** *Old-fashioned F* **to d. and carry one** (*when walking*) boiter **(e)** *Sl* **to d. sb one** (*hit*) flanquer un gnon à qn

dotage ['dəʊtɪdʒ] *n* gâtisme *m*; **to be in one's d.** être gâteux

dote [dəʊt] *vi* être gâteux

▶ **dote on, dote upon** *vipo* (*sb*) adorer

doting ['dəʊtɪŋ] *adj attrib* (*parents, grandparents*) qui montre une tendresse *ou* une indulgence exagérée; **a d. husband** un mari qui gâte sa femme

dot matrix (printer) *n* imprimante *f* matricielle, matricielle *f*

dotted ['dɒtɪd] *adj* **(a)** (*contour*) pointillé; **d. line** (ligne *f* en) pointillé *m*, ligne pointillée; **to sign on the d. line** (*on form*) signer à l'endroit indiqué; *Fig* donner son consentement; **tear along the d. line** déchirer en suivant les pointillés **(b)** *Mus* (*note*) pointé

dottle ['dɒt(ə)l] *n* (*in pipe*) culot *m*

dotty ['dɒtɪ] *adj F* toqué, piqué; **he's d. about her** il est toqué *ou* fou d'elle; **I'm not d. about him** je ne raffole pas de lui; **she wasn't d. about moving house** l'idée de déménager ne l'enchantait pas

double[1] ['dʌb(ə)l] **1** *adj* **(a)** (*having two, two together*) double; **'all' is spelt 'a, d. l'** 'all' s'écrit 'a, deux l'; **d. two d. three** (*when giving telephone number, address*) vingt-deux trente-trois; **to reach d. figures** (*of inflation etc*) atteindre les deux chiffres; *Br Univ* **she took a d. first in English and History** elle a deux licences avec mention très bien, une en anglais et l'autre en histoire; *Am* **to go on a d. date** sortir à deux couples; *F* **d. ace** (*in dicing, dominoes*) double-as *m*, *pl* doubles-as; *Mus* **d. bassoon** contrebasson *m*; **d. bed** grand lit *m*, lit pour deux personnes; **d. bedroom** chambre *f* pour deux personnes; *Cin* **d. bill** *or* **feature** double programme *m*; **d. boiler** *or* **saucepan** bain-marie *m*, *pl* bains-marie; **d. chin** double menton *m*; *Br* **d. cream** crème *f* épaisse, *Can* crème à fouetter; *Comptr* **d. density (disk)** disquette *f* (à) double densité; *Tennis* **d. fault** double faute *f*; *Tennis* **to d. fault** faire une double faute; *Biol* **d. helix** double hélice *f*; *Am* **d. indemnity** (*in insurance*) indemnité *f* double; *Med* **d. incontinence** incontinence *f* double; **d. knitting (wool)** grosse laine *f*; *St Exch* **d. option** stellage *m*; *Journ* **d. page spread** page *f* centrale, double page; (*advert*) pub *f* double page; **d. pneumonia** pneumonie *f* double; **to have d. pneumonia** faire une pneumonie double; *Typ* **d. quotes** guillemets *mpl*; **d. sided** (*disk etc*) à deux faces, à double face; **d. sink** évier *m* à deux bacs; *Typ* **d. spacing** double interligne *m*; *Comptr* **d. strike** double passage *m* (de la tête d'impression); **d. strike printing** impression *f* à double frappe; **d. time** *Ind* = multiplication *f* par deux du salaire horaire (des employés travaillant pendant le week-end etc); *US Mil* pas *m* redoublé, pas de course; **in d. time** au pas de gymnastique, au pas de course; *Typ* **d. underlining** double soulignement *m*; **d. whisky, d. Scotch** double (dose *f* de) whisky *m*; **to have a d. yolk** (*of egg*) avoir deux jaunes

(b) (*misleading, ambiguous*) double; **with a d. meaning** à deux *ou* double sens; (*ambiguous*) ambigu, -uë; **to play a d. game** jouer double jeu; **to lead a d. life** mener une double vie; **to apply a d. standard** utiliser deux poids, deux mesures

2 *adv* **to see d.** voir double; **to fold a sheet (of paper) d.** plier une feuille en deux; **bent d.** (*of person*) courbé en deux; **bent d. with pain/laughter** plié en deux de douleur/rire; **d. the number** le double, deux fois autant; **it took me d. the time I expected** ça m'a pris le double du temps que je pensais; **to pay d. (the price)** payer le double (du prix); **I am d. your age** je suis deux fois plus âgé que vous, j'ai deux fois votre âge

3 *n* **(a)** (*of person*) double *m*, *F* sosie *m*; *Th, Cin* doublure *f*

(b) *F* (*hotel room*) chambre *f* à deux personnes

(c) (*measure of drink*) double *m*; **make mine a d.** un double pour moi

(d) *Tennis* **men's/women's/mixed doubles** double *m* messieurs/dames/mixte; **a doubles match** un double; **to play doubles** jouer des doubles

(e) *Horseracing* pari *m* couplé; **to bring off a d.** réussir un double

(f) *Cards* (*at bridge*) contre *m*; (*at dominoes*) double *m*; *Billiards* doublé *m*; **d. or quits** quitte ou double

(g) on *or* **at the d.** *Mil* au pas de gymnastique, au pas de course; *Fig* (*quickly*) en moins de deux; (*immediately, right away*) tout de suite, sur-le-champ

double[2] **1** *vt* **(a)** (*increase*) (*amount, salary etc*) doubler; (*figure*) porter au double, multiplier par deux; **to d. the stakes** doubler la mise **(b)** (*fold*) (*paper, blanket etc*) plier en deux; (*thread*) doubler **(c)** *Cards* (*at bridge*) contrer; *Billiards* **to d. the red** doubler la rouge **(d)** *Naut* (*headland*) doubler **2** *vi* **(a)** (*of population, salary etc*) doubler; **to d. in value** doubler de valeur **(b) to d. as** servir de; **the smallest bedroom doubles as my study** la chambre la plus petite se sert également de bureau; *Th* **to d. as sb** jouer qn en plus d'un rôle principal

▶ **double back 1** *vtsep* (*blanket etc*) replier, rabattre **2** *vi* **to d. back (on one's tracks)** (*of person, hunted animal etc*) revenir sur ses pas; **to d. back on itself** (*of road*) tourner en épingle à cheveux

▶ **double for** *vipo* remplacer; *Th* doubler; *Cin* (*of stuntman*) être la doublure de

▶ **double over 1** *vi* se plier; **to d. over with pain** se plier en deux de douleur, se tordre de douleur **2** *vtsep* replier, rabattre

▶ **double up 1** *vi* **(a)** (*bend over*) se plier (en deux), se courber (en deux); **to d. up with laughter/pain** se tordre de rire/douleur **(b)** (*share room*) partager une chambre **2** *vtsep* **(a)** (*paper, material etc*) plier en deux **(b)** (*of blow, pain etc*) (*person*) faire plier en deux

double-acting *adj MecE* à double effet

double agent *n* agent *m* double

double-barrelled ['dʌb(ə)l'bærəld] *adj* (*shotgun*) à deux coups; **d. name** patronymique *m* double (*par exemple Mr J. Wynn-Jones*)

double bass *n Mus* contrebasse *f*

double bind *n* impasse *f*; *Psych* double contrainte *f*; **to be caught in a d.** être dans une impasse

double-blind *adj Med* **d. test** test *m* à double insu

double bluff *n* = technique *f* consistant à faire croire qu'on bluffe alors qu'on dit la vérité; **it was a d. on her part** elle voulait lui/nous/*etc* faire croire qu'elle bluffait

double-book **1** *vt* (*seat, room*) réserver pour deux personnes différentes, sur-réserver; **we've been double-booked again** nous sommes encore en double réservation; **I've double-booked myself for next Friday** (*doing two things*) je me suis engagé à faire deux choses différentes vendredi prochain **2** *vi* (*of hotel, airline*) faire une/des double(s) réservation(s)

double-booking *n* double réservation *f*

double-bottomed ['dʌb(ə)l'bɒtəmd] *adj* (*saucepan, suitcase etc*) à double fond; (*dinghy etc*) à double coque

double-breasted ['dʌb(ə)l'brestɪd] *adj* (*jacket*) croisé

double-check *vti* revérifier

double click *n Comptr* double-clic *m*

double-click *vi Comptr* cliquer deux fois, faire un double-clic

double-clutch *vi US Aut* faire un double débrayage

double-cross[1] *vt F* doubler, trahir

double-cross[2] *n F* trahison *f*, tromperie *f*

double-crosser ['dʌb(ə)l'krɒsər] *n* traître *m*

double-dealer *n* fourbe *m*

double-dealing **1** *n* duplicité *f* **2** *adj* déloyal

double-decker *n* **(a)** *Br* (*bus*) autobus *m* à impériale **(b)** *esp Am* (*sandwich*) sandwich *m* double

double-declutch *vi Br Aut* faire un double débrayage

double-declutching ['dʌb(ə)ldiː'klʌtʃɪŋ] *n Br Aut* double débrayage *m*

double Dutch *n Br Fig* charabia *m*; **to talk d.** baragouiner; *Fig* **it's all d. to me** (*what they're saying*) je ne comprends rien à ce baragouin, pour moi c'est du charabia; (*this topic*) c'est de l'hébreu pour moi

double-edged *adj* (*sword, compliment, argument*) à deux tranchants

double entendre [duːb(ə)lɑːn'tɑːndrə] *n Pej* ambiguïté *f*, équivoque *f*

double entry book-keeping *n Com* comptabilité *f* en partie double

double exposure *n Phot* surimpression *f*

double-faced ['dʌb(ə)l'feɪst] *adj* **(a)** *Tex* réversible **(b)** *Pej* (*person*) à double face, hypocrite
double-glaze *vt* **to have the windows double-glazed** poser du double vitrage; **they've just had their house double-glazed** ils viennent de faire poser du double vitrage chez eux
double-glazed *adj* à double vitrage
double-glazing *n* double vitrage *m*; **to put in d.** installer *ou* poser du double vitrage
double-headed *adj* à deux têtes, *Spec* bicéphale; *TV* (*programme*) animé par deux présentateurs; *Her* **d. eagle** aigle *f* à deux têtes; **d. coin** pièce *f* de monnaie à deux faces
double-header *n Am Sp* = deux matchs disputés l'un après l'autre
double-jointed *adj* (*person, limb*) désarticulé
double-lock *vt* (*door etc*) fermer à double tour
double negative *n Gram* double négation *f*
double occupancy *n* (*of a hotel room*) occupation *f* double
double-park *vti Aut* stationner en double file
double parking *n* stationnement *m* en double file
double-pointed *adj Knitting* **d. needle** aiguille *f* à double pointe
double-quick *adj, adv* **in d. time, d.** *Mil* au pas de gymnastique; *F* (*very quickly*) en moins de rien; (*immediately, right away*) tout de suite, sur-le-champ
double-space *vt* (*write/type*) (*text*) écrire/taper en double interligne, mettre en double interligne; **double-spaced** en double interligne
double-speak *n* propos *mpl* ambigus *ou* équivoques; **rationalization is just d. for more unemployment** rationalisation n'est qu'un euphémisme pour plus de chômage
double-stop *vi* (**-pp-**) *Mus* (*on violin*) faire des doubles-cordes
double-stopping *n Mus* double-corde *f*
doublet ['dʌblɪt] *n* **(a)** *Ling* doublet *m* **(b)** *Hist* (*jacket*) pourpoint *m*, justaucorps *m*
double take *n* **(a)** *TV, Cin* double prise *f* **(b)** *F* **to do a d.** marquer un temps d'arrêt
double talk *n* propos *mpl* ambigus *ou* équivoques
double-think *n* raisonnement *m* contradictoire
double vision *n* double vision *f*; **to have d.** voir double
double whammy ['wæmɪ] *n F* **the Tories' d.** les deux fléaux des Conservateurs; **to be caught in a d.** être dans une impasse
double white line *n* (*on a road*) double ligne *f* blanche (*d'interdiction de doubler*); (*in France*) ≈ ligne blanche
double yellow line *n Br* (*on a road*) double ligne *f* jaune (*qui indique une zone de stationnement interdit*)
doubling ['dʌblɪŋ] *n* (*of number etc*) doublement *m*
doubly ['dʌb(ə)lɪ] *adv* doublement; **to be d. careful/interested** redoubler de prudence/d'intérêt
doubt¹ [daʊt] *n* doute *m*; **to be in d.** (*of person*) être en *ou* dans le doute; (*of future, event*) être douteux *ou* incertain; **I'm in no d. as to ...** je ne doute absolument pas de ...; **to raise doubts in sb's mind** soulever des doutes dans l'esprit de qn; **the whole thing raised doubts about his abilities** toute cette affaire a mis ses capacités en question; **when in d.** dans le doute; **to cast doubt(s) on sth** mettre qch en doute; **to have one's doubts about sth** avoir des doutes sur *ou* au sujet de qch; **I have my doubts whether this is true** je doute que cela soit vrai; **beyond (a shadow of a) d.** hors de doute; **the facts have been established beyond (all) d.** ces faits ont été avérés sans le moindre doute; **no d. he will come** il viendra sans doute; **there is** *or* **seems to be no d. that ...** il ne semble faire aucun doute que ...; **there is no d. about her guilt** il n'y a aucun doute sur sa culpabilité; **there is some d. about her guilt** il y a des doutes quant à sa culpabilité; **is there any d. in your mind?** est-ce qu'il y a un doute dans votre esprit?; **do you have any doubts?** est-ce que vous avez des doutes?; (*about getting married etc*) est-ce que vous hésitez?; **I have no doubts** je n'ai aucun doute; **to leave no (room for) d.** ne laisser aucun doute (**that** sur le fait que); **without (a** *or* **any** *or* **the slightest) d.** sans aucun doute
doubt² **1** *vt* (*person*) douter de; (*person's word*) douter de, mettre en doute; **I d. we'll be hearing** *or* **I d. if we'll hear from him again** je doute que nous entendions à nouveau parler de lui; **I d. it** j'en doute; **he made me d. the evidence of my own eyes** il m'a fait douter de ce que je voyais de mes propres yeux; **I d. whether** *or* **if he will come** je doute qu'il vienne **2** *vi* (*have doubts*) douter
doubter ['daʊtər] *n* sceptique *mf*
doubtful ['daʊtfʊl] *adj* **(a)** (*undecided*) (*person*) indécis, incertain; (*future, outcome, weather*) incertain; **to be d. of** *or* **about sth** avoir des doutes sur qch; **I'm d. about going** j'hésite à y aller; **I'm d. about the wisdom/advisability of it** je doute que ce soit bien sage/conseillé; **it is d. whether ...** il est douteux *ou* à douter que ...
(b) (*questionable*) (*character, appearance*) équivoque, suspect; (*origin, decision, food*) douteux; **in d. taste** d'un goût douteux; **John's a bit d. for Saturday** il n'est pas sûr qu'on puisse compter sur John samedi; **she's a d. starter (for the race)** il n'est pas certain qu'elle prenne le départ (de la course); *Fin* **d. debt** client *m* douteux, créance *f* douteuse
doubtfully ['daʊtfʊlɪ] *adv* (*to say*) d'un ton dubitatif, dubitativement; (*to watch*) d'un air dubitatif; (*to stand etc*) en hésitant, d'une façon indécise
doubting ['daʊtɪŋ] *adj* incrédule, sceptique; *Bible* **d. Thomas** Thomas l'incrédule; **you're always such a d. Thomas** tu es toujours tellement sceptique
doubtless(ly) ['daʊtlɪs(lɪ)] *adv* **(a)** (*certainly*) sans aucun doute **(b)** (*probably*) sans doute, sûrement
douche¹ [du:ʃ] *n* **(a)** (*cleansing*) douche *f*; *Med* lavage *m* interne; (*as contraceptive*) douche vaginale; **to be like a d. of cold water** faire l'effet d'une douche froide **(b)** *Med* (*instrument*) poire *f* à injection
douche² *vt* doucher
dough [dəʊ] *n* **(a)** (*for bread etc*) pâte *f* **(b)** *Old-fashioned Sl* (*money*) fric *m*, pognon *m*
doughboy ['dəʊbɔɪ] *n US Hist* soldat *m* américain de la première guerre mondiale
doughnut ['dəʊnʌt] *n Culin* beignet *m*, *Can* beigne *m*; **jam d.** beignet à la confiture
doughty ['daʊtɪ] *adj Arch, Lit* vaillant
doughy ['dəʊɪ] *adj* **(a)** (*bread*) pâteux **(b)** *Fig* (*face*) terreux
dour [dʊər] *adj* austère, sévère
douse [daʊs] *vt* **(a)** (*splash*) (*person, object*) arroser, asperger (**with** de); (*plunge*) plonger, tremper; **he doused himself with** *or* **in aftershave** il s'est aspergé d'après-rasage **(b)** (*extinguish*) (*light, fire*) éteindre
dove [dʌv] **1** *n* (*bird*) colombe *f*; **ring d.** (pigeon *m*) ramier *m*, palombe *f*; **d. of peace** colombe de la paix; *Pol* **the doves and the hawks** les colombes et les faucons **2** *adj* **d.(-coloured** *or* **-grey)** colombin, gorge-de-pigeon *inv*
dovecote ['dʌvkɒt] *n* colombier *m*, pigeonnier *m*
Dover ['dəʊvər] *n* Douvres; **the Straits of D.** le Pas de Calais
dovetail¹ ['dʌvteɪl] *n Carp* queue-d'aronde *f*, *pl* queues-d'aronde; **d. (joint)** assemblage *m* à queue-d'aronde
dovetail² **1** *vt Carp* assembler à queue-d'aronde; **dovetailed joint** assemblage *m* à queue-d'aronde; *Fig* **to d. two schemes (together** *or* **into each other)** harmoniser deux projets **2** *vi* (*of schemes etc*) se rejoindre, se raccorder (**with** à)
dovish ['dʌvɪʃ] *adj esp US Pol* (*person*) partisan de la manière douce; (*speech*) conciliateur
dowager ['daʊədʒər] *n* douairière *f*; **d. duchess** duchesse douairière; *F* **d.'s hump** = bosse *f* qui se développe chez les femmes d'un certain âge suite à une carence de calcium
dowdiness ['daʊdɪnɪs] *n* manque *m* d'élégance *ou* de chic
dowdy ['daʊdɪ] *adj* peu élégant; (*dress, image*) démodé
dowel ['daʊəl] *n Carp, Tech* (*location device*) téton *m* (de positionnement); **d. (pin)** (*wooden*) cheville *f*, goujon *m*, tourillon *m*
dowelling ['daʊəlɪŋ] *n* (*material*) bois *m* à goujons *ou* tourillons
dower ['daʊər] *n* **d. house** maison *f* assignée en douaire
Dow-Jones ['daʊ'dʒəʊnz] *n St Exch* **D. average** *or* **index** index *m* Dow Jones
Down [daʊn] *n Med* **D.'s syndrome** mongolisme *m*, *Spec* trisomie *f*; **D.'s syndrome baby** bébé *m* mongolien *ou Spec* trisomique
down¹ [daʊn] **1** *adv* **(a)** (*motion*) vers le bas; **I'll be d. in a minute** je descends dans une minute; **to lay d. one's arms** mettre bas les armes; **to shoot** *or* **bring d. an aircraft** abattre *ou F* descendre un avion; **to fall d.** tomber à terre *ou* par terre; **d. to the ground** jusqu'à terre; *F* **it suits me d. to the ground** ça me va parfaitement; **d. with traitors!** à bas les traîtres!; **d. with it!** (*of medicine etc*) avalez!; **d.!** (*to dog*) couché!; **d. you go!** allez, descends!
(b) (*in crossword*) verticalement; **I can't get five d.** je ne trouve pas le cinq vertical
(c) (*position, level*) **d. below** en bas, en contre-bas; **d. there** là-bas; **d. here** ici; **further d.** plus bas; **d. under** aux antipodes; *US* **d. South** dans les États du sud; **the blinds were d.** les stores étaient baissés; **to lay sth face d.** placer qch face en dessous *ou* à l'envers; **head d.** la tête en bas; *Fig* **to hit a man when he's d.** frapper un homme à terre; **she's d. with flu** elle est grippée; *F* **that gets me d.** ça me déprime; *Tel* **the lines are d.** les lignes sont coupées; **the wind is d.** le vent est tombé *ou* s'est apaisé; **the river is d.** la

rivière est basse; **the price of gold is d.** le prix de l'or a baissé; **he's £20 d. on the deal** il en est pour 20 livres de sa poche; **bookings are d. on last week's** les réservations sont en baisse par rapport à la semaine dernière; **takings are several hundred pounds d. on last year** les recettes ont baissé de plusieurs centaines de livres par rapport à l'année dernière; *Fin* **to be d. 12% as against last year** être en baisse de 12% par rapport à l'année précédente; **your team is five-two d.** ton équipe est en train de perdre par cinq à deux

(d) (*order, time*) **everyone from the boss d.** tout le monde, y compris le patron; **from prince d. to beggar** du prince jusqu'au mendiant; **I'm d. to my last cigarette/cheque** j'en suis à ma dernière cigarette/mon dernier chèque; **d. to recent times** jusqu'au temps présent; **d. to here** (en descendant) jusqu'ici; **one d., nine to go!** un de moins, plus que neuf!

(e) (*in writing*) **to put** *or* **get sth d. (in writing)** coucher *ou* mettre qch par écrit; **if I was you, I'd get that d. in writing** *or* **on paper** (*as opposed to taking sb's word for it*) à ta place, j'essaierais d'obtenir ça noir sur blanc; **there's nothing d. on paper yet** il n'y a encore rien d'officiel; **but there's nothing d. on paper to that effect** mais il n'y a aucun écrit à cet effet; **she's d. for 20 boxes** (*has reserved*) elle a réservé 20 boîtes; **she's d. for £20** (*has agreed to donate*) elle est inscrite pour une cotisation de 20 livres; **he's d. for the 100 metres** il est inscrit pour le 100 mètres; **I've got you d. to present the bouquet** tu as été désigné pour offrir le bouquet

(f) (*phrases*) **to be d. on sb** en vouloir à qn; **to be d. (in the mouth)** être découragé *ou* déprimé; **you look very d.** tu as l'air très déprimé; *Comptr* **to be d.** être en panne; **it's d. to you whether or not we go** (*it's your decision*) c'est à toi de décider si nous y allons ou pas; **this is all d. to you!** (*your fault*) tout cela est de ta faute!; **our lack of cash is all d. to the repairs to the roof** (*is attributable to*) notre manque d'argent est entièrement dû aux réparations du toit; **it was d. to his hard work that we managed to finish** c'est grâce à son travail acharné que nous avons réussi à terminer; **money d., cash d.** argent (au) comptant *ou* sur table; **you can have it for £50 d.** c'est à vous pour 50 livres au comptant; **to go d. by the bows** (*of ship*) piquer de l'avant

2 *prep* **to slide d. sth** glisser le long de qch; **the tears ran d. his face** les larmes lui coulaient le long des joues; **d. the side of his trousers/the box** le long de son pantalon/de la boîte; **to go d. the street/a hill** descendre la rue/une colline; **to fall d. the stairs** tomber en bas de l'escalier; *F* **get that d. you** (*food, drink*) avale ça!; *F* **he's gone d. the pub** il est allé au pub; *F* **to go d. the shops** aller en courses; **they live further d. the street** ils habitent plus bas dans cette rue; *Lit* **d. the centuries/years** au long des siècles/années; *Rail* **d. the line** en aval

3 *adj* **(a)** (*depressed*) découragé, déprimé

(b) *Old-fashioned Rail* **d. train** train descendant

(c) *Comptr* **d. arrow** flèche *f* vers le bas

4 *n F* **to have a d. on sb** en vouloir à qn

down² *vt* **(a)** (*person*) terrasser; *Boxing* (*opponent*) abattre; (*aircraft*) descendre, abattre **(b)** *Ind* **to d. tools** cesser le travail **(c)** *F* **to d. a drink** s'envoyer un verre; **he downed his beer and left** il a descendu sa bière et est parti; **to d. sth in one (go)** *or* **in a oner** avaler qch d'un coup

down³ *n* (*on bird, person, fruit*) duvet *m*; (*on plant*) poil *m*, coton *m*, duvet *m*

down⁴ *n Geog* (*usu pl*) **downs** chaîne *f* de collines crétacées; *Br* **the (North/South) Downs** les Downs *mpl*

down-and-out 1 *adj* **to be d.** être sans le sou **2** *n* clochard, -arde

down-at-heel *adj* **(a)** (*shoe*) éculé **(b)** (*person*) miteux

downbeat ['daʊnbiːt] **1** *n Mus* (temps *m*) frappé *m* **2** *adj F* **(a)** (*gloomy*) (*ending, story*) triste; (*speech, person*) pessimiste **(b)** (*relaxed*) relaxe

downcast ['daʊnkɑːst] *adj* **(a)** (*person*) abattu, déprimé; **there's no need to be so d.** il ne faut pas se laisser abattre *ou* se décourager comme ça; **to look d.** avoir l'air découragé **(b)** (*look, eyes etc*) baissé

downdraught, *US* **down draft** ['daʊndrɑːft] *n Met* courant *m* d'air descendant; *Aut* **d. carburettor** carburateur *m* inversé

downer ['daʊnər] *n Sl* **(a)** (*drug*) tranquillisant *m* **(b)** (*depressing situation, experience*) **to be on a d.** avoir le moral à zéro, être au trente-sixième dessous; **she's a real d.** elle vous met le moral à zéro; **it was a real d. to find out I hadn't even got an interview** ça m'a mis le moral complètement à zéro de savoir que je n'avais même pas obtenu d'entretien

downfall ['daʊnfɔːl] *n* (*of person*) ruine *f*; (*of government etc*) écroulement *m*, effondrement *m*; **drink brought about** *or* **was his d.** la boisson l'a perdu

downgrade¹ ['daʊngreɪd] *n esp Am* descente *f*, déclivité *f*; *Fig* **to be on the d.** baisser, être sur le déclin *ou F* sur le retour

downgrade² *vt* (*move to lower position*) (*employee*) rétrograder, déclasser à une échelle de salaire inférieure; (*goods*) classer dans une catégorie inférieure; **he was downgraded to area manager** il a été rétrogradé au rang de responsable régional; **the hurricane has been downgraded to a storm** l'ouragan n'est maintenant plus qu'une tempête

downgrading ['daʊngreɪdɪŋ] *n* (*of employee*) déclassement *m* à une échelle de salaire inférieure, rétrogradation *f*; (*of goods*) classement *m* dans une catégorie inférieure

downhearted [daʊn'hɑːtɪd] *adj* découragé, déprimé; **don't be d.!** ne te décourage pas!, ne te laisse pas abattre!; **to become d.** se décourager

downhill ['daʊn'hɪl] **1** *n* **(a)** descente *f*, pente *f* **(b)** *Ski* descente *f* **2** *adj* (*slope*) descendante; **the d. journey** la descente **3** *adv* **to go d.** (*of road, car*) descendre; *Fig F* (*of person*) être sur le déclin; (*of business etc*) péricliter; (*of sb's work*) devenir moins bon; **it's d. all the way** ça descend tout le long du chemin; *Hum* **it's d. all the way after you're 40** après 40 ans, c'est le déclin; **after January it'll be d. all the way** (*easier*) après janvier le pire sera passé

downhill skier *n* descendeur, -euse

downhill skiing *n* ski *m* alpin *ou* de descente

Downing Street ['daʊnɪŋstriːt] *n Br Pol* = résidence officielle du Premier ministre (no. 10) et du Ministre des Finances (no. 11); **there has been no confirmation from D.** le Premier ministre n'a pas apporté de confirmation

download¹ ['daʊnləʊd] *n Comptr* téléchargement *m*

download² **1** *vt* télécharger; **d. font** police *f* téléchargeable **2** *vi* se télécharger

downloadable [daʊn'ləʊdəb(ə)l] *adj Comptr* téléchargeable

down-market 1 *adj* (*car, house etc*) bas de gamme; (*person*) ordinaire; (*district, accent*) populaire **2** *adv* **to move d.** passer au bas de gamme; (*go to a cheap restaurant etc*) donner dans le populaire

down payment *n Fin* acompte *m*, versement *m* à la commande; **to make a d.** verser un acompte **(on sth** pour qch**)**

downpipe ['daʊnpaɪp] *n Constr* tuyau *m* de descente

downplay [daʊn'pleɪ] *vt* minimiser

downpour ['daʊnpɔːr] *n* forte pluie *f*, averse *f*

downright ['daʊnraɪt] **1** *adv* (*idiotic etc*) tout à fait, complètement; (*rude, disgusting, nosy*) carrément **2** *adj* **(a)** (*complete, absolute*) (*stupidity, carelessness, dishonesty*) absolu; (*lie*) éclatant; **d. fool** parfait *ou* franc imbécile **(b)** (*blunt, frank*) (*person, language*) direct, franc, *f* franche

downshift ['daʊnʃɪft] *vi Aut* rétrograder

downside ['daʊnsaɪd] *n* désavantage *m* **(to sth** de qch**)**; **there's a d. to everything** toute médaille a son revers; **on the d., however, the situation has worsened in the South** mais par contre la situation a empiré dans le sud; **on the d., we'll have to sleep in the train** le désavantage, c'est que nous devrons dormir dans le train

downsize [daʊn'saɪz] **1** *vt Electron* microniser; (*project*) réduire l'envergure de; (*of designers*) (*car*) réduire les dimensions de; **downsized car** voiture aux dimensions réduites **2** *vi* (*of company*) réduire ses effectifs

downsizing [daʊn'saɪzɪŋ] *n* **(a)** *Electron* micronisation *f* **(b)** (*of company*) réduction *f* des effectifs

downspout ['daʊnspaʊt] *n* tuyau *m* de descente

downstage ['daʊnsteɪdʒ] *Th* **1** *adv, adj* sur le devant (de la scène), à l'avant-scène; **to stand d. of sb** se tenir plus en avant que qn sur la scène; **take two paces d.** fais deux pas vers le devant de la scène **2** *n* avant-scène *f*

downstairs 1 [daʊn'steəz] *adv* **(a)** (*down the stairs*) en bas; **to come/go d.** descendre (l'escalier); **to run d.** descendre (l'escalier) en courant **(b)** (*on a lower floor*) en bas; **our neighbours d.** nos voisins d'en-dessous **2** ['daʊnsteəz] *adj* **the d. rooms** les pièces d'en bas *ou* du bas **3** ['daʊnsteəz] *n* l'étage *m* du bas

downstate ['daʊnsteɪt] *US* **1** *adj* **in d. New York** dans le sud de l'État de New York **2** *adv* au sud de l'État

downstream 1 *adv* [daʊn'striːm] en aval, à l'aval **(from** de**)**; **a few miles d. from here** quelques miles en aval d'ici **2** *adj* ['daʊnstriːm] d'aval; *TV* **d. keyer** incrustateur *m* après mélange; *Petr* **d. operations** opérations *fpl* en aval

downstroke ['daʊnstrəʊk] *n* **(a)** (*in writing*) plein *m* **(b)** *MecE* course *f* descendante; (*of piston*) mouvement *m* de descente **(c)** *Orn* (*of wing*) abaissée *f*

downswept ['daʊnswept] *adj Av* (*wings*) surbaissé

downswing ['daʊnswɪŋ] *n* (*in economy etc*) tendance *f* à la baisse

down time *n* (*of machine*) temps *m* de non-disponibilité *ou* d'immobilisation; (*unproductive time*) perte *f* de temps

down-to-earth *adj* (*person, approach, attitude*) terre(-)à(-)terre *inv*, réaliste

downtown ['daʊn'taʊn] *Am* **1** *adv* dans/vers (le centre de) la ville; **he gave me a lift d.** il m'a descendu en ville; **to live d.** habiter en ville **2** *adj* **d. New York** le centre de New York; **d. theatres** théâtres *mpl* du centre **3** *n* (*of town*) centre *m*

downtrodden ['daʊntrɒd(ə)n] *adj* (**a**) *Fig* (*people, wife etc*) opprimé (**b**) (*grass etc*) piétiné

downturn ['daʊntɜːn] *n* (*in inflation, unemployment figures*) baisse *f*; (*in economy*) ralentissement *m*; **to take a d.** (*of economy*) ralentir; (*of inflation, unemployment*) baisser; **their fortunes took a sudden d. when ...** leur fortune a connu un soudain revers quand ...

downward ['daʊnwəd] **1** *adj* (*movement, path*) descendant; **to take a d. glance** *or* **look at sth** jeter un coup d'œil par en dessous à qch; *Fig* **to be on the d. path** aller à sa perte; *Fin* **d. movement** mouvement *m* de baisse; **d. trend** (*in prices etc*) tendance *f* à la baisse **2** *adv* = **downwards**

downward-compatible *adj Comptr* compatible vers le bas

downwards ['daʊnwədz] *adv* vers le bas, en descendant; (*on river*) en aval; (*to look*) en bas; **to slope d.** descendre; **to lay sth face d.** placer qch face en dessous; **from the twelfth century d.** à partir du *ou* depuis le douzième siècle; **children of five and d.** enfants de cinq ans et au-dessous; **every member of the cabinet, from the Prime Minister d.** tout le monde, du Premier ministre au dernier membre du gouvernement

downwind **1** *adv* [daʊn'wɪnd] *Av* (*to land*) vent arrière; **to move d. of an animal** se déplacer sous le vent d'un animal; *Hum* **it's best to stand d. of old Mr Wilson** il vaut mieux ne pas trop s'approcher du vieux M. Wilson **2** *adj* ['daʊnwɪnd] *Av* (*landing*) vent arrière

downy ['daʊnɪ] *adj* duveteux, duveté; (*fruit*) velouté, duveté

dowry ['daʊrɪ] *n* dot *f*

dowse[1] [daʊz] *vi* faire de la radiesthésie; **to d. for water** chercher de l'eau à l'aide d'une baguette de sourcier

dowse[2] [daʊs] *vt* = **douse**

dowser ['daʊzər] *n* sourcier *m*, radiesthésiste *mf*

dowsing ['daʊzɪŋ] *n* radiesthésie *f*; **d. rod** baguette *f* divinatoire de sourcier

doyen ['dɔɪjən] *n* doyen *m* (d'âge)

doyenne ['dɔɪjen] *n* doyenne *f* (d'âge)

doz (*abbr* **dozen**) d(ou)z

doze[1] [dəʊz] *n* petit somme; **to have a d.** faire un petit somme; **to fall into a d.** s'assoupir

doze[2] *vi* somnoler

▶ **doze off** *vi* s'assoupir

dozen ['dʌz(ə)n] *n* (①**A12**,1,h,i; **B57**,E,2] (**a**) (*inv*) douzaine *f*; **a d. eggs** une douzaine d'œufs; **half a d., a half d.** une demi-douzaine; **£5 a d./half d.** cinq livres la douzaine/demi-douzaine; **six d. bottles of wine** six douzaines de bouteilles de vin; **by the d.** à la douzaine

(**b**) (*pl* **dozens**) **they arrived in their dozens** ils arrivèrent par douzaines; **dozens of people have asked me about it** des dizaines de personnes me l'ont demandé; **to have dozens of things to do** avoir des tas de choses à faire; **dozens and dozens of times** maintes et maintes fois; **a baker's d., thirteen to the d.** treize à la douzaine; *F* **to talk nineteen to the d.** bavarder comme une pie

dozenth ['dʌz(ə)nθ] *adj* douzième

dozily ['dəʊzɪlɪ] *adv* (*to watch*) d'un œil somnolent; (*to answer*) d'une voix endormie

doziness ['dəʊzɪnɪs] *n* (**a**) somnolence *f*; (**b**) *Br F* (*stupidity*) bêtise *f*

dozy ['dəʊzɪ] *adj* (**a**) somnolent, assoupi; **to feel d.** avoir envie de dormir (**b**) *Br F* (*not very bright*) nunuche

DP [diː'piː] *n Comptr* (*abbr* **data processing**) traitement *m* des données, informatique *f*; **DP manager** chef *m* des traitements

D Phil [diː'fɪl] *n Univ abbr* **Doctor of Philosophy**

DPP [diːpiː'piː] *n Br Jur abbr* **Director of Public Prosecutions**

dpt *abbr* **department**

Dr (a) (*abbr* **doctor**) Dr. (**b**) (*abbr* **Drive**) av.

drab [dræb] **1** *adj* (**a**) (*colour*) terne; (*clothing*) de couleur terne (**b**) *Fig* (*surroundings, routine*) morne, monotone; (*existence*) terne, monotone; (*person*) insignifiant **2** *n* (**a**) (*colour*) olivâtre *m* (**b**) (*material*) (*grey*) tissu *m* gris; (*brown*) tissu brun

drably ['dræblɪ] *adv* de façon terne; **d. coloured** aux couleurs ternes *ou* mornes

drabness ['dræbnɪs] *n* (*of surroundings, existence*) monotonie *f*; **the d. of her clothes** ses vêtements ternes

drachm [dræm] *n* (*measurement*) drachme *f*

drachma, *pl* **-mas** ['drækmə, -məz] *n* drachme *f*

draconian [drə'kəʊnɪən] *adj* draconien

draft[1] [drɑːft] *n* (**a**) (*of letter*) brouillon *m*; (*of law*) projet *m*; (*of treaty*) avant-projet *m*, *pl* avant-projets; *Archit, MecE etc* dessin *m* schématique, tracé *m*; **rough d.** (*of map etc*) ébauche *f*; **do you want it in d.?** tu le veux au brouillon?; **first d. of a novel** premier jet *m* d'un roman; **d. agreement** projet *m* de contrat; **d. budget** projet de budget; **d. contract** projet de contrat; *Comptr* **d. mode** mode *m* rapide *ou* brouillon, mode d'impression rapide, mode liste rapide; *Comptr* **d. printout** brouillon; *Comptr* **d. quality** (*of printout*) qualité *f* brouillon *ou* listing, qualité liste rapide; *Comptr* **d. quality printing** impression *f* en qualité brouillon *ou* en qualité liste rapide

(**b**) *Com* traite *f*; **banker's d.** chèque *m* bancaire

(**c**) *US Mil* (*conscription*) conscription *f*; **to be d. age** être en âge de faire son service

(**d**) *Mil* (*group*) (*of troops*) détachement *m*; (*of recruits*) contingent *m*

draft[2] *vt* (**a**) (*letter*) faire le brouillon de; (*deed, project*) rédiger; *Pol* **to d. a bill** établir un projet de loi (**b**) *US Mil* (*conscript*) appeler sous les drapeaux (**c**) *Mil* (*detach*) (*troops*) détacher, envoyer en détachement; (*soldier*) affecter (**to** à); **to d. troops into ...** faire passer des troupes dans ...; *Fig* **could we d. in some outside help?** est-ce que nous pourrions obtenir de l'aide à l'extérieur?; **she had been drafted in from the Foreign Office** on l'avait fait venir du Ministère des affaires étrangères

draft[3] *n US* = **draught**[1]

draft board *n* = conseil *m* de révision

draft card *n* ordre *m* d'incorporation

draft dodger, draft evader *n F* réfractaire *m*

draftsman, draftsmanship *etc US* = **draughtsman, draughtsmanship** *etc*

drafty ['drɑːftɪ] *adj US* = **draughty**

drag[1] [dræg] *n* (**a**) (*in aerodynamics*) résistance *f* de l'air; *Av* traînée *f*; *Billiards* effet *m* rétrograde; **d. coefficient** coefficient *m* aérodynamique, coefficient de pénétration dans l'air, Cx *m*; **d. factor** coefficient *m* de traînée; *Aut* **d. link** biellette *f* de direction; *Aut* **d. link bar** bielle *f* pendante

(**b**) *F* (*bore*) (*person*) raseur, -euse; **it's an awful d.** c'est la barbe, c'est barbant; **the party was a d.** la soirée était rasante; **I don't want to be a d. but ...** je ne voudrais pas être rasoir, mais ...; **what a d. for you!** quelle barbe!

(**c**) *Sl* **to have a d.** (*on cigarette*) tirer une taffe; **she took a quick d. on her cigarette** elle tira vivement sur sa cigarette

(**d**) *Sl* (*women's clothes worn by man*) costume *m* féminin (porté par un homme); **he was in d.** il portait des vêtements de femme

(**e**) *esp US F* **the (main) d.** la rue principale; *Am Aut* **d. (race)** concours *m* d'accélération

(**f**) *Am F* **to have d.** (*influence*) avoir du piston

(**g**) (*in hunting*) voie *f* artificielle; **d. (hunt)** chasse *f* à courre où la meute suit une piste artificielle, drag *m*

(**h**) (*brake*) **to put a d. on a wheel** enrayer une roue; *Fig* **she was a d. on his career** elle entravait sa carrière, elle le freinait dans sa carrière; **I don't want to be a d. on you** (*in career, on walk, climb etc*) je ne veux pas te freiner

(**i**) (*trek*) **it's a long d. to the top of the hill** c'est une sacrée tirée jusqu'en haut de la colline

(**j**) (*for dredging*) drague *f*; (*for retrieving lost object*) araignée *f*; *Naut* grappin *m* à main; (*for helping drowning person*) gaffe *f* de sauvetage

drag[2] (**-gg-** [drægd]) **1** *vt* (**a**) (*pull*) traîner, tirer; (*by force*) (*sb*) entraîner de force *ou* contre sa volonté; **to d. one's feet** traîner les pieds; *Fig* **to d. one's feet** *or* **heels** tarder (**over doing** à faire); **she dragged her feet over the decision** elle a tardé à se décider; *Fig* **I wish you'd stop dragging your feet** je voudrais bien que tu arrêtes d'atermoyer; **he dragged himself to the door** il se traîna jusqu'à la porte; **to d. its anchor** (*of ship*) déraper; *Fig* **I don't want to d. you through it** je ne veux pas te faire subir ça; *Fig* **he dragged me to the football match** il m'a traîné au match de football; *Fig* **to d. sb through the courts** traîner qn devant les tribunaux

(**b**) (*search*) (*pond, river*) draguer

(**c**) *Comptr* (*with mouse*) faire glisser; **d. and drop** glisser-lâcher

2 *vi* (**a**) (*of skirt etc*) traîner (à terre)

(**b**) (*progress slowly*) (*of lawsuit, Th of scene etc*) traîner en longueur; (*of conversation*) languir; (*of work*) se traîner; **time is dragging** les heures se traînent; **the meeting finally dragged to a close at 10 pm** la réunion s'est enfin terminée à 10 heures

(**c**) *Tech* offrir de la résistance; (*of brakes*) frotter (sur les roues) (**d**) *F* **to d. on** *or* **at a cigarette** tirer des bouffées d'une cigarette

(**e**) (*search*) draguer (**for sth** pour retrouver qch)

(**f**) *Fishing* pêcher à la drague; **to d. for oysters** pêcher les huîtres à la drague

▶ **drag along 1** *vtsep* (*sb, sth*) traîner **2** *vi* (*of dress*) traîner; (*of person*) être à la traîne

▶ **drag apart** *vtsep* séparer

▶ **drag away** *vtsep* (*sb*) entraîner, emmener de force; (*sb, sth*) arracher (**from** de); **I couldn't d. myself away** j'étais cloué sur place; **if you could d. yourself away from the television** si tu pouvais t'arracher de devant la télévision

▶ **drag behind 1** *vtsep* traîner derrière (soi) **2** *vi* être à la traîne; **stop dragging behind** arrête de traîner comme ça

▶ **drag down** *vtsep* (**a**) (*person, object*) entraîner en bas; (*by force*) (*person*) faire descendre de force; *also Fig* **he dragged me down with him** il m'a entraîné dans sa chute; **to d. sb down to one's level** faire descendre qn à son niveau (**b**) (*of illness etc*) (*person*) déprimer

▶ **drag in** *vtsep* (**a**) (*pull in*) traîner; (*by force*) faire entrer de force (**b**) *F* (*refer to*) faire allusion à; **why do you always have to d. in my one mistake?** pourquoi est-ce que tu te crois obligé de faire sans arrêt allusion à ma seule erreur?

▶ **drag into** *vtaspo* (*involve*) **don't d. me into this!** ne me mêle pas à ça!; **he keeps dragging her name into the conversation** il n'arrête pas de glisser son nom dans la conversation

▶ **drag off** *vtsep* = **drag away**

▶ **drag on** *vi* (*of meeting, business etc*) s'éterniser, traîner en longueur; **to let a matter d. on** laisser traîner une affaire; **the play dragged on and on** la pièce n'en finissait pas; **the exams seemed to d. on for ages** les examens semblaient n'en plus finir

▶ **drag out** *vtsep* (**a**) (*heavy object, person*) traîner à l'extérieur; (*by force*) (*person*) faire sortir de force; **to d. sb out of bed** tirer qn de son lit; **to d. the truth/a confession out of sb** arracher la vérité/des aveux à qn; **I finally managed to d. out of him the reason why he was so upset** j'ai finalement réussi à lui faire dire pourquoi il était si retourné (**b**) (*speech, presentation, matter*) faire traîner; *Lit* **to d. out a wretched existence** traîner une existence misérable

▶ **drag up** *vt* (**a**) (*object, person*) entraîner *ou* tirer jusqu'en haut; *F* **you dragged me up to London for this?** et c'est pour ça que tu m'as fait venir à Londres? (**b**) *F* (*refer to*) (*sth*) déterrer (**c**) *F* (*raise badly*) **those children are being dragged up** ces enfants sont élevés n'importe comment; **where were <u>you</u> dragged up?** où as-tu été élevé?

drag act *n Sl* numéro *m* de travesti(s)

drag artist *n Sl* artiste *m* de travesti

dragging ['drægɪŋ] **1** *adj* **d. step** pas traînant **2** *n* (**a**) (*of something heavy behind one etc*) traînement *m*; *Naut* **d. of the anchor** dérapage *m* (**b**) (*of pond, river*) dragage *m*

draggy ['drægɪ] *adj F* (**a**) (*boring*) (*evening, party*) ennuyeux, barbant (**b**) (*listless*) pas dans son assiette; **to feel a bit d.** ne pas être dans son assiette

dragnet ['drægnet] *n* (**a**) (*organized by police*) cordon *m* de police; **twenty suspects were picked up in the d.** vingt personnes suspectes furent arrêtées dans la rafle (**b**) *Fishing* seine *f*, drège *f*

dragon ['drægən] *n* (**a**) *Myth, Fig F* dragon *m*; *Mil* **d.'s teeth** (*anti-tank defence*) rangées *fpl* de tétraèdres de béton; *Sl* **to chase the d.** (*smoke heroin*) chasser le dragon (**b**) (*lizard*) dragon *m*

dragonfly ['drægənflaɪ] *n* libellule *f*

dragoon[1] [drə'gu:n] *n Mil* dragon *m*

dragoon[2] *vt F* **to d. sb into doing sth** forcer qn à faire qch

drag queen *n Sl* travelo *m*

dragrope ['drægrəʊp] *n* (**a**) *Mil* bricole *f*, combleau *m* (**b**) *Av* (*of hot-air balloon*) guide-rope *m*, *pl* guide-ropes

drag show *n Sl* spectacle *m* de travesti

dragster ['drægstər] *n Aut* dragster *m*

drain[1] [dreɪn] *n* (**a**) (*in street*) égout *m*; (*of house*) canalisation *f* sanitaire; **a smell of drains** une odeur d'égout; **the drains are overflowing** les égouts débordent; **to pour sth down the d.** (dé)verser qch dans les égouts; *Fig* **to throw money down the d.** jeter son argent par la fenêtre; *F* **that's five years' work down the d.** voilà cinq années de travail perdues; *F* **that's my holiday down the d.** mes vacances sont à l'eau; *F* **to laugh like a d.** rire à gorge déployée

(**b**) (*loss*) (*of energy etc*) perte *f*, fuite *f*; (*of capital etc*) drainage *m*; **this constant d. on our resources** cette hémorragie continuelle de nos ressources; **the car is a continual d. on our resources** la voiture nous cause constamment des dépenses; **the brain d.** l'exode *m ou* la fuite des cerveaux

(**c**) *MecE etc* tuyau *m* d'écoulement; *Med* drain *m*; **overflow d.** (tube *m* de) trop-plein *m*, *pl* trop-pleins; *Aut etc* **d. hole** vis *m* de purge, trou *m* d'évacuation; *Aut etc* **d. plug** bouchon *m* de vidange

drain[2] **1** *vt* (**a**) (*liquid*) (*from field, pond*) évacuer; **d. the water from the vegetables** égoutter les légumes; *Med* **to d. pus from a wound** faire sortir le pus d'une blessure; *Fig* **to d. wealth from a country** drainer les richesses d'un pays

(**b**) (*glass, pond, radiator etc*) vider; (*land, swamp, Med wound, abscess*) drainer; (*sump*) vidanger; *Culin* (*vegetables etc*) égoutter; **well/poorly-drained soil** sol perméable/peu perméable; *Fig* **to d. a country of its wealth** épuiser les richesses d'un pays; **the company is being drained of its top executives** la société perd ses cadres supérieurs

(**c**) *Fig* (*person*) épuiser; **to d. sb's energy** épuiser qn; **to feel drained** (*of energy*) être épuisé; (*of emotions*) être vidé; **to be drained of emotion** ne plus ressentir aucune émotion; **to d. sb of their strength** épuiser les forces de qn

2 *vi* (*of dishes*) égoutter; (*of sink, washing machine*) se vider; **the river drains into the sea** la rivière se jette dans la mer; **the colour drained from her face** elle est devenue blême

▶ **drain away 1** *vtsep* (*remove*) (*oil, water etc*) faire couler **2** *vi* (*of water*) s'écouler; (*of strength, enthusiasm, energy etc*) s'épuiser; (*of fear, tension*) s'envoler, s'en aller

▶ **drain off 1** *vtsep* (*water, oil*) évacuer **2** *vi* (*of water*) s'écouler

drainage ['dreɪnɪdʒ] *n* (**a**) = **draining**; *Agr* **d. ditch** rigole *f* d'écoulement; *Geog* **d. area** *or* **basin** bassin *m* hydrographique; *Med* **d. tube** drain *m* (**b**) *Constr* (*for draining land etc*) système *m* d'écoulement des eaux; (*drains*) système d'égouts; **main d.** tout-à-l'égout *m inv*; *Agr* **soil with good d.** sol *m* perméable; **to improve the d. of the soil** rendre le sol plus perméable (**c**) (*water*) eaux *fpl* de surface; (*sewage*) eaux d'égout

drainer ['dreɪnər] *n* égouttoir *m*

draining ['dreɪnɪŋ] *n* (*of water*) écoulement *m*; (*of swamp*) drainage *m*, assèchement *m*; *Agr* (*of land*) drainage, assainissement *m*; (*of bottles etc*) égouttement *m*; (*of sump etc*) vidange *f*; *Med* (*of wound*) drainage; **d. board** égouttoir *m* (d'évier)

drainpipe ['dreɪnpaɪp] *n* tuyau *m* d'écoulement *ou* de drainage; *F* **d. trousers, drainpipes** pantalon *m* étroit *ou* en tuyau de poêle

drake [dreɪk] *n* (*bird*) canard *m* mâle; **wild d.** malard *m*

DRAM ['di:ræm] *n Comptr* (*abbr* **dynamic random access memory**) DRAM *f*

dram [dræm] *n* (**a**) *Pharm* drachme *f* (= un seizième d'once, = 1,77 grammes) (**b**) *esp Scot F* (*of whisky*) goutte *f*; **to take a d.** prendre un petit verre (de whisky)

drama ['dra:mə] *n* (**a**) *Th* (*play*), *Fig* drame *m*; *Fig* **to make a d. out of sth** faire un drame de qch; **there's no need to make such a d. out of it** ce n'est pas la peine d'en faire tout un drame; **she always has to make a d. out of everything** elle est toujours à dramatiser

(**b**) (*art form*) l'art *m* dramatique, le théâtre; **the masterpieces of French d.** les chefs-d'œuvre du théâtre français; **to teach d.** donner des cours d'art dramatique *ou* de théâtre; **d. documentary** drame *m* reconstitué; **d. series** série *f* dramatique; **d. studio** studio *m* d'enregistrement

(**c**) *Fig* (*excitement*) action *f*; **packed with d., full of d.** (*film etc*) plein d'action *ou* de rebondissements; **the d. of the situation is heightened by the fact that …** le caractère dramatique de la situation est renforcé par le fait que …

dramadoc ['dra:mədɒk] *n TV etc F* drame *m* reconstitué

drama school *n* école *f* d'art dramatique, école de théâtre

drama student *n* étudiant, -ante en art dramatique

dramatic [drə'mætɪk] *adj* (**a**) (*book, ending, actor etc*) dramatique; **the d. works of Corneille** le théâtre de Corneille (**b**) *Fig* (*substantial*) (*developments, rise, decline, change etc*) considérable, très important (**c**) *Fig* (*theatrical*) (*gesture, effect*) théâtral

dramatically [drə'mætɪklɪ] *adv* (**a**) *Th* (*to end*) sur un coup de théâtre; **d., the play doesn't work** du point de vue dramatique, la pièce ne tient pas debout (**b**) *Fig* (*substantially*) considérablement (**c**) *Fig* (*theatrically*) théâtralement; **the room is decorated rather d. in red and black** la pièce est décorée avec beaucoup d'effet en rouge et noir

dramatics [drə'mætɪks] *n* [①A10,c] **amateur d.** théâtre *m* amateur; *Pej* **this is no time for d.** ce n'est pas le moment de faire un drame *ou* de dramatiser

dramatis personae ['dræmətɪspɜ:'səʊnaɪ] *npl Th* personnages *mpl*

dramatist ['dræmətɪst] *n Th* auteur *m* dramatique, dramaturge *mf*

dramatization [dræmətaɪˈzeɪʃən] *n Rad, TV, Th* (*of novel etc*) adaptation *f*; *Fig* (*of event*) dramatisation *f*

dramatize [ˈdræmətaɪz] **1** *vt Rad, TV, Th* (*novel*) adapter; *Fig* (*event*) dramatiser; **there's no need to d. it** il ne faut pas en faire un drame **2** *vi* **novel that would d. well** (*for stage/screen/radio*) roman qui s'adapterait bien à la scène/à l'écran/à la radio; *Fig* **there's no need to d.** il ne faut pas en faire un drame; **he tends to d.** il a tendance à dramatiser

drape¹ [dreɪp] **1** *vt* (*table, window, neckline, material*) draper (**with, in** de); **to d. sth over sth** draper qch sur qch; **the hall was draped in black** la salle était tendue de noir; **she was draped over the sofa** elle s'était étalée sur le canapé; **she draped herself round him** elle l'a enlacé; **he had a coat draped over his arm** il avait un manteau sur le bras **2** *vi* (*of material*) se draper

drape² *n* **(a)** (*of dress etc*) drapé *m* **(b) drapes** tentures *fpl*; *Am* (*curtains*) rideaux *mpl*

draper [ˈdreɪpər] *n Old-fashioned Br* marchand, -ande de tissus; **d.'s shop** magasin *m* de tissus

drapery [ˈdreɪpərɪ] *n* **(a)** *Old-fashioned Br* (*trade*) commerce *m* des tissus; (*shop*) magasin *m* de tissus **(b)** (*hangings*) tentures *fpl*

drastic [ˈdræstɪk] *adj* (*action*) énergique; (*measures, solution, change*) radical, drastique; (*cuts*) draconien, sombre; (*remedy*) drastique; (*decline, rise, improvement, change*) dramatique; (*shortage*) dramatique, critique; (*need*) urgent; **things are getting d.** la situation devient critique; **that's quite a d. haircut you've got** tu as la boule à zéro; **that's a bit d.** (*of proposal etc*) c'est un peu exagéré; **d. reductions** (*notice in shop*) soldes monstres

drastically [ˈdræstɪklɪ] *adv* (*to act*) énergiquement; (*shortened, improved etc*) radicalement; **to be d. short of sth** manquer dramatiquement de qch; **they're not d. different** ils ne sont pas fondamentalement différents; **d. reduced prices** prix cassés

drat [dræt] *int Old-fashioned F* **d. (it)!** sacristi!, nom de nom!; **d. the child!** au diable cet enfant!

dratted [ˈdrætɪd] *adj Old-fashioned F* (*boy etc*) maudit

draught¹, *US* **draft** [drɑːft] *n* **(a)** (*wind*) courant *m* d'air; **I'm in a d., I feel a d.** je suis dans un courant d'air; **d. excluder** bourrelet *m*; **d.-proof** à l'épreuve des courants d'air; *Fig F* **we're (all) feeling the d.** les choses vont mal (pour tout le monde) **(b)** (*of chimney*) tirage *m* **(c)** *Lit* (*drink*) trait *m*, gorgée *f*; **he took a long d. of beer** il a bu une grande gorgée de bière **(d)** *Med Arch* potion *f*; **poisoned d.** potion empoisonnée **(e)** *Naut* (*of ship*) tirant *m* d'eau **(f) beer on d., d. beer** bière *f* à la pression **(g) d. animal** bête *f* de trait **(h)** (*for playing draughts*) pion *m*

draught² *n, vt* = **draft**[1,2]

draughtboard [ˈdrɑːftbɔːd] *n* damier *m*

draughts [ˈdrɑːfts] *n* [ⓘ**A10**,d] *Br* (jeu *m* de) dames *fpl*; **to play d.** jouer aux dames; **a game of d.** une partie de dames

draughtsman, *US* **draftsman,** *pl* **-men** [ˈdrɑːftsmən] *n* **(a)** *Ind* (*of plans, drawings etc*) dessinateur *m* industriel **(b)** *Art* dessinateur *m*

draughtsmanship, *US* **draftsmanship** [ˈdrɑːftsmənʃɪp] *n* **(a)** *Ind* l'art *m* du dessin industriel **(b)** (*ability to draw well*) talent *m* de dessinateur; **a fine piece of d.** un très bon dessin; **the d. is excellent** c'est très bien dessiné; **d. was never his strong point** le dessin n'a jamais été son fort

draughtswoman, *US* **draftswoman,** *pl* **-women** [ˈdrɑːftswʊmən, -wɪmɪn] **(a)** *Ind* (*of plans, drawings etc*) dessinatrice *f* industrielle **(b)** *Art* dessinatrice *f*

draughty, *US* **drafty** [ˈdrɑːftɪ] *adj* (*room, corridor etc*) plein de courants d'air; (*street corner*) exposé à tous les vents; **it's d. here** il y a des courants d'air ici

draw¹ [drɔː] *n* **(a)** (*game*) partie *f* nulle; *Fb, Boxing* match *m* nul; **it ended in a d.** ils ont fait partie/match nul(le); (*of competition*) ils ont fini à égalité; *Fb* **a one-all/nil-nil d.** un match nul un à un/zéro à zéro; **it's a d. so far** pour l'instant ils sont à égalité

(b) (*lottery*) loterie *f*, tombola *f*; (*selection of winners, competitors*) tirage *m* (au sort); *Sp* (*list*) = tableau *m* des concurrents à chaque tour d'une série d'épreuves de championnat/*etc*; **an easy/difficult d.** un tirage favorable/défavorable; *Fb* **the d. for the World Cup** le tirage de la Coupe du Monde; *F* **that's just the luck of the d.** c'est la vie!

(c) (*attraction*) attraction *f*; *Th* pièce *f* qui fait recette; **the match/film was a big d.** le match/film a remporté un grand succès; **she was a big d.** elle a attiré beaucoup de monde

(d) to take a d. at one's pipe tirer une bouffée de sa pipe; **she had a quick d. on her cigarette** elle tira vivement sur sa cigarette; *F* **to be quick on the d.** (*with gun*) avoir la gâchette facile; (*with answers*) avoir la répartie facile; **to be a fast d.** avoir la gâchette facile; **the fastest d. in the West** le tireur le plus rapide de l'Ouest

draw² (*pt* **drew** [druː]; *pp* **drawn** [drɔːn]) **1** *vt* **(a)** *Art* (*landscape, figure etc*) dessiner; *Geom* (*circle, plan*) tracer; (*triangle, hexagon*) tracer, construire; (*line*) tirer, tracer; **to d. a map** dessiner une carte; (*of surveyor*) dresser une carte; **to d. sb's picture** faire le portrait de qn; *Fig* **the author has drawn the characters skilfully** l'auteur a tracé les personnages avec adresse

(b) (*pull*) (*person*) attirer (**towards** vers); (*cart*) tirer; (*bow*) tendre; (*blind*) baisser; **to d. the curtains** tirer les rideaux; **drawn by a locomotive** remorqué par une locomotive; **to d. breath** souffler; *Fig* **I haven't drawn breath all day** (*I've been very busy*) je n'ai pas arrêté de la journée; **she drew his head down towards her** elle attira sa tête vers elle; **to d. a comb/brush through one's hair** se donner un coup de peigne/brosse

(c) (*extract*) retirer, ôter (**sth from** *or* **out of sth** qch de qch); (*screw*) ôter, enlever; (*cork*) retirer, tirer, faire sauter; (*tooth, nail etc*) arracher; **to d. one's sword** tirer l'épée, dégainer; **to d. one's revolver** (*from holster/pocket*) sortir son revolver de l'étui/de sa poche, dégainer; **to d. a gun on sb** sortir un révolver et le pointer sur qn; **to d. a knife (on sb)** sortir un couteau (et en menacer qn); **to d. a card (from the pack)** tirer une carte; *Cards* **to d. trumps** faire tomber les atouts; **to d. money from the bank** retirer de l'argent de la banque; **to d. blood** (*of weapon*) faire couler le sang; (*of dog*) mordre jusqu'au sang; (*of cat*) griffer jusqu'au sang; *Fig* (*of remark, criticism*) avoir un effet dévastateur; **to d. water from the river/the well** puiser *ou* tirer de l'eau à la rivière/au puits; **to d. wine (from a barrel)** tirer du vin (d'un tonneau); **to d. lots for sth** tirer qch au sort; **to d. straws** tirer à la courte paille; **to be drawn** (*of winning number, bonds*) sortir au tirage; **to d. a team/player against another** tirer une équipe/un joueur au sort contre un(e) autre; **it was the second time Czechoslovakia had been drawn against Scotland** c'était la deuxième fois que la Tchécoslovaquie tombait contre l'Écosse; **to d. a confession from sb** arracher un aveu à qn; **to d. a conclusion from sth** tirer *ou* déduire une conclusion de qch

(d) *Sp* **to d. a game with sb** faire match nul avec qn; (*in chess etc*) faire partie nulle avec qn; **the match was drawn** ils ont fait match nul

(e) (*receive*) (*salary, Mil rations*) toucher; **to d. supplies from sb** s'approvisionner chez qn

(f) (*attract*) (*criticism, praise, person's gaze*) attirer; **to d. a crowd** (*of incident*) créer un attroupement; (*of play*) attirer le public; **to feel drawn to sb** se sentir attiré par qn; *Mil* **to d. the enemy's fire** attirer sur soi le feu de l'ennemi; **to d. sb's fire** (*of policeman, Fig deliberately*) faire diversion; *Fig* (*accidentally*) s'attirer les foudres de qn; **his accusation drew an instant denial** son accusation provoqua un démenti immédiat; **the government refused to be drawn** le gouvernement refusa de se commettre; **she would not be drawn on what she intended to do** elle a refusé de faire connaître ses intentions

(g) (*take, derive*) (*strength, comfort, consolation etc*) tirer (**from** de); **our members are drawn from all walks of life** nos membres appartiennent à tous les milieux

(h) *Fin* (*cheque*) libeller, rédiger; **to d. a cheque on** tirer *ou* disposer un chèque sur; **to d. a bill on** tirer une traite sur

(i) *Culin* (*chicken etc*) vider

(j) *Naut* **to d. twenty feet of water** (*of ship*) tirer *ou* jauger vingt pieds d'eau, avoir vingt pieds de tirant d'eau

(k) *Med* (*abscess*) faire aboutir

(l) *Metal* (*wire, tubes etc*) étirer, tirer

(m) to d. tea faire infuser du thé

2 *vi* **(a)** *Art* dessiner

(b) *Sp* faire match nul; (*in chess etc*) faire partie nulle; **they drew two all** ils ont fait deux partout; **they drew for third place** ils ont fait troisième ex æquo

(c) (*move*) **to d. ahead of sb** devancer qn; **to d. level with a competitor** arriver à (la) hauteur d'un concurrent; **to d. to an end** tirer *ou* toucher à sa fin; **to d. near** (*of elections, Christmas*) se rapprocher; (*of person*) se rapprocher, s'approcher (**to sb** de qn); **the bird flew away as they drew near** à leur approche l'oiseau s'est envolé; **as they drew nearer, they could see ...** en s'approchant, ils ont vu ...; **to d. to a halt** (*stop*) s'arrêter

(d) (*of chimney, pipe etc*) tirer; (*of pump*) aspirer

(e) (*in dominoes*) **to d. (from the pool)** piocher

(f) (*infuse*) (*of tea*) infuser

(g) *Fin* **to d. at sight** tirer à vue

▶ **draw alongside 1** *vi* (*of vehicle*) **to d. alongside of a car/the platform** (*and stop*) se ranger à côté d'une voiture/le long du quai; **the police car drew alongside and signalled him to stop** la voiture de police a roulé à sa hauteur et lui a fait signe d'arrêter **2** *vipo* (*and stop*) se ranger à côté de; (*keep moving*) rouler à la hauteur de; **the train drew alongside the platform** le train s'est rangé le long du quai

▶ **draw apart 1** *vtsep* séparer, écarter **2** *vi* (*of people*) se séparer, s'écarter; (*in relationship*) s'éloigner l'un de l'autre; **they drew apart from the rest of the crowd** ils se sont écartés du reste de la foule

▶ **draw aside 1** *vtsep* (*person*) tirer *ou* prendre à l'écart; (*chair, suitcase*) tirer en arrière; (*curtain, sheet*) tirer, écarter **2** *vi* s'écarter

▶ **draw away 1** *vtsep* (*person*) entraîner, détourner (**from sth** de qch); **she drew us away from the other guests** elle nous a entraîné à l'écart des autres invités; **to d. one's hand away** retirer sa main **2** *vi* **(a)** (*of car etc*) s'éloigner; *Sp* **the first half-dozen runners are now beginning to d. away** les six premiers coureurs commencent à devancer les autres; *Sp* **to d. away from a competitor** prendre de l'avance sur un concurrent **(b)** (*recoil*) reculer, avoir un mouvement de recul

▶ **draw back 1** *vtsep* **(a)** (*pull*) (*table, chair etc*) tirer en arrière; (*sheet, veil etc*) tirer, écarter; *Mil* (*troops*) retirer; **she drew her hand back from the fire** elle a retiré sa main du feu; **to d. back the curtains** ouvrir les rideaux

(b) (*attract back*) **what drew you back to your home town?** qu'est-ce qui t'a poussé à revenir dans ta ville natale?; **I'm increasingly being drawn back to folk music** je reviens de plus en plus à la musique folk

2 *vi* **(a)** (*recoil*) reculer; **to d. back from making a decision** ne pas vouloir prendre une décision; **caution made him d. back from telling anyone about his new job** par prudence il résista à l'envie de parler à quiconque de son nouveau travail

(b) (*from commitment etc*) faire marche arrière

▶ **draw in 1** *vtsep* **(a)** (*net*) haler à bord; (*of cat etc*) (*claws*) rentrer, rétracter; (*of horseman*) (*reins, bridle*) serrer; *Fig F* **to d. in one's horns** faire des économies **(b)** (*air*) aspirer **(c)** (*involve*) (*person*) impliquer; **they're arguing and I don't want to be drawn in** ils se disputent et je ne veux pas y être mêlé **2** *vi* **(a)** (*of days, nights*) diminuer, raccourcir **(b)** (*of train, bus*) arriver

▶ **draw into 1** *vipo* (*arrive at*) **the train drew into the station** le train entra en gare; **a car drew into the kerb** une voiture s'est rangée le long du trottoir **2** *vtaspo* (*involve*) **to get drawn into an argument** être mêlé à une dispute; **to d. sb into conversation** entamer une conversation avec qn; **to d. sb into the conversation** faire entrer qn dans la conversation

▶ **draw off** *vtsep* (*liquid*) soutirer

▶ **draw on 1** *vi* **(a)** (*approach*) approcher; **evening was drawing on** la nuit approchait

(b) (*go past slowly*) s'avancer; **as the day gradually drew on** au fur et à mesure que la journée avançait; **as time drew on his health improved** avec le temps sa santé s'améliora

2 *vipo* **(a)** (*use*) se servir de; **to d. on one's savings** prendre sur ses économies; **to d. on the reserves** puiser dans les réserves; **to d. on sb's experiences for a novel** s'inspirer des expériences de qn pour un roman

(b) (*pipe, cigarette*) tirer sur

(c) *F* **to d. on sb** sortir un revolver et le pointer sur qn

3 *vtsep* (*put on*) mettre; **she drew on a pair of gloves** elle a enfilé une paire de gants

▶ **draw out 1** *vtsep* **(a)** (*sth from sth*) sortir, retirer; (*nail*) arracher; **to d. money out (of the bank)** retirer de l'argent (de la banque)

(b) (*person*) faire sortir de sa réserve; **I managed to draw her out (of herself)** j'ai réussi à la faire sortir de sa réserve

(c) (*prolong*) (*meal, speech*) prolonger; (*situation*) tirer en longueur, (faire) traîner; *Mus* (*note*) tenir; **they drew the meeting out on purpose** ils ont fait exprès de faire traîner la réunion

(d) *Metal* (*stretch*) (*iron*) étirer; (*gold*) étendre

2 *vi* **(a)** (*of bus, train etc*) partir; **the train drew out of the station** le train a quitté la gare; *Aut* **to d. out in order to overtake** déboîter pour doubler

(b) (*of days*) se prolonger

▶ **draw to** *vtsep* (*curtains*) tirer, fermer

▶ **draw together 1** *vtsep* (*people, objects*) rassembler, réunir; **the child's illness had drawn them together** la maladie de l'enfant les avait rapprochés **2** *vi* se rassembler

▶ **draw up 1** *vtsep* **(a)** (*pull*) tirer vers le haut; (*heavy object*) hisser; (*water from well*) tirer; **he drew the blankets up to his chin** il ramena les couvertures jusqu'à son menton; **to d. oneself up** se redresser; **she drew herself up to her full height** elle s'est dressée de toute sa hauteur; *Naut* **to d. up a boat (on the beach)** tirer un bateau à sec; **to d. up a chair** approcher une chaise (**to** de)

(b) (*prepare*) (*document*) dresser, rédiger; (*account, budget, itinerary*) établir; (*programme, procedure*) dresser, établir; (*plan*) élaborer; **document drawn up before a lawyer** acte passé devant (un) notaire; *Jur* **to d. up a will** dresser un testament; **to d. up a commercial bill** créer un effet de commerce; **to d. up an invoice** rédiger une facture

(c) (*arrange in formation*) (*troops, chairs*) ranger, aligner

2 *vi* **(a)** (*of car etc*) s'arrêter, stopper; **to d. up at the kerb** se ranger le long du trottoir

(b) (*of troops*) se mettre en rang, s'aligner; **to d. up in line** se mettre en ligne

(c) to d. up to the table s'approcher de la table

drawback [ˈdrɔːbæk] *n* **(a)** (*disadvantage*) inconvénient *m*, désavantage *m* (**to** de) **(b)** *Admin* remboursement *m* (à la sortie) des droits d'importation

drawbar [ˈdrɔːbɑː] *n Aut* crochet *m* (d'attelage)

drawbridge [ˈdrɔːbrɪdʒ] *n* **(a)** (*over moat*) pont-levis *m*, *pl* ponts-levis **(b)** *Constr* pont basculant *ou* à bascule

drawcard [ˈdrɔːkɑːd] *n Am* = **drawing card**

drawcord [ˈdrɔːkɔːd] *n* (*of curtains etc*) cordon *m*

drawdown [ˈdrɔːdaʊn] *n Fin* tirage *m*

drawee [drɔːˈiː] *n Com* (*of bill of exchange*) tiré *m*, payeur *m*

drawer [ˈdrɔːər] *n* **(a)** *Art* dessinateur, -trice; **she's a good d.** (*of child, amateur*) elle dessine bien **(b)** *Fin* tireur *m*; (*of bill*) souscripteur *m* **(c)** (*of water*) puiseur, -euse **(d)** [drɔːr] tiroir *m*; **chest of drawers** commode *f*; *Old-fashioned* **bottom d.** (*trousseau*) trousseau *m* (de mariage); *Old-fashioned F* **they're not really (out of the) top d.** ils n'appartiennent pas vraiment à l'élite; *Com* **cash d.** tiroir-caisse *m*, *pl* tiroirs-caisses

drawers [ˈdrɔː(ə)z] *npl Old-fashioned* **(pair of) drawers** (*for women*) culotte *f*; (*for men*) caleçon *m*

drawing [ˈdrɔːɪŋ] *n* **(a)** *Art* (*picture, art*) dessin *m*; **to make a d. of sth** dessiner qch; **her talent for d.** son talent pour le dessin; **line d.** dessin au trait; **rough d.** ébauche *f*, croquis *m*; **pencil d.** dessin au crayon; *Ind, MecE* **engineering d.** dessin industriel; **sectional d.** (vue *f* en) coupe *f*; **d. office** atelier *m* *ou* bureau *m* d'études

(b) (*pulling*) (*of cart*) tirage *m*

(c) (*extraction*) (*of water*) puisage *m*; (*of teeth*) extraction *f*; (*of lots*) tirage *m*

(d) (*attraction*) attraction *f* (**towards** vers); *Am* **d. card** (*of festival etc*) attraction *f*, clou *m*; **she's always a big d. card** elle attire toujours beaucoup de monde; **d. power** pouvoir *m* d'attraction

(e) *Com, Fin* **drawings** prélèvements *mpl*, levées *fpl*; *Fin* **d. rights** droits *mpl* de tirage

(f) *Culin* (*of poultry*) vidage *m*

(g) *Metal* (*of metal*) étirage *m*

drawing board *n* planche *f* à dessin; *Fig* **still on the d.** (*plan, project*) encore à l'étude; **(it's time to go) back to the d.** il n'y a plus qu'à tout recommencer

drawing book *n* cahier *m* de dessin

drawing off *n* (*of wine*) soutirage *m*

drawing paper *n* papier *m* à dessin

drawing pin *n Br* punaise *f*

drawing program *n Comptr* programme *m* de dessin, logiciel *m* de dessin

drawing room *n* salon *m*; *Am Rail* compartiment *m* salon

drawing up *n* (*of deed, document, will*) rédaction *f*; (*of constitution, plan*) élaboration *f*; (*of account, budget, itinerary etc*) établissement *m*

drawl[1] [drɔːl] *n* voix *f* traînante; **to speak with a d./a Texan d.** parler d'une voix traînante/avec un accent Texan; **to speak with an affected d.** traîner la voix avec affectation

drawl[2] **1** *vi* traîner la voix en parlant, parler d'une voix traînante **2** *vt* **…, he drawled …**, dit-il d'une voix traînante; **to d. one's vowels** traîner sur les voyelles

▶ **drawl out** *vtsep* = **drawl**[2] **2**

drawling [ˈdrɔːlɪŋ] **1** *adj* (*voice, tone*) traînant **2** *n* affectation *f* de langueur dans le débit

drawn [drɔːn] *adj* **(a)** (*face*) hagard; **to look d.** avoir les traits tirés; **d. features** traits tirés **(b) with d. sword(s)** sabre *m* au clair; *Sewing* **d.(-thread) work** ouvrage *m* *ou* travail *m* à jour(s) **(c)** (*battle*) indécis; **d. match** partie *f* nulle *ou* remise

drawsheet [ˈdrɔːʃiːt] *n Med* alaise *f*, alèse *f*

drawstring [ˈdrɔːstrɪŋ] *n* cordon *m*; **d. trousers, trousers with a d. waist** pantalon *m* qui se ferme par un cordon autour de la taille

dray [dreɪ] *n* (*cart*) haquet *m*, camion *m*

drayhorse [ˈdreɪhɔːs] *n* cheval *m* de roulage

drayman, *pl* **-men** [ˈdreɪmən] *n* conducteur *m* de haquet

dread[1] [dred] **1** *n* terreur *f*, épouvante *f*; **I have a d. of dentists** j'ai la hantise des dentistes; **she has a terrible d. of heights** elle a effroyablement peur du vide; **I have this d. that he'll**

find out where I am j'ai la hantise qu'il apprenne où je suis; she waited in d. for the phone to ring angoissée, elle attendait que le téléphone sonne; to be or stand in d. of sb/sth craindre ou redouter qn/qch 2 adj attrib Old-fashioned redouté

dread² vt (sb, sth) redouter, appréhender, craindre; I'm dreading Monday je redoute la journée de lundi; I'm dreading my driving test j'appréhende de passer le permis de conduire; to d. that ... redouter que (ne) ... + sub; I d. to think! je n'ose même pas y penser!; I d. having them both here j'appréhende de les avoir tous les deux en même temps; the dreaded Monday finally arrived le lundi si redouté est finalement arrivé; she said the dreaded words elle prononça les mots tant redoutés

dreadful ['dredfʊl] adj (a) (pain, noise etc) atroce, épouvantable; it is d. that nothing can be done c'est affreux qu'on ne puisse rien faire; to feel/look d. ne pas se sentir/avoir l'air bien du tout; I really feel d. about it! ça m'ennuie terriblement!; the shops were d. (very busy) c'était l'horreur dans les magasins; I'm a d. dancer je danse atrocement mal; to be d. at maths être nul en maths (b) F (intensive) terrible; it's a d. bore! c'est assommant!; it's a d. pity or shame c'est vraiment dommage (c) Fml (causing dread) terrible, redoutable

dreadfully ['dredfʊlɪ] adv (a) terriblement, horriblement; I was d. frightened j'avais horriblement peur; the children behaved d. les enfants se sont terriblement ou horriblement mal conduits; she suffers d. from backache son dos la fait atrocement souffrir (b) F (intensive) terriblement; d. ugly affreusement laid; our neighbours are d. noisy nos voisins sont terriblement bruyants; I am d. sorry je regrette infiniment

dreadlocks ['dredlɒks] npl dreadlocks fpl

dream¹ [dri:m] n rêve m, songe m; to have a d. faire un rêve; to have a d. about sb/sth rêver de qn/qch; to have beautiful/bad dreams faire de beaux/mauvais rêves; sweet dreams! faites de beaux rêves!; to see sth in a d. voir qch en rêve ou en songe; to go about in a d. être comme dans un rêve; my d. house, the house of my dreams la maison de mes rêves; a d. holiday des vacances de rêve; it is my d. to go to Australia je rêve d'aller en Australie; I've always had this d. that one day I would have ... j'ai toujours rêvé d'avoir ...; it's everybody's d. to win the lottery tout le monde rêve de gagner à la loterie; I've long cherished a d. to be my own boss je caresse depuis longtemps le rêve de me mettre à mon compte; F a d. of a car la voiture rêvée; it's a d. c'est le rêve; it's a d. come true c'est un rêve devenu réalité, mon rêve s'est réalisé; it worked like a d. cela a réussi à merveille; F in your dreams! tu peux toujours rêver!; d. sequence (in film) scène f de rêve; Sp, Pol d. team/ticket équipe f/combinaison f rêvée; d. world monde m imaginaire; Austr in the d. time (of native people) au temps où l'homme n'était pas encore arrivé sur la terre; Fig F il y a des siècles

dream² (pt, pp dreamt [dremt], dreamed [dri:md]) 1 vi (a) (in sleep, daydream) rêver; to d. of or about sb/sth rêver de qn/qch; you must have been dreaming! vous l'avez rêvé!; to d. of one's youth rêver à sa jeunesse; F d. on! tu peux toujours rêver!

(b) (think) I wouldn't d. of doing it jamais je ne m'aviserais de faire cela; I wouldn't d. of it! je n'y songerais même pas!; no one would have dreamt of suspecting him personne n'aurait songé à le soupçonner

2 vt I dreamt (that) you were ill j'ai rêvé que vous étiez malade; little did I d. that ... je ne songeais guère que ...; I never dreamt you would take me seriously je n'aurais jamais pensé que tu me prendrais au sérieux; you must have dreamt it! vous l'avez rêvé!

▶ **dream away** vtsep (one's time) passer à rêver; he'll d. his whole life away il passera sa vie à rêver

▶ **dream up** vtsep F (idea etc) inventer, imaginer; what have you dreamed up now? qu'est-ce que tu as encore inventé?

dreamboat ['dri:mbəʊt] n Old-fashioned F (attractive man, woman) canon m

dreamer ['dri:mər] n rêveur, -euse

dreamily ['dri:mɪlɪ] adv (to look at, smile) d'un air rêveur; (to say) d'un ton rêveur; (to wander) comme dans un rêve; to think d. of the future rêvasser à l'avenir

dreaming ['dri:mɪŋ] n rêves mpl; this d. will get you nowhere ça ne te mènera à rien de rêver comme ça

dreamland ['dri:mlænd] n le pays ou le monde des rêves, le pays des songes

dreamless ['dri:mlɪs] adj (sleep) sans rêves

dreamlessly ['dri:mlɪslɪ] adv (to sleep) d'un sommeil sans rêves

dreamlike ['dri:mlaɪk] adj (unreal) onirique

dreamy ['dri:mɪ] adj (a) (person, mood) rêveur, -euse, songeur, -euse; d. look/smile air/sourire rêveur; the d. look in her eye son regard rêveur (b) F (wonderful) magnifique, superbe

drearily ['drɪərɪlɪ] adv tristement; (to look at) d'un air morne; (to say) d'un ton morne

dreariness ['drɪərɪnɪs] n (of life, countryside etc) caractère m morne; (of book, speech etc) platitude f, monotonie f; the d. of the weather la grisaille

dreary ['drɪərɪ] adj (weather, countryside) triste, morne; (speech, routine, person etc) morne, ennuyeux; (diet) monotone; we had a d. time (of it) ce n'était pas très gai

dredge¹ [dredʒ] n (a) (boat) (bateau m) dragueur m (b) (machine) drague f; d. bucket godet m de drague (c) Fishing d. (net) (filet m de) drague f

dredge² 1 vt (canal) draguer, dévaser; to d. away mud enlever la vase avec une drague; to d. one's memory for sth chercher qch dans ses souvenirs ou sa mémoire 2 vi to d. for sth draguer à la recherche de qch

dredge³ vt Culin saupoudrer (with de); to d. flour over meat saupoudrer la viande de farine

▶ **dredge up** vtsep (silt) enlever avec une drague; (submerged object) pêcher ou recueillir avec une drague; Fig (scandal) déterrer; to d. sth up out of one's memory ressortir qch de sa mémoire; where did you d. these old photographs up from? où as-tu été repêcher ces vieilles photos?

dredger¹ ['dredʒər] n (a) (boat) (bateau m) dragueur m (b) (machine) drague f; bucket d. drague à godets; grab d. drague à benne piocheuse (c) (person) (ouvrier m) dragueur m; oyster d. dragueur d'huîtres

dredger² n Culin (for sugar etc) saupoudroir m

dredging ['dredʒɪŋ] n (of canal etc) dragage m

dregs [dregz] npl (a) (solid particles) (in glass) lie f, fond m; (of coffee) marc m; to drink sth to the d. boire qch jusqu'à la lie; Fig the d. of society les bas-fonds mpl de la société (b) (remainder, residue) fond m

drench [drentʃ] vt (soak) tremper, mouiller (with de); (earth) (of gardener) arroser abondamment; (of rain) détremper; to d. sb with water/a hosepipe arroser qn d'eau/avec un tuyau; to get drenched (with rain) se faire tremper, F se faire saucer; drenched to the skin trempé jusqu'aux os; to be drenched with sweat être en nage

drenching ['drentʃɪŋ] 1 adj (rain) battant, diluvien 2 n we got a d. nous avons été trempés, F nous nous sommes fait saucer

Dresden ['drezdən] n Dresde; D. (china) porcelaine f de Saxe

dress¹ [dres] n (a) (for woman) robe f; ball d. robe de bal; d. material tissu m pour robes; d. shield dessous-de-bras m inv

(b) (attire) costume m; to wear Western d. s'habiller à l'occidentale; it's a d. affair il faudra se mettre en tenue de soirée; evening d. tenue f de soirée; d. shirt chemise f de soirée; d. suit habit m (de soirée); to be casual in one's d. s'habiller de façon décontractée; to have no d. sense ne pas savoir s'habiller ou choisir ses vêtements; Mil mess d., formal d., d. uniform uniforme m de cérémonie ou de soirée; in full d. (of men) en grande tenue; (of women) en grande toilette; Mil en grande tenue, en uniforme de parade; Mil (full) d. parade parade f en grande tenue

dress² (dressed [drest]) 1 vt (a) (put clothes on) (person) habiller, vêtir; Th (play) costumer; to d. oneself, to get dressed s'habiller; to be dressed in black/silk être vêtu de noir/soie; dressed in rags vêtu ou couvert de haillons; dressed for the country/for climbing en tenue de campagne/d'escalade; I'm not dressed for it je ne suis pas habillé pour; well/badly dressed bien/mal habillé; to be plainly or simply dressed avoir une mise simple, être simplement vêtu; esp Mil to be improperly dressed ne pas porter la tenue réglementaire; dressed as a clown/a witch (for a party) déguisé en clown/en sorcière; F dressed to kill sur son trente et un

(b) (decorate) orner, parer (sth with sth qch de qch); Naut (ship) pavoiser; dressed over all (of ship) sous le grand pavois; Com to d. the window faire la vitrine; TV etc to d. set habiller le décor; Old-fashioned to d. sb's hair coiffer qn

(c) Mil (troops, tents etc) aligner

(d) Med (wound) panser

(e) Tech (prepare, finish) (surface, hide) apprêter; (land, fields) engraisser; (leather) corroyer; (stone) dresser, tailler; (wood) dresser, corroyer; (ore) trier; Culin (poultry, meat) habiller; (dish) accommoder; (salad) assaisonner, garnir; dressed poultry volaille prête à cuire ou parée; dressed crab crabe servi dans sa carapace; to d. timber roughly dégrossir le bois; dressed timber bois dégrossi

2 *vi* s'habiller; **she dresses like a man** elle s'habille comme un homme; **to d. in black** s'habiller de noir; **to d. (for dinner)** (*of man*) se mettre en habit; (*of woman*) se mettre en robe du soir; **they always d. for dinner** ils s'habillent toujours pour le dîner

▶ **dress down 1** *vtsep F* (*reprimand*) passer un savon à **2** *vi* s'habiller plus simplement qu'à l'accoutumée

▶ **dress up 1** *vtsep* **(a)** (*put elegant clothes on*) **to d. oneself up** se faire beau/belle, s'habiller; **to be all dressed up, to be dressed up to the nines** être sur son trente et un **(b)** (*put fancy dress on*) **you could d. yourself up as Batman** tu pourrais te déguiser en Batman; **to d. sb up** costumer qn, déguiser qn **(as sth** en qch); *Fig* **we'll have to d. it up a bit** il faudra améliorer un peu la présentation; *Fig* **however you d. it up** de quelque façon qu'on le présente **2** *vi* **(a)** (*wear elegant clothes*) se faire beau/belle, s'habiller **(b)** (*wear fancy dress*) se déguiser

dressage ['dresɑːʒ] *n Horseriding* dressage *m* (supérieur)

dress circle *n Th* premier balcon *m*

dress designer *n* styliste *mf*, modéliste *mf*

dresser¹ ['dresər] *n* **(a)** (*for plates etc*) buffet *m*; **(Welsh) d.** vaisselier *m* **(b)** *Am* (*dressing table*) table *f* de toilette, coiffeuse *f*

dresser² *n* **(a) to be a smart d.** s'habiller avec chic **(b)** *Th* habilleur, -euse **(c)** (*tool*) (*for wood*) raboteuse *f*; (*for stone*) rabotin *m*

dressing ['dresɪŋ] *n* **(a)** (*putting clothes on*) habillement *m*; **d. case** nécessaire *m*, trousse *f* de toilette; **d. gown** robe *f* de chambre, peignoir *m*; **d. room** (*in home*) cabinet *m* de toilette; *Th, Cin* (*of actor, actress*) loge *f*; *Sp* vestiaire *m*; **d. table** table *f* de toilette, coiffeuse *f*; **d.-table set** garniture *f* de toilette

(b) *Naut* (*of ship*) pavoisement *m*

(c) *Mil* (*of troops*) alignement *m*

(d) *Med* (*of wound*) pansement *m*; **to apply a d.** mettre *ou* faire un pansement; **surgical d. case** trousse *f* de pansement; *Mil* **d. station** poste *m* de secours

(e) *Agr* engrais *m*; **a heavy d. of manure** un gros apport de fumier; **surface d., top d.** engrais en couverture, couche *f* d'engrais

(f) *Culin* **(salad) d.** assaisonnement *m*, sauce *f*; **French d.** vinaigrette *f*

(g) *Tech* (*of hide*) apprêt *m*; (*of stone*) dressage *m*, taille *f*; (*of wood*) dressage, corroyage *m*; (*of ore*) préparation *f* mécanique; *Tex* apprêt, empois *m*; *Culin* (*of poultry*) habillage *m*; (*of dish*) assaisonnement *m*

(h) *Am Culin* (*stuffing*) farce *f*

dressing down *n F* verte semonce *f*, savon *m*; **to give sb a d.** passer un savon à qn; **to get a d.** se faire passer un savon

dressing up *n* déguisement *m*; **d. clothes** (vêtements *mpl* de) déguisement; **d. box** malle *f* à déguisements

dressmaker ['dresmeɪkər] *n* (*female*) couturière *f*; (*male*) couturier *m*

dressmaking ['dresmeɪkɪŋ] *n* (*by tailor, dress designer*) couture *f*; *Ind* confection *f* de robes

dress rehearsal *n Th, Fig* (répétition *f*) générale *f*

dress-run *n TV, Th etc* répétition *f* générale

dressy ['dresɪ] *adj* **(a)** (*clothes*) chic, élégant; (*party*) habillé; **it's a bit d. for a barbecue** c'est un peu trop habillé pour un barbecue; **I wanted something a bit more d.** je cherchais quelque chose d'un peu plus habillé **(b)** *Pej* (*person*) trop (élégamment) habillé

drib [drɪb] *n only used in* **in dribs and drabs** petit à petit, peu à peu

dribble¹ ['drɪb(ə)l] *n* **(a)** (*of water etc*) petite(s) goutte(s) *f(pl)*; *Fig* **supplies are coming through in dribbles** les approvisionnements sont livrés au compte-gouttes; **there's only a d. left** il n'en reste que quelques gouttes **(b)** (*of person, dog*) bave *f* **(c)** *Fb etc* dribble *m*

dribble² 1 *vi* **(a)** (*of baby etc*) baver

(b) (*of water etc*) dégoutter, tomber goutte à goutte; **the wine dribbled down his chin** le vin lui coula le long du menton; **half the flour/water had dribbled out** la moitié de la farine/l'eau s'était échappée; *Fig* **to d. in/out** (*of people*) entrer/sortir au compte-gouttes; **news has started to dribble back** des nouvelles commencent à filtrer

(c) *Billiards* **to d. into the pocket** (*of ball*) rouler doucement dans la blouse

(d) *Fb etc* dribbler

2 *vt* **(a) to d. (out)** (*liquid*) laisser couler goutte à goutte; **I had dribbled juice all down my tie** je m'étais mis plein de jus de fruit sur la cravate; **d. some oil over it** versez quelques gouttes d'huile dessus

(b) *Fb etc* (*ball*) dribbler

(c) *Billiards* **to d. the ball into the pocket** faire rouler tout doucement la bille dans la blouse

dribbler ['drɪblər] *n Fb etc* dribbleur *m*

dribbling ['drɪblɪŋ] *n* **(a)** (*of baby etc*) écoulement *m* de bave; **people were disgusted by his d.** les gens étaient dégoûtés de le voir baver comme ça **(b)** *Fb etc* dribbling *m*

driblet ['drɪblɪt] *n* (*of water etc*) gouttelette *f*, petite goutte; *Fig* petite somme *f* d'argent; **in driblets** goutte à goutte, au compte-gouttes; *Fig* au compte-gouttes

dried [draɪd] *adj* séché

dried-up *adj* (*river bed, lake etc*) asséché; (*grass, bread*) sec; *Fig Pej* **a d. old maid** une vieille bique au cœur asséché

drier ['draɪər] *n* = **dryer**

drift¹ [drɪft] *n* **(a)** (*movement*) mouvement *m*; (*of current*) direction *f*, sens *m*; (*of business, events*) cours *m*; (*of plane, ship*) dérive *f*; (*of missile etc*) dérivation *f*; *Constr* (*of borehole*) déviation *f*; *Electron* glissement *m*; **carried along by the d. of the current** emporté par le courant; *Fig* **policy of d.** politique *f* de laisser-faire; **the d. towards war** la descente vers la guerre; *Met* **d. ice** glaces *fpl* flottantes; *Fishing* **d. (net)** filet *m* traînant; **the d. from the land** la lente désertification des campagnes; **the d. towards the cities** l'exode *m* rural; *Sch* **the d. away from science** le désintéressement envers la science

(b) (*meaning*) (*of person's words*) sens *m* général, portée *f*; **I catch** *or* **follow his d.** je vois où il veut en venir; *F* **I get the/your d.** je pige

(c) (*of sand, leaves etc*) amoncellement *m*; *Geog* apport(s) *mpl*; (*of snow*) congère *f*

(d) *Min* (*of gallery*) direction *f*; (*passage*) (galerie *f* de) chassage *m*; (*exploratory*) galerie d'exploration

drift² 1 *vi* **(a)** (*of boat*) dériver, aller à la dérive; *Av* déporter; (*of questions, events*) tendre **(towards sth** vers qch); *Fig* **she's been drifting** elle ne s'est pas fixée; **you can't go on drifting like this** tu ne peux pas continuer à te laisser porter par les événements comme ça; **to d. from job to job** aller d'un travail à un autre; **to let things d.** laisser aller les choses; **to d. apart** (*of friends*) se perdre de vue; (*of married couple*) devenir peu à peu des étrangers l'un pour l'autre; **wisps of smoke were drifting across the sky** la fumée formait des traînées dans le ciel; **conversation drifted from one subject to another** la conversation passait d'un sujet à un autre; **a few tramps had drifted in in search of warmth** attirés par la chaleur, quelques vagabonds étaient entrés; **the cigarette smoke was drifting into his eyes** la fumée de cigarette lui venait dans les yeux; **to d. into war/crime** être entraîné dans la guerre/vers le crime; **the yacht drifted onto a sandbank** le yacht a dérivé et s'est échoué sur un banc de sable; **the audience started to d. towards the exit** les spectateurs se dirigeaient lentement vers la sortie; **to d. with the current** se laisser aller au fil de l'eau; *Fig* se laisser porter par les événements

(b) (*of sand etc*) s'amonceler, s'amasser; (*of snow*) se former en congères, s'amasser; **some snow had drifted in through the open door** de la neige s'était infiltrée par la porte ouverte

2 *vt* **(a)** (*logs*) flotter; (*of current*) (*sth*) entraîner

(b) (*of wind*) (*snow, sand*) amonceler, entasser; **the wind was drifting snow in through the window** de la neige entrait par la fenêtre, portée par le vent

▶ **drift off 1** *vi* **to d. off (to sleep)** s'assoupir **2** *vipo Naut, Av* **to d. off course** dévier de son cap

drifter ['drɪftər] *n* **(a)** *Fishing* bateau *m* de pêche à filets traînants **(b)** *Fig* personne *f* qui se laisse aller; **he's been a d. all his life** il ne s'est jamais fixé; **she's a bit of a d.** elle n'a pas vraiment de but dans la vie

drifting ['drɪftɪŋ] **1** *adj* (*ship etc*) à la dérive; (*cloud*) traînant; **d. snow** neige *f* soulevée par le vent; **d. banks of fog/cloud** des traînées de brouillard/de nuages **2** *n* (*caused by current*) entraînement *m* par le courant; (*caused by wind*) entraînement par le vent; (*formation of drifts*) (*of snow*) amoncellement *m*; **caused by the d. of the snow across the road** causé par la neige soulevée par le vent en travers de la route

driftwood ['drɪftwʊd] *n* (*in the sea*) bois *m* flottant *ou* flotté; (*on the shore*) bois rejeté *ou* refoulé par la mer

drill¹ [drɪl] *n* **(a)** *Carp, Metal* (*for wood, metal*) foret *m*, mèche *f*; (*for metal*) foreuse *f*, drille *f*; (*power-driven*) perceuse *f*; (*of dentist*) fraise *f*; **electric d.** perceuse électrique; **hand d.** perceuse à main; **percussion d.** perceuse à percussion; **spoon d.** cuiller *f*, cuillère *f*; **d. chuck** mandrin *m* (de tour) porte-mèche; **d. bit** foret, mèche; **d. hole** trou *m* à la foreuse; *Petr* trou de forage

(b) *Min, Constr* perforateur *m*, perforatrice *f*; (*for taking borings*) sondeuse *f*, sonde *f*; (*for oil*) trépan *m*; **d. (bit)** burin *m*

(c) (*training*) exercice(s) *mpl*; *Fig* **to know the d.** savoir ce qu'il faut faire *ou* comment s'y prendre; *F* **what's the d.?** (*what do you want me to do?*) qu'est-ce qu'il y a à faire?; (*for working the photocopier etc*) comment on fait?; *Sch* **verb d.** exercices oraux sur les verbes; *Mil* **firing d.** instruction *f* du tir; **recruit d.** école *f* du soldat; **rifle d.** maniement *m* du fusil; **d. ground** terrain *m* d'exercice *ou* de manœuvres; **d. sergeant** sergent *m* instructeur

drill² **1** *vt* **(a)** (*well etc*) forer; (*wood, metal*) faire un trou dans; (*hole*) percer; (*tooth*) fraiser

(b) *Min* (*rock etc*) (per)forer

(c) *Gym etc* (*people*) faire faire l'exercice à; *Mil* (*soldiers*) instruire, exercer; *Naut* **well-drilled crew** équipage bien exercé; *F* **to d. sb (in what to do/say)** faire la leçon à qn (sur ce qu'il faut faire/dire); **I can't d. (it) into him that ...** je ne peux pas lui faire comprendre que ...; **it had always been drilled into her that ...** on lui avait enfoncé dans la tête que ...; **to d. good manners into sb** enseigner les bonnes manières à qn; *Sch* **to d. pupils in French verbs** faire faire aux élèves des exercices oraux sur les verbes français

2 *vi* **(a)** *Petr* forer; **to d. for oil** forer pour trouver du pétrole

(b) (*do exercises*) s'exercer, s'entraîner; (*of troops*) faire l'exercice

drill³ *n Agr* **(a)** (*row*) rayon *m*, sillon *m*; **to sow the grain in drills** semer la graine en rayons **(b)** (*machine*) semoir *m* (à cuillers); **d. harrow** herse *f* à semer

drill⁴ *vt Agr* semer en rayons

drill⁵ *n Tex* coutil *m*; (*for denims etc*) treillis *m*

drilling ['drɪlɪŋ] *n* **(a)** *Metal* forage *m*, perçage *m*; *Min* (*of rock etc*) perforation *f*; *Min* (*of well*) forage *m*, sondage *m*; **d. machine** foreuse *f* **(b)** *Petr* forage *m*; **d. rig** installation *f* de forage; **offshore d. rig** île *f* de forage; **d. mud** boue *f* (de forage); **d. operations** opérations *fpl* de forage; **d. platform** plate-forme *f* de forage **(c)** (*of tooth*) fraisage *m* **(d)** *Mil* exercices *mpl*, manœuvres *fpl*

drily ['draɪlɪ] *adv* = **dryly**

drink¹ [drɪŋk] *n* **(a)** boisson *f*; (*said by waiter, barkeeper etc*) consommation *f*; (*alcoholic*) verre *m*, *F* pot *m*; **to give sb food and d.** donner à boire et à manger à qn; **to give sb a d.** donner à boire à qn; **to have a d.** boire *ou* prendre quelque chose; **I'd love a d. of water** je voudrais bien un verre d'eau; **will you join me in a d.?** tu prends un verre avec moi?; **pour yourself a d.** sers-toi un verre *ou* à boire; **we're going for a d.** nous allons prendre un verre *ou F* un pot; **how about a d. after work?** on prend un verre *ou F* un pot après le travail?; **to pay for the drinks** payer les consommations; **I haven't had a d. in six months** je n'ai pas bu d'alcool depuis six mois; **long d.** = gin/vodka/*etc* allongé de jus d'orange/de limonade/*etc*; **short d.** = gin/whisky/*etc* non dilué; **strong d.** (*spirits*) boissons fortes; **soft drinks** boissons sans alcool; **to take to d.** s'adonner à la boisson, se mettre à boire; **to have a d. problem** (trop) boire; **to smell of d.** sentir l'alcool; **to be the worse for d.** être plein *ou* ivre; **he can't hold his d.** (*gets drunk quickly*) il ne tient pas l'alcool; (*vomits*) il vomit le moindre verre d'alcool; *F* **I didn't mean it, it was the d. talking** je n'étais pas sérieux, j'avais juste un peu trop bu; **to be under the influence of d.** avoir trop bu; *Jur* **to drive a car while under the influence of d.** conduire en état d'ébriété; **to drive sb to d.** pousser qn à l'ivrognerie; **drinks dispenser** *or* **machine** distributeur *m* automatique de boissons

(b) *F* **the d.** (*sea*) la baille; **to fall into the d.** tomber à la baille

drink² (*pt* **drank** [dræŋk]; *pp* **drunk** [drʌŋk], *Arch* **drunken** ['drʌŋkən]) **1** *vt* (*water etc*) boire; **will you have something to d.?** voulez-vous boire *ou* prendre quelque chose?; **what are you drinking?** qu'est-ce que tu prends *ou* bois?; **to d. sb's health** boire à la santé de qn; **to d. sb under the table** faire rouler qn sous la table; **the wine is best drunk at room temperature** ce vin se boit chambré; **fit to d.** bon à boire, potable

2 *vi* **(a)** (*take in liquid*) boire; **to d. straight from the bottle** boire à la bouteille

(b) (*take alcohol*) boire, être adonné à la boisson; **I don't d.** je ne bois pas; **to d. heavily** s'alcooliser; **you're drinking yourself to death** l'alcool est en train de te détruire; **to d. oneself into debt** s'endetter à cause de la boisson; **don't d. and drive** ≈ boire ou conduire, il faut choisir; **to d. like a fish** boire comme un trou; **to d. to sb** boire à la santé de qn; **to d. to sth** arroser qch; **I'll d. to that!** et comment!

(c) (*of wine*) **the wine is now drinking superbly** ce vin a atteint toute sa saveur; **it won't d. quite as well in two years' time** dans deux ans il aura perdu de sa saveur

► **drink away** *vtsep* (*one's pay*) boire

► **drink down** *vtsep* (*water etc*) boire, avaler

► **drink in** *vtsep* (*person's words*) boire; (*scenery, fresh air*) se délecter de, se repaître de

► **drink off** *vtsep* (*glass*) boire d'un coup; (*bottle*) avaler

► **drink up 1** *vtsep* finir (de boire); **I want you to d. that all up!** (*not leave any*) bois tout! **2** *vi* **d. up!** videz vos verres!

drinkable ['drɪŋkəb(ə)l] *adj* buvable; (*water*) potable; **the wine's very d.** ce vin se laisse boire

drink-driver *n Br F* conducteur *m* ivre; **he's a notorious d.** tout le monde sait qu'il conduit souvent en état d'ébriété

drink-driving *n Br F* **he was arrested for d.** il a été arrêté pour conduite en état d'ébriété

drinker ['drɪŋkər] *n* buveur, -euse; **I'm not much of a d.** je ne bois pas beaucoup; **wine/beer/tea drinkers** buveurs de vin/de bière/de thé; **he's a heavy** *or* **hard d.** il boit beaucoup; **she's a social d.** elle ne boit que pour les grandes occasions

drinking ['drɪŋkɪŋ] **1** *adj* **I'm not a d. man** je n'ai pas l'habitude de boire **2** *n* **(a)** boire *m*; **d. fountain** fontaine *f* publique; **d. glass** verre *m* à boire; **d. straw** paille *f*; **d. trough** abreuvoir *m* **(b)** (*to excess*) ivrognerie *f*, alcoolisme *m*; **they'd been doing some heavy d.** ils avaient beaucoup bu; **it was her d. that destroyed the marriage** c'est son alcoolisme qui a détruit leur mariage; **d. bout** beuverie *f*; **d. companions** compagnons *mpl* de boisson; **d. song** chanson *f* à boire

drinking chocolate *n* chocolat *m* en poudre

drinking laws *npl* = lois *fpl* sur les débits de boissons

drinking water *n* eau *f* potable

drip¹ [drɪp] *n* **(a)** (*sound*) **the d. of water** le bruit de l'eau qui tombe *ou* qui s'écoule; **the d. of a tap** le bruit d'un robinet qui goutte

(b) (*drop*) goutte *f*; **there's a d. coming from the ceiling** le plafond goutte, il tombe des gouttes du plafond; **you're getting drips all over the floor** tu fais tomber des gouttes partout sur le sol; **the drips from the trees** les gouttes qui tombent/tombaient des arbres; **the d. method of making coffee** la méthode filtre de faire le café; *Mktg* **d. advertising** publicité *f* continue, publicité goutte à goutte; *Tech* **d. feed** (*for oil*) distributeur *m* compte-gouttes; *Tech* **d.-feed lubricator** (graisseur *m*) compte-gouttes *m inv*; **d. mat** dessous *m* de bouteille *ou* de verre

(c) *Med* goutte-à-goutte *m inv*; **he's on a d.** il est sous perfusion

(d) *Sl* (*feeble person*) **he's/she's a d.** c'est un mou/une molle, c'est un ramolli/une ramollie

drip² (**-pp-**) **1** *vi* (*of rain, water*) tomber goutte à goutte, (dé)goutter; **the perspiration was dripping from his forehead** la sueur lui dégouttait du front, son front était ruisselant de sueur; **just leave it to d.** (*of shirt etc*) laisse-le s'égoutter; **the tap has been dripping all night** le robinet a fui *ou* goutté toute la nuit; *Fig* **to be dripping with jewels** être couvert de bijoux **2** *vt* (*liquid*) faire dégoutter, laisser tomber goutte à goutte; **you're dripping water/paint everywhere!** tu mets des gouttes d'eau/de peinture partout!; **the ceiling was dripping water** le plafond gouttait, des gouttes d'eau tombaient du plafond

drip-dry *adj* (*shirt etc*) ne nécessitant aucun repassage

drip-feed *vt* (*pt, pp* **drip-fed**) *Med* (*patient*) nourrir *ou* alimenter par perfusion

drip-feeding *n* alimentation *f* par perfusion

dripping ['drɪpɪŋ] **1** *adj* ruisselant; (*tap*) qui goutte; **to be d. wet** être trempé; **d. with perspiration/blood** ruisselant de sueur/sang; **2** *n* **(a)** égouttement *m* **(b)** *Br Culin* graisse *f* de rôti; **bread and d.** tartine *f* à la graisse; **d. pan** lèchefrite *f*

drippy ['drɪpɪ] *adj F* (*person*) mou, *f* molle; (*film, novel*) (*inane*) plat, fade; (*sentimental*) mélo

drive¹ [draɪv] *n* **(a)** *Aut* (*trip*) promenade *f* en voiture; (*in taxi*) course *f*; **a 50-km d.** un parcours *ou* un trajet de 50 km; **it's an hour's d. away** c'est à une heure en voiture; **to go for** *or* **take a d.** aller faire une promenade *ou* un (petit) tour en voiture, faire une promenade en voiture; **it's a very pleasant d. to the coast** la route est très belle jusqu'à la côte; *Aut* **test d.** conduite *f* d'essai

(b) (*of cattle*) conduite *f*; (*of deer*) battue *f*; *Am* (*guiding of logs*) (transport *m* du bois par le) flottage *m*, *Can* drave *f*; (*logs*) train *m* (de bois flotté)

(c) *MecE* (mouvement *m* de) propulsion *f*; (*by component*) commande *f*, transmission *f*, actionnement *m*; *Aut* (*for any shaft*) entraînement *m*; (*on automatic gearbox*) conduite *f* normale; **belt/chain d.** entraînement *ou* transmission par courroie/chaîne; **gear d.** commande par engrenages; *Aut* **direct d.** prise *f* directe; *Aut* **d. belt** courroie *f* d'entraînement; (*for interdependent parts*) courroie de commande; *Aut* **d. shaft** arbre *m* d'entraînement *ou* de commande

(d) *Aut* (*location of steering wheel*) conduite *f*; **left-hand d.** conduite à gauche; **car with left-hand d.** voiture avec conduite à gauche (**e**) (*shot*) *Golf, Tennis* drive *m*; *Cr* coup *m* droit long et appuyé

(**f**) *Fig* (*initiative*) énergie *f*, dynamisme *m*; **to have plenty of d.** être énergique *ou* entreprenant

(**g**) (*campaign*) (*to increase sales etc*) campagne *f*; (*against stronghold, abuse*) offensive *f*; **membership d.** campagne *f* pour attirer des membres

(**h**) *Psy* (*urge*) (*sexual etc*) pulsions *fpl*

(**i**) (*of house*) allée *f*; **the car's sitting in the d.** la voiture est garée dans l'allée

(**j**) *Cards* (*for bridge, whist*) tournoi *m*

(**k**) *Comptr* (*for disk*) lecteur *m*, unité *f*; **d. a:/b:** unité de disque a:/b:; **d. door** porte *f* de l'unité de disquette

drive² (*pt* **drove** [drəʊv]; *pp* **driven** ['drɪv(ə)n]) **1** *vt* (**a**) (*car, train*) conduire; (*racing car*) conduire, piloter; *Sp* (*trotting horse*) driver; **can you d. a car?** savez-vous conduire?; **to d. sb to a place** conduire qn en voiture quelque part; **I haven't driven all this way just to …** je n'ai pas fait tout ce chemin juste pour …

(**b**) (*cattle*) conduire, mener; (*deer etc*) rabattre; (*prisoners*) faire aller (devant soi); (*log train*) diriger; **thousands of people have been driven from their homes** des milliers de personnes ont été obligées de quitter leur maison; **to d. the enemy from his position** déloger l'ennemi; **the wind is driving the rain against the window panes** le vent abat la pluie contre les vitres; **the waves drove the ship onto the rocks** les vagues ont poussé le navire contre les rochers

(**c**) (*force*) (*sb to do sth*) pousser; **I was driven to resign** j'ai été forcé de démissionner; **he won't be driven** on ne le mène pas comme on veut; **to d. sb mad** *or* **out of his/her mind** rendre qn fou/folle; **she drove me to it** c'est elle qui m'y a poussé; **to d. sb to despair** réduire qn au désespoir; **to be driven by ambition** être mû par l'ambition

(**d**) (*one's employees*) surmener; **to d. oneself too hard** se surmener; **she drives herself as hard as she drives us** elle se surmène autant qu'elle nous surmène

(**e**) **to d. a bargain** conclure un marché; **to d. a hard bargain** chercher à gagner le dernier centime

(**f**) **to d. the ball** *Cr* chasser la balle; *Tennis* jouer un drive, driver; *Golf* driver

(**g**) *MecE* (*machine*) actionner, faire marcher; (*of part*) (*component*) actionner; *Comptr* (*of program*) commander, piloter; **to be driven by electricity** fonctionner à l'électricité

2 *vi* (**a**) *Aut* conduire; **can you d.?** savez-vous conduire?; **I don't d.** (*I never learned*) je n'ai pas mon permis; **who was driving?** qui était au volant?; **to d. to work** aller *ou* se rendre au travail en voiture; **to d. slowly/fast** rouler lentement/vite; **to d. on the right (of the road)** circuler à droite, tenir la droite; **car that drives well** voiture facile à conduire

(**b**) **the rain driving against the window panes** la pluie qui fouette les vitres; *Lit* **to d. before the wind** (*of clouds etc*) chasser devant le vent

▶ **drive along** *vi* rouler (en voiture); **I was driving along slowly** je roulais lentement; **to d. along the road** rouler sur la route

▶ **drive at** *vipo* **what are you driving at?** où voulez-vous en venir?; **what do you think she was driving at?** où croyez-vous qu'elle voulait en venir?

▶ **drive away 1** *vtsep* (**a**) (*dog, intruder*) chasser, éloigner, écarter; (*lover, spouse*) faire partir; (*friend*) éloigner; (*doubt, suspicion*) écarter; (*fear*) chasser (**b**) *Aut* (*person*) emmener en voiture; **the men came in a car and drove her away** des hommes sont arrivés et l'ont emmenée en voiture; **they were driven away in a taxi** ils ont été conduits en taxi **2** *vi* partir *ou* s'en aller en voiture; (*of car, bus*) s'éloigner; **he jumped into his car and drove away** il a sauté dans sa voiture et s'en est allé

▶ **drive back 1** *vtsep* (**a**) (*repel*) (*attack, demonstrators*) repousser; (*of flames*) faire reculer (**b**) *Aut* (*person*) reconduire *ou* ramener en voiture **2** *vi Aut* rentrer en voiture

▶ **drive down 1** *vtsep* (**a**) *Econ* (*prices, inflation etc*) faire baisser (**b**) *Aut* **to d. sb down to London** conduire qn à Londres **2** *vi Aut* (*from north to south*) se rendre en voiture; **how did you get here? – we drove down** comment êtes-vous venus? – nous sommes venus *ou* descendus en voiture; **to d. down to Marseilles** descendre à Marseille en voiture; **she had driven down from Inverness the day before** elle était descendue d'Inverness en voiture la veille

▶ **drive home** *vtsep* (**a**) (*nail*) enfoncer, renfoncer (**b**) (*make understood*) **to d. sth home to sb** faire comprendre qch à qn, *F* faire rentrer qch dans la tête de qn; **d. it home to them that they mustn't speak to strangers** fais-leur comprendre qu'ils ne doivent pas parler à des inconnus (**c**) *Aut* **to d. sb home** reconduire qn chez lui

▶ **drive in 1** *vtsep* (*nail*) enfoncer **2** *vi Aut* (*into garage*) entrer (en voiture); **he had driven in from the countryside** il était venu de la campagne en voiture

▶ **drive into 1** *vipo Aut* (*garage*) entrer dans (en voiture); **I'm driving into town** je vais en ville en voiture **2** *vtaspo* **to d. a nail into the wall** enfoncer un clou dans le mur; **he drove his fist into the other man's face** il a mis un coup de poing à l'autre

▶ **drive off 1** *vtsep* (**a**) (*repel*) (*attack, attackers*) repousser; (*mosquitoes*) chasser (**b**) *Aut* (*person*) emmener en voiture; **they were driven off in a taxi** ils ont été conduits en taxi **2** *vi* (**a**) *Aut* partir *ou* s'en aller en voiture; (*of car, bus*) s'éloigner; **he jumped into his car and drove off** il a sauté dans sa voiture et s'en est allé (**b**) *Golf* commencer la partie

▶ **drive on 1** *vi Aut* continuer (sa route); **the policeman told us to d. on** le gendarme nous a dit de circuler **2** *vtsep* (*sb*) pousser (**to do sth** à faire qch)

▶ **drive out 1** *vtsep* (*sb, sth*) chasser; **I will not be driven out of my home** on ne me chassera pas de ma maison; **we're being driven out of business by the supermarkets** les supermarchés nous font faire faillite **2** *vi Aut* **he had driven out from Glasgow** il était venu de Glasgow en voiture; **he drove out of the petrol station** il est sorti de la station d'essence

▶ **drive through 1** *vtaspo Constr* **to d. a tunnel through rock** percer *ou* forer un tunnel dans le rocher; **to d. a railway through the desert** tracer *ou* construire une ligne de chemin de fer à travers le désert; **to d. one's sword through sb's body** passer son sabre à travers le corps à qn **2** *vi Aut* passer en voiture; **we'll just d. through** (*not stop*) nous ne ferons que passer en voiture **3** *vipo Aut* (*town*) traverser en voiture

▶ **drive up 1** *vi Aut* s'approcher; **they've just driven up** ils viennent de s'approcher; **a car drove up to the door** une voiture vint s'arrêter devant la porte **2** *vtsep Econ* (*prices, inflation etc*) faire monter

driveability [draɪvə'bɪlɪtɪ] *n* (*of vehicle*) facilité *f ou* agrément *m* de conduite

drive-in *n Am Aut* (*cinema*) cinéma *m* en plein air auquel on assiste en voiture, drive-in *m inv*, *Can* ciné-parc *m*, *pl* cinés-parcs; (*restaurant*) restaurant *m* où les clients sont servis dans leurs voitures; **d. bank** banque *f* dont les guichets sont accessibles aux clients depuis leurs voitures

drivel¹ ['drɪv(ə)l] *n F* bêtises *fpl*, balivernes *fpl*; **to talk d.** radoter; **the film was absolute d.** le film n'était qu'un tas de balivernes

drivel² *vi* (**-ll-**, *US* **-l-**) *F* radoter; **what are you drivelling (on) about?** qu'est-ce que tu radotes?

driveline ['draɪvlaɪn] *n Aut* chaîne *f* cinématique

drivelling, *US* **driveling** ['drɪv(ə)lɪŋ] *adj F* radoteur, -euse; **you d. idiot!** espèce d'idiot!

driven ['drɪv(ə)n] *adj* (**a**) **d. snow** neige *f* vierge (**b**) (*person*) mû comme par une obsession (**c**) *Tech* **electrically d.** actionné par l'électricité

driver ['draɪvər] *n* (**a**) (*of car, bus*) conducteur, -trice, chauffeur, -euse; (*of taxi, truck*) chauffeur, -euse; (*of train*) mécanicien *m*; (*of tram*) mécanicien, wattman *m*; (*of horse-drawn vehicle*) conducteur, -trice; (*of horse-drawn carriage*) cocher *m*; *Sp* (*of trotting horse*) driver *m*; **he's a very good/bad d.** il conduit très bien/mal; *Aut* **d. alertness monitor** contrôleur *m* de vigilance du conducteur; *Am* **d.'s license** permis *m* de conduire; **d.'s seat** siège *m* du conducteur; *Fig* **to be in the d.'s seat** mener l'affaire; **that win really puts them in the d.'s seat** cette victoire les met dans une position dominante

(**b**) *Comptr* (*software*) programme *m* de gestion, pilote *m*, gestionnnaire *m* (de périphérique)

(**c**) (*of cattle*) conducteur *m*

(**d**) **log d.** flotteur *m*, driver *m*, *Can* draveur *m*

(**e**) *Golf* driver *m*

drive-time programme *n Rad* émission *f* aux heures de grande écoute en voiture

drivetrain ['draɪvtreɪn] *n Aut* chaîne *f* cinématique

driveway ['draɪvweɪ] *n* (*of house*) allée *f*

driving ['draɪvɪŋ] **1** *adj* (**a**) *MecE* (*wheel etc*) moteur, -trice; *Aut* **d. axle** essieu *m* moteur; **d. belt** courroie *f* de commande; **d. force** force *f* motrice; *Fig* **the d. force behind the scheme** le moteur du projet; **d. gear** (engrenage *m* de) transmission *f*, pignon *m* d'entraînement; **d. shaft** arbre *m* de transmission; **d. wheel** roue *f* motrice; (*of locomotive etc*) roue de transmission

(**b**) (*rain*) battant; **d. snow** neige fouettée par le vent

2 *n* (**a**) (*of car etc*) conduite *f*; **d. is fun** c'est amusant de conduire; **his d. is awful** il conduit affreusement mal; **d.**

conditions conditions *fpl* de conduite; **d. lamp** feu *m* de route; **d. lessons** leçons *fpl* de conduite

(b) **log d.** flottage *m* du bois, *Can* drave *f*

(c) *Golf* **d. iron** grand fer *m*, driver *m*

driving instructor *n* moniteur, -trice d'auto-école, moniteur *m* de conduite

driving licence *n Br* permis *m* de conduire

driving mirror *n* rétroviseur *m*

driving school *n* auto-école *f*, *pl* auto-écoles

driving seat *n* siège *m* du conducteur; *Fig* **to be in the d.** mener l'affaire

driving test *n* (examen *m* pour) permis *m* de conduire; **to pass/fail one's d.** avoir/rater son permis (de conduire)

drizzle[1] ['drɪz(ə)l] *n* bruine *f*, crachin *m*; **the rain came down in a steady d.** il tombait un crachin persistant

drizzle[2] *vi* bruiner; **it was drizzling** il bruinait, il faisait de la bruine

drizzly ['drɪz(ə)lɪ] *adj* (*day*) bruineux

drogue [drəʊg] *n* (a) *Naut* cône-ancre *m*, *pl* cônes-ancres (b) *Av* (*for slowing descent*) parachute *m* de queue

droll [drəʊl] *adj* drôle, comique; *Iron* **oh, very d.!** très drôle!

dromedary ['drɒmədə(ə)rɪ] *n* dromadaire *m*

drone[1] [drəʊn] *n* (a) (*bee*) abeille *f* mâle, faux-bourdon *m*, *pl* faux-bourdons; *Fig Pej* (*parasite*) fainéant *m*, parasite *m* (b) (*noise*) (*of bee, conversation, traffic*) bourdonnement *m*; (*of plane*) ronronnement *m*; *Mus* (*of bagpipe*) bourdon *m*; *Fig* (*of speaker etc*) débit *m* monotone (c) *Mil, Av* avion *m* téléguidé, drone *m*

drone[2] 1 *vi* (*of bee etc*) bourdonner; (*of plane*) ronronner; *Fig* (*of person*) parler d'un ton monotone; **a droning sound** un bourdonnement; **a droning voice** une voix monotone 2 *vt* (*sth*) dire d'un ton monotone

▶ **drone on, drone away** *vi* **he droned on for hours** il n'a pas cessé de parler de sa voix monotone; **to d. on** *or* **away about sth** parler de qch ad nauseam

drool [dru:l] *vi* (*dribble*) baver; *Fig* (*gloat*) baver d'admiration; *Fig* **the sight of her in her bikini made him d.** ça le faisait baver de la voir dans son bikini

▶ **drool over** *vipo* (*sth*) baver d'admiration à la vue de

droop[1] [dru:p] *n* **he could tell from the d. of her shoulders/head** il savait à ses épaules tombantes/à la façon dont elle penchait la tête

droop[2] 1 *vi* (*of head*) (se) pencher; (*of shoulders, moustache*) tomber; (*of eyelids*) s'abaisser; (*of feathers*) pendre; (*of flower*) baisser la tête; *Fig* (*of person*) languir; **his spirits drooped at the thought** cette pensée le démoralisa 2 *vt* (*head*) baisser, pencher

drooping ['dru:pɪŋ] *adj* (*shoulders, moustache*) tombant; (*head*) baissé, penché; (*eyelids*) abaissé; (*flower*) qui commence à faner; *Fig* (*person*) languissant; **to revive sb's d. spirits** remonter le moral à qn

droopy ['dru:pɪ] *adj* (*moustache*) tombant; *Fig* (*weak, not very well*) patraque, mal fichu

drop[1] [drɒp] *n* (a) (*of water, blood*) goutte *f*; (*of wine*) doigt *m*, larme *f*; *Culin* (*of vinegar*) filet *m*; (*of necklace, chandelier etc*) pendant *m*, pendeloque *f*; **d. by d.** goutte à goutte; *Fig* **it's only a d. in the ocean** *or* **bucket** ce n'est qu'une goutte d'eau dans la mer; *Pharm* **drops** gouttes; *F* **to take a d.** boire un verre; **you've had a d. too much (to drink)** tu as un peu trop bu; **he likes a wee d.** il aime bien prendre la goutte; **I haven't touched a d. since** je n'y ai pas touché depuis; **acid d.** bonbon *m* acidulé; **chocolate d.** pastille *f* de chocolat

(b) (*fall*) (*in price, enrolments etc*) chute *f*, baisse *f*; (*in pressure*) perte *f*, chute; **a d. of a couple of inches** un différence de niveau de quelques centimètres; **a d. of a hundred metres** (*sharp*) un à-pic de cent mètres; **careful, it's a long d.** attention, c'est haut; **d. in the ground** dénivellation *f* du terrain; *Fig* **at the d. of a hat** sans hésiter, sans la moindre hésitation; (*without any warning*) sur-le-champ, immédiatement; **he gets angry at the d. of a hat** il se met en colère pour un oui pour un non

(c) *Av* parachutage *m*, droppage *m*

(d) *Old-fashioned F* **the d.** (*hanging*) la potence; **he's for the d.** il est bon pour la potence; *Fig Hum* son compte est bon

(e) *Th* **d. (curtain)** rideau *m* d'entr'acte

(f) *Rugby* **d. goal** drop-goal *m*, *pl* drop-goals, drop *m*; **d. kick** coup *m* tombé, coup de pied à ras de terre; *Tennis* **d. shot** volée *f* amortie, amorti *m*

(g) *Metal* **d. forge** *or* **hammer** marteau-pilon *m*, *pl* marteaux-pilons; **d. handlebars** (*on bicycle*) guidon *m* renversé, aile *f* de dérive; **d.-leaf table** table *f* à battants

(h) (*for spies to leave letters etc*) boîte aux lettres *f*, planque *f*

(i) *F* **to have/get the d. on sb** (*have advantage*) avoir/prendre l'avantage sur qn

(j) (*length*) (*of curtain, blind, earring*) hauteur *f*

drop[2] (-pp- [drɒpt]) 1 *vi* (a) (*of object*) tomber; (*of person*) se laisser tomber; (*of ground*) s'abaisser, s'affaisser; *Med* (*of womb etc*) descendre; **the book dropped from** *or* **out of her hands** le livre lui tomba des mains; **his jaw dropped** il en est resté bouche bée; **to d. into a chair** s'affaler dans un fauteuil; **I'm ready to d.** (*with fatigue*) je tombe de fatigue, je ne tiens plus sur mes jambes; (*with sleep*) je tombe de sommeil; **people are dropping like flies** (*succumbing quickly to flu etc*) les gens tombent comme des mouches; **to d. (down) dead** tomber (raide) mort; *Sl* **d. dead!** va te faire voir!; **he can d. dead for all I care** il peut aller se faire voir; **he's dropped to sixth place** il est descendu à la sixième place; **to d. to the rear** passer à l'arrière; *F* **let it d.!** n'en parlons plus!; **I'm not going to let it d.** (*grievance etc*) je ne vais pas laisser passer cela

(b) (*of liquid*) tomber doucement (**from** de); (*of rain*) tomber

(c) (*of prices, temperature, voice etc*) baisser; (*of prices*) reculer; (*of wind*) tomber; (*of speed*) diminuer

2 *vt* (a) (*object*) laisser tomber, lâcher; (*bomb*) lancer; (*parachutist*) lâcher; *Naut* (*anchor*) jeter, mouiller; *Comptr* (*icon*) lâcher; **d. it!** (*to dog*) lâche ça!; **he dropped it from the balcony to his accomplice** il l'a lancé à son complice depuis le balcon; **to d. a word in sb's ear** glisser *ou* couler un mot à l'oreille de qn; **to d. a letter into the pillar box** mettre une lettre à la poste; **to d. sb a line/a card** envoyer *ou* écrire un mot/une carte à qn

(b) (*lower*) (*one's eyes, veil, curtain*) baisser; (*one's arms*) laisser tomber; **to d. a curtsey** faire une révérence; **to d. the hem of a dress** allonger une robe; *Av* **to d. a wing** piquer de l'aile

(c) (*set down*) *Aut* (*person*) déposer, descendre (de voiture); *Naut* (*pilot*) débarquer

(d) (*give up, stop*) (*work*) abandonner, délaisser; (*pursuit*) cesser, lâcher; **to d. the idea of doing sth** renoncer à (l'idée de) faire qch; **I've dropped the idea** j'y ai renoncé; **let's d. the subject** ne parlons plus de cela!; *F* **d. it!** en voilà assez!; **just d. it, okay?** laisse tomber, hein?; **to d. everything** laisser tout tomber; *Sch* **to d. maths** arrêter les maths; **to d. sb** laisser tomber qn; *F* **to d. sb like a hot brick** *or* **potato** laisser tomber qn du jour au lendemain; *Sp* **to d. a player** laisser tomber un équipier; **she's been dropped from the team** elle a été écartée de l'équipe; *Jur* **to d. the charges** abandonner l'accusation (**against** contre)

(e) (*omit*) (*letter, syllable*) omettre, supprimer; (*when speaking*) (*the r etc*) ne pas prononcer; **cases in which the article is dropped** cas où l'on supprime l'article; **you can d. the 'sir' when we're on our own** vous pouvez laisser tomber les 'monsieurs' quand nous sommes seuls

(f) (*lose*) (*money, Sp points, serve, stitch*) perdre

(g) *Zool* (*of sheep etc*) (*young*) mettre bas

▶ **drop away** *vi* (*of support, attendance etc*) diminuer

▶ **drop back** *vi* = **drop behind 1**

▶ **drop behind 1** *vi* (*in race*) se laisser distancer; (*with work*) prendre du retard (**with** dans); **she dropped behind to talk to John** elle est passée vers l'arrière pour parler à John 2 *vipo* (*sb*) se laisser distancer par

▶ **drop by** *vi* passer (chez qn); **I thought I'd d. by for a chat** je me suis dit que je passerais pour bavarder deux minutes

▶ **drop down** *vi* (a) (*of person*) (*accidentally*) tomber par terre; (*deliberately*) se mettre par *ou* à terre; **to d. down dead** tomber (raide) mort; **they dropped down into the Second Division** ils sont descendus en deuxième division (b) (*of flap etc*) s'abaisser

▶ **drop in 1** *vtsep* (*sth*) laisser tomber dedans, mettre dedans; **d. this letter in the box for me** mets cette lettre à la boîte; *F* **you dropped me right in it** tu m'as mis dans la merde 2 *vi* **to d. in at the butcher's** passer chez le boucher; **to d. in on sb** (*for a few minutes*) faire une petite visite à qn; (*arrive unexpectedly*) venir en visite chez qn à l'improviste; **I'll d. in on my way home** (*to see you*) je passerai (chez toi) en rentrant; **they're always dropping in on us** ils nous tombent toujours dessus à l'improviste

▶ **drop off 1** *vi* (a) (*fall, become detached*) (*of leaves etc*) tomber, se détacher; **I feel as if my arm is going to d. off** (*because this case is so heavy etc*) j'ai l'impression que mon bras va lâcher

(b) *F* **to d. off (to sleep)** s'assoupir, s'endormir; **it was two o'clock before I finally dropped off** je ne me suis pas endormi avant deux heures du matin; **she dropped off for a few hours** elle a dormi quelques heures

(c) (*decline*) (*of membership, attendance etc*) diminuer

2 *vtsep* (a) (*deposit*) (*letter, parcel etc*) déposer

(b) (*let out of car*) (*person*) déposer; **where do you want to be dropped off?** où veux-tu que je te dépose?

▶ **drop out 1** *vtsep* laisser tomber dehors; **he dropped it out of the window** il l'a laissé tomber par la fenêtre **2** *vi* **(a)** (*from pocket, briefcase etc*) tomber **(b)** *F* (*from school*) abandonner ses études; (*from class*) abandonner *ou* laisser tomber (un cours); (*from contest*) se retirer; (*from society*) rejeter la société; **he dropped out at the age of 14** il a abandonné ses études à 14 ans; **to d. out of university** laisser tomber l'université

▶ **drop round** *vi* = **drop in 2**

drop arm *n Aut* bielle *f* pendante

drop-deadline *n F* délai *m* de rigueur

drop-down menu *n Comptr* menu *m* déroulant

drop-forge *vt Metal* étamper, estamper

drop-forging *n Metal* **(a)** (*process*) estampage *m* **(b)** (*result*) pièce *f* emboutie *ou* étampée

drophead ['drɒphed] *n Aut* capote *f* rabattable; **d. coupé** coupé *m* décapotable *ou* cabriolet

drop-in centre *n Br* centre *m* de permanence (*où on est reçu sans rendez-vous*)

droplet ['drɒplɪt] *n* gouttelette *f*

drop letter *n Typ* lettrine *f*

dropout ['drɒpaʊt] *n* **(a)** *F Sch, Univ* étudiant, -ante qui abandonne ses études; (*from society*) marginal, -ale **(b)** (*on a tape*) blanc *m*, perte *f* de signal

dropped [drɒpt] *adj* **(a)** *Aut etc* (*axle etc*) surbaissé **(b)** *Rugby* **d. goal** drop-goal *m*, *pl* drop-goals

dropper ['drɒpər] *n* compte-gouttes *m inv*

dropping ['drɒpɪŋ] *n* **(a)** (*of object*) descente *f*, chute *f*; *Av* (*of parachutist, package*) largage *m*, droppage *m*; *Av* **d. zone** zone *f* de largage *ou* de droppage **(b)** (*reduction*) (*of prices*) baisse *f*, chute *f* **(c)** (*omission*) (*of word*) suppression *f* **(d)** (*abandonment*) (*of project, course*) abandon *m* **(e)** *Aut* (*of chassis*) surbaissement *m* **(f)** *Vet* **d. (of young)** mise *f* bas

dropping off *n* (*of attendance etc*) diminution *f*

dropping out *n F Sch, Univ* abandon *m*; (*from society*) désinsertion *f* sociale

droppings ['drɒpɪŋz] *npl* (*of animals, birds*) fiente *f*; (*of sheep*) crottes *fpl*

dropsical ['drɒpsɪk(ə)l] *adj Med* hydropique

dropsy ['drɒpsɪ] *n Med* hydropisie *f*

drop test *n Aut* essai *m* de chute

dross [drɒs] *n* **(a)** *Metal* scories *fpl*, crasse *f* **(b)** (*waste*) impuretés *fpl*, déchets *mpl*; *F* (*rubbish*) rebut *m*

drought [draʊt] *n* sécheresse *f*

drove [drəʊv] *n* **(a)** (*of cattle etc*) troupeau *m* en marche **(b)** **droves** (*of people*) foules *fpl* (de personnes en marche); **to arrive** *or* **come in droves** (*of sightseers, tourists etc*) arriver en foule

drover ['drəʊvər] *n* conducteur *m ou* toucheur *m* de bestiaux

drown [draʊn] **1** *vt* **(a)** (*kill*) noyer; **to d. oneself** se noyer; **to be drowned** (*by accident*) se noyer; (*on purpose*) être noyé; **drowned at sea** noyé en mer; *Fig* **to d. one's sorrows (in drink)** noyer son chagrin dans la boisson

(b) (*flood*) (*meadow, city*) inonder, submerger; **eyes drowned in tears** yeux noyés de larmes; **don't d. it!** (*when adding water etc to alcoholic drink*) ne le noie pas!

(c) (*make inaudible*) (*sound*) étouffer; **the noise of the waterfall drowned her voice** le bruit de la cascade a couvert sa voix

2 *vi* se noyer; *Fig* (*be unable to cope*) être dépassé; **I'm drowning in a sea of paper** je suis dans la paperasse jusqu'au cou

▶ **drown out** *vtsep* (*sound*) couvrir; (*person*) couvrir la voix de

drowned [draʊnd] *adj* **(a)** (*person, animal*) noyé; **a d. man/woman** un noyé/une noyée; *Fig* **he came home like a d. rat** il est rentré trempé comme une soupe **(b)** (*land*) inondé

drowning ['draʊnɪŋ] **1** *adj* **a d. man** un homme qui se noie **2** *n* **(a)** **(case of) d.** noyade *f*; **to save sb from d.** sauver qn qui se noie, sauver qn de la noyade **(b)** (*of fields*) inondation *f*

drowse [draʊz] *vi* somnoler

drowsily ['draʊzɪlɪ] *adv* (*to look at*) d'un air somnolent, à demi endormi; (*to say*) d'une voix endormie *ou* ensommeillée, à demi endormi; (*to think, reflect*) à moitié endormi

drowsiness ['draʊzɪnɪs] *n* somnolence *f*; **may cause d.** (*notice on bottle of cough mixture etc*) peut entraîner une somnolence

drowsy ['draʊzɪ] *adj* (*person*) somnolent; (*atmosphere*) engourdi; (*voice*) endormi, ensommeillé; **to be** *or* **feel d.** avoir envie de dormir, avoir sommeil

drub [drʌb] *vt* **(-bb-)** (*sb, the enemy*) battre, rosser

▶ **drub into** *vtaspo* **to d. sth into sb** faire entrer qch de force dans la tête de qn

drubbing ['drʌbɪŋ] *n* (*with stick, fists*) volée *f* de coups; *Fig* défaite *f*; **to give an opponent a d.** battre un adversaire à plates coutures

drudge[1] [drʌdʒ] *n* femme *f*/homme *m* de peine; **the household d.** la cendrillon

drudge[2] *vi* trimer, peiner

drudgery ['drʌdʒərɪ] *n* travail *m* pénible *ou* ingrat, corvée(s) *f(pl)*; **just two more weeks of d.** plus que deux semaines à trimer; **the d. of housework** le caractère pénible *ou* ingrat des tâches ménagères

drug[1] [drʌg] *n* **(a)** (*medication*) médicament *m*, drogue *f*; **d. company** compagnie *f* de produits pharmaceutiques

(b) (*narcotic*) drogue *f*, stupéfiant *m*; **hard/soft drugs** drogues dures/douces; **to take** *or* **be on** *or F* **do drugs** se droguer; **to be arrested on d. charges** (*for using/possessing/dealing*) être arrêté pour utilisation/possession/trafic de stupéfiants; **athletes who take drugs** les athlètes qui se dopent; **the whole question of drugs in sport** tout le problème du dopage dans le sport; *Fig* **computer games are a d.** les jeux électroniques sont une véritable drogue; *Fig Mktg* **d. on the market** produit *m* invendable; **to be a d. on the market** être invendable; **truth d.** sérum *m* de vérité; **d. money** narco-dollars *mpl*; **d. taking** toxicomanie *f*; *Sp* dopage *m*

drug[2] *vt* **(-gg-)** (*person, guard dog, wild animal, horse*) droguer; (*horse*) (*to increase performance*) doper; **to d. oneself** prendre de la drogue; (*habitually*) se droguer; **they had drugged his wine/food** on avait mis un narcotique dans son vin/sa nourriture; *F* **he's drugged up to the eyeballs** (*after operation*) il est bourré de médicaments; **to be in a drugged sleep** dormir profondément sous l'effet d'un narcotique

drug abuse *n* usage *m* de stupéfiants

drug addict *n* toxicomane *mf*

drug addiction *n* toxicomanie *f*

drug baron *n* nabab *m* de la drogue

drug dealer *n* dealer *m*

drug dependency *n* dépendance *f* à l'égard des drogues, toxicomanie *f*; *Med Spec* pharmacodépendance *f*

druggist ['drʌgɪst] *n Am* pharmacien, -ienne; **wholesale d.** pharmacien, -ienne en gros

druggy ['drʌgɪ] *n F* camé, -ée

drug peddling *n* trafic *m* de drogue

drug pusher *n* revendeur, -euse de drogue

drug pushing *n* trafic *m* de drogue

drug smuggler *n* trafiquant, -ante de drogue

drug smuggling *n* trafic *m* de drogue

drug squad *n* (*of police force*) brigade *f* des stupéfiants

drugstore ['drʌgstɔːr] *n Am* drugstore *m*

drug trafficker *n* narco-traffiquant, -ante

drug trafficking *n* trafic *m* de drogue

druid ['druːɪd] *n* druide *mf*

drum[1] [drʌm] *n* **(a)** *Mus* tambour *m*; **the drums** la batterie; **to beat the d.** battre du tambour; **to play the drums** jouer de la batterie; **big** *or* **bass d.** grosse caisse *f*; *Fig* **to bang** *or* **beat the d. for sb/sth** battre le tambour pour qn/qch; **d. kit** batterie *f* **(b)** (*container*) tonneau *m* en fer, fût *m*; (*for oil*) bidon *m*, tambour *m* **(c)** *MecE etc* tambour *m*; (*of winch*) cylindre *m*; **concrete mixing d.** mélangeur *m* à béton, bétonnière *f*; **cable d.** tambour, dévidoir *m* (*de câble électrique*) **(d)** (*for laser printer*) tambour *m*; **d. kit** kit *m* tambour; **d. plotter** traceur *m* à tambour

drum[2] **(-mm-) 1** *vi Mus* jouer de la batterie; *Mil* battre du tambour; **he drummed with** *or* **for the Beatles** il était batteur *ou* il jouait de la batterie pour les Beatles; **to d. on the window panes** (*of person, rain*) tambouriner sur les vitres; **her fingers were drumming on the table** elle tapotait sur la table **2** *vt* **to d. a tune on sth** tambouriner un air sur qch; **she was drumming her fingers on the table** elle tapotait sur la table

▶ **drum into** *vtaspo* **to d. sth into sb** enfoncer qch dans la tête de qn; **d. it into them that they mustn't take sweets from strangers** mets-leur bien dans la tête qu'ils ne doivent pas accepter de bonbons offerts par des inconnus

▶ **drum out** *vtsep* **(a)** *Mil, Hist* (*soldier*) renvoyer **(of** de) **(b)** *Fig* (*from a club etc*) (*person*) expulser avec ignominie

▶ **drum up** *vtsep* (*supporters*) racoler; (*friends*) battre le rappel de; **to d. up customers** rechercher de la clientèle; **to d. up support for sth** rechercher du soutien pour qch

drumbeat ['drʌmbiːt] *n* coup *m* de tambour

drumhead ['drʌmhed] *n Mus* dessus *m* de tambour; *Mil* **d. court-martial** conseil *m* de guerre (*tenu sur le champ de bataille*); *Mil, Rel* **d. service** office *m* divin en plein air

drum major *n Mil* tambour-major *m*, *pl* tambours-majors

drum majorette *n US* majorette *f*

drummer ['drʌmər] *n* (*of drum*) tambour *m*; (*of kettle-drum*) timbalier *m*; (*playing jazz, rock*) batteur *m*; **d. boy** tambour; *Fig* **to march to a different d.** suivre son propre chemin

drumming ['drʌmɪŋ] *n* **(a)** (*sound*) (*of rain, fists*), *Mus* tambourinage *m*; **the d. of her fingers on the table was driving me crazy** la façon qu'elle avait de tapoter sur la table me rendait fou **(b)** (*action*) (*of woodpecker*) tambourinage *m*; *Mus* **his d. has improved** il s'est amélioré à la batterie

drum roll *n* roulement *m* de tambour

drumstick ['drʌmstɪk] *n* **(a)** *Mus* baguette *f* de tambour *ou* de timbale **(b)** *Culin* (*of chicken*) pilon *m*

drunk [drʌŋk] **1** *pp see* **drink²**

2 *adj* ivre, soûl, gris; *Fig* enivré (**with success** par le succès); **to get d.** se soûler (**on sth** à qch); **to make** *or* **get sb d.** soûler qn; **d. drivers** les personnes qui conduisent en état d'ivresse; **d. as a lord** soûl comme un Polonais; *Jur* **d. and disorderly** = en état d'ivresse manifeste dans un lieu public; *Fig* **d. with joy/power** ivre de joie/puissance; **he is d. with power** le pouvoir lui a monté à la tête

3 *n* homme *m* soûl/femme *f* soûle; (*habitual*) ivrogne *mf*; **the city centre was full of drunks** le centre-ville était plein de gens soûls *ou* ivres; **some old d. came up to me** un vieil ivrogne s'est approché de moi

drunkard ['drʌŋkəd] *n* ivrogne *mf*

drunken ['drʌŋk(ə)n] *adj* (*person*) ivre; (*fury, stupor*) alcoolique; (*party, celebration*) bien arrosé; (*laughter, voice*) d'ivrogne; **d. brawl** querelle *f* d'ivrognes; **d. state** état *m* d'ivresse; *Jur* **d. driving** conduite *f* en état d'ébriété

drunkenly ['drʌŋk(ə)nlɪ] *adv* (*to sing, speak*) d'une voix d'ivrogne; **to stagger d.** tituber; **to quarrel d.** avoir une querelle d'ivrognes; **he slumped d. onto his chair** complètement soûl, il s'est affalé sur sa chaise

drunkenness ['drʌŋk(ə)nnɪs] *n* ivresse *f*; (*habitual*) ivrognerie *f*

drunkometer [drʌŋ'kɒmɪtər] *n US* alcootest *m*

drupe [dru:p] *n Bot* drupe *f*

dry¹ [draɪ] **1** *adj* (**drier, driest**) **(a)** (*weather, cold, bread, clothing etc*) sec, *f* sèche; (*well, spring*) tari, à sec; (*river*) asséché; *Ind, Ch etc* (*process, analysis*) par voie sèche; **tomorrow will be d. and bright** demain sera une journée sans pluie et ensoleillée; **to be** *or* **feel d.** (*of thirsty person*) avoir la gorge sèche; **to pump a well d.** épuiser l'eau d'un puits; **to run** *or* **go d.** (*of river*) s'assécher; (*of spring, well*) s'épuiser, (se) tarir; (*of pump*) se désamorcer; **to run d.** (*of speaker*) être à sec; **I've run d.** (*of author*) mon inspiration s'est tarie; **to be kept d.** (*notice on container*) garder au sec; *F* **d. as a bone, bone d.** sec comme une allumette; **d. battery** *or* **cell** pile *f* sèche; **d. country** pays *m* aride; *Fig* pays sec (*où les boissons alcoolisées sont prohibées*); *Fig* **to go d.** (*prohibit alcohol*) prohiber la consommation des boissons alcoolisées; **there wasn't a d. eye in the house** tout le monde pleurait; *Fishing* **d. fly** mouche *f* sèche; **d. land** (*as opposed to sea*) terre *f* ferme; **d. measure** mesure *f* sèche; **to have d. skin** avoir la peau sèche; *Met* **d. spell** éclaircie *f*; **d. stone walling** murs *mpl* en pierres sèches; (*process*) construction *f* en pierres sèches; **d. weather tyre** pneu *m* temps sec; **d. work** (*causing thirst*) travail *m* qui donne soif

(b) (*drinks*) **d. martini** martini *m* bianco; **d. wine** vin *m* sec; **medium d. wine** vin demi-sec, *pl* vins demi-secs; **extra d. champagne** champagne *m* brut

(c) (*dull, boring*) (*subject*) aride; (*book, lecture*) ennuyeux; **to be as d. as dust** être ennuyeux comme la pluie

(d) (*ironic*) (*person*) pince-sans-rire; (*wit, humour*) teinté d'ironie; **he has a d. manner** il est plutôt pince-sans-rire

(e) *Br Pol F* dur

(f) *Av, Naut* **d. lease** location *f* d'avion/de bateau sans carburant ni équipage

2 *n* **(a)** *Br Pol F* dur *m*, dure *f*

(b) *Austr F* **the d.** la saison sèche

(c) **to stay in the d.** rester au sec *ou* à couvert

dry² (**dried** [draɪd]) **1** *vt* sécher; (*clothes*) faire sécher; (*skin*) dessécher; **to d. the dishes** essuyer la vaisselle; **to d. one's eyes** s'essuyer les yeux; **to d. one's hair** se sécher les cheveux; **to d. one's tears** sécher ses larmes **2** *vi* **(a)** (*of clothes, paint, cement*) sécher; (*of skin*) se dessécher; **to put sth out to d.** mettre qch à sécher dehors; **it's my turn to d.** (*when doing the dishes*) c'est à moi d'essuyer la vaisselle; **ink that dries black** encre qui vire au noir en séchant **(b)** *F* (*of actor*) oublier ses lignes

▸ **dry off** **1** *vi* (*of varnish, paint etc*) sécher; (*of person*) se sécher **2** *vtsep* (*person*) sécher; **come and d. yourself off in front of the fire** viens te sécher devant le feu

▸ **dry out** **1** *vi* **(a)** *F* (*of alcoholic*) se faire désintoxiquer **(b)** (*of moisture*) s'évaporer, sécher; (*of skin, wooden furniture*) se déssécher; (*of soil, wood*) sécher; **leave your wet things in the bathroom to d. out** laisse tes affaires à sécher dans la salle de bain **2** *vtsep* **(a)** *F* (*alcoholic*) désintoxiquer **(b)** (*water*) faire évaporer; (*skin*) dessécher; (*ground, football pitch, wood*) sécher

▸ **dry up** **1** *vi* (*of well, pool etc*) se dessécher, tarir; *Fig* (*of funds, conversation*) tarir; (*of inspiration*) se tarir; (*of author etc*) épuiser son inspiration; (*of speaker, actor etc*) oublier son texte; **the well has dried up** le puits est à sec; *Sl* **d. up!** (*be quiet!*) la ferme!, ta gueule! **2** *vtsep* (*dishes*) essuyer; (*roads, ground*) sécher; (*skin*) dessécher

dryad ['draɪæd] *n Myth* dryade *f*

dry-clean *vt* nettoyer à sec

dry-cleaner *n* nettoyeur *m* à sec, teinturier *m*; **take it to the d.'s** portez-le à la teinturerie *ou* au pressing

dry-cleaning *n* **(a)** (*process*) nettoyage *m* à sec; **d. is not recommended** (*on label*) le nettoyage à sec n'est pas recommandé **(b)** (*clothes*) vêtements *mpl* laissés chez le teinturier; **pick up the d. for me** va me chercher les vêtements chez le teinturier

dry dock *n Naut* cale *f* sèche; **to be in d.** (*of ship*) être en cale sèche

dry-dock **1** *vt* (*ship*) mettre en cale sèche **2** *vi* (*of ship*) entrer en cale sèche

dryer ['draɪər] *n* **(a)** (*device*) *Ind* sécheur *m*, séchoir *m*; **hair d.** (*hand-held*) séchoir (à cheveux), sèche-cheveux *m inv*; (*on stand*) casque *m* sèche-cheveux; **clothes-d.** (*hanging from ceiling, folding etc*) séchoir; **spin d.** essoreuse *f* (centrifuge); **tumble d.** séchoir rotatif (à air chaud); *Phot* **plate d.** sèche-cliché *m*, *pl* sèche-clichés **(b)** (*in paint etc*) siccatif *m*

dry-eyed *adj* les yeux secs, l'œil sec

dry goods *npl Am* étoffes *fpl* et articles *mpl* de mercerie

dry ice *n* neige *f* carbonique

drying ['draɪɪŋ] **1** *adj* **(a)** (*wind*) (*which dries up skin*) desséchant; **a good d. wind** (*for clothes*) un bon vent pour sécher le linge **(b)** **quick-d.** (*oil, varnish*) siccatif **2** *n* séchage *m*; (*of skin*) dessèchement *m*; (*with a cloth*) essuyage *m*; **d. rack** (*for clothes*) séchoir *m*

drying out **(a)** *F* (*of alcoholic*) désintoxication *f* **(b)** (*of skin*) dessèchement *m*; (*of soil, wood, clothes*) séchage *m*

drying up **(a)** (*of stream, river etc*) tarissement *m* **(b)** (*of dishes*) essuyage *m*; **I'll do the d.** je vais essuyer (la vaisselle)

dryly ['draɪlɪ] *adv* (*with irony*) avec une pointe d'ironie, d'un air de pince-sans-rire

dryness ['draɪnɪs] *n* **(a)** (*of region, weather, ground*) sécheresse *f* **(b)** (*of speech*) aridité *f* **(c)** (*of tone*) ironie *f*; **the d. of her wit** son humour pince-sans-rire

dry-roasted [draɪ'rəʊstɪd] *adj* (*peanuts*) grillé à sec

dry rot *n* (*in timber*) pourriture *f* sèche

dry run *n Mil* exercices *mpl* d'entraînement avec munitions à blanc; *Fig* coup *m* d'essai, test *m* à sec

DSC [di:es'si:] *n Br Mil abbr* **Distinguished Service Cross**

D. Sc. [di:es'si:] *n Univ abbr* **Doctor of Science**

DSM [di:e'sem] *n Br Mil abbr* **Distinguished Service Medal**

DSO [di:e'səʊ] *n Br Mil abbr* **Distinguished Service Order**

DSS [di:e'ses] *n Br Admin abbr* **Department of Social Security**

DST [di:es'ti:] *n Am* (*abbr* **daylight saving time**) HAE *f*

DTI [di:ti:'aɪ] *n Br Admin abbr* **Department of Trade and Industry**

DTP [di:ti:'pi:] *n Comptr* (*abbr* **desktop publishing**) PAO *f*

DTs [di:'ti:z] *npl F* (*abbr* **delirium tremens**) **to have the DTs** (*of alcoholic*) faire une crise de delirium tremens

dual ['dju:əl] *adj* **(a)** double; **to have d. nationality** avoir la double nationalité; **to have a d. function** *or* **purpose** avoir une double fonction; *Aut* **d.-control car** voiture *f* à double commande; **d. ownership** copropriété *f*; *Aut* **d. wheels** roues *fpl* jumelées **(b)** *Math* dual

dual carriageway *n Br Aut* route *f* à deux chaussées

dualism ['dju:əlɪz(ə)m] *n* dualité *f*; *Phil* dualisme *m*

duality [dju:'ælɪtɪ] *n* dualité *f*; *Psy* (*of personality*) dédoublement *m*

dual personality *n Psy* dédoublement *m* de la personnalité

dual-purpose *adj* à double emploi

dual-venturi ['dju:əlven'tjʊərɪ] *adj Aut* à double venturi

dub¹ [dʌb] *n Cin, TV* (*sound*) repiquage *m*; (*video*) copie *f*; (*action*) doublage *m*

dub² *vt* (**-bb-**) (*film*) (*into foreign language*) doubler (**into** en); (*original voice soundtrack*) sonoriser; (*sound*) post-synchroniser; (*video*) faire une copie de dans un autre format

dub³ *vt* (**-bb-**) **(a)** **to d. sb (a) knight** armer *ou* adouber qn chevalier; *Fig* **he was dubbed the king of tennis** on l'a surnommé le roi du tennis **(b)** (*leather*) préparer au dégras

dubbin¹ ['dʌbɪn] *n* (*for leather*) dégras *m*

dubbin² *vt* (*shoes*) enduire de dégras

dubbing ['dʌbɪŋ] *n Cin, TV* (*into foreign language*) doublage *m*; (*of original voice soundtrack*) sonorisation *f*; (*of sound*) post-synchronisation *f*, repiquage *m* du son, mixage *m*; **d. mixer** mélangeur *m* de son, ingénieur *m* du son; **d. suite** studio *m* de doublage

dubiety [dju:'baɪətɪ] *n Fml* = **dubiousness**

dubious ['dju:bɪəs] *adj* **(a)** (*uncertain*) (*person*) qui doute; (*outcome*) incertain; **d. expression** air *m* de doute; **she looked d.** elle avait l'air d'avoir des doutes; **d. as to what he should do** ne sachant trop ce qu'il devait faire; **I'm still a bit d.** j'ai encore quelques doutes; **we were d. about the scheme** nous avions des doutes sur le projet; **it is d. whether they will succeed in persuading him** il est incertain qu'ils réussissent à le persuader

(b) *Pej* (*suspect, questionable*) (*origin*) douteux; (*advantage*) contestable; (*distinction, honour*) triste; (*compliment*) équivoque; (*company*) douteux, louche; **financiers of d. character** financiers véreux

dubiously ['dju:bɪəslɪ] *adv* (*to say*) d'un ton de doute; (*to look at*) d'un air de doute

dubiousness ['dju:bɪəsnɪs] *n* **(a)** (*uncertainty*) (*of outcome*) incertitude *f*; (*in voice, of expression*) doute *m*; **their increasing d. about the whole enterprise** leurs doutes croissants à propos de toute cette affaire **(b)** (*suspect nature*) (*of origin, proposal, person's background*) caractère *m* douteux; (*of advantage*) caractère contestable; (*of compliment etc*) caractère équivoque; **the d. of this distinction** ce triste honneur

ducal ['dju:k(ə)l] *adj usu attrib* ducal

ducat ['dʌkət] *n Hist* (*coin*) ducat *m*

duchess ['dʌtʃɪs] *n* duchesse *f*

duchesse ['du:ʃes] *n Culin* **d. potatoes** pommes *fpl* (de terre) duchesse

duchy ['dʌtʃɪ] *n* duché *m*

duck¹ [dʌk] *n* **(a)** (*bird*) canard *m*; (*female*) cane *f*; *Culin* canard; **wild d.** canard sauvage; *Culin* **Peking d.** canard à la Pékinoise; *Culin* **Bombay d.** poisson *m* sec assaisonné de cari; **d. pond** mare *f* aux canards; **d.-egg blue** bleu *m* pâle; *Fig* **to take to sth like a d. to water** mordre à qch; **criticism runs off him like water off a d.'s back** les critiques glissent sur lui comme de l'eau sur les plumes d'un canard; **to play at ducks and drakes** faire des ricochets (sur l'eau); *Fig* **to play ducks and drakes with one's money** jeter l'argent par les fenêtres; *F* **d.'s arse** (*hairstyle*) = coiffure *f* masculine populaire dans les années cinquante (cheveux courts plaqués vers l'arrière)

(b) *Eng Dial* (*form of address*) **what do you want, ducks?** (*to woman*) et pour vous, ma petite dame?; (*to man*) et pour le monsieur, qu'est-ce que ce sera?

(c) *Cr* zéro *m*; **to be out for a d., to make a d.** faire chou blanc; **to break one's d.** marquer son premier point

duck² **1** *vi* **(a)** (*to avoid being hit*) baisser la tête, se baisser; **to d. behind a tree/car** se cacher derrière un arbre/une voiture; **to d. out of sight** se cacher

(b) (*under water*) plonger sous l'eau; **he ducked under the surface** il a plongé sous la surface de l'eau

2 *vt* **(a)** (*one's head*) baisser subitement; **to d. a blow** esquiver un coup

(b) *Fig* (*obligations, embarrassing question etc*) se dérober à; (*problem*) contourner; **to d. the issue** s'esquiver; (*in reply*) user de faux-fuyants; **to d. a challenge** ne pas relever un défi

(c) (*under water*) (*person*) plonger dans l'eau, faire faire le plongeon à

duck³ *n* (*movement*) (*to avoid being hit etc*) mouvement *m* instinctif de la tête; *Boxing* esquive *f*

duck⁴ *n Tex* coutil *m*; *Old-fashioned* **ducks** (*trousers*) pantalon *m* de coutil *ou* de toile

▶ **duck out** *vi* se défiler; **to d. out of doing sth** éviter de faire qch; **I managed to d. out of it** j'ai réussi à me défiler, j'ai réussi à y couper

duck-billed ['dʌkbɪld] *adj* **d. platypus** ornithorynque *m*

duckboards ['dʌkbɔ:dz] *npl* caillebotis *m*

duckie ['dʌkɪ] *n, adj* = **ducky**

ducking ['dʌkɪŋ] *n* (*under water*) plongeon *m* (involontaire); **to give sb a d.** faire boire la tasse à qn; **to get** *or* **take a d.** boire la tasse

duckling ['dʌklɪŋ] *n* canardeau *m*; (*male*) caneton *m*; (*female*) canette *f*; *Culin* caneton; **the Ugly D.** le vilain petit Canard

duckweed ['dʌkwi:d] *n* (*plant*) lentille *f* d'eau

ducky ['dʌkɪ] **1** *n Eng Dial* (*to man*) mon petit chou; (*to woman*) ma cocotte **2** *adj US F* tout mignon

duct [dʌkt] *n* **(a)** (*tube*) conduit *m*; *Constr etc* (*for cables etc*) caniveau *m*, -eaux; **air d.** manche *f* à air, gaine *f* de ventilation **(b)** *Anat* canal *m*, -aux, vaisseau *m*, -eaux; **tear d.** conduit *m* lacrymal

ductile ['dʌktaɪl] *adj* (*metal*) ductile; *Fig Lit* (*character*) malléable

ductility [dʌk'tɪlɪtɪ] *n* (*of metal*) ductilité *f*; *Fig Lit* (*of character*) malléabilité *f*

dud [dʌd] *F* **1** *n* (*person*) incapable *mf*; *Mil* (*shell*) obus *m* non éclaté; **several fireworks were duds** plusieurs pièces d'artifice ont foiré; **I'm a d. at history** je suis nul en histoire; **the note was a d.** le billet était faux **2** *adj Mil* **d. shell** obus *m* non éclaté; **d. cheque** chèque *m* sans provision *ou* en bois; **d. note** faux billet *m*; **it was a d. idea** c'était nul comme idée

dude [dju:d, du:d] *n US F* **(a)** (*dandy*) gommeux *m* **(b)** (*man*) type *m*; **a real cool d.** un type formidable **(c)** (*vacationer on ranch*) hôte *m* d'un ranch-hôtel; **d. ranch** ranch-hôtel *m*

dudgeon ['dʌdʒən] *n only used in* **in high d.** sur ses grands chevaux

duds [dʌdz] *npl F* (*clothes*) fringues *fpl*

due [dju:] **1** *adj* **(a)** (*owed*) *Com, Fin* (*debt*) exigible; (*bill*) échu; **bill d. on 1st May** effet *m* payable le premier mai; **balance d.** solde *m* dû; **debts d. to us** dettes *fpl* actives; **debts d. by us** dettes passives; **bond d. for repayment** obligation *f* amortie; **to fall** *or* **become d.** (*of bill etc*) échoir, devenir payable; **falling d.** échéance *f*; **are you d. any money from him?** est-ce qu'il te doit de l'argent?; **the money d. to you** l'argent qui vous est dû; **d. date** échéance *f*; **on the d. date** à l'échéance, à terme échu; **redemption before d. date** remboursement *m* anticipé; **you're d. an apology** je vous dois/il vous doit/*etc* une excuse; **they are d. our thanks** ils méritent nos remerciements; **I'm (still) d. three days' holiday** j'ai encore trois jours de congé à prendre; **I'm d. (for) a rise** j'attends une augmentation de salaire

(b) (*merited, proper*) dû, juste, mérité; **to give sb d. warning** avertir qn dans les formes; **with d. care** avec tout le soin requis; **he was received with d. ceremony** il fut reçu avec tout le cérémonial qui lui était dû; **in d. form** en bonne et due forme, en due forme; **after d. consideration** après mûre réflexion; **with all d. respect** avec tout le respect que je vous dois; **to treat sb with d. respect** *or* **the respect d. to him/her** traiter qn avec le respect qui lui est dû; **all in d. time** chaque chose en son temps; **in d. course** (*be told about something, learn of decision etc*) en temps voulu; (*come into inheritance, sit an exam*) le moment venu; **the impostor was unmasked in d. course** l'imposteur a finalement été démasqué

(c) d. to (*caused by*) causé par, attribuable à, à cause de; (*as a result of*) par suite de, en raison de; **it is d. to his negligence** c'est sa négligence qui en est (la) cause, c'est dû à sa négligence; **what is it d. to?** à quoi cela tient-il?, à quoi est-ce que c'est dû?; **d. to fog the boat arrived late** par suite du brouillard, le bateau est arrivé en retard; **d. to circumstances beyond our control** en raison de circonstances indépendantes de notre volonté

(d) (*expected*) **the train/he is d. (to arrive) at two o'clock** le train/il doit arriver à deux heures; **there's a bus d. now** un bus doit arriver d'un moment à l'autre; **when is the baby d.?** pour quand la naissance est-elle prévue?, quand le bébé doit-il naître?

2 *adv* **d. north** droit vers le nord, plein nord

3 *n* **(a)** (*what is owed*) dû *m*; **to give sb their d.** donner à qn ce qui lui est dû *ou* ce qui lui revient; *Fig* **to give him his d., he did apologize** pour lui rendre justice, il faut reconnaître qu'il s'est excusé

(b) dues (*for membership*) droits *mpl*, frais *mpl*; (*club subscription*) cotisation *f* annuelle; *esp Am Fig* **she's paid her dues** (*merits respect*) elle mérite le respect; (*has worked hard*) elle a peiné pour en arriver où elle en est; *Naut* **harbour dues** droits de port

duel¹ ['djʊəl] *n* duel *m*; *Fig* lutte *f*; **a d. to the death** un duel à mort; **to fight a d.** se battre en duel

duel² *vi* (**-ll-**, *US* **-l-**) se battre en duel

duelling, *US* **dueling** ['djʊəlɪŋ] *n* le duel; **d. pistols** pistolets *mpl* de combat

duellist, *US* **duelist** ['djʊəlɪst] *n* duelliste *m*

duet [dju:'et] *n* duo *m*; (*for piano*) morceau *m* à quatre mains

duettist [dju:'etɪst] *n Mus* duettiste *mf*

duff¹ [dʌf] *n Culin* (**plum**) **d.** pudding *m* aux raisins

duff² *adj Br F* nul; **it was a d. idea** c'était nul comme idée

▶ **duff up** *vtsep Br Sl* (*beat up*) rosser; **to get duffed up** se faire rosser

duffel ['dʌf(ə)l] *n* **d. (coat)** duffle-coat *m*, *pl* duffle-coats, *Can* corvette *f*; **d. bag** sac *m* marin *ou* de campeur

duffer ['dʌfər] *n F* **(a)** (*incompetent person*) bousilleur, -euse; *Sch* cancre *m*; **to be a d. at** (*history etc*) être nul en **(b) an old d.** (*old man*) un vieux croulant

duffle ['dʌf(ə)l] *n* = **duffel**

dug¹ [dʌg] *pt, pp see* = **dig²**

dug² *n* (*of cow*) pis *m*; *Pej* (*of woman*) mamelle *f*, tétine *f*

dugout ['dʌgaʊt] *n* **(a)** (*canoe*) canot *m* creusé dans un tronc d'arbre, pirogue *f* **(b)** (*shelter*) *Mil* tranchée-abri *f*, *pl* tranchées-abris; *Fb* banc *m* abri de touche

duke [dju:k] *n* **(a)** duc *m* **(b)** *Old-fashioned Sl* **dukes** (*fists*) poings *mpl*; **put up your dukes** en garde!

▶ **duke out** *vtsep US Old-fashioned* **to d. it out** se bagarrer (**with** avec)

dukedom ['dju:kdəm] *n* **(a)** (*territory*) duché *m* **(b)** (*title*) titre *m* de duc; (*rank*) dignité *f* de duc

dulcet ['dʌlsɪt] *adj attrib Lit, Iron* (*sound*) doux, suave, agréable; **to say sth in d. tones** dire qch d'un ton suave; *Hum* **I recognize those d. tones** je reconnais le son harmonieux de cette voix

dulcimer ['dʌlsɪmər] *n Mus* tympanon *m*

dull[1] [dʌl] *adj* **(a)** (*not intelligent*) (*person*) lent, lourd; **to be d.-witted** avoir l'esprit lourd *ou* engourdi; *Prov* **all work and no play makes Jack a d. boy** on s'abrutit à ne penser qu'au travail

(b) (*boring*) (*book, film, person*) ennuyeux; (*life*) monotone; (*party*) assommant; (*style*) terne; **things have been pretty d. since she left** c'est plutôt monotone depuis qu'elle est partie; **as d. as ditchwater** ennuyeux comme la pluie; **deadly d.** abrutissant, assommant; **it's deadly d. here** on s'ennuie à mourir ici; **never a d. moment!** pas le temps de s'ennuyer!

(c) (*not sharp*) (*pain*) sourd; (*sound*) sourd, étouffé; (*blunt*) (*edge*) émoussé; **to become d.** (*of tool, senses etc*) s'émousser

(d) (*not bright*) (*colour, surface*) terne, mat; (*glow*) faible, terne; (*eyes*) sans éclat; (*voice*) terne; (*weather, sky, cloud*) sombre; **paper with a d. finish** papier mat *ou* non satiné

(e) *Com, Fin* (*market*) calme, inactif; **business is d.** les affaires ne marchent pas fort

dull[2] **1** *vt* **(a)** (*the mind*) engourdir, alourdir **(b)** (*make less sharp*) (*pain*) endormir, calmer; (*pleasure*) rendre moins vif; (*sound*) amortir, assourdir; (*tool, the senses*) émousser; **sorrow is dulled by the passage of time** le temps émousse la douleur **(c)** (*make less bright*) (*colours*) ternir; (*surface*) dépolir; (*metal*) mater; (*eyes*) faire perdre son éclat à; (*voice*) ternir **2** *vi* **(a)** (*become less sharp*) (*of senses, eyesight*) s'émousser **(b)** (*become less bright*) (*of colour*) se ternir; (*of metal etc*) se dépolir; (*of eyes*) perdre son éclat

dullard ['dʌləd] *n Fml* lourdaud, -aude; *Sch* cancre *m*

dullness ['dʌlnɪs] *n* **(a)** (*of mind*) lourdeur *f* d'esprit **(b)** (*tedium*) ennui *m*, tristesse *f*; (*of life, speech*) monotonie *f*; **a film of such d.** un film aussi ennuyeux **(c)** (*lack of sharpness*) (*of blade etc*) manque *m* de tranchant; (*of point, senses*) émoussement *m*; (*of pain*) caractère *m* sourd **(d)** (*lack of brightness*) (*of colour, eyes*) manque *m* d'éclat; (*of sound, light*) faiblesse *f*; (*of voice*) caractère *m* terne; **the d. of the weather** la grisaille **(e)** *Com, Fin* (*of business*) stagnation *f*; (*of market*) inactivité *f*

dully ['dʌllɪ] *adv* **(a)** (*stupidly*) lourdement, lentement **(b)** (*boringly*) d'une manière ennuyeuse **(c)** (*not sharply*) (*to echo*) sourdement, faiblement; (*to throb*) sourdement **(d)** (*not brightly*) (*lit, to gleam*) faiblement; **..., she said d.** ..., dit-elle d'une voix terne

duly ['dju:lɪ] *adv* **(a)** (*properly*) dûment; **d. appointed** (*member*) régulièrement désigné **(b)** (*as expected*) comme prévu; **rent d. paid** loyer payé exactement; **and all the shops were d. shut** et tous les magasins étaient bien entendu fermés

dumb [dʌm] *adj* **(a)** (*unable or unwilling to speak*) muet, *f* muette; **I was struck d. with astonishment** la stupeur m'a rendu muet; **d. animals** les bêtes *fpl*; **d. insolence** silence insolent; **d. show** pantomime *f*; *Comptr* **d. terminal** terminal *m* passif **(b)** *esp Am F* (*stupid*) (*person, mistake*) bête; (*worthless*) nul; **to play** *or* **act d.** faire le niais; **d. blonde** blonde *f* évaporée; **d. cluck** imbécile *mf*; **I don't want to go to some d. theatre!** je ne veux pas aller au théâtre, c'est nul!

dumbbell ['dʌmbel] *n* **(a)** (*weight*) haltère *m* **(b)** *esp Am Sl* (*idiot*) lourdaud, -aude

dumbfound [dʌm'faʊnd] *vt* abasourdir, ahurir, ébahir

dumbfounded [dʌm'faʊndɪd] *adj* abasourdi, ahuri, ébahi (**at** de); **I'm d.** je n'en reviens pas; **we were d. at the news** la nouvelle nous frappa de stupeur

dumbly ['dʌmlɪ] *adv* (*to follow, stare*) sans rien dire; **to be d. obedient** obéir silencieusement

dumbness ['dʌmnɪs] *n* **(a)** mutisme *m*; **deaf and d.** surdi-mutité *f* **(b)** *F* (*stupidity*) sottise *f*, bêtise *f*

dumbo ['dʌmbəʊ] *n F* andouille *f*, imbécile *mf*

dumbstruck ['dʌmstrʌk] *adj* = **dumbfounded**

dumbwaiter [dʌm'weɪtər] *n* (*food stand*) guéridon *m*; (*revolving*) plateau *m* tournant; (*lift*) monte-plats *m inv*

dumdum ['dʌmdʌm] *n* **(a)** *Mil* **d.** (**bullet**) (balle *f*) dum-dum *f*, *pl* dum-dums **(b)** *F* (*idiot*) idiot, -ote

dummy ['dʌmɪ] **1** *n* **(a)** (*in clothes shop window*), *Sewing* mannequin *m*; (*of ventriloquist*) marionnette *f*; *F* **standing there like a stuffed d.** planté comme un piquet

(b) (*imitation object*) objet *m*/paquet *m*/bouteille *f*/*etc* factice; (*book*) maquette *f*; **it's just a d.** ce n'en est pas un vrai

(c) *Offensive* (*person who cannot speak*) muet *m*; *Fig Pej* (*idiot*) abruti, -ie, lourdaud, -aude

(d) *Br* (*for baby*) tétine *f*

(e) *Cards* (*player or hand at bridge, whist*) mort *m*; **to be** *or* **play d.** faire le mort; **d. bridge** bridge *m* à trois personnes; **d. whist** whist *m* avec un mort

(f) *Fb etc* feinte *f*

2 *adj* (*fake*) factice; **d. run** *Mil, Av* incursion aérienne sans bombardement; *Fig F* coup *m* d'essai

dump[1] [dʌmp] *n* **(a)** (*for refuse*) (lieu *m* de) décharge *f*; **refuse** *or* **rubbish** *or US* **garbage d.** décharge **(b)** *F* (*house etc*) taudis *m*; **what a d.!** (*of place*) quel trou!, quel bled!; (*of office etc*) quelle saloperie de boîte! **(c)** (*store*) dépôt *m*; *Mil* **ammunition d.** dépôt de munitions, parc *m* à munitions; *Com* **d. bin** panier *m* de présentation en vrac **(d)** *Comptr* cliché *m* mémoire; (**memory**) **d.** vidage *m* (de) mémoire; (**screen**) **d.** impression *f* écran **(e)** *Am Rail* **d. car** wagon *m* à bascule **(f)** *Sl* **to take** *or* **have a d.** (*defecate*) chier

dump[2] **1** *vt* **(a)** (*put down*) (*lorryload of sand etc*) décharger, déverser; (*package etc*) laisser tomber lourdement; (*sb, sth*) (*on chair etc*) déposer rudement; *Av* (*cargo*) se délester de; **I'm just going home to d. my suitcase** je vais déposer ma valise chez moi; **d. your bags in the corner** déposez *ou* laissez vos sacs dans le coin; **can we d. the kids here for the weekend?** est-ce que nous pouvons laisser les enfants ici ce week-end?

(b) (*throw away, dispose of*) (*refuse*) jeter à la voirie; (*waste in the sea*) déverser; *F* (*car, unwanted object etc*) se débarrasser de; (*lover, boyfriend etc*) plaquer

(c) *Com* **to d. goods on a foreign market** faire du dumping, écouler des marchandises à perte à l'étranger

(d) *Comptr* (*memory*) vider

2 *vi Com* faire du dumping

▶ **dump on** *vipo Am F* **(a)** (*criticize*) (*sb, sth*) s'en prendre à **(b)** (*tell one's problems to*) (*sb*) se décharger de ses problèmes sur

dumper ['dʌmpər] *n Br Constr etc* **d.** (**truck**) tombereau *m*, dumper *m*

dumping ['dʌmpɪŋ] *n* **(a)** **'no d.'** (*sign*) 'décharge interdite'; *Constr* **d. ground** (lieu *m* de) décharge *f*; *Fig* **people use the home as a d. ground for their elderly parents** les gens utilisent la maison de retraite pour se débarrasser de leurs parents âgés; **they just use this house as a d. ground** ici ce n'est qu'un dépôt pour eux **(b)** *Com* (*of goods*) dumping *m* **(c)** *Comptr* (*of memory*) vidage *m*

dumpling ['dʌmplɪŋ] *n* **(a)** *Culin* (*in stew*) boulette *f* de pâte; **apple d.** pomme *f* enrobée dans de la pâte et cuite au four **(b)** *Fig F* (*plump person*) boulot, -otte, petit gros *m*, petite grosse *f*; **he's become a bit of a d.** il est devenu un peu boulot

dumps [dʌmps] *npl F* (*depression*) cafard *m*, idées *fpl* noires; **to be down in the d.** broyer du noir, avoir le cafard

dumpster ['dʌmpstər] *n Am* benne *f* à ordures

dump truck *n Constr etc* tombereau *m*, dumper *m*

dumpy ['dʌmpɪ] *adj* (*person etc*) boulot, -otte

dun[1] [dʌn] **1** *adj* brun grisâtre; (*horse*) gris louvet **2** *n* (*horse*) cheval *m* gris louvet

dun[2] *vt* (-nn-) *Old-fashioned* (*debtor*) importuner, harceler; **dunned by his creditors** pressé par ses créanciers; **a dunning letter** une lettre de relance *ou* de poursuite

dunce [dʌns] *n Sch* cancre *m*; **the d. of the class, the class d.** le dernier de la classe; **to be a d. at physics** être nul en physique; **d.'s cap** bonnet *m* d'âne

dunderhead ['dʌndəhed] *n F* imbécile *mf*

dune [dju:n] *n* (**sand**) **d.** dune *f*; **d. buggy** buggy *m*

dung [dʌŋ] *n* **(a)** (*excrement*) crotte *f*; (*of wild animal*) fumées *fpl*; (*of cow*) bouse *f*; (*of horse*) crottin *m*; **d. beetle** bousier *m* **(b)** *Agr* (*manure*) fumier *m*, engrais *m*

dungaree [dʌŋgə'ri:] *n* **(a)** **dungarees** (*with bib*) salopette *f*; (*workman's*) bleu(s) *m*(*pl*) (de travail); **to be wearing (a pair of) dungarees** porter une salopette, être en salopette; (*workman's*) porter un *ou* des bleu(s) (de travail), être en bleu(s) (de travail) **(b)** *Tex* treillis *m*

dungeon ['dʌndʒ(ə)n] *n* **(a)** (*prison*) cachot *m* **(b)** *Hist* (*tower*) donjon *m*

dunghill ['dʌŋhɪl] *n* tas *m* de fumier, fumier *m*

dunk [dʌŋk] **1** *vt* (*bread, croissant*) (*in coffee etc*) tremper **2** *vi* faire trempette

Dunkirk [dʌn'kɜ:k] *n* Dunkerque *f*

dunlin ['dʌnlɪn] *n* (*bird*) bécasseau *m* variable

dunno [dʌ'nəʊ] *Sl* (= **don't know**) sais pas!

dunnock ['dʌnək] *n* (*bird*) accenteur *m* mouchet

duo ['dju:əʊ] *n* **(a)** *Mus* duo *m* **(b)** (*two people*) couple *m*

duodecimal [dju:əʊ'desɪm(ə)l] **1** *adj* duodécimal **2** *npl* **duodecimals** (*system*) système *m* de numérotation duodécimal

duodenal [dju:əʊ'di:n(ə)l] *adj Anat, Med* (*ulcer etc*) duodénal

duodenum, *pl* **-na, -nums** [dju:əʊ'di:nəm, -nə, -nəmz] *n Anat* duodénum *m*

dupe[1] [dju:p] *n* dupe *f*

dupe[2] *vt* duper, tromper; **to be duped** se laisser duper; **to d. sb into doing sth** duper qn pour qu'il fasse qch; **she duped him into believing that …** elle lui a fait gober que …

duple ['dju:p(ə)l] *adj Mus* **d. time** mesure *f* à deux temps

duplex ['dju:pleks] **1** *adj El, Tel* (*line*) duplex *inv*; (*operation etc*) en duplex **2** *adj, n Am* **d. (house)** maison *f* jumelée, *Can* duplex *m*; **d. (apartment)** (appartement *m*) duplex

duplicate[1] ['dju:plɪkət] **1** *adj* (en) double; **I have a d. key** j'ai un double de la clé; **d. set of tools** outils *mpl* de rechange; **d. receipt** quittance *f* double **2** *n* (*of work of art etc*) double *m*; (*of cheque etc*) duplicata *m*; (*of written document*) double, contrepartie *f*; **in d.** en double (exemplaire), en deux exemplaires, *Fml* en duplicata

duplicate[2] ['dju:plɪkeɪt] *vt* **(a)** (*make a copy of*) (*key*) faire un double de; (*document*) copier, reproduire en double exemplaire **(b)** (*on duplicator*) reprographier, polycopier; **to d. sth** tirer plusieurs exemplaires de qch au duplicateur, polycopier qch **(c)** (*do again*) refaire; **that's just duplicating what they've already done** cela revient à refaire ce qu'ils ont déjà fait

duplicating ['dju:plɪkeɪtɪŋ] *n* (*of document*) reproduction *f*; **d. machine** duplicateur *m*, machine *f* à polycopier

duplication [dju:plɪ'keɪʃən] *n* reproduction *f*; **unnecessary d. of work** répétition *f* inutile du travail

duplicator ['dju:plɪkeɪtər] *n* duplicateur *m*, machine *f* à polycopier

duplicity [dju:'plɪsɪtɪ] *n* duplicité *f*

durability [djʊərə'bɪlɪtɪ] *n* durabilité *f*; *Ind* résistance *f*

durable ['djʊərəb(ə)l] **1** *adj* (*peace*) durable; (*fabric*) résistant; *Com* **d. goods** biens *mpl* durables **2** *npl* **(consumer) durables** biens *mpl* durables

duration [djʊ'reɪʃən] *n* durée *f*; (*of life*) étendue *f*; **the peace was of short d.** la paix fut de courte durée; **for the d.** *Mil* (*to enlist*) pour la durée de la guerre; *Fig* jusqu'à la Saint-Glinglin

duress [djʊ'res] *n Jur* contrainte *f*, coercition *f*; **to act under d.** agir sous la contrainte

Durex® ['djʊəreks] *n* préservatif *m*

during ['djʊərɪŋ] *prep* pendant, durant; **d. the whole week** toute la semaine; **d. the winter** au cours de *ou* pendant l'hiver; **d. the journey** en cours de route; **d. the last year** dans le courant de l'année dernière; **killed d. a brawl** tué au cours d'une rixe; **d. that time** pendant ce temps

durum ['djʊərəm] *n* **d. wheat** blé *m* dur

dusk [dʌsk] *n* crépuscule *m*; **at d.** à la nuit tombante, à la tombée de la nuit

duskiness ['dʌskɪnɪs] *n* **(a)** (*darkness of skin*) teint *m* mat **(b)** *Lit* (*dimness*) demi-jour *m*, pénombre *f*

dusky ['dʌskɪ] *adj* **(a)** (*dark*) (*complexion*) mat; (*dark-skinned*) au teint mat **(b)** *Lit* (*dim*) crépusculaire

dust[1] [dʌst] *n* **(a)** (*dirt, powder*) poussière *f*; (*of marble*) sciure *f*; **these ornaments just collect the d.** ces bibelots ne sont que des nids à poussière; **to raise a cloud of d.** soulever un nuage de poussière; *Fig* **to bite the d.** (*die, fail*) mordre la poussière; (*of hopes*) s'envoler; *Fig* **to throw d. in sb's eyes** jeter de la poudre aux yeux à qn; *Fig* **to blow the d. off sth** dépoussiérer qch; *Old-fashioned F* **to kick up** *or* **raise a d.** (*a fuss*) faire du foin; *Fig* **once the d. has settled** une fois que les choses seront revenues à la normale, une fois que la situation se sera apaisée; **all their hopes had turned to d. and ashes** tous leurs espoirs s'étaient anéantis; *F* **when there's work to be done you can't see him for d.!** dès qu'il y a du travail, il n'y a plus personne!; **… or you won't see me for d.!** … ou tu ne me reverras pas de sitôt!; **brick d.** poussière de brique; *Phys* **cosmic d.** poussière cosmique; **d. bag** (*for vacuum cleaner*) (*disposable*) sac *m* à poussière; (*fixed*) sac tissu; *Am* **d. ball** *or* **bunny** *or* **kitten** mouton *m*; **to take a d. bath** (*of bird*) s'ébrouer dans la poussière; **d. cap** capuchon *m* anti-poussière; *Old-fashioned* **d. coat** cache-poussière *m inv*; *Am* **d. cloth** chiffon *m* à poussière; *MecE* **d. collector** capteur *m* de poussières; **d. trap** nid *m* à poussière; *Ind* attrape-poussières *m inv*

(b) (*action*) **to give the table a d.** passer un coup de chiffon sur la table (pour enlever la poussière)

dust[2] *vt* **(a)** (*remove dust from*) (*room, furniture*) épousseter **(b)** (*sprinkle*) **to d. a cake with sugar, to d. sugar over a cake** saupoudrer un gâteau de sucre; **sugar-dusted doughnuts** beignets saupoudrés de sucre; *F* **to d. a gun for fingerprints** examiner un revolver pour y relever des empreintes digitales

▶ **dust down, dust off** *vtsep* (*furniture*) épousseter; *Fig* (*legislation, lecture*) dépoussiérer; (*one's French etc*) rafraîchir, dérouiller; **to d. oneself off** *or* **down** se brosser (pour enlever la poussière); **she dusted the crumbs off the chair** elle brossa la chaise pour en enlever les miettes

dustbin ['dʌstbɪn] *n Br* poubelle *f*

Dust Bowl *n US* **the D.** le désert de poussière

dust bowl *n Geog* zone *f* semi-aride *ou* semi-désertique

dustcart ['dʌstkɑ:t] *n Br* camion *m* d'enlèvement des ordures ménagères, camion des boueux

dustcloud ['dʌstklaʊd] *n* nuage *m* de poussière

dust cover *n* (*for chair etc*) housse *f*; (*for book*) chemise *f*, jaquette *f*

dust devil *n Met* tourbillon *m* de poussière

duster ['dʌstər] *n* **(a)** *Br* (*cloth*) chiffon *m* (à poussière); *Sch* (*for blackboard*) (*cloth*) chiffon (à effacer); (*pad*) tampon *m* (à effacer); **feather d.** plumeau *m* **(b)** *Naut Sl* (*flag*) pavillon *m*; **red d.** = pavillon marchand **(c)** *Am* **d. (coat)** manteau *m* léger, *Old-fashioned* cache-poussière *m inv*

dustiness ['dʌstɪnɪs] *n* état *m* poudreux *ou* poussiéreux

dusting ['dʌstɪŋ] *n* **(a)** (*of room, furniture etc*) époussetage *m*; **to give a room a d.** épousseter une pièce; **have you done the d.?** tu as fait la poussière? **(b)** (*of cake etc*) saupoudrage *m*; **the cake had a d. of chocolate powder** le gâteau était saupoudré de chocolat; **there was a d. of snow on the pavement** le trottoir était saupoudré de neige

dusting powder *n* (*talc*) (poudre *f* de) talc *m*; *Med* poudre antiseptique

dust jacket *n* (*for book*) chemise *f*, jaquette *f*

dustman, *pl* **-men** ['dʌstmən] *n Br* éboueur *m*, *F* boueur *m*, boueux *m*

dustpan ['dʌstpæn] *n* pelle *f* (à poussière)

dustproof ['dʌstpru:f] *adj* imperméable à la poussière

dustsheet ['dʌstʃi:t] *n* (*for furniture*) housse *f*

dust storm *n* tempête *f* de poussière

dust-up *n F* (*quarrel*) coup *m* de torchon, querelle *f*; (*brawl*) bagarre *f*; **to have a d. with sb** se quereller/se bagarrer avec qn; **they've had a bit of a d.** le torchon a brûlé entre eux

dusty ['dʌstɪ] *adj* poussiéreux, couvert de poussière; **to get d.** se couvrir de poussière; *Old-fashioned Sl* **it's not so d.** (*not bad*) c'est pas mal du tout; *Old-fashioned F* **a d. answer** une réponse un peu sèche

Dutch [dʌtʃ] **1** *adj* **(a)** hollandais; (*cheese etc*) de Hollande; (*government*) néerlandais; *Fig F* **to talk to sb like a D. uncle** faire la morale à qn; **D. auction** enchères *fpl* au rabais; **D. barn** hangar *m* à récoltes; **D. cap** (*contraceptive*) diaphragme *m*; **D. courage** bravoure *f* après boire; **I'll need a little D. courage** il faut que je boive un peu pour me donner du courage; *Am* **D. door** porte *f* à double vantail; **D. elm disease** maladie *f* des ormes; *Am* **D. oven** cocotte *f*; *F* **D. treat** = régal *m* où chacun paie son écot; **as long as it's a D. treat** tant que chacun paie sa part *ou* son écot

(b) *US* **(Pennsylvania) D.** allemand de Pennsylvanie

2 *n* **(a) the D. (people)** les Hollandais *mpl*

(b) *Ling* hollandais *m*; **Cape D.** afrikaans *m*

3 *adv F* **to go D.** payer son écot; **let's go D.** payons chacun notre part

dutch [dʌtʃ] *n Br Sl* (*wife*) **my old d.** ma femme, ma vieille

Dutchman, *pl* **-men** ['dʌtʃmən] *n* Hollandais *m*, Néerlandais *m*; *F* **if that's a real diamond (then) I'm a D.** si c'est un vrai diamant je mange mon chapeau

Dutchwoman, *pl* **-women** ['dʌtʃwʊmən, -wɪmɪn] *n* Hollandaise *f*, Néerlandaise *f*

dutiable ['dju:tɪəb(ə)l] *adj* (*goods purchased abroad*) soumis aux droits de douane, imposable, taxable

dutiful ['dju:tɪfʊl] *adj* (*son, daughter*) obéissant; **a d. husband** un mari plein d'égards pour sa femme

dutifully ['dju:tɪfʊlɪ] *adv* avec soumission

duty ['dju:tɪ] *n* **(a)** (*obligation*) devoir *m* (**to** envers); **to do one's d.** faire son devoir; **to fail in one's d.** manquer à son devoir (**as a** de); **to do one's d. by sb** remplir son devoir envers qn; **I shall make it my d. to …** je considérerai de mon devoir de …; **it is your d. to …** il est de ton devoir de …; **from** *or* **out of a sense of d.** par devoir; **to have no sense of d.** n'avoir aucun sens du devoir; *Hum* **I must go, d. calls** je dois y aller, le devoir m'appelle; **to pay a d. call** faire une visite de politesse

(b) (*task*) (*usu pl*) **duties** fonction(s) *fpl*, attributions *fpl*; *Mil* mission *f*; **public duties** fonctions publiques; **to take up** *or* **assume one's duties** entrer en fonctions *ou* en charge; **to hand over one's duties** (*resign*) résigner ses fonctions; (*transfer them*) remettre ses fonctions (**to** à); **to carry out** *or* **perform one's duties** exercer ses fonctions

(c) to be on d. être de service; (*in factory, playground etc*) être de surveillance; *Naut* être de service *ou* de corvée; *Mil,*

Naut etc **while on d.** pendant le service; **to be off d.** ne pas être de service; **to do d. for sb** remplacer qn (dans son service); **to do d. for sth** servir de qch; *Mil* **tour of d.** tour *m* de service; *US* **active d.** service actif; **fatigue d.** corvée *f*; **d. chart** *or* **roster** tableau *m* de service; *Journ* **d. editor** rédacteur *m* en chef de service; **d. manager** directeur *m* (qui est) de service; **d. officer** officier *m* de service

(d) *Fin* (*tax*) droit *m*; **customs d.** droit(s) de douane; **liable to d.** passible de droits; **to pay d. on sth** payer une taxe sur qch; **d. paid** franc de douane, droits acquittés

duty-bound *adj pred* tenu; **you are d. to do it** votre devoir vous y oblige, vous y êtes tenu; **I feel d. to ...** je me sens tenu par mon devoir de ...

duty-free 1 *adj* exempt de droits (de douane); (*wine, cigarettes etc for personal use*) hors taxe; **d. allowance** quantité *f* de marchandises hors taxe autorisée; **d. entry** admission *f* en franchise; **d. goods** marchandises *fpl* franches de douane, marchandises hors taxe; **d. sales** ventes *fpl* hors taxe; **d. shop** magasin *m* hors taxe; **d. zone** zone *f* en franchise **2** *n* (*purchase*) achat *m* hors taxe **3** *adv* **how much wine can I bring back d.?** quelle quantité de vin est-ce que j'ai le droit de ramener hors taxe?

duty-paid goods *npl* marchandises *fpl* libérées *ou* acquittées

duvet ['du:veɪ] *n* couette *f*, *Swiss* duvet *m*; **d. cover** housse *f* de couette

dux [dʌks] *n Scot Sch* premier, -ière de la classe/l'école

DV [di:'vi:] *Adv* (*abbr* **deo volente**) si Dieu le veut

dwarf¹, *pl* **dwarfs, dwarves** [dwɔ:f, dwɔ:vz] **1** *n* (*person*), *Myth* nain *m*, naine *f* **2** *adj* (*plant, tree*) nain

dwarf² *vt* (a) écraser; *Fig* (*sb's achievements, success*) éclipser; **tower that dwarfs the main building** tour dont la hauteur écrase le corps de bâtiment; **the church is dwarfed by the skyscraper** l'église est écrasée par le gratte-ciel; **at nearly six feet, Jack dwarfed his classmates** avec son mètre 80, Jack semblait un géant par rapport à ses camarades de classe **(b)** (*stunt growth of*) (*plant*) rabougrir

dwarfish ['dwɔ:fɪʃ] *adj* (*legs*) de nain; (*man, stature*) très petit

dwell¹ [dwel] *vi* (*pt, pp* **dwelt** [dwelt]) **(a)** *Lit* **to d. in a place** habiter (dans) un lieu **(b)** *Fig* (*remain*) rester; **to let one's eye d. on sb** arrêter son regard sur qn; *Lit* **this hope dwells within our hearts** cet espoir repose dans notre cœur

dwell² *n MecE* dwell *m*; **d. angle** angle *m* de dwell *ou* de fermeture

▶ **dwell on, dwell upon** *vipo* (*brood about*) remâcher, ressasser; (*memories*) s'attarder sur; (*discuss*) (*in speech, book*) s'appesantir sur; (*syllable etc*) appuyer sur; **don't d.** *or* **don't let your mind d. on it** essaie de ne pas y penser

dweller ['dwelər] *n* habitant, -ante (**in, on** de); **city-d.** citadin, -ine; **flat-d.** personne *f* qui habite dans un appartement

dwelling¹ ['dwelɪŋ] *n* **d. (place)** domicile *m*, demeure *f*, *Lit* lieu *m* de séjour; **d. house** maison *f* d'habitation

-dwelling² *suff* **tree-d.** arboricole, qui vit sur les arbres; **ocean/cave-d.** qui vit dans l'océan/dans les caves

DWEM [dwem] *n* (*abbr* **dead white European male**) écrivain/ musicien/*etc* européen blanc mort depuis longtemps

dwindle ['dwɪnd(ə)l] *vi* **to d. (away)** diminuer; **to d. to nothing** se réduire à rien

dwindling ['dwɪnd(ə)lɪŋ] **1** *adj* (*audience, funds, membership*) en baisse; (*enthusiasm*) faiblissant; **a d. number of people** de moins en moins de gens **2** *n* (*of supplies, enthusiasm, support*) baisse *f*, diminution *f*; *Fin* (*of capital*) déperdition *f*

dye¹ [daɪ] *n* (*for clothes, hair*) teinture *f*; **fast d.** (*on label*) bon teint; *Lit* **villain of the deepest d.** fieffé coquin *m*; *Phot* **d. solution** bain *m* colorant

dye² (*prp* **dyeing**) **1** *vt* teindre; **to d. sth black/red** teindre qch en noir/rouge; **to have a dress dyed** faire teindre une robe; **to d. one's hair** se teindre les cheveux **2** *vi* (se) teindre; **material that dyes well** tissu qui prend bien la teinture

dyed-in-the-wool ['daɪdɪnðə'wʊl] *adj Fig* invétéré, inébranlable; **a d. Englishman/conservative** un Anglais/ conservateur bon teint

dyeing ['daɪɪŋ] *n* **(a)** (*of material, hair*) teinture *f* **(b)** (*trade*) teinturerie *f*

dyer ['daɪər] *n* teinturier *m*; **d. and cleaner** teinturier dégraisseur

dyestuff ['daɪstʌf] *n* matière *f* colorante, colorant *m*

dyeworks ['daɪwɜ:ks] *npl* (*usu with sing verb*) teinturerie *f*

dying ['daɪɪŋ] **1** *adj* (*person*) mourant, agonisant; *Fig* (*industry, ideology*) agonisant; (*traditions*) en voie de disparition; **in a d. voice** d'une voix éteinte; **d. words** dernières paroles; **with his d. breath** de sa voix agonisante; **it was my mother's d. wish that ...** les dernières volontés de ma mère étaient que ...; **I shall remember it to my d. day** je m'en souviendrai jusqu'à la mort; *Fig F* **to look like a d. duck (in a thunderstorm)** avoir l'air pitoyable

2 *n* **(a)** (*death throes*) agonie *f*; (*death*) mort *f*

(b) (*pl*) **the dead and the d.** les morts *mpl* et les moribonds *mpl*; **prayers for the d.** prières *fpl* des agonisants

dyke¹ [daɪk] *n* **(a)** *HydE* digue *f*, levée *f*; (*embankment*) chaussée *f* surélevée *ou* en remblai **(b)** (*ditch*) fossé *m*, chenal *m*, -aux

dyke² *vt HydE* (*river*) endiguer; (*land*) protéger par des digues

dyke³ *n F* (*lesbian*) gouine *f*

dynamic [daɪ'næmɪk] **1** *adj Phys, Fig* dynamique; *Fig* **to have a d. personality** être plein de dynamisme; *Comptr* **d. data exchange** échange *m* dynamique de données; *Comptr* **d. RAM** mémoire *f* RAM dynamique **2** *n* dynamique *f*

dynamically [daɪ'næmɪklɪ] *adv* dynamiquement

dynamics [daɪ'næmɪks] *npl* [①**A10,c**] (*usu with sing verb*) *Phys, Fig* dynamique *f*; **the d. of change/progress** la dynamique du changement/progrès

dynamism ['daɪnəmɪz(ə)m] *n Phys, Fig* dynamisme *m*

dynamite¹ ['daɪnəmaɪt] *n* dynamite *f*; *F* **subject that is political d.** sujet explosif sur le plan politique; **it/she could be political d. for the Government** ça/elle pourrait faire des dégâts au niveau du gouvernement; *F* **this information is d.** cette information c'est de la dynamite; *F* **it's d.!** (*marvellous*) c'est du tonnerre!; *F* **this new band is d.** ce nouveau groupe déménage

dynamite² *vt* (*rocks etc*) faire sauter à la dynamite; (*building etc*) dynamiter

dynamiting ['daɪnəmaɪtɪŋ] *n* dynamitage *m*

dynamo, *pl* **-os** ['daɪnəməʊ, -əʊz] *n El* dynamo *f*; *Fig* **she's a human d.** elle a une énergie extraordinaire

dynastic [dɪ'næstɪk] *adj* dynastique

dynasty ['dɪnəstɪ, *Am* 'daɪnəstɪ] *n* dynastie *f*

dyne [daɪn] *n Phys* (*unit of force*) dyne *f*

dysentery ['dɪsəntrɪ] *n Med* dysenterie *f*; **to have d.** avoir la dysenterie

dysfunction [dɪs'fʌŋkʃən] *n Med* (*of organ*) insuffisance *f*

dyslectic [dɪs'lektɪk], **dyslexic** [dɪs'leksɪk] *adj, n Med* dyslexique *mf*

dyslexia [dɪs'leksɪə] *n Med* dyslexie *f*; **to have d.** être dyslexique

dysmenorrhoea, *US* **dysmenorrhea** [dɪsmenə'rɪə] *n Med* dysménorrhée *f*

dyspepsia [dɪs'pepsɪə] *n Med* dyspepsie *f*; **acid d.** aigreurs *fpl*

dyspeptic [dɪs'peptɪk] **1** *n Med* dyspepsique *mf*, dyspeptique *mf* **2** *adj* **(a)** *Med* dyspepsique, dyspeptique **(b)** *Fig* (*bad-tempered*) ronchon, grognon

dysphasia [dɪs'feɪzɪə] *n Med* dysphasie *f*

dystrophy ['dɪstrəfɪ] *n Med* dystrophie *f*

E

E, e [iː] *n* **(a)** (*letter*) E, e *m* **(b)** *Mus* mi *m*; **key of E flat** clef *f* de mi bémol **(c)** *Sl* (*ecstasy*) ecstasy *f* **(d)** *F* **to give sb the big E** (*reject*) plaquer qn

e (*abbr* **east**) E.

each [iːtʃ] [①A35,c; B14,B,1,a] **1** *adj* chaque; **e. day** chaque jour, tous les jours; **e. one of us** chacun/chacune de nous *ou* d'entre nous

2 *pron* **(a)** (*both or all*) chacun, -une; **e. of us** chacun/chacune de nous *ou* d'entre nous; **we e. earn £10, we earn £10 e.** nous gagnons 10 livres chacun; **peaches at 25p e.** pêches à 25 pence chacune *ou* 25 pence pièce; **a little of e.** un peu de chaque

(b) (*reciprocal*) **e. other** l'un l'autre, l'une l'autre, *pl* les uns les autres, les unes les autres; **separated from e. other** séparés l'un de l'autre/les uns des autres; **to fight e. other** se battre; **we can help e. other** nous pouvons nous aider l'un l'autre, nous pouvons nous aider mutuellement, nous pouvons nous entraider; **they flatter e. other** ils se flattent réciproquement *ou* mutuellement

eager [ˈiːgər] *adj* (*desire, hope*) vif; (*look*) avide; (*voice, face*) exalté; (*supporter*) fervent; **to be e. for sth** désirer qch vivement; **the crowd were e. for blood** la foule était assoiffée de sang; **the audience were still e. for more when the show ended** le public en voulait encore quand le spectacle s'est terminé; **to be e. to do sth** être impatient de faire qch; **to be e. to please** être très désireux de plaire; **they were e. to learn** ils étaient avides d'apprendre; **I didn't want to seem too e.** (*in relationship etc*) je ne voulais pas sembler trop empressé; *F* **to be an e. beaver** être zélé; **I've never seen such an e. beaver** je n'ai jamais vu quelqu'un d'aussi zélé

eagerly [ˈiːgəlɪ] *adv* (*to listen*) avidement; (*to ask, smile*) avec empressement; (*to wait*) impatiemment; (*to study, work*) avec passion; **to desire sth e.** désirer qch passionnément; **her e. awaited second album** son deuxième album impatiemment attendu

eagerness [ˈiːgənɪs] *n* (*to see sb*) impatience *f*; (*to make oneself useful etc*) empressement *m*; (*to learn sth etc*) vif désir *m*; **to show e. in doing sth** montrer un intérêt très vif à faire qch; **to show** *or* **have no e. for sth** n'avoir aucunement envie de qch; **he thought he detected a certain lack of e. in her voice** il lui sembla déceler un certain manque d'ardeur dans sa voix; **e. to succeed** ardent désir de réussir

eagle [ˈiːg(ə)l] *n* **(a)** (*bird*) aigle *m*; *Rel* **e. lectern** aigle *m* **(b)** *Her* aigle *f*; **double-headed e.** aigle à deux têtes **(c)** *US Mil* aigle *m* (= *insigne de grade de colonel*) **(d)** *Golf* eagle *m*, *Can* aiglon *m*

eagle-eyed [iːg(ə)ˈlaɪd] *adj* aux yeux d'aigle

eaglet [ˈiːglɪt] *n* (*bird*) aiglon *m*

ear [ɪər] *n* **(a)** oreille *f*; *Anat* **the external** *or* **outer/middle/internal** *or* **inner e.** l'oreille externe/moyenne/interne; **deaf in one e.** sourd d'une oreille; *Med* **e., nose and throat specialist** oto-rhino(-laryngologiste) *mf*; **e., nose and throat department** service *m* d'oto-rhino-laryngologie; **she was smiling** *or* **grinning from e. to e.** elle avait un sourire épanoui jusqu'aux oreilles; **to go in one e. and out the other** (*of words*) entrer par une oreille et sortir par l'autre; **your ears must have been burning** les oreilles ont dû vous siffler; **up to one's ears in work** accablé de travail; **up to one's ears in debt** endetté jusqu'au cou; *F* **to be (thrown) out on one's e.** se faire jeter dehors *ou* sur le pavé; **after only two months in the job he found himself out on his e. again** après seulement deux mois de travail il s'est retrouvé de nouveau sur le pavé

(b) (*hearing*) **to have sharp ears** avoir l'ouïe fine; *Mus* **to have a good/poor e.** avoir de l'oreille/ne pas avoir d'oreille; **to have an e. for music** avoir l'oreille musicale; *Mus* **to play by e.** jouer sans notes; *Fig* **to play it by e.** aller au pifomètre, improviser; **to have an e. for poetry** avoir le sens de la poésie; **to have an e.** *or* **a good e. for languages** avoir une bonne oreille pour les langues; **to have sb's e.** être dans les faveurs *ou* les petits papiers de qn; **to keep one's ears open** *or* **one's e. to the ground** se tenir aux écoutes; **I'm all ears** je suis tout ouïe; **to close one's ears to the truth** fermer l'oreille à la vérité; **word reached their e. of the enemy's plan** les projets de l'ennemi leur sont venus à l'oreille

(c) *Tech* (*of vase*) anse *f*, oreille *f*; (*of bell*) anse

(d) (*of seashell*) oreillette *f*

(e) (*of wheat etc*) épi *m*; **wheat in the e.** blé *m* en épi

earache [ˈɪəreɪk] *n* mal *m* d'oreille(s); *Med* otalgie *f*; **to have e.** avoir mal à l'oreille/aux oreilles

eardrops [ˈɪədrɒps] *npl Med* gouttes *fpl* pour les oreilles

eardrum [ˈɪədrʌm] *n Anat* tympan *m*

-eared [ɪəd] *suff* **long/short-e.** aux oreilles longues/courtes

earflap [ˈɪəflæp] *n* (*of cap*) oreillette *f*

earful [ˈɪəfʊl] *n* **I got an e. of water** j'ai pris de l'eau plein l'oreille; *F* **to give sb an e.** (*reprimand*) donner une verte semonce à qn, passer un savon à qn; *F* **a right** *or* **real e.** un bon savon

earhole [ˈɪəhəʊl] *n Br F* trou *m* de l'oreille

earl [ɜːl] *n* comte *m*

earldom [ˈɜːldəm] *n* **(a)** (*land*) comté *m* **(b)** (*title*) titre *m* de comte

ear lobe *n Anat* lobe *m* de l'oreille

early [ˈɜːlɪ] **(earlier, earliest) 1** *adj* **(a)** (*in the day*) matinal; **in the e. morning** de bon matin; **e. morning walk** promenade *f* matinale; **I'm not a great believer in e. rising** se lever de bonne heure, ce n'est pas pour moi; **to be an e. riser** être matinal, se lever de bon matin; **an e. bird** un lève-tôt, un matinal; *Prov* **the e. bird catches the worm** l'avenir appartient à ceux qui se lèvent tôt; **e. edition** (*of newspaper*) première édition *f*, premier tirage *m*; **e. morning call** appel *m* matinal; **e. morning tea** thé *m* du matin

(b) (*at beginning of period of time*) **in (the) e. summer, in the e. part of summer** dans les *ou* aux premiers jours de l'été, au début de l'été; **in the e. afternoon** au début de l'après-midi; **to have an e. dinner** dîner de bonne heure; **I'm going to have an e. night** je vais me coucher de bonne heure; **in the e. nineteenth century** au début du XIXe siècle; **in the e. sixties** au début des années soixante; **e. medieval music** musique *f* du début du moyen-âge; **e. youth** première jeunesse *f*; **e. Debussy/Racine** première(s) œuvre(s) *f(pl)* de Debussy/Racine; **at an e. age** tout jeune; **from the earliest age** dès la plus tendre enfance; **from (the) earliest times** depuis les temps les plus reculés; **it's e. days yet** il est encore tôt

(c) (*first*) **the e. Church** l'Église *f* primitive; **e. Christians** les premiers chrétiens *mpl*; **the earliest legends** les premières légendes *fpl*; **a very e. example of …** un des premiers exemples de …; **this e. pottery** ces exemples des premières formes de poterie; **e. music** (*from Middle Ages*) musique *f* médiévale; (*earlier*) première forme *f* de musique; *Art* **the e. masters** les primitifs *mpl*; **e. radios didn't have loudspeakers** les premières radios n'avaient pas de haut-parleurs; **my earliest recollections** mes souvenirs les plus lointains; **he received his e. education at …** il reçut sa première éducation à …

(d) (*ahead of time*) **you're e.** tu es en avance; **I am half an hour e.** je suis en avance d'une demi-heure

(e) (*premature*) précoce, hâtif; (*death*) prématuré; **e. beans** haricots *mpl* de primeur; **e. vegetables/fruit/produce** primeurs *fpl*; **we're having an e. winter** l'hiver est précoce; **Easter is e. this year** Pâques est tôt cette année; **e. redemption** amortissement *m* anticipé; **e. retirement** préretraite *f*; **to take e. retirement** prendre la retraite anticipée

(f) (*future*) **at an e. date** prochainement, à une date prochaine; **at an earlier date** à une date plus rapprochée; **to take an e. opportunity to do sth** faire qch à la première occasion; **at the earliest possible moment** dans le plus bref délai possible; **at your earliest convenience** dès que possible

(g) (*previous*) **at an earlier date** à une date antérieure

2 *adv* (**a**) (*in the day*) de bonne heure, tôt; **e. in the morning** le matin de bonne heure, de grand matin; **e. in the evening** tôt dans la soirée; **to get up e.** se lever de bonne heure; **as e. as possible** le plus tôt possible

(**b**) (*at beginning of period of time etc*) **e. in the winter** au début *ou* à l'entrée de l'hiver; **e. in the year** au début de l'année; **e. on it was apparent that ...** dès l'abord il est apparu que ...; **e. in (his) life** dans ses jeunes années, dans sa jeunesse; **e. in his career** au début de sa carrière; **as e. as the tenth century** dès le dixième siècle; **e. in the list** tout au commencement de la liste

(**c**) (*ahead of time*) en avance; **too e.** trop tôt; **to arrive five minutes (too) e.** arriver avec cinq minutes d'avance; **they left the party e.** ils ont quitté la soirée tôt

(**d**) (*prematurely*) **to die e.** (*young*) mourir jeune; (*sooner than expected*) mourir prématurément; **this flower blooms very e.** cette fleur s'épanouit très précocement

(**e**) (*soon*) **next week at the earliest** la semaine prochaine au plus tôt

(**f**) (*previously*) **earlier** plus tôt; **as I mentioned earlier** (*in time*) comme je l'ai mentionné plus tôt; (*in writing*) comme je l'ai mentionné ci-dessus *ou* plus haut

early adopter *n Mktg* réceptif *m* précoce

early closing *n* (*practice*) (*of shop etc*) fermeture *f* l'après-midi

early-closing *adj Br Com* **e. day** jour *m* où les magasins ferment tôt

early follower *n Mktg* suiveur *m* immédiat

early-purchase discount *n Mktg* discompte *m* sur achat dans un bref délai

early warning system *n Mil* réseau *m* de radars de guet *ou* de pré-alerte

earmark¹ ['ɪəmɑːk] *n Agr* (*of sheep etc*) marque *f* à l'oreille; *Fig* **to have all the earmarks of embezzlement/another of her silly ideas** porter tous les signes d'un détournement de fonds/d'une de ses idées stupides

earmark² *vt* (**a**) (*assign*) (*funds*) donner à une affectation spéciale; **to e. funds for a project** assigner des fonds à un projet; **the land has been earmarked for a new school** le terrain a été affecté à la construction d'une nouvelle école; **the building is earmarked for closure** il est prévu que ce bâtiment soit fermé; *F* **to e. sth for oneself** se réserver qch (**b**) (*mark the corner of*) (*document, cheque*) faire une marque au coin de (**c**) *Agr* (*sheep etc*) marquer à l'oreille

earmuff ['ɪəmʌf] *n* protège-oreilles *m inv*, cache-oreilles *m inv*

earn [ɜːn] *vt* (**a**) (*money*) gagner; **how much do you e.?** combien gagnez-vous?; **to e. one's living by writing** gagner sa vie de sa plume; *Fin* **to e. interest** (*of money*) produire des intérêts

(**b**) (*deserve*) (*rest, respite*) mériter; (*sb's affection, respect*) gagner; **to e. sb's love** gagner le cœur de qn; **you've earned it** (*this break, rise etc*) tu l'as bien mérité; **his conduct earned him universal praise/many votes** sa conduite lui valut les éloges de tous/de nombreuses voix; **it earned her nothing but criticism** cela ne lui a valu que des critiques; **this action earned her many enemies** cette action lui a valu de nombreux ennemis, par cette action elle s'est attiré de nombreux ennemis; **her attitude has earned her a lot of friends/supporters** son attitude lui a gagné de nombreux amis/partisans

earned [ɜːnd] *adj Fin* **e. income** revenus *mpl* salariaux, traitements *mpl*

earner ['ɜːnər] *n* (**a**) (*person*) (**wage**) **e.** salarié, -ée; **she's not a big e.** elle ne gagne pas beaucoup; **the high/low earners** les gros/petits salaires *mpl* (**b**) *Br F* (*activity, business*) **a nice little e.** une bonne petite affaire, un bon plan

earnest ['ɜːnɪst] **1** *adj* (*person, effort, discussion*) sérieux; (*expression*) pénétré, grave; (*demand, voice*) pressant; (*request*) fervent; (*desire, wish*) profond **2** *n* (**a**) **in e.** sérieusement; **to be in e.** être sérieux; **are you in e.?** (*in what you're saying*) parlez-vous sérieusement?; **to speak in e.** parler sérieusement; **she's leaving him in e. this time** cette fois elle le quitte pour de bon; **to set to work in e.** se mettre sérieusement à l'ouvrage (**b**) *Old-fashioned Com etc* arrhes *fpl*

earnestly ['ɜːnɪstlɪ] *adv* (*to speak, discuss, consider*) sérieusement; (*to hope, believe*) sincèrement; (*to desire*) profondément; (*to pray*) avec ferveur

earnestness ['ɜːnɪstnɪs] *n* (*of discussion*) caractère *m* sérieux; (*of tone, person*) gravité *f*, sérieux *m*; (*of hope, desire*) sincérité *f*; (*of request*) ferveur *f*

earning ['ɜːnɪŋ] *n* (*act*) gain *m*; **e. capacity** (*of business*) rapport *m*; (*of person*) revenu *m* potentiel

earnings ['ɜːnɪŋz] *npl* (**a**) (*salary*) salaire *m*; **my e.** ce que je gagne; **e. related** (*pensions, benefits etc*) proportionnel au salaire (**b**) (*profits*) profits *mpl*, bénéfices *mpl*

earphone ['ɪəfəʊn] *n Rad, Tel* écouteur *m*

earpiece ['ɪəpiːs] *n Tel* (*of handset*) écouteur *m*; (*in TV studio*) écouteur auriculaire

ear-piercing ['ɪəpɪəsɪŋ] **1** *adj* (*scream*) à vous percer les tympans **2** *n* (*for earrings*) **do you know anywhere in town that does e.?** connais-tu un endroit en ville où l'on peut se faire percer les oreilles?

earplug ['ɪəplʌg] *n* (*for sleeping*) boule *f* Quiès®; (*for protection from noise*) protège-tympan *m inv*

ear protector *n* (*against cold*) protège-tympan *m inv*; (*against noise*) casque *m* anti-bruit

earring ['ɪərɪŋ] *n* boucle *f* d'oreille

earshot ['ɪəʃɒt] *n* **within/out of e.** à portée/hors de portée de voix

ear-splitting ['ɪəsplɪtɪŋ] *adj* à vous déchirer *ou* crever les tympans

earth¹ [ɜːθ] *n* (**a**) (*planet*) terre *f*; (*world*) monde *m*; **the e.** *or* **E.** (*planet*) la Terre; **the e.'s crust/atmosphere** l'écorce *f*/l'atmosphère *f* terrestre; **on e.** sur terre; *Bible* **on e. as it is in heaven** sur la terre comme au ciel; *F* **where/why on e. ...?** où/pourquoi diable ...?; **what on e. have you done to your hair?** que diable as-tu fait à tes cheveux?; **there's no reason on e.** il n'y a absolument aucune raison; **it wouldn't cost the e.** ça ne coûterait pas les yeux de la tête; **to pay the e. for sth** payer qch les yeux de la tête; **he promised people the e.** il a promis la lune aux gens; **e. creature** (*in science fiction*) créature *f* terrestre; **e. orbit** (*of satellite*) orbite *f* terrestre; **e. satellite** satellite *m* terrestre; *TV* **e. station** station *f* terrestre

(**b**) (*ground*) sol *m*; *Fig* **to come back to e. (with a bump)** revenir (brutalement) sur terre; **it brought her down to e. with a bit of a bump** ça l'a ramenée sur terre un peu brutalement; **the e. moved** la terre a tremblé; *Hum* **did the e. move for you?** (*while making love*) est-ce que tu as eu le grand frisson?

(**c**) *Agr etc* (*soil*) terre *f*; **loose/heavy e.** terre(s) meuble(s)/lourde(s); **e. floor** (*of hut etc*) sol *m* en terre battue

(**d**) *Br El* terre *f*, masse *f*; (*terminal*) mise *f* à terre; **dead e.** contact *m* parfait avec le sol; **e. to frame** (*of car etc*) contact à la masse; **e. cable** câble *m* de terre; *Aut* câble de masse; **e. connection** prise *f* de terre; **e. wire** fil *m* de terre

(**e**) (*of fox*) terrier *m*, tanière *f*; **to go to e.** (*of fox, fugitive*) se terrer; **I've been trying to get in touch with him but he seems to have gone to e.** j'ai essayé de le joindre mais on dirait qu'il s'est volatilisé; **to run to e.** (*fox*) chasser jusqu'à son terrier; (*fugitive*) dépister; (*person*) dénicher; (*mistake in the figures*) découvrir la source de

earth² **1** *vt* (**a**) *Br El* mettre à la terre (**b**) (*in hunting*) poursuivre jusqu'à son terrier (**c**) = **earth up 2** *vi* (*of fox*) se terrer

▶ **earth up** *vtsep* (*in gardening*) (*plant*) butter, chausser

earthbound ['ɜːθbaʊnd] *adj* (**a**) (*mundane*) terre à terre *inv* (**b**) **e. spirit** esprit *m* qui ne peut pas quitter le monde des vivants (**c**) (*heading towards earth*) qui se dirige vers la terre

earthen ['ɜːθ(ə)n] *adj* (**a**) (*crockery etc*) en *ou* de terre (cuite) (**b**) (*floor*) en terre battue

earthenware ['ɜːθ(ə)nweər] *n* poterie *f* (de terre); **glazed e.** faïence *f*; (*stoneware*) grès *m* flambé; **e. jug** cruche *f* en *ou* de terre (cuite)

earthfall ['ɜːθfɔːl] *n* éboulement *m* de terres

earthiness ['ɜːθɪnɪs] *n* truculence *f*, *Pej* grossièreté *f*

earthlight ['ɜːθlaɪt] *n Astron* (*of moon*) lumière *f* cendrée

earthling ['ɜːθlɪŋ] *n* (*in science fiction*) habitant, -ante de la terre, terrien, -enne

earthly ['ɜːθlɪ] **1** *adj* terrestre; **the E. Paradise** le Paradis terrestre; *F* **there's no e. reason for ...** il n'y a pas la moindre raison au monde pour ...; *F* **it's of no e. use to me** ça ne me sert *ou* ne me servirait absolument à rien; *F* **he hasn't got an e. chance** *or* **hope** il n'a pas la moindre chance **2** *n Br F* **he hasn't got an e.** il n'a pas la moindre chance

earthman, *pl* **-men** ['ɜːθmæn, -mɛn] *n* (*in science fiction*) terrien *m*

earthmover ['ɜːθmuːvər] *n* bulldozer *m*

earthmoving ['ɜːθmuːvɪŋ] *n* **e. equipment** engins *mpl* de terrassement

earthquake ['ɜːθkweɪk] *n also Fig* tremblement *m* de terre, séisme *m*; **e. survivor** survivant *m ou* rescapé *m* d'un tremblement de terre

earth sciences *npl* sciences *fpl* de la terre

earth-shaking ['ɜːθʃeɪkɪŋ] *adj* = **earth-shattering**

earth-shattering *adj* (**a**) (*discovery, news*) stupéfiant; (*defeat*) accablant (**b**) (*explosion, crash etc*) assourdissant

earthwoman, *pl* **-women** ['ɜːθwʊmən, -wɪmɪn] *n* (*in science fiction*) terrienne *f*
earthwork ['ɜːθwɜːk] *n* **e. embankment** terrassement *m* en remblai; **earthworks** (*banked earth*) travaux *mpl* en terre *ou* de terrassement; (*prehistoric*), *Mil* fortifications *fpl* en terre
earthworm ['ɜːθwɜːm] *n* lombric *m*, ver *m* de terre
earthy ['ɜːθɪ] *adj* (**a**) terreux; **to have an e. smell** sentir la terre (**b**) (*coarse*) (*person*) truculent; (*humour, language*) truculent, vert; **an e. laugh** un gros rire (**c**) **e. common sense** sens *m* pratique
ear trumpet *n* cornet *m* acoustique
earwax ['ɪəwæks] *n* cire *f* sécrétée par les oreilles, *Fml* cérumen *m*
earwig ['ɪəwɪg] *n* (*insect*) perce-oreille *m*, *pl* perce-oreilles
ease¹ [iːz] *n* (**a**) (*facility*) (*when speaking, moving etc*) facilité *f*; (*of manners, movements etc*) aisance *f*; **the e. with which they adapted** la facilité avec laquelle ils se sont adaptés; **with e.** (*to defeat, adapt*) facilement; (*to answer*) aisément; (*to speak*) avec facilité; **with the utmost** *or* **the greatest of e.** avec la plus grande facilité, le plus facilement du monde; **the e. with which we entered the building** la facilité avec laquelle nous sommes entrés dans le bâtiment; **e. of use** confort *m ou* facilité d'emploi
(**b**) (*peace*) (*mental*) tranquillité *f*; (*physical*) repos *m*, bien-être *m*; **to be at e.** (*mentally*) avoir l'esprit tranquille; **to be at e. with sb/in a place** être à l'aise avec qn/dans un endroit; **to be** *or* **feel ill at e.** (*awkward*) être mal à l'aise; (*worried*) être inquiet (**about** au sujet de); **a nation at e. with itself** une nation qui s'accepte; **to be at one's e.** (*relaxed*) être à son aise; (*calm*) être tranquille; **to put sb at e.** mettre qn à l'aise; **set your mind at e.** rassurez-vous, soyez tranquille; **to take one's e.** se mettre à l'aise; *Mil etc* **to stand at e.** se mettre *ou* se tenir au repos; **at e.!** repos!
(**c**) (*leisure*) loisir *m*; (*idleness*) oisiveté *f*; **a life of e.** une vie d'oisiveté
ease² **1** *vt* (**a**) (*alleviate*) (*suffering, pain*) adoucir, calmer, soulager; (*the mind*) tranquilliser; **to e. sb's anxiety/fears** calmer les inquiétudes/craintes de qn
(**b**) (*free*) débarrasser, délivrer (**sb of** *or* **from sth** qn de qch); **to e. oneself of a burden** se soulager d'un fardeau
(**c**) (*relax*) (*rope, spring*) détendre, relâcher; (*screw*) desserrer; (*pressure*) soulager; (*tension*) réduire; **to e. the congestion in a street** décongestionner la circulation d'une rue
(**d**) (*move carefully, slowly*) déplacer doucement; **to e. a box open** ouvrir doucement une boîte; **to e. one's way through the crowd** se faufiler à travers la foule
(**e**) *Sewing* (*dress, item of clothing*) donner plus d'ampleur à; *MecE* (*part*) donner du jeu à
2 *vi* (*of pain, pressure etc*) s'atténuer; (*of tension, St Exch market etc*) se détendre; **the wind/rain has eased** le vent/la pluie s'est calmé(e); **the situation has eased** la situation s'est détendue
▶ **ease off** **1** *vtsep* (**a**) (*release*) enlever doucement; **she eased the lid off the jar** elle a doucement enlevé le couvercle de sur le pot (**b**) *Naut* (*let out*) (*rigging*) filer, choquer **2** *vi* (**a**) (*work less*) moins travailler, *Pej* se relâcher (**b**) (*diminish*) (*of pain*) s'atténuer; (*of rain*) se calmer; *St Exch* (*of rates*) se détendre (**c**) *Naut* s'éloigner un peu du rivage
▶ **ease up** *vi* (**a**) = **ease off 2** (*a*), (*b*) (**b**) (*slow down*) ralentir
easel ['iːz(ə)l] *n* (*of painter*) chevalet *m*
easily ['iːzɪlɪ] *adv* (**a**) (*without difficulty*) facilement, sans difficulté; **you can e. imagine my disappointment** vous concevez sans peine ma déception; **he is not e. satisfied** il n'est pas facile à satisfaire; *Sp etc* **he came in first e.** il est arrivé bon premier; **the car holds six people e.** six personnes tiennent à l'aise dans cette voiture; **that's e. said** c'est vite dit
(**b**) (*in relaxed manner*) à son aise; **to take things** *or* **life e.** prendre les choses comme elles viennent, prendre la vie comme elle vient, *Pej* se laisser vivre, se la couler douce
(**c**) (*undoubtedly*) **e. larger** largement plus grand; **e. the best/worst/biggest** de loin le meilleur/le pire/le plus gros; **he is e. forty** il a bien quarante ans; **it's e. 20 kilometres to the next village** il y a bien 20 kilomètres jusqu'au prochain village
(**d**) (*possibly*) **the information could e. be wrong** les informations pourraient très bien être fausses
easiness ['iːzɪnɪs] *n* (**a**) (*of task*) facilité *f*; **I was surprised at the e. with which the door opened** j'ai été surpris par la facilité avec laquelle la porte s'est ouverte (**b**) (*easy-going nature*) (*of person*) décontraction *f*; (*of approach*) caractère *m* décontracté; **his e. with children** la facilité de ses rapports avec les enfants
easing ['iːzɪŋ] *n* (**a**) (*of suffering, pressure*) atténuation *f*; (*caused by medication*) soulagement *m*; (*of beam etc*) allègement *m* (**b**) (*relaxation*) (*of conflict, pressure*) atténuation *f*; (*of restrictions*) allègement *m*; **e. of tension** (*political etc*) détente *f*; *Com* **e. of the market** détente du marché
easing off *n* (**a**) (*of pain*) atténuation *f*; **there had been no e. of the pain** la douleur ne s'était pas atténuée (**b**) (*from work*) relâchement *m*
east [iːst] **1** *n* est *m*; **house facing the e.** maison orientée à l'est; **on the e., to the e.** à l'est (**of** de); **to pray to the e.** prier en direction de l'est; **the E.** (*the Orient*) l'Orient *m*; (*Eastern Europe*) l'Est; **the Middle E.** le Moyen-Orient; **the Far E.** l'Extrême-Orient; **the e. of England** l'est de l'Angleterre
2 *adv* à l'est; **e. of the Rhine** à l'est du Rhin; **to travel e.** voyager vers l'est; **to face e.** (*of house*) être orienté à l'est
3 *adj* (*coast etc*) est *inv*; (*wind*) d'est; (*wall, window*) qui fait face à l'est; **e. end** (*of church*) chevet *m*; **the E. End** = les quartiers *mpl* pauvres et populeux de la partie est (*de Londres, de Glasgow*); **the E. Side** = les quartiers est (*de New York*)
East Africa *n* Afrique *f* orientale
eastbound ['iːstbaʊnd] *adj* (*train etc*) allant vers l'est; (*traffic, carriageway*) en direction de l'est
Easter ['iːstər] *n* Pâques *m*; **at E.** à Pâques; **to celebrate E.** fêter Pâques; **E. Day, E. Sunday** le jour *ou* le dimanche de Pâques; **E. Monday** le lundi de Pâques; **E. week** (*following Easter*) la semaine de Pâques; (*Holy Week*) la semaine sainte; **E. egg** œuf *m* de Pâques
Easter Island *n* l'île *f* de Pâques
easterly ['iːstəlɪ] **1** *adj* (*wind*) d'est, qui vient de l'est; (*current*) qui se dirige vers l'est; (*point*) situé à *ou* vers l'est; **in an e. direction** vers l'est **2** *adv* vers l'est **3** *n* vent *m* d'est
eastern ['iːstən] *adj* est *inv*, de l'est; (*of Far East*) oriental, -aux; **the e. side of the country** la partie est *ou* orientale du pays; *Rel* **the E. Church** l'Église *f* d'Orient
Easterner ['iːstənər] *n* (*from Far East*) oriental, -ale; (*from North America*) habitant, -ante des *US* États *ou Can* provinces de l'est
Eastern Europe *n* Europe *f* de l'Est
Eastern Standard Time *n Am* heure *f* normale de l'est
Eastern Townships *npl Can* Cantons *mpl* de l'Est
Eastertide ['iːstətaɪd] *n* Pâques *m*
East Europe *n esp Am* Europe *f* de l'Est
east-facing ['iːstfeɪsɪŋ] *adj* orienté à l'est
East Germany *n Hist* Allemagne *f* de l'Est
East India Company *n Hist* compagnie *f* des Indes Orientales
East Indies *npl* Indes *fpl* orientales
eastward ['iːstwəd] **1** *adj* (*in the east*) à l'est, dans l'est; (*in an eastward direction*) du côté de l'est **2** *adv* = **eastwards**
eastwards ['iːstwədz] *adv* à l'est; (*with motion*) vers l'est
easy ['iːzɪ] (**easier, easiest**) **1** *adj* (**a**) (*not difficult*) (*work*) facile, aisé; (*question, test*) facile; (*method, solution*) simple; **e. to please** pas difficile; **to be e. to annoy/upset** s'énerver/se vexer facilement; **he's e. to keep entertained** un rien l'amuse; **e. to get on with** d'un commerce facile; **e. to live with** facile à vivre; **don't worry, it's e. to do on your first day** ne t'inquiète pas, ça arrive à tout le monde le premier jour; **that is e. to see** cela se voit; **it is e. for him to …** il lui est facile de …; **it's e. to say …** on a vite fait de dire …; **this will make your job easier** ceci vous facilitera la tâche; **it makes life much easier not having to fill in these forms** ça facilite bien les choses de ne pas avoir à remplir ces formulaires; **within e. reach of …** à distance commode de …; **it's within e. walking distance** on peut facilement y aller à pied; *F* **as e. as ABC** *or* **as falling off a log** *or* **as pie** simple comme bonjour; **it isn't e. being a mother** ce n'est pas facile d'être mère; **the e. way out** *or* **option** la solution de facilité; **there are no e. answers** c'est un problème qui est loin d'être facile à résoudre; *F* **e. money** argent *m* gagné sans peine; **to have an e. time (of it)** se la couler douce; **by e. stages** (*travel*) à petites étapes; **learn how to drive/French in five e. steps** *or* **stages** apprendre à conduire/le français sans peine en cinq leçons; **the film is very e. on the eye** le film est reposant à regarder; **he's/she's e. on the eye** il/elle n'est pas mal du tout; *Com* **by e. payments, on e. terms** avec facilités de paiement; *Sp etc* **to come in an e. first** arriver bon premier
(**b**) (*easy-going, relaxed*) (*person*) d'un caractère facile; (*manners etc*) libre, dégagé; (*style*) facile, naturel; (*grace*) naturel; **they're usually fairly e. about deadlines** d'habitude ils sont assez accommodants sur les délais; **the e. familiarity of her welcome instantly reassured them** la familiarité dégagée de son accueil les a immédiatement rassurés; *F* **I'm e.!** (*I don't mind*) ça m'est égal!; *Old-*

fashioned **woman of e. virtue** femme *f* de mœurs faciles *ou* légères; *Sl* **an e. lay** une femme/fille facile

(c) (*movement*) aisé, souple; **e. fit** *MecE* ajustage *m* lâche; (*of jeans, clothes*) lâche, de coupe confortable; **my coat is an e. fit** mon manteau est de coupe confortable

(d) (*comfortable*) (*pace*) tranquille; (*life*) sans souci; **to be e. in one's mind** avoir l'esprit tranquille; **at an e. pace** tranquillement; **with an e. conscience** la conscience tranquille; *F* **to be on e. street** ne pas avoir de problèmes financiers

(e) *Com* (*market*) tranquille; **prices are (getting) easier** on accuse une détente dans les prix; **cotton was easier** le coton a accusé une détente

2 *adv* **(a) to take things** *or* **it e.** (*in relaxed manner*) prendre les choses en douceur; **to take things** *or* **life e.** (*lead a life of ease*) mener une vie tranquille; (*not overdo things*) ralentir; **take it e.!** doucement!; (*don't get upset*) ne vous en faites pas!; **you'll have to go e. for a bit** il va falloir ralentir *ou* freiner un peu; **to go e. with sth/sb** ménager qch/qn; **e. does it!** (allez-y) doucement!; **go e. on the electricity/the curry powder** allez-y doucement avec l'électricité/le curry; **e. (ahead)!** (*in rowing*) (en avant) doucement!; *Mil* **stand e.!** repos!

(b) *F* (*without difficulty*) **I can do it e.** cela me sera facile; **(it's) easier said than done** c'est plus facile à dire qu'à faire; *prov* **e. come e. go** ce qui vient de la flûte s'en va par le tambour

easy chair *n* fauteuil *m*

easy-going *adj* **(a)** (*not given to anger*) qui prend les choses tranquillement; (*not worrying*) qui ne se fait pas de bile, décontracté; (*undemanding*) accommodant, coulant, peu exigeant; (*permissive*) qui a la conscience élastique; **try to be more e. on yourself** essaie d'être moins exigeant envers toi-même; **they take an e. attitude to such cases** ils adoptent une attitude plus lâche dans de tels cas **(b)** (*horse*) à l'allure douce

eat [iːt] (*pt* **ate** [et, *esp Am* eɪt]; *pp* **eaten** ['iːt(ə)n]) **1** *vt* **(a)** (*bread, soup etc*) manger; **to e. one's breakfast** déjeuner, prendre son petit déjeuner; **to e. one's dinner/supper** dîner/ souper; **to e. a good dinner** faire un bon dîner; **to e. a card** (*credit card*) avaler une carte; **fit to e.** bon à manger, mangeable; **I don't e. meat** je ne mange pas de viande; **to e. one's fill** manger à sa faim; **he won't e. you** il ne vous mangera pas; *F* **(I'm so hungry) I could eat a horse**! j'ai une faim de loup!; *F* **we e. teams like you for breakfast** nous ne faisons qu'une seule bouchée d'équipes comme la vôtre; **to e. one's words** se rétracter; **if it comes off, I'll e. my hat** si ça réussit, je mange mon chapeau; **to e. sb out of house and home** ruiner qn en nourriture; **she ate her way through six packets of biscuits** elle a réussi à engloutir six paquets de biscuits

(b) *F* (*trouble*) **what's eating you?** qu'est-ce qui vous inquiète *ou* tracasse?

2 *vi* **(a)** manger; **to e. like a horse** manger comme un ogre; **to e. like a bird** avoir un appétit d'oiseau, manger trois fois rien; **he eats out of my hand** (*of bird*) il vient manger dans ma main; *Fig* (*of person*) il fait tout ce que je veux; **treat them right and you'll have them eating out of your hand** traite-les bien et tu en feras ce que tu voudras

(b) (*have meal*) dîner; **we e. at seven** nous dînons à sept heures; **to e. well** bien manger; **let's e.!** on mange?; **have you eaten?** est-ce que tu as mangé?

▶ **eat away** *vtsep* (*erode*) (*rocks, cliff, self-confidence*) éroder, miner; (*foundations*) saper; (*part of body*) ronger; (*of acid*) dissoudre

▶ **eat away at** *vipo* = **eat away, eat into**

▶ **eat in** *vi* (*of hotel guest*) consommer sur place

▶ **eat into** *vipo* **(a)** (*attack*) ronger; **rust had eaten into the metal** la rouille avait rongé le métal; **to e. into wood** (*of insect, worm*) ronger le bois **(b)** (*diminish*) entamer; **these expenses had eaten into their savings** ces dépenses avaient entamé leurs économies

▶ **eat off** *vtsep F* **to e. one's head off** s'empiffrer

▶ **eat out 1** *vi* **(a)** (*eat in restaurant*) manger au restaurant **(b)** (*of hotel guest*) déjeuner/dîner à l'extérieur **2** *vtsep F* **to e. one's heart out** se ronger le cœur; **e. your heart out, USA!** = dommage pour les États-Unis!

▶ **eat up 1** *vtsep* **(a)** (*eat completely*) (*cake etc*) manger jusqu'à la dernière miette; **e. up your bread!** finis ton pain! **(b)** (*consume*) consumer sans profit; *F* **stove that eats up the coal** poêle qui mange beaucoup de charbon; **to e. up the miles** (*of car etc*) dévorer la route; **jealousy is eating him up** la jalousie le dévore; **to be eaten up with** (*pride*) être dévoré de; (*ambition*) être consumé par **(c)** (*exhaust*) (*provisions*) épuiser **2** *vi* (*eat everything*) finir son assiette; **e. up!** (*there's lots more*) vas-y, mange!

eatable ['iːtəb(ə)l] **1** *adj* comestible; (*fit to eat*) mangeable, bon à manger; **fruit that is quite e.** fruit qui se laisse manger **2** *npl esp Hum* **eatables** provisions *fpl* de bouche, comestibles *mpl*

eater ['iːtər] *n* **(a)** (*person*) mangeur, -euse; **he isn't as good an e. as his sister** il ne mange pas aussi bien que sa sœur; **to be a fussy e.** être difficile (sur la nourriture); **to be a messy e.** manger salement; **small/big e.** petit/gros mangeur **(b)** (*apple*) pomme *f* à couteau *ou* de dessert

eatery ['iːtərɪ] *n F* (café-)restaurant *m*

eating ['iːtɪŋ] *n* manger *m*; **healthy e.** alimentation *f* saine; **these birds make good e.** ces oiseaux sont bons à manger; **e. apple** pomme *f* à couteau *ou* de dessert; **e. habits** habitudes *fpl* alimentaires, hygiène *f* alimentaire; **e. house, e. place** restaurant *m*; **cheap e. house** gargote *f*

eats [iːts] *npl F* bouffe *f*; **plenty of e.** plein à bouffer; **let's get some e.** allons chercher de la bouffe

eau-de-Cologne ['əʊdəkə'ləʊn] *n* eau *f* de Cologne

eaves [iːvz] *npl Constr* avant-toit *m*

eavesdrop ['iːvzdrɒp] *vi* (**-pp-**) écouter aux portes; **to e. on a conversation** tendre l'oreille pour écouter une conversation privée; **I found myself eavesdropping on their conversation** j'ai entendu leur conversation sans le vouloir; **stop eavesdropping!** arrête d'espionner le monde!

eavesdropper ['iːvzdrɒpər] *n* oreille *f* indiscrète

ebb[1] [eb] *n* **(a)** (*of tide*) reflux *m*; **the e. and flow** le flux et le reflux; **the e. and flow of marital life** les hauts et les bas de la vie conjugale; **the e. and flow of political change** les fluctuations de la vie politique; **the tide is on the e.** la marée baisse **(b)** (*of fortune, life*) déclin *m*; **to be at a low e.** (*of patient*) être très bas; (*be depressed*) être déprimé; (*of business*) être au ralenti; **her spirits were at a low e. /their lowest e.** elle était abattue/très abattue; **their funds were at a low/their lowest e.** ils étaient à bout de ressources

ebb[2] *vi* **(a)** (*of tide*) baisser; **to e. and flow** monter et baisser **(b)** = **ebb away**

▶ **ebb away** *vi* (*of enthusiasm, courage, strength*) faiblir, baisser; (*of rage, indignation*) se calmer; (*of support*) s'amenuiser; (*of time, water*) s'écouler; **his life was ebbing away** il baissait d'heure en heure

ebbing ['ebɪŋ] *adj* **(a)** (*water*) qui reflue **(b)** (*fortunes etc*) sur le déclin; (*popularity*) en baisse; (*strength, enthusiasm*) faiblissant

ebb tide *n* marée *f* descendante, jusant *m*

ebony ['ebənɪ] *n* **(a)** (*wood*) (bois *m* d')ébène *f*; **e. box** boîte *f* en bois d'ébène **(b) e. (tree)** ébénier *m* **(c)** (*colour*) ébène *f*; **e. skin** peau *f* noire d'ébène

ebullience [ɪ'bʌlɪəns] *n* bouillonnement *m*, effervescence *f*; **the e. of youth** l'exubérance *f* de la jeunesse

ebullient [ɪ'bʌlɪənt] *adj* enthousiaste, exubérant; **they were in (an) e. mood** *or* **in e. spirits** ils étaient d'une humeur exubérante

EC [iː'siː] **1** *n* (*abbr* **European Community**) CE *f*; **EC directive** directive *f* européenne **2** *adj attrib* de la CE

eccentric [ek'sentrɪk] **1** *adj* **(a)** (*person, behaviour*) excentrique **(b)** *Math, Astron* (*circle, orbit etc*) excentrique; *MecE* (*camshaft*) excentré; **e. shaft** arbre *m* à excentrique **2** *n* **(a)** (*person*) excentrique *mf*, original, -ale **(b)** *MecE* excentrique *m*

eccentrically [ek'sentrɪklɪ] *adv MecE* excentriquement; (*to dress, behave*) de manière excentrique, excentriquement

eccentricity [eksen'trɪsɪtɪ] *n* **(a)** (*of character, behaviour etc*) excentricité *f*; **eccentricities** (*of person*) excentricités **(b)** *Math* (*of ellipse*) excentricité *f*; *MecE* excentricité, désaxage *m*

ecclesiastic [ɪkliːzɪ'æstɪk] *n Fml* ecclésiastique *m*

ecclesiastical [ɪkliːzɪ'æstɪk(ə)l] *adj* ecclésiastique

ECG [iːsiː'dʒiː] *n Med* **(a)** (*abbr* **electrocardiogram**) ECG *m* **(b)** (*abbr* **electrocardiograph**) électrocardiographe *m*

ECGD [iːsiːdʒiː'diː] *n* (*abbr* **Export Credit Guarantee Department**) COFACE *f*

echelon ['eʃəlɒn] *n* **(a)** (*level*) **the higher** *or* **upper echelons of industry/the Civil Service** les niveaux supérieurs de l'industrie/de l'administration **(b)** *Mil* échelon *m*; **in e.** en échelon

echo[1], *pl* **-oes** ['ekəʊ, -əʊz] *n* écho *m*; **this room has a bit of an e./a good e.** il y a un peu d'écho/un bon écho dans cette pièce; **to cheer sb to the e.** applaudir qn à tout rompre; *Fig* **there are echoes of the 18th century in this novel** il y a des accents du XVIIIe siècle dans ce roman; **echoes of Churchill/Godard** du Churchill/du Godard; **her words found an e. in many hearts** ses mots ont fait vibré la corde sensible dans beaucoup de cœurs

echo[2] **1** *vt* répéter (en écho); **to e. sb's words** répéter ce que qn a dit; **to e. sb's opinions** se faire l'écho des opinions de qn; **'we're going to the beach', she said – 'beach?' he echoed** 'nous allons à la plage' dit-elle – 'à la plage?', répéta-t-il; *Fig* **the yellow of the walls is echoed in the curtains** le jaune des murs se trouve rappelé dans les rideaux **2** *vi* faire écho; **the woods echoed with the songs of birds** les bois retentissaient des chants des oiseaux; **room that does not e.** pièce *f* sourde; **his voice echoes through the room** sa voix résonne dans la salle

echo chamber *n* chambre *f* sonore

echo sounder *n* écho-sondeur *m*, *pl* écho-sondeurs

echo sounding *n* sondage *m* par ultra-sons

éclair [eɪ'kleər] *n Culin* éclair *m*; **chocolate e.** éclair au chocolat

eclectic [ɪ'klektɪk] *adj, n* éclectique *mf*; **an e. blend** un mélange varié

eclecticism [ɪ'klektɪsɪz(ə)m] *n* éclectisme *m*

eclipse¹ [ɪ'klɪps] *n* **(a)** *Astron* éclipse *f*; **solar/lunar e.** éclipse de soleil/de lune; **total/partial e.** éclipse totale/partielle **(b)** *Naut (of lighthouse)* éclipse *f* **(c)** *Fig (overshadowing)* éclipse *f*; **the e. of this team by a younger one** l'éclipse de cette équipe par une équipe plus jeune; **to suffer** *or* **go into an e.** être éclipsé

eclipse² *vt* **(a)** *Astron, Naut etc* éclipser **(b)** *Fig (overshadow, supersede)* éclipser

ecofreak ['i:kəʊfri:k] *n F* écologiste *mf* enragé(e)

eco-friendly ['i:kəʊfrendlɪ] *adj (product)* qui ne nuit pas à l'environnement; *(lifestyle, person)* qui respecte l'environnement

ecological [i:kə'lɒdʒɪk(ə)l] *adj* écologique

ecologically [i:kə'lɒdʒɪklɪ] *adv* écologiquement; **to be e. harmful/sound** nuire/ne pas nuire à l'environnement

ecologist [ɪ'kɒlədʒɪst] *n* écologiste *mf*

ecology [ɪ'kɒlədʒɪ] *n* écologie *f*

econometric [ɪkɒnə'metrɪk] *adj* économétrique; **e. modelling** modélisation *f* économétrique

econometrics [ɪkɒnə'metrɪks] *n* [①A10,c] économétrie *f*

economic [i:kə'nɒmɪk] *adj* **(a)** *Econ* économique; **e. geography** géographie *f* économique; **e. circumstances** conjoncture *f*; **e. forecast** prévisions *fpl* économiques; **e.-forecasting firm** organisme *m* spécialisé dans les prévisions économiques; **e. recovery** reprise *f* économique, redressement *m* économique; **e. trend** tendance *f* de l'économie **(b)** *Br (profitable)* rentable; **to make sth e.** rentabiliser qch **(c)** *F (inexpensive)* économique

economical [i:kə'nɒmɪk(ə)l] *adj (person)* économe; *(apparatus etc)* économique; *(style)* concis, sobre; **to be e. with sth** économiser qch; **to be e. with the truth** dire la vérité avec parcimonie; **it is more e. to buy larger packets** c'est plus économique d'acheter des paquets plus grands; **e. speed** *(of ship etc)* vitesse *f* économique

economically [i:kə'nɒmɪklɪ] *adv* économiquement; **e. written** écrit avec concision; **e. viable** économiquement viable, rentable; **to use sth e.** *(electricity, fuel)* économiser qch

economics [i:kə'nɒmɪks] *n* [①A10,c] **(a)** *Econ* les sciences *fpl* économiques; **socialist/supply-side e.** économie *f* socialiste/de l'offre **(b)** *(financial pros and cons)* aspects *mpl* économiques *ou* financiers; **the e. of town planning** les aspects financiers de l'urbanisme

economist [ɪ'kɒnəmɪst] *n Econ* économiste *mf*

economize [ɪ'kɒnəmaɪz] **1** *vi* économiser, faire des économies; **to e. on sth** économiser sur qch **2** *vt (time, money etc)* économiser, ménager

economizer [ɪ'kɒnəmaɪzər] *n Aut* économiseur *m*

economy [ɪ'kɒnəmɪ] *n* **(a)** *(careful use, saving) (of money, resources etc)* économie *f*; **e. in fuel consumption** économie de combustible; **to practise e.** économiser; **try to practise e. in your use of the photocopier** essaie d'utiliser la photocopieuse avec parcimonie; **to make economies** faire des économies; **it's a false e.** ce n'est pas vraiment rentable; **with e. of effort** sans effort inutile; **e. of style** concision *f* de style; **economies of scale** économies d'échelle **(b)** *Econ (of country)* économie *f*, régime *m* économique; *Old-fashioned* **political e.** économie politique; **(centrally) planned e.** économie planifiée

economy brand *n* marque *f* économique

economy class *n Naut, Av* classe *f* économique; **to travel e.** voyager en classe économique

economy drive *n* campagne *f* de réduction des dépenses

economy fare *n* tarif *m* économique

economy measure *n* mesure *f* de réduction des dépenses; **as an e.** par mesure d'économie

economy mode *n Aut (with automatic gears)* mode *m* économique

economy pack *n Com* paquet *m* économique

economy size *n* format *m* économique

ecosphere ['i:kəʊsfɪər] *n* écosphère *f*

ecosystem ['i:kəʊsɪstəm] *n* écosystème *m*

eco-tourism [i:kəʊ'tʊərɪz(ə)m] *n* tourisme *m* écologique

ecru ['ekru:] *n, adj Tex* écru *m*

ECSC [i:si:es'si:] *n Admin (abbr* **European Coal and Steel Community***)* CECA *f*

ecstasy ['ekstəsɪ] *n* **(a)** *(joyful feeling)* joie *f* délirante, ravissement *m*; **an e. of delight** un transport de joie; **to be in an e. of joy** se pâmer de joie; **to go into/be in ecstasies over sth** s'extasier/être en extase devant qch; **to send sb into ecstasies** faire tomber qn en extase **(b)** *Rel, Psy etc* extase *f* **(c)** *Sl (drug)* ecstasy *f*

ecstatic [ek'stætɪk] *adj* extatique; **he was e. about** *or* **over the news/their arrival** la nouvelle/leur arrivée le rendait fou de joie

ecstatically [ek'stætɪklɪ] *adv* avec extase; *(to look at)* d'un air extasié; **e. happy** heureux jusqu'au ravissement

ECT [i:si:'ti:] *n (abbr* **electroconvulsive therapy***)* traitement *m* par électrochocs

ectopic [ek'tɒpɪk] *adj Obst* **e. pregnancy** grossesse *f* extra-utérine, grossesse ectopique

ectoplasm ['ektəʊplæz(ə)m] *n Biol, Spiritualism* ectoplasme *m*

ECU *n* **(a)** ['eɪkju:, *occ* i:si:'ju:] *(abbr* **European Currency Unit***)* écu *m* **(b)** [i:si:'ju:] *abbr* **electronic control unit**

Ecuador ['ekwədɔ:r] *n* (la République de) l'Équateur *m*

Ecuadoran [ekwə'dɔ:rən], **Ecuadorian** [ekwə'dɔ:rɪən] **1** *adj* écuadorien, équatorien **2** *n* Écuadorien, -ienne, Équatorien, -ienne

ecumenical [i:kjʊ'menɪk(ə)l] *adj Rel (council)* œcuménique

ecumenism [i:'kju:mənɪz(ə)m], **ecumenicism** [i:kju:'menɪsɪz(ə)m] *n Rel* œcuménisme *m*

eczema ['eksɪmə] *n Med* eczéma *m*; **to have** *or* **suffer from e.** avoir *ou* faire de l'eczéma

ed (a) *(abbr* **edition***)* éd(it) **(b)** *abbr* **editor (c)** *abbr* **edited**

eddy¹ ['edɪ] *n (of water, wind)* remous *m*, tourbillon *m*; *(of leaves, dust)* tourbillon; *El* **e. currents** courants *mpl* de Foucault, courants parasites

eddy² *vi (of water)* faire des remous; *(of wind, smoke, snow)* tourbillonner, tournoyer; *(of crowds)* tournoyer

edelweiss ['eɪd(ə)lvaɪs] *n (plant)* édelweiss *m*

edema [ɪ'di:mə] *n US* œdème *m*

Eden ['i:d(ə)n] *n Bible* **(the Garden of) E.** l'Éden *m*, le Paradis terrestre

EDF [i:di:'ef] *n (abbr* **European Development Fund***)* FED *m*

edge¹ [edʒ] *n* **(a)** *(of blade)* fil *m*, tranchant *m*; *(of tool)* angle *m*; *(of skate)* carre *f*; *(of stone etc)* arête *f*, angle; **sharp/rounded e.** arête vive/mousse; **inside/outside e.** dedans *m*/dehors *m*; **knife with a keen e. on it** couteau à tranchant aigu; **to put an e. on a tool** aiguiser *ou* affiler un outil; **to take the e. off** *(blade, appetite etc)* émousser; *(pleasure)* gâter; *(argument)* couper tout l'effet de

(b) *(rim, border, limit) (of table)* bord *m*, rebord *m*; *(of plank, medal, book)* tranche *f*; *(of wood)* lisière *f*, bordure *f*, orée *f*; *(of river)* bord, rive *f*; *(of plain)* limite *f*; *(of road, path)* bordure, bord; *(sewn onto material)* liséré *m*; **it fell off the e. of the table** il est tombé de la table; **it fell off the e.** il est tombé; **gilt edges** tranches dorées; **with gilt edges** doré sur tranches; **to be on the e. of ...** *(new age)* être à l'orée de ...; *(final conflict, great discoveries)* être au bord de ...; **at the e. of the road** au bord *ou* en bordure de la route; **the flag had a golden fringe round the e.** le drapeau était bordé d'une frange dorée; *Phot etc* **white e.** *(of print)* liséré blanc; **at the water's e.** au bord de l'eau; **at the e. of a precipice** au bord d'un précipice; **on e.** *(of brick)* de chant, de can; **to set sth on e.** *(tilt)* mettre qch de chant *ou* de can

(c) *(idioms) F* **to have an** *or* **the e. on sb** être avantagé par rapport à qn; **to have an e. to one's voice** avoir une voix coupante; **to speak with a sarcastic/nervous/contemptuous e. to one's voice** parler avec une pointe de sarcasme/de nervosité/de mépris dans la voix; **on e.** *(of person)* énervé, nerveux; **to set sb on e.** crisper qn, énerver qn; **to set** *or* **put sb's teeth on e.** faire grincer des dents à qn; **to set sb's nerves on e.** taper sur les nerfs de qn; **to send sb over the e.** porter le coup de grâce à qn; **a movie that will have you on the e. of your seat** un film au suspense insoutenable; **to give sb the rough e. of one's tongue** dire son fait à qn

edge² **1** *vt* **(a)** *Tech (sharpen) (knife, tool)* affiler, aiguiser; *(millstone)* repiquer

(b) *(border) (material)* border **(with** de); *(skirt etc)* lisérer

(c) *(move slowly)* **to e. one's way into a room/through the crowd** se faufiler dans une pièce/à travers la foule; **to e. one's chair nearer** rapprocher *ou* avancer sa chaise peu à peu

2 *vi* (*move slowly*) **to e. towards sb/sth** s'approcher tout doucement de qn/qch; **to e. through the crowd/past the guards** se faufiler à travers la foule/devant les gardes; **could you possibly e. a little closer?** pourriez-vous vous rapprocher un petit peu?; **the drivers were edging forwards in the traffic jam** les conducteurs avançaient lentement dans l'embouteillage

▶ **edge away** *vi* (*move away slowly*) s'éloigner *ou* s'écarter tout doucement (**from sb** de qn)

▶ **edge out 1** *vi* (*move cautiously*) **I opened the window and edged out** j'ai ouvert la fenêtre et me suis doucement glissé dehors; **the driver/car edged out** le conducteur/la voiture se dégagea lentement **2** *vtsep* **(a) to e. one's way out** se frayer un chemin; **she edged her way out onto the ledge** elle gagna le rebord de la fenêtre avec précaution **(b)** (*supplant*) évincer; **to e. sb out of the chairmanship** évincer qn de la présidence

▶ **edge past 1** *vi* (*move past cautiously*) passer prudemment **2** *vipo* **I edged past her** je suis passé discrètement à côté d'elle

▶ **edge up 1** *vi* (*climb slowly*) (*of prices*) grimper petit à petit **2** *vtaspo* **they edged their way up the cliff** ils ont escaladé la falaise à grand peine

edge cutter *n* (*for grass*) coupe-bordure *m*, *pl* coupe-bordure(s)

edged [edʒd] *adj* (*tool, weapon etc*) tranchant, acéré

-edged [edʒd] *suff* **double-e.** à double tranchant; *Fig* **a double-e. weapon** une arme à double tranchant; **sharp-e.** au tranchant affilé *ou* bien aiguisé; **a razor-e. knife/tongue** un couteau/une langue bien affilé(e)

edge trimmer *n* (*for grass*) coupe-bordure *m*, *pl* coupe-bordure(s)

edgeways ['edʒweɪz], **edgewise** ['edʒwaɪz] *adv* **(a)** (*on its edge*) de chant; **to lay** *or* **set a plank e.** placer une planche de chant; *F* **I can't get a word in e.** je n'arrive pas à placer un mot (dans la conversation) **(b)** (*from side*) latéralement, de côté; **seen e. (on)** vu de côté

edginess ['edʒɪnɪs] *n* nervosité *f*

edging ['edʒɪŋ] *n* **(a)** (*action*) (*of dress*) pose *f* d'un liséré *ou* d'une ganse; (*of lawn*) entretien *m* de la bordure **(b)** (*border*) *Sewing* liséré *m*, passement *m*, ganse *f*; (*of flower bed*) bordure *f*

edging shears *npl* cisaille *f* à bordures

edging tool *n* coupe-gazon *m inv*, tranche-gazon *m inv*, molette *f*

edgy ['edʒɪ] *adj* (*person*) énervé; **to get e.** s'énerver

edible ['edɪb(ə)l] *adj* comestible; (*fit to eat*) bon à manger, mangeable; **it was so hot it was barely e.** c'était si chaud que c'était à peine mangeable; **it's very e.** c'est très bon; **e. oil** huile *f* comestible

edict ['i:dɪkt] *n Jur, Pol* édit *m*; *Hist* **the E. of Nantes** l'Édit de Nantes

edification [edɪfɪ'keɪʃən] *n Fml* édification *f*, instruction *f*; *esp Iron* **for your e.** pour votre édification

edifice ['edɪfɪs] *n* édifice *m*

edify ['edɪfaɪ] *vt Fml* édifier

edifying ['edɪfaɪɪŋ] *adj Fml* (*spectacle, book etc*) édifiant

Edinburgh ['edɪnbrə] *n* Édimbourg

edit¹ ['edɪt] *vt* **(a)** *Publishing, Journ* (*prepare*) préparer pour la publication; (*work*) donner une édition annotée de; (*series of texts etc*) diriger; (*be in charge of*) (*newspaper, magazine*) rédiger, diriger; **edited by ...** (*series, newspaper etc*) sous la direction de ... **(b)** *Cin* (*film*) monter; **edited master** (*of film, tape*) master *m* monté, montage *m* original **(c)** *Comptr* (*text on screen*) éditer

edit² *n Publishing* révision *f*; *TV* point *m* de montage; (*in newspaper, text*) correction *f*, révision *f*

▶ **edit in** *vtsep* insérer

▶ **edit out** *vtsep* (*scene*) couper; (*from text*) supprimer; (*write out of TV series*) faire disparaître; **he was edited out of the film when he broke his contract** on a coupé toutes les scènes du film où il apparaissait quand il a rompu son contrat

editable ['edɪtəb(ə)l] *adj* pouvant être édité

editing ['edɪtɪŋ] *n* **(a)** *Publishing* (*of text*) préparation *f*, édition *f*; (*of newspaper, magazine*) rédaction *f*; **a textbook on e.** un manuel d'édition **(b)** *Cin* (*of film*) montage *m*; (*removal*) (*of scene, passage etc*) suppression *f* **(c)** *Comptr* édition *f*

editing desk *n TV* table *f ou* banc *m* de montage

editing function *n* fonction *f* d'édition

editing table *n TV* table *f* de montage

editing terminal *n TV* terminal *m* de montage

editing window *n Comptr* fenêtre *f* d'édition

edition [ɪ'dɪʃən] *n Publishing, Journ* édition *f*; **the earlier editions of the newspapers** les premières éditions des journaux; **this error was corrected in later editions** cette erreur a été corrigée dans les éditions ultérieures; **the hardback/paperback e.** l'édition reliée/de poche; **in Tuesday's e. of the programme** dans l'émission de mardi; **school e.** édition scolaire; **cheap e.** édition populaire; **book in its fourth e.** livre à sa quatrième édition

edition time *n* (*for newspaper*) bouclage *m*, heure *f* de l'édition, tombée *f*

editor ['edɪtər] *n* **(a)** *Publishing, Journ* (*of text*) éditeur *m*; (*of critical edition*) auteur *m*; (*in charge of publication*) surveillant *m* de la publication; (*of series, dictionary*) directeur *m*; (*of magazine, newspaper*) rédacteur *m* en chef, directeur; **news e.** rédacteur au service des informations; **series e.** directeur de la publication; **sports/political/fashion e.** rédacteur sportif/politique/de mode; **editors' conference** conférence *f* de rédaction **(b)** *Cin* (*of film*) monteur *m*; *TV, Rad* **programme e.** réalisateur *m* **(c)** *Comptr* (*software*) éditeur *m*; **e. program** programme *m* éditeur

editorial [edɪ'tɔ:rɪəl] **1** *adj Publishing, Journ* de rédaction; **that's an e. decision** c'est une décision qui appartient à la rédaction; **e. advertisement** reportage *m* publicitaire; **e. advertising** publicité *f* rédactionnelle; **e. conference** conférence *f* de rédaction; **e. content** contenu *m* rédactionnel; **e. department** (*in press*) service *m* de la rédaction, rédaction *f*, direction *f* de la rédaction; **e. director** (*of newspaper*) rédacteur *m* en chef, directeur *m* de la rédaction; (*of publishing company*) directeur de la rédaction; **e. freedom** liberté *f* des rédacteurs; **e. interference** ingérence *f* rédactionnelle; **e. office** (salle *f* de) rédaction *f*; **e. opinion** (*in press*) avis *m* éditorial; **e. policy** politique *f* éditoriale; (*in press*) politique *f* de la rédaction; **the e. staff** la rédaction

2 *n Journ* éditorial *m*, *F* édito *m*; **e. writer** éditorialiste *mf*

editorialist [edɪ'tɔ:rɪəlɪst] *n Am* éditorialiste *mf*

editorialize [edɪ'tɔ:rɪəlaɪz] *vi* émettre des opinions personnelles, être subjectif; **as the Times editorialized, ...** comme l'affirmait l'éditorial du Times, ...

editorship ['edɪtəʃɪp] *n* rédaction *f*, direction *f*; **the series was produced under the general e. of ...** la série a été produite sous la direction générale de ...

edit suite *n TV* régie *f ou* salle *f* de montage

EDP [i:di:'pi:] *n* (*abbr* **electronic data processing**) informatique *f*; **E. department** service *m* informatique

educable ['edjʊkəb(ə)l] *adj* éducable

educate ['edjʊkeɪt] *vt* **(a)** *Sch* (*person*) donner de l'instruction à, instruire; **he was educated in France/at Oxford** il a fait ses études en France/à Oxford; **to have one's child educated** faire faire des études à son enfant; **to be impossible to e.** être inéducable **(b)** (*train, develop*) (*sb, sb's taste/mind*) former; **the series aims to e. the viewers in the ways of this strange people** cette série a pour objectif d'instruire les téléspectateurs sur les coutumes de ce peuple étrange; **she was educated always to think of others before herself** on lui a enseigné à toujours penser aux autres avant elle-même

educated ['edjʊkeɪtɪd] *adj* (*person*) instruit, lettré; **half-e.** peu instruit; **an e. guess** une supposition éclairée; **self-e.** autodidacte; **he was well e. in the ways of the locals** il était bien renseigné sur le mode de vie des gens de la région

education [edjʊ'keɪʃən] *n* **(a)** (*instruction*) enseignement *m*, instruction *f*; **to study E.** étudier les Sciences de l'Éducation; **the e. of young people in the use of birth control methods** l'éducation des jeunes pour l'utilisation des méthodes contraceptives; **he has had a good e.** il a reçu une bonne instruction; **to receive a classical/literary e.** recevoir une éducation *ou* un enseignement classique/littéraire; **to get oneself an e.** faire des études; **he never completed his e.** il n'a jamais fini *ou* terminé ses études; **it was an e. working over there** c'était instructif de travailler là-bas; **adult e.** enseignement des adultes; **compulsory e.** enseignement obligatoire; **full-time e.** enseignement à temps complet; **further e.** enseignement post-scolaire; **higher** *or* **university e.** (*system*) enseignement supérieur; (*of person*) études *fpl* supérieures; **primary/secondary e.** enseignement primaire/secondaire; *Br* **Department of E. and Science** = Ministère *m* de l'Éducation nationale; *Br* **(local) e. authority** = Direction *f* de l'enseignement

(b) (*learning*) éducation *f*; **a man without e.** un homme sans éducation; **gaps in one's e.** des lacunes dans son éducation

Education Act *n* Loi *f* sur l'Enseignement

educational [edjʊ'keɪʃən(ə)l] *adj* (*institution, work*) d'éducation, d'enseignement; (*role, function*) éducatif, éducateur; (*programme, publisher*) scolaire; (*method*) éducatif, pédagogique; **working over there was very e.**

c'était très instructif de travailler là-bas; **it was an e. experience/visit** c'était une expérience/visite instructive; **for e. purposes** dans un but pédagogique; **e. adviser** conseiller *m* d'orientation; **e. film** film *m* éducatif; **e. holiday** vacances *fpl* studieuses; **e. psychologist** (*practical*) psychologue *mf* scolaire; (*academic*) psychopédagogue *mf*; **e. qualification** diplôme *m*; **e. software** logiciel *m* didactique; **e. tour** Éductour *m*, voyage *m* d'études

education(al)ist [edjʊ'keɪʃənɪst, -əlɪst] *n* éducateur, -trice, pédagogue *mf*

educationally [edjʊ'keɪʃən(ə)lɪ] *adv* du point de vue de l'éducation *ou* de l'enseignement; **e. subnormal** (*child*) arriéré

education correspondent *n* correspondant, -ante sur les questions d'éducation

education page *n* page *f* éducation

education supplement *n* supplément *m* éducation

educative ['edjʊkətɪv] *adj* (*function, purpose*) éducatif; (*experience, remark*) instructif

educator ['edjʊkeɪtər] *n esp Am* éducateur, -trice

Edwardian [ed'wɔːdɪən] *adj* qui a rapport à l'époque du roi Édouard VII; **the E. era** la Belle Époque

Edward the Confessor ['edwəd] *n* Édouard *m* le Confesseur

EEC [iːiː'siː] *n* (*abbr* **European Economic Community**) CEE *f*

EEG [iːiː'dʒiː] *n Med* **(a)** (*abbr* **electroencephalogram**) EEG *m* **(b)** (*abbr* **electroencephalograph**) = appareil *m* à EEG

eel [iːl] *n* anguille *f*; **e. basket** *or* **pot** nasse *f* à anguilles; *Br Culin* **jellied eels** anguilles en gelée

eelworm ['iːlwɜːm] *n* anguillule *f*

EEPROM ['iːprɒm] *n Comptr* (*abbr* **electrically erasable programmable ROM**) EEPROM *f*

eerie ['ɪərɪ] *adj* (*calm, sound*) inquiétant, sinistre; (*atmosphere*) qui donne des frissons; **an e. silence** (*after explosion, in empty house etc*) un silence de mort; **I had the e. feeling that I was being watched** j'avais l'étrange impression qu'on m'observait; **it was e. to think that …** cela donnait des frissons *ou* la chair de poule de penser que …

eerily ['ɪərɪlɪ] *adv* étrangement, à donner des frissons; **e. quiet** (*house etc*) d'un calme inquiétant; **the cat's eyes glowed e. in the dark** les yeux du chat brillaient d'une lueur surnaturelle dans le noir; **the whole town was e. silent** dans toute la ville régnait un silence inquiétant *ou* sinistre

eeriness ['ɪərɪnɪs] *n* (*of place, sound etc*) étrangeté *f* surnaturelle

eery ['ɪərɪ] *adj* = **eerie**

eff [ef] *vi Br Sl Euph* **he's always effing and blinding** il n'arrête pas de jurer

▶ **eff off** *vi Br Sl Euph* **e. off!** va te faire foutre!; **she told him to e. off** elle lui a dit d'aller se faire foutre

efface [ɪ'feɪs] *vt* effacer; (*memory of sth*) oblitérer, effacer; (*remnants of past*) faire disparaître; **to e. oneself** s'effacer

effacement [ɪ'feɪsmənt] *n* effacement *m*

effect[1] [ɪ'fekt] *n* **(a)** (*result*), *Phys* effet *m*; (*of deed*) résultat *m*, conséquence *f*; **the e. of heat on metals** l'action de la chaleur sur les métaux; **the e. of this action was to bring prices down** cette action a eu pour effet de faire baisser les prix; **to have an e. on sb/sth** faire *ou* produire de l'effet sur qn/qch, affecter qn/qch; **to have no e.** ne faire *ou* ne produire aucun effet; **let's see what e. the addition of hydrogen has** voyons l'effet que produit l'addition d'hydrogène; **to take e.** (*of regulation, law etc*) entrer en vigueur; (*of drug*) agir, opérer; (*of vaccination*) prendre; **law that comes into e. today** loi qui entre en vigueur à partir d'aujourd'hui; **to no e.** en vain, sans résultat; **to put sth into e.** (*plan*) mettre qch à exécution; (*decision*) donner suite à qch

(b) (*purpose, meaning*) (*of document*) sens *m*, teneur *f*; **to the e. that …** (*clause*) portant que …; **we have made provisions to this e.** nous avons pris des dispositions dans ce sens; **that is what he said or words to that e.** voilà ce qu'il a dit, ou quelque chose d'approchant

(c) (*simulation*) **moonlight e.** effet *m* de lune; **clever use of lighting created the e. of a thunderstorm** une utilisation adroite de la lumière donnait l'impression qu'il y avait un orage; **stage effects** jeux *mpl* scéniques; *Cin, TV etc* **(special) effects** trucage *m*, effets spéciaux; **sound effects** bruitage *m*

(d) (*impression*) effet *m*, impression *f*; **the combination of colours creates** *or* **has a pleasing e.** le mélange des couleurs laisse une impression agréable; **for effect** (*to impress*) pour faire de l'effet; **words meant for e.** phrases à effet

(e) in e. en fait, en réalité; **that is in e. a refusal** c'est de fait un refus

(f) (*always pl*) (*belongings*) *Fml* **personal effects** effets *mpl ou* biens *mpl* personnels; **household effects**, *Jur* **movable effects** biens mobiliers

effect[2] *vt* (*repair, change*) effectuer; (*plan, wish, saving*) réaliser; (*plan, law*) exécuter; (*reconciliation*) parvenir à; **to e. an entry** entrer de force; **to e. a cure for sth** apporter un remède à qch; **to e. a solution to sth** apporter une solution à qch; *Mil* **to e. a retreat** battre en retraite; **to e. a payment** effectuer un paiement

effective [ɪ'fektɪv] **1** *adj* **(a)** (*efficient, having desired effect*) efficace; (*speech*) qui fait de l'effet; (*response*) plein d'à-propos; **the medicine was e.** le médicament a produit son effet; **an e. argument** un argument de poids; **she is an e. speaker** ses paroles font de l'effet *ou* portent

(b) (*actual*) *Econ etc* (*yield, return*) effectif; (*value*) réel; *El* (*charge*) efficace; (*frequency*) utile; **this resulted in the e. silencing of all opposition** (*was tantamount to*) cela a eu en effet pour résultat de faire taire les opposants; *MecE* **e. power** rendement *m*; **e. range** (*of firearm*) portée *f* utile; *Av* rayon *m* d'action; *Electron* étendue *f* de mesure

(c) (*striking*) (*contrast*) frappant, saisissant

(d) to become e. (*of law etc*) entrer en vigueur; *Admin* **e. date** date *f* d'entrée en vigueur; **e. as from October 10** applicable à partir du 10 octobre

2 *npl Mil* **effectives** effectifs *mpl*

effectively [ɪ'fektɪvlɪ] *adv* **(a)** (*really, in effect*) en fait, en réalité; **the country was e. ruled by the military** en fait *ou* en réalité, le pays était dirigé par les militaires; **the match was e. over** c'était comme si le match était déjà terminé **(b)** (*efficiently*) efficacement; **the building has been designed very e.** le bâtiment a été conçu avec un grand souci d'efficacité; **he spoke e. in favour of the government's motion** il a fait un éloge percutant *ou* persuasif de la motion du gouvernement **(c)** (*strikingly*) d'une façon frappante

effectiveness [ɪ'fektɪvnɪs] *n* **(a)** (*efficiency*) efficacité *f* **(b)** (*of colour scheme, design*) effet *m* percutant; **the e. of the white houses outlined against a darkening sky** l'effet de contraste percutant *ou* (*stronger*) saisissant des maisons blanches qui se découpaient sur un ciel de plus en plus sombre

effectual [ɪ'fektjʊəl] *adj* **(a)** *Fml* efficace **(b)** *Jur* (*contract*) valide; (*ruling*) en vigueur

effectually [ɪ'fektjʊəlɪ] *adv* efficacement

effeminacy [ɪ'femɪnəsɪ] *n* caractère *m* efféminé

effeminate [ɪ'femɪnət] *adj* efféminé

effervesce [efə'ves] *vi* **(a)** être en effervescence; (*start to effervesce*) entrer en effervescence; (*of drinks*) pétiller **(b)** *Fig* (*of person*) pétiller de joie *ou* d'animation

effervescence [efə'vesəns] *n* **(a)** (*of liquid*) effervescence *f* **(b)** *Fig* (*of youth etc*) pétillement *m*

effervescent [efə'vesənt] *adj* **(a)** effervescent; (*drink*) gazeux, pétillant **(b)** *Fig* (*person, mood*) effervescent; **to be e. with enthusiasm/joy** pétiller d'enthousiasme/de joie

effete [ɪ'fiːt] *adj* (*person*) mou, veule; (*nation, civilization etc*) amorphe

efficacious [efɪ'keɪʃəs] *adj Fml* efficace

efficacy ['efɪkəsɪ], **efficaciousness** [efɪ'keɪʃəsnɪs] *n* efficacité *f*

efficiency [ɪ'fɪʃənsɪ] *n* (*of method, organization*) efficacité *f*; (*of machine, business etc*) (*output*) rendement *m*; (*functioning*) bon fonctionnement *m*; (*of person*) capacité *f*, compétence *f*; **e. expert** expert *m* en organisation

efficient [ɪ'fɪʃənt] *adj* (*method, work, organization*) efficace; (*machine*) (*productive*) à bon rendement, performant; (*functioning well*) d'un fonctionnement sûr; (*person*) performant, capable, compétent; (*software*) performant; **to be e. at sth** faire qch avec compétence; **to be e. in one's work** se montrer capable dans son travail; **e. use of one's time** utilisation rationnelle de son temps; **energy e.** (*machine*) qui ne consomme pas beaucoup d'énergie

efficiently [ɪ'fɪʃəntlɪ] *adv* (*effectively*) efficacement; (*competently*) avec compétence; **to organize one's time e.** utiliser son temps de manière rationnelle; **this car runs more e. than any of its competitors** cette voiture a un meilleur rendement que toutes ses concurrentes

effigy ['efɪdʒɪ] *n* effigie *f*; **to burn/hang sb in e.** brûler/pendre qn en effigie

effing ['efɪŋ] *Br Sl Euph* **1** *adj* foutu; **this e. weather** ce temps de merde **2** *adv* **how e. stupid!** quelle connerie! **3** *n* (*swearing*) **there's too much e. and blinding** on entend trop de grossièretés

efflorescence [eflə'resəns] *n* **(a)** *Bot* floraison *f* **(b)** *Ch, Med etc* efflorescence *f*

efflorescent [eflə'resənt] *adj Bot, Ch* efflorescent

effluence ['efluəns] *n Lit* émanation *f*, effluence *f*

effluent ['efluənt] **1** *adj* effluent **2** *n* effluent *m*

effluvium, *pl* **-ia** [e'fluːvɪəm, -ɪə] *n* effluve *m*, émanation *f*, *Pej* émanation désagréable *ou* fétide

effort [ˈefət] *n* **(a)** effort *m*; **physical e.** effort physique; **without e.** sans effort; **to make an e. to do sth** faire (un) effort pour faire qch; **he made no e. to contact us** il n'a fait aucun effort pour nous joindre; **put some e. into it!** fais un effort!; **she put all her e. into her work** elle s'est jetée corps et âme dans son travail; **their efforts were rewarded** leurs efforts ont été récompensés; *Fml* **we make every e. to ensure our products reach you in perfect condition** nous faisons tout ce qui est en notre pouvoir pour que nos produits vous parviennent en bon état; *F* **it's an e. to get up so early** il faut vraiment faire un effort pour se lever si tôt; **wasted e.** peine *f* perdue
(b) *F* (*attempt*) tentative *f*; **that's not a bad e.** ce n'est pas mal réussi; **some of my first efforts at making pots were pretty awful** certains de mes premiers essais en poterie étaient plutôt ratés; **literary/artistic e.** œuvre *f* littéraire/ artistique; *F* **what do you think of his latest e.?** qu'est-ce que vous pensez de sa dernière performance?
(c) *Phys* (*of traction etc*) effort *m*, poussée *f*, travail *m*
(d) *Sl* (*thing, gadget*) truc *m*; **there's this sort of lever e.** il y a une espèce de levier

effortless [ˈefətlɪs] *adj* (*victory, success etc*) facile; (*skill, grace*) aisé; **she won with an almost e. ease** elle a gagné avec une facilité presque absolue

effortlessly [ˈefətlɪslɪ] *adv* sans effort; **to be e. graceful/ skilful** être naturellement gracieux/talentueux; **her voice soars e. to the high notes** elle peut chanter très haut sans aucun effort

effrontery [ɪˈfrʌntərɪ] *n* effronterie *f*; **she had the e. to correct me!** elle a eu l'audace de me corriger!

effusion [ɪˈfjuːʒən] *n* effusion *f*

effusive [ɪˈfjuːsɪv] *adj* (*person*) démonstratif, expansif; (*style*) exubérant; (*compliments*) sans fin; (*welcome, speech*) enthousiaste; **to be e. in one's thanks** se confondre en remerciements; **to be e. in one's praise/congratulations** louer/féliciter qn avec grand enthousiasme

effusively [ɪˈfjuːsɪvlɪ] *adv* avec effusion; **to thank sb** se confondre en remerciements; **to praise/congratulate/welcome sb e.** louer/féliciter/accueillir qn avec enthousiasme

effusiveness [ɪˈfjuːsɪvnɪs] *n* effusion *f*; **the e. of his praise** l'enthousiasme *m* de ses louanges

EFL [iːeˈfel] *n Sch* (*abbr* **English as a Foreign Language**) = anglais *m* langue étrangère; **to have an E. qualification** = avoir une qualification en anglais langue étrangère

EFT [iːefˈtiː] *n Comptr* (*abbr* **electronic funds transfer**) transfert *m* de fonds électronique

EFTA [ˈeftə] *n* (*abbr* **European Free Trade Association**) AELE *f*

EFTPOS [ˈeftpɒs] *n Comptr* (*abbr* **electronic funds transfer at point of sale**) transfert *m* de fonds électronique sur point de vente

eg [iːˈdʒiː] (*abbr* **exempli gratia**) ex

EGA [iːdʒiːˈei] *n Comptr* (*abbr* **enhanced graphics adaptor**) EGA *m*

egalitarian [ɪgælɪˈteərɪən] **1** *adj* égalitaire **2** *n* égalitariste *mf*

egalitarianism [ɪgælɪˈteərɪənɪz(ə)m] *n* égalitarisme *m*

egg [eg] *n* (*of hen, animal, insect etc*) œuf *m*; (*of louse*) lente *f*; **bacon and eggs** œufs au jambon *ou* au bacon; *F* **as sure as eggs is eggs** aussi sûr que deux et deux font quatre; *F* **you've got e. on your chin** (*fly is undone*) ta braguette est ouverte; *Fig F* **to have e. on one's face** être couvert de ridicule; *Old-fashioned F* **a bad e.** (*person*) un vaurien; *Old-fashioned F* **a good e.** (*person*) un gars épatant; *Prov* **don't put all your eggs in one basket** il ne faut pas mettre tous ses œufs dans le même panier; **e. custard** crème *f* anglaise; **e. flip** (*with milk*) lait *m* de poule; (*with alcohol*) lait de poule alcoolisé; **e. mayonnaise** œuf *m* mayonnaise; **e. nog** lait *m* de poule alcoolisé; **e. sandwich** sandwich *m* à l'œuf; **e. spoon** cuillère *f* à œufs; **e. tooth** (*of bird*) dent *f* d'éclosion; **e. white** blanc *m* d'œuf; **e. yolk** jaune *m* d'œuf

► **egg on** *vtsep* **to e. sb on (to do sth)** pousser *ou* inciter qn (à faire qch); **don't e. him on** ne l'encourage pas

egg-and-spoon *adj* **e. race** = course *f* dans laquelle les coureurs doivent porter un œuf dans une cuillère

eggbeater [ˈegbiːtər] *n Culin* batteur *m ou* fouet *m* à œufs

egg cup *n* coquetier *m*

egghead [ˈeghed] *n Hum, Pej* intello *mf*, cerveau *m*

egg-laying **1** *adj* ovipare **2** *n* ponte *f*

eggplant [ˈegplɑːnt] *n esp Am* aubergine *f*

egg-shaped *adj* ovoïde, ovoïdal, -aux

eggshell [ˈegʃel] *n* **(a)** coquille *f* (d'œuf); *Cer* **e. china** coquille d'œuf; **e. finish** (*on paint*) fini *m* coquille d'œuf; **e. blue** (*paint*) bleu *m* semi-mat **(b)** (*colour*) (couleur *f*) coquille *f* d'œuf, blanc *m* cassé

egg timer *n* sablier *m*

eggwhisk [ˈegwɪsk] *n* = **eggbeater**

eggy [ˈegɪ] *adj F* (*stained*) taché *ou* souillé de jaune d'œuf; **an e. taste/smell** un goût/une odeur d'œuf

egis [ˈiːdʒɪs] *n US* = **aegis**

eglantine [ˈegləntaɪn] *n* (*plant*) églantier *m*

ego [ˈiːgəʊ, ˈegəʊ] *n* **the e.** l'ego *m inv*; *Psy* le moi, l'ego; **you've got an enormous e.** tu as un ego démesuré; **it gave my e. a boost** mon ego en est ressorti gonflé; **his bruised e.** son ego blessé; **to feed/deflate sb's e.** entretenir/rabaisser l'ego de qn; *F* **e. trip** autosatisfaction *f*; **it was a real e. trip for her** c'était une occasion pour elle de donner libre cours à sa vanité

egocentric [iːgəʊˈsentrɪk] *adj* égocentrique

egocentricity [iːgəʊsenˈtrɪsɪtɪ] *n* égocentrisme *m*

egoism [ˈiːgəʊɪz(ə)m] *n* égoïsme *m*

egoist [ˈiːgəʊɪst] *n* égoïste *mf*

egoistic(al) [iːgəʊˈɪstɪk, -ɪk(ə)l] *adj* égoïste

egoistically [iːgəʊˈɪstɪklɪ] *adv* égoïstement

egomania [iːgəʊˈmeɪnɪə] *n* manie *f* égocentrique

egotism [ˈiːgəʊtɪz(ə)m] *n* égotisme *m*

egotist [ˈiːgəʊtɪst] *n* égotiste *mf*

egotistic(al) [iːgəʊˈtɪstɪk, -ɪk(ə)l] *adj* égotiste

egregious [ɪˈgriːdʒəs] *adj Fml Pej* (*idiot*) fameux; **e. blunder** maladresse *f* insigne

egress [ˈiːgres] *n* **(a)** *Fml* (*exit*) sortie *f*, issue *f* **(b)** *Astron* émersion *f*

egret [ˈiːgrɪt] *n* (*bird*) aigrette *f*

Egypt [ˈiːdʒɪpt] *n* Égypte *f*

Egyptian [ɪˈdʒɪpʃən] **1** *adj* égyptien, d'Égypte **2** *n* Égyptien, -ienne

eh [eɪ, e] *int* eh!, hé!, hein?

EIB [iːaɪˈbiː] *n* (*abbr* **European Investment Bank**) BEI *f*

eider [ˈaɪdər] *n* **e. (duck)** eider *m* à duvet

eiderdown [ˈaɪdədaʊn] *n* **(a)** (*quilt*) édredon *m* **(b)** (*feathers*) duvet *m* d'eider

eight [eɪt] *num adj, n* **(a)** (*numeral*) huit *m*; **at e. (o'clock)** à huit heures; **at the age of e., at e. (years old)** à huit ans; **at e.-thirty** à huit heures et demie; **a boy of e.** un garçon de huit ans; *Cards* **the e. of spades** le huit de pique; **to take an e. in gloves** avoir une pointure de huit (pour les gants); *F* **to have had one over the e.** avoir bu un coup de trop; **e.-hour day** journée *f* de huit heures
(b) *Sp* (*in rowing*) (*team*) équipe *f* de huit rameurs; (*boat*) canot *m* à huit rameurs; **to reach the last e.** (*in knockout competition*) être en huitième de finale; *Am* **e. ball** (*game*) = variante *f* du billard; (*ball*) bille *f* noire (qui porte le numéro huit); *Am Fig F* **to be behind the e. ball** être dans une situation délicate

eight-bit byte *n* octet *m*

eight-bit character *n* caractère *m* à huit bits

eighteen [eɪˈtiːn] *num adj, n* dix-huit *m*; **she is e. (years old)** elle a dix-huit ans; **at e. thirty (hours)** à dix-huit heures trente

eighteenth [eɪˈtiːnθ] **1** *adj* dix-huitième; **Louis the E.** Louis Dix-huit **2** *n* **(a)** **(on) the e. of May** le dix-huit mai; **on the e.** le dix-huit **(b)** (*fraction*) dix-huitième *m*

eightfold [ˈeɪtfəʊld] **1** *adj* octuple; **an e. increase** une augmentation à l'octuple **2** *adv* huit fois autant; **to increase e.** octupler

eighth [eɪtθ] **1** *adj* huitième; **in the e. place** huitièmement; **Henry the E.** Henri Huit; *esp Am Mus* **e. note** croche *f* **2** *n* **(a)** **(on) the e. of April** le huit avril; **on the e.** le huit **(b)** (*fraction*) huitième *m*; **three eighths** trois huitièmes

eightieth [ˈeɪtɪɪθ] *adj, n* quatre-vingtième *m*, *Swiss Belg* huitantième *m*, *Swiss Can* octantième *m*

eighty [ˈeɪtɪ] *num adj, n* [ⓘB56,A,d] quatre-vingts *m Swiss Belg* huitante *m*, *Swiss Can* octante *m*; **e.-one** quatre-vingt-un; **page e.** page quatre-vingt; **in the eighties** (*decade*) dans les années quatre-vingt; **she is in her eighties** elle a quatre-vingts ans passés

Eire [ˈeərə] *n* Eire *f*

eisteddfod [aɪˈstedfəd] *n* = festival *m* gallois de poésie et de musique

either [ˈaɪðər, *esp Am* ˈiːðər] **1** *adj, pron* [ⓘA37,f] **(a)** (*each of the two*) l'un(e) et l'autre; **on e. side** de chaque côté, des deux côtés
(b) (*one or other*) l'un(e) ou l'autre; **e. of them** soit l'un(e), soit l'autre; **I don't believe e. of you** je ne vous crois ni l'un ni l'autre; **I do not want e. of them** je ne veux ni l'un(e) ni l'autre; **e. candidate may win** l'un ou l'autre candidat pourra l'emporter; **there is no evidence e. way** les preuves manquent de part et d'autre
2 *conj, adv* **(a)** [ⓘA68,a,v,b] **e. … or …** (ou) … ou …, soit …, soit …; **e. you or your brother** (ou) vous ou votre frère, soit vous, soit votre frère; **it's e. that motorbike or me!** c'est cette moto ou moi!; **e. come in or go out!** entrez ou sortez!
(b) **not … e.** ne … non plus; **if you don't go, I won't go e.** si vous n'y allez pas je n'irai pas non plus; **she's caught**

cold, and she isn't very strong e. elle s'est enrhumée, elle qui n'est déjà pas si forte

either-or *adj* **an e. situation** = une situation dans laquelle il faut choisir entre deux maux le moindre

ejaculate [ɪ'dʒækjʊleɪt] **1** *vi* **(a)** *Physiol* éjaculer **(b)** *Old-fashioned, Lit (exclaim)* s'écrier **2** *vt (cry)* pousser; **'help!', he ejaculated** 'à l'aide!' s'écria-t-il

ejaculation [ɪdʒækjʊ'leɪʃən] *n* **(a)** *Physiol* éjaculation *f* **(b)** *Old-fashioned, Lit (exclamation)* cri *m*, exclamation *f*; **an e. of surprise/joy/horror** un cri de surprise/de joie/d'horreur

eject [ɪ'dʒekt] **1** *vt* **(a)** *(troublemaker etc)* expulser **(from** de) **(b)** *(of volcano etc) (lava)* projeter; *(flames etc)* jeter, émettre; *(of tape recorder, rifle)* éjecter **2** *vi Av (of pilot)* s'éjecter

ejection [ɪ'dʒekʃən] *n* **(a)** *(of person)* expulsion *f*; *(of tape, cartridge, pilot)* éjection *f*; *esp Am* **e. seat** siège *m* éjectable **(b)** *(by volcano) (of flames, lava)* projection *f*

ejector [ɪ'dʒektər] *n* **(a)** *Av* **e. seat** siège *m* éjectable; **to use the e. seat** s'éjecter **(b)** *(on firearm)* éjecteur *m*

▶ **eke out** [iːk] *vtsep* **(a) to e. out a living** gagner péniblement sa vie; **they eked out a miserable existence on the barren land** ils tiraient leur maigre subsistance du sol aride **(b)** *(supplement) (one's income etc)* suppléer à l'insuffisance de **(c)** *(make last) (rations)* économiser, faire durer

El [el] *n US Rail (abbr* **elevated railroad)** chemin *m* de fer *ou* métro *m* aérien

elaborate[1] [ɪ'læbərət] *adj (style)* travaillé; *(plan, arrangements, inspection etc)* minutieux; *(description, explanation)* détaillé; *(dress etc)* recherché; *(hairstyle, pattern, design)* compliqué; *(work)* soigné; *(excuse)* alambiqué; *(apparatus, network etc)* complexe; **I haven't cooked anything e.** je n'ai pas préparé quelque chose de compliqué; **the cake was a very e. affair** c'était un gâteau très élaboré

elaborate[2] [ɪ'læbəreɪt] **1** *vi* donner plus de détails **(on sth** sur qch); **could you e.?** est-ce que vous pouvez être plus précis? **2** *vt (formulate) (plan)* élaborer; *(flesh out)* développer

elaborately [ɪ'læbərətlɪ] *adv (planned, drawn)* minutieusement, de façon détaillée; *(designed)* avec recherche

elaboration [ɪlæbə'reɪʃən] *n (working out from scratch)* élaboration *f*; *(fleshing out)* développement *m*

élan [eɪ'lɑn] *n Lit* élan *m*, impétuosité *f*

eland ['iːlənd] *n (animal)* éland *m*; **common e.** éland du Cap

elapse [ɪ'læps] *vi (of time)* s'écouler, passer; **years have elapsed since then** des années ont passé depuis

elapsed time *n Comptr* temps *m* écoulé

elastic [ɪ'læstɪk] **1** *adj Phys (body)* élastique; *(movement)* souple; **e. band** élastique *m*, (bande *f* en) caoutchouc *m*; *Pej* **e. conscience** conscience *f* élastique; *Econ* **e. supply/demand** offre *f*/demande *f* élastique **2** *n* **(a)** élastique *m* **(b)** *esp Am (rubber band)* (bande *f* en) caoutchouc *m*

elasticated [ɪ'læstɪkeɪtɪd] *adj (clothing)* extensible

elasticity [iːlæs'tɪsɪtɪ] *n Phys (of body)* élasticité *f*; *(of wood, metal)* flexibilité *f*; *Med (of muscles)* tonicité *f*; **e. of interpretation** *(of law)* élasticité; *Econ* **the e. of supply and demand** l'élasticité de l'offre et de la demande

elastomer [ɪ'læstəmər] *n Ch* élastomère *m*

Elastoplast ® [ɪ'læstəplɑːst] *n* sparadrap *m*

elate [ɪ'leɪt] *vt* exalter

elated [ɪ'leɪtɪd] *adj* transporté, exalté; **to feel e.** se sentir plein de joie; **to be e. with success** être enivré de succès

elation [ɪ'leɪʃən] *n* exaltation *f*

Elba ['elbə] *n* **(the island of) E.** l'île *f* d'Elbe

elbow[1] ['elbəʊ] *n (of arm, sleeve, pipe)* coude *m*; **to lean one's e. on sth** s'accouder sur qch; *Fig* **to stand e. to e.** être coude à coude; **to be at sb's e.** être *ou* se tenir aux côtés de qn; **to be out at the elbows** *(of person)* être déguenillé; *(of jacket etc)* être troué aux coudes; **I'm up to my elbows in work** je suis submergé de travail; **to rub elbows with all sorts of people** fréquenter *ou* coudoyer toutes sortes de gens; *F* **to give sb the e.** *(of employer)* virer qn; *(of boyfriend etc)* plaquer qn; *F* **to get the e.** *(of employee)* se faire jeter; *(of boyfriend etc)* se faire plaquer; *F* **to bend** *or* **lift the e.** *(drink)* lever le coude; *F* **e. grease** huile *f* de coude; **use a bit of e. grease!** mets un peu d'huile de coude!; **e. joint** *Anat* articulation *f* du coude; *MecE* raccord *m* coudé

elbow[2] *vt* pousser du coude; **to e. sb aside** écarter qn d'un coup de coude; **to e. one's way through the crowd** se frayer un passage à travers la foule en jouant des coudes; *Fig* **she just elbowed aside anyone in the office who might have opposed her** elle a joué des coudes pour écarter quiconque au bureau se serait opposé à elle

▶ **elbow out** *vtsep (remove) (person)* évincer; **there have been attempts to e. him out as chairman** on a essayé de l'évincer de la présidence

elbow-length *adj* **e. gloves** gants *mpl* longs (montant jusqu'au coude)

elbow-rest *n* accoudoir *m*

elbowroom ['elbəʊrʊm] *n Fig* **to have (enough) e.** avoir ses coudées franches; **give me some more e.** laisse-moi les coudées franches

elder[1] ['eldər] [ⓘA19,g,iv] **1** *adj (of two people)* aîné, plus âgé; **my e. brother** mon frère aîné; **Pliny the E.** Pline l'Ancien; **e. statesman** doyen *m* des hommes politiques **2** *n* **(a)** aîné, -ée; **he is my e. by two years** il est de deux ans mon aîné; **children should obey their elders** les enfants devraient obéir à leurs aînés **(b)** *Hist, Rel (of tribe, church, village)* ancien *m*

elder[2] *n* **e. (tree)** sureau *m*

elderberry ['eldəberɪ] *n (fruit)* baie *f* de sureau; **e. wine** vin *m* de sureau

elderflower ['eldəflaʊər] *n* fleur *f* de sureau

elderly ['eldəlɪ] **1** *adj* d'un certain âge, assez âgé; *Fig* **an e. typewriter** une machine à écrire qui a fait son temps **2** *npl* **the e.** les personnes *fpl* âgées

eldest ['eldɪst] **1** *adj* [ⓘA19,g,iv] aîné; **my e. daughter** ma fille aînée, mon aînée; **their e. son** leur fils aîné **2** *n* aîné, -ée

elect[1] [ɪ'lekt] **1** *adj* élu; **the president e.** le président élu **2** *npl Rel* **the e.** les élus *mpl*

elect[2] *vt* **(a)** *Pol* élire; **to e. sb to the presidency** élire qn à la présidence; **to get elected** être élu; **she was elected president** elle a été élue présidente **(b)** *Fml (choose)* choisir **(to do** de faire)

election [ɪ'lekʃən] *n (of candidate etc)* élection *f*; **to hold an e.** procéder à une élection; **to stand for e.** poser sa candidature, se porter candidat; **e. agent** directeur, -trice de campagne électorale; **e. campaign** campagne *f* électorale; **e. committee** comité *m* électoral; **e. promise** promesse *f* électorale; **e. results** résultat *m* des élections

electioneer [ɪlekʃə'nɪər] *vi* faire de la propagande électorale

electioneering [ɪlekʃə'nɪərɪŋ] *n* propagande *f* électorale

elective [ɪ'lektɪv] **1** *adj* **(a)** *Pol (office etc)* électif; *(body etc)* électoral **(b)** *esp Am Sch, Univ (subject)* facultatif **(c)** *Med* **e. surgery** chirurgie *f* de confort **2** *n esp Am Sch, Univ (course)* cours *m* facultatif; **I'm taking two electives in psychology** je suis deux cours facultatifs en psychologie

elector [ɪ'lektər] *n* électeur, -trice, votant, -ante; *Hist (of Holy Roman Empire)* électeur

electoral [ɪ'lektər(ə)l] *adj* électoral, -aux; **e. body** corps *m* électoral; **e. college** collège *m* électoral; **e. reform** réforme *f* électorale; **e. roll** liste *f* électorale

electorate [ɪ'lektərət] *n Pol* corps *m* électoral, électeurs *mpl*

electret microphone [ɪ'lektrət] *n* microphone *m* à électret

electric [ɪ'lektrɪk] *adj (light, cooker, car etc)* électrique; *Fig* **the atmosphere of the meeting was e.** l'atmosphère de la réunion était électrique; **the effect of her words was e.** ses mots ont eu un effet électrisant; **e. blanket** couverture *f* chauffante; **e. blue** bleu *m* électrique; **e. charge** charge *f* électrique; **e. eye** cellule *f* photoélectrique; **e. fence** clôture *f* électrique; **e. field** champ *m* électrique; **e. generator** générateur *m*, génératrice *f*; **e. guitar** guitare *f* électrique; **e. headlamp adjustment** réglage *m* électrique des projecteurs; **e. heater** radiateur *m* électrique; **e. motor** moteur *m* électrique; **e. ray** raie *f* électrique; **e. wave** onde *f* électrique; **e. window** glace *f ou* vitre *f* électrique

electrical [ɪ'lektrɪk(ə)l] *adj* électrique; **e. appliance** appareil *m* électrique; **e. failure** panne *f* d'électricité; **e. fault** défaut *m* dans le système électrique

electrical engineer *n* électrotechnicien, -ienne, ingénieur *m* en électricité

electrical engineering *n* électrotechnique *f*; **e. industry** industrie *f* de l'équipement électrique

electrically [ɪ'lektrɪklɪ] *adv* électriquement; *Fig* **an e. charged atmosphere** une atmosphère électrique; **e. controlled window** vitre *f* à commande électrique; *Comptr* **e. erasable ROM** mémoire *f* morte effaçable électriquement

electric chair *n US Jur* chaise *f* électrique

electric eel *n* anguille *f* électrique, gymnote *m*

electrician [ɪlek'trɪʃən] *n* électricien, -ienne; **e.'s screwdriver** tournevis *m* d'électricien

electricity [ɪlek'trɪsɪtɪ] *n* électricité *f*; **lit by e.** éclairé à l'électricité; **many homes are without e.** *(temporarily)* de nombreux foyers sont privés d'électricité; *(not installed)* de nombreux foyers n'ont pas l'électricité; **e. meter** compteur *m* d'électricité; *Fig* **you could feel the e. in the air** il y avait de l'électricité dans l'air

Electricity Board *n Br* ≈ EDF *f* (Électricité de France)

electric power station *n* centrale *f* électrique

electrics [ɪ'lektrɪks] *npl Br F (of car etc)* circuits *mpl* électriques

electric shock *n* décharge *f* électrique; **e. treatment** électrochocs *mpl*; **I got an e. from the switch** j'ai reçu une décharge en touchant l'interrupteur

electrification [ɪlektrɪfɪ'keɪʃən] *n* (*of railways etc*) électrification *f*
electrify [ɪ'lektrɪfaɪ] *vt* **(a)** (*convert to electricity*) (*railway line etc*) électrifier **(b)** (*charge with electricity*) (*fence, Fig auditorium*) électriser
electrifying [ɪ'lektrɪfaɪɪŋ] *adj* (*effect etc*) électrisant
electrocardiogram [ɪlektrəʊ'kɑːdɪəʊgræm] *n Med* électrocardiogramme *m*
electrocardiograph [ɪlektrəʊ'kɑːdɪəʊgræf] *n Med* électrocardiographe *m*
electrocardiography [ɪlektrəʊkɑːdɪ'ɒgrəfɪ] *n Med* électrocardiographie *f*
electrochemistry [ɪlektrəʊ'kemɪstrɪ] *n* électrochimie *f*
electroconvulsive [ɪlektrəʊkən'vʌlsɪv] *adj Med* **e. therapy** traitement *m* par électrochocs
electrocute [ɪ'lektrəkjuːt] *vt* électrocuter; **to e. oneself** s'électrocuter
electrocution [ɪlektrə'kjuːʃən] *n* électrocution *f*
electrode [ɪ'lektrəʊd] *n* électrode *f*; **e. gap** écartement *m* des électrodes; **e. holder** porte-électrodes *m inv*
electrodynamics [ɪlektrəʊdaɪ'næmɪks] *n* [①**A10**,c] électrodynamique *f*
electroencephalogram [ɪlektrəʊen'sefələʊgræm] *n Med* électroencéphalogramme *m*
electroencephalograph [ɪlektrəʊen'sefələʊgræf] *n Med* appareil *m* à EEG
electrolysis [ɪlek'trɒlɪsɪs] *n* électrolyse *f*
electrolyte [ɪ'lektrəʊlaɪt] *n El* électrolyte *m*
electrolytic [ɪlektrəʊ'lɪtɪk] *adj* électrolytique
electromagnet [ɪlektrəʊ'mægnɪt] *n* électro-aimant *m, pl* électro-aimants
electromagnetic [ɪlektrəʊmæg'netɪk] *adj* (*field, wave etc*) électromagnétique
electromagnetism [ɪlektrəʊ'mægnɪtɪz(ə)m] *n* électromagnétisme *m*
electromotive [ɪlektrəʊ'məʊtɪv] *adj* électromoteur, -trice; **e. force** force *f* électromotrice
electron [ɪ'lektrɒn] *n Phys* électron *m*; **positive/negative e.** électron positif/négatif; **e. beam** faisceau *m* d'électrons; **e. gun** canon *m* à électrons; **e. microscope** microscope *m* électronique
electronic [ɪlek'trɒnɪk] *adj* électronique; **e. brain** cerveau *m* électronique; **e. card lock** serrure *f* à carte perforée; **e. computer** calculateur *m* électronique; **e. control unit** centrale *f* électronique; **e. fuel injection** injection *f* à commande numérique, injection électronique; **e. key card** carte-clé *f, pl* cartes-clés; **e. key encoding machine** programmateur *m* de cartes-clés électroniques; **e. lock** serrure *f* électronique; **e. music** musique *f* électronique; **e. news gathering** journalisme *m* électronique de télévision; **e. news-sheet** bulletin *m* électronique; **e. organ** orgue *m* électronique; **e. purse** porte-monnaie *m* électronique; *Aut* **e. ride control** contrôle *m* électronique de confort; **e. route finder** guide *m* électronique d'itinéraire; **e. sports gathering** captation *f* sportive électronique; **e. wallet** porte-monnaie *m* électronique
electronically [ɪlek'trɒnɪklɪ] *adv* électroniquement
electronic banking *n Fin* bancatique *f*, banque *f* électronique
electronic data processing *n Comptr* traitement *m* électronique de l'information
electronic funds transfer *n Fin* transfert *m* électronique de fonds; **e. at point of sale** transfert électronique de fonds au point de vente
electronic mail *n Comptr* courrier *m* électronique
electronic mailbox *n Comptr* boîte *f* à *ou* aux lettres électronique
electronic money *n* monnaie *f* électronique; (*concept*) monétique *f*
electronic payment *n* télépaiement *m*
electronic publishing *n* éditique *f*, édition *f* électronique
electronics [ɪlek'trɒnɪks] *n* [①**A10**,c] **(a)** électronique *f*; **e. company** électronicien *m*; **e. engineer** ingénieur *m* électronicien, électronicien, -ienne; **e. industry** industrie *f* électronique **(b)** (*of machine*) système *m* électronique
electronic tagging *n* système *m* électronique de surveillance de personnes
electroplate¹ [ɪ'lektrəʊpleɪt] *n Metal* **(a)** (*material*) (métal *m*) plaqué *m* **(b)** (*no pl*) (*articles*) articles *mpl* plaqués; (*plated with silver*) articles argentés
electroplate² *vt Metal* plaquer; (*with silver*) argenter
electro-sensitive [ɪ'lektrəʊ'sensɪtɪv] *adj* électrosensible
electroshock [ɪ'lektrəʊʃɒk] *adj Med* **e. therapy** *or* **treatment** traitement *m* par électrochocs
electrostatic [ɪlektrəʊ'stætɪk] *adj Phys* (*generator etc*) électrostatique
electrostatics [ɪlektrəʊ'stætɪks] *n* [①**A10**,c] *Phys* électrostatique *f*
electrotechnic(al) [ɪlektrəʊ'teknɪk, -ɪk(ə)l] *adj El* électrotechnique
electrotherapy [ɪlektrəʊ'θerəpɪ] *n Med* électrothérapie *f*
electrotype¹ [ɪ'lektrəʊtaɪp] *n Typ* galvanotype *m*
electrotype² *vt Typ* galvanotyper
elegance ['elɪgəns] *n* élégance *f*
elegant ['elɪgənt] *adj* **(a)** (*appearance, person etc*) élégant; **e. furniture** meubles *mpl* d'un goût raffiné **(b)** *Am F* (*excellent*) excellent, de premier ordre
elegantly ['elɪgəntlɪ] *adv* élégamment, avec élégance; **e. proportioned** aux proportions élégantes
elegiac [elɪ'dʒaɪək] *Lit* **1** *adj* élégiaque **2** *npl* **elegiacs** vers *mpl* élégiaques
elegy ['elɪdʒɪ] *n* élégie *f*
element ['elɪmənt] *n* **(a)** (*aspect*) **e. of uncertainty/danger/chance** part *f* d'incertitude/de danger/de chance; **there is an e. of risk involved** cela comporte un risque; **disturbing e.** élément *m* d'instabilité; **the personal/time e.** le facteur humain/temps; **the film has all the elements of a hit movie** le film a tous les ingrédients d'un film à succès; **a key e. in selling is ...** un des facteurs clés dans la vente est ...
(b) (*part of whole*) élément *m*, partie *f*; *El* (*of kettle, fire etc*) résistance *f*; **elements** (*basics*) (*of science*) rudiments *mpl*; *Comptr* **data e.** élément d'information; **the hooligan e. (in our society/in a football crowd)** les hooligans (dans notre société/parmi les spectateurs d'un match de football); **undesirable elements (in society)** éléments indésirables (de la société)
(c) *Ch* corps *m* simple
(d) *Met* **the four elements** les quatre éléments *mpl*; **to brave the elements** braver les éléments; **exposed to the elements** exposé aux intempéries; *Fig* **to be in one's e.** être dans son élément; *Fig* **to be out of one's e.** ne pas être dans son élément
(e) *Rel* **the elements (of bread and wine)** les espèces *fpl*
elemental [elɪ'ment(ə)l] *adj* **(a)** (*belonging to the elements*) qui appartient aux éléments *ou* aux forces de la nature; (*spirit*) élémentaire; (*rage, fury*) déchaîné; **e. forces** forces *fpl* des éléments **(b)** (*primitive*) élémentaire, primitif **(c)** *Ch* élémentaire **(d)** (*basic*) fondamental, essentiel; **to be e. to sth** être essentiel à qch
elementary [elɪ'ment(ə)rɪ] *adj* élémentaire; *Sch* **e. algebra** rudiments *mpl* d'algèbre
elementary school *n esp Am Sch* école *f* primaire
elephant ['elɪfənt] *n* éléphant *m*; **e. calf,** *F* **baby e.** éléphanteau *m*; **e. seal** éléphant de mer
elephantiasis [elɪfæn'taɪəsɪs] *n Med* éléphantiasis *f*
elephantine [elɪ'fæntaɪn] *adj* (*proportions etc*) éléphantesque; (*movement etc*) lourd et gauche; *Fig* (*humour*) lourd
elevate ['elɪveɪt] *vt* **(a)** (*raise*) élever, hausser; *Mil* (*gun*) pointer en hauteur; *Rel* (*host, mind*) élever; **to e. sb to a high rank** élever qn à un haut rang **(b)** (*exalt*) (*sb*) exalter; (*sb's soul*) élever; **they had elevated their legends into a religion** ils avaient élevé leurs légendes au rang de religion
elevated ['elɪveɪtɪd] *adj* **(a)** (*raised, exalted*) élevé; **e. position** position *f* élevée; **e. thoughts** hautes pensées *fpl*; **he has an e. opinion of himself** il a une haute opinion de lui-même **(b)** (*overhead*) surélevé; **e. motorway** autoroute *f* surélevée; **e.** *Br* **railway** *or US* **railroad** chemin *m* de fer *ou* métro *m* aérien; *TV, Cin* **e. shot** plongée *f*
elevating ['elɪveɪtɪŋ] **1** *adj* (*discourse etc*) édifiant; **the experience was far from e.** l'expérience n'a rien eu de bien inspirant **2** *n* élévation *f*, levage *m*
elevation [elɪ'veɪʃən] *n* **(a)** (*of sth to certain height, of sb to superior position*) élévation *f*; *Rel* **the E. (of the Host)** l'Élévation **(b)** *Geog* (*height*) **e. above sea level** altitude *f ou* hauteur *f* au-dessus du niveau de la mer **(c)** (*hill*) élévation *f*, éminence *f* **(d)** *Astron* (*of star*) élévation *f* **(e)** *Mil* (*of gun*) hausse *f*, pointage *m* en hauteur; **angle of e.** angle *m* de hausse; **e. mechanism** dispositif *m* de pointage en hauteur **(f)** *Archit etc* élévation *f*; **front e.** façade *f*; **side e.** façade latérale; **rear e.** derrière *m* **(g)** (*nobility, refinement*) (*of style*) élévation *f*, dignité *f*; (*of character*) noblesse *f*, grandeur *f*
elevator ['elɪveɪtər] *n* **(a)** (*lifting device*) élévateur *m*; *US* (*for goods*) monte-charge *m inv*; **bucket e.** élévateur à godets; **grain e.** élévateur *m* à grains; (*silo*) silo *m*; **e. shoe** chaussure *f* à semelle compensée **(b)** *Am* (*lift*) ascenseur *m*; **e. attendant** liftier *m* **(c)** *Av* gouvernail *m* de profondeur *ou* d'altitude; **e. angle** angle *m* de braquage
eleven [ɪ'lev(ə)n] *num adj, n* **(a)** (*numeral*) onze *m*; **the e. o'clock train** le train de onze heures **(b)** *Sp* (*team*) onze *m*; **the French e.** le onze de France
elevenses [ɪ'lev(ə)nzɪz] *npl Br F* collation *f ou* casse-croûte *m inv* de onze heures (du matin)
eleventh [ɪ'lev(ə)nθ] **1** *adj* onzième; *Fig* **at the e. hour** au

dernier moment, à la dernière heure **2** *n* (**a**) **on the e. of May** le onze mai; **on the e.** le onze (**b**) (*fraction*) onzième *m*

eleventh-hour *adj* de la dernière heure *ou* chance, de dernière minute; **an e. rescue attempt** une tentative de sauvetage de dernière heure

elf, *pl* **elves** [elf, elvz] *n Myth* elfe *m*, lutin *m*, lutine *f*

elfin ['elfɪn] *adj* (*grace, features*) d'elfe, de lutin; (*music*) féerique

elfish ['elfɪʃ] *adj* (**a**) = **elfin** (**b**) (*mischievous*) espiègle

elicit [ɪ'lɪsɪt] *vt* (**a**) (*extract*) (*truth*) découvrir; (*facts*) tirer au clair; (*answer from sb*) obtenir; **to e. sth from sb** tirer qch de qn (**b**) (*give rise to*) (*response*) provoquer

elide [ɪ'laɪd] *vt Ling* élider

eligibility [elɪdʒɪ'bɪlɪtɪ] *n* (**a**) (*entitlement*) éligibilité *f* (**b**) (*of suitor etc*) acceptabilité *f*

eligible ['elɪdʒɪb(ə)l] *adj* (**a**) (*entitled*) éligible; **to be e.** avoir droit (**for** à); **she wasn't e. for a tax rebate/early retirement** elle n'avait pas droit à une réduction d'impôts/la retraite anticipée; **e. for promotion** qualifié pour une promotion (**b**) (*worthy of being chosen*) digne d'être élu *ou* choisi, acceptable; **e. bachelor/young man** bon parti *m*

eliminate [ɪ'lɪmɪneɪt] *vt* (*toxic substances, names from list, poverty etc*) éliminer; (*hypothesis, possible explanation*) écarter; (*possibility of error, risk etc*) supprimer; *Euph* (*kill*) supprimer; *Math* **to e. x** éliminer x; **the police have eliminated him from their enquiries** la police l'a écarté de son enquête; *Sp* **they were eliminated in the first round** ils ont été éliminés au premier round

eliminating [ɪ'lɪmɪneɪtɪŋ] *adj attrib* éliminateur, -trice; *Sp* **e. heats/rounds** épreuves *fpl* éliminatoires

elimination [ɪlɪmɪ'neɪʃən] *n* élimination *f*; **in spite of her e. from the list** bien qu'elle ait été éliminée de la liste; **by (a) process of e.** en procédant par élimination

eliminator [ɪ'lɪmɪneɪtər] *n* éliminateur *m*; **the next match will be the e.** le prochain match décidera de qui sera éliminé

elision [ɪ'lɪʒən] *n* [①B2] *Ling* (*of vowel etc*) élision *f*

élite [eɪ'li:t] *n* élite *f*; **the é. of society** l'élite de la société; *Mil* **é. regiment** corps *m* d'élite

elitism [eɪ'li:tɪz(ə)m] *n* élitisme *m*; **the e. of his attitude** son attitude élitiste

elitist [eɪ'li:tɪst] *adj, n* élitiste *mf*

elixir [ɪ'lɪksər] *n* élixir *m*; **the e. of life** l'élixir de longue vie

Elizabethan [ɪlɪzə'bi:θ(ə)n] **1** *adj* (*house, literature etc*) élisabéthain **2** *n* = Britannique *mf* vivant sous le règne de la reine Élisabeth 1ère

Elizabeth I [ɪ'lɪzəbəθðə'fɜ:st] *n* Élisabeth *f* 1ère

elk [elk] *n* (**Scandinavian**) **e.** élan *m*; (**American**) **e.** wapiti *m*

ell [el] *n Arch* (*measurement*) aune *f*

ellipse [ɪ'lɪps] *n Math* ellipse *f*

ellipsis, *pl* **-ipses** [ɪ'lɪpsɪs, -si:z] *n Gram* ellipse *f*

ellipsoid [ɪ'lɪpsɔɪd] *n Math* ellipsoïde *m*

elliptic(al) [ɪ'lɪptɪk, -ɪk(ə)l] *adj Gram, Math, Fig* elliptique

elliptically [ɪ'lɪptɪklɪ] *adv* elliptiquement

elm [elm] *n* (*tree, wood*) orme *m*; **e. grove** ormaie *f*

elocution [elə'kju:ʃən] *n* élocution *f*, diction *f*; **e. lessons** cours *mpl* de diction

elocutionist [elə'kju:ʃənɪst] *n* (*teacher*) professeur *m* de diction

elongate ['i:lɒŋgeɪt] **1** *vt* allonger, étendre; (*line, platform*) prolonger **2** *vi* s'allonger, s'étendre

elongated ['i:lɒŋgeɪtɪd] *adj* allongé

elongation [i:lɒŋ'geɪʃən] *n* (**a**) allongement *m*; (*of line*) prolongement *m* (**b**) *Astron* élongation *f*

elope [ɪ'ləʊp] *vi* s'enfuir (pour se marier); **they eloped together** ils se sont enfuis pour se marier

elopement [ɪ'ləʊpmənt] *n* fuite *f*

eloquence ['eləkwəns] *n* éloquence *f*

eloquent ['eləkwənt] *adj* éloquent; **to be an e. speaker** être éloquent, avoir de l'éloquence; *Fig* **an e. gesture** un geste éloquent; **the state of the economy is an e. indictment of this policy** la situation économique en dit long sur cette politique

eloquently ['eləkwəntlɪ] *adv* éloquemment; **to pause e.** faire une pause éloquente

else [els] **1** *adv* **or e.** (*otherwise*) autrement; (*if not, then*) ou bien; **come tomorrow or e. it will be too late** venez demain, autrement il sera trop tard; **he must be joking or e. he's mad** il plaisante, ou bien alors il est fou; **do what I tell you or e.!** fais ce que je te dis, sinon!

2 *adj, adv* (**a**) (*with -one/body*) **anyone** *or* **anybody e.** toute autre personne, n'importe qui d'autre; **he is no more stupid than anyone e.** il n'est pas plus bête qu'un autre; **can I speak to anyone e.?** y a-t-il quelqu'un d'autre à qui je puisse parler?; **it couldn't be anyone e.'s** ça ne pouvait être celui de personne d'autre; **I couldn't find anyone e. to help me** je n'ai pu trouver personne d'autre pour m'aider; **someone** *or* **somebody e.** quelqu'un d'autre; **you are taking me for someone e.** vous me prenez pour quelqu'un d'autre; **everyone** *or* **everybody e. knows it** tous les autres le savent; **you're kind to everyone e., why are you so horrible to me?** tu es gentil avec tout le monde, pourquoi es-tu si horrible avec moi?; **no one e., nobody e.** personne d'autre, aucun autre; **I knew nobody e. would do it for me** je savais que personne d'autre ne le ferait pour moi; **no one e. could do it** il n'y a que lui/elle/*etc* qui puisse le faire

(**b**) (*with -thing*) **anything e.** n'importe quoi d'autre; **have you anything e. to do?** avez-vous autre chose à faire?; **he wouldn't accept anything e.** il n'a rien voulu accepter d'autre; **anything e. I produce is impossible to sell** tout ce que je fais d'autre est invendable; **anything e., madam?** (*in shop*) et avec cela, madame?; **something e.** quelque chose d'autre, autre chose; **is there something e. you want me to do?** y a-t-il quelque chose d'autre *ou* autre chose que tu voudrais que je fasse?; **I was thinking of something e.** je pensais à autre chose; *F* **she's/it's something e.!** elle est/c'est génial!; **everything e.** tout le reste; **nothing e.** rien d'autre; **nothing e., thank you** c'est tout, merci

(**c**) (*with -where*) **somewhere e.** autre part, ailleurs; **I'm sure somewhere e. will give them a room** je suis sûr qu'ailleurs on leur donnera une chambre; **anywhere e.** n'importe où (ailleurs); **anywhere e. would have turned them away** n'importe où ailleurs on les aurait renvoyés; **can I find some anywhere e.?** puis-je en trouver ailleurs?; **everywhere e.** partout ailleurs; **everywhere e. was shut** (*other shops*) tous les autres magasins étaient fermés; **nowhere e.** nulle part ailleurs; **nowhere e. was willing to accept them** nulle part ailleurs on ne voulait les accepter

(**d**) (*with interr pronouns*) **who e.?** qui d'autre?, qui encore?; **you think they'll give the prize to Whippleton? — who e.?** tu crois qu'ils attribueront le prix à Whippleton? — à qui d'autre veux-tu qu'ils le donnent?; **what e.?** quoi encore?, quoi de plus?; **do you use fresh pasta for this dish? – what e.?** utilises-tu des pâtes fraîches pour ce plat? – que veux-tu que j'utilise d'autre?; **what e. can I say?** qu'est-ce que je peux dire de plus?; **where e.?** (*did you go, look etc*) où encore?; (*did you think you would find it, her etc*) où est-ce que tu pensais le/la/*etc* trouver sinon là?; **when e.?** à quel autre moment/date?; **when e. has this happened?** quand cela est-il déjà arrivé?; **how e.?** de quelle autre manière?; **did you come by taxi? – how e.?** tu es venu en taxi? – comment serais-je venu sinon?; **why e.?** pour quelle autre raison?

(**e**) (*with little/(not) much*) **little e.** pas grand-chose d'autre; **he eats bread but little e.** il ne mange guère que du pain; **there isn't much e. to be done** il ne reste pas beaucoup à faire; (*we've no choice*) il n'y a pas grand chose d'autre à faire; *Fml* **much e. could be said on this topic** on pourrait encore en dire long sur ce sujet; *Fml* **much e. remained to be done** il restait encore beaucoup à faire

elsewhere ['elsweər] *adv* ailleurs, autre part; **e. the weather will be fine** ailleurs, il fera beau; **her ambitions lie e.** ses ambitions se situent à un autre niveau

ELT [i:el'ti:] *n Sch* (*abbr* **English Language Teaching**) = enseignement *m* de l'anglais à des étudiants étrangers

elucidate [ɪ'lu:sɪdeɪt] **1** *vt* élucider, éclaircir; (*reference*) clarifier, éclaircir **2** *vi* s'expliquer, être plus clair; **can you e.?** peux-tu être plus clair?

elucidation [ɪlu:sɪ'deɪʃən] *n* élucidation *f*, éclaircissement *m* (**of** de)

elude [ɪ'lu:d] *vt* (*question*) éluder; (*blow*) esquiver, éviter; (*death, police, capture*) échapper à; (*justice*) se soustraire à; **to e. sb's grasp** échapper aux mains de qn; *Fig* **to e. sb** (*mentally*) échapper à qn

elusive [ɪ'lu:sɪv] *adj* (*enemy, happiness*) insaisissable; (*answer*) évasif; (*concept*) flottant; (*memories*) fugitif; (*scent, perfume*) indéfinissable; **but for him success remained e.** mais le succès lui a échappé

elusiveness [ɪ'lu:sɪvnɪs] *n* (*of enemy, happiness*) nature *f* insaisissable; (*of answer*) caractère *m* évasif; (*of scent, perfume*) caractère indéfinissable; **a concept of great e.** un concept extrêmement flottant

elver ['elvər] *n* (*young eel*) civelle *f*

elvish ['elvɪʃ] *adj* = **elfish**

Elysian [ɪ'lɪzɪən] *adj Myth* élyséen; **E. fields** champs *mpl* Elysées

em [em] *n Typ* em *m*

'em [əm] *pron F* = **them**

emaciate [ɪ'meɪsɪeɪt] *vt* (*body*) émacier, dessécher

emaciated [ɪ'meɪsɪeɪtɪd] *adj* émacié, décharné

emaciation [ɪmeɪsɪ'eɪʃən] *n* (*of body*) émaciation *f*, dessèchement *m*

e-mail[1] [ˈiːmeɪl] *n* courrier *m ou* messagerie *f* électronique; **e. box** boîte *f* à *ou* aux lettres électronique
e-mail[2] *vt* **to e. sth to sb** envoyer qch à qn par courrier électronique; **can I e. you?** est-ce que je peux vous contacter par courrier électronique?
emanate [ˈemənert] **1** *vi* émaner (**from** de); (*of light*) provenir (**from** de) **2** *vt* dégager
emanation [eməˈneɪʃən] *n* émanation *f*; (*of light*) émission *f*
emancipate [ɪˈmænsɪpeɪt] *vt* (*minor, women etc*) émanciper; (*slave*) affranchir; **an emancipating realization** une réflexion émancipatrice
emancipated [ɪˈmænsɪpeɪtɪd] *adj* émancipé; (*slave*) affranchi
emancipation [ɪmænsɪˈpeɪʃən] *n* émancipation *f*; (*of slave*) affranchissement *m*
emasculate [ɪˈmæskjʊleɪt] *vt* émasculer, châtrer; *Fig* émasculer
emasculation [ɪmæskjʊˈleɪʃən] *n* émasculation *f*, castration *f*
embalm [ɪmˈbɑːm] *vt* embaumer
embalmer [ɪmˈbɑːmər] *n* embaumeur *m*
embalming [ɪmˈbɑːmɪŋ] *n* embaumement *m*; **e. fluid** fluide *m* de thanatopraxie
embankment [ɪmˈbæŋkmənt] *n Rail etc* talus *m*, remblai *m*; (*to contain river*) digue *f*; (*alongside river etc*) berge *f*, quai *m*
embargo[1], *pl* **-oes** [emˈbɑːgəʊ, -əʊz] *n* embargo *m*; **to be under (an) e.** être sous embargo; (*of ship*) être séquestré; **to put an e. on** (*goods etc*) mettre un embargo sur; **to lift the e.** lever l'embargo; **trade/oil/arms e.** embargo commercial/pétrolier/sur les armes
embargo[2] *vt* mettre l'embargo sur
embark [emˈbɑːk] **1** *vt Naut* embarquer, prendre à bord **2** *vi Naut, Av* s'embarquer; *Fig* **to e. (up)on** (*adventure etc*) s'embarquer dans
embarkation [embɑːˈkeɪʃən] *n Naut, Av* embarquement *m*; **e. card** carte *f* d'accès à bord *ou* d'embarquement
embarrass [ɪmˈbærəs] *vt* embarrasser
embarrassed [ɪmˈbærəst] *adj* embarrassé, gêné; **an e. silence** un silence embarrassé
embarrassing [ɪmˈbærəsɪŋ] *adj* embarrassant, gênant; **a financially e. situation** un embarras financier; **how e.!** comme ça a dû être/c'est/ce serait embarrassant!
embarrassingly [ɪmˈbærəsɪŋlɪ] *adv* d'une manière embarrassante *ou* gênante; **there were e. few in the audience** le public était si réduit que c'en était embarrassant; **e., we seem to have omitted the principal's name** il semble que nous ayons oublié le nom du directeur, ce qui est plutôt embarrassant
embarrassment [ɪmˈbærəsmənt] *n* **(a)** (*feeling*) embarras *m*, gêne *f*; **much to my e.** à mon grand embarras; **blushing with e.** rouge de confusion; **to be in a state of financial e.** avoir des embarras d'argent **(b)** (*person, thing*) source *f* d'embarras
embassy [ˈembəsɪ] *n* (*building*) ambassade *f*; **the French E.** l'ambassade de France; **e. staff** personnel *m* d'ambassade
embattled [ɪmˈbæt(ə)ld] *adj* (*engaged in battle*) pris d'assaut; *Fig* (*under attack*) assiégé
embed [ɪmˈbed] *vt* (**-dd-**) **(a)** (*nail in wall*) enfoncer; (*frame in wall*) encastrer; (*diamond in gold etc*) incruster; **to be embedded in sth** (*of hook, tooth etc*) être enfoncé dans qch; **embedded in concrete** noyé dans le béton; **to be embedded in sb's memory** être gravé dans la mémoire de qn; **to be embedded in sb's mind** être ancré dans l'esprit de qn; **to be embedded in sb's personality** être enraciné dans la personnalité de qn **(b)** *Comptr* intégrer, imbriquer
embedded [ɪmˈbedɪd] *adj Comptr* **e. command** commande *f* intégrée *ou* imbriquée; *Ling* **e. clause** proposition *f* imbriquée; **a deeply e. feeling of inferiority** un sentiment d'infériorité profondément ancré
embellish [ɪmˈbelɪʃ] *vt* orner, embellir; (*prose*) embellir; *Fig* (*account, story*) enjoliver
embellishment [ɪmˈbelɪʃmənt] *n* embellissement *m*, ornement *m*; (*of story*) enjolivure *f*
ember [ˈembər] *n* (*usu pl*) **embers** braise *f*, charbons *mpl* ardents
embezzle [ɪmˈbez(ə)l] **1** *vt* (*funds*) détourner, distraire, s'approprier **2** *vi* commettre des détournements de fonds
embezzlement [ɪmˈbezəlm(ə)nt] *n* détournement *m* de fonds, appropriation *f* de fonds
embezzler [ɪmˈbezlər] *n* détourneur *m* de fonds
embitter [ɪmˈbɪtər] *vt* (*sb*) aigrir, remplir d'amertume; (*character*) aigrir; (*quarrel etc*) envenimer
embittered [ɪmˈbɪtəd] *adj* (*person*) aigri (**by** par); (*laugh*) amer
embittering [ɪmˈbɪtərɪŋ] *adj* (*experience*) qui aigrit
emblazon [ɪmˈbleɪz(ə)n] *vt Her* blasonner, décorer d'armoiries; **emblazoned with the arms of the town** peint aux armes de la ville; **she didn't want to see her name emblazoned across the front page of the Sun** elle ne voulait pas voir son nom étalé en première page du Sun
emblem [ˈembləm] *n* (*symbol*) emblème *m*; *Her* emblème, devise *f*; *Aut* (*on radiator*) écusson *m*; **sporting e.** insigne *m* sportif
emblematic [embləˈmætɪk] *adj* emblématique
embodiment [ɪmˈbɒdɪmənt] *n* incarnation *f*, personnification *f*; **he is the e. of kindness** il est la bonté même
embody [ɪmˈbɒdɪ] *vt* (**embodied**; **embodying**) **(a)** (*give form to*) incarner **(b)** (*personify*) (*quality*) personnifier **(c)** (*incorporate*) (*clause in law*) incorporer; (*principles in treatise*) renfermer, rédiger
embolden [ɪmˈbəʊldən] *vt* **(a)** enhardir (**sb to do sth** qn à faire qch) **(b)** *Typ* (*characters*) renforcer, graisser
embolism [ˈembəlɪz(ə)m] *n Med* embolie *f*
embolus [ˈembələs] *n Med* embole *m*
embonpoint [ɒmbɒnˈpwæn] *n Hum* embonpoint *m*, rondeurs *fpl*
emboss [ɪmˈbɒs] *vt* (*metal*) travailler en relief, bosseler; (*metal, leather*) repousser, estamper
embossed [ɪmˈbɒst] *adj* (*metal*) gravé en relief, travaillé en bosse; (*metal, leather*) estampé, repoussé; (*paper*) gaufré; **e. work** travail *m* en relief *ou* en repoussé
embossing [ɪmˈbɒsɪŋ] *n* **(a)** (*technique, activity*) (*of metal*) bosselage *m*; (*of leather*) estampage *m*, repoussage *m*; **e. punch** repoussoir *m*; **e. press** (*in paper making*) presse *f* à imprimer en relief **(b)** (*result*) relief *m*, repoussé *m*, bosselure *f*
embrace[1] [ɪmˈbreɪs] *n* étreinte *f*; (*of lovers*) étreinte amoureuse; **to hold sb in a warm e.** étreindre qn chaleureusement; *Poet* **winter's iron e.** l'étreinte glacée de l'hiver
embrace[2] **1** *vt* **(a)** (*sb*) étreindre; (*in official ceremony*) donner une accolade à; **to e. one another tenderly** s'étreindre tendrement **(b)** (*adopt*) (*religion*) embrasser; (*cause*) adopter **(c)** (*include*) embrasser, contenir (**in** dans); (*subjects*) comprendre; **the view from the terrace embraces the whole valley** de la terrasse la vue s'étend sur toute la vallée *ou* embrasse toute la vallée **2** *vi* (*of two people*) s'embrasser
embrasure [ɪmˈbreɪʒər] *n* **(a)** *Archit* embrasure *f*, ébrasement *m* **(b)** *Mil* embrasure *f*, sabord *m*
embrocation [embrəˈkeɪʃən] *n Med* embrocation *f*
embroider [ɪmˈbrɔɪdər] **1** *vt* **(a)** *Sewing* broder **(b)** (*exaggerate*) (*account, report*) enjoliver **2** *vi* **(a)** *Sewing* broder **(b)** (*exaggerate*) broder, enjoliver, *F* en rajouter
▶ **embroider on** *vipo* (*truth, facts*) enjoliver
embroidering [ɪmˈbrɔɪdərɪŋ] *n* = **embroidery**
embroidery [ɪmˈbrɔɪdərɪ] *n* **(a)** *Sewing* broderie *f*; **e. frame/thread** métier *m*/fil *m* à broder **(b)** (*added details*) (*of account, report*) enjolivement *m*, fioriture *f*; **their e. on the facts** les enjolivements qu'ils avaient apportés aux faits
embroil [ɪmˈbrɔɪl] *vt* (*usu passive*) (*involve*) **embroiled in a quarrel** entraîné dans une querelle; **to become** *or* **get embroiled in sth** se trouver impliqué à qch; **I wouldn't get embroiled with her if I was you** à ta place je ne me compliquerais pas la vie avec elle, *F* à ta place je ne me laisserais pas embringuer avec elle
embroilment [ɪmˈbrɔɪlmənt] *n* (*involvement*) implication *f*
embryo, *pl* **-os** [ˈembrɪəʊ, -əʊz] *n Biol, Fig* embryon *m*; **in e.** (*foetus, plan*) à l'état embryonnaire; **e. research** recherche *f* portant sur les embryons
embryogenesis [embrɪəʊˈdʒenɪsɪs] *n Med* embryogénèse *f*
embryology [embrɪˈɒlədʒɪ] *n* embryologie *f*
embryonic [embrɪˈɒnɪk] *adj Biol* embryonnaire; *Fig* (*plan, idea etc*) à l'état embryonnaire
embus [ɪmˈbʌs] *Mil* **1** *vt* (*troops*) embarquer dans un autocar **2** *vi* monter dans un autocar
emcee [ˈemˈsiː] *F* **1** *n* maître *m* de cérémonies; *Rad, TV* animateur, -trice **2** *vt* (*show*) animer
emend [ɪˈmend] *vt* corriger
emendation [iːmenˈdeɪʃən] *n* **(a)** (*action*) (*of text*) correction *f* **(b)** (*proposed alteration*) variante *f* proposée
emerald [ˈem(ə)rəld] *n* **(a)** *Miner* émeraude *f* **(b)** (*colour*) **e. (green)** (vert *m* d')émeraude *m*; *Lit* **the E. Isle** la verte Irlande
emerge [ɪˈmɜːdʒ] *vi* (*appear*) (*from liquid, the shadow, fog*) émerger (**from** de); (*from hole, from behind sth etc*) déboucher (**from** de); (*from house, hole, darkness*) sortir; (*arise*) (*of difficulty etc*) se dresser, surgir; (*of truth, facts*) émerger, se faire jour; **the moon is emerging from behind the clouds** la lune sort de derrière les nuages; **she emerged as an important politician** elle est devenue une personnalité politique importante; **from these facts it emerges that …** de ces faits il ressort que …; **it later emerged that …** il est apparu par la suite que …; **he was**

soon to e. from his father's shadow il allait bientôt sortir de l'ombre de son père

emergence [ɪ'mɜːdʒəns] *n* (*of theory etc*) émergence *f*; (*of new state, new leader*) apparition *f*; **they still awaited the e. of a convincing account of the events** ils attendaient encore qu'un récit convaincant des événements se fasse jour

emergency [ɪ'mɜːdʒənsɪ] *n* circonstance *f* critique, cas *m* urgent; *Med* urgence *f*; **to provide for emergencies** parer aux éventualités *ou* à l'imprévu; **this is an e.** c'est une urgence; **to meet an e.** faire face à une situation critique; **in an e., in case of e.** en cas d'urgence; **state of e.** état *m* d'urgence; **to declare a state of e.** déclarer l'état d'urgence; **national e.** catastrophe *f* nationale; **e. aid** secours *mpl* d'urgence; **e. brake** frein *m* de secours; **e. fund** fonds *m* de secours; **e. goods** produits *mpl* de dépannage; *Cin etc* **e. light/lighting** éclairage *m* de sécurité; *Med* **e. operation** opération *f* à chaud; **e. rations** vivres *mpl* de réserve; **e. regulations** mesures *fpl* d'exception; **e. repairs** réparations *fpl* d'urgence; **e. supply** en-cas *m inv*; **e. tank** réservoir *m* auxiliaire; **e. telephone** téléphone *m* d'urgence, poste *m* d'appel d'urgence; **e. ward** salle *f* des urgences

emergency exit *n* sortie *f ou* issue *f* de secours

emergency landing *n Av* atterrissage *m* forcé

emergency services *npl* services *mpl* d'urgence

emergent [ɪ'mɜːdʒənt] *adj* (*talent, ability*) naissant; **e. nations** nations *fpl* en voie de développement

emeritus [ɪ'merɪtəs] *adj Univ* **e. professor** professeur *m* honoraire

emery ['emərɪ] *n* émeri *m*; **e. board** lime *f* émeri; **e. cloth** toile *f* d'émeri; **e. paper** papier *m* (d')émeri; **e. powder** poudre *f* d'émeri; **e. wheel** meule *f* (en) émeri

emetic [ɪ'metɪk] *adj, n Med* émétique *m*

emf, EMF [iːe'mef] *n El* (*abbr* **electromotive force**) force *f* électromotrice

emigrant ['emɪgrənt] *adj, n* émigrant, -ante

emigrate ['emɪgreɪt] *vi* émigrer

emigrating ['emɪgreɪtɪŋ] *adj* émigrant

emigration [emɪ'greɪʃən] *n* émigration *f*

emigré ['emɪgreɪ] *n* émigré, -ée; **e. writer** écrivain *m* émigré

eminence ['emɪnəns] *n* (**a**) (*position of importance*) position *f* éminente; (*of office*) grandeur *f*, distinction *f*; **to rise to e.** parvenir à une haute position (**b**) (*raised ground*) éminence *f*, élévation *f* (**c**) *Rel* **E.** (*title of cardinal*) Éminence *f*; **Your E.** Votre Éminence

eminent ['emɪnənt] *adj* éminent; **in view of his e. suitability for the job** du fait qu'il convient tout à fait pour le poste

eminently ['emɪnəntlɪ] *adv* éminemment; **an e. respectable family** une famille éminemment honorable *or* des plus honorables; **an e. suitable place** un endroit *ou* une place parfaitement adapté(e) (**for** à); **what an e. sensible idea!** quelle sage idée!; **an e. believable story** une affaire tout à fait crédible

emir [e'mɪər] *n* émir *m*

emirate ['emɪreɪt] *n* émirat *m*

emissary ['emɪsərɪ] *n* émissaire *m*

emission [ɪ'mɪʃən] *n* (**a**) (*action*) (*of gas, heat, light etc*) émission *f*, dégagement *m*; (*of pollutant*) émission; *Banking etc* (*of bank notes*) émission; *Aut* **e. limit** seuil *m* d'émission (**b**) (*substance*) émanation *f*; **nocturnal emissions** pollutions *fpl* nocturnes

emit [ɪ'mɪt] *vt* (*heat, light etc*) émettre, dégager; (*signal, sigh, cry, Banking paper money*) émettre; (*smell*) exhaler, dégager; (*sparks*) lancer, jeter; (*sound*) rendre

emitter [ɪ'mɪtər] *n Nucl Phys* émetteur *m*

Emmy ['emɪ] *n US TV* ≈ Sept *m* d'Or

emollient [ɪ'mɒlɪənt] *adj, n Med* émollient *m*

emolument [ɪ'mɒljʊmənt] *n* (*usu pl*) **emoluments** émoluments *mpl*, appointements *mpl*, honoraires *mpl*

e-money *n* monnaie *f* électronique

emote [ɪ'məʊt] *vi* donner dans l'emphase

emotion [ɪ'məʊʃən] *n* émotion *f*; **to show one's emotions** laisser paraître ses émotions; **to appeal to the emotions** faire appel aux sentiments; **to be in control of one's emotions** maîtriser ses émotions; **full of e.** plein d'émotion, ému; **she felt a mixture of emotions** ses sentiments étaient partagés

emotional [ɪ'məʊʃən(ə)l] *adj* (**a**) (*reaction*) émotif; (*problems*) émotionnel; (*motive*) affectif; **e. shock** choc *m* émotif *ou* émotionnel; **she's an e. wreck** elle a de gros problèmes émotionnels; **he was something of an e. cripple** il était quelque peu handicapé sur le plan affectif; **why is my life such an e. mess?** pourquoi ma vie affective est-elle si compliquée?; **for e. reasons** pour des raisons émotives (**b**) (*liable to emotion*) émotif; **to be e.** (*of person*) s'attendrir facilement; **he got very e.** (*tearful*) il a pris ça très à cœur; (*tearfully angry*) il a pris ça très mal (**c**) (*full of emotion*) (*plea, ceremony etc*) émouvant

emotionalism [ɪ'məʊʃənəlɪz(ə)m] *n* sentimentalisme *m*; **it's a piece of e.** c'est du sentimentalisme; **the e. of his writing** son style sentimentaliste

emotionally [ɪ'məʊʃən(ə)lɪ] *adv* (**a**) **to be e. involved with sb** être attaché à qn; **I'm too e. involved with the whole situation** cette situation me touche de trop près; **I don't want to get e. involved** je ne veux pas m'attacher; **e. disturbed/exhausted** troublé/vidé sur le plan émotionnel; **e. deprived** en manque d'affection (**b**) (*with strong emotion*) avec beaucoup d'émotion

emotionless [ɪ'məʊʃənlɪs] *adj* (*person*) indifférent; (*face, look*) impassible; (*style*) sobre

emotive [ɪ'məʊtɪv] *adj* qui déchaîne les passions; **e. speech/language** discours *m*/langage *m* sensationnaliste; **racism is a very e. issue** le racisme est un sujet qui déchaîne les passions; **an e. word** un mot chargé

empanel [ɪm'pæn(ə)l] *vt* (**-ll-**, *US* **-l-**) *Jur* **to e. a juror** inscrire un juré sur la liste du jury

empathetic [empə'θetɪk] *adj* compatissant; **to feel e. towards sb** éprouver de la compassion pour qn

empathetically [empə'θetɪklɪ] *adv* avec compassion

empathize ['empəθaɪz] *vi* compatir; **to e. with sb** avoir de la compassion pour qn; **to e. with sb's suffering/problems** compatir à la souffrance/aux problèmes de qn

empathy ['empəθɪ] *n* empathie *f*; **to feel e. for sb** éprouver de l'empathie pour qn

emperor ['empərər] *n* empereur *m*

emperor moth *n Ent* saturnie *f*, *F* paon *m* de nuit

emperor penguin *n* manchot *m* empereur

emphasis ['emfəsɪs] *n* (**a**) (*insistence*) insistance *f*; **to lay** *or* **place e. on** (*fact*) appuyer *ou* insister sur; (*word*) souligner; **too much e. is placed on individualism** l'individualisme l'emporte trop souvent; **the e. is on written work** l'accent est mis sur le travail écrit (**b**) (*stress*) (*in words*) force *f*, accentuation *f*; *Gram* mise *f* en relief; *Ling* accent *m*

emphasize ['emfəsaɪz] *vt* (*stress*) (*word, fact*) accentuer, appuyer sur; (*draw attention to*) (*fact*) attirer l'attention sur; (*quality etc*) faire ressortir, mettre en relief; **she emphasized the need for caution** elle a bien insisté sur la nécessité d'être prudent; **you should e. the first syllable** il faut accentuer la première syllabe

emphatic [ɪm'fætɪk] *adj* (**a**) (*manner, gesture*) énergique; (*speaker*) vigoureux; (*refusal, response*) positif, net; (*victory*) net; **he was quite e. on that point** il s'est montré très catégorique sur ce point (**b**) *Ling* (*syllable*) accentué

emphatically [ɪm'fætɪk(e)lɪ] *adv* (**a**) (*to say*) énergiquement; (*to refuse*) carrément, catégoriquement; (*to deny*) catégoriquement; **they had been e. defeated** ils avaient été largement battus (**b**) (*intensive*) **he is most e. a leader** c'est un chef s'il en fut jamais; **e. yes!** tout à fait, oui!

emphysema [emfɪ'siːmə] *n Med* emphysème *m*; (*pulmonary*) emphysème pulmonaire

empire ['empaɪər] *n* empire *m*; *Hist* **the (British) E.** l'Empire britannique; *Fig* **a shipbuilding e.** un empire dans le monde de la construction navale; *Archit etc* **E. style** style *m* Empire; **E. furniture** meubles *mpl* Empire; *Br Hist* **E. troops** (*of British Empire*) armée *f* coloniale

empire-builder *n also Fig* constructeur *m* d'empires

empire-building *n also Fig* construction *f* d'empires

empiric [em'pɪrɪk] **1** *adj* = **empirical 2** *n* empiriste *mf*

empirical [em'pɪrɪk(ə)l] *adj* empirique; **e. evidence** preuve *f* empirique

empiricism [em'pɪrɪsɪz(ə)m] *n* empirisme *m*

emplacement [ɪm'pleɪsmənt] *n Mil* (*of gun*) emplacement *m*

emplane [ɪm'pleɪn] *Mil* **1** *vi* monter en avion **2** *vt* (*sb, troops*) faire monter en avion

employ¹ [ɪm'plɔɪ] *n Fml* emploi *m*; **to be in sb's e.** être au service de qn, être employé par qn

employ² *vt* (**a**) (*give work to*) employer; **to e. sb as secretary** employer qn comme secrétaire (**b**) (*occupy*) **to e. oneself, to be employed** s'occuper, être occupé (**in doing sth** à faire qch); **she employed herself by tidying up the room** elle s'est occupée en rangeant la pièce (**c**) (*use*) (*means, time, technique*) employer; (*force, argument*) se servir de; (*one's skills, tact*) user de

employable [ɪm'plɔɪəb(ə)l] *adj* susceptible d'être employé; **qualifications make you more e.** il est plus facile de se faire embaucher quand on a des qualifications

employed [ɪm'plɔɪd] **1** *adj* employé **2** *npl* **employers and e.** le patronat et le salariat

employee [ɪmplɔɪ'iː, em'plɔɪiː] *n* employé, -ée; **employees** effectif *m*, salariés *mpl*; **relations between management and employees** relations entre la direction et le personnel

employee association *n* comité *m* d'entreprise
employee buyout *n* reprise *f* de l'entreprise par les salariés, RES *f*
employee contributions *npl* cotisations *fpl* salariales, charges *fpl* sociales salariales
employee file *n* fichier *m* salarié
employee profit-sharing scheme *n* intéressement *m* aux résultats; **to provide an e.** intéresser les employés aux bénéfices
employee representative *n* délégué *m* du personnel
employee's contributions *n* cotisations *fpl ou* retenues *fpl* salariales, charges *fpl* sociales salariales
employer [ɪm'plɔɪər] *n* patron, -onne, *Fml* employeur, -euse; **she's a good e. (to work for)** c'est une bonne patronne; **this company is the town's largest e.** c'est cette entreprise qui emploie le plus de gens dans la ville; **(body of) employers** patronat *m*; **employers' association** organisation *f* patronale, syndicat *m* patronal; **e.'s contributions** cotisations *fpl ou* retenues *fpl* patronales; **e.'s liability** responsabilité *f* patronale; **e. 's organization** syndicat *m* patronal
employment [ɪm'plɔɪmənt] *n* **(a)** (*work*) emploi *m*, travail *m*; **to be looking for e.** chercher un emploi *ou* du travail; **to be without e.** être sans emploi *ou* sans travail; **to be in e.** avoir un emploi; **the firm gives e. to 2,000 (people)** l'entreprise emploie 2 000 personnes; **e. agency** *or* **bureau** bureau *m ou* agence *f* de placement; (*for manual workers*) service *m* d'embauche; **e. law** code *m ou* législation *f* du travail; **e. tax** taxe *f* sur les salaires **(b)** (*act of giving work*) embauche *f*; **the e. of 200 more staff** l'embauche de 200 employés supplémentaires **(c)** (*use*) (*of money, force etc*) usage *m*
emporium [ɪm'pɔːrɪəm] *n Old-fashioned, Lit* (*shop*) grand magasin *m*
empower [ɪm'paʊər] *vt* **(a)** (*sb*) donner du pouvoir à; *Jur* donner pouvoir *ou* procuration à **(b)** (*authorize*) **to e. sb to do sth** autoriser qn à faire qch, donner *ou* conférer plein(s) pouvoir(s) à qn pour faire qch
empress ['emprɪs] *n* impératrice *f*
emptiness ['emptɪnɪs] *n* (*of room, existence etc*) vide *m*; (*of feelings, way of life, words*) vacuité *f*; **to feel an e.** (*after bereavement, divorce etc*) sentir un vide
empty[1] ['emptɪ] **1** *adj* **(a)** vide **(of** de); (*street*) désert; (*building*) inoccupé; (*stomach*) creux; (*wagon*) sans chargement; **to come back e.** (*of lorry etc*) revenir à vide; **you shouldn't run on an e. stomach** tu ne devrais pas courir à jeun; *Com* **e. weight** poids *m* à vide **(b)** *Fig* (*existence*) vide; (*words, threats, pleasure*) vain; **word e. of meaning** mot vide de sens; **to feel e.** (*after bereavement etc*) sentir un vide **2** *n Com* (*crate*) caisse *f* vide; (*bottle*) bouteille *f* vide; **returnable empties** (*bottles*) bouteilles consignées
empty[2] **1** *vt* (*glass etc*) vider **(into** dans); (*truck*) décharger; *Min* verser; (*streets*) dépeupler; (*cesspool, tank etc*) vidanger; **he emptied (the contents of) the bucket over her head** il a vidé le seau sur sa tête; **she emptied the cigarette butts into a plant pot** elle a versé les mégots dans un pot de fleurs; **she emptied the water out of her boots** elle a vidé l'eau qui était dans ses bottes **2** *vi* (*of river etc*) se déverser **(into** dans); (*of theatre etc*) se vider; **the crowd emptied onto the streets** la foule s'est répandue dans les rues
▶ **empty out** *vtsep* (*pockets*) vider; **he emptied (the contents of) his pockets out onto the table** il a vidé le contenu de ses poches sur la table
empty-handed *adv* les mains vides; **to leave e.** repartir les mains vides; **to return e.** rentrer les mains vides, rentrer bredouille
empty-headed *adj* sans cervelle
emptying ['emptɪɪŋ] *n* (*of glass etc*) vidage *m*; (*of barrel etc*) vidange *f*; (*of wagon*) déchargement *m*; (*of streets*) dépeuplement *m*
EMS [iːiː'mes] *n* **(a)** (*abbr* **European Monetary System**) SME *m* **(b)** (*abbr* **engine management system**) EMS *f* **(c)** *Comptr* (*abbr* **expanded memory specification**) mémoire *f* paginée, spécifications *fpl* de la mémoire paginée
emu ['iːmjuː] *n* (*bird*) émeu *m*
emulate ['emjʊleɪt] *vt* (*imitate*) imiter; (*try to equal or surpass*) (*sb*) être l'émule de; *Comptr* émuler; **to e. sb's success** égaler le succès de qn
emulation [emjʊ'leɪʃən] *n also Comptr* émulation *f*
emulator ['emjʊleɪtər] *n also Comptr* émulateur *m*
emulsifier [ɪ'mʌlsɪfaɪər] *n* émulsifiant *m*
emulsify [ɪ'mʌlsɪfaɪ] *vt* émulsionner
emulsion [ɪ'mʌlʃən] *n* **(a)** émulsion *f*; *Phot* **plate e.** émulsion pour plaques **(b) e. (paint)** peinture *f* mate
enable [ɪ'neɪb(ə)l] *vt* **to e. sb to do sth** mettre qn à même *ou* en état de faire qch; *Jur* habiliter qn à faire qch; **this legacy enabled him to retire** cet héritage lui permit de prendre sa retraite
enabling [ɪ'neɪb(ə)lɪŋ] *adj Jur* habilitant; **e. act** loi *f* d'habilitation; **e. legislation** décret *m* d'application
enact [ɪ'nækt] *vt* **(a)** (*act out*) (*tragedy, play*) jouer, représenter; **the political drama currently being enacted** le drame politique qui se joue *ou* se déroule actuellement **(b)** *Jur* (*law*) décréter; (*measure*) ordonner, décréter
enactment [ɪ'næktmənt] *n* **(a)** (*of play*) représentation *f* **(b)** *Jur* (*of law*) établissement *m*, promulgation *f*; (*decree*) ordonnance *f*, décret *m*; **by legislative e.** par un texte législatif
enamel[1] [ɪ'næm(ə)l] *n* **(a)** *Art etc* émail *m*, *pl* émaux; **e. saucepan** casserole *f* émaillée; **e. ware** ustensiles *mpl* en fer émaillé; **e. work** émaillure *f*; (*painting on enamel*) peinture *f* sur émail **(b)** *Anat* (*of teeth*) émail *m* **(c)** (*varnish*) vernis *m*, émail *m*, *pl* émails; **e. paint** peinture *f* au vernis
enamel[2] *vt* (**-ll-**, *US* **-l-**) émailler
enamelled [ɪ'næm(ə)ld] *adj* **(a)** (*covered with enamel*) (*brick etc*) émaillé; (*tile*) vernissé; **e. saucepan** casserole *f* émaillée **(b)** (*painted*) peint en émail
enamelling [ɪ'næm(ə)lɪŋ] *n* (*art*) émaillure *f*; (*painting*) peinture *f* en émail
enamour [ɪ'næmər] *vt* **his behaviour did little to e. me of him** son comportement ne me l'a guère rendu plus sympathique
enamoured [ɪ'næməd] *adj* passionné **(of sth** pour qch), amoureux **(of sb** de qn); **to become e. of sb** s'éprendre de qn; **I am scarcely e. of the suggestion** cette suggestion ne m'enchante guère
encage [ɪn'keɪdʒ] *vt Fml* (*animal*) encager
encamp [ɪn'kæmp] **1** *vt* (*army*) (faire) camper; **the army had been encamped outside the city for nearly three months** l'armée campait aux portes de la ville depuis près de trois mois **2** *vi* camper
encampment [ɪn'kæmpmənt] *n* campement *m*, camp *m*; **an army e.** un campement militaire
encapsulate [ɪn'kæpsjʊleɪt] *vt* **(a)** (*summarize*) résumer; **this film encapsulates the atmosphere of the times** ce film contient *ou* renferme l'atmosphère de l'époque **(b)** *Pharm* capsuler
encase [ɪn'keɪs] *vt* **(a)** (*provide with covering*) envelopper; **encased in concrete** noyé dans le béton **(b)** (*put in case*) encaisser, enfermer **(in** dans)
encash [ɪn'kæʃ] *vt Br Banking* (*cheque*) encaisser
encashment [ɪn'kæʃmənt] *n Br Banking* (*of cheque*) encaissement *m*
encaustic [en'kɔːstɪk] **1** *adj Art* (*painting etc*) à l'encaustique; (*paint*) encaustique; *Cer* **e. tile** carreau *m* céramique **2** *n Art* encaustique *f*
encephalitis [ensefə'laɪtɪs] *n Med* encéphalite *f*
enchant [ɪn'tʃɑːnt] *vt* **(a)** (*delight*) enchanter, ravir; **he was less than enchanted by the prospect** l'idée ne l'enchantait guère **(b)** (*put under a spell*) ensorceler
enchanted [ɪn'tʃɑːntɪd] *adj* **(a)** (*delighted*) enchanté **(with** de) **(b)** (*under a spell, magic*) enchanté, ensorcelé; **an e. wood** une forêt enchantée
enchanter [ɪn'tʃɑːntər] *n* enchanteur *m*
enchanting [ɪn'tʃɑːntɪŋ] *adj* (*smile, scenery*) enchanteur, -eresse; (*voice, person*) ravissant, charmant; (*idea, thought*) délicieux; **an e. little cottage** une charmante petite maison de campagne
enchantingly [ɪn'tʃɑːntɪŋlɪ] *adv* à ravir; (*to sing, to smile etc*) de façon enchanteresse; **she looked quite e. beautiful** elle était belle à ravir
enchantment [ɪn'tʃɑːntmənt] *n* **(a)** (*delight*) ravissement *m*, enchantement *m*; **he professed his e.** il a déclaré qu'il était enchanté; *Lit* **distance lends e. (to the view)** tout paraît beau (vu) de loin; **it filled us with a sense of e.** cela nous a remplis de ravissement *ou* jetés dans le ravissement **(b)** (*placing under spell*) enchantement *m*, ensorcellement *m*
enchantress [ɪn'tʃɑːntrɪs] *n* enchanteresse *f*
encircle [ɪn'sɜːk(ə)l] *vt* ceindre, encercler; (*army*) cerner, entourer; **she encircled him with her arms** elle a mis ses bras autour de lui
encirclement [ɪn'sɜːkəlmənt] *n* encerclement *m*; *Mktg* **e. attack** attaque *f* par encerclement; *Mktg* **e. strategy** stratégie *f* d'encerclement
encircling [ɪn'sɜːk(ə)lɪŋ] **1** *n* encerclement *m* **2** *adj Mil* **e. movement** manœuvre *f* d'encerclement
encl (*abbr* **enclosure**) p. j.
enclave ['enkleɪv] *n* enclave *f*
enclose [ɪn'kləʊz] *vt* **(a)** (*include*) inclure, (r)enfermer **(in** dans); **to e. sth in a letter** joindre qch à une lettre; **letter enclosing a cheque** lettre contenant un chèque; **enclosed herewith** sous ce pli; **enclosed please find ...** veuillez

trouver ci-inclus *ou* ci-joint ... **(b)** *(surround)* *(field)* clôturer (**with** de); *(the enemy, town)* entourer, investir; **garden enclosed with** *or* **in** *or* **by high walls** jardin entouré *ou* ceint de hauts murs **(c)** *(cover)* *(electric motor etc)* blinder; *(mechanism)* enfermer *(dans un carter)*

enclosed [ɪn'kləʊzd] *adj* **(a)** *(in letter)* joint, ci-joint, ci-inclus; **the e. documents** les pièces jointes **(b)** *(field etc)* clos, enclos; *(army)* entouré, cerné; *(city)* investi; *Rel* *(order, monk etc)* cloîtré; *(existence, way of life)* reclus; **e. space** espace *m* clos **(c)** *MecE etc* *(covered)* recouvert, enfermé; *(mechanism)* en carter

enclosure [ɪn'kləʊʒər] *n* **(a)** *(area)* enclos *m*, clos *m*, enceinte *f*; *Br Hist* enclosure *f*; *Horseracing* **the e.** le pesage; **the public enclosures** la pelouse **(b)** *(fence, wall etc)* enceinte *f*, clôture *f* **(c)** *Com* *(in letter)* pièce *f* annexée *ou* incluse, annexe *f*; **enclosures** pièces jointes

encode [en'kəʊd] *vt* *(text etc)* chiffrer; *Comptr* encoder

encoder [en'kəʊdər] *n* *Comptr* encodeur *m*

encoding [en'kəʊdɪŋ] *n* *Comptr* codage *m*, encodage *m*

encomium, *pl* **-ia** [ɪn'kəʊmɪəm, -ɪə] *n* *Lit* apologie *f*, panégyrique *m*

encompass [ɪn'kʌmpəs] *vt* **(a)** *(include)* englober, envelopper, renfermer (**with, within** dans); **their repertoire encompasses most musical styles** leur répertoire englobe la plupart des genres musicaux; **the state education system encompasses children of all ability levels** le système d'éducation nationale regroupe des enfants de tous les niveaux d'aptitude **(b)** *Fml* *(surround)* entourer (**with** de); *(of army, enemy)* encercler, cerner

encore¹ ['ɒŋkɔːr] *Th* **1** *n* **(a)** *(song etc)* = chanson *f* ou morceau *m* exécuté(e) à la fin d'un spectacle ou d'un concert etc par un artiste que l'on a bissé; **to call for an e.** *(of audience)* bisser; **to give an e.** *(of pianist, singer etc)* bisser; **to play/sing an e.** jouer/chanter un morceau supplémentaire; *(repeating sth)* bisser un morceau **(b)** *(shout)* bis *m* **2** *int* **e.!** bis!

encore² *vt Th* *(passage, actor etc)* bisser

encounter¹ [ɪn'kaʊntər] *n* **(a)** *(meeting)* *(of friends etc)* rencontre *f*; *Psy* **e. group** atelier *m* thérapeutique **(b)** *(confrontation)* rencontre *f* (hostile); *(fight)* combat *m*; *Sp, Journ* confrontation *f*; **the e. between colonised and coloniser** la confrontation entre colonisés et colonisateurs

encounter² *vt* *(sb, obstacle)* rencontrer; *(difficulties)* éprouver; *(the enemy)* affronter; *(resistance)* recontrer, trouver; *(storm, objection)* essuyer

encourage [ɪn'kʌrɪdʒ] *vt* **(a)** *(sb)* encourager; **to e. sb to do sth** encourager *ou* inciter qn à faire qch; **don't e. him!** ne l'encourage pas! **(b)** *(support)* *(good works)* appuyer; *(the arts, commerce)* favoriser; *(belief)* encourager; **they encouraged their daughter's ambition** ils ont encouragé leur fille à réaliser ses ambitions

encouragement [ɪn'kʌrɪdʒmənt] *n* encouragement *m*; **to give** *or* **offer sb e.** encourager qn; **to get** *or* **receive e. from sb** être encouragé par qn; **her success was a great e. to us** sa réussite nous a beaucoup encouragés; *Iron* **he doesn't need any e.** il n'a pas besoin qu'on l'encourage; **to draw e. from sth** trouver des motifs d'encouragement dans qch

encouraging [ɪn'kʌrɪdʒɪŋ] *adj* *(news, person)* encourageant; **he wasn't very e. to me** il ne s'est pas montré très encourageant à mon égard; **it is e. to see the progress that has been made** c'est encourageant de constater les progrès qui ont été faits

encouragingly [ɪn'kʌrɪdʒɪŋlɪ] *adv* *(to say sth)* d'une manière encourageante; *(to smile)* d'un air encourageant; **he looked e. healthy** sa bonne mine était encourageante

▶ **encroach on, encroach upon** [ɪn'krəʊtʃ] *vipo* *(land etc)* empiéter sur; *(sb's rights)* usurper; *Jur* léser; **the sea is encroaching on the land** la mer gagne du terrain

encroachment [ɪn'krəʊtʃmənt] *n* **(a) e. upon sb's rights** usurpation *f* des droits de qn, empiètement *m* sur les droits de qn **(b)** *(of sea)* ingression *f*

encrust [ɪn'krʌst] *vt* **(a)** *(decorate)* **encrusted with diamonds** incrusté de diamants **(b)** *(cover with hard outer layer)* couvrir (d'une croûte), incruster (**with** de); **encrusted with mud/blood** couvert de boue/sang

encrypt [en'krɪpt] *n* *Comptr* crypter, chiffrer

encryption [en'krɪpʃən] *n* *Comptr* chiffrement *m*

encumber [ɪn'kʌmbər] *vt* **(a)** encombrer (**with** de); *(sb, movement)* gêner; **the party remains encumbered by the legacy of its Stalinist past** le parti pâtit encore du legs encombrant de son passé stalinien **(b)** *Jur* **encumbered estate** *(with debts)* propriété *f* grevée de dettes; *(with mortgage)* propriété grevée d'hypothèques

encumbrance [ɪn'kʌmbrəns] *n* **(a)** embarras *m*; **to be an e. to sb** *(physically)* encombrer qn; *(financially)* être à la charge de qn; **to be an e. to sb's plans** gêner les projets de qn; **the suitcase was something of an e.** la valise était plutôt encombrante **(b)** *Jur* *(of inheritance)* charges *fpl*; **to free an estate from encumbrances** dégrever une propriété

encyclic [ɪn'sɪklɪk] *adj Cathol* encyclique

encyclical [ɪn'sɪklɪk(ə)l] *Cathol* **1** *n* encyclique *f* **2** *adj* *(letter)* encyclique

encyclop(a)edia [ɪnsaɪklə'piːdɪə] *n* encyclopédie *f*; **an e. entry** un article d'encyclopédie; **e. salesman** représentant *m* en encyclopédies

encyclop(a)edic [ɪnsaɪklə'piːdɪk] *adj* encyclopédique

encyclop(a)edist [ɪnsaɪklə'piːdɪst] *n* encyclopédiste *mf*

end¹ [end] *n* **(a)** *(extremity, limit etc in space)* *(of stick, road etc)* bout *m*, extrémité *f*; *(of football pitch)* camp *m*; *(limit)* limite *f*, borne *f*; *(of book)* fin *f*; *(of procession etc)* queue *f*; *(of beam)* about *m*; *(of mast)* tronçon *m*; *(of cable)* tronche *f*; *(remnant)* *(of candle)* bout; *(of cigarette)* bout, mégot *m*; **the e. of the table** le bout de la table; **to the ends of the earth** jusqu'au bout du monde; **from one e. of the country to the other** d'un bout à l'autre du pays; **to come to the e. of the road** arriver au bout de la route; *(in one's career)* arriver au bout de sa carrière; *(in one's life)* arriver au bout de sa vie; *(be unable to make progress)* être dans une impasse; *Fb etc* **to change ends** changer de camp; **the third from the e.** le troisième avant la fin; *Tel* **at the other e. of the line** à l'autre bout de la ligne, au bout du fil; **what's the weather like at your e.?** quel temps fait-il chez vous?; **the problem's at the supplier's e.** le problème est chez le fournisseur; **it's at the other e. of town** c'est à l'autre bout de la ville; **at the northern e. of the park/town/lake** à l'extrémité nord du parc/de la ville/du lac; **e. to e.** bout à bout; **from e. to e.** d'un bout à l'autre; **on e.** *(of barrel etc)* debout, sur bout; **to stand a box (up) on e.** dresser une boîte debout; **e. on** bout à bout; **the deep/shallow e.** *(of swimming pool)* le grand/le petit fond

(b) *(limit in time, quantity etc)* fin *f*; *(of process etc)* terme *m*; **five hours on e.** cinq heures de suite *ou* d'affilée; **for hours on e.** pendant des heures et des heures; **we shall never hear the e. of it** on n'entendra jamais la fin; **and that's the e. of it!** et voilà tout!; **let that be an e. to the matter!** qu'on en finisse là!, qu'on n'en parle plus!; **there's no e. to it** cela n'en finit pas; *F* **no e. of ...** infiniment de ...; *F* **it'll do you no e. of good** ça te fera énormément de bien; *F* **it helped me no e.** ça m'a énormément aidé; **to make an e. of, to put an e. to** *(sth)* en finir avec; *(evil etc)* mettre fin à; *(competition)* supprimer; **to draw to an e.** tirer *ou* toucher à sa fin; **to come to an e.** prendre fin; **to come to an abrupt e.** terminer abruptement; **to come to the e. of the supplies/what one wants to say** arriver au bout des réserves/de ce qu'on a à dire; **to come to a bad** *or* *F* **sticky e.** mal finir; **to bring sth to an e.** mettre fin à qch; **the war was at an e.** la guerre était terminée; **to be at the e. of one's resources** être au bout de ses ressources; **I am at the e. of my patience** je suis à bout de patience; **at the e. of** *(month, winter, century, contract, class)* à la fin de; *(six months etc)* au bout de; **at the e. of the day** à la fin de la journée; *Fig* en fin de compte, au bout du compte; **in the e.** à la longue, à la fin; **you'll get used to it in the e.** tu t'y habitueras à la longue; **she gave me the money back in the e.** elle m'a rendu l'argent à la fin, elle a fini par me rendre l'argent; **he always pays me back in the e.** il finit toujours par me rendre ce qu'il me doit; **e. of the world** fin du monde; **it's not the e. of the world** ce n'est pas la fin du monde; *Rel* **world without e.** pour les siècles des siècles; **until the e. of time** jusqu'à la fin des temps; **the e. of one's life** la fin *ou* le terme de la vie; **to meet one's e.** trouver la mort; **e. result** résultat *m* final

(c) *(aim, purpose)* fin *f*, but *m*, dessein *m*; **an e. in itself** une fin en soi; **to attain** *or* **achieve one's end(s)** en arriver *ou* parvenir à ses fins, atteindre son but; **to this e.** à ces fins; **to no good e.** avec de mauvaises intentions; **with this e. in view** avec cet objectif en vue; *Fml* **to what e.?** dans quel but?; *Prov* **the e. justifies the means** la fin justifie les moyens

(d) *(technical uses)* **east e.** *(in church architecture)* chevet *m*; *Aut* **big e.** tête *f* de bielle; *Aut* **small e.** pied *m* de bielle; *Rail* **the e. carriage** le wagon de queue; *Rail* **e. of line** tête *f* de ligne; *Tech* **e. piece** embout *m*

(e) *(idioms)* **his hair was standing on e.** ses cheveux se dressaient sur sa tête *ou* se hérissaient; *F* **to keep one's e. up** *(stay cheerful)* ne pas se laisser démonter; *(contribute)* y mettre du sien; *Fig* **to make (both) ends meet** joindre les deux bouts; *Fig* **to get hold of the wrong e. of the stick** mal comprendre; *Fig* **to begin at the wrong e.** ne pas commencer par le commencement; *Fig* **I don't know one e. of a tennis racket/a computer from the other** je ne sais même pas à quoi ressemble une raquette de tennis/un ordinateur; *F* **you're the e.!** tu es impossible!

end² **1** *vt* (*work, task etc*) finir, terminer, achever; (*speech*) conclure; (*meeting*) clore; **to e. one's days peacefully** terminer ses jours en paix; **to e. a speech with a quotation** terminer un discours avec une citation; *F* **to e. it all** en finir; **the war to e. all wars** la dernière des dernières (guerres), la der des ders; **it's the horror film to e. all horror films** c'est le nec plus ultra des films d'horreur; **a headache to e. all headaches** une migraine de première

2 *vi* **(a)** finir, se terminer (**in** dans, en); (*of subscription*) expirer; **to e. happily** (*of story*) avoir une fin heureuse, bien se terminer; **the path ends at the lakeside** le chemin aboutit au bord du lac; **to e. in a point** (*of stick*) se terminer en pointe; **it ended in a fight** ça a fini en bagarre, ça s'est terminé par une bagarre; **this will e. in tears!** ça va se finir par des larmes!; **to e. in bitterness/acrimony** se terminer dans l'amertume/l'acrimonie; **his extravagance will e. by ruining him** son extravagance aboutira à sa ruine; **I must e. by thanking Mr Brown** pour conclure je dois remercier M. Brown; **the film ends with her saying ...** le film se termine sur elle disant ...; **let us e. with a song** finissons par une chanson; **the story ends on a happy note** l'histoire se termine sur une note gaie; **how will it all e.?** (*what is the world coming to?*) comment tout cela va-t-il se terminer?; **will this torment/the bad weather never e.?** ce tourment/ce mauvais temps n'en finira donc jamais?; *Prov* **all's well that ends well** tout est bien qui finit bien

(b) (*of word*) se terminer (**in -er/***etc* en -er/*etc*); **a word ending in s** un mot qui se termine par s

▶ **end up** *vi* (*finish*) finir; **no one thought she'd e. up in prison** personne ne pensait qu'elle finirait en prison; **we ended up going to see a movie** en fin de compte nous sommes allés voir un film; **he ended up dead** il a fini par se faire tuer; **our luggage ended up in Hong Kong** nos bagages se sont retrouvés à Hong Kong; **she'll e. up killing someone if she carries on driving like that** elle finira par tuer quelqu'un si elle continue à conduire comme ça

end-all *n see* **be-all**

endanger [ɪn'deɪndʒər] *vt* (*sb, sth*) mettre en danger; (*one's life*) exposer, risquer; (*interests, health, chances*) compromettre

endangered [ɪn'deɪndʒəd] *adj attrib* menacé; **e. species** espèce *f* menacée; **an e. way of life** un mode de vie qui menace de disparaître

endear [ɪn'dɪər] *vt* (*sb, sth*) rendre cher (**to** à); **he has endeared himself to all** il s'est fait aimer de tous; **her outspokenness did not e. her to the régime** sa franchise ne l'a pas rendue populaire auprès du régime; **the melancholy of his songs endears him to many a listener** la mélancolie de ses chansons le fait apprécier de nombreux auditeurs

endearing [ɪn'dɪərɪŋ] *adj* (*person, smile, look*) attachant; (*quality*) sympathique; (*word*) tendre; **he has a less than e. habit of ...** il a l'habitude peu plaisante de ...

endearingly [ɪn'dɪərɪŋlɪ] *adv* d'une manière attachante; **he's e. coy/modest** il est d'une pudeur/modestie attachante

endearment [ɪn'dɪəmənt] *n* **term of e.** terme *m* affectif; **endearments** mots *mpl* tendres

endeavour¹, *US* **endeavor** [ɪn'devər] *n* effort *m*; **to wish sb good luck in their endeavours** souhaiter bonne chance à qn dans ses entreprises; **to use** *or* **make every e. to ...** faire tout son possible *ou* tous les efforts possibles pour ...; **in an e. to persuade them** dans une tentative pour les persuader; **in the field of human e.** dans l'histoire des réussites humaines

endeavour², *US* **endeavor** *vt* **to e. to do sth** s'efforcer *ou* tenter de faire qch, chercher à faire qch

endemic [en'demɪk] **1** *adj Bot, Med, Fig* endémique **2** *n Med* endémie *f*

endgame ['endgeɪm] *n Chess* fin *f* de partie; *Mktg* objectif *m* (mercatique)

ending ['endɪŋ] *n* **(a)** (*of nuclear tests etc*) cessation *f*; (*of restrictions*) levée *f* **(b)** (*of story etc*) fin *f*, conclusion *f*; **happy e.** dénouement *m* heureux; **a surprise e.** une fin surprenante **(c)** *Gram* (*of word*) terminaison *f*, désinence *f*; **feminine/masculine/neuter e.** terminaison féminine/masculine/neutre; **accusative/genitive/***etc* **e.** désinence de l'accusatif/du génitif/*etc*; **verb/noun/***etc* **e.** désinence *ou* flexion *f* verbale/nominale/*etc*; **case e.** flexion casuelle

endive ['endaɪv] *n Culin* **(a)** (**curly**) **e.** chicorée *f* frisée **(b)** *Am* (*chicory*) endive *f*

end key *n Comptr* touche *f* fin

endless ['endlɪs] *adj* **(a)** (*in space*) infini, sans bornes; (*journey, list etc*) interminable, sans fin; *Tech* (*cable, screw*) sans fin; **e. space** l'infini *m*

(b) (*in time*) interminable, sans fin; (*discussion, meeting*) à n'en plus finir, interminable; (*pain*) continuel, incessant; (*chatter*) intarissable; **it's an e. task, it's e.** cela n'en finit pas; **after what seemed like an e. wait** après une attente qui m'a/lui a/*etc* semblé une éternité

(c) (*in number*) innombrable; **a seemingly e. number of ...** un nombre apparemment infini de ...; **to take e. pains to do sth** se donner une peine infinie à faire qch; **the possibilities are e., there are e. possibilities** les possibilités sont innombrables

endlessly ['endlɪslɪ] *adv* (*to speak, discuss*) interminablement; (*to repeat, revise sth*) sans cesse; (*to stretch out*) à l'infini, à perte de vue

endnote ['endnəʊt] *n Comptr* note *f* de fin de document, NfD *f*

endocardium [endəʊ'kɑːdɪəm] *n Anat* endocarde *m*

endocarp ['endəʊkɑːp] *n Bot* endocarpe *m*

endocrine ['endəʊkraɪn] *Physiol* **1** *adj* (*gland*) endocrine **2** *n* (glande *f*) endocrine *f*

endocrinology [endəʊkraɪ'nɒlədʒɪ] *n Med* endocrinologie *f*

end-of-month *adj* de fin de mois; **e. statement** relevé *m* de fin de mois

end-of-year *adj* de fin d'année; **e. bonus** gratification *f* de fin d'année

endogamy [en'dɒgəmɪ] *n* endogamie *f*

endogenous [en'dɒdʒɪnəs] *adj* endogène

endometrium [endəʊ'miːtrɪəm] *n Anat* endomètre *m*

endomorph ['endəʊmɔːf] *n* endomorphe *mf*

endorphin ['endɔːfɪn] *n Physiol* endorphine *f*

endorse [ɪn'dɔːs] *vt* **(a)** *Admin, Fin etc* (*document, cheque*) endosser; (*passport*) viser; (*bill*) avaliser **(b)** *Br Admin* **to e. a driving licence** = décompter des points sur un permis de conduire **(c)** (*approve*) (*action*) appuyer, sanctionner; (*decision*) souscrire à; (*opinion*) soucrire à, sanctionner; *Jur* (*appeal*) approuver; *Pol* **to e. sb as a candidate, to e. sb's candidature** appuyer la candidature de qn; (*by party*) investir qn; **I e. all you have done** j'approuve tout ce que vous avez fait; *Com* **our products are endorsed by leading athletes** nos produits sont signés par les plus grands athlètes

endorsee [endɔː'siː] *n Fin* endossataire *mf*

endorsement [ɪn'dɔːsmənt] *n* **(a)** *Admin, Fin etc* (*of cheque*) endossement *m*, endos *m*; (*of bill*) aval *m*; (*on passport*) mention *f* spéciale; (*in insurance*) avenant *m*; *Fin* **e. fee** commission *f* d'endos **(b)** *Br Admin* (*on driving licence*) contravention *f* inscrite sur le permis de conduire **(c)** (*approval*) (*of action*) approbation *f*; (*of opinion*) adhésion *f* (**of** à)

endorser [ɪn'dɔːsər] *n Fin* endosseur *m*

endoscope ['endəʊskəʊp] *n Med* endoscope *m*

endoscopic [endəʊ'skɒpɪk] *adj Med* endoscopique

endoscopy [en'dɒskəpɪ] *n Med* endoscopie *f*

endosperm ['endəʊspɜːm] *n Bot* endosperme *m*

endow [ɪn'daʊ] *vt* **(a)** doter; **endowed with great talents** doué de grands talents; **woman endowed with great beauty** femme dotée d'une grande beauté; *F Hum* **to be well endowed** (*of man, woman*) avoir tout ce qu'il faut **(b)** *Fin* (*sb, company*) doter (**with** de); (*hospital bed, university chair etc*) fonder

endowment [ɪn'daʊmənt] *n* **(a)** *Fin* (*action, fund*) dotation *f*; (*bequeathed to home*) fondation *f*; (**ordinary**) **e. assurance** assurance mixte; (**pure**) **e. assurance** *or* **policy** assurance *f* en cas de vie, assurance à capital différé; **e. mortgage** hypothèque *f* associée à une assurance-vie **(b)** (*talent*) don *m* (naturel), talent *m*

endpaper ['endpeɪpər] *n* (*of book*) page *f* de garde

end piece *n Tech* embout *m*

end product *n* produit *m* fini *ou* final; *Fig* (*consequence*) suite *f*, résultat *m*

end titles *npl TV, Cin* générique *m* de fin

endue [ɪn'djuː] *vt Lit* revêtir (**with** de)

endurable [ɪn'djʊərəb(ə)l] *adj* supportable

endurance [ɪn'djʊərəns] *n* résistance *f*; **physical e.** endurance *f* (physique); **to have great powers of e.** avoir une grande endurance; **beyond e.** insupportable, intolérable; **it was boring/irritating him beyond e.** cela l'ennuyait/l'irritait atrocement *ou* insupportablement; **e. test** *MecE* test *m* de résistance; *Sp* épreuve *f* d'endurance; *Fig* **this is a real e. test** c'est une véritable épreuve d'endurance

endure [ɪn'djʊər] **1** *vt* endurer; (*insults etc*) supporter; **it was more than she could e.** c'était plus qu'elle ne pouvait supporter; **it is something I (just) can't e.** c'est une chose que je ne supporte pas; **these days she just endures him** à présent elle le souffre avec patience **2** *vi* rester; (*of relationship*) durer; (*of work of art*) (bien) supporter le passage du temps; **monuments which e. to this day** des monuments qui subsistent jusqu'à ce jour; **their names will e. forever in our hearts** leurs noms resteront pour toujours dans nos cœurs

enduring [ɪnˈdjʊərɪŋ] *adj* (*influence, memory, friendship*) durable, qui dure, permanent; (*peace*) stable; (*evil*) persistant, qui persiste

enduro [ɪnˈdjʊərəʊ] *n* (*motor race*) enduro *m*

end-user *n* utilisateur *m* final; (*of foodstuffs*) consommateur *m* final, utilisateur final; *Mktg* **e. specialist** spécialiste *mf* du marché utilisateur final

endways [ˈendweɪz], **endwise** [ˈendwaɪz] *adv* **(a)** (*end up*) de chant, debout; **e. on** avec le bout en avant; **I could only see the object e. on** je ne voyais que la face latérale de l'objet; **the house stands e. on to the road** la maison est perpendiculaire à la route **(b)** (*end to end*) bout à bout; **to put things together e.** mettre des choses bout à bout **(c)** (*lengthways*) longitudinalement; **we'll have to take it through e.** il faudra que nous le passions dans le sens de la longueur

enema [ˈenəmə] *n Med* lavement *m*; **they gave him an e.** ils lui ont administré un lavement

enemy [ˈenəmɪ] **1** *n* [①A11,g,i] ennemi, -e; **to be one's own (worst) e.** se desservir soi-même; **to make enemies** se faire des ennemis; *Mil etc* **the e.** (*no pl*) l'ennemi; *Fig* **the e. at the gates** l'ennemi qui menace **2** *adj* (*country, ship etc*) ennemi; **e. alien** ressortissant, -ante d'un pays ennemi

enemy-occupied *adj Mil* **e. territory** territoire *m* occupé par l'ennemi

energetic [enəˈdʒetɪk] *adj* (*person, action*) énergique; **I'll join you later if I'm feeling e.** je vous rejoindrai plus tard si je m'en sens l'énergie; **I'm not feeling very e.** je ne me sens pas beaucoup d'énergie

energetically [enəˈdʒetɪklɪ] *adv* énergiquement, avec énergie; (*to deny, reply etc*) énergiquement

energetics [enəˈdʒetɪks] *n* [①A10,c] *Phys* énergétique *f*

energize [ˈenədʒaɪz] *vt* **(a)** (*sb*) donner de l'énergie à, stimuler; **an energizing effect** un effet énergisant *ou* stimulant **(b)** *El* alimenter; (*dynamo*) amorcer; (*core of coil*) aimanter

energy [ˈenədʒɪ] *n* **(a)** (*vitality*) énergie *f*, vigueur *f*; **to have no e.** ne pas avoir d'énergie; **I don't have the e.** (*to do it, go out etc*) je n'en ai pas l'énergie; **to run out of e.** ne plus avoir d'énergie; **I am running out of e.** je n'ai plus beaucoup d'énergie; **man of considerable e.** homme très énergique; **to devote** *or* **apply all one's e.** *or* **energies to a task** consacrer *ou* apporter *ou* appliquer tous ses efforts *ou* toute son énergie à une tâche; **to shout/work/***etc* **with all one's e.** crier/travailler/*etc* de toutes ses forces; **to conserve one's energies** économiser ses forces

(b) *Phys* énergie *f*; **e. consumed** puissance *f* absorbée; **kinetic e.** énergie cinétique; **atomic e.** énergie atomique; **e.-absorbing bumper** pare-chocs *m* à absorption d'énergie; **to save e.** faire des économies d'énergie; **the e. crisis** la crise de l'énergie

Energy Minister *n Pol* ministre *m* de l'Énergie

energy-saving *adj* (*device*) d'économie d'énergie, pour économiser l'énergie, qui économise l'énergie

Energy Secretary *n Br Pol* ministre *m* de l'Énergie

enervate [ˈenəveɪt] *vt* (*body, the will*) affaiblir

enervating [ˈenəveɪtɪŋ] *adj* (*climate*) débilitant

enervation [enəˈveɪʃən] *n* (*state*) mollesse *f*

enfeeble [ɪnˈfiːb(ə)l] *vt* (*of pain, age*) affaiblir

enfilade[1] [ˈenfɪleɪd] *n Mil* tir *m* d'enfilade

enfilade[2] *vt Mil* enfiler, prendre en enfilade

enfold [ɪnˈfəʊld] *vt* envelopper (**sth in sth** qch dans qch); **to e. sb in one's arms** étreindre qn, serrer qn dans ses bras

enforce [ɪnˈfɔːs] *vt* **(a)** (*put into effect*) (*a law etc*) mettre en vigueur, appliquer; (*rights*) faire valoir; (*the law*) faire respecter, faire obéir; (*ruling*) imposer, faire observer; **such a law would be impossible to e.** une telle loi serait impossible à appliquer; **to e. compliance with the law/regulations** faire respecter la loi/les réglementations; **to e. obedience** se faire obéir **(b)** *Fml* (*reinforce*) (*argument*) donner de la force à, faire valoir

enforceable [ɪnˈfɔːsəb(ə)l] *adj* (*ruling, policy*) applicable; (*contract*) exécutoire

enforced [ɪnˈfɔːst] *adj* (*silence, inactivity etc*) forcé

enforcement [ɪnˈfɔːsmənt] *n Jur* (*of law*) exécution *f*, mise *f* en vigueur, application *f*; **law e. officers** fonctionnaires *mpl* chargés de l'application de la loi

enfranchise [ɪnˈfræntʃaɪz] *vt* **(a)** (*give vote to*) admettre au suffrage, accorder le droit de vote à **(b)** (*free*) (*slave*) affranchir

enfranchisement [ɪnˈfræntʃɪzmənt] *n* **(a)** *Pol* (*of citizen*) admission *f* au suffrage **(b)** (*freeing*) (*of slave*) affranchissement *m*

ENG [iːenˈdʒiː] *n* (*abbr* **electronic news gathering**) journalisme *m* électronique de télévision

engage [ɪnˈgeɪdʒ] **1** *vt* **(a)** *Fml* (*employ, hire*) (*domestic employee etc*) engager; (*workers*) embaucher; *Naut* (*men*) recruter; **to e. sb's services** employer les services de qn

(b) (*occupy*) (*sb*) occuper; (*attention*) fixer; (*sb's affection*) attirer, gagner; **to e. sb in conversation** entrer en conversation avec qn, engager la conversation avec qn; **to be engaged in doing sth** être occupé à faire qch

(c) *Mil* **to e. the enemy** attaquer l'ennemi; **to e. an enemy aircraft** ouvrir le feu sur un appareil ennemi

(d) *MecE* (*cog, gear*) mettre en prise; **to e. first (gear)** mettre en première (vitesse); **to e. the clutch** embrayer

(e) *Fml* (*pledge*) **to e. oneself to do sth** s'engager à faire qch

2 *vi* **(a)** (*take part*) **to e. in** (*sport etc*) s'adonner à; **to e. in conversation** commencer une conversation

(b) *Mil* attaquer; **to e. in an action** se lancer dans une action

(c) *MecE* (*of cog wheel*) (s')engrener, (s')engager (**with** avec); (*of clutch*) s'embrayer

(d) *Fml* (*pledge*) s'engager (**to do** à faire)

engaged [ɪnˈgeɪdʒd] *adj* **(a)** **to be e.** (**to be married**) être fiancé(e); **to get e.** se fiancer; **the e. couple** les fiancés *mpl* **(b)** (*busy*) **heavily e.** très occupé; **to be deeply e. in conversation** être en pleine conversation; **I am (otherwise) e.** je suis pris **(c)** *Br Tel* **the number is e.** la ligne est occupée; **to get the e. tone** *or* **signal** entendre le signal de ligne occupée **(d)** (*on lavatory door*) occupé **(e)** *MecE* (*gear wheels*) en prise

engagement [ɪnˈgeɪdʒmənt] *n* **(a)** (*to be married*) fiançailles *fpl*; **e. ring** anneau *m ou* bague *f* de fiançailles

(b) (*meeting etc*) rendez-vous *m*; **owing to a previous** *or* **prior e.** en raison d'un engagement antérieur; **public e.** engagement *m* à paraître en public; **she has many social engagements** elle est très demandée; **to have an e.** être pris, être occupé; **e. book** agenda *m*

(c) (*obligation*) engagement *m*, promesse *f*, obligation *f*; **to make an e./a formal e. to do sth** s'engager/s'engager formellement à faire qch; *Com* **to carry out** *or* **meet one's engagements** faire face à ses engagements, remplir ses engagements

(d) *Mil* (*action*) combat *m*, engagement *m*; (*of unit*) intervention *f*

(e) *MecE* mise *f* en prise; (*of clutch*) embrayage *m*; (*of pinion with wheel etc*) prise *f*

(f) (*employment*) (*of domestic staff, actor*) engagement *m*; *Naut* (*of men*) recrutement *m*

engaging [ɪnˈgeɪdʒɪŋ] *adj* (*smile*) engageant, attrayant, attirant; (*tone*) liant, engageant; **to have an e. manner** être liant

engagingly [ɪnˈgeɪdʒɪŋlɪ] *adv* d'une manière engageante; (*to smile*) gentiment; **e. honest/modest** d'une honnêteté/modestie engageante

engender [ɪnˈdʒendər] *vt* (*effect*) faire naître, produire; (*illness, feeling*) engendrer; **it engendered some respect for her among her colleagues** cela fit naître chez ses collègues un certain respect à son égard

engine [ˈendʒɪn] *n* **(a)** *MecE etc* moteur *m*; (*for ship*) machine *f*; *Comptr* (*in laser*) mécanique *f*, base *f*, cœur *m*; *Fig* **the e. of progress/reform/***etc* le moteur du progrès/de la réforme/*etc*; **car e.** moteur de voiture; *Br* **petrol** *or US* **gas e.** moteur à essence; **e. block** bloc *m* moteur, bloc-cylindre *m*; *Aut* **e. braking** frein-moteur *m*; **e. bulkhead** pare-feu *m* de moteur; **e. compartment** compartiment *m* moteur; **e. immobilizer** (dispositif *m*) antidémarrage *m*; **e. management system** commande *f* électronique du moteur; **e. mounting** support *m* moteur; **e. oil** huile *f* moteur; *Aut etc* **e. trouble** panne *f* de moteur

(b) (*Br* **railway** *or Am* **railroad**) **e.** locomotive *f*; **circular e. shed** rotonde *f*

(c) *Arch* (*machine, device*) machine *f*, appareil *m*

engine driver *n Br* (*of locomotive*) conducteur *m*, mécanicien *m*

engineer[1] [endʒɪˈnɪər] *n* **(a)** (*technical specialist*) ingénieur *m*; (*mechanic, repairer*) dépanneur *m*; **civil e.** ingénieur civil; **marine e.** ingénieur du génie maritime; **mechanical e.** ingénieur mécanicien; **mining e.** ingénieur des mines; **consulting e.** ingénieur conseil; **production e.** ingénieur (chargé) de la production; *Tel* **telephone e.** technicien *m* des télécommunications *ou* du téléphone

(b) *Naut* ingénieur *m*, mécanicien *m*; **chief e.** chef *m* mécanicien; **e. officer** ingénieur mécanicien; **second e.** officier *m* mécanicien en second

(c) *Av* **flight e.** (*on military aircraft*) mécanicien *m* navigant; (*on civil aircraft*) mécanicien de bord; **aircraft e.** mécanicien de piste (**d**) *Mil* soldat *m* du génie, sapeur *m*; **the engineers** le génie, l'arme *f* du génie; *Br* **the Royal Engineers,** *US* **the Corps of Engineers** = le Génie

(**e**) *Am Rail* (*driver*) (*of locomotive*) conducteur *m*, mécanicien *m*

(**f**) *Fig* (*instigator*) (*of plan, plot*) âme *f*, instigateur *m*; **her ex-husband was the e. of her downfall** son ex-mari a été l'instigateur de sa ruine

engineer[2] *vt* (**a**) *usu Pej* (*cause, bring about*) (*coup, sb's downfall, defeat*) machiner; (*situation*) manigancer; *Sp* (*goal*) amener; **she engineered his escape** elle a organisé son évasion; **he had carefully engineered the seating arrangements** il avait disposé les convives avec soin (**b**) (*build*) (*bridges, roads*) construire (en qualité d'ingénieur); **the bridge has been superbly engineered** le pont est un superbe travail d'ingénierie

engineering [endʒɪ'nɪərɪŋ] *n* (**a**) *Tech* ingénierie *f*, technique *f* *ou* science *f* de l'ingénieur; **a degree in e.** une licence en ingénierie; **a tremendous feat of e.** une remarquable prouesse technique; **agricultural e.** génie *m* agricole *ou* rural; **civil e.** génie civil; **industrial e.** organisation *f* industrielle; **light e.** petite mécanique *f*; **marine e.** génie maritime; **mechanical e.** mécanique; **precision e.** mécanique de précision; **production e.** technique de la production; *Mktg* **e. attributes** qualités *fpl* techniques; **e. consultant** ingénieur *m* conseil; **e. department** service *m* technique; **e. and design department** bureau *m* d'études; **e. test** test *m* technique; **e. works** atelier *m* de constructions mécaniques

(**b**) *usu Pej* (*planning*) machinations *fpl*, manœuvres *fpl*; **he had participated in the e. of her downfall** il avait participé aux machinations *ou* manœuvres qui ont conduit à sa ruine

engine house *n* bâtiment *m* des machines *ou* des moteurs; (*for fire engines*) dépôt *m*

engineman, *pl* **-men** ['endʒɪnmən, -men] *n Am Rail* mécanicien *m*

engine room *n* salle *f* des machines; *Naut* chambre *f* des machines

engine shed *n* dépôt *m* des locomotives

England ['ɪŋglənd] *n* l'Angleterre *f*; **in E.** en Angleterre; **to go to E.** aller en Angleterre; *Sp* **the E. team** l'équipe d'Angleterre; **an E. player** un joueur de l'équipe d'Angleterre

English ['ɪŋglɪʃ] **1** *adj* anglais; **E. born** *or* **by birth** de naissance anglaise; *Archit* **early E. (style)** premier style *m* gothique; *Culin* **E. breakfast** petit déjeuner *m* à l'anglaise; **E. history** histoire *f* d'Angleterre; *Am* **E. muffin** muffin *m*; *Fig* **an E. rose** *le type idéal de la femme anglaise; qualification souvent donnée à la princesse Diana, par ex.* she's blonde, doe-eyed, sylph-like and softly spoken — just the sort of E. rose type Paul goes for; **E. service** (*in restaurant*) service *m* à l'anglaise

2 *npl* **the E.** les Anglais *mpl*

3 *n Ling* anglais *m*; **she speaks excellent E.** elle parle un anglais excellent, son anglais est excellent; **E.E., British E.** l'anglais d'Angleterre; **American/Australian/Indian/Nigerian E.** l'anglais américain/australien/indien/nigérian; **the King's/Queen's E.** l'anglais correct; **E. speaking** anglophone, de langue anglaise; **to study E.** étudier l'anglais; **to speak E.** parler anglais; **in E.** en anglais; **E. teacher** professeur *m* d'anglais

English Channel *n* **the E.** la Manche

Englishman, *pl* **-men** ['ɪŋglɪʃmən] *n* Anglais *m*; *Prov* **an E.'s home is his castle** tout homme est maître chez lui

Englishwoman, *pl* **-women** ['ɪŋglɪʃwʊmən, -wɪmɪn] *n* Anglaise *f*

engrave [ɪn'greɪv] *vt* graver; **to e. on wood** graver sur bois; **engraved on the memory** gravé dans la mémoire; *Fig* **to be engraved on tablets of stone** être parole d'évangile

engraved [ɪn'greɪvd] *adj attrib* gravé

engraver [ɪn'greɪvə*r*] *n* (*person*) graveur *m*

engraving [ɪn'greɪvɪŋ] *n* (*process, print*) gravure *f*; (*print*) estampe *f*; **line e.** gravure au burin

engross [ɪn'grəʊs] *vt* (**a**) (*sb*) absorber, occuper; **engrossed in her reading** plongée dans sa lecture, toute à sa lecture; **to become engrossed in sth** s'absorber *ou* s'abstraire dans qch (**b**) *Jur* (*document*) (*draw up*) rédiger; (*copy*) grossoyer

engrossing [ɪn'grəʊsɪŋ] *adj* (*study, article, work*) absorbant; (*film, account, book*) captivant

engrossment [ɪn'grəʊsmənt] *n* (**a**) (*absorption*) (*of attention*) absorption *f* (**in** dans); **her total e. in the project meant she** ... ce projet l'absorbait tellement qu'elle ... (**b**) *Jur* rédaction *f* de la grosse

engulf [ɪn'gʌlf] *vt* engloutir, engouffrer; **to be engulfed by the waves** sombrer dans les flots; **engulfed by the flames** englouti par les flammes; **the house was suddenly engulfed in darkness** la maison a été soudain plongée dans l'obscurité; **a feeling of despair engulfed him** le désespoir l'a terrassé

enhance [ɪn'hɑːns, -'hæns] *vt* (*quality of life, performance, chances*) améliorer; (*sth's worth*) rehausser; (*ability, effect*) renforcer; (*pleasure*) accroître; (*sb's beauty*) mettre en valeur; (*reputation*) agrandir; *Fin* (*pension*) augmenter; *Comptr* améliorer

enhancement [ɪn'hɑːnsmənt, -'hæns-] *n* (*of value*) rehaussement *m*; (*of pleasure*) augmentation *f*; *Comptr* **computer e.** amélioration *f* par ordinateur

enharmonic [enhɑː'mɒnɪk] *adj Mus* enharmonique

enigma [ɪ'nɪgmə] *n* énigme *f*; (*person*) personne *f* énigmatique *ou* mystérieuse

enigmatic [enɪg'mætɪk] *adj* énigmatique, mystérieux

enigmatically [enɪg'mætɪklɪ] *adv* énigmatiquement, mystérieusement

enjoin [ɪn'dʒɔɪn] *vt Fml* enjoindre (**sth on sb** qch à qn); **to e. sb to do sth** enjoindre à qn de faire qch

enjoy [ɪn'dʒɔɪ] **1** *vt* (**a**) (*take pleasure from*) aimer, prendre plaisir à; (*pipe, meal*) savourer; (*music, film, play etc*) aimer; **I don't think you would e. the concert** je ne pense pas que tu aimerais le concert *ou* que le concert te plairait; **I couldn't e. the film knowing what was really happening there** je n'ai pas pu apprécier le film en sachant ce qui se passait réellement là-bas; **you won't e. the party** tu ne t'amuseras pas à la soirée; **he's someone who really enjoys his food** c'est quelqu'un qui aime la bonne chère; **to e. the fine weather** jouir du beau temps; **to e. life** profiter de la vie; **to e. oneself** s'amuser, se divertir; **they enjoyed themselves hiding in the bushes** ils se sont amusés à se cacher dans les buissons; **e. yourself!** amusez-vous bien!; **to e. doing sth** aimer faire *ou* trouver du plaisir à faire qch; **I e. cooking** j'aime (bien) faire la cuisine; **I enjoyed seeing them make fools of themselves** j'ai pris plaisir à les voir se ridiculiser; **I don't e. being woken up in the middle of the night** je n'aime pas qu'on me réveille en plein milieu de la nuit

(**b**) *esp Fml* (*benefit from*) (*wealth, sb's confidence*) jouir de, posséder; **to e. good health/a high standard of living** jouir d'une bonne santé/d'un haut niveau de vie; *Hum* **to e. bad health** se complaire dans ses maux

2 *vi Am* **e.!** (*before meal*) bon appétit!

enjoyable [ɪn'dʒɔɪəb(ə)l] *adj* (*stay, trip, wine*) agréable; **that was a very e. meal** c'était très bon; **we had a most e. evening** nous avons passé une soirée des plus agréables

enjoyably [ɪn'dʒɔɪəblɪ] *adv* agréablement; **we spent the week most e.** nous avons passé une semaine des plus agréables

enjoyment [ɪn'dʒɔɪmənt] *n* (**a**) (*pleasure*) plaisir *m*; **to get e. out of sth/doing sth** retirer du plaisir de qch/à faire qch; **to take great e. in doing sth** prendre un grand plaisir à faire qch; **the noise spoiled our e. of the music** le bruit nous a empêchés de profiter pleinement de la musique (**b**) *Fml* (*benefit*) (*of right etc*) jouissance *f*

enlarge [ɪn'lɑːdʒ] **1** *vt* (**a**) (*increase in size*) agrandir; (*property*) étendre; (*wealth*) accroître, augmenter; (*hole*) élargir; *Med* (*heart, liver*) hypertrophier; *Phot* (*photograph*) agrandir; **to have** *or* **get a photograph enlarged** faire agrandir une photo (**b**) (*develop*) (*idea*) développer **2** *vi* (**a**) (*increase in size*) s'agrandir; (*of property*) s'étendre; (*of wealth*) augmenter; (*of hole*) s'élargir, s'agrandir; *Med* (*of heart, liver*) s'hypertrophier (**b**) (*speak or write at greater length*) **to e. on** (*subject, importance of sth*) s'étendre sur

enlarged [ɪn'lɑːdʒd] *adj* (*majority*) accru; (*photograph*) agrandi; *Med* (*tonsil, liver*) hypertrophié; **e. edition** (*of reference book*) édition *f* augmentée

enlargement [ɪn'lɑːdʒmənt] *n* (**a**) (*increase*) agrandissement *m*; (*of property*) extension *f*; (*of wealth*) accroissement *m*; (*of hole*) élargissement *m* (**b**) *Phot* (*print, action*) agrandissement *m* (**c**) *Med* (*of heart, spleen*) hypertrophie *f*

enlarger [ɪn'lɑːdʒə*r*] *n Phot* agrandisseur *m*

enlighten [ɪn'laɪt(ə)n] *vt* (*sb*) éclairer (**on, as to** sur); **can somebody e. me as to what is going on?** est-ce que quelqu'un peut m'expliquer ce qui se passe?; **the programme didn't really e. me as to why ...** l'émission ne m'a pas vraiment éclairé sur la raison pour laquelle ...

enlightened [ɪn'laɪt(ə)nd] *adj* (*person, criticism*) éclairé; *Hist* **e. despot** despote *m* éclairé; **to be sexually e.** (*liberal*) avoir les idées larges sur le plan de la sexualité; (*knowledgeable*) avoir de bonnes connaissances en matière de sexualité

enlightenment [ɪn'laɪtənmənt] *n* (**a**) éclaircissement *m* (**on** sur); **for your e.** pour votre édification (**b**) *Hist* **the (Age of) E.** le Siècle des lumières

enlist [ɪn'lɪst] **1** *vt* (*supporters*) recruter; *Mil* (*soldier*) enrôler, engager; (*sb's support, help, sympathy*) s'assurer; **to e. sb's**

support for a cause rallier qn à une cause; **she enlisted the help of two bystanders** elle a obtenu de l'aide de la part de deux spectateurs **2** *vi Mil* (*of soldier*) s'engager

enlisted [ɪnˈlɪstɪd] *adj Mil* enrôlé, engagé, appelé (sous les drapeaux); *US* **e. man** simple soldat *m*; **e. men** hommes *mpl* de troupe

enlistment [ɪnˈlɪstmənt] *n Mil* engagement *m*

enliven [ɪnˈlaɪv(ə)n] *vt* (*sb, conversation*) animer; (*party*) égayer, animer; **she had been enlivened by the visit of her grandson** la visite de son petit-fils l'avait égayée

en masse [ˈɒnˈmæs] *adv* en masse, tous ensemble

enmesh [ɪnˈmeʃ] *vt* (*sb*) prendre dans un piège; (*in net*) prendre au filet; *Fig* **to be enmeshed in a situation** être empêtré dans une situation

enmity [ˈenmɪtɪ] *n* inimitié *f*, hostilité *f*; **she felt no e. for** *or* **towards him** elle ne ressentait aucune inimitié *ou* hostilité à son égard; **religious and ethnic enmities** hostilités religieuses et ethniques

ennoble [ɪˈnəʊb(ə)l] *vt* **(a)** (*raise to the nobility*) (*commoner*) anoblir **(b)** (*make nobler*) (*sb, character*) ennoblir

ennoblement [ɪˈnəʊb(ə)lmənt] *n* **(a)** (*of commoner*) anoblissement *m* **(b)** (*of character etc*) ennoblissement *m*

ennobling [ɪˈnəʊblɪŋ] *adj* (*effect, experience*) ennoblissant

ennui [ɒnˈwiː] *n* ennui *m*; **this feeling of e.** cet ennui

enormity [ɪˈnɔːmɪtɪ] *n* (*of crime*) énormité *f*; **enormities** énormités, atrocités *fpl*

enormous [ɪˈnɔːməs] *adj* (*building, hands, sum, difference, improvement*) énorme; (*gratitude, patience, whisky*) immense; (*power, intelligence*) colossal, -aux; (*loss*) gigantesque; (*idiot, stupidity*) monumental, -aux

enormously [ɪˈnɔːməslɪ] *adv* énormément; **I was e. grateful** j'étais infiniment reconnaissant

enormousness [ɪˈnɔːməsnɪs] *n* immensité *f*; (*of problems*) énormité *f*

enough [ɪˈnʌf] **1** *adj, n* assez (de); **(not) e. money** (pas) assez d'argent; **will this be e.?** est-ce que ça suffira?; **I've had e. of it/them** (*fed up with*) j'en ai assez; **I've had e. to drink** j'ai assez bu; **that's e. for me** cela me suffit; **that's e.** (*to eat, drink*) c'est assez, ça suffit; (*of your behaviour*) en voilà assez!, ça suffit!; **e. is e.** il ne faut pas exagérer; **he started to help her but then decided that e. was e.** il a d'abord essayé de l'aider mais il a ensuite décidé qu'il en avait déjà assez fait; **more than e.** plus qu'il n'en faut, plus que suffisant; **there was more than e.** il y en avait de reste; **you've said more than e. already** tu en as déjà largement assez dit; **have you e. to pay?** avez-vous de quoi payer?; **wages that are not e. to live on** salaire qui ne suffit pas pour vivre; **he has e. to live on** il a de quoi vivre; **e. said!** assez parlé!; **e. of this nonsense!** assez de ces bêtises!; **one word was e. to prove that ...** il a suffi d'un mot pour prouver que ...; **it was e. to drive you crazy** c'était à vous rendre fou; *Prov* **e. is as good as a feast** assez vaut (un) festin

2 *adv* [①A25,d,v] **(a)** (*sufficiently*) assez; **good e.** assez bon; **fair e.!** ça va!, d'accord!; **it's a good e. reason** c'est une raison comme une autre; **she is not strong e.** elle n'est pas assez forte; **to be near e. to see** être assez près pour voir; **I haven't been here long e. to say** cela ne fait pas assez longtemps que je suis ici pour le savoir; **he didn't try (hard) e.** il n'a pas assez essayé

(b) (*intensive*) **you know well e. what I mean** vous savez très bien ce que je veux dire; **curiously** *or* **oddly e., nobody knew anything about it** chose curieuse, personne n'en savait rien

en passant [ɒnpæˈsɒn] *adv Chess, Fig* en passant

enplane [enˈpleɪn] *vt* embarquer

enquire [ɪŋˈkwaɪər] *vti* = **inquire**

enquiry [ɪnˈkwaɪ(ə)rɪ] *n* = **inquiry**

enrage [ɪnˈreɪdʒ] *vt* (*sb*) rendre furieux, exaspérer; **she was enraged by the government's complacency** la complaisance du gouvernement la rendait furieuse *ou* l'exaspérait

enrapture [ɪnˈræptʃər] *vt* éblouir, émerveiller

enraptured [ɪnˈræptʃəd] *adj* ébloui, émerveillé

enrich [ɪnˈrɪtʃ] *vt* (*person, language etc*) enrichir; (*soil*) fertiliser, amender; *Aut* **to e. the mixture** enrichir le mélange

enriched [ɪnˈrɪtʃd] *adj* **e. with gold** rehaussé d'or; **e. with vitamin C** enrichi à la vitamine C; *Nucl Phys* **e. uranium** uranium *m* enrichi

enriching [ɪnˈrɪtʃɪŋ] *adj* (*experience*) enrichissant

enrichment [ɪnˈrɪtʃmənt] *n* enrichissement *m*; (*of soil*) fertilisation *f*, amendement *m*

enrol, *US* **enroll** [ɪnˈrəʊl] **(enrolled; enrolling) 1** *vt* (*recruits*) enrôler, encadrer; (*workers*) embaucher; (*students*) immatriculer; **to e. oneself** (*in army*) s'enrôler, s'engager (**in** dans); (*in a society*) s'inscrire **2** *vi* s'enrôler, s'engager; (*in a society*) s'inscrire (**in** dans); (*for course*) s'inscrire (**for** à); **to e. for a course of lectures** s'inscrire pour une série de conférences

enrolment, *US* **enrollment** [ɪnˈrəʊlmənt] *n* (*of soldiers etc*) enrôlement *m*; (*of workers*) embauche *f*; (*of students*) immatriculation *f*

Ens *abbr* **Ensign**

ensconce [ɪnˈskɒns] *vt* **to e. oneself** (*in armchair*) s'installer confortablement; (*in corner*) se nicher; **she was ensconced in her favourite chair** elle était confortablement installée dans son fauteuil préféré

ensemble [ɒnˈsɒmb(ə)l] *n* (*clothing etc*), *Mus* ensemble *m*

enshrine [ɪnˈʃraɪn] *vt Rel* enchâsser (**in** dans); *Fig* **this right is enshrined in the constitution** ce droit fait partie intégrante de la constitution

ensign [ˈensaɪn] *n* **(a)** (*flag*) drapeau *m*; *Naut* pavillon *m* national; *Br Naut* **white e.** = pavillon de la Marine anglaise et du Royal Yacht Squadron; *Br Naut* **red e.** = pavillon marchand **(b)** *US* (*officer*) enseigne *m* (*de vaisseau de deuxième classe*)

ensilage [enˈsaɪlɪdʒ] *n Agr* ensilage *m*, silotage *m*

enslave [ɪnˈsleɪv] *vt* réduire à l'esclavage, asservir

enslavement [ɪnˈsleɪvmənt] *n* (*of nation etc*) réduction *f* à l'esclavage, asservissement *m*

ensnare [ɪnˈsneər] *vt* (*animal*) prendre au piège; *Pej* (*of woman*) attirer dans ses filets; **she used her beauty to e. him into marrying her** elle s'est servi de sa beauté comme d'un appât pour qu'il l'épouse; **he was ensnared by her charms** il a été enjôlé par ses charmes

ensue [ɪnˈsjuː] *vi* s'ensuivre; **a long silence ensued** il se fit un long silence

ensuing [ɪnˈsjuːɪŋ] *adj* (*in the past*) qui a/ont suivi(s), suivant; (*in the future*) qui suivra/suivront; (*negotiations*) ultérieur, postérieur

en suite [ˈɒnˈswiːt] **1** *n* (*bathroom*) salle *f* de bain particulière **2** *adv* **with a bathroom e.** avec salle de bain particulière **3** *adj* (*bathroom*) particulier

ensure [ɪnˈʃʊər] *vt* assurer; **I have taken steps to e. that ...** j'ai pris des mesures pour que ... + *sub*; **it is the police's job to e. that the public are protected** c'est à la police de faire en sorte que le public soit protégé

ENT [iːenˈtiː] *n Med* (*abbr* **ear nose and throat**) O. R. L. *f*

entail¹ [ˈenteɪl] *n* **(a)** *Jur* (*act*) substitution *f* **(b)** (*property*) bien *m* substitué **(c)** (*inheritance*) héritage *m* inéluctable

entail² [enˈteɪl] *vt* **(a)** (*involve*) (*expenditure*) entraîner, occasionner; (*a lot of work*) imposer; (*difficulties*) comporter; (*in logic*) entraîner; **it entailed my going to London** cela exigeait que je me rende à Londres; **the job entails working unsociable hours** ce travail nécessite que l'on travaille en dehors des heures régulières **(b)** *Jur* **to e. an estate** substituer un bien (**on sb** au profit de qn); **entailed estate** bien *m* substitué

entangle [ɪnˈtæŋg(ə)l] *vt* **(a)** (*catch*) empêtrer; **to get** *or* **become entangled in sth** (*of person, animal*) s'empêtrer dans qch; (*of string, raincoat belt, hair*) s'enchevêtrer dans qch **(b)** (*mix up*) (*hair, thread*) emmêler; (*wire*) enchevêtrer; **to get** *or* **become entangled** s'emmêler, s'embrouiller **(c)** *Fig* embarrasser, empêtrer; **to become entangled in lies/sb's problems** s'empêtrer dans des mensonges/les problèmes de qn; **to get entangled with sb** (*emotionally*) avoir une liaison avec qn; **he got himself entangled with criminals** il s'est retrouvé mêlé à *ou F* embringué avec des criminels

entanglement [ɪnˈtæŋg(ə)lmənt] *n* **(a)** embrouillement *m*, enchevêtrement *m*; *Mil* **barbed wire e.** réseau(x) *m(pl)* de fil de fer barbelé **(b)** *Fig* **e. with the law/the police** accrochage *m* avec la loi/la police; **emotional entanglements** complications *fpl* sentimentales; **an e. with a woman** une liaison avec une femme

entente [ɒnˈtɒnt] *n* entente *f*; *Hist* **e. cordiale** entente cordiale

enter¹ [ˈentər] **(-r-) 1** *vt* **(a)** (*go or come into*) (*house, country etc*) entrer dans; **to e. the war** entrer en guerre; **the bullet had entered his heart** la balle lui avait pénétré dans le cœur; **it never entered my head that ...** il ne m'est pas venu à l'esprit que ...

(b) (*join*) **to e. the Army/Navy** entrer dans l'armée/dans la marine; **to e. the Church** entrer dans les ordres; **to e. a university/convent** entrer à une université/dans un couvent; **to e. sb's service** entrer au service de qn

(c) (*begin*) **to e. one's sixtieth year** entrer dans sa soixantième année

(d) (*include, register*) **to e. a name on a list** inscrire *ou* porter un nom sur une liste; **to e. sb for an exam** inscrire qn à un examen; **to e. sb for a race** inscrire qn au nombre des participants d'une course; **to e. a horse for a race** engager un cheval dans une course; *Com* **to e. goods** (*in customs*) déclarer des marchandises en douane; *Acct* **to e. an item in the ledger** inscrire *ou* porter un article au grand livre; *Acct* **to e. sth to** *or* **against sb** porter *ou* inscrire qch au compte de qn; *Acct* **to e. sth in the accounts** compatibiliser qch; **to e. a protest** protester formellement

(**e**) (*take part in*) (*race, competition*) participer à

(**f**) *Comptr* (*data*) entrer, introduire

2 *vi* (**a**) entrer (**through** par); *Th* **e. Hamlet** entre Hamlet

(**b**) (*take part*) **to e. for a race** se faire inscrire pour une course; **to e. for an examination** se présenter à un examen; **are you going to e.?** (*for competition, exam*) est-ce que tu vas te présenter?

enter[2] *n Comptr* touche *f* (d')entrée; **press e.** appuyer sur la touche entrée; **e. key** touche *f* (d')entrée

▶ **enter into** *vipo* (**a**) (*begin*) (*service, relationship*) entrer en; (*business, dispute*) entrer dans; (*negotiations*) engager; (*agreement*) conclure, passer; (*contract*) passer; **to e. into partnership with sb** s'associer avec qn; *Lit* **to e. into holy matrimony** se marier; **to e. into** (**a**) **conversation with sb** engager une conversation avec qn (**b**) (*have part in*) (*decision*) peser sur, influencer; **money doesn't e. into it** l'argent n'entre pas en jeu *ou* en ligne de compte (**c**) **to e. into the spirit of the game** entrer dans le jeu

▶ **enter on** *vipo* (**a**) (*commence*) débuter (dans), commencer, entamer; **she has entered on a new career** elle a commencé une nouvelle carrière (**b**) *Jur* (*property*) entrer en possession de, prendre possession de

▶ **enter up** *vtsep Com* **to e. up an item in the ledger** inscrire *ou* porter un article au grand livre

▶ **enter upon** *vipo* = **enter on**

enteric [en'terɪk] *adj Med* entérique; **e. fever** fièvre *f* typhoïde, paratyphoïde *f*

entering ['entərɪŋ] *n Comptr* (*of command, character*) entrée *f*; (*of data*) entrée *f*, introduction *f*; **e. of an order** enregistrement *m* d'une commande

enteritis [entə'raɪtɪs] *n Med* entérite *f*

enterprise ['entəpraɪz] *n* (**a**) (*undertaking*) entreprise *f* (difficile) (**b**) *Com* (*business*) entreprise *f*; **free e.** la libre entreprise; **private e.** l'entreprise privée (**c**) (*initiative*) **to show e.** faire preuve d'un esprit entreprenant; **man of great e.** homme entreprenant; **to lack e.** manquer d'initiative; **to be full of e., to have a lot of e.** être très entreprenant

enterprising ['entəpraɪzɪŋ] *adj* entreprenant; (*imaginative*) plein d'imagination; (*solution*) imaginatif, ingénieux

enterprisingly ['entəpraɪzɪŋlɪ] *adv* d'une façon entreprenante; (*to repair sth*) ingénieusement

entertain [entə'teɪn] **1** *vt* (**a**) (*amuse*) divertir, amuser; **she entertained us with stories of her travels** elle nous a divertis en nous racontant ses histoires de voyages; **to keep sb entertained** divertir *ou* amuser qn

(**b**) *esp Fml* **to e. guests** recevoir (des invités); **we are entertaining them to dinner next Tuesday** nous les avons invités à dîner mardi prochain

(**c**) (*consider, accept*) (*proposition, opinion*) admettre, accueillir; (*request*) faire un accueil favorable à; **he wasn't prepared to e. the idea** il se refusait à considérer cette idée

(**d**) (*harbour*) (*fears, suspicions*) éprouver; (*hope, idea, doubts*) nourrir; (*illusion*) chérir, caresser

2 *vi* offrir une réception; **they e. a great deal** ils reçoivent beaucoup (de monde)

entertainer [entə'teɪnər] *n* (**a**) *Th etc* artiste *mf* de cabaret, fantaisiste *mf*; (*comedian*) comique *mf*; **TV e.** animateur, -trice de la télé (**b**) (*of guests*) **they never were big entertainers** ils n'ont jamais beaucoup reçu

entertaining [entə'teɪnɪŋ] **1** *adj* divertissant; (*funny, amusing*) amusant **2** *n* (*of guests*) réception *f*; **they do a lot of e.** ils reçoivent beaucoup; **he never liked e.** il n'a jamais aimé recevoir

entertainingly [entə'teɪnɪŋlɪ] *adv* d'une manière divertissante; (*in funny or amusing way*) d'une manière amusante

entertainment [entə'teɪnmənt] *n* (**a**) (*amusement*) divertissement *m*, amusement *m*; **much to the e. of the crowd** au grand amusement de la foule; **to be good e. value** être amusant *ou* divertissant

(**b**) *Th etc* spectacle *m*, divertissement *m*; **the e. business** l'industrie *f* du spectacle; **entertainments director** (*at holiday centre etc*) directeur *m* de l'animation; **entertainments guide** guide *m* des spectacles; **entertainments officer** (*on ship*) = officier *m* chargé des spectacles, animateur *m*; **entertainments team** équipe *f* d'animation; **e. tax** taxe *f* sur les spectacles

(**c**) (*hospitality*) hospitalité *f*; (*reception*) réception *f*, fête *f*; *Com* **e. allowance** indemnité *f* de représentation; *Com* **e. expenses** frais *mpl* de représentation

enthral, *US* **enthrall** [ɪn'θrɔːl] *vt* (**enthralled; enthralling**) (*of spectacle, speaker*) captiver, passionner; (*of object, beauty*) fasciner; (*of prospect, idea*) enthousiasmer, exalter; **we were enthralled by his stories** nous étions captivés par ses histoires

enthralling [ɪn'θrɔːlɪŋ] *adj* (*spectacle, speaker etc*) captivant, passionnant; (*object, beauty*) fascinant; (*prospect, idea*) exaltant, enthousiasmant

enthrallingly [ɪn'θrɔːlɪŋlɪ] *adv* d'une manière captivante; **e. beautiful** d'une beauté fascinante

enthrone [ɪn'θrəʊn] *vt* (*king*) mettre sur le trône; (*bishop*) introniser

enthronement [ɪn'θrəʊnmənt] *n* intronisation *f*

enthuse [ɪn'θjuːz] **1** *vi* s'enthousiasmer (**over, about** pour) **2** *vt* enthousiasmer

enthusiasm [ɪn'θjuːzɪæz(ə)m] *n* enthousiasme *m* (**for, about** pour); **to show/feel little e. for sth** faire preuve de/se sentir peu d'enthousiasme pour qch

enthusiast [ɪn'θjuːzɪæst] *n* enthousiaste *mf*; (*of golf etc*) fanatique *mf*; (*of music*) passionné, -ée; **Harold, long an e. of privatization** Harold, partisan *ou* adepte de longue date de la privatisation; **a great Shakespeare e.** un grand amateur de Shakespeare

enthusiastic [ɪnθjuːzɪ'æstɪk] *adj* enthousiaste; (*angler etc*) passionné; **to be very e. about sth** être très enthousiaste à l'égard de qch; **to become e. about sth** s'enthousiasmer pour qch; *Iron* **don't sound so e.!** tu pourrais te montrer un peu plus enthousiaste!

enthusiastically [ɪnθjuːzɪ'æstɪklɪ] *adv* avec enthousiasme; **to accept e.** accepter d'enthousiasme

entice [ɪn'taɪs] *vt* attirer, séduire; **to e. sb to do sth** convaincre *ou* persuader qn de faire qch; **she'll never be able to e. him away from his wife** elle n'arrivera jamais à le séduire au point de lui faire quitter sa femme; **to e. sb away from a company** appâter qn pour qu'il quitte une entreprise; **they used a prostitute to e. him into the bar** ils se sont servi d'une prostituée pour le séduire et l'attirer dans le bar; **she used it to e. the mouse out from under the cooker** elle s'en est servi pour faire sortir la souris de sous la cuisinière

enticement [ɪn'taɪsmənt] *n* (**a**) *Jur* (*act*) séduction *f* (**b**) (*charm*) attrait *m*, charme *m* (**c**) (*lure*) appât *m*; **to offer an e.** offrir une gratification

enticing [ɪn'taɪsɪŋ] *adj* (*offer, idea etc*) séduisant, tentant, attrayant; (*publicity poster*) tentant; (*dish*) alléchant; (*smile*) charmeur, séduisant; **the water doesn't look very e.** l'eau n'est pas très tentante

enticingly [ɪn'taɪsɪŋlɪ] *adv* d'une manière séduisante *ou* attrayante; **the sky was e. blue** le ciel était d'un bleu tentant; **she smiled at him e.** elle lui adressa un sourire charmeur *ou* séduisant; **the food smelt e. good** la nourriture dégageait une odeur alléchante; **the holiday was e. cheap** le prix de ces vacances était tentant *ou* attrayant

entire [ɪn'taɪər] *adj* (**a**) (*whole*) entier, tout; **the e. population** la population (tout) entière; **the e. day** toute la journée; **she read the e. book in an afternoon** elle a lu le livre en entier *ou* tout le livre en l'espace d'un après-midi; **she didn't say one new thing in the e. speech** elle n'a pas dit une seule chose nouvelle dans tout le discours; **the e. business had proved to be a complete waste of time** toute l'affaire s'est résumée à une pure perte de temps; **to enjoy sb's e. confidence** jouir de l'entière confiance de qn (**b**) (*intact*) entier, intact

entirely [ɪn'taɪəlɪ] *adv* entièrement, tout à fait, complètement; **to agree e. with sb** être entièrement *ou* tout à fait d'accord avec qn; **almost e.** presque entièrement *ou* complètement; **you are e. mistaken** vous vous trompez du tout au tout

entirety [ɪn'taɪərətɪ] *n* intégralité *f*, intégrité *f*; (*of domain etc*) totalité *f*; **in its e.** en entier, intégralement, dans son entier; **to consider sth in its e.** considérer qch dans son entier; **the skeleton had been preserved in its e.** le squelette avait été intégralement conservé

entitle [ɪn'taɪt(ə)l] *vt* (**a**) (*give right to*) donner le droit à (**to** à); **to e. sb to do sth** donner (le) droit à qn de faire qch; **to be entitled to sth** avoir droit à qch; **to be entitled to do sth** avoir le droit de faire qch; **the very least I am entitled to is an explanation** je pourrais quand même avoir une explication, c'est la moindre des choses!; *Jur* **to be entitled to inherit** être apte *ou* habilité à hériter (**b**) (*give title to*) (*book, chapter, song etc*) intituler (**c**) (*give aristocratic title to*) **to e. sb duke/prince/***etc* donner à qn le titre de duc/prince/*etc*

entitlement [ɪn'taɪt(ə)lmənt] *n* = ce qui revient de droit à qn; (*money*) allocation *f* (*à laquelle on a droit*); (**annual**) **holiday e.** congé *m* annuel (*auquel on a droit*)

entity [ˈentɪtɪ] *n* entité *f*
entomb [ɪnˈtuːm] *vt* (*bury*) mettre dans la tombe, mettre au tombeau; (*of ruins etc*) (*sb*) ensevelir
entombment [ɪnˈtuːmmənt] *n* mise *f* au tombeau; (*by ruins*) ensevelissement *m*
entomological [entəməˈlɒdʒɪk(ə)l] *adj* entomologique
entomologist [entəˈmɒlədʒɪst] *n* entomologiste *mf*
entomology [entəˈmɒlədʒɪ] *n* entomologie *f*
entourage [ɒntuːˈrɑːʒ] *n* entourage *m*
entr'acte [ɒnˈtrækt] *n Th* entracte *m*
entrails [ˈentreɪlz] *npl* entrailles *fpl*; *Fig* **to study the e.** prendre les augures
entrain [ɪnˈtreɪn] *Mil* **1** *vt* (*troops etc*) embarquer, faire embarquer en train **2** *vi* s'embarquer (en train)
entrance¹ [ˈentrəns] *n* **(a)** (*way in*) entrée *f*; **main e.** entrée principale; **the e. is at the rear** (*of bus etc*) l'entrée s'effectue par l'arrière; **e. gate** grille *f* d'entrée; **e. hall** (*of house*) vestibule *m*; (*of large house, hotel*) hall *m* **(b)** (*act of entering*) entrée *f*; *Th, Fig* **to make one's e.** faire son entrée; **to force an e. into a house** forcer l'entrée d'une maison; **to gain e. to a building** s'introduire *ou* pénétrer dans un immeuble **(c)** (*admission*) (*to association, club etc*) admission *f*; (*to cinema*) entrée *f*; **to refuse sb e.** (*to association, restaurant*) refuser l'accès à qn
entrance² [ɪnˈtrɑːns] *vt* (*person*) extasier, ravir, transporter; **to be entranced by …** s'extasier sur …, être en extase devant …; **I was entranced by the music** j'étais transporté par la musique; **they all sat entranced** ils étaient tous fascinés
entrance examination *n* examen *m* d'entrée
entrance fee *n* droit *m* d'entrée; (*to association, club*) droit d'inscription
entrance qualifications/requirements *npl Univ* conditions *fpl* d'admission
entrancing [ɪnˈtrɑːnsɪŋ] *adj* (*beauty, sight*) enchanteur, -eresse; (*story*) passionnant; (*melody*) ravissant
entrancingly [ɪnˈtrɑːnsɪŋlɪ] *adv* à ravir; (*to sing, to smile etc*) de façon enchanteresse; **to be e. beautiful** être beau à ravir
entrant [ˈentrənt] *n* (*in race, competition*) inscrit, -ite; (*in examination*) candidat, -ate; (*in profession*) débutant, -ante; *Com* (*on market*) acteur *m*
entrap [ɪnˈtræp] *vt* (**-pp-**) *also US Jur* prendre au piège, piéger; **to e. sb into doing sth** prendre qn au piège *ou* piéger qn pour qu'il fasse qch; **he claimed that his client had been entrapped into committing a crime** il prétendait que son client avait été piégé et forcé à commettre un crime
entrapment [ɪnˈtræpmənt] *n US Jur* = coup *m* monté par la police pour piéger un criminel
entreat [ɪnˈtriːt] *vt* **to e. sb to do sth** prier *ou* implorer *ou* supplier qn de faire qch; **they entreated him to stay** ils l'implorèrent *ou* le supplièrent de rester; *Lit* **be merciful, I e. you** ayez pitié, je vous en implore *ou* supplie
entreating [ɪnˈtriːtɪŋ] *adj* (*tone, look*) suppliant, implorant
entreatingly [ɪnˈtriːtɪŋlɪ] *adv* d'un air suppliant *ou* implorant
entreaty [ɪnˈtriːtɪ] *n Fml* prière *f*, supplication *f*; **at sb's urgent e.** sur les vives instances de qn; **look of e.** regard suppliant
entrée [ˈɒntreɪ] *n* **(a)** *Culin* (*dish before the main course*) entrée *f*; *US* (*as main course*) plat *m* de résistance **(b)** (*right of entry*) entrée *f* (**to, into** dans)
entrench [ɪnˈtrentʃ] *vt Mil*, (*camp, town*) retrancher; *Fig* **to e. oneself behind** *or* **in sth** se retrancher *ou* se terrer derrière qch
entrenched [ɪnˈtrentʃt] *adj Mil, Fig* retranché; (*views, ideas*) arrêté; (*customs*) enraciné; **an e. position** une position de retranchement
entrenchment [ɪnˈtrentʃmənt] *n Mil, Fig* retranchement *m*
entrepôt [ˈɒntrəpəʊ] *n* entrepôt *m*
entrepreneur [ɒntrəprəˈnɜːr] *n* entrepreneur *m*
entrepreneurial [ɒntrəprəˈnɜːrɪəl] *adj* (*skills, talents*) d'entrepreneur; (*person, class*) qui a l'esprit d'entreprise; **his e. success** son succès en tant qu'entrepreneur
entrepreneurship [ɒntrəprəˈnɜːʃɪp] *n* esprit *m* d'entreprise
entropy [ˈentrəpɪ] *n* entropie *f*
entrust [ɪnˈtrʌst] *vt* **to e. sth to sb** confier qch à qn; **to e. a secret/a child to sb** confier un secret/un enfant à qn; **to e. sb with** (*task etc*) charger qn de; (*mission*) investir qn de; **to e. sb with the task** *or* **job of doing sth** charger qn de faire qch; **to e. sb with the care of sth** commettre qch à la garde de qn; **to be entrusted with the sale of sth** être chargé de la vente de qch
entry [ˈentrɪ] *n* **(a)** (*act of entering*) entrée *f* (**(in)to** dans); (*to world of politics etc*) début *m* (**(in)to** dans); **to gain e. to a house** pénétrer dans une maison; *Jur* **illegal e. (of a dwelling)** violation *f* de domicile; **to make one's e.** faire son entrée; (*of actor*) entrer en scène; (*of new politician, artist*) faire ses débuts; **right of free e.** droit *m* de passer librement les frontières; **no e.** entrée interdite; (*in one way street*) sens interdit
(b) (*way in*) entrée *f* (**to** de)
(c) (*writing down*) (*of a record*) enregistrement *m*; (*of name in a list, in bookkeeping*) inscription *f*; (*item*) article *m*, poste *m*, écriture *f*; (*in dictionary, encyclopaedia*) article; *Acct* **single/double e.** comptabilité *f* en partie simple/double; **to make an e.** (*in bookkeeping*) porter un article à compte; (*in journal etc*) inscrire quelque chose; **author/subject entries** (*in cataloguing*) fiches *fpl* auteur/sujet; *Naut* **e. in the log** élément *m* du journal de bord
(d) *Sp etc* (*of competitor*) inscription *f*; (*list of competitors*) liste *f* de concurrents; **there are twenty entries** il y a vingt participants; **a big/small e.** une forte/faible participation
entry card *n* (*for entry to a country*) fiche *f* de police (au débarquement)
entry form *n* feuille *f* d'inscription
entryism [ˈentrɪɪz(ə)m] *n Pol* entrisme *m*, noyautage *m*
entryist [ˈentrɪɪst] *n, adj Pol* entriste *mf*
entry-level *adj* (*car, computer*) d'entrée de gamme
entryphone [ˈentrɪfəʊn] *n* interphone *m*
entry tax *n* taxe *f* d'entrée
entry visa *n* visa *m* d'entrée
entwine [ɪnˈtwaɪn] **1** *vt* **to e. sth round sth** enlacer qch autour de qch; **to become entwined** (*of one thing, ribbon etc*) s'enlacer; (*of two or more things, ribbons etc*) s'entrelacer; **with arms entwined** les bras entrelacés; **her hair was entwined with ribbons** ses cheveux étaient entrelacés de rubans **2** *vi* s'enlacer (**round** autour de); (*of two or more things*) s'entrelacer
E-number *n* additif *m* (dont le code commence par E)
enumerate [ɪˈnjuːməreɪt] *vt* (*reasons, one's services etc*) énumérer, détailler, dénombrer
enumeration [ɪnjuːməˈreɪʃən] *n* énumération *f*, dénombrement *m*, recensement *m*
enunciate [ɪˈnʌnsɪeɪt] **1** *vt* **(a)** (*pronounce clearly*) (*sounds, words*) prononcer, articuler **(b)** *Fml* (*state clearly*) (*opinion etc*) énoncer, déclarer **2** *vi* **to e. clearly** articuler distinctement
enunciation [ɪnʌnsɪˈeɪʃən] *n* **(a)** (*pronunciation*) articulation *f*; (*of word*) prononciation *f* **(b)** *Fml* (*of opinion etc*) énonciation *f*; *Math* (*of problem*) énoncé *m*
enuresis [enjʊˈriːsɪs] *n Med* énurésie *f*
envelop [ɪnˈveləp] *vt* (**-p-**) envelopper (**in** dans, de); **enveloped in mist/cloud** (*countryside*) enveloppé *ou* voilé de brume/par les nuages
envelope [ˈenvələʊp, *occ* ˈɒnvələʊp] *n* **(a)** (*for letter*) enveloppe *f*; **window e.** enveloppe à fenêtre; **to put a letter in an e.** mettre une lettre sous enveloppe; **in a sealed e.** sous pli cacheté; **in the same e.** sous le même pli; **e. file** chemise *f* (de carton) **(b)** (*covering*) enveloppe *f*; *Biol* (*of organ*) enveloppe, tunique *f*
envelopment [ɪnˈveləpmənt] *n* enveloppement *m*
envenom [ɪnˈvenəm] *vt* envenimer
enviable [ˈenvɪəb(ə)l] *adj* enviable, digne d'envie; **in the e. position of being offered two jobs** dans la position enviable de se voir proposer deux emplois
enviably [ˈenvɪəblɪ] *adv* d'une manière enviable; **e. rich/well-read** d'une richesse/culture enviable
envious [ˈenvɪəs] *adj* envieux; **I'm so e.!** comme je t'/l'/*etc* envie!; **my sister's got a big house but I'm not e.** ma sœur a une grande maison, mais je ne l'envie pas; **e. glances** regards *mpl* d'envie; **to be e. of sb/sth** envier qn/qch; **to look at sb with e. eyes** regarder qn d'un œil jaloux; **to make sb e.** rendre qn jaloux
enviously [ˈenvɪəslɪ] *adv* (*to speak*) avec envie; (*to look at sth*) d'un œil jaloux
environment [ɪnˈvaɪrənmənt] *n* **(a)** (*surroundings*) milieu *m*; **in an office/a hospital e.** dans un bureau/milieu hospitalier; **natural e.** milieu naturel **(b)** *Ecol* **the e.** l'environnement *m*; **Department** *or* **Ministry of the E.** = ministère *m* de (la Protection de la Nature et de) l'Environnement **(c)** *Comptr* environnement *m*
environmental [ɪnvaɪrənˈment(ə)l] *adj* (*conditions*) qui ont rapport à l'environnement; (*change*) de l'environnement; (*brought about by the environment*) produit par l'environnement; **chemicals that cause e. damage** produits chimiques nuisibles à l'environnement; **the company must improve its e. performance** la société doit améliorer ses performances en matière d'environnement; **e. (protection) group** groupe *m* écologiste, groupe de protection de l'environnement; **e. impact** impact *m* sur l'environnement
environmentalist [ɪnvaɪrənˈmentəlɪst] **1** *n* écologiste *mf* **2** *adj* (*issues, politics*) écologique
environmentally [ɪnvaɪrənˈmentəlɪ] *adv* du point de vue de

l'environnement; **e. friendly** qui ne nuit pas à l'environnement, non polluant, non nuisible à l'environnement; **E. Sensitive Area** = zone *f* de protection de la nature désignée par la CE où les agriculteurs doivent utiliser des méthodes traditionnelles

environment-friendly *adj* (*product*) qui ne nuit pas à l'environnement; **to be e.** ne pas nuire à l'environnement

environs [ɪn'vaɪrənz] *npl* (*of town*) environs *mpl*, alentours *mpl*; **New York and its e.** New York et ses environs

envisage [ɪn'vɪzɪdʒ] *vt* (*difficulty etc*) envisager; **I can easily e. something of the kind happening** j'envisage sans peine qu'arrive une chose de ce genre

envision [en'vɪʒən] *vt Am* envisager

envoy ['envɔɪ] *n* (*person*) envoyé, -ée

envy[1] ['envɪ] *n* (**a**) envie *f*, jalousie *f*; **to be green with e.** être dévoré d'envie; **to do sth out of e.** faire qch par envie *ou* jalousie; **to excite sb's e.** exciter *ou* s'attirer l'envie de qn (**b**) (*object of envy*) **to be the e. of sb** être un objet d'envie pour qn

envy[2] *vt* (*person*) envier, porter envie à; **I don't e. you** je ne t'envie pas; **to e. sb sth** envier qch à qn; **I don't e. him having to catch such an early train** je ne l'envie pas d'avoir à prendre le train de si bonne heure; **a job to e.** un métier digne d'envie

enzyme ['enzaɪm] *n Biol, Ch* enzyme *f*, diastase *f*

EOC [iːəʊ'siː] *n Br Admin* (*abbr* **Equal Opportunities Commission**) = organisme *m* désigné par le gouvernement pour veiller à l'application des dispositions relatives aux droits des femmes au travail

Eocene ['iːəʊsiːn] *adj, n Geol* éocène *m*

E&OE [iːənd'əʊiː] *Com* (*abbr* **errors and omissions excepted**) s. e. & o.

eon ['iːən] *n US* = **aeon**

EP [iː'piː] *n* (*abbr* **extended-play (record)**) disque *m* double durée

EPA [iːpiː'eɪ] *n US* (*abbr* **Environmental Protection Agency**) Agence *f* pour la Protection de l'Environnement

epaulette, *US* **epaulet** [epɒ'let] *n Mil* épaulette *f*

ephedrine ['efɪdrɪn] *n Pharm* éphédrine *f*

ephemera, *pl* **-ae, -as** [ɪ'femərə, -iː, -əz] *n* (**a**) chose *f* éphémère (**b**) (*insect*) éphémère *m*

ephemeral [ɪ'femərəl] *adj* éphémère; (*passion*) fugitif; (*beauty*) passager

ephemerid [ɪ'femərɪd] *n* (*insect*) éphémère *m*

epic ['epɪk] **1** *adj* épique **2** *n* (*poem*) poème *m* épique, épopée *f*; (*film*) film *m* à grand spectacle

epicarp ['epɪkɑːp] *n Bot* épicarpe *m*

epicene ['epɪsiːn] *adj Fml* androgyne

epicentre, *US* **epicenter** ['epɪsentər] *n* (*of earthquake*) épicentre *m*

epicure ['epɪkjʊər] *n* (*gourmet*) gourmet *m*, gastronome *mf*

epicurean [epɪkjʊ'riːən] *adj, n, Phil, Fig* épicurien, -ienne

epicyclic [epɪ'saɪklɪk] *adj Tech* **e. gear** engrenage *m* épicycloïdal

epidemic [epɪ'demɪk] **1** *adj* (*disease*) épidémique; *Fig* **corruption has reached e. proportions** la corruption prend des allures d'épidémie **2** *n Med, Fig* épidémie *f*

epidemiological [epɪdiːmɪə'lɒdʒɪk(ə)l] *adj Med* (*evidence, research, study*) épidémiologique

epidemiologist [epɪdiːmɪ'ɒlədʒɪst] *n Med* épidémiologiste *mf*

epidemiology [epɪdiːmɪ'ɒlədʒɪ] *n Med* épidémiologie *f*

epidermis [epɪ'dɜːmɪs] *n Anat* épiderme *m*

epidural [epɪ'djʊər(ə)l] **1** *adj Anat* épidural **2** *n Med* péridurale *f*; **she had an e.** on lui a fait une péridurale

epiglottis [epɪ'glɒtɪs] *n Anat* épiglotte *f*

epigram ['epɪgræm] *n Liter* épigramme *f*

epigrammatic [epɪgrə'mætɪk] *adj* épigrammatique

epigraph ['epɪgræf] *n* épigraphe *f*

epilepsy ['epɪlepsɪ] *n* épilepsie *f*

epileptic [epɪ'leptɪk] **1** *n* épileptique *mf* **2** *adj* épileptique; **e. fit** crise *f* épileptique *ou* d'épilepsie

epilogue ['epɪlɒg] *n Liter, Fig* épilogue *m*

Epiphany [ɪ'pɪfənɪ] *n Rel* Épiphanie *f*

epiphyte ['epɪfaɪt] *n Bot* (plante *f*) épiphyte *m*

episcopacy [ɪ'pɪskəpəsɪ] *n* épiscopat *m*

Episcopal [ɪ'pɪskəp(ə)l] *adj Am Scot* **the E. Church** l'Église *f* épiscopale

episcopal [ɪ'pɪskəp(ə)l] *adj* épiscopal; **e. palace** évêché *m*; **e. ring** anneau *m* pastoral

Episcopalian [ɪpɪskə'peɪlɪən] **1** *n Am Scot* membre *m* de l'Église épiscopale **2** *adj* de l'Église épiscopale

episcopalian [ɪpɪskə'peɪlɪən] *adj, n* épiscopalien, -ienne

episcopate [ɪ'pɪskəpeɪt] *n* épiscopat *m*

episiotomy [əpiːzɪ'ɒtəmɪ] *n Obst* épisiotomie *f*

episode ['epɪsəʊd] *n* (*of story etc*) épisode *m*; (*incident*) incident *m*

episodic [epɪ'sɒdɪk] *adj* épisodique

epistemic [epɪ'stiːmɪk] *adj Phil, Ling* épistémique

epistemology [ɪpɪstɪ'mɒlədʒɪ] *n Phil* épistémologie *f*

epistle [ɪ'pɪs(ə)l] *n* (**a**) *Rel* épître *f*; **e. side** (*of altar*) côté *m* de l'épître (**b**) *Arch, Hum* (*letter*) épître *f*, lettre *f*

epistolary [ɪ'pɪstələrɪ] *adj* (*style, novel*) épistolaire

epitaph ['epɪtæf] *n* épitaphe *f*

epithelium [epɪ'θiːlɪəm] *n Anat* épithélium *m*

epithet ['epɪθet] *n* (①A17-18) épithète *f*

epitome [ɪ'pɪtəmɪ] *n* (**a**) (*perfect example*) **to be the e. of sth** incarner qch; **he is the e. of elegance** il est l'élégance même (**b**) *Arch* (*summary*) épitomé *m*, abrégé *m*

epitomize [ɪ'pɪtəmaɪz] *vt* (*embody*) incarner; **this situation epitomizes what we're up against** cette situation est le parfait exemple de ce contre quoi nous luttons

epizootic [epɪzəʊ'ɒtɪk] *Vet* **1** *adj* (*disease*) épizootique **2** *n* épizootie *f*

epoch ['iːpɒk] *n* époque *f*, âge *m*; **to mark an e.** faire époque, faire date

epoch-making *adj* (*discovery, event*) qui fait époque, qui fait date

eponymous [ɪ'pɒnɪməs] *adj Lit* éponyme

EPOS ['iːpɒs] *n Com* (*abbr* **electronic point of sale**) point *m* de vente électronique

epoxy [ɪ'pɒksɪ] *Ch* **1** *adj* **e. resin** résine *f* époxyde **2** *n* époxyde *m*

EPROM ['iːprɒm] *n Comptr* (*abbr* **erasable programmable ROM**) EPROM *f*, mémoire *f* morte programmable et effaçable

Epsom ['epsəm] *n Pharm* **E. salts** sel *m* d'Epsom

equability [ekwə'bɪlɪtɪ, iːk-] *n* (*of climate, temperature*) uniformité *f*; (*of moods*) égalité *f*

equable ['ekwəb(ə)l] *adj* (*climate, temperature*) uniforme, régulier; **e. temperament** humeur égale; **an e. companion** un compagnon/une compagne à l'humeur égale

equably ['ekwəblɪ] *adv* d'humeur égale; (*to reply, say*) calmement

equal[1] ['iːkwəl] **1** *adj* (**a**) (*same*) égal (**to, with** à); **e. numbers of boys and girls** un nombre égal de garçons et de filles; **to finish e. first/second** finir premier/deuxième ex æquo; **on e. terms** à conditions égales; **to be on e. terms** *or* **on an e. footing with sb** être sur un pied d'égalité avec qn; **in e. measure** en quantité égale; **e. distribution of taxes** péréquation *f* de l'impôt; **all things** *or* **other things being e.** si tout se déroule normalement, si tout va bien; **to be an e. opportunity employer** offrir des chances égales d'emploi à tous; **e. pay for e. work** à travail égal, salaire égal; *Math* **e. sign** signe *m* égal *ou* d'égalité

(**b**) (*of sufficient calibre etc*) **to be e. to (doing) sth** être à la hauteur de (faire) qch; **I don't feel e. to (doing) it** (*I'm too tired etc*) je ne m'en sens pas le courage *ou* la force; (*I'm not good enough*) je ne m'en sens pas à la hauteur; **cinema e. to any in London** cinéma à l'instar des cinémas de Londres

2 *n* égal, -ale; **the service is the e. of a five star hotel** le service est du niveau d'un hôtel cinq étoiles; **your equals** vos pareils, vos égaux; **you won't find her e.** vous ne trouverez pas son semblable; **she's easily his e. at tennis/chemistry** elle l'égale facilement au tennis/en chimie; **to treat sb as an e.** traiter qn d'égal à égal

equal[2] *vt* (**-ll-,** *US* **-l-**) (**a**) (*be equal to*) égaler, être égal à (**in** en); **nothing can e. this splendour** rien ne saurait égaler cette splendeur; **no one has equalled her record** personne n'a égalé son record; **not to be equalled** sans égal, qui n'a pas son égal; **her clumsiness is only equalled by her lack of manners** sa maladresse n'a d'égal que ses mauvaises manières; **I've never seen anything to e. it** je n'ai jamais rien vu qui l'égale (**b**) *Math* (*total*) faire; **four fives e.** *or* **four times five equals twenty** quatre fois cinq font vingt; **let x e. 20** soit x égal à 20

equality [ɪ'kwɒlɪtɪ] *n* égalité *f* (**with sb** avec qn); **e. of opportunity** égalité des chances

equalization [iːkwəlaɪ'zeɪʃən] *n* (**a**) égalisation *f*; *Admin* (*of contributions*) péréquation *f* (**b**) *MecE* équilibrage *m*

equalize ['iːkwəlaɪz] **1** *vt* égaliser (**sth with sth** qch avec qch); (*salaries*) faire la péréquation de; (*chances*) équilibrer; (*forces etc*) compenser, équilibrer **2** *vi Sp* égaliser

equalizer ['iːkwəlaɪzər] *n El* égaliseur *m* de potentiel; (*for sound*) égaliseur; *MecE* compensateur *m*; *Sp* (*point*) point *m* égalisateur; (*goal*) but *m* égalisateur

equalizing ['iːkwəlaɪzɪŋ] *adj* (*current etc*) compensateur; (*pressure*) de compensation; *Sp* **the e. goal** le but égalisateur

equally ['iːkwəlɪ] *adv* (**a**) (*to an equal degree*) tout aussi; **it would be e. wrong/mistaken/rash/***etc* **to ...** ce serait tout aussi faux/erroné/imprudent/*etc* de ...; **I'm e. interested in**

the Baroque period la période baroque m'intéresse tout autant; **she worked e. hard** elle a travaillé tout aussi dur **(b)** (*in equal amounts*) **to contribute e. to the expenses** contribuer pour une part égale à la dépense; **the money was divided e. between the children** l'argent a été partagé de façon égale entre les enfants **(c)** (*likewise*) **e., they may be telling the truth** il se pourrait tout aussi bien qu'ils disent la vérité

equal rights *npl* droits *mpl* égaux

equals sign *n* signe *m* égal

equanimity [iːkwəˈnɪmɪtɪ, ek-] *n Fml* égalité *f* d'âme, équanimité *f*; **to disturb sb's e.** troubler la sérénité de qn; **to recover one's e.** se ressaisir; **with e.** d'une âme égale, avec équanimité

equate [ɪˈkweɪt] *vt* **(a)** (*make equal*) rendre égal **(to, with** à); *Math* (*two expressions etc*) mettre en équation **(b)** (*think of as equal*) **I e. communism with the Soviet Union** j'assimile le communisme à l'Union Soviétique; **to e. Jupiter with Zeus** donner Jupiter comme l'équivalent de Zeus; **to e. Picasso with Michelangelo** voir en Picasso l'égal de Michel-Ange

equating [ɪˈkweɪtɪŋ] *n* **(a)** (*making equal*) égalisation *f*; *Math* mise *f* en équation **(b)** (*thinking of as equal*) assimilation *f*

equation [ɪˈkweɪʒən] *n* **(a)** *Math, Ch, Astron* équation *f*; *Math* **simple/quadratic e.** équation du premier/deuxième degré **(b)** (*making equal*) (*of expenditure to income etc*) égalisation *f* **(c)** (*thinking of as equal*) assimilation *f*; **the e. of fame with success** l'assimilation de la célébrité au succès

equator [ɪˈkweɪtər] *n* équateur *m* (de la terre); **at the e.** sous l'équateur

equatorial [ekwəˈtɔːrɪəl] *adj* équatorial

equerry [ˈekwərɪ] *n* écuyer *m*

equestrian [ɪˈkwestrɪən] **1** *adj usu attrib* (*statue etc*) équestre; *Sp* **e. event** tournoi *m* équestre; **e. performances** exercices *mpl* d'équitation **2** *n* cavalier, -ière; (*in circus*) écuyer, -ère

equidistant [iːkwɪˈdɪstənt] *adj Fml* équidistant **(from** de)

equilateral [iːkwɪˈlæt(ə)rəl] *adj Geom* équilatéral, -aux

equilibrium [iːkwɪˈlɪbrɪəm] *n* équilibre *m*, aplomb *m*; **stable/unstable e.** équilibre stable/instable; **to lose one's e.** perdre l'équilibre; **to maintain one's (inner) e.** garder son équilibre; **to keep sth in e.** maintenir qch en équilibre; **in a state of e.** en équilibre

equine [ˈiːkwaɪn, ˈekwaɪn] **1** *adj* équin; (*race, face*) chevalin **2** *n* équidé *m*

equinoctial [iːkwɪˈnɒkʃəl, ek-] *adj Met* (*line, year etc*) équinoxial; (*storm etc*) d'équinoxe; **e. tides** marées *fpl* d'équinoxe, grandes marées

equinox [ˈiːkwɪnɒks, ˈek-] *n Met* équinoxe *m*; **spring** *or* **vernal e.** équinoxe du printemps, point *m* vernal; **autumn(al) e.** équinoxe d'automne

equip [ɪˈkwɪp] *vt* **(-pp-) (a)** (*provide with equipment*) (*soldier, expedition, kitchen etc*) équiper; (*house*) meubler, monter; (*factory*) outiller, monter; **to e. sb with sth** munir *ou* équiper qn de qch; **to e. oneself with sth** s'équiper *ou* se munir de qch **(b)** (*prepare*) préparer **(to do sth** pour faire qch); **her training had not equipped her for such an eventuality** sa formation ne l'avait pas parée à une telle éventualité

equipage [ˈekwɪpɪdʒ] *n Horseriding* (*vehicle*) équipage *m*

equipment [ɪˈkwɪpmənt] *n* **(a)** (*items*) équipement *m*; (*in house*) appareils *mpl*; (*in factory*) installations *fpl*, matériel *m*; **camping e.** matériel de camping; **electrical e.** équipement électrique; **emergency e.** matériel *ou* installations de secours; **heavy e.** matériel lourd; **kitchen e.** ustensiles *mpl* de cuisine; **laboratory/office e.** matériel de laboratoire/bureau; *Mil* **regulation** *or* **standard e.** matériel réglementaire; **sports e.** équipement sportif; **surplus e.** matériel en excédent; **e. allowance** subvention *f* pour l'achat de matériel

(b) *Fig* **intellectual e.** capacité *f* intellectuelle

(c) (*act*) (*of expedition*) équipement *m*; (*of house*) aménagement *m*; (*of factory*) outillage *m*; (*of laboratory etc*) installation *f*

equipped [ɪˈkwɪpt] *adj* **(a)** (*soldier, expedition etc*) équipé **(with** de); **the aircraft is e. to take aerial photographs** *or* **for aerial photography** l'avion est équipé pour prendre des photos aériennes **(b)** (*prepared*) préparé; **she is well e. to succeed/for the job** elle est préparée pour réussir/pour ce travail; (*possessing adequate skills*) elle a les qualités requises pour réussir/pour ce travail

equitable [ˈekwɪtəb(ə)l] *adj* équitable

equitably [ˈekwɪt(ə)blɪ] *adv* équitablement

equitation [ekwɪˈteɪʃən] *n Fml* équitation *f*

equity [ˈekwɪtɪ] *n* **(a)** (*fairness*) équité *f* **(b)** *Jur* équité *f* **(c)** (*of shareholders*) capitaux *mpl ou* fonds *mpl* propres, avoir *m* des actionnaires; (*of company*) capital *m* actions; *Fin* **equities** actions *fpl* ordinaires; **the equities market** le marché des actions ordinaires; *St Exch* **e. trading** marché *m* des actions; *St Exch* **e. unit trust** sicav *m* actions **(d)** *Br Th* **E.** (*actors' union*) = le syndicat des artistes de la scène

equity loan *n* prêt *m ou* titre *m* participatif

equivalence [ɪˈkwɪvələns] *n* équivalence *f*

equivalent [ɪˈkwɪvələnt] **1** *adj* équivalent; **to be e. to sth** être équivalent à qch, équivaloir à qch; **to be e. in meaning/weight to sth** avoir un sens/un poids équivalent à celui de qch; **that would be e. to saying that ...** cela reviendrait à dire que ... **2** *n* équivalent *m*; **to drink the e. of one glass of wine** boire la valeur d'un verre de vin; **the Soviet e. of the FBI** l'équivalent soviétique du FBI; **to be an acceptable e.** être un substitut acceptable

equivocal [ɪˈkwɪvək(ə)l] *adj* **(a)** (*ambiguous*) (*reply, attitude*) équivoque, ambigu, -uë; (*word*) à double sens, équivoque; **he was rather e.** il s'est montré plutôt ambigu **(b)** (*uncertain*) incertain, douteux

equivocally [ɪˈkwɪvəklɪ] *adv* d'une manière équivoque

equivocate [ɪˈkwɪvəkeɪt] *vi* user d'équivoque, tergiverser

equivocation [ɪkwɪvəˈkeɪʃən] *n* tergiversation *f*; **to resort to equivocation(s)** user d'équivoque, tergiverser

ER [iːˈɑːr] **(a)** *Br* (*abbr* **Elizabeth Regina**) la Reine Elizabeth **(b)** *US* (*abbr* **Emergency Room**) urgences *fpl*

er [ə, ɜː] *int* euh

ERA [iːɑːˈreɪ] *n US* (*abbr* **Equal Rights Amendment**) = modification *f* proposée à la constitution relative aux droits de la femme et aux droits des citoyens, indépendamment de leur race ou de leur religion

era [ˈɪərə] *n Hist, Geol etc* ère *f*; **the end of an e.** la fin d'une époque; **to mark an e.** faire date; **the post-war e.** l'après-guerre *m*

eradicate [ɪˈrædɪkeɪt] *vt* (*prejudice, evil*) extirper, déraciner; (*disease*) éradiquer, faire disparaître; (*resistance, poverty*) éliminer

eradication [ɪrædɪˈkeɪʃən] *n* (*of prejudice, evil etc*) extirpation *f*; (*of disease*) éradication *f*; (*of resistance, poverty*) élimination *f*

erase [ɪˈreɪz] *vt* (*written material, sth on tape, disk, file*) effacer; (*with eraser*) gommer; (*memory*) oblitérer; **the e. button** le bouton d'effacement

erase head *n Comptr* tête *f* d'effacement

eraser [ɪˈreɪzər] *n* (*rubber*) gomme *f* (à effacer); **ink e.** gomme à encre

erasing [ɪˈreɪzɪŋ] *n* effacement *m*

erasure [ɪˈreɪʒər] *n* **(a)** (*act*) effacement *m* **(b)** (*what is erased*) mot *m*/chiffre *m*/*etc* effacé; **there were a number of mysterious erasures** un certain nombre de choses avaient été mystérieusement effacées

ere [eər] *Arch, Lit* **1** *prep* avant; **e. now** (*in the past*) auparavant; (*by this time*) déjà; **e. long** bientôt **2** *conj* avant que + *sub*; **e. you forget** avant que tu (n')oublies

erect[1] [ɪˈrekt] *adj* (*person*) droit, debout; (*carriage*) droit; (*penis, nipples etc*) en érection; (*dog's ears*) dressé; **with head e.** la tête haute *ou* relevée; **to stand e.** se tenir droit

erect[2] *vt* (*building, theory*) ériger; (*statue*) élever **(to** à); (*scaffolding, altar, mast*) dresser; (*machine*) installer; (*tent*) monter

erectile [ɪˈrektaɪl] *adj Physiol* (*tissue*) érectile

erection [ɪˈrekʃən] *n* **(a)** (*act*) (*of building*) construction *f*, érection *f*; (*of statue*) érection; (*of mast*) dressage *m*; (*of machine*) installation *f* **(b)** *Physiol* (*of organ*) érection *f*; **to have/get an e.** avoir une érection **(c)** *often Pej* (*building, structure*) bâtisse *f*, construction *f*, édifice *m*

erectness [ɪˈrektnɪs] *n* attitude *f* droite; **the e. of his bearing** sa posture droite

erector [ɪˈrektər] *n* **(a)** (*person*) (*of buildings*) constructeur *m* **(b)** *Anat* **e. (muscle)** (muscle *m*) érecteur *m*

erg [ɜːg] *n Phys* erg *m*

ergo [ˈɜːgəʊ, ˈeəgəʊ] *adv Fml, Hum* ergo, donc

ergonomic [ɜːgəˈnɒmɪk] *adj* ergonomique

ergonomically [ɜːgəˈnɒmɪklɪ] *adv* **e. designed** (*chair etc*) d'une conception ergonomique

ergonomics [ɜːgəˈnɒmɪks] *n* [①**A10**,c] ergonomie *f*

ergot [ˈɜːgɒt] *n Agr, Pharm* ergot *m*

ergotism [ˈɜːgətɪz(ə)m] *n Med* ergotisme *m*

Erie [ˈɪərɪ] *n* **Lake E.** le lac Érié

erigeron [ɪˈrɪdʒərən] *n Bot* (*plant*) érigéron *m*

Erin [ˈerɪn] *n Arch, Lit* Irlande *f*

Eritrea [erɪˈtreɪə] *n* Erythrée *f*

Eritrean [erɪˈtreɪən] *n* Erythréen, -enne

ERM [iːɑːˈrem] *n Fin* (*abbr* **Exchange Rate Mechanism**) mécanisme *m* de change

erm [ɜːm] *int* euh

ermine [ˈɜːmɪn] *n* hermine *f*

erode [ɪˈrəʊd] **1** *vt* (*of elements*) éroder; (*of acid, corrosive substance*) ronger, corroder; (*confidence*) miner, entamer; *Fig* **the power of the church has been eroded** le pouvoir de l'église a été miné; **our savings have been eroded by inflation** nos économies se sont trouvées grignotées par l'inflation **2** *vi* (*of metal*) s'éroder, se corroder; (*of confidence, popularity*) baisser, se détériorer; (*of prices*) s'effriter

erogenous [ɪˈrɒdʒɪnəs] *adj* érogène; **e. zone** zone *f* érogène

Eros [ˈɪərɒs] *n* Éros *m*

erosion [ɪˈrəʊʒən] *n* (*marine etc*) érosion *f*; *Fig* (*of confidence, popularity*) détérioration *f*; **wind e.** érosion éolienne; **soil e.** érosion du sol; *Fig* **the e. of real earnings by inflation** la diminution du salaire réel causée par l'inflation; **e. of prices** effritement *m* des prix

erosive [ɪˈrəʊzɪv] *adj* érosif

erotic [ɪˈrɒtɪk] *adj* (*art, book, film etc*) érotique

erotica [ɪˈrɒtɪkə] *npl* écrits *mpl*/dessins *mpl*/*etc* érotiques

erotically [ɪˈrɒtɪklɪ] *adv* érotiquement; **to be e. charged** avoir un contenu érotique

eroticism [ɪˈrɒtɪsɪz(ə)m] *n* érotisme *m*

err [ɜːr] *vi* (**a**) (*make mistake*) faire erreur, *esp Lit* errer; **to e. in one's judgement** faire une erreur de jugement; *Prov* **to e. is human** l'erreur est humaine (**b**) (*sin*) pécher; **he does not e. on the side of modesty** il ne pèche pas par la modestie; **let's e. on the side of caution and do …** par mesure de prudence, faisons …; **it's better to e. on the side of generosity** il vaut mieux pécher par générosité, il vaut mieux être trop généreux que pas assez (**c**) (*stray*) s'égarer, s'écarter (**from** de); *sometimes Hum* **to e. from the straight and narrow** s'égarer du droit chemin

errand [ˈerənd] *n* commission *f*, course *f*; **to send sb on an e.** envoyer qn faire une commission *ou* une course; **to go on** *or* **run errands** (aller) faire des commissions *ou* des courses; *Lit* **e. of mercy** mission *f* humanitaire; **e. boy** garçon *m* de courses, garçon livreur

errant [ˈerənt] *adj* (*erring*) dévoyé; **e. ways** vie *f* dévoyée; **e. husband** mari *m* infidèle

errata [ɪˈrɑːtə] *npl Typ* errata *mpl*

erratic [ɪˈrætɪk] *adj* (**a**) (*irregular*) irrégulier; (*light*) intermittent, discontinu; **e. working** (*of machine*) irrégularité *f* de marche; *Aut* **e. driving** conduite mal assurée (**b**) (*person*) capricieux, bizarre, velléitaire; (*life*) désordonné; (*changes of mood*) imprévisible; **her playing is e.** (*of sportswoman, musician*) son jeu est inégal; **the road/river follows an e. course** la route/rivière suit un cours irrégulier (**c**) *Med* (*pain*) erratique

erratically [ɪˈrætɪklɪ] *adv* sans méthode, sans règle; **to work e.** (*of person*) travailler irrégulièrement; (*of machine*) fonctionner irrégulièrement *ou* par à-coups; **to play e.** (*of sportsman, musician*) avoir un jeu inégal; *Aut* **to drive e.** conduire d'une façon mal assurée

erratum, *pl* **-ta** [ɪˈrɑːtəm, -tə] *n* erratum *m*, *pl* errata

erring [ˈɜːrɪŋ] *adj* (*sinning*) dévoyé, égaré; (*mistaken*) tombé dans l'erreur; (*husband, wife*) infidèle; **e. ways** vie *f* dévoyée

erroneous [ɪˈrəʊnɪəs] *adj esp Fml* (*calculation, premise, conclusion*) erroné, faux; (*supposition*) faux

erroneously [ɪˈrəʊnɪəslɪ] *adv esp Fml* à tort; **e. accused of …** accusé à tort de …

erroneousness [ɪˈrəʊnɪəsnɪs] *n esp Fml* erreur *f*, fausseté *f*

error [ˈerər] *n* (**a**) (*mistake*) erreur *f*, faute *f*; **to make an e.** faire *ou* commettre une erreur; **to make an e. in one's calculations** faire une erreur de calcul; **e. of judgement** erreur de jugement; **printing** *or* **printer's e.** faute d'impression; *Com* **errors and omissions excepted** sauf erreur ou omission

(**b**) *Tech* erreur *f*, aberration *f*, déviation *f*; *Comptr* erreur; **allowable e.** erreur permise, tolérance *f*

(**c**) (*being wrong*) **to do sth in e.** faire qch par erreur; **to be in e.** être dans l'erreur, avoir tort; **to fall into e.** tomber dans l'erreur

(**d**) (*wrongdoing*) écart *m* (de conduite); **errors of youth** erreurs *fpl ou* écarts de jeunesse; **he has seen the e. of his ways** il est revenu de ses égarements; **to show sb the e. of his ways** montrer à qn qu'il est dans le mauvais chemin

error code *n Comptr* code *m* d'erreur

error correction *n Comptr* correction *f* d'erreurs

error message *n Comptr* message *m* d'erreur

error routine *n Comptr* sous-programme *m* de correction d'erreurs

ersatz [eəˈzæts, ˈɜːzæts] **1** *n* ersatz *m*, succédané *m* **2** *adj Pej* **e. coffee** succédané *m* de café; *Fig* **e. religion** ersatz *m* de religion

Erse [ɜːs] *Ling* **1** *n* (**a**) (*Gaelic*) erse *m*, gaélique *m* (**b**) (*Irish Gaelic*) irlandais *m* **2** *adj* (*see n*) (**a**) gaélique (**b**) irlandais

erstwhile [ˈɜːstwaɪl] *adj attrib Arch, Lit* (*pupil, friend, belief etc*) ancien

eructate [ˈiːrʌkteɪt] *vi Fml* éructer

eructation [iːrʌkˈteɪʃən] *n Fml* éructation *f*

erudite [ˈerʊdaɪt] *adj* érudit, savant

erudition [erʊˈdɪʃən] *n* érudition *f*; **work of monumental e.** vrai monument d'érudition

erupt [ɪˈrʌpt] *vi* (**a**) (*of volcano*) entrer en éruption (**b**) (*of violence, anger, sound*) éclater; (*of person*) exploser; **the stadium erupted in a huge roar** le stade a éclaté d'un énorme rugissement (**c**) (*of teeth*) percer; (*of spot*) sortir; **his face erupted in spots** son visage s'est couvert de boutons

eruption [ɪˈrʌpʃən] *n* (**a**) (*of volcano*) éruption *f*; **volcano in e.** volcan *m* en éruption (**b**) (*of anger, joy etc*) éruption *f*, éclat *m* (**c**) (*of teeth*) éruption *f*; (*of spots*) éruption, poussée *f*

erysipelas [erɪˈsɪpɪləs] *n Med* érysipèle *m*

erythema [erɪˈθiːmə] *n Med* erythème *m*

erythrocyte [eˈrɪθrəʊsaɪt] *n Physiol* érythrocyte *m*

ESA [iːeˈseɪ] *n* (*abbr* **European Space Agency**) ASE *f*

escalate [ˈeskəleɪt] **1** *vi* (**a**) (*of prices etc*) monter (en flèche) (**b**) (*of conflict etc*) s'aggraver; **small incidents can easily e. into a world war** de simples incidents (militaires) peuvent facilement mener à une guerre mondiale **2** *vt* intensifier; **to e. the situation** aggraver la situation

escalation [eskəˈleɪʃən] *n* (**a**) (*of prices etc*) augmentation *f* (rapide), montée *f* en flèche; (*of interest rates*) escalade *f* (**b**) (*of war, situation*) escalade *f*

escalator [ˈeskəleɪtər] *n* (**a**) (*moving stairway*) escalier *m* mécanique, escalator *m* (**b**) *Econ* **e.** (**clause**) clause *f* d'échelle mobile

escalope [ˈeskəlɒp] *n Culin* escalope *f*

escapade [ˈeskəpeɪd] *n* escapade *f*, frasque *f*, fredaine *f*

escape[1] [ɪsˈkeɪp] *n* (**a**) (*flight*) fuite *f*, évasion *f*; **to make one's e.** s'échapper, se sauver; **to make good one's e.** réussir à s'échapper; **to have a narrow e.** l'échapper belle; **to have a miraculous e.** échapper comme par miracle; *Fig* **the cinema provided an e. from their daily routine** le cinéma leur offrait un moyen de s'évader de leur routine quotidienne (**b**) (*of gas, water etc*) échappement *m*, fuite *f*, dégagement *m* (**c**) *HydE* déversoir *m* (**d**) *Comptr* échappement *m*

escape[2] **1** *vi* (**a**) (*of person*) échapper, s'échapper, prendre la fuite; **to e. from prison** s'évader de prison; **escaped prisoner** évadé, -ée; **the lion escaped from the zoo** le lion s'est échappé du zoo; **to e. by the skin of one's teeth** échapper tout juste; **to e. uninjured** s'en tirer indemne; **he escaped with a fright** il en a été quitte pour la peur; **he was lucky to e. with his life** il a eu de la chance de s'en sortir vivant; *Fig* **to e. from reality** s'évader *ou* s'échapper de la réalité

(**b**) (*of gases, fluids*) s'échapper, fuir

2 *vt* (**a**) (*of person, animal*) (*danger*) échapper à; **he narrowly escaped death** il a échappé tout juste à la mort; **he just escaped being killed** il a bien failli être tué, il a manqué (de) se faire tuer; **they escaped punishment/justice** ils ont échappé à la punition/justice

(**b**) (*go unnoticed by*) échapper à; **nothing escapes her eagle eye** rien n'échappe à son regard perçant; **to e. notice** échapper à l'attention, passer inaperçu

(**c**) (*of name, date etc*) échapper à; **his name escapes me** son nom m'échappe

(**d**) (*of sound*) **a cry escaped him** un cri lui a échappé

escape clause *n Com etc* clause *f* échappatoire

escapee [eskeɪˈpiː] *n* évadé, -ée

escape hatch *n Naut* trappe *f* de secours

escape key *n Comptr* touche *f* d'échappement

escapement [ɪsˈkeɪpmənt] *n* (*of clock, piano etc*) échappement *m*

escaper [ɪsˈkeɪpər] *n* fugitif, -ive

escape route *n* (*from fire etc*) itinéraire *m* de sortie de secours; (*of criminal*) itinéraire ménagé pour s'échapper

escape valve *n MecE etc* soupape *f* d'échappement *ou* de trop-plein

escape velocity *n Astronaut* vitesse *f* de libération de l'attraction terrestre

escape wheel *n Tech* roue *f* d'échappement

escapism [ɪsˈkeɪpɪz(ə)m] *n* évasion *f* (de la réalité); **the movie is pure e.** ce film permet de s'évader totalement de la réalité

escapist [ɪsˈkeɪpɪst] **1** *n* **she had always been a bit of an e.** elle avait toujours un peu cherché à s'évader de la réalité **2** *adj* (*film, story*) qui permet de s'évader de la réalité; **e. literature** littérature *f* d'évasion

escapologist [eskəˈpɒlədʒɪst] *n* prestidigitateur *m* spécialiste de l'évasion

escapology [eskəˈpɒlədʒɪ] *n* art *m* de l'évasion

escarpment [ɪsˈkɑːpmənt] *n* escarpement *m*

eschatology [eskəˈtɒlədʒɪ] *n Rel* eschatologie *f*
eschew [ɪsˈtʃuː] *vt Lit (notions, ideas)* éviter; **to e. violence** s'abstenir de recourir à la violence; **to e. sb's company** fuir *ou* éviter qn
escort¹ [ˈeskɔːt] *n* **(a)** *(for convoy etc)* escorte *f*; *(for tourists etc)* guide *m*; *(woman from agency)* hôtesse *f*; *Old-fashioned (to woman)* cavalier *m*; *(to man)* cavalière *f*; *(ship)* escorteur *m*, bâtiment *m* d'escorte; **a police e.** une escorte de police **(b)** *(act of escorting)* escorte *f*; **under the e. of ...** sous l'escorte de ...; **to conduct a prisoner under e.** conduire un prisonnier sous escorte
escort² [ɪsˈkɔːt] *vt (convoy)* escorter, faire escorte à, servir d'escorte à; *(lady)* servir de cavalier à; *(prisoner)* conduire sous escorte; **to be escorted to safety** être escorté jusqu'à un lieu sûr
escort agency *n* agence *f* d'hôtesses
escort duty *n Mil* service *m* d'escorte
escort fighter *n Mil, Av* chasseur *m* d'escorte
escrow [ˈeskrəʊ] *n Banking* argent *m*/biens *mpl* placé(s) en dépôt légal; **to put money in e.** placer de l'argent en dépôt légal; **e. account** compte *m* bloqué
escutcheon [ɪsˈkʌtʃ(ə)n] *n Her* écu *m*, écusson *m*
Eskimo, *pl* -os, -o [ˈeskɪməʊ, -əʊz] **1** *adj* esquimau, *(occ* -aude *in feminine)*, -aux, eskimo *inv* **2** *n* Esquimau, -aude
ESL [iːeˈsel] *n Sch (abbr* **English as a Second Language***)* anglais *m* deuxième langue
esophagus [ɪˈsɒfəgəs] *n US Anat* œsophage *m*
esoteric [esəʊˈterɪk] *adj* ésotérique
ESP [iːesˈpiː] *n* **(a)** *(abbr* **extrasensory perception***)* perception *f* extra-sensorielle **(b)** *Sch (abbr* **English for Specific** *or* **Special Purposes***)* anglais *m* appliqué
esp *(abbr* **especially***)* spécialt
espadrille [ˈespədrɪl] *n* espadrille *f*
espalier [ɪsˈpælɪər, -ɪeɪ] *n Bot* espalier *m*
esparto [esˈpɑːtəʊ] *n Bot* **e. (grass)** sparte *m*, alfa *m*
especial [ɪsˈpeʃəl] *adj* spécial, particulier; **of e. importance** d'une importance toute particulière
especially [ɪsˈpeʃəlɪ] *adv* surtout; **we were e. lucky with the weather** le temps nous était particulièrement favorable; **he likes birds, e. parrots** il aime les oiseaux, spécialement les perroquets; **I did it e. for you** je l'ai fait spécialement *ou* exprès pour vous; **I was e. pleased to hear about your success** cela m'a fait tout particulièrement plaisir d'apprendre la nouvelle de votre succès; **these figures are surprisingly good, e. given recent developments** ces chiffres sont étonnamment bons, surtout si l'on considère les derniers développements
Esperanto [espəˈræntəʊ] *n* espéranto *m*
espionage [ˈespɪənɑːʒ] *n* espionnage *m*
esplanade [espləˈneɪd] *n* esplanade *f*; *(in seaside town)* digue *f*
espousal [ɪsˈpaʊz(ə)l] *n* **the e. of a cause** l'adhésion *f* à une cause
espouse [ɪsˈpaʊz] *vt (cause, belief etc)* épouser, embrasser
espresso [esˈpresəʊ] **1** *n* (café *m*) expresso *m*; **e. machine** machine *f* à expresso **2** *adj* expresso
espy [ɪsˈpaɪ] *vt Arch, Lit* apercevoir, aviser
Esq *Old-fashioned abbr* **Esquire**
Esquire [ɪsˈkwaɪər] *n Old-fashioned (respectful title)* **David Thomas, E.** = Monsieur David Thomas
essay¹ [ˈeseɪ] *n* **(a)** *(piece of writing) Liter* essai *m*; *Sch* composition *f*; *(for younger students)* rédaction *f* **(b)** *Fml (attempt)* essai *m*, tentative *f* **(at** de)
essay² [eˈseɪ] *vt Fml* tenter; **to e. a smile** tenter de sourire
essayist [ˈeseɪɪst] *n Liter* essayiste *mf*, auteur *m* d'essais
essence [ˈesəns] *n* **(a)** *Phil, Rel etc* essence *f*; *(of question)* fond *m*; *(of speech)* essentiel *m*; **the very e. of authority/bravery/stupidity** l'autorité/le courage/la stupidité même; **in e.** essentiellement; **speed/time is of the e.** la vitesse/le temps est le facteur prioritaire; **diplomacy is of the e.** la diplomatie s'impose *ou* est de rigueur; **the e. of the matter is that ...** le fond de l'affaire c'est que ... **(b)** *Ch, Culin etc* essence *f*, extrait *m*; **meat e.** extrait de viande; **vanilla e.** extrait de vanille
essential [ɪˈsenʃəl] **1** *adj* **(a)** *(basic) (difference etc)* essentiel **(b)** *(indispensable)* essentiel, indispensable; **e. foodstuffs** denrées *fpl* de première nécessité; **an e. part** *or* **feature** un élément essentiel; **it is e. to do that** il est essentiel *ou* absolument nécessaire de faire cela; **the e. thing** l'essentiel *m*; **prudence is e.** la prudence s'impose; **e. information** *(on package label)* mentions *fpl* obligatoires **2** *n (usu pl)* **reduced to its essentials** dépouillé; **to concentrate on the essentials** s'attacher à l'essentiel; **one of the essentials of a business man** une des qualités indispensables à un homme d'affaires
essentially [ɪˈsenʃ(ə)lɪ] *adv* essentiellement; **her analysis is e. correct** pour l'essentiel son analyse est correcte
essential oil *n* huile *f* essentielle
EST [iːesˈtiː] *n Am (abbr* **Eastern Standard Time***)* HNE *f*
est (a) *Com (abbr* **established***)* établi, fondé; **A. Jones, est 1885** A. Jones, établi en 1885 **(b)** *(abbr* **estimated***)* estimatif
establish [ɪsˈtæblɪʃ] *vt* **(a)** *(set up) (government)* établir; *(system)* établir, édifier; *(business)* fonder; *(agency)* créer; *(company)* constituer; *(peace)* mettre sur pied; **to e. close relations with sb** nouer des relations avec qn; **to e. oneself in business** s'établir dans les affaires; *Pej* **to e. oneself in sb's house** s'installer *ou* s'incruster chez qn; *Com* **established 1885** établi en 1885
(b) *(make firm) (one's faith)* affermir; *(power)* asseoir; *(rule of law)* instaurer; *Jur (will)* confirmer, ratifier; **to e. one's right** faire apparaître son bon droit; **to e. a reputation** se faire une réputation; **to e. sb's reputation as an author** faire la réputation de qn comme auteur; **the film established her as an important director** le film a établi sa réputation de metteur en scène important
(c) *(prove, become clear about) (fact, sb's innocence etc)* établir; **research has established links between the two diseases** la recherche a permis d'établir des liens entre les deux maladies
(d) *Rel, Pol (Church)* ériger en Église d'État
established [ɪsˈtæblɪʃt] *adj* établi; *(friendship)* solide; *(fact)* avéré; *(reputation)* solide, bien établi; **once the company becomes e.** quand la société sera bien établie; **when you become e. as an opera singer** quand ta réputation de chanteur d'opéra sera faite; **e. scientific fact** fait acquis à la science; *Rel, Pol* **the e. Church** l'Église *f* établie; **the e. religion** la religion d'État; **the e. order** l'ordre *m* établi
establishing shot [ɪsˈtæblɪʃɪŋ] *n TV, Cin* plan *m* de situation *ou* de mise en place *ou* d'ensemble
establishment [ɪsˈtæblɪʃmənt] *n* **(a)** *(established order)* **the E.** *(national institutions)* les institutions *fpl*; *(dominant group)* le groupe dirigeant; *(prevailing values)* l'ordre *m* établi; **the liberal/academic/*etc* E.** les sommités *fpl* libérales/académiques/*etc*; **E. figure** membre *m* de la classe dirigeante; **to be against the E., to be anti-E.** être anticonformiste; **to revolt against the E.** se révolter contre l'ordre établi; *Rel* **the (Church) E.** l'Église *f* établie
(b) *Com (company etc)* établissement *m*; **business e.** maison *f* de commerce; **a family e.** *(hotel, restaurant)* un établissement familial
(c) *(staff)* personnel *m*; *Mil etc (of unit etc)* effectif *m*; *Fml* **to be on the e.** faire partie du personnel; *Mil* **peacetime e.** effectifs *mpl* de paix
(d) *Pol (of government, Church)* établissement *m*; *(of system)* création *f*; *Com (of business)* fondation *f*; *(of company)* constitution *f*
(e) *(of fact etc)* constatation *f*; *(of one's faith)* affermissement *m*; *Jur (of will)* homologation *f*
estate [ɪsˈteɪt] *n* **(a)** *Jur (possessions)* bien *m*; *(of deceased person)* succession *f*, biens; *(of bankrupt)* actif *m*; **e. duty** droits *mpl* de succession
(b) *(land)* terre *f*, propriété *f*; **country house and e. for sale** à vendre château et domaine; *Br* **(housing) e.** lotissement *m*; *(council houses)* groupe *m* de H.L.M.; *Br* **(industrial) e.** zone *f* industrielle; *Br* **e. (car)** familiale *f*, break *m*
(c) *Lit, Arch (state)* état *m*, condition *f*; **man's e.** l'âge *m* d'homme; **of high/low e.** *(social condition)* de haut rang/d'humble condition
(d) *Pol* **the third e.** le tiers (état); **the fourth e.** le quatrième pouvoir; *Fr Hist* **the Estates (of the Realm)** les états *mpl*, les ordres *mpl* (de l'ancien régime)
estate agency *n* agence *f* immobilière
estate agent *n* agent *m* immobilier
esteem¹ [ɪsˈtiːm] *n* estime *f*, considération *f*; **to hold sb in high e.** avoir qn en haute estime; **to hold sb in low e.** avoir peu d'estime *ou* de considération pour qn; **to go up/down in sb's e.** monter/baisser dans l'estime *ou* la considération de qn
esteem² *vt* **(a)** *(regard highly) (sb)* estimer; *(sth)* priser; **to e. sth lightly** faire peu de cas de qch; **highly esteemed** *(person)* fort estimé **(b)** *Fml (consider)* estimer, regarder **(sth as sth** qch comme qch); **to e. it an honour that ...** se sentir honoré que ...; **I would e. it a favour if you did this** je vous serais reconnaissant de le faire
esteem needs *n Mktg* besoin *m* d'estime
ester [ˈestər] *n Biol, Ch* ester *m*
esthete, esthetic *etc US* = **aesthete, aesthetic** *etc*
estimable [ˈestɪməb(ə)l] *adj* estimable, digne d'estime
estimate¹ [ˈestɪmət] *n* **(a)** *(rough calculation) (of contents of sth, of force of sth)* appréciation *f*, évaluation *f*, calcul *m*; **it's**

only an e. ce n'est qu'une estimation; **rough e.** approximation *f* grossière; **at a rough e.** à vue de nez; **at the lowest e.** au bas mot **(b)** *Com* devis *m* (estimatif); **to ask for an e.** demander un devis; **to give** *or* **put in an e. for decorating work** donner un devis pour des travaux de décoration, soumissionner des travaux de décoration; *Pol* **the Estimates** les prévisions *fpl* budgétaires; **building e.** devis de construction; **free e.** devis gratuit; **preliminary e.** devis de prévision

estimate² ['estɪmeɪt] *vt* (*costs etc*) estimer, évaluer; **to e. sth at £10,000** estimer *ou* calculer qch à 10 000 livres; **his fortune is estimated at …** on évalue sa fortune à …; **I e. that it will take three years** j'estime que cela prendra trois ans

estimated ['estɪmeɪtɪd] *adj* (*cost*) estimatif; (*value*) estimé; **it will cost an e. £500,000** on estime que cela coûtera 500 000 livres; **it is only an e. figure** ce n'est qu'une estimation; **e. time of arrival** heure d'arrivée prévue

estimation [estɪ'meɪʃən] *n* **(a)** (*rough calculation*) estimation *f*, appréciation *f*, évaluation *f*; (*of costs etc*) calcul *m* **(b)** (*judgement*) jugement *m*; **in my e.** d'après moi, à mon avis **(c)** (*regard*) estime *f*, considération *f*; **she is rising in the e. of the public** elle monte dans l'estime du public; **he's gone down in my e.** il est descendu dans mon estime *ou* ma considération

estimator ['estɪmeɪtər] *n Fin* expert *m*

Estonia [es'təʊnɪə] *n* Estonie *f*

Estonian [es'təʊnɪən] **1** *adj* estonien **2** *n* Estonien, -ienne

estrange [ɪs'treɪndʒ] *vt* s'aliéner l'affection de; **to become estranged from sb** se détacher de qn; **the quarrel estranged her from her family** cette dispute l'a brouillée avec sa famille

estranged [ɪs'treɪndʒd] *adj* **an e. couple** des époux séparés; **her e. husband** son mari dont elle est séparée; **their e. son** leur fils avec qui ils sont brouillés

estrangement [ɪs'treɪndʒmənt] *n* (*of person*) aliénation *f*; (*of two people*) brouille *f* (**between** entre); (*of married couple*) séparation *f*

estrogen ['i:strədʒən] *n US Biol, Ch* œstrogène *m*

estrous ['i:strəs] *adj US Biol* (*cycle*) œstral

estrus ['i:strəs] *n US Biol* œstrus *m*

estuary ['estjʊ(ə)rɪ] *n* estuaire *m*; **the Thames e.** l'estuaire de la Tamise

ETA [i:ti:'eɪ] *n Av* (*abbr* **estimated time of arrival**) heure *f* d'arrivée prévue

et al [et'æl] (*abbr* **et alii**) et autres

etc [et'setrə] *adv* (*abbr* **et cetera**) etc; *F* **you have to fill in the form in duplicate etc etc** il faut remplir le formulaire en deux exemplaires et cætera, et cætera

et cetera [et'setrə] *adv* et cætera

etceteras [et'setrəs] *npl* extras *mpl*

etch [etʃ] **1** *vt Art, Typ* (*drawing etc*) graver à l'eau-forte; (*plate*) graver; **to e. away the metal** enlever le métal à l'eau-forte; *Fig* **the scene was etched in his memory** la scène était gravée dans sa mémoire **2** *vi Art* faire de la gravure à l'eau-forte

etcher ['etʃər] *n Art* graveur *m* à l'eau-forte

etching ['etʃɪŋ] *n Art* (*art*) art *m* de graver à l'eau-forte; (*individual work*) gravure *f* à l'eau-forte, eau-forte *f*, *pl* eaux-fortes; *Hum* **come up and see my etchings** monte, je vais te montrer ma collection d'estampes japonaises

ETD [i:ti:'di:] *n* (*abbr* **estimated time of departure**) heure *f* de départ prévue

eternal [ɪ'tɜ:n(ə)l] **1** *adj* éternel; (*continual*) continuel, sans fin; **e. life** la vie éternelle; **e. quarrelling/complaints/gossip** querelles/plaintes/commérages incessant(e)s; *Fig* **the e. triangle** l'éternel triangle *m* **2** *n* **the E.** l'Éternel *m*

eternally [ɪ'tɜ:n(ə)lɪ] *adv* éternellement; **I shall be e. grateful to you** je vous serai éternellement reconnaissant

eternity [ɪ'tɜ:nɪtɪ] *n* éternité *f*; *F* **I waited an e.** j'ai attendu pendant une éternité; *Br* **e. ring** = bague *f* entièrement sertie de pierres symbolisant l'éternité du mariage

ethane ['i:θeɪn] *n Ch* éthane *m*

ether ['i:θər] *n* **(a)** *Phys, Ch* éther *m* **(b)** *Arch, Lit* **the e.** (*heavens*) la voûte éthérée

ethereal [ɪ'θɪərɪəl] *adj* éthéré; (*form*) léger, impalpable

ethereally [ɪ'θɪərɪəlɪ] *adv* **e. beautiful** d'une beauté éthérée

etherize ['i:θəraɪz] *vt Med* éthériser

ethic ['eθɪk] **1** *adj Gram* **e. dative** datif *m* éthique **2** *n* (*set of values*) éthique *f*; **work e.** conception *f* du travail

ethical ['eθɪk(ə)l] *adj* éthique, moral, *Liter* **e. writer** moraliste *m*; *Pharm* **e. drug** = remède *m* vendu uniquement sur l'ordonnance d'un médecin; **it's not e.** (*morally wrong*) ce n'est pas moral; **the doctor's behaviour was not e.** (*against professional ethics*) le comportement du médecin n'était pas conforme au code déontologique

ethically ['eθɪklɪ] *adv* d'après (les doctrines de) l'éthique; **e. questionable** d'une éthique douteuse; **she has behaved quite e.** son comportement a été tout à fait éthique *ou* moral

ethics ['eθɪks] *n* [①A10,c] *Phil* éthique *f*, morale *f*; (*of profession*) déontologie *f*; **e. code, code of e.** code *m* déontologique

Ethiopia [i:θɪ'əʊpɪə] *n* Éthiopie *f*

Ethiopian [i:θɪ'əʊpɪən] **1** *adj* éthiopien **2** *n* Éthiopien, -ienne

ethnic ['eθnɪk] **1** *adj* ethnique; **e. cleansing** purification *f* ethnique; **e. community/minority** communauté *f*/minorité *f* ethnique; **e. tourism** (*travel to ancestral country*) tourisme *m* ethnique **2** *n US* membre *m* d'une minorité ethnique

ethnically ['eθnɪklɪ] *adv* du point de vue ethnique

ethnographer [eθ'nɒgrəfər] *n* ethnographe *mf*

ethnography [eθ'nɒgrəfɪ] *n* ethnographie *f*

ethnological [eθnə'lɒdʒɪk(ə)l] *adj* ethnologique

ethnologically [eθnə'lɒdʒɪklɪ] *adv* ethnologiquement

ethnologist [eθ'nɒlədʒɪst] *n* ethnologue *mf*

ethnology [eθ'nɒlədʒɪ] *n* ethnologie *f*

ethological [i:θə'lɒdʒɪk(ə)l] *adj* éthologique

ethology [ɪ'θɒlədʒɪ] *n* éthologie *f*

ethos ['i:θɒs] *n* (*of people*) génie *m*; (*of company, class*) culture *f*

ethyl ['eθɪl] *n Ch* éthyle *m*; **e. alcohol** alcool *m* éthylique

ethylene ['eθɪli:n] *n Ch* éthylène *m*

etiolate ['i:tɪəʊleɪt] *vt* (*plant*) étioler

etiological [i:tɪə'lɒdʒɪk(ə)l] *adj US* étiologique

etiology [i:tɪ'ɒlədʒɪ] *n US* étiologie *f*

etiquette ['etɪket] *n* étiquette *f*; **court e.** cérémonial *m* de cour; **e. demands that …** l'étiquette veut *ou* exige que …; **professional e.** usages *mpl* professionnels

Etonian [i:'təʊnɪən] *n Sch* élève *m* (du collège) d'Eton; **Old E.** ancien élève d'Eton

Etruscan [ɪ'trʌskən] **1** *adj* étrusque **2** *n* Étrusque *mf*

etymological [etɪmə'lɒdʒɪk(ə)l] *adj* étymologique

etymologically [etɪmə'lɒdʒɪklɪ] *adv* étymologiquement

etymologist [etɪ'mɒlədʒɪst] *n* étymologiste *mf*

etymology [etɪ'mɒlədʒɪ] *n* étymologie *f*

EU [i:'ju:] *n* (*abbr* **European Union**) UE *f*

eucalyptus, *pl* **-ti, -tuses** [ju:kə'lɪptəs, -taɪ, -təsɪz] *n* (*tree*) eucalyptus *m*; *Pharm* **e. oil** essence *f* d'eucalyptus

Eucharist (the) [ðə'ju:kərɪst] *n Rel* l'eucharistie *f*; **to receive the E.** recevoir l'eucharistie

Euclidean [ju:'klɪdɪən] *adj* (*geometry*) euclidien

eugenics [ju:'dʒenɪks] *n* [①A10,c] eugénique *f*, eugénisme *m*

eulogist ['ju:lədʒɪst] *n* panégyriste *mf*

eulogize ['ju:lədʒaɪz] *vt* (*sb, sth*) faire l'éloge *ou* le panégyrique de

eulogy ['ju:lədʒɪ] *n* panégyrique *m*; **to pronounce a e. on sb** faire l'éloge *ou* le panégyrique de qn

eunuch ['ju:nək] *n* eunuque *m*

euphemism ['ju:fɪmɪz(ə)m] *n* euphémisme *m*

euphemistic [ju:fɪ'mɪstɪk] *adj* euphémique

euphemistically [ju:fɪ'mɪstɪklɪ] *adv* par euphémisme; **e. known as …** auquel on se réfère par euphémisme sous le terme de …

euphonious [ju:'fəʊnɪəs] *adj* euphonique

euphonium [ju:'fəʊnɪəm] *n Mus* saxhorn *m* basse, basse *f* (des cuivres)

euphony ['ju:fənɪ] *n* euphonie *f*

euphorbia [ju:'fɔ:bɪə] *n Bot* (*plant*) euphorbe *f*

euphoria [ju:'fɔ:rɪə] *n* euphorie *f*

euphoric [ju:'fɒrɪk] *adj* euphorique

Eurasia [jʊə'reɪʃə, -ʒə] *n* Eurasie *f*

Eurasian [jʊə'reɪʃən, -ʒən] **1** *adj* eurasien; (*fauna etc*) eurasiatique **2** *n* Eurasien, -ienne

eureka [ju:'ri:kə] *int* eurêka

eurhythmics [ju:'rɪðmɪks] *n* [①A10,c] gymnastique *f* rythmique

Euro- ['jʊərəʊ] *pref* euro-

Eurobank ['jʊərəʊbæŋk] *n* eurobanque *f*

Eurobond ['jʊərəʊbɒnd] *n* euro-obligation *f*

Eurocheque ['jʊərəʊtʃek] *n* eurochèque *m*

Eurocommunism ['jʊərəʊkɒmjʊnɪz(ə)m] *n Pol* eurocommunisme *m*

Eurocrat ['jʊərəʊkræt] *n* eurocrate *mf*

Eurocurrency ['jʊərəʊkʌrənsɪ] *n* eurodevise *f*

Eurodollar ['jʊərəʊdɒlər] *n* eurodollar *m*

Eurofranc ['jʊərəʊfræŋk] *n* eurofranc *m*

Euroloan ['jʊərəʊləʊn] *n* eurocrédit *m*

Euromarket ['jʊərəʊmɑ:kɪt] *n* marché *m* des eurodevises

Euro MP *n* (*abbr* **European Member of Parliament**) membre *m* du parlement européen

Europe ['jʊərəp] *n* Europe *f*; **in E.** en Europe

European [jʊərə'pi:ən] **1** *adj* européen; **E. Commission** Commission *f* européenne; **E. Community** Communauté *f* européenne; **E. Court of Human Rights** Cour *f* européenne des droits de l'homme; **E. Court of Justice** Cour *f* de justice européenne; **E. Currency Unit** unité *f* monétaire européenne; **E. Development Fund** Fonds *m* européen de développement; **E. Economic Community** Communauté *f* économique européenne; **E. Free Trade Association** Association *f* européenne de libre-échange; **E. Investment Bank** Banque *f* européenne d'investissement; **E. Monetary System** Système *m* monétaire européen; **E. Parliament** Parlement *m* européen; *US* **E. plan** = tarif *m* d'hôtel qui n'inclut pas les repas; **E. Regional Development Fund** Fonds *m* européen de développement régional; **E. Union** Union *f* européenne

2 *n* Européen, -éenne

Europeanize [jʊərə'piːənaɪz] *vt* européaniser

European-style option *n St Exch* option *f* européenne

Eurosceptic ['jʊərəʊskeptɪk] *n* eurosceptique *mf*

Eurotourism ['jʊərəʊtʊərɪz(ə)m] *n* eurotourisme *m*

Eurotunnel ['jʊərəʊtʌnəl] *n* Eurotunnel *m*

Eurovision ['jʊərəvɪʒən] *n* Eurovision *f*; **the E. song contest** le concours Eurovision de la chanson

Eustachian [juː'steɪʃən] *adj Anat* **E. tube** trompe *f* d'Eustache

euthanasia [juːθə'neɪzɪə] *n* euthanasie *f*

evacuate [ɪ'vækjʊeɪt] *vt* (*place, population*) évacuer; *MecE* (*exhaust gases*) refouler; *Phys* (*create vacuum in*) faire le vide dans; **children were evacuated to the countryside** les enfants ont été évacués vers la campagne; *Physiol* **to e. the bowels** vider les intestins

evacuation [ɪvækjʊ'eɪʃən] *n* (*of place, people, bowels*) évacuation *f*; *MecE* (*of exhaust gases*) refoulement *m*; *Phys* (*creation of vacuum*) production *f* du vide

evacuee [ɪvækjʊ'iː] *n* évacué, -ée; **e. children** enfants évacués

evade [ɪ'veɪd] *vt* (*blow*) éviter, esquiver; (*danger*) éviter; (*creditors*) esquiver; (*justice, responsibility*) se soustraire à; (*obstacle, the law*) éluder, tourner; (*question, problem*) éluder; (*sb's vigilance*) déjouer; (*one's pursuers, detection*) échapper à, se dérober à; **to e. customs duty on sth** passer qch en fraude; **to e. tax** frauder le fisc; **success evades him** le succès lui échappe

evader [ɪ'veɪdər] *n* **tax e.** fraudeur, -euse du fisc

evaluate [ɪ'væljʊeɪt] *vt* (*danger, strength*) évaluer; (*damages*) évaluer, estimer le montant de

evaluation [ɪvæljʊ'eɪʃən] *n* évaluation *f*

evanescent [evə'nesənt] *adj* évanescent, éphémère

evangelical [iːvæn'dʒelɪk(ə)l] *Rel* **1** *adj* (*relating to Gospels*) évangélique; **e. preacher** évangéliste *mf*; **an e. Christian/church/sect** un chrétien/une église/une secte évangélique; **he's one of these e. Christians** c'est un de ces évangélistes; **e. zeal** zèle religieux; *Fig* **an e. vegetarian/communist** un végétarien/communiste à tout crin **2** *n* protestant, -ante évangélique

evangelicalism [iːvæn'dʒelɪkəlɪz(ə)m] *n Rel* évangélisme *m*

evangelism [ɪ'vændʒɪlɪz(ə)m] *n Rel* évangélisme *m*, prédication *f* de l'Évangile

evangelist [ɪ'vændʒɪlɪst] *n Rel* évangéliste *mf*

evangelize [ɪ'vændʒɪlaɪz] *Rel* **1** *vt* évangéliser; (*person*) prêcher l'Évangile à **2** *vi* prêcher l'Évangile; *Fig* **to e. for a cause** prêcher une cause; **he has been evangelizing about jazz for years** il prêche les mérites du jazz depuis des années

evaporate [ɪ'væpəreɪt] **1** *vt* (*liquid*) (faire) évaporer; **evaporated milk** lait *m* condensé (non sucré) **2** *vi* (*of liquid etc*) s'évaporer; (*of acid*) se volatiliser; *Fig* (*of money*) disparaître comme par enchantement; (*of enthusiasm, hope etc*) s'envoler

evaporation [ɪvæpə'reɪʃən] *n* (*of liquid*) évaporation *f*; (*of acid*) volatilisation *f*; (*of fears*) disparition *f*

evaporator [ɪ'væpəreɪtər] *n Ind* évaporateur *m*

evasion [ɪ'veɪʒən] *n* **(a)** (*escape*) évasion *f*, fuite *f*; (*act of dodging a commitment*) dérobade *f*; **by skilful e. of the more difficult questions** en se dérobant adroitement aux questions plus difficiles; **tax e.** fraude *f* fiscale **(b)** (*subterfuge*) subterfuge *m*, échappatoire *f*, faux-fuyant *m*, *pl* faux-fuyants; **without e.** sans détours

evasive [ɪ'veɪsɪv] *adj* (*person*) évasif; (*personality*) fuyant; **to give an e. answer** faire une réponse évasive, répondre évasivement; *Mil etc* **to take e. action** faire une manœuvre d'évitement

evasively [ɪ'veɪsɪvlɪ] *adv* (*to answer*) évasivement

evasiveness [ɪ'veɪsɪvnɪs] *n* caractère *m* évasif; **her e. increased our suspicions** ses propos évasifs ont renforcé nos soupçons

EVC [iːviː'siː] *n Mktg* (*abbr* **economic value to the customer**) valeur *f* économique apporté au consommateur

Eve [iːv] *n* Ève *f*; *Br Culin* **E.'s pudding** = compote *f* de pommes recouverte de génoise

eve [iːv] *n* **(a)** (*day before*) veille *f*; **Christmas E.** la veille de Noël; **New Year's E.** la Saint-Sylvestre; **on the e. of ...** à la veille de ...; *Fig* **to be on the e. of success** être à la veille du succès **(b)** *Arch, Lit* (*evening*) soir *m*

even[1] ['iːv(ə)n] *adj* **(a)** (*surface, ground etc*) uni, égal; **to be e. with sth** être au niveau de *ou* à ras de qch; **to make e.** (*foundations of building*) araser; (*surface*) aplanir; (*edges of two planks etc*) affleurer

(b) (*regular*) (*pulse*) égal, régulier; **e. temperature** température égale; **e. disposition** caractère *m* calme; **to make e.** (*spacing*) égaliser

(c) (*equal*) **he has an e. chance of succeeding** il a une chance sur deux de réussir; **the chances** *or* **odds are about e. that ...** il y a à peu près une chance sur deux que ...; *Sp* **to be e.** être à égalité; **they are an e. match** ils sont à partie égale; *Fig* **to get e. with sb** prendre sa revanche sur qn; **to be e. with sb** être quitte avec qn; **I'll get e. with him yet** je la lui rendrai; *Horseracing* **e. money** pari *m* avec enjeu égal; **horse quoted at e. money** cheval coté à égalité; *Fig* **I'll give you e. money that ...** je te parie que ..., je suis prêt à te parier que ...; *Sl* **to be e. Stevens** être quitte; *Sl* **to go e. Stevens with sb** partager fifty-fifty avec qn

(d) (*fair*) **with an e. hand** impartialement; **e. bargain** marché *m* équitable *ou* juste

(e) (*number*) pair; **odd or e.** pair ou impair; *Comptr* **e. parity** parité *f*

even[2] *adv* **(a)** même; **it isn't e. amusing any more** ce n'est même plus amusant; **or e. ...** ou même ...; **e. the cleverest** même les plus habiles; **e. the children knew** même les enfants savaient; **I never e. saw it** je ne l'ai même pas vu; **without e. speaking** sans même dire un mot; **e. then she wouldn't believe me** même alors elle ne voulait pas me croire; **this would be sad, tragic e.** ça serait triste, tragique même

(b) (*with comparatives*) encore; **that would be e. worse/better** ce serait encore pis/mieux; **e. more/less** encore plus/moins; **bring a friend — e. better, bring two** amène un ami — mieux encore, amène-en deux; **e. sadder than usual** encore plus triste que d'habitude

(c) (*giving conditions*) même; **e. supposing that ...** même en supposant que ...; **e. if** même si; **e. if she came** même si elle venait; **e. though** bien que; **e. though he has a car** bien qu'il ait une voiture; **e. with a computer the work would take months** même avec un ordinateur, le travail prendrait des mois; **e. so** cependant, quand même

(d) (*with time*) **e. as I speak** au moment même où je parle; **e. now** à l'instant même; **e. now, four years later, I still haven't got over it** aujourd'hui encore, quatre ans plus tard, je ne m'en suis pas encore remis; **e. then** (*already*) déjà (à cette époque)

even[3] *vt* **(a)** (*make smooth*) (*surface etc*) aplanir, niveler, égaliser; (*two planks etc*) affleurer; (*foundations of a wall*) araser **(b)** (*make equal*) rendre égal; *Typ* (*spacing*) égaliser; **to e. the odds** égaliser les chances

▶ **even out 1** *vi* (*become smooth, flat*) s'aplanir, s'égaliser, se niveler; (*of curve on graph*) s'aplanir; **the road goes uphill and then evens out** la route monte puis s'aplanit; **prices finally evened out** les prix ont fini par s'égaliser; **that should e. out over the lifetime of the entire project** cela devrait s'équilibrer sur la durée totale du projet **2** *vtsep* (*make more equal, fairer*) (*taxation etc*) répartir également; **that evens things out** on est quitte(s)

▶ **even up** *vtsep* **(a)** (*make equal*) (*score etc*) égaliser; **that will e. things up** (*financially*) on sera quitte(s); (*in competition*) cela équilibrera les choses **(b)** (*sum*) arrondir au chiffre supérieur; **let's e. it up to a pound** arrondissons la somme à une livre

even-handed *adj* équitable, juste, impartial

evening ['iːvnɪŋ] *n* **(a)** [①**B58,B,3**] soir *m*; (*duration*) soirée *f*; **tomorrow e.** demain soir; **yesterday e.** hier soir; **in the e.** le soir; **what do you do in the evenings?** qu'est-ce que vous faites le soir?; **at nine o'clock in the e.** à neuf heures du soir; **I'm going out this e.** je sors ce soir; **to have an e. out** sortir; **(on) that e.** ce soir-là; **(on) the e. before, (on) the previous e.** la veille au soir; **the next e.** le lendemain soir; **one** *or* **on a fine summer e.** (par) un beau soir d'été; **long winter evenings** longues soirées d'hiver; **every e.** tous les soirs; **every Monday e.** tous les lundis soir; **on the e. of Monday, 29th March** dans la soirée du lundi 29 mars; **all (the) e.** toute la soirée; **during the e.** pendant la soirée; *Fig Lit* **in the e. of life** au déclin de la vie; *Sp* **e. fixture/match** nocturne *f*

(b) (*evening party*) soirée *f*; **musical/cultural e.** soirée musicale/culturelle; **e. dress** *or* **wear** (*for men*) tenue *f* de soirée; (*for women*) robe *f* du soir; **in e. dress** en tenue de soirée

evening class *n* cours *m* du soir

evening gown *n* robe *f* de soirée *ou* du soir

evening paper *n* journal *m* du soir
evening performance *n Th* représentation *f* de soirée
evening prayers *npl Rel* office *m* du soir
evening primrose oil *n* huile *f* d'onagre
evening service *n Rel* service *m* du soir
evening star *n Astron* étoile *f* du soir
evenly ['i:v(ə)nlɪ] *adv* **(a)** (*to stretch, knit*) uniment; **spread the glue e.** étaler la colle régulièrement **(b)** (*to breathe*) régulièrement; (*to say sth*) calmement **(c)** (*fairly*) (*to divide*) également; **e. matched** (*of equal size*) de grandeur égale; (*of equal strength*) de force égale
evenness ['i:vənnɪs] *n* **(a)** (*smoothness*) caractère *m* plat *ou* égal *ou* nivelé **(b)** (*regularity*) égalité *f*; (*of movement*) régularité *f* **(c)** (*calm*) (*of character*) calme *m*; (*of mood*) égalité *f*
even-numbered ['i:vən'nʌmbəd] *adj* (portant un nombre) pair
evens ['i:v(ə)nz] *npl* (*in betting*) **to lay e.** parier à l'égalité; **horses quoted at e.** chevaux cotés à égalité; **the bookmakers are offering e.** les bookmakers offrent un enjeu égal
evensong ['i:v(ə)nsɒŋ] *n Church of Eng* office *m* du soir
event [ɪ'vent] *n* **(a)** (*occurrence*) événement *m*; **it is going to be quite an e.** ça va être un véritable événement; **in the course of events** par la suite; **to be swept along by the tide** *or* **course of events** être emporté par le cours des événements; **as recent events have shown** comme l'ont montré de récents événements; *F* **a happy e.** (*birth*) un heureux événement; **when's the happy e.?** quand l'heureux événement doit-il avoir lieu?; *Com* **coat e.!** soldes de manteaux!; *Mktg* **e. advertising** publicité *f* par l'événement; **e. attraction** (*in tourism*) attrait *m* touristique lié à une manifestation; **e. management** organisation *f* de manifestations; *Mktg* **e. promotion** communication *f* événementielle
(b) (*outcome*) issue *f*, résultat *m*; **in either e.** dans l'un ou l'autre cas; **wise after the e.** sage après coup; **at all events, in any e.** en tout cas; **in the e. of his refusing** au cas *ou* dans le cas où il refuserait, pour le cas où il refuserait; **in the e. of (his) death** en cas de décès; **in the e. of rain** au cas où il pleuvrait, en cas de pluie
(c) *Sp* (*meeting*) réunion *f* sportive; (*individual category, contest*) épreuve *f*; *Boxing, Fencing etc* rencontre *f*; **sporting e.** manifestation *f* sportive; **what was your best e.?** quelle a été ta meilleure discipline?
even-tempered *adj* (*person*) d'humeur égale; **of an e. disposition** d'humeur égale
eventer [ɪ'ventər] *n Horseriding* participant, -ante au concours complet
eventful [ɪ'ventfʊl] *adj* (*life, journey, day*) mouvementé, plein d'incidents
eventide ['i:v(ə)ntaɪd] *n Lit* soir *m*; **e. home** maison *f* de retraite
eventing [ɪ'ventɪŋ] *n Horseriding* concours *m* complet d'obstacles
eventual [ɪ'ventjʊəl] *adj* **(a)** (*final*) final, définitif; **his prodigality and his e. ruin** sa prodigalité et sa ruine finale **(b)** *Com* (*possible*) éventuel; **the e. profits from his new deal** les profits éventuels de sa nouvelle affaire
eventuality [ɪventjʊ'ælɪtɪ] *n* éventualité *f*; **in that e.** dans cette éventualité
eventually [ɪ'ventjʊəlɪ] *adv* (*in the end*) finalement, en fin de compte; (*at future date*) par la suite; **he e. became a judge** il finit par être nommé juge; **they e. reached the castle** ils ont fini par arriver au château; **I'll get round to mending that door e.** je finirai par réparer cette porte un de ces jours; **don't worry, I will do it e.** ne t'en fais pas, tôt ou tard je le ferai
▸ **eventuate in** [ɪ'ventjʊeɪt] *vipo Fml* conduire à
ever ['evər] *adv* **(a)** jamais; **I don't know if I'll e. see him again** je ne sais pas si je le reverrai un jour; **have you e. eaten caviar?** as-tu déjà mangé du caviar?; **I seldom if e. read French** je lis rarement du français, pour ne pas dire jamais; **if I e. catch him** si jamais je l'attrape; **nothing e. happens** il n'arrive jamais rien; **hardly e., scarcely e.** presque jamais; **he's a liar if e. there was one** c'est un menteur s'il en fût jamais; **it started to rain faster than e.** il s'est mis à pleuvoir de plus belle; **without e. having thought of it** sans jamais y avoir pensé; **the best mother that e. was** la meilleure mère qui fût jamais; **it was the best/worst e.** c'était le meilleur/pire de tous; *Sl* **did you e.!** par exemple!
(b) (*always*) toujours; **all she e. does is criticize** elle ne fait que critiquer; **e.-increasing influence** influence toujours plus grande; **e. the gentleman, he opened the door for her** en gentleman, comme toujours, il lui a ouvert la porte; **she was as cheerful as e.** elle était aussi gaie qu'à l'habitude; **for e.** pour toujours, à jamais; **to go away for e.** partir sans retour *ou* pour toujours; *Rel* **for e. and e.** à tout jamais, pour l'éternité; **Scotland for e.!** vive l'Écosse!; **to live for e.** vivre éternellement; **they lived happily e. after** ils vécurent heureux à tout jamais; *Old-fashioned* **yours e., e. yours** (*letter ending*) bien cordialement à vous, tout(e) à vous
(c) (*intensive*) **it was the funniest sight e.** c'était à se tordre; *F* **e. so pretty** joli comme tout; *F* **it was e. so long ago** ça fait tellement longtemps; *F* **e. so many times** je ne sais combien de fois; *F* **thank you e. so much, thanks e. so** merci mille fois; *F* **I'm e. so pleased** j'en suis tellement content; *F* **e. so slightly …** légèrement …; *Fml* **be he e. so clever/handsome** si intelligent/beau qu'il soit; *F* **e. such a lot of money** une somme d'argent tellement importante; *F* **as if I e. would!** comme si j'étais capable d'une chose pareille!; *Old-fashioned* **as quickly as e. you can** aussi vite que possible
(d) (*in what/where/etc questions*) **what e. shall we do?** qu'est-ce que nous allons bien faire?; **what e.'s the matter with you?** mais qu'est-ce que vous avez donc?; **what e. can it be?** qu'est-ce que ça peut bien être?; **when e. will he come?** quand donc viendra-t-il?; **where e. have you been?** d'où venez-vous donc?; **who e. told you that?** qui est-ce qui a bien pu vous dire cela?; **why e. not?** mais pourquoi pas?; **how e. are we going to get back?** comment allons-nous bien pouvoir rentrer?; **how e. you manage I don't know** je me demande comment vous faites
(e) e. since (then) dès lors, depuis; **I have been here e. since lunch** je suis là depuis le déjeuner; **he came to Scotland in 1960 and he's been here e. since** il est arrivé en Écosse en 1960 et il y est toujours resté
(f) *esp Am Sl* **is he/she/it/***etc* **e.!** (*generous, stupid, a beautiful day etc*) et comment!; **was I e. grateful for your help!** je te suis vraiment reconnaissant de m'avoir donné un coup de main!
evergreen ['evəgri:n] **1** *adj Bot* à feuilles persistantes; **e. oak** chêne *m* vert; *Fig* **e. topic** question *f* toujours d'actualité; *Fin* **e. facility** = possibilité *f* de prêt permanent **2** *n* (*tree*) arbre *m* à feuilles persistantes; (*song*) classique *m*
everlasting [evə'lɑ:stɪŋ] **1** *adj* **(a)** (*eternal*) éternel; *Bible* **the e. Father** le Père éternel; **e. flower** immortelle *f*; **e. pea** pois *m* vivace; **Henry, to his e. credit, said nothing** Henry n'a rien dit, ce qui est tout à son honneur **(b)** (*material*) inusable, solide **(c)** (*continual*) perpétuel, continuel, sans fin **2** *n* **the E.** l'Éternel *m*
everlastingly [evə'lɑ:stɪŋlɪ] *adv* (*eternally*) éternellement; (*continually*) perpétuellement
evermore [evə'mɔ:r] *adv Lit* toujours; **for e.** à jamais
every ['evrɪ] *adj* [①**A35-36**,c; **B14**,B,1,a] **(a)** (*indicating regular occurrence*) chaque, tout, tous les …; **e. week** toutes les semaines, chaque semaine; **e. day** chaque jour, tous les jours; **it's not e. day you get married** ce n'est pas tous les jours qu'on se marie; **confidence is increasing e. day** la confiance s'accroît de jour en jour; **e. other** *or* **second day** tous les deux jours, un jour sur deux; **e. other Sunday** un dimanche sur deux; **e. other line/page** une ligne/page sur deux, toutes les deux lignes/pages; **e. second or third day** tous les deux ou trois jours; **e. third man was chosen** on choisissait un homme sur trois; **at e. quarter past the hour** toutes les heures, au quart; **e. few minutes** toutes les cinq minutes; **e. so often, e. now and again** *or* **then** de temps en temps, de temps à autre; **e. mile/few miles or so** tous les miles/deux ou trois miles
(b) (*each*) chaque; **e. one** chacun, *f* chacune; **e. one of us was there** nous étions tous là; **they are my friends, e. one of them** ils sont tous mes amis; **I've checked e. single one** j'ai vérifié chacun d'entre eux; **at e. opportunity** chaque fois que c'est/c'était possible; **from e. side** de tous (les) côtés; **of e. kind** *or* **sort** de toute sorte; **of e. variety/age** de toutes les variétés/tous les âges; **e. word he says is a lie** tout ce qu'il dit est mensonge; **I have copied e. word of it** je l'ai copié mot pour mot; **e. time (that) she comes** chaque fois qu'elle vient; **perseverance wins e. time** la persévérance l'emporte toujours; **e. man for himself** chacun pour soi; (*in danger*) sauve qui peut!; **e. person has this right** chacun a ce droit; **e. man Jack of them** tous sans exception
(c) (*intensive*) **he was e. inch a republican** il était républicain jusqu'au bout des ongles; **I have e. reason to believe that …** j'ai tout lieu de croire que …; **you have e. right to be angry** tu as tout à fait le droit d'être en colère; **e. bit as good/intelligent as …** tout aussi bon/intelligent que …; **she's e. bit as much to be pitied as he is** elle est tout autant à plaindre que lui; **I shall give you e. assistance** je vous aiderai de tout mon pouvoir; **I look forward with e.**

confidence to the future j'envisage l'avenir avec une pleine confiance; **there's e. chance that he'll pull through** il a toutes les chances de s'en sortir; **we have e. hope that ...** nous avons grand espoir que ...; *Am* **e. which way I look** où que je regarde; *Am* **to look e. which way for sb** chercher qn partout; *Am* **(from) e. which way** de tous les côtés

(d) *esp Fml* **her e. action** chacune de ses actions; **they hung on his e. word** ils ne perdaient pas un seul mot de ce qu'il disait; **his desire to meet your e. wish** son désir d'aller au-devant de chacun de vos désirs

everybody [ˈevrɪbɒdɪ] *indef pron* [①A36,c] tout le monde; **e. has his/her** *or* **their own way of doing things** chacun/chacune a sa manière de faire les choses; **e. else** tous les autres; **I don't know about e. else, you guys, but I'm going home** je ne sais pas ce que vous comptez faire, les mecs, mais moi je rentre chez moi; **I don't know about e. else, but I'll be there** je ne sais pas ce que les autres comptent faire, mais moi je serai là; **e. knows that** tout le monde *ou* n'importe qui sait cela; **not e. can do it** ce n'est pas tout le monde qui pourrait le faire; **e. who is anybody** toutes les personnes importantes; **e. seems to know e. else** tout le monde semble se connaître

everyday [ˈevrɪdeɪ] *adj attrib* **(a)** (*daily*) journalier, quotidien; **e. occurrence** (*happening every day*) fait *m* journalier; (*ordinary*) fait banal; **it's an e. occurrence** cela arrive tous les jours; **e. life** la vie quotidienne; **e. routine** train-train *m* quotidien **(b)** (*used every day*) de tous les jours; **for e. wear** pour porter tous les jours **(c)** (*ordinary*) usuel, ordinaire; **e. expression** expression *f* courante; **e. English** l'anglais de tous les jours; **words in e. use** mots d'usage courant

everyone [ˈevrɪwʌn] *indef pron* = **everybody**

everyplace [ˈevrɪpleɪs] *adv Am F* = **everywhere**

everything [ˈevrɪθɪŋ] *indef pron* [①A36,d,ii] tout; **he has eaten e.** il a tout mangé; **e. I did seemed to go wrong** tout ce que je faisais semblait mal tourner; **(a place for e. and) e. in its place** chaque chose à sa place; **e. good** tout ce qu'il y a de bon; **they sell e.** on y vend de tout; *Com* **e. for cyclists** tout ce qui concerne le cyclisme; **money is not e.** l'argent n'est pas tout; **beauty isn't e.** il n'y a pas que la beauté (qui compte); **she's e. to me** elle est tout pour moi; *F* **to call sb e.** traiter qn de tous les noms; *F* **we're in a bad way with strikes and e.** ça marche mal à cause des grèves et de tout ça

everywhere [ˈevrɪweər] *adv* partout, en tous lieux; **to look e. for sb/sth** chercher qn/qch partout; **e. you go** partout où vous allez, où que vous alliez; **e. you look there is poverty** de quelque côté que l'on se tourne, on voit la pauvreté; **e. in France** partout en France

evict [ɪˈvɪkt] *vt* (*tenant*) évincer, expulser **(from** de); (*from meeting, court-room*) expulser; **evicted tenant** locataire *m* évincé

eviction [ɪˈvɪkʃən] *n Jur* (*of tenant*) éviction *f*, expulsion *f*; **e. notice, e. order** avis *m* d'expulsion

evidence[1] [ˈevɪdəns] *n* **(a)** (*non-legal use*) (*reason for belief*) évidence *f*; **if you can't believe the e. of your eyes!** si vous n'êtes pas convaincu par ce que vous voyez devant vous!; **there was clear e. that ...** il était clair *ou* manifeste que ...; **there is no e. to suggest a link between the two diseases** il n'y a aucune preuve suggérant qu'il y ait un lien entre les deux maladies; **they gave no e. of this** ils n'en laissaient paraître aucun signe; **on the e. of their past performances** si l'on en juge par leurs performances passées; **on this e., the answer would seem to be 'yes'** autant qu'on puisse en juger ici, la réponse semblerait être 'oui'

(b) (*indication*) signe *m*, marque *f*; **to bear e. of sth** porter la marque de qch; **there was no e. of his stay in the house** rien ne montrait qu'il eût séjourné dans la maison; **the books were e. of her interest in the subject** les livres étaient le signe *ou* l'indication de son intérêt pour le sujet; **to be in e.** (*of person, thing*) être en évidence; **the army was much in e. on the streets** l'armée était très fortement présente dans les rues

(c) *Jur* preuve *f*; (*testimony*) témoignage *m*; **there wasn't enough e. to convict them** il n'y avait pas suffisamment de preuves pour qu'on les condamne; **internal e.** preuves intrinsèques; **external e.** preuves extrinsèques; **oral e.** preuve orale; **written/documentary e.** preuve littérale/documentaire; **to give e.** témoigner, déposer (en justice); **to give e. in sb's favour** témoigner en faveur de qn; **to call sb in e.** appeler qn en témoignage; **the e. was strongly against him** les témoignages pesaient contre lui; **whatever you say may be given in e.** tout ce que vous direz pourra être retenu contre vous; **to turn** *Br* **King's/Queen's** *or US* **State's e.** témoigner contre ses complices (*sous promesse de pardon*)

evidence[2] *vt Fml* témoigner de; **as evidenced by ...** comme en témoigne ...

evident [ˈevɪdənt] *adj* évident; (*fact, truth*) patent; **it was e. that ...** il était évident *ou* clair que ...; **that was far from e.** c'était loin d'être évident

evidently [ˈevɪdəntlɪ] *adv* **(a)** (*clearly*) à l'évidence, manifestement; **he was e. afraid** il était évident *ou* clair qu'il avait peur; **e. worried** manifestement inquiet; **e., such a dangerous criminal must be caught** il est évident qu'un criminel aussi dangereux doit être arrêté; **I got held up – e.** j'ai été retardé – c'est ce qu'il semblerait **(b)** (*apparently*) **e. he's been away** il semblerait qu'il ait été absent; **e. not** il semble bien que non

evil [ˈiːv(ə)l] **1** *adj* **(a)** (*person, look*) mauvais, malveillant; (*spirit*) malfaisant, malin; (*moment*) funeste; **the E. One** le Malin; **e. influence** influence *f* néfaste; **e. eye** mauvais œil *m*; **e. intentions** mauvaises intentions *fpl*; **e. tongue** mauvaise langue *f*; **to silence e. tongues** faire taire la médisance; **house of e. repute** lieu *m* mal famé; **e. omen** présage *m* de malheur; *Lit* **to fall on e. days** tomber dans l'infortune *ou* dans le malheur; *F* **to put off the e. hour** (*of visit to dentist etc*) repousser le moment fatal

(b) (*smell*) mauvais, nauséabond

2 *n* mal *m*, *pl* maux; **to choose the lesser of two evils** choisir entre deux maux le moindre; **a social e.** une plaie sociale; **to speak e. of sb** dire du mal de qn; **the evils of drink** les effets néfastes de la boisson

evildoer [ˈiːv(ə)lduːər] *n Lit* malfaiteur *m*

evil-looking [ˈiːv(ə)llʊkɪŋ] *adj* (*man*) louche; (*knife*) vilain

evilly [ˈiːvɪlɪ] *adv* (*to laugh, leer etc*) avec malveillance; (*to look at sb*) d'un mauvais œil, d'un air méchant

evil-minded *adj* malintentionné, malveillant

evil-smelling *adj* nauséabond

evince [ɪˈvɪns] *vt Fml* (*quality, talent etc*) montrer, témoigner; (*curiosity, enthusiasm etc*) manifester

eviscerate [ɪˈvɪsəreɪt] *vt* **(a)** éviscérer, éventrer **(b)** *Fig* (*literary work etc*) émasculer

evisceration [ɪvɪsəˈreɪʃən] *n* éviscération *f*

evocation [evəˈkeɪʃən] *n* évocation *f*

evocative [ɪˈvɒkətɪv] *adj* évocateur, -trice **(of** de)

evoke [ɪˈvəʊk] *vt* **(a)** (*conjure up*) (*memory*) évoquer **(b)** (*provoke*) **this remark evoked a smile** cette observation a provoqué *ou* suscité un sourire

evolution [iːvəˈluːʃən] *n* **(a)** *Biol, Fig* (*of species, project etc*) évolution *f*, développement *m*; **the theory of e.** la théorie de l'évolution des espèces; *Fig* **the e. of events** le déroulement des événements; **her e. from journalist to revolutionary leader** son passage de la carrière de journaliste à celle de dirigeante d'un groupe révolutionnaire **(b)** (*manoeuvre*) (*of acrobat, troops etc*) évolution *f*

evolutionary [iːvəˈluːʃən(ə)rɪ] *adj Biol* (*character, symptom, disease*) évolutif

evolutionism [iːvəˈluːʃənɪz(ə)m] *n Biol* évolutionnisme *m*

evolutionist [iːvəˈluːʃənɪst] *adj, n Biol* évolutionniste *mf*

evolve [ɪˈvɒlv] **1** *vt* (*plan*) dérouler, développer; (*theory, truth*) développer, déduire **(from** de); **some species evolved wings** des ailes se sont développées chez certaines espèces **2** *vi* (*of events*) se dérouler; (*of situation, race etc*) se développer, évoluer; **the scheme evolved from a pilot project** ce programme a été développé à partir d'un projet-pilote; **medicine has evolved into a sophisticated science** la médecine est devenue une science sophistiquée

ewe [juː] *n* brebis *f*

ewer [ˈjuːər] *n Old-fashioned* pot *m* à eau; (*on washstand*) broc *m* de toilette

ex[1] [eks] *prep* **(a)** *Com* (*out of*) **price ex works** prix *m* départ usine, prix sortie d'usine **(b)** *Fin* (*without*) **shares quoted ex dividend/ex coupon** actions cotées dividende détaché/coupon détaché

ex[2] *n F* (*former husband, girlfriend etc*) ex *mf inv*

ex- [eks] *pref* (*former*) ancien, ex-; **ex-minister** ex-ministre *m*; **an ex-teacher** un ancien professeur; **ex-wife** ex-femme *f*; **ex-husband** ex-mari *m*; **all her ex-boyfriends** tous ses ex

exacerbate [egˈzæsəbeɪt] *vt* **(a)** (*pain, situation, sb's difficulties etc*) exacerber, aggraver **(b)** (*person*) irriter, exaspérer

exact[1] [ɪgˈzækt] *adj* exact, précis; **at the e. moment when ...** au moment précis *ou* au moment même où ...; **she was very e. in her reporting of events** elle a été très précise dans son compte-rendu des événements; **in the south of France, the Dordogne, to be more e.** dans le sud de la France, en Dordogne, pour être plus précis; **to give e. details** donner des détails précis *ou* des précisions, préciser; **an e. replica** une réplique exacte; **those were her e. words** c'est ce qu'elle a dit mot pour mot; **the e. word to describe Joanna** le mot juste pour décrire Joanna; **that wasn't the e. word he used** ce n'est pas exactement le mot qu'il a employé; **to**

tender the e. amount (*on bus*) faire l'appoint; **the e. opposite** exactement le contraire; *Fml* **to be e.** (*in payments*) être exact; (*in business*) être strict

exact² *vt* (*take*) (*tax*) exiger (**from** de); (*ransom, promise*) extorquer (**from** à); (*insist on*) (*obedience*) exiger, réclamer (**from** de)

exacting [ɪg'zæktɪŋ] *adj* (*person*) exigeant; (*work*) astreignant

exaction [ɪg'zækʃən] *n Fml* (*of taxes, money*) exaction *f*; (*of promise*) extorsion *f*

exactitude [ɪg'zæktɪtju:d] *n Fml* (*of report*) exactitude *f*, précision *f*; (*of reasoning, calculation*) exactitude, justesse *f*; **to say sth with e.** dire qch précisément *ou* exactement

exactly [ɪg'zæktlɪ] *adv* (**a**) exactement, précisément; (*of time*) juste; **I don't know e. what happened** je ne sais pas au juste ce qui est arrivé; **I don't e. know where he is** je ne sais pas exactement où il se trouve; **I'm not e. sure what you mean** je ne suis pas tout à fait sûr de ce que tu veux dire; **where e. in France did you go?** où exactement êtes-vous allés en France?; **that's e. right!** c'est exactement cela!; **but that's e. what I mean!** mais c'est précisément ce que je veux dire!; **it's e. the same thing** c'est exactement la même chose; **at e. the right/wrong moment** exactement *ou* juste au bon/mauvais moment; **e.!** précisément!, parfaitement!; **e. so!** exactement!; **it is e. five** il est cinq heures juste; **not e.** pas précisément; **she didn't e. agree, but ...** elle n'était pas vraiment d'accord, mais ...; **he is not e. a scholar** ce n'est pas precisément un savant

(**b**) (*with precision*) précisément, exactement; **e. calibrated** précisément étalonné

exactness [ɪg'zæktnɪs] *n* exactitude *f*

exact sciences *npl* sciences *fpl* exactes

exaggerate [ɪg'zædʒəreɪt] **1** *vt* exagérer; (*faults*) agrandir, amplifier; (*incident*) grandir; (*account, report*) charger **2** *vi* exagérer; **let's not e.!** n'exagérons rien!

exaggerated [ɪg'zædʒəreɪtɪd] *adj* exagéré; (*praise*) outré; **e. behaviour** comportement *m* excessif; **to have an e. opinion of oneself** avoir une trop haute opinion de soi-même; **to attach e. importance to sth** prêter une importance excessive à qch

exaggeratedly [ɪg'zædʒəreɪtɪdlɪ] *adv* exagérément

exaggeration [ɪgzædʒə'reɪʃən] *n* exagération *f*; **it would be no e. to say that ...** on pourrait dire sans exagérer *ou* sans exagération que ...; **without e.** sans exagération; **that's an e.!** vous exagérez!/ils exagèrent!/*etc*

exalt [ɪg'zɔ:lt] *vt* (**a**) (*praise*) (*sb's virtues*) exalter, vanter; **to e. sb to the skies** porter qn jusqu'aux nues (**b**) (*raise in rank*) élever

exalted [ɪg'zɔ:ltɪd] (**a**) (*sentiment*) exalté; (*tone*) élevé (**b**) (*rank*) élevé; (*person*) haut placé

exam [ɪg'zæm] *n* = **examination (a)**

examination [ɪgzæmɪ'neɪʃən] *n* (**a**) *Sch etc* examen *m*; **competitive e.** concours *m*; **to take** *or* **sit an e.** passer *ou* subir un examen; **to pass/fail an e.** être reçu/refusé à un examen

(**b**) (*inspection*) examen *m*; *Med* (*of vagina, rectum*) toucher *m*; (*of machines etc*) inspection *f*, visite *f*; (*of accounts*) vérification *f*; (*of report*) dépouillement *m*; *Jur* (*of files etc*) compulsation *f*; **on e.** après examen, examen fait; **on further e.** après un examen plus approfondi; **the matter is under e.** l'affaire est à l'étude; **to undergo a medical e.** passer une visite médicale

(**c**) *Jur* (*of accused*) interrogatoire *m*; (*of witness*) audition *f*; (*of case*) instruction *f*; **to be put under e.** (*accused*) subir un interrogatoire; (*witness*) être entendu; **he admitted, under e., ...** il a admis, lors de l'interrogatoire/l'audition, ...

examination paper *n* sujet *m* d'examen, questions *fpl* d'examen

examination result *n* résultat *m* d'examen

examine [ɪg'zæmɪn] *vt* (**a**) (*inspect*) (*machine*) examiner, inspecter; (*in Customs*) (*baggage*) fouiller, examiner; (*accounts*) vérifier; (*passport*) contrôler; (*files etc*) compulser, étudier, examiner; (*inventory, account*) dépouiller; *Med* (*patient*) examiner; **to e. one's conscience** faire son examen de conscience; **to e. a question thoroughly** examiner une question à fond (**b**) *Sch etc* (*pupil*) examiner, faire passer un examen à; **to e. a candidate in Latin** examiner un candidat en latin (**c**) *Jur etc* (*accused*) interroger, faire subir un interrogatoire à; (*witness*) interroger, entendre; (*case*) instruire

examinee [ɪgzæmɪ'ni:] *n Sch etc* candidat, -ate

examiner [ɪg'zæmɪnər] *n* (**a**) (*of baggage etc*) inspecteur, -trice; (*of files etc*) compulseur *m* (**b**) *Sch etc* examinateur, -trice; **the examiners** le jury (d'examen)

examining [ɪg'zæmɪnɪŋ] *adj Sch etc* **e. body** jury *m* d'examen; *Jur* **e. magistrate** = juge *m* d'instruction

example [ɪg'zɑ:mp(ə)l] *n* (**a**) exemple *m*; **to give an e.** donner un exemple; **to give just one e., ...** pour ne donner *ou* citer qu'un exemple, ...; **to quote sth as an e.** citer qch à titre d'exemple; **she showed me some examples of her work** elle m'a montré des spécimens de son travail; **a perfect e. of what not to do in a crisis** un exemple parfait de ce qu'il ne faut pas faire dans une crise; **for e.** par exemple; **large towns, (as) for e. London** les grandes villes, telles que Londres (par exemple); **by way of e.** en guise d'exemple

(**b**) (*model*) exemple *m*; **to set an e.** donner l'exemple; **to set a good/bad e. for sb** donner le bon/mauvais exemple à qn; **I wish you would set a better e. for your sister** j'aimerais bien que tu donnes un peu mieux l'exemple à ta sœur; **to be an e.** *or* **a good e. to sb** être un exemple *ou* un bon exemple pour qn; **their father wasn't a very good e.** leur père n'a pas été un très bon exemple; **let that be an e. to you!** que ça te serve d'exemple!; **to make an e. of sb** faire un exemple de qn, punir qn pour l'exemple; **to take sb as an e.** prendre exemple sur qn; **to follow sb's e.** suivre l'exemple de qn

exasperate [ɪg'zɑ:spəreɪt] *vt* exaspérer, irriter; **exasperated at** *or* **by his insolence** exaspéré par son insolence; **an exasperated look/voice** un regard/une voix exaspéré(e); **an exasperated gesture** un geste d'exaspération

exasperating [ɪg'zɑ:spəreɪtɪŋ] *adj* exaspérant, irritant

exasperatingly [ɪg'zɑ:spəreɪtɪŋlɪ] *adv* d'une manière exaspérante *ou* irritante; **to be e. slow/obstinate** être d'une lenteur/obstination exaspérante; **they had come e. close to winning** ils avaient frôlé la victoire de si près que c'en était exaspérant

exasperation [ɪgzɑ:spə'reɪʃən] *n* exaspération *f*; **to drive sb to e.** pousser qn à bout; **shut up!, she screamed in e.** tais-toi!, cria-t-elle, exaspérée

excavate ['ekskəveɪt] **1** *vt* (*tunnel*) excaver, creuser; (*soil*) fouiller; (*canal*) approfondir; (*ruins etc*) déterrer; *Archeol* **to e. a site** faire des fouilles **2** *vi Archeol* faire des fouilles; *Constr* procéder à une/des excavation(s)

excavation [ekskə'veɪʃən] *n* (**a**) (*action*) excavation *f*; (*of ground, soil*) approfondissement *m*; **the e. of a site** les fouilles *fpl* conduites dans un site (**b**) (*site*) terrain *m* excavé; *Archeol* fouille *f*; **the excavations at Pompeii** les fouilles de Pompéi

excavator ['ekskəveɪtər] *n* (**a**) *Constr* (*machine*) excavateur *m*, excavatrice *f*, pelleteuse *f* (**b**) *Archeol* (*person*) personne *f* qui fait des fouilles

exceed [ɪk'si:d] *vt* (*limits etc*) excéder, dépasser; (*hopes, fears, ambitions*) dépasser; (*other products*) surpasser (**in** en); **not exceeding ten pounds** ne dépassant pas dix livres; **not exceeding 250 gr.** (*parcels etc*) jusqu'à 250 g.; **do not expose to temperatures exceeding 50°C** ne pas exposer à des températures excédant 50°C; **to e. one's instructions** aller au-delà des instructions reçues; **to e. one's rights/one's powers** outrepasser ses droits/sa compétence; *Aut* **to e. the speed limit** dépasser *ou* excéder la limitation de vitesse; **he was fined for exceeding the speed limit** il a eu une contravention pour excès de vitesse; **the outcome exceeded all our hopes** le résultat a dépassé toutes nos espérances; **demand exceeded supply** la demande a excédé l'offre

exceedingly [ɪk'si:dɪŋlɪ] *adv* extrêmement

excel [ɪk'sel] (**-ll-**) **1** *vi* exceller (**at doing sth** à faire qch); **to e. at a game** exceller à un jeu; **at school she excelled in chemistry** à l'école, elle excellait en chimie **2** *vt* (*person*) surpasser; **to e. oneself** se surpasser; *Iron* **he's excelled himself this time** il s'est surpassé cette fois-ci

excellence ['eksələns] *n* qualité *f*, supériorité *f*, excellence *f*; **students are expected to strive for e.** on demande aux étudiants de s'efforcer à atteindre l'excellence; **centre of e.** centre *m* d'excellence

excellency ['eksələnsɪ] *n* (*title*) **Your E.** Votre Excellence *f*; **his E. the French Ambassador** Son Excellence l'ambassadeur de France

excellent ['eksələnt] *adj* excellent, parfait

excellently ['eksələntlɪ] *adv* admirablement; **she had done e. in her exams** elle avait excellé à ses examens, elle avait obtenu d'excellents résultats à ses examens

except¹ [ɪk'sept] **1** *prep* sauf, excepté, à l'exception de; **nobody e. him** personne excepté *ou* sauf lui; **all e. the doctor** tous, à l'exception du docteur, tous, sauf le docteur; **nobody heard it e. (for) me** personne ne l'a entendu sauf moi; **e. by agreement between the parties** sauf accord entre les parties; **they could do nothing e. pray** ils ne pouvaient rien faire d'autre que prier; **e. when** sauf quand; **e. for** à part, si ce n'est; **e. for getting a few scratches, she came out of it uninjured** à part quelques égratignures, elle s'en est tirée indemne; **we would have lost e. for you** sans toi nous aurions perdu; **the dress is ready e. for the buttons** la robe est prête, à l'exception des boutons; **you cannot obtain such permission e. by paying a bribe to local officials** on ne peut obtenir une telle permission qu'en soudoyant les autorités locales

2 *conj* **e. (that)** excepté que, si ce n'est que; **he came out of it unscathed, e. that he lost his hat** il en est sorti indemne, si ce n'est qu'il a perdu son chapeau; **I would go, e. I'm busy** j'irais bien, mais je suis occupé

except² *vt* excepter, exclure (**from** de); **present company excepted** les présents exceptés

excepting [ɪk'septɪŋ] *prep* à l'exception de, sauf; **not e. my wife** sans excepter ma femme

exception [ɪk'sepʃən] *n* **(a)** exception *f*; **to make an e. (of sth/for sb)** faire une exception (pour qch/qn); *Prov* **the e. proves the rule** l'exception confirme la règle; **without e.** sans (aucune) exception; **with the e. of ...** à l'exception de ..., exception faite de ...; **with a few exceptions** sauf de rares exceptions, à quelques exceptions près; **with certain exceptions** sauf exceptions **(b) to take e. to sth** (*object*) trouver à redire à qch; (*take offence*) se formaliser *ou* s'offenser de qch; **to take e. to sb's doing sth** trouver mauvais que qn fasse qch; **I take great e. to that remark** je trouve cette remarque très offensante

exceptionable [ɪk'sepʃənəb(ə)l] *adj Fml* (*usu with negative*) critiquable; (*offensive*) offensant; **nothing e.** rien de critiquable/d'offensant; **to find nothing e. in sth** ne rien trouver à redire à qch; (*offensive*) ne rien trouver d'offensant à qch

exceptional [ɪk'sepʃən(ə)l] *adj* (*unusual, outstanding*) exceptionnel

exceptionally [ɪk'sepʃən(ə)lɪ] *adv* (*unusually*) exceptionnellement, extraordinairement; **an e. fine day** un jour exceptionnellement beau; **e. cheap** d'un prix exceptionnellement bas; **e., no bail was granted** à titre exceptionnel, il n'a pas été accordé de remise en liberté sous caution; **e. gifted child** enfant remarquablement doué; **an e. well-made film** un film d'une qualité exceptionnelle

excerpt ['eksɜːpt] *n Liter, Mus* extrait *m* (**from** de)

excess [ɪk'ses] *n* **(a)** (*of light, enthusiasm etc*) excès *m*; **to eat/drink to e.** manger/boire à l'excès; **indulgence carried to e.** indulgence poussée trop loin; **to commit excesses** commettre des excès; (*cruel acts*) commettre des cruautés; **to be given to e.** avoir le goût des excès; **to indulge in e.** tomber dans l'excès **(b)** (*quantity, sum etc*) excédent *m*; **to pay the e. (on one's ticket)** prendre un supplément; **sum in e.** somme *f* en surplus; **sum in e. of 50** somme au-dessus de 50 **(c)** *Br Fin* (*in insurance*) franchise *f*

excess baggage *n Av* excédent *m* de bagages

excess fare *n Rail* supplément *m*

excessive [ɪk'sesɪv] *adj* (*heat, fine, expenses, amount*) excessif; (*zeal, desire*) immodéré; (*virtue*) outré, exagéré; (*ambition*) démesuré; **to be an e. drinker/smoker** boire/fumer à l'excès

excessively [ɪk'sesɪvlɪ] *adv* (*expensive, hot*) excessivement; (*clever, stupid, polite*) extrêmement, particulièrement; (*to eat, drink*) à l'excès; **it was hot/damaged, but not e. so** il faisait chaud/il était endommagé, mais pas trop; **to be e. generous** être (par) trop généreux; **he's not e. intelligent** il n'est pas particulièrement intelligent

excess luggage *n Av* excédent *m* de bagages

excess profit *n* surprofit *m*

excess supply *n* suroffre *f*

excess weight *n* excédent *m* de poids

exchange¹ [ɪks'tʃeɪndʒ] *n* **(a)** (*of prisoners, blows etc*) échange *m*; **e. of views** échange de vues; **we had an angry** *or* **heated e.** nous avons eu des mots; **in e. (for sth)** en échange (de qch); **car taken in part e.** reprise *f*; *Admin* **e. of posts** (*of two officials, civil servants*) permutation *f*; *Nucl Phys* **e. reaction** réaction *f* d'échange; *Med* **e. transfusion** transfusion *f* d'échange

(b) *Fin* (*of currency*) change *m*; **foreign e.** change; **dollar e.** change du dollar *ou* en dollars; *US* **exchanges** (*bills*) lettres *fpl* de change, traites *fpl*; **e. bank** banque *f* s'occupant d'opérations de change; **(foreign) e. broker** cambiste *m*; **e. control** contrôle *m* des changes; **e. index** indice *m* boursier; **(foreign) e. office** bureau *m* de change; **at the current rate of e.** au cours du jour, au taux du change du jour

(c) *Fin* **(Stock) E.** bourse *f* (des valeurs); **commodities e.** bourse de commerce; **corn e.** bourse des céréales; *US Mil* **post e.** économat *m* de l'armée

(d) (telephone) e. central *m* téléphonique; **local e. area** = réseau *m* urbain; **e. office** bureau *m* central (téléphonique)

exchange² *vt* (*blows, words, prisoners*) échanger; (*foodstuffs etc*) troquer; **to e. sth for sth** échanger/troquer qch pour *ou* contre qch, faire un échange de qch pour *ou* contre qch; **records exchanged for money** (*sign*) rachat de disques; **to e. glances** échanger un regard/des regards; **to e. views** échanger ses vues; *Admin* **to e. posts with sb** permuter avec qn

exchangeable [ɪks'tʃeɪndʒəb(ə)l] *adj* échangeable (**for** pour, contre); **a voucher which is e. for goods** un bon qui peut être échangé contre des marchandises

exchange gain *n Fin* gain *m* de change

exchange loss *n Fin* perte *f* de change

exchange rate *n* cours *m ou* taux *m* du change; **e. parity** parités *fpl* du change; **e. stability** stabilité *f* des changes; **e. swap** swap de change

Exchange Rate Mechanism *n EC* mécanisme *m* de change

exchange student *n Sch* étudiant, -ante qui participe à un échange

exchange visit *n Sch* échange *m*

exchequer [eks'tʃekər] *n Br Admin* **the E.** (*money*) le Trésor public; (*government department*) = le Ministère des Finances; **the Chancellor of the E.** = le Ministre des Finances

excise¹ ['eksaɪz] *n Admin* (*tax*) contributions *fpl* indirectes, *Belg* accise *f*; (*department*) service *m* des contributions indirectes, régie *f*; *Br* **Customs and E.** la Régie; **e. duties** droits *mpl* de régie; **e. documents** documents *mpl* administratifs de régie; **e. officer** receveur *m* des douanes

excise² [ɪk'saɪz] *vt Surg* (*tumour etc*) exciser; *Fig* (*passage*) couper (**from a book** d'un livre)

exciseman, *pl* **-men** ['eksaɪzmən] *n Br Hist* employé *m* de l'excise *ou* de la régie

excision [ɪk'sɪʒən] *n* excision *f*, coupure *f*; *Surg* excision, abscission *f*, ablation *f*

excitable [ɪk'saɪtəb(ə)l] *adj* **(a)** (*person, temperament*) émotif; **young children tend to be easily e.** les jeunes enfants ont tendance à être facilement surexcités; **they are an easily e. people** c'est un peuple exubérant; **be careful with him, he's rather easily e.** fais attention avec lui, il est assez excitable **(b)** *El, Physiol* excitable

excite [ɪk'saɪt] *vt* **(a)** (*get worked up*) agiter, énerver, surexciter; **don't e. him** ne l'énerve pas; **easily excited** surexcitable

(b) (*arouse enthusiasm in*) enthousiasmer, *F* emballer; **the idea/prospect clearly excited them** il était évident que l'idée/la perspective les animait *ou* enthousiasmait; **it really excites me** ça m'emballe vraiment; **what excites you in life?** qu'est-ce qui vous passionne dans la vie?

(c) (*stimulate*) exciter, animer; (*feeling, passion*) stimuler; (*sexually*) exciter; *Physiol* (*nerve*) exciter, stimuler

(d) (*give rise to*) provoquer, exciter, soulever; (*feeling, admiration, fear*) inspirer, provoquer; (*interest*) susciter; (*sb's curiosity*) piquer

(e) *El* (*dynamo, relay etc*) exciter, amorcer

excited [ɪk'saɪtɪd] *adj* **(a)** (*worked up*) énervé, surexcité, agité; (*impatient*) impatient; (*upset*) troublé; **e. children** enfants surexcités; **e. crowd** foule surexcitée *ou* en émoi; (*impatient*) foule impatiente; **to get e.** s'exciter; (*to get angry*) s'énerver; **don't get e.!** ne vous énervez pas!, du calme!; **he gets e. over nothing** il s'emballe pour un rien; **it's nothing to get e. about** il n'y a pas de quoi en faire toute une histoire

(b) (*enthusiastic*) animé, enthousiaste; **she was very e. about her trip to Canada** elle était très excitée *ou* animée à l'idée de son voyage au Canada; **the medical world is very e.** (*by discovery etc*) le monde médical est très enthousiaste; **doctors are e. by this discovery** les médecins sont enthousiasmés par cette découverte; **she was not in the least bit e. at the thought of his visit/about going to university** elle n'était pas du tout enthousiaste *ou F* emballée à l'idée de sa visite/à l'idée d'aller à l'université; **I can't get e. about it** ça ne me dit vraiment rien; **I don't understand what everyone's getting so e. about** je ne comprends pas ce qu'ils ont tous à s'exciter *ou F* s'emballer comme ça; **he was e. at the prospect of earning all this money** la perspective de gagner tout cet argent l'enthousiasmait *ou F* l'emballait

(c) *El, Physiol* excité; **e. state** *Nucl Phys* état *m* excité *ou* d'excitation; *El* état d'amorçage

excitedly [ɪk'saɪtɪdlɪ] *adv* (*to speak, laugh*) avec animation; (*to wait*) avec une impatience fébrile; **she was jumping up and down e.** elle sautait dans tous les sens, très animée; **she was watching the road e., waiting for the car to appear** elle regardait la route anxieusement, guettant la voiture; **he was waving his arms e.** il agitait les bras frénétiquement

excitement [ɪk'saɪtmənt] *n* **(a)** (*agitation*) agitation *f*; **he mustn't have too much e.** il ne faut pas qu'il s'agite; **to**

avoid e. éviter les sensations fortes; **to be in a state of e.** (*of person*) être surexcité

(**b**) (*enthusiasm, excited state*) animation *f*, enthousiasme *m*; **the thirst for e.** la soif des sensations fortes; **the e. of departure** l'émoi *m* du départ; **to cause great e.** faire (grande) sensation; **there is some e. in the city** il y a un certain émoi dans la ville; **a sense** *or* **feeling of e.** un sentiment d'exaltation; **there was an air of e. surrounding the event** l'événement baignait dans une atmosphère exaltée; **in the e. of the moment** dans l'excitation du moment; **we had a bit of e. at the office this morning** il y a eu de l'animation au bureau ce matin; **I wouldn't want to miss the e.** je ne veux pas rater ça; **it put the e. back into life for him** ça a remis du sel dans sa vie; **all the e. has gone out of my life** ma vie a perdu tout son piquant

(**c**) *Physiol* (*of organ*) surexcitation *f*

exciting [ɪk'saɪtɪŋ] *adj* (**a**) (*film, story, person etc*) passionnant; (*idea, prospect, proposal*) enthousiasmant; (*situation, scene*) sensationnel; (*full of suspense*) plein de suspense; **e. developments in medical research** développements passionnants dans la recherche médicale; **it was e. for him to be involved in such a project** c'était exaltant *ou* excitant pour lui de faire partie d'un tel projet; *Sp* **an e. finish** une arrivée palpitante; **an e. game** une partie mouvementée (**b**) *El* **e. coil** bobine *f* inductrice; **e. dynamo** dynamo *f* d'excitation

excitingly [ɪk'saɪtɪŋlɪ] *adv* d'une manière sensationnelle; (*to dress*) avec originalité; **e. different** d'une originalité enthousiasmante *ou* électrisante; **the most e. dangerous thing she had ever done** la chose la plus follement dangereuse qu'elle ait jamais faite; **the match finished as e. as it had started** le match s'est terminé de façon aussi palpitante qu'il avait commencé; **e., nobody knew exactly what might happen** ce qui était excitant *ou* exaltant, c'est que personne ne savait ce qui allait se passer

exclaim [ɪks'kleɪm] **1** *vi* s'écrier, s'exclamer; **to e. in anger/surprise/delight** pousser une exclamation de colère/surprise/ravissement **2** *vt* **leave me alone, he exclaimed** laissez-moi, s'est-il écrié

exclamation [ekskləˈmeɪʃən] *n* exclamation *f*; *Br* **e. mark,** *US* **e. point** point *m* d'exclamation

exclamatory [eks'klæmət(ə)rɪ] *adj* exclamatif

exclude [ɪks'klu:d] *vt* exclure (**from** de); (*draught*) empêcher d'entrer; (*doubt, suspicion*) écarter; **to e. sb from a society** (*expel*) exclure qn d'une société; (*not allow to join*) refuser à qn l'entrée d'une société; **the figures e. deaths from other causes** ces chiffres ne tiennent pas compte des morts provoquées par d'autres causes; **to e. sb from voting/working** dénier le droit de vote/de travailler à qn; **excluding ...** à l'exclusion de ...; **this excludes all possibility of doubt** le doute n'est plus permis

exclusion [ɪks'klu:ʒən] *n* (**a**) exclusion *f* (**from** de); **to the e. of ...** à l'exclusion de ... (**b**) (*refusal to allow to join*) refus *m* d'admission (**from** à); **the e. of blacks from certain jobs** l'exclusion des noirs de certains postes; **the e. of women from voting** la dénégation du droit de vote aux femmes

exclusion order *n* ordre *m* d'exclusion; **to serve an e. on sb** frapper qn d'un ordre d'exclusion

exclusive [ɪks'klu:sɪv] **1** *adj* (**a**) (*right etc*) exclusif; **to have e. rights in a production** avoir l'exclusivité d'une production; **you don't have an e. right to use this park!** vous n'avez pas l'exclusivité de ce parc!; *Journ* **e. interview** interview exclusive

(**b**) (*only*) seul, unique; **it has been his e. occupation for ten years** cela a été son occupation unique pendant dix ans

(**c**) (*expensive, upper-class*) huppé; (*club, social circle etc*) très fermé; (*boutique*) de luxe; (*clothing, jewellery*) de grande marque

(**d**) (*in logic*) exclusif; **two qualities that are mutually e.** deux qualités qui s'excluent

(**e**) (*with numbers, dates etc*) exclusivement; **chapters one to twenty e.** chapitres un à vingt exclusivement

(**f**) (*not including extras*) sans compter les extras; **rent £6000 a year e.** loyer 6 000 livres par an, contributions et charges non comprises

(**g**) (*not including*) **e. of** non compris; **e. of wrappings** sans compter l'emballage, emballage non compris; **price of dinner e. of wine** prix du dîner, vin non compris; **all prices are e. of postage and packing** les prix indiqués ne tiennent pas compte des frais d'envoi et d'emballage; **e. of tax** hors taxe, HT

2 *n Journ* article *m* en exclusivité; **a Times e.** une exclusivité du Times

exclusively [ɪks'klu:sɪvlɪ] *adv* exclusivement; **to be published e. in the Sunday Express** paraître en exclusivité dans le Sunday Express; **brought to you e. on ITV** diffusé en exclusivité sur ITV

exclusivity [eksklu:'sɪvɪtɪ] *n* (**a**) (*of restaurant, area*) caractère *m* huppé; (*of club, social circle*) caractère fermé (**b**) *Com* (*of dealership etc*) exclusivité *f*; **e. clause** clause *f* d'exclusivité; **e. arrangement** accord *m* d'exclusivité

excommunicate[1] [ekskə'mju:nɪkeɪt] *vt* excommunier

excommunicate[2] [ekskə'mju:nɪkət] *adj, n* excommunié, -ée

excommunication [ekskəmju:nɪ'keɪʃən] *n* excommunication *f*

ex-con *n Sl* ancien taulard *m*

excrement ['ekskrɪmənt] *n* excrément *m*

excrescence [eks'kresəns] *n* excroissance *f*

excrescent [eks'kresənt] *adj Fml* (**a**) (*outward-growing*) qui forme une excroissance (**b**) (*superfluous*) superflu, redondant

excreta [ɪks'kri:tə] *npl* excrétions *fpl*

excrete [ɪks'kri:t] *vt* excréter; (*of plant*) sécréter

excretion [ɪks'kri:ʃən] *n* excrétion *f*; (*of plant*) sécrétion *f*

excruciating [ɪks'kru:ʃɪeɪtɪŋ] *adj* (*pain*) atroce, horrible; **she was in e. pain** elle souffrait atrocement *ou* horriblement; *F* **e. music** musique *f* atroce

excruciatingly [ɪks'kru:ʃɪeɪtɪŋlɪ] *adv* atrocement; **e. painful** atrocement douloureux; *F* **e. funny** (*story*) tordant; *F* **e. boring** à en mourir d'ennui; **e. embarrassing/shy** horriblement embarrassant/timide

exculpate ['ekskʌlpeɪt] *vt Fml* disculper, exonérer (**from** de)

exculpation [ekskʌl'peɪʃən] *n Fml* disculpation *f*, exonération *f* (**from** de)

excursion [ɪks'kɜ:ʃən] *n* (**a**) (*journey*) excursion *f*; *Aut, Cycling etc* randonnée *f*; **to make** *or* **go on an e.** faire une excursion; **a shopping e.** un tour dans les magasins; *Old-fashioned Rail* **e. ticket** billet *m* d'excursion; **e. fare** tarif *m* excursion (**b**) (*digression*) (*in speech*) digression *f*; **after a brief e. into sculpture she returned to painting** après une brève incursion dans la sculpture, elle est retournée à la peinture

excursionist [ɪks'kɜ:ʃənɪst] *n* excursionniste *mf*

excusable [ɪks'kju:zəb(ə)l] *adj* (*error etc*) excusable, pardonnable

excusably [ɪks'kju:zəblɪ] *adv* de manière excusable; **she was e. reluctant to help** on pouvait l'excuser de ne pas vouloir aider

excuse[1] [ɪks'kju:s] *n* (**a**) (*justification*) excuse *f*; **there is no e. for his behaviour** sa conduite est inexcusable; **there was no e. for doing that** il n'y avait aucun prétexte à faire cela; **ignorance of the law is no e.** nul n'est censé ignorer la loi; **that's no e.!** ce n'est pas une excuse!

(**b**) (*pretext*) excuse *f*, prétexte *m*; **poor** *or* **feeble e.** faible excuse; **I'm not interested in excuses** tes excuses ne m'intéressent pas; **their e. was that they'd forgotten** leur prétexte était qu'ils avaient oublié; **to make excuses** s'excuser; **I make no excuses for these views** je ne ressens pas le besoin de justifier ces opinions; **stop making excuses for him** arrête de lui trouver des excuses; **to look for an e.** chercher des excuses; (*in order not to do sth*) chercher des faux-fuyants *ou* une échappatoire; **to look for an e. to celebrate** chercher un prétexte pour faire la fête; **to find an e. for sth** trouver une excuse à qch; **any e. to get out of the house!** tout prétexte est bon pour sortir de la maison; **he's just using his broken leg as an e. to ...** il se sert du fait qu'il a une jambe cassée comme excuse pour ...

(**c**) (*example*) **a poor e. for a letter** un semblant de lettre; **a poor e. for a car** un vieux tacot délabré

excuse[2] [ɪks'kju:z] *vt* (**a**) (*forgive*) excuser, pardonner; **to e. sb's laziness, to e. sb's being lazy** excuser la paresse de qn; **e. my being late** excusez-moi d'être en retard; **e. me yawning** je vous demande pardon si je bâille; **to e. sb's absence** excuser l'absence de qn; **he may be excused for laughing** il est excusable d'avoir ri; **you could be excused for thinking it was spring** on aurait pu facilement penser que c'était le printemps; **if you will e. the expression** si vous voulez me pardonner l'expression; **if you will e. me I have to finish my work** si vous voulez bien m'excuser, il faut que je finisse mon travail; **e. me!** (*let me past, sorry*) pardon!, excusez-moi!; **e. me?** (*what did you say?*) pardon?; **e. me, it was yesterday that ...** (*expressing contradiction*) pardon, c'était hier que ...

(**b**) (*exempt*) exempter, dispenser (**from doing sth** de faire qch); **to e. sb from attendance** excuser qn; **may I be excused?** (*leave the table*) puis-je sortir de table?; *Sch* est-ce que je peux sortir?; *Mil, Naut* **to be excused a fatigue** être exempté d'une corvée

(**c**) (*justify*) excuser; **his youth excuses him** sa jeunesse l'excuse *ou* peut lui servir d'excuse

(**d**) **to e. oneself** (*give excuse*) s'excuser; **I excused myself** (*apologized for leaving*) je me suis excusé de devoir partir

excuse-me *n* = danse *f* où on change de partenaire lorsque quelqu'un s'approche en disant 'excusez-moi'

ex-directory *adj Br Tel* **e. number** numéro *m* ne figurant pas dans l'annuaire, numéro se trouvant sur la liste rouge; **they** *or* **their number must be e.** ils doivent être sur la liste rouge; **to go e.** (*of subscriber*) se faire inscrire sur la liste rouge

ex dividend *adv* coupon échu

execrable ['eksɪkrəb(ə)l] *adj* exécrable, abominable

execrably ['eksɪkrəblɪ] *adv* exécrablement, abominablement

execrate ['eksɪkreɪt] *vt Fml* **(a)** (*abhor*) exécrer **(b)** (*curse*) maudire

execration [eksɪ'kreɪʃən] *n Fml* **(a)** (*abhorrence*) exécration *f* **(of** de); **to hold sth/sb in e.** avoir qch/qn en exécration **(b)** (*curse*) malédiction *f*

executable file ['eksɪkju:təb(ə)l] *n Comptr* fichier *m* exécutable

execute ['eksɪkju:t] *vt* **(a)** (*carry out*) (*task, order*) exécuter; (*plan*) mettre à exécution; (*operation*) accomplir; *Fin* (*transfer*) effectuer; *Jur* (*will*) exécuter; (*deed*) souscrire, signer; *Mus* (*piece*) exécuter, jouer; *Admin* **executed on ...** fait le ... **(b)** (*put to death*) exécuter **(c)** *Comptr* exécuter

execute cycle *n Comptr* cycle *m* d'exécution

execute file *n Comptr* fichier *m* exécutable

execution [eksɪ'kju:ʃən] *n* **(a)** (*of project, order*) exécution *f*; (*of purpose, goal etc*) accomplissement *m*; *Jur* (*of deed*) souscription *f*; (*of will*) exécution; *Mus* (*of piece of music*) exécution; (*of musician*) jeu *m*; **to put** *or* **carry a plan into e.** mettre un projet à exécution; **in the e. of one's duty** dans l'exercice de ses fonctions; *St Exch* **e. at market** exécution *f* au prix du marché **(b)** *Jur* (*seizure of property*) saisie-exécution *f*, *pl* saisies-exécutions **(c)** (*killing*) (*of criminal*) exécution *f*; **e. by firing squad** exécution par un peloton d'exécution **(d)** *Comptr* exécution *f*

executioner [eksɪ'kju:ʃənər] *n* bourreau *m*

executive [ɪg'zekjʊtɪv] **1** *adj* **(a)** (*in business*) (*post etc*) de cadre; (*in politics*) (*power*) exécutif; **executives** encadrement *m*, cadres *mpl*; **e. briefcase** attaché-case *m*; **e. chef** cuisinier *m* en chef, maître-coq *m*; **e. committee** comité *m* de direction; **e. decision** décision *f* prise par un cadre; *Fig* décision capitale; *Mil* **e. duties** service *m* de détail; **e. housekeeper** (*in hotel*) gouvernante *f* générale; **e. jet** avion *m* de société; **chief e. officer** président-directeur *m* général; **e. recruitment agency** association *f* pour l'emploi des cadres, APEC *f*; *US Pol* **e. session** séance *f* à huis clos; **e. travel** voyages *mpl* d'affaires

(b) (*luxury*) de luxe; **e. suite** (*in hotel*) suite *f* de luxe; **e. model** *or* **version** (*of car etc*) modèle *m ou* version *f* de (grand) luxe

2 *n* **(a)** (*in business*) cadre *m*; **sales e.** directeur *m* commercial

(b) (*of government*) (pouvoir *m*) exécutif *m*

(c) (*of political party, union*) bureau *m*, comité *m* central; **the union's national e.** le bureau national du syndicat

executive board *n* directoire *m*

executive class *n* classe *f* affaires

executive director *n* directeur *m* administratif, directeur gérant

executive officer *n Admin* cadre *m* supérieur; *Naut* second *m*, commandant *m* en second

executive producer *n Cin* producteur *m* délégué

executive secretary *n* secrétaire *mf* de direction

executor [ɪg'zekjʊtər] *n Jur* exécuteur, -trice testamentaire; **literary e.** exécuteur littéraire

executrix, *pl* **-trices** [ɪg'zekjʊtrɪks, -trɪsi:z] *n Jur* exécutrice *f* testamentaire

exegesis [eksɪ'dʒi:sɪs] *n* exégèse *f*

exegetical [eksɪ'dʒetɪk(ə)l] *adj* exégétique

exemplary [ɪg'zemplərɪ] *adj* **(a)** (*outstanding*) (*conduct*) exemplaire; (*husband*) modèle **(b)** (*serving as example*) (*punishment*) exemplaire; *Jur* **e. damages** dommages-intérêts *mpl* exemplaires

exemplification [ɪgzemplɪfɪ'keɪʃ(ə)n] *n* exemplification *f*; **in e. of his remarks** pour exemplifier ses remarques

exemplify [ɪg'zemplɪfaɪ] *vt* **(a)** (*show by example*) exemplifier, illustrer **(b)** (*serve as example of*) (*rule*) servir d'exemple à; (*problem*) être un exemple de

exempt¹ [ɪg'zempt] *adj* exempt, dispensé, exempté **(from** de); (*from tax*) exempt, franc, *f* franche; **he was declared e. from any blame** il a été délivré de toute responsabilité; *Mil* **to be e. from fatigues** être dispensé *ou* exempté des corvées

exempt² *vt* exempter, dispenser **(from** de); **to e. sb from doing sth** exempter *ou* dispenser qn de faire qch; *Mil* **exempted from military service** exempté *ou* dispensé du service militaire; **to e. books from VAT** exempter les livres de TVA; **to e. sb from responsibility for sth** délivrer qn de la responsabilité de qch

exemption [ɪg'zem(p)ʃən] *n* (*from tax, military service*) exemption *f*, dispense *f*; **e. clause** clause *f* d'exonération; **e. from customs duty** franchise *f* douanière; **e. from liability** exonération *f* de responsabilité; **e. from VAT** exonération *f* de TVA

exercise¹ ['eksəsaɪz] *n* **(a)** (*physical*) exercice *m*; **outdoor e.** exercice au grand air; **to take e.** prendre de l'exercice; **I don't get much e.** je ne fais pas beaucoup d'exercice; *Gym* **physical exercises** exercices physiques; **breathing exercises** gymnastique *f* respiratoire, exercices respiratoires

(b) (*mental, educational*) exercice *m*; **school/grammar e.** exercice scolaire/de grammaire; **piano exercises** exercices pour piano

(c) *Mil, Naut* exercice *m*; **tactical exercises** évolutions *fpl* tactiques; **to be on e.** être à l'exercice

(d) (*activity*) **religious exercises** pratiques *fpl* religieuses; **it was an interesting e.** c'était une expérience intéressante; **sending an ambassador would be a pointless e.** envoyer un ambassadeur ne servirait à rien; **it was just an e. in public relations** ce n'était que pour les apparences *ou* pour l'effet d'annonce

(e) (*use, practice*) (*of faculty, duty*) exercice *m*; (*of profession, religion*) pratique *f*; **in the e. of one's duties/rights** dans l'exercice de ses fonctions/droits; *St Exch* **e. of an option** levée *f* d'une prime

exercise² **1** *vt* **(a)** (*train etc*) (*body, mind*) exercer; (*troops*) faire faire l'exercice à; **to e. a horse** exercer un cheval; (*take for a walk*) promener un cheval **(b)** (*practise*) (*right*) exercer, user de; (*profession*) exercer, pratiquer; **to e. one's influence in sb's favour** user de son influence en faveur de qn; **to e. one's will/authority** faire acte de volonté/d'autorité; **we must e. caution/restraint** nous devons user de prudence/de retenue; *Fin* **to e. an option** lever une prime, exercer une option **(c)** *Fml* (*bother*) (*sb*) tracasser; *Old-fashioned* (*sb's patience*) mettre à l'épreuve **2** *vi* prendre de l'exercice; (*train*) s'entraîner

exerciseable ['eksəsaɪzɪb(ə)l] *adj St Exch* exerçable

exercise bike *n* vélo *m* d'appartement

exercise book *n* cahier *m*

exercise class *n* cours *m* de gymnastique

exercise date *n St Exch* date *f* d'échéance

exercise price *n St Exch* (*of share*) prix *m* d'exercice

exercise yard *n* (*of prison*) préau *m*

exert [ɪg'zɜ:t] *vt* **(a)** (*use*) (*force*) employer, faire usage de; (*influence, pressure, authority*) exercer **(b) to e. oneself** se remuer, se donner du mal; **to e. oneself to do sth** faire des efforts pour faire qch; *Iron* **don't e. yourself!** ne te donne pas trop de mal, surtout!

exertion [ɪg'zɜ:ʃən] *n* **(a)** (*of force*) usage *m*, emploi *m*; **he was accused of undue e. of influence** il a été accusé d'exercer une influence abusive **(b)** (*effort*) effort *m*

exeunt ['eksɪənt] *vi Th* **e. Romeo and Juliet** Roméo et Juliette sortent

exfoliate [eks'fəʊlɪeɪt] *vi Biol, Geol* s'exfolier

exfoliating [eks'fəʊlɪeɪtɪŋ] *adj Biol, Geol* exfoliant; **e. cream** crème *f* exfoliante

exfoliation [eksfəʊlɪ'eɪʃən] *n Biol, Geol* exfoliation *f*

ex gratia [eks'greɪʃɪə] *adj, adv Fml, Jur* à titre de faveur, à titre gracieux; **e. payment** paiement *m* à titre gracieux

exhalation [eksə'leɪʃən] *n* **(a)** (*of breath*) expiration *f*; **on e.** lors de l'expiration **(b)** (*thing exhaled*) effluve *m*, exhalaison *f*

exhale [eks'heɪl] **1** *vt* (*air from lungs*) expirer; (*one's last breath, smoke, gas etc*) exhaler **2** *vi* expirer

exhaust¹ [ɪg'zɔ:st] *n Aut, MecE* **(a)** échappement *m*; (*what is ejected*) gaz *m* d'échappement; **e. emission** émission *f* de gaz d'échappement; **e. fumes** gaz *mpl* d'échappement; **e. stroke** course *f* d'échappement **(b)** (*pipe*) (tuyau *m* d')échappement *m*; **e. manifold** conduits *mpl ou* collecteur *m* d'échappement

exhaust² *vt* **(a)** (*tire*) (*person*) épuiser, éreinter, exténuer; **to e. oneself in useless efforts** se consumer en efforts inutiles; **this/he is exhausting me** cela/il m'épuise **(b)** (*use up*) (*reserves, topic of conversation*) épuiser; **to e. sb's patience** venir à bout de la patience de qn

exhausted [ɪg'zɔ:stɪd] *adj* **(a)** (*person*) épuisé, exténué, éreinté; **I'm e.** je n'en peux plus, je suis épuisé *ou* exténué; **this baby's got me e.** ce bébé m'épuise **(b)** (*land, resources*) épuisé; **my patience is e.** je suis à bout de patience

exhaustible [ɪg'zɔ:stɪb(ə)l] *adj* limité; **her patience is easily e.** elle est vite à bout de patience

exhausting [ɪg'zɔ:stɪŋ] *adj* (*effort, climate*) épuisant; (*work, person*) épuisant, éreintant

exhaustion [ɪg'zɔːstʃən] *n* **(a)** *(of person, animal)* **(state of) e.** épuisement *m*; **mental e.** extrême fatigue *f* mentale; **to be in a state of complete e.** être complètement à bout de forces; **I was ready to drop with e.** je tombais de fatigue **(b)** *(of resources, land)* épuisement *m* **(c)** *Phys (of gas)* aspiration *f*
exhaustive [ɪg'zɔːstɪv] *adj (list)* exhaustif; *(analysis, description)* détaillé, minutieux; *(investigation, enquiry, search)* approfondi; **in e. detail** très en détail; **to make an e. study of a subject** traiter un sujet à fond
exhaustively [ɪg'zɔːstɪvlɪ] *adv (detailed, to list)* exhaustivement; *(to describe)* minutieusement; *(to study)* à fond; **this is an e. researched book** ce livre est le résultat de recherches approfondies *ou* très poussées
exhaust pipe *n* (tuyau *m* d')échappement *m*
exhibit¹ [ɪg'zɪbɪt] *n* **(a)** *Art etc* objet *m* exposé; **how many exhibits will there be?** combien d'objets seront exposés?; **we'll need more exhibits** nous aurons besoin d'autres objets à exposer **(b)** *Jur (in criminal proceedings)* pièce *f* à conviction
exhibit² **1** *vt* **(a)** *Art etc (of artist) (paintings etc)* exposer **(b)** *Jur (items of supporting evidence)* exhiber, produire **(c)** *(show) (object)* exhiber, montrer, faire voir; *(in shop window)* exposer; *(courage, bad grace etc)* faire preuve de; **to e. signs of stress/anxiety** donner des signes de tension/d'anxiété; **parking permits must be clearly exhibited on the windscreen** les permis de stationnement doivent être disposés bien en vue derrière le pare-brise; **he exhibited no remorse** il n'a manifesté aucun remords **2** *vi (of artist)* exposer
exhibition [eksɪ'bɪʃən] *n* **(a)** *(event)* exposition *f*; **Ideal Home E.** = Salon *m* des Arts ménagers; **e. insurance** assurance *f* foire; **e. stand** stand *m* d'exposition
(b) *(display) (of merchandise etc)* exposition *f*, étalage *m*; *(of talent)* manifestation *f*; *(of procedure etc)* démonstration *f*; *Jur (of items in evidence)* production *f*; *F* **to make an e. of oneself** se donner en spectacle; **it was a disgraceful e.** ce fut un spectacle de mauvais goût; **to give an e. of bad manners/bad temper** faire montre d'impolitesse/de mauvaise humeur; **I've never seen such an e. of bad manners** je n'ai jamais vu une telle impolitesse
(c) *US Sch* = séance *f* musicale etc donnée par les élèves et à laquelle sont invités les parents
(d) *Br Univ (award)* bourse *f*
exhibition centre *n* parc *m* des expositions
exhibition hall *n* salle *f ou* hall *m* d'exposition
exhibitionism [eksɪ'bɪʃənɪz(ə)m] *n* **(a)** *(showing off)* désir *m* de se faire remarquer **(b)** *Psy (exposing oneself)* exhibitionnisme *m*
exhibitionist [eksɪ'bɪʃənɪst] *n* **(a)** **he's an e.** *(shows off)* il aime se faire remarquer **(b)** *Psy* exhibitionniste *mf*
exhibitor [ɪg'zɪbɪtər] *n* **(a)** *Art (at exhibition)* exposant, -ante **(b)** *Br Cin* exploitant, -ante
exhilarate [ɪg'zɪləreɪt] *vt (of mountain air)* vivifier; *(of experience, news etc)* faire exulter; **they had been exhilarated by the thought that ...** ils exultaient à la pensée que ...
exhilarated [ɪg'zɪləreɪtɪd] *adj* exultant, fou de joie; *(laugh, cry)* d'exultation; **they felt e. by the news** la nouvelle les faisait exulter; **to feel e.** *(physically, after sauna etc)* se sentir grisé
exhilarating [ɪg'zɪləreɪtɪŋ] *adj (air, wind, walk etc)* vivifiant; *(experience, ride)* grisant; *(news)* réjouissant
exhilaration [ɪgzɪlə'reɪʃən] *n* gaieté *f* de cœur, joie *f* de vivre; **a mood/an atmosphere of e.** une humeur/une atmosphère joyeuse; **the thought filled him with e.** cette pensée le faisait exulter; **this feeling of e.** cette exultation
exhort [ɪg'zɔːt] *vt (person)* exhorter, encourager **(to do** à faire); **to e. sb to greater efforts** exhorter qn à plus d'efforts
exhortation [ɪgzɔː'teɪʃən] *n* exhortation *f* **(to do** à faire)
exhumation [ekshjuː'meɪʃən] *n* exhumation *f*; **e. order** permis *m* d'exhumer
exhume [eks'hjuːm] *vt* exhumer, déterrer
exigency ['eksɪdʒənsɪ], **exigence** ['eksɪdʒəns] *n Fml* **(a)** *(necessity)* exigence *f*, nécessité *f* **(b)** *(situation)* cas *m* pressant, situation *f* urgente **(c)** **exigencies** *(requirements)* exigences *fpl*, impératifs *mpl*
exigent ['eksɪdʒənt] *adj Fml* **(a)** *(urgent)* urgent, pressant **(b)** *(demanding)* exigeant
exiguity [eksɪ'gjuːɪtɪ] *n Fml (of accommodation etc)* exiguïté *f*; *(of income etc)* modicité *f*
exiguous [ɪg'zɪgjʊəs] *adj Fml* exigu, -uë, fort petit; *(diet)* maigre; *(income)* modique
exile¹ ['eksaɪl] *n* **(a)** *(banishment)* exil *m*, bannissement *m*; **to send sb into e.** envoyer qn en exil, bannir qn; **to go into e.** partir en exil *ou* pour l'exil; *(voluntarily)* s'exiler; **he lives in e. in Madrid** il vit en exil à Madrid; **government in e.** gouvernement en exil **(b)** *also Fig (person)* exilé, -ée
exile² *vt* exiler **(from** de)
exist [ɪg'zɪst] *vi* **(a)** *(be in existence)* exister; *(of conditions etc)* régner; **fairies don't e.** les fées n'existent pas; **a legend/tradition exists that ...** il y a une légende/tradition selon laquelle ...; **to cease to e.** cesser d'exister; **to continue to e.** subsister; **the Institute exists to carry out research** la raison d'être de l'Institut est d'effectuer des recherches; **these old shops still e. in a few places** ces vieilles boutiques existent encore dans quelques endroits; *F* **as far as you're concerned I don't e., do I?** en ce qui te concerne, c'est comme si je n'existais pas, hein?
(b) *(live)* se maintenir en vie; **I can't e. on that** cela ne me suffit pas pour vivre; **they managed to e. on a handful of rice a day** ils parvenaient à se maintenir en vie avec une poignée de riz par jour
existence [ɪg'zɪstəns] *n* **(a)** *(state of existing)* existence *f*; **the e. of these laws is not enough** l'existence de ces lois ne suffit pas; **to be in e.** exister; **the oldest manuscript in e.** le plus ancien manuscrit existant; **it's the only one still in e.** c'est le seul qui existe encore; **to come into e.** naître; *Lit* **to call sth into e.** créer qch; **to spring into e.** naître soudainement; **to go out of e.** disparaître, cesser d'exister **(b)** *(life)* existence *f*, vie *f*; **to lead a pleasant e.** mener une existence agréable
existent [ɪg'zɪstənt] *adj* **(a)** *(that exists)* existant; **these conditions have been e. since ...** ces conditions existent depuis ... **(b)** *(current)* actuel
existential [egzɪs'tenʃəl] *adj Phil* existentiel, -elle
existentialism [egzɪs'tenʃəlɪz(ə)m] *n Phil* existentialisme *m*
existentialist [egzɪs'tenʃəlɪst] *adj, n Phil* existentialiste *mf*
existing [ɪg'zɪstɪŋ] *adj* existant, actuel; *(equipment)* existant; **in e. circumstances** dans les circonstances actuelles *ou* présentes; *Mktg* **e. customer** client *m* actuel; *Mktg* **e. market** marché *m* existant, marché actuel
exit¹ ['eksɪt] *n* **(a)** *(way out) (from theatre etc)* sortie *f*, issue *f*; *(from highway)* sortie; *(roadway)* bretelle *f* de sortie; **e. only** *(passage etc)* réservé à la sortie
(b) *(act of going out)* sortie *f*; **to make a hurried e.** sortir en vitesse; *Th* **to make one's e.** sortir, quitter la scène; **the audience must have free e. at all times** le public doit pouvoir sortir librement à tout moment; **e. barrier** *(in store)* barrière *f* à la sortie; **e. door** porte *f* de sortie; *Mktg* **e. interview** *(for lost customers)* enquête *f* sur les clients perdus; *Pol* **e. poll** = sondage *m* effectué lorsque les électeurs viennent de voter; **e. sign** panneau *m* indiquant une/la sortie; **e. staircase** escalier *m* de sortie
(c) *Comptr* sortie *f*; **e. routine** routine *f* de sortie
exit² **(-t-)** **1** *vi* **(a)** *Th* faire sa sortie; **e. Macbeth** Macbeth sort **(b)** *(leave)* sortir **(c)** *Comptr* sortir **2** *vt Comptr (program, session etc)* sortir de
exit permit *n Admin* permis *m* de sortie
exit visa *n Admin* visa *m* de sortie
exocrine ['eksəʊkraɪn] *adj Physiol* exocrine; **e. gland** glande *f* exocrine
exodus ['eksədəs] *n* **(a)** *Bible (of the Jews etc)* exode *m*; **(the Book of) Exodus** l'Exode **(b)** *Fml, Hum (departure) (of group of people etc)* départ *m*, sortie *f*; **a mass e. towards the beaches** un exode en direction des plages; **there was a general e.** il y eut une sortie générale; *Fin* **e. of capital** évasion *f ou* fuite *f* des capitaux
ex officio ['eksə'fɪʃɪəʊ] *Admin* **1** *adj (member)* de droit, à titre d'office **2** *adv (to act)* d'office
exonerate [ɪg'zɒnəreɪt] *vt* **(a)** *(absolve)* **to e. sb (from blame)** disculper *ou* justifier qn **(b)** *(exempt)* exonérer, décharger **(sb from an obligation** qn d'une obligation)
exoneration [ɪgzɒnə'reɪʃən] *n* **(a)** **e. (from blame)** disculpation *f*, justification *f* **(b)** *(exemption)* exonération *f*, décharge *f* **(from** de)
exorbitance [ɪg'zɔːbɪt(ə)ns] *n (of prices, demands)* énormité *f*
exorbitant [ɪg'zɔːbɪt(ə)nt] *adj* exorbitant, exagéré, excessif; *(interest)* usuraire; **e. price** prix exorbitant
exorbitantly [ɪg'zɔːbɪt(ə)ntlɪ] *adv (priced)* d'une manière exorbitante; **e. expensive** excessivement cher, d'un prix exorbitant
exorcism ['eksɔːsɪz(ə)m] *n Rel* exorcisme *m*
exorcist ['eksɔːsɪst] *n Rel* exorciste *m*
exorcize ['eksɔːsaɪz] *vt Rel* exorciser; *(demon, possessed etc)* conjurer; *(spirit, fears)* faire disparaître
exotic [ɪg'zɒtɪk] **1** *adj* exotique; **a taste for the e.** le goût de l'exotique; **she is e.-looking** elle a un charme exotique; **an e.-sounding name** un nom aux consonances exotiques **2** *n Bot* plante *f* exotique
exotica [ɪg'zɒtɪkə] *npl* objets *mpl* exotiques
exotically [ɪg'zɒtɪklɪ] *adv* exotiquement; **e. flavoured/coloured** aux saveurs/couleurs exotiques

exoticism [ɪg'zɒtɪsɪz(ə)m] *n* exotisme *m*
expand [ɪks'pænd] **1** *vt* (*production, output*) augmenter; (*gas*) dilater; (*boundaries of empire*) étendre; (*idea, algebraic formula, chest*) développer; (*mind, circle of friends, range of products*) élargir; (*wings*) déployer; **it's an idea that could easily be expanded into a novel** c'est une idée qu'on pourrait facilement développer pour en faire un roman; **the police force is to be expanded** les effectifs de la police doivent être augmentés
2 *vi* **(a)** (*of solid, air, gas*) se dilater; (*of balloon*) se gonfler; (*of steam*) se détendre; (*of chest*) se développer; (*of sail etc*) s'étendre, se déployer; (*of company*) s'agrandir; *MecE* (*of belt*) s'allonger; **they want to e. into plastics** ils veulent se développer en s'introduisant sur le marché des plastiques; **as the Empire expanded** à mesure que l'Empire grandissait *ou* s'étendait
(b) (*talk, write at greater length*) préciser sa pensée; **could you e.?** est-ce que vous pourriez préciser ce que vous voulez dire par là?
▶ **expand on, expand upon** *vipo* (*talk, write at greater length about*) développer; **I'd like to e. on that** j'aimerais développer ce point
expandable [ɪks'pændɪb(ə)l] *adj Comptr* extensible
expanded [ɪks'pændɪd] *adj* étendu; (*wings*) déployé; **e. polystyrene** polystyrène *m* expansé; *Comptr* **e. memory** mémoire *f* paginée *ou* expansée; *Comptr* **e. memory specification** spécifications *fpl* de la mémoire paginée
expander [ɪks'pændər] *n* **(a)** *Gym* **(chest) e.** extenseur *m* **(b)** *Aut* (*in brake drum*) came *f* de frein
expanding [ɪks'pændɪŋ] *adj* **(a)** (*market, sector, field*) en expansion; (*gas*) qui se dilate; (*balloon etc*) qui se gonfle, qui enfle; (*commerce*) qui se développe, qui prend de l'extension; (*demand, production*) croissant; (*interests, circle of friends*) qui s'élargit; **the e. universe** l'univers *m* en expansion **(b)** (*watch strap, headband*) extensible; (*suitcase*) à soufflets
expanse [eks'pæns] *n* (*of country, water etc*) étendue *f*; **a vast e.** (*of water, snow etc*) une vaste étendue; (*of sand*) une mer; **a wide e. of cloudless sky** une immensité de ciel sans nuages
expansion [ɪks'pænʃən] *n* **(a)** (*making larger*) (*of gas*) dilatation *f*; (*of subject, chest etc*) développement *m*; *Comptr* **e. slot** emplacement *m* pour carte d'extension **(b)** (*becoming larger*) (*of solid, liquid, commerce etc*) expansion *f*; (*of gas, metal etc*) dilatation *f*; (*of flower, heart*) épanouissement *m*; *Econ* relance *f*; **colonial/territorial e.** expansion coloniale/territoriale **(c)** *MecE* **e. joint** fourreau *m* compensateur, (joint *m*) compensateur *m*; (*in concrete work*) joint de dilatation; **e. bit** foret *m ou* mèche *f* extensible
expansion card *n Comptr* carte *f* d'extension
expansionism [ɪks'pænʃənɪz(ə)m] *n Pol* expansionnisme *m*
expansionist [ɪks'pænʃənɪst] *adj, n Pol* expansionniste *mf*
expansion tank *n Aut* vase *m ou* réservoir *m* d'expansion
expansive [ɪks'pænsɪv] *adj* **(a)** (*force*) expansif; (*gas*) expansible, dilatable **(b)** (*person*) expansif; **in an e. mood** en veine d'épanchement; **to welcome sb with an e. gesture** accueillir qn à bras ouverts
expansively [ɪks'pænsɪvlɪ] *adv* (*to welcome*) chaleureusement; **to gesture e. towards the skyline/paintings** désigner l'horizon/les tableaux d'un grand geste
expansiveness [ɪks'pænsɪvnɪs] *n* **(a)** (*of gas*) expansibilité *f* **(b)** (*of person*) expansivité *f*, nature *f* expansive
expat [eks'pæt] *adj, n Br F* expatrié, -ée
expatiate [eks'peɪʃɪeɪt] *vi Fml* discourir (longuement) (**on** sur)
expatriate[1] [eks'pætrɪət] *n* expatrié, -ée; **an e. Scot** un Écossais expatrié
expatriate[2] [eks'pætrɪeɪt] *vt* (*person*) expatrier
expatriation [ekspætrɪ'eɪʃən] *n* expatriation *f*
expect [ɪks'pekt] **1** *vt* **(a)** (*anticipate*) (*person, letter, phonecall etc*) attendre; (*event*) s'attendre à; (*sb's arrival etc*) compter sur; **to e. sb for dinner** attendre qn à dîner; **the delivery isn't expected until Thursday** on n'attend pas la livraison avant jeudi; **I expected as much** je m'y attendais; **I expected more from you** je m'attendais à mieux de ta part; **I knew what to e.** je savais à quoi m'attendre; **to e. the worst** s'attendre au pire; **as one might e., as might be expected** comme on doit s'y attendre, comme de raison; **she played with the brilliance (which) we have come to e. (from her)** elle a joué avec le brio auquel elle nous a maintenant habitués; **to e. that sb will do sth/that sth will happen** s'attendre à ce que qn fasse qch/à ce que qch arrive; **I half expected him to say no** je m'attendais plus ou moins à ce qu'il dise non; **I fully expected him to agree** je comptais bien qu'il soit d'accord; **to e. to do sth** compter *ou* espérer faire qch; **I don't e. them to be pleased** je ne m'attends pas à ce qu'ils soient contents; **the movie was better than I expected (it to be)** le film était meilleur que je ne m'y attendais; **she was angry – well, what did you e.?** elle était en colère – et alors, ça t'étonne?; **some slight initial difficulty is to be expected** il faut s'attendre à rencontrer quelques légères difficultés initiales; **that's only to be e.** ce n'est pas du tout surprenant; **he is not expected to recover** on ne s'attend pas à ce qu'il se rétablisse; **they arrived later than expected** ils sont arrivés plus tard que prévu; **she's expecting a baby** elle attend un bébé
(b) (*require*) **to e. sth from sb** exiger qch de qn; **I e. you to be punctual** je vous demande d'arriver à l'heure; **I don't e. you to be perfect** je ne te demande pas d'être parfait; **it is expected that the candidate will be willing to undertake some travel** on attend du candidat qu'il soit disposé à voyager; **how do you e. me to do it?** comment voulez-vous que je le fasse?; **where do they e. them to go if there's nowhere else?** où veulent-ils qu'ils aillent si c'est le seul endroit?; **is it too much to e. a little courtesy?** est-ce qu'un peu de courtoisie est trop demander?; **it's too much to e. of a child** c'est trop attendre d'un enfant; **I know what is expected of me** je sais ce qu'on attend de moi; **people e. too much from marriage** les gens attendent trop du mariage
(c) (*suppose*) **to e. (that)** penser que; **I e. he'll pay** je pense qu'il payera; **I e. so/not** je crois bien que oui/que non
2 *vi F* **she's expecting** elle attend un bébé
expectancy [ɪks'pektənsɪ] *n* **(a)** (*expectation*) attente *f*; **an air/atmosphere of e.** un air/une atmosphère d'expectative *f*; **a look of e.** un regard plein d'espoir; **eager e.** vive impatience *f*; **life e.** espérance *f* de vie; *Mktg* **e.-value model** modèle *m* de valeur attendue **(b)** *Jur* (*of inheritance etc*) expectative *f*
expectant [ɪks'pekt(ə)nt] *adj* **(a)** (*expecting*) (qui est) dans l'attente (**of sth** de qch); (*crowd, face*) impatient; (*air, hush*) d'expectative; **the e. look on the children's faces** l'expectative qui se lisait sur le visage des enfants; **e. mother** femme *f* enceinte, future mère *f* **(b)** *Jur* (*property, heir etc*) en expectative
expectantly [ɪks'pekt(ə)ntlɪ] *adv* dans l'expectative, dans l'attente; **fans waiting e. at the stage door** des fans qui attendent à la sortie des artistes, pleins d'espoir; **he looked at me e.** il m'a regardé avec l'air d'attendre quelque chose
expectation [ekspek'teɪʃən] *n* **(a)** (*thing expected*) attente *f*, espérance *f*; **to come up to/fall short of sb's expectations** remplir *ou* répondre à/tromper l'attente de qn; **it didn't come up to e.** il n'a pas été à la hauteur de ce qu'on attendait; **to succeed beyond one's expectations** réussir au delà de ses espérances; **contrary to all expectations** contrairement à *ou* contre toute attente; **to have high expectations of sb/sth** attendre beaucoup de qn/qch; **in (the) e. of** dans l'attente de
(b) (*anticipation*) **with eager e.** avec une vive impatience; **to live in e.** vivre dans l'expectative
(c) *Jur* expectative *f* d'héritage; **expectations** espérances *fpl*; **uncle from whom one has expectations** oncle *m* à héritage
(d) (*probability*) (*of event*) probabilité *f*; **there is every/no e. that we shall be seeing them again soon** il y a de grandes chances/peu de chance pour que nous les revoyions bientôt; **e. of life** espérance *f* de vie
expected [ɪks'pektɪd] *adj* attendu; (*hoped for*) espéré; *Mktg* **e. product** produit *m* attendu; *Mktg* **e. service** service *m* attendu
expectorant [ɪks'pektərənt] *adj, n Med* expectorant *m*
expectorate [eks'pektəreɪt] *Fml, Med* **1** *vt* (*mucus*) expectorer **2** *vi* cracher
expectoration [ekspektə'reɪʃən] *n Fml, Med* expectoration *f*
expedience [ɪks'piːdɪəns], **expediency** [ɪks'piːdɪənsɪ] *n* **(a)** (*convenience*) (*of measure etc*) convenance *f*, opportunité *f*; **I questioned the e. of doing …** j'ai douté qu'il soit opportun de faire …; **on grounds of e.** pour des raisons de convenance **(b)** *Pej* (*opportunism*) opportunisme *m*
expedient [ɪks'piːdɪənt] **1** *adj* **(a)** (*convenient*) expédient, convenable; **do what you think e.** faites ce que vous jugerez à propos **(b)** *Pej* (*opportunist*) opportun **2** *n* expédient *m*, moyen *m*
expedite ['ekspɪdaɪt] *vt* **(a)** *Fml* (*hasten*) (*measure*) activer, pousser, hâter; (*procedure*) accélérer; **I'll do what I can to e. matters** je ferai ce que je pourrai pour accélérer les choses **(b)** *Old-fashioned* (*deal with speedily*) (*matter*) expédier, dépêcher
expedition [ekspə'dɪʃən] *n* **(a)** (*trip*) expédition *f*; **an e. to the North Pole** une expédition au pôle nord; *F* **a shopping e.** une expédition dans les magasins; *F* **getting here was quite an e.** ça a été toute une expédition pour arriver jusqu'ici **(b)** *Old-fashioned, Fml* (*promptness*) promptitude *f*

expeditionary [ekspə'dɪʃ(ə)nərɪ] *adj Mil (unit etc)* expéditionnaire

expeditious [ekspə'dɪʃəs] *adj Fml (procedure)* expéditif; *(reply)* prompt

expeditiously [ekspə'dɪʃəslɪ] *adv Fml* promptement

expel [ɪks'pel] *vt* **(-ll-)** *(person)* expulser; *(foreign body, enemy etc)* chasser, expulser; *(liquid, gas)* chasser, refouler; *(breath)* exhaler; *Admin (foreigner)* expulser, refouler; **to e. a pupil (from school)** renvoyer un élève (de l'école)

expend [ɪks'pend] *vt (time, resources)* consacrer, employer; *(money)* dépenser, employer; *(ammunition)* utiliser; **to e. one's energies on sth** consacrer ses énergies à qch; **all our stocks have been expended** toutes nos réserves sont épuisées

expendable [ɪks'pendəb(ə)l] *adj* **he/it is e.** il n'est pas irremplaçable *ou* indispensable; **the general considered these troops to be e.** le général considérait qu'on pouvait sacrifier ces troupes

expenditure [ɪks'pendɪtʃər] *n* **(a)** *(of money, energy etc)* dépense *f*; *(of ammunitions)* consommation *f* **(b)** *(amount)* dépense(s) *f(pl)*; **heavy e.** une forte dépense, de fortes dépenses; **e. on arms** les dépenses pour l'armement

expense [ɪks'pens] *n* **(a)** *(cost)* dépense *f*, frais *mpl*; *(of energy)* dépense; *(of funds)* utilisation *f*; *(of fuel, ammunition)* consommation *f*; **regardless of e.** sans regarder à la dépense; **at great/little e.** à grands/peu de frais; **at no extra e.** sans supplément de frais; **at my own e.** à mes propres frais; **book published at author's e.** livre édité à compte d'auteur; **to go to great e.** faire beaucoup de dépenses; **they didn't want to go to the e. of hiring a car** ils ne voulaient pas faire les frais de louer une voiture; **don't go to any e. over ...** ne faites pas de frais pour ...; **they went to considerable e.** ils ont dépensé des sommes considérables; **to put sb to e.** faire faire des dépenses à qn; **no e. was spared to ...** on n'a pas regardé à la dépense pour ...; *Fig* **a joke at my e.** une plaisanterie à mes dépens; **at the e. of the poor/his social life** aux dépens des pauvres/de sa vie sociale

(b) *Com* **expenses** frais *mpl*, dépenses *fpl*; **to meet/cover sb's expenses** rembourser/couvrir les frais de qn; **it's on expenses** c'est la société qui paie, ça va sur la note de frais; **to offer sb £100 and expenses** offrir à qn 100 livres, plus les frais; **travelling expenses** frais de déplacement, indemnité *f* de voyage; **living expenses** frais de séjour; **general expenses** frais généraux; **incidental expenses** faux frais; **to incur expenses** faire des dépenses; **to have all expenses paid** être défrayé de tout; **an all-expenses-paid trip to Paris** un voyage à Paris tous frais payés; **expenses claim form** note *f* de frais

(c) *(financial burden)* **to be a great e. to sb** être une grande charge pour qn

expense account *n* note *f* de frais; *Acct* compte *m* de charges

expensive [ɪks'pensɪv] *adj (object)* cher, coûteux; *(shop, restaurant)* cher; *(procedure, habit)* dispendieux; *(pastime, treatment)* onéreux; *(mistake)* qui coûte cher; **he has e. tastes** il a des goûts dispendieux *ou* de luxe; **that butcher's very e.** ce boucher est très cher; **to be** *or* **come e.** revenir cher; **that can be e.** ça peut être cher; **travelling is e.** les voyages coûtent cher

expensively [ɪks'pensɪvlɪ] *adv (to dress)* coûteusement; *(to eat, decorate)* à grands frais; **e. priced** coûteux, cher; **to live e.** mener la vie large, vivre dispendieusement; **try not to have it done too e.** essaie de ne pas le faire faire à trop grands frais

expensiveness [ɪks'pensɪvnɪs] *n (of commodity, life etc)* cherté *f*; **the e. of his tastes** ses goûts dispendieux

experience¹ [ɪks'pɪərɪəns] *n* **(a)** expérience *f*; **to gain e. of life** faire l'apprentissage de la vie; **practical e.** pratique *f*; **driving e.** expérience de la route; **he still lacks e.** il manque encore de pratique; **she has several years' e.** elle a plusieurs années d'expérience; **have you had any previous e.?** avez-vous déjà travaillé dans ce métier?; **I have enough business e. to ...** j'ai assez de pratique des affaires pour ...; **a man of e.** un homme d'expérience; **e. shows that ...** l'expérience démontre que ...; **to know sth from e.** savoir qch par expérience; **to learn from e.** tirer les leçons de l'expérience; **I know from bitter e. that ...** je sais, pour l'avoir éprouvé cruellement, que ...; **he was clearly speaking from e.** de toute évidence, il parlait en connaissance de cause *ou* il parlait d'expérience; **in my e.** d'après mon expérience; **my e. has been that** *or* **in my e. people appreciate politeness** j'en ai fait l'expérience, les gens apprécient la politesse; **I had no e. of looking after disabled people** je ne m'étais jamais occupé de personnes handicapées; **the black e. in this country** la condition des noirs dans ce pays; **I lost a lot of money but I'll just have to put it down to e.** j'ai perdu beaucoup d'argent mais au moins ça me servira de leçon; **well, it's all e.** voilà qui est à mettre au compte de l'expérience; *Mktg* **e.-curve pricing** tarification *f* en fonction de la courbe d'expérience; *Mktg* **e. quality** qualité *f* reconnue après achat

(b) *(individual event)* expérience *f*; **to have a nasty e.** faire une mauvaise expérience; **the journey was an e.** le voyage a été enrichissant; *Iron* le voyage a été une drôle d'expérience; **it was his first e. of love** c'était la première fois qu'il tombait amoureux

experience² *vt (emotions, feeling, pain)* ressentir; *(real hunger, poverty, success)* connaître, faire l'expérience de; *(difficulties, problems)* avoir

experienced [ɪks'pɪərɪənst] *adj* qui a de l'expérience, expérimenté, chevronné; *(observer)* averti; *(eye)* exercé; **to be e. in sth** avoir l'expérience de qch, s'y connaître en qch; **to be politically e.** avoir de l'expérience en matière de politique; **e. in business** rompu aux affaires; **a more e. doctor** un médecin plus expérimenté; **sexually e.** qui a de l'expérience en matière de sexualité

experiment¹ [ɪks'perɪmənt] *n* expérience *f*; **to carry out** *or* **do an e.** faire *ou* procéder à une expérience; **as an e., by way of e.** à titre d'essai *ou* d'expérience

experiment² *vi* expérimenter, faire une expérience/des expériences **(on** sur**)**; **an artist should be prepared to e.** un artiste devrait être prêt à toutes les expériences; **to e. with** *(new technique, style)* s'essayer à; *(philosophy, religion)* goûter à; **to e. with drugs** faire l'expérience de la drogue; **to e. with smoking** goûter à la cigarette

experimental [ɪksperɪ'ment(ə)l] *adj* **(a)** *(subject)* d'expérience; *(physics, evidence, method)* expérimental; **this new reactor is at the e. stage** ce nouveau réacteur est à l'essai *ou* en cours d'expérimentation; **e. research** recherche (expérimentale); **e. rocket** fusée expérimentale **(b)** *(based on experiment) (knowledge)* expérimental, -aux, fondé sur l'expérience

experimentally [ɪksperɪ'ment(ə)lɪ] *adv* **(a)** *(as experiment)* à titre d'essai **(b)** *(to discover sth)* expérimentalement

experimentation [ɪksperɪmen'teɪʃən] *n* expérimentation *f*

expert ['ekspɜːt] **1** *adj* expert, habile; **to be e. in** *or* **at sth** être expert en qch; **to be e. in** *or* **at doing sth** être habile à faire qch; **e. advice** avis autorisé; **an e. opinion** une opinion avisée; **e. panel** jury d'experts; *Jur* **e. witness** expert *m* cité comme témoin **2** *n* spécialiste *mf*; *(professional, with qualifications)* expert *m*; **I'm no e.** je ne suis pas un expert; *Jur* **medical e.** médecin *m* légiste; **according to the experts** selon les experts; **to be an e. at doing sth** être habile à faire qch; **she is an e. in this field** elle est expert en la matière; **the eye of an e.** un œil expert; **e.'s report** expertise *f*

expertise [ekspɜː'tiːz] *n (technical, financial etc)* connaissances *fpl*; *(as a cook, carpenter etc)* savoir-faire *m*, adresse *f*, habileté *f* **(in** à**)**

expertly ['ekspɜːtlɪ] *adv* habilement, de manière experte

expert system *n Comptr* système *m* expert

expiate ['ekspɪeɪt] *vt (sin)* expier

expiation [ekspɪ'eɪʃən] *n* expiation *f*; **in e. of his crime** pour expier *ou* en expiation de son crime

expiration [ekspɪ'reɪʃən] *n* **(a)** *(expiry) (of lease)* cessation *f*, expiration *f*; *(of option)* échéance *f*; *(of term)* fin *f*; *(of insurance policy)* expiration, déchéance *f*; **date of e.** *(of guarantee etc)* date *f* d'expiration **(b)** *Physiol (of air from lungs)* expiration *f*

expire [ɪks'paɪər] **1** *vi* **(a)** *(of law, treaty, deadline etc)* expirer, venir à expiration; **expired policy** *(in insurance)* police déchue; **this passport expires on ...** ce passeport expire le ...; **expired passport** passeport périmé **(b)** *Lit (die)* expirer, mourir; *(of hope)* s'évanouir **2** *vt Physiol (air from lungs)* expirer, exhaler

expiring [ɪks'paɪərɪŋ] *adj* **(a)** *Jur (lease, contract)* qui expire, qui est à son terme **(b)** *Lit (dying)* expirant, qui se meurt; **with an e. voice** d'une voix mourante

expiry [ɪks'paɪərɪ] *n (of term, contract, deadline)* expiration *f*, fin *f*; *(of period)* terme *m*; **e. date** échéance *f*, date *f* d'échéance, date d'expiration; **e. date of a contract** échéance d'un contrat

explain [ɪks'pleɪn] **1** *vt* **(a)** *(make clear)* expliquer; **that explains everything** voilà qui explique tout; **that is easily explained** cela s'explique facilement; **that explains his embarrassment** cela explique son embarras; **she explained to us how the system works** elle nous a expliqué comment le système fonctionne; **I explained that we were tourists** j'ai expliqué que nous étions des touristes

(b) *(justify) (one's behaviour etc)* justifier

(c) **to e. oneself** *(make oneself understood)* s'expliquer;

(*justify oneself*) se justifier; **I don't understand, please e. yourself** je ne comprends pas, veuillez vous expliquez
2 *vi* donner des explications; **you'd better e.** allons, expliquez-vous

▶ **explain away** *vtsep* donner une explication satisfaisante de; **how did he manage to e. away the broken vase?** quelle raison a-t-il trouvée pour expliquer que le vase soit cassé?; **he tried to e. away the women's underwear in the car** il a essayé de fournir une raison expliquant la présence de dessous féminins dans la voiture; **e. that away, if you can!** explique donc ça!; **he tried to e. away his absence from the meeting** il a essayé de justifier son absence à la réunion

explainable [ɪks'pleɪnəb(ə)l] *adj* (*behaviour etc*) explicable; **it's easily e.** cela s'explique facilement; **to become e.** s'expliquer

explanation [ekspləˈneɪʃən] *n* explication *f*, éclaircissement *m*; **to give explanations** fournir des explications; **to give an e. of one's behaviour** justifier sa conduite; **one e. is that ...** l'une des explications est que ...; **the e. is that ...** cela s'explique par le fait que ...; **I hope you've got a good e. for this!** j'espère que vous avez une explication satisfaisante à me donner à propos de ceci!; **she wasn't able to offer any e. of why it had happened** elle a été incapable d'expliquer pourquoi c'était arrivé

explanatory [ɪks'plænət(ə)rɪ] *adj* explicatif; **e. notes** commentaires *mpl*

expletive [ɪks'pliːtɪv] **1** *n* **(a)** (*swear word*) juron *m* **(b)** *Gram etc* particule *f* explétive, explétif *m* **2** *adj Gram etc* explétif

explicable [eks'plɪkəb(ə)l] *adj* explicable; **to become e.** s'expliquer; **this phenomenon is not e. by sociological factors alone** ce phénomène ne peut s'expliquer par les seuls facteurs sociologiques

explicit [eks'plɪsɪt] *adj* explicite; **to be more e. (in one's statements)** préciser (ses affirmations); **to make sth e.** rendre qch explicite; **e. sex and violence** (*on television etc*) de la violence et du sexe montrés de façon explicite; **sexually e. scenes** scènes au contenu sexuel non voilé; **e. language** (*vulgar*) langage susceptible d'offenser la pudeur

explicitly [eks'plɪsɪtlɪ] *adv* explicitement, de manière explicite

explode [ɪks'pləʊd] **1** *vt* **(a)** (*detonate etc*) (*shell*) faire éclater; (*mine*) faire sauter; (*gas*) faire exploser **(b)** (*show to be false*) démontrer la fausseté de; (*theory*) discréditer; (*myth*) detruire **(c)** (*in diagram*) éclater **2** *vi* (*of boiler, shell etc*) éclater; (*of mine*) sauter; (*of gas, dynamite etc*) exploser, détoner; (*of car, plane etc*) exploser; *Fig* **to e. with laughter** éclater de rire; *Fig* **he'll e.** (*with anger*) il va exploser (de colère), il va sortir de ses gonds; (*with repressed feeling*) il va craquer; (*with overeating*) il va exploser; *Fig* **the population exploded after the war** il y a eu une explosion démographique après la guerre

exploded [ɪks'pləʊdɪd] *adj* **(a)** (*shell*) éclaté; (*mine*) qui a sauté **(b)** (*theory*) abandonné, reconnu pour faux **(c)** (*in technical drawing*), *Phot* **e. view** vue *f* éclatée

exploit[1] ['eksplɔɪt] *n* exploit *m*, haut fait *m*

exploit[2] [eks'plɔɪt] *vt* **(a)** (*take unfair advantage of*) exploiter; **immigrant workers are being exploited** les travailleurs immigrés se font exploiter **(b)** (*use*) (*mine, forest etc*) exploiter; (*talents*) mettre à profit; (*scandal*) exploiter

exploitation [eksplɔɪ'teɪʃən] *n* exploitation *f*

exploration [ekspləˈreɪʃən] *n* **(a)** (*trip*) exploration *f*; **voyage of e.** voyage *m* de découverte; **Magellan called here on his explorations** au cours de ses explorations, Magellan est passé par ici **(b)** (*act*) (*of terrain*) exploration *f*, reconnaissance *f*; **e. work** travaux *mpl* de recherches; **the e. of a possibility** l'étude *f* d'une possibilité **(c)** *Med* (*of wound*) exploration *f*

explorative [ɪks'plɒrətɪv] *adj* explorateur, -trice

exploratory [ɪks'plɒrət(ə)rɪ] *adj* (*well, poll*) d'exploration; (*voyage*) de découverte; (*dialogue*) préliminaire; *Med* **e. surgery** opération *f* exploratoire; *Med* **e. test** exploration *f*

explore [ɪks'plɔːr] *vt* **(a)** (*region, town*) explorer; (*continent*) aller à la découverte dans; (*country*) faire l'exploration de; (*terrain*) tâter; (*possibility, idea*) étudier; (*theory*) étudier en détail; **to e. sth with one's hands/tongue** explorer qch de ses mains/de la langue; *Com* **to e. the market** prospecter le marché **(b)** *Med* (*wound*) explorer, sonder

explorer [ɪks'plɔːrər] *n* (*person*) explorateur, -trice

explosion [ɪks'pləʊʒən] *n* (*of gases, shell etc*) explosion *f*; (*of gas*) déflagration *f*; (*noise*) détonation *f*; *Fig* (*of anger, joy*) débordement *m*; (*of laughter, artistic creativity, new writing*) explosion; **to cause an e.** provoquer une explosion; *Fig* **population e.** explosion démographique

explosive [ɪks'pləʊsɪv] **1** *adj* **(a)** explosif, détonant; **e. device** engin *m* explosif; *Nucl Phys* **e. fission** fission *f* explosive; **e. mixture** mélange *m* détonant; *Fig* **an e. situation/combination** une situation/combinaison explosive **(b)** *Ling* (*consonant*) explosif **2** *n* **(a)** (*material*) explosif *m* **(b)** *Ling* (consonne *f*) explosive *f*

exponent [ɪks'pəʊnənt] *n* **(a)** (*of system etc*) interprète *mf*; (*of theory, idea, opinion*) avocat *m*, défenseur *m*; *Mus* (*of work*) interprète, exécutant, -ante; (*of sport*) protagoniste *mf*; **the leading exponents of this genre** les principaux représentants de ce genre **(b)** *Math* (*of quantity*) exposant *m*

exponential [ekspəʊ'nenʃəl] *adj* exponentiel; *Math* **e. curve** courbe *f* exponentielle

exponentially [ekspəʊ'nenʃəlɪ] *adv* de manière exponentielle

export[1] ['ekspɔːt] *n* **(a)** (*product*) article *m* d'exportation; **coffee is an important e.** le café est une des exportations principales; **exports** (*of country*) exportations *fpl*; **visible/invisible exports** exportations visibles/invisibles
(b) (*trade*) exportation *f*; **the e. of coal** l'exportation de charbon; **for e. only** réservé à l'exportation; **e. agent** agent *m* exportateur; **e. ban** interdiction *f* d'exportation; **e. bid** offre *f* export; **e. company** entreprise *f* exportatrice; **e. credit guarantee** garantie *f* de crédit à l'exportation; **E. Credit Guarantee Department** COFACE *f*; **e. department** service *m* des exportations, service export, service commercial export; **e. director** directeur *m* export; **e. duty** droit(s) *m(pl)* de sortie; **e. earnings** recettes *fpl* d'exportation; **e. financing** financement *m* des exportations; **e. guarantee** garantie *f* à l'exportation; **e. licence** licence *f* d'exportation; **e. management company** société *f* de portage; **e. manager** directeur *m* export; **e. market** marché *m* à l'export, marché à l'exportation; **e. order** commande *f* export; **e. restrictions** restrictions *fpl* aux exportations; **e. sales** ventes *fpl* export; **e. sales director** directeur *m* des ventes export; **e. tariff** tarif *m* export; **e. tax** taxe *f* à l'exportation; **e. tourism** tourisme *m* d'exportation; **e. trade** commerce *m* d'exportation; **a flourising e. trade** une exportation florissante

export[2] [eks'pɔːt] **1** *vt* **(a)** (*goods, Fig way of life*) exporter **(b)** *Comptr* exporter **2** *vi* exporter; **exporting country** pays *m* exportateur

exportable [eks'pɔːtəb(ə)l] *adj* exportable

exportation [ekspɔː'teɪʃən] *n* exportation *f*

exporter [eks'pɔːtər] *n* exportateur, -trice (**of** de)

expose [ɪks'pəʊz] *vt* **(a)** (*put in unprotected position*) exposer; (*new born child*) abandonner; *Phot* (*film*) exposer; **to be exposed to the weather** être exposé aux intempéries; **to e. sb/oneself to danger** exposer qn/s'exposer au danger; **to e. one's flank to the enemy** prêter le flanc à l'ennemi; **to e. oneself to ridicule/sb's anger** s'exposer à la risée publique/à la colère de qn
(b) (*lay bare*) (*wire etc*) mettre à découvert *ou* à nu *ou* à jour
(c) (*display*) (*one's ignorance, feelings*) afficher; (*goods for sale*) étaler; *Rel* (*the Blessed Sacrament*) exposer; **to e. oneself** faire de l'exhibitionnisme; **a man exposed himself to her** un exhibitionniste l'a approchée
(d) (*reveal*) (*secret*) éventer; (*crime*) dévoiler; (*criminal activity, network*) mettre à jour; (*traitor*) démasquer; **they're trying to e. him as ...** ils essaient de démontrer que c'est ...; **he feared being exposed as a homosexual** il craignait que son homosexualité ne soit découverte *ou* mise à jour

exposé [eks'pəʊzeɪ] *n* (*article, documentary, book etc*) exposé *m*; (*of scandal etc*) révélation *f*

exposed [ɪks'pəʊzd] *adj* **(a)** (*to sight, elements*) exposé; (*gears*) à découvert; *Phot* (*film*) exposé, impressionné; *Mil* **e. position** endroit exposé; *Fig* **this leaves the Prime Minister in an e. position** cela laisse le premier ministre dans une position fragile; **to be e.** (*of troops*) être en l'air **(b)** (*laid bare*) à nu

exposition [ekspə'zɪʃən] *n* **(a)** (*explanation*) exposé *m*, exposition *f*, présentation *f*; (*in novel*), *Mus* exposition **(b)** (*exhibition*) exposition *f* **(c)** *Rel* exposition *f*

expostulate [ɪks'pɒstjʊleɪt] *vi* vitupérer (**about** contre); **to e. with sb about sth** faire des remontrances à qn sur *ou* à propos de qch

expostulation [ɪkspɒstjʊ'leɪʃən] *n* (*to person*) vitupérations *fpl*, remontrance(s) *f(pl)*

exposure [ɪks'pəʊʒər] *n* **(a)** (*to air, cold, danger*) exposition *f*; (*of new born child*) abandon *m*; *Fin* exposition *f* aux risques; **to die of e.** mourir de froid; *Nucl Phys* **e. (to radiation)** irradiation *f*
(b) (*display*) (*of goods for sale*) exposition *f*, étalage *m*; (*on market*) exposition; *Jur* **indecent e.** outrage *m* public à la pudeur
(c) *Journ etc* **press e.** couverture *f* médiatique; **to get a lot of e.** recevoir une importante couverture médiatique;

politicians eager for e. les hommes politiques anxieux de paraître dans les médias

(d) (*of crime etc*) dévoilement *m*; (*of crook*) dénonciation *f*; **to threaten sb with e.** menacer de mettre à jour les activités de qn

(e) *Phot* (*shot*) prise *f* de vue; **time e.** pose *f*; **a 36-e. film** une pellicule 36 poses

(f) (*outlook of building, place*) exposition *f*, orientation *f*

exposure counter *n Phot* compteur *m* de prises de vue

exposure meter *n Phot* posemètre *m*

exposure time *n Phot* temps *m* de pose

expound [ɪks'paʊnd] *vt* (*doctrine, principles*) exposer; *Rel* (*Holy Scriptures*) interpréter

express[1] [ɪks'pres] **1** *adj* **(a)** (*clear*) (*law, stipulation etc*) exprès, *f* expresse; (*order*) formel, explicite; **for this e. purpose** dans ce but même; **it was her e. instruction that we …** elle nous a formellement *ou* explicitement demandé de … **(b)** *US* (*rapid*) **e. company** compagnie *f* de messageries **(c)** (*image*) exact, fidèle (**of** de) **2** *adv* sans arrêt; **to send a letter e.** envoyer une lettre par *ou* en exprès; **lift that goes e. to the twentieth floor** ascenseur qui monte directement au vingtième étage **3** *n* **(a)** (*train*) express *m*, rapide *m* **(b)** *US F* (*freight company*) compagnie *f* de messageries

express[2] *vt* **(a)** (*one's feelings, intention*) exprimer; (*one's will, desire*) manifester; (*opinion*) émettre; (*wish*) formuler; (*gratitude*) témoigner; **a millionaire has expressed an interest in (buying) the castle** un millionnaire s'est déclaré intéressé par le château; **well/badly expressed** bien/mal rendu; **to e. oneself** s'exprimer; *Math* **to e. sth as an equation** exprimer qch sous forme d'équation **(b)** (*remove*) (*oil etc*) extraire (**out of, from** de); (*milk*) exprimer **(c)** (*letter*) envoyer par *ou* en exprès; *US* (*package*) (*by freight company*) envoyer *ou* expédier par les messageries

express delivery *n* envoi *m* par exprès

express freight *n* fret *m* express

expression [ɪks'preʃən] *n* **(a)** (*of face, eyes*) expression *f*; **he had a strange e. (on his face)** il avait une drôle d'expression

(b) (*phrase*) expression *f*, locution *f*; **it's just an e.** ce n'est qu'une expression; *Math* **algebraical e.** expression *ou* formule *f* algébrique

(c) (*act of expressing*) (*of thought, joy etc*) expression *f*, manifestation *f*; **beyond e.** au delà de toute expression, inexprimable; **freedom of e.** liberté *f* d'expression; **these feelings found e. in her poetry** sa poésie a su exprimer ces sentiments; **he raised his fist in an e. of defiance** il brandit le poing en signe de défi

(d) (*feeling*) **with e.** (*to sing, act*) avec expression

expressionism [ɪks'preʃənɪz(ə)m] *n Art* expressionnisme *m*

expressionist [ɪks'preʃənɪst] *adj, n Art* expressionniste *mf*

expressionless [ɪks'preʃənlɪs] *adj* (*voice*) sans expression; (*face*) impassible, sans expression; **there was something rather e. about her performance** quelque chose dans sa performance manquait d'expression

expressive [ɪks'presɪv] *adj* (*face, eyes*) expressif, plein d'expression; (*gesture, silence*) éloquent; (*person*) démonstratif; (*language*) expressif; **attitude e. of disdain** attitude qui exprime le dédain

expressively [ɪks'presɪvlɪ] *adv* avec expression

expressiveness [ɪks'presɪvnɪs] *n* (*of face etc*) caractère *m* expressif, force *f* d'expression

express letter *n* lettre *f* exprès

expressly [ɪks'preslɪ] *adv* **(a)** (*clearly*) expressément, formellement; **e. forbidden** expressément *ou* formellement défendu; **I e. told you to buy a lettuce** je t'ai bien dit d'acheter une salade **(b)** (*with a clear purpose*) **to do sth e. to …** faire qch dans le seul but de …

express messenger *n* messager *m* exprès; **by e.** par exprès

express train *n* (train *m*) express *m*, rapide *m*

expressway [ɪks'presweɪ] *n Am* autoroute *f*, voie *f* rapide

expropriate [eks'prəʊprɪeɪt] *vt* (*owner, property*) exproprier

expropriation [ekspræʊprɪ'eɪʃən] *n* expropriation *f*

expulsion [ɪks'pʌlʃən] *n* (*from country, political party etc*) expulsion *f*; (*from school*) renvoi *m*

expunge [ɪks'pʌndʒ] *vt Fml* (*name from list*) effacer, rayer; (*passage from book*) supprimer; (*memory, thought*) effacer

expurgate ['ekspɜːgeɪt] *vt* (*book*) expurger; (*text*) épurer; (*passage etc*) supprimer; **expurgated edition** édition expurgée

expurgation [ekspɜː'geɪʃən] *n* (*of book*) expurgation *f*; (*of text*) épuration *f*; (*of passage*) suppression *f*

exquisite ['ekskwɪzɪt] *adj* **(a)** (*food, wine, afternoon*) exquis; (*pleasure etc*) vif; **the relief was e.** ce fut un merveilleux soulagement **(b)** (*delicate*) très sensible, délicat, subtil **(c)** (*torture*) raffiné; (*pain*) exquis

exquisitely [eks'kwɪzɪtlɪ] *adv* **(a)** (*delicately*) d'une manière exquise; **e. done** (*of needlework etc*) perlé **(b)** (*extremely*) extrêmement; **an e. warm afternoon** un après-midi délicieusement chaud

exquisiteness [eks'kwɪzɪtnɪs] *n* **(a)** (*delicacy, subtlety*) (*of work of art*) perfection *f* délicate; (*of hearing*) finesse *f* **(b)** (*extreme degree*) (*of pleasure etc*) caractère *m* vif; (*of pain*) acuité *f*

ex-serviceman, *pl* **-men** *n* militaire *m* en retraite

ex-servicewoman, *pl* **-women** *n* femme *f* militaire en retraite

ex ship *adv* ex navire

ext *Tel abbr* **extension**

extant [eks'tænt] *adj* existant encore, qui existe encore

extemporaneous [ɪkstempə'reɪnɪəs] *adj Fml* improvisé, impromptu

extemporaneously [ɪkstempə'reɪnɪəslɪ] *adv Fml* (*to speak etc*) impromptu

extempore [ɪks'tempərɪ] *Fml* **1** *adv* (*to speak*) impromptu, sans préparation **2** *adj* (*speech*) improvisé, impromptu; (*speaker*) qui parle sans préparation

extemporization [ɪkstempəraɪ'zeɪʃən] *n* improvisation *f*

extemporize [ɪks'tempəraɪz] **1** *vt* (*speech*) improviser **2** *vi* (*speak*) improviser, parler à l'impromptu; *Mus* improviser (**on the organ/***etc* à l'orgue/*etc*)

extend [ɪks'tend] **1** *vt* **(a)** (*stretch*) (*body, arm*) étendre, allonger; **the giraffe extended its neck** la girafe a allongé *ou* tendu le cou; **to e. an aerial/telescope** développer une antenne/un télescope

(b) (*prolong*) (*period of time, rail ticket, contract*) prolonger; *Com* (*expiry of bill*) proroger; (*research*) continuer; **the deadline has been extended until 25th May** la date limite a été repoussée au 25 mai

(c) (*broaden, lengthen, increase*) (*line*) prolonger; (*boundaries*) étendre, porter plus loin; (*sense of word*) étendre; (*knowledge*) accroître; (*power, lands*) agrandir, augmenter; (*agreement, scope*) élargir; (*house, room*) agrandir; (*frontiers of state*) reculer; **we are going to e. our premises** nous allons nous agrandir

(d) (*offer*) (*hand*) tendre; (*thanks, sympathy*) présenter; (*support*) offrir; **to e. a welcome to sb** souhaiter la bienvenue à qn; *Banking* **to e. credit to sb** accorder un crédit à qn

(e) *Sp etc* (*push to limit*) (*horse, runner etc*) faire rendre son maximum à, pousser; **to e. oneself** donner son maximum; **they haven't really been extended by any of their opponents** aucun de leurs adversaires ne les a vraiment poussés au bout de leurs limites

2 *vi* **(a)** (*in space*) s'étendre, s'allonger; **to e. beyond the wall** s'avancer au-delà du mur; **the government's concern with austerity does not e. to its own departments** la volonté du gouvernement de mener une politique d'austérité ne s'étend pas jusqu'à ses propres départements

(b) (*of period of time*) se prolonger, continuer; **enquiries extending over a number of years** investigations prolongées pendant un grand nombre d'années

extendable [ɪks'tendɪb(ə)l] *adj* (*aerial, pole*) télescopique; (*ladder*) à coulisse; (*contract of employment*) renouvelable

extended [ɪks'tendɪd] *adj* **(a)** (*body, arm*) étendu, allongé; *Mil* **in e. order** en ordre dispersé; *Horseriding* **e. trot** trot *m* allongé; **I'm fully e. at the moment** (*with financial commitments*) je n'ai pas de disponibilités en ce moment; **to be fully e. in a job** mettre ses talents pleinement à profit dans un travail **(b)** (*in time*) (*long*) long, prolongé; (*prolonged*) prolongé; **e. maintenance insurance** assurance *f* maintenance étendue; **e. warranty** garantie *f* prolongée **(c)** (*increased*) augmenté, agrandi; *Comptr* **e. ASCII** ASCII *m* étendu; *Comptr* **e. memory** mémoire *f* étendue

extended family *n* famille *f* au sens large

extended-play record *n* disque *m* double durée

extender lens [ɪks'tendə] *n* bague *f* rallonge

extending [ɪks'tendɪŋ] *adj* (*table*) à rallonges; (*ladder*) à coulisse

extension [ɪks'tenʃən] *n* **(a)** (*act of stretching out*) (*of arm*) extension *f*; (*of canal, railway etc*) prolongement *m*; (*of factory etc*) agrandissement *m*, extension; *Surg* (*of broken leg*) extension; *Av* (*of landing gear*) sortie *f*; **e. ladder** échelle *f* à coulisse; **e. piece** *MecE* pièce *f* formant prolongement; (*of table, jack etc*) (r)allonge *f*

(b) (*development*) extension *f*, accroissement *m*; **there has been a considerable e. of his business** son commerce a pris une extension considérable

(c) (*extra part*) (*of table etc*) (r)allonge *f*; (*of cable*) allonge *f*; (*on building*) annexe *f*; **we're having an e. built (onto the house)** nous faisons agrandir la maison; **an e. is being added to the museum** on construit une annexe au musée

(d) *Tel* poste *m* supplémentaire; *Tel* **e. 35** poste 35; **e.**

loudspeaker haut-parleur *m* séparé; **e. number** (*of telephone*) numéro *m* de poste
(**e**) *Gram* (*of subject, attribute*) complément *m*
(**f**) (*in time*) (*of leave, railway ticket etc*) prolongation *f*; **to get/give an e.** (*of deadline*) obtenir/accorder un délai
(**g**) *Sch etc* **e. courses** formation *f* continue
extension cable *n* câble *m* de raccordement
extensive [ɪks'tensɪv] *adj* (**a**) étendu, vaste; (*repairs, alterations, reworking*) considérable, important; **e. knowledge** vastes connaissances *fpl*; **e. researches** travaux *mpl* approfondis; **there was e. damage to both wings** les deux ailes ont été très endommagées; **to make e. use of sth** faire un usage considérable de qch (**b**) (*agriculture*) extensif
extensively [ɪks'tensɪvlɪ] *adv* (*to travel, read etc*) énormément; (*rewritten, revised etc*) largement; **to use sth e.** se servir beaucoup de qch, faire un usage considérable de qch; **it was e. damaged/repaired** il a subi des dommages/réparations considérables
extensor [ɪks'tensə] *n Anat* (*muscle*) extenseur *m*
extent [ɪks'tent] *n* (*of lands, knowledge etc*) étendue *f*; (*of damage etc*) importance *f*; **credit to the e. of £500** crédit jusqu'à concurrence de 500 livres; **to an e., to a certain e., to some e.** jusqu'à un certain point, dans une certaine mesure; **to a great e., to a large e.** en grande partie, dans une large mesure; **to such an e. that ...** à tel point que ...; **to what e. is this true?** jusqu'à quel point est-ce vrai?; **to the e. that he can play a few tunes, he is a musician** dans la mesure où il peut jouer quelques airs, c'est un musicien; **the e. to which the strike affected production is unclear** les conséquences de la grève sur la production sont mal définies
extenuate [ɪks'tenjʊeɪt] *vt* (*crime*) atténuer, amoindrir
extenuating [ɪks'tenjʊeɪtɪŋ] *adj* **e. circumstances** circonstances *fpl* atténuantes
extenuation [ɪkstenjʊ'eɪʃən] *n* **to say sth in e. of an offence/an act** dire qch pour atténuer la gravité d'un délit/d'un acte
exterior [ɪks'tɪərɪər] **1** *adj* extérieur (**to** à), en dehors (**to** de); *Math* **e. angle** angle *m* externe; **e. wall** mur *m* extérieur **2** *n* (**a**) extérieur *m*, dehors *mpl*; **on the e.** à l'extérieur; **house with an imposing e.** maison aux dehors imposants; **despite her stern e. she is very likeable** malgré un extérieur *ou* une apparence sévère elle est très sympathique (**b**) *Th, Cin* extérieur *m*
exteriorize [ɪks'tɪərɪəraɪz] *vt* extérioriser
exterminate [ɪks'tɜːmɪneɪt] *vt* (*insects, population etc*) exterminer; (*belief, disease*) supprimer
extermination [ɪkstɜːmɪ'neɪʃən] *n* extermination *f*; (*of belief*) suppression *f*; (*of disease*) éradication *f*
exterminator [ɪks'tɜːmɪneɪtər] *n* (*person*) exterminateur, -trice; **a rodent e.** un employé de la dératisation
extern [eks'tɜːn] *n US Med* externe *mf*
external [ɪks'tɜːn(ə)l] **1** *adj* (*wall, reality, world, trade, debt*) extérieur; (*angle, damage*) externe; (*interference, pressure*) du dehors, de l'extérieur; (*affairs*) étranger, -ère, extérieur; (*student*) libre; **in e. appearance** en apparence; **to judge sth by (its) e. appearance** juger qch d'après ses apparences; *Med* **for e. use only** à usage externe; *Comptr* **e. command** commande *f* externe; *Comptr* **e. device** dispositif *m* externe, périphérique *m*; (*printer*) imprimante *f*; *Comptr* **e. drive** unité *f* (de disque) externe; **e. modem** modem *m* externe; *Aut* **e. temperature display** indicateur *m* de température extérieure
2 *n* (*usu pl*) (**a**) (*appearance*) **externals** extérieur *m*, formes *fpl* extérieures, dehors *mpl*; **to judge by externals** juger les choses selon les apparences
(**b**) (*inessential things*) **externals** choses *fpl* secondaires
external examiner *n Univ* examinateur, -trice de l'extérieur
external financing *n Fin* fonds *mpl* extérieurs
externalize [ɪks'tɜːnəlaɪz] *vt* (*feelings*) exprimer
externally [ɪks'tɜːn(ə)lɪ] *adv* (*damaged, calm*) extérieurement; **to apply e.** appliquer en usage externe
extinct [ɪks'tɪŋkt] *adj* (*animal, plant*) disparu, qui n'existe plus; (*office, title*) aboli, tombé en désuétude; (*volcano, passion*) éteint; **to become e.** (*of race*) s'éteindre, disparaître; (*of way of life*) disparaître, se perdre
extinction [ɪks'tɪŋkʃən] *n* (*of fire, race*) extinction *f*; (*of hope*) anéantissement *m*; **to hunt an animal to e.** chasser un animal jusqu'à extinction de la race; **race threatened with e.** race *f* en passe de disparaître
extinguish [ɪks'tɪŋgwɪʃ] *vt* (*fire, cigarette, candle*) éteindre; (*hope, race*) anéantir
extinguisher [ɪks'tɪŋgwɪʃər] *n* (**a**) (*for fire*) (appareil *m*) extincteur *m* (d'incendie), appareil d'extinction; **foam e.** extincteur à mousse (**b**) (*for candle*) éteignoir *m*
extirpate ['ekstɜːpeɪt] *vt Fml* (*evil*) extirper, déraciner
extirpation [ekstɜː'peɪʃən] *n Fml* (*of evil*) extirpation *f*, éradication *f*
extn *Tel* (*abbr* **extension**) poste
extol, *US* **extoll** [ɪks'təʊl] *vt* (*Br & US* **extolled, extolling**) *esp Lit* exalter, vanter, prôner; (*sb's beauty*) célébrer, chanter; **she was extolling the virtues of central heating** elle vantait les vertus du chauffage central; **to e. sb to the skies** porter qn aux nues
extort [ɪks'tɔːt] *vt* (*money etc*) extorquer (**from sb** à qn); (*promise, confession*) arracher (**from sb** à qn)
extortion [ɪks'tɔːʃən] *n* (*of money etc*) extorsion *f*; (*of promise, confession*) arrachement *m*; **£15 for this? that's sheer e.!** 15 livres pour ça? c'est du vol!
extortionate [ɪks'tɔːʃənɪt] *adj* (**a**) (*price*) exorbitant (**b**) (*person*) extorsionnaire, rapace
extortioner [ɪks'tɔːʃənər], **extortionist** [ɪks'tɔːʃənɪst] *n* extorqueur, -euse
extra ['ekstrə] **1** *adj* (**a**) (*additional*) de plus, supplémentaire; **an e. pint of milk** une pinte de lait supplémentaire *ou* de plus; **it costs 15p e.** ça coûte 15 pence de plus; **I took an e. £5, just in case** j'ai pris 5 livres de plus, au cas où; **e. trains** des trains supplémentaires; **500 e. police officers** 500 officiers de police supplémentaires; **e. charge** supplément *m* (de prix); **no e. charge** sans supplément de prix; **at no e. cost** sans supplément; **e. pay** prime *f*, supplément *m* de salaire; *Mil, Naut* supplément de solde; **e. work** (*hours*) heures *fpl* supplémentaires; (*work*) surcroît *m* de travail; **e. time** *Ind etc* heures supplémentaires; *Br Sp* prolongation *f*; *Br Sp* **to go into e. time** jouer les prolongations; **as an e. precaution** pour plus de précaution; *Sch* **e. subject** matière *f* facultative; **to make an e. effort** faire un surcroît d'effort
(**b**) (*spare*) de réserve, de rechange; **bring some e. batteries** prends des piles de rechange; **these ones are e., take them!** ceux-là sont en trop, prends-les!
2 *adv* (**a**) (*more than usual*) plus que d'ordinaire, extra-; **to be e. kind/polite** être particulièrement gentil/poli; **an e. special wine for those e. special occasions** un grand vin pour les grandes occasions; **this is an e. special cake for your birthday** voici un gâteau exceptionnel pour ton anniversaire; **e. strong binding/rope** reliure *f*/corde *f* extra-solide; **e. white/fast** extra-blanc/-rapide; **e. smart** ultra-chic; **e. large** (*clothing*) grand patron
(**b**) (*in addition*) en plus; **meals taken in the bedroom are charged (for) e.** il y a un supplément pour les repas servis dans la chambre; **I had to pay e. for the sun roof** il a fallu que je paye un supplément pour le toit ouvrant; **packing e.** emballage en sus; **a few e.** quelques-uns en plus
3 *n* (**a**) (*on restaurant bill*) supplément *m*; (*of newspaper*) édition *f* spéciale; (*on car*) option *f*
(**b**) *Cin, Th* (*actor*) figurant, -ante; **to be** *or* **work as an e.** faire de la figuration
(**c**) **extras** (*expenses*) frais *mpl ou* dépenses *fpl* supplémentaires; (*on invoice*) suppléments *mpl*; **extras bill** facture *f* des extras
(**d**) (*luxuries*) **little extras** petits à-côtés *mpl*, extras *mpl*
extra- ['ekstrə] *pref* (*outside*) extra-; **extragalactic** extragalactique; **extravascular** extravasculaire
extract¹ ['ekstrækt] *n* (**a**) (*of substance*) extrait *m*, concentré *m*; **malt/beef e.** extrait de malt/de bœuf; **meat e.** concentré de viande (**b**) *Liter etc* extrait *m*; **selected extracts** (*from author, works*) morceaux *mpl* choisis
extract² [ɪks'trækt] *vt* (*tooth*) extraire, arracher; (*oil, metal, data, passage from book etc*) extraire (**from** de); (*letter from pocket etc*) tirer (**from** de); (*passage from book*) extraire (**from** de); **to e. money/a confession from sb** arracher de l'argent/un aveu à qn, tirer de l'argent/un aveu de qn; *Math* **to e. the square root of a number** extraire la racine carrée d'un nombre
extraction [ɪks'trækʃən] *n* (**a**) (*removal*) (*of juice from lemon etc*) extraction *f*; (*of nail, tooth*) arrachage *m*; **she needs two extractions and three fillings** il faut lui arracher deux dents et en plomber trois; **e. of stone from a quarry** extraction de la pierre d'une carrière (**b**) (*origin*) extraction *f*, origine *f*; **of humble e.** de basse extraction; **of Italian e.** d'origine italienne
extractor [ɪks'træktər] *n* (**a**) (*tool*) pince *f*; (*in dentistry*) davier *m*; *Surg* (*of stones etc*) extracteur *m*; **e. hood** (*for stove*) hotte *f* (d'aération) (**b**) (*person*) (*of teeth etc*) extracteur *m*
extractor fan *n* aérateur *m*
extracurricular ['ekstrəkə'rɪkjʊlər] *adj Sch* hors-programme *inv*; **e. activities** activités *fpl* périscolaires
extraditable [ekstrə'daɪtəb(ə)l] *adj* (*person*) passible d'extradition; (*crime, offence*) qui justifie l'extradition
extradite ['ekstrədaɪt] *vt Jur* (*criminal*) (*hand over*) extrader; (*obtain extradition of*) obtenir l'extradition de; **the**

authorities were unable to e. him from the USA les autorités n'ont pas réussi à obtenir son extradition des États-Unis

extradition [ekstrə'dɪʃən] *n* extradition *f*; **the Spanish government is seeking/has obtained his e.** le gouvernement espagnol a demandé/obtenu son extradition; **e. treaty** accord *m* d'extradition

extra-dry *adj* (*wine*) très sec

extra-fine *adj* extra-fin

extrajudicial ['ekstrədʒuː'dɪʃəl] *adj* extrajudiciaire

extramarital ['ekstrə'mærɪt(ə)l] *adj* extra-conjugal

extramural ['ekstrə'mjʊər(ə)l] *adj Sch* **e. lecturer** = conférencier *m* en dehors de la Faculté accrédité pour certains cours; **e. course** cours *m* de formation continue; *Br Univ* **Department of E. Studies** Département *m* de la formation continue

extraneous [ɪks'treɪnɪəs] *adj* (*considerations*) en dehors de la question; (*details*) sans rapport; **to be e. to sth** n'avoir aucun rapport avec qch

extraordinarily [ɪks'trɔːd(ə)nərɪlɪ] *adv* extraordinairement; **it was an e. brave/foolish action** c'était un acte particulièrement courageux/inconscient

extraordinary [ɪks'trɔːd(ə)nrɪ] *adj* **(a)** (*remarkable*) (*extent, success, coincidence, story*) extraordinaire; (*behaviour, suggestion, idea*) surprenant, singulier, étrange; (*appearance*) surprenant, bizarre; **the e. thing is that ...** ce qu'il y a d'étrange *ou* de singulier c'est que ...; **that's e., he was here only an hour ago!** c'est incroyable, il était là il y a une heure à peine!; **I find it e. that you did not inform the police** je trouve incroyable *ou* extraordinaire que vous n'ayez pas prévenu la police; **they went to e. lengths to conceal the truth** ils se sont donné un mal fou pour cacher la vérité

(b) (*special*) extraordinaire; **ambassador e.** ambassadeur *m* extraordinaire; **e. powers** pouvoirs *mpl* extraordinaires; *Fin* **e. general meeting** assemblée *f* générale extraordinaire; *Acct* **e. income** produits *mpl* exceptionnels; *Acct* **e. item** poste *m* extraordinaire

extrapolate [ek'stræpəleɪt] *vti* extrapoler; **to e. from sth** extrapoler à partir de qch; **we can e. a prediction** nous pouvons extrapoler et établir une prévision

extrasensory ['ekstrə'sensərɪ] *adj* extra-sensoriel; **e. perception** perception *f* extra-sensorielle; **to have e. perception** avoir des dons de perception extra-sensorielle

extraterrestrial ['ekstrətɪ'restrɪəl] *adj, n* extra-terrestre *mf*

extraterritorial ['ekstrəterɪ'tɔːrɪəl] *adj* (*privilege*) d'exterritorialité

extravagance [ɪks'trævəgəns] *n* **(a)** (*excessive, wasteful expenditure*) folles dépenses *fpl*, prodigalités *fpl*; **the e. of your tastes** tes goûts dispendieux *ou* de luxe; **it was real e.** c'était de la folie; **she accused the government of e.** elle a accusé le gouvernement de dilapider le trésor public; **a piece of e., an e.** une dépense inutile, une folie **(b)** (*exaggeration*) extravagance *f*

extravagant [ɪks'trævəgənt] *adj* **(a)** (*wasteful*) (*person*) dépensier, gaspilleur; (*tastes*) dispendieux; **it was very e. of them to come by taxi** ils ont fait une folie en venant en taxi; **don't be so e. with the butter** ne gaspillez pas le beurre; **he considered two baths a week (to be) e.** il trouvait que deux bains par semaine, c'était du gaspillage **(b)** (*exaggerated*) extravagant; (*claim*) exagéré, déraisonnable; (*praise*) outré; (*style*) exagéré; (*price*) exorbitant, prohibitif; **e. claims have been made for the drug** des propriétés abusives ont été attribuées à ce médicament

extravagantly [ɪks'trævəgəntlɪ] *adv* **(a)** (*excessively*) **e. priced items** des articles à des prix exorbitants; **he spent money e.** il jetait l'argent par la fenêtre; **to live e.** vivre sur un grand pied, dépenser sans compter; **e. furnished house** maison meublée avec un luxe exagéré **(b)** (*exaggeratedly*) d'une façon extravagante; **to talk/act e.** dire/faire des folies *ou* des extravagances

extravaganza [ekstrævə'gænzə] *n* (*lavish show*) grand spectacle *m*

extravasation [ɪkstrævə'seɪʃən] *n Med* épanchement *m*

extravert ['ekstrəvɜːt] *adj, n* = **extrovert**

extreme [ɪks'triːm] **1** *adj* **(a)** (*heat, difficulty, pleasure etc*) extrême; (*nationalism*) outrancier; (*opinions, views*) extrême, extrémiste; **to be in e. danger** *or* **peril** être en (très) grand danger; **to be in e. pain** souffrir à l'extrême; **to behave with e. awkwardness** se conduire avec la dernière gaucherie; **an e. case** un cas exceptionnel; **the question is one of e. delicacy** le problème est délicat entre tous; *Cin, TV* **e. close-up** plan *m* très rapproché; *Cin, TV* **e. long shot** plan très éloigné

(b) (*far*) extrême; **the e. opposite** l'extrême opposé; **at the e. end of the quay** tout au bout du quai; *Pol* **the e. left** l'extrême gauche; **on the e. left of the photograph** à l'extrême gauche de la photo

(c) (*final*) **the e. penalty** le dernier supplice; *Cathol* **e. unction** extrême-onction *f*

2 *n* extrême *m*; **they were rude in the e.** ils étaient mal polis à l'extrême; **to go from one e. to the other** passer d'un extrême à l'autre; **to go to the e. of calling the police** aller jusqu'à appeler la police; **now he's going to the other e. and ...** il est passé d'un extrême à l'autre et maintenant ...; **to go to extremes** pousser les choses à l'extrême; **extremes of temperature** extrêmes de température

extremely [ɪks'triːmlɪ] *adv* extrêmement; **to be e. witty** avoir énormément d'esprit

extremism [ɪks'triːmɪz(ə)m] *n Pol* extrémisme *m*

extremist [ɪks'triːmɪst] *adj, n Pol* extrémiste *mf*

extremity [ɪks'tremɪtɪ] *n* **(a)** (*end*) extrémité *f*, point *m* extrême; **the southernmost e. of Europe** l'extrême sud de l'Europe **(b) the extremities** (*of the body*) les extrémités *fpl* **(c)** (*need*) gêne *f*; **how had they arrived at such an e.?** comment étaient-ils parvenus à de telles extrémités?; **to be reduced to the last e.** en être réduit à la dernière extrémité

extricate ['ekstrɪkeɪt] *vt* dégager, tirer **(sb from a critical position** qn d'un mauvais pas); **to e. oneself from a danger** se tirer d'un danger; **to e. oneself from a conversation** se dégager d'une conversation; **to e. oneself from difficulties** se débrouiller, se tirer d'affaire

extrinsic [eks'trɪnsɪk] *adj* extrinsèque

extrovert ['ekstrəvɜːt] **1** *n* extraverti, -ie, extroverti, -ie; **a bit (too much) of an e.** un peu (trop) extraverti; **she's much more of an e. than her sister** elle est bien plus extravertie que sa sœur, c'est une extravertie bien plus que sa sœur **2** *adj* extraverti, extroverti; **to have e. tendencies** être d'un naturel extraverti

extrude [eks'truːd] **1** *vt* expulser, faire jaillir **(from** de); *Metal* filer, profiler; *Ind* (*plastics*) boudiner (à chaud); **extruded section** *or* **shape** profilé *m* **2** *vi Geol* (*of rock etc*) s'épancher

extrusion [eks'truːʒən] *n* expulsion *f*; (*of secretion*) émission *f*; *Geol* épanchement *m*; *Metal* extrusion *f*, filage *m* (à chaud); *Ind* (*of plastics*) boudinage *m*, extrusion

exuberance [ɪg'zjuːb(ə)rəns] *n* exubérance *f*; (*of person*) exubérance, gaieté *f* débordante; (*of vegetation*) luxuriance *f*, richesse *f*

exuberant [ɪg'zjuːb(ə)rənt] *adj* (*person*) exubérant, débordant de vie; (*imagination*) exubérant; (*vegetation*) luxuriant, riche; (*health, vitality*) débordant; **she felt e. at the news** la nouvelle la remplit d'une joie exubérante

exuberantly [ɪg'zjuːb(ə)rəntlɪ] *adv* avec exubérance; **e. cheerful** d'une gaieté exubérante; **e. healthy** débordant de santé

exude [ɪg'zjuːd] **1** *vt* exsuder; *Fig* **she exudes health** elle respire la santé; **he exudes (an air of) confidence/well-being/charm** un halo de confiance en soi/de bien-être/de charme se dégage de tout son être **2** *vi* exsuder, suinter; (*of sap*) couler, s'écouler

exult [ɪg'zʌlt] *vi* **(a)** (*rejoice*) exulter, se réjouir **(at, in** de); **they exulted at their enemies' confusion** ils exultaient de voir la confusion dans laquelle se trouvaient leurs ennemis; **to e. in the name of 'Mad Mitch'** porter le nom singulier de 'Mad Mitch' **(b)** (*triumph*) **to e. over sb** triompher de qn

exultant [ɪg'zʌltənt] *adj esp Lit* (*feeling*) joyeux; (*cry*) de triomphe; **to be e. at sth** (*of person*) exulter de qch

exultantly [ɪg'zʌltəntlɪ] *adv* (*to speak etc*) d'un air triomphant

exultation [egzʌl'teɪʃən] *n* exultation *f*; **to sing in e.** chanter le cœur plein de joie

ex voto [eks'vəʊtəʊ] *n Rel* **ex v. (offering)** ex-voto *m inv*

ex warehouse *adv* départ entrepôt

ex works *adv* départ usine

eye[1] [aɪ] *n* **(a)** (*of human, animal*) œil *m*, *pl* yeux; **to have blue eyes** avoir les yeux bleus; **a man with green eyes** un homme aux yeux verts; **to have good eyes** avoir de bons yeux; **to open/close one's eyes** ouvrir/fermer les yeux; **to open one's eyes wide** ouvrir les yeux tout grands; **to have the sun/the light in one's eyes** avoir le soleil/la lumière dans les yeux; **I've got something in my e.** j'ai quelque chose dans l'œil; **with tears in one's eyes** les larmes aux yeux; **dry your eyes** essuyez vos larmes; **he could not keep his eyes open** il dormait debout; **at e. level** à la hauteur des yeux; **e. contact** échange *m* de regards; **to maintain e. contact with sb** soutenir le regard de qn; **to make e. contact with sb** regarder qn (droit) dans les yeux; **to try to make e. contact with sb** chercher le regard de qn; **she always avoids e. contact (with me)** elle évite tout le temps mon regard; **to look sb straight in the e.** regarder qn droit dans les yeux; *Zool* **simple e.** œil simple, ocelle *m*; *Zool* **compound e.** œil composé *ou* à facettes

(b) (*idioms of observation, awareness etc*) **as far as the e.**

can see à perte de vue; **to keep one's eyes and ears open** avoir l'œil et l'oreille aux aguets; **to keep one's eyes open** *or F* **peeled** *or F* **skinned** avoir *ou* ouvrir l'œil; *Fig* **to open sb's eyes** ouvrir les yeux à qn, dessiller les yeux à qn (**to** sur); *Fig* **to do sth with one's eyes open** faire qch en connaissance de cause; **I could do it with my eyes shut** je pourrais le faire les yeux fermés; **to shut** *or* **close one's eyes to sb's faults** fermer les yeux sur les défauts de qn; **to be all eyes** être tout yeux; **all eyes were upon her** elle était au centre de tous les regards, tous les regards étaient posés sur elle; **to strike/catch the e.** frapper/attirer l'œil *ou* les regards; **to catch sb's e.** (*of person, thing*) attirer l'attention de qn; *Parl* **to catch the Speaker's e.** obtenir la parole; **it pleases/delights the e.** cela charme/réjouit les yeux *ou* les regards; **he has eyes in** *or* **at the back of his head** il a des yeux d'Argus; **he has eyes for nobody but her** il n'a d'yeux que pour elle; **to set** *or* **lay eyes on sth** poser les yeux sur qch, apercevoir qch, voir qch; **it was the biggest fish I'd ever laid eyes on** c'était le plus gros poisson que j'aie jamais vu; **to see sth with one's own eyes** voir qch de ses propres yeux; **it took place before my (very) eyes** cela s'est passé sous mes yeux; **to see sth in one's mind's e.** voir qch en imagination *ou* en idée; *Fig* **where are your eyes?** êtes-vous aveugle?; **use your eyes!** ouvre les yeux!; **to run** *or* **cast one's e. over sth** jeter un coup d'œil sur qch; **to look at sth with a critical/experienced e.** regarder qch d'un œil critique/exercé; **with jealous eyes** d'un œil jaloux; **you can see that with half an e.** cela saute aux yeux; **anyone with half an e. can see it's a fake** du premier coup d'œil n'importe qui verrait que c'est un faux; **with half an e. on the weather** sans quitter le ciel des yeux; **to keep an e. on sth/sb** surveiller qch/qn; **keep your e. on him!** ne le quittez pas des yeux!; **I couldn't keep my eyes off him/it** je ne pouvais pas en détacher mes yeux; **to keep an e. out for sth** être à l'affût de qch; **keep an e. out for anyone trying to sell it** soyez à l'affût au cas où quelqu'un essaierait de le vendre; **keep an e. on the children/potatoes** surveille les enfants/les pommes de terre; **a neighbour is keeping an e. on the house while we're away** un de nos voisins a l'œil sur la maison quand nous sommes absents; **to keep one's e. on the ball** suivre *ou Golf* fixer la balle; **keep your eyes on the road** regarde la route; **to have one's e. on sth/sb** (*be watching*) avoir qch/qn à l'œil; (*have in mind, be thinking of acquiring*) avoir l'œil sur qch/qn; **the police have had their e. on him for some time** cela fait un certain temps que la police l'a à l'œil; **under the (watchful) e. of …** sous la surveillance de …

(**c**) (*point of view, perception*) **everyone is equal in the eye(s) of the law** tout le monde est égal devant la loi; **in the eyes of all he is guilty** aux yeux de tous il est coupable; **through sb else's eyes** du point de vue de qn d'autre; **to be very much in the public e.** occuper une position très en vue; **to have an e. for a horse** s'y connaître en chevaux, être bon juge des chevaux; **to have an e. for a bargain** savoir reconnaître une bonne affaire; **with the e. of a painter** d'un œil de peintre; **an e. for detail/colour** l'œil pour le détail/la couleur

(**d**) (*idiomatic expressions*) **to be up to the** *or* **one's eyes in work/debt** avoir du travail/des dettes par-dessus la tête; **to see e. to e. with sb** voir les choses du même œil que qn; **for your eyes only** confidentiel; *F* **that's one in the e. for him!** ça lui fait les pieds!; *Old-fashioned F* **my e.!** mon œil!; *Bible* **an e. for an e., a tooth for a tooth** œil pour œil, dent pour dent; *Bible* **to pass through the e. of a needle** passer par le trou d'une aiguille; *Fig* **at the e. of the hurricane** dans un havre de paix, dans un îlot préservé; **to make eyes at sb,** *F* **to give sb the (glad) e.** lancer des œillades *ou* faire de l'œil à qn; *F* **to make sheep's eyes at sb** lancer des œillades amoureuses à qn; **with an e. to …** en vue de …; **he does everything with an e. for** *or* **on** *or* **to the main chance** il fait tout avec son propre intérêt en vue

(**e**) (*specialist uses*) (*bud*) œil *m*, *pl* yeux, bourgeon *m*; (*on potato*) germe *m*; (*in grafting*) œilleton *m*; (*hole*) (*of needle, rigging*) œil, *pl* œils; (*of support, prop*) collet *m*, œillet *m*; (*with screw thread*) piton *m*; *Met* (*of storm*) œil; *Mil* **eyes right/left!** tête (à) droite/(à) gauche!; *Mil* **eyes front!** fixe!; *Sp* **to get one's e. in** se faire la main; **eyes** (*on peacock's tail*) yeux *mpl*, miroirs *mpl*; **bird's eyes** (*in mahogany etc*) tourbillons *mpl*; **e. end** (*of cable*) œil, piton; *Electron* **electric** *or* **magic e.** cellule *f* photoélectrique, œil magique

(**f**) *F* (*private detective*) détective *m ou* enquêteur *m* privé

eye[2] *vt* (**eyed; eyeing**) (*look at*) regarder, observer (**with suspicion** d'un air soupçonneux); (*weigh up*) (*person, obstacle etc*) mesurer des yeux; **to e. sb up and down** regarder qn de la tête aux pieds

▶ **eye up** *vtsep* (**a**) (*with sexual interest*) **to e. up the girls/boys** reluquer les filles/les garçons; **he eyed her up** il l'a déshabillée du regard (**b**) (*estimate strength etc of*) (*opponent etc*) jauger (d'un coup d'œil)

eyeball[1] ['aɪbɔːl] *n* globe *m* oculaire; *Fig* **to come e. to e.** (*of two people*) s'affronter; **to come e. to e. with sb** affronter qn; **an e. to e. confrontation** un affrontement direct

eyeball[2] *vt F* regarder en face

eye bank *n Med* banque *f* des yeux

eyebath ['aɪbɑːθ] *n Br Med* (**a**) œillère *f* (**b**) (*liquid*) bain *m* d'œil

eyebrow ['aɪbraʊ] *n* sourcil *m*; *Fig* **he never raised an e.** (*in disapproval, astonishment*) il n'a pas sourcillé; *Fig* **(some) eyebrows were raised at this suggestion** (*in disapproval*) cette proposition a suscité des grimaces de désapprobation; (*in astonishment*) cette proposition a suscité de l'étonnement; **e. pencil** crayon *m* à sourcils; **e. tweezers** pince *f* à épiler

eye camera *n* caméra *f* oculaire

eye-catching *adj* (*design, dress, title*) accrocheur, -euse; (*advertisement*) tapageur, -euse

eyecup ['aɪkʌp] *n Am* = **eyebath** (**a**)

-eyed [aɪd] *suff* **blue-e.** aux yeux bleus; **wide-e.** aux grands yeux

eye drops *npl Med* gouttes *fpl* pour les yeux

eyeful ['aɪfʊl] *n* **to get an e. of mud/sand/water** recevoir de la boue/du sable/de l'eau plein les yeux; *F* **to get an e.** (*look*) se rincer l'œil; *F* **she's quite an e.** elle vaut le coup d'œil

eyeglass ['aɪglɑːs] *n* (*monocle*) monocle *m*; **watchmaker's e.** loupe *f* d'horloger

eyeglasses ['aɪglɑːsɪz] *npl US* (*spectacles*) lunettes *fpl*

eyehole ['aɪhəʊl] *n* (**a**) (*in mask*) **eyeholes** ouvertures *fpl* pour les yeux (**b**) (*small opening*) petite ouverture *f*, judas *m*; *Tech* trou *m* de regard *ou* de visite

eye hospital *n Med* clinique *f ou* centre *m* ophtalmologique

eyelash ['aɪlæʃ] *n* cil *m*; **e. curlers** recourbe-cils *m inv*

eyelet ['aɪlɪt] *n* œillet *m*

eyelevel ['aɪlev(ə)l] *adj* **e. grill** gril *m* à la hauteur des yeux

eyelid ['aɪlɪd] *n* paupière *f*; *Fig* **he didn't bat an e.** il n'a pas sourcillé

eye light *n* petit projecteur *m* pour le regard

eye-line *n TV etc* direction *f* du regard

eyeliner ['aɪlaɪnər] *n* eye-liner *m*

eye movement camera *n* caméra *f* oculaire

eye-opener *n* (**a**) **that was an e. for him** cela lui a ouvert les yeux, ça a été une révélation pour lui (**b**) *Am* (*drink*) petit verre *m* du matin

eye-opening *adj* qui ouvre les yeux, révélateur, -trice; **it was very e.** ça a été très révélateur

eyepatch ['aɪpætʃ] *n* cache *m* (sur l'œil); **eyepatches** caches (pour les yeux)

eyepiece ['aɪpiːs] *n Opt* (*of microscope etc*) oculaire *m*, viseur *m*; (*on camera*) œilleton *m*, oculaire *m* de visée; *Metal* (*of furnace*) lunette *f* de regard; (*of gas mask*) lunette *f*

eyeshade ['aɪʃeɪd] *n* visière *f*

eye shadow *n* ombre *f* à paupières

eyesight ['aɪsaɪt] *n* vue *f*; **to lose one's e.** perdre la vue; **to have good e.** avoir une bonne vue *ou* de bons yeux; **my e. is failing** ma vue baisse

eye socket *n* orbite *f*

eyesore ['aɪsɔːr] *n* **the building is an e.** le bâtiment est une horreur *ou* blesse la vue

eyespot ['aɪspɒt] *n* (*of butterfly etc*) ocelle *f*

eyestrain ['aɪstreɪn] *n* **to suffer from e.** avoir les yeux fatigués; **you'll give yourself e.** tu vas te fatiguer les yeux

eye test *n* examen *m* de la vue

eyetooth, *pl* **-teeth** ['aɪtuːθ, -tiːθ] *n* (dent *f*) canine *f*; **to cut one's eyeteeth** faire ses canines; *F* (*come to end of childhood*) sortir de sa première enfance; **I'd give my eyeteeth to go with them** je donnerais n'importe quoi pour aller avec eux

eyewash ['aɪwɒʃ] *n Pharm* collyre *m*; *Fig* **that's a lot** *or* **load of e.** (*nonsense*) tout ça c'est du boniment

eyewitness ['aɪwɪtnɪs] *n* témoin *m* oculaire (**of** de); **an e. account** le récit d'un témoin oculaire

eyrie ['ɪərɪ] *n* (*of eagle*) aire *f*

F

F, f [ef] *n* **(a)** (*letter*) F, f *m*; *Br F* **the F word** = le mot de Cambronne **(b)** *Mus* fa *m*; **F clef** clef *f* de fa
FA [e'feɪ] *n* **(a)** *Br Fb* (*abbr* **Football Association**) = fédération *f* anglaise de football; **FA Cup** coupe *f* de la fédération anglaise de football **(b)** *Sl* **sweet FA** rien du tout, nib de nib
fa [fɑː] *n Mus* fa *m*
fab [fæb] *adj Old-fashioned Br F* sensass; **the f. Four** = les Beatles *mpl*
Fabian ['feɪbɪən] *adj Pol* fabien, -ienne
fable ['feɪb(ə)l] *n* fable *f*, conte *m*
fabled ['feɪb(ə)ld] *adj* de la fable; *Fig* légendaire
fabric ['fæbrɪk] *n* **(a)** *Tex etc* tissu *m*, étoffe *f*; **dress fabrics** tissus pour robes; **silk, woollen and cotton fabrics** soieries *fpl*, lainages *mpl* et cotonnades *fpl* **(b)** (*of building, system*) structure *f*; **the f. of society** l'édifice *m* social; **the urban f.** le tissu urbain
fabricate ['fæbrɪkeɪt] *vt* (*news, story, alibi*) forger, fabriquer; (*document*) contrefaire
fabrication [fæbrɪ'keɪʃən] *n* (*of news, story, alibi*) fabrication *f*; (*of document*) contrefaçon *f*; **it's pure f.** c'est de la pure fabrication; **a pure f.** (*lie*) une histoire inventée de toutes pièces
fabulous ['fæbjʊləs] *adj* **(a)** (*marvellous*) prodigieux, fabuleux; (*price*) fou, *f* folle; **we had a f. evening** on a passé une soirée merveilleuse *ou* fabuleuse **(b)** (*fairy story*) fabuleux; (*character, city*) légendaire
fabulously ['fæbjʊləslɪ] *adv* (*rich etc*) fabuleusement, prodigieusement
façade [fæ'sɑːd] *n Archit, Fig* façade *f*; **they put on a f. of family happiness** ils adoptent une façade de bonheur familial
face¹ [feɪs] *n* **(a)** figure *f*, visage *m*; *F* **shut your f.!** ferme-la!, la ferme!; **you should have told him to shut his f.** tu aurais dû lui dire de la fermer *ou* boucler; **to hide one's f. in shame** se cacher le visage de honte; **to set one's f. against sth** s'opposer résolument à qch; **he won't show his f. here again!** il ne remettra pas les pieds ici!; **I told him so to his f.** je le lui ai dit en face; **I shall never be able to look her in the f. again** je ne pourrai jamais plus la regarder en face; *Fig, F* **I'm just going to put my f. on** je vais me maquiller; **her f. doesn't fit** (*in job, company etc*) sa tête ne nous/leur/*etc* revient pas; **the f. of Britain is changing** le visage de la Grande-Bretagne est en train de changer; **the unacceptable f. of capitalism** le visage inacceptable du capitalisme; **Communism with a human f.** le communisme à visage humain; **in the f. of danger** devant le danger; **in the f. of an enemy** en face d'un ennemi; **in the f. of this threat, he ...** confronté à cette menace, il ...; **full-f. portrait** portrait *m* de face; **f. level vent** aérateur *m* (vers visage)
(b) (*expression*) mine *f*, physionomie *f*; **to pull a long f.** tirer une tête longue comme ça, *F* tirer une tête de six pieds de long; **to make** *or* **pull faces** faire des grimaces (**at** à); **to keep a straight f.** garder son sérieux; **to put a good f. on it** faire contre mauvaise fortune bon cœur
(c) (*appearance*) (*of sth*) apparence *f*, aspect *m*; **on the f. of it** au premier aspect, à première vue; **f. value** valeur *f* nominale; **I took him at (his) f. value** je l'ai jugé sur les apparences; **to take what sb says at f. value** prendre ce que qn dit pour argent comptant; **to save/lose f.** sauver/perdre la face; **loss of f.** humiliation *f*
(d) *F* (*cheek*) culot *m*, front *m*, toupet *m*
(e) (*surface*) (*of the earth*) surface *f*; **they disappeared from** *or* **off the f. of the earth** ils ont disparu de la surface du globe; **my keys can't just have disappeared off the f. of the earth!** mes clés n'ont pas pu se volatiliser tout de même!
(f) (*side*) (*of coin, cliff, polyhedron, golf club etc*) face *f*; (*of material*) endroit *m*; (*of document*) recto *m*; (*of building*) devant *m*, façade *f*; (*of crystal*) facette *f*, plan *m*; (*of hammer*) plat *m*; (*on valve seat*) portée *f*; **bearing f.** (sur)face portante; **the north f. of the Eiger** la face nord de l'Eiger; **f. up/down** face en dessus/en dessous; **the toast landed f. up/down** le toast est tombé du bon/mauvais côté; *Min* **(coal) f.** front *m* de taille (du charbon)
(g) (*of clock, watch*) cadran *m*
(h) *Typ* (*of character*) œil *m*; **bold/light f.** (caractère *m*) gras *m*/maigre *m*
face² **1** *vt* **(a)** (*confront*) (*difficulties, enemy*) affronter, faire face à; (*danger*) braver, affronter; **to f. facts** regarder les choses en face; **let's f. it** voyons les choses comme elles sont; **f. it** sois réaliste; **f. it — you've lost/she's not coming back** accepte-le — tu as perdu/elle ne reviendra pas; **the problem that faces us** le problème qui se pose à nous, le problème auquel nous sommes confrontés; **to be faced with a difficulty** se heurter à une difficulté; **to be faced with a decision** être confronté à une décision; **to f.** *or* **be faced with a crisis/a grim future** être confronté à une crise/un avenir lugubre; **he dared not f. me** il n'a pas osé me rencontrer face à face; *Fig* **to f. the music** faire front
(b) (*look towards*) faire face à; **to f. the front** regarder devant soi; **sunflowers always f. the sun** le tournesol est toujours tourné vers le soleil; **hotel facing the square** hôtel en façade sur la place; **the picture facing page 10** la gravure en regard de la page 10; **facing each other** l'un en face de l'autre; *Rail* **seat facing the direction of travel** place *f* dans le sens de la marche
(c) *Metal etc* (*dress*) dresser, planer, surfacer; *Constr* (*cover*) (*wall etc*) revêtir (**with** de)
2 *vi* **the house faces north** la maison est exposée au nord *ou* regarde le nord; **terrace facing south** terrasse orientée au sud; **to f. both ways** faire face des deux côtés; *Fig* ménager la chèvre et le chou; *Mil* **right/left f.!** face à droite/ à gauche!
▶ **face about** *vi Mil* faire demi-tour
▶ **face down** *vtsep* (*confront*) (*enemy, critic*) faire face à
▶ **face on to** *vipo* (*garden, street*) donner sur
▶ **face out** *vtsep* (*deal with, confront*) (*problems, difficult situation*) faire face à; (*threat*) défier; (*oppose, resist*) (*person*) résister à; **to f. it out** ne pas broncher; **to f. out opposition** résister à l'opposition
▶ **face up to** *vipo* **(a)** (*confront*) (*person, danger*) affronter; **to f. up to one's fears** faire face à ses craintes; **you have to f. up to him over his treatment of you** il faut que tu lui dises en face que tu n'aimes pas la façon dont il te traite **(b)** (*accept*) regarder en face, faire face à; **to f. up to one's responsibilities** faire face à ses responsabilités
▶ **face with** *vtaspo* **to f. sb with sth** (*confront with*) confronter qn à qch; **why don't you f. them with it?** (*what they said or did*) pourquoi est-ce que tu ne le leur dis pas en face?; **he confessed when faced with the evidence/the dead man's wife** il a avoué lorsqu'il a été confronté aux preuves/à la femme du défunt
face card *n Am Cards* figure *f*
face cloth *n* = gant *m* de toilette
face cream *n* crème *f* pour le visage
face flannel *n* = gant *m* de toilette
face guard *n Sp* masque *m* protecteur
faceless ['feɪslɪs] *adj Fig* anonyme
face-lift *n* **(a)** lifting *m*; **to have a f.** se faire faire un lifting **(b)** *Fig* (*of facade of building*) restauration *f*; (*of flat, house*) rénovation *f*, retapage *m*; **Glasgow's had a f.** Glasgow a été remis à neuf
face mask *n Sp* masque *m* protecteur; (*cosmetic*) masque
face pack *n* masque *m*; **to give oneself a f.** se faire un masque
face powder *n* poudre *f* pour le visage
facer ['feɪsər] *n Br F* **that's a f.!** quelle tuile!
face-saving *adj* (*agreement, compromise etc*) qui sauve la face
face scrub *n* (*cosmetic*) exfoliant *m*
face shot *n TV, Cin* plan *m* de visage
facet¹ ['fæsɪt] *n* **(a)** (*of diamond, insect's eye*) facette *f* **(b)** *Fig* (*of situation*) aspect *m*; **there are several facets to this problem/question** ce problème/cette question a plusieurs facettes
facet² *vt* (**-tt-**, *US* **-t-**) (*precious stone*) facetter

facetious [fə'siːʃəs] *adj* (*person, remark*) facétieux, plaisant, bouffon; **I was being f.** je plaisantais; **there's no need to be so f.** il n'y a pas de quoi se moquer

facetiously [fə'siːʃəslɪ] *adv* facétieusement; (*to say sth*) d'un ton facétieux; **do you have to behave so f.?** faut-il absolument que tu fasses le bouffon?

facetiousness [fə'siːʃəsnɪs] *n* caractère *m* facétieux, bouffonnerie *f*; (*mood*) humeur *f* facétieuse; **I find his f. a bit tiresome** je trouve ses bouffonneries un peu lassantes; **there's no need for f.** il n'y a pas de quoi se moquer

face-to-face *adj* (*meeting*) face-à-face; **a f. encounter** un face-à-face; **to bring sb f. with sb/the consequences of one's actions** confronter qn avec qn/aux conséquences de ses actions; **to come f. with sb** se trouver face à face avec qn; **to meet sb f.** rencontrer qn face à face

facetted ['fæsɪtɪd] *adj* à facettes

facia ['feɪʃə] *n Br Aut* tableau *m* de bord

facial ['feɪʃ(ə)l] **1** *adj* (*nerve, tic*) facial; (*expression, hair*) du visage **2** *n* soins *mpl* du visage; **to have a f.** se faire faire des soins du visage

facile ['fæsaɪl, -ɪl] *adj* **(a)** (*simplistic*) simpliste **(b)** *Old-fashioned Pej* facile; **to be a f. liar** être habile à controuver des mensonges

facilitate [fə'sɪlɪteɪt] *vt* (*action*) faciliter

facilitator [fə'sɪlɪteɪtə*r*] *n Mktg* auxiliaire *mf*

facility [fə'sɪlɪtɪ] *n* **(a)** (*ease*) facilité *f*; **f. in speaking/writing** facilité à parler/écrire; **to do sth with great f.** faire qch avec une grande facilité; **to have a f. at** *or* **for doing sth** avoir de la facilité à *ou* pour faire qch

(b) (*means*) (*usu pl*) **facilities** aménagements *mpl*; **the building has limited facilities for the handicapped** le bâtiment est doté d'aménagements limités pour les handicapés; **storage/cooking facilities** installations *fpl* de stockage/cuisine; **transport facilities** moyens *mpl* de transport; **play/educational facilities** équipements *mpl* récréatifs/scolaires; **the village has few shopping facilities** le village ne compte pas beaucoup de magasins; **we have no facilities for it** nous ne sommes pas équipés pour cela; **facilities for payment** facilités *mpl* de paiement; **they are given every f. for improving their French** on leur accorde toutes facilités de se perfectionner en français; *Av* **ground facilities** installations au sol; *Euph* **can I use the facilities?** (*toilet*) est-ce que je peux utiliser les toilettes?; *TV etc* **facilities man** technicien *m*, prestataire *m*

(c) *esp Am* (*establishment*) établissement *m*; (*hotel*) hôtel *m*; **training/research f.** établissement de formation/recherche

facing ['feɪsɪŋ] **1** *n* **(a)** *Sewing* (*material*) revers *m*; (*on outside*) parement *m*; (*on inside*) parementure *f*; *Constr* (*of wall etc*) revêtement *m*; *Mil* **regimental facings** = parements *mpl* (de la manche ou du col) servant à distinguer les différents corps; *Constr* **f. brick** brique *f* de parement **(b)** (*in shop*) frontal *m*, frontale *f* **2** *adj* (*page*) ci-contre

facsimile [fæk'sɪmɪlɪ] *n* **(a)** (*copy*) fac-similé *m*, *pl* fac-similés; *Jur* (*of will etc*) copie *f* figurée; **to reproduce sth in f., to make a f. of sth** faire un fac-similé de qch; **f. signature** signature autographiée **(b)** *Telecom* télécopie *f*; **f. machine** télécopieur *m*

fact [fækt] *n* fait *m*; **f. and fiction** le réel et l'imaginaire; **scientific facts** les vérités *fpl* scientifiques; **to stick to the facts** s'en tenir aux faits; **just give me the facts** donnez-moi simplement les faits; **the f. that you're a woman** le fait que vous soyez une femme; **the f. (of the matter) is that ...** le fait est que ...; **owing to the f. that ...** du fait que ...; **it's a f. that ...** il est de fait que ...; **to know for a f. that ...** savoir pertinemment que ...; **apart from the f. that ...** hormis que ...; **in f.** de fait; **in point of f.** en fait; *Jur* **the jury only decides issues of f.** les jurés ne sont juges que du fait; **the facts of life** les choses de la vie; **it's a f. of life** c'est une réalité

fact-finding *adj* (*mission etc*) d'information, d'enquête

faction[1] ['fækʃən] *n* (*group*) faction *f*

faction[2] *n Cin, TV* docudrame *m*

factious ['fækʃəs] *adj* factieux

factitious [fæk'tɪʃəs] *adj* factice, artificiel

factor ['fæktə*r*] *n* **(a)** facteur *m*; *Math* diviseur *m*, facteur; *Tech* (*of drag, amplification etc*) coefficient *m*; *Math* **the highest common f.** le plus grand commun diviseur; *Econ* **f. of production** facteur de production, intrant *m*, input *m*; **demand f.** facteur de consommation; **f. of safety, safety f.** marge *f* de sécurité; *Tech* **load f.** coefficient de charge; **the human f.** l'élément *m* humain **(b)** *Com* (*agent*) agent *m*, dépositaire *m*; *Scot* (*of estate*) intendant *m*

factor analysis *n* analyse *f* factorielle

factoring ['fæktərɪŋ] *n Com* affacturage *m*; **f. company** société *f* d'affacturage

factory ['fækt(ə)rɪ] *n* usine *f*; **munitions f.** fabrique *f* de munitions; **biscuit f.** biscuiterie *f*; **f. inspector** inspecteur *m* du travail; **f. inspectorate** Inspection *f* du Travail; **f. manager** directeur *m* d'usine; **f. price** prix *m* usine; **f. retail outlet** magasin *m* d'usine; **f. shop** magasin *m* d'usine; **f. workers** ouvriers *mpl* en usine

factory farm *n Agr* exploitation *f* d'élevage industriel

factory farming *n Agr* élevage *m* industriel

factory ship *n Fishing* navire-usine *m*, *pl* navires-usines

factotum [fæk'təʊtəm] *n* factotum *m*, homme *m*/femme *f* à tout faire

fact sheet *n* prospectus *m*

factual ['fæktʃʊəl] *adj* (*account, information, description*) factuel, reposant sur les faits; (*knowledge*) des faits

factually ['fæktʃʊəlɪ] *adv* en ce qui concerne les faits; (*to report, describe etc*) objectivement

facultative ['fækəltətɪv] *adj* facultatif, -ive

faculty ['fækəltɪ] *n* **(a)** (*of mind, body*) faculté *f*, pouvoir *m*; **the f. of speech** le don de la parole; **to be in possession of all one's faculties** jouir de toutes ses facultés **(b)** (*ability*) facilité *f*, talent *m*; **to have a f. for doing sth** avoir des facilités pour faire qch; **to have the f. of observation** être observateur **(c)** *Univ* (*departments*) faculté *f*; *Am* (*teaching staff*) professorat *m*, corps *m* enseignant

fad [fæd] *n* lubie *f*; **it's only a passing f.** ce n'est qu'une toquade, ce n'est qu'un engouement passager; **the f. for macrobiotic food** la lubie pour les aliments macrobiotiques; **to have a f. about sth** se toquer de qch

faddiness ['fædɪnɪs] *n* **his f.** ses goûts *mpl* difficiles

faddy ['fædɪ] *adj* capricieux, maniaque; **he's f. about his food, he's a f. eater** il est difficile sur la nourriture

fade[1] [feɪd] **1** *vi* **(a)** (*of flowers*) se faner, se flétrir; (*of colours*) passer; (*of material*) se décolorer, déteindre; (*of hope*) s'éteindre; (*of light, sound*) s'affaiblir; **the light is fading** (*daylight*) le jour baisse; *TV, Cin* **to f. to black** faire un fondu au noir; **colours that f. into each other** couleurs qui se fondent; **summer fades into autumn** peu à peu l'automne succède à l'été; **to f. from memory** s'effacer de la mémoire **(b)** *TV, Cin* faire un fondu **2** *vt* **(a)** faner, décolorer; **curtains faded by the sun** rideaux décolorés par le soleil **(b)** *TV, Cin* fondre

fade[2] *n* **(a)** *TV, Cin* fondu *m* **(b)** (*of drum brakes*) fading *m*, évanouissement *m*

► **fade away** *vi* (*of light, sound*) s'affaiblir; *Fig* (*of person*) dépérir

► **fade in 1** *vi* (*of scene in film*) ouvrir en fondu; (*of music*) commencer en fondu sonore **2** *vtsep TV, Cin* ouvrir en fondu; **to f. the music in** introduire la musique en fondu sonore

► **fade out 1** *vi* (*of scene in film*) se terminer en fondu; (*of music*) se terminer en fondu sonore **2** *vtsep TV, Cin* fermer en fondu; (*music*) terminer par un fondu sonore

faded ['feɪdɪd] *adj* (*flower, memory*) fané, flétri; (*material*) décoloré; (*beauty, colour*) défraîchi, passé; (*photograph*) jauni

fade-in *n* (*of scene, music*) ouverture *f* en fondu

fade-out *n* (*of scene, music*) fermeture *f* en fondu

fader ['feɪdə*r*] *n TV, Cin* potentiomètre *m*

fading ['feɪdɪŋ] **1** *adj* (*flower*) qui se fane; (*light*) pâlissant **2** *n* **(a)** (*of plant*) flétrissure *f*; (*of material*) décoloration *f* **(b)** *Rad* fading *m* **(c)** *Cin* fondu *m*

faecal, *US* **fecal** ['fiːk(ə)l] *adj* fécal; **f. matter** matières *fpl* fécales, déjections *fpl*

faeces, *US* **feces** ['fiːsiːz] *npl Physiol* fèces *fpl*, matières *fpl* fécales

► **faff about, faff around** [fæf] *vi Br F* perdre son temps à des bricoles; **stop faffing about with the radio** arrête de tripoter la radio

fag[1] [fæg] *n* **(a)** *Br F* (*unpleasant job*) corvée *f* **(b)** *Am Pej, Sl* (*homosexual*) pédé *m*, pédale *f* **(c)** *Br F* (*cigarette*) clope *m*, sèche *f*; *Br F* **f. end** (*of cigarette*) mégot *m*, clope; *Fig* (*of material, winter etc*) bout *m*; (*of day, film*) fin *f* **(d)** *Eng Sch* (*pupil*) = jeune élève *m* attaché au service d'un grand

fag[2] *vi* **(-gg-) (a)** *Eng Sch* **to f. for a senior** (*of pupil*) faire les corvées d'un grand **(b)** *Old-fashioned F* (*work hard*) travailler dur, s'échiner

► **fag out** *vtsep F* (*of work etc*) éreinter; **fagged out** épuisé, éreinté

fagged [fægd] *adj Br F* **I can't be f.** ça ne me dit pas; **I could never really be f. about things like that** ces trucs-là ne m'ont jamais trop rien dit; **I don't know how he can be f. doing that** je ne sais pas comment il peut s'embêter à faire ça

faggot ['fægət] *n* **(a)** *Am Pej Sl* (*homosexual*) pédé *m*, pédale *f* **(b)** *Br Culin* boulette *f* (de viande) **(c)** (*bundle of wood*) fagot *m*

fah [fɑː] *n Mus* = **fa**

Fahrenheit [ˈfærənhaɪt] *adj Phys* (*scale, thermometer*) Fahrenheit; **ten degrees F.** dix degrés Fahrenheit

faience [faɪˈjɑːns] *n Cer* faïence *f*

fail[1] [feɪl] *n* **(a)** (*in exam*) échec *m*; **she got three passes and two fails** elle a réussi trois examens et en a raté deux; **he had never had a single f. in his life** il n'avait jamais raté un examen de sa vie **(b)** *Comptr* (*when logging in*) erreur *f* **(c) without f.** sans faute

fail[2] **1** *vi* **(a)** (*not succeed*) (*of person*) ne pas réussir, échouer, manquer son coup; (*in exam*) échouer; (*of negotiations etc*) ne pas aboutir; (*of play*) faire fiasco; (*of business*) faire faillite; (*of project*) échouer; **he failed in his attempt to …** il a échoué dans sa tentative de …; **I f. to see why/how …** je ne vois pas pourquoi/comment …; **the discussions have failed to bring any progress** les discussions n'ont pas réussi à produire le moindre progrès; **the high proportions of pupils who are failing** la forte proportion d'élèves qui échouent à leurs examens

(b) (*be inadequate*) manquer, faire défaut; (*of health, patient*) décliner; (*of health, light, memory, strength*) baisser; (*of eyesight*) faiblir, baisser; (*of brakes, heart, support*) lâcher; (*of engine*) tomber en panne; **his parachute failed** son parachute ne s'est pas ouvert; **if all else fails** en désespoir de cause; **to f. in one's duty** manquer à son devoir; **to f. to do sth** négliger de faire qch; **she was charged with failing to report an accident** elle a été inculpée pour avoir manqué de signaler un accident; **he failed to mention that …** il a omis de faire remarquer que …; **the cheque failed to arrive** le chèque n'est pas arrivé; **the engine failed to start** le moteur a refusé de démarrer; **she never fails to visit me on Sundays** elle ne manque jamais de me rendre visite le dimanche; **it never fails** (*it always happens*) ça ne manque jamais; (*of remedy*) ça ne rate jamais

2 *vt Sch* (*candidate*) refuser, recaler; (*exam*) être refusé *ou* recalé à; (*essay*) rater; **to f. a drugs test** être positif au contrôle anti-dopage; **words f. me** les mots me manquent; **his nerve failed him** le courage lui a fait défaut, il a manqué de courage; **I won't f. you** vous pouvez compter sur moi; **he had failed her before** il lui avait déjà fait faux bond; **his memory/eyesight was beginning to f. him** sa mémoire/vue commençait à lui faire défaut

failed [feɪld] *adj* (*candidate*) refusé, recalé; *Com* (*company*) en faillite; (*project, scheme*) qui n'a pas abouti; (*artist, politician*) raté; *Comptr* **f. logon** ouverture *f* de session avortée

failing [ˈfeɪlɪŋ] **1** *adj* (*sight, strength etc*) défaillant, baissant; **to be in f. health** avoir une santé défaillante **2** *n* (*fault*) faiblesse *f*, défaut *m*; **with all her failings** malgré tous ses défauts **3** *prep* à *ou* au défaut de; **f. a satisfactory reply** faute de réponse satisfaisante; **f. which** faute de quoi; **f. all else** en désespoir de cause; **call me at home or f. that at the office** appelle-moi à la maison ou, à défaut, au bureau

failsafe [ˈfeɪlseɪf] *adj* (*system*) protégé contre les incidents; **f. device** *or* **system** dispositif *m* de sécurité positive

failure [ˈfeɪljər] *n* **(a)** (*lack of success*) insuccès *m*, non-réussite *f*; (*in exam, of play*) échec *m*; *Com* faillite *f*; **the experiment was** *or* **proved** *or* **turned out a f.** l'expérience n'a pas réussi *ou* a raté; **the expedition ended in f.** l'expédition s'est soldée par un échec; **the team's f. to win the championship was a great surprise** cela a été une grande surprise que l'équipe n'ait pas remporté le championnat; **the f. of his new film** l'échec qu'a rencontré son nouveau film

(b) (*person*) raté, -ée; (*play etc*) four *m*, fiasco *m*; **I'm a complete f. as a teacher** comme professeur, je suis complètement raté; *Sch* **there are too many failures** trop de candidats ont été recalés

(c) (*neglect*) manque *m*; **f. to keep a promise** manquement *m* à une promesse; **f. to pay a bill** défaut *m* de paiement d'un effet; **your f. to apologise is inexcusable** tu es inexcusable de ne pas avoir demandé pardon; **he was angry at her f. even to write** il était en colère qu'elle n'écrive même pas

(d) (*of machine*) panne *f*; (*of software, hardware*) panne, défaillance *f*; (*of organ*) insuffisance *f*; *El* **power f.** panne de courant; **f. rate** taux *m* de panne

fain [feɪn] *adv Arch, Lit* volontiers

faint[1] [feɪnt] *adj* **(a)** (*weak*) (*hope, light, sound, possibility etc*) faible; (*praise*) tiède; (*colour*) pâle, délavé; (*sound, touch, bruise etc*) léger; (*idea*) vague, peu précis; (*mark etc*) à peine visible; (*inscription*) indistinct; **to give a f. smile** (*not be amused or pleased*) sourire du bout des lèvres; **I could detect a f. smile on her lips** j'ai décelé un petit sourire sur ses lèvres; **a f. tinge of blue** une légère nuance bleuâtre; **I haven't the faintest (idea)** je n'en ai pas la moindre idée; **the sound of the footsteps grew fainter** le bruit des pas s'affaiblit

(b) to feel *or* **be f.** se sentir mal; **I was feeling f. with hunger** j'avais tellement faim que la tête me tournait; **to be f. with tiredness** tomber de fatigue

(c) *Arch, Lit* (*timid*) timide; *Prov* **f. heart never won fair lady** jamais honteux n'eut belle amie

faint[2] *n Med* évanouissement *m*, défaillance *f*; **to fall down in a f.** tomber évanoui

faint[3] *vi Med* **to f. (away)** s'évanouir, défaillir; **she fainted with pain** elle s'évanouit de douleur

faint-hearted [feɪntˈhɑːtɪd] *adj* pusillanime

faint-heartedly [feɪntˈhɑːtɪdlɪ] *adv* avec pusillanimité

faint-heartedness [feɪntˈhɑːtɪdnɪs] *n* pusillanimité *f*

fainting [ˈfeɪntɪŋ] *n* évanouissement *m*; **f. fit** évanouissement

faintly [ˈfeɪntlɪ] *adv* (*to hear, shine*) faiblement; (*uneasy, amused, ridiculous*) légèrement; (*to remember, see*) vaguement; **f. visible** à peine visible; **to smile f.** esquisser un sourire; **it is f. possible that …** il y a une faible possibilité pour que …

faintness [ˈfeɪntnɪs] *n* (*of voice, sound etc*) faiblesse *f*; (*of breeze etc*) légèreté *f*; *Med* malaise *f*; **have you been suffering from f.?** avez-vous souffert d'évanouissements?; **it's the f. of the writing that's the problem** le problème c'est que l'écriture est pâle

fair[1] [feər] *n* foire *f*; **world f.** exposition *f* universelle; *Br* **(fun) f.** fête *f* foraine; **village f.** kermesse *f*

fair[2] **1** *adj* **(a)** (*just*) juste, équitable; (*price*) raisonnable; (*wage*) équitable; (*fight*) loyal; **to get a f. trial** être jugé de façon équitable; **f. play** jeu *m* loyal, franc jeu, fair-play *m inv*; **fair's f.** il faut être juste; **that's only f.** ce n'est que juste; **it's not f.** ce n'est pas juste; **it isn't f. to expect children to …** ce n'est pas raisonnable de demander à des enfants de …; **f. enough!** ça va!, d'accord!; **it's all f. and above board** *or* **all f. and square** c'est de bonne guerre; **he is strict but f.** il est sévère mais juste *ou* sans parti pris; **it is only f. to say that …** il faut dire que …; **but, to be f.** (*honest, reasonable*) mais, pour être honnête; **as is only f.** comme il se doit; *Sl* **f. do's** ce n'est que justice; **a f. example** un bon exemple; **a f. exchange** un échange équitable; *Prov* **f. exchange is no robbery** tout le monde est content; **f. game** proie *f* facile; **everyone deserves their f. share** chacun mérite d'avoir ce qui lui est dû; **he got more than his f. share!** il a eu plus que ce qui lui revenait!; **he's had more than his f. share of criticism/problems** il a eu largement sa part de critiques/problèmes; **by f. means or foul** d'une manière ou d'une autre; *Prov* **all's f. in love and war** à la guerre comme à la guerre

(b) (*quite good*) assez bon; **a f. amount of** pas mal de; **he has a f. chance of success** il a des chances de réussir; **in f. condition** acceptable; **a f. idea** une bonne idée; **a f. number of …** un nombre respectable de …; **a f. pace** un bon pas *ou* rythme; **f. to middling** comme ci comme ça; **in a f. way to recovering** en bonne voie de rétablissement

(c) (*wind etc*) propice, favorable; **f. weather** beau temps

(d) *esp Lit, Arch* (*attractive*) beau, *f* belle; **the fair(er) sex** le beau sexe; *Hum* **to make sth with one's own f. hands** faire qch de ses propres mains, *Hum* faire qch tout seul comme un grand

(e) (*specious*) spécieux; **f. promises/words** de belles promesses/paroles

(f) (*light-coloured*) (*person, hair*) blond; (*skin*) blanc, *f* blanche

(g) *Sl* (*intensive*) **we had a f. old time of it at the party** nous nous sommes drôlement bien amusés à la fête

2 *adv* **(a)** (*to act*) loyalement; **to play f.** jouer franc jeu; **to fight f.** se battre loyalement; **you can't say fairer than that** il n'y a pas plus équitable

(b) (*completely*) complètement; **struck f. (and square) on the chin** frappé en plein menton

fair copy *n* copie *f* au propre; **to make a f. of a letter** passer *ou* recopier une lettre au propre

fairground [ˈfeəgraʊnd] *n* champ *m* de foire

fair-haired *adj* blond, aux cheveux blonds; *US Fig* **f. boy** chouchou *m*

fairing [ˈfeərɪŋ] *n Av, Aut* carénage *m*

fairish [ˈfeərɪʃ] *adj* **(a)** (*hair*) plutôt blond **(b)** (*quite good*) assez bon

fairly [ˈfeəlɪ] *adv* **(a)** (*to judge etc*) équitablement, avec justice; **to treat sb f.** traiter qn équitablement *ou* avec impartialité

(b) (*to act, play etc*) honnêtement; (*to fight*) loyalement; **to come by sth f. (and squarely)** obtenir qch par des moyens honnêtes; **to win f. and squarely** (*clearly, easily*) remporter une nette victoire; (*without dishonest means*) vaincre honnêtement

(c) (*quite*) (*rich, skilful etc*) assez; **f. good wine** vin passablement *ou* assez bon; **it is f. certain that** ... il est à peu près certain que ...; **to do sth f. well** faire qch d'une façon acceptable *ou* passable

(d) (*well*) bien; **once the ship was f. under way** une fois le navire en bonne route; **we f. raced through the work** nous avons fait notre travail à bonne allure

(e) *F* (*completely*) complètement, absolument

fair-minded *adj* équitable, juste

fairness ['feənɪs] *n* (a) (*of decision*) impartialité *f*; (*of person*) équité *f*, impartialité; (*of law, share*) équité; **in all f.** en toute justice; **in f. to him, he did help us a lot** pour lui rendre justice, il faut dire qu'il nous a beaucoup aidé (b) *Arch, Lit* (*beauty*) beauté *f* (c) (*of hair*) blondeur *f*; (*of skin*) blancheur *f*

fair-sized *adj* assez grand

fairway ['feəweɪ] *n* (a) *Golf* fairway *m* (b) *Naut* chenal *m*, passe *f*, passage *m*

fair-weather *adj* (*boat*) qui convient seulement pour le beau temps; **f. friends** amis *mpl* des beaux jours

fairy ['feərɪ] 1 *n* (a) fée *f*; **the wicked f.** la fée Carabosse (b) *Sl, Pej* (*homosexual man*) pédé *m*, tapette *f*, tante *f* 2 *adj* féerique; **f. footsteps** pas légers; **f. queen** reine *f* des fées; **f. godmother** marraine *f* fée; *Fig* marraine gâteau; **f. lights** guirlande *f* lumineuse (pour sapin de Noël); **f. story** *or* **tale** conte *m* de fées; *Fig* (*lie*) histoires *fpl* à dormir debout

fairyland ['feərɪlænd] *n* pays *m* *ou* royaume *m* des fées; *Fig* (*imaginary world*) féerie *f*; **at night the garden became a f.** le soir, le jardin se transforma en pays enchanté

faith [feɪθ] *n* (a) (*trust*) foi *f*; **to have (every) f. in sb/sth** avoir (entièrement) confiance en qn/qch; **I don't have much f. in doctors** je ne fais pas beaucoup confiance aux médecins; **to have f. in God** avoir foi en Dieu; **to put one's f. in sb** accorder toute sa confiance à qn; **an act of f.** un acte de foi

(b) (*religion*) religion *f*, foi *f*, croyance *f*; **what f. are you?** de quelle religion êtes-vous?; **to be of the Catholic/Jewish f.** être de religion catholique/juive; **the Christian f.** la foi chrétienne; **to lose one's f.** perdre la foi

(c) (*loyalty*) **to keep f. with sb** tenir ses engagements envers qn; **to break f. with sb** manquer de foi *ou* de parole à qn; **good f.** bonne foi; **to say sth in good f.** dire qch en toute bonne foi; **to do sth in all good f.** faire qch en tout honneur; **bad f.** perfidie *f*

faithful ['feɪθfʊl] 1 *adj* (*friend etc*) fidèle, loyal, -aux; (*copy*) exact, juste; (*translation, description, account*) fidèle; **to remain f. to sb/one's promises** rester fidèle à qn/ses promesses; **f. in every detail** exact jusqu'au moindre détail 2 *Rel* **the f.** les fidèles *mpl*; (*Islam*) les croyants *mpl*; *Pol* **the party f.** les fidèles du parti

faithfully ['feɪθfʊlɪ] *adv* (a) (*loyally*) fidèlement, loyalement; **yours f.** (*in formal letter*) recevez l'expression de mes/nos sentiments distingués; **he promised f. to come tomorrow** il a promis formellement de venir demain (b) (*to copy*) exactement; (*to translate, follow instructions*) fidèlement

faithfulness ['feɪθfʊlnɪs] *n* (a) (*loyalty*) fidélité *f*, loyauté *f* (**to** envers) (b) (*accuracy*) (*of report etc*) fidélité *f*, exactitude *f*

faith healer *n* guérisseur *m* par la prière

faith healing *n* guérison *f* par la prière

faithless ['feɪθlɪs] *adj* (a) *Rel* (*lacking faith*) infidèle, sans foi (b) (*to husband, wife etc*) infidèle (**to** à); (*to party, friend etc*) déloyal, -aux

faithlessness ['feɪθlɪsnɪs] *n* (a) (*lack of trust*) manque *m* de confiance (b) (*to husband, wife etc*) infidélité *f* (**to** à); (*to party, friend*) déloyauté *f*

fake[1] [feɪk] 1 *n* (*object*) article *m* faux *ou* truqué; **it's a f.** c'est un faux; **he's a f.** c'est un bluffeur 2 *adj* faux, *f* fausse

fake[2] 1 *vt* (*calculations etc*) truquer; (*signature*) contrefaire; (*illness*) simuler; **faked balance sheet** bilan truqué; **to f. a story** inventer une histoire; **she faked her own death** elle a fait croire à sa propre mort; **it's all faked** (*in cinema etc*) c'est du trucage 2 *vi* (*pretend*) faire semblant, jouer la comédie

faker ['feɪkər] *n F* (*who pretends*) comédien, -ienne

faking ['feɪkɪŋ] *n* **it's just f.** c'est de la comédie

fakir ['feɪkɪər, fə'kɪər] *n* fakir *m*

falcon ['fɔːlkən] *n* (*bird*) faucon *m*

falconer ['fɔːlkənər] *n* fauconnier *m*

falconry ['fɔːlkənrɪ] *n* fauconnerie *f*

Falkland ['fɔːlklənd] *n* **the F. Islands, the Falklands** les (îles *fpl*) Malouines *fpl*, les îles Falkland

fall[1] [fɔːl] *n* (a) (*of body etc*) chute *f*; (*in wrestling*) tomber *m*; *Th* (*of curtain*) baisser *m*; (*of snow, rain*) précipitations *fpl*; **a f. of earth/rock** (*actual earth, rocks*) un éboulis de terre/pierres; **there's been another f.** il y a encore eu un éboulement; **to have a f.** faire une chute; **a bad f.** une mauvaise chute; **there has been a heavy f. of snow** il est tombé beaucoup de neige; *Fig* **to be heading** *or* **riding for a f.** courir à sa perte; *esp Am F* **f. guy** (*dupe*) pigeon *m*; (*scapegoat*) bouc *m* émissaire, souffre-douleur *m inv*

(b) *Am* (*autumn*) automne *m*

(c) (*waterfall*) (*usu pl*) **falls** chute *f* (d'eau); **Victoria Falls** les Chutes Victoria; **Niagara Falls** les Chutes du Niagara

(d) (*lowering*) (*of water*) décrue *f*, baisse *f*; (*of tide*) reflux *m*, jusant *m*; (*of voice*) cadence *f*

(e) (*decrease*) (*in weight, number etc*) diminution *f*; (*of barometer, in pressure etc*) chute *f*; (*in temperature, interest, income, frequency*) baisse *f*; *Com, Fin* (*of prices, shares*) baisse; (*of currency*) dépréciation *f*; **f. in prices** baisse de prix

(f) (*slope*) (*of road etc*) pente *f*

(g) (*ruin*) (*of person*) perte *f*, ruine *f*; **after this f. from grace** après être tombé en disgrâce

(h) (*capture*) (*of city*) chute *f*; (*of empire etc*) chute, déchéance *f*; **the F. of the Roman Empire** la chute de l'Empire romain; **the F. of the Bastille** la prise de la Bastille

(i) *Rel* **the F. (of Man)** la chute

fall[2] *vi* (*pt* **fell** [fel]; *pp* **fallen** [fɔːlən]) (a) (*from a height*) tomber; *Astron* (*of star*) filer; **to f. to the ground** tomber à terre; **she fell to her death** elle a fait une chute mortelle; **to f. off a ladder** tomber d'une échelle; **to f. 20 feet** tomber de 20 pieds; **the water falls over 800m to the valley below** l'eau tombe dans une cascade de plus de 800 m de haut jusque dans la vallée; **the cliff falls sheer to the ocean below** la falaise descend à pic vers l'océan; **to f. out of the window** tomber par la fenêtre; **to f. on one's feet** retomber sur ses pieds; *Fig* avoir de la chance; **to f. short of a target** manquer la cible; **to f. short of a past performance** être loin d'une performance passée; **to f. into a trap** tomber *ou* donner dans un piège; **to f. into sb's hands** tomber entre les mains de qn; **night is falling** la nuit tombe; **rain/snow had fallen overnight** il avait plu/neigé pendant la nuit; **his hair fell to his shoulders** (*hung down*) ses cheveux lui descendaient *ou* tombaient jusqu'aux épaules; **his hair keeps falling into his eyes** ses cheveux n'arrêtent pas de lui tomber dans les yeux

(b) (*from standing or perpendicular position*) **to f. to the ground** tomber par terre; **to f. on one's knees** tomber à genoux; **to f. (in battle)** tomber au champ d'honneur; *Fig* **the scheme fell flat** le projet est tombé à l'eau

(c) (*collapse*) (*of building*) s'écrouler, s'effondrer; **to f. to pieces** *or* **bits** tomber en morceaux; **when Liège fell** lorsque Liège capitula; **the government has fallen** le gouvernement a été renversé *ou* est tombé

(d) (*diminish*) (*of price etc*) diminuer, baisser, chuter; (*of exchange etc*) baisser, se déprécier; (*of wind*) tomber; *Fig* **his stock is falling** son crédit est en baisse; **the thermometer/temperature has fallen ten degrees** le thermomètre/la température a baissé *ou* chuté de dix degrés

(e) (*become lower*) (*of ground*) aller en pente, s'incliner; (*of tide etc*) baisser; **her eyes fell** elle a baissé les yeux; **his face fell** sa figure s'allongea; **my spirits fell** j'ai perdu tout courage; **to f. from one's position** déchoir de sa position; **to f. to the bottom of the league/list** tomber en bas du classement/de la liste; **to f. in sb's estimation** baisser dans l'estime de qn

(f) *Rel* (*sin*) tomber, pécher; **to f. from grace** perdre la grâce; *Fig* **to f. from grace with sb** tomber en disgrâce auprès de qn

(g) (*alight*) **a shadow fell on the wall** une ombre se projeta sur le mur; **his eye fell on a box/a curious headline** son regard est tombé sur une boîte/un titre curieux

(h) (*occur*) tomber; **Christmas falls on a Thursday** Noël tombe un jeudi; **the accent falls on the last syllable** l'accent tombe sur la dernière syllabe; **it fell to me to break the bad news** c'est à moi qu'il est revenu d'annoncer la mauvaise nouvelle; **these facts f. under another category** ces faits entrent dans une autre catégorie; **that falls outside the scope of our investigation** ceci dépasse les limites de notre enquête

(i) (*enter into given state*) **to f. under suspicion** (*of person*) devenir l'objet des soupçons, devenir suspect; **the country has fallen on hard times** le pays connaît des jours difficiles; **I soon fell in with their ways** (*became used to their way of doing things*) je me suis vite accoutumé à leur manière de faire; (*learnt routine*) j'ai bientôt appris la routine; **to f. in love with sb/sth** tomber amoureux de qn/qch; **to f. into a habit** contracter une habitude; **to f. into error** être induit en erreur; **to f. into despair** sombrer dans le désespoir; **to f. into line with** s'aligner sur

(j) (*become*) **to f. asleep** s'endormir; **to f. ill** *or* **sick** tomber malade; **to f. silent** (*of person, guns*) se taire; **the room fell**

silent le silence se fit dans la salle; **to f. vacant** *(of post)* se trouver vacant; **to f. (a) victim to …** être victime de …

(k) *(begin)* **they fell to work/discussing (again)** ils se (re)mirent au travail/à discuter

▶ **fall about** *vi (fall in different directions)* tomber de côté et d'autre; **to f. about (laughing)** se tordre de rire

▶ **fall apart** *vi (fall to pieces)* se désintégrer, tomber en morceaux; *(of marriage)* se désintégrer, sombrer

▶ **fall away** *vi* **(a)** *(of ground)* s'affaisser **(b)** *(crumble)* se désintégrer; *(of plaster, paint)* s'écailler **(c)** *(of attendance)* diminuer; *(of followers etc)* déserter **(d)** *(of prejudice etc)* disparaître

▶ **fall back** *vi* **(a)** *(fall)* tomber à la renverse *ou* en arrière; **to f. back on the cushions** *(after trying to get up)* retomber sur les coussins; *(sink back)* se basculer en arrière sur les coussins; *(from standing position)* tomber à la renverse sur les coussins **(b)** *(of troops)* se replier, reculer; **to f. back a pace** reculer d'un pas **(c)** *St Exch, Fin* **to f. back two points** se replier de deux points

▶ **fall back on** *vipo (resort to)* avoir recours à; **she fell back on the usual clichés** elle a eu recours aux clichés habituels; **to have some money to f. back on** avoir de l'argent en réserve au cas où; **he knew he could always f. back on his parents** il savait qu'il pouvait compter sur ses parents

▶ **fall behind** *vi (of runner, political party etc)* être à la traîne, se faire distancer, rester en arrière; **to f. behind with the rent** être en retard pour payer son loyer; **to f. behind with one's work** prendre du retard dans son travail

▶ **fall down** *vi* **(a)** *(fall to ground)* tomber à terre *ou* par terre **(b)** *(of building etc)* s'écrouler, s'effondrer **(c)** *(fail)* échouer; **that's where their argument falls down** c'est sur ce point que leurs arguments ne tiennent plus debout; **where the whole thing falls down is …** là où plus rien ne tient debout *ou* où tout s'écroule c'est …; **I fell down badly on the first question** j'ai complètement raté la première question; **to f. down on the job** louper le travail

▶ **fall for** *vipo F* **(a)** *(fall in love with) (sb)* tomber amoureux de; **I've fallen for that antique chair** j'ai eu le coup de foudre pour cette vieille chaise **(b)** *(be deceived by) (story etc)* se laisser prendre à; **to f. for it** s'y laisser prendre; **I'm not falling for that one!** ça ne prend pas!, à d'autres!

▶ **fall in** *vi* **(a)** *(of building, roof etc)* s'écrouler, s'effondrer; *(of trench etc)* s'ébouler; **I was running along the edge of the pool when I fell in** je courais le long de la piscine quand je suis tombé dedans **(b)** *Mil (of troops)* former les rangs; **f. in!** rassemblement!

▶ **fall in with** *vipo* **(a)** *(person) (meet up with)* rencontrer par hasard; *(associate with)* fréquenter; **my son fell in with a bad crowd** mon fils s'est mis à avoir de mauvaises fréquentations **(b)** *(agree with) (suggestion)* accepter; *(request)* accéder à; **I fell in with the plans for a picnic** j'ai accepté le projet d'un pique-nique

▶ **fall off** *vi* **(a)** *(fall from something)* tomber; **I picked the violin up and the neck fell off** j'ai pris le violon et le manche est tombé **(b)** *(of followers etc)* faire défection; *(of profits)* diminuer; *(of speed)* ralentir; *(of wind)* tomber; *(of zeal)* se relâcher; *(of popularity)* baisser **(c)** *(of skills, standards, quality)* baisser **(d)** *Naut* abattre sous le vent

▶ **fall on** *vipo* **(a)** *(of blame, responsibility, suspicion)* retomber sur **(b)** *(attack) (enemy)* attaquer; *(food)* se jeter sur; **they fell on each other in delighted relief** vivement soulagés, ils tombèrent dans les bras l'un de l'autre

▶ **fall out** *vi* **(a)** *(fall from inside sth)* tomber dehors; *(of hair)* tomber **(b)** *Mil (of troops)* rompre les rangs; **f. out!** rompez! **(c)** *(quarrel)* se brouiller, se fâcher **(with** avec); **they have fallen out** ils sont fâchés *ou* brouillés **(d)** *(occur)* se passer, se dérouler; **as things fell out** en fin de compte

▶ **fall over 1** *vi (of person)* tomber (par terre); *(of thing)* se renverser, être renversé **2** *vipo (stumble on)* trébucher sur; **move that suitcase before someone falls over it** déplace cette valise avant que quelqu'un ne se prenne les pieds dedans; *F* **publishers were falling over each other for her new book** les éditeurs se disputaient avec acharnement son nouveau livre; **he was falling over himself to please her** il se mettait en quatre pour lui plaire

▶ **fall through** *vi (of scheme etc)* ne pas aboutir, échouer, *F* tomber à l'eau

▶ **fall to** *vi Old-fashioned F (begin eating)* s'attaquer au repas

▶ **fall upon** *vipo* = **fall on**

fallacious [fə'leɪʃəs] *adj* erroné

fallacy ['fæləsɪ] *n* erreur *f*; *(in logic)* sophisme *m*; **it is a f. that …** ce serait une erreur de croire que …; **the f. of this argument is that …** ce qui est faux dans ce raisonnement, c'est que …

fallback ['fɔːlbæk] **1** *n* solution *f* de remplacement **2** *adj* de remplacement, alternatif

fallen ['fɔːlən] **1** *adj (leaf, tree etc)* tombé; *(angel)* déchu; *(idol)* tombé en disgrâce; *Old-fashioned* **f. woman** femme déchue, fille perdue; *Med* **f. arches** voûtes plantaires affaissées **2** *npl Mil, Lit* **in memory of the f.** en mémoire des soldats tombés au combat

fallibility [fælɪ'bɪlɪtɪ] *n* faillibilité *f*

fallible ['fælɪb(ə)l] *adj* faillible

falling ['fɔːlɪŋ] **1** *adj (piece of masonry, tile)* qui tombe; *(darkness etc)* tombant; *(temperature, membership, standards)* en baisse; *Com (prices)* qui baisse; *(market)* avec tendance à la baisse; **f. rocks** chute *f* de pierres; *Arch* **f. sickness** épilepsie *f*; *Astron* **f. star** étoile *f* filante **2** *n* chute *f*; *(of prices, barometer etc)* baisse *f*

falling away *n (of support)* affaiblissement *m*; *(of supporters)* défection *f*, désertion *f*

fall(ing)-off *n (of support)* affaiblissement *m*; *(of supporters)* désertion *f*, défection *f*; *(of figures, rate etc)* diminution *f*, baisse *f*; *(of power, popularity)* déclin *m*; *(of zeal)* relâchement *m*; *(of orders, business)* ralentissement *m*

Fallopian [fə'ləʊpɪən] *adj Anat* **F. tubes** trompes *fpl* de Fallope

fallout ['fɔːlaʊt] *n* retombées *fpl* (radioactives); *Fig* **the political f. from the scandal** les retombées politiques du scandale

fallow¹ ['fæləʊ] *Agr* **1** *n* jachère *f* **2** *adj (land)* en jachère; **to lie f.** être en jachère; *Fig* **a f. period** une période de régénération

fallow² *adj* **f. deer** daim *m*

false [fɔːls] **1** *adj* **(a)** *(incorrect)* faux, *f* fausse; *(idea)* erroné; **to give sb a f. impression of sth** donner à qn une fausse impression sur qch; **to put a f. interpretation on sb's actions/words** mal interpréter les actions/paroles de qn; **one f. move and he would have killed me** si j'avais fait un faux mouvement, il m'aurait tué; **to put sb in a f. position** donner de qn l'image qu'il est en tort; **f. alarm** fausse alerte *f*; *F* canard *m*; **f. claim** *(made for product)* promesse *f* mensongère; **f. dawn** premières lueurs *fpl* de l'aube; *Ling* **f. friend** faux ami *m*; **f. invoice** fausse facture *f*; **f. modesty** fausse modestie *f*; *(about sexual matters)* fausse pudeur *f*; *Mus, Fig* **f. note** fausse note *f*; *Fig* **to strike a f. note** créer une fausse note; **f. report** fausse nouvelle *f*; **f. trade description** description *f* commerciale erronée *ou* mensongère; **f. start** faux départ *m*; *Sp* **to get off to a f. start** faire un faux départ

(b) *(dishonest)* hypocrite; *(unfaithful)* infidèle; *(promise etc)* mensonger; **he turns on the charm for them — it's all so f.** il veut leur faire du charme — quelle hypocrisie!; **to be in a f. position** être dans une situation délicate; **under f. pretences** par des moyens frauduleux; *(by lying)* sous des prétextes fallacieux; **f. witness** faux témoin *m*; **to bear f. witness** rendre faux témoignage

(c) *(not real) (beard, nose etc)* faux, *f* fausse, artificiel, postiche; *(action etc)* feint, prétendu; *(coin, seal, document)* faux, contrefait; **f. bottom** *(of box etc)* double fond; **it's a f. economy** ce n'est pas vraiment rentable; **f. name** faux nom *m*; **(a set of) f. teeth** fausses dents *fpl*, dentier *m*

2 *adv Lit, Old-fashioned* **to play sb f.** trahir qn; **his memory played him f.** sa mémoire l'a trahi *ou* lui a joué des tours

false-hearted [fɔːls'hɑːtɪd] *adj Lit* fourbe

falsehood ['fɔːlshʊd] *n* **(a) to distinguish truth from f.** distinguer le vrai du faux **(b)** *Fml (lie)* mensonge *m*; **to tell a f.** dire un mensonge

falsely ['fɔːlslɪ] *adv* faussement; **to smile f.** affecter un sourire; *esp Lit* **to act f.** agir déloyalement

falseness ['fɔːlsnɪs] *n* **(a)** *(of report, manner etc)* fausseté *f* **(b)** *Old-fashioned (of lover etc)* infidélité *f*

falsers ['fɔːlsəz] *npl Br F Hum (teeth)* râtelier *m*, dentier *m*

falsetto [fɔːl'setəʊ] *Mus* **1** *n* **(a)** *(voice)* voix *f* de fausset; **to sing (in) f.** chanter en fausset **(b)** *(singer)* fausset *m* **2** *adj (voice)* de fausset

falsies ['fɔːlsɪz] *npl F (padding for breasts)* bonnet *m* rembourré

falsifiable [fɔːlsɪ'faɪb(ə)l] *adj Phil* falsifiable

falsification [fɔːlsɪfɪ'keɪʃən] *n* falsification *f*

falsify ['fɔːlsɪfaɪ] *vt* **(falsified; falsifying) (a)** *(make false) (document)* falsifier; *(balance sheet)* fausser; *(facts etc)* dénaturer **(b)** *(disprove)* prouver la fausseté de

falsity ['fɔːlsɪtɪ] *n* = **falseness**

falter ['fɔːltər] **1** *vi (of voice)* hésiter, trembler; *(of person)* chanceler; *(in one's belief, conviction)* vaciller; *(of courage, determination)* défaillir; **his steps faltered as he neared the room** ses pas se firent hésitants tandis qu'il s'approchait de la pièce; **he faltered in his speech** il eut un moment d'hésitation **2** *vt* dire d'une voix hésitante; **he faltered his**

way through his speech (*nervously*) il a prononcé son discours d'une voix hésitante; (*losing thread*) il n'a pas arrêté de perdre le fil de son discours

▶ **falter out** *vtsep* (*excuse etc*) balbutier

faltering [ˈfɔːltərɪŋ] *adj* (*voice etc*) hésitant; (*courage, memory etc*) défaillant; (*legs*) chancelant; **to speak in a f. voice** parler d'une voix mal assurée; **to reply in f. Spanish** répondre dans un espagnol mal assuré; **with f. steps** d'un pas mal assuré *ou* chancelant; **a child's first f. steps** les premiers pas hésitants d'un enfant

fame [feɪm] *n* renom *m*, renommée *f*; **to win f.** se faire un grand nom; **to rise** *or* **come to f. as an explorer** atteindre la renommée en tant qu'explorateur; **to seek f. and fortune** rechercher la gloire et la fortune; **house of ill f.** maison mal famée; **not Chandler of Philip Marlowe f.?** le Chandler célèbre pour son Philip Marlowe?

famed [feɪmd] *adj* célèbre, bien connu (**for** pour); **she was f. for her rudeness** elle était bien connue pour son impolitesse

familiar [fəˈmɪlɪər] **1** *adj* (**a**) (*well-known*) familier, bien connu; **a f. face** un visage familier; **she looks f.** je l'ai déjà vue quelque part; **an experience that will be f. to everyone** une expérience bien connue de tous; **it strikes one as f.** (*seen before*) cela laisse une impression de déjà vu; (*heard before*) cela laisse une impression de déjà entendu; **to be on f. ground** être sur son terrain; **an all too f. story of drug addiction and homelessness** (c'est) toujours ce même problème de drogue et de sans-abris; **his voice sounded f. to me** il me sembla reconnaître sa voix; **there was something f. about him/it** il/cela me disait quelque chose

(**b**) (*acquainted*) **to be f. with sth/s. b.** bien connaître qch/qn; **to be f. with the customs** être au courant des usages; **to become more f. with s. b. /sth** se familiariser avec qn/qch

(**c**) (*intimate*) familier, intime; *Ling* familier; **to adopt a f. tone** prendre un ton familier *ou* d'intimité; **to be on f. terms with s. b.** avoir des rapports d'intimité avec qn; *Old-fashioned* **you are rather too f.** vous prenez trop de privautés; **don't let the pupils get too f. (with you)** ne laissez pas les élèves prendre trop de familiarités (avec vous)

2 *n* (**a**) **f. (spirit)** (*in witchcraft*) démon *m* familier

(**b**) *Old-fashioned* (*friend*) familier *m*, intime *m*

familiarity [fəmɪlɪˈærɪtɪ] *n* (**a**) (*intimacy*) familiarité *f*; *Prov* **f. breeds contempt** la familiarité engendre *ou* fait naître le mépris (**b**) (*acquaintance*) connaissance *f* (**with** de); **her f. with French** sa connaissance du français

familiarization [fəmɪlɪəraɪˈzeɪʃən] *n* **after a period of f. with ...** après une période de familiarisation avec ...; **greater f. with the details of the proposal** une connaissance plus poussée des détails de la proposition; **f. trip** (*for sales agents*) voyage *m* d'études *ou* de familiarisation

familiarize [fəˈmɪlɪəraɪz] *vt* (**a**) (*acquaint*) **to f. s. b. with sth** faire connaître qch à qn, familiariser qn avec qch; **to f. oneself with a language/the rules** se familiariser avec une langue/le règlement (**b**) (*make known*) rendre familier; **science-fiction had long familiarized us with the idea** la science-fiction nous avait depuis longtemps rendu cette idée familière *ou* habitués à cette idée

familiarly [fəˈmɪlɪəlɪ] *adv* familièrement; **f. known as ...** communément connu comme ...

family [ˈfæmlɪ, -ɪlɪ] *n* (**a**) [ⓘA11,g,i] famille *f*; **large f.** famille nombreuse; **a friend of the f., a f. friend** un ami de la famille; **they don't want (to have** *or* **start) a f. yet** ils ne veulent pas encore avoir un enfant *ou* fonder de famille; **to be one of the f.** être de la maison; *F* **we've got f. coming to stay** nous allons avoir de la famille en visite; *F* **she's like f.** c'est comme si elle était de la famille; **it runs in the f.** cela tient de famille; **disease that runs in the f.** maladie *f* héréditaire; **the painting has been in the f. for generations** ce tableau est dans la famille depuis des générations; **we will keep it in the f.** (*of heirloom, land etc*) ça restera dans la famille; (*of scandal*) ça ne sortira pas de la famille; **you can see the f. resemblance** *or* **likeness** on ne peut pas ne pas remarquer un air de famille; *F* **she's in the f. way** elle est enceinte; **to get** *or* **put s. b. in the f. way** mettre qn enceinte; **f. business** entreprise *f* familiale; **f. butcher** boucher *m* du coin; **a f. dinner** un dîner en famille; **a f. celebration** une fête de famille; *Mktg* **f. expenditure survey** étude *f* sur les dépenses des familles; *F* **f. get-together** réunion *f* familiale; **f. hotel** hôtel *m* de famille; **sorry, it's a f. joke** désolé, c'est une plaisanterie qu'on ne peut comprendre que si l'on fait partie de la famille; **f. life** vie *f* familiale; **f. likeness** air *m* de famille; **f. portraits** portraits *mpl* d'ancêtres; *Com* **f.-size(d) jar/packet** pot *m*/paquet *m* familial; **f. programme** émission *f* tout public, programme *m* familial; **f. rate** tarif *m* famille; **f. room** chambre *f* 'famille'; **unsuitable for f. viewing** non approprié aux enfants; **I wouldn't call it f. viewing** ce n'est pas exactement un spectacle à conseiller aux enfants; **this film is not f. viewing** ce n'est pas un film tout public

(**b**) *Biol, Ling* (*of plants, words etc*) famille *f*

family allowance *n Br Admin* allocation *f* familiale

family car *n* familiale *f*

family doctor *n* médecin *m* de famille

family income supplement *n Br, Admin* allocations *fpl* familiales

family man *n* père *m* de famille; (*man who takes interest in his family*) = homme *m* attaché à sa famille

family name *n* [ⓘB8,10] nom *m* de famille

family planning *n Med* limitation *f* des naissances, planning *m* familial; **f. clinic** clinique *f* du planning familial

family-run *adj* (*hotel, restaurant*) géré en famille, familial

family saloon *n* berline *f* familiale

family tree *n* arbre *m* généalogique

famine [ˈfæmɪn] *n* (*food shortage*) famine *f*; **to die of f.** mourir de faim; **f. prices** prix *mpl* exorbitants *ou* faramineux

famished [ˈfæmɪʃt] *adj* affamé; *F* **to be** *or* **feel f.** (*hungry*) mourir de faim, être affamé

famous [ˈfeɪməs] **1** *adj* (**a**) célèbre, renommé (**for** pour, par); **many f. names have stayed here** beaucoup de personnages célèbres ont séjourné ici; **f. in history** célèbre dans l'histoire; **town f. for its monuments** ville célèbre *ou* renommée pour *ou* par ses monuments; *Iron* **f. last words!** c'est cela, oui! (**b**) *Old-fashioned F* (*excellent*) parfait, fameux **2** *npl* **the f.** les célébrités *fpl*

famously [ˈfeɪməslɪ] *adv* (**a**) **the castle has often been the scene of important events, most f. when ...** le château a souvent été la scène d'événements importants, le plus célèbre d'entre eux ayant eu lieu quand ... (**b**) *Old-fashioned F* (*very well*) fameusement, à merveille; **I get on f. with him** on s'entend à merveille

fan¹ [fæn] *n* (**a**) (*hand-held*) éventail *m*; *Archit* **f. vaulting** voûte(s) *f(pl)* en éventail; *Bot* **f. palm** palmier-éventail *m* (**b**) (*mechanical*) ventilateur *m*; *Ind* soufflet *m*; *Sl* **when the shit** *or* **it hits the f.** quand la merde me/nous/lui/*etc* tombera dessus; *Aut* **radiator f.** ventilateur *m* (**c**) *Agr* (*winnowing machine*) tarare *m*

fan² *vt* (**-nn-**) (**a**) (*blow air on*) (*person*) éventer; (*fire, embers*) souffler sur; *Fig* (*stir up*) (*passions*) attiser, exciter; (*quarrel*) attiser, envenimer; **these remarks had fanned the flames of nationalist feeling** ces remarques avaient exacerbé le sentiment nationaliste; **to f. the embers of s. b.'s passion** raviver les flammes de la passion de qn; **terraces fanned by cool sea breezes** terrasses rafraîchies par les brises de mer (**b**) *Agr* (*winnow*) (*grain*) vanner

fan³ *n F* (*enthusiast*) (*of television, sport etc*) fanatique *mf*, fana *mf*; (*of singer, actor*) fan *mf*; **a f. of sb/sth** un fana de qn/qch; **I'm a big f. (of hers)** je suis un de ses fans les plus fervents; **I'm not a great f. of his** il est loin d'être mon idole; **football f.** fana de football; *F* **f. mail** (*of film star etc*) courrier *m* des admirateurs et admiratrices

▶ **fan out 1** *vi* (*spread out*) se déployer *ou* s'étaler en éventail **2** *vtsep* (*spread out*) étaler (en éventail)

fan(-assisted) oven [ˈfæn(əsɪstɪd)] *n* four *m* à chaleur pulsée

fanatic [fəˈnætɪk] *adj, n* fanatique *mf*

fanatical [fəˈnætɪk(ə)l] *adj* fanatique

fanatically [fəˈnætɪklɪ] *adv* fanatiquement

fanaticism [fəˈnætɪsɪz(ə)m] *n* fanatisme *m*

fan belt *n Aut* courroie *f* de ventilateur

fanciable [ˈfænsɪəb(ə)l] *adj F* attirant

fancied [ˈfænsɪd] *adj* (*imaginary*) imaginaire

fancier [ˈfænsɪər] *n* (*of dogs etc*) connaisseur, -euse

fanciful [ˈfænsɪfʊl] *adj* (**a**) (*unrealistic*) (*project, idea etc*) chimérique; **he was being rather f.** (*being unrealistic*) il se faisait des idées, il rêvait; (*indulging his imagination*) il se laissait porter par son imagination (**b**) (*imaginative*) (*person*) capricieux, fantasque; (*work etc*) fantaisiste; (*portrait*) plein de fantaisie

fancifully [ˈfænsɪfʊlɪ] *adv* d'une manière fantasque; (*decorated*) de manière fantaisiste; **somewhat f. described as ...** désigné sous le terme plutôt fantaisiste de ...

fan club *n* (**a**) fan-club *m* (**b**) *St Exch* club *m* des amis

fan-cooled [ˈfænkuːld] *adj* refroidi par ventilateur

fancy¹ [ˈfænsɪ] **1** *n* (**a**) (*imagination*) imagination *f*, fantaisie *f*; (*imagined thing*) chose *f* imaginaire; **the realm of f.** le domaine de l'imaginaire *ou* de l'imagination; **it's only f.!** c'est pure imagination!; **idle fancies** vaines imaginations

(**b**) (*whim*) fantaisie *f*, caprice *m*; **just as the f. takes me** comme l'idée me prend, *F* comme ça me chante

(**c**) (*liking*) **he took a f. to the house** la maison lui a plu; **to take an immediate f. to sth** s'enticher de qch; **to take a f. to**

sb (*become fond of*) prendre qn en affection; (*become sexually attracted to*) s'éprendre *ou* s'enticher de qn; **it took** *or* **caught my f. at once** cela m'a séduit du premier coup

2 *adj* (*jewels, gadget, hat*) de fantaisie; (*writing style*) recherché; **just a bottle of ordinary wine, nothing f.** juste une bouteille de vin ordinaire, rien de spécial; **f. biscuits** biscuits assortis; **f. footwork** beau jeu de jambes; *Fig* **I had to do a bit of f. footwork** j'ai dû faire des pieds et des mains; **f. price** prix excessif *ou* exorbitant; *F* **to cut out the f. stuff** élaguer, faire moins de fantaisies

fancy² *vt* **(a)** (*imagine*) s'imaginer, se figurer; *F* **f. now!, just f.!, f. (that)!** figurez-vous ça!; **f. meeting you!** tiens, toi ici!; **f. him not knowing that!** il ne sait pas ça! incroyable!

(b) (*have impression*) **to f. (that)** croire *ou* penser que; **I f. I have seen her before** j'ai l'impression de l'avoir déjà vue; **he fancied he heard footsteps** il a cru entendre des pas

(c) *F* (*feel desire for*) **to f. sb** être attiré par qn; **he fancies you** tu lui plais; **I like him as a person but I don't f. him** je l'aime bien en tant que personne mais il ne m'attire pas; **he fancies her rotten** elle lui plaît vachement

(d) *F* (*have good opinion of*) **to f. oneself** être infatué de sa petite personne, se gober; **he fancies himself as a speaker** il se croit orateur; **I don't f. their chances of winning** je ne crois pas qu'ils aient des chances de gagner; **they were not fancied to win** personne ne pensait qu'ils gagneraient; *Horseracing* **strongly fancied horse** cheval très coté

(e) *Br F* **to f. sth** (*like*) bien aimer qch; (*feel like*) avoir envie de qch; **I don't f. his offer** son offre ne me dit rien; **I f. a bit of chicken** je mangerais volontiers un morceau de poulet, j'ai envie d'un morceau de poulet; **I wouldn't f. being in her shoes** je ne voudrais pas être à sa place; **I don't f. going** ça ne me dit rien d'y aller, je n'ai pas envie d'y aller; **she wasn't sure if she fancied the idea** elle n'était pas sûre que l'idée la tentait; **I didn't really f. the sound of her second novel** son deuxième roman ne m'a trop rien dit

fancy dress *n* déguisement *m*; **to go to a party in f.** aller à une fête déguisé; **I didn't realise it was f.** je ne savais pas qu'il fallait se déguiser; **f. party** fête *f* travestie

fancy-free *adj* **to be f.** avoir le cœur libre

fancy goods *npl* nouveautés *fpl*

fancy man *n F, Pej* amant *m*, jules *m*

fancy woman *n F, Pej* maîtresse *f*, poule *f*

fancywork ['fænsɪwɜːk] *n Sewing* broderie *f*; (*crochet work*) crochet *m*

fanfare ['fænfeər] *n* fanfare *f*

fanfold ['fænfəʊld] *adj Comptr* **f. paper** papier continu plié en accordéon

fang [fæŋ] *n* (*of dog etc*) croc *m*; (*of viper*) crochet *m*; (*of vampire*) canine *f*

fan heater *n* radiateur *m* soufflant

fanlight ['fænlaɪt] *n* imposte *f*

fanny ['fænɪ] *n* **(a)** *Br Vulg* (*vagina*) chatte *f* **(b)** *Am F* (*buttocks*) derrière *m*, fesses *fpl*; **f. pack** banane *f* **(c)** *Br Sl Euph* **sweet f. adams** rien du tout, nib de nib

fan-shaped *adj* en éventail

fantabulous [fæn'tæbjʊləs] *adj F* sensass

fantail ['fænteɪl] *n* (*bird*) pigeon *m* paon

fantailed ['fænteɪld] *adj* **f. pigeon** pigeon *m* paon

fantasia [fæn'teɪzɪə] *n Mus* fantaisie *f*

fantasize ['fæntəsaɪz] **1** *vi* fantasmer (**about** sur); **he fantasized about being able to read people's minds** son fantasme était de pouvoir lire les pensées; **she was still fantasizing about making love to Robert Redford when …** elle fantasmait encore qu'elle faisait l'amour avec Robert Redford quand … **2** *vt* **to f. that …** imaginer que …

fantastic [fæn'tæstɪk] *adj* **(a)** *F* (*excellent*) formidable, fantastique; **we had a f. time** nous nous sommes superbement bien amusés

(b) (*enormous*) (*price, size etc*) énorme; *Com* **f. reductions** baisses *fpl* phénoménales *ou* fantastiques; **a f. sum** une somme faramineuse

(c) (*unbelievable*) (*person, thing*) bizarre; (*thing*) fantastique, grotesque; (*animals*) fantastique; (*claim*) grotesque, absurde; **that's the most f. thing I've ever heard** c'est la chose la plus grotesque *ou* absurde que j'aie jamais entendue; **what is absolutely f. about all this is that …** ce qu'il y a de vraiment fantastique dans toute cette histoire c'est que …; **it sounds f., but it's true** (*unbelievable*) ça paraît inouï mais c'est vrai; **it's f. to suppose/claim that …** (*absurd*) c'est absurde de penser/de prétendre que …

fantastically [fæn'tæstɪklɪ] *adv* **(a)** *F* **f. beautiful/old/mean** incroyablement beau/vieux/méchant **(b) somewhat f., the story ends with …** l'histoire se termine d'une manière un peu invraisemblable avec …

fantasy ['fæntəsɪ, -zɪ] *n* **(a)** (*imagined event*) vision *f* bizarre; (*idea*) idée *f* fantasque; (*proposal*) extravagance *f*; **sexual f.** fantasme *m* sexuel; **his f. was to own a house in the country** son rêve était d'avoir une maison à la campagne **(b)** (*imagination*) fantaisie *f*; **you live in a f. world!** tu vis dans un monde imaginaire!; **he has a strong sense of f.** il a énormément de fantaisie; **the realm of f.** le domaine de l'imaginaire **(c)** (*work*) *Art* œuvre *f* fantastique; *Mus* fantaisie *f*

fanzine ['fænziːn] *n* fanzine *m*

far¹ [fɑːr] *adv* [ⓘA19,g,i](**farther, -est** ['fɑːðər, -ɪst]; **further, -est** ['fɜːðər, -ɪst]) **(a)** (*distance*) loin; **to go f.** aller loin; **how f. did you go?** jusqu'où êtes-vous allé?; **I got as f. as Birmingham** je suis allé jusqu'à Birmingham; *Fig* **this young man will go f.** ce jeune homme ira loin; **a pound does not go very f. nowadays** on ne va pas loin avec une livre de nos jours; **to go so f. as to do sth** aller jusqu'à faire qch; **I'll go so f. as to say that …** j'irai jusqu'à dire que …; **things went so f. that …** les choses sont allées si loin que …; *Fig* **to go too f.** aller trop loin; **that is going too f.** cela passe la mesure; **to live f. away** (*from here*) habiter loin d'ici; (*from there*) habiter loin; **her thoughts were f. away** sa pensée était ailleurs; **it isn't f. off** ce n'est pas loin; **f. from …** loin de …; **not f. from …** à peu de distance de …; *Fig* **f. from it** loin de là; *Fig* **not f. from it** peu s'en faut; **f. be it from me to …** loin de moi l'idée de …; **f. from admiring him I loathe him** bien loin de l'admirer je le déteste; **f. out at sea** au (grand) large; **f. beneath/above us** loin au-dessous/au-dessus de nous; **f. and wide** *or* **near** de tous côtés; **they searched f. and wide for a suitable site** ils ont cherché partout un emplacement convenable; **the story so f.** = résumé *m* des chapitres précédents; **how f. have you got?** (*with your reading etc*) où en êtes-vous?; **as f. as the eye can see** à perte de vue; **as f. as I can judge …** pour autant que je puisse en juger …; **as f. as I know** autant que je sache; **I will help you as f. as I can** *or* **as f. as possible** je vous aiderai de mon mieux; **as f. as I can see** pour autant que je puisse en juger; **in so f. as …** dans la mesure où …; **by f.** de loin; **by f. the best** de beaucoup *ou* de loin le meilleur

(b) (*time*) **so f.** jusqu'ici; **so f. so good** jusqu'ici tout va bien; **have you seen him? – not so f.** l'avez-vous vu? – pas encore; **as f. back as I can remember** aussi loin que je puisse me rappeler; **as f. back as 1900** déjà en 1900; **she is not f. off sixty** elle n'est pas loin de la soixantaine; **to work f. into the night** travailler fort avant dans la nuit

(c) (*much*) beaucoup; **it is f. better** c'est beaucoup mieux; **she's f. too intelligent to do that** elle est bien trop intelligente pour faire ça; **to be f. too many/little/***etc* être beaucoup trop nombreux/petit/*etc*; **f. and away the best** de beaucoup *ou* de loin le meilleur; **the night was f. advanced** la nuit était fort avancée

far² *adj* [ⓘA19,g,i] (**farther, -est** ['fɑːðər, -ɪst]; **further, -est** ['fɜːðər, -ɪst]) **(a)** (*distant*) lointain, éloigné; **a f. country** un pays lointain; **in the f. distance** tout au loin **(b)** (*other*) **the f. end** (*of plank etc*) l'autre bout, le bout le plus éloigné; **the f. bank of the river** la rive opposée de la rivière; *Pol* **the f. left/right** l'extrême-gauche/-droite *f*

farad ['færæd] *n El* farad *m*

faraway ['fɑːrəweɪ] *adj* lointain, éloigné; (*country*) lointain; **his eyes had a f. look** il avait le regard perdu dans le vague

farce [fɑːs] *n Th* farce *f*; **knockabout f.** grosse farce; *Fig* **the trial was a f.** le procès relevait de la farce *ou* était grotesque; **this is an absolute f.!** c'est grotesque!; **the whole thing was a f.** tout a tourné à la farce; **their marriage had been little more than a loveless f.** leur mariage n'avait été qu'une comédie sans amour

farcical ['fɑːsɪk(ə)l] *adj Th* bouffon, burlesque; *Fig* (*incident, idea, accusation*) absurde, grotesque; **the whole thing is becoming f.** c'est en train de tourner à la farce

farcically ['fɑːsɪklɪ] *adv* d'une manière absurde *ou* grotesque

fare¹ [feər] *n* **(a)** *Rail, Av* prix *m* du voyage; (*in bus*) prix du trajet; (*in taxi*) prix de la course; **half f.** demi-place *f*, *pl* demi-places; **single f.** aller *m* (simple); **return f.** aller et retour *m*; **to pay one's f.** payer son billet; (*in taxi*) payer sa course; **fares, please!** (*in bus*) = tickets, s'il vous plaît!; **rail/bus fares are going up** les billets de train/les tickets de bus augmentent; **f. structure** structure *f* tarifaire **(b)** (*taxi passenger*) client, -ente **(c)** *esp Fml* (*food*) chère *f*; **traditional f.** cuisine *f* traditionnelle; **good f.** bonne chère; **prison f.** régime *m* de prison

fare² *vi* **how is he faring?** comment ça marche pour lui?, comment se débrouille-t-il?; (*after operation etc*) comment va-t-il?; **she fared badly** elle ne s'en est pas bien tirée; **she fared well** elle s'en est bien tirée, elle s'est bien débrouillée; **he went out to see how the lambs were faring** il est sorti pour voir ce que devenaient les agneaux

Far East *n* Extrême-Orient *m*

farewell [feə'wel] *int, n* adieu *m*; **to bid sb f.** dire adieu à qn; **to say** *or* **make one's farewells** faire ses adieux; **a f. dinner** un dîner d'adieu
far-fetched ['fɑː'fetʃt] *adj (idea, example, story)* tiré par les cheveux
far-flung *adj* **(a)** *(large) (empire etc)* très étendu **(b)** *(distant) (countries)* lointain; *(villages, places)* éloigné
farinaceous [færɪ'neɪʃəs] *adj* farineux, farinacé; **f. foods** farineux *mpl*, féculents *mpl*
farm¹ [fɑːm] *n* **(a)** *Agr* ferme *f*, exploitation *f* agricole; **I work on a f.** je travaille dans une ferme; **dairy f.** ferme laitière; **fish f.** établissement *m* piscicole; **poultry f.** exploitation avicole; **sheep/trout f.** élevage *m* de moutons/truites; **stud f.** haras *m*; **f. animals** animaux *mpl* de ferme; **f. buildings** bâtiments *mpl* de la ferme; *(outhouses)* dépendances *fpl*; **f. hand** *or* **labourer** *or* **worker** ouvrier *m* agricole; **f. holiday** vacances *fpl* à la ferme; **f. horse** cheval *m* de ferme; **f. machinery** machines *fpl* agricoles
(b) *(installation)* **sewage f.** champs *mpl* d'épandage; **f. tourism** tourisme *m* 'fermier' *ou* agricole
(c) *(centre)* **health f.** établissement *m* de cure
farm² **1** *vt (land)* cultiver, exploiter; **to f. 400 acres** = exploiter 160 hectares **2** *vi* être cultivateur
▶ **farm out** *vtsep F (send to other people) (children)* confier à l'extérieur; **she farmed out the children to their aunty** elle a confié les enfants à leur tante; **to f. out work** donner du travail à des collaborateurs extérieurs; *(subcontract)* sous-traiter du travail
farmer ['fɑːmər] *n* agriculteur, -trice, cultivateur, -trice; **(tenant) f.** fermier, -ière; **sheep f.** éleveur, -euse de moutons; **poultry f.** aviculteur, -trice
farmhouse ['fɑːmhaʊs] *n* (maison *f* de) ferme *f*
farming ['fɑːmɪŋ] **1** *adj* **f. communities** agglomérations *fpl* rurales **2** *n* agriculture *f*; **the f. of the land** la culture de la terre; **mixed f.** polyculture *f*; **sheep f.** élevage *m* de moutons; **poultry f.** aviculture *f*
farmstead ['fɑːmsted] *n* ferme *f*
farmyard ['fɑːmjɑːd] *n* cour *f* de ferme
Faroe ['feərəʊ] *n* **the F. Islands, the Faroes** les îles *fpl* Féroé
far-off *adj (place)* lointain, éloigné; *(country)* lointain; *(time)* reculé; **the day was not f. when ...** le jour était proche où ...
far-out *adj F (avant-garde)* avant-gardiste; *(fantastic)* super
far-reaching ['fɑː'riːtʃɪŋ] *adj* de grande envergure, d'une grande portée; **to have a f. influence** avoir une grande portée
farrier ['færɪər] *n Br* maréchal-ferrant *m*, *pl* maréchaux-ferrants
farrow¹ ['færəʊ] *n (piglets)* portée *f* de cochons
farrow² **1** *vt (of sow) (piglets)* mettre bas **2** *vi (of sow)* **to f. (down)** faire des petits, cochonner
far-seeing *adj* clairvoyant; *(providing for the future)* prévoyant; **to be f.** voir loin
far-sighted *adj* **(a)** *(providing for the future) (person)* prévoyant; *(decision etc)* avisé, sage **(b)** *(long-sighted)* hypermétrope; *(because of old age)* presbyte
far-sightedness ['fɑː'saɪtɪdnɪs] *n* **(a)** *(of government, leader)* prévoyance *f*, perspicacité *f*; *(of decision)* sagesse *f* **(b)** *(long-sightedness)* hypermétropie *f*; *(because of old age)* presbytie *f*
fart¹ [fɑːt] *n F* pet *m*; *Fig* **a boring old f.** un vieux rasoir; **you stupid f.!** espèce de con!
fart² *vi F* péter, lâcher un pet
▶ **fart about, fart around** *vi F* **(a)** *(play the fool)* déconner **(b)** *(waste time)* glander; **he's been farting about with the car for days** il a passé des journées entières à trifouiller la voiture; **if you hadn't spent so much time farting about with your make-up** si tu n'avais pas autant traîné en te maquillant
farther ['fɑːðər] *(comp of* **far)** [①**A19**,g,i] **1** *adv* **(a)** *(place)* plus loin **(than** que); **f. off** plus éloigné, plus loin; **they stopped a little f. on** ils se sont arrêtés un peu plus loin; **f. on in the book** plus loin dans le livre; **I can go no f.** je ne saurais aller plus loin; *(exhausted)* je n'en peux plus!; **f. down/west** plus bas/à l'ouest; **before she could get any f. with her story ...** avant qu'elle ne puisse continuer son histoire ... **(b)** *(time)* **f. (back)** plus en arrière; **f. back than 1500** avant 1500 **2** *adj* plus lointain; **at the f. end of the room** à l'autre bout de la salle
farthest ['fɑːðɪst] *(superl of* **far)** [①**A19**,g,i] **1** *adv* le plus loin; **this is the f. east they reached** voici le point le plus à l'est qu'ils ont atteint **2** *adj* **(a)** *(distant)* **f. (off)** le plus éloigné, le plus reculé **(b)** *(distance etc)* le plus long
farthing ['fɑːðɪŋ] *n Br Hist (coin)* quart *m* d'un penny; *Fig F* **not to have a f.** n'avoir pas le sou; *Old-fashioned F* **I don't care a brass f.** je m'en moque éperdument
FAS *Com (abbr* **free alongside ship)** FLQ, FAS, franco quai
fascia, *pl* **-s** ['feɪʃə, -z] *n* **(a)** *Archit* bandelette *f*, bande *f*; *(on shop front)* enseigne *f* en forme d'entablement **(b)** tableau *m* de bord; **f. panel** planche *f* de bord
fascicle ['fæsɪk(ə)l], **fascicule** ['fæsɪkjuːl] *n Typ* fascicule *m*
fascinate ['fæsɪneɪt] *vt (person)* fasciner; **insects f. him** les insectes le fascinent; **to be fascinated by sth** être fasciné par qch
fascinating ['fæsɪneɪtɪŋ] *adj* fascinant
fascination [fæsɪ'neɪʃən] *n* fascination *f*, attrait *m*; **I don't understand the f. of tennis** je ne comprends pas l'attrait que peut avoir le tennis; **the sport has** *or* **holds a f. for millions** ce sport fascine des millions de gens; **he has always had a f. for dinosaurs** les dinosaures ont toujours exercé une fascination sur lui, il a toujours été fasciné par les dinosaures; **she watched/listened in f.** elle regardait/écoutait, fascinée
fascism ['fæʃɪz(ə)m] *n Pol* fascisme *m*
fascist ['fæʃɪst] *adj, n Pol* fasciste *mf*
fash [fæʃ] *vt Scot (person)* agacer, ennuyer; **dinna f. yersel** ne te fais pas de bile
fashion¹ ['fæʃən] *n* **(a)** *(in clothes etc)* mode *f*, vogue *f*; **in f.** à la mode, en vogue; **out of f.** passé de mode, démodé; **in the latest f.** à la dernière mode; **to set the f.** lancer la mode; **to follow f.** suivre la mode; **to become the f., to come into f.** devenir à la mode; **to go out of f.** se démoder; **the Costa del Sol was going out of f. with British holidaymakers** la Costa del Sol n'était plus aussi à la mode pour les vacanciers britanniques; **it's all the f.** c'est la grande vogue; **it's the latest f.** c'est la dernière mode; **f. editor** rédacteur, -trice de mode; **f. magazine** journal *m* de mode; **f. model** mannequin *m*; **f. parade** défilé *m* de mode; **f. show** présentation *f* de collections; **f. victim** bête *f* de mode; **f. writer** chroniqueur *m* de mode, critique *m* de mode
(b) *(manner)* manière *f*; **crabs walk in a peculiar f.** les crabes marchent d'une façon étrange; **we rubbed noses, Eskimo f.** nous nous sommes frotté le nez à la manière des esquimaux; **after a f.** tant bien que mal; **he loved her, after a f.** il l'aimait plus ou moins
fashion² *vt* façonner, former; *(dress etc)* confectionner; **to f. a log into a canoe** façonner un tronc d'arbre en canot
fashionable ['fæʃənəb(ə)l] *adj* à la mode, en vogue; **a f. film director** un metteur en scène en vogue; **a f. part of town** un quartier très en vogue *ou* à la mode *ou* branché
fashionably ['fæʃənəblɪ] *adv (dressed)* à la mode
fashion designer *n Com* styliste *mf*, modéliste *mf*; *(big name, director of fashion house)* couturier *m*
fashion house *n* maison *f* de haute couture
fast¹ [fɑːst] **1** *adj* **(a)** *(rapid)* rapide; *Phot (film)* rapide; **you're a f. walker** vous marchez vite; **he likes f. cars** il aime les voitures qui vont vite; *Sp* **a f. time** *(in race etc)* un bon temps, un bon chrono; *F* **he pulled a f. one on me** il m'a joué un mauvais tour; **he's a f. worker** il travaille vite; **f. forward (button)** *(on tape recorder)* avance *f* rapide; *Aut* **f. idle** ralenti *m* accéléré; **the f. lane** *(on motorway)* la voie rapide; *Fig* **life in the f. lane** la vie à cent à l'heure; *Mktg* **f. mover** *(product)* article *m* à forte rotation; *Rail* **f. train** rapide *m*
(b) *(clock, watch)* en avance; **my watch is** *or F* **I'm five minutes f.** ma montre avance *ou* j'avance de cinq minutes
(c) *(secure) (stake etc)* ferme, fixe, solide; *(grip etc)* ferme; *(door, lid etc)* bien fermé; *(colour)* solide, résistant; **these colours are not f.** ces couleurs ne résistent pas; *Naut* **to make f. (to a buoy)** prendre le corps-mort; **to make f. (alongside)** s'amarrer
(d) *(immoral)* **f. living** débauche *f*; **f. woman** femme légère
2 *adv* **(a)** *(rapidly)* vite, rapidement; **she was walking faster than me** elle marchait plus vite *ou* rapidement que moi; **not so f.!** pas si vite!, doucement!; **bad news travels f.** les mauvaises nouvelles courent vite
(b) *(securely)* ferme, solidement; **to hold f.** tenir ferme, tenir bon; **to stick f.** bien tenir; *(be stuck)* rester pris, rester collé; **the door was shut f.** la porte était bien fermée; *Tex* **f. dyed** grand teint *inv*; **to be f. asleep** dormir d'un sommeil profond; *F* **to play f. and loose** jouer double jeu **(with sb** avec qn); **to play f. and loose with sb's emotions** se jouer des émotions de qn; **to play f. and loose with the statistics** truquer *ou* falsifier les statistiques
fast² *n* jeûne *m*; *Rel* **f. day** jour *m* de jeûne; **to break one's f.** rompre le jeûne
fast³ *vi* jeûner; *Med* être à la diète
fastback ['fɑːstbæk] *n Aut* arrière *m* profilé; *(car)* voiture *f* à l'arrière profilé
fasten ['fɑːs(ə)n] **1** *vt* **(a)** *(attach)* attacher **(to** à); **to f. papers together with a clip** attacher des papiers (ensemble) avec une agrafe; **to f. one's eyes/attention on sth** fixer le regard/son attention sur qch

(b) (*hold*) fixer; **to f. a door with a bolt** fermer une porte au verrou, verrouiller une porte; **to f. one's seat-belt** accrocher *ou* attacher sa ceinture; **to f. one's buttons** se boutonner; **to f. one's coat** boutonner son manteau

2 *vi* s'attacher, se fixer; (*of garment*) s'agrafer, se boutonner (**at the back** par derrière); (*of door etc*) se verrouiller; (*of attention, eyes*) se fixer; **door that fastens with a bolt** porte qui se ferme au verrou

▶ **fasten down** *vtsep* fixer (en place); (*tent, furniture*) fixer au sol; (*patient*) accrocher

▶ **fasten on, fasten onto** *vipo* (a) (*seize*) s'accrocher à; (*of eyes*) se fixer sur (b) (*evidence, statement, idea etc*) s'accrocher à; **she fastened on(to) this kiss as evidence of his affection** elle se raccrochait à ce baiser comme à une preuve de son affection; **she quickly fastened on(to) this excuse** elle saisit l'excuse à la volée; **the assessor fastened on(to) the irregularities in the accounts** le contrôleur des impôts s'obstinait sur les irrégularités que contenaient les comptes

▶ **fasten up** 1 *vtsep* (*one's dress etc*) agrafer, boutonner 2 *vi* **this dress fastens up at the back** cette robe se boutonne *ou* s'agrafe dans le dos

▶ **fasten upon** *vipo* = **fasten on, fasten onto**

fastener ['fɑːs(ə)nər] *n* attache *f*; (*of garment*) (*hook*) agrafe *f*; (*of purse*) fermoir *m*; (*of window etc*) fermeture *f*; (*of French window*) espagnolette *f*; (**snap**) **f.** (bouton *m* à) pression *f*; (**zip**) **f.** fermeture à glissière, fermeture éclair®

fastening ['fɑːs(ə)nɪŋ] *n* (*device*) = **fastener**; **fastenings** attaches *fpl*

fast food *n* restauration *f* rapide; **f. chain** chaîne *f* de restauration rapide; **f. restaurant** fast-food *m*, sandwicherie *f*, brasserie *f*

fast-forward 1 *vt* (*cassette*) mettre en avance rapide 2 *vi* (*of tape*) se dérouler en avance rapide; (*of person*) (faire) avancer; **I'm just waiting for the tape to f.** j'attends que la cassette ait fini de se dérouler

fastidious [fæ'stɪdɪəs] *adj* difficile (**about sth** sur qch); (*about manners, hygiene, details*) pointilleux; (*about appearance*) méticuleux; (*about choice of friends*) exigeant, difficile; **she's always been a very f. eater** elle a toujours été très difficile sur la nourriture

fastidiously [fæ'stɪdɪəslɪ] *adv* méticuleusement

fastidiousness [fæ'stɪdɪəsnɪs] *n* (*about appearance, details*) méticulosité *f*; **I was unused to such f. about hygiene** je n'étais pas accoutumé à ce qu'on soit aussi pointilleux sur l'hygiène; **because of his f. about what he eats** parce qu'il est difficile sur la nourriture

fasting ['fɑːstɪŋ] *n* jeûne *m*; *Med* diète *f* (absolue)

fast-moving *adj* rapide; **f. consumer goods** biens *mpl* de consommation à forte rotation

fastness ['fɑːstnɪs] *n* (a) (*of colour, dye*) solidité *f* (b) (*of moorings etc*) sûreté *f*, fiabilité *f* (c) *Lit* (*stronghold*) **mountain f.** forteresse *f*

FAT *Comptr* (*abbr* **file allocation table**) Fat *f*

fat[1] [fæt] *adj* (**fatter**; **fattest**) (a) (*person*) gros, *f* grosse, gras, *f* grasse, corpulent; (*meat*) gras; (*tissue*) adipeux; *F* (*cheque, salary*) gros; **to get f.** engraisser; *Fig* **to grow f. on sth/at the expense of others** s'engraisser de qch/aux dépens d'autrui; *F* **a f. lot of good that'll do you!** cela vous fera une belle jambe!; *F* **that was a f. lot of good** *or* **use!** on est bien aidé avec ça!; *F* **a f. lot of difference that has made!** ça a bien avancé les choses!; *F* **a f. lot you know about it!** comme si vous en saviez quelque chose!; *F* **f. chance he's got!** il est mal barré!; *esp US F* **f. cat** (*rich person*) richard *m*; **a f. volume** un gros tome; **f. wallet** portefeuille *m* bien garni

(b) (*land*) riche, fertile, gras; (*clay, lime etc*) gras

fat[2] *n* graisse *f*; (*of meat*) gras *m*; **fats** matières *fpl* grasses; **animal/vegetable f.** graisse animale/végétale; *Fig, F* **the f.'s in the fire!** ça va chauffer!; **to live off the f. of the land** vivre comme un coq en pâte; **f. content** teneur *f* en graisse *ou* en lipides; **f. intake** ration *f* de corps gras

fatal ['feɪt(ə)l] *adj* (a) (*blow, accident, disease*) mortel; **this condition can prove f.** cela peut être mortel (b) (*disastrous*) **f. decision** décision *f* funeste; **f. error** *or* **mistake** erreur *f* fatale, faute *f* capitale; *Comptr* **f. error** erreur *f* fatale (c) *Lit* (*ordained by fate*) fatal, -als; **the f. hour** l'heure *f* fatale

fatalism ['feɪtəlɪz(ə)m] *n* fatalisme *m*

fatalist ['feɪtəlɪst] *n* fataliste *mf*

fatalistic [feɪtə'lɪstɪk] *adj* fataliste

fatality [fə'tælɪtɪ] *n* (a) (*fatal accident*) accident *m* mortel; **there were no fatalities** (*deaths*) il n'y a pas eu de mort (b) (*fatal nature*) caractère *m* funeste (**of** de)

fatally ['feɪt(ə)lɪ] *adv* (*wounded*) mortellement; **f. ill** condamné; **f. damaged** qui a subi un tort irréparable; **to be f. damaging to sth, to f. damage sth** causer un tort irréparable à qch

fate [feɪt] *n* destin *m*, sort *m*; **stroke of f.** coup *m* du destin *ou* du sort; **f. decreed that ...** le sort a voulu que ...; *Myth* **the Fates** les Parques *fpl*; **to leave sb to their f.** abandonner qn à son sort; **to meet one's f.** trouver la mort; **to escape one's f.** échapper à son destin; **to suffer** *or* **share a similar f.** avoir le même sort; **a f. worse than death** un destin pire que la mort

fated ['feɪtɪd] *adj* (a) (*destined*) destiné, condamné (**to do sth** à faire qch); **this was f. to be the last time they would ever meet** le sort a voulu que ce soit la dernière fois qu'ils se voyaient (b) (*doomed*) voué à la destruction

fateful ['feɪtfʊl] *adj* (a) (*words*) fatidique (b) (*day*) fatidique; (*event*) fatal, -als

fathead ['fæthed] *n F* imbécile *mf*

fatheaded [fæt'hedɪd] *adj F* abruti, bête

father[1] ['fɑːðər] *n* (a) père *m*; **from f. to son** de père en fils; **he's his f.'s son** c'est bien le fils de son père; **on the f.'s side** du côté paternel; **like a f.** paternellement; **he was like a f. to me** il était comme un père pour moi; **like f. like son** tel père tel fils

(b) *Lit* (*ancestor*) **our fathers** nos ancêtres *mpl*, nos aïeux *mpl*

(c) (*founder*) (*of science, art etc*) père *m*, fondateur *m*; **the Fathers of the Church** les Pères de l'Église

(d) *Rel* (*God*) Père *m*; **God the F.** Dieu le Père; **Our F. which** *or* **who art in Heaven** notre Père qui êtes aux cieux

(e) *Rel* (*priest*) père *m*; **the Holy F.** (*Pope*) le Saint-Père; **f. confessor** père spirituel, directeur *m* (de conscience); **F. O'Riley** (*in monastic order*) le Père O'Riley; (*priest*) l'abbé O'Riley; **yes, F.** oui, mon Père

(f) (*senior*) (*of the House etc*) doyen *m*; *Typ etc* **f. of chapel** chef *m* de l'atelier

father[2] *vt* (*child*) engendrer; (*steam engine etc*) inventer; (*project, idea*) concevoir

Father Christmas *n* le père Noël

father figure *n* = personne *f* qui tient le rôle du père; **to be a f. to sb** jouer le rôle du père pour qn

fatherhood ['fɑːðəhʊd] *n* paternité *f*

father-in-law, *pl* **fathers-in-law** *n* beau-père, *pl* beaux-pères

fatherland ['fɑːðəlænd] *n* patrie *f*

fatherless ['fɑːðəlɪs] *adj* sans père, orphelin, -ine de père

fatherly ['fɑːðəlɪ] *adj* (*person, tone, manner etc*) paternel; **to behave in a f. way towards sb** se montrer paternel envers qn

Father's Day *n* la fête des pères

Father Time *n* le Temps

fathom[1] ['fæðəm] *n Naut* (*measurement*) brasse *f*

fathom[2] *vt Naut* sonder; *Fig* (*mystery*) pénétrer, sonder; **I can't f. him (out)** je ne le comprends pas; **I can't f. out why he did it at all** je n'arrive pas à me figurer pourquoi il a fait cela

fatigue[1] [fə'tiːg] *n* (a) (*tiredness*) fatigue *f*; **to be suffering from f.** être épuisé; **mental f.** fatigue cérébrale; **to be dropping with f.** tomber de fatigue; *Tech* **metal f.** fatigue des métaux (b) *Mil* **f. (duty)** corvée *f*; **to put sb on f.** mettre qn de corvée; **cookhouse f.** corvée de cuisine(s); **f. dress, fatigues** treillis *m*; **f. party** (détachement *m* de) corvée

fatigue[2] *vt* (*metal etc*) fatiguer; (*person*) fatiguer; (*stronger*) épuiser; **to f. oneself doing sth** se fatiguer/s'épuiser à faire qch

fatiguing [fə'tiːgɪŋ] *adj* fatigant; (*stronger*) épuisant

fatness ['fætnɪs] *n* (*of person*) embonpoint *m*, corpulence *f*; (*of stomach, bum*) grosseur *f*; (*of flesh etc*) adiposité *f*

fatso ['fætsəʊ] *n F* gros *m*; (*woman*) grosse (bonne femme) *f*; (*more insulting*) gros lard *m*; (*woman*) grosse vache *f*; **it's f. food** ça fait grossir

fatted ['fætɪd] *adj prov* **to kill the f. calf** tuer le veau gras

fatten ['fæt(ə)n] 1 *vt* (*sheep, calves etc*) engraisser 2 *vi* engraisser

▶ **fatten up** *vtsep* = **fatten 1**; *F* (*person*) faire grossir, engraisser; **we'll have to f. you up a bit** il va falloir qu'on t'engraisse un peu

fattening ['fæt(ə)nɪŋ] 1 *adj* (*food*) qui fait grossir 2 *n* (*of animals*) engraissement *m*, engraissage *m*

fatty ['fætɪ] 1 *adj* graisseux; (*tissue etc*) adipeux; (*meat*) gras; **f. foods** aliments *mpl* gras; *Ch* **f. acid** acide *m* gras 2 *n F* gros *m*; (*woman*) grosse (bonne femme) *f*; **hey, f.!** ohé, mon gros!/ma grosse!; **they always called him f.** ils l'appelaient toujours le gros

fatuity [fæ'tjuːɪtɪ] *n* sottise *f*, imbécillité *f*; **the utter f. of his efforts/the enterprise** l'absurdité de ses efforts/de l'entreprise

fatuous ['fætjʊəs] *adj* imbécile, idiot; (*attempt*) ridicule; (*smile*) béat

fatuously [ˈfætjʊəslɪ] *adv* sottement, d'un air imbécile
fatuousness [ˈfætjʊəsnɪs] *n* = **fatuity**
faucet [ˈfɔːsɪt] *n Am* robinet *m*
fault¹ [fɔːlt] *n* **(a)** (*flaw*) défaut *m*; **in spite of all his faults** malgré tous ses défauts *ou* travers; **scrupulous to a f.** scrupuleux à l'excès; **to find f. with sb/sth** trouver à redire contre qn/à qch; **she's always finding f.** elle trouve toujours quelque chose à redire
(b) *Tech* (*inherent*) problème *m*, défaut *m*; **a f. has developed on the line** il y a un problème sur la ligne; *Ordinat* **f. diagnosis software** logiciel *m* d'aide au diagnostic de panne; **f. warning sensor** détecteur *m* d'anomalie
(c) (*guilt*) faute *f*; **to be at f.** être en faute, être coupable; **you were at f. in not warning us** vous avez eu tort de ne pas nous prévenir; **his memory was at f.** sa mémoire lui a fait défaut; **whose f. is it?** à qui la faute?; **I am afraid it was (all) my f.** je crains bien que ce ne soit de ma faute; **it's his own silly f.** c'est de sa faute, à cet imbécile; **through no f. of mine** sans que je sois en cause
(d) *Tennis* faute *f*; **double f.** double faute; **foot f.** faute de pied
(e) *Geol* faille *f*; **f. line/plane** ligne *f*/plan *m* de faille
fault² *vt* (*person*) prendre en défaut; (*sth*) trouver un défaut dans; **I can't f. her research** je ne trouve aucune erreur dans ses recherches
fault-finder *n* (*person*) critiqueur, -euse; (*device*) détecteur *m* de fuites
fault-finding **1** *adj* (*critical*) ergoteur, pinailleur **2** *n* **(a)** (*criticism*) disposition *f* à critiquer; **I'd had enough of her petty f.** j'en avais assez de ses pinailleries **(b)** *Tech* localisation *f* des défauts
faultiness [ˈfɔːltɪnɪs] *n* défectuosité *f*, imperfection *f*
faultless [ˈfɔːltlɪs] *adj* (*work, performance, craftmanship etc*) sans faute, impeccable; (*dress, behaviour*) impeccable, irréprochable
faultlessly [ˈfɔːltlɪslɪ] *adv* impeccablement
fault-tolerant *adj Comptr* quasi insensible aux défaillances, tolérant les pannes
faulty [ˈfɔːltɪ] *adj* (*work, device etc*) défectueux; (*style etc*) incorrect; (*reasoning etc*) erroné; (*logic*) défaillant; *Gram* (*construction etc*) vicieux; **f. workmanship** mauvaise construction *f*
faun [fɔːn] *n Myth* faune *m*
fauna [ˈfɔːnə] *n* (*of region, country*) faune *f*
faux pas [ˈfəʊˈpɑː] *n* faux pas *m*, gaffe *f*
favour¹, *US* **favor** [ˈfeɪvər] *n* **(a)** (*approval*) faveur *f*, approbation *f*; **to be in/out of f.** (*of person*) être bien/mal vu; *F* avoir/ne pas avoir la cote; (*of style*) être à la mode/démodé; **to look on sth/sb with f.** être favorable à qch/qn, être bien disposé envers qch/qn; **to find f. with sb** trouver grâce aux yeux de qn; (*of theory, explanation*) être favorablement reçu auprès de qn; **to gain sb's f.** gagner la faveur de qn; **to be restored** *or* **to return to f.** rentrer en grâce; **to fall out of f. with sb** perdre les bonnes grâces de qn, tomber en défaveur aux yeux de qn; **this method has rather fallen out of f. in recent years** cette méthode a été plus ou moins abandonnée au cours de ces dernières années
(b) (*service*) service *m*; **to ask sb a f., to ask a f. of sb** solliciter un service *ou* une faveur de qn; **as a f.** à titre gracieux; **as a personal f.** à titre personnel; **to do sb a f.** faire une faveur à qn, obliger qn; **you could at least do me the f. of listening** tu pourrais au moins me faire la faveur d'écouter; **will you do me a great f.?** voulez-vous me rendre un grand service?; *Br Sl* **do me a f.!** (*you must be joking!*) tu te fous de moi!; *F* **why don't you do everyone a f. and shut up?** tu vas faire plaisir à tout le monde et la fermer, d'accord?; **she's not doing herself any favours by being so arrogant** son arrogance la dessert
(c) (*preference*) partialité *f*, préférence *f*; **to show f. towards sb** favoriser qn; **to speak in sb's f.** parler en faveur de qn; **he has everything in his f.** tout lui sourit; **design C has everything in its f.** le projet C a tous les avantages; **in f. of ...** en faveur de ...; **all those in f. raise your hand** (*in meeting, debate etc*) que tous ceux qui sont pour lèvent la main; **this route was abandoned in f. of a more direct one** cette route a été abandonnée pour une autre qui était plus directe; **to be in f. of sth** être partisan de qch, préconiser qch; **he's in f. of introducing subsidies** il est favorable à *ou* partisan de la mise en place de subventions; **a point in sb's/sth's f.** un élément en faveur de qn/qch; *Fin* **balance in your f.** solde en votre faveur
(d) *Arch* (*ribbon etc*) faveur *f*, cocarde *f*
(e) *Lit, Hum* **favours** (*of woman*) faveurs *fpl*; **she was rather too free with her favours** elle était un peu trop prodigue de ses faveurs
favour², *US* **favor** *vt* **(a)** (*approve of*) (*sth*) approuver, préférer; (*project*); être pour; (*person*) accorder une préférence à; **I f. allowing more time for the planning stage** je suis partisan d'accorder plus de temps au stade préparatoire
(b) (*bestow favour on*) (*person*) favoriser; **to f. sb with a smile** gratifier qn d'un sourire; *Iron* **we have not, as yet, been favoured with a reply** on ne nous a pas encore fait la faveur de nous répondre
(c) (*give advantage to*) (*person*) avantager, montrer de la partialité pour; (*sth*) faciliter; **to be favoured by circumstances** avoir les circonstances en sa faveur; **the town is uniquely favoured as a holiday destination** cette ville est exceptionnellement avantagée en tant que destination de vacances
(d) (*of fact etc*) (*theory etc*) soutenir
favourable, *US* **favorable** [ˈfeɪv(ə)rəb(ə)l] *adj* favorable; (*weather, wind etc*) propice; (*reception etc*) bienveillant; (*terms etc*) bon, avantageux; (*report etc*) bon, rassurant; **in a f. light** sous un jour favorable; *Com* **on f. terms** à des conditions avantageuses
favourably, *US* **favorably** [ˈfeɪv(ə)rəblɪ] *adv* favorablement; **to be f. disposed to(wards) sb/sth, to look f. on sb/sth** être favorable à qn/qch, être bien disposé à l'égard de qn/qch; **I hope everything goes f. for you** j'espère que tout ira bien pour toi; **to compare f. with sth** n'avoir rien à envier à qch; **I was f. impressed** j'ai été favorablement impressionné
favoured, *US* **favored** [ˈfeɪvəd] *adj* **(a)** (*person*) favorisé, avantagé; **he is one of our most f. clients** c'est un de nos clients privilégiés; **most-f. nation status** statut *m* de nation la plus favorisée; **the f. few** les élus *mpl* **(b)** *Old-fashioned* **ill-f.** laid, de mauvaise mine
favourite, *US* **favorite** [ˈfeɪv(ə)rɪt] **1** *n* favori, *f* favorite, préféré, -ée; (*song*) succès *m*, tube *m*; *Sp* **to back the f.** jouer le favori; **chocolate cake is a firm f. with children** c'est vraiment le gâteau au chocolat que les enfants préfèrent; **it's a great f. of mine** c'est l'un de mes livres/disques/opéras/*etc* préférés *ou* favoris; **he's a great f. with the old ladies** les vieilles dames l'affectionnent particulièrement; **roast duck? (that's) my f.!** du canard rôti? c'est mon plat préféré! **2** *adj* favori, préféré; *US Pol* **a f. son** un candidat favorisé par les électeurs du même état que lui
favouritism, *US* **favoritism** [ˈfeɪv(ə)rɪtɪz(ə)m] *n* favoritisme *m*
fawn¹ [fɔːn] **1** *n* **(a)** (*deer*) faon *m* **(b)** (*colour*) couleur *f* fauve **2** *adj* **f. (-coloured)** fauve
fawn² *vi* **to f. on sb** se mettre à plat ventre devant qn
fawning [ˈfɔːnɪŋ] **1** *adj* (*flattering*) adulateur, -trice; (*servile*) servile **2** *n* adulation *f*
fax¹ [fæks] *n* **(a)** **f. (machine)** télécopieur *m*, fax *m*; **to send sth by f.** envoyer qch par fax *ou* par télécopie; **f. board** carte *f* fax, carte de télécopie; **f. modem** modem-fax *m*, *pl* modems-fax, modem-télécopieur *m*, *pl* modems-télécopieurs; **f. shot** publicité *f* directe par télécopie; **f. software** logiciel *m* de télécopie; **f. user** utilisateur *m* de télécopieur **(b)** (*copy, message*) fax *m*; **to send sb a f.** envoyer un fax à qn; **f. message** message *m* par fax; **f. number** numéro *m* de fax
fax² *vt* (*document*) faxer, télécopier, envoyer par fax *ou* télécopie; (*person*) envoyer un fax *ou* une télécopie à
▶ **fax back** *vtsep* (*return by fax*) renvoyer par fax *ou* par télécopie (**to** à); **I'll f. you back** je vous réponds par fax
faxable [ˈfæksəb(ə)l] *adj* (*document*) faxable, télécopiable; **are you f.?** est-ce qu'on peut vous joindre par fax?
faze [feɪz] *vt F* (*person*) déconcerter
FBI [efbiːˈaɪ] *n US* (*abbr* **Federal Bureau of Investigation**) FBI *m*, ≈ Police *f* Judiciaire; **FBI agent** agent *m* du FBI
FC [efˈsiː] *n* (*abbr* **Football Club**) Club *m* de Football
FCL-FCL *Com* (*abbr* **full container load-full container load**) FCL-FCL
FCL-LCL *Com* (*abbr* **full container load-less than container load**) FCL-LCL
FD (*abbr* **floppy disk**) disquette *f*
FDA [efdiːˈeɪ] *n US* (*abbr* **Food and Drug Administration**) = office *f* du contrôle pharmaceutique et alimentaire
FDD (*abbr* **floppy disk drive**) unité *f* de disquette
fealty [ˈfɪəltɪ] *n Hist* fidélité *f*
fear¹ [fɪər] *n* **(a)** crainte *f*, peur *f*; **my greatest f. was that they would forget** ce que je craignais le plus, c'est qu'ils oublient; **f. seized her** la peur l'envahit; **deadly f.** effroi *m*; **in f. and trembling** tremblant de peur; **to be overcome by** *or* **with f.** être en proie à la frayeur; **to be** *or* **stand** *or* **go in f. of sb/sth** avoir peur de *ou* redouter *ou* craindre qn/qch; **to go in f. of one's life** craindre pour sa vie; **there are fears for her life** sa vie est en danger; **for f. of waking the baby** de crainte

de réveiller le bébé; **for f. of making a mistake** de crainte d'erreur; **there is no f. that he will come back** il n'y a pas de danger qu'il revienne; **without f. or favour** sans distinction de personnes; *F* **no f.!** pas de danger!, jamais de la vie!

(b) *(respect)* *(of God, the law etc)* respect *m*, crainte *f*; *F* **to put the f. of God into sb** *(reprimand)* faire à qn une semonce dont il se souviendra longtemps; *(frighten)* inspirer une peur bleue à qn

fear[2] **1** *vt* **(a)** *(sb, sth)* craindre, redouter; *(event)* appréhender, craindre; **what they most feared** ce qu'ils craignaient le plus; **he fears failure above all else** l'échec est ce qu'il craint *ou* redoute par-dessus tout; **she is an adversary to be feared** c'est une adversaire redoutable; **it is to be feared that ...** il est à craindre que ...; *Fml* **I f. it is too late** j'ai peur *ou* je crains qu'il ne soit trop tard; *Fml* **I f. he will not come** je crains qu'il ne vienne pas; **I f. so/not** je crains que oui/que non; *Fml* **I f. he's out** je crains qu'il ne soit pas là; *Fml* **I f. I'm late** je crois bien être en retard; **I f. the worst!** je crains *ou* redoute le pire!

(b) *(respect)* *(God etc)* craindre

2 *vi* avoir peur; **we'll be here tomorrow, never f.** nous serons là demain, n'aie pas peur; *Old-fashioned* **f. not** *or* **never f., help is at hand** n'ayez crainte, l'assistance ne saurait tarder; **to f. for sb/sth** s'inquiéter au sujet de qn/qch; **I was beginning to f. for her sanity** je commençais à m'inquiéter pour son état mental; **we feared for our lives** nous craignions pour nos vies

feared [fɪəd] *adj* *(person etc)* redouté

fearful ['fɪəfʊl] *adj* **(a)** *(consequences, doubt)* affreux, effrayant; *(pain, accident)* atroce, affreux; *esp Old-fashioned F* *(terrible)* affreux; **he's a f. bore** il est affreusement rasoir; **a f. mess** un désordre effrayant *ou* formidable **(b)** *(person)* peureux, craintif; **don't look so f.!** n'aie pas l'air aussi apeuré!; **f. of ...** qui craint *ou* a peur de ...; **f. of what would happen ...** par crainte de ce qui arriverait ...

fearfully ['fɪəfʊlɪ] *adv* **(a)** *(frighteningly)* affreusement, terriblement **(b)** *esp Old-fashioned F* *(very)* affreusement; **f. clever/interesting** terriblement intelligent/intéressant **(c)** *(out of fear)* peureusement

fearfulness ['fɪəfʊlnɪs] *n* **(a)** *(of noise etc)* caractère *m* terrifiant; **the f. of his appearance** son aspect terrifiant **(b)** *(of person)* *(fear)* crainte *f*; *(concern)* appréhension *f*

fearless ['fɪəlɪs] *adj* intrépide, courageux; **f. of ...** sans peur de ...; **he was f. of danger** il ne reculait devant aucun danger

fearlessly ['fɪəlɪslɪ] *adv* intrépidement

fearlessness ['fɪəlɪsnɪs] *n* intrépidité *f*, courage *m*

fearsome ['fɪəsəm] *adj* *(weapon, opponent)* effrayant, redoutable; *(bark, growl)* effrayant

feasibility [fi:zə'bɪlɪtɪ] *n* *(of plan etc)* faisabilité *f*; **to doubt the f. of a suggestion** douter qu'une suggestion puisse être mise en pratique; **the f. of finding backers** la possibilité de trouver des garants; *Mktg* **f. stage** phase *f* de faisabilité

feasibility study *n* étude *f* de faisabilité

feasible ['fi:zəb(ə)l] *adj* **(a)** *(plan etc)* faisable, réalisable, praticable **(b)** *(story etc)* vraisemblable

feast[1] [fi:st] *n* **(a)** *(large meal)* festin *m*, banquet *m*; *Fig* **a f. for the eyes/the senses** un plaisir pour les yeux/les sens **(b)** *Rel etc* **f. (day)** (jour *m* de) fête *f*

feast[2] **1** *vi* faire festin, festoyer; **to f. (up)on sth** se régaler de qch **2** *vt* *Old-fashioned* *(person)* régaler, fêter; **to f. one's eyes on sth** repaître ses yeux de qch

feasting ['fi:stɪŋ] *n Lit* festoiement *m*

feat [fi:t] *n* **(a)** *(exploit)* exploit *m*; **f. of arms** fait *m* d'armes **(b)** *(achievement)* tour *m* de force; **a remarkable f. of modern technology** une remarquable prouesse technologique; **feats of engineering** triomphes *mpl* de l'ingénieur; **f. of skill** tour *m* d'adresse

feather[1] ['feðə*r*] *n* **(a)** plume *f*; *(of tail, wing)* penne *f*; *(on arrow)* (em)penne *f*; **as light as a f.** léger comme une plume; **in fine f.** dans une forme éblouissante; *Fig* **to show the white f.** manquer de courage; *prov* **you could have knocked me down with a f.** je n'en revenais pas; *Fig* **that's a f. in her cap** elle peut en être fière; *Fig* **to smoothe sb's ruffled feathers** rasséréner qn; *Fig* **to make the feathers fly** déclencher les hostilités; **f. bed** lit *m* de plume; *Fig* sinécure *f*; **f. cut** coupe *f* en dégradé **(b)** *(in rowing)* nage *f* plate

feather[2] **1** *vt* **(a)** *(arrow)* empenner; *Fig* **to f. one's nest** faire sa pelote *ou* son beurre **(b)** *(in rowing)* *(oar)* ramener à plat; **f. your oars!** avirons à plat! **(c)** *Av* *(propeller)* mettre en drapeau **2** *vi* *(in rowing)* nager plat

featherbed ['feðəbed] *vt Econ* protéger par des subventionnements excessifs; *Fig* *(children)* élever dans du coton

featherbedding ['feðəbedɪŋ] *n Econ* subventionnement *m* excessif

feather boa *n* boa *m* en plumes

featherbrain ['feðəbreɪn] *n F* tête *f* de linotte; **he's a real f.** c'est une vraie tête de linotte

featherbrained ['feðəbreɪnd] *adj F* étourdi; *(scheme, idea)* insensé

feather duster *n* plumeau *m*

feather-edge *n Carp etc* biseau *m*

feather-edged *adj* taillé en biseau, biseauté

feathering ['feðərɪŋ] *n* **(a)** *(of birds)* plumage *m* **(b)** *(of arrow)* empennage *m* **(c)** *(in rowing)* nage *f* plate **(d)** *Av* *(of propeller)* mise *f* en drapeau

featherstitch ['feðəstɪtʃ] *n Sewing* point *m* d'épines

featherweight ['feðəweɪt] *n Boxing* poids *m* plume; *Fig* **he's a bit of a f.** il ne fait pas vraiment le poids

feathery ['feðərɪ] *adj* *(snow, wheat etc)* plumeux; **it has a light, f. feel to it** c'est doux et léger comme la plume

feature[1] ['fi:tʃə*r*] *n* **(a)** *(of face)* trait *m*; **prominent features** traits accusés

(b) *(of landscape, person, car)* caractéristique *f*; *(of software)* fonction *f*; **a f. of the course is ...** un des aspects de la formation est ...; **paper that makes a f. of sports** journal qui fait une large place aux sports; **to make a f. of the fact that ...** attirer l'attention sur le fait que ...; **they decided to make a f. of the huge pillar in the dining area** ils ont décidé de mettre en valeur l'énorme pilier qui se trouve dans la salle à manger; **physical features of a country** topographie *f* d'un pays; **distinguishing f.** trait *m* distinctif; **distinguishing features** *(in passport)* signes *mpl* particuliers; **main features** grands traits; **prominent** *or* **salient f.** trait saillant; **the redeeming f.** *(of sth)* le beau côté; **special f.** particularité *f*

(c) *Cin* **f. (film)** long métrage *m*; **double-f. programme** programme *m* à deux longs métrages

(d) *Journ* *(item)* article *m* vedette; *(news report etc)* grand reportage *m*; **f. article** article *m* de fond; **features department** service *m* des rubriques; **features editor** rédacteur *m* de rubrique, journaliste *mf* responsable d'une rubrique; **features writer** grand reporter *mf*, éditorialiste *mf*

feature[2] **1** *vt* **(a)** *Cin* *(person)* représenter; **film featuring John Wayne** film avec John Wayne en vedette **(b)** *Journ* *(news item)* mettre en manchette; **the story was featured in all the main newspapers** cette affaire a fait la manchette de tous les grands quotidiens **(c)** *(have as special feature)* présenter, comporter; **the new model features four-wheel drive** le nouveau modèle comporte quatre roues motrices **2** *vi* **(a)** *Cin* *(of actor)* faire une apparition **(b)** *(appear)* figurer

feature-length *adj Cin* *(cartoon etc)* long métrage *inv*

featureless ['fi:tʃəlɪs] *adj* sans caractéristiques bien marquées

feature writer *n Journ* éditorialiste *mf*

Feb *abbr* **February**

febrile ['fi:braɪl] *adj Med, Fig* fébrile

February ['februərɪ] *n* [①A75-6,B-C; B58-9,B-C] février *m*; **in F.** au mois de février, en février; **(on) the first/the seventh of F.** le premier/le sept février

fecal, feces *US* = **faecal, faeces**

feckless ['feklɪs] *adj* **(a)** *(irresponsible)* *(person)* étourdi, irréfléchi; *(lifestyle)* inconscient, irresponsable **(b)** *(ineffectual)* *(person)* propre à rien, incapable; *(attempt)* inepte

fecklessness ['feklɪsnɪs] *n* **(a)** *(irresponsibility)* étourderie *f* **(b)** *(of plan)* ineptie *f*

fecund ['fi:kənd] *adj esp Fml* fécond

fecundity [fɪ'kʌndɪtɪ] *n* fécondité *f*

Fed *abbr* **Federal**

fed[1] [fed] *n US F* agent *m* du FBI

fed[2] *pt, pp see* **feed[2]**

federal ['fedərəl] **1** *adj* *(government etc)* fédéral **2** *n US Hist* fédéral *m*, nordiste *m*

federalism ['fedərəlɪz(ə)m] *n* fédéralisme *m*

federalist ['fedərəlɪst] *adj, n* fédéraliste *mf*

federalize ['fedərəlaɪz] *vt* **(a)** fédéraliser **(b)** *US* *(put under federal control)* charger le gouvernement fédéral du contrôle de

Federal Reserve (Board) *n US Fin* banque *f* centrale (des États-Unis)

federate[1] ['fedərət] *adj* *(state etc)* fédéré

federate[2] ['fedəreɪt] **1** *vt* fédérer **2** *vi* se fédérer

federation [fedə'reɪʃən] *n* fédération *f*; **employers' f.** association *f* patronale

fedora [fɪ'dɔ:rə] *n* feutre *m*

fed up *adj F* **to be f.** en avoir ras le bol *ou* marre; **I was getting pretty f.** je commençais à en avoir sérieusement marre *ou* ras le bol; **to be f. to the back teeth with sb/sth** en avoir plein le dos de qn/qch; **she sounded pretty f.** elle avait l'air d'en avoir marre; **I'm f. with it** j'en ai marre

fee [fi:] *n* **(a)** (*of physician, lawyer etc*) honoraires *mpl*; (*of actor*) cachet *m*; (*of company director*) jeton *m* de présence; **for a small f.** moyennant une légère redevance; **is there a f. for joining?** est-ce que l'inscription est payante?; **school fees** frais *mpl* de scolarité; **boarding-school fees** pension *f*; **entrance f.** droit *m* d'entrée; **membership fee(s)** droit d'inscription; **registration f.** (*for conference etc*) droit d'inscription; (*for letter*) taxe *f* de recommandation; **f. note** note *f* d'honoraires **(b)** *Jur* **property held in f. simple** propriété sans conditions *ou* libre **(c)** *Hist* (*fief*) fief *m*

feeble ['fi:b(ə)l] *adj* **(a)** (*weak*) faible; *F* **that's pretty f.** (*as an excuse, attempt*) c'est un peu léger; (*as a joke*) ce n'est pas très drôle **(b)** *F* (*ineffectual*) mou, *f* molle, peu capable; (*film*) faible, médiocre

feeble-minded 1 *adj* d'esprit faible, arriéré **2** *npl* **the f.** les débiles *mpl* mentaux

feeble-mindedness ['fi:b(ə)l'maɪndɪdnɪs] *n* faiblesse *f* d'esprit, arriération *f*

feebleness ['fi:b(ə)lnɪs] (*of person*) faiblesse *f*; (*of excuse*) pauvreté *f*, faiblesse; (*of film, book, play*) médiocrité *f*, faiblesse

feebly ['fi:blɪ] *adv* **(a)** (*weakly*) faiblement **(b)** (*ineffectually*) mollement; **to say sth f.** dire qch d'un ton peu convaincu

feed[1] [fi:d] *n* **(a)** (*animal food*) nourriture *f*, pâture *f*; (*for horses etc*) fourrage *m*; *F* (*meal*) repas *m*; **to have a good f.** bien manger; **horse off his f.** cheval qui boude sur son avoine; *F* **to be off one's f.** (*of baby*) bouder sur la nourriture; **it's time for baby's f.** il faut donner à manger au bébé

(b) (*portion*) (*of food for animals*) mesure *f*, ration *f*; **f. of oats** picotin *m* d'avoine

(c) *Th etc* (*actor*) acteur, -trice qui donne la réplique; (*of comedian*) faire-valoir *m*; **f. line** réplique *f*

(d) *Tech* (*of machine etc*) (*process*) alimentation *f*; (*device*) appareil *m ou* système *m* d'alimentation; (*pipe*) conduit *m* d'alimentation

feed[2] (*pt, pp* **fed** [fed]) **1** *vt* **(a)** (*give food to*) (*person*) nourrir, donner à manger à; (*family etc*) nourrir; (*country etc*) approvisionner; (*army*) ravitailler; (*dog etc*) faire manger; (*livestock*) affourrager; (*breastfeed*) allaiter; (*of mother bird*) (*chicks*) donner la becquée à; **to f. the birds** donner à manger aux oiseaux, nourrir les oiseaux; **he can f. himself already** il arrive déjà à manger tout seul; **we were well fed** nous étions bien nourris; **the animals are fed a diet of fruit** les animaux sont nourris de fruits; **we were fed bread and water** on nous donnait de l'eau et du pain; **they were fed to the lions** ils ont été jetés en pâture aux lions; **field that feeds three cows** champ qui nourrit trois vaches; **manure feeds the ground** le fumier nourrit la terre; **to f. the mind/sb's anger/sb's obsession** nourrir l'esprit/la colère de qn/l'obsession de qn

(b) (*supply with*) *Tech* (*machine, fire etc*) alimenter; (*furnace etc*) charger; *Comptr* (*paper*) faire avancer, alimenter; *Comptr* **to f. data into a computer** entrer des données dans un ordinateur; **to f. coins into a parking meter** mettre des pièces dans un parcmètre; **to f. sb with false information** fournir de fausses informations à qn; *Fb etc* **to f. the forwards** alimenter les avants

(c) *Th* (*actor*) donner la réplique à

2 *vi* manger; (*of cattle, sheep*) paître, brouter; **to f. on sth** se nourrir *ou* vivre de qch

▶ **feed back 1** *vtsep* (*information*) envoyer; (*send back again*) retransmettre **2** *vi* **to f. back into a system** être incorporé à un système

▶ **feed in** *vtsep Comptr* introduire en machine *ou* en mémoire; **to f. sth into the computer** entrer qch dans l'ordinateur, mettre qch en mémoire

▶ **feed up** *vtsep* (*animals*) engraisser

feedback ['fi:dbæk] *n* **(a)** *Electron etc* réaction *f*, rétroaction *f*; *F* feed-back *m inv* **(b)** (*of information*) retour *m*, remontée *f*; (*reaction*) réactions *fpl*; **we haven't had much f.** nous n'avons pas eu beaucoup d'écho; **positive/negative f.** réactions positives/négatives

feed belt *n* (*of machine gun*) bande-chargeur *f* (souple), *pl* bandes-chargeurs

feeder ['fi:dər] *n* **(a)** (*person*) (*of machine etc*) alimenteur, -euse; (*of furnace etc*) chargeur, -euse; (*eater*) mangeur, -euse; **heavy f.** gros mangeur

(b) (*feeding bottle*) biberon *m*; *Br* (*bib*) (*for baby*) bavette *f*, bavoir *m*

(c) *Geog* (*of river*) affluent *m*; *HydE* canal *m* d'alimentation *ou* d'amenée; (*road*) route *f* de raccordement; *Rail* embranchement *m*; (*for gas etc*) canalisation *f*; *El* câble *m ou* ligne *f* d'alimentation; *Br Sch* **f. (primary) school** = école *f* primaire d'où arrivent les élèves d'un collège donné; **f. airline** compagnie *f* aérienne d'apport; **f. flight** vol *m* d'apport; **f. network** (*for airport*) réseau *m* d'apport

(d) (*device*) dispositif *m* d'alimentation

feeding ['fi:dɪŋ] *n* **(a)** (*of person, machine etc*) alimentation *f*; (*of livestock*) affourragement *m*; **f. bottle** biberon *m*; *Med* **f. cup** biberon *m*, canard *m*; **f. frenzy** (*of sharks*) = frénésie *f* causée par la présence de nourriture; *Zool* **f. grounds** = endroit *m* où les animaux viennent trouver leur nourriture; *Ind* **f. mechanism** mécanisme *m* alimentateur; **f. time** (*at zoo etc*) (heure *f* des) repas *mpl* **(b)** *MecE* avance *f*, avancement *m*

feed pipe *n* tuyau *m* d'alimentation

feed pump *n* pompe *f* d'alimentation

feel[1] [fi:l] **(a)** (*act of touching*) toucher *m*; **rough to the f.** rude au toucher; **to have a f. of sth** toucher qch, tâter qch; **to have a f. in a drawer for sth** chercher qch à tâtons dans un tiroir; *Fig* **I don't like the f. of this** ça ne me dit rien qui vaille; *Sl* **to give sb a (quick) f.** tripoter qn

(b) (*texture*) (*of paper etc*) toucher *m*; **it has a nice f. to it** (*fabric*) c'est agréable au toucher; (*place*) il y a une bonne atmosphère; (*name*) ça sonne bien; **there's a funny f. to this gearstick** le levier de vitesses fait un peu drôle; **to recognize sth by the f. of it** reconnaître qch au toucher

(c) (*sensation*) sensation *f*; **the f. of a collar round my neck/of silk against your skin** la sensation d'un col autour de mon cou/de la soie contre la peau

(d) (*knack*) **he has the f. of his car** il a sa voiture bien en main; **you'll soon get the f. of the work** vous allez bientôt vous habituer au travail; **to have a f. for translation** avoir le sens de la traduction; **you need to have a f. for it** il faut l'avoir en soi

feel[2] (*pt, pp* **felt** [felt]) **1** *vt* **(a)** (*touch*) (*sth with one's hand*) toucher; (*pulse, pocket etc*) tâter; (*organ*) palper; **to f. one's way** (*in darkness*) avancer à tâtons; *Fig* explorer le terrain, y aller doucement; *Fig* **to f. one's way towards sth** avancer vers qch à tâtons; **to f. one's way into sth** se faire à qch; **to f. one's way around** essayer de s'y retrouver; **he felt her scalp to see if there was a lump** il tâta son crâne pour voir s'il y avait une bosse

(b) [①**A40**,**C**,**1**,**a**; **B33**,**2**,**b**,**i**] (*be conscious of, experience*) sentir; (*bitterness, pain, joy etc*) éprouver, ressentir; **I felt the floor tremble** *or* **trembling** j'ai senti trembler le sol; **she felt his arms around her** elle sentait ses bras l'entourant; **f. the weight of that!** pèse un peu ça!; **to f. the heat** être sensible à la chaleur; **to f. the cold** être sensible au froid, être frileux; **to make one's authority felt** affirmer son autorité, faire sentir son autorité; **she felt nothing, only emptiness** elle ne ressentait rien, seulement un vide; **do you f. anything for her?** est-ce que tu éprouves *ou* ressens quelque chose à son égard?; **I f. it in my bones that I shall succeed** quelque chose en moi me dit que je réussirai; **I felt it necessary to intervene** j'ai jugé nécessaire d'intervenir; **what do you f. about ...?** qu'est-ce que vous pensez de ...?; **what I f. about it is ...** mon sentiment là-dessus, c'est que ...; **I felt that he could have tried harder** j'avais le sentiment qu'il aurait pu faire plus d'efforts; **to f. a fool** se sentir bête *ou* stupide; **to f. a new woman/man** se sentir comme neuve/neuf

2 *vi* **(a)** (*of person*) **to f. hot/cold** avoir chaud/froid; **to f. ill/tired** se sentir malade/fatigué; **I f. really stupid** je me sens vraiment stupide; **to f. sick** *Br* (*about to vomit*) avoir envie de vomir; *Am* (*ill*) ne pas se sentir bien, se sentir malade; **she felt sick when she thought of ...** ça la rendait malade de penser à ...; **he felt really bad about leaving her** ça l'ennuyait vraiment de la laisser; **they felt betrayed** ils se sont sentis trahis; **my foot feels better** mon pied va mieux; **how do you f.?, how are you feeling?** comment te sens-tu?; **to f. all the better for it** s'en trouver mieux; **I f. ten years younger** je me sens dix ans de moins; **not to f. oneself** ne pas être dans son assiette; **I f. quite myself again** je me sens tout à fait rétabli; **to f. up to doing sth** (*well enough*) se sentir assez bien pour faire qch; (*competent enough*) se sentir de taille à faire qch; **to f. certain/convinced that ...** être certain/convaincu que ...; **how would you f. if I were to offer you a job?** qu'est-ce que vous diriez si je vous offrais un emploi?; **how would you f. if she left you?** qu'est-ce que tu ressentirais si elle te quittait?; **how do you think I f.?** (*that's a stupid question*) qu'est-ce que tu crois?; **how would <u>you</u> f.?** (*if sb did that to you*) qu'est-ce que tu ressentirais, toi?; **she feels strongly about it** elle a des idées très arrêtées là-dessus; **I f. as if ...** j'ai l'impression que ...; **I felt as if I'd seen him before** j'avais l'impression de l'avoir déjà vu; **I felt as if** *or F* **like I was wasting my time** j'avais l'impression de perdre mon temps; **to f. like a fool** se sentir bête *ou* stupide; **to f. like a new man/woman** se sentir comme neuf/neuve (**b**) (*want sth/to do sth*) **to f. like doing sth** se sentir d'humeur à faire qch; **I felt like crying** j'avais envie de pleurer; **if you f. like it** si ça vous dit, si le cœur vous en dit; **I don't f. like it** ça ne me dit rien; **I f. like a cup of tea** j'ai envie d'une tasse de thé

(**c**) (*of things*) **to f. hard/soft** être dur/doux au toucher; **the wall/her forehead felt hot** le mur/son front était chaud au toucher; **his legs/head felt heavy** il se sentait les jambes/ la tête lourde(s); **the atmosphere felt tense** on sentait une certaine tension dans l'air; **my hands f. cold** j'ai froid aux mains; **my arm feels as if it's broken** j'ai l'impression que je me suis cassé le bras; **the room feels damp** la pièce (me) paraît humide; **it feels like ...** cela donne la sensation de ...; **it feels like (it's going to) rain** on dirait qu'il va pleuvoir; **it felt good to be alive** c'était bon d'être en vie; **it feels different/dead now she's gone** c'est différent/mort depuis qu'elle est partie; **what did it f. like when you won?** qu'est-ce que vous avez ressenti en gagnant?

(**d**) (*explore, touch with fingers*) **to f. in one's pockets for sth** chercher qch dans ses poches; **he felt on the ground for his keys** il cherchait ses clefs à tâtons sur le sol

▶ **feel about, feel around** *vi* (*search by touching*) chercher à tâtons; **to f. about** *or* **around for sth** chercher qch à tâtons

▶ **feel for** *vipo* (*feel sympathy for*) éprouver de la compassion à l'égard de; **I f. for her** elle a toute ma sympathie; **to feel for sb in their sorrow** partager la douleur de qn; **I really felt for you then** je t'ai sincèrement plaint à ce moment

▶ **feel up** *vtsep Sl* (*touch sexually*) peloter

feeler ['fiːlər] *n* (**a**) *Biol* (*of insect etc*) antenne *f*; (*of snail*) corne *f*; (*of mollusc etc*) tentacule *m* (**b**) *Fig* (*tentative enquiry etc*) ballon *m* d'essai; **to put out feelers** lancer un ballon d'essai, tâter le terrain; **peace feelers** sondages *mpl* de paix (**c**) *MecE* **f. (gauge)** calibre *m* d'épaisseur (à lames)

feel-good factor *n* sentiment *m* de bien-être

feeling ['fiːlɪŋ] **1** *adj* (*person*) sensible

2 *n* (**a**) **(sense of) f.** toucher *m*; **to have no f. in one's arm** avoir le bras mort; **to lose the f. in one's arm/leg** ne plus avoir aucune sensation dans le bras/la jambe

(**b**) (*sensation*) sensation *f*

(**c**) (*emotion*) sentiment *m*; **there is a f. of grief/joy throughout the country** le chagrin/la joie règne dans tout le pays; **a f. of emptiness** une impression de vide; **to hurt sb's feelings** blesser qn; **I don't want anybody to have hurt feelings about it** je ne veux pas que cela blesse qui que soit; **her feelings are hurt** elle est blessée; **she had a f. of elation** elle éprouvait un sentiment d'allégresse; **his feelings towards me** ses sentiments envers moi; **to have no feelings** n'avoir aucun cœur; **I know the f.!** je sais ce que c'est!; **I had a f. I might find you here** je pensais bien vous trouver ici; **I've got a nasty** *or* **unpleasant f. that ...** j'ai la désagréable impression que ...; **no hard feelings!** sans rancune!; **with f.** (*to speak etc*) (*emotionally*) avec émotion; (*warmly*) chaleureusement; (*angrily*) avec emportement; (*to sing etc*) avec expression *ou* âme

(**d**) (*opinion*) **what are your feelings about fox-hunting?** qu'est-ce que vous pensez de la chasse au renard?; **I don't have any strong feelings about it** ça m'est plus ou moins égal; **feelings are running very high** les esprits sont très échauffés; **public f. ran high against the proposal** le sentiment populaire s'élevait contre cette proposition; **there is a general f. that ...** l'impression règne (dans le public) que ..., le sentiment général est que ...

(**e**) (*sensitivity*) sensibilité *f*; **to have a f. for music/nature** être sensible à la musique/la nature; **to have a f. for sth** (*do well*) être doué pour qch

feelingly ['fiːlɪŋlɪ] *adv* (*to speak*) avec émotion; (*warmly*) chaleureusement; (*to sing, play*) avec expression

feet *npl see* **foot**[1]

feign [feɪn] *vt* (*anger etc*) feindre, simuler; (*surprise*) affecter; **to f. illness** feindre *ou* simuler la maladie; **to f. sleep** faire semblant de dormir

feigned [feɪnd] *adj* (*illness*) simulé; (*surprise*) feint

feint[1] [feɪnt] *n Mil* fausse attaque *f*; *Boxing, Fencing etc* feinte *f*; **his anger is only a f.** sa colère n'est qu'une simulation

feint[2] *vi Mil* faire une fausse attaque; *Boxing etc* feinter; *Boxing* **to f. with the right** feinter du droit

feint[3] *n* **f.-ruled paper** papier *m* réglé

feistiness ['faɪstɪnɪs] *n esp Am* (**a**) (*spirit, energy*) fougue *f*, impétuosité *f* (**b**) (*pugnacity*) attitude *f* contestataire

feisty ['faɪstɪ] *adj esp Am* (**a**) (*full of energy*) impétueux, fougueux (**b**) (*pugnacious*) contestataire

feldspar ['feldspɑːr] *n Miner* feldspath *m*

felicitous [fɪ'lɪsɪtəs] *adj Lit* (*choice, decision*) heureux; (*word, expression etc*) bien trouvé, à propos

felicity [fɪ'lɪsɪtɪ] *n Lit* (**a**) (*happiness*) félicité *f*, bonheur *m* (**b**) (*aptness*) (*of remark, expression etc*) à-propos *m*, bien-trouvé *m*; (*of choice, decision*) caractère *m* heureux

feline ['fiːlaɪn] **1** *adj* félin; **f. grace** grâce *f* féline, grâce de chat **2** *n* félin *m*

fell[1] [fel] *vt* (*opponent etc*) abattre, terrasser; (*tree*) abattre, couper; **felled wood** *or* **timber** abattis *m*, bois *m* gisant, vente *f*

fell[2] *pt see* **fall**[2]

fell[3] *adj* **at one f. swoop** d'un seul coup

fell[4] *n Eng Dial* (*hill, mountain*) colline *f*; **the Fells** (*moorland*) le lande; **f. walking** randonnée *f* en basse montagne

fell[5] *n* (*animal skin*) peau *f*

fella, feller ['felə, -ər] *n F* mec *m*, type *m*; *Br* (*boyfriend*) copain *m*, mec, *Can* chum *m*

fellatio [fə'leɪʃɪəʊ] *n* fellation *f*

felling ['felɪŋ] *n* (*of cow, forest*) abattage *m*; (*of timber*) abattage, coupe *f*

fellow ['feləʊ] *n* (**a**) (*comrade*) camarade *mf*, compagnon *m*; **f. being** *or* **creature** semblable *mf*; **f. citizen** concitoyen, -enne; **f. countryman/countrywoman** compatriote *mf*; **f. feeling** sympathie *f*; **f. passenger/sufferer** compagnon de voyage/ misère; **f. soldier** compagnon d'armes, camarade de régiment; **f. student** camarade d'études; **f. traveller** (*on train etc*), *Pol* compagnon de route

(**b**) (*colleague*) semblable *mf*, pareil *m*; (*one of a pair*) pendant *m*; **a vase and its f.** un vase et son pendant

(**c**) (*at university*) (*professor*) = professeur *m* permanent; (*postgraduate student*) chargé, -ée de cours; (*of learned society*) membre *m*

(**d**) *Br F* (*boyfriend*) copain *m*, mec *m*, *Can* chum *m*

(**e**) *Old-fashioned, F* (*man*) homme *m*, gars *m*; **a good f.** un brave garçon; **a decent f.** un bon gars; **he's a queer f.** c'est un drôle de type; **the poor little f.** le pauvre petit

Fellow of the Royal Society *n* = membre *m* de la Société royale (de Londres)

fellowship ['feləʊʃɪp] *n* (**a**) (*friendship*) **(good) f.** amitié *f*, camaraderie *f* (**b**) (*association*) association *f*, corporation *f* (**c**) (*at university*) bourse *f* universitaire (*avec obligation de faire un cours, des recherches*); (*of learned society*) titre *m* de membre

felon ['felən] *n Jur Arch* criminel, -elle

felonious [fe'ləʊnɪəs] *adj Jur Arch* criminel; **f. act** action *f* qui constitue un crime

felony ['felənɪ] *n Jur Arch* crime *m*; **to compound a f.** pactiser avec un crime

felspar ['felspɑːr] *n* = **feldspar**

felt[1] [felt] *n Tex etc* feutre *m*; **tarred f.** feutre bitumé

felt[2] *vt Tex* (*wool, hairs*) feutrer; *Constr* (*roof etc*) couvrir de feutre bitumé

felt[3] *pt, pp see* **feel**[2]

felt-tip *n* **f. (pen)** (stylo *m*) feutre *m*

female ['fiːmeɪl] **1** *adj* (*person*) féminin; (*voice etc*) de femme; (*animal, plant etc*) femelle; *Tech* femelle; **male and f. patients** malades *mpl* hommes et femmes; **male and f. heirs** héritiers *mpl* mâles et femelles; **f. executive** femme *f* cadre; *Tech* **male-f. coupling/connection/adapter** accouplement *m*/accordement *m*/adaptateur *m* mâle-femelle; **f. screw** écrou *m* **2** *n* (**a**) (*person*) *Jur* femme *f*; *F Pej* gonzesse *f*; *Th* **f. impersonator** travesti *m* (**b**) (*animal, plant*) femelle *f*

feminine ['femɪnɪn] [①A16,E; B6-7,A-B] **1** *adj* féminin; *Gram* **this word is f.** ce mot est féminin **2** *n Gram* féminin *m*; **in the f.** au féminin

femininity [femɪ'nɪnɪtɪ] *n* féminité *f*

feminism ['femɪnɪz(ə)m] *n* féminisme *m*

feminist ['femɪnɪst] *adj, n* féministe *mf*

femoral ['femərəl] *adj Anat* fémoral

femur, *pl* **femurs, femora** ['fiːmər, -əz, 'femərə] *n Anat* fémur *m*

fen [fen] *n* marais *m*, marécage *m*; **the Fens** = les plaines *fpl* marécageuses de l'est de l'Angleterre

fence[1] [fens] *n* (**a**) (*for delimiting an area*) clôture *f*; (*more solid, for preventing entry*) barrière *f*; **sunk f.** saut *m* de loup; *Fig* **to sit on the f.** ménager la chèvre et le chou; **to get** *or* **come off the f.** arrêter de ménager la chèvre et le chou; *Fig* **to be on the other side of the f.** être de l'autre côté de la barricade, avoir une opinion contraire; **I don't often find myself on the same side of the f. as you** je n'ai pas souvent les mêmes opinions que toi; *esp Am Fig* **to mend one's fences** (*of politician*) regagner la confiance des électeurs; *Am Fig* **to mend one's fences with sb** se remettre en bons termes avec qn; **f. post** poteau *m* de clôture

(**b**) *Horseriding* (*in steeplechasing*) obstacle *m*, haie *f*; (*in showjumping*) obstacle, barrière *f*

(**c**) *Tech* (*of circular saw etc*) guide *m*; (*of machine tool etc*) garde *f*

(**d**) *Sl* (*receiver of stolen property*) receleur, -euse (d'objets volés)

fence² 1 *vt* (*field*) clôturer 2 *vi* (a) *Sp* faire de l'escrime; *Fig* **to f. with a counsel** répondre en éludant les questions d'un avocat; *Fig* **stop fencing!** arrête d'éluder la question! (b) *Sl* (*receive stolen property*) faire du recel
▶ **fence in** *vtsep* (*land etc*) clôturer
▶ **fence off** *vtsep* séparer par une clôture
fence-mending *n esp Am Fig* reprise *f* des relations
fencer ['fensər] *n Sp* escrimeur, -euse
fencing ['fensɪŋ] *n* (a) (*barrier etc*) clôture *f*, barrière *f*; (*material*) matériaux *mpl* pour clôture; **wire f.** treillage *m* en fil de fer (b) (*action*) (*of land etc*) action *f* de clôturer (c) *Sp* escrime *f*; **f. bout** *or* **match** assaut *m* d'armes; **f. master** maître *m* d'armes; **f. school** salle *f* d'escrime *ou* d'armes (d) *Sl* (*receiving*) recel *m*
fend [fend] *vi* **to f. for oneself** se débrouiller
▶ **fend off** *vtsep* (*blow, questions etc*) parer, détourner; (*attack*) parer
fender ['fendər] *n Am Aut* garde-boue *m inv*; (*protecting wall, door, post etc*) bouteroue *f*; (*for fireplace*) garde-cendre *m inv*; *Am Rail* (*on train engine, tram*) pare-choc(s) *m inv*; (*for clearing track*) chasse-pierres *m inv*; *Naut* bourrelet *m* de défense; *Am Aut F* **it was just a f. bender** (*minor accident*) il n'y a eu que de la tôle froissée
fenland ['fenlænd] *n* pays *m* marécageux
fennel ['fen(ə)l] *n Bot, Culin* fenouil *m*
feral ['ferəl] *adj Fml* (*cat, dog etc*) devenu sauvage
ferment¹ ['fɜːment] *n* (a) (*yeast etc*) ferment *m* (b) (*fermentation*) (*of liquid*) fermentation *f*; *Fig* (*commotion*) effervescence *f*, agitation *f*; **the whole town was in a (state of) f.** toute la ville était en effervescence *ou* dans un état d'agitation
ferment² [fə'ment] 1 *vi* (*of liquids etc, Fig of sedition*) fermenter; (*of wine*) travailler 2 *vt* (*liquid*) laisser fermenter
fermentation [fɜːmen'teɪʃən] *n* (*of liquid etc*) fermentation *f*; (*of wine*) travail *m*; *Fig* agitation *f*
fern [fɜːn] *n* (*plant*) fougère *f*; **hillside covered with f.** coteau couvert de fougères
ferocious [fə'rəʊʃəs] *adj* (*animal, person, look etc*) féroce
ferociously [fə'rəʊʃəslɪ] *adv* férocement, avec férocité
ferocity, ferociousness [fə'rɒsɪtɪ, fə'rəʊʃəsnɪs] *n* férocité *f*
ferret¹ ['ferɪt] *n* (*animal*) furet *m*
ferret² (-t-) 1 *vi* (a) (*hunt*) chasser au furet (b) *F* **to f. (about) in one's pockets** fouiller dans ses poches (**for sth** pour trouver qch); **what are you ferreting for?** qu'est-ce que tu cherches? 2 *vt* (*rabbits etc*) chasser au furet
▶ **ferret out** *vtsep* (*dislodge*) (*sb, sth*) dénicher; (*secret, the truth*) déterrer
ferreting ['ferɪtɪŋ] *n* (*hunting*) chasse *f* au furet
ferrety ['ferɪtɪ] *adj* de furet; *Pej* **f. eyes/face** yeux *mpl*/visage *m* de fouine
ferric ['ferɪk] *adj Ch* ferrique; **f. ammonium salt** sel *m* ferrico-ammonique
Ferris wheel ['ferɪswiːl] *n* (*at fairground*) grande roue *f*
ferrite ['feraɪt] *n* ferrite *f*
ferroconcrete ['ferəʊ'kɒŋkriːt] *n* béton *m* armé
ferromagnetic ['ferəʊmæg'netɪk] *adj* ferromagnétique
ferrous ['ferəs] *adj Ch* (*oxide etc*) ferreux; **f. sulphide** pyrite *f* de fer
ferrule ['ferəl, -uːl] *n* (*of walking stick*) bout *m* ferré, embout *m*
ferry¹ ['ferɪ] *n* (*boat*) bac *m*, ferry *m*; **to take the f.** prendre le bac *ou* le ferry; **passenger/car f.** bac *ou* ferry à piétons/à voitures; **train f.** bac transbordeur; **air f.** avion *m* transbordeur; **f. port** port *m* de ferry; **f. service** ligne *f* de bac *ou* de ferry
ferry² *vt* **to f. sb/a car across a river** passer qn/une voiture en bac *ou* en ferry de l'autre côté de la rivière; **to f. voters to the polls** transporter des électeurs aux urnes; **she ferries her children backwards and forwards to school by car** elle fait la navette pour conduire ses enfants à l'école et les en ramener
ferryboat ['ferɪbəʊt] *n* bac *m*, ferry *m*
ferrying ['ferɪɪŋ] *n* transport *m* en *ou* par bac *ou* ferry
ferryman, *pl* **-men** ['ferɪmən] *n* passeur *m*
fertile ['fɜːtaɪl] *adj* (*soil, woman, imagination etc*) fertile, fécond (**in** en); (*man*) fécond; (*egg*) fécondé
fertility [fɜː'tɪlɪtɪ] *n* (*of soil, person's imagination, woman etc*) fertilité *f*, fécondité *f*; **f. drug** médicament *m* de traitement de la stérilité; **f. treatment** traitement *m* de la stérilité; **f. symbol** symbole *m* de fertilité
fertilization [fɜːtɪlaɪ'zeɪʃən] *n* (*of egg etc*) fertilisation *f*, fécondation *f*; *Biol* **self f.** autofécondation *f*
fertilize ['fɜːtɪlaɪz] *vt* (a) (*egg, plant etc*) fertiliser, féconder (b) *Agr* (*soil*) fertiliser, engraisser
fertilizer ['fɜːtɪlaɪzər] *n Agr* engrais *m*; **artificial fertilizers** engrais chimiques
fervent ['fɜːvənt] *adj* (*prayer, supporter, belief*) ardent, fervent; (*wish, desire*) ardent
fervently ['fɜːvəntlɪ] *adv* (*to plead, believe, pray etc*) avec ferveur; (*to wish, support etc*) avec ardeur
fervid ['fɜːvɪd] *adj* = **fervent**
fervour, *US* **fervor** ['fɜːvər] *n* (*of prayer, speech, belief*) ferveur *f*; (*of wish, supporter*) ardeur *f*
fester ['festər] *vi* (*of wound etc*) suppurer, s'envenimer; (*of conflict, resentment*) s'envenimer; (*of dislike, sense of injustice*) s'aviver
festering ['festərɪŋ] *adj* (*wound etc*) ulcéreux, suppurant; (*conflict, resentment*) qui s'envenime; (*dislike, sense of injustice*) aggravé, de plus en plus vif
festival ['festɪv(ə)l] *n* (*of music, drama etc*) festival *m*, -als; (*religious*) fête *f*; *esp Rel* **harvest f.** = office *m* d'action de grâces (célébré après la rentrée des récoltes); **film f.** festival du film; **street f.** fête de quartier
festive ['festɪv] *adj* (*day etc*) de fête; **the f. season** l'époque *f* des fêtes; **to be in (a) f. mood** (*of person*) avoir le cœur en fête
festivity [fes'tɪvɪtɪ] *n* fête *f*, réjouissance *f*, festivité *f*; **an air/atmosphere of f.** un air/une atmosphère de fête; **festivities** festivités, réjouissances
festoon¹ [fes'tuːn] *n* feston *m*, guirlande *f*
festoon² *vt* festonner (**with** de); (*flowers etc*) disposer en festons
feta ['fetə] *n* **f. (cheese)** feta *f*
fetal ['fiːt(ə)l] *adj* = **foetal**
fetch [fetʃ] 1 *vt* (a) (*go to get*) aller chercher; **to f. water from the river** aller puiser de l'eau dans la rivière; **to f. sb from the airport** aller chercher qn à l'aéroport; **I'll f. you** je viendrai te chercher; **f.!** (*to dog*) va chercher!
(b) *Com* rapporter; (*specific price*) atteindre; **it fetched a high price** cela s'est vendu cher; **it fetched £100,000** cela a atteint les 100 000 livres; **I'd be surprised if it fetched that much** cela m'étonnerait que cela rapporte autant *ou* que cela se vende aussi cher
(c) (*hit*) **to f. sb a blow** flanquer un coup à qn
(d) *Lit* (*utter*) (*sigh, moan*) pousser
2 *vi* **I'm not going to f. and carry for you!** je ne vais pas être ta bonne à tout faire!
▶ **fetch back** *vtsep* (*bring back*) (*sb*) ramener; (*sth*) rapporter
▶ **fetch up** 1 *vi* (*reach*) **to f. up at a port** parvenir *ou* arriver à un port; **the kite fetched up in the branches of a tree** le cerf-volant est resté accroché dans les branches d'un arbre; *F* **they finally fetched up at our house** ils ont finalement abouti chez nous; *F* **the car fetched up against a wall** la voiture s'est (finalement) arrêtée en heurtant un mur 2 *vtsep* (a) (*bring from lower place*) (*sb*) faire monter; (*sth*) remonter (b) *F* (*vomit*) dégueuler
fetching ['fetʃɪŋ] *adj* (*woman, air*) séduisant, attrayant; (*hat, smile*) ravissant
fête¹ [feɪt] *n* fête *f*; **village f.** fête communale
fête² *vt* (*person, event*) fêter; (*person*) faire fête à
fetid ['fetɪd, 'fiːtɪd] *adj* fétide, puant
fetish ['fetɪʃ] *n* (*magic object*), *Psy* fétiche *m*; **he has a f. for black silk** il est obsédé par la soie noire; **to make a f. of sth** être obsédé par qch
fetishism ['fetɪʃɪz(ə)m] *n Psy* fétichisme *m*
fetishist ['fetɪʃɪst] *n Psy* fétichiste *mf*
fetishistic [fetɪ'ʃɪstɪk] *adj Psy* fétichiste
fetlock ['fetlɒk] *n* (*of horse*) (*hair*) fanon *m*; **f. (joint)** boulet *m*
fetter¹ ['fetər] *n* (*usu pl*) **fetters** (*of prisoner etc*) chaînes *fpl*, fers *mpl*; **in fetters** enchaîné, dans les fers; **to put sb in fetters** mettre qn aux fers; *Fig* **to place fetters on sb/on sb's freedom** entraver qn/la liberté de qn; **the fetters of marriage** les chaînes du mariage
fetter² *vt* (*person*) enchaîner; (*horse*) entraver; *Fig* (*unions etc*) garrotter
fettle ['fet(ə)l] *n* **to be in fine** *or* **good f.** être en condition *ou* en forme
fetus ['fiːtəs] *n* = **foetus**
feud¹ [fjuːd] *n* (*between families, clans etc*) inimitié *f*; **blood f.** vendetta *f*; **family f.** querelle *f* familiale
feud² *vi* se quereller (**over** au sujet de); **the feuding parties** les opposants *mpl*, les parties *fpl* en conflit
feudal ['fjuːd(ə)l] *adj Hist* (*system, service etc*) féodal; *Pej* (*attitude, approach to sth*) moyenâgeux
feudalism ['fjuːdəlɪz(ə)m] *n* le système féodal; **under late f.** pendant les dernières années du système féodal
feudally ['fjuːd(ə)lɪ] *adv* féodalement
fever ['fiːvər] *n Med* (*high temperature, disease*) fièvre *f*; **high f.** forte fièvre; **she's got** *or* **she is running a f.** elle a de la fièvre; *Fig* **to be in a f. of excitement** être animé d'une excitation fébrile *ou* fiévreuse; **expectation had reached f.**

pitch l'attente était fiévreuse; **things are at f. pitch** l'atmosphère est enfiévrée; **gold f.** fièvre de l'or

fevered ['fi:vəd] *adj* enfiévré, fiévreux; **f. brow** front *m* fiévreux; **a f. imagination** une imagination enfiévrée

feverish ['fi:vərɪʃ] *adj Med* fiévreux, fébrile; **to be f.** avoir de la fièvre, être fiévreux *ou* fébrile; **to feel f.** se sentir fiévreux; *Fig* **f. activity** activité fébrile *ou* fiévreuse

feverishly ['fi:vərɪʃlɪ] *adv* fiévreusement, fébrilement

feverishness ['fi:vərɪʃnɪs] *n Med* état *m* fébrile; (*of activity*) fébrilité *f*

few [fju:] [①A5,C,1,d] **1** *adj* **(a)** (*not many*) (*people, things*) peu de; **to have f. friends** avoir peu d'amis; **very f. opportunities** très peu d'occasions; **with f. exceptions** à de rares exceptions près; **on the f. occasions I've spoken to her** les rares fois où je lui ai parlé; **his visits/tourists are f. and far between** ses visites/les touristes sont rarissimes; **trains every f. minutes** trains toutes les deux ou trois minutes; **every f. days** tous les deux ou trois jours; **too f. points** pas suffisamment de points; **f. in number** peu nombreux; **f. novelists have equalled her** peu de romanciers l'ont égalée

(b) (*some*) **a f.** quelques; **I have only a f. pounds** je n'ai que quelques livres; **he had a good f. enemies** il avait pas mal d'ennemis; **in a f. minutes** dans quelques minutes; **quite a f. minutes passed** un bon moment s'est écoulé; **in the next f. days** dans les jours qui suivent/suivaient

2 *pron* **(a)** (*not many*) (*people etc*) peu; **there are very/too f. of us** nous sommes très peu/trop peu nombreux; **f. (of them) could speak French** peu parmi eux parlaient français; **there are so f. of them** ils sont tellement peu nombreux

(b) (*some*) **a f. of these cakes/oranges** quelques-uns de ces gâteaux/quelques-unes de ces oranges; **a f. of the survivors** quelques-uns des survivants; **I know a f. of them** j'en connais quelques-uns; **a f. of us** quelques-uns d'entre nous; **I've seen/read a f.** j'en ai vu/lu quelques-uns; *F* **you've had a f. too many** (*drunk too much*) tu as un peu trop bu; **she only knew a f. (of them)** elle ne connaissait que quelques-uns d'entre eux

3 *npl* **the f.** la minorité; **the fortunate f.** les heureux élus *mpl*; **the f. who came** les rares personnes qui sont venues

fewer ['fju:ər] **1** *adj* [①A10,b,iii] (*comp of* **few**) moins de; **there are f. trees here** il y a moins d'arbres ici; **no f. than thirty** pas moins de trente; **the houses became f.** les maisons devenaient plus rares *ou* moins nombreuses; **f. and f. people** de moins en moins de gens **2** *pron* moins; **there are f. (of them) than I thought** il y en a moins que je n'avais pensé

fewest ['fju:ɪst] **1** *adj* (*superl of* **few**) le moins de; **the f. people possible** le moins de gens possible; **the area where there are the f. houses** la région où il y a le moins de maisons **2** *pron* **the region where the f. live** la région où vit le moins grand nombre de gens

fey [feɪ] *adj* **(a)** (*charming*) qui possède un charme éthéré **(b)** (*silly*) un peu idiot **(c)** *Scot* (*foreseeing death*) qui a des pressentiments de mort *ou* des visions de l'au-delà; (*having second sight*) doué de seconde vue

fez [fez] *n* (*hat*) fez *m*

fiancé, *f* **fiancée** [fɪ'ɒnseɪ] *n* fiancé, -ée

fiasco [fɪ'æskəʊ] *n* fiasco *m*; **to be a f.** (*of play*) faire un four, être un fiasco

fib[1] [fɪb] *n F* petit mensonge *m*; **that's a f.!** ce n'est pas vrai!, c'est des histoires!; **you're telling me fibs** tu me racontes des histoires; **I told them a f. about having to do some work** je leur ai raconté qu'il fallait que je travaille

fib[2] *vi* (**-bb-**) *F* (*lie*) dire des petits mensonges; **you're fibbing to me again** tu es encore en train de me raconter des histoires; **I'm sure he was fibbing about how much he earns** je suis sûr qu'il a menti *ou* raconté des histoires à propos de l'argent qu'il gagne; **I fibbed to them about having to do some work** je leur ai raconté qu'il fallait que je travaille

fibber ['fɪbər] *n F* menteur, -euse; **she's a terrible f.** elle raconte tout le temps des histoires; **what a f. you are!** quel menteur tu fais!

fibre, *US* **fiber** ['faɪbər] *n* fibre *f*; **(dietary) f.** fibres (alimentaires); **muscle/moral f.** fibre musculaire/morale; **every f. of his being revolted at the idea** chaque fibre de son être se révoltait à cette idée; **glass f.** fibre de verre; **vegetable f.** crin *m* végétal; **wood f.** fibre de bois; **a high-f. diet** une alimentation riche en fibres

fibreboard, *US* **fiberboard** ['faɪbəbɔ:d] *n* panneau *m* de fibres agglomérées

fibreglass, *US* **fiberglass** ['faɪbəglɑ:s] *n* fibre *f* de verre; **f. canoe** canoë *m* en fibre de verre

fibre optic cable *n* câble *m* en fibres optiques

fibre optics *n* [①A10,c] technologie *f* des fibres optiques

fibrescope, *US* **fiberscope** ['faɪbəskəʊp] *n Med, Opt* fibroscope *m*

fibrillation [faɪbrɪ'leɪʃən] *n* fibrillation *f*

fibroid ['faɪbrɔɪd] **1** *adj* (*tumour etc*) fibroïde **2** *n Med* fibrome *m*

fibroma, *pl* **-mata** [faɪ'brəʊmə, -mətə] *n Med* fibrome *m*

fibrosis [faɪ'brəʊsɪs] *n Med* fibrose *f*

fibrositis [faɪbrəʊ'saɪtɪs] *n Med* fibrosite *f*

fibrous ['faɪbrəs] *adj* (*tissue etc*) fibreux

fibula ['fɪbjʊlə] *n Anat* péroné *m*

fickle ['fɪk(ə)l] *adj* inconstant, capricieux; (*character*) changeant, versatile; (*esp romantically*) volage; (*weather*) capricieux

fickleness ['fɪk(ə)lnɪs] *n* inconstance *f*, humeur *f* volage; **the f. of luck** les caprices *mpl* de la chance

fiction ['fɪkʃən] *n* **(a)** (*creation of imagination*) fiction *f*, création *f* de l'imagination; *Jur* **legal f.** fiction légale; **these tales are pure f.** tous ces contes sont totalement imaginaires **(b)** (*in library, bookshop*) romans *mpl*; **light f.** romans de lecture facile; **a piece of f.** une œuvre de fiction; *Fig* **his entire statement is a piece of f.** sa déposition est fabriquée de toutes pièces; **f. writer** romancier, -ière

fictional ['fɪkʃən(ə)l] *adj* fictif; **a f. autobiography** une autobiographie romancée

fictionalize ['fɪkʃənəlaɪz] *vt* romancer

fictitious [fɪk'tɪʃəs] *adj* (*character, events*) fictif; (*account*) inventé; *Com* **f. assets** actif *m* fictif; **her statement is entirely f.** sa déposition est fabriquée de toutes pièces

fictitiously [fɪk'tɪʃəslɪ] *adv* fictivement

fiddle[1] ['fɪd(ə)l] *n F* **(a)** (*violin*) violon *m*; (*musician*) (joueur, -euse de) violon; **bass f.** contrebasse *f*; *Fig* **to play second f.** jouer un rôle secondaire **(to sb** auprès de qn) **(b)** *Br* (*swindle*) combine *f*, magouille *f*; **to be on the f.** faire du fricotage

fiddle[2] **1** *vi* **(a)** (*play violin*) jouer du violon; *Pej* racler du violon; *Fig* **to f. while Rome burns** = s'occuper de choses futiles au lieu de lutter contre une calamité

(b) (*play, fidget*) **to f. (about** *or* **around) with** jouer avec, tripoter, trifouiller; (*details etc*) chipoter sur, ergoter sur; **to f. with one's watch** jouer avec sa montre; **don't f. with the switch** laisse l'interrupteur tranquille, ne tripote pas l'interrupteur; **she fiddled with a few knobs** elle a manipulé quelques boutons; **stop fiddling about** *or* **around and get down to some work!** arrête de tourner en rond et mets-toi au travail!

(c) *Br F* (*swindle*) combiner, fricoter

2 *vt Br F* (*tamper with*) (*meter etc*) bricoler; (*obtain dishonestly*) carotter; **to f. the accounts** truquer les comptes; **he fiddled a week's leave** il a carotté huit jours de permission; **he fiddled it** *or* **things so that ...** il s'est arrangé pour que ... + *sub*

fiddlededee [fɪd(ə)lɪdɪ'di:] *int Old-fashioned F* bah!, turlututu!

fiddle-faddle ['fɪd(ə)lfæd(ə)l] *Old-fashioned F* **1** *n* bagatelles *fpl*, balivernes *fpl*, fadaises *fpl* **2** *int* = **fiddlededee**

fiddler ['fɪdlər] *n F* **(a)** *Mus* joueur, -euse de violon; *Pej* violoneux *m* **(b)** *Br* (*swindler*) combinard, -arde

fiddlesticks ['fɪd(ə)lstɪks] *int Old-fashioned F* (*nonsense*) balivernes!, quelle blague!; (*annoyance*) zut de zut!

fiddling ['fɪdlɪŋ] **1** *adj* (*insignificant*) futile, insignifiant **2** *n* **(a)** *F, Pej* (*on violin*) raclage *m* **(b)** (*fidgeting*) trifouillage *m*, tripotage *m*; **his f. with the details of my reports** la manière qu'il avait de chipoter *ou* d'ergoter sur les détails de mes rapports **(c)** *Br F* (*dishonest dealing*) combines *fpl*, fricotage *m*; **a lot of f. goes on around here** ça magouille *ou* ça fricote pas mal par ici

fiddly ['fɪdlɪ] *adj* (*work*) délicat, minutieux; (*details*) minutieux; **it was f. getting this nut off** ça a été délicat d'enlever cet écrou

fidelity [fɪ'delɪtɪ] *n* **(a)** (*of person, to person*) fidélité *f* **(b)** (*of translation, sound reproduction*) fidélité *f*; **f. to the original** fidélité à l'original; *Rad etc* **high f.** haute fidélité

fidget[1] ['fɪdʒɪt] *n* **(a)** (*usu pl*) **the fidgets** l'agitation *f* nerveuse; **to have the fidgets** ne pas tenir en place **(b)** (*person*) **he's a f.** il ne tient pas en place; **what a f. you are!** mais tu ne tiens donc pas en place!; **don't be such a f.!** mais tiens-toi donc tranquille!

fidget[2] *vi* (**-t-**) être agité, ne pas tenir en place; (*become excited*) s'énerver; **to f. around with sth** tripoter qch; **don't f.!** (*to child*) tiens-toi tranquille!

fidgetiness ['fɪdʒɪtɪnɪs] *n* agitation *f* nerveuse

fidgety ['fɪdʒɪtɪ] *adj* agité, qui ne tient pas en place; (*excited*) nerveux, impatient

fiduciary [fɪ'dju:ʃərɪ] *Jur, Fin* **1** *adj* fiduciaire **2** *n* héritier *m* fiduciaire; (*trustee*) dépositaire *m*

fief [fi:f] *n Hist Fig* fief *m*

field¹ [fiːld] *n* (a) (*land*) champ *m*; (*under pasture*) pré *m*; (*of oil, gas, coal, diamonds etc*) gisement *m*; **to work in the fields** travailler dans les champs; **to cut across the fields** couper à travers champs; **f. of wheat** champ de blé; **strawberry f.** plantation *f* de fraisiers; **in the open f.** en plein champ; *Av* **landing f.** terrain *m* d'atterrissage

(b) *Mil* **f.** (**of battle**) champ *m* de bataille; **in the f.** en campagne; **to hold the f.** se maintenir sur ses positions; (*of theory etc*) faire autorité; **to take the f.** entrer en campagne; **f. of honour** champ d'honneur; **f. battery** batterie *f* de campagne; **f. exercise** exercice *m* en campagne, manœuvre *f*; **f. gun** canon *m* de campagne; **f. rations** ration *f* de guerre; **f. service** service *m* en campagne; **f. telegraph** télégraphe *m* militaire

(c) *Sp* (*ground*) *Fb, Cr etc* terrain *m*; (*for baseball*) champ *m*; *Cr* (*bowlers*) chasseurs *mpl*

(d) (*in race*), *Horseracing* **the f.** les partants *mpl*; **big f.** champ *m* fourni; **a strong f.** un bel éventail de concurrents; *Fig* **there are three candidates in the f.** trois candidatures ont été déposées; **well ahead of the rest of the f.** loin devant les autres; **to lead the f.** *Sp* mener le peloton; *Fig* (*of theory, ideas etc*) faire autorité; **our company leads the f. when it comes to fitted kitchens** notre entreprise est en tête du marché pour ce qui est des cuisines encastrées; *F* **to play the f.** (*keep options open*) ne pas s'engager; (*in relationships*) (*of man*) courir le jupon; (*of woman*) courir les hommes

(e) (*domain*) (*of operation etc*) théâtre *m*, champ *m*; (*of science*) domaine *m*; **in the political f.** sur le plan politique; **she is the leading artist in her f.** elle est la plus grande artiste dans son domaine; **they were first in the f. with miniaturized TVs** ils ont été les premiers à commercialiser les télévisions miniaturisées; **that's not my f.** ce n'est pas mon domaine; **to work in the f.** (*not in office etc*) travailler sur le terrain; **to test a product in the f.** essayer un produit sur le terrain; **f. agent** agent *m* sur le terrain; **f. engineer** ingénieur *m* de chantier *ou* sur le terrain; **f. experiment** expérience *f* sur le terrain; *Mktg* **f. interviewing** sondage *m* sur le terrain; **f. research** études *fpl* sur le terrain; **f. research executive** responsable *mf* des études sur le terrain; **f. sales manager** directeur *m* des ventes sur le terrain; **f. sales personnel** personnel *m* de vente sur le terrain; **f. study** étude *f* sur le terrain *ou* sur les lieux; **f. trials** (*of vehicle*) essais *mpl* sur le terrain; *Sch etc* **f. trip** voyage *m* d'étude (sur le terrain)

(f) *Opt, Phot etc* champ *m*; **f. of view** *or* **of vision** champ visuel; *Phys* **f. of force** champ de force; **magnetic f.** champ magnétique; **f. coil** bobine *f* d'excitation *ou* d'inducteur, bobine inductrice

(g) *Her* champ *m*, sol *m*; *Art* (*of painting etc*) champ, fond *m*; (*of medal*) champ

(h) *Comptr* (*in database*) champ *m*; **f. delimiter** délimiteur *m* de champ; **f. separator** séparateur *m* de champs; **f. size** taille *f* de champ

field² **1** *vt* (a) *Sp* (*team*) réunir; *Mil etc* **to be able to f. 50,000 men** pouvoir mettre 50 000 hommes en ligne; *Pol* **to f. 500 candidates** présenter 500 candidats (b) *Cr* **to f. a ball** arrêter (et relancer) une balle; **to f. a question** (**well**) bien répondre à une question **2** *vi Cr* tenir le champ

field artillery *n* artillerie *f* de campagne

field day *n Mil* jour *m* de grandes manœuvres *ou* de revue; *esp Am Sp* réunion *f* athlétique; *Fig* **to have a f.** (*enjoy oneself*) s'en donner à cœur joie

fielder [ˈfiːldər] *n Cr etc* chasseur *m*

field events *npl* (*in athletics*) concours *mpl*

field glasses *npl* jumelles *fpl*

field hockey *n Am* hockey *m* sur gazon

field hospital *n* ambulance *f* divisionnaire

field marshal *n* = maréchal *m* (de France)

fieldmouse, *pl* **-mice** [ˈfiːldmaʊs, -maɪs] *n* mulot *m*

field officer *n* officier *m* supérieur

field work *n* (*research etc*) travaux *mpl ou* recherches *fpl* sur le terrain *ou* sur les lieux

field worker *n* travailleur *m* sur le terrain

fiend [fiːnd] *n* (a) (*demon*) démon *m*, diable *m* (b) (*evil person*) monstre *m* (de cruauté) (c) *F* (*fanatic*) **fresh-air f.** maniaque *mf ou* fanatique *mf* du plein air; *Old-fashioned* **dope f.** toxicomane *mf*

fiendish [ˈfiːndɪʃ] *adj* diabolique, satanique; *Fig* diabolique; (*weather*) atroce, abominable; **to take a f. pleasure in sth** prendre un plaisir diabolique à qch

fiendishly [ˈfiːndɪʃlɪ] *adv* diaboliquement; **to laugh f.** avoir un rire diabolique; *F* **f. difficult** d'une difficulté infernale; **f. complicated/expensive** affreusement compliqué/cher; **a f. clever plan/piece of software/virus** un plan/logiciel/virus drôlement malin; *F* **it was f. cold** il faisait un froid de tous les diables

fierce [ˈfɪəs] *adj* (a) (*person*) redoutable; (*animal*) féroce; (*fire etc*) ardent; (*heat*) torride; (*battle, competition, opposition*) acharné; (*critic, opponent*) ardent; (*wind etc*) furieux, violent; **to give sb a f. look** jeter un regard féroce à qn; **f. encounter** rencontre violente; **there was f. criticism of the policy** la politique a suscité des critiques violentes; **she was f. in her defence of him** elle le défendait avec acharnement; **f. fighting** lutte *f* acharnée; *Aut etc* **f. brake** frein *m* brutal (b) *Am F* (*unpleasant*) désagréable; **the weather has been f.** il a fait un temps de chien

fiercely [ˈfɪəslɪ] *adv* (*to lash out, criticize*) violemment; (*to glare*) d'un œil féroce; (*to defend, fight*) avec acharnement; **to be f. opposed to sth** être ardemment opposé à qch; **the sun beat down f.** le soleil frappait très fort

fierceness [ˈfɪəsnɪs] *n* (*of person, opposition, criticism*) violence *f*, véhémence *f*; (*of animal*) férocité *f*; (*of fire etc*) ardeur *f*; (*of battle*) acharnement *m*; (*of wind etc*) fureur *f*; *Aut etc* (*of brakes*) brutalité *f*; **the f. of her tone** son ton véhément

fieriness [ˈfaɪərɪnɪs] *n* (a) (*of sun*) ardeur *f*; **the f. of the seasoning** l'assaisonnement très relevé *ou* épicé (b) (*of character*) ardeur *f*, fougue *f*, impétuosité *f*, emportement *m*

fiery [ˈfaɪərɪ] *adj* (a) brûlant, enflammé; (*alcoholic drink*) extrêmement fort, brûlant; **f. coal(s)** charbons *mpl* ardents; **f. furnace** fournaise *f* ardente; **f. red** rouge *m* ardent, rouge feu; **f. sky** ciel *m* embrasé; **f. taste** saveur *f* très épicée, goût *m* piquant (b) (*person, character*) fougueux, emporté, impétueux; **f. temper** tempérament *m* fougueux *ou* emporté; **to make f. speeches against sb** vomir feu et flamme contre qn

fiery cross *n esp US* = symbole *m* du Ku Klux Klan

FIFA [ˈfiːfə] *n* (*abbr* **International Association Football Federation**) Fédération *f* Internationale de Football Association

fife [faɪf] *n Mus* fifre *m*

FIFO [ˈfiːfəʊ] *Com* (*abbr* **first in, first out**) PEPS

fifteen [fɪfˈtiːn, ˈfɪftiːn] *n* (a) quinze *m*; **she is f.** (**years old**) elle a quinze ans; **the plane will land at f. thirty** (**hours**) l'avion va atterrir à quinze heures trente (b) *Rugby* **the French f.** le quinze de France

fifteenth [fɪfˈtiːnθ, ˈfɪftiːnθ] **1** *adj* quinzième; **Louis the F.** Louis Quinze; (**on**) **the f.** (**of the month**) le quinze du mois **2** *n* (a) (*person, thing*) quinzième *mf* (b) (*fraction*) quinzième *m*

fifth [fɪfθ] **1** *adj* cinquième; **Henry the F.** Henri Cinq; *US Jur, Hum* **to plead the F. Amendment, to take the F.** (**Amendment**) = refuser de répondre pour ne pas dire quelque chose pouvant être utilisé contre soi; *Aut* **f. wheel** (*trailer coupling*) sellette *f*; (*on test car*) cinquième roue *f*; *Am* **to feel like a f. wheel** avoir l'impression d'être la cinquième roue du carrosse; *Br Sch* **f. form** = classe *f* de seconde **2** *n* (a) (*of month*) cinq *m*; **on the f.** le cinq (b) (*person, thing*) cinquième *mf* (c) (*fraction*) cinquième *m* (d) *Mus* quinte *f*

fifth column *n Pol* cinquième colonne *f*

fifth columnist *n* = espion, -onne qui sert l'ennemi d'une ville assiégée

fifth-generation *adj Comptr* de la cinquième génération

fifthly [ˈfɪfθlɪ] *adv* cinquièmement

fifth-rate *adj F* médiocre

fiftieth [ˈfɪftɪəθ] **1** *adj* cinquantième **2** *n* (a) (*person, thing*) cinquantième *mf* (b) (*fraction*) cinquantième *m*

fifty [ˈfɪftɪ] *adj, n* cinquante *m*; **f. -one** cinquante et un; **f. -two** cinquante-deux; **about f. books** une cinquantaine de livres; **the fifties** les années cinquante; **to be f.** avoir cinquante ans; **to be in one's fifties** avoir entre cinquante et soixante ans; **to be over f.** avoir cinquante ans passés, avoir plus de cinquante ans

fifty-fifty *adj, adv* (*partnership*) à parts égales; **to split the profits f.** partager les bénéfices à parts égales; **to go f. on sth** partager le coût de quelque chose à parts égales; **her chances are f.** (*of surviving*) elle a cinquante pour cent de chances de s'en tirer; (*of winning*) elle a cinquante pour cent de chances de gagner

fig¹ [fɪg] *n* (a) (*fruit*) figue *f*; **fresh** *or* **green figs** figues fraîches; **dried figs** figues sèches; *Old-fashioned F* **he doesn't give** *or* **care a f. what you think** il se fiche éperdument de ce que tu penses; **f. leaf** feuille *f* de figuier; *Art* feuille de vigne; *Fig* **it's just a f. leaf** ce n'est qu'une couverture (b) **f.** (**tree**) figuier *m*

fig² (*abbr* **figure**) (*in book etc*) fig; **see f. 21b** voir fig 21b

fight¹ [faɪt] *n Boxing, Mil etc* combat *m*; (*brawl*) bagarre *f*; (*argument*) dispute *f*; **f. to the death** lutte *f* à mort; **they had a f.** (*in which they hit each other*) ils se sont battus; (*they argued*) ils se sont disputés; **to get into a f. with sb** se battre avec qn; (*argue*) se disputer avec qn; **I don't want us to get into a f. over this, but ...** je ne veux pas que nous nous disputions pour ça, mais ...; **do you want a f.?** tu veux te battre?; **a fair f.** un combat loyal; **the f. for life** la lutte pour la vie; **her f. against cancer** sa lutte contre le cancer; **to carry on a stubborn f. against s. b.** soutenir une lutte opiniâtre contre qn; **to show some f.** résister, offrir de la résistance; **I won't give in without a f.** je ne vais pas me laisser faire sans me battre; *Sp* **to put up a good f.** bien se défendre; **there was no f. left in him** il n'avait plus le cœur à se battre; **he still has a lot of f. left in him** il n'a pas dit son dernier mot; **you'll have a f. on your hands** (*it will be difficult*) tu vas avoir du mal; **the f. for the leadership of the party** la lutte pour la tête du parti

fight² (*pt, pp* **fought** [fɔːt]) **1** *vi* (*physically*) se battre; (*struggle*) lutter; (*argue*) se disputer; *Mil* **he fought in Russia** il s'est battu en Russie; **to f. against the enemy** combattre l'ennemi; **to f. against adversity/disease** lutter contre l'adversité/la maladie; **to f. against sleep** lutter contre le sommeil; **to f. for s. b.** se battre pour qn; **to f. for sth** (*on behalf of*) se battre pour qch; (*to get something*) se battre pour obtenir qch; **to f. for breath** lutter pour respirer; **to f. for one's rights/freedom** se battre *ou* lutter pour ses droits/sa liberté; **she fought to clear her name** elle s'est battue pour prouver son innocence; **to f. on two fronts** se battre sur deux fronts; **two dogs fighting over a bone** deux chiens qui se disputent un os; **to f. fair** se battre loyalement; **they were fighting over some islands/who would sleep where** ils se battaient pour des îles/pour décider qui allait dormir où; **to be fighting for one's life** (*of someone seriously ill, competitor*) lutter pour sa vie; **to f. to the finish** se battre jusqu'au dernier moment; **to go down fighting** se battre jusqu'au bout

2 *vt* (*person*) se battre avec *ou* contre; (*enemy, fire, new measure, decision*) combattre; (*illness, temptation*) lutter contre; (*match*) disputer; *Boxing* **to f. the champion** affronter le champion; **I'll f. you in the courts** je vous traînerai en justice; **I'll f. you for custody** je me battrai contre toi pour obtenir la garde des enfants; **to f. a battle** livrer (une) bataille; **to f. a duel** se battre en duel; *Fig* **to f. a losing battle** livrer *ou* mener une bataille perdue d'avance; **to f. a losing battle to do sth** tenter vainement de faire qch; *Rel etc* **to f. the good fight** combattre pour la bonne cause; *Fig* **to f. sb's battles** prendre le parti de qn; **I'm not going to f. your battles for you** c'est à vous de vous débrouiller; **he fought his way through the crowd** il se fraya un chemin à travers la foule; **to f. one's way out** se frayer un passage pour sortir; **to f. one's way to the top** (*of one's profession*) se battre pour atteindre le sommet; **to f. an action (at law)** se défendre dans un procès; **to f. an election** se présenter à une élection; **she will be fighting a popular businessman** (*in election*) elle sera opposée à un homme d'affaires populaire; **to f. an emotion** lutter contre une émotion; **f. it!** résiste!

▶ **fight back 1** *vtsep* **(a)** (*suppress*) (*emotion etc*) lutter contre; (*tears*) refouler **(b) to f. one's way back again** remonter le courant **2** *vi* (*retaliate*) riposter, résister; **to f. back against an illness** lutter contre une maladie

▶ **fight down** *vtsep* (*suppress*) (*passion, resistance etc*) vaincre; (*impulse, urge*) réprimer

▶ **fight off** *vtsep* (*repel*) (*enemy, attack, sb's advances etc*) repousser; (*illness etc*) combattre; (*inflation*) juguler; **to f. off one's fear** lutter contre *ou* combattre sa peur

▶ **fight out** *vtas* **to f. it out** se mesurer l'un à l'autre; **you'll have to f. that out with him** tu régleras ça avec lui

fighter [ˈfaɪtər] *n* **(a)** (*person who fights*) combattant *m*; (*boxer*) boxeur *m*; *Fig* **she's a f.** c'est une battante **(b)** *Mil, Av* **f. (aircraft** *or* **plane)** chasseur *m*, avion *m* de chasse; **f. squadron/pilot** escadron *m*/pilote *m* de chasse

fighter-bomber *n* chasseur-bombardier *m*, *pl* chasseurs-bombardiers

fighter model *n Mktg* modèle *m* d'attaque

fight game *n* boxe *f*

fighting [ˈfaɪtɪŋ] **1** *adj Mil* **f. men** combattants *mpl*; **f. forces** effectifs *mpl* sous les armes; **f. unit/strength** unité *f*/effectif *m* de combat; **f. cock** coq *m* de combat; **that's f. talk!** tu cherches la bagarre?/il cherche la bagarre!/*etc*; *F* **I still have a f. chance** j'ai encore de bonnes chances; **to be f. fit** être dans une forme éblouissante; **to get f. drunk** se saouler et chercher la bagarre **2** *n Mil* combat *m*; *Boxing* boxe *f*; **there was a lot of f. at my school** il y avait beaucoup de bagarre dans mon école; **the f. on the eastern front** les combats sur le front est

figment [ˈfɪgmənt] *n* **a f. of the imagination** un phénomène imaginaire; **it's a f. of your imagination** tu te fais des idées, c'est le fruit de ton imagination; **is this a f. of my imagination or ...?** est-ce que je me fais des idées, ou bien ...?

figurative [ˈfɪgərətɪv] *adj* **(a)** (*language etc*) figuré, métaphorique; **in the f. sense** au (sens) figuré **(b)** (*art*) figuratif; **f. writing** écriture *f* en images

figuratively [ˈfɪgərətɪvlɪ] *adv* **(a)** (*to speak, write*) au figuré, métaphoriquement; **f. speaking, ...** métaphoriquement parlant, ... **(b)** *Art* figurativement

figure¹ [ˈfɪgər, *Am* ˈfɪgjər] *n* **(a)** (*number*) chiffre *m*; **it's difficult to give an exact f.** il est difficile de donner un chiffre exact; **figures** (*for project etc*) détails *mpl* chiffrés; (*involving calculation*) calculs *mpl*; (*statistics*) statistiques *fpl*; **there must be a mistake in the figures** il doit y avoir une erreur dans les calculs; **the figures for 1975** les statistiques de 1975; *Com* **sales figures** chiffres *mpl* de vente; **unemployment figures** le taux de chômage; **in round figures** en chiffres ronds; **to put a f. on sth** (*assess price, cost*) évaluer le prix/coût de qch; (*assess quantity*) évaluer le nombre de qch; **to be good at figures** être bon en calcul; **to fetch a high f.** se vendre cher; **his score barely managed to get into double figures** son score s'élevait tout juste à un nombre à deux chiffres; **our takings have reached four figures** nous avons décroché les quatre chiffres; **to get inflation down to single figures** réduire l'inflation à un taux inférieur à dix pour cent

(b) (*shape*) figure *f*; (*of person*) silhouette *f*; **to have a good f.** être bien fait de sa personne; (*of woman*) avoir une jolie silhouette; **to look after/keep one's f.** soigner/garder sa ligne; **to be f. -conscious** faire attention à sa ligne

(c) (*human form*) forme *f* humaine; **a fine f. of a man** un bel homme; **a fine f. of a woman** une belle femme; *Art* **reclining f.** corps *m* au repos

(d) (*person, character*) personnage *m*; **a distinguished f.** une personnalité; **a f. of fun** un objet de ridicule; **a hate f., a f. of hate** un objet de haine; **the central f. of a painting** le personnage principal d'un tableau

(e) (*appearance*) apparence *f*, air *m*; **to cut a sorry f.** faire piètre figure; **to cut an elegant f.** être élégant de sa personne; **to cut a pathetic f.** avoir l'air lamentable

(f) (*illustration*) illustration *f*; **see f. 21b** (*in book*) voir figure 21b; **geometrical f.** figure *f* géométrique

(g) (*pattern*) figure *f*; (*on material*) dessin *m*; **the figures of a dance** les figures d'une danse

figure² **1** *vi* **(a)** (*appear*) figurer; **his name figures on the list** son nom figure sur la liste

(b) (*calculate*) calculer

(c) *esp Am F* (*make sense*) sembler logique *ou* normal; **that doesn't f.** ce n'est pas logique, ça n'a pas de sens; **that figures** ça colle

2 *vt* **(a)** *esp Am* (*think*) **I figured that she might be feeling lonely** je me suis dit qu'elle se sentait peut-être seule

(b) *esp Am* (*estimate*) **I f. that it will take three years** j'estime que cela prendra trois ans

(c) (*put pattern on*) (*silk etc*) brocher, gaufrer; (*cotton etc*) imprimer

(d) (*bass*) chiffrer

(e) *esp Lit* (*imagine*) (*person, landscape etc*) figurer, représenter; **f. to yourself a happy family** imaginez une famille heureuse

▶ **figure on** *vipo esp Am F* s'attendre à; (*plan on*) compter sur; **to f. on doing sth** avoir l'intention de *ou* compter faire qch; **I didn't f. on this happening** je ne m'attendais pas à ce que cela se produise; **he didn't f. on a woman for the position** (*did not consider hiring one*) il ne pensait pas à une femme pour le poste; (*did not think one would get it*) il ne s'attendait pas à ce qu'une femme obtienne le poste

▶ **figure out** *F* **1** *vtsep* (*work out*) (*amount*) calculer; (*problem*) résoudre; **he couldn't f. out what she meant** il n'arrivait pas à comprendre ce qu'elle voulait dire; **we couldn't f. out what to do next** nous n'arrivions pas à décider ce que nous devions faire; **we couldn't f. out where we were** nous n'arrivions pas à découvrir où nous étions; **we figured out that they must have paid more than we did** nous avons réalisé qu'ils avaient dû payer plus que nous; **she can't f. you out at all** elle n'arrive pas du tout à te comprendre

2 *vi Am* **it will f. out at about $100** cela coûtera une centaine de dollars

▶ **figure up** *vi Am* (*amount*) **to f. up to sth** s'élever à qch

-figure [ˈfɪgər] *suff* **three/four/***etc***-f.** à trois/quatre/*etc* chiffres; **four-f. number** nombre *m* à quatre chiffres

figured [ˈfɪgəd] *adj* **(a)** (*material, velvet etc*) façonné; (*silk etc*) broché **(b)** *Mus* (*counterpoint*) figuré; (*bass*) chiffré

figurehead [ˈfɪgəhed] *n* (*on ship*) figure *f* de proue; *Fig, Pej* (*man*) homme *m* de paille; **she's just a f.** elle n'agit qu'en prête-nom

figure-hugging *adj* moulant
figure of eight *n* (*shape*) (figure *f* en forme de) huit *m*; *Sp* **to cut figures of eight** (*in skating etc*) faire des huits; **to draw figures of eight** décrire des huits
figure of speech *n* (*expression*) façon *f* de parler; (*in rhetoric*) figure *f* de rhétorique; **it's just a f.** ce n'est qu'une façon de parler
figure skater *n Sp* patineur, -euse artistique
figure skating *n Sp* patinage *m* artistique
figurine ['fɪgəriːn] *n Art etc* figurine *f*
Fiji ['fiːdʒiː] *n* **F., the F. Islands** les îles *fpl* Fidji
Fijian [fiː'dʒiːən] **1** *adj* fidjien **2** *n* Fidjien, -ienne
filament ['fɪləmənt] *n* **(a)** *El* filament *m*; **f. lamp** lampe *f* à incandescence **(b)** *Biol* filament *m*, filet *m*
filbert ['fɪlbət] *n* aveline *f*; (*hazelnut*) grosse noisette *f*
filch [fɪltʃ] *vt F* faucher, piquer (**sth from sb** qch à qn)
file[1] [faɪl] *n* (*tool*) lime *f*; **nail f.** lime à ongles
file[2] *vt* (*metal etc*) limer; **to f. one's nails** se limer les ongles
file[3] *n* **(a)** (*folder*) classeur *m*; (*documents*) dossier *m*; **the f. on James Brown, the James Brown f.** le dossier James Brown; **to keep a f. on sb/sth** constituer un dossier sur qn/qch; **have we got anything on f. about it?** y a-t-il quelque chose là-dessus dans les dossiers?; **files** archives *fpl*; **we have placed your report on our files** nous avons classé votre rapport dans nos dossiers; **card-index f.** fichier *m*; **card f.** fichier sur cartes; **f. divider** (*in filing cabinet*) carte-guide *f*, *pl* cartes-guides, guide-classement *m*, *pl* guide-classements; **f. separator** (*in filing cabinet*) carte-guide; **f. trolley** bac *m* roulant
(b) *Comptr* fichier *m*; **f. allocation table** table *f* des fichiers; **f. compression** compression *f* de fichiers; **f. conversion** conversion *f* de fichier(s); **f. extension** extension *f* de fichier; **f. sharing** partage *m* de fichier(s)
file[4] **1** *vt* **(a)** (*classify*) (*documents, letters etc*) classer; **it was filed under 'jazz'** c'était classé dans la catégorie 'jazz'; **the books are filed according to author** les livres sont classés par auteur
(b) to f. a petition (*of court official*) déposer une requête; (*of plaintiff*) enregister une requête; **to f. one's petition (in bankruptcy)** déposer son bilan; **to f. a claim for damages** intenter une action en dommages-intérêts; **to f. an insurance claim** faire une déclaration de sinistre; **to f. a story** (*of journalist*) boucler un sujet; **to f. copy** (*of journalist*) rapporter une copie
(c) *esp US Admin* (*document, complaint*) déposer (**with sb** auprès de qn)
2 *vi* **to f. for divorce** faire une demande de divorce
file[5] *n* (*line*) file *f*; **in single** *or* **Indian f.** en file indienne; **to walk in single f.** marcher à la file *ou* en file indienne; *Mil* **in f.** (en rang) par deux
file[6] *vi Mil etc* (*walk in line*) marcher à la file *ou* en ligne de file; **to f. off** défiler; **to f. past** défiler; **to f. past sb/sth** défiler devant qn/qch; **to f. in/out** entrer/sortir un à un
▶ **file away** *vtsep* **(a)** (*documents etc*) classer, archiver; *Fig* (*mentally*) enregistrer **(b)** = **file down (a)**
▶ **file down** *vtsep* **(a)** (*remove by filing*) (*rough edge etc*) enlever à la lime, limer **(b)** (*smooth by filing*) (*surface*) polir à la lime, limer; (*of blacksmith etc*) (*horseshoe*) raboter
▶ **file off** *vtsep* = **file down (a)**
file cabinet *n Am* armoire *f* de classement
file card *n* fiche *f* (de classeur)
file clerk *n esp Am* employé, -ée préposé(e) au classement
file-compatible *adj Comptr* compatible du point de vue des fichiers
file copy *n* exemplaire *m* d'archives
file management *n Comptr* gestion *f ou* tenue *f* de fichiers; **f. system** système *m* de gestion de fichiers
file manager *n Comptr* gestionnaire *m* de fichiers
filename ['faɪlneɪm] *n Comptr* nom *m* de fichier
file number *n* (*of document in file*) cote *f*
filer ['faɪlər] *n Comptr* classeur *m*, gestionnaire *m* de fichiers et de répertoires
file server *n Comptr* serveur *m* de fichiers
filial ['fɪlɪəl] *adj Fml* filial
filibuster[1] ['fɪlɪbʌstər] *n* **(a)** *esp US Pol* obstruction *f*; **a six hour f.** un discours obstructionniste de six heures **(b)** *Hist* (*pirate*) flibustier *m*
filibuster[2] *vi esp US Pol* faire de l'obstruction; **filibustering tactics** manœuvres *fpl ou* tactiques *fpl* obstructionnistes
filigree ['fɪlɪgriː] *n* filigrane *m*; **f. work** (travail *m* en) filigrane
filing[1] ['faɪlɪŋ] *n* **(a)** (*of metal etc*) limage *m* **(b)** (*small pieces of metal etc*) (*usu pl*) **filings** limaille *f*
filing[2] *n* **(a)** (*of documents, letters etc*) classement *m*; (*for long-term storage*) archivage *m*; **f. by subject** classement *m* idéologique **(b)** *Jur* (*of petition*) (*by court official*) enregistrement *m*; (*of claim*) (*by plaintiff*) dépôt *m*
filing cabinet *n* armoire *f* de classement
filing clerk *n Br* employé, -ée préposé(e) au classement
filing system *n* méthode *f* de classement
filing tray *n* corbeille *f* pour correspondance à classer
Filipino [fɪlɪ'piːnəʊ] **1** *adj* philippin **2** *n* Philippin, -ine
fill[1] [fɪl] *n* **(a) to have had one's f. of sth** en avoir assez de qch; **to eat one's f.** manger à sa faim; **the horse ate its f. of straw** le cheval s'est rassasié de paille **(b)** *Tech* matériau *m* de remplissage; *Constr* remblai *m*; **a f. of tobacco** une pipée de tabac
fill[2] **1** *vt* **(a)** (*jug etc*) remplir, emplir (**with** de); (*pipe*) bourrer; (*cart etc*) charger; **to f. sb's glass** servir à boire à qn; (*to the brim*) verser une rasade à qn; **to f. the air with one's cries** remplir l'air de ses cris; **a smell of cooking filled the house** une odeur de cuisine envahissait la maison; **to f. one's head with useless things** se farcir la tête de choses inutiles; **to be filled with admiration** être rempli d'admiration; **the thought filled him with jealousy** cette pensée le remplissait de jalousie; **to be filled with hope** être plein d'espoir; **to be filled with fear/envy** être dévoré de peur/d'envie
(b) (*plug*) (*opening, gap etc*) combler, boucher; (*tooth*) plomber; (*of employer*) (*vacancy*) pourvoir à; **to f. the woodwork** (*before painting*) mastiquer les boiseries; **I'm having two teeth filled tomorrow** on va me faire deux plombages demain; **two places remain to be filled** deux postes restent à pourvoir; **the position has already been filled** le poste a déjà été pourvu
(c) (*occupy*) (*time*) occuper; **a position she has filled for some time** un poste qu'elle occupe depuis quelque temps; **to f. sb's shoes** (*take on sb's responsibilities*) prendre les fonctions de qn; **it's going to be difficult to f. his shoes** ça va être difficile de trouver quelqu'un pour le remplacer; **the thoughts that filled his mind** les pensées qui occupaient son esprit; **reading fills my evenings** la lecture remplit mes soirées
(d) (*fulfil*) (*order, prescription*) exécuter; *esp Am* **to f. every requirement** répondre à tous les besoins
(e) (*pour*) verser
2 *vi* **(a)** (*of tank, bath, container, hall etc*) se remplir; (*of hole*) se combler; **her eyes filled with tears** ses yeux se sont remplis de larmes
(b) (*of sails*) se gonfler
▶ **fill in** **1** *vtsep* **(a)** (*make level*) (*hole*) combler, boucher; (*ditch*) remblayer; (*block off*) (*door*) condamner
(b) (*complete*) (*form*) remplir; **to f. in a gap in one's knowledge** combler un vide *ou* une lacune dans ses connaissances; **to f. in the blanks** remplir les blancs
(c) (*insert*) (*date etc*) insérer
(d) *F* **to f. sb in on the details** mettre qn au courant des détails; **she quickly filled us in on what had been happening** elle nous a rapidement mis au courant de ce qui s'était passé
(e) (*use up*) **to f. in time** occuper son temps
2 *vi* **to f. in for sb** remplacer qn; **I'm filling in while she's on holiday** je la remplace pendant ses vacances
▶ **fill out** **1** *vtsep* **(a)** (*pad out*) (*speech etc*) étoffer **(b)** (*complete*) (*form*) remplir **2** *vi* (*of sails*) se gonfler; (*of person*) s'étoffer; (*of adolescent female*) prendre des formes; **her cheeks are filling out** ses joues se remplissent, elle prend des joues
▶ **fill up** **1** *vtsep* **(a)** (*with liquid*) (*glass*) remplir jusqu'au bord; *Aut F* **f. her up** (faites) le plein **(b)** (*plug*) (*hole with putty etc*) boucher **(c)** (*complete*) (*form*) remplir **2** *vi* **(a)** (*become full*) (*of tank, container etc*) se remplir (**with** de); (*of hole*) se combler, se remplir **(b)** (*fill tank etc*) **to f. up with petrol/water** faire le plein d'essence/d'eau
filler ['fɪlər] *n* **(a)** (*person*) remplisseur, -euse; (*machine*) remplisseuse *f*; **oil f.** entonnoir *m*; *Aut* **f. cap** bouchon *m* de remplissage **(b)** (*substance*) (matière *f* de) remplissage *m*; (*of cigar*) tripe *f*; (*for wood etc*) bouche-pores *m inv*; (*before painting*) mastic *m*; *Fig* (*between main acts etc*) bouche-trou *m*, *pl* bouche-trous; (*in media*) bouche-trou, passe-partout *m inv*; *TV* **f. light** éclairage *m* d'appoint; *TV* **f. mike** micro *m* d'appoint; **f. paste** mastic *m* de bouchage **(c) f. (word)** mot *m* de remplissage
fillet[1] ['fɪlɪt] *n* **(a)** *Culin* (*of beef, sole*) filet *m*; (*of veal*) rouelle *f*; **f. steak** filet de bœuf **(b)** (*for hair*) ruban *m*
fillet[2] *vt* (**-t-**) *Culin* (*fish*) détacher les filets de; **filleted sole** filets *mpl* de sole
filling ['fɪlɪŋ] **1** *adj* (*food*) nourrissant **2** *n* **(a)** (*of hole*) comblement *m*; (*of tooth*) plombage *m* **(b)** (*substance*) (matière *f* de) remplissage *m*; (*in dentistry*) plombage *m*; *Carp* mastic *m*; *Constr* remplissage; (*rubble*) blocage *m*; (*liquid*) coulis *m*; *Culin* (*for pie, sandwich*) garniture *f*; **cake with a chocolate f.** gâteau fourré au chocolat

filling station *n* station-service *f*, *pl* stations-service; (*small*) poste *m* d'essence

fillip ['fɪlɪp] *n* (*stimulus*) stimulant *m*, encouragement *m*; **to give a f. to business** stimuler *ou* doper les affaires

fill-up *n Aut* plein *m*; **do you want a f.?** (*more to drink*) je te remplis ton verre?

filly ['fɪlɪ] *n* **(a)** (*horse*) pouliche *f* **(b)** *Old-fashioned F* (*girl*) jeune fille *f*

film¹ [fɪlm] *n* **(a)** *Cin* film *m*; (*celluloid strip*) bande *f*; **full-length/short f.** long/court métrage *m*; **news f.** actualités *fpl*; **to shoot** *or* **make a f.** tourner un film; **the films** (*cinema*) le cinéma; **to be in films** faire du cinéma; **f. actor/actress** acteur/actrice de cinéma; **f. archives** cinémathèque *f*; **f. camera** caméra *f*; **f. editor** monteur *m*; **the f. industry** l'industrie *f* cinématographique *ou* du cinéma; **f. releasing company** éditeur *m* de film; **f. scanner** lecteur *m* de télécinéma, analyseur *m* de film

(b) *Phot* pellicule *f*, film *m*; **I've run out of f.** ma pellicule est finie; **a roll of f.** un rouleau de pellicule, une pellicule; **colour f.** pellicule *ou* film couleur(s); **f. cassette** cartouche *f* de pellicule *ou* de film; **f. laboratory** laboratoire *m* de film, labo *m*; **f. reel** bobine *f* de film

(c) (*layer*) (*of ice, oil*) pellicule *f*, couche *f*; (*of plastic*) film *m*; (*of mist, smoke etc*) voile *m*; *Med* (*over eye*) taie *f*; **wrapped in plastic f.** emballé dans un film en plastique

film² **1** *vt Cin* (*scene*) filmer, tourner; (*novel*) porter à l'écran; (*person, interview etc*) filmer **2** *vi* **(a)** *Cin, TV* filmer; **we start filming next week** on commence à tourner la semaine prochaine **(b)** = **film over**

▶ **film over** *vi* se couvrir d'une pellicule; *Med* (*of eyes*) se couvrir d'une taie

film clip *n* séquence *f ou* extrait *m* de film

film club *n* ciné-club *m*

film critic *n* critique *m* de cinéma

film director *n* réalisateur *m*, metteur *m* en scène

film festival *n* festival *m* cinématographique *ou* du cinéma

filmic ['fɪlmɪk] *adj* filmique

filming ['fɪlmɪŋ] *n Cin* tournage *m*; **to get permission for f.** obtenir l'autorisation de tourner

filmless camera ['fɪlmlɪs] *n* caméra *f* sans film

film library *n* cinémathèque *f*

film maker *n* réalisateur *m* de films, cinéaste *mf*

film-making *n* production *f* cinématographique

film producer *n* producteur *m* de cinéma

film rights *npl* droits *mpl* film

film script *n* scénario *m*, script *m*

film set *n* plateau *m* de cinéma

film setter *n* photocomposeuse *f*

film star *n* vedette *f* de cinéma

film strip *n* (*stills*) film *m* fixe; (*short piece of film*) extrait *m* de film

film studio *n* studio *m* de cinéma

film test *n* bout *m* d'essai

filmy ['fɪlmɪ] *adj* (*eye*) couvert d'une taie; (*lace, cloud etc*) léger, diaphane

Filofax® ['faɪləʊfæks] *n* organiseur *m*

filter¹ ['fɪltər] *n* **(a)** filtre *m*; (*for oil etc*) épurateur *m*; (*cigarette*) cigarette *f* à filtre; *Br* **a packet of Regal® f.** un paquet de Regal filtres; **coffee f.** filtre à café; *HydE* **f. bed** bassin *m* de filtration; **f. coffee** (*as opposed to espresso etc*) café-filtre *m*, *pl* cafés-filtre; *Aut* **f. element** cartouche *f* filtrante; **f. paper** papier *m* filtre; **f. tip** bout *m* filtre **(b)** *Opt, Phot* **colour f.** filtre *m* de couleur, écran *m* filtre **(c)** *El, Electron etc* **frequency f.** filtre *m* de fréquences; **f. circuit** circuit *m* de filtrage **(d)** *Br Aut* **f. (signal)** (*on traffic light*) flèche *f* de dégagement

filter² **1** *vt* (*water etc*) filtrer; (*air etc*) épurer **2** *vi* **(a)** (*of water etc*) filtrer (**through** à travers); (*seep*) suinter **(b)** *Br Aut etc* changer de file; **to f. to the right/left** prendre la voie de dégagement vers la droite/la gauche **(c)** *F* **to f. into a building** entrer par petits groupes dans un immeuble

▶ **filter down** *vi* filtrer; **the information finally filtered down to them** les informations ont fini par filtrer jusqu'à eux

▶ **filter out** **1** *vtsep* (*remove with filter*) (*impurities*) séparer par filtrage; *Fig* (*in selection procedure etc*) éliminer; **f. out the solids** retenir les solides par filtrage **2** *vi* (*leave slowly*) quitter lentement; **information is beginning to f. out that ...** des informations commencent à filtrer selon lesquelles ...; **to f. out of a building** sortir par petits groupes d'un édifice

▶ **filter through** **1** *vi* (*pass slowly*) passer lentement; **the news soon filtered through** les nouvelles n'ont pas tardé à filtrer **2** *vipo* **the light filtered through the branches** la lumière filtrait à travers les branches

filterable ['fɪltərəb(ə)l] *adj Med* (*virus*) filtrant

filtering ['fɪltərɪŋ] *n* filtrage *m*, filtration *f*

filter lane *n* voie *f* de dégagement

filth [fɪlθ] *n* **(a)** (*dirt*) immondices *mpl*; (*excreta*) ordure *f*; **to live in f.** vivre dans la saleté **(b)** (*obscenity*) **to talk f.** dire des obscénités; **what are you reading that f. for?** pourquoi est-ce que tu lis ces cochonneries?; **this isn't art, it's f.!** ce n'est pas de l'art, c'est de la pornographie!

filthy ['fɪlθɪ] **1** *adj* **(a)** (*very dirty*) (très) sale; **your hands are f.!** tes mains sont dégoûtantes!; **to get f.** (*of person*) se salir; (*of part of machine*) s'encrasser; **my hands got f.** je me suis sali les mains; **my jacket got f.** j'ai sali ma veste

(b) *F* **he gave me a f. look** il m'a jeté un sale regard, il m'a regardé d'un sale œil; *F* **in a f. temper** d'une humeur massacrante; *esp Br F* **f. weather** temps *m* de chien

(c) (*obscene*) (*language, talk etc*) ordurier, obscène; (*suggestion*) obscène, dégoûtant; (*person*) dégoûtant; **you've got a f. mind!** tu as l'esprit mal tourné!; **you f. beast!** espèce de gros dégoûtant!

2 *adv F* **f. dirty** dégoûtant; **f. rich** pourri de fric; **the f. rich** les gros richards *mpl*

filtration [fɪl'treɪʃən] *n* filtration *f*, filtrage *m*

fin [fɪn] *n* **(a)** (*of fish, whale etc*) nageoire *f*; (*of shark*) aileron *m*; **fins** (*for swimmer, diver*) palmes *fpl* **(b)** (*of boat*) dérive *f*; (*of plane*) empennage *m*; (*of bomb etc*) ailette *f*; *Aut etc* (*of radiator etc*) ailette; **cooling fins** ailettes de refroidissement; **stabilizer f.** aileron stabilisateur

finagle [fɪ'neɪg(ə)l] *vt F* = **wangle**

final ['faɪn(ə)l] **1** *adj* **(a)** (*last*) final, -als, dernier; **f. details/preparations** derniers détails/préparatifs; **to make a f. effort** faire un dernier effort; **to put the f. touches to sth** mettre la dernière main à qch; *Com* **f. acceptance** réception *f* définitive; *Com, Fin* **f. date (for payment)** date *f* limite; **f. demand** (*for payment*) dernier avis *m*, dernier rappel *m*; *St Exch* **f. dividend** dividende *m* définitif; **f. edition** (*of newspaper*) dernière édition *f*; *Com* **f. hand-over** réception *f* définitive; **f. instalment** dernier versement, versement de libération; **f. offer** dernière proposition *f*; *Fin* **f. settlement** solde *m* de tout compte; **f. warning** dernier avertissement

(b) (*definitive*) définitif; *Jur* **f. judgment** jugement *m* définitif *ou* sans appel; **f. text** texte définitif; **the umpire's decision is f.** la décision de l'arbitre est sans appel; **take this as f.** tenez-le-vous pour dit

(c) *Gram, Phil* (*clause, cause*) final

2 *n* **(a)** *Sp* **the f.** *or* **finals** la finale; **to be through to the final(s)** être en finale; *Fb* **cup f.** finale de coupe

(b) *Univ* **to sit** *or* **take one's finals** = passer son dernier examen de licence

finale [fɪ'nɑːlɪ] *n Mus* finale *m*; *Th etc* conclusion *f*; **grand f.** apothéose *f*; **there was a grand f. to the match** le match s'est terminé en apothéose

finalist ['faɪnəlɪst] *n* finaliste *mf*

finality [faɪ'nælɪtɪ] *n* **(a)** (*of decision*) caractère *m* définitif, irrévocabilité *f*; **to say sth with f.** dire qch d'un ton irrévocable *ou* sans appel **(b)** *Phil* finalité *f*

finalization [faɪnəlaɪ'zeɪʃən] *n* (*of details, plans etc*) mise *f* au point

finalize ['faɪnəlaɪz] *vt* (*details, plans etc*) mettre au point; (*deal, arrangement*) conclure; **details of the visit have yet to be finalized** les détails de la visite restent à préciser

finally ['faɪn(ə)lɪ] *adv* **(a)** (*lastly*) à la fin, en dernier; **and f., I would like to thank Mr Smith** et enfin *ou* et pour finir, j'aimerais remercier M Smith **(b)** (*at last*) finalement, enfin **(c)** (*irrevocably*) définitivement

finance¹ [faɪ'næns, fɪ-] *n* **(a)** finance *f*; (*funding*) finances *fpl*; **high f.** la haute finance; **f. company** société *f* de crédits, société *f* financière; **f. (department)** service *m* financier; **f. director** directeur *m* financier **(b)** (*funds*) fonds *mpl*; **his finances are low** ses fonds sont bas; **what state are your finances in?** comment vont tes finances?; **it's a problem of f.** c'est un problème financier; **where are they going to get the f. from?** où vont-ils trouver les fonds nécessaires?

finance² *vt* (*project*) financer; (*person, company etc*) financer, commanditer; *Acct* **financed from cashflow** autofinancé

financial [faɪ'nænʃəl, fɪ-] *adj* (*difficulty, planning, scandal etc*) financier; *Rad, TV* **f. news** chronique *f* financière; **f. correspondent** correspondant, -ante sur les questions financières; **f. accounting** comptabilité *f* générale; **f. centre** place *f* financière; **f. circles** sphères *fpl* de la finance; **f. controller** contrôleur *m* financier; *Acct* **f. costs** frais *mpl* financiers; **f. department** service *m* financier; **f. director** directeur *m* financier; **f. engineering** ingénierie *f* financière; *St Exch* **f. future** instrument *m* financier à terme; **f. healthcheck** diagnostic *m* financier; **f. institution**

établissement *m* financier; **f. management** direction *f ou* gestion *f* financière; **f. management accounting** comptabilité-gestion *f* financière; **f. manager** directeur *m* financier; **f. market** marché *m* financier; **f. marketplace** marché *m* financier; (*centre*) place *f* financière; **f. pages** pages *fpl* financières; **f. period** période *f* comptable; **f. position** position *f* financière; **f. services** services *mpl* financiers; **f. statement** bilan *m* financier; **f. statements** document *m* de synthèse; **f. transaction** opération *f* financière; **f. transactions** flux *m* financier; *Br* **f. year** exercice *m*, exercice comptable, année *f* budgétaire

financially [faɪˈnænʃəlɪ, fɪ-] *adv* financièrement; **f. successful** aux finances prospères

financier [faɪˈnænsɪər, fɪ-] *n* financier *m*

financing [faɪˈnænsɪŋ, fɪ-] *n* (*of project etc*) financement *m*; **f. plan** plan *m* de financement

finch [fɪntʃ] *n* (*bird*) fringillidé *m*

find[1] [faɪnd] *n* découverte *f*, trouvaille *f*; (*artist, actor etc*) découverte; **he's quite a f.** c'est une perle rare; **it's quite a f.** c'est une fameuse trouvaille

find[2] (*pt, pp* **found** [faʊnd]) **1** *vt* **(a)** (*discover by chance*) trouver, découvrir; **to f. happiness with sb** trouver *ou* rencontrer le bonheur auprès de qn; **to f. sb at home** *or* **in** trouver qn chez lui; **they found him dead** on l'a trouvé mort; **I found her waiting in the hall** je l'ai trouvée qui attendait dans le vestibule; **we must leave everything as we f. it** il faut tout laisser dans l'état où nous l'avons trouvé; **I often f. myself smiling** je me surprends souvent à sourire; **I found myself in London** (*instead of Manchester etc*) je me suis retrouvé à Londres; **they found an unexpected supporter in Mr Smith** ils ont trouvé en M. Smith un partisan inattendu

(b) (*discover by searching*) **to try to f. sth** chercher qch; **to f. an answer/a solution** trouver une réponse/une solution; **f. some paper** allez chercher du papier; *Comptr* **to f. and replace** trouver et remplacer; **I ran to f. a doctor** j'ai couru chercher un médecin; **the (lost) key has been found** la clef a été retrouvée; **she was nowhere to be found** elle était introuvable; **you won't f. a better motorbike at this price** vous ne trouverez pas une meilleure moto à ce prix; **to f. a job for sb** trouver un emploi à qn; **to f. sth for sb to do** trouver qch à faire à qn; **to f. a leak in a main** localiser une fuite dans une conduite; **the bullet found its mark** la balle a atteint son but; **I can f. no reason for …** je ne vois pas de raison pour …; **he keeps finding excuses** il arrive toujours à trouver des excuses; **to f. it in one's heart to do sth** avoir le cœur de faire qch; **he couldn't f. it in his heart to tell her** il n'avait pas le cœur de lui dire; **to f. favour with sb** gagner la faveur de qn; **to f. one's balance** trouver son équilibre; **to f. one's way** trouver son chemin; *Fig* trouver sa voie; **such ideas can easily f. their way into the minds of the young** de telles idées peuvent facilement entrer dans les jeunes esprits; **to f. a way to do sth** trouver moyen de faire qch; **to f. oneself** (*one's true self*) se trouver

(c) (*learn, be told*) apprendre; (*come to realize, discover*) constater; **you will f. that I am right** vous verrez que j'ai raison; **I was surprised to f. that …** j'ai été surpris de constater que …; **after his death his family found that …** après sa mort sa famille a appris que …

(d) (*experience*) **to f. some difficulty in doing sth** éprouver quelque difficulté à faire qch; **they will f. it easy/difficult** cela leur sera facile/difficile; **to f. it impossible/necessary to do sth** se trouver dans l'impossibilité/la nécessité de faire qch; **I found it almost impossible to understand him** j'ai eu un mal fou à le comprendre; **how do you f. this wine?** comment trouvez-vous ce vin?; **how did you f. the meal?** le repas vous a-t-il plu?; **I f. her rather offhand/friendly** je la trouve plutôt désinvolte/aimable

(e) *Jur* **to f. sb guilty/innocent** déclarer qn coupable/innocent

(f) (*provide*) **to f. the money for an undertaking** procurer les capitaux *ou* fournir l'argent pour une entreprise; **to f. half the costs for a project** financer la moitié des coûts d'un projet; **wages £20, all found** gages 20 livres, tout fourni

2 *vi Jur* **to f. for/against sb** prononcer *ou* rendre un verdict en faveur de/contre qn

► **find out 1** *vtsep* **(a)** (*discover*) (*facts*) se rendre compte de; (*truth*) découvrir; **we found out that she was French** nous avons découvert qu'elle était française; **did you f. anything out?** est-ce que vous avez découvert quoi que ce soit?

(b) to f. sb out (*learn truth about*) découvrir le vrai caractère de qn; (*catch doing wrong*) prendre qn en défaut; **we've been found out** nous nous sommes faits prendre; **they had found her out for the liar she was** ils avaient découvert quelle menteuse elle était; **she had been found out transferring money into her own account** on avait découvert qu'elle transférait de l'argent sur son propre compte

2 *vi* (*discover*) **I'll f. out** je le saurai; **your mother had better not f. out!** j'espère pour toi que ta mère ne l'apprendra pas!; **to f. out about sth** se renseigner sur qch; **I have found out all about it** j'ai tout appris à ce sujet

find command *n Comptr* commande *f* de recherche

finder [ˈfaɪndər] *n* **(a)** (*of lost item*) **there's a reward for the f.** la personne qui le trouvera recevra une récompense; **well it's yours then, finders keepers** eh bien c'est à toi maintenant, puisque tu l'as trouvé **(b)** (*of telescope*) chercheur *m*

finding [ˈfaɪndɪŋ] *n* (*usu pl*) **findings** (*of scientist, enquiry, investigation etc*) résultat *m*; (*of tribunal, jury, committee, report*) conclusion *f*; **he published his findings in a scientific journal** il a fait publier les résultats de ses recherches dans un journal scientifique; **his f. is that …** il est arrivé à la conclusion que …

fine[1] [faɪn] *n Jur* amende *f*; **to impose a f. on sb** infliger une amende à qn; **to pay a f.** payer une amende; **parking f.** amende pour stationnement illégal

fine[2] *vt Jur* condamner à une amende; **to f. sb £20** frapper qn d'une amende de 20 livres

fine[3] *adj* **(a)** (*excellent*) excellent, magnifique; **meat/wine of the finest quality** viande/vin de premier choix; **a f. athlete** un excellent athlète; **that's f.!** c'est parfait!; **that's f. by** *or* **with me** ça me va; **she's/everything is f.** elle/tout va bien; **we had a f. time** nous nous sommes bien amusés; *Iron* **he had a f. time explaining what he was doing there** il a passé un mauvais quart d'heure quand il a fallu qu'il explique ce qu'il faisait là-bas; *Iron* **you're a f. one, you are!** vous êtes joli, vous!; *Iron* **you're a f. one to talk!** vous pouvez bien parler!

(b) *F* (*intensive*) **he was in a f. (old) temper!** ce qu'il rageait!; **this is another f. mess you've got us into!** tu nous a encore mis dans un beau pétrin!

(c) (*beautiful*) beau, bel, *f* belle; **a f. piece of writing** un bon écrit; **the f. arts** les beaux-arts *mpl*

(d) (*weather*) beau; **when the weather is f.** quand il fait beau; **a f. day** une belle journée; **it's turned out f. again** aujourd'hui encore il fait beau

(e) (*noble, admirable*) **to appeal to sb's finer feelings** faire appel aux sentiments élevés de qn; **she's a f. woman** c'est une femme admirable

(f) *Old-fashioned* **a f. lady** (*elegant*) une dame élégante; (*of high rank*) une grande dame

(g) (*texture, hair, rain etc*) fin; (*gravel etc*) menu, fin

(h) (*pointed*) effilé; (*writing*) délié, mince; (*needle*) fin; (*blade*) affilé, aigu; (*pen*) pointu; **f. print** petits caractères *mpl*; **to read the f. print** lire ce qui est écrit en petits caractères; **not to put too f. a point on it** pour parler carrément

(i) (*subtle*) fin; **a f. distinction** une distinction subtile; **she's got washing the car down to a f. art** elle est passée maître dans l'art de laver la voiture; **there's a f. line between eccentricity and madness** il n'y a qu'un pas de l'excentricité à la folie

(j) (*pure*) (*metals, oil etc*) fin; **gold twenty-two carats f.** or à vingt-deux carats de fin

fine[4] *int* (*agreed*) bon!, entendu!, d'accord!

fine[5] *adv* **(a) to get on** *or* **do f.** (*in new job etc*) se débrouiller très bien; (*be well*) aller bien; **to get on f.** (*of two people*) bien s'entendre **(b) to chop meat f.** hacher menu la viande; *Fig* **to cut it (a bit) f.** calculer un peu juste; **that's cutting it a bit f.** là tu calcules/il calcule/*etc* un peu juste; *Billiards* **to cut the ball too f.** prendre la bille trop fin *ou* trop fine

► **fine down** *vtsep* **(a)** (*refine*) (*beer*) clarifier **(b)** (*make thinner*) (*metal, wood*) amincir, désépaissir; (*plans, proposals*) dégrossir

fine-cut *adj* **(a)** (*features*) finement *ou* délicatement ciselé **(b)** (*tobacco*) haché fin

fine-drawn *adj* **(a)** (*features etc*) fin **(b)** (*distinction*) subtil **(c)** (*wire*) finement étiré; (*thread*) délié

fine-grained [ˈfaɪnˈgreɪnd] *adj* (*wood, leather*) à grain fin

fine-looking *adj* beau, *f* belle

finely [ˈfaɪnlɪ] *adv* **(a)** (*excellently*) magnifiquement **(b)** (*skilfully*) habilement **(c)** (*delicately*) délicatement; **f. drawn features** traits *mpl* fins **(d)** (*in small size*) **f. powdered** finement pulvérisé; **f. chopped** haché fin; **f. ground** moulu très fin

fineness [ˈfaɪnnɪs] *n* **(a)** (*excellence*) qualité *f* supérieure, excellence *f* **(b)** (*splendour*) (*of dress etc*) splendeur *f*, magnificence *f* **(c)** (*in texture*) (*of hair, material etc*) finesse *f* **(d)** (*purity*) (*of gold*) titre *m*, aloi *m*

finery [ˈfaɪnərɪ] *n* parure *f*; **decked out in all his f.** paré de ses plus beaux atours
fine-spun *adj* **(a)** *Tex* au fil ténu *ou* délié **(b)** *(reasoning etc)* subtil
finesse [fɪˈnes] *n* **(a)** *(skill) (of style etc)* finesse *f*, délicatesse *f* **(b)** *(ruse)* finesse *f*, ruse *f* **(c)** *Cards* impasse *f*
fine-tooth *adj (comb)* fin; *Fig* **to go through sth with a f. comb** passer qch au peigne fin
fine-tune *vt (radio, engine etc)* régler avec précision; *Fig (plan, proposals)* peaufiner
finger[1] [ˈfɪŋgər] *n* **(a)** *(of hand, glove etc)* doigt *m*; **first** *or* **index f.** index *m*; **middle f.** médius *m*, doigt du milieu; **ring f.** annulaire *m*; **little f.** auriculaire *m*; **to eat sth with one's fingers** manger qch avec les doigts; **to keep one's fingers crossed** croiser les doigts; **they could be counted on the fingers of one hand** on pourrait les compter sur les doigts de la main; *Fig* **he's got them (wrapped) round his little f.** il fait d'eux ce qu'il veut; **the f. (of suspicion) is pointed at him** on le montre d'un doigt suspicieux; **he has a f. in every pie** il est mêlé à tout; **I've been working my fingers to the bone** je me suis tué à la tâche; **don't you dare lay a f. on him** je vous défends de le toucher; *Fig* **I can't quite put my f. on it** je n'arrive pas à mettre le doigt dessus; **to lay** *or* **put one's f. on the source of the trouble** mettre le doigt sur la source du mal; **she wouldn't lift a f. to help you** elle ne remuerait pas le petit doigt pour vous aider; **he's so lazy, I've never seen him lift a f.** il est si paresseux, je ne l'ai jamais vu faire le moindre effort; *Br F* **get** *or* **pull** *or* **take your f. out!** remue-toi!, *Sl* bouge ton cul!; *F* **to put the f. on sb** *(inform on)* balancer qn; **to give sb the f.** *(rude gesture)* = faire un bras d'honneur à qn; *Culin* **f. biscuit** biscuit *m* à la cuiller; **f. exercises** exercices *mpl* de doigté; **f. food** = petits fours *mpl ou* amuse-gueule *m*; *Mus* **f. hole** *(of flute etc)* trou *m*; **f. painting** peinture *f* aux doigts; **she's being doing f. paintings all afternoon** elle a peint avec ses doigts tout l'après-midi; **f. plate** *(on door etc)* plaque *f* de propreté
(b) *(measure etc)* **f. of brandy** doigt *m* de cognac; **f. of cake** petit morceau *m* (rectangulaire) de gâteau
finger[2] *vt* **(a)** *(feel)* toucher, tâter; **stop fingering that food!** arrête de tripoter la nourriture! **(b)** *Mus (piece of music)* doigter; **to f. the piano** tapoter sur le piano **(c)** *Sl (inform on)* balancer
finger board *n (of violin etc)* touche *f*
finger bowl *n* rince-doigts *m inv*
finger buffet *n Culin* = buffet *m* où sont servis des petits fours *ou* amuse-gueule etc que l'on mange avec les doigts
fingering [ˈfɪŋgərɪŋ] *n Mus* doigté *m*
fingermark [ˈfɪŋgəmɑːk] *n* trace *f* de doigt
fingernail [ˈfɪŋgəneɪl] *n* ongle *m* (de la main)
fingerprint[1] [ˈfɪŋgəprɪnt] *n* empreinte *f* digitale; **f. identification** dactyloscopie *f*; **to take sb's fingerprints** prendre les empreintes digitales de qn; **f. expert** expert *m* en empreintes digitales
fingerprint[2] *vt (person)* prendre les empreintes digitales de; **the police fingerprinted him** la police a pris ses empreintes digitales
fingerstall [ˈfɪŋgəstɔːl] *n Med* doigtier *m*
fingertip [ˈfɪŋgətɪp] *n* bout *m* du doigt; **he is a Frenchman to his fingertips** il est français jusqu'au bout des ongles; **to have sth at one's fingertips** savoir qch sur le bout des doigts; **f. control** commande *f* au doigté
finicky [ˈfɪnɪkɪ] *adj (person)* méticuleux, *Pej* tatillon, vétilleux; *(style, layout)* alambiqué; *(job, task)* minutieux; *(device, recipe)* compliqué; **to be a very f. eater** être très difficile sur la nourriture; **this is a f. dish to make** c'est un plat très délicat à préparer; **there are all these f. little bits and pieces** il y a toutes ces petites pièces embêtantes à manier
finish[1] [ˈfɪnɪʃ] *n* **(a)** *(end)* fin *f*; *Sp (of race)* arrivée *f*; **she was exhausted by the f.** sur la fin elle était épuisée; *Sp* **he has a fast f.** il a un bon finish; *Sp* **it's going to be a close f.** l'arrivée va être serrée; *F* **that was the f. (of him)** ce fut le coup de grâce; **to be in at the f.** être là pour voir la fin
(b) *(workmanship) (of work etc)* fini *m*; *Tech (operation)* finition *f*; *(surface)* apprêt *m*; **paint with a gloss/matt f.** peinture vernie/mate; **paper with a gloss/matt f.** papier glacé/mat; **all the woodwork has been given a pine f.** toute les boiseries ont été teintées imitation pin; **car with a metallic/silver f.** voiture métallisée/argentée
finish[2] **1** *vt* **(a)** *(end)* finir, terminer, achever; *(cake, food)* finir; *(meal)* finir, terminer; **to f. doing sth** terminer *ou* finir de faire qch; **you can f. telling me tomorrow** tu peux me raconter la fin demain; **to f. what one was saying** finir ce qu'on avait à dire; **when do you f. work?** à quelle heure est-ce que tu finis?; **f. your soup!** finis ta soupe!
(b) *(ruin, kill) (person)* achever; **he's finished!** il est fini *ou* achevé!; **this defeat has finished the team's chances** cette défaite a mis un terme aux chances de l'équipe; **she was finished as a singer** sa carrière de chanteuse était finie; **you're finished here** *(I'm sacking you)* tu es viré
(c) *(put finishing touches) (to piece of work etc)* perfectionner, donner du fini à; *Tex (fabric)* apprêter; *Metal (part)* usiner; *Sewing* **to f. a buttonhole** brider une boutonnière; **the wood/paintwork hasn't been very well finished** le bois/la peinture n'a pas un très bon fini
2 *vi* se terminer, s'achever; **they finished long before the others** ils ont fini *ou* terminé bien avant les autres; **the meeting finished in a brawl** le meeting se termina par des coups; **when do you f.?** *(leave work)* quand est-ce que tu finis?; **have you finished?** *(eating, shouting etc)* tu as terminé?; **to f. in a point** *(of blade, shape etc)* se terminer en pointe; **the book finishes with him returning to the family house** à la fin du livre il retourne à la maison familiale; **I'd like to f. on an optimistic note** je voudrais terminer *ou* finir sur une note optimiste; **he finished by calling me a liar** il a fini par me traiter de menteur; *Sp* **to f. fourth** finir *ou* arriver quatrième; *Sp* **where did she f.?** à quelle place est-ce qu'elle a fini?
▶ **finish off 1** *vtsep* **(a)** *(complete) (task)* terminer; *Sewing* **to f. off a buttonhole** brider une boutonnière
(b) *(have the last of) (cake, milk etc)* finir
(c) *F (kill)* achever; *(exhaust)* achever, épuiser; *(ruin) (company, industry)* faire la ruine de; *(hopes)* ruiner, anéantir; **to f. off a wounded animal** donner le coup de grâce à une bête; **this fly killer will soon f. them off!** ce tue-mouches aura bientôt raison d'elles!; **cirrhosis of the liver finally finished him off** une cirrhose du foie a fini par avoir raison de lui
2 *vi (end)* finir, terminer; **we should be finishing off soon** nous devrions bientôt avoir fini *ou* terminé; **they finished off with some fruit/a song** ils ont fini avec des fruits/une chanson
▶ **finish up 1** *vtsep* **(a)** *(complete)* finir, terminer; **f. up your soup!** finis ta soupe! **(b)** *(have the last of)* finir; **don't f. up the pie** ne mange pas toute la tourte **2** *vi (end up)* finir; **we finished up in a ditch** nous avons fini dans un fossé; **I'm going to f. up a nervous wreck!** je vais finir par m'user les nerfs!; **I'm going to f. up hating him** je vais finir par le détester
▶ **finish with** *vipo* **(a)** *(stop using)* ne plus avoir besoin de; **have you finished with the dictionary/mustard?** est-ce que tu as fini avec le dictionnaire/la moutarde?; **I've finished with it** je n'en ai plus besoin
(b) *(stop doing)* en avoir fini avec; **I've finished with acting** j'en ai fini avec le théâtre; **I've finished with trying to help people** plus jamais je n'essaierai d'aider les gens
(c) *(finish dealing with)* **I haven't finished with you!** je n'en ai pas fini avec toi!; **wait until I've finished with him!** *(threat)* attendez que je lui aie réglé son compte!
(d) *(end relationship with)* rompre avec; **I've finished with you** tout est fini entre nous; **I've finished with men for ever!** les hommes et moi, c'est fini!
finished [ˈfɪnɪʃt] *adj* **(a)** *(item etc)* fini, apprêté; *(product)* ouvré; **machine f.** apprêté à la machine; **badly f. goods** marchandises mal finies; **beautifully/professionally f.** d'un fini magnifique/professionnel **(b)** *(appearance etc)* soigné, fini; *(performance)* au point, parfait **(c)** *(ruined)* **he's f. as a boxer** sa carrière de boxeur est finie; **if I can't raise the money I'm f.!** si je n'arrive pas à trouver l'argent je suis fichu!
finisher [ˈfɪnɪʃər] *n Ind, Sp (person)* finisseur, -euse; *Sp* **he's a fast f.** c'est un bon finisseur, il a un bon finish
finishing [ˈfɪnɪʃɪŋ] **1** *adj* dernier; **the f. stroke** le coup de grâce; **f. touches** finitions *fpl*; **to put the f. touches to sth** mettre la dernière main à qch **2** *n* **(a)** *(completion) (of task etc)* achèvement *m*; *Sp* **f. line** ligne *f* d'arrivée **(b)** *Tech* finition *f*; *(of leather, paper)* apprêtage *m*; **f. coat** *(of paint etc)* dernière couche *f*; *Ind* **f. shop** atelier *m* de finitions
finishing school *n* = école *f* d'arts d'agrément pour les jeunes filles
finite [ˈfaɪnaɪt] **1** *adj (universe)* fini, limité; *(resources, means)* limité; *Gram (verb)* à un mode fini; **a f. number of possibilities** un nombre limité de possibilités **2** *n* **the f. and the infinite** le fini et l'infini
fink [fɪŋk] *n Am F, Pej* **(a)** *(unpleasant person)* salaud *m* **(b)** *(strikebreaker)* jaune *m* **(c)** *(informer)* balance *f*, indic *m*
Finland [ˈfɪnlənd] *n* Finlande *f*
Finn [fɪn] *n* [①A20,d] Finlandais, -aise, Finnois, -oise
finnan [ˈfɪnən] *n Culin* **f. haddie** haddock *m*
Finnish [ˈfɪnɪʃ] [①A20,d] **1** *adj* finlandais, finnois **2** *n Ling* finlandais *m*, finnois *m*
fiord [fjɔːd] *n Geog* fjord *m*, fiord *m*
fir [fɜːr] *n* **(a)** **f. (tree)** sapin *m*; **Douglas f.** sapin de Douglas;

Scots f. pin *m* d'Écosse; **f. cone** pomme *f* de pin (**b**) (*wood*) (bois *m* de) sapin *m*; (*pine*) (bois de) pin *m*

fire[1] ['faɪər] *n* (**a**) (*in hearth etc*) feu *m*; **to make** *or* **light a f.** faire du feu; **to set** *or* **lay a f.** préparer un feu; **wolves are afraid of f.** les loups ont peur du feu; *Fig* **to go through f. and water for sb** subir des épreuves pour qn; *Fig* **to play with f.** jouer avec le feu; *Fig* **to fight f. with f.** combattre le mal par le mal; **gas/electric f.** radiateur *m* à gaz/électrique; **to throw sth into the f.** jeter qch au feu; **open f.** feu de cheminée; **a roaring f.** une belle flambée; **blacksmith's f.** feu de forge; *Cer* **f. clay** argile *f* réfractaire; **f. irons** garniture *f* de foyer; **f. screen** pare-feu *m*, *pl* pare-feux, pare-étincelles *m inv*; **f. worship** culte *m* du feu

(**b**) (*large, destructive*) incendie *m*; **bush f.** feu *m* de brousse; **to cause** *or* **start a f.** provoquer un incendie; **to catch f.** prendre feu; **f.!** au feu!; **on f.** en feu; **to set f. to sth, to set sth on f.** mettre le feu à qch; *F* **my singing isn't going to set the world** *or Br* **the Thames on f.** la façon dont je chante n'a rien de fantastique; *F* **to get on like a house on f.** (*of work etc*) marcher rondement; (*of two people*) s'entendre à merveille; **f. blanket** couverture *f* pare-flamme; *Naut, Av* **f. bulkhead** cloison *f* pare-feu; **f. damage** dégâts *mpl* causés par le feu; **f. door** porte *f* coupe-feu; **f. drill** exercice *m* d'évacuation en cas d'incendie; **f. hazard** risque *m* d'incendie; **that old gas cooker must be a f. hazard** cette vieille cuisinière à gaz doit présenter un risque d'incendie; **f. hose** tuyau *m* de pompe à incendie; **f. hydrant** bouche *f* d'incendie; **f. insurance** assurance *f* contre l'incendie; **f. master** capitaine *m* des pompiers; **f. notice** (*in hotel etc*) consignes *fpl* en cas d'incendie; **f. raiser** incendiaire *mf*; **f. regulations** réglementations *fpl* anti-incendie; (*posted in hotel room*) consignes *fpl* d'incendie; **f. safety** sécurité *f* incendie; **f. sale** vente *f* de marchandises qui ont été endommagées dans un incendie

(**c**) *Mil etc* (*act*) feu *m*, tir *m*; (*shots*) coups *mpl* de feu; **individual f., f. at will** tir *ou* feu à volonté; **to open f.** ouvrir le feu; **to hold one's f.** (*stop firing*) arrêter de tirer, cesser le feu; (*postpone firing*) ne pas tirer; **to cease f.** cesser le feu; **to return (sb's) f.** riposter (au tir de qn); **under enemy f.** sous le feu de l'ennemi; **we are under f.** on nous tire dessus; **to come under f.** être exposé aux tirs (**from sb** de qn); *Fig* **to be/come under f.** être exposé à de sévères critiques (**from** de la part de); **to draw sb's f.** attirer sur soi les tirs de qn; *Mil, Fig* **between two fires** entre deux feux; *Fig* **to hang f.** (*of project etc*) être en attente; **f. power** puissance *f* de tir; *Comptr* **f. button** (*on joystick*) bouton *m* feu

(**d**) (*of diamond*) lumière *f*, éclat *m*

(**e**) (*enthusiasm*) enthousiasme *m*; (*ardour*) fougue *f*; **the f. of youth** l'enthousiasme de la jeunesse; **the speech lacked f.** le discours manquait de mordant; **he lacks the f. of his predecessor** il n'a pas l'ardeur de son prédécesseur

fire[2] 1 *vt* (**a**) *Fml, Lit* (*set on fire*) mettre le feu à

(**b**) (*fill with enthusiasm*) animer, enthousiasmer; (*the imagination*) exciter; **she was fired with an intense desire to help others** elle était animée d'un désir intense d'aider autrui; **to be fired with enthusiasm for sth** brûler d'enthousiasme pour qch; **the speech had fired them with enthusiasm** le discours les avait remplis d'un enthousiasme ardent

(**c**) *Cer* (*pottery etc*) cuire

(**d**) (*heat*) (*locomotive etc*) chauffer; (*boiler*) allumer; **oil-fired/gas-fired central heating** chauffage *m* central au mazout/au gaz

(**e**) (*fuel mix in engine*) enflammer

(**f**) *Mil etc* (*shot, salvo*) tirer; (*rifle, pistol*) décharger; (*rocket, torpedo*) lancer; (*cannon*) tirer un coup de; **to f. a gun at sb** tirer un coup de fusil sur qn; **without firing a shot** sans tirer un seul coup de feu; *Fig* **to f. a question at sb** poser une question à qn à brûle-pourpoint

(**g**) *F* (*dismiss*) (*employee etc*) virer, saquer; **you're fired!** vous êtes viré!

2 *vi* (**a**) (*of spark plug*) s'allumer; (*of engine*) tourner; **to f. on all (four) cylinders** tourner rond; *Fig* **I'm not firing on all (four) cylinders this morning** je ne tourne pas tout à fait rond ce matin

(**b**) *Mil etc* (*of person*) tirer; (*of shot*) partir; **we could hear the guns firing** on entendait le bruit des canons; **the revolver failed to f.** le revolver a fait long feu; **to f. at** *or* **on sb/sth** tirer sur qn/qch; **to f. at sb with a revolver** tirer un coup de revolver sur qn; **f.!** feu!; **to f. at will** tirer à volonté; **we were fired on** nous avons reçu des coups de feu, on nous a tiré dessus

▶ **fire away** *vi Mil etc* tirer à feu continu (**at** sur); *Fig* **f. away!** allez-y!, commencez!

▶ **fire off** *vtsep Mil etc* (*round etc*) tirer; *Fig* (*questions*) poser à brûle-pourpoint; **she fired off a letter of complaint** elle a envoyé une lettre de réclamation sur-le-champ

fire alarm *n* sirène *f* d'incendie

fire-and-brimstone *adj* (*sermon, preacher*) annonçant les feux de l'enfer

firearm ['faɪərɑːm] *n* arme *f* à feu; **firearms training** formation *f* à l'utilisation des armes à feu

fireball ['faɪəbɔːl] *n* (**a**) *Met* éclair *m* en boule (**b**) *Astron* bolide *m* (**c**) *Fig* **she's a real f.** elle déborde d'énergie

fireboat ['faɪəbəʊt] *n* bateau-pompe *m*, *pl* bateaux-pompes

firebox ['faɪəbɒks] *n* foyer *m*, boîte *f* à feu

firebrand ['faɪəbrænd] *n* (**a**) (*burning wood*) tison *m*, brandon *m* (**b**) (*agitator*) brandon *m* de discorde

firebreak ['faɪəbreɪk] *n* (*in forest etc*) coupe-feu *m inv*

firebrick ['faɪəbrɪk] *n* brique *f* réfractaire

fire brigade *n Br* (corps *m* de) sapeurs-pompiers *mpl*, *F* pompiers *mpl*

firebug ['faɪəbʌg] *n F* incendiaire *mf*, pyromane *mf*

fire chief *n Am* capitaine *m* des pompiers

firecracker ['faɪəkrækər] *n Am* pétard *m*

firedamp ['faɪədæmp] *n Min* grisou *m*; **f. explosion** coup *m* de grisou

fire department *n Am* (corps *m* de) sapeurs-pompiers *mpl*; *F* pompiers *mpl*

firedog ['faɪədɒg] *n* (*in fireplace*) chenet *m*

fire-eater *n* (**a**) (*at fair etc*) avaleur *m* de feu (**b**) *F* (*aggressive person*) batailleur, -euse

fire engine *n* voiture *f* de pompiers

fire escape *n* escalier *m* de secours

fire-extinguisher *n* extincteur *m* (d'incendie)

fire fighter *n* pompier *m*

fire fighting *n* lutte *f* contre l'incendie

fire-fighting *adj* **f. equipment** matériel *m* de lutte contre l'incendie

firefly ['faɪəflaɪ] *n* (*insect*) luciole *f*

fireguard ['faɪəgɑːd] *n* (**a**) (*in front of open fire*) écran *m* pare-étincelles, garde-feu *m inv*, devant *m* de cheminée (**b**) = **firebreak**

firehouse ['faɪəhaʊs] *n US* poste *m* d'incendie; (*with living quarters*) caserne *f* de (sapeurs-)pompiers

firelight ['faɪəlaɪt] *n* **to read by f.** lire à la lumière du feu; **in the f.** à la lumière du feu

firelighter ['faɪəlaɪtər] *n* allume-feu *m inv*

fireman, *pl* **-men** ['faɪəmən] *n* (**a**) (*firefighter*) (sapeur-) pompier *m* (**b**) *Rail* (*of steam engine*) chauffeur *m*

fire marshal *n US* capitaine *m* des pompiers

fireplace ['faɪəpleɪs] *n* cheminée *f*

fireplug ['faɪəplʌg] *n esp US* bouche *f* d'incendie

fireproof[1] ['faɪəpruːf] *adj* incombustible; (*treated against fire*) ignifugé; **f. cabinet** armoire *f* ignifugée; *Culin* **f. dish** plat *m* allant au feu; **f. door** porte *f* coupe-feu; **f. material** matière *f* ignifugée

fireproof[2] *vt* rendre ininflammable, ignifuger

fireside ['faɪəsaɪd] *n* coin *m* du feu; **sitting by the f.** assis au coin du feu; **f. chair** chaise *f* de coin du feu; **f. chat** (*of politician etc*) causerie *f* au coin du feu

fire station *n* caserne *f* des pompiers

firestorm ['faɪəstɔːm] *n* tempête *f* de feu

fire tender *n* voiture *f* de pompiers

firetrap ['faɪətræp] *n* **this building's a real f.** ce bâtiment est un véritable piège (en cas d'incendie)

fire truck *n* voiture *f* de pompiers

firewall ['faɪəwɔːl] *n Am Aut* pare-feu *m* de moteur

firewarden ['faɪəwɔːdən] *n Am* guetteur, -euse d'incendies

firewatcher ['faɪəwɔːtʃər] *n Br* guetteur, -euse d'incendies

firewatching ['faɪəwɔːtʃɪŋ] *n Br* surveillance *f* contre les incendies

firewater ['faɪəwɔːtər] *n F* gnole *f*, gnôle *f*, gniole *f*

firewood ['faɪəwʊd] *n* bois *m* de chauffage; **bundle of f.** fagot *m*; **to go out in search of f.** aller chercher du bois; **to chop sth up for f.** couper qch en morceaux pour en faire du bois de chauffage

firework ['faɪəwɜːk] *n* (**a**) (*device*) pièce *f* d'artifice; **f. display** feu *m* d'artifice (**b**) (*display*) (*usu pl*) **fireworks** feu *m* d'artifice; **grand display of fireworks** grand feu d'artifice; *Fig F* **there'll be fireworks** il va y avoir du grabuge

firing ['faɪərɪŋ] *n* (**a**) *Mil etc* (*of rocket*) tir *m*; (*shooting*) tir, feu *m*; **heavy f. could be heard** on entendait une vive fusillade; **they could hear the f. of the guns** ils entendaient les coups de feu; **f. line** ligne *f* de tir; **f. party** *or* **squad** (*for execution*) peloton *m* d'exécution; (*for ceremonial duties*) peloton chargé de tirer la salve d'honneur; **f. pin** percuteur *m*; **f. position** (*of weapon*) position *f* de tir; (*of person*) position du tireur; **f. practice** exercice *m* de tir; **f. range** (*place*) stand *m* de tir; **within f. range** à portée de fusil

(**b**) (*heating*) (*of oven, locomotive etc*) chauffage *m*, chauffe *f*; **coal/oil f.** chauffe au charbon/mazout

(c) *Cer* (*of bricks, pottery etc*) cuisson *f*; **they'll be given a second f.** elles seront cuites une deuxième fois

(d) (*of engine*) allumage *m*; **f. order** *or* **sequence** (*of cylinders*) ordre *m* d'allumage

firm[1] [fɜːm] *n* [①A11,g,i] *Com* maison *f* (de commerce), entreprise *f*, firme *f*; **the firm's giving us a rise** la firme nous accorde une augmentation; **a large f.** une grosse entreprise; **f. of auditors** cabinet *m* comptable; **f. of solicitors** étude *f* de notaires

firm[2] **1** *adj* **(a)** (*flesh, mattress, handshake etc*) ferme; (*post, nail, foundations etc*) solide; **as f. as a rock** inébranlable; **to rule with a f. hand** gouverner d'une main ferme; **to walk with a f. step** *or* **tread** marcher d'un pas assuré; **I'm on firmer ground when it comes to the marketing side** je suis plus à mon affaire pour ce qui touche au marketing

(b) (*intention, person etc*) ferme; (*voice*) ferme, assuré; (*friendship*) solide; (*date*) fixe; (*evidence*) convaincant; **a f. favourite for the Derby/with the crowd** un grand favori dans le Derby/auprès de la foule; **there has been no f. news** il n'y a aucune nouvelle certaine; **to be f. about sth** tenir bon sur qch; **she was polite but f.** elle a été polie mais ferme; **to have a f. belief that …** avoir la ferme conviction que …; **I'm a f. believer in corporal punishment** je suis résolument partisan du châtiment corporel; **I'm a f. believer in the value of a high fibre diet** je crois fermement à la valeur d'un régime riche en fibres

(c) (*offer, sale, order*) ferme; **these shares remain f. at …** ces actions se maintiennent à …; **the dollar remained f. against the yen** le dollar est resté fort contre le yen

2 *adv* **to stand f.** tenir bon *ou* ferme; **to stand f. about sth** tenir bon sur qch; **to hold f.** tenir bon, résister; **to hold f. to one's principles/beliefs** être fidèle à ses principes/croyances

firm[3] **1** *vt* **to f. the soil** affermir *ou* tasser le sol **2** *vi* = **firm up 2**

▶ **firm up 1** *vtsep* (*make firm*) raffermir; (*details*) préciser **2** *vi* (*become firm*) (*of price, muscles etc*) se raffermir

firmament [ˈfɜːməmənt] *n Lit* firmament *m*; *Fig* **one of the brightest stars in the Hollywood f.** l'une des plus grandes stars de l'univers hollywoodien

firmly [ˈfɜːmlɪ] *adv* (*tied, to deny*) fermement; (*to nail down, screw on*) solidement; (*to walk*) d'un pas assuré; (*to say*) d'un ton ferme, fermement; (*to act*) avec fermeté; **I f. believe that …** j'ai la ferme conviction que …; **to deal f. with sb** traiter qn fermement *ou* avec fermeté; **she remains f. entrenched in her views** elle demeure fermement retranchée derrière ses opinions

firmness [ˈfɜːmnɪs] *n* **(a)** (*solidity*) fermeté *f*; (*of character etc*) force *f*; (*of tread*) assurance *f* **(b)** (*of intention, person, voice etc*) fermeté *f*; (*of friendship*) solidité *f*; **the f. of her voice** l'assurance qu'il y avait dans sa voix **(c)** *Com, Fin etc* (*of shares etc*) stabilité *f*

firmware [ˈfɜːmweə(r)] *n Comptr* microprogrammation *f*, microprogrammes *mpl* constructeurs

first [fɜːst] **1** *adj* [①B56,B,a-b] (*in time, order*) premier; **the f. (day) of the month** le premier (jour) du mois; **twenty-f.** vingt et unième; **eighty-f.** quatre-vingt-unième; **ninety-f.** quatre-vingt-onzième; **one hundred and f.** cent unième; **the f. of April** le premier avril; **the f. three years** les trois premières années; **Charles the F.** Charles Premier *m*; **to use** *or* **wear sth for the f. time** étrenner qch; **it was my f. flight** c'était mon baptême de l'air; **to be the f. person to do sth** être le premier/la première à faire qch; **English is my f. language** l'anglais est ma langue maternelle; **English is my f. foreign language** l'anglais est ma première langue; **to have news at f. hand** tenir une nouvelle de première main; **America's f. lady** l'épouse *f* du Président des États-Unis; **the f. lady of British cinema** la plus grande dame du cinéma britannique; **to put f. things f.** commencer par le commencement; **f. things f.!** commençons par le commencement!; **f. things f., let's talk about financing** avant tout, parlons du financement; **I don't know the f. thing** *or* **have the f. idea about motorbikes** je ne connais absolument rien aux motos; **f. thing in the morning** (*as soon as I get up*) dès que je me lève; (*as soon as I arrive at the office etc*) dès que j'arrive; (*immediately the shop etc opens*) à l'ouverture; **at the f. attempt** au premier *ou* de prime abord; **at f. light** aux premières lueurs du jour; **at f. sight** à première vue; *Gram* **in the f. person** à la première personne; **in the f. place, I didn't ask for your help** d'abord *ou* pour commencer, je ne t'ai rien demandé; **why didn't you tell me that in the f. place?** pourquoi ne me l'as-tu pas dit dès le début?; **of the f. water** de la plus belle eau; **on the f. floor** *Br* au premier étage; *Am* au rez-de-chaussée; **f. cousin** cousin, -ine germain(e); **f. draft** premier jet *m*; **f. edition** édition *f* originale; *Mktg* **f. entry** premier lancement *m*; *Aut* **f. gear** première *f* (vitesse); **f. love** premier amour; *Mktg* **f. mover** premier entré *m*; *Mktg* **f. mover advantage** avantage *m* du premier entré; *Th etc* **f. night, f. performance** première *f*; *Jur* **f. offence** premier délit *m*; **f. offender** personne *f* qui commet un délit pour la première fois; *Parl* **f. reading** (*of bill*) première lecture *f*; *Cin* **f. showing** première exclusivité *f*; *Mus* **f. violin/trombone** premier violon *m*/trombone *m*; *Br Sch* **f. year** *or* **form** = (classe de) sixième *f*

2 *n* **(a)** (*person, thing*) premier, *f* première; **we were the very f. to arrive** nous sommes arrivés les tout premiers; **we were the f. to tell him** nous avons été les premiers à le lui dire; **she was the f. to finish** elle a terminé la première; **you'll be the f. to know** vous serez le premier à le savoir; *Sp etc* **to come in an easy f.** arriver bon premier; **to be the f. to do sth** être le premier/la première à faire qch; *Univ* **to get a f.** avoir une licence avec mention très bien; **the inflatable life jacket was a Scottish f.** (*it was invented there*) le gilet de sauvetage gonflable est une invention écossaise; **this is a f. for France** (*the first time it has won the competition*) c'est une première pour la France; **it's the f. I've heard of it!** première nouvelle!

(b) (*beginning*) commencement *m*; **from f. to last** depuis le début jusqu'à la fin; **from the f.** dès le commencement *ou* début; **at f.** d'abord

(c) *Aut* (*gear*) première *f* (vitesse); **in f.** en première (vitesse); **to put the car into f.** se mettre en première, passer la première

3 *adv* **(a)** (*firstly*) d'abord; **I shall f. have to give it careful consideration** il faudra d'abord que j'examine cela soigneusement; **f. make sure the parts are clean** premièrement, assurez-vous que les parties sont propres; **do this f.** (*before anything else*) commence par ça; **what should I do f.?** par quoi est-ce que je dois commencer?; **f. and foremost** avant toute chose; **f. of all** pour commencer, en premier lieu; *F* **f. off, why did you do it?** pour commencer *ou* et d'abord, pourquoi est-ce que tu as fait cela?; **f. forget that …** commencez par oublier que …

(b) (*for the first time*) pour la première fois; **when did you f. see him?** quand l'avez-vous vu pour la première fois?

(c) (*rather*) plutôt; **I'll see him damned f.** qu'il aille plutôt au diable

(d) (*before others*) le premier, la première; **he arrived/left/died f.** il est arrivé/parti/mort le premier; **you go f.!** (*in queue*) passez devant!; **to claim the right to speak f.** réclamer la priorité de parole; **to come f.** passer en premier; **to come f. in an examination** être reçu premier à un examen; **f. come f. served** premier arrivé, premier servi; **it's a case of f. come f. served** les premiers arrivés sont les premiers servis; **tickets were handed out on a f. come f. served basis** les billets ont été distribués par ordre d'arrivée; **ladies f.!** place aux dames!; **women and children f.!** les femmes et les enfants d'abord!; **to fall head f.** tomber la tête la première; **he was carried out feet f.** on l'a emporté les pieds devant

first aid *n Med* secourisme *m*, premiers secours *mpl*; **to give/receive f.** donner/recevoir les premiers secours

first-aid *adj Med* **f. certificate** brevet *m* de secourisme; **f. class** cours *m* de secourisme; **f. kit** trousse *f* de secours; **f. post** poste *m* de (premier) secours; **I've had f. training** j'ai une formation de secouriste

first aider *n* secouriste *mf*

first-born *adj, n esp Lit* (*boy*) premier-né *m*, *pl* premiers-nés; (*girl*) première-née *f*, *pl* premières-nées

first(-)class 1 *adj* **(a)** (*compartment, ticket*) de première (classe); (*item*) de première qualité; (*hotel, player, performance etc*) de premier ordre; *Univ* **f. honours (degree)** licence *f* avec mention très bien; **the food was f.** la nourriture était excellente **(b)** (*postal service*) à tarif normal; **f. mail** courrier *m* envoyé au tarif normal; *Am* (*sealed letter*) lettre *f* close; **f. stamp** timbre *m* au tarif normal **2** *adv* **to travel f.** voyager en première; **to send a letter f.** envoyer une lettre au tarif normal

first-day *adj Philat* **f. cover** (enveloppe *f* de) premier jour *m* (d'émission)

first-degree *adj Med* **f. burns** brûlures *fpl* au premier degré; *US Jur* **f. murder** assassinat *m*

first-foot[1] *n Scot* = première personne *f* à se rendre chez quelqu'un pour souhaiter la bonne année

first-foot[2] *vi Scot* **to f. sb** = être le premier à se rendre chez qn pour souhaiter la bonne année

first-hand *adj, adv* (*news*) de première main; **she had the news f.** elle a appris la nouvelle de première main; **to experience sth f.** faire l'expérience personnelle de qch

first-in first-out *adj Comptr, Ind* premier entré, premier sorti

first lieutenant *n Mil* lieutenant *m* en premier
firstly ['fɜːstlɪ] *adv* premièrement, en premier lieu; **f. she rang the office** elle téléphona d'abord au bureau
first mate *n Naut* second *m*
first name *n* prénom *m*; **I am on first-name terms with my boss** j'appelle mon patron par son prénom; **I'm not on first-name terms with her but we say hello** je ne fais pas partie de ses intimes, mais nous nous saluons
first-nighter [fɜːst'naɪtər] *n Th* habitué, -ée des premières
first-off *n Mktg* produit *m* vedette
first officer *n Naut* second *m*; *Av* co-pilote *m*
first-past-the-post *adj Pol* **f. system** scrutin *m* à un tour
first-rate *adj* excellent, de première classe; **of f. quality** de toute première qualité; **f. idea** fameuse idée *f*; **I feel f.!** je suis en pleine forme!
first-strike *adj* (*missile, capability etc*) de première frappe
first-time *adj Com* **f. buyer** (*of property*) personne *f* achetant une propriété pour la première fois, nouvel acheteur *m*; **f. user** nouvel utilisateur *m*
first view¹ *n TV etc* dérushage *m*
first-view² *vt TV etc* dérusher
First World War *n* première guerre *f* mondiale
firth [fɜːθ] *n Geog Scot* estuaire *m*; **the F. of Forth** le golfe du Forth
fiscal ['fɪsk(ə)l] **1** *adj Fin* (*resources, control*) fiscal, -aux; (*policy*) budgétaire; *Am* **f. period** période *f* comptable; *Am* **f. year** exercice *m*, exercice comptable, année *f* budgétaire **2** *n Scot* (**procurator**) **f.** procureur *m* général
fish¹, *pl* **fishes** *or* **fish** [fɪʃ, 'fɪʃɪz] *n* **(a)** [ⓘA12,1,g] poisson *m*; **I don't like f.** (*as food*) je n'aime pas le poisson; *Br* **f. and chips** poisson frit avec des frites; *Fig F* **I've other f. to fry** j'ai d'autres chats à fouetter; *Fig* **there are plenty more f. in the sea** un(e) de perdu(e), dix de retrouvé(e)s; **to feel like a f. out of water** ne pas se sentir dans son élément; **a big f. in a small pond** une gloire locale; **at university she was a small f. in a big pond** à l'université, elle se sentait complètement perdue dans la masse; *Fig* **neither f. nor fowl** ni chair ni poisson; **f. bone** arête *f* (de poisson); **f. cake** croquette *f* de poisson; *Culin* **f. course** *or* **dish** plat *m* de poisson; **f. farm** établissement *m* piscicole; **f. farmer** pisciculteur *m*; **f. farming** pisciculture *f*; *Br* **f. fingers,** *Am* **f. sticks** bâtonnets *mpl* de poisson; **f. kettle** poissonnière *f*; *Culin* **f. knife** couteau *m* à poisson; **f. knife and fork** couverts *mpl* à poisson; **f. market** marché *m* au poisson; **f. meal** farine *f* de poisson; **f. pond** étang *m*; (*for breeding fish*) vivier *m*; **f. shop** poissonnerie *f*; *Culin* **f. slice** truelle *f* à poisson; **f. tank** vivier *m*
(b) *Astron* **the Fish(es)** les Poissons *mpl*
fish² **1** *vi* pêcher; **to f. for trout/pearls** pêcher la truite/des perles; **to go fishing** aller à la pêche; *F* **to f. for compliments** chercher des compliments **2** *vt* **(a)** (*salmon etc*) pêcher **(b)** (*river*) pêcher dans **(c)** (*remove*) **to f. sth/sb from somewhere** tirer qch/qn de quelque part; **they fished the body from the pond** ils ont repêché le corps de l'étang
▶ **fish out** *vtsep* (*remove from water*) repêcher; **to f. out a dead body** (re)pêcher un cadavre; **she put her hand in the drawer and fished out a twenty-dollar bill** elle a mis la main dans le tiroir et en a sorti un billet de vingt dollars; **he fished a pencil out of his pocket** il a fouillé dans sa poche et en a tiré un crayon
▶ **fish up** *vtsep* (*bring up from water*) repêcher; (*dead body*) (re)pêcher; (*mine*) relever; (*information*) dénicher
fish-and-chip *adj Br* **f. shop** = boutique *f* qui vend du poisson frit et des frites
fisherman, *pl* **-men** ['fɪʃəmən] *n* pêcheur *m*; **f.'s bend** (*knot*) nœud *m* de grappin
fishery ['fɪʃərɪ] *n* (*fishing ground*) pêcherie *f*; (*fishing industry*) pêche *f*; **f.-protection vessel** garde-pêche *m inv*
fish-eye *Phot* **1** *adj* **f. lens** objectif *m* ultra grand angle, objectif fish eye **2** *n F* grand-angle *m*
fish-hook *n* hameçon *m*
fishing ['fɪʃɪŋ] *n* pêche *f*; **there's good f. to be had here** il y a du poisson par ici; **trout f.** pêche à la truite; **pearl f.** pêche des perles; **fly f.** pêche à la mouche; **f. boat** *or* **smack** bateau *m* de pêche; **f. ground** pêcherie *f*; **f. line** ligne *f* (de pêche); **f. net** filet *m* de pêche; **f. port** port *m* de pêche; **f. rights** droits *mpl* de pêche; **f. rod** canne *f* à pêche; **f. tackle** articles *mpl* de pêche; **f. trip** partie *f* de pêche; **f. vessel** navire *m* de pêche, pêcheur *m*; **f. village** village *m* de pêcheurs
fishmonger ['fɪʃmʌŋgər] *n esp Br* (*person*) poissonnier, -ière; **f.'s** (**shop**) poissonnerie *f*
fishnet ['fɪʃnet] **1** *n esp Am Fishing* filet *m* de pêche **2** *adj* **f. stockings** bas *mpl* résille
fishplate ['fɪʃpleɪt] *n Rail* éclisse *f*
fishpole mike *n* micro *m* sur perche
fishwife, *pl* **-wives** ['fɪʃwaɪf, -waɪvz] *n* marchande *f* de poisson; **she swears like a f.** elle jure comme un charretier
fishy ['fɪʃɪ] *adj* **(a)** (*smell, taste*) de poisson **(b)** *F* (*suspicious*) (*business etc*) louche; **f. story** histoire qui ne tient pas debout; **there's something f. going on here** il y a quelque chose de louche
fissile ['fɪsaɪl] *adj* fissile
fission ['fɪʃən] *n* **(a)** *Phys* fission *f*; **nuclear/thermal f.** fission nucléaire/thermique **(b)** *Biol* scissiparité *f*
fissure¹ ['fɪʃər] *n* (*in wall, rock etc*) fissure *f*, fente *f*
fissure² **1** *vt* (*rock etc*) fissurer, fendre **2** *vi* (*of rock etc*) se fissurer, se fendre
fist [fɪst] *n* poing *m*; **to clench one's f., to make a f.** serrer le poing; **to shake one's f.** *or* **fists at sb** menacer qn du poing; **he went for them with his fists** il tomba sur eux à coups de poing
fistful ['fɪstfʊl] *n* (*of money etc*) poignée *f*
fisticuffs ['fɪstɪkʌfs] *npl Old-fashioned, Hum* coups *mpl* de poing
fistula ['fɪstjʊlə] *n Med* fistule *f*
fit¹ [fɪt] *n* (*of madness etc*) accès *m*; (*of coughing*) quinte *f*; (*apoplexy*) crise *f* d'apoplexie; (**epileptic**) **f.** crise d'épilepsie; **to have** *or F* **throw a f.** piquer une crise; *F* **he'll have a f. when he finds out** il en aura une congestion quand il le saura; **in a f. of temper** dans un mouvement de colère; **f. of crying** crise de larmes; **f. of laughter** accès de rire; **to be in fits** (**of laughter**) avoir le fou rire; **to have sb in fits** donner le fou rire à qn; **in a f. of carelessness** dans un moment d'inattention; **to work by fits and starts** travailler par à-coups
fit² *adj* (**fitter; fittest**) **(a)** (*appropriate*) bon, propre (**for sth** à qch); **f. to eat** bon à manger, mangeable; **f. to drink** buvable, potable; **I've nothing f. to wear** je n'ai rien à me mettre; **story that is not f. to be repeated** histoire qu'il ne serait pas convenable de répéter; **a meal f. for a king** un repas digne d'un roi; **I'm not f. to be seen** je ne suis pas présentable; **to think f.** *or* **see f. to do sth** trouver bon de faire qch; **do as you see** *or* **think f.** faites comme bon vous semble; **this is no f. way to behave** ce comportement est inacceptable; **this is no f. way to run a company** ce n'est pas comme ça qu'on dirige une entreprise; **he's not f. to polish my boots** il n'est même pas bon à cirer mes chaussures
(b) (*capable*) capable; **f. to do sth** capable de faire qch; **that's all he's f. for** il n'est bon qu'à cela; **she's not a f. mother** c'est une mère indigne
(c) (*ready*) **I felt f. to drop** je me sentais prêt à tomber (de fatigue); **she worked until she was f. to drop** elle a travaillé jusqu'à tomber de fatigue
(d) (*healthy*) en forme; **to get f.** retrouver la forme; **I'm a lot fitter** je suis bien plus en forme; **to be** (**fighting**) **f.** être en forme; **to keep f.** se maintenir en forme; **he is not yet f. to go back to work** il n'est pas encore en état de reprendre son travail; **f. for duty** bon pour le service; *Mil* valide; *F* **to be as f. as a fiddle** être en parfaite santé, se porter comme un charme
fit³ *n* **your coat is a perfect/poor f.** votre manteau vous va parfaitement/ne vous va pas très bien; **easy/tight f.** coupe *f* confortable/ajustée; **it was a tight f. but everyone squeezed in** il n'y avait pas beaucoup de place mais tout le monde a tenu
fit⁴ *v* (**-tt-**) **1** *vt* **(a)** (*be suitable for*) s'accorder avec; **to make the punishment f. the crime** proportionner la peine au délit
(b) (*of clothes*) **to fit sb** aller à qn; **it fits/they f. me** elle me va/elles me vont; **it fitted her perfectly** il était exactement à sa taille; **key that fits the lock** clef qui va à la serrure
(c) (*install*) adapter, ajuster (**sth to sth** qch à qch); **to f. a nozzle on the end of a pipe** adapter un ajutage à l'extrémité d'un tuyau; **to f. a handle to a broom** emmancher un balai; **to f. one part into another** emboîter une pièce dans une autre; **to f. a carpet** poser une moquette; **I'm going to be fitted for my new dress** je vais faire l'essayage de ma nouvelle robe
(d) (*assemble*) **to f. parts together** monter *ou* assembler des pièces; **to f. a machine together** assembler une machine
(e) (*equip*) munir, pourvoir (**sth with sth** qch de qch); **fitted with two propellers** pourvu de deux hélices
(f) (*insert*) **to f. sth/sb into/onto sth** mettre *ou F* caser qch/qn dans/sur qch; **we can f. another two (people) inside** il y a de la place pour deux personnes de plus
2 *vi* aller; **the lid doesn't f.** ce n'est pas le bon couvercle; **your dress fits well/badly** votre robe vous va/ne vous va pas bien; **she no longer fits into her dress** elle n'entre plus dans sa robe; **I can't f. into these jeans any more** je n'arrive plus à rentrer dans ce jean; **to f.** (**together**) s'ajuster, s'adapter;

to f. into sth (*of piece etc*) s'emboîter dans qch; **all her tools easily fitted into the bag** tous ses outils tenaient largement dans le sac; **we won't all f. into the car** nous ne tiendrons pas tous dans la voiture; **the photos just f. onto the page** les photos tiennent juste sur la page; **the phrase/colour has to f.** l'expression/la couleur doit bien aller avec le reste; *F* **his face didn't fit** on n'aimait pas sa gueule

▶ **fit in 1** *vtsep* (*find room, time for*) **I can't f. any more clothes in** je ne peux plus mettre aucun vêtement; **the hairdresser says she can f. me in tomorrow** la coiffeuse dit qu'elle peut s'arranger pour me prendre demain; **I'll check my diary and see if I can f. you in** je vais regarder mon agenda et voir si je trouve un moment pour toi

2 *vi* **(a)** (*go into place*) tenir; **there's no way they'll all f. in** ils ne tiendront jamais tous; **to f. in between two things** s'emboîter entre deux choses

(b) (*harmonize*) **to f. in with sth** (*of piece of furniture, building, colour*) être en accord avec qch; **your plans don't f. in with mine** vos projets ne cadrent pas avec les miens; **to f. in with sb's plans** (*of person*) s'adapter aux projets de qn; **he doesn't f. in there** il n'y est pas dans son élément; **you'll have to make more of an effort to f. in** il va falloir que tu t'efforces un peu plus pour t'adapter *ou* t'intégrer

(c) (*agree*) correspondre (**with** à); *F* coller (**with** avec); **that doesn't f. in with what I was told** ça ne correspond pas à ce qu'on m'a dit; *F* ça ne colle pas avec ce qu'on m'a dit

▶ **fit out** *vtsep* équiper (**sth with sth** qch de qch); (*ship*) armer; (*new ship*) équiper; **to f. sb out** équiper qn (**with clothes/***etc* de vêtements/*etc*)

▶ **fit up** *vtsep* **(a)** (*provide*) doter, pourvoir, munir (**with** de); **they fitted me up with an artificial leg** ils m'ont mis une jambe artificielle **(b)** *F* **to f. sb up (for a crime)** monter un coup contre qn; **they claim to have been fitted up by the Serious Crimes Squad** ils se prétendent tous victimes d'un coup monté organisé par la Brigade criminelle

fitful ['fɪtfʊl] *adj* (*sleep, night*) agité; **to make f. progress** progresser par à-coups

fitfully ['fɪtfəlɪ] *adv* (*to sleep*) d'un sommeil agité; (*to work*) par à-coups

fitment ['fɪtmənt] *n* **(a)** *Br* (*piece of furniture*) élément *m* **(b)** (*of machine*) accessoire *m*

fitness ['fɪtnɪs] *n* **(a)** (*health*) forme *f* (physique); **f. centre** club *m* de gymnastique; **f. freak** fana *mf* de la forme; **f. room** salle *f* de musculation **(b)** (*suitability*) (*of person*) aptitude *f* (**for a job**/*etc* à un emploi/*etc*); (*of remark*) justesse *f*, à-propos *m*; **her f. for government** *or* **power** son aptitude à gouverner

fitted ['fɪtɪd] *adj* **(a)** (*garment*) ajusté; **f. carpet** moquette *f*; **f. kitchen** cuisine *f* encastrée; **f. sheet** drap *m* housse; **f. wardrobe/cooker** garde-robe *f*/four *m* encastré(e) **(b)** (*suitable*) (*of person, thing*) **to be f. for sth** convenir à qch

fitter ['fɪtər] *n* **(a)** *MecE, Aut etc* ajusteur *m*, assembleur, -euse; **electrical f.** installateur *m* d'appareils électriques **(b)** *Sewing* essayeur, -euse

fitting ['fɪtɪŋ] **1** *adj* convenable, approprié (**to** à); (*remark*) à propos; **it was a f. tribute to a great athlete** c'était un hommage mérité rendu à un grand athlète; **it was only f. he should score the winning goal** ce n'était que justice qu'il marque le but gagnant; **a f. end for a murderer** une fin appropriée pour un meurtrier

2 *n* **(a)** (*of clothes*) essayage *m*; *Com* **made in three fittings** fabriqué en trois tailles; (*of shoes*) fabriqué en trois largeurs; **f. room** cabine *f* d'essayage

(b) (*usu pl*) **fittings** (*of office etc*) installations *fpl*; (*of bathroom etc*) accessoires *mpl*; **door fittings** ferrures *fpl* de porte; **brass fittings** garnitures *fpl* en cuivre; *El* **light f.** appareil *m* d'éclairage; **ceiling f.** plafonnier *m*; **wall f.** applique *f*; *Ind* **f. shop** atelier *m* d'ajustage

fittingly ['fɪtɪŋlɪ] *adv* convenablement, à propos; **f., he was buried in his home town** comme il convenait, il a été enterré dans sa ville natale; **f. he died the sort of violent death he had inflicted on so many others** ce n'est que justice qu'il soit mort de la même mort violente qu'il avait infligée à tant d'autres

fitting out *n* (*of expedition etc*) équipement *m*; (*of ship*) armement *m*

five [faɪv] **1** *adj, n* (*numeral*) cinq *m*; **f.-o'clock shadow** barbe *f* d'un jour; *Br* **a f.-pound note** un billet de cinq livres; **he leaves his office at f.** il quitte son bureau à cinq heures; **f. and a quarter inch disk** disquette *f* de cinq pouces un quart **2** *npl Sp* **fives** (*game*) = balle *f* au mur

five-day week *n* semaine *f* de cinq jours

five-door model *n Aut* (version *f*) cinq portes *f*

five-finger *adj Mus* **f. exercises** exercices *mpl* de doigté

fivefold ['faɪvfəʊld] **1** *adj* quintuple; **a f. increase/rise** une augmentation au quintuple **2** *adv* au quintuple; **to increase f.** quintupler, augmenter au quintuple

fiver ['faɪvər] *n F Br* billet *m* de cinq livres, *US* billet de cinq dollars; *Br* **it'll cost you a f.** ça te coûtera cinq livres

five-seater *n Aut* cinq places *f*

five-speed gearbox *n Aut* boîte *f* cinq-vitesses, boîte de vitesses cinq rapports

fivespot ['faɪvspɒt] *n US F* billet *m* de cinq dollars

five-star *adj* (*hotel*) cinq étoiles, quatre étoiles-luxe; **f. accommodation** hébergement *m* en hôtel cinq étoiles

five-year *adj* quinquennal

Five-Year Plan *n Econ* Plan *m* quinquennal

fix[1] [fɪks] *n* **(a)** *F* (*difficulty*) embarras *m*, difficulté *f*; **to be in a f.** être dans le pétrin; **to get into a f.** se mettre dans l'embarras *ou* dans le pétrin; **I'm in a bit of a f. financially** j'ai quelques difficultés financières **(b)** *Sl* (*of drug*) dose *f*; (*injection*) piqûre *f* (de drogue); **to give oneself a f.** se piquer, se shooter; *F, Fig* **my daily f. of television news** ma dose quotidienne de journaux télévisés **(c)** *Av, Naut* position *f*; **to get a f. on a ship/***etc* déterminer la position d'un navire/*etc* **(d)** *F* (*set-up*) **the match/quiz was a f.** le match/jeu était truqué; **it's a f.!** c'est de l'arnaque!

fix[2] *vt* **(a)** (*attach securely*) fixer; (*bait to a line etc*) accrocher; **to f. sth in one's memory** se graver qch dans la mémoire; **to f. one's attention on sth** fixer son attention sur qch; **to f. one's eye(s) on sb** fixer qn (du regard)

(b) (*decide*) (*limits, interest rates etc*) fixer, établir; (*meeting place*) choisir; (*itinerary, date, price etc*) fixer; (*meeting etc*) arranger; **there's nothing fixed yet, nothing is fixed yet** il n'y a encore rien de décidé *ou* de fixé

(c) (*repair*) réparer, retaper; (*prepare*) (*meal etc*) préparer; **to f. sth with sb** arranger qch avec qn; **I've fixed it with her** je me suis arrangé avec elle; *F* **I'll f. him!** je lui ferai son affaire!; **just wait while I f. my hair** attends que je me coiffe

(d) (*set up*) (*camp*) établir

(e) (*bribe*) graisser la patte à; (*rig*) (*match, jury etc*) truquer

(f) *Ch, Phot etc* (*mercury, dye etc*) fixer

(g) *US Dial* **to be fixing to do sth** envisager de faire qch

▶ **fix on 1** *vtsep* (*attach*) fixer **2** *vipo* (*choose, decide*) (*holiday destination, dress, house etc*) se décider pour; (*date, itinerary, price, time*) fixer

▶ **fix up** *vtsep F* **(a)** (*assemble, put up*) (*tent*) monter; **they fixed up a temporary telephone** ils ont installé une ligne de téléphone provisoire; **to f. up a room as a study** transformer une pièce en bureau

(b) (*arrange*) (*business, meeting*) arranger; **it's all fixed up** c'est une affaire réglée, tout est arrangé; **I've already fixed up to go out tonight** j'ai déjà prévu de sortir ce soir

(c) (*improve*) (*car, bike*) réparer, retaper; (*house, apartment*) retaper; **you should f. yourself up a bit** tu devrais t'arranger un peu

(d) (*provide*) **to f. sb up with a job/room** trouver un travail/une chambre pour *ou* à qn; **I've fixed you up with a date** je t'ai arrangé un rendez-vous; **they've been trying to f. me up with her for weeks** ça fait des semaines qu'ils essaient de me monter un plan avec elle

fixated [fɪk'seɪtɪd] *adj* **to be f. on** *or* **with sth** être obsédé par qch; **he was still f. by the idea** cette idée l'obsédait encore

fixation [fɪk'seɪʃən] *n Psy* fixation *f*; **to have a mother f.** faire une fixation sur sa mère

fixative ['fɪksətɪv] *adj, n Art* fixatif *m*

fixed [fɪkst] *adj* **(a)** fixe; (*rule*) établi, absolu; (*smile*) figé; **f. annual payment** annuité *f* constante; *Acct* **f. asset** actif *m* immobilisé; *Acct* **f. asset account** compte *m* d'immobilisations; **f. assets** immobilisations *fpl*; **f. costs** charges *fpl* fixes, charges de structure, coûts *mpl* fixes; **f. disk** disque *m* fixe; **of f. length** de longueur constante; **to have f. ideas** avoir des idées (bien) arrêtées; **f. income** revenu *m* fixe; **f. income investment** placement *m* à revenus fixes; **f. interest** intérêt *m* fixe; **to have no f. plans** ne pas avoir de projets bien déterminés; **f. point** point *m* fixe, point de repère; **f. point arithmetic** arithmétique *f* en virgule fixe; **f. price** prix *m* fixe *ou* forfaitaire; **f. rate** prix *m* fixe

(b) *F* **how are you f. for money/for condoms?** tu as assez d'argent/de capotes?; **how are you f. for time?** tu as du temps libre?; **how are you f. for accommodation/transport?** est-ce que tu as un endroit où loger/un moyen de transport?; **how are we f. for disks?** on a des disquettes?

(c) *Ch* (*oil, salt*) fixe

(d) *F Pej* (*rigged*) truqué

fixed-centre holiday *n* vacances *fpl* avec hébergement fixe

fixedly ['fɪksɪdlɪ] *adv* fixement

fixed-price menu *n* menu *m* à prix fixe

fixed-rate *adj* à taux fixe
fixed-term *adj Com* à terme fixe; **f. bill** effet *m* à date fixe; **f. contract** contrat *m* à durée déterminée, CDD *m*; **f. credit** crédit *m* à durée déterminée
fixer [ˈfɪksər] *n* **(a)** *F* (*person*) combinard *m* **(b)** *Art* fixatif *m*; *Phot* fixateur *m*
fixing [ˈfɪksɪŋ] *n* **(a)** (*repairing*) réparation *f* **(b)** *Com* (*of prices etc*) établissement *m*; *Phot* **f. solution/bath** solution *f*/bain *m* de fixage **(c)** (*usu pl*) *Am* **fixings** (*trimmings*) accessoires *mpl*; (*food*) accompagnements *mpl*, garnitures *fpl*; **roast turkey with all the fixings** dinde rôtie avec tout ce qui s'ensuit
fixity [ˈfɪksɪtɪ] *n* fixité *f*; *Fml* **f. of purpose** détermination *f*
fixture [ˈfɪkstʃər] *n* **(a)** (*installation*) appareil *m* fixe; **fixtures** (*of house etc*) aménagements *mpl*; (*electrical etc*) appareils; **fixtures and fittings** agencements *mpl*, installations *fpl* fixes; **£3000 for fixtures and fittings** 3.000 livres de reprise; **bathroom fixtures and fittings** installations et accessoires de salles de bain; *F* **he's become a f. here** il fait partie des meubles à présent; **she was something of a f. at his parties** elle apparaissait inévitablement à chacune de ses soirées; **she was becoming a f.** elle commençait à faire partie des meubles
(b) *Br Sp* rencontre *f* (prévue), match *m* (prévu); **f. list** calendrier *m* (de la saison)
fizz¹ [fɪz] *n* **(a)** (*sound*) (*of champagne etc*) pétillement *m*; (*of steam*) sifflement *m*; (*fizziness*) gaz *m* **(b)** *F* (*soft drink*) boisson *f* gazeuse; (*champagne*) champagne *m*
fizz² *vi* (*of champagne*) pétiller; (*of steam, firework*) siffler; **the champagne fizzed out of the bottle** le champagne est sorti de la bouteille en pétillant; **the coke fizzed up and spilled onto the table** le coca a moussé et s'est répandu sur la table
fizzle [ˈfɪz(ə)l] *vi* (*of wine*) pétiller; (*of gas burner etc*) siffler
▶ **fizzle out** *vi F* (*of plan*) tomber à l'eau; (*of enthusiasm, interest, desire*) tomber; (*of hope*) s'envoler; (*of story, film*) finir en queue de poisson; **the evening fizzled out** la soirée se traîna lamentablement
fizzy [ˈfɪzɪ] *adj* (*mineral water, drink*) gazeux; (*wine*) mousseux
fjord [fjɔːd] *n Geog* fjord *m*, fiord *m*
Fla *abbr* **Florida**
flab [flæb] *n F* (*fat*) graisse *f*; **he was trying to get rid of his f.** il essayait de perdre sa graisse
flabbergast [ˈflæbəgɑːst] *vt F* abasourdir, ahurir; **I was flabbergasted** j'en étais sidéré
flabbiness [ˈflæbɪnɪs] *n* (*of flesh, skin*) flaccidité *f*, manque *m* de fermeté; (*of person*) flaccidité; (*of person's grip*) mollesse *f*; (*of prose, writing, novel*) prolixité *f*; (*of argument, idea*) manque de rigueur
flabby [ˈflæbɪ] *adj* (*muscles etc*) flasque, mou, *f* molle; (*cheeks*) pendant; (*person*) grassouillet; (*grip*) mou; *Fig* (*prose*) prolixe; (*reasoning, ideas, morals*) qui manque de rigueur
flaccid [ˈflæsɪd] *adj* mou, *f* molle; (*flesh*) flasque
flag¹ [flæg] *n* **(a)** (*cloth, emblem*) drapeau *m*; *Naut* pavillon *m*; *Fig* **to fly the f. for one's country** défendre les couleurs de son pays; *also Fig* **to show the f.** faire acte de présence; **black f.** (*of pirate*) pavillon noir; **yellow f.** pavillon de quarantaine; *Naut, Com* **f. of convenience** pavillon de complaisance; **f. airline** compagnie *f* aérienne nationale; **f. carrier** (*airline etc*) compagnie de transports nationale; **f. signals** signalisation *f* par fanions **(b)** (*of taxi*) drapeau *m*; **taxi with the f. up** taxi *m* libre **(c)** *Comptr* (*marker*) drapeau *m*, marqueur *m* **(d)** (*for file, folder*) papillon *m*
flag² *vt* **(a)** = **flag down (b)** (*mark*) marquer; (*error in text etc*) marquer, signaler
flag³ *vi* (*of sail*) battre; (*of plant*) s'étioler, languir; (*of person*) s'alanguir; (*of conversation*) traîner, languir; (*of attention, courage, determination*) faiblir; **our spirits were flagging** notre moral faiblissait; **his strength was flagging** ses forces baissaient
flag⁴ *n* = **flagstone**
flag⁵ *vt Constr* (*pave*) daller; (*pavement etc*) paver de carreaux
flag⁶ *n* (*plant*) iris *m*
▶ **flag down** *vtsep* (*stop*) arrêter, stopper
▶ **flag out** *vtsep Sp* (*racetrack*) jalonner
▶ **flag up** *vtsep* (*mark, indicate*) marquer; (*mistake*) signaler, marquer
flag captain *n Naut* commandant *m* du navire amiral
Flag Day *n* (*in United States*) le 14 juin
flag day *n* (*for charity*) = jour *m* de quête pour une œuvre de bienfaisance
flagellate¹ [ˈflædʒəleɪt] *adj, n Zool* flagellé *m*
flagellate² *vt* flageller, fouetter
flagellation [flædʒəˈleɪʃən] *n* flagellation *f*
flageolet [ˈflædʒəlet, flædʒəˈlet] *n Mus, Culin* flageolet *m*
flagged [flægd] *adj* (*floor*) dallé
flagging¹ [ˈflægɪŋ] *adj* (*conversation etc*) languissant; (*courage, determination, attention*) faiblissant; (*strength, health*) baissant; **to revive sb's f. spirits** remonter le moral à qn
flagging² *n* (*paving*) dallage *m*
flag officer *n Naut* officier *m* général
flagon [ˈflægən] *n* **(a)** (*large bottle*) grosse bouteille *f* (ventrue), bonbonne *f* **(b)** (*jug*) pot *m* (à anse)
flagpole [ˈflægpəʊl] *n* mât *m* de drapeau; *Fig, F* **to run sth up the f.** proposer qch pour voir les réactions
flagrant [ˈfleɪgrənt] *adj* (*offence, miscarriage of justice, lie*) flagrant; **a f. injustice** une injustice criante; **this f. disobedience** cet acte de désobéissance effronté; **what a f. cheek!** ça alors, quel culot!
flagrante delicto (in) [ɪnfləˈgræntɪdɪˈlɪktəʊ] *adv Jur* en flagrant délit
flagrantly [ˈfleɪgrəntlɪ] *adv* d'une manière flagrante; **f. unfair** d'une injustice criante; **f. dishonest** d'une malhonnêteté flagrante
flagship [ˈflægʃɪp] *n Naut* (navire *m*) amiral *m*; *Fig* **the London store is the f. of the chain** le magasin de Londres est le plus important de la chaîne; **this latest model is the f. of their new range** ce dernier modèle est le produit vedette de leur nouvelle gamme; **the Conservatives' f. council** le conseil municipal qui est le fleuron du parti Conservateur
flagstaff [ˈflægstɑːf] *n* mât *m* de drapeau; *Naut* mât de pavillon
flagstone [ˈflægstəʊn] *n* dalle *f*; **f. pavement** dallage *m* en pierre
flag-waving *n Pej, F* (*patriotic remarks*) déclarations *fpl* cocardières; **f. speech** discours *m* cocardier
flail¹ [fleɪl] *n Agr* fléau *m*
flail² **1** *vt* **(a)** *Agr* battre au fléau **(b)** **he flailed his fists at me** il balançait les poings dans ma direction; **the animal was flailing its legs in the air** l'animal battait l'air de ses pattes **2** *vi* (*of rope, cable*) se balancer violemment; **I dodged my assailant's flailing arms** j'ai esquivé les coups de mon assaillant
▶ **flail about, flail around** *vi* (*wave wildly*) (*of arms, legs*) s'agiter dans tous les sens; **she was flailing about in the water** elle se débattait des mains et des pieds dans l'eau
flair [ˈfleər] *n* (*skill*) aptitude *f* (**for** à); (*skill in detecting things etc*) flair *m*; (*energy etc*) dynamisme *m*; **to have a f. for languages/cooking** avoir le don des langues/pour cuisiner; **to dress/write with f.** (*stylishness*) s'habiller/écrire avec style; **he had no f. for business** il n'avait pas le sens des affaires; **they have a real f. for making the right choices** ils ont vraiment le don de faire les bons choix
flak [flæk] *n* **(a)** (*artillery*) artillerie *f* anti-aérienne; (*fire*) tir *m* contre-avions; **f. jacket** gilet *m* de protection **(b)** *F* (*criticism*) critique *f*; **she got a lot of f. for this decision** on l'a beaucoup critiquée pour cette décision
flake¹ [fleɪk] *n* **(a)** (*of snow, oat, corn*) flocon *m*; (*of metal etc*) écaille *f*, éclat *m*, paillette *f*; (*of paint, plaster*) écaille; **soap flakes** savon *m* en paillettes; **a f. of skin** un petit morceau de peau morte **(b)** *Am F* (*crazy person*) barjo *mf*
flake² *vi* (*of metal, paint etc*) s'écailler; (*of arms, nose*) peler; **my skin was flaking** je pelais
▶ **flake away, flake off** *vi* (*of metal, paint etc*) s'écailler; **the skin on my nose is flaking off** mon nez pèle, j'ai le nez qui pèle
▶ **flake out** *vi F* (*fall asleep*) s'endormir; **I just want to f. out on the sofa** j'ai envie de m'effondrer sur le canapé et roupiller; **she's gone upstairs to f. out** elle est montée roupiller; **to be flaked out** (*exhausted*) être vidé *ou* crevé; (*asleep*) roupiller
flaking [ˈfleɪkɪŋ] *adj* (*paint*) qui s'écaille; (*skin*) qui se détache
flaky [ˈfleɪkɪ] *adj* **(a)** (*mineral etc*) écailleux; (*paint*) écaillé; *Culin* **f. pastry** pâte *f* feuilletée; **her skin was all dry and f.** elle avait la peau toute sèche qui pelait **(b)** *Am F* (*crazy*) barjo
flamboyance [flæmˈbɔɪəns] *n* (*of personality, manner, clothes, car*) extravagance *f*; (*of physical gesture*) caractère *m* magistral
flamboyant [flæmˈbɔɪənt] *adj* (*personality, generosity, manner, clothes, car*) extravagant; (*physical gesture*) magistral
flamboyantly [flæmˈbɔɪəntlɪ] *adv* (*to behave, dress*) avec extravagance; (*designed*) aux lignes extravagantes
flame¹ [fleɪm] *n* **(a)** flamme *f*; **in flames** en flammes, en feu; **to go up in flames** être détruit par le feu; *Fig* (*of hopes, chances*) s'envoler, partir en fumée; **to burst into flame(s)**

s'enflammer, se mettre à flamber; **f. cutter** (*in metalworking*) chalumeau *m* à découper; *Agr* **f. gun** agriflamme *m*; **f. red** rouge feu *inv*; **f. red hair** chevelure *f* flamboyante; **f. tree** flamboyant *m*

(b) (*light*) éclat *m*

(c) *Lit* (*passion*) passion *f*, ardeur *f*; *F* (*lover*) béguin *m*; **he is an old f. of mine** c'est un de mes anciens amoureux; **the f. of passion** les feux de la passion; **the f. of enthusiasm** la flamme de l'enthousiasme; **to keep the f. of freedom burning** ne pas laisser s'éteindre la flamme de la liberté

flame² **1** *vi* (a) (*of fire etc*) flamber, flamboyer; *Lit* (*of passions etc*) brûler; **her cheeks flamed** ses joues s'empourprèrent (b) (*of diamond etc*) briller **2** *vt Culin* flamber

▶ **flame up** *vi* (*blaze*) s'enflammer; *F* (*get angry*) se mettre en colère; **to f. up at sb/a suggestion** se mettre en colère contre qn/à une suggestion

flame-coloured *adj* ponceau *inv*, couleur de feu *inv*

flamenco [flə'meŋkəʊ] *n Mus* flamenco *m*

flameproof ['fleɪmpruːf] *adj* ininflammable; (*material*) ignifugé; *El* antidéflagrant

flamethrower ['fleɪmθrəʊər] *n Mil etc* lance-flammes *m inv*

flaming ['fleɪmɪŋ] **1** *adj* (a) (*fire*) flambant, flamboyant (b) (*sun*) ardent; (*sunset*) flamboyant; (*sky*) embrasé; **f. red** rouge feu *inv*; *F* **in a f. temper** d'une humeur massacrante (c) *Br F* (*intensifier*) sacré; **you f. idiot!** sacré imbécile!; **a f. cheek** un culot monstre **2** *adv Br F* complètement, carrément; **he's so f. stupid** il est complètement stupide; **he's so f. brillant** il est carrément génial; **it was f. expensive** c'était super cher

flamingo, *pl* **-o (e)s** [flə'mɪŋgəʊ, -əʊz] *n* (*bird*) flamant *m*

flammable ['flæməb(ə)l] *adj* inflammable

flan [flæn] *n Culin* tarte *f*; **f. case** fond *m* de tarte

Flanders ['flɑːndəz] *n* Flandre *f*

flange¹ [flændʒ] *n* (*of tube, pipe*) bourrelet *m*, collerette *f*; (*of piece of sheet metal*) collet *m*, rebord *m*; (*of wheel*) boudin *m*, rebord; (*of beam*) aile *f*; *Rail* (*of rail*) patin *m*; **cooling f.** ailette *f* de refroidissement; **f. coupling** raccordement *m* à bride

flanged [flændʒd] *adj* (*tube*) à bride(s); (*wheel*) à boudin; (*rail*) à patin; (*beam*) à aile; (*piece of sheet metal*) à bord tombé; *Aut* (*radiator*) à ailettes

flank¹ [flæŋk] *n* (a) (*of person, animal*) flanc *m*; *Culin* (*of beef*) flanchet *m* (b) (*of mountain etc*) côté *m*, flanc *m* (c) *Mil* (*of army etc*) flanc *m*; **left/right f.** aile *f* gauche/droite; **to protect one's flanks** se couvrir sur les flancs; **to launch a f. attack** lancer une attaque de côté; *Mktg* **f. attack** attaque *f* latérale

flank² *vt* (a) flanquer; **to f. sth with *or* by sth** flanquer qch de qch; **flanked by two policemen** encadré de deux gendarmes (b) *Mil* (*the enemy*) prendre de flanc; (*trench*) enfiler; **flanking movement** attaque *f* par le/les flanc(s)

flanker ['flæŋkər] *n* (a) *Rugby* avant-aile *m*, *pl* avant-ailes (b) *Mktg* produit *m* de protection latérale; **f. brand** marque *f* de protection latérale, marque dérivée

flannel ['flæn(ə)l] **1** *n* (a) *Tex* (*material*) flanelle *f*; **flannels** (*trousers*) pantalon *m* de flanelle (b) *Br* **(face) f.** = gant *m* de toilette (c) *Br F* (*wordy language*) blabla(bla) *m*; (*flattery*) flatteries *fpl* **2** *adj* (*trousers etc*) de flanelle **3** *vi Br F* faire du baratin; **stop flannelling** arrête ton baratin

flannelette [flænə'let] *n* pilou *m*, veloutine *f*

flap¹ [flæp] *n* (a) (*movement, sound*) (*of wing*) battement *m*, coup *m*; (*of sail*) claquement *m*

(b) (*piece of material etc*) (*of envelope, dustcover for book, tent*) rabat *m*; (*of pocket*) patte *f*; (*of table*) abattant *m*; (*of cellar door*) trappe *f*; (*on studio light*) volet *m*; *Av* volet; *MecE* clapet *m* (à charnière); **desk with a writing f.** secrétaire *m*; **a f. of skin** un lambeau de peau; *Aut* **f. valve** (*in throttle*) valve *f* papillon, papillon *m*

(c) *F* (*panic*) affolement *m*; **to get into a f.** s'affoler, se mettre dans tous ses états; **to be in a f.** ne plus savoir où donner de la tête; **there's a big f. on** c'est la panique, c'est l'affolement total

flap² **(-pp-)** **1** *vt* (*wings*) battre; (*hands, piece of paper*) agiter; **the bird flaps its wings** l'oiseau bat des ailes; **to f. one's arms about** agiter les bras **2** *vi* (a) (*of sail*) battre, claquer; (*of wings*) battre; **the eagle flapped off/away** l'aigle s'envola/s'éloigna en battant des ailes; **when she started talking to me it really set his ears flapping** quand elle a commencé à me parler il a tendu l'oreille (b) *F* (*panic*) s'affoler, se mettre dans tous ses états; **once he stopped flapping about** une fois son affolement passé

flapjack ['flæpdʒæk] *n Culin* (a) *Am* (*pancake*) crêpe *f* (b) *Br* (*biscuit*) biscuit *m* à l'avoine

flapper ['flæpər] *n* = jeune femme *f* (des années 20)

flapping ['flæpɪŋ] *n* (*of wings*) battement *m*; (*of sail*) claquement *m*

flare¹ [fleər] *n* (a) (*bright flame*) flamboiement *m*; (*of jet engine etc*) flammes *fpl* (b) (*signal*) feu *m* de signal; (*rocket*) fusée *f* éclairante; **f. pistol** pistolet *m* de signalisation; **f. path** piste *f* éclairée (c) (*of pipe etc*) évasement *m*; (*of skirt*) godet *m*; **(pair of) flares** (*trousers*) pantalon *m* (à) pattes d'éléphant

flare² **1** *vi* (a) (*of lamp, light etc*) flamboyer (b) (*of skirt etc*) s'évaser; (*of nostrils*) se dilater **(with** de**)** (c) (*of temper*) s'échauffer; **tempers flared at the council meeting** le ton est monté pendant la réunion du conseil **2** *vt* (*pipe, skirt etc*) évaser; (*nostrils*) dilater

▶ **flare up** *vi* (a) (*of candle etc*) s'enflammer brusquement (b) (*of anger, fighting etc*) éclater; (*of person*) s'emporter; (*of medical condition, skin condition*) se déclencher; **he flares up at the slightest thing** il monte comme une soupe au lait

flared [fleəd] *adj* (*skirt, pipe etc*) evasé; **f. trousers** pantalon *m* à pattes d'éléphant

flare-up *n* (a) (*with flames*) flambée *f* soudaine (b) (*outbreak*) (*of war*) déclenchement *m*; (*of anger*) éruption *f*; (*renewal of anger, war*) recrudescence *f*; (*argument*) altercation *f*; (*of person*) flambée *f ou* éclat *m* de colère; (*of violence*) explosion *f*; **there has been a new f. in the Balkans** il y a eu une nouvelle recrudescence des combats dans les Balkans

flash¹ [flæʃ] *n* (a) (*light*) éclair *m*; (*of diamond etc*) éclat *m*; (*of firearm*) lueur *f*, éclair; **a f. of lightning** un éclair; **f. of wit** saillie *f*; **f. of inspiration** éclair de génie; **(as) quick as a f.** vif comme l'éclair; **in a f.** en un rien de temps, en un clin d'œil; **it came to her in a f.** ça lui est venu subitement; *Fig* **a f. in the pan** un feu de paille; **f. welding** (*in metalwork*) soudure *f* par étincelage

(b) *Phot* flash *m*, *pl* flashes; **f. gun** flash *m*; **f. photography** photographie *f* au flash; **I took this one with a f.** celle-ci je l'ai prise au flash *ou* avec le flash

(c) *Am F* (*torch*) torche *f* (électrique)

(d) *Journ* flash *m*; **news f.** flash d'information

(e) *Br Mil* (*badge*) écusson *m*

flash² **1** *vi* (a) (*of light, diamonds*) briller; (*of light on police car etc*) clignoter; (*of eyes*) jeter des éclairs; (*with enthusiasm*) briller; **the light flashed once then went out** la lumière s'est allumée puis s'est éteinte; **his eyes flashed with anger** ses yeux lançaient des éclairs de colère

(b) (*move fast*) **to f. past** passer comme un éclair; **she flashed past me on a skateboard** elle m'a doublé en skateboard à la vitesse de l'éclair; **he flashed through the exercises** il a fait les exercices à toute vitesse; **the days seemed to f. by** les journées ont passé à toute vitesse; **it flashed across my mind that ...** l'idée m'est venue tout d'un coup que ...; **my life flashed before me** ma vie a défilé devant mes yeux; **a look of panic flashed across his face** une expression de panique passa rapidement sur son visage; **a smile flashed across her lips** un sourire se dessina soudain sur ses lèvres

(c) *Br F* (*expose oneself*) s'exhiber **(at** devant**)**

2 *vt* (a) (*smile, look*) lancer **(at sb** à qn**)**; **to f. a light in sb's eyes** diriger une lumière dans les yeux de qn; **she flashed her headlights at us** elle nous a fait un appel de phares; **she flashed a mirror to signal for help** elle a fait des signaux avec un miroir pour appeler à l'aide; **he was flashing a fat wad of money** il exhibait un gros paquet de billets; **to f. a piece of news all over Europe** répandre une nouvelle en éclair à travers l'Europe; **she flashed a report to head office** elle a envoyé un rapport-éclair au siège social

(b) (*show quickly*) montrer rapidement; (*picture etc on screen*) projeter; **he flashed a photo in front of me** il m'a passé une photo sous les yeux; **he flashed a £50 note at them** il leur passa un billet de cinquante livres sous le nez

flash³ *adj Br F* (*showy*) tape-à-l'œil *inv*, voyant, extravagant; **f. Harry** (*fancy dresser*) m'as-tu-vu *m*; (*spiv*) filou *m*

▶ **flash around** *vtas F* (*show off*) montrer, exhiber; **he likes flashing his money around** il aime étaler sa richesse; **don't f. your money around here!** ne montre *ou* n'exhibe pas ton argent ici!

▶ **flash back** *vi Cin* (*of film*) revenir en arrière, faire un retour en arrière *ou* un flash-back; (*of mind*) remonter (dans le passé); **my thoughts flashed back to the last time we had all been together** j'ai soudain repensé à la dernière fois où nous étions tous ensemble

▶ **flash forward** *vi* (*of film*) faire un saut en avant

flashback ['flæʃbæk] *n Cin* retour *m* en arrière, flash-back *m*; **their story is told in f.** leur histoire est racontée par flash-backs *ou* par retours en arrière; *Fig* **he had a f. to that fateful day** cette journée fatidique lui revint soudain à l'esprit

flashbulb ['flæʃbʌlb] *n Phot* ampoule *f* (de) flash

flash burn *n Nucl, Phys* brûlure *f* par irradiation

flashcard ['flæʃkɑːd] *n* étiquette *f*

flashcube ['flæʃkjuːb] *n Phot* flash *m* cube

flasher ['flæʃər] *n* **(a)** *Br F* (*man exposing himself*) exhibitionniste *m* **(b)** *Aut F* (*lamp*) clignotant *m*; **f. unit** centrale *f* clignotant

flash flood *n Met* crue *f* subite

flashily ['flæʃɪlɪ] *adv* **f. dressed** habillé tapageusement

flashing¹ ['flæʃɪŋ] **1** *adj* (*signal, light, torch*) clignotant; (*eyes, gems*) étincelant **2** *n* (*of diamond*) éclat *m*; (*of mirror*) miroitement *m*; (*of signal*) clignotement *m*

flashing² *n* (*on roof*) revêtement *m*

flashlamp ['flæʃlæmp] *n* torche *f* (électrique)

flashlight ['flæʃlaɪt] *n* **(a)** *Phot* flash *m*; **f. photography** photographie *f* au flash **(b)** *esp Am* (*torch*) torche *f* (électrique)

flashover ['flæʃəʊvər] *n El* étincelle *f* de rupture

flash pack *n* (*discounted*) emballage *m* comportant une réduction de prix

flash point *n Tech* (*of oil etc*) point *m* d'inflammabilité; *Fig* situation *f* explosive *ou* critique

flashy ['flæʃɪ] *adj Pej* (*clothes, car, jewellery*) voyant, tapageur, -euse; (*taste*) tapageur; **f. young man** jeune homme habillé tapageusement; **you and your f. friends** toi et tes copains aux goûts tapageurs

flask [flɑːsk] *n* flacon *m*; *Ch* fiole *f*; (*spherical*) ballon *m*; **brandy f.** flacon à cognac; **(vacuum) f.** thermos® *m ou f*; **a f. of tea** un(e) thermos de thé

flat¹ [flæt] **1** *adj* **(a)** plat; (*roof*) plat, en terrasse; (*curve etc*) aplati; (*surface*) plat, uni; (*nose*) camus; *Med* (*feet*) plat; (*picture*) sans relief; (*in painting*) (*colour*) mat; *Archit* (*vault*) plat; (*arch*) déprimé; **to beat sth f.** aplatir qch; **the city had been bombed f.** les bombardements avaient rasé la ville; **as f. as a pancake** plat comme une galette; *F* **to go into a f. spin** (*of person*) s'affoler; **f. bed** (*of lorry*) plateau *m*; **f. blade screwdriver** tournevis *m* à lame plate, tournevis plat; **f. cap** casquette *f*; **f. chest** poitrine *f* plate; **f. country** pays *m* plat; *Comptr* **f. file** fichier *m* non structuré; *Aut* **f. 4** 4 cylindres à plat; **f. race** course *f* plate *ou* de plat; *Horseracing* **f. racing** le plat; *Comptr, TV* **f. screen** écran *m* plat; **f. screen tube** tube *m* cathodique plat; **f. sheets** (*in bookbinding*) feuilles *fpl* à plat; **f. shoes** chaussures *fpl* plates; *Aut* **f. spot** point *m* mort; **f. tyre** pneu *m* à plat; (*punctured*) pneu crevé

(b) (*absolute*) net, *f* nette; (*denial*) formel, absolu; (*refusal*) net, catégorique; **to give a f. refusal** refuser net; *F* **and that's f.!** voilà qui est net!; **I'm not going and that's f.** je n'y vais pas, un point c'est tout

(c) (*existence etc*) monotone, ennuyeux; (*style etc*) terne; (*voice*) terne, blanc; (*drink*) éventé, plat; (*battery*) à plat; **to go f.** (*of drink*) s'éventer; *Naut* **f. calm** calme *m* plat; **business has been a bit f. lately** les affaires sont calmes ces derniers temps

(d) *Com etc* (*unchanging*) **f. rate** taux *m ou* tarif *m* uniforme; **f. fare, f.-rate fare** (*on bus etc*) tarif unique; **f.-rate subscription** abonnement *m* à forfait

(e) (*sound*) sourd; *Mus* bémol *inv*; **symphony in D f.** symphonie en ré bémol; **you're f.** (*singing*) vous chantez en dessous du ton; (*playing*) vous jouez en dessous du ton; **her voice went a bit f. at the end** elle a fini un peu en dessous du ton

2 *adv* **(a)** (*in level position*) à plat; *also Fig* **to knock sb f.** faire tomber qn à la renverse; **to fall f. on one's face** tomber à plat ventre; *F* (*be humiliated*) essuyer une humiliation; **to fall f.** (*of joke etc*) manquer son effet, tomber à plat; (*of play etc*) faire un four; **stretched out f. on the ground** étendu à plat sur le sol; **to fold f.** se plier; **he pressed himself f. against the wall** il s'est collé au mur

(b) (*absolutely*) nettement, positivement; *F* **he told me f. that ...** il m'a dit carrément que ...; **to turn sb down f.** envoyer qn balader, envoyer qn sur les roses; *F* **to be f. broke** être à sec; **to work f. out** travailler d'arrache-pied; **to go f. out** (*run*) filer à toute allure; *Fig* **she was going f. out for the championship** elle mettait tout en jeu pour le championnat; **to lie f. out** être allongé à plat; **to be f. out** (*exhausted*) être à plat

(c) (*exactly*) **in twenty seconds f.** en vingt secondes pile; **in less than ten seconds f.** en moins de dix secondes

(d) *Mus* (*to sing, play etc*) en dessous du ton

3 *n* **(a)** (*of sword etc*) plat *m*; **the f. of the hand** le plat de la main

(b) (*land*) plaine *f*; (*left exposed at low tide*) sèche *f*

(c) **on the f.** (*horizontally*) horizontalement; *Rail* (*track*) en palier; *Sp* sur le plat

(d) *Horseracing* **the f.** (*season*) la saison du plat; (*racing*) les courses *fpl* de plat, le plat

(e) *esp Br* (*rooms*) appartement *m*; **furnished/unfurnished f.** appartement meublé/non meublé; **service f.** appartement avec service; **f. swapping** échange *m* d'appartement

(f) *Th* (*scenery*) panneau *m* de décor

(g) *Mus* bémol *m*

(h) *F* (*flat tyre*) pneu *m* à plat; (*punctured*) pneu crevé

flatbed ['flætbed] *adj* **f. truck** *or Br* **lorry** semi-remorque *m* à plateau; *Comptr* **f. plotter** traceur *m* à plat; *Comptr* **f. scanner** scanneur *m* à plat

flat-bottomed ['flæt'bɒtəmd] *adj* à fond plat

flatcar ['flætkɑːr] *n Am Rail* wagon *m* en plateforme

flat-chested ['flæt'tʃestɪd] *adj* plat

flatfish, *pl* **-fishes** *or* **-fish** ['flætfɪʃ, -fɪʃɪz] *n* poisson *m* plat

flatfoot ['flætfʊt] *n* **(a)** *Med* pied *m* plat **(b)** *Old-fashioned Br F* (*policeman*) agent *m* de police, *F* poulet *m*

flat-footed *adj* **(a)** *Med* à pied plat, aux pieds plats **(b)** *Br Fig, F* (*clumsy, inelegant*) maladroit

flatiron ['flætaɪən] *n* fer *m* à repasser

flatlet ['flætlɪt] *n esp Br* petit appartement *m*, studio *m*

flatly ['flætlɪ] *adv* **(a)** (*absolutely*) nettement, carrément; (*to refuse*) net; (*to deny*) absolument; (*to say*) sèchement **(b)** (*monotonously*) d'une façon monotone; **the speaker's voice droned f. on** l'orateur continuait de sa voix lassante et monotone

flatmate ['flætmeɪt] *n Br* colocataire *mf* (*d'un appartement*); **we used to be flatmates** avant nous partagions un appartement

flatness ['flætnɪs] *n* **(a)** (*of surface etc*) nature *f* plate; (*of countryside*) absence *f* de relief; (*of curve etc*) aplatissement *m* **(b)** (*of refusal*) netteté *f* **(c)** (*of existence etc*) monotonie *f*; (*of style etc*) insipidité *f*, platitude *f*; (*of beer etc*) évent *m*; (*of colour*) caractère *m* terne; (*of sound*) caractère sourd; **there was a f. in his voice which suggested that ...** le détachement que l'on décelait dans sa voix suggérait que ...

flatten ['flæt(ə)n] **(-n-) 1** *vt* **(a)** aplatir; (*road*) aplanir; (*of wind, rain*) (*corn etc*) coucher; **to f. oneself against a wall** se plaquer *ou* se coller contre un mur; *F* **to f. sb** (*in fight*) mettre la pâtée à qn; (*humiliate*) écraser qn **(b)** (*make dull*) rendre fade *ou* insipide; (*make less striking*) atténuer **(c)** *Mus* (*note*) bémoliser **2** *vi* **(a)** s'aplatir **(b)** (*become dull*) devenir fade *ou* insipide; (*of colour*) se ternir

▶ **flatten out** *vi* **(a)** *Av* reprendre le vol horizontal; (*after dive*) se redresser; (*of inflation, unemployment etc*) se stabiliser **(at** à**)** **(b)** (*of terrain, slope*) s'aplanir

flattened ['flæt(ə)nd] *adj* **(a)** aplati; (*nose*) épaté **(b)** *Mus* (*note*) bémolisé

flatter ['flætər] **1** *vt* flatter; **the portrait/dress flatters her** ce portrait/cette robe la flatte *ou* l'avantage; **he flatters himself that he will succeed** il est persuadé de sa réussite; **I f. myself on my goulash/my ability to judge people** je me flatte de faire un bon goulasch/de savoir juger les gens; *F* **don't f. yourself!** tu rêves! **2** *vi* être flatteur

flatterer ['flætərər] *n* flatteur, -euse; (*who exaggerates*) flagorneur, -euse

flattering ['flætərɪŋ] *adj* (*words, photo etc*) flatteur, -euse; (*exaggerated*) adulatoire; **it is f. to be asked to give this speech** c'est flatteur d'être sollicité pour faire ce discours; **to speak in f. terms of sb, to make f. remarks about sb** parler de qn en termes flatteurs; **I didn't get a very f. impression of the city/your boss** la ville/ton patron ne m'a pas fait une impression très favorable

flatteringly ['flætərɪŋlɪ] *adv* (*to speak*) en termes flatteurs; **the photograph had been f. lit** la photo avait été prise dans une lumière flatteuse

flattery ['flætərɪ] *n* flatterie *f*; (*exaggerated*) flagornerie *f*; **f. will get you nowhere!** ça ne vous apportera rien de flatter les gens!

flat top *n* **(a)** *US Naut F* porte-avions *m inv* **(b)** (*hairstyle*) (coupe *f* en) brosse *f*

flatulence ['flætjʊləns] *n Med* flatuosité *f*; **to suffer from f.** avoir des vents; **to cause f.** provoquer des flatuosités

flatulent ['flætjʊlənt] *adj* **(a)** *Med* (*person*) qui souffre de flatuosités **(b)** *Fig* (*style*) boursouflé

flatware ['flætweər] *n Am* vaisselle *f* plate

flaunt [flɔːnt] *vt* (*wealth, knowledge*) étaler, afficher, faire parade de; (*jewels*) étaler, arborer; (*bad manners, ignorance*) afficher

flautist ['flɔːtɪst] *n Mus* flûtiste *mf*

flavour¹, *US* **flavor** ['fleɪvər] *n* saveur *f*, goût *m*; (*of tea etc*) arôme *m*; (*of ice cream etc*) parfum *m*; **what f. (of) ice cream did you want?** quel parfum tu voulais?; *F* à quoi tu voulais ta glace?; **it comes in six different flavours** il existe en six parfums différents; *Culin* **f. enhancer** agent *m* de sapidité; **her stories have a Mediterranean f.** ses histoires sentent bon la Méditerranée; **there was a f. of regret about his remarks** ses remarques contenaient une pointe de regret;

her book gives the true f. of the Mexican hinterland son livre fleure bon l'arrière-pays mexicain; *F* **I'm not f. of the month** je ne suis pas en odeur de sainteté; **she's definitely f. of the month** décidément, elle a la cote ce mois-ci

flavour², *US* **flavor** *vt* (*dish etc*) assaisonner, parfumer; **to f. a sauce with garlic** relever une sauce avec de l'ail; **vanilla flavoured** (parfumé) à la vanille

flavouring, *US* **flavoring** ['fleɪvərɪŋ] *n* (*savoury*) assaisonnement *m*; (*sweet*) parfum *m*; **artificial f.** arôme *m* artificiel

flavourless, *US* **flavorless** ['fleɪvəlɪs] *adj* (*food etc*) sans saveur, fade, insipide; (*wine*) plat

flaw¹ [flɔː] *n* **(a)** défaut *m*, imperfection *f*; (*in plan*) point *m* faible; **there is one f. in their argument** il y a une faille dans leur argument; **to have a f. in one's character** avoir un défaut **(b)** *Jur* (*in document etc, making it null and void*) vice *m* de forme

flaw² *vt* **(a)** (*spoil*) endommager, défigurer; **the plan is flawed by the lack of ...** le point faible de ce plan est le manque de ... **(b)** (*find fault with*) **I can't f. his argument/reasoning** je ne trouve pas de défaut à son argument/raisonnement

flawed [flɔːd] *adj* (*reasoning*) défectueux; (*novel, film*) qui a des défauts; (*sweater, scarf, fabric*) qui a un/des défaut(s); (*wood*) gercé; (*diamond*) qui a un crapaud *ou* un défaut

flawless ['flɔːlɪs] *adj* sans défaut, parfait; (*technique*) impeccable

flawlessly ['flɔːlɪslɪ] *adv* parfaitement

flawlessness ['flɔːlɪsnɪs] *n* perfection *f*

flax [flæks] *n* (*plant*) lin *m*; **f. field** linière *f*

flaxen ['flæksən] *adj* (*hair*) blond de lin *inv*, blond filasse *inv*

flay [fleɪ] *vt* **(a)** (*skin*) (*animal*) écorcher; **to be flayed alive** être écorché vif **(b)** (*whip*) fouetter; *Fig* **the critics flayed him** les critiques l'ont éreinté

flea [fliː] *n* (*insect*) puce *f*; **to have fleas** avoir des puces; *Fig F* **she sent him away with a f. in his ear** elle l'a envoyé promener; **f. collar** collier *m* anti-puces; **f. market** marché *m* aux puces

fleabag ['fliːbæg] *n Sl* **(a)** *Br* (*person*) pouilleux, -euse; (*animal*) sac *m* à puces **(b)** *US* (*hotel*) hôtel *m* pouilleux

fleabite ['fliːbaɪt] *n* **(a)** morsure *f* de puce **(b)** *Fig* (*trifle*) vétille *f*, bagatelle *f*

flea-bitten *adj* (*dog, cat, person*) plein de puces; (*hotel*) pouilleux; (*old jacket*) miteux

fleapit ['fliːpɪt] *n Br Old-fashioned Sl* (*cinema*) cinéma *m* pouilleux

fleck¹ [flek] *n* **(a)** (*mark*) (*of light etc*) petite tache *f*; (*of colour, paint*) moucheture *f* **(b)** (*particle*) (*of dust*) particule *f*

fleck² *vt* tacheter; **flecked with clouds** moucheté de nuages; **hair flecked with grey** cheveux qui grisonnent; **flecked material** tissu moucheté

fled *see* flee

fledged [fledʒd] *adj* (*bird*) qui a toutes ses plumes; *see* **fully-fledged**

fledgling ['fledʒlɪŋ] *n* **(a)** (*young bird*) oisillon *m* **(b)** (*beginner*) novice *mf*; **f. lawyer** avocat novice; **a f. industry/state** une industrie/un état jeune

flee [fliː] (*pt, pp* **fled**) **1** *vi* (*of person*) s'enfuir, prendre la fuite; (*of time etc*) voler; (*of hope*) s'envoler; **to f. from a place** s'enfuir d'un endroit; **to f. from temptation/persecution** fuir la tentation/les persécutions; **to f. to America** s'enfuir en Amérique **2** *vt* (*country etc*) s'enfuir de; (*person, temptation etc*) fuir

fleece¹ *n* **(a)** (*of sheep*) toison *f*; *Liter* **the Golden F.** la Toison d'or **(b)** *Tex* (*material*) molleton *m*; **f. lining** doublure *f* de molleton

fleece² *vt F* (*cheat, overcharge*) écorcher; **I've been fleeced** je me suis fait estamper

fleece-lined *adj* doublé de molleton

fleecing ['fliːsɪŋ] *n F* (*overcharging*) estampage *m*

fleecy ['fliːsɪ] *adj* (*wool*) floconneux; (*material etc*) laineux; (*cloud*) moutonné

fleeing ['fliːɪŋ] *adj* (*army etc*) en fuite

fleet¹ [fliːt] *n* **(a)** *Naut* flotte *f*; (*naval unit*) escadre *f*; **the F.** = la Marine nationale; **the Atlantic F.** l'escadre de l'Atlantique; **merchant f.** flotte de commerce; **fishing f.** flottille *f* de pêche **(b)** (*of cars, taxis*) parc *m*; **air f.** flotte aérienne; **a f. of coaches took the tourists to their hotel** une caravane de cars a amené les touristes à leur hôtel

fleet² *adj Lit* vite, leste; **f. of foot** au pied léger

fleet admiral *n US* amiral *m*

Fleet Air Arm *n Br* = Aéronavale *f*

fleet-footed *adj Lit* au pied léger

fleeting ['fliːtɪŋ] *adj* (*time, moment*) fugitif, fugace; (*beauty*) passager; (*happiness*) éphémère; (*relationship*) de courte durée; **for a f. moment** l'espace d'un instant; **to pay sb a f. visit** faire une courte visite à qn; **to catch a f. glimpse of sth** entrevoir qch, apercevoir qch; **to give sb a f. glance** lancer un regard fugace à qn

fleetingly ['fliːtɪŋlɪ] *adv* (*to glimpse, appear*) un court instant; **she has been f. involved with a number of men** elle a eu un certain nombre d'aventures de courte durée

Fleet Street [fliːt] *n Br Journ* = rue *f* où se trouvait le siège des principaux journaux britanniques; *Fig* (*press*) la presse nationale; **the F. papers** les journaux *mpl* nationaux; **F. journalist** journaliste *mf* de la presse nationale

Fleming ['flemɪŋ] *n* Flamand, -ande

Flemish ['flemɪʃ] **1** *adj* flamand **2** *n Ling* flamand *m*

flesh¹ [fleʃ] *n* **(a)** (*of person, fruit*) chair *f*; **to put on f.** (*of animal*) prendre chair; (*of person*) grossir, prendre de l'embonpoint; **to put some f. on an idea** étoffer *ou* développer une idée; **f. wound** blessure *f* légère *ou* en séton; **there he was in the f.** c'était lui en chair et en os; **to make sb's f. creep** *or* **crawl** donner la chair de poule à qn; **his own f. and blood** la chair de sa chair; **it is more than f. and blood can stand** *or* **bear** c'est plus que la nature humaine ne saurait endurer; **I'm only f. and blood!** je ne suis pas un surhomme!; *F* **to press the f.** serrer des mains

(b) (*as opposed to spirit*) *Rel* **to mortify the f.** mortifier sa chair; *Rel, Lit* **to go the way of all f.** payer sa dette à la nature; *Rel, Lit* **the sins of the f.** le péché de la chair; *Rel, prov* **the spirit is willing but the f. is weak** l'esprit est prompt, mais la chair est faible

(c) (*colour*) **f. colour** couleur *f* chair; *Th etc* **f. tights** collant *m* chair; *Art* **f. tints** carnations *fpl*

(d) *Arch* (*meat*) viande *f*; **f.-eating animals** les animaux *mpl* carnivores; *Rel* **to eat f.** faire gras

▶ **flesh out 1** *vtsep* (*plan, character, remarks*) étoffer **2** *vi* (*become fatter*) s'étoffer

flesh-coloured *adj* (*tights etc*) (couleur) chair

fleshpots ['fleʃpɒts] *npl Lit, Hum* **the f.** les lieux *mpl* de perdition

fleshy ['fleʃɪ] *adj* (*limb, fruit etc*) charnu; (*leaf*) succulent

fleur-de-lis, *pl* **fleurs-de-lis** ['flɜːdə'liː] *n Her* fleur *f* de lis

flew *see* **fly³**

flex¹ [fleks] **1** *vt* (*one's arm, knees etc*) fléchir; (*one's muscles*) faire jouer; *Fig* **he's just flexing his muscles** ce n'est qu'une démonstration d'autorité de sa part **2** *vi* (*of spring*) fléchir

flex² *n Br El* cordon *m*, câble *m*

flexibility [fleksɪ'bɪlɪtɪ] *n* (*of material, plan, person*) flexibilité *f*; (*of character*) souplesse *f*

flexible ['fleksɪb(ə)l] *adj* (*material, plans*) flexible, souple; (*character, principles*) souple; **when would you like the appointment? – I'm very f.** quand désirez-vous prendre rendez-vous? – je suis disponible à peu près tout le temps; **f. ticket** billet *m* sans condition; **f. working hours** horaire *m* à la carte, *Can* horaire flexible

flexion ['flekʃən] *n* **(a)** (*of spring etc*) flexion *f*, courbure *f* **(b)** (*bend*) courbe *f*

flexitime ['fleksɪtaɪm], **flextime** ['flekstaɪm] *n Ind etc* horaire *m* à la carte, *Can* horaire flexible; **we're on f.** nous avons des horaires à la carte

flexor ['fleksər] *n Anat* (*muscle*) fléchisseur *m*

flibbertigibbet [flɪbətɪ'dʒɪbɪt] *n F* écervelé, -ée, évaporé, -ée, hurluberlu *m*

flick¹ [flɪk] *n* **(a)** (*of whip, tail etc*) petit coup *m*; (*with finger*) chiquenaude *f*; **a f. of the wrist** un tour de main; **at the f. of a switch** juste en appuyant sur un bouton; *Br* **f. knife** (*with folding blade*) couteau *m* à cran (d'arrêt); (*with retractable blade*) couteau à lame rentrable; *Aut* **f. wipe** balayage *m* unique **(b)** *Old-fashioned Br F* (*film*) film *m*; **the flicks** (*cinema*) le ciné, le cinoche; **to go to the flicks** aller au ciné *ou* au cinoche

flick² *vt* (*with whip etc*) (*horse etc*) effleurer; (*with finger*) donner une chiquenaude à; **he had to keep flicking the hair out of his eyes** il n'arrêtait pas de chasser du doigt les cheveux qui lui tombaient dans les yeux; **she was flicking cigarette ash all over the floor** elle faisait tomber de la cendre de cigarette partout; **she flicked the dust from her shoulders** du doigt elle fit envoler la poussière qui se trouvait sur ses épaules; **to f. a duster over sth** donner un coup de torchon à qch

▶ **flick away** *vtsep* chasser; (*with fingers*) repousser d'une chiquenaude

▶ **flick off** *vtsep* (*with fingers*) enlever d'une chiquenaude; **to f. sth off with a duster** faire envoler qch d'un coup de torchon; **he flicked the dandruff off his collar** il secoua les pellicules qui se trouvaient sur son col

▶ **flick on** *vtsep* **to f. on the lights** allumer; *Aut* allumer les phares

▶ **flick out** *vi* sortir; **the snake's tongue was flicking in and**

out la langue du serpent sortait et rentrait à petits coups rapides

► **flick through** *vipo* (*book*) feuilleter; (*photographs*) jeter un œil parmi

flicker¹ ['flɪkər] *n* petit mouvement *m* vacillant; (*of eyelids*) battement *m*; *Cin* scintillement *m*; *TV* papillotement *m*; *Fig* **without a f.** sans un battement de cil; **a f. of light** une petite lueur tremblotante; **a f. of recognition** une lueur de reconnaissance; **a f. of hope/a smile** l'ombre d'un espoir/ d'un sourire; **a f. of interest/annoyance** une pointe d'intérêt/d'énervement

flicker² *vi* (*of flame etc*) trembloter, vaciller; (*of eyelids*) cligner; (*of light*) clignoter; (*of snake's tongue*) onduler; (*of instrument needle etc*) osciller; *Cin* scintiller; **the candle flickered out** la bougie vacilla et s'éteignit; **a smile flickered on his lips** un sourire erra sur ses lèvres

flicker-free *adj* (*screen*) anti-scintillements

flickering ['flɪkərɪŋ] *adj* (*light*) clignotant; (*shapes, images, candle*) vacillant

flier ['flaɪər] *n* (**a**) (*pilot etc*) aviateur, -trice; **I'm not a good f.** (*passenger*) je n'aime pas prendre l'avion (**b**) *F* (*fall*) **to take a f. over the handlebars** faire un vol plané par-dessus le guidon (**c**) (*leaflet*) feuille *f* volante, prospectus *m* (**d**) (*in race*) (*of sprinter*) départ *m* en flèche; (*of racing car*) départ sur les chapeaux de roues (**e**) **to take a f.** (*financial risk*) prendre un risque financier

flight¹ [flaɪt] *n* (**a**) (*act of flying*) (*of bird, plane etc*) vol *m*; (*of projectile, star etc*) course *f*; **these birds are not capable of f.** ces oiseaux ne peuvent pas voler; **very graceful in f.** très gracieux en vol; **once we're in f.** quand nous serons à notre altitude de croisière; *Av* **level f.** vol horizontal *ou* en palier; *Fig* **f. of fancy** essor *m* de l'imagination; **f. feather** (*of bird*) penne *f*

(**b**) (*distance*) (*of bird etc*) volée *f*, distance *f* parcourue; (*of birds etc*) migration *f*; (*of projectile*) trajectoire *f*; *Av* **it's an hour's f. from London** c'est à une heure de vol de Londres

(**c**) (*specific trip*) vol *m*; **f. A200 to Brussels** vol A200 pour Bruxelles; **I don't want to miss my f.** je ne veux pas rater mon avion; **my f. is at 2.15** mon avion est à 2h15; **how was your f.?** comment s'est passé le vol?; **f. clearance** autorisation *f* de vol; **f. only** vol *m* 'sec'

(**d**) (*group*) (*of birds etc*) vol *m*, volée *f*; (*of planes*) escadrille *f*; *Fig* **in the top f.** parmi les tout premiers; *Av* **the Queen's/ King's F.** = avions *mpl* au service de la famille royale

(**e**) **f. (of stairs)** escalier *m*; **you go up two flights** tu montes de deux étages *ou* de deux volées d'escalier; **they live six flights up from me** ils habitent six étages au-dessus de chez moi; **he lives up four flights (of stairs)** il habite au quatrième; *Sp* **f. of hurdles** (*in obstacle race*) série *f* de haies

(**f**) (*on arrow, dart*) plume *f*

flight² *n* (*escape*) fuite *f*; **his sudden f. from the room** sa sortie précipitée de la pièce; **in the course of her f. from justice** alors qu'elle fuyait la justice; **to take (to) f.** prendre la fuite; **to put the enemy to f.** mettre l'ennemi en fuite; **in full f.** en pleine déroute; *Fin* **the f. of capital** l'exode *m* *ou* la fuite des capitaux

flight attendant *n* (*male*) steward *m*; (*female*) hôtesse *f* de l'air

flight control *n* (*of individual aircraft*) conduite *f*; (*from ground*) contrôle *m* de la navigation aérienne; *Mil* contrôle des missions aériennes

flight crew *n* équipage *m*

flight deck *n* (*on aircraft*) poste *m* de pilotage; (*on aircraft carrier*) pont *m* d'envol

flight engineer *n* mécanicien *m* de bord, ingénieur *m* de vol

flight formation *n* formation *f* de vol

flightiness ['flaɪtɪnɪs] *n* inconstance *f*

flightless ['flaɪtlɪs] *adj* (*bird*) coureur

flight lieutenant *n Br Mil, Av* capitaine *m* aviateur

flight log *n* journal *m* de vol

flight mechanic *n* mécanicien *m* navigant

flight number *n* numéro *m* de vol

flight path *n* trajectoire *f* de vol

flight pattern *n* formation *f* de vol

flight personnel *n* personnel *m* navigant

flight plan *n* plan *m* de vol

flight recorder *n* enregistreur *m* de vol

flight simulator *n* simulateur *m* de vol

flight time *n* durée *f* de vol; (*take-off time*) heure *f* du vol

flighty ['flaɪtɪ] *adj* inconstant; (*emotionally*) volage

flimsily ['flɪmzɪlɪ] *adv* d'une manière peu solide; **f. constructed** d'une construction peu solide

flimsiness ['flɪmzɪnɪs] *n* (**a**) (*of dress, cloth*) légèreté *f*; (*of building, plane*) manque *m* de solidité; (*of walls, wooden beams*) minceur *f* (**b**) (*of excuse etc*) faiblesse *f*, pauvreté *f*

flimsy ['flɪmzɪ] **1** *adj* (**a**) fragile, peu solide; (*paper etc*) fin, fragile; (*dress, cloth*) léger (**b**) (*excuse*) faible, pauvre; (*evidence, alibi*) peu convaincant; (*novel, plot*) faible; **to condemn sb on the flimsiest evidence** condamner qn sur les preuves les plus faibles **2** *n* (**a**) (*paper*) papier *m* pelure (**b**) *Journ* (*copy*) copie *f* (*de reporter*)

flinch [flɪntʃ] *vi* (**a**) (*shy away*) **not to f. from doing sth** ne pas hésiter à faire qch; **she didn't f. from carrying out her duty** elle ne s'est pas dérobée à l'accomplissement de son devoir (**b**) (*with pain*) tressaillir (**with** de); **to bear pain without flinching** supporter la douleur sans broncher; **I flinched at the thought of it** d'y penser m'a fait tressaillir; **the very thought of telling her about it made him f.** la simple pensée de lui en parler le faisait frémir

fling¹ [flɪŋ] *n* (**a**) (*throw*) jet *m*, coup *m* (**b**) *F* (*attempt*) **I'll have a f. at it** je vais essayer; **to give sth a f., to have a f. at sth** essayer qch; **to have a f. at doing sth** essayer de faire qch; **he had given French a f. a few years before** il avait essayé de se mettre au français quelques années auparavant (**c**) (*dance*) (**highland**) **f.** = pas *m* seul écossais (**d**) *F* (*impulsive behaviour*) **to have one's f.** faire la fête; **the summer seemed to be having one last f.** l'été semblait avoir un dernier sursaut (**e**) *F* (*affair*) **to have a f.** avoir une aventure (**with sb** avec qn)

fling² *vt* (*pt, pp* **flung** [flʌŋ]) jeter; (*ball etc*) lancer; **to f. sb into prison** jeter qn en prison; **to f. oneself into sb's arms/ an armchair** se jeter dans les bras de qn/un fauteuil; **to f. oneself into a task** se lancer dans une tâche; **to f. one's arms around sb** jeter ses bras autour de qn

► **fling about** *vtsep* (*objects*) jeter de côté et d'autre; **to f. one's arms about** gesticuler violemment; **to f. one's money about** mener grand train

► **fling away** *vtsep* (*throw*) jeter de côté; (*get rid of*) se débarrasser de; **to f. one's money away** gaspiller son argent

► **fling back** *vtsep* (*sheets, blanket*) rejeter; **to f. back one's head** rejeter la tête en arrière

► **fling down** *vtsep* (*to the ground, floor*) jeter par terre; (*blinds, hatch*) refermer brusquement; *Fig* (*ultimatum*) imposer; **he flung the books down on the table** il a jeté les livres sur la table; **f. down my keys, will you?** lance-moi mes clés, s'il te plaît

► **fling off** *vtsep* (**a**) (*rid oneself of*) (*impositions, restrictions*) se débarrasser de; *Lit* **to f. off the yoke of tyranny** secouer le joug de la tyrannie (**b**) (*take off*) (*one's coat etc*) retirer brusquement

► **fling open** *vtsep* (*window, door etc*) ouvrir toute grande

► **fling out** *vtsep* (**a**) (*throw out*) jeter dehors; (*get rid of*) (*unwanted object*) jeter, balancer; (*bill, legislation, case*) rejeter; *F* **to f. sb out** flanquer qn à la porte; **she flung him out of the house** elle l'a flanqué à la porte, elle l'a viré de chez elle (**b**) (*extend*) **to f. out one's arm** étendre le bras d'un grand geste; **he flung out a fist and knocked his assailant out** il balança son poing et mis son assaillant K.-O.; **he flung out a foot and turned the ball into the net** il tendit le pied et dévia la balle vers le filet

► **fling up** *vtsep* (**a**) (*throw in air*) jeter en l'air; **he flung the bag up to her** il lui a envoyé le sac (**b**) *F* (*possibility*) entraîner; **what did your investigations f. up?** qu'ont produit vos recherches?

flint [flɪnt] *n Miner* silex *m*; (*for making fire*) pierre *f* à feu; (*for cigarette lighter*) pierre à briquet; **f. glass** flint(-glass) *m*; *Hist* **f. tools** outils *mpl* en silex taillés

flinty ['flɪntɪ] *adj* (**a**) (*of or resembling flint*) de silex (**b**) *Fig* (*heart*) de pierre, dur; (*person*) au cœur de pierre; (*expression, manner*) dur; **cold f. eyes** un regard froid et dur

flip¹ [flɪp] *n* (*flick*) chiquenaude *f*, pichenette *f*; **f. card** (*as prompt*) aide-mémoire *m* texte, *pl* aide-mémoires texte; *F* **f. side** (*of record*) face *f* B; (*of policy, situation*) envers *m*; **there is, of course, a f. side to the expansion of industry** l'expansion de l'industrie a, comme toute médaille, son revers; **f. of the tail** coup *m* de queue

flip² (**-pp-**) **1** *vt* (**a**) (*flick*) (*record, pancake, card etc*) retourner vivement; **to f. a coin** (*to decide*) jouer à pile ou face; **she flipped the coin into the air** elle lança la pièce en l'air; **he flipped the leaflet into the bin** il balança le prospectus dans la poubelle; *F* **to f. one's lid** (*get very angry*) sortir de ses gonds, piquer une crise; (*go crazy*) perdre la boule; **he absolutely flipped his lid at us** il a piqué une drôle de crise contre nous

(**b**) *El* (*switch*) basculer

(**c**) *F* (*turn over*) (*record*) retourner

2 *vi Sl* (**a**) (*get very angry*) sortir de ses gonds, piquer une crise; (*go crazy*) perdre la boule

(**b**) (*become ecstatic*) flasher, flipper (**over** sur)

flip³ *adj F* (*flippant*) léger, désinvolte, cavalier

► **flip open** *vtsep* ouvrir

▶ **flip out** *vi* (a) *esp Am F* (*get very angry*) sortir de ses gonds, piquer une crise (b) (*of end of lorry*) déraper

▶ **flip over 1** *vtsep* (*turn over*) (*record*) retourner; **to f. over the pages of a magazine** feuilleter les pages d'un magazine **2** *vi* (*turn over*) se retourner

▶ **flip through** *vipo* (*book*) feuilleter; (*photos, posters, wallpaper samples etc*) jeter un coup d'œil à

flip-flop *n* (a) (*sandal*) (*usu pl*) **flip-flops** tongs *fpl* (b) (*jump*) saut *m* périlleux; (*change of opinion*) volte-face *f inv*; **to do a f. (over an issue)** faire volte-face sur une question, retourner sa veste sur une question (c) *Electron* **f. (circuit)** (circuit *m*) basculeur *m* monostable

flippancy ['flɪpənsɪ] *n* légèreté *f*, désinvolture *f*

flippant ['flɪpənt] *adj* désinvolte, cavalier

flippantly ['flɪpəntlɪ] *adv* (*to say*) d'un ton *ou* d'une manière désinvolte

flipper ['flɪpər] *n* (*of whale, seal*) nageoire *f*; (*of scuba diver etc*) palme *f*

flipping ['flɪpɪŋ] *Br F* **1** *adj* fichu; **don't be such a f. idiot!** arrête donc de faire l'imbécile! **2** *adv* sacrément; **it's f. hot** il fait sacrément chaud; **he's so f. stupid** il est bête comme ses pieds

flip-top *adj* **f. pack** paquet *m* dur

flirt¹ [flɜːt] *n* (*man*) flirteur *m*; (*woman*) flirteuse *f*

flirt² *vi* faire du charme (**with sb** à qn); **to f. with danger/Marxism** flirter avec le danger/le Marxisme; **to f. with an idea/death** jouer avec une idée/la mort

flirtation [flɜː'teɪʃən] *n* flirt *m*; **to have a f. with sb** flirter avec qn; **to have a f. with danger/an idea** jouer avec le danger/une idée

flirtatious [flɜː'teɪʃəs] *adj F* charmeur; (*look, smile*) enjôleur; **to be f. with sb** faire du charme à qn

flirtatiously [flɜː'teɪʃəslɪ] *adv* (*to say sth*) d'un ton charmeur; **she smiled f. at him** elle lui fit un sourire enjôleur

flit¹ [flɪt] *n Br F* **to do a (moonlight) f.** déménager à la cloche de bois

flit² *vi* (**-tt-**) (a) (*of bird etc*) **to f. by** passer légèrement; **to f. about** aller et venir d'un pas léger; *Fig* **to f. from one thing to another** passer d'une chose à l'autre (b) *Scot, North Eng* (*move house*) déménager (c) *Br F* (*leave stealthily*) déménager à la cloche de bois

flitch [flɪtʃ] *n* (*of bacon*) flèche *f*

float¹ [fləʊt] *n* (a) (*of boiler, carburettor etc*) flotteur *m*; **f. chamber,** *US* **f. bowl** (*in engine*) chambre *f* du flotteur

(b) *Fishing* (*on fishing line, net*) flotteur *m*, bouchon *m*

(c) *Biol* (*of aquatic plant*) flotteur *m*; (*of fish*) vessie *f* natatoire

(d) (*raft*) radeau *m*; (*floating logs*) train *m* (de bois); (*swimming aid*) flotteur *m*

(e) *Th* **the floats** (*footlights*) la rampe

(f) (*vehicle, in carnival etc*) char *m* de carnaval; *Br* **milk f.** voiture *f* de livraison du lait

(g) *Com esp Am* (*petty cash*) petite caisse *f*; *esp Br* (*in cash till etc*) fond *m* de caisse; (*advance*) avance *f*; **they gave me a f. of £200 for the trip** (*advance*) ils m'ont donné un viatique de 200 livres, ils m'ont donné 200 livres pour le voyage

(h) *esp US Culin* (*drink*) = soda *m*, jus *m* de fruit ou milk-shake *m* dans lequel on ajoute une boule de glace

float² 1 *vi* (a) (*in water*) flotter; (*of boat*) être à flot; *Swimming* faire la planche; **to f. down the stream** descendre le courant

(b) (*move as if in water*) **to f. to the surface** revenir à la surface; **to f. in the air** planer dans l'air; **she floated out of the room** elle est sortie de la pièce d'un pas léger; **he seems to just f. through life** (*has no worries*) il semble ne jamais avoir de soucis; (*has no goals*) il semble se laisser porter par les événements

(c) *MecE* (*of part of machine*) avoir du jeu

2 *vt* (a) (*timber etc*) flotter; (*launch*) (*ship*) mettre à flot *ou* à l'eau; (*refloat*) (*ship*) renflouer

(b) *Com* (*company etc*) lancer; *Fin* (*loan*) émettre, lancer; (*idea, rumour*) lancer; (*proposal*) introduire; **to f. sth on the Stock Exchange** introduire qch en Bourse

▶ **float about, float around** *vi* (*of news etc*) circuler, courir; (*in a daze etc*) flotter; **there were rumours floating about that ...** le bruit courait que ...; *F* **he's floating around somewhere** il traîne dans les parages; *F* **he just floats around all day** il traîne sans rien faire toute la journée

▶ **float off 1** *vi* (*of ship etc*) se déséchouer **2** *vipo* (*of ship etc*) **the boat floated off the sandbank at high tide** à marée haute, le bateau s'est dégagé du banc de sable **3** *vtsep* (*wrecked ship etc*) renflouer, déséchouer; **they floated the boat off the sandbank** ils ont remis à flot *ou* renfloué le bateau échoué sur un banc de sable

floating ['fləʊtɪŋ] **1** *adj* (a) flottant, à flot; **this ship is, in effect, a f. hotel** en fait, ce bateau est un hôtel flottant; **f. bridge** pont *m* de bateaux *ou* de radeaux; **f. crane** ponton-grue *m*, *pl* pontons-grues; *Culin* **f. island** île *f* flottante

(b) (*population*) flottant, fluctuant; *Fin* (*exchange rate*) flottant; (*capital*) circulant, mobile; *MecE* (*bearing*) flottant; *Acct* **f. assets** actif *m* circulant; *Banking* **f. charge** nantissement *m* général; **f. exchange rate** taux *m* de change flottant; *Med* **f. kidney** rein *m* mobile *ou* flottant; *Comptr* **f. point** virgule *f* flottante; **f. point arithmetic** arithmétique *f* en virgule flottante; **f. rate bond** obligation *f* à intérêt variable *ou* à revenu variable; *Banking* **f. rate note** effet *m* à taux flottant; *Anat* **f. ribs** côtes *fpl* flottantes; *Pol* **f. vote** (*voters*) indécis *mpl*, électorat *m* flottant; **f. voter** électeur *m* indécis, électrice *f* indécise

2 *n* (*of ship*) mise *f* à flot; (*of wrecked ship etc*) renflouage *m*; (*of timber*) flottage *m*; *Com* (*of company etc*) lancement *m*; *Fin* (*of loan*) émission *f*

floating off *n* (*of wrecked ship etc*) renflouage *m*

flock¹ [flɒk] *n* (*of sheep, geese*) troupeau *m*; (*of animals*) bande *f*; (*of birds*) volée *f*; **a pastor and his f.** un pasteur et ses ouailles *fpl*; **a f. of visitors** une foule de visiteurs

flock² *vi* (*gather*) s'attrouper, s'assembler; **everybody is flocking to see the exhibition** tout le monde vient en masse pour voir l'exposition; **in summer people f. to the sea** en été les gens vont en foule au bord de la mer; **people flocked towards the park** les gens se sont dirigés en foule vers le parc; **crowds flocked to the stadium** des foules de gens sont allés au stade

flock³ *n* (*material*) bourre *f* (de laine); **f. mattress** matelas *m* en bourre de laine; **f. wallpaper** papier *m* tontisse

▶ **flock together** *vi* s'assembler

floe [fləʊ] *n* (**ice**) **f.** masse *f* de glaces flottantes, banquise *f*

flog [flɒg] *vt* (**-gg-**) (a) (*person*) flageller, fouetter; (*with stick*) frapper à coups de bâton; **to f. a horse** cravacher un cheval; *F, Fig* **to f. a dead horse** se dépenser en pure perte; *F, Fig* **to f. a subject to death** s'étendre indéfiniment sur une question; **we've flogged the subject to death** nous avons épuisé le sujet (b) *Br F* (*sell*) vendre; (*sell off quickly*) bazarder; (*stolen goods etc*) fourguer

▶ **flog off** *vtsep Br F* (*sell off*) bazarder

flood¹ [flʌd] *n* inondation *f*; **the river was in f.** la rivière débordait; **the victims of the f.** les inondés *mpl*; *Bible* **the F.** le Déluge; **the floods of the Nile** les crues *fpl* du Nil; **a f. of light** des flots *mpl* de lumière; **floods of tears/abuse** un torrent de larmes/d'injures; **f. plain** plaine *f* d'inondation; **f. (tide)** flux *m*, marée *f* montante; **f. water** inondation *f*; **the f. waters receded** les inondations ont diminué

flood² 1 *vt* (*land, the bathroom etc*) inonder; *Naut* (*hold*) noyer; *Agr* (*for irrigation*) irriguer; *Aut* (*carburettor*) noyer; (*engine*) étouffer, noyer; **the river flooded its banks** la rivière est sortie de son lit, la rivière a débordé; **to be flooded** (*of ship*) être envahi par l'eau; (*of house*) être inondé; **to f. the market with ...** inonder le marché de ...; **to be flooded with letters/telephone calls** être submergé de lettres/de coups de téléphone; **flooded with light** (*room*) inondé de lumière

2 *vi* (*of river etc*) (*overflow*) déborder; (*be in flood*) être en crue; *Fig* **the sun's rays came flooding through the window** les rayons du soleil entraient à flots par la fenêtre; **spectators were flooding into the stadium** les spectateurs affluaient dans le stade

▶ **flood back** *vi* (*return to memory*) revenir (à l'esprit); **it all came flooding back** tout m'est/leur est/*etc* soudain revenu; **all the feelings came flooding back** un flot d'émotions familières m'envahit/l'envahit/*etc*; **it all comes flooding back** tout me/te/*etc* revient, tout à coup

▶ **flood in** *vi* (*of light, water*) arriver à flots; (*of correspondence, people, thanks*) affluer

▶ **flood out 1** *vtsep* (*force to leave*) forcer à partir; **many families have been flooded out** les inondations ont forcé beaucoup de familles à évacuer leur maison **2** *vi* (*of people*) sortir à flots; **light flooded out of the open casement** des flots de lumière s'échappaient de la fenêtre ouverte; **money flooded out of the country** il y eut d'énormes fuites de capitaux

flooded ['flʌdɪd] *adj* (*land*) inondé; (*carburettor*) noyé

floodgate ['flʌdgeɪt] *n* vanne *f* (de décharge), porte *f* d'écluse; **to open/close the floodgates** lever/mettre les vannes; *Fig* **to open the floodgates to immigration/immorality/***etc* ouvrir les vannes de l'immigration/l'immoralité/*etc*

flooding ['flʌdɪŋ] *n* (*of land etc*) inondation *f*; (*of river etc*) débordement *m*; *Agr* (*for irrigation*) irrigation *f*; *Naut* (*of hold*) noyage *m*; **road liable to f.** (*road sign*) route inondable; **there has been f. in many parts of the country** il y a eu des inondations dans de nombreuses régions

floodlight¹ [ˈflʌdlaɪt] *n* projecteur *m*; *Phot* (lampe *f*) flood *f*; **under** *or* **by f.** à la lumière des projecteurs

floodlight² *vt* (*pt, pp* **floodlighted** *or* **floodlit**) illuminer aux projecteurs

floodlighting [ˈflʌdlaɪtɪŋ] *n* illumination *f* aux projecteurs; (*lights*) projecteurs *mpl*

floodlit [ˈflʌdlɪt] *adj* illuminé (aux projecteurs)

floor¹ [flɔːr] *n* **(a)** sol *m*; (*wooden*) plancher *m*; (*of Stock Exchange, the House*) parquet *m*; (*of studio*) plateau *m*; **parquet f.** parquet *m*; **tiled f.** carrelage *m*; *F* **to wipe the f. with sb** battre qn à plate(s) couture(s); **to take the f.** (*at meeting*) prendre la parole; (*at dance*) se joindre aux danseurs; **Mr Taylor has the f.** la parole est à M. Taylor; **questions from the f.** (*at meeting*) questions du public; **to give sb the f.** donner la parole à qn; **dance f.** piste *f* de danse; *Ind* **the factory** *or* **shop f.** l'atelier *m*; *TV* **f. assistant** assistant *m* de plateau; *TV* **f. crew** personnel *m* de plateau; *TV* **f. manager** régisseur *m* de plateau; *Aut* **f. shift** levier *m* (de vitesses) au plancher; **f. show** spectacle *m* de cabaret; **f. tile** dalle *f* de sol

(b) (*storey*) étage *m*; **house on two floors** maison avec étage; *Br* **ground f.** rez-de-chaussée *m*; **first f.** *Br* premier étage, *Am* rez-de-chaussée; **to live on the fifth f.** *Br* habiter au cinquième, *Am* habiter au quatrième; **we live on the same f.** nous habitons sur le même palier, nous sommes voisins de palier; **on the f. above/below** à l'étage du dessus/dessous; **we're ten floors up** nous sommes au dixième étage; **their offices are two floors down** leurs bureaux sont deux étages plus bas; **f. clerk** (*in hotel*) responsable *m* d'étage; **f. housekeeper** (*in hotel*) gouvernante *f* d'étage; **f. manager** (*in department store*) chef *m* de rayon; **f. plan** (*of building*) plan *m* d'étage; **f. waiter** (*in hotel*) garçon *m* d'étage

(c) (*of ocean*) fond *m*; *Min* (*of gallery*) sole *f*; **on the ocean f.** au fond de l'océan; **the forest f.** le sol de la forêt

floor² *vt* **(a)** (*room*) (*with floorboards*) planchéier; (*with wooden blocks*) parqueter; (*with tiles*) carreler **(b)** (*knock down*) (*opponent*) terrasser, envoyer au tapis **(c)** *F* (*of problem, question*) **to f. sb** réduire qn à quia, clouer le bec à qn

floorboard [ˈflɔːbɔːd] *n* planche *f*

floorcloth [ˈflɔːklɒθ] *n* serpillière *f*

flooring [ˈflɔːrɪŋ] *n* **(a)** (*action*) (*with floorboards*) planchéiage *m*; (*with wooden blocks*) parquetage *m*; (*with tiles*) carrelage *m*; (*with large slabs*) dallage *m* **(b)** (*floor*) plancher *m*; (*tiles*) carrelage *m*

floor-mounted gearstick *n* levier *m* (de vitesses) au plancher

floor polish *n* cire *f ou* encaustique *f* à parquet

floorspace [ˈflɔːspeɪs] *n* (*of room etc*) surface *f* (couverte), superficie *f*; (*of vehicle*) surface au plancher; **there was barely enough f. for all of them** il y avait tout juste assez d'espace pour eux tous

floorwalker [ˈflɔːwɔːkər] *n US* inspecteur, -trice, surveillant, -ante (de magasin)

floozie, floozy [ˈfluːzɪ] *n F* pouffiasse *f*

flop¹ [flɒp] *n F* (*failure*) four *m*, fiasco *m*, bide *m*; (*novel, product*) bide; (*person*) (*in life*) raté, -ée; (*in film, play*) nul, *f* nulle; **it was a f.** ça a fait un four *ou* un bide, c'était un fiasco

flop² *adv* **to fall f.** faire patapouf

flop³ *vi* **(-pp-)** **(a)** (*fall*) faire plouf, faire floc; (*of person*) se laisser tomber, s'affaler; (*into water*) tomber; **to f. down on(to) a seat** tomber lourdement sur un siège, se laisser tomber comme un sac sur un siège **(b)** *F* (*fail*) échouer; (*of play, novel, product etc*) faire un bide; (*of jokes, sketch*) tomber à plat

flophouse [ˈflɒphaʊs] *n Am Sl* asile *m* de nuit

floppy [ˈflɒpɪ] **1** *adj* (*hat, bow etc*) pendant, souple; (*garment*) lâche, trop large; **with f. ears** à oreilles pendantes; *Comptr* **f. disk** disquette *f*, disque *m* souple; **f. (disk) controller** contrôleur *m* d'unité de disquette; **f. (disk) drive** unité *f* de disquettes **2** *n Comptr* disquette *f*, disque *m* souple; **on f.** sur disquette

floptical [ˈflɒptɪk(ə)l] *adj Comptr* **f. disk** disque/disquette *m/f* optique; **f. drive** unité *f* de disque/disquette optique

flora [ˈflɔːrə] *n* (*of country, region*) flore *f*; **the f. and fauna of a region** la flore et la faune d'une région

floral [ˈflɔːrəl] *adj* floral, -aux; **dress with a bold f. design** robe *f* à grands ramages; **f. tribute** couronne *f* de fleurs

floret [ˈflɔːrɪt] *n Bot* fleuron *m*

florid [ˈflɒrɪd] *adj* (*style etc*) fleuri, orné à l'excès; (*complexion*) coloré

Florida [ˈflɒrɪdə] *n* Floride *f*

florin [ˈflɒrɪn] *n Br Hist* (*coin*) pièce *f* de deux shillings

florist [ˈflɒrɪst] *n* fleuriste *mf*; **f.'s (shop)** magasin *m* de fleurs; **to go to the f.'s** aller chez le fleuriste

floss¹ [flɒs] *n Tex* **f. silk** bourre *f* de soie; **(dental) f.** fil *m* (de soie) dentaire

floss² *vt* **to f. one's teeth** se passer du fil dentaire entre les dents

flotation [fləʊˈteɪʃən] *n Com* (*of company*) lancement *m*; *Fin* (*of loan*) émission *f*

flotilla [fləˈtɪlə] *n Naut* flottille *f*; (*of small boats*) escadrille *f*

flotsam [ˈflɒtsəm] *n* épave(s) *f(pl)* flottante(s); **f. and jetsam** choses *fpl* refoulées par la mer; **sometimes the f. and jetsam of a wrecked ship would be washed up on the shore** parfois les restes d'une épave, refoulés par la mer, venaient s'échouer sur la rive; *Fig* **the f. of the war/of society** (*people*) les laissés-pour-compte *mpl* de la guerre/de la société

flounce¹ [flaʊns] *n* **(a)** (*of indignation, impatience*) mouvement *m* vif; **with a f. of her long skirt, she marched out of the room** elle sortit de la pièce d'un pas ferme en faisant voltiger sa longue jupe **(b)** *Sewing* volant *m*

flounce² **1** *vi* **to f. in/out/off** entrer/sortir/partir brusquement; **don't you go flouncing off!** ne te sauve pas si vite! **2** *vt Sewing* garnir de volants; **flounced skirt** jupe *f* à volants

flounder¹ [ˈflaʊndər] *n* (*fish*) flet *m*, carrelet *m*

flounder² *vi* (*in water, mud etc*) patauger; **to f. about in the water** se débattre dans l'eau; **to f. along** avancer en trébuchant; **to f. in a speech/course** patauger dans un discours/cours

flour¹ [ˈflaʊər] *n Culin* farine *f*; (*of sulphur*) fleur *f*; *Culin* **to dust sth with f.** (en)fariner qch; **potato f.** fécule *f* de pommes de terre; **f. dredger** saupoudroir *m* à farine; **f. mill** minoterie *f*

flour² *vt Culin* (en)fariner, saupoudrer de farine

flourbin [ˈflaʊəbɪn] *n* farinière *f*, huche *f*, maie *f*

flourish¹ [ˈflʌrɪʃ] *n* **(a)** (*in writing, style*) fioriture *f*; (*after signature*) parafe *m* **(b)** (*gesture*) grand geste *m*; (*of sword*) brandissement *m*; **with a f. of his sword/umbrella** en brandissant son épée/parapluie; **to raise one's hat with a f.** saluer d'un grand coup de chapeau; **to carry things off with a f.** faire les choses avec panache **(c)** *Mus* fioriture(s) *f(pl)*, ornement *m*; (*of trumpets*) fanfare *f*

flourish² **1** *vi* (*of plant*) croître, se développer; (*of person, business etc*) être florissant, prospérer; (*of arts*) fleurir; **to f. in sandy soil** se plaire dans un terrain sablonneux; **trade is flourishing** le commerce est prospère **2** *vt* (*sword, stick, newspaper etc*) brandir

flourishing [ˈflʌrɪʃɪŋ] *adj* (*plant, industry etc*) florissant; (*business*) prospère

floury [ˈflaʊərɪ] *adj* **(a)** (*hands etc*) enfariné, couvert de farine **(b)** (*potatoes, texture etc*) farineux; (*rolls*) saupoudré de farine

flout [flaʊt] *vt* (*person's authority, convention etc*) faire fi de; (*person*) passer outre à la volonté de

flow¹ [fləʊ] *n* **(a)** (*movement*) (*of liquid*) coulée *f*; (*of river, blood*) écoulement *m*; *El* (*of current*) passage *m*; (*of air, fuel etc*) passage, arrivée *f*; (*of tide*) flot *m*, flux *m*; *Fin* (*of capital*) mouvement *m*; (*of information*) circulation *f*; **a steady f. of immigrants** un courant ininterrompu d'immigration; **a f. of ideas/proposals** un flot d'idées/de propositions; **f. of money** flux monétaire; **the speaker was interrupted in full f.** l'orateur a été interrompu en plein discours; **to follow the f. of sb's argument** suivre le fil de l'argumentation de qn; **to go with the f.** suivre le mouvement; *Comptr* organigramme *m*; *Comptr* **f. path** branche *f* de traitement

(b) (*volume*) (*of liquid*) volume *m*; (*of river, pump, electric current*) débit *m*; **the f. of traffic** le flux de la circulation; **there was a heavy f. of traffic** il y avait beaucoup de circulation

(c) (*stream*) courant *m*, cours *m* (d'eau); (*of lava*) coulée *f*; (*of blood etc*) flot *m*; *Physiol* **menstrual f.** règles *fpl*

(d) *Sewing* (*of garment*) drapé *m*

flow² *vi* **(a)** (*of water, river*) couler, s'écouler; (*of electric current, blood in veins*) circuler; (*of traffic, crowd*) s'écouler; (*of hair etc*) flotter; (*of tide*) monter, remonter; **to f. into the sea** se verser dans la mer; **lava that flows down the mountain** lave qui s'écoule le long de la montagne; **the tears flowed down her cheeks** les larmes coulaient sur ses joues; **blood flowed from the wound** le sang s'écoulait de la blessure; **blood flowing to the head** sang qui afflue à la tête; *prov* **land flowing with milk and honey** pays *m* de cocagne, terre *f* d'abondance; **you can feel the energy f.** on sent circuler l'énergie; **the work is flowing nicely** le travail suit bien son cours; **the ideas are really flowing today** les idées affluent aujourd'hui

(b) (*of literary style, prose*) couler; **to keep the conversation flowing** entretenir la conversation; **these two**

paragraphs don't f. ces deux paragraphes ne s'enchaînent pas bien; **the film flows very nicely** tout s'enchaîne vraiment bien dans le film

(c) (*result*) dériver, découler (**from** de); **God from whom all blessings f.** Dieu, de qui découlent toutes les grâces

▶ **flow away** *vi* (*of liquid*) s'écouler; **the small craft flowed away on the tide** le petit bateau s'éloigna dans le flot de la marée

▶ **flow back** *vi* (*of water*) refluer; (*in pipe etc*) regorger

▶ **flow in** *vi* (*of liquid*) entrer; (*of people, money*) affluer; **the stream flowed in to the river** le ruisseau se jetait dans la rivière

▶ **flow out** *vi* (*of liquid*) sortir, s'écouler; (*of people*) partir; (*of money*) disparaître; **people flew out of the country in their thousands** les gens quittèrent le pays par milliers

flowchart ['fləʊtʃɑːt] *n* organigramme *m*

flower[1] ['flaʊər] *n* (**a**) fleur *f*; **to put flowers on a grave** fleurir une tombe; **no flowers by request** ni fleurs ni couronnes; **in f.** (*of plant*) en fleur; **in full f.** en plein épanouissement; **to burst into f.** fleurir; *Fig* **in the (first) f. of youth** dans la première fleur de la jeunesse; **f. arrangement** (*art*) l'art *m* de composer des bouquets; (*example*) composition *f* florale; **f. arranging** art *m* de composer les bouquets; **f. children** hippies *mpl* (des années soixante); **f. garden** jardin *m* d'agrément; **f. girl** (*in street*) marchande *f* de fleurs; (*at wedding*) = jeune fille *f* qui porte les fleurs dans un cortège; **f. head** capitule *m*; **f. market** marché *m* aux fleurs; *Hist* **f. power** = message *m* pacifiste des hippies, dans les années soixante; **f. seller** (*in street*) marchand, -ande de fleurs; **f. show** exposition *f* florale, floralies *fpl*; **f. vase** vase *m* à fleurs

(**b**) *Ch* **flowers of sulphur** fleurs *fpl* de soufre

(**c**) *Fig* (*best part*) (*of an army etc*) fine fleur *f*, crème *f*

flower[2] *vi* (*of plant*) (*action*) fleurir; (*state*) être en fleur; (*of art etc*) fleurir, s'épanouir

flowerbed ['flaʊəbed] *n* plate-bande *f*, *pl* plates-bandes; (*round*) corbeille *f*

flowered ['flaʊəd] *adj* (*material, wallpaper etc*) à fleurs

-flowered ['flaʊəd] *suff* **white/yellow/***etc***-f.** à fleurs blanches/jaunes/*etc*; **many-f.** multiflore

flowering ['flaʊərɪŋ] **1** *adj* (**a**) (*in flower*) (*garden, plant*) fleuri, en fleur (**b**) (*that flowers*) (*shrub*) à fleurs **2** *n* (*of plant*) fleuraison *f*; *Fig* **her late f. as an artist** son épanouissement tardif en tant qu'artiste

flowerpot ['flaʊəpɒt] *n* pot *m* de fleurs; (*ornamental*) cache-pot *m inv*

flowery ['flaʊərɪ] *adj* (**a**) (*meadow*) fleuri; (*dress, carpet*) à fleurs (**b**) *Pej* (*style etc*) fleuri; **f. phrases** fleurs *fpl* de rhétorique

flowing ['fləʊɪŋ] *adj* (*style etc*) coulant, fluide; (*movement*) fluide; (*hair*) tombant (dans le cou); (*beard*) long; **a fast f. stream** un ruisseau au cours rapide

flowline ['fləʊlaɪn] *n* (*on organization chart*) ligne *f* de jonction de symboles

flowmeter ['fləʊmiːtər] *n* (*for liquid etc*) débitmètre *m*, indicateur *m* d'écoulement *ou* de débit

flown *see* **fly**[3]

flu [fluː] *n Med* grippe *f*; **I've got (the) f.** j'ai la grippe, je suis grippé; **f. epidemic** épidémie *f* de grippe; **a bad dose** *or* **case of (the) f.** une mauvaise grippe

flub[1] [flʌb] *n Am F* gaffe *f*, bourde *f*

flub[2] (**-bb-**) *Am F* **1** *vi* faire une gaffe, gaffer **2** *vt* **to f. a question** répondre de travers à une question

fluctuate ['flʌktjʊeɪt] *vi* (**a**) fluctuer; (*of pulse, heartbeat*) être irrégulier; (*of conditions etc*) varier; **prices f. between ... and ...** les prix oscillent entre ... et ... (**b**) (*of person*) (*in one's opinions etc*) vaciller, balancer

fluctuating ['flʌktjʊeɪtɪŋ] *adj* (*temperature etc*) variable; (*prices etc*) oscillant, fluctuant; (*heartbeat*) irrégulier; (*interest*) variable, fluctuant

fluctuation [flʌktjʊ'eɪʃən] *n* (*of temperature etc*) variations *fpl*; (*of support, interest*) fluctuation(s) *f(pl)*; *Fin* **exchange f.** fluctuation(s) *f(pl)* du change

flue [fluː] *n* (**a**) *Constr* tuyau *m* de cheminée, conduit *m* de fumée; **f. boiler** chaudière *f* à tubes-foyers; **f. brush** torche-tubes *m inv*, hérisson *m* (**b**) *Mus* bouche *f* (de tuyau d'orgue); **f. pipe** tuyau *m* à bouche; **f. stop** jeu *m* de flûte

fluency ['fluːənsɪ] *n* (*of speech, style*) facilité *f*; **her f. in French** son aisance à s'exprimer en français

fluent ['fluːənt] *adj* (*speech etc*) coulant, facile; **to be a f. speaker** avoir la parole facile; **he is a f. speaker of French, he speaks f. French, he is f. in French** il parle le français couramment

fluently ['fluːəntlɪ] *adv* (*to speak a language, read a language*) couramment; (*to express oneself*) avec facilité, avec aisance

fluff[1] [flʌf] *n* (**a**) (*of fabric*) duvet *m*; (*of wool*) coton *m*; **a bit of f.** une peluche; *Old-fashioned Br F* (*girl*) une poule; (**pieces of**) **f.** (*under bed etc*) moutons *mpl* (**b**) (*of rabbit etc*) fourrure *f* douce; (*of chicks*) duvet *m* (**c**) *Th F* (*mistake*) raté *m*

fluff[2] *vt* (**a**) = **fluff out, fluff up** (**b**) *F* (*entrance, line, exam, interview*) rater, louper; *Sp* **to f. a shot** rater un coup

▶ **fluff out, fluff up** *vtsep* (*one's hair, cushions*) faire bouffer; **to f. up its feathers** (*of bird*) hérisser ses plumes; **f. up the potatoes with a fork** fouetter la purée avec une fourchette

fluffy ['flʌfɪ] *adj* (*sheet*) pelucheux; (*woollen material*) (*naturally*) duveteux; (*after wear*) pelucheux; (*chick, beard, moustache etc*) duveteux; (*clouds*) cotonneux; (*mashed potatoes, cake*) léger et mousseux; **f. hair** cheveux flous

fluid ['fluːɪd] **1** *adj* (*substance*) fluide, liquide; *MecE* (*transmission*) fluide; (*style etc*) coulant, facile; (*movement, grace*) fluide, coulant; (*opinions etc*) changeant, inconstant; **my plans are still f.** mes projets ne sont pas encore définis; **industry in a f. state** industrie en voie de transformation rapide; **f. clutch** embrayage *m* hydrodynamique; **f. situation** situation *f* fluide **2** *n* fluide *m*, liquide *m*; **body fluids** sécrétions *fpl*; *Med* **fluids only** liquides uniquement

fluidity [fluː'ɪdɪtɪ] *n* (*of style etc*) fluidité *f*, aisance *f*; (*of opinions etc*) caractère *m* changeant *ou* fluctuant

fluid ounce *n* = 0,03 litres *mpl*

fluke[1] [fluːk] *n* (**a**) (*fish*) flet *m* (**b**) **f.** (**worm**) (*in liver*) douve *f*

fluke[2] *n* (**a**) *Naut* (*of anchor*) patte *f*, aile *f* (**b**) (*of whale*) **flukes** nageoires *fpl*

fluke[3] *n F* (*coincidence*) hasard *m*; (*stroke of luck*) coup *m* de veine, coup de pot; **it was a pure f.** c'était un véritable coup de veine *ou* de pot; (*just coincidence*) c'était un pur hasard; **his success was due to a f.** c'est un hasard qu'il ait réussi; **by a pure f.** purement par hasard

fluky ['fluːkɪ] *adj F* **f. shot** coup *m* de veine, coup de pot

flume [fluːm] *n* (**a**) (*of watermill*) buse *f* (**b**) (*for logs etc*) canal *m* d'amenée; (*water chute in amusement park*) toboggan *m* (**c**) *US* (*ravine*) ravin *m*

flummox ['flʌməks] *vt F* réduire à quia

flung *see* **fling**[2]

flunk [flʌŋk] *esp Am F* **1** *vi* (*in exam*) se faire recaler, se faire coller **2** *vt* (**a**) (*of teacher*) (*person in exam*) recaler, coller (**b**) (*of student*) (*exam*) rater, se faire coller *ou* recaler à

flunkey ['flʌŋkɪ] *n Pej* laquais *m*

fluorescence [flʊə'resəns] *n* fluorescence *f*

fluorescent [flʊə'resənt] *adj* fluorescent; **f. lighting** éclairage *m* fluorescent

fluoridation [flʊərɪ'deɪʃən] *n Ch* fluoration *f*

fluoride ['flʊəraɪd] *n Ch* fluorure *f*; **f. toothpaste** dentifrice *m* au fluor

fluorine ['flʊəriːn] *n Ch* fluor *m*

fluoroscope ['flʊərəskəʊp] *n Med* fluoroscope *m*

flurry[1] ['flʌrɪ] *n* (**a**) (*of snow*) rafale *f* (**b**) (*agitation*) agitation *f*, bouleversement *m*, émoi *m*; **f. of excitement/protest** vague *f* d'excitation/de protestations

flurry[2] *vt* **to get flurried** perdre la tête

flush[1] *vt* (*in hunting*) (*partridge etc*) (faire) lever, faire partir

flush[2] *n* (**a**) (*of lavatory*) chasse *f* (d'eau); (*of drain*) curage *m*; **to pull the f.** tirer la chasse (d'eau) (**b**) (*of light, beauty etc*) éclat *m*; (*of emotion etc*) accès *m*; (*of enthusiasm*) élan *m*; **in the first f. of victory** dans l'ivresse de la victoire; **in the first f. of youth** dans le premier éclat de la jeunesse (**c**) (*redness of face*) rougeur *f*; *Med* suffusion *f*; **the words brought a f. to her cheeks** ces mots l'ont fait rougir

flush[3] **1** *vt* (**a**) (*water*) faire jaillir; **to f. a drain** donner une chasse à un égout; **to f. the lavatory** tirer la chasse d'eau; **to f. sth down the lavatory** jeter qch dans les toilettes (et tirer la chasse d'eau) (**b**) (*redden*) faire rougir; **the exercise had flushed their cheeks** l'exercice leur avait fait monter le sang au visage **2** *vi* (**a**) (*of person*) rougir (**with** de); **he** *or* **his face flushed** il a rougi; **she flushed crimson** elle est devenue écarlate (**b**) (*in lavatory*) (*of person*) tirer la chasse d'eau; **the lavatory isn't flushing properly** la chasse d'eau ne fonctionne pas bien

flush[4] *n Cards* (*in poker*) flush *m*, longue couleur *f*; **straight f.** séquence *f* flush

flush[5] **1** *adj* (**a**) (*surface etc*) de niveau; (*door, lock etc*) encastré; (*screw, nail*) noyé; (*rivet*) à tête noyée *ou* perdue; **f. mounted** monté à fleur; **to be f. with sth** être à fleur de qch, être de niveau avec qch; **f. with the ground** à ras de sol (**b**) *F* **to be f. (with money)** (*of person*) être en fonds **2** *adv Typ* **f. left/right** justifié à gauche/droite

▶ **flush away** **1** *vtsep* (*dispose of in lavatory*) jeter dans les toilettes (et tirer la chasse d'eau) **2** *vi* **it wouldn't f. away** ça ne voulait pas partir

▶ **flush out** *vtsep* (**a**) (*force to emerge*) forcer à sortir, faire sortir de force; (*force to reveal oneself*) faire se trahir; **they used tear gas to f. the students out** ils ont utilisé des gaz lacrymogènes pour faire sortir les étudiants (**b**) (*clean*)

rincer par circulation d'eau; **to f. out a drain** donner une chasse à un égout

flushed [flʌʃt] *adj* (*face*) empourpré, congestionné; **f. with anger/joy** rouge de colère/plaisir; **f. with success** exalté par le succès

fluster[1] ['flʌstər] *n* agitation *f*, trouble *m*; **in a f.** paniqué

fluster[2] **1** *vt* (*person*) décontenancer; (*cause to panic*) faire perdre la tête à; (*make nervous*) rendre nerveux; **to get flustered** se troubler, perdre contenance **2** *vi* **he doesn't f. easily** il ne se trouble pas facilement, il ne perd pas facilement contenance

flustered ['flʌstəd] *adj* (*look*) paniqué; (*reaction*) de panique; **it was a rather f. Jim that came out of the meeting** Jim était plutôt décontenancé quand il est sorti de la réunion

flute[1] [flu:t] *n* **(a)** *Mus* flûte *f*; **transverse f.** flûte traversière; *Th* **the Magic F.** la Flûte Enchantée; **f. (player)** joueur, -euse de flûte, flûtiste *mf*; **f. stop** (*on organ*) jeu *m* de flûte **(b)** (*groove*) (*of column*) cannelure *f*; **f. (glass)** flûte *f*

fluted ['flu:tɪd] *adj* (*wood etc*) à cannelures; (*column*) cannelé

fluting ['flu:tɪŋ] *n* (*no pl*) (*grooves*) cannelures *fpl*

flutist ['flu:tɪst] *n esp Am Mus* flûtiste *mf*

flutter[1] ['flʌtər] *n* **(a)** (*of bird*) volettement *m*, trémoussement *m*; (*of wings, eyelids*) battement *m*; (*of heart*) palpitation *f*; (*of flag etc*) flottement *m*; (*of sound*) pulsation *f*; (*on tape*) pompage *m*; **she thinks she can get whatever she wants with a f. of her eyelashes** elle croit pouvoir obtenir tout ce qu'elle veut d'un simple battement de cils

(b) *Fig* (*agitation*) agitation *f*, trouble *m*; **to be in a f. of excitement** *or F* **all in a f.** être tout en émoi

(c) *Br F* (*bet*) petite spéculation *f*; **to have a little f.** faire un ou deux petits paris; (*in gambling house etc*) risquer de petites sommes au jeu; **to have a f. on the horses** risquer de petites sommes au tiercé

flutter[2] **1** *vi* (*of birds, insects*) (*fly*) voleter; (*flap wings*) battre des ailes; (*of flag etc*) flotter, s'agiter (au vent); (*of heart*) palpiter; (*of pulse*) battre irrégulièrement; **to make sb's heart f.** faire tressaillir le cœur de qn; **the letter fluttered to the ground** la lettre a volé par terre; **the pigeons fluttered off** *or* **away** les pigeons s'éloignèrent en voletant; **he was fluttering about nervously** il s'agitait nerveusement; **she fluttered happily round the house** elle virevoletait gaiement dans toute la maison **2** *vt* **to f. its wings** (*of bird*) battre des ailes; **she fluttered her eyelashes at him** elle l'a regardé en battant des cils

fluvial ['flu:vɪəl] *adj* fluvial

flux [flʌks] *n* **(a)** *Med* (*of blood etc*) flux *m* **(b)** (*constant change*) changement *m* continuel; **to be in a (constant) state of f.** être sujet à des changements fréquents **(c)** *Phys* flux *m* **(d)** *Metal* fondant *m*, flux *m*; **gold f.** (*in glassmaking*) aventurine *f*

fluxion ['flʌkʃən] *n Med* (*of blood etc*) fluxion *f*

fluxmeter ['flʌksmi:tər] *n Phys* fluxmètre *m*

fly[1], *pl* **flies** [flaɪ, -z] *n* **(a)** (*insect*) mouche *f*; **they were dying** *or* **dropping like flies** ils tombaient comme des mouches; **he wouldn't hurt a f.** il ne ferait pas de mal à une mouche; *F* **a f. in the ointment** un cheveu (sur la soupe); *Fig* **to catch flies** bayer aux corneilles; *F* **there are no flies on her** elle n'est pas bête; **I wish I could be a f. on the wall** (*at that interview, meeting etc*) si je pouvais être une petite souris; *TV* **f.-on-the-wall documentary** documentaire *m* intimiste, documentaire avec caméra cachée; **f. agaric** amanite *f* tue-mouches, fausse oronge *f*; **f. orchid** (*plant*) ophrys *f* mouche; **f. spray** insecticide *m*; **f. swat(ter)** tapette *f* tue-mouches; **f. whisk** chasse-mouches *m inv*

(b) *Fishing* mouche *f*; **wet f.** mouche mouillée *ou* noyée; **wet/dry-f. fishing** pêche *f* à la mouche noyée/sèche

fly[2] *n* **(a)** (*often in pl*) **flies, f.** (*of trousers*) braguette *f*; **your flies are** *or* **f. is undone** *or* **open** ta braguette est ouverte **(b)** **f. (sheet)** (*of tent*) (*flap*) auvent *m*; (*roof*) double toit *m*; **f. sheet** (*handbill*) prospectus *m* **(c)** *Th* **the flies** les cintres *mpl*

fly[3] (*pt* **flew** [flu:]; *pp* **flown** [fləʊn]) **1** *vi* **(a)** (*of bird etc*) voler; **a flock of geese flew across the sky** un troupeau d'oies traversa le ciel à tire d'aile; *Fig, F* **the bird has flown** l'oiseau s'est envolé; **to f. high** voler haut; *Fig* (*of person*) avoir de l'ambition

(b) *Av* (*of aircraft, pilot, missile*) voler; (*of passenger*) prendre l'avion, voyager en avion; **he flew for** *or* **with the RAF** il volait pour la RAF; **I've never flown before** c'est la première fois que je prends l'avion; **it's cheaper to f.** il est moins cher de prendre l'avion; **I've never flown in a 747** je n'ai jamais voyagé en 747; **to f. blind** voler sans visibilité; **to f. over London** survoler Londres; **to f. across the Channel** traverser la Manche en avion; **we flew 400 miles** nous avons parcouru 640 kilomètres en avion; **who did you f. with?** (*which airline*) avec quelle compagnie est-ce que tu as voyagé?; **to f. direct** effectuer un vol direct; **to f. via London** faire escale à Londres; **we f. to over a dozen destinations** (*of airline*) nous desservons plus d'une douzaine de destinations; **we f. to Berlin four days a week** nous avons des vols pour Berlin quatre jours par semaine; **the airline only flies to Hong Kong via Karachi** tous les vols de la compagnie à destination de Hong-Kong s'effectuent via Karachi; **they don't f. from Heathrow any more** ils n'ont plus de vols au départ de Heathrow

(c) (*of hair etc*) flotter; (*of flag*) flotter, battre; **the American flag flew above the building** le drapeau américain flottait au-dessus du bâtiment

(d) (*move quickly etc*) (*of person etc*) courir *ou* aller à toute vitesse; (*flee*) s'enfuir; (*of time*) filer; (*of cork etc*) voler, sauter en l'air; **the insults were really flying** les insultes fusaient de toutes parts; **to f. to sb's aid** courir à l'aide de qn; *F* **it's late, I must f.** il se fait tard, il faut que je me sauve; *F* **I flew home to change** j'ai filé à la maison pour me changer; **time is flying** le temps vole; **the door flew open** la porte s'ouvrit en coup de vent; **to f. into a rage** *or F* **off the handle** s'emporter, sortir de ses gonds; **to f. into a temper** se mettre en colère; **to f. at sb** (*attack them*) se jeter sur qn; **to let f.** (*lose one's temper*) s'emporter; (*arrow*) décocher; (*string of insults*) lâcher; **to let f. at sb** (*abuse, reprimand*) passer un savon à qn, sonner les cloches à qn; (*hit*) flanquer un coup à qn; *F* **to send sb/sth flying** envoyer rouler qn/qch; **to f. (in)to pieces** *or* **to bits** éclater, voler en éclats; *Fig* **to f. in the face of the evidence/current thinking** aller à l'encontre de l'évidence/des idées actuelles; **to f. in the face of reason/logic** défier la raison/toute logique

2 *vt* **(a)** *Av* (*plane*) piloter; (*person, object*) emmener en avion, transporter par avion; **we'll f. it to you tomorrow** nous vous l'enverrons par avion demain; **we were flown to Norway** on nous a emmenés en Norvège en avion; **to f. ABC airlines** voyager avec la compagnie aérienne ABC; **several airlines f. this route** plusieurs compagnies aériennes empruntent cette route; **he had flown three missions** il avait effectué trois missions en vol; **I'd never flown the Atlantic before** je n'avais jamais traversé l'Atlantique en avion auparavant; **her employers flew her to the States** ses employeurs l'ont envoyée aux États-Unis en avion; **we're flying them home on the first flight** nous les rapatrions par le premier vol

(b) *Naut* (*flag*) déployer; **the ship was flying the Italian flag** le bateau arborait le pavillon italien

(c) **to f. a kite** faire voler un cerf-volant; *Fig* lancer un ballon d'essai; *esp Am* **go f. a kite!** (*go away*) fiche-moi le camp!; (*I'm not going to do it*) va te faire voir!

(d) (*flee*) **to f. the country** s'enfuir du pays; *esp Am* **to f. the coop** disparaître; **to f. the nest** (*of fledgling, child*) quitter le nid

fly[4] *adj Br Sl* malin, *f* -igne; (*scheme*) rusé, astucieux; **he's very f.** c'est un malin; **on the f.** en douce

▶ **fly about, fly around** *vi* (*of bird*) voler çà et là; (*of butterfly etc*) voltiger; *Fig* (*of rumours*) courir; **there are lots of figures flying about** *or* **around** on entend tellement de chiffres différents

▶ **fly away** *vi* (*of bird etc*) s'envoler

▶ **fly by** *vi* **(a)** (*of time*) passer à toute vitesse; **the time has flown by!** comme le temps a passé!; **as the days flew by** à mesure que les jours s'enfuyaient **(b)** *Av* (*of aircraft*) passer

▶ **fly in 1** *vi* **(a)** (*arrive by aircraft*) arriver en avion **(b)** (*approach*) (*of pilot, aircraft*) arriver; **the planes flew in over the coast** les avions sont arrivés en survolant la côte **2** *vtsep* (*transport by aircraft*) amener en avion; **the air force flew in supplies/reinforcements** les forces aériennes ont amené des ravitaillements/du renfort

▶ **fly off 1** *vi* (*of bird, aircraft etc*) s'envoler; (*leave in aircraft*) partir en avion; (*of button, lid etc*) sauter **2** *vtsep* (*transport by aircraft*) envoyer par avion; **they were flown off by helicopter** ils ont été évacués par hélicoptère

▶ **fly out 1** *vi* **(a)** (*of bird*) sortir en volant **(b)** (*leave in aircraft*) partir en avion; **a medical team flew out to the disaster area** une équipe médicale s'est rendue en avion sur la région sinistrée **(c)** (*be ejected*) être éjecté; **the knife flew out of his hand** le couteau lui a échappé de la main **2** *vtsep* (*transport by aircraft*) emmener en avion; **her husband's employer flew her out to be with him** l'employeur de son mari l'a envoyée le retrouver par avion

▶ **fly past** *vi* **(a)** (*of bird, aircraft*) passer (en volant); *Mil, Av* (*in formation*) exécuter un défilé aérien; *Fig* **he flew past on a bicycle** il est passé à toute vitesse en bicyclette **(b)** (*of time*) passer vite

▶ **fly up** *vi* **(a)** (*of bird etc*) s'envoler; **I flew up from London on Saturday** j'ai pris l'avion depuis Londres samedi **(b)**

(*become vertical*) (*of arm etc*) s'élever; **the other end of the broom flew up** l'autre extrémité du balai s'est relevée

flyaway ['flaɪəweɪ] *adj* **(a) f. hair** cheveux légers et indisciplinés **(b)** (*person*) léger, étourdi

flyblown ['flaɪbləʊn] *adj* (*meat*) plein *ou* couvert d'œufs de mouches

flyby ['flaɪbaɪ] *n Mil, Av* défilé *m* aérien

fly-by-night *F Pej* **1** *adj* (*company etc*) douteux, véreux **2** *n* (*dishonest person*) personne *f* qui file à l'anglaise pour éviter de payer; (*who doesn't pay rent*) déménageur *m* à la cloche de bois; (*firm*) entreprise *f* douteuse *ou* véreuse

flycatcher ['flaɪkætʃər] *n* (*bird*) gobe-mouches *m inv*, *Am* moucherolle *f*; **spotted f.** gobe-mouches gris

fly cruise *n* forfait *m* avion et croisière

fly-drive **1** *n* forfait *m* avion + location de voiture **2** *adj Com* **f. holiday** vacances *fpl* en formule avion-voiture

flyer ['flaɪər] *n* = **flier**

fly-half *n Rugby* demi *m* d'ouverture

flying ['flaɪɪŋ] **1** *adj* **(a)** (*bird, fish etc*) volant; (*ribbon, hair etc*) volant, léger; **they were hurt by f. glass** ils ont été blessés par des bris de verre; **f. ambulance** avion-ambulance *m, pl* avions-ambulances; **f. machine** machine *f* volante; **unidentified f. object** objet *m* volant non identifié; **f. saucer** soucoupe *f* volante

(b) (*rapid*) **to take a f. leap** *or* **jump over sth** franchir qch d'un saut; *Fig, F* **to take a f. jump** aller se faire voir; *Mil* **f. column** colonne *f* mobile, groupement *m* mobile; **f. squad** (*police*) brigade *f* volante; *Sp* **f. start** départ *m* en flèche; **we got off to a f. start** (*in a project etc*) nous nous sommes lancés à toute allure *ou* à fond de train; **to pay a f. visit to London** faire une visite éclair à Londres

(c) to pass an exam with f. colours réussir un examen haut la main

(d) *Constr* **f. buttress** arc-boutant *m, pl* arcs-boutants

(e) (*fleeing*) en fuite

2 *n* **(a)** (*flight*) vol *m*; (*of plane*) pilotage *m*; *Av* (*activity*) aviation *f*; **he loves f.** (*as pilot*) il adore piloter; (*as passenger*) il adore prendre l'avion; **I don't like f.** (*as passenger*) je n'aime pas prendre l'avion; **I haven't done much f.** (*as pilot*) je n'ai pas beaucoup volé; (*as passenger*) je n'ai pas pris l'avion très souvent; **night f.** vol *m* de nuit; **f. club** aéro-club *m, pl* aéro-clubs; **f. lessons** leçons *fpl* de pilotage aérien; **f. time** heures *fpl* de vol; **200 hours f. time** 200 heures de vol

(b) (*of flag*) déploiement *m*

flying boat *n Av* hydravion *m*

flying bomb *n Hist* bombe *f* volante

flying corps *n US Av* corps *m* d'armée aérien

flying doctor *n* médecin *m* volant

Flying Dutchman *n Liter, Mus* Vaisseau *m* fantôme

flying fox *n Zool* roussette *f*

flying picket *n Ind* piquet *m* de grève volant

fly-kick *n Rugby* coup *m* de pied à suivre

flyleaf ['flaɪli:f] *n* (*of book*) feuille *f* de garde *f*

flyover ['flaɪəʊvər] *n* **(a)** *Br* (*elevated road*) autopont *m*; **f. crossing** croisement *m* à niveaux différents **(b)** *Am Av* survol *m*; (*ceremonial*) défilé *m* aérien

flypaper ['flaɪpeɪpər] *n* papier *m* tue-mouches

fly-past *n Mil Av* défilé *m* aérien

flypost ['flaɪpəʊst] *vi* coller illicitement des affiches

flyposting ['flaɪpəʊstɪŋ] *n* affichage *m* illégal

fly rail *n* forfait *m* avion + train

fly-tipping *n Br* dépôt *m* d'ordures illégal

flyweight ['flaɪweɪt] *n Boxing* (*boxer, category*) poids *m* mouche; **f. champion** champion *m* poids mouche

flywheel ['flaɪwi:l] *n MecE etc* volant *m* (de commande)

FM [e'fem] *n Rad* (*abbr* **frequency modulation**) FM *f*; **a station on FM, an FM station** une station FM

f-number *n Phot* échelle *f* d'ouverture

FO [e'fəʊ] *n Br Admin* (*abbr* **Foreign Office**) ministère *m* des affaires étrangères

foal[1] [fəʊl] *n* poulain *m*, pouliche *f*; (*of donkey*) ânon *m*, bourriquet *m*; **mare in** *or* **with f.** jument *f* pleine

foal[2] **1** *vi* pouliner **2** *vt* (*colt, filly*) mettre bas

foam[1] [fəʊm] *n* **(a)** (*on sea*) écume *f*; (*on beer*) mousse *f*; **waves white with f.** vagues moutonneuses; **to break into f.** (*of wave*) déferler; **f.-flecked** moucheté d'écume; **f. bath** bain *m* moussant **(b)** (*from mouth*) bave *f*, écume *f* **(c)** (*artificial substance*) mousse *f*; **f. fire extinguisher** extincteur *m* à mousse carbonique; **polystyrene f.** mousse *f* en polystyrène; **f.-backed** doublé de mousse; **f. rubber** caoutchouc *m* mousse

foam[2] *vi* (*of sea etc*) écumer; (*of beer etc*) mousser; **to f. at the mouth** avoir l'écume aux lèvres; (*of dog etc*) baver; *F, Fig* (*be furious*) écumer (de rage); **he was foaming at the mouth about the latest price rises** il écumait de rage en évoquant les dernières hausses de prix

► **foam up** *vi* mousser, faire de la mousse

foaming ['fəʊmɪŋ] *adj* (*sea, horse etc*) écumant; (*sea*) moutonnant; (*blood, saliva*) spumeux; (*beer etc*) moussant; *Hum* **f. ale** bière *f*

foamy ['fəʊmɪ] *adj* (*sea*) écumant; (*drink*) mousseux

fob [fɒb] *n* (*chain*) chaîne *f*; **f. (pocket)** gousset *m* (de pantalon); **f. (watch)** montre *f* de gousset

► **fob off** *vtsep* **(a) to f. sb off** se débarrasser de qn; **they fobbed him off with some excuse** ils lui ont donné la première excuse venue; **she'll try to f. it off on(to) some unsuspecting buyer** elle essaiera de le vendre *ou F* fourguer à un acheteur peu soupçonneux **(b) to f. sth off as sth** faire passer qch pour qch

f.o.b, FOB [efəʊ'bi:] *adj Com* (*abbr* **free on board**) f. à b., FAB, FOB; **F. port of embarkation** FAB port d'embarquement

focal ['fəʊk(ə)l] *adj* **(a)** *Phys, Opt, Math* focal; **f. length** distance *f ou* longueur *f* focale; **f. point** (*of mirror etc*) foyer *m*; *Fig* (*of discussion etc*) point *m* central; (*of room*) point de mire; *Phot* **f. plane shutter** obturateur *m* focal **(b)** *Med* (*infection*) focal

fo'c'sle ['fəʊks(ə)l] *n* = **forecastle**

focus[1], *pl* **foci, focuses** ['fəʊkəs, 'fəʊsaɪ, 'fəʊkəsɪz] *n* **(a)** *Opt, Math etc* (*of lens etc*) foyer *m*; **in f.** (*of image*) net, au point; (*of instrument*) réglé; **out of f.** (*of image*) flou, pas au point; (*of instrument*) non réglé, déréglé; **to bring sth into f.** (*image*) mettre qch au point; **to bring a problem into f.** mieux définir un problème, clarifier la nature d'un problème; **these unemployment figures bring the economic crisis into an even sharper f.** ces chiffres du chômage mettent la crise économique encore plus en relief; *Phot* **fixed-f. camera** appareil *m* à mise au point fixe; **f. control** (*on camera*) mise *f* au point; **f. knob** bouton *m* de mise au point; **f. puller** responsable *m* point, assistant caméraman *m*

(b) (*of discontent, unrest*) foyer *m*; (*of interest, attention*) centre *m*; *Med* (*of illness*) siège *m*; **she was the f. of attention** elle était le centre d'attention; *Med* **f. of infection** foyer *m* d'infection; **these proposals have been the f. of much concern** ces propositions ont fait l'objet de profondes inquiétudes; **the organization will provide some kind of a f. for opposition to the project** l'organisation fournira un point de ralliement à l'opposition au projet; **this became a f. of people's discontent** le mécontentement s'est concentré là-dessus

focus[2] **(-s-)** **1** *vt* **(a)** (*rays of light etc*) concentrer **(in** dans; **on** sur); (*rays*) faire converger; (*one's interest, concern*) centrer; (*one's energies*) concentrer; **all eyes were focused on him** il était le point de mire de tous les regards; **to f. one's attention on sth** concentrer son attention sur qch; **to f. attention on sth** attirer l'attention des gens sur qch **(b)** (*microscope, camera etc*) mettre au point **2** *vi* **(a)** (*with eyes*) fixer; **to f. on sth** (*with eyes*) fixer qch; (*of debate, speaker etc*) se concentrer sur qch; *Phot* **to f. on an object** mettre au point sur un objet **(b)** (*of light, sound etc*) converger **(on** sur)

focus group *n Mktg* groupe *m* test réuni pour une étude; **f. interviewing** entretien *m* avec les membres du groupe test

fodder[1] ['fɒdər] *n* fourrage *m*; **green/dry f.** fourrage (en) vert/(en) sec

fodder[2] *vt* (*animal*) donner le fourrage à

foe [fəʊ] *n Lit* ennemi *m*, adversaire *m*

foetal ['fi:t(ə)l] *adj Biol* fœtal; **f. heartbeat** rythme *m* cardiaque du fœtus; **to lie in a f. position** être allongé en position fœtale

foetid ['fi:tɪd] *adj* = **fetid**

foetus, *pl* **-uses** ['fi:təs, -əsɪz] *n Biol* fœtus *m*

fog[1] [fɒg] *n* **(a)** *Met* brouillard *m*; **in the f.** dans le brouillard; *Fig* **I'm in a f.** je ne sais plus où j'en suis; **she was in a complete f. about what she was supposed to be doing** elle ignorait complètement ce qu'elle était censée faire; **he is in a f. on anything related to economics** il est complètement perdu pour tout ce qui touche à l'économie; *Met* **f. bank** nappe *m* de brouillard; *Av etc* **f. dispersal** dénébulation *f*; **f. light** projecteur *m* pour le brouillard; *Aut* (phare *m*) antibrouillard *m*; **f. signal** *Naut* signal *m*, -aux de brume; *Rail* pétard *m* **(b)** *Phot* (*on negative*) voile *m*

fog[2] **(-gg-)** **1** *vt* **(a)** *Fig* (*ideas*) brouiller; (*person, issue*) embrouiller; **I am a bit fogged** je ne sais plus très bien où j'en suis; **don't be fogged by all the long words he uses** ne vous laissez pas embrouiller par ses grands mots **(b)** *Phot* (*negative*) voiler **(c)** (*mirror etc*) embuer, couvrir de buée **2** *vi* **(a)** = **fog up** **(b)** *Phot* (*of negative*) se voiler

► **fog up** *vi* (*of spectacles, windows*) se couvrir de buée, s'embuer

fogbound ['fɒgbaʊnd] *adj* (*airport*) bloqué par le brouillard

fogey ['fəʊgɪ] *n F* **old f.** vieille baderne *f*; **I'm afraid I'm**

turning into a bit of an old f. je crois que je suis en train de m'encroûter; **he dresses like such an old f.** il s'habille tellement vieux jeu; **young f.** pépère *m*

fogginess ['fɒgɪnɪs] *n* (a) (*of weather*) temps *m* brumeux (b) (*of person's ideas*) confusion *f*; *Phot* voile *m*

foggy ['fɒgɪ] *adj* (a) (*weather, climate etc*) brumeux; **on a f. day** par un jour de brouillard; **it's f.** il y a du brouillard; **due to f. conditions** pour cause de brouillard; **the roads are rather f.** il y a du brouillard sur les routes (b) (*photograph etc*) voilé; **to have only a f. idea of sth** n'avoir qu'une vague idée de qch; *F* **I haven't the foggiest (idea)!** je n'en ai pas la moindre idée!

foghorn ['fɒghɔːn] *n Naut* corne *f* de brume, sirène *f*; *F* **voice like a f.** voix *f* de stentor

foglamp ['fɒglæmp] *n* (phare *m*) antibrouillard *m*

foible ['fɔɪb(ə)l] *n* (*idiosyncrasy*) particularité *f*; (*weakness*) point *m* faible

foil[1] [fɔɪl] *n* (a) (*metal sheet, gold etc*) feuille *f*; **silver f.** feuille d'argent; *Culin* **cooking** *or* **kitchen f.** papier *m* aluminium; **sandwiches wrapped in f.** sandwiches enveloppés dans du papier aluminium (b) (*person, thing*) repoussoir *m*; **to serve as a f. to sb's beauty** servir de repoussoir à la beauté de qn (c) *Av, Naut* (*of hydrofoil*) patin *m*, aile *f* (d) *Archit* (*of arch etc*) lobe *m*

foil[2] *n Fencing* (a) fleuret *m* (b) **foils** (*fencing*) escrime *f* au fleuret

foil[3] *vt* (*thwart*) (*attempt etc*) faire échouer; (*plan, plot*) contrecarrer; **to be foiled at all points** (*of person*) échouer sur toute la ligne; **foiled again!** encore raté!; **once again they have been foiled by their own incompetence** une fois encore ils ont échoué à cause de leur propre incompétence

foist [fɔɪst] *vt* refiler (**sth on sb** qch à qn); **to f. oneself on sb** s'imposer à qn *ou* chez qn; **I try not to f. my opinions/ideas on people** j'essaie de ne pas imposer mes opinions/idées à autrui

fold[1] [fəʊld] *n* (a) (*crease*) (*in paper, skirt etc*) pli *m*; **folds of fat** bourrelets *mpl* de graisse (b) *Geol* pli *m*, plissement *m*

fold[2] **1** *vt* (a) (*sheet of paper etc*) plier; **to f. sth in two** *or* **in half** plier qch en deux; **to f. sth in paper** envelopper qch dans du papier; **to f. sb in one's arms** enlacer qn, serrer qn dans ses bras; **to f. one's arms** (se) croiser les bras; **with folded arms** les bras croisés; **to f. one's hands** joindre les mains (b) *Culin* **f. the whites into the mixture** incorporer petit à petit les blancs dans le mélange **2** *vi* (a) (*of screen etc*) se (re)plier (b) *F* (*of business*) cesser ses activités; *Th* **the play folded after a week** la pièce a été retirée au bout d'une semaine

fold[3] *n* (a) *Agr* (**sheep**) **f.** parc *m* à moutons (b) *Fig* (*of Church, family*) sein *m*; **to return to the f.** (*of member of family*) rentrer au bercail; (*of politician etc*) rentrer dans les rangs; **to welcome sb back to the f.** accueillir l'enfant prodigue; **they welcomed Paul back to the f.** ils ont accueilli Paul comme l'enfant prodigue

fold[4] *vt Agr* (*sheep*) (em)parquer

▶ **fold away 1** *vi* (*of table etc*) se replier, être escamotable **2** *vtsep* (*store*) plier et ranger; **f. your clothes away neatly** plie tes affaires et range-les; **I slept on a campbed which I folded away every morning** je dormais sur un lit de camp que je repliais tous les matins

▶ **fold back 1** *vtsep* (*collar etc*) rabattre; (*bedcovers, page*) replier **2** *vi* (*of door etc*) se rabattre

▶ **fold down 1** *vtsep* (*bedcovers*) replier **2** *vi* (*of seat etc*) se rabattre; (*of sofa*) se déplier

▶ **fold in** *vtsep Culin* **to f. in the whites of the eggs** incorporer les blancs d'œufs

▶ **fold over** *vtsep* plier; **she had folded the top of the paper over** elle avait replié le haut de la feuille par-dessus

▶ **fold under** *vtsep* (*edges*) replier en dessous

▶ **fold up 1** *vtsep* (*seat, table*) (re)plier; (*screen*) replier, fermer **2** *vi* se (re)plier

-fold [fəʊld] *suff* **three/eleven/twenty/** *etc*-**f.** (*in three/eleven etc parts*) en trois/onze/vingt/ *etc* parties; (*to increase*) (par) trois/onze/vingt/ *etc* fois

foldaway ['fəʊldəweɪ] *adj* (*bed, table*) pliant, escamotable; (*seat*) pliant, rabattable

foldback ['fəʊldbæk] *n TV etc* ré-injection *f*, retour *m*, play-back *m*

folder ['fəʊldər] *n* (a) (*for papers etc*) chemise *f* (b) *Com* (*leaflet*) prospectus *m* (plié) (c) (*device*) plioir *m* (d) *Comptr* (*directory*) dossier *m*

folding ['fəʊldɪŋ] **1** *adj* (*seat*) pliant, rabattable; (*bed*) pliant, escamotable; (*joint, shutter*) brisé; **f. camera** appareil *m* à soufflet; **f. door** porte *f* pliante; **f. machine** (*for documents*) machine *f* à plier les documents; *esp Am F* **f. money** billet *mpl*; **f. screen** paravent *m*; **f. stool** pliant *m*; **f. table** table *f* pliante *ou* escamotable; (*with extending sections*) table à battants; **car with a f. top** voiture *f* décapotable; **f. tray** (*in plane etc*) tablette *f* (*qui se relève*) **2** *n* (*of material etc*) pliage *m*; (*in bookbinding*) (*of pages*) pliure *f*; *Geol* (*of land*) plissement *m*

foldout ['fəʊldaʊt] *n* dépliant *m*

foliage ['fəʊlɪɪdʒ] *n* feuillage *m*, frondaison *f*; **f. plant** plante *f* à feuillage

foliate ['fəʊlɪeɪt] *adj Bot* feuillu

foliation [fəʊlɪ'eɪʃən] *n* (a) (*of plant*) foliation *f*, feuillaison *f* (b) *Archit* (ornementation *f* en) rinceaux *mpl* (c) *Geol* (*of rock*) foliation *f* (d) (*of book*) foliotage *m*

folic ['fəʊlɪk] *adj* **f. acid** acide *m* folique

folio, *pl* **-os** ['fəʊlɪəʊ, -əʊz] **1** *n* (*in bookbinding*) (*sheet*) folio *m*, feuille *f*; *Typ* (*page number*) numéro *m*; (**book in**) **f.** (livre *m*) in-folio *m inv* **2** *adj* **f. book** (livre *m*) in-folio *m inv*

folk [fəʊk] *n* (*pl* **folk,** *esp Am* **folks**) [①A11,f,ii] (*people*) gens *mfpl*; (*music*) folk *m*; **I don't care what f. think** je me moque de ce que les gens pensent; **country f.** campagnards *mpl*; **my f., your f.** les miens, ma famille/les vôtres, votre famille; *esp Am F* **hi, folks!** salut, tout le monde!; **f. concert/festival** concert *m*/festival *m* de folk; **f. dance** danse *f* folklorique; **f. medicine** médecine *f* populaire; **f. museum** musée *m* folklorique, musée des arts et traditions populaires, musée du folklore; **f. music** musique *f* folk *ou* folklorique; **f. singer** chanteur, -euse de chansons folkloriques; (*modern*) folk-singer *m*, *pl* folk-singers; **f. song** chanson *f* traditionnelle *ou* folklorique; (*modern*) folk-song *m*, *pl* folk-songs; **f. tale** conte *m* folklorique

folklore ['fəʊklɔːr] *n* folklore *m*

folksy ['fəʊksɪ] *adj F* (*friendly*) sociable; (*smile, greeting, cheerfulness*) bon enfant; (*dress*) traditionnel

foll (*abbr* **following**) suiv

follicle ['fɒlɪk(ə)l] *n Anat, Bot etc* follicule *m*

follow ['fɒləʊ] **1** *vt* (a) (*person, car, suspect etc*) suivre; **to f. sb about** suivre qn partout; **to f. sb up the stairs/into a room** monter l'escalier/entrer dans une pièce à la suite de qn; *F* **to f. one's nose** y aller à l'instinct

(b) (*go along*) (*path, road, itinerary*) suivre; **the road follows the coast** la route longe la côte

(c) (*succeed*) succéder à; **the years f. one another** les années se succèdent *ou* se suivent; **as sure as day follows night** aussi sûr que deux et deux font quatre; **in the months that followed his resignation** dans les mois qui ont suivi sa démission; **George IV was followed by William IV** Guillaume IV a succédé à George IV; **dinner followed by a dance** dîner suivi d'un bal; **how do you expect me to f. that?** comment veux-tu passer après un truc comme ça?; **following our correspondence** (comme) suite à notre échange de lettres

(d) (*imitate, adhere to*) (*person*) être le disciple de; (*the old masters*) imiter; (*person's example, teaching, pattern, fashion*) suivre; (*diet*) s'assujettir à, suivre; **to f. instructions** suivre les consignes

(e) (*practise, carry out*) (*profession*) exercer, suivre; (*career*) poursuivre; **to f. suit** (*do the same*) faire de même; **you're not following the music** vous ne suivez pas la musique

(f) (*understand*) (*explanation etc*) suivre, comprendre; **I don't quite f. you** je ne vous comprends *ou* suis pas très bien; **I didn't f. why they killed him** je n'ai pas compris pourquoi ils l'ont tué

(g) (*pay attention to*) (*speech etc*) prêter attention à; (*events, news, programme*) suivre; **I don't f. the tennis any more** je ne suis plus le tennis

(h) (*support*) **to f. a football team** être supporter d'une équipe de foot

2 *vi* (a) (*come after*) (*of person, event*) suivre, venir après; **my husband is following later** mon mari viendra plus tard; **in the days that followed** dans les jours qui ont suivi; **a long silence followed** un long silence s'ensuivit; **roast beef with strawberries to f.** du rosbif suivi par des fraises; **proceed as follows** procéder comme suit; **our method is as follows** notre méthode est la suivante; **what follows is a brief account** ce qui suit est un bref compte-rendu

(b) (*result*) s'ensuivre, résulter (**from** de); **it follows that ...** il s'ensuit que ...; **it does not f. that ...** ça ne veut pas nécessairement dire que ... + *ind*; **it follows from this that ...** il en résulte que ...; **I don't see how that conclusion follows** je ne vois pas comment tu arrives/il arrive/etc à cette conclusion; (*in logic etc*) je ne vois pas comment cette conclusion s'ensuit; **that doesn't f.** pas nécessairement, pas forcément

(c) (*understand*) suivre; **I don't f.** je ne suis pas

▶ **follow on** *vi* (a) (*come after*) suivre; **you go ahead, we'll f. on** partez en avant, nous vous suivons; **she said she wo**

f. on later elle a dit qu'elle nous rejoindrait plus tard **(b)** (*result*) **it follows on from this that ...** il en résulte que ...; **I don't see how that follows on at all** je ne vois pas du tout comment on en arrive là **(c)** *Cr* = reprendre la garde du guichet au commencement de la seconde partie du match (au lieu d'alterner avec l'autre équipe)

▶ **follow out** *vtsep* (*orders*) exécuter; (*instructions*) suivre; (*investigation*) procéder à

▶ **follow through 1** *vtsep* (*execute*) **to f. a project through (to the end)** poursuivre un projet jusqu'à sa conclusion; **she seems incapable of following anything through** on dirait qu'elle est incapable de mener quoi que ce soit à bien **2** *vi Sp* suivre le coup

▶ **follow up 1** *vtsep* (*take further*) poursuivre; *Com* (*letter*) faire suivre d'une seconde lettre; (*person*) relancer; (*advantage*) poursuivre; (*enquiry, order etc*) donner suite à; (*opportunity*) saisir; (*success*) exploiter; (*victory etc*) donner suite immédiate à; (*tip-off*) suivre; **to f. up a clue** suivre une piste **2** *vi* (*add to previous action*) continuer; (*in selling*) faire de la relance; **he followed up with a right to the jaw** il a continué avec un droit à la mâchoire; **it's up to you now to f. up** c'est à toi d'agir maintenant

follower ['fɒləʊər] *n* **(a)** (*supporter*) partisan, -ane, disciple *mf*; (*of football club*) supporter *m*; **as followers of this programme will be aware ...** comme les personnes qui suivent cette émission le savent, ...; **she had never really been much of a f. of the arts** elle ne s'était jamais beaucoup intéressée à l'art **(b)** (*servant*) (*of prince etc*) serviteur *m*; **the King and his followers** le roi et sa suite **(c)** *Mktg* suiveur *m*

following ['fɒləʊɪŋ] **1** *adj* suivant; **on the f. day** le jour suivant, le jour d'après, le lendemain; **the f. Monday** le lundi suivant; **the f. resolution** la résolution que voici *ou* suivante; **the f. persons** les personnes dont les noms suivent, les personnes suivantes; **two days f.** deux jours de suite; *TV, Cin* **f. pan** pano *m* de poursuite; *Naut* **f. wind** vent *m* arrière

2 *n* **(a)** *Pol etc* (*of leader*) parti *m*; (*of prince*) suite *f*; **to have a big f.** avoir un grand nombre de partisans *ou* de disciples; **television programme that commands a wide f.** émission télévisée très suivie; **a team with a large f.** une équipe qui a beaucoup de supporters

(b) the f. (*things, points*) ce qui suit; (*people*) les personnes suivantes *ou* dont les noms suivent; **the f. is the full list** voici la liste complète

3 *prep* après, à la suite de

follow-me product *n Mktg* produit *m* tactique

follow-my-leader *n Br* jeu *m* de la queue leu leu

follow-on *n Cr* **to try to avoid** *or* **save the f.** = s'efforcer de marquer le nombre de points requis pour ne pas avoir à reprendre la garde du guichet

follow-the-leader *n Am* = **follow-my-leader**

follow-through *n Sp* fin *f* du coup

follow-up *n* suite *f*; *Com etc* (*of advertising etc*) relance *f*; *Med* examens *mpl* de contrôles à long terme; **f. of orders** suivi *m* des commandes; **f. action** suite; **to take f. action on sth** donner suite à qch; *Med* **f. care** soins *mpl* post-hospitaliers; **f. interview** (*for job, research*) deuxième entretien *m*; *Com etc* **f. letter** lettre *f* de relance; **f. publicity** publicité *f* de rappel; **f. story** suite *f*; **f. system** système *m* de relance; **f. visit** (*medical*) visite *f* de contrôle; (*in selling*) visite de relance

folly ['fɒlɪ] *n* **(a)** folie *f*, sottise *f*; **an act of f., a f.** une folie; **it would be the height of f. to ...** ce serait la plus grande folie de ...; **this decision is sheer f. on the part of the government** c'est de la folie furieuse pour le gouvernement d'avoir pris cette décision **(b)** *Archit* folie *f*

foment [fə'ment] *vt* **(a)** (*discord, discontent*) fomenter **(b)** *Med* (*wound*) fomenter

fomentation [fəʊmen'teɪʃən] *n* **(a)** (*of discord, discontent*) fomentation *f* **(b)** *Med* (*of wound*) fomentation *f*

fond [fɒnd] *adj* **(a) to be f. of sb/sth** (*to like*) bien aimer qn/qch; **they are f. of each other** ils s'aiment bien; **I'm f. of you but I don't love you** je t'aime bien mais c'est tout; **he was very f. of me** il me portait beaucoup d'affection; **to become f. of sb** s'attacher à qn; **to be f. of music** être amateur de musique; **f. of sweets** friand de sucreries; **to be passionately f. of reading** adorer la lecture; **I'm not f. of being told I'm an idiot** je n'apprécie pas qu'on me traite d'idiot; **he is rather too f. of the sound of his own voice** il aime un peu trop s'écouter parler; **he was f. of the odd whisky** il aimait bien prendre un petit whisky de temps à autre

(b) (*loving*) (*person, embrace*) affectueux, tendre; (*smile*) attendri; **f. parents** (*loving*) parents pleins d'affection; (*indulgent*) parents indulgents; **with f. regards** (*in letter*) bien amicalement

(c) (*memory*) agréable

(d) (*foolish*) **in the f. hope of catching a glimpse of my idol** dans le fol espoir d'apercevoir mon idole; **she still retained the f. belief that he would return** elle persistait à croire qu'il reviendrait

fondant ['fɒndənt] *n* fondant *m*

fondle ['fɒnd(ə)l] *vt* (*person*) caresser, câliner; (*of lover, mother*) faire des câlins à; (*dog, cat etc*) caresser; **he was fondling her leg under the table** il lui caressait la jambe sous la table

fondly ['fɒndlɪ] *adv* **(a)** (*lovingly*) (*to smile, stroke etc*) tendrement, affectueusement **(b)** (*naively*) (*to hope, believe etc*) naïvement; **I f. believed that ...** j'ai naïvement cru que ...

fondness ['fɒndnɪs] *n* **(a)** (*affection*) affection *f*, tendresse *f* **(for** pour, envers**)** **(b)** (*liking*) penchant *m*, prédilection *f*, goût *m* **(for sth** pour qch); (*strong liking*) goût profond **(for sth** de qch)

fondue ['fɒndu:] *n Culin* fondue *f*; **beef/cheese f.** fondue bourguignonne/savoyarde

font[1] [fɒnt] *n Rel* fonts *mpl* baptismaux

font[2] *n Typ, Comptr* police *f*, fonte *f*; **f. cartridge** cartouche *f* de polices; **f. cassette** cassette *f* de polices de caractères, cassette de fontes

fontanel(le) [fɒntə'nel] *n Anat* fontanelle *f*

food [fu:d] *n* **(a)** (*no pl*) nourriture *f*; (*as opposed to drink*) manger *m*; (*for expedition*) vivres *mpl*; *Agr* (*for animals*) pâture *f*; (*for poultry*) mangeaille *f*; **f. and drink** le boire et le manger; *Mktg* **f. and non-f.** alimentaire et non-alimentaire; **there's some f. in the fridge** il y a à manger dans le frigidaire; **f. is expensive here** la nourriture est chère ici; **take some f. for the journey** prenez de quoi manger pendant le voyage; **hotel where the f. is good** hôtel où la cuisine *ou* la table est bonne; **to be off one's f.** ne pas avoir d'appétit; **to hunt** *or* **search for f.** (*of animal*) chercher sa nourriture; **f. for the mind** nourriture de l'esprit; **to give sb f. for thought** donner à penser à qn; **f. allergy** allergie *f* alimentaire; **f. counter** (*in large store*) buffet *m*; **f. critic** critique *m* gastronomique; **f. counter,** (*in large store*) **f. hall** *or* **department** rayon *m* d'alimentation; **f. critic** critique *m* gastronomique; **f. hygiene regulations** réglementation *f* sur l'hygiène alimentaire; *Am* **f. product** produit *m* alimentaire; **f. stamp** ticket *m* alimentaire; **f. value** valeur *f* nutritive

(b) (*type of food*) aliment *m*; **canned** *or Br* **tinned foods** aliments de conserve (en boîte); **health foods** (*for special diet*) produits *mpl* diététiques; (*natural foods*) produits alimentaires naturels; **skin f.** aliment pour la peau

food chain *n* **(a)** *Biol* chaîne *f* alimentaire **(b)** (*stores*) chaîne *f* de restauration

foodie ['fu:dɪ] *n F* fana *mf* de bouffe; (*stress on cooking*) fana de cuisine

food industry *n* industrie *f* alimentaire

food mixer *n* mixer *m*

food poisoning *n* intoxication *f* alimentaire

food processor *n* robot *m* de cuisine

foodstore ['fu:dstɔ:r] *n* magasin *m* d'alimentation

foodstuff ['fu:dstʌf] *n* (*usu pl*) **foodstuffs** produits *mpl* alimentaires *ou* d'alimentation

fool[1] [fu:l] **1** *n* imbécile *mf*, idiot, -ote; *Hist* (*jester*) fou *m*; **to play** *or* **act the f.** faire l'idiot; **to make a f. of oneself** se couvrir de ridicule; **no one likes being made a f. of** personne n'aime être ridiculisé; **I felt such a f.** je me sentais vraiment idiot; **you'd be a f. to buy it** tu serais bête de l'acheter; **only a f. would pay that much for it** il faudrait être bête pour le payer aussi cher; **what f. was responsible for this decision?** quel est l'idiot *ou* l'imbécile qui a pris cette décision?; *F* **silly f.!** espèce d'idiot!; **what a f.!** quel idiot!; **he's no f.** il n'est pas bête; **he's a bigger f. than I thought** il est plus bête que je ne le pensais; **more f. you!** (*for believing them, buying it etc*) ce que tu es bête!; **if you agreed to that then more f. you** si tu as accepté c'est que tu es vraiment bête; **like a f., I agreed** comme un idiot, j'ai accepté; **any f. knows that** le premier imbécile venu sait cela; **some f. doctor** un imbécile de docteur; *Prov* **there's no f. like an old f.** un vieux fou est le pire des fous; **to make a f. of sb** (*make look ridiculous*) exposer qn au ridicule, ridiculiser qn; (*tease*) se moquer de qn; **she's nobody's** *or* **no-one's f.** c'est une maline *ou* une rusée; **to go on a f.'s errand** y aller pour des prunes *ou* pour le roi de Prusse; **I went on a f.'s errand trying to buy a turkey on Christmas Eve** j'ai essayé de trouver une dinde la veille de Noël mais il n'y a pas eu moyen; **the sales trip promised to be nothing but a f.'s errand** ce voyage d'affaires avait l'air d'être une belle perte de temps en perspective; **to send sb on a f.'s errand** envoyer qn décrocher la lune; **All Fools' Day, April**

Fools' Day le premier avril; **they're living in a f.'s paradise** ils rêvent tout éveillés *ou* debout; *Bot* **f.'s parsley** petite ciguë *f*

2 *adj esp Am* stupide; **what a damn f. idea!** quelle idée stupide!

fool² **1** *vi* **(a)** (*act foolishly*) faire l'idiot; **stop fooling!** assez de bêtises!; **I'm becoming tired of your fooling** je commence à en avoir assez de tes bêtises

(b) (*not be serious*) dire des blagues; **I was only fooling** je plaisantais

2 *vt* (*deceive*) duper; (*tease*) faire marcher; **you can't f. me** on ne m'a pas comme ça; **to (allow oneself to) be fooled** se laisser duper; **to be fooled into doing sth** être amené à faire qch par duperie; **he fooled me into believing it** il me l'a fait croire; **he had tried to f. her into providing him with an alibi** il avait essayé de l'embobiner pour qu'elle lui fournisse un alibi; **they had me completely fooled** ils m'ont bien eu; **you didn't have me fooled for a moment** je n'ai pas été dupe un seul instant; **at that point I knew I had them fooled** à ce moment-là j'ai su qu'ils avaient mordu; *Iron* **her?, a socialist?, you could've fooled me!** elle?, une socialiste?, je ne l'aurais pas cru!

fool³ *n Br Culin* marmelade *f* à la crème; **gooseberry f.** marmelade de groseilles (à maquereau) à la crème

▶ **fool about, fool around** *vi* **(a)** (*act foolishly*) faire l'imbécile; **to f. about** *or* **around with sth** (*with electrical appliance etc*) tripoter qch; (*with gun*) jouer avec qch; **I still enjoy fooling around with my old train set** j'aime encore bien m'amuser avec mon vieux train électrique; **she fooled around with drugs** elle a touché à la drogue

(b) (*waste time*) traîner; **this is no time to f. around, young man** ce n'est pas le moment de traîner, jeune homme

(c) (*have affair*) faire des infidélités à sa femme/son mari; **if I thought my husband/wife was fooling around ...** si je pensais que mon mari/ma femme me trompait ...; **to f. around with sb** coucher avec qn; **if I found that he'd been fooling around while I was away** si j'apprenais qu'il m'avait fait des infidélités pendant que j'étais en voyage

▶ **fool with** *vipo Am* (*handle or play with carelessly*) (*electrical appliance etc*) tripoter; (*gun*) jouer avec; **to f. with drugs** toucher à la drogue; **don't f. with me!** ne me cherche pas!; **nobody fools with Mental Mickey** on ne plaisante pas avec Mental Mickey

foolery ['fu:lərɪ] *n* **(a)** (*stupidity*) **(piece of) f.** sottise *f*, folie *f* **(b)** (*playing the fool*) bouffonnerie *f*, pitreries *fpl*

foolhardiness ['fu:lhɑ:dɪnɪs] *n* témérité *f*, imprudence *f*

foolhardy ['fu:lhɑ:dɪ] *adj* téméraire, imprudent; **he was brave to the point of being f.** il était d'un courage qui frôlait la témérité *ou* l'imprudence

foolish ['fu:lɪʃ] *adj* (*stupid*) bête; (*imprudent*) insensé; **don't be so f.!** ne sois pas bête!; **it is f. of him to ...** c'est fou de sa part de ...; **a f. hope** un fol espoir; **to do something f.** faire une bêtise; **to look f.** avoir l'air penaud; **to make sb look f.** tourner qn en ridicule, ridiculiser qn; **to feel f.** se sentir idiot

foolishly ['fu:lɪʃlɪ] *adv* bêtement; **she looked at him rather f.** elle le regardait d'un air plutôt bête; **f., he decided to invade the country** il prit la folle décision d'envahir le pays

foolishness ['fu:lɪʃnɪs] *n* (*of person*) bêtise *f*; (*of plan, decision, idea etc*) stupidité *f*; **it is sheer f. to believe that ...** il est absolument stupide de croire que ...; **they've described the project as nothing but f.** ils ont qualifié le projet d'absurdité; *Old-fashioned* **what f. is this?** qu'est-ce que c'est que ces bêtises?

foolproof ['fu:lpru:f] *adj* (*mechanism*) indéréglable, indétraquable, de sûreté, à toute épreuve; (*scheme*) à toute épreuve, sûr; (*method, system*) infaillible; **it's f.** (*scheme etc*) il n'y a aucun risque, ça marche à tous les coups; **if this plan of yours is so f.** si ton plan est aussi sûr

foolscap ['fu:lskæp] *n esp Br* (*paper*) papier *m* ministre

fool's gold *n Miner* pyrite *f* de fer

foot¹, *pl* **feet** [fʊt, fi:t] *n* **(a)** (*of human, animal with cloven hoof*) pied *m*; (*of dog, cat, bird etc*) patte *f*; **the fore/hind feet** (*of horse*) le bipède antérieur/postérieur; **to put one's feet up** (*have a rest*) se reposer; **she put her feet up on the table** elle a mis les pieds sur la table; **to put one's f. in the door** (*of salesperson etc*) coincer son pied dans la porte; **to set f. on an island** mettre pied sur une île; **I shall never set f. in his house again** jamais je ne remettrai les pieds chez lui; **to rise to one's feet** (*stand*) se lever; (*in debate*) prendre la parole; **he jumped to his feet** d'un bond il fut debout; **to be on one's feet** se tenir debout; **she is on her feet all day** elle est sur ses jambes du matin au soir; **to be on one's feet again** être de nouveau sur pied; **he's constantly getting under my feet** je l'ai toujours dans les pattes; **on f.** à pied; **to go on f.** aller à pied; **under f.** sous les pieds; **to trample** *or* **tread sth under f.** fouler qch aux pieds; **f. control** commande *f* au pied; **feet first** les pieds devant; *Vet* **f. rot** fourchet *m*, piétin *m*

(b) (*idioms*) *F* **to have/get cold feet** avoir la frousse; **to have one's feet firmly on the ground** avoir les pieds sur terre; **to have one f. in the grave** avoir un pied dans la tombe; **not to put a f. wrong** ne faire aucune erreur; **to catch sb on the wrong f.** prendre qn au dépourvu; *Tennis etc* prendre qn à contre-pied; **to start** *or* **get off on the wrong f.** (*of two people*) faire un mauvais départ; **to put one's best f. forward** (*get on with task*) abattre la besogne; (*make rapid progress*) avancer vite *ou* à toute allure; **to put one's f. down** (*be firm*) faire preuve de fermeté; (*stop sth*) mettre le holà; *Aut F* mettre le pied au plancher; *F* **to put one's f. in it** mettre les pieds dans le plat, faire une gaffe; **to sit at sb's feet** être le disciple de qn; **to set sb on their feet** (re)mettre qn sur pied, (r)établir qn; **to begin to find one's feet** (*in new job, situation etc*) commencer à s'adapter; **to get a f. in the door** établir un premier contact; **it's not much of a job but it's a f. in the door** ce n'est pas terrible comme travail, mais ça fait un contact; **to have feet of clay** être un colosse aux pieds d'argile; *F* **my f.!** mon œil!

(c) (*no pl*) *Arch, Mil* (*infantry*) fantassins *mpl*, soldats *mpl* d'infanterie; **a regiment of f.** un régiment d'infanterie; **the 42nd F.** le 42ème d'infanterie

(d) (*lower part*) (*of stocking*) pied *m*; (*of table*) bout *m*, pied; (*of bed, tombstone, glass*) pied; (*of lake*) extrémité *f* inférieure; (*of column etc*) base *f*; (*of mountain, ladder*) pied, bas *m*; *Typ* (*of letter*) pied; **at the f. of the stairs** au bas *ou* en bas de l'escalier; **at the f. of the page/list** au bas de la page/liste

(e) *Liter* (*in poetry*) pied *m*

(f) (*measurement*) pied *m* anglais (= 30,48 cm); **square f.** pied carré; **cubic f.** pied cube; **to be five f.** *or* **feet high/thick** avoir cinq pieds de haut(eur)/d'épaisseur; **three f.** *or* **feet six (inches)** trois pieds six pouces; **a f. of water** un pied d'eau; **at 2,000 feet (above sea level)** à 2000 pieds (au-dessus du niveau de la mer)

foot² *vt* **(a)** *F* **to f. it** (*walk*) marcher **(b)** *F* (*pay*) **to f. the bill** payer la note *ou* les dépenses **(c)** *Am F* = **foot up**

▶ **foot up** *vtsep Am F* (*add up*) (*bill*) additionner

footage ['fʊtɪdʒ] *n* **(a)** (*length*) longueur *f* (en pieds) **(b)** *Cin* (*length of film*) métrage *m* **(c)** *Cin* (*sequence, film*) séquences *fpl*

foot-and-mouth *adj, n Vet* **f.-(disease)** fièvre *f* aphteuse

football ['fʊtbɔ:l] *n* **(a)** (*soccer*) football *m*; *F* foot *m*; (*American*) football; **f. club** club *m* de football; **f. fan** *or* **supporter** supporteur, -trice d'une équipe de football; **f. ground** terrain *m* de football; **f. hooligan** hooligan *m ou* houligan *m* (de football); **f. hooliganism** hooliganisme *m* commis lors de match(e)s de football; **f. league** championnat *m* de football; **f. pitch** terrain *m* de football; **f. player** joueur, -euse de football, footballeur, -euse; *Br* **f. pools** = loto *m* sportif; **f. season** saison *f* de football; *Br Rail* **f. special** train *m* mis en service spécialement pour un match de foot

(b) (*ball*) ballon *m* (de football); *Fig* **it has become a political f.** ça fait l'objet d'un match entre politiciens

footballer ['fʊtbɔ:lər] *n* footballe(u)r, -euse

footbath ['fʊtbɑ:θ] *n* bain *m* de pieds

footbrake ['fʊtbreɪk] *n Aut* frein *m* à pédale *ou* à pied

footbridge ['fʊtbrɪdʒ] *n* pont *m* pour piétons; (*narrow*) passerelle *f*

footer ['fʊtər] *n* **(a)** *Comptr* bas *m* de page **(b)** *Old-fashioned Br F* (*soccer*) foot *m*

footfall ['fʊtfɔ:l] *n* (bruit *m* de) pas *m*; **I heard a light f.** j'ai entendu un pas léger

foot fault *n Tennis* faute *f* de pied

foot-fault *Tennis* **1** *vi* faire une faute de pied **2** *vt* (*of umpire*) **to f. a player** pénaliser un joueur pour faute de pied

footgear ['fʊtgɪər] *n* (grosses) chaussures *fpl*

foothills ['fʊthɪlz] *npl* collines *fpl* basses *ou* avancées; (*of mountain range*) avant-monts *mpl*

foothold ['fʊthəʊld] *n* prise *f* pour le pied; **to get a f.** prendre pied; **to keep one's f.** préserver l'équilibre; **to lose one's f.** perdre pied; *Fig* **enemy troops gained a f. on the island** les troupes ennemies ont pris pied sur l'île

footing ['fʊtɪŋ] *n* **(a)** **to lose one's f.** (*in bathing etc*) perdre pied; **to miss one's f.** poser le pied à faux **(b)** (*situation*) (*of person*) position *f*, condition *f*; (*of institution etc*) condition, état *m*; **on a war f.** (*of troops*) sur le pied de guerre; (*of country, economy*) en état de guerre; **to be on a sound f.** (*of company, economy*) être sain *ou* ferme *ou* bien établi; **to place two people on the same f.** mettre deux personnes sur le même rang; **to be on an equal f.** être de pair *ou* sur un pied d'égalité **(with** avec); **to be on a friendly f. with** avoir des rapports amicaux avec qn

▶ **footle about, footle around** [ˈfuːt(ə)l] *vi F* (*waste time*) traînailler; **to f. about** *or* **around with sth** jouer avec qch, tripoter qch

footlights [ˈfʊtlaɪts] *npl Th* rampe *f*

footling [ˈfuːtlɪŋ] *adj F* insignifiant

footloose [ˈfʊtluːs] *adj* (*person*) libre; (*existence*) sans attaches; **to be f. and fancy-free** être libre comme l'air

footman, *pl* **-men** [ˈfʊtmən] *n* valet *m* de pied

footnote [ˈfʊtnəʊt] *n* note *f* de bas de page; *Fig* détail *m*; **he is now little more than a f. to the history of the period** il n'a guère plus qu'un rôle d'arrière-plan dans l'histoire de l'époque

foot passenger *n* voyageur *m* à pied, passager *m* à pied, passager piéton

footpath [ˈfʊtpɑːθ] *n* sentier *m* (pour piétons); (*alongside canal, railway*) banquette *f*, accotement *m*; (*in street*) trottoir *m*

foot patrol *n Mil* patrouille *f* à pied

footplate [ˈfʊtpleɪt] *n Rail* (*of railway engine*) plate-forme *f*, *pl* plates-formes, tablier *m*

footplateman, *pl* **-men** [ˈfʊtpleɪtmən] *n Rail* mécanicien *m* de locomotive

foot-pound *n* (*pl* **foot-pounds**) *Phys* (*measurement*) pied-livre *m*, *pl* pieds-livres

footprint [ˈfʊtprɪnt] *n* (**a**) empreinte *f* de pas; **footprints in the sand** (empreintes de) pas *mpl* sur le sable (**b**) *Comptr* encombrement *m* (**c**) (*of satellite*) empreinte *f*

foot pump *n* pompe *f* à pied

footrest [ˈfʊtrest] *n* (*on chair, motorcycle*) repose-pied(s) *m inv*; *Med* porte-pieds *m inv*, repose-pied(s); (*on bicycle*) cale-pied(s) *m inv*

foot scraper *n* gratte-pieds *m inv*

foot-second *n* (*pl* **foot-seconds**) *Phys* (*measurement*) pied *m* par seconde

Footsie *n* [ˈfʊtsɪ] ≈ indice *m* CAC 40

footsie *n F* **to play f. with sb** faire du pied à qn

footslog [ˈfʊtslɒg] *vi* (**-gg-**) marcher, faire la route à pied

foot soldier *n* soldat *m* d'infanterie, fantassin *m*

footsore [ˈfʊtsɔːr] *adj* qui a mal aux pieds; **they arrived f. and weary** ils sont arrivés les pieds en compote et épuisés

footstall [ˈfʊtstɔːl] *n Archit* socle *m*

footstep [ˈfʊtstep] *n* (**a**) (*sound*) pas *m*; **I hear footsteps** j'entends des pas *ou* un bruit de pas (**b**) (*footprint*) (empreinte *f* de) pied *m ou* pas *m*; *Fig* **to follow** *or* **tread** *or* **walk in sb's footsteps** marcher sur les traces *ou* pas de qn; *Fig* **to follow in one's father's footsteps** suivre les traces de son père

footstool [ˈfʊtstuːl] *n* tabouret *m* (pour les pieds)

footwarmer [ˈfʊtwɔːmər] *n* chancelière *f*

footway [ˈfʊtweɪ] *n* chemin *m* (pour piétons)

footwear [ˈfʊtweər] *n* chaussures *fpl*

footwell [ˈfʊtwel] *n Aut* place *f* aux pieds

footwork [ˈfʊtwɜːk] *n* (*in dancing, sports etc*) jeu *m* de pieds *ou* de jambes; *Fig* **it required some rather fancy f. on his part** il a dû faire des pieds et des mains

fop [fɒp] *n Pej* bellâtre *m*, dandy *m*

foppish [ˈfɒpɪʃ] *adj* (*man*) qui met trop de recherche à sa toilette; (*clothes, manners*) d'une élégance affectée; (*taste, elegance*) de bellâtre, de dandy

FOR [efəʊˈɑːr] *Com* (*abbr* **free on rail**) franco wagon

for [fɔːr, **unstressed** fər] **1** *prep* (**a**) (*representing*) **A f. Andrew** A comme André; **what's the Russian f. 'book'?** comment dit-on 'livre' en russe?

(**b**) (*as*) **to have sb f. a teacher** avoir qn comme professeur; **f. the first time** pour la première fois

(**c**) (*in return for*) **you can hire a car f. five pounds a day** on peut louer une voiture pour cinq livres par jour; **to sell sth f. ten francs** vendre qch dix francs; **three f. £5** trois pour 5 livres; **to be paid f. one's services** recevoir un paiement pour ses services; **oh, f. some peace and quiet!** que ne donnerais-je pour la paix!

(**d**) (*in favour of*) **he is f. free trade** il est partisan du libre-échange, il est pour le libre-échange; **I'm all f. it** je suis tout à fait pour; *Jur* **judgment f. the plaintiff** arrêt *m* en faveur du demandeur

(**e**) (*purpose*) **garments f. men** vêtements pour hommes; **can you give me something f. the pain?** est-ce que vous pouvez me donner quelque chose pour *ou* contre la douleur?; **f. books on gardening try Jackson's bookshop** pour trouver des livres sur le jardinage, essayez la librairie Jackson

(**f**) (*in trouble*) *F* **he's f. it!** [ˈfɔːrɪt,]; **he's in f. it!** [ˈɪnfɔrɪt] qu'est-ce qu'il va prendre!; **I really thought I was in f. it** j'ai bien crû que mon compte était bon

(**g**) (*because of*) **to choose sb f. his/her ability** choisir qn en raison de sa compétence; **he's well known f. his views on taxation** il est célèbre pour ses opinions sur l'impôt; **she couldn't sleep f. the pain** elle ne pouvait pas dormir à cause de la douleur; **I feel all the better f. it** je me sens vraiment mieux, ça m'a fait du bien; **I'm a few million poorer and I'm all the better f. it** j'y ai laissé quelques millions et je ne m'en porte que mieux

(**h**) (*considering*) **f. all the use he is he might as well go and play** pour ce qu'il fait d'utile il peut aussi bien aller jouer; **f. all the sense it made** pour ce que c'était clair

(**i**) (*direction*) **ship (bound) f. America** navire à destination de l'Amérique; **the train f. London** le train pour *ou* à destination de *ou* en direction de Londres; **I'm leaving f. France** je pars pour la France; **his feelings f. you** ses sentiments envers vous *ou* à votre égard; **to swim f. sth** nager vers qch

(**j**) [①B29,9] (*extent*) **the road is lined with trees f. two miles** la route est bordée d'arbres pendant deux mil(l)es; **bends f. one mile** (*on sign*) virages sur un mil(l)e; **I'm going away f. a fortnight** je pars pour quinze jours; **he will be away f. a year** il sera absent pendant un an; **she won't be back f. a month** elle ne sera pas de retour avant un mois; **we have food f. three days** nous avons des vivres pour trois jours; **I lived there f. five years** j'y ai vécu (pendant) cinq ans; **I have not seen him f. three years** il y a trois ans que je ne l'ai vu; **I have been here f. three days** il y a trois jours que je suis ici, je suis ici depuis trois jours; **I had known him f. years** je le connaissais depuis des années, il y avait des années que je le connaissais; **f. now, f. the time being** pour l'instant, pour le moment

(**k**) (*intention, destination*) **this box is f. you** cette boîte est pour vous; **it's f. you** (*letter, phone call*) c'est pour toi; **your job f. tomorrow** votre travail pour demain; **you are the man f. me/the job** vous êtes l'homme qu'il me faut/qui convient pour ce poste; **that is just the thing f. you** c'est juste ce qu'il vous faut; **there's no time f. that** il n'y a pas de temps pour ça; **it'll do f. temporary accommodation** ça ira comme logement provisoire

(**l**) (*to the amount of*) **a cheque f. £50** un chèque de 50 livres; **put me down f. £5** inscrivez-moi pour 5 livres

(**m**) (*with regard to*) **he is big f. his age** il est grand pour son âge; **not bad f. a beginner!** pour un débutant ce n'est pas si mal!; **f. sheer impudence his remarks are hard to beat** pour ce qui est de l'effronterie, ses commentaires sont imbattables; **as f. him** quant à lui; **as f. that** pour ce qui est de cela; **f. myself, f. my part** pour moi, quant à moi, pour ma part; **this shop is better f. books** ce magasin est mieux pour les livres

(**n**) (*in spite of*) **f. all that** malgré tout, malgré cela, tout de même; *esp Lit* **f. all that he wanted to believe them** pour autant qu'il veuille les croire; **she loved him, f. all his faults** elle l'aimait malgré tous ses défauts

(**o**) (*owing to*) **were it not f. her** *or* **but f. her, I should have died** sans elle, je serais mort

(**p**) (*corresponding to, in opposition to*) **they sell twenty red bikes f. every black one** pour chaque vélo noir vendu, il y en a vingt rouges

(**q**) (*introducing an infinitive clause*) **it is easy/difficult/impossible f. him to come** il lui est facile/difficile/impossible de venir; **it is too late f. us to set off** il est trop tard pour que nous partions; **they made way f. him to pass** on se rangea pour le laisser passer; **I have brought it f. you to see** je l'ai apporté pour que vous le voyiez; **it is not f. me to decide/to criticize him** ce n'est pas à moi de décider/de le critiquer; **it is usual f. the mother to accompany her daughter** il est d'usage que la mère accompagne sa fille; **it's no good f. him to talk** il a beau dire; (*because he is similarly guilty etc*) il peut bien dire; **f. that to be done** pour que ça soit fait; **it took an hour f. the taxi to get to the station** le taxi a mis une heure pour aller jusqu'à la gare; **the best plan will be f. you to go away for a time** le mieux sera que vous vous absentiez pour quelque temps; **it would be a disgrace f. you to back out now** vous retirer maintenant serait honteux

2 *conj Lit* car; **f. it was too late** car il était trop tard

forage[1] [ˈfɒrɪdʒ] *n* (*animal food*) fourrage(s) *m(pl)*; **to go on the f.** (*search for provisions*) chercher de la nourriture; **to have a f. for sth** (*search for sth*) fouiller *ou* fourrager pour trouver qch; *Mil* **f. cap** calot *m*

forage[2] *vi* fourrager; **to f. for sth** fourrager *ou* fouiller pour trouver qch; **never mind me, I'll f. for myself** ne t'occupe pas de moi, je me débrouillerai

▶ **forage about, forage around** *vi* (*rummage*) fourrager, fouiller (**in** dans)

foray[1] [ˈfɒreɪ] *n* razzia *f*, incursion *f*, raid *m*; **she was on one of her forays round the bookshops** elle procédait à l'une de ses excursions dans les librairies; *Fig* **to make a brief f. into**

the business world faire une courte incursion dans le monde des affaires

foray² *vi* faire des incursions *ou* des raids

forbear¹ [ˈfɔːbeər] *n* = **forebear**

forbear² [fɔːˈbeər] (*pt* **forbore** [fɔːˈbɔːr]; *pp* **forborne** [fɔːˈbɔːn]) *Lit* **1** *vt* s'abstenir de **2** *vi* **to f. from doing sth** s'abstenir de *ou* se garder de faire qch

forbearance [fɔːˈbeərəns] *n* **(a)** patience *f*, *Lit* longanimité *f*; **to show f. towards sb** montrer de l'indulgence envers qn **(b)** *Fml* **your f. from doing this** le fait que vous vous soyez abstenu de faire ceci

forbearing [fɔːˈbeərɪŋ] *adj* patient, indulgent

forbid [fəˈbɪd] *vt* (*pt* **forbade** [fəˈbæd, -ˈbeɪd]; *pp* **forbidden** [fəˈbɪd(ə)n]) **(a)** (*prohibit*) défendre, interdire; (*custom etc*) proscrire; *Jur* prohiber; **I f. it!** je l'interdis!; **to f. sb sth** défendre qch à qn; **to f. sb to do sth** défendre *ou* interdire à qn de faire qch; **I am forbidden (to drink) tea** le thé m'est défendu; **smoking is strictly forbidden** il est formellement interdit de fumer; **to be forbidden from doing sth** ne pas avoir le droit de faire qch; **he was forbidden from seeing her again** on lui a interdit de la revoir

(b) (*prevent*) empêcher; **my condition forbids strenuous exercise** mon état ne me permet pas de me livrer à des exercices violents; **Heaven f. that I should do such a thing!** Dieu me préserve de faire une telle chose!; **God f.!** à Dieu ne plaise! (**that** que + *sub*)

forbidden [fəˈbɪd(ə)n] *adj* défendu, interdit; **f. fruit** fruit *m* défendu; **to tread on f. ground** empiéter sur un terrain défendu; *Fig* toucher à un sujet tabou

forbidding [fəˈbɪdɪŋ] *adj* (*face, aspect*) sinistre; (*character*) mal avenant; (*sky, weather*) sombre; (*rock, building*) menaçant; (*look, stare*) sombre, menaçant; **a text of f. density/complexity** un texte d'une densité/complexité rébarbative

forbiddingly [fəˈbɪdɪŋlɪ] *adv* **the castle towered f. over the town** le château, menaçant, dominait la ville; **f. difficult/complex** d'une difficulté/complexité rébarbative

force¹ [fɔːs] *n* **(a)** (*strength, violence*) force *f*; **by sheer** *or* **brute f.** de vive force; **by sheer f. of will** à force de volonté; **by f. of circumstance(s)** par la force des choses; **f. of habit** force de l'habitude; **f. of personality** force de personnalité; **to use f. against the strikers** avoir recours à la force contre les grévistes; **armed f.** force armée

(b) (*authority*) influence *f*, autorité *f*; **f. of example** influence de l'exemple; **moral f.** force morale

(c) (*effort*) énergie *f*; (*power*) (*of blow, wind etc*) intensité *f*; (*of imagination etc*) vigueur *f*; **a blow with plenty of f. behind it** un coup bien appuyé *ou* bien asséné; **considerable f. would be needed to break the door down** il faudrait une force considérable pour défoncer la porte; **the full f. of the explosion** toute la force de l'explosion; **the forces of Nature** les forces de la Nature; **a f. for good** une influence positive; **to be a f. for change** être le moteur du changement; **the forces at work here** les forces en jeu ici; **several forces conspired to bring about his downfall** plusieurs facteurs ont conspiré pour provoquer sa chute

(d) *Phys* force *f*, effort *m*; **f. exerted by an engine** effort d'un moteur; **f. of gravity** (force de la) pesanteur *f*; *Met* **f. ten on the Beaufort scale** force dix sur l'échelle de Beaufort

(e) *Mil etc* (*group*) force *f*, troupe *f*, élément(s) *m(pl)*; **a f. of 20,000 men** une troupe de 20 000 hommes; **an armed f.** une force (armée); **the (armed) forces** les forces armées; **he was in the forces** il était dans l'armée; **forces slang** argot *m* militaire; **the police f.**, *F* **the F.** la Police; **a strong f. of police** un gros détachement de police; **two different police forces** deux forces de police différentes; **we turned out in (full) f.** nous sommes venus en masse

(f) (*value*) (*of argument*) poids *m*; (*sense*) (*of word, document*) signification *f*; (*of word, expression*) valeur *f*; **I mean it with the full f. of the word** je le dis avec toute la force du mot

(g) (*of law, rule etc*) **to be in f.** être en vigueur; **to put the law into f.** appliquer la loi; **to come into f.** entrer en vigueur

force² *vt* **(a)** (*compel*) **to f. sb to do sth** *or* **into doing sth** forcer *ou* obliger qn à faire qch; **no one's forcing you!** (*to go etc*) personne ne t'y force *ou* oblige!; **I am forced to conclude that ...** je suis forcé de conclure que ...; **to be forced to give way** céder à la force; **that forced me to think** cela m'a obligé à réfléchir; **to f. sb into/out of the room** faire entrer/sortir qn de force; **to f. sth on sb** imposer qch à qn; **to f. drink on sb** contraindre qn à boire; **to f. a promise/confession from sb** arracher une promesse/confession à qn

(b) (*obtain, produce etc by effort*) (*break open*) (*door, window*) forcer, enfoncer; (*lock*) forcer; **to f. sb's hand** forcer la main à qn; **to f. the issue** précipiter les choses; **to f. the pace** forcer l'allure *ou* le pas; **she forced a smile** elle s'est forcée à sourire; **to f. (the meaning of) a word** forcer le sens d'un mot; **to f. legislation through Parliament** forcer le Parlement à voter une législation; **to f. a plant** forcer une plante; *Aut* **to f. the engine** trop pousser le moteur; **to f. a car/sb off the road** faire sortir une voiture/qn de la route; **to f. one's way into a house** pénétrer de force dans une maison; **to f. one's way through the crowd** se frayer un passage à travers la foule; **to f. sth into sth** faire entrer qch de force dans qch; **to f. oneself on sb** s'imposer à qn; **compressed air forces the liquid up the pipe** l'air comprimé fait monter le liquide dans le tuyau

▶ **force back** *vtsep* (*enemy forces etc*) repousser, faire reculer; (*air, water, tears etc*) refouler; (*impulse, laugh*) réprimer

▶ **force down** *vtsep* faire descendre de force; (*suitcase lid*) fermer de force; **to f. prices down** faire baisser les prix; *Av* **the plane was forced down** on a forcé l'avion à atterrir; **to f. down food/medicine/***etc* avaler un aliment/un médicament/*etc* à contre-cœur; **to f. food/medicine/***etc* **down sb** faire avaler un aliment/un médicament/*etc* de force à qn

▶ **force open** *vtsep* (*door, window*) ouvrir de force, forcer; (*lock*) forcer; **it took all his strength to f. open the dog's jaws** il a dû y aller de toutes ses forces pour réussir à ouvrir la mâchoire du chien

▶ **force out** *vtsep* faire sortir de force; (*in engine*) (*exhaust gas*) refouler au dehors; **shopkeepers were forced out of the town centre by the rising rents** la hausse des loyers a chassé les petits commerçants du centre ville; **to be forced out of business** être forcé à fermer boutique; **to f. out a few words of congratulation** féliciter qn du bout des lèvres

▶ **force up** *vtsep* faire monter de force; (*prices*) faire monter

forced [fɔːst] *adj* forcé; (*laugh*) forcé, faux; **to give a f. laugh** rire du bout des lèvres, avoir un rire forcé; **f. labour** travail *m* forcé; *Mil* **f. march** marche *f* forcée; **f. sale** vente *f* forcée; **f. vegetables/fruit** légumes *mpl*/fruits *mpl* forcés, primeurs *fpl*

forced feeding *n* (*of goose etc*) gavage *m*

forced landing *n Av* atterrissage *m* forcé

force-feed *vt* (*pt, pp* **-fed** [-fed]) (*goose*) gaver; (*person*) nourrir de force

forceful [ˈfɔːsfʊl] *adj* (*personality*) énergique; (*argument, case*) puissant; (*language*) musclé; (*reason*) bon

forcefully [ˈfɔːsfʊlɪ] *adv* (*to speak, act*) énergiquement; (*to express oneself, reason, write*) avec vigueur; (*to argue*) énergiquement, avec force; **I was f. struck by it** ça m'a fortement marqué

force-land *vi Av* faire un atterrissage forcé

forcemeat [ˈfɔːsmiːt] *n Culin* farce *f*

forceps [ˈfɔːseps] *npl* **(pair of) f.** pince *f*, *Surg* forceps *m*; (*in dentistry*) davier *m*; *Obst* **f. delivery** accouchement *m* au forceps

forcible [ˈfɔːsɪb(ə)l] *adj* **(a)** (*entry etc*) de force; *Jur* **f. entry** (*offence*) entrée *f* par effraction **(b)** (*argument*) vigoureux, plein de force; (*reminder*) brutal

forcibly [ˈfɔːsɪblɪ] *adv* **(a)** (*by force*) de force; **to detain sb f.** retenir qn de force **(b)** (*convincingly*) vigoureusement; **she argued f. for their release** elle a argumenté énergiquement *ou* avec force en faveur de leur libération; **they put their case very f.** ils se sont défendus avec force *ou* vigueur; **we were all f. reminded of our own mortality** nous avons été brutalement rappelés à notre condition de mortels

forcing [ˈfɔːsɪŋ] *n* **(a)** (*of lock*) forcement *m*; (*of door*) enfoncement *m*; *Culin* **f. bag** poche *f* à douille **(b)** (*in gardening*) forçage *m*, culture *f* forcée; **f. frame** châssis *m*; **f. house** (*for plants*) forcerie *f*; *Fig, F* **it's just an academic f. house** dans cette boîte, tout ce qui compte ce sont les résultats aux examens

ford¹ [fɔːd] *n* (*in river*) gué *m*

ford² *vt* (*river*) guéer, traverser à gué

fordable [ˈfɔːdəb(ə)l] *adj* (*river*) guéable

fore [fɔːr] **1** *adj Naut* (de l')avant; **f. hatch** panneau *m* avant; **f.-and-aft sail** voile *f* aurique; **f.-and-aft bulkhead** cloison *f* médiane; *Mil* **f.-and-aft cap** calot *m*; **f.-and-aft movement** (*of engine*) déplacement *m* longitudinal

2 *n Naut* avant *m*; **at the f.** au mât de misaine; *Fig* **to the f.** (*prominent*) en vue, en évidence, en vedette; **this question has been very much to the f. in the talks** cette question a été au tout premier plan au cours des discussions; **to come to the f.** (*of person*) commencer à être connu; **this issue came to the f. during last year's negotiations** ce problème a été mis en évidence lors des négociations de l'an dernier; **to bring to the f.** (*aspect, problem, importance of sth*) mettre en évidence, souligner; (*theory, philosophy*) mettre au premier plan

3 *adv Naut* de l'avant; **f. and aft** de l'avant à l'arrière

4 *int Golf* gare devant!

forearm¹ ['fɔːrɑːm] *n* avant-bras *m inv*

forearm² [fɔːr'ɑːm] *vt* (*person*) prémunir; **he came forearmed** il est venu prémuni *ou* préparé; **she would always ensure that she was forearmed before going** elle prenait toujours soin de se prémunir avant d'y aller

forebear¹ ['fɔːbeər] *n* aïeul *m*, *pl* aïeux, aïeule *f*, ancêtre *mf*; *Fig* ancêtre *mf*

forebode [fɔː'bəʊd] *vt* **to f. disaster** présager *ou* laisser prévoir le désastre

foreboding [fɔː'bəʊdɪŋ] *n* (*intuition*) (mauvais) pressentiment *m*; **she was filled with (a sense of) f.** elle était envahie par un mauvais pressentiment; **to have a f. that ...** avoir le pressentiment que ...; **she thought with f. of what the future would hold** elle songea avec appréhension à ce que l'avenir lui réservait

forecast¹ ['fɔːkɑːst] *n* prévision *f*; **his f. was wrong/right** ses prévisions étaient fausses/exactes; **forecasts of higher interest rates** des prévisions d'augmentation des taux d'intérêts; **racing f.** pronostic *m* des courses; **(weather) f.** prévisions météorologiques, *F* météo *f*; **long/short-range f.** prévision à longue échéance/sur période courte

forecast² *vt* (*pt, pp* **forecast(ed)**) (*events, storm etc*) prévoir; *Sp* (*result*) pronostiquer; **I wouldn't like to f. a winner** je ne voudrais pas avoir à prédire qui va gagner; **f. balance sheet** bilan *m* prévisionnel

forecaster ['fɔːkɑːstər] *n* pronostiqueur, -euse; *Econ* expert *m*; **weather f.** météorologiste *mf*

forecasting ['fɔːkɑːstɪŋ] *n* (*of result etc*) pronostication *f*; (*of weather, economic matters, sports*) prévision *f*; **f. firm** société *f* de prévisions; **f. model** modèle *m* de prévisions

forecastle ['fəʊks(ə)l] *n Naut* gaillard *m*; (*in merchant vessel*) poste *m* de l'équipage

foreclose [fɔː'kləʊz] *Jur* **1** *vt* **to f. the mortgage** saisir l'immeuble hypothéqué **2** *vi* (*on a mortgage*) saisir l'immeuble hypothéqué; (*on a loan*) récupérer le prêt; **to f. on a loan** interrompre un crédit, rompre un crédit avant son terme; **the bank has foreclosed on us** la banque nous a saisi l'immeuble hypothéqué/a décidé de récupérer le prêt

foreclosure [fɔː'kləʊʒər] *n Jur* (*on a mortgage*) saisie *f* (d'une hypothèque), forclusion *f*

forecourt ['fɔːkɔːt] *n* avant-cour *f*, *pl* avant-cours; (*of garage, station*) devant *m*; (*of car dealer*) parc *m* d'exposition

foredoomed [fɔː'duːmd] *adj* condamné d'avance (**to** à)

forefather ['fɔːfɑːðər] *n Lit* aïeul *m*, *pl* aïeux; *Fig* ancêtre *m*

forefinger ['fɔːfɪŋgər] *n* index *m*

forefoot, *pl* **-feet** ['fɔːfʊt, -fiːt] *n* (*of dog, cat, bird*) patte *f* de devant; (*animal with cloven hoof*) pied *m* antérieur

forefront ['fɔːfrʌnt] *n* **to bring sth to the f.** mettre qch au premier plan; **this question is still in the f.** cette question occupe toujours le premier plan

foregather [fɔː'gæðər] *vi* = **forgather**

forego [fɔː'gəʊ] *vt* = **forgo**

foregoing ['fɔːgəʊɪŋ] *adj esp Fml* précédent, antérieur; (*previously cited*) cité ci-avant; **the f.** ce qui précède

foregone ['fɔːgɒn] *adj* **it was a f. conclusion** c'était prévu d'avance

foreground ['fɔːgraʊnd] *n Art, Phot etc* premier plan *m*; **in the f.** au premier plan; **they must be hoping that this issue will fade from the f.** ils doivent espérer que ce problème ne restera pas longtemps au premier plan; *TV, Cin* **f. matte** cache *m* d'avant-plan; *Comptr* **f. processing** traitement *m* en avant-plan; *Comptr* **f. program** programme *m* prioritaire

forehand ['fɔːhænd] *Tennis* **1** *adj* **f. stroke** coup *m* droit; **f. drive** drive *m* de coup droit **2** *n* coup *m* droit; **to have a strong/weak f.** avoir un coup droit puissant/faible; **to play a f.** jouer un coup droit; **to serve to one's opponent's f.** servir sur le coup droit adverse

forehead ['fɒrɪd, 'fɔːhed] *n Anat* front *m*

foreign ['fɒrɪn] *adj* **(a)** (*from different country, countries*) étranger; **she looked f.** elle paraissait étrangère; **a f.-sounding name** un nom aux consonances étrangères; **f. countries, f. parts** pays étrangers, l'étranger *m*; **our relations with f. countries** nos rapports avec l'extérieur; **I don't like f. food** je n'aime pas la cuisine étrangère; **f. investment** investissement *m* à l'étranger; *esp US* **the f. service** le corps diplomatique; **f. trade** commerce *m* extérieur; **f. travel** voyages à l'étranger

(b) (*not belonging*) étranger (**to** à); **such feelings are f. to his nature** de tels sentiments lui sont étrangers; **lying is f. to her nature** ce n'est pas dans sa nature de mentir; *Med etc* **f. body** corps *m* étranger

foreign affairs *n Pol* les affaires *fpl* étrangères

foreign aid *n* aide *f* aux pays étrangers; (*from point of view of recipient*) aide de l'étranger

foreign-built *adj* (*car*) de marque étrangère; (*ship*) construit à l'étranger

foreign correspondent *n Journ etc* correspondant, -ante à l'étranger

foreign currency *n* devises *fpl* étrangères; **f. account** compte *m* en devises étrangères; **f. earnings** apport *m* de devises étrangères; **f. holding** avoir *m* en devises étrangères; **f. option** option *f* de change; **f. reserves** réserves *fpl* en devises

foreigner ['fɒrɪnər] *n* étranger, -ère; **I feel like a f. here** je me sens étranger ici

foreign exchange *n* devises *fpl* étrangères; **f. broker** *or* **dealer** cambiste *mf*; **f. gain** gain *m* de change; **f. loss** perte *f* de change; **f. market** marché *m* des changes; **f. risk** risque *m* de change

foreign legion *n* légion *f* étrangère

foreign minister *n Pol* ministre *m* des affaires étrangères

foreignness ['fɒrɪnnɪs] *n* air *m* étranger; (*of place*) caractère *m* étranger; (*exotic nature*) exotisme *m*; **the f. of the food/their way of life** la nourriture/leur mode de vie bien à part; **given the f. of this concept to our culture** étant donné que ce concept est étranger à notre culture

Foreign Office *n Br Pol* = Ministère *m* des Affaires étrangères

Foreign Secretary *n Br Pol* = Ministre *m* des Affaires étrangères

foreknowledge [fɔː'nɒlɪdʒ] *n esp Fml* connaissance *f* anticipée; **to have f. of sth** avoir connaissance à l'avance de qch

foreland ['fɔːlənd] *n* cap *m*, promontoire *m*

foreleg ['fɔːleg] *n* patte *f* de devant; (*of horse*) jambe *f* de devant

forelock ['fɔːlɒk] *n* (*of person*) mèche *f* (de cheveux) sur le front; **to touch** *or* **tug one's f.** = porter la main à son front (pour saluer qn); *Fig* faire une révérence

foreman, *pl* **-men** ['fɔːmən] *n* **(a)** *Ind etc* contremaître *m*; *Typ* prote *m*; (*of gang of workmen*) chef *m* d'équipe *ou* de brigade; **works f.** conducteur *m* de travaux **(b)** (*of jury*) président *m*

foremast ['fɔːmɑːst] *n Naut* mât *m* de misaine

forementioned ['fɔː'menʃənd] *adj Jur, Admin* précité

foremost ['fɔːməʊst] **1** *adj* (*in importance*) le plus important; (*in place*) le plus en avant; **of the f. importance** de la plus haute importance **2** *adv* **to rank f.** se classer parmi les premiers; **I shall only leave this room feet f.** je ne quitterai cette pièce que les pieds devant

forename ['fɔːneɪm] *n* prénom *m*

forenoon ['fɔːnuːn] *n esp Scot, Irish* matinée *f*; **in the f.** dans *ou* pendant la matinée

forensic [fə'rensɪk, fɒ-] **1** *adj Jur* (*medicine, chemistry*) légal; **f. evidence** expertise *f* médico-légale; **f. laboratory** laboratoire *m* médico-légal; **f. medicine** *or* **science** médecine *f* légale; **f. scientist** expert *m* légiste; (*medical*) médecin *m* légiste **2** *n F* (*department*) service *m* médico-légal; **did f. come up with anything?** est-ce que le service médico-légal a trouvé quelque chose?

foreordain ['fɔːrɔː'deɪn] *vt Fml* prédestiner (**sb to sth** qn à qch; **sb to do sth** qn à faire qch)

foreplay ['fɔːpleɪ] *n* (*sexual*) préliminaires *mpl*; **he doesn't go in much for f.** il n'est pas très porté sur les préliminaires

forequarter ['fɔːkwɔːtər] *n* (*of cow etc*) quartier *m* de devant; **forequarters of a horse** avant-main *m ou* avant-train *m* d'un cheval

forerunner ['fɔːrʌnər] *n* ancêtre *m*; (*person*) précurseur *m*

foresail ['fɔːseɪl, 'fɔːs(ə)l] *n Naut* (voile *f* de) misaine *f*

foresee [fɔː'siː] *vt* (*pt* **foresaw** [fɔː'sɔː]; *pp* **foreseen** [fɔː'siːn]) (*misfortune, event, development*) prévoir; **I f. difficult times/a problem** j'entrevois des moments difficiles/un problème; **it was an accident which should have been foreseen** c'était un accident qu'on aurait dû prévoir

foreseeable [fɔː'siːəb(ə)l] *adj* (*future, consequence, result etc*) prévisible; **not in the f. future** pas dans un avenir prévisible

foreshadow [fɔː'ʃædəʊ] *vt* (*event etc*) annoncer, présager

foreshore ['fɔːʃɔːr] *n* laisse *f* de mer; (*beach*) plage *f*

foreshorten [fɔː'ʃɔːt(ə)n] *vt Art* (*object*) dessiner en raccourci *ou* en perspective; **foreshortened figure** figure vue en raccourci; **the distances are foreshortened** les distances sont réduites (par la perspective)

foreshortening ['fɔː'ʃɔːt(ə)nɪŋ] *n Art* raccourci *m*

foresight ['fɔːsaɪt] *n* **(a)** prévoyance *f*; **lack of f.** manque *m* de prévoyance, imprévoyance *f*; **with f. this could all have**

been avoided avec un peu de prévoyance tout ceci aurait pu être évité **(b)** *(on gun)* guidon *m*, bouton *m* de mire

foreskin [ˈfɔːskɪn] *n Anat* prépuce *m*

forest¹ [ˈfɒrɪst] *n* forêt *f*; **deciduous/coniferous f.** forêt à feuilles caduques/de conifères; **f.-covered hills** collines boisées; *Fig* **a f. of masts/telegraph poles** une forêt de mâts/poteaux télégraphiques; **f. fire** feu *m* de forêt; *esp Am* **f. ranger** garde *m* forestier

forest² *vt (region)* boiser **(with** de)

forestall [fɔːˈstɔːl] *vt (attempt, criticism)* anticiper, devancer; *(rivals)* devancer

forestay [ˈfɔːsteɪ] *n Naut* étai *m* de misaine

forested [ˈfɒrɪstɪd] *adj* boisé **(with** de)

forester [ˈfɒrɪstə(r)] *n* (garde *m*) forestier *m*

forestry [ˈfɒrɪstrɪ] *n* sylviculture *f*

Forestry Commission *n Br Admin* = service *m* des Eaux et Forêts

foretaste [ˈfɔːteɪst] *n* avant-goût *m*, *pl* avant-goûts; **to give** *or* **offer sb a f. of sth** donner un avant-goût de qch à qn

foretell [fɔːˈtel] *vt (pt, pp* **foretold** [fɔːˈtəʊld]) *(of person)* prédire

forethought [ˈfɔːθɔːt] *n* prévoyance *f*; **to do sth with a lack of f.** manquer de prévoyance en faisant qch; **if you had given it some f.** si tu y avais un peu réfléchi à l'avance

forever [fəˈrevə(r)] **1** *adv* **(a)** *(until end of time)* pour toujours, à jamais; **a good bike should last f.** un vélo de bonne qualité devrait durer pour toujours; **to live f.** vivre éternellement *ou* pour toujours; **nobody lives f.** personne n'est éternel; **nothing lasts f.** tout a une fin; *(object, possession)* rien n'est éternel; **the journey seemed to last f.** le voyage a semblé durer une éternité

(b) *(ceaselessly)* sans cesse, sans arrêt; **he was f. changing his mind** il changeait sans cesse *ou* sans arrêt d'avis

2 *n F* **to take f. to do sth** prendre *ou* mettre une éternité à faire qch; **it took me f. to persuade him to come** ça m'a pris une éternité pour le persuader de venir

forewarn [fɔːˈwɔːn] *vt* prévenir, avertir; **to f. sb of sth** prévenir *ou* avertir qn de qch; *Prov* **forewarned is forearmed** un homme averti en vaut deux

forewoman, *pl* **-women** [ˈfɔːwʊmən, -wɪmɪn] *n* **(a)** *Ind etc* contremaîtresse *f*; *F* première *f* **(b)** *Jur (of jury)* président *m*, présidente *f*

foreword [ˈfɔːwɜːd] *n (to book)* avant-propos *m inv*, préface *f*

forex [ˈfɒreks] *n, adj abbr* **foreign exchange**

forfaiting [ˈfɔːfeɪtɪŋ] *n Banking* forfaitage *m*, forfaitisation *f*

forfeit¹ [ˈfɔːfɪt] *adj Hist, Jur* confisqué; **his lands were f.** on lui a confisqué ses terres

forfeit² *n* **(a)** *Jur (fine)* amende *f*; *(for non-performance of contract)* dédit *m*; **to have to pay a f.** être mis à l'amende **(b)** *(in game)* gage *m*; **to play forfeits** jouer aux gages

forfeit³ *vt* **(a)** *(have confiscated) (object)* perdre par confiscation; *(right)* être déchu de **(b)** *(lose) (sb's respect)* perdre; **to f. one's life** payer de sa vie; **to f. one's honour** forfaire à l'honneur; **he had forfeited his independence in return for financial security** il avait sacrifié son indépendance au profit de la sécurité financière

forfeiture [ˈfɔːfɪtʃə(r)] *n* **(a)** *Jur (act of having confiscated) (of property)* perte *f* par confiscation; *Jur, Fin (of shares, right)* déchéance *f*, forfaiture *f* **(b)** *esp Fml (loss) (of sb's respect, one's life, honour etc)* perte *f*

forgather, foregather [fɔːˈgæðə(r)] *vi Fml* se réunir

forge¹ [fɔːdʒ] *n* atelier *m* de forgeron, forge *f*; **f. hammer** marteau-pilon *m*, *pl* marteaux-pilons

forge² *vt* **(a)** *(of blacksmith etc) (horseshoe etc)* forger; *Metal (iron)* forger, cingler; *Fig* **to f. an alliance/a friendship** forger une alliance/une amitié **(b)** *(counterfeit) (signature, banknotes, cheque)* contrefaire; *(document, passport)* faire un faux de

▶ **forge ahead** *vi* **(a)** *(press forward)* faire des progrès; *(in race, election campaign)* prendre de l'avance; *(in business, undertaking)* aller de l'avant; **to f. ahead with one's plans** aller de l'avant dans ses projets, mener ses projets de l'avant **(b)** *(outstrip competitors)* dépasser tous ses concurrents; **to f. ahead of one's rivals** prendre de l'avance sur ses rivaux

forged [fɔːdʒd] *adj* **(a)** *Metal (iron)* forgé **(b)** *(document, banknote, signature)* faux, *f* fausse, contrefait; **f. document** faux *m*; *(identity paper)* faux papier

forger [ˈfɔːdʒə(r)] *n (of banknotes)* contrefacteur *m*, faussaire *mf*; *(of signature etc)* faussaire *mf*

forgery [ˈfɔːdʒərɪ] *n* **(a)** *(activity)* contrefaçon *f*; *(of documents)* falsification *f*; *Jur* **to be guilty of f.** être coupable de faux **(b)** *(thing forged)* faux *m*; **it's a f.** *(of signature)* c'est une fausse signature; **it's a clever/obvious f.** c'est une contrefaçon bien/mal réussie; **it's a f. of my signature** c'est une contrefaçon de ma signature

forget [fəˈget] *(pt* **forgot** [fəˈgɒt]; *pp* **forgotten** [fəˈgɒt(ə)n]; *prp* **forgetting) 1** *vt* **(a)** [①A43,b,iii] *(fact, person, knowledge)* oublier; *(one's French)* désapprendre; **to f. to do sth** oublier *ou* omettre de faire qch; **don't f. to ...** n'oubliez *ou* ne manquez pas de ...; **to f. how to do sth** oublier comment on fait qch, ne plus savoir faire qch; **to f. oneself** s'oublier; **have I forgotten anyone?** est-ce que j'ai oublié quelqu'un?; **to f. sb's birthday** oublier (de souhaiter) l'anniversaire de qn; **to f. one's manners** oublier ses bonnes manières; **have you forgotten your manners?** où sont tes bonnes manières?; *(to child)* veux-tu être poli!; **f. it!** *(in reply to apology, thanks)* il n'y a pas de quoi!; **f. it, it wasn't important** *(what I said)* non, non, ça n'a pas d'importance; **look, f. it will you?** *(stop talking about it)* écoute, laisse tomber, d'accord?; **they can f. it!** *(they're being unreasonable)* ils peuvent faire une croix dessus *ou F* aller se faire voir!; *(they've no chance)* ils peuvent faire une croix dessus!, *F* ils sont foutus!; **you can f. the holiday** *(we can't afford it)* tu peux laisser tomber l'idée d'aller en vacances; **he's only ten years old, don't f.** n'oubliez pas qu'il n'a que dix ans; **to be forgotten** tomber dans l'oubli; **he felt that he had been forgotten by his friends** il avait l'impression que ses amis l'avaient oublié; **it's best forgotten** il vaut mieux ne plus en parler; **it's all been forgotten now** tout ça c'est du passé; **things best forgotten** choses qu'il vaut mieux oublier

(b) *(leave by mistake) (handkerchief, gloves etc)* oublier; **I forgot my hat on the train** j'ai oublié mon chapeau dans le train

2 *vi* oublier; **before I f.** *(can you do sth?)* avant que j'oublie *ou* que je n'oublie; **to f. about sth/sb** oublier qch/qn; **he warned me of the danger but I forgot (all) about it** il m'a averti du danger mais je n'y ai plus pensé; **and you can f. about going to London!** et ce n'est pas la peine de songer à aller à Londres!

forgetful [fəˈgetfʊl] *adj* **(a) to be very f.** avoir très mauvaise mémoire **(b)** *(negligent)* oublieux **(of** de); **to be f. of one's duty** être oublieux de *ou* négliger son devoir

forgetfulness [fəˈgetfʊlnɪs] *n* manque *m* (habituel) de mémoire; **a moment of f.** un moment de distraction

forget-me-not *n (plant)* myosotis *m*

forging [ˈfɔːdʒɪŋ] *n Metal (activity)* travail *m* de forge; *(forged item)* pièce *f* forgée; **f. mill** forge *f*; **f. press** marteau-pilon *m*, *pl* marteaux-pilons

forgivable [fəˈgɪvəb(ə)l] *adj* excusable, pardonnable

forgivably [fəˈgɪvəblɪ] *adv* de façon excusable *ou* pardonnable; **he was f. angry/surprised** il est compréhensible *ou* naturel qu'il ait été en colère/surpris; **f. so, in my opinion** ce qui est tout à fait compréhensible *ou* naturel, à mon avis

forgive [fəˈgɪv] *(pt* **forgave** [fəˈgeɪv]; *pp* **forgiven** [fəˈgɪv(ə)n]) **1** *vt* **(a)** *(sth)* pardonner; *Arch, Rel (mistake, insult)* remettre; **to f. sb sth** pardonner qch à qn; **to f. sb a debt** faire grâce d'une dette à qn; **if you'll f. the pun** pardonnez-moi ce jeu de mots; **she was not prepared to f. his rudeness** elle n'était pas prête à lui pardonner sa grossièreté

(b) to f. sb pardonner à qn; **he asked me to f. him** il m'a demandé pardon, il m'a demandé de le pardonner; **am I forgiven?** est-ce que tu me pardonnes?; **I'll never f. him for what he did** je ne lui pardonnerai jamais ce qu'il a fait; **one might perhaps be forgiven for thinking that ...** il n'est pas interdit de penser que ...; **f. me for intruding/interrupting** excusez-moi de vous déranger/interrompre

2 *vi* pardonner; **f. and forget** il faut oublier et pardonner

forgiveness [fəˈgɪvnɪs] *n* **(a)** *(act) (of sins)* rémission *f*; **to ask sb's f.** demander pardon à qn; **she pleaded for his f.** elle l'a imploré pour qu'il la pardonne **(b)** *(quality)* indulgence *f*; **to show f.** faire preuve d'indulgence, se montrer indulgent

forgiving [fəˈgɪvɪŋ] *adj* indulgent **(of** envers)

forgo, forego [fɔːˈgəʊ] *vt (pt* **forwent** [fɔːˈwent]; *pp* **forgone** [fɔːˈgɒn]) renoncer à; **to f. doing sth** s'abstenir de faire qch

forgotten [fəˈgɒt(ə)n] *adj* oublié; **the f. man of Scottish football** le laissé-pour-compte du football écossais

fork¹ [fɔːk] *n* **(a)** *(for food)* fourchette *f*; *Agr* fourche *f*; **f. lunch** buffet *m*; **garden f.** fourche à bêcher; *Mus* **tuning f.** diapason *m* **(b)** *(sth with shape of fork) (of water diviner)* baguette *f* divinatoire; *(to support branch etc)* poteau *m* fourchu; **f. of lightning** zigzag *m* (d'éclair); *Cycling* **front f.** fourche *f* avant *ou* de direction **(c)** *(division) (in road)* bifurcation *f*, jonction *f*; *(of branches)* fourche *f*; **take the left f.** prenez la route/le sentier de gauche

fork² **1** *vi (of tree etc)* fourcher; *(of road)* faire une fourche, bifurquer; **follow the road until it forks** suivez la route jusqu'à la bifurcation *ou* fourche; **f. right for York** *(on sign)* prenez à droite pour York **2** *vt Agr* (*earth, hay*) fourcher; **they were forking hay onto the truck** ils chargeaient du foin à la fourche dans le camion

▶ **fork in** *vtsep* (*compost*) enfouir en fourchant

▶ **fork off** *vi* (*of road, driver*) bifurquer

▶ **fork out** *F* **1** *vtsep* (*provide, often unwillingly*) **to f. out money** allonger *ou* abouler de l'argent **2** *vi* (*pay out money*) **to f. out for sth** casquer pour qch; **he had to f. out (for it)** il a dû allonger la monnaie, il a dû casquer; **come on, f. out** (*what you owe me*) allez, aboule

▶ **fork over** *vtsep* (*flower bed*) retourner légèrement à la fourche

forked [fɔːkt] *adj* (*branch, pipe*) fourchu, bifurqué, en fourche; (*road*) qui bifurque, à bifurcation; (*tongue*) fourchu; (*lightning*) ramifié

forkful [ˈfɔːkfʊl] *n* **(a)** (*of food etc*) fourchetée *f* **(b)** (*of hay etc*) fourchée *f*

fork-lift *n* **f. (truck)** chariot *m* (élévateur) à fourche

forlorn [fəˈlɔːn] *adj Lit* **(a)** (*place*) désert, abandonné; (*look*) triste; *Am* **f. of hope** privé de tout espoir; **to look f.** avoir l'air triste; **a f. expression** une expression de tristesse **(b)** (*desperate*) (*attempt*) désespéré; **it's a f. hope** c'est une aventure désespérée; **to do sth in the f. hope that …** faire qch dans le maigre espoir que …

form[1] [fɔːm] *n* **(a)** (*shape*) (*of object*) forme *f*, configuration *f*; (*of person, animal*) silhouette *f*; **to take f.** prendre forme

(b) (*manifestation*), *Biol, Gram, Liter, Mus* forme *f*; **f. and content** (*of book etc*) la forme et le fond; **work that lacks f.** œuvre qui manque de forme; **tonic taken in the f. of pills** remontant pris sous (la) forme de pilules; **what f. did the lesson take?** quelle forme la leçon a-t-elle prise?; **poverty in every f.** la misère sous toutes ses formes; **it's a f. of disease** c'est une forme spéciale de maladie; **the different forms of worship** les différentes pratiques religieuses

(c) (*formality*) formalité *f*; *Jur etc* **in due** *or* **proper f.** en bonne (et due) forme; **a receipt in due f.** une quittance régulière; **to go through the f. of refusing** faire semblant de refuser; **for f.'s sake** pour la forme; **as a matter of f.** par manière d'acquit; **it is a mere matter of f.** c'est une pure formalité; *F* **to know the f.** (*what to do*) savoir ce qu'il faut faire; **it is good f.** c'est de bon ton; **good f. demands that …** la politesse exige que …; **it is not good f., it's bad f.** c'est de mauvais ton, ça fait mauvais genre; **it is bad f. to ask a lady her age** ce n'est pas poli de demander son âge à une dame; **it would have been good f. to at least tell me** la moindre des politesses aurait été de me le dire

(d) (*formula*) (*of legal document etc*) formule *f*, forme *f*; **correct f. of words** tournure *f* de phrase correcte; **forms of address** (*when writing*) formules de politesse; (*when speaking*) titres *mpl* de politesse

(e) (*printed document with spaces*) formulaire *m*; **order f.** bulletin *m* de commande; **f. letter** lettre *f* type

(f) *esp Sp* (*condition*) forme *f*, condition *f*; *Horseracing* (*of horse*) performances *fpl*; (*in newspaper etc*) (*of horses*) tableau *m* des performances; **to be in/out of f.** être/ne pas être en forme; **to be in good f.** (*at a party etc*) être en train *ou* en forme; **in excellent f.** dans une forme excellente; **he felt in good f.** il se sentait en forme; **on present f.** (*the company will make a profit etc*) si l'on en juge par la situation actuelle; *Horseracing* **to study (the) f.** étudier les performances des chevaux

(g) *Br Sl* **he's got f.** (*a criminal record*) son casier judiciaire n'est pas vierge; **has he got f.?** est-ce qu'il a un casier judiciaire?

(h) *Br Sch* (*class*) classe *f*; **first f.** (classe *f* de) sixième *f*; **sixth f.** (classe de) première *f*

(i) *Br Old-fashioned* (*bench*) banc *m*, banquette *f*

(j) (*mould*) *Metal* forme *f*, moule *m*; *Constr etc* (*for reinforced concrete*) coffrage *m*, coffre *m*; *US Typ* (*frame*) forme

(k) (*of hare*) gîte *m*, forme *f*

form[2] **1** *vt* **(a)** (*shape*) former, faire, façonner; (*the mind*) développer; (*character*) former; (*idea etc*) se former, se faire; (*doubts*) concevoir; **to f. the impression that …** avoir l'impression que …

(b) (*habit etc*) contracter; (*relationship*) établir; (*plan*) arrêter; **to f. a friendship** (*of two people*) devenir amis; **to f. a friendship with sb** devenir ami avec qn; **to f. a successful partnership** former une association réussie; **he had formed a plan to …** il avait projeté de …

(c) (*constitute*) former, faire; (*government, organisation*) constituer; (*company etc*) former, organiser; (*republic etc*) instituer, établir; (*new word etc*) former, faire; **to f. a obstacle to sth** faire obstacle à qch; **Portugal formed the last remaining obstacle** le Portugal constituait le dernier obstacle; **the walls f. a square** les murs forment un carré; **to f. part of sth** faire partie de qch; **they formed themselves into a committee** ils se constituèrent en comité; **the past tense is formed by the addition of -ed** le passé se forme par l'addition de -ed

2 *vi* **(a)** (*of ideas, opinions*) prendre forme, se former; (*of character, personality*) se former; (*of company*) se constituer; (*of friendship, relationship*) naître

(b) *Mil* **to f. into a line** se mettre en ligne

▶ **form up** *vi Mil* se former en rangs

formal [ˈfɔːm(ə)l] **1** *adj* **(a)** (*welcome, reception, occasion etc*) cérémonieux, solennel; (*invitation*) officiel; **a f. dinner** un grand dîner; **f. dress** (*evening dress*) tenue *f* de soirée; **is it f.?** (*the party, dance etc*) est-ce que c'est habillé?

(b) *esp Pej* (*person*) compassé, formaliste; (*tone, manner*) guindé; (*language*) soutenu; **f. style** style *m* empesé *ou* compassé

(c) (*procedure, notification*) formel, en règle; (*order, denial, agreement*) formel; (*contract*) en due forme; (*logic, grammar*) formel; (*garden*) à la française; **f. demand** mise *f* en demeure; **f. notice** mise *f* en demeure; **f. request for payment** mise *f* en demeure de payer; **to give sb a f. warning** avertir qn dans les formes; **a purely f. arrangement** un arrangement purement formel; **a f. similarity** une similarité de forme; **she had no f. schooling** elle n'a pas fait d'études conventionnelles; **f. religion** religion *f* officielle

2 *n Am* (*dress*) robe *f* de soirée; (*occasion*) soirée *f* de cérémonie; (*with dancing*) bal *m* de cérémonie

formaldehyde [fɔːˈmældɪhaɪd] *n Ch* formaldéhyde *m*, aldéhyde *m* formique

formalin [ˈfɔːməlɪn] *n Ch* formol *m*

formalism [ˈfɔːməlɪz(ə)m] *n* formalisme *m*

formality [fɔːˈmælɪtɪ] *n* **(a)** (*procedure*) formalité *f*; **legal formalities** formes *fpl ou* formalités juridiques; **a mere f.** une pure formalité; **to dispense with the formalities** se dispenser des formalités **(b)** (*stiffness*) (*of speech*) compassement *m*; **the f. of the dance** le caractère cérémonieux du bal

formalize [ˈfɔːməlaɪz] *vt* (*contract, relations etc*) donner une forme officielle à; *Ling, Phil* (*grammar, proposition*) formaliser

formally [ˈfɔːməlɪ] *adv* **(a)** (*with formality*) cérémonieusement; **they greeted her f.** ils l'ont accueillie cérémonieusement; **to dress f.** s'habiller strictement; (*in evening dress*) porter une tenue de soirée **(b)** (*openly, officially*) officiellement; **the organization f. renounced violence** l'organisation a officiellement renoncé à la violence **(c)** (*procedurally*) **f. correct** correct quant à la forme, dans les formes; **the institute is f. subordinate to the Department** sur le papier l'institut est subordonné au Département

format[1] [ˈfɔːmæt] *n* (*of book, disk, TV programme etc*) format *m*; (*of meeting, evening etc*) organisation *f*

format[2] *vt* **(-tt-)** *Comptr* (*disk*) formater; (*page, text*) mettre en forme, formater

formation [fɔːˈmeɪʃən] *n* **(a)** (*act of creating*) (*of plural, coal, new policy, character etc*) formation *f*; (*of opinions, child's mind*) développement *m*; (*of company etc*) constitution *f*, formation; (*of republic etc*) établissement *m* **(b)** *Mil etc* (*arrangement*) (*of troops*) formation *f*, dispositif *m*; **battle f.,** *US* **combat f.** formation de combat; **close f.** ordre *m* serré; **to break f.** décrocher; *Av* **f. flying** vol *m* de groupe; **f. dancing** = danse *f* de salon dans laquelle les couples s'entrecroisent **(c)** *Mil* (*unit*) unité *f*; **armoured f.** formation blindée **(d)** *Geol* **granite f.** formation *f* granitique

formative [ˈfɔːmətɪv] **1** *adj* (*experience, influence etc*) formateur, -trice; **the f. years** les années de formation **2** *n Ling* élément *m* formateur

formatted [ˈfɔːmætɪd] *adj* (*disk*) formaté; (*text, page*) mis en forme, formaté

formatting [ˈfɔːmætɪŋ] *n Comptr* (*of disk*) formatage *m*; (*of page, text*) mise *f* en forme, formatage; **f. command** commande *f* de formatage; **f. instructions** instructions *fpl* pour le formatage

form document *n Comptr* document *m* canevas

former[1] [ˈfɔːmər] **1** *adj* **(a)** (*previous*) antérieur, -eure, précédent; (*pupil, servant, colleague etc*) ancien; **my f. pupils** mes anciens élèves; **a f. convict** un repris de justice; **in f. times** autrefois; **in a f. life** dans une vie antérieure; **he is a mere shadow of his f. self** il n'est plus que l'ombre de lui-même

(b) [①A72,9] (*as opposed to the latter*) premier; **I prefer the f. alternative to the latter** je préfère la première alternative à la deuxième

2 [①A72,9] *pron* **the f.** celui-là, *f* celle-là, *pl* ceux-là, celles-

là; **the f. ..., the latter ...** le premier ..., le second ...; **of the two methods I prefer the f.** des deux méthodes je préfère celle-là
-former ['fɔːmər] *suff Br Sch* **first/second/***etc***-f.** élève *mf* de sixième/cinquième/*etc*
formerly ['fɔːməlɪ] *adv* autrefois, jadis; **Mr Martin, f. a liberal** M. Martin, autrefois libéral; **Mrs Boyle, f. Miss Reid** Madame Boyle, auparavant Mademoiselle Reid; **f. of London** résidant auparavant à Londres; **Burkina Faso, f. Upper Volta** le Burkina Faso, ancienne Haute-Volta
form feed *n Comptr* avancement *m* du papier
formic ['fɔːmɪk] *adj Ch* (*acid*) formique
Formica® [fɔː'maɪkə] *n* Formica® *m*; **F. work top** plan *m* de travail en Formica®
formidable ['fɔːmɪdəb(ə)l] *adj* (*opponent, difficulty, appearance, weapon*) redoutable; (*performance, talent, defence*) formidable
formidably [fɔː'mɪdəblɪ] *adv* (*armed, difficult*) redoutablement; (*talented, thorough, equipped*) formidablement, remarquablement
forming ['fɔːmɪŋ] *n* **(a)** (*of company etc*) constitution *f*, formation *f* **(b)** *Metal* formage *m*, façonnage *m*
forming up *n Mil* rassemblement *m*
formless ['fɔːmlɪs] *adj* informe, sans forme; (*desire, idea*) indéfini, flou
form master *n Br* = professeur *m* principal
Formosa [fɔː'məʊsə] *n Hist* Formose *f*
form room *n Br* salle *f* de classe, classe *f*
form teacher *n Br* = professeur *m* principal
formula, *pl* **-as, -ae** ['fɔːmjʊlə, -əz, -iː] *n* **(a)** (*scheme, plan*) formule *f*; **an infallible f. for success/happiness** une recette infaillible pour réussir/trouver le bonheur; **a f. acceptable to all parties** une formule qui soit acceptable à tous les partis; **these romantic novels are all done to the same f.** ces romans à l'eau de rose sont tous écrits selon la même formule; *Aut* **F. 1** Formule 1 **(b)** (*equation, recipe*), *Ch etc* (*pl usu* **formulae**) formule *f*; **gentle f.** (*shampoo, make-up remover etc*) formule douce **(c)** (*for feeding baby*) lait *m* en poudre
formulaic [fɔːmjʊ'leɪɪk] *adj Fml* stéréotypé
formulate ['fɔːmjʊleɪt] *vt* **(a)** (*law, doctrine, theory etc*) formuler; (*plan, strategy, policy*) élaborer **(b)** (*one's opinion, objections*) formuler, exprimer; (*one's response*) formuler; **difficult to f. in words** difficile à exprimer en paroles
formulation [fɔːmjʊ'leɪʃən] *n* **(a)** (*development*) (*of plan, policy*) formulation *f*, élaboration *f* **(b)** (*putting into words, expressing*) expression *f* **(c)** (*wording*) formulation *f*
formwork ['fɔːmwɜːk] *n* (*for reinforced concrete*) coffrage *m*
fornicate ['fɔːnɪkeɪt] *vi* forniquer
fornication [fɔːnɪ'keɪʃən] *n* fornication *f*
fornicator ['fɔːnɪkeɪtər] *n* (*man*) fornicateur *m*; *F* coureur *m* de jupons; (*woman*) coureuse *f*
forsake [fə'seɪk] *vt* (*pt* **forsook** [fə'sʊk]; *pp* **forsaken** [fə'seɪk(ə)n]) *esp Lit* **(a)** (*abandon*) (*person*) abandonner, délaisser; (*shelter*) abandonner; **his habitual assurance had forsaken him** son assurance habituelle l'avait abandonné **(b)** (*renounce*) (*belief, career etc*) renoncer à, abandonner; (*conduct, life of ease*) renoncer à
forsooth [fə'suːθ] *Arch, Lit* **1** *adv* (*in truth*) en vérité **2** *int* par exemple!, ma foi!
forswear [fɔː'sweər] *vt* (*pt* **forswore** [fɔː'swɔːr]; *pp* **forsworn** [fɔː'swɔːn]) *Fml* **(a)** renoncer à; *Rel* abjurer, renier **(b)** *Jur* **to f. oneself** se parjurer
forsythia [fɔː'saɪθɪə] *n* (*shrub*) forsythia *m*
fort [fɔːt] *n Mil* fort *m*, forteresse *f*; *F* **to hold the f.** (*look after house etc*) garder la maison; (*look after office, shop etc*) tenir la boutique
forte[1] [fɔːt, 'fɔːtɪ] *n* (*strong point*) fort *m*
forte[2] ['fɔːtɪ] *Mus* **1** *adj, adv* forte *inv* **2** *n* forte *m*
forth [fɔːθ] *adv* **(a)** (*forwards*) en avant; **to walk back and f.** marcher de long en large, faire les cent pas; **the ferry goes back and f. between ...** le ferry fait la navette entre ...; *Arch* **from this time f.** désormais, dorénavant; **from that/this day f.** à partir de ce jour/d'aujourd'hui **(b) and so f.** (*etcetera*) et ainsi de suite, et cetera
forthcoming [fɔːθ'kʌmɪŋ] *adj* **(a)** (*imminent*) prochain, à venir; (*book, film*) qui va sortir; **the f. session** la prochaine session **(b)** (*available*) **to be f.** ne pas se faire attendre; **the money will be f.** on trouvera l'argent nécessaire; **no answer was f.** aucune réponse n'est venue **(from** de); **the promised help was not f.** les secours promis ont fait défaut **(c)** (*person*) (*sociable*) sociable, expansif; (*frank*) ouvert, franc, *f* franche; **not (very) f.** réservé, renfermé **(about** au sujet de)
forthright ['fɔːθraɪt] *adj* (*person, reply*) franc, *f* franche
forthrightness ['fɔːθraɪtnɪs] *n* franchise *f* **(about** au sujet de)
forthwith [fɔːθ'wɪθ] *adv Fml* tout de suite, immédiatement, aussitôt; **the council must be summoned f.** il faut convoquer le conseil d'urgence; **to dispense with sb's services f.** se dispenser sur-le-champ *ou* immédiatement des services de qn
fortieth ['fɔːtɪɪθ] **1** *adj* quarantième **2** *n* **(a)** (*person, thing*) quarantième *mf* **(b)** (*fraction*) quarantième *m*
fortification [fɔːtɪfɪ'keɪʃən] *n* fortification *f*
fortified ['fɔːtɪfaɪd] *adj* **(a)** (*wine*) viné **(b)** *Mil* fortifié; **f. town** ville *f* fortifiée, place *f* forte
fortify ['fɔːtɪfaɪ] *vt* **(a)** (*ship etc*) renforcer, fortifier; (*person*) fortifier; *Fig* (*person, person's resolve*) affermir, fortifier; **to f. oneself for the coming struggle** rassembler ses forces pour la lutte à venir; **fortified with the rites of the Church** muni des sacrements de l'Église; **to f. oneself against the cold** se prémunir contre le froid **(b)** (*wine*) viner; (*food*) augmenter la valeur nutritive de **(c)** *Mil* (*place*) fortifier
fortifying ['fɔːtɪfaɪɪŋ] *adj* fortifiant; (*drink etc*) remontant
fortissimo [fɔː'tɪsɪməʊ] *Mus* **1** *adv* fortissimo **2** *n* fortissimo *m inv*
fortitude ['fɔːtɪtjuːd] *n* force *f* morale
fortnight ['fɔːtnaɪt] *n esp Br* quinzaine *f*, quinze jours *mpl*; **today f.** (d')aujourd'hui en quinze; **a f. tomorrow** demain en quinze; **in a f.'s time** dans une quinzaine (de jours); **a f. ago** il y a quinze jours; **to adjourn a case for a f.** remettre une cause à quinzaine; **to take a f.'s holiday** prendre quinze jours de vacances
fortnightly ['fɔːtnaɪtlɪ] *esp Br* **1** *adj* bimensuel, semi-mensuel **2** *adv* (*to appear*) bimensuellement, tous les quinze jours; (*to meet*) tous les quinze jours
FORTRAN ['fɔːtræn] *n Comptr* FORTRAN *m*
fortress ['fɔːtrɪs] *n* forteresse *f*; (*town*) place *f* forte; **the place was built like a f.** l'endroit était construit comme une forteresse; **f. city** ville *f* à fortifications
fortuitous [fɔː'tjuːɪtəs] *adj esp Fml* fortuit, imprévu
fortuitously [fɔː'tjuːɪtəslɪ] *adv esp Fml* fortuitement, par hasard
fortunate ['fɔːtjənət, -tʃ-] *adj* **(a)** (*person etc*) **to be f.** avoir de la chance; **to be f. enough to ...** avoir la chance de ...; **I consider myself f. to know her** j'ai la chance de la connaître; **we've been quite f. in the weather** nous avons eu de la chance pour ce qui est du temps; **we've been quite f. in our choice** nous avons fait un choix très heureux; **the less f. among them** les moins fortunés d'entre eux **(b)** (*occasion etc*) propice, favorable, heureux; **a f. choice of words** une tournure heureuse; **it was f. that you remembered** encore heureux que tu t'en sois souvenu; **how f.!** quel bonheur!, quelle chance!
fortunately ['fɔːtjənətlɪ, -tʃ-] *adv* heureusement, par bonheur; **we're quite f. situated as far as the shops are concerned** nous sommes plutôt bien lotis en ce qui concerne les magasins
fortune ['fɔːtʃən] *n* **(a)** (*prosperity*) prospérité *f*, richesse *f*; (*riches*) richesses *fpl*, biens *mpl*; **a man of f.** un homme riche; **to make a** *or* **one's f.** faire fortune; **you must be making a f.** tu dois gagner un argent fou; **she has made and lost several fortunes** elle a fait fortune plusieurs fois dans sa vie; **to come into a f.** hériter une fortune; **her jewels are worth a f.** ses bijoux valent une fortune; *F* **it cost me a (small) f.** cela m'a coûté un argent fou *ou* une fortune *ou* les yeux de la tête *ou F* la peau des fesses; **to spend a (small) f. on books/decorating the house** dépenser une fortune en livres/pour décorer la maison; **her face is her f.** son visage est son grand atout
(b) (*luck*) fortune *f*; (*chance*) hasard *m*, chance *f*; (*destiny*) destinée *f*, sort *m*; *Myth* le Sort, le Destin; **ill f.** malchance *f*, mauvais sort; **piece of good f.** coup *m* de chance, bonheur *m*; **by (sheer) good f.** par bonheur; **f. favours** *or* **is kind to him** la fortune lui sourit; **the fortunes of war** le sort des armes; **he followed the team's changing fortunes** il a suivi l'équipe bon an mal an; **despite its changing fortunes over the years, the company ...** en dépit des adversités qu'elle a rencontré au fil des ans, la compagnie ...; **to tell fortunes** dire la bonne aventure; **to tell sb's f.** dire la bonne aventure à qn; **to tell s.b's f. by the cards** tirer les cartes à qn; *Am* **f. cookie** = friandise *f* chinoise avec un message à l'intérieur
fortune-hunter *n* (*man*) coureur *m* de dot; (*woman*) croqueuse *f* de diamants
fortune-teller *n* diseur, -euse de bonne aventure; (*with cards*) tireur, -euse de cartes
fortune-telling *n* la bonne aventure; (*with cards*) cartomancie *f*
forty ['fɔːtɪ] *adj, n* quarante *m*; **f.-one** quarante et un; **f.-two** quarante-deux; **about f. guests** une quarantaine d'invités; **to be f. (years old)** avoir quarante ans; *prov* **life begins at f.** la vie commence à quarante ans; **the forties** les années

quarante; **to be in one's forties** avoir passé la quarantaine; *F* **to have f. winks** piquer *ou* faire un petit somme

forty-five *n* (*record*) (disque *m*) quarante-cinq tours *m*

fortyish ['fɔːtɪɪʃ] *adj* d'une quarantaine d'années; **I'd say she was f.** je lui donne la quarantaine *ou* une quarantaine d'années; **he was balding, f. and plump** il perdait ses cheveux et avait la quarantaine rondouillarde

forum ['fɔːrəm] *n* tribune *f* libre, forum *m*; *Antiq* (*square*) forum *m*; **a f. in which workers can put forward their views** un forum permettant aux ouvriers d'exprimer leurs opinions

forward¹ ['fɔːwəd, *Naut* 'fɒrəd] **1** *adj* (**a**) (*of place*) de devant, situé en avant; *Naut* (de l')avant, sur l'avant; (*movement etc*) en avant; *Aut* **f. gears** marches *fpl* avant; **f. motion** marche *f* (en) avant; **f. and backward movement** mouvement *m* d'avant en arrière; *Rugby* **f. pass** passe *f* en avant, en-avant *m*; *Mil* **f. positions** premières positions *fpl*; **f. post** avant-poste *m*; *Comptr* **f. search** recherche *f* vers l'avant; *Naut* **f. turret** tourelle *f* avant

(**b**) (*of time*) (*plants*) avancé, précoce; (*child*) précoce, en avance; *Admin* **f. planning** planification *f*; **a f. thinking company** une entreprise tournée vers l'avenir

(**c**) (*impudent, bold*) effronté, hardi; **it would have been thought f. of a woman to …** cela aurait été considéré comme effronté de la part d'une femme de …

(**d**) *Fin* (*price etc*) à terme; **f. account** compte *m* à terme; **f. buying** achat *m* à terme; **f. deals** opérations *fpl* à terme; **f. exchange** change *m* à terme; *Mktg* **f. integration** intégration *f* en aval; *Mktg* **f. invention** invention *f* de produits totalement nouveaux; **f. rate** cours *m* à terme; *Com* **f. requirement** commande *f* prévisionnelle; **f. sale** vente *f* à terme

2 *adv* (*occ* **forwards** ['fɔːwədz]) (**a**) (*of time*) **from this/that day f.** à partir d'aujourd'hui/de ce jour-là

(**b**) (*of direction*) en avant; **to go** *or* **move f.** (s')avancer; **to step f.** faire un pas en avant; **f.!** en avant!; *Mil* **f. march!** en avant, marche!

(**c**) (*of position*) à l'avant; **the seat is too far f.** la banquette est trop avancée *ou* trop en avant; **we're sitting too far f.** tu es assis trop en avant; *Naut* **f. of the beam** sur l'avant du travers; **the crew's quarters are f.** le logement de l'équipage est à l'avant

(**d**) *Com* (**carried**) **f.** report *m*; *Com* **charges f.** frais *mpl* à percevoir à la livraison; *Com, Fin* **to sell f.** vendre à terme

3 *n Fb etc* (*player*) avant *m*

forward² *vt* (**a**) (*send*) (*letter*) faire suivre; (*goods etc*) expédier, envoyer, *Spec* transiter; **please f.** (*on letter*) prière de faire suivre, à faire suivre; **to f. sth to sb** faire parvenir qch à qn; **we'll f. your complaint/report to the relevant department** nous transmettrons votre plainte/rapport au service correspondant (**b**) (*promote*) (*person's interests etc*) favoriser

forwarder ['fɔːwədər] *n Com* transitaire *m*; **f. and consolidator** transitaire-groupeur *m*

forwarding ['fɔːwədɪŋ] *n* (*sending*) expédition *f*, envoi *m*; **f. address** nouvelle adresse *f*; *Com* **f. agent** (agent *m*) transitaire *m*; *Com* **f. instructions** indications *fpl* concernant l'expédition

forward-looking *adj* progressiste

forwardness ['fɔːwədnɪs] *n* (**a**) (*eagerness*) empressement *m*, ardeur *f* (**b**) (*boldness*) hardiesse *f*, présomption *f*

forwards ['fɔːwədz] *adv see* **forward¹ 2**

forwent *see* **forgo**

Fosbury flop ['fɒzbərɪ] *n Sp* Fosbury *m*

fossil ['fɒs(ə)l] **1** *n* fossile *m*; *F, Pej* **an old f.** (*person*) une vieille croûte, un vieux fossile **2** *adj* (*plant, bones etc*) fossile; **f. fuel** combustible *m* fossile

fossilization [fɒsɪlaɪ'zeɪʃən] *n* fossilisation *f*

fossilize ['fɒsɪlaɪz] **1** *vt* fossiliser **2** *vi* se fossiliser; *Fig* (*of person*) s'encroûter, se fossiliser

fossilized ['fɒsɪlaɪzd] *adj* fossilisé; (*ideas, attitudes etc*) fossile

foster¹ ['fɒstər] *vt* (**a**) (*child*) prendre en famille d'accueil; **to f. a child** (**out**) mettre un enfant en famille d'accueil (**b**) (*promote*) (*idea, hope, belief etc*) entretenir, nourrir; (*person's plans, sense of responsibility*) encourager, favoriser; (*the arts etc*) protéger; **to f. friendship between peoples** stimuler l'amitié entre les peuples

foster² *adj* **f. child** = enfant *mf* placé(e) dans une famille d'accueil; **f. home** famille *f* d'accueil; **placing of children in f. homes** placement familial des enfants; **f. father** père *m* nourricier; *Admin* = assistant *m* familial; **f. mother** mère *f* nourricière; *Admin* = assistante *f* familiale; **f. parents** famille d'accueil

fostering ['fɒstərɪŋ] *n* (**a**) (*of child*) prise *f* en famille d'accueil; (*fostering out*) mise *f* en famille d'accueil (**b**) (*of the arts etc*) patronage *m*, encouragement *m*

fought *see* **fight²**

foul¹ [faʊl] **1** *adj* (**a**) (*disgusting*) (*smell*) infect, nauséabond; (*thoughts*) immonde, impur, corrompu; (*language*) grossier, ordurier; (*water*) croupi; *F* **that soup was f.!** cette soupe était infecte!; *F* **what f. weather!** quel sale temps!, quel temps infect!; *Naut* **f. weather** gros temps; **to be f. to sb/about sth** être infect *ou* abject avec qn/au sujet de qch; **f. air** air vicié; **f. breath** mauvaise haleine; *esp Lit* **f. deed** infamie *f*; **f.-smelling/-tasting** qui a une odeur/un goût infect(e); *F* **I'm in a f. temper today** je suis d'une humeur massacrante aujourd'hui; **she has a f. temper** elle a un sale caractère; **she's got a f. tongue** elle a une langue de vipère

(**b**) (*gun, spark plug*) encrassé; **f. bottom** (*of anchorage*) mauvais fond *m*; (*of ship*) carène *f* sale

(**c**) *Sp etc* (*unfair*) déloyal, illicite; **f. play** *Sp* jeu déloyal; (*criminal behaviour*) action criminelle; (*underhand dealings*) intrigue *f*; **f. play is not suspected** on ne croit pas à un crime; **f. shot** (*in basketball*) coup *m* franc

2 *n Sp* coup *m* illicite *ou* déloyal; *Fb, Rugby* faute *f*

3 *adv* (**a**) **it smells f.!** ça pue!; **it tastes perfectly f.** c'est infect; **it looks f.** c'est horrible *ou* atroce; *F* **to feel f.** ne pas se sentir bien

(**b**) (*unfairly*) irrégulièrement, déloyalement; *Old-fashioned* **to fight f.** se battre déloyalement; *Naut* **to run f. of another ship** (*collide with*) entrer en collision avec *ou* aborder *ou* heurter un autre navire; **to fall** *or* **run f. of the law/sb** avoir des démêlés avec la justice/qn

foul² **1** *vt* (**a**) (*dirty*) (*place, reputation etc*) salir, souiller; (*of dog*) (*pavement*) souiller; (*gun barrel, spark plugs*) encrasser (**b**) (*obstruct, jam*) (*ropes etc*) s'emmêler dans; (*collide with*) (*ship*) entrer en collision avec, (se) heurter contre; **weeds fouled the anchor** l'ancre était prise *ou* coincée dans des algues; **the ropes fouled the propeller** les cordes avaient bloqué l'hélice (**c**) *Sp* (*another player*) commettre une faute contre **2** *vi* (**a**) (*of gun barrel etc*) s'encrasser; (*of pump*) s'engorger (**b**) *Naut* (*of anchor, rope etc*) se coincer; (*of anchor*) surjaler; *MecE* (*of moving part*) toucher

▶ **foul up** **1** *vtsep* (**a**) (*put out of order*) (*machine*) dérégler (**b**) *F* (*ruin*) (*plan*) gâcher; **it will f. things up if he finds out** ça va tout gâcher s'il l'apprend **2** *vi* (**a**) *Sl* (*of person*) merder; **don't f. up again/this time!** tâche de ne plus merder/ne pas merder cette fois! (**b**) (*of gun barrel etc*) s'encrasser; (*of pump*) s'engorger

fouler ['faʊlər] *n Sp* **he's a persistent f.** il commet des fautes sans arrêt

fouling ['faʊlɪŋ] *n* (**a**) (*of pipes*) engorgement *m*; (*of spark plugs*) encrassement *m* (**b**) *Sp* **a lot of f.** beaucoup de jeu déloyal

foully ['faʊlɪ] *adv* (**a**) (*to speak etc*) grossièrement (**b**) (*to behave*) bassement, ignoblement; *Lit* **he was f. murdered** il fut ignoblement assassiné

foul-mouthed ['faʊl'maʊðd] *adj* (*person*) au langage ordurier, grossier, -ière; (*reply, tirade*) ordurier, grossier

foulness ['faʊlnɪs] *n* (**a**) (*dirtiness*) saleté *f*; (*of air etc*) fétidité *f*; **the f. of the smell** l'odeur infecte, la puanteur (**b**) (*of language etc*) grossièreté *f*, obscénité *f* (**c**) (*of a deed, behaviour*) infamie *f*, ignominie *f*

foul-tempered *adj* **to be f.** avoir un sale caractère

foul-up *n F* (*mistake*) cafouillage *m*; **there's been a f.** quelque chose a cloché *ou* cafouillé, il y a eu un cafouillage

found¹ [faʊnd] *vt* (**a**) (*city, hospital, dynasty*) fonder; (*college, club, organisation etc*) fonder, créer; (*company, business etc*) établir, créer; **to f. a fortune** (*lay foundations of fortune*) établir les bases d'une fortune; (*make fortune*) bâtir une fortune (**on** sur) (**b**) (*suspicions, hope, social order etc*) baser, fonder (**on** sur); **founded on fact** (*of novel etc*) reposant sur des faits véridiques

found² **1** *pt, pp see* **find² 2** *adj* (*with adv prefixed*) (*ship etc*) **well-f.** bien équipé (**in** de)

found³ *vt Metal* (*metals*) fondre; (*casting*) mouler

foundation [faʊn'deɪʃən] *n* (**a**) (*action*) (*of city etc*) fondation *f*; (*of empire*) établissement *m*, institution *f*; (*of company*) établissement *m*, création *f*; (*of hospital*) fondation et dotation *f*

(**b**) *Constr* (*base*) (*of building*) fondement *m*, fondation *f*; (*of road*) assiette *f*; (*of machine etc*) assise *f*; *Fig* **to lay the foundation(s) of an alliance** jeter les bases d'une alliance; **the foundations of modern society** les assises *ou* fondations de la société moderne; *Constr* **to lay the f. stone** poser la première pierre; *Sch* **f. course** année *f* préparatoire

(**c**) (*basis*) (*of theory etc*) fondement *m*, base *f*; (*of doubt*) motif *m*, cause *f*; **rumour without f.** bruit dénué de fondement

(**d**) (*institution*) institution *f* dotée, fondation *f*; (*legacy*) capital *m* légué pour œuvres de bienfaisance, fondation; **a charitable f.** une institution charitable; **the Ford f.** la fondation Ford; **f. scholar** élève *m* boursier

(e) (*in clothing*) **embroidery on a silk f.** broderie *f* sur fond de soie; *Old-fashioned* **f. garment** (*girdle*) gaine *f*; (*full-length*) combiné *m*

(f) **f. (cream)** fond *m* de teint

founder[1] ['faʊndər] *n* (*of hospital etc*) fondateur *m*; **f. member** (*of club etc*) membre *m* fondateur

founder[2] *n Metal* fondeur *m*

founder[3] **1** *vi* (*of hopes, horse*) s'effondrer; (*of talks, negotiations*) avorter; (*of project, scheme*) péricliter; (*of ship*) sombrer, couler; **to f. on the rocks** s'échouer sur les rochers **2** *vt* (*horse*) courbaturer

foundering ['faʊndərɪŋ] *n* (*of hopes*) effondrement *m*

founding[1] ['faʊndɪŋ] **1** *adj* (*member*) fondateur, -trice; **f. father** fondateur *m*; *US Hist* **F. Father** = membre *m* de la Convention constituante de 1787 **2** *n* = **foundation (a)**

founding[2] *n Metal* fonderie *f*, moulage *m*

foundling ['faʊndlɪŋ] *n Old-fashioned* enfant *mf* trouvé(e); *Hist* **f. hospital** hospice *m* des enfants trouvés

foundry ['faʊndrɪ] *n Metal* (*iron etc*) fonderie *f*; **f. iron** fonte *f* de moulage

fount[1] [faʊnt] *n Lit* (*spring*) source *f* (d'eau); *Fig* (*of happiness etc*) source

fount[2] [faʊnt, fɒnt] *n Typ* fonte *f*

fountain ['faʊntɪn] *n* (*natural*) fontaine *f*, source *f* (d'eau); (*man-made*) fontaine; (*in park etc*) jet *m* d'eau; **a f. of water shot from the broken pipe** un jet d'eau jaillit du tuyau cassé; **f. pen** stylo *m* à plume

fountainhead ['faʊntɪnhed] *n esp Fig* source *f*

four [fɔːr] **1** *adj, n* quatre *m*; **twenty-f.** vingt-quatre; **f. fives** *or* **five fours are twenty, f. times five is twenty** quatre fois cinq *ou* cinq fois quatre font vingt; **at f. thirty** à quatre heures et demie; **to be f. (years old)** avoir quatre ans; **scattered to the f. corners of the earth** éparpillé aux quatre coins du monde; **open to the f. winds** ouvert aux quatre vents; **to get down/run on all fours** se mettre/courir à quatre pattes

2 *n Sp* **a f.** (*in rowing*) un quatre; **would you like to make up a f.?** (*for a game of bridge*) voudriez-vous vous joindre à nous pour faire une partie à quatre?; *Cr* **to hit a f.** marquer quatre points; *Golf* **a f.-ball (match)** une partie à quatre joueurs et quatre balles

four-colour *adj Typ etc* à quatre couleurs; **f. work** (*process*) quadrichromie *f*

four-cornered *adj* à quatre coins; (*quadrangular*) quadrangulaire

four-cycle *adj Am* (*engine, cylinder etc*) à quatre temps

four-door *adj Aut* à quatre portes; **f. model** quatre portes *f*; **f. saloon** berline *f* à quatre portes

four-engined ['fɔːr'endʒɪnd] *adj* (*plane*) quadrimoteur

four-eyes ['fɔːraɪz] *n F* binoclard, -arde

four-figure *adj Math* (*number, sum*) à quatre chiffres; (*logarithm*) à quatre décimales

fourfold ['fɔːfəʊld] **1** *adj* **a f. increase** une augmentation au quadruple **2** *adv* quatre fois autant, au quadruple; **to increase f.** quadrupler

four-footed ['fɔː'fʊtɪd] *adj* (*animal*) quadrupède, à quatre pattes; *F* **a f. friend** un ami à quatre pattes

four-handed ['fɔː'hændɪd] *adj* **(a)** *Cards* (*game*) à quatre (personnes) **(b)** *Mus* (*piece*) à quatre mains

four-in-hand *n* (*carriage*) véhicule *m* à quatre chevaux

four-leaf *adj* **f. clover** trèfle *m* à quatre feuilles

four-leaved *adj* (*plant*) quadrifolié; **f. clover** trèfle *m* à quatre feuilles

four-legged *adj* (*animal*) quadrupède; (*table*) à quatre pieds; **our f. friends** nos amis les bêtes

four-letter *adj F* **f. word** gros mot *m*, obscénité *f*; *Iron* **life is a f. word** la vie est une connerie; **for some people, 'socialism' seems to be a f. word** pour certains, il semble que le mot 'socialisme' soit tabou

four-part *adj Mus* à quatre parties; (*singing*) à quatre voix

four-phase *adj El* (*system*) tétraphasé

four-poster **1** *n* lit *m* à colonnes *ou* à baldaquin **2** *adj* (*bed*) à colonnes

fourscore [fɔː'skɔːr] *adj Arch, Lit* quatre-vingt

four-seater *n Aut* voiture *f* à quatre places

foursome ['fɔːsəm] *n* (*four people*) groupe *m* de quatre personnes; (*two couples*) deux couples; *Golf* (*game*) partie *f* (de) double *ou* à deux contre deux; **to go out in a f.** (*of four people*) sortir à quatre; (*of two couples*) sortir à deux couples; **to make up a f.** (*of four people*) former un groupe de quatre personnes; (*of two couples*) former deux couples; (*be the fourth person*) faire le quatrième

four-speed *adj Aut* à quatre vitesses

foursquare ['fɔː'skweər] **1** *adj* **(a)** (*refusal*) carré **(b)** (*building*) solide **2** *adv* (*to refuse*) carrément; (*to build*) solidement; **to stand f. behind sb** soutenir qn fermement *ou* résolument

four-star *n Br* (*petrol*) super *m*; **f. unleaded** super sans plomb

four-stroke *adj* (*engine*) à quatre temps

fourteen ['fɔː'tiːn] *adj, n* quatorze *m*; **she is f.** elle a quatorze ans; **the plane will arrive at f. thirty (hours)** l'avion arrivera à quatorze heures trente

fourteenth [fɔː'tiːnθ] **1** *adj* quatorzième; **Louis the F.** Louis Quatorze **2** *n* **(a)** (*of month*) quatorze *m*; **(on) the f. of May** le quatorze mai **(b)** (*fraction*) quatorzième *m* **(c)** (*person, thing*) quatorzième *mf*

fourth [fɔːθ] **1** *adj* quatrième; **Henry the F.** Henri Quatre; **he's f. in his class** il est le quatrième de sa classe; **the f. estate** (*press*) la presse; *Aut* **in f. (gear)** en quatrième (vitesse); *Br Sch* **the f. year** *or* **form** = la classe de troisième; *Cards etc* **to make a f.** faire le quatrième; *Pol* **the F. World** le quart-monde **2** *n* **(a)** (*of month*) quatre *m*; **on the f.** le quatre; **the f. of January, January the f.** le quatre janvier **(b)** (*fraction*) quart *m*; **three-fourths of the globe** les trois quarts du globe **(c)** (*person, thing*) quatrième *mf* **(d)** *Mus* quarte *f*

fourthly ['fɔːθlɪ] *adv* quatrièmement, en quatrième lieu

Fourth of July *n US* = anniversaire *m* du jour de l'indépendance

four-wheel *adj* (*vehicle*) à quatre roues; **tractor with f. drive** tracteur à quatre roues motrices; **does it have f. drive?** est-ce qu'il a quatre roues motrices?; **it's a f. drive** c'est un quatre-quatre; **f. steering** quatre roues *fpl* directrices

four-wheeled *adj* à quatre roues

four-wheeler *n* voiture *f* à quatre roues

fowl[1] [faʊl] *n* **(a)** (*domesticated bird*) volaille *f*; **to keep fowl(s)** élever de la volaille *ou* des volailles; *Culin* **boiling f.** poule *f* (au pot); *Vet* **f. pest** peste *f* aviaire *ou* des poules; **f. pox** diphtérie *f* aviaire **(b)** (*wild bird*) (*pl* **fowl**) gibier *m* ailé **(c)** *Lit* (*bird*) oiseau *m*

fowling ['faʊlɪŋ] *n* **to go f.** aller à la chasse au gibier ailé; **f. piece** fusil *m* de chasse

fox[1] [fɒks] *n* renard *m*; **red f.** renard commun; **Arctic f.** renard bleu; **silver f.** renard argenté; *F* **an old f.** (*cunning man*) un vieux renard, un vieux madré; *F* **a sly f.** un fin renard, un roublard; **f. brush** queue *f* de renard; **f. cub** renardeau *m*; **f. fur** (fourrure *f*) renard; **f. fur coat** manteau *m* en renard

fox[2] *vt* **(a)** (*mystify*) (*person*) mystifier, tromper; **you've got me foxed** je suis perplexe; **it foxes me why he did it** je n'arrive pas à saisir pourquoi il a fait ça; **she was absolutely foxed by the problem** le problème la laissait complètement perplexe **(b)** (*trick, deceive*) tromper, duper **(c)** (*discolour*) (*pages of book*) tacher de roux; (*engraving*) maculer

foxglove ['fɒksglʌv] *n* (*plant*) digitale *f* (pourprée)

foxhole ['fɒkshəʊl] *n* **(a)** renardière *f*, terrier *m* de renard **(b)** *Mil* abri *m* individuel; (*for sniper*) trou *m* de tirailleur

foxhound ['fɒkshaʊnd] *n* fox-hound *m*, *pl* fox-hounds

foxhunt ['fɒkshʌnt] *n* chasse *f* au renard

foxhunting ['fɒkshʌntɪŋ] *n* chasse *f* au renard

foxiness ['fɒksɪnɪs] *n* **(a)** (*craftiness*) roublardise *f* **(b)** *Am F* (*of woman*) air *m* sexy

foxtail ['fɒksteɪl] *n* **(a)** queue *f* de renard **(b)** (*plant*) **f. (grass)** vulpin *m*

fox-terrier *n* fox-terrier *m*, *pl* fox-terriers; *F* fox *m*

foxtrot[1] ['fɒkstrɒt] *n* (*dance*) fox-trot *m inv*

foxtrot[2] *vi* **(-tt-)** danser le fox-trot

foxy ['fɒksɪ] *adj* **(a)** (*crafty*) rusé, astucieux, *esp Pej* roublard **(b)** *Am F* (*woman*) sexy; **a f. lady** une nana sexy

foyer ['fɔɪeɪ, 'fwæjeɪ] *n Th* foyer *m* du public; *Cin* (hall *m* d')entrée *f*; (*of hotel*) hall (de réception)

FPA [efpiː'eɪ] *n* (*abbr* **Family Planning Association**) = association *f* pour le planning familial

Fr *abbr* **(a)** *Rel* **(Father)** Père **(b)** **France** **(c)** *Fin* **franc**

fracas ['frækaː] *n* remue-ménage *m*; **to cause a f.** faire du remue-ménage

fractal ['frækt(ə)l] *n* fractal *m*

fraction ['frækʃən] *n* **(a)** [①A70,16,2; B56,C,1] *Math* fraction *f*; **vulgar** *or* **common f.** fraction ordinaire; **compound f.** fraction de fraction; **decimal f.** fraction décimale

(b) (*small part*) petite portion *f*, petite partie *f*; **the new method takes only a f. of the time** la nouvelle méthode prend bien moins de temps; **he escaped death by a f. of a second** il a été à deux doigts de la mort; **a f. too small/large** un tout petit peu trop petit/grand; **a f. earlier/too late** un tout petit peu plus tôt/trop tard; **she won by a f.** elle a gagné d'un rien

(c) *Fin* (*of share*) fraction *f*, rompu *m*

(**d**) *Ch* (*of distillation*) fraction *f*
(**e**) *Pol* (*of party*) fraction *f*, groupe *m* fractionnaire

fractional ['frækʃən(ə)l] *adj* (**a**) *Math* fractionnaire; *Fig* **the difference is only f.** la différence est minime (**b**) *Ch* fractionné; **f. distillation** distillation *f* fractionnée

fractionally ['frækʃən(ə)lɪ] *adv* légèrement, un tout petit peu

fractionate ['frækʃəneɪt] *vt Ch, Ind* (*petroleum etc*) fractionner

fractionize ['frækʃənaɪz] *vt Math* fractionner

fractious ['frækʃəs] *adj* de mauvaise humeur; (*tone of voice, expression*) irrité; (*baby*) pleurnicheur; **to be f.** *or* **in a f. mood** être de mauvaise humeur; (*baby*) pleurnicher

fractiousness ['frækʃəsnɪs] *n* mauvaise humeur *f*; (*of baby*) pleurnicherie *f*, pleurnichage *m*; **the f. of her voice** l'irritation qu'il y avait dans sa voix

fracture[1] ['fræktʃər] *n* (**a**) *Med* fracture *f*; **to set a f.** réduire une fracture (**b**) (*of axle etc*) fracture *f*, rupture *f*; *Geol* cassure *f*, fracture

fracture[2] **1** *vt* (**a**) *Med* (*bone*) fracturer; **fractured skull** crâne fracturé; **fractured ribs** côtes enfoncées (**b**) (*break*) casser, briser **2** *vi* (**a**) *Med* (*of bone, limb*) se fracturer (**b**) (*break*) se casser, se briser

fragile ['frædʒaɪl] *adj* (**a**) (*cup, peace*) fragile *Mktg* **f. market-share trap** risque *m* de fragiliser les parts de marché (**b**) (*person*) (*weak*) fragile, faible; (*delicate*) délicat; **she was a f. child** c'était une enfant fragile; **he's become very f. recently** il s'est beaucoup affaibli ces derniers temps; **emotionally f.** fragile sur le plan émotionnel; **he sounded rather f. over the phone** il avait l'air plutôt abattu au téléphone; *F* **I'm feeling a bit f. this morning** (*hung over*) j'ai mal aux cheveux ce matin

fragilely ['frædʒaɪllɪ] *adv* fragilement

fragility [frə'dʒɪlɪtɪ] *n* (**a**) (*of ornament, peace*) fragilité *f* (**b**) (*of person*) (*weakness*) fragilité *f*, faiblesse *f*; (*delicateness*) délicatesse *f*; **emotional f.** fragilité émotionnelle

fragment[1] ['frægmənt] *n* (**a**) (*of porcelain etc*) fragment *m*, morceau *m*; (*of paper*) morceau; (*of mortar shell*) éclat *m*; (*of story, account*) fragment; **to fly into fragments** voler en morceaux *ou* en éclats (**b**) *Liter* fragment *m*; (*of book*) extrait *m*; (*of author*) œuvre *f* inachevée

fragment[2] [fræg'ment] **1** *vi* se fragmenter **2** *vt* réduire en fragments, briser en morceaux; **the family structure/the party has been fragmented** la structure familiale/le parti a été fragmenté(e)

fragmentary ['frægmənt(ə)rɪ] *adj* fragmentaire

fragmentation [frægmən'teɪʃən] *n* fragmentation *f*; *Mil* **f. bomb** bombe *f ou* grenade *f* à fragmentation

fragrance ['freɪgrəns] *n* parfum *m*; **bubble bath with the f. of bilberries** bain moussant (parfumé) à la myrtille

fragrant ['freɪgrənt] *adj* parfumé, odorant, fragrant; (*scent*) embaumé; **to be** *or* **smell f.** sentir bon; **woods f. with wild strawberries** bois qui embaument les fraises sauvages

frail [freɪl] *adj* (**a**) (*person*) faible, frêle; **a f. old man** un vieil homme frêle *ou* fragile; **to be in f. health** avoir une santé délicate (**b**) (*object*) peu solide, fragile; (*beauty*) éphémère; (*happiness*) précaire; (*hope*) fragile

frailness ['freɪlnɪs] *n* (**a**) (*of person*) faiblesse *f*; (*of character*) faiblesse morale; **the f. of his health** sa santé délicate (**b**) (*of glass etc*) fragilité *f*; (*of beauty*) caractère *m* éphémère; (*of happiness*) précarité *f*

frailty ['freɪltɪ] *n* (**a**) = **frailness** (**a**) (**b**) (*moral flaw*) faible *m*, défaut *m*; **human f.** faiblesse *f* des hommes

frame[1] [freɪm] *n* (**a**) (*of picture, mirror etc*) cadre *m*, encadrement *m*; (*of window, door*) chambranle *m*, châssis *m* dormant; (*picture*) *TV* trame *f* (double); *Cin* (*of film*) image *f*; (*of comic strip*) case *f*
(**b**) (*framework*) (*of person, animal, wing of plane*) ossature *f*; (*of building, bridge etc*) charpente *f*; (*of bicycle etc*) cadre *m*; (*of railway engine, car*) châssis *m*; (*of machine*) bâti *m*; (*of umbrella*) monture *f*; (*of racket*) armature *f*; (*of bed*) châlit *m*; (*of ship*) membrure *f*, carcasse *f*; (*in gardening*) châssis; **his huge f. filled the doorway** sa large carrure s'encadrait dans la porte; **man of gigantic f.** homme bâti comme un colosse; (**spectacle**) **frames** monture (de lunettes); **glasses with metal frames** lunettes à monture de métal; *Am* **f. house** maison *f* en bois
(**c**) **f. of mind** état *m ou* disposition *f* d'esprit; **he is in a bad f. of mind** il est mal disposé; **f. of reference, reference f.** *Math* système *m* de coordonnées, référentiel *m*; *Fig* système *m* de référence
(**d**) (*in embroidery*) (*floor standing*) métier *m* (à broder); (*hand-held*) tambour *m* (à broder)
(**e**) *Sp* (*in snooker*) (*wooden device*) triangle *m*; (*game*) partie *f*

frame[2] *vt* (**a**) (*surround*) (*picture etc*) encadrer; *TV* (*the picture*) cadrer, centrer; **black hair framed her face** des cheveux noirs encadraient son visage (**b**) (*compose*) (*poem etc*) composer; (*law*) rédiger; (*one's thoughts*) mettre de l'ordre dans; (*opinion*) formuler; (*answer, reply*) composer, formuler (**c**) *F* (*falsely incriminate*) (*person*) monter une accusation *ou* un coup contre; **I've been framed** c'est un coup monté (contre moi); **she was framed by the police for a bank robbery** la police a monté un coup contre elle et l'a accusée d'avoir dévalisé une banque

frame format *n Comptr* (*of network*) protocole *m*

framer ['freɪmər] *n* (*of pictures*) encadreur *m*

frame-up *n Sl* (*false incrimination*) coup *m* monté

framework[1] ['freɪmwɜːk] *n* (*of building, ship*) charpente *f*, carcasse *f*; (*of novel, play*) charpente; (*of negotiations*) structure *f*; **a political/legal/constitutional f.** un cadre politique/légal/constitutionnel; **it comes within the f. of the UN** cela entre dans le cadre de l'ONU

framing ['freɪmɪŋ] *n* (**a**) (*of picture etc*) encadrement *m*; (**picture**) **f.** encadrement *m* (**b**) (*structuring*) (*of poem etc*) composition *f* (**c**) *F* (*false incrimination*) accusation *f* à tort (**d**) **metal f.** (*for window*) vitrière *f*

franc [fræŋk] *n* (*currency*) franc *m*

France [frɑːns] *n* France *f*; **in F.** en France

franchise ['fræntʃaɪz] *n* (**a**) (*granted by public body*) concession *f*; (*granted by manufacturer*) franchise *f*; (*shop, outlet*) établissement *m* en franchise; **f. agreement** accord *m* de franchise; **f. holder** franchisé, -ée (**b**) *Pol* droit *m* de vote

franchisee [fræntʃaɪ'ziː] *n Com* franchisé, -ée

franchising ['fræntʃaɪzɪŋ] *n Com* franchisage *m*

franchisor ['fræntʃaɪzər] *n Com* franchiseur, -euse

Franciscan [fræn'sɪskən] *n, adj* franciscain *m*

Francis of Assisi ['frɑːnsɪs] *n* saint François d'Assise

francophile ['fræŋkəʊfaɪl] *adj, n* francophile *mf*

francophobe ['fræŋkəʊfəʊb] *adj, n* francophobe *mf*

francophone ['fræŋkəʊfəʊn] *adj, n* francophone *mf*

frangible ['frændʒɪb(ə)l] *adj* cassant, fragile

frangipane ['frændʒɪpɑːn] *n* frangipane *f*

Franglais [frɒn'gle] *n* franglais *m*

Frank [fræŋk] *n Hist* Franc *m*, Franque *f*

frank[1] [fræŋk] *adj* (*person, answer*) franc, *f* franche, sincère; (*speech*) direct, ouvert; (*discussion, exchange of views*) à cœur ouvert; **to be quite f. with you** pour être franc avec vous; **I don't think you're being f. with me** je ne crois pas que tu me dises la vérité

frank[2] *vt* (*letter*) affranchir (*à la machine*); (*by post office*) oblitérer

frankfurter ['fræŋkfɜːtər] *n* saucisse *f* de Francfort

frankincense ['fræŋkɪnsens] *n* encens *m* (mâle)

franking ['fræŋkɪŋ] *n* (*of letter*) affranchissement *m* (*à la machine*); **f. machine** machine *f* à affranchir, affranchisseuse *f*

Frankish ['fræŋkɪʃ] *adj Hist* franc, *f* franque

frankly ['fræŋklɪ] *adv* franchement; **f. incredible** tout bonnement incroyable; **I tell you f. that ...** je vous dis carrément que ...; (**quite**) **f. no!** franchement, non!; **I'll speak f. to you** je vais vous parler franchement *ou* à cœur ouvert

frankness ['fræŋknɪs] *n* franchise *f*, sincérité *f*; **I admire her f. in telling him** j'admire la franchise *ou* la sincérité avec laquelle elle le lui a dit

frantic ['fræntɪk] *adj* (*rush, pace*) frénétique, forcené; **f. efforts** efforts effrénés; **in a f. attempt to ...** dans une folle tentative pour ...; **everyone was quite f. in their efforts to meet the deadline** tout le monde se déchaînait *ou* travaillait comme des fous pour essayer de respecter la date limite; **the last month had been absolutely f.** le mois précédent avait été complètement fou; **f. with pain/worry** fou, *f* folle de douleur/d'inquiétude; **it drives him f.** cela le met hors de lui; **I'm f.** je suis hors de moi; **I was f. when I heard she'd had an accident** j'ai paniqué en apprenant qu'elle avait eu un accident

frantically, *esp US* **franticly** ['fræntɪklɪ] *adv* (*to work, try*) frénétiquement, avec frénésie; **to rush f. around** courir frénétiquement dans tous les sens; **she was f. trying to help** elle essayait désespérément d'apporter son aide; **f. worried** fou, *f* folle d'inquiétude; *F* affreusement, terriblement; **I'm f. busy** je ne sais plus où donner de la tête

frat [fræt] *adj US F* = **fraternity** (**c**)

fraternal [frə'tɜːn(ə)l] *adj* fraternel

fraternally [frə'tɜːn(ə)lɪ] *adv* fraternellement

fraternity [frə'tɜːnɪtɪ] *n* (**a**) (*brotherliness*) fraternité *f* (**b**) (*group engaged in same activity*) confrérie *f*; **the banking/medical f.** la confrérie des banquiers/des médecins; **the sporting f.** la grande famille du sport (**c**) *US Univ* = organisation *f* d'étudiants; **f. house** maison *f* communautaire (où résident des étudiants appartenant à une même organisation)

fraternization [frætənaɪ'zeɪʃən] *n* fraternisation *f* (**with** avec); **f. with the enemy is forbidden** il est interdit de fraterniser avec l'ennemi

fraternize ['frætənaɪz] *vi* fraterniser (**with** avec); **they tend not to f. with each other** ils ont tendance à ne pas fraterniser

fraud [frɔːd] *n* (**a**) (*deception*) supercherie *f*, tromperie *f*; *Jur* fraude *f*, dol *m*; **to obtain sth by f.** obtenir qch frauduleusement *ou* par fraude; **guilty of f.** coupable de manœuvres frauduleuses; **he had carried out a wages f.** il avait fraudé sur les salaires; **the f. squad** la brigade de (la police chargée de) la répression des fraudes (**b**) (*person*) imposteur *m*; (*thing, place*) farce *f*, attrape *f*; **this place is a f.** cet endroit ne répond pas à la réputation qu'on lui a faite

fraudulence ['frɔːdjʊləns] *n* (*of transaction*) caractère *m* frauduleux; (*of concerns, sentiments*) fausseté *f*

fraudulent ['frɔːdjʊlənt] *adj* (*false*) (*sympathy, feelings*) faux, *f* fausse, affecté; (*charge, accusation*) faux; *Jur* (*bankrupt, transaction*) frauduleux

fraudulently ['frɔːdjʊləntlɪ] *adv* frauduleusement

fraught [frɔːt] *adj* (**a**) plein (**with problems** de problèmes); **the voyage was f. with danger** la traversée a été remplie *ou* pleine d'embûches; **an atmosphere f. with emotion/tension** une atmosphère chargée d'émotion/de tension; **things have been rather f.** l'atmosphère est assez tendue; **a f. day** une journée stressante (**b**) (*distressing*) pénible; **it's a f. subject** c'est un thème ardu (**c**) (*person*) (*distressed*) désespéré; (*anxious*) inquiet

fray[1] [freɪ] *n* (*brawl*) bagarre *f*, échauffourée *f*, mêlée *f*; **in the thick of the f.** au plus épais de la mêlée; **to enter the f.** descendre dans l'arène; **to return to the f.** rentrer en lice; **ready for the f.** prêt à entrer dans la mêlée

fray[2] **1** *vt* (*material etc*) érailler, effiler **2** *vi* (**a**) (*of material*) (*at edges*) s'effilocher, s'effiler; (*at collar, seams*) s'élimer (**b**) (*of nerves*) être à vif; (*of tempers*) s'échauffer

frayed [freɪd] *adj* (**a**) (*cloth, garment etc*) (*at edges*) effiloché, effrangé; (*at collar, seams*) élimé; (*rope*) usé (**b**) (*nerves*) à vif; **my nerves are f.** je suis à bout de nerfs; **tempers were getting a little f.** tout le monde commençait à être à bout de nerfs

frazzle ['fræz(ə)l] *n F* **to be worn to a f.** (*of person*) être complètement éreinté; **a joint cooked** *or* **burnt to a f.** un rôti calciné; **you look burnt to a f.** (*by sun*) tu as l'air d'avoir pris un de ces coups de soleil

frazzled ['fræzəld] *adj F* (**a**) (*mentally*) à bout de nerfs; **his nerves were still f.** il était encore à bout de nerfs (**b**) (*burnt*) calciné; **I got f. on the beach** je me suis pris un gros coup de soleil sur la plage

freak[1] [friːk] *n* (**a**) **f. (of nature)** monstre *m*, phénomène *m*; **a circus f.** un phénomène de cirque; **what kind of a f. would do something like that?** il faut être taré pour faire un truc pareil!; **people treat me as some kind of f.** (*because of what I think, do etc*) les gens me trouvent anormal; **by some f. (of fortune) he won** par un coup de chance il a gagné; **f. accident** accident *m* bizarre; **f. show** exhibition *f* de monstres; **f. storm** orage *m* inattendu; **f. weather** temps *m* anormal (**b**) (*enthusiast*) fana *mf*; **jazz/film f.** fana de jazz/cinéma

freak[2] *vi* = **freak out 1**

▶ **freak out** *F* **1** *vi* (**a**) (*become angry*) piquer une crise (**at** contre; **about** à propos de); (*be shocked, scared*) flipper, avoir les boules; (*become mentally unbalanced*) être déboussolé; (*of drug taker*) se défoncer; **mum'll f. out when she sees that mess** Maman va piquer une crise quand elle verra tout ce désordre (**b**) (*dance etc with abandon*) s'éclater (**to the music** sur la musique) **2** *vtsep* (*person*) (*shock, scare*) mettre les boules à, faire flipper; (*mentally unbalance*) rendre dingue

freakish ['friːkɪʃ] *adj* (**a**) (*weather etc*) insolite, anormal (**b**) (*imagination, idea, appearance, hairdo*) bizarre; (*stronger*) délirant; **f. notion** délire *m*

freaky ['friːkɪ] *adj* (*person, appearance etc*) bizarre; (*stronger*) délirant

freckle ['frek(ə)l] *n* tache *f* de rousseur; **she's got freckles** elle a des taches de rousseur

freckled ['frek(ə)ld] *adj* (**a**) (*person, face, arm etc*) couvert de taches de rousseur (**b**) (*animal's coat*) tacheté

freckly ['freklɪ] *adj F* = **freckled**

Frederick the Great ['fred(ə)rɪk] *n Hist* Frédéric *m* le Grand

free[1] [friː] **1** *adj* (**a**) (*unrestricted*) (*person, animal, movement, translation*) libre; *Ch* (*gas*) (à l'état) libre, non combiné; **to set f.** (*prisoner, hostage*) relâcher, remettre en liberté; (*slave*) affranchir; (*person*) (*from relationship, contract*) libérer; (*bird*) laisser s'envoler; **to break f.** (*of bonds*) se dégager (**of** de); (*escape*) s'échapper; **to be allowed to go f.** être mis en liberté, être relâché; **to be (entirely) f. to do sth** être (entièrement) libre de faire qch; **I am f. to do what I please** je suis libre de mes mouvements; **f. from** *or* **of sth** débarrassé de qch; **the area is now f. of** *or* **from contamination** cette zone a été complètement décontaminée; **to remain f. of** *or* **from sth** être préservé de qch; **to be f. of sb** être débarrassé de qn; **to be f. from care** *or* **worry** *or* **anxiety** être sans souci; **she's f. and graceful in all her actions** elle fait tout avec aisance et grâce; **as f. as the air** *or* **a bird** libre comme l'air; *Fig* **it's a f. country** on est en démocratie; **with his f. hand** avec sa main libre; *Fig* **to have a f. hand** avoir pleine liberté d'action, avoir ses coudées franches (**to do** pour faire); **to give** *or* **allow sb a f. hand** donner carte blanche à qn; **to make a f. choice** décider librement *ou* en toute liberté; **f. climbing** escalade *f* libre, libre *m*; *Sch* **f. composition** composition *f* libre; *Com* **f. agent** agent *m* indépendant; *Fig* **to be a f. agent** être libre de ses mouvements; **f. diving** plongée *f* sous-marine autonome; **f. end** (*of rope*) extrémité *f* libre; **right of f. entry** droit *m* de passer librement les frontières; **f. fall** (*of weight, parachutist*) chute *f* libre; **f. love** union *f* libre; *Jur* **f. pardon** grâce *f*; *Com* **f. port** port *m* franc; **f. press** presse *f* libre; **f. speech** libre parole *f*; **f. spirit** esprit *m* libre; *Liter* **f. verse** vers *mpl* libres; *Pol* **f. vote** vote *m* libre; *Cycling* **f. wheel** roue *f* libre; **f. will** libre arbitre *m*; **of one's own f. will** de (son) propre gré; *Pol* **the f. world** le monde libre; *Com* **f. zone** zone *f* franche

(**b**) (*unoccupied*) libre; *Tel* (*line*) libre; **is this table f.?** est-ce que cette table est libre?; **I am f. tomorrow** je suis libre demain; **to have some time f.** avoir du temps libre; **f. time** temps *m* libre, loisir *m*

(**c**) (*without charge*) (*concert, sample etc*) gratuit; *Th* (*ticket*) de faveur; **it came f. with the magazine** c'était en prime pour l'achat du magazine; *Fig* **there's no such thing as a f. lunch** tout se paie; **f. demonstration** démonstration gracieuse; **admission f.** entrée gratuite; *Com* **delivery f.** livré franco *inv*; **post f.** franco de port; *Com* **f. alongside ship** franco long du quai; *Com* **f. at** franco rendu; *Com* **f. at frontier** franco frontière; *Com* **f. carrier** franco transporteur; *Com* **f. destination** franco rendu point de destination; *Com* **f. of average** franc de toute avarie; **f. of customs duty** franco de douane; *Fin* **f. of duty** (*in customs*) exempt de droits d'entrée; **to import sth f. of duty** faire entrer qch en franchise; **f. of packing charges** franco d'emballage; **f. of tax** franc d'impôts; *Fin* **interest f. of tax** intérêts nets *ou* exempts d'impôt; **f. of VAT** en franchise de TVA; **f. on board** franco à bord; *Com* **f. on rail** franco wagon; **f. copy** (*in publishing*) spécimen *m*; *Com* **f. gift** prime *f*, cadeau *m*; **f. trial** essai *m* gratuit; **f. trial period** période *f* d'essai gratuit

(**d**) (*generous*) (*person*) libéral, généreux; **to be f. with one's time** être généreux de son temps; **to be f. with one's money** être prodigue de son argent; **he was very f. with his advice** il a été très prodigue en conseils

(**e**) *esp Pej* (*uninhibited*) **you'll like it here, things are f. and easy** tu te plairas ici, on ne fait pas de façons; **things are a bit too f. and easy here** ici on est un peu trop sans gêne *ou* désinvolte; **he's pretty f. and easy as a boss** il est plutôt décontracté comme patron; **to make f. with sth** se servir de qch sans se gêner; **he made very f. with my whisky** il ne se gênait pas pour boire mon whisky; **to be rather f. in one's conversation** tenir des propos peu convenables; *F* **feel f.** faites comme chez vous; *F* **may I take another? – feel f.** puis-j'en reprendre? – je vous en prie; **feel f. to speak your mind** n'hésitez pas à dire ce que vous pensez

2 *adv* (**a**) (*without charge*) franco, gratuitement; **catalogue sent f. on request** catalogue gratuit sur demande; **the museum is open f. on Saturdays** l'entrée du musée est gratuite le samedi; **for f.**, *F* **f. gratis and for nothing** gratis; **to get sth for f.** obtenir qch gratis; **you are allowed to bring in half a litre f.** (*exempt from duty*) il y a une tolérance d'un demi-litre

(**b**) (*followed by a present participle*) **f. flowing** qui coule abondamment; **f. flowering** qui fleurit abondamment

free[2] *vt* (**freed**; **freeing**) (**a**) (*prisoner, caged animal etc*) libérer, relâcher; (*of rescuer*) (*hostage, prisoner*) délivrer; (*slave, colony*) affranchir; (*sth stuck, one's foot etc*) dégager; (*funds*) dégager; (*time, space*) libérer; **to f. sb's hands** (*untie*) détacher les mains de qn; **to f. oneself from sb's grasp** se dégager des mains de qn; **to f. sb from an obligation** libérer qn d'une obligation; **to f. oneself from one's commitments** se libérer *ou* se délier de ses engagements; **to f. sb to do sth** libérer qn pour qu'il puisse faire qch; **to f. the franc** libéraliser le cours du franc (**b**) (*clear obstructions from*) débarrasser (**from, of** de); (*path etc*) dégager; *MecE etc* (*part*) dégager; (*blocked filter*) désobstruer; (*pump*) dégorger; **to f. a property** (**from mortgage**) déshypothéquer une propriété

▶ **free up** *vtsep* (*funds*) dégager; (*time, space*) libérer; **this will f. up sales people to do more actual selling** cela donnera plus de temps au personnel de vente pour se consacrer à la vente même

-free [fri:] *suff* sans; **sugar/gluten/***etc***-f.** sans sucre/gluten/*etc*

free association *n Psy* association *f* d'idées; (*word association*) association libre

freebie, freebee ['fri:bi:] *n F* (*for customer etc*) cadeau *m*; (*perk*) à-côté *m*; **it was a f. with the magazine** c'était un cadeau offert avec le magazine

freeboard ['fri:bɔ:d] *n Naut* (franc-)bord *m*

freeborn ['fri:bɔ:n] *adj* libre de naissance, né libre

freedom ['fri:dəm] *n* (**a**) liberté *f*; **in f.** en liberté; **we have less f. now** nous sommes moins libres maintenant; **f. to do sth** liberté de faire qch; **f. to overfly a country without landing** droit *m* de survol d'un État; **f. of information/speech/worship** liberté d'information/d'expression/de culte; **f. of action** liberté d'action; **freedoms of the air** libertés *fpl* de l'air; **f. of movement** liberté de mouvement; **f. of the press** liberté *f* de la presse; **f. fighter** guérillero *m*, révolutionnaire *mf*

(**b**) (*frankness*) (*of a conversation etc*) franchise *f*; *Pej* (*uninhibitedness*) sans-gêne *m*, familiarité *f*; **to speak with complete f.** parler en toute liberté

(**c**) (*exemption*) exemption *f*, franchise *f*; **f. from tax** exemption d'impôts; **with my new f. from worry** désormais libéré de mes inquiétudes

(**d**) (*free use*) **the f. of sth** le libre usage de qch; **the f. of the seas** la liberté de la haute mer; **f. of the city** droit *m* de cité; (*honorary citizenship*) citoyenneté *f* d'honneur d'une ville; **to receive the f. of a city** être nommé citoyen/citoyenne d'honneur d'une ville; **to give sb the f. of one's library** mettre sa bibliothèque à la disposition de qn

free enterprise *n Econ* libre entreprise *f*

Freefone® ['fri:fəʊn] *n Br Tel* appel *m* gratuit, numéro *m* vert; **call F. 123** composez le numéro vert 123

free-for-all *n F* **f.** (**fight**) rixe *f*, bagarre *f*, mêlée *f*; **when the food arrived the queue quickly turned into a f.** quand la nourriture est arrivée la file d'attente a tourné en pagaille générale

free-form *adj Art* à forme libre; **f. jazz** free-jazz *m*

Free France *n Hist* la France libre

Free French *n Hist* Français *mpl* libres

freehand ['fri:hænd] *adj, adv Art* à main levée

free-handed [fri:'hændɪd] *adj* généreux

freehold ['fri:həʊld] *Jur* **1** *adj* tenu en propriété perpétuelle et libre **2** *n* (*property*) propriété *f* foncière perpétuelle et libre; **to buy the f.** acheter en pleine propriété

freeholder ['fri:həʊldər] *n* propriétaire *m* foncier (à perpétuité)

free house *n Br Com* = débit *m* de boissons qui est libre de vendre les produits de n'importe quelle brasserie

freeing ['fri:ɪŋ] *n* (*of prisoner*) libération *f*; (*of slave*) affranchissement *m*; (*of funds, resources*) dégagement *m*

free kick *n Fb* coup *m* franc

freelance[1] ['fri:lɑ:ns] **1** *n* indépendant, -ante, free-lance *mf inv*; (*esp journalist etc*) indépendant, -ante, pigiste *mf*; **to work as a f.** travailler en indépendant *ou* free-lance; (*esp journalist*) travailler comme pigiste *ou* en indépendant, travailler à la pige

2 *adj* (*contributor, worker*) free-lance, indépendant; (*esp journalist etc*) qui travaille à la pige, free-lance; (*rates*) du travail free-lance; *Journ* **f. work** travail indépendant *ou* à la pige *ou* (en) free-lance

3 *adv* **to work f.** travailler en indépendant *ou* en free-lance; (*esp journalist*) travailler comme pigiste *ou* en indépendant, travailler à la pige

freelance[2] *vi* travailler en indépendant *ou* en free-lance; (*esp journalist*) faire de la pige, travailler comme pigiste *ou* en indépendant

freelancer ['fri:lɑ:nsər] *n* free-lance *mf*; (*esp journalist*) pigiste *mf*

freeload ['fri:ləʊd] *vi esp Am F* parasiter

freeloader ['fri:ləʊdər] *n esp Am F* pique-assiette *mf inv*, parasite *m*

freely ['fri:lɪ] *adv* (**a**) (*copiously, abundantly*) librement; **to give f. to sb** faire des libéralités à qn; **to give out advice f.** se répandre en conseils; **the wine was flowing f.** le vin coulait à flots (**b**) (*without hindrance*) librement; (*to speak, act etc*) en toute liberté; **to speak f. to sb** parler à qn à cœur ouvert; **f. available** (*for sale*) en vente libre; (*easy to get hold of*) qu'on peut se procurer facilement; **I f. admit that ...** j'avoue sans peine que ...

freeman, *pl* **-men** ['fri:mən] *n* (**a**) *Hist* homme *m* libre (**b**) (*of city*) citoyen *m* d'honneur; **to be made a f. of the city** être nommé citoyen d'honneur

free market *n Econ* économie *f* de marché

freemason ['fri:meɪs(ə)n] *n* franc-maçon, *pl* francs-maçons

freemasonry ['fri:meɪs(ə)nrɪ] *n* franc-maçonnerie *f*

Freepost® ['fri:pəʊst] *n Br* correspondance-réponse *f*

free radical *n Med* radical *m* libre

free-range *adj* (*eggs, chicken*) de ferme

freesia ['fri:ʒə] *n* (*plant*) freesia *m*

free-spoken *adj* (*person*) franc, *f* franche, qui parle ouvertement

freestanding ['fri:'stændɪŋ] *adj* (*wall etc*) auto-portant; *Archit* (*column*) isolé; (*clinic, restaurant, machine*) autonome

freestyle ['fri:staɪl] *n Swimming* nage *f* libre; (*wrestling*) lutte *f* libre

freethinker ['fri:θɪŋkər] *n Old-fashioned* libre penseur, -euse

free trade *n Econ* libre-échange *m*; **f. area** zone *f* de libre-échange

free-trader *n Econ* libre-échangiste *mf*, *pl* libre-échangistes

freeware *n Comptr* freeware *m*, logiciel *m* public; **f. programs** freewares *mpl*, logiciels *mpl* publics

freeway ['fri:weɪ] *n US* autoroute *f* (gratuite)

freewheel[1] ['fri:wi:l] *vi* (**a**) *Cycling* être en roue libre; *Aut* rouler au point mort; **to f. down a hill** descendre une côte en roue libre/au point mort (**b**) *esp Am* (*travel in carefree fashion*) se laisser aller, aller sans but précis

freewheel[2] *n* roue *f* libre

freewheeling ['fri:wi:lɪŋ] *adj F* (*discussion*) libre; **her f. approach to such serious matters** sa façon un peu légère *ou* désinvolte de traiter des questions aussi sérieuses; **to lead a f. existence** rouler sa bosse

freeze[1] [fri:z] *n* (**a**) *Met* gel *m*, gelée *f*; **the big f.** la grande gelée; **we had a big f. last winter** il a gelé très fort l'hiver dernier (**b**) (*act of fixing*) **price and wage f.** blocage *m* des prix et des salaires; **to put a f. on further changes/expenditure** bloquer le processus de changement/les dépenses

freeze[2] (*pt* **froze** [frəʊz]; *pp* **frozen** [frəʊz(ə)n]) **1** *v impers* **it's freezing** il gèle

2 *vi* (**a**) (*of liquid*) geler; (*of food, washing on line*) se congeler; **the river has frozen** la rivière est prise *ou* a gelé; **the earth had frozen hard** la terre avait gelé; **the sausages had f. together** les saucisses s'étaient congelées et ne formaient plus qu'un bloc; **his hand had frozen to the ice axe** le gel avait collé sa main au piolet; **the gears had frozen together** les vitesses étaient gelées; **it has frozen solid** (*mud*) elle est dure de gel; (*food*) il est congelé; (*milk*) il est gelé; **to f. to death** mourir de froid; *F* **I'm freezing** je meurs de froid, je gèle; *F* **we froze in our thin clothes** on n'était pas assez couvert, on s'est caillé; **the smile froze on his lips** le sourire se figea sur ses lèvres

(**b**) (*of person*) (*not move*) rester cloué sur place, se figer; (*stiffen*) se raidir, se guinder; (*become speechless*) rester sans voix; **f.!** on ne bouge plus!; **I froze at the sound of his voice** je me suis immobilisé au son de sa voix

3 *vt* (**a**) geler, congeler; (*meat*) congeler; **to f. the blood (in one's veins)** glacer le sang *ou* le cœur; **she froze them with a look** d'un regard elle les glaça sur place; **to be frozen to death** mourir de froid

(**b**) *Fin* (*credit, currency, prices*) geler; (*wages*) bloquer; **to f. assets** immobiliser des actifs

(**c**) *Med* insensibiliser par anesthésie locale

(**d**) **to f. a film** faire un arrêt sur image

▶ **freeze out** *vtsep F* (*exclude*) (*person*) évincer; (*rival*) supplanter; **to f. sb out of the conversation** exclure qn de la conversation

▶ **freeze over** *vi* **the pond has/is frozen over** l'étang a/est gelé d'un bout à l'autre

▶ **freeze up** *vi* (*become frozen*) geler; *Fig* (*of person*) rester sans voix; **the river has frozen up** la rivière est prise *ou* gelée; **the radiator froze up** le radiateur a gelé

freeze-dry *vt* (*serum etc*) lyophiliser

freeze-frame *n Cin* arrêt *m* sur image

freezer ['fri:zər] *n* congélateur *m*; **f. (compartment)** (*in refrigerator*) freezer *m*; **chest f.** congélateur bahut

freeze-up *n Met* gelée *f*

freezing ['fri:zɪŋ] **1** *adj* (*weather, room, temperature etc*) glacial, -als; **it's f. in here!** ça caille ici!; **I'm f.** je gèle

2 *adv* **f. cold** glacé; **the weather's f. cold** il fait un temps glacial; **I'm f. cold** je suis gelé; **a f. cold shower** une douche glacée

3 *n* (**a**) (*becoming frozen*) congélation *f*, gel *m*; **the temperature was below f.** la température était inférieure à zéro (**b**) (*making frozen*) (*of liquid etc*) réfrigération *f*; (*of meat*) congélation *f*; **f. compartment** (*in refrigerator*) freezer *m*; **f. instructions** (*for food*) consignes *fpl* pour la congélation; **f. mixture** mélange *m* réfrigérant

(**c**) *Fin* (*of wages etc*) blocage *m*; (*of credit, prices*) gel *m*

freezing point *n Phys* point *m* de congélation; **the thermometer is at f.** le thermomètre est à zéro

freight[1] [freɪt] *n* (**a**) (*transport*) fret *m*, transport *m* (de marchandises); **air f.** transport par air

(**b**) (*cargo of ship*) fret *m*, cargaison *f*, chargement *m*; *Rail, Av* marchandises *fpl* (transportées); **f. bill** connaissement *m*; *Am Rail* **f. car** wagon *m* à *ou* de marchandises; **f. consolidator** groupeur *m*; **f. depot** dépôt *m* de fret; *Av* **f. plane** avion-cargo *m*, *pl* avions-cargos, avion *m* de fret; *Av* **f. terminal** terminal *m* de fret; **f. ton** tonneau *m* de fret; **f. train** train *m* de marchandises

(**c**) (*price of transport*) fret *m*; **f. charges** tarifs *mpl* de fret; **f. price** prix *m* de transport

freight[2] *vt* (**a**) (*load*) (*vessel*) charger (**b**) (*hire*) (*ship*) (af)fréter; (*of owner*) donner à fret (**c**) *esp Am* (*transport*) transporter

freightage ['freɪtɪdʒ] *n* fret *m*; (*transport*) transport *m*

freight collect *adv Com* port avancé

freighter ['freɪtər] *n* (**a**) (*ship*) cargo *m*, navire *m* de charge; *Am Rail* wagon *m* de marchandises; *Av* avion-cargo *m*, *pl* avions-cargos, avion *m* de fret (**b**) (*hirer*) (*of ship*) affréteur *m* (**c**) *Am* (*of goods carried overland*) consignateur, -trice (**d**) (*operator of transport company*) entrepreneur *m* de transports, exportateur *m*

freight forward *adv Com* port avancé

freight forwarder *n* agent *m* de fret, transitaire *m*

freight forwarding *n* transit *m*

freightliner ['freɪtlaɪnər] *n Rail* train *m* de marchandises en conteneurs, train *m* conteneur

French [frentʃ] **1** *adj* français; (*dish, fashion etc*) à la française; (*class, teacher*) de français; *F* **to take F. leave** filer à l'anglaise; **the F. Ambassador** l'ambassadeur, -drice de France; **F. bean** haricot *m* vert; **F. bread** pain *m* à la française; **F. chalk** craie *f* de tailleur; *Culin* **F. dressing** vinaigrette *f*; *esp Am Culin* **F. fried potatoes** pommes *fpl* de terre frites; **F. fries** frites *fpl*; *Mus* **F. horn** cor *m* d'harmonie; **F. kiss** patin *m*; *Hum* **'F. lessons (given)'** = offre de services de nature sexuelle; *Br Sl* **F. letter** capote *f* anglaise; **F. loaf** *or* **stick** baguette *f*; **F. pleat** (*hairstyle*) chignon *m*; **F. polish** vernis *m* au tampon; **F. service** (*in restaurant*) service *m* à la française *ou* au guéridon; *Culin* **F. toast** = pain *m* perdu; *Br* **F. windows,** *Am* **F. doors** porte-fenêtre *f*, *pl* portes-fenêtres

2 *n* (**a**) *Ling* français *m*; **to speak F.** parler français; **to learn/know F.** apprendre/savoir parler le français; **say it in F.** dites-le en français; **her F. is excellent** elle parle très bien (le) français; **Canadian F.** français canadien *ou* du Canada; *Hum* **excuse my F.** passez-moi l'expression

(**b**) **the F.** *pl* (*people*) les Français *mpl*

(**c**) *Sl* (*blow-job*) pipe *f*

French Canada *n Geog* le Canada français

French Canadian *n* (*person*) Canadien, -ienne français(e); (*language*) français *m* canadien

French Foreign Legion *n Mil* Légion *f* étrangère

Frenchify ['frentʃɪfaɪ] *vt Pej* (*one's style etc*) franciser

Frenchman, *pl* **-men** ['frentʃmən] *n* Français *m*

French-polish *vt* (*table etc*) vernir au tampon

French-speaking *adj* (*native speaker*) francophone; (*who can speak French*) qui parle français; **the F. world** la francophonie

French Switzerland *n Geog* la Suisse Romande

French West Indies *n Geog* Antilles *fpl* Françaises

Frenchwoman, *pl* **-women** ['frentʃwʊmən, -wɪmɪn] *n* Française *f*

Frenchy ['frentʃɪ] *n Old-fashioned F* Français, -aise

frenetic [frə'netɪk] *adj* (*person, action etc*) frénétique

frenetically [frə'netɪklɪ] *adv* frénétiquement

frenzied ['frenzɪd] *adj* (*person*) affolé, forcené; (*rage*) fou, *f* folle; (*applause, activity*) frénétique; (*attack, mob*) déchaîné; **f. with worry/rage** fou d'inquiétude/de rage; **there was a f. look in her eye** elle avait un regard halluciné

frenzy ['frenzɪ] *n* (*of despair etc*) frénésie *f*, folie *f*; **in a f. of excitement/hatred** dans un accès d'excitation/de haine; **to work oneself into a f.** (*get angry, upset*) se mettre dans tous ses états; **the children worked themselves into a f.** (**of excitement**) les enfants se sont mis dans un état de surexcitation folle

frequency ['fri:kwənsɪ] *n* (**a**) fréquence *f*; **to recur with increasing f.** se faire de plus en plus fréquent; **the increasing f. of his absences** ses absences de plus en plus fréquentes; *Math* **f. of errors** répartition *f* des erreurs; **f. marketing programme** programme *m* mercatique de fidélisation (**b**) *Phys* fréquence *f*; *El* **high/low f.** haute/basse fréquence; *Rad* **very high f.** très haute fréquence; **f. band** bande *f* de fréquences; **f. modulation** modulation *f* de fréquence; **f. range** gamme *f* de fréquences

frequent[1] ['fri:kwənt] *adj* (*visits etc*) fréquent; (*visitor*) assidu; (*customer*) habituel; (*widespread*) très répandu; (*explanation, state of affairs etc*) commun, habituel; **he became a f. visitor to our house** c'est devenu un habitué de la maison; **it is a f. occurrence** cela se produit souvent; **it is a f. sight in the summer months** on en voit souvent pendant les mois d'été; **this bird is a f. visitor to our shores** cet oiseau visite régulièrement nos rivages; **f. theatregoers** des gens qui vont souvent au théâtre; **the doctor recommended f. changes of the dressing** le docteur a recommandé que le pansement soit changé souvent; **it's quite a f. practice** c'est une coutume assez répandue; *Mktg* **f. flyer club** club *m* de fidélité de compagnie aérienne; *Mktg* **f. flyer programme** programme *m* de fidélisation des passagers de compagnies aériennes; *Mktg* **f. user card** carte *f* de fidélité; *Mktg* **f. user programme** programme *m* de fidélisation

frequent[2] [frɪ'kwent] *vt* fréquenter; (*theatres, pubs etc*) hanter

frequenter [frɪ'kwentər] *n* (*of a house etc*) habitué, -ée, familier *m*; **a great f. of public houses** un pilier de bar

frequently ['fri:kwəntlɪ] *adv* fréquemment; **I f. can't remember my address** il m'arrive fréquemment de ne pas pouvoir me souvenir de mon adresse; **how f.?** avec quelle fréquence?, *F* tous les combien?; **I can't say how f. it happened** je ne saurais pas dire à quelle fréquence cela se produisait

fresco, *pl* **-o (e)s** ['freskəʊ, -əʊz] *n Art* fresque *f*; **to paint in f.** peindre à fresque; **f. painter** fresquiste *mf*

fresh [freʃ] **1** *adj* (**a**) (*fruit, eggs, fish, colour etc*) frais, *f* fraîche; (*person*) (*full of vigour*) vigoureux, alerte; (*refreshed*) (*after sleep, rest*) dispos; (*horse*) fougueux, animé; (*complexion*) frais, fleuri; **as f. as a daisy** frais et dispos; **a f.-faced youth** un jeune homme au teint frais; **I felt fresher after a shower** une douche m'a rafraîchi

(**b**) (*new*) nouveau, -el, *f* -elle; (*news, blood, footprints*) frais, *f* fraîche; **a f. change of clothes/socks** des habits/chaussettes de rechange; **f. dangers to face** de nouveaux dangers à affronter; **to make a f. start on a problem** reprendre un problème à zéro; **to put f. courage into sb** ranimer le courage de qn; **to put f. water in the fish tank** changer l'eau de l'aquarium; **f. outbreak of fire/disease** reprise *f* du feu/de la maladie; **it is still f. in my mind** je l'ai encore frais à la mémoire; **the wound was f.** la plaie était récente; **f. from London** nouvellement arrivé de Londres; **and now, f. from his tour of the States, we present ...** et maintenant, tout juste rentré de sa tournée aux États-Unis, nous vous présentons ...; **the bread was f. from the oven** le pain sortait du four; **f. paragraph** nouveau paragraphe; **f. troops** troupes fraîches

(**c**) (*air*) frais, *f* fraîche, pur; (*cool*) frais; **it's f. this morning** il fait frais ce matin; **in the f. air** au grand air, en plein air; **to let f. air into a room** aérer une pièce; *F* **f.-air fiend** fanatique *mf* d'air frais; (*outdoor person*) fanatique du grand air; *Naut* **f. breeze** bonne brise; **f. water** eau douce

(**d**) *esp Am F* (*impudent*) effronté; **to get f. with a girl** prendre des libertés avec une jeune fille; **don't (you) get f. with me!** ne te fiche pas de moi!

2 *adv* (*arrived, painted etc*) fraîchement, nouvellement, récemment; **f.-cut flowers** fleurs nouvellement cueillies; *esp Am* **to be f. out of sth** ne plus avoir de qch; **f.-frozen** congelé à la fabrication; (*fish*) congelé sur le bateau

freshen ['freʃən] **1** *vi* (*of temperature*) (se) rafraîchir; (*of wind, weather*) fraîchir **2** *vt* (*air, one's memory etc*) rafraîchir; *esp Am* **can I f. your drink?** est-ce que je vous sers un autre verre?

▶ **freshen up 1** *vi* (*wash*) faire un brin de toilette **2** *vtsep* (**a**) (*renew*) (*makeup*) retoucher; **to f. up the paint** (r)aviver la couleur; **to f. up one's lipstick** se remettre du rouge à lèvres; **to f. oneself up** faire un brin de toilette (**b**) (*change air in*) (*room*) aérer

fresher ['freʃər] *n Br F* = **freshman**

freshly ['freʃlɪ] *adv* (*with pp only*) fraîchement; **f. picked peaches** des pêches fraîchement cueillies; **f. baked** sortant du four; **f. squeezed orange juice** orange *f* pressée

freshman, *pl* **-men** ['freʃmən] *n Univ F* étudiant, -ante de première année

freshness ['freʃnɪs] *n* (**a**) (*of fruit, fish etc*) fraîcheur *f* (**b**) (*of event*) caractère *m* récent; (*of impression, approach etc*) fraîcheur *f* (**c**) (*of wind etc*) fraîcheur *f* (**d**) (*liveliness*) vigueur *f*, vivacité *f* (**e**) *esp Am F* (*impudence*) effronterie *f*

freshwater ['freʃwɔːtər] *adj (fish etc)* d'eau douce; **f. fishing** pêche *f* en eau douce

fret[1] [fret] *n F* **to be in a f.** être dans tous ses états; *(extremely worried)* se faire du mauvais sang *ou* de la bile

fret[2] (-tt-) **1** *vi (worry)* s'inquiéter, se tourmenter; **don't f.!** *(don't worry)* ne vous inquiétez pas!; *(don't upset yourself)* ne vous faites pas de bile!, ne vous faites pas de mauvais sang!; **child fretting for his mother** enfant qui réclame sa mère en pleurnichant; **she's fretting because her pony is missing** elle est dans tous ses états parce que son poney a disparu; **children always tend to f. in hospital** les enfants ont toujours tendance à se tourmenter quand ils sont à l'hôpital

2 *vt* **(a)** *(worry)* **don't f. yourself!** ne te tracasse pas!; **to f. one's life away** passer sa vie à se tracasser *ou* se tourmenter

(b) *(wear away)* ronger; **to f. a rope** érailler un cordage

fret[3] *n Mus (on guitar etc)* touchette *f*, touche *f*

fret[4] *vt Carp (wood)* découper; **f. saw** scie *f* à découper

fretful ['fretfʊl] *adj (anxious) (person)* inquiet, qui se fait du mauvais sang; *(voice)* inquiet; *(peevish)* grincheux; **f. baby** bébé agité

fretfully ['fretfʊlɪ] *adv (to speak, complain)* d'un ton grincheux; *(to look at sb)* d'un air chagrin

fretfulness ['fretfʊlnɪs] *n* irritabilité *f*

fretting ['fretɪŋ] *n* **(a)** *(worrying)* inquiétude *f* **(over** à propos de); *(being upset)* agitation *f*; **I wish he'd stop his f.!** si seulement il pouvait arrêter de se faire du mauvais sang! **(b)** *(of rope etc)* usure *f*

fretwork ['fretwɜːk] *n Carp (technique)* découpage *m*; *(finished work)* travail *m* ajouré, bois *m* découpé *ou* chantourné

Freudian ['frɔɪdɪən] *adj Psy* freudien; **F. slip** lapsus *m*

FRG [efɑː'dʒiː] *n (abbr* **Federal Republic of Germany)** RFA *f*

friable ['fraɪəb(ə)l] *adj (soil etc)* friable

friar ['fraɪər] *n Cathol* moine *m*, frère *m*, religieux *m*; **F. Bernard** Frère Bernard; **Grey Friars** Franciscains *mpl*; **Black Friars** Dominicains *mpl*; **White Friars** Carmes *mpl*; *Pharm* **f.'s balsam** baume *m* de benjoin

friary ['fraɪərɪ] *n* monastère *m*

fricassee[1] [frɪkə'siː] *n Culin* fricassée *f*; *(of rabbit or hare)* gibelotte *f*

fricassee[2] *vt Culin* fricasser

fricative ['frɪkətɪv] *Ling* **1** *adj (consonant)* fricatif **2** *n* fricative *f*

friction ['frɪkʃən] *n* **(a)** *Phys* friction *f*, frottement *m*; *(of two bodies)* frottement; *(of scalp etc)* friction *f*; *Aut* **f. clutch** embrayage *m* à friction; *Aut* **f. cylinder** cylindre *m* de friction; **f. drive** entraînement *m* par friction; *Comptr* **f. feed** avancement *m* par friction; **f. glove** *(for massage)* gant *m* de crin; *Aut* **f. lining** garniture *f* de friction; *Aut* **f. plate** plateau *m* de friction; *Am* **f. tape** chatterton *m* **(b)** *(disagreement)* friction *f*, désaccord *m*; **there's f. between them** il y a du tirage entre eux

Friday ['fraɪdɪ] *n* [①**A75-6,B-C; B58-9,B-C**] vendredi *m*; **he's coming (on) F.** il viendra vendredi; **he comes every F.** il vient tous les vendredis; **(Man) F.** *Liter* Vendredi; *Fig* factotum *m*, homme *m* à tout faire; *F* **girl F.** aide *f* de bureau

fridge [frɪdʒ] *n F* frigo *m*

fridge-freezer *n F* frigo *m* avec congélateur

fried [fraɪd] **1** *adj* frit; **they eat a lot of f. food** ils mangent beaucoup de friture; **f. eggs** œufs *mpl* sur le plat; **f. potatoes** pommes *fpl* de terre sautées **2** *pt, pp see* **fry**[1]

friend [frend] *n* **(a)** ami, *f* amie; *(acquaintance)* connaissance *f*; **we're the best of friends** nous sommes les meilleurs amis du monde; **let's be friends again** faisons la paix; **I'm offering you a bargain, my f.** *(to stranger)* cher ami, c'est une affaire que je vous propose; **I am speaking to you as a f.** je vous parle en ami(e); **that's what friends are for** c'est à ça que servent les amis; **she's been a good f. to us** elle a beaucoup fait pour nous; **we're just good friends** nous sommes bons amis, c'est tout!; **school f.** ami(e) *ou* camarade *mf* d'école; **man f.** *(pl* **men friends)** ami homme, *pl* amis hommes; **woman f.** *(pl* **women friends)** amie femme, *pl* amies femmes; *Old-fashioned* **lady f.** petite amie *f*; **to be friends with sb** être ami avec qn; **they've been friends for years** ils sont amis depuis des années; **to be more than friends** être plus qu'amis; **to make friends** *(with others)* se faire des amis; **they made friends** *(with each other)* ils sont devenus amis; **I made friends with them** nous sommes devenus amis, je suis devenu ami avec eux; *Prov* **a f. in need is a f. indeed** au besoin on connaît l'ami; **he has been a real f. in need** il ne m'a/l'a/*etc* pas abandonné dans le besoin; **you'd better be** *or* **stay friends with them** vous feriez bien de ne pas vous brouiller avec eux; **let us part friends** séparons-nous (en) bons amis; **he's no f. of mine** *(he's an enemy)* je ne le compte pas parmi mes amis; *(he means me no good)* il ne me veut pas de bien; **Britain is no f. of those who seek to ...** la Grande-Bretagne n'est pas favorable à ceux qui cherchent à ...; *Fig* **to have friends in high places** *or* **at court** avoir des protections *ou* des relations *ou* des amis influents; *Fig* **a f. at court** un ami en haut lieu *ou* bien placé; **f. or foe?** *(said by sentry)* qui va là?

(b) *(supporter) (of law and order etc)* ami, *f* amie, partisan *m*; *(of the arts etc)* patron, -onne; **f. of the poor** bienfaiteur, -trice des pauvres; **she's no f. of trade unionism** elle n'est pas favorable au syndicalisme; **the Friends of Canterbury Cathedral** la Société des Amis *ou* les Amis de la Cathédrale de Cantorbéry

(c) *Rel* **F.** *(Quaker)* Quaker, -eresse, Ami, -ie; **the Society of Friends** la Société des Amis

friendless ['frendlɪs] *adj* sans amis; **I am totally f. now** je n'ai plus aucun ami

friendliness ['frendlɪnɪs] *n* amabilité *f* **(to, towards** envers); **to show great f. towards sb** se montrer très aimable envers qn

friendly ['frendlɪ] **1** *adj* **(a)** *(people, smile, slap on the back, welcome)* amical; *(city, neighbours, face)* sympathique; *(well disposed)* favorable, favorablement disposé; *(dog)* gentil; *(quarrel, argument)* entre amis; **you should try to be a bit more f. to people** tu devrais essayer d'être un peu plus aimable; **why is he so f. all of a sudden?** pourquoi est-il aussi aimable tout à coup?; **to be f. with sb** être ami avec qn; **she's very f. with the boss all of a sudden** elle est très copine avec le patron tout d'un coup; **they became very f.** *(to each other)* ils se sont pris d'amitié l'un pour l'autre; **to get too f. with sb** se montrer trop familier avec qn; **piece of f. advice** avis amical; **someone ought to have a f. word with him and explain that ...** quelqu'un devrait lui expliquer gentiment que ...; **f. gathering** réunion d'amis; **in a f. manner** *or* **way** *(to talk, argue, smile)* amicalement; **to be on f. terms with sb** être en bons termes avec qn; **he gave me a f. wave** il m'a fait un signe amical de la main

(b) *(software, layout etc)* convivial

(c) *Mil* **to come under f. fire** tomber sous les tirs des siens; **f. forces** troupes amies *ou* alliées; **is this aircraft f.?** est-ce que cet avion est des nôtres?; **f. nation** pays ami; *Br Fin* **f. society** société *f* de mutualité

2 *n Sp* match *m* amical

-friendly ['frendlɪ] *suff* **ozone-f.** qui préserve la couche d'ozone; **environment-f.** qui respecte l'environnement

Friendly Islands (the) *npl* Tonga *m*, les îles *fpl* des Amis

friendship ['frendʃɪp] *n* amitié *f*; **to form a f. with sb** se lier (d'amitié) avec qn; **to lose sb's f.** perdre l'amitié de qn; **her f. means more to me than anything** notre amitié est ce qu'il y a de plus important pour moi; *esp Fml* **to enjoy the f. of sb** cotoyer qn

fries [fraɪz] *npl esp Am F* **(French) f.** frites *fpl*

Friesian ['friːʒən] **1** *adj* frison **2** *n* **(a)** *(person)* Frison, -onne; *(cow)* frisonne *f* **(b)** *Ling* frison *m*

frieze [friːz] *n* **(a)** *Archit* frise *f* **(b)** *(of wallpaper)* bordure *f*

frig [frɪg] *Vulg* **1** *vt (have sex with)* baiser avec **2** *vi (of woman)* se masturber, se toucher

▶ **frig about, frig around** *vi Sl (waste time)* traînailler, glandouiller; *(play the fool)* déconner

▶ **frig off** *vi Sl* **f. off!** va te faire foutre!

frigate ['frɪgət] *n* **(a)** *Naut* frégate *f*, escorteur *m* **(b) f. (bird)** frégate *f*

frigging ['frɪgɪŋ] *Sl* **1** *adj* foutu; **this f. car** cette foutue bagnole, cette putain de bagnole; **what a f. waste of time!** putain, quelle perte de temps!; **he's a f. nuisance** il est chiant comme pas deux **2** *adv* foutrement

fright [fraɪt] *n* **(a)** peur *f*, effroi *m*; **to take f.** s'effrayer **(at** de); **to give sb a f.** faire peur à qn; **to get** *or* **be given the f. of one's life** avoir une peur bleue; *F* **I got an awful f.** j'ai eu une sacrée peur **(b)** *F* **what a f. you look!** tu es à faire peur!; **that dress makes you look a real f.!** tu es moche à faire peur dans cette robe!

frighten ['fraɪt(ə)n] **1** *vt* effrayer, faire peur à; **it frightens him/her** cela lui fait peur; **it frightens me that so many people believe him** ça m'effraie que tant de personnes le croient; **he is easily frightened** il s'effraie pour un rien; **these animals are easily frightened** ces animaux s'effarouchent d'un rien; **to f. sb into doing sth** faire peur à qn pour qu'il fasse qch; **to f. sb out of doing sth** faire peur à qn et le dissuader de faire qch; *F* **to f. the life** *or* **the living daylights out of sb** faire mourir qn de peur; *F* **to f. sb out of their wits, to f. the wits out of sb** rendre qn fou de peur; **you f. me to death** vous me faites mourir de peur

2 *vi* **I don't f. easily** c'est difficile de me faire peur; **he frightens easily** il s'effraie pour un rien

▶ **frighten away** *or* **off** *vtsep* (*scare*) (*animal*) effaroucher; (*person*) faire peur à, faire fuir

frightened ['fraɪt(ə)nd] *adj* (*look, voice etc*) apeuré; **to be** *or* **feel f.** avoir peur (**of** de); **I wasn't as f. as you were** je n'avais pas aussi peur que vous; **he's a very f. man** il a très peur; **I was f. of waking her** j'avais peur de la réveiller; **f. out of one's wits** terrifié; **f. to death** mort de peur

frightening ['fraɪt(ə)nɪŋ] *adj* effrayant

frighteningly ['fraɪt(ə)nɪŋlɪ] *adv* à faire peur; **they were f. close** ils se rapprochaient dangereusement; **they look f. similar** ils se ressemblent tellement que c'en est effrayant; **f. expensive** terriblement cher, hors de prix

frightful ['fraɪtfʊl] *adj* effroyable, épouvantable, affreux

frightfully ['fraɪtfʊlɪ] *adv* affreusement; **he is f. ugly** il est laid à faire peur; **I am f. sorry** je regrette énormément; **f. rich/stupid/expensive** incroyablement riche/stupide/cher; *F Hum* **f. f.** *maniérisme utilisé pour décrire les manières et l'accent de la haute bourgeoisie britannique*; *par ex.* his family have several thousand acres in Hertfordshire, keep racehorses, are absolutely loaded and are terribly f. f.

frightfulness ['fraɪtfʊlnɪs] *n* atrocité *f*

frigid ['frɪdʒɪd] *adj* (*sexually*) frigide; *Geog etc* glacial, -als, (très) froid; (*style, smile, atmosphere*) glacial; (*response, silence*) glacé

frigidity [frɪ'dʒɪdɪtɪ] *n* (*sexual*) frigidité *f*; (*of style, response, atmosphere*) froideur *f*

frigidly ['frɪdʒɪdlɪ] *adv* (*to answer, reply etc*) d'un ton glacial; **f. polite** d'une politesse glaciale

frill [frɪl] *n* (*on clothing etc*) volant *m*, ruche *f*; *Culin* (*on ham etc*) papillote *f*; **shirt f.** jabot *m*; *Fig* **a plain meal without frills** un repas simple sans présentation compliquée

frilled [frɪld] *adj* (*ribbon etc*) froncé, ruché; (*shirt*) à jabots; **f. lizard** iguane *m* australien

frilly ['frɪlɪ] *adj* froncé, ruché; (*style, language*) fleuri

fringe[1] [frɪndʒ] *n* **(a)** (*of tablecloth, scarf etc*) frange *f*

(b) *esp Br* (*of hair*) frange *f*

(c) (*edge*) bordure *f*, bord *m*; **the outer fringe(s) of London** la banlieue excentrique de Londres; **to live on the f. of society** vivre en marge de la société; **to be on the radical f. of a party** appartenir à la frange radicale d'un parti; **f. benefits** avantages *mpl* accessoires; (*for employees*) compléments *mpl* de salaire en nature, avantages *mpl* sociaux; *Pol* **f. group** frange *f*; *Pol* **f. meeting** réunion *f* parallèle; **f. theatre** (petit) théâtre *m* expérimental, théâtre off

fringe[2] *vt* (*carpet etc*) franger; **eyes fringed with black lashes** yeux bordés de cils noirs

frippery ['frɪpərɪ] *n* (*usu pl*) **fripperies** (*ornaments*) colifichets *mpl*

Frisbee® ['frɪsbɪ] *n* frisbee *m*; **to play F.** jouer au frisbee

Frisco ['frɪskəʊ] *n Am F* San Francisco

frisk[1] [frɪsk] *n* **(a)** (*search*) fouille *f*; **to give sb a f.** fouiller qn **(b)** (*movement*) **with a f. of its tail** en donnant un coup de queue

frisk[2] **1** *vt* **(a)** (*search*) (*suspect etc*) fouiller; **to be frisked for weapons/alcohol** être fouillé pour vérifier qu'on ne cache pas d'armes/d'alcool **(b)** (*of dog etc*) **to f. its tail** remuer la queue **2** *vi* (*of lambs etc*) s'ébattre, gambader, folâtrer

▶ **frisk about** *vi* = **frisk**[2] **2**

friskiness ['frɪskɪnɪs] *n* vivacité *f*

frisking ['frɪskɪŋ] *n* (*of suspect, traveller*) fouille *f*; **to get a f. from a policeman, to be given a f. by a policeman** se faire fouiller par un policier

frisky ['frɪskɪ] *adj* vif; (*horse*) qui fait des cabrioles; **to feel f.** (*of person*) se sentir plein d'entrain; *F* (*sexually*) avoir le feu au derrière; *F* **to get f.** s'échauffer; **for an old man, he was still remarkably f.** il avait un tempérament encore très ardent pour son âge

fritillary [frɪ'tɪlərɪ] *n* **(a)** (*plant*) fritillaire *f* **(b)** (*butterfly*) damier *m*

fritter ['frɪtər] *n Culin* beignet *m*; **apple/banana f.** beignet aux pommes/à la banane

▶ **fritter away** *vtsep F* (*fortune*) dissiper; (*money, time*) gaspiller; **to f. away one's money on clothes/jewellery** gaspiller son argent dans des vêtements/des bijoux; **I feel as if I've just frittered away the day** j'ai l'impression d'avoir perdu ma journée

frivolity [frɪ'vɒlɪtɪ] *n* frivolité *f*

frivolous ['frɪvələs] *adj* (*person etc*) frivole; (*remark*) frivole, futile; (*objection, criticism*) futile

frivolously ['frɪvələslɪ] *adv* (*to behave, say sth*) frivolement

frivolousness ['frɪvələsnɪs] *n* (*of person*) frivolité *f*; (*of objection etc*) futilité *f*

frizz [frɪz] **1** *vt* (*hair*) crêper, frisotter **2** *vi* (*of hair*) frisotter

frizziness ['frɪzɪnɪs] *n* **the f. of my hair** mes cheveux crépus

frizzle ['frɪz(ə)l] **1** *vi* (*of meat etc in frying pan*) grésiller **2** *vt Culin* (*burn*) laisser brûler

frizzy ['frɪzɪ] *adj* (*hair*) crêpelé, crépu

FRN [efɑː'ren] *n Banking* (*abbr* **floating-rate note**) effet *m* à taux flottant

fro [frəʊ] *adv* **to go to and f.** aller et venir

frock [frɒk] *n* (*for child, woman*) robe *f*; (*of monk*) froc *m*, bure *f*; **f. coat** redingote *f*

frog[1] [frɒg] *n* **(a)** (*animal*) grenouille *f*; *F* **to have a f. in one's throat** avoir un chat dans la gorge **(b)** *Br Offensive Sl* **F.** (*French person*) Français, -aise

frog[2] *n Mil etc* **(a)** (*for sword*) porte-epée *m inv*; (*for bayonet*) porte-baïonnette *m inv* **(b)** (*braid*) brandebourg *m*

frogged [frɒgd] *adj* (*uniform, tunic etc*) orné de brandebourgs

Froggie ['frɒgɪ] *n Br Offensive Sl* (*French person*) Français, -aise

frogging ['frɒgɪŋ] *n* (*on uniform etc*) brandebourgs *mpl*

frogman, *pl* **-men** ['frɒgmən] *n* homme-grenouille *m*, *pl* hommes-grenouilles

frogmarch ['frɒgmɑːtʃ] *vt* (*person*) emmener de force; **they frogmarched her out of the room** ils l'ont fait sortir de la pièce de force

frogspawn ['frɒgspɔːn] *n* (*no pl*) œufs *mpl* de grenouille

frolic[1] ['frɒlɪk] *n* (*of young animal, child etc*) ébats *mpl*; **to have a f. in the fields** s'ébattre *ou* gambader dans les champs

frolic[2] *vi* (**frolicked**) s'ébattre

from [frɒm, **unstressed** frəm] *prep* **(a)** (*place*) de; **he returned f. London** il est revenu de Londres; **f. Paris to London** de Paris à Londres; **f. town to town** de ville en ville; **f. here** d'ici

(b) (*origin*) **to take/remove/steal/***etc* **sth f. sb** prendre/ôter/voler/*etc* qch à qn; **to take sth f. somewhere** prendre qch quelque part; **to remove sth f. somewhere** enlever qch de quelque part; **where do you come f.?, where are you f.?** d'où viens-tu?; **a train/plane f. Manchester** un train/avion en provenance de Manchester; **wheat f. Russia** blé (venant) de Russie; **a quotation f. Shakespeare** une citation tirée de Shakespeare; **he grabbed a revolver f. the table** il saisit un revolver sur la table; **I have brought it to you f. a friend** je vous l'apporte de la part d'un ami; **tell her that f. me** dites-lui cela de ma part; **f. ...** (*on parcel*) expéditeur/expéditrice ...

(c) (*range*) **the bird lays f. four to six eggs** l'oiseau pond de quatre à six œufs; **wine f. four francs a bottle** vins à partir de quatre francs la bouteille; **every flavour of ice-cream f. vanilla to pistachio** tous les parfums de glace de la vanille à la pistache

(d) (*time*) depuis, dès, à partir de; **f. that day** depuis ce jour, à partir de ce jour; **f. tomorrow on** à partir de demain; **house let f. June 1st** maison louée à compter du premier juin; **f. his childhood** depuis *ou* dès son enfance; **she remembered him f. her childhood** elle se souvenait de lui dans son enfance; **he remembered the name f. his time with the BBC** il se souvenait du nom de l'époque où il était à la BBC; **f. morning till night** du matin au soir

(e) (*distance*) **not far f. ...** pas loin de ...; **ten kilometres f. Paris** à dix kilomètres de Paris

(f) (*change*) **f. bad to worse** de mal en pis; **the price has been increased f. fifty pence to sixty pence** on a augmenté le prix de cinquante pence à soixante pence

(g) (*because of*) **to act f. conviction** agir par conviction; **I know him f. seeing him at the club** je le reconnais pour l'avoir vu au cercle; **f. his looks you might suppose that ...** à le voir on dirait que ...; **f. what I heard ...** d'après ce que j'ai entendu dire ...; **f. what I can see ...** à ce que je vois ...

(h) (*with adv, prep*) **f. above** d'en haut; **I saw him f. a long way off** je l'ai vu de loin; **f. among the trees ...** de parmi les arbres ...; **take one f. among ...** prenez-en un parmi ...

(i) (*after adv*) **to come down f. one's room** descendre de sa chambre; **to move away f. sb** s'éloigner de qn

frond [frɒnd] *n* (*of fern*) fronde *f*; (*of palm tree*) feuille *f*

front[1] [frʌnt] **1** *n* **(a)** devant *m*; (*of building*) façade *f*; (*of shop*) devanture *f*; (*of car*) avant *m*; (*of shirt*) devant; **carriage at the f. of the train** voiture en tête du train; **at the f. of the book** au début du livre; **I spilled soup all down my f.** je me suis renversé de la soupe dessus; **f. of house** (*in theatre*) salle *f*; (*in hotel*) accueil *m*; **f. -of-house manager** (*in hotel*) directeur *m* administratif, directeur de l'hébergement; *Th* **out f.** dans la salle; *Br* **the f.** (*promenade at seaside*) la promenade; *Br* **house on the f.** maison faisant face à la mer (**b**) (*first row*) premier rang *m*; **to push one's way to the f.** se frayer un chemin jusqu'au premier rang; *Fig* se pousser (en avant)

(**c**) (*outward appearance*) **to put on a bold f.** faire bonne contenance; **it's only a f. on his part** (*way of behaving etc*) ce n'est qu'une façade; **the company was just a f. for their arms dealing operation** la société n'était qu'une couverture pour leur trafic d'armes; *Br F* **to have the f. to do sth** (*nerve*) avoir l'effronterie *ou* le front de faire qch; **f. (man)** prête-nom *m*, *pl* prête-noms, homme *m* de paille; (*presenter*) présentateur *m*; **to act as a f. man for sb** servir de prête-nom *ou* d'homme de paille à qn; **f. organization** couverture *f*, façade *f*

(**d**) *Mil, Pol, Met* front *m*; *Pol* **common f.** front commun; **popular f.** front populaire; *Fig* **to make progress on all fronts** faire des progrès sur tous les fronts; *Met* **warm/cold f.** front chaud/froid

(**e**) **in f.** devant, en avant; (*in race, contest*) en tête; **Manchester United are now five points in f.** Manchester United mène par cinq points; **to send sb on in f.** envoyer qn devant; **in f. of,** *US* **f. of** devant; (*opposite*) en face de; **he was standing right in f. of me** (*facing me*) il se trouvait juste en face de moi; (*in queue, crowd etc*) il se trouvait juste devant moi; **it's right in f. of you** (*what you are looking for*) c'est juste devant vous; **he opened it/talked about it in f. of her** il l'a ouvert/en a parlé devant elle

(**f**) *F* **I want the money up f.** je veux mon argent avant; **to pay up f.** payer d'avance; *F* **he was very up f. about it** il a été franc sur ce point

2 *adj* (*garden, teeth*) de devant; **the f. part of the brain** la partie antérieure du cerveau; **f. carriage** (*of train*) voiture *f* de tête; **f. desk** réception *f*; **f. door** porte *f* d'entrée; **f. -loading washing machine** machine *f* à laver avec chargement frontal; **f. office** réception *f*, bureau *m* d'accueil; *Banking* front-office *m*; **f.-office manager** chef *m* de la réception; *Journ* **f. cover** (*of magazine*) couverture *f*, première *f* de couverture, *F* première de couve; **to appear on the front cover** faire la Une; **f. panel** (*with LEDs*) face *f* avant; **f. room** chambre *f* sur la rue; **in the f. row** au premier rang; *Rugby* **f.-row forward** avant *m* de première ligne; *Th* **f.-row seat** siège *m* de premier rang; *Aut* **f. seat** siège avant; *Th; Fig* **to have a f.(-row) seat** être aux premières loges; **f. view** vue *f* de face; *Archit* élévation *f* du devant; **f. wheel** (*of car, bicycle*) roue *f* avant; *Aut* **f.-wheel drive** traction *f* avant

front[2] **1** *vi* (**a**) (*of building*) **the house fronts north** la maison est exposée *ou* orientée au nord (**b**) *Mil* faire front; **left f.!** à gauche front!, à gauche, gauche! **2** *vt* (**a**) (*building*) donner une (nouvelle) façade à (**b**) (*government*) diriger; *TV* (*programme*) présenter; *Mus* **to f. a band** (*lead it*) diriger un orchestre

▶ **front on, front onto** *vipo* (*of building*) (*be opposite*) faire face à; (*point towards*) être tourné vers; **the river and the houses fronting on it** (*overlooking*) le fleuve et les maisons donnant dessus

frontage ['frʌntɪdʒ] *n* (**a**) (*of building*) longueur *f* de façade; (*of shop*) devanture *f*; **premises with frontages on two streets** local avec façades sur deux rues (**b**) (*of river etc*) terrain *m* en bordure (**c**) (*land at front of building etc*) espace *m* sur le devant d'un immeuble

frontal[1] ['frʌnt(ə)l] *n* (**a**) *Rel* devant *m* d'autel, fronteau *m* (**b**) (*of building*) façade *f*

frontal[2] *adj Anat* frontal; *Archit* (*view etc*) de face; *Mil* (*attack etc*) de front; **to launch a f. attack** attaquer de front; *Mktg* **f. attack** attaque *f* frontale; *Aut* **f. impact** choc *m* frontal; **f. impact test** test *m* de choc frontal

front bench *n Br Parl* = le banc des ministres et celui des membres du cabinet fantôme

front-bench *adj Br Parl* **f. MP = frontbencher;= f. spokesperson** (*of cabinet*) porte-parole *m* du gouvernement; (*of shadow cabinet*) porte-parole du cabinet fantôme; **f. team** (*cabinet*) équipe *f* ministérielle; (*shadow cabinet*) cabinet fantôme

frontbencher ['frʌnt'bentʃər] *n Br Parl* = membre *m* de la Chambre siégeant aux premières banquettes (réservées aux ministres et aux membres du cabinet fantôme)

front-end *adj Comptr* **f. processor** (ordinateur *m*) frontal *m*

frontier ['frʌntɪər] *n* frontière *f*; **natural frontiers** frontières naturelles; **the frontiers of human knowledge** les bornes *fpl* des connaissances humaines; **f. guard** garde-frontière *m*, *pl* gardes-frontière; **f. town** ville *f* frontière

frontispiece ['frʌntɪspi:s] *n Typ* frontispice *m*

front line *n Mil* ligne *f* de contact *ou* de feu

front-line *adj Mil* **f. troops** troupes *fpl* du front; *Mktg* **f. person** combattant *m* de front

front-loader *n* (*washing machine*) machine *f* à laver avec chargement frontal

front page *n* première page *f*; *F* **to make the f., to be f. news** faire la une; **f. article** article *m* de une

frontrunner ['frʌntrʌnər] *n* (*leader*) coureur/cheval/ concurrent *m* de tête; (*in election etc*) favori, -ite

frosh [frɒʃ] *n US Univ F* étudiant, -ante de première année

frost[1] [frɒst] *n Met* gelée *f*, gel *m*; **there was a f. last night** il a gelé la nuit dernière; **there was f. on the ground** il y avait du gel par terre; **ground f.** gelée blanche; **heavy/light f.** grosse/petite gelée; **ten degrees of f.** dix degrés au-dessous de zéro

frost[2] **1** *vt* (**a**) (*windows etc*) givrer (**b**) *esp Am Culin* (*cake etc*) glacer (**c**) (*damage by frost*) (*fruit tree etc*) geler (**d**) (*in glassmaking*) (*glass*) dépolir **2** *vi* = **frost over, frost up**

▶ **frost over, frost up** *vi* (*of windscreen etc*) se givrer, se couvrir de givre

frostbite ['frɒstbaɪt] *n Med* (*of feet etc*) engelure *f*; **to have f.** avoir des engelures

frostbitten ['frɒstbɪt(ə)n] *adj* (**a**) (*nose etc*) gelé (**b**) (*plant*) brûlé par le froid, grillé (par la gelée)

frostbound ['frɒstbaʊnd] *adj* (*earth*) gelé

frosted ['frɒstɪd] *adj* (**a**) (*windscreen*) givré (**b**) *esp Am Culin* (*cake*) glacé (**c**) (*glass*) dépoli

frost-free *adj* (*refrigerator, freezer*) à dégivrage automatique

frostily ['frɒstɪlɪ] *adv* (*to say*) sur un ton glacial; **to greet sb f.** faire un accueil glacé à qn; **she smiled f.** elle fit un sourire glacial

frostiness ['frɒstɪnɪs] *n* (**a**) (*of the morning etc*) froid *m* glacial (**b**) (*of person*) manière *f* glaciale; **the f. of her smile/ behaviour** son sourire/comportement glacial

frosting ['frɒstɪŋ] *n esp Am Culin* (*on cake*) glaçage *m*; *Fig* **the f. on the cake** la cerise sur le gâteau

frostproof ['frɒstpru:f] *adj* résistant à la gelée

frosty ['frɒstɪ] *adj* (**a**) (*night, air etc*) glacial, -als (**b**) (*welcome, smile, greeting*) glacial, -als; **f. answer** réponse glacée (**c**) (*window*) couvert de givre; (*ground*) gelé

froth[1] [frɒθ] *n* (**a**) (*foam*) écume *f*; (*on beer, coke etc*) mousse *f* (**b**) *Pej* (*empty words*) paroles *fpl* creuses

froth[2] *vi* écumer, mousser; (*of beer, coke etc*) mousser; (*of waves*) moutonner; **he was frothing at the mouth** il avait l'écume aux lèvres; **the frothing water** (*of sea*) les eaux écumantes

▶ **froth up** *vi* mousser

frothy ['frɒθɪ] *adj* (**a**) écumeux, mousseux; (*waves*) moutonneux; (*beer, coke etc*) mousseux (**b**) (*speech, play, style*) léger; *Pej* vide, creux

frown[1] [fraʊn] *n* froncement *m* de sourcils; (*disapproving look*) air *m* désapprobateur; (*stern look*) regard *m* sévère; **to say sth with a f.** dire qch en fronçant les sourcils

frown[2] *vi* (*of person*) froncer les sourcils, se renfrogner; **she frowned disapprovingly/in annoyance** elle fronça les sourcils d'un air désapprobateur/irrité; **to f. at sb** regarder qn en fronçant les sourcils

▶ **frown on, frown upon** *vipo* (*disapprove of*) (*suggestion etc*) désapprouver; **such behaviour was frowned upon** un tel comportement était mal vu

frowning ['fraʊnɪŋ] *adj* (*expression*) renfrogné

frowsty ['fraʊstɪ] *adj Br F* (*room*) qui sent le renfermé; (*smell, atmosphere*) de renfermé

frowzy ['fraʊzɪ] *adj F* (**a**) (*musty*) (*room*) qui sent le renfermé (**b**) (*person, clothes etc*) peu soigné

froze *see* **freeze**[2]

frozen ['frəʊz(ə)n] **1** *adj* (**a**) gelé, glacé; (*meat, peas etc*) congelé, surgelé; **f. foods** (produits *mpl*) surgelés *mpl ou* congelés *mpl*; *F* **my hands are f.** j'ai les mains gelées *ou* glacées; **I've got f. waiting for you** je me suis gelé à vous attendre (**b**) *Fin* (*assets etc*) non liquide, gelé; **f. account** compte *m* bloqué; **f. credit** crédit *m* bloqué **2** *pp see* **freeze**[2]

fructify ['frʌktɪfaɪ] **1** *vi* fructifier **2** *vt* faire fructifier

fructose ['frʌktəʊs] *n Ch* fructose *m*

frugal ['fru:g(ə)l] *adj* (*person, life*) frugal; (*meal etc*) frugal, -aux, sobre; (*thrifty*) économe; **to be f. with sth** ménager qch

frugality [fru:'gælɪtɪ] *n* (*of person, life*) frugalité *f*; (*of meal*) frugalité, sobriété *f*; (*thriftiness*) économie *f*

frugally ['fru:g(ə)lɪ] *adv* frugalement

fruit[1] [fru:t] *n* (**a**) fruit *m*; **would you like some f.?** prendrez-vous un fruit?; **apples and other fruit(s)** les pommes et autres fruits; **eat more f.** mangez plus de fruits; *Br* **soft f.,** *Am* **small f.** petits fruits; **to bear f.** (*of tree*) donner des fruits, porter fruit; *Fig* (*of labour*) porter ses fruits; **my enquiries bore f.** mes recherches furent couronnées de succès; **f. basket** (*for display etc*) corbeille *f* à fruits; **f. bowl** (*for display etc*) coupe *f* à fruits; **f. bud** bourgeon *m* à fruit; **f. cup** (*drink*) boisson *f* glacée avec fruits; **f. dish** compotier *m*; (*for display*) coupe *f* à fruits; **f. drop** bonbon *m* acidulé; **f. farmer**

or **grower** fruiticulteur, -trice; **f. farming** culture *f* fruitière; **f. juice** jus *m* de fruit; **f. knife** couteau *m* à fruit(s); *Br* **f. machine** machine *f* à sous; **f. salad** *or* **cocktail** macédoine *f ou* salade *f* de fruits; **f. shop** fruiterie *f*; **f. stall** étalage *m* de fruit; **f. tree** arbre *m* fruitier

(b) *Fig* fruit *m*; *Lit* **the fruits of the earth** les fruits de la terre; *Lit* **the f. of her womb** le fruit de ses entrailles

(c) *Old-fashioned Br F* **yes, my old f.** oui, mon vieux

(d) *Am Offensive Sl* (*homosexual*) pédé *m*

fruit² *vi* (*of tree*) porter des fruits

fruit bat *n Zool* chauve-souris *f* frugivore

fruit-bearing *adj* (*tree etc*) frugifère, fructifère

fruitcake [ˈfruːtkeɪk] *n* **(a)** *Culin* cake *m* **(b)** *esp Br F* (*eccentric, mad person*) cinglé, -ée, fou, *f* folle; **he's as nutty as a f.** il est complètement cinglé

fruit-eating *adj* (*animal*) frugivore

fruiterer [ˈfruːtərər] *n esp Br Old-fashioned* fruitier, -ière; **f.'s (shop)** fruiterie *f*

fruit fly *n Ent* mouche *f* à fruits

fruitful [ˈfruːtfʊl] *adj* **(a)** (*work, discussion etc*) fructueux **(b)** (*tree etc*) fructueux, productif; (*soil etc*) fertile, fécond

fruitfully [ˈfruːtfʊlɪ] *adv* fructueusement; **they had spent the day f.** la journée avait été fructueuse pour eux

fruitfulness [ˈfruːtfʊlnɪs] *n* **(a)** *Fig* (*of work, discussion etc*) caractère *m* fructueux **(b)** (*of tree etc*) productivité *f*; (*of earth etc*) fertilité *f*

fruiting [ˈfruːtɪŋ] *adj* (*tree etc*) frugifère, fructifère

fruition [fruːˈɪʃən] *n* (*of plan, hope*) réalisation *f*; **to come to f.** porter ses fruits; **to bring sth to f.** mener qch à bien

fruitless [ˈfruːtlɪs] *adj* (*discussions, negotiations*) stérile, infructueux; (*efforts, attempt*) infructueux, vain; **at least the trip won't have been entirely f.** au moins le voyage n'aura pas tout à fait servi à rien

fruity [ˈfruːtɪ] *adj* **(a)** (*taste etc*) de fruit; (*wine*) fruité, fruiteux **(b)** *F* **a f. voice** une voix (trop) étoffée; **a f. laugh** un rire généreux **(c)** *esp Br Old-fashioned* (*novel, scandal etc*) corsé **(d)** *Am Offensive Sl* (*homosexual*) de pédé **(e)** *US* (*crazy*) toqué, cinglé

frump [frʌmp] *n* femme *f* mal attifée; **she's a f.** elle est ficelée comme l'as de pique

frumpish [ˈfrʌmpɪʃ], **frumpy** [ˈfrʌmpɪ] *adj* (*clothes*) tarte, moche; **f. woman** femme mal attifée *ou F* mal fagotée

frustrate [frʌsˈtreɪt] *vt* **(a)** (*upset, annoy*) (*person*) décevoir, frustrer **(b)** (*thwart*) (*person*) contrecarrer; (*plan*) faire échouer; **to f. sb's hopes** frustrer qn dans son espoir, frustrer l'espoir de qn

frustrated [frʌsˈtreɪtɪd] *adj* (*writer etc*) frustré; **(sexually) f.** frustré

frustrating [frʌsˈtreɪtɪŋ] *adj* (*experience etc*) frustrant

frustration [frʌsˈtreɪʃən] *n* **(a)** (*emotion*) frustration *f* **(b)** (*of person's plans*) anéantissement *m*; (*of hopes, ambitions*) frustration *f*

fry¹ [fraɪ] **(fried) 1** *vt Culin* (*fish etc*) (faire) frire; **to f. an egg** faire cuire un œuf sur le plat **2** *vi* **(a)** (*of food*) frire **(b)** *esp US Sl* (*of convict*) mourir *ou* finir sur la chaise électrique

fry² *n* (*no pl*) (*of fish*) frai *m*, fretin *m*, alevin *m*; **small f.** menu fretin; *Fig* (*insignificant people*) menu fretin, gens *mpl* insignifiants; (*children*) gosses *mpl*; **salmon f.** saumoneaux *mpl* dans la deuxième année

fry³ *n* (*offal*) issues *fpl*; (*of lamb, pig*) fressure *f*

fryer [ˈfraɪər] *n Culin* **(a)** (*person*) = personne *f* qui fait de la friture **(b)** (*frying pan*) poêle *f* à frire; **(deep) f.** friteuse *f* **(c)** (*chicken*) poulet *m* à frire

frying [ˈfraɪɪŋ] *n* friture *f*; **f. pan** poêle *f* (à frire); *Prov* **to jump out of the f. pan into the fire** tomber de Charybde en Scylla

fry-pan *n Am* poêle *f* à frire

fry-up *n Br Culin F* = bacon, saucisses, tomates *etc* frits ensemble

f-stop *n Phot* ouverture *f* du diaphragme

ft (*abbr* **foot/feet**) p., pd.

FT 100 index [efˈtiː] *n St Exch* indice *m* FT 100

FTSE [eftiːesˈiː] *n* (*abbr* **Financial Times Stock Exchange**) ≈ indice *m* CAC 40

fuchsia [ˈfjuːʃə] *n* (*plant*) fuchsia *m*

fuck¹ [fʌk] *Vulg* **1** *n* **(a)** (*intercourse*) baise *f*; **they had a quick f.** ils ont baisé *ou* tiré un coup en vitesse; **to be a good f.** bien baiser; **to be an easy f.** coucher avec tout le monde

(b) (*as intensifier*) **what the f. is that?** qu'est-ce que c'est que ça, bordel de merde?; **who the f. told you about it/did this?** quel est le connard qui t'en a parlé/qui a fait ça?; **as stupid/rich as f.** foutrement con/riche; **he ran like f.** il a couru comme un dératé; **shut the f. up!** ferme ta gueule putain *ou* bordel!; **get the f. out of here!** casse-toi connard!; **for f.'s sake!** bordel!, putain!; **f. knows why I agreed to come!** putain *ou* bordel, pourquoi est-ce que j'ai accepté de venir?; **not to care** *or* **give a f.** n'en avoir rien à foutre **(about sth** de qch); **why should I give a f. about what you think?** qu'est-ce que ça peut me foutre, ce que tu penses?; **she'd like you to apologize – like f. I will!** elle voudrait que tu t'excuses – qu'elle aille se faire foutre!; **did you invite them? – like f. I did!** tu les as invités? – tu déconnes ou quoi?; **like f. I'm going to help that bastard!** qu'il aille se faire foutre, ce connard, je ne l'aiderai pas!; **get to f.!** va te faire foutre!

2 *int* merde!, bordel!

fuck² *Vulg* **1** *vt* **(a)** (*person*) baiser **(b) f. it!** merde!; **f. this!** et puis merde!; **f. you!, go f. yourself!** va te faire foutre!, je t'emmerde!; **f. him!** qu'il aille se faire foutre!; **f. what he thinks/says!** je m'en fous de ce qu'il pense/dit!; **f. me!** putain!; **f. the President!** aux chiottes le Président!; **f. all** que dalle; **she does f. all work** elle en fout pas une rame **2** *vi* baiser

▶ **fuck about, fuck around** *Vulg* **1** *vi* (*play the fool*) déconner; (*waste time*) glander; **to f. about** *or* **around with sth** (*car, radio*) trifouiller qch; **if you spent less time fucking about** *or* **around with your computer program ...!** si tu passais moins de temps sur ton putain de logiciel ...! **2** *vtas* (*person*) (*treat badly*) emmerder; (*waste time of*) faire tourner en bourrique

▶ **fuck off** *Vulg* **1** *vi* (*go away*) se casser; **to tell sb to f. off** dire à qn d'aller se faire foutre, envoyer qn se faire foutre; **f. off!** va te faire foutre! **2** *vtsep* (*annoy*) (*person*) emmerder, faire chier; **she's been feeling really fucked off about work recently** le boulot la fait vraiment chier ces temps-ci

▶ **fuck over** *vtas Am Vulg* **to f. sb over** (*cheat*) baiser qn, arranger la gueule à qn; **I really got fucked over on that one** là je me suis vraiment fait baiser *ou* arranger la gueule; **he had been fucked over for a thousand dollars** il s'était fait baiser de mille dollars

▶ **fuck up** *Vulg* **1** *vtsep* (*ruin*) foutre en l'air, niquer; (*person*) foutre en l'air; **I think I've fucked up the exam/the meringue** je crois que j'ai loupé ce putain d'examen/cette putain de meringue; **she was badly fucked up by her parents** ses parents l'ont complètement foutue en l'air; **to be fucked up** (*of person*) être à côté de ses pompes **2** *vi* (*bungle sth*) déconner, merder

fucked [fʌkt] *adj Vulg* (*car, stereo etc*) foutu, naze; **I'm f.!** (*exhausted*) je suis mort *ou* crevé!; **his knee/heart/eye is f.** son genou/cœur/œil est naze *ou* niqué; **his chances of winning the race were completely f.!** il n'avait plus une chance de gagner cette putain de course

fucker [ˈfʌkər] *n Vulg* **(a) stupid f.** connard *m*; **old f.** vieux con *m* **(b)** (*thing, object*) connerie *f*; **I can't get the f. out** je n'arrive pas à retirer cette connerie **(c)** (*sexually*) baiseur, -euse

fuckface [ˈfʌkfeɪs] *n Vulg* tête *f* de con

fucking [ˈfʌkɪŋ] *Vulg* **1** *adj* foutu; **this f. car** cette voiture de mes deux, cette putain de voiture; **I've cut my f. finger** bordel *ou* putain, je me suis coupé le doigt; **he's a f. idiot!** c'est un connard!; **you're a f. liar!** tu n'es qu'un connard de menteur!; **that's a f. lie!** c'est des conneries!; **you haven't got a f. clue, have you?** tu n'y connais foutrement rien, hein?; **f. hell!** bordel de merde!; **who the f. hell does she think she is?** mais merde, pour qui elle se prend?; **why/when the f. hell did you do that?** pourquoi/quand est-ce que tu as fait ça putain *ou* bordel?

2 *adv* (*cold, expensive, good*) vachement; (*stupid*) foutument; **it's f. cold** putain, il fait vachement froid; **you're f. out of your mind!** bordel, ça va vraiment pas dans ta tête!; **what did you f. expect?** mais qu'est-ce que tu croyais putain *ou* bordel?

3 *n* baise *f*

fuck-up *n Vulg* gâchis *m*; **the whole thing was a complete f.** tout a merdé; **to make a f. of sth** (*task, job*) saloper qch; (*marriage*) foutre qch en l'air; **I made a real f. of the exam/interview** j'ai complètement merdé à l'examen/l'entretien

fuddle [ˈfʌd(ə)l] *vt* (*person*) embrouiller; **he had fuddled his brain with drink and drugs** l'alcool et la drogue lui avaient embrouillé le cerveau

fuddled [ˈfʌd(ə)ld] *adj F* **(a)** (*drunk*) soûl; **to get f.** se soûler, s'enivrer; **slightly f.** un peu gris **(b)** (*confused*) embrouillé

fuddy-duddy [ˈfʌdɪdʌdɪ] *F* **1** *n* vieil encroûté *m*; **don't be such an old f.!** arrête de t'encroûter comme ça! **2** *adj* vieux jeu *inv*

fudge¹ [fʌdʒ] *n* **(a)** *Culin* fondant *m* **(b)** *Journ* (*late news*) dernières nouvelles *fpl* **(c)** (*evasion*) **his answer was a f.** sa réponse n'était qu'une dérobade

fudge² *F* **1** *vt* (*botch*) (*piece of work etc*) bousiller; (*falsify*) (*accounts etc*) truquer; **to f. an issue** (*avoid*) éluder une question **2** *vi* se dérober; **I've had enough of their fudging** j'en ai assez de leurs dérobades

fuel¹ [ˈfjʊəl] *n* combustible *m*; (*for engine*) carburant *m*; **domestic** *or* **household f.** combustible de ménage; *Fig* **to add f. to the flames** jeter de l'huile sur le feu; *Fig* **to add fresh f. to a quarrel** alimenter une querelle; **f. bill** (*of household*) facture *f* de chauffage; (*of region*) dépenses *fpl* énergétiques; **f. consumption** consommation *f* d'énergie; (*of car*) consommation de carburant; **f. costs** (*of household*) coûts *mpl* de chauffage; (*of region*) coûts de l'énergie; *Nucl Phys* **f. element** élément *m* combustible; **f. gauge** jauge *f* de carburant; **f. injection** alimentation *f* par injection, injection *f* (de combustible); **f. injection system** système *m* d'injection (de combustible); **f. injector** injecteur *m* de carburant; **f. level** niveau *m* de carburant; **f. oil** mazout *m*; **f. pipe** tuyau *m* d'alimentation en carburant; **f. pressure** pression *f* de carburant; **f. pump** pompe *f* à carburant *ou* d'alimentation; *Nucl Phys* **f. rod** assemblage *m* d'éléments combustibles; **f. tank** réservoir *m* à carburant; **f. tank shield** bouclier *m* de réservoir de carburant; **f. tax** taxe *f* sur les carburants; **f. temperature gauge** jauge *f* de température du carburant

fuel² (**-ll-**, *US* **-l-**) **1** *vt* (*furnace etc*) alimenter, charger; (*vehicle, machine etc*) ravitailler *ou* alimenter en carburant; *Fig* (*speculations*) nourrir; (*doubts, hatred, argument*) alimenter **2** *vi* se ravitailler en carburant

fuel/air mixture *n* mélange *f* air/carburant

fuel-injected [ˈfjʊəlɪndʒektɪd] *adj Aut etc* à injection

fuelling, *US* **fueling** [ˈfjʊəlɪŋ] *n* ravitaillement *m* en combustible *ou* en carburant; **f. stop** escale *f* de ravitaillement (en combustible *ou* carburant)

fug [fʌg] *n esp Br F* forte odeur *f* de renfermé; (*in smoke-filled room*) air *m* empesté de tabac; **there's a terrible f. in here** ce que ça pue le renfermé/le tabac là-dedans!; **quite a f. had built up during the meeting** l'air s'était empesté de tabac pendant la réunion

fuggy [ˈfʌgɪ] *adj esp Br F* (*room etc*) qui sent le renfermé; (*atmosphere*) confiné

fugitive [ˈfjuːdʒɪtɪv] **1** *n* fugitif, -ive, fuyard, -arde; (*refugee*) réfugié, -ée; **f. from justice** fugitif recherché par la justice **2** *adj* **(a)** (*prisoner*) fugitif, fuyard **(b)** *esp Lit* (*happiness*) fugitif, fugace; (*smile, impression, thought*) fugitif

fugue [fjuːg] *n Mus, Psy* fugue *f*

fulcrum, *pl* **-cra, -crums** [ˈfʌlkrəm, -krə, -krəmz] *n* (*of lever*) pivot *m*

fulfil, *US* **fulfill** [fʊlˈfɪl] *vt* (*Br* **fulfils,** *US* **fulfills**; *Br, US* **fulfilled, fulfilling**) (*task, prophecy*) accomplir; (*expectations*) répondre à, remplir; (*wish*) satisfaire; (*prayer, plea*) exaucer; (*obligation, duties*) remplir, s'acquitter de; (*conditions, instructions, purpose, contract*) remplir; (*requirements, need, purpose*) répondre à, satisfaire à; (*promise*) exécuter; (*commandment*) obéir à; (*ambition, plan, potential*) réaliser; **to f. oneself** se réaliser; **administrative work doesn't f. me** le travail de bureau ne me permet pas de me réaliser; **to feel fulfilled** (*of person*) sentir qu'on s'est réalisé

fulfilling [fʊlˈfɪlɪŋ] *adj* (*work etc*) épanouissant

fulfilment, *US* **fulfillment** [fʊlˈfɪlmənt] *n* (*of prophecy, duty, wish etc*) accomplissement *m*; (*of prayer, plea*) exaucement *m*; (*of plan, contract*) exécution *f*; *Jur* (*of condition*) accomplissement; (*of ambition*) réalisation *f*; (*of promise*) exécution; **to find** *or* **achieve f.** se réaliser; **to have a feeling** *or* **sense of f.** avoir un sentiment de plénitude

full [fʊl] **1** *adj* **(a)** (*receptacle, cupboard*) plein, rempli; (*room*) comble; (*bus etc*) plein; (*day*) chargé; (*sail*) plein, gonflé; (*disk*) saturé; **f. to the brim** rempli jusqu'au bord *ou* à ras bord; **f. to overflowing** plein à déborder; **don't speak with your mouth f.** ne parle pas la bouche pleine; **to be f. (up)** (*of person*) être repu *ou* rassasié; **on a f. stomach** le ventre plein; **the bus is f. up** l'autobus est au complet; **the sails are f.** les voiles portent bien; **to be f. of sth** être plein de qch; **the (news)papers were f. of it** les journaux ne parlaient que de ça; **to become f.** (*of disk*) arriver à saturation; **to have one's pockets f. of money** avoir les poches pleines d'argent; **her eyes were f. of tears** ses yeux étaient remplis de larmes; **f. of holes** plein de trous

(b) look f. of hatred regard chargé de haine; **to be f. of hope** être rempli d'espoir; **to be f. of ideas** être plein d'idées; **to be f. of life/energy/vitality** être plein de vie/d'énergie/de vitalité; **to be f. of praise for sb** ne pas tarir d'éloges sur qn; **to be f. of one's own importance** être pénétré de sa propre importance; *Pej* **f. of oneself** plein de soi-même

(c) (*written notes, details etc*) ample, copieux; **she received her f. share of the money** elle a eu sa bonne part de l'argent; **in the fullest detail** dans le plus grand détail; **to ask for fuller information about sth** demander des précisions sur qch

(d) (*complete*) complet, entier; **the f. horror of the situation** toute l'horreur de la situation; **in f. flower** en pleine fleur; **roses in f. bloom** roses épanouies; **to be in f. cry** (*of hounds*) donner de la voix; *Fig* **the press was in f. cry after the minister** la presse se déchaînait contre le ministre; **in f. flow** en plein discours; *Mil, Fig* **in f. flight/retreat** en pleine déroute/retraite; *Mil, Fig* **at f. strength** au grand complet; **below f. strength** pas au complet; **in f. uniform** en grande tenue; **to be in f. swing** (*of party, sales etc*) battre son plein; **in f. view of the police/the enemy** sous les yeux de la police/de l'ennemi; **to lead a f. life** mener une vie bien remplie; **I waited two f. hours** *or* **a f. two hours** j'ai attendu deux bonnes heures; **we were under f. sail** nous avions toutes voiles dehors; **to give f. scope to sb** donner libre carrière à qn; **to give f. scope to sb's talents** donner libre champ aux talents de qn; **f. amount** somme totale; **at f. blast** à fond; **f. cargo** plein chargement; *Phot* **in f. colour** tout en couleur; *Com* **f. container load** conteneur *m* chargé complètement; **f. employment** plein emploi *m*; **f. employment policy** politique *f* de plein emploi; *Cards* **f. hand** *or* **house** (*in poker*) main *f* pleine; *Mktg* **f. launch** lancement *m* définitif; *Aut* **f. licence** permis *m* tous véhicules; *Sch* **f. marks** dix sur dix/vingt sur vingt/*etc*; *Fig* **f. marks for all those who spotted the mistake** bravo à tous ceux qui ont trouvé l'erreur; **f. meal** repas complet; **f. member** membre *m* titulaire; **f. moon** pleine lune; **f. pay** paie entière; **leave on f. pay** congé *m* à solde entière; **f. payment** paiement *m* intégral; **to make f. payment for a share** libérer entièrement une action; **f. price** prix fort; **to pay the f. price for sth** payer le prix fort pour qch; **to pay f. price/fare** payer place entière; *Am* **f. professor** professeur *m* titulaire; **f. session** (*of a committee etc*) réunion *f* plénière; *TV, Cin* **f. shot** plan *m* d'ensemble, plan général; *Com* **f. set of bills of lading** jeu *m* complet de connaissements; **(at) f. speed** à toute vitesse, à fond; *Naut* **f. speed ahead!** en avant toute!; *Fig* **it's f. speed ahead** maintenant on peut y aller; **f. text** texte intégral; **f. warranty** garantie *f* totale; **f. weight** poids *m* juste

(e) (*face*) plein, rond; (*sleeve etc*) large, bouffant; **f. face portrait** portrait de face; **a f. figure** (*of woman*) une silhouette généreuse; **f. lips** grosses lèvres, lèvres charnues; **f. skirt** jupe *f* bouffante; **f. voice** voix pleine *ou* ronde

2 *n* **to publish a letter in f.** publier une lettre intégralement; **money refunded in f.** (*on notice etc*) on rembourse intégralement l'argent *ou* l'argent en totalité; **to pay in f.** payer intégralement; **name in f.** nom et prénoms; **to write out a word in f.** écrire un mot en toutes lettres; **to the f.** tout à fait; **to live life to the f.** vivre sa vie pleinement; **to indulge one's tastes to the f.** donner libre cours à ses goûts

3 *adv* **(a)** (*completely*) **to turn a tap f. on** *or* **on f.** ouvrir un robinet en grand; **to turn the radio f. on** *or* **on f.** mettre la radio à fond; **to drive (one's car) f. out** (*at top speed*) conduire à toute vitesse; **to work f. out** travailler à toute vitesse; **I know it f. well** je le sais bien *ou* parfaitement

(b) (*right*) **lying f. in the sun** couché en plein (au) soleil; **hit f. in the face** atteint en pleine figure

fullback [ˈfʊlbæk] *n Sp* arrière *m*; **at f.** à l'arrière

full beam *n* **on f.** en feux de route, en pleins phares

full-blooded *adj* **(a)** (*racially*) de race pure; (*horse*) de sang, pur-sang *inv*; **f. Indians** Indiens de race pure **(b)** (*vigorous*) vigoureux

full-blown *adj* **(a)** (*rose etc*) épanoui, en pleine fleur **(b)** (*crisis*) de la plus grande envergure; **a f. argument** une vraie dispute **(c)** *Fig* (*doctor etc*) qualifié; **she is a f. lawyer** elle a (obtenu) tous ses diplômes; **to have f. AIDS** avoir le sida (à son stade symptomatique)

full board *n* pension *f* complète

full-bodied [ˈfʊlˈbɒdɪd] *adj* (*wine*) corsé, qui a du corps

full-cost pricing *n Mktg* fixation *f* du prix en fonction du coût

full-cream *adj* **f. milk** lait *m* entier

full-dress *adj* (*attire*) de cérémonie, de parade; *Mil, Naut* **f. uniform** tenue *f* numéro un; **f. debate** débat *m* solennel

full duplex *n* full duplex *m*, voie *f* bidirectionnelle simultanée; **to send sth f.** transmettre qch en full duplex

fuller [ˈfʊlər] *n* **f.'s earth** terre *f* à foulon

full-faced [ˈfʊlˈfeɪst] *adj* (*person*) à la figure ronde, au visage plein

full-fare paying passenger *n* voyageur *m* à haute contribution

full-fledged *adj Am* = **fully-fledged**

full-frontal 1 *adj* **(a) f. nudity** nudité *f* vue de face **(b)** (*attack, assault*) de front **2** *n* nudité *f* vue de face, nu *m* de face **3** *adv* nu de face

full-grown *adj* (*tree*) qui a atteint son développement complet; (*person, cow*) adulte

full house *n Th etc* salle *f* comble; **we're going to have a f. this weekend** (*at home*) la maison va être pleine de monde ce week-end

full-length[1] *adj* (*portrait*) en pied; (*mirror*) qui permet de se voir en pied; (*evening dress*) long; **f. film** long métrage *m*; **a f. novel** un vrai roman; *TV, Cin* **f. shot** plan *m* général

full-length[2] *adv* de tout mon/ton/son/*etc* long

full name *n* (*on form*) nom *m* en toutes lettres; **what is your f.?** quels sont vos nom et prénoms?

ful(l)ness ['fʊlnɪs] *n* **(a)** (*of receptacle*) état *m* plein; **out of the f. of his heart** comme son cœur débordait; **to speak out of the f. of one's grief** parler le cœur débordant de chagrin **(b)** (*of strength*) plénitude *f*, perfection *f*, totalité *f*; **in the f. of time** avec le temps **(c)** (*of skirt, report etc*) ampleur *f*; (*of detail*) abondance *f*; (*of figure*) rondeur *f*; (*of style etc*) richesse *f*

full-page *adj* (*illustration*) hors texte; **f. advertisment** publicité *f* pleine page

full point *n Typ* (*in punctuation*) point *m*

full-scale *adj* **(a)** = **full-sized) (b)** (*reform*) complet, intégral; (*panic, drought, retreat*) total; (*attack, war*) de grande envergure; (*emergency*) absolu

full-screen menu *n Comptr* menu *m* plein écran

full-size(d) *adj* (*drawing, model etc*) grandeur nature; (*tree*) adulte; (*keyboard, wheel*) aux dimensions standard; (*violin, bicycle*) d'adulte

full stop *n Typ* (*in punctuation*) point *m*

full-strength *adj* de force normale

full time *n Sp, Fb etc* fin *f* de match

full-time 1 *adv* (*work*) à plein temps, à temps complet **2** *adj* (*work, employee, job*) à temps complet, à plein temps; **f. contract** contrat *m* à temps plein; *Fig* **looking after the baby is a f. job** s'occuper du bébé ne laisse pas une minute de libre

fully ['fʊlɪ] *adv* **(a)** (*completely*) (*involved, occupied in sth, taken up*) entièrement; (*satisfied, justified, convinced*) pleinement, entièrement; (*to understand*) parfaitement; (*to treat subject etc*) à fond; **to be f. aware** *or* **conscious of the fact that ...** être parfaitement conscient du fait que ...; **I f. expect to be back here on Monday** je pense vraiment être de retour lundi; **f. licensed** (*hotel, restaurant etc*) qui a obtenu une licence pour la vente d'alcool; **f. paid** payé intégralement; **f. paid up** (*capital*) intégralement libéré; **f. loaded** (*van, plane etc*) en pleine charge; **this topic is dealt with more f. below** ce thème est traité plus en détail ci-après

(b) (*at least*) **it takes f. two hours** cela prend bien *ou* au moins deux heures

fully-fashioned ['fʊlɪ'fæʃənd] *adj* (*stockings, sweater*) bien ajusté

fully-fledged *adj* (*bird*) qui a toutes ses plumes; *F* (*doctor etc*) qualifié; **now you're a f. actor!** maintenant tu es un acteur pour de bon!

fulmar ['fʊlmər] *n* (*bird*) pétrel *m* glacial

fulminate ['fʌlmɪneɪt] *vi* fulminer (**against** contre)

fulmination [fʌlmɪ'neɪʃən] *n* malédiction *f*, imprécation *f*

fulsome ['fʊlsəm] *adj* (*praise*) enthousiaste; (*excessive*) excessif, exagéré; (*welcome, greeting*) plein d'effusion; **to be f. in one's praise of sb/sth** porter qn/qch aux nues

fulsomely ['fʊlsəmlɪ] *adv* **to praise sb/sth f.** porter qn/qch aux nues; **'it's gorgeous!', she said f.** 'c'est magnifique!', dit-elle pleine d'enthousiasme

fumarole ['fju:mərəʊl] *n Geol* fumerolle *f*

fumble ['fʌmb(ə)l] **1** *vi* (*in enclosed space*) fouiller (au hasard); (*on floor, in dark etc*) tâtonner; **to f. (about** *or* **around) in a drawer for sth** fouiller dans un tiroir pour trouver qch; **to f. (about** *or* **around) in a dark room for sth** chercher qch à tâtons dans une pièce obscure; **to f. for words** chercher ses mots; **to f. with sth** manier qch maladroitement **2** *vt* manier maladroitement; (*opportunity*) gâcher; **to f. a question** répondre à une question en bafouillant; *Sp* **to f. the ball** mal attraper la balle

fumbling ['fʌmblɪŋ] *adj* maladroit, gauche

fume[1] [fju:m] *n* (*vapour*) vapeur *f*; (*gas*) gaz *m*; **petrol fumes** vapeurs d'essence; *Aut* **exhaust fumes** gaz d'échappement

fume[2] *vi F* (*be angry*) rager; **I was fuming** je rageais (**at** contre), j'étais exaspéré (**at** par)

fumigate ['fju:mɪgeɪt] *vt* (*flat etc*) désinfecter par fumigation

fumigation [fju:mɪ'geɪʃən] *n* fumigation *f*

fumigator ['fju:mɪgeɪtər] *n* (*device*) appareil *m* fumigatoire

fumitory ['fju:mɪtərɪ] *n* (*plant*) fumeterre *f*

fun [fʌn] *n* amusement *m*, gaieté *f*; (*joking*) plaisanterie *f*; **to have f.** s'amuser, se divertir; **to get a lot of f. out of doing sth** bien s'amuser en faisant qch; **we had lots of** *or* **great** *or* **good f.** on s'est bien amusé; **to have f. at sb's expense** s'amuser aux dépens de qn; **there'll be f. and games** ça va chauffer, il va y avoir du grabuge; **it was great f.** c'était très amusant; **he is great f.** *or* **full of f.** il est très drôle; **she's f. to be with** on s'amuse avec elle; **to make f. of** *or* **poke f. at sb/sth** se moquer de qn/qch, rire de qn/qch; **to say sth in f.** dire qch en plaisantant; **in f.** (*as a joke*) par plaisanterie; **for f.** (*for enjoyment*) pour se distraire; **I did it for the f. of the thing** *or* **of it** je l'ai fait pour le plaisir; **where's the f. in that?** je ne vois pas ce que ça a d'agréable; **it wasn't much f. walking home in the rain** rentrer à pied sous la pluie n'avait rien d'une partie de plaisir; **it won't be half as much f. without you** ce ne sera pas si drôle sans toi; **all the f.'s gone out of it** ce n'est plus drôle du tout; *esp Am F* **a f. party** une soirée où l'on s'amuse bien; **she's a f. person to be with** on s'amuse bien avec elle; **I don't want to spoil your f.** je ne veux pas vous empêcher de vous amuser; **to take the f. out of sth** rendre qch plus drôle du tout; **to put the f. back into sth** redonner tout son charme à qch; **that's half the f. as far as I'm concerned** c'est là tout le charme de la chose pour moi; **to join in the f.** s'amuser avec tout le monde; *Iron* **that's when the f. began** (*trouble*) c'est là que ça a commencé à barder; **all the f. of the fair** toutes les attractions de la foire; **what f.!** comme c'est amusant!; *Iron* très amusant!; **f.-loving** qui aime s'amuser; **f. fur** fourrure *f* synthétique; **a f.-packed** *or* **-filled holiday** des vacances pendant lesquelles on n'a pas le temps de s'ennuyer; **f. run** = course *f* organisée au profit d'une œuvre de bienfaisance

function[1] ['fʌŋkʃən] *n* **(a)** (*of body, machine, institution*) fonction *f*; (*of person*) fonction, charge *f*; **in his f. as a magistrate** en sa qualité de magistrat; **he combines the functions of servant and gardener** il tient le double emploi de domestique et de jardinier; **to discharge one's functions** s'acquitter de ses fonctions; **my f. in life** ma raison d'être; **the spring performs the f. of a shock absorber** le ressort joue le rôle d'(un) *ou* fait fonction d'amortisseur; *Comptr* **f. key** touche *f* de fonction

(b) (*occasion*) (*reception*) réception *f*, réunion *f*; (*public ceremony*) cérémonie *f* publique; **society f.** réception mondaine; **f. room** salle *f* de réception *ou* de réunion; **functions manager** (*at hotel*) responsable *m* des réceptions

(c) *Math etc* fonction *f*; *also Fig* **to be a f. of sth** être fonction de qch

function[2] *vi* (*operate, work*) fonctionner; **to f. as sth** (*fill a role*) faire fonction de qch

functional ['fʌŋkʃən(ə)l] *adj* **(a)** (*furniture etc*) fonctionnel, utilitaire **(b)** (*operational*) **to be f.** fonctionner; **I'm barely f. before ten o'clock** je ne suis guère opérationnel avant dix heures; **f. illiterate** = personne *f* dont l'analphabétisme l'empêche de faire face aux situations courantes; **f. disorder** trouble *m* fonctionnel **(c)** *Math, Med* fonctionnel

functionally ['fʌŋkʃən(ə)lɪ] *adv* **to be f. illiterate** = être analphabète au point de ne pas pouvoir faire face aux situations courantes; **to be f. equivalent to sth** avoir la même fonction que qch; **the human appendix is f. unnecessary** l'appendice humain est inutile du point de vue fonctionnel

functionary ['fʌŋkʃənərɪ] *n often Pej* fonctionnaire *mf*

functioning ['fʌŋkʃənɪŋ] *n* (*of machine etc*) fonctionnement *m*

fund[1] [fʌnd] *n* [①**A10**,f] **(a)** *Fin etc* fonds *m*, caisse *f*; **to start a f.** lancer une souscription **(b) funds** fonds *mpl*, ressources *fpl* pécuniaires; (*of government*) fonds publics; **to be in funds** être en fonds; **funds are low** les fonds sont bas; **to be short of** *or* **low on funds** être à court d'argent; *Banking* **'no funds'** 'défaut de provision,' 'manque de fonds'; **f.-holder** rentier, -ière **(c)** (*supply*) (*of wit*) fonds *m*; (*of information*) source *f*; **unfailing f. of humour** des ressources d'humour intarissables; **a f. of anecdotes** un stock d'anecdotes

fund[2] *vt Fin* (*project*) financer; (*company etc*) pourvoir de fonds; (*public debt*) consolider; **to f. money** placer de l'argent dans les fonds publics; *Acct* **funded from cashflow** autofinancé

fundamental [fʌndə'ment(ə)l] **1** *adj* **(a)** fondamental, -aux, essentiel; (*question*) principal, de fond; **of f. importance** d'une importance capitale; **to be f. to one's understanding/the success of sth** être fondamental pour *ou* essentiel à la compréhension/essentiel au succès de qch **(b)** *Mus* **f. note** note *f* fondamentale **2** *n* **(a) fundamentals** principe(s) *m(pl)*; (*of science*) notions fondamentales *fpl*, fondements *mpl*; (*of system*) partie *f* essentielle; **to reach agreement on fundamentals** réaliser un accord sur les points essentiels; **let's get down to fundamentals** allons à l'essentiel **(b)** *Mus* son *m* fondamental

fundamentalism [fʌndə'mentəlɪz(ə)m] *n Rel* fondamentalisme *m*

fundamentalist [fʌndəˈmentəlɪst] *adj, n Rel* fondamentaliste *mf*

fundamentally [fʌndəˈmentəlɪ] *adv* (*honest, incorrect, important*) fondamentalement; **f., there's nothing wrong with the idea** l'idée en soi n'est pas mauvaise; **f., it's a question of who's got more money** au fond, ce qui importe c'est qui a le plus d'argent

funded [ˈfʌndɪd] *adj Fin* (*assets*) en rentes; **f. capital** capitaux *mpl* investis; **f. debt** dette *f* consolidée

funding [ˈfʌndɪŋ] *n* **(a)** (*for project*) financement *m*; **f. plan** plan *m* de financement **(b)** (*of debt*) consolidation *f*; (*of annuity*) assiette *f*

fund management *n Fin* gestion *m* de capitaux *ou* de portefeuille *ou* de fonds

fund manager *n* dirigeant *m* d'OPCVM, gérant *m* de portefeuille

fund-raiser *n* **(a)** (*professional*) = personne *f* employée par une œuvre de bienfaisance pour rassembler des fonds **(b)** (*event*) = match *m*/concert *m*/*etc* au profit d'une œuvre de bienfaisance

fund-raising 1 *n* collecte *f* de fonds pour une œuvre de bienfaisance; **Nadia is in charge of f.** Nadia est chargée de rassembler les fonds **2** *adj* **f. scheme** projet *m* visant à rassembler des fonds; **f. dinner** dîner *m* de bienfaisance

funeral [ˈfjuːnərəl] *n* funérailles *fpl*, obsèques *fpl*; (*including burial*) enterrement *m*; **to attend sb's f.** assister à l'enterrement de qn; *F* **that's your f.!** ça c'est votre problème!; **f. ceremony** cérémonie *f* funèbre; **f. director** entrepreneur *m* de pompes funèbres; *Mus* **f. march** marche *f* funèbre; **f. parlour** *or US* **home** établissement *m* de pompes funèbres; **f. procession** cortège *m* funebre; **f. pyre** bûcher *m*; **f. service** office *m* des morts

funereal [fjuːˈnɪərɪəl] *adj* lugubre, funèbre, triste; (*voice*) lugubre, sépulcral; (*pace*) lent; **to proceed at a f. pace** avancer à un pas d'enterrement

funfair [ˈfʌnˈfeər] *n* (*travelling*) fête *f* foraine, foire *f*; (*fixed*) parc *m* d'attractions

fungible [ˈfʌndʒɪb(ə)l] *adj St Exch* fongible

fungicide [ˈfʌndʒɪsaɪd] *n* fongicide *m*

fungoid [ˈfʌŋgɔɪd] *adj* **(a)** *Bot* fongoïde **(b)** *Med* fongueux

fungous [ˈfʌŋgəs] *adj Med* fongueux

fungus, *pl* **-uses, -i** [ˈfʌŋgəs, -əsɪz, -gaɪ, -dʒaɪ] *n* **(a)** *Bot* champignon *m*; (*on walls*) moisissure *f*; *Hum* **face f.** (*moustache*) moustache *f*, bacchantes *fpl*; (*beard*) barbe *f* **(b)** *Med* fongus *m*

funicular [fjuːˈnɪkjʊlər] *n, adj* (*railway*) funiculaire *m*

funk¹ [fʌŋk] *n Old-fashioned esp Br Sl* (*fright*) frousse *f*; **to be in a (blue) f.** avoir une peur bleue, avoir une frousse de tous les diables; **to get into a f.** caner; *Mil F* **f. hole** abri *m*, planque *f*

funk² *Old-fashioned esp Br Sl* **1** *vt* **to f. sth/doing sth** avoir peur de qch/de faire qch; **to f. it** caner, se dégonfler **2** *vi* caner, se dégonfler

funk³ *n Mus* funk *m*; **f. band** groupe *m* funk

funky [ˈfʌŋkɪ] *adj* **(a)** *Mus* funky, funk **(b)** *Am F* (*smelly*) puant **(c)** *esp Am Old-fashioned F* (*fashionable*) cool, branché **(d)** *esp Br Old-fashioned Sl* (*cowardly*) froussard

funnel¹ [ˈfʌn(ə)l] *n* **(a)** (*of locomotive, steamship*) cheminée *f* **(b)** (*for filling*) entonnoir *m*; *Ind* **(loading) f.** trémie *f*, hotte *f* **(c)** (*for ventilation*) tuyau *m ou* cheminée *f* d'aération

funnel² **(-ll-) 1** *vi* **the crowd funnelled into a narrow passage/through the gates** la foule s'est engouffrée dans un passage étroit/entre les grilles **2** *vt* (*direct*) canaliser; **to f. a liquid into a bottle** verser un liquide dans une bouteille à l'aide d'un entonnoir; **complaints are funnelled to the head office** les réclamations sont canalisées vers le bureau central

funnelling [ˈfʌn(ə)lɪŋ] *n Mktg* (*in questionnaire construction*) entonnoir *m*

funnily [ˈfʌnɪlɪ] *adv* **(a)** (*amusingly*) comiquement **(b)** (*curiously*) curieusement, bizarrement; **f. enough ...** chose curieuse ...

funniness [ˈfʌnɪnɪs] *n* **(a)** (*amusing nature*) (*of person*) caractère *m* amusant *ou* drôle **(b)** (*strangeness*) bizarrerie *f*

funny [ˈfʌnɪ] **1** *adj* **(a)** (*amusing*) drôle, amusant; **it was really too f.!, it was too f. for words!** c'était vraiment trop drôle!, c'était tordant!; **she's a very f. woman** (*comic, actress*) elle est très drôle; **none of your f. tricks!, don't try to be f.!** pas de farces!; **the f. thing about it is ...** le comique de la chose c'est que ...; **f. bone** (*of elbow*) petit juif *m*; *Cin* **f. film** film *m* comique

(b) (*strange*) curieux, bizarre; **he is a f. person** c'est un drôle d'homme; **he was f. that way** il était comme ça; **a f. idea** une drôle d'idée; **well, that's f.!** voilà qui est curieux *ou* étrange; **f., I thought I'd locked the door** tiens, c'est drôle, je pensais avoir fermé la porte à clé; **(it's) f. you should say that** c'est drôle que vous disiez cela; **it's a f. thing but ...** c'est drôle, mais ...; **there's something f. about the entire business** il y a quelque chose de louche dans cette affaire; *F* **no f. business!** pas de blagues!, pas de bêtises!; **this butter tastes/smells f.** ce beurre a un drôle de goût/une drôle d'odeur; **it feels f.** ça fait drôle; **the engine sounds f.** le moteur fait un drôle de bruit; **his voice sounded f.** il avait une drôle de voix; *F* **I came over all f.** je me suis senti(e) tout(e) drôle; **I've got a f. feeling in my stomach** j'ai un peu mal au cœur; **I had a f. feeling we were going to meet again** j'avais comme l'impression que nous nous reverrions; **he went a bit f. in his old age** il devint un peu bizarre dans sa vieillesse; *Sl* **f. farm** maison *f* de fous; *F* **f. money** des sommes mirobolantes *ou* astronomiques; *F* **f. peculiar or f. ha-ha?** comment ça, drôle? bizarre ou rigolo?

2 *npl esp Am F* **the funnies** (*in magazine*) bandes *fpl* dessinées, pages *fpl* comiques

fur¹ [fɜːr] *n* **(a)** *Com* fourrure *f*; *Zool* poil *m*; *F* **to make the f. fly, to set the f. flying** (*make a scene*) faire une scène violente; (*fight*) se battre avec acharnement; **furs** (*of animals*) peaux *fpl*; **f. coat** manteau *m* de fourrure; **f. farm** élevage *m* d'animaux à fourrure; **f. lined boot** bottillon *m* fouré; **f.-lined coat** manteau doublé de fourrure; **f. skins** peaux *fpl*; **f. trade** commerce *m* de fourrures, pelleterie *f* **(b)** (*deposit*) (*in kettle, boiler*) tartre *m*; *Med* (*on tongue*) enduit *m*

▶ **fur up** *vi* (*of boiler etc*) s'incruster, s'entartrer; *Med* (*of tongue*) se charger, s'empâter

furbish [ˈfɜːbɪʃ] *vt* **(a)** (*polish*) (*piece of métal*) fourbir, polir, astiquer **(b)** (*renovate*) (*furniture*) remettre à neuf

furious [ˈfjʊərɪəs] *adj* furieux; (*look*) furibond; (*battle, activity, efforts etc*) acharné, forcené; (*storm, sea, wind*) déchaîné; **to drive at a f. speed** conduire à une allure folle; **to get f.** entrer en fureur; **to be f. with sb/oneself** être furieux contre qn/soi-même

furiously [ˈfjʊərɪəslɪ] *adv* furieusement; (*to work*) avec acharnement; (*to fight*) avec acharnement, avec furie; (*to drive*) à une allure folle; **the fire was blazing f.** l'incendie faisait rage

furl [fɜːl] *vt* (*umbrella, flag etc*) rouler; *Naut* (*sail*) serrer, ferler

furlong [ˈfɜːlɒŋ] *n* (*measurement*) furlong *m* (= 201 mètres); **a race over seven furlongs** une course de 1 400 mètres

furlough [ˈfɜːləʊ] *n Mil etc* congé *m*, permission *f*; **to be/go on f.** être/aller en permission

furnace [ˈfɜːnɪs] *n* **(a)** fourneau *m*, four *m*; *Fig* fournaise *f*; **this room is like a f.** cette pièce est une (vraie) fournaise **(b)** **(central-heating) f.** calorifère *m*

furnish [ˈfɜːnɪʃ] *vt* **(a)** (*house, flat etc*) meubler; **to f. one's room/home/flat** se meubler **(b)** *esp Fml* (*provide*) (*information*) fournir, donner; (*funds*) pourvoir; (*reasons*) produire, alléguer; (*opportunity*) offrir, présenter, fournir; (*needs*) pourvoir à; **to f. sb with sth** fournir qch à qn, pourvoir *ou* munir qn de qch; **to f. an army (with provisions)** fournir une armée en provisions

furnished [ˈfɜːnɪʃt] *adj* **(a)** (*flat, room*) meublé; **to live in f. rooms** loger en meublé **(b)** (*provided*) pourvu, fourni, équipé **(with** de); **well f. shop** magasin bien achalandé

furnishing [ˈfɜːnɪʃɪŋ] *n* **f. fabrics** tissus *mpl* d'ameublement

furnishings [ˈfɜːnɪʃɪŋz] *npl* (*furniture*) (*of house*) ameublement *m*; **soft f.** (*fabrics*) tissus *mpl* d'ameublement; (*carpets and curtains*) tapis *mpl* et rideaux *mpl*

furniture [ˈfɜːnɪtʃər] *n* **(a)** (*in house etc*) meubles *mpl*, mobilier *m*; **a piece of f.** un meuble; *F* **I feel as if I'm part of the f.** j'ai l'impression de faire partie des meubles; **dining-room f.** mobilier *ou* meubles de salle à manger; **f. polish** encaustique *f* pour les meubles; **f. remover** déménageur *m*; **f. shop** magasin *m* d'ameublement; **f. van** camion *m* de déménagement **(b)** (*of door, coffin etc*) ferrures *fpl*

furore [fjʊˈrɔːreɪ], *US* **furor** [ˈfjʊərɔːr] *n* (*uproar*) tumulte *m* (**over** au sujet de); (*enthusiasm*) enthousiasme *m* démesuré; **to cause** *or* **create a f.** (*cause uproar*) provoquer un tumulte; (*be very popular*) faire fureur; **there's been a great f. over those scenes** ces scènes ont provoqué un énorme tumulte

furred [fɜːd] *adj* (*boiler etc*) entartré, encrusté; **f. tongue** langue chargée

furrier [ˈfʌrɪər] *n* pelletier, -ière, fourreur *m*

furring [ˈfɜːrɪŋ] *n* (*in boiler etc*) tartre *m*

furrow¹ [ˈfʌrəʊ] *n* (*in field, Fig in stone*) sillon *m*; *Fig* (*on face*) ride *f* profonde, sillon; *Fig* **to plough a lonely f.** (*of inventor, reformer etc*) poursuivre seul une idée; (*keep oneself to oneself*) faire bande à part

furrow² *vt* **(a)** (*earth*) creuser des sillons dans; *Lit* **the boats furrowed the seas** les bateaux sillonnaient les mers **(b)**

(*forehead etc*) rider profondément; **his brow is furrowed with wrinkles** des rides profondes lui sillonnent le front

furrowed [ˈfʌrəʊd] *adj* (*forehead, brow*) coupé de rides profondes; **f. with concentration** plissé de concentration

furry [ˈfɜːrɪ] *adj* **(a)** (*animal*) à poil; (*tail, ears*) poilu; (*insect*) velu; (*moss etc*) qui ressemble à (de) la fourrure; **f. toy** peluche *f*; **the husky has a f. coat** le husky a de longs poils; **a f. little kitten** un chaton tout doux **(b)** (*boiler, kettle*) entartré; **f. tongue** langue chargée

further[1] [ˈfɜːðər] (*comp of* **far**) [①A19,g,i] **1** *adv* **(a)** (*distance*) plus loin (**than** que); (*extent*) davantage, plus; **to penetrate f. into the country** pénétrer plus avant dans le pays; **I can go no f.** je ne peux pas aller plus loin; (*I'm exhausted*) je n'en peux plus; *F* **this mustn't go any f.** ceci ne doit pas se propager; **to move f. away** s'éloigner; **I didn't question him any f.** je ne l'ai pas interrogé davantage; **until you hear f.** jusqu'à nouvel avis; **I've nothing f. to say** je n'ai rien d'autre à dire; **to go no f. into the matter** en rester là; **to add water to the wine to make it go f.** allonger le vin d'eau; **that doesn't get us much f.** cela ne nous avance pas beaucoup; **f. back** (*in time*) à une période plus reculée; **f. back than the last century** antérieurement au siècle dernier

(b) (*moreover*) d'ailleurs, de plus; **we would f. add that ...** nous nous permettons d'ajouter en outre que ...

(c) *Fml* **f. to** (*following*) suite à

2 *adj* **(a)** (*of two*) **at the f. end of the room** à l'autre bout *ou* au fond de la salle; **the f. bank of the river** la rive opposée de la rivière; **the f. of the two villages** le plus éloigné des deux villages

(b) (*additional*) additionnel, supplémentaire; **upon f. consideration** après plus ample(s) réflexion(s); **do you have any f. instructions?** est-ce que vous avez d'autres consignes?; **one or two f. details** encore un ou deux détails; **without f. loss of time** sans perdre plus de temps; **to await f. news** attendre de plus amples nouvelles; **until f. notice** jusqu'à nouvel ordre; **without f. warning** sans plus d'avertissement; *Br* **f. education** enseignement *m* postscolaire; **f. information** renseignements *mpl* complémentaires (**about** au sujet de); *Com* **I would like to place a f. order** je voudrais passer une nouvelle commande; *esp Mil* **to await f. orders** attendre les ordres

further[2] *vt* (*cause, person's interests*) servir; (*one's attempts, efforts, career*) favoriser

furtherance [ˈfɜːðərəns] *n* (*of work etc*) avancement *m*; **for the f.** *or* **in f. of sth** pour servir qch

furthermore [fɜːðəˈmɔːr] *adv* en outre, de plus, par ailleurs

furthermost [ˈfɜːðəməʊst] *adj* (*place etc*) le plus lointain, le plus reculé, le plus éloigné; *Lit* **to the f. ends of the earth** jusqu'au bout du monde

furthest [ˈfɜːðɪst] (*superl of* **far**) [①A19,g,i] **1** *adv* **he went f.** il est allé le plus loin; **when it's f. from the sun** lorsqu'il se trouve le plus éloigné du soleil; **this is the f. north I've ever been** c'est le plus au nord que j'aie jamais été **2** *adj* **the f. part of the cave** la partie la plus reculée de la caverne

furtive [ˈfɜːtɪv] *adj* (*manner, person*) sournois, cachottier; (*smile, look etc*) furtif, dérobé

furtively [ˈfɜːtɪvlɪ] *adv* (*see adj*) sournoisement; furtivement

fury [ˈfjʊərɪ] *n* **(a)** (*of person*) furie *f*, fureur *f*; (*of wind etc*) déchaînement *m*, violence *f*; **to be in a f.** (*of person*) être furieux, être en furie *ou* fureur; **to get into a f.** entrer en furie *ou* fureur, s'emporter; *F* **to work like f.** travailler avec acharnement; **to run like f.** courir comme un dératé **(b)** *Myth* **the Furies** les Furies *fpl*

furze [fɜːz] *n* (*plant*) ajonc *m*

fuse[1], *US* **fuze** [fjuːz] *n Mil etc* (*for shell etc*) fusée *f*; (*for bomb*) amorce *f*; *Min* étoupille *f*, mèche *f*; **safety f.** cordeau *m* (bickford); **time f.** fusée à retard(ement); **to set a f.** régler une fusée; *Fig* **the incident which lit the f. of the revolution** l'incident qui a déclenché la révolution; *Fig, F* **to have a short f.** démarrer au quart de tour

fuse[2], *US* **fuze** *vt Mil etc* (*bomb*) amorcer

fuse[3] *n El* (**safety**) **f.** fusible *m* (de sécurité); *F* plomb *m*; **to blow a f.** faire sauter un plomb; *Fig, F* (*of person*) sortir de ses gonds; **the f. has blown** *or F* **gone** le plomb a sauté; **f. box** boîte *f* à fusibles; **f. wire** fil *m* à fusible

fuse[4] **1** *vt* **(a)** (*melt*) (*metal etc*) fondre, mettre en fusion; **to f. two pieces together** réunir deux pièces par fusion **(b)** (*join*) fusionner, amalgamer **(c)** *Br El* (*circuit*) faire sauter les plombs de; **to f. the lights** faire sauter les plombs **2** *vi* **(a)** (*of metals etc*) fondre; **the parts had fused together** les pièces avaient fondu et s'étaient collées les unes aux autres **(b)** (*of parties etc*) fusionner **(c)** *Br El* **the lights have fused** les plombs ont sauté

fused [fjuːzd] *adj El* muni d'un fusible

fuselage [ˈfjuːzəlɑːʒ] *n Av* fuselage *m*

fusilier [fjuːzɪˈlɪər] *n Mil* fusilier *m*

fusillade [fjuːzɪˈleɪd] *n Mil* **a f.** (**of shots**) une fusillade; **a f. of criticism/questions** une avalanche de critiques/questions

fusion [ˈfjuːʒən] *n* **(a)** *Phys* fusion *f*; (*of metal*) fonte *f*; *Phys* **cold f.** fusion à froid; *Nucl, Phys* **controlled f.** fusion contrôlée; *Mil* **f. bomb** bombe *f* thermonucléaire **(b)** (*amalgamation*) (*of banks etc*) fusionnement *m*; *Pol* (*of parties etc*) fusion *f*

fuss[1] [fʌs] *n* (*exaggeration*) histoires *fpl*; **what's all the f. about?** qu'est-ce que c'est que toutes ces histoires?; (*what's wrong*) qu'est-ce qui cloche?; **without any f.** (*to get married*) sans cérémonies; (*to get through customs*) sans aucun problème; **can you have him ejected from the studio without too much f.?** est-ce que vous pouvez le faire évacuer du studio discrètement?; **I don't want any f. made when I retire** je ne veux pas qu'on fasse tout un cinéma quand je prendrai ma retraite; **a lot of f. about** *or* **over nothing** beaucoup de bruit pour rien; **if you knew the f. your letter caused** si tu savais le remue-ménage que ta lettre a provoqué; **a great f.** bien des cérémonies; **to make a f.**, *F* **to kick up a f.** (*complain loudly*) faire un tas d'histoires, faire tout un cinéma; **don't make such a f. about it** ne faites pas tant d'histoires; **I don't see what all the f. is about** (*I think it's a harmless, poor quality film/product etc*) je ne vois pas pourquoi on fait un tel cinéma; **to make a f. of** *or* **over sb** être aux petits soins pour qn; (*talk about with excessive admiration*) faire grand cas de qn; **he likes to be made a f. of** *or* **over** (*of person*) il aime qu'on fasse grand cas de lui; (*of dog*) il aime qu'on le caresse

fuss[2] **1** *vi* faire des embarras *ou* des histoires; **stop fussing!** arrête de faire des histoires!; **she never stops fussing with her hair** elle ne cesse pas d'arranger nerveusement ses cheveux **2** *vt* (*person*) tracasser, agiter; *F* **I'm not fussed** ça ne me fait rien

▶ **fuss about, fuss around** *vi* (*be busy*) s'affairer

▶ **fuss over** *vipo* (*person*) être aux petits soins pour

fussily [ˈfʌsɪlɪ] *adv* **(a)** (*to arrange things*) d'une manière tatillonne; (*to say sth*) d'un air important **(b) f. dressed** vêtu avec trop de recherche; **the room was rather f. decorated** la décoration de la pièce était surchargée

fussiness [ˈfʌsɪnɪs] *n* **(a)** (*of person*) (*behaviour*) tendance *f* à faire beaucoup d'embarras; (*character*) esprit *m* tracassier; **his f. about food is ridiculous** il est si difficile sur la nourriture que c'en est ridicule; **her f. about details** l'attention exagérée qu'elle porte aux détails **(b)** (*of dress, decor etc*) manque *m* de simplicité

fusspot [ˈfʌspɒt] *n Br F Pej* (*finicky person*) (*about preparing food, cleaning house*) tatillon, -onne; (*about getting wet, dirty etc*) chichiteux, -euse; (*worrier*) tracassier, -ière; **don't be such a f. about a little bit of rain** ne sois pas aussi chichiteux, ce n'est qu'une petite pluie; **don't be such a f., leave the housework for one day** ne sois pas aussi tatillon, laisse tomber le ménage pour aujourd'hui; **don't be such a f., I'm sure he is safe** ne te tracasse pas comme ça, je suis sûr qu'il est en sécurité

fussy [ˈfʌsɪ] *adj* **(a)** (*person*) (*who worries*) tracassier, qui fait des histoires; (*who is finicky, particular*) tatillon, -onne; **I'm not the f. kind** je ne suis pas difficile; **I'm not f.** cela m'est égal; **we can't afford to be too f.** nous ne pouvons pas nous permettre d'être trop difficiles; **to be f. about one's food** être difficile sur la nourriture **(b)** (*dress, decor*) surchargé; (*style*) qui manque de simplicité, surchargé

fustian [ˈfʌstɪən] *n Tex* futaine *f*; *Fig Lit* (*pompousness*) grandiloquence *f*, emphase *f*

fustiness [ˈfʌstɪnɪs] *n* **(a)** (*smell*) odeur *f* de moisi **(b)** *Fig* (*of theory etc*) caractère *m* démodé

fusty [ˈfʌstɪ] *adj* **(a)** (*house, clothes*) qui sent le renfermé; (*smell*) de renfermé **(b)** *Fig* (*ideas etc*) suranné, démodé

futile [ˈfjuːtaɪl] *adj* **(a)** (*vain*) inutile; (*attempt, protest*) vain **(b)** (*trifling*) (*remark etc*) futile; **f. ideas** idées creuses

futility [fjuːˈtɪlɪtɪ] *n* futilité *f*; (*of efforts etc*) inutilité *f*; **an exercise in f.** une vaine entreprise

futon [ˈfuːtɒn] *n* futon *m*

future [ˈfjuːtʃər] **1** (①A49-50; B29,6-7] *adj* futur; (*events*) à venir; **my f. wife** ma future épouse; **at some f. date** dans l'avenir; **for f. reference** à titre d'information; *Com* **goods for f. delivery** marchandises livrables ultérieurement; *Fin* **to sell for f. delivery** vendre livrable à terme; *Gram* **f. tense** temps *m* futur

2 *n* **(a)** avenir *m*; **in (the) f., for the f.** à l'avenir; **in the near f.** dans un proche avenir, sous peu; **in the distant f.** dans un avenir lointain; **at some point** *or* **stage in the f.** un jour; **what does the f. hold for us?** qu'est-ce que l'avenir nous réserve?; **the public transport of the f.** les transports en commun de l'avenir; **you're looking at the f.** (*when you look* *at this car/computer/etc*) voilà la voiture/l'ordinateur/*etc* de demain *ou* de l'avenir

(**b**) (*of person*) avenir *m*; **job with a (good) f.** situation d'avenir; **to ruin one's f.** briser son avenir; **she has a brilliant f. (before her)** elle a un bel avenir devant elle

(**c**) *St Exch* contrat *f* à terme; **futures** opérations *fpl* à terme; **futures contract** contrat *m* à terme; **futures exchange** marché *m* à terme; **futures market** marché *m* à terme; **futures trading** negociations *fpl* à terme

(**d**) [①A49-50; B29,6-7] *Gram* (temps *m*) futur *m*; **f. perfect** futur antérieur; **verb in the f.** verbe au futur

future-proof[1] *adj esp Comptr* évolutif

future-proof[2] *vt esp Comptr* rendre évolutif

futurism ['fju:tʃərɪz(ə)m] *n Art* futurisme *m*

futurist ['fju:tʃərɪst] *adj, n Art* futuriste *mf*; **f. research firm** société *f* spécialisée dans les prévisions futuristes

futuristic ['fju:tʃə'rɪstɪk] *adj* futuriste

futurologist [fju:tʃə'rɒlədʒɪst] *n* futurologue *mf*

futurology [fju:tʃə'rɒlədʒɪ] *n* futurologie *f*

fuze [fju:z] *n, vt US* = **fuse**[1,2]

fuzz[1] [fʌz] *n* (**a**) (*on blankets etc*) peluches *fpl*, bourre *f* (**b**) (*on peach, skin*) duvet *m*

fuzz[2] *npl Sl* **the f.** (*the police*) les flics *mpl*

fuzziness ['fʌzɪnɪs] *n* (**a**) (*of outline, recording etc*) manque *m* de netteté; (*of photo etc*) flou *m* (**b**) **the f. of my hair** mes cheveux crépus

fuzzy ['fʌzɪ] *adj* (**a**) (*outline etc*) sans netteté; (*recording*) qui manque de netteté; (*idea, look*) flou, vague; *Art, Phot* flou; **everything looks f. to me** j'ai une vue confuse de tout; **I feel a bit f.-headed** je n'ai pas les idées très claires; **f. logic** logique *f* floue (**b**) (*hair*) crépu; (*cloth etc*) floconneux

fwd *abbr* **forward**

G

G, g [dʒiː] *n* **(a)** *(letter)* G, g *m* **(b)** *Mus* sol *m*; **G clef** clef *f* de sol; **in G minor** en sol mineur **(c)** *US (thousand dollars)* = mille dollars **(d) G-suit** combinaison *f* spatiale **(e)** *Phys* **G** conductance *f* **(f)** *Austr Cin* **G.** visible par tous
g *(abbr* **gramme***)* gr.
G-string *n Mus* corde *f* de sol; *(of stripper)* cache-sexe *m inv*
Ga *abbr* **Georgia**
gab¹ [gæb] *n F (chat, talk)* **we had a good g. on the phone** on a taillé une bonne bavette au téléphone; **to have the gift of the g.** avoir la langue bien pendue; *(be convincing talker)* avoir du bagou(t)
gab² *vi* **(-bb-)** *F Pej (chat)* bavarder, *Pej* papoter; *(gossip)* caqueter, jaser
gabardine [gæbəˈdiːn, ˈgæbədiːn] *n* gabardine *f*
gabble¹ [ˈgæb(ə)l] *n* bredouillement *m (de paroles prononcées trop vite)*; **to speak in a g.** bredouiller; **to listen to the g. of voices** écouter le bruit des conversations; **there was an incomprehensible g. coming from the garden** on entendait une conversation inintelligible dans le jardin
gabble² **1** *vi* bredouiller, manger ses mots **2** *vt (speech)* débiter à toute vitesse
▶ **gabble away** *vi* baragouiner; **two foreigners were gabbling away to each other** deux étrangers baragouinaient dans leur langue
▶ **gabble out** *vtsep* = **gabble² 2**
gaberdine [gæbəˈdiːn, ˈgæbədiːn] *n* gabardine *f*
gable [ˈgeɪb(ə)l] *n Archit* **g. (end)** pignon *m*; **g. roof** comble *m* sur pignon(s); **g. window** faîtière *f*
gabled [ˈgeɪb(ə)ld] *adj Archit (house)* à pignon(s); *(wall)* en pignon; *(roof)* sur pignon(s)
Gabon [gæˈbɒn] *n* Gabon *m*
Gabonese [gæbəˈniːz] **1** *adj* gabonais **2** *n* Gabonais, -aise
▶ **gad about** [gæd] *vi* courir le monde; **he spent a year gadding about Europe** il a passé un an à parcourir l'Europe; **she's been out gadding about (town) all night** elle a passé toute la nuit à faire la fête (en ville)
gadfly [ˈgædflaɪ] *n (insect)* taon *m*; *Fig* casse-pieds *mf inv*
gadget [ˈgædʒɪt] *n* gadget *m*; **it's just another g.** c'est un gadget de plus; **what's that g. for?** à quoi sert ce truc-là?
gadgetry [ˈgædʒɪtrɪ] *n* gadgets *mpl*
Gaelic [ˈgeɪlɪk] **1** *adj* gaélique **2** *n Ling* gaélique *m*
gaff¹ [gæf] *n* **(a)** *Fishing* gaffe *f* **(b)** *Naut* corne *f*; **g. topsail** voile *f* de flèche
gaff² *vt Fishing* gaffer
gaff³ *n F* **to blow the g.** vendre la mèche; **to blow the g. on** *(sb's plans)* dévoiler; *(corruption)* dénoncer; **to blow the g. on sb** dénoncer qn, vendre qn
gaffe [gæf] *n (blunder)* gaffe *f*, bourde *f*
gaffer [ˈgæfər] *n* **(a)** *Br F (foreman)* contremaître *m*, chef *m* d'équipe; *(boss, owner)* patron *m*, singe *m*; *Cin, TV* chef *m* électricien, gaffer *m*; *TV, Cin* **g. grip** pince *f* pour projecteur **(b)** *F (old man)* vieux *m*
gag¹ [gæg] *n* **(a)** *(on mouth)* bâillon *m*; *Surg* ouvre-bouche *m inv*; *Fig* **the law was used as a g. on the freedom of the press** la loi servait à bâillonner la presse **(b)** *Th, Cin F (joke)* blague *f*; *(visual)* gag *m*; **to do sth for a g.** faire qch pour rire *ou* pour s'amuser
gag² **(-gg-) 1** *vt (put a gag on) (person, the press)* bâillonner **2** *vi F (retch)* avoir des haut-le-cœur; **to make sb g.** donner envie de vomir à qn
gaga [ˈgɑːgɑː] *adj F* gaga *inv*, gâteux; **to go g.** devenir gaga *ou* gâteux
gage¹ [geɪdʒ] *n Old-fashioned (pledge)* gage *m*, garantie *f*
gage² *n, vt Am* = **gauge**
gage³ *n* = **greengage**
gagging [ˈgægɪŋ] *n (of person, press)* bâillonnement *m*
gaggle¹ [ˈgæg(ə)l] *n (of geese)* troupeau *m*; *Fig* **a g. of young schoolgirls** un troupeau de jeunes élèves
gaggle² *vi (of goose)* cacarder
gagman, *pl* -men [ˈgægmən] *n Am Cin, Th* auteur *m* de gags, gagman *m*, *pl* gagmen

gaiety [ˈgeɪətɪ] *n* **(a)** *(cheerfulness)* gaieté *f* **(b)** *Old-fashioned (festivities) (usu pl)* **gaieties** réjouissances *fpl*
gaily [ˈgeɪlɪ] *adv* **(a)** *(happily)* gaiement, allègrement **(b)** *(with bright colours)* de couleurs gaies; **g. coloured** aux couleurs gaies *ou* vives
gain¹ [geɪn] *n* **(a)** *(profit)* gain *m*, profit *m*, avantage *m*; **to do sth for g.** faire qch par intérêt; **my g. is your loss** le profit de l'un est le dommage de l'autre **(b)** *(increase)* augmentation *f*; *(in value)* hausse *f*; *Fin* **g. in value** plus-value *f*; **g. in weight** prise *f* de poids; **there has been a net g. in their income** leurs revenus ont nettement augmenté; *St Exch* **there has been a g. of 100 points on the Dow Jones** l'indice Dow Jones a gagné 100 points; *Pol* **Labour made important gains in London** le parti travailliste a beaucoup progressé à Londres **(c)** *Electron* gain *m*
gain² **1** *vt* **(a)** *(acquire) (reputation)* acquérir; *(sympathy)* gagner; **you will g. nothing by it** vous n'y gagnerez rien; **to g. permission** obtenir une permission; **to g. sb's affection** gagner l'affection de qn; **to g. experience** acquérir de l'expérience; **to g. entrance** *or* **admission** s'introduire; **to g. the impression that ...** avoir l'impression que ...; **to g. an advantage** obtenir un avantage; **we have not so much lost a daughter as gained a son, we're not losing a daughter, we're gaining a son** nous n'avons pas perdu une fille mais gagné un fils

(b) *(acquire more of)* gagner, prendre; *(time)* gagner; *(strength)* (re)prendre; **to g. weight** prendre du poids; **to g. popularity** devenir plus populaire; **he has gained prestige through this action** cette action a rehaussé son prestige; **the party has gained support** le parti a gagné des voix; **to g. ground** *(of racer, pursuer)* gagner du terrain **(on** sur); *(of a custom)* se répandre, se développer; **to g. share** *(of market)* gagner des parts de marché

(c) *(win)* **to g. a victory** remporter une victoire; **they gained two points** ils ont gagné deux points; **to g. the upper hand** prendre le dessus

(d) *(of clock)* **to g. five minutes a day** avancer de cinq minutes par jour

2 *vi* **(a)** *(benefit)* **to g. by** bénéficier de, être aidé par; **we have all gained by his hard work** nous avons tous bénéficié de son labeur; **we have gained by having her in the team** cela nous a aidés de l'avoir dans l'équipe; **I had a good teacher and I think I gained by that** j'ai eu un bon professeur et je crois que ça m'a servi

(b) *(increase)* **to g. in popularity/experience** gagner en popularité/acquérir de l'expérience; **to g. in self-confidence** gagner *ou* prendre de l'assurance; **to g. in number** devenir plus nombreux

(c) *(of clock)* avancer

(d) *(of racer, pursuer)* gagner du terrain

▶ **gain on** *vipo (adversary, competitor)* gagner du terrain sur
gainer [ˈgeɪnər] *n* gagnant, -ante
gainful [ˈgeɪnfʊl] *adj* profitable, rémunérateur, -trice; **to be in g. employment** avoir un emploi rémunéré
gainfully [ˈgeɪnfʊlɪ] *adv* **to be g. employed** *(doing sth useful)* faire quelque chose d'utile; *(earning money)* avoir un emploi rémunéré
gainsay [geɪnˈseɪ] *vt (pp, pt* **gainsaid** [geɪnˈsed]*)* *usu Lit* contredire; **there's no gainsaying his honesty/skill** son honnêteté/son adresse est indéniable
gait [geɪt] *n* démarche *f*; *(of horse)* train *m*; **unsteady g.** pas *m* mal assuré
gaiter [ˈgeɪtər] *n* **(a)** *Clothing* guêtre *f* **(b)** *Aut* soufflet *m*
gal¹ *abbr* **gallon(s)**
gal² [gæl] *n Old-fashioned F (girl)* fille *f*
gala [ˈgɑːlə] *n* gala *m*; **swimming g.** grand concours *m* de natation; **in g. dress** en habit de gala; **g. evening** soirée *f* de gala; **g. performance** représentation *f* de gala
galactic [gəˈlæktɪk] *adj Astron (pole etc)* galactique
Galahad [ˈgæləhæd] *n Myth* **Sir G.** Galaad *m*; *Fig* personne *f* noble et généreuse, seigneur *m*
Galapagos [gəˈlæpəgəs] *n* **the G. (Islands)** les (îles *fpl*) Galapagos *fpl*

galaxy [ˈgæləksɪ] *n* (**a**) *Astron* galaxie *f*; **the G.** (*Milky Way*) la Voie Lactée (**b**) *Fig* (*of famous people, film stars etc*) pléiade *f*

gale [geɪl] *n* grand (coup *m* de) vent *m*, vent fort; **the roof was blown off in a g.** un grand coup de vent a emporté le toit; **it's blowing a g.** le vent souffle en tempête; *Fig* **a g. of laughter** un éclat de rire; *Met* **g. force winds** vents forts; *Met* **g. warning** avis *m* de tempête

galena [gəˈliːnə] *n Miner* galène *f*

Galilean [gælɪˈliːən] *Bible* **1** *adj* galiléen **2** *n* Galiléen, -éenne

Galilee [ˈgælɪliː] *n* Galilée *f*; **the Sea of G.** la mer *ou* le lac de Galilée

Galileo [gælɪˈleɪəʊ] *n* Galilée *m*

gall¹ *abbr* **gallon(s)**

gall² [gɔːl] *n* (*impudence*) effronterie *f*, culot *m*, toupet *m*; **she had the g. to …** elle a eu le culot *ou* le toupet de …

gall³ *n* (*sore*) (*on horse etc*) écorchure *f*; *Fig* **the criticism was a g. to his pride** la critique l'a piqué au vif

gall⁴ *vt* (**a**) (*make sore*) écorcher (*par frottement*) (**b**) (*annoy*) irriter, exaspérer

gall⁵ *n Bot* galle *f*, cécidie *f*

gallant *adj* (**a**) [ˈgælənt] (*brave*) brave, vaillant; **the ship and her g. crew** le navire et son valeureux équipage; **g. deed** acte de bravoure (**b**) [gəˈlænt] (*with women*) galant

gallantly *adv* (**a**) [ˈgæləntlɪ] (*bravely*) bravement, vaillamment (**b**) [gəˈlæntlɪ, ˈgæləntlɪ] (*with women*) galamment, en homme galant

gallantry [ˈgæləntrɪ] *n* (**a**) (*bravery*) vaillance *f*, bravoure *f*; **a medal for g.** une médaille de bravoure (**b**) (*with women*) galanterie *f*

gall bladder *n* vésicule *f* biliaire

galleon [ˈgælɪən] *n Naut, Hist* galion *m*

gallery [ˈgælərɪ] *n* (**a**) (*in hall etc*) galerie *f*; **strangers'** *or* **public g.** (*in Houses of Parliament*) tribune *f* du public; **press g.** tribune de la presse; *Th* **the g.** (*seats*) la (troisième) galerie, *F* le paradis; *Fig* **to play to the g.** jouer pour la galerie (**b**) (*private*), *Com* (**art**) **g.** galerie *f*; (*museum*) musée *m* (d'art) (**c**) *Min* galerie *f* (**d**) **shooting g.** stand *m* de tir (**e**) *Am* (*balcony*) balcon *m*; (*veranda*) véranda *f*

galley [ˈgælɪ] *n* (**a**) (*ancient ship*) galère *f*; (*rowing boat*) yole *f*; **g. slave** galérien *m* (**b**) *Naut, Av* (*kitchen*) cuisine *f* (**c**) *Typ* galée *f*; **g.** (**proof**) (épreuve *f* en) placard *m*

Gallic [ˈgælɪk] *adj* (**a**) (*French*) (*flair, charm, sophistication*) français; **a G. shrug** un haussement d'épaules (**b**) *Hist* (*of Gaul*) gaulois; **the G. Wars** la guerre des Gaules

gallicism [ˈgælɪsɪz(ə)m] *n Ling* gallicisme *m*

gallicize [ˈgælɪsaɪz] **1** *vt* franciser **2** *vi* se franciser

galling [ˈgɔːlɪŋ] *adj* irritant, exaspérant; **it was g. to reflect that …** ça me/la/*etc* rendait malade de penser que …

gallium [ˈgælɪəm] *n Ch* gallium *m*

▶ **gallivant about, gallivant around** [ˈgælɪvænt] *F* **1** *vi* partir en vadrouille; **he goes out gallivanting around every night** il est en vadrouille toutes les nuits **2** *vipo* (*travel around*) **I'm fed up with gallivanting about the country** j'en ai marre de toujours être par monts et par vaux; **he's gallivanting around the South of France** il est parti en vadrouille dans le Midi

gallon [ˈgælən] *n* gallon *m* (= 4,54 l, *US* = 3,78 l); *Aut* **miles per g.** = consommation *f* d'essence aux cent kilomètres; *F* **they drink gallons of beer** ils boivent de la bière à tire-larigot

gallop¹ [ˈgæləp] *n* (**a**) (*pace*) galop *m*; **at a g.** au galop (allongé); (**at**) **full g.** au grand galop (**b**) (*ride*) galopade *f*; **to have** *or* **go for a g.** faire une galopade

gallop² (**-p-**) **1** *vi* (*of horse*) galoper; (*of horse, rider*) aller au galop; **to g. away** *or* **off** partir au galop; **he came galloping down the steps** (*of person*) il a descendu les escaliers quatre à quatre *ou* au grand galop; *Fig* **to g. through one's work/a task** expédier un travail/une tâche; *Fig* **to g. through prayers** réciter les prières à toute vitesse **2** *vt* (*horse*) faire galoper

galloping [ˈgæləpɪŋ] *adj* (*horse*) au galop; *Fig* **at a g. pace** à la vitesse grand V; *Econ* **g. inflation** inflation galopante

Gallo-Roman [ˈgæləʊˈrəʊmən] *adj* gallo-romain, *pl* gallo-romains

gallows [ˈgæləʊz] *npl* (*often with sing verb*) potence *f*, gibet *m*; *Old-fashioned* **g. bird** gibier *m* de potence; **g. humour** humour *m* noir; **g. tree** gibet

gallstone [ˈgɔːlstəʊn] *n Med* calcul *m* biliaire; **to have gallstones** avoir des calculs

Gallup [ˈgæləp] *n* **G. poll** sondage *m* Gallup

galore [gəˈlɔːr] *adv F* à gogo; **children g.** une flopée d'enfants; **books/money g.** des livres/de l'argent à gogo

galoshes [gəˈlɒʃɪz] *npl* bottes *fpl* en caoutchouc

…lumph [gəˈlʌmf] *vi F* galoper lourdement (et bruyamment)

…anic [gælˈvænɪk] *adj* galvanique

…ism [ˈgælvənɪz(ə)m] *n* galvanisme *m*

…tion [gælvənaɪˈzeɪʃən] *n* galvanisation *f*

galvanize [ˈgælvənaɪz] *vt* galvaniser; *Fig* **to g. sb/sth into life** galvaniser qn/qch

galvanized [ˈgælvənaɪzd] *adj* **g. iron** fer *m* galvanisé

galvanizing [ˈgælvənaɪzɪŋ] *adj* **g. effect** effet *m* de galvanisation; *Fig* **the imminent danger had a g. effect on us** la proximité du danger nous a galvanisés

galvanometer [gælvəˈnɒmɪtər] *n* galvanomètre *m*

Gambia (the) [ðəˈgæmbɪə] *n* la Gambie; **the G. (River)** la Gambie

gambit [ˈgæmbɪt] *n Chess* gambit *m*; *Fig* tactique *f*, stratagème *m*; *Fig* **opening g.** manœuvre *f* d'approche; **a g. to get their sympathy** un stratagème pour gagner leur sympathie

gamble¹ [ˈgæmb(ə)l] *n* (*risk*) risque *m*; **I know it's a g. but …** je sais que c'est risqué mais …; **to take a g.** prendre un risque; **it's a g. but it may pay off** c'est un risque *ou* c'est risqué mais ça peut être payant

gamble² **1** *vi* jouer de l'argent; **I don't g.** je ne joue pas pour de l'argent; **to g. on a throw of the dice** miser sur un coup de dé(s); **to g. on the Stock Exchange** jouer en bourse, spéculer; **to g. on a rise in prices** jouer à la hausse; *Fig* **they're gambling on there not being an inspector on the train** ils misent sur le fait qu'il n'y aura pas de contrôleur dans le train; *Fig* **she's gambling on getting home by 8 o'clock** elle compte rentrer avant 8 heures; *Fig* **Napoleon gambled and lost** Napoléon a joué et perdu

2 *vt* **to g. one's money on horses** jouer son argent aux courses; *Fig* **the government has gambled its political future on the plan's success** le gouvernement a joué son avenir sur le succès du projet

▶ **gamble away** *vtsep* (*fortune*) perdre au jeu

gambler [ˈgæmblər] *n* joueur, -euse (pour de l'argent)

gambling [ˈgæmblɪŋ] *n* jeu *m*, jeux *mpl* d'argent; **g. on the Stock Exchange** la spéculation en Bourse; **my father was a g. man** mon père jouait; **g. debts** dettes *fpl* de jeu; *Pej* **g. den** *or* **house** *or US* **joint** tripot *m*

gambol¹ [ˈgæmb(ə)l] *n* cabriole *f*, gambade *f*

gambol² *vi* (**-ll-**, *US* **-l-**) gambader, cabrioler

gambrel [ˈgæmbrəl] *n Archit* toit *m* en croupe

game¹ [geɪm] *n* (**a**) (*activity, sport*) jeu *m*; **g. of skill/chance** jeu d'adresse/de hasard; **outdoor games** jeux de plein air; *Br Sch* **games** sports *mpl*; **games teacher** professeur *m* d'éducation physique; *Br Sch* **he's good at games** il est bon en sport, c'est un sportif; **the children were playing a g. of cowboys and Indians** les enfants jouaient aux cowboys et aux Indiens

(**b**) (*contest*) *Sp* match *m*; (*friendly*) (*of cards, chess, golf, snooker etc*) partie *f*; (*part of a game of cards*) manche *f*; (*in tennis match*) jeu *m*; **how's the g. going?** comment marche la partie?; **we're having a g. of football after work** on va jouer au football après le travail; **anyone for darts/tennis? – I'll give you a g.** quelqu'un veut faire une partie de fléchettes/de tennis? – oui, moi; **you might get a g.** (*if someone is absent*) tu pourras peut-être jouer; **he played 65 games for England** il a joué 65 fois pour l'Angleterre; **we had a good g.** (*played well*) nous avons bien joué; **he plays a good g. of cards/billiards** il joue bien aux cartes/au billard; *Tennis* **g., set and match** jeu, set et match; *Chess* **opening/middle/end g.** début *m*/milieu *m*/fin *f* de partie; *TV* **games channel** chaîne *f* de jeux; *Comptr* **games port** port *m* (de connexion pour) jeux, sortie *f* jeux; **games room** salle *f* de jeux; *Comptr* **games software** ludiciel *m*, logiciel *m* ludique

(**c**) *Fig* **to play the g.** jouer le jeu, jouer selon les règles; **that's not playing the g.** ce n'est pas loyal; **to beat sb at his own g.** battre qn à son propre jeu; **two can play at that g.** on peut jouer à deux à ce petit jeu-là; *F* **what's his g.?** où veut-il en venir?, à quoi joue-t-il?; **I know your (little) g.!** je sais bien où vous voulez en venir!; **so that's your g.!** voilà donc ce que vous manigancez!; **politics is just a g. to him** la politique n'est qu'un jeu pour lui; **it isn't a g.!** (*it's serious*) ce n'est pas un jeu!; **to play games with sb** jouer avec qn; **let's stop playing games and come to the point** trêve de plaisanteries, passons aux choses sérieuses; **to play a dangerous g.** jouer un jeu dangereux; **he's up to his old games again** voilà qu'il refait des siennes; **the g.'s up** l'affaire est à l'eau; **the g. is not worth the candle** le jeu n'en vaut pas la chandelle; **I've been in this g. a long time** j'ai été de la partie pendant longtemps; *F* **how long have you been in the newspaper g.?** ça fait combien de temps que tu es dans les journaux?; *Br Sl* **to be on the g.** (*be a prostitute*) faire le trottoir; **to spoil sb's little g.** déjouer les plans de qn; **what a g.!** (*a lot of trouble*) quel cinéma!; **they were just playing a g., pretending to be angry** ils faisaient semblant d'être en colère

(**d**) *Hunting, Culin* gibier *m*; **small g.** menu gibier; **big g.** les grands fauves *mpl*; **big-g. hunting** la chasse aux grands fauves; **g. pie** pâté *m* de gibier en croûte

game² *vi* jouer (de l'argent)
game³ *adj F* (*brave*) courageux; **to be g. (to do sth)** (*willing*) être partant (pour faire qch); **I'm g.!** d'accord (j'en suis)!, je suis partant!; **he's g. for anything** il est toujours partant, *Pej* il est prêt à tout *ou* capable de tout
game⁴ *adj* = **gammy**
game birds *n* gibier *m* à plumes
gamecock ['geɪmkɒk] *n* coq *m* de combat
gamekeeper ['geɪmki:pər] *n* garde-chasse *m*, *pl* gardes-chasse(s)
game licence *n* permis *m* de chasse
gamely ['geɪmlɪ] *adv* courageusement
gameplan ['geɪmplæn] *n Chess, Fig* stratégie *f*; *Mktg* stratégie (de mercatique)
game point *n Tennis* balle *f* de jeu
game reserve *n* réserve *f* naturelle; (*for hunting*) réserve de chasse
gameshow ['geɪmʃəʊ] *n TV* jeu *m* télévisé; *Rad* jeu radiophonique
gamesmanship ['geɪmzmənʃɪp] *n* astuce *f*; **this is just g.** ce n'est qu'une astuce pour déstabiliser son adversaire
gamete ['gæmi:t, gæ'mi:t] *n Biol* gamète *m*
game theory *n Psy, Mktg* théorie *f* des jeux
gameware ['geɪmweər] *n Comptr* ludiciel *m*
gamey ['geɪmɪ] *adj* = **gamy**
gaming ['geɪmɪŋ] *n* jeu *m*; **g. house/table** maison *f*/table *f* de jeu
gamma ['gæmə] *n* (*in Greek alphabet*) gamma *m*
gamma ray *n* rayon *m* gamma
gamma-ray *adj Med* **g. therapy** gammathérapie *f*
gammon ['gæmən] *n* (*bacon*) quartier *m*; (*ham*) jambon *m* fumé; **g. steak** tranche *f* épaisse de jambon fumé
gammy ['gæmɪ] *adj F* **a g. leg** une patte folle
gamp [gæmp] *n Br Old-fashioned F* parapluie *m*, pépin *m*
gamut ['gæmət] *n* (*of colours*), *Mus, Fig* gamme *f*; **this character runs the whole g. of emotions** ce personnage passe par toute la gamme des émotions
gamy ['geɪmɪ] *adj* faisandé
gander ['gændər] *n* **(a)** (*male goose*) jars *m* **(b)** *Br Sl* (*look*) coup *m* d'œil; **just take a g.!** mate-moi ça!
gang [gæŋ] *n* [①A11,g,i] (*of criminals*) bande *f*, gang *m*; (*of children*) bande; (*of workmen*) équipe *f*; (*of prisoners*) convoi *m*; **can I join your g.?** (*of children*) je peux faire partie de votre bande?; *F* **the whole g.** (*of friends, colleagues*) toute la bande; *Pol, Hist* **the G. of Four** la Bande des Quatre; **g. war(fare)** guerre *f* des gangs
▶ **gang up** *vi F* former un gang; **to g. up with sb** s'allier avec qn; **to g. up on sb** se liguer contre qn
gangbang ['gæŋbæŋ] *n Sl* (*group rape*) viol *m* collectif
ganger ['gæŋər] *n Br Rail* chef *m* d'équipe
Ganges (the) [ðə'gændʒi:z] *n* le Gange
gangland ['gæŋlænd] *n* (*area*) (*in big city*) territoire *m* contrôlé par des gangsters; (*underworld*) le milieu; **a g. boss** un chef de gang; **a g. killing** un règlement de compte (entre gangsters); **g. warfare** guerre *f* des gangs
gangling ['gæŋglɪŋ] *adj* dégingandé; **a g. youth** un jeune dégingandé
ganglion, -ia ['gæŋglɪən, -ɪə] *n Anat* ganglion *m*
gangplank ['gæŋplæŋk] *n Naut* passerelle *f*; **to make sb walk the g.** forcer qn à marcher sur la planche (*de telle sorte qu'il tombe dans la mer*)
gang rape *n* viol *m* collectif
gang-rape *vt* commettre un viol collectif sur; **women who have been gang-raped** les femmes qui ont été victimes de viols collectifs; **they gang-raped her** ils l'ont violée
gangrene ['gæŋgri:n] *n Med* gangrène *f*, nécrose *f*; **to have g.** avoir la gangrène
gangrenous ['gæŋgrɪnəs] *adj* gangreneux, gangrené; **to go g.** (*of wound*) se gangrener
gangster ['gæŋstər] *n* gangster *m*; **g. film** film *m* de gangsters
gangsterism ['gæŋstərɪz(ə)m] *n* gangstérisme *m*
gangway ['gæŋweɪ] *n* **(a)** (*passage*) passage *m*; (*of bus etc*) couloir *m* central; **when you set the chairs out leave a g.** laissez un passage entre les chaises quand vous les installerez; **g.!** dégagez, s'il vous plaît! **(b)** *Naut* (*gangplank*) passerelle *f* de service; *Av* (*for plane*) passerelle; **g. port** sabord *m* de coupée
ganja ['gændʒə] *n* (*marijuana*) ganja *f*
gannet ['gænɪt] *n* (*bird*) fou *m* (de Bassan); *Hum Fig* (*glutton*) goinfre *mf*
gantry ['gæntrɪ] *n* **(a)** (*for travelling crane*) pont *m* roulant; (*for rocket*) portique *m* de lancement; *Rail* **signal g.** portique de signalisation; **g. crane** grue *f* à portique; **travelling g.** portique roulant **(b)** (*for barrel*) chantier *m*
gaol [dʒeɪl] *n, vt Br* = **jail**
gaolbird ['dʒeɪlbɜ:d] *n Br* = **jailbird**
gaolbreak ['dʒeɪlbreɪk] *n Br* évasion *f* de prison
gaolbreaker ['dʒeɪlbreɪkər] *n Br* évadé, -ée de prison
gaoler ['dʒeɪlər] *n Br* = **jailer**
gap [gæp] *n* **(a)** (*hole, opening*) (*which needs mending*) trou *m*; (*in floorboards*) interstice *m*; (*created deliberately*) trouée *f*, ouverture *f*; (*in a wall*) brèche *f*; (*in clouds*) trou; (*in trees*) trouée; (*of spark plug, points*) écartement *m*; (*in piston ring*) jeu *m* à la coupe (des segments); **that fills a g.** (*of snack*) ça cale bien; **a g. in the bookshelf** un vide sur l'étagère; **the demolition of the house left a g. in the street** la démolition de la maison a laissé un espace vide dans la rue; **a g. of 2 cm** un intervalle de 2 cm; **leave a g. of six centimetres between the chairs** laissez un espace de six centimètres entre les chaises; **there's a g. in the curtains** les rideaux bâillent; **the g. in his teeth** l'écart entre ses dents; **there were gaps in his teeth** il avait les dents écartées; **the shelling had opened great gaps in the ranks** le bombardement avait éclairci les rangs; *Aut* **(spark) g.** intervalle *m* d'allumage; *Com* **g. in the market** créneau *m*; *Mktg* **g. analysis** étude *f* des créneaux; *Mktg* **g. level** écart *m* de performance
(b) (*difference*) différence *f*; **age g.** différence d'âge; **the g. between us and our competitors** l'écart entre nos concurrents et nous; **to close the g.** réduire l'écart; **there is a vast g. in ability between the two teams** il y a une grande différence de niveau entre les deux équipes; **the g. between rich and poor has widened** le fossé entre les riches et les pauvres s'est élargi
(c) (*in time*) écart *m*; **there is a g. of two years in the records** il y a un trou de deux ans dans les archives; **after a g. of over twenty years** après un intervalle de plus de vingt ans
(d) *Fig* (*in memory etc*) trou *m*, lacune *f*, vide *m*; **his death leaves a g. in all of our lives** sa mort laisse un vide dans nos vies; **to fill the gaps in one's education** combler les lacunes de son éducation; **there are a lot of gaps in her account of the event** il y a beaucoup d'omissions dans sa version des événements
(e) *Geog* (*opening in hills, mountains*) trouée *f*; *esp US* (*pass*) col *m*
(f) (*in recording*) blanc *m* sonore; (*in recorded tape*) plage *f* de silence
gape¹ [geɪp] *n* **I could tell from his astonished g. that ...** je savais à son air éberlué que ...; **with a g. of disbelief** la bouche ouverte *ou* bée en signe d'incrédulité
gape² *vi* **(a)** (*stare*) être *ou* rester bouche bée; **to g. in admiration/astonishment** être bouche bée d'admiration/ d'étonnement; **to g. at sb/sth** regarder qn/qch bouche bée; **what are you gaping at?** qu'est-ce que tu regardes bouche bée?; **stop gaping!** remets-toi! **(b) to g. (open)** (*of thing*) s'ouvrir (tout grand); (*of seam etc*) bâiller; (*of hole*) être béant
gaping ['geɪpɪŋ] *adj attrib* (*hole etc*) béant
gappy [gæpɪ] *adj* (*list etc*) incomplet; *F* **g. teeth** dents *fpl* écartées; **g. smile** sourire *m* édenté
gap-toothed ['gæptu:θt] *adj* aux dents écartées
garage¹ ['gærɑ:ʒ, -rɪdʒ] *n Aut* garage *m*; (*multistorey*) parking *m*; **g. attendant** gardien *m* de parking; **g. mechanic** mécanicien *m* (de garage), *F* garagiste *m*; **g. proprietor** *or* **owner** garagiste; **there is g. space for two cars** il y a de la place pour garer deux voitures
garage² *vt* (*car*) rentrer; (*for longer period*) remiser
garage sale *n esp Am* = brocante *f* chez un particulier
garb¹ ['gɑ:b] *n Lit* costume *m*, habit *m*; **in clerical g.** en habit ecclésiastique
garb² *vt* (*usu passive*) *Lit* habiller, vêtir (**in** de); **garbed all in black** tout de noir vêtu
garbage ['gɑ:bɪdʒ] *n* **(a)** *esp Am* (*waste*) ordures *fpl* (ménagères); **g. heap** tas *m* d'ordures; **g. can** poubelle *f*; **g. disposal unit** broyeur *m* à ordures; **g. man** *or* **collector** (é)boueur *m*; *Comptr* **g. in, g. out** mauvaises données à l'entrée égale mauvais résultats à la sortie **(b)** *Fig* (*nonsense*) bêtises *fpl*; **he's talking g.** il dit n'importe quoi
garbanzo [gɑ:'bænzəʊ] *n Am* pois *m* chiche
garble ['gɑ:b(ə)l] *vt* (*news, quotation*) fausser; (*facts*) dénaturer; (*text*) altérer; **garbled account** compte rendu *m* trompeur *ou* mensonger; **garbled message** message *m* confus
Garda, *pl* **Gardai** ['gɑ:də, 'gɑ:di:] *n* **(a)** (*police force*) police *f* (*de la République d'Irlande*) **(b)** (*policeman*) policier *m* (*de la République d'Irlande*)
garden¹ ['gɑ:d(ə)n] *n* jardin *m*; **back/front g.** jardin de derrière/de devant; **g. of remembrance** = jardin en souvenir des défunts; **public garden(s)** jardin public, parc *m*; *F* **to**

lead sb up the g. path duper qn, faire marcher qn; **g. city** cité-jardin *f, pl* cités-jardins; **g. furniture/chair** meubles *mpl*/chaise *f* de jardin; **g. hose** tuyau *m* d'arrosage; **g. plants** plantes *fpl* de jardin; **g. produce** produits *mpl* maraîchers; **g. suburb** cité-jardin *f, pl* cités-jardins; **g. tools** outils *mpl* de jardinage

garden² *vi* (*usu continuous*) jardiner, faire du jardinage

garden centre *n* jardinerie *f*

gardener ['gɑːdnər] *n* jardinier, -ière; **he's a keen g.** c'est un adepte du jardinage

garden flat *n* appartement *m* au rez-de-chaussée avec jardin

gardenia [gɑː'diːnɪə] *n* (*flower*) gardénia *m*

gardening ['gɑːdnɪŋ] *n* jardinage *m*; **g. book** livre *m* de jardinage; **g. expert** spécialiste *mf* du jardinage; **g. programme** émission *f* sur le jardinage; **g. tools** outils *mpl* de jardinage

garden party *n* réception *f* en plein air, garden-party *f, pl* garden-parties

gargantuan [gɑː'gæntjʊən] *adj* gargantuesque

gargle¹ ['gɑːg(ə)l] *n Med* gargarisme *m*

gargle² *vi Med* se gargariser

gargoyle ['gɑːgɔɪl] *n Archit etc* gargouille *f*

garish ['geərɪʃ] *adj* **(a)** (*clothes*) voyant; (*wallpaper*) criard; (*taste*) vulgaire **(b)** (*light, colour*) cru

garishly ['geərɪʃlɪ] *adv* de façon criarde

garishness ['geərɪʃnɪs] *n* **(a)** (*of clothes*) aspect *m* voyant *ou* tapageur; (*of wallpaper*) aspect criard; (*of taste*) vulgarité *f* **(b)** (*of light, colour*) crudité *f*

garland¹ ['gɑːlənd] *n* guirlande *f*

garland² *vt* parer de guirlandes, enguirlander; **garlanded with flowers** paré de guirlandes de fleurs

garlic ['gɑːlɪk] *n* ail *m, pl* ails *ou* aulx; **clove of g.** gousse *f* d'ail; **head of g.** bulbe *m* d'ail; **g. bread** = pain *m* au beurre et à l'ail servi chaud; **g. butter** beurre *m* à l'ail; **g. press** presse-ail *m inv*; **g. sausage** saucisson *m* à l'ail

garlicky ['gɑːlɪkɪ] *adj* qui sent l'ail; (*taste*) d'ail

garment ['gɑːmənt] *n Fml* vêtement *m*; **the g. industry** l'industrie *f* du vêtement

garner ['gɑːnər] *vt* (*collect*) (*information*) recueillir

garnet ['gɑːnɪt] *n Miner* grenat *m*; **g. necklace** collier *m* de grenat

garnish¹ ['gɑːnɪʃ] *n Culin etc* garniture *f*

garnish² *vt* garnir, orner (**with** de); *Culin* (*dish*) garnir

garnishee [gɑːnɪ'ʃiː] *n Jur* **g. order** ordonnance *f* de saisie-arrêt

garnishing ['gɑːnɪʃɪŋ] *n* garnissage *m*; *Culin* garniture *f*

garret ['gærət] *n* mansarde *f*; **to live in a g.** habiter sous les combles

garrison¹ ['gærɪs(ə)n] *n Mil* garnison *f*; **g. duty** service *m* de place *ou* de garnison; **g. town** ville *f* de garnison

garrison² *vt Mil* (*station*) mettre en garnison; **troops garrisoned at Lille** troupes en garnison à Lille; **to g. a town** (*provide with a garrison*) mettre une garnison dans une ville

garrotte¹, *US* **garrote** [gə'rɒt] *n* **(a)** (*device*) garrot *m* **(b)** (*execution*) supplice *m* du garrot

garrotte², *US* **garrote** *vt* **(a)** (*strangle*) étrangler (*avec un fil, une corde etc*) **(b)** (*execute*) faire subir le supplice du garrot à

garrotting, *US* **garroting** [gə'rɒtɪŋ] *n* **(a)** (*strangling*) strangulation *f* (*avec un fil, une corde*) **(b)** (*execution*) supplice *m* du garrot

garrulity [gæ'ruːlɪtɪ], **garrulousness** ['gærʊləsnɪs] *n* loquacité *f*

garrulous ['gærʊləs] *adj* loquace, bavard

garrulously ['gærʊləslɪ] *adv* avec volubilité, de façon loquace

garter ['gɑːtər] *n* jarretière *f*; *Am* (*suspender*) (*for stockings*) jarretelle *f*; *Am* (*for socks*) fixe-chaussette *m, pl* fixe-chaussettes; *Br* **Knight of the (Order of the) G.** chevalier *m* de l'Ordre de la Jarretière; *Am* **g. belt** porte-jarretelles *m inv*; *Knitting* **g. stitch** point *m* mousse

gas¹, *pl* **gases** [gæs, 'gæsɪz] *n* **(a)** gaz *m inv*; **to pay the g. bill** *or* **for the g.** payer le gaz; **the g. has been cut off** le gaz a été coupé; **to cook with** *or* **by g.** faire la cuisine au gaz; **to have g.** (*as anaesthetic*) se faire anesthésier au gaz; **town g.** gaz de ville; **g. burner** bec *m* de gaz; **g. cooker** *or* **stove** cuisinière *f* à gaz; **g. cylinder** bouteille *f* de gaz; **g. explosion** (*in home or street*) explosion *f* due à une fuite de gaz; **g. field** gisement *m* de gaz; **g. fire** radiateur *m* à gaz; **g. fitter** poseur *m ou* ajusteur *m* d'appareils à gaz; **g. furnace** fourneau *m* à gaz; **g. holder** *or* **tank** gazomètre *m*, réservoir *m* à gaz; **g. leak** fuite *f* de gaz; **g. lighter** (*for fire, cooker*) allume-gaz *m inv*; (*for cigarettes etc*) briquet *m* (à gaz); **g. mantle** manchon *m* à incandescence; **g. meter** compteur *m* à gaz; **g. oven** four *m* à gaz; **to put one's head in a g. oven** mettre la tête dans un four à gaz; **she threatened to put her head in a g. oven** elle a menacé de se suicider; *Comptr* **g. plasma screen** écran *m* à plasma; *Br* **g. poker** allume-gaz *m* inv; **g. ring** (*small stove*) réchaud *m* à gaz (à un feu); (*on a cooker*) brûleur *m* à couronne; **g. tap** robinet *m* du gaz; **g. turbine** turbine *f* à gaz; **g. turbine engine** moteur *m* à turbine à gaz

(b) *Mil* gaz *m* de combat; **g. attack** attaque *f* aux gaz; **g. warfare** guerre *f* chimique

(c) *Min* grisou *m*; **g. explosion** coup *m* de grisou

(d) *Am* (*gasoline*) essence *f*; **to fill up with g.** faire le plein d'essence; **to step on the g.** (*press on accelerator*) appuyer sur le champignon; *Fig* (*hurry*) se presser, *F* se grouiller; *F* **g. guzzler** voiture *f* qui consomme beaucoup

(e) *F* (*worthless talk*) bavardage *m*, verbiage *m*

(f) *esp Am* **what a g.!** (*situation, activity*) quelle rigolade!; **we did it for a g.** on l'a fait pour rigoler

gas² **(-ss-) 1** *vt* (*person*) asphyxier (*avec un gaz*); (*deliberately*) gazer; **to g. oneself** (*deliberately*) se suicider au gaz; (*accidentally*) être asphyxié **2** *vi F* (*chat*) bavarder, jaser

gasbag ['gæsbæg] *n F* bavard, -arde; (*boaster*) vantard, -arde

Gas Board *n Br Admin* compagnie *f* du gaz

gas chamber *n* chambre *f* à gaz

Gascony ['gæskənɪ] *n* la Gascogne

gas-cooled [gæs'kuːld] *adj* **g. reactor** réacteur *m* à refroidissement par gaz

gaseous ['gæsɪəs, 'geɪsɪəs, geɪʃɪəs] *adj* gazeux

gas-fired [gæs'faɪəd] *adj* au gaz

gas gangrene *n Med* gangrène *f* gazeuse

gash¹ [gæʃ] *n* (*on body*) coupure *f*, entaille *f*; (*on face*) balafre *f*; (*in earth's surface etc*) fente *f*; **the iceberg had ripped a great g. in the ship's side** l'iceberg avait fait une grande déchirure sur le côté du bateau

gash² *vt* (*wound*) entailler, couper; (*face*) balafrer; **to g. one's chin** se faire une entaille au menton

gasholder ['gæshəʊldər] *n* réservoir *m* à gaz

gasify ['gæsɪfaɪ] **1** *vt* gazéifier **2** *vi* se gazéifier

gas industry *n* industrie *f* du gaz

gasket ['gæskɪt] *n MecE* (*of joint*) joint *m* d'étanchéité, garniture *f*; *Aut* (*of cylinder head*) joint de culasse; **to blow a g.** *Aut* faire sauter un joint de culasse; *Fig F* se mettre en rage, piquer une colère; *F* **he just about blew a g.** il a pété les plombs

gas lamp *n* (*in street*) réverbère *m*

gaslight ['gæslaɪt] *n* lumière *f* du gaz; **by g.** à la lumière du gaz

gas main *n* tuyau *m* à gaz, conduite *f* de gaz; (*big*) gazoduc *m*

gasman, *pl* **-men** ['gæsmæn, -men] *n F* contrôleur *m ou* employé *m* du gaz, gazier *m*

gas mask *n* masque *m* à gaz

gasoline ['gæsəliːn] *n Am* essence *f*

gasometer [gæ'sɒmɪtər] *n* gazomètre *m*, réservoir *m* à gaz

gasp¹ [gɑːsp] *n* (*of surprise*) hoquet *m*, sursaut *m*; **there were gasps of admiration from the audience** il y a eu des sursauts d'admiration dans le public; **..., she said with a g.** ..., dit-elle le souffle coupé; **to be at one's last g.** agoniser, être à l'agonie; *Fig F* être sur le point de rendre son dernier soupir; **to give one's last g.** rendre le dernier soupir; **to defend sth to the last g.** défendre qch jusqu'à son dernier souffle

gasp² **1** *vi* (*with surprise, fright, horror*) avoir le souffle coupé (**with** de); **to make sb g.** couper le souffle à qn; **to g. for breath** *or* **for air** haleter, suffoquer; *F* **I'm gasping (for a drink)** je meurs de soif; *F* **I'm gasping (for a cigarette)** je meurs d'envie de fumer une cigarette **2** *vt* dire d'une voix entrecoupée; **she managed to g. her name** elle a réussi à dire son nom d'une voix entrecoupée

▶ **gasp out** *vtsep* = **gasp² 2**

gasper ['gɑːspər] *n F* (*cigarette*) tige *f*

gas-permeable *adj* **g. (contact) lenses** lentilles *fpl* semi-rigides

gas pipe *n* tuyau *m* à gaz, conduite *f* de gaz; (*big*) gazoduc *m*

gassed [gæst] *adj F* (*drunk*) bourré

gassing ['gæsɪŋ] *n* **(a)** (*of person*) (*deliberate*) gazage *m* **(b)** *F* (*talk*) bavardage *m*

gas station *n Am* station-service *f, pl* stations-service

gassy ['gæsɪ] *adj* (*beer etc*) trop gazeux

gas tank *n Am Aut* réservoir *m* (d'essence)

gastrectomy [gæs'trektəmɪ] *n Med* gastrectomie *f*

gastric ['gæstrɪk] *adj* gastrique; **g. flu** grippe *f* gastro-intestinale; **g. juices** sucs *mpl* gastriques; **g. ulcer** ulcère *m* gastrique

gastritis [gæs'traɪtɪs] *n Med* gastrite *f*; **to have g.** avoir *ou* faire une gastrite

gastro-enteritis [gæstrəʊentə'raɪtɪs] *n Med* gastro-entérite *f, pl* gastro-entérites

gastroenterology [gæstrəʊentə'rɒlədʒɪ] *n* gastro-entérologie *f*

gastronome [ˈgæstrənəʊm] *n* gastronome *mf*
gastronomic(al) [gæstrəˈnɒmɪk, -ɪk(ə)l] *adj* gastronomique
gastronomy [gæsˈtrɒnəmɪ] *n* gastronomie *f*
gastropod [ˈgæstrəpɒd] *n* (*mollusc*) gastéropode *m*
gasworks [ˈgæswɜːks] *npl* (*usu with sing verb*) usine *f* à gaz
gate[1] [geɪt] *n* **(a)** (*of castle, city, factory*) porte *f*; (*of manor house*) portail *m*; **the gate(s) of hell** les portes de l'enfer
(b) (*of garden*) portail *m*; (*metal*) grille *f*; (*of field*) barrière *f*; *Ski* porte *f*; *Av* **g. 15** (*at airport*) porte 15; *Sp* **(starting) g.** starting-gate *m*, *pl* starting-gates; **g. lounge** salle *f* d'embarquement
(c) (*at stadium*) entrée *f*; **to pay at the g.** payer à l'entrée; *Sp* **the g.** (*spectators*) le public; *Sp* **the g. (money)** la recette, les entrées
(d) *HydE* **(lock) g.** vanne *f* (d'écluse)
(e) *Aut* (*for gearstick*) grille *f* (*de changement de vitesse*); **g. pattern** (*of gearbox*) disposition *f* de grille, type *m* de grille
(f) *Electron* porte *f*; **(logic) g.** porte logique
gate[2] *vt Br Sch, Univ* **to be gated** se faire consigner
gâteau [ˈgætəʊ] *n* gros gâteau *m* à la crème
gate-crash 1 *vi* resquiller **2** *vt* **to g. a party** aller à une soirée sans y être invité
gate-crasher [ˈgeɪtkræʃər] *n* resquilleur, -euse
gatefold [ˈgeɪtfəʊld] *n* page *f* qui se déplie, dépliant *m* (*dans un magazine*)
gatehouse [ˈgeɪthaʊs] *n* **(a)** (*of an estate*) loge *f* **(b)** (*of a castle*) corps-de-garde *m inv*
gatekeeper [ˈgeɪtkiːpər] *n* **(a)** gardien, -ienne **(b)** *Mktg* contrôleur *m*, relais *m*, filtre *m* **(c)** *Rail* garde-barrière *mf*, *pl* gardes-barrière(s)
gate-leg(ged) [ˈgeɪtleg, -d] *adj* (*table*) à abattants
gatepost [ˈgeɪtpəʊst] *n* montant *m* (de barrière); *F* **between you, me and the g.** entre nous soit dit
gateway [ˈgeɪtweɪ] *n* **(a)** porte *f*, entrée *f*; *Fig* **the g. to the Continent** la porte du Continent; **a g. to a successful career** un passeport pour une carrière réussie **(b)** *Comptr* passerelle *f* de connexion
gather [ˈgæðər] **1** *vt* **(a)** (*collect*) (*people*) assembler, rassembler; (*things*) rassembler; (*flowers*) cueillir; (*information*) recueillir; (*wood, papers*) ramasser; (*strawberries etc*) cueillir, faire la cueillette de; (*one's skirts*) serrer autour de ses jambes; (*in bookbinding*) (*pages of a book*) rassembler; **to g. the harvest** rentrer la moisson; **to g. honey from the flowers** (*of bees*) butiner les fleurs; **we are gathered here today …** nous sommes rassemblés ici aujourd'hui …; **to g. one's thoughts** rassembler ses pensées; **to g. all one's strength (in order) to do sth** rassembler toutes ses forces pour faire qch; **to g. one's hair into a bun/a ponytail/bunches** se faire un chignon/une queue de cheval/des couettes; *Lit Euph* **to be gathered to one's fathers** expirer
(b) (*accumulate*) **to g. dirt** s'encrasser; **to g. dust** ramasser la poussière; **to g. force** (*of argument*) gagner du terrain; **to g. momentum, to g. speed** prendre de la vitesse; **to g. strength** (*of person*) reprendre des forces
(c) (*pull together*) *Sewing* (*skirt etc*) froncer; **to g. the blankets round one** se serrer dans les couvertures; **he gathered her in his arms** il l'a serrée dans ses bras
(d) (*conclude, understand*) conclure; **so far as I can g.** à ce que je sache; **I g. from the papers that …** à en croire les journaux …; **I g. he has been ill** j'ai appris qu'il a été malade; **I g. from the evidence given that …** je déduis *ou* j'infère de ces témoignages que …; **as you may/must already have gathered** comme vous l'avez peut-être/sûrement déjà compris; **I had (already) gathered as much** (*it was not news to me*) j'avais déjà compris; **prices have gone up – so I g.** les prix ont augmenté – c'est bien ce qu'il me semble
2 *vi* **(a)** (*of people*) se réunir, s'assembler, se rassembler; **a crowd gathered** une foule se forma
(b) (*of objects, dust*) s'accumuler, s'amonceler; **tears were gathering in her eyes** ses yeux se remplissaient de larmes; **the clouds are gathering** les nuages s'amoncellent; **a storm is gathering** un orage se prépare
(c) *Med* (*of abscess*) mûrir, aboutir; **the pus gathers** le pus s'accumule
▶ **gather in** *vtsep* **(a)** (*collect*) (*crops, harvest*) rentrer; (*sheep*) faire rentrer; (*exam papers, questionnaires*) ramasser **(b)** *Sewing* froncer
▶ **gather round 1** *vipo* se rassembler autour de **2** *vi* s'approcher; **g. round!** approchez-vous!
▶ **gather together 1** *vtsep* (*collect*) (*belongings, children etc*) rassembler **2** *vi* (*assemble*) se rassembler
▶ **gather up** *vtsep* (*collect*) (*belongings, things*) ramasser; **she gathered up her skirts** elle a serré sa jupe autour de ses jambes; **to g. up one's hair** attacher *ou* relever ses cheveux; **he gathered her up in his arms** il l'a serrée dans ses bras

gathered [ˈgæðəd] *adj Sewing* (*flounce etc*) froncé, à fronces; **g. pages** (*in bookbinding*) feuilles *fpl* assemblées
gathering [ˈgæðərɪŋ] **1** *n* **(a)** (*people*) (*in a hall etc*) assemblée *f*, réunion *f*; (*in a street*) rassemblement *m*, attroupement *m*; **the g. of the clans** le rassemblement des clans; **a small g. was listening to him** quelques personnes attroupées l'écoutaient **(b)** (*of information, data*) collecte *f*; (*of fruit etc*) cueillette *f*; *Sewing* (*pleats*) fronces *fpl* **2** *adj attrib* **in the g. darkness** dans la nuit grandissante; **with g. force** avec une force croissante
gathers [ˈgæðəz] *npl Sewing* fronces *fpl*
GATT [gæt] *n* (*abbr* **General Agreement on Tariffs and Trade**) GATT *m*, AGETAC *m*
gauche [gəʊʃ] *adj* gauche, maladroit
gaucheness [ˈgəʊʃnɪs] *n* gaucherie *f*, maladresse *f*
gaudily [ˈgɔːdɪlɪ] *adv* d'une manière voyante; (*painted*) avec des couleurs criardes
gaudiness [ˈgɔːdɪnɪs] *n* (*of colour etc*) éclat *m* criard
gaudy [ˈgɔːdɪ] *adj* (*colour*) voyant, criard; (*display*) de mauvais goût
gauge[1] [geɪdʒ] *n* **(a)** (*size*) (*of screw etc*) calibre *m*; *Rail* (*of track*) écartement *m* **(b)** (*standardization device*) étalon *m*; (*for liquid*) jauge *f*; **wire g.** calibre *m* pour fils métalliques **(c)** (*control instrument*) indicateur *m*; *MecE* **water/oil g.** indicateur *ou* jauge *f* de niveau d'eau/d'huile; **pressure g.** manomètre *m*; *Aut* **(petrol** *or* **fuel) g.** jauge d'essence; *Fig* **an opinion poll is a useful g. of public opinion** un sondage constitue un indicateur utile de l'opinion
gauge[2] *vt* (*screw etc*) calibrer; (*oil*) jauger, mesurer; **in order to g. the amount of petrol/water necessary to …** pour évaluer la quantité d'essence/d'eau nécessaire à …; *Fig* **to g. a situation** évaluer une situation; **it was difficult to g. how interested they were/their enthusiasm** il était difficile de juger dans quelle mesure ils étaient intéressés/de juger de leur enthousiasme
gauging [ˈgeɪdʒɪŋ] *n* **g. rod** *or* **stick** jauge *f*
Gaul [gɔːl] *n Antiq* **(a)** (*region*) Gaule *f* **(b)** (*inhabitant*) Gaulois, -oise
Gaullist [ˈgəʊlɪst] *adj, n Pol* gaulliste *mf*
gaunt [gɔːnt] *adj* **(a)** (*person, face*) maigre, décharné **(b)** (*place*) désolé
gauntlet[1] [ˈgɔːntlɪt] *n* **(a)** (*part of armour*) gantelet *m*, gant *m*; *Fig* **to throw** *or* **fling down the g.** jeter le gant; *Fig* **to take up the g.** relever le gant **(b) g. (glove)** gant *m* à crispins *ou* à manchette
gauntlet[2] *n* **to run the g.** *Mil* passer par les baguettes; *Naut* courir la bouline; *Fig* soutenir un feu roulant (de critiques adverses); **they had to run the g. of enemy fire** ils ont dû soutenir le feu roulant de l'ennemi; **he had to run the g. of their abuse** il a dû soutenir le feu roulant de leurs injures
gauntness [ˈgɔːntnɪs] *n* (*of person, face*) maigreur *f*; (*of place*) désolation *f*; **the g. of his face** son visage hâve
gauze [gɔːz] *n* gaze *f*; *Med* **(antiseptic) g.** gaze aseptique; *Med* **g. bandage** bande *f* de gaze; **(wire) g.** toile *f* métallique
gave *see* **give[2]**
gavel [ˈgæv(ə)l] *n* (*of auctioneer, Am of judge*) marteau *m*
gavotte [gəˈvɒt] *n Mus* gavotte *f*
Gawd [gɔːd] *n Sl* = **God**
gawk[1] [gɔːk] *n F* lourdaud, -aude
gawk[2] *vi F* = **gawp**
gawker [ˈgɔːkər] *n Am* badaud *m*, curieux, -euse
gawkiness [ˈgɔːkɪnɪs] *n* gaucherie *f*, *F* air *m* empoté
gawky [ˈgɔːkɪ] *adj* gauche, *F* empoté
gawp [gɔːp] *vi F* rester bouche bée, gober les mouches; **to g. at sth** regarder qch d'un air bête; **stop gawping!** ne reste pas planté là à regarder
gay [geɪ] **1** *adj* **(a)** (*homosexual*) homosexuel, gay *inv*; **the g. community** la communauté homosexuelle *ou* gay; **g. club/disco/magazine** club/discothèque/magazine pour homosexuels; **g. lib** mouvement *m* de libération des homosexuels **(b)** *esp Old-fashioned* (*happy*) gai, allègre; (*laugh*) enjoué; (*colour*) vif, gai; **to have a g. old time** bien s'amuser **2** *n* homosexuel, -elle
gayness [ˈgeɪnɪs] *n* (*homosexuality*) homosexualité *f*
gaze[1] [geɪz] *n* regard *m* fixe; **she turned her g. on the dog** elle a tourné son regard vers le chien; **to meet sb's g.** regarder qn dans les yeux; **exposed to the public g.** exposé aux regards inquisiteurs de tous
gaze[2] *vi* regarder fixement; **they gazed around them** ils ont regardé autour d'eux; **to g. at** *or* **on sb/sth** fixer *ou* contempler *ou* considérer qn/qch
gazebo [gəˈziːbəʊ] *n* belvédère *m*
gazelle [gəˈzel] *n* (*animal*) gazelle *f*
gazette[1] [gəˈzet] *n* (*official journal*) journal *m* officiel; **the Police G.** ≈ la Gazette des tribunaux

gazette² *vt* (*bankruptcy, appointment etc*) annoncer *ou* publier dans un journal officiel
gazetteer [gæzɪ'tɪər] *n* répertoire *m* géographique
gazump [gə'zʌmp] *vt Br F* **to g. sb** = revenir sur une promesse de vente faite à qn pour accepter une offre plus élevée; **we were gazumped** le propriétaire est revenu sur la promesse de vente qu'il nous avait faite
gazumping [gə'zʌmpɪŋ] *n Br F* = fait de revenir sur une promesse de vente pour accepter une offre plus élevée
GB ['dʒi:bi:] *n* **(a)** (*abbr* **Great Britain**) *Aut* **GB plate** plaque *f* GB; *Aut* **GB sticker** autocollant *m* GB **(b)** *Comptr* (*abbr* **gigabyte**) Go *m*
GBH [dʒi:bi:'eɪtʃ] *n Jur* (*abbr* **grievous bodily harm**) = coups *mpl* et blessures *fpl* graves
GCE [dʒi:si:'i:] *Br Sch* (*before 1988*) (*abbr* **General Certificate of Education**) **1** *adj* **G. examination** = examen *m* du diplôme général d'enseignement; **G. O level** ≈ brevet *m* élémentaire du premier cycle; **G. A level** ≈ baccalauréat *m* **2** *n* **G. in Maths** = diplôme *m* général d'enseignement en maths
GCHQ [dʒi:si:eɪtʃ'kju:] *n Br* (*abbr* **Government Communications Headquarters**) centre *m* de renseignement du gouvernement britannique
GCSE [dʒi:si:es'i:] *n Br Sch* (*abbr* **General Certificate of Secondary Education**) = première partie *f* de l'examen de fin d'études secondaires
GDP [dʒi:di:'pi:] *n Econ* (*abbr* **gross domestic product**) P. I. B. *m*
GDR [dʒi:di:'ɑ:r] *n* (*abbr* **German Democratic Republic**) RDA *f*
Gds *abbr* **Gardens**
gear¹ [gɪər] *n* **(a)** (*speed*) vitesse *f*; (*mechanism*) appareil *m*, mécanisme *m*; *MecE etc* (*gearwheel*) engrenage *m*; **in g.** (*car*) embrayé, en prise; *Sl* **get your arse in g.!** remue-toi!; **out of g.** (*car*) au point mort; **to throw** *or* **put out of g.** (*car*) débrayer; *Fig* (*plan, process*) perturber; **a ten-g. racing bike** un vélo de course à dix vitesses; *Aut* **neutral g.** point *m* mort; *Aut* **first** *or* **bottom g.** première vitesse; *Aut* **top g.** quatrième/cinquième vitesse; *Fig* **we're not operating in top g.** nous ne sommes pas à notre maximum *ou* au top de notre forme; **to change** *or Am* **shift g.** *Aut, Fig* changer de vitesse; *Cycling* changer de vitesse *ou* de braquet; *Aut* **g. changes** changements *mpl* de vitesse; *Br Aut* **g. lever** levier *m* de changement de vitesse, levier de vitesses; *MecE* **g. ratio** rapport *m* d'engrenages *ou* des dentures
(b) (*equipment*) équipement *m*; *Naut* apparaux *mpl*; (*for camping, fishing, photography*) équipement, matériel *m*; *Fig F* **he arrived with all his g.** (*his belongings*) il est arrivé avec tout son attirail
(c) *F* (*clothes*) fringues *fpl*
(d) (*harness*) (*of draught horse*) harnais *m*, harnachement *m*
gear² *vt MecE* engrener, embrayer
▶ **gear down** **1** *vi* (*of factory etc*) ralentir la production **2** *vtsep* **(a)** **to g. down production** ralentir la production **(b)** *MecE* démultiplier
▶ **gear to** *vtaspo* (*intend for*) **to g. sth to sth** adapter qch en fonction de qch; **wages geared to the cost of living** salaires indexés sur le coût de la vie; **this book is geared to the needs of students** ce livre est spécialement adapté aux besoins des étudiants
▶ **gear up** **1** *vi* (*prepare*) se préparer; **the shops are gearing up for Christmas** les magasins se préparent pour Noël **2** *vtsep* **(a)** (*prepare*) préparer; **businesses were getting geared up for the single European market** les entreprises se préparaient en vue du marché unique européen **(b)** *MecE* multiplier
gearbox ['gɪəbɒks] *n Aut* boîte *f* de vitesses; **g. ratio** rapport *m* de boîte
gearing ['gɪərɪŋ] **(a)** *MecE etc* (*gears*) engrenage *m*, embrayage *m*, système *m ou* jeu *m* d'engrenages; (*drive*) transmission *f* **(b)** *Fin* ratio *m* d'endettement
gearing down *n MecE* démultiplication *f*
gearing up *n MecE* multiplication *f*; *Cycling* développement *m*
gearshift ['gɪəʃɪft] *n Am Aut* (*lever*) levier *m* de vitesses; (*action*) changement *m* de vitesse; **automatic g.** changement de vitesse automatique
gearstick ['gɪəstɪk] *n* levier *m* de vitesses
gearwheel ['gɪəwi:l] *n MecE* engrenage *m*; *Cycling* pignon *m*
gecko, *pl* **-os, -oes** ['gekəʊ, -əʊz] *n* gecko *m*
gee¹ [dʒi:] *int* (*to horse*) **g. up!** hue!
gee² *int Am* **g. (whiz(z))!** ça alors!, mince alors!
gee-gee ['dʒi:dʒi:] *n F* (*in children's language*) (*horse*) dada *m*
geek [gi:k] *n F* crétin, -ine, débile *mf*
geese [gi:s] *npl see* = **goose²**
geezer ['gi:zər] *n Br F* type *m*; **old g.** vieux type; **funny old g.** drôle *m* de bonhomme
Geiger counter ['gaɪgər] *n* compteur *m* Geiger
geisha ['geɪʃə] *n* geisha *f*
gel¹ [dʒel] *n Ch* colloïde *m* (coagulé); (*for hair, eyes*) gel *m*
gel² *vi* (**-ll-**) se coaguler; *Fig* (*of ideas, plans*) prendre corps *ou* forme; *Fig* **the musicians didn't g.** la cohésion ne s'est pas faite entre les musiciens
gelatine ['dʒelətiːn] *n* gélatine *f*; *Phot* **g. paper** papier *m* gélatine
gelatinize [dʒɪ'lætɪnaɪz] **1** *vt* gélatiniser **2** *vi* se gélatiniser
gelatinous [dʒɪ'lætɪnəs] *adj* gélatineux
geld [geld] *vt* (*animal*) châtrer; (*horse*) hongrer
gelding ['geldɪŋ] *n* (*animal*) animal *m* châtré; (*horse*) (cheval *m*) hongre *m*
gelignite ['dʒelɪgnaɪt] *n* gélignite *f*
gem [dʒem] *n* **(a)** (*precious stone*) pierre *f* précieuse; **g. stone** pierre gemme **(b)** *Fig* (*marvellous thing or person*) perle *f*; **he's a g. of a husband** c'est la perle des maris; **the g. of the collection** le joyau de la collection **(c)** *Typ* diamant *m*
Gemini ['dʒemɪnaɪ] *npl Astron* les Gémeaux *mpl*; *Astrol* **I'm a G.** je suis Gémeaux
Gen *Mil* (*abbr* **General**) gal
gen [dʒen] *n Br F* renseignements *mpl*, tuyaux *mpl* (**on sth** sur qch)
▶ **gen up** *vtsep Br F* (*provide with information*) (*person*) rencarder (**on** sur)
▶ **gen up on** *vipo Br F* se rencarder sur
gender ['dʒendər] *n* **(a)** [①B5-6,3,A] *Gram* genre *m*; **to agree in g.** s'accorder en genre (**with** avec) **(b)** (*sex*) sexe *m*; **the male/female g.** le sexe masculin/féminin; **it is not a question of g.** ce n'est pas une question de sexe
gender-bender *n F* **(a)** (*person*) travesti, -ie **(b)** *Comptr* commutateur *m*, changeur *m* de genre
gender-changer *n Comptr* commutateur *m*, changeur *m* de genre
gene [dʒi:n] *n Biol* gène *m*; *Fig* **music's in his genes** chez lui la musique, c'est héréditaire; **it's in his genes** c'est inné, il est né comme ça; **g. pool** patrimoine f génétique
genealogical [dʒi:nɪə'lɒdʒɪk(ə)l] *adj* généalogique; **g. chart** *or* **tree** arbre *m* généalogique
genealogist [dʒi:nɪ'ælədʒɪst] *n* généalogiste *mf*
genealogy [dʒi:nɪ'ælədʒɪ] *n* généalogie *f*
genera ['dʒenərə] *npl see* **genus**
general ['dʒen(ə)r(ə)l] **1** *adj* **(a)** (*paralysis, improvement etc*) général; **the rain has been pretty g.** il a plu un peu partout; **g. effect** effet *m* d'ensemble; **the g. tone of her remarks was that ...** ce qui ressortait de ses remarques c'est que ...; **he made himself a g. nuisance** il a été embêtant à tout point de vue; **I had a g. tidy-up** j'ai fait du rangement un peu partout; **a word in g. use** un mot couramment employé; **to come into g. use** se généraliser; **as a g. rule** en règle générale; **in g. terms** en termes généraux; **speaking in a g. way** d'une manière générale; *Banking* **g. account manager** chargé *m* de clientèle grand public; *Admin* **g. business** (*on agenda*) questions *fpl* diverses; *Rel* **g. confession** confession *f* en commun; *Am* **g. delivery** poste *f* restante; **g. manager** directeur *m* à responsabilités générales; **General Manager, European Operations** Directeur des Opérations européennes; **g. meeting** assemblée *f* générale; *Mil* **g. officer** (officier *m*) général *m*; **g. overheads** frais *mpl* d'administration générale; *Com* **g. partnership** société *f* commerciale en nom collectif; **the g. public** le grand public; **g. strike** grève *f* générale; **g. wholesaler** grossiste *m* généraliste
(b) (*in titles*) **inspector g.** inspecteur *m* général *ou* en chef; *Fr Hist* **Estates G.** États *mpl* généraux
2 *n* **(a)** **in g.** en général; **what effect will this have in g.?** quel effet général est-ce que cela va avoir?; **to argue from the g. to the particular** arguer du général au particulier
(b) *Mil* général *m*; (*rank*) général d'armée; *Rel* (*of religious order*) général; **g. staff** état-major *m*, *pl* états-majors
General Agreement on Tariffs and Trade *n* Accord *m* général sur les tarifs douaniers et le commerce
general anaesthetic *n Med* anesthésie *f* générale
General Assembly *n* (*of United Nations*) Assemblée *f* générale
general election *n Pol* élections *fpl* générales
general hospital *n Med* hôpital *m* (*qui traite toutes les maladies*)
general-interest station *n TV* station *f* généraliste
generalissimo [dʒenərə'li:si:məʊ] *n Mil* généralissime *m*
generality [dʒenə'rælɪtɪ] *n* **(a)** (*statement*) **to confine oneself to generalities** s'en tenir aux généralités **(b)** (*quality*) (*of remarks, opinions*) caractère *m* général **(c)** *Fml* (*majority*) **the g. of mankind** la plupart des hommes

generalization [dʒen(ə)rəlaɪ'zeɪʃən] *n* généralisation *f*; **to make generalizations** généraliser

generalize ['dʒen(ə)rəlaɪz] **1** *vi* **(a)** généraliser, faire des généralisations; **I don't like generalizing, but ...** je n'aime pas faire de généralisations, mais ... **(b)** *Med* (*of disease*) généraliser **2** *vt* **(a)** (*conclusion, facts etc*) généraliser à partir de **(b)** (*make widespread*) (*custom etc*) généraliser; **to become generalized** (*of practice*) se généraliser

generalized ['dʒen(ə)rəl] *adj* généralisé

general knowledge *n* culture *f* générale

generally ['dʒenrəlɪ] *adv* **(a)** (*widely*) généralement; **the word is g. understood to mean ...** le mot veut généralement dire ...; **this information is not g. available** le public n'a pas accès à ces informations; **it is not g. known that ...** beaucoup de gens ignorent que ...

(b) (*taken overall*) dans l'ensemble; **to make oneself g. useful** se rendre généralement utile; **she behaved in a g. antisocial manner** d'une manière générale, elle s'est comportée de façon antisociale

(c) (*as a general rule*) en règle générale, généralement, en général; **g. speaking** d'une manière générale; **the roads are g. crowded at this time** en général, les routes sont très encombrées à cette heure-ci

general practice *n Med* médecine *f* générale

general practitioner *n Med* (médecin *m*) généraliste *mf*, omnipraticien, -ienne

general-purpose *adj* universel, à usages multiples

generalship ['dʒen(ə)rəlʃɪp] *n Mil* (*skill*) l'art *m* d'être général; **his g.** la compétence de général dont il a fait preuve

generate ['dʒenəreɪt] *vt* (*result, electric current, heat etc*) produire; (*income*) créer; (*feeling, reaction, response*) provoquer, engendrer; (*interest, ideas*) faire naître; *Comptr* créer, générer; *Math* engendrer; *Ling* générer; **tourism generated three million pounds for the region** le tourisme a rapporté trois millions de livres à la région; **environment that generates crime** environnement qui engendre la délinquance

generating ['dʒenəreɪtɪŋ] **1** *adj* générateur, -trice; *El* **g. station** centrale *f* électrique **2** *n* génération *f*

generation [dʒenə'reɪʃən] *n* **(a)** [①A11,g,i] (*period, people, computers etc*) génération *f*; **from g. to g.** de génération en génération, de père en fils; **for generations there had always been a doctor in the family** ils étaient médecins de père en fils; **people of my g. will remember ...** les gens de ma génération se souviendront ...; **he's my g.** il est de ma génération; **we're a different g.** nous appartenons à des générations différentes; **the younger/older g.** la jeune/ l'ancienne génération; **the g. gap** l'écart *m ou* le fossé entre les générations

(b) (*production*) (*of ideas etc*) génération *f*, formation *f*; *El, Phys etc* (*of heat etc*) génération, production *f*; *Math* génération; *Ling* production, génération; *Comptr* création *f*, génération

-generation *suff* **second-g. immigrant** immigrant de la deuxième génération; **third-g. fax machines** télécopieurs de la troisième génération

generative ['dʒenərətɪv] *adj Ling* génératif

generator ['dʒenəreɪtər] *n El* génératrice *f*, dynamo *f*; (*backup device*) groupe *m* électrogène; *Comptr* (programme *m*) générateur *m*; *Tech* (*of heat etc*) générateur; **tourism is a major g. of income** le tourisme est une source importante de revenus

generatrix, *pl* **-ices** ['dʒenəreɪtrɪks, -ɪsiːz] *n Math* génératrice *f*

generic [dʒɪ'nerɪk] **1** *adj* (*term, noun*) générique; **g. advertising** publicité *f* générique; **g. market** marché *m* générique; **g. drug** médicament *m* générique **2** *n Mktg* produit *m* générique

generically [dʒɪ'nerɪklɪ] *adv* génériquement; **they are g. distinct** ils se distinguent en genre

generosity [dʒenə'rɒsɪtɪ] *n* (*with money, gifts*) générosité *f*, libéralité *f*; (*of spirit*) grandeur *f*, magnanimité *f*; **in a spirit of g.** (*to act*) par générosité; **thanks to the g. of Mr Jones** grâce à la générosité de M. Jones

generous ['dʒen(ə)rəs] *adj* (*person*) (*with money, gifts*) généreux; (*remarks, comments*) bienveillant; **he has a g. nature** c'est une âme généreuse; **he's a bit too g. with his advice** il n'est pas avare de conseils; **that's a g. interpretation of his motives** c'est faire preuve de bienveillance que d'interpréter ainsi ses raisons; **to be g. in victory** se montrer magnanime; **to be g. in defeat** être bon perdant; **g. mark** (*for homework etc*) note généreuse; **she's g. with her money** elle n'est pas avare de son argent; **a g. helping of food/measure of whisky** une portion généreuse de nourriture/un bon verre de whisky; **he took a g. helping of the stew** il s'est servi amplement de ragoût; *F* **she's built on g. lines** elle a des formes généreuses

generously ['dʒen(ə)rəslɪ] *adv* (*to give, donate etc*) généreusement; **he g. congratulated her on her victory** bon joueur, il l'a félicitée pour sa victoire; **he helped himself g. to the stew** il s'est servi amplement de ragoût; **she g. offered to help** elle a généreusement proposé son aide; **her g. proportioned figure** ses formes généreuses

genesis ['dʒenɪsɪs] *n* genèse *f*, origine *f*; *Bible* **(the Book of) G.** la Genèse

genetic [dʒɪ'netɪk] *adj Biol* génétique; **g. code** code *m* génétique; **g. engineering** génie *m* génétique; **g. fingerprint** empreinte *f* génétique; **g. fingerprinting** détermination *f* de l'empreinte génétique

genetically [dʒɪ'netɪklɪ] *adv Biol* génétiquement; **to g. alter a mouse** faire des manipulations génétiques sur une souris

geneticist [dʒɪ'netɪsɪst] *n Biol* généticien, -ienne

genetics [dʒɪ'netɪks] *n* [①A10,c] *Biol* génétique *f*

Geneva [dʒɪ'niːvə] *n* Genève *f*; **Lake G.** le lac Léman; *Hist* **the G. Convention** la Convention de Genève

Genghis Khan ['geŋgɪs'kɑːn] *n* Gengis Khan

genial ['dʒiːnɪəl] *adj* (*person, tone, manner*) plein de bienveillance, affable, plein de bonne humeur

geniality [dʒiːnɪ'ælɪtɪ] *n* bienveillance *f*, bonne humeur *f*

genially ['dʒiːnɪəlɪ] *adv* affablement, avec affabilité

genie, *pl* **genii** ['dʒiːnɪ, 'dʒiːnɪaɪ] *n* djinn *m*, génie *m*

genital ['dʒenɪt(ə)l] **1** *adj* génital; *Med* **g. herpes** herpès *m* génital **2** *npl* **genitals** organes *mpl* génitaux externes

genitalia [dʒenɪ'teɪlɪə] *npl* organes *mpl* génitaux externes

genitive ['dʒenɪtɪv] [①A15-16,D] *Gram* **1** *n* génitif *m*; **in the g.** au génitif **2** *adj* génitif; **g. case** génitif *m*

genito-urinary [dʒenɪtəʊ'jʊərɪnərɪ] *adj Med* génito-urinaire

genius ['dʒiːnɪəs] *n* **(a)** (*pl* **geniuses** ['dʒiːnɪəsɪz]) (*person*) génie *m*; **she's a mathematical g.** c'est un génie en mathématiques

(b) (*no pl*) (*great talent*) génie *m*; **man/work of g.** homme *m*/œuvre *f* de génie; **to show g.** faire preuve de génie; **that goal was pure g.** ce goal, c'était du génie pur et simple

(c) (*no pl*) (*aptitude*) aptitudes *fpl* naturelles; **to have a g. for business** avoir le génie des affaires; **to have a g. for doing sth** avoir le don de faire qch

(d) *Lit* (*no pl*) (*of a nation, era*) génie *m*

(e) *Lit* (*pl* **genii** ['dʒiːnɪaɪ]) (*spirit*) (*of place etc*) génie *m ou* esprit *m* tutélaire; **she is his good/evil g.** c'est son bon/ mauvais génie

Genoa ['dʒenəʊə] *n* Gênes *f*

genocidal [dʒenə'saɪd(ə)l] *adj* génocide

genocide ['dʒenəsaɪd] *n* génocide *m*

Genoese [dʒenəʊ'iːz] **1** *adj* génois **2** *n* Génois, -oise

genome *n Bibl* ['dʒiːnəʊm] génome *m*

genotype ['dʒenəʊtaɪp] *n Biol* génotype *m*

genre ['ʒɒnrə] *n* genre *m*; **g. film** film *m* de genre; **g. painting** tableau *m* de genre

gent [dʒent] *n Br F* **(a)** monsieur *m*; **he's a real g.** c'est un gentleman; **gents' footwear** chaussures pour hommes **(b) gents** (*toilets*) toilettes *fpl* pour hommes; **where's the gents?** où sont les toilettes?

genteel [dʒen'tiːl] *adj* **(a)** *Pej* (*affected*) maniéré **(b)** *Old-fashioned* (*respectable*) comme il faut; **g. poverty** pauvreté *f* digne; **g. society** société *f* comme il faut

gentian ['dʒenʃɪən] *n* (*plant*) gentiane *f*; **g. bitter** (amer *m* de) gentiane; **g. blue** bleu *m* gentiane

Gentile ['dʒentaɪl] *adj, n* gentil, -ile

gentility [dʒen'tɪlɪtɪ] *n* **(a)** *Pej* (*affectation*) prétention *f* au bon ton **(b)** *Old-fashioned* (*respectability*) respectabilité *f*; **the g.** (*people*) la haute bourgeoisie; **shabby g.** la misère en habit noir

gentle ['dʒent(ə)l] *adj* (**gentler, gentlest**) **(a)** (*delicate, kind*) doux, *f* douce; (*reprimand*) peu sévère; (*tap on shoulder etc*) léger; (*exercise*) modéré; (*slope*) doux, faible; **to be g. with sb** être doux avec qn; **g. as a lamb** doux comme un agneau; **the gentle(r) sex** le sexe faible; **a g. breeze** une petite brise; **a g. giant** un bon géant **(b)** *Old-fashioned* (*noble*) **of g. birth** bien né

gentlefolk ['dʒent(ə)lfəʊk] *npl Old-fashioned* personnes *fpl* de bonne famille

gentleman, *pl* **-men** ['dʒent(ə)lmən] *n* **(a)** (*well-bred man*) homme *m* bien élevé, gentleman *m*; **g.'s agreement** gentleman's agreement *m*; **to act** *or* **behave like a g.** se conduire en gentleman; **he's no g.** il est mal élevé; **thank you, you're a g.** merci, vous êtes un gentleman

(b) (*man*) monsieur *m*, homme *m*; **Ladies and Gentlemen!** (*to audience*) mesdames et messieurs!; **there's a g. to see you** il y a un monsieur qui voudrait vous parler; **this young gentleman's lost** ce petit jeune homme est perdu; *Com* **gentlemen's hairdresser** coiffeur *m* pour hommes; **gentlemen** (*on toilet*) messieurs; **g.'s g.** valet *m* de chambre; **gentlemen's club** club *m* dont l'accès est réservé aux hommes; *Hum* **g. of the road** (*tramp*) clochard *m*; *Old-fashioned* **g. friend** (*of woman*) ami *m*

(**c**) (*nobleman etc*) gentilhomme *m*, *pl* gentilshommes; **g.** (**of independent means**) rentier *m*; **G. in waiting** gentilhomme de service (*près du roi*)
(**d**) *Old-fashioned Sp* amateur *m*

gentleman-farmer *n* gentleman-farmer *m*, *pl* gentlemen-farmers

gentlemanly ['dʒent(ə)lmənlı] *adj* bien élevé; **it would have been more g. to say nothing** un homme bien élevé *ou* un gentleman n'aurait rien dit

gentleness ['dʒent(ə)lnıs] *n* douceur *f*

gently ['dʒentlı] *adv* (*to handle etc*) doucement; (*to remind, imply, dissuade*) gentiment; **to speak g.** parler d'un ton doux *ou* avec douceur; **to deal g. with sb** traiter qn avec douceur; **g. (does it)!** allez-y doucement!; **the road slopes g. down to the beach** la route descend en pente douce jusqu'à la plage

gentrification [dʒentrıfı'keıʃən] *n Br* embourgeoisement *m*

gentrified ['dʒentrıfaıd] *adj Br* (*area, street*) qui s'est embourgeoisé

gentry ['dʒentrı] *n* (*no pl*) petite noblesse *f*; **landed g.** aristocratie *f* terrienne

genuflect ['dʒenjʊflekt] *vi* faire une génuflexion

genuflection, genuflexion [dʒenjʊ'flekʃən] *n* génuflexion *f*

genuine ['dʒenjʊın] *adj* (**a**) (*manuscript etc*) authentique, véritable; *Com* (*article*) garanti d'origine; (*champagne*) authentique; (*diamond*) véritable (**b**) (*sincere*) sincère, franc, *f* franche; (*belief*) sincère; (*friend*) loyal; *Com* **g. buyer** acheteur *m* sérieux; **I think he's being g.** je crois qu'il est sincère; **she comes across as a g. person** elle donne l'impression d'être une personne sincère; **it was a g. mistake on her part** elle ne l'a pas fait exprès; **a g. surprise** une véritable surprise

genuinely ['dʒenjʊınlı] *adv* (**a**) authentiquement (**b**) (*to believe, be sorry etc*) sincèrement; **g. surprised** vraiment surpris

genuineness ['dʒenjʊınnıs] *n* (**a**) (*of manuscript etc*) authenticité *f* (**b**) (*sincerity*) sincérité *f*

genus, *pl* **genera** ['dʒi:nəs, 'dʒenərə] *n Biol* genre *m*

geo- ['dʒi:əʊ] *pref* géo(-)

geode ['dʒi:əʊd] *n Geol* géode *f*

geodemographic [dʒi:əʊdeməʊ'græfık] *adj Mktg* géodémographique

geodesic [dʒi:əʊ'di:sık] *adj* géodésique; **g. dome** dôme *m* géodésique

geodesy [dʒı'ɒdısı] *n* géodésie *f*

geographer [dʒı'ɒgrəfər] *n* géographe *mf*

geographic(al) [dʒıə'græfık, -ık(ə)l] *adj* géographique; **a g. survey** un relevé topographique; *Mktg* **g. pricing** tarification *f* géographique

geographically [dʒıə'græfıklı] *adv* géographiquement

geography [dʒı'ɒgrəfı] *n* géographie *f*; **I haven't quite got a grasp of the g. of the building** je ne m'oriente pas encore très bien dans le bâtiment; *Euph* **I'll show you the g. of the house** (*where toilets are*) je vais vous montrer où sont les petits coins; **g. (book)** livre *m* de géographie

geologic(al) [dʒıə'lɒdʒık, -ık(ə)l] *adj* géologique; **g. survey** relevé *m* géologique

geologically [dʒıə'lɒdʒıklı] *adv* géologiquement

geologist [dʒı'ɒlədʒıst] *n* géologue *mf*

geology [dʒı'ɒlədʒı] *n* géologie *f*

geometer [dʒı'ɒmıtər] *n* géomètre *mf*

geometric(al) [dʒıə'metrık, -ık(ə)l] *adj* géométrique; **g. design** dessin *m* géométrique; **g. progression** progression *f* géométrique

geometrically [dʒıə'metrıklı] *adv* géométriquement

geometrician [dʒıɒmı'trıʃən] *n* géomètre *mf*

geometry [dʒı'ɒmıtrı] *n* géométrie *f*

geomorphologic(al) [dʒi:əʊmɔ:fə'lɒdʒık, -ık(ə)l] *adj* géomorphologique

geomorphology [dʒi:əʊmɔ:'fɒlədʒı] *n* géomorphologie *f*

geophysical [dʒi:əʊ'fızık(ə)l] *adj* géophysique

geophysicist [dʒi:əʊ'fızısıst] *n* géophysicien, -ienne

geophysics [dʒi:əʊ'fızıks] *n* [①**A10**,c] géophysique *f*

geopolitics [dʒıəʊ'pɒlıtıks] *n* [①**A10**,c] géopolitique *f*

Geordie ['dʒɔ:dı] *Br F* **1** *n* (*resident*) habitant, -ante de Newcastle-upon-Tyne ou de sa région; (*by birth*) originaire *mf* de Newcastle-upon-Tyne ou de sa région; (*dialect*) dialecte *m* parlé dans la région de Newcastle-upon-Tyne **2** *adj* (*dialect etc*) de Newcastle-upon-Tyne

George [dʒɔ:dʒ] *n* (**a**) *Old-fashioned F* **by G.!** sapristi!; **G. Cross** médaille *f* récompensant des actes de bravoure; **G. Medal** médaille décernée à des civils pour des actes de bravoure (**b**) *Av F* (*automatic pilot*) George *m*

georgette [dʒɔ:'dʒet] *n Tex* crêpe *m* georgette

Georgia ['dʒɔ:dʒıə] *n* Géorgie *f*

Georgian[1] ['dʒɔ:dʒıən] *adj Br Hist* (**a**) du règne des quatre rois Georges; **a G. house** une maison datant de l'époque 1720-1830 (**b**) (*of George V*) du règne de Georges V

Georgian[2] *Geog* **1** *adj* géorgien **2** *n* Géorgien, -ienne

geoscience [dʒi:əʊ'saıəns] *n* sciences *fpl* de la terre

geosphere ['dʒi:əʊsfıər] *n* géosphère *f*

geostationary [dʒi:əʊ'steıʃənərı] *adj* géostationnaire; **g. orbit** orbite *f* géostationnaire

geothermal [dʒi:əʊ'θɜ:məl] *adj* géothermique

geotropism [dʒı'ɒtrəpız(ə)m] *n* géotropisme *m*

geranium [dʒə'reınıəm] **1** *n* (**a**) (*plant*) géranium *m* (**b**) (*colour*) **g. (red)** vermeil *m* **2** *adj* **g. (red)** vermeil

gerbil ['dʒɜ:bıl] *n* gerbille *f*

geriatric[1] [dʒerı'ætrık] *n Med* malade *mf* gériatrique; *Pej* (*old person*) vieux croulant *m*, vieille croulante *f*

geriatric[2] *adj* des vieillards; **g. medicine** gériatrie *f*; **g. ward** service *m* de gériatrie

geriatrician [dʒerıə'trıʃən] *n* gériatre *mf*

geriatrics [dʒerı'ætrıks] *n sing* [①**A10**,c] *Med* gériatrie *f*

germ [dʒɜ:m] *n* (**a**) *Med* (*of disease*) germe *m*, microbe *m*; **I don't want your germs!** je ne veux pas de tes microbes!; **g. warfare** guerre *f* bactériologique (**b**) *Biol* (*of organism*) germe *m*; **g. cell** gamète *m*; *Fig* **the g. of an idea** le germe d'une idée

German ['dʒɜ:mən] **1** *adj* allemand; *Hist* **West/East G.** ouest-/est-allemand **2** *n* (**a**) Allemand, -ande; *Hist* **West/East G.** Allemand de l'Quest/de l'Est (**b**) *Ling* allemand *m*; **High/Low G.** haut/bas allemand

German Democratic Republic *n Hist* République *f* démocratique Allemande

germander [dʒɜ:'mændər] *n* (*plant*) germandrée *f*

germane [dʒɜ:'meın] *adj Fml* se rapportant (**to** à)

germanic [dʒɜ:'mænık] *adj* germanique

Germanist ['dʒɜ:mənıst] *n Ling* germaniste *mf*

Germanize ['dʒɜ:mənaız] *vt* germaniser

German measles *npl Med* rubéole *f*

German shepherd *n esp Am* (*dog*) berger *m* allemand

Germany ['dʒɜ:mənı] *n* Allemagne *f*; *Hist* **West/East G.** l'Allemagne de l'Ouest/de l'Est; **the two Germanies** les deux Allemagnes

germ-free *adj* (*environment*) stérile

germicidal [dʒɜ:mı'saıd(ə)l] *adj* germicide

germicide ['dʒɜ:mısaıd] *n* germicide *m*

germinate ['dʒɜ:mıneıt] **1** *vi* (*of seed, Fig of idea*) germer **2** *vt* (*seeds*) faire germer

germination [dʒɜ:mı'neıʃən] *n* germination *f*

gerontocracy [dʒerɒn'tɒkrəsı] *n* gérontocratie *f*

gerontologist [dʒerɒn'tɒlədʒıst] *n* gérontologue *mf*

gerontology [dʒerɒn'tɒlədʒı] *n* gérontologie *f*

gerrymander ['dʒerımændər] *Pol* **1** *vti* **to g. (constituencies)** faire du tripatouillage électoral **2** *n* tripatouillage *m* électoral

gerrymandering [dʒerı'mændərıŋ] *n Pol* tripatouillage *m* électoral

gerund ['dʒerənd] *n* [①**A42-44**] *Gram* gérondif *m*, nom *m* verbal; **in the g.** au gérondif

gerundive [dʒı'rʌndıv] *Gram* **1** *adj* du gérondif **2** *n* adjectif *m* verbal

gesso ['dʒesəʊ] *n Art* (*coating*) (*for frescos*) enduit *m* de plâtre; (*substance*) plâtre *m* de Paris, gypse *m*

gestalt [gə'ʃtælt] *n Psy* gestalt *f*; **g. therapy** gestalt-thérapie *f*

Gestapo [gəs'tɑ:pəʊ] *n* Gestapo *f*

gestate [dʒes'teıt] *vi* être en gestation

gestation [dʒes'teıʃən] *n Physiol, Fig* gestation *f*; **g. period** période *f* de gestation

gesticulate [dʒes'tıkjʊleıt] *vi* gesticuler

gesticulation [dʒestıkjʊ'leıʃən] *n* gesticulation *f*

gesture[1] ['dʒestʃər] *n* geste *m*; **to make a g.** faire un geste; **with a sweeping g.** d'un geste large; **g. of defiance** geste de défi; *Fig* **as a g. of friendship** en témoignage d'amitié; **a g. towards peace** un geste indiquant une volonté de paix

gesture[2] **1** *vi* faire des gestes; **she gestured to them to be silent** elle leur a fait signe de se taire **2** *vt* exprimer par gestes; **he gestured us over** il nous a fait signe d'approcher

get [get] (*pt* **got** [gɒt]; *pp* **got,** *Arch, Am also* **gotten** ['gɒt(ə)n]; *prp* **getting** ['getıŋ]) **1** *vt* (**a**) (*obtain*) procurer, obtenir; **to g. sth for sb** procurer qch à qn; (*buy*) acheter qch pour qn; **where did you g. that?** où avez-vous trouvé/acheté cela?; **where can we g. some information?** où est-ce que nous pouvons obtenir des informations?; **to g. something to eat** (*find*) trouver de quoi manger; (*eat in restaurant etc*) manger quelque chose; **we g. our eggs from the farm next door** nous achetons nos œufs à la ferme d'à-côté; **I got this car cheap** j'ai eu *ou* j'ai acheté cette voiture à un bon prix; **if you're going to buy shoes, g. good ones** si tu achètes des chaussures, prends-en de bonnes; **to g. a job** trouver un travail; **I haven't got the right answer** je n'ai pas trouvé la solution; **to g. sb's permission to do sth** obtenir la permission de qn de faire qch; **to g. one's own way** faire valoir sa volonté; **I'll do it if I g. the time/a moment** je le ferai si j'ai le temps/si je trouve un moment; **I've got six more to g.** (*in collection*) il m'en manque six; **you g. a fine view from here** il y a une vue magnifique d'ici; **you g. a lot of people marrying young here** il y a beaucoup de gens qui se marient jeunes par ici; **we don't g. many accidents here** nous n'avons pas beaucoup d'accidents par ici; **I finally got her on her own** *or* **alone** j'ai fini par réussir à la voir en tête à tête; **you need to g. (yourself) a good lawyer** il te faut un bon avocat

(b) (*receive*) (*present, medal etc*) recevoir; (*prize*) gagner, remporter; **what did you g. for your birthday?** qu'est-ce que tu as eu pour ton anniversaire?; **I got your letter last week** j'ai eu *ou* reçu ta lettre la semaine dernière; **I didn't g. a reply** je n'ai pas eu de réponse; **room that gets no sun** pièce où le soleil ne donne pas; **we g. quite a lot of rain in summer** il pleut beaucoup en été; **he gets his shyness from his mother** il tient sa timidité de sa mère; **I got the idea from a book** j'ai trouvé l'idée dans un livre; **I need all the advice I can g.** j'ai besoin de tous les conseils qu'on peut me donner; **to g. ten years** prendre dix ans de prison; **to g. £15 000 a year** gagner 15 000 livres par an; **to g. 10% interest** recevoir 10% d'intérêt; **to g. a good price for sth** obtenir un bon prix pour qch; **what did you g. for your car?** combien est-ce que tu as vendu ta voiture?; **she got very little from her lessons** elle a très peu appris de ses leçons

(c) *Rad, TV* **we can't g. Moscow/Channel 4** nous ne pouvons pas avoir Moscou/Channel 4; **we can only g. three channels here** nous ne pouvons recevoir que trois chaînes ici; **we g. the Guardian** (*newspaper*) nous achetons le Guardian; *Tel* **I had a job getting you** j'ai eu du mal à vous joindre; *Tel* **I couldn't g. her at the office** je n'ai pas pu l'avoir au bureau; *Tel* **g. me Washington 330 330** (*to operator*) appelez-moi Washington 330 330; **could you g. the phone/the door?** (*answer*) est-ce que tu peux décrocher?/ouvrir la porte?

(d) (*catch*) prendre, attraper; (*train, bus*) prendre; (*cold, illness*) attraper; (*note down, record*) noter; *F* **we'll g. them yet!** on les aura!; **I'll g. you for that** je te revaudrai ça; **you've got me this time** (*caught me*) cette fois-ci vous m'avez eu; (*I don't know the answer*) je donne ma langue au chat; **the piranhas got him in the end** les piranhas ont fini par l'avoir

(e) (*hit*) (*with fist, foot*) atteindre; (*with bullet, arrow, stone etc*) toucher; **he got a bullet in his shoulder** il a reçu une balle dans l'épaule

(f) *F* (*move emotionally*) émouvoir; **the play didn't really g. me** la pièce ne m'a pas fait grand-chose

(g) *F* (*annoy*) mettre en boule; **that gets me** *or* **gets my goat** ça me met en boule; **what gets me is that ...** ce qui me met en boule, c'est que ...

(h) *F* (*understand*) comprendre; **I don't g. your meaning** je ne vous comprends pas; **if you g. my meaning** si tu vois ce que je veux dire; **g. me?** tu y es?, tu piges?; **oh, I g. you!** ah! j'ai pigé!; **I don't g. it** je ne comprends pas; **to g. a joke** comprendre une blague; **g. it?** (*do you understand the joke?*) tu piges?

(i) *Sl* (*consider*) **g. a load of this!** (*listen*) écoute un peu ça!; **g. him!** (*he looks outrageous*) regarde-le, celui-là!; (*he made an outrageous remark*) écoute-le, celui-là!; **g. him, riding around in a Rolls when he's on the dole!** tu te rends compte, il roule en Rolls alors qu'il touche le chômage!

(j) (*fetch*) aller chercher; **he went and got a book from the library** il est allé chercher un livre à la bibliothèque; **go and g. a doctor** allez chercher un médecin; **g. me the big screwdriver** allez me chercher le gros tournevis; **can I g. you anything?** (*to sb ill etc*) est-ce vous avez besoin de quelque chose?; **g. him a chair, someone** est-ce quelqu'un peut lui apporter une chaise?

(k) (*prepare*) faire, préparer; **can I g. you an omelette?** est-ce que je peux vous faire une omelette?; **she got herself some breakfast** elle s'est préparé un petit déjeuner; **to g. lunch (ready)** préparer le déjeuner

(l) (*move, send*) faire parvenir, faire transporter; **you'll never g. that box through the door** tu n'arriveras jamais à faire passer cette boîte par la porte; **they got her to the airport on time** ils l'ont amenée à l'aéroport à l'heure; **I got a message to them** je leur ai fait parvenir un message; **how can I g. it to you?** comment puis-je vous le faire parvenir?; **how am I to g. this parcel home?** (*by myself*) comment vais-je faire pour transporter ce paquet chez moi?; **to g. the children to bed** coucher les enfants, mettre les enfants au lit; *Fig* **where has all this got us?** (*our hard work, arguing*) où est-ce que tout ça nous a menés?; **this is getting us nowhere** (*of method, argument*) ça ne nous mène nulle part, ça ne nous mène à rien; **to g. sb on(to) a subject** amener qn à parler sur un sujet

(m) (*cause to be*) **to g. sth dry/wet** sécher/mouiller qch; **to g. sth clean/dirty** nettoyer/salir qch; **to g. sb angry** mettre qn en colère; **to g. sb nervous** rendre qn nerveux; **I got myself terribly agitated** je me suis rendu malade; **they've got me so I don't know whether I'm coming or going** c'en est à un tel point que je ne sais plus où j'en suis; **I couldn't g. the drawer open** je n'arrivais pas à ouvrir le tiroir; **to g. the answer right** trouver la bonne réponse; **I got his name wrong** j'ai fait erreur sur son nom; **you've got him worried** tu l'as fait s'inquiéter; **to g. people interested (in sth)** intéresser les gens (à qch)

(n) [①A55,b,iv] (*with pp or inf or prp*) (*cause*) **to g. sth done by sb, to g. sb to do sth** faire faire qch à *ou* par qn; **to g. sth mended** faire réparer qch; **to g. oneself noticed** se faire remarquer; **g. him to read it** faites-le-lui lire; **to g. sb to agree** décider qn à consentir; **you'll never g. him to admit to it** tu ne le lui feras jamais admettre; **we must g. him to come and see us** il faut le persuader de venir nous voir; **I can't g. the door to shut** je n'arrive pas à fermer la porte; **to g. one's work finished** venir à bout de son travail; **to g. one's dress torn** déchirer sa robe; **to g. sb doing sth** faire faire qch à qn; **if you want to g. him going ...** (*angry*) si tu veux le mettre en colère ...; (*cause him to talk a lot*) si tu veux le faire parler ...; **once he gets going there's no stopping him** quand il commence, il n'y a plus moyen de l'arrêter; *Aut* **to g. the engine running** mettre le moteur en marche; **that got him guessing** ça l'a intrigué

(o) (*do eventually*) **to g. to do sth** finir par faire qch; **you'll g. to like him** vous finirez par l'aimer; **to g. to know sth** apprendre qch; **when you g. to know him** quand on le connaît mieux; **they got to be friends** ils sont devenus amis; **she got to be very rich** elle est devenue très riche

(p) (*have opportunity to do*) **to g. to do sth** avoir l'occasion de faire qch; **as a diplomat she got to visit many countries** en tant que diplomate elle a pu visiter *ou* a eu l'occasion de visiter de nombreux pays; **I didn't g. to speak to him in person** je n'ai pas pu lui parler en personne; **I finally got to see the Taj Mahal** j'ai finalement réussi à voir le Taj Mahal

(q) [①A54-5,b,iii] (*have*) **to have got** avoir; **have you got any children?** avez-vous des enfants?; **I haven't got any** je n'en ai pas; **have you got a light?** avez-vous du feu?; **what have you got there?** qu'avez-vous là?; **she's (really) got something** elle a (vraiment) quelque chose; **it's got something** (*of play, poem, song etc*) il y a quelque chose là-dedans; **he's got measles** il a la rougeole; **what's that got to do with it!** qu'est-ce que cela a à voir?; *F* **you've got it!** vous y êtes!, c'est ça

(r) [①A58,e] (*must*) **to have got to do sth** être obligé de *ou* devoir faire qch; **it has got to be done** il faut que cela soit fait; **have you really got to work on Sundays?** est-ce que vous êtes vraiment obligé de travailler le dimanche?; **but that's got to be the right answer!** c'est forcément la bonne réponse!

2 *vi* **(a)** (*reach, make one's way*) arriver, se rendre (**to** à); **how does one g. there?** comment fait-on pour y aller?; **when I got home** quand je suis arrivé à la maison; **how do I g. to the station?** (*asking one's way*) où se trouve la gare?; **to g. there** (*reach a place*) arriver; (*reach a goal*) y arriver, réussir; **we're not getting anywhere, we're getting nowhere** nous n'aboutissons à rien, nous n'arrivons à rien, nous n'allons nulle part; **to g. to the top of a tree/ladder** monter jusqu'en haut d'un arbre/d'une échelle; **where has he got to?** où est-ce qu'il est passé?; **where have you got to?** (*in your work etc*) où en êtes-vous?; **she got to the door and turned round** elle est allée jusqu'à la porte et s'est retournée; **to g. to one's feet** se lever; **to g. to university** aller à l'université; **they only got as far as Marseilles** ils ne sont pas allés plus loin que Marseille; **he got as far as saying ...** il a été jusqu'à dire ...; **we got onto (the subject of) divorce** nous en sommes venus à parler de divorce; **it got to the point where they weren't speaking to one another** c'en est venu au point qu'ils ne se parlaient plus; **eventually we got to talking about politics** nous avons fini par en venir à parler de politique; *Sl* **it really gets to me** (*annoys me*) ça me met hors de moi; (*thrills me*) ça me fait quelque chose

(b) (*move*) **to g. behind a tree** se mettre derrière un arbre; **she got inside the barrel** elle est rentrée dans le tonneau

(c) to g. to work (*start working*) se mettre au travail; (*reach workplace*) arriver à son (lieu de) travail (**d**) (*with adj complement*) (*become*) devenir; **to g. old** devenir vieux, vieillir; **I'm getting used to it** je commence à m'y habituer; **to g. angry** se mettre en colère; **to g. better** (*improve*) s'améliorer; (*after illness*) se remettre

(**e**) [ⓘ**A53**,16,b] (*with pp*) **to g. dressed** s'habiller; **to g. married** se marier; **to g. shaved** (*by self*) se raser; (*by barber*) se faire raser; **to g. killed** se faire tuer; **to g. drowned** se noyer; **to g. caught** (*by police etc*) se faire prendre; (*by rain etc*) être surpris; **he got sacked** il s'est fait renvoyer; **to g. started** commencer

(**f**) (*with prp*) (*start*) **to g. going** (*leave*) partir, se mettre en route; (*start work*) se mettre au travail; (*hurry*) se dépêcher; **let's g. going** *or F* **cracking** allons-y!; **to g. talking with sb** entrer en conversation avec qn

▶ **get about** *vi* (**a**) (*move around*) circuler; **he gets about a great deal** il se déplace beaucoup; **she can't g. about very easily** (*of invalid*) elle se déplace difficilement; **I don't g. about so much these days** (*of old person*) je ne sors plus tellement ces temps-ci (**b**) (*of news etc*) se répandre, circuler; **it got about that she was planning to resign** le bruit s'est répandu qu'elle projetait de démissionner

▶ **get across 1** *vi* (**a**) (*succeed in crossing*) traverser

(**b**) (*communicate*) communiquer; **she can't g. across to her audience** elle ne peut pas communiquer avec son public; **our message is not getting across** notre message ne passe pas; *Th* **the play didn't g. across to the audience** la pièce n'a pas passé la rampe

2 *vtas* (**a**) (*over water, over street*) (*person*) faire traverser; **we couldn't g. the supplies across** (*across the river*) nous ne pouvions pas faire passer les vivres de l'autre côté; **it was easy to g. the people across** (*across the border*) il était facile de faire passer les gens

(**b**) *F* (*communicate*) **I couldn't g. it across to him** je n'ai pas réussi à le lui faire comprendre; **we're not getting our message across** notre message ne passe pas

▶ **get ahead** *vi* (**a**) (*make progress*) avancer; **you'll never g. ahead unless you work hard** tu n'arriveras à rien si tu ne travailles pas dur (**b**) (*move in front*) prendre la tête

▶ **get along** *vi* (**a**) (*leave*) s'en aller, partir; **it's time for me to be getting along, it's time I was getting along** il est temps que je parte; *F* **g. along with you!** (*go away*) allez-vous-en!; (*that's silly, not true*) allons donc!, vous plaisantez!

(**b**) (*progress*) **how are you getting along in your new job?** comment ça va, ton nouveau travail?; **how are you getting along in the new house?** comment ça va, dans la nouvelle maison?; **we've got along all right without their help/them** nous nous sommes bien débrouillés sans leur aide/eux

(**c**) (*be on good terms*) (bien) s'entendre (**with** avec); **I wish I got along better with my neighbours** j'aimerais bien m'entendre mieux avec mes voisins

▶ **get around 1** *vi* (**a**) (*be active*) bouger; (*gain experience*) rouler sa bosse; **old people find it hard to g. around** les personnes âgées ont du mal à se déplacer; **she gets around a great deal** (*travels*) elle voyage beaucoup; **you g. around, don't you!** tu sors beaucoup, hein!

(**b**) (*spread*) se répandre; **the word got around that he had some information** on a raconté qu'il avait des informations

2 *vipo* (*avoid, circumvent*) (*difficulties*) couper à, échapper à; **there's no getting around it, we'll have to tell her** il n'y a pas d'autre moyen, il va falloir que nous le lui disions; **there's no getting around the fact that he lied to us** il reste qu'il nous a menti

▶ **get around to** *vipo* **to g. around to doing sth** trouver le temps de faire qch; **I'll g. around to it one day** je trouverai le temps de le faire un de ces jours; **could you g. around to telling me why you're here?** est-ce que tu pourrais enfin me dire pourquoi tu es ici?

▶ **get at** *vipo* (**a**) (*reach, have access to*) (*place, person*) atteindre; **the study is locked and I can't g. at my books** le bureau est fermé à clef et je ne peux pas accéder à mes livres; **it's on the top shelf where the children can't g. at it** c'est sur l'étagère du haut où les enfants ne peuvent pas l'atteindre; **to g. at the truth** découvrir la vérité; *F* **just let me g. at him!** si jamais il me tombe sous la main!

(**b**) (*imply*) **what are you getting at?** où voulez-vous en venir?

(**c**) *F* (*suborn*) (*witness*) suborner

(**d**) *F* (*criticize unfairly*) (*person*) attaquer; **she's always getting at her husband** elle est toujours à dénigrer son mari; **you're not being got at, no one's getting at you** on ne s'en prend pas à toi, personne ne s'en prend à toi

▶ **get away 1** *vi* (*leave*) partir; (*escape*) s'échapper, se sauver; **to g. away for a few days** s'absenter pendant quelques jours; **g. away!** allez-vous-en!; *F* **g. away (with you)!** (*stop joking*) tu plaisantes!, ça ne prend pas!; **car that gets away quickly** voiture qui a une bonne reprise **2** *vtas* (*remove*) (*person*) emmener; (*object*) s'emparer de

▶ **get away from 1** *vipo* (*leave, escape from*) (*place*) quitter; **to g. away early from the office** quitter le bureau de bonne heure; **I couldn't g. away from him** (*he wouldn't stop talking*) je ne pouvais pas m'en défaire; **how wonderful to g. away from it all!** quel plaisir de tout quitter!; *Fig* **there's no getting away from it** il faut bien l'admettre

2 *vtaspo* (*remove from*) **g. that child away from the road!** éloignez cet enfant de la route!; **g. me away from here!** fais-moi sortir d'ici!; **g. your dog away from my garden!** faites sortir votre chien de mon jardin!; **they managed to g. him away from the TV** ils ont fini par l'arracher de devant la télévision; **to g. sth away from sb** prendre qch à qn

▶ **get away with** *vipo* (**a**) (*escape with*) **the burglars got away with £10000** les cambrioleurs sont repartis avec *ou* ont raflé 10000 livres

(**b**) (*be let off with*) s'en tirer avec; **he got away with a small fine** il s'en est tiré avec une petite amende

(**c**) (*not be punished for*) **that child gets away with murder** on laisse tout faire à ce gamin; **children who play truant mustn't be allowed to g. away with it** les enfants qui font l'école buissonnière doivent être punis; **she pretended she was a doctor and she got away with it** elle a fait semblant d'être médecin et ça a marché; **her skirt is really tiny but she gets away with it** sa jupe est vraiment très courte mais elle peut se le permettre

▶ **get back 1** *vi* (**a**) (*return*) revenir, retourner; **when did you g. back?** quand est-ce que tu es rentré?; **I got back from Italy yesterday** je suis rentré d'Italie hier; **to g. back home** rentrer chez soi; **to g. back into bed** se recoucher

(**b**) (*move away, step back*) reculer (**from** de); **g. back or I'll shoot!** reculez ou je tire!

2 *vtsep* (**a**) (*recover*) (*sth*) récupérer; (*one's strength*) reprendre; **I'll g. the book back from her tomorrow** je lui demanderai de rendre le livre demain; **to g. one's money back** (*loan returned*) récupérer son argent; (*reimbursed*) se faire rembourser

(**b**) (*return*) (*sth*) rendre; **g. the file back to me as soon as possible** (*in person*) rendez-moi le dossier dès que possible; (*by post etc*) faites en sorte que je récupère le dossier dès que possible

(**c**) (*put back*) (*sth*) remettre; **to g. sth back into its box** faire rentrer qch dans sa boîte

▶ **get back at** *vipo* (*have revenge on*) se venger de

▶ **get back to** *vipo* (**a**) (*return to*) retourner à; **to g. back to London** rentrer à Londres; **to g. back to work** (*after illness*) reprendre le travail; (*after short break*) se remettre au travail; **to g. back to nature** retourner à la nature (**b**) (*contact again*) recontacter; **can we g. back to you on that later?** est-ce que nous pouvons vous donner une réponse à ce sujet plus tard?

▶ **get behind 1** *vi* (*become delayed*) prendre du retard; **to g. behind with** *or* **in one's work** prendre du retard dans son travail; **to g. behind with the rent** être en retard pour payer son loyer **2** *vipo* (**a**) (*move to the back of*) se mettre derrière; **g. behind that tree** mets-toi derrière cet arbre (**b**) *esp Am F* (*support, sympathize with*) appuyer

▶ **get by 1** *vi* (**a**) (*pass*) passer (**b**) *F* (*manage*) se débrouiller; **we just g. by** on s'en tire, sans plus; **he thinks he'll g. by without studying** il croit qu'il va s'en tirer sans étudier; **you can g. by on a few dollars a day** vous pouvez vous en tirer avec quelques dollars par jour **2** *vipo* (**a**) (*move past*) **can you g. by the washing machine?** est-ce que vous avez assez de place pour passer à côté de la machine à laver? (**b**) (*escape attention of*) (*censor, editor*) échapper à

▶ **get down 1** *vi* (**a**) (*from wall, tree etc*) descendre (**from, off** de)

(**b**) (*lower one's body*) **g. down or she'll see us!** baisse-toi sinon elle va nous voir!; **to g. down on one's knees** se mettre à genoux; **g. down!** (*to dog*) couché!

(**c**) (*leave table*) quitter la table, sortir de table; **may I g. down?** est-ce que je peux quitter la table?

2 *vtsep* (**a**) (*bring, fetch down*) (*book from shelf etc*) descendre

(**b**) (*reduce*) (*temperature, inflation etc*) faire baisser; **to g. one's weight down** perdre du poids

(**c**) (*make a note of*) noter (**in writing, on paper** par écrit)

3 *vtas* (**a**) (*depress*) déprimer; **this rain is getting me down** cette pluie me déprime

(**b**) (*swallow*) avaler; **try and g. this down (you)** essaye d'avaler ça

▶ **get down to** *vipo* (*tackle*) se mettre à; **to g. down to work** se mettre au travail; **to g. down to doing sth** se mettre à faire qch; **we'd better g. down to the facts** il faut en venir aux faits; **we eventually got down to details** nous avons fini par en arriver aux détails; **when you g. down to it, there's very little difference between them** en fin de compte, il y a très peu de différence entre eux

▶ **get in 1** *vi* **(a)** (*gain entrance*) entrer; **how did the thieves g. in?** comment est-ce que les voleurs sont entrés?; **water had got in everywhere** l'eau avait pénétré partout

(b) (*arrive*) (*of train etc*) arriver; **when does the London train g. in?** à quelle heure est-ce que le train de Londres arrive?; **we got in at about eleven** (*home*) nous sommes rentrés (chez nous) vers onze heures

(c) *Pol* (*be elected*) être élu; **the Conservatives didn't g. in** les conservateurs n'ont pas été élus

2 *vipo* (*enter*) **g. in the car!** monte dans la voiture!; **the smoke got in our eyes** la fumée nous est venue dans les yeux

3 *vtsep* **(a)** (*summon*) (*doctor, police etc*) faire venir

(b) (*bring in, bring inside*) (*washing, harvest etc*) rentrer; (*dog*) faire rentrer; **shouldn't Jack be in on this meeting? – of course, could you get him in?** on n'a pas besoin de Jack pour cette réunion? – si, bien sûr, tu peux lui demander de venir?

(c) (*plant in the ground*) planter, mettre en terre

(d) (*manage to do*) réussir à faire; **she got in some last-minute revision before the exam** elle a réussi à faire des révisions de dernière minute avant l'examen; **I'd like to g. in some golf over the weekend** j'aimerais trouver le temps de faire un peu de golf ce week-end

(e) (*insert*) faire pénétrer; **I couldn't g. a word in** je n'ai pas pu placer un mot, je n'ai pas pu en placer une

(f) (*stock up with*) (*food, coal etc*) faire provision de; **to g. coal in for the winter** faire une provision de *ou* faire rentrer du charbon pour l'hiver; **to g. in a round of drinks** (*in pub*) payer une tournée; **I'll g. the pints in** je m'occupe des bières

4 *vtas* **(a)** (*assure of admission*) permettre d'entrer; **a press card should g. you in** une carte de presse devrait vous permettre d'entrer; **these exam results will g. you in** (*to university*) les notes que vous avez obtenues à l'examen vous permettront d'être admis

(b) (*ensure election of*) (*person, party*) assurer l'élection de; **her reputation for integrity got her in** sa réputation d'intégrité a assuré son élection

▶ **get into 1** *vipo* **(a)** (*gain entrance to*) (*house etc*) entrer dans; (*car, train etc*) monter dans; **to g. into Parliament** être élu député; **to g. into university** entrer à la faculté

(b) (*put on*) (*clothes*) mettre, enfiler; (*overcoat etc*) mettre, enfiler, endosser; **I can't g. into this dress any more** je n'entre plus dans cette robe

(c) (*affect*) **I don't know what's got into her** je ne sais pas ce qu'elle a *ou* ce qui lui prend

(d) (*become involved in*) **to g. into (a) conversation** entamer une conversation; **to g. into a fight** se bagarrer; **to g. into trouble** s'attirer des ennuis; **I got into trouble at school today** je me suis fait disputer à l'école aujourd'hui; **to g. into debt** s'endetter

(e) to g. into the way of doing sth prendre l'habitude de faire qch; **the system may seem difficult but you'll soon g. into it** le système peut sembler difficile mais tu t'y feras vite

(f) *F* (*become interested in*) (*music etc*) commencer à s'intéresser à; **it's a hard book to g. into** c'est un livre dans lequel il est difficile de rentrer

(g) (*phrases*) **to g. into a panic** être pris de panique; **to g. into a rage** se mettre en rage; **to g. into a bad habit** acquérir *ou* prendre une mauvaise habitude

2 *vtaspo* **(a)** (*insert into*) **to g. sth into sth** (faire) (r)entrer qch dans qch; **to g. the key into the lock** mettre *ou* introduire la clef dans la serrure; **to g. an article into a paper** faire accepter un article par un journal; **to g. an idea into one's head** se mettre une idée en tête; **when are you going to g. it into your thick head that that isn't how things work?** quand est-ce que tu te mettras dans la tête que les choses ne se passent pas comme ça?

(b) you got me into this mess tu m'as mis dans ce pétrin; **to g. sb into a rage** mettre quelqu'un en rage; **to g. sb into a good mood** mettre qn de bonne humeur; *F* **he got me into jazz** c'est lui qui m'a fait connaître le jazz

▶ **get in with** *vipo* **(a)** (*ingratiate oneself with*) s'insinuer dans les bonnes grâces de, se mettre bien avec; **if you want to g. in with him ...** si tu veux te mettre bien avec lui ... **(b)** (*associate with*) (*person, group etc*) fréquenter; **he has got in with ...** il fréquente ...; **she got in with the wrong crowd at school** elle avait de mauvaises fréquentations à l'école

▶ **get off 1** *vi* **(a)** (*descend from vehicle*) descendre; *Fig* **I told him where to g. off** (*rebuked him*) je lui ai dit ses quatre vérités

(b) (*let go of sth*) lâcher; **hey! g. off! that's <u>my</u> book!** hé! laisse ça! c'est mon livre!

(c) (*go unpunished*) s'en tirer; **to g. off lightly** s'en tirer à bon compte

(d) (*leave, especially referring to work*) quitter, sortir; **I'd like to g. off early tomorrow** j'aimerais bien quitter (le travail) tôt *ou* sortir tôt (du travail) demain

(e) to g. off (to sleep) s'endormir

(f) to g. off to a late start commencer avec du retard; **to g. off to a good/bad start** bien/mal commencer

2 *vipo* **(a)** (*descend from*) descendre de; **to g. off a bike** descendre d'une bicyclette; **g. off that wall!** descends de ce mur!; **g. off the grass!** ne marche pas sur la pelouse!

(b) (*let go of*) **g. off me!** laisse-moi tranquille!, lâche-moi!

(c) (*be exempted from*) couper à, échapper à; **he managed to g. off military service** il s'est débrouillé pour couper au service militaire

3 *vtas* **(a)** (*remove*) (*lid etc*) enlever; (*stain*) faire partir; **g. your feet off the table!** enlève tes pieds de sur la table!; **g. your hands off me/that cake** ne me touche pas/ne touche pas ce gâteau; **we got his clothes off** nous lui avons enlevé ses vêtements; *Fig* **to g. sth off one's chest** vider son sac

(b) (*send*) (*letter*) expédier, envoyer; **to g. the children off to bed** envoyer les enfants au lit; **to g. a baby off (to sleep)** endormir un bébé; *Naut* **to g. a ship off** (*from sandbank etc*) renflouer un bateau, remettre un bateau à flot

(c) (*save from punishment*) **to g. sb off** tirer qn d'affaire; *Jur* (*person standing trial*) faire acquitter qn

(d) (*have as holiday*) **to g. a day/week off** prendre un jour/une semaine de congé; **can you g. tomorrow afternoon/next week off?** est-ce que tu peux prendre un congé demain après-midi/la semaine prochaine?

(e) *F* (*obtain*) **to g. sth off sb** obtenir qch de qn; **I got that story off the woman next door** je tiens cette histoire de la voisine; **I got this cold off the woman next door** la voisine m'a passé son rhume

(f) (*free from*) **to g. sb off doing sth** dispenser qn de faire qch; **those burns got him off work** ces brûlures l'ont dispensé d'aller travailler

(g) that got the meeting off to a late start la réunion a commencé en retard à cause de ça

▶ **get off on** *vipo F* prendre son pied avec

▶ **get off with** *vipo* **(a)** (*a fine etc*) s'en tirer avec; **he got off with it for years before the police caught him** on l'a laissé tranquille pendant des années avant que la police ne l'arrête **(b)** *Br F* **to g. off with sb** (*have sex with*) coucher avec qn; **did you g. off with anybody at the party?** (*meet anybody*) tu as rencontré quelqu'un d'intéressant à la soirée?; **to g. off with each other** (*kiss etc*) se peloter

▶ **get on 1** *vi* **(a)** (*board*) monter

(b) (*succeed, progress*) réussir, progresser; **to g. on in life** *or* **in the world** arriver dans la vie

(c) (*continue with work, journey*) continuer; **right, let's g. on, shall we?** bien, si on continuait?

(d) (*cope, manage*) **how are you getting on?** (*how are you*) comment ça va?; (*at work*) comment va votre travail?; **how did you g. on?** (*in exam, at dentist's*) comment ça s'est passé?; **I was getting on perfectly well without you** je me débrouillais très bien sans vous; **I'll let you know how he's getting on** je vous donnerai de ses nouvelles

(e) (*have good relationship*) s'entendre; **to g. on well/badly with sb** bien/mal s'entendre avec qn

(f) (*become late*) se faire tard; **time's getting on** l'heure tourne

(g) (*age*) **to be getting on (in years)** prendre de l'âge

2 *vtas* (*put on*) (*clothing*) mettre, enfiler; **I can't g. these trousers on any more** je n'entre plus dans ce pantalon; **she's just getting her coat on** elle est en train de mettre *ou* d'enfiler son manteau; **I can't g. the lid on** je n'arrive pas à mettre le couvercle

3 *vipo* **(a)** (*board, enter*) (*bus, train, plane etc*) monter dans

(b) (*climb onto*) (*chair, ladder*) monter sur; (*with some effort*) grimper sur

(c) how did these papers g. on my desk? comment est-ce que ces papiers se sont retrouvés *ou* sont arrivés sur mon bureau?

▶ **get on at** *vipo* harceler; **he keeps getting on at me to have my hair cut** il est toujours après moi pour que je me fasse couper les cheveux; **you'll have to really g. on at her if you want her to do something** il va falloir que tu sois toujours derrière elle si tu veux qu'elle fasse quelque chose

▶ **get on for** *vipo* (*approach*) **he must be getting on for forty** il doit approcher de *ou* friser la quarantaine; **it's getting on for midnight** il est presque minuit; **there were getting on**

for 200 people at the wedding il y avait près de 200 personnes au mariage

▶ **get onto** *vipo* **(a)** *(contact)* contacter, se mettre en contact avec, se mettre en rapport avec; **I'll g. onto the bank about it** je vais contacter la banque à ce sujet; **I'll g. onto him to finish the work** je vais le contacter pour lui dire de finir le travail **(b)** *(locate, find name of) (person)* trouver le nom *ou* les coordonnées de; **how did you g. onto me?** comment est-ce que vous avez trouvé mon nom? **(c)** *(move forward to)* en arriver à; **they eventually got onto (the subject of) money** ils ont fini par en arriver à parler d'argent **(d)** = **get on 3**

▶ **get on with** *vipo* **(a)** *(have good relationship with)* s'entendre bien avec; **I don't g. on with my parents** je ne m'entends pas avec mes parents **(b)** *(continue with)* **how are you getting on with the painting?** alors, ça avance la peinture?; **just g. on with what you are supposed to be doing** *(said by teacher etc)* continuez ce que vous avez à faire; **let Dad g. on with his work** laissez Papa travailler en paix; **I wish the press would let me g. on with my life** si la presse pouvait me laisser vivre en paix; **I've got enough work to be getting on with** j'ai assez de travail à faire, j'ai assez de pain sur la planche

▶ **get out 1** *vi* **(a)** *(leave)* sortir; *(from car)* descendre; *F* **g. out you bastard!** fiche(-moi) le camp espèce de salaud!

(b) *(be released from prison, hospital)* sortir; **when does she g. out?** quand est-ce qu'elle sort?; **how did the news g. out?** comment la nouvelle s'est-elle répandue?; **the secret got out** le secret a transpiré

(c) *(leave one's house, flat)* sortir (de chez soi); **he ought to g. out more** il devrait sortir plus

2 *vtsep* **(a)** *(bring out) (tools, books etc)* sortir; **to g. one's car out** *(from garage)* sortir sa voiture; **to g. a book out from the library** emprunter un livre à la bibliothèque; **he could hardly g. a word out** c'est à peine s'il a pu sortir un mot; **we have to g. this report out by Monday** nous devons sortir ce rapport pour lundi

(b) *(free) (hostages etc)* libérer

(c) *(remove)* enlever; *(nail etc)* arracher; *(cork)* retirer; *(stain)* faire disparaître

(d) *Cr (batsman)* renverser le guichet à

▶ **get out of 1** *vipo* **(a)** *(leave)* sortir de; *(car)* descendre de; **let's g. out of here** partons d'ici; **he managed to g. out of the country** *(of criminal, refugee)* il a réussi à quitter le pays; **to g. out of bed** se lever; **to g. out of prison/the army** sortir de prison/quitter l'armée; **to g. out of sb's way** s'écarter du chemin de qn, faire place à qn; *Sl* **g. the hell out of here!** fiche(-moi) le camp!

(b) *(extricate oneself from)* se faire exempter de; **to g. out of doing sth** se faire exempter de faire qch; **he always gets out of doing the washing up** il arrive toujours à couper à la corvée de vaisselle; **to g. out of a difficulty** se tirer d'une position difficile; **I'd like to see her g. out of this one** j'aimerais bien voir comment elle va s'en tirer cette fois

(c) *(become unaccustomed to)* **to g. out of (the habit of) doing sth** perdre l'habitude de faire qch

2 *vtaspo* **(a)** *(bring out of)* sortir de; **g. the phone book out of the drawer** sors l'annuaire du tiroir; **she got the nail out of her shoe** elle a retiré le clou de sa chaussure; **to g. a secret out of sb** arracher un secret à qn; **I can't g. anything out of him** je ne peux rien en tirer; **we finally got the truth out of her** nous avons fini par lui arracher la vérité; **I can't g. the idea out of my mind** je ne peux pas chasser cette idée de mon esprit; **to g. money out of sb** soutirer de l'argent à qn; **I got ten pounds out of it** j'y ai gagné dix livres; **to g. sb out of a difficulty** tirer qn d'affaire; **the firemen got us out of the building** les pompiers nous ont fait sortir du bâtiment; **to g. a stain out of a carpet** enlever une tache d'un tapis

(b) *(derive from)* **I didn't g. much out of my lessons** je n'ai pas tiré grand-chose de mes leçons; **he could have got more out of the experience** il aurait pu tirer davantage de l'expérience

▶ **get over 1** *vi* **(a)** *(over road etc)* traverser; **to g. over to France/America** aller en France/Amérique; **to g. over to visit sb** *(in another city, country etc)* aller rendre visite à qn; **we'll try to g. over next weekend** *(to visit)* nous essayerons de venir vous voir le week-end prochain; **the wall was low, it was easy to g. over** le mur était bas, il a été facile de le franchir

(b) *(communicate)* **to g. over to sb** se faire comprendre de qn

2 *vipo* **(a)** *(cross) (wall etc)* escalader, passer par-dessus; *(road, river etc)* franchir

(b) *(recover from) (illness)* se remettre de; *(difficulties)* venir à bout de; *(surprise)* revenir de; **she can't g. over it** *(illness, emotional shock, trauma)* elle ne s'en remet pas; *(surprise, shock etc)* elle n'en revient pas; *(loss)* elle est inconsolable; **it will take her a long time to g. over it** elle s'en ressentira longtemps, ça lui prendra longtemps pour s'en remettre

(c) *(overcome) (fear etc)* surmonter

3 *vtsep (communicate)* faire passer; **she got her point over very well** elle a très bien fait passer ce qu'elle voulait dire

4 *vtas (to other side of something)* faire passer; **we got the children over the road** nous avons fait traverser la route aux enfants

▶ **get over with** *vtas (complete)* terminer, finir; **she got her work over with as quickly as possible** elle a fini son travail aussi vite que possible; **when I g. my exams over with I'll be able to relax** quand j'aurai terminé mes examens, je pourrai me détendre; **let's get it over with as quickly as possible** finissons-en au plus vite

▶ **get round 1** *vi* **(a) it would take a day to g. round** *(round the exhibition, museum)* ça prendrait une journée pour en faire le tour

(b) the doctor said she'd g. round as soon as she could le docteur a dit qu'elle viendrait *ou* passerait dès qu'elle pourrait; **I didn't manage to g. round to each pupil in the class** je n'ai pas réussi à m'occuper de chaque élève de la classe

(c) *(of news, rumour)* se répandre; **news gets round pretty quickly in small towns** les nouvelles circulent vite dans les petites villes

2 *vipo* **(a)** *(exhibition, museum)* faire le tour de; *(corner)* passer

(b) *(circumvent) (difficulty, regulations etc)* contourner; *(persuade) (person)* embobiner; **there's no getting round it** *(you'll have to own up)* il n'y a pas moyen d'y couper; **will you be able to g. round your dad?** est-ce que tu réussiras à persuader ton père?; **how did they g. round the regulations?** comment est-ce qu'ils ont réussi à contourner les réglementations?

3 *vtas* **(a)** *(bring, take)* **I'll g. the books round (to you) as soon as I can** je t'apporterai les livres dès que je le pourrai

(b) *(persuade)* **we eventually got him round to our way of thinking** nous avons finalement réussi à le convaincre

▶ **get round to** *vipo* = **get around to**

▶ **get through 1** *vi* **(a)** *(arrive)* **the road was blocked and no one could g. through** la route était bloquée et personne ne pouvait passer; **the message didn't g. through** le message n'est pas passé; **only a few trains got through to the besieged city** seuls quelques trains sont arrivés jusqu'à la ville assiégée; **the news got through to them** la nouvelle leur est parvenue

(b) *Tel* obtenir la communication **(to sb** avec qn); *Fig (communicate)* se faire comprendre **(to sb** de qn); *Fig* **I'm not getting through (to you), am I?** je ne me fais pas bien comprendre, hein?

(c) *Am (finish)* finir, terminer; **the class doesn't usually g. through until six o'clock** la leçon ne se termine généralement pas avant six heures

(d) *(pass exam)* être reçu

2 *vipo* **(a)** *(pass through) (hole etc)* passer à travers; **I thought I'd never g. through the day** j'ai cru que la journée n'en finirait jamais; **they got through the day without a single argument** ils ne se sont pas disputés une seule fois de toute la journée; **the Government may have difficulty getting through another six months** le gouvernement aura peut-être du mal à tenir encore six mois; **I couldn't g. through another winter in Moscow** je ne pourrais pas passer un hiver de plus à Moscou; **you won't g. through the roadblock** tu n'arriveras pas à franchir le barrage routier

(b) *(succeed in) (exam)* être reçu à, réussir

(c) *(finish) (work etc)* achever, arriver au bout de; *(food, drink etc)* consommer; **to g. through a lot of work** abattre beaucoup de travail

(d) *(use up)* **he gets through eight shirts a week** il salit huit chemises par semaine; **we'll never g. through all this food** nous ne viendrons jamais à bout de toute cette nourriture; **she gets through her wages very quickly** elle dépense son salaire très rapidement

3 *vtas* **(a)** *(transport, send successfully)* faire parvenir; **they got the food supplies through** ils ont réussi à faire parvenir les provisions alimentaires (à destination); **to g. sth through customs** (faire) passer qch à la douane; **they got a message through** ils ont fait passer un message; **you'll never g. that desk through** tu n'arriveras jamais à faire passer ce bureau; *Parl* **to g. a bill through** faire adopter un projet de loi

(b) I finally got it through to him that I wasn't interested j'ai fini par lui faire comprendre que je n'étais pas intéressé

(c) *(cause to succeed)* **it was your essay that got you through (the exam)** c'est grâce à ta dissertation que tu as réussi l'examen

(d) *(enable to endure)* **I need four cups of coffee to g. me through the day** il me faut mes quatre tasses de café par jour

▶ **get together 1** *vi* *(of people)* se réunir, se rassembler **(to do** pour faire); **the two countries got together to deal with coastal pollution** les deux pays ont collaboré pour s'attaquer au problème de la pollution côtière **2** *vtsep* *(collect)* *(objects)* rassembler; *(friends etc)* réunir; **g. your things together, we're going** rassemble tes affaires, nous partons; **to g. some money together** réunir une somme d'argent; **let me g. my thoughts together** laissez-moi rassembler mes idées

▶ **get under 1** *vipo* *(get into position beneath)* *(table etc)* se mettre sous; **they got under the fence and escaped** ils sont passés sous la clôture et se sont enfuis **2** *vtaspo* *(place beneath)* mettre *ou* placer sous; **I can't g. the carpet under the table** je n'arrive pas à placer le tapis sous la table

▶ **get up 1** *vi* **(a)** *(get out of bed)* se lever; *(stand up)* se lever, se mettre debout; **g. up!** levez-vous!; **to g. up from a chair/the table** se lever de sa chaise/de table

(b) *Met* **the wind/a storm was getting up** le vent/une tempête se levait

2 *vipo* *(climb)* *(stairs)* monter; *(ladder)* monter à; *(mountain)* faire l'ascension de

3 *vtsep* **(a) to g. up speed** prendre de la vitesse

(b) *(organize)* *(party etc)* organiser; *Pol* **to g. up a petition** organiser *ou* faire une pétition

4 *vtas* **(a)** *(move up)* monter; **how are we going to g. this desk up to the fifth floor?** comment allons-nous monter ce bureau jusqu'au cinquième étage?; **to g. sb up the stairs** *(help climb)* aider qn à monter l'escalier

(b) *(rouse)* faire (se) lever; **have you got the children up?** est-ce que tu as fait lever les enfants?

(c) to g. oneself up as sb/sth *(dress up)* se déguiser en qn/qch

(d) *Vulg* **to g. it up** *(achieve an erection)* bander; **he couldn't g. it up** il n'a pas réussi à bander

▶ **get up to** *vipo* **(a)** *(reach)* arriver à; **it took ages to g. up to the top of the hill** ça a pris une éternité pour arriver en haut de la colline; **I've got up to chapter 5** j'en suis au chapitre 5; **where have you got up to?** *(in your reading etc)* où en êtes-vous? **(b)** *(do)* **those children are always getting up to something** *or* **to some mischief** ces enfants sont toujours en train de faire des bêtises; **what have you been getting up to?** qu'est-ce que tu as fabriqué?; **the dog's been getting up to his usual tricks** le chien a encore fait des siennes

getatable, get-at-able [get'ætəb(ə)l] *adj F* accessible, d'accès facile

getaway ['getəweɪ] *n* *(of criminal)* fuite *f*; **to make one's g.** s'enfuir; **g. car** voiture *f* utilisée pour prendre la fuite

Gethsemane [geθ'semənɪ] *n* Gethsémani *m*

get-rich-quick *adj F* **a g. scheme** un stratagème pour s'enrichir rapidement

get-together *n F* réunion *f*; **I'm having a g. with some friends** je vois quelques amis; **you and I must have a little g. one day** il faut qu'on se voie un de ces jours tous les deux

get-up *n F* **(a)** *(clothes)* accoutrement *m*, tenue *f*; *(fancy dress)* déguisement *m*; **what a g.!** quel accoutrement! **(b)** *Com* *(of merchandise)* présentation *f*

get-up-and-go *n F* allant *m*, entrain *m*; **where's your g.?** allez, remue-toi!

get-well *adj* **g. card** = carte *f* que l'on envoie à un malade pour lui souhaiter un prompt rétablissement

gewgaw ['gju:gɔ:] *n* babiole *f*

geyser ['gi:zər] *n* **(a)** *Geol* geyser *m* **(b)** *Old-fashioned Br* *(water heater)* chauffe-eau *m inv* à gaz

Ghana ['gɑ:nə] *n* Ghana *m*

Ghanaian, Ghanian [gɑ:'neɪən, 'gɑ:nɪən] **1** *adj* ghanéen **2** *n* Ghanéen, -éenne

ghastliness ['gɑ:stlɪnɪs] *n* *(of crime)* horreur *f*

ghastly ['gɑ:stlɪ] *adj* **(a)** *(experience)* horrible, affreux, épouvantable; *F* **what g. weather!** quel temps épouvantable *ou* abominable!; **a g. mistake** une erreur monstrueuse **(b)** *(pale)* blême; *(pallor)* mortel; *(light)* blafard; **he looked g.** il avait l'air d'un déterré

ghee [gi:] *n Culin* beurre *m* clarifié

Ghent [gent] *n* Gand *m*

gherkin ['gɜ:kɪn] *n* cornichon *m*; **pickled gherkins** cornichons au vinaigre

ghetto ['getəʊ] *n* ghetto *m*; *F* **g. blaster** mini-stéréo *f* portable

ghillie ['gɪlɪ] *n* = **gillie**

ghost¹ [gəʊst] *n* **(a)** fantôme *m*, spectre *m*; **to believe in ghosts** croire aux revenants *ou* fantômes; **you look as if you've seen a g.** comme tu es pâle, tu as l'air d'avoir reçu un sacré choc; **to be the mere g. of one's former self** n'être plus que l'ombre de soi-même; **not the g. of a chance** pas la moindre chance; **g. of a smile** esquisse *f* de sourire; **g. ship** vaisseau *m* fantôme; *Mktg* **g. shopping** achats *mpl* simulés pour audit; **g. story** histoire *f* de revenants; **g. town** ville *f* fantôme

(b) *Rel* **the Holy G.** l'Esprit *m* Saint, le Saint-Esprit

(c) *Arch* *(soul)* âme *f*; *(still used in)* **to give up the g.** *(die)* rendre l'âme, expirer; *Fig F* **the car finally gave up the g. yesterday** la voiture a finalement rendu l'âme hier

(d) *Opt* spectre *m* secondaire, image *f* blanche; *TV* écho *m*

ghost² *Liter* **1** *vi* servir de nègre **(for an author** à un écrivain) **2** *vt* *(sb's speeches)* écrire; **to g. a book** servir de nègre à l'auteur d'un livre; **ghosted work** ouvrage écrit par un nègre

ghosting ['gəʊstɪŋ] *n TV* images *fpl* fantôme

ghostly ['gəʊstlɪ] *adj* spectral

ghostwrite ['gəʊstraɪt] *vt* = **ghost² 2**

ghostwriter ['gəʊstraɪtər] *n* nègre *m*

ghoul [gu:l] *n* **(a)** *(evil spirit)* goule *f*; *Fig* *(person)* personne *f* qui a des goûts macabres *ou* morbides; **a crowd of ghouls had gathered at the scene of the accident** une foule d'amateurs de spectacles macabres s'était assemblée sur la scène de l'accident **(b)** *Old-fashioned* *(grave robber)* déterreur *m* de cadavre

ghoulish ['gu:lɪʃ] *adj* **(a)** *(humour etc)* macabre **(b)** *Myth* de goule

GHQ [dʒi:eɪtʃ'kju:] *n Mil* (*abbr* **General Headquarters**) = Q. G. *m inv*

GHz (*abbr* **gigahertz**) GHz *m*

GI [dʒi:'aɪ] *n F* **GI (Joe)** soldat *m* américain, G. I. *m inv*; **GI bride** = femme *f* étrangère ayant épousé un G. I.

giant ['dʒaɪənt] **1** *n Myth, Fig* géant *m*; *esp Sp* **g. killer** = équipe *f*/sportif *m* qui remporte une victoire inattendue contre un adversaire de haute stature; *Geol* **g.'s kettle** marmite *f ou* chaudière *f* de géant(s) **2** *adj* *(oak, package)* géant; **with g. strides** à pas de géant

giantess [dʒaɪən'tes] *n* géante *f*

Gib [dʒɪb] *n F* Gibraltar *m*

gibber ['dʒɪbər] *vi* *(like a monkey, an idiot)* produire des sons inarticulés; *(of foreigners speaking amongst themselves)* baragouiner; **he was gibbering with rage/fear** il bégayait de rage/frayeur; **it reduced him to a gibbering wreck** il en est devenu bègue; *F* **gibbering idiot** espèce de crétin

gibberish ['dʒɪbərɪʃ] *n* baragouin *m*, charabia *m*; **to talk g.** raconter n'importe quoi

gibbet ['dʒɪbɪt] *n* gibet *m*, potence *f*

gibbon ['gɪbən] *n* *(monkey)* gibbon *m*

gibbous ['gɪbəs] *adj Astron* **g. moon** lune *f* gibbeuse

gibe¹ [dʒaɪb] *n* raillerie *f*, quolibet *m*; **to make a g.** lancer une raillerie *ou* un quolibet **(at** à)

gibe² *vi* **to g. at sb** railler qn, se moquer de qn

giblets ['dʒɪblɪts] *npl* *(of poultry)* abats *mpl*, abattis *mpl*

Gibraltar [dʒɪ'brɔ:ltər] *n* Gibraltar *m*

giddily ['gɪdɪlɪ] *adv* **(a)** *(to rise)* de manière vertigineuse **(b)** *(frivolously)* étourdiment

giddiness ['gɪdɪnɪs] *n* **(a)** *(vertigo)* étourdissement *m*, vertige *m*; **fits of g.** des étourdissements, des vertiges **(b)** *(frivolousness)* frivolité *f*

giddy ['gɪdɪ] *adj* **(a)** *(dizzy)* *(person)* étourdi; **to be** *or* **feel g.** avoir le vertige; **I feel g.** la tête me tourne; **it makes me (feel) g.** cela me donne le vertige **(b)** *(height)* vertigineux, qui donne le vertige **(c)** *(frivolous)* frivole; **g. round of pleasures** tourbillon *m* de plaisirs; *Br Old-fashioned* **oh my g. aunt!** ciel!

gift [gɪft] *n* **(a)** *(to individual)* cadeau *m*; **it was a g.** c'était un cadeau; *(of bargain)* c'était donné; *F* *(easy victory)* c'était un jeu d'enfants; **I wouldn't have it as a g.** je n'en voudrais pas même si on m'en faisait cadeau; *Prov* **never look a g. horse in the mouth** à cheval donné on ne regarde pas la bouche

(b) *(donation)* don *m*; **a g. of £2 000** un don de 2 000 livres; **to make a g. of sth to sb** faire don de qch à qn; *Jur* **as a g.** en cadeau; **in the g. of sb** à la discrétion de qn

(c) *Com* *(on presentation of coupons)* prime *f*; **free g.** cadeau *m*

(d) *(talent)* don *m*; **to have a g. for mathematics** avoir le don *ou F* la bosse des mathématiques

gifted ['gɪftɪd] *adj* doué; *(artist)* de talent

gift shop *n* boutique *f* de cadeaux

gift token *n* chèque-cadeau *m*, *pl* chèques-cadeaux

gift voucher *n* chèque-cadeau *m*, *pl* chèques-cadeaux
giftwrap ['gɪftræp] *vt* emballer (*et faire un paquet-cadeau*); **shall I g. it?** je vous fais un paquet-cadeau?
giftwrapped ['gɪftræpt] *adj Com* (*article*) sous paquet-cadeau; **would you like it g.?** c'est pour offrir?, je vous fais un paquet-cadeau?
giftwrapping ['gɪftræpɪŋ] *n* (*paper, ribbons etc*) emballage-cadeau *m*
gig¹ [gɪg] *n* **(a)** (*carriage*) cabriolet *m* **(b)** *Naut* yole *f*
gig² *n Mus F* concert *m*
giga- ['gɪgə] *pref* giga-
gigabyte ['gɪgəbaɪt] *n Comptr* gigaoctet *m*
gigahertz ['gɪgəhɜːts] *n* gigahertz *m*
gigantic [dʒaɪ'gæntɪk] *adj* géant, gigantesque; (*building, bridge*) colossal
gigantically [dʒaɪ'gæntɪklɪ] *adv* de façon démesurée
giggle¹ ['gɪg(ə)l] *n* petit rire *m*; (*of young girl*) gloussement *m*, rire *m* bébête; **to have (a fit of) the giggles** avoir le fou rire; **to give a nervous g.** avoir un petit rire nerveux; *F* **to do sth for a g.** faire qch pour se marrer *ou* pour rigoler; **the evening was a g. from start to finish** on s'est marré toute la soirée; **she was a real g. as usual** elle était tordante comme d'habitude
giggle² *vi* avoir un petit rire; (*nervously*) rire nerveusement; (*of young girls*) glousser, rire bêtement; **what are you giggling about?** qu'est-ce qui vous fait rire?
giggling ['gɪg(ə)lɪŋ] **1** *adj* qui pousse de petits rires; (*nervously*) qui rit avec nervosité; (*young girl*) qui glousse, qui rit bêtement **2** *n* petits rires *mpl*; (*nervous*) petits rires nerveux; (*of young girl*) rires bébêtes, gloussements *mpl*
giggly ['gɪg(ə)lɪ] *adj* qui se met à rire bêtement pour un rien; **to get** *or* **go all g.** se mettre à rire bêtement; **to be in a g. mood** être d'humeur joyeuse
GIGO [dʒiːaɪdʒiː'əʊ] *Comptr Sl abbr* **garbage in, garbage out**
gigolo ['dʒɪgələʊ] *n* gigolo *m*
gigot ['dʒɪgət] *n* gigot *m*
gild [gɪld] *vt* (*pt* **gilded**; *pp* **gilded,** *occ* **gilt** [gɪlt]) dorer; *Fig* **to g. the lily** surcharger; *Lit* **gilded youth** la jeunesse dorée
gilding ['gɪldɪŋ] *n* dorure *f*
gill¹ [gɪl] *n* (*usu pl*) **(a)** (*of fish*) **gills** ouïes *fpl*, branchies *fpl* **(b)** **gills** (*of mushroom*) lamelles *fpl* **(c)** *F* **to be** *or* **look green about the gills** (*look ill*) avoir le teint verdâtre *ou* jaune; (*through disgust, shock etc*) être vert; **he went green about the gills** (*looked ill*) son teint est devenu verdâtre *ou* jaune; (*through disgust, shock etc*) il est devenu vert
gill² [dʒɪl] *n* (*measure*) quart *m* de pinte (= 0,142 l.)
gillie ['gɪlɪ] *n Scot* serviteur *m* (*de chasseur, pêcheur etc*)
gillyflower ['dʒɪlɪflaʊər] *n* **(a)** (*wallflower*) giroflée *f* jaune *ou* des murailles **(b)** (**clove**) **g.** œillet *m* giroflée
gilt¹ [gɪlt] *pp see* **gild**
gilt² *adj* (*frame etc*) doré
gilt³ *n* (*gold*) dorure *f*, doré *m*; *St Exch* **gilts** fonds *mpl* d'État, *F* valeurs *fpl* de tout repos *ou* de père de famille; *F* **that takes the g. off the gingerbread** voilà qui enlève le charme *ou* l'attrait
gilt-edged ['gɪlt'edʒd] *adj* **(a)** (*book*) doré sur tranche **(b)** *St Exch* **gilt-edge(d) stock(s)** fonds *mpl* d'État, *F* valeurs *fpl* de tout repos *ou* de père de famille
gimbals ['dʒɪmb(ə)lz] *npl Av, Naut etc* (suspension *f* à) cardan *m*
gimcrack ['dʒɪmkræk] *adj Old-fashioned* (*furniture*) de pacotille; (*house*) en carton; (*jewellery*) en toc; (*scheme, theory etc*) à la noix
gimlet ['gɪmlɪt] *n* **(a)** *Carp* (*tool*) vrille *f*, foret *m* à bois; *Fig* **g. eyes** yeux *mpl* perçants **(b)** (*cocktail*) = mélange *m* de gin ou de vodka et de jus de citron vert
gimme ['gɪmiː] *Sl* = **give me**
gimmick ['gɪmɪk] *n* truc *m*, astuce *f*; **advertising g.** astuce *ou* truc publicitaire
gimmickry ['gɪmɪkrɪ] *n* astuces *fpl*
gimmicky ['gɪmɪkɪ] *adj* plein d'astuces; **a bit too g.** trop artificiel
gin¹ [dʒɪn] *n* **(a)** (*drink*) gin *m*; (*made in Holland*) genièvre *m*; *F Hum* **g. palace** troquet *m* **(b)** *Cards* **g. rummy** rami *m*
gin² *n* **(a)** (*trap*) piège *m* **(b)** *Tex* (**cotton**) **g.** égreneuse *f* de coton
ginger ['dʒɪndʒər] **1** *n* **(a)** *Bot, Culin* gingembre *m*; **preserved** *or* **crystallized g.** gingembre confit; **g. ale** boisson *f* à base de gingembre; **g. beer** limonade *f* au gingembre; **g. biscuit** *or* **nut** *or* **snap** biscuit *m* au gingembre; **g. wine** vin *m* de gingembre **(b)** *F* (*liveliness*) énergie *f*; *Br Pol* **g. group** groupe *m* de pression **(c)** (*redhead*) **hi g.!** ohé, poil de carotte! **(d)** *Scot F* (*fizzy drink*) boisson *f* gazeuse **2** *adj F* (*hair*) poil-de-carotte *inv*
▶ **ginger up** *vtsep F* (*apathetic person*) secouer les puces à; (*film, text, storyline etc*) donner du punch à; **we need something to g. up the party** il nous faut quelque chose pour mettre un peu d'animation dans la soirée
gingerbread ['dʒɪndʒəbred] **1** *n Culin* pain *m* d'épice **2** *adj Culin* **g. man** bonhomme *m* de *ou* en pain d'épice
gingerly ['dʒɪndʒəlɪ] *adv* avec précaution; (*trying not to make a noise*) doucement; **he stepped g. between the cowpats** il a avancé précautionneusement entre les bouses de vache
gingery ['dʒɪndʒərɪ] *adj* **(a)** (*taste*) de gingembre **(b)** (*hair, colour*) qui tire sur le roux
gingham ['gɪŋəm] *n Tex* vichy *m*; **g. curtains/dress** rideaux/robe en vichy
gingivitis [dʒɪndʒɪ'vaɪtɪs] *n Med* gingivite *f*
ginormous [dʒaɪ'nɔːməs] *adj F* gigantesque, hénaurme
ginseng ['dʒɪnseŋ] *n* ginseng *m*
gippo ['dʒɪpəʊ] *n Br Old-fashioned Offensive Sl* romanichel, -elle
gippy ['dʒɪpɪ] *adj F* **to have a g. tummy** avoir la courante
gipsy ['dʒɪpsɪ] *n* **(a)** bohémien, -ienne, *Pej* romanichel, -elle; (*Spanish*) gitan, -ane; **g. caravan** roulotte *f*; **g. music** musique *f* tzigane **(b)** *Ent* **g. moth** zigzag *m*
gipsyish ['dʒɪpsɪɪʃ] *adj* comme un bohémien *ou Pej* un romanichel; (*dark-skinned*) brun de peau
giraffe [dʒɪ'ræf, -'rɑːf] *n* girafe *f*
gird [gɜːd] *vt* (*pt, pp* **girded, girt** [gɜːt]) *Arch, Lit* **(a)** (*wrap around with a belt*) ceindre; **to g. up one's loins** se ceindre les reins; **to g. (on) one's sword** ceindre son épée **(b)** (*surround*) ceindre (**with** de)
girder ['gɜːdər] *n Constr* poutre *f* (métallique)
girdle¹ ['gɜːd(ə)l] *n* (*corset*) gaine *f*; (*belt*) ceinture *f*
girdle² *vt Lit* ceindre, entourer
girdle³ *n* = **griddle**
girl [gɜːl] *n* fille *f*; (*young woman*) jeune fille, jeune femme *f*; **little g.** petite fille, fillette *f*; **when I was a g.** quand j'étais petite; **g.'s name** prénom *m* féminin *ou* de fille; **girls' school** école *f* de filles; *Br Sch* **old g.** ancienne élève *f*; **a French/an Indian g.** une jeune Française/Indienne; **his g.** (*daughter*) sa fille; *Old-fashioned* (*girlfriend*) sa petite amie; **the Smith(s') g.** la fille (des) Smith; **that's my g.!** (*well done*) bravo!, très bien!; *Old-fashioned* **my dear g.!** ma chère!; *Old-fashioned F* **the old g.** la vieille femme, *Pej* la vieille; (*wife*) ma femme, la bourgeoise; (*mother*) ma mère; (*boss*) la patronne; (*car*) ma vieille voiture *ou* bagnole; *Old-fashioned* **hello, old g.!** salut, ma vieille!
girlfriend ['gɜːlfrend] *n* (*of boy, man*) petite amie *f*; (*of girl, woman*) amie, *F* copine *f*
Girl Guide *n Br* éclaireuse *f*
girlhood ['gɜːlhʊd] *n* (*childhood*) enfance *f*; (*young womanhood*) jeunesse *f*; **in my g.** dans ma jeunesse, quand j'étais jeune fille
girlie ['gɜːlɪ] *n F* **(a)** (*effeminate boy*) fillette *f* **(b)** **g. magazine** magazine *m* de femmes à poil
girlish ['gɜːlɪʃ] *adj* **(a)** (*behaviour*) de fille; (*figure*) de jeune fille; **g. laughter** un rire de (petite) jeune fille **(b)** (*boy*) efféminé; **g. good looks** air enfantin *ou* de très jeune fille
girlishly ['gɜːlɪʃlɪ] *adv* (*to behave, dress*) comme une petite fille
Girl Scout *n Am* éclaireuse *f*
giro ['dʒaɪrəʊ] *n Br Banking* **National G.** = service *m* de chèques postaux; **bank g.** virement *m* bancaire; **g. account** compte *m* chèque postal, CCP *m*; **g. cheque** chèque *m* de virement; **I haven't had my g. (cheque) yet** (*unemployment benefit*) mon allocation de chômage ne m'a pas encore été payée; **g. transfer** transfert *m* par CCP
girt *see* **gird**
-girt [gɜːt] *suff Lit* **sea-g. isle** île *f* encerclée par les mers
girth [gɜːθ] *n* **(a)** (*circumference*) (*of tree etc*) circonférence *f*; (*of chest, waist*) tour *m*; **of considerable g.** (*of person*) d'une belle corpulence **(b)** (*on harness*) sangle *f*; **saddle g.** sangle de selle
gismo ['gɪzməʊ] *n* = **gizmo**
gist [dʒɪst] *n* (*of conversation*) essentiel *m*; (*of question*) point *m* essentiel; **to get the g. (of the matter)** saisir l'essentiel; **could you just give me the g. (of it) now?** pourrais-tu m'en donner l'essentiel?; **I got the g. of what she was saying** j'ai compris l'essentiel de ce qu'elle disait; **the g. of what she was saying was ...** elle a dit en substance ...
git [gɪt] *n Br Sl* con, *f* conne **stupid g.** espèce de con/conne!
give¹ [gɪv] *n* élasticité *f*; (*in mechanism etc*) jeu *m*
give² (*pt* **gave** [geɪv]; *pp* **given** ['gɪv(ə)n]) **1** *vt* **(a)** (*present, bestow, pledge, provide*) **to g. sth to sb, to g. sb sth** donner qch à qn; **to g. sb a present** faire *ou* donner un cadeau à qn; **to g. an example** donner un exemple; **to g. a discount** accorder un escompte; *Fml* **to g. a dinner** (*in honour of sb*) donner un dîner; **to g. sb one's hand** (*to hold*) donner *ou* tendre la main à qn; **to g. sb a note from sb** remettre à qn

un petit mot de qn; **to g. no sign of life** ne donner aucun signe de vie; **to g. sb sth to eat/drink** donner à manger/à boire à qn; **to g. sb six months' imprisonment** condamner qn à six mois de prison; **he was given life** il a été condamné à perpétuité; **to g. a child a name** donner un nom à un enfant; **to g. sb a job to do** assigner une tâche à qn; **g. her my love** embrasse-la pour moi; **to g. sb one's support** prêter son appui à qn; *Euph* **she gave herself to him** elle s'est donnée à lui; **g. me the good old days!** parlez-moi du bon vieux temps!; **g. me British weather any day!** rien ne vaut le climat de la Grande-Bretagne!

(b) (*in exchange*) donner; **to g. a good price for sth** donner *ou* payer un bon prix pour qch; **I'll g. you £10 for it** je vous en donnerai 10 livres; **to g. sth in exchange for sth** donner qch en échange de *ou* contre qch; **to g. one's life for one's beliefs** donner sa vie pour ses convictions; **I would g. a lot** *or* **a great deal to know ...** je donnerais beaucoup pour savoir ...

(c) (*devote*) **to g. oneself to one's studies** se consacrer entièrement *ou* s'adonner à ses études; **to g. one's attention to sth** porter son attention sur qch; **he gave it considerable thought** il y a beaucoup réfléchi; **I've given you six years of my life** je t'ai donné six ans de ma vie; **she gave this job the best years of her life** elle a consacré à ce travail les plus belles années de sa vie

(d) (*do*) **to g. a laugh** rire, laisser échapper un rire; **to g. a sigh** soupirer, pousser un soupir; **to g. a jump** sauter, faire un saut; (*with surprise*) sursauter; **to g. sb's hand a squeeze** serrer la main à qn; **to g. sb a smile** faire un sourire à qn; **he gave me an odd look** il m'a lancé un regard singulier; **she gave her hair a comb** elle s'est donnée un coup de peigne; **he gave his face a wash** il s'est lavé le visage; **he gave the table a wipe** il a essuyé la table

(e) (*reason, explanation, opinion, answer, reference number*) donner; **the answer (that) he gave me** la réponse qu'il m'a faite *ou* donnée; **he gave his age as twenty** il a déclaré avoir vingt ans; **to g. a decision** faire connaître sa décision; *Jur* rendre un arrêt; **don't g. me that!** (*don't try to fool me*) ne me raconte pas d'histoires!, à d'autres!; **don't g. me that stuff about how hard your life is** épargne-moi le récit de tous tes malheurs

(f) (*grant*) **she gave him her hand (in marriage)** elle lui a accordé sa main; **to g. sb an interview** accorder une interview à qn; **we were given a choice** on nous a fait choisir; **g. me a break!** fais-moi des vacances!, lâche-moi les baskets!; **g. me a chance!** donne-moi une chance!; **g. me five minutes** accorde-moi cinq minutes; **I can g. you 10 minutes** je peux te consacrer *ou* t'accorder 10 minutes; **we'll get there in two hours, g. or take a few minutes** on fera le trajet en deux heures, à quelques minutes près; **g. us a song!** chante-nous quelque chose!; **aren't you going to g. me a kiss?** tu ne vas pas m'embrasser?; **married? those two? I'll g. it a year at the outside** mariés? ces deux-là? je leur donne un an au grand maximum; **he's keen, I'll g. you that** il est très enthousiaste, je te le concède

(g) (*perform, execute*) (*concert etc*) donner; **she gave an outstanding performance** (*of actress*) son interprétation était remarquable; **I g. you our host** (*in proposing toast*) je bois à la santé de notre hôte

(h) (*pass on*) **he gave me his cold** il m'a donné *ou* passé son rhume; **that gave me the idea of travelling** cela m'a donné l'idée de voyager; **don't go giving him ideas!** ne va pas lui mettre des idées dans la tête!

(i) (*cause*) (*embarrassment, pleasure*) faire, causer; **to g. oneself trouble** se donner du mal; **to g. sb to believe** *or* **understand that ...** faire croire *ou* donner à entendre à qn que ...

(j) (*yield*) rendre; **investment that gives 10%** placement qui rend *ou* rapporte 10%; **this lamp gives a poor light** cette lampe éclaire mal; **to g. an average of ...** donner une moyenne de ...

(k) *F* (*hit etc*) **to g. it (to) sb** (*beat up*) rosser qn; (*reprimand*) laver la tête à qn; **g. it to them!** allez-y!; **I gave him what for!** (*reprimanded him*) je lui ai passé un savon!; **caviare on toast? I'll g. him caviare on toast!** (*in annoyance at request*) du caviar et des toasts! je vais lui en donner, moi, du caviar et des toasts!

2 *vi* **(a)** (*give gift etc*) donner, offrir; *Prov* **it is better** *or* **more blessed to g. than to receive** donner vaut mieux que recevoir; **please g. generously** (*to charity collection*) soyez généreux; **to g. generously of one's time** donner beaucoup de son temps; **to g. and take** faire des concessions; **to g. as good as one gets** rendre coup pour coup

(b) (*of cloth, elastic*) se détendre; *Fig* (*of person*) céder; **something's got to g.** ça va exploser; **the springs don't g. enough** les ressorts manquent de souplesse; **the door will g. if you push hard enough** la porte cédera si vous la poussez assez fort

(c) *esp Am F* **what gives?** (*hi!*) salut!; (*what's going on?*) qu'est-ce qui se passe?; (*what's the news?*) quoi de neuf?

(d) *Sl* **g.!** (*tell me etc*) vide ton sac!

▶ **give away** *vtsep* **(a)** (*give for nothing*) donner, faire cadeau de; **I'm practically giving them away!** (*said by salesman*) c'est pratiquement donné!; **you couldn't g. them away** tu n'arriveras pas à t'en débarrasser (même si tu en faisais cadeau) **(b)** (*at ceremony*) **to g. away the prizes** distribuer les prix; **to g. the bride away** conduire la mariée à l'autel **(c)** (*betray, reveal*) (*of person*) trahir, vendre; (*of accent, clothes etc*) trahir; **to g. oneself away** se trahir; **to g. the game** *or* **show away** vendre la mèche; **I'm not going to g. anything away** (*that might help you*) je ne veux rien vous révéler

▶ **give back** *vtsep* (*sth*) rendre, restituer (**to sb** à qn); (*echo*) renvoyer; (*image*) refléter; **to g. sb back his liberty** rendre la liberté à qn

▶ **give in 1** *vtsep* (*hand over*) donner, remettre; **I gave the wallet in to the police** j'ai remis le portefeuille à la police; **to g. in one's name** donner son nom; **to g. in one's examination paper** remettre sa copie d'examen **2** *vi* (*under pressure*) céder; (*in fight, battle*) se rendre; (*of rebel*) se soumettre; (*not know the answer*) renoncer, abandonner; **to g. in to intimidation** se laisser intimider; **you g. in too easily** tu abandonnes trop facilement; **to g. in to sb** céder à qn

▶ **give off** *vtsep* (*emit*) (*smell*) dégager, émettre; (*heat*) émettre, répandre; *Ch* (*gas*) dégager

▶ **give onto** *vipo* (*of window, door etc*) (*garden, street*) donner sur

▶ **give out 1** *vtsep* **(a)** (*distribute*) (*supplies, books etc*) distribuer **(b)** (*emit*) (*smell*) dégager; (*heat*) répandre; (*sound*) émettre **(c)** (*make known*) **it was given out that ...** on a annoncé *ou* dit que ... **2** *vi* **(a)** (*become used up*) manquer, faire défaut; (*of supplies*) s'épuiser; **my strength/patience was giving out** j'étais à bout de forces/patience; **my luck has finally given out** finalement, la chance a tourné **(b)** (*of radio, car etc*) tomber en panne

▶ **give over 1** *vtsep* **(a)** (*transfer*) remettre (**to sb** entre les mains de qn) **(b)** (*devote*) (*afternoon, rest of the evening etc*) consacrer (**to** à) **(c)** (*usu passive*) (*abandon*) **given over to despair** abandonné *ou* en proie au désespoir **2** *vi F* (*stop*) **g. over, will you?** vraiment, ça suffit!; **g. over kicking your sister** arrête de donner des coups de pieds à ta sœur

▶ **give up 1** *vtsep* **(a)** (*abandon*) (*possessions, pretensions*) abandonner; (*plan etc*) renoncer à; **to g. up the idea of doing sth** renoncer à (l'idée de) faire qch; **he gave up all hope of being promoted** il a abandonné tout espoir d'être promu; **to g. up smoking** cesser de fumer; **to g. up one's job** quitter son emploi; **to g. up the game/struggle** abandonner la partie/renoncer à la lutte; **to g. sth up as a bad job** renoncer à qch (en raison du manque de résultats); **to g. sb up (for lost)** considérer qn comme perdu; **the doctors have given him up** les médecins disent qu'il est perdu; **I'd given you up!** (*given up waiting*) je ne vous attendais plus!; **he gave himself up to grief** il s'est laissé aller au désespoir

(b) (*surrender*) (*prisoner*) livrer; **to g. up one's seat to sb** céder sa place à qn; **to g. oneself up** se constituer prisonnier, se rendre; **I want to g. myself up** je veux me rendre; **she gave herself up to her studies** elle s'est consacrée entièrement à ses études; **his mornings were given up to business** ses matinées étaient consacrées aux affaires

2 *vi* **(a)** (*surrender*) se rendre; **I g. up** (*I don't know the answer*) j'abandonne, je donne ma langue au chat

(b) (*abandon a course of action, struggle etc*) abandonner, laisser tomber; **you mustn't g. up now** tu ne peux pas abandonner maintenant; **I g. up!** (*you're or it's etc hopeless*) j'abandonne!

▶ **give up on** *vipo* (*stop having faith in*) **even his mother had given up on him** même sa mère avait perdu tout espoir à son sujet; **don't g. up on me** ne me laisse pas tomber

▶ **give way** *vi* **(a)** (*collapse*) s'effondrer; (*of ladder*) se casser, se rompre; (*of cable*) céder, partir; **the ground gave way under our feet** le sol s'est affaissé *ou* s'est dérobé sous nos pieds; **my legs are giving way (under me)** mes jambes fléchissent *ou* mollissent *ou* se dérobent sous moi; **his health is giving way** sa santé s'affaiblit

(b) (*yield*) **to g. way to sb** (*in argument*) céder à qn; **to g. way to despair/grief** s'abandonner au désespoir/à la douleur; **to g. way (to a car)** céder le passage (à une voiture); *Aut* **g. way** cédez le passage (**c**) (*be superseded by*) **her tears gave way to laughter** le rire l'a emporté sur ses larmes; **natural fibres have given way to synthetics** les fibres naturelles ont été remplacées par les synthétiques

give-and-take *n* (*mutual concession*) concessions *fpl* (mutuelles); **there has to be some g.** il faut que chacun fasse des concessions, il faut que chacun y mette du sien

giveaway ['gɪvəweɪ] *n F* (**a**) (*revelation*) révélation *f* involontaire; (*clue*) indice *m*; **her remark about inflation was the g.** sa remarque sur l'inflation l'a trahie; **it was a dead g.** c'était un geste/un mot/*etc* qui en disait long (**b**) *Com* (*free gift*) prime *f*, cadeau *m*; **g. paper** journal *m* gratuit; **g. price** prix *m* défiant toute concurrence

given ['gɪv(ə)n] **1** *adj* (**a**) (*specific*) donné, déterminé; **in a g. time** dans une période donnée; **at any g. time** à tout moment; **at a g. point** à un point donné; **g. name** prénom *m*, nom *m* de baptême (**b**) (*apt, likely*) **to be g. to forgetfulness** avoir tendance à être distrait; **I'm g. to losing my temper** c'est dans ma nature de me mettre en colère **2** *prep* **g. these facts, explain why ...** à partir de ces données, expliquez pourquoi ...; **g. her age** (*considering it*) étant donné son âge; **g. a triangle ABC** soit un triangle ABC

giver ['gɪvər] *n* (*of blood, organ*) donneur, -euse; (*of money*) donateur, -trice

give way sign *n* signal *m* de priorité

giving ['gɪvɪŋ] *adj* (*person*) généreux, -euse; **of a g. nature** d'une nature généreuse

gizmo ['gɪzməʊ] *n esp Am F* machin *m*, truc *m*, bidule *m*

gizzard ['gɪzəd] *n* gésier *m*; *Fig F* **that sticks in my g.** je ne peux pas avaler *ou* digérer ça

glacé ['glæseɪ] *adj Culin* **g. cherries** cerises *fpl* confites

glacial ['gleɪsɪəl, -ʃəl] *adj* (**a**) *Geol* (*erosion, valley etc*) glaciaire (**b**) (*wind, Fig manner etc*) glacial, -als

glaciation [gleɪsɪ'eɪʃən, -ʃɪ'eɪ-] *n* glaciation *f*

glacier ['glæsɪər, 'gleɪs-, *Am* 'gleɪʃər] *n Geol* glacier *m*

glad [glæd] *adj* (**gladder, gladdest**) (**a**) (*person*) heureux, content; **to be g. to hear sth** apprendre qch avec plaisir, être heureux *ou* content d'apprendre qch; **I'm g. you like him** je suis content que vous l'aimiez; **I'm (so) g.** (*to know that you're better etc*) ça me fait plaisir (de l'apprendre); **he is only too g. to help you** il ne demande pas mieux que de vous aider; **they would be g. of your help** ils seraient bien heureux d'avoir votre aide; **to be g. of an opportunity to do sth** se réjouir de l'occasion de faire qch; **it makes my heart g. to hear him** cela me réjouit le cœur de l'entendre

(**b**) (*smile*) de contentement; (*shout*) de plaisir; **g. news,** *Lit* **g. tidings** bonne nouvelle *f*; *Old-fashioned F* **to give sb the g. eye** faire de l'œil à qn; *US* **to give sb the g. hand** faire un accueil chaleureux à qn (*souvent dans un but intéressé*); *F Hum* **to put on one's g. rags** se mettre sur son trente et un

gladden ['glæd(ə)n] *vt* (*person*) rendre heureux; **it gladdens my heart to see them** cela me réjouit le cœur de les voir

glade [gleɪd] *n esp Lit* (*in forest*) clairière *f*

glad-hand *vt US* (*welcome warmly*) faire un accueil chaleureux à; (*of politician etc*) serrer la main à (*souvent dans un but intéressé*)

gladiator ['glædɪeɪtər] *n* gladiateur *m*

gladiatorial [glædɪə'tɔːrɪəl] *adj* (*combats*) de gladiateurs; *Fig* **g. politics** = politique *f* qui fait de la confrontation son moyen d'action

gladiolus, *pl* **-li** [glædɪ'əʊləs, -laɪ] *n* glaïeul *m*

gladly ['glædlɪ] *adv* (*willingly*) avec plaisir, volontiers; **I accept g.** j'accepte avec grand plaisir

gladness ['glædnɪs] *n* joie *f*, allégresse *f*

Gladstone ['glædstən] *n* **G. bag** = petit sac *m* de voyage

Glam *abbr* **Glamorganshire**

glam [glæm] *adj F* = **glamorous**

glamorize ['glæməraɪz] *vt* rendre séduisant *ou* attrayant; **to g. war** présenter la guerre de telle sorte qu'elle apparaisse attrayante; **a TV programme that glamorizes violence** une émission de télé qui rend la violence attrayante; **an advertising campaign that seeks to g. smoking** une campagne publicitaire qui cherche à redorer l'image des fumeurs

glamorous ['glæmərəs] *adj* (*person*) chic et élégant; (*dress*) habillé; (*job, football club etc*) prestigieux, -ieuse; (*job as model etc*) qui fait rêver; **a g. grandmother** une grand-mère sophistiquée; **working in the film industry is not always g.** il n'y a pas que des métiers de prestige dans le cinéma

glamour, *US also* **glamor** ['glæmər] *n* (*of person*) glamour *m*, chic *m* fascinant; (*of name, lifestyle*) prestige *m*; (*of ceremony etc*) éclat *m*; **the false g. of war** la fascination trompeuse qu'exerce la guerre; **g. is back in fashion** le chic revient à la mode; *F* **g. boy** beau mec *m*, beau mâle *m*; *F* **g. girl** belle fille *f*, pin up *f*

glam-rock *n Mus* glam-rock *m*

glance¹ [glɑːns] *n* (*quick look*) regard *m*, coup *m* d'œil; **at a g.** d'un coup d'œil; **at first g.** à première vue, au premier coup d'œil; **to give sth a g., to have a g. at sth** jeter un coup d'œil sur qch; **at-a-g. list** aide-mémoire *m inv*

glance² *vi* (*look quickly*) **to g. at sb/sth** jeter un regard sur qn/qch, lancer un coup d'œil à qn/sur qch; **to g. around** jeter un coup d'œil autour de soi; **to g. through** *or* **over sth** (*examine*) parcourir rapidement qch; **to g. through a book** parcourir *ou* feuilleter un livre; **he glanced up briefly when I came in** il a brièvement levé la tête quand je suis entré

▶ **glance off 1** *vi* (*of bullet etc*) ricocher **2** *vipo* ricocher sur; (*of light*) se refléter sur; **the blow glanced off his helmet** le coup a ricoché sur son casque

glancing ['glɑːnsɪŋ] *adj* (*blow*) oblique; **she caught him with a g. blow** elle lui a donné un coup sur le côté

gland¹ [glænd] *n* glande *f*

gland² *n MecE* **packing g.** bague *f* de presse-étoupe

glanders ['glændəz] *npl* (*with sing verb*) *Vet* morve *f*

glandular ['glændjʊlər] *adj Physiol, Med* glandulaire; *Med* **g. fever** mononucléose *f* infectieuse

glans [glænz], *pl* **glandes** ['glændiːz] *n Anat* gland *m*

glare¹ [gleər] *n* (**a**) (*angry stare*) regard *m* fixe et furieux (**b**) (*of sun, headlight etc*) éclat *m*, lumière *f* éblouissante; *Fig* **in the full g. of publicity** sous le feu croisé des médias

glare² *vi* (**a**) (*stare angrily*) fixer un regard furieux *ou* furibond (**at sb** sur qn) (**b**) (*of sun etc*) être aveuglant

glaring ['gleərɪŋ] *adj* (**a**) (*eyes*) furieux (**b**) (*light*) éblouissant, éclatant; (*sun*) aveuglant; (*colour etc*) voyant (**c**) *Fig* (*fact etc*) manifeste, patent, qui saute aux yeux; (*error, injustice, omission*) flagrant; (*abuse*) scandaleux, choquant

glaringly ['gleərɪŋlɪ] *adv* **it's g. obvious** ça saute aux yeux

glasnost ['glɑːznɒst] *n Pol* glasnost *f*

glass [glɑːs] *n* (**a**) (*material*) verre *m*; **the g. industry** l'industrie *f* du verre; *Prov* **people who live in g. houses shouldn't throw stones** il faut être sans défauts pour critiquer autrui; **g. with care** (*notice on parcel*) fragile; **g. bottle** bouteille de *ou* en verre; **g. case** vitrine *f*; **to keep/display sth in a g. case** *or* **under g.** garder/exposer qch sous verre; **g. door** porte vitrée, porte de *ou* en verre; **g. eye** œil *m* de verre; *Boxing etc F* **g. jaw** mâchoire *f* fragile; **g. partition** cloison de *ou* en verre; **g. roof** (*of station etc*) verrière *f*; **g. manufacture** verrerie *f*

(**b**) (*single piece*) (*of window*) vitre *f*, carreau *m*; (*of car*) glace *f*, vitre; (*of watch, lamp*) verre *m*

(**c**) (*cup*) verre *m*; **wine g.** verre à vin; **g. of wine** verre de vin; **to sell wine by the g.** vendre le vin au verre

(**d**) (*no pl*) (*glassware*) verrerie *f*

(**e**) (*lens*) (*of optical instrument*) lentille *f*

(**f**) (*telescope*) (**field**) **g.** lunette *f* d'approche, longue-vue *f*, *pl* longues-vues

(**g**) (*mirror*) (**looking**) **g.** glace *f*, miroir *m*

(**h**) *Old-fashioned* (*barometer*) baromètre *m* (à cadran); **the g. is falling** le baromètre baisse

(**i**) (*in gardening*) **grown under g.** (*in cold frame*) cultivé sous verre *ou* sous châssis; (*in glasshouse*) cultivé en serre

▶ **glass in** *vtsep* (*balcony etc*) entourer d'une cloison vitrée

glass-blower *n* souffleur *m* de verre

glass-blowing *n* soufflage *m* de verre

glasscloth ['glɑːsklɒθ] *n* torchon *m* (pour essuyer les verres)

glass cutter *n* (*person*) vitrier *m*; (*tool*) coupe-verre *m inv*, diamant *m* (*de vitrier*)

glass cutting *n* taille *f* du verre

glasses ['glɑːsɪz] *npl* [ⓘ**A10**,e] (*spectacles*) lunettes *fpl*

glass fibre *n* fibre(s) *f(pl)* de verre; **g. cable** câble *m* en fibre(s) de verre

glassful ['glɑːsfʊl] *n* (*of water etc*) (plein) verre *m*

glasshouse ['glɑːshaʊs] *n* (**a**) *Br* (*in garden*) serre *f* (**b**) *Br Mil F* prison *f* militaire, *F* trou *m* (**c**) *US* (*factory*) verrerie *f*

glasspaper ['glɑːspeɪpər] *n* papier *m* de verre

glassware ['glɑːsweər] *n* verres *mpl*; (*stylish*) verrerie *f*

glass wool *n* laine *f* de verre

glassworks ['glɑːswɜːks] *npl* (*usu with sing verb*) verrerie *f*; (*for crystal*) cristallerie *f*

glassy ['glɑːsɪ] *adj* (*smooth*) vitreux; **g. look/eye** regard/œil terne

Glaswegian [glæz'wiːdʒɪən] **1** *n* (*resident*) habitant, -ante de Glasgow; (*by birth*) originaire *mf* de Glasgow **2** *adj* de Glasgow

glaucoma [glɔː'kəʊmə] *n Med* glaucome *m*; **to have g.** avoir un glaucome

glaucous ['glɔːkəs] *adj* glauque

glaze¹ [gleɪz] *n* (**a**) *Cer* vernis *m* (luisant) (**b**) *Culin* glaçage *m* (**c**) *Art* vernis *m* (**d**) *US* (*ice*) verglas *m*

glaze² *vt* (**a**) (*window, house*) vitrer (**b**) *Cer* (*pottery*) vernisser; (*tiles etc*) vitrifier (**c**) *Culin* glacer (**d**) *Art* (*painting*) glacer; *Phot* (*print*) émailler

▶ **glaze over** *vi* (*of eyes*) devenir vitreux
glazed [gleɪzd] *adj* **(a)** (*door*) vitré **(b)** *Cer* verni; (*brick*) vitrifié **(c)** *Culin* glacé **(d)** (*eye, look*) vitreux
glazier ['gleɪzɪər] *n* vitrier *m*
glazing ['gleɪzɪŋ] *n* **(a)** (*fitting of windows etc*) pose *f* des vitres **(b)** (*no pl*) (*windows*) vitrerie *f*; *Cer* vernissage *m*
GLC [dʒi:el'si:] *n* (*abbr* **Greater London Council**) = anciennement, conseil *m* municipal du grand Londres
gleam¹ [gli:m] *n* (*of light*) rayon *m*, trait *m*; (*of knife etc*) reflet *m*; **there's a strange g. in his eye** il y a une drôle de lueur dans son regard; *Hum* **when you were just a g. in your father's eye** bien avant ta naissance
gleam² *vi* luire, reluire; (*of water*) miroiter; (*of eyes*) briller; **she polished the silverware until it gleamed** elle a astiqué l'argenterie jusqu'à ce qu'elle reluise
gleaming ['gli:mɪŋ] *adj* luisant; (*surface of water*) miroitant; (*silverware etc*) reluisant; **g. eyes** yeux brillants
glean [gli:n] **1** *vt* (*corn, information etc*) glaner; **I couldn't g. much from the brochure** je n'ai pas pu tirer grand-chose de la brochure **2** *vi Agr* faire la glane
gleaner ['gli:nər] *n Agr* glaneur, -euse
gleaning ['gli:nɪŋ] *n* **gleanings** (*of crops*) glanes *fpl*; *Fig* **gleanings from the newspapers** informations *fpl* glanées dans les journaux
glebe [gli:b] *n Rel* terre *f* assignée à un bénéfice
glee [gli:] *n* **(a)** (*delight*) joie *f*, allégresse *f*; (*malicious pleasure*) jubilation *f*; **the children gave shouts of g.** les enfants ont poussé des cris de joie; **she announced it with some g.** elle l'a annoncé avec un malin plaisir **(b)** *Mus* petit chant *m* à trois ou quatre parties (*pour voix d'hommes*)
glee club *n esp Am* chorale *f*
gleeful ['gli:fʊl] *adj* joyeux, allègre; (*maliciously*) plein d'une joie malicieuse
gleefully ['gli:fʊlɪ] *adv* allègrement, plein de joie; (*maliciously*) avec une joie malicieuse
glen [glen] *n* vallée *f*; (*narrower*) gorge *f*
glengarry [glen'gærɪ] *n Scot* **g. (bonnet)** = béret *m* écossais
glib [glɪb] *adj* (*answer*) spécieux; (*speaker*) qui a du bagou(t); **his explanation was a bit too g.** son explication était un peu trop facile
glibly ['glɪblɪ] *adv* (*to reply*) spécieusement; (*to speak*) avec aisance
glibness ['glɪbnɪs] *n* (*of excuse, reply*) spéciosité *f*; (*of person*) bagou(t) *m*
glide¹ [glaɪd] *n* **(a)** (*movement*) glissement *m*; (*in dancing*) glissade *f*, glissé *m* **(b)** (*of glider*) vol *m* plané; (*of aircraft*) descente *f* en (vol) plané; **g. path** (*of aircraft*) trajectoire *f* d'atterrissage **(c)** *Mus* port *m* de voix **(d)** *Ling* son *m* transitoire
glide² *vi* **(a)** (*slide*) glisser; **to g. (along) over the water** glisser sur l'eau **(b)** (*of birds*) planer; (*of aircraft*) planer, faire un vol plané; (*in glider*) faire du vol à voile
glider ['glaɪdər] *n Av* planeur *m*; **g. pilot** pilote *m* de planeur
gliding ['glaɪdɪŋ] *n Av* vol *m* plané *m*; (*sport*) vol à voile; **g. club** club *m* de vol à voile
glimmer¹ ['glɪmər] *n* (*of candle etc*) faible lueur *f*; (*of water etc*) reflet *m*; **g. of hope/intelligence** lueur d'espoir/d'intelligence; **not a g. of interest** pas le moindre intérêt
glimmer² *vi* jeter une faible lueur; (*of water*) miroiter
glimmering ['glɪmərɪŋ] *adj* (*water*) miroitant; **a g. light** une faible lueur
glimpse¹ [glɪmps] *n* vision *f* momentanée; **to catch a g. of sb/sth** entrevoir qn/qch; **she had only caught a g. of her assailant** elle n'avait fait qu'entrevoir son assaillant; **a g. of the future** un aperçu de ce que sera le futur
glimpse² *vt* entrevoir
glint¹ [glɪnt] *n* (*of light*) (*flash*) éclair *m*; (*continuous*) scintillement *m*; (*of knife etc*) reflet *m*; **hair with glints of gold** chevelure à *ou* aux reflets d'or
glint² *vi* étinceler; (*on water*) miroiter; **the blade glinted in the sunlight** la lame miroita/miroitait au soleil; **his eyes were glinting with fury** ses yeux étincelaient de fureur
glissando [glɪ'sændəʊ] *n Mus* glissando *m*
glisten ['glɪs(ə)n] *vi* (re)luire, scintiller; (*of sea*) miroiter; **his forehead glistened with sweat** la sueur perlait sur son front
glistening ['glɪs(ə)nɪŋ] *adj* luisant, scintillant; (*sea*) miroitant
glitch [glɪtʃ] *n F* (*problem etc*) pépin *m*; *Comptr* défaillance *f* subite
glitter¹ ['glɪtər] *n* scintillement *m*; *Fig* (*of occasion etc*) éclat *m*
glitter² *vi* briller, scintiller, (re)luire; **her eyes glittered with excitement** ses yeux brillaient *ou* scintillaient de joie; *Prov* **all that glitters is not gold** tout ce qui brille n'est pas or
glitterati [glɪtə'rɑ:ti:] *npl F* **the g.** le beau monde
glittering ['glɪtərɪŋ] *adj* scintillant; (*occasion*) brillant; *Fig* **the g. world of showbusiness** le monde de lumière du show-business
glitz [glɪts] *n F* (*of showbusiness etc*) tape-à-l'œil *m*
glitzy ['glɪtsɪ] *adj F* (*party etc*) tape-à-l'œil *inv*
gloaming ['gləʊmɪŋ] *n Lit* crépuscule *m*; **in the g.** au crépuscule
gloat¹ [gləʊt] *vi* jubiler; **don't g.** ne te réjouis pas; **to g. about sth** se réjouir à l'idée de qch
gloat² *n* **to have a g. about sth** se réjouir à l'idée de qch
▶ **gloat over** *vipo* **to sit gloating over one's possessions** jubiler à la vue de ses possessions; **to g. over sb's misfortune** se réjouir du malheur de qn; **he was gloating over his victory/success** il jubilait en pensant à sa victoire/son succès
gloating ['gləʊtɪŋ] *adj* (*eye*) avide; (*smile, look*) jubilant
glob [glɒb] *n F* (*of cream etc*) petite boule *f*
global ['gləʊb(ə)l] *adj* **(a)** (*worldwide*) mondial, -aux; *Com* **g. market(place)** marché *m* global; *Mktg* **g. marketing** mercatique *f* globale *ou* internationale; *Mktg* **g. player** acteur *m* international; **g. village** village *m* planétaire; **g. war(fare)** guerre *f* mondiale; **g. warming** réchauffement *m* de la planète **(b)** (*comprehensive*) global, -aux; *Comptr* **g. change** changement *m* global; *Comptr* **g. search and replace** recherche *f* et remplacement global
globalization [gləʊb(ə)laɪ'zeɪʃən] *n* **(a)** (*making worldwide*) mondialisation *f* **(b)** (*generalization*) globalisation *f*
globalize ['gləʊb(ə)laɪz] *vt* **(a)** (*make worldwide*) mondialiser **(b)** (*generalize*) globaliser
globally ['gləʊbəlɪ] *adv* **(a)** (*generally*) globalement **(b)** (*worldwide*) mondialement; **the problem of over-population must be dealt with g.** on doit résoudre le problème de la surpopulation à l'échelle planétaire
globe [gləʊb] *n* (*sphere*) sphère *f*; (*with map*) globe *m* terrestre; (*lampshade*) globe (de lampe); *Anat* (*of eye*) globe; **to go round the g.** faire le tour du globe; **g. artichoke** artichaut *m*; *Met* **g. lightning** éclair *m* en boule
globe-fish *n* poisson-globe *m*, *pl* poissons-globes
globetrotter ['gləʊbtrɒtər] *n F* globe-trotter *m*, *pl* globe-trotters
globetrotting ['gləʊbtrɒtɪŋ] *n F* voyages *mpl* dans le monde entier
globular ['glɒbjʊlər] *adj* (*globe-shaped*) globulaire; (*composed of globules*) globuleux
globule ['glɒbju:l] *n* (*of fat etc*) globule *m*; (*of wax, molten metal*) gouttelette *f*
globulin ['glɒbjʊlɪn] *n Biol, Ch* globuline *f*
glockenspiel ['glɒkənʃpi:l] *n Mus* glockenspiel *m*
glomerulus [glɒ'merʊləs] *n Anat* glomérule *m*
gloom [glu:m] *n* **(a)** (*darkness*) obscurité *f*, ténèbres *fpl* **(b)** (*melancholy*) mélancolie *f*, tristesse *f* empreinte de pessimisme; **to cast** *or* **throw a g. over** *or* **on the company** jeter une ombre *ou* un voile de tristesse sur l'assemblée; **there is g. in the City** la Bourse de Londres est pessimiste
gloomily ['glu:mɪlɪ] *adv* avec mélancolie, mélancoliquement
gloominess ['glu:mɪnɪs] *n* **(a) the g. of the sky** le ciel gris; **the g. of the weather** ce temps maussade **(b)** (*melancholy*) tristesse *f*, mélancolie *f*
gloomy ['glu:mɪ] *adj* **(a)** (*dark*) sombre, *Lit* ténébreux; **the weather is g.** il fait sombre; **to turn g.** s'assombrir **(b)** (*melancholy*) morne, sombre; (*stronger*) lugubre; (*prediction etc*) sombre; **to become g.** (*of person*) devenir sombre, se rembrunir; **g. thoughts** de noires pensées; *Fig* **to paint a g. picture** faire un tableau plutôt sombre
glorification [glɔ:rɪfɪ'keɪʃən] *n* glorification *f*
glorified ['glɔ:rɪfaɪd] *adj* **(a)** *Rel* glorifié; (*body*) glorieux **(b) it's just a g. motor scooter** ce n'est qu'un scooter amélioré; **in fact he's just a g. janitor** en fait ce n'est qu'un simple concierge
glorify ['glɔ:rɪfaɪ] *vt* glorifier, célébrer; (*God*) rendre gloire à; **the book glorifies war** ce livre glorifie la guerre
glorious ['glɔ:rɪəs] *adj* **(a)** (*reign, martyr*) glorieux; (*victory*) éclatant; (*action*) remarquable; *Br Hist* **the G. Revolution** la (seconde) Révolution d'Angleterre; **the G. Twelfth** = le 12 août, début de la chasse à la grouse **(b)** (*splendid, beautiful*) resplendissant, radieux; **g. in her youth and beauty** resplendissante de jeunesse et de beauté **(c)** (*excellent*) magnifique, splendide; **what g. weather!** quel temps superbe!
gloriously ['glɔ:rɪəslɪ] *adv* **(a)** glorieusement **(b)** *F* **g. drunk** ivre bien comme il faut
glory ['glɔ:rɪ] *n* **(a)** (*honour*) gloire *f*; **the athletes get all the g.** ce sont les athlètes qui remportent toute la gloire; **to give g. to God** rendre gloire à Dieu; **g. be to God!** gloire à Dieu!; *Old-fashioned F* **g. be!** oh mon Dieu!; (*thank heavens*) Dieu soit loué!

(**b**) (*thing*) sujet *m* de gloire; **to be the g. of the age** faire la gloire du siècle; *esp Br F* **g. hole** (*room, cupboard*) capharnaüm *m*, débarras *m*

(**c**) (*splendour*) (*of spectacle etc*) splendeur *f*, éclat *m*; **in all her g.** parée de ses plus beaux atours; **Spain, in the days of her g.** l'Espagne, au temps de sa splendeur; **the glories of the Irish countryside** les splendeurs de la campagne irlandaise

(**d**) *Rel* gloire *f*; **the saints in g.** les glorieux *mpl*

(**e**) (*halo*) (*of saint*) gloire *f*

▶ **glory in** *vipo* (*rejoice in*) se glorifier de; **to g. in one's freedom** profiter pleinement de sa liberté; **the dog gloried in the name of Marmaduke** le chien portait le nom ronflant de Marmaduke

Glos *abbr* **Gloucestershire**

gloss[1] [glɒs] *n Liter* glose *f*

gloss[2] *vt Liter* (*text*) annoter

gloss[3] *n* (*shine*) lustre *m*, vernis *m*, brillant *m*; *Tex* cati *m*; *Fig* (*veneer*) (*of legality etc*) vernis *m*; *Fig* **to take the g. off sth** gâcher qch; **g. (paint)** peinture *f* brillante

gloss[4] *vt* (*make shine*) lustrer

▶ **gloss over** *vipo* (**a**) (*deal hurriedly with*) ne pas s'étendre sur; (*sb's shortcomings*) glisser *ou* passer sur (**b**) (*conceal, cover up*) dissimuler

glossary ['glɒsərɪ] *n* glossaire *m*, lexique *m*

glossiness ['glɒsɪnɪs] *n* lustre *m*, vernis *m*

glossy ['glɒsɪ] **1** *adj* lustré, brillant; (*paper*) glacé; (*coat*) (*of dog*) lustré; *Phot* (*paper*) brillant; **g. magazine** magazine *m* féminin de luxe; *Phot* **g. print** épreuve *f* sur papier brillant **2** *n* (*pl* **glossies**) *Journ* magazine *m* quadri sur papier glacé; (*women's magazine*) magazine *m* féminin de luxe; **the glossies** la presse féminine de luxe

glottal ['glɒt(ə)l] *adj Ling* glottal; *Anat* glottique; *Ling* **g. stop** coup *m* de glotte

glottis ['glɒtɪs] *n Anat* glotte *f*

glove[1] [glʌv] *n* gant *m*; **to put on one's gloves** mettre ses gants, se ganter; **to take off one's gloves** enlever ses gants, se déganter; **it fits like a g.!** ça me/te/lui/*etc* va comme un gant; *Fig* **the gloves were off** on n'a pas mis de gants, on y est allé carrément; *Aut* **g. compartment** boîte *f* à gants; **g. counter** *or* **department** (*in large store*) rayon *m* des gants, ganterie *f*; **g. maker** *or* **manufacturer** gantier, -ière

glove[2] *vt* ganter

glovebox ['glʌvbɒks] *n Aut* boîte *f* à gants

glove puppet *n* marionnette *f* (à gaine), pupazzo *m*

glover ['glʌvər] *n* gantier, -ière

glow[1] [gləʊ] *n* (**a**) (*light*) lueur *f*; (*of hot metal*) rougeoiement *m*, incandescence *f*; **the g. of the setting sun** l'embrasement *m* du ciel au couchant (**b**) (*of complexion*) **to have a healthy g. in one's cheeks** avoir les joues bien rouges; **g. of health** bonne mine *f*; **a g. of pleasure** une rougeur de plaisir (**c**) *Fig* (*warm feeling*) **it gave him a g. of pride** cela le faisait rayonner d'orgueil; **he felt a warm g. spread over him as the whisky went down** il sentit une sensation de chaleur dans tout le corps après avoir bu le whisky; **it gives you a warm g.** (*of news, scene etc*) ça vous fait chaud au cœur

glow[2] *vi* (*of light, fire, hot metal*) rougeoyer; (*of person, face*) rayonner; **her face was glowing with pleasure** son visage rayonnait de plaisir; **to g. with enthusiasm** brûler d'enthousiasme; **to be glowing with health** être rayonnant de santé; **his cheeks were glowing** il avait les joues en feu

glower ['glaʊər] *vi* avoir un air renfrogné; **(to g. at sb** (*with disapproval or anger*) lancer un/des regard(s) noir(s) à qn

glowering ['glaʊərɪŋ] *adj* (*expression*) renfrogné; **to give sb a g. look** lancer à qn un regard noir

glowing ['gləʊɪŋ] *adj* (**a**) (*metal*) (chauffé au) rouge, incandescent, rougeoyant (**b**) (*coal, embers, cigarette*) rougeoyant; (*eyes*) de braise (**c**) (*complexion*) rayonnant; (*cheeks*) rouge (**d**) (*colours, words*) chaleureux; (*description*) en termes chaleureux; *Fig* **to paint sth in g. colours** présenter qch sous un jour des plus favorables; **the reviews were g.** les critiques étaient très élogieuses; **to speak in g. terms of sb** faire les louanges de qn

glow-worm *n* ver *m* luisant

gloxinia [glɒk'sɪnɪə] *n* (*plant*) gloxinia *m*

glucose ['glu:kəʊs] *n* glucose *m*

glue[1] [glu:] *n* colle *f* (forte), glu *f*; *F* **he sticks to me like g.** il me suit partout comme un petit chien

glue[2] *vt* (**glued; gluing**) coller (à la colle forte); **to g. sth on** *or* **to sth** coller qch sur qch; **I glued it on** je l'ai collé dessus; **to g. two things together** coller deux choses (ensemble); *Fig* **with her face glued to the window** le visage collé à la fenêtre; *Fig* **they were glued to the television** ils étaient rivés à la télévision; *Fig* **keep your eyes glued to the road** gardez les yeux rivés *ou* fixés sur la route

▶ **glue down** *vtsep* coller

glue ear *n Med* otite *f* séreuse

gluepot ['glu:pɒt] *n* pot *m* de colle

glue-sniffer *n* sniffeur, -euse (de colle)

glue-sniffing ['glu:snɪfɪŋ] *n* inhalation *f* de colle; **to be into g.** sniffer de la colle

gluey ['glu:ɪ] *adj* gluant, poisseux

glug[1] [glʌg] *n F* **g. (g.)** glouglou *m*

glug[2] *vi* (**-gg-**) *F* faire glouglou

glum [glʌm] *adj* (*face, expression*) renfrogné, maussade; (*appearance*) morne, maussade

glumly ['glʌmlɪ] *adv* d'un air maussade

glumness ['glʌmnɪs] *n* air *m* maussade

glut[1] [glʌt] *n Com* (*on market*) encombrement *m*; (*of commodity*) surabondance *f*

glut[2] *vt* (**-tt-**) (**a**) *Com* (*market*) encombrer, inonder; **the market is glutted with ...** le marché regorge de ... (**b**) **to g. oneself** se rassasier, se gorger (**on** de)

glutamine ['glu:təmɪn] *n* glutamine *f*

gluten ['glu:tən] *n* gluten *m*

glutinous ['glu:tɪnəs] *adj* glutineux

glutted ['glʌtɪd] *adj* (*market*) encombré

glutton ['glʌt(ə)n] *n* (*person*) glouton, -onne, goinfre *m*, *Arg* morfal, -ale; **she's a g. for work** c'est un bourreau de travail; **you're a g. for punishment** tu cherches les complications

gluttonous ['glʌtənəs] *adj* glouton

gluttonously ['glʌtənəslɪ] *adv* gloutonnement

gluttony ['glʌtənɪ] *n* gloutonnerie *f*, goinfrerie *f*

glycaemia [glaɪ'si:mɪə] *n Med* glycémie *f*

glycerin(e) ['glɪsərɪn, -i:n] *n Ch etc* glycérine *f*

glycerol ['glɪsərɒl] *n Ch etc* glycérol *m*

glyceryl trinitrate ['glɪsərɪltraɪ'naɪtreɪt] *n Pharm* trinitine *f*

glycol ['glaɪkɒl] *n Ch* glycol *m*

G-man, -men ['dʒi:mæn, -men] *n US F* = agent *m* du F. B. I.

GMT [dʒi:em'ti:] *n* (*abbr* **Greenwich Mean Time**) G. M. T. *m*

gnarled [nɑ:ld] *adj* (**a**) (*tree*) (*knotty*) noueux; (*twisted*) tordu (**b**) (*hands, fingers*) noueux; (*old man, woman*) fripé

gnash [næʃ] *vt* **to g. one's teeth** grincer des dents

gnashing ['næʃɪŋ] *n* grincement *m*; *Lit, Hum* **there was much weeping and g. of teeth** il y eut moult pleurs et grincements de dents

gnat [næt] *n* (*insect*) moucheron *m*

gnaw [nɔ:] *vt* (*pt* **gnawed**; *pp* **gnawed, gnawn**) (*of rodent*) ronger; **to g. a bone** (*of dog*) ronger un os; *Fig* **gnawed by hunger** tenaillé par la faim; **gnawed by remorse** rongé par le remords

▶ **gnaw at, gnaw into, gnaw through** *vipo* ronger

gnawing ['nɔ:ɪŋ] *adj* (*hunger, anxiety*) dévorant; **the g. pains of hunger** les tiraillements *mpl* de la faim

gneiss [naɪs] *n Geol* gneiss *m*

gnome [nəʊm] *n Myth* gnome *m*; (**garden**) **g.** = statue *f* de nain qui décore un jardin; *F Pej* **the gnomes of Zurich** les banquiers *mpl* internationaux de Zurich

gnomic ['nəʊmɪk] *adj Lit* gnomique

gnostic ['nɒstɪk] *adj, n Rel, Hist* gnostique *mf*

gnosticism ['nɒstɪsɪz(ə)m] *n Rel, Hist* gnosticisme *m*

GNP [dʒi:en'pi:] *n Econ* (*abbr* **Gross National Product**) P. N. B. *m*

gnu [nu:] *n* (*animal*) gnou *m*

go[1] [gəʊ] **1** *n* (*pl* **goes**) (**a**) (*activity*) **to be always on the go** être toujours à trotter *ou* à courir, *F* avoir la bougeotte; **to keep sb on the go** faire trimer qn; **it's all go** on n'a pas une minute à soi, ça n'arrête pas

(**b**) (*energy*) **to be full of** *or* **have plenty of go** avoir de l'allant

(**c**) (*try*) coup *m*, essai *m*; **to make a go of it** (*succeed*) y réussir; **(it's) your go!** (*in game*) à vous de jouer!; **to have a g. (at doing sth)** essayer (de faire qch); **can I have a go?** je peux essayer?; **let's have a go!** tentons le coup!, allons-y!; (*let me try*) laisse-moi essayer; **she had a go at me** (*abused me verbally*) elle s'en est prise à moi; *F* **to have a go** (*stop or arrest criminal*) tenter quelque chose (*alors qu'on n'est pas de la police*); **(it's) no go!** rien à faire!; **at one go** d'un (seul) coup; **£1 a go** (*at fair etc*) une livre la partie *ou* le tour; **to have a go on the dodgems** faire un tour d'autos tamponneuses; **he wouldn't let me have** *or* **give me a go** (*on his bicycle etc*) il ne voulait pas me laisser l'essayer; **you've had three goes already** (*attempts*) tu as déjà essayé trois fois; (*on bicycle etc*) tu as déjà fait trois tours

(**d**) *Old-fashioned* **it's all the go** (*fashionable*) ça fait fureur *ou* rage

2 *adj Astronaut* **all systems are go** tout est paré et en ordre de marche (pour le départ)

go[2] (**he goes**; *pt* **went** [went]; *pp* **gone** [gɒn]) **1** *vi* (**a**) aller; **to go to a place** aller *ou* se rendre à un endroit; **to go to Paris/to the country** aller à Paris/à la campagne; **to go to France/**

Japan aller en France/au Japon; **to go home** aller *ou* rentrer chez soi; **to go to church/Mass** aller à l'église/à la messe; **to go to the doctor's** aller chez le médecin; **to go to prison** aller en prison; **to go to the lavatory** aller aux toilettes; **do you need to go?** (*to toilet*) tu as besoin de faire pipi?; **I went before I came** (*to toilet*) j'ai fait (pipi) avant de venir; **to go to sb's house** aller chez qn; **to go on foot/by train/by car** aller à pied/par le train/en voiture; **there he goes!** le voilà (qui passe)!; *Mil* **who goes there?** qui va là?; **the car was going very slowly/fast** la voiture allait très lentement/vite; **to go at 100 km an hour** faire 100 km *ou* du cent à l'heure; **you go first** (*after you*) à vous l'honneur, vous d'abord; (*you leave first*) partez le premier *ou* devant; **to go up/down/across a street** remonter/descendre/traverser une rue; **which road goes to London?** quelle est la route de Londres?; *Fig* **where do we go from here?** et maintenant?; **to go one's own way** faire à sa guise; **there you go!** (*handing sth to sb*) voilà!; **it's expensive, but there you go** (*that's how it is*) c'est cher mais c'est comme ça; **there you go again!** vous voilà reparti!; **to go riding** (aller) se promener à cheval; **to go hunting/fishing** aller à la chasse/à la pêche; **to go looking for sth** partir à la recherche de qch

(b) (*be active, function*) marcher; **to set** *or* **get a piece of machinery going** mettre une machine en marche *ou* en mouvement; *F* **get going!** file!, vas-y!; **my watch has stopped going** ma montre ne marche plus; **the bell went 10 minutes ago** la cloche a sonné il y a dix minutes; **enough timber to keep three sawmills going** assez de bois pour alimenter trois scieries; **to keep the conversation going** entretenir la conversation; **when he gets going he never stops** quand il est lancé *ou* une fois lancé, il ne sait pas s'arrêter

(c) (*progress*) **everything's going well** tout marche bien; **things are going badly** cela va mal; **how are things going?, how is it going?** comment ça va?; **if all goes well** si tout va bien; **the rehearsal went well/badly** la répétition a bien/mal marché; **the way things are going** au train où vont les choses; **I forget how the tune goes** l'air m'échappe; **how does the chorus go?** quelles sont les paroles du refrain?; **how does it go?** (*of tune, music*) c'est comment?; **as things go today** par les temps qui courent; **that's not dear as things go today** ce n'est pas cher au prix où sont les choses; **which way will the decision go?** que décidera-t-on?; **I don't know how things will go** je ne sais pas comment cela tournera

(d) (*of time*) passer; **there were only five minutes to go before ...** il ne restait que cinq minutes avant ...; **how's the time going?** combien de temps nous reste-t-il?; **it has just gone eight** il est un peu plus de huit heures

(e) (*be the rule*) **what she says goes** c'est elle qui commande; **anything goes** (*do, wear etc whatever you like*) on fait ce qu'on veut

(f) *F* (*make sound, perform action*) **to go crack/bang** faire crac/pan; **go like this with your left foot** fais comme ça du pied gauche; **and then he went, 'oh, I forgot'** et alors il a dit 'oh, j'ai oublié'

(g) (*match*) **these colours don't go** ces couleurs jurent; **these colours go perfectly** ces couleurs vont parfaitement ensemble

(h) (*leave*) partir, s'en aller; **after** *or* **when I had gone** après mon départ, aprés que je sois parti; **we must go** *or* **must be going** il est temps de partir; **let me go** laissez-moi partir; **go!** (*go away*) allez vous-en!; *Sp* (*in race etc*) partez!; **from the word go** dès le début; **that old chair will have to go** il va falloir se débarrasser de cette vieille chaise; **a hundred employees will have to go** il va falloir mettre cent employés à la porte; *Euph* **his wife went first** (*died*) sa femme est partie avant lui; *Euph* **when I am gone, after I have gone** (*died*) quand je ne serai plus là

(i) (*disappear*) disparaître; **my hat has gone** mon chapeau a disparu; **it's all gone** il n'y en a plus; **that's the way the money goes** voilà comme l'argent file; **most of my money goes on food** la plus grande partie de mon argent passe dans la nourriture; **her sight is going** elle est en train de perdre la vue

(j) (*break*) (se) casser; **the spring went** le ressort s'est cassé; **the batteries are going** les piles sont presque mortes; *El* **a fuse went** un plomb a sauté; **my dress is going at the seams** ma robe s'use aux coutures

(k) (*be on sale, available*) **they are going at ten francs each** on les vend dix francs pièce; **the lot went for £20** (*at auction*) le lot fut adjugé à 20 livres; **going! going! gone!** (*at auction*) une fois! deux fois! adjugé!; **let's see if there's any lunch going** allons voir si le déjeuner est prêt; **there are drinks going in the drawing room** on sert l'apéritif dans le salon; **there's a job going at the factory** il y a une place à l'usine

(l) (*introducing an action*) **to go and do sth** aller faire qch; **to go to dinner with sb** aller dîner avec qn; (*at their place*) aller dîner chez qn; **to go to** *or* **and see sb** aller voir qn; **go and see** *or esp Am* **go see what's happening** va voir ce qui se passe; **to go and look for sth** aller chercher qch; *F* **and then he went and got married!** et puis, il a eu l'idée de se marier!; *F* **what did you have to go and tell him for?** qu'est-ce qui t'a pris d'aller le lui dire?; *F* **you've gone and done it now!** vraiment, tu as tout gâché!; **he went (forward) to help her, but ...** il a fait un mouvement pour l'aider, mais ...

(m) [①**A49-50,c**] (*aux forming future*) **I'm going to tell you a story** je vais vous raconter une histoire; **the shortage is not going to last** la disette ne durera pas; **I'm going to have my own way** je vais faire comme je l'entends; **I'm not going to be cheated** je ne me laisserai pas abuser; **I was going to walk** (*intention*) j'avais l'intention d'y aller à pied; **I'm going to go to France for my holiday** je compte passer mes vacances en France; **he knew it was going to be difficult** il savait que ce serait difficile; **she was going to telephone the police when she was shot** elle s'apprêtait à téléphoner à la police quand la balle l'a frappée

(n) (*fit*) **too big to go into the basket** trop grand pour entrer dans le panier; **the key won't go in(to) the lock** la clef n'entre pas dans la serrure; **the piano won't go through the door** le piano ne passe pas par la porte; *Math* **six into twelve goes twice** douze divisé par six fait deux; **four into three won't go** trois n'est pas divisible par quatre

(o) (*belong*) **where does this book go?** où va ce livre?; **the scissors go in the drawer** les ciseaux vont *ou* se rangent dans le tiroir

(p) (*be given*) **the proceeds will go to charity** les bénéfices iront à des œuvres de charité; **the estate will go to his eldest son** la propriété va revenir à son fils aîné

(q) (*contribute*) **the qualities that go to make a great man** les qualités qui font un grand homme; **ingredients that go to make a good dish** ingrédients qui contribuent à faire un bon plat; **these reforms go some way to(wards) improving the situation** ces réformes contribuent à améliorer la situation; **this money will go to(wards) building a new school** cet argent servira à construire une nouvelle école; **to go to prove sth** servir à prouver qch; **it only goes to show that ...** cela montre bien que ...

(r) (*extend*) s'étendre; **the garden goes down to the river** le jardin s'étend jusqu'à la rivière; **that's true, as far as it goes** c'est vrai jusqu'à un certain point; **her essay's quite good, as far as it goes** malgré ses faiblesses, sa dissertation n'est pas mauvaise

(s) (*become*) devenir; **to go Communist** devenir communiste; **you'll just have to go hungry** il va falloir que tu supportes la faim; **while half the world go hungry** tandis que la moitié du monde n'a rien à manger *ou* connaît la faim; **he went cold all over** son sang s'est glacé; **the tea's gone cold** le thé a refroidi; **to go red** rougir; **to go white** blanchir; **my hair is going grey** mes cheveux grisonnent *ou* deviennent gris; **to go to the bad** mal tourner

2 *vt F* **that's really going it!** (*that's fast*) ça, c'est de la vitesse!; **to go it alone** agir tout seul; (*in business*) se lancer tout seul; *F* **I could really go a beer** je me paierais bien une bière; **to go 10** (*in gambling*) risquer 10; *Cards* **to go no/two/three trumps** annoncer sans/deux/trois atout(s); **to go one better** surenchérir (**than sb** sur qn)

▶ **go about 1** *vi* (*move*) circuler; (*of rumour*) courir; *Naut* (*turn*) virer de bord; **policemen usually go about in pairs** en général, les policiers circulent par deux; **you can't go about saying things like that!** il ne faut pas raconter des choses pareilles!; **someone has been going about saying that ...** quelqu'un a été raconter que ...; **she's been going about with that Smith boy** on l'a vue traîner avec le fils Smith

2 *vipo* **(a)** (*country*) parcourir; **to go about the streets** circuler dans les rues

(b) (*tackle*) **how to go about it** comment s'y prendre; **how do I go about getting a licence?** que dois-je faire pour obtenir un permis?

(c) (*one's work, business*) vaquer à

▶ **go across 1** *vi* traverser; **she's gone across to Mrs McGinty's** elle est en face, chez Mme McGinty **2** *vipo* (*bridge etc*) traverser

▶ **go after** *vipo* (*pursue*) essayer d'obtenir; (*person*) courir après; **she really goes after what she wants** elle fait tout pour obtenir ce qu'elle veut

▶ **go against** *vipo* (*conflict with, act contrary to*) aller contre;

to go against sb's wishes contrarier les désirs de qn; **this goes against everything I believe in** ceci est contraire à tout ce en quoi je crois; **the judgement/decision went against them** le jugement/la décision leur a été défavorable

▶ **go ahead** *vi* **(a)** *(proceed)* continuer, poursuivre; **may I say something? – go ahead** puis-je dire quelque chose? – allez-y; **to go ahead with sth** commencer qch; **he went ahead and did it** *(without hesitating)* il l'a fait sans l'ombre d'une hésitation; *(despite warnings)* rien ne l'a arrêté; **the building work was finally able to go ahead** la construction a pu commencer; **they went straight a.** ils sont allés droit devant eux; **the project is going a.** *(has been approved)* le projet a été accepté; **they're going ahead with the project after all** ils ont finalement décidé de mener le projet à bien

(b) *(go in front)* avancer; **you go (on) ahead** *(I'll follow later)* partez devant; **to go ahead of sb** devancer qn

▶ **go along** *vi* **(a)** *(walk, ride, drive etc)* avancer; **as we go along** en chemin; **we were going along quite slowly when …** nous avancions plutôt lentement quand … **(b)** *(proceed)* **I check the figures as I go along** je vérifie les chiffres au fur et à mesure; **you'll have to make it up as you go along** il faudra que tu improvises au fur et à mesure **(c)** *(go to meeting, party etc)* aller

▶ **go along with** *vipo (agree with) (person)* coopérer avec; *(sth)* approuver, accepter; **she wouldn't go along with it** elle n'était pas d'accord

▶ **go around** *vi* = **go about 1**

▶ **go at** *vipo (sb, sth)* s'attaquer à; **to go at it hard** ne pas y aller de main morte; **he was still going at it when I left** *(working hard)* il était encore à la tâche quand je suis parti; **they went at the task with a will** ils se sont mis à la tâche avec beaucoup de détermination

▶ **go away** *vi (leave)* s'en aller, partir; **go away!** va-t'en!; **to go away on business/for the weekend** s'absenter pour affaires/pour le week-end; **to go away with sth** emporter qch

▶ **go back** *vi* **(a)** *(return)* revenir, s'en retourner; *(turn back)* retourner (en arrière); *(move back)* reculer; **go back! it's dangerous!** recule! c'est dangereux!; **to go back home** retourner *ou* rentrer chez soi; **to go back to Paris** retourner à Paris; **he's never gone back** *(to that place)* il n'y est jamais retourné; **let's go back the way we came** reprenons le même chemin qu'à l'aller; **to go back two paces** faire deux pas en arrière; **to go back to the beginning** reprendre depuis le début; **he went back to his reading** il s'est replongé dans sa lecture; **to go back to sleep** se rendormir; **to go back to one's old ways** retomber dans ses anciennes habitudes; **to go back to doing sth** *(resume task, habit)* se remettre à faire qch; **he went back to teaching** il est revenu à l'enseignement

(b) *(date back)* remonter **(to** à); **there are records going back to 1700** il y a des récits qui remontent à 1700; **we go back a long way** *(our acquaintance)* ça fait longtemps qu'on se connaît

(c) *(extend)* **the garden goes back 40 metres behind the house** le jardin s'étend sur 40 mètres derrière la maison

(d) the clocks go back tonight on retarde les pendules d'une heure cette nuit

▶ **go back on** *vipo (abandon, alter) (decision, promise)* revenir sur

▶ **go before 1** *vi* précéder; *Euph* **those who have gone before** *(the dead)* ceux qui nous ont précédés **2** *vipo (tribunal, committee etc)* se présenter devant; *Jur* comparaître devant; **the case goes before the court/the judge tomorrow** l'affaire passe au tribunal/devant le juge demain; **it goes before the committee tomorrow** elle passe en commission demain

▶ **go below** *vi Naut* descendre

▶ **go by 1** *vi* **(a)** *(pass)* passer; **to watch people going by** regarder passer les gens; *Fig* **to let an opportunity go by** laisser passer une occasion

(b) *(elapse)* s'écouler; **half an hour went by** une demi-heure s'est écoulée; **as the years go by** à mesure que les années passent

2 *vipo* **(a)** *(judge on the basis of)* juger d'après; **don't go by what he says/his opinion** ne juge pas d'après ce qu'il dit/ne tiens pas compte de ses opinions; **to go by appearances** juger d'après les apparences

(b) *(follow)* **to go by the rules** suivre *ou* respecter les règles; **promotion goes by seniority** l'avancement se fait à l'ancienneté; **go by your sister's example** suis l'exemple de ta sœur

(c) *(be known by)* **to go by a different/false name** être connu sous un nom différent/un faux nom; **the product goes by the name of 'Bango' in France** ce produit est vendu sous le nom de 'Bango' en France

▶ **go down 1** *vi* **(a)** *(descend)* descendre; *(of sun)* se coucher; *(of ship)* sombrer; **going down!** *(in lift)* on descend!, pour descendre!; **go down and answer the door** descends ouvrir; **to go down on one's knees** se mettre à genoux; *Sl* **to go down on sb** *(perform oral sex on)* sucer qn; *F* **to go down with flu** attraper la grippe; **to have gone down in the world** avoir connu des jours meilleurs; **the captain went down with his ship** le capitaine a sombré avec son navire; **I'm not going to go down without a fight** *(be defeated)* je me battrai jusqu'à la fin

(b) *(decrease) (of floods, temperature)* baisser, s'abaisser; *(of wind)* baisser, tomber; *(of prices, value)* baisser; **to go d. in sb's estimation** baisser dans l'estime de qn

(c) *(be received)* **to go down well** *(of drink)* se laisser boire; *(of food)* se laisser manger; *(of entertainment, speech, suggestion)* plaire, être bien reçu; **he went down in history as a tyrant** l'histoire a retenu de lui l'image d'un tyran

(d) *(shrink) (of swelling)* désenfler, se dégonfler; *(of tyre, balloon)* se dégonfler

(e) *(extend)* continuer; *(to end of page etc)* aller jusqu'à; **the mineshaft goes down three hundred metres** le puits de mine a trois cents mètres de profondeur

(f) *Br Univ (esp Oxford and Cambridge)* **to go down (from university)** *(at end of studies)* quitter l'université; *(at end of term)* partir en vacances

(g) *Cards (bridge)* chuter

(h) *US F* **what's going down?** *(happening)* qu'est-ce qui se passe?

2 *vipo (descend) (hill, ladder, street)* descendre; *Sch* **to go down a class/a grade** descendre d'une classe; **some of his food went down the wrong way** il a avalé de travers; **my weight has gone down a few pounds** j'ai perdu quelques kilos; *Fig* **I don't want to go down that road** je ne veux pas m'engager là-dedans

▶ **go for** *vipo* **(a)** *(attack) (person)* attaquer, tomber sur; **go for him!** *(to dog)* attaque!; **they went for each other in court** *(physically)* ils se sont empoignés devant le tribunal; *(verbally)* ils se sont disputés *ou F* engueulés devant le tribunal

(b) *(strive to attain)* essayer d'obtenir; **if you really want the job, go for it!** si tu veux vraiment le poste, mets-y le paquet!; **with his next jump, he's going for the gold** avec son prochain saut, il vise la médaille d'or

(c) *(like)* être porté sur, être attiré par; **I don't go for him much** *(don't like him)* je ne l'aime pas tellement; *(don't think him attractive)* il ne m'attire pas spécialement; **tabloid newspapers go for stories like those** la presse à scandales adore ce genre d'histoires

(d) *(choose)* prendre; **I'll go for the blue one** je prendrai le bleu

(e) she's got a lot going for her elle a bien des atouts dans son jeu; **the third proposal has a lot going for it** la troisième proposition a bien des avantages

(f) the same goes for you ça s'applique à vous aussi

▶ **go forth** *vi Rel* **go forth and multiply** croissez et multipliez; *Lit* **the word went forth that …** on a fait savoir que …; *Hum* **the word has gone forth that the boss would like …** le patron a fait savoir qu'il voudrait …

▶ **go forward** *vi* (s')avancer; **the clocks go forward tomorrow** on avance les pendules demain; **if this scheme goes forward …** si ce projet est accepté …

▶ **go in 1** *vi* **(a)** *(enter)* entrer, rentrer; **let's go in!** entrons!; **it's too big, it won't go in** c'est trop grand, ça ne rentrera pas **(b)** *(of sun)* se cacher **(c)** *Cr* prendre son tour au guichet **(d)** *Mil etc F (attack)* attaquer **2** *vipo (enter) (house, room etc)* entrer dans, rentrer dans

▶ **go in for** *vipo* **(a)** *(use, produce, show interest in)* **they don't go in for injections so much nowadays** ils ne sont pas tellement pour les piqûres de nos jours; **why do scientists go in for all that jargon?** pourquoi est-ce que les scientifiques utilisent tout ce jargon?; **this publisher doesn't really go in for fiction** cet éditeur ne fait pas tellement dans le roman; **we don't go in for pop music** nous ne sommes pas très musique pop

(b) *(engage in)* s'adonner à, se consacrer à; **he doesn't go in for team sports** il n'est pas très porté sur les sports d'équipe; **to go in for painting** *(as hobby)* faire de la peinture; **to go in for teaching** *(as career)* entrer dans l'enseignement

(c) *(enter)* **to go in for an examination** se présenter à un examen; **to go in for a competition** prendre part à un concours

▶ **go into** *vipo* **(a)** *(enter)* entrer dans, rentrer dans; **she's gone into hospital** elle est (r)entrée à l'hôpital; **to go into fits of laughter** avoir des crises de fou rire; **to go into the**

army s'engager (dans l'armée); (*be called up*) partir au régiment; **to go into teaching** (*as career*) entrer dans l'enseignement; **to go into a convent** entrer au couvent

(**b**) (*examine*) (*question*) examiner, étudier; **I shall go into the matter** je vais m'occuper de l'affaire; **to go into the reasons (given) for sth** rechercher les raisons de qch

(**c**) (*explain, provide the reasons for*) expliquer; **to go into details** entrer dans les détails

(**d**) (*embark on*) (*description*) s'embarquer dans, se lancer dans

(**e**) (*collide with*) entrer dans

▶ **go in with** *vipo* (*person in a business etc*) se joindre à

▶ **go off 1** *vi* (**a**) (*leave*) partir, s'en aller; *Th* quitter la scène; *F* **she's gone off and left him** elle l'a quitté; **he went off with the woman next door** il est parti avec la voisine; **to go off with sth** emporter qch, enlever qch

(**b**) (*deteriorate*) (*of milk*) tourner; (*of butter*) rancir; (*of fish, meat*) se gâter; (*of tennis player etc*) perdre sa forme

(**c**) (*proceed*) **everything went off well** tout a bien marché, tout s'est bien passé; **how did the concert go off?** comment le concert s'est-il passé?

(**d**) (*cease working, be disconnected*) **the power/light went off** l'électricité a été coupée/la lumière s'est éteinte

(**e**) (*of gun*) partir, se décharger; (*of bomb*) éclater; **the pistol didn't go off** le coup n'est pas parti; **the firework went off in my face** la fusée m'a explosé dans la figure

(**f**) (*of alarm*) se déclencher; (*of alarm clock*) sonner

(**g**) (*go to sleep*) s'endormir

2 *vipo* (*lose liking for*) (*sth*) perdre le goût de; **I've gone off cheese** je ne mange plus de fromage; **I've completely gone off him** (*husband, boyfriend*) je me suis complètement détaché de lui; (*actor, singer, writer*) je ne l'aime plus du tout; **funny how you can go off people** c'est drôle comme on se lasse des gens parfois; **I've gone off the idea** cette idée ne me dit plus rien

▶ **go on 1** *vi* (**a**) (*continue*) continuer (**doing sth** à faire qch); **and that's not all, he went on** et ce n'est pas tout, a-t-il poursuivi; **go on with what you were doing** continuez ce que vous étiez en train de faire; **I must go on with my work** il me faut continuer mon travail; **as time went on her intentions became clear** à mesure que le temps passait, ses intentions devenaient plus claires; **the lecture went on rather a long time** le cours a duré assez longtemps; **I have enough to be going on with** j'en ai assez pour le moment; **to go on to another question** passer à une autre question; **go on, take one** allez, prends-en un; **go on, try it** allez, essaie-le; **can I? – yes, go on** est-ce je peux? – oui, vas-y; *Old-fashioned F* **go on (with you)!** allons donc!

(**b**) (*talk excessively, unreasonably*) parler à n'en plus finir (**about** de); **how he goes on!** impossible de l'arrêter!; **once he starts he goes on and on** une fois qu'il est parti, il n'y a plus moyen de l'arrêter; **what are you going on about now?** qu'est-ce que vous racontez?; **she went on a bit** elle s'est un peu étendue sur la question; **he's always going on at me** il est toujours à me faire des remontrances

(**c**) (*happen*) **this has been going on for years** cela fait des années que ça dure; **what's going on here?** qu'est-ce qui se passe ici?

(**d**) (*begin to operate, be connected*) se mettre en marche; (*of streetlight*) s'allumer

(**e**) *Th* (*walk on stage*) entrer en scène; **the band went on at 10 o'clock** le groupe est entré en scène à 10 heures

(**f**) (*fit*) **I can't get the lid to go on** je n'arrive pas à mettre le couvercle; **these shoes won't go on** ces chaussures ne vont pas; **these jeans won't go on any more** je ne rentre plus dans ce jean

2 *vipo* (**a**) (*enter*) (*boat, train*) monter dans

(**b**) (*embark on*) **to go on a journey/a holiday** partir en voyage/en vacances; **to go on a diet** se mettre au régime; **to go on social security** s'inscrire au chômage

(**c**) (*approach*) aller sur; **she's two going on three** elle va sur ses trois ans

(**d**) (*be guided by*) se fonder sur; **the police have nothing to go on** la police n'a rien sur quoi se fonder

▶ **go on for** *vipo* (*approach*) approcher de, aller sur; **he's going on for forty** il va sur ses quarante ans

▶ **go out** *vi* (**a**) (*leave house etc*) sortir; **to go out for a meal** aller au restaurant; **she's gone out to get a paper** elle est sortie (pour) acheter un journal; **to go out for a walk** sortir se promener; **we don't go out much in the evenings** nous ne sortons pas beaucoup le soir; **she was dressed to go out** elle était en tenue de ville; **she's decided to go out to work** elle a décidé de travailler à l'extérieur; **what time did he go out to work?** à quelle heure est-il parti travailler?; *Ind* **to go out (on strike)** se mettre en grève; **the magic seemed to have gone out of their marriage** leur mariage semblait avoir perdu de son charme; **her heart went out to them** elle a ressenti de la compassion pour eux; **my heart goes out to you** je partage votre douleur; *Iron* j'en ai les larmes aux yeux

(**b**) (*date*) **they've been going out (together) for a month** ils sortent ensemble depuis un mois; **to go out with sb** sortir avec qn, fréquenter qn; **he went out with her for two years before they got married** il l'a fréquentée pendant deux ans avant de l'épouser

(**c**) (*of fire, light*) s'éteindre; **the lights go out at midnight** on éteint les lumières à minuit; *F* **I went out like a light** (*fell asleep*) je me suis endormi tout de suite

(**d**) (*of tide*) baisser, se retirer

(**e**) (*become unfashionable*) passer de mode, se démoder

(**f**) *Sp* (*be eliminated*) être éliminé, *F* se faire sortir; **I bet they go out in the next round** je parie qu'ils vont être éliminés à la prochaine manche; **Lendl went out to Becker** Lendl s'est fait sortir par Becker

(**g**) (*of letter*) être envoyé

(**h**) *TV, Rad* (*of programme*) être diffusé

▶ **go over 1** *vi* (**a**) (*cross*) **I went over and tapped him on the shoulder** je suis allé vers lui et je lui ai tapé sur l'épaule

(**b**) (*transfer allegiance*) **to go over to the enemy** passer à l'ennemi; **to go over to the other side** changer de parti; **he's thinking of going over to cigars** il songe à passer aux cigares

(**c**) (*be received*) **to go over well/badly** (*of suggestion, joke*) bien/mal passer; (*of play*) être bien/mal reçu; *F* **to go over big** avoir un grand succès

(**d**) (*turn upside down*) se retourner

2 *vipo* (**a**) (*pass across*) **to go over a bridge** passer un pont; **to go over a river** passer par-dessus une rivière; **the ball went over the wall** la balle est passée par-dessus le mur

(**b**) (*examine*) (*accounts, report*) examiner, revoir; (*papers etc*) passer en revue; (*document*) relire; (*lesson*) repasser, revoir; **to go over sth in one's mind** repasser qch dans son esprit

(**c**) (*discuss*) parler de; *Fig* **we are just going over the same old ground** on ressasse les mêmes choses

(**d**) (*rehearse*) refaire; (*bars of music*) rejouer; (*sing*) rechanter

▶ **go round 1** *vi* (**a**) (*make a detour*) faire un détour

(**b**) (*spin*) tourner; **my head's going round** la tête me tourne

(**c**) (*visit*) **I said I'd go round (and see her)** j'ai dit que j'irais la voir; **he's gone round to a friend's** il est allé chez un ami

(**d**) (*circulate*) (*of rumour*) circuler, courir; (*of bottle, cold, flu*) circuler

(**e**) (*suffice*) **the food only just went round** il y avait juste assez de nourriture pour tout le monde; **to make the food go round** ménager la nourriture; **there isn't enough to go round** il n'y en a pas assez pour tout le monde

2 *vipo* (**a**) (*make a detour by*) **to go round the long way** faire un long détour

(**b**) (*tour*) (*museum*) faire le tour de; **I hate going round the shops** j'ai horreur de faire les boutiques; **they went round the neighbourhood looking for their cat** ils ont fait le tour du quartier pour chercher leur chat

(**c**) (*be sufficient for*) suffire pour; **will the soup go round twenty?** est-ce qu'il y aura assez de soupe pour vingt?

▶ **go through 1** *vi* (**a**) (*travel through, penetrate*) passer, traverser; **the gates were open and we went through** les barrières étaient ouvertes et nous sommes passés

(**b**) (*be completed, accepted*) (*of deal*) être conclu; (*of divorce*) être prononcé; *Parl* (*of bill*) passer

2 *vipo* (**a**) (*penetrate*) traverser

(**b**) (*suffer*) (*trials and tribulations*) subir, essuyer; **he went through agony** (*wondering what had happened*) il était au supplice; **in spite of all she had gone through** malgré tout ce qu'elle avait enduré

(**c**) (*complete*) (*formalities*) remplir

(**d**) (*examine*) (*documents*) examiner; (*lesson, accounts*) revoir

(**e**) (*search*) (*suitcases*) fouiller; **to go through sb's pockets** fouiller dans les poches de qn, *F* faire les poches à qn

(**f**) (*use up*) (*money*) dépenser; (*supplies, paper, toner etc*) utiliser; (*food*) consommer; **to go through all one's money** dépenser tout son argent; **have we gone through the salmon already?** est-ce qu'on a déjà fini le saumon?

▶ **go through with** *vipo* (*carry out*) réaliser, exécuter, aller jusqu'au bout de; **she decided that she couldn't go through**

with the wedding elle a décidé qu'elle ne pouvait pas se marier; **I mean to go through with it** j'ai l'intention d'aller jusqu'au bout

▶ **go together** *vi* (a) (*harmonize*) aller ensemble (b) (*date*) sortir ensemble; **they've been going together for a long time** ils sortent ensemble depuis longtemps

▶ **go under 1** *vi* (a) (*of drowning man*) couler, s'enfoncer; (*of ship*) couler, sombrer (b) (*go bankrupt*) faire faillite (c) (*under anaesthetic*) s'endormir **2** *vipo* **to go under a false/different name** utiliser *ou* prendre un faux nom/un nom différent; **since the divorce she's been going under her old name** depuis le divorce, elle utilise son nom de jeune fille; **a glue that goes under the name of Stikit** une colle qui s'appelle Stikit

▶ **go up** *vi* (a) (*climb, rise*) monter; **to go up to bed** monter se coucher; **to go up in a helicopter** monter en hélicoptère; **going up!** (*in lift*) on monte!, pour monter!; *Th* **before the curtain goes up** avant le lever du rideau; **a shout went up from the crowd** un cri s'éleva de la foule; *Br Univ* **to go up (to Oxford/***etc***)** entrer à l'université (d'Oxford/*etc*); **to go up in the world** faire son chemin

(b) (*of prices, temperature etc*) monter; **bread is going up** (*in price*) le pain augmente; **to go up in sb's estimation** monter dans l'estime de qn

(c) (*explode, be destroyed*) sauter; **to go up in flames** se mettre à flamber; *Fig* **their plans went up in smoke** leurs projets sont partis en fumée

▶ **go up to** *vipo* (a) (*approach*) **to go up to sb/sth** se diriger vers qn/qch; **the path goes up to the front door** le chemin mène à la porte d'entrée (b) (*go as far as*) **the book only goes up to the end of the war** le livre ne va que jusqu'à la fin de la guerre; **I will go up to £100** je veux bien aller jusqu'à 100 livres

▶ **go with** *vipo* (a) (*accompany*) aller de pair avec; **mathematical ability usually goes with skill at chess** des capacités en mathématiques vont souvent de pair avec un don pour les échecs; **a company car goes with the job** ce poste donne droit à une voiture de fonction

(b) (*harmonize with*) s'accorder avec, aller avec; (*of colours*) se marier avec; **the carpet doesn't go with the furniture** le tapis n'est pas assorti aux meubles; **this behaviour doesn't go with what I know about her** un tel comportement ne cadre pas avec ce que je sais d'elle

(c) (*date*) (*person*) sortir avec, fréquenter; **is she going with someone?** est-ce qu'elle sort avec quelqu'un?

(d) (*have sex with*) coucher avec

▶ **go without 1** *vi* (*not have sth*) **I'd rather go without** je préfère m'en passer; **as children they often went without** lorsqu'ils étaient enfants, ils ont souvent été privés; **they went without so that the children got enough to eat** ils ont dû se priver pour que les enfants aient assez à manger **2** *vipo* (*not have*) se passer de; **I went without breakfast so I wouldn't be late** je me suis passé de petit déjeuner pour ne pas être en retard

goad¹ [gəʊd] *n also Fig* aiguillon *m*

goad² *vt* (*cattle*) aiguillonner, piquer; (*sb's curiosity*) piquer, stimuler; **to g. sb into doing sth** talonner qn jusqu'à ce qu'il fasse qch

▶ **goad on** *vtsep* aiguillonner; **don't g. him on!** arrête de l'exciter!

go-ahead *F* **1** *adj* (*enterprising*) entreprenant **2** *n* **to give sb the g.** donner le feu vert à qn; **to give sth the g.** donner le feu vert pour qch

goal [gəʊl] *n* (a) (*aim*) but *m*, objectif *m*; **to achieve a g.** atteindre un but, réaliser un objectif; **my g. is in sight** j'approche de mon but *ou* du but (b) *Fb etc* but *m*; (*structure*) but, cages *fpl*; **Macleod was in g. for Rangers** Macleod était dans les buts des Rangers; **g. kick** coup *m* de pied au but; **g. line** ligne *f* de but; **g. scorer** buteur *m*; **the leading** *or* **top g. scorer** le meilleur buteur

goalkeeper ['gəʊlki:pər], *F* **goalie** ['gəʊlɪ] *n Fb etc* gardien *m* de but, goal *m*

goalless ['gəʊllɪs] *adj Fb etc* **g. draw** match *m* nul 0-0

goalmouth ['gəʊlmaʊθ] *n Fb etc* entrée *f* de but; **there was no shortage of g. incident** il y avait beaucoup d'action devant les cages

goalpost ['gəʊlpəʊst] *n Fb etc* montant *m ou* poteau *m* (de but); *Fig* **to move** *or* **shift the goalposts** changer les règles du jeu

goat [gəʊt] *n* (a) chèvre *f*; **she g.** chèvre, *F* bique *f*; **he g.** bouc *m*; **g.'s milk** lait *m* de chèvre; **g.'s (milk) cheese** fromage *m* de chèvre; *Fig F* **it really gets my g.!** ça me met en boule!, ça me tape sur les nerfs!; *Fig* **to act** *or* **play the g.** faire l'idiot (b) *Pej* **silly old g.** (*old man*) imbécile *m*; *F* **a randy old g.** un obsédé (sexuel)

goatee [gəʊ'ti:] *n* (*beard*) barbiche *f*, bouc *m*

goatherd ['gəʊthɜ:d] *n* chevrier, -ière

goatskin ['gəʊtskɪn] *n* (a) peau *f* de chèvre *ou F* de bique (b) (*bottle*) outre *f* (en peau de bouc)

goatsucker ['gəʊtsʌkər] *n Am* (*bird*) engoulevent *m*

gob¹ [gɒb] *n* (a) *Br F* (*spittle*) crachat *m*, *Vulg* mollard *m*; **a g. of spit** un crachat (b) *esp Br Sl* (*mouth*) gueule *f*; **shut your g.!** ferme-la!, ta gueule!

gob² *vi Br Sl* (*spit*) cracher (**at** sur)

gobble¹ ['gɒb(ə)l] *vt* (a) (*eat*) avaler gloutonnement, dévorer, *F* bouffer; **don't g. (your food)!** (*to child*) n'avale pas si vite (b) *Vulg Sl* **to g. sb** (*perform oral sex on*) sucer qn

gobble² *n* (*of turkey*) glouglou *m*

gobble³ *vi* (*of turkey*) glouglouter

▶ **gobble down** *vtsep* (*eat quickly*) avaler gloutonnement, *F* bouffer

▶ **gobble up** *vtsep* (*eat quickly*) engloutir, engouffrer, *F* bouffer; *Fig* (*money, pay rise*) engloutir; *Fig* **the empire gobbled up these territories** l'empire a absorbé ces territoires

gobbledegook, gobbledygook ['gɒb(ə)ldɪgu:k] *n F* charabia *m*

go-between *n* intermédiaire *mf*; **to act** *or* **serve as a g.** servir d'intermédiaire (**to** à)

goblet ['gɒblɪt] *n* verre *m* à pied; *Lit* (*drinking cup*) coupe *f*

goblin ['gɒblɪn] *n* lutin *m*

gobo ['gəʊbəʊ] *n* (*camera matte*) drapeau *m*

gobshite ['gɒbʃaɪt] *n Sl* (*bastard*) trouduc *m*

gob-smacked ['gɒbsmækt] *adj Br Sl* **I was g.** j'en étais tout estomaqué

gobstopper ['gɒbstɒpər] *n Br* gros bonbon *m* rond

go-by *n F* **to give sb the g.** snober qn

GOC [dʒi:əʊ'si:] *n Mil* (*abbr* **general officer commanding**) général *m* commandant en chef

go-cart *n* (a) (*child's toy*) petit chariot *m*; *Sp* kart *m*; **g. racing** karting *m* (b) *Am* (*baby-walker*) trotteur *m*; (*push-chair*) poussette *f*

God [gɒd] *n* Dieu *m*; *Rel* **G. the Father, G. the Son and G. the Holy Ghost** Dieu le père, le fils et le Saint-Esprit; **a man of G.** un homme de Dieu; **to play G.** se prendre pour Dieu; **G. willing** s'il plaît à Dieu; **I wish to G. ...** plût à Dieu ...; **in G.'s name, in the name of G.** au nom de Dieu; *F* **for G.'s sake!, for the love of G.!** pour l'amour de Dieu!; *F* **what in G.'s name are you doing?** que faites-vous là, grand Dieu!; *F* **G. knows** Dieu seul le sait; *F* **she's G. knows where** elle est Dieu sait où; *F* **oh G.!, my G.!** mon Dieu!; **G. forbid** à Dieu ne plaise!; *F* **he thinks he's G.'s gift to women** il croit que toutes les femmes vont tomber à ses pieds; **he's not exactly G.'s gift to women** ce n'est pas vraiment l'homme dont rêvent toutes les femmes; **act of G.** force *f* majeure; **an act of G.** un cas de force majeure

god [gɒd] *n* dieu *m*; **the g. of war** le dieu de la guerre; **a river g.** une divinité de la rivière; **to make a g. of money** diviniser l'argent; *Th F* **the gods** (*gallery*) *F* le poulailler

god-awful *adj F* dégueulasse

god-botherer ['gɒdbɒðərər] *n F* cul-bénit *m*, *pl* culs-bénits

godchild, *pl* **-children** ['gɒdtʃaɪld, -tʃɪldrən] *n* filleul, -eule

goddamn ['gɒd'dæm] *esp US Sl* **1** *int* nom de Dieu! **2** *adj* (*also* **god-damned**) fichu, sacré; **don't be such a g. fool!** ne sois donc pas si bête!

goddaughter ['gɒddɔ:tər] *n* filleule *f*

goddess ['gɒdɪs] *n* déesse *f*; *Fig* **a g. of the screen, a screen g.** une idole du grand écran

godfather ['gɒdfɑ:ðər] *n* parrain *m*

god-fearing ['gɒdfi:rɪŋ] *adj* (*person*) très religieux; **decent g. folk** les gens croyants bien comme il faut

godforsaken ['gɒdfəseɪk(ə)n] *adj* (*place, town*) perdu; **what a g. place!** quel bled!

godhead ['gɒdhed] *n* divinité *f*

godless ['gɒdlɪs] *adj* (*person, action etc*) impie

godlike ['gɒdlaɪk] *adj* divin, de dieu

godliness ['gɒdlɪnɪs] *n* piété *f*

godly ['gɒdlɪ] *adj* dévot, pieux; **to lead a g. life** vivre pieusement

godmother ['gɒdmʌðər] *n* marraine *f*

godparent ['gɒdpeərənt] *n* (*woman*) marraine *f*; (*man*) parrain *m*; **my godparents** mon parrain et ma marraine

godsend ['gɒdsend] *n* aubaine *f*; **this money is a g. to him** cet argent est un don du ciel; **the president's gaffe was a g. to the opposition** la gaffe du président a été une aubaine pour l'opposition

godson ['gɒdsʌn] *n* filleul *m*

godsquad ['gɒdskwɒd] *n F* bondieusards *mpl*

goer ['gəʊər] *n* (a) **to be a good/bad g.** (*of horse*) courir bien/mal; (*of car*) marcher bien/mal (b) *F* **she's a real g.!** (*promiscuous*) c'est une femme facile; (*good in bed*) c'est un bon coup!

-goer ['gəʊər] *suff* **church/cinema/theatre-g.** personne qui va souvent à l'église/au cinéma/au théâtre
GO-error [gəʊ] *n Mktg* erreur *f* d'adoption
gofer, gopher ['gəʊfər] *n* **(a)** *esp Am F (menial assistant)* (*male*) grouillot *m*, homme *m* à tout faire; (*female*) bonne *f* à tout faire **(b)** *Comptr* (serveur *m*) gopher *m*
go-getter ['gəʊgetər] *n F* battant, -ante
go-getting ['gəʊgetɪŋ] *adj F (person, approach)* entreprenant, dynamique
goggle ['gɒg(ə)l] *vi* (*of person*) rouler de gros yeux; (*of eyes*) être saillant; **to g. at sb/sth** regarder qn/qch en roulant de gros yeux
gogglebox ['gɒg(ə)lbɒks] *n Br F* télé *f*
goggle-eyed *adj F* qui a les yeux en boules de loto; **they watched g.** ils regardaient, les yeux en boules de loto
goggles ['gɒg(ə)lz] *npl* (*for motorcyclist*) lunettes *fpl* protectrices *ou* de moto; (*for skier*) lunettes (de ski); (*for diver, swimmer*) lunettes (de plongée); *Ind* lunettes de travail; (*for welder*) lunettes (protectrices); *Hum* (*spectacles*) carreaux *mpl*
go-go *adj* **g. dancer** danseuse *f* (*dans une boîte de nuit etc*)
going ['gəʊɪŋ] **1** *adj* **(a)** (*functioning*) qui marche; **to start** *or* **set sth g.** mettre qch en marche; **the business is a g. concern** c'est une affaire qui marche; **to be sold as a g. concern** à vendre avec fonds
(b) (*current*) **the g. price** *or* **rate** le prix courant *ou* actuel
2 *n* **(a)** (*progress*) **that's very good g.!** voilà qui n'est pas mal du tout!; **it was slow g.** (*walking, climbing*) on progressait lentement; (*working, learning*) ça avancait lentement; **it was hard g.** (*walking, climbing*) on progressait difficilement; (*learning, working*) c'était dur; *Typ* **g. to press** mise *f* sous presse
(b) (*leaving*) départ *m*
(c) *Horseracing etc* (*condition of ground*) état *m* du sol; **the g. is rough** le chemin est rude; *Horseracing* **good/heavy g.** bon terrain/terrain lourd; *Fig* **heavy g.** (*of film, book etc*) indigeste; *Fig* **it's heavy g. getting him to talk** on a du mal à le faire parler; *Fig* **while the g. is good** tant que c'est favorable; **to get out while the g.'s good** partir pendant que la voie est libre
-going ['gəʊɪŋ] *suff* **(a) theatre/cinema-g.** fréquentation *f* des théâtres/des cinémas **(b) slow/fast-g.** qui marche lentement/vite
going-away *adj* **g. dress** robe *f* de voyage de noce; **a g. party/present** une soirée/un cadeau d'adieu
going back *n* (*return*) retour *m*; (*retreat*) recul *m*; **g. on one's word** manque *m* de parole; **there's no g. now** il n'y a pas moyen de revenir en arrière
going-concern status *n Com* continuité *f* d'exploitation
going-over *n F* **to give sb a g.** (*beating*) tabasser qn; (*criticism*) sonner les cloches à qn; **the burglars had given the flat a real g.** les cambrioleurs avaient laissé l'appartement sens dessus dessous; **the auditors gave the accounts a thorough g.** les experts ont soigneusement examiné les comptes
going-rate pricing *n Mktg* alignement *m* sur les prix du marché
goings-on ['gəʊɪŋzɒn] *npl F* (*events*) événements *mpl*; (*behaviour*) conduite *f*; **the g. of the Royals** les activités *fpl* des membres de la famille royale; **there were strange g.** il se passait de drôles de choses; **what extraordinary g.!** quelles histoires extraordinaires!
goitre, *US* **goiter** ['gɔɪtər] *n Med* goitre *m*
go-kart *n Sp* kart *m*; **g. racing** karting *m*
gold [gəʊld] **1** *n* **(a)** or *m*; **to pay sb in g.** payer qn en or; **g. brooch/necklace** broche/collier en or; **g. braid** (*on uniform etc*) galon *m* doré; **g. bullion** or en barres *ou* en lingots; **g. coin** pièce *f* d'or; **g. content** teneur *f* en or; **g. currency** *or* **money** monnaie *f* d'or; **g. filling** (*in tooth*) obturation *f* à l'or *ou* en or; **g. lamé dress** robe lamée d'or; **g. leaf** *or* **foil** feuille *f* d'or, or en feuille; **g. plate** plaqué *m* or; *Mus* **g. record** disque *m* d'or; *Fin* **g. reserve** réserve *f* d'or
(b) *Sp* **g.** (**medal**) médaille *f* d'or; **to win g., to win a g. medal** gagner la médaille d'or
(c) (*colour*) or *m*; **the reds and golds of autumn** les rouges et les ors de l'automne
2 *adj* (*made of gold*) en or; (*gold-coloured*) doré; **g. dress** robe couleur d'or *ou* dorée; **g. paint** peinture dorée
goldcrest ['gəʊldkrest] *n* (*bird*) roitelet *m* huppé
gold-digger *n* chercheur *m* d'or; *Pej Fig* (*woman*) croqueuse *f* de diamants
gold dust *n* poussière *f* d'or; *Fig* **to be g.** valoir de l'or
golden ['gəʊld(ə)n] *adj* **(a)** (*made of gold*) en or; *Myth* **the G. Fleece** la Toison d'or; *Bible, Fig* **to worship the g. calf** adorer le veau d'or; *Fig* **g. goose** poule *f* aux œufs d'or; *Fin* **g. handshake/parachute** (grosse) indemnité *f* de départ; *Fig* **to give sb a g. hello** faire un pont d'or à qn; *Com Fig* **g. share** action *f* privilégiée
(b) (*gold-coloured*) d'or; **G. Delicious** golden *f*; **g. hair** cheveux d'or; **the G. State** = la Californie; **g. syrup** = sirop *m* de sucre roux
(c) (*excellent, best*) **the g. age** l'âge *m* d'or; **g. boy/girl** (*of tennis etc*) enfant *mf* chéri/chérie; **the g. mean** le juste milieu; **a g. opportunity** une occasion en or; **the g. rule** la règle d'or
(d) (*commemorating 50 years*) **g. jubilee** jubilé *m*; **g. wedding** noces *fpl* d'or
golden eagle *n* aigle *m* royal
Golden Gate Bridge *n* **the G.** le Golden Gate
golden oldie *n Mus F* vieux tube *m*; *F* **he's a g.** il a de beaux restes
golden pheasant *n* faisan *m* d'or
goldenrod ['gəʊld(ə)nrɒd] *n Bot* (*plant*) verge *f* d'or
gold fever *n* fièvre *f* de l'or
goldfield ['gəʊldfi:ld] *n* champ *m* *ou* région *f* aurifère
goldfinch ['gəʊldfɪntʃ] *n* chardonneret *m*
goldfish ['gəʊldfɪʃ] *n* poisson *m* rouge; **g. bowl** bocal *m* à poissons rouges; *Fig* **it's like living in a g. bowl** c'est comme être en vitrine
Goldilocks ['gəʊldɪlɒks] *n* Boucles d'Or *f*
gold mine *n also Fig* mine *f* d'or
gold-plated *adj* plaqué or
gold-rimmed *adj* **g. spectacles** lunettes *fpl* à monture dorée
gold rush *n Hist* ruée *f* vers l'or
goldsmith ['gəʊldsmɪθ] *n* orfèvre *m*
gold standard *n Econ* étalon-or *m*
gold-tipped *adj* à bout doré
golf[1] [gɒlf] *n Sp* golf *m*; **g. ball** balle *f* de golf; (*on typewriter*) boule *f*; **g. ball (typewriter)** machine *f* à écrire à boule; **g. club** (*for hitting ball*) canne *f* *ou* crosse *f* de golf, club *m*; (*association*) club de golf; **g. course/links** terrain *m* *ou* parcours *m* de golf, golf *m*; **g. umbrella** parapluie *m* de golf
golf[2] *vi* jouer au golf; **I went golfing yesterday** hier, j'ai fait du golf *ou* j'ai joué au golf
golfer ['gɒlfər] *n* golfeur, -euse, joueur, -euse de golf
golfing ['gɒlfɪŋ] *n* golf *m*; **g. holiday** stage *m* de golf
Goliath [gə'laɪəθ] *n Bible, Fig* Goliath *m*
golliwog ['gɒlɪwɒg] *n* = poupée *f* en étoffe représentant un Noir
golly ['gɒlɪ] *int Old-fashioned F* fichtre!, mince (alors)!
goloshes [gə'lɒʃɪz] *npl* = **galoshes**
gonad ['gɒnæd, 'gəʊ-] *n Biol* gonade *f*
gondola ['gɒndələ] *n* **(a)** (*boat*) gondole *f* **(b)** *Av* (*of airship, balloon*) nacelle *f*; *Am* (*cable car*) nacelle *ou* cabine *f* de téléphérique **(c)** *Am Rail* **g. (car)** wagon *m* plat **(d)** (*in supermarket etc*) gondole *f*
gondolier [gɒndə'lɪər] *n* gondolier *m*
gone [gɒn] **1** *pp see* **go**[2] **2** *adj* **(a) to be g.** (*dead*) être mort, être parti; **when I'm g.** quand je ne serai plus là; *F* **oh well, that's that g.!** (*of broken machine etc*) bon, ben c'est foutu! **(b) to be pretty far g.** (*drunk*) être complètement bourré; (*on drugs*) être complètement camé; (*of dying patient*) être très mal; *F* **to be six months g.** (*pregnant*) être enceinte de six mois; **how far g. is she?** (pregnant) elle est enceinte de combien? **(c)** *F* **g. on sb** amoureux *ou F* toqué de qn **(d)** (*past*) **it's g. ten o'clock** il est plus de dix heures, il est dix heures passées
goner ['gɒnər] *n F* mourant, -ante; **I thought she was a g.** je pensais qu'elle allait mourir; **if the engine fails now, we'll all be goners** si le moteur tombe en panne, on va tous crever *ou* on est tous foutus; *Fig* **I'm a g. if she finds out where I've been** je suis fichu *ou* foutu si elle apprend où je suis allé
gong [gɒŋ] *n* **(a)** *Mus etc* gong *m*; **to sound the g.** faire retentir le gong **(b)** *Br F* (*medal*) médaille *f*; **he was wearing all his gongs** il exhibait toute sa batterie de cuisine
gonna ['gənə] *F* = **going to**
gonorrhoea, *US* **gonorrhea** [gɒnə'rɪə] *n Med* blennorragie *f*; **to have g.** avoir *ou* faire une blennorragie
goo [gu:] *n F* **(a)** (*sticky substance*) substance *f* visqueuse **(b)** (*sentimentality*) mièvrerie *f*
good [gʊd] **1** *adj* **(better, best) (a)** (*of fine quality*) bon, *f* bonne; **a g. wine** un bon vin; **to have a g. ear (for music)** avoir de l'oreille; **g. handwriting** belle écriture; **she was wearing her g. dress** elle portait sa belle robe; **we only use the g. cutlery when we have guests** nous n'utilisons nos beaux couverts que lorsque nous avons des invités; **he has a g. style, but ...** son style est agréable, mais ...; **g. weather** beau temps; **g. to eat** bon à manger; **the leaves are g. to eat as well as the root** les feuilles, de même que la racine, sont comestibles *ou* bonnes à manger; **this fruit is a bit bashed, but it's still g. to eat** ce fruit est un peu écrasé, mais il est encore bon; **is the meat still g.?** est-ce que la viande est

encore bonne?; *F* **that's a g. one!** (*of story, joke*) elle est bien bonne, celle-là!; **he's too g. for that job** il mérite une meilleure situation; **I suppose he thinks he's too g. for us** j'imagine qu'il se trouve trop bien pour nous; **if it's g. enough for you, it's g. enough for me** si ça vous va, alors ça me va aussi; **this isn't g. enough!** (*you will have to do better*) c'est insuffisant!; **it's looking g.** ça a l'air de bien se passer; (*is going to succeed*) ça se présente bien; **he's looking g.** (*of boxer, athlete, candidate in election*) il a toutes ses chances; **g. living, the g. life** la belle vie

(b) (*appropriate*) bon, *f* bonne; **g. opportunity** bonne occasion; **to be in a g. position to do sth** être bien placé pour faire qch; **it is not always g. to …** il n'est pas toujours bon de …

(c) (*pleasant, enjoyable*) heureux; **g. news** bonnes *ou* heureuses nouvelles; **to have a g. time** (bien) s'amuser; **to show sb a g. time** faire passer un bon moment à qn; **a g. time was had by all** tout le monde s'est bien amusé; **too g. to be true** trop beau pour être vrai; **it's g. to be alive!** que la vie est belle!; **it's g. to know you've got friends** ça fait plaisir de savoir qu'on a des amis; **it's g. to see you** je suis/nous sommes content(s) de te voir; **it's been g. seeing you again** ça m'a/nous a fait plaisir de vous revoir

(d) (*attractive*) **she looks g. in that hat** ce chapeau lui va bien; **that pizza looks g.** cette pizza a l'air bonne; **the vase looks g. there** le vase rend très bien là; **(that) sounds g.!** (*good idea*) bonne idée!; **g. looks** beauté *f*; **to have a g. figure** être bien fait

(e) (*beneficial*) **this medicine is very g. for coughs** ce remède est très bon pour la toux; **beer is not g. for me** la bière ne me vaut rien; **you'll accept, if you know what's g. for you** tu accepteras, si tu as deux sous de bon sens; **to drink more than is g. for one** boire plus que de raison; **it will be g. for them to have some company** ça leur fera du bien d'avoir de la compagnie; **it isn't g. for people to live alone** il n'est pas bon de vivre seul; **it's g. for your health** c'est bon pour la santé; **he's not g. for her** il a une mauvaise influence sur elle; **to be g. for business** être bon pour les affaires

(f) (*skilful, effective etc*) bon, *f* bonne; **to be g. with one's hands** être adroit *ou* habile de ses mains; **to be g. with children** (*of person*) savoir y faire avec les enfants; **to be g. at maths** être bon *ou* fort en math; **to be g. at sport** être bon en sport; **to be g. for doing sth** (*of equipment, medicine, chemical etc*) être bien pour faire qch; **to be g. on French history/contract law** (*of author*) être bon en histoire de France/sur le droit des contrats; **to be g. on sth** (*of book*) être complet sur qch; **to be g. in bed** être bien au lit; **g. for nothing** bon à rien

(g) (*morally good*) bon, *f* bonne; **g. Christian** bon chrétien, bonne chrétienne; **to lead a g. life** vivre en homme de bien, pratiquer le bien; **he proved to be a g. friend** il s'est montré un véritable ami; **g. nature** bon naturel *m*; **they take advantage of his g. nature** ils profitent de son bon caractère; **the G. Book** la sainte Bible

(h) (*well-behaved*) sage; **answer would you, there's a g. boy** sois gentil, réponds; **be g.!** (*to child*) sois sage!; **g. dog!** (*encouraging*) oh, le beau chien!; (*congratulating*) c'est bien, le chien!; **he's g. with children** (*of dog, pony etc*) il est très doux avec les enfants; **g. conduct** *or* **behaviour** bonne conduite *f*; **as g. as gold** sage comme une image

(i) (*kind*) aimable; **that's very g. of you** c'est bien aimable *ou* gentil de votre part; **he was very g. about it** il s'est montré très compréhensif; **would you be g. enough to …?** auriez-vous l'amabilité *ou* la gentillesse de …?; **she has always been g. to me** elle s'est toujours montrée bonne pour moi; **life has been g. to me** j'ai eu de la chance dans la vie; **he's a g. sort** *or* **chap** c'est un brave type; **to do sb a g. turn** rendre service à qn

(j) (*valid*) **a g. reason** une bonne raison, une raison valable; **he** *or* **his credit is g. for £25 000** on peut lui faire jusqu'à 25 000 livres de crédit; **he should be g. for a couple of hundred pounds** on devrait pouvoir en tirer quelques centaines de livres; **how much is he g. for?** de combien dispose-t-il?; **this car ought to be g. for another five years** cette voiture devrait me faire encore cinq ans; **this pass is g. for another six months** cette carte d'abonnement est encore valable six mois; *F* **she's g. for another ten years yet** elle est bonne pour encore dix ans

(k) (*substantial*) **it makes a g. meal for four** ça fait un bon repas pour quatre; **to earn g. money** bien gagner sa vie; **you've got a g. chance** tu as une bonne chance; **of a g. size** de bonne taille; **a g. way into the first act** bien après le début du premier acte; **it's a g. distance** *or* **way (from here)** c'est assez loin d'ici; **I was a g. way into the book when I realized that …** j'avais déjà bien avancé dans ma lecture quand je me suis rendu compte que …

(l) (*thorough*) bon; **a g. spanking/beating** une bonne fessée/correction; **to have a g. look (at sb/sth)** bien regarder qn/qch; **to have a g. cry** pleurer un bon coup **(about sth** à propos de qch); **I had a g. sleep last night** j'ai bien dormi la nuit dernière; **we had a g. laugh (about it)** on (en) a ri un bon coup

(m) to make g. (*of person*) prospérer, faire son chemin; **an immigrant made g.** un immigrant qui a fait son chemin; **to make g. a loss** remplacer ce qu'on a perdu; **to make g. one's losses** compenser ses pertes; **to make g. a deficiency** pallier une insuffisance; **to make g. an injustice/damage** réparer une injustice/des dégâts; **to make g. one's promise** remplir *ou* tenir sa promesse; **he made g. his escape** il a réussi son évasion

(n) (*expressions with 'as'*) **it's as g. a way as any other** c'est une façon qui en vaut une autre; **it's as g. a place as any to stay** qu'on séjourne là ou ailleurs, ça ne fait pas de différence; **this is as g. as you can get** c'est ce qui se fait de mieux; **to give as g. as one gets** rendre coup pour coup; **this method is as g. if not better** cette méthode est aussi bonne, pour ne pas dire meilleure; **it's as g. as new** il/elle est comme neuf/neuve; **to make sth as g. as new** remettre qch à neuf; **it's as g. as settled** c'est comme si c'était fait; **are you married? – as g. as** (*I'm living with sb*) tu es marié? – non, mais c'est tout comme; **it is as g. as saying that …** ça revient à dire que …; **he as g. as told me it would be a disaster** il m'a quasiment dit que ce serait un désastre; **he as g. as called me a liar to my face** c'est comme s'il m'avait traité de menteur

(o) (*used affectionately*) **g. old Anne, I knew she wouldn't let us down!** cette brave Anne, je savais bien qu'elle ne nous laisserait pas tomber!; **g. old London** le bon vieux Londres; **the g. old days** le bon vieux temps; *Old-fashioned* **his g. lady (wife)** son épouse; **your g. lady** votre dame; *Old-fashioned* **my g. man** mon brave

(p) (*greetings, exclamations*) **g. morning/afternoon!** bonjour (monsieur/*etc*)!; *Fml* **g. day** (*hello*) bonjour; (*goodbye*) au revoir; **g. night!** (*when going to bed*) bonne nuit!; (*when leaving*) bonsoir!; **very g.!** (*well done, congratulations etc*) très bien!, parfait!; **very g., sir!** bien, monsieur!; *esp Fml* (*I'll do as you say*) très bien, je m'en charge; **g. for you!**, *esp Austr* **g. on you!** tant mieux pour toi; **g. Lord!** grand Dieu!; **g. heavens!, g. gracious!** bon sang!; **g. grief!** fichtre!

(q) (*with quantity, number*) **a g. half** une bonne moitié; **a g. two hours** deux bonnes heures; **a g. while, a g. time** pas mal de temps; **a g. round sum** une somme rondelette; **a g. twenty years ago** il y a bien vingt ans; **a g. deal, a g. many** beaucoup; **a g. few** pas mal; **a g. few people** pas mal de gens; **to come in a g. third** arriver bon troisième

2 *adv* **(a)** bien; **a g. long break** une pause bien longue; **to have a g. long soak in the bath** rester des heures dans le bain

(b) *F* **they beat us g. and proper** ils nous ont écrasés; **he was g. and mad** il était absolument furieux; **I'll do it when I'm g. and ready** je le ferai quand ça me chantera; **I like my coffee g. and strong** j'aime le café bien fort; **make sure it's stuck on g. and hard** vérifie que c'est vraiment bien collé; **put the paint on g. and thick** appliquer la peinture en couches bien épaisses

(c) *esp Dial F* (*well*) bien; **she sure sings g.** elle chante bien, c'est sûr; **how are you? – g. thanks** comment allez-vous? – bien, merci

3 *n* **(a)** (*morally good behaviour*) bien *m*; **to return g. for evil** rendre le bien pour le mal; **to do g.** faire le bien; **he's up to no g.** il prépare un mauvais coup; **to come to no g.** finir mal; **there is g. and bad everywhere** il y a du bien et du mal partout; **there's g. and bad in everyone** il y a du bon et du mauvais en chacun de nous; **to see the g. in sb/sth** voir le bon côté de qn/qch

(b) (*benefit, use*) **I did it for your own g.** je l'ai fait pour votre bien; **for the g. of one's health** pour sa santé; **to act for the common g.** agir dans l'intérêt commun; **it will do you g. (to spend a week in the country)** cela vous fera du bien (de passer une semaine à la campagne); **what g. will that do you?, what g. will it be to you?** à quoi cela vous avancera-t-il?; **that won't be much g.** ça ne servira pas à grand-chose; **for all the g. it will do** pour la différence que cela fera; **what's the g. of (doing) that?** à quoi bon (faire) cela?; **it's no g. talking about it** inutile d'en parler; **that's no g.** (*pointless*) cela ne sert à rien; (*worthless*) ça ne vaut rien; **he's no g.** il est nul; **it's no g. complaining** se plaindre ne sert à rien (**c**) (*profit*) **to be five pounds to the g.** avoir cinq livres de gagné *ou* de profit; **it is all to the g.** c'est autant de gagné

(**d**) **for g.** (**and all**) (*permanently*) pour de bon; **he is gone for g.** il est parti pour de bon; **to settle down for g.** se fixer définitivement

(**e**) **the g. and the bad** (*pl*) (*people*) les bons et les méchants

4 *int* bien; **g., that's settled then** eh bien, c'est arrangé alors; **I feel better today – g.!** je me sens mieux aujourd'hui – tant mieux!

goodbye ['gʊd'baɪ] *int, n* au revoir *m*; **g. for now!** à bientôt!; **to say g. to sb** dire au revoir à qn; **she said her goodbyes** elle a dit au revoir; (*for good*) elle a fait ses adieux; **it was g. to Paris for the time being** il fallait dire au revoir à Paris pour le moment; **that was g. to £5000** j'ai dû dire adieu à mes 5 000 livres; **he can say g. to any hope of an ambassadorship** il peut dire adieu à ses espoirs de devenir ambassadeur; **to give sb a g. kiss/hug** embrasser qn/serrer qn dans ses bras pour lui dire au revoir; **g. present** cadeau *m* d'adieu

good-for-nothing 1 *adj* (*person*) qui n'est bon à rien; **her g. husband** son bon à rien de mari **2** *n* bon *m* à rien, bonne *f* à rien, vaurien, -ienne

Good Friday *n* vendredi saint

good-hearted [gʊd'hɑːtɪd] *adj* qui a bon cœur; (*gesture*) généreux

Good Housekeeping seal *n* label *m* britannique de bonne qualité

good-humoured, *US* **-humored** [gʊd'hjuːməd] *adj* (*person*) d'un caractère agréable, facile à vivre; (*on particular occasion*) de bonne humeur; (*smile, air*) bon enfant *inv*; (*answer*) plaisant; (*joke etc*) sans malice; **he is always g.** il a bon caractère; **in that g. way of hers** avec sa bonne humeur habituelle

good-humouredly, *US* **-humoredly** [gʊd'hjuːmədlɪ] *adv* avec bonhomie; (*to laugh*) avec bonne humeur

goodish ['gʊdɪʃ] *adj F* (**a**) (*quite good*) assez bon, passable (**b**) (*number etc*) assez grand; **it's a g. step from here** c'est à un bon bout de chemin d'ici; **it's a g. size** c'est assez grand; **add a g. pinch of salt** ajoutez une bonne pincée de sel

good-looker *n F* **he's/she's a g.** il/elle est beau/belle

good-looking *adj* (**better-looking, best-looking**) beau, *f* belle; **he's very g.** il est beau garçon; **she's quite g.** elle n'est pas mal; **hey, g.!** (*to woman*) eh, ma jolie!; (*to man*) eh, beau gosse!

goodly ['gʊdlɪ] *adj Old-fashioned, Lit* (*portion etc*) large, ample; (*number*) considérable; **a g. sum (of money)** une belle somme (d'argent)

good-natured [gʊd'neɪtʃəd] *adj* (*person*) accommodant, d'un caractère agréable; (*laugh*) jovial

good-naturedly [gʊd'neɪtʃədlɪ] *adv* avec bonhomie

goodness ['gʊdnɪs] *n* (**a**) (*of person*) bonté *f*; *Fml* **would you have the g. to inform me next time?** auriez-vous la bonté de m'informer la prochaine fois?

(**b**) (*of thing*) bonne qualité *f*; **contains all the g. of full cream milk** (*in advert*) contient toutes les bonnes choses du lait entier; **to extract all the g. out of sth** extraire tout ce qu'il y a de bon de qch; **it's where the g. is** (*in fruit etc*) c'est ce qu'il y a de plus nutritif

(**c**) (*as euphemism*) **g. gracious (me)!** bonté divine!, mon Dieu!; **g. (me)!** mon Dieu!, oh là là!; **thank g.!** Dieu merci!; **for goodness' sake, be quiet!** taisez-vous, pour l'amour de Dieu!; **I wish to g. he'd shut up!** je prie le ciel qu'il se taise!; **g. (only) knows what I'm going to do** Dieu seul sait ce que je dois faire

goodnight [gʊd'naɪt] *n* **after they had said their goodnights** (*and gone to bed*) après qu'ils se furent dit bonne nuit; (*and left*) après qu'ils se furent dit bonsoir; **to give sb a g. kiss** donner un baiser à qn pour lui dire bonne nuit

goods [gʊdz] *npl* (**a**) *Jur* biens *mpl*, effets *mpl*; **g. and chattels** possessions *fpl* (**b**) *Com, Econ* marchandises *fpl*; **manufactured g.** produits *mpl* manufacturés; **leather g.** articles en cuir, maroquinerie *f*; **to deliver the g.** livrer la marchandise *ou* les marchandises; *Fig* (*keep one's promise*) remplir ses engagements, tenir parole; *Fig* **a computer that can deliver the g.** un ordinateur qui tient ses promesses; *Fig* **to come up with the g.** faire le nécessaire; *Rail* **g. train/station/depot** train *m*/gare *f*/dépôt *m* de marchandises; **g. vehicle** poids *m* lourd, véhicule *m* utilitaire

Good Samaritan *n Bible, Fig* bon Samaritain *m*

good-tempered *adj* d'un caractère facile, qui a bon caractère; (*reply, discussion*) aimable

good-till-cancelled order *n St Exch* ordre *m* à révocation

good-time *adj F* qui ne pense qu'à s'amuser; **g. girl** fille *f* rigolote; (*sexually*) fille facile; (*prostitute*) fille de joie

goodwill ['gʊd'wɪl] *n* (**a**) (*benevolence*) bienveillance *f*, bon vouloir *m* (**towards** pour, envers); **a gesture of g.** un geste de bonne volonté; **a g. mission** une mission de conciliation; **a g. tour** un voyage d'amitié; **to retain sb's g.** conserver les bonnes grâces de qn (**b**) (*willingness*) bonne volonté *f* (**c**) *Com* fonds *m* de commerce, actif *m* incorporel

goody ['gʊdɪ] *F* **1** *n* (**a**) (*person*) brave type *m*; (*too good*) petit saint *m*; **the goodies and the baddies** les bons *mpl* et les méchants (**b**) *Culin* **goodies** gourmandises *fpl* **2** *int* (**g.**) **g.!** chouette!

goody-goody *F Pej* **1** *n* petit saint *m*, petite sainte *f* **2** *adj* de petit saint; **she's awfully g.** elle prend toujours des airs de petite sainte

goody-two-shoes *n* = **goody-goody 1**

gooey ['guːɪ] *adj F* (**a**) (*sticky*) gluant, collant (**b**) (*sentimental*) à l'eau de rose

goof[1] [guːf] *n F* (**a**) (*blunder*) gaffe *f*, bourde *f*; *TV etc* **g. sheet** pense-bête *m*, *pl* pense-bêtes (**b**) (*idiot*) cave *m*

goof[2] *vi F* gaffer, faire une gaffe *ou* une bourde

▶ **goof about, goof around** *vi F* faire l'idiot

▶ **goof off** *vi US F* (*evade work, waste time*) glander, glandouiller

goofball ['guːfbɔːl] *n Am Sl* (**a**) (*fool*) cave *m* (**b**) (*drug*) somnifère *m*

goofy ['guːfɪ] *adj F* (**a**) (*stupid*) loufoque (**b**) *Br* (*teeth*) en avant

googly ['guːglɪ] *n Cricket* = balle *f* lancée avec de l'effet qui prend le batteur à contre-pied alors qu'il pensait l'avoir bien anticipée; *Fig* **to bowl sb a g.** essayer de tromper qn

gook [guːk] *n US* (**a**) *Offensive Sl* (*Oriental*) Chinetoque *mf* (**b**) *F* (*muck*) saleté *f*, crasse *f*

goolies ['guːlɪz] *npl Br Sl* couilles *fpl*

goon [guːn] *n F* (**a**) (*stupid person*) imbécile *mf* (**b**) *Am* (*criminal*) gorille *m*

goosander [guː'sændər] *n* (*bird*) harle *m* bièvre

goose[1], *pl* **geese** [guːs, giːs] *n* (**a**) (*bird*) oie *f*; *Fig* **you've cooked your g., your g. is cooked** tu es fichu; *Fig* **to kill the g. that lays the golden egg** tuer la poule aux œufs d'or; *Fig* **all his geese are swans** à l'entendre, tout ce qu'il fait tient du prodige; **goose('s) egg** œuf *m* d'oie; **g. fat** graisse *f* d'oie; **to get g. pimples** *or* **g. flesh,** *Am* **to have g. bumps** avoir la chair de poule; *Mil* **g. step** pas *m* de l'oie (**b**) *Old-fashioned F* (*silly person*) niais *m*, niaise *f*; **I'm not such a g.** je ne suis pas si bête que ça

goose[2] *vt Sl* pincer les lesses à

gooseberry ['gʊzb(ə)rɪ] *n* (*fruit*) groseille *f* à maquereau, groseille verte; **g. (bush)** groseillier *m*; **I told her children were found under a g. bush** je lui ai dit que les petites filles naissent dans les roses et les petits garçons dans les choux; *Culin* **g. fool** crème *f* de groseilles (à maquereau); *Br F* **to play g.** tenir la chandelle

goosegog ['gʊzgɒg] *n Br F* groseille *f* à maquereau

goose-step *vi* (**-pp-**) *Mil* faire le pas de l'oie

GOP [dʒiːəʊ'piː] *n US Pol* (*abbr* **Grand Old Party**) = Parti *m* républicain

gopher ['gəʊfər] *n* (**a**) (*rodent*) (**pocket**) **g.** géomys *m* (**b**) (*ground squirrel*) spermophile *m* (**c**) = **gofer**

gorblimey [gɔː'blaɪmɪ] *int Eng Dial* nom d'un chien!

Gordian ['gɔːdɪən] *adj Fig* **to cut the G. knot** trancher le nœud gordien

gore[1] [gɔːr] *n* (*blood*) sang *m*; **blood and g.** du sang et encore du sang; **there's plenty of g. in this movie** ce film est sanglant à souhait; *Lit* **he lay in his g.** il baignait dans son sang

gore[2] *vt* (*of bull*) blesser avec les cornes, encorner; **gored to death** tué d'un coup/à coups de corne

gorge[1] [gɔːdʒ] *n* (**a**) *Geog* gorge *f*, défilé *m* (**b**) *Lit* (*throat*) gorge *f*; **it makes my g. rise** cela me soulève le cœur

gorge[2] **1** *vi* se gorger, se repaître, se rassasier, *F* s'empiffrer (**on** de) **2** *vt* (*person*) rassasier; **to g. oneself** se gaver, *F* s'empiffrer

gorgeous ['gɔːdʒəs] *adj* magnifique; (*weather*) superbe, magnifique; (*meal*) somptueux; *Lit* (*palaces*) fastueux; *F* **hello g.!** (*usu to young woman*) bonjour, ma beauté!

gorgeously ['gɔːdʒəslɪ] *adv* magnifiquement, somptueusement

gorgon ['gɔːgən] *n Myth* gorgone *f*

gorilla [gə'rɪlə] *n* (*animal, F bodyguard*) gorille *m*

gormless ['gɔːmlɪs] *adj Br F* idiot, imbécile; **he's g.** c'est une nouille

gorse [gɔːs] *n Bot* (*shrub*) ajoncs *mpl*; **g. bush** ajonc *m*

gory ['gɔːrɪ] *adj* sanglant, ensanglanté; (*film*) sanglant; **in g. detail** avec les détails les plus sanglants; *Fig* **spare me the g. details** épargne-moi les détails

gosh [gɒʃ] *int F* zut (alors)!, mince (alors)!

goshawk ['gɒshɔːk] *n* (*bird*) autour *m*

gosling ['gɒzlɪŋ] *n* oison *m*

go-slow *n Br Ind* grève *f* du zèle
gospel ['gɒsp(ə)l] *n* évangile *m*; *Mus* gospels *mpl*; **St Mark's G., the G. according to St Mark** l'Évangile selon saint Marc; *Fig* **to take sth as g.** accepter qch comme parole d'évangile; *Fig* **it's the g. truth** c'est parole d'évangile; *Rel* **the g. for the day** l'évangile du jour; **to preach the g.** prêcher l'évangile; *Fig* **to preach the g. of monetarism** prêcher le monétarisme; **g. oath** serment *m* prêté sur l'évangile
gospeller ['gɒspələr] *n* **(hot) g.** évangélisateur, -trice
gospel music *n Mus* gospels *mpl*
gospel singer *n* chanteur, -euse de gospels
gossamer ['gɒsəmər] **1** *n* **(a)** (*spider's web*) fils *mpl* de la Vierge, filandres *fpl*; **g. thread** filandre **(b)** *Tex* gaze *f* légère **2** *adj* (*cloth*) très léger, arachnéen
gossip¹ ['gɒsɪp] *n* **(a)** (*person*) bavard, -arde; (*ill-natured*) commère *f*, cancanier, -ière **(b)** (*talk*) bavardage *m*; (*ill-natured*) commérage(s) *m(pl)*, *F* cancans *mpl*, potins *mpl*; **to have a good g.** se raconter les derniers potins; *Journ* **g. column** chronique *f* mondaine, échos *mpl*; **g. columnist** *or* **writer** échotier *m*, rédacteur, -trice mondain(e)
gossip² *vi* bavarder; (*ill-naturedly*) *F* cancaner, potiner; **to g. about sb** faire des commérages sur qn
gossiping ['gɒsɪpɪŋ] **1** *n* bavardage *m*; (*ill-natured*) commérage *m* **2** *adj attrib* cancanier
gossipmonger ['gɒsɪpmʌngər] *n* commère *f*
gossipy ['gɒsɪpɪ] *adj* (*style*) anecdotique; (*person*) cancanier, -ière; **g. letter** lettre pleine de petits potins
got *see* **get**
Gothic ['gɒθɪk] **1** *adj Archit, Art, Ling etc* gothique; *Liter* **g. novel** roman *m* gothique; **g. film** film *m* d'horreur **2** *n* **(a)** *Art* gothique *m* **(b)** *Ling* gotique *m*, gothique *m*
gotta ['gɒtə, 'gɒdə] *F* = **got to**
gotten *Am, Arch see* **get**
gouache [gʊ'ɑːʃ] *n Art* gouache *f*
gouge¹ [gaʊdʒ] *n Carp, Surg* gouge *f*
gouge² *vt Carp* (*wood*) gouger
▶ **gouge out** *vtsep* (*groove, channel etc*) creuser; **to g. sb's eye out** arracher un œil à qn
goulash ['guːlæʃ] *n Culin* goulasch *m*, goulache *m*
gourd ['gʊəd] *n* **(a)** (*plant*) gourde *f* **(b)** (*container*) gourde *f*, calebasse *f* **(c)** *F* **out of one's g.** maboul
gourmand ['gʊəmənd] *n* (*glutton*) glouton, -onne *f*; (*gourmet*) gourmet *m*
gourmet ['gʊəmeɪ] *n* gourmet *m*, gastronome *mf*; **g. cooking** cuisine *f* gastronomique; **g. restaurant** restaurant *m* gastronomique
gout [gaʊt] *n Med* goutte *f*; **to have g.** avoir la goutte
gouty ['gaʊtɪ] *adj* (*person, joint etc*) goutteux
Gov **(a)** *abbr* **government** **(b)** *abbr* **governor**
govern ['gʌvən] **1** *vt* **(a)** (*rule*) (*state etc*) gouverner, régir; (*province etc*) administrer **(b)** (*control*) *MecE* gouverner; *Gram* (*the accusative etc*) se construire avec; **laws that g. chemical reactions** lois qui régissent les réactions chimiques **(c)** (*restrain*) (*emotions*) maîtriser, contenir **2** *vi* (*rule*) gouverner
governance ['gʌvənəns] *n Lit* **(a)** (*act, manner*) (*of state etc*) gouvernement *m*; (*of province etc*) administration *f* **(b)** (*control*) emprise *f*
governess ['gʌvənɪs] *n* gouvernante *f*
governing ['gʌvənɪŋ] **1** *adj* **(a)** *Pol etc* gouvernant; **g. body** conseil *m* d'administration; **the g. party/coalition** le parti/la coalition au pouvoir **(b)** *Fig* dominant; **the g. concept of his philosophy** le principe qui sous-tend toute sa philosophie **2** *n* gouvernement *m*
government ['gʌv(ə)nmənt] *n* **(a)** [①A11,g,i] *Pol* gouvernement *m*; **form of g.** régime *m*; **g. action** action *f* gouvernementale; **g. advertising** publicité *f* d'intérêt général; **g. bond** obligation *f* du gouvernement; **g. finance** financement *m* par l'État; **g. grant** subvention *f* d'État; **g. expenditure** dépenses *fpl* publiques; **g. intervention** intervention *f* du gouvernement; *Mil* **it's g. issue** c'est fourni par le gouvernement; **g. loan** emprunt *m* d'État; **g. market** marché *m* de l'État; **g. monopoly** monopole *m* d'État; **g. offices** bureaux *mpl* du Gouvernement; **g. organization** collectivité *f* publique; **g. restraints** *or* **restrictions** restrictions *fpl* gouvernementales; **g. revenue** recettes *fpl* publiques; **g. sector** secteur *m* public; **g. spending** dépenses *fpl* publiques; **g. stocks** rentes *fpl* de l'État, bons *mpl* du Trésor
(b) (*cabinet*) ministère *m*; **to form a g.** former un gouvernement *ou* un ministère
(c) **G. house** (*governor's residence*) résidence *f* officielle du gouverneur
governmental [gʌvən'ment(ə)l] *adj* gouvernemental
government-sponsored [gʌvənmənt'spɒnsəd] *adj* parrainé par le gouvernement
governor ['gʌv(ə)nər] *n* **(a)** (*of colony, bank, US state*) gouverneur *m*; (*of prison, reform school etc*) directeur *m*; (*member of board of governors of a school etc*) membre *m* du conseil d'administration; *Br F* **the g.** (*boss*) le patron, le singe; *F* **where to, g.?** on va où, patron? **(b)** *Tech* (*device*) régulateur *m*; (*of speed*) modérateur *m*
governor general *n* gouverneur *m* général
governorship ['gʌvənəʃɪp] *n* (*post*) poste *m* de gouverneur; (*function*) fonctions *fpl* de gouverneur
Govt *abbr* **government**
gown [gaʊn] *n* **(a)** (*woman's*) robe *f* **(b)** (*of magistrate, academic etc*) robe *f*, toge *f*; (*of surgeon*) blouse *f*; *Univ* **town and g.** = les gens *mpl* de la ville et les étudiants *mpl*
goy, *pl* goys, goyim [gɔɪ, -z, 'gɔɪɪm] *n* goy *m*, *pl* goyim
GP [dʒiː'piː] *n Br Med* (*abbr* **general practitioner**) (médecin *m*) généraliste *mf*, omnipraticien, -ienne
GPO [dʒiːpiː'əʊ] *n Br* (*abbr* **General Post Office**) Poste *f* principale
gr (*abbr* **gramme(s)**) g.
grab¹ [græb] *n* **(a)** (*movement*) **to make a g. at sth** faire un mouvement vif pour saisir qch; *F* **to be up for grabs** être à prendre; (*be on market, for sale*) être à vendre; **they're getting rid of all the furniture, so those chairs are up for grabs** ils se débarrassent de tous leurs meubles, alors ces chaises sont à qui veut les prendre; **is that last chocolate up for grabs?** est-ce que je peux prendre le chocolat qui reste?; **you can take it if you like, it's up for grabs** vous pouvez le prendre si vous voulez, il est là pour ça; **g. bag** gros sac plein de cadeaux (*utilisé pour la pêche miraculeuse*); *Fig* fourre-tout *m inv*
(b) *Constr* **g. (bucket)** benne *f* preneuse *ou* piocheuse
(c) *Aut* (*of brakes*) blocage *m*
grab² (-bb-) **1** *vt* **to g. (hold of) sth/sb** saisir qch (d'un geste brusque), empoigner qch/qn; **he grabbed a revolver from the table** il a saisi un revolver sur la table; **she grabbed the letter from my hands** elle m'a arraché la lettre des mains; **he grabbed me by the lapels** il m'a empoigné par le revers; **to g. a rope** (*to save oneself*) se raccrocher à un cordage; **to g. a chance/an opportunity** saisir une chance/une occasion; **to g. sb's attention** retenir *ou* (*stronger*) accaparer l'attention de qn; **I'll g. something to eat on the way** j'avalerai quelque chose en chemin; *F Fig* **how does that g. you?** (*my suggestion*) ça te dit?; **the idea doesn't g. me** ça ne me dit rien
2 *vi* **to g. at sb** s'agripper à qn; **to g. at sth** se saisir de qch, se jeter sur qch; **don't g.!** (*esp to children*) ne m'arrache/ne lui arrache/*etc* pas les choses/la nourriture/*etc* des mains!
grabby ['græbɪ] *adj F* **don't be so g.** (*don't grab things*) ne te jette pas sur les choses; (*don't grab me*) ne t'agrippe pas à moi; **he's very g.** (*of child picking things up*) il touche à tout
grace¹ [greɪs] *n* **(a)** (*of movement, dancer etc*) grâce *f*; (*of language*) élégance *f*; *Mus* **g. note** note *f* d'agrément
(b) (*of manners*) grâce *f*; **to do sth with (a) good/bad g.** faire qch de bonne/mauvaise grâce; **to have the (good) g. to apologize** avoir la bonne grâce de faire des excuses; **the social graces** le savoir-vivre
(c) (*favour*) faveur *f*; **to be in/get into sb's good graces** être dans/entrer dans les bonnes grâces de qn; *Rel* **the g. of God** la grâce de Dieu; **there, but for the g. of God, go I** je remercie le ciel de m'avoir épargné; **in a state of g.** en état de grâce; **to fall from g.** perdre la grâce; *Old-fashioned* **in the year of g. 1066** en l'an de grâce 1066; *Comptr* **g. log in** connexion *f* de grâce
(d) *Fin* (*for payment of a bill*) **days of g.** délai *m*; **to give a creditor seven days' g.** accorder à un créancier sept jours de grâce *ou* de faveur; *Com* **period of g.** jours *mpl* de grâce
(e) (*prayer*) (*before meal*) bénédicité *m*; (*after meal*) grâces *fpl*; **to say g.** réciter le bénédicité
(f) (*address*) **His G.** (*the duke*) Monsieur (le duc de …); (*the archbishop*) Monseigneur (l'archevêque de …); **Her G.** (*the duchess*) Madame (la duchesse de …)
(g) *Myth* **the Graces** les Grâces *fpl*
(h) *Arch* (*pardon*) grâce *f*, pardon *m*
grace² *vt* **(a)** (*honour*) honorer (**with** de); **to g. a meeting with one's presence** honorer une réunion de sa présence **(b)** (*ornament*) embellir, orner
grace-and-favour *adj Br* (*residence etc*) = prêté gratuitement par le souverain à un sujet qui lui a rendu service
graceful ['greɪsfʊl] *adj* **(a)** (*person, movement*) gracieux; **g. figure** silhouette élégante; **she is a g. dancer** elle danse avec grâce **(b)** (*speech*) gracieux, poli, bien tourné
gracefully ['greɪsfʊlɪ] *adv* avec grâce, avec élégance
gracefulness ['greɪsfʊlnɪs] *n* grâce *f*, élégance *f*

graceless ['greɪslɪs] *adj* (*inelegant*) gauche, inélégant; *F* (*rude*) effronté

gracious ['greɪʃəs] **1** *adj* **(a)** (*kind, polite*) poli, affable; (*generous, noble-minded*) courtois; **to be g. to sb** être affable avec *ou* envers qn; **to be g. in accepting sth** accepter qch avec courtoisie; **our g. King/Queen** notre gracieux souverain **(b)** (*God*) plein de grâce *ou* de miséricorde **(to** envers) **(c)** (*living, house etc*) luxueux **2** *int* **g. (me)!, good(ness) g.!** miséricorde!, mon Dieu!; **good g. no!** jamais de la vie!

graciously ['greɪʃəslɪ] *adv* (*to accept, allow*) gracieusement, de bonne grâce; (*to reply, behave*) avec politesse; *Fml* **to be g. pleased to do sth** daigner faire qch

graciousness ['greɪʃəsnɪs] *n* **(a)** (*kindness*) gentillesse *f*; (*politeness*) courtoisie *f* **(b)** (*of God*) bonté *f*, miséricorde *f* **(c)** (*of life, house etc*) luxe *m*

gradate [grə'deɪt] **1** *vi* se dégrader **(into** en) **2** *vt* (*colours*) dégrader

gradation [grə'deɪʃən] *n* **(a)** *Art* (*of colours*) gradation *f* **(b)** (*degree*) (*on thermometer etc*) degré *m*; **gradations of meaning** nuances *fpl* de sens

grade¹ [greɪd] *n* **(a)** (*of hierarchy etc*) grade *m*, rang *m*; (*of administration*) échelon *m* **(b)** (*quality*) (*of paper, coffee, flour*) qualité *f*; (*of potato*) calibre *m*; (*of oil*) grade *m*; *Fig* **to make the g.** se montrer à la hauteur; *Com* **g. label** étiquette *f* de calibrage **(c)** *esp Am* (*gradient*) pente *f* **(d)** *esp Am Sch* (*mark*) note *f*; **to get high grades** avoir de bonnes notes **(e)** *Am Sch* (*year at school*) classe *f*; *US* **the grades** = l'école *f* primaire **(f)** *Agr* **g. cattle, grades** bétail *m* amélioré par croisement

grade² *vt* **(a)** (*classify*) (*produce, oil, jobs*) classer; (*potatoes*) calibrer; *Am Sch* **to g. essays** noter des dissertations **(b)** *Am Rail* (*track*) ménager *ou* régulariser la pente de; *Constr* (*land*) niveler **(c)** *Agr* (*breed etc*) améliorer

▶ **grade down** *vtsep* (*move to lower category*) classer dans une catégorie inférieure

▶ **grade up** *vtsep* **(a)** (*move to higher category*) classer dans une catégorie supérieure **(b)** *Agr* (*breed etc*) améliorer

grade crossing *n Am Rail* passage *m* à niveau; **g. gate** barrière *f* de passage à niveau

graded ['greɪdɪd] *adj* calibré; **g. exercises** exercices gradués; **g. tax** (*upwards*) impôt *m* progressif; (*downwards*) impôt dégressif

grade school *n US* = école *f* primaire

gradient ['greɪdɪənt] *n* **(a)** *Constr etc* inclinaison *f*; (*of ground*) dénivellation *f*; **downward g.** pente *f*, déclivité *f*; **upward g.** rampe *f*, montée *f*; **a g. of 1 in 6, a 1 in 6 g.** une dénivellation d'un sixième; **steep/low g.** forte/faible pente **(b)** *Math, Phys* (*of temperature etc*) gradient *m*

grading ['greɪdɪŋ] *n* **(a)** (*classification*) (*of oil, tasks, exercises*) classement *m*, gradation *f*; (*of potatoes*) calibrage *m*; (*of ore etc*) triage *m*; *Am Sch* (*marking*) correction *f* **(b)** *Am Constr, Rail* (*of slope*) (a)ménagement *m*

gradual ['grædjʊ(ə)l] **1** *adj* progressif, graduel; **a g. process** un processus graduel; **a g. slope** une pente douce; **a g. transition** une transition progressive **(from ... to ...** de ... à ...) **2** *n Rel* graduel *m*

gradually ['grædjʊ(ə)lɪ] *adv* petit à petit, progressivement; **it happened very g.** ça s'est produit très progressivement; **g. you'll be able to type without looking at the keyboard** graduellement *ou* petit à petit *ou* progressivement, tu seras capable de taper sans regarder le clavier

graduate¹ ['grædjʊət] **1** *n* diplômé, -ée; *Univ* = licencié, -ée; **biology g.** = licencié, -ée en biologie; *Am Sch* **high school g.** = titulaire *mf* du baccalauréat **2** *adj Am Univ* (*postgraduate*) **g. school** = université *f* de troisième cycle; **g. studies** études *fpl* de troisième cycle

graduate² ['grædjʊeɪt] **1** *vi* obtenir son diplôme; *Univ* (*complete one's degree*) obtenir sa licence; (*receive one's degree certificate*) recevoir son diplôme de licence; **he graduated from Oxford** il a fait ses études à Oxford; **I graduated in 1989** j'ai eu ma licence en 1989; *Am Sch* **to g. from high school** terminer ses études au lycée; *Fig* **to g. from sth to sth** passer de qch à qch; **she learnt on a cheap violin before graduating to a better instrument** elle a appris à jouer avec un violon bon marché avant de passer à un meilleur instrument

2 *vt* **(a)** (*scale, thermometer etc*) graduer; **graduated in centimetres** gradué en centimètres

(b) *Am Sch, Univ* remettre un diplôme/un diplôme de licence à

graduated ['grædjʊeɪtɪd] *adj* (*thermometer etc*) gradué; **a g. pay rise/tax increase** une augmentation de salaire/des impôts progressive; **g. income tax** impôt *m* progressif; *Aut* **g. tint shadeband** nuancier *m*

graduation [grædjʊ'eɪʃən] *n* **(a)** *Univ* remise *f* des diplômes; (*by student*) réception *f* d'un diplôme; *Fig* **my g. to the post of supervisor** ma promotion au poste de surveillant; *Univ* **g. ceremony** cérémonie *f* de remise des diplômes **(b)** (*of thermometer etc*) graduation *f*; (*of tax*) progressivité *f*; **graduations** degrés *mpl*, grades *mpl*

graffiti [græ'fiːtiː] *npl* graffiti *mpl* **a piece of g.** un graffiti; **there's some g. on the wall** il y a des graffiti sur le mur; **g. artist** tagger *m*, graffiteur, -euse; **g. writer** tagger

graft¹ [grɑːft] *n* **(a)** (*from a plant*) greffon *m*; (*from a tree*) ente *f* **(b)** *Surg* greffe *f*; **bone/skin g.** greffe osseuse/de peau; **I had to have a skin g.** on a dû me faire une greffe de peau

graft² *vt* (*onto a plant*) greffer; (*onto a tree*) enter; *Surg* greffer **(onto** sur); *Fig* **this piece was grafted onto the symphony later** ce morceau a été rajouté à la symphonie plus tard; **the tower was grafted onto the original Norman edifice** la tour a été ajoutée à l'édifice norman d'origine

graft³ *n F* **(a)** *Am* (*bribery etc*) pot-de-vin *m* **(b)** *Br* (*work*) **to achieve sth by hard g.** réussir qch en travaillant dur

graft⁴ *vi F* **(a)** *Am* (*engage in bribery etc*) (*give*) verser des pots-de-vin; (*take*) recevoir des pots-de-vin **(b)** *Br* (*work hard*) travailler dur

grafter ['grɑːftər] *n Br F* (*hard worker*) bosseur, -euse

grafting ['grɑːftɪŋ] *n* (*in horticulture, arboriculture*) greffe *f*, greffage *m*; *Surg* greffe; **skin g.** greffe de peau

Grail [greɪl] *n* **the G., the Holy G.** le Saint-Graal; *Fig* **the G. of full employment/world peace** la croisade pour parvenir au plein emploi/instaurer la paix mondiale

grain [greɪn] *n* **(a)** (*of wheat, pepper, salt, sand etc*) grain *m*; *Fig* **there's not a g. of truth in what he says** il n'y a pas un grain de vérité dans ce qu'il dit; *Fig* **not a g. of common sense** pas un grain *ou* pas deux sous de bon sens, pas une once de bon sens

(b) (*no pl*) (*cereals*) céréales *fpl*; **a shipment of g.** une cargaison de céréales; **g. alcohol** alcool *m* de grain; **g. crop** récolte *f* de céréales, récolte céréalière; **g. elevator** élévateur *m* pour le grain; **g. market** marché *m* céréalier

(c) (*measurement*) grain *m* (= 0,0648 g.)

(d) (*of wood, photo etc*) grain *m*; (*of wood, meat*) fil *m*; (*of leather*) grain, grenure *f*; **against** *or* **across the g.** contre le fil, à contre-fil; *Fig* **it goes against the g. for me to do it** ça m'est difficile de le faire, c'est contre ma nature de le faire

grainy ['greɪnɪ] *adj Phot* granuleux

gram [græm] *n* gramme *m*

grammage ['græmɪdʒ] *n* (*of paper*) grammage *m*

grammar ['græmər] *n* **(a)** grammaire *f*; **that's not good g.** ce n'est pas grammaticalement correct **(b) g. (book)** grammaire *f*; **a French g.** une grammaire française

grammarian [grə'meərɪən] *n* grammairien, -ienne

grammar school *n Sch Br* = lycée *m*; *US* = école *f* primaire

grammatical [grə'mætɪk(ə)l] *adj* **(a)** grammatical, -aux; **g. mistake** faute de grammaire **(b)** (*correct*) grammaticalement correct

grammatically [grə'mætɪklɪ] *adv* grammaticalement

gramme [græm] *n* gramme *m*

gramophone ['græməfəʊn] *n Old-fashioned Br* gramophone *m*; **g. record** disque *m*

grampus ['græmpəs] *n* (*killer whale*) épaulard *m*, orque *f*

gran [græn] *n esp Br F* (*grandmother*) grand-mère *f*, (*in children's language*) mamie *f*, mémé *f*

granary ['grænərɪ] *n Agr* grenier *m*; *Com* entrepôt *m* de grain; **Egypt was the g. of the ancient world** l'Égypte était le grenier de l'antiquité; *Br Culin* **g. bread/loaf** = pain *m* complet avec des morceaux de blé non moulu

grand [grænd] **1** *adj* **(a)** (*imposing*) grandiose, imposant, magnifique; **to do things on a g. scale** faire les choses en grand; **to entertain on a g. scale** recevoir des gens en grande pompe; **to invest on a g. scale** faire de gros investissements; **to build on a g. scale** réaliser de grands projets de construction; **in g. style** en grande pompe; **it was all part of his g. design** tout cela faisait partie de son grand projet; **the g. manner of the aristocracy** le faste de l'aristocratie; **the mayor looked very g. in his robes** le maire avait un air très imposant avec ses vêtements de cérémonie; **the g. old man of trade unionism/Scottish folk music** le patriarche du syndicalisme/de la musique folklorique écossaise; **a g. lady** une grande dame; **lexicographer is just a g. name for someone who writes dictionaries** lexicographe est simplement un mot pompeux pour désigner une personne qui écrit des dictionnaires; **g. concert** grand concert; *Mus, Fig* **g. finale** apothéose *f*; *Hist* **G. Tour** tour *m* d'Europe; **g. tour** (*of mansion etc*) visite *f*; *Hum* **would you like a g. tour of the house?** veux-tu que je te fasse visiter la maison?

(b) *F* (*excellent*) (*food, accommodation*) excellent;

(*weather*) magnifique; **I'm not feeling too g.** je ne suis pas dans mon assiette; **she sounded absolutely g. when I spoke to her on the phone** elle avait l'air en pleine forme quand je l'ai eue au téléphone; **to have a g. time** bien s'amuser; *Iron* **we had a g. old time trying to find the house!** on s'est marré pour trouver la maison!

(**c**) (*overall*) **g. total** total *m* général; **a g. total of £21.52** une somme totale de 21 livres 52 pence

(**d**) (*in titles*) **g. duchess** grande-duchesse *f, pl* grandes-duchesses; **g. duke** grand-duc *m, pl* grands-ducs; **g. master** (*of order, in chess*) grand maître *m*; (*of freemasons*) vénérable *m*

2 *n* (**a**) *F Am* (*thousand dollars*) mille dollars *mpl*; *Br* (*thousand pounds*) mille livres *fpl*; **two g.** *Am* deux mille dollars; *Br* deux mille livres

(**b**) *Mus* piano *m* à queue

grandad [ˈgrændæd] *n F* papi *m*, pépé *m*

grandaddy [ˈgrændædɪ] *n* = **grandad**; *Fig* **the g. of them all** (*of car, locomotive etc*) l'ancêtre *mf*

grandchild, *pl* **-children** [ˈgræntʃaɪld, -tʃɪldrən] *n* (*boy*) petit-fils *m, pl* petits-fils; (*girl*) petite-fille *f, pl* petites-filles; **that will be something to tell your grandchildren** voilà quelque chose que tu pourras raconter à tes petits-enfants

granddad [ˈgrændæd] *n F* papi *m*, pépé *m*

granddaughter [ˈgrændɔːtər] *n* petite-fille *f, pl* petites-filles

grandee [grænˈdiː] *n Hist* grand *m* (*d'Espagne*); *Fig* **Tory grandees** = personnes *fpl* influentes du parti conservateur

grandeur [ˈgrændjər] *n* (**a**) (*of person*) grandeur *f*, noblesse *f*, éminence *f* (**b**) (*of building, surroundings etc*) splendeur *f*, magnificence *f*; **the g. of the landscape** la majesté du paysage; **an air of g.** quelque chose de grandiose; **faded g.** (*of house, furnishings etc*) splendeur passée

grandfather [ˈgrænfɑːðər, ˈgrænd-] *n* grand-père, *pl* grands-pères; **g. clock** horloge *f* comtoise *ou* de parquet

grandfatherly [ˈgrændfɑːðəlɪ] *adj* de grand-père

grandiloquence [grænˈdɪləkwəns] *n* grandiloquence *f*, emphase *f*

grandiloquent [grænˈdɪləkwənt] *adj* grandiloquent

grandiose [ˈgrændɪəʊs, -əʊz] *adj* (*building etc*) grandiose, magnifique; (*term, theory, title etc*) pompeux; (*idea, scheme*) grandiose

grand jury *n US Jur* = jury *m* qui décide si une affaire doit être portée devant les tribunaux ou non

grand larceny *n US Jur* vol *m* qualifié

grandly [ˈgrændlɪ] *adv* (**a**) (*impressively*) de façon grandiose *ou* impressionnante (**b**) (*pompously*) pompeusement

grandma [ˈgrænmɑː, ˈgrænd-, ˈgræm-] *n F* mamie *f*, mémé *f*

grandmother [ˈgrænmʌðər, ˈgrænd-] *n* grand-mère *f, pl* grands-mères

Grand National *n Br Horseracing* = course *f* hippique la plus célèbre de Grande-Bretagne

grandnephew [ˈgrænˈnefjʊ, ˈgrænd-] *n* petit-neveu *m, pl* petits-neveux

grandness [ˈgrændnɪs] *n* grandeur *f*; *Pej* caractère *m* pompeux

grandniece [ˈgrænˈniːs, ˈgrænd-] *n* petite-nièce *f, pl* petites-nièces

grand opera *n* grand opéra *m*

grandpa [ˈgrænpɑː] *n F* papi *m*, pépé *m*

grandparent [ˈgrænpeərənt, ˈgrænd-] *n* (*male*) grand-père *m*; (*female*) grand-mère *f*; **grandparents** grands-parents; **children are often looked after by a g.** les enfants sont souvent gardés par un de leurs grands-parents

grand piano *n* piano *m* à queue

grand slam *n Cards, Tennis* grand chelem *m*; *Tennis* **Grand Slam tournament** tournoi *m* du Grand Chelem

grandson [ˈgrænsʌn, ˈgrænd-] *n* petit-fils *m, pl* petits-fils

grandstand¹ [ˈgrænstænd, ˈgrænd-] *n Sp* tribune *f* (d'honneur); *Sp* **g. finish** arrivée *f* palpitante; **to have a g. view of sth** être bien placé pour voir qch

grandstand² *vi Am Fig* faire le mariolle

grange [greɪndʒ] *n* (**a**) *Br* (*country house*) petit manoir *m* (**b**) *Arch* (*granary*) grange *f*

granite [ˈgrænɪt] *n* granit(e) *m*; **g. building** édifice en granit(e)

granitic [grəˈnɪtɪk] *adj* granitique, graniteux

grannie, granny [ˈgrænɪ] *n F* mamie *f*, mémé *f*; **an old g.** une vieille mémé; **g. flat** = partie *f* d'une maison aménagée indépendamment pour héberger un parent âgé; **g. knot** nœud *m* de ménagère *ou* de soldat

Granny Smith *n* (*apple*) granny-smith *f inv*

grant¹ [grɑːnt] *n* (**a**) (*financial aid*) subvention *f*; *Univ* bourse *f* d'études; **I can't live on my g.** je n'arrive pas à m'en sortir avec seulement ma bourse d'études; **to make a g. to sb** accorder une subvention/une bourse d'études à qn; **to receive a g.** être subventionné, recevoir une subvention; *Univ* recevoir *ou* se voir accorder une bourse d'études (**b**) (*action*) *Com* (*of patent*) délivrance *f*; *Jur* (*of property etc*) cession *f*

grant² *vt* (**a**) (*permission*) donner; (*interview, audience, request etc*) accorder; (*authorization, patent*) délivrer; *Jur* (*property etc*) faire cession de; **he was granted permission to ...** il reçut la permission de ...; **the countries that have been granted autonomy** les pays qui se sont vus accorder l'autonomie; **God g. that ...** Dieu veuille que ...; **to take sth for granted** considérer qch comme allant de soi *ou* comme normal; **you take too much for granted** vous présumez trop; **he takes it for granted that he can borrow my books** il se croit permis d'emprunter mes livres; **we take all this for granted** tout cela nous semble normal; **she felt that she was being taken for granted** elle avait le sentiment qu'elle ne comptait pas; **I'm tired of the way everybody just takes me for granted** j'en ai assez que personne ne fasse attention à moi; **the party has been accused of taking its members for granted** on a accusé le parti de ne pas tenir compte de ses membres

(**b**) (*subsidy*) accorder, allouer (**to** à)

(**c**) (*admit*) admettre; **it must be granted that ...** il faut reconnaître que ...; **I g. you that he is lazy** il est paresseux, je vous l'accorde; **I'll g. you that** je vous l'accorde

grant-in-aid *n* subvention *f*

grant-maintained *adj Br Sch* **g. school** = école *f* privée qui reçoit une subvention de l'État

granular [ˈgrænjʊlər] *adj* (*surface, texture*) granulaire, granuleux

granulate [ˈgrænjʊleɪt] *vt* (*powder etc*) granuler, grener, grainer; (*sugar*) cristalliser

granulated [ˈgrænjʊleɪtɪd] *adj* **g. sugar** sucre *m* cristallisé

granulation [grænjʊˈleɪʃən] *n* granulation *f*

granule [ˈgrænjʊl] *n* grain *m*, granule *m*; **coffee/tea granules** granules de café/thé

grape [greɪp] *n* grain *m* de raisin; **a (variety of) g.** un raisin; **to eat grapes** manger du raisin; **to pick grapes** faire les vendanges, cueillir le raisin; **g. harvest** vendange(s) *f(pl)*; **g. hyacinth** muscari *m*; **g. juice** jus *m* de raisin; **g. picker** vendangeur, -euse

grapefruit [ˈgreɪpfruːt] *n* pamplemousse *m*; **g. (tree)** pamplemoussier *m*; **g. juice** jus *m* de pamplemousse

grapeshot [ˈgreɪpʃɒt] *n* (*ammunition*) mitraille *f*

grapevine [ˈgreɪpvaɪn] *n* (**a**) vigne *f*, treille *f* (**b**) *Fig* téléphone *m* arabe; **I heard on the g. that ...** j'ai entendu par le téléphone arabe que ...

graph¹ [grɑːf] *n* graphique *m*, diagramme *m*; **g. paper** papier *m* millimétré

graph² *vt* faire la représentation graphique de

graphic [ˈgræfɪk] **1** *adj* (**a**) *Math* (*also* **graphical**) (*representation etc*) graphique; **g. character** caractère *m* graphique (**b**) (*vivid*) (*description etc*) très vivant; (*shocking*) cru (**c**) *Art* (*design etc*) graphique **2** *n* graphique *m*

graphically [ˈgræfɪklɪ] *adv* (**a**) *Math* (*to solve a problem*) graphiquement (**b**) (*vividly*) de façon très vivante; (*in a shocking way*) crûment

graphical user interface [ˈgræfɪk(ə)l] *n Comptr* interface *f* utilisateur graphique

graphic art *n* art *m* graphique

graphic artist *n* graphiste *mf*

graphic design *n* conception *f* graphique

graphic designer *n* graphiste *mf*

graphic equalizer *n* (*on hi-fi*) égaliseur *m* graphique

graphic interface *n Comptr* interface *f* graphique

graphics [ˈgræfɪks] *n* [①**A10**,c] (**a**) (*art*) arts *mpl* graphiques (**b**) *Comptr* graphismes *mpl*, graphiques *mpl*; **g. accelerator card** carte *f* accélérateur graphique; **g. capability** aptitude *f* graphique; **g. card** carte graphique; **g. designer** concepteur *m* graphiste; **g. digitizer** convertisseur *m* numérique de graphiques; **g. generator** générateur *m* graphique; **g. mode** mode *m* graphique; **g. resolution** résolution *f* graphique; **g. software** logiciel *m* graphique *ou* de graphisme, (logiciel) grapheur *m*

graphite [ˈgræfaɪt] *n* graphite *m*, mine *f* de plomb

graphologist [græˈfɒlədʒɪst] *n* graphologue *mf*

graphology [græˈfɒlədʒɪ] *n* graphologie *f*

grapnel [ˈgræpnəl] *n Naut* grappin *m*, crochet *m*; *Av* (*of balloon*) ancre *f*

grapple¹ [ˈgræp(ə)l] *n* = **grapnel**

grapple² **1** *vi* (*fight*) lutter corps à corps; *Fig* **to g. with** (*difficulty, problem, computer, machine etc*) se débattre avec; **to g. with inflation** être aux prises avec l'inflation **2** *vt Am* (*sb*) empoigner; **to g. sb to the floor** mettre qn à terre

grappling [ˈgræp(ə)lɪŋ] *n Naut* **g. iron** *or* **hook** grappin *m*, crochet *m*

grasp¹ [grɑːsp] *n* (**a**) (*hold*) prise *f*; **to wrest sth from sb's g.** arracher qch des mains de qn; **to have a strong g.**

(*handshake*) avoir de la poigne; *Fig* **to have sth within one's g.** avoir qch à sa portée; *Fig* **it is now within everyone's g.** (*financially etc*) c'est maintenant à la portée de tout le monde; *Fig* **to let an opportunity slip from one's g.** rater une occasion **(b)** *Fig* (*understanding*) compréhension *f*; **to have a good g. of modern history** avoir une bonne connaissance de l'histoire moderne; **his g. of the problem was poor** il dominait mal le problème

grasp² *vt* **(a)** (*hold firmly*) saisir, empoigner; **to g. sb's hand** serrer la main à qn; **I grasped his arm** je l'ai agrippé par le bras; *Fig* **to g. the opportunity** saisir l'occasion **(of doing sth** de faire qch) **(b)** *Fig* (*understand*) comprendre, saisir; **to g. the importance of sth** saisir l'importance de qch

▸ **grasp at** *vipo* (*attempt to take hold of*) tenter de saisir *ou* d'atteindre; *Fig* (*seize*) (*opportunity, offer*) saisir avidement; *Fig* **to g. at straws** se raccrocher à de faux espoirs

grasping ['grɑːspɪŋ] *adj* (*mean*) avide, cupide

grass¹ [grɑːs] *n* **(a)** (*plant*) herbe *f*; *Fig* **she doesn't let the g. grow under her feet** elle ne perd pas son temps; **g. box** (*on lawn mower*) panier *m* à herbes; *Tex* **g. cloth** (toile *f* de) ramie *f*; **g. seed** (*for lawn*) graine *f* pour gazon; (*as feed*) graine fourragère; **the g. roots** (*of political party etc*) la base; **the feeling at the g. roots is that …** le sentiment à la base est que …; *F* **g. widow** (*whose husband is away*) femme *f* dont le mari est absent *ou* en voyage; (*who is divorced or separated*) femme divorcée/séparée (de son mari); **I'm a g. widow this weekend** je suis célibataire ce week-end

(b) (*lawn*) pelouse *f*, gazon *m*; *Tennis* gazon; **keep off the g.** défense de marcher sur le gazon *ou* sur la pelouse, pelouse interdite; *Prov* **the g. is always greener (on the other side of the fence)** c'est toujours mieux ailleurs; *Tennis* **she plays well on g.** elle joue bien sur gazon; *Tennis* **g. court** court *m* en gazon

(c) (*pasture*) herbage *m*; **to put** *or* **turn a horse out to g.** mettre un cheval à l'herbe; *Fig* **to put sb out to g.** mettre qn à la retraite; **to be (out) at g.** (*of animal*) être au vert; **to put land under g.** enherber une terre, mettre une terre en herbe

(d) *F* (*marijuana*) herbe *f*

(e) *Br Sl* (*informer*) balance *f*, indicateur *m*

grass² **1** *vt* **(a)** (*cover with grass*) (*field*) mettre en herbe, enherber; (*garden*) gazonner **(b)** *Sl* (*inform on*) **to g. sb** balancer, dénoncer **2** *vi Br Sl* (*inform*) parler; **to g. on sb** balancer *ou* dénoncer qn

▸ **grass over** *vtsep* (*garden*) gazonner; (*field*) mettre en herbe, enherber

grass(-)green *adj* (*colour*) vert gazon *inv*

grasshopper ['grɑːshɒpər] *n* sauterelle *f*

grassland ['grɑːslænd] *n* prairies *fpl*, prés *mpl*

grass-root(s) *adj* de base, qui émane de la base; **there is no g. support for their policy** il n'y a pas de soutien de la base pour leur politique; **the g. feeling is that …** le sentiment à la base est que …; **at g. level** à la base; *Mktg* **g. forecasting** prévision *f* de la base

grass snake *n* couleuvre *f* (à collier)

grassy ['grɑːsɪ] *adj* herbu, herbeux; (*lane*) vert; (*plain*) verdoyant

grate¹ [greɪt] *n* (*of hearth*) grille *f*; (*fireplace*) foyer *m*, âtre *m*; **a fire in the g.** un feu dans la cheminée

grate² **1** *vt* **(a)** (*cheese, carrot, nutmeg etc*) râper **(b)** (*scrape*) **to g. sth on sth** frotter qch contre qch (avec un grincement); **to g. one's teeth** grincer des dents **2** *vi* **(a)** (*of machinery*) grincer; (*of chalk on blackboard*) crisser **(b)** (*irritate*) taper sur les nerfs **(on sb** à qn); **it really grates (on me)** ça me tape vraiment sur les nerfs; **to g. on the ear** (*of music, particular accent*) écorcher l'oreille; (*of noise*) faire mal aux oreilles

grateful ['greɪtfʊl] *adj* reconnaissant **(to sb for sth** à *ou* envers qn de qch); **I'm g. for all you've done** je vous suis reconnaissant de tout ce que vous avez fait, *esp Fml* je vous sais gré de tout ce que vous avez fait; **he gave her a g. smile** il lui a adressé un sourire reconnaissant; **I would be g. if you could let me know as soon as possible** je vous serais reconnaissant de m'informer dès que possible; **I was g. it wasn't me** j'étais bien content que ce ne soit pas moi; **I suppose we should be g. for that** on devrait s'en estimer heureux

gratefully ['greɪtfʊlɪ] *adv* avec reconnaissance; **to smile g.** faire un sourire reconnaissant

grater ['greɪtər] *n* râpe *f*

gratification [grætɪfɪ'keɪʃən] *n* satisfaction *f*, plaisir *m*; **to do sth for one's own g.** faire qch pour sa propre satisfaction; **she had the g. of knowing that she'd been proved right** elle avait la satisfaction de savoir qu'on lui avait donné raison

gratified ['grætɪfaɪd] *adj* satisfait, content **(with** de); (*smile*) de satisfaction

gratify ['grætɪfaɪ] *vt* **(a)** (*please*) (*person*) faire plaisir à **(b)** (*satisfy*) (*passion etc*) satisfaire, contenter; **to g. sb's whims** satisfaire les caprices de qn

gratifying ['grætɪfaɪɪŋ] *adj* satisfaisant

grating¹ ['greɪtɪŋ] **1** *adj* (*noise*) discordant, grinçant; (*voice*) éraillé; **g. laugh** ricanement *m*; **g. sound** grincement *m* **2** *n Culin* râpage *m*; **gratings** (*of cheese*) fromage *m* râpé; (*of chocolate*) copeaux *mpl*

grating² *n* (*bars*) (*of window*) grille *f*

gratis ['grɑːtɪs] **1** *adj* gratis, gratuit **2** *adv* gratis, gratuitement

gratitude ['grætɪtjuːd] *n* gratitude *f*, reconnaissance *f* **(to** envers); **to show one's g.** témoigner de sa reconnaissance

gratuitous [grə'tjuːɪtəs] *adj* (*unnecessary*) gratuit, sans raison; **g. violence** violence *f* gratuite

gratuitously [grə'tjuːɪtəslɪ] *adv* gratuitement, sans raison

gratuity [grə'tjuːɪtɪ] *n Fml* (*tip*) pourboire *m*; **no gratuities** pourboires interdits

grave¹ [greɪv] *n* tombe *f*, tombeau *m*; **(mass) g.** fosse *f* commune; (*in wartime*) charnier *m*; **to be in one's g.** être dans la tombe; **she worked herself into an early g.** elle s'est tuée au travail; **he took his secret with him to the g.** il a emporté son secret dans la tombe; **he drank himself into an early g.** l'alcool l'a prématurément tué; **he's drinking himself into an early g.** il se détruit à force de boire; *Fig* **he must have turned in his g.** il a dû se retourner dans sa tombe; **it would make her turn in her g.** elle se retournerait dans sa tombe; **someone has just walked over my g.** j'ai eu un frisson; **to be digging one's own g.** creuser sa propre tombe; **to have one foot in the g.** avoir un pied dans la tombe; **from beyond the g.** d'outre-tombe

grave² *adj* (*serious*) grave, sérieux; (*tone*) solennel; (*situation*) grave; (*error*) lourd; **to make a g. mistake** se tromper lourdement; **g. news** de graves nouvelles

grave³ [grɑːv] *adj Ling* **g. accent** accent *m* grave

gravedigger ['greɪvdɪgər] *n* fossoyeur *m*

gravel¹ ['græv(ə)l] *n* gravier *m*; **g. pit** carrière *f* de gravier; **g. path** allée *f* de gravier

gravel² *vt* **(-ll-,** *US* **-l-) (a)** (*cover with gravel*) couvrir de gravier; **gravelled path** allée *f* de gravier **(b)** *esp US F* (*perplex*) (*person*) embarrasser

gravelly ['græv(ə)lɪ] *adj* (*containing gravel*) graveleux; (*river bed*) pierreux; **g. voice** voix râpeuse

gravely ['greɪvlɪ] *adv* (*to say*) gravement, solennellement; **g. ill** gravement malade; **to be g. mistaken** se tromper lourdement; **g. wounded** grièvement blessé

graven ['greɪvən] *adj Arch, Lit* **g. on his memory** gravé dans sa mémoire; *Bible* **g. image** image *f* sculptée, idole *f*

graveness ['greɪvnɪs] *n* (*of manner, tone*) gravité *f*

grave robber *n* déterreur *m* de cadavres

Graves' disease ['greɪvzdɪziːz] *n Med* maladie *f* de Basedow

graveside ['greɪvsaɪd] *n* **at the g.** près de la tombe; **his next of kin were there at the g.** ses proches étaient présents à l'enterrement

gravestone ['greɪvstəʊn] *n* pierre *f* tombale

graveyard ['greɪvjɑːd] *n* (*for people, Fig for cars*) cimetière *m*; *Fig* **this town is a g.** cette ville est mortelle; **this department has been the g. of more than one young hopeful's ambitions** ce service a mis fin aux ambitions de plus d'un jeune; **g. shift** = équipe *f* de nuit (à partir de minuit)

graving ['greɪvɪŋ] *n Naut* **g. dock** bassin *m* de radoub

gravitate ['grævɪteɪt] *vi Phys* graviter **(towards** vers; **round** autour de); *Fig* **most of the guests had gravitated towards the bar/kitchen** la plupart des invités s'étaient rapprochés du bar/de la cuisine; **at a party she gravitates towards anybody who can help her career** dans les soirées, elle est tout de suite attirée par les personnes qui peuvent l'aider dans sa carrière; **he had gravitated towards a pro-European position** il s'était rallié à la cause européenne

gravitation [grævɪ'teɪʃən] *n Phys* gravitation *f*; *Fig* **there was a general g. towards the bar** tout le monde s'est dirigé vers le bar; *Phys* **law of g.** loi *f* de la gravitation

gravitational [grævɪ'teɪʃən(ə)l] *adj Phys* gravitationnel; (*field*) de gravitation; **g. pull** gravitation *f*

gravity ['grævɪtɪ] *n* **(a)** *Phys* gravité *f*, pesanteur *f*; **law of g.** loi *f* de la pesanteur; *Tech* **g. feed** alimentation *f* en charge *ou* par gravité **(b)** (*of person*) gravité *f*, sérieux *m*; (*of situation, injury*) gravité

gravy ['greɪvɪ] *n* **(a)** *Culin* jus *m*; (*thickened*) sauce *f* (au jus); **g. boat** saucière *f* **(b)** *US Sl* (*money*) (*gained easily*) bénef *m*; (*gained illegally*) profit *m* illicite; **to get on the g. train** trouver le filon; **she's been on the g. train for years** elle a eu la vie facile pendant des années; **it's just a g. train for him and his friends** c'est une véritable mine d'or pour lui et ses amis

gray [greɪ] *adj, n, vi esp US* = **grey**

grayling ['greɪlɪŋ] *n* **(a)** *(fish)* ombre *m* (de rivière) **(b)** *(butterfly)* (papillon *m*) agreste *m*

graze¹ [greɪz] *Agr* **1** *vi* *(of cattle etc)* paître, brouter; **to g. on grass** brouter l'herbe; **to g. in a field** paître au champ **2** *vt* *(of farmer)* *(herd)* (faire) paître; *(field)* mettre en pâturage; *(of cattle etc)* *(field)* pâturer; *(grass)* brouter, paître

graze² *n* écorchure *f*; *(slighter)* éraflure *f*

graze³ *vt* **(a)** *(scrape)* *(knees etc)* écorcher; *(slighter)* érafler **(b)** *(brush past)* effleurer; **the bullet grazed his shoulder** la balle lui rasa l'épaule

grazing ['greɪzɪŋ] *n Agr* **(a)** *(of herd etc)* pâturage *m*; **g. rights** droit *m* de pâturage *ou* de pacage **(b) g. (land** *or* **ground)** pâture *f*, pacage *m*

grease¹ [gri:s] *n Culin, MecE etc* graisse *f*; *MecE* *(dirty)* cambouis *m*; **g. box** boîte *f* à graisse *ou* de graissage; **g. gun** pistolet *m* graisseur; *Av, Aut F* **g. monkey** mécano *m*; **g. nipple** graisseur *m*; **g. stain** *(on clothing etc)* tache *f* de gras *ou* de graisse

grease² *vt Tech* *(machine)* graisser, lubrifier; *Culin* *(cake tin)* beurrer; *Fig F* **to g. sb's palm** graisser la patte à qn

▶ **grease back** *vtsep* **to g. back one's hair** se gominer les cheveux

greased [gri:st] *adj F* **like g. lightning** en quatrième vitesse; **he's like g. lightning** c'est un rapide

greasepaint ['gri:speɪnt] *n* maquillage *m* (de théâtre); **stick of g.** crayon *m* gras (de maquillage); *Fig* **the smell of g.** le mirage du théâtre

greaseproof ['gri:spru:f] *adj* *(paper)* sulfurisé

greaser ['gri:sər] *n* **(a)** *Br esp Aut Sl* *(mechanic)* mécano *m* **(b)** *Old-fashioned Br Sl* *(motorcyclist)* motard *m* **(c)** *US Offensive Sl* *(Mexican)* Mexicain, -aine

greasiness ['gri:sɪnɪs] *n* **(a)** état *m* graisseux *ou* gras **(b)** *F* *(of manner)* onctuosité *f*

greasy ['gri:sɪ] *adj* **(a)** *(containing, covered in grease)* graisseux, huileux; *(sausage etc)* gras; *(grease-stained)* taché de graisse; **his hands felt g.** il avait les mains grasses; **you'll get your jacket all g.** tu vas mettre plein de graisse sur ta veste; **g. hair** cheveux gras; **g. complexion** peau grasse; **g. pole** *(at village fête etc)* mât *m* de cocagne; *Sl* **g. spoon** *(café)* boui-boui *m*, *pl* bouis-bouis **(b)** *(slippery)* *(road etc)* glissant **(c)** *F* *(manner)* onctueux, mielleux

great [greɪt] **1** *adj* **(a)** *(large, important)* grand; **a g. crowd** une foule nombreuse *ou* énorme; **a g. deal of time/money** beaucoup de temps/d'argent; **I expect a g. deal from my staff** j'attends beaucoup de mon personnel; **you're expecting a g. deal if you think that ...** tu espères trop si tu crois que ...; **a g. many people** beaucoup de gens *ou* de monde; **the g. majority, the greater part** la plupart, la majeure partie **(of** de); **to a g. extent, in g. part** en grande partie; **to reach a g. age** parvenir à un âge avancé; **his greatest fault** son plus grand défaut, son défaut capital; **to take g. care** prendre grand soin **(of** de); **g. difference** grande *ou* forte différence; **the g. divide between rich and poor/the two communities** le fossé immense qui sépare les riches et les pauvres/les deux communautés; **to take a g. interest in sb/sth** s'intéresser beaucoup à qn/qch; **with g. pleasure/with the greatest of pleasure** avec grand/avec le plus grand plaisir; **it gives me g. pleasure to inform you that ...** j'ai l'immense plaisir de vous informer que ...; **they are g. friends** ce sont de grands amis; **it is no g. matter** ce n'est pas une grosse affaire; **to have no g. opinion of sb** ne pas avoir une haute opinion de qn; **the g. thing is that ...** le grand avantage *ou* ce qui est bien, c'est que ...; *Zool* **the g. apes** les grands singes *mpl*; **g. artist** grand artiste; **a g. man** un grand homme; *Old-fashioned F* **G. Scott!** grands dieux!

(b) *(in proper names)* **Alexander the G.** Alexandre le Grand; **the G. Bear** la grande ourse

(c) *F* *(very good)* **to have a g. time** bien s'amuser; **(that's) g!** parfait!, (c'est) super!; *Iron* bravo!; **he's a g. guy** c'est un gars super; **a g. idea** une idée géniale; **isn't he g.!** qu'est-ce qu'il est bien!; **to be g. at tennis** être excellent au tennis; **she's g. at making the past come alive** elle arrive merveilleusement bien à faire revivre le passé; **I'm not g. on Roman history** je ne suis pas très fort *ou* calé en histoire romaine; *Iron* **she's a g. one for borrowing things without asking people** elle est spécialiste pour emprunter les choses sans demander l'autorisation

(d) *(enthusiastic)* **she's a g. hillwalker** elle fait beaucoup de randonnée; **I'm a g. reader** je lis énormément; **to be a g. believer in sth** croire beaucoup en qch

2 *adv F* **(a)** *(well)* très bien; **I feel g.!** je me sens super bien!; **I don't feel g. about what I did** je ne me sens pas très fier de ce que j'ai fait; **you look g. in that suit** il te va vraiment bien ce costume; **you look g.** *(very healthy)* tu as vraiment bonne mine; **he's doing g.** *(in health)* il se porte à merveille

(b) *(intensifier)* **a g. big dog** un énorme chien; **be careful with your g. clumsy feet!** fais attention avec tes grands pieds maladroits!; **you g. fat slob!** espèce de gros lard!

3 *n* **(a)** *(person)* grand *m*, grande *f*; **one of the greats of world cinema** un des grands du cinéma mondial **(b) the g. and the good** *(pl)* les gens influents

great-aunt *n* grand-tante *f*, *pl* grands-tantes

Great Britain *n* Grande-Bretagne *f*

greatcoat ['greɪtkəʊt] *n* **(a)** pardessus *m* **(b)** *Mil* *(worn by cavalry)* manteau *m*; *(worn by infantry)* capote *f*

Great Dane *n* danois *m*

Greater London [greɪtə] *n* Londres *m* et son agglomération

Greater Manchester *n* Manchester *m* et son agglomération

greater than sign *n* signe *m* plus grand que, signe supérieur à

greatest ['greɪtɪst] *n* **to be the g.** *(best)* être le/la meilleur

great-grandchild, *pl* **-children** *n* *(boy)* arrière-petit-fils *m*, *pl* arrière-petits-fils; *(girl)* arrière-petite-fille *f*, *pl* arrière-petites-filles; **great-grandchildren** arrière-petits-enfants

great-granddaughter *n* arrière-petite-fille *f*, *pl* arrière-petites-filles

great-grandfather *n* arrière-grand-père *m*, *pl* arrière-grands-pères, bisaïeul *m*

great-grandmother *n* arrière-grand-mère *f*, *pl* arrière-grands-mères, bisaïeule *f*

great-grandparents *npl* arrière-grands-parents *mpl*, bisaïeuls *mpl*

great-grandson *n* arrière-petit-fils *m*, *pl* arrière-petits-fils

great-greatgrandfather *n* arrière-arrière-grand-père *m*, trisaïeul *m*

great-greatgrandmother *n* arrière-arrière-grand-mère *f*, trisaïeule *f*

great-hearted [greɪt'hɑ:tɪd] *adj* généreux

Great Lakes *npl* **the G.** the Grands Lacs *mpl*

greatly ['greɪtlɪ] *adv* très; **to be g. influenced/surprised/amused** être très influencé/surpris/amusé; **g. irritated** très *ou* fortement irrité; **the difficulties have been g. exaggerated** on a beaucoup exagéré les difficultés; **he has g. improved since last year** il a fait beaucoup de progrès depuis l'année dernière; **I would g. prefer ...** je préférerais nettement ...; **to contribute g. to a result** largement contribuer à un résultat; **g. though I admired/respected him ...** j'avais beau l'admirer/le respecter beaucoup ...

great-nephew *n* petit-neveu *m*, *pl* petits-neveux

greatness ['greɪtnɪs] *n* **(a)** *(of person, action etc)* grandeur *f*; *(of thought)* élévation *f*, noblesse *f*; **g. of soul** grandeur d'âme **(b)** *(extent, size)* grandeur *f*, importance *f*

great-niece *n* petite-nièce *f*, *pl* petites-nièces

Great Plains *npl* **the G.** les Grandes Plaines *fpl*

great-uncle *n* grand-oncle *m*, *pl* grands-oncles

Great Wall of China *n* **the G.** la grande muraille de Chine

Great War *n* **the G.** la Grande Guerre

grebe [gri:b] *n* *(bird)* grèbe *m*; **great crested g.** grèbe huppé

Grecian ['gri:ʃən] *adj* grec, *f* grecque; **in the G. style** à la grecque

Greece [gri:s] *n* Grèce *f*

greed [gri:d] *n* **(a)** *(for material things)* avidité *f*, cupidité *f*; **g. for fame/power** la recherche avide de célébrité/pouvoir; **it's sheer g.!** c'est de l'avidité pure et simple **(b)** *(gluttony)* gourmandise *f*

greedily ['gri:dɪlɪ] *adv* **(a)** *(to hoard, keep for oneself etc)* avidement, cupidement **(b)** *(to eat)* goulûment; *(to look, say)* avec gourmandise

greediness ['gri:dɪnɪs] *n* = **greed**

greedy ['gri:dɪ] *adj* **(a)** *(for material things)* avide, cupide **(b)** *(gluttonous)* gourmand; *Sl* **g. guts** goinfre *m*

Greek [gri:k] **1** *adj* grec, *f* grecque; **the G. Church** l'Église grecque **2** *n* **(a)** *(person)* Grec *m*, Grecque *f* **(b)** *Ling* grec *m*; **modern G.** le grec moderne; *F* **it's all G. to me** c'est de l'hébreu pour moi

green [gri:n] **1** *adj* **(a)** *(colour)* vert; **to paint sth g.** peindre qch en vert; *Lit* **to keep sb's memory g.** entretenir la mémoire de qn; **to give sb the g. light** donner le feu vert à qn **(to do sth** pour faire qch); **to go** *or* **turn g.** *(of traffic lights)* passer au vert; *(of person)* verdir, blêmir; *(of lawn, fields)* verdir; **to grow g.** verdir; *(of grass)* verdoyer; **she has** *Br* **g. fingers** *or Am* **a g. thumb** elle a la main verte; *Agr* **the g. revolution** la révolution verte; **g. with envy** vert de jalousie, pâle d'envie; **to make sb g. with envy** faire pâlir qn d'envie

(b) *F* *(young, inexperienced)* jeune, inexpérimenté; *(naive)* naïf, *f* naïve; **he's not as g. as he looks** il n'est pas si niais qu'il en a l'air; **she's as g. as grass** *(person)* elle est extrêmement naïve

(c) *Pol* *(consumer, policy etc)* vert, écologiste; **g.**

marketing mercatique *f* écologique, marketing *m* vert, écolomercatique *f*, écomarketing *m*; *Mktg* **g. product** produit *m* vert *ou* écologique; **g. tourism** tourisme *m* vert
2 *n* **(a)** (*colour*) vert *m*
(b) (*of trees, plants etc*) verdure *f*
(c) (*vegetables*) **greens** légumes *mpl* verts
(d) (*grassy area*) pelouse *f*, gazon *m*; **village g.** pelouse communale, pré *m* communal; **the g.** la pelouse; *Golf* le green; **bowling g.** (terrain *m* pour) jeu *m* de boules; **g. keeper** (*of bowling green, golf course*) préposé, -ée à l'entretien des pelouses
(e) *Pol* (*person*) écologiste *mf*

green² green wellies = green wellington boots; symbol of landed aristocracy or rural upper-middle class: Examples: the green welly brigade was much in evidence at the village fête; the meeting was attended by agricultural labourers and small tenant farmers—there was not a green welly in sight

greenback ['gri:nbæk] *n US F* billet *m* vert

green bean *n* haricot *m* vert

green belt *n* (*land*) zone *f* verte

Green Berets *npl* bérets *mpl* verts

green card *n Admin* = permis *m* de travail; (*in insurance*) carte *f* verte, attestation *f* d'assurance

green channel *n* (*at airport etc*) file *f* 'rien à déclarer'

greenery ['gri:nəri] *n* verdure *f*

green-eyed *adj* aux yeux verts; *Lit* **the g. monster** (*jealousy*) la jalousie

greenfield ['gri:nfi:ld] *n* **g. site** (*for factory etc*) terrain *m* non-bâti

greenfinch ['gri:nfintʃ] *n* (*bird*) verdier *m*

greenfly ['gri:nflai] *n* (*insect*) puceron *m*; **to have g.** (*of plant*) avoir des pucerons; **g. spray** produit *m* à vaporiser contre les pucerons

greengage ['gri:ngeidʒ] *n* reine-claude *f*, *pl* reines-claudes

greengrocer ['gri:ngrəusər] *n esp Br* marchand, -ande de fruits et légumes; **g.'s (shop)** magasin *m* de fruits et légumes

greenhorn ['gri:nhɔ:n] *n F* blanc-bec *m*, *pl* blancs-becs; *Mil* bleu *m*

greenhouse ['gri:nhaus] *n* serre *f*; **the g. effect** l'effet *m* de serre; **g. gas** gaz *m* à effet de serre

greening ['gri:niŋ] *n* **the recent g. of the Labour Party** la récente conversion du Parti travailliste à l'écologie

greenish ['gri:niʃ] *adj* verdâtre

Greenland ['gri:nlənd] *n* Groenland *m*; **in G.** au Groenland

Greenlander ['gri:nləndər] *n* Groenlandais, -aise

greenmail ['gri:nmeil] *n Fin* greenmail *m*

greenness ['gri:nnis] *n* (*of fruit etc*) immaturité *f*; (*inexperience*) inexpérience *f*; (*naivety*) naïveté *f*, simplicité *f*; (*of countryside etc*) vert *m*, verdure *f*; **the g. of the wood made the fire difficult to light** le feu avait du mal à prendre parce que le bois était vert

Green Paper *n Br Pol* livre *m* blanc

Green Party *n* (*in UK*) parti *m* écologiste

green pea *n* petit pois *m*

green pepper *n* poivron *m* vert

green pound *n EC* livre *f* verte

greenroom ['gri:nru:m] *n TV* salle *f* de détente; *Th* foyer *m* des artistes

green salad *n* salade *f* verte

greenstick ['gri:nstik] *adj Med* **g. fracture** fracture *f* en bois vert

greenstuff ['gri:nstʌf] *n* **(a)** *Br* (*vegetables*) légumes *mpl* verts **(b)** *US Sl* (*paper money*) billets *mpl*

greensward ['gri:nswɔ:d] *n Lit* pelouse *f*, (tapis *m* de) gazon *m*

Greenwich ['grinidʒ, -itʃ, 'gren-] *n* Greenwich; **G. Mean Time** temps *m* universel; **G. meridian** méridien *m* de Greenwich

greenwood ['gri:nwud] *n Lit* bois *m*, forêt *f* (*en été*)

greet¹ [gri:t] **1** *vt* (*person*) saluer; (*welcome*) accueillir avec quelques paroles aimables; **to g. a speech with cheers** acclamer un discours; **the announcement was greeted with cheers** l'annonce a été saluée par des acclamations; **his words were greeted with resentful silence** ses mots ont été accueillis par un silence désapprobateur; **the first thing to g. my ear was ...** la première chose que j'ai entendue a été ...; **to g. the eyes** s'offrir à l'œil **2** *vi Scot* (*cry*) pleurer

greet² *n Scot* (*cry*) **to have a g.** pleurer (**about sth** à cause de qch)

greeting ['gri:tiŋ] *n* salutation *f*, salut *m*; **to send greetings to sb** envoyer ses salutations à qn; **New Year/Christmas greetings** vœux *mpl* de bonne année/Noël; **greetings card** carte *f* de vœux

gregarious [gri'geəriəs] *adj* (*person*) sociable; *Zool, Bot* grégaire

gregariously [gri'geəriəsli] *adv Zool* (*to live*) en groupe; **she was not g. inclined** elle n'avait pas le tempérament grégaire

gregariousness [gri'geəriəsnis] *n* (*of person*) sociabilité *f*; *Zool, Bot* grégarisme *m*, instinct *m* grégaire

Gregorian [gri'gɔ:riən] *adj Rel* (*chant, calendar etc*) grégorien

gremlin ['gremlin] *n F* lutin *m*; *Fig* **to get all the gremlins out of the system** se débarrasser de toutes les petites bêtises qui ralentissent le système

grenade [grə'neid] *n Mil* grenade *f*; **g. launcher** lance-grenade *m*, *pl* lance-grenades; **g. attack** attaque *f* à la grenade

grenadier [grenə'diər] *n Mil* grenadier *m*

grenadine ['grenədi:n] *n* (*syrup*) grenadine *f*

grew *see* **grow**

grey¹, *US* **gray** [grei] **1** *adj* **(a)** gris; **to turn** *or* **go g.** grisonner; *Fig* **it's a g. area** c'est une zone d'ombre; *Com* **g. import** importation *f* grise; *Com, Fin* **g. market** marché *m* gris; *Anat* **g. matter** substance *f ou* matière *f* grise; *Hum* **to exercise the g. matter** faire marcher sa matière grise; *esp US* **g. power** = pouvoir *m* (économique, social etc) des personnes âgées; *Comptr* **g. scale** niveau *m* de gris
(b) (*complexion*) blême; **to turn g.** blêmir
(c) (*outlook etc*) sombre, morne; **a g. dismal morning** un matin gris et triste; **a g. existence** une existence morne
2 *n* **(a)** (*colour*) gris *m*; **hair touched with g.** cheveux grisonnants; *Comptr* **shades of g.** niveaux de gris
(b) (*horse*) cheval *m* gris

grey², *US* **gray** *vi* (*of hair*) grisonner; **to be greying at the temples** avoir les tempes grisonnantes, grisonner aux tempes

greybeard ['greibiəd] *n esp Lit* (*old man*) vieillard *m* sage, *Pej* vieux barbon *m*

grey-eyed *adj* aux yeux gris

grey-haired, -headed [grei'heəd, -'hedid] *adj* aux cheveux gris; (*greying*) grisonnant

greyhound ['greihaund] *n* lévrier *m*; **g. racing** courses *fpl* de lévriers; **g.(-racing) track** cynodrome *m*

greying ['greiiŋ] *adj* grisonnant; **a g. population** une population vieillissante

greyish ['greiiʃ] *adj* grisâtre

greylag ['greilæg] *n* **g. (goose)** oie *f* cendrée

greyness ['greinis] *n* **(a)** (*colour*) teinte *f* grise; **the g. of London** la grisaille de Londres **(b)** (*depressing quality*) caractère *m* morne *ou* sombre, tristesse *f*

Grey Panthers *npl esp US* = groupe *m* de pression composé de personnes âgées

grey squirrel *n* écureuil *m* gris

grey wolf *n* loup *m* gris

grid [grid] *n* **(a)** (*bars etc*), *El* grille *f*, grillage *m* **(b)** = **gridiron** **(c)** (*on map*) quadrillage *m*; **g. reference** coordonnées *fpl*; **g. system** réseau *m* de quadrillage; **g. lines** droites *fpl* du quadrillage; *El* **the national g.** le réseau électrique national; **g. layout** (*of town*) quadrillage, damier *m* **(d)** *Sp* (*of motor racing circuit*) **(starting) g.** ligne *f* de départ

griddle ['grid(ə)l] *n Culin* tôle *f* (*sur laquelle on cuit des galettes*); **g. cake** galette *f*

gridiron ['gridaiən] *n Am Fb* terrain *m* de football

gridlock ['gridlɒk] *n Am* (*on road*) embouteillage *m*; *Fig* impasse *f*

grief [gri:f] *n* chagrin *m*, douleur *f*; **to die of g.** mourir de chagrin; **to come to g.** (*of person*) (*in undertaking*) échouer; (*have an accident*) avoir un accident; (*of rider*) faire une chute; (*of plan etc*) échouer, mal tourner; **she came to g. in the written exam** elle a échoué à l'écrit; *F* **good g.!** mon Dieu!

grief-stricken ['gri:fstrik(ə)n] *adj* accablé de douleur *ou* de chagrin

grievance ['gri:vəns] *n* **(a)** (*feeling of having been wronged*) grief *m*; **to have a g. against sb** avoir un grief contre qn; **to air** *or* **state one's grievances** conter *ou* exprimer ses doléances **(b)** (*wrong*) doléance *f*; **to redress a g.** réparer un tort; *Ind etc* **g. procedure** procédure *f* pour porter plainte

grieve [gri:v] **1** *vi* se chagriner, s'affliger (**over** *or* **about sth** de qch); **the whole nation grieved at his death** la nation entière pleura sa mort; **he was grieving for his lost daughter** il pleurait sa fille perdue; **she is still grieving** elle a encore de la peine **2** *vt* (*person*) chagriner, affliger; **we are grieved to learn ...** nous apprenons avec peine ...; **it grieves me to ...** cela me peine de ...

grieved [gri:vd] *adj* chagriné, affligé (**at** de); **deeply g.** navré (**at** de)

grievous ['gri:vəs] *adj Fml* **(a)** (*causing grief*) douloureux, pénible; (*news*) affligeant, douloureux; (*loss*) cruel **(b)** (*wound etc*) grave; *Jur* **g. bodily harm** coups *mpl* et blessures *fpl* graves; *Jur* **to cause g. bodily harm** causer de graves blessures

grievously [ˈgriːvəslɪ] *adv (seriously)* gravement; *(wounded)* grièvement

griffin [ˈgrɪfɪn] *n Myth* griffon *m*

griffon [ˈgrɪfən] *n* **(a)** *(dog)* griffon *m* **(b)** *Myth* griffon *m* **(c)** *(bird)* **g. (vulture)** vautour *m* griffon

grift [grɪft] *vt Am Sl* escroquer

grifter [ˈgrɪftər] *n Am Sl* escroc *m*

grill[1] [grɪl] *n Br Culin* **(a)** *(food)* grillade *f*; **a mixed g.** un assortiment de grillades **(b)** *(room in restaurant)* grill-room *m, pl* grill-rooms; *(restaurant)* rôtisserie *f*

grill[2] *n Br Culin (device)* gril *m*; **to cook sth under the g.** cuire qch sur le *ou* au gril

grill[3] **1** *vt* **(a)** *Br (cook) (meat etc)* faire griller **(b)** *F (interrogate) (prisoner etc)* cuisiner **2** *vi Br Culin* griller

grill(e) [grɪl] *n (bars) (of gate)* grille *f*; **(counter) g.** *(in bank etc)* grille de comptoir; *Aut* **(radiator) g.** calandre *f*

grilled [grɪld] *adj Br Culin* grillé; **g. meat** viande *f* grillée, grillade *f*

grilling [ˈgrɪlɪŋ] *n* **(a)** *Br (of food)* cuisson *f* sur le *ou* au gril **(b)** *F (interrogation)* **to give sb a g.** cuisiner qn

grillroom [ˈgrɪlrʊm] *n (in restaurant)* grill-room *m, pl* grill-rooms; *(restaurant)* rôtisserie *f*

grim [grɪm] *adj (countryside, surroundings)* sinistre, lugubre; *(news, report)* sombre; *(face)* sévère; *(smile)* sardonique; *(humour)* macabre; **to hold on like g. death** se cramponner **(to sb/sth** à qn/qch); **g. determination** volonté inflexible; **to look g.** *(of person) (serious)* avoir une mine sévère; *(very ill)* avoir très mauvaise mine; **things are looking g.** ça s'annonce mal; **the g. prospect of another famine** la perspective sinistre d'une autre famine; *F* **how do you feel? – pretty g.!** comment ça va? – plutôt mal; *F* **I thought it was pretty g.** *(not well done, of poor quality)* je l'ai trouvé plutôt minable

grimace[1] [grɪˈmeɪs] *n* grimace *f*; **to make a g.** faire la grimace

grimace[2] *vi* grimacer, faire la grimace

grime [graɪm] *n* saleté *f*; *(dust)* poussière *f* de charbon *ou* de suie

griminess [ˈgraɪmɪnɪs] *n* saleté *f*, noirceur *f*

grimly [ˈgrɪmlɪ] *adv* sinistrement, de façon lugubre; *(to fight, hold on)* avec acharnement

grimness [ˈgrɪmnɪs] *n (of surroundings, landscape)* caractère *m* sinistre *ou* lugubre; *(of face)* sévérité *f*; *(of struggle)* acharnement *m*; **the g. of the situation in Rwanda** la situation désespérée au Rwanda; **the g. of the news from the front** les sombres nouvelles du front

grimy [ˈgraɪmɪ] *adj* sale, encrassé, noirci; *(with soot)* noir (de suie)

grin[1] [grɪn] *n* **(a)** *(smile)* large sourire *m*; **to give a broad g.** avoir la bouche fendue jusqu'aux oreilles **(b)** *(grimace)* grimace *f* (qui découvre les dents)

grin[2] *vi* **(-nn-)** **(a)** *(smile)* sourire; *(broadly)* faire un large sourire; **he grinned broadly** son visage s'est épanoui en un large sourire, il fit un large sourire; *Fig* **to g. and bear it** (tâcher de) garder le sourire, *F* encaisser (sans broncher) **(b)** *(grimace)* grimacer en montrant les dents

grind[1] [graɪnd] *n* **(a)** *F (work)* labeur *m* monotone et continu; **the daily g.** métro, boulot, dodo; **what a g.!** quelle corvée! **(b)** *(erotic dance)* déhanchement *m* **(c)** *(sound)* grincement *m*, crissement *m*

grind[2] *(pt, pp* **ground** [graʊnd]) **1** *vt* **(a)** *(pulverize) (grain, coffee, pepper)* moudre; *Am (meat)* hacher; *also Fig* **to g. sth to dust** pulvériser qch; **to g. sth under one's heel** écraser qch avec le talon; *Fig* écraser qch; *Fig* **to g. the faces of the poor** opprimer les pauvres; **to g. one's teeth** grincer des dents

(b) *(polish) (glass)* dépolir; *Opt* **to g. lenses** polir des lentilles

(c) *(sharpen)* aiguiser, affûter; *(on grindstone)* passer à la meule

(d) to g. a barrel organ jouer de l'orgue de Barbarie; **to g. a pepper mill** moudre du poivre

2 *vi* **(a)** *(of wheels)* grincer, crisser; *(of gears)* craquer; **to g. to a halt** *(of vehicle)* s'immobiliser; *(of machine, Fig production)* stopper; **the whole country ground to a halt** *or* **standstill during the General Strike** le pays a été complètement paralysé pendant la grève générale

(b) *Old-fashioned F (work hard)* bûcher, turbiner; *Sch* bachoter

▶ **grind away** *vi* **(a)** *(working)* progresser laborieusement; **to g. away at sth** travailler laborieusement à qch **(b)** *F (sexually)* s'envoyer en l'air

▶ **grind down 1** *vtsep* **(a)** *(opposition)* écraser; **a people ground down by poverty** un peuple accablé par une pauvreté extrême; *F* **don't let the bastards g. you down!** ne te laisse pas enfoncer par ces salauds! **(b)** *(pulverize) (grain, coffee)* moudre **(c)** *(sharpen)* aiguiser, affûter **2** *vi (of substance)* **it grinds down easily** c'est facile à moudre

▶ **grind on** *vi (proceed relentlessly)* ne pas en finir; *(of negotiations, speech)* traîner en longueur, s'éterniser; **the accordion music ground on in the background** en fond sonore on entendait l'accordéon, interminable et monotone

▶ **grind out** *vtsep* **(a)** *(produce without originality) (articles, poems)* pondre; **to g. out a tune** jouer un air avec monotonie; **he ground out the same jokes night after night** il a débité les mêmes plaisanteries soir après soir **(b)** *(cigarette)* écraser

▶ **grind up** *vtsep (pulverize)* pulvériser; **to g. sth up small** moudre qch fin

grinder [ˈgraɪndər] *n* **(a)** *(device)* appareil *m* broyeur, broyeuse *f*; *(for coffee)* moulin *m* à café; *(for sharpening)* meule *f*; *Fig* **to put sb through the g.** faire passer un mauvais quart d'heure à qn **(b)** *(person)* broyeur, -euse; *(of knives etc)* rémouleur *m* **(c)** *(molar)* molaire *f* **(d)** *US F (sandwich)* gros sandwich *m*

grinding [ˈgraɪndɪŋ] **1** *adj (boredom, monotony etc)* mortel; *(worry, insecurity)* accablant; **g. poverty** extrême pauvreté; **g. sound** *(of machine, car, lift)* grincement *m*; *(of gears)* craquement *m*; **to come to a g. halt** *(of vehicle)* s'immobiliser en grinçant; *(of machine, Fig production)* stopper; **to bring sth to a g. halt** *(production)* stopper qch; *(country, rail network)* paralyser qch **2** *n (of corn)* mouture *f*; *(sound) (of machine, factory)* grincement *m*; *(of gears)* craquement *m*

grindingly [ˈgraɪndɪŋlɪ] *adv* **g. boring/monotonous** ennuyeux/monotone à mourir

grindstone [ˈgraɪndstəʊn] *n* meule *f*; *Fig F* **he keeps our noses to the g.** il ne nous laisse aucun répit; **it's going to be noses to the g.** il va y avoir du boulot

gringo [ˈgrɪŋgəʊ] *n usu Pej (English speaker in Latin America)* gringo *m*

grip[1] [grɪp] *n* **(a)** *(hold, grasp)* prise *f*; *(of wheels on road)* adhérence *f*; **to have a strong g.** *(of person)* avoir une bonne poigne; **your g. is wrong** *(on tennis racket, golf club etc)* tu ne tiens pas ta raquette/ton club comme il faut; *Fig* **I can't get to grips with Shakespeare** je n'arrive pas à comprendre Shakespeare; **to come to grips with sb** *(physically)* s'en prendre à qn; **to get a g. on sth** avoir une prise sur qch; *Fig* **to get a g. on the situation** *(bring under control)* prendre la situation en mains; *Fig* **to get** *or* **take** *or* **keep a g. on oneself** se maîtriser; **to have a firm g. on sth** *(physically)* tenir qch bien en main; *Fig* **although he has officially retired, Sir Charles retains a firm g. on financial decisions** bien qu'il soit officiellement à la retraite, Sir Charles est toujours très impliqué dans les décisions financières; *Br Fig F* **get a g.!** *(control yourself)* reprends-toi!; *(behave normally, be realistic)* arrête de déconner!; **to lose one's g.** *(on rope etc)* lâcher prise; *Fig (mentally)* baisser; **I must be losing my g.** je vieillis, je baisse; **to lose one's g. on reality** perdre le sens des réalités; **he was beginning to lose his g. on the situation** il commençait à perdre le contrôle de la situation; **in the g. of a disease/despair/pessimism** en proie à une maladie/au désespoir/au pessimisme; *Fig* **the country was in the g. of the worst winter for years** le pays connaissait l'hiver le plus rigoureux qu'il avait connu depuis des années

(b) *(handle) (of oar, handlebars)* poignée *f*; *(of pistol)* poignée, crosse *f*; *Tennis (of racket)* manche *m*

(c) *MecE etc (device)* pince *f*

(d) (hair) g. pince *f* (à cheveux)

(e) *Old-fashioned Am (bag)* mallette *f*

(f) *TV, Cin* **grip(s)** machiniste *m* (de plateau)

grip[2] **(-pp-) 1** *vt (seize)* saisir, prendre; *(hold)* empoigner, agripper; **to g. sth in a vice** serrer qch dans un étau; **the tyres g. the road well** les pneus adhèrent bien (à la route); *Fig* **to be gripped by panic** être pris *ou* saisi de panique; **the region has been gripped by cold weather** la région a été saisie par une vague de froid; *Fig* **the play gripped the audience** la pièce a captivé les spectateurs **2** *vi (of tyre)* adhérer

gripe[1] [graɪp] *n* **(a)** *F (complaint)* sujet *m* de mécontentement; **what's your g.?** de quoi est-ce que tu te plains?; **they've always got some g.** ils sont toujours en train de râler **(b)** *(pain)* **gripes** coliques *fpl*; **g. water** médicament *m* pour coliques infantiles

gripe[2] *vi F (complain)* ronchonner, râler **(about sth** à propos de qch)

griping [ˈgraɪpɪŋ] **1** *adj* **g. pains** coliques *fpl* **2** *n F (complaining)* plaintes *fpl*

gripping [ˈgrɪpɪŋ] *adj (book, story)* passionnant

grisly [ˈgrɪzlɪ] *adj (murder, discovery)* macabre, sinistre; *(story, sight)* effrayant, épouvantable

grist [grɪst] *n* blé *m* à moudre; *Fig* **it's all g. to their mill** cela apporte de l'eau à leur moulin

gristle ['grɪs(ə)l] *n* (*in meat*) nerfs *mpl*
gristly ['grɪslɪ] *adj* (*meat*) nerveux
grit¹ [grɪt] *n* **(a)** (*particles*) grès *m*, sable *m*; (*for icy roads*) sable; *MecE etc* impuretés *fpl* **(b)** *Fig* (*courage, determination*) cran *m*, courage *m*; **to have a lot of g.** avoir beaucoup de cran **(c)** (*stone*) grès *m* (dur)
grit² (-tt-) **1** *vt* **(a)** (*put grit on*) (*slippery road surface etc*) sabler **(b) to g. one's teeth** grincer des dents; *Fig* **you'll just have to g. your teeth** il va falloir que tu prennes ton mal en patience **2** *vi* (*put grit on roads*) sabler (les routes)
grits [grɪts] *npl US* (*dish*) gruau *m* d'avoine
gritstone ['grɪtstəʊn] *n* grès *m* (dur)
gritter ['grɪtər] *n Br* (*vehicle*) camion *m* de sablage
gritting ['grɪtɪŋ] *n Br* (*of roads*) sablage *m*; **g. lorry** camion *m* de sablage
gritty ['grɪtɪ] *adj* **(a)** (*soil*) cendreux; (*texture*) graveleux **(b)** *F* (*brave*) qui a du cran, résolu; **g. determination** détermination farouche **(c)** (*realistic*) (*writing etc*) très réaliste; **g. realism** (*of book, film etc*) réalisme cru
grizzle ['grɪz(ə)l] *vi esp Br F* (*complain*) ronchonner, râler; (*whine*) pleurnicher, geindre
grizzled ['grɪz(ə)ld] *adj* (*hair, person*) grisonnant
grizzling ['grɪzlɪŋ] *n esp Br F* (*whining*) pleurnicherie *f*, pleurnichement *m*
grizzly ['grɪzlɪ] **1** *adj* **(a)** (*hair, person*) grisonnant **(b)** *F* (*whining*) grognon **(c) g. bear** grizzli *m*, grizzly *m* **2** *n* (*bear*) grizzli *m*, grizzly *m*
groan¹ [grəʊn] *n* (*of pain*) gémissement *m*; (*at boring story, bad joke*) grognement *m* désapprobateur; (*of disappointment, dismay*) grognement; (*of tree, timber*) grincement *m*; **to give** *or* **utter a deep g.** pousser un profond gémissement
groan² **1** *vi* (*in pain*) gémir, pousser un gémissement; (*complain*) geindre; (*at bad joke, in dismay*) grogner; (*of tree, timber*) grincer; **to g. inwardly** étouffer une plainte *ou* un gémissement; **to g. under the weight of sth** grincer sous le poids de qch; **the cart is groaning under the load** la charrette grince sous le fardeau **2** *vt* (*say*) gémir
groats [grəʊts] *npl* (*of oats, wheat*) gruau *m* d'avoine/de froment
grobag® ['grəʊbæg] *n* = sac *m* de terreau que l'on perfore et qui sert directement de pépinière
grocer ['grəʊsər] *n* épicier, -ière; **the g.'s will be closed** l'épicerie sera fermée; **to go to the g.'s** aller à l'épicerie *ou* chez l'épicier
groceries ['grəʊsərɪz] *npl* (articles *mpl* d')épicerie *f*
grocery ['grəʊsərɪ] *n* (*shop*) épicerie *f*; **to be in the g. business** être dans l'épicerie
grog [grɒg] *n* (*drink*) grog *m*
groggy ['grɒgɪ] *adj F* chancelant, titubant; (*boxer*) groggy; **to feel g.** avoir les jambes en coton; **I'm feeling a bit g.** je ne suis pas dans mon assiette
grogshop ['grɒgʃɒp] *n Austr F* = magasin *m* où l'on vend des boissons alcoolisées
groin [grɔɪn] *n* **(a)** *Anat* aine *f*; **g. injury** blessure *f* à l'aine; *Euph* **she kicked him in the g.** elle lui a donné un coup de pied dans les parties **(b)** *Archit* (*of vault*) arête *f*
grommet ['grɒmɪt] *n MecE* bague *f* d'étoupe; *Naut* erse *f*, erseau *m*
groom¹ [gru:m] *n* **(a)** (*of horse*) palefrenier *m* **(b)** (*at wedding*) marié *m* **(c)** (*of King's Bed Chamber etc*) gentilhomme *m*, valet *m*
groom² *vt* **(a)** (*horse*) panser **(b)** *Fig* (*candidate*) préparer, former (*en vue d'un poste ou d'une fonction dans la politique etc*); **the dictator groomed his successor for power** le dictateur a préparé son successeur au pouvoir
groomed [gru:md] *adj* **well-g.** (*horse*) bien entretenu; (*person*) bien soigné, soigné de sa personne
grooming ['gru:mɪŋ] *n* **(a)** (*of horse*) pansage *m* **(b)** (*of person*) **good g. is very important** il est important d'avoir une bonne présentation **(c)** *Fig* (*of candidate*) préparation *f*
groove¹ [gru:v] *n* **(a)** (*slot*) rainure *f*; (*of gun etc*) rayure *f*; (*of column etc*) cannelure *f*; (*on record*) sillon *m* sonore; (*for sliding shutter etc*) coulisse *f*, glissière *f* **(b)** *Fig* (*routine*) routine *f*; **to get into a g.** s'encroûter, devenir routinier
groove² **1** *vt* rainer; (*gun etc*) rayer; (*column*) canneler **2** *vi F* (*dance*) danser; **to g. to the beat** danser en rythme
groovy ['gru:vɪ] *adj Old-fashioned F* sensass
grope¹ [grəʊp] *n* **(a)** (*in dark etc*) tâtonnement *m* **(b)** *F* (*sexual*) pelotage *m*; **they were having a g.** ils se pelotaient; **all he's interested in is a quick g.** tout ce qui l'intéresse c'est d'avoir quelqu'un à peloter en vitesse
grope² **1** *vi* tâtonner; **to g. for sth** chercher qch à tâtons *ou* à l'aveuglette; **to g. for a word** chercher un mot **2** *vt* **(a) to g. one's way** avancer à tâtons, se diriger en tâtonnant (**towards sth** vers qch) **(b)** *F* (*sexually*) peloter
groper ['grəʊpər] *n* (*fish*) mérou *m*
groping ['grəʊpɪŋ] **1** *adj* tâtonnant **2** *n* **(a)** (*in dark etc*) tâtonnement *m* **(b)** (*sexual*) pelotage *m*
grosbeak ['grəʊsbi:k] *n* (*bird*) gros-bec *m*, *pl* gros-becs
grosgrain ['grəʊgreɪn] *n Tex* gros-grain *m*
gross¹ [grəʊs] *n inv* [①A12,1,hi] (*twelve dozen*) douze douzaines *fpl*, grosse *f*
gross² **1** *adj* **(a)** (*fat*) gras, *f* grasse
(b) (*blatant*) (*error*) grossier; (*ignorance*) crasse; (*injustice, carelessness, idiocy*) flagrant; (*abuse*) choquant; **g. negligence** faute *f* grave
(c) (*vulgar*) (*joke, person*) grossier; *esp Am F* **that's g.**! (*excessive*) c'est trop
(d) *Com, Fin* (*profit, income*) brut; **g. amount** montant *m* brut; *Am* **g. holiday** *or* **vacation propensity** tendance *f* touristique générale; **g. income** (*in accounts*) produit *m* brut; (*of individual*) revenu *m* brut; **g. margin** marge *f* brute; **g. operating profit** bénéfice *m ou* résultat *m* brut d'exploitation; **g. profit** bénéfice *m* brut; **g. profit margin** marge *f* commerciale brute; **g. weight** poids *m* brut, brut *m*
(e) *Naut* (*displacement*) global, total; **g. ton** tonne *f* de jauge; **g. (register) tonnage** (tonnage *m* de) jauge *f* brute, tonnage *m* brut
2 *n* (*whole amount*) montant *m* brut
gross³ *vt Com etc* (*of company*) gagner brut; (*of sale*) produire brut
gross domestic product *n Econ* produit *m* intérieur brut
grossed-up price ['grəʊstʌp] *n* prix *m* fort, plein tarif *m*
grossly ['grəʊslɪ] *adv* **(a)** (*vulgarly*) grossièrement **(b)** (*exaggerated, negligent*) énormément; **to be g. mistaken** se tromper grossièrement; **his skills have been g. overrated** ses capacités ont été vraiment surestimées
gross national product *n Econ* produit *m* national brut
grossness ['grəʊsnɪs] *n* **(a)** (*obesity*) obésité *f* **(b)** (*of abuse, stupidity, error etc*) énormité *f* **(c)** (*vulgarity*) grossièreté *f*
grot [grɒt] *n F* (*muck*) crasse *f*
grotesque [grəʊ'tesk] **1** *adj* (*bizarre*) grotesque **2** *n Art* grotesque *m*
grotesquely [grəʊ'tesklɪ] *adv* grotesquement
grotto, *pl* **-oes, -os** ['grɒtəʊ, -əʊz] *n* grotte *f*
grotty ['grɒtɪ] *n Br F* dégueulasse; (*ill*) vaseux
grouch¹ [graʊtʃ] *n F* **(a)** (*person*) râleur, -euse **(b)** (*complaint*) plainte *f*; **to have a g. about sth** se plaindre de qch; **to have a g. against sb** en vouloir à qn
grouch² *vi F* râler, ronchonner (**to sb** après qn; **about sth** à propos de qch)
grouchy ['graʊtʃɪ] *adj F* râleur, ronchonneur
ground¹ [graʊnd] *adj* **(a)** (*coffee, wheat*) moulu; **g. rice** semoule *f* de riz; *Am* **g. beef/meat** bœuf *m*/viande *f* haché(e) **(b)** (*steel*) meulé; (*glass*) dépoli
ground² *n* **(a)** (*earth etc*) sol *m*, terre *f*; **sitting on the g.** assis par terre; **to pick sth up off the g.** ramasser qch par terre; **to fall to the g.** tomber à *ou* par terre; **above/below g.** sur/sous terre; **curtains down to the g.** rideaux qui pendent jusqu'à terre; **burnt (down) to the g.** brûlé de fond en comble; *F* **that suits me** *Br* **down to the g.** *or US* **from the g. up** (*of arrangement etc*) ça me convient parfaitement; *Fig* **to cut the g. from under sb's feet** couper l'herbe sous le pied à qn; **the plane didn't get off the g.** l'avion n'a pas décollé, l'avion n'a pas quitté le sol; *Fig* **the idea never got off the g.** l'idée n'a jamais abouti à rien; *Fig* **the idea may take a while to get off the g.** l'idée risque de mettre du temps à prendre forme; **when the project eventually did get off the g.** quand le projet a enfin démarré; *Fig* **to work oneself into the g.** se tuer au travail; *Fig* **he's driven this car into the g.** il a usé cette voiture jusqu'au bout; **to go to g.** (*of fox*), *Fig* se terrer; **to run a fox to g.** traquer un renard jusqu'à son terrier; *Fig* **to run sb to g.** (*criminal, person sought by police*) traquer qn; **I finally ran him to g. in the library** j'ai fini par le trouver à la bibliothèque; **g. arrangements** (*at airport*) services *mpl* au sol; *Mil* **g. attack** attaque *f* terrestre; *Aut* **g. clearance** hauteur *f* du châssis au-dessus du sol, garde *f* au sol; *Mil* **g. forces** forces *fpl* terrestres; *Met* **g. frost** gelée *f* blanche; **g. handling agency** agence *f* de réceptif, agence réceptive; **g. handling agent** agent *m* de réceptif; *TV, Cin* **g. lamp** lampe *f* de rampe; *TV* **g. station** station *f* terrestre; *TV* **g. transmitter** émetteur *m* terrestre
(b) (*land, for sport*) terrain *m*; *Fig* **to find common g. for negotiations** trouver un terrain d'entente en vue de négocier; *Fig* **to be on firm g.** être sûr de soi; *Fig* **to be on shaky g.** marcher sur des œufs; *Fig* **to change** *or* **shift one's g.** changer de tactique; *Fig* **to break new** *or* **fresh g.** faire œuvre de pionnier, innover; **to cover a lot of g.** (*travel a great distance*) faire beaucoup de chemin *ou* de kilomètres; *Fig* (*deal with many subjects*) couvrir de très nombreux domaines; **to cover a lot of g. looking for sb** rechercher qn

dans un vaste rayon; **to gain g.** gagner du terrain, progresser; (*of idea*) faire son chemin; **to lose g.** (*of troops, company, government*) perdre du terrain; **we are losing g. to the competition** la concurrence gagne du terrain; **to give g.** (*of troops, company, government*) céder du terrain; **to stand** *or* **hold one's g.** tenir bon, tenir ferme; *Fig* **to confront/defeat sb on his own g.** affronter/battre qn sur son propre terrain; **g. rent** loyer *m* de la terre; (*as source of income*) rente *f* foncière

(**c**) **grounds** (*of school, hospital, country house*) parc *m*; **the school has extensive grounds** l'école est entourée d'un immense parc; **country house with extensive grounds** château avec domaine

(**d**) (*of sea*) fond *m*; *Naut* **to touch g.** (*of ship*) talonner, heurter le fond

(**e**) (*background*) (*of painting*) fond *m*, champ *m*; **light colour on a dark g.** couleur claire sur un fond sombre

(**f**) **grounds** (*reasons*) raison *f*, cause *f*, motif *m*; (*of suspicions etc*) base *f*; **g.** *or* **grounds for complaint** raisons de se plaindre; **she has no g. for complaint** elle n'a aucune raison de se plaindre; **to have (good) g.** *or* **grounds for doing sth** avoir de bonnes raisons de faire qch; **they had no grounds for treating her like that** ils n'avaient pas le droit de la traiter de cette manière; **... and with good g.** ... et avec raison; **what grounds have you for saying that?** qu'est-ce qui vous permet d'affirmer cela?; **it gives us grounds to suspect that ...** cela nous donne des raisons de suspecter que ...; **on what grounds?** à quel titre?; **on personal/medical/moral grounds** pour des raisons personnelles/médicales/morales; **on grounds of ill-health** pour raisons de santé; *Jur* **grounds for divorce** motifs de divorce; *Jur* **grounds for appeal** voies *fpl* de recours

(**g**) *Am El* terre *f*, masse *f*; **to connect to g.** (*pole*) mettre à la masse, relier à la terre; *Am Aut* **g. cable** câble *m* de masse

(**h**) **grounds** (*of coffee*) marc *m*

(**i**) *Mus* **g. bass** basse *f* contrainte; **g. note** son *m* fondamental

ground³ 1 *vt* (**a**) (*base*) fonder, baser, appuyer (**on** *or* **in sth** sur qch); (*belief*) asseoir (**on** sur) (**b**) **to g. sb in sth** (*give a grounding in*) former qn en qch (**c**) *Am El* (*current*) mettre à la masse, relier à la terre (**d**) (*ship*) échouer; (*airplane*) interdire de vol; *F* **to be grounded** (*of teenager*) ne pas avoir le droit de sortir; *Mil* **g. arms!** reposez armes! **2** *vi* (*of ship*) échouer, s'échouer (**on** sur); (*of balloon*) atterrir

groundbait ['graʊndbeɪt] *n Fishing* amorce *f* de fond

ground connection *n Am El* prise *f* de terre

ground control *n Av, Astronaut* contrôle *m* au sol

ground crew *n* personnel *m* au sol, personnel non navigant

grounded ['graʊndɪd] *adj* (**a**) (*based*) (*argument, belief etc*) fondé; **well/ill g.** (*belief*) bien/mal fondé (**b**) *Am El* (mis) à la masse, relié à la terre

ground floor *n Br* rez-de-chaussée *m inv*; *Fig* **to get in on the g.** (*of a project*) participer dès le début; *Fin* (*buy shares*) acheter des actions dès leur émission

groundhog ['graʊndhɒg] *n* marmotte *f* d'Amérique; *Am* **g. day** = jour *m* où la marmotte d'Amérique, sortant de son terrier, indique que le printemps est arrivé

grounding ['graʊndɪŋ] *n* (**a**) (*of argument on sth*) fondement *m* (**b**) *Am El* (*of current*) mise *f* à la terre *ou* à la masse (**c**) (*of ship*) échouage *m*; (*of airplane*) interdiction *f* de vol; (*of balloon*) atterrissage *m* (**d**) **to have a good g. in Latin** avoir de bonnes bases en latin

groundless ['graʊndlɪs] *adj* (*suspicion etc*) mal fondé, sans fondement

ground level *n* rez-de-chaussée *m inv*; **at g.** au rez-de-chaussée

ground line *n Fishing* ligne *f* de fond

groundnut ['graʊndnʌt] *n Br* arachide *f*; **g. oil** huile *f* d'arachide

ground operator *n* (*organizes services, transfers etc*) voyagiste *m ou* agence *f* de réceptif, réceptif *m*

ground personnel *n* personnel *m* au sol, personnel non navigant

ground plan *n Constr* plan *m* horizontal, projection *f* horizontale

ground rule *n* règle *f* de base; **to establish the ground rules** fixer les règles de base

groundsel ['graʊndsəl] *n* (*weed*) séneçon *m*

groundsheet ['graʊndʃiːt] *n* (*of tent*) tapis *m* de sol

groundsman, *pl* **-men** ['graʊndzmən] *n Sp* responsable *m* de l'entretien d'un terrain de sport

groundspeed ['graʊndspiːd] *n Av* vitesse *f* au sol

ground staff *n* (**a**) *Sp* personnel *m* responsable de l'entretien d'un terrain de sport (**b**) (*at airport*) personnel *m* au sol

groundswell ['graʊndswel] *n Naut* lame *f* de fond; *Fig* **g. of public opinion** grand mouvement *m* d'opinion publique; **there has been a g. of support for the proposal** il y a eu un raz-de-marée en faveur de la proposition

ground-to-air *adj Mil* (*missile etc*) sol-air *inv*

ground-to-ground *adj Mil* (*missile etc*) sol-sol *inv*

groundwork ['graʊndwɜːk] *n* (*initial work*) travail *m* préparatoire; *Fig* **to do** *or* **lay the g. for a project/economic reform** jeter les fondations d'un projet/de réformes économiques; **I've laid the g., the rest is up to you** j'ai préparé le terrain, le reste dépend de toi

group¹ [gruːp] *n* [①A11,g,i] (**a**) (*of people, companies*), *Mus* groupe *m*; (*of things*) groupe, ensemble *m*; **to form a g.** se grouper; **(arranged) in groups of three** répartis en groupes de trois; **g. of accounts** classe *f* de comptes; **political g.** groupe(ment) *m* politique; **g. booking** réservation *f* de groupe; **g. decision** décision *f* collective; **g. discount** remise *f* pour les groupes; *Psy* **g. dynamics** dynamique *f* de groupe; **g. fare** tarif *m* de groupe; **g. interview** entretien *m* de groupe; **g. leader** responsable *mf* de groupe; **g. manager** chef *m* de groupe; **g. meeting** (*for marketing survey*) réunion *f* de groupe; **g. organizer** organisateur, -trice groupe; **g. photograph** photographie *f* de groupe; *Med* **g. practice** (*doctors*) cabinet *m* médical; (*dentists*) cabinet dentaire; **g. product manager** chef *m* de groupe de produits; **g. rate** tarif *m* groupe; **g. sex** sexe *m* de groupe *TV, Cin* **g. shot** plan *m* de groupe (de personnages); **g. subscription** abonnement *m* collectif; *Psy* **g. therapy** psychothérapie *f* de groupe; **g. travel** voyages *mpl* en groupe; *Fin* **g. turnover** chiffre *m* d'affaires du groupe

(**b**) *Mil, Av* (*unit*) groupe *m*; *Br Mil* **g. captain** colonel *m* (d'aviation)

group² 1 *vt* grouper **2** *vi* se grouper (**round** autour de)

groupage ['gruːpɪdʒ] *n* groupage *m*; *Com* **g. bill** connaissement *m* de groupage

grouped consignment [gruːpt] *n Com* envoi *m* groupé

grouper ['gruːpər] *n* (*fish*) mérou *m*

group fader ['feɪdər] *n TV, Cin* potentiomètre *m* général

groupie ['gruːpɪ] *n F* groupie *f*

grouping ['gruːpɪŋ] *n* (**a**) (*putting together*) (*of packages, consignments etc*) groupage *m*; (*of figures etc*) groupement *m* (**b**) (*group*) groupe *m*; **political g.** groupement *m* politique

groupware ['gruːpweər] *n Comptr* logiciel *m* de groupe, synergiciel *m*

grouse¹ [graʊs] *n inv* (*bird*) tétras *m*, grouse *f*; **red g.** lagopède *m* (rouge) d'Écosse; **black g.** tétras lyre; **g. shooting** chasse *f* à la grouse

grouse² *n* (*grumble*) grogne *f*; (*complaint*) plainte *f*; **he enjoys a good g.** il aime ronchonner

grouse³ *vi* ronchonner, grogner (**at, about** contre)

grouser ['graʊsər] *n* râleur, -euse

grousing ['graʊsɪŋ] *n* ronchonneries *fpl*; **I've had enough of your g.!** j'en ai assez de t'entendre ronchonner!

grout¹ [graʊt] *n Constr etc* coulis *m*, mortier *m* clair *ou* liquide; **cement g.** lait *m ou* laitance *f* de ciment

grout² *vt Constr* jointoyer

grove [grəʊv] *n* futaie *f*, bosquet *m*; **beech g.** hêtraie *f*; **olive g.** oliveraie *f*; *Lit* **the groves of Academe** les hautes sphères de l'université

grovel ['grɒv(ə)l] *vi* (**-ll-**, *US* **-l-**) être à quatre pattes; **what are you doing grovelling around on the floor?** qu'est-ce que tu fais à quatre pattes?; *Fig* **to g. to** *or* **before sb** ramper devant qn

grovelling, *US* **groveling** ['grɒv(ə)lɪŋ] **1** *adj* (*humble*) servile; **a g. apology** une excuse obséquieuse **2** *n* servilité *f*; (*before sb*) obséquiosité *f*

grow [grəʊ] (*pt* **grew** [gruː]; *pp* **grown** [grəʊn]) **1** *vi* (**a**) (*of plants, hair*) pousser; (*of seeds*) germer; **to g. back** (*of plants, hair*) repousser; **she let her hair g. long** elle a laissé pousser ses cheveux, elle s'est laissé pousser les cheveux; **olives do not g. in England** les oliviers ne poussent pas en Angleterre

(**b**) (*of person, animal*) grandir; (*of company*) s'agrandir; **you've grown** tu as grandi; **you've grown really tall** qu'est-ce que tu as grandi; **this variety of tree will g. fairly tall in five years** cette variété d'arbre atteint une taille assez importante en cinq ans; **she has grown two inches** elle a grandi de 5 cm

(**c**) (*increase*) augmenter, s'accroître; **the crowd grew** la foule augmenta *ou* grossit; **the economy has grown by 5% in the last two years** la croissance de l'économie a été de 5% au cours des deux dernières années; **his influence grew** son influence a grandi; **support for the strike is growing** la grève est de plus en plus soutenue; **the rumour was growing** la rumeur grandissait; **to g. in wisdom/beauty** grandir en sagesse/beauté (**d**) (*become*) devenir; **to g. old** vieillir; **to g. younger** rajeunir; **to g. big/bigger** (*of person*) grandir; (*of animal, database, crowd, tumor*) grossir; (*of town, company*) s'agrandir; (*of plant, tree*) pousser; (*of problem*) s'accroître; **to g. smaller** (*of person*) rapetisser; (*of swelling, problem*) diminuer; **the noise grew louder** le bruit a augmenté *ou* s'est amplifié; **to g. alarmed/excited** s'alarmer/s'exciter; **to g. angry** se fâcher; **to g. less** diminuer; **it is growing dark** il commence à faire sombre

(**e**) (*reach point*) **I have grown to think that ...** j'en suis venu à penser que ...; **they grew to like the house** ils ont fini par aimer la maison

2 *vt* (**a**) (*roses, vegetables*) cultiver; **soil that will not g. asparagus** sol peu propice aux asperges

(**b**) (*beard*) se laisser pousser; **to g. one's hair (long)** se laisser pousser les cheveux, laisser pousser ses cheveux; **the stag grows fresh antlers every year** de nouveaux andouillers poussent au cerf chaque année

▶ **grow apart** *vi* (*of people*) s'éloigner; **we gradually grew apart as we got older** nous nous sommes progressivement éloignés l'un de l'autre en vieillissant

▶ **grow in** *vi* (*of hair*) repousser; (*of nail*) s'incarner

▶ **grow into** *vipo* (**a**) (*become*) devenir; **she had grown into a woman** elle était devenue femme; **the company grew into a huge organization** l'entreprise est devenue une énorme société (**b**) (*become big enough for*) **he has grown into his brother's shirts** les chemises de son frère lui vont maintenant

▶ **grow on** *vipo F* **that picture grows on me** plus je regarde ce tableau plus il me plaît; **this music grows on you** plus on écoute cette musique plus on l'aime; **it's grown on me** je me suis mis à l'aimer petit à petit; **it will g. on you** tu finiras par l'aimer; **the idea was beginning to g. on me** l'idée commençait à me séduire

▶ **grow out** *vi* **she let the dye grow out** elle a laissé pousser ses cheveux jusqu'à ce que les traces de teinture aient disparu

▶ **grow out of** *vipo* (**a**) (*become too large for*) ne plus rentrer dans; **he's grown out of his shoes** ses chaussures sont maintenant trop petites pour lui (**b**) (*become too old for*) **to g. out of doing sth** passer l'âge de faire qch; **she grew out of her dolls** elle a passé l'âge de jouer à la poupée; **it's just a phase, he'll g. out of it** ce n'est qu'une tocade, ça lui passera; **to g. out of one's friends** ne plus avoir grand-chose en commun avec ses amis

▶ **grow up** *vi* (**a**) (*become adult*) grandir; **I want to be a doctor when I g. up** je veux être docteur quand je serai grand; **we didn't have television when I was growing up** nous n'avions pas la télévision quand j'étais petit

(**b**) (*behave like adult*) **I wish you'd g. up!** j'aimerais bien que tu cesses tes gamineries!; **g. up!** (*be realistic*) reviens sur terre!

(**c**) (*develop*) se développer, se faire jour; **a theory has grown up that ...** une théorie s'est fait jour selon laquelle ...; **a custom has grown up** la coutume s'est établie; **a legend grew up around these events** une légende s'est développée autour de ces événements; **the town grew up around the castle** la ville s'est développée autour du château; **a close friendship gradually grew up between them** une étroite amitié s'est développée entre eux petit à petit

grower ['grəʊər] *n* (**a**) (*person*) cultivateur, -trice (**b**) (*plant*) **fast/slow g.** plante *f* qui pousse vite/lentement

growing ['grəʊɪŋ] **1** *adj* (**a**) (*child*) en pleine croissance; (*town, population etc*) en pleine expansion (**b**) (*increasing*) (*debt*) qui augmente; (*opinion, belief*) de plus en plus répandu; (*discontent, opposition, problem*) grandissant; **there was a g. fear that ...** on craignait de plus en plus que ...; **there is g. support for this party** le parti a de plus en plus d'adhérents; **there are g. problems** il y a de plus en plus de problèmes **2** *n* **g. pains** douleurs *fpl* de croissance

-growing ['grəʊɪŋ] *suff* **wheat/potato-g.** culture *f* du blé/de la pomme de terre; **a potato-g. region** une région à pommes de terre; (*plant*) **fast/slow-g.** qui pousse vite/lentement

growl[1] [graʊl] *n* (*of dog, bear, tiger etc*) grondement *m*, grognement *m*

growl[2] *vti* (**a**) (*of dog, lion etc*) grogner, gronder (**at** contre) (**b**) (*of person*) grogner, grommeler (**at sb** contre qn)

growling ['graʊlɪŋ] *n* (*of dog, bear etc*) grognement *m*, grondement *m*

grown[1] [grəʊn] *adj* grand; **a g. woman** une femme adulte; **when fully g. these animals can ...** lorsqu'ils ont atteint l'âge adulte, ces animaux peuvent ...

grown[2] *pp see* **grow**

grown-up 1 ['grəʊnʌp] *n* grand *m*, grande personne *f*; **the grown-ups** les grands, les grandes personnes **2** [grəʊn'ʌp] *adj* adulte; **he's very g. for his age** il est très mûr pour son âge

growth [grəʊθ] *n* (**a**) (*of person, plant*) croissance *f*; *Med* **(human) g. hormone** hormone *f* somatotrope *ou* de croissance, somatotrophine *f*

(**b**) (*increase*) accroissement *m*; (*of business*) croissance *f*; (*of business, company, population*) expansion *f*; **(economic) g.** croissance économique; **to go for g.** favoriser la croissance; **rate of g.** taux *m* d'expansion *ou* de croissance; **the recent g. in the number of small businesses** l'augmentation récente du nombre de petites entreprises; **a g. area** un secteur en expansion; **alternative medicine has really been a g. area in recent years** les médecines parallèles ont connu un boum ces dernières années; *Mktg* **g. developer** stimulateur *m* de croissance; **g. industry** industrie *f* en expansion; *Mktg* **g. inhibitor** inhibiteur *m* de croissance; **g. market** marché *m* porteur; *St Exch* **g. shares** *or* **stock** actions *fpl* susceptibles d'une hausse rapide, valeurs *fpl* d'avenir *ou* de croissance; **g. strategy** stratégie *f* de croissance

(**c**) (*something that has grown*) **the entrance was covered by a dense g. of weeds** l'entrée était envahie par les mauvaises herbes; **g. of hair** poussée *f* de cheveux; **with a week's g. (of beard) on his chin** le menton couvert d'une barbe de huit jours; **yearly g.** (*of plant*) pousse *f* annuelle

(**d**) (*tumour*) grosseur *f*, excroissance *f*; **benign/malignant g.** tumeur *f* bénigne/maligne; **I have a g. on my neck** j'ai une grosseur au cou

growth-share matrix *n Mktg* matrice *f* croissance-part de marché

groyne [grɔɪn] *n* brise-lames *m inv*

grub [grʌb] *n* (**a**) (*larva*) larve *f*; (*maggot*) asticot *m*, *F* ver *m* (blanc) (**b**) *Sl* (*food*) bouffe *f*; **g.'s up!** à la bouffe! (**c**) *Rugby* **g. kick** coup *m* de pied (bas) à suivre

▶ **grub about, grub around** *vi* (*search*) fouiller, farfouiller; **I was grubbing about in the dirt looking for my key** j'étais en train de farfouiller par terre dans les saletés pour trouver ma clef

▶ **grub out** *vtsep* (*roots etc*) extirper

▶ **grub up** *vtsep* (*root*) extirper; (*plant*) déraciner; (*of bird, animal*) déterrer

grubbiness ['grʌbɪnɪs] *n* (*dirtiness*) saleté *f*, malpropreté *f*; *Fig* (*immorality*) bassesse *f*

grubby ['grʌbɪ] *adj* (*dirty*) crasseux, malpropre; *Fig* (*immoral*) sordide, bas; *Fig* **I felt g. when I found out he was married** je me suis méprisée quand j'ai appris qu'il était marié; **it's normal to feel g. after being raped** c'est normal de se sentir sali aprés un viol; **I don't want him getting his g. hands on these documents** je ne veux pas que ce malpropre ait quoi que ce soit à faire avec ces documents

grubstake ['grʌbsteɪk] *n Am* = provisions *fpl* données à un prospecteur contre un pourcentage de ses profits

Grub Street *n* le monde du journalisme

grudge[1] [grʌdʒ] *n* rancune *f*; **to bear sb a g., to have a g. against sb** tenir rancune à qn, en vouloir à qn; **she's not one to bear a g.** elle n'est pas du genre rancunier; **g. match** règlement *m* de compte

grudge[2] *vt* (**a**) (*give unwillingly*) **to g. sb sth** donner qch à contrecœur à qn; **she grudged them every penny she gave them** elle leur donnait chaque penny à contrecœur; **to g. sb the food they eat** lésiner sur la nourriture de qn (**b**) (*resent*) **to g. sb their pleasures** mal supporter que qn passe du bon temps; **she grudges him his success** elle lui en veut à cause de son succès; **I don't g. spending money but ...** je ne répugne pas à dépenser mais ...; **I g. having to get up so early** je supporte très mal d'avoir à me lever si tôt

grudging ['grʌdʒɪŋ] *adj* (*praise, gift*) fait/donné à contrecœur

grudgingly ['grʌdʒɪŋlɪ] *adv* (*to do sth*) à contrecœur, à regret

gruel ['gru:əl] *n* gruau *m* (d'avoine); (*thin*) brouet *m*

gruelling, *US* **grueling** ['gru:əlɪŋ] *adj* (*race, interview*) éreintant, épuisant; (*match*) âprement disputé; **we had a g. time** ça a été très dur

gruesome ['gru:səm] *adj* horrible, abominable; *Hum* **the g. twosome** les deux terreurs *fpl*

gruesomely ['gru:səmlɪ] *adv* horriblement, abominablement

gruff [grʌf] *adj* (*tone*) bourru, brusque; **a g. voice** une grosse voix

gruffly ['grʌflɪ] *adv* d'un ton bourru

gruffness ['grʌfnɪs] *n* brusquerie *f*; **the g. of his tone** son ton bourru

grumble[1] ['grʌmb(ə)l] *n* grommellement *m*, grognement *m*; **his letter contained the usual grumbles** sa lettre contenait les plaintes habituelles; **to obey without a g.** obéir sans murmurer; *F* **to have a good old g.** rouspéter un bon coup

grumble² **1** *vi* grommeler, grogner, *F* rouspéter; *Fig* (*of thunder*) gronder; **(we) mustn't g.** il ne faut pas se plaindre; **to g. about the food** se plaindre de la nourriture; **to g. at sb** grommeler *ou* rouspéter contre qn; **my stomach's grumbling** j'ai l'estomac qui gargouille **2** *vt* **I do all the work here, he grumbled** c'est moi qui fait tout ici, a-t-il grommelé
grumbler ['grʌmblər] *n* grognon *m*, ronchonneur, -euse, *F* rouspéteur, -euse
grumbling ['grʌmblɪŋ] **1** *adj* grognon; **the g. crowd waited impatiently** la foule attendait avec des ronchonnements d'impatience; **g. noises** des ronchonnements *mpl*; **g. appendix** appendicite *f* chronique **2** *n F* rouspétance *f*
grummet ['grʌmɪt] *n* = **grommet**
grump [grʌmp] *n F* **(a)** (*person*) grincheux, -euse **(b)** *Old-fashioned* **to have the grumps** être grincheux
grumpily ['grʌmpɪlɪ] *adv* (*to agree, wonder, say*) en ronchonnant; (*to look at*) d'un air ronchon
grumpiness ['grʌmpɪnɪs] *n* mauvaise humeur *f*
grumpy ['grʌmpɪ] **1** *adj* (*person*) ronchon, grincheux; (*attitude, tone*) renfrogné; (*answer*) grincheux; **a g. old man** un vieux grincheux **2** *n* **what's wrong, g.?** qu'est-ce qui ne va pas, grincheux?
grunge [grʌndʒ] *n F* **(a)** (*dirt*) crasse *f* **(b)** (*fashion*) grunge *m*
grungy ['grʌndʒɪ] *adj F* (*town*) nul; (*flat, hotel*) miteux; (*sweater, trainers*) crasseux; (*mood*) désagréable
grunt¹ [grʌnt] *n* (*of pig, person*) grognement *m*; **to give a g.** pousser *ou* faire entendre un grognement
grunt² **1** *vi* (*of pig, person*) grogner, pousser un grognement **2** *vt* **to g. an answer** grogner une réponse
grunt³ *n US Mil Sl* (*private*) bidasse *m*
grunting ['grʌntɪŋ] *n* grognement(s) *m(pl)*
gryphon ['grɪfən] *n* = **griffin**
GST [dʒi:es'ti:] *n Can Fin* (*abbr* **goods and services tax**) TPS *f* (*taxe sur les produits et services*)
gt (*abbr* **great**) grand
Guadeloupe [gwɑ:də'lu:p] *n Geog* Guadeloupe *f*
guano ['gwɑ:nəʊ] *n* guano *m*
guarantee¹ [gærən'ti:] *n* **(a)** *Com* (*document, promise*) garantie *f*; **a clock with a 12-month g.** une horloge garantie 12 mois; **this camera's still got two months' g. left** cet appareil-photo est encore garanti deux mois; **it's still under g.** il est encore sous garantie; **g. certificate** certificat *m* de garantie; **g. commission** commission *f* de garantie **(b)** (*security*) garantie *f*, caution *f*; **to leave sth as a g.** laisser qch en garantie; **g. fund** fonds *m* de garantie **(c)** (*assurance*) garantie *f*
guarantee² *vt* (*stand surety for*) se porter garant *ou* caution pour; (*debt, product*) garantir; **watch guaranteed for two years** montre garantie deux ans; **it's guaranteed not to rust** c'est garanti anti-rouille; **I can't g. that she'll come** je ne garantis pas qu'elle viendra; **to g. sb against loss** garantir qn contre les pertes
guaranteed [gærən'ti:d] *adj* (*success*) garanti, assuré; **g. by** (*on financial document*) pour aval, bon pour aval; **g. bond** obligation *f* garantie
guarantor [gærən'tɔ:r] *n* garant, -ante, caution *f*; (*of bill*) donneur d'aval *m*, avaliste *mf*; **to stand as g. for sb** se porter garant *ou* caution pour qn
guaranty ['gærəntɪ] *n* = **guarantee¹**
guard¹ [gɑ:d] *n* **(a)** (*readiness*) garde *f*; **to be on one's g.** être *ou* se tenir sur ses gardes; **to be on one's g. against sth** être sur ses gardes contre qch; **to put sb on his g.** mettre qn en garde; **to be caught off one's g.** être pris au dépourvu; *Fencing, Boxing* **on g.!** en garde!
(b) (*of sentry etc*) **to be on g. (duty)** être en *ou* de faction, être de garde; **to go on g., to mount g.** monter la garde; **to come off g.** descendre de garde; **to keep g.** monter la garde, être de garde; **to keep a prisoner under g.** garder un prisonnier à vue; **he was marched off under g.** il fut emmené sous escorte
(c) (*no pl*) *Mil* (*men*) garde *f*; **one of the old g.** un vieux de la vieille; **g. of honour** garde d'honneur; **to form a g. of honour** faire une haie d'honneur; **to set a g. on a bridge** faire surveiller un pont
(d) (*person*) *Mil* soldat *m* de garde; *Br Rail* chef *m* de train; *US* **(prison) g.** gardien *m* de prison; *Br Mil* **the Guards** les Gardes *mpl* du corps; *Br Mil* **a Guards officer** un officier de la Garde; *Br Rail* **g.'s van** wagon *m* du chef de train; (*for luggage etc*) fourgon *m*
(e) (*device*) dispositif *m* protecteur, protection *f*; (*on machine*) protecteur *m*; *Fencing* (*of foil*) garde *f*; **(fire) g.** garde-feu *m inv*
guard² *vt* **(a)** (*entrance etc*) garder; **to g. sb from** *or* **against a danger** garder *ou* protéger qn d'un danger **(b)** **to g. one's tongue** tenir sa langue **(c)** *Tech* (*gears etc*) protéger
▶ **guard against** *vipo* (*be careful to avoid*) se garder de; **to g. against colds** se protéger *ou* se prémunir contre les rhumes; **to g. against an error** prendre garde à ne pas commettre une erreur
guard dog *n* chien *m* de garde
guarded ['gɑ:dɪd] *adj* **(a)** (*speech, reply, comments etc*) prudent; **he was very g.** il est resté très prudent **(b)** (*mechanism*) protégé **(c)** (*prisoner*) gardé à vue; (*building*) gardé, surveillé
guardedly ['gɑ:dɪdlɪ] *adv* avec circonspection, avec prudence
guardhouse ['gɑ:dhaʊs] *n Mil* corps *m* de garde
guardian ['gɑ:dɪən] *n* gardien, -ienne; *Jur* (*of minor*) tuteur, -trice; **g. angel** ange *m* gardien
guardianship ['gɑ:dɪənʃɪp] *n* garde *f*; *Jur* gestion *f* tutélaire, tutelle *f*
guardrail ['gɑ:dreɪl] *n* garde-fou *m*, *pl* garde-fous, parapet *m*; (*on ship*) bastingage *m*
guardroom ['gɑ:dru:m] *n Mil* **(a)** (*for guards*) corps *m* de garde **(b)** (*for prisoners*) salle *f ou* poste *m* de police
guardsman, *pl* **-men** ['gɑ:dzmən] *n Mil* **(a)** *Br* (*soldier*) soldat *m* de la Garde; (*officer*) officier *m* de la Garde **(b)** *US* **(National) G.** soldat *m* de la Garde Nationale
Guatemala [gwætɪ'mɑ:lə] *n Geog* Guatemala *m*
Guatemalan [gwætɪ'mɑ:lən] *Geog* **1** *adj* guatémaltèque **2** *n* Guatémaltèque *mf*
guava ['gwɑ:və] *n* **(a)** (*fruit*) goyave *f* **(b)** **g. (tree)** goyavier *m*
gubernatorial [gu:bənə'tɔ:rɪəl] *adj esp US* (*residence*) du gouverneur; (*election*) au poste de gouverneur
gudgeon¹ ['gʌdʒən] *n* (*fish*) goujon *m*
gudgeon² *n MecE* goujon *m*, tourillon *m*, axe *m*; *Br* **g. pin** (*in engine*) axe de pied de bielle; (*in machine*) tourillon de la crosse
guelder-rose ['geldə'rəʊz] *n* (*shrub*) boule-de-neige *f*, *pl* boules-de-neige
gueridon ['gerɪdən] *n* guéridon *m*
Guernsey ['gɜ:nzɪ] *n* **(a)** *Geog* Guernesey *f* **(b)** (*sweater*) jersey *m*; (*cow*) vache *f* de Guernesey
guer(r)illa [gə'rɪlə] *n* **(a)** *Mil* guérillero *m*; **g. attacks** attaques *fpl* de guérilleros; **g. war/warfare** guérilla *f*; **band of guer(r)illas** guérilla; **g. leader** chef *m* de guérilla **(b)** *Mktg* **g. attack** guérilla *f*
guess¹ [ges] *n* conjecture *f*, estimation *f*; **to have** *or* **make a g.** deviner; **that was a lucky g.!** je suis/tu es/*etc* tombé juste!; **it was just a lucky g.** c'était un coup de chance; **your g. is as good as mine** j'en sais autant que toi; **it's anybody's g.** qui sait?, Dieu seul le sait; **it's my g. …** à mon avis …; **I give you three guesses** tu as droit à trois essais; **at a g. I'd say he's German** a priori je dirais qu'il est allemand; **at a rough g. I'd say he's forty** je dirais qu'il a quarante ans; **at a g., there will be 40 people at the party** je pense qu'il y aura environ 40 personnes à la soirée; **40 at a rough g.** environ quarante
guess² **1** *vt* **(a)** deviner; (*estimate*) (*the length of sth etc*) estimer; **g. who did it!** devine qui a fait ça!; **I guessed him to be twenty-five** je lui ai donné vingt-cinq ans; **to g. sth from sb's manner** deviner qch d'après l'attitude de qn; **g. what! I saw Ian yesterday** tu sais quoi? j'ai vu Ian hier; **g. who** devine qui?; **you've guessed it!** vous l'avez deviné!
(b) *esp Am* (*think*) croire, penser; **I g. you're right** tu as raison; **I g. so/not** je crois que oui/non
2 *vi* deviner; **to g. right** deviner juste; **to g. wrong** se tromper; **you'll never g.** tu ne devineras jamais; **to keep sb guessing** laisser qn dans l'ignorance; **to g. at sth** (essayer de) deviner qch; **we could only g. at their plans** nous ne pouvions qu'essayer de deviner leurs intentions; **I couldn't begin to g.** je n'en ai pas la moindre idée; *Iron* **I would never have guessed** je n'aurais jamais deviné
guessing ['gesɪŋ] *n* estimation *f*; **g. games** devinettes *fpl*
guesstimate ['gestɪmɪt] *n F* calcul *m* au pif
guesswork ['geswɜ:k] *n* estimation *f*, conjecture *f*; **it's pure** *or* **sheer g.** c'est de la pure conjecture; **by g.** au jugé; **by sheer** *or* **pure g.** à vue de nez
guest¹ [gest] *n* **(a)** invité, -ée; (*at meal*) convive *mf*; *also Iron* **be my g.!** faites comme chez vous!; **with a g. appearance from …** avec comme invité, -ée d'honneur …; **to make a g. appearance in a programme** être invité dans une émission; **g. artist** invité, -ée; **g. night** (*in club etc*) = soirée *f* d'un club où les non-membres sont invités; **g. room** chambre *f* d'ami(s); **g. speaker** invité, -ée; *Cin, TV* **g. star …** (*in credits*) avec la participation de …; **our thanks to this week's g. star, Billy Connolly** nous remercions Billy Connolly qui nous a fait la gentillesse d'être avec nous cette semaine
(b) (*at hotel*) client, -iente; **the landlord and his guests** l'hôtelier et ses hôtes; **g. book** registre *m*; **g. comments** commentaires *mpl* clients; **g. folio** fiche *f* client; **g. history**

card fiche *f* Kardex; **g. history file** fichier *m* clients; **g. list** liste *f* des clients; **g. occupancy** taux *m* d'occupation des lits
guest² *vi TV, Rad* **to g. on sb's show** faire une apparition dans l'émission de qn; *Mus* **another guitarist guested on one of the numbers** un autre guitariste a participé à l'un des morceaux
guesthouse ['gesthaʊs] *n* **(a)** (*hotel*) pension *f* de famille **(b)** (*of monastery etc*) hôtellerie *f*
guff [gʌf] *n F* bêtises *fpl*, âneries *fpl*
guffaw¹ [gʌ'fɔː] *n* gros rire *m*
guffaw² *vi* s'esclaffer
GUI ['guːiː] *n Comptr* (*abbr* **graphical user interface**) interface *f* utilisateur graphique
Guiana [gaɪ'ɑːnə] *n* (*region*) Guyane *f*
guidance ['gaɪdəns] *n* **(a)** direction *f*, conduite *f*; **under the g. of ...** sous la direction de ...; **sent for your g.** envoyé à titre d'indication **(b)** (*of missile*) guidage *m*; **g. system** système *m* de guidage
guide¹ [gaɪd] *n* **(a)** (*person*) guide *m*; *Br* **(Girl) G.** guide *f*, éclaireuse *f* **(b)** (*book*) guide *m*; (*of railways*) indicateur *m*; **g. to Switzerland** guide de la Suisse; **the book is a useful g. to the world of finance** le livre constitue un guide utile du monde de la finance **(c)** (*indication*) indication *f*, exemple *m*; **as a g.** à titre indicatif **(d) g. rope** câble *m* de guidage; *Av* guiderope *m*; *Rail* **g. rail** contre-rail *m*, *pl* contre-rails
guide² *vt* guider, conduire; **to g. a child's first steps** guider les premiers pas d'un enfant; **I will be guided by your advice** je suivrai vos conseils
guidebook ['gaɪdbʊk] *n* guide *m*
guided ['gaɪdɪd] *adj* **(a)** (*tour etc*) guidé **(b)** *Mil* **g. missile** engin *m* guidé
guide dog *n* chien *m* d'aveugle
guideline ['gaɪdlaɪn] *n* **(a)** (*indication*) directive *f* **(on** concernant); **as a general** *or* **rough g.** en règle générale **(b)** (*line*) ligne *f*
guidepost ['gaɪdpəʊst] *n* poteau *m* indicateur
guiding ['gaɪdɪŋ] *adj attrib* (*principle*) directeur, -trice; **without his g. hand** sans ses conseils; *Fig* **g. star** *or* **light** guide *m*
guild [gɪld] *n* **(a)** *Hist* corporation *f*; **merchant g.** guilde *f* de commerçants **(b)** (*organization*) association *f*, confrérie *f*; **church** *or* **parish g.** cercle *m* paroissial
guilder ['gɪldər] *n* florin *m*
guildhall ['gɪldhɔːl] *n* **(a)** (*of a guild*) salle *f* de réunion d'une guilde **(b)** (*town hall*) hôtel *m* de ville
guile [gaɪl] *n* ruse *f*; **she is without g.** elle est candide
guileless ['gaɪllɪs] *adj* (*naive*) candide
guillemot ['gɪlɪmɒt] *n* (*bird*) guillemot *m*
guillotine¹ ['gɪlətiːn] *n* **(a)** (*for execution*) guillotine *f*; **to be executed by g.** être guillotiné; **to go to the g.** aller à la guillotine, être mené à la guillotine **(b)** (*for cutting paper*) massicot *m* **(c)** *Parl* = imposition *f* d'une limite de temps pour les débats parlementaires
guillotine² *vt* **(a)** (*execute*) guillotiner **(b)** (*cut*) (*paper etc*) massicoter **(c)** *Parl* (*bill*) imposer une limite de temps pour la discussion de
guilt [gɪlt] *n* **(a)** culpabilité *f* **(for sth** pour qch); **the g. does not lie with him alone** il n'est pas le seul coupable **(b)** (*feeling*) culpabilité *f*; **to feel g.** ressentir de la culpabilité; **g. feelings, feelings of g.** sentiments *mpl* de culpabilité; **g. complex** complexe *m* de culpabilité
guiltily ['gɪltɪlɪ] *adv* coupablement, d'un air coupable; **she looked away g.** elle a détourné les yeux d'un air coupable
guiltless ['gɪltlɪs] *adj* innocent **(of sth** de qch)
guilty ['gɪltɪ] *adj* **(a)** coupable **(of** de); **g. person** coupable *mf*; **he is not the only g. party** il n'est pas le seul coupable; *Jur* **to plead g./not g.** plaider coupable/non coupable; *Jur* **to find sb g./not g.** déclarer qn coupable/non coupable; *Jur* **verdict of g./not g.** verdict *m* de culpabilité/d'acquittement **(b)** (*feeling guilt*) **I feel g. about not telling them** je me sens coupable *ou* je culpabilise de ne pas leur avoir dit; **you're making me feel g.** tu me culpabilises; **she looked very g.** elle avait un air très coupable; **g. conscience** mauvaise conscience *f*; (*more serious*) conscience chargée **(c)** (*act*) coupable
Guinea ['gɪnɪ] *n* **(a)** *Geog* Guinée *f* **(b)** *Br Arch* **g.** (pièce *f* d'or d'une) guinée *f* (*= 21 shillings (£1.05)*)
guinea fowl ['gɪnɪ] *n* (*bird*) pintade *f*
guinea pig *n* cobaye *m*, cochon *m* d'Inde; *Fig* **to be a g. pig** servir de cobaye
guise [gaɪz] *n* dehors *m*, apparence *f*; **under** *or* **in the g. of friendship** sous l'apparence *ou* sous le masque de l'amitié; **under the g. of religion** sous le manteau *ou* le couvert de la religion; **it's the same idea in a new g.** c'est la même idée présentée sous une autre forme
guitar [gɪ'tɑːr, *Am also* 'gɪtɑːr] *n Mus* guitare *f*; **to play the g.** jouer de la guitare; **g. player** guitariste *mf*
guitarist [gɪ'tɑːrɪst] *n Mus* guitariste *mf*
gulch [gʌltʃ] *n Am* ravin *m*
gulf [gʌlf] *n* **(a)** *Geog* golfe *m*; **the (Persian) G.** le Golfe **(b)** (*abyss*) gouffre *m*, abîme *m*; *Fig* **there is a g. between the two ideologies** un abîme sépare les deux idéologies
Gulf Stream *n* **the G.** le Gulf Stream
Gulf War *n* **the G.** la guerre du Golfe
gull¹ [gʌl] *n* (*bird*) mouette *f*; (*bigger*) goéland *m*; *Aut* **g.-wing doors** portes *fpl* papillon
gull² *vt Arch, Lit* (*person*) duper, rouler
gullet ['gʌlɪt] *n Anat* œsophage *m*; *F* (*throat*) gosier *m*; *Fig F* **it really sticks in my g.** ça me reste en travers du gosier
gulley ['gʌlɪ] *n* = **gully**
gullibility [gʌlɪ'bɪlɪtɪ] *n* crédulité *f*
gullible ['gʌlɪb(ə)l] *adj* crédule
gully ['gʌlɪ] *n Geol* petit ravin *m*
gulp¹ [gʌlp] *n* **(a)** (*act of gulping*) coup *m* de gosier; **to swallow sth at one g.** avaler qch d'un coup; **he confessed with a g. that ...** il admit, la gorge serrée, que ... **(b)** (*mouthful*) grosse bouchée *f*; (*of drink*) goulée *f*
gulp² **1** *vt* **(a)** (*swallow*) = **gulp down (b)** (*say nervously, with shock*) **me?, she gulped** moi, dit-elle la voix étranglée **2** *vi* essayer d'avaler; **he gulped** sa gorge se serra; **G.!** (*as in comic strip*) gulp!, glup!
▶ **gulp back** *vtsep* **to g. back one's tears** avaler *ou* refouler ses larmes
▶ **gulp down** *vtsep* (*swallow*) avaler à grosses bouchées; (*oyster etc*) avaler; **he gulped it down** (*in one mouthful*) il n'en fit qu'une bouchée; (*drinking*) il n'en fit qu'une gorgée
gum¹ [gʌm] *n* **(a)** *Bot* gomme *f*; (*adhesive*) colle *f*, gomme **(b) g. arabic** gomme *f* arabique **(c) (chewing) g.** chewing-gum *m*; **two sticks of g.** deux chewing-gums; **(wine/fruit/***etc***) g.** boule *f* de gomme **(d) g. tree** gommier *m*; *Fig F* **to be up a g. tree** être dans le pétrin
gum² *vt* **(-mm-) (a)** (*coat with adhesive*) (*paper*) gommer, encoller **(b)** (*stick with adhesive*) (*page in book etc*) coller; **to g. two pages together** coller deux feuilles **(c)** = **gum up**
gum³ *n Anat* gencive *f*; **g. disease** gingivite *f*
gum⁴ *int Old-fashioned Br F* **by g.!** fichtre!, mazette!
▶ **gum up** *vtsep MecE* (*piston*) gommer; (*file*) encrasser; *F* **to g. up the works** enrayer le mécanisme; *Fig* compliquer les choses
gumboil ['gʌmbɔɪl] *n* abcès *m* à la gencive, *Spec* parulie *f*
gumboot ['gʌmbuːt] *n* botte *f* en *ou* de caoutchouc
gumdrop ['gʌmdrɒp] *n* (*sweet*) boule *f* de gomme
gummed [gʌmd] *adj* (*label etc*) gommé
gummy ['gʌmɪ] *adj* **(a)** gommeux; (*sticky*) gluant **(b) he gave her a g. smile** il lui sourit, découvrant ses gencives encore sans dents
gumption ['gʌmʃən, 'gʌmp-] *n F* jugeote *f*, sens *m* pratique; **she's got plenty of g.** c'est une débrouillarde
gumshield ['gʌmʃiːld] *n Boxing etc* protège-dents *m inv*
gumshoe ['gʌmʃuː] *n* **(a)** (*rubber overshoe*) caoutchouc *m* **(b)** *F* (*detective*) privé *m*
gun¹ [gʌn] *n* **(a)** *Mil* (*artillery*) canon *m*, pièce *f* (d'artillerie); **the guns** l'artillerie *f*, le canon; **the big guns** la grosse artillerie, les grosses pièces; *F* **big g.** (*important person*) gros manitou *m*, grosse légume *f*; **do you hear the guns?** entendez-vous le canon?; **21-g. salute** salve de 21 coups de canon; *F* **it was blowing great guns** il faisait un vent à décorner les bœufs; *F* **to be going great guns** (*of work, sale*) marcher très fort; **to jump the g.** (*in race*) faire un faux départ; *Fig* s'emballer; **g. carriage** affût *m* (de canon); (*at military funeral*) prolonge *f* d'artillerie

(b) (*rifle*) fusil *m*; (*handgun*) revolver *m*, pistolet *m*; **machine g.** mitrailleuse *f*; *Fig* **to stick to one's guns** ne pas en démordre; **a party of six guns** (*hunters*) une bande de six chasseurs; **g. barrel** canon *m* de fusil/revolver; **g. room** salle *f* aux fusils

(c) *Tech etc* **(grease) g.** seringue *f*, injecteur *m* (à graisse); **(spray) g.** pistolet *m* (à peinture); *Electron* **(electron) g.** canon *m* à électrons
gun² **(-nn-) 1** *vt Aut* (*engine*) (faire) emballer **2** *vi F* **to g. along** (*of car, driver*) foncer
▶ **gun down** *vtsep* (*kill*) abattre
▶ **gun for** *vipo* (*only in continuous tenses*) **(a)** (*want to reprimand, punish*) en avoir après; **he's gunning for us** il nous en veut, il en a après nous **(b)** (*try to get*) pourchasser; **he's gunning for the heavyweight title** il vise le titre poids lourd
gunboat ['gʌnbəʊt] *n* aviso-torpilleur *m*, *pl* avisos-torpilleurs; **g. diplomacy** politique *f* de la canonnière
guncotton ['gʌnkɒt(ə)n] *n* fulmicoton *m*
gundeck ['gʌndek] *n Naut* batterie *f*
gun dog *n* chien *m* d'arrêt

gunfight [ˈgʌnfaɪt] *n* fusillade *f*, échange *m* de coups de feu
gunfighter [ˈgʌnfaɪtər] *n* (*in Western film, novel*) bandit *m* armé
gunfire [ˈgʌnfaɪər] *n Mil* (*of artillery*) canonnade *f*, feu *m* (des pièces); (*of smaller guns*) coups *mpl* de feu; **we heard g.** nous avons entendu des coups de feu
gunge [gʌndʒ] *n* (*no pl*) *F* crasse *f* graisseuse
gung-ho [gʌŋˈhəʊ] *adj* (*enthusiastic*) tout feu tout flamme; (*ready to fight*) belliqueux
gunk [gʌŋk] *n F* = **gunge**
gun licence *n* permis *m* de port d'armes
gunmaker [ˈgʌnmeɪkər] *n* armurier *m*
gunman, *pl* **-men** [ˈgʌnmən] *n* **(a)** (*terrorist*) terroriste *m*; (*robber*) bandit *m* armé **(b)** *US* = **gunmaker**
gunmetal [ˈgʌnmet(ə)l] *n* **(a)** (*bronze*) bronze *m* à canon **(b)** (*colour*) **g. (grey)** gris métallisé *m inv*; **a car with a g. finish** une voiture gris métallisé
gun mike *n* micro *m* canon
gunnel [ˈgʌn(ə)l] *n* = **gunwale**
gunner [ˈgʌnər] *n* artilleur *m*; *Naut* (*warrant officer*) canonnier *m*; **(machine) g.** mitrailleur *m*
gunnery [ˈgʌnərɪ] *n Mil* (*guns*) artillerie *f*; **g. officer** officier *m* d'artillerie
gunny [ˈgʌnɪ] *n esp US* (*material*) toile *f* de jute; **g. (sack)** sac *m* en jute
gunplay [ˈgʌnpleɪ] *n esp US* coups *mpl* de revolver
gunpoint [ˈgʌnpɔɪnt] *n* **at g.** sous la menace d'un pistolet/d'un fusil; **to hold sb at g.** menacer qn d'un pistolet/d'un fusil
gunport [ˈgʌnpɔːt] *n Naut* sabord *m* de batterie
gunpowder [ˈgʌnpaʊdər] *n* poudre *f* (à canon); *Br Hist* **the G. Plot** la Conspiration des Poudres
gunrunner [ˈgʌnrʌnər] *n* trafiquant, -ante d'armes
gunrunning [ˈgʌnrʌnɪŋ] *n* trafic *m* d'armes
gunship [ˈgʌnʃɪp] *n* **(helicopter) g.** hélicoptère *m* de combat
gunshot [ˈgʌnʃɒt] *n* coup *m* de feu; (*of rifle*) coup de fusil; **within/out of g.** à/hors de portée de fusil; **g. wound** blessure *f* par balle; **to receive a g. wound** être blessé par balle
gun-shy *adj* (*dog*) qui a peur des coups de feu
gunslinger [ˈgʌnslɪŋər] *n US F* bandit *m* armé
gunsmith [ˈgʌnsmɪθ] *n* armurier *m*; **g.'s (shop)** armurerie *f*
gunstock [ˈgʌnstɒk] *n* fût *m* (de fusil)
gun turret *n* tourelle *f*
gunwale [ˈgʌn(ə)l] *n Naut* plat-bord *m*, *pl* plats-bords; **full to the gunwales** plein à ras bord
guppy [ˈgʌpɪ] *n* (*fish*) guppy *m*
gurgle¹ [ˈgɜːg(ə)l] *n* (*of liquid*) glouglou *m*; (*of stream*) murmure *m*; *Fig* (*of pleasure, delight*) gloussement *m*, roucoulement *m*; **happy gurgles could be heard coming from the baby's cot** on entendait l'enfant gazouiller dans son berceau; *Fig* **gurgles of laughter** des gloussements
gurgle² **1** *vi* (*of liquid*) glouglouter, faire glouglou; (*of stream*) murmurer, gargouiller; (*of person*) glousser, roucouler; (*of baby*) gazouiller; **he gurgled with laughter** il eut un rire perlé **2** *vt* **she gurgled her delight** elle roucoula de plaisir
gurgling [ˈgɜːg(ə)lɪŋ] *adj* (*liquid in bottle*) glougloutant, qui fait glouglou; (*stream*) murmurant; **a g. laugh** un rire perlé
Gurkha [ˈgɜːkə] *n* Go(u)rkha *m*; *Br Mil* **G. regiment** régiment *m* de Go(u)rkhas
gurnard [ˈgɜːnəd], **gurnet** [ˈgɜːnɪt] *n* (*fish*) grondin *m*
guru [ˈgʊruː] *n Rel, Fig* gourou *m*
gush¹ [gʌʃ] *n* (*of spring, fountain*) jaillissement *m*; (*of tears*) torrent *m*; (*of blood*) jet *m*, flot *m*; *Fig* **a g. of words** un flot de paroles; *Fig* **a g. of enthusiasm** un élan d'enthousiasme; **a g. of anger/emotion** une bouffée de colère/d'émotion
gush² **1** *vi* **(a)** (*spurt, pour*) jaillir, couler à flots; **tears gushed from her eyes** un torrent de larmes coulait de ses yeux **(b)** *Pej* (*talk effusively*) faire de longs discours sentimentaux, *F* la faire au sentiment; **she gushed over their baby** elle s'attendrissait sur leur bébé **2** *vt* **(a) to g. water/oil** lancer des jets d'eau/un jet de pétrole **(b) 'how wonderful to see you!', she gushed** 'qu'est-ce que ça me fait plaisir de te voir!', s'exclama-t-elle
▶ **gush forth, gush out** *vi* = **gush² 1(a)**
gusher [ˈgʌʃər] *n* **(a)** *Pej* (*person*) personne *f* trop exubérante **(b)** *Petr* source *f* (de pétrole) jaillissante, puits *m* jaillissant
gushing [ˈgʌʃɪŋ] *adj* **(a)** (*water*) jaillissant; **the car was swept away by a g. torrent of water** la voiture a été emportée par un véritable torrent d'eau; **a g. stream fed by melting snow** les flots déchaînés d'un ruisseau grossi par la fonte des neiges **(b)** *Pej* (*person*) trop exubérant; (*compliments*) très élogieux
gushy [ˈgʌʃɪ] *adj Pej* = **gushing (b)**
gusset [ˈgʌsɪt] *n Sewing* soufflet *m*; (*in sleeve*) gousset *m*
gust¹ [gʌst] *n* **g. (of wind)** rafale *f*, bourrasque *f*; *Naut* grain *m*; **g. of rain** ondée *f*, giboulée *f*; **a g. of hot air** une bouffée d'air chaud; *Fig* **a g. of anger** une bouffée de colère
gust² *vi* (*of wind*) souffler par rafales
gustatory [gʌsˈteɪtərɪ] *adj Fml* gustatif
gusto [ˈgʌstəʊ] *n* délectation *f*, goût *m*; **to eat sth with g.** manger qch en savourant; **to do sth with g.** faire qch avec grand plaisir
gusty [ˈgʌstɪ] *adj* (*weather*) venteux; (*wind*) soufflant en rafales; (*day*) de grand vent
gut¹ [gʌt] *n* **(a)** (*intestine*) (*of animal*) boyau *m*; (*of human*) intestin *m*; *Fig F* **to sweat** *or* **work one's guts out** se casser les reins; *Fig F* **she hates my guts** elle ne peut pas me saquer *ou* m'encadrer; *Fig F* **I'll have his guts for garters** je vais le massacrer; *Fig* **it's just a g. feeling** c'est une intuition; *Fig* **g. reaction** réaction *f* viscérale
(b) *Fig F* (*courage*) **to have guts** avoir du cran, avoir du cœur au ventre; **I didn't have the guts to tell them** je n'ai pas eu le courage de le leur dire; **he hasn't any guts** il manque de cran
(c) *F* (*stomach*) bide *m*; **pull in your g.** rentre ton bide; **to have sore guts** avoir mal au bide; **g. ache** mal *m* de bide
(d) (*for violins etc*) corde *f* de boyau
gut² *vt* (-tt-) **(a)** (*animal*) étriper; (*fish, poultry*) vider **(b) the house had been gutted by the fire** la maison avait été ravagée par l'incendie; **she gutted the house and completely redecorated it** elle a cassé tout l'intérieur de la maison et a tout refait
gutless [ˈgʌtlɪs] *adj F* (*cowardly*) lâche
gutsy [ˈgʌtsɪ] *adj F* **(a)** (*brave*) qui a du cran, courageux **(b)** (*powerful*) (*prose etc*) vigoureux **(c)** (*greedy*) goinfre
gutter¹ [ˈgʌtər] *n* **(a)** (*in street*) caniveau *m*; (*on roof*) gouttière *f*, chéneau *m*; *Fig* **to end up in the g.** finir sous les ponts; *Fig* **to drag oneself out of the g.** se sortir de la misère; **the language of the g.** la langue de la rue; **g. tile** tuile *f* creuse **(b)** *Typ* gouttière *f*, petits fonds *mpl* (*de deux pages en vis-à-vis*)
gutter² *vi* (*of candle*) vasciller
guttering [ˈgʌtərɪŋ] *n Constr* (*on building*) gouttières *fpl*
gutter pipe *n* tuyau *m* de descente
gutter press *n F Pej* presse *f* à scandales
guttersnipe [ˈgʌtəsnaɪp] *n Old-fashioned Pej* gamin, -ine des rues
guttural [ˈgʌtərəl] **1** *adj* guttural, -aux **2** *n Ling* gutturale *f*
guv [gʌv], **guv'nor** [ˈgʌvnər] *n Br Sl* **the g.** (*boss*) le patron, le singe; *Old-fashioned* (*father*) le vieux, le paternel; **all right, g.** d'accord, chef
guy¹ [gaɪ] *n* **(a)** *F* (*man*) type *m*, mec *m*; **a great g.** un type *ou* mec super; **a tough g.** un dur; **I didn't like the look of those guys** ces types avaient une sale tête **(b)** *esp Am F* (*as second person plural*) **hurry up, you guys!** allez, dépêchez-vous!; **what are you guys doing tonight?** vous faites quoi, vous, ce soir?; **ok guys, let's go** ok, les amis, on y va; **do you guys want to go out?** vous voulez sortir?; **hi guys!** salut vous! **(c)** *Br* (*effigy*) = effigie *f* burlesque de Guy Fawkes, le chef de la Conspiration des Poudres (1605)
guy² *vt Old-fashioned* se moquer de, *F* charrier, mettre en boîte
guy³ *n* **g. (rope)** corde *f* de tente
Guyana [gaɪˈænə] *n* (*country*) Guyana *f*
Guyanese [gaɪəˈniːz] **1** *adj* guyanais **2** *n* Guyanais, -aise
guzzle [ˈgʌz(ə)l] *F* **1** *vt* (*food*) bâfrer, bouffer; (*drink*) descendre; *esp Am* **to g. gas** (*of car*) bouffer de l'essence **2** *vi* (*of eater*) s'empiffrer, goinfrer; (*of drinker*) boire avidement
guzzler [ˈgʌzlər] *n F* (*of food*) bâfreur, -euse, goinfre *m*; (*of drink*) soiffard, -arde
gym [dʒɪm] *n F* **(a)** (*place*) gymnase *m*; (*in hotel etc*) salle *f* de sport *ou* de musculation *ou F* de muscu **(b)** (*activity esp at school*) gym *f*; **we have g. today** on a gym aujourd'hui; **g. shoes** (chaussures *fpl* de) tennis *mpl*
gymkhana [dʒɪmˈkɑːnə] *n Br* (*for horses*) concours *m* hippique; *esp Am Aut* gymkhana *m*
gymnasium, *pl* **-iums, -ia** [dʒɪmˈneɪzɪəm, -ɪəmz, -ɪə] *n Sp* gymnase *m*
gymnast [ˈdʒɪmnæst] *n* gymnaste *mf*
gymnastic [dʒɪmˈnæstɪk] *adj* gymnastique
gymnastics [dʒɪmˈnæstɪks] *n* [①**A10**,c] gymnastique *f*; **to do g.** faire de la gymnastique; *Fig* **mental/verbal g.** gymnastique intellectuelle/verbale
gymslip [ˈdʒɪmslɪp] *n esp Br Sch* tunique *f*
gynaecologic(al), *US* **gynecologic(al)** [gaɪnɪkɒˈlɒdʒɪk, -ɪk(ə)l] *adj* gynécologique
gynaecologist, *US* **gynecologist** [gaɪnɪˈkɒlədʒɪst] *n* gynécologue *mf*
gynaecology, *US* **gynecology** [gaɪnɪˈkɒlədʒɪ] *n* gynécologie *f*

gyp [dʒɪp] *n Br F* **to give sb g.** (*of aching tooth etc*) faire souffrir qn
gypsum ['dʒɪpsəm] *n Miner* gypse *m*
gypsy ['dʒɪpsɪ] *n* = **gipsy**
gyrate [dʒaɪ'reɪt] *vi* tourner; (*less regularly*) (*of dancers*) tournoyer
gyration [dʒaɪ'reɪʃən] *n* giration *f*
gyratory ['dʒaɪrətrɪ, -ərɪ, dʒaɪ'reɪtərɪ] *adj* giratoire; **g. (traffic) system** (système *m* de circulation en) sens *m* giratoire
gyrfalcon ['dʒɜːfɔːlkən] *n* (*bird*) gerfaut *m*
gyro ['dʒaɪrəʊ] **1** *adj* gyroscopique; **g. control** commande *f* gyroscopique **2** *n* **(a)** = **gyroscope (b)** = **gyrocompass**
gyrocompass ['dʒaɪrəʊkʌmpəs] *n Naut* gyrocompas *m*, compas *m* gyroscopique
gyromagnetic [dʒaɪrəʊmæg'netɪk] *adj* gyromagnétique
gyropilot ['dʒaɪrəʊpaɪlət] *n Av* pilote *m* automatique, gyropilote *m*; *Naut* (*compass*) gyropilote
gyroplane ['dʒaɪrəpleɪn] *n Av* autogyre *m*
gyroscope ['dʒaɪrəskəʊp] *n* gyroscope *m*, gyro *m*
gyroscopic [dʒaɪrə'skɒpɪk] *adj* gyroscopique
gyrostat ['dʒaɪrəstæt] *n* gyrostat *m*

H, h [eɪtʃ] *n* (*letter*) H, h *mf*; **to drop one's h's** ['eɪtʃɪz] ne pas prononcer (correctement) les h; **H bomb** bombe *f* H.

ha [hɑː] *int* ha!, ah!; *F* **ha bloody ha!** ha ha ha!, très drôle!

habeas corpus ['heɪbɪəs'kɔːpəs] *n Jur* (**writ of**) **h.** habeas corpus *m*

haberdasher ['hæbədæʃər] *n Old-fashioned Com* (**a**) *Br* (*for sewing articles*) mercier *m*, -ière (**b**) *Am* (*for men's clothes*) chemisier *m*

haberdashery ['hæbədæʃərɪ] *n Old-fashioned Com* (**a**) *Br* (*sewing articles*) mercerie *f* (**b**) *Am* (*men's clothes*) chemiserie *f*

habit ['hæbɪt] *n* (**a**) (*custom, practice*) habitude *f*, coutume *f*; (*picking nose, biting nails etc*) habitude; **bad habits** mauvaises habitudes; **to be in the** *or* **make a h. of doing sth** avoir l'habitude de faire qch; **I try not to make a h. of working late** j'essaye de ne pas prendre l'habitude de travailler tard; **don't make a h. of it** ne recommence pas; **it's a h. with him** c'est une habitude chez lui; **to get into the h. of doing sth** prendre l'habitude de faire qch; **to get sb into the h. of doing sth** habituer qn à faire qch; **to get into bad habits** prendre de mauvaises habitudes; **to get out of a h.** perdre une habitude; **from force of h.** poussé par l'habitude; **to do sth by sheer force of h.** faire qch (simplement) par habitude

(**b**) *F* (*addiction*) accoutumance *f*; **to have a (drug) h.** être dépendant (d'une drogue), *F* être accro; **a cocaine/heroin h.** une accoutumance à la cocaïne/à l'héroïne

(**c**) (*costume*) (*of monk, nun*) habit *m*; **riding h.** tenue *f* d'équitation

habitable ['hæbɪtəb(ə)l] *adj* habitable; **to make a room h.** rendre une pièce habitable

habitat ['hæbɪtæt] *n* habitat *m*

habitation [hæbɪ'teɪʃən] *n* (**a**) (*occupation*) (*of house*) habitation *f*; **fit for h.** habitable; **unfit for h.** inhabitable; **there were no signs of h.** l'endroit ne semblait pas habité (**b**) (*dwelling place*) habitation *f*, demeure *f*

habit-forming *adj* (*drug*) qui crée une accoutumance

habitual [hə'bɪtjʊəl] *adj* (**a**) (*customary*) habituel (**b**) (*liar, drunk*) invétéré; **h. criminal** *or* **offender** récidiviste *mf*

habitually [hə'bɪtjʊəlɪ] *adv* habituellement, d'habitude

habituate [hə'bɪtjʊeɪt] *vt* **to h. sb to sth/to doing sth** habituer *ou* accoutumer qn à qch/à faire qch; **to become habituated to sth/to doing sth** s'habituer à qch/à faire qch

hack¹ [hæk] *n* (*cut*) taillade *f*, entaille *f*; (*blow*) (*with foot, arm*) coup *m*; *Fb etc* (*kick*) coup de pied

hack² **1** *vt* (**a**) (*cut*) hacher; **to h. sb/sth to pieces** mettre *ou* tailler qn/qch en pièces; *Fig* **my article has been hacked to pieces** mon article a été massacré; **to h. sb to death** lacérer qn à mort; **to h. one's way through the jungle** se frayer un chemin à coups de machette dans la jungle

(**b**) *Fb etc* **to h. sb's shins** donner délibérément à qn un coup de pied sur le tibia; **to h. the ball** donner un petit coup de pied dans le ballon

(**c**) *esp Am F* **he can't h. it** (*cope*) il ne s'en sort pas, il est complètement dépassé

2 *vi* (**a**) (*cut*) taillader, entailler; **to h. (away) at a tree** entailler un arbre à coups de hache; **to h. at one's meat** taillader son morceau de viande; **to h. away at a text** sabrer un texte *ou* des passages d'un texte

(**b**) (*cough*) émettre une toux sèche

(**c**) (*kick*) **to h. at sb's shins** essayer de donner un coup de pied/des coups de pied dans le tibia de qn

hack³ *n* (**a**) *F Pej* (*journalist*) journaleux, -euse, tâcheron *m*; **there were all the usual Labour Party hacks** on y trouvait tous les habitués du parti travailliste; **h. writer, literary h.** écrivaillon *m*; **a h. reporter** un obscur journaliste de la rubrique des chiens écrasés (**b**) (*horse for hire*) cheval *m*, -aux de louage; (*for riding*) cheval de selle; *F* (*nag*) rosse *f* (**c**) *Am F* (*taxi*) taxi *m*; (*taxi driver*) chauffeur *m* de taxi

hack⁴ *vi Br* (*ride*) se promener à cheval

▶ **hack about** *vtsep* (*often passive*) (*body*) mutiler; **the piece of wood had been hacked about** on avait tailladé ce morceau de bois; **the article had been hacked about a bit** on avait pas mal remanié l'article

▶ **hack down** *vtsep* (*tree*) abattre

▶ **hack into** *vipo Comptr* **to h. into a database** s'introduire en fraude dans une base de données, *F* pirater une base de données

▶ **hack off** *vtsep* (**a**) (*chop off*) trancher (**b**) *F* (*annoy*) **I'm feeling thoroughly hacked off** je suis très embêté

▶ **hack up** *vtsep* (*chop up*) mettre en pièces

hacker ['hækər] *n Comptr F* pirate *m* informatique

hacking¹ ['hækɪŋ] **1** *n* (**a**) *Fb etc* coups *mpl* de pied (sur le tibia) (**b**) *F* (**computer**) **h.** piratage *m* informatique **2** *adj* **h. cough** toux *f* sèche et pénible

hacking² *n Br* (*riding*) promenade(s) *f(pl)* à cheval; **h. jacket** veste *f* d'équitation

hackle ['hæk(ə)l] *n* (*of bird*) plume *f* du cou; **hackles** camail *m*; **his hackles rose** (*of dog, Fig of person*) il s'est hérissé; *Fig* **to get one's hackles up** se hérisser, monter sur ses ergots; *Fig* **his hackles are up** il se prépare pour la bagarre; *Fig* **to make sb's hackles rise** hérisser qn

hackney ['hæknɪ] *n* (**a**) (*taxi*) **h. cab** *or* **carriage** fiacre *m* (**b**) (*carriage for hire*) cabriolet *m* de louage (**c**) (*horse*) cheval *m* de selle; (*trotter*) trotteur *m*

hackneyed ['hæknɪd] *adj* (*language*) rebattu, usé, banal, -als; **a h. argument** un argument éculé; **h. phrase** formule *f* stéréotypée, cliché *m*

hacksaw ['hæksɔː] *n* scie *f* à métaux

hackwork ['hækwɜːk] *n F* **to do h.** (*of writer*) écrire au kilomètre; **it's just h.** (*routine work*) c'est du travail alimentaire; **the report was a piece of shoddy h.** ce rapport, c'était du travail d'écrivaillon

had *see* **have²**

haddock ['hædək] *n* (*fish*) aiglefin *m*, églefin *m*; *Culin* **smoked h.** haddock *m*

Hades ['heɪdiːz] *n Myth* les Enfers *mpl*

hadn't [hæd(ə)nt] = **had not**, *see* **have²**

Hadrian's Wall ['heɪdrɪənzwɔːl] *n* le Mur d'Hadrien

haema- ['hiːmə] *pref Med etc* héma-

haemato- ['hiːmə'tɒ, -təʊ] *pref Med etc* hémato-

haematology, *US* **hematology** [hiːmə'tɒlədʒɪ] *n Med* hématologie *f*

haematoma, *US* **hematoma,** *pl* **-omas, -omata** [hiːmə'təʊmə, -əʊməz, -əʊmətə] *n Med* hématome *m*

haemo- ['hiːməʊ, -mə] *pref Med etc* hémo-

haemoglobin, *US* **hemoglobin** [hiːməʊ'gləʊbɪn] *n Med* hémoglobine *f*

haemophilia, *US* **hemophilia** [hiːməʊ'fɪlɪə] *n Med* hémophilie *f*

haemophiliac, *US* **hemophiliac** [hiːməʊ'fɪlɪæk] *n Med* hémophile *mf*

haemophilic, *US* **hemophilic** [hiːməʊ'fɪlɪk] *adj Med* hémophile

haemorrhage¹, *US* **hemorrhage** ['hemərɪdʒ] *n Med, Fig* hémorragie *f*

haemorrhage², *US* **hemorrhage** *vi Med* faire une hémorragie; *Fig* (*disappear, fade fast*) (*of support etc*) s'évanouir, se dissiper; **party membership was haemorrhaging badly** les effectifs du parti diminuaient de façon spectaculaire; **foreign capital would h. if ...** il y aurait une hémorragie *ou* fuite de capitaux si ...

haemorrhoids, *US* **hemorrhoids** ['hemərɔɪdz] *npl Med* hémorroïdes *fpl*; **to have h.** avoir des hémorroïdes

haemostat, *US* **hemostat** ['hiːməʊstæt] *n Med* (*instrument*) pince(s) *f(pl)* hémostatique(s)

haft [hɑːft] *n* (*of tool etc*) manche *m*, poignée *f*

hag [hæg] *n* (*witch*) (vieille) sorcière *f*; *F* (*unpleasant old woman*) vieille taupe *f*, vieux chameau *m*

haggard ['hægəd] *adj* (**a**) (*gaunt*) hâve; (*face*) décharné (**b**) (*wild*) (*face*) égaré, hagard

haggis ['hægɪs] *n Scot Culin* = panse *f* de brebis farcie (d'un hachis d'abats et de farine d'avoine très épicé)

haggle ['hæg(ə)l] *vi* marchander, *F* chipoter; **I'm not going to h.** je ne vais pas chipoter; **to h. about** *or* **over the price of sth** chicaner sur le prix de qch

haggler ['hæglər] *n* (*over details etc*) chipoteur, -euse
haggling ['hæg(ə)lɪŋ] *n* marchandage *m*
hagiographer [hægɪ'ɒgrəfər] *n* hagiographe *mf*
hagiography [hægɪ'ɒgrəfɪ] *n* hagiographie *f*
hag-ridden *adj* (*by nightmares*) tourmenté par des cauchemars; (*by an idea etc*) obsédé, tourmenté
Hague (the) [ðə'heɪg] *n* la Haye
hah [hɑː] *int* ha!, ah!
ha-ha¹ [hɑː'hɑː] *int* ha, ha!
ha-ha² ['hɑːhɑː] *n* (*ditch*) saut-de-loup *m*, *pl* sauts-de-loup
haiku ['haɪkuː] *n* haïku *m*
hail¹ [heɪl] *n Met* grêle *f*; **h. of blows/stones** grêle *ou* volée *f* de coups/pierres; **a h. of bullets** une pluie de balles; **a h. of fire** un déluge de feu; **a h. of abuse** une pluie d'injures; **to be met by a h. of insults** être reçu sous *ou* par une pluie d'insultes
hail² **1** *v impers Met* grêler; **it's hailing** il grêle **2** *vt* **to h. blows on sb** donner une volée de coups à qn; **to h. insults/abuse/obscenities on sb** asséner des insultes/des injures/des obscénités à qn
hail³ **1** *int Arch, Lit* salut!; **h., Caesar!** Avé César!; **h., Mary, full of grace!** je te salue, Marie, pleine de grâce! **2** *n Old-fashioned* **within h.** à portée de (la) voix
hail⁴ **1** *vt* **(a)** *Old-fashioned* (*greet*) (*person*) saluer **(b)** (*attract attention of*) (*person, ship, taxi*) héler; **within hailing distance** à portée de (la) voix **(c)** (*acclaim*) acclamer; **he has been hailed as the new ...** il a été acclamé comme le nouveau ...; **the bridge was hailed as an engineering marvel** le pont a été salué comme une merveille de technicité; **the plan was hailed as the solution to their problems** le projet a été salué comme la solution à tous leurs problèmes **2** *vi* **where does he h. from?** d'où vient-il?; **to h. from a port** (*of ship*) (*be based at*) venir *ou Spéc* dépendre d'un port; (*come from*) venir *ou* arriver d'un port
▶ **hail down 1** *vi* **blows/missiles hailed down on our heads** nous avons reçu une volée de coups/une pluie de missiles; **criticism hailed down on him** il a subi une avalanche *ou* un déluge de critiques **2** *vtsep* (*throw*) **they hailed stones down on us** ils nous ont bombardés de cailloux; **they hailed insults down on the President** ils ont déversé un flot d'insultes à l'intention du président
hail-fellow-well-met *adj* **to be h. with everyone** être à tu et à toi avec tout le monde
Hail Mary *n Cathol* Avé Maria *m inv*; **to say two Hail Marys** dire deux Avé Maria
hailstone ['heɪlstəʊn] *n* grêlon *m*
hailstorm ['heɪlstɔːm] *n* averse *f* de grêle
hair [heər] *n* **(a)** (*of human head*) cheveux *mpl*; (*single*) cheveu *m*; **the h.** les cheveux, la chevelure; **to have fair h.** avoir les cheveux clairs; **woman with short h.** femme aux cheveux courts; **I like your h.** j'aime bien ta coiffure; **to wash one's h.** se laver la tête; **to have** *or* **get one's h. cut** se faire couper les cheveux; **to do one's h.** se coiffer; **to have one's h. done** aller chez le coiffeur; **if you harm** *or* **touch a h. on that child's head ...** si tu touches un cheveu de cet enfant ...; **it was enough to make your h. stand on end** c'était à faire dresser les cheveux sur la tête; *F* **keep your h. on!** calmez-vous!; *F* **to get in sb's h.** taper sur les nerfs de qn, enquiquiner qn; **to comb one's h.** se peigner; **h. crack** (*in metal*) gerçure *f*; **h. cream** crème *f* pour les cheveux; **h. tonic** *or* **lotion** lotion *f* capillaire; **h. trigger** (*of firearm*) détente *f* très sensible

(b) (*individual hair, of human face and body, animals, plants*) poil *m*; **(body) h.** (*of human*) poil; **(facial) h.** (*of human*) poil du visage, duvet *m*; **removal of unwanted h.** épilation *f*, dépilation *f*; *Fig* **h. of the dog** (*for hangover*) antidote *m*; *F* **that'll put hairs on your chest** ça te rendra plus viril, ça fera de toi un homme

(c) (*coat*) (*of animal*) poil *m*, pelage *m*; (*of horse*) crin *m*; (*of pig*) soie *f*; **h. mattress** matelas *m* de crin

(d) *Opt* (*of gun sight etc*) cheveu *m*, fil *m*; **cross hairs** réticule *m*
hairball ['heəbɔːl] *n* (*in cat's stomach*) boule *f* de poils
hairband ['heəbænd] *n* bandeau *m*
hairbrush ['heəbrʌʃ] *n* brosse *f* à cheveux
haircut ['heəkʌt] *n* **(a)** (*act*) coupe *f* de cheveux; **to have a h.** se faire couper les cheveux **(b)** (*hairstyle*) coupe *f* de cheveux, coiffure *f*
hairdo ['heəduː] *n F* coiffure *f*
hairdresser ['heədresər] *n* coiffeur, -euse; **to go to the h.'s** aller chez le coiffeur
hairdressing ['heədresɪŋ] *n* coiffure *f*; **h. salon** salon *m* de coiffure; **h. trainee** apprenti coiffeur *m*, apprentie coiffeuse *f*
hair dryer *n* (*held in hand*) sèche-cheveux *m inv*, séchoir *m*; (*on stand*) casque *m*
-haired [heəd] *suff* **short/grey/***etc***-h.** aux cheveux courts/gris/*etc*
hair gel *n* gel *m*
hairgrip ['heəgrɪp] *n esp Br* pince *f* à cheveux
hair lacquer *n* laque *f*
hairless ['heəlɪs] *adj* (*bald*) chauve; (*face*) glabre, imberbe; (*body, animal*) sans poils
hairline ['heəlaɪn] *n* **(a)** (*of person*) racine *f* des cheveux; **his h. is receding** son front commence à se dégarnir, il commence à se dégarnir **(b)** *Typ* délié *m* **(c)** *Tech* (*in metal*) gerçure *f*; **h. crack** légère fêlure *f*; *Med* **h. fracture** fêlure *f* **(d)** *Opt* (*of gun sight etc*) cheveu *m*, fil *m*; **hairlines** réticule *m*
hairnet ['heənet] *n* filet *m*, résille *f*
hair oil *n* brillantine *f*
hairpiece ['heəpiːs] *n* mèche *f* postiche
hairpin ['heəpɪn] *n* épingle *f* à cheveux; **h. bend** (*on road*) virage *m* en épingle à cheveux
hair-raising *adj* effrayant; (*adventure*) effroyable; (*account*) à vous faire dresser les cheveux sur la tête
hair restorer *n* lotion *f* capillaire (contre la calvitie)
hair's-breadth *n* épaisseur *f* d'un cheveu; **he escaped death by a h.** il a été à deux doigts de la mort, il a frisé la mort; **to be within a h. of disaster** être à un cheveu de la ruine
hair shirt *n Rel* haire *f*, cilice *m*
hair slide *n Br* barrette *f*
hair-splitting **1** *n* ergotage *m*; (*dispute*) chicane *f* **2** *adj* (*distinction etc*) (trop) subtil
hair spray *n* laque *f*
hairspring ['heəsprɪŋ] *n* (*of watch, clock etc*) spiral *m*, *pl* spiraux
hairstyle ['heəstaɪl] *n* coiffure *f*
hairstylist ['heəstaɪlɪst] *n* coiffeur, -euse
hairy ['heərɪ] *adj* **(a)** (*hands, chest etc*) velu, poilu; (*person*) hirsute **(b)** *F* (*dangerous*) périlleux; (*frightening*) effrayant; **things are getting rather h.** la situation devient assez désespérée
Haiti ['heɪtɪ, 'haɪ-] *n* Haïti *m ou f*
Haitian ['heɪʃən, 'heɪtɪən] **1** *adj* haïtien **2** *n* Haïtien, -ienne
hake [heɪk] *n* (*fish*) merluche *f*, colin *m*
halal [hæ'læl] *adj Muslim Rel* hal(l)al *inv*
halberd ['hælbəd] *n Mil, Hist* hallebarde *f*
halcyon ['hælsɪən] *n* **(a)** *Lit* **h. days** bon vieux temps *m*, jours *mpl* heureux **(b)** (*kingfisher*) halcyon *m*
hale [heɪl] *adj* vigoureux, robuste, encore gaillard; **to be h. and hearty** être frais et gaillard
half, *pl* **halves** [hɑːf, hɑːvz] **1** *n* [①A5,B] **(a)** moitié *f*; (*of beer, hour*) demi *m*; **to fold/cut sth in h.** *or* **into halves** plier/couper qch en deux; **two halves** (*in arithmetic*) deux demis; **three and a h.** trois et demi; **what is h. of twelve?** quelle est la moitié de douze?; **h. a dozen** une demi-douzaine; **a h. of lager** un demi de blonde; *Fig* **h. the time he isn't there** les trois quarts du temps, il n'est pas là; **h. of them were students** la moitié d'entre eux étaient étudiants; **the first h. of the year** la première moitié de l'année; **she gave each of us h.** elle nous en a donné la moitié à chacun; **I'll be with you in h. a second** *or Br F* **h. a tick** je suis à vous dans une seconde; **I've got h. a mind to complain** j'ai bien envie de faire une réclamation; *F* **my better** *or* **other h.** ma (chère) moitié; *F* **how the other h. lives** comment vivent les autres; **bigger by h.** plus grand de moitié; *F* **she is too clever by h.** elle est beaucoup trop maligne; *F* **you haven't heard the h. of it!** tu n'en sais pas encore le quart!; **but that's h. the fun of it!** mais c'est le plus amusant!; **that was h. the point of going there** c'était tout l'intérêt d'y aller; **they don't do things by halves** ils ne font pas les choses à moitié; **to go halves with sb** partager avec qn; *Br* **one and two halves** (*on bus, train*) un tarif normal, deux tarifs enfant; *Rail* **outward/return h.** (*of ticket*) coupon *m* d'aller/de retour; **chicken halves** (*portions*) demi-poulets *mpl*

(b) (*time*) **h. an hour** une demi-heure; **h. past twelve** midi/minuit et demi; **it is h. past two** *or F* **h. two** il est deux heures et demi; **I waited for two and a h. hours** j'ai attendu pendant deux heures et demi

(c) *Sp* (*player*) demi *m*; **the first/second h. (of the game)** la première/seconde mi-temps; **in our h. (of the pitch)** dans notre camp

2 *adj* demi; **at h. price** à moitié prix; *Br F* **h. seas over** gris, soûl, ivre

3 *adv* à moitié; **she only h. understands** elle ne comprend qu'à moitié; **he h. opened the door** il entrouvrit la porte; **the bottle was h. full/empty** la bouteille était à moitié *ou* à demi pleine/vide; **you're h. right** tu n'as pas tout à fait tort; **h. laughing, h. crying** moitié riant, moitié pleurant; **I was h. afraid that you wouldn't come** j'avais quelque crainte que vous ne veniez pas; **h. as big** moitié moins grand; **h. as big**

again plus grand de moitié; **it was not h. as expensive as I thought it would be** c'était bien moins cher que je ne le pensais; **he gets h. as much money as you** il reçoit moitié moins d'argent que vous; *Br F* **it isn't h. bad** ce n'est pas mal du tout; *Br F* **it isn't h. cold!** il fait rudement froid!; *Br F* **he doesn't h. say some stupid things!** il dit vraiment n'importe quoi *ou* des âneries!; *Br F* **not h.!** et comment!

4 *pref* **h. dressed** à demi vêtu; **h. naked/asleep/dead** à moitié nu/endormi/mort; **h. done** (*work*) fait à moitié; (*cooked meat etc*) à moitié cuit

half-a-crown *n Br Arch* demi-couronne *f*

half-and-half 1 *adj, adv* moitié l'un moitié l'autre, *F* moitié-moitié; **how shall I mix them? – h.** comment faut-il les mélanger? – à doses égales; **how do you like your coffee? – h.** comment prenez-vous le café? – moitié café, moitié lait 2 *n Am* (*milk and cream*) = mélange *m* de lait et de crème liquide

halfback ['hɑːfbæk] *n* (a) *Old-fashioned Fb* demi-arrière *m, pl* demi-arrières (b) (*in rugby*) demi *m*

half-baked *adj F* (*poorly planned*) nul; (*idea*) qui ne tient pas debout, ridicule

half bearing *n* demi-palier *m*

half-binding *n* demi-reliure *f*

half-blood *n* = **halfbreed**

half board *n* demi-pension *f*

halfbreed ['hɑːfbriːd] *n* (a) *Old-fashioned Offensive Sl* (*person*) métis, -isse (b) (*horse*) cheval *m* demi-sang, *pl* chevaux demi-sang *ou* demi-sangs

half-brother *n* demi-frère *m, pl* demi-frères; *Jur* (*through mother*) frère utérin; (*through father*) frère consanguin

half-caste *adj, n Old-fashioned usu Offensive* métis, -isse

half-circle *n* demi-cercle *m, pl* demi-cercles; *Naut* **to turn a h.** faire demi-tour

half(-)cock *n* **at h.** (*rifle etc*) à moitié armé, sur le cran de sûreté; *Fig F* **to go off at h.** mal partir, mal démarrer

half-crown *n* = **half-a-crown**

half day *n Admin* demi-journée *f*

half duplex *n Comptr* semi-duplex *m*; **to send sth h.** transmettre qch en semi-duplex

half-fare ticket *n* billet *m* demi-tarif

halfhearted ['hɑːf'hɑːtɪd] *adj* sans enthousiasme; (*effort*) timide, hésitant

halfheartedly ['hɑːf'hɑːtɪdlɪ] *adv* sans enthousiasme

halfheartedness ['hɑːf'hɑːtɪdnɪs] *n* tiédeur *f*, manque *m* d'enthousiasme

half-height bulkhead *n Aut* cloison *f* basse de séparation

half-height drive *n Comptr* unité *f* demi-hauteur

half-hour *n* demi-heure *f*; **on the h.** à la demie

half-hourly 1 *adv* toutes les demi-heures 2 *adj* **there is a h. train service** il y a des trains toutes les trente minutes; **he needs his h. break** il lui faut faire une pause toutes les trente minutes; **at h. intervals** toutes les demi-heures, toutes les trente minutes

half-length *n* (a) *Horseracing* demi-longueur *f, pl* demi-longueurs (b) **h. portrait** portrait *m* en buste

half-life *n Nucl Phys etc* (*of isotope etc*) demi-vie *f, pl* demi-vies

half-light *n* demi-jour *m, pl* demi-jours

half-mast *n Br* **at h.** à mi-mât; **flag at h.** pavillon *m* en berne; *Hum* **to be at h.** (*of trousers*) arriver à mi-mollet; (*of socks*) descendre

half-moon *n* (a) demi-lune *f, pl* demi-lunes (b) (*of fingernail*) lunule *f*

half-nelson *n* (*in wrestling*) simple prise *f* de tête à terre

half-note *n esp Am Mus* blanche *f*

half-pay *n* demi-salaire *m*; (*in civil service*) demi-traitement *m*; *Mil* demi-solde *f*; **on h.** à mi-salaire/à demi-traitment/en demi-solde

halfpenny ['heɪpnɪ, 'hɑːfpenɪ] *n Br Arch* demi-penny *m*, sou *m*; *F* **it isn't worth a h.** ça ne vaut pas un sou!; **he's down to his last h.** il ne lui reste que quelques sous

half-price 1 *adj* (*ticket*) demi-tarif 2 *adv* (à) demi-tarif; **children get in h.** les enfants payent demi-tarif

half-shaft *n* demi-arbre *m*

half-sister *n* demi-sœur *f, pl* demi-sœurs; *Jur* (*through mother*) sœur utérine; (*through father*) sœur consanguine

half-size *n* (*in dress*) demi-taille *f*; (*in shoes*) demi-pointure *f*; **we don't stock half-sizes of that shoe** nous n'avons pas les demi-pointures de ce modèle en stock

half-staff *n Am* = **half-mast**

half-term *n Br Sch* congé *m* de mi-trimestre

half-timbered *adj Archit* (*house*) à colombages

half time *n Fb etc* (la) mi-temps; **the h. results** le score à la mi-temps

half-title *n Typ* (*of book*) faux-titre *m, pl* faux-titres

halftone [hɑːftəʊn] *n* (a) *Art* demi-teinte *f, pl* demi-teintes; *Phot* similigravure *f* (tramée) (b) *Am Mus* demi-ton *m, pl* demi-tons

half-track *n Aut* (auto)chenille *f*, half-track *m*

half-truth *n* demi-vérité *f, pl* demi-vérités

half volley *n Tennis* demi-volée *f*

halfway [hɑːfweɪ] *adv* (a) à mi-chemin; (*of piston*) à mi-course; **h. between the two towns** à mi-chemin entre les deux villes; **h. to Paris** à mi-chemin de Paris; **we're h. there** nous sommes à mi-chemin, nous avons fait la moitié du chemin; (*in project etc*) nous sommes à mi-chemin; **h. up (the hill)** à mi-côte, à mi-pente; **I was h. up/down the stairs** j'étais à mi-hauteur de l'escalier; **the lift got stuck h. up** l'ascenseur s'est bloqué à mi-hauteur; **h. through the project** à mi-projet; **we're h. through the year and ...** six mois ont déjà passé et ...; **we're h. through the summer holidays/week** nous sommes à la moitié des grandes vacances/de la semaine; **it happened h. through the holidays** ça s'est passé en plein milieu des vacances; **we're h. through the work** nous avons fait la moitié du travail; **to meet sb h.** (*in distance*) aller à la rencontre de qn à mi-chemin; **let's meet up h. in Bath** disons que chacun fait la moitié du chemin et qu'on se retrouve à Bath; **let's meet h.** (*in distance*) faisons chacun la moitié du chemin; **I'll meet you h.** (*in price*) faisons moitié-moitié, trouvons un compromis; (*in concessions asked for*) faisons un arrangement

(b) (*partly*) à peu près; **haven't you got a h. acceptable shirt?** tu n'as pas une chemise à peu près convenable?

halfway house *n Hist* (*inn*) maison *f ou* auberge *f* à mi-chemin; (*rehabilitation centre*) (*for drug addicts etc*) centre *m* de réadaptation; *Fig* (*compromise*) juste milieu *m*

halfway line *n Fb* ligne *f* médiane

halfwit ['hɑːfwɪt] *n* faible *mf* d'esprit, simple *mf* d'esprit

halfwitted [hɑːf'wɪtɪd] *adj* faible d'esprit, simple

half year *n* semestre *m*

half-yearly 1 *adj* semestriel; **h. result** demi-résultat *m*, résultat à six mois 2 *adv* une fois par semestre, tous les six mois

halibut ['hælɪbət] *n* (*fish*) flétan *m*

halitosis [hælɪ'təʊsɪs] *n Med* mauvaise haleine *f*; **to suffer from h.** avoir mauvaise haleine

hall [hɔːl] *n* (a) **(entrance) h.** (*of house*) entrée *f*; (*of hotel*) hall *m*; **h. porter** concierge *m*; **h. stand** portemanteau *m* (b) *Am* (*corridor*) couloir *m*, corridor *m* (c) (*room, building*) salle *f*; **(dining) h.** (*of stately home*) salle à manger; *Univ* réfectoire *m*; **the servants' h.** l'office *m*; *Br Univ* **h. (of residence)** résidence *f* universitaire, maison *f* d'étudiants; *Br Univ* **to eat in h.** manger au réfectoire *ou* RU; *Br Univ* **to live in h.** loger en résidence universitaire (d) (*manor house*) manoir *m*; **she works up at the h.** elle travaille au château; **Ludgely H.** (*in name*) le château de Ludgely

hallelujah [hælɪ'luːjə] *int, n* alléluia *m*

hallmark[1] ['hɔːlmɑːk] *n* (*on silver*) (cachet *m* de) contrôle *m*, poinçon *m*; *Fig* **the h. of genius** l'empreinte *f* du génie; **to bear all the hallmarks of ...** porter l'empreinte de ..., avoir tous les signes de ...

hallmark[2] *vt* (*silver*) contrôler, poinçonner

hallo [hə'ləʊ] *int* = **hello**

Hall of Fame *n esp Am* = Panthéon *m*; **she was inducted into the Country Music H.** elle a été admise parmi les grands de la musique country

hallow[1] ['hæləʊ] *n Old-fashioned Rel* **All Hallows' (Day)** (le jour de) la Toussaint

hallow[2] *vt Rel* sanctifier, consacrer; **hallowed** ['hæləʊd, *occ* 'hæləʊɪd] **be Thy name** que Ton nom soit sanctifié

hallowed ['hæləʊd] *adj* béni, sanctifié; **h. ground** terre sainte

Hallowe'en [hæləʊ'iːn] *n* = veille *f* de la Toussaint, *Can* halloween *f*

hallucinate [hə'luːsɪneɪt] 1 *vt* **he was hallucinating that his skin had turned green** dans ses hallucinations, il se voyait avec la peau verte 2 *vi* avoir des hallucinations

hallucination [həluːsɪ'neɪʃən] *n* hallucination *f*

hallucinatory [hə'luːsɪnət(ə)rɪ] *adj* hallucinatoire

hallucinogen [hə'luːsɪnədʒen] *n* hallucinogène *m*

hallucinogenic [həluːsɪnəʊ'dʒenɪk] *adj* hallucinogène

hallway ['hɔːlweɪ] *n* (a) vestibule *m*, entrée *f* (b) *Am* (*corridor*) couloir *m*

halo, *pl* **-os, -oes** ['heɪləʊ, -əʊz] *n* (a) (*of saint*) auréole *f*, nimbe *m*; *Hum* **your h.'s slipping!** tu te dévergondes! (b) *Astron, Opt, Phot* halo *m*; (*of moon*) auréole *f*; *Mktg* **h. effect** effet *m* de halo

halogen ['hælədʒən] *adj, n Ch* halogène *m*; **h. headlights** phares *mpl* halogènes

halt[1] [hɒlt] *n* (a) (*act of stopping*) arrêt *m*, interruption *f* (momentanée), halte *f*, pause *f*; **a brief h. at an inn** une brève halte dans une auberge; **to bring to a h.** (*process etc*) arrêter; (*movement, action*) provoquer l'interruption momentanée de; (*vehicule, crowd etc*) arrêter, faire stopper; **to come to a h.** marquer un temps d'arrêt, s'interrompre momentanément, s'arrêter, stopper; (*on journey*) faire halte; (*in a speech*) rester sans rien dire; **to call a h.** (demander à) faire une halte; **to call a h. to sth** arrêter qch; *Aut* **h. sign** stop *m* **(b)** *Br Rail* (*small station*) halte *f*

halt² **1** *vi* faire halte, s'arrêter; **to h. at ...** faire un arrêt à ..., s'arrêter à ...; *Mil* **company h.!** compagnie halte!; *Mil* **h.! who goes there** halte! qui va là? **2** *vt* (*person*) faire faire (une) halte à; (*sth*) (*for good*) arrêter, mettre un terme *ou* un point final à; (*temporarily*) interrompre

halt³ *Arch, Bible* **1** *adj* boiteux **2** *npl* **the h. and the lame** les estropiés *mpl*

halter¹ ['hɔːltər] *n* **(a)** (*for horse*) licou *m* **(b)** (*clothing*) **h. (top)** (corsage *m ou* haut *m*) bain-de-soleil *m inv*; **h.-neck dress** robe *f* dos nu, dos-nu *m, pl* dos-nus **(c)** (*rope*) (*for hanging person*) corde *f*

halting ['hɔːltɪŋ] *adj* (*words, speech etc*) hésitant; (*style*) heurté

haltingly ['hɔːltɪŋlɪ] *adv* en hésitant

halve [hɑːv] *vt* **(a)** (*cut*) diviser en deux (moitiés), couper en deux (moitiés) **(b)** (*share*) partager en deux **(c)** (*reduce*) (*expenses, costs etc*) réduire de moitié

halves [hɑːvz] *npl see* **half**

halyard ['hæljəd] *n Naut* drisse *f*

ham¹ [hæm] *n* **(a)** *Culin* jambon *m*; **h. and eggs** œufs *mpl* au jambon; **h. sandwich** sandwich *m* au jambon **(b)** *F* (*buttocks*) **the hams** les fesses *fpl*, le derrière **(c)** *Th, Cin etc F* **h. (actor)** cabotin *m*; **h. acting** cabotinage *m* **(d)** *Rad F* (*enthusiast*) **(radio) h.** radioamateur *m*

ham² (-mm-) *Th, Cin etc F* **1** *vi* jouer comme un pied **2** *vt* **he hams all his parts** il charge tous ses rôles, *F* il en fait trop

▶ **ham up** *vtsep Th, Cin etc F* **to h. it up** jouer comme un pied

Hamburg ['hæmbɜːg] *n* Hambourg

Hamburger ['hæmbɜːgər] *n* (*person*) Hambourgeois, -oise

hamburger ['hæmbɜːgər] *n Culin* hamburger *m*; *Am* (*meat*) viande *f* hachée

ham-fisted ['hæm'fɪstɪd] *adj F* maladroit

Hamitic [hə'mɪtɪk] *adj* chamitique

hamlet ['hæmlɪt] *n* hameau *m*

hammer¹ ['hæmər] *n* **(a)** (*tool*) marteau *m*; (*heavy*) masse *f*; *Pol* **the h. and sickle** la faucille et le marteau; **to go at it h. and tongs** (*work etc energetically*) y aller de bon cœur, ne pas y aller de main morte; (*quarrel*) se quereller; (*fight*) se bagarrer; *Sp* **throwing the h., h. throwing** lancement *m* du marteau; **h. thrower** lanceur *m* de marteau **(b)** (*of auctioneer*) marteau *m*; **to come under the h.** être mis aux enchères **(c)** (*in clock, alarm, piano etc*) marteau *m* **(d)** *Anat* (*of inner ear*) marteau *m* **(e)** (*of firearm*) chien *m*

hammer² **1** *vt* marteler; *F* (*beat*) (*person*) tabasser; (*of boxer etc*) (*opponent*) cogner dur sur; (*defeat*) (*opponent, other side*) battre à plate(s) couture(s), écraser; (*criticize*) (*person, book etc*) massacrer, descendre; **to h. a nail into sth** enfoncer un clou dans qch avec un marteau; **to h. into shape** (*pot etc*) façonner à coups de marteau; *Fig F* (*plan etc*) perfectionner; *F* **to h. sth into sb** faire entrer qch dans la tête de qn; **I'll h. it into her** je veux lui faire entrer ça dans la tête; **to h. prices** écraser les prix

2 *vi* **(a)** travailler avec un marteau, travailler au marteau; **to h. at** *or* **on the door** frapper à la porte à coups redoublés

(b) *F* **to h. down the motorway** foncer sur l'autoroute

▶ **hammer along** *vi F* (*in car*) foncer

▶ **hammer away** *vi* **(a)** (*with hammer*) **they've been hammering away all evening** ils ont donné des coups de marteau toute la soirée; **to h. away at sth** marteler qch **(b)** (*of heart*) battre très fort (dans la poitrine) **(c)** *Fig* **to h. away at sth** (*at agreement*) travailler d'arrache-pied à qch; **to h. away at the keyboard** frapper de toutes ses forces sur le clavier

▶ **hammer home** *vtsep* **(a)** (*sth*) enfoncer (à l'aide d'un marteau); **make sure you h. the nails home** assure-toi que tu as bien enfoncé les clous **(b)** *Fig* (*insist on*) **to h. sth home** insister sur qch, répéter cent fois qch

▶ **hammer in** *vtsep* (*nail*) enfoncer à coups de marteau

▶ **hammer out** *vtsep* **(a)** (*in metalwork*) (*gold etc*) étendre sous le marteau; (*copper*) panner; **to h. out a dent in sth** débosseler qch **(b) to h. out a tune (on the piano)** pianoter un air; **to h. out a message on the pipes** tapoter un message sur les conduits **(c)** *Fig F* (*draw up*) élaborer, mettre au point; **unions and management hammered out an agreement** les syndicats et le patronat sont parvenus à un accord

hammerhead ['hæməhed] *n* **(a) h. (shark)** requin *m* marteau **(b)** (*bird*) ombrette *f* (du Sénégal)

hammering ['hæmərɪŋ] *n* (*with hammer*) martelage *m*; (*noise*) martèlement *m*; (*of iron*) battage *m*; *F* (*with fists*) volée *f* de coups; **to give sb a h.** (*hit*) cogner dur sur qn, rouer qn de coups; (*defeat*) battre qn à plate(s) couture(s), écraser qn; **to give sb/a book a h.** (*criticize*) descendre qn/un livre; **our team got a h.** notre équipe a été battue à plate(s) couture(s)

hammertoe ['hæmətəʊ] *n Med* orteil *m* en marteau *ou* en cou de cygne

hammock ['hæmək] *n* hamac *m*

hammy ['hæmɪ] *adj Th, Cin etc F* (*acting*) outrancier; **h. actor** cabotin *m*, acteur *m* qui en fait trop

hamper¹ ['hæmpər] *n* panier *m*; (*for oysters etc*) bourriche *f*; **Christmas h.** panier rempli de gourmandises de Noël

hamper² *vt* (*person*) embarrasser, gêner, entraver; **to h. the progress of business** entraver la marche des affaires; **high winds hampered the rescue work** les sauveteurs ont été gênés dans leur travail par la force des vents; **they were hampered in their efforts (to do sth) by the terrible weather** ils furent gênés dans leurs efforts (pour faire qch) par le mauvais temps; **she was hampered by her long cloak** elle était empêtrée dans son grand manteau

hamster ['hæmstər] *n* hamster *m*

hamstring¹ ['hæmstrɪŋ] *n* tendon *m* du jarret; **h. injury** lésion *f* du tendon du jarret

hamstring² *vt* (*pt, pp* **hamstringed** *or* **-strung**) **(a)** (*cut hamstrings of*) (*person, horse*) couper le(s) jarret(s) à **(b)** *Fig* paralyser; (*financially*) (*person*) couper les moyens à; **we are hamstrung by a lack of funds** nous sommes paralysés par l'absence de fonds suffisants

hand¹ [hænd] *n* **(a)** (*part of body*) main *f*; **on one's hands and knees** à quatre pattes; **give me your h.** donnez-moi la main; **to hold in one's h.** (*sword, hat*) tenir à la main; (*grain*) tenir dans la main; (*success*) tenir entre les mains; **to hold hands** se tenir (par) la main; **keep your hands to yourself** ne touche pas, enlève *ou* retire tes mains de là; **to lay hands on sth** mettre la main sur qch; **to lay hands on sb** faire violence à qn; **to pass sth from h. to h.** passer qch de main en main; **I can't put my h. on it** je n'arrive pas à mettre la main dessus; **to take sb by the h.** prendre qn par la main; **he writes with his left h.** il écrit de la main gauche; **I only have one pair of hands!** je n'ai que deux mains!; **made/done by h.** fait à la main; **to wash clothes by h.** laver du linge à la main; **by h.** (*on letter etc*) = remise par porteur (sans timbre); **to send/deliver a letter by h.** envoyer/distribuer une lettre par porteur; **sword in h.** sabre au poing; **hands off!** n'y touchez pas!; (*off me*) bas les pattes!; **hands up!** haut les mains!; *Old-fashioned* **h. glass** (*for reading*) loupe *f*; (*mirror*) miroir *m* de sac; *TV etc* **h. cue** signal *m* de départ de la main; **h. microphone** micro *m* portatif

(b) (*responsibility, control, ownership etc*) **to have a h. in sth** être impliqué dans qch, être mêlé à qch; **I had no h. in this crime** je n'ai absolument rien à voir avec ce crime; **the h. of God** le doigt de Dieu; **I see Moriarty's h. in this** je reconnais la griffe de Moriarty dans cette affaire; **to have one's hands full** (*literally*) avoir les mains prises; *Fig* (*be busy*) avoir du pain sur la planche, être débordé; **I've got my hands full trying to cope as it is** j'ai déjà assez à faire comme ça; **to fall into enemy hands** tomber aux mains *ou* entre les mains de l'ennemi; **in the wrong hands this knowledge could be very dangerous** si elles tombaient aux mains de personnes malintentionnées, ces connaissances pourraient être très dangereuses; **to be in good hands** être en (de) *ou* entre (de) bonnes mains; **to put oneself in sb's hands** se confier à qn; **it's in your own hands what happens next** la suite dépend de vous; **to put a matter in the hands of a lawyer** confier une affaire à un avocat; **the matter's in their hands now** désormais, l'affaire est entre leurs mains; **it's out of my hands** je ne peux (plus) rien y faire; **the case is off our hands** l'affaire ne dépend plus de nous; **to get sth off one's hands** se débarrasser de qch; **to change hands** (*of goods etc*) changer de mains; (*of business etc*) changer de propriétaire

(c) (*skill*) **to try one's h. at sth** essayer de faire qch, s'essayer à qch; **to get one's h. in** se faire la main; **to keep one's h. in** garder la main; **she can turn her h. to anything** c'est une femme qui peut tout faire

(d) (*idioms*) *Fml* **he asked for her h. (in marriage)** il lui a demandé sa main; *F* **he never does a h.'s turn** il ne fait jamais rien de ses dix doigts; *F* **to give sb a big h.** (*applaud*) applaudir vivement qn; **to give** *or* **lend sb a (helping) h.** aider qn, donner un coup de main à qn; **to lend a h.** mettre la main à la pâte; *Fig* **to have one's hands tied** avoir les mains liées; **I could beat you at tennis with one h. tied**

behind my back je pourrais te battre au tennis même avec une main dans le dos; *F* **to put** *or* **dip one's h. in the till** puiser dans la caisse; **to be h. in glove with sb** être d'intelligence *ou Péj* de mèche avec qn; *F* **to make money h. over fist** s'enrichir rapidement; **to be living from h. to mouth** vivre au jour le jour; *Sp etc* **to win hands down** gagner haut la main; **to beat sb hands down** battre qn à plate(s) couture(s)

(e) (*phrases with* **at**) **to be (near) at h.** (*of object etc*) être à portée de la main *ou* sous la main; (*of event etc*) approcher, être proche; **the hour is at h.** l'heure est proche; **there is always a doctor at h.** il y a toujours un médecin de service; **to suffer at the hands of …** souffrir aux mains de *ou* entre les mains de …

(f) (*phrases with* **in**) **to walk h. in h. with sb** marcher avec qn la main dans la main; **to work h. in h. with sb** agir de concert avec qn; **to have so much money in h.** avoir tant d'argent disponible; **stock in h.** marchandises en magasin; **I've five minutes in h.** j'ai encore cinq minutes; **the matter in h.** l'affaire en question; **work in h.** travail en cours *ou* en chantier; **the situation is well in h.** la situation est bien en main; **to take sb in h.** prendre qn en main

(g) (*phrases with* **on**) **work on h.** travail en cours *ou* à faire; **to have sb/sth on one's hands** avoir qn/qch à sa charge *ou F* sur les bras; **to have an hour on one's hands** avoir une heure à tuer; **to have time on one's hands** avoir du temps libre; **she's got a lot on her hands at the moment** elle est très occupée en ce moment; **I'm on h. if you need me** je suis à votre disposition si vous avez besoin de moi; **on the one h.** d'une part; **on the other h.** d'autre part

(h) (*phrases with* **out of**) **these birds will eat out of your h.** ces oiseaux te mangeront dans la main; *Fig* **I'll soon have him eating out of my h.** bientôt, il me mangera dans la main; **to do sth out of h.** faire qch sur-le-champ; **to shoot sb out of h.** abattre qn sans autre forme de procès; **to get out of h.** (*of situation, inflation etc*) échapper à notre/leur/ *etc* contrôle; (*of children, class etc*) perdre toute discipline

(i) (*phrases with* **to**) **to come to h.** tomber sous la main; **you can use anything that comes to h.** tu peux utiliser tout ce qui te tombe sous la main; **your parcel came to h. this morning** votre paquet m'est parvenu ce matin; **use whatever is to h.** utilisez ce que vous avez sous la main; **the first excuse to h.** le premier prétexte venu

(j) (*worker*) ouvrier, -ière; *Naut* matelot *m*; *Ind etc* **to take on hands** embaucher de la main-d'œuvre; *Naut* **the (ship's) hands** l'équipage *m*; **all hands on deck!** tout le monde sur le pont!; **to be lost with all hands** (*of ship*) périr corps et biens; **an old h. (at sth)** un expert (en/dans qch), un spécialiste (en/de qch); **an old h. at doing sth** un expert *ou* spécialiste pour ce qui est de faire qch; **he was an old h. at spotting such tricks** c'était un expert dans l'art de reconnaître de telles ruses

(k) (*handwriting*) écriture *f*; **in one's own h.** (*write a letter*) de sa propre main; *Arch, Jur* **to set one's h. to a deed** apposer sa signature à un acte

(l) *Cards* (*cards received*) jeu *m*; (*player*) joueur, -euse; (*round*) partie *f*; **to have a good h.** avoir un beau jeu, avoir du jeu; **first/fourth h.** (*player*) premier *m*/dernier *m* en cartes; **to show one's h.** faire voir son jeu

(m) (*measurement*) paume *f*; **horse fifteen hands high** cheval de quinze paumes

(n) *Typ* index *m*; (*of signpost, barometer*) indicateur *m*; (*of clock, watch*) aiguille *f*; **the little h. is pointing to three** la petite aiguille est sur le trois

(o) (*of bananas*) régime *m*

hand[2] *vt* passer, remettre, donner (**sth to sb** qch à qn); **he handed her the letter to read** il lui a donné la lettre à lire; *Fig* **to h. sth to sb on a plate** apporter à qn qch sur un plateau; *Fig F* **to h. it to sb** reconnaître la supériorité de qn; **you've got to h. it to him** devant lui, chapeau!; **you've got to h. it to these Russians, they know how to dance!** il faut reconnaître que ces Russes savent danser!

▶ **hand around** *vtsep* = **hand round**

▶ **hand back** *vtsep* (*return*) repasser; **she handed me back the bottle** elle m'a repassé la bouteille

▶ **hand down** *vtsep* **(a)** (*give*) **h. me down that bottle** descends-moi cette bouteille **(b)** (*help down*) **to h. sb down** donner la main à qn pour l'aider à descendre **(c)** (*bequeath etc*) (*necklace, tradition*) transmettre (**from** de; **to** en); **all her clothes had been handed down from her older sisters** tous ses vêtements venaient de ses sœurs aînées **(d)** *Jur* **to h. down a sentence** prononcer une sentence

▶ **hand in** *vtsep* remettre, déposer; **to h. in one's resignation** démissionner; **to h. in a piece of homework** rendre un devoir; **to h. a piece of lost property in (to the police)** remettre un objet trouvé (à la police)

▶ **hand off** *vtsep Rugby* (*player*) raffûter

▶ **hand on** *vtsep* (*custom*) transmettre; (*news*) passer (**to** à)

▶ **hand out** *vtsep* **(a)** (*distribute*) (*leaflets, biscuits*) distribuer **(b)** (*give*) donner; **he's always handing out advice** il se permet de donner des conseils, *F* il est sans cesse à donner des conseils; **he's fond of handing it out, but can't take it** (*criticism*) il se permet de critiquer les autres mais il déteste qu'on le critique

▶ **hand over 1** *vtsep* **(a)** (*give*) donner, remettre

(b) (*deliver*) remettre, livrer; **she handed over the documents to a lawyer** elle a remis les documents à un avocat

(c) (*surrender*) (*property*) céder; **h. over your wallet!** donne ton portefeuille!; **to h. sb over to justice** livrer qn à la justice, remettre qn aux mains de la justice

(d) (*transfer*) (*power*) transmettre; **we now h. you over to our foreign affairs correspondent** nous passons maintenant la parole au responsable des affaires étrangères; **to h. over the command to …** remettre le commandement à …

2 *vi* **(a)** (*transfer*) **I now h. over to the weatherman** je passe maintenant la parole au présentateur de la météo; **when will she h. over to the new president?** quand va-t-elle laisser la place au nouveau président?

(b) *F* (*give*) **I know you have it, so h. over!** passe-le moi, je sais que tu l'as!

▶ **hand round** *vtsep* (*circulate*) (*bottle etc*) faire passer, faire circuler; **to h. round a hat** faire passer (à la ronde) un chapeau

hand- [hænd] *pref* à la main; **h.-sewn** cousu (à la) main; **h.-operated** à commande manuelle

handbag [ˈhændbæg] *n* sac *m* à main, *Can* sacoche *m*

hand baggage *n* bagage(s) *m(pl)* à main

handball [ˈhændbɔːl] *n Sp* (*game*) hand-ball *m*

hand ball *n Fb* (*foul*) (faute *f* de) main *f*

hand basin *n* lavabo *m*

handbell [ˈhændbel] *n* sonnette *f*, clochette *f*

handbill [ˈhændbɪl] *n* prospectus *m*

handbook [ˈhændbʊk] *n* **(a)** (*for traveller, tourist*) guide *m*; (*for use in museum etc*) livret *m* **(b)** *Sch etc* (*of science etc*) manuel *m*

handbrake [ˈhændbreɪk] *n* frein *m* à main; **h.-on light** voyant *m* de frein à main, témoin *m* de frein parking

handcart [ˈhændkɑːt] *n* charrette *f* à bras

handclap [ˈhændklæp] *n* **to give sb a slow h.** = siffler qn

hand controls *npl* commandes *fpl* manuelles

hand cream *n* crème *f* pour les mains

handcuff [ˈhændkʌf] *vt* (*person*) mettre *ou* passer les menottes à, menotter; **to h. sb to sb** attacher qn à qn d'autre avec des menottes; **to h. sb to sth** attacher qn à qch avec des menottes

handcuffs [ˈhændkʌfs] *npl* menottes *fpl*

handful [ˈhændfʊl] *n* **(a)** (*of sand etc*) poignée *f* **(b)** (*small number*) petit nombre *m*; **there was** *or* **were only a h. of people there** il n'y avait là que quelques personnes **(c)** *F* (*difficult person*) **that child is a real h.** cet enfant-là me donne du fil à retordre

hand grenade *n Mil* grenade *f* (à main)

handgrip [ˈhændgrɪp] *n Cycling etc* poignée *f*

handgun [ˈhændgʌn] *n* revolver *m*, pistolet *m*

hand-held *adj Cin, TV* **h. camera** caméra *f* portable; *Comptr* **h. scanner** scanneur *m* (à) main

handhold [ˈhændhəʊld] *n* prise *f*

handicap[1] [ˈhændɪkæp] *n* **(a)** (*disadvantage*) handicap *m*, désavantage *m*; *Med* handicap; **to have a severe h.** avoir un lourd handicap **(b)** *Sp* handicap *m*; **(weight) h.** (*of racehorse*) surcharge *f*, handicap; **time/distance h.** handicap en temps/ distance

handicap[2] *vt* **(-pp-)** **(a)** (*disadvantage*) handicaper, désavantager; **their lack of preparation handicapped them** ils ont été désavantagés par leur manque de préparation **(b)** *Sp* handicaper

handicapped [ˈhændɪkæpt] **1** *adj* handicapé **2** *npl* **the (physically/mentally) h.** les handicapés *mpl* (physiques/ mentaux)

handicraft [ˈhændɪkrɑːft] *n* (*usu pl*) **(a)** (*trade*) artisanat *m*, métier *m* manuel **(b)** (*result*) artisanat *m*, produit *m* artisanal

handily [ˈhændɪlɪ] *adv* commodément; **h. shaped** d'une forme très pratique; **they h. left their fingerprints** ils ont laissé leurs empreintes, ce qui était bien pratique

handiness [ˈhændɪnɪs] *n* **(a)** (*of tool etc*) commodité *f*; **the h. of the house for the shops** l'emplacement très commode de la maison près des magasins **(b)** (*skill with hands*) adresse *f*, dextérité *f*, habileté *f* (manuelle)

handing down *n* (*of tradition*) transmission *f*

handing over *n* (*of hostages, keys*) remise *f* (**to** aux mains de); *Jur* (*of property*) cession *f*; (*of power*) transmission *f*

handiwork ['hændɪwɜːk] *n* **(a)** (*action*) travail *m* manuel **(b)** (*result*) ouvrage *m*, travail *m*, œuvre *f*; **the repair/fruit bowl is Jenny's h.** c'est Jenny qui a fait la réparation/la corbeille à fruits; *Iron* **is this your h.?** c'est ton œuvre?; **this quarrel (of theirs) is your h.** c'est de ta faute s'ils se disputent

hand-job *n Sl* **to give sb a h.** branler qn

handkerchief ['hæŋkətʃɪf] *n* mouchoir *m*

hand-knit(ted) *adj* (*sweater etc*) tricoté (à la) main

handle[1] ['hænd(ə)l] *n* **(a)** (*of broom, knife, tool etc*) manche *m*; (*of pump*) bras *m*, balancier *m*; (*of wheelbarrow*) bras; (*of stretcher*) brancard *m*; (*of frying pan*) queue *f*; (*of sword, lever, box, suitcase etc*) poignée *f*; (*of tap*) clef *f*; (*of basket, bucket etc*) anse *f*; **(door) h.** poignée; *F* **to fly off the h.** s'emballer; **to get a h. on a problem** savoir comment s'y prendre pour résoudre un problème; **you're giving him a h. against you** vous lui donnez des armes *ou* un avantage contre vous

(b) *F* (*title*) titre *m*; (*CB radio user's call name*) indicatif *m*, code *m*; **to have a h. to one's name** avoir un nom à rallonge(s)

handle[2] **1** *vt* **(a)** (*touch, hold*) tâter, toucher; **to h. a material** tâter *ou* toucher un tissu; **h. with care** (*on package*) = fragile; **to h. stolen goods** recéler des objets volés; *Fb* **to h. the ball** toucher la balle, faire une main

(b) (*operate*) (*object*) manier, manipuler; (*ship, sails etc*) manœuvrer; (*ship*) gouverner; (*car*) conduire; **how to h. a gun** comment se servir d'un fusil

(c) (*treat*) traiter; **to h. sb roughly** malmener qn, rudoyer qn; **the author handles the subject well** l'auteur traite bien le sujet

(d) (*manage, cope with*) **to h. a situation** prendre en main une situation; **you handled that very well** vous vous en êtes très bien sorti; **to h. a crisis** résoudre une crise; **don't worry, I'll h. this/him** ne vous inquiétez pas, je vais m'en occuper/je vais m'occuper de lui; **to h. oneself (well) in a crisis** bien se comporter *ou* se conduire en cas de crise; *F* **I can't h. interviews** je n'arrive pas à affronter les interviews; *F* **he can't h. it when people get aggressive** il n'arrive pas à faire face aux gens agressifs; **she can h. would-be Romeos** elle sait comment faire avec ce genre de dragueurs; *F* **could you h. another potato?** tu reprendras bien une autre pomme de terre?

(e) (*deal with*) **we h. a lot of business for them** nous travaillons beaucoup pour eux; **who handles your business in ...?** qui s'occupe de votre entreprise en ...?; **we don't h. that sort of business** nous ne nous occcupons pas de ce genre d'affaires; **to h. large orders** s'occuper de grosses commandes; **to h. a lot of money** brasser beaucoup d'argent; **we h. 10 000 passengers a week** 10 000 passagers passent par nos services chaque semaine; **we don't h. that kind of material/product any more** nous ne faisons plus ce genre de matériel/produit; **who handles your products in France?** qui distribue vos produits en France?; **to h. figures/words** manier les chiffres/les mots

2 *vi* **to h. well** (*of car, boat*) être agréable à conduire; **how does it h.?** elle/il est comment?

handlebar ['hænd(ə)lbɑːr] *n* (*usu pl*) **handlebars** guidon *m*; *F* **h. moustache** moustaches *fpl* en guidon (de bicyclette)

handler ['hændlər] *n Com* manutentionnaire *mf*; (*of spy*) contact *m*; **(dog) h.** maître *m* (de) chien

handling ['hændlɪŋ] *n* **(a)** (*touching, holding*) manipulation *f*, action *f* de toucher; (*of stolen goods*) recel *m*

(b) (*of tool*) maniement *m*; (*of explosives*) manipulation *f*; (*of a ship*) manœuvre *f*

(c) (*of a car*) maniabilité *f*, comportement *m* routier

(d) (*treatment*) (*of person, subject etc*) traitement *m*; **rough h.** traitement brutal

(e) (*of crisis, situation*) prise *f* en main; (*of funds*) maniement *m*

(f) *Com* manutention *f*, distribution *f*; **h. charges** frais *mpl* de manutention; *Admin* frais d'administration; **h. fee** frais *mpl* d'administration

(g) *Fb* (faute *f* de) main *f*

hand lotion *n* lait *m* pour les mains

hand luggage *n* bagages *mpl* à main

handmade [hænd'meɪd] *adj* fait *ou* fabriqué à la main, fait main

handmaid ['hændmeɪd], **handmaiden** ['hændmeɪd(ə)n] *n Old-fashioned* servante *f*

hand-me-down *n F* **hand-me-downs, h. clothes** vêtements usagés *ou* d'occasion, frusques *fpl*; **I used to wear my brother's hand-me-downs** je récupérais les vêtements usagés de mon frère

hand-out, handout ['hændaʊt] *n* **(a)** *Pej* (*alms*) aumône *f*; (*food*) = nourriture *f* distribuée aux pauvres; **I don't want to live off hand-outs** je ne veux pas vivre de la charité des autres; **state** *or* **government h.** aumône du gouvernement **(b)** *Journ* compte rendu *m* communiqué à la presse, communiqué *m*; *Sch, Univ* notes *fpl* (polycopiées), polycopié *m* (*donné aux élèves etc*) **(c)** *Com* (*brochure*) prospectus *m*, brochure *f*, tract *m*; (*sample*) cadeau *m* publicitaire

handover ['hændəʊvər] *n* (*of hostage, ransom*) remise *f*; **h. of power** passation *f* de pouvoirs

hand-pick *vt* (*fruit etc*) cueillir à la main; **the volunteers have been hand-picked** les volontaires ont été triés sur le volet

hand-picked ['hænd'pɪkt] *adj* (*fruit etc*) cueilli à la main; (*person, team*) trié sur le volet

hand puppet *n Th* marionnette *f*

handrail ['hændreɪl] *n* (*of staircase etc*) rampe *f*, main *f* courante; (*of bridge etc*) garde-fou *m*, *pl* garde-fous, garde-corps *m inv*; *Naut, Rail* rambarde *f*

handsaw ['hændsɔː] *n* scie *f* à main

handset ['hændset] *n Tel* combiné *m*

hands-free conversation *n Tel* conversation *f* 'mains libres'

handshake ['hændʃeɪk] *n* **(a)** poignée *f ou* serrement *m* de main **(b)** *Comptr* dialogue *m* d'établissement de liaison; **h. message** message *m* d'établissement de liaison, message de prise de contact

handshaking ['hændʃeɪkɪŋ] *n Comptr* établissement *m* d'une liaison

hand signal *n Aut* signe *m* de la main

hands-off *adj Pol* non-interventionniste; **the director has a h. style of management** le directeur est partisan de laisser de l'autonomie à son personnel, *Pej* le directeur a un sens très large de la délégation de pouvoir

handsome ['hænsəm] *adj* **(a)** (*good-looking*) beau, *f* belle; **a h. man** un bel homme; **she was a h. woman** c'était une belle femme; **a h. building** une belle construction **(b)** (*conduct etc*) gracieux, généreux; (*praise, apology*) sincère, sans réserve; **he received very h. treatment** on l'a traité d'une façon très généreuse **(c)** (*considerable*) (*price*) bon; (*gift*) généreux; **h. fortune** belle fortune; **to make a h. profit** faire *ou* réaliser de beaux bénéfices; **a h. sum** une coquette somme

handsomely ['hænsəmlɪ] *adv* **(a)** (*dressed, furnished etc*) bien **(b)** (*to act*) généreusement; (*to treat, praise, apologize*) avec sincérité, sans réserve; (*to pay*) libéralement

handsomeness ['hænsəmnɪs] *n* **(a)** (*of person, monument etc*) beauté *f* **(b)** (*of an action*) générosité *f*; (*of reward*) libéralité *f*; (*of an apology*) sincérité *f*

hands-on *adj* (*experience*) pratique; **h. exhibition** (*at museum*) = exposition *f* où les gens sont encouragés à toucher aux objets; **the director has a h. style of management** le directeur s'implique vraiment

handspring ['hændsprɪŋ] *n Gym* saut *m* de mains

handstand ['hændstænd] *n Gym* **to do a h.** faire un équilibre sur les mains, faire l'arbre droit

hand-to-hand **1** *adj* (*fighting*) corps-à-corps **2** *adv* **to fight h.** se battre au corps-à-corps

hand-to-mouth *adj, adv* **to live h., to lead a h. existence** tirer le diable par la queue

hand-tooling *n* **(a)** *Tech* (*on a lathe etc*) travail *m* à la main **(b)** (*in bookbinding*) dorure *f* à froid faite à la main

handwork ['hændwɜːk] *n* travail *m* fait à la main, travail manuel

handwriting ['hændraɪtɪŋ] *n* écriture *f*; **h. expert** graphologue *mf*; *Comptr* **h. recognition** reconnaissance *f* de l'écriture manuscrite

handwritten ['hændrɪt(ə)n] *adj* (*letter etc*) manuscrit

handy ['hændɪ] *adj* **(a)** (*useful*) (*tool etc*) pratique; (*ship*) maniable; **that would come in very h.** ça serait bien utile; **a h. tip** un bon conseil **(b)** (*convenient*) commode; **the flat's h. for the shops** l'appartement est tout près des commerces **(c)** (*within reach*) à portée (de la main); **I always keep my tools h.** j'ai toujours mes outils sous la main **(d)** (*skilful*) (*with one's hands*) adroit, habile (*de ses mains*); **he's very h. about the house** (*good at making, repairing things*) c'est un bon bricoleur; **h. at sth/at doing sth** adroit à qch/à faire qch; **to be h. with one's fists** savoir se servir de ses poings

handyman, *pl* **-men** ['hændɪmæn, -men] *n* (*employee*) homme *m* à tout faire *ou* à toutes mains; (*DIY expert etc*) bricoleur *m*; *Am* **h.'s special** = maison *f* qui a besoin de beaucoup de travaux

hang[1] [hæŋ] *n* **(a)** (*of clothing*) tombé *m*; (*of material*) drapé *m* **(b)** *F* **to get the h. of sth** (*understand*) comprendre qch, piger qch; **when you've got the h. of it** (*acquired skill*) quand tu auras attrapé le coup; **I haven't got the h. of this new keyboard yet** je ne connais pas encore très bien ce nouveau clavier!; **when you've got the h. of things** (*in new* *office, job etc*) quand vous serez au courant (**c**) *F* **I don't give** *or* **care a h.** je m'en moque *ou* m'en fiche

hang² (*pt, pp* **hung** [hʌŋ]) **1** *vt* (**a**) (*suspend*) pendre, accrocher, suspendre (**on, from** à); (*door*) monter; **to h. a coat on a hook** pendre *ou* suspendre un manteau à une patère; **to h. sth on the wall** accrocher qch au mur; **they hung banners from their windows** ils ont accroché des bannières à leurs fenêtres; **to h. a picture** suspendre un tableau; (*exhibit*) exposer un tableau (*au Salon etc*); **to h. wallpaper** poser du papier peint

(**b**) (*droop*) **to h. one's head** baisser la tête

(**c**) (*decorate*) **to h. a room with tapestries** tendre une salle de tapisseries; **hall hung with flags** salle ornée de drapeaux

(**d**) *Culin* (*meat, game*) faire faisander

(**e**) **to h. fire** (*of troops etc*) suspendre le feu; *Fig* (*of decision etc*) traîner (en longueur), faire traîner les choses

(**f**) (*pt, pp* **hanged** [hæŋd]) (*criminal*) pendre; **he hanged himself** il s'est pendu; *Br Pol F Pej* **the h. 'em and flog 'em brigade** = les partisans *mpl* de la peine de mort et des châtiments corporels; *F* **I'm hanged if I know!** je n'en sais fichtre *ou* foutre rien!; **h. it!** zut!, mince alors!; *Prov* **as well be hanged for a sheep as for a lamb** quitte à avoir des ennuis, autant que ça en vaille la peine; *Hist* **to be hanged, drawn and quartered** être pendu, éventré et écartelé; *Fig* **he was hanged, drawn and quartered by the press** il s'est fait étriper par la presse

2 *vi* (**a**) (*be suspended*) pendre, être suspendu; *Culin* (*of game*) se faisander; **picture hanging on the wall** tableau pendu *ou* accroché au mur; **he was hanging by his arms from the tree** il était suspendu à l'arbre par les bras; **to h. out of the window** (*of person*) se pencher par la fenêtre; (*of object*) pendre à la fenêtre

(**b**) (*of drapery, clothes etc*) tomber, se draper; **to h. loose** *or* **limply** pendiller, *F* pendouiller; **his clothes h. loosely on him** il flotte dans ses vêtements; *esp Am Sl* **h. loose!** relax, Max!; **this door hangs badly** cette porte est mal suspendue (sur ses gonds); **time hangs heavy (on my hands)** le temps me pèse *ou* me semble long

(**c**) (*of criminal*) être pendu; **to h. for murder** être pendu pour meurtre; *Fig F* **if he doesn't like it he can go h.** si ça ne lui plaît pas, qu'il aille se faire pendre; *Old-fashioned* **you'll h. for this!** tu seras pendu pour ça!

▶ **hang about, hang around 1** *vi F* (**a**) (*wait*) poireauter; **to keep sb hanging about** faire poireauter qn; **h. about, that's not what I said!** eh, minute! ce n'est pas ce que j'ai dit!

(**b**) (*waste time*) traîner, flâner; **to h. about the house doing nothing** traîner à la maison sans rien faire; **young men hanging about on street corners** jeunes qui traînent dans les rues; **don't h. about or we'll never finish!** ne perds pas de temps ou nous n'aurons jamais fini!; *F* **you don't h. about, do you!** vous êtes un/une rapide, vous!; *F* **this car doesn't h. about** cette voiture est un vrai bolide

(**c**) (*associate*) **to h. about with sb** traîner avec qn

2 *vipo* (*frequent*) (*place*) fréquenter, traîner dans

▶ **hang back** *vi* (*not go forward*) rester en arrière; (*hesitate*) hésiter; **to h. back from doing sth** renâcler à faire qch

▶ **hang down** *vi* pendre (**from sth** de qch)

▶ **hang in** *vi esp Am F* (*persevere, not lose heart*) tenir bon, persévérer; **just h. in there** courage, tenez bon

▶ **hang on 1** *vi* (**a**) (*hold*) se cramponner, s'accrocher; **h. on tight!** cramponne-toi bien!

(**b**) *F* (*wait*) patienter, attendre; *Tel* **h. on!** ne quittez pas!; **h. on for a moment** attendez un moment, patientez un instant

(**c**) (*survive*) supporter, *F* tenir le coup; **to h. on by the skin of one's teeth** s'en sortir de justesse

2 *vipo* (**a**) (*hold*) **to h. on sb's arm** (*of thing*) pendre au bras de qn; (*of person*) se pendre au bras de qn

(**b**) (*be attentive to*) **to h. on sb's lips** *or* **words** être pendu aux lèvres de qn; **the children hung on his every word** les enfants buvaient ses paroles *ou* étaient suspendus à chacune de ses paroles

(**c**) (*depend on*) dépendre de, tenir à; **everything hangs on his answer** tout dépend de sa réponse

▶ **hang on to** *vipo* (**a**) (*hold tightly*) se cramponner à, ne pas lâcher; **he hung on to the cliff face** il s'est agrippé à la paroi de la falaise (**b**) (*keep*) garder; **I'd h. on to those documents if I were you** si j'étais toi, je garderais précieusement ces documents; **he hung on to these outdated ideas** il se raccrochait à ces idées démodées; **to h. on to an opinion** persister dans son opinion; **he hung on to his version of events** il a maintenu sa version des faits

▶ **hang out 1** *vtsep* (*suspend*) (*object*) pendre *ou* mettre au dehors; **to h. out the washing** étendre le linge; **to h. out a flag** arborer un pavillon **2** *vi* (**a**) (*be suspended*) pendre (au dehors); **the rocks h. out over the gully** les rochers surplombent le ravin; **his shirt was hanging out** sa chemise dépassait; *Sl* **to let it all h. out** se défouler (**b**) *F* (*live*) crécher; (*frequent*) traîner; **to h. out with one's friends** traîner avec ses amis

▶ **hang over** *vipo* (*hover over*) planer *ou* peser sur; **a thick fog hangs over the town** un épais brouillard plane sur la ville; **a heavy silence hung over the meeting** un lourd silence pesait sur l'assemblée; **to have a threat hanging over one** avoir une menace qui pèse sur soi; **a question mark is hanging over the outcome of the debate** il reste un point d'interrogation quant à l'issue du débat; **I have an appointment with the dentist hanging over me** il y a une visite chez le dentiste qui me pend au nez; **we've got the threat of eviction hanging over us** nous risquons d'être expulsés d'une minute à l'autre

▶ **hang together** *vi* (**a**) (*of people*) rester unis (**b**) (*of statements etc*) s'accorder, *F* tenir debout

▶ **hang up 1** *vtsep* (*hat, picture etc*) accrocher, pendre, suspendre; *Fig* **to h. up one's boots/racket** (*retire*) raccrocher **2** *vi Tel* raccrocher (l'appareil); **to h. up on sb** raccrocher au nez de qn

hangar ['hæŋər] *n esp Av* hangar *m*

hangdog ['hæŋdɒg] *adj* **h. look** air *m* de chien battu

hanger ['hæŋər] *n* (**coat** *or* **clothes**) **h.** cintre *m*

hanger-on, *pl* **hangers-on** *n* parasite *m*, pique-assiette *m inv*

hang-glide *vi* faire du deltaplane

hang-glider *n* (*craft*) deltaplane *m*; (*person*) libériste *mf*

hang-gliding *n* (sport *m* du) deltaplane *m*; **to go h.** faire du deltaplane

hanging ['hæŋɪŋ] **1** *adj* (*hook etc*) pendant; *Geog* (*valley*) suspendu; (*paragraph*) en sommaire; **h. cupboard** armoire *f* murale; **h. indent** retrait *m* en sommaire, alinéa *m* négatif; **h. wardrobe** penderie *f*

2 *n* (**a**) (*execution*) pendaison *f*; *F* **h. judge** = juge *m* féroce, qui condamne les accusés à la potence; *Fig* **it's not a h. offence** ce n'est pas un crime gravissime

(**b**) (*of picture etc*) suspension *f*; (*of door*) montage *m*, accrochage *m*; (*of wallpaper*) pose *f*; *Art* **h. committee** = comité *m* de réception *ou* jury *m* d'admission des tableaux

(**c**) (**wall**) **hangings** tenture(s) *f(pl)*, tapisserie(s) *f(pl)*

Hanging Gardens of Babylon *npl* jardins *mpl* suspendus de Babylone

hangman, *pl* **-men** ['hæŋmən] *n* (**a**) bourreau *m* (**b**) (*game*) le pendu

hangnail ['hæŋneɪl] *n* envie *f*

hang-out *n F* (*haunt*) repaire *m*, nid *m*, endroit *m* favori

hangover ['hæŋəʊvər] *n* (**a**) (*from drinking*) **to have a h.** avoir la gueule de bois, *Hum* avoir mal aux cheveux (**b**) (*practice, belief etc*) reliquat *m*; **a h. from the past** un reliquat du passé

hang-up *n* (**a**) *F* (*complex*) complexe *m*; **he's got a h. about driving** il fait un blocage, il ne veut pas conduire; **you've got a lot of hang-ups** tu es très complexé (**b**) *Comptr* arrêt *m* imprévu

hank [hæŋk] *n* (*of wool etc*) écheveau *m*; (*of thread*) peignée *f*

hanker ['hæŋkər] *vi* **to h. after** *or* **for sth** avoir bien envie de qch, soupirer après qch, convoiter qch

hankering ['hæŋkərɪŋ] *n* vif désir *m*, grande envie *f* (**after, for** de); **to have a h. for sth** avoir grande envie de qch

hankie, hanky ['hæŋkɪ] *n F* mouchoir *m*

hanky-panky ['hæŋkɪ'pæŋkɪ] *n F* (**a**) (*sexual activity*) batifolage *m*, galipettes *fpl* (**b**) (*underhand behaviour*) coup *m* fourré, entourloupette *f*

Hanoverian [hænə'vɪərɪən] **1** *adj* hanovrien **2** *n* Hanovrien, -ienne

Hansard ['hænsɑːd] *n Br Parl* = compte *m* rendu officiel des débats parlementaires

Hanseatic [hænsɪ'ætɪk] *adj Hist* **the H. League** la Ligue hanséatique

hansom ['hænsəm] *n Hist* **h.** (**cab**) cab *m*

Hants [hænts] *abbr* **Hampshire**

ha'penny, *pl* **ha'pence** ['heɪpənɪ, -pəns] *n Br F* = **halfpenny**

haphazard [hæp'hæzəd] *adj* (*attempt*) au petit bonheur (la chance); (*arrangement*) fortuit; **to choose in a h. way** choisir à l'aveuglette

haphazardly [hæp'hæzədlɪ] *adv* au petit bonheur (la chance), à l'aveuglette

hapless ['hæplɪs] *adj Arch, Lit* infortuné, malheureux

happen ['hæp(ə)n] **1** *vi* (*take place*) arriver, se passer, se produire; **it happened ten years ago** cela s'est passé il y a dix ans; **did anyone see what happened?** (*of accident, incident*) quelqu'un a-t-il vu ce qui s'est passé *ou* est arrivé?; **it happens over and over again** c'est toujours la même chose; **don't let it h. again!** que cela n'arrive plus!, que cela ne se reproduise pas!; **it couldn't h. here** ce n'est pas ici que ça arriverait; **I don't like what's happening in this country** je n'aime pas ce qui se passe dans ce pays; **just as if nothing had happened** comme si de rien n'était; **whatever happens** quoi qu'il arrive; **as it happens** justement, précisément; **as often happens** comme il est fréquent; **what has happened to him?** (*what has occurred?*) qu'est-ce qui lui est arrivé?; (*what has become of him?*) qu'est-ce qu'il est devenu?; **if anything happens to me** (*if I die*) s'il m'arrive quelque chose; **what's happened to my pen?** (*where is it?*) qu'est-ce qu'on a fait de mon stylo?; (*what's wrong with it?*) qu'est-il arrivé à mon stylo?

2 *vt* (*chance*) **I happened to pass that way** il se trouve que je passais par là; **a taxi happened to be passing** par hasard *ou* par bonheur, un taxi passait; **I h. to know that ...** il se trouve que je sais que ...; **do you h. to know whether ...?** sauriez-vous par hasard si ...?; **it just so happens that ...** il se trouve justement que ...; **if you h. to find it** s'il arrive que vous le trouviez; **she happens to be my sister** il se trouve qu'elle est ma sœur

▶ **happen along, happen by** *vi* (*arrive by chance*) arriver par hasard

▶ **happen on, happen upon** *vipo* (*come across*) (*person, object*) tomber sur

happening ['hæp(ə)nɪŋ] *n* événement *m*; *Th* happening *m*

happenstance ['hæp(ə)nstæns] *n esp Am* **it was h.** c'était le hasard, c'était le fait d'un heureux hasard

happily ['hæpɪlɪ] *adv* **(a)** heureusement; **they laughed h.** ils rirent de bon cœur; **we were sitting there quite h. watching television** nous étions installés tout tranquillement devant la télévision; **to live h.** vivre heureux; **a h. married couple** un ménage heureux; **they lived h. ever after** (*at end of fairy story*) = ils furent heureux et eurent beaucoup d'enfants; **he'll quite h. say one thing and do the opposite** ça ne le gêne pas de dire une chose et de faire exactement le contraire **(b)** (*fortunately*) heureusement

happiness ['hæpɪnɪs] *n* bonheur *m*, félicité *f*

happy ['hæpɪ] *adj* **(a)** (*content*) heureux; **to be h. to do sth** être heureux *ou* content de faire qch; **h. to oblige** ravi de rendre service; **to make sb h.** rendre qn heureux; **his money hasn't made him h.** l'argent n'a pas fait son bonheur; **a h. life** une vie heureuse; **a h. ending** une fin heureuse; **to have a h. ending** bien se terminer; **to be as h. as the day is long** être heureux comme un poisson dans l'eau; **as h. as a lark** *or* **a sandboy** gai comme un pinson; **those were h. days** c'était le bon temps; **in happier circumstances** dans des circonstances plus favorables; **in happier times** en des jours meilleurs; **I'm very h. with his work** je suis très satisfait *ou* content de son travail; **I'm not at all h. about it** cela ne me plaît pas du tout; **if you are h. with these conditions ...** si vous êtes satisfait de ces conditions ...; **give me a good book and I'm h.** un bon livre suffit à me satisfaire; **to keep sb h.** satisfaire qn; **this game keeps the children h. for hours** avec ce jeu, les enfants sont contents pendant des heures; *Old-fashioned F* **to be h.** (*drunk*) être un peu gris; **h. birthday!** joyeux *ou* bon anniversaire!; **h. Christmas!** joyeux Noël!; *F* **h. days** (*as toast*) à votre santé!

(b) (*wording etc*) bien choisi, à propos; (*coincidence*) heureux

happy families *n Cards* jeu *m* des sept familles

happy-go-lucky *adj* (*person*) sans souci, insouciant; **to do sth in a h. fashion** faire qch au petit bonheur

happy hour *n* (*in bar*) = moment *m* pendant lequel les boissons sont moins chères

happy medium *n* juste milieu *m*

Hapsburg ['hæpsbɜːg] *n Hist* Habsbourg

harangue¹ [hə'ræŋ] *n* harangue *f*

harangue² *vt* haranguer; **to h. sb into doing sth** sermonner qn pour qu'il fasse qch

harass ['hærəs, hə'ræs] *vt* **(a)** *Mil* (*enemy forces*) harceler, tenir en alerte **(b)** (*pester*) (*person*) tracasser, tourmenter, harceler; (*sexually*) harceler; **to h. sb to do sth** harceler qn pour qu'il fasse qch; **to h. sb into doing sth** harceler qn jusqu'à ce qu'il fasse qch; **he was harassing me for money** il me harcelait pour que je lui donne de l'argent

harassed [hə'ræst] *adj* stressé

harassment ['hærəsmənt, hə'ræs-] *n* (*pestering*), *Mil* harcèlement *m*; **police h.** tracasseries *fpl* policières; **sexual h.** harcèlement sexuel

harbinger ['hɑːbɪndʒər] *n Lit* avant-coureur *m*, *pl* avant-coureurs; **the riot was a h. of things to come** la bagarre annonçait ce qui allait arriver

harbour¹, *US* **harbor** ['hɑːbər] *n Naut* port *m*; **h. dues** droits *mpl* de mouillage *ou* de port; **h. lights** feux *mpl* (d'entrée) de port; **h. master** capitaine *m ou* officier *m* de port; (*of small port*) lieutenant *m* de port; **h. terminal** gare *f* maritime

harbour², *US* **harbor** *vt* (*person*) héberger, donner asile à; (*criminal*) receler, cacher; (*dirt*) attirer, garder, retenir; (*suspicions*) entretenir, nourrir; **to h. a grudge against sb** garder rancune à qn

hard [hɑːd] **1** *adj* **(a)** (*substance etc*) dur; (*snow*) durci; **to become** *or* **get h.** (*of cement etc*) durcir; **to become harder** durcir *ou* se durcir davantage; *Fig* **h. fact** fait *m* brut; **the h. facts** la dure réalité; **the h. fact is that there isn't enough money** la vérité, c'est qu'il n'y a pas assez d'argent; **the argument was not backed up by any h. fact** l'argument ne s'appuyait sur rien de concret; **there's no h. evidence** il n'y a pas de preuve tangible; **h. cash** liquide *m*, espèces *fpl*; *Br F* **h. luck!, h. lines! h. cheese!** pas de chance!, quelle guigne!; *Metal* **h. lead** plomb *m* aigre; *Pol* **the h. left** l'extrême gauche *f*; **h. line** (*attitude*) ligne *f* dure; **the president takes a h. line on drugs** le président a pris une position très ferme concernant la drogue; *Anat* **h. palate** palais *m* dur, voûte *f* du palais

(b) (*difficult*) difficile; (*task*) pénible; **to learn the h. way** apprendre à ses dépens; **I learnt it the h. way** j'en ai bavé et maintenant, je le sais; **to do things the h. way** (*through choice*) se compliquer la vie; (*due to circumstances*) en baver; **h. work** (*working hard*) travail *m* assidu; (*hard task*) (*difficult*) tâche *f* difficile; (*strenuous*) travail *m* ingrat; **he's not afraid of h. work** le travail ne lui fait pas peur; **it was h. work to convince him** j'ai eu fort à faire pour le convaincre; **it is h. work for me to ..., I find it h. work to ...** j'ai beaucoup de peine *ou* bien du mal à ...; **it was h. work!** (que) c'était dur!; **the hardest part of the job is done** le plus dur est fait; **to play h. to get** faire languir qn, faire durer le plaisir; **to be h. to please** être exigeant *ou* difficile à contenter; **to be h. of hearing** être dur d'oreille; **the h. of hearing** les malentendants *mpl*; **the laws make it h. to leave the country** à cause des lois, il est difficile de quitter le pays; **I find it h. to believe that ...** j'ai peine à croire que ... + *sub*; **it is h. to understand** c'est difficile à comprendre; **it's h. to say** c'est difficile à dire; **that book was h. to read** ce livre était difficile à lire; **to have a h. fight** *or* **struggle on one's hands** avoir une lourde tâche devant soi

(c) (*severe, harsh*) (*person, manner etc*) dur, sévère (**to, towards** envers); (*master*) sévère, exigeant; (*heart*) dur; *Phot* (*print*) heurté, contrasté; **a h. man** (*tough*) un dur; **he's h.** (*a hard man*) c'est un dur; **to be h. on sb** être sévère envers qn; **it's hardest on the children** le plus dur, c'est pour les enfants; **it's h. to lose a child** c'est une épreuve de perdre un enfant; **to say h. things to sb** avoir des mots très durs pour qn, dire des choses très dures à qn; **it's a h. blow for him** c'est un coup terrible pour lui; **no h. feelings?** tu ne m'en veux pas?; **a h. life** une vie difficile *ou* dure; **times are h.** les temps sont durs *ou* difficiles; **he's been giving her a h. time** il lui en a fait voir de toutes les couleurs; **to have a h. time of it** en voir de dures; **to be as h. as nails** ne pas avoir de cœur; (*physically*) être un vrai dur

(d) (*intense*) **to try one's hardest** faire tout son possible; **to be a h. worker** travailler dur; **a h. winter** un hiver rude *ou* rigoureux; **a h. frost** une forte gelée; *Horseriding* **h. gallop** galop *m* soutenu; *Com* **h. sell** méthode *f* de vente agressive; *Com* **to give sth the h. sell** promouvoir qch de façon très agressive

(e) h. drinker gros *ou* grand buveur *m*; *Tech* **h. light** lumière *f* crue; **h. liquor** spiritueux *mpl*; *F* **a drop of the h. stuff** une goutte d'alcool *ou* d'eau-de-vie; **h. water** eau *f* calcaire; *Tech* eau dure

(f) *Comptr, Typ* **h. carriage return** retour *m* chariot obligatoire; **h. hyphen** trait *m* d'union insécable; **h. page break** fin *f* de page obligatoire; *Comptr* **h. reset** réinitialisation *f* totale de la machine; **h. return** retour *m* obligatoire; **h. space** espace *m* insécable

2 *adv* **(a)** (*vigorously*) fort; **as h. as one can** de toutes ses forces; **to hit** *or* **strike h.** cogner dur; **to push/pull h.** pousser/tirer fort; **to jam on the brakes h.** serrer les freins à bloc; **to look** *or* **gaze** *or* **stare h. at sb** regarder fixement qn; **we can't find it – well, look harder!** nous ne le trouvons pas – et bien cherchez mieux!; **you didn't look very h.!** tu n'as pas bien cherché; **to try h.** faire de son mieux; **to try harder** faire plus d'efforts; **to think h.** réfléchir profondément; **to work h. at sth** travailler dur à qch; **she works too h.** elle se surmène; **to be h. at work** être en plein travail; **he works h. and plays h.** il se dépense beaucoup dans son travail et dans ses loisirs; **to play h.** (*roughly*) avoir un jeu (très) physique; **to drink h.** boire beaucoup; **it's raining h.** il pleut à verse; **to turn h. to the left** braquer à gauche, faire un virage très sec vers la gauche; **to swim h. for the shore** nager de toutes ses forces vers le rivage; *Naut* **h. over!** la barre toute!

(**b**) (*with difficulty*) difficilement, avec peine; **you'd be h. pushed** *or* **pressed** *or* **put to find a shop open at this time** tu vas avoir du mal à trouver une boutique ouverte à cette heure-ci; **she took the news h.** elle a très mal pris la nouvelle; *Old-fashioned* **it will go h. with him if …** cela sera sérieux (pour lui) si …

(**c**) (*near*) **to follow h. (up)on** *or* **after** *or* **behind sb** suivre qn de près; **his resignation followed h. (up)on this news** sa démission a suivi tout de suite cette nouvelle; *Old-fashioned* **h. by** tout près, tout contre

(**d**) *F* (*harshly*) **to feel h. done by** se sentir traité de façon injuste

hard-and-fast *adj* (*rule etc*) absolu

hardback ['hɑːdbæk] **1** *n* livre *m* cartonné; **the book is only available in h.** ce livre n'est disponible qu'en version cartonnée **2** *adj* (*book*) cartonné

hard-bitten *adj F* (*person*) dur à cuire

hardboard ['hɑːdbɔːd] *n Constr* carton *m* dur, Isorel® *m*

hard-boiled *adj* (**a**) *Culin* **h. egg** œuf *m* dur (**b**) *F* (*person*) dur à cuire

hard consonant *n Ling* (*strong*) consonne *f* dure

hard copy *n Comptr* copie *f* sur papier

hard core *n Constr* empierrement *m*; (*of people*) noyau *m* dur; (*in politics, economics*) tendance *f* dure; **there is a h. of resistance to the reforms** il y a un noyau de résistance à ces réformes

hard-core *adj* (*reactionary, supporter*) de la tendance dure; *Mktg* **h. loyal** fidèle *m* absolu; **h. pornography** pornographie *f* hard

hard court *n Tennis* court *m* en dur

hardcover ['hɑːdkʌvər] *n esp Am* = **hardback**

hard currency *n Fin* devise *f ou* monnaie *f* forte

hard disk *n Comptr* disque *m* dur; **h. activity light** voyant *m* d'activité du disque dur; **h. cache** cache *m ou* antémémoire *f* de disque dur; **h. drive** unité *f* de disque dur; **h. driver** gestionnaire *m* de disque dur

hard drive *n Comptr* unité *f* de disque dur

hard drugs *npl* drogues *fpl* dures

hard-earned *adj* (*money etc*) péniblement gagné; (*prize*) bien mérité; **don't waste your h. wages** ne gaspille pas l'argent que tu as péniblement gagné

harden ['hɑːd(ə)n] **1** *vt* (**a**) (*sth*) durcir, endurcir; (*steel etc*) tremper; *Med* (*muscles etc*) scléroser; **to h. oneself** *or* **to become hardened to the cold** s'endurcir *ou* s'aguerrir au froid; **to h. sb's heart** endurcir le cœur à qn (**to sb** à l'égard de qn) (**b**) *Metal* = **case-harden** (**c**) = **harden off 2** *vi* (**a**) (*of substance*) (se) durcir, s'endurcir; (*of person, constitution*) s'endurcir, s'aguerrir; **attitudes have hardened** les attitudes se sont durcies; **scientific opinion has hardened to the view that …** de plus en plus, les scientifiques sont d'avis que … (**b**) *Fin* (*of shares etc*) se raffermir; **prices are hardening** les prix sont en hausse

▶ **harden off** *vtsep* **to h. off seedlings** fortifier de jeunes plantes

▶ **harden up** *vi Fin* (*of shares etc*) se raffermir

hardened ['hɑːd(ə)nd] *adj* (*substance*) durci, endurci; (*steel, glass*) trempé; (*criminal*) endurci

hardener ['hɑːd(ə)nər] *n* (*for paint, glue*) durcisseur *m*

hardening ['hɑːd(ə)nɪŋ] *n* (**a**) durcissement *m*, endurcissement *m*, affermissement *m*; *Metal* (*of steel*) trempe *f*; *Med* **h. of the arteries** artériosclérose *f*; *Fig* **a h. of attitudes** un durcissement des attitudes; *Fin* **a h. of prices** un raffermissement des prix (**b**) *Metal* = **case-hardening**

hard-faced, -featured [hɑːd'feɪst, -'fiːtʃəd] *adj* (*person*) aux traits durs *ou* sévères

hard-fought *adj* vivement contesté

hard hat *n* (*hat*) *Constr* casque *m*; *Horseriding* bombe *f*; (*worker*) ouvrier *m* de la construction *ou* du bâtiment

hard-hat *adj esp US* = caractéristique des attitudes conservatrices et des préjugés attribués aux ouvriers de la construction

hard-headed *adj* (**a**) (*tough*) dur, réaliste; (*realism*) sans concession; (*attitude*) réaliste; **h. business man** homme d'affaires réaliste (**b**) *esp Am* (*stubborn*) obstiné, têtu

hard-hearted ['hɑːd'hɑːtɪd] *adj* (*person*) impitoyable, au cœur dur; (*attitude*) impitoyable

hard-hit *adj* gravement atteint *ou* touché; **one particularly h. village** un village touché de façon particulièrement dure

hard-hitting [hɑːd'hɪtɪŋ] *adj* (*boxer*) qui frappe dur; (*critic, speech*) très dur; **the speech was a h. attack on this policy** le discours était une attaque directe contre cette politique

hardiness ['hɑːdmɪs] *n* robustesse *f*, vigueur *f*

hard labour *n Jur* travaux *mpl* forcés; **fifteen years' h.** quinze ans de travaux forcés

hardline ['hɑːdlaɪn] *adj Pol etc* (*Conservative etc*) convaincu; (*policy*) intransigeant

hardliner [hɑːd'laɪnər] *n Pol etc* dur *m*, dure *f*

hardly ['hɑːdlɪ] *adv* [①A72,a,iv] (*scarcely*) à peine, ne … guère; **she can h. read** c'est à peine si elle sait lire; **I need h. say …** il va sans dire …; **h. anyone/anything** presque personne/rien; **h. ever** presque jamais; **she would h. set her own house on fire** elle n'aurait sûrement pas mis le feu à sa propre maison; **he could h. have said that** il n'aurait sûrement pas dit cela

hardness ['hɑːdnɪs] *n* (**a**) (*of substance, water*) dureté *f*; (*of steel*) trempe *f*; (*of print, painting*) tons *mpl* heurtés (**b**) (*of task, problem*) difficulté *f*; **h. of hearing** surdité *f* (**c**) (*harshness*) (*of rule etc*) sévérité *f*, rigueur *f*; (*of person*) caractère *m* insensible, dureté *f*; **h. of heart** sécheresse *f* de cœur (**d**) *Fin* (*of market, shares*) raffermissement *m*

hard-nosed ['hɑːdnəʊzd] *adj esp Am F* = **hard-headed**

hard-on *n Sl* **to have a h.** bander, avoir la trique

hard-packed *adj* **h. snow** congère *f*

hard porn *n* (porno *m*) hard *m*

hard-pressed, -pushed [hɑːd'prest, -'pʊʃt] *adj* (*troops, personnel*) très sollicité; (*funds, finances*) qui s'épuisent; (*debtor*) aux abois, fort embarrassé; (*tolerance, patience*) presqu'à bout; **to be h. to do sth** avoir du mal à faire qch; **to be h. for time** manquer de temps; **to be h. for money** être à court d'argent

hard sauce *n esp Am Culin* = sauce *f* au beurre, au sucre et au brandy ou au rhum servie avec le pudding

hard-sectored ['hɑːdsektəd] *adj* (*disk*) à secteurs pré-définis

hardship ['hɑːdʃɪp] *n* (**a**) (*circumstance*) privation *f*, (dure) épreuve *f*; **he has suffered great hardship(s)** il en a vu de dures; **h. grant/fund** = argent *m* disponible en cas d'urgence (**b**) (*suffering*) souffrance *f*; (*deprivation*) privation *f*; **to live in h.** vivre dans la misère

hard shoulder *n Aut* bande *f* d'arrêt d'urgence

hardtack ['hɑːdtæk] *n Naut* biscuit *m* de mer

hardtop ['hɑːdtɒp] *n Aut* hard-top *m*

hard-up *adj F* **to be h. (for money)** être fauché *ou* à sec; *F* **to be h. for volunteers/suggestions** manquer de bénévoles/suggestions

hardware ['hɑːdweər] *n* (*no pl*) (**a**) *Com* quincaillerie *f*; **h. dealer** quincaillier, -ière; **h. shop** *or* **store** quincaillerie (**b**) *Comptr* matériel *m*, hardware *m*; **h. problem** problème *m* de matériel (**c**) (*weapons*) armement *m*; *Sl* (*gun*) pêtard *m*, soufflant *m*

hard-wearing *adj* (*garment etc*) de bon usage; (*material*) durable

hard-wired ['hɑːdwaɪəd] *adj* câblé

hard-won *adj* (*trophy, victory*) âprement disputé, remporté de haute lutte

hardwood ['hɑːdwʊd] *n* bois *m* dur

hard-working *adj* laborieux, travailleur, -euse, assidu

hardy ['hɑːdɪ] *adj* (**a**) (*robust*) robuste; *Bot* résistant; (*shrub*) vivace; (*plant*) de pleine terre; **h. annual** *Bot* plante *f* annuelle de pleine terre; *Fig F* question *f* qui revient régulièrement sur le tapis (**b**) (*courageous*) hardi, courageux, audacieux

hare[1] [heər] *n* lièvre *m*; **doe h.** hase *f*; *Fig* **to run with the h. and hunt with the hounds** ménager la chèvre et le chou; (*play double game*) jouer double jeu; **to start a h.** (*in hunting*) lever un lièvre; (*in conversation*) donner un nouveau tour à la conversation; *Sp* **h. and hounds** = jeu *m* de piste, rallye *m*; **h. coursing** chasse *f* à courre au lièvre

hare[2] *vi F* (*of person*) courir comme un lièvre *ou* à toutes jambes; **to h. off after sb** s'élancer à la poursuite de qn

harebell ['heəbel] *n* (*plant*) campanule *f*

harebrained ['heəbreɪnd] *adj* écervelé, étourdi; **h. scheme** projet *m* insensé

harelip ['heəlɪp] *n Med* bec-de-lièvre *m*, *pl* becs-de-lièvre

harem [hɑː'riːm, 'heərəm] *n* harem *m*

haricot ['hærɪkəʊ] *n* **h. (bean)** haricot *m* blanc

hark [hɑːk] *vi esp Arch, Lit* prêter l'oreille (**at, to** à); **h.!** écoutez!; *F* **h. at him!** comme il y va!

▶ **hark back** *vi* (*recall*) **to h. back (to the past)** ressasser le passé; **to h. back to sth** (*in conversation*) ramener la conversation sur qch

harlequin ['hɑːlɪkwɪn] *n Th* arlequin *m*; **h. coat** habit *m* bigarré

harlot ['hɑːlət] *n Arch, Lit* prostituée *f*

harm[1] [hɑːm] *n* mal *m*; (*to reputation etc*) tort *m*; **to do h. to sb** faire du mal/du tort à qn; **what h. has she done you?** quel mal vous a-t-elle fait?; **it will do more h. than good** cela fera plus de mal que de bien; **that won't do any h.** cela ne gâtera rien; **it won't do him any h.** cela ne lui fera pas de mal; **to see no h. in sth** ne pas voir de mal à qch; **you will come to no h.** il ne vous arrivera pas de mal; **out of h.'s way** (*of fragile object etc*) à l'abri du danger, en sûreté; (*of dangerous object etc*) mis dans l'impossibilité de nuire à personne; **they put the china in a cupboard, out of h.'s way** ils ont mis la porcelaine à l'abri dans un placard; **put these chemicals where they'll be out of h.'s way** mets ces produits chimiques en lieu sûr; **there's no h. in saying so** il n'y a pas de mal à le dire; **there's no h. in trying** on peut toujours essayer

harm² *vt* (*person*) (*physically*) faire du mal à; (*non-physically*) faire du mal *ou* du tort à, causer du tort à, nuire à; (*reputation*) salir; (*person's interests*) léser; (*health*) nuire à

harmful ['hɑːmfʊl] *adj* (*substances*) nocif; (*remarks*) nuisible; (*ideas, influence*) malfaisant, pernicieux; **it's h. to your health** cela nuit à votre santé; **in small doses the drug is not h.** à petites doses, ce médicament n'est pas dangereux; **it had a h. effect on her education** cela a eu des conséquences fâcheuses sur son éducation; **h. side-effects** effets secondaires dangereux

harmfully ['hɑːmfʊlɪ] *adv* de façon nuisible *ou* dangereuse, dangereusement

harmfulness ['hɑːmfʊlnɪs] *n* nocivité *f*, nature *f* nuisible

harmless ['hɑːmlɪs] *adj* (*animal, person*) inoffensif; (*pastime*) innocent; (*drug, sex scenes etc*) anodin; **to render h.** (*explosives*) désamorcer; (*chemical*) neutraliser; **it was just a bit of h. fun** c'était pour rire; **h. gossip** propos inoffensifs

harmlessly ['hɑːmlɪslɪ] *adv* sans faire de mal; (*to enjoy oneself*) innocemment; (*to tease*) gentiment

harmonic [hɑː'mɒnɪk] **1** *adj* harmonique; **h. series** *Mus* échelle *f* harmonique; *Math* série *f* harmonique; *Math, Phys* **h. motion** mouvement *m* sinusoïdal **2** *n* **(a)** *Mus* (*of root*) harmonique *m*; (*on stringed instrument*) harmonique, son *m* flûté; **harmonics** sons harmoniques; (*science*) harmonie *f* **(b)** *Math, Phys* (*of wave motion*) harmonique *m*

harmonica [hɑː'mɒnɪkə] *n* harmonica *m*

harmonious [hɑː'məʊnɪəs] *adj* **(a)** (*combination, relationship*) harmonieux **(b)** (*music*) mélodieux

harmoniously [hɑː'məʊnɪəslɪ] *adv* harmonieusement; (*to work, live*) en harmonie

harmonium [hɑː'məʊnɪəm] *n Mus* harmonium *m*

harmonization [hɑːmənaɪ'zeɪʃən] *n* harmonisation *f*

harmonize ['hɑːmənaɪz] **1** *vt* **(a)** *Mus* (*melody*) harmoniser **(b)** (*ideas etc*) harmoniser; (*texts etc*) faire s'accorder; (*colours etc*) allier, harmoniser **(with** avec) **2** *vi* **(a)** *Mus* (*of singer*) chanter en harmonie; (*of musician*) jouer en harmonie **(b)** (*of sounds, colours etc*) s'harmoniser; (*of people, ideas etc*) se mettre en harmonie, s'accorder **(with** avec); **colours that h. well (with one another)** couleurs qui vont bien ensemble

harmony ['hɑːmənɪ] *n* **(a)** *Mus* harmonie *f*; **to study h.** étudier l'harmonie; **songs full of h.** chants mélodieux **(b)** (*of people, ideas etc*) harmonie *f*, accord *m*; (*of voices, instruments*) concert *m*; (*of texts*) concordance *f*; **to live in perfect h. (with sb)** vivre en parfaite intelligence (avec qn); **in h. with ...** en accord avec ...; **to be in h. with sb/sth** être en harmonie avec qn/qch

harness¹ ['hɑːnɪs] *n* **(a)** (*of horse*) harnais *m*, harnachement *m*; **draught h.** harnais d'attelage; *Fig* **to get back into h. (again)** (*of person*) reprendre le collier; *Fig* **to die in h.** mourir à la peine *ou* au travail *ou* à la tâche; **to work in h. (with sb)** travailler de concert (avec qn); **h. horse** cheval *m* d'attelage; *US Horseracing* **h. race** course *f* de trot; **h. room** sellerie *f* **(b)** *Av* **(parachute) h.** ceinture *f ou* harnais *m* (de parachutiste); *Ind, Aut etc* **(safety) h.** harnais (de sécurité) **(c)** *Tex* (*of loom*) harnais *m*

harness² *vt* **(a)** (*horse*) harnacher; **to h. a horse to a cart** atteler un cheval à une charrette; *Fig* **to be harnessed to sth** être étroitement lié à qch **(b)** (*waterfall etc*) aménager; **to h. atomic energy for industrial purposes** mettre l'énergie nucléaire au service de l'industrie

harnessing ['hɑːnɪsɪŋ] *n* **(a)** (*of a horse*) harnachement *m* **(b)** (*of waterfall etc*) aménagement *m*; (*of energy*) exploitation *f*

harp [hɑːp] *n Mus* harpe *f*

▶ **harp on** *vi* revenir sans arrêt sur la même chose; **he's always harping on about inflation** il est toujours en train de nous rebattre les oreilles avec l'inflation

harpist ['hɑːpɪst] *n Mus* harpiste *mf*

harpoon¹ [hɑː'puːn] *n* harpon *m*, lance *f*; **h. gun** (*on deck of ship*) canon *m* lance-harpon; (*hand held*) fusil *m* à harpon

harpoon² *vt* harponner

harpsichord ['hɑːpsɪkɔːd] *n Mus* clavecin *m*

harpsichordist ['hɑːpsɪkɔːdɪst] *n Mus* claveciniste *mf*

harpy ['hɑːpɪ] *n Myth* harpie *f*; *F* **old h.** vieille mégère *f*; **h. eagle** (*bird*) harpie

harridan ['hærɪd(ə)n] *n Lit* vieille sorcière *f*

harrier ['hærɪər] *n* (*bird*) busard *m*

harrow¹ ['hærəʊ] *n Agr* herse *f*

harrow² *vt Agr* (*soil*) herser; *Fig* **to h. sb's feelings, to h. sb** déchirer le cœur à qn

harrowed ['hærəʊd] *adj attrib Fig* (*appearance*) meurtri

harrowing ['hærəʊɪŋ] *adj* (*story etc*) poignant, navrant; (*cry*) déchirant; (*experience*) très douloureux, cruel

Harry ['hærɪ] *n Old-fashioned Br F* **to play old H. with sb** en faire voir des vertes et des pas mûres à qn; **to play old H. with sb's health** ruiner la santé de qn

harry ['hærɪ] *vt* (*enemy forces*) attaquer, harceler; **he was being harried by his creditors** il était harcelé par ses créanciers

harsh [hɑːʃ] *adj* **(a)** (*rough to the touch*) dur, rêche, rude; (*taste*) âpre; (*sound*) strident; (*voice*) rude, rauque **(b)** (*severe, brutal*) (*character*) bourru; (*treatment*) dur; (*master, answer, climate, winter*) rude; (*punishment*) sévère, rude; (*light*) cru; **to say h. things to sb** dire des choses (très) dures à qn; **she was very h. about them** elle a été très dure à leur égard; **to be h. on sb** être dur avec qn; **h. words** mots durs

harshly ['hɑːʃlɪ] *adv* (*to answer etc*) durement, rudement; (*to treat sb*) sévèrement

harshness ['hɑːʃnɪs] *n* **(a)** (*roughness to the touch*) dureté *f*, rudesse *f*; (*of light*) dureté, crudité *f*; (*of style, voice*) aspérité *f*; (*of climate etc*) rudesse; **the h. of these sounds** ces sons stridents **(b)** (*severity*) (*of punishment, law*) sévérité *f*

hart [hɑːt] *n* cerf *m*; (*in hunting*) cerf âgé de plus de cinq ans

harum-scarum ['heərəm'skeərəm] *F* **1** *adj* étourdi, écervelé **2** *adv* étourdiment **3** *n* écervelé, -ée

harvest¹ ['hɑːvɪst] *n* **(a)** (*of corn*) moisson *f*; (*of fruit*) récolte *f*, cueillette *f*; (*of wine*) vendange *f*; *Fig* récolte; **a good/poor h.** une bonne/mauvaise récolte; **to get in the h.** faire la moisson; **to help with the h.** aider à la moisson; *Fig* **it yielded a rich h. of information** on a récolté beaucoup d'informations **(b)** (*time of year*) (temps *m ou* époque *f* de la) moisson; **at h. (time)** à l'époque de la moisson

harvest² **1** *vt* (*corn*) moissonner; (*fruit*) récolter, faire la cueillette de; *Fig* récolter; (*market*) exploiter **2** *vi* rentrer *ou* faire la moisson

harvester ['hɑːvɪstər] *n* **(a)** (*person*) moissonneur, -euse **(b)** (*machine*) moissonneuse *f*

harvest festival *n Rel* action *f* de grâces (*après la rentrée des récoltes*)

harvest home *n* (*festival*) fête *f* de la moisson

harvesting ['hɑːvɪstɪŋ] *n* (rentrée *f* de la) moisson *f*

harvest moon *n* lune *f* de la moisson

harvest mouse *n* souris *f* des moissons

harvest thanksgiving *n Rel* action *f* de grâces (*après la rentrée des récoltes*)

has-been *n F Pej* (*person*) ringard *m*, ringarde *f*; **he's a h.** il est fini, c'est un ringard

hash¹ [hæʃ] *n* **(a)** *Culin* hachis *m*; *Am* **h. browns** pommes de terre *fpl* sautées **(b)** *F* (*mess*) **to make a h.(-up) of sth** faire un beau gâchis de qch; **he made a h. of everything** il a tout bousillé *ou* saboté; **to settle sb's h.** régler son compte à qn **(c)** *Sl* (*hashish*) hasch *m* **(d)** *Typ* **h. (sign)** caractère # *m*, dièse *f*

hash² *vt* **(a)** *Culin* **to h. meat** hacher de la viande (en petits morceaux) **(b)** *F* = **hash up**

▶ **hash over** *vtsep esp Am F* (*discuss sth*) discuter

▶ **hash up** *vtsep F* (*mess up*) (*sth*) bousiller

hashed index [hæʃt] *n Comptr* index *m* de totalisation

hashish ['hæʃiːʃ] *n* hachisch *m*

hasn't ['hæz(ə)nt] = **has not,** *see* **have²**

hasp [hɑːsp] *n* (*on door*) loquet *m*; (*on book etc*) fermoir *m*; **(staple) h.** (*for padlocking*) moraillon *m*

hassle¹ ['hæs(ə)l] *n F* **(a)** (*inconvenience*) problème *m*, embêtement *m*; **it's too much h. going by train** c'est trop d'embêtements d'aller par le train; **all the h. of filling out the form** tous les embêtements pour remplir le formulaire **(b)** (*argument*) dispute *f*; **I don't want any h., right?** pas d'histoires, d'accord?; **the police give us a lot of h.** la police nous fait des tas d'histoires

hassle² *vt F* (*person*) ennuyer, embêter; **he keeps hassling me for money** il n'arrête pas de m'embêter pour que je lui donne de l'argent

hassock ['hæsək] *n Rel* agenouilloir *m*

haste [heɪst] *n* hâte *f*, célérité *f*; **to do sth in h.** faire qch à la hâte *ou* en hâte; **a note written in h.** un billet écrit à la hâte; *Fml* **to make h.** se hâter, se presser, se dépêcher **(to do sth** de faire qch); *Prov* **more h. less speed** plus on se hâte moins on avance

hasten ['heɪs(ə)n] *esp Lit, Fml* **1** *vt* (*one's pace etc*) accélérer; (*person's departure*) hâter, presser, avancer; **to h. the hour when ...** hâter l'heure où ... **2** *vi* se hâter, se dépêcher, se presser (**to do sth** de faire qch); **I don't agree with him, I h. to add** je m'empresse d'ajouter que je ne suis pas d'accord avec lui

hastily ['heɪstɪlɪ] *adv* **(a)** (*quickly*) à la hâte, précipitamment **(b)** (*rashly*) de façon irréfléchie; (*to speak*) sans réfléchir; (*to judge sth*) à la légère, trop vite

hastiness ['heɪstɪnɪs] *n* **(a)** (*speed*) précipitation *f*, hâte *f* **(b)** (*rashness*) irréflexion *f*

hasty ['heɪstɪ] *adj* **(a)** (*departure, farewell*) précipité; (*sketch*) fait à la hâte; (*meal*) sommaire; **I sent him a h. note** je lui ai envoyé un billet écrit à la hâte; **to be too h. in doing sth** mettre trop de hâte à faire qch; **a h. decision** une décision hâtive; **to jump to a h. conclusion** conclure à la légère **(b)** (*short-tempered*) vif; **to have a h. temper** s'emporter facilement

hat [hæt] *n* chapeau *m*; **paper h.** chapeau en papier; *Fig* **I'm saying that with my lawyer's h. on** je dis ça en ma qualité de juriste; *Fig* **she wears several different hats in the company** elle remplit plusieurs rôles dans la société; **to put on/take off one's h.** mettre/enlever son chapeau; *Fig* **I take my h. off to him/you/***etc*! chapeau!; **hats off!** chapeaux bas!; *Fig* **to hang up one's h.** raccrocher; *Fig* **to pass the h. round** faire passer le chapeau (à la ronde), faire la quête (**for sb/sth** pour qn/qch); *Fig* **to throw one's h. in the ring** se porter candidat; *Old-fashioned F* **my h.!** mon Dieu!; *F* **to talk through one's h.** parler à tort et à travers; *Fig F* **to keep sth under one's h.** garder qch pour soi; *F* **if that comes off I'll eat my h.** si ça réussit, je mange mon chapeau; *F* **that's old h.** c'est vieux jeu

hatband ['hætbænd] *n* ruban *m* de chapeau

hatbox ['hætbɒks] *n* carton *m* à chapeau

hatch¹ [hætʃ] *n* **(a)** *Naut* descente *f*, écoutille *f*; **h. (cover)** panneau *m* de descente, panneau (d'écoutille); **cargo h.** panneau de chargement *ou* de déchargement; *F* **down the h.!** (*when drinking*) cul sec! **(b)** (*trap door*) trappe *f*, panneau *m* d'accès; **(service** *or* **serving) h.** passe-plats *m inv*; *Av etc* **(escape) h.** panneau d'évacuation **(c)** *HydE* vanne *f* d'écluse

hatch² *n Agr* **(a)** (*of egg, clutch of birds*) éclosion *f* **(b)** (*clutch of birds*) couvée *f*

hatch³ **1** *vt* (*chickens*) faire éclore; (*eggs*) incuber, (faire) couver; (*in fish farming, of fish*) (*eggs*) incuber; *Fig* **to h. a plot** ourdir *ou* tramer un complot **2** *vi* (*of young birds, eggs*) éclore; **newly hatched chickens** poussins qui sortent de la coquille

hatch⁴ *vt* (*drawing*) hacher, hachurer

▶ **hatch out** *vi* = **hatch³ 2**

hatchback ['hætʃbæk] *n Aut* **(a)** (*car*) voiture *f* à hayon (arrière) **(b)** (*part, door*) hayon *m* (arrière)

hatchery ['hætʃərɪ] *n Agr* couvoir *m*, couveuse *f*; (*in fish farming*) appareil *m* à éclosion

hatchet ['hætʃɪt] *n* hachette *f*; *Fig* **to bury the h.** enterrer la hache de guerre; *Journ etc F* **h. job** démolissage *m*; *F* **to do a h. job on sb/sth** démolir qn/qch; **h. face** visage *m* en lame de couteau; *F* **h. man** (*hired killer*) tueur *m* (à gages); *Pol, Ind etc* homme *m* de main

hatching ['hætʃɪŋ] *n* (*in drawing*) hachure(s) *f(pl)*

hatchway ['hætʃweɪ] *n Naut* descente *f*, écoutille *f*

hate¹ [heɪt] *n* **(a)** (*hatred*) haine *f*; **h. mail** lettres *fpl* d'injures **(b)** (*object of dislike*) objet *m* d'aversion; **her pet h.** sa bête noire

hate² *vt* (*sb, sth*) haïr, détester, exécrer; **I h. him** je le déteste, je le hais; **I h. classical music** je déteste la musique classique; **I h. myself for agreeing to it** je m'en veux d'y avoir consenti; **I h. it when he's in a bad mood** je déteste quand il est de mauvaise humeur; **to h. to do sth** détester (de) faire qch; **to h. doing sth** détester faire qch; **she hates having her hair washed** elle déteste qu'on lui lave les cheveux; **he hates to be contradicted** il ne peut pas souffrir qu'on le contredise; **she hates being kissed** elle a horreur qu'on l'embrasse; **I'd h. anyone to find out** je ne supporterais pas que quelqu'un l'apprenne; *F* **I h. to tell you, but I think you've missed your train** je regrette de devoir te le dire mais je pense que tu as raté ton train

hated ['heɪtɪd] *adj* détesté, haï

hateful ['heɪtfʊl] *adj* (*person, thing*) odieux, détestable

hatefully ['heɪtfʊlɪ] *adv* odieusement, détestablement

hater ['heɪtər] *n* ennemi *m* (**of** de); **to be an animal-h.** détester les animaux

hatless ['hætlɪs] *adj* (*person*) sans chapeau, tête nue

hatpeg ['hætpeg] *n* patère *f*

hatpin ['hætpɪn] *n* épingle *f* à chapeau

hatrack ['hætræk] *n* porte-chapeaux *m inv*

hatred ['heɪtrɪd] *n* haine *f* (**of sb** de *ou* contre qn)

hatshop ['hætʃɒp] *n* (*for men*) chapellerie *f*; (*for women*) boutique *f* de modiste

hatstand ['hætstænd] *n* porte-chapeaux *m inv*

hatter ['hætər] *n* chapelier, -ière; *prov* **he's as mad as a h.** il a un grain, il travaille du chapeau

hat trick *n* (*by conjuror*) tour *m ou* coup *m* du chapeau; *Fb etc* trois buts *mpl* marqués de suite par le même joueur; *Cr* mise *f* hors jeu de trois batteurs avec trois balles de suite; *Fig* **that's my h.** jamais deux sans trois; **are you going for the h.?** alors, jamais deux sans trois?

haughtily ['hɔːtɪlɪ] *adv* hautainement, d'une manière hautaine *ou* arrogante

haughtiness ['hɔːtɪnɪs] *n* hauteur *f*, arrogance *f*

haughty ['hɔːtɪ] *adj* hautain, arrogant

haul¹ [hɔːl] *n* **(a)** (*pull*) **to give a h. on sth** tirer sur qch

(b) (*fish caught*) prise *f*, pêche *f*; *Fig* (*of thieves etc*) butin *m*; **drugs h.** saisie *f* de drogue; **to make** *or* **get a good h.** (*of fishermen*) faire (une) bonne pêche; *Fig* (*of thieves etc*) faire son butin; **you've got a good h.!** (*of birthday etc presents etc*) c'est un joli tas de cadeaux que tu viens de recevoir!

(c) *F* (*distance, journey*) parcours *m*, trajet *m*; *Av etc* **short/long h.** étape *f ou* distance *f* courte/longue; **there's still a long h. ahead** il reste un long chemin à parcourir; **it's a long h. from Glasgow to Naples** (*by road*) c'est un long trajet de Glasgow à Naples; **it's a real h.** c'est un sacré trajet

haul² **1** *vt* **(a)** (*pull*) tirer; (*load*) traîner; (*boat, train*) remorquer; *F* **to h. sb over the coals** réprimander qn, *F* passer un savon à qn **(b)** *Com* (*transport by road*) (*goods*) transporter par camions **2** *vi* **(a)** (*pull*) tirer, traîner; **they all hauled together** ils ont tous tiré ensemble; *Naut* **to h. on a rope** haler sur une manœuvre **(b)** *Naut* (*sail, move etc*) **to h. alongside** accoster

▶ **haul down** *vtsep* (*bring down*) (*sth*) descendre; *Naut* (*sails etc*) haler bas, affaler; (*flag*) rentrer

▶ **haul in** *vtsep* (*bring in*) (*sth*) tirer en dedans; *Naut* (*sail, nets*) haler en dedans; *F* (*suspects, people for questioning*) emmener; *F* **they hauled in some experts to back up their case** ils ont amené des experts pour les soutenir

▶ **haul up** *vtsep* **(a)** (*hoist*) (*sth*) monter; *Naut* (*flag*) hisser; **to h. up a boat** (*on ship*) rentrer une embarcation; (*on the beach*) haler un bateau à sec **(b)** (*call to account*) **to h. sb up** demander des comptes à qn (**for sth** de qch); **to be hauled up before the court** être traîné devant les tribunaux; **he was hauled up before the headmaster** il a dû se présenter devant le principal

haulage ['hɔːlɪdʒ] *n* **(a)** *Com* (*transportation*) (transport *m* par) roulage *m*, charriage *m*, camionnage *m*; **road h.** transports *mpl* routiers; **h. contractor** entrepreneur *m* de transports **(b)** *Com* (*costs*) frais *mpl* de roulage *ou* de transport

haulier ['hɔːlɪər], *US* **hauler** ['hɔːlər] *n Com* camionneur *m*, entrepreneur *m* de transports, transporteur *m*; (*driver*) routier *m*

hauling ['hɔːlɪŋ] *n Naut* halage *m*; **h. rope** câble *m* de halage

haunch [hɔːntʃ] *n* **(a)** *Anat* hanche *f*; **haunches** arrière-train *m*; **sitting** *or* **squatting on his haunches** (*person*) accroupi; (*dog*) assis **(b)** *Culin* (*of venison*) cuissot *m*

haunt¹ [hɔːnt] *n* retraite *f*, repaire *m*; (*of group of people*) rendez-vous *m*; **this pub was one of his haunts** ce pub était l'un de ses repaires; **the h. of existentialists** le lieu de rendez-vous des existentialistes

haunt² *vt* **(a)** (*of ghost*) (*house etc*) hanter **(b)** (*of person, animal*) (*place, person*) fréquenter **(c)** (*of thoughts etc*) (*person*) obséder, poursuivre; (*mind, sleep*) troubler, hanter; **to be haunted by memories** être obsédé par des souvenirs; **a lack of finance haunted the project** le problème du manque de moyens les a hantés tout le long du projet; **these problems have returned to h. us** ces problèmes nous minent une fois de plus

haunted ['hɔːntɪd] *adj* (*castle, room etc*) hanté; **he has a h. look** il a l'air égaré

haunting ['hɔːntɪŋ] *adj* (*melody, memory*) qui vous hante; (*memory etc*) obsédant

Havana [hə'vænə, -'vɑː-] *n* **(a)** la Havane **(b) a H. (cigar)** un havane

have¹ [hæv] *n F* **the haves and the h.-nots** les riches *mpl* et les pauvres

have² *vt* [①**A54-55**,b] (*pr* **have**; *3rd person* **has** [hæz]; *pl* **have**; *pr sub sing, pl* **have**; *past, past sub* **had** [hæd]; *pl* **had**; *prp* **having**; *pp* **had**; **have not, has not, had not** *are frequently shortened into* **haven't, hasn't, hadn't**; **I have, he has, we have** *etc into* **I've, he's, we've** *etc*; **I had** *etc into* **I'd** *etc*) **(a)** avoir; **a week has seven days** une semaine a sept jours; **he had no friends** il n'avait pas d'amis; **all I h.** tout ce que je possède *ou* que j'ai; **she has a shop** elle tient *ou* a une boutique; **he has big hands** il a de grosses mains; **my bag**

has no name on it ma valise ne porte pas de nom; **she had the pen in her desk** le stylo était dans son bureau; **I h. nothing to do** je n'ai rien à faire; **I h. work to do** j'ai à travailler *ou* du travail; **to h. a right** avoir un droit, jouir d'un droit; **I h. it!** (*solution*) j'y suis!; *Br F* **come on!, let's be having you!** (*come forward*) allez, venez par ici!; (*hurry up!*) allez!, dépêche-toi; *F* **he had it coming to him** c'est bien fait pour lui, il l'a bien mérité; *Sl* **I'm not having any** (*I don't believe it*) ça ne prend pas avec moi; (*I'm not getting involved*) je ne vais pas m'en mêler

(b) (*invite etc*) **we're having visitors tomorrow** nous attendons des invités demain; **to h. friends to dinner** avoir des amis à dîner

(c) (*obtain*) **there was no work to be had** on ne pouvait pas obtenir de travail; **they were the cheapest seats to be had** ce sont les places les moins chères qu'on pouvait trouver; **to h. one's wish** obtenir ce que l'on désire

(d) (*receive etc*) **to h. news from sb** recevoir des nouvelles de qn; **I h. it on good authority** je l'ai appris de bonne source; **I will let you h. it for £5** je vous le céderai pour cinq livres; **let me h. your keys** donnez-moi vos clefs; **you shall h. it back tomorrow** je vous le rendrai demain; *F* **I let him h. it** (*verbally*) je lui ai dit son fait; (*physically*) je lui ai flanqué un coup; *F* **I've had it!** (*if sb finds out*) je suis foutu!; (*I'm exhausted*) je suis crevé!; *F* **this coat has had it** (*is worn out*) ce manteau est foutu; *F* **the car has just about had it** la voiture va bientôt rendre l'âme; *F* **he's had it** (*dead, dying*) il a sa dose; *F* **I've had it up to here with him** j'en ai jusque-là de ce type-là; *F* **I've had it up to here with you** j'en ai marre de toi

(e) (*take*) (*meal*) prendre; **to h. tea with sb** prendre le thé avec qn; **what will you h., sir? – I'll h. lasagne, please** que prendra monsieur? – donnez-moi *ou* je prendrai les lasagnes

(f) (*in numerous verbal phrases*) **to h. measles** avoir la rougeole, *F* faire une rougeole; **to h. a cold** avoir un rhume, être enrhumé; **to h. the choice** avoir le choix; **to h. an idea** avoir une idée; **to h. a dream** faire un rêve; **to h. a game** faire une partie; **to h. a fall** faire une chute; **to h. a lesson** prendre une leçon; **to h. a bath** prendre un bain; **to h. a wash** se laver; **to h. a shave** se raser; **to h. a cigarette** fumer une cigarette

(g) (*experience*) **I had a pleasant evening** j'ai passé une soirée agréable; **I didn't h. any trouble in finding it** je n'ai eu aucune peine à le trouver; **we had a rather strange adventure** il nous est arrivé une aventure assez étrange; **to h. fine/wet weather** avoir du beau temps/de la pluie

(h) (*claim*) **public opinion has it that he is not telling the truth** on pense généralement qu'il ne dit pas la vérité; **she has it that John has been having an affair** elle prétend que John a une liaison; **rumour has it that ...** le bruit court que ...; **as Plato has it** comme dit Platon, comme l'a écrit Platon

(i) (*hold*) **to h. sb in one's power** avoir qn en son pouvoir; **he had me by the throat** il me tenait à la gorge

(j) *F* (*outwit*) **to be had** donner dans le panneau, *F* donner dedans; **you've been had!** on vous a eu!; (*for a purchase*) on vous a refilé un rossignol; **you h. me there!** là, je donne ma langue au chat!

(k) (*give birth to*) avoir; **our cat has had kittens** notre chatte a fait des petits

(l) **he had two children by her** il a eu d'elle deux enfants

(m) *Sl* (*have sexual intercourse with*) prendre, coucher avec

(n) [①**A40**,B,1,a; **B34**,d] (*causative*) **to h. sth done** faire faire qch; **to h. sb do sth** faire faire qch à qn; **to h. one's hair cut** se faire couper les cheveux; **three houses had their windows shattered** trois maisons ont eu leurs fenêtres brisées; **I had my watch stolen** je me suis fait voler ma montre; **to h. a tooth out** se faire arracher une dent; **I shall h. everything ready** je veillerai à ce que tout soit prêt

(o) (*want*) **which one will you h.?** lequel voulez-vous?; **she won't h. him** elle ne veut pas de lui; **as luck would h. it he arrived too late** la malchance voulut qu'il arrivât trop tard; **what would you h. me do?** (*despairing*) que voulez-vous que j'y fasse?; **I'll h. you know that ...** sachez que ...

(p) (*allow*) **I will not h. such conduct** je ne supporterai pas une conduite pareille; **I won't h. you coming in here** je ne veux pas que vous entriez ici; *F* **he wouldn't h. it** (*that he was wrong*) il n'a pas voulu me/nous/*etc* écouter, il ne voulait pas en convenir; *F* **we tried to give the dog a bath but he wasn't having any of it!** nous avons essayé de donner un bain au chien, mais rien n'y a fait; **I'm not having any of your nonsense** pas de bêtises

(q) (*place*) mettre; **I'll h. the television in that corner** (*when I get one*) je mettrai la télé dans ce coin; (*to person holding it*) mettez la télé dans ce coin; *Horseracing* **to h. something on a horse** (*a bet*) miser (de l'argent) sur un cheval

(r) (*be compelled*) **to h. to do sth** devoir faire qch, être obligé *ou* forcé de faire qch; **I had to go away** j'ai dû m'en aller; **I don't h. to work** je n'ai pas besoin de travailler; *Iron* **of course you <u>had</u> to go and tell him!** bien sûr, il a fallu que tu ailles le lui dire!; **the clock will h. to be mended** la pendule a besoin d'une réparation; **I don't like housework but it has to be done** je n'aime pas faire le ménage mais il faut bien que quelqu'un le fasse; **first the potatoes h. to be washed** il faut d'abord laver les pommes de terre

(s) [①**A48**,11,d; **B25-26**,C] (*as auxiliary*) **to h. been/given/done** avoir été/donné/fait; **to h. come** être arrivé; **to h. hurt oneself** s'être blessé; **I h. lived in London for three years** j'habite Londres depuis trois ans; **well, you <u>have</u> grown!** ce que tu as grandi!; **you h. forgotten your gloves – so I h.!** vous avez oublié vos gants – en effet! *ou* tiens, c'est vrai!; **you h. been in prison before – I haven't!** vous avez déjà fait de la prison – c'est faux!; **you've forgotten, haven't you?** vous avez oublié, n'est-ce pas?; **you haven't forgotten, h. you?** vous n'avez pas oublié, n'est-ce pas?

(t) [①**A40**,B,1,a] (*with* **better, sooner**) **I had better say nothing** je ferais mieux de ne rien dire; **I'd sooner leave at once** j'aimerais bien mieux partir tout de suite

▶ **have around** *vtas* **(a)** (*keep available*) garder *ou* avoir sous la main; **I h. the documents around somewhere** les documents sont là quelque part, j'ai les documents quelque part; **she's a useful person to h. around** il est bon de l'avoir sous la main; **I don't like having children around** je n'aime pas la compagnie des enfants **(b)** (*invite*) inviter; **we must h. them around for dinner** il faudra qu'on les invite à dîner

▶ **have away** *vtas Br Sl* (*have sexual intercourse*) **to h. it away (with sb)** s'envoyer en l'air (avec qn)

▶ **have back** *vtas* **(a)** (*invite*) **we're having them back on Saturday** (*in return*) nous leur rendons leur invitation samedi prochain; (*for second visit*) nous les réinvitons samedi prochain **(b)** (*invite after an event*) **after the movie we had them back for coffee** après le cinéma, nous les avons invités à venir prendre le café chez nous

▶ **have down** *vtas* (*invite from upstairs, north*) inviter

▶ **have in** *vtas* **(a)** (*summon*) appeler, faire venir; **we had to h. the doctor in** nous avons dû faire venir le médecin; **we're having the painters in next week** les peintres viennent la semaine prochaine **(b)** (*invite*) inviter, recevoir; **let's h. him in to discuss it** (*ask to come in*) demandons-lui de venir nous en parler; **she had friends in for tea** elle a reçu quelques amis pour le thé **(c)** *F* **to h. it in for sb** (*have a grudge against*) en avoir après qn, garder à qn un chien de sa chienne; **they had it in for me from the day I arrived** ils en ont eu après moi dès mon arrivée

▶ **have off** *vtas* **(a)** (*remove*) retirer; **the barber nearly had my ear off** le coiffeur a failli me couper l'oreille **(b)** (*have removed*) faire retirer; **she's having the plaster off next week** on lui retire son plâtre la semaine prochaine **(c)** *Br Sl* (*have sexual intercourse*) **to h. it off (with sb)** s'envoyer en l'air (avec qn)

▶ **have on 1** *vtsep* (*wear*) porter; **they had nothing on** ils étaient nus; **she had her black dress on** elle avait *ou* portait sa robe noire

2 *vtas* **(a)** *F* (*fool*) (*person*) faire marcher; **I was only having you on** c'était juste pour te faire marcher

(b) (*have arranged*) **he has a lot on this week** il est très occupé cette semaine; **I h. something else on tonight** j'ai d'autres projets pour ce soir

(c) (*install, put on*) installer, mettre; **they soon had the roof-rack on** très vite, ils ont installé *ou* mis la galerie; **she had her coat on in no time** en un clin d'œil, elle a mis son manteau

3 *vtaspo* **to h. sth on sb** avoir qch sur qn; **the police h. nothing on him** la police n'a rien sur lui

▶ **have out** *vtas* **(a)** (*remove*) (*object*) retirer; (*of dentist*) (*tooth*) extraire, arracher **(b)** (*have extracted*) (*tooth*) se faire arracher **(c)** (*resolve*) **to h. it out with sb** mettre les choses au point avec qn; **let's h. this out once and for all** mettons les choses au point une fois pour toutes

▶ **have over** *or* **round** *vtas* = **have around (b)**

▶ **have up** *vtas* **(a)** (*usu passive*) (*bring to court*) **to be had up (for vagrancy/etc)** passer devant le tribunal (pour vagabondage/*etc*) **(b)** (*erect, install*) installer, mettre en place; **they had the decorations up in a few hours** ils ont installé les décorations en quelques heures **(c)** (*invite from downstairs, the south*) inviter; **we'd better h. him up for a chat** (*ask to come up*) on devrait lui demander de venir; **he**

had them up (to his flat) for tea il les a invités à venir prendre le thé
haven ['heɪv(ə)n] *n* (*shelter*) abri *m*, asile *m*, refuge *m*; *Lit* (*port*) havre *m*, port *m*; **safe h.** enclave *f* de protection; **to provide a safe h. for sb** offrir une terre d'asile à qn; (*within a war zone*) offrir un refuge à qn
have-not *n* démuni, -ie; **the have-nots of our society** les (plus) démunis de notre société
haven't ['hæv(ə)nt] = **have not,** *see* **have**[2]
haversack ['hævəsæk] *n* havresac *m* (*de camping;*); *Mil* musette *f*
havoc ['hævək] *n* ravage *m*, dégâts *mpl*, dévastation *f*; **to cause** *or* **wreak h.** (*in a country etc*) faire de grands dégâts *ou* de grands ravages; **to play h. with** (*harvest etc*) ravager; (*person's health etc*) déranger, détraquer; (*person's plans etc*) désorganiser complètement
haw [hɔː] *n Bot* cenelle *f*
Hawaii [hə'waiː] *n* Hawaï *m*, Hawaii *m*
Hawaiian [hə'waɪən] **1** *adj* hawaïen; *Mus* **H. guitar** guitare *f* hawaïenne **2** *n* Hawaïen, -ïenne
hawk[1] [hɔːk] *n* **(a)** (*bird*) faucon *m*; **he has eyes like a h.** (*sharp eyesight*) il a des yeux d'aigle *ou* de lynx; (*misses nothing*) rien ne lui échappe; **to watch sb/sth like a h.** ne pas lâcher qn/qch des yeux, ne pas quitter qn/qch du regard **(b)** *Pol* faucon *m*; **hawks and doves** faucons et colombes *fpl* **(c)** *Ent* **h. moth** sphinx *m*, crépusculaire *m*, smérinthe *m*
hawk[2] *vi* (*hunt*) chasser au faucon
hawk[3] *vt* (*sell*) (*goods*) colporter; (*rumour etc*) répandre; **to h. one's wares** (*in market etc*) vendre ses marchandises à la criée; (*from door to door*) faire du porte-à-porte; *Hum* (*of prostitute*) offrir ses services
hawk[4] *vi* (*clear throat*) se racler la gorge; (*spit*) cracher
▶ **hawk up** *vtsep* expectorer
hawker[1] ['hɔːkər] *n* (*hunter*) fauconnier *m*
hawker[2] *n* (*seller*) colporteur *m*, démarcheur, -euse
hawk-eyed *adj* (*sharp-sighted*) aux yeux d'aigle; (*who misses nothing*) à qui rien n'échappe
hawking[1] ['hɔːkɪŋ] *n* (*hunting*) chasse *f* au faucon, fauconnerie *f*
hawking[2] *n* (*selling*) colportage *m*
hawkish ['hɔːkɪʃ] *adj Pol etc* belliciste; **h. politician** faucon *m*
hawknosed ['hɔːknəʊzd] *adj* (*person*) au nez aquilin
hawser ['hɔːzər] *n Naut* haussière *f*, aussière *f*; (*for mooring only*) amarre *f*; **steel h.** aussière/amarre en fil d'acier
hawthorn ['hɔːθɔːn] *n* (*shrub*) aubépine *f*
hay [heɪ] *n* foin *m*; **to make h.** faire le(s) foin(s), faner; *Prov* **to make h. while the sun shines** battre le fer pendant qu'il est chaud; *Sl* **to hit the h.** se coucher; **h. rake** râteau *m*, fauchet *m*
haycart ['heɪkɑːt] *n* fourragère *f* de foin
haycock ['heɪkɒk] *n* tas *m ou* meulette *f* de foin
hayfever ['heɪfiːvər] *n Med* rhume *m* des foins
hayfork ['heɪfɔːk] *n* fourche *f* à foin
haying ['heɪɪŋ] *n* fenaison *f*
hayloft ['heɪlɒft] *n* fenil *m*
haymaker ['heɪmeɪkər] *n* **(a)** (*person*) faneur, -euse; (*machine*) faneuse *f*, tourne-foin *m inv* **(b)** *F* (*punch*) uppercut *m*, swing *m*
haymaking ['heɪmeɪkɪŋ] *n* fenaison *f*
hayrack ['heɪræk] *n* râtelier *m* d'écurie
hayrick ['heɪrɪk] *n* meule *f* de foin; (*square*) barge *f*
hayseed ['heɪsiːd] *n Am F* (*yokel*) péquenaud *m*
haystack ['heɪstæk] *n* = **hayrick**
haywire ['heɪwaɪər] *adj F* confus, embrouillé; **to go h.** (*of plan*) louper, finir en queue de poisson; (*of mechanism etc*) se détraquer; **he's gone h.** (*crazy*) il déménage, il perd la boule
hazard[1] ['hæzəd] *n* **(a)** (*danger*) risque *m*, danger *m*, péril *m*; *Aut etc* (*place*) point *m* dangereux; **ice presents another h. for drivers** le verglas est un danger supplémentaire pour les automobilistes; *Aut* **h. lights** feux *mpl* de détresse **(b)** *Golf* accident *m* de terrain; *Mktg* **h. forecasting** prévision *f* événementielle
hazard[2] *vt* (*one's life, fortune*) risquer, hasarder; **to h. an opinion** risquer une opinion; **to h. a guess** tenter de deviner
hazardous ['hæzədəs] *adj* (*risky*) hasardeux, chanceux; (*dangerous*) (*journey, job etc*) dangereux; (*uncertain*) (*project, undertaking*) incertain, hasardeux, aventureux
haze[1] [heɪz] *n* (*mist*) brume *f* légère; **a h. of uncertainty surrounded the affair** une atmosphère d'incertitude entourait l'affaire; **she** *or* **her mind was in a h.** son esprit était embrouillé; **to see everything through an alcohol-induced h.** voir tout sous l'emprise de l'alcool
haze[2] *vt Am Univ* (*new student etc*) brimer, bizuter
hazel ['heɪz(ə)l] **1** *n* **(a) (tree)** noisetier *m*, coudrier *m*, avelinier *m* **(b)** (*colour*) (couleur *f* de) noisette *f* **2** *adj* (couleur) noisette *inv*; **h. eyes** yeux (couleur) noisette
hazelnut ['heɪz(ə)lnʌt] *n Bot* noisette *f*, aveline *f*
hazily ['heɪzɪlɪ] *adv* vaguement
haziness ['heɪzɪnɪs] *n* (*of atmosphere, mind*) état *m* brumeux *ou* nébuleux; (*of memory*) imprécision *f*
hazing ['heɪzɪŋ] *n Am Univ* bizutage *m*
hazy ['heɪzɪ] *adj* (*air etc*) brumeux, embrumé; (*outline*) flou, estompé; (*idea etc*) nébuleux, flou; (*memory, knowledge*) vague; **to be h. about** (*knowledge*) n'avoir qu'une connaissance imprécise de; (*memory*) n'avoir qu'un souvenir vague de
h & c (*abbr* **hot and cold**) eau *f* courante chaude et froide
HD [eɪtʃ'diː] *Comptr* **(a)** (*abbr* **hard disk**) DD **(b)** (*abbr* **high density**) HD
HDD *Comptr* (*abbr* **hard disk drive**) unité *f* de disque dur
HDTV ['eɪtʃdiːtiːviː] *n TV* (*abbr* **high definition television**) TVHD *f*
he [hiː] **1** *pers pron* (*of person, male animal, Lit of certain things personified*) **(a)** [①A26-27,a,c] (*unstressed*) il; **he loves her** il l'aime; **what is he saying?** que dit-il?; **here he comes** le voici *ou* voilà qui vient *ou* arrive; **he's a strange man** c'est un homme étrange **(b)** (*stressed*) lui; **he and I** lui et moi; **I am as tall as he (is)** je suis aussi grand que lui; *esp Lit* **he who believes** celui qui croit **2** *n* **(a)** *F* (*male*) mâle *m*; **it's a he** (*of newborn child*) c'est un garçon; (*of animal*) c'est un mâle **(b)** (*children's game*) (jeu *m* de) chat *m*; **you're he!** c'est toi le chat!
he- [hiː] *pref* **he-bear** ours *m* mâle; **he-goat** bouc *m*
head[1] [hed] **1** *vt* **(a)** (*lead*) (*procession*) conduire, mener, venir en tête de; (*party*) être à la tête de, diriger; (*the poll*) venir en tête de; **she headed the attack on the Government's economic policy** elle menait l'attaque contre la politique économique du gouvernement; **to h. the list** être *ou* venir en tête de (la) liste

(b) (*direct*) diriger; **they are heading the country into chaos** ils conduisent le pays au chaos; **just h. me towards the nearest bar** dirigez-moi vers le bar le plus proche; *Naut* **to h. the ship for Southampton** mettre le cap sur Southampton

(c) (*put a title on*) **the article is headed ...** l'article est intitulé ...

(d) *Old-fashioned* (*skirt around*) (*lake*) contourner par l'amont; (*river*) contourner par sa source

(e) *Fb* (*ball*) jouer de la tête

2 *vi* (*go*) **to h. east** *or* **to the East** (*of ship*) aller vers l'Est; **where are you heading** *or* **headed?** où allez-vous?; **you're heading in the right direction** vous allez dans la bonne direction; **he was headed** *or* **heading for an early death** il allait mourir jeune
head[2] *n* **(a)** tête *f*; **from h. to foot** *or* **toe** de la tête aux pieds, des pieds à la tête; *Fig* **he gave orders over my h.** il a donné des ordres sans me consulter; *Fig* **to be in over one's h.** (*in difficult situation*) être dépassé; **to stand on one's h.** faire le poirier; *F* **I could do it standing on my h.** c'est simple comme bonjour; **that's the kind of thing he could do standing on his h.** c'est le genre de choses qu'il peut faire les yeux fermés; **to stand** *or* **turn sth on its h.** poser qch la tête en bas; *Fig* retourner qch; **recent events have turned the situation on its h.** les événements récents ont retourné la situation; **to fall** *or* **go** *or* **turn h. over heels** faire la culbute; **to fall h. over heels in love with sb** tomber follement amoureux de qn; **to be a h. taller than sb** avoir une tête de plus que qn; **she stands h. and shoulders above me** elle fait une tête de plus que moi; *Fig* **she's h. and shoulders above the other athletes** elle est bien supérieure aux autres athlètes; *Horseracing* **to win by a h.** (*of horse*) gagner d'une tête; **to win by a short h.** gagner de justesse; **they'll have your h. (on a plate) for this** ils auront ta tête pour ça; **to let sb have their h.** lâcher les rênes à qn; *Lit* **his blood will be upon your h.** la responsabilité de sa mort pèsera sur vos épaules; **on your own h. be it** assumez-en la responsabilité; **to cut off sb's h.** décapiter qn, couper la tête à qn; *F* **to shout one's h. off** crier à tue-tête *ou* à pleins poumons; *F* **to talk one's h. off** bavarder comme une pie; *F* **to bite** *or* **snap sb's h. off** rembarrer qn; **a fine h. of hair** une belle chevelure; **to have a (good) h. for heights** ne pas avoir le vertige; **I haven't got a h. for heights** j'ai le vertige; **to have a good** *or* **strong h. for drink** bien supporter l'alcool; **the wine went (straight) to my h.** le vin m'a fait tourner la tête, le vin m'est monté à la tête; **all the praise went to his h.** toutes les louanges lui sont montées à la tête; **to have one's h. in the clouds** être dans les nuages *ou* dans la lune; *Fig* **to bang** *or* **bash** *or* **knock one's h. against a (brick) wall** se heurter à un mur; *Fig* **to bury** *or* **have one's h. in the sand** se cacher la tête dans le sable; *esp Am Sl* **to give sb h.** (*oral sex*) sucer qn

(**b**) (*intellect, mind*) **to do sums in one's h.** calculer de tête; **to have a good h. for business** avoir le sens des affaires, s'entendre aux affaires; **to have a good h. for figures** être à l'aise avec les chiffres; **to let the h. be ruled by the heart** laisser son cœur gouverner sa raison; **to get sth into one's h.** se mettre qch dans la tête; **I can't get that into his h.** je n'arrive pas à le lui faire comprendre; **he has taken it into his h. that ...** il s'est mis dans la tête *ou* en tête que ...; **it never entered my h. that ...** je n'aurais jamais pensé que ...; **to put ideas into sb's h.** donner des idées à qn; **to put an idea into sb's h.** mettre une idée dans la tête à qn; **his name has gone right** *or* **clean out of my h.** j'ai complètement oublié son nom; **the girl's got a good h. on her shoulders** cette fille a la tête sur les épaules; *Prov* **he's an old h. on young shoulders** il est très mûr pour son âge; **we put our heads together** nous avons réfléchi ensemble; *Prov* **two heads are better than one** deux conseils valent mieux qu'un; **I think he made it up out of his own h.** je crois que c'est lui qui a inventé ça; **not off the top of my h.** (*I'd have to check*) pas au pied levé; **she made some figures up off the top of her h.** elle a inventé des chiffres; **off the top of my h., I'd say somewhere like Paris** à tout hasard, je dirais un endroit comme Paris; **to be over the heads of the audience** (*of speech, lecture etc*) dépasser l'entendement de l'auditoire; **it's (way) over his h.** il n'y comprend rien (du tout); *F* **to lose one's h.** perdre la tête *ou F* la boule *ou F* la boussole; *F* **to keep one's h.** (*in crisis*) garder la tête sur les épaules; *F* **to be off one's h.** être fou *ou F* timbré *ou F* toqué; *F* **to go off one's h.** devenir fou; *F* **he's not quite right in the h., he's a bit soft in the h.** il est faible d'esprit *ou F* un peu timbré; *F* **to be out of one's h.** (*on drugs, alcohol*) se défoncer

(**c**) *F* (*headache*) **I've got a bad h.** *or* **an awful h.** j'ai mal à la tête *ou* un de ces maux de tête; (*after drinking*) j'ai mal aux cheveux

(**d**) *Culin* **sheep's h.** tête *f* de mouton; **calf's h.** tête de veau; **potted h.** fromage *m* de tête

(**e**) (*antlers*) (*of stag*) bois *mpl*, tête *f*; **deer of the first/second h.** cerf *m* à la première/deuxième tête

(**f**) (*top part, end*) (*of pin, hammer, violin, flower, volcano, piston, boil, tennis racket*) tête *f*; (*of cabbage, cane, stick*) pomme *f*; (*of asparagus*) pointe *f*; (*of celery*) pied *m*; (*of lance etc*) fer *m*; (*of page, stairs*) haut *m*; (*heading of page*) en-tête *m, pl* en-têtes; (*of column, rocket, still*) chapiteau *m*; *Typ* (*of chapter etc*) tête, intitulé *m*; (*of mineshaft*) bouche *f*; (*of cylinder*) tête, culasse *f*; (*of torpedo*) cône *m*; (*of cask etc*) fond *m*; (*of drum*) peau *f*; (*of bed*) chevet *m*, tête; (*of the table*) haut bout *m*; (*of river*) source *f*; (*in bookkeeping*) rubrique *f*; (*on beer*) mousse *f*, *F* faux col *m*; (*on fermenting liquid*) chapeau *m*; **beer with no h.** bière éventée; **at the h. of the lake** à l'extrémité du lac; **to come to a h.** atteindre un paroxysme; **things are coming to a h.** la crise est proche; **to bring matters to a h.** forcer une décision; *Min* **h. frame** chevalement *m*; *Aut* **h. gasket** joint *m* de culasse; *HydE* **h. gate** (*of lock*) porte *f* d'amont

(**g**) (*heading, grouping*) rubrique *f*; **under this h.** sous cette rubrique

(**h**) *Naut F* (*latrine*) latrines *fpl*

(**i**) = **headland**

(**j**) (*front or chief place*) **at the h. of a procession** à la *ou* en tête d'un cortège; **to be at the h. of the list** venir en tête de liste; **at the h. of the queue** en tête de file; **to sit at the h. of the table** présider la table

(**k**) (*person in charge*) (*of family, the Church, business*) chef *m*; **h. (of department)** *Sch* chef de département; (*in company*) chef de service; (*in store*) chef de rayon; **h. of section** chef de service; **h. barman** chef barman; **h. cashier** chef caissier; *Com* **h. clerk** premier commis *m*, chef de bureau; **h. concierge** chef concierge; **h. foreman** chef d'atelier; **h. gardener** jardinier *m* en chef; **h. housekeeper** (*in hotel*) gouvernante *f* générale; **h. office** (*of company, organization*) siège *m* social; **it's h. office on the phone** c'est le siège au téléphone; **h. porter** chef concierge; **h. receptionist** chef de réception; **h. waiter** maître *m* d'hôtel; *F* **h. cook and bottlewasher** = homme *m*/femme *f* qui mène toute l'affaire

(**l**) (*no pl*) (*unit*) **six h. of cattle** six têtes de bétail; **thirty h. of oxen** trente bœufs

(**m**) (*person*) **to pay so much per h.** *or* **a h.** payer tant par tête *ou* par personne

(**n**) (*of coin*) face *f*; *Art etc* **coin bearing the h. of George III** pièce (frappée) à l'effigie de Georges III; **heads or tails?** pile ou face?; **heads I win, tails you lose** pile je gagne, face tu perds, je gagne de toutes les façons *ou* de toute façon; *F* **I can't make h. or tail of this** je n'y comprends rien de rien, ça n'a ni queue ni tête

(**o**) *Phys etc* (*of a fluid, gas etc*) charge *f*, pression *f*; **h. of water** (*pressure*) charge *ou* pression d'eau; **full h. of steam** charge *ou* pression de vapeur; *Phys* **loss of h.** perte *f* de pression

(**p**) (*on tape recorder, disk drive*) tête *f*; **h. crash** crash *m* *ou* écrasement *m* de tête

▶ **head back** *vi* rentrer, retourner; **it's time we were heading back** il est temps que nous rentrions

▶ **head for** *vipo* (*go towards*) **to h. for a place** s'avancer *ou* se diriger vers un endroit; *Naut* avoir le cap sur un endroit; **we were heading for ...** nous étions en route pour ...; **let's h. for home** rentrons; **where are you headed for?** vers où *ou* dans quelle direction allez-vous?; **the country is heading for civil war** le pays va droit à la guerre civile; **you're heading for trouble** vous allez avoir des ennuis; **they're heading for disaster** ils vont *ou* courent à la catastrophe; **to be heading for a fall** aller tout droit vers un échec

▶ **head in** *vtsep Fb* **to h. the ball in** marquer (un but) de la tête

▶ **head off** *vtsep* (*divert*) (*person, enemy troops*) barrer la route à; (*fugitives*) intercepter; (*question*) parer; **I'll h. them off at the pass** je les intercepterai au col

▶ **head up** *vtsep* (*team etc*) diriger

headache ['hedeɪk] *n* (**a**) mal *m* de tête, *pl* maux de tête; **to have a h.** avoir mal à la tête; *Fig F* **you give me a h.** vous me cassez la tête (**b**) *F* (*worry, problem*) embêtement *m*, casse-tête *m*, plaie *f*; **it can be a h. finding somewhere to park** certains jours, c'est une plaie de trouver à se garer; **this injury is another h. for the team's manager** cette blessure, c'est un nouveau casse-tête pour le manager de l'équipe

headband ['hedbænd] *n* bandeau *m*

headboard ['hedbɔːd] *n* dosseret *m*

head boy *n Br Sch* = élève *m* choisi parmi les grands pour maintenir la discipline etc

headbutt[1] ['hedbʌt] *n* coup *m* de tête; **to give sb a h.** donner un coup de tête à qn

headbutt[2] *vt* donner un coup de tête à

headcase ['hedkeɪs] *n Br F* cinglé, -ée

headcheese ['hedtʃiːz] *n Am Culin* fromage *m* de tête

head cold *n Med* rhume *m* de cerveau

headcount ['hedkaʊnt] *n* dénombrement *m* des personnes présentes; **let's do a h.** on va les compter

headdress ['heddres] *n* coiffe *f*

headed ['hedɪd] *adj* **h. (note)paper** papier *m* à en-tête

-headed ['hedɪd] *suff* **big/two/***etc***-h.** qui a la grosse tête/qui a deux têtes/*etc*

header ['hedər] *n* (**a**) *Typ, Comptr* en-tête *m* (**b**) *Fb* tête *f*, coup *m* de tête (**c**) *F* (*fall*) **to take a (flying) h.** (*into water*) tomber (à l'eau) la tête la première; (*on to ground*) tomber (par terre) la tête la première (**d**) *Constr* boutisse *f*

header tank *n Aut* réservoir *m* en charge, réservoir supérieur

headfirst ['hed'fɜːst] *adv* (*to fall*) la tête la première; **he was hanging h. from the window** il était suspendu à la fenêtre la tête en bas

headgear ['hedgɪər] *n* (*no pl*) couvre-chef *m*; **all kinds of h.** toutes sortes de couvre-chefs

head girl *n Br Sch* = élève *f* choisie parmi les grandes pour maintenir la discipline etc

head-hunt *vt Com* **to be head-hunted** être recruté par un chasseur de têtes; **we'll have to h. someone** il va falloir y aller à la manière d'un chasseur de têtes

head-hunter *n* (*tribal warrior*), *Com* chasseur *m* de têtes

head-hunting *n* (*recruitment*) recrutement *m* de cadres par approche directe; **a h. firm** un cabinet de chasseurs de têtes

headiness ['hedɪnɪs] *n* (**a**) (*of wine etc*) qualité *f* capiteuse (**b**) (*rashness*) impétuosité *f*; **the h. of the moment** la griserie *ou* l'ivresse *f* du moment

heading ['hedɪŋ] *n* (**a**) (*in book etc*) (*of chapter, article*) tête *f*; (*of article*) rubrique *f*; (*of page etc*) en-tête *m, pl* en-têtes; (*in bookkeeping*) poste *m*, rubrique; **it falls under the h. of ...** c'est à mettre à la rubrique de ...; **this subject comes under the h. of rhetoric** cette discipline fait partie de la rhétorique (**b**) *Fb* jeu *m* de tête (**c**) *Min* (*head of tunnel*) avancée *f*, avancement *m*; (*tunnel*) galerie *f* d'avancement (**d**) *Constr* **h. (course)** assise *f* de boutisses

headlamp ['hedlæmp] *n* (*of car*) phare *m*; (*of locomotive*) feu *m* d'avant; **h. washer** lave-phare *m*; **h. wash/wipe** lave-essuie-phare *m*; **h. wiper** essuie-phare *m*

headland ['hedlənd] *n Geog* cap *m*, promontoire *m*

headless ['hedlɪs] *adj* (**a**) sans tête; (*body*) décapité; *prov* **to run about like a h. chicken** courir dans tous les sens, paniquer (**b**) *Biol* (*animal etc*) acéphale

headlight ['hedlaɪt] *n* (*of car*) phare *m*; (*of locomotive*) feu *m* d'avant

headline¹ ['hedlaɪn] *n* (**a**) *Journ* titre *m*, gros titre; **to get into** *or* **hit the headlines** faire la une, faire les gros titres; **pollution has been in the headlines a lot recently** la pollution a beaucoup fait la une récemment; *Rad, TV* **... and here are the headlines** ... et voici les grands titres (de l'actualité); **the disappearance of a dog isn't normally h. news** la disparition d'un chien ne fait pas normalement la une de l'actualité; **h. writer** titreur *m* (**b**) *Typ* en-tête *m*, *pl* en-têtes, ligne *f* de tête

headline² **1** *vt Journ* mettre en vedette *ou* en première page; **the story was headlined 'Tragic accident'** l'histoire s'intitulait 'un accident tragique' **2** *vi Mus etc* (*be chief attraction of a show*) être en vedette

headlining ['hedlaɪnɪŋ] *n* (*in car*) garnissage *m* de plafond

headlong ['hedlɒŋ] **1** *adv* **to fall h. (on the floor)** tomber de tout son long (par terre); **to rush h. to one's ruin** courir à sa ruine; **they rushed h. into the deal** ils se sont jetés à corps perdu dans l'affaire; **they rushed h. into marriage** ils se sont mariés trop vite et sans réfléchir **2** *adj* (*fall*) la tête la première; **to take a h. dive** piquer une tête; **there was a h. rush to buy the shares** tout le monde s'est précipité pour acheter les actions; **h. flight** sauve-qui-peut *m inv*

head louse, *pl* **head lice** *n* pou *m*, *pl* poux

headman, *pl* **-men** ['hedmən] *n* (*of tribe etc*) chef *m*

headmaster [hed'mɑːstər] *n* (*of school*) directeur *m*; (*of comprehensive*) principal *m*; (*of high school*) proviseur *m*

headmistress [hed'mɪstrɪs] *n* (*of school*) directrice *f*; (*of comprehensive*) principale *f*; (*of high school*) proviseur *m*

head of state *n* chef *m* d'État

head-on *adj, adv* de front; **to meet sb h.** prendre qn de front; **they met h. over the issue of taxation** ils se sont affrontés sur la question des impôts; *Mktg* **h. attack** attaque *f* frontale; **h. collision** collision *f* frontale *ou* de plein fouet; **h. confrontation** affrontement *m* direct

headphones ['hedfəʊnz] *npl Tel, Rad* casque *m*, écouteurs *mpl*

headphone talkback ['tɔːkbæk] *n* micro *m* sur casque, casque *m* interphone

headquarter ['hedkwɔːtər] *Am* **1** *vi* (*of company*) **to h. in Glasgow** établir son siège à Glasgow **2** *vt* **to be headquartered in Glasgow** avoir son siège à Glasgow

headquarters [hed'kwɔːtəz] *npl* (*often with sing verb*) (**a**) (*of private company, bank*) siège *m* social; (*of organization, government office*) bureau *m* principal; (*of UN etc*) administration *f* centrale; **to have its h. at ...** siéger *ou* avoir son siège à ... (**b**) *Mil* (*of lower units*) poste *m* de commandement; (*of higher units*) quartier *m* général; (*staff*) état-major *m*, *pl* états-major; **company/platoon h.** (*staff*) groupe *m* de commandement de la compagnie/de la section

head register *n Mus* voix *f* de tête

headrest ['hedrest] *n* appui-tête *m*, *pl* appuis-tête, appuie-tête *m inv*

head restraint *n* (*in car*) repose-tête *m inv*, appui-tête *m*, *pl* appuis-tête, appuie-tête *m inv*

headroom ['hedruːm] *n* hauteur *f*; (*of arch*) échappée *f*; (*in car*) hauteur au plafond; (*under bridge*) hauteur (de passage); **there wasn't enough h. for the bus** il n'y avait pas un dégagement suffisant au-dessus du bus

headscarf ['hedskɑːf] *n* foulard *m*

headset ['hedset] *n Rad, TV* casque *m*, écouteurs *mpl*

headship ['hedʃɪp] *n Br Sch* (*of school*) direction *f*

head shot *n TV, Cin* gros plan *m* de tête

headshrinker ['hedʃrɪŋkər] *n* (*savage*) réducteur *m* de têtes; *F Hum* (*psychiatrist*) psychiatre *mf*, psy *mf*

headstall ['hedstɔːl] *n* (*for horse*) têtière *f*, licou *m*

headstand ['hedstænd] *n Gym* poirier *m*; **to do a h.** faire le poirier

head start *n* (*in race*) avantage *m* dès le départ; **to give sb a h.** (*in race*) laisser partir qn devant, donner de l'avance à qn; *Fig* **to have a h.** avoir un avantage dès le départ

headstone ['hedstəʊn] *n* (**a**) (*on grave*) pierre *f* tombale (**b**) *Archit, Constr* clef *f* de voûte

headstrong ['hedstrɒŋ] *adj* volontaire, têtu, entêté

head teacher *n Br Sch* directeur, -trice

head-up *adj Mil, Av* **h. display** affichage *m* tête haute

head voice *n Mus* voix *f* de tête

headway ['hedweɪ] *n* progrès *m*; **to make h.** avancer, faire des progrès; (*of ship*) faire route; **to make no h.** ne pas avancer; **the two sides have made some h. in their negotiations** les deux parties ont avancé dans leurs négociations

headwind ['hedwɪnd] *n Naut* vent *m* contraire, vent debout

headword ['hedwɜːd] *n* (*in dictionary*) entrée *f*

heady ['hedɪ] *adj* (*vin*) capiteux; (*perfume*) capiteux, troublant; (*height etc*) vertigineux; **the h. heights of international finance** les sommets de la finance internationale; **to be h. with success** être grisé par le succès; **the h. times during the revolution** les moments grisants de la révolution

heal [hiːl] **1** *vt* guérir (**sb of a disease** qn d'une maladie); *Med, Fig* (*wound*) guérir, cicatriser; *Fig* **to h. the breach (between two people)** amener une réconciliation (entre deux personnes) **2** *vi* (*of wound*) se cicatriser, se refermer; **the wound hasn't healed properly** la blessure ne s'est pas bien cicatrisée *ou* n'a pas bien cicatrisé

▶ **heal over, heal up** *vi* = **heal 2**

healer ['hiːlər] *n* guérisseur, -euse; *Prov* **time is a great h.** le temps guérit toutes les blessures

healing ['hiːlɪŋ] **1** *adj* (*remedy etc*) curatif; (*ointment, plant, remedy*) cicatrisant **2** *n* guérison *f*; (*of wound*) cicatrisation *f*, guérison

health [helθ] *n* santé *f*; **exercise is good for the** *or* **one's h.** l'exercice est bon pour la santé; **good h.** bonne santé; **ill** *or* **poor h.** mauvaise santé; **to be in good h.** être en bonne santé *ou* bien portant; **to be in bad** *or* **poor h.** se porter mal, être mal portant; *Fig* **the economy is in good h.** l'économie se porte bien; **to restore sb to (full** *or* **good) h.** rendre la santé à qn; **to endanger one's h.** mettre en danger sa santé; **to regain one's h.** recouvrer la santé; **to suffer from ill h.** être de santé fragile; **the Department of H.** = le Ministère de la Santé; **to drink to sb's h.** boire à la santé de qn; **(your very) good h.!** (à votre) santé!; **public h.** santé *ou* hygiène *f* publique; **(public) h. officer** *or* **inspector** inspecteur *m* de la santé publique; *Br Admin* **(local) h. authority** = organisme *m* régional responsable de l'administration de la santé publique; **h. checks** contrôles *mpl* sanitaires; **h. and fitness centre** centre *m* de sport et de remise en forme; **h. and safety committee** comité *m* d'hygiène et de sécurité; **h. and safety regulations** réglementation *f* sur l'hygiène et la sécurité; *Br* **H. Service** services *mpl* de santé; **the epidemic has put terrible strain on the h. services** l'épidémie a mis les services médicaux à rude épreuve

health care *n* soins *mpl* médicaux

health centre *n* centre *m* de soins, dispensaire *m*

health certificate *n* certificat *m* sanitaire

health cover *n Fin* assurance *f* médicale

health farm *n* = établissement *m* à la campagne où l'on suit un régime, fait du sport etc pour se remettre en forme

health food *n* produits *mpl* diététiques; (*natural foods*) produits naturels; **h. shop** magasin *m* de produits diététiques

health-giving *adj* (*effect etc*) bienfaisant, salutaire; (*air etc*) tonifiant, vivifiant

health hazard *n* risque *m* pour la santé

healthily ['helθɪlɪ] *adv* sainement, salubrement

healthiness ['helθɪnɪs] *n* (*of place, climate*) salubrité *f*; (*of person*) bonne santé; (*of relationship*) caractère *m* sain

health insurance *n* assurance *f* médicale *ou* maladie; **h. scheme** caisse *f* de maladie

health resort *n* station *f* climatique; (*by sea*) station balnéaire

health risk *n* risque *m* pour la santé

health tourism *n* tourisme *m* de santé

health visitor *n Br* infirmière *f* visiteuse

healthy ['helθɪ] *adj* (*person, animal*) en bonne santé, bien portant; (*skin, lungs, relationship*) sain; (*plant*) robuste; (*climate, food etc*) salubre, sain; **a h. appetite** un solide appétit; **h. eating habits** bonne alimentation *f*; **to look healthier** avoir meilleure mine; **h. living** une vie saine; **a h. interest in the opposite sex** un intérêt naturel à l'égard du sexe opposé; **to have a h. respect for sb/sth** avoir beaucoup de respect pour qn/qch; **to have a h. disregard for traditions** avoir un mépris louable des traditions; **it isn't h. for a child to spend so much time reading** il n'est pas sain pour un enfant de passer tant de temps à lire; **a h. democracy** une démocratie qui se porte bien; **a h. economy** une économie saine *ou* prospère; **to make a h. profit** faire de bons bénéfices; **it is a h. sign that ...** il est encourageant que ... + *sub*

heap¹ [hiːp] *n* (**a**) (*pile*) (*of wood, stones etc*) tas *m*, monceau *m*, amas *m*, amoncellement *m*; **the books were in a h. on the floor** les livres étaient en tas sur le sol; *Fig* **at the top/bottom of the h.** en haut/au bas de l'échelle (sociale); **h. of junk** tas de ferraille; **a h. of rubble** un tas de ruines; **to lie in a h.** être en tas; **to fall in a h.** (*of person*) s'affaisser (*sur soi-même*); *F* **to be struck all of a h.** en rester abasourdi *ou* stupéfait

(**b**) *F* (*large number*) (*usu pl*) **she had heaps of children** elle avait une ribambelle d'enfants; **I've got heaps of things to do** j'ai un tas de choses à faire; **you've got heaps of time** vous avez largement le temps; **to have heaps of room/money** avoir plein de place/d'argent

(c) *Sl* (*car*) **this old h.** cette vieille bagnole, ce vieux tas de ferraille

heap² *vt* (a) (*pile*) (*wood, stones etc*) entasser, amonceler, mettre en tas; **to h. riches/praise on sb** couvrir qn de richesses/d'éloges; **to h. scorn on sb/sb's proposal** ridiculiser qn/la proposition de qn; **to h. insults on sb('s head)** accabler qn d'injures (b) (*cover, fill*) **the table was heaped with food** la table était couverte de victuailles; **the lorry was heaped with food supplies** le camion regorgeait de provisions; **she heaped my plate with cherries** elle a rempli mon assiette de cerises

▶ **heap up** *vtsep* (*make pile of*) empiler, entasser

heaped [hiːpt] *adj* (*container, bowl*) entassé, amoncelé; *Culin* **a h. teaspoonful/tablespoonful** (*in recipe*) une bonne cuillère à café/à soupe

heaps [hiːps] *adv F* (*a lot*) vachement

hear [hɪər] (*pt, pp* **heard** [hɜːd]) **1** *vt* (a) [①**A40**,C,1,a; **B33**,2,b,i] (*perceive*) entendre; **I heard a ring** j'ai entendu sonner; **let's h. it** (*tell us*) dites donc, racontez-nous ça; **let's h. it for ...** (*applaud*) applaudissons ...; **I heard my name (mentioned)** j'ai entendu dire mon nom; **to h. sb speak** entendre parler qn, entendre qn parler; **I could hardly make myself heard/h. myself speak** je pouvais à peine me faire entendre; *Iron* **he hears what he wants to h.** il n'entend que ce qu'il veut; *F* **I've heard that one before!** j'ai déjà entendu ça (quelque part)!; **you heard!** ne faites pas celui/celle qui n'a pas entendu!

(b) (*listen to*) écouter; *Jur* (*witness, testimony*) entendre; **h. me out** écoutez-moi jusqu'au bout; **h.! h.!** (*at meeting*) très bien! très bien!; *esp Am F* **I h. you, I h. what you're saying** je comprends, j'ai compris; *Rel* **to h. Mass** assister à la messe; **to h. sb's confession** entendre qn en confession; **to h. a prayer** exaucer *ou* écouter *ou* entendre une prière; *Jur* **to h. a case** juger une affaire; **the case was heard in camera** l'audience a eu lieu à huis clos; **when is your case going to be heard?** quand ton affaire va-t-elle être jugée *ou* passer au tribunal?

(c) (*learn*) (*piece of news*) apprendre; (*the truth*) apprendre, savoir; **I heard it from a friend** je l'ai su par un ami, je l'ai appris par un ami; **I heard a rumour that she was in Spain** j'ai entendu une rumeur selon laquelle elle serait en Espagne; **I have heard that ...** j'ai appris *ou* on m'a appris que ...; **I h. you're getting married** j'apprends que tu vas te marier; **for six months we heard nothing** (*received no news*) pendant six mois nous n'avons pas eu de nouvelles; **she was very famous for a while then we heard no more about her** elle a été célèbre pendant un moment puis on n'a plus entendu parler d'elle; **let me h. how you get on** donnez-moi de vos nouvelles; **from what I h.** à ce qu'on dit; **I have heard a great deal about him** on m'a beaucoup parlé de lui; **I don't want to h. any more about it** je ne veux plus en entendre parler; **I've heard nothing but good about them** je n'ai entendu que du bien à leur propos; **to h. tell of ...** entendre parler de ...

2 *vi* (a) (*have hearing*) entendre (bien); **I can't h. properly** je n'entends pas bien

(b) (*receive news, word*) **to h. from sb** recevoir des nouvelles de qn; **you'll h. from me!** (*as threat*) vous aurez de mes nouvelles!; **you'll be hearing from my lawyer!** mon avocat vous contactera!, on en reparlera devant les tribunaux!; **to h. about sb/sth** avoir des nouvelles de qn/qch, entendre parler de qn/qch; **haven't you heard?** vous ne savez pas?

▶ **hear of** *vipo* (a) (*learn about*) (*person, thing*) entendre parler de; **he has not been heard of since** depuis on n'en a plus entendu parler; **this is the first I have heard of it** c'est la première fois que j'en entends parler; **I only heard of it yesterday** je n'en ai eu connaissance qu'hier; **I never heard of such a thing!** a-t-on jamais entendu une chose pareille!, je n'ai jamais vu une chose pareille! (b) (*in neg*) (*allow*) **I won't h. of you going to a hotel** il est hors de question que vous alliez à l'hôtel; **I won't h. of it** je ne veux pas en entendre parler

hearer [ˈhɪərər] *n* auditeur, -trice; **hearers** auditoire *m*

hearing [ˈhɪərɪŋ] *n* (a) (*ability to hear*) ouïe *f*; **my h. is very bad** mon ouïe est très faible; **loud noise can permanently damage your h.** trop de bruit peut endommager l'ouïe de façon irréversible; **he has very little h. left** son ouïe est défaillante, il n'entend presque plus; **the h. impaired** les malentendants *mpl*; *Med* **h. aid** audiophone *m*

(b) (*range*) **within h.** à portée de voix; **out of h.** hors de portée de voix; **it was said in my h.** on l'a dit devant moi *ou* en ma présence

(c) (*act of listening*) audition *f*, audience *f*; **he was refused a h.** on a refusé de l'entendre; **to condemn sb without a h.** condamner qn sans l'écouter; **we should give her a fair h. first** on devrait l'entendre d'abord

(d) *Jur* **h. of witnesses** audition *f* des témoins; **the h. of the case** l'audience *f*; (*by judge alone*) l'audition de la cause par le juge; **the case comes up for h. tomorrow** l'affaire passera en jugement demain

(e) (*meeting*) séance *f*; (*investigation*) (*of Senate etc*) enquête *f*

hearken [ˈhɑːk(ə)n] *vi Arch, Lit* écouter

hearsay [ˈhɪəseɪ] *n* ouï-dire *m inv*; **that's only h.** ce ne sont que des on-dit; **I know it** *or* **have it only from h.** je ne le sais que par ouï-dire; *Jur* **h. evidence** déposition *f* sur la foi d'autrui

hearse [hɜːs] *n* corbillard *m*, fourgon *m* mortuaire

heart [hɑːt] *n* (a) *Anat* cœur *m*; *Med* **to have h. trouble, to have a weak** *or* **bad h.** être cardiaque; **to press** *or* **clasp sb to one's h.** serrer *ou* presser qn sur son cœur

(b) *Fig* (*seat of the emotions*) **to have a big h.** avoir très bon cœur; **h. of gold** cœur d'or; **h. of stone** cœur de pierre; **you've got no h.** tu n'as pas de cœur; **have a h.!** ayez un peu de cœur!; **it did my h. good to see her again** ça m'a fait chaud au cœur de la revoir; **her h.'s in the right place** (*she is kind*) elle a bon cœur; (*has good intentions*) elle a de bonnes intentions; **his h. was full** *or* **heavy** il avait le cœur gros; **with a heavy h.** le cœur serré *ou* gros; **my h. sank at the news** cette nouvelle m'a désespéré; *F* **my h. was in my boots** j'étais complètement découragé; **to have one's h. in one's mouth** avoir un serrement de cœur; **to break sb's h.** briser le cœur à qn; **it was enough to break your h.** c'était à fendre le cœur *ou* l'âme; **to cry one's h. out** pleurer toutes les larmes de son corps; **to be sick at h.** avoir le cœur gros *ou* serré; **to wear one's h. on one's sleeve** ne pas cacher ses préférences

(c) (*representing romantic love*) **to win sb's h.** gagner le cœur de qn; **to lose one's h. to sb** tomber amoureux de qn; **affairs** *or* **matters of the h.** affaires *fpl* de cœur

(d) (*representing sincerity, one's deepest preferences*) **in my h. of hearts** au plus profond de mon cœur; **from the bottom of one's h.** (*thank sb, congratulate sb*) de tout son cœur; **to love sb with all one's h.** aimer qn de tout son cœur; **to have sb's welfare at h.** avoir à cœur le bonheur de qn; **she's a socialist at h.** au fond, elle est socialiste; **a cause close to my h.** une cause qui me tient à cœur; **to take sth to h.** prendre qch à cœur; **to have set one's h. on sth/on doing sth** avoir qch à cœur/avoir *ou* prendre à cœur de faire qch; **I have set my h. on it** j'y tiens; **he's a man after my own h.** c'est un homme qui me ressemble, il est comme moi; **to one's h.'s content** à cœur joie, à souhait; **to eat/drink to one's h.'s content** manger/boire tout son soûl; **to be all h.** être plein de bonne volonté; *Iron* **you're all h.** tu es charmant!

(e) (*enthusiasm, courage*) **to put (all) one's h. into it** y aller de tout son cœur; **his/my h. isn't in it** le cœur n'y est pas; **to put one's h. and soul** *or* **to throw oneself h. and soul into sth** se donner corps et âme à qch; **to put new h. into sb** donner du courage *ou* du cœur à qn; **to take h.** (re)prendre courage; **to lose h.** se décourager; **she didn't have the h. to tell him** elle n'a pas eu le cœur de le lui dire

(f) **to learn/know sth (off) by h.** apprendre/savoir qch par cœur

(g) (*centre*) (*of cabbage*) cœur *m*; (*of tree*) cœur, vif *m*; (*of cable*) âme *f*, mèche *f*; **h. of oak** homme *m* courageux; **the h. of the matter** le fond du problème; **in the h. of** (*town, country*) au cœur de; (*forest*) au (beau) milieu de

(h) *Cards* **heart(s)** cœur *m*; **to play a h./hearts** jouer du cœur/cœur; **king/queen of hearts** roi *m*/dame *f* de cœur

heartache [ˈhɑːteɪk] *n* chagrin *m ou* peine *f* de cœur

heart attack *n* crise *f* cardiaque

heartbeat [ˈhɑːtbiːt] *n* battement *m ou* pulsation *f* du cœur; *Fig* **a h. away from sth** à un cheveu de qch

heartbreak [ˈhɑːtbreɪk] *n* peine *f* immense, chagrin *m*; (*romantic*) chagrin d'amour; **I've had my share of heartbreak(s)** j'ai eu ma part de chagrins d'amour

heartbreaker [ˈhɑːtbreɪkər] *n* (*man*) bourreau *m* des cœurs; (*woman*) mangeuse *f* d'hommes

heartbreaking [ˈhɑːtbreɪkɪŋ] *adj* navrant, accablant, déchirant; (*sigh, news*) à fendre le cœur; (*sight*) navrant; **it was h.** c'était à fendre l'âme; **h. cries** cris déchirants

heartbroken [ˈhɑːtbrəʊk(ə)n] *adj* **to be h.** avoir le cœur brisé

heartburn [ˈhɑːtbɜːn] *n Med* brûlures *fpl* d'estomac

heart disease *n* maladie *f* de cœur

hearten [ˈhɑːt(ə)n] *vt* (*person*) encourager, donner du courage à

heartening [ˈhɑːt(ə)nɪŋ] *adj* (*advice, words*) encourageant

heart failure *n* arrêt *m* cardiaque

heartfelt [ˈhɑːtfelt] *adj* (*emotion, vow*) sincère, qui vient *ou* part du cœur; **to express one's h. thanks to sb** adresser de sincères remerciements à qn

hearth, *pl* **hearths** [hɑːθ, hɑːθs] *n* foyer *m*, âtre *m*; **without h. and home** sans feu ni lieu; **h. rug** devant *m* de foyer

hearthstone [ˈhɑːθstəʊn] *n* pierre *f* de la cheminée, (marbre *m* du) foyer *m*

heartily [ˈhɑːtɪlɪ] *adv* **(a)** (*cordially*) (*to greet*) cordialement; (*to welcome, applaud*) chaleureusement; (*to work, laugh*) de bon cœur; (*to rejoice*) sincèrement; *F* **to be h. sick of sth** être profondément dégoûté de qch **(b)** (*to eat*) de bon appétit, avec appétit

heartiness [ˈhɑːtɪnɪs] *n* **(a)** (*cordiality*) (*of welcome*) cordialité *f*, chaleur *f*; (*of consent*) sincérité *f* **(b)** (*vigour*) (*of appetite*) vigueur *f*

heartland [ˈhɑːtlænd] *n Pol, Econ, Geog* centre *m*, cœur *m*; **the country's industrial h.** le centre industriel du pays; **this is Tory h.** c'est une place forte du parti conservateur

heartless [ˈhɑːtlɪs] *adj* (*person*) sans cœur, insensible; (*action, remark*) dur, cruel; **it was h. of you to say that** c'était cruel de ta part de dire ça

heartlessly [ˈhɑːtlɪslɪ] *adv* sans cœur, sans pitié; (*cruelly*) cruellement

heartlessness [ˈhɑːtlɪsnɪs] *n* manque *m* de cœur, insensibilité *f*; (*cruelty*) cruauté *f*

heart-lung *adj Med* **h. machine** cœur-poumon *m* artificiel; **h. transplant** greffe *f* cœur-poumon

heart murmur *n* souffle *m* au cœur, souffle cardiaque

heart-rending [ˈhɑːtrendɪŋ] *adj* = **heartbreaking**

heart-searching *n* **after much h.** après avoir longuement réfléchi

heart share *n Mktg* préférence *f*

heartsick [ˈhɑːtsɪk] *adj esp Lit* écœuré; **to be** *or* **feel h.** avoir le cœur serré *ou* gros

heartstrings [ˈhɑːtstrɪŋz] *npl Fig* **to tug at sb's h.** serrer le cœur de qn

heart surgery *n* chirurgie *f* du cœur; (*operation*) opération *f* du cœur

heart-throb *n F* (*person*) idole *f*, coqueluche *f*; **he thinks he's a real h.** il se prend pour Johnny

heart-to-heart 1 *adj* (*conversation*) intime, à cœur ouvert; **to have a h. talk with sb** parler avec qn à cœur ouvert **2** *n* conversation *f* intime *ou* à cœur ouvert; **I think it's time we had a h.** il est temps que nous parlions franchement

heart transplant *n* greffe *f* du cœur, g. cardiaque **h. patient** greffé, -ée du cœur

heart-warming *adj* réconfortant, qui réchauffe le cœur; **it was h. to see father and child getting on so well** ça vous réchauffait le cœur de voir le père et l'enfant s'entendre si bien

hearty [ˈhɑːtɪ] **1** *adj* **(a)** (*cordial*) cordial, -aux; (*sentiment*) sincère, qui part du cœur; (*laugh*) jovial; **my heartiest congratulations** mes félicitations les plus chaleureuses; **h. cheers** acclamations nourries; **she has a h. dislike of hypocrisy** elle a une sainte horreur de l'hypocrisie **(b)** (*vigorous*) vigoureux, robuste, bien portant; **he is still (hale and) h.** il est encore gaillard **(c)** (*substantial*) (*meal*) copieux, abondant; **h. appetite** gros appétit, *F* rude appétit; **he's a h. eater** c'est un gros mangeur **2** *n* joyeux luron *m*; *Arch, Naut* **my hearties** les gars

heat¹ [hiːt] *n* **(a)** chaleur *f*; (*of sun, fire*) ardeur *f*; **in the h. of the day** au plus chaud de la journée; *Culin* **cook at a low h.** cuire à faible température *ou* à feu doux; **we've been without h. for over a week** (*heating*) nous n'avons plus de chauffage depuis plus d'une semaine; *Fig F* **if you can't take the h., get out of the kitchen** si tu ne peux pas t'y faire, laisse tomber; **h. shield** (*of spaceship etc*) bouclier *m* thermique; **h. treatment** *Ind* traitement *m* thermique; *Med* thermothérapie *f*

(b) (*passion*) **to reply with some h.** répondre avec (une certaine) vivacité; **to take the h. out of the situation** dédramatiser la situation; **in the h. of the moment** sur le moment; **in the h. of the argument** dans le feu de la discussion; **in the h. of battle** dans le feu de la bataille; **to do sth in the h. of one's passion** faire qch dans le feu de la passion

(c) *Sl* (*pressure*) **to turn up the h.** (*in interrogation etc*) faire pression, mettre la pression; **until the h. is off** jusqu'à ce que les choses se calment

(d) (*of female animal*) chaleur *f*, rut *m*; **to be on** *or* **in h.** être en chaleur

(e) *Sp* (épreuve *f*) éliminatoire *f*; **it was a dead h.** ils ont fini à égalité *ou* ex æquo

heat² 1 *vt* (*water, house etc*) chauffer; **to h. sth to (a temperature of) 80°** porter qch à 80°; **to h. a house with gas** chauffer une maison au gaz **2** *vi* (*of water etc*) chauffer

▶ **heat up 1** *vtsep* (*warm*) (*food etc*) (faire) réchauffer **2** *vi* (*of water*) chauffer; (*of room*) se réchauffer; (*of discussion etc*) s'échauffer

heat-conducting *adj* thermoconducteur, -trice

heat constant *n Phys* constante *f* calorifique

heated [ˈhiːtɪd] *adj* **(a)** (*swimming pool, apartment*) chauffé; (*towel rail*) chauffant; **h. (rear) window** lunette *f* (arrière) chauffante; **h. seat** siège *m* chauffant **(b)** (*passionate, angry*) (*discussion*) chaud, animé; **to become h.** (*of discussion, person*) s'échauffer; **things got a bit h.** l'atmosphère a commencé à s'échauffer

heatedly [ˈhiːtɪdlɪ] *adv* avec chaleur, avec emportement

heat engine *n Tech* machine *f ou* moteur *m* thermique

heater [ˈhiːtər] *n* **(a)** (*for room etc*) radiateur *m*; (*for water*) chauffe-eau *m inv*; *Tech* réchauffeur *m*; *Electron* filament *m* incandescent; **(immersion) h.** thermoplongeur *m* **(b)** *US Sl* (*pistol etc*) revolver *m*

heat exchange *n Phys* échange *m* de chaleur

heat exchanger *n Tech* échangeur *m* de chaleur

heat exhaustion *n Med* épuisement *m* dû à la chaleur

heath [hiːθ] *n* **(a)** (*tract of land*) bruyère *f*, lande *f* **(b)** (*heather*) bruyère *f*

heat haze *n* brume *f* de chaleur

heathen [ˈhiːð(ə)n] **1** *adj* (*pagan*) païen, -ïenne **2** *npl Lit* **the h.** les païens *mpl*; *Old-fashioned* (*barbarians*) les barbares *mpl*

heathenish [ˈhiːðənɪʃ] *adj* (*pagan*) païen, -ïenne

heathenism [ˈhiːðənɪz(ə)m] *n* paganisme *m*

heather [ˈheðər] *n* (*shrub*) bruyère *f*, brande *f*

Heath Robinson [hiːθˈrɒbɪnsən] *adj* de bric et de broc

heating [ˈhiːtɪŋ] **1** *adj attrib* **h. apparatus** appareil *m* de chauffage; **h. bill** facture *f* de chauffage; *MecE etc* **h. coil** serpentin *m* de chauffage, réchauffeur *m*; *El etc* **h. element** *or* **unit** élément *m* chauffant; **h. engineer** chauffagiste *m*; **h. power** puissance *f ou* pouvoir *m* calorifique; *El* puissance de chauffage; **h. system** (système *m* de) chauffage *m* **2** *n* (*system*) chauffage *m*; **there's no h. in the bathroom** il n'y a pas de chauffage dans la salle de bain; **to put the h. on** mettre le chauffage

heat loss *n Phys* déperdition *f* de chaleur

heatproof [ˈhiːtpruːf] *adj* (*clothing, material*) résistant à la chaleur; (*varnish, dish etc*) allant au feu; (*asbestos*) incombustible; **is it h.?** (*dish*) est-ce que ça va au feu?

heat prostration *n Med* épuisement *m* dû à la chaleur

heat pump *n Tech* pompe *f* à chaleur

heat rash *n Med* boutons *mpl* de chaleur

heat-resistant, -resisting [ˈhiːtrɪzɪstənt, -rɪzɪstɪŋ] *adj* résistant à la chaleur; *Tech* thermorésistant

heat-seeking [ˈhiːtsiːkɪŋ] *adj* (*missile*) guidé par la chaleur

heatsink [ˈhiːtsɪŋk] *n* dissipateur *m* thermique *ou* de chaleur

heatstroke [ˈhiːtstrəʊk] *n Med* coup *m* de chaleur

heatwave [ˈhiːtweɪv] *n Met* vague *f* de chaleur, canicule *f*

heave¹ [hiːv] *n* **(a)** effort *m*; **with a mighty h.** avec un énorme effort; *Naut* **h. of the sea** houle *f* **(b)** (*retch*) haut-le-cœur *m inv*

heave² (*pt, pp* **heaved** *or esp Naut* **hove** [həʊv]) **1** *vt* **(a)** (*lift*) (*load*) faire un effort pour lever *ou* soulever; (*pull*) faire un effort pour tirer; (*push*) faire un effort pour pousser; (*drag*) faire un effort pour traîner; (*throw*) faire un effort pour lancer; **he heaved the sacks of coal onto the truck** il a hissé les sacs de charbon dans le camion (à grand-peine); **she heaved herself out of her chair** elle s'est soulevée de la chaise avec effort; *Naut* **to h. the anchor** lever l'ancre; **to h. a sigh of relief** pousser un soupir de soulagement

(b) *Naut* **to h. the ship ahead/astern** virer le navire de l'avant/de l'arrière

2 *vi* **(a) h.!** (*push*) poussez!; (*pull*) tirez!; (*lift*) soulevez!; **they heaved on the rope** ils ont tiré très fort sur la corde

(b) (*swell*) (se) gonfler, se soulever; (*of sea*) s'agiter, se soulever; (*of ship*) se soulever sur la lame; (*of bosom*) palpiter

(c) (*retch*) (*of person*) avoir des haut-le-cœur; (*of stomach*) se soulever

(d) *Naut* (*of land, ship*) **to h. in sight** paraître (à l'horizon)

▶ **heave to** *Naut* **1** *vi* se mettre en panne *ou* à la cape; (*in gale*) caranguer **2** *vtas* mettre en panne

heave-ho 1 *int Naut* oh hisse! **2** *n F* **to give sb the h.** (*of employer*) sacquer qn, virer qn; (*of boyfriend etc*) plaquer qn; **to get** *or* **be given the h.** se faire jeter

heaven [ˈhev(ə)n] *n* ciel *m*, *pl* cieux; **in h.** au ciel; *Fig* (*overjoyed*) au paradis, aux anges; **to go to h.** aller au ciel *ou* en *ou* au paradis; **this is h.!** c'est merveilleux!; **it's h. on earth** c'est le paradis sur terre; **to move h. and earth to do**

sth remuer ciel et terre pour faire qch; **the heavens opened** il s'est mis à pleuvoir à torrents; *F* **it stinks to high h.** ça pue; **(good) heavens!, heavens above!** bon Dieu!; **thank h. (for that)!** Dieu merci!; **h. (alone) knows!** Dieu seul le sait!; **h. knows why/when/***etc* ... Dieu seul sait pourquoi/quand/*etc* ...; **for h.'s sake!** pour l'amour de Dieu!, pour l'amour du ciel!; **where in the name of h.** *or* **in h.'s name is he?** où diable est-il?; **h. forbid!** que le ciel nous (en) préserve!

heavenly ['hev(ə)nlɪ] *adj* **(a)** *(from God) (gift, mercy etc)* du ciel; *(music etc)* céleste; *Astron* **h. body** astre *m*; **our h. Father** notre Père céleste **(b)** *F (wonderful)* divin; **what h. peaches!** quelles pêches délicieuses!; **to have a h. evening** passer une soirée merveilleuse

heaven-sent *adj* providentiel

heavily ['hevɪlɪ] *adv* **(a)** *(to fall, lean)* lourdement; *(to walk)* lourdement, d'un pas pesant; **time hangs h. on his hands** le temps lui pèse

(b) *(to a considerable extent)* fortement, fort; **h. underlined** souligné d'un gros trait; **to drink/smoke h.** boire/fumer beaucoup; **it was raining h.** il pleuvait fort, il pleuvait beaucoup; **to rely** *or* **depend h. on sth** dépendre beaucoup de qch; **to lose h.** perdre gros; **to be h. defeated** subir une lourde défaite; **h. indebted** fortement endetté; **the secret service was h. involved in training guerillas** les services secrets étaient lourdement impliqués dans la formation des guérilleros; **to be h. hit** *(by financial misfortune etc)* être gravement atteint; **to be h. taxed** être fortement imposé

(c) *(deeply) (to sigh, sleep)* profondément

(d) *(with difficulty) (to breathe)* péniblement

heaviness ['hevɪnɪs] *n* **(a)** *(of body, gait)* lourdeur *f*, pesanteur *f*; *(of burden)* poids *m*; *(of food)* lourdeur **(b)** *(of limbs)* engourdissement *m*; **h. of heart** serrement *m* de cœur

heavy ['hevɪ] **1** *adj* **(a)** *(in weight)* lourd, pesant; *(step)* pesant, lourd, alourdi; *(style)* lourd; *Phys (body)* grave; *Nucl Phys (atom)* lourd; **h. blow** coup violent; **fate had dealt her a h. blow** le destin lui avait porté un coup très rude; **h. meal** repas lourd à digérer; **h. with sleep** lourd de sommeil

(b) *(large, thick) (coat, shoes)* gros, *f* grosse; **h. beard** forte barbe; **h. features** gros traits; **h. losses** lourdes *ou* fortes pertes; *Naut* **h. armament** artillerie *f* lourde; **h. industry** industrie *f* lourde; **h. wire** fil *m* (de) grosse épaisseur

(c) *(intense)* **h. rain** forte pluie; **a h. shower** une grosse averse; *Mil* **h. fire** feu nourri, feu intense; *Med* **a h. cold** un gros rhume; *Med* **h. period(s)** règles *fpl* abondantes; **h. sleep** profond sommeil, sommeil de plomb

(d) *(oppressive) (smell)* fort; *(smell of perfume)* lourd; *(sky)* sombre, morne; **air h. with scent** air chargé de parfums; **h. responsibility** lourde responsabilité; **h. fine** lourde amende; **to rule with a h. hand** gouverner de façon très autoritaire

(e) *(hard) (work)* pénible, difficile, dur; *(breathing)* pénible; *(task)* lourd; *(day)* chargé; *(football pitch etc)* lourd; *F* **to be h. on electricity/petrol** consommer beaucoup d'électricité/d'essence; **she did the h. work** c'est elle qui a fait le gros travail; **this book is h. reading** *or* **going** ce livre est indigeste; **to find it h. going** trouver cela difficile; **h. soil** sol *m* gras; **h. user** gros utilisateur *m*; **he made h. weather of it** il s'est noyé dans un verre d'eau; **to make h. weather of sth** faire une montagne de qch, se compliquer la vie (en ce qui concerne qch); **h. sea** forte mer, grosse mer

(f) *Th (serious)* **h. part** rôle sérieux; **h. father** père *m* autoritaire; *Fig F* **to come the h. father** prendre un ton de père autoritaire; *(stronger)* jouer les Père Fouettard

(g) *(eater, drinker)* gros; **to be a h. sleeper** avoir le sommeil lourd; **to be a h. smoker** fumer beaucoup

(h) *Sl (tense, frightening) (situation etc)* difficile, menaçant

2 *adv* **to weigh h.** *(of time, duty etc)* peser lourd; **food that lies h. on the stomach** nourriture lourde *ou* indigeste *ou* qui pèse sur l'estomac

3 *n* **(a)** *F (thug)* dur *m*

(b) *Th (serious part)* rôle *m* sérieux; *(role of villain)* rôle de scélérat

(c) *Journ F* **heavies** journaux *mpl* sérieux

heavy-duty *adj (machine)* à grand *ou* fort rendement, de grande puissance; *(clothing)* résistant; *(boots)* solide, robuste; *Aut (tyre)* tout-terrain; **h. oil** huile *f* HD

heavy-eyed *adj* aux yeux battus

heavy goods vehicle *n Aut* poids lourd *m*; **h. driver** conducteur *m* de poids lourd; **h. licence** permis *m* poids lourds

heavy-handed [hevɪ'hændɪd] *adj* **(a)** *(clumsy)* maladroit, gauche **(b)** *(harsh)* oppressif, cruel

heavy-hearted [hevɪ'hɑːtɪd] *adj* qui a le cœur lourd *ou* gros; **to feel h.** avoir le cœur gros

heavy-laden *adj* **(a)** lourdement chargé **(b)** *(with cares)* accablé de soucis

heavy metal *n Ch* métal *m* lourd; *Mus* heavy metal *m*; **h. band** *or* **group** groupe *m* de heavy metal

heavy water *n Phys* eau *f* lourde

heavyweight ['hevɪweɪt] **1** *n* **(a)** *Boxing* poids lourd *m* **(b)** *(serious, important person)* personne *f* de poids *ou* d'influence; **he is not a literary h.** ce n'est pas un grand de la littérature **2** *adj* **(a)** *Boxing* (catégorie (des)) poids lourd(s); **h. champion** champion *m* (de la catégorie (des)) poids lourd(s) **(b)** *Tex* lourd

Hebrew ['hiːbruː] **1** *adj Bible* hébreu, *f* hébraïque **2** *n* **(a)** *Bible (person)* Hébreu *m* **(b)** *Ling* hébreu *m*

Hebridean [hebrɪ'diːən] *adj* des Hébrides

Hebrides (the) [ðə'hebrɪdiːz] *n* les Hébrides *fpl*

heck [hek] *F* **1** *int* sapristi!, zut! **2** *n* **what the h. are you doing here?** que diable fais-tu là?; **a h. of a lot** *(quantity)* tout un tas; **not a h. of a lot** *(not greatly)* pas tellement, pas beaucoup, pas des masses

heckle ['hek(ə)l] **1** *vt (at public meetings) (speaker)* interpeller; **he was heckled non-stop** il s'est fait chahuter tout le temps **2** *vi* chahuter

heckler ['heklər] *n Pol etc* **there were two hecklers in the audience** il y avait deux membres du public qui faisaient du chahut

heckling ['hek(ə)lɪŋ] *n* chahut *m*

hectare ['hektɑːr] *n (measurement)* hectare *m*

hectic ['hektɪk] *adj* **(a)** *(busy)* agité, fiévreux; *(existence, morning)* mouvementé; **to lead a h. existence** mener une vie trépidante; **it gets very h. in the post office at Christmas** c'est la bousculade à la poste à Noël; **we had a h. time** nous ne savions où donner de la tête **(b)** *Med (fever)* hectique

hectically ['hektɪklɪ] *adv* fiévreusement

hectolitre, *US* **hectoliter** ['hektəliːtər] *n* hectolitre *m*, *F* hecto *m*

hector ['hektər] **1** *vt (person)* rudoyer **2** *vi* prendre des tons autoritaires

hectoring ['hektərɪŋ] *adj (tone etc)* autoritaire, impérieux

he'd [hiːd] **(a) = he had,** *see* **have**[2] **(b) = he would,** *see* **will**[2]

hedge[1] [hedʒ] *n* **(a)** haie *f*; *Fig* **to buy sth as a h. against inflation** acheter qch pour se mettre à l'abri de l'inflation; **h. clippers** *or* **shears** taille-haies *m inv* **(b)** *St Exch* couverture *f*; **h. ratio** ratio *m* de couverture

hedge[2] **1** *vt (field)* mettre une haie autour de; *St Exch (position)* protéger, couvrir; **to h. one's bets** *(in betting)* répartir les risques; *Fig (cover oneself)* se couvrir, éviter de se compromettre; **the laws are hedged about with exceptions** les lois sont remplies d'exceptions **2** *vi* **(a)** *(in discussion)* se réserver, éviter de se compromettre **(b)** *Horseracing* parier pour et contre **(c)** *St Exch* se couvrir **(against** contre)

▶ **hedge in** *vtsep (surround) (field)* entourer d'une haie; *(person)* entourer; **hedged in with difficulties** entouré de difficultés

▶ **hedge off** *vtsep (separate with a hedge) (field)* séparer par une haie **(from** de)

hedgehog ['hedʒhɒg] *n* hérisson *m*; *Am (porcupine)* porc-épic *m*, *pl* porcs-épics; **to curl up like a h.** se pelotonner, se recroqueviller (sur soi-même)

hedgehop ['hedʒhɒp] *vi* **(-pp-)** *Av F* voler en rase-mottes, faire du rase-mottes

hedgerow ['hedʒrəʊ] *n* bordure *f* d'arbres *ou* d'arbustes formant une haie; **animals of the hedgerows** animaux qui vivent dans les haies

hedging ['hedʒɪŋ] *n* **(a)** *(care of hedges)* entretien *m* des haies; **h. and ditching** entretien des haies et des fossés **(b)** *(hedges)* bordure *f* **(c)** *Horseracing* répartition *f* des risques **(d)** *St Exch* couverture *f* **(e)** *(in discussion etc)* hésitation *f* à prendre des décisions

hedonism ['hiːdənɪz(ə)m, 'hed-] *n* hédonisme *m*

hedonist ['hiːdənɪst, 'hed-] *n* hédoniste *mf*

hedonistic [hiːdə'nɪstɪk, hed-] *adj* hédoniste

heebie-jeebies ['hiːbɪ'jiːbɪz] *npl F* **to have the h.** *(be nervous)* avoir la frousse; **he gives me the h.** *(revolts me)* il me hérisse; *(scares me)* il me donne la chair de poule

heed[1] [hiːd] *n esp Lit* **to give** *or* **pay h. to sth/sb** faire attention à qch/qn; **to take h.** prendre garde; **to take h. of a warning** tenir compte d'un avertissement

heed[2] *vt esp Lit* tenir compte de; **his advice was not heeded** on n'a tenu aucun compte de ses conseils

heedful ['hiːdfʊl] *adj Fml* **to be h. of ...** être attentif à ...

heedless ['hiːdlɪs] *adj* **to be h. of** *(what is happening)* être inattentif à; *(the future etc)* être peu soucieux de; **they continued, h. of her warning/the danger** ils ont continué sans se soucier de son avertissement/du danger

heedlessly [ˈhiːdlɪslɪ] *adv* étourdiment, avec insouciance
hee-haw[1] [ˈhiːhɔː] *n* hi-han *m*
hee-haw[2] *vi* braire, faire hi-han
heel[1] [hiːl] *n* **(a)** (*of foot*) talon *m*; **to have the police at one's heels** avoir la police à ses trousses; **to tread on sb's heels** marcher sur les talons de qn; **to follow close on sb's heels** suivre qn de près, emboîter le pas à qn; **to take to one's heels** prendre ses jambes à son cou; *F* **to cool** *or* **kick one's heels** poireauter; **to turn on one's h.** tourner les talons; **to be down at h.** (*of shoes*) être éculé; (*of person*) avoir l'air miteux; **to come to h.** (*of dog*) venir au pied; *F* (*of person, state*) se soumettre; **h.!** (*to dog*) au pied!; **to bring sb to h.** rappeler qn à l'ordre
(b) (*of shoe, sock*) talon *m*; **high heels** talons hauts; **she was wearing heels** elle portait des talons; **h. bar** talon-minute *m*
(c) (*of bread*) croûton *m*
(d) *esp Am Sl* (*contemptible person*) chameau *m*, salaud *m*
(e) *Tech etc* (*of tool*) talon *m*; *Naut* (*of mast*) pied *m*, caisse *f*; (*of rudder*) talon
(f) (*of hoof of horse etc*) derrière *m* du sabot
heel[2] *vt* **(a)** (*shoe*) (*fit with a heel*) mettre un talon à; (*repair*) réparer le talon de; **to get one's shoes heeled** (faire) refaire le talon de ses chaussures **(b)** *Rugby* (*ball*) talonner
heel[3] *n Naut* (*of ship*) bande *f*, gîte *f*, inclinaison *f*
heel[4] *vi Naut* (*of ship*) avoir *ou* donner de la bande, prendre de la gîte
▶ **heel over** *vi* = **heel**[4]
heel and toe *n Aut* talon-pointe *m*
heelpiece [ˈhiːlpiːs] *n* (*of shoe*) contrefort *m* du talon
heeltap [ˈhiːltæp] *n* (*in shoe*) rondelle *f* en cuir (*pour talon*)
heft [heft] *vt Am F, Br Dial* **(a)** (*lift*) soulever **(b)** (*guess weight of*) soupeser
hefty [ˈheftɪ] *adj F* **(a)** (*person*) fort, solide, costaud **(b)** (*heavy*) lourd, pesant; **a h. blow** un coup violent **(c)** (*substantial*) gros, important; **a h. bill** une note de taille
Hegelian [heˈgeɪlɪən] *adj, n* hégélien, -ienne
hegemony [hɪˈgemənɪ] *n* hégémonie *f*
hegira [hɪˈdʒaɪrə] *n Muslim Rel* hégire *f*
heifer [ˈhefər] *n Agr* génisse *f*
heigh-ho [ˈheɪˈhəʊ] *int* eh bien!
height [haɪt] *n* **(a)** hauteur *f*; (*of person*) taille *f*, stature *f*; **wall two metres in h.** mur qui a deux mètres de haut; **a h. of 20 metres** une hauteur de 20 mètres; **overall h.** (*of vehicle*) hauteur totale; **what's your h.?, what h. are you?** combien mesurez-vous?; **of average h.** de taille moyenne
(b) (*of an arch*) flèche *f*, montée *f*
(c) (*altitude*) altitude *f*; **h. above sea level** altitude au-dessus du niveau de la mer; *Av* **cruising h.** altitude de croisière; **the plane was gaining/losing h.** l'avion prenait/perdait de l'altitude; **to have a good head for heights** ne pas avoir le vertige; **I'm scared of heights** j'ai le vertige; *Av* **h. indicator** altimètre *m*
(d) *Fig* (*highest point*) (*of career, glory etc*) apogée *m*; (*of eloquence*) sommet *m*; **at the h. of his glory** au faîte de la gloire; **it's the h. of madness!** c'est de la folie pure!; **this is the h. of insolence!** c'est de la plus haute insolence!; **at the h. of the storm** au plus fort de l'orage; **an actress at the h. of her career** une actrice à l'apogée de sa carrière; **at the h. of summer** en plein été; **the season is at its h.** la saison bat son plein; **it's the h. of fashion** c'est la dernière mode *ou* le dernier cri
height-adjustable *adj* réglable en hauteur
heighten [ˈhaɪt(ə)n] **1** *vt* **(a)** (*increase etc*) (*pleasure*) accroître, augmenter; (*contrast*) accentuer; (*colour etc*) relever, faire ressortir; (*impression, speculation*) renforcer; **to h. the interest in sth** augmenter l'intérêt pour qch; **to h. public awareness** sensibiliser le public; **the riots have heightened racial tensions in the city** les émeutes ont accentué *ou* aggravé les tensions raciales dans la ville **(b)** (*increase height of*) (*wall etc*) surélever, rehausser **2** *vi* (*of tension*) s'accroître
heightened [ˈhaɪt(ə)nd] *adj* accru; (*sensitivity*) exacerbé; **there is a h. awareness of the dangers of pollution** il y a une prise de conscience accrue des dangers de la pollution
heightening [ˈhaɪt(ə)nɪŋ] *n* **(a)** (*increase etc*) (*of pleasure*) accroissement *m*; **there has been a h. of speculation** il y a eu un renforcement de la spéculation **(b)** (*raising of height*) (*of wall etc*) surélévation *f*, rehaussement *m*
heights [haɪts] *npl* (*area of high ground*) éminence *f*, hauteurs *fpl*
heinous [ˈheɪnəs] *adj Fml* (*crime*) odieux, atroce, abominable
heir [eər] *n* héritier *m*; **to be h. to an estate** être l'héritier d'une propriété; **the h. to the throne** l'héritier du trône; **h. apparent** héritier présomptif; **h. presumptive** héritier présomptif (*sauf naissance d'un héritier en ligne directe*)
heir-at-law, *pl* **heirs-at-law** *n Jur* héritier *m* légitime
heiress [ˈeərɪs] *n* héritière *f*
heirloom [ˈeəluːm] *n* héritage *m*; **a family h.** (*furniture*) un meuble de famille; (*jewellery*) un bijou de famille
heist [haɪst] *n esp Am Sl* fric-frac *m*, casse *m*; **to pull a h.** faire un casse
Helen of Troy [ˈhelɪnəvˈtrɔɪ] *n* Hélène *f* de Troie
helianthus [hiːlɪˈænθəs] *n* (*flower*) hélianthe *m*, tournesol *m*
helical [ˈhelɪk(ə)l] *adj MecE* (*gear etc*) hélicoïdal, -aux; (*spring*) hélicoïde, en hélice; **h. shell** coquille *f* contournée
helicopter [ˈhelɪkɒptər] *n Av* hélicoptère *m*; **h. pilot** pilote *m* d'hélicoptère; *Mil* **h. gunship** hélicoptère de combat
▶ **helicopter in** *vtsep* (*troops, supplies*) amener en hélicoptère, héliporter
▶ **helicopter out** *vtsep* (*people*) emmener en hélicoptère, héliporter
heliograph [ˈhiːlɪəgræf] *n* (*for signalling*) héliographe *m*
heliotrope [ˈhiːlɪətrəʊp] **1** *n* (*flower*) héliotrope *m* **2** *adj* (*colour*) héliotrope *inv*
helipad [ˈhelɪpæd] *n Av* zone *f* d'atterrissage pour hélicoptère
heliport [ˈhelɪpɔːt] *n Av* héliport *m*
helium [ˈhiːlɪəm] *n Ch* hélium *m*; **h. balloon** ballon *m* gonflé à l'hélium
helix, *pl* **helices** [ˈhiːlɪks, ˈhiːlɪsiːz] *n* **(a)** *Math* hélice *f*, *Archit etc* spirale *f* **(b)** *Anat* (*of the ear*) hélix *m* **(c)** (*snail*) hélice *f*, colimaçon *m*
hell [hel] **1** *n* **(a)** enfer *m*; *Myth* les enfers
(b) *F* (*unpleasant state/experience*) **it was h. working in the mine** c'était l'enfer de travailler dans la mine; **it can be h. trying to park here** quelquefois, c'est l'enfer pour se garer ici; **to make sb's life h.** *or* **a h. on earth** faire un enfer de la vie de qn; **I feel like h.** je suis au trente-sixième dessous, je me sens horriblement mal; **to give sb h.** (*tell off*) passer un savon à qn, engueuler qn; (*give a hard time*) faire une vie d'enfer à qn; **these shoes are giving me h.** ces chaussures me font un mal de chien; **it was all h. let loose** c'était infernal; **all h. broke loose** c'était l'horreur; **there'll be h. to pay if your mother finds out** ça va barder si ta mère l'apprend
(c) *F* (*idioms*) **go to h.!** va au diable!; (*stronger*) va te faire voir!; **to h. with him!** qu'il aille au diable!; **get the h. out of here!** fiche-moi le camp d'ici!; *Br* **it's as cold as h.** il fait un froid de canard; **to run like h.** courir comme un dératé; **to work like h.** travailler comme un malade; **like h. (I will)!, the h. I will!** jamais de la vie!; **(you can wait) till h. freezes over** tu peux attendre jusqu'à la saint-Glinglin; **I wish to h. I could remember** si seulement je pouvais me souvenir; **come h. or high water** contre vents et marées; **to go h. for leather** (*running*) courir ventre à terre; (*driving*) conduire comme un fou; (*working, playing music*) travailler/jouer comme un malade; **to do sth for the h. of it** faire qch sans raison particulière; **I did it for the h. of it** je l'ai fait parce que cela me chantait; **why don't you just do it for the h. of it?** et si tu le faisais juste comme ça?; **to play merry h. with sth** foutre qch en l'air; *esp Am* **the whole country's going to h. in a handcart** tout fout le camp dans ce pays
(d) *F* (*intensifier*) **a h. of a price** un prix salé *ou* démentiel *ou* ahurissant; **you've got a h. of a nerve!** tu as un culot du diable!; **there was a** *or* **one h. of a fight** il y a eu une bagarre terrible, *très F* il y a eu une putain de bagarre; **he's a h. of a guy** c'est un type formidable *ou* un mec super; **it was a h. of a good film** c'était un sacrément bon film; **we had a h. of a time** (*bad*) on en a bavé; (*good*) on s'est super marrés; **you'll have a h. of a time** (*bad*) tu vas en baver; (*good*) tu vas te marrer; **I had a h. of a time getting here** (*bad*) j'en ai bavé pour arriver jusqu'ici, ça a été l'enfer pour arriver ici; **a h. of a lot of ...** énormément de ...; **not a h. of a lot** pas des masses; **what the h. do you think you're doing?** qu'est-ce que tu fous?; **what the h.'s going on?** qu'est-ce qui se passe, nom de Dieu?; **who the h. are you?** qui diable êtes-vous?; **what the h., you only live once** que diable, on ne vit qu'une fois
2 *int F* **(oh) h.!** zut alors!; (*stronger*) merde alors!; *F* **h.'s bells!, h.'s teeth!, h. and damnation!** (sacré) nom de nom!
he'll [hiːl] = **he will,** *see* **will**[2]
hellbender [ˈhelbendər] *n US F* (*drinking bout*) (séance *f* de) beuverie *f*
hellbent [ˈhelbent] *adj F* **to be h. on doing sth** vouloir à tout prix faire qch; **the human race seems h. on self-destruction** la race humaine semble vouloir s'autodétruire à tout prix
hellcat [ˈhelkæt] *n F* sorcière *f*, mégère *f*
hellebore [ˈhelɪbɔːr] *n* (*plant*) ellébore *m*
Hellene [ˈheliːn] *n* Hellène *mf*

Hellenic [he'lenɪk] *adj* (*people*) hellène; (*language, history*) hellénique

hellfire ['helfaɪər] *n* feu *m* de l'enfer; **h. preacher** prédicateur *m* annonçant les feux de l'enfer

hellhole ['helhəʊl] *n F* (*bar, club etc*) bouge *m*, boui-boui *m*

hellish ['helɪʃ] *F* **1** *adj* (*unpleasant*) infernal; **I feel h.** je ne me sens vraiment pas bien **2** *adv* terriblement, *F* vachement

hellishly ['helɪʃlɪ] *adv F* diaboliquement, *F* vachement

hello [he'ləʊ] *int* bonjour!, *F* salut!; (*in evening*) bonsoir!, *F* salut!; *Tel* allô; **h. there, wake up!** (*calling attention*) holà! réveille-toi!; **h., what's this?** (*indicating surprise*) tiens!, qu'est-ce que c'est que ça?; **to say h.** dire bonjour; **say h. to him for me** dis-lui bonjour de ma part; **she gave them a cheery 'h.'** elle leur a lancé un 'bonjour' joyeux

hell-raiser *n F* chahuteur *m*

hell-raising *n F* vie *f* de patachon, vie de bâton de chaise; **his h. days** sa vie de patachon

helluva ['heləvə] *F* = **hell of a,** *see* **hell 1 (d)**

helm [helm] *n Naut* gouvernail *m*, timon *m*; **the man at the h.** *Naut* l'homme de barre; *Fig* l'homme qui tient le gouvernail *ou* qui dirige l'entreprise; *Naut, Fig* **to be at the h.** être à la barre; *Fig* **to take (over) the h.** prendre la direction des affaires

helmet ['helmɪt] *n* (*of soldier, fireman etc*) casque *m*; **(crash) h.** casque protecteur

helmsman, *pl* **-men** ['helmzmən] *n Naut* homme *m* de barre, timonier *m*

help[1] [help] *n* **(a)** aide *f*, assistance *f*; (*when in danger etc*) secours *m*, aide; **with God's h.** avec l'aide de Dieu, grâce à Dieu; **to shout for h.** crier au secours, appeler à l'aide; **he's past h.** (*is dying*) il est perdu; (*is crazy, stupid*) on ne peut rien pour lui; **can I be of (any) h.?** puis-je vous aider?; **to be of h. to sb** être d'un grand secours à qn; **some students need h. to decide which course to take** certains étudiants ont besoin qu'on les aide à choisir leur cursus; **she needs h.** (*from a psychiatrist etc*) il faut qu'elle voie un psychiatre, elle a des problèmes psychologiques; **if you think that's funny, you need h.** si tu trouves ça drôle, c'est que tu dois avoir un problème; **to give h. to sb** aider qn; (*at accident etc*) porter secours à qn; **to provide some financial h.** offrir une aide financière; **the map wasn't much h.** la carte n'a pas servi à grand-chose; **for all the h. you've been** pour ce que tu nous as aidés; **I had h.** (*I didn't do it on my own*) on m'a aidé; *F* **a (fat) lot of h. <u>you</u> are** tu parles d'une aide!; **to come to sb's h.** venir au secours de qn

(b) to be a h. to sb rendre service à qn; **my daughter's been a great h.** ma fille m'a bien rendu service; **that was a big h. (to me)** ça m'a beaucoup aidé; *Iron* **you're a great h.!** merci pour ton aide!

(c) (*helper*) aide *mf*; *esp Br* **daily h.** femme *f* de ménage; *esp Br* **home h.** aide *f* ménagère; **mother's h.** aide *f* familiale

(d) *esp Am* (*pl* **help**) (*worker*) **a hired h.** un ouvrier *ou* (*white collar*) employé intérimaire; **we need more h.** on a besoin de plus de personnel

(e) (*alternative*) **there was no h. for it** il n'y avait rien d'autre à faire

(f) *Comptr* **h. button** case *f* d'aide; **h. function** fonction *f* d'aide; **h. menu** menu *m* d'aide; **h. screen** écran *m* d'aide; **h. window** fenêtre *f* d'aide

help[2] **1** *vt* **(a)** [①A40,C,1,a] (*person*) aider; **to h. one another** s'entraider; **can I** *or* **may I h. you?** puis-je vous aider?; (*in shop, restaurant*) que désirez-vous?; (*on telephone*) que puis-je faire pour vous?; *Jur* **do you swear to tell the truth, so h. you God?** jurez-vous de dire la vérité, que Dieu vous vienne en aide?; **so h. me God!** (*it's the truth*) c'est la vérité!; *F* **so h. me** je jure; **come and h. me** venez m'aider *ou* me donner un coup de main; **he helped me with my homework** il m'a aidé à faire mes devoirs; **to h. sb (to) do sth** aider qn à faire qch; **he helped the old lady up the stairs** il a aidé la vieille dame à monter l'escalier; **to h. sb on/off with their coat** aider qn à mettre/enlever son manteau; **to h. sb out of a difficulty** aider qn à se tirer d'une difficulté; **he helped the ball into the goal** il a donné un petit coup au ballon pour le faire entrer dans les buts; *Prov* **God helps those who h. themselves** aide-toi et le ciel t'aidera; **it helped me knowing that someone was waiting for me** ça m'a aidé de savoir que quelqu'un m'attendait; **a man is helping the police with their enquiries** un homme est interrogé par la police; **it helped to give the impression that ...** cela a contribué à donner l'impression que ..., à cause de cela, on avait l'impression que ...; **h.!** (*when in danger etc*) au secours!; **h.!, I'm late!** mon Dieu!, je suis en retard!

(b) (*improve*) (*digestion, progress*) faciliter; **that doesn't h. the situation, that doesn't h. much** cela ne nous avance pas (beaucoup); *Iron* **to h. matters, we had a puncture** pour ne rien arranger, nous avons crevé

(c) (*at table*) (*person*) servir; **to h. sb to soup/wine** servir du potage/verser du vin à qn; **h. yourself** servez-vous; **to h. oneself to sth** (*serve*) se servir en *ou* de qch; *F, Iron* (*steal*) voler *ou* prendre *ou* chiper qch

(d) (*prevent*) (*with negation expressed or implied*) **it can't be helped!** tant pis!, il n'y a rien à faire, on n'y peut rien; **I can't h. laughing** je ne peux pas m'empêcher de rire; **I couldn't h. overhearing** je n'ai pu m'empêcher de surprendre la conversation; **I can't h. wondering** je ne peux pas m'empêcher de poser la question; **I can't h. it** c'est plus fort que moi, je ne peux pas m'en empêcher; (*it can't be helped*) je n'y peux rien; **they can't h. being born there** ils n'ont pas demandé à naître là; **I'm not going back if I can h. it** si j'ai le choix, je n'y retournerai pas

2 *vi* **(a)** aider; **can I h.?** est-ce que je peux faire quelque chose?; **I was only trying to h.!** je voulais seulement vous/les/*etc* aider!; **he offered to h. with the clearing up** il a proposé de nous/les/*etc* aider à ranger; **it helps if you can speak the language** c'est plus facile si on parle la langue; **forgetting the map didn't h. (much)** le fait d'avoir oublié la carte n'a pas arrangé les choses; **it's near the post office if that helps** (*of information*) c'est près du bureau de poste si ça peut vous aider; **every little helps** les petits ruisseaux font les grandes rivières

(b) (*avoid*) **don't be away longer than you can h.** tâchez d'être absent le moins de temps possible

▶ **help out 1** *vi* (*help*) aider; **everyone helped out with the cleaning up** tout le monde a aidé à nettoyer; **I could h. out with the cooking** je pourrais vous/les/*etc* aider à faire les repas **2** *vtas* (*help*) aider; **I need £20, can you h. me out?** j'ai besoin de 20 livres, est-ce que tu peux me les avancer?; **they helped him out with food and money** ils l'ont aidé en lui donnant de la nourriture et de l'argent, ils lui ont donné de la nourriture et de l'argent pour l'aider

help desk *n* service *m* d'assistance téléphonique

helper ['helpər] *n* aide *mf*; (*assistant*) assistant, -ante; **voluntary h.** bénévole *mf*

helpful ['helpfʊl] *adj* **(a)** (*person*) secourable, serviable; **he always tries to be h.** il essaie toujours de rendre service; **he was not being very h.** il n'a pas fait grand-chose pour nous aider; (*wasn't telling us much*) il ne disait pas grand-chose **(b)** (*book, advice*) utile; **this dictionary is not very h.** ce dictionnaire ne sert pas à grand-chose

helpfully ['helpfʊlɪ] *adv* **she very h. offered/lent us ...** elle a eu la gentillesse *ou* l'amabilité de nous offrir/prêter ...; **it's very h. indexed** l'index est très utile; **it's h. explained in the brochure** c'est très bien expliqué dans la brochure; *Iron* **someone had very h. let the battery run down** quelqu'un a eu l'amabilité de décharger la pile

helpfulness ['helpfʊlnɪs] *n* **(a)** (*of person*) serviabilité *f* **(b)** (*of book etc*) utilité

helping ['helpɪŋ] **1** *adj* **to lend a h. hand** aider; **to give sb a h. hand** donner un coup de main à qn **2** *n* (*of food*) portion *f*; **two helpings of soup** deux assiettées *fpl* de soupe; **I had two helpings** *or* **a second h.** j'en ai repris, je me suis resservi

helpless ['helplɪs] *adj* (*powerless*) faible, impuissant; (*orphan etc*) sans appui, délaissé; (*handicapped person*) infirme; (*ship*) désemparé; **I am h. in the matter** je n'y puis *ou* peux rien; **a h. onlooker** un spectateur impuissant; **we were h. to prevent what was happening** nous ne pouvions rien faire contre ce qui se passait; **I was h. with laughter** je n'en pouvais plus de rire; *F* **he's one of the h. sort** il est incapable de se débrouiller; **carry it yourself, you're not h.** débrouille-toi, tu peux très bien le porter tout seul

helplessly ['helplɪslɪ] *adv* (*to struggle*) en vain; **to gesture h.** lever les mains en signe d'impuissance; **to watch h.** regarder en spectateur impuissant; **they were h. convulsed with laughter** ils n'en pouvaient plus de rire

helplessness ['helplɪsnɪs] *n* impuissance *f*; **because of his h. around the house** parce qu'il est incapable de se débrouiller tout seul chez lui

helpline ['helplaɪn] *n Tel* (*for information*) ligne *f* d'assistance; (*for battered women*) = SOS femmes battues; (*for victims of child abuse*) = SOS enfants martyrs

helter-skelter ['heltə'skeltər] **1** *adv* (*to run, flee*) pêle-mêle, à la débandade **2** *adj* **h. flight** fuite désordonnée, débandade *f* **3** *n Br* (*at fairground*) toboggan *m*

hem[1] [hem] *n Sewing* **(a)** (*of garment*) bord *m*; (*turned over part*) ourlet *m*; **let the h. down** j'ai rallongé ma jupe en en défaisant l'ourlet **(b)** = **hemline**

hem[2] *vt Sewing* ourler, faire l'ourlet de

hem[3] *int* hem!, hum!

hem⁴ *vi* = **hum² 1(b)**
▸ **hem in** *vtsep* (*surround*) (*enemy troops*) entourer, cerner; (*place*) investir; **hemmed in by high mountains** enserré entre de hautes montagnes
hema- ['hi:mə] *pref US Med* = **haema-**
he-man, *pl* **-men** ['hi:mæn, -men] *n F* homme *m* viril
hemato- [hi:mə'təʊ] *pref US Med* = **haemato-**
hemicycle ['hemɪsaɪk(ə)l] *n Archit* hémicycle *m*
hemiplegia [hemɪ'pli:dʒɪə] *n Med* hémiplégie *f*
hemisphere ['hemɪsfɪər] *n* hémisphère *m*; *Geog* **the northern/southern h.** l'hémisphère nord *ou* boréal/sud *ou* austral; **left/right h.** (*of brain*) hémisphère gauche/droit
hemispherical [hemɪ'sferɪk(ə)l] *adj* hémisphérique
hemline ['hemlaɪn] *n Sewing* bas *m* de l'ourlet; **hemlines are coming down** la mode rallonge; **daring hemlines** des jupes très courtes
hemlock ['hemlɒk] *n* ciguë *f*
hemo- ['hi:məʊ] *pref US Med* = **haemo-**
hemp [hemp] *n* **(a)** (*plant*) chanvre *m*; *Tex* chanvre, filasse *f* **(b)** *Pharm etc* **Indian h.** chanvre *m* indien, hachisch *m*
hemstitch¹ ['hemstɪtʃ] *n Sewing* ourlet *m* à jour
hemstitch² *vt* (*handkerchief etc*) ourler à jour
hen [hen] *n* **(a)** (*chicken*) poule *f*; *F* **h. party** soirée *f* entre femmes; (*before marriage*) = soirée où une femme enterre sa vie de jeune fille **(b)** (*female bird*) femelle *f*; **h. bird** oiseau *m* femelle; **h. pheasant** (poule *f*) faisane *f* **(c)** *Scot F* (*form of address to woman*) **here's your change, h.** voilà votre monnaie ma petite dame
henbane ['henbeɪn] *n* (*plant*) jusquiame *f*, herbe *f* aux poules
hence [hens] *adv* **(a)** (*referring to consequence*) de là, d'où, en conséquence; **h. his anger** de là *ou* d'où sa fureur **(b)** (*referring to time*) dorénavant, désormais, à partir d'aujourd'hui; **five years h.** dans cinq ans **(c)** *Arch, Lit* (*referring to place*) **(from) h.** d'ici; **five miles h.** à deux lieues d'ici
henceforth [hens'fɔ:θ], **henceforward** [hens'fɔ:wəd] *adv Fml* désormais, dorénavant, à l'avenir
henchman, *pl* **-men** ['hentʃmən] *n Pol etc Pej* acolyte *m*
hencoop ['henku:p] *n* cage *f* à poules
henhouse ['henhaʊs] *n* poulailler *m*
henna ['henə] **1** *n* (*shrub, dye*) henné *m* **2** *vt* **to h. one's hair** se faire un henné; **hennaed hair** cheveux teints au henné
henpecked ['henpekt] *adj* **h. husband** mari mené par le bout du nez; **he's h.** sa femme le mène par le bout du nez
henroost ['henru:st] *n* **(a)** (*perch*) juchoir *m*, perchoir *m* **(b)** = **henhouse**
Henry the Eighth, Henry VIII ['henrɪ ðɪ:eɪtθ] *n* Henri *m* VIII
hep [hep] *adj Old-fashioned F* à la page, dans le vent
heparin ['hepərɪn] *n Pharm* héparine *f*
hepatic [he'pætɪk] *adj Anat etc* hépatique
hepatitis [hepə'taɪtɪs] *n Med* hépatite *f*; **h. A/B/C** hépatite A/B/C
hepatology [hepə'tɒlədʒɪ] *n Med* hépatologie *f*
heptagon ['heptəgən] *n Math* heptagone *m*
her¹ [①**A26**,a-c; **B17-18**,2] (*unstressed* [hər]; *stressed* [hɜ:r]) *pers pron* (*of person, female animal, certain things personified*) **(a)** (*unstressed*) (*direct*) la; (*before a vowel sound*) l'; (*indirect*) lui; (*reflexive, after preposition*) elle; **I hate h.** je la déteste; **have you seen h.?** l'avez-vous vue?; **I shall tell h. so** je le lui dirai; **look at h.** regardez-la; **tell h.** dites-lui; **I am thinking of h.** je pense à elle; **I remember h.** je me souviens d'elle; **she closed the door behind h.** elle referma la porte derrière elle; *Fml* **Poland's friends deserted h.** (*country*) la Pologne a été abandonnée par ses amis; **the enemy sank h.** (*ship*) il a été coulé par l'ennemi; *F* **I'll get h. started** (*car etc*) je vais la faire démarrer
(b) (*stressed*) elle; *Lit* (*with dem force*) celle; **I can forgive her son but not <u>her</u>** je peux pardonner à son fils, mais pas à elle; *Lit* **to h. who should take offence at this I would say ...** à celle qui s'en offenserait je dirais ...; **who better than h. to break the news?** qui, mieux qu'elle, saurait annoncer la nouvelle?
(c) (*complement of verb* **to be**) **it's h.!** c'est elle!; **that's h.!** la voilà!
her² *poss adj* [①**A30**,8; **A42**,3; **B19-20**,E,1] son, *f* sa, *pl* ses; **h. hat** son chapeau; **h. dress/dresses** sa robe/ses robes; **h. father and mother** son père et sa mère; *Admin* ses père et mère; **h. eyes are blue** elle a les yeux bleus; **she has hurt h. hand** elle s'est fait mal à la main; **H. Majesty** sa Majesté; *Fml* **France reassured h. allies** la France rassura ses alliés; **the ship and h. crew** le navire et son équipage
her³ *n F* **it's a h. not a him** (*of baby*) c'est une fille, pas un garçon; (*of animal*) c'est une femelle, pas un mâle
herald¹ ['herəld] *n* **(a)** héraut *m*; **the Heralds' College** le Collège héraldique (*à Londres*) **(b)** *Fig* (*of spring etc*) présage *m*
herald² *vt Fml, Lit* (*arrival etc*) annoncer, proclamer; **these negotiations h. a new era for world peace** ces négociations marquent le début d'une ère nouvelle pour la paix mondiale; **to h. the dawn** annoncer l'aube
heraldic [hɪ'rældɪk] *adj* héraldique; **h. bearing** armoirie *f*, blason *m*
heraldry ['herəldrɪ] *n* héraldique *f*; (*coat of arms*) blason *m*; **book of h.** armorial *m*, -aux
herb [hɜ:b] *n* (*plant*) herbe *f*; *Culin* **herbs** (fines) herbes; **herbs and spices** condiments *mpl*; **medicinal herbs** plantes *fpl* médicinales; **h. tea** infusion *f*, tisane *f* (*d'herbes*); **h. garden** = carré *m* où poussent les herbes fines
herbaceous [hɜ:'beɪʃəs] *adj Bot* herbacé; **h. border** bordure *f* de plantes herbacées
herbage ['hɜ:bɪdʒ] *n* (*plants*) herbes *fpl*, herbage(s) *m(pl)*
herbal ['hɜ:b(ə)l] **1** *n Old-fashioned* (*book*) herbier *m* **2** *adj* (*drink*) fait avec des plantes; (*remedy*) à base d'herbes *ou* de plantes; **h. infusion** infusion *f*, tisane *f*; **h. tea** tisane; **h. medicine** médecine *f* par les plantes, phytothérapie *f*; **h. cigarettes** cigarettes *fpl* aux plantes
herbalist ['hɜ:bəlɪst] *n* herboriste *mf*
herbarium [hɜ:'beərɪəm] *n* herbier *m*
herbicide ['hɜ:bɪsaɪd] *n* herbicide *m*
herbivore ['hɜ:bɪvɔ:r] *n* (*animal*) herbivore *m*
herbivorous [hɜ:'bɪvərəs] *adj* (*animal*) herbivore
Herculean [hɜ:kjʊ'li:ən] *adj* (*effort, strength*) herculéen
Hercules ['hɜ:kjʊli:z] *n Myth, Astron* Hercule *m*; *Fig* (*strong man*) hercule *m*; **H. monitor** moniteur *m* Hercules
herd¹ [hɜ:d] *n* (*of cattle, elephants etc*) troupeau *m*; (*of deer*) troupeau, *Spec* harde *f*; (*of horses etc*) troupe *f*, bande *f*; (*of people*) troupeau, foule *f*; **the h. instinct** (*in animals, people*) l'instinct grégaire; **the common h.** le peuple, *Pej* la canaille, la populace
herd² *vt* (*cattle*) garder, surveiller; *F* (*tourists etc*) diriger; **the cattle were herded into the barn** on a fait entrer le bétail dans la grange; **the candidates were then all herded into the waiting room** on a alors entassé les candidats dans la salle d'attente; **the prisoners were herded onto trucks** on a entassé les prisonniers dans des camions
▸ **herd together 1** *vi* (*of animals*) (*live in herds*) vivre en troupeaux; (*form a herd*) s'assembler en troupeau; *F* (*of people*) se regrouper **2** *vtsep* (*cattle etc*) rassembler en troupeau
herder ['hɜ:dər] *n esp US* = **herdsman**
herdsman, *pl* **-men** ['hɜ:dzmən] *n esp Br* gardien *m* de troupeau
here [hɪər] **1** *adv* [①**A23**,3,b] **(a)** (*this place*) ici; **come h.!** (venez) ici!; **in h., please** par ici, s'il vous plaît; **near h.** près d'ici; **over h.** par ici; **from h. to there** d'ici à là-bas; **Mr Green's not h. today** M. Green n'est pas là aujourd'hui; **over h. in Scotland** ici, en Écosse; **h. and now** immédiatement, tout de suite; **it's h. to stay** (*of fashion*) cela restera; **h. lies ...** (*on tombstone*) ci-gît ...; *Lit* **h. below** (*on this earth*) ici-bas
(b) (*point in time, argument etc*) **I think we could break h. for lunch** je crois que nous pouvons nous arrêter là pour déjeuner; **h. I am referring to taxation** (*at this point*) c'est aux impôts que je fais allusion; **we disagree h.** c'est là que nous ne sommes pas d'accord; **h.'s what you have to do** voilà ce que tu as à faire
(c) h.'s your hat! voici *ou* voilà votre chapeau!; **h. you are!** (*on seeing, finding sb*) vous voici!, vous voilà!; (*giving sth*) tenez!; **h. we are!** (*on finding sth*) voilà! j'ai trouvé!; (*on arriving somewhere*) nous y sommes!, nous voilà arrivés! *ou* rendus!; **h. she comes!** la voici (qui vient)!; **h. I am!** me voici!, me voilà!; **h. is** *or* **h. we have a woman who ...** voici une femme qui ...; **my friend h. will tell you** mon ami que voici vous le dira; *F* **this h. ...** ce..., *f* cette ...; **h. goes!** allons-y!; **h. we go (again)!** (*said with a sigh*) c'est reparti!; (*annoyed*) encore?
(d) (*esp over drink etc*) **h.'s to you!** à votre santé!; **h.'s to the success of your venture!** à votre succès!
(e) h. and there partout, ça et là, *Lit* par-ci, par-là; **h., there and everywhere** (un peu) partout; **neither h. nor there** ni ici ni ailleurs; *Fig* **that's neither h. nor there** cela n'a aucun rapport
2 *int* **(a)** (*at roll call*) présent!
(b) (*to attract sb's attention*) **h.! come and look at this** eh! viens voir ça!; **h., take this** tiens, prends ça
(c) (*to express annoyance*) **h., that's my chair!** eh, c'est ma chaise!; **h., stop that!** écoute, tu arrêtes un peu!
3 *n* **the h. and now** le présent
hereabout(s) ['hɪərəbaʊt, -s] *adv* près d'ici, par ici
hereafter [hɪər'ɑ:ftər] **1** *adv Fml* **(a)** (*of position*) (*in book, writings etc*) ci-après, ci-dessous **(b)** *esp Jur* (*of time*) dorénavant, désormais **(c)** (*after death*) dans l'autre monde **2** *n Lit* **the h.** l'au-delà *m*; **in the h.** dans l'autre monde, dans l'au-delà

hereby [hɪə'baɪ, 'hɪəbaɪ] *adv Fml* par ceci, par ce moyen, par là; *Jur* par la présente *ou* les présentes; **the council h. declares that ...** le conseil déclare par le présent acte que ...
hereditary [hɪ'redɪt(ə)rɪ] *adj (disease etc)* héréditaire
heredity [hɪ'redɪtɪ] *n* hérédité *f*
herein [hɪər'ɪn] *adv Lit, Jur* **(a)** *(of place, position)* ici, en ce lieu; *(in document)* dans ce document; **the letter enclosed h.** la lettre ci-incluse **(b)** *(in this matter)* sur ce point
heresy ['herəsɪ] *n Rel, Fig* hérésie *f*; **it smacks of h.** *(of opinion)* c'est une hérésie
heretic ['herətɪk] *n Rel, Fig* hérétique *mf*
heretical [hɪ'retɪk(ə)l] *adj Rel, Fig* hérétique
hereto [hɪə'tuː, 'hɪətuː] *adv Jur* **annexed h., h. annexed** ci-joint
heretofore ['hɪətʊ'fɔːr] *adv Arch, Lit* jusqu'ici; **as h.** comme par le passé
hereunder [hɪər'ʌndər] *adv Jur etc* ci-dessous
hereupon ['hɪərəpɒn] *adv Jur etc* là-dessus; **h. he left** sur ce *ou* là-dessus, il partit
herewith [hɪə'wɪθ] *adv* **(a)** = **hereby (b)** *Com* **price list h. enclosed** prix-courant ci-inclus *ou* sous ce pli
heritable ['herɪtəb(ə)l] *adj* **(a)** *Biol (disease)* héréditaire **(b)** *Jur (right)* héréditaire; *(property)* = dont on peut hériter; *(person)* capable d'hériter
heritage ['herɪtɪdʒ] *n* héritage *m*, patrimoine *m*; *(of nation, humanity)* patrimoine; **h. site** site *m* patrimoine; **h. tourism** tourisme *m* culturel; **h. trail** = parcours *m* touristique qui va d'un lieu historique à un autre
hermaphrodite [hɜː'mæfrədaɪt] *adj, n Zool, Bot* hermaphrodite *m*
hermaphroditic [hɜːmæfrə'dɪtɪk] *adj* hermaphrodite
hermetic [hɜː'metɪk] *adj* hermétique; *Fig* **the university was a h. world** l'université était un monde très fermé *ou* hermétique
hermetically [hɜː'metɪklɪ] *adv (sealed)* hermétiquement
hermit ['hɜːmɪt] *n* ermite *m*; **to live like a h.** vivre en solitaire *ou* en ermite; **h. crab** bernard-l'ermite *m*
hermitage ['hɜːmɪtɪdʒ] *n* ermitage *m*
hernia ['hɜːnɪə] *n Med* hernie *f*; **to have a h.** avoir une hernie
hero, *pl* **-oes** ['hɪərəʊ, -əʊz] *n* héros *m*; **a sporting h.** un champion sportif; **h. worship** adoration *f*, idolâtrie *f*; *F* **my h.!** mon héros!
Herod ['herəd] *n Hist* Hérode *m*
heroic [hɪ'rəʊɪk] *adj* héroïque; **h. deed** acte *m* d'héroïsme; *Liter* **h. poem** poème *m* épique; *Liter* **h. verse/couplet** vers *m* décasyllabe/distique *m* héroïque
heroically [hɪ'rəʊɪklɪ] *adv* héroïquement
heroics [hɪ'rəʊɪks] *npl* **(a)** *Pej (behaviour)* coup *m* d'éclat; *(in opera)* emphase *f* **(b)** *(heroic efforts)* efforts *mpl* héroïques
heroin ['herəʊɪn] *n Ch, Pharm* héroïne *f*; **h. addict** héroïnomane *mf*
heroine ['herəʊɪn] *n* héroïne *f*
heroism ['herəʊɪz(ə)m] *n* héroïsme *m*
heron ['herən] *n (bird)* héron *m*
hero-worship *vt (person)* idolâtrer
herpes ['hɜːpiːz] *n Med* herpès *m*; **to have h.** avoir de l'herpès; **h. simplex** herpès simplex; **h. virus** virus *m* de l'herpès; **h. zoster** zona *m*
herring ['herɪŋ] *n (fish)* hareng *m*; **h. boat** harenguier *m*; **h. fleet** flotille *f* de harenguiers
herringbone ['herɪŋbəʊn] *n* **(a) h. (pattern)** dessin *m* à chevrons **(b)** *Sewing* **h. (stitch)** point *m* croisé, point d'épine **(c)** *Ski* montée *f* en ciseaux *ou* en pas de canard
hers [hɜːz] *poss pron* [①A30,8; B20,E,2] le sien, la sienne, *pl* les siens, les siennes; **this book is h.** ce livre est à elle *ou* lui appartient; **a friend of h.** un(e) de ses ami(e)s, un(e) ami(e) à elle; **it's no business of h.** ce n'est pas son affaire
herself [hɜː'self] *pers pron* [①A29] **(a)** *(emphatic)* elle-même; **she did all the work h.** elle a fait tout le travail elle-même *ou* toute seule; **she's looking (quite) h. again** *(after illness)* elle paraît complètement remise; **she's not h. today** elle n'est pas elle-même aujourd'hui, elle n'est pas dans son état normal aujourd'hui

(b) [①B26,D] *(reflexive)* se; **she hurt h.** elle s'est fait mal

(c) *(after preposition)* elle(-même); **'well, well!' she said to h.** 'eh bien!' se dit-elle; **she isn't being honest with h.** elle n'est pas honnête avec elle-même; **she kept one for h.** elle s'en est gardé un/une pour elle; **she painted a picture of h.** elle a fait son autoportrait; **she was living by h.** elle vivait seule

Herts [hɑːts] *abbr* **Hertfordshire**
hertz [hɜːts] *n El* hertz *m*
he's [hiːz] **(a)** = **he is,** *see* **be (b)** = **he has,** *see* **have²**
hesitancy ['hezɪtənsɪ] *n* hésitation *f*
hesitant ['hezɪtənt] *adj* hésitant, irrésolu; **I would be h. to ...** j'hésiterais à ...; **he's a very h. speaker** il hésite beaucoup en parlant
hesitantly ['hezɪtəntlɪ] *adv* avec hésitation
hesitate ['hezɪteɪt] **1** *vi (in speaking, acting)* hésiter; **without hesitating** sans hésiter **2** *vt* **to h. to do sth** hésiter à faire qch
hesitation [hezɪ'teɪʃən] *n* hésitation *f*; **without (the slightest) h.** sans (la moindre) hésitation; **he has no h. about it** il n'a pas le moindre doute à ce sujet
hessian ['hesɪən] *n Tex* toile *f* de jute
hetero ['hetərəʊ] *adj, n F* = **heterosexual**
heterodox ['hetərəʊdɒks] *adj* hétérodoxe
heterogeneous [hetərə'dʒiːnɪəs] *adj* hétérogène; *Mktg* **h. shopping goods** produits *mpl* d'achat réfléchi hétérogènes
heterosexual [hetərəʊ'seksjʊəl] *adj, n* hétérosexuel, -elle
het up [he'tʌp] *adj Br F (annoyed)* fâché, en rogne; *(upset, tense)* énervé, à cran; **don't get h. about it** ne t'en fais pas pour cela
heuristic [hjʊ'rɪstɪk] **1** *adj* heuristique; **h. model** modèle *m* heuristique **2** *n* [①A10,c] **heuristics** heuristique *f*
hew [hjuː] *vt (pt* **hewed** [hjuːd]; *pp* **hewed, hewn** [hjuːn]) *(with axe, chisel etc)* couper, tailler; *(stone)* tailler, équarrir, dresser; **to h. coal** abattre le charbon
▶ **hew down** *vtsep (cut down) (tree)* abattre
▶ **hew off** *vtsep (branch)* abattre
▶ **hew out** *vtsep* creuser; **the cavern had been hewn out of the rock** la caverne a été creusée dans la pierre
hewer ['hjuːər] *n (of stones)* tailleur *m*
hex¹ [heks] *n Am F (spell)* sortilège *m*, (mauvais) sort *m*; **to put a h. on sb/sth** jeter un sort à qn/qch
hex² *vt Am F* jeter un sort à
hex³ *Comptr* **1** *n* notation *f* hexadécimale; **in h.** en hexadécimal **2** *adj* **h. code** code *m* hexadécimal, notation *f* hexadécimale; **h. file** fichier *m* hexadécimal
hexadecimal [heksə'desəm(ə)l] *adj Comptr* hexadécimal
hexagon ['heksəgən] *n Math* hexagone *m*
hexagonal [hek'sægən(ə)l] *adj* hexagonal
hexameter [hek'sæmɪtər] *n Liter* hexamètre *m*
hey [heɪ] *int* **(a)** *(to attract attention)* hé!, holà! **(b) h. presto!** passez muscade!, le tour est joué!; **h., that's a good idea!** hé, c'est une bonne idée, ça!
heyday ['heɪdeɪ] *n* apogée *m*; **in its h. it was one of the busiest ports in the world** à son heure de gloire, c'était l'un des ports les plus importants du monde; **to be in the h. of youth** être dans *ou* à la fleur de l'âge
HGH [eɪtʃdʒiːeɪtʃ] *n Biol (abbr* **human growth hormone)** hormone *f* de croissance
HGV [eɪtʃdʒiː'viː] *n Br Admin (abbr* **heavy goods vehicle)** poids lourd *m*; **HGV licence** permis *m* poids lourd
hi [haɪ] *int* **(a)** *F (hello)* salut! **(b)** *(to attract attention)* hé!, là-bas!, ohé!
hiatus, *pl* **-uses** [haɪ'eɪtəs, -əsɪz] **(a)** *Fml (gap in series, text etc)* lacune *f* **(b)** *Fml (pause in conversation etc)* silence *m*; *(pause in negotiation etc)* interruption *f*; **apart from a h. between 1923 and 1925** mis à part une interruption entre 1923 et 1925; *Med* **h. hernia** hernie *f* hiatale **(c)** *Gram* hiatus *m*
hibernate ['haɪbəneɪt] *vi* hiberner
hibernation [haɪbə'neɪʃən] *n also Comptr* hibernation *f*; **to go into h.** hiberner
hibiscus [hɪ'bɪskəs] *n (plant)* ketmie *f*, hibiscus *m*
hiccup¹, hiccough ['hɪkʌp] *n* **(a)** hoquet *m*; **to have (the) hiccups** avoir le hoquet **(b)** *Fig (problem)* problème *m*, *F* hic *m*; **there's been some sort of h. with the delivery** il y a eu un hic à la livraison
hiccup², hiccough *vi* hoqueter
hick [hɪk] *Am F* **1** *n* paysan *m*, rustaud *m* **2** *adj* **a h. town** un bled
hickey ['hɪkɪ] *n Am F* **(a)** *(spot)* bouton *m*; *(love bite)* suçon *m* **(b)** *(gadget)* machin *m*, truc *m*
hickory ['hɪkərɪ] *n (tree or wood)* noyer *m* (blanc) d'Amérique, hickory *m*
hid *see* **hide²**
hidden ['hɪd(ə)n] **1** *pp see* **hide² 2** *adj (difficulty, treasure etc)* caché; **I have h. reserves** j'ai encore des réserves; *Fin* **h. reserves** réserve *f* latente; *Com* **h. defects** défauts *ou* vices *mpl* cachés; **h. extras** dépenses *fpl* supplémentaires inattendues; **no h. extras** garanti tout compris; **she has h. talents** elle a des talents cachés; *Fig* **h. hand** influence *f* occulte
hide¹ [haɪd] *n Br (place for hunter etc)* affût *m*, cachette *f*
hide² *(pt* **hid** [hɪd]; *pp* **hidden** ['hɪd(ə)n]) **1** *vt* cacher; *(feelings, emotions)* dissimuler; **to h. sth from sb** cacher qch à qn; *(not divulge information)* taire qch à qn; **I've got nothing to h.** je n'ai rien à cacher; **to h. one's face** se cacher le visage; **where has she hidden herself?** où est-elle allée se cacher *ou F* se fourrer?; **they hid him from the police** ils l'ont

caché pour que la police ne le trouve pas; **to h. sth from sight** soustraire qch aux regards; **trees h. the house from sight** les arbres cachent la maison; **clouds hid the sun** des nuages voilaient le soleil; *Fig* **to h. one's light under a bushel** cacher son talent; *Fig* **he doesn't exactly h. his light under a bushel** il ne se prend pas pour le quart de la moitié d'un citron, ce n'est pas la modestie qui l'étouffe

2 *vi* se cacher (**from sb** de qn); **have you been hiding from me?** tu te caches?; **she was hiding in a corner** (*of shy person*) elle restait dans son coin; **to h. behind an excuse/statistics** prétexter une excuse/les statistiques; *Fig* **to h. behind sb** se réfugier derrière qn

hide[3] *n* (*skin*) (*of animal*) peau *f*, dépouille *f*; *Com* (*leather*) cuir *m*; *F* **to save one's h.** sauver sa peau; *F* **I haven't seen h. nor hair of her** je ne l'ai pas vue du tout

▶ **hide away 1** *vi* = **hide**[2] *2* **2** *vtas* = **hide**[2] **1**

▶ **hide out** *vi* (*be in hiding*) se cacher, se terrer

hide-and-seek, *Am* **hide-and-go-seek** *n* cache-cache *m*; **to play h.** jouer à cache-cache

hideaway ['haɪdəweɪ] *n* cachette *f*, *F* planque *f*

hidebound ['haɪdbaʊnd] *adj* (*person*) aux vues étroites, plein de préjugés; (*attitude*) rigide; **the country's h. legal profession** les hommes de loi conservateurs et bornés de ce pays

hideous ['hɪdɪəs] *adj* (*appearance etc*) hideux, affreux, effroyable; (*crime*) horrible, odieux; **what a h. painting!** quelle peinture abominable!

hideously ['hɪdɪəslɪ] *adv* hideusement, affreusement

hideousness ['hɪdɪəsnɪs] *n* laideur *f*; **the h. of his wounds/the crime** ses blessures abominables/le crime abominable

hide-out *n* cachette *f*, *F* planque *f*; **so this is your h.!** alors, c'est ici que tu te caches!

hidey-hole ['haɪdɪhəʊl] *n F* cachette *f*

hiding[1] ['haɪdɪŋ] *n* **to go into h.** se cacher; **to be in h.** se tenir caché, se cacher; **to live in h.** vivre dans la clandestinité; **to come out of h.** sortir de sa cachette; (*stop living in hiding*) sortir de la clandestinité; **h. place** cachette *f*

hiding[2] *n F* (*beating*) raclée *f*, rossée *f*, volée *f*; **to give sb a good h.** donner une raclée à qn; **to be on a h. to nothing** n'avoir aucune chance (de réussir)

hierarchic(al) [haɪə'rɑːkɪk, -ɪk(ə)l] *adj* hiérarchique; **in h. order** par ordre hiérarchique

hierarchy ['haɪərɑːkɪ] *n* hiérarchie *f*

hieroglyph ['haɪərəglɪf] *n* hiéroglyphe *m*

hieroglyphic [haɪərə'glɪfɪk] *adj* hiéroglyphique

hieroglyphics [haɪərə'glɪfɪks] *n* [①**A10,c**] (*system*) hiéroglyphes *mpl*; (*characters*) signes *mpl* hiéroglyphiques; *Fig F* (*bad handwriting*) hiéroglyphes

hifalutin(g) [haɪfə'luːtɪn, -tɪŋ] *adj F* = **highfalutin(g)**

hi-fi ['haɪ'faɪ] **1** *n* hi-fi *f inv* **2** *adj* hi-fi *inv*

higgledy-piggledy ['hɪg(ə)ldɪ'pɪg(ə)ldɪ] *adv F* en pagaïe, pêle-mêle

high [haɪ] **1** *adj* **(a)** haut, élevé; **built on h. ground** construit sur un terrain élevé; **this house is much higher (up) than the village** cette maison est située à beaucoup plus haute altitude que le village; **the highest mountain in the country** la plus haute montagne du pays; **wall two metres h.** mur haut de deux mètres, mur d'une hauteur de deux mètres, mur de deux mètres de hauteur; **at h. water** *or* **tide** à marée haute; **h. neck** (*on garment*) col montant; **h. cheekbones** pommettes saillantes; **with one's head h.** la tête haute; **h. beam** (*on car*) feux *mpl* de route; (*in gym*) poutre *f*

(b) (*in number, degree*) (*price*) élevé; (*percentage*) gros; (*speed*) grand; **to fetch a h. price** se vendre cher; **to pay a h. price** payer le prix fort; **to make a higher bid** faire une offre supérieure, surenchérir; **highest bidder** surenchérisseur *m*; *Cards, Fig* **to play for h. stakes** jouer gros (jeu); *Cards* **h. cards** honneurs *mpl*; **ore with a h. mineral content** minerai à haute teneur; **cheese is h. in calcium** le fromage est riche en calcium; **h. latitudes** hautes latitudes; **highest speed** vitesse maximum, vitesse de pointe; **to have a h. opinion of sb** avoir une haute opinion de qn, tenir qn en haute estime; **of the highest importance** de première importance; **h. end** (*of market*) haut *m*; **to be h. farce** tourner à la farce; **h. quality** bonne qualité; **a h. fever** une forte *ou* grosse fièvre; **h. winds** vents forts; *Jur* **h. treason** haute trahison *f*

(c) (*superior, advanced*) haut; **of h. rank** de haut rang; **she is h. up in the government** elle est haut placée dans le gouvernement; **to be in a h. position** être haut placé; **she's acting all h. and mighty** elle agit avec beaucoup d'arrogance; **higher posts** postes *ou* emplois supérieurs; **higher education** études *fpl* supérieures; **higher mathematics** mathématiques *fpl* supérieures; *Jur* **higher court** instance *f* supérieure; *Br Rel* **H. Church** Haute Église *f* (*de l'église anglicane*); *Mil* **h. command** haut commandement *m*; **h. school** *US* = établissement *f* d'enseignement supérieur; *Br* = lycée *m*; **h. fashion** haute couture *f*; **h. resolution** haute résolution *f*; **h. resolution screen** écran *m* à haute résolution; **h. society** haute société *f*

(d) (*noble*) (*principles, character etc*) élevé, noble; **h. ideals** idéaux élevés; **she has very h. moral standards** elle a des principes (de moralité) très élevés

(e) (*strong*) **h. colour** couleur *f* vive; **h. explosive** explosif *m* puissant

(f) (*good*) **to be in h. spirits** être plein d'entrain; **our spirits were h.** nous avions le moral; **the h. life** la vie mondaine; **the h. point of the match** le point culminant du match; **one of the h. points of the evening** un des points forts de la soirée

(g) *Mus etc* **h. voice** voix élevée *ou* haute; (*thin*) voix grêle; **h. note** note *f* aiguë; *Fig* point *m* culminant

(h) (*principal*) *Br* **the H. Street** la Grand-rue, la Grande rue; **the h. table** la table d'honneur; *Sch, Univ* la table des professeurs (*au réfectoire*); *Rel* **H. Mass** grand-messe *f*, grande messe *f*; **h. altar** maître-autel *m*, *pl* maîtres-autels; *Rel* **h. priest/priestess** grand(e) prêtre/prêtresse; *Fig* **the h. priests of fashion** les grands noms de la mode; *Naut* **the h. seas** la haute mer

(i) (*of time*) **h. noon** plein midi; **h. summer** plein été; **it's h. time he went to school** il est grand temps qu'il aille à l'école; *Br Com* **the h. season** la haute saison; *Br* **h. tea** = dîner *m* pris assez tôt dans la soirée

(j) (*meat etc*) avancé; (*bad*) avarié; (*game*) faisandé; **to get h.** (*of game*) se faisander; **to smell h.** avoir une forte odeur

(k) *F* (*person*) **to be h.** (*drugged*) planer; *Fig* (*euphoric*) être dans un état d'euphorie; **h. on cocaine** défoncé à la cocaïne; *Fig* **they were h. on success** ils ne se sentaient plus après ce succès

(l) *F* (*lively*) **to have a h. old time** faire la noce

(m) **h. and dry** (*of ship*) échoué au plein; (*pulled up on beach etc*) à sec; *F* **to be left h. and dry** (*of person*) être laissé en plan

2 *adv* **(a)** (*to aim, jump etc*) haut, en haut; **higher (up)** plus haut; **higher and higher** de plus en plus haut; **to rise h. in public esteem** monter très haut dans l'estime du public; **to hunt h. and low for sth** chercher qch partout; **higher up the river** en amont

(b) (*in bidding etc*) **to go as h. as £2,000** aller jusqu'à 2 000 livres; *Cards etc* **to play** *or* **stake h.** jouer gros jeu

(c) **to run h.** (*of sea*) être grosse *ou* houleuse; (*of prices*) être élevés; **feelings are running h.** les passions s'exacerbent; (*between countries*) la tension monte; **tempers were running h.** les esprits s'échauffaient

(d) *Comptr* **h. memory** mémoire *f* haute; **h. memory area** zone *f* de mémoire haute; **to have memory loaded h.** avoir chargé en mémoire haute

3 *n* **(a)** (*high point*) **highs and lows** (*of share prices etc*) hausses *fpl* et baisses *fpl*; (*of career etc*) hauts *mpl* et bas *mpl*; **prices have reached a new h.** les prix ont atteint un nouveau maximum

(b) *Met* aire *f* anticyclonique

(c) *F* **to be on a h.** (*from drugs etc*) planer; (*from success etc*) être sur son petit nuage

(d) *Rel* **the Most H.** le Très-Haut, le Tout-Puissant; **on h.** en haut, dans le ciel; *Rel, Fig* **from on h.** d'en haut

high-ability *adj* **h. children** enfants *mpl* surdoués

high-angle *adj Cin* **h. shot** plan *m* en plongée

highball ['haɪbɔːl] *n* = whisky-soda *m* avec de la glace servi dans un grand verre

high blood pressure *n Med* hypertension *f*

highborn ['haɪbɔːn] *adj* de haute naissance

highboy ['haɪbɔɪ] *n Am* (*furniture*) commode *f* haute

highbrow ['haɪbraʊ] *F* **1** *n* intello *mf* **2** *adj* intello

highchair ['haɪtʃeər] *n* (*for baby*) chaise *f* haute

high-class *adj* (*merchandise etc*) de premier ordre, de première qualité; (*hotel*) de grande classe; (*prostitute*) de luxe

High Commission *n Admin* = représentation *f* officielle d'un pays, équivalente à une ambassade

High Commissioner *n* = représentant *m* officiel d'un pays, équivalent à un ambassadeur

High Court *n Jur* Tribunal *m* de grande instance

high-definition TV *n* télévision *f* haute définition

high-density *adj Comptr* (*disk, graphics, printing*) haute densité; **h. housing** habitations *fpl* à forte concentration de population; (*in high-rise buildings*) grands ensembles *mpl*

high-diving *n* plongeon *m* de haut vol, haut vol *m*

highfalutin(g) [haɪfə'luːtɪn, -ɪŋ] *adj F* (*style, language*) ampoulé, prétentieux, pompeux

high-fibre *adj Culin* riche en fibres

high fidelity *n* haute fidélité *f*
high-fidelity *adj* de haute fidélité
high-flier, -flyer *n* (*successful person*) ambitieux, -euse; (*company*) société *f* qui va de l'avant; **she's a real h.** elle ira loin
high-flown *adj* (*style, language*) ampoulé, pompeux
high-flying *adj* (*successful*) ambitieux, qui ira loin
high frequency *n Phys etc* haute fréquence *f*
high-frequency *adj El* (*current*) à haute fréquence; (*amplifier*) de haute fréquence
High German *n Ling* haut allemand *m*
high-grade *adj* (*ore etc*) à haute teneur; (*merchandise*) de première qualité, de (premier) choix; *Aut* **h.** *Br* **petrol** *or Am* **gasoline** supercarburant *m*
high-handed [haɪ'hændɪd] *adj* (*person, behaviour etc*) trop autoritaire, tyrannique; **was there any need to be so h. about it?** était-il nécessaire de te montrer si autoritaire?
high hat *n* **(a)** *Mus* cymbales *fpl* (*montées sur un pied*) **(b)** *Old-fashioned F* (*person*) arrogant *m*, snob *mf* **(c)** *Cin, TV* petit pied *m* de caméra, pied de sol
high-heeled [haɪ'hi:ld] *adj* **h. shoes** chaussures *fpl* à hauts talons, talons *mpl* hauts
high-income *adj* à haut revenu; **h. group** groupe *m* des gros salaires, groupe des salaires élevés
high-involvement *adj Mktg* (*purchasing*) à forte participation des consommateurs
highjack, highjacker *etc* = **hijack, hijacker** *etc*
high jump *n Sp* saut *m* en hauteur; *Br Fig F* **you'll be for the h. jump** tu vas te faire engueuler; (*you'll be thrown out*) tu vas te faire virer
high jumper *n Sp* sauteur, -euse en hauteur
highland ['haɪlənd] **1** *n* pays *m* montagneux; **the Highlands** (*of Scotland*) les Highlands *mpl* **2** *adj* des montagnes; (*from Scotland*) des Highlands; **H. cattle** vaches *fpl* rousses (*race bovine des Highlands*)
highlander ['haɪləndər] *n* montagnard, -arde; **H.** (*from Scotland*) Highlander *m*, habitant, -ante de la Haute Écosse; *Mil* = soldat *m* d'un régiment écossais
high-level *adj* (*discussion*) à haut niveau; (*official, officer*) de haut niveau; *Comptr* **h. language** langage *m* de haut niveau; **h. programming language** langage *m* de programmation évolué
highlight¹ ['haɪlaɪt] *n* **(a)** (*important moment*) grand moment *m*; (*of celebration etc*) clou *m*; (*of match etc*) point *m* culminant; *TV, Sp* **they didn't show the whole match, just the highlights** ils n'ont pas retransmis tout le match, seulement les meilleurs moments **(b) highlights** (*in a painting*) rehauts *mpl*, clairs *mpl* **(c) highlights** (*in hair*) reflets *mpl*, mèches *fpl* **(d)** *Comptr* relief *m*
highlight² *vt* **(a)** (*problem, need*) souligner **(b)** (*with coloured marker*) surligner **(c)** *Comptr* (*text block*) mettre en relief; **to be highlighted** (*of text*) apparaître en surimpression *ou* en surbrillance
highlighted ['haɪlaɪtɪd] *adj Comptr* lumineux, contrasté; **h. command** article *m* contrasté
highlighter ['haɪlaɪtər] *n* **(a)** (*coloured marker*) surligneur *m*, stylo *m* surligneur, marqueur *m* surligneur **(b)** (*for hair*) shampooing-reflets *m*, shampooing éclaircissant
highly ['haɪlɪ] *adv* **(a) h. placed official** haut fonctionnaire *m*; **to be h. placed** être haut placé; **his services are h. paid** on paie très cher ses services; **to think h. of sb** avoir une haute opinion de qn **(b)** (*extremely*) fort, très, fortement; **h. amusing** très amusant; **h. displeased** fort mécontent; **h. seasoned** fortement assaisonné; **h. coloured** (*painting, style*) haut en couleur; (*account, report*) coloré, haut en couleur; **to be h. sexed** avoir une forte libido; **h. strung** (*person*) très sensible, *F* hypersensible
high-margin product *n* produit *m* à forte marge
high-minded *adj* aux sentiments nobles, généreux; (*action, nature*) magnanime; **to be too h.** avoir trop de principes
high-mindedness ['haɪ'maɪndɪdnɪs] *n* noblesse *f* de sentiments, grandeur *f* d'âme; (*of action etc*) magnanimité *f*
Highness ['haɪnɪs] *n* (*title*) Altesse *f*; **His/Her Royal H.** son Altesse Royale
high-octane *adj* (*fuel*) à indice d'octane élevé
high-performance *adj* (à) haute performance; **h. car** voiture *f* (à) haute performance; **h. chip** puce *f* à haute performance; **h. engine** moteur *m* (à) haute performance
high-pitched *adj* **(a)** (*sound*) aigu, -uë; (*voice*) aigu, criard **(b)** *Constr* **h. roof** comble *m* à forte inclinaison *ou* à forte pente
high-powered *adj* (*engine, car, telescope*) très puissant; (*microscope*) à fort grossissement; *Fig* (*person*) dynamique et compétent; **a h. businessman** un homme d'affaires de poids; **she is something h. in the City** elle a un poste important à la Cité de Londres; **a h. job** un poste très important, *F* un super boulot
high-pressure *adj* **(a)** *Tech* (*cylinder, machine*) à haute pression, à haute tension; *Met* (*area*) anticyclonique, de hautes pressions **(b)** *Pej* (*salesman*) agressif
high-principled *adj* aux principes élevés
high-profile *adj* (*politician etc*) en vue; (*company*) connu; (*campaign etc*) de grande envergure
high-quality *adj* haut de gamme
high-resolution *adj Phot, TV etc* (*screen, graphics*) à haute résolution
high-rise *Archit* **1** *n* tour *f* **2** *adj* **h. building** tour *f*
high-risk *adj* (*occupation, category etc*) à haut(s) risque(s)
highroad ['haɪrəʊd] *n* **(a)** *Old-fashioned* grand-route *f* **(b)** *Fig* **on the h. to success** sur la route du succès
high-sounding *adj* (*title*) pompeux, ronflant
high-speed *adj* ultra-rapide; (*machine*) à marche rapide; (*engine*), *Phot* grande vitesse; **h. access** accès *m* rapide; *Comptr* **h. bus** bus *m* rapide; **h. printer** imprimante *f* rapide; **h. camera** caméra *f* grande vitesse; **h. train** train *m* à grande vitesse, TGV *m*
high-spirited *adj* plein d'ardeur *ou* de feu; (*horse*) fougueux
high street *n Br* **prices on the h.** prix *mpl* dans le commerce
high-street *adj Br* **h. shops** commerces *mpl*; **prices in the h. shops** prix dans le commerce; **a h. bank** une banque populaire, une banque de dépôt
high-strung *adj* (*character, person*) très sensible
hightail ['haɪteɪl] *vt esp Am F* **to h. it** se tirer en vitesse; **he hightailed it out of town** il a fichu le camp de la ville; **he hightailed it back to the ranch** il est retourné au ranch en quatrième vitesse
high-tech ['haɪtek] *adj, n* = **hi-tech**
high technology *n* haute technologie *f*
high-tensile steel *n* acier *m* à haute résistance élastique
high-tension *adj El* (*wire*) à haute tension; **h. cable** câble *m* haute tension; **h. coil** bobine *f* haute tension
high-up *F* **1** *n* gros bonnet *m*, grosse légume *f* **2** *adj* (*judge, politician etc*) haut placé
high value added *adj* à haute valeur ajoutée
high-viscosity *adj* (*oil*) à haute viscosité
high voltage *n* haute tension *f*
highway ['haɪweɪ] *n* **(a)** *esp Am* (*main road*) route *f* nationale, autoroute *f*; *US* **h. patrolman** motard *m* de la police; **highways and byways** chemins *mpl* et sentiers *mpl*; **that price is h. robbery!** un prix pareil, c'est du vol pur et simple **(b)** *Br Admin* (*public road*) voie *f* publique; **h. engineer** = ingénieur *m* des Ponts et Chaussées; **H. Code** Code *m* de la Route
highwayman, *pl* **-men** ['haɪweɪmən] *n Hist* voleur *m* de grand(s) chemin(s)
high wire *n* (*for tightrope walker*) corde *f* raide
hijack¹ ['haɪdʒæk] *n* détournement *m*
hijack² *vt* (*plane in flight*) détourner; (*vehicle*) s'emparer de force de; *Fig* **the government hijacked the opposition's policy** le gouvernement s'est approprié la politique de l'opposition
hijacker ['haɪdʒækər] *n* (*of aircraft*) pirate *mf* de l'air; (*of vehicle*) pirate de la route; **the hijackers of the Israeli Boeing** les pirates de l'air du Boeing israélien
hijacking ['haɪdʒækɪŋ] *n* (*of aircraft*) (*general practice*) piraterie *f* aérienne; (*single incident*) détournement *m*; (*of vehicle*) = vol *m* à main armée d'un véhicule et de son contenu
hike¹ [haɪk] *n* **(a)** (*walk*) (longue) promenade *f* à pied, randonnée *f*; **to go on** *or* **for a h.** faire une (longue) promenade à pied, faire une randonnée; *Am F* **he can take a h.!** il peut aller se faire voir! **(b)** (*in interest rates etc*) augmentation *f*, hausse *f*
hike² *vi* (*walk*) faire une (longue) promenade à pied, faire une randonnée
▸ **hike up** *vtsep* (*trousers, skirt*) remonter; (*interest rates*) augmenter; **to h. oneself up on to sth** se hisser jusqu'à qch
hiker ['haɪkər] *n* randonneur, -euse (*à pied*)
hiking ['haɪkɪŋ] *n* randonnée *f* pédestre; **h. boots** bottes *fpl* de randonnée, chaussures *fpl* de marche; **to go on a h. holiday** partir en vacances faire de la randonnée
hilarious [hɪ'leərɪəs] *adj* (*very amusing*) hilarant, *F* marrant; **it was h.!** c'était à se tordre (de rire)!
hilariously [hɪ'leərɪəslɪ] *adv* (*unlikely, old-fashioned looking*) à vous faire tordre de rire; (*to laugh*) aux éclats; **it was h. funny** c'était à se tordre (de rire)
hilariousness [hɪ'leərɪəsnɪs] *n* (*of scene, joke*) caractère *m* hilarant
hilarity [hɪ'lærɪtɪ] *n* hilarité *f*
hill [hɪl] *n* **(a)** colline *f*; (*sloping ground*) coteau *m*; **up h. and**

down dale par monts et par vaux; *Fig F* **to be over the h.** commencer à se faire vieux; *Am F* **it ain't worth a h. of beans, it doesn't amount to a h. of beans** (*of opinion etc*) ça ne vaut pas tripette; **to be as old as the hills** (*of joke, person etc*) dater de *ou* remonter à Mathusalem; *Mil* **h. 304** la cote 304; **h. country** pays *m* de collines; **h. station** (*in India*) station *f* de montagne **(b)** (*on road*) côte *f*; (*uphill*) montée *f*; (*downhill*) descente *f*; **steep h.** (*uphill*) montée abrupte; (*downhill*) descente abrupte; *Aut* **h. start** départ *m* en côte

hillbilly ['hɪlbɪlɪ] *n US F Pej* villageois, -oise un peu rustaud(e); **h. music** country musique *f* (*du sud-est des États-Unis*)

hill-climbing *n* randonnée *f* (*en pays de collines*); (*of vehicle*) montée *f*

hillfarm ['hɪlfɑːm] *n* ferme *f* à flanc de coteau

hilliness ['hɪlɪnɪs] *n* vallonnement *m*

hillock ['hɪlək] *n* petite colline *f*; (*smaller*) butte *f*, tertre *m*

hillside ['hɪlsaɪd] *n* flanc *m* de coteau, coteau *m*

hilltop ['hɪltɒp] *n* sommet *m* de (la) colline

hill-walker *n* randonneur, -euse (en pays de collines)

hill-walking *n* randonnée *f* (en pays de collines)

hilly ['hɪlɪ] *adj* (*country*) montagneux; (*terrain*) accidenté; (*road*) montueux, à fortes pentes

hilt [hɪlt] *n* (*of sword*) poignée *f*; (*of dagger, knife etc*) manche *m*; *Fig* **right up to the h.** jusqu'au bout; **to back** *or* **support sb to the h.** soutenir qn sans réserve *ou* à fond; **mortgaged up to the h.** (*person*) endetté jusqu'au cou, qui doit rembourser des emprunts énormes; (*property*) fortement hypothéqué

him [hɪm] *pers pron* **(a)** [①**A26**,a-c; **A42**,3] (*direct*) le; (*before a vowel sound*) l'; **I hate h.** je le déteste; **do you love h.?** l'aimez-vous?; **have you seen h.?** l'avez-vous vu?; **I remember h.** je me souviens de lui

(b) (*indirect and reflexive, after prepositions*) lui; **I shall tell h. so** je le lui dirai; **tell h. I have come** dites-lui que je suis là; **we are thinking of h.** nous pensons à lui; **he took his luggage with h.** il a pris ses bagages avec lui; **he closed the door behind h.** il a fermé la porte derrière lui; **I object to h. borrowing the car** je m'oppose à ce qu'il emprunte la voiture

(c) (*as complement of verb* **to be**) **it's h.!** c'est lui!

(d) (*stressed*) lui; *Lit* (*with dem force*) celui; **we can forgive his parents but not <u>him</u>** nous pouvons pardonner à ses parents, mais pas à lui; **who better than h. to break the news?** qui, mieux que lui, pourrait annoncer la nouvelle?; *Lit* **to h. who should take offence at this I would say ...** à celui qui s'en offenserait, je dirais ...

Himalayan [hɪmə'leɪən] *adj* himalayen, -enne

Himalayas [hɪmə'leɪəz] *npl* **the H.** (les montagnes *fpl* de) l'Himalaya *m*

himself [hɪm'self] *pers pron* [①**A29**] **(a)** (*emphatic*) lui-même; **he doesn't want to do it h.** il ne veut pas le faire lui-même; **he's not (quite) h. again yet** (*after illness*) il n'est pas encore complètement remis; **he's not h. today** il n'est pas lui-même aujourd'hui, il n'est pas dans son état normal aujourd'hui; **I spoke to the author h.** j'ai parlé à l'auteur lui-même *ou* en personne

(b) [①**B26**,D] (*reflexive*) se; **he hurt h.** il s'est fait mal; **he lives by h.** il vit seul; **'well, well!', he said to h.** 'eh bien!', se dit-il; **he kept one for h.** il s'en est gardé un/une

(c) (*used impersonally*) soi(-même); **everyone for h.** chacun pour soi

hind¹ [haɪnd] *n* (*female deer*) biche *f*; **h. calf** faon *m* femelle

hind² *adj* de derrière, postérieur; **h. legs/feet** pattes *fpl* de derrière; *F* **to get up on one's h. legs** (*of person*) se lever (pour prononcer un discours)

hinder¹ ['haɪndər] *adj* de derrière, postérieur

hinder² ['hɪndər] *vt* **(a)** (*impede*) gêner, embarrasser; (*movement*) entraver; (*delay*) retarder **(b)** (*prevent*) empêcher, retenir (**from doing** de faire)

Hindi ['hɪndɪ] *n Ling* hindi *m*

hindmost ['haɪndməʊst] *adj* dernier; *prov* **devil take the h.!** chacun pour soi; **it's a case of devil take the h.** vu les circonstances, c'est chacun pour soi

hindquarters ['haɪndkwɔːtəz] *npl* arrière-train *m*

hindrance ['hɪndrəns] *n* empêchement *m*, obstacle *m*, entrave *f*; **he is a h.** il gêne; **they were more of a h. than a help** ils nous/les/*etc* gênaient plus qu'ils ne nous/les/*etc* aidaient

hindsight ['haɪndsaɪt] *n* recul *m*, sagesse *f* que donne le recul; **with (the benefit of) h.** après coup, avec le recul; **with all the advantages of h.** avec tous les avantages que donne le recul

Hindu [hɪn'duː] **1** *adj* hindou **2** *n* Hindou, -oue

Hinduism ['hɪnduːɪz(ə)m] *n* hindouisme *m*

Hindustan [hɪndʊ'stɑːn] *n Geog* Hindoustan *m*

Hindustani [hɪndʊ'stɑːnɪ] *Ling* **1** *n* hindoustani *m* **2** *adj* hindi

hinge¹ [hɪndʒ] *n* charnière *f*; (*of door*) gond *m*; **the door came off its hinges** la porte est sortie de ses gonds; **(stamp) h.** charnière

hinge² **1** *vt* (*mount on hinges*) (*door etc*) monter sur ses gonds; (*put hinges on*) (*box etc*) mettre des charnières à **2** *vi Tech* tourner, pivoter (**on** autour de); **to h. forward** (*of seat etc*) basculer vers l'avant

▶ **hinge on, hinge upon** *vipo* (*depend on*) dépendre de; **everything hinges on his answer** tout dépend de sa réponse

hinged [hɪndʒd] *adj* (*door, lid etc*) à charnière(s); **h. flap** (*of counter etc*) battant *m* rabattable; (*of aircraft*) volet *m* articulé

hint¹ [hɪnt] *n* **(a)** (*allusion*) allusion *f* (indirecte); **broad h.** allusion évidente *ou* claire; **gentle h.** allusion discrète; **to give** *or* **drop sb a h.** toucher un mot à qn; **to know how to take a h.** comprendre à demi-mot; **we can take a h.** nous avons compris l'allusion; **he can't take a h.** il faut lui mettre les points sur les i

(b) (*sign*) signe *m*, indication *f*, suggestion *f*; **not a h. of surprise** pas une ombre de surprise; **not the slightest h. of ...** pas le moindre soupçon de ...; **there was a h. of garlic in the stew** il y avait un soupçon d'ail dans le ragoût

(c) (*piece of advice*) petit conseil *m*; **the book is full of useful hints on how to save money** le livre est plein de tuyaux pour faire des économies; **can you give me some hints?** (*about how I should proceed*) pouvez-vous me donner quelques conseils?; (*about the right answer*) pouvez-vous me mettre sur la voie?

hint² *vt* **to h. that ...** insinuer que ...; **to h. to sb that ...** laisser entendre à qn que ...

▶ **hint at** *vipo* faire (une) allusion à

hinterland ['hɪntəlænd] *n* arrière-pays *m*

hip¹ [hɪp] *n* **(a)** *Anat* hanche *f*; **to have narrow/wide hips** avoir les hanches fines/larges; **he stood with his hands on his hips** il était debout, les mains sur les hanches; *esp Am Fig* **he shoots from the h.** il ne prend pas de gants; **h. bath** bain *m* de siège; **h. flask** flacon *m* (de poche); **h. pocket** poche *f* revolver; **h. joint** articulation *f* de la hanche; *Med* **h. replacement operation** mise *f* en place d'une prothèse de la hanche; **h. size** *or* **measurement** tour *m* de hanches **(b)** *Constr* **h. (piece** *or* **rafter)** (*of roof*) arêtier *m*, arête *f*

hip² *n* (*fruit*) cynor(r)hodon *m*, fruit *m* du rosier

hip³ *adj F* (*trendy*) à la page, dans le vent

hip⁴ *int* **h.! h.!, hurray!** hip! hip! hourra!

hipbone ['hɪpbəʊn] *n* os *m* iliaque

hip-huggers ['hɪp'hʌgəz] *npl Am* = **hipster (b)**

-hipped [hɪpt] *suff* **broad-h.** aux hanches fortes; **narrow-h.** aux hanches fines *ou* étroites

hippie ['hɪpɪ] *adj, n* hippie *mf*; *Hum* **ageing h.** vieillisant(e) hippie

hippo ['hɪpəʊ] *n F* hippopotame *m*

Hippocrates [hɪ'pɒkrətiːz] *n* Hippocrate *m*

Hippocratic [hɪpə'krætɪk] *adj Med* hippocratique; **H. oath** serment *m* d'Hippocrate

hippodrome ['hɪpədrəʊm] *n* hippodrome *m*; (*not for racing*) arène *f*

hippopotamus, *pl* **-muses, -mi** [hɪpə'pɒtəməs, -məsɪz, -maɪ] *n* hippopotame *m*

hippy¹ ['hɪpɪ] *adj* (*with large hips*) aux hanches larges

hippy² *adj, n* = **hippie**

hipster ['hɪpstər] *n* **(a)** *esp Am Old-fashioned* beatnick *mf* (*des années 40 et 50*) **(b)** *Br* **hipsters** (*trousers*) pantalon *m* (à) taille basse

hire¹ ['haɪər] *n* **(a)** *Br* (*of car, room*) location *f*; **for h.** (*sign on taxi*) libre; **for** *or* **on h.** à louer; **h. car** voiture *f* de location; **h. charges** frais *mpl* de location **(b)** *Am* (*of labour*) embauche *f*; (*of servant*) louage *m* **(c)** *Lit* (*wages*) salaire *m*, gages *mpl*

hire² **1** *vt* **(a)** *Br* (*car etc*) louer **(b)** (*take on*) (*lawyer, private detective etc*) s'assurer les services de, engager **(c)** *Am* (*worker*) embaucher, engager; (*domestic staff*) prendre à son service **2** *vi esp Am* (*take on workers*) embaucher

▶ **hire out** *vtsep Br* louer, donner en location (**to sb** à qn)

hired ['haɪəd] *adj* **(a)** *Br* (*car etc*) de location **(b)** **h. gun/killer** tueur *m* à gages; *Am* **h. man** (*servant*) domestique *m*; **h. man** *or* **hand** (*farmworker*) ouvrier *m* agricole

hireling ['haɪəlɪŋ] *n Pej* laquais *m*

hire-purchase *n Br Com* location-vente *f*; **h. agreement** contrat *m* de location-vente; **to buy sth on h.** acheter qch en location-vente

hiring ['haɪ(ə)rɪŋ] *n* **(a)** *Br* (*of a car etc*) location *f* **(b)** (*of staff etc*) embauche *f*; *F* **he does the h. and firing** il est chargé des embauches et des licenciements

hirsute ['hɜːsjuːt] *adj Lit* hirsute, velu, poilu

his¹ [hɪz] *poss adj* [①**A30**,8; **A42**,3; **B19-20**,E,1] son, *f* sa, *pl* ses; **one**

of h. friends un de ses amis, un ami à lui; **h. father and mother** son père et sa mère; *Admin* ses père et mère; **h. own son** son propre fils; **he has hurt h. hand** il s'est fait mal à la main; **h. eyes are brown** il a les yeux bruns; **I object to h. borrowing the car** je m'oppose à ce qu'il emprunte la voiture; **H. Majesty** Sa Majesté

his² *poss pron* [①A30,8; **B20**,E,2] le sien, la sienne, *pl* les siens, les siennes; **he took my pen as well as h.** il a pris mon stylo avec le sien; **this book is h.** ce livre est à lui, c'est son livre à lui; **a friend of h.** un de ses amis, un ami à lui; **it is no business of h.** cela ne le regarde pas; **it's no business of h. to tell me what to do** ce n'est pas à lui de me dire quoi faire

Hispanic [hɪs'pænɪk] **1** *adj* hispanique **2** *n US* Hispano-Américain, -aine

Hispano-American [hɪ'spænəʊə'merɪk(ə)n] **1** *adj* hispano-américain **2** *n* Hispano-Américain, -aine

hiss¹ [hɪs] *n* **(a)** (*sound*) sifflement *m*; *Th etc* sifflets *mpl*; (*on tape*) bruit *m* parasite, bruit de piste **(b)** *Ling* sifflante *f*

hiss² *vti* (*of person, steam, geese etc*) siffler; (*of steam, gas*) chuinter; **to h. (at) an actor** siffler un acteur; **to be hissed** être sifflé

hissing ['hɪsɪŋ] **1** *adj* **h. noise** sifflement *m*; (*of gas*) chuintement *m* **2** *n* sifflement *m*; (*of gas*) chuintement *m*

histamine ['hɪstəmɪn, -miːn] *n Physiol* histamine *f*

histogram ['hɪstəgræm] *n* histogramme *m*

historian [hɪs'tɔːrɪən] *n* historien, -ienne

historic [hɪs'tɒrɪk] *adj* **(a)** historique; **h. building** monument *m* historique **(b)** [①**B28**,F,4] *Gram* **past h.** passé *m* simple

historical [hɪs'tɒrɪk(ə)l] *adj* **(a)** (*character, event, novel*) historique; **h. background** contexte *m* historique; **of purely h. interest** d'intérêt purement historique; **h. record/account** historique *m*; **h. research** recherche *f* en histoire **(b)** *Ling* **h. linguistics** linguistique *f* diachronique

historically [hɪs'tɒrɪklɪ] *adv* historiquement

historiographer [hɪstɔːrɪ'ɒgrəfər] *n* historiographe *mf*

historiography [hɪstɔːrɪ'ɒgrəfɪ] *n* historiographie *f*

history ['hɪst(ə)rɪ] *n* **(a)** (*of country, ship etc*) histoire *f*; **French h.** l'histoire de France; **ancient/modern h.** l'histoire ancienne/moderne; *Fig* **that's h.** c'est du passé; **that's ancient h.** c'est une vieille histoire, c'est de l'histoire ancienne; **we're making h.** nous faisons l'histoire, nous entrons dans l'histoire; *Sch* **h. book/teacher/***etc* livre *m*/professeur *m*/*etc* d'histoire; **Shakespeare's h. plays** les pièces *fpl* historiques de Shakespeare

(b) (*book*) histoire *f*; (*chronological account*) historique *m*

(c) (*tradition*) tradition *f*; **there is a long h. of cultural links between these cities** il existe une longue tradition de liens culturels entre ces villes; **there is a h. of heart disease in her family** il y a des antécédents de maladie cardiaque dans sa famille

history file *n Comptr* fichier *m* historique

histrionic [hɪstrɪ'ɒnɪk] *adj* **(a)** histrionique **(b)** *Th Lit* théâtral

histrionics [hɪstrɪ'ɒnɪks] *npl Pej* démonstrations *fpl* affectées (*de colère etc*); **I've had enough of his h.** j'en ai assez de ses simagrées *ou F* son cinéma; **it is mere h. on her part** elle nous joue la comédie

hit¹ [hɪt] *n* **(a)** (*blow*) coup *m*; *Fig F* **that's a h. at you** c'est à vous que s'adresse l'allusion

(b) *Fencing* touche *f*, coup *m*; *Billiards* touche; *Baseball* coup de batte; *Hockey* coup de crosse; *Hockey* **free h.** coup franc; **to score a h.** *Fencing* toucher; (*in shooting*) atteindre la cible; *Fig* **to score a h. against sb** marquer des points contre qn; **to score a direct h.** (*of bomber, tank etc*) taper dans le mille; **to score a direct h. on sth** (*of bomber etc*) toucher qch en plein dans le mille; (*of bomb*) tomber en plein dans qch; **built to withstand a direct h.** construit pour résister à une bombe; **the ship suffered two direct hits from missiles** le bateau a été touché par deux missiles

(c) *Th, TV etc* (*success*) succès *m*; *Mus* **h. (record)** tube *m*; **she had a h. with her song 'Bye, Bye'** sa chanson 'Bye, Bye' a été un tube; **Frank Sinatra's greatest hits** les plus grands succès de Frank Sinatra; **to make** *or* **score a h. with sb** faire bonne impression à qn; (*romantically*) avoir une touche avec qn; **one-h. wonder** (*group, singer*) groupe/chanteur qui n'a eu qu'un seul tube; *Old-fashioned* **h. parade** hit parade *m*, palmarès *m*; *Th* **h. show** spectacle *m* à succès

(d) *esp US Sl* (*murder*) meurtre *m*

(e) (*of drugs*) flash *m*

hit² (*pt, pp* **hit**; *prp* **hitting**) **1** *vt* **(a)** (*of person*) frapper; *Comptr* (*key*) appuyer sur; (*of bullet*) (*person*) atteindre; (*of car etc*) (*tree, bus*) percuter; **to h. sb in the face** frapper qn au visage; **to h. one's foot against a stone** se cogner le pied contre une pierre; (*and stumble*) buter contre une pierre; **to h. one's head on the ceiling** se cogner la tête contre le plafond; **to h. a reef** (*of ship, boat*) heurter un récif; **the bullet hit her in the arm** la balle l'a touchée au bras; **to h. the target** (*with gun, missile etc*) toucher la cible; *Am F* **that really hit the spot** (*is just what was needed*) c'est juste ce qu'il me fallait; *Journ F* **to h. the headlines** défrayer la chronique; *Fig* **to h. the nail on the head** tomber juste; *Fig* **to h. the roof** être furieux; *Sl* **to h. the bottle** picoler; *Sl* **to h. the hay** *or US* **the sack** se pieuter; **it suddenly hit me that ...** j'ai réalisé tout d'un coup que ...; **he didn't know what had hit him** il se demandait ce qui lui était arrivé

(b) (*reach*) atteindre; *Fencing, Billiards* toucher; **to h. the wrong note** (*on the piano etc*), *Fig* faire une fausse note; (*in singing*) chanter faux; **I can't h. those high notes any more** je n'arrive plus à chanter ces notes aiguës; **to h. ninety (miles an hour)** faire du 140 km/h; **to h. an all-time low** (*of investment, relationship etc*) être au plus bas; **to h. rock-bottom** atteindre son point le plus bas

(c) (*affect*) **to be hard hit** (*by losses etc*) être sérieusement touché; **the strike has hit several factories** la grève a atteint plusieurs usines

(d) *US F* (*borrow from*) **he hit his friend for $100** il a tapé son ami de 100 dollars

(e) (*guess*) **you've hit it!** vous y êtes!, vous avez mis le doigt dessus!

(f) *F* (*arrive at*) (*place, town*) arriver à; **the circus hits town tomorrow night** le cirque arrive en ville demain soir; **to h. the beach** (*of troops*) atteindre la plage; **let's h. the beach!** allons à la plage!; **when it hits the shops** quand il arrivera sur le marché; **to h. the trail** *or* **the road** (*start*) se mettre en route; *Fig* **to h. the ground running** être opérationnel immédiatement

(g) (*encounter*) (*problem, difficulty*) buter sur; **the tunnellers hit rock** les ouvriers qui creusaient le tunnel sont tombés sur de la roche; **we hit a terrible snowstorm** nous nous sommes trouvés dans une tempête de neige terrible; **to h. a sticky** *or* **bad patch** rencontrer des difficultés

(h) *esp US Sl* (*murder*) buter

2 *vi* frapper; (*collide*) se heurter; **to h. hard** frapper fort, *F* cogner fort; *Fig* **the remark hit home** la remarque a eu l'effet escompté

▶ **hit back 1** *vi* **(a)** (*return blow*) rendre coup pour coup **(at sb** à qn) **(b)** *Fig* (*answer accusation, criticism etc*) riposter, répondre **2** *vtas* (*return blow to*) **to h. sb back** donner un coup en retour à qn

▶ **hit off** *vtsep* **(a)** (*imitate*) (*in satirical drawing*) caricaturer; (*impersonate*) imiter **(b)** *F* **to h. it off** (*get on well*) bien s'entendre (**with** avec)

▶ **hit on** *vipo* = **hit upon**

▶ **hit out** *vi* **(a)** (*punch etc*) frapper; **she hit out at her attackers** elle a frappé ses agresseurs; **he hit out in all directions** il donnait des coups dans tous les sens **(b)** (*verbally*) attaquer (verbalement); **to h. out at sb** s'en prendre à qn

▶ **hit upon** *vipo* (*discover*) (*idea, method etc*) trouver

hit-and-run 1 *adj* **(a)** *Aut* **h. accident** accident *m* dont l'auteur s'est enfui; **h. driver** chauffard *m* qui a pris la fuite; **h. offence** délit *m* de fuite **(b)** *Mil* **h. raid** raid *m* éclair **2** *n* (*accident*) accident *m* avec délit de fuite

hitch¹ [hɪtʃ] *n* **(a)** (*difficulty*) empêchement *m*, anicroche *f*, contretemps *m*; **there's a h. somewhere** il y a quelque chose qui cloche; **there's been a h.** il y a eu un problème; **without a h.** sans anicroches, sans accroc; *Rad, TV etc* **technical h.** incident *m* technique **(b)** (*knot*) nœud *m*; **half h.** demi-clef *f* **(c)** *Am F* (*length of time*) **a three-year h. in the army** (une période de) trois ans dans l'armée; **to do a three-year h. in prison** faire trois ans de prison **(d)** (*movement*) saccade *f*, secousse *f*; (*of horse*) léger boitement *m*

hitch² 1 *vt* **(a)** (*attach*) accrocher, attacher; *Naut* amarrer (**to** à); **she hitched her horse to a post** elle a attaché son cheval à un poteau; **they hitched the horses to the cart** ils ont attelé les chevaux à la charrette **(b)** *F* (*hitchhike*) **to h. a lift** *or* **ride** faire du stop, *Can* faire du pouce; **we hitched a ride to Paris** on nous a pris en stop jusqu'à Paris **(c)** *F* **to get hitched** (*married*) se caser **2** *vi* **(a)** *F* = **hitchhike (b)** (*of person*) **to h. on to sth** s'accrocher à qch

▶ **hitch up** *vtsep* **(a)** (*harness*) (*horse*) harnacher **(b)** (*lift*) (*trousers, skirt*) remonter

hitchhike ['hɪtʃhaɪk] *vi* faire de l'auto-stop *ou* du stop, *Can* faire du pouce; **to h. to Paris** aller à Paris en stop

hitchhiker ['hɪtʃhaɪkər] *n* auto-stoppeur, -euse

hitchhiking ['hɪtʃhaɪkɪŋ] *n* (auto-)stop *m*

hi-tech ['haɪtek] **1** *adj* de haute technologie, de pointe; (*furniture*) hi-tech; **they've adopted a h. approach** ils ont eu recours à la technologie de pointe; **we're very h. here** nous faisons un usage intensif de l'automatisation *ou* de l'informatique ici **2** *n* technologie *f* de pointe, hi-tech *f*; *Archit* hi-tech

hither ['hɪðər] *adv Arch, Lit* ici; **h. and thither** çà et là; *Hum* **to give sb a 'come h.' look** jeter un coup d'œil coquin à qn

hitherto [hɪðə'tuː] *adv* jusqu'ici, jusqu'à présent

hit list *n* liste *f* de victimes potentielles; *Fig* liste de personnes/sociétés/*etc* qu'on a dans le colimateur

hit man *n* tueur *m* à gages

hit-or-miss 1 *adj* (*method*) aléatoire, *F* au pif, au pifomètre; **it was all rather h.** c'était au pifomètre *ou* au pif; **in a h. sort of way** au pifomètre, au pif; **to reply in a h. sort of way** répondre au hasard *ou* au petit bonheur; **their method is rather h.** ils font les choses au pif **2** *adv* (*to answer*) au petit bonheur, *F* au pif

HIV [eɪtʃaɪ'viː] *n Med* (*abbr* **human immuno-deficiency virus**) HIV *m*, VIH *m*; **to be H. positive** être séropositif; **to be H. negative** être séronégatif; **H. cases** cas de séropositivité; **H. patients** patients séropositifs; **H. deaths** morts liées à la séropositivité

hive[1] [haɪv] *n* (*for bees*) ruche *f*; *Fig* **a h. of industry** une véritable ruche *ou* fourmilière

hive[2] **1** *vt* (*swarm*) mettre dans une ruche **2** *vi* (*of swarm*) entrer dans la ruche

▶ **hive off 1** *vtsep* (*separate*) détacher *ou* séparer (d'un tout); **to h. off work** sous-traiter, donner du travail en sous-traitance; *Br Com* **part of the industry was hived off to private ownership** une partie de cette industrie a été privatisée **2** *vi* (*split off*) se séparer (**from** de)

hives [haɪvz] *npl Med* urticaire *f*; **to have h.** avoir de l'urticaire

hiya ['haɪjə, haɪ'jɑː] *int F* salut!

HM [eɪtʃ'em] *Br abbr* **His/Her Majesty**

h'm [hm] *int* (*expressing doubt*) heu!, hum!

HMG [eɪtʃem'dʒiː] *Br Admin abbr* **His/Her Majesty's Government**

HMI [eɪtʃem'aɪ] *Br* (*abbr* **His/Her Majesty's Inspector**) inspecteur *m* de l'éducation nationale (britannique)

HMS [eɪtʃe'mes] *Br Naut abbr* **His/Her Majesty's Ship**

HMSO [eɪtʃeme'səʊ] *n Br* (*abbr* **Her/His Majesty's Stationery Office**) = Imprimerie *f* Nationale

HO *n Br* (*abbr* **Home Office**) = Ministère *m* de l'Intérieur

ho [həʊ] *int* **(a)** *Old-fashioned* (*to attract attention*) hé!, ohé!; *Naut* **land ho!** terre! **(b) ho! ho!** (*laughter*) ha! ha!

hoar [hɔːr] *n* gelée *f* blanche

hoard[1] [hɔːd] *n* amas *m*; (*of provisions, food etc*) réserve *f*; **h. of money** trésor *m*, *F* magot *m*; **he has a whole h. of stories** il a une réserve d'histoires assez extraordinaire

hoard[2] *vt* (*corn, information*) amasser; (*provisions, food etc*) mettre *ou* tenir en réserve; (*causing shortage for others*) accaparer; (*money*) thésauriser

▶ **hoard up** *vtsep* = **hoard**[2]

hoarder ['hɔːdər] *n* (*animal*) animal *m* prévoyant; **petrol hoarders were arrested** ceux qui accaparaient l'essence ont été arrêtés; **she's a real h.** elle garde absolument tout, elle ne jette absolument rien

hoarding[1] ['hɔːdɪŋ] *n* (*of provisions*) mise *f* en réserve

hoarding[2] *n* **(a)** *Br* (*for advertising*) panneau *m* d'affichage **(b)** (*fencing*) clôture *f* en planches; (*around worksite etc*) palissade *f*

hoarfrost ['hɔːfrɒst] *n* gelée *f* blanche

hoarse [hɔːs] *adj* (*voice etc*) enroué, rauque; **to be h.** être enroué; **to shout oneself h.** s'enrouer à force de crier

hoarsely ['hɔːslɪ] *adv* d'une voix rauque *ou* enrouée

hoarseness ['hɔːsnɪs] *n* enrouement *m*

hoary ['hɔːrɪ] *adj* **(a)** *Lit* (*hair*) blanchi, chenu; *Bot, Ent* (*foliage, insect*) couvert d'un duvet blanc **(b)** (*old*) vieux, *f* vieille

hoax[1] [həʊks] *n* canular *m*, farce *f*; *Journ F* canular, canard *m*; (**bomb**) **h.** fausse alerte *f* à la bombe; **it turned out to be a h.** finalement, c'était un canular; **to play a h. on sb** faire un canular à qn

hoax[2] *vt* monter *ou* faire un canular à

hoax caller *n* mauvais plaisant *m* (*qui donne de fausses informations par téléphone*)

hoaxer ['həʊksər] *n* farceur, -euse; (*hoax caller*) (*in bomb hoax etc*) mauvais plaisant *m* (*qui donne de fausses informations par téléphone*)

hob [hɒb] *n* (*on electric cooker*) plaque *f*; (*on hearth*) plaque de côté

hobble[1] ['hɒb(ə)l] *n* **(a)** (*limp*) boitillement *m*; *Hist* **h. skirt** jupe *f* entravée **(b)** (*for horses etc*) entrave *f*

hobble[2] **1** *vi* boitiller, clopiner; **to h. along** marcher en boitillant **2** *vt* (*horse etc*) entraver

hobby ['hɒbɪ] *n* passe-temps *m inv*, hobby *m*, violon *m* d'Ingres; **to take up a h.** se trouver un hobby; **to take up sth as a h.** se mettre à qch pendant son temps libre

hobbyhorse ['hɒbɪhɔːs] *n* (*toy*) (*of merry-go-round*) cheval *m* de bois; (*rocking-horse*) cheval à bascule; *Fig* dada *m*, cheval de bataille; *Fig* **to get on one's h.** enfourcher son dada *ou* son cheval de bataille

hobgoblin ['hɒbgɒblɪn] *n Myth* lutin *m*

hobnail ['hɒbneɪl] *n* clou *m*, fer *m* (*pour les chaussures*); **hobnail(ed) boot** chaussure *f* ferrée

hobnob ['hɒbnɒb] *vi* (**-bb-**) *F* **to h. with sb** frayer avec qn

hobo ['həʊbəʊ] *n Am* **(a)** (*tramp*) clochard *m* **(b)** (*itinerant worker*) ouvrier *m* saisonnier

Hobson ['hɒbsən] *n* **it's H.'s choice** je n'ai pas/il n'a pas/*etc* vraiment le choix (*se dit d'une situation où le choix n'est qu'apparent*)

hock[1] [hɒk] *n* (*of horse*) jarret *m*

hock[2] *n* (*wine*) vin *m* du Rhin

hock[3] *n F* **in h.** (*of watch etc*) en gage, *F* au clou, *F* chez ma tante; (*of person*) (*in debt*) endetté; **to put sth in h.** (*pawn*) mettre qch en gage; **to be in h. to the bank** devoir de l'argent à la banque

hock[4] *vt F* (*pawn*) mettre au clou

hockey ['hɒkɪ] *n Sp* **(a)** *Br* hockey *m* (sur gazon); **to play h.** jouer au hockey; **h. stick** crosse *f* de hockey **(b)** *Am* (*ice hockey*) hockey *m* (sur glace), *Can* hockey

hockshop ['hɒkʃɒp] *n Am F* crédit *m* municipal, mont-de-piété *m*, *pl* monts-de-piété

hocus-pocus ['həʊkəs'pəʊkəs] *n* **(a)** (*formula used by conjurers*) abracadabra **(b)** (*trickery*) tromperie *f*, supercherie *f*

hod [hɒd] *n* **(a)** (*of bricklayer*) oiseau *m*, hotte *f*; **h. carrier** aide-maçon *m* **(b)** (*for coal*) seau *m*, caisse *f*

hodgepodge ['hɒdʒpɒdʒ] *n esp Am* = **hotchpotch**

Hodgkin's disease ['hɒdʒkɪnz] *n Med* maladie *f* de Hodgkin

hoe[1] [həʊ] *n* houe *f*, binette *f*; (**weeding**) **h.** sarcloir *m*; (**Dutch**) **h.** griffe-bineuse *f*, *pl* griffes-bineuses

hoe[2] *vt* (**hoed; hoeing**) (*soil*) biner; (*weeds*) sarcler

hoedown ['həʊdaʊn] *n esp Am* bal *m* populaire

hog[1] [hɒg] *n* **(a)** (*castrated pig*) porc *m* châtré; *Am* (*pig*) porc, cochon *m*, pourceau *m*; *F* **to go the whole h.** aller jusqu'au bout; **they went the whole h. for the party** (*didn't stint*) ils n'ont pas fait les choses à moitié; *US Fig F* **to live high on the h.** mener joyeuse vie **(b)** *Fig* (*glutton*) goinfre *m*, glouton *m*

hog[2] *vt* (**-gg-**) *F* (*take, use etc more than one's fair share of*) prendre plus que sa part de; **to h. the television** monopoliser la télé; **to h. the limelight** accaparer la vedette; *Aut* **to h. the road** prendre toute la place; *Aut* **to h. the centre lane** monopoliser la voie centrale

Hogmanay [hɒgmə'neɪ] *n Scot* la Saint-Sylvestre

hogshead ['hɒgzhed] *n* (*barrel*) tonneau *m*, barrique *f*

hogtie ['hɒgtaɪ] *vt US* (*animal*) lier les quatre pattes de; *Fig* (*the economy etc*) entraver

hogwash ['hɒgwɒʃ] *n* (*swill*) eaux *fpl* grasses (*que l'on donne aux porcs*); *F* (*nonsense*) foutaise *f*

hogweed ['hɒgwiːd] *n* (*plant*) berce *f* commune

hoi polloi ['hɔɪpə'lɔɪ] *npl Pej* **the h.** la foule *f*, les masses *fpl*

hoist[1] [hɔɪst] *n* **(a)** (*act*) levage *m*; *F* **to give sb a h.** (**up**) aider qn à monter; (*from beneath also*) faire la courte échelle à qn **(b)** (*device*) appareil *m ou* engin *m* de levage; (*winch*) treuil *m*, grue *f*, palan *m*; *Min* bourriquet *m*; (*for goods*) monte-charge *m inv*

hoist[2] *vt* (*load*) lever, hisser; *Naut* (*ship's boat, flag*) hisser; **to h. boats in/out** embarquer/débarquer les canots; **h. away!** hissez!; **she hoisted herself on to the wall** elle s'est hissée sur le mur; *Fig* **to be hoist with one's own petard** tomber dans son propre piège

hoity-toity ['hɔɪtɪ'tɔɪtɪ] **1** *int* ta, ta, ta!, taratata! **2** *adj* qui se donne des airs, qui fait l'important; **she can get quite h.** elle fait l'importante quelquefois

hokey-cokey [həʊkɪ'kəʊkɪ] *n Br* **to do the h.** danser une ronde (*où chacun imite l'autre*)

hokum ['həʊkəm] *n Am F* (*in film etc*) niaiseries *fpl*; (*nonsense*) bêtises *fpl*, âneries *fpl*

hold[1] [həʊld] *n* **(a)** (*grip*) prise *f*; *Boxing* tenu *m*; (*in wrestling*) prise; **to have h. of sb/sth** tenir qn/qch; **to catch** *or* **get** *or* **take h. of sb/sth** saisir *ou* empoigner qn/qch; **to get h. of sth** (*find*) mettre la main sur qch; **where did you get h. of that?** où vous êtes-vous procuré cela?; **they prevented us from getting h. of the code** ils nous ont empêchés de nous emparer du code; **to get h. of the wrong idea** mal comprendre; **it's difficult to get h. of this book** (*find a copy of it*) ce livre est difficile à trouver; **to relax one's h.** relâcher son étreinte; **to let go one's h.** lâcher prise; **to lose one's h. on reality** perdre le sens des réalités; **to have a h. on** *or* **over sb** avoir prise *ou* de l'emprise sur qn; **to gain a firm h. over sb** acquérir un grand pouvoir sur qn; **no holds barred** tous les coups sont permis; **a no-holds-barred argument/contest**

une dispute/compétition où tous les coups sont permis; **a no-holds-barred discussion** une discussion très franche

(b) (*in rockclimbing etc*) point *m* d'appui

(c) on h. (*of project*) en suspens; **to put sth on h.** mettre qch en suspens; **the road building programme is on h.** la construction de la route est interrompue; *Tel* **to put sb on h.** mettre qn en attente *ou* en parcage; *Tel* **to be on h.** (*of caller*) attendre, être en attente

hold² (*pt, pp* **held** [held]) **1** *vt* **(a)** (*grip*) (*child etc*) tenir; **to h. sth in one's hand** tenir qch à la main; (*something very small*) tenir qch dans la main; **to h. sth/sb tight(ly)** serrer qch/qn, tenir qch/qn serré; **they held (each other's) hands** ils se tenaient (par) la main; **to h. one's sides with laughter** se tenir les côtes de rire; **to h. one's nose** se boucher le nez; **to h. sth in position** tenir *ou* maintenir qch en place; **four screws h. the shelf to the wall** l'étagère est fixée au mur par quatre vis; **the table is held in place by steel bolts** la table est maintenue par des boulons d'acier

(b) (*detain etc*) *Jur* **to be held on remand** être incarcéré (*en détention provisoire*); **to h. sb prisoner** retenir qn prisonnier; **to h. sb (as) hostage** retenir qn en otage; **she was held without trial for six weeks** elle est restée en prison six semaines sans avoir été jugée

(c) (*command etc*) **to h. one's ground** tenir bon, ne pas lâcher pied; **to h. one's own** se maintenir, se défendre; *Mil* **to h. a fort** défendre une forteresse; **to h. a position** tenir une position; **to h. the stage** (*of actor*) captiver son auditoire; *Fig* (*in discussion etc*) occuper le devant de la scène; *Naut etc* **to h. course** tenir la route; **car that holds the road well** voiture qui tient bien la route

(d) (*carry*) porter; **to h. one's head high** garder la tête haute; **to h. oneself straight/well** se tenir droit/bien

(e) (*contain*) contenir, renfermer; **barrel that holds twenty litres** tonneau d'une contenance de vingt litres; **car that holds six people** voiture à six places; **to h. water** (*of cask etc*) être étanche; *Fig* (*of theory, story etc*) tenir debout; **the theory doesn't h. water** la théorie ne tient pas (debout); **to be able to h. one's drink** bien supporter l'alcool; **what the future holds for us** ce que l'avenir nous réserve; **sport held no interest for them** pour eux, le sport ne présentait aucun intérêt

(f) (*conduct etc*) (*meeting*) tenir; (*party etc*) donner; **the meeting will be held at 8pm** la réunion aura lieu à 8 heures du soir; **to h. a conversation with sb** s'entretenir avec qn; **the two sides held talks** des discussions ont eu lieu entre les deux parties; **to h. a surgery for one's patients** recevoir ses patients

(g) (*restrain*) **to h. one's breath** retenir sa respiration *ou* son souffle; **there's no holding him** (une fois lancé) il n'y a pas moyen de l'arrêter; **h. your tongue!** taisez-vous!; *F* **h. it!, h. your horses!** arrêtez!, attendez!, stop!; **h. it!** (*at photographer's*) ne bougez plus!, on ne bouge plus!; *Mil* **to h. the enemy** contenir l'ennemi; **to h. the front page** garder la une

(h) (*keep*) (*airline seat*) bloquer; **to h. sb's interest** retenir l'attention de qn; **the film doesn't h. the attention for long** le film ne retient pas l'attention très longtemps; **to h. one's audience** retenir l'attention de son auditoire; **to h. sb to their promise** obliger *ou* contraindre qn à tenir sa promesse; **we can h. a room for you until tomorrow** la chambre vous sera réservée jusqu'à demain, on vous gardera la chambre jusqu'à demain; *Am* **h. the onions** (*in restaurant*) sans oignons

(i) (*possess*) (*title*) avoir, posséder; (*opinion*) avoir; (*position, post*) occuper; (*record, shares*) détenir; (*passport*) être porteur *ou* détenteur de; **to h. 5% of the shares in a company** détenir 5% du capital d'une société; **she had held (government) office before** elle avait déjà assumé des fonctions au gouvernement; *Com* **to h. sb's commercial bill** détenir un effet sur qn

(j) (*consider*) **to h. sth lightly** faire peu de cas de qch, attacher peu d'importance à qch; **to h. sth sacred** tenir qch pour sacré; **to h. sb responsible** tenir qn responsable; **to be held in respect** être respecté de tous; **to h. that ...** soutenir que ...

(k) *Mus* **to h. a note** tenir *ou* prolonger une note

(l) *Tel* **h. the line!** ne quittez pas!; **h. all my calls** ne me passez aucun appel

2 *vi* **(a)** (*of rope etc*) tenir (bon); **h. tight!** tenez bon!; *Aut* **tyres that h. in the wet** pneus qui tiennent bien la route par temps de pluie

(b) (*last*) (*of agreement etc*) durer, persister; (*of weather*) se maintenir; **if your luck holds** si votre chance dure

(c) (*be valid*) **to h. (good** *or* **true)** être vrai *ou* valable; **the same holds true in respect of ...** il en est de même pour ...

(d) *Tel* attendre

hold³ *n* (*of ship*) cale *f*; (*for luggage on plane*) soute *f*; **h. baggage** bagages *mpl* de soute

▶ **hold against** *vtaspo* (*dislike for*) **to h. sth against sb** tenir rigueur de qch à qn; **I won't h. it against you** je ne t'en voudrai pas

▶ **hold back 1** *vi* **(a)** (*stay in the background*) rester en arrière **(b)** (*restrain oneself*) se retenir; **to h. back from doing sth** attendre avant de faire qch; (*stronger*) se retenir de faire qch; **buyers are holding back** les acheteurs s'abstiennent **2** *vtsep* **(a)** (*restrain*) (*person, anger, tears*) retenir; (*anger, tears, crowd*) contenir **(b)** (*impede*) freiner, entraver; **lack of investment is holding industry back** l'absence d'investissements freine l'industrie **(c)** (*withhold*) (*truth*) cacher, dissimuler; **he's holding something back** il cache quelque chose

▶ **hold down** *vtsep* **(a)** (*restrain*) (*person*) maintenir à terre; **to h. down interest rates** empêcher l'augmentation des taux d'intérêt **(b) to h. down a job** (*occupy*) avoir un emploi; (*keep*) garder un emploi; **although she is a student, she holds down a full-time job** bien qu'elle étudie, elle occupe un poste à plein temps; **he never holds down a job for more than a week** il ne peut jamais garder un emploi plus d'une semaine

▶ **hold forth** *vi* (*speak pompously*) disserter (**on sth** sur qch); **he's always got something to h. forth about** il trouve toujours quelque chose sur quoi disserter

▶ **hold in** *vtsep* (*laughter*) réprimer; (*emotion*) maîtriser; (*anger*) contenir; (*horse*) serrer la bride à, contenir; **to h. one's stomach** *or* **oneself in** rentrer son ventre; **to h. oneself in** (*emotionally*) se maîtriser

▶ **hold off 1** *vtsep* **(a)** (*keep away*) (*enemy*) tenir à distance; **he held off his assailants** il a tenu ses assaillants en respect; **she held the press off by promising to make a statement** elle a fait attendre les journalistes en leur promettant un communiqué **(b)** (*refrain from*) (*decision, choice etc*) remettre à plus tard; **to h. off doing sth** attendre pour faire qch; **they held off buying a new car** ils ont repoussé l'achat d'une nouvelle voiture **2** *vi* (*keep away*) se tenir à distance (**from** de); (*refrain from doing sth, from deciding*) différer, surseoir; **the rain is holding off** jusqu'ici il ne pleut pas

▶ **hold off from** *vipo* (*decision, choice etc*) remettre à plus tard; **to h. off from doing sth** attendre avant de faire qch

▶ **hold on 1** *vi* **(a)** (*endure*) tenir, résister **(b)** (*wait*) attendre, patienter; **h. on (a minute)!** (*not so fast*) pas si vite!; *Tel* **h. on a moment** ne quittez pas **(c)** (*keep one's grip*) se tenir; **h. on (tight)!** (*on bus, motorbike etc*) tiens-toi bien! **2** *vtsep* (*keep attached*) (*piece of wood etc*) fixer; **the tiles are held on with glue** les carreaux sont maintenus en place par de la colle

▶ **hold on to** *vipo* **(a)** (*grip*) (*thing*) s'agripper à; *Fig* (*idea, hope etc*) se raccrocher à **(b)** (*keep*) garder; **h. on to that book** (*it may be valuable*) garde ce livre précieusement; **she held on to her money** elle se cramponnait à son argent

▶ **hold out 1** *vtsep* **(a)** (*stretch out*) (*one's hand*) tendre **(b)** (*offer*) (*hope*) offrir, laisser; **the doctor doesn't h. out much hope** le docteur ne laisse pas beaucoup d'espoir **2** *vi* **(a)** (*resist*) tenir (le coup); **to h. out against an attack** résister à une attaque; **to h. out for a higher price** espérer un prix plus élevé **(b)** (*of supplies etc*) durer

▶ **hold out on** *vipo* (*not give information to*) **you've been holding out on me** (*I didn't know you played the piano etc*) tu m'as caché des choses

▶ **hold over** *vtsep* **(a)** (*postpone*) remettre (à plus tard); (*decision*) ajourner; (*payment*) arriérer **(b) to h. sth over sb** (*threaten with*) menacer qn de qch

▶ **hold to** *vipo* (*abide by*) s'en tenir à; **to h. to a belief** rester attaché à une croyance; **to h. to one's decision** s'en tenir à *ou* maintenir sa décision

▶ **hold together 1** *vtsep* (*two objects*) maintenir ensemble; (*party, alliance*) maintenir la cohésion de; **the two pieces of wood are held together by nails** les deux morceaux de bois sont cloués ensemble **2** *vi* (*of objects*) tenir (ensemble); (*of ideas*) être cohérent; **the story doesn't h. together** l'histoire ne tient pas debout

▶ **hold up 1** *vtsep* **(a)** (*support*) soutenir; **these ropes h. the tent up** ces cordes maintiennent la tente bien droite

(b) (*raise*) lever (en l'air); **to h. one's head up (with pride)** lever la tête (avec fierté); **she held the book up** (*so that everyone could see*) elle brandit le livre; *Fig* **to h. sb up as an example** citer qn comme exemple; **to h. sb up to ridicule** tourner qn en ridicule

(c) (*delay*) (*person*) retenir, retarder; (*train, kick-off etc*) retarder; (*traffic, agreement, decision*) bloquer; **the car was held up at the traffic lights** la voiture a dû s'arrêter au feu rouge; **our departure was held up by bad weather** notre départ a été retardé par le mauvais temps; **goods held up at customs** marchandises retenues à la douane; **financial difficulties are holding the project up** le projet est freiné par des difficultés financières

(**d**) (*in order to rob*) (*person, bank*) attaquer; (*train*) attaquer à main armée

2 *vi* (**a**) (*stay in place*) (*of shelf etc*) tenir (en place); (*of good weather*) se maintenir; **the old building is still holding up** le vieux bâtiment est toujours debout; **I hope the good weather holds up** j'espère que le beau temps va durer; **she's holding up well under the pressure** elle supporte bien la pression; **my finances are holding up well** je tiens le coup financièrement

(**b**) (*of theory etc*) tenir debout

▶ **hold with** *vipo* (*usu neg*) **I don't h. with such behaviour/his opinions** je n'approuve pas une telle conduite/ses opinions

holdall ['həʊldɔːl] *n Br* sac *m* de voyage, fourre-tout *m inv*

holder ['həʊldər] *n* (**a**) (*person*) (*of passport, permit etc*) possesseur *m*, détenteur, -trice; (*of ticket*) possesseur; (*of degree, record, shares*) détenteur, -trice; (*of opinion, belief*) tenant *m*; *Fin* (*of bonds, bill*) porteur, -euse; (*of right, post, account, degree etc*) titulaire *mf*; (*of championship*) tenant; *Sp* **the present h.** (*of the title*) l'actuel tenant du titre (**b**) (*device*) support *m*; (**drill**) **h.** porte-foret *m*, *pl* porte-forets; (**soap**) **h.** porte-savon *m*, *pl* porte-savons; **pot plant h.** cache-pot *m*, *pl* cache-pots; (**cigarette**) **h.** porte-cigarettes *m inv*

holding ['həʊldɪŋ] *n* (**a**) *Agr* (*property*) terre *f* affermée, ferme *f*; *Fin* effets *mpl* en portefeuille; (*shares in company*) participation *f*; **he has holdings in several companies** il est actionnaire de plusieurs sociétés; **h. company** holding *m*, société *f* de gestion

(**b**) (*action*) (*of congress etc*) tenue *f*; *Mus* (*of note*) tenue; (*lengthening*) prolongation *f*

(**c**) (*delay*) *Av* attente *f*; **h. letter/h. reply** réponse *f* d'attente; *Mil* **h. operation** (*containment*) opération *f* de fixation; *Fig* **we need a h. operation** il faut trouver un moyen de retarder les choses; *Av* **h. pattern** circuit *m* d'attente

hold-up *n* (**a**) (*delay*) arrêt *m*; (*on road*) embouteillage *m*; **there's been a h. on the line** (*on the Tube etc*) il y a eu des perturbations sur la ligne; **there have been no hold-ups with the project** le projet n'a eu à souffrir d'aucun retard (**b**) (*armed robbery*) attaque *f* à main armée, hold-up *m*; **this is a h.** c'est un hold-up

hole¹ [həʊl] *n* (**a**) (*in the ground*) trou *m*, creux *m*, cavité *f*; *Golf* trou; (*of rabbit*) terrier *m*; (*of fox*) tanière *f*; (*of mouse etc*) trou; **to dig a h.** creuser un trou; **what a h.!** (*of room etc*) quel gourbi!; (*of house*) quel taudis!; (*of town*) quel bled!; *Golf* **h. in one** trou réussi en un coup

(**b**) (*opening*) trou *m*; (*in metal plate etc*) perforation *f*; (*of drive belt etc*) point *m*; (*of flute*) perce *f*; (*in theory etc*) point faible; **a h. in the law** un vide juridique; *Comptr* (**punch**) **h.** perforation *f*; *Med* **h. in the heart** trou dans le cœur; **h. in the wall** restaurant/café/endroit exigu; **to make a h. in** faire un trou dans *ou* à; (*piece of clothing*) trouer; *Fig* **to make a h. in one's savings** (*of expenditure*) faire un (gros) trou dans ses économies; **this jersey is full of holes** ce tricot est tout troué *ou* est plein de trous; **to pick holes in a theory** relever les points faibles d'une théorie

(**c**) *F* (*difficult situation*) situation *f* difficile; **to be** *or* **find oneself in a h.** être *ou* se trouver dans une situation délicate

hole² **1** *vt* (**a**) (*make a hole in*) trouer, faire un trou dans; **the ship was holed below the water line** le navire avait des avaries au-dessous de la ligne de flottaison; **the building had been holed by shellfire** le bâtiment a été endommagé par les obus (**b**) (*put into a hole*) **to h. the ball** *Golf* envoyer *ou* mettre la balle dans le trou; *Billiards* bloquer; *Fig* **holed in one!** vous avez deviné juste! **2** *vi* (*of stockings etc*) se trouer, se percer

▶ **hole out** *vi Golf* mettre la balle dans le trou

▶ **hole up** *vi F* (*hide*) se terrer

hole-and-corner *adj F* clandestin; (*affair*) un peu louche

hole-in-the-wall machine *n Banking* guichet *m* automatique

hole punch *n* perforatrice *f*

holey ['həʊlɪ] *adj F* (tout) troué, plein de trous

holiday¹ ['hɒlɪdɪ, -deɪ] *n* (**a**) *Br* vacances *fpl*; **a month's h.** un mois de vacances; **how much h. do you get?** combien est-ce que tu as de vacances?; **the summer holidays** les grandes vacances; **to be on h.** être en vacances; **to take a h.** prendre des vacances; **when are you going on h.?** quand est-ce que vous allez prendre vos vacances?; **where are you going on h.** *or* **for your holidays?** où allez-vous pour vos vacances?; **camping h.** vacances passées à faire du camping; **ski** *or* **skiing h.** vacances de neige; **h. brochure** catalogue *m* de vacances; **h. centre** centre *m* de vacances; **h. club** club *m* de vacances; **h. entitlement** nombre *m* de jours de vacances auquel un employé a droit, droit *m* aux vacances; **h. market** marché *m* du tourisme; **h. period** période *f* de fêtes; **h. spot** lieu *m* de vacances, villégiature *f*; **h. tummy** turista *f*, diarrhée *f* du voyageur; **h. village** village *m* de vacances *ou* de loisirs; **h. worker** vacataire *mf*

(**b**) *Br* (*day off*) (jour *m* de) congé *m*; *Sch* **half h.** demi-journée *f* de congé; **I'm going to take a h. today** je vais prendre un jour de congé aujourd'hui

(**c**) (*day of festival*) (jour *m* de) fête *f*, jour férié; **public** *or* *Br* **bank h.** fête légale

holiday² ['hɒlɪdeɪ] *vi Br* passer les vacances

holiday camp *n Br* camp *m* de vacances; (*for children*) colonie *f* de vacances

holiday cottage *n Br* gîte *m*

holiday home *n Br* résidence *f* secondaire

holiday-maker *n Br* vacancier, -ière; (*in summer*) estivant, -ante

holiday resort *n Br* lieu *m* de vacances, villégiature *f*

holiday season *n Br* période *f* des vacances

holier-than-thou ['həʊlɪəðən'ðaʊ] *adj* (*attitude etc*) hypocritement pieux

holiness ['həʊlɪnɪs] *n* sainteté *f*; **His/Your H.** (*of the Pope*) Sa/Votre Sainteté

holism ['həʊlɪz(ə)m] *n Phil, Med* holisme *m*

holistic [həʊ'lɪstɪk] *adj Phil, Med* holistique

Holland ['hɒlənd] *n* Hollande *f*

holland ['hɒlənd] *n Tex* toile *f* de Hollande, toile bise

holler¹ ['hɒlər] *n esp Am F* braillement *m*

holler² *vi esp Am F* crier à tue-tête, brailler

hollow ['hɒləʊ] **1** *adj* (**a**) creux; (*cheek*) creux, rentré; (*eye*) cave; *Mil, Hist* **h. square** carré *m*; *Fig* **to feel h.** (*emotionally*) se sentir vide *ou* vidé; (*hungry*) avoir le ventre *ou* l'estomac creux; *Fig* **he's got h. legs** (*can eat a lot*) il mange comme quatre, il a le ver solitaire; (*can drink a lot*) il boit comme un trou

(**b**) (*sound*) sourd; **in a h. voice** d'une voix caverneuse; **a h. laugh** un ricanement

(**c**) (*insincere*) (*promise, friendship etc*) faux, *f* fausse, trompeur, -euse; (*worthless*) qui sonne creux; **a h. victory** une victoire sans signification

2 *adv* (**a**) **to sound h.** sonner creux

(**b**) *Br F* **to beat sb h.** battre qn à plate(s) couture(s)

3 *n* (*of hand, tree, in field etc*) creux *m*; (*larger depression in ground*) dépression *f* (*du sol*); *Geog* (*basin*) cuvette *f*

▶ **hollow out** *vtsep* (*carve, scrape out etc*) creuser, évider; **to h. out the ground** (*of water*) raviner le terrain

hollow-cheeked [hɒləʊ'tʃiːkt] *adj* aux joues creuses

hollow-eyed *adj* aux yeux caves

hollowness ['hɒləʊnɪs] *n* (**a**) (*of tree etc*) creux *m*, cavité *f* (**b**) (*of voice*) timbre *m* caverneux (**c**) (*of promise etc*) manque *m* de sincérité; (*worthlessness*) (*of victory etc*) absence *f* de signification

holly ['hɒlɪ] *n* **h.** (**tree**) houx *m*; **h. berry** cenelle *f*

hollyhock ['hɒlɪhɒk] *n* (*plant*) rose *f* trémière

holm¹ [həʊm] *n Eng Dial* (*island*) petite île *f*, îlot *m* (*de rivière*)

holm² *n* (*tree*) **h.** (**oak**) yeuse *f*, chêne *m* vert

holocaust ['hɒləkɔːst] *n* holocauste *m*; *Hist* **the H.** l'Holocauste; **a H. survivor/victim** un survivant/une victime de l'Holocauste

hologram ['hɒləgræm] *n Phot* hologramme *m*

holograph ['hɒləgræf] *n* document *m* /testament *m* (h)olographe

hols [hɒlz] *npl Br F* vacances *fpl*, vacs *fpl*

holster ['həʊlstər] *n* étui *m* (de revolver); (*for rifle*) fonte *f*

holy ['həʊlɪ] **1** *adj* (**holier, holiest**) saint, sacré; (*person*) saint, pieux; *Fig F* **to swear by all that is h.** jurer sur ce qu'on a de plus sacré; *Fig* **to have a h. fear of sth** avoir une peur bleue de qch; *F* **that child is a h. terror** cet enfant est une terreur; **the H. Bible** la sainte Bible; **h. bread** pain *m* bénit; **the H. City** la Ville sainte; **H. Communion** Sainte communion *f*; *Sl* **h. cow!, h. smoke!, h. mackerel!** sapristi!; **the H. Father** le Saint-Père, le pape; **the H. Ghost** *or* **Spirit** le Saint-Esprit; **h. ground** terre *f* sacrée; *F Pej* **H. Joe** grenouille *f* de bénitier; **the H. Land** la Terre Sainte; **h. matrimony** les liens *mpl* sacrés du mariage; **h. orders** les ordres *mpl*; **h. place** lieu *m* saint; **the H. Roman Empire** le Saint-Empire romain germanique; **the H. Trinity** la Sainte Trinité; **h. war** guerre *f* sainte; **h. water** eau *f* bénite; **H. Week** la semaine sainte

2 *n* **the H. of Holies** le Saint des Saints

homage ['hɒmɪdʒ] *n* hommage *m*; **to pay** *or* **do h. to sb** rendre hommage à qn

homburg ['hɒmbɜːg] *n* **h.** (**hat**) chapeau *m* mou, feutre *m* souple

home[1] [həʊm] **1** *n* **(a)** *(house)* maison *f*; *(flat)* appartement *m*; *Biol (of animal, plant)* habitat *m*; **this is my h.** ici, c'est chez moi; **a house without love is not a h.** sans l'amour, une maison n'est pas un foyer; **to come from a broken h.** avoir des parents divorcés; **a happy h.** une famille heureuse; **I've come straight from h.** je viens (directement) de chez moi; *Br* **the Ideal H. Exhibition,** *US* **the H. Show** ≈ le Salon des Arts Ménagers; **to have a h. of one's own** avoir un chez-soi *ou* un foyer; **to own one's own h.** être propriétaire (de sa maison); **television brings the world into your own h.** la télévision vous apporte le monde à domicile; *Iron* **don't you have a h. to go to?** vous avez l'intention de passer la nuit ici?; **to buy some things for the h.** acheter des choses pour sa maison/son appartement; **to make one's h. in France** s'établir en France; **Glasgow is her second h.** Glasgow est sa deuxième patrie; **it's a h. from h.** on y est comme chez soi; **there's no place like h.** on n'est nulle part si bien que chez soi; **to leave h.** quitter la maison; *(for good)* partir (définitivement); **to be away from h.** être parti *ou* absent *ou* en voyage; **at h.** à la maison, chez soi; *Sp (to play)* à domicile; **to stay at h.** rester à la maison; **to find no one at h.** trouver la maison vide; **how are things at h.?** comment ça va chez vous?; **these children have problems at h.** ces enfants ont des problèmes chez eux; **I don't feel at h. here** je me sens dépaysé ici, je ne me sens pas chez moi ici; **he is at h. on** *or* **with any topic** il est à l'aise sur tous les sujets; **make yourself at h.** fais comme chez toi; **he insulted me in my own h.!** il m'a insulté sous mon propre toit!; **to come from a good h.** venir d'une bonne famille; **good h. wanted for three kittens** *(on notice)* on recherche de gentils maîtres pour trois chatons

(b) *(country, region)* patrie *f*, pays *m* (natal), terre *f* natale; **at h. and abroad** dans notre pays et à l'étranger; **our policy at h. and abroad** notre politique intérieure et extérieure; **to take an example nearer h.** sans aller chercher si loin; **Greece, the h. of the arts** la Grèce, patrie des beaux-arts; **Valencia is the h. of paella** Valence est le pays de la paella

(c) *(for old people etc)* asile *m*, hospice *m*; **old people's h.** maison *f* de retraite; **she didn't want her father to go into a h.** elle ne voulait pas que son père aille à l'hospice; **children's h.** home *m* d'enfants

(d) *(in games)* le but

(e) *(in compounds)* **h. address** adresse *f* personnelle; *Obst* **h. birth** accouchement *m* à la maison; **first-time h. buyer** personne *f* qui achète une maison pour la première fois; **h. improvements** travaux *mpl* d'amélioration du logement; **h. journey** voyage *m* de retour; *Sp* **h. leg** match *m* à domicile; **h. life** vie *f* de famille; *Fin* **h. loan** crédit *m* immobilier; **h. purchase loan** crédit *m* épargne logement; *Econ* **h. market** marché *m* intérieur; *Sp* **h. match** match à domicile; *TV, Journ* **h. news** nouvelles *fpl* nationales; **h. owner** propriétaire *mf* d'une maison/d'un appartement; **h. ownership is increasing** le nombre des personnes propriétaires de leur logement augmente; *Econ* **h. products** produits *mpl* nationaux *ou* domestiques; *Baseball* **h. run** coup *m* de circuit; **to hit a h. run** faire un coup de circuit; **h. sales** ventes *fpl* sur le marché intérieur; *Sp* **the h. straight** *or* **stretch** la dernière ligne droite; *Sp* **h. team** *or* **side** équipe *f* qui reçoit; **a h. truth** une vérité bien sentie; **to tell sb a few h. truths** dire son fait *ou* ses quatre vérités à qn; **h. user** utilisateur *m* domestique; *Sp* **h. win** victoire *f* à domicile

(f) *Comptr (key)* (touche *f*) début *m*

2 *adv* **(a)** *(to/at one's house)* à la maison, chez soi; **to go/come h.** rentrer (à la maison); *(after period of absence)* retourner/revenir dans sa famille; **on her way h.** en rentrant *ou* en retournant/revenant chez elle; **to bring work h.** emporter du travail à la maison; **to be h.** être de retour; **he's h. again!** il est de retour!; **we'll be h. soon** nous serons bientôt arrivés chez nous

(b) *(to/in one's country)* au pays; **to go/come h.** retourner au pays; **to send sb h.** renvoyer qn chez lui; *(repatriate)* rapatrier qn

(c) **his speech went h.** son discours fit forte impression; **her remarks/criticisms hit h.** ses remarques/critiques ont fait mouche; **it will come h. to him some day** il s'en rendra compte un jour; **to drive sth h. to sb** faire entrer qch dans la tête à qn; **to push an attack h.** pousser à fond une attaque; **to push h. one's advantage** profiter au maximum d'un avantage

(d) *(all the way)* à fond; **to screw a piece h.** visser *ou* serrer une pièce à bloc; **she drove the knife h. with all her strength** elle enfonça le couteau de toutes ses forces; **the bolt slid h.** le verrou glissa dans la serrure

home[2] *vi (of pigeon)* revenir au colombier; **to h. on** *or* **towards ...** *(of aircraft, missile etc)* mettre le cap sur ..., se diriger vers *ou* sur ...

▶ **home in** *vi (approach or reach target) (of airplane, missile etc)* arriver au but

▶ **home in on** *vipo (aim for)* viser; **to h. in on a target** *(of missile)* se diriger en plein vers un objectif; *Fig* **she homed in on this error** elle a relevé *ou* repéré cette erreur, elle n'a pas manqué de relever cette erreur

home-baked *adj (bread, cake)* fait *ou* cuit à la maison; *(bread)* de ménage

home banking *n Comptr* banque *f* à domicile

homebird ['həʊmbɜːd] *n F (person)* casanier, -ière

homebody ['həʊmbɒdɪ] *n esp Am F* casanier, -ière

home(-)brew *n (beer)* bière *f* brassée à la maison

home-brewed ['həʊm'bruːd] *adj (beer)* brassé à la maison

homecoming ['həʊmkʌmɪŋ] *n* retour *m* (au foyer *ou* à la maison); *(to one's country)* retour au pays

home computer *n* ordinateur *m* domestique

home computing *n* informatique *f* à domicile

home cooking *n* cuisine *f* familiale; *(in restaurant)* cuisine bourgeoise

Home Counties *n Br Geog* comtés *mpl* avoisinant Londres

home delivery *n* livraison *f* à domicile

home economics *n* [①A10,c] *Sch* économie *f* domestique

home economist *n* spécialiste *mf* d'économie domestique

home ground *n Sp* terrain *m* du club; *Fig* **to be on h.** être en terrain familier

home-grown *adj (from garden)* du jardin; *(from one's own country)* du pays; *Fig* **many people prefer Japanese cars to the h. product** beaucoup de gens préfèrent les voitures japonaises à celles qu'on fabrique chez eux

Home Guard *n Br Hist (in Second World War)* section *f* de volontaires de l'armée britannique restée sur le territoire pour le défendre en cas d'invasion

home help *n Br Admin (person)* aide *f* ménagère

home key *n Comptr* touche *f* début

homeland ['həʊmlænd] *n esp Lit* patrie *f*; *(in South Africa)* bantoustan *m*, homeland *m*

homeless ['həʊmlɪs] **1** *adj* sans foyer, sans abri; **to be h.** être à la rue *ou* sur le pavé **2** *npl* **the h.** les sans-abri *mpl*, les sans-logis *mpl*

homelessness ['həʊmlɪsnɪs] *n* = fait de ne pas avoir de logis; **h. among the young is growing** de plus en plus de jeunes sont sans abri

homeloving ['həʊmlʌvɪŋ] *adj* casanier, -ière

homely ['həʊmlɪ] *adj* **(a)** *(food)* simple, ordinaire; *(tastes)* modeste; *(atmosphere)* accueillant; *Br (person)* simple **(b)** *Am (plain) (person)* au physique ingrat

home-made *adj (cake, wine)* fait à la maison; *(bread)* de ménage; **the bookshelves looked rather h.** les étagères semblaient plutôt artisanales

homemaker ['həʊmmeɪkər] *n Am* **(a)** femme *f*/homme *m* d'intérieur, ménagère *f* **(b)** *(social worker)* aide *f* ménagère

Home Office *n Br Pol* = Ministère *m* de l'Intérieur

homeopath ['həʊmɪəʊpæθ] *n* homéopathe *mf*

homeopathic [həʊmɪəʊ'pæθɪk] *adj* homéopathique

homeopathy [həʊmɪ'ɒpəθɪ] *n* homéopathie *f*

home party selling *n Mktg* vente *f* domiciliaire

Homer ['həʊmər] *n* Homère *m*; *Prov* **even H. nods, H. sometimes nods** même les meilleurs font des erreurs

homer ['həʊmər] *n* **(a)** *Am Baseball F* coup *m* de circuit **(b)** *F (homing pigeon)* pigeon *m* voyageur **(c)** *Br F (work)* = travail *m* exécuté par un ouvrier à l'insu de son patron

Homeric [həʊ'merɪk] *adj (poem, hero)* homérique

home rule *n Pol* autonomie *f*

Home Secretary *n Br Pol* = Ministre *m* de l'Intérieur

home shopping *n Comptr, Tel* téléachat *m*

homesick ['həʊmsɪk] *adj* **(a)** *(for one's country)* nostalgique, qui a le mal du pays; **to feel h.** avoir le mal du pays **(b)** *(for one's home)* **a h. little boy** un petit garçon qui s'ennuie de ses parents; **are you h.?** tu t'ennuies de chez toi?

homesickness ['həʊmsɪknɪs] *n* mal *m* du pays, nostalgie *f*

homespun ['həʊmspʌn] **1** *adj* **(a)** *(simple)* simple, sans apprêt; **h. philosophy** philosophie *f* simpliste **(b)** *Tex (cloth)* fait à la maison **2** *n Tex* tissu *m* fait à la maison

homestead ['həʊmsted] *n* **(a)** *Agr* ferme *f (avec dépendances)* **(b)** *US Jur (land granted)* concession *f* statutaire de 160 acres

home town *n* ville *f* natale

home video *n* **to watch sb's home videos** regarder les cassettes de vidéo filmées par qn

homeward ['həʊmwəd] **1** *adj* qui se dirige vers sa maison; *(from abroad)* qui se dirige vers son pays; **h. journey** *or Naut* **voyage** voyage *m* de retour; **h. leg** *(of a journey)* dernière étape *f* **2** *adv* = **homewards**

homeward-bound *adj Naut (ship)* à destination de son port d'attache, retournant au port, sur le retour; *(container)* de retour; **to be h.** *(of person)* rentrer chez soi

homewards ['həʊmwədz] *adv* (*to one's house*) vers sa maison, vers sa demeure; (*from abroad*) vers son pays

homework ['həʊmwɜːk] *n* **(a)** *Sch* devoirs *mpl*; *Fig F* **it was plain that the chairman had not done his h.** il était évident que le président ne maîtrisait pas son sujet **(b)** (*paid work*) travail *m* à domicile

homeworker ['həʊmwɜːkər] *n* travailleur, -euse à domicile

homey ['həʊmɪ] *adj esp Am* accueillant

homicidal [hɒmɪ'saɪd(ə)l] *adj* homicide, meurtrier

homicide ['hɒmɪsaɪd] *n* **(a)** (*crime*) homicide *m*; *Jur* **wilful** *or* **culpable h.** homicide volontaire; *Jur* **justifiable h., h. in self defence** homicide en état de légitime défense **(b)** *esp Am* (*person*) homicide *mf*

homily ['hɒmɪlɪ] *n* homélie *f*; *Fig* sermon *m*

homing ['həʊmɪŋ] *adj Tech* directionnel, de radioguidage; **h. device** appareil *m ou* dispositif *m* autodirecteur, autodirecteur *m*; *Zool* **h. instinct** instinct *m* de retour; **h. pigeon** pigeon *m* voyageur

hominy ['hɒmɪnɪ] *n Am Culin* **h. (grits)** maïs *m* concassé et bouilli

homo ['həʊməʊ] *n F Pej* homo *m*, pédé *m*

homoeopath, homoeopathic *etc* = **homeopath, homeopathic** *etc*

homogeneity [hɒməʊdʒɪ'niːɪtɪ] *n* homogénéité *f*

homogeneous [hɒməʊ'dʒiːnɪəs] *adj* homogène; *Mktg* **h. shopping goods** produits *mpl* d'achat réfléchi homogènes

homogenize [hɒ'mɒdʒənaɪz] *vt* (*milk*) homogénéiser

homograft ['hɒməgrɑːft] *n Med* allogreffe *f*, autogreffe *f*

homograph ['hɒməgræf] *n Ling* homographe *m*

homologous [hə'mɒləgəs] *adj Biol, Math etc* homologue

homonym ['hɒmənɪm] *n Ling* homonyme *m*

homophobe ['hɒməʊfəʊb] *n* adversaire *mf* des homosexuels

homophobia [hɒməʊ'fəʊbɪə] *n* haine *f* des homosexuels

homophobic [hɒməʊ'fəʊbɪk] *adj* anti-homosexuel

homophone ['hɒməfəʊn] *n* homophone *m*

homosexual [hɒməʊ'seksjʊəl] *adj, n* homosexuel, -elle

homosexuality [hɒməʊseksjʊ'ælɪtɪ] *n* homosexualité *f*

Hon *Br Parl* **the H.** *abbr* **the Honourable**

hone [həʊn] *vt* aiguiser, affiler; *Fig* (*sense of humour*) aiguiser; *Fig* **finely honed musicianship** sens aigu de la musique

honest ['ɒnɪst] *adj* **(a)** (*trustworthy*) honnête, probe, droit; (*in business*) loyal; **he has an h. face** il a une figure d'honnête homme

(b) (*sincere, truthful*) sincère, de bonne foi; **the h. truth** la vérité vraie; **I gave you an h. answer** je t'ai répondu avec sincérité; **is that your h. opinion?** est-ce que c'est ce que tu penses vraiment?; **to be h. (with you)** pour être franc; **if you're h. (with yourself)** si tu étais sincère avec toi-même; **an h. piece of work** un travail consciencieux; *Sl* **I couldn't help it, h.** c'était plus fort que moi, je t'assure

(c) (*legitimate*) juste, légitime; (*means*) légitime; **to earn an h. living** gagner honnêtement sa vie; **an h. day's work** une bonne journée de travail; **he's never done an h. day's work in his life** (*real work*) il n'a jamais rien fait de ses dix doigts; (*honest work*) il n'a jamais rien fait d'honnête; **an h. day's pay for an h. day's work** toute peine mérite salaire

(d) *Old-fashioned, Hum* **to make an h. woman of sb** faire de qn une honnête femme (*en l'épousant*)

(e) *Old-fashioned* (*usu used condescendingly*) (*respectable*) brave; **they are h. folk** ce sont de braves gens

honestly ['ɒnɪstlɪ] **1** *adv* **(a)** (*in legitimate manner*) honnêtement **(b)** (*sincerely*) sincèrement; **quite h.** en toute sincérité; **I can h. say that …** je peux dire en toute sincérité que …; **do you h. believe that?** est-ce que tu le crois vraiment?; **I didn't do it, h.!** ce n'est pas moi qui l'ai fait, je t'assure! **2** *int* (*expressing indignation*) **h.! some people!** y'a des gens, je te jure!

honesty ['ɒnɪstɪ] *n* **(a)** (*trustworthiness*) honnêteté *f*; *Prov* **h. is the best policy** l'honnêteté est la meilleure des tactiques; **h. system** (*in hotels*) système *m* faisant appel à l'honnêteté du client **(b)** (*sincerity*) sincérité *f*, bonne foi *f*; (*of a speech*) franchise *f*; **in all h.** en toute sincérité **(c)** (*plant*) lunaire *f*, *F* monnaie-du-pape *f*

honey ['hʌnɪ] *n* **(a)** miel *m*; **clear/thick h.** miel liquide/solide; **comb h.** miel en rayon; *Fig* **he was all h.** il a été tout sucre et tout miel; **h. bear** kinkajou *m*; **h. coloured** miellé, couleur de miel **(b)** *esp Am* (*term of endearment*) chéri, *f* chérie **(c)** *esp Am* (*nice person*) amour *m*; (*excellent thing*) bijou *m*; **she's a real h., isn't she?** c'est un amour, tu ne trouves pas?; **it's a h. of an apartment** cet appartement est un bijou

honeybee ['hʌnɪbiː] *n* abeille *f*

honeybun(ch) ['hʌnɪbʌn, -tʃ] *n US F* (*term of endearment*) mon chéri, ma chérie, mon amour

honeycomb[1] ['hʌnɪkəʊm] *n* rayon *m* de miel; (*for eating*) gâteau *m* de miel; *Tex* nid *m* d'abeilles; *Geol* **h. structure/formation** structure *f*/formation *f* alvéolée *ou* alvéolaire

honeycomb[2] *vt* **to be honeycombed with sth** être criblé de qch; **the city was honeycombed with narrow streets** la ville était un dédale de rues étroites

honeydew ['hʌnɪdjuː] *n* miellée *f*, miellure *f*; **h. melon** melon *m* d'hiver

honeyed ['hʌnɪd] *adj* (*tones, words*) mielleux

honeymoon[1] ['hʌnɪmuːn] *n* (*of couple*) lune *f* de miel; *Fig* état *m* de grâce; **h. (trip)** voyage *m* de noces; **they're on their h.** ils sont en voyage de noces; **h. couple** couple *m* en voyage de noces; **h. suite** suite *f* nuptiale; *Fig* **the h. is over** c'est la fin de l'état de grâce

honeymoon[2] *vi* être en voyage de noces; (*go on honeymoon*) aller en voyage de noces

honeymooners ['hʌnɪmuːnəz] *npl* couple *m* en voyage de noces

honeypot ['hʌnɪpɒt] *n* **(a)** pot *m* à miel **(b)** *Sl* (*vagina*) minette *f*

honeysuckle ['hʌnɪsʌk(ə)l] *n* (*shrub*) chèvrefeuille *m*

honk[1] [hɒŋk] *n* **(a)** (*of goose*) cri *m* **(b)** (*of car horn*) coup *m* de klaxon

honk[2] **1** *vi* **(a)** (*of goose, seal etc*) pousser un cri **(b)** (*of car horn etc*) retentir; **she honked twice on the horn** elle a donné deux coups de klaxon **2** *vt* **to h. the horn** klaxonner

honk[3] *vi Br Sl* (*vomit*) dégueuler

honky ['hɒŋkɪ] *n esp Am Offensive Sl* (*white person*) blanc *m*, blanche *f*

honky-tonk ['hɒŋkɪ'tɒŋk] *n Am F* **(a)** (*bar*) **h. (joint)** bouge *m*, boui-boui *m* **(b)** *Mus* musique *f* de bastringue

honorarium, *pl* **-ia, -iums** [ɒnə'reərɪəm, -ɪə, -ɪəmz] *n* (*of doctor, lawyer*) honoraires *mpl*

honorary ['ɒnərərɪ] *adj* (*without pay*) bénévole; (*without duties*) honorifique; (*president*) d'honneur; (*member*) honoraire; *Univ* **h. degree** diplôme *m* à titre honorifique; **to have an h. doctorate** être docteur honoris causa; **h. membership** honorariat *m*; *Mil* **h. rank** grade *m* honorifique

honor, honorable *etc US* = **honour, honourable** *etc*

honorific [ɒnə'rɪfɪk] *adj* (*title*) honorifique

honour[1], *US* **honor** ['ɒnər] *n* **(a)** (*respect*) honneur *m*; **to put up a statue in h. of sb** ériger une statue à la gloire de qn; **dinner in your h.** dîner en votre honneur; **in h. of the occasion** pour l'occasion; **to do sb h.** honorer qn; **you would do yourself h.** ce serait tout à ton honneur; *Prov* **h. where h. is due** à tout seigneur tout honneur; *US Mil* **honor guard** garde *f* d'honneur; (*soldier*) soldat *m* de la garde d'honneur

(b) (*privilege*) honneur *m*; **to consider it an h. to do sth** considérer comme un honneur de faire qch; **it is a great h. to be selected for the team** c'est un grand honneur que d'être sélectionné pour l'équipe; **it was an h. to have worked with her** cela a été un honneur que de travailler avec elle; *Fml* **whom have I the h. of addressing?** à qui ai-je l'honneur de parler?; *Fml* **I don't believe I've had the h.** je ne crois pas avoir eu l'honneur d'être présenté; **we had the h. of a visit from the president** nous avons eu l'honneur de recevoir la visite du président; **to have the h.** *Golf* avoir l'honneur; (*at bowls*) avoir la boule; *Fml* **may I have the h.?** (*at dance*) me ferez-vous l'honneur de cette danse?

(c) (*good name*) honneur *m*; **to come out of an affair with h.** se tirer honorablement d'une affaire; **she acquitted herself with h.** (*of player*) elle s'en est tirée honorablement; **their courage does them h.** leur courage leur fait honneur; **to make it a point of h. to do sth** mettre son (point d')honneur à faire qch; **I'm h. bound to …** l'honneur m'oblige à …; **I felt h. bound to stay** je sentis que l'honneur me commandait de rester; **man of h.** homme *m* d'honneur; **to swear on one's h.** jurer sur son honneur; **to put sb on their h.** faire promettre à qn sur son honneur; **you're on your h.** tu as promis sur ton honneur; **to give one's word of h.** engager sa parole (d'honneur); **on my (word of) h.!** je vous donne ma parole (d'honneur)!, sur l'honneur!; *Prov* **(there is) h. among thieves** les loups ne se mangent pas entre eux; **h. is satisfied** l'honneur est sauf; **h. system** = système *m* d'autodiscipline (*dans les écoles, les prisons, les hôtels etc*)

(d) *Old-fashioned* (*chastity*) honneur *m*; *Old-fashioned, Hum* **to defend one's h.** défendre son honneur

(e) (*award*) distinction *f* honorifique; **honours list** *Sch* tableau *m* d'honneur; *Br Admin* = liste *f* des personnes choisies pour recevoir le titre de MBE *etc*; *Univ* **honours course** programme *m* d'études approfondies au niveau de la licence; **honours degree** ≈ licence *f*

(f) (*civilities*) **to receive sb with full honours** recevoir qn avec tous les honneurs qui lui sont dus; *F Hum* **to do the honours** (*serve food, drinks*) servir; (*do introductions*) faire les présentations; *Hist* **the honours of war** les honneurs de la guerre; **he was buried with full military honours** il a été enterré avec tous les honneurs militaires

(g) *Cards* (*at bridge etc*) **honours** honneurs *mpl* (*as, roi, dame et valet*)

(h) (*person*) **to be an h. to one's country** faire honneur à sa patrie

(i) *Jur* (*in title*) **Your/His H.** Votre Honneur/Monsieur le juge, Monsieur le président

honour[2], *US* honor *vt* **(a)** (*sb, sb's memory*) honorer; *Iron* **the manager honoured us with his presence today** le directeur nous a fait l'honneur de sa présence aujourd'hui; *Iron* **we are honoured!** quel honneur!; **I'm honoured that you have chosen me** je suis très honoré que vous m'ayez choisi; **our honoured guest** notre invité d'honneur **(b)** (*bill, signature etc*) honorer; (*credit card*) accepter

honourable, *US* honorable ['ɒnərəb(ə)l] **1** *adj* honorable; **he is an h. man** c'est un homme d'honneur; **to receive (an) h. mention** (*in competition*) recevoir une mention spéciale; *Old-fashioned, Hum* **are his intentions h.?** ses intentions sont-elles honorables?; **it's the h. thing to do** c'est la solution la plus honorable **2** *n* **(a)** *Br Parl* **the H., the Hon.** = titre *m* donné aux membres du Parlement britannique; **the H. member for Caithness** l'honorable député du Caithness **(b)** *Br* (*in aristocracy*) = titre donné aux benjamins des familles nobles britanniques; **her fiancé is an h.** son fiancé est un membre de l'aristocratie

honourably, *US* honorably ['ɒnərəblɪ] *adv* honorablement; (*to behave etc*) d'une manière honorable; (*to treat prisoners*) décemment

Hons [ɒnz] *Univ abbr* **Honours**, *see* **honour[1] (e)**

hooch [huːtʃ] *n Am Sl* (*drink*) gnôle *f*

hood[1] [hʊd] *n* **(a)** (*of anorak, duffle coat, monk's etc*) capuchon *m*; (*with eye-holes*) (*of thief, Ku Klux Klan*) cagoule *f*; *Univ* épitoge *f*; (*over hawk's head*) chaperon *m*; **the kidnappers put a h. over her head** les ravisseurs lui ont couvert la tête avec un sac **(b)** (*soft top of car*) capote *f*; *US* (*bonnet*) capot *m* **(c)** (*over cooker, fireplace etc*) hotte *f*; (*of hairdryer*) casque *m*; *Phot* (*over lens*) pare-soleil *m*; (*any protective cover, acoustic etc*) couvercle *m*

hood[2] *n esp US Sl* (*gangster*) truand *m*

hooded ['hʊdɪd] *adj* **(a)** (*monk*) encapuchonné; (*executioner, thief*) au visage masqué; (*eyes*) aux paupières tombantes; (*eyelid*) tombant; **h. men** hommes en cagoule **(b)** (*jacket*) avec une cagoule

hooded crow *n Orn* corneille *f* mantelée

hoodlum ['huːdləm] *n esp US F* (*ruffian, yobbo*) voyou *m*

hoodoo ['huːduː] *n F* (*bad luck*) poisse *f*, guigne *f*; (*person*) porte-malheur *m*; **to put a h. on sb** porter la poisse à qn

hoodwink ['hʊdwɪŋk] *vt F* berner; **I've been hoodwinked** je me suis fait avoir; **to h. sb into believing sth** faire croire qch à qn; **I was hoodwinked into signing** on m'a raconté des bobards pour me faire signer

hooey ['huːɪ] *n F* **that's all h.** ce ne sont que des sornettes; **don't talk h.** arrête de dire des bêtises

hoof[1], *pl* **hooves** [huːf, huːvz] *n* (*of horse etc*) sabot *m*; (*of devil*) pied *m* fourchu; **500 cattle on the h.** 500 têtes de bétail sur pied; *Fig* **to do things on the h.** improviser; *Fig* **on the h.** (*on ad hoc basis*) au coup par coup; **I had lunch on the h.** à midi j'ai mangé sur le pouce; *US* **h. and mouth disease** fièvre *f* aphteuse

hoof[2] *vt F* **to h. it** (*walk*) aller à pinces; (*to dance*) danser; **to h. sb out** chasser qn à coups de pied

hoofbeat ['huːfbiːt] *n* **hoofbeats** (*of horses*) bruit *m* de la cavalcade

hoofed [huːft] *adj* (*animal*) à sabots

hoofer ['huːfər] *n F Hum* danseur *m*, danseuse *f* (*de métier*)

hoofprint ['huːfprɪnt] *n* trace *f* de sabot

hoo-ha ['huːhɑː] *n F* raffut *m*; **there was a lot of h. in the press about ...** la presse a fait tout un plat de ...; **the announcement caused a great h. at the school** cette nouvelle a fait beaucoup de bruit à l'école; **when all the h. about the Royal Wedding/government scandal has died down** quand le mariage princier/le scandale au sein du gouvernement ne sera plus à la une de l'actualité; **now that all the h. is over we can get down to serious business** maintenant que le calme est revenu, nous pouvons nous occuper de choses sérieuses

hook[1] [hʊk] *n* **(a)** crochet *m*; (*for clothes*) patère *f*; (*for meat*) croc *m*; (*on fishing line*) hameçon *m*; *Sewing* **h. and eye** agrafe *f*; *Av, Naut* **arrester h.** crosse *f* d'appontage

(b) *Boxing* crochet *m*; *Golf* hook *m*; *Boxing* **a left/right h.** un crochet du gauche/droit

(c) *Geog* pointe *f* de terre; (*larger*) cap *m*

(d) (*phrases*) *F* **he swallowed it** *or* **fell for it h. line and sinker** il a tout gobé; *F* **he's fallen for her h. line and sinker** il est fou d'elle; **we must do it by h. or by crook** nous devons le faire, coûte que coûte; **to leave the phone off the h.** décrocher le *ou* son téléphone; **your phone was off the h.** tu avais décroché ton téléphone; (*accidentally*) tu avais mal raccroché ton téléphone; **to put the phone back on the h.** reposer le combiné (sur son support); *F* **that lets you off the h.** te voilà tiré d'affaire; *F* **thanks for getting me off the h.** merci de m'avoir tiré d'affaire; *F* **he owned up and got me off the h.** (*vindicated me*) son aveu m'a innocenté; *US Sl* **to get the h.** (*be sacked*) se faire vider *ou* virer; *Br Sl* **to sling one's h.** foutre le camp; **once she's got her hooks into him ...** une fois qu'elle lui aura mis le grappin dessus ...

hook[2] **1** *vt* **(a)** accrocher (**to sth** à qch); **to h. the shutters open** accrocher les volets après les avoir ouverts; **to h. the shutters back** ouvrir les volets et les attacher au mur; **he got his sweater hooked on a nail** il a accroché son tricot à un clou; **the two bits of wire had become hooked together** les deux fils de fer s'étaient pris l'un dans l'autre; **he hung with his legs hooked around the trapeze** il se suspendit par les jambes au trapèze; **she had her feet hooked up under her chair** elle avait calé ses pieds sous sa chaise; **h. one end of the wire around ...** fixer une extrémité du fil de fer autour de ...; **to h. a fish** faire mordre le poisson à l'hameçon; *F* **she's hooked herself a husband** elle a décroché un mari; *F* **she'll never manage to h. him** elle n'arrivera jamais à lui mettre le grappin dessus

(b) *Boxing* envoyer un crochet à; **to h. sb to the jaw** envoyer un crochet dans la mâchoire de qn

(c) *Rugby* (*of hooker*) talonner; (*in kicking*) envoyer à gauche; *Golf* **to h. the ball** faire un hook

2 *vi* **(a)** (*of dress etc*) s'agrafer

(b) *Boxing* envoyer des crochets; *Golf* faire un/des hook(s)

▶ **hook on** **1** *vi* s'accrocher (**to** à) **2** *vtsep* (*caravan to car etc*) accrocher (**to** à)

▶ **hook up** **1** *vi* **(a)** (*of dress etc*) s'agrafer; (*of wires*) se raccorder **(b)** *TV etc* **we're now going to h. up with ...** nous vous proposons maintenant une émission en duplex avec ... **2** *vtsep* **(a)** (*dress, bra*) agrafer; **could you h. me up please?** tu peux agrafer ma robe/*etc*? **(b)** (*trailer etc*) accrocher (**to** à) **(c) to h. up two computers** connecter deux ordinateurs

hookah ['hʊkə] *n* narguilé *m*

hooked [hʊkt] *adj* **(a)** (*nose*) crochu **(b)** (*having hooks*) à crochets **(c)** *F* **to be h. on** (*drugs etc*) se droguer à, être dépendant de; (*Italian cinema, jazz, tennis etc*) être mordu de, être fana de; (*person*) être fou de; (*novelist etc*) être fana de; **to be h.** (*on drugs*) se droguer; **he's completely h.** il est complètement accro; **one bite and I was h.** une bouchée et j'étais conquis

hooker ['hʊkər] *n* **(a)** *Rugby* talonneur *m* **(b)** *esp Am F* (*prostitute*) putain *f*

hookey ['hʊkɪ] *n esp US F* = **hooky**

hook-nosed ['hʊknəʊzd] *adj* au nez crochu

Hook of Holland *n* Hoek *m* van Holland

hook-up *n TV* duplex *m*; (*programme*) émission *f* en duplex; **you can have a direct computer h. with your Paris office** votre ordinateur peut être relié directement à celui de Paris

hookworm ['hʊkwɜːm] *n* ankylostome *m*

hooky ['hʊkɪ] *n esp US F* **to play h.** sécher les cours

hooligan ['huːlɪgən] *n* voyou *m*, hooligan *m*

hooliganism ['huːlɪgənɪz(ə)m] *n* hooliganisme *m*

hoop [huːp] *n* **(a)** (*on barrel*) cercle *m*; (*toy, for skirt, in circus etc*) cerceau *m*; (*in croquet*) arceau *m*; **h. earrings** anneaux *mpl* **(b)** (*coloured ring on plumage, fur etc, stripe*) rayure *f*; (*around animal's neck*) collier *m* **(c)** *Fig F* **to put sb through the hoops** mettre qn à l'épreuve; **to go through the hoops** passer l'épreuve du feu; **I've really been through the hoops for you** j'ai sué sang et eau pour toi

hooped [huːpt] *adj* (*skirt*) à cerceaux

hoop-la ['huːplɑː] *n* **(a)** *Br* (*game*) jeu *m* des anneaux; **h. stall** stand *m* du jeu des anneaux **(b)** *US F* = **hoo-ha**

hoopoe ['huːpəʊ] *n* (*bird*) huppe *f*

hooray [hʊ'reɪ] **1** *int, n* = **hurrah** **2** *n Br F Pej* **H. Henry** fils *m* de famille, jeune homme *m* de la haute (*expansif et bruyant*)

hoosegow ['huːsgaʊ] *n US Sl* (*prison*) taule *f*

hoot[1] [huːt] *n* **(a)** (*of owl*) hululement *m* **(b)** (*mocking*) huée *f*; **hoots of laughter** des hurlements *mpl* de rire; **she gave a great h. of laughter** elle partit d'un grand éclat de rire **(c)** *Aut* coup *m* de klaxon; *Rail* coup de sifflet; *Naut* coup de sirène; **when you hear three hoots on the factory hooter** quand la sirène de l'usine retentit trois fois **(d)** *F* **it was a h.!** (*hilarious*) c'était tordant!; **he's a h.!** il est d'un drôle! **(e)** *F* **not to give** *or* **care a h.** *or* **two hoots about sb/sth** se ficher éperdument de qn/qch; **I don't give a h.** je m'en fiche comme de l'an quarante; **it doesn't matter two hoots** ça n'a strictement aucune importance

hoot[2] **1** *vi* **(a)** (*of owl*) hululer **(b) to h. with laughter** hurler de rire; **they all hooted with** *or* **in derision** ils poussèrent tous des huées (**c**) *Aut* klaxonner, donner un coup/des coups de klaxon; *Rail* siffler; *Naut* donner un coup/des coups de sirène **2** *vt* (*actor, speaker*) huer; (*play*) siffler; **the speaker was hooted down** l'orateur fut réduit au silence par les huées; **he was hooted off the stage** on lui a fait quitter la scène sous les huées

hootenanny ['hu:tnænɪ] *n US* improvisation *f* collective de musique folklorique

hooter ['hu:tər] *n Br* (**a**) *Naut, Ind* sirène *f*; *Aut* klaxon *m* (**b**) *F* (*nose*) pif *m*

hooting ['hu:tɪŋ] *n* (**a**) (*of owl*) hululement *m* (**b**) (*of person*) (*jeering*) huées *fpl*; (*laughter*) hurlements *mpl* de rire (**c**) (*of cars*) coups *mpl* de klaxon

hoover®[1] ['hu:vər] *n* aspirateur *m*

hoover[2] **1** *vt* (*carpet etc*) passer l'aspirateur sur; (*room*) passer l'aspirateur dans **2** *vi* passer l'aspirateur

► **hoover up** *vtsep* enlever avec l'aspirateur; **I'll just h. it up** je vais (y) donner un coup d'aspirateur

hoovering ['hu:vərɪŋ] *n* **to do the h.** passer l'aspirateur; **when you've finished with the h.** quand tu auras passé l'aspirateur; **there's still a lot of h. to do** nous n'avons pas/je n'ai pas/*etc* encore fini de passer l'aspirateur

hooves [hu:vz] *npl see* **hoof**[1]

hop[1] [hɒp] *n Bot* houblon *m*; **hops** (*for brewing*) houblon; **h. grower** houblonnier *m*; **h. field** houblonnière *f*; **h. picker** cueilleur, -euse de houblon; **h. picking** cueillette *f* du houblon

hop[2] *n* (**a**) (*jump*) saut *m*; (*on one foot*) saut à cloche-pied (**b**) *Sp* **h. skip and jump** triple saut *m* (**c**) *Fig F* **to catch sb on the h.** prendre qn au dépourvu; **to keep sb on the h.** ne pas laisser chômer qn (**d**) *Av* **it's just a short h. from London to Paris** il n'y a qu'un saut de Londres à Paris (**e**) *F* (*dance*) fête *f* (**f**) *Am F* (*drug*) came *f*

hop[3] **1** *vi* (**a**) (*jump*) sautiller; **to h. (on one leg)** sauter à cloche-pied

(**b**) **to h. out of bed** sauter du lit; **to h. into bed with sb** coucher avec qn; *F* **h. in!** (*into car etc*) montez!; **he hopped off the bus/his bike** il sauta du bus/de son vélo; **he hopped on the bus/his bike** il sauta dans le bus/sur son vélo; **I hopped across to France for the weekend** j'ai fait un saut en France pour le week-end; **he hopped onto the first London-bound plane/train** il a sauté dans le premier avion/train pour Londres; *F* **she's just hopped out for a second** elle est sortie deux minutes

2 *vt F* **h. it!** fiche le camp!; **to h. a ride on a train** voyager en train clandestinement (*en sautant dans un wagon de marchandises/sur le toit*); **can I h. a ride?** je peux monter avec vous?

► **hop off** *vi Br F* (*clear off*) ficher le camp; **he's hopped off (with the silver)** il a filé (avec l'argenterie)

hope[1] [həʊp] *n* (**a**) (*no pl*) espoir *m*; **to be full of h.** être plein d'espoir; **to lose** *or* **to give up h.** perdre (l')espoir; **there is little/no h. of finding it** il y a peu d'espoir/il n'y a aucun espoir de le trouver; **to put one's h. in the future** compter sur l'avenir; **to live in the h. that ...** caresser l'espoir que ...; *F* **we live in h.!** c'est l'espoir qui fait vivre!; **in the h. of ...** dans l'espoir de ...; *Am* **h. chest** trousseau *m* (*de mariage*)

(**b**) (*individual instance*) **my last h.** mon dernier espoir, ma dernière planche de salut; **to have hopes of doing sth** avoir bon espoir de faire qch; **do you still have hopes of ...?** est-ce que vous avez toujours l'espoir de ...?; **to have hopes of sth** avoir l'espoir de qch; **to have no hopes of sth/doing sth** n'avoir pas d'espoir *ou* aucun espoir de qch/faire qch; **to have hopes of doing sth** avoir l'espoir de faire qch; **I'm not getting my hopes up** je ne veux pas (commencer à) me faire des idées; **these events have raised hopes of a peaceful solution** ces événements ont fait naître l'espoir d'une solution pacifique; **the team's hopes were high** les espoirs de l'équipe étaient grands; **they had high hopes for their daughter** ils avaient de grandes espérances pour leur fille; **to set one's hopes on sb/sth** mettre tout son espoir en qn/qch; *Iron* **what a h.!, some h.!** (si vous) comptez là-dessus!; **she hasn't got a h.** *or F* **a h. in hell of winning** elle n'a aucun espoir de gagner

hope[2] **1** *vi* espérer; **to h. for sth** espérer qch; **don't h. for too much** n'en attends pas trop; **we'll just have to h. for the best** nous n'avons plus qu'à espérer que tout aille pour le mieux; **to h. for better days** attendre des jours meilleurs; **we must h. against hope** il faut espérer malgré tout; **hoped-for victory** victoire espérée *ou* désirée

2 *vt* [①**A46,9,a,iii**] **I h. to see you again** j'espère vous revoir; **I h. (that) your brother is better** j'espère que votre frère va mieux; **I h. you are right** je souhaite que vous ayez raison; *F* **I h. to God** *or* **to hell that ...** je prie le ciel que ... + *sub*; **I h. and pray that ...** je prie Dieu que ... + *sub*; **I h. so** j'espère que oui, j'espère bien; **I h. not** j'espère que non; **I should h. so!** j'espère bien!; **I should h. not!** j'espère bien que non!; **hoping to hear from you** (*in letter*) dans l'attente (d'avoir) de vos nouvelles

hopeful ['həʊpful] **1** *adj* (**a**) (*person*) plein d'espoir; **we must remain h.** il faut continuer d'espérer; **to be h. that ...** avoir bon espoir que ... (**b**) (*promising*) **the situation looks more h.** la situation est plus encourageante *ou* porte à l'optimisme **2** *n F* (*person*) (*looking for a job*) candidat *m*; **young h.** jeune espoir *mf*

hopefully ['həʊpfulɪ] *adv* (**a**) (*to speak, wait etc*) avec bon espoir, avec optimisme (**b**) *F* (*with luck*) **h. the sun will shine tomorrow** espérons qu'il fera du soleil demain; **do you think he'll come? – h.** est-ce que vous pensez qu'il viendra? – espérons-le; **h. not** espérons que non

hopefulness ['həʊpf(ʊ)lnɪs] *n* (*of person*) confiance *f*, optimisme *m*

hopeless ['həʊplɪs] *adj* (**a**) (*without hope*) (*person*) sans espoir, désespéré; (*situation*) désespéré; (*project*) qui n'a aucune chance de réussir; **to give sth up as h.** renoncer à faire qch (parce ce qu'on a peu de chance de réussir); **it's h.!** ça (ne) sert à rien!; **it is h. to try to ...** il est tout à fait inutile de ...; **to be in a h. condition** (*of patient etc*) être dans un état désespéré; **a h. cause** (*in politics etc*) une cause que l'on sait perdue d'avance; **h. grief** douleur *f* inconsolable

(**b**) *F* (*very bad*) **I'm a h. singer** je chante très mal; **you're h.!** espèce d'idiot!; **to be h. at maths/at cooking** être nul en maths/en cuisine; **a h. drunkard** un ivrogne invétéré

hopelessly ['həʊplɪslɪ] *adv* (**a**) (*to live*) sans espoir; (*to sob*) plein de désespoir; (*to shake one's head, sigh*) découragé; (*stronger*) plein de désespoir (**b**) (*beaten*) à plates coutures; (*in love*) éperdument; **h. drunk** fin soûl; **h. lost/out of control** complètement perdu/incontrôlable; **h. naive** d'une naïveté désespérante; **the government is h. out of touch** le gouvernement a totalement perdu contact (avec le pays)

hopelessness ['həʊplɪsnɪs] *n* (*despair*) désespoir *m*; (*of situation*) état *m* désespéré; **a feeling of h.** un sentiment d'impuissance

hophead ['hɒphed] *n US Sl* toxicomane *mf*, drogué, -ée

hopper ['hɒpər] *n* (**a**) *F* (*insect*) sauterelle *f* (**b**) *Tech* trémie *f*, huche *f*, hotte *f*; *Agr* (*for sowing*) semoir *m*; (*for feeding poultry*) trémie; **h. barge** marie-salope *f*, *pl* maries-salopes; *Rail* **h. car** wagon-trémie *m*

hopping ['hɒpɪŋ] *adv F* **to be h. mad** être fou de colère

hopscotch ['hɒpskɒtʃ] *n* marelle *f*

Horatian [hə'reɪʃən] *adj Liter* d'Horace

horde [hɔ:d] *n* (*of barbarians*), *Fig* horde *f*

horizon [hə'raɪz(ə)n] *n* horizon *m*; **on the h.** à l'horizon; **studying has opened up new horizons for her** les études lui ont ouvert des horizons nouveaux; **reading broadened my horizons** la lecture a élargi mes horizons; *Astron, Av, Naut* **celestial h.** horizon astronomique; *Av, Naut* **h. bar** barre *f* d'horizon

horizontal [hɒrɪ'zɒnt(ə)l] **1** *adj* horizontal, -aux; *Gym* **h. bar** barre *f* fixe; *US* **h. increase in salaries of 10%** augmentation *f* uniforme de 10% sur toutes les rétributions; *Mktg* **h. integration** intégration *f ou* concentration *f* horizontale; **h. market** marché *m* horizontal; *F* **I was h. for a few days with the flu** je suis resté couché *ou* au lit pendant quelques jours avec la grippe **2** *n* horizontale *f*

horizontally [hɒrɪ'zɒntəlɪ] *adv* horizontalement

hormonal [hɔ:'məʊn(ə)l] *adj Physiol* hormonal

hormone ['hɔ:məʊn] *n Physiol* hormone *f*; **h. replacement therapy** hormonothérapie *f*

horn[1] [hɔ:n] *n* (**a**) (*of cattle, ram, snail etc*) corne *f*; (*of stag beetle*) antenne *f*; (*of owl*) aigrette *f*; **horns** (*of deer*) bois *mpl*; *Fig* **to draw in one's horns** restreindre son ardeur, rabattre (de) ses prétentions; (*economize*) se serrer la ceinture, faire des économies, diminuer ses dépenses; **to be (caught) on the horns of a dilemma** être en proie à un dilemme; *Lit* **h. of plenty** corne d'abondance

(**b**) (*of moon*) corne *f*; (*of estuary*) branche *f*; **Cape H., the H.** le cap Horn; **the H. of Africa** la corne de l'Afrique

(**c**) (*material*) corne *f*; **h. comb** peigne *m* en corne

(**d**) *Mus* cor *m Sl* (*brass or woodwind instrument*) trompette *f*; **English/French h.** cor anglais/d'harmonie; **to sound** *or* **blow the h.** sonner du cor; *Am Fig* **to blow one's own h.** se vanter; **h. player** corniste *mf*; **the h. section, the horns** les cors

(**e**) (*on car*) klaxon *m*; **to sound one's h.** klaxonner

(**f**) (*of loud speaker*) pavillon *m*

horn[2] *vt* (*gore*) encorner, donner un coup de corne à

► **horn in** *vi US Sl* (*interrupt, intrude*) intervenir sans façon, ramener sa fraise (**on a conversation** dans une conversation); **I don't want him horning in on this deal** je veux pas qu'il fourre son nez dans cette affaire

hornbeam [ˈhɔːnbiːm] *n* (*tree*) charme *m*
hornbill [ˈhɔːnbɪl] *n* (*bird*) calao *m*
horned [hɔːnd] *adj* (*animal*) à cornes
hornet [ˈhɔːnɪt] *n* (*insect*) frelon *m*; *Fig* **to stir up a h.'s nest** mettre le feu au poudre
hornpipe [ˈhɔːnpaɪp] *n Naut, Mus* matelote *f*
horn-rimmed *adj* (*spectacles*) à monture lourde, à grosse monture
horny [ˈhɔːnɪ] *adj* **(a)** (*like horn*) corné; (*beak etc*) de corne, en corne; (*hand etc*) calleux; **to grow h.** se racornir **(b)** *Sl* (*sexually*) **to be h.** (*in general*) ne penser qu'à ça; (*of man also*) être un chaud lapin; (*be sexually aroused*) être tout excité; **to get h.** s'exciter **(c)** *US Sl* (*sexy*) bandant
horology [hɒˈrɒlədʒɪ] *n* **(a)** (*clockmaking*) horlogerie *f* **(b)** (*measuring time*) horométrie *f*
horoscope [ˈhɒrəskəʊp] *n* horoscope *m*; **to cast sb's h.** faire *ou* dresser l'horoscope de qn; **my h. said that …** (*in newspaper etc*) d'après mon horoscope …
horrendous [hɒˈrendəs] *adj* affreux, horrible
horrendously [hɒˈrendəslɪ] *adv F* (*expensive etc*) affreusement, horriblement
horrible [ˈhɒrəb(ə)l] *adj* **(a)** horrible, affreux, atroce; (*noise*) épouvantable; (*weather*) abominable; **how h.!** quelle horreur! **(b)** (*unkind*) atroce; **to be h. to sb** être méchant *ou* horrible avec qn; **to say h. things about sb** dire des horreurs *ou* des choses terribles sur qn
horribly [ˈhɒrɪblɪ] *adv* horriblement, affreusement; (*to behave*) de façon abominable
horrid [ˈhɒrɪd] *adj* **(a)** horrible, affreux; **he's such a h. little man!** c'est un affreux petit bonhomme; **h. sight** chose *f* horrible à voir **(b)** *F* (*unkind*) méchant, ignoble; **to be h. to sb** être ignoble envers qn, être odieux avec qn; **to say h. things about sb** dire des méchancetés de qn
horridly [ˈhɒrɪdlɪ] *adv F* (*to behave*) méchamment, de façon odieuse *ou* ignoble
horrific [hɒˈrɪfɪk, hə-] *adj* horrible; **h. injuries** blessures horribles
horrify [ˈhɒrɪfaɪ] *vt* horrifier
horrifying [ˈhɒrɪfaɪɪŋ] *adj* horrifiant
horror [ˈhɒrər] *n* (*feeling, terrifying thing*) horreur *f*; **paralysed with h.** glacé d'horreur; **to my h.** à ma grande horreur; **to have a h. of sth/doing sth** avoir horreur de qch/faire qch; **he had a h. of being seen naked** il avait horreur qu'on le voie nu; *F* **it gives me the horrors** cela me donne le frisson; *F* **that child's a little h.** cet enfant est un petit monstre; **h. film** *or* **movie** film *m* d'horreur; *Liter* **h. story** histoire *f* d'épouvante; *Fig F* **h. stories about hotels where nothing worked** des histoires terribles sur des hôtels où rien ne marchait
horror-stricken, horror-struck *adj* saisi *ou* glacé *ou* frappé d'horreur
horse [hɔːs] *n* **(a)** cheval *m*, -aux; *Horseracing* **to put some money on the horses** jouer aux courses; **draught h.** cheval de trait; **to fall off one's h.** tomber de cheval; *Fig* **to get up on one's high h.** monter sur ses grands chevaux **(about sth** à propos de qch); *F* **to eat like a h.** manger comme quatre; **I could eat a h.!** j'ai une faim de loup!; *Fig* **to hear sth from the h.'s mouth** apprendre qch de source sûre; *F* **hold your horses!** ne t'emballe pas!, doucement!, du calme!; **h. blanket** *or* **rug** couverture *f* de cheval; **h. brass** médaillon *m* de cuivre (*fixé sur le harnachement du cheval*); **h. collar** collier *m* de cheval; **h. dealer** *or* **trader** maquignon *m*; *F* **h. doctor** vétérinaire *mf*; **h. fair** foire *f* aux chevaux; **h. laugh** gros rire *m* bruyant; **h. meat** viande *f* de cheval; *Am Cin, TV F* **h. opera** western *m*; **h. sense** gros bon sens *m*; **h. racing** courses *fpl* de chevaux; **h. riding** équitation *f*; **h. show** concours *m* hippique; *also Fig* **h. trading** maquignonnage *m*; **h. trailer** van *m* à chevaux
(b) (*in breeding*) cheval *m* mâle, cheval entier; **stud h.** étalon *m*; **to take a mare to h.** faire couvrir une jument
(c) *Mil, Hist* (*pl*) cavalerie *f*, troupes *fpl* montées; **regiment of h.** régiment *m* de cavalerie; **h. artillery** artillerie *f* montée; *Br* **the (Royal) H. Guards** la Garde Royale (à cheval)
(d) *Gym* **(vaulting) h.** cheval(-sautoir) *m*; **pommel h.** cheval d'arçons
(e) (*for sawing*) chevalet *m*, tréteau *m*, chèvre *f*
(f) *MecE F* = **horsepower**
(g) *Sl* (*heroin*) héro *f*, blanche *f*
▶ **horse about, horse around** *vi* (*play roughly*) faire l'imbécile
-horse [hɔːs] *suff* **one/two-h.** à un cheval/deux chevaux; *see* **one-horse**
horseback [ˈhɔːsbæk] *n* **on h.** à (dos de) cheval; **to ride on h.** aller à cheval
horsebox [ˈhɔːsbɒks] *n* (*trailer*) van *m*; *Rail* wagon *m* à chevaux
horsebreaker [ˈhɔːsbreɪkər] *n* dresseur, -euse de chevaux
horse chestnut *n Culin* marron *m* d'Inde; *Bot* (*tree*) marronier *m* (d'Inde)
horse-drawn *adj* tiré par des chevaux; **h. vehicle** véhicule *m* attelé
horseflesh [ˈhɔːsfleʃ] *n* **(a)** (*horses*) chevaux *mpl*; **to be a good judge of h.** bien s'y connaître en chevaux **(b)** (*meat*) chair *f ou* viande *f* de cheval
horsefly [ˈhɔːsflaɪ] *n* taon *m*
horsehair [ˈhɔːsheər] *n* crin *m* (de cheval); *Tex* tissu *m* de crin; **h. mattress** matelas *m* de crin
horseman, *pl* **-men** [ˈhɔːsmən] *n* cavalier *m*, écuyer *m*; **to be a good h.** bien monter à cheval, être bon cavalier; **the four horsemen of the apocalypse** les quatre cavaliers de l'apocalypse
horsemanship [ˈhɔːsmənʃɪp] *n* équitation *f*, art *m* de monter à cheval; **we admired her h.** nous avons admiré l'art avec lequel elle montait à cheval, nous avons admiré son talent de cavalière
horseplay [ˈhɔːspleɪ] *n* **they were having a bit of h. in the pool** ils faisaient les imbéciles dans la piscine; **it's just harmless h.** c'est une bagarre pour rire; **no h.!** jeux de mains, jeux de vilains!
horsepower [ˈhɔːspaʊər] *n MecE etc* puissance *f* en chevaux; (*measurement*) cheval-vapeur *m*, *pl* chevaux-vapeur; **actual h.** puissance effective en chevaux
horseradish [ˈhɔːsrædɪʃ] *n* (*plant*) raifort *m*; *Culin* **h. sauce** sauce *f* au raifort
horseshoe [ˈhɔːsʃuː, ˈhɔːʃ-] *n* fer *m* à cheval; **h. brooch/table** broche *f*/table *f* en (forme de) fer à cheval
horsewhip[1] [ˈhɔːswɪp] *n* cravache *f*
horsewhip[2] *vt* **(-pp-)** (*person*) cravacher
horsewoman, *pl* **-women** [ˈhɔːswʊmən, -wɪmɪn] *n* cavalière *f*, amazone *f*, écuyère *f*; **she's a good h.** elle est bonne cavalière, elle monte bien
horsy, horsey [ˈhɔːsɪ] *adj* (*appearance*) chevalin; (*keen on horses*) fou/*f* folle de chevaux; **she's terribly h.** elle ne parle que chevaux; **h. face** figure chevaline
horticultural [hɔːtɪˈkʌltʃər(ə)l] *n* (*implement*) horticole, d'horticulture; **h. show** exposition *f* d'horticulture *ou* horticole
horticulture [ˈhɔːtɪkʌltʃər] *n* horticulture *f*
horticulturist [hɔːtɪˈkʌltʃərɪst] *n* horticulteur, -trice
hose[1] [həʊz] *n* **(a)** (*pl* **hoses**) (*pipe*) tuyau *m*; *MecE* **(flexible) h.** tuyau flexible; (*in car*) durite *f*; **air h.** tuyau d'air flexible; *Aut* **h. clip** collier *m* de durite; **garden h.** tuyau d'arrosage; **h. reel** chariot *m* à tuyaux **(b)** (*no pl*) *Com* (*stockings etc*) (*for women*) bas *mpl*; *Hist* (*for men*) chausses *fpl*; **half h.** chaussettes *fpl* (*d'hommes*)
hose[2] *vt* **(a)** (*car etc*) laver au jet **(b)** (*lawn*) arroser (au jet d'eau)
▶ **hose down** *vtsep* = **hose**[2] **(a)**
▶ **hose out** *vtsep* (*clean out*) laver au jet
hosepipe [ˈhəʊzpaɪp] *n* tuyau *m*, flexible *m*; **h. ban** = interdiction *f* d'utiliser les tuyaux d'arrosage pendant les périodes de sécheresse
hosier [ˈhəʊzɪər] *n Com* bonnetier, -ière
hosiery [ˈhəʊzɪərɪ] *n Com* (*stockings and socks*) bas *mpl* et chaussettes *fpl*; **h. (trade)** bonneterie *f*; **h. counter** *or* **department** rayon *m* des bas (et chaussettes)
hospice [ˈhɒspɪs] *n* hospice *m*; (*for terminally ill*) hospice (pour malades en phase terminale); (*part of hospital*) pavillon *m* des incurables
hospitable [hɒsˈpɪtəb(ə)l] *adj* (*climate*) hospitalier, accueillant; (*person*) accueillant
hospitably [hɒsˈpɪtəblɪ] *adv* avec hospitalité
hospital [ˈhɒspɪt(ə)l] *n* **(a)** **[①A6,d,i]** hôpital *m*, -aux; **to be in h.** être à l'hôpital; **she had to go (in)to** *Br* **h.** *or US* **the h.** elle a dû aller à l'hôpital; **to send sb to** *Br* **h.** *or US* **the h.** hospitaliser qn; **h. bed** lit *m* d'hôpital; **h. radio** radio *f* diffusant dans les hôpitaux; **h. ship** navire-hôpital *m*, *pl* navires-hôpitaux; **h. train** train *m* sanitaire; **h. treatment/staff** traitement *m*/personnel *m* hospitalier **(b) Chelsea H.** l'hôpital *m* de Chelsea (*pour les vieux soldats*); **Greenwich H.** l'Hospice *m* de Greenwich (*pour les invalides de la marine*)
hospitality [hɒspɪˈtælɪtɪ] *n* hospitalité *f*; *Old-fashioned Euph* **to enjoy His/Her Majesty's h.** faire de la prison; **h. business** hôtellerie *f*; **h. industry** industrie *f* hôtelière; **h. management** gestion *f* hôtelière; **h. tray** plateau *m* de courtoisie
hospitalization [hɒspɪtəlaɪˈzeɪʃən] *n* hospitalisation *f*
hospitalize [ˈhɒspɪtəlaɪz] *vt* (*sick person*) hospitaliser; **a couple of thugs hospitalized him** deux voyous l'ont envoyé à l'hôpital

host¹ [həʊst] *n* **(a)** (*in private house*) hôte *m*; *Com* (*in hotel etc*) hôtelier *m*; (*in inn*) aubergiste *m*; *TV etc* (*of chat show, games show*) animateur, -trice; **he was the perfect h.** il a été un hôte parfait **(b)** *Biol* hôte *m*; **h. organism** hôte **(c)** *Comptr* **h. file** fichier *m* serveur; **h. system** système *m* serveur *ou* hôte; **h. computer** ordinateur-serveur *m*

host² *vt* (*party*) donner; *TV etc* (*programme*) présenter; (*games show*) animer

host³ *n* **(a)** (*great number*) **a (whole) h.** (*of servants etc*) (toute) une armée; **a h. of good restaurants** une quantité de bons restaurants **(b)** *Arch, Lit* (*throng*) armée *f*, multitude *f*

host⁴ *n Rel* (*consecrated bread*) hostie *f*

hostage ['hɒstɪdʒ] *n* otage *m*; **as (a) h.** en otage, pour otage; **to take sb h.** prendre quelqu'un en otage; **she is being held h.** elle est gardée en otage; **h. taker** preneur, -euse d'otage; **h. taking** prise *f* d'otage(s); *Fig* **that's a h. to fortune** c'est la porte ouverte à tous les ennuis

hostel ['hɒstəl] *n* (*for the homeless, students*) foyer *m*; **youth h.** auberge *f* de jeunesse

hosteller, *US* **hosteler** ['hɒstələr] *n* **(youth) h.** ajiste *mf*

hostelling, *US* **hosteling** ['hɒstəlɪŋ] *n* **(youth) h.** ajisme *m*

hostelry ['hɒstəlrɪ] *n Arch* hostellerie *f*; *Br Hum* pub *m*; bar *m*

hostess ['həʊstɪs] *n* **(a)** (*in private house, night club*) hôtesse *f*; (*hotel-keeper etc*) hôtelière *f*; *TV etc* (*of chat show etc*) animatrice *f* **(b)** *Av* **(air) h.** hôtesse *f* de l'air

hostile ['hɒstaɪl, *Am* 'hɒst(ə)l] **1** *adj* (*attitude, climate, environment*) hostile; (*act*) d'hostilité; **to be h. to sb/sth** (*opposed*) être hostile à qn/qch; *Mil* **h. forces** forces *fpl* ennemies; *St Exch* **h. takeover** prise *f* de contrôle inamicale **2** *n US* ennemi *m*

hostility [hɒs'tɪlɪtɪ] *n* **(a)** hostilité *f* **(to** contre**)**; **to feel no h. towards sb** n'avoir aucune animosité contre qn **(b)** **hostilities** (*war*) hostilités *fpl*

hot [hɒt] **1** *adj* **(hotter, hottest)** **(a)** chaud; (*sun*) ardent; (*fire*) vif; *Nucl Phys* radioactif; **boiling h.** bouillant; **burning h.** brûlant; **to be very h.** (*of person*) avoir très chaud; (*of water, plate etc*) être très chaud; (*of weather*) faire très chaud; **it was a h. day** il faisait chaud; **to get** *or* **become h.** (*of person*) commencer à avoir chaud; (*of water, plate etc*) devenir chaud, chauffer; (*of weather*) commencer à faire chaud; **to keep a dish h.** tenir un plat au chaud; *F* **to get all h. and bothered** devenir tout rouge; *F* **to get h. under the collar** (*with embarrassment*) être embarrassé; (*with anger*) se mettre en colère; *F* **it's all h. air** ce ne sont que des balivernes; *F* **he's full of h. air** il ne raconte que des foutaises; **to sell like h. cakes** se vendre comme des petits pains; *Med* **h. flush** bouffée *f* de chaleur; **a h. meal** un repas chaud; *Fig F* **h. potato** sujet *m* délicat; *F* **to drop sb like a h. potato** laisser tomber qn comme une vieille chaussette *ou* savate; *Geol* **h. spring** source *f* d'eau chaude; *Fig F* **to be in h. water** être dans le pétrin; *Fig F* **to get into h. water** s'attirer *ou* se créer des ennuis

(b) *Culin* (*spicy etc*) (*pepper*) fort; (*mustard*) piquant, fort; (*food*) épicé; **not all Indian food is h.** la cuisine indienne n'est pas nécessairement relevée

(c) (*fresh*) **h. gossip/news** les tous derniers cancans/les toutes dernières nouvelles; **news h. from the press** nouvelles de dernière heure; **a book h. from the press** un livre qui sort tout juste de l'imprimerie

(d) (*close*) **to be h. on the scent** *or* **trail** être sur la bonne piste; **to be in h. pursuit of sb** suivre qn de près; **you're getting h.** (*in guessing game*) tu brûles

(e) (*angry, emotional*) **to have a h. temper** s'emporter facilement; **the political climate has become noticeably hotter in recent weeks** le climat politique est devenu sensiblement plus chaud depuis quelques semaines

(f) *F* (*good*) super; **that record wasn't so h.** ce disque n'était pas super; **that isn't such a h. idea** ce n'est pas terrible *ou* fameux comme idée; **I'm not very h. on history** (*knowledgeable about*) je ne suis pas très calé en histoire; **they're very h. on formal qualifications** (*attach importance to*) ils insistent beaucoup sur les diplômes; **they're not very h. on hygiene** (*fussy about*) ils ne sont pas très portés sur l'hygiène; **to be h. stuff** (*sexy*) (*of woman*) être canon; (*of man*) être super (bien); **he's h. stuff at tennis** au tennis, c'est un as; **how are you? – not so h.** comment ça va? – pas terrible *ou* fameux

(g) *Horseracing etc* **h. favourite** grand favori *m*; **h. tip** tuyau *m* de première

(h) *F* (*dangerous, difficult*) (*stolen goods etc*) recherché par la police; **the place was getting too h. for me** je me trouvais dans un véritable guêpier; **the situation was too h. to handle** la situation était trop délicate pour qu'on s'en mêle; **to make things** *or* **it too h. for sb** rendre la vie infernale à qn; **the presence of the army made things h. for the smugglers** la présence de l'armée a rendu les choses très difficiles pour les contrebandiers; *US F* **h. seat** (*electric chair*) chaise *f* électrique; *Fig* **to be in the h. seat** (*be responsible*) avoir toute la responsabilité; (*have to answer difficult questions*) être sur la sellette; **the man in the England h. seat** (*manager of football team etc*) l'homme qui a la tâche difficile de diriger l'équipe d'Angleterre

(i) *Tel* **h. line** numéro *m* d'urgence; (*USA to Kremlin*) téléphone *m* rouge; **h. line number** numéro *m* de téléphone accessible 24 heures sur 24

(j) *Fin* **h. money** capitaux *mpl* fébriles

2 *adv* **to blow h. and cold** (*of person*) changer d'avis sans cesse; (*in moods*) être d'humeur changeante; **she's blowing h. and cold over him** un jour, elle l'aime, un jour, elle ne l'aime pas

▶ **hot up** *F* **1** *vtsep Aut* (*engine*) gonfler; **to h. up the pace** (*increase*) forcer l'allure **2** *vi* (*of campaign etc*) s'échauffer; (*of competition, love affair, discussion*) s'intensifier; (*of race*) s'animer; **things are beginning to h. up** l'affaire se corse

hot-air *adj Av* **h. balloon** montgolfière *f*, ballon *m* à air chaud

hotbed ['hɒtbed] *n* **(a)** *Fig* (*of rebellion, intrigue etc*) foyer *m* **(b)** (*in gardening*) couche *f*

hot-blooded *adj* ardent, passionné; **to be h.** avoir le sang chaud; **the Italians are a h. race** les Italiens sont un peuple qui a le sang chaud

hotchpotch ['hɒtʃpɒtʃ] *n* mélange *m* confus; **this book's a bit of a h.** (*good and bad*) ce livre est de qualité inégale; (*mixture*) ce livre est un patchwork

hot cross bun *n Br* = brioche *f* à la canelle

hotdog ['hɒtdɒg] *n Culin* hot-dog *m*

hot-dog *vi Ski* faire du ski acrobatique

hot-dogging ['hɒtdɒgɪŋ] *n Ski* ski *m* acrobatique

hotel [həʊ'tel] *n* hôtel *m*; **at** *or* **in my h.** à mon hôtel; **to stay at a h.** descendre dans un hôtel; **private** *or* **residential h.** = pension *f* de famille; **h. accommodation** hébergement *m* à l'hôtel; **h. administration** gestion *f* hôtelière; **h. and catering industry** industrie *f* de l'hôtellerie et de la restauration; **h. bed** lit *m* d'hôtel; **h. bedroom** chambre *f* d'hôtel; **h. business** hôtellerie *f*; **h. chain** chaîne *f* hôtelière; **h. clerk** employé *m* d'hôtel; **h. group** groupe *m* hôtelier; **h. industry** industrie hôtelière, hôtellerie; **h. keeper** hôtelier, -ière; **h. lobby** hall *m* d'hôtel, hall d'entrée d'un hôtel; **h. management** gestion *f* hôtelière; **h. manager** gérant, -ante *ou* directeur, -trice d'hôtel; **h. occupancy** taux *m* d'occupation des hôtels; **h. reception** réception *f* d'hôtel; **h. receptionist** réceptionniste *mf* d'hôtel; **h. register** agenda *m ou* livre *m* de réservation; **h. school** école *f* hôtelière; **h. tax** taxe *f* sur l'hôtellerie; **h. taxi** taxi *m* d'hôtel; **the h. trade** l'industrie hôtelière, l'hôtellerie; **h. transfer** transfert *m* (de la gare/l'aéroport à l'hôtel)

hotelier [həʊ'teljeɪ] *n* hôtelier, -ière

hotel keeping *n* hôtellerie *f*

hotfoot¹ ['hɒtfʊt] *adv* (*to set off, arrive*) à toute vitesse, en (toute) hâte

hotfoot² *vt F* **to h. it** galoper, aller à toute allure

hothead ['hɒthed] *n* exalté, -ée

hot-headed *adj* (*rash*) exalté, impétueux; (*quick-tempered*) emporté, violent

hothouse ['hɒthaʊs] *n* serre *f* chaude; *Fig* (*of new talent etc*) pépinière *f*; **h. plant** plante *f* de serre chaude; *Fig* (*person*) plante de serre

hot key *n Comptr* touche *f* personnalisée

hotly ['hɒtlɪ] *adv* **(a)** (*to reply, protest*) vivement; **h. contested** âprement disputé **(b)** (*to pursue*) avec acharnement

hotplate ['hɒtpleɪt] *n* (*for cooking*) plaque *f* chauffante; (*on table*) chauffe-plat *m*, *pl* chauffe-plats

hotpot ['hɒtpɒt] *n esp Br Culin* = ragoût *m* de viande aux pommes de terre cuit à l'étuvée

hotrod ['hɒtrɒd] *n Aut F* bolide *m*, voiture *f* gonflée

hots [hɒts] *npl Sl* **to have the h. for sb** (*of woman*) mouiller pour qn; (*of man*) bander pour qn

hot-shoe *n Phot* sabot-contact *m*

hotshot ['hɒtʃɒt] *US F* **1** *adj* magnifique, terrible; **a h. chess player** un joueur d'échecs super-doué **2** *n* (*expert*) as *m*, crack *m*

hot spot *n Phys* point *m* chaud; *Fig* (*dangerous area*) point chaud; (*in city*) quartier *m* chaud

hot-tempered *adj* colérique, coléreux

Hottentot ['hɒt(ə)ntɒt] **1** *adj* hottentot **2** *n* Hottentot, -ote

hot-water bottle *n* bouillotte *f*

hound¹ [haʊnd] *n* **(a)** (*in hunting*) chien *m* de meute; *F* (*dog*) chien; **the hounds** (*pack*) la meute *f*; **as if all the hounds of hell were after him** comme s'il avait tous les diables de l'enfer à ses trousses; **to ride to hounds** chasser à courre **(b)** *Sp* (*in paper chase*) coureur *m*, poursuivant *m* **(c)** *Old-fashioned F Pej* (*contemptible person*) canaille *f*

hound² *vt Fig* **she was hounded by the press** elle était traquée *ou* poursuivie par la presse; **hounded from place to place** pourchassé d'un endroit à un autre; **he was hounded out of France** il fut chassé de France
▸ **hound down** *vtsep (person)* traquer jusqu'à la capture; **wherever you are we'll h. you down** où que vous soyez, on vous aura; **he's been hounded down** il s'est fait prendre
hour [ˈauər] *n* **(a)** [①A75,A; B58,A] *(period)* heure *f*; **an h. and a half** une heure et demie; **half an h.**, *esp Am* **a half hour** une demi-heure; **a quarter of an h.** un quart d'heure; **h. by h.** d'heure en heure; **to pay sb by the h.** payer qn à l'heure; **to be paid £5 an h.** être payé 5 livres de l'heure; *Ind etc* **output per h.** rendement *m* à l'heure; **there's a train every h. on the h.** il y a un train toutes les heures (à l'heure juste); **to take hours over sth** mettre des heures à faire qch; *F* **we've been waiting (for) hours** ça fait des heures que nous attendons; **h. hand** *(of watch, clock)* petite aiguille *f*
(b) *(in timetables)* **office hours** heures *fpl* de bureau; **what are your hours?, what hours do you work?** quels sont vos horaires de travail?; **to keep late hours** rentrer à des heures indues; *(go to bed late)* se coucher très tard; **they keep odd** *or* **unusual hours** ils ont des horaires bizarres; **to work long hours** faire de longues journées (de travail); **after hours** *(of office)* après les heures de travail; *Br (of pub)* après l'heure de la fermeture
(c) *(time of day)* **at this h.?!** à cette heure-ci?!; **in the small** *or* **early hours** en pleine nuit; **well on into the small hours** très avant dans la nuit; **people come and go at all hours** les gens vont et viennent à toute heure; **till all hours** jusqu'à des heures impossibles
(d) *(moment)* heure *f*, moment *m*; **in the h. of need/death** à l'heure du besoin/de la mort; **his h. has come** son heure est venue; **I thought my final h. had come** j'ai cru ma dernière heure arrivée; **her last hours** ses dernières heures; **he was the man of the h.** c'était l'homme du moment
-hour [ˈauər] *suff* **one/two/***etc***-h.** d'une/de deux/*etc* heure(s); **an eight-h. day** une journée de travail de huit heures; **a 30-h. week** une semaine de trente heures; **a three-h. delay** un retard de trois heures; **to put a twenty-four h. watch/guard on sb/sth** surveiller qn/qch vingt-quatre heures sur vingt-quatre
hourglass [ˈauəglɑːs] *n* sablier *m*; **h. figure** silhouette *f* de rêve
hourlong [ˈauəlɒŋ] *adj (meeting)* d'une heure
hourly [ˈauəlɪ] **1** *adj* de toutes les heures; *(train service etc)* à chaque heure; *(output, yield, wage)* horaire, à l'heure; **at h. intervals** toutes les heures; **h. rate** taux horaire; **there is an h. train from platform 8** il y a un train toutes les heures sur le quai numéro 8 **2** *adv* toutes les heures
-hourly [ˈauəlɪ] *suff* **two/three/***etc***-h.** toutes les deux/trois/*etc* heures
house¹, *pl* **houses** [haʊs, ˈhaʊzɪz] *n* **(a)** maison *f*; **at his h.** chez lui; **we invited him to our h.** nous l'avons invité chez nous; **from h. to h.** de porte en porte; **to keep h. for sb** tenir *ou* diriger la maison de qn; **they keep open h.** on est toujours les bienvenus chez eux; **to set up h.** s'installer; *(of young unmarried couple)* se mettre en ménage; *Fig* **the government should put** *or* **set its own h. in order before criticizing others** le gouvernement devrait balayer devant sa porte avant de critiquer les autres; *F* **they got on like a h. on fire** ils se sont immédiatement entendus comme larrons en foire; *F* **he's progressing like a h. on fire** il a fait des progrès du feu de Dieu; *F* **it's coming on like a h. on fire** ça marche du feu de Dieu; *Br F* **the bus goes all round the houses** le bus fait tout le tour de la ville; *Fig F* **to go all round the houses** *(avoid being direct in talking)* tourner autour du pot; **the son/daughter of the h.** le fils/la fille de la maison; **to move h.** déménager; *also Fig* **h. of cards** château *m* de cartes; **h. agent** agent *m* immobilier; **h. guest** invité, -ée; **h. painter** peintre *m* en bâtiments; **h. party** partie *f* de campagne; *(guests)* invités *mpl* à une partie de campagne
(b) *(institution)* **the h. of God** *(church)* la maison de Dieu; **h. of prayer** *or* **worship** église *f*; *(Protestant)* temple *m*; *Br* **the H.** *(parliament)* le Parlement
(c) *Com etc (company)* maison *f*; **banking h.** établissement *m* bancaire; **publishing h.** maison d'édition; **h. bill** double *m* de connaissement; **in h.** dans les locaux de la compagnie; *Naut* **h. flag** pavillon *m* d'armateur *ou* de compagnie (de navigation); **h. magazine** journal *m* d'entreprise; **h. manager** *(of hotel)* gérant *m*; *see* **in-house**
(d) *(restaurant etc)* **to have a drink on the h.** prendre une consommation aux frais du patron *ou* de la maison; **h. rule** règle *f* de la maison; **h. speciality,** *F* **h. special** spécialité *f* (de la) maison; **h. phone** *(in hotel)* téléphone *m* intérieur
(e) *Br Sch* = groupe *m* d'élèves qui rivalise avec un autre pour les activités sportives etc
(f) *Med* **h. surgeon/physician** chirurgien *m*/médecin *m* de garde
(g) *Astrol* maison *f*
(h) *(of crane)* cabine *f*; *Naut (on deck)* rouf *m*; *(at helm)* kiosque *m*
(i) *(household)* maison *f*; *(dynasty)* famille *f*, maison; **the H. of Stuart/Bourbon** les Stuarts *mpl*/les Bourbons *mpl*; **the whole h. was down with flu** toute la maisonnée avait la grippe
(j) *Th* salle *f*, auditoire *m*, assistance *f*; **is there a doctor in the h.?** y a-t-il un médecin dans la salle?; **a full h.** une salle pleine; **h. full** complet; **to play to an empty h.** jouer devant des banquettes vides, jouer devant une salle vide; **to play to packed houses** jouer devant une salle comble, faire salle comble; **there wasn't a dry eye in the h.** tout le monde pleurait dans la salle; *Old-fashioned Cin* **the first h.** la première séance; **h. lights** éclairages *mpl* de la salle
house² [haʊz] *vt* **(a)** *(person)* loger, héberger; *(population)* pourvoir au logement de; **a building that can h. ten families** un bâtiment qui peut loger dix familles **(b)** *(of museum etc) (collection)* contenir; *(locomotive)* mettre à l'abri *ou* à couvert; **the gears are housed in a steel case** l'engrenage est contenu dans un carter d'acier; **this section houses the main engines** dans cette section se trouvent les moteurs principaux
house arrest *n Jur* assignation *f* à domicile; **to be placed under h.** être placé en résidence surveillée (à son domicile)
houseboat [ˈhaʊsbəʊt] *n* house-boat *m*, *pl* house-boats, péniche *f* (aménagée)
housebound [ˈhaʊsbaʊnd] *adj* obligé de rester à la maison; *(invalid)* immobilisé à la maison
housebreaker [ˈhaʊsbreɪkər] *n (burglar)* cambrioleur *m*
housebreaking [ˈhaʊsbreɪkɪŋ] *n (burglary)* cambriolage *m*, vol *m* avec effraction
housecoat [ˈhaʊskəʊt] *n (woman's)* robe *f* d'intérieur
house detective *n* détective *m* d'hôtel
housefly [ˈhaʊsflaɪ] *n* mouche *f* domestique *ou* commune
houseful [ˈhaʊsfʊl] *n* **to have a h. of guests** avoir sa maison pleine d'invités
household [ˈhaʊshəʊld] *n* **(a)** *(people in house)* (membres *mpl* de la) maison *f*; *(economically, statistically)* ménage *m*; **there are five people in this h.** *(in house)* cinq personnes habitent dans cette maison; *(in family)* cette famille compte cinq personnes; **h. appliances** électro-ménager *m*; **h. articles** articles *mpl* pour le ménage; **h. budget** budget *m* du ménage; **h. chores** *or* **duties** *or* **tasks** tâches *fpl* ménagères, travaux *mpl* ménagers; **h. consumption** consommation *f* des ménages; **h. expenses** frais *mpl* de *ou* du ménage; **h. goods** articles pour le ménage, produits *mpl* ménagers; **h. unit** foyer *m*; **not for h. use** *(on industrial cleaner etc)* usage industriel uniquement; **her name is a h. word, she is a h. name** son nom est connu de tous
(b) *(servants)* domestiques *mfpl*
(c) *Br* **the H.** la Maison du souverain; **the H. troops** la Garde
householder [ˈhaʊshəʊldər] *n (owner)* propriétaire *mf* d'une/de la maison; *(tenant)* locataire *mf*
househusband [ˈhaʊshʌzbənd] *n* homme *m* au foyer
housekeeper [ˈhaʊskiːpər] *n* femme *f* de charge; *(of priest etc)* gouvernante *f*; *(at castle etc)* économe *f*, intendante *f*; *(in hotel)* gouvernante; **to be a good h.** *(at home)* être une bonne maîtresse de maison
housekeeping [ˈhaʊskiːpɪŋ] *n (art)* économie *f* domestique; *(work)* soins *mpl* du ménage; *Comptr (file management)* aménagement *m*; **h. (allowance** *or* **money)** argent *m* du *ou* pour le ménage; **she knows nothing about h.** ce n'est pas une femme d'intérieur; **h. book** carnet *m* de dépenses
housemaid [ˈhaʊsmeɪd] *n Old-fashioned* bonne *f*, femme *f* de chambre; *Med F* **h.'s knee** hygroma *m* du genou
houseman, *pl* **-men** [ˈhaʊsmən] *n Br Med (at hospital)* interne *m*; *(in hotel)* homme *m* de ménage
house martin *n (bird)* hirondelle *f* des fenêtres
housemaster, housemistress [ˈhaʊsmɑːstər, -mɪstrɪs] *n Br Sch (in boarding school)* = professeur *m* chargé de la surveillance d'un internat; *(in day school)* = professeur chargé d'un groupe d'élèves
House of Commons *n Br Parl* Chambre *f* des Communes
House of Lords *n Br Parl* Chambre *f* des Lords
House of Representatives *n US, Austr* ≈ Chambre *f* des représentants
house plant *n Bot* plante *f* d'intérieur, plante d'appartement
house-proud *adj* **she is very h.** c'est une femme d'intérieur méticuleuse, *Pej* c'est une véritable maniaque du ménage
houseroom [ˈhaʊsruːm] *n* place *f* *(pour loger qn, qch)*; *F* **I wouldn't give it h.** je n'en voudrais pas même si on m'en faisait cadeau

house-sit *vi* **to h. for sb** s'occuper de la maison de qn pendant son absence
Houses of Parliament *npl Br Parl* Parlement *m*
house-style book *n* guide *m* du style maison; (*for design*) charte *f* graphique; (*editorial*) charte rédactionnelle
house-to-house *adj* (*enquiry, selling etc*) à domicile; **h. canvassing** porte-à-porte *m*; **the police made a h. search** la police a fait une fouille maison par maison, la police a perquisitionné maison après maison
housetop ['haʊstɒp] *n* toit *m*; *Fig* **to shout** *or* **proclaim sth from the housetops** crier qch sur tous les toits
house-train *vt Br* (*dog etc*) dresser à la propreté; **house-trained** (*dog etc*) propre; *F Hum* **she got him (properly) house-trained** (*taught clean habits*) elle lui a appris la propreté; (*taught basic housekeeping*) elle lui a appris à se débrouiller à la maison
house-warming *n* **h. (party)** pendaison *f* de crémaillère, soirée *f* pour pendre la crémaillère; **to give** *or* **have a h.** pendre la crémaillère
housewife, *pl* **-wives** *n* **(a)** ['haʊswaɪf, -waɪvz] femme *f* au foyer **(b)** ['hʌzɪf, -vz] *Br Old-fashioned* (*sewing kit*) trousse *f* de couture
housewifely ['haʊswaɪflɪ] *adj* de femme au foyer
housewifery ['haʊswɪf(ə)rɪ] *n Old-fashioned* économie *f* domestique; (*work*) soins *mpl* du ménage
house wine *n* cuvée *f* de la maison *ou* du patron, vin *m* de la maison
housework ['haʊswɜːk] *n* travaux *mpl* domestiques *ou* de ménage; **to do the h.** faire le ménage
housey-housey ['haʊsɪ'haʊsɪ] *n Br* (jeu *m* de) loto *m*
housing ['haʊzɪŋ] *n* **(a)** (*of people*) logement *m*; *Br* **h. association** association *f* pour l'aide au logement; *Br Admin* **h. benefit** allocation *f* logement; *Br* **h. estate** résidence *f*; *Pej* cité *f*; *Am* **h. project, h. market** marché *m* de l'immobilier; **the h. problem** *or* **shortage** la crise du logement; **h. stock** parc *m* immobilier **(b)** (*for machine, mechanism etc*) boîtier *m*; (*bigger*) coffre *m*; (*of gears, differential*) carter *m*
hove *see* **heave²**
hovel ['hɒv(ə)l] *n Pej* taudis *m*, masure *f*
hover ['hɒvər] *vi* **(a)** (*of bird, insect*) planer, se balancer; (*of helicopter*) effectuer un vol stationnaire; **the helicopter hovered just above us** l'hélicoptère s'immobilisa au-dessus de nos têtes
(b) *Fig* (*of person*) tourner en rond; (*waiting to pounce, do sth*) guetter; **danger is hovering over him** le danger le menace; **a waitress was hovering near our table** une serveuse tournait autour de notre table; **I don't like him hovering over me** je n'aime pas qu'il soit sur mon dos; **don't just h. in the background** ne reste pas dans ton coin; **to h. between two courses of action** hésiter entre deux possibilités; **a smile hovered on his lips** l'ombre d'un sourire passa sur ses lèvres; **she hovered between life and death** elle oscilla *ou* resta entre la vie et la mort; **he seemed to be hovering on the brink of saying something** il semblait hésiter à dire quelque chose
▶ **hover around 1** *vipo* (*move about, near*) **to h. around sb** errer *ou* rôder autour de qn; **prices are hovering around the £3.50 mark** les prix oscillent autour de 3 livres 50 **2** *vi* (*move about nearby*) tourner
hovercraft ['hɒvəkrɑːft] *n inv* aéroglisseur *m*, *F* hovercraft *m*
hoverport ['hɒvəpɔːt] *n* hoverport *m*, gare *f* des aéroglisseurs
hovertrain ['hɒvətreɪn] *n* aérotrain *m*
how [haʊ] **1** *adv* **(a)** [①**A68-69**,2,a; **A69**,b,iv] (*in what manner*) comment; **h. do you spell this word?** comment écrit-on ce mot?; *F* **h. the devil …?, h. on earth …?, h. in the world …?** comment diable …?; **h. did they find out?** comment est-ce qu'ils l'ont su *ou* appris?; **tell me h. he did it** dites-moi comment il (l')a fait; **h. was she dressed?** comment est-ce qu'elle était habillée?, qu'est-ce qu'elle portait?; **h. is it that …?** comment se fait-il que …?; **h. so?** comment ça?; *F* **h. come?** comment cela se fait-il?, et comment ça se fait?; **h. come she didn't tell you?** comment ça se fait qu'elle ne te l'ait pas dit?; **h.'s that?** (*how can that be?*) comment ça?; (*repeat that*) pardon?; *Cr* = appel *m* à l'arbitre, pour savoir si le guichet est sauf ou si la balle a été bien attrapée; **suppose I offer you another £500, h.'s that?** et si je t'offre 500 livres en plus, qu'est-ce que tu en dis?; **h.'s that for a sandwich?** qu'est-ce que tu dis de ce sandwich?; **h.'s that for size?** (*of jacket etc*) ça va comme taille?; *F* **and h.!** et comment!; **h. could you?** (*shame on you*) vous n'avez pas honte?; **I don't know h. he can say that!** je ne sais pas comment il peut dire une chose pareille!; **to learn h. to do sth** apprendre à faire qch; **h. do you like this wine?** comment trouvez-vous ce vin?; **h. do you like your steak?** comment voulez-vous votre steak?; **here's h.!** (*toast*) santé!
(b) (*to what extent*) **h. much/many** combien (de); **h. many times?, h. often?** combien de fois?; **h. many are there of you?** vous êtes combien (de personnes)?; **h. long have you been here?** depuis combien de temps êtes-vous là?; **h. long is the flight?** quelle est la durée du vol?; **you know h. useful he is to me** vous savez à quel point il m'est utile; **you don't know h. right you are** vous ne savez pas combien vous dites vrai, vous ne savez pas à quel point vous avez raison; **h. early would you like to be woken?** à quelle heure voulez-vous qu'on vous réveille?; **h. wide is this room?** quelle est la largeur de cette pièce?; **h. old are you?** quel âge avez-vous?; **h. likely is that to happen?** quelle est la probabilité d'un tel événement?; **h. keen are you on fish?** aimez-vous le poisson?
(c) (*greetings, enquiries after health etc*) **h. are you?** comment allez-vous?, *F* comment ça va?; **h. do you do?** (*when being introduced*) enchanté (de faire votre connaissance); (*hello*) bonjour; *F* **h. are things?** comment ça va?; *F* **h. are you doing?** comment vas-tu?; *F* **h.'s it going?** comment ça se passe?; **h.'s your leg?** et (comment va) ta jambe?; **h.'s business?** comment vont les affaires?; *F* **h.'s life?** comment vas-tu?
(d) (*in exclamations*) comme, que; **h. pretty she is!** comme elle est jolie!; **h. disgusting!** quelle horreur!; **h. kind (of you)!** comme *ou* que c'est gentil (de votre part); **h. she has changed!** comme elle a changé!; **h. I wish I could!** si seulement je pouvais!; **h. surprised he was when …!** quelle ne fut pas sa surprise lorsque …!
(e) *F* (*introducing indirect statement*) que; **I told him h. there had been a great storm** je lui ai dit qu'il y avait eu un gros orage
(f) h. about …? (*making suggestion*) et si …?; **h. about a game of cards/going out for a meal?** et si on faisait une partie de cartes/allait au restaurant?; **h. about you?** et vous?
2 *n* **the hows, whys and wherefores** les comment et les pourquoi, tous les détails
howdy ['haʊdɪ] *int Am F* salut!
how-d'ye-do [haʊdjə'duː] *n Old-fashioned F* **here's a (fine) h.!** en voilà une histoire!, quelle histoire!
however [haʊ'evər] *adv* **(a)** (*on the other hand*) toutefois, cependant, pourtant; **if, h., you don't agree** si toutefois cela ne vous convient pas; **there are more important matters, h.** il y a des problèmes plus importants, pourtant
(b) [①**A69**,b,iv] (*in whatever degree*) quelque … que …+ *sub*, si … que …+ *sub*; **h. good his work is** si excellent que soit son travail; **h. poor** si pauvre qu'il soit/qu'elle soit/*etc*; **h. hard she tried, she couldn't do it** elle a eu beau faire (tout ce qu'elle a pu), elle n'y est pas parvenue; **h. much I try/you cry** même si j'essaie/tu pleures; **h. much it rains** même s'il pleut des cordes
(c) [①**A69**,b,iv] (*in whatever way*) de quelque manière que …+ *sub*; **h. that may be** quoi qu'il en soit; **h. did she find out?** comment est-ce qu'elle l'a su?
howitzer ['haʊɪtsər] *n Mil* obusier *m*
howl¹ [haʊl] *n* (*of person, wolf etc*) hurlement *m*; (*of baby*) braillement *m*; (*of wind*) mugissement *m*; *Electron* hurlement d'amplificateur; **to give a h. of pain/rage** hurler de douleur/rage; **there were howls of laughter** on riait à gorge déployée
howl² 1 *vi* (*of animals, people*) hurler; (*of wind*) mugir, rugir; *Electron* (*of loudspeaker*) hurler; **to h. with laughter** rire à gorge déployée; **to h. with pain/rage** hurler de douleur/rage **2** *vt* (*shout*) hurler
▶ **howl down** *vtsep* (*person*) faire taire en poussant des huées; *Fig* (*suggestion*) rejeter; **the speaker was howled down** sous les huées, l'orateur fut contraint de se taire
howler ['haʊlər] *n* **(a)** *F* (*mistake*) grosse gaffe *f*, bourde *f* énorme; **schoolboy h.** perle *f* (*d'écolier*) **(b) h. monkey** singe *m* hurleur
howling ['haʊlɪŋ] **1** *adj attrib* **(a)** (*baby, wolf*) qui hurle; (*crowd*) hurlant; (*gale, wind*) furieux; **I'm not going out in this h. gale** je ne sortirai pas sous un vent pareil **(b)** *F* (*very great*) énorme; (*success*) fou, *f* folle **2** *n* hurlement *m*; (*of baby*) braillement *m*; (*of wind, gale*) mugissement *m*
hoyden ['hɔɪd(ə)n] *n Old-fashioned Pej* garçon *m* manqué
hoydenish ['hɔɪd(e)nɪʃ] *adj Old-fashioned Pej* garçonnier, -ière
HP, hp [eɪtʃ'piː] *n* **(a)** *MecE* (*abbr* **horsepower**) CV *m* **(b)** *Br Com abbr* **hire-purchase**
HQ, hq [eɪtʃ'kjuː] *n Mil* (*abbr* **headquarters**) Q. G. *m*
HR [eitʃ'ɑː] *n* (*abbr* **human resources**) ressources *fpl* humaines, RH *fpl*; **HR department** direction *f* des ressources humaines, DRH *f*
hr (*abbr* **hour**) h.

HRH [eɪtʃɑːˈreɪtʃ] *Br* (*abbr* **His/Her Royal Highness**) SAR
HRT [eɪtʃɑːˈtiː] *n Med* (*abbr* **hormone replacement therapy**) HTS *f*
HT *n* (*abbr* **high tension**) HT *f*; **HT cable** fil *m* HT
ht *abbr* **height**
hub [hʌb] *n* **(a)** (*of wheel, propeller*) moyeu *m* **(b)** *Fig* centre *m* d'activité; **the h. of the universe** le centre de l'univers; **h. airport** aéroport *m* 'hub' *ou* central; **h. and spoke system** système *m* d'aéroports central et d'apport extérieur
hubbub [ˈhʌbʌb] *n* remue-ménage *m*, vacarme *m*; **h. of voices** brouhaha *m* de voix
hubby [ˈhʌbɪ] *n Br F* (petit) mari *m*
hubcap [ˈhʌbkæp] *n Aut* enjoliveur *m*
hubris [ˈhjuːbrɪs] *n Lit* orgueil *m* démesuré
huckleberry [ˈhʌk(ə)lberɪ] *n Am* (*fruit*) airelle *f*, myrtille *f*
huckster [ˈhʌkstər] *n* **(a)** *Old-fashioned* (*hawker*) colporteur *m* **(b)** (*profiteer*) mercanti *m*, profiteur *m*; **political h.** politicien *m* magouilleur
HUD [eɪtʃjuːˈdiː] *abbr* **(a)** *Mil, Av* **head-up display (b)** *US Admin* **((Department of) Housing and Urban Development)** Ministère *m* de la Ville
huddle¹ [ˈhʌd(ə)l] *n* (*of things*) tas *m* confus; (*of people*) (petit) groupe *m*; *Fig* **to go into a h.** se réunir en petit comité
huddle² **1** *vi* **(a)** se blottir; **to h. in a corner/round the fire** se blottir dans un coin/autour du feu **(b)** *Am F* (*meet and confer*) se réunir en petit comité **2** *vt* = **huddle up 2**
▶ **huddle together 1** *vi* (*of people, animals*) s'entasser, se serrer les uns contre les autres **2** *vtsep* **houses huddled together** maisons blotties les unes contre les autres
▶ **huddle up 1** *vi* (*of person*) se pelotonner **2** *vtsep* (*usu pass*) **huddled up in bed** couché en chien de fusil; **huddled up in a corner** blotti dans un coin
hue¹ [hjuː] *n* (*colour*) teinte *f*, nuance *f*
hue² *n* **h. and cry** clameur *f* de haro; **a h. and cry was raised against this reform** cette réforme provoqua un tollé général
huff¹ [hʌf] *n F* **to be in a h.** être froissé *ou* fâché; **to get into a h.** prendre la mouche, s'offusquer; **he went off in a h.** il prit la mouche et s'en alla
huff² *vi* **he huffed and puffed** il soufflait et haletait; (*showed annoyance*) il ronchonnait
huffily [ˈhʌfɪlɪ] *adv F* d'un air pincé
huffy [ˈhʌfɪ] *adj F* (*annoyed*) fâché, vexé
hug¹ [hʌg] *n* **(a)** (*sign of affection*) étreinte *f*; **to give sb a h.** serrer qn dans ses bras, étreindre qn; **give me a h.** prends-moi dans tes bras **(b)** (*in wrestling*) prise *f*; (*of bear*) étreinte *f*
hug² *vt* **(-gg-) (a)** (*person*) étreindre, embrasser, serrer; **she hugged the child to her** elle a serré l'enfant sur son cœur; **clothes that h. the figure** vêtements qui moulent la silhouette; *Fig* **to h. sb to death** embrasser qn jusqu'à l'étouffer; *Fig* **to h. oneself for doing sth** se féliciter d'avoir fait qch **(b)** (*of bear*) étouffer, enserrer **(c)** (*keep close to*) (*wall*) longer, serrer; **to h. the ground** raser le sol; *Naut* **to h. the coast** suivre la côte de près; *Aut* **to h. the kerb** serrer le trottoir
huge [hjuːdʒ] *adj* immense, énorme; (*success*) immense, formidable; (*man*) colossal; (*difference*) énorme, capital; **h. undertaking** vaste entreprise
hugely [ˈhjuːdʒlɪ] *adv* énormément; (*amusing*) extrêmement
hugeness [ˈhjuːdʒnɪs] *n* énormité *f*, immensité *f*
hugger-mugger [ˈhʌgəmʌgər] *adj Old-fashioned* (*confused*) (*collection*) sans ordre; (*arrangement*) confus
-hugging [ˈhʌgɪŋ] *suff* **hip/figure/***etc***-h.** (*of clothes*) qui moule les hanches/la silhouette/*etc*
Huguenot [ˈhjuːgənɒt, -nəʊ] *n Rel, Hist* Huguenot, -ote
hulk [hʌlk] *n* **(a)** *Naut* carcasse *f* de navire; *Hist* (*prison ship*) ponton *m* **(b)** *Fig* (*person*) mastodonte *m*
hulking [ˈhʌlkɪŋ] *adj attrib* gros, lourd; **h. great man** mastodonte *m*, colosse *m*
hull¹ [hʌl] *n* **(a)** (*of ship, flying boat, tank*) coque *f*; (*in marine insurance*) corps *m*; **h. insurance** assurance *f* sur corps **(b)** (*of pea, bean*) cosse *f*, gousse *f* **(c)** (*of strawberry, raspberry*) calice *m*
hull² *vt* **(a)** (*peas*) écosser; (*oats*) baller; (*rice, barley*) décortiquer **(b)** *Naut* (*ship*) percer la coque de
hullabaloo [hʌləbəˈluː] *n* tintamarre *m*, vacarme *m*
hullo [hʌˈləʊ] *int* = **hello**
hum¹ [hʌm] *n* **(a)** (*of bee*) bourdonnement *m*; (*of machine*) ronflement *m*; (*of plane, top*) vrombissement *m*; (*of voices*) bruit *m* sourd, murmure *m*; (*of conversation*) rumeur *f*; *Rad etc* bourdonnement, ronflement **(b)** *Br Sl* (*bad smell*) puanteur *f*
hum² **(-mm-) 1** *vi* **(a)** (*of person*) fredonner, chantonner; (*of insect etc*) bourdonner; (*of top*) ronfler, vrombir; (*of aircraft*) vrombir; *Rad* (*of set*) ronronner, ronfler; **town humming with activity** ville bourdonnante d'activité; *Fig* **to make things h.** faire marcher rondement les choses **(b)** (*say 'hum'*) dire hum; **to h. and haw** (*mumble*) bredouiller, bafouiller; (*hesitate*) hésiter (*à prendre un parti*) **(c)** *Br Sl* (*smell bad*) chlinguer, puer **2** *vt* (*tune*) fredonner, chantonner
hum³ *int* hmm!, hum!
human [ˈhjuːm(ə)n] **1** *adj* (*body, race etc*) humain; **he's only h.** il est humain après tout; **it's only h.** c'est humain; **h. being** être *m* humain; **not fit for h. consumption** impropre à la consommation, non comestible; **not fit for h. habitation** inhabitable; **h. error** erreur *f* humaine; **h. growth hormone** hormone *f* somatotrope *ou* de croissance, somatotrophine *f*; *esp Journ* **h. interest story** histoire *f* (*de la vie quotidienne*); **h. nature** la nature humaine; **h. resources** ressources *fpl* humaines; **h. resources management** gestion *f* des ressources humaines; **h. resources manager** gestionnaire *m* des ressources humaines; **h. rights** droits *mpl* de l'homme
2 *n* être *m* humain; **humans** les humains *mpl*, les êtres humains
humane [hjuːˈmeɪn] *adj* **(a)** (*kind*) humain; **h. society** (*organization*) = société *f* visant à promouvoir certaines valeurs humaines **(b)** (*killing*) qui évite de faire souffrir, humain
humanely [hjuːˈmeɪnlɪ] *adv* humainement, avec humanité
humanism [ˈhjuːmənɪz(ə)m] *n Phil* humanisme *m*
humanist [ˈhjuːmənɪst] *n Phil* humaniste *m*
humanistic [hjuːməˈnɪstɪk] *adj Phil* humaniste
humanitarian [hjuːmænɪˈteərɪən] *adj, n* humanitaire *mf*
humanity [hjuːˈmænɪtɪ] *n* **(a)** humanité *f*; *F* **the club was packed with sweaty h.** le club était plein d'une foule transpirante **(b)** *Univ* **the humanities** les humanités *fpl*, les lettres *fpl*, les sciences *fpl* humaines
humanize [ˈhjuːmənaɪz] *vt* humaniser
humankind [hjuːm(ə)nˈkaɪnd] *n* humanité *f*
humanly [ˈhjuːm(ə)nlɪ] *adv* humainement; **to do everything h. possible** faire tout ce qui est humainement possible
humanoid [ˈhjuːmənɔɪd] *adj, n* humanoïde *mf*
humble¹ [ˈhʌmb(ə)l] *adj* **(a)** (*meek*) humble; **h. prayer** humble prière *f*; **to offer a h. apology** faire de plates excuses; **in my h. opinion** à mon humble avis; *Old-fashioned* **Your h. servant** (*ending letter*) je reste votre humble serviteur **(b)** (*unpretentious*) (*cottage, background*) modeste; **to be of h. origin** être d'origine modeste; *Fig* **to eat h. pie** admettre son erreur; **to be forced to eat h. pie** être forcé de se rétracter
humble² *vt* (*person*) humilier, mortifier; (*sb's pride*) rabattre; **to h. oneself** s'humilier
humblebee [ˈhʌmb(ə)lbiː] *n* (*insect*) bourdon *m*
humbleness [ˈhʌmb(ə)lnɪs] *n* humilité *f*
humbling [ˈhʌmb(ə)lɪŋ] **1** *adj* (*experience*) humiliant **2** *n* (*of person*) humiliation *f*
humbly [ˈhʌmb(ə)lɪ] *adv* **(a)** (*weekly*) humblement, avec humilité; **if I may h. suggest ...** si je peux me permettre de suggérer ... **(b)** (*to live etc*) modestement
humbug [ˈhʌmbʌg] *n* **(a)** *F* (*nonsense*) bêtises *fpl*; (*deceptive, insincere*) foutaises *fpl*; **h.!** c'est du pipeau! **(b)** *F* (*person*) (*hypocrite, impostor*) charlatan *m* **(c)** *Br* (*sweet*) berlingot *m*, = bêtise *f* de Cambrai
humdinger [ˈhʌmdɪŋər] *n F* quelque chose d'extraordinaire *ou* de fantastique; **a h. of a speech** un discours formidable *ou* sensationnel
humdrum [ˈhʌmdrʌm] **1** *adj* monotone, banal, -als; (*existence*) monotone; **h. daily life** train-train *m* quotidien **2** *n* (*of existence etc*) monotonie *f*
humerus, *pl* **-i** [ˈhjuːmərəs, -aɪ, -iː] *n Anat* humérus *m*
humid [ˈhjuːmɪd] *adj* humide
humidifier [hjuːˈmɪdɪfaɪər] *n* humidificateur *m*
humidify [hjuːˈmɪdɪfaɪ] *vt* (*air*) humidifier
humidity [hjuːˈmɪdɪtɪ] *n* humidité *f*
humidor [ˈhjuːmɪdɔːr] *n* boîte *f* à cigares (pourvue d'un humidificateur)
humiliate [hjuːˈmɪlɪeɪt] *vt* humilier
humiliating [hjuːˈmɪlɪeɪtɪŋ] *adj* humiliant, mortifiant
humiliation [hjuːmɪlɪˈeɪʃən] *n* humiliation *f*
humility [hjuːˈmɪlɪtɪ] *n* humilité *f*
humming [ˈhʌmɪŋ] **1** *adj* bourdonnant; **h. top** toupie *f* d'Allemagne; **h. noise** bourdonnement *m* **2** *n* **(a)** = **hum¹** *(a)* **(b) h. and hawing** hésitation *f*
hummingbird [ˈhʌmɪŋbɜːd] *n* colibri *m*, oiseau-mouche *m*, *pl* oiseaux-mouches
hummock [ˈhʌmək] *n* **(a)** (*in ground*) tertre *m*, mamelon *m*, monticule *m* **(b)** (*in ice field*) hummock *m*
humor [ˈhjuːmər] *n, vt US* = **humour[1,2]**
humorist [ˈhjuːmərɪst] *n* (*writer*) écrivain *m* humoristique, humoriste *m*; (*comedian*) humoriste, comique *m*; (*joker*) farceur *m*

humorous ['hju:m(ə)rəs] *adj* comique, drôle; (*writer etc*) humoriste, humoristique; (*drawing, remark etc*) humoristique
humorously ['hju:m(ə)rəslı] *adv* avec humour
humour¹, *US* **humor** ['hju:mər] *n* **(a)** (*funniness*) humour *m*; **the h. of the situation** le côté comique de la situation **(b)** (**sense of**) **h.** sens *m* de l'humour; **to have no sense of h.** ne pas avoir le sens de l'humour; **to have a good sense of h.** avoir le sens de l'humour **(c)** *Fml* (*mood, temper*) humeur *f*, disposition *f*; **to be in the h. for doing sth** être disposé à faire qch; **good h.** bonne humeur
humour², *US* **humor** *vt* (*indulge*) se prêter *ou* se plier à tous les caprices de; (*be nice to*) ménager; **are you only saying that just to h. me?** est-ce que tu dis ça simplement pour me faire plaisir?
humourless, *US* **humorless** ['hju:məlıs] *adj* dépourvu d'humour
hump¹ [hʌmp] *n* **(a)** (*on flat surface, of hunchback, camel*) bosse *f*; **to have a h.** être bossu; **h. in the road** dos *m* d'âne; *Fig* **we're over the h. now** (*past the worst*) le plus difficile est passé maintenant **(b)** *Br F* **to have the h.** (*be sulking*) faire la tête, bouder; **what's he got the h. about?** pourquoi est-ce qu'il fait la tête?
hump² **1** *vt* **(a)** *F* (*carry*) (*load*) porter sur son dos **(b)** *Sl* (*have sexual intercourse with*) sauter, baiser **2** *vi Sl* (*have sexual intercourse*) baiser
humpback ['hʌmpbæk] *n* **(a)** = **hunchback** **(b)** **h.** (**whale**) baleine *f* à bosse **(c)** *Br* **h.** (**bridge**) pont *m* en dos d'âne
humpbacked ['hʌmpbækt] *adj* bossu; *Br* **h. bridge** pont *m* en dos d'âne
humph [hʌmf, hm] *int* hum! hmm!
humus ['hju:məs] *n* (*soil*) humus *m*; (*with fertilizer*) terreau *m*
Hun [hʌn] *n* **(a)** *F* (*in First World War*) Boche *m* **(b)** *Hist* **the Huns** (*from Asia*) les Huns *mpl*
hunch¹ [hʌntʃ] *n* **(a)** (*intuition*) **to have a h.** avoir un pressentiment **(b)** (*hump*) bosse *f*
hunch² *vt* **to h. one's back** arrondir le dos; **to h. one's shoulders** voûter les épaules
▶ **hunch up** *vtsep* = **hunch²**; **to sit hunched up** se tenir le dos rond
hunchback ['hʌntʃbæk] *n* bossu, -ue; **to have a h.** être bossu; **the H. of Notre Dame** le bossu de Notre Dame
hunchbacked ['hʌntʃbækt] *adj* bossu
hundred ['hʌndrəd] *adj, n* [①**A12**,1h,i; **B56**,A,c-d] **(a)** (*numeral*) cent *m*; **one** *or* **a h.** cent; **a h. and one** cent un; **about a h. houses** une centaine de maisons; **two h. apples** deux cents pommes; **to live to be a h.** vivre jusqu'à cent ans; **they were dying in (their) hundreds** ils mouraient par centaines; **the temperature was in the hundreds** il faisait plus de 40°; *Culin* **hundreds and thousands** vermicelles *mpl* (*en sucre*); **to drive at a h. kilometres an hour** faire du cent à l'heure; **one** *or* **a h. per cent** cent pour cent; **to be a h. per cent certain** être sûr à cent pour cent; **I'm not feeling a h. per cent** je ne me sens pas dans mon assiette; **I'm not feeling a h. per cent yet** je ne suis pas encore complètement remis; **to sell by the h.** (*of new product*) se vendre par centaines; *Sp* **the h. metre race, the h. metres** le cent mètres
(b) *F* (*large number*) **not a h. miles away** pas si loin d'ici; **a h. and one details** mille et un détails; **I've told you hundreds of times** je vous l'ai dit je ne sais combien de fois; **a h. to one it will be a failure** ça fera un four à coup sûr
hundredfold ['hʌndrədfəʊld] *adj* centuple; **to increase a h.** centupler
hundredth ['hʌndrədθ] **1** *adj* centième; **the two h. anniversary of ...** le bicentenaire de ...; *F* **for the h. time, no!** pour la centième fois, c'est non!; *Th* **h. performance** centième *f* **2** *n* **(a)** (*person, thing*) centième *mf* **(b)** (*fraction*) centième *m*; **three hundredths** trois centièmes
hundredweight ['hʌndrədweıt] *n* **(a)** *Br* poids *m* de 112 livres, = 50 kg 802, *Can* = quintal *m*; **two h., two hundredweights** = un quintal, *Can* = deux quintaux **(b)** *Am* poids *m* de 100 livres, = 45 kg 359
Hundred Years' War *n Hist* guerre *f* de cent ans
hung¹ [hʌŋ] *pt, pp see* **hang²**
hung² *adj* **(a)** **h. jury** jury *m* aux opinions partagées; **it was a h. jury** le jury ne parvenait pas à se départager; **h. parliament** parlement *m* sans majorité **(b)** *Sl* **to be well h.** (*man*) être bien membré; **h. like a horse** bien monté
Hungarian [hʌŋ'geərıən] **1** *adj* hongrois **2** *n* **(a)** Hongrois, -oise **(b)** *Ling* hongrois *m*
Hungary ['hʌŋgərı] *n* Hongrie *f*
hunger¹ ['hʌŋgər] *n* faim *f*; **to have a h. for sth** avoir un ardent désir de qch, avoir soif de qch; **h. pains** *or* **pangs** tiraillements *mpl* d'estomac; **h. strike/striker** grève *f*/gréviste *mf* de la faim; **to go on h. strike** faire la grève de la faim
hunger² *vi esp Lit* avoir faim
▶ **hunger after, hunger for** *vipo esp Lit* être affamé de, avoir soif de
hung-over *adj F* **to be h.** avoir la gueule de bois
hungrily ['hʌŋgrılı] *adv* avidement, voracement; **she eyed the food h.** elle regardait la nourriture d'un air vorace; *Fig* **they stared h. at the women** ils fixaient les femmes avec avidité
hungry ['hʌŋgrı] *adj* **(a)** affamé, qui a faim; **to be** *or* **feel h.** avoir faim; **to be ravenously h.** *or* **as h. as a wolf** *or US* **a bear** avoir une faim de loup; **I was getting h.** je commençais à avoir faim; **to look h.** avoir l'air affamé; **it's h. work** ça donne faim **(b)** *Fig* (*look, eye*) avide; **to be h. for knowledge** être avide de connaissances; **to be h. for love** avoir soif d'amour
hung up *adj Sl* **to be h. up on sb** être obsédé par qn; **to be h. up about sth** être obsédé par qch
hunk [hʌŋk] *n* **(a)** (*of bread*) quignon *m*; (*of meat, cheese etc*) gros morceau *m* **(b)** *F* (*attractive man*) beau mec *m*, mec bien foutu
hunky ['hʌŋkı] *adj F* (*man*) (*with good body*) bien foutu; (*big and strong*) (bien) baraqué
hunky-dory ['hʌŋkı'dɔ:rı] *adj F* excellent, au poil
hunt¹ [hʌnt] *n* **(a)** *Sp* (*activity*) chasse *f*; (*people*) équipage *m* de chasse; (*area*) terrain *m* de chasse; **fox/tiger h.** chasse au renard/au tigre **(b)** (*search*) recherche *f*; **he continued his h. for work** il continuait à chercher un emploi; **local people joined in the h. for the child** des gens de la région se sont joints aux recherches pour retrouver l'enfant; **I've had a good h. for my gloves** j'ai cherché mes gants partout; **the h. is on for ...** on recherche ...
hunt² **1** *vi Sp* chasser; **to h. for sth/sb** (*search for*) chercher (à découvrir) qch/qn; **to h. for treasure** aller à la recherche d'un trésor; **to h. high and low for sth** chercher partout qch **2** *vt* **(a)** (*fox, deer etc*) chasser; (*whales*) pêcher, chasser; **to h. a criminal** (*try to locate*) poursuivre un criminel, être à la recherche d'un criminel; **h. the slipper** (*game*) jeu *m* de cache-cache **(b)** (*ride, walk over*) (*piece of land*) parcourir, battre **(c)** (*use in hunting*) (*horse*) monter à la chasse; (*pack*) diriger, conduire
▶ **hunt about, hunt around** *vi* (*search*) chercher partout; **to h. about for sth** chercher qch partout
▶ **hunt down** *vtsep* **(a)** (*chase*) (*animal*) traquer, forcer; (*person*) traquer **(b)** (*find*) dénicher
▶ **hunt out** *vtsep* (*find*) (*person*) débusquer; (*object*) déterrer, dénicher (à force de recherches); **I've hunted out her phone number for you** je t'ai trouvé son numéro de téléphone
▶ **hunt up** *vtsep* (*find*) dénicher
hunted ['hʌntıd] *adj* **he had a h. look** il avait l'air persécuté
hunter ['hʌntər] *n* **(a)** *Sp* (*person*) chasseur *m* **(b)** (*horse*) cheval *m* de chasse, hunter *m* **(c)** (*watch*) (montre *f* à) savonnette *f*; **half h.** montre à guichet
hunter-killer *adj* **h. submarine** sous-marin *m* nucléaire d'attaque
hunting ['hʌntıŋ] **1** *adj* **h. man** fervent *m* de la chasse à courre, grand chasseur *m* **2** *n* **(a)** *Sp* chasse *f*; (*of game*) poursuite *f*; (*science*) vénerie *f*; **fox h.** chasse au renard; **h. dog** chien *m* de chasse; **h. lodge** pavillon *m* de chasse; **h. horn** cor *m ou* trompe *f* de chasse; **h. ground** terrain *m* de chasse; **the Happy H. Grounds** le Paradis des Peaux-Rouges; **a happy h. ground for collectors** un paradis pour les collectionneurs **(b)** *Aut* (*engine surge*) pompage *m*
Huntington's chorea ['hʌntıŋtənzkɒ'rıə] *n Med* chorée *f* de Huntington
huntress ['hʌntrıs] *n* chasseuse *f*, *Lit* chasseresse *f*
huntsman, *pl* **-men** ['hʌntsmən] *n* chasseur *m* (à courre); (*in charge of hounds*) veneur *m*, piqueur *m*
hurdle¹ ['hɜ:d(ə)l] *n* **(a)** (*in athletics*), *Horseracing* haie *f*; **h. race** course *f* de haies; **400-metre hurdles** 400 mètres haies **(b)** *Fig* (*obstacle*) obstacle *m*; **to overcome a h.** franchir un obstacle; **the next h. will be to persuade the managing director** le prochain obstacle sera de persuader le directeur général **(c)** (*fence*) claie *f*, clôture *f*
hurdle² **1** *vt* **(a)** (*jump over*) (*obstacle*) sauter; *Sp* (*fence*) franchir **(b)** (*surround with fences*) entourer de claies **2** *vi Sp* courir une course de haies
hurdler ['hɜ:dlər] *n* (*athlete*) coureur, -euse de haies; (*horse*) sauteur *m*
hurdling ['hɜ:d(ə)lıŋ] *n* (*in athletics*), *Horseracing* course *f* de haies; (*part of competition*) courses de haies; **the world 400m h. champion** le champion du monde du 400m haies
hurdy-gurdy ['hɜ:dı'gɜ:dı] *n Mus* orgue *m* de Barbarie
hurl [hɜ:l] *vt* (*object*) lancer avec force *ou* violence (**at** contre); (*insults*) lancer (**at sb** à qn); **to h. oneself at sb** se ruer sur qn; **he hurled himself off the bridge** il s'est jeté du pont; **to**

h. oneself into the fray se jeter à corps perdu dans la mêlée; **to h. abuse** vociférer des injures

▶ **hurl back** *vtsep* (a) (*object*) relancer avec force *ou* violence (b) *Lit* (*repulse*) (*enemy*) refouler, repousser

▶ **hurl down** *vtsep* jeter

hurley ['hɜːlɪ] *n* = **hurling**

hurling ['hɜːlɪŋ] *n Sp* (*Irish game*) = variété *f* de jeu de hockey

hurly-burly ['hɜːlɪ'bɜːlɪ] *n F* charivari *m*, tohu-bohu *m*

hurrah [hʊ'rɑː], **hurray** [hʊ'reɪ] *int, n* hourra *m*; **h. for the holidays!** vive(nt) les vacances!

hurricane ['hʌrɪkən, -keɪn] *n Met* ouragan *m*; (*in West Indies*) hurricane *m*; **it was blowing a h.** le vent soufflait en ouragan; **h. lamp** lampe-tempête *f*, *pl* lampes-tempête; **h. warning** avis *m* d'ouragan

hurried ['hʌrɪd] *adj* (*step*) pressé, précipité; (*work*) fait à la hâte; **a few h. words** (*written*) quelques mots écrits à la hâte; (*spoken*) quelques mots dits à la hâte; **to have a h. conversation** échanger rapidement quelques mots; **to make a h. decision** décider à la va-vite; **a h. departure** un départ précipité; **a h. meal** un repas pris à la hâte

hurriedly ['hʌrɪdlɪ] *adv* à la hâte, en toute hâte, précipitamment

hurry[1] ['hʌrɪ] *n* hâte *f*, précipitation *f*; **to be in a h.** être pressé; **to do sth in a h.** faire qch à la hâte; **to leave in a h.** sortir à la hâte *ou* en courant; **in her h. she forgot her keys** dans sa précipitation, elle a oublié ses clefs; **they were in a h. to complete the work** ils étaient pressés de terminer le travail; **there's no h.** rien ne presse, ça ne presse pas; **to be in no h.** ne pas être pressé, avoir (tout) le temps; **he was in no h. to leave** il n'était pas pressé de partir; **you won't see her again in a h.** vous ne la reverrez pas de sitôt; **I won't do that again in a h.** je ne suis pas près de recommencer, je ne recommencerai pas de sitôt; **are you in a h. for it?** c'est urgent?; **so what's the h.?** qu'est-ce qui presse tant?; **what's your h.?** pourquoi est-ce que vous êtes aussi pressé?

hurry[2] **1** *vt* (*person*) presser; (*work*) hâter, activer, presser; **don't h. him** ne le presse pas; **she was hurried to hospital** elle a été transportée à l'hôpital en (toute) hâte; **work that cannot be hurried** travail qui demande du temps; **it can't be hurried** il faut le temps; **don't h. your meal** ne mangez pas trop vite

2 *vi* (a) se dépêcher, se hâter, se presser (**to do** de faire); **don't h.** ne vous pressez pas; **there's no need to h.** nous avons tout le temps

(b) (*go quickly*) presser le pas; **she hurried home** elle s'est dépêchée de rentrer; **to h. into/out of a room** entrer dans une pièce/sortir d'une pièce en toute hâte; **to h. after sb** courir après qn

▶ **hurry along 1** *vi* marcher d'un pas pressé; **h. along please** (*we're closing*) dépêchez-vous, s'il vous plaît **2** *vtsep* (*person*) faire se dépêcher; (*work*) accélérer; **he hurried them along** (*walking*) il les a fait marcher plus vite; **h. him along!** dis-lui de se presser!

▶ **hurry away 1** *vi* partir précipitamment **2** *vtsep* **he hurried the children away from the scene of the accident** il a vite éloigné les enfants du lieu de l'accident

▶ **hurry back** *vi* revenir *ou* retourner à la hâte; **she'll soon come hurrying back** elle reviendra vite; **promise to h. back afterwards** promets de revenir vite après

▶ **hurry off 1** *vi* partir précipitamment **2** *vtsep* **they hurried her off to hospital** ils l'ont emmenée à l'hôpital en (toute) hâte

▶ **hurry on 1** *vi* (*proceed quickly*) continuer à la hâte; **she hurried on with the housework** elle a continué le ménage à la hâte **2** *vtsep* (*person*) faire hâter le pas à; (*work*) activer

▶ **hurry up 1** *vi* se dépêcher, se hâter; **h. up!** dépêche-toi!; **h. up and get dressed** dépêche-toi de t'habiller; **h. up with that packing** dépêche-toi de faire ces bagages; **h. up with the iron** dépêche-toi avec le fer **2** *vtsep* (*person*) faire se dépêcher; (*work*) activer, accélérer; **I'll go and h. them up** je vais leur dire de se dépêcher

hurt[1] [hɜːt] **1** *n* (a) (*physical*) mal *m* (b) (*emotional harm*) **to cause h. to sb** blesser qn, faire de la peine à qn; **what h. can it do you?** quel tort cela peut-il vous faire? **2** *adj* (*look, feelings*) blessé

hurt[2] (*pt, pp* **hurt**) **1** *vt* (a) (*cause physical pain or injury to*) (*person*) faire (du) mal à, blesser; **to h. oneself** se faire (du) mal; **to h. one's foot** se blesser au pied; **to get hurt** se blesser; **are you hurt?** êtes-vous blessé?; *Fig* **it wouldn't h. him to have to wait for a change** ça ne lui ferait pas de mal de devoir attendre pour changer; **the scandal will h. their prospects** le scandale nuira à leurs chances

(b) (*emotionally*) faire de la peine à; **to h. sb's feelings** blesser qn, peiner qn, offenser qn; **it hurt me when they did that** ça m'a fait de la peine quand ils ont fait ça; **he is easily hurt** il s'offense facilement; **the thing that hurts me most** ce qui me fait le plus mal

2 *vi* (a) (*cause physical pain*) faire mal; **it hurts** ça fait mal; **where does it h.?** où est-ce que ça vous fait mal?; **my foot hurts** mon pied me fait mal; *F* **I h. all over** j'ai mal partout; *Fig* **just one drink won't h.** juste un verre ne te fera pas de mal; **it wouldn't h. to make a few more photocopies** ça ne fera pas de mal de faire quelques photocopies de plus

(b) (*emotionally*) faire souffrir; **it hurts when you say that ...** ça fait mal de t'entendre dire que ...

hurtful ['hɜːtfʊl] *adj* (*remark*) blessant, offensant; **what a h. thing to say!** comme c'est blessant de dire une chose pareille!; **he was very h.** il a été très blessant

hurtle ['hɜːt(ə)l] **1** *vi* **to h. along** (*of car, person etc*) aller à toute vitesse; **a girl on roller skates hurtled into me** une fille en patins à roulettes m'est rentrée dedans; **the rocks hurtled down** les rochers ont dévalé la pente avec fracas **2** *vt* (*throw*) (*rocks etc*) lancer

husband[1] ['hʌzbənd] *n* mari *m*, époux *m*; **h. and wife** les (deux) époux, les conjoints *mpl*; **h. and wife run the hotel together** les deux époux s'occupent ensemble de l'hôtel; **to live as h. and wife** vivre maritalement

husband[2] *vt Fml* (*resources, strength*) ménager, économiser; (*resources*) bien gérer

husband-and-wife *adj* **h. team** équipe *f* formée par deux époux; **h. business** entreprise *f* appartenant à deux époux *ou* à un couple marié

husbandry ['hʌzbəndrɪ] *n* (a) *Agr* agronomie *f*, économie *f* rurale, agriculture *f*; **animal h.** élevage *m* (b) *Fml* (*management*) gestion *f*

hush[1] [hʌʃ] *n* (*quiet*) silence *m*, calme *m*; **there was a h. when** *or* **as ...** il y a eu un silence quand ...; *F* **h. money** = argent *m* donné à qn pour acheter son silence; *F* **he wanted h. money** il exigeait de l'argent pour se taire

hush[2] **1** *vt* (*baby, child*) calmer, faire taire; (*person*) imposer silence à; *F* **I wish you'd h. your noise** j'espère que tu vas te taire **2** *vi* se taire, faire silence

hush[3] *int* chut!, silence!

▶ **hush up** *vtsep* (*scandal etc*) étouffer

hushed [hʌʃt] *adj* **h. conversation** conversation étouffée *ou* discrète; **to talk in h. tones** chuchoter, parler à voix basse; **a h. silence** un silence profond; **they stared in h. amazement** frappés de stupeur, ils regardaient sans (pouvoir) rien dire

hush-hush *adj F* top-secret, -ète, ultra-secret, -ète

husk[1] [hʌsk] *n* (*of seed, grain*) tégument *m*, pellicule *f*; (*of peas etc*) cosse *f*, gousse *f*; (*of nuts*) brou *m*; (*of chestnut*) hérisson *m*; (*of coffee bean*) coque *f*; (*of corn on the cob*) enveloppe *f*; **husks** (*of grain*) vannure *f*

husk[2] *vt* (*seed*) vanner; (*peas*) écosser; (*rice, barley*) perler, monder; (*corn*) éplucher

huskily ['hʌskɪlɪ] *adv* (*to speak*) d'une voix rauque; (*because of sore throat*) d'une voix enrouée

huskiness ['hʌskɪnɪs] *n* **the h. of her voice** (*because of sore throat*) sa voix enrouée; (*natural*) sa voix rauque

husky[1] ['hʌskɪ] *adj* (a) **h. voice** (*because of sore throat*) voix *f* enrouée *ou* voilée; (*naturally*) voix rauque (b) (*strong*) fort, *F* costaud

husky[2] *n* (*dog*) chien *m* de traîneau, husky *m*

hussar [hʊ'zɑːr] *n Mil* hussard *m*

hussy ['hʌsɪ] *n Old-fashioned F* coquine *f*, friponne *f*; **you little h.!** petite coquine!

hustings ['hʌstɪŋz] *npl* plate-forme *f* électorale; **to be (out) on the h.** faire des discours électoraux sur le terrain; **he's hopeless on the h.** comme orateur sur le terrain, il est nul

hustle[1] ['hʌs(ə)l] *n* (*energetic activity*) grande activité *f*, effervescence *f*; **h. and bustle** tourbillon *m* d'activité; **the h. and bustle of London** l'activité incessante de Londres

hustle[2] **1** *vt* (a) (*shove, push*) bousculer, pousser, presser; **to be hustled away** être emmené précipitamment; **I was hustled into a small room** on m'a fait entrer précipitamment dans une petite pièce

(b) (*hurry*) **to h. things on** faire avancer les choses, *F* faire activer les choses; **to h. sb into a decision** forcer qn à se décider (sans lui donner le temps de respirer); **I won't be hustled** je ne veux pas qu'on me bouscule

2 *vi* (a) (*hurry*) se dépêcher, se presser

(b) (*shove*) **to h. through the crowd** se frayer un passage à travers la foule

(c) *Am Sl* (*swindle*) arnaquer

(d) *Am Sl* (*of prostitute*) faire le trottoir

hustler ['hʌslər] *n* (a) *F* (*energetic person*) (*with lots of business activities*) brasseur *m* d'affaires; (*problem-solver etc*) débrouillard *m* (b) *esp Am Sl* (*swindler*) arnaqueur *m* (c) *Am Sl* (*prostitute*) prostituée *f*

hut [hʌt] *n* hutte *f*, cabane *f*

hutch [hʌtʃ] *n* **(a)** (*for rabbit*) clapier *m*, lapinière *f* **(b)** *Am* (*cupboard*) vaisselier *m*
hutments ['hʌtmənts] *npl Mil* baraquements *mpl*
hyacinth ['haɪəsɪnθ] *n* **(a)** (*flower*) jacinthe *f*; **wood** *or* **wild h.** jacinthe des bois **(b)** (*colour*) bleu jacinthe *m inv*, bleu violet *m inv*; **a h. dress** une robe bleu violet **(c)** *Miner* hyacinthe *f*
hyaena [haɪ'i:nə] *n* = **hyena**
hybrid ['haɪbrɪd] *adj, n Biol, Ling etc* hybride *m*
hybridism ['haɪbrɪdɪz(ə)m] *n Biol* hybridisme *m*
hybridization [haɪbrɪdaɪ'zeɪʃən] *n Biol* hybridation *f*
hybridize ['haɪbrɪdaɪz] **1** *vt* hybrider **2** *vi* s'hybrider
hydra ['haɪdrə] *n* **(a)** (*pl* **hydrae** ['haɪdrɪ]) (*animal*) hydre *f* **(b)** *Myth* **H.** Hydre *f* de Lerne; *Fig* **h.-headed** à plusieurs têtes
hydrangea [haɪ'dreɪndʒə] *n* (*shrub*) hortensia *m*
hydrant ['haɪdrənt] *n* prise *f* d'eau; **fire h.** bouche *f* d'incendie
hydrate¹ ['haɪdreɪt] *n Ch* hydrate *m*
hydrate² *vt Ch* hydrater
hydration [haɪ'dreɪʃən] *n Med* hydratation *f*
hydraulic [haɪ'drɔ:lɪk] *adj* (*force, brake, power etc*) hydraulique; **h. cylinder** *or* **ram** vérin *m* hydraulique; **h. jack** (*for lifting car*) cric *m* hydraulique; **h. engineering** technique *f* hydraulique, hydraulique *f*
hydraulics [haɪ'drɔ:lɪks] *n* [①A10,c] hydraulique *f*
hydro ['haɪdrəʊ] *n* **(a)** *Br* (*centre for hydrotherapy*) établissement *m* hydrothérapique **(b)** *Can F* (*power*) énergie *f* hydraulique; (*power station*) centrale *f* hydraulique; **to pay the h. bill** payer la note d'électricité
hydrocarbon [haɪdrəʊ'kɑ:bən] *n Ch* hydrocarbure *m*
hydrochloric [haɪdrəʊ'klɒrɪk] *adj Ch* (*acid*) chlorhydrique
hydrochloride [haɪdrəʊ'klɔ:raɪd] *n Ch* chlorhydrate *m*
hydrodynamics [haɪdrəʊdaɪ'næmɪks] *n* [①A10,c] hydrodynamique *f*
hydroelectric [haɪdrəʊɪ'lektrɪk] *adj* hydroélectrique; **h. dam** barrage *m* hydroélectrique; **h. power** énergie *f* hydraulique
hydroelectricity [haɪdrəʊɪlek'trɪsɪtɪ] *n* hydroélectricité *f*
hydrofoil ['haɪdrəfɔɪl] *n* hydrofoil *m*
hydrogen ['haɪdrədʒən] *n Ch* hydrogène *m*; **h. bomb** bombe *f* à hydrogène; **h. engine** moteur *m* hydrogène; **h. peroxide** eau *f* oxygénée
hydrography [haɪ'drɒgrəfɪ] *n* hydrographie *f*
hydrolastic suspension [haɪdrə'læstɪk] *n* suspension *f* hydroélastique
hydrolysis [haɪ'drɒlɪsɪs] *n Ch* hydrolyse *f*
hydrometer [haɪ'drɒmɪtər] *n* hydromètre *m*
hydrometry [haɪ'drɒmɪtrɪ] *n Phys* hydrométrie *f*
hydropathy [haɪ'drɒpəθɪ] *n* hydropathie *f*
hydrophobia [haɪdrə'fəʊbɪə] *n Med* **(a)** (*rabies*) hydrophobie *f* **(b)** (*fear*) phobie *f* de l'eau
hydrophobic [haɪdrə'fəʊbɪk] *adj* hydrophobe
hydroplane ['haɪdrəpleɪn] *n* **(a)** (*boat*) hydroglisseur *m* **(b)** *esp US* (*seaplane*) hydravion *m*
hydroponics [haɪdrəʊ'pɒnɪks] *n* [①A10,c] culture *f* hydroponique
hydrostat ['haɪdrəʊstæt] *n* hydrostat *m*
hydrostatics [haɪdrəʊ'stætɪks] *n* [①A10,c] hydrostatique *f*
hydrotherapy [haɪdrəʊ'θerəpɪ] *n Med* hydrothérapie *f*
hydroxide [haɪ'drɒksaɪd] *n Ch* hydroxyde *m*, hydrate *m*
hyena [haɪ'i:nə] *n* (*animal*) hyène *f*; **laughing h.** hyène rieuse; **to laugh like a h.** rire comme un bossu
hygiene ['haɪdʒi:n] *n* hygiène *f*
hygienic [haɪ'dʒi:nɪk] *adj* hygiénique
hygienically [haɪ'dʒi:nɪklɪ] *adv* hygiéniquement
hymen ['haɪmen] *n* **(a)** *Anat* hymen *m* **(b)** *Myth* **H.** Hyménée *f*
hymn [hɪm] *n* **(a)** *Rel* hymne *m ou f*, cantique *m*; **h. book** livre *m* de cantiques; **there will be h. singing** on chantera des hymnes **(b)** (*anthem, poem etc*) hymne *m*
hymnal ['hɪmn(ə)l] *n Fml* livre *m* de cantiques
hype¹ [haɪp] *n* **(a)** *F Pej* (*publicity*) battage *m* publicitaire, matraquage *m* publicitaire; **it's all h.** c'est du matraquage **(b)** *Sl* (*hypodermic needle*) aiguille *f* hypodermique
hype² *vt F* **to h. a product** faire du matraquage publicitaire pour un produit
▶ **hype up** *vtsep F* (*publicize*) **to h. sth up** faire de la publicité à outrance pour qch; **to h. up a new film/rock group** lancer un nouveau film/groupe de rock à grand renfort de publicité; **it's been so hyped up in the media** on a fait un tel battage médiatique; **I don't want to h. it up too much, but …** (*overstate*) je ne voudrais pas exagérer mais …
hyped up [haɪp'tʌp] *adj* **(a)** *F* (*heavily publicized*) lancé à grand renfort de publicité **(b)** *F* (*excited*) tout excité **(c)** *Sl* (*on drugs*) camé
hyper ['haɪpər] *adj F* (*over-excited*) tout excité; (*generally overactive etc*) hyper-dynamique
hyper- ['haɪpər] *pref* hyper-
hyperacidity [haɪpərə'sɪdɪtɪ] *n* hyperacidité *f*
hyperactive [haɪpə'ræktɪv] *adj* hyperactif
hyperbola [haɪ'pɜ:bələ] *n Math* hyperbole *f*
hyperbole [haɪ'pɜ:bəlɪ] *n Liter* hyperbole *f*
hyperbolic(al) [haɪpə'bɒlɪk, -ɪk(ə)l] *adj* (*in rhetoric*), *Math* hyperbolique
hypercritical [haɪpə'krɪtɪkəl] *adj* hypercritique
hyperemotivity [haɪpərɪməʊ'tɪvɪtɪ] *n* hyperémotivité *f*
hyperglycaemia [haɪpəglaɪ'si:mɪə] *n Med* hyperglycémie *f*
hyperglycaemic [haɪpəglaɪ'si:mɪk] *adj Med* hyperglycémique; (*drug*) hyperglycémiant
hypermarket ['haɪpəmɑ:kɪt] *n Br* hypermarché *m*, grande surface *f*
hypersensitive [haɪpə'sensɪtɪv] *adj* très *ou* trop susceptible
hypersensitivity [haɪpəsensɪ'tɪvɪtɪ] *n* (*emotional*) (extrême) susceptibilité *f*
hypertension [haɪpə'tenʃən] *n Med* hypertension *f*
hypertext ['haɪpətekst] *n Comptr* hypertexte *m*
hyperthyroid [haɪpə'θaɪrɔɪd] *adj Med* hyperthyroïdien, -ienne
hyperthyroidism [haɪpə'θaɪrɔɪdɪz(ə)m] *n Med* hyperthyroïdie *f*
hyphen ['haɪf(ə)n] *n* trait *m* d'union
hyphenate ['haɪfəneɪt] *vt* (*word*) mettre un trait d'union à; **hyphenated word** mot *m* composé; **is that hyphenated?** est-ce que ça prend un trait d'union?; *US* **hyphenated American** étranger naturalisé (*Germano-Américain, Hispano-Américain etc*)
hyphenation [haɪfə'neɪʃən] *n* syllabation *f*; (*in printing*) césure *f*, coupure *f* des mots; *Comptr* **h. help** aide *f* à la césure; *Comptr* **h. logic** logique *f* de césure; *Comptr* **h. menu** menu *m* de césure; *Comptr* **h. program** programme *m* de césure, logiciel *m* de syllabation
hypnosis [hɪp'nəʊsɪs] *n* hypnose *f*; **under h.** sous hypnose
hypnotic [hɪp'nɒtɪk] *adj Psy, Pharm* hypnotique; **h. state** état *m* d'hypnose; **in a h. trance** en état d'hypnose; **to have a h. effect on sb** hypnotiser qn; **she had a h. fascination for him** il était totalement fasciné par elle
hypnotism ['hɪpnətɪz(ə)m] *n* hypnotisme *m*
hypnotist ['hɪpnətɪst] *n* hypnotiseur, -euse
hypnotize ['hɪpnətaɪz] *vt* hypnotiser
hypo- ['haɪpəʊ] *pref* hypo-
hypoallergenic [haɪpəʊælə'dʒenɪk] *adj* hypoallergénique, anallergique
hypocalorific [haɪpəkælə'rɪfɪk] *adj* hypocalorique, hypoénergétique
hypochondria [haɪpə'kɒndrɪə] *n Med* hypocondrie *f*
hypochondriac [haɪpə'kɒndrɪæk] **1** *n* hypocondriaque *mf*, malade *mf* imaginaire **2** *adj* hypocondriaque; **h. region** (*of abdomen*) hypocondre *m*
hypocrisy [hɪ'pɒkrɪsɪ] *n* hypocrisie *f*
hypocrite ['hɪpəkrɪt] *n* hypocrite *mf*, tartufe *m*
hypocritical [hɪpə'krɪtɪk(ə)l] *adj* hypocrite
hypocritically [hɪpə'krɪtɪklɪ] *adv* hypocritement
hypodermic [haɪpə'dɜ:mɪk] **1** *adj* **(a)** (*injection, syringe, needle etc*) hypodermique **(b)** *Anat* sous-cutané **2** *n* (*syringe*) seringue *f* hypodermique; (*needle*) aiguille *f* hypodermique; (*injection*) piqûre *f* hypodermique
hypoglycaemia [haɪpəʊglaɪ'si:mɪə] *n Med* hypoglycémie *f*
hypoglycaemic [haɪpəʊglaɪ'si:mɪk] *adj Med* hypoglycémique; (*drug*) hypoglycémiant
hypoid ['haɪpɔɪd] *adj MecE* hypoïde
hypotenuse [haɪ'pɒtənju:z] *n Math* hypoténuse *f*
hypothalamus [haɪpə'θæləməs] *n* hypothalamus *m*
hypothermia [haɪpəʊ'θɜ:mɪə] *n Med* hypothermie *f*
hypothesis [haɪ'pɒθəsɪs] *n* [①A14,10] hypothèse *f*; **working h.** hypothèse de travail
hypothesize [haɪ'pɒθəsaɪz] **1** *vi* faire *ou* formuler des hypothèses **2** *vt* **to h. that …** admettre comme hypothèse que …
hypothetical [haɪpə'θetɪk(ə)l] *adj* hypothétique, supposé
hypothetically [haɪpə'θetɪklɪ] *adv* hypothétiquement, par hypothèse
hypothyroid [haɪpəʊ'θaɪrɔɪd] *adj Med* hypothyroïdien, -ienne
hypothyroidism [haɪpəʊ'θaɪrɔɪdɪz(ə)m] *n Med* hypothyroïdie *f*
hypotonic [haɪpəʊ'tɒnɪk] *adj* hypotonique
hysterectomy [hɪstə'rektəmɪ] *n Surg* hystérectomie *f*; **to have a h.** subir une hystérectomie
hysteria [hɪs'tɪərɪə] *n* **(a)** crise *f* de nerfs; *Med* hystérie *f* **(b)** *F* (*great amusement*) fou rire *m*
hysteric [hɪs'terɪk] *n Med* hystérique *mf*
hysterical [hɪs'terɪk(ə)l] *adj* **(a)** *Med* hystérique; **h. pregnancy** grossesse *f* nerveuse **(b)** (*very emotional*) en proie à une crise de nerfs; (*laughter*) nerveux, énervé; (*reaction*) hystérique; **h. sobbing** sanglots *mpl* convulsifs; **she was h.** elle était dans tous ses états **(c)** *F* (*very amusing*) écroulant, tordant **(d)** *F* (*very amused*) **h. laughter** fou rire *m*
hysterically [hɪs'terɪklɪ] *adv* **(a)** (*very emotionally*) sans

pouvoir maîtriser ses émotions; **he was waving his arms h.** il agitait ses bras de façon incontrôlée; **to weep h.** avoir une crise de larmes; **to laugh h.** être pris d'un rire nerveux **(b)** *F* **h. funny** écroulant, tordant **(c)** *F* **to laugh h.** (*with great amusement*) avoir le fou rire

hysterics [hɪs'terɪks] *npl* **(a)** *Med* hystérie *f* **(b)** (*emotional reaction*) crise *f* de nerfs; **to go into h.** avoir une crise de nerfs **(c)** *F* (*great amusement*) fou rire *m*; **to be in h.** être écroulé de rire; **she had us in h.** elle nous a fait tordre de rire; **to send sb into (a fit of) h.** faire tordre qn de rire

I

I¹, i [aɪ] *n* (*letter*) I, i *m*
I² **1** *pers pron* [①A26,a; B17,1,a] (**a**) (*unstressed*) je, (*preceding vowel*) j'; **I sing** je chante; **I accuse** j'accuse; **here I am** me voici; **what have I said?** qu'ai-je dit? (**b**) (*stressed*) moi; **he and I both like jazz** lui et moi, nous aimons le jazz; **I too have a twin sister** moi aussi, j'ai une jumelle **2** *n* **another I** un autre moi(-même)
Ia *abbr* **Iowa**
iambic [aɪ'æmbɪk] *Liter* **1** *adj* (*verse*) iambique; **i. foot** iambe *m*; **i. pentameter** pentamètre *m* iambique **2** *n* (*line, poem*) iambe *m*
IATA [aɪ'ɑːtə, iː'ɑːtə] *n Av* (*abbr* **International Air Transport Association**) IATA *f*
IBC [aɪbiː'siː] *n* (*abbr* **inside back cover**) troisième *f* de couverture
I-beam *n Comptr* pointeur *m* en I
Iberia [aɪ'bɪərɪə] *n Hist* Ibérie *f*
Iberian [aɪ'bɪərɪən] **1** *adj* (*people*) ibérien, ibérique; **the I. Peninsula** la péninsule ibérique **2** *n* Ibère *mf*
ibex, *pl* **-exes** ['aɪbeks, -eksɪz] *n* bouquetin *m* des Alpes
ibid ['ɪbɪd] *adv* (*abbr* **ibidem**) ibid
ibis, *pl* **-ises** ['aɪbɪs, -ɪsɪz] *n* ibis *m*
IBM-compatible [aɪbiːemkəm'pætɪb(ə)l] *n, adj* compatible *m* IBM
IBOR ['aɪbɔːr] *n* (*abbr* **interbank offered rate**) TIO *m*
IBS [aɪbiː'es] *n Med* (*abbr* **irritable bowel syndrome**) colite *f*
IC [aɪ'siː] *n Comptr* (*abbr* **integrated circuit**) circuit *m* intégré; **IC card** carte *f* à circuits intégrés
ICAO [aɪsiːeɪ'əʊ] *n Av* (*abbr* **International Civil Aviation Organization**) OACI *f*
ice¹ [aɪs] *n* (**a**) (*frozen water*) glace *f*; *Met* (*on road*) verglas *m*; **my feet are as cold as i.** j'ai les pieds glacés; **with i.?** (*in drink*) avec des glaçons *ou* de la glace?; *Fig* **to be on** *or* **skate on thin i.** être sur *ou* toucher à un sujet délicat; *Fig* **to put a project on i.** mettre un projet en veilleuse; **that cuts no i. with me** ça ne marche pas avec moi; **i. house** glacière *f*; **i. machine** distributeur *m* de glaçons; *esp US* **i. man** livreur *m* de glace; *Th* **i. show** spectacle *m* sur glace; **i. water** eau *f* avec glaçons
(**b**) *Br Culin* (*ice-cream*) glace *f*; **strawberry i.** glace à la fraise
(**c**) *Sl* (*diamonds*) cailloux *m*
ice² *vt* (**a**) *Culin* (*cake*) glacer (**b**) *Sl* (*kill*) refroidir
▶ **ice over** *vi* (*of pond*) geler; (*of road*) se couvrir de verglas
▶ **ice up** *vi* (*of windscreen, propeller*) se givrer
ice age *n Geol* période *f* glaciaire
iceberg ['aɪsbɜːg] *n* (**a**) iceberg *m*; *Fig* **this is just the tip of the i.** ce n'est que la partie visible de l'iceberg; **i. lettuce** = laitue *f* croquante (**b**) *Fig* (*unemotional person*) glaçon *m*
icebound ['aɪsbaʊnd] *adj* (*ship, port*) bloqué par les glaces
icebox ['aɪsbɒks] *n* (**a**) (*for storing food*) glacière *f*; (*in fridge*) compartiment *m* à glace, freezer *m* (**b**) *Am Old-fashioned* (*fridge*) réfrigérateur *m*
icebreaker ['aɪs'breɪkər] *n Naut* brise-glace *m*; *Fig* **if you're looking for an i.** si tu veux briser la glace
ice bucket *n* seau *m* à glace
icecap ['aɪskæp] *n* calotte *f* glaciaire
ice-cold *adj* (*water, house*) glacé; (*wind*) glacial
ice-cream *n* glace *f*; **strawberry/chocolate i.** glace à la fraise/ au chocolat; **i. cone** *or* **cornet** cornet *m*; **i. man** marchand *m* de glaces; *esp Am* **i. parlor** salon *m* de dégustation de glaces
ice cube *n* glaçon *m*
iced [aɪst] *adj* (**a**) (*very cold*) (*coffee, tea*) glacé; **i. water** eau *f* avec glaçons (**b**) (*decorated*) (*cake*) glacé
ice dancer *n Sp* danseur, -euse sur glace
ice dancing *n* danse *f* sur glace
ice floe *n Geog* banquise *f*
ice hockey *n Sp* hockey *m* sur glace, *Can* hockey
Iceland ['aɪslənd] *n* Islande *f*
Icelander ['aɪsləndər] *n* Islandais, -aise
Icelandic [aɪs'lændɪk] **1** *adj* islandais **2** *n Ling* islandais *m*
ice lolly *n Br* sucette *f* glacée; (*ice-cream*) esquimau® *m*
ice pack *n* (*for headache, ankle*) sachet *m* de glace
ice pick *n* (*in mountaineering*) piolet *m*; *Culin* pic *m* à glace
ice rink *n* patinoire *f*
ice scraper *n* (*for car window*) raclette *f* (antigivre)
ice skate *n* patin *m* (à glace)
ice-skate *vi* faire du patin à glace
ice skater *n* patineur, -euse
ice skating *n* patinage *m* (sur glace)
ichthyology [ɪkθɪ'ɒlədʒɪ] *n* ichtyologie *f*
ichthyosaurus [ɪkθɪə'sɔːrəs] *n* ichtyosaure *m*
icicle ['aɪsɪk(ə)l] *n* stalactite *f*, glaçon *m*
icily ['aɪsɪlɪ] *adv* (**a**) (*to say, reply etc*) d'un ton glacial; (*to look at*) d'un air glacial; **we were greeted i.** nous avons eu un accueil glacial (**b**) (*bitterly*) **it's i. cold** il fait un froid glacial
iciness ['aɪsɪnɪs] *n* (*of wind, water*) température *f* glaciale; **because of the i. of the steps** parce que les marches étaient verglacées; *Fig* **the i. of her voice** son ton glacial
icing ['aɪsɪŋ] *n* (**a**) *esp Br Culin* (*action, decoration*) glaçage *m*; *Fig* **the i. on the cake** (*final touch*) la cerise sur le gâteau; *Br* **i. sugar** sucre *m* glace (**b**) *Av* (*formation of ice*) givrage *m*
ICJ [aɪsiː'dʒeɪ] *n* (*abbr* **International Court of Justice**) CIJ *f*
icky ['ɪkɪ] *adj US F* (*repulsive*) dégoûtant; (*sticky*) collant
icon ['aɪkɒn] *n Rel, Comptr* icône *f*; *Fig* **a 60's i.** le symbole des années soixante; **i. bar** barre *f* d'icônes; **i. drag** glisser *m* d'icônes; **i. drag and drop** glisser-lâcher *m* d'icônes; **i. drop** lâcher *m* d'icônes; **i. editor** éditeur *m* d'icônes
iconize ['aɪkɒnaɪz] *vt Comptr* représenter en icône
iconoclast [aɪ'kɒnəklæst] *n* iconoclaste *mf*
iconoclastic [aɪkɒnə'klæstɪk] *adj* iconoclaste
ICU [aɪsiː'juː] *n Med abbr* **intensive care unit**
icy ['aɪsɪ] *adj* (**a**) (*covered in ice*) couvert de glace; (*road*) verglacé (**b**) (*very cold*) (*water, wind*) glacial; (*hands*) glacé (**c**) *Fig* (*welcome, stare, tone of voice*) glacial
ID¹ ['aɪ'diː] *n* (*abbr* **identification**) pièce *f* d'identité; **have you got any ID?** est-ce que vous avez une pièce d'identité?; **ID card** carte *f* d'identité
ID² *vt* (*abbr* **identify**) identifier
I'd [aɪd] (**a**) = **I had** *see* **have²** (**b**) = **I would** *see* **would**
Ida *abbr* **Idaho**
IDE [aɪdiː'iː] *n Comptr* (*abbr* **intelligent disk enhancement**) IDE
idea [aɪ'dɪə] *n* (**a**) (*individual notion*) idée *f*; **I can't bear the i. (of it)** je ne supporte pas cette idée; **a bright i.** une idée lumineuse; **whose i. was it to do that?** qui a eu l'idée de faire cela?; **what a funny i.!** quelle drôle d'idée!; **what a good i.!** quelle bonne idée!; **I've got a good i.** j'ai une idée; **to be full of ideas** être *ou* avoir plein d'idées; **I got the i. from a film** c'est en voyant un film que l'idée m'est venue; **to get ideas into one's head** se faire des idées; **what put that i. into your head?** qu'est-ce qui vous a donné cette idée?; **don't say that, you'll give her ideas!** ne dis pas ça, tu vas lui donner des idées!; **what an i.!** en voilà une idée!; **the (very) i.!** quelle idée!; **get the i.?** vous comprenez?; **what's the (big) i.?** qu'est-ce qui te prend?
(**b**) (*conception*) conception *f*; **it's not my i. of fun** je ne trouve pas ça drôle; **her i. of a joke is …** le genre de plaisanterie qu'elle aime c'est …; **if this is your i. of a joke** si tu trouves que c'est drôle; **you've got a funny i. of loyalty** tu as une conception bizarre de la loyauté
(**c**) (*understanding, impression*) **I have an i. that I've seen him before** j'ai l'impression de l'avoir déjà vu; **I had no i. that …** je ne savais pas que …; **you have no i. how anxious I was** tu ne peux pas t'imaginer à quel point j'étais inquiet; **can you give me an** *or* **some i.?** (*of how much it will be, how long it will take etc*) est-ce que vous pouvez me donner une idée?; **he has some i. of chemistry** il a des notions de chimie; **you don't have much i. about women, do you?** tu ne connais pas grand-chose aux femmes, hein?; **to get the i. that …** s'imaginer que …
(**d**) (*plan*) **I had some i. of going as far as Paris** j'avais dans l'idée de pousser jusqu'à Paris; **I thought the i. was for them to come here** il n'était pas prévu que ce serait eux qui

viendraient ici?; **i. chairman** (*at group discussion*) directeur *m* de réunion de groupe synectique; **i. committee** comité *m* synectique; **ideas person** boîte *f* à idées

(**e**) (*aim*) **the general i. is to ...** l'idée est de ...; **the i. is to get the ball into the net** le but est de mettre le ballon dans le panier

ideal [aɪ'di:əl] **1** *adj* idéal; **it's i.!** c'est l'idéal!, c'est le rêve!; **in an i. world** dans l'idéal **2** *n* (**a**) (*perfect example*) idéal *m, pl* -als, -aux; **the i. of beauty** l'idéal de la beauté (**b**) (*principle*) idéal *m, pl* -als, -aux; **a man with no ideals** un homme sans idéaux; **with such high ideals you'll never be satisfied** si tu es aussi idéaliste, tu ne seras jamais satisfait

idealism [aɪ'dɪəlɪz(ə)m] *n* idéalisme *m*

idealist [aɪ'dɪəlɪst] *n* idéaliste *mf*

idealistic [aɪdɪə'lɪstɪk] *adj* idéaliste

idealize [aɪ'dɪəlaɪz] *vt* idéaliser

ideally [aɪ'di:əlɪ] *adv* (**a**) (*in ideal case*) dans l'idéal (**b**) (*extremely well*) (*qualified, suited*) parfaitement; **the flat is i. situated** l'appartement est extrêmement bien situé; **they're i. matched** ils vont parfaitement bien ensemble; **she's i. positioned to benefit from the situation** elle est dans une position idéale pour tirer parti de la situation

ident ['aɪdent] *n TV, Rad* indicatif *m*, identification *f*

identical [aɪ'dentɪk(ə)l] *adj* identique (**to** à); **i. twins** vrais jumeaux, *f* vraies jumelles

identically [aɪ'dentɪk(ə)lɪ] *adv* identiquement

identifiable [aɪdentɪ'faɪəb(ə)l] *adj* identifiable; **he is i. by ...** on peut l'identifier grâce à ...

identification [aɪdentɪfɪ'keɪʃən] *n* (**a**) (*of body, criminal*) identification *f*; *Av, Naut* **i. marks** (lettres *fpl* et numéros *mpl* d')immatriculation *f*; **i. papers** pièces *fpl* ou papiers *mpl* d'identité; **i. parade** séance *f* d'identification (*où l'on demande à un témoin de reconnaître le suspect dans un groupe*) (**b**) (*documents*) papiers *mpl* d'identité; **have you got any i.?** avez-vous une pièce d'identité?; (*to person claiming to be police officer, gas man etc*) est-ce que vous avez de quoi prouver votre identité? (**c**) (*association*) **i. of sth with sth** identification *f* de qch avec qch

identifier [aɪ'dentɪfaɪər] *n Comptr* identificateur *m*

identify [aɪ'dentɪfaɪ] **1** *vt* (**a**) (*recognize, put a name to*) (*body, person, bird, plant etc*) identifier; (*car, wallet etc*) reconnaître (**b**) (*associate*) **to i. sth with sth** identifier qch à qch; **to be identified with sth** être associé à qch; **to i. oneself with a cause** s'identifier à *ou* avec une cause, s'assimiler à une cause **2** *vi* s'identifier (**with sb** à qn); **I can't i. with the way she feels** je ne peux pas me mettre à sa place; **I can't i. with his problems** j'ai du mal à comprendre ses problèmes de l'intérieur

identifying [aɪ'dentɪfaɪɪŋ] *adj* **i. marks** signes *mpl* particuliers

Identikit® [aɪ'dentɪkɪt] *n* **I. (picture)** portrait-robot *m, pl* portraits-robots

identity [aɪ'dentɪtɪ] *n* (**a**) identité *f*; **to prove one's i.** établir son identité; **mistaken i.** erreur *f* sur la personne, quiproquo *m* (**b**) (*quality of being identical*) identité *f*

identity bracelet *n esp Mil* bracelet *m* d'identité

identity card *n Admin* carte *f* d'identité

identity crisis *n Psy* crise *f* d'identité

identity disc *n Mil* plaque *f* d'identité

identity papers *npl* papiers *mpl* d'identité

identity parade *n* séance *f* d'identification (*où l'on demande à un témoin de reconnaître le suspect dans un groupe*)

ideogram ['ɪdɪəgræm], **ideograph** ['ɪdɪəgræf] *n* idéogramme *m*

ideological [aɪdɪə'lɒdʒɪk(ə)l] *adj* idéologique

ideologically [aɪdɪə'lɒdʒɪk(ə)lɪ] *adv* **i., they are poles apart** en termes d'idéologie, ils sont aux antipodes; **an i. motivated attack** une attaque qui a des motifs idéologiques

ideologist [aɪdɪ'ɒlədʒɪst] *n* idéologue *mf*

ideologue ['aɪdɪəlɒg] *n* idéologue *mf*

ideology [aɪdɪ'ɒlədʒɪ] *n* idéologie *f*

ides [aɪdz] *npl Hist* ides *fpl*

idiocy ['ɪdɪəsɪ] *n* (**a**) (*stupidity*) idiotie *f*, stupidité *f* (**b**) *Old-fashioned* (*mental backwardness*) (**congenital**) **i.** idiotie *f* (congénitale)

idiolect ['ɪdɪəʊlekt] *n Ling* idiolecte *m*

idiom ['ɪdɪəm] *n* (**a**) (*expression*) locution *f*, expression *f* idiomatique (**b**) (*dialect*) dialecte *m*, idiome *m* (**c**) *Art, Mus* style *m*

idiomatic [ɪdɪə'mætɪk] *adj* [①**A3**; **B2**] idiomatique; **i. phrase** expression *f* idiomatique

idiomatically [ɪdɪə'mætɪklɪ] *adv* (*to express oneself*) de façon idiomatique

idiosyncrasy [ɪdɪəʊ'sɪŋkrəsɪ] *n* particularité *f*, petite manie *f*

idiosyncratic [ɪdɪəʊsɪŋ'krætɪk] *adj* particulier

idiot ['ɪdɪət] *n* (**a**) imbécile *mf*, idiot, -ote; **what an i. I've been!** comme j'ai été bête!; **you i.!** espèce d'imbécile *ou* d'idiot!; **some i. has ...!** il y a un imbécile qui a ...!; **to make sb look like an i.** faire passer qn pour un imbécile (**b**) *Old-fashioned* (*mentally retarded person*) idiot, -ote, imbécile *mf*

idiot board *n TV* pense-bête *m, pl* pense-bêtes

idiot box *n F* (*television*) télé *f*

idiotic [ɪdɪ'ɒtɪk] *adj* bête, idiot; **that's i.** c'est stupide, c'est idiot; **don't be i.!** ne sois pas bête!

idiotically [ɪdɪ'ɒtɪklɪ] *adv* bêtement, idiotement

idiotism ['ɪdɪətɪz(ə)m] *n Am* (*of language*) idiotisme *m*

idle[1] ['aɪd(ə)l] *adj* (**a**) (*unoccupied*) (*person*) inoccupé, oisif, désœuvré; (*machinery*) à l'arrêt; **to be** *or* **stand i.** (*of person*) rester à ne rien faire; (*of machine*) ne pas servir; **to lie i.** (*of money*) dormir; **in my i. moments** à mes heures perdues; **when you've got an i. moment, could you ...** quand tu auras un moment, pourrais-tu ...; **i. capital** capital *m* improductif; **i. period** période *f* d'inactivité; *Aut* **i. screw** vis *f* de ralenti; *Aut* **i. speed** vitesse *f ou* régime *m* de ralenti; **the i. rich** les riches désœuvrés

(**b**) (*lazy*) paresseux, fainéant, indolent

(**c**) (*futile*) (*threat, suggestion*) en l'air; (*gossip, rumour*) sans fondement; (*boast*) mal placé; **it is i. to speculate** il est vain de spéculer; **i. talk** paroles *fpl* en l'air, balivernes *fpl*

(**d**) (*casual*) (*glance*) en passant; (*remark*) fait en passant; **out of i. curiosity** par simple curiosité

idle[2] *vi* (**a**) *Aut* (*of engine*) tourner au ralenti (**b**) (*be lazy*) fainéanter, musarder

▶ **idle away** *vtsep* (*waste*) **to i. one's time away** passer son temps à ne rien faire; **we idled away the afternoon chatting** nous avons passé l'après-midi à discuter tranquillement

idleness ['aɪd(ə)lnɪs] *n* (**a**) (*of person*) (*inaction*) inaction *f*, désœuvrement *m*; (*laziness*) paresse *f*, fainéantise *f* (**b**) (*futility*) (*of threat, boast*) futilité *f*

idler ['aɪdlər] *n* (**a**) (*lazy person*) paresseux, -euse (**b**) *MecE* (*wheel*) roue *f* folle; (*pulley*) poulie *f* folle

idling ['aɪdlɪŋ] **1** *adj* **i. speed** ralenti *m* **2** *n* (**a**) (*time-wasting*) fainéantise *f*; **that's more than enough i. for one day** assez fainéanté pour aujourd'hui (**b**) (*of engine*) (marche *f* au) ralenti *m*

idly ['aɪd(ə)lɪ] *adv* (**a**) (*not working*) sans rien faire, sans travailler; **to stand i. by** rester là à ne rien faire (**b**) (*lazily*) paresseusement; (*casually*) nonchalamment; **to do sth i.** faire qch pour passer le temps (**c**) (*futilely*) inutilement; (*to speculate etc*) vainement

idol ['aɪd(ə)l] *n* idole *f*; **to make an i. of wealth** idolâtrer l'argent

idolater, idolatress [aɪ'dɒlətər, -trɪs] (**a**) *Rel* idolâtre *mf* (**b**) *Fig* adorateur, -trice (**of** de)

idolatrous [aɪ'dɒlətrəs] *adj* (*worship, beliefs etc*) idolâtre

idolatry [aɪ'dɒlətrɪ] *n Rel, Fig* idolâtrie *f*

idolize ['aɪdəlaɪz] *vt* idolâtrer

idolizing ['aɪdəlaɪzɪŋ] **1** *adj* plein d'adoration **2** *n* idolâtrie *f*

idyll ['ɪdɪl] *n* idylle *f*

idyllic [ɪ'dɪlɪk, aɪ-] *adj* idyllique

ie ['aɪ'i:] (*abbr* **id est**) c.-à.-d.

IEEE [aɪi:i:'i:] *Comptr* (*abbr* **Institute of Electronic and Electrical Engineers**) IEEE

if [ɪf] **1** *conj* (**a**) [①**A50-1,13**; **B31-32,3**] si; **if not** sinon; **if he does it, he will be punished** s'il le fait, il sera puni; **let him do it if he dare(s)!** qu'il ose seulement!; **if a child can do it so can I** si un enfant peut le faire, je peux le faire aussi; **if I know Sophie, she won't have done it!** comme *ou* telle que je connais Sophie, elle ne l'aura pas fait!; **if (it is) necessary** s'il le faut, si c'est nécessaire, au besoin; **if (it is) possible** si (c'est) possible; **if (it be) so** s'il en est ainsi; **if so, when?** si oui, quand?; **modifications, if any, will have to be made later** les modifications éventuelles devront être apportées plus tard; **go and see her, if only to please me** allez la voir, ne serait-ce que pour me faire plaisir; **if and when they arrive we will decide what to do** s'ils arrivent et seulement à ce moment-là, nous déciderons ce que nous ferons; **if I were** *or* **was you** si j'étais toi, à ta place; **if it were so** même s'il en était ainsi; **even if he did say so** même s'il a dit cela; **what if I did/she has?** et alors?; **if I had only known!** (*exclamatory*) si seulement j'avais su!; **if only he comes in time!** pourvu qu'il vienne à temps!; **if only!** si seulement!; **as if by chance** comme par hasard; **he looks as if he is drunk** on dirait qu'il est soûl; **he said he would do it – as if!** il a dit qu'il le ferait – mon œil!; **as if I would allow it!** comme si j'allais le permettre!

(**b**) (*concessive*) **pleasant weather, if rather cold** temps agréable, bien qu'un peu froid; **it is well-paid, if uninteresting work** c'est un travail bien payé à défaut d'être intéressant; **if anything it's better/worse** en fait c'est mieux/pire

(c) (*introducing a noun clause*, = **whether**) si; **I asked if it was true** j'ai demandé si c'était vrai

(d) (*for second occurrence in a clause*) que; **if he agrees and (if) we have time** s'il est d'accord et que nous avons le temps

2 *n* si *m inv*; **the agreement is full of ifs and buts** l'accord n'est qu'une suite de conditions; **if ... and it's a very big if, ...** si ... et il n'y a rien de moins sûr, ...

IFA [aɪef'eɪ] *npl Mil* (*abbr* **intermediate-range nuclear forces**) FNI *fpl*

IFC [aɪef'siː] *n* (*abbr* **Inside Front Cover**) deuxième *f* de couverture

iffy ['ɪfɪ] *adj F* (a) (*uncertain*) (*situation*) aléatoire; **the picnic/project is looking very i.** le pique-nique/projet semble très compromis; **the car's a bit i. these days** la voiture n'est pas très fiable ces jours-ci; **I'm still a bit i. about the whole thing** (*haven't made my mind up*) j'hésite encore; **that sky looks a bit i.** le ciel est un peu menaçant; **the ice is a bit i.** (*on pond*) la glace n'a pas l'air très sûre; **it's still a bit i. but I think I will be going to the conference** je ne suis pas complètement sûr mais je pense que j'irai à la conférence (b) (*suspect*) (*person, appearance*) louche

if-then operation *n Comptr* opération *f* 'si-alors'

igloo ['ɪgluː] *n* igloo *m*

igneous ['ɪgnɪəs] *adj* éruptif, igné

ignite [ɪg'naɪt] **1** *vt* (*fuel etc*) enflammer, mettre feu à; (*explosive charge*) allumer; *Fig* (*situation, conflict*) enflammer **2** *vi* prendre feu, s'enflammer; *Fig* (*of situation, conflict*) s'enflammer

ignition [ɪg'nɪʃən] *n* (a) *Aut* allumage *m*; **to switch off the i.** couper l'allumage; **the key was still in the i.** la clé était encore sur le contact; **i. cable** *or* **lead** fil *m* d'allumage *ou* de bougie; **i. coil** bobine *f* d'allumage; **i. cycle** cycle *m* d'allumage; **i. key** clé *f* de contact; **i. lock** antivol-contact *m*; **i. spark** étincelle *f* d'allumage; **i. switch** contact *m*; **i. system** circuit *m* d'allumage (b) (*of explosive charge etc*) ignition *f*

ignoble [ɪg'nəʊb(ə)l] *adj* ignoble, vil

ignominious [ɪgnə'mɪnɪəs] *adj* ignominieux, honteux

ignominiously [ɪgnə'mɪnɪəslɪ] *adv* ignominieusement, honteusement

ignominy ['ɪgnəmɪnɪ] *n* ignominie *f*, honte *f*

ignoramus [ɪgnə'reɪməs] *n* ignorant, -ante, ignare *mf*

ignorance ['ɪgnərəns] *n* (a) ignorance *f*; **out of** *or* **through i.** par ignorance; **to keep sb in i. of sth** laisser qn dans l'ignorance de qch; **I am in complete i. of his intentions** j'ignore tout de ses intentions; **in a situation like this, i. is bliss** dans ce genre de situation, il vaut mieux ne pas savoir; *Jur* **i. of the law is no excuse** nul n'est censé ignorer la loi (b) (*ill manners*) manque *m* d'éducation

ignorant ['ɪgnərənt] *adj* (a) (*lacking knowledge*) (*person*) ignorant; (*question, remark*) qui trahit l'ignorance; **to be i. of sth** ignorer qch; *Fml* **he is i. of the world** (*unworldly, naïve*) il ne connaît pas les choses du monde; **i. people like him** des ignorants de son espèce (b) (*ill-mannered*) (*person, remark*) grossier

ignorantly ['ɪgnərəntlɪ] *adv* (*to believe*) par ignorance; (*to talk*) avec ignorance

ignore [ɪg'nɔːr] *vt* (*take no notice of*) (*person, instructions*) ignorer; (*facts*) méconnaître; (*letter, invitation*) ne pas répondre à; (*insult*) ne pas relever; (*order, advice*) ne tenir aucun compte de; (*signal, red light*) ne pas respecter; **just i. him!** ne fais pas attention à lui!; **I'll i. that!** (*what you said*) je ferai comme si je n'avais rien entendu!

iguana [ɪ'gwɑːnə] *n* iguane *m*

ikon ['aɪkɒn] *n Rel, Comptr* icône *f*

ilex, *pl* **ilexes** ['aɪleks, 'aɪleksɪz] *n* ilex *m*

ilium ['ɪlɪəm] *n Anat* os *m* iliaque

ilk [ɪlk] *n* (a) *Scot* **Moray of that i.** Moray du domaine de Moray (b) **of that i.** de ce genre, *Pej* de cette espèce

Ill *abbr* **Illinois**

ill[1] [ɪl] **1** *adj* (a) (*unwell*) malade; **to be i.** être malade; **to look i.** avoir mauvaise mine; **to feel i.** ne pas se sentir bien; **it makes me feel i.** ça me rend malade; **to fall** *or* **be taken i.** tomber malade; **he was seriously i. last year** il a été gravement malade l'année dernière; **a very i. woman** une femme très malade

(b) (*bad*) (*repute*) mauvais; (*deed, nature etc*) méchant, mauvais; *Prov* **it is an i. wind that blows nobody any good** à quelque chose malheur est bon; **i. breeding** manque *m* de savoir-vivre; **to be in i. health** ne pas être en bonne santé; **he retired due to i. health** il a pris sa retraite pour raisons de santé; **i. luck** *or* **fortune** malchance *f*; **house of i. repute** maison *f* close; **woman of i. repute** femme *f* de mauvaise vie; **he hasn't suffered any i. effects** (*after eating, drinking sth*) il n'a pas été malade; (*from being imprisoned etc*) il n'a pas eu de séquelles; **i. feeling** rancune *f*; **i. will** malveillance *f*

2 *adv* mal; *Lit* **to take sth i.** prendre qch en mauvaise part; **to be i. provided with sth** être mal pourvu de qch; **I can i. afford the expense** je peux difficilement me permettre cette dépense; **it i. becomes you to ...** il vous sied mal de ..., vous êtes mal venu de ...; **to be** *or* **feel i. at ease** (*uncomfortable*) être mal à l'aise; (*anxious*) être *ou* se sentir inquiet (**about** au sujet de)

3 *n* (a) (*evil*) mal *m*; **to speak/think i. of sb** dire/penser du mal de qn

(b) (*wrong*) dommage *m*, tort *m*; **I have suffered no i. at his hands** il ne m'a fait aucun tort

(c) (*misfortune*) **ills** maux *mpl*, malheurs *mpl*

ill[2] *abbr* **illustration**

I'll [aɪl] (a) = **I will** *see* **will**[2] (b) = **I shall** *see* **shall**

ill-advised ['ɪləd'vaɪzd] *adj* (*person*) malavisé (**to do** de faire); (*action*) peu judicieux

ill-assorted *adj* disparate

ill-behaved *adj* qui se conduit *ou* se tient mal

ill-bred ['ɪl'bred] *adj* mal élevé; **an i. young man** un malappris

ill-concealed *adj* mal dissimulé

ill-considered *adj* (*action, view etc*) peu réfléchi; (*measure etc*) hâtif

ill-defined ['ɪldɪ'faɪnd] *adj* mal défini

ill-disposed *adj* (a) (*unfriendly, unhelpful*) **to be i. towards sb** être mal disposé envers qn; **to be i. towards an idea/a proposal** ne pas être favorable à une idée/une proposition (b) (*disinclined*) **to be i. to do sth** être peu disposé à faire qch

illegal [ɪ'liːg(ə)l] *adj* illégal; (*immigrant*) clandestin; (*parking*) interdit; *Comptr* (*file name, character*) non autorisé; **it is i. to ...** il est illégal de ...

illegality [ɪlɪ'gælɪtɪ] *n* illégalité *f*

illegally [ɪ'liːg(ə)lɪ] *adv* illégalement

illegible [ɪ'ledʒɪb(ə)l] *adj* illisible

illegibly [ɪ'ledʒɪblɪ] *adv* illisiblement

illegitimacy [ɪlɪ'dʒɪtɪməsɪ] *n* illégitimité *f*

illegitimate [ɪlɪ'dʒɪtɪmət] *adj* (*child, conclusion, act*) illégitime

illegitimately [ɪlɪ'dʒɪtɪmətlɪ] *adv* illégitimement

ill-equipped *adj* mal équipé; *Fig* **to be i. to do sth** ne pas être apte à faire qch

ill-fated *adj* (*person*) infortuné; (*day, mission*) fatal, fatidique; **the i. expedition** l'expédition frappée par le destin

ill-fitting *adj* (*garment, lid, window*) mal ajusté

ill-founded ['ɪl'faʊndɪd] *adj* (*rumour*) mal fondé, sans fondement

ill-gotten ['ɪl'gɒtn] *adj* **i. gains** biens *mpl* mal acquis *ou* acquis malhonnêtement

ill-humoured, *US* **-humored** ['ɪl'hjuːməd] *adj* de mauvaise humeur

illiberal [ɪ'lɪbər(ə)l] *adj* peu libéral; (*narrow-minded*) borné; (*ungenerous*) peu généreux, mesquin

illiberality [ɪlɪbə'rælɪtɪ] *n* (*in opinions*) étroitesse *f* d'esprit; (*lack of generosity*) manque *m* de libéralité

illicit [ɪ'lɪsɪt] *adj* illicite; **i. still** alambic *m* clandestin

illicitly [ɪ'lɪsɪtlɪ] *adv* illicitement

illimitable [ɪ'lɪmɪtəb(ə)l] *adj* illimité

ill-informed *adj* (a) (*having the wrong information*) (*person*) mal renseigné (b) (*having insufficient information*) peu informé; **we continue to be i. about their intentions** nous ne sommes toujours pas sûrs de savoir quelles sont leurs intentions; **he made an i. attack on the government** il a attaqué le gouvernement en utilisant des arguments sans fondement

ill-intentioned ['ɪlɪn'tenʃənd] *adj* malintentionné (**towards** envers)

illiquid [ɪ'lɪkwɪd] *adj* peu liquide

illiteracy [ɪ'lɪt(ə)rəsɪ] *n* analphabétisme *m*

illiterate [ɪ'lɪt(ə)rət] **1** *adj* (a) (*unable to read or write*) illettré, analphabète (b) (*lacking culture*) (*person*) qui n'a aucune culture; (*usage, style*) incorrect; **you should ignore the i. ravings of such people** vous ne devriez pas faire attention aux inepties mal écrites de ces gens-là **2** *n* illettré, -ée, analphabète *mf*

ill-judged ['ɪl'dʒʌdʒd] *adj* (*action*) malavisé, peu sage

ill-mannered *adj* grossier, malappris; **to be i.** être mal élevé

ill-natured ['ɪl'neɪtʃəd] *adj* (*person*) d'un mauvais caractère, désagréable; (*remark, criticism etc*) désagréable; **to be i.** avoir mauvais caractère

illness ['ɪlnɪs] *n* (ⓘ**A10**,d) maladie *f*

illogical [ɪ'lɒdʒɪk(ə)l] *adj* illogique

illogicality [ɪlɒdʒɪ'kælɪtɪ] *n* manque *m* de logique, illogisme *m*

illogically [ɪ'lɒdʒɪk(ə)lɪ] *adv* sans logique; **the i. ordered universe** l'univers désordonné

ill-prepared *adj* mal préparé
ill-starred *adj Lit* (*person*) infortuné; (*day*) malheureux, néfaste
ill-suited ['ɪl'su:tɪd] *adj* (*couple*) mal assorti; **such clothes were i. to a hot climate** ces vêtements n'étaient pas adaptés à un climat chaud; **arts graduates are i. to this job** les diplômés en lettres ne sont pas aptes à ce travail
ill-tempered *adj* (*person*) (*in general*) grincheux; (*on specific occasion*) de mauvaise humeur, grincheux; **to be i.** (*in general*) avoir mauvais caractère; **why must he always be so i.?** pourquoi faut-il qu'il soit toujours d'aussi mauvaise humeur?
ill-timed ['ɪl'taɪmd] *adj* (*remark*) mal à propos, hors de propos, inopportun; (*arrival*) inopportun
ill-treat *vt* (*person, dog*) maltraiter
ill-treatment *n* mauvais traitement *m*
illuminate [ɪ'lu:mɪneɪt] *vt* **(a)** (*room etc*) éclairer; (*building*) illuminer **(b)** *Fig* (*subject, question*) éclairer, élucider **(c)** *Art* (*manuscript*) enluminer
illuminated [ɪ'lu:mɪneɪtɪd] *adj* **(a)** (*sign*) lumineux **(b)** *Art* (*manuscript*) enluminé
illuminating [ɪ'lu:mɪneɪtɪŋ] **1** *adj* (*speech, interview*) qui éclaire la situation; (*comparison, remark, example*) éclairant; **the programme was very i.** l'émission m'a appris beaucoup de choses **2** *n* **(a)** (*of building*) illumination *f* **(b)** *Art* (*of manuscript*) enluminure *f*
illumination [ɪlu:mɪ'neɪʃən] *n* **(a)** (*of room etc*) éclairage *m*; (*of building*) illumination *f*; *esp Br* **the illuminations** (*decorative outdoor lights*) les illuminations **(b)** *Art* (*of manuscript*) enluminure *f* **(c)** *Opt* (*of lens etc*) éclat *m*; *Phys* **(degree of) i.** éclairement *m* **(d)** *Rel etc* (*enlightenment*) illumination *f*
illuminator [ɪ'lu:mɪneɪtər] *n Art* enlumineur, -euse
illumine [ɪ'lu:mɪn] *vt Lit* illuminer
ill-use[1] ['ɪl'ju:s] *n* mauvais traitement *m*
ill-use[2] ['ɪl'ju:z] *vt* **(a)** (*physically*) maltraiter **(b)** (*behave badly towards*) ne pas bien traiter; **he feels he's been ill-used** il a le sentiment qu'il n'a pas été bien traité
illusion [ɪ'lu:ʒən] *n* illusion *f*; **to be under the i. that ...** s'imaginer que ...; **I have no illusions** *or* **am under no i. on that score** je ne me fais aucune illusion à ce sujet
illusionist [ɪ'lu:ʒənɪst] *n* illusionniste *mf*
illusory [ɪ'lu:s(ə)rɪ] *adj* illusoire, trompeur
illustrate ['ɪləstreɪt] *vt* **(a)** (*book, newspaper*) illustrer; **illustrated by Cruikshank** (*on title page etc*) illustré par *ou* illustrations de Cruikshank; **illustrated magazine** (journal *m ou* magazine *m*) illustré *m* **(b)** (*explain, give example of*) illustrer; **to i. my point** pour illustrer ce que je veux dire; **the lecture will be illustrated by slides** la conférence sera accompagnée de diapositives
illustration [ɪlə'streɪʃən] *n* **(a)** (*picture*) (*in book etc*) illustration *f*, gravure *f* **illustrations** (*in book*) iconographie *f* **(b)** (*publishing process*) illustration *f*; **he/she works in i.** il est illustrateur/elle est illustratrice **(c)** *Fig* (*of principle etc*) illustration *f*, exemple *m*; **to be an i. of sth** illustrer qch; **by way of i.** à titre d'exemple
illustrative ['ɪləstr(ə)tɪv] *adj* illustratif; **this incident is i. of his state of mind** cet incident reflète bien son état d'esprit
illustrator ['ɪləstreɪtər] *n* illustrateur, -trice
illustrious [ɪ'lʌstrɪəs] *adj* illustre, célèbre
illustriously [ɪ'lʌstrɪəslɪ] *adv* de façon illustre
ILO [aɪe'ləʊ] *n Ind* (*abbr* **International Labour Organization**) O. I. T. *f*
I'm [aɪm] = **I am** *see* **be**
image ['ɪmɪdʒ] *n* **(a)** (*copy*) image *f*; **God created man in his own i.** Dieu créa l'homme à son image; **he's the (very** *or* **living** *or F* **spitting) i. of his father** c'est le portrait de son père, *F* c'est son père tout craché
(b) (*representation*) portrait *m*; (*sculpture*) image *f* (sculptée); (*of god etc*) représentation *f*, statue *f*; (*for worship*) idole *f*
(c) (*mental picture*) image *f*
(d) (*of politician, party etc*) image *f*; **its i. is that of a dirty industrial city** cette ville a la réputation d'être une ville industrielle sale; **he/it needs a bit of i. building** il a besoin de rehausser un peu son image de marque; *Mktg* **i. pricing** fixation *f* de prix en fonction de l'image
(e) *Liter* image *f*, métaphore *f*
(f) *Opt* image *f*; **i. enhancement** correction *f* de l'image, retouche *f* d'images; **i. enhancer** correcteur *m* d'images; **i. bank** banque *f* d'images **i. refresh rate** taux *m* de rafraîchissement d'images
image distortion *n Electron, TV* distorsion *f* d'image
image file *n* fichier *m* d'images
image-maker *n Mktg* responsable *mf* des relations publiques
image processing *n* traitement *m* de l'image
imager ['ɪmɪdʒər] *n Comptr* imageur *m*
imagery ['ɪmɪdʒ(ə)rɪ] *n Liter, Cin etc* images *fpl*
imaginable [ɪ'mædʒɪnəb(ə)l] *adj* imaginable; **the finest thing i.** la plus belle chose qu'on puisse imaginer
imaginary [ɪ'mædʒɪn(ə)rɪ] *adj* imaginaire
imagination [ɪmædʒɪ'neɪʃən] *n* imagination *f*; **to have no i.** n'avoir aucune imagination; **it's your i.!** tu te fais des idées!; **use your i.!** fais preuve d'un peu d'imagination!; **it's all in your i.** tout ça c'est dans ta tête
imaginative [ɪ'mædʒɪnətɪv] *adj* (*person, story etc*) imaginatif; (*solution, excuse, reason*) plein d'imagination
imaginativeness [ɪ'mædʒɪnətɪvnɪs] *n* (*of person*) imagination *f*, esprit *m* inventif; (*of story, solution, reason, excuse etc*) caractère *m* imaginatif
imagine [ɪ'mædʒɪn] **1** *vt* **(a)** (*picture in one's mind*) imaginer; **I can just i. her saying/doing that** je la vois très bien dire/faire ça; **I just can't i. you in that hat** je ne t'imagine *ou* te vois pas du tout avec ce chapeau; **I can't i. living anywhere else** je n'imagine pas vivre ailleurs; **to be always imagining things** se faire des idées; **I was beginning to i. all sorts of things!** je commençais à m'imaginer des tas de choses; **you're imagining things** tu rêves; **that child is always imagining things** c'est un enfant très imaginatif; **you must have imagined it** tu as dû rêver; **as may (well) be imagined** comme on peut (se) l'imaginer; *F* **i. meeting you here!** ça alors, toi ici!; **just i. my despair** tu imagines à quel point j'étais désespéré; **you can't i. it!** vous n'avez pas idée!; **well, what did you i.?** qu'est-ce que tu croyais?, qu'est-ce que tu t'imaginais?
(b) (*suppose*) imaginer; **I i. them to be fairly rich** j'imagine qu'ils sont assez riches; **don't i. that I'm satisfied** n'allez pas croire que je sois satisfait; **I i. that you must be very tired** j'imagine *ou* je suppose que vous devez être fatigué
2 *vi* **he ate all of it, can you i.?** il a tout mangé, tu t'imagines?; **I can i.** je veux bien le croire!, j'imagine!
imagined [ɪ'mædʒɪnd] *adj* imaginé, imaginaire
imaging device ['ɪmɪdʒɪŋ] *n Comptr* imageur *m*
imaginings [ɪ'mædʒɪnɪŋz] *npl* **the i. of a fevered mind** les élucubrations d'un esprit enfiévré
imam [ɪ'mɑ:m] *n* imam *m*
imbalance [ɪm'bæləns] *n* déséquilibre *m*
imbecile ['ɪmbɪsi:l] **1** *n F, Med* imbécile *mf* **2** *adj attrib* imbécile
imbecilic [ɪmbɪ'sɪlɪk] *adj* = **imbecile 2**
imbecility [ɪmbɪ'sɪlɪtɪ] *n* **(a)** *F* (*stupidity*) stupidité *f*, imbécillité *f* **(b)** *Med* imbécillité *f*
imbibe [ɪm'baɪb] **1** *vt Fml* (*of person*) (*knowledge, ideas*) absorber, assimiler; (*drink*) boire, avaler; **to i. the atmosphere** s'imprégner de l'atmosphère **2** *vi F Hum* boire trop, *F* picoler
imbroglio [ɪm'brəʊlɪəʊ] *n Lit* imbroglio *m*
imbue [ɪm'bju:] *vt Lit* (*sb*) imprégner (**with an idea** d'une idée); **to be imbued with melancholy/hope** (*of novel etc*) être empreint de mélancolie/d'espoir
IMF [aɪe'mef] *n Econ* (*abbr* **International Monetary Fund**) F. M. I. *m*
imitable ['ɪmɪtəb(ə)l] *adj* imitable
imitate ['ɪmɪteɪt] *vt* **(a)** (*copy*) (*sb*) imiter, copier; **to i. sb's style** imiter le style de qn **(b)** (*mimic*) (*sb*) singer, mimer; (*call of bird etc*) imiter; **to i. its surroundings** (*of insect etc*) prendre l'aspect de son milieu
imitation [ɪmɪ'teɪʃən] *n* **(a)** (*action*) imitation *f*; **in i. of sb/sth** à l'imitation de *ou* imitant qn/qch; *Prov* **i. is the sincerest form of flattery** l'imitation est la flatterie la plus sincère qui soit **(b)** (*copy*) copie *f*, imitation *f*; *Com* imitation; **beware of imitations** méfiez-vous des contrefaçons; **in i. marble/crocodile skin** en imitation marbre/crocodile; **i. jewellery** bijoux *mpl* en faux *ou* en toc; **i. leather** imitation *f* cuir; **i. pearls** fausses perles *fpl*
imitative ['ɪmɪtətɪv] *adj* (*sound etc*) imitatif; **manner/style i. of sb** manière *f*/style *m* qui imite qn; *Mktg* **i. product** produit *m* d'imitation
imitator ['ɪmɪteɪtər] *n* (*copier*) imitateur, -trice; **the Beatles had their imitators** les Beatles ont eu des imitateurs
immaculate [ɪ'mækjʊlət] *adj* **(a)** (*dress, desk, room*) impeccable; *Lit* (*snow, white*) immaculé; *Fig* **her attendance record is i.** elle n'a pas été absente une seule fois **(b)** (*morally pure*) (*reputation*) sans tache; *Rel* **the I. Conception** l'Immaculée Conception *f*
immaculately [ɪ'mækjʊlətlɪ] *adv* (*dressed*) impeccablement; **the children behaved i.** les enfants se sont admirablement bien tenus
immanent ['ɪmənənt] *adj Phil* immanent
immaterial [ɪmə'tɪərɪəl] *adj* **(a)** (*unimportant, irrelevant*) sans importance; **that fact is (quite) i.** cela n'a aucune importance **(b)** (*ghost etc*) immatériel, incorporel
immature [ɪmə'tjʊər] *adj* **(a)** (*young, undeveloped*) *Biol*

immature; (*fruit etc*) (qui n'est) pas mûr (**b**) (*childish*) immature, qui manque de maturité; **stop being so i.!** arrête de te comporter comme un gamin!; **i. work** œuvre *f* de jeunesse *ou* d'apprenti
immaturity [ɪmə'tjʊərɪtɪ] *n* (**a**) (*youth, lack of development*) (*of person*), *Biol* immaturité *f* (**b**) (*childishness*) immaturité *f*, manque *m* de maturité; (*of work of art*) manque de maturité
immeasurable [ɪ'meʒərəb(ə)l] *adj* (*space, complexity etc*) incommensurable; (*time*) infini; **to have an i. influence on sth** avoir une influence énorme sur qch
immeasurably [ɪ'meʒərəblɪ] *adv* (*difficult, painful, bad*) extrêmement, *Lit* incommensurablement; **she influenced her contemporaries i.** elle a énormément influencé ses contemporains
immediacy [ɪ'mi:dɪəsɪ] *n* caractère *m* immédiat (**of** de); (*of danger*) imminence *f*; (*of need*) urgence *f*
immediate [ɪ'mi:dɪət] *adj* (**a**) (*urgent, imminent*) (*need*) pressant, urgent; (*danger*) imminent; **my i. objective** mon objectif premier; **what are your i. plans?** que proposez-vous de faire d'abord?; **I have no i. plans to retire** je n'ai pas l'intention de prendre ma retraite dans un futur proche (**b**) (*instant*) (*answer, delivery etc*) immédiat; **house for sale with i. possession** maison à vendre avec jouissance immédiate (**c**) (*closest*) (*neighbour, surroundings*) immédiat, proche; **the i. family** les proches parents; **in the i. future** dans un avenir immediat
immediately [ɪ'mi:dɪətlɪ] **1** *adv* (**a**) (*without delay*) immédiatement, tout de suite; **he is i. recognizable** on le reconnaît immédiatement *ou* tout de suite; **the distinction isn't i. obvious** la distinction n'est pas évidente tout de suite; **please send ... i.** veuillez (bien) envoyer immédiatement *ou* d'urgence ...; **i. after** aussitôt après (**b**) (*directly*) immédiatement, directement; **it does not affect me i.** cela ne me touche pas directement (**c**) (*in space*) juste; **i. after the traffic lights** juste après le feu **2** *conj Br* dès que; **i. I saw her I knew ...** dès que je l'ai vue j'ai su que ...
immemorial [ɪmɪ'mɔ:rɪəl] *adj Lit* immémorial; **from time i.** depuis des temps immémoriaux
immense [ɪ'mens] *adj* (*expanse, success, satisfaction etc*) immense; (*quantity*) énorme; **of i. size** de taille immense
immensely [ɪ'menslɪ] *adv* (*large, rich*) immensément; (*to enjoy oneself*) énormément; **to be i. successful** avoir énormément de succès; **i. entertaining** extrêmement divertissant; **she is i. fat** elle est absolument énorme
immensity [ɪ'mensɪtɪ] *n* (**a**) (*of universe, fortune etc*) immensité *f* (**b**) (*of problem, task*) énormité *f*
immerse [ɪ'mɜ:s] *vt* (**a**) (*in liquid*) plonger; *Rel* baptiser par immersion (**b**) **to i. oneself in sth** (*become absorbed by*) se plonger dans qch; **to be immersed in one's work/thoughts** être plongé *ou* absorbé dans son travail/ses pensées
immersion [ɪ'mɜ:ʃən] *n* (**a**) (*in liquid*) immersion *f*; *Rel* baptême *m* par immersion; **i. (water) heater** chauffe-eau *m inv* à immersion (**b**) (*mental*) absorption *f* (**in** dans); **to learn a language by i.** apprendre une langue par immersion; **i. course** cours *m* en immersion
immigrant ['ɪmɪgrənt] *adj, n* (*in the process of emigrating*) immigrant, -ante; (*who has emigrated*) immigré, -ée; **i. families** familles *fpl* immigrées; **i. workers** travailleurs *mpl* immigrés
immigrate ['ɪmɪgreɪt] *vi* immigrer
immigration [ɪmɪ'greɪʃən] *n* immigration *f*; **to go through i.** (*at port, airport etc*) passer à l'immigration; **i. control** contrôle *m* de l'immigration; **i. department** service *m* de l'immigration; **i. laws** lois *fpl* sur l'immigration; **i. officer** agent *m* du service de l'immigration; **i. quotas** quotas *mpl* d'immigration
imminence ['ɪmɪnəns] *n* imminence *f* (**of** de)
imminent ['ɪmɪnənt] *adj* (*danger, disaster, arrival etc*) imminent
immobile [ɪ'məʊbaɪl] *adj* immobile
immobility [ɪmə'bɪlɪtɪ] *n* immobilité *f*
immobilize [ɪ'məʊbɪlaɪz] *vt* (*wounded limb, traffic etc*), *Fin* immobiliser
immobilizer [ɪ'məʊbɪlaɪzər] *n* (*for vehicle*) antidémarrage *m* codé
immoderate [ɪ'mɒd(ə)rət] *adj* (*drinking*) immodéré; (*feeling, attitude, display of grief*) exagéré, excessif; (*behaviour*) excessif; (*thirst*) anormal; (*gaiety*) exagéré
immoderately [ɪ'mɒd(ə)rətlɪ] *adv* immodérément
immodest [ɪ'mɒdɪst] *adj* (**a**) (*indecent*) (*person, dress, behaviour*) impudique (**b**) (*vain*) présomptueux
immodestly [ɪ'mɒdɪstlɪ] *adv* (**a**) (*indecently*) impudiquement (**b**) (*vainly*) présomptueusement
immolate ['ɪməʊleɪt] *vt Lit* immoler
immoral [ɪ'mɒrəl] *adj* immoral; (*novel etc*) contraire à la morale; *Jur* **for i. purposes** aux fins de débauche; *Jur* **living on i. earnings** (*of pimp*) proxénétisme *m*
immorality [ɪmə'rælɪtɪ] *n* immoralité *f*; (*sexual*) débauche *f*
immorally [ɪ'mɒrəlɪ] *adv* immoralement, de façon immorale
immortal [ɪ'mɔ:t(ə)l] **1** *adj* immortel; **the i. memory of ...** le souvenir impérissable de ... **2** *n* immortel, -elle
immortality [ɪmɔ:'tælɪtɪ] *n* immortalité *f*
immortalize [ɪ'mɔ:təlaɪz] *vt* (*person, author's name, sb's memory etc*) immortaliser
immovable [ɪ'mu:vəb(ə)l] **1** *adj* (*object*) (qui est) impossible à déplacer; *Fig* (*opposition*) inébranlable; (*person*) inflexible; *Rel* **i. feast** fête *f* fixe; *Fig* **they were i.** ils sont restés inflexibles; *Jur* **i. property** immeubles *mpl*, biens *mpl* immobiliers **2** *npl Jur* **immovables** immeubles *mpl*, biens *mpl* immobiliers
immune [ɪ'mju:n] *adj* (**a**) *Med* immunisé (**to** contre) (**b**) *Fig* **i. to criticism** imperméable à la critique; **no-one was i. from criticism** personne n'a échappé aux critiques; **i. from taxation** exempt d'impôts; **i. from prosecution** à l'abri de poursuites judiciaires
immune system *n* système *m* immunitaire
immunity [ɪ'mju:nɪtɪ] *n* (**a**) *Med* immunité *f* (**to** contre) (**b**) (*exemption*) exemption *f* (**from** de); **they were guaranteed i. from prosecution** on leur a assuré qu'ils seraient à l'abri de poursuites judiciaires
immunization [ɪmjʊnaɪ'zeɪʃən] *n Med* immunisation *f* (**against** contre)
immunize ['ɪmjʊnaɪz] *vt Med* immuniser (**against** contre)
immunodeficiency [ɪmjʊnəʊdɪ'fɪʃənsɪ] *n Med* immunodéficience *f*
immunoglobulin [ɪmjʊnəʊ'glɒbjʊlɪn] *n Med* immunoglobuline *f*
immunological [ɪmjʊnəʊ'lɒdʒɪk(ə)l] *adj Med* immunologique
immunology [ɪmjʊ'nɒlədʒɪ] *n Med* immunologie *f*
immunosuppressant [ɪmjʊnəʊsə'presənt] *n Med* immunosuppresseur *m*
immunosuppressive [ɪmjʊnəʊsə'presɪv] *adj Med* immunosuppresseur
immunotherapy [ɪmjʊnəʊ'θerəpɪ] *n Med* immunothérapie *f*
immure [ɪ'mjʊər] *vt Arch, Lit* (**a**) (*shut away*) (*sb*) enfermer, cloîtrer; **he had immured himself in the library** il s'était enfermé dans la bibliothèque; **immured in silence** cloîtré dans le silence (**b**) (*wall up*) (*victim*) emmurer
immutability [ɪmju:tə'bɪlɪtɪ] *n Fml* immutabilité *f*, caractère *m* immuable
immutable [ɪ'mju:təb(ə)l] *adj* immuable
immutably [ɪ'mju:təblɪ] *adv* immuablement
imp [ɪmp] *n* diablotin *m*, lutin *m*; *F* (**little**) **i.** (*boy*) petit garnement *m*, galopin *m*; (*girl*) petite coquine *f*
impact[1] ['ɪmpækt] *n* (**a**) (*shock*) choc *m*; (*of bullet*) impact *m*; **on i.** (*of projectile*) au moment de l'impact; **i. adhesive** colle *f* forte instantanée; *Aut* **i. test** essai *m* au choc (**b**) *Fig* (*of speech, play, advertising campaign etc*) impact *m*; **the play has lost none of its i.** la pièce n'a pas du tout perdu de son impact; **he seems to have made quite an i. on you** il semble avait fait une forte impression sur vous
▶ **impact on** *vipo* (*trade figures, section of population etc*) avoir un impact sur, affecter
impact bar *n Aut* barre *f* de renfort
impacted [ɪm'pæktɪd] *adj Surg* (*fracture*) avec impaction *ou* incongruence; **i. tooth** dent *f* barrée
impact printer *n Comptr* imprimante *f* à impact
impair [ɪm'peər] *vt* (*sight, hearing, mental faculties*) affaiblir; (*strength*) faire perdre, diminuer; (*relations, person's authority, chances*) compromettre; **his health has been (seriously) impaired by the expedition** sa santé s'est (gravement) détériorée à la suite de l'expédition
impairment [ɪm'peəmənt] *n* (*of sight, hearing, memory*) affaiblissement *m*; (*of health, relations*) dégradation *f*; (*of strength*) diminution *f*; **without i. of quality** sans perte de qualité
impala [ɪm'pɑ:lə] *n* (*antelope*) impala *m*
impale [ɪm'peɪl] *vt* empaler; **to be impaled** (*on railings etc*) être empalé, s'empaler
impalpable [ɪm'pælpəb(ə)l] *adj* (**a**) (*intangible*) impalpable, intangible (**b**) (*to the mind*) insaisissable
impanel [ɪm'pænəl] *vt* = **empanel**
impart [ɪm'pɑ:t] *vt Fml* (**a**) (*lend*) (*courage etc*) donner; (*movement*) imprimer, communiquer (**to** à); (*heat, light*) transmettre (**b**) (*transmit*) (*knowledge*) communiquer; (*news*) faire connaître, annoncer; (*secret*) confier; (*truth*) transmettre (**to** à)
impartial [ɪm'pɑ:ʃəl] *adj* (*person, conduct*) impartial (**towards** envers); **to be i.** être impartial *ou* équitable
impartiality [ɪmpɑ:ʃɪ'ælɪtɪ] *n* impartialité *f* (**towards** envers)
impartially [ɪm'pɑ:ʃəlɪ] *adv* impartialement, avec impartialité; (*to judge*) équitablement

impassable [ɪm'pɑːsəb(ə)l] *adj* (*river, barrier, pass*) infranchissable; (*road*) impraticable
impasse ['æmpɑːs] *n* impasse *f*; **we have reached an i.** nous sommes dans une *ou* l'impasse
impassioned [ɪm'pæʃənd] *adj* (*orator, speech, defence etc*) passionné; (*style*) chaleureux
impassive [ɪm'pæsɪv] *adj* (*person, face*) impassible
impassively [ɪm'pæsɪvlɪ] *adv* impassiblement
impatience [ɪm'peɪʃəns] *n* impatience *f* (**to do** de faire); **i. to leave** hâte *f* de partir; **there was a note of i. in his voice** on sentait l'impatience dans sa voix; *Fml* **he was known for his i. of sloppy work** il avait la réputation de mal supporter le travail brouillon
impatient [ɪm'peɪʃənt] *adj* (*person, tone*) impatient; (*reply*) vif, emporté; **to get** *or* **grow i.** s'impatienter; **to get i. with sb** s'impatienter contre qn; **I am getting so i. with this photocopier!** je perds complètement patience avec cette photocopieuse!; **to be i. for change/reform** avoir soif de changement/réforme; **to be i. to do sth** être impatient *ou* brûler de faire qch; *Lit* **he was i. of those less intelligent than himself** il supportait mal ceux qui étaient moins intelligents que lui
impatiently [ɪm'peɪʃəntlɪ] *adv* (*to wait*) avec impatience; (*to answer*) sur un ton *ou* d'un ton d'impatience
impeach [ɪm'piːtʃ] *vt* **(a)** *Jur* (*accuse*) accuser (**of** *or* **with a crime** d'un crime); *Br* **to i. sb for high treason** inculper qn pour haute trahison; *US* **to i. a public official** = mettre un haut fonctionnaire en accusation devant le Congrès **(b)** *Fml* (*call into question*) (*truth, sb's integrity*) attaquer, mettre en doute; *Jur* (*witness*) récuser, reprocher; (*evidence*) révoquer
impeachable [ɪm'piːtʃəb(ə)l] *adj US Jur* = passible d'une mise en accusation devant le Congrès
impeachment [ɪm'piːtʃmənt] *n Jur* (*of minister etc*) mise *f* en accusation *US* impeachment *m*
impeccable [ɪm'pekəb(ə)l] *adj* (*house, room etc*) impeccable; *Fig* (*conduct, management, manners*) irréprochable; **he speaks i. English** il parle un anglais impeccable
impeccably [ɪm'pekəblɪ] *adv* (*to behave*) irréprochablement; (*dressed*) impeccablement
impecunious [ɪmpɪ'kjuːnɪəs] *adj Fml* impécunieux
impedance [ɪm'piːdəns] *n El* impédance *f*
impede [ɪm'piːd] *vt* (*progress, activity, sb's efforts etc*) entraver, gêner; (*traffic*) gêner; **to i. the enemy's movements** gêner les déplacements de l'ennemi; **she was impeded by her skirt** sa jupe entravait ses mouvements
impediment [ɪm'pedɪmənt] *n* obstacle *m* (**to** à); **speech i.** défaut *m* de prononciation
impedimenta [ɪmpedɪ'mentə] *npl Hum, Mil Fml* impedimenta *mpl*
impel [ɪm'pel] *vt* (**-ll-**) **(a)** (*motivate, oblige*) obliger, forcer (**sb to do sth** qn à faire qch) **(b)** (*push*) projeter (en avant)
impeller [ɪm'pelər] *n MecE* rotor *m*; (*of water pump*) turbine *f*; (*of converter*) roue *f* pompe
impending [ɪm'pendɪŋ] *adj* (*danger, arrival, downfall etc*) imminent
impenetrability [ɪmpenɪtrə'bɪlɪtɪ] *n* impénétrabilité *f*
impenetrable [ɪm'penɪtrəb(ə)l] *adj* (*defences, mystery, mist*) impénétrable; (*jargon*) incompréhensible
impenitence [ɪm'penɪtəns] *n Fml* impénitence *f*
impenitent [ɪm'penɪtənt] *adj, n Fml* impénitent, -ente
impenitently [ɪm'penɪtəntlɪ] *adv* sans repentir
imperative [ɪm'perətɪv] **1** *adj* **(a)** (*need etc*) urgent; **it is i. that he should come** il est impératif qu'il vienne **(b)** (*tone*) impérieux, péremptoire **(c)** *Gram* (*mood*) impératif **2** *n* [①**A39**,8; **B32**,4] *Gram* (mode *m*) impératif *m*; **in the i.** à l'impératif
imperceptible [ɪmpə'septɪb(ə)l] *adj* (*movement, difference, improvement etc*) imperceptible; (*sound, difference*) insaisissable
imperceptibly [ɪmpə'septɪblɪ] *adv* imperceptiblement
imperfect [ɪm'pɜːfɪkt] **1** *adj* **(a)** (*not perfect*) imparfait; *Com* (*goods*) qui a un défaut; **it's slightly i.** (*of item for sale*) il a un léger défaut **(b)** *Gram* (*tense*) imparfait **2** *n* [①**B28**,F,2] *Gram* imparfait *m*; **verb in the i.** verbe *m* à l'imparfait
imperfection [ɪmpə'fekʃən] *n* **(a)** (*flaw*) imperfection *f*, défectuosité *f* **(b)** (*state of being imperfect*) caractère *m* imparfait
imperfectly [ɪm'pɜːfɪktlɪ] *adv* imparfaitement
imperial [ɪm'pɪərɪəl] *adj* **(a)** (*government, crown etc*) impérial; **His/Her I. Majesty** Sa Majesté Impériale **(b)** *Br* (*weights and measures*) utilisé traditionellement dans les pays anglo-saxons **(c)** (*commanding*) majestueux, altier
imperialism [ɪm'pɪərɪəlɪz(ə)m] *n* impérialisme *m*
imperialist [ɪm'pɪərɪəlɪst] *adj, n* impérialiste *mf*
imperialistic [ɪmpɪərɪə'lɪstɪk] *adj* impérialiste
imperially [ɪm'pɪərɪəlɪ] *adv* **(a)** *Pol* impérialement **(b)** (*in a commanding manner*) impérieusement
imperil [ɪm'perɪl] *vt* (**-ll-**, *US* **-l-**) (*sb's life etc*) mettre en danger; (*one's reputation*) compromettre
imperious [ɪm'pɪərɪəs] *adj* (*person, tone, character*) impérieux, dictatorial
imperiously [ɪm'pɪərɪəslɪ] *adv* (*to speak, act*) impérieusement
imperishable [ɪm'perɪʃəb(ə)l] *adj* impérissable
impermanent [ɪm'pɜːmənənt] *adj* impermanent
impermeable [ɪm'pɜːmɪəb(ə)l] *adj* imperméable
impersonal [ɪm'pɜːsən(ə)l] *adj* **(a)** (*style etc*) impersonnel **(b)** [①**B27-8**,E] *Gram* (*verb*) impersonnel
impersonally [ɪm'pɜːsən(ə)lɪ] *adv* impersonnellement, de façon impersonnelle
impersonate [ɪm'pɜːsəneɪt] *vt* (*pretend to be*) se faire passer pour; *Th, TV etc* (*imitate*) imiter
impersonation [ɪmpɜːsə'neɪʃən] *n* (*pretence of being*) usurpation *f* d'identité (**of** de); *Th, TV etc* (*imitation*) imitation *f*; **to do an i. of sb** imiter qn
impersonator [ɪm'pɜːsəneɪtər] *n* (*imposter*) imposteur *m*; *Th, TV etc* (*mimic*) imitateur, -trice
impertinence [ɪm'pɜːtɪnəns] *n* impertinence *f*, insolence *f*; **an i., a piece of i.** une impertinence
impertinent [ɪm'pɜːtɪnənt] *adj* **(a)** (*person, remark*) impertinent, insolent (**to sb** envers qn) **(b)** *esp Jur* (*not relevant*) non pertinent
impertinently [ɪm'pɜːtɪnəntlɪ] *adv* **(a)** (*to say, look at sb*) de façon impertinente, impertinemment **(b)** *esp Jur* de façon non pertinente
imperturbable [ɪmpə'tɜːbəb(ə)l] *adj* imperturbable
impervious [ɪm'pɜːvɪəs] *adj* **(a)** insensible (**to criticism** à la critique); **she is i. to reason** on ne peut pas la raisonner **(b)** (*material etc*) **to be i. to light/water** ne pas laisser passer la lumière/être imperméable
impetigo [ɪmpɪ'taɪgəʊ] *n Med* impétigo *m*; **to have i.** avoir un impétigo
impetuosity [ɪmpetjʊ'ɒsɪtɪ] *n* = **impetuousness**
impetuous [ɪm'petjʊəs] *adj* (*person, character, action*) impétueux; (*decision*) hâtif
impetuously [ɪm'petjʊəslɪ] *adv* impétueusement, avec impétuosité
impetuousness [ɪm'petjʊəsnɪs] *n* (*of person, action*) impétuosité *f*
impetus ['ɪmpɪtəs] *n* **(a)** élan *m*; **to give an i. to sth** donner de l'élan à qch; **to gain i.** prendre *ou* gagner de l'importance; **to lose i.** perdre de son élan **(b)** *Phys* vitesse *f* acquise
impiety [ɪm'paɪətɪ] *n* impiété *f*
▶ **impinge on** [ɪm'pɪndʒ] *vipo* **(a)** (*affect*) affecter; **it impinges in a big way on all our lives** ça affecte énormément notre vie à tous; **to i. on sb's conscious mind** venir à la conscience de qn; **it didn't even i. on his consciousness** il ne s'en est même pas rendu compte; **in so far as it impinges on our department** dans la mesure où cela affecte *ou* a des répercussions sur notre service **(b)** (*infringe on*) (*sb's rights etc*) empiéter sur
impingement [ɪm'pɪndʒmənt] *n* (*on sb's rights etc*) empiètement *m*
impious ['ɪmpɪəs] *adj* impie
impiously ['ɪmpɪəslɪ] *adv* avec impiété
impish ['ɪmpɪʃ] *adj* (*laughter, face*) de petit diable, d'espiègle; (*child, remark*) espiègle, malicieux
impishly ['ɪmpɪʃlɪ] *adv* comme un petit diable
impishness ['ɪmpɪʃnɪs] *n* espièglerie *f*
implacable [ɪm'plækəb(ə)l] *adj* implacable (**towards** à, pour, à l'égard de)
implacably [ɪm'plækəblɪ] *adv* implacablement
implant[1] ['ɪmplɑːnt] *n Surg* implant *m*
implant[2] [ɪm'plɑːnt] *vt* **(a)** (*insert*), *Med* implanter (**in** dans) **(b)** *Fig* (*opinion, principle*) inculquer (**in sb** à qn); (*idea*) implanter (**in sb** dans la tête de qn); **from his youth this ideal had been implanted in his mind** dès sa jeunesse cet idéal lui avait été inculqué
implausible [ɪm'plɔːzɪb(ə)l] *adj* peu plausible, invraisemblable
implausibly [ɪm'plɔːzɪblɪ] *adv* invraisemblablement; **to end i.** (*of book, film etc*) se terminer de façon peu vraisemblable
implement[1] ['ɪmplɪmənt] *n* outil *m*, instrument *m*; **gardening implements** outils de jardinage; **kitchen implements** ustensiles *mpl* de cuisine
implement[2] ['ɪmplɪment] *vt* (*treaty, plan, agreement, technique, decision*) mettre en application; (*promise*) exécuter; (*change*) introduire
implementation [ɪmplɪmen'teɪʃən] *n* (*of treaty, plan, agreement, technique, decision*) mise *f* en œuvre; (*of promise*) exécution *f*; (*of change*) introduction *f*; *Mktg* **i. stage** (*of product development*) phase *f* de mise en œuvre
implicate ['ɪmplɪkeɪt] *vt* **(a)** impliquer, mêler (**sb in a crime** qn dans un crime); **without implicating anyone** sans compromettre personne **(b)** *Fml* (*imply*) impliquer, renfermer

implication [ɪmplɪ'keɪʃən] *n* implication *f*; **by i.** implicitement; **the full i. of what he said was not lost on us** nous avons tout de suite vu ce que ses paroles impliquaient

implicit [ɪm'plɪsɪt] *adj* **(a)** (*implied*) (*condition, meaning etc*) implicite; (*recognition*) tacite **(b)** (*absolute*) (*obedience*) absolu; **i. faith** confiance *f* aveugle **(in** dans**)**

implicitly [ɪm'plɪsɪtlɪ] *adv* **(a)** implicitement; **to i. recognize a country** reconnaître un pays de manière tacite **(b)** (*absolutely*) (*to obey*) aveuglément; **to trust sb i.** faire totalement confiance à qn

implied [ɪm'plaɪd] *adj* implicite; **i. meaning** sous-entendu *m*, *pl* sous-entendus

implode [ɪm'pləʊd] *vi* imploser

implore [ɪm'plɔːr] *vt* (*sb*) implorer, supplier **(to do sth** de faire qch**)**; (*forgiveness*) implorer

imploring [ɪm'plɔːrɪŋ] *adj* (*look, tone*) implorant, suppliant

imploringly [ɪm'plɔːrɪŋlɪ] *adv* (*to say*) d'un ton suppliant; (*to look at sb*) d'un air suppliant

implosion [ɪm'pləʊʒən] *n* implosion *f*

imply [ɪm'plaɪ] *vt* **(a)** (*of person*) sous-entendre; **you seem to i. that ...** ce que vous dites laisse supposer que ...; **are you implying that I stole the money?** est-ce que tu sous-entends que j'ai volé l'argent?; **your silence implies that you are guilty** votre silence laisse à penser que vous êtes coupable **(b)** (*of circumstance*) (*presuppose*) impliquer; **the new deadline implies a lot of hard work** les nouvelles échéances impliquent qu'il va falloir travailler dur

impolite [ɪmpə'laɪt] *adj* impoli **(to, towards** envers**)**

impolitely [ɪmpə'laɪtlɪ] *adv* impoliment

impoliteness [ɪmpə'laɪtnɪs] *n* impolitesse *f*

impolitic [ɪm'pɒlɪtɪk] *adj* peu judicieux

imponderability [ɪmpɒndərə'bɪlɪtɪ] *n* impondérabilité *f*

imponderable [ɪm'pɒndərəb(ə)l] **1** *adj* (*reasons, motives*) impondérable **2** *n* impondérable *m*

import[1] ['ɪmpɔːt] *n* **(a)** *Com* (*item*) article *m* d'importation, importation *f*; (*activity*) importation; **i. and export** l'importation et l'exportation *f*; **imports** importations; *Fig* **the art of lacemaking was an i. from France** l'art de la (fabrication de la) dentelle nous est venu de France; **i. ban** interdiction *f* d'importation; **to impose an i. ban on sth** interdire qch d'importation; **i. bonus** prime *f* d'importation; **i. controls** contrôles *mpl* à l'importation; **i. duty** droit *m* d'entrée, taxe *f* d'importation; **i. licence** licence *f* d'importation; **i. permit** permis *m* d'importer, permis d'importation; **i. quotas** contingents *mpl* d'importation; **i. restrictions** restrictions *fpl* à l'importation; **i. trade** commerce *m* d'importation; **i. wholesaler** grossiste *m* importateur

(b) *Fml* (*meaning*) (*of word*) sens *m*, signification *f*; (*of document etc*) teneur *f*

(c) *Fml* (*importance*) (*of event, discovery*) importance *f*; (*of remark*) portée *f*; **a matter of great i.** une affaire de première importance

import[2] [ɪm'pɔːt] *vt* **(a)** *Com* (*goods*) importer **(from** de**)**; **imported goods** marchandises *fpl* importées *ou* d'importation **(b)** *Comptr* importer **(from** depuis**)** **(c)** *Fml* (*mean*) signifier, vouloir dire

importance [ɪm'pɔːtəns] *n* importance *f*; **to be of i.** avoir de l'importance; **of vital/strategic i.** d'une importance capitale/stratégique; **it is of the utmost i. to remember that ...** il est absolument essentiel de se rappeler que ...; **it is of no great i.** cela importe peu; **a detail of no i.** un détail sans importance; **to attach i. to sth** mettre *ou* attacher de l'importance à qch; *Pej* **to be full of one's own i.** être imbu de sa personne; *Mktg* **i.-performance analysis** analyse *f* importance-performance

important [ɪm'pɔːtənt] *adj* important; (*difference*) considérable; **what is more i.?** qu'est-ce qui est le plus important?; **to become more i.** (*of issue, nation etc*) prendre de l'importance; **it is i. to know that ...** il est important de savoir que ...; **it is i. for you to know that ..., it is i. that you should know that ...** il est important que vous sachiez que ...; **his children/hobbies are very i. to him** ses enfants/passe-temps sont très importants pour lui; *Pej* **he was trying to look i.** il essayait de se donner l'air important

importantly [ɪm'pɔːtəntlɪ] *adv* (*to look at*) d'un air important; (*to say*) d'un ton important; **but, more i. ...** mais, ce qui est plus important ...

importation [ɪmpɔː'teɪʃən] *n* **(a)** (*of goods*) importation *f* **(b)** (*imported article*) importation *f*, article *m* d'importation **(c)** *Comptr* importation *f*

importer [ɪm'pɔːtər] *n* importateur, -trice; **i. margin** marge *f* de l'importateur

import-export *n* import-export *m*; **i. (trade)** import-export *f*

importing ['ɪmpɔːtɪŋ] **1** *adj* (*country*) importateur, -trice **2** *n* (*of goods*) importation *f*

importunate [ɪm'pɔːtjʊnɪt] *adj Fml* (*creditor, visitor*) importun

importune [ɪm'pɔːtjuːn] *vt Fml* importuner

importunity [ɪmpɔː'tjuːnɪtɪ] *n Fml* importunité *f*

impose [ɪm'pəʊz] **1** *vt* (*silence, one's will, restrictions etc*) imposer **(on sb** à qn**)**; **his bearing imposes respect** il en impose; **to i. a tax on sugar** taxer le sucre; **to i. a fine on sb** condamner qn à (payer) une amende; **to i. the maximum penalty provided** appliquer le maximum de la peine; **to i. oneself on a situation/a political party** (*exert strong influence over*) s'imposer dans une situation/un parti politique **2** *vi* (*take advantage*) abuser; **I hope I'm not imposing** (*by staying*) j'espère que je ne m'impose pas; **to i. on** *or* **upon sb** abuser de l'amabilité de qn; **to i. on** *or* **upon sb's kindness** abuser de la bonté de qn

imposing [ɪm'pəʊzɪŋ] *adj* (*air, tone*) imposant; (*spectacle, building*) impressionnant

imposition [ɪmpə'zɪʃən] *n* **(a)** (*of task, tax*) imposition *f*; (*of fine*) fait *m* d'infliger **(b)** (*abuse*) **I told him I thought it was a bit of an i. asking me to ...** je lui ai dit que je trouvais qu'il abusait un peu de ma bonté en me demandant de ... **(c)** (*tax*) imposition *f*, impôt *m*, taxe *f* **(d)** *Old-fashioned Br Sch* (*punishment*) punition *f*

impossibility [ɪmpɒsɪ'bɪlɪtɪ] *n* impossibilité *f*; **it's a physical i.** c'est matériellement impossible

impossible [ɪm'pɒsɪb(ə)l] **1** *adj* **(a)** (*task, demand*) impossible; **it is i. for me to do it** il m'est impossible de le faire; **to make it i. for sb to do sth** mettre qn dans l'impossibilité de faire qch; **it's not i. that ...** il n'est pas impossible que ...; **(it's) i. to say** *or* **tell** c'est impossible à dire **(b)** (*unbelievable*) (*story, account*) invraisemblable **(c)** *F* (*intolerable*) (*life, person*) impossible; **you're i.!** vous êtes impossible! **2** *n* impossible *m*; **to attempt the i.** tenter l'impossible

impossibly [ɪm'pɒsɪblɪ] *adv* (*long, difficult*) incroyablement; **he's i. stupid** est-il possible d'être aussi stupide!; *F* **the children were behaving i.** les enfants étaient vraiment impossibles

impostor [ɪm'pɒstər] *n* imposteur *m*

imposture [ɪm'pɒstʃər] *n* imposture *f*, tromperie *f*

impotence ['ɪmpətəns] *n* **(a)** (*powerlessness*) impuissance *f*; (*weakness*) faiblesse *f*, impotence *f* **(b)** (*sexual*) impuissance *f*

impotent ['ɪmpətənt] *adj* **(a)** (*powerless*) impuissant; (*weak*) impotent, faible **(b)** (*sexually*) impuissant

impound [ɪm'paʊnd] *vt* **(a)** *Jur* (*confiscate*) confisquer, saisir **(b)** (*put in pound*) (*animal, car etc*) mettre en fourrière

impounding [ɪm'paʊndɪŋ] *n* **(a)** *Jur* (*of goods*) arrêt *m*, saisie *f* **(b)** (*putting in pound*) (*of animals, cars etc*) mise *f* en fourrière

impoverish [ɪm'pɒvərɪʃ] *vt* (*person, country, soil*) appauvrir

impoverished [ɪm'pɒvərɪʃt] *adj* appauvri, pauvre

impoverishment [ɪm'pɒvərɪʃmənt] *n* appauvrissement *m*

impracticability [ɪmpræktɪkə'bɪlɪtɪ] *n* impraticabilité *f*

impracticable [ɪm'præktɪkəb(ə)l] *adj* infaisable, impraticable

impractical [ɪm'præktɪk(ə)l] *adj* (*person*) qui n'a pas le sens *ou* l'esprit pratique; (*project, suggestion*) peu réaliste; **he's completely i.** il n'a aucun sens pratique

imprecation [ɪmprɪ'keɪʃən] *n* imprécation *f*

imprecise [ɪmprɪ'saɪs] *adj* imprécis, vague

imprecision [ɪmprɪ'sɪʒən] *n* imprécision *f*, manque *m* de précision

impregnable [ɪm'pregnəb(ə)l] *adj* **(a)** (*fortress*) imprenable; **i. to attack** imprenable **(b)** *Fig* (*truth, argument*) invincible

impregnate ['ɪmpregneɪt] *vt* **(a)** *Biol* féconder **(b)** *Tech* imprégner, imbiber **(sth with sth** qch de qch**)**; **allow the oil to i. the wood** laissez le bois s'imprégner d'huile

impregnation [ɪmpreg'neɪʃən] *n* **(a)** *Biol* fécondation *f* **(b)** *Tech* (*of fabric, wood etc*) imprégnation *f*

impresario [ɪmpre'sɑːrɪəʊ] *n* impresario *m*

impress[1] ['ɪmpres] *n Fml, Lit* **(a)** (*imprint*) empreinte *f*, impression *f* **(b)** *Fig* (*distinctive style etc*) marque *f* distinctive

impress[2] [ɪm'pres] **1** *vt* **(a)** (*create strong impression on*) impressionner, faire une impression à; **I was deeply impressed by it** j'ai été très impressionné, cela m'a fait une grande impression; *F* **I'm not impressed!** c'est pas terrible!; **she wasn't impressed by my excuse** mon excuse ne l'a pas vraiment convaincue; **he impressed me favourably** il m'a fait bonne impression; **she impressed me as hard-working** elle m'a fait l'impression d'être travailleuse

(b) (*make understood*) faire bien comprendre **(sth on** *or* **upon sb** qch à qn**)**; (*idea*) inculquer **(on** *or* **upon sb** à qn**)**; **you must i. on him that ...** il faut bien lui faire comprendre que ...

(c) (*imprint*) **to i. sth on** *or* **upon sth** imprimer qch sur qch; **to i. sth with a seal** faire une impression sur qch avec un cachet; *Fig* **to i. sth on the mind** graver qch dans la mémoire; *Fig* **to i. sb with the idea that …** inculquer à qn l'idée que …

2 *vi* (*of person, remark*) faire impression

impression [ɪmˈpreʃən] *n* **(a)** (*effect*) impression *f*; **to make an i.** faire impression; **to make a good/bad i.** faire bonne/mauvaise impression **(on** sur); **my argument was making no i. on her** (*having no effect*) mon argument ne lui faisait aucun effet

(b) (*idea, opinion*) impression *f*; **I'm under the i. that I've seen him before** j'ai l'impression de l'avoir déjà vu; **I don't know where she got that i. from** je ne sais pas où elle est allée chercher ça; **I had the i. that you liked her** j'avais l'impression que tu l'aimais bien; **to create** *or* **give the i. that …** donner *ou* produire l'impression que …; **my first i. wasn't favourable** ma première impression n'a pas été favorable

(c) (*imprint*) (*of seal*) empreinte *f*, impression *f*; **to take an i. of sth** prendre l'empreinte *ou* l'impression de qch; **i. cylinder** cylindre *m* de rotative

(d) (*re-print*) (*of book etc*) tirage *m*

(e) (*imitation*) imitation *f*; **to do impressions** faire des imitations; **this is my i. of you eating** je t'imite en train de manger

impressionable [ɪmˈpreʃənəb(ə)l] *adj* (*person*) influençable; (*age*) impressionnable

impressionism [ɪmˈpreʃənɪz(ə)m] *n Art* impressionnisme *m*

impressionist [ɪmˈpreʃənɪst] **1** *adj Art* impressionniste **2** *n Art* impressionniste *mf*; (*mimic*) imitateur, -trice

impressionistic [ɪmpreʃəˈnɪstɪk] *adj* impressionniste

impressive [ɪmˈpresɪv] *adj* (*spectacle, language*) impressionnant

impressively [ɪmˈpresɪvlɪ] *adv* d'une manière impressionnante

imprimatur [ɪmprɪˈmɑːtər] *n* imprimatur *m*

imprint[1] [ˈɪmprɪnt] *n* **(a)** (*of seal, animal's feet etc*) empreinte *f*; **to take an i. of a credit card** passer une carte de crédit dans la facturette; **the events left their i. on her mind** les événements sont restés gravés dans son esprit **(b)** **(publisher's) i.** (*mark*) marque *f* de l'éditeur; **i. page** page *f* qui porte la marque de l'éditeur; **XYZ books is an i. of JMG Publishers** XYZ fait partie des Éditions JMG

imprint[2] [ɪmˈprɪnt] *vt* imprimer; **to i. sth with sth** marquer *ou* empreindre qch de qch; **the shape of an animal's foot was imprinted in the earth** l'empreinte du pied d'un animal était restée dans la terre; **to i. sth on the memory** graver *ou* fixer qch dans la mémoire

imprinter [ˈɪmprɪntər] *n* (*for credit card payment*) pressographe *m*

imprison [ɪmˈprɪzən] *vt* emprisonner, mettre en prison; **to keep sb imprisoned** garder qn prisonnier

imprisonment [ɪmˈprɪzənmənt] *n* emprisonnement *m*; **ten days' i.** dix jours d'emprisonnement *ou* de prison

improbability [ɪmprɒbəˈbɪlɪtɪ] *n* improbabilité *f*

improbable [ɪmˈprɒbəb(ə)l] *adj* improbable; **it's highly i. that he'll come** il est très improbable *ou* très peu probable qu'il vienne

improbably [ɪmˈprɒbəblɪ] *adv* invraisemblablement; **quite i., he won** contre toute attente, il a gagné; **he was wearing an i. large hat** il portait un chapeau d'une grandeur invraisemblable

impromptu [ɪmˈprɒmptjuː] **1** *adv* (*to do sth*) sans préparation, impromptu **2** *adj* (*poem, speech*) impromptu; **to make an i. speech** improviser un discours **3** *n Th, Mus* impromptu *m*

improper [ɪmˈprɒpər] *adj* **(a)** (*incorrect*) (*use, purpose*) impropre; *Math* **i. fraction** expression *f* fractionnaire **(b)** (*indecent*) (*suggestion, remark*) indécent, inconvenant **(c)** (*not fitting*) (*behaviour, dress*) déplacé; **it would be i. to refuse** il serait de mauvaise grâce de refuser; **i. practices** pratiques *fpl* irrégulières

improperly [ɪmˈprɒpəlɪ] *adv* **(a)** (*incorrectly*) (*to use a tool, one's power*) improprement **(b)** (*indecently*) (*to behave*) d'une manière inconvenante, avec indécence **(c)** (*inappropriately*) (*to speak, behave*) d'une façon déplacée; **to be i. dressed** ne pas porter une tenue convenable

impropriety [ɪmprəˈpraɪətɪ] *n* **(a)** (*unsuitable expression, gesture etc*) inconvenance *f*, indécence *f*; **to be guilty of improprieties** avoir commis des inconvenances **(b)** (*incorrectness*) (*of language etc*) impropriété *f*; (*of behaviour*) inconvenance *f*, indécence *f*

improve [ɪmˈpruːv] **1** *vt* (*one's French, the flavour, translation etc*) améliorer; (*invention, system*) apporter des perfectionnements à; (*wine etc*) bonifier; (*one's knowledge*) étendre, élargir; (*one's taste*) affiner; *Agr* (*soil*) bonifier, enrichir; **to i. the appearance of sb/sth** embellir qn/qch; *esp Hum* **to i. one's mind** se cultiver **2** *vi* (*of situation, sb's health etc*) s'améliorer; (*of wine etc*) s'améliorer, se bonifier; *Com* (*of prices, markets*) monter; **business is improving** les affaires reprennent

▶ **improve on, improve upon** *vi po* (*sth*) (*make better*) améliorer; *Com* **to i. on sb's offer** offrir plus que qn

improved [ɪmˈpruːvd] *adj* (*situation etc*) amélioré; (*invention*) perfectionné; *Com* (*offer*) supérieur

improvement [ɪmˈpruːvmənt] *n* **(a)** (*in situation, health etc*) amélioration *f* **(in** de); (*of invention*) perfectionnement *m*; **to be an i. on sb/sth** surpasser qn/qch; **the weather is a bit of an i. on what it was yesterday** il fait légèrement meilleur aujourd'hui qu'hier; **we should see something of an i. in the weather tomorrow** le temps devrait s'améliorer demain; **my new car is a great i. on the old one** ma nouvelle voiture est bien supérieure à l'ancienne; **the cakes were an i. on my first attempt** les gâteaux étaient mieux réussis que la première fois; **her new boyfriend's a bit of an i.** son nouveau petit ami est un peu mieux que le(s) précédent(s)

(b) (*usu pl*) *Constr etc* **improvements** améliorations *fpl*, embellissements *mpl*; **we're making some improvements to the house** nous rénovons la maison; *Br* **i. grant** subvention *f* pour la rénovation d'une maison

improvidence [ɪmˈprɒvɪdəns] *n* **(a)** (*rashness*) imprévoyance *f* **(b)** (*carelessness with money*) prodigalité *f*

improvident [ɪmˈprɒvɪdənt] *adj* **(a)** (*rash*) imprévoyant **(b)** (*careless with money*) prodigue

improvidently [ɪmˈprɒvɪdəntlɪ] *adv* (*see adj*) **(a)** de façon imprévoyante **(b)** de façon prodigue

improving [ɪmˈpruːvɪŋ] *adj* (*book etc*) édifiant; (*influence, environment*) bénéfique

improvisation [ɪmprəvaɪˈzeɪʃən] *n* improvisation *f*

improvise [ˈɪmprəvaɪz] **1** *vt* improviser; **hastily improvised** sommairement organisé; **improvised speech** discours improvisé *ou* impromptu; **they improvised bandages from bedsheets** ils ont fait des bandages de fortune avec des draps; **improvised raft** radeau *m* de fortune **2** *vi* improviser; **to i. on the piano** improviser au piano; **you will have to i.** (*make do*) il faudra que vous vous débrouilliez avec ce qu'il y a

improviser [ˈɪmprəvaɪzər] *n* improvisateur, -trice

imprudence [ɪmˈpruːdəns] *n* imprudence *f*; (*with money*) manque *m* de prévoyance

imprudent [ɪmˈpruːdənt] *adj* imprudent; **i. with money** imprudent dans ses dépenses; **she's rather i. in her choice of friends** elle choisit mal ses amis; **i. action** imprudence *f*

imprudently [ɪmˈpruːdəntlɪ] *adv* imprudemment

impudence [ˈɪmpjʊdəns] *n* impudence *f*, insolence *f*

impudent [ˈɪmpjʊdənt] *adj* impudent, insolent; **he's an i. fellow** c'est un insolent

impudently [ˈɪmpjʊdəntlɪ] *adv* avec impudence *ou* insolence

impugn [ɪmˈpjuːn] *vt Fml* (*sb's honour, motives*) mettre en doute *ou* en question; *Jur* (*sb's evidence*) récuser

impulse [ˈɪmpʌls] *n* **(a)** (*desire*) envie *f*; *Psy* (*sexual etc*) pulsion *f*; **to feel an i. to do sth** avoir une soudaine envie de faire qch; **a sudden i. made me start running** instinctivement, j'ai commencé à courir; **to act on i.** agir spontanément *ou* sur le coup d'une impulsion; **I did it on i.** j'ai fait ça sur un coup de tête; **i. goods** produits *mpl* d'achat impulsif

(b) (*stimulation, force*) impulsion *f*; *Fig* **to give an i. to trade** donner une impulsion au commerce

(c) *Phys* quantité *f* de mouvement; *El* **electrical impulses** impulsions *fpl* électriques; *Physiol* **nerve i.** signal *m* nerveux

impulse buy *n* achat *m* impulsif *ou* spontané

impulse buyer *n* acheteur *m* impulsif

impulse buying *n* achats *mpl* faits sur un coup de tête

impulsion [ɪmˈpʌlʃən] *n* impulsion *f*

impulsive [ɪmˈpʌlsɪv] *adj* **(a)** (*person, gesture, decision, remark*) impulsif; **i. action** acte *m* impulsif, coup *m* de tête; **i. buy** achat *m* non prémédité; **i. buyer** acheteur *m* impulsif **(b)** *MecE* impulsif, propulsif; **i. force** force *f* impulsive *ou* projective

impulsively [ɪmˈpʌlsɪvlɪ] *adj* (*to act*) par impulsion, de façon impulsive

impulsiveness [ɪmˈpʌlsɪvnɪs] *n* caractère *m* impulsif

impunity [ɪmˈpjuːnɪtɪ] *n* impunité *f*; **to do sth with i.** faire qch impunément *ou* en toute impunité

impure [ɪmˈpjʊər] *adj* impur

impurity [ɪmˈpjʊərɪtɪ] *n* (*of water etc, Fig of thoughts*) impureté *f*

imputation [ɪmpjuːˈteɪʃən] *n* imputation *f*

impute [ɪmˈpjuːt] *vt* (*action etc*) imputer, attribuer **(to sb** à qn)

in [ɪn] **1** *prep* [①A67; B51-54] **(a)** (*of place*) en, à, dans; **in France** en France; **in Japan** au Japon; **in the United States** aux États-Unis; **in Paris** à Paris; **in the provinces** en province; **to be in town/in the country** être en ville/à la campagne; **in his country** dans son pays; **in prison** en prison; **in church** à l'église; **in bed** au lit; **in the house/city** dans la maison/ville; **in the water** dans l'eau; **the key is in the door** la clef est sur la porte; **in this book** dans ce livre; **in my hand** dans ma main; **with a cigar in his mouth** un cigare à la bouche; **in the distance** au loin; **in your place** à votre place; **wounded in the shoulder** blessé à l'épaule

(b) (*among*) **in the crowd** dans la foule; **the temperature was in the nineties** la température était dans les 30 degrés; **this illness is rare in men** cette maladie est rare chez les hommes; **this is a common theme in Shakespeare's work** c'est un thème fréquent dans les œuvres de Shakespeare

(c) (*regarding*) **an expert in economics** un expert en économie politique; **two metres in length** long de deux mètres; **in certain repects he was right** à certains égards il avait raison

(d) (*of ratio*) **one in ten** un sur dix; **once in ten years** une fois tous les dix ans

(e) (*of time, age*) **in 1927** en 1927; **in the thirties** dans les années trente; **in the night** pendant la nuit; **in the afternoon/evening** l'après-midi/le soir; **at four o'clock in the afternoon** à quatre heures de l'après-midi; **the baby usually goes for a sleep in the afternoon** d'habitude le bébé dort (dans) *ou* pendant l'après-midi; **in spring/summer/ autumn/winter** au printemps/en été/en automne/en hiver; **in (the month of) April** au mois d'avril, en avril; **in the future** à l'avenir; **never in my life have I met ...** jamais de ma vie je n'ai rencontré ...; **in my time** de mon temps; **he's in his sixties** il a la soixantaine; **to do sth in three hours** (*within*) faire qch en trois heures; **he'll be here in three hours** il sera là dans trois heures; **in a little while** dans un petit moment; **I haven't seen you in years** je ne t'ai pas vu depuis des années, ça fait des années que je ne t'ai pas vu

(f) (*introducing a gerund*) en; **in crossing the river** en traversant la rivière; **we had no problem/difficulty in doing it** nous n'avons eu aucun problème/aucune difficulté à le faire

(g) (*of condition, state*) **in good health** en bonne santé; **in a good mood** de bonne humeur

(h) (*clothed in, surrounded by*) **in his shirt** en chemise; **in slippers** en pantoufles; **dressed in white** habillé de *ou* en blanc; **the man in black** l'homme en noir; **wrapped in paper** enveloppé de papier; *Culin* **beef in a red wine sauce** bœuf avec une *ou* accompagné d'une sauce au vin rouge; **fish in breadcrumbs** poisson pané

(i) (*of weather, light*) **to go out in the rain/snow** sortir par la pluie/la neige; **in this warm weather** par ce temps chaud; **to work in the rain** travailler sous la pluie; **in the sun** au soleil; **in the dark** dans l'obscurité

(j) (*engaged in*) **in politics** en politique; **to be in politics** être dans la politique; **killed in action** tué au combat; **in the navy** dans la marine; **she's been in a lot of films** elle a joué dans beaucoup de films; **he wasn't in that race** il n'a pas pris part à cette course

(k) (*due to*) dans; **in their hurry/panic** dans leur hâte/ panique; **the fence blew down in the storm** la barrière est tombée pendant la tempête

(l) (*of manner*) **in a gentle voice** d'une voix douce; **in a businesslike manner** d'une façon professionnelle; **in the French style** à la française; **to be in fashion** être à la mode

(m) (*of medium*) **to write in French** écrire en français; **in writing** par écrit; **to talk in whispers** parler en chuchotant; **they were paid in gold/cash** ils étaient payés en or/liquide

(n) (*of arrangement*) **to stand in a circle** se tenir en cercle; **in alphabetical order** par ordre alphabétique; **line up in twos** mettez-vous par deux

(o) (*of form*) **I've nothing in your size** je n'ai rien à *ou* dans votre taille; **do you have it in a 5?** est-ce que vous l'auriez dans le 39?; **in the form of a pill** sous forme de pilule; **she was curled up in a ball** elle était roulée en boule; **do you have it in red/silk?** est-ce que vous l'avez en rouge/ soie?

(p) (*of degree, extent*) **in large quantities** en grandes quantités; **in part** en partie; **in places** par endroits

(q) (*of purpose*) **in reply to ...** en réponse à ...; **in honour of ...** en l'honneur de ...; **in search of ...** à la recherche de ...; **in the cause of humanity** pour la cause de l'humanité

(r) (*with reflexive pronoun*) **this product is not a poison in itself** ce produit n'est pas un poison en soi

(s) (*of character, ability*) **I didn't think she had it in her** je ne l'en croyais pas capable; **he had it in him to be cruel** il était capable de cruauté; **it's not in her nature to be cruel** ce n'est pas dans sa nature d'être cruelle

(t) *Mus* en; **symphony in B minor** symphonie en si mineur

2 *conj* **in that** parce que, puisque, vu que; **in so far as** dans la mesure où

3 *adv* **(a)** (*inside building, room, boundary etc*) (*at home*) à la maison, chez soi; (*in one's office etc*) dans son bureau *etc*; **is he in?** est-ce qu'il est là?; **is your mother in?** est-ce que votre mère est à la maison?; **we've got the builders in** nous avons des ouvriers à la maison; *F* **what's he in for?** (*in prison*) pourquoi est-ce qu'il fait de la tôle?; (*in hospital*) pourquoi est-ce qu'il est à l'hôpital?; *Agr* **the harvest is in** la moisson est rentrée; **to be in** (*of bus, plane etc*) être arrivé; **the train is in** le train est en gare *ou* est arrivé; *Tennis* **the ball is in** la balle est bonne

(b) (*indoors, inside*) à l'intérieur, dedans; **in with you!** (*come in*) allons, rentrez!; (*go in*) allez-y!

(c) (*in a situation*) **the Liberals were in** (*in power*) le parti libéral était au pouvoir; **stripes are in this year** (*in fashion*) les rayures sont à la mode cette année; *F* **to be (well) in with sb** (*in favour*) être en bons termes avec qn, être dans les petits papiers de qn; **my luck is in** je suis en veine; *Cr* **to be in** battre la balle, *F* être à la batte

(d) (*phrases*) **I'm in for a thousand pounds** (*have invested etc*) j'ai engagé mille livres; **we're in for a storm** nous aurons sûrement de l'orage; **he's in for a surprise** il va être surpris, il va avoir une surprise; *F* **he's in for it** qu'est-ce qu'il va prendre!; *F* **to have it in for sb** avoir une dent contre qn; **to be in at the start/finish of sth** assister au début/à la fin de qch; **to be in on a secret** être dans le secret; **I wasn't in on it** je n'étais pas dans le coup; **to go in and out** entrer et sortir; **she and I were always in and out of each other's house** nous étions tout le temps fourrées l'une chez l'autre; **to be all in** (*exhausted*) être complètement crevé

4 *adj* **(a)** (*fashionable*) **it's the in thing these days** c'est la mode aujourd'hui; **the in people** *or* **crowd** les gens à la mode *ou F* dans le coup

(b) (*exclusive*) **an in joke** une plaisanterie de coterie

5 *n* **(a)** *F* **to know the ins and outs of a matter** connaître une affaire dans tous ses détails

(b) *US F* (*influence*) **to have an in** avoir de l'influence; **he has an in with the senator** il a ses entrées chez le sénateur

(c) (*where film clip begins*) entrée *f*

inability [ɪnəˈbɪlɪtɪ] *n* incapacité *f* (**to do sth** de faire qch); (*powerlessness*) impuissance *f* (**to do sth** à faire qch)

inaccessibility [ɪnæksesɪˈbɪlɪtɪ] *n* inaccessibilité *f*

inaccessible [ɪnækˈsesɪb(ə)l] *adj* (*place, poetry, person*) inaccessible (**to** à); **senior civil servants are i. to the public** le public n'a pas accès auprès des hauts fonctionnaires

inaccuracy [ɪnˈækjʊrəsɪ] *n* (*of rifle, storyteller*) imprécision *f*, manque *m* de précision; (*of report, account*) inexactitude *f*, manque de précision; (*of translation*) infidélité *f*; **full of inaccuracies** (*work*) plein d'inexactitudes

inaccurate [ɪnˈækjʊrət] *adj* (*calculation, idea*) inexact; (*account, translation*) inexact, infidèle

inaccurately [ɪnˈækjʊrətlɪ] *adv* (*to calculate, judge, quote, translate etc*) inexactement, de façon inexacte

inaction [ɪnˈækʃən] *n* inaction *f*

inactive [ɪnˈæktɪv] *adj* (*person, volcano*) inactif; (*mind*) inerte

inactivity [ɪnækˈtɪvɪtɪ] *n* inactivité *f*

inadequacy [ɪnˈædɪkwəsɪ] *n* (*of income*) insuffisance *f*; (*of system etc*) imperfection *f*; *Psy* (*of person*) complexe *m* d'infériorité; *Fml* **because of his i. to the task** en raison de son incapacité à faire ce travail

inadequate [ɪnˈædɪkwət] *adj* (*not enough*) (*funds, salary, preparations, ventilation etc*) insuffisant; (*unsuitable*) (*diet, precautions*) inadéquat; **that is an i. explanation of his behaviour** cela ne suffit pas à justifier son comportement; **to be i.** (*of thing*) être insuffisant (**for** pour); **she makes me feel i.** elle me donne des complexes; **I feel so i. in a situation like this** dans une situation comme celle-ci je me sens tellement peu à la hauteur

inadequately [ɪnˈædɪkwətlɪ] *adv* (*ventilated, informed, supplied*) insuffisamment; **they were i. equipped for climbing a mountain** ils n'avaient pas l'équipement adéquat pour faire une ascension; **the vehicle was felt to perform i. on rough terrain** la performance du véhicule sur terrain accidenté a été jugée insuffisante

inadmissible [ɪnədˈmɪsɪb(ə)l] *adj* (*theory, claim*) inadmissible; *Jur* (*evidence*) irrecevable

inadvertence [ɪnədˈvɜːtəns] *n* inattention *f*; **through i.** par inadvertance

inadvertent [ɪnədˈvɜːtənt] *adj* (*mistake etc*) involontaire

inadvertently [ɪnədˈvɜːtəntlɪ] *adv* par inadvertance

inadvisability [ɪnədvaɪzəˈbɪlɪtɪ] *n* (*of action*) imprudence *f*

inadvisable [ɪnədˈvaɪzəb(ə)l] *adj* imprudent, déconseillé

inalienable [ɪnˈeɪlɪənəb(ə)l] *adj* (*property, right*) inaliénable

inane [ɪˈneɪn] *adj* (*person, action*) inepte, stupide; (*smile*) bête, niais; (*answer*) inepte, saugrenu; **i. remark** ineptie *f*

inanely [ɪˈneɪnlɪ] *adv* bêtement, stupidement

inanimate [ɪn'ænɪmət] *adj* (*body, style etc*) inanimé, sans vie
inanition [ɪnə'nɪʃən] *n Med* inanition *f*
inanity [ɪ'nænɪtɪ] *n* (*of remark*) inanité *f*; (*of person*) stupidité *f*
inapplicable [ɪn'æplɪkəb(ə)l] *adj* inapplicable (**to** à); **'delete where i.'** 'rayez la mention inutile'
inappropriate [ɪnə'prəʊprɪət] *adj* (*behaviour, music*) peu approprié, qui ne convient pas (**to** à); (*word*) impropre; (*speech, joke, remark*) déplacé; **his clothes were i. to the climate** ses vêtements n'étaient guère appropriés au climat; **her dress was i. to this formal occasion** sa robe convenait mal au caractère officiel de l'occasion
inappropriately [ɪnə'prəʊprɪətlɪ] *adv* (*to behave*) de façon inconvenante; **to be i. dressed** ne pas porter des vêtements appropriés
inapt [ɪn'æpt] *adj* (*inappropriate*) peu approprié (**to** à)
inaptitude [ɪn'æptɪtju:d] *n* (*inability*) incapacité *f*
inarticulate [ɪnɑ:'tɪkjʊlɪt] *adj* (**a**) (*person*) qui manque de facilité à s'exprimer; (*sound*) inarticulé; *esp Lit* (*desire*) inexprimé; **he's so i.** il a tellement de mal à s'exprimer; **i. with rage** bégayant de colère; **I was seized by an i. rage** j'ai été pris d'une rage telle que je pouvais à peine m'exprimer (**b**) *Biol* (*without joints*) inarticulé
inartistic [ɪnɑ:'tɪstɪk] *adj* (*production of play, arrangement of flowers etc*) peu artistique; (*person*) dépourvu de sens artistique; **I'm fairly i.** je n'ai pas beaucoup de sens artistique
inasmuch [ɪnəz'mʌtʃ] *conj Fml* **i. as** dans la mesure où
inattention [ɪnə'tenʃən] *n* inattention *f*, manque *m* d'attention; **i. to detail** inattention aux *ou* manque d'attention pour les détails
inattentive [ɪnə'tentɪv] *adj* (*audience, child at school*) inattentif, distrait; (*husband, waiter etc*) peu attentionné, peu prévenant (**to, towards sb** à l'égard de qn), inattentif (**to sb's needs** aux besoins de qn); **to be i. to** (*detail, consequences of one's action, comfort of guests*) ne pas faire attention à
inattentively [ɪnə'tentɪvlɪ] *adv* sans prêter attention, distraitement
inaudible [ɪn'ɔ:dɪb(ə)l] *adj* inaudible; (*sound*) imperceptible, inaudible
inaudibly [ɪn'ɔ:dɪblɪ] *adv* de manière inaudible
inaugural [ɪ'nɔ:gjʊrəl] **1** *adj* (*meeting*) inaugural, -aux; (*speech*) inaugural, d'inauguration **2** *n US* (*speech*) discours *m* inaugural *ou* d'inauguration
inaugurate [ɪ'nɔ:gjʊreɪt] *vt* (*building*) inaugurer; (*conference, exhibition*) ouvrir; *Fig* (*new era*) inaugurer, commencer; (*new system, tradition etc*) instaurer; (*head of state*) faire prêter serment à (*lors de la prise de fonctions*); **he will be inaugurated today** il prêtera serment aujourd'hui
inauguration [ɪnɔ:gjʊ'reɪʃən] *n* (*of building etc*) inauguration *f*; (*of new system etc*) instauration *f*; *US* **I. Day** = jour *m* où le président prend ses fonctions; **i. ceremony** (*for building, bridge etc*) cérémonie *f* d'inauguration
inauspicious [ɪnɔ:'spɪʃəs] *adj* (*circumstances*) défavorable; (*moment*) malencontreux; **an i. sign** un mauvais signe; **the project got off to an i. start** le projet a mal commencé
inauspiciously [ɪnɔ:'spɪʃəslɪ] *adv* de façon peu propice
in-between **1** *adj* intermédiaire, au milieu **2** *n* **but what happens if you're an i.?** et qu'est-ce qu'on fait si on est entre les deux?
inborn ['ɪn'bɔ:n] *adj* (*instinct, merit*) inné, naturel; *Med* congénital, -aux
inbound ['ɪnbaʊnd] *adj* **i. and outbound telemarketing** télémercatique *f* active et passive; **i. and outbound telesales** téléventes *fpl* actives et passives; **i. tourism** tourisme *m* récepteur, tourisme réceptif; **i. travel** tourisme *m* récepteur
inbred ['ɪn'bred] *adj* (**a**) (*dog, horse etc*) consanguin; **they are so i. that ...** la consanguinité chez eux est telle que ... (**b**) (*innate*) inné
inbreed ['ɪn'bri:d] *vi* (*pt, pp* **inbred**) se reproduire entre eux
inbreeding ['ɪn'bri:dɪŋ] *n* (*of animals*) accouplement *m* d'animaux consanguins; (*of people*) unions *fpl* consanguines
in-built *adj* = **built-in**
Inc [ɪŋk] *US Com* (*abbr* **Incorporated**) = SARL
Inca ['ɪŋkə] **1** *n* Inca *mf* **2** *adj* inca *inv*
incalculable [ɪn'kælkjʊləb(ə)l] *adj* (*consequences, harm*) incalculable; (*loss, help*) inestimable
incalculably [ɪn'kælkjʊləblɪ] *adv* de façon inestimable
in camera *adv, adj Jur* à huis clos
incandescence [ɪnkæn'desəns] *n* incandescence *f*
incandescent [ɪnkæn'desənt] *adj* incandescent; (*light, light bulb etc*) à incandescence
incantation [ɪnkæn'teɪʃən] *n* incantation *f*
incapability [ɪnkeɪpə'bɪlɪtɪ] *n* incapacité *f*
incapable [ɪn'keɪpəb(ə)l] *adj* (*unable*) incapable (**of** de); **I'm not i.!** je ne suis pas impotent!; **i. of movement** (*of person*) incapable de bouger; *Fml* **the essay is i. of improvement** (*cannot be improved upon*) cette dissertation ne peut pas être améliorée, tant elle est parfaite; *Jur* **declared i. of managing his own affairs** en état d'incapacité légale; *Jur* **i. of succeeding to an estate** incapable de prendre la succession d'un domaine
incapacitate [ɪnkə'pæsɪteɪt] *vt* (**a**) rendre incapable (**for work** de travailler); (*vehicle*) mettre hors d'état de marche; **the alcohol had temporarily incapacitated him** l'alcool avait temporairement inhibé ses facultés (**b**) *Jur* frapper d'incapacité
incapacity [ɪnkə'pæsɪtɪ] *n* (**a**) incapacité *f*, incompétence *f* (**b**) *Jur* incapacité *f*
in-car *adj Aut* **i. listening** écoute *f* de la radio en voiture; **i. stereo** système *m* autoradio
incarcerate [ɪn'kɑ:səreɪt] *vt Fml* incarcérer
incarceration [ɪnkɑ:sə'reɪʃən] *n Fml* incarcération *f*, emprisonnement *m*
incarnate¹ [ɪn'kɑ:neɪt] *adj* incarné; **the devil i.** le diable incarné; **perfection/wisdom i.** la perfection/la sagesse incarnée
incarnate² ['ɪnkɑ:neɪt] *vt* incarner
incarnation [ɪnkɑ:'neɪʃən] *n Rel, Fig* (*of Christ, an idea*) incarnation *f*; **to be the i. of wisdom** (*of person*) être l'incarnation de la sagesse; **in a previous i.** dans une vie antérieure; *Fig* **in a previous i. he was an MP** à une époque il était député
incautious [ɪn'kɔ:ʃəs] *adj* imprudent; (*remark etc*) inconsidéré; **in an i. moment** dans un moment d'inattention
incautiously [ɪn'kɔ:ʃəslɪ] *adv* imprudemment
incendiary [ɪn'sendɪərɪ] **1** *adj* (*bomb, device, Fig remarks, speech*) incendiaire **2** *n* (**a**) (*arsonist*) incendiaire *mf*; *Fig* (*agitator*) trublion *m*, agitateur, -trice (**b**) (*bomb*) bombe *f* incendiaire
incense¹ ['ɪnsens] *n* encens *m*; **i. bearer** thuriféraire *m*; **i. burner** encensoir *m*; **i. stick** bâton *m* d'encens
incense² [ɪn'sens] *vt* rendre furieux
incensed [ɪn'senst] *adj* furieux; **to become** *or* **get i.** être furieux (**with** contre, **about** au sujet de)
incentive [ɪn'sentɪv] *n* encouragement *m*; *Com, Ind* (*payment*) prime *f*; *Mktg* stimulation *f*, *F* stim *f*; (*reduction, freebie*) stimulant *m*, stimulateur *m*; **there is no i. for students here to work hard** il n'y a rien ici qui incite *ou* encourage les étudiants à travailler dur; **i. to buy** incitation *f ou* stimulation *f* à l'achat; **i. bonus** prime d'encouragement; **i. company** (*in tourism*) agence *f* spécialisée dans le voyage de stimulation; **i. fare** tarif *m* de stimulation; **i. marketing** mercatique *f* de stimulation; *Com, Ind* **i. pay** primes *fpl* de rendement; **i. scheme** (*for buyers*) programme *m* de stimulation; (*for workers*) système *m* de primes; **i. tourism** tourisme *m* de stimulation; **i. travel** voyages *mpl* de motivation; **i. trip** voyage *m* de stimulation
inception [ɪn'sepʃən] *n Fml* (*of company, scheme etc*) commencement *m*, début *m*
incessant [ɪn'sesənt] *adj* (*noise*) incessant, continuel; (*worry*) éternel
incessantly [ɪn'sesəntlɪ] *adv* sans cesse, sans relâche, continuellement
incest ['ɪnsest] *n* inceste *m*
incestuous [ɪn'sestjʊəs] *adj* incestueux; *Fig* **the i. world of writers** le monde très fermé *ou* en vase clos des écrivains
inch [ɪntʃ] *n* (*measurement*) pouce *m* (= 2,54 cm); **he's every i. a** *or* **the soldier** il a tout du militaire; **she won't give (way) an i.** elle ne reculera pas d'une semelle; **by inches, i. by i.** peu à peu, petit à petit; **I know every i. of the neighbourhood** je connais le quartier comme ma poche; **give her an i. and she'll take a mile** tu lui en donnes jusqu'au coude, elle en demande long comme le bras; **to be within an i. of doing** être à deux doigts de faire; **to beat sb to within an i. of their life** battre qn en le laissant pour mort; **I'll beat him to within an i. of his life!** je vais l'étrangler!
▶ **inch along, inch forward** **1** *vi* avancer tout doucement **2** *vtsep* (*sth*) faire avancer tout doucement; **she inched her way along the window ledge** elle se déplaça tout doucement le long du rebord de la fenêtre
incidence ['ɪnsɪdəns] *n* (**a**) (*frequency*) (*of thefts etc*) fréquence *f*; (*of disease*) incidence *f*; **the i. of cancer has increased** les cas de cancer se sont multipliés (**b**) *Opt, Electron, Av etc* **angle of i.** angle *m* d'incidence
incident¹ ['ɪnsɪdənt] *n* incident *m*; **a journey full of incident(s)** un voyage mouvementé
incident² *adj* (**a**) *Opt, Electron* (*light beam etc*) incident (**b**) *Fml* (*related*) inhérent (**to** à)
incidental [ɪnsɪ'dent(ə)l] **1** *adj* (*minor*) (*event, circumstance,*

effect) secondaire; (*extra, supplementary*) (*advantage, benefit*) supplémentaire; **to be i. to sth** être occasionné par *ou* découler de qch; **the disruption i. to the reorganization** le désordre occasionné par la restructuration; **i. costs** frais *mpl* accessoires; **i. expenses** faux *ou* menus frais *mpl*, frais accessoires; **i. music** (*for film*) musique *f* de film; (*for play*) musique de scène **2** *n* détail *m*; **incidentals** (*expenses*) faux frais *mpl*

incidentally [ɪnsɪ'dentəlɪ] *adv* **(a)** (*by the way*) soit dit en passant *ou* entre parenthèses; **i., how is he?** au fait, comment va-t-il? **(b)** (*accidentally, secondarily*) incidemment

incinerate [ɪn'sɪnəreɪt] *vt* incinérer

incineration [ɪnsɪnə'reɪʃən] *n* incinération *f*

incinerator [ɪn'sɪnəreɪtər] *n Ind etc* incinérateur *m*; (*in crematorium*) four *m* crématoire

incipient [ɪn'sɪpɪənt] *adj* naissant, dans ses débuts; **i. madness** folie naissante

incise [ɪn'saɪz] *vt Art etc* (*inscription etc*) graver

incision [ɪn'sɪʒən] *n* incision *f*; **to make an i. in sth** inciser qch, pratiquer une incision dans qch

incisive [ɪn'saɪsɪv] *adj* (*remark, style*) incisif; (*mind*) pénétrant

incisively [ɪn'saɪsɪvlɪ] *adv* de façon incisive

incisor [ɪn'saɪzər] *n Anat* incisive *f*

incite [ɪn'saɪt] *vt* inciter (**to sth** à qch; **to do sth** à faire qch); **to i. racial hatred** inciter à la haine raciale; **to i. sb to crime/violence** inciter *ou* pousser qn au crime/à la violence

incitement [ɪn'saɪtmənt] *n* (*of people, actions*) incitation *f*, encouragement *m* (**to sth** à qch)

incivility [ɪnsɪ'vɪlɪtɪ] *n Fml* incivilité *f*

incl **(a)** (*abbr* **inclusive**) inclus; **from 14th-23rd November i.** du 14 au 23 novembre inclus; **i. of gas and electricity** gas et électricité compris **(b)** (*abbr* **including**) avec

inclemency [ɪn'klemənsɪ] *n Fml* inclémence *f*, rigueur *f*

inclement [ɪn'klemənt] *adj Fml* (*weather*) inclément

inclination [ɪnklɪ'neɪʃən] *n* **(a)** (*desire*) envie *f* (**for sth** de qch; **to do** de faire); **to have an i. for sth** avoir un penchant pour qch; **she had no i. to help him** elle n'avait pas du tout envie de l'aider; **to have lost all i. for sth** n'avoir plus envie de qch; **to show little i. to do sth** se montrer peu enclin à faire qch; **to follow one's inclinations** faire ce à quoi on est naturellement enclin

(b) (*tendency*) tendance *f* (**towards sth** à qch; **to do** à faire); **my i. would be to …** j'aurais tendance à …, je serais porté à …; **my i. would be to say yes, but …** je serais enclin à dire oui, mais …; **she is by i. a cautious person** c'est quelqu'un de très prudent par nature

(c) (*angle*) (*of head, body*) inclination *f*; *Math* (*of plane*) inclinaison *f*

incline¹ ['ɪnklaɪn] *n* pente *f*

incline² [ɪn'klaɪn] **1** *vt* **(a)** (*motivate, cause*) inciter; **this inclines me to believe them** ceci me porte *ou* m'encourage à les croire; **her remarks don't i. me to be sympathetic** ses remarques ne m'incitent pas à être compréhensif **(b)** (*head*) incliner, pencher **2** *vi* **(a)** (*of person*) avoir un penchant (**to sth** pour qch, **to do** à faire), avoir tendance (**to do** à faire); **to i. to the belief that …** être porté *ou* avoir tendance à croire que … **(b)** (*of thing*) s'incliner, pencher (**to** à; **towards** vers)

inclined [ɪn'klaɪnd] *adj* **(a)** (*person*) (*temporarily*) disposé (**to** à); (*permanently*) enclin (**to** à); **to feel** *or* **be i. to do sth** (*tend to*) avoir tendance à faire qch; (*have desire to*) avoir envie de faire qch; **I am i. to think that he's right** je suis porté *ou* j'ai tendance à croire qu'il a raison; **to be well i. towards sb** être bien disposé envers qn; **if ever you should feel so i.** si jamais l'envie vous en prenait; **prices are i. to fall** les prix ont tendance à baisser; **he's i. to put on weight** il a tendance à grossir; **i. to laziness** *or* **to be lazy** enclin à la paresse; **I'm not musically i.** (*I don't like music*) je ne suis pas très porté sur la musique; (*I have no talent*) je n'ai pas de talent musical; **if you're that way i.** (*if you want to*) si cela vous dit; *F* **he's the other way i.** (*in his sexual orientation*) il est de l'autre bord

(b) *Math* (*plane*) incliné

include [ɪn'klu:d] *vt* inclure, comprendre; **the speech included several references to Soviet history** le discours comportait plusieurs références à l'histoire de l'Union Soviétique; **the committee includes politicians from all parties** le comité comprend des politiciens de tous les partis; **men above seventy are not included** les hommes de plus de soixante-dix ans ne sont pas compris; **the price does not i. accommodation** le prix ne comprend pas l'hébergement; **there are five of us, not including the children** nous sommes cinq, sans compter les enfants; **including me** moi y compris; **if you i. Christmas Day** en comptant le jour de Noël; **up to and including …** jusqu'à … inclus; **to i. sb among one's friends** compter qn parmi *ou* au nombre de ses amis

▶ **include out** *vtsep F Hum* **i. me out** ne compte pas sur moi

included [ɪn'klu:dɪd] *adj* (y) compris; **all his property was sold, his house i.** tous ses biens furent vendus, y compris sa maison; **i. in the price are two excursions** deux excursions sont comprises dans le prix; **service i.** (*on bill*) service compris; **batteries not i.** les piles ne sont pas comprises

inclusion [ɪn'klu:ʒən] *n* inclusion *f*

inclusive [ɪn'klu:sɪv] *adj* **five i. of the driver** cinq y compris le chauffeur; **from the 4th to the 12th February i.** du 4 au 12 février inclusivement; **i. of costs** frais inclus; **i. of tax** toutes taxes comprises, TTC; **i. terms** (*at hotel etc*) (prix *m*) tout compris; **i. tour** voyage *m* organisé *ou* à forfait, inclusive tour *m*

inclusively [ɪn'klu:sɪvlɪ] *adv* inclusivement

incognito [ɪnkɒg'ni:təʊ] **1** *adj, adv* **to be/travel i.** être/voyager incognito **2** *n* (*name, disguise*) incognito *m*; **to travel under an i.** voyager incognito

incoherence [ɪnkəʊ'hɪərəns] *n* incohérence *f*

incoherent [ɪnkəʊ'hɪərənt] *adj* (*speech, reasoning*) incohérent; (*style*) décousu; **to be i.** (*of person*) tenir des propos incohérents

incoherently [ɪnkəʊ'hɪərəntlɪ] *adv* d'une manière incohérente

incombustible [ɪnkəm'bʌstɪb(ə)l] *adj* incombustible

income ['ɪnkəm] *n* **(a)** revenu *m*, revenus *mpl*; **source of i.** source *f* de revenu; **their combined i.** leurs revenus additionnés; **i. from investments** revenu(s) provenant de placements; **to have a private i. of £15 000 a year** avoir quinze mille livres de rente; **to be on a low/high i.** avoir un faible revenu/un revenu élevé **(b)** *Com* (*receipts*) recettes *fpl*, revenus *mpl*, rentrées *fpl*; *Acct* **i. account** compte *m* de produits; *Acct* **i. from operations** produits *mpl* de gestion courante, produits d'exploitation

income bracket, income group *n* tranche *f* de salaire *ou* de revenus

incomer ['ɪnkʌmər] *n* nouvel arrivant, nouvelle arrivante

incomes policy *n Pol* politique *f* des revenus

income statement *n Am Acct* compte *m* de résultat

income support *n Br* aide *f* sociale; **to be on i.** recevoir une aide sociale

income tax *n* impôt *m* sur le revenu; **i. inspector** inspecteur *m* des impôts; **i. return** déclaration *f* de revenu *ou* d'impôts

incoming ['ɪnkʌmɪŋ] **1** *adj* (*government*) nouveau; (*plane, missile*) entrant; *Tel* **i. call** appel *m* de l'extérieur; **this telephone takes i. calls only** ce téléphone ne permet que de recevoir des appels; **i. fax** télécopie *f* en entrée; **i. mail** courrier *m* à l'arrivée; **i. message** message *m* entrant; **the i. president** le président élu; **i. tide** marée montante; **i. tour operator** voyagiste *m* de réceptif **2** *npl Com, Fin* **incomings** recettes *fpl*, revenus *mpl*, rentrées *fpl*

incommensurable [ɪnkə'menʃərəb(ə)l] *adj* incommensurable (**with** avec); *Math* (*number*) irrationnel

incommensurate [ɪnkə'menʃərət] *adj* pas en rapport, pas en proportion (**with** avec)

incommode [ɪnkə'məʊd] *vt Fml* incommoder, déranger

incommodious [ɪnkə'məʊdɪəs] *adj Fml* incommode

incommunicado [ɪnkəmju:nɪ'kɑ:dəʊ] *adv* **to be held i.** être tenu au secret

incomparable [ɪn'kɒmpərəb(ə)l] *adj* incomparable, sans pareil

incomparably [ɪn'kɒmpərəblɪ] *adv* incomparablement; **i. beautiful** d'une beauté incomparable

incompatibility [ɪnkəmpætɪ'bɪlɪtɪ] *n* (*of people, theories, medication etc*) incompatibilité *f* (**with** avec; **between** entre)

incompatible [ɪnkəm'pætɪb(ə)l] *adj* incompatible (**with** avec)

incompetence [ɪn'kɒmpɪtəns] *n also Jur* incompétence *f*

incompetent [ɪn'kɒmpɪtənt] **1** *adj* **(a)** (*person*) incompétent, incapable **(b)** *Jur* (*judge, court*) (*to hear case, carry out act*) incompétent; **I am i. to act** je n'ai pas qualité pour agir **2** *n* incompétent, -ente

incomplete [ɪnkəm'pli:t] *adj* (*not complete*) incomplet; (*not finished*) inachevé

incompletely [ɪnkəm'pli:tlɪ] *adv* incomplètement

incompleteness [ɪnkəm'pli:tnɪs] *n* (*of novel, painting etc*) inachèvement *m*; (*of collection of works*) état *m* incomplet

incomprehensible [ɪnkɒmprɪ'hensɪb(ə)l] *adj* (*situation, speech, person*) incompréhensible; (*writing*) indéchiffrable

incomprehensibly [ɪnkɒmprɪ'hensɪblɪ] *adv* de manière incompréhensible

incomprehension [ɪnkɒmprɪ'henʃən] *n* incompréhension *f*

inconceivable [ɪnkən'si:vəb(ə)l] *adj* inconcevable

inconceivably [ɪnkən'si:vəblɪ] *adv* inconcevablement

inconclusive [ɪnkən'klu:sɪv] *adj* (*reasoning, evidence*) peu concluant; **it was all very i.** cela n'a donné aucun résultat

inconclusively [ɪnkən'klu:sɪvlɪ] *adv* d'une manière peu concluante

incongruity [ɪnkɒŋ'gruːɪtɪ] *n* incongruité *f*

incongruous [ɪn'kɒŋgrʊəs] *adj* (*behaviour, remark, building*) incongru; (*combination*) bizarre; **the bright red is very i. in this room** le rouge vif détonne fortement dans cette pièce; **they are such an i. couple** ils sont tellement bizarrement assortis

incongruously [ɪn'kɒŋgrʊəslɪ] *adv* de manière incongrue, incongrûment

inconsequence [ɪn'kɒnsɪkwəns] *n* inconséquence *f*

inconsequent [ɪn'kɒnsɪkwənt] *adj* = **inconsequential**

inconsequential [ɪnkɒnsɪ'kwenʃəl] *adj* (**a**) (*unimportant*) (*matter, remarks*) sans importance (**b**) (*not following*) (*reasoning, ideas*) décousu

inconsiderate [ɪnkən'sɪdərɪt] *adj* (*person*) qui manque d'égards (pour les autres); (*remark, action*) déplacé; **it was most i. of you to do that** tu n'as guère fait preuve de considération en faisant cela; **don't be so i.** pense un peu aux autres

inconsiderately [ɪnkən'sɪdərətlɪ] *adv* **to behave i. to sb** manquer d'égards *ou* de considération envers qn; **he had i. locked the door** il avait fermé la porte à clef sans se soucier des autres

inconsistency [ɪnkən'sɪstənsɪ] *n* (**a**) (*lack of logicality*) (*of person, argument*) incohérence *f* (**b**) (*inconsistent argument, action*) incohérence *f*; **his book is full of inconsistencies** son livre est bourré d'incohérences (**c**) (*uneven quality*) (*of artist's work etc*) irregularité *f*, manque *m* de régularité

inconsistent [ɪnkən'sɪstənt] *adj* (**a**) (*remark*) en contradiction, contradictoire (**with** avec); **his words are i. with his conduct** ce qu'il dit est en contradiction *ou* ne cadre pas avec ce qu'il fait (**b**) (*person*) incohérent; **you're being i.** (*in saying that*) tu te contredis; (*in doing that*) tu n'es pas cohérent; **they're i. in what they say** leurs dires sont contradictoires (**c**) (*irregular*) (*work*) irrégulier; **his films are very i. in quality** la qualité de ses films est très irrégulière

inconsistently [ɪnkən'sɪstəntlɪ] *adv* (*to behave*) de façon incohérente; (*to assert*) de façon contradictoire

inconsolable [ɪnkən'səʊləb(ə)l] *adj* inconsolable

inconspicously [ɪnkən'spɪkjʊəslɪ] *adv* de manière discrète

inconspicuous [ɪnkən'spɪkjʊəs] *adj* (*person*) discret, -ète, qui passe inaperçu; (*error, spot*) qui passe inaperçu; **to remain i.** rester dans l'ombre; **I tried to look i.** j'ai essayé de me faire discret

inconstancy [ɪn'kɒnstənsɪ] *n* (*of person, character*) inconstance *f*; (*of weather etc*) instabilité *f*, caractère *m* changeant

inconstant [ɪn'kɒnstənt] *adj* (*person, character*) inconstant, volage

incontestable [ɪnkən'testəb(ə)l] *adj* incontestable, indéniable

incontestably [ɪnkən'testəblɪ] *adv* incontestablement

incontinence [ɪn'kɒntɪnəns] *n Med* incontinence *f*; **i. pads** couches *fpl* pour adultes

incontinent [ɪn'kɒntɪnənt] *adj Med* incontinent

incontrovertible [ɪnkɒntrə'vɜːtɪb(ə)l] *adj* (*truth*) incontestable; (*evidence*) irrécusable; (*argument*) irréfutable

inconvenience[1] [ɪnkən'viːnjəns] *n* dérangement *m*; (*more serious*) désagrément *m*; **to cause i. to sb, to be an i. to sb** incommoder qn, déranger qn; **I'm putting you to a great deal of i.** je vous donne beaucoup d'embarras; **without the slightest i.** sans le moindre dérangement; **we apologize for any i.** nous vous prions de nous excuser pour tout désagrément éventuel; **the i. of living so far from town** les inconvénients qu'il y a à vivre si loin de la ville

inconvenience[2] *vt* déranger, causer du dérangement à

inconvenient [ɪnkən'viːnjənt] *adj* (*time*) inopportun; (*visitor*) gênant; (*house*) incommode, malcommode; **this isn't an i. time, is it?** tu es sûr que je ne te dérange pas?; **it's a bit i. just now, could you call back later?** je n'ai pas vraiment le temps tout de suite, tu pourrais me rappeler plus tard?; **if it is not i. to you** si cela ne vous gêne *ou* dérange pas; **Friday's a bit i.** vendredi ne me convient pas tellement; **it's very i. living so far from town** c'est très incommode d'habiter aussi loin de la ville; **the house is very i. for the shops** la maison est mal située par rapport aux commerces

inconveniently [ɪnkən'viːnjəntlɪ] *adv* (*to arrive*) à un moment inopportun; **the announcement was i. timed** le moment de l'annonce a été mal choisi; **i. located** mal situé

inconvertible [ɪnkən'vɜːtɪb(ə)l] *adj Fin* inconvertible

incorporate [ɪn'kɔːpəreɪt] **1** *vt* (**a**) (*include, add*) inclure, incorporer (**with** à, avec; **in** dans); **to i. a paragraph in(to) a chapter** incorporer un paragraphe dans un chapitre; **her work incorporates all the latest discoveries** ses travaux incluent toutes les découvertes les plus récentes

(**b**) *Com* (*company*) constituer en société commerciale; (*banks*) réunir en société

(**c**) (*merge*) regrouper pour former un tout; **these organizations were incorporated into a national fire brigade** ces organismes ont été regroupés pour constituer une brigade nationale de pompiers

2 *vi* (**a**) s'incorporer

(**b**) *Com* se constituer en société commerciale

incorporated [ɪn'kɔːpəreɪtɪd] *adj US Com* **i. company** association *f* constituée en société commerciale; **Sanders I.** Sanders SARL

incorporation [ɪnkɔːpə'reɪʃən] *n* (**a**) *Com, Jur* (*of company*) constitution *f* en société commerciale (**b**) (*inclusion*) incorporation *f* (**with** à, avec; **in(to)** dans)

incorrect [ɪnkə'rekt] *adj* (**a**) (*statement, account etc*) inexact; (*figures*) faux, *f* fausse; (*translation*) incorrect (**b**) (*style, behaviour etc*) incorrect

incorrectly [ɪnkə'rektlɪ] *adv* (**a**) (*reported, stated*) inexactement; (*to speak*) incorrectement; (*invoiced*) indûment; **i. addressed** (*letter*) mal adressé (**b**) (*to behave etc*) incorrectement

incorrigible [ɪn'kɒrɪdʒɪb(ə)l] *adj* (*child, laziness etc*) incorrigible

incorruptible [ɪnkə'rʌptɪb(ə)l] *adj* (*metal, judge*) incorruptible

incoterms ['ɪnkəʊtɜːmz] *npl Com* termes *mpl* commerciaux, incoterms *mpl*

increase[1] ['ɪnkriːs] *n* (**a**) (*in price, takings, salary, speed etc*) augmentation *f*; (*in pain, population*) accroissement *m*; (*in zeal, attention*) renouvellement *m*; **i. in the cost of living** augmentation du coût de la vie; **sales have shown an i. over the last six months** les ventes ont progressé ces six derniers mois; **i. in value** (*of property etc*) plus-value *f*; **I've had an i. in salary** j'ai été augmenté; **to be on the i.** être en augmentation *ou* en hausse (**b**) *Knitting* augmentation *f*

increase[2] [ɪn'kriːs] **1** *vi* (*of prices, speed, unemployment etc*) augmenter; (*of noise, dissatisfaction*) grandir, s'agrandir; (*of pain, population*) s'accroître; **to i. in size** s'agrandir; **to i. in price** augmenter; **to i. in value** prendre de la valeur; **his paintings have increased in value fivefold** la valeur de ses tableaux a quintuplé; **to i. in volume** (*of substance*) augmenter de volume; **the volume of traffic increases every year** le volume de la circulation augmente chaque année

2 *vt* (**a**) (*speed, production, salaries*) augmenter; (*number, expenses*) grossir, augmenter; (*one's wealth*) accroître, augmenter; (*prices*) majorer, augmenter; (*distance*) allonger, augmenter; (*dissatisfaction*) accentuer, augmenter; **to i. sb's salary** augmenter (le salaire de) qn; **to i. the dose** (*of medicine*) augmenter la dose; **to i. one's efforts** redoubler d'efforts; **increased cost of living** augmentation *f* du coût de la vie; **to i. the size of sth** agrandir qch

(**b**) *Knitting* **i. two in the next row** augmenter de deux mailles au rang suivant

increasing [ɪn'kriːsɪŋ] *adj* (*numbers, use, difficulty*) croissant; **an i. number of people are opting for …** de plus en plus de gens choisissent …; *Fin* **i. rate** tarif *m* progressif

increasingly [ɪn'kriːsɪŋlɪ] *adv* (*difficult, big etc*) de plus en plus; **i., people are saying that …** de plus en plus, les gens disent que …

incredible [ɪn'kredɪb(ə)l] *adj* (**a**) (*unbelievable*) incroyable; **I find it i. that she didn't know** je n'arrive pas à croire qu'elle n'était pas au courant (**b**) *F* (*excellent*) incroyable, époustouflant

incredibly [ɪn'kredɪblɪ] *adv* incroyablement; **he's i. stupid** il est d'une sottise incroyable; **i., she agreed** elle a consenti, ce qui est incroyable

incredulity [ɪnkrɪ'djuːlɪtɪ] *n* incrédulité *f*

incredulous [ɪn'kredjʊləs] *adj* incrédule (**of** à l'égard de); (*smile*) d'incrédulité

incredulously [ɪn'kredjʊləslɪ] *adv* (*to look at sb*) d'un air incrédule; (*to say*) d'un ton incrédule

increment ['ɪnkrɪmənt] *n* augmentation *f*; **to rise in annual increments of £1,000** (*of salary*) augmenter de mille livres par an; **unearned i.** (*of land, shares*) plus-value *f*

incremental compiler [ɪnkrɪ'ment(ə)l] *n Comptr* compilateur *m* incrémentiel

incriminate [ɪn'krɪmɪneɪt] *vt* (*implicate*) incriminer, mettre en cause; **I don't want to i. myself** je ne veux rien dire qui me fasse apparaître comme coupable; **you've just incriminated yourself** vous venez de vous compromettre

incriminating [ɪn'krɪmɪneɪtɪŋ] *adj* (*circumstance, statement etc*) compromettant

incrimination [ɪnkrɪmɪ'neɪʃən] *n* mise *f* en cause, incrimination *f*

incriminatory [ɪn'krɪmɪnətərɪ] *adj* compromettant

incrustation [ɪnkrʌs'teɪʃən] *n* (*action*) entartrage *m*; (*deposit*) tartre *m*, dépôt *m* calcaire.

incubate ['ɪnkjʊbeɪt] **1** *vt* (*eggs*) couver, incuber **2** *vi* (*of eggs*) incuber; (*of disease*) couver

incubation [ɪnkjʊ'beɪʃən] *n* incubation *f*; *Med* **i. period** (*for illness*) durée *f* d'incubation
incubator ['ɪnkjʊbeɪtər] *n* (*for eggs, bacteria*) incubateur *m*; (*for premature babies*) couveuse *f*
incubus ['ɪnkjʊbəs] *Myth* incube *m*; *Fig Lit* cauchemar *m*
in-cue *n TV, Rad* signal *m* de départ
inculcate ['ɪnkʌlkeɪt] *vt* inculquer; **to i. sth in sb, to i. sb with sth** inculquer qch à qn
inculcation [ɪnkʌl'keɪʃən] *n* inculcation *f*
incumbent[1] [ɪn'kʌmbənt] *n* **(a)** (*of administrative position*) titulaire *mf* **(b)** *Rel* bénéficiaire *m*, titulaire *m* (*d'une charge*)
incumbent[2] *adj* **(a)** (*necessary*) **to be i. on sb to do sth** incomber *ou* appartenir à qn de faire qch **(b)** (*official*) en place
incunabulum, *pl* **incunabula** [ɪnkju:'næbjʊləm, -jʊlə] *n* incunable *m*
incur [ɪn'kɜ:r] *vt* (**-rr-**) (*risk*) courir; (*blame, cost*) encourir; (*loss*) subir; (*sb's anger, hatred*) s'attirer; (*debts*) contracter
incurable [ɪn'kjʊərəb(ə)l] *adj* (*disease*) incurable, inguérissable; *Fig* (*optimist, bigot*) invétéré, incorrigible; **an i. romantic** un romantique incorrigible
incurably [ɪn'kjʊərəblɪ] *adv* **to be i. ill** avoir une maladie incurable; *Fig* **i. lazy/optimistic** d'une paresse/d'un optimisme incorrigible; **I'm i. romantic** je suis un romantique incorrigible
incurious [ɪn'kjʊərɪəs] *adj* sans curiosité
incursion [ɪn'kɜ:ʃən] *n* incursion *f* (**into** dans)
Ind (a) (*abbr* **Independent**) indépendant **(b)** *abbr* **Indiana**
indebted [ɪn'detɪd] *adj* **(a)** (*owing money*) endetté; **to be heavily i. to sb** devoir une forte somme à qn **(b)** *Fig* redevable (**to sb for sth** à qn de qch); **I am i. to Mr Martin for this information** c'est à M. Martin que je dois ce renseignement
indebtedness [ɪn'detɪdnɪs] *n* endettement *m*; *Fig* dette *f* (**to** envers)
indecency [ɪn'di:sənsɪ] *n* indécence *f*; *Jur* (**public act of**) **i.** (*assault*) attentat *m* à la pudeur; (*exposure*) outrage *m* public à la pudeur
indecent [ɪn'di:sənt] *adj* indécent; *Fig F* (*sum of money, salary*) scandaleux; **i. behaviour** attentat *m* aux mœurs; **to do sth with i. haste** faire qch avec une rapidité scandaleuse
indecent assault *n* attentat *m* à la pudeur
indecent exposure *n* outrage *m* public à la pudeur
indecently [in'di:səntlɪ] *adv* de manière indécente; *Fig F* (*rich*) scandaleusement
indecipherable [ɪndɪ'saɪfərəb(ə)l, -frəb(ə)l] *adj* indéchiffrable
indecision [ɪndɪ'sɪʒən] *n* indécision *f*
indecisive [ɪndɪ'saɪsɪv] *adj* **(a)** (*argument*) peu concluant; (*battle, election*) indécis **(b)** (*person*) indécis, irrésolu; **she was i. about whether to go or stay** elle ne savait pas si elle devait partir ou rester
indecisiveness [ɪndɪ'saɪsɪvnɪs] *n* indécision *f*
indeclinable [ɪndɪ'klaɪnəb(ə)l] *adj Gram* indéclinable
indecorous [ɪn'dekərəs] *adj* (*person*) inconvenant; (*departure, retreat etc*) peu digne
indecorously [ɪn'dekərəslɪ] *adv* (*to behave*) de manière incorrecte *ou* inconvenante; (*to retreat, leave*) de façon peu digne
indecorum [ɪndɪ'kɔ:rəm] *n* incorrection *f*, inconvenance *f*
indeed [ɪn'di:d] *adv* **(a)** (*certainly*) en effet, vraiment; **he was i. a man of genius** c'était vraiment un homme de génie; **I may i. be wrong** il se peut toutefois que j'aie tort
(b) (*intensive*) **I am very glad i.** je suis très très content; **thank you very much i.** merci infiniment, merci mille fois
(c) (*what is more*) même, à vrai dire; **I think so, i. I am sure of it** je le pense et même j'en suis sûr
(d) (*with affirmation or negation*) **you've been to Venice haven't you? – i. I have!** tu es allé à Venise, n'est-ce pas? – oui, j'y suis allé; **you haven't been to Venice – i. I have!** tu n'es jamais allé à Venise – si, j'y suis déjà allé!; **yes i.!** mais certainement!, pour sûr!; **i. not!** certes non!; **it does i.!, i. it does!** (*surprise me, mean that etc*) certainement!
(e) (*interrogatively*) **I have lived in Paris – i.?** j'ai vécu à Paris – vraiment?; **have you i.?** (*expressing doubt, lack of interest, mockery*) ah oui?
indefatigable [ɪndɪ'fætɪgəb(ə)l] *adj* infatigable
indefatigably [ɪndɪ'fætɪgəblɪ] *adv* infatigablement
indefensible [ɪndɪ'fensɪb(ə)l] *adj* (*theory, argument*) indéfendable; (*behaviour*) inexcusable
indefinable [ɪndɪ'faɪnəb(ə)l] *adj* (*feeling, quality etc*) indéfinissable
indefinite [ɪn'defɪnɪt] *adj* **(a)** (*period of time, number*) indéterminé; (*leave, strike*) illimité **(b)** (*ideas, promises etc*) indéfini, vague **(c)** [①**A5**,C,1; **B4**,B] *Gram* (*article, pronom*) indéfini
indefinitely [ɪn'defɪnɪtlɪ] *adv* (*to postpone sth*) indéfiniment; **I could go on i.** je pourrais continuer à l'infini
indelible [ɪn'delɪb(ə)l] *adj* (*ink*) indélébile, ineffaçable; *Fig* (*mark, memory*) indélébile
indelibly [ɪn'delɪblɪ] *adv* de façon indélébile; *Fig* **i. printed on her mind** à jamais gravé dans son esprit
indelicacy [ɪn'delɪkəsɪ] *n* (*of person*) indélicatesse *f*, manque *m* de délicatesse; (*of remark, behaviour*) inconvenance *f*
indelicate [ɪn'delɪkət] *adj* (*person*) indélicat, qui manque de délicatesse; (*remark, behaviour*) inconvenant
indelicately [ɪn'delɪkətlɪ] *adv* de façon inconvenante
indemnification [ɪndemnɪfɪ'keɪʃən] *n* **(a)** (*action*) indemnisation *f*, dédommagement *m* (**of sb for sth** de qn de qch) **(b)** (*money*) indemnité *f*, dédommagement *m*
indemnify [ɪn'demnɪfaɪ] *vt* **(a)** (*protect*) garantir (**from, against** contre) **(b)** (*compensate*) indemniser, dédommager (**for a loss** d'une perte)
indemnity [ɪn'demnɪtɪ] *n* **(a)** (*protection*) (*against loss etc*) garantie *f*, assurance *f* **(b)** (*compensation*) indemnité *f*, dédommagement *m*
indent[1] ['ɪndent] *n* **(a)** *Typ* alinéa *m* **(b)** *Old-fashioned Br Com* commande *f* de marchandises **(c)** (*notch*) entaille *f*; (*in metal*) bosselure *f*
indent[2] [ɪn'dent] **1** *vt* **(a)** *Typ* (*line*) renfoncer, mettre en retrait *ou* à l'alinéa; **indented line** ligne *f* en alinéa *ou* en retrait; **indented paragraph** paragraphe *m* en retrait **(b)** (*put notches in*) denteler, entailler; (*surface*) bosseler, bossuer; *Carp* (*beam*) endenter **(c)** *Old-fashioned Br Com* **to i. sb for sth** facturer qch à qn **2** *vi Old-fashioned Br Com* **to i. on sb for sth** commander qch à qn
indentation [ɪnden'teɪʃən] *n* **(a)** (*made in sand by wheels etc*) trace *f*, impression *f* **(b)** (*action*) (*of edges of sth*) découpage *m* **(c)** (*notched, jagged edge*) dentelure *f*; (*notch*) entaille *f* **(d)** *Typ* = **indent**[1] **(a)**
indenture[1] [ɪn'dentʃər] *n Jur* contrat *m* synallagmatique, contrat bilatéral; **indentures** (*of apprentice*) contrat d'apprentissage
indenture[2] *vt Jur* **(a)** (*bind by contract*) lier par contrat **(b)** *Arch* (*of parent or guardian*) mettre en apprentissage (**to sb** chez qn); (*of employer*) engager par un brevet d'apprentissage
independence [ɪndɪ'pendəns] *n* indépendance *f* (**from** à l'égard de); (*of state*) indépendance, autonomie *f*; *US* **I. Day** fête *f* de l'Indépendance
independent [ɪndɪ'pendənt] **1** *adj* (*person, inquiry etc*) indépendant; (*state, country*) indépendant, autonome; **to be i. of sb/sth** ne pas dépendre de qn/qch; **person of i. means** rentier, -ière; **an i. thinker** un libre-penseur; **his children are i. now** ses enfants peuvent maintenant pourvoir eux-mêmes à leurs besoins; *Br Admin* **i. school** = école *f* libre; *Aut* **i. suspension** suspension *f* indépendante **2** *n Pol etc* indépendant, -ante
independently [ɪndɪ'pendəntlɪ] *adv* **(a)** (*to behave etc*) avec indépendance; **to live i.** être indépendant **(b)** (*without being connected*) indépendamment; **i. of that** indépendamment de cela
in-depth *adj* (*study etc*) approfondi, en profondeur; **i. article** article *m* de fond
indescribable [ɪndɪ'skraɪbəb(ə)l] *adj* (*anger, poverty*) indescriptible; (*joy*) indicible
indescribably [ɪndɪ'skraɪbəblɪ] *adv* (*angry, painful etc*) atrocement; (*happy*) indiciblement; **it was i. awful** c'était absolument affreux
indestructible [ɪndɪ'strʌktəb(ə)l] *adj* indestructible
indeterminable [ɪndɪ'tɜ:mɪnəb(ə)l] *adj* indéterminable
indeterminate [ɪndɪ'tɜ:mɪnət] *adj* (*space etc, Math quantity*) indéterminé
indeterminately [ɪndɪ'tɜ:mɪnətlɪ] *adv* (*to continue*) de façon indéterminée; **an i. long period** une période indéterminée; **an i. large number of factors** un nombre de facteurs indéterminé
index[1] ['ɪndeks], *pl* **indexes, indices** ['ɪndeksɪz, 'ɪndɪsi:z] *n* **(a)** (*pl* **indexes**) (*of book*) index *m*, table *f* alphabétique **(b)** (*pl* **indexes**) (*catalogue*) fichier *m*, répertoire *m*; *St Exch* **i. option** option *f* sur indice **(c)** (*pl* **indices**) *Math etc* indice *m*; (*exponent*) exposant *m*; *Opt* **i. of refraction** indice de réfraction; *Com, Econ* **i. number** indice **(d) i. finger** index *m* **(e)** (*pl* **indices**) *Fig* (*sign*) indice *m*, signe *m* (indicateur)
index[2] *vt* **(a)** (*create index of*) (*book*) dresser l'index de; *Comptr* (*database*) indexer **(b)** (*put into index*) (*article etc*) répertorier, classer **(c)** (*of wages, pension*) **indexed to inflation** indexé sur l'inflation
indexation [ɪndek'seɪʃən] *n* indexation *f*
index card *n* fiche *f*; **i. box** boîte *f* à fiches
indexing ['ɪndeksɪŋ] *n Comptr* indexation *f*
index-link *vt* indexer; **to i. a pension to the cost of living** indexer une retraite sur le coût de la vie
index-linked *adj* (*wages, pension*) indexé

index-linking *n* indexation *f*

India ['ɪndɪə] *n* Inde *f*; **I. ink** encre *m* de Chine; **I. paper** papier *m* bible, papier pelure; **I. rubber** (*eraser*) gomme *f* à effacer; (*material*) caoutchouc *m*, gomme élastique

Indian ['ɪndɪən] **1** *adj* **(a)** (*of, from India*) de l'Inde, indien; **I. elephant** éléphant *m* d'Inde; **I. ink** encre *m* de Chine; **the I. Ocean** l'océan *m* Indien

(b) (*of Native Americans*) (*customs, handicrafts etc*) indien, amérindien; (*leader, chief*) indien; **I. club** (*for exercise*) massue *f* de gymnastique; **I. corn** maïs *m*; **I. file** file *f* indienne; *Am Pej* **to be an I. giver** = demander le retour de qch qu'on a donné; **I. hemp** chanvre *m* indien; **I. reserve** réserve *f* indienne; **I. summer** été *m* indien; *Fig* période *f* de succès *ou* de bonheur tardif

2 *n* **(a)** (*inhabitant, native of India*) Indien, -ienne

(b) (*Native American*) Indien, -ienne (d'Amérique), Amérindien, -ienne

indicate ['ɪndɪkeɪt] **1** *vt* **(a)** (*point to, show*) indiquer, montrer; **to i. sth with one's hand** indiquer qch de la main; **at the time indicated** à l'heure dite *ou* indiquée; *Aut* **to i. a left/right turn** mettre son clignotant pour indiquer que l'on va tourner à gauche/droite

(b) (*denote*) indiquer, dénoter; **an expression that indicated determination** un visage plein de détermination

(c) (*state*) (*opposition, intention to do sth*) faire connaître; **he has indicated that ...** il a fait savoir que ...

(d) (*need*) *Med* **plenty of rest is indicated** il est recommandé de bien se reposer; **strong measures were clearly indicated** il était évident que la situation exigeait des mesures rigoureuses

2 *vi Aut* mettre son clignotant

indication [ɪndɪ'keɪʃən] *n* **(a)** (*act of pointing out*) indication *f* **(of sth to sb** de qch à qn) **(b)** (*sign*) indice *m*, signe *m*, indication *f*; **there is every i. that he was speaking the truth** tout porte à croire qu'il disait vrai; **there is no i. of a struggle** il n'y a aucun signe de lutte; **all the indications are that ...** tout porte à croire que ...; **he gave early indications of his talent** son talent se révéla de bonne heure; **to take sth as an i. that** interpréter qch comme une indication du fait que **(c)** (*warning, statement*) **to give clear i. of one's intentions** faire connaître clairement ses intentions

indicative [ɪn'dɪkətɪv] [①A39,8; B,2] **1** *n Gram* indicatif *m*; **in the i.** à l'indicatif **2** *adj* **(a)** (*suggestive*) révélateur **(of** de) **(b)** *Gram* **i. mood** mode *m* indicatif

indicator ['ɪndɪkeɪtər] *n* **(a)** (*on instrument, gauge etc*) index *m*, aiguille *f*; *Aut* clignotant *m*; (*LED, on machine*) indicateur *m*; *Naut, Av* (*for speed etc*) indicateur, compteur *m*; **i. light** signal *m* lumineux; (*on monitor*) voyant *m* **(b)** (*indication, guide*) indicateur *m*, indice *m* **(c)** *Rail etc* **i. board** tableau *m* *ou* indicateur *m* des arrivées et des départs

indict [ɪn'daɪt] *vt Jur* inculper (**for** pour)

indictable [ɪn'daɪtəb(ə)l] *adj Jur* (*person*) passible de poursuite en justice; **i. offence** délit *m*

indictment [ɪn'daɪtmənt] *n Jur* **(a)** (*of person*) inculpation *f*; (*by public prosecutor*) réquisitoire *m*; *Fig* **it is an i. of our education system that the illiteracy rate is so high** le taux d'analphabétisme élevé en dit long sur notre système éducatif **(b)** (*document*) acte *m* d'accusation

indie ['ɪndɪ] *adj Mus F* indépendant

Indies (the) [ðɪ'ɪndɪz] *npl Hist* (*South and Southeast Asia*) les Indes *fpl*

indifference [ɪn'dɪfrəns, -fərəns] *n* **(a)** (*lack of interest*) indifférence *f* (**to** *or* **towards sth/sb** pour qch/à l'égard de qn); **it's a matter of complete i. to me** cela m'est parfaitement indifférent **(b)** (*of talent etc*) médiocrité *f*

indifferent [ɪn'dɪfrənt, -fərənt] *adj* **(a)** (*not interested*) indifférent (**to** à); **I am** *or* **feel i. about him** il m'est indifférent **(b)** (*meal, cooking, painter*) médiocre

indifferently [ɪn'dɪfrəntlɪ] *adv* **(a)** (*disinterestedly*) avec indifférence **(b)** (*to cook, paint etc*) médiocrement

indigence ['ɪndɪdʒəns] *n Fml* indigence *f*

indigenous [ɪn'dɪdʒɪnəs] *adj* (*plant, product, population etc*) indigène (**to** à)

indigent ['ɪndɪdʒənt] *adj Fml* indigent

indigestible [ɪndɪ'dʒestɪb(ə)l] *adj* indigeste

indigestion [ɪndɪ'dʒestʃən] *n* indigestion *f*; **to have (an attack of) i.** avoir une indigestion

indignant [ɪn'dɪgnənt] *adj* (*person, air*) indigné; (*shout*) d'indignation; **to be** *or* **feel i. at sth** être indigné *ou* s'indigner de qch; **to make sb i.** indigner qn

indignantly [ɪn'dɪgnəntlɪ] *adv* avec indignation; (*to look*) d'un air indigné

indignation [ɪndɪg'neɪʃən] *n* indignation *f*

indignity [ɪn'dɪgnɪtɪ] *n* indignité *f*; **to suffer indignities** souffrir des affronts; **the i. of it!** quelle honte!

indigo, *pl* **indigo(e)s** ['ɪndɪgəʊ, 'ɪndɪgəʊz] **1** *n* **(a)** (*dye*) indigo *m*; **i. (blue)** (*colour*) indigo **(b)** *Bot* **i. (plant)** indigotier *m* **2** *adj* indigo *inv*

indirect [ɪndɪ'rekt] *adj* **(a)** [①A61,21] (*influence, result etc*) indirect; *Gram* **i. speech** discours *m* indirect; **i. object** complément *m* d'objet indirect; *Mktg* **i. promotional expenditure** coûts *mpl* de promotion indirects **(b)** (*route, approach, ways*) détourné; (*answer, costs, tax*) indirect

indirectly [ɪndɪ'rektlɪ] *adv* indirectement

indiscernible [ɪndɪ'sɜːnɪb(ə)l] *adj* (*not visible*) indiscernable; *Fig* (*reason*) obscur; (*difference*) imperceptible

indiscipline [ɪn'dɪsɪplɪn] *n* indiscipline *f*

indiscreet [ɪndɪ'skriːt] *adj* indiscret, -ète; **an i. admission** une indiscrétion

indiscreetly [ɪndɪ'skriːtlɪ] *adv* indiscrètement; (*to behave*) imprudemment

indiscretion [ɪndɪ'skreʃən] *n* **(a)** (*lack of discretion*) manque *m* de discrétion, indiscrétion *f* **(b)** (*unwise act*) écart *m* de conduite; (*unwise remark*) indiscrétion *f*; **to be guilty of an i.** (*blunder*) commettre une inconséquence; (*sexual*) se compromettre

indiscriminate [ɪndɪ'skrɪmɪnɪt] *adj* (*revenge*) aveugle, qui ne fait pas de distinction; **he's an i. reader** il lit tout ce qui lui tombe sous la main; **he was i. in his praise** il a distribué des compliments sans discernement; **i. slaughter** tuerie *f* générale

indiscriminately [ɪndɪ'skrɪmɪnɪtlɪ] *adv* (*to hit, blame, kill*) sans distinction; **he reads i.** il lit tout ce qui lui tombe sous la main; **to fire i. into the crowd** tirer dans la foule sans faire de distinction

indispensable [ɪndɪ'spensəb(ə)l] *adj* (*person, thing*) indispensable

indisposed [ɪndɪ'spəʊzd] *adj Fml* **(a)** (*ill*) indisposé, souffrant; **to be** *or* **feel i.** être indisposé *ou* souffrant **(b)** (*not inclined*) peu enclin, peu disposé (**to do sth** à faire qch)

indisposition [ɪndɪspə'zɪʃən] *n Fml* **(a)** (*illness*) indisposition *f* **(b)** (*lack of inclination*) peu *m* d'inclination (**to do sth** à faire qch)

indisputable [ɪndɪ'spjuːtəb(ə)l] *adj* incontestable, indiscutable; **it is the i. truth** c'est incontestable

indisputably [ɪndɪ'spjuːtəblɪ] *adv* indiscutablement, incontestablement

indissoluble [ɪndɪ'sɒljʊb(ə)l] *adj* (*union, friendship*) indissoluble

indistinct [ɪndɪ'stɪŋkt] *adj* (*object, noise etc*) indistinct, peu distinct; (*sound*) confus; (*memory*) vague

indistinctly [ɪndɪ'stɪŋktlɪ] *adv* (*to see, talk*) indistinctement; (*to feel*) vaguement

indistinguishable [ɪndɪ'stɪŋgwɪʃəb(ə)l] *adj* que l'on ne peut distinguer (**from** de), indiscernable; **the forgery was i. from the real thing** le faux et l'original étaient indiscernables, on ne pouvait distinguer le faux de l'original; **the two insects are i.** les deux insectes ne peuvent pas être distingués

individual [ɪndɪ'vɪdjʊəl] **1** *adj* **(a)** (*for a single person or thing*) individuel; **his pupils get i. attention** il s'occupe de ses élèves individuellement; **every room has its own i. shower** chaque chambre est équipée de sa propre douche; **i. tuition** cours *mpl* particuliers **(b)** (*taken separately*) **i. animals vary in size** la taille varie selon les individus; **i. cases will be decided on their merits** chaque cas sera étudié individuellement **(c)** (*unique*) personnel; **she always has a very i. hairstyle** elle est toujours coiffée de façon très personnelle **2** *n* individu *m*; **a private i.** un simple particulier

individualism [ɪndɪ'vɪdjʊəlɪz(ə)m] *n* individualisme *m*

individualist [ɪndɪ'vɪdjʊəlɪst] *n* individualiste *mf*

individualistic [ɪndɪvɪdjʊə'lɪstɪk] *adj* individualiste

individuality [ɪndɪvɪdjʊ'ælɪtɪ] *n* individualité *f*

individualize [ɪndɪ'vɪdjʊəlaɪz] *vt* (*to make distinctive*) individualiser; (*adapt to individual needs*) adapter aux besoins de chaque individu

individually [ɪndɪ'vɪdjʊəlɪ] *adv* individuellement, séparément; **he spoke to us all i.** il nous a parlé à tous un par un

indivisible [ɪndɪ'vɪzɪb(ə)l] *adj* indivisible

Indochina ['ɪndəʊ'tʃaɪnə] *n* Indochine *f*

indoctrinate [ɪn'dɒktrɪneɪt] *vt* endoctriner; **to i. sb with an idea** inculquer une idée à qn

indoctrination [ɪndɒktrɪ'neɪʃən] *n* endoctrinement *m*

Indo-European ['ɪndəʊjʊərə'piːən] **1** *adj Ling* indo-européen **2** *n* **(a)** Indo-Européen, -enne **(b)** *Ling* indo-européen *m*

indolence ['ɪndələns] *n* indolence *f*

indolent ['ɪndələnt] *adj* indolent

indolently ['ɪndələntlɪ] *adv* indolemment

indomitable [ɪn'dɒmɪtəb(ə)l] *adj* indomptable; (*courage etc*) invincible

Indonesia [ɪndəʊ'niːzɪə, -ʒə] *n* Indonésie *f*

Indonesian [ɪndəʊ'niːzɪən, -ʒ(ə)n] **1** *adj* indonésien **2** *n* **(a)** Indonésien, -ienne **(b)** *Ling* indonésien *m*

indoor ['ɪndɔːr] *adj* (*plant*) d'appartement; (*photography*) en intérieur; **i. aerial** antenne *f* intérieure; **i. athletics** athlétisme *m* en salle; **i. games** (*sport*) sports *mpl* en salle; (*party games*) jeux *mpl* de société; **i. (swimming) pool** piscine *f* couverte; **i. visitor attraction** centre *m* d'intérêt couvert

indoors [ɪn'dɔːz] *adv* (*inside house*) à la maison; (*inside building*) à l'intérieur; **to go i.** (r)entrer; **to stay i.** rester à l'intérieur; **don't stay i., go out and play!** ne reste donc pas enfermé, va jouer dehors!; **this job's better, at least it's i.** ce poste est mieux, au moins je/tu/il/*etc* travaille(s) à l'intérieur; *Br Sl* **her i.** (*the wife*) la bourgeoise

indorse [ɪn'dɔːs] *vt* = endorse

indrawn ['ɪndrɔːn] *adj* (*air*) aspiré; **i. breath** aspiration *f*; **he watched with i. breath** il regardait en retenant son souffle

indubitable [ɪn'djuːbɪtəb(ə)l] *adj* indubitable

indubitably [ɪn'djuːbɪtəblɪ] *adv* indubitablement

induce [ɪn'djuːs] *vt* **(a)** (*persuade*) persuader (**to do** à faire); **nothing will i. him to change his mind** rien ne le fera changer d'idée **(b)** (*bring about*) (*sleep, vomiting, feeling*) provoquer; *El etc* (*current etc*) amorcer, induire; **a drug-induced state** un état provoqué par la drogue **(c)** *Obst* **to i. labour** provoquer l'accouchement, déclencher le travail; *Obst* **she's had to be induced** on a dû lui faire une piqûre pour provoquer l'accouchement *ou* déclencher le travail **(d)** (*in logic*) (*law etc*) induire

inducement [ɪn'djuːsmənt] *n* (*incentive*) **the company was offered several inducements to relocate in the area** l'entreprise s'est vu offrir plusieurs avantages pour l'inciter à se relocaliser dans la région; **what inducements were used to persuade him to co-operate?** comment l'a-t-on incité à coopérer?; **fears for his daughter's safety will be enough of an i.** le fait qu'il craint pour la sécurité de sa fille sera une motivation suffisante; **an i. of $10,000** (*bribe*) un pot de vin de 10 000 dollars

induct [ɪn'dʌkt] *vt* **(a)** (*install in office*) installer dans sa charge; *Rel* (*minister*) mettre en possession d'un bénéfice **(b)** (*initiate*) initier (**into** à); **he was inducted into the Freemasons** il a été initié à la franc-maçonnerie **(c)** *US Mil* **to be inducted** (*into the army*) être appelé sous les drapeaux

inducted gas [ɪn'dʌktɪd] *n Aut* gaz *m* aspiré

induction [ɪn'dʌkʃən] *n* **(a)** (*of minister, official*) installation *f* **(b)** *Obst* (*of labour*) déclenchement *m* **(c)** (*in logic*), *Math* induction *f* **(d)** *El* induction *f*; **i. coil** bobine *f* d'induction, bobine de self; **i. loop** circuit *m* d'induction

inductive [ɪn'dʌktɪv] *adj* **(a)** (*reasoning*) inductif, par induction **(b)** *El* (*current etc*) inducteur

indulge [ɪn'dʌldʒ] **1** *vt* **(a)** (*sb*) être trop gentil avec; (*spoil*) gâter; (*hope*) nourrir; (*passion*) se livrer à, donner libre cours à; **they indulged his every whim** ils lui cédaient tous ses caprices; **to i. oneself** se faire plaisir

(b) *Com* (*payer of bill of exchange*) accorder un délai à

2 *vi* **to i. in** (*activity*) s'adonner à, se livrer à; **to i. in a cigar** se permettre un cigare; **to i. in a glass of port** s'offrir un verre de porto; **to i. in speculation** se laisser aller à des spéculations (**on, about** sur); **I used to drink a lot but nowadays I rarely i.** je buvais beaucoup mais maintenant c'est rare que je me le permette; *F* **thanks, but I don't i.** (*drink, smoke*) merci, mais je ne bois/fume pas

indulgence [ɪn'dʌldʒəns] *n* **(a)** (*doting, leniency*) indulgence *f* (**to** envers), *Pej* complaisance *f* (**to** envers) **(b)** (*act, activity*) **because of his i. in his favourite pastime** parce qu'il s'adonnait *ou* se livrait à son passe-temps préféré; **i. in rich food** excès *mpl* de table **(c)** (*treat*) **Belgian chocolates are my only i.** les chocolats belges sont mon seul péché mignon; **I allow myself the occasional i.** de temps en temps je me fais plaisir **(d)** *Cathol* indulgence *f*

indulgent [ɪn'dʌldʒənt] *adj* indulgent (**to** envers, pour); **over-i. father** père *m* trop indulgent

indulgently [ɪn'dʌldʒəntlɪ] *adv* avec indulgence

industrial [ɪn'dʌstrɪəl] *adj* (*area, city, activity etc*) industriel; (*conflict*) ouvrier, du travail; **for i. use only** usage *m* industriel uniquement; **in i. quantities** en quantités *fpl* industrielles; **i. accident** accident *m* du travail; **i. accident insurance** assurance *f* contre les accidents du travail; **i. arbitrator** prud'homme *m*; **i. complex** complexe *m* industriel; **i. disease** maladie *f* professionnelle *ou* du travail; **i. espionage** espionnage *m* industriel; **i. marketer** mercaticien *m* industriel; **i. marketing** mercatique *f* industrielle; *Med* **i. medicine** médecine *f* du travail; **i. statistics** statistiques *fpl* sur l'industrie; **i. unrest** agitation *f* ouvrière

industrial action *n Br* actions *fpl* revendicatives; **to take i.** se mettre en grève

industrial estate *n Br* zone *f* industrielle, ZI *f*

industrialism [ɪn'dʌstrɪəlɪz(ə)m] *n* industrialisme *m*

industrialist [ɪn'dʌstrɪəlɪst] *n* industriel *m*

industrialization [ɪndʌstrɪəlaɪ'zeɪʃən] *n* industrialisation *f*

industrialize [ɪn'dʌstrɪəlaɪz] **1** *vt* industrialiser **2** *vi* s'industrialiser

industrialized [ɪn'dʌstrɪəlaɪzd] *adj* **i. nations** pays *mpl* industrialisés

industrializing [ɪn'dʌstrɪəlaɪzɪŋ] *adj* (*country, economy*) en voie d'industrialisation

industrial relations *npl* relations *fpl* entre le patronat et les travailleurs

Industrial Revolution *n* la Révolution industrielle

industrials [ɪn'dʌstrɪəlz] *npl St Exch* valeurs *fpl* industrielles *ou* des sociétés industrielles

industrial tribunal *n Br* = conseil *m* de prud'hommes

industrious [ɪn'dʌstrɪəs] *adj* industrieux, travailleur

industriously [ɪn'dʌstrɪəslɪ] *adv* assidûment

industriousness [ɪn'dʌstrɪəsnɪs] *n* assiduité *f* (au travail), application *f*

industry ['ɪndʌstrɪ] *n* **(a)** industrie *f*; **i. has declined in this country** l'industrie a décliné dans ce pays; **heavy/light i.** l'industrie lourde/légère; **i. expert** expert *m* de l'industrie; **i. forecast** prévision *f* de l'industrie; **i. sector** secteur *m* industriel *ou* secondaire **(b)** (*diligence*) assiduité *f* (au travail), application *f*

industry-standard *adj* normalisé

inebriate[1] [ɪn'iːbrɪət] *Fml* **1** *adj* ivre; **in his i. state** dans son état d'ébriété *ou* d'ivresse **2** *n* ivrogne *mf*

inebriate[2] [ɪn'iːbrɪeɪt] *vt* enivrer

inebriated [ɪn'iːbrɪeɪtɪd] *adj* ivre

inebriation [ɪniːbrɪ'eɪʃən] *n* **(a)** (*act of making drunk*) enivrement *m* **(b)** (*drunkenness*) ivresse *f*, ébriété *f*

inedible [ɪn'edɪb(ə)l] *adj* non comestible; (*too disgusting to eat*) immangeable

ineducable [ɪn'edjʊkəb(ə)l] *adj* inéducable

ineffable [ɪn'efəb(ə)l] *adj Fml* (*joy etc*) ineffable, indicible

ineffective [ɪnɪ'fektɪv] *adj* (*means, remedy, speech, leader*) inefficace; (*speaker*) terne; (*style*) plat, terne

ineffectively [ɪnɪ'fektɪvlɪ] *adv* (*to protest, plead*) vainement; (*to chair a meeting*) de manière inefficace; **the dart bounced i. off the rhino's hide** la flèche a rebondi sur la peau du rhinocéros sans produire aucun effet

ineffectual [ɪnɪ'fektjʊəl] *adj* (*effort, reasoning, person*) inefficace

inefficacious [ɪnefɪ'keɪʃəs] *adj Fml* inefficace

inefficacy [ɪn'efɪkəsɪ] *n* inefficacité *f*

inefficiency [ɪnɪ'fɪʃənsɪ] *n* (*of method, machine, organization, person*) manque *m* d'efficacité, inefficacité *f*

inefficient [ɪnɪ'fɪʃənt] *adj* (*measure, person etc*) inefficace

inefficiently [ɪnɪ'fɪʃəntlɪ] *adv* inefficacement

inelastic [ɪnɪ'læstɪk] *adj* sans élasticité; *Fig* rigide, raide

inelegant [ɪn'elɪgənt] *adj* inélégant

inelegantly [ɪn'elɪgəntlɪ] *adv* inélégamment

ineligible [ɪn'elɪdʒɪb(ə)l] *adj* (*candidate*) inéligible; **to be i. for sth** ne pas avoir droit à qch; **he's i. to vote** il n'a pas le droit de voter; **i. for military service** inapte au service militaire

ineluctable [ɪnɪ'lʌktəb(ə)l] *adj Lit* inéluctable

inept [ɪn'ept] *adj* inepte

ineptitude [ɪn'eptɪtjuːd] *n* ineptie *f*

ineptly [ɪn'eptlɪ] *adv* de façon inepte

inequality [ɪnɪ'kwɒlɪtɪ] *n* (*social, economic*) inégalité *f*

inequitable [ɪn'ekwɪtəb(ə)l] *adj* inéquitable

ineradicable [ɪnɪ'rædɪkəb(ə)l] *adj* indéracinable, inextirpable

inert [ɪ'nɜːt] *adj* inerte; *Ch* **the i. gases** les gaz *mpl* inertes

inertia [ɪ'nɜːʃɪə] *n Phys, F* (*of person*) inertie *f*; *Br Com* **i. selling** = pratique *f* illégale consistant à envoyer des marchandises non commandées; **i. switch** contacteur *m* à inertie

inertia-reel *adj Aut* **i. seat-belt** ceinture *f* (de sécurité) à enrouleur

inescapable [ɪnɪ'skeɪpəb(ə)l] *adj* incontournable

inessential [ɪnɪ'senʃəl] **1** *adj* non essentiel **2** *n* chose *f* superflue; **that's one of the inessentials** ça fait partie du superflu

inestimable [ɪn'estɪməb(ə)l] *adj* (*value, benefit etc*) inestimable

inevitability [ɪnevɪtə'bɪlɪtɪ] *n* caractère *m* inévitable

inevitable [ɪn'evɪtəb(ə)l] **1** *adj* (*unavoidable*) inévitable; (*conclusion*) incontournable; **his promotion is i.** il va de soi qu'il sera promu; **the i. conclusion** (*of a play, novel*) le dénouement fatal **2** *n* **the i.** l'inévitable *m*

inevitably [ɪn'evɪtəblɪ] *adv* inévitablement; **he's i. late** il est immanquablement en retard

inexact [ɪnɪg'zækt] *adj* (*lacking clarity*) imprécis; (*inaccurate*) inexact; **it's an i. science** ce n'est pas une science exacte

inexactitude [ɪnɪg'zæktɪtjuːd] *n* (*inaccuracy*) inexactitude *f*; (*lack of clarity*) imprécision *f*

inexactly [ɪnɪg'zæktlɪ] *adv* (*inaccurately*) inexactement; (*with a lack of clarity*) de façon imprécise
inexactness [ɪnɪg'zæktnɪs] *n* (*inaccuracy*) inexactitude *f*; (*lack of clarity*) imprécision *f*
inexcusable [ɪnɪk'skju:zəb(ə)l] *adj* inexcusable, impardonnable; **that was i. of you** tu es impardonnable
inexcusably [ɪnɪk'skju:zəblɪ] *adv* inexcusablement, impardonnablement; **i. rude/slow** d'une grossièreté/lenteur inexcusable
inexhaustible [ɪneg'zɔ:stɪb(ə)l] *adj* inépuisable; (*source*) intarissable; (*patience*) inépuisable, sans limite; **she had an i. supply of jokes** elle avait un stock de blagues inépuisable
inexorable [ɪn'eksərəb(ə)l] *adj* inexorable
inexorably [ɪn'eksərəblɪ] *adv* inexorablement
inexpedient [ɪnɪk'spi:dɪənt] *adj* inopportun, malavisé
inexpensive [ɪnɪk'spensɪv] *adj* peu coûteux, bon marché *inv*; **i. to run** (*house, car*) économique
inexpensively [ɪnɪk'spensɪvlɪ] *adv* bon marché, à bas prix; (*to live*) économiquement, à peu de frais
inexperience [ɪnɪk'spɪərɪəns] *n* inexpérience *f*
inexperienced [ɪnɪk'spɪərɪənst] *adj* **(a)** (*person*) inexpérimenté, sans expérience; **she is still i.** elle manque encore d'expérience; **he's i. in handling staff** il n'a pas l'habitude de diriger le personnel **(b)** (*eye, ear*) inexercé
inexpert [ɪn'ekspɜ:t] *adj* inexpert; **he was i. in such matters** il ne connaissait pas grand-chose à ces choses; **her i. handling of the situation** la façon maladroite dont elle a géré l'affaire
inexpertly [ɪn'ekspɜ:tlɪ] *adv* maladroitement, de façon maladroite
inexpiable [ɪn'ekspɪəb(ə)l] *adj Fml* inexpiable
inexplicable [ɪnɪk'splɪkəb(ə)l] *adj* inexplicable
inexplicably [ɪnɪk'splɪkəblɪ] *adv* inexplicablement
inexpressible [ɪnɪk'spresɪb(ə)l] *adj* (*pleasure*) inexprimable
inexpressive [ɪnɪk'spresɪv] *adj* inexpressif, sans expression
inextinguishable [ɪnɪk'stɪŋgwɪʃəb(ə)l] *adj* inextinguible
in extremis [ɪnɪk'stri:mɪs] *adv* **(a)** (*as a last resort*) en dernier recours **(b)** *esp Rel* (*at the point of death*) sur le point de mourir, à l'article de la mort
inextricable [ɪnek'strɪkəb(ə)l] *adj* **(a)** (*situation*) inextricable **(b)** (*ties, links*) indissoluble
inextricably [ɪnek'strɪkəblɪ] *adv* (*see adj*) **(a)** inextricablement **(b)** indissolublement
infallibility [ɪnfælɪ'bɪlɪtɪ] *n Rel etc* infaillibilité *f*
infallible [ɪn'fælɪb(ə)l] *adj* infaillible, immanquable
infallibly [ɪn'fælɪblɪ] *adv* infailliblement, immanquablement
infamous ['ɪnfəməs] *adj* (*person*) infâme; (*behaviour*) abominable, infâme; (*place*) mal famé
infamously ['ɪnfəməslɪ] *adv* (*to behave*) de manière infâme
infamy ['ɪnfəmɪ] *n* infamie *f*
infancy ['ɪnfənsɪ] *n* **(a)** (*early childhood*) petite enfance *f*; *Fig* (*of an art, industry*) débuts *mpl*; **from i.** dès la plus tendre enfance; *Fig* **science was in its i.** la science en était à ses balbutiements **(b)** *Jur* (*minority*) minorité *f*
infant ['ɪnfənt] **1** *n* **(a)** (*until the age of two*) nourrisson *m*; *Br* (*under the age of seven*) jeune enfant *mf*; **i. prodigy** enfant prodige **(b)** *Jur* (*minor*) mineur, -eure **2** *adj* (*child*) en bas âge; *Fig* **an i. science** une science naissante
infant class *n Br Sch* classe *f* enfantine
infanticide [ɪn'fæntɪsaɪd] *n* **(a)** (*crime*) infanticide *m* **(b)** (*person*) infanticide *mf*
infantile ['ɪnfəntaɪl] *adj* **(a)** (*of infants*) (*mind, imagination*) d'enfant; *Med* (*illness*) infantile; *Med* **i. paralysis** paralysie *f* infantile **(b)** *Pej* (*childish*) (*reasoning, remark etc*) puéril
infantilism [ɪn'fæntɪlɪz(ə)m] *n Fml* infantilisme *m*
infant mortality *n* mortalité *f* infantile; **i. rate** taux *f* de mortalité infantile
infantry ['ɪnfəntrɪ] *n Mil* infanterie *f*; (*foot soldiers*) fantassins *mpl*
infantryman, *pl* **infantrymen** ['ɪnfəntrɪmən] *n* soldat *m* d'infanterie, fantassin *m*
infant school *n Br Sch* école *f* pour les enfants de cinq à huit ans
infarct ['ɪnfɑ:kt] *n Med* infarctus *m*
infarction [ɪn'fɑ:kʃən] *n Med* infarctus *m*
infatuated [ɪn'fætjʊeɪtɪd] *adj* entiché (**with** de); **to become i. with sb/sth** s'enticher de qn/de qch
infatuation [ɪnfætjʊ'eɪʃən] *n* engouement *m*, *F* toquade *f*; **to have an i. for sb** s'enticher de qn; **it's just (an) i.** ce n'est qu'une toquade
infect [ɪn'fekt] *vt* **(a)** (*water supply, area, food, Med person*) contaminer; (*wound, limb*), *Comptr* infecter; **to i. sb with a disease** (*involuntarily*) transmettre une maladie à qn; (*voluntarily*) inoculer une maladie à qn; *Fig* **to i. sb with one's enthusiasm** communiquer son enthousiasme à qn **(b)** *Fig* (*corrupt, taint*) (*air, morals etc*) corrompre, vicier
infected [ɪn'fektɪd] *adj* (*clothing, food, area*) contaminé; (*wound, limb, disk etc*) infecté; **to become i.** (*of wound*) s'infecter
infection [ɪn'fekʃən] *n Med* (*with disease*) contamination *f*; (*in part of body*) infection *f*; **source of i.** foyer *m* d'infection; **to spread/prevent i.** répandre/empêcher l'infection
infectious [ɪn'fekʃəs] *adj Med* (*disease*) infectieux, contagieux; *F* (*person*) contagieux; *Fig* (*laughter, optimism, pessimism etc*) communicatif
infectiousness [ɪn'fekʃəsnɪs] *n* **(a)** *Med* (*of disease*) nature *f* infectieuse **(b)** *Fig* (*of enthusiasm, hope etc*) caractère *m* communicatif
infelicitous [ɪnfɪ'lɪsɪtəs] *adj Lit* (*remark, event*) malheureux
infelicity [ɪnfɪ'lɪsɪtɪ] *n Lit* **(a)** (*remark*) expression *f* malheureuse **(b)** (*unhappiness*) malheur *m*
infer [ɪn'fɜ:r] *vt* (**-rr-**) **(a)** inférer, déduire, conclure (**sth from sth** qch de qch; **that** que) **(b)** *F* = **imply**
inference ['ɪnfərəns] *n* **(a)** (*method*) inférence *f*; **by i.** par déduction **(b)** (*conclusion*) déduction *f*, conclusion *f*
inferior [ɪn'fɪərɪər] **1** *adj* inférieur; (*work*) de second ordre; **the expensive screwdriver was i. to the cheap one** le tournevis cher était de moins bonne qualité que celui qui était bon marché; **her second novel is a much i. work** son deuxième roman est bien moins bon; **i. quality** qualité *f* inférieure; **to be in an i. position** être dans une position inférieure *ou* subordonnée; *Astron* **the i. planets** les planètes *fpl* inférieures; *Typ* **i. letter** petite lettre *f* inférieure **2** *n* **(a)** inférieur, -eure; **one's inferiors** les personnes *fpl* inférieures à soi **(b)** *Typ* petite lettre *f* inférieure
inferiority [ɪnfɪərɪ'ɒrɪtɪ] *n* infériorité *f* (**to** par rapport à); *Psy* **i. complex** complexe *m* d'infériorité
infernal [ɪn'fɜ:n(ə)l] *adj* **(a)** *F* (*diabolical*) infernal, diabolique; **that i. little man!** cet homme infernal *ou* insupportable! **(b)** *F* (*extreme*) (*noise, heat etc*) infernal; **it's an i. nuisance** c'est diablement embêtant **(c)** (*of hell*) infernal; **the i. regions** l'enfer *m*
infernally [ɪn'fɜ:n(ə)lɪ] *adv F* diablement; **it's i. hot** il fait une chaleur d'enfer *ou* à crever
inferno, *pl* **infernos** [ɪn'fɜ:nəʊ, ɪn'fɜ:nəʊz] *n* **(a)** (*hell*) enfer *m*; *Liter* **Dante's I.** l'Enfer de Dante **(b)** (*fire*) brasier *m*; **the house was a raging i.** la maison était un véritable brasier
infertile [ɪn'fɜ:taɪl] *adj* (*person, ovum*) stérile; (*land*) stérile, infertile
infertility [ɪnfɜ:'tɪlɪtɪ] *n* (*of person*) stérilité *f*; (*of soil*) infertilité *f*, stérilité; **i. clinic** = clinique *f* pour traiter les couples stériles
infest [ɪn'fest] *vt* (*of vermin etc*) infester; **to be infested by rats/cockroaches** être infesté de rats/cafards
infestation [ɪnfes'teɪʃən] *n Med* infestation *f*; *Bot* (*of plants by parasites etc*) invasion *f*
-infested [ɪn'festɪd] *suff* **rat-/cockroach-infested** infesté de rats/cafards
infidel ['ɪnfɪdəl] *adj, n* infidèle *mf*
infidelity [ɪnfɪ'delɪtɪ] *n* **(a)** (*of spouse, lover*) infidélité *f* **(b)** (*disloyalty*) (*of servant etc*) infidélité *f*, déloyauté *f*
infighting ['ɪnfaɪtɪŋ] *n* (*within group*) querelles *fpl* intestines; *Boxing* corps à corps *m*; **political i.** querelles politiques intestines
infill ['ɪnfɪl] *n Constr* remplissage *m*
infiltrate ['ɪnfɪltreɪt] **1** *vt* **(a)** *Pol etc* (*of subversives etc*) (*trade union*) noyauter; (*enemy*) s'infiltrer chez **(b)** (*cause to enter*) (*liquid etc*) faire pénétrer (**into** dans); **we've infiltrated someone into the party** l'un des nôtres a réussi à s'infiltrer dans le parti **(c)** (*of liquid*) (*substance*) s'infiltrer *ou* pénétrer dans, imprégner **2** *vi* (*of fluid, spies etc*) s'infiltrer (**into** dans; **through** à travers)
infiltration [ɪnfɪl'treɪʃən] *n* **(a)** (*by spies, troops etc*) infiltration *f*; *Pol* **the i. of the Labour Party by Trotskyists** le noyautage du Parti travailliste par les Trotskistes **(b)** (*of liquid etc*) infiltration *f* (**into** dans, **through** à travers)
infiltrator ['ɪnfɪltreɪtər] *n* (*of political party etc*) agent *m* qui s'infiltre
infinite ['ɪnfɪnɪt] **1** *adj* infini; **of i. importance** d'une extrême importance; **to go to i. pains to do sth** se donner infiniment de mal pour faire qch; *Rel, Hum* **in his i. wisdom** dans son infinie sagesse **2** *n* **the i.** l'infini *m*
infinitely ['ɪnfɪnɪtlɪ] *adv* infiniment
infinitesimal [ɪnfɪnɪ'tesɪməl] *adj* (*quantity*) infinitésimal; (*majority*) infime; *Math* **i. calculus** calcul *m* infinitésimal
infinitive [ɪn'fɪnɪtɪv] *n* [①**A40-42; B32-35**,H] *Gram* infinitif *m*; **in the i.** à l'infinitif
infinity [ɪn'fɪnɪtɪ] *n* **(a)** (*of space etc*) infinité *f* **(b)** *Math etc* infini *m*; **to i.** à l'infini; *Phot* **to focus on** *or* **for i.** mettre au point sur l'infini
infirm [ɪn'fɜ:m] *adj* **(a)** (*person*) infirme, débile **(b)** *Fml* (*mind, judgement*) irrésolu

infirmary [ɪnˈfɜːmərɪ] *n* **(a)** (*hospital*) hôpital *m*, -aux **(b)** (*in school, prison etc*) infirmerie *f*

infirmity [ɪnˈfɜːmɪtɪ] *n* **(a)** (*weakness*) (*of body*) infirmité *f* **(b)** (*affliction*) infirmité *f*; **the infirmities of old age** les infirmités de la vieillesse **(c)** (*lack of resolve*) **i. of purpose** irrésolution *f*

in flagrante delicto [ɪnfləˈgræntɪdɪˈlɪktəʊ] *adv Jur* en flagrant délit

inflame [ɪnˈfleɪm] **1** *vt* **(a)** (*stir up*) (*desire*) allumer; (*quarrel*) envenimer; (*crowd*) enflammer **(b)** *Med* (*wound*) enflammer **2** *vi Med* (*of wound, tissue*) s'enflammer

inflamed [ɪnˈfleɪmd] *adj* **(a)** *Med* (*wound, eye etc*) enflammé; **to become i.** s'enflammer **(b)** *Fig* enflammé (**with** de); **i. with passion** brûlant d'amour

inflammable [ɪnˈflæməb(ə)l] *adj* (*substance etc*) inflammable; *Fig* (*person, crowd*) prompt à s'échauffer; *Fig* **the situation is highly i.** la situation est explosive

inflammation [ɪnfləˈmeɪʃən] *n Med* inflammation *f*

inflammatory [ɪnˈflæmətərɪ] *adj* **(a)** (*speech, leaflet*) incendiaire **(b)** *Med* (*disease*) inflammatoire

inflatable [ɪnˈfleɪtəb(ə)l] **1** *adj* (*balloon etc*) gonflable; (*raft*) pneumatique **2** *n* (*boat*) bateau *m* pneumatique

inflate [ɪnˈfleɪt] **1** *vt* **(a)** (*fill with air*) (*balloon, tyre, sail*) gonfler; **to i. the lungs with air** (*one's own*) remplir ses poumons d'air; (*when giving artificial respiration*) souffler dans les poumons **(b)** *Fin* (*prices*) faire monter; *Com* (*account*) grossir, charger; (*expense account, figures*) gonfler; *Econ* **to i. the currency** accroître artificiellement la circulation fiduciaire **2** *vi* se gonfler; *Fig* **to i. with pride** se gonfler d'orgueil

inflated [ɪnˈfleɪtɪd] *adj* **(a)** (*balloon, tyre etc*) gonflé; **to become i.** (*with air etc*) se gonfler; *Fig* **i. with pride** bouffi d'orgueil; *Fig* **to have an i. opinion of oneself** avoir une opinion trop flatteuse *ou* surfaite de soi-même **(b)** *Fin* (*price*) exagéré **(c)** *Liter* (*style*) enflé

inflation [ɪnˈfleɪʃən] *n* **(a)** *Econ* inflation *f*; **rate of i.** taux *m* d'inflation; **i.-proof** (*pension etc*) protégé contre les effets de l'inflation **(b)** (*of balloon, tyre etc*) gonflage *m*

inflationary [ɪnˈfleɪʃənərɪ] *adj Econ* inflationniste; **i. spiral** spirale *f* inflationniste

inflect [ɪnˈflekt] **1** *vt* **(a)** *Gram* (*noun, adjective*) décliner; (*verb*) conjuguer **(b)** (*voice*) moduler; *Mus* (*note*) altérer **(c)** *Opt* (*light beam*) infléchir **2** *vi Gram* prendre une marque flexionnelle

inflected [ɪnˈflektɪd] *adj Ling* (*language*) à flexions, flexionnel; (*vowel*) infléchi

inflection [ɪnˈflekʃən] *n* = **inflexion**

inflexibility [ɪnfleksɪˈbɪlɪtɪ] *n* (*of person, government etc*) inflexibilité *f*; *Tech* rigidité *f*

inflexible [ɪnˈfleksɪb(ə)l] *adj* (*person, government etc*) inflexible; *Tech* rigide; **i. code of morals** morale *f* rigide *ou* inflexible

inflexion [ɪnˈflekʃən] *n* **(a)** *Gram* (*of word*) flexion *f* **(b)** (*of voice*) inflexion *f*; *Mus* (*of note*) altération *f* **(c)** *Opt, Math* inflexion *f*

inflict [ɪnˈflɪkt] *vt* (*suffering, losses, Jur punishment*) infliger (**sth on sb** qch à qn); (*wound*) faire (**on** à); (*unhappiness*) causer, occasionner (**on** à); *F Hum* **to i. oneself on sb** s'imposer

infliction [ɪnˈflɪkʃən] *n* (*action*) action *f* d'infliger; **to take pleasure in the i. of pain** prendre du plaisir à infliger de la douleur

in-flight *adj Av* en vol; **i. catering** restauration *f* aérienne; **i. entertainment** distractions *fpl* en vol; **i. magazine** magazine *m* distribué dans les avions; **i. meal** repas *m* servi pendant le vol; **i. service** service *m* à bord (d'un avion)

inflorescence [ɪnfləˈresəns] *n Bot* inflorescence *f*

inflow [ˈɪnfləʊ] *n* (*act of flowing in*) (*of water*) arrivée *f*; (*of people, goods, cash*) afflux *m*; (*of new ideas*) flot *m*; **i. of capital** afflux *m* de capitaux; **i. of money** rentrée *f* d'argent; **i. pipe** (*for water*) arrivée d'eau

influence¹ [ˈɪnflʊəns] *n* influence *f* (**upon, on** sur); **to exert** *or* **exercise an i. on sb** exercer une influence sur qn, influencer qn; **to be a good/bad/great i. on sb** avoir une bonne/mauvaise/grande influence sur qn; **to use one's i. with sb** user de son influence auprès de qn; **man of i.** homme *m* influent; **he owes his position to i.** il doit sa situation à des personnalités influentes; **to have i.** avoir de l'influence; **to have great i. over sb** avoir beaucoup d'influence sur qn; **to be under sb's i.** être sous l'influence de qn; **under the i. of drink,** *F* **under the i.** sous l'empire de la boisson

influence² *vt* influencer; **she's too easily influenced** elle se laisse influencer trop facilement

influencer [ˈɪnflʊənsər] *n Mktg* préconisateur *m*

influential [ɪnflʊˈenʃəl] *adj* influent; **to be i.** (*of person*) avoir de l'influence, *F* avoir le bras long; (*of factor etc*) avoir du poids, jouer un rôle; **he was i. in getting her a job** il a fait jouer son influence pour l'aider à obtenir du travail

influenza [ɪnflʊˈenzə] *n Med* grippe *f*, influenza *f*

influx [ˈɪnflʌks] *n* (*of water etc*) arrivée *f*; (*of people, goods, cash*) afflux *m*; (*of gas*) afflux; (*of new ideas*) flot *m*; **a sudden i. of tourists** un soudain afflux de touristes; *Econ* **i. of gold** entrée *f ou* afflux d'or

info [ˈɪnfəʊ] *n F* renseignements *mpl*, tuyaux *mpl*

infomercial [ɪnfəʊˈmɜːʃəl] *n Am* publicité *f* télévisée sous forme de reportage, publi-rédactionnel *m* télévisuel

inform [ɪnˈfɔːm] **1** *vt* **(a)** (*tell*) **to i. sb of sth** informer qn de qch; **to i. sb about sth** (*provide with information*) renseigner qn sur qch; **to keep sb informed of what is happening** tenir qn au courant de ce qui se passe; **why was I not informed (of this)?** pourquoi est-ce que je n'en ai pas été informé?; **to i. the police** avertir la police; **we are writing to i. you of the dispatch of …** nous vous avisons de l'envoi de …; **I regret to have to i. you that …** j'ai le regret de vous annoncer que …; **we are informed that …** on nous fait savoir que …

(b) *Lit* (*pervade*) (*literary work etc*) imprégner

2 *vi Jur* **to i. against** *or* **on sb** dénoncer qn

informal [ɪnˈfɔːməl] *adj* **(a)** (*person, manner, attitude*) simple, décontracté; (*speech, language, words*) familier; (*clothes*) décontracté; (*reception, dinner*) sans cérémonie; **he's very i. for a prime minister** il est très décontracté pour un premier ministre; **British offices tend to be more i. than German ones** en Grande-Bretagne l'ambiance dans les bureaux tend à être plus décontractée qu'en Allemagne; **dress: i.** (*on invitation*) tenue de ville

(b) (*unofficial*) (*meeting*) non-officiel; (*arrangement*) officieux; **I had an i. chat with the boss** j'ai discuté un peu avec le patron; **the two leaders had i. talks** les deux dirigeants ont eu des entretiens non-officiels

informality [ɪnfɔːˈmælɪtɪ] *n* (*of person*) simplicité *f*, décontraction *f*; (*of occasion*) absence *f* de formalité *ou* de cérémonie; (*of talks*) caractère *m* non-officiel

informally [ɪnˈfɔːməlɪ] *adv* **(a)** (*to dine*) sans cérémonie, sans formalités; (*to dress*) simplement; **i. known as …** familièrement connu sous le nom de … **(b)** (*to discuss*) officieusement, à titre non-officiel

informant [ɪnˈfɔːmənt] *n* informateur, -trice; **I have it from a reliable i.** je le tiens de source sûre

informatics [ɪnfɔːˈmætɪks] *n* [①A10,c] informatique *f*

information [ɪnfəˈmeɪʃən] *n* **(a)** (*news, facts etc*) renseignement(s) *m(pl)*, information(s) *f(pl)*; **a bit** *or* **piece of i.** un renseignement, une information; **I'm afraid your i. is wrong** je crains qu'on vous ait mal renseigné; **to ask for i. on** *or* **about sb/sth** demander des renseignements sur qn/qch; **for further i. write to …** pour de plus amples informations écrire à …; **why don't you ask at i.?** pourquoi est-ce que tu ne demandes pas aux renseignements?; **for my own i.** pour ma propre information; **I am sending you this brochure for your i.** je vous envoie cette brochure à titre d'information; **for your i., I'm not stupid** sachez que je ne suis pas complètement idiot; **for your i., I've done the dishes for the past week!** je t'apprendrai que j'ai fait la vaisselle toute cette semaine!; **his head is full of useless i.** il encombre sa mémoire de choses inutiles; **I can't retain i. as well as I could** ma mémoire n'est pas aussi bonne qu'avant; **i. gathering** collecte *f* d'informations; **i. market** marché *m* des informations; **i. pack** dossier *m* d'information; **i. sheet** fiche *f* explicative

(b) *Comptr* information *f*; **i. carrier** support *m* d'information; **i. retrieval** recherche *f* documentaire *ou* des informations; **i. retrieval system** système *m* de recherche documentaire; **i. storage** mémorisation *f* des informations; **i. system** système *m* informatique; **i. theory** théorie *f* de l'information

(c) *Jur* dénonciation *f* (**against sb** contre qn), délation *f* (**against sb** de qn); **to lay i. against sb with the police** dénoncer qn à la police, informer contre qn

(d) *Am Tel* renseignements *mpl*

information bureau *n* bureau *m* de renseignements, centre *m* d'information; (*for tourists*) syndicat *m* d'initiative

information desk *n* (*in hotel etc*) bureau *m* des renseignements

information processing *n* traitement *m* de l'information; **i. industry** industrie *f* de l'informatique

information science *n* sciences *fpl* informatiques, informatique *f*

information scientist *n* informaticien, -ienne

information (super)highway *n* autoroute *f* de l'information

information technology *n* informatique *f*

informative [ɪnˈfɔːmətɪv] *adj* (*programme, book, lecture*)

instructif; (*book*) éducatif; **he wasn't very i.** il ne nous a pas appris grand-chose; *Mktg* **i. advertising** publicité *f* informative
informed [ɪn'fɔːmd] *adj* (*person*) bien renseigné *ou* informé; **the i. opinion is that ...** les experts pensent que ...; **the i. consumer** le consommateur averti; **an i. estimate/decision** une évaluation faite/une décision prise en connaissance de cause
informer [ɪn'fɔːmər] *n Pej* indicateur *m*; **to turn i.** dénoncer ses complices
infotainment [ɪnfəʊ'teɪnmənt] *n TV* émissions *fpl* d'information divertissantes
infraction [ɪn'frækʃən] *n Fml* = **infringement**
infra dig ['ɪnfrə'dɪg] *adj F* rabaissant; **it would be i. for us to reply** ce serait au-dessous de nous de répondre, ce serait se rabaisser que de répondre
infrared [ɪnfrə'red] *adj Phys* infrarouge; **i. keyboard** clavier *m* à infrarouge; *Med* **i. lamp** lampe *f* à rayons infrarouges; *Comptr* **i. mouse** souris *f* à infrarouge; **i. radiation** *or* **rays** radiation *f* infrarouge, infrarouge *m*; **i. remote control** télécommande *f* à infrarouge
infrastructure ['ɪnfrəstrʌktʃər] *n* infrastructure *f*
infrequency [ɪn'friːkwənsɪ] *n* rareté *f*
infrequent [ɪn'friːkwənt] *adj* rare, peu fréquent
infrequently [ɪn'friːkwəntlɪ] *adv* rarement; **not i.** assez souvent
infringe [ɪn'frɪndʒ] *vt* (*law, rule*) enfreindre, violer, transgresser; **to i. (an author's) copyright** empiéter sur les droits d'un auteur
▶ **infringe on** *vipo* (*person's rights*) empiéter sur
infringement [ɪn'frɪndʒmənt] *n* (*of rule*) infraction *f*; (*of law, right*) violation *f*; **i. of sb's rights** infraction *ou* atteinte *f* aux droits de qn; **minor i. of the law/regulations** contravention *f*; **i. of copyright** non-respect *m* des droits *f* d'auteur
infuriate [ɪn'fjʊərɪeɪt] *vt* rendre furieux, enrager
infuriated [ɪn'fjʊərɪeɪtɪd] *adj* furieux
infuriating [ɪn'fjʊərɪeɪtɪŋ] *adj* exaspérant; **at times I find him i.** quelquefois il me met hors de moi; **it's i. the way she's always right** ça me met hors de moi qu'elle ait toujours raison
infuriatingly [ɪn'fjʊərɪeɪtɪŋlɪ] *adv* (*to answer*) d'une façon exaspérante; **to be i. slow/difficult** être d'une lenteur/difficulté exaspérante
infuse [ɪn'fjuːz] **1** *vt* **(a)** (*instil*) (*energy, new life, courage*) insuffler **(into sb** à qn) **(b)** (*soak*) (*tea, herbs*) infuser, faire infuser **2** *vi* (*of tea*) infuser
infuser [ɪn'fjʊːzər] *n* infusoir *m*
infusion [ɪn'fjuːʒən] *n* **(a)** (*liquid*) (*of camomile etc*) tisane *f*, infusion *f*; *Pharm* infusé *m* **(b)** (*action*) (*of tea, herbs*) infusion *f*; (*of energy, new life etc*) injection *f*
ingenious [ɪn'dʒiːnɪəs] *adj* (*person, device*) ingénieux
ingeniously [ɪn'dʒiːnɪəslɪ] *adv* ingénieusement
ingenuity [ɪndʒɪ'njuːɪtɪ] *n* (*of person, invention*) ingéniosité *f*
ingenuous [ɪn'dʒenjʊəs] *adj* **(a)** (*naive*) ingénu, candide, naïf, *f* naïve **(b)** (*frank*) franc, *f* franche, sincère
ingenuously [ɪn'dʒenjʊəslɪ] *adv* **(a)** (*naively*) ingénument, naïvement, avec candeur **(b)** (*frankly*) franchement, sincèrement
ingenuousness [ɪn'dʒenjʊəsnɪs] *n* **(a)** (*naivety*) ingénuité *f*, naïveté *f*, candeur *f* **(b)** (*frankness*) franchise *f*, sincérité *f*
ingest [ɪn'dʒest] *vt Physiol* (*food*) ingérer
ingestion [ɪn'dʒestʃən] *n Physiol* ingestion *f*
inglenook ['ɪŋg(ə)lnʊk] *n* coin *m* du feu
inglorious [ɪn'glɔːrɪəs] *adj* (*shameful*) (*defeat etc*) déshonorant, honteux
ingloriously [ɪn'glɔːrɪəslɪ] *adv* (*to retreat*) sans gloire; (*to be defeated*) honteusement
ingot ['ɪŋgət] *n* (*of gold, silver*) lingot *m*
ingrained [ɪŋ'greɪnd] *adj* **(a) i. with dirt** encrassé; **i. dirt** crasse *f* **(b)** (*deep-seated*) (*prejudice, distrust, belief etc*) enraciné; (*habit*) invétéré, enraciné; **certain habits are i. in one's nature** certaines habitudes sont enracinées dans la nature de chacun
ingratiate [ɪn'greɪʃɪeɪt] *vt* **to i. oneself with sb** s'insinuer dans les bonnes grâces de qn
ingratiating [ɪn'greɪʃɪeɪtɪŋ] *adj* doucereux; **to act/speak in an i. manner** agir/parler d'une manière doucereuse
ingratiatingly [ɪn'greɪʃɪeɪtɪŋlɪ] *adv* d'une manière doucereuse
ingratitude [ɪn'grætɪtjuːd] *n* ingratitude *f*
ingredient [ɪn'griːdɪənt] *n* ingrédient *m*; *Fig* **what are the ingredients of her success?** qu'est-ce qui fait son succès?
ingress ['ɪngres] *n Jur* entrée *f*
ingrowing ['ɪngrəʊɪŋ], **ingrown** ['ɪngrəʊn] *adj Med* **i. toenail** ongle *m* incarné
inhabit [ɪn'hæbɪt] *vt* (*house, town*) habiter, habiter dans; **a fictitious world inhabited by strange people** un monde fictif peuplé de gens étranges
inhabitable [ɪn'hæbɪtəb(ə)l] *adj* habitable
inhabitant [ɪn'hæbɪtənt] *n* habitant, -ante
inhabited [ɪn'hæbɪtɪd] *adj* habité, peuplé
inhalant [ɪn'heɪlənt] *n Med* produit *m* à prendre en inhalation
inhalation [ɪnhə'leɪʃən] *n* **(a)** (*of chloroform etc*) inhalation *f* **(b)** (*of perfume*) aspiration *f*
inhale [ɪn'heɪl] **1** *vt Med* (*ether etc*) inhaler; (*perfume*) aspirer, humer; (*cigarette smoke*) respirer, avaler **2** *vi* respirer; (*in smoking*) avaler la fumée
inhaler [ɪn'heɪlər] *n* **(a)** *Med* (*device*) inhalateur *m* **(b)** (*smoker*) = fumeur, -euse qui avale la fumée de sa cigarette
inhaling [ɪn'heɪlɪŋ] *n* inhalation *f*
inherent [ɪn'hɪərənt, -'herənt] *adj* inhérent, propre **(in** à); **i. stability** (*of plane, ship etc*) stabilité *f* propre; **an i. fault in the design** une anomalie inhérente à la conception; **power i. in an office** pouvoir *m* inhérent à une fonction; *Com* **i. vice** vice *m* inhérent
inherently [ɪn'hɪərəntlɪ, -'herəntlɪ] *adv* fondamentalement; **i. lazy** né paresseux
inherit [ɪn'herɪt] **1** *vt* (*house, money etc, Fig character, looks*) hériter (de); **to i. sth from sb** hériter (de) qch de qn **2** *vi* **to i. equally** hériter de parts égales; **to i. jointly** cohériter
inheritance [ɪn'herɪtəns] *n* **(a)** (*act of inheriting*) succession *f*; **the title came to him by right of i.** il a hérité du titre de plein droit; **law of i.** droit *m* successif **(b)** (*money, jewels etc*), *Fig* patrimoine *m*, héritage *m*; *Biol* (*genetic*) patrimoine; **to come into an i.** faire un héritage
inheritance tax *n* droits *mpl* de succession
inherited [ɪn'herɪtɪd] *adj* (*property, characteristic, taste, wealth*) hérité
inhibit [ɪn'hɪbɪt] *vt* **(a)** (*progress, growth etc*) entraver **(b)** *Psy* (*feeling*) inhiber **(c)** *Med* (*secretion etc*) inhiber **(d)** *Jur etc* **to i. sb from doing sth** interdire *ou* défendre à qn de faire qch
inhibit code *n Comptr* code *m* inhibiteur
inhibited [ɪn'hɪbɪtɪd] *adj* inhibé; **i. person** inhibé, -ée; **she's not inhibited** elle n'a pas d'inhibitions
inhibiting [ɪn'hɪbɪtɪŋ] *adj* (*influence etc*) inhibiteur, -trice
inhibition [ɪn(h)ɪ'bɪʃən] *n* **(a)** *Med, Psy* inhibition *f*; **to have no inhibitions** avoir aucune inhibition **(about confessing** pour ce qui est d'avouer) **(b)** *Jur etc* défense *f* expresse, prohibition *f*
inhibitive [ɪn'hɪbɪtɪv] *adj Med* inhibiteur
inhibitor [ɪn'hɪbɪtər] *n Mktg, Aut, Med* inhibiteur *m*
inhibitory [ɪn'hɪbɪt(ə)rɪ] *adj* **(a)** (*nerve, reflex*) inhibiteur **(b)** (*warrant*) prohibitif
in-home placement testing *n Mktg* test *m* à domicile par des consommateurs-témoins
inhospitable [ɪnhɒ'spɪtəb(ə)l, ɪn'hɒs-] *adj* (*person, climate, region etc*) inhospitalier
inhospitably [ɪnhɒ'spɪtəblɪ] *adv* d'une manière inhospitalière
in-house 1 *adj* **to have an i. accountant/computer** avoir un comptable/un ordinateur sur place; **i. magazine** revue *f* d'entreprise; **i. newspaper** journal *m* interne; **i. publication** publication *f* interne; **i. travel agency** implant *m* **2** *adv* **to do sth i.** faire qch sur place; **to keep a job i.** faire un travail sur place
inhuman [ɪn'hjuːmən] *adj* inhumain; (*custom*) barbare
inhumane [ɪnhjuː'meɪn] *adj* inhumain, cruel
inhumanity [ɪnhjuː'mænɪtɪ] *n* (*of person, action*) inhumanité *f*, cruauté *f*, barbarie *f*; **man's i. to man** la cruauté de l'homme envers son prochain
inimical [ɪ'nɪmɪk(ə)l] *adj* (*people*) ennemi, hostile; (*conditions*) défavorable, contraire **(to** à)
inimitable [ɪ'nɪmɪtəb(ə)l] *adj* inimitable
inimitably [ɪ'nɪmɪtəblɪ] *adv* d'une manière inimitable
iniquitous [ɪ'nɪkwɪtəs] *adj* inique
iniquitously [ɪ'nɪkwɪtəslɪ] *adv* iniquement
iniquity [ɪ'nɪkwɪtɪ] *n* iniquité *f*
initial[1] [ɪ'nɪʃəl] **1** *adj* initial, premier; **her i. delight** son plaisir initial; **the disease is only in the i. stages** la maladie n'en est qu'à son stade initial; **the i. difficulties** les difficultés du début; *Typ* **i. letter** lettre initiale, lettrine *f*; *Ling* **in i. position** en position initiale; *Com* **i. stock** stock *m* de départ **2** *n* **(a) initials** initiales *f*; (*to alteration of cheque etc*) paraphe *m*; (*of supervisor etc*) visa *m*; (*on garment etc*) monogramme *m* **(b)** *Typ* lettre *f* initiale, lettrine *f*
initial[2] *vt* **(-ll-**, *US* **-l-)** (*treaty, correction etc*) parapher; (*legal document*) viser, mettre son paraphe au bas de
initialization [ɪnɪʃəlaɪ'zeɪʃən] *n* initialisation *f*
initialize [ɪ'nɪʃəlaɪz] *vt Comptr* initialiser
initially [ɪ'nɪʃəlɪ] *adv* au départ, au début
initiate[1] [ɪ'nɪʃɪeɪt] *vt* **(a)** (*begin*) (*negotiations etc*) commencer, ouvrir; (*project etc*) lancer, amorcer; (*measures etc*) instaurer; (*new policy etc*) inaugurer; (*reform*) être l'initiateur de; *Jur* **to i. proceedings against sb** entamer des poursuites contre qn

(**b**) (*induct*) initier; **to i. sb into a secret society** admettre qn dans une société secrète

initiate² [ɪ'nɪʃɪət] *n* initié, -ée

initiated [ɪ'nɪʃɪeɪtɪd] **1** *adj* initié **2** *npl* **the i.** les initiés *mpl*

initiation [ɪnɪʃɪ'eɪʃən] *n* (**a**) (*induction*) initiation *f* (**into** à); **i. ceremony** cérémonie *f* d'initiation (**b**) (*beginning*) (*of undertaking*) commencement(s) *m(pl)*, début(s) *m(pl)*

initiative [ɪ'nɪʃɪətɪv, ɪ'nɪʃətɪv] *n* initiative *f*; **to take the i.** prendre l'initiative (**in doing sth** de faire qch); **to do sth on one's own i.** faire qch de sa propre initiative; **to show/lack i.** faire preuve/manquer d'initiative; **use your i.!** fais preuve d'un peu d'initiative!; **we need sb with i.** nous avons besoin de quelqu'un qui a de l'initiative

initiator [ɪ'nɪʃɪeɪtər] *n* initiateur, -trice

inject [ɪn'dʒekt] *vt* (*drug, Fig capital*) injecter (**into** dans); (*give injection to*) faire une piqûre à (**with sth** de qch); **to i. sb with morphine** faire une piqûre de morphine à qn; **to i. a fluid into a cavity, to i. a cavity with a fluid** injecter un liquide dans une cavité; **to i. drugs** (*of addict*) s'injecter de la drogue, se piquer; *Fig* **to i. new life into sth** donner un nouvel essor à qch; **she tried to i. a little humour into the meeting** elle a essayé d'introduire une note d'humour dans la réunion

injectable [ɪn'dʒektəb(ə)l] *adj* (*drug*) injectable

injection [ɪn'dʒekʃən] *n* (*action*) injection *f*; *Med* **an i.** une injection, une piqûre; **tetanus/polio i.** piqûre *f ou* vaccin *m* antitétanique/antipoliomyélitique; **to give sb an i.** faire une injection *ou* une piqûre à qn; *Fig* **i. of capital into a business** injection *ou* apport *m* de capital dans une entreprise; *Constr* **i. pump** pompe *f* à injection; *Aut* (**fuel**) **i. pump** pompe d'injection (de carburant); **i. moulding** (*of plastics*) moulage *m* par injection

injector [ɪn'dʒektər] *n Aut* injecteur *m*

injudicious [ɪndʒʊ'dɪʃəs] *adj* peu judicieux, malavisé

injudiciously [ɪndʒʊ'dɪʃəslɪ] *adv* d'une façon peu judicieuse

Injun ['ɪndʒən] *n US Offensive F* Indien, -ienne (d'Amérique); **honest I.!** vrai de vrai!, sans blague!

injunction [ɪn'dʒʌŋkʃən] *n* (**a**) *Jur* arrêt *m* de suspension, arrêt de sursis; **I shall ask for an i.** je vais demander un sursis (**b**) (*command*) injonction *f*, ordre *m*, recommandation *f*; **to give sb strict injunctions to do sth** enjoindre formellement à qn de faire qch

injure ['ɪndʒər] *vt* (**a**) (*physically*) blesser; **to i. oneself** se blesser, se faire du mal; **she injured her head** elle s'est blessée à la tête; *Fig* **to i. sb's pride** blesser qn dans son amour-propre (**b**) (*harm*) (*sb*) nuire à, faire tort à, léser; *Jur* porter préjudice à; (*sb's reputation*) nuire à, faire du tort à; (*sb's interests*) compromettre; **to i. one's health** s'abîmer la santé

injured ['ɪndʒəd] **1** *adj* (**a**) (*physically*) blessé; **badly/slightly i.** gravement/légèrement blessé (**b**) *Fig* (*offended*) offensé, outragé; (*deceived*) trompé, trahi; **the i. party** l'offensé, -ée; *Jur* la partie lésée; **in an i. (tone of) voice** d'une voix offensée; **i. pride** orgueil *m* blessé **2** *npl* **the i.** les blessés *mpl*

injurious [ɪn'dʒʊərɪəs] *adj* (**a**) (*harmful*) nuisible, préjudiciable (**to** à); **i. to (the) health** nuisible à la santé (**b**) *Fml* (*language*) injurieux, offensant

injury ['ɪndʒ(ə)rɪ] *n* (**a**) (*physical*) (*to body*) blessure *f*, *Spec* lésion *f*; **to do oneself an i.** se blesser, se faire du mal; **wearing a seat belt can prevent i.** le port de la ceinture de sécurité peut éviter des blessures; **he escaped without i.** il n'a pas été blessé (**b**) (*wrong*) tort *m*, préjudice *m*; *Jur* lésion *f*; **to do sb an i.** faire du tort à qn

injury time *n Sp* arrêts *mpl* de jeu; **he scored nine minutes into i.** il a marqué un but neuf minutes après le début des arrêts de jeu

injustice [ɪn'dʒʌstɪs] *n* (**a**) (*of law, system etc*) injustice *f* (**b**) (*unjust act, remark*) injustice *f*; **you do him an i.** vous êtes injuste envers lui

ink¹ [ɪŋk] *n* (**a**) encre *f*; **written in i.** écrit à l'encre; **i. bottle** bouteille *f* d'encre; **i. cartridge** cartouche *f* d'encre; **i. channel** (*in printer*) canal *m* encreur; **i. pad** tampon *m* (encreur); **i. pot** encrier *m*; **i. stain** tache *f* d'encre (**b**) (*of squid, octopus*) noir *m*, encre *f*; **i. bag** *or* **sac** glande *f ou* poche *f* du noir

ink² *vt Typ* (*letters, plate*) encrer

▶ **ink in** *vtsep Art* (**a**) (*pencil lines*) tracer à l'encre (**b**) (*drawing*) mettre à l'encre

▶ **ink out** *vtsep* (*word etc*) oblitérer *ou* rayer *ou* biffer à l'encre

inkblot ['ɪŋkblɒt] *n* (*on paper*) pâté *m*; *Psy* (*in Rorschach test*) tache *f* d'encre; **i. test** test *m* de la tache d'encre

inking ['ɪŋkɪŋ] *n Typ* (*of rollers*) encrage *m*

ink-jet *n* (*printer*) imprimante *f* à jet d'encre

inkling ['ɪŋklɪŋ] *n* soupçon *m*; **to give sb an i. of sth** faire entrevoir qch à qn; **she gave me no i. of her intentions** elle ne m'a aucunement communiqué ses intentions; **could you give me an i. of what it's about?** est-ce que tu pourrais me donner une idée de ce dont il s'agit?; **he had an i. of the truth** il entrevoyait la vérité; **he has no i. of the matter, he doesn't have an i.** il ne se doute de rien; **she had no i. of what they were up to** elle ne se doutait pas le moins du monde de ce qu'ils préparaient

inkstand ['ɪŋkstænd] *n* (grand) encrier *m*

inkwell ['ɪŋkwel] *n* encrier *m* (*de pupitre*)

inky ['ɪŋkɪ] *adj* (**a**) (*stained with ink*) taché d'encre; (*blotted with ink*) barbouillé d'encre (**b**) **i. (black)** noir comme (de) l'encre; **the night was i. black** il faisait nuit noire

inlaid [ɪn'leɪd] *adj* (*furniture, brooch etc*) incrusté (**with** de); (*with wood*) marqueté; (*floor*) parqueté; **i. work** (*wood*) marqueterie *f*; **i. enamel work** nielle *f*

inland ['ɪnlænd, 'ɪnlənd] **1** *adj* (**a**) (*away from sea*) intérieur; **i. clearance depot** dépôt *m* de dédouanement intérieur; **i. freight** fret *m* intérieur; **i. haulage** transport *m* routier; **i. navigation** navigation *f* intérieure *ou* fluviale; **i. waterway** voie *f* navigable *ou* fluviale; **i. waterway transport** transport *m* fluvial

(**b**) *Br* (*mail*) intérieur; **i. postage rates** (tarif *m* d')affranchissement *m* en régime intérieur

2 *adv* vers l'intérieur, dans les terres; **to go i.** pénétrer vers l'intérieur *ou* dans les terres; **the town is situated a few miles i.** la ville est située à quelques kilomètres dans les terres

Inland Revenue *n* le fisc

in-law *n* parent *m* par alliance; **in-laws** (*mother & father of spouse*) beaux-parents *mpl*; (*family of spouse*) belle-famille *f*

inlay¹ ['ɪnleɪ] *n* (**a**) (*of mother-of-pearl etc*) incrustation *f*; (*piece of marquetry*) marqueterie *f* (**b**) (*in dentistry*) (*of metal, ceramic etc*) inlay *m*, incrustation *f*

inlay² ['ɪnleɪ, ɪn'leɪ] *vt* (*pt, pp* **inlaid**) incruster (**with** de); (*table etc*) (*with wood*) marqueter; **to i. with enamel** nieller; **table inlaid with mother-of-pearl** table incrustée de nacre

inlet ['ɪnlet] *n* (**a**) (*in shore etc*) petit bras *m* de mer; (*small bay*) crique *f*, anse *f* (**b**) *Tech* (*opening*) (*for air etc*) (orifice *m* d')entrée *f*, (orifice d')admission *f*; (*of ventilator etc*) ouïe *f*; *Aut* **i. manifold** conduits *mpl* d'admission, collecteur *m* d'admission; **i. pipe** (*for steam etc*) tuyau *m* d'arrivée; *Aut* **i. valve** soupape *f* d'admission; (*of fuel pump*) soupape *f* d'alimentation

in-line engine *n Aut* moteur *m* en ligne

inmate ['ɪnmeɪt] *n* (*in prison*) détenu, -ue; (*in mental hospital*) interné, -ée

in memoriam [ɪnmɪ'mɔːrɪəm] *prep* en mémoire de

inmost ['ɪnməʊst] *adj* le plus profond; **our i. thoughts** nos pensées les plus secrètes; **our i. feelings** nos sentiments les plus intimes; **our i. being** le plus profond de nous-mêmes

inn [ɪn] *n* (**a**) auberge *f* (**b**) *Eng Jur* **Inns of Court** = les quatre Écoles de droit de Londres qui seules confèrent le droit d'être avocat

innards ['ɪnədz] *npl* (*of person, animal*) entrailles *fpl*, intestins *mpl*; (*of machine*) entrailles

innate [ɪ'neɪt] *adj* inné; **i. common sense** bon sens *m* naturel *ou* foncier; *Phil* **i. ideas** idées *fpl* innées

inner ['ɪnər] **1** *adj* (*chamber, courtyard, calm, lining*) intérieur; (*layer, Anat ear etc*) interne; **i. conviction** conviction *f* intime; **i. harbour** arrière-port *m*, *pl* arrière-ports; **i. London** Londres intra-muros; *Rel* **the i. man** (*soul*) l'âme *f*; *Hum* **here's something for the i. man** (*stomach*) voilà de quoi boucher un trou; *Aut, Cycling* **i. tube** chambre *f* à air; **the i. circle** le cercle intime (d'amis); (*of political party*) le groupe dirigeant; **i. suburbs** première couronne *f* **2** *n* (*of target*) premier cercle *m* autour de la mouche

inner city *n* les vieux quartiers *mpl* du centre-ville

inner-city *adj* **i. crime** crimes *mpl* se produisant dans les quartiers pauvres; **i. children** enfants *mpl* des quartiers pauvres

innermost ['ɪnəməʊst] *adj* = **inmost**

inning ['ɪnɪŋ] *n Baseball* tour *m* de batte

innings ['ɪnɪŋz] *n inv Cr* tournée *f*, tour *m* de batte (*de chaque équipe ou de chaque membre de l'équipe*); *Fig* **she had a good i.** (*of sb recently dead*) elle a bien profité de la vie; (*of participant in game show etc*) elle ne s'en est pas mal sortie

innkeeper ['ɪnkiːpər] *n* aubergiste *mf*, hôtelier, -ière

innocence ['ɪnəsəns] *n* (**a**) (*of defendant*) innocence *f* (**b**) (*inexperience, naiveté*) naïveté *f*, innocence *f*; **to lose one's i.** perdre son innocence; **to take advantage of sb's i.** abuser de l'innocence de qn; **in all i.** en toute innocence

innocent ['ɪnəsənt] **1** *adj* (**a**) (*not guilty*) innocent; **i. of a crime** innocent d'un crime; **an i. person** un(e) innocent(e); **the bomb killed several i. bystanders** la bombe a tué plusieurs innocents qui se trouvaient là; *F* **to act all i.** faire l'innocent

(b) (*pure*) innocent; **as i. as a newborn babe** innocent comme l'enfant qui vient de naître

(c) (*naive*) naïf, *f* naïve

(d) (*harmless*) (*game, fun*) innocent; (*remark, question etc*) sans malice, innocent

(e) *Fml* (*devoid*) dépourvu (**of** de)

2 *n* innocent, -ente; **I was a real i. then** j'étais vraiment innocent à l'époque; **don't come the i. with me** ne fais pas l'innocent avec moi; *Cathol* **Holy Innocents' Day** la fête des saints Innocents

innocently [ˈɪnəsəntlɪ] *adv* innocemment, en toute innocence

innocuous [ɪˈnɒkjʊəs] *adj* inoffensif; **an i. remark** une remarque anodine

innocuously [ɪˈnɒkjʊəslɪ] *adv* (*to remark etc*) de façon inoffensive *ou* anodine

innocuousness [ɪˈnɒkjʊəsnɪs] *n* (*of remark, joke etc*) caractère *m* anodin; *Med* innocuité *f*

innovate [ˈɪnəveɪt] *vi* innover (**in** à, en, dans)

innovating company *n Mktg* entreprise *f* innovatrice

innovation [ɪnəˈveɪʃən] *n* innovation *f*

innovative [ˈɪnəveɪtɪv, -vətɪv] *adj* (in)novateur, -trice; *Mktg* **i. product** produit *m* novateur

innovator [ˈɪnəveɪtər] *n* (in)novateur, -trice

innuendo, *pl* **-o(e)s** [ɪnjʊˈendəʊ, -əʊz] *n* **(a)** (*insinuation*) insinuation *f*; **to discredit sb by i.** discréditer qn par sous-entendus **(b)** (*in jokes*) allusion *f* grivoise; **the play is full of i.** la pièce est pleine de sous-entendus **(c)** *Jur* insinuation *f*, mot *m* couvert (*destiné à atteindre qn dans son honneur*)

innumerable [ɪˈnjuːmərəb(ə)l] *adj* innombrable, sans nombre; **the successes have been i.** les réussites ne se comptent plus

innumeracy [ɪˈnjuːmərəsɪ] *n* fait *m* de ne pas savoir compter

innumerate [ɪˈnjuːmərət] *adj* qui ne sait pas compter

inoculate [ɪˈnɒkjʊleɪt] *vt Med* inoculer, vacciner (**contre** against); **to i. sb with a virus** inoculer un virus à qn

inoculation [ɪnɒkjʊˈleɪʃən] *n Med* inoculation *f*

inoffensive [ɪnəˈfensɪv] *adj* **(a)** (*odour etc*) qui n'a rien de désagréable; (*remark, humour etc*) qui n'a rien d'offensant **(b)** (*harmless*) (*animal, person*) inoffensif

inoperable [ɪnˈɒpərəb(ə)l] *adj* **(a)** *Med* inopérable **(b)** (*system*) qui ne peut pas être exploité, inexploitable

inoperative [ɪnˈɒpərətɪv] *adj* inopérant

inopportune [ɪnˈɒpətjuːn] *adj* inopportun, intempestif

inopportunely [ɪnˈɒpətjuːnlɪ] *adv* inopportunément, mal à propos

inordinate [ɪnˈɔːdɪnət] *adj* démesuré, excessif, immodéré

inordinately [ɪnˈɔːdɪnətlɪ] *adv* démesurément, excessivement; **to wait an i. long time** attendre excessivement longtemps

inorganic [ɪnɔːˈgænɪk] *adj* inorganique

in(-)patient *n Med* patient *m* hospitalisé, patiente *f* hospitalisée

in-plant agency *n Am* (*travel agency*) implant *m*

inpoint [ˈɪnpɔɪnt] *n* (*on tape, film*) point *m* d'entrée

input¹ [ˈɪnpʊt] *n* **(a)** (*of factory*) besoins *mpl* (*en personnel, matières premières etc*), *Spec* intrant *m*; (*of machine*) consommation *f*; *El, Electron* (*current etc*) puissance *f* à l'entrée *ou* d'alimentation; (*terminal*) entrée *f*; **i. socket** (*for power*) prise *f* d'alimentation; *Acct* **i. tax** TVA *f* récupérée; *El* **i. transformer** courant *m ou* transformateur *m* d'entrée

(b) *Comptr* (*of data*) entrée *f*, introduction *f*; **i. box** case *f* de saisie; **i. buffer** mémoire *f* tampon de saisie; **i. (data)** données *fpl* introduites, données en entrée; **i. device** périphérique *m* d'entrée; **i. file** fichier *m* d'entrée; **i. mask** masque *m* de saisie; **i./output** entrée/sortie *f*; **i./output port** port *m* d'entrée/sortie; **i. port** port *m* d'entrée; **i. program** programme *m* d'introduction; **i. terminal** terminal *m* d'entrée (de données)

(c) (*contribution to discussion etc*) contribution *f*

input² *vt Comptr* (*data*) entrer

inquest [ˈɪnkwest] *n* enquête *f*; *Fig* (*into reasons for failure of project etc*) analyse *f*

inquire [ɪnˈkwaɪər] **1** *vt* s'informer de (**of sb** auprès de qn); **to i. of sb what is happening** s'informer auprès de qn de ce qui se passe **2** *vi* se renseigner (**about** sur); **I'd like to i. about ...** je voudrais des renseignements sur ...; **i. within** s'adresser ici

▸ **inquire after** *vipo* (*sb*) demander des nouvelles de; **to i. after sb's health** s'informer de la santé de qn

▸ **inquire into** *vipo* faire des recherches sur; *Jur* (*affair*) enquêter *ou* faire une enquête sur; **to i. into the reasons for sth** chercher à connaître les raisons de qch

inquiring [ɪnˈkwaɪərɪŋ] *adj* (*mind*) curieux; (*look*) interrogateur

inquiringly [ɪnˈkwaɪərɪŋlɪ] *adv* (*to look up, to raise one's eyebrows*) d'un air interrogateur; (*to say*) d'un ton interrogateur; **to look i. at sb** interroger qn du regard

inquiry [ɪnˈkwaɪərɪ] *n* **(a)** (*official investigation*) recherche *f*, investigation *f*; (*by police*) enquête *f*; **a man is helping the police with their inquiries** la police est en train d'interroger un individu; **to conduct** *or* **hold an i. into sth** procéder à une enquête sur qch

(b) (*request for information*) demande *f* de renseignements; **to make inquiries** se renseigner; **to make inquiries about sb** prendre des renseignements sur qn; (*less official*) s'informer *ou* se renseigner sur qn; **to make inquiries after sb** s'enquérir de qn; **to make inquiries into sth** faire des recherches sur qch; **as a result of her inquiries** à la suite de ses recherches; **on i.** renseignements pris; *Br* **(private) i. agent** détective *m* (privé); **i. desk** *or* **office, inquiries** bureau *m* de renseignements

inquisition [ɪnkwɪˈzɪʃən] *n Rel, Hist* **the I.** l'Inquisition *f*; *F* **the interview turned into an i.** l'entrevue s'est transformée en inquisition

inquisitive [ɪnˈkwɪzɪtɪv] *adj* **(a)** (*mind, child*) curieux; (*look*) plein de curiosité **(b)** *Pej* (*prying*) indiscret; (*gaze*) inquisiteur

inquisitively [ɪnˈkwɪzɪtɪvlɪ] *adv* (*with curiosity*) avec curiosité; (*to look*) d'un œil inquisiteur; (*to say sth*) sur un ton inquisiteur

inquisitiveness [ɪnˈkwɪzɪtɪvnɪs] *n* curiosité *f*

inquisitor [ɪnˈkwɪzɪtər] *n* **(a)** *Jur* enquêteur, -euse **(b)** *Rel, Hist, Fig F* inquisiteur *m*

inquisitorial [ɪnkwɪzɪˈtɔːrɪəl] *adj* inquisitorial

inroad [ˈɪnrəʊd] *n usu pl* **(a) to make inroads into** (*capital, savings*) entamer, ébrécher; (*opposition's support*) entamer; **they were making inroads into the cheese** ils avaient attaqué le fromage **(b)** *Mil* (*attack*) incursion *f*

inrush [ˈɪnrʌʃ] *n* (*of water, air etc*) irruption *f*; (*of passengers etc*) afflux *m*

ins (a) (*abbr* **insurance**) asse. **(b)** (*abbr* **inches**) pouces, ppo.

insalubrious [ɪnsəˈluːbrɪəs] *adj* insalubre, malsain

insane [ɪnˈseɪn] **1** *adj* **(a)** (*person*) fou, *f* folle; **to become** *or* **go i.** perdre la raison; **to drive sb i.** rendre qn fou; **to be i. with grief/jealousy** être fou de douleur/jalousie; *Am* **i. asylum** hospice *m ou* asile *m* d'aliénés **(b)** *F* (*desire, scheme etc*) insensé, fou, *f* folle; **an i. idea** une idée folle **2** *npl* **the i.** les aliénés *mpl*

insanely [ɪnˈseɪnlɪ] *adv* comme un fou/une folle/des fous/*etc*; **he was i. jealous** (*by nature*) il était d'une jalousie maladive; **he became i. jealous every time he saw ...** il devenait fou de jalousie chaque fois qu'il voyait ...

insanitary [ɪnˈsænɪt(ə)rɪ] *adj* insalubre, malsain

insanity [ɪnˈsænɪtɪ] *n* **(a)** *Med* folie *f*, démence *f*, *Fml* aliénation *f* mentale **(b)** *F* (*of course of action etc*) folie *f*; **it's sheer i. doing that** c'est de la folie pure et simple (que) de faire cela

insatiable [ɪnˈseɪʃ(ɪ)əb(ə)l] *adj* (*appetite, desire etc*) insatiable

insatiably [ɪnˈseɪʃ(ɪ)əblɪ] *adv* insatiablement

inscribe [ɪnˈskraɪb] *vt* (*carve*) inscrire, graver (**sth on stone** qch sur la pierre); (*write*) écrire; *Fig* graver (**in sb's memory** dans la mémoire de qn); **to i. a tomb with a name** graver un nom sur un tombeau

inscription [ɪnˈskrɪpʃən] *n* **(a)** (*of name etc*) inscription *f* **(b)** (*message*) (*on monument etc*) inscription *f*; (*on coin*) inscription, légende *f*; (*in book etc*) dédicace *f*

inscrutability [ɪnskruːtəˈbɪlɪtɪ] *n* inscrutabilité *f*

inscrutable [ɪnˈskruːtəb(ə)l] *adj* (*look, face*) impénétrable, énigmatique; (*remark*) énigmatique; **to remain i.** (*of person*) rester impassible

insect [ˈɪnsekt] *n* insecte *m*; **i. bite** piqûre *f* d'insecte; **i. eater** insectivore *m*; **i. powder** poudre *f* insecticide; **i. repellent** lotion *f ou* crème *f* anti-insectes

insecticide [ɪnˈsektɪsaɪd] *adj, n* insecticide *m*

insectivore [ɪnˈsektɪvɔːr] *n* insectivore *m*

insectivorous [ɪnsekˈtɪvərəs] *adj* insectivore

insecure [ɪnsɪˈkjʊər] *adj* **(a)** (*person*) qui manque d'assurance (sur le plan affectif); **to feel i.** (*because of circumstances*) éprouver un sentiment d'insécurité **(b)** (*unstable*) (*government*) fragile; (*job, arrangement, future*) précaire; **financially i.** financièrement vulnérable **(c)** (*place*) exposé **(d)** (*not solid, tight etc*) (*fastening, border*) peu sûr; (*grip, hold*) lâche

insecurity [ɪnsɪˈkjʊərɪtɪ] *n* insécurité *f*; (*of job, future*) précarité *f*; *esp Mil* (*of position*) caractère *m* exposé; **to have a feeling of i.** éprouver un manque d'assurance *ou* un sentiment d'insécurité

inseminate [ɪnˈsemɪneɪt] *vt* inséminer

insemination [ɪnsemɪˈneɪʃən] *n Biol* insémination *f*

insensate [ɪnˈsenseɪt] *adj Lit* **(a)** (*insensitive*) insensible **(b)** (*senseless*) insensé

insensibility [ɪnsensɪˈbɪlɪtɪ] *n* **(a)** (*unconsciousness*) inconscience *f* **(b)** (*indifference*) insensibilité *f* (**to** à), indifférence *f* (**to** pour)

insensible [ɪnˈsensɪb(ə)l] *adj Fml* **(a)** (*indifferent*) insensible (**to** à) **(b)** (*unaware*) inconscient (**of** de); **he was quite i. of the danger he was in** il ne se doutait pas du danger qui le menaçait **(c)** (*unconscious*) sans connaissance, inconscient; **to become i.** perdre connaissance

insensitive [ɪn'sensɪtɪv] *adj* (*person, approach*) dur, insensible; (*remark*) indélicat; **he can be amazingly i.** il peut manquer de tact *ou* de délicatesse à un point incroyable; **to be i. to sth** être insensible à qch

insensitiveness [ɪn'sensɪtɪvnɪs], **insensitivity** [ɪnsensɪ'tɪvɪtɪ] *n* insensibilité *f*

inseparable [ɪn'sepərəb(ə)l] *adj* inséparable (**from** de)

inseparably [ɪn'sepərəblɪ] *adv* inséparablement

insert¹ ['ɪnsɜːt] *n* (**a**) *Cin* scène-raccord *f*, *pl* scènes-raccords; (*in magazine etc*) encart *m* (**b**) *Typ etc* (*in proofs*) insertion *f*; **i. mark** signe *m* d'insertion (**c**) *Comptr* insertion *f*; **i. key** touche *f* d'insertion; **i. mode** mode *m* (d')insertion; **i. point** point *m* d'insertion (**d**) *Sewing* incrustation *f*

insert² [ɪn'sɜːt] *vt* (**a**) (*key in lock etc*) introduire, enfoncer; (*page in book etc*) insérer; (*clause in contract etc*) insérer, introduire, apposer; **to i. an ad (in the newspaper)** mettre une petite annonce dans le journal (**b**) *Typ* (*line*) intercaler (**c**) *Comptr* insérer

insertion [ɪn'sɜːʃən] *n* (**a**) (*act of inserting*) insertion *f*, introduction *f* (**of sth into sth** de qch dans qch); (*of advert in newspaper*) insertion (**b**) (*thing inserted*) *Typ* insertion *f*; *Sewing* incrustation *f*; (*of lace etc*) entre-deux *m inv*; *Typ* **i. mark** renvoi *m*

inset¹ ['ɪnset] *n* (**a**) (*in bookbinding*) (*of 4 or 8 pages*) encart *m*, carton *m*; (*leaf, advertisement*) encartage *m* (**b**) *Typ* (*map etc*) hors-texte *m inv*, médaillon *m*; *TV, Cin* médaillon (**c**) *Sewing* incrustation *f*

inset² ['ɪn'set] *vt* (*pt, pp* **inset** *or* **insetted**) (**a**) (*in bookbinding*) (*leaves, advertisements*) encarter (**b**) *Typ* insérer en cartouche *ou* en médaillon (**c**) *Sewing* (*piece of fabric etc*) insérer; (*lace etc*) faire des incrustations de (**d**) *Typ* (*indent*) (*line, new paragraph*) renfoncer

inshore ['ɪn'ʃɔːr] *Naut* **1** *adv* près de la côte; (*to head*) vers la côte; **to keep close i.** naviguer près de la côte **2** *adj* (*navigation, fishing*) côtier; **i. waters** eaux *fpl* près de la côte; **i. wind** vent *m* du large

inside 1 *n* ['ɪn'saɪd] (**a**) (*of garment etc*) (côté *m*) intérieur *m*; (*of house etc*) intérieur; **the door opens from (the) i.** la porte s'ouvre de l'intérieur; **the door had been locked from the i.** la porte était verrouillée de l'intérieur; **on the i.** à l'intérieur; **a scar on the i. of his leg** une cicatrice sur la face interne de sa jambe; **to walk on the i. (of the pavement)** marcher loin de la chaussée; **a motorbike was coming up on the i.** une moto arrivait sur la droite *ou* (*in Britain*) la gauche; *F* **to know the i. of an affair** connaître les dessous d'une affaire

(**b**) *F* **insides** (*internal organs*) entrailles *fpl*; **to have pains in one's inside(s)** avoir mal au ventre

(**c**) **i. out** (*sweater etc*) à l'envers; **to turn sth i. out** mettre qch à l'envers; *Fig* **to turn everything i. out** mettre tout sens dessus dessous; *Fig* **to know sth i. out** savoir qch à fond; *Fig* **to know Paris i. out** connaître Paris comme sa poche

2 *adj* ['ɪnsaɪd] (*wall, door, pocket etc*) intérieur; *Constr* (*measurement, stair etc*) dans œuvre; (*diameter*) interne; **i. lane** (*of road*) (*in France, USA etc*) voie *f* de droite; (*in Britain*) voie de gauche; **to be in the i. lane** (*in athletics race*) être sur le couloir intérieur; **i. back cover** troisième *f* de couverture; **i. front cover** deuxième *f* de couverture; **i. leg measurement** entrejambe *m*; *Horseracing* **to be on the i. track** tenir la corde; **it's an i. job** (*of burglary etc*) c'est un coup monté par quelqu'un de la maison; **to have an i. accomplice** avoir un complice à l'intérieur; **i. information** renseignements *mpl* privés; **I speak with i. knowledge** ce que je dis je le sais de bonne source; **i. margin** marge *f* de reliure; **to know the i. story** connaître les dessous de l'histoire

3 *adv* [ɪn'saɪd] (**a**) à l'intérieur; **he took the box and looked i.** il a pris la boîte et a regardé dedans *ou* à l'intérieur; **there's nothing i.** il n'y a rien dedans *ou* à l'intérieur; **i. she was angry** intérieurement elle était en colère; **i. and out** au dedans et au dehors, à l'intérieur et à l'extérieur; **to push sb i.** pousser qn à l'intérieur *ou* dedans; **come i.!** entrez!; *Sl* **to put sb/be i.** (*in prison*) mettre qn/être en tôle *ou* taule

(**b**) (*of time*) (*within*) **i. of three hours** en moins de trois heures

4 *prep* [ɪn'saɪd] (**a**) (*of place*) (*house etc*) à l'intérieur de, dans; **i. the country/company** au sein du pays/de la société; **the telephone is just i. the door** le téléphone est juste derrière la porte; *F* **get this i. you** avale-ça; *Th F* **to get right i. a part** entrer dans la peau d'un personnage

(**b**) (*of time*) **i. a week/an hour** en moins d'une semaine/d'une heure

inside centre *n Rugby* premier centre *m*

inside left *n Fb* intérieur *m ou F* inter *m* gauche

insider [ɪn'saɪdər] *n* initié, -ée; *Fin* **i. dealing** *or* **trading** délit *m ou* opération *f* d'initié

insidious [ɪn'sɪdɪəs] *adj* insidieux

insidiously [ɪn'sɪdɪəslɪ] *adv* insidieusement

insight ['ɪnsaɪt] *n* (**a**) (*perspicacity*) perspicacité *f*; **i. into character** finesse *f* psychologique; **to have a lot of i.** être très perspicace (**b**) (*understanding*) aperçu *m*; **to get an i. into sth** avoir un aperçu de qch; **the book offers several valuable insights into ...** le livre donne un bon aperçu de ...

insightful ['ɪnsaɪtfʊl] *adj* perspicace

insignia [ɪn'sɪgnɪə] *npl* (*of royal family etc*) insignes *mpl*; *Mil* **i. of rank** insignes du grade

insignificance [ɪnsɪg'nɪfɪkəns] *n* insignifiance *f*; **my problems fade into i. beside yours** mes problèmes semblent totalement insignifiants à côté des tiens

insignificant [ɪnsɪg'nɪfɪkənt] *adj* insignifiant

insincere [ɪnsɪn'sɪər] *adj* peu sincère, faux, *f* fausse, *Lit* insincère

insincerity [ɪnsɪn'serɪtɪ] *n* manque *m* de sincérité, fausseté *f*

insinuate [ɪn'sɪnjʊeɪt] *vt* (**a**) (*suggest indirectly*) insinuer; **are you insinuating that ...?** est-ce que vous insinuez que ...? (**b**) *Fml* (*manoeuvre*) **to i. one's hand/body into an opening** glisser sa main/se glisser dans une ouverture; **to i. oneself into a room** s'introduire dans une pièce; **to i. oneself into sb's favour** s'insinuer dans les bonnes grâces de qn

insinuation [ɪnsɪnjʊ'eɪʃən] *n* (**a**) (*indirect suggestion*) insinuation *f* (**b**) *Fml* (*of hand, body*) introduction *f*

insipid [ɪn'sɪpɪd] *adj* (*food*) insipide, fade; (*style, conversation*) fade, plat, insipide; (*person*) insipide

insipidity [ɪnsɪ'pɪdɪtɪ], **insipidness** [ɪn'sɪpɪdnɪs] *n* insipidité *f*, fadeur *f*

insist [ɪn'sɪst] **1** *vi* insister (**on doing** pour faire); **to i. on a point** insister *ou* appuyer sur un point; **I won't i.** je n'insiste pas; **very well, if you i.** très bien, si tu insistes; **he insists on your coming** il insiste pour que vous veniez; **he insisted on paying** il a tenu à payer; **let me pay for the meal, I i. (on it)!** laisse-moi payer l'addition, j'insiste!; **show me what you've got there, I i.!** montre-moi ce que tu as dans les mains, je l'exige!; **to i. upon one's innocence** affirmer son innocence avec insistance; **to i. on one's rights** revendiquer ses droits; **i. on the best** exigez la meilleure qualité

2 *vt* (**a**) (*maintain*) soutenir, maintenir; **people insisted that they had seen him** des gens affirmaient l'avoir vu; **he insisted that it was so** il maintenait qu'il en était ainsi

(**b**) **I i. that you let me pay** j'insiste, laisse-moi payer; **I i. that you show me what you have in your hand** j'exige que tu me montres ce que tu as dans la main

insistence [ɪn'sɪstəns] *n* insistance *f*; **because of his i. on paying** parce qu'il tenait à payer; **he did it at her i.** il l'a fait parce qu'elle a insisté; **her i. that she was telling the truth didn't convince me** quoi qu'elle ait bien insisté qu'elle disait la vérité, elle ne m'a pas convaincu

insistent [ɪn'sɪstənt] *adj* qui insiste, insistant; (*demands*) instant; (*noise*) incessant; **to be i. about sth** insister sur qch; **to be very i.** insister beaucoup; **don't be too i.** n'insistez pas trop

insistently [ɪn'sɪstəntlɪ] *adv* instamment, avec insistance

in situ [ɪn'sɪtjuː] *adv* in situ

insofar [ɪnsəʊ'fɑːr] *adv US* **i. as** dans la mesure où

insole ['ɪnsəʊl] *n* (*of shoe*) (*inner sole*) première semelle *f*; (*separate piece*) (*of cork, felt etc*) semelle intérieure

insolence ['ɪnsələns] *n* insolence *f* (**to** envers)

insolent ['ɪnsələnt] *adj* insolent (**to** envers); **an i. boy** un (jeune) insolent

insolently ['ɪnsələntlɪ] *adv* insolemment

insolubility [ɪnsɒljʊ'bɪlɪtɪ] *n* insolubilité *f*

insoluble [ɪn'sɒljʊb(ə)l] *adj* (**a**) (*salt etc*) insoluble (**b**) (*problem*) insoluble, qu'on ne peut pas résoudre

insolvency [ɪn'sɒlvənsɪ] *n* insolvabilité *f*

insolvent [ɪn'sɒlvənt] **1** *adj* (*debtor, company*) insolvable; **to declare oneself i.** se déclarer insolvable; *Com* déposer son bilan **2** *n* débiteur *m*/compagnie *f* insolvable

insomnia [ɪn'sɒmnɪə] *n* insomnie *f*

insomniac [ɪn'sɒmnɪæk] *n* insomniaque *mf*

insomuch [ɪnsəʊ'mʌtʃ] *adv* = **inasmuch**

inspect [ɪn'spekt] *vt* (**a**) (*examine*) examiner, regarder de près; **my mother inspected our hands (to see if they were clean)** ma mère a regardé si nos mains étaient propres (**b**) (*carry out official inspection of*) (*school etc*) inspecter; (*accounts of business, machine etc*) contrôler, vérifier (**c**) *Mil* (*regiment*) passer en revue; **to be inspected** (*of troops*) être passé en revue

inspecting officer *n* inspecteur *m*

inspection [ɪn'spekʃən] *n* (**a**) (*of documents etc*) examen *m*, vérification *f*; (*of tickets, goods etc*) contrôle *m*; **on close** *or* **closer i.** en y regardant de plus près; **i. copy** (*in publishing*) spécimen *m*

(**b**) (*of school, factory etc*) (*by official*) (visite *f* d')inspection *f*; (*of head, hands etc*) (*by nurse*) inspection; (*of machinery, vehicle*) contrôle *m*, vérification *f*; **tour of i.** visite d'inspection; **sanitary i.** contrôle *m* sanitaire; **medical i.** visite médicale; *Tech* **i. hole** *or* **port** orifice *m ou* trou *m ou* regard *m* de visite; *MecE* **i. panel** panneau *m* de visite; **i. pit** (*in garage*) fosse *f* d'inspection

(**c**) *Mil* revue *f*; **to make** *or* **hold an i.** passer une revue

inspector [ɪn'spektər] *n* (*of schools, police, mines*) inspecteur *m*; *Br* (*on train, bus etc*) contrôleur, -euse; *Br* **i. of taxes** inspecteur *ou* contrôleur *m* des contributions directes

inspectorate [ɪn'spektərət] *n* (**a**) (*inspectors*) corps *m* d'inspecteurs (**b**) (*post*) inspectorat *m*

inspiration [ɪnspɪ'reɪʃən] *n* (**a**) (*stimulus*) inspiration *f*; **he is the i. of the movement** c'est l'âme du mouvement; **she's an i. to us all** elle est notre modèle à tous; **to lack i.** (*of poet etc*) manquer d'inspiration; **to provide the i. for sth** fournir l'inspiration pour qch; **to have a sudden i.** avoir une inspiration subite (**b**) *Fml* (*inhalation*) inspiration *f*

inspirational [ɪnspɪ'reɪʃənəl] *adj* (**a**) (*inspiring*) qui inspire, inspirant (**b**) (*inspired*) inspiré

inspire [ɪn'spaɪər] *vt* (**a**) (*stimulate*) inspirer; **to i. a thought/a feeling in sb** inspirer une pensée/un sentiment à qn; **to i. sb with confidence** inspirer (de la) confiance à qn; **to i. sb with hope** donner de l'espoir à qn; **inspired with hope** animé d'espoir; **the programme inspired her to study biology** l'émission l'a poussée à étudier la biologie; **her example inspired us to ...** son exemple nous a incités à ...; **I don't know what inspired me to turn back** je ne sais pas ce qui m'a poussé à revenir sur mes pas; *Iron* **what inspired you to do that?** qu'est-ce qui t'a pris de faire ça? (**b**) *Fml* (*inhale*) inspirer

inspired [ɪn'spaɪəd] *adj* (*poet, cook etc*) inspiré, plein d'inspiration; (*decision*) inspiré; *F* **no one was (feeling) i.** personne n'était très inspiré; **to make an i. guess** bien tomber, tomber juste; **it was just an i. guess** c'était un coup de chance

inspiring [ɪn'spaɪərɪŋ] *adj* (*speech, example etc*) qui inspire, inspirant; *F* **the menu wasn't very i.** le menu n'avait rien de bien tentant

inst [ɪnst] (*abbr* **instant**) *Old-fashioned Com* (*in letter*) **on the 5th i.** le 5 courant

instability [ɪnstə'bɪlɪtɪ] *n* (*of government, economy etc*) instabilité *f*; *MecE* déséquilibre *m*; *Met* instabilité (atmosphérique); (*of bridge etc*) manque *m* de solidité; (*of character*) mobilité *f*, instabilité

install, *US* **instal** [ɪn'stɔːl] *vt* (**a**) (*machine, electricity, software*) installer (**b**) (*settle*) **she installed herself in an armchair/in front of the TV** elle s'est installée dans un fauteuil/devant la télé (**c**) *Rel, Fml* (*bishop, person in position*) installer

installation [ɪnstə'leɪʃən] *n* (**a**) (*of central heating, machine, bishop, software*) installation *f*; **i. manual** manuel *m* d'installation; **i. program** programme *m* d'installation (**b**) (*thing installed*) installation *f*

installer [ɪn'stɔːlər] *n Comptr* disquette *f* d'installation

instalment, *US* **installment** [ɪn'stɔːlmənt] *n* (**a**) *Com etc* (*part payment*) versement *m*; **to pay in** *or* **by instalments** payer par versements, échelonner *ou* fractionner les paiements; **payable in monthly instalments** payable par mensualités; **final i.** paiement *m* pour solde; *Am* **i. plan** vente *f* à tempérament; *Am* **to buy sth on the i. plan** acheter qch à crédit (**b**) (*of work published in parts*) fascicule *m*, livraison *f*; (*of work published in periodical, Rad, TV of soap opera etc*) épisode *m*

instance¹ ['ɪnstəns] *n* (**a**) (*example*) cas *m*; **in many instances** dans bien des cas; **in the present i., in this i.** dans le cas présent; **for i.** par exemple (**b**) **in the first i.** en (tout) premier lieu (**c**) *Fml* (*urging*) **to do sth at sb's i.** *or* **at the i. of sb** faire qch à *ou* sur la demande de qn

instance² *vt* citer en exemple; **his cruelty is well instanced by ...** sa cruauté est bien illustrée par ...

instant¹ ['ɪnstənt] *adj* (**a**) (*action, dislike etc*) immédiat; (*solution*) instantané; *Fml* **this calls for i. remedy** il faut y remédier tout de suite *ou* sur-le-champ; *Phot* **i. camera** appareil *m* photo à développement instantané; *TV* **i. replay** reprise *f*; (*in slow motion*) ralenti *m* (**b**) (*quickly prepared*) (*coffee*) instantané; **i. potatoes** purée *f* en flocons/en poudre (**c**) *Lit* (*urgent*) pressant, urgent (**d**) *Old-fashioned* (*in letter*) (*of current month*) courant

instant² *n* (**a**) (*moment*) instant *m*, moment *m*; **come this i.!** venez immédiatement!; **I just arrived this (very) i.** j'arrive à l'instant; **not an i. too soon** juste à temps; **in an i.** dans un instant; **the i. I saw him** dès que je l'ai vu (**b**) *F* (*instant coffee*) café *m* instantané

instantaneous [ɪnstən'teɪnɪəs] *adj* instantané; *Phot* **i. exposure** pose *f* instantanée, instantané *m*

instantaneously [ɪnstən'teɪnɪəslɪ] *adv* instantanément

instantly ['ɪnstəntlɪ] *adv* tout de suite, immédiatement, sur-le-champ; **she would have died i.** elle serait morte immédiatement; **i. recognizable** immédiatement reconnaissable

instead [ɪn'sted] *adv* (**a**) (*in place of sth*) à la place; (*in sb's place*) à ma/sa/*etc* place; **if John can't come, take me i.** si Jean ne peut pas venir, emmenez-moi à sa place; **use the hammer i.** utilise le marteau à la place (**b**) **i. of** (*thing*) au lieu de; (*person*) à la place de; **i. of doing sth** au lieu de faire qch

instep ['ɪnstep] *n* (*of foot*) cou-de-pied *m*, *pl* cous-de-pied; (*of shoe*) cambrure *f*; **to have a high i.** (*of person*) avoir le pied très cambré

instigate ['ɪnstɪgeɪt] *vt* (*of person*) (*inquiry, negotiations, changes, rebellion etc*) être à l'origine de; (*of event, development etc*) (*rebellion, change*) provoquer; (*incite*) (*person*) inciter, pousser (**to do** à faire)

instigation [ɪnstɪ'geɪʃən] *n* instigation *f*, incitation *f*; **at sb's i.** à l'instigation de qn

instigator ['ɪnstɪgeɪtər] *n* instigateur, -trice

instil, *US* **instill** [ɪn'stɪl] *vt* (*Br* **instils,** *US* **instills,** *Br & US* **instilled, instilling**) (*pride, courage etc*) inspirer (**into sb** à qn); (*idea*) faire pénétrer (**into sb** dans l'esprit de qn)

instinct ['ɪnstɪŋkt] *n* instinct *m*; **by** *or* **from i.** d'instinct, par instinct; **to follow one's instincts** suivre son instinct; **my i. was to run away** mon instinct m'a dit de fuir; **to have an i. for business** avoir le sens des affaires; **she has a strong business i.** elle a un fort instinct pour les affaires

instinctive [ɪn'stɪŋktɪv] *adj* instinctif

instinctively [ɪn'stɪŋktɪvlɪ] *adv* instinctivement, d'instinct

institute¹ ['ɪnstɪtjuːt] *n* institut *m*; **i. for the blind** établissement *m* pour aveugles

institute² *vt* (**a**) (*set up*) (*order, law*) instituer, établir; (*club etc*) fonder, constituer (**b**) (*initiate*) (*search*) lancer; *Jur* (*enquiry*) ordonner, instituer; **to i. (legal) proceedings against sb** entamer *ou* engager des poursuites contre qn

institution [ɪnstɪ'tjuːʃən] *n* (**a**) (*organization, society*) (*for education etc*) institution *f*; (*public, financial etc*) établissement *m*; (*for old people*) hospice *m*; (*for mental patients*) asile *m* (**b**) (*action*) (*of enquiry etc*) établissement *m*; (*of law etc*) institution *f*; (*of committee*) constitution *f*; (*of state*) création *f*; (*of search*) lancement *m* (**c**) (*established practice etc*) institution *f*; *Fig* **to become a national i.** (*of person, event etc*) devenir une institution nationale; **the i. of marriage is under threat** le mariage est une institution menacée

institutional [ɪnstɪ'tjuːʃən(ə)l] *adj* institutionnel; **he needs i. care** il a besoin d'être hospitalisé; **i. advertising** publicité *f* institutionnelle; *Fin* **i. buying** achats *mpl* institutionnels; **i. food** nourriture *f* de cantine; *Fin* **i. investors** investisseurs *mpl* institutionnels, *F* zinzin *m*; **i. life** la vie en collectivité

institutionalize [ɪnstɪ'tjuːʃənəlaɪz] *vt* (**a**) (*put in a home etc*) placer dans un établissement spécialisé (**b**) (*turn into an institution*) institutionnaliser

institutionalized [ɪnstɪ'tjuːʃənəlaɪzd] *adj* (**a**) (*person*) marqué par la vie en collectivité; **after years in a psychiatric hospital, she had become completely i.** après des années en hôpital psychiatrique, elle était devenue complètement dépendante; **things are less i. in this establishment** cet établissement a un caractère moins institutionnel (**b**) (*practice*) établi

in-store *adj Mktg* **i. advertising space** espace *m* de PLV, espace de publicité sur le lieu de vente; **i. demonstration** démonstration *f* sur le lieu de vente

instruct [ɪn'strʌkt] *vt* (**a**) (*teach, train*) **to i. sb in sth** enseigner qch à qn (**b**) (*command*) ordonner (**to do** de faire); **I am instructed by the Board to inform you that ...** la Direction me charge de vous faire savoir que ... (**c**) *Br Jur* **to i. a solicitor** donner ses instructions à un avoué; **to i. counsel** constituer avocat (**d**) *Fml* (*inform*) informer (**that** que)

instruction [ɪn'strʌkʃən] *n* (**a**) (*no pl*) (*training*) instruction *f*, enseignement *m*; **we received i. in using the machines** on nous a appris comment utiliser les machines

(**b**) (*usu pl*) **instructions** (*orders*) instructions *fpl*, directives *fpl*; (*to sentry etc*) consigne *f*; (*to representative etc*) mandat *m*; *Comptr* (*in program*) instructions; **instructions (for use)** (*for machine, cleaning product etc*) mode *m ou* notice *f* d'emploi; **to give sb instructions to do sth** ordonner à qn de faire qch; **strict instructions** des instructions formelles, des ordres formels; **I gave strict instructions that I wasn't to be disturbed** j'ai donné l'ordre formel qu'on ne me dérange pas; **to carry out instructions** exécuter des ordres; **to act in accordance with/contrary to instructions** se conformer/ne pas se conformer aux instructions reçues; **our instructions were to arrest him** nous avions reçu l'ordre de l'arrêter; **to follow sb's instructions** suivre les instructions de qn; **to obey sb's instructions** obéir aux ordres de qn; *Com* **we await your instructions** nous attendons vos instructions; *Br Jur* **to give instructions to a solicitor** donner ses instructions à un avoué; **i. book(let)** livret *m* d'instruction(s); *Comptr* **i. code** code *m* d'instruction; **i. manual** (*for machine etc*) manuel *m* d'entretien; *Comptr* **i. set** jeu *m* d'instructions

instructive [ɪn'strʌktɪv] *adj* instructif

instructor [ɪn'strʌktər] *n* enseignant, -ante, professeur *m*; *Am Univ* assistant, -ante; *Mil* instructeur *m*; *Ski, Aut* moniteur, -trice; **swimming/judo/riding i.** professeur *m* de natation/de judo/d'équitation

instructress [ɪn'strʌktrɪs] *n* maîtresse *f*, professeur *m*; *Ski Aut* monitrice *f*

instrument¹ ['ɪnstrʊmənt] *n* **(a)** *Tech, Surg, Mus etc* instrument *m*; **aircraft instruments** instruments de bord; **flying/landing on instruments, i. flying/landing** vol *m*/atterrissage *m* aux instruments *ou* sans visibilité; *Av, Aut* **i. board** *or* **panel** *or* **display** tableau *m* de bord **(b)** *Fml* (*means, agent*) instrument *m*; **to serve as the i. of sb's vengeance** servir d'instrument à la vengeance de qn **(c)** *Jur* (*legal document*) instrument *m*, acte *m* juridique; *Com* **i. to order** papier *m* à ordre

instrument² ['ɪnstrʊmənt] **1** *vt* **(a)** *Mus* (*opera etc*) orchestrer, instrumenter **(b)** *Tech* (*workshop etc*) équiper *ou* munir d'outils **2** *vi Jur* instrumenter

instrumental [ɪnstrʊ'ment(ə)l] **1** *adj* **(a)** (*contributing*) **to be i. in doing sth** contribuer à faire qch, jouer un rôle décisif dans qch **(b)** *Tech* **by i. means** avec des instruments de mesure; **i. error** erreur *f* (de lecture) due à l'instrument **(c)** *Mus* instrumental **2** *n Mus* version *f* instrumentale

instrumentalist [ɪnstrʊ'mentəlɪst] *n Mus* instrumentiste *mf*

instrumentation [ɪnstrʊmen'teɪʃən] *n Mus, Aut* instrumentation *f*

insubordinate [ɪnsə'bɔːdɪnət] *adj* insubordonné, insoumis

insubordination [ɪnsəbɔːdɪ'neɪʃən] *n* insubordination *f*, insoumission *f*

insubstantial [ɪnsəb'stænʃəl] *adj* **(a)** (*thin, flimsy*) (*reason*) qui manque de substance; (*argument*) vide, creux; (*book etc*) creux, qui manque de substance; **an i. breakfast** un petit déjeuner frugal **(b)** (*unreal*) (*fear*) imaginaire

insufferable [ɪn'sʌfərəb(ə)l] *adj* insupportable, intolérable

insufferably [ɪn'sʌfərəblɪ] *adv* insupportablement, intolérablement

insufficiency [ɪnsə'fɪʃənsɪ] *n* insuffisance *f*

insufficient [ɪnsə'fɪʃənt] *adj* (*amount, resources, justification etc*) insuffisant; (*facilities*) inadéquat; **the sum is i. to cover our costs** la somme ne suffit pas à couvrir nos frais; **i. evidence** preuves *fpl* insuffisantes; *Fin* **i. funds** provision *f* insuffisante, insuffisance *f* de provision

insufficiently [ɪnsə'fɪʃəntlɪ] *adv* insuffisamment

insular ['ɪnsjʊlər] *adj* **(a)** (*narrow*) (*mind*) étroit, borné; (*life etc*) d'insulaire; **to be very i. in one's views** être très étroit d'esprit **(b)** *Geog* (*climate etc*) insulaire

insularity [ɪnsjʊ'lærɪtɪ] *n Pej* (*of country*) manque *m* d'ouverture sur l'extérieur; **the i. of their views** leur étroitesse *f* d'esprit

insulate ['ɪnsjʊleɪt] *vt El* (*wire etc*) isoler; (*pipe, water tank etc*) calorifuger; *Rad etc* (*soundproof*) insonoriser; **to i. against vibration** protéger contre les vibrations; *Fig* **insulated from the outside world** protégé contre le monde extérieur

insulated ['ɪnsjʊleɪtɪd] *adj El* isolé; (*handle, screwdriver etc*) isolant; (*against loss of heat*) calorifugé; (*soundproofed*) insonorisé

insulating ['ɪnsjʊleɪtɪŋ] *adj* isolant; (*against loss of heat*) calorifuge; (*soundproofing*) insonore; *El* **i. material** isolant *m*; **i. properties** propriétés *fpl* isolantes; **i. tape** ruban *m* isolant, chatterton *m*

insulation [ɪnsjʊ'leɪʃən] *n* **(a)** (*action, state*) (*of wires etc*) isolation *f*, isolement *m*; **heat** *or* **thermal i.** isolation thermique; **sound i.** (*of room etc*) insonorisation *f* **(b)** (*substance*) (*for wires, against heat loss etc*) isolant *m*

insulator ['ɪnsjʊleɪtər] *n El, Constr* (*substance*) isolant *m*; *El* (*device*) isolateur *m*

insulin ['ɪnsjʊlɪn] *n Med* insuline *f*; **i. treatment** insulinothérapie *f*

insulin-dependent *adj Med* insulinodépendant

insult¹ ['ɪnsʌlt] *n* (*abuse*) insulte *f*; (*affront*) affront *m*, insulte; **and to add i. to injury ...** et comme si ça ne suffisait pas ...; **it's an i. to the intelligence** c'est une insulte à l'intelligence

insult² [ɪn'sʌlt] *vt* (*abuse*) insulter; (*affront*) faire affront *ou* injure à, insulter; **to i. sb's intelligence** (*of book, film etc*) être une insulte à l'intelligence de qn; (*of person*) prendre qn pour un/une imbécile; **to feel insulted** se sentir insulté

insulting [ɪn'sʌltɪŋ] *adj* (*gesture, expression*) insultant, offensant, injurieux; (*person*) injurieux; **it is i. to suggest that ...** il est insultant de suggérer que ...; **it's i.!** c'est une insulte!; **to use i. language** employer un langage injurieux; **to be guilty of i. behaviour towards sb** s'être conduit insolemment à l'égard de qn; *Jur* (*to magistrate, policeman*) être coupable d'outrages à qn

insultingly [ɪn'sʌltɪŋlɪ] *adv* d'une façon insultante *ou* offensante

insuperable [ɪn'suːpərəb(ə)l] *adj* (*difficulty, obstacle etc*) insurmontable

insuperably [ɪn'suːpərəblɪ] *adv* **i. difficult** impossible

in-supplier *n Mktg* fournisseur *m* agréé

insupportable [ɪnsə'pɔːtəb(ə)l] *adj* insupportable

insurable [ɪn'ʃʊərəb(ə)l, ɪn'ʃɔːr-] *adj* assurable

insurance [ɪn'ʃʊərəns, -ʃɔːrəns] *n* **(a)** *Com* assurance *f*; **to take out i. on sth** prendre une assurance sur qch; **to take out i. against a risk** prendre une assurance *ou* s'assurer contre un risque; **he's in i.** il est dans les assurances; **i. against loss of trade** assurance *f* courant d'affaires, assurance perte de l'exploitation; **i. adviser** assureur-conseil *m*; **i. group** groupe *m* d'assurance; **i. portfolio** portefeuille *m* d'assurances
(b) (*premium*) prime *f* d'assurance; **to pay the i. on a car** payer l'assurance d'une voiture
(c) *Fig* (*protection*) garantie *f*; **to buy gold as (an) i. against inflation** acheter de l'or pour se prémunir contre l'inflation

insurance agent *n* agent *m* d'assurance(s)

insurance banker *n* bancassureur *m*

insurance broker *n* courtier *m* d'assurance(s)

insurance certificate *n* certificat *m* d'assurance

insurance claim *n* demande *f* d'indemnité; (*for more serious damage*) déclaration *f* de sinistre *ou* de dommages

insurance company *n* compagnie *f* d'assurance(s)

insurance cover *n* couverture *f* d'assurance

insurance inspector *n* inspecteur *m* d'une société d'assurances

insurance policy *n* police *f* d'assurance; **to take out an i. policy** souscrire une police d'assurance

insurance premium *n* prime *f* d'assurance

insure [ɪn'ʃʊər, -ʃɔːr] *vt* **(a)** (*of insurance company*) (*car, valuables etc*) assurer; (*of client*) (*goods etc*) (faire) assurer; **I'm insured** je suis assuré; **to i. one's life** s'assurer *ou* se faire assurer sur la vie **(b)** *esp US* = **ensure**

▶ **insure against** *vipo* (*risk, theft, fire*) s'assurer *ou* se faire assurer contre; (*danger*) se garantir de; **to i. against loss** couvrir une perte

insured [ɪn'ʃʊəd, -ʃɔːd] **1** *adj* assuré; **i. value** valeur *f* assurée **2** *n* **the i.** (*person*) l'assuré, -ée

insurer [ɪn'ʃʊərər, -ʃɔːrər] *n* assureur *m*

insurgent [ɪn'sɜːdʒənt] **1** *adj* insurgé, révolté **2** *n* insurgé, -ée, révolté, -ée

insurmountable [ɪnsə'maʊntəb(ə)l] *adj* (*difficulty, obstacle*) insurmontable

insurrection [ɪnsə'rekʃ(ə)n] *n* insurrection *f*

insurrectionary [ɪnsə'rekʃənərɪ] **1** *adj* insurrectionnel **2** *n* insurgé, -ée

insurrectionist [ɪnsə'rekʃənɪst] *n* insurgé, -ée

intact [ɪn'tækt] *adj* intact

intaglio [ɪn'tɑːlɪəʊ] *n* (*gem*) intaille *f*; **i. engraving** gravure *f* en creux

intake ['ɪnteɪk] *n* **(a)** (*opening*) (*for water, electricity*) prise *f*; (*for steam*) arrivée *f*, adduction *f*, admission *f*; (*in engine*) (*for air*) arrivée, prise; *Min* galerie *f* d'appel d'air; *HydE* aire *f* d'alimentation; **he gave a sharp i. of breath when he heard the news** il a eu le souffle coupé quand il a entendu la nouvelle; *Aut* **i. pipe** conduit *m* d'admission **(b)** (*of alcohol, calories etc*) consommation *f* **(c)** *Sch* (*of pupils, students*) admission(s) *f(pl)*; *Mil* (*of recruits*) contingent *m*

intangible [ɪn'tændʒɪb(ə)l] **1** *adj* (*benefit*) intangible; (*quality*) indéfinissable; *Acct* **i. assets** valeurs *fpl* immatérielles, actif *m* incorporel; *Acct* **i. fixed assets** immobilisations *fpl* incorporelles; *Jur* **i. property** biens *mpl* incorporels **2** *npl Acct* **intangibles** valeurs *fpl* immatérielles, actif *m* incorporel

integer ['ɪntɪdʒər] *n Math* (nombre *m*) entier *m*

integral ['ɪntɪgr(ə)l] **1** *adj* **(a)** (*essential*) indispensable **(to** pour); **to be** *or* **form an i. part of sth** faire partie intégrante de qch **(b)** *Math* **i. number** nombre *m* entier; **i. calculus** calcul *m* intégral **(c)** *Tech* (*forming a part*) incorporé **(with** à), qui fait partie intégrante **(with** de); *Aut* **i. body shell** coque *f* autoporteuse; **i. power supply** accumulateur *m* incorporé **2** *n Math* intégrale *f*

integrate ['ɪntɪgreɪt] **1** *vt* **(a)** (*incorporate*) (*minority*) intégrer **(into** à); *US* **to i. a school** imposer la déségrégation raciale dans une école **(b)** *(bring together)* regrouper **(into** en), combiner **(c)** *Math (function)* intégrer **2** *vi (social milieu, ethnic group etc)* s'intégrer; *US (carry out racial integration)* pratiquer la déségrégation raciale

integrated ['ıntıgreıtıd] *adj* **(a)** intégré; **an i. transport system** un système de transports cohérent; *Comptr* **i. package** logiciel *m ou* progiciel *m* intégré, intégré *m* **(b)** *(school)* qui pratique la déségrégation raciale

integrated circuit *n Electron* circuit *m* intégré; **i. card** carte *f* à circuit intégré

integration [ıntı'greıʃən] *n* **(a)** intégration *f*; **the i. of ethnic minorities** l'intégration des minorités ethniques; **racial i.** déségrégation *f* raciale **(b)** *Math* **i. by parts** intégration *f* par parties

integrative growth ['ıntıgreıtıv] *n Com* croissance *f* par intégration

integrator ['ıntıgreıtər] *n Comptr* intégrateur *m*

integrity [ın'tegrıtı] *n* **(a)** *(honesty) (of person)* intégrité *f*, honnêteté *f*, probité *f*; *(of motive)* honnêteté; **woman/man of i.** femme/homme intègre **(b)** *(wholeness) (of text, computer data)* intégrité *f*

integument [ın'tegjʊmənt] *n Biol* tégument *m*

intellect ['ıntılekt] *n* intelligence *f*, intellect *m*; **a man of i.** un homme intelligent; **he was one of the best intellects of his time** c'était un des plus grands esprits de son époque

intellectual [ıntı'lektjʊəl, -tʃʊəl] **1** *adj* intellectuel **2** *n* intellectuel, -elle

intellectually [ıntı'lektjʊəlı, -tʃʊəlı] *adv* intellectuellement

intelligence [ın'telıdʒəns] *n* **(a)** *(mental capacity)* intelligence *f*; *(mind)* esprit *m*; **a person of some i.** une personne assez intelligente; **use your i.!** réfléchis un peu **(b)** *Mil, Pol (information)* renseignements *mpl*; **I. (service)** service *m* de renseignements

intelligence officer *n Mil, Pol* officier *m* de renseignements

intelligence quotient *n Psy* quotient *m* intellectuel

intelligence test *n* test *m* d'intelligence

intelligent [ın'telıdʒənt] *adj* intelligent

intelligently [ın'telıdʒəntlı] *adv* intelligemment, avec intelligence

intelligentsia [ınteli'dʒentsıə] *n* intelligentsia *f*

intelligibility [ıntelıdʒı'bılıtı] *n* intelligibilité *f*

intelligible [ın'telıdʒıb(ə)l] *adj* intelligible; **he was hardly i.** on le comprenait à peine

intelligibly [ın'telıdʒıblı] *adv* intelligiblement

intemperance [ın'temp(ə)rəns] *n* intempérance *f*

intemperate [ın'temp(ə)rıt] *adj Fml (person)* intempérant; *(climate)* rude; **person of i. habits** personne *f* intempérante; *(excessive drinker)* personne qui s'adonne à la boisson

intend [ın'tend] *vt* **(a)** *(plan)* **to i. to do sth** avoir l'intention de faire qch, compter faire qch; **was that intended?** était-ce fait à dessein?, était-ce intentionnel?; **the play was intended to shock** la pièce voulait choquer; **that's exactly what I intended** c'était exactement mon intention; **what the author intended and what his readers understood** ce que l'auteur a voulu dire et ce que ses lecteurs ont compris; **I i. to be obeyed** je veux qu'on m'obéisse; **I didn't i. her to see it yet** je ne voulais pas qu'elle le voie déjà; **I intended it as a compliment** mon intention était de vous/lui/*etc* faire un compliment

(b) *(aim, destine)* **a book intended for students** un livre destiné aux étudiants; **this remark is intended for you** cette observation s'adresse à vous

intended [ın'tendıd] **1** *adj* **(a)** *(hoped-for)* voulu **(b)** *(intentional)* intentionnel **2** *n Old-fashioned, Hum F* **his/her i.** sa fiancée/son fiancé, sa future/son futur

intense [ın'tens] *adj (feeling, anxiety)* vif, *f* vive; *(heat, book, colour, activity etc)* intense; *(pain)* vif, intense; *(bombardment, campaign)* intensif; *(hatred)* profond; **i. expression** expression *f* concentrée; **she's too i.** elle est trop sérieuse

intensely [ın'tenslı] *adv* **(a)** *(greatly) (amusing, entertaining, boring etc)* extrêmement; **it was i. hot** il faisait une chaleur intense; **i. blue eyes** yeux *mpl* d'un bleu intense **(b)** *(to look at)* avec intensité, intensément

intensification [ıntensıfı'keıʃən] *n (of sound etc)* intensification *f*; *Phot (of negative)* renforcement *m*

intensifier [ın'tensıfaıər] *n Ling* intensif *m*

intensify [ın'tensıfaı] **1** *vt (feeling)* intensifier, augmenter, accroître; *(colour)* renforcer **2** *vi* s'intensifier, augmenter

intensity [ın'tensıtı] *n* **(a)** *(of passion, anger)* intensité *f*; *(of pain)* violence *f* **(b)** *Phys (of sound, current etc)* intensité *f*; *Ch (of reaction)* énergie *f*; *Phot (of negative)* densité *f*

intensive [ın'tensıv] *adj* intensif; *Sch etc* **i. course** cours *m* accéléré; *Med* **i. care (unit)** service *m* de soins intensifs; *Med* **to be in i. care** être dans le service de soins intensifs; **i. farming** exploitation *f* intensive

intensively [ın'tensıvlı] *adv* intensivement

intent[1] [ın'tent] *n* intention *f*, dessein *m*, but *m*; **with good i.** dans une bonne intention; *Jur* **with i. to defraud** dans l'intention de frauder; **declaration of i.** déclaration *f* d'intention; **to all intents (and purposes)** quasiment

intent[2] *adj* **(a) to be i. on doing sth** *(determined)* être résolu *ou* déterminé à faire qch; **they left i. on murder** ils sont partis, déterminés à commettre un meurtre; **a woman i. on success** une femme déterminée à réussir **(b) to be i. on sth** *(engrossed in)* être tout entier à *ou* absorbé par qch **(c)** *(intense) (look)* profond

intention [ın'tenʃən] *n* intention *f*; **I had no i.** *or* **not the slightest i. of accepting** je n'avais nullement l'intention d'accepter; **to have every i. of doing sth** être résolu à faire qch, avoir la ferme intention de faire qch; **I have every i. of calling her!** *(I won't forget)* j'ai bien l'intention de l'appeler; **was (it) your i. to …?** est-ce qu'il était de ton intention de …?; **he acted with the best and most honourable intentions** il a agi en tout bien (et) tout honneur; **her intentions were good** elle avait de bonnes intentions; *Old-fashioned* **his intentions are honourable** *(towards her)* il a l'intention de l'épouser; *Mktg* **i.-to-buy scale** échelle *f* des intentions d'achat

intentional [ın'tenʃən(ə)l] *adj* intentionnel, voulu; **it wasn't i.** je ne l'ai pas/il ne l'a pas/*etc* fait exprès

intentionally [ın'tenʃən(ə)lı] *adv* intentionnellement; **he didn't do it i.** il ne l'a pas fait exprès *ou* intentionnellement; **I i. didn't invite her** c'est intentionnellement que je ne l'ai pas invitée

intently [ın'tentlı] *adv (to listen, look at, study)* attentivement; *(to think)* profondément

inter [ın'tɜːr] *vt* **(-rr-)** *Fml (bury)* inhumer, enterrer

interact [ıntər'ækt] *vi (of chemicals)* interagir; *esp Psy* **to encourage a child to i. with its environment** encourager les échanges d'un enfant avec son environnement; **a situation in which therapist and patient i.** une situation où il y a interaction entre le thérapeute et son patient; **a person who doesn't i. well with others** une personne qui a du mal dans ses rapports avec les autres; **the way the two characters in the novel i.** l'interaction entre les deux personnages dans ce roman

interaction [ıntər'ækʃən] *n* interaction *f*

interactive [ıntər'æktıv] *adj* interactif; **i. CD** CD-interactif *m*; **i. learning** apprentissage *m* interactif; **i. marketing** mercatique *f* interactive; **i. television** télévision *f* interactive; **i. terminal** terminal *m* (informatique) interactif

interactiveness, interactivity [ıntər'æktıvnıs, ıntəræk'tıvıtı] *n* interactivité *f*

inter alia [ıntər'eılıə] *adv Fml* entre autres

interbank ['ıntəbæŋk] *adj attrib* interbancaire; **i. market** marché *m* interbancaire; **i. money** argent *m* de gré à gré entre banques; **i. transfer** virement *m* interbancaire

interbreed [ıntə'briːd] *(pt, pp* **interbred) 1** *vt* **(a)** *(breed from same stock)* croiser *(des animaux consanguins)* **(b)** *(crossbreed)* croiser **2** *vi* **(a)** *(in same family group)* se reproduire entre eux **(b)** *(crossbreed)* se reproduire par croisement, se croiser

interbreeding [ıntə'briːdıŋ] *n* **(a)** *(in same family)* reproduction *f* entre membres d'une même famille; *(of animals)* reproduction par accouplements consanguins **(b)** *(crossbreeding)* croisement *m*

intercede [ıntə'siːd] *vi* intercéder **(with sb** auprès de qn; **for sb, on sb's behalf** en faveur de qn, pour qn)

intercept [ıntə'sept] **1** *vt (letter, enemy plane, person, Fb pass)* intercepter **2** *vi Fb* intercepter une passe

intercept interview *n Mktg* entretien *m* spontané

interception [ıntə'sepʃən] *n (of letter, message etc), Fb* interception *f*

interceptor [ıntə'septər] *n* **(a)** *(person) (of message etc)* personne *f* qui intercepte **(b)** *Av, Mil* **i. (aircraft)** avion *m* d'interception, intercepteur *m*

intercession [ıntə'seʃən] *n* intercession *f*

interchange[1] ['ıntətʃeındʒ] *n* **(a)** *(of compliments, things, ideas)* échange *m* **(b)** *Constr (on motorway)* échangeur *m*

interchange[2] [ıntə'tʃeındʒ] *vt (compliments etc)* échanger **(with** avec); *(two parts of machine etc)* intervertir; **all parts of these machines can be interchanged** toutes les pièces de ces machines sont interchangeables

interchangeable [ıntə'tʃeındʒəb(ə)l] *adj* interchangeable

interchangeably [ıntə'tʃeındʒəblı] *adv (to use)* indifféremment

intercharacter spacing [ıntə'kærəktə] *n Typ* espacement *m* entre les caractères

inter-city [ıntə'sıtı] **1** *adj Br Rail (service, train)* de grandes lignes; **i. travel** déplacements sur les grandes lignes **2** *n Br Rail (train)* train *m* de grandes lignes

intercom [ˈɪntəkɒm] *n Tel F* interphone *m*; **to speak over the i.** parler dans l'interphone
intercommunicate [ɪntəkəˈmjuːnɪkeɪt] *vi* (*of rooms etc*) communiquer
intercommunion [ɪntəkəˈmjuːnjən] *n Rel* intercommunion *f*
intercompany [ɪntəˈkʌmpənɪ] *adj* interentreprise
interconnect [ɪntəkəˈnekt] *El, Comptr* **1** *vt* (*circuits, computers*) interconnecter **2** *vi* être interconnectés
interconnecting doors [ɪntəkəˈnektɪŋ] *npl* portes *fpl* de chambres communiquantes
interconnection [ɪntəkəˈnekʃən] *n El, Comptr* interconnexion *f*
intercontinental [ɪntəkɒntɪˈnent(ə)l] *adj* inter-continental; **i. ballistic missile** missile *m* balistique intercontinental
intercooled [ˈɪntəkuːld] *adj* (*engine*) refroidi
intercooler [ˈɪntəkuːlər] *n Aut* intercooler *m*, refroidisseur *m* intermédiaire
intercostal [ɪntəˈkɒst(ə)l] *adj Anat* intercostal
intercourse [ˈɪntəkɔːs] *n* **(a)** **(sexual) i.** rapports *mpl* sexuels; **to have i. with sb** avoir des rapports sexuels avec qn **(b)** *Old-fashioned* (*dealings*) commerce *m*, relations *fpl*, rapports *mpl*; **social i.** la fréquentation du monde
intercut [ɪntəˈkʌt] *vt TV, Cin* insérer
intercut shot *n TV, Cin* plan *m* de coupe
interdenominational [ˈɪntədɪnɒmɪˈneɪʃən(ə)l] *adj Rel* interconfessionnel
interdepartmental [ˈɪntədiːpɑːtˈment(ə)l] *adj* (*in company*) entre différents services; (*in university*) entre différents départements
interdependence [ɪntədɪˈpendəns] *n* interdépendance *f*
interdependent [ɪntədɪˈpendənt] *adj* interdépendant
interdict¹ [ˈɪntədɪkt] *n* **(a)** *Jur* défense *f*, interdiction *f* **(b)** *Rel* interdit *m*
interdict² [ɪntəˈdɪkt] *vt* **(a)** *Jur* interdire, prohiber **(b)** *Rel* (*town*) frapper d'interdit; (*priest*) interdire, frapper d'interdit
interdiction [ɪntəˈdɪkʃən] *n* **(a)** (*action*) interdiction *f* **(b)** (*result*) *Jur* interdiction *f*; *Rel* interdit *m*
interdisciplinary [ɪntəˈdɪsɪplɪnərɪ] *adj* interdisciplinaire
interest¹ [ˈɪnt(ə)rɪst] *n* **(a)** (*curiosity*) intérêt *m* **(in** à**)**; **to take/have an i. in sb/sth** s'intéresser à qn/qch; **to show an i. in sth** montrer un intérêt pour qch; **her i. in Latin America** son intérêt pour l'Amérique latine; **to take no further i. in sth, to lose i. in sth** se désintéresser de qch; **two people have shown an i. in (buying) the house** deux personnes sont intéressées par la maison; **there's little i. in these old chairs nowadays** on ne s'intéresse pas beaucoup à ces vieilles chaises de nos jours

(b) (*interesting aspect*) intérêt *m*; **this may be of i. to you** ceci peut vous intéresser; **what he does is of no i. to me** ça ne m'intéresse pas de savoir ce qu'il fait; **there was little of i. on television** il n'y avait pas grand-chose d'intéressant à la télévision; **buildings of historical/architectural i.** bâtiments d'intérêt historique/architectural; **a little garlic will give i. to a stew** l'ail donnera un peu de piquant aux ragoûts

(c) (*activity, subject of interest*) **I have many interests** beaucoup de choses m'intéressent; **her interests include skiing and photography** le ski et la photographie font partie de ses centres d'intérêt

(d) (*participation*) intérêt *m*, participation *f*; **to have a direct i. in sth** être concerné directement par qch; **I have no financial i. in the business** je ne suis pas intéressé dans cette entreprise; **to have a controlling i. in a company** avoir une participation majoritaire dans une société

(e) (*group*) **the oil/steel interests in the country** l'industrie pétrolière/sidérurgique du pays; **i. group** association *f*, groupe *m* d'intérêt

(f) (*benefit*) intérêt *m*, avantage *m*; **the public i.** l'intérêt public; **it would not be in the public i.** ça ne serait pas dans l'intérêt public; **to act in/against one's (own) interest(s)** agir dans/contre son propre intérêt; **to act in sb's best interest(s)** agir dans l'intérêt de qn; **we look after British interests** nous défendons les intérêts britanniques; **it's in my i. to do it** j'ai intérêt à le faire; **it's not in their i. to offend her** ce n'est pas dans leur intérêt de l'offenser, ils n'ont pas intérêt à l'offenser; **in the interests of justice/peace** dans l'intérêt de la justice/paix; **in the interests of safety/hygiene** par mesure de sécurité/d'hygiène; **in the interests of accuracy** pour être tout à fait précis

(g) *Fin* intérêt(s) *m(pl)*; **i. on arrears** intérêt *m* de retard; **i. on capital** rémunération *f* de capital; **to pay i. on a loan** payer des intérêts sur un prêt; **to bear** *or* **yield i.** porter intérêt *ou* des intérêts; **to yield 5% i.** rapporter du 5% *ou* un intérêt de 5%; **i. and dividend income** produits *mpl* financiers; **i. accrued** fraction *f* d'intérêt; **i. charges** frais *mpl* financiers; **i. due** intérêts dus *ou* exigibles; **i. due and payable** intérêts exigibles; **i. paid** intérêts versés; **i. payable** intérêt exigible; **i. rate** taux *m* d'intérêt; *St Exch* **i. rate swap** échange *f* de taux d'intérêt; *Fig* **to repay an injury with i.** rendre le mal avec usure
interest² *vt* intéresser; **we couldn't i. her in the idea** nous ne sommes pas parvenus à susciter son intérêt pour cette idée; **we couldn't i. her in a game of cards** nous n'avons pas réussi à la convaincre de venir jouer aux cartes avec nous; **can I i. you in a drink?** puis-je vous proposer un verre?; **it might i. you to learn** *or* **know that ...** ça t'intéressera peut-être d'apprendre *ou* de savoir que ...
interest-bearing *adj* productif d'intérêts, qui produit intérêt
interested [ˈɪnt(ə)rɪstɪd] *adj* **(a)** (*curious*) intéressé; **to be i. in painting/music** s'intéresser à la peinture/à la musique; **I am not i.** cela ne m'intéresse pas; **he wasn't i.** (*in the offer, suggestion*) il n'était pas intéressé, ça ne l'intéressait pas; **anyone i.?** il y en a que ça intéresse?, est-ce que quelqu'un est intéressé?; **I should be i. to hear the end of the story** je serais curieux d'apprendre la fin de l'histoire **(b)** (*involved*) intéressé; **the i. parties** les parties *fpl* intéressées; **to act from i. motives** agir par calcul; *Jur* **i. party** ayant droit *m*, *pl* ayants droit
interest-free *adj* (*credit*) gratuit; **i. loan** prêt *m* sans intérêt
interesting [ˈɪnt(ə)rɪstɪŋ] *adj* (*book, job etc*) intéressant
interestingly [ˈɪnt(ə)rɪstɪŋlɪ] *adv* de façon intéressante; **i. enough ...** ce qui est intéressant c'est que ...; **i., a number of her supporters voted against her** il est intéressant de noter qu'un certain nombre de ses partisans ont voté contre elle
interface¹ [ˈɪntəfeɪs] *n Comptr, Fig* interface *f*; **the patient–doctor i.** les relations médecin-patient; **the extent of the i. between these two subjects** l'étendue des rapports entre ces deux sujets; **i. bus** bus *m* d'interface; **i. cable** câble *m* de connexion; **i. card** carte *f* d'interface; **i. switching** (*on laser printer*) commutation *f* d'interface
interface² *Comptr* **1** *vi* avoir une interface **(with** avec**)**; **this device interfaces with most PC's** ce dispositif permet une interface avec la plupart des ordinateurs individuels **2** *vt* (*two computers*) mettre en interface, interfacer
interfacing [ˈɪntəfeɪsɪŋ] *n* **(a)** *Comptr* interfaçage *m* **(b)** *Sewing* entoilage *m*
interfere [ɪntəˈfɪər] *vi* **(a)** (*of person*) s'ingérer, s'immiscer, intervenir **(in a matter** dans une affaire**)**; (*in quarrel*) s'interposer; **to i. in sb's affairs** se mêler des affaires de qn; **don't i. in what doesn't concern you** ne vous mêlez pas de ce qui ne vous regarde pas; **he's always interfering** il fourre son nez partout, il est toujours à se mêler de ce qui ne le regarde pas; **do not i. with the doors** ne pas gêner la fermeture des portes; **someone has interfered with the clock** on a touché à la pendule; *Euph* **was she interfered with?** (*sexually*) est-ce qu'on a abusé d'elle?

(b) (*of thing*) **to i. with** (*sb's plans*) gêner, contrarier; (*traffic, person's movements*) gêner, entraver; (*progress of business*) entraver; **pleasure should not be allowed to i. with business** il ne faut pas que les plaisirs empiètent sur les affaires

(c) *Phys etc* interférer; *Ch* perturber; *Electron, Rad* **to i. with a signal** brouiller *ou* parasiter un signal
interference [ɪntəˈfɪərəns] *n* **(a)** (*by person*) intervention *f*, intrusion *f*, ingérence *f* **(in** dans**)**; *Sp* (*from opponent*) obstruction *f* **(b)** *Phys* interférence *f*; *Ch* perturbation *f*; *Electron, Rad* interférence(s), parasite(s) *m(pl)*, brouillage *m*; *Opt* **i. figure** *or* **pattern** figure *f* d'interférence
interfering [ɪntəˈfɪərɪŋ] *adj* (*person*) importun, qui se mêle de ce qui ne le regarde pas; **he's so i.** il fourre son nez partout
interferon [ɪntəˈfɪərɒn] *n Biol* interféron *m*
interim [ˈɪntərɪm] **1** *n* **in the i.** entre-temps **2** *adj* (*government, report etc*) intérimaire; **the i. period** l'intérim *m*; *Fin* **i. dividend** acompte *m* sur dividende, dividende *m* intérimaire *ou* intermédiaire; *Jur* **i. order** avant faire droit *m inv*; *Acct* **i. profit and loss statement** compte *m* de résultat prévisionnel; *Acct* **i. statement** bilan *m* intérimaire
interior [ɪnˈtɪərɪər] **1** *adj* (*side, trade*) intérieur; (*regions etc*) de l'intérieur; *Math* (*angle*) interne; **i. decoration** décoration *f* d'intérieur; **i. decorator** décorateur *m*; *TV, Cin* **i. shot** scène *f* d'intérieur; *Aut* **i. trim** habillage *m* intérieur **2** *n* **(a)** (*of country, region, building*) intérieur *m* **(b)** *Art* (tableau *m* d')intérieur *m*
interior-sprung *adj* **i. mattress** matelas *m* à ressorts
interject [ɪntəˈdʒekt] *vt* (*remark etc*) lancer; (*protest*) émettre
interjection [ɪntəˈdʒekʃən] *n* **(a)** (*action*) (*of remark etc*) action *f* de lancer; (*of protest*) action d'émettre **(b)** (*word, phrase*) interjection *f*
interlace [ɪntəˈleɪs] **1** *vt* (*wires, branches*) entrecroiser; (*speech etc*) entremêler **(with** de**)** **2** *vi* s'entrelacer, s'entrecroiser

interlaced [ɪntəˈleɪst] *adj Comptr* (*display, monitor*) entrelacé
interlard [ɪntəˈlɑːd] *vt* (*speech, story*) entrelarder (**with** de)
interleave [ɪntəˈliːv] *vt* (*book*) interfolier; (*sheets*) intercaler
interlibrary [ɪntəˈlaɪbrərɪ] *adj* **i. loan** prêt *m* inter-bibliothèque
interline [ɪntəˈlaɪn] **1** *vt* (**a**) (*document, manuscript*) interligner (**b**) *Sewing* mettre une doublure intermédiaire à **2** *adj* (**a**) **i. sale** (*between airlines*) vente *f* inter-compagnie (**b**) *Typ* **i. spacing** interligne *m*
interlining [ˈɪntəlaɪnɪŋ] *n* (**a**) *Sewing* doublure *f* intermédiaire (**b**) (*between airlines*) accord *m* inter-compagnie
interlock [ɪntəˈlɒk] **1** *vt* (*mechanism*) enclencher; (*cogs*) engrener; (*parts of mechanism*) emboîter; (*fingers*) entrelacer **2** *vi* (*of mechanism*) s'enclencher; (*of parts*) s'emboîter
interlocking [ɪntəˈlɒkɪŋ] *adj* (*parts*) emboîtable; *MecE* (*gears*) qui s'engrènent *ou* s'enclenchent
interlocutor [ɪntəˈlɒkjʊtə(r)] *n Fml* interlocuteur, -trice
interloper [ˈɪntələʊpə(r)] *n* intrus, -use
interlude [ˈɪntəluːd] *n Th, Fig* intermède *m*; **musical i.** interlude *m*, intermède musical
intermarriage [ɪntəˈmærɪdʒ] *n* (*between families etc*) mariage *m* (*entre les membres de différentes familles/castes/races/etc*); (*within a family*) mariage consanguin
intermarry [ɪntəˈmærɪ] *vi* (*between families etc*) se marier (*entre membres de différentes familles/castes/races/etc*); (*within a family*) se marier entre membres d'une même famille; **they began to i.** ils commencèrent à se marier entre eux
intermediary [ɪntəˈmiːdɪərɪ] **1** *n* intermédiaire *mf*; **to act as i.** servir d'intermédiaire **2** *adj* intermédiaire
intermediate [ɪntəˈmiːdɪət] *adj* (*size etc*) intermédiaire; *Sch* (*class etc*) (de niveau) moyen; **i. stops** (*during journey*) arrêts *mpl* intermédiaires; *El* **i. frequency** fréquence *f* moyenne; **i.-range nuclear forces** forces *fpl* nucléaires intermédiaires
interment [ɪnˈtɜːmənt] *n* enterrement *m*, inhumation *f*
intermezzo [ɪntəˈmetsəʊ] *n Mus, Th* intermezzo *m*
interminable [ɪnˈtɜːmɪnəb(ə)l] *adj* interminable
interminably [ɪnˈtɜːmɪnəblɪ] *adv* interminablement
intermingle [ɪntəˈmɪŋg(ə)l] **1** *vt* entremêler (**with** de); (*colours*) mélanger **2** *vi* se mêler (**with** à), se mélanger (**with** avec)
intermission [ɪntəˈmɪʃən] *n* (**a**) *Cin, Th, Mus etc* entracte *m* (**b**) (*pause*) interruption *f*, pause *f*; *Med* (*in fever*) intermission *f*; **without i.** sans arrêt
intermittent [ɪntəˈmɪtənt] *adj* intermittent; *Aut* **i. facility** (*of wipers*) intermittence *f*
intermittently [ɪntəˈmɪtəntlɪ] *adv* par intermittence, de façon intermittente
intermodal [ɪntəˈməʊdəl] *adj Can* (*transport etc*) intermodal; **i. travel** voyages *mpl* par différents moyens de transport
intern[1] [ˈɪntɜːn] *n Am Med* (*in hospital*) interne *mf*
intern[2] [ɪnˈtɜːn] *vt* interner
internal [ɪnˈtɜːn(ə)l] *adj* (**a**) intérieur, interne; *Med* (*haemorrhage, organ, ear etc*) interne; (*disorder*) organique; **the i. workings of the mind** les opérations *fpl* secrètes de l'esprit; *Tel* **i. cable** câble *m* d'immeuble; *Comptr* **i. command** commande *f* interne; *Comptr* **i. drive** unité *f ou* lecteur *m* interne; *Med* **i. injuries** lésions *fpl* internes; **i. modem** modem *m* interne; **i. telephone** téléphone *m* intérieur
(**b**) (*within a country*) (*trade*) intérieur; (*legislation*) national, interne; (*within a company*) (*regulation, investigation*) interne; **i. company document** document *m* interne à l'entreprise; *Pol* **i. exile** exil *m* (*dans le pays où l'on réside*); **i. flight** vol *m* intérieur; **i. mail** courrier *m* interne; **i. marketing** mercatique *f* interne; **i. promotion** promotion *f* interne; **i. security** sécurité *f* intérieure; **i. travel** voyages *mpl* à l'intérieur d'un même pays
(**c**) (*value, proof*) intrinsèque
(**d**) **i. student** étudiant, -ante d'une université
internal combustion engine *n MecE* moteur *m* à combustion interne, moteur à explosion
internal exam *n Univ* examen *m* propre à une université
internal examiner *n* examinateur, -trice (*qui fait passer un examen dans l'université où il/elle enseigne*)
internalize [ɪnˈtɜːnəlaɪz] *vt* intérioriser
internally [ɪnˈtɜːn(ə)lɪ] *adv* intérieurement; *Pharm* **not to be taken i.** à usage externe
internal revenue *n US* recettes *fpl* fiscales; (*authority*) fisc *m*
international [ɪntəˈnæʃən(ə)l] **1** *adj* international; **i. law** droit *m* international; **i. tourism destination** destination *f* touristique internationale; **i. trade fair** foire *f* internationale; *Com* **i. trading corporation** société *f* de commerce international, SCI *f* **2** *n* (**a**) *Sp* (*player*) (joueur, -euse) international, -ale; (*match*) match *m* international (**b**) *Pol, Hist* **the I.** l'Internationale *f*
International Air Transport Association *n* Association *f* internationale de transport aérien
International Chamber of Commerce *n* chambre *f* de commerce internationale
International Court of Justice *n* Cour *f* internationale de justice
International Date Line *n* ligne *f* de changement de date *ou* de changement de jour
Internationale (the) [ðiːɪntənæʃjəˈnɑːl] *n* (*socialist anthem*) l'Internationale *f*
internationalism [ɪntəˈnæʃənəlɪz(ə)m] *n* internationalisme *m*
internationalize [ɪntəˈnæʃənəlaɪz] *vt* internationaliser
International Labour Organization *n* Organisation *f* internationale du travail
internationally [ɪntəˈnæʃənəlɪ] *adv* internationalement; **an i. recognized qualification** un diplôme reconnu sur le plan international
International Monetary Fund *n* Fonds *m* monétaire international
interne [ˈɪntɜːn] *n Am* = **intern**[1]
internecine [ɪntəˈniːsaɪn] *adj* de destruction réciproque
internee [ɪntɜːˈniː] *n* interné, -ée
Internet [ˈɪntənet] *n Comptr* Internet *m*; **I. surfer** internaute *mf*; **I. surfing** navigation *f* dans l'Internet, surf *m* sur l'Internet
internist [ɪnˈtɜːnɪst] *n esp Am Med* spécialiste *mf* des maladies organiques
internment [ɪnˈtɜːnmənt] *n* internement *m*; **i. camp** camp *m* d'internement
internship [ˈɪntɜːnʃɪp] *n Am Med* (*position*) internat *m*
interpenetrate [ɪntəˈpenɪtreɪt] *vi* s'interpénétrer
interpenetration [ɪntəpenɪˈtreɪʃən] *n* interpénétration *f*
interpersonal [ɪntəˈpɜːsən(ə)l] *adj* interpersonnel
interplanetary [ɪntəˈplænɪt(ə)rɪ] *adj* interplanétaire
interplay [ˈɪntəpleɪ] *n* interaction *f*
Interpol [ˈɪntəpɒl] *n* Interpol *m*
interpolate [ɪnˈtɜːpəleɪt] *vt* (**a**) (*insert*) (*remark, question*) glisser; (*word, passage*) intercaler; **interpolated sheet** (*in bookbinding*) feuille *f* intercalaire (**b**) (*change*) (*text*) altérer par interpolation
interpolation [ɪntɜːpəˈleɪʃən] *n* (*remark, question*) remarque *f*/question *f* glissée dans un discours; (*word, passage*) mot *m*/passage *m* intercalé dans un texte; (*intended to change meaning*) interpolation *f*
interpose [ɪntəˈpəʊz] *vt* interposer; **to i. a remark** (*in conversation*) faire une observation
interpret [ɪnˈtɜːprɪt] **1** *vt* interpréter; **to i. sb's words as a threat** interpréter les paroles de qn comme une menace **2** *vi* faire l'interprète; **can you i. for me?** est-ce que vous pouvez me servir d'interprète?
interpretation [ɪntɜːprɪˈteɪʃən] *n* interprétation *f*; **to put the wrong i. on sth** donner une fausse interprétation à qch; **she wasn't sure what i. to put on the remarks** elle ne savait pas trop comment elle devait interpréter ces remarques; *Can* **i. centre** (*at historic site etc*) centre *m* d'interprétation
interpretative [ɪnˈtɜːprɪtətɪv] *adj* interprétatif
interpreter [ɪnˈtɜːprɪtə(r)] *n* (**a**) (*person*) interprète *mf*; **to act as i.** servir d'interprète (**b**) *Comptr* (*program*) interpréteur *m*
interpreting [ɪnˈtɜːprɪtɪŋ] *n* (*occupation*) interprétation *f*; **i. assignment** mission *f* d'interprète
interpretive [ɪnˈtɜːprɪtɪv] *adj* interprétatif
interracial [ɪntəˈreɪʃəl] *adj* (*marriage, conflict etc*) entre des races différentes
interregnum [ɪntəˈregnəm], *pl* **-ums, -a** [-əmz, -ə] *n* interrègne *m*
interrelated [ɪntərɪˈleɪtɪd] *adj* (*facts*) étroitement liés, en corrélation; **i. costs** coûts *mpl* interdépendants; **i. demand** demande *f* en rapport
interrelation [ɪntərɪˈleɪʃən] *n* corrélation *f*
interrogate [ɪnˈterəgeɪt] *vt* (*sb*) interroger, questionner; (*of police*) faire subir un interrogatoire à; *Comptr* (*database*) interroger
interrogation [ɪnterəˈgeɪʃən] *n* (**a**) interrogatoire *m*; *Comptr* (*of database*) interrogation *f*; **under i.** en train de subir un interrogatoire; *Mil* **i. centre** (*for prisoners of war*) centre *m* où les interrogatoires ont lieu (**b**) *Gram* **i. mark**, *Am* **i. point** point *m* d'interrogation
interrogative [ɪntəˈrɒgətɪv] **1** *adj* (**a**) (*tone, look etc*) interrogateur, -trice (**b**) *Gram* (*pronoun etc*) interrogatif **2** *n* [①**A31**; **B15-16**,**C**] *Gram* (*pronoun etc*) interrogatif *m*; (*symbol*) point *m* d'interrogation
interrogatively [ɪntəˈrɒgətɪvlɪ] *adv* interrogativement; d'un air interrogateur
interrogator [ɪnˈterəgeɪtə(r)] *n* interrogateur, -trice
interrogatory [ɪntəˈrɒgətərɪ] *adj* (*tone, look etc*) interrogateur, -trice

interrupt[1] [ɪntəˈrʌpt] **1** *vt* **(a)** (*stop*) (*action, conversation etc*) interrompre; **am I interrupting something?** est-ce que je vous dérange?; **to i. sb** interrompre qn, couper la parole à qn **(b)** (*block*) (*rail etc services*) interrompre; (*communications, supplies*) couper; (*electrical circuit*) interrompre; (*rhythm*) rompre; (*view*) gêner **2** *vi* interrompre; **don't interrupt!** (*when I'm talking*) ne me coupe pas la parole!, ne m'interromps pas!; (*when sb is talking*) ne coupe pas la parole aux gens!, n'interromps pas les gens!; **I'm sorry to i.** (*intrude*) je suis désolé de vous interrompre

interrupt[2] [ˈɪntərʌpt] *n Comptr* interruption *f*; **i. function** fonction *f* d'interruption

interruption [ɪntəˈrʌpʃən] *n* interruption *f*; **without i.** sans interruption; **I want no more interruptions** (*let me finish speaking*) je ne veux plus qu'on m'interrompe; (*leave me in peace*) je ne veux plus être dérangé

interscholastic [ɪntəskəˈlæstɪk] *adj* interscolaire, inter-écoles

intersect [ɪntəˈsekt] **1** *vt* (*of street*) croiser; **Maple Street is intersected by Elm Avenue** Maple Street et Elm Avenue se croisent; **line that intersects another** ligne qui en coupe une autre; **to i. one another** (*of lines, surfaces*) se couper, s'entrecroiser **2** *vi* (*of lines*) se couper; (*of streets*) se croiser

intersection [ɪntəˈsekʃən] *n* **(a)** *Math* (*of two planes etc*) intersection *f*; **(point of) i.** point *m* d'intersection **(b)** *esp Am* (*of roads*) croisement *m*

interspace [ɪntəˈspeɪs] *vt Typ* espacer

intersperse [ɪntəˈspɜːs] *vt* parsemer (**with** de); **to i. a speech with quotations** émailler un discours de citations; **plain-clothes officers were interspersed in the crowd** des policiers en civil étaient dispersés dans la foule; **carnations are interspersed among the roses** les roses sont parsemées d'œillets; **there will be sunshine interspersed with showers** il y aura une alternance d'averses et d'éclaircies

interstate [ˈɪntəsteɪt] **1** *adj* (*commerce etc*) (*in United States, Australia etc*) entre États; **i. carrier** transporteur *m* inter-État **2** *n US Aut* autoroute *f*

interstellar [ɪntəˈstelə*r*] *adj Astron* interstellaire

interstice [ɪnˈtɜːstɪs] *n* interstice *m*

intertribal [ɪntəˈtraɪb(ə)l] *adj* entre tribus

intertwine [ɪntəˈtwaɪn] **1** *vt* entrelacer; **his fate seemed intertwined with hers** son destin semblait lié au sien **2** *vi* s'entrelacer; **she found them intertwined** elle les a trouvés enlacés dans les bras l'un de l'autre

interurban [ɪntərˈɜːbən] *adj* interurbain

interval [ˈɪntəvəl] *n* **(a)** (*time*) intervalle *m*; *esp Br Th* entracte *m*; *Fb etc* mi-temps *f inv*, pause *f*; **it rained at intervals** il a plu par intervalles; **I completed the job at intervals over a period of two months** j'ai effectué le travail en plusieurs fois sur une période de deux mois; **I saw him at intervals during my stay** je l'ai vu de temps en temps au cours de mon séjour; **at regular intervals** à intervalles réguliers; **at five-minute intervals, at intervals of five minutes** toutes les cinq minutes; **rainy weather with bright intervals** temps pluvieux avec éclaircies; **after an i. of time** après un certain temps; **an hour's i. between two lectures** une heure de battement entre deux conférences

(b) (*space*) écart *m*, espace *m*, intervalle *m*; **at two-metre intervals** à deux mètres d'écart, à un intervalle de deux mètres; **there are trees growing at regular intervals along the road** des arbres jalonnent la route

(c) *Mus* intervalle *m*

intervene [ɪntəˈviːn] *vi* **(a)** (*take action*) intervenir (**in** dans); **the government intervened to save the company** le gouvernement est intervenu pour sauver l'entreprise **(b)** (*of event*) survenir; **the war intervened** la guerre est survenue; **ten years intervened** dix ans s'écoulèrent

intervening [ɪntəˈviːnɪŋ] *adj* (*period*) intermédiaire; **during the i. period** entre-temps; **the i. events** les événements qui survinrent entre-temps *ou* dans l'intervalle; **during the i. week** pendant la semaine qui s'écoula entre-temps

intervention [ɪntəˈvenʃən] *n* (*by government, individual etc*) intervention *f*; **i. price** prix *m* d'intervention

interventionism [ɪntəˈvenʃənɪz(ə)m] *n* interventionnisme *m*

interventionist [ɪntəˈvenʃənɪst] **1** *adj* interventionniste **2** *n* interventionniste *mf*

interview[1] [ˈɪntəvjuː] *n* **(a)** (*for job, place at university etc*) entrevue *f*, entretien *m*; (*in survey etc*) entretien *m*; **a job i., an i. for a job** un entretien pour un emploi; **to invite sb to an** *or* **for (an) i.** convoquer qn à un entretien **(b)** *Journ, TV* interview *f*; **he rarely gives interviews** il donne *ou* accorde rarement des interviews

interview[2] **1** *vt* **(a)** (*for job, place at university etc*) faire passer un entretien *ou* une entrevue à; (*in survey*) interroger, enquêter; (*criminal, suspect etc*) interroger; **who interviewed you?** qui t'a fait passer l'entretien?; **she's being interviewed tomorrow** elle est convoquée pour un entretien demain **(b)** *Journ, TV* interviewer **2** *vi* **(a)** (*of job interviewer etc*) faire passer des entretiens; **he doesn't i. well** (*of job candidate etc*) il n'est pas très bon aux entretiens **(b)** *Journ, TV* **the new Minister interviews well** le nouveau ministre passe bien aux interviews

interviewee [ɪntəvjuːˈiː] *n Journ, TV* personne *f* interviewée; (*for job*) candidat, -ate (*à qui l'on fait passer un entretien*)

interviewer [ˈɪntəvjuːə*r*] *n Journ, TV etc* interviewer *m*, intervieweur, -euse; (*for research, in canvassing*) enquêteur, -euse; **her skills as an i.** (*of job applicants*) ses qualités pour faire passer les entretiens *ou* pour examiner les candidats

inter-war [ˈɪntəˈwɔːr] *adj* **the i. years** *or* **period** l'entre-deux-guerres *m*; **i. politics** la politique de l'entre-deux-guerres

interweave [ɪntəˈwiːv] (*pt* **interwove** [ɪntəˈwəʊv]; *pp* **interwoven** [ɪntəˈwəʊv(ə)n]) **1** *vt* **(a)** *Tex* (*gold thread with wool etc*) tisser ensemble; (*branches etc*) entrelacer; **material interwoven with gold threads** tissu broché d'or **(b)** *Fig* (*stories*) mêler; **to i. sth into sth** mêler qch à qch; **closely interwoven systems** systèmes étroitement liés l'un à l'autre **2** *vi* (*of branches*) s'entrelacer; *Fig* (*of stories, narratives*) s'entremêler

interword spacing [ɪntəˈwɜːd] *n Typ* espacement *m* entre les mots

intestate [ɪnˈtesteɪt] *Jur* **1** *adj* intestat *inv*; **she died i.** elle est morte intestat; **i. estate** *or* **succession** succession *f* ab intestat **2** *n* intestat *mf*

intestinal [ɪntesˈtaɪn(ə)l, ɪnˈtestɪn(ə)l] *adj Anat* intestinal

intestine [ɪnˈtestɪn] *n Anat* intestin *m*; **the large i.** le gros intestin; **the small i.** l'intestin grêle

intimacy [ˈɪntɪməsɪ] *n* **(a)** intimité *f*; **in the i. of the family** dans l'intimité de la famille **(b)** (*intimate remark etc*) familiarité *f* **(c)** *Fml* (*sexual intercourse*) rapports *mpl* sexuels; **evidence that i. took place** preuves *fpl* de relations intimes

intimate[1] [ˈɪntɪmɪt] **1** *adj* (*friendship, friend, restaurant etc*) intime; **they're very i.** ils sont très intimes; **a few i. friends** quelques intimes; **the i. nature of their conversation** la nature intime de leur conversation; **to be i. with sb** (*know well*) être intime avec qn; *Fml* (*have sexual intercourse*) avoir des relations intimes avec qn; **to have an i. knowledge of sth** avoir une connaissance approfondie de qch **2** *n* intime *mf*

intimate[2] [ˈɪntɪmeɪt] *vt* **(a)** (*suggest, hint at*) laisser entendre (**sth to sb** qch à qn) **(b)** *Fml* (*make known*) (*order*) intimer; (*one's intentions*) signifier; **to i. sth to sb** notifier qch à qn

intimately [ˈɪntɪmətlɪ] *adv* intimement; **i. connected** étroitement lié; **to know sb i.** (*well*) connaître qn intimement

intimation [ɪntɪˈmeɪʃən] *n* **(a)** *Fml* (*hint*) indication *f*; **she gave me no i. of her intentions** elle ne m'a rien laissé entrevoir de ses intentions; **they had no i. of the difficulties ahead** ils étaient loin de se représenter les difficultés qui les attendaient **(b)** *Arch* (*notice*) **an i. of death** un avis de décès

intimidate [ɪnˈtɪmɪdeɪt] *vt* intimider; **I'm not going to be intimidated by her** je ne vais pas me laisser intimider par elle; **to i. sb into doing sth** intimider qn pour qu'il fasse qch

intimidating [ɪnˈtɪmɪdeɪtɪŋ] *adj* intimidant

intimidation [ɪntɪmɪˈdeɪʃən] *n* intimidation *f*; *Jur* menaces *fpl*

into [ˈɪntʊ, ˈɪntə] *prep* (①**A67**) **(a)** (*motion, direction*) dans; **to go i. a house** entrer dans une maison; **to fall i. the hands of the enemy** tomber entre les mains de l'ennemi *ou* aux mains de l'ennemi; **the door opens i. the garden** la porte donne sur le jardin; **to come i. a property** (*by inheritance*) hériter d'un bien; **to get i. difficulties** s'attirer des ennuis; **to walk i. a door/sb** rentrer dans une porte/qn; **to cut i. a piece of cheese** couper dans un morceau de fromage; **to speak i. a microphone** parler dans un micro; **I'd like to get i. television** j'aimerais bien rentrer *ou* entrer à la télévision

(b) (*change, result*) en; **to change sth i. sth** changer *ou* transformer qch en qch; **to grow i. a man** devenir un homme; **to divide i. four** diviser en quatre; **to break sth i. pieces** briser qch en morceaux; **to burst i. tears** fondre en larmes; **to go i. a coma** tomber dans le coma; **they cajoled her i. agreeing** ils lui ont arraché son accord à force de cajoleries

(c) (*with time, age etc*) **to work far i. the night** travailler très tard dans la nuit; **he was well i. his sixties before he retired** il avait la soixantaine bien sonnée quand il est parti à la retraite; **it was well i. January before we got any snow** le mois de janvier était bien entamé quand nous avons eu la première neige

(d) *Math* **three i. six goes two** six divisé par trois font deux

(e) *F* **to be i. sb/sth** (*like*) bien aimer qn/qch; **he's i. drugs** (*uses*) il se drogue; **he's really i. her/jogging/French cooking** il est fou d'elle/de jogging/de cuisine française;

she's i. the green movement elle est à fond *ou* elle donne à fond dans le mouvement écolo; **I'm not i. computers/wearing ties** l'informatique/les cravates, ce n'est pas mon truc; **I'm not really i. that sort of thing** ces choses-là, ce n'est pas mon truc; **I'm not i. computers the way you are** je ne suis pas aussi amateur d'informatique que toi; **we're not i. cheating people** (*that's not our style*) nous ne cherchons pas à rouler les gens; **if that's what you're i.!** si c'est ton truc!

(**f**) *Am* (*in debt to*) **he's i. them for $5 000** il leur doit cinq mille dollars

intolerable [ɪn'tɒlərəb(ə)l] *adj* intolérable, insupportable

intolerably [ɪn'tɒlərəblɪ] *adv* (*boring, vain*) insupportablement; **it was i. hot** il faisait une chaleur intolérable *ou* insupportable; **they are i. rude** ils sont d'une grossièreté intolérable *ou* insupportable

intolerance [ɪn'tɒlərəns] *n* intolérance *f* (**of, towards** à l'égard de); *Med* **i. of a drug/foodstuff** intolérance à un remède/un aliment

intolerant [ɪn'tɒlərənt] *adj* intolérant (**of** à l'égard de); **to be very i.** être d'une extrême intolérance; *Med* **to be i. of a drug** ne pas tolérer *ou* supporter un médicament

intolerantly [ɪn'tɒlərəntlɪ] *adv* avec intolérance, de façon intolérante

intonation [ɪntə'neɪʃən] *n* intonation *f*

intone [ɪn'təʊn] *vt* (**a**) (*speak*) débiter (**b**) *Rel* (*litany*) psalmodier

intoxicate [ɪn'tɒksɪkeɪt] *vt* (*make drunk*) enivrer, rendre ivre; *Fig* griser

intoxicated [ɪn'tɒksɪkeɪtɪd] *adj* (*drunk*) ivre; **to become i.** s'enivrer (**with** de); *Fig* **i. with power** ivre de pouvoir; **i. by their first taste of freedom** grisés par leur première expérience de la liberté

intoxicating [ɪn'tɒksɪkeɪtɪŋ] *adj* (*wine, perfume*) enivrant; *Fig* (*experience, freedom*) grisant; **i. liquors** spiritueux *mpl*

intoxication [ɪntɒksɪ'keɪʃən] *n* (**a**) (*drunkenness*) ivresse *f*; *Fig* griserie *f* (**b**) *Med* intoxication *f*

intra-Community ['ɪntrəkə'mju:nɪtɪ] *adj attrib* intracommunautaire; **i. trade** échange *m* intracommunautaire

intra-company [ɪntrə'kʌmpanɪ] *adj* intra-entreprise

intractability [ɪntræktə'bɪlɪtɪ] *n* (*of person*) opiniâtreté *f*, inflexibilité *f*; (*of illness, problem*) caractère *m* rebelle

intractable [ɪn'træktəb(ə)l] *adj Fml* (*person*) (*about specific question*) intraitable; (*child*) insoumis; (*illness*) rebelle; (*problem*) très difficile

intramural [ɪntrə'mjʊərəl] *adj esp Am Sch etc* **i. athletics competition** épreuves *fpl* d'athlétisme entre membres d'un même établissement scolaire

intramuscular [ɪntrə'mʌskjʊlər] *adj* (*injection*) intramusculaire

intransigence [ɪn'trænsɪdʒəns] *n* intransigeance *f*

intransigent [ɪn'trænsɪdʒənt] *adj, n* intransigeant, -ante

intransitive [ɪn'trænsɪtɪv] *Gram* **1** *adj* (*verb*) intransitif **2** *n* intransitif *m*

intransitively [ɪn'trænsɪtɪvlɪ] *adv* intransitivement

intra-state carrier [ɪntrə'steɪt] *n* transporteur *m* intra-État

intrauterine [ɪntrə'ju:təraɪn] *adj Anat* intra-utérin; **i. device** stérilet *m*

intravenous [ɪntrə'vi:nəs] *adj Med* intraveineux; **i. injection** (injection *f*) intraveineuse *f*

intravenously [ɪntrə'vi:nəslɪ] *adv Med* par voie intraveineuse

in-tray *n* bac *m* du courrier à traiter *ou* du courrier reçu

intrepid [ɪn'trepɪd] *adj* intrépide

intrepidity [ɪntre'pɪdɪtɪ] *n* intrépidité *f*

intrepidly [ɪn'trepɪdlɪ] *adv* intrépidement

intricacy ['ɪntrɪkəsɪ] *n* complexité *f*; **the intricacies of the law** les complexités de la loi

intricate ['ɪntrɪkət] *adj* (*mechanism, drawing, design*) compliqué; (*question, plot*) complexe

intricately ['ɪntrɪkətlɪ] *adv* d'une manière compliquée; **an i. detailed drawing** un dessin extrêmement détaillé

intrigue[1] ['ɪntri:g] *n* (**a**) (*plot, plotting*) intrigue *f* (**b**) *Old-fashioned* (*love affair*) aventure *f*

intrigue[2] [ɪn'tri:g] **1** *vt* intriguer; **I'm greatly intrigued by the idea** l'idée m'intrigue énormément **2** *vi* intriguer (**against sb** contre qn)

intriguing [ɪn'tri:gɪŋ] *adj* intrigant; **I find all this very i.** tout cela m'intrigue beaucoup

intrinsic [ɪn'trɪnsɪk] *adj* (*worth*) intrinsèque

intrinsically [ɪn'trɪnsɪklɪ] *adv* intrinsèquement

intro ['ɪntrəʊ] *n F* = **introduction (b)**

introduce [ɪntrə'dju:s] *vt* (**a**) (*present*) présenter (**to sb** à qn); **to i. oneself** se présenter; **I don't think we've been introduced** je ne crois pas que nous avons été présentés; **we've introduced ourselves** nous nous sommes déjà présentés; *Cin* **introducing Franella Floozie** et pour la première fois à l'écran Franella Floozie; **to be introduced to society** (*of débutante*) faire son entrée dans le monde

(**b**) (*initiate*) **to i. sb to sth** faire connaître qch à qn; **he introduced me to Greek** il m'a initié au grec; **they introduced me to drugs/Rabelais** ils m'ont fait connaître la drogue/Rabelais

(**c**) (*put in, bring in*) (*key into lock, new species, disease*) introduire; **to i. a subject** mettre une question sur le tapis; **to i. sb into sb's presence** introduire qn auprès de qn

(**d**) (*have adopted*) (*law, usage*) établir, faire adopter; (*fashion, new machinery, methods etc*) introduire; *Parl* **to i. a bill** déposer un projet de loi

(**e**) *Gram* (*of conjunction, adverb*) (*phrase*) introduire

(**f**) *Com* (*product*) lancer; *St Exch* (*shares*) introduire

introduce-a-friend scheme *n Mktg* offre-ami *f, pl* offres-ami

introduction [ɪntrə'dʌkʃən] *n* (**a**) (*presentation*) présentation *f* (**of sb to sb** de qn à qn); **to make the introductions** faire les présentations

(**b**) (*of book*) avant-propos *m inv*, introduction *f*; *Mus* introduction

(**c**) (*book for beginners*) introduction *f* (**to** à); (*to chemistry, biology etc*) manuel *m* élémentaire (**to** de), introduction (**to** à)

(**d**) (*act of initiation*) introduction *f*, premier contact *m* (**to sth** avec qch); **this was my i. to Shakespeare** ça a été mon premier contact avec Shakespeare; **this record would be a good i. to her work** ce disque constituerait une bonne introduction à son œuvre

(**e**) (*act of bringing in, putting in*) (*of new species, disease, key into lock*) introduction *f*

(**f**) (*of custom etc*) introduction *f*; **the sport is a recent i. from the United States** ce sport est récemment arrivé des États-Unis

(**g**) *Parl* (*of bill*) introduction *f*

introductory [ɪntrə'dʌktərɪ] *adj* (qui sert) d'introduction; (*page, paragraph*) liminaire; **after a few i. words** après quelques mots d'introduction; **i. music** introduction *f* musicale, musique *f* d'ouverture; *Com* **i. price** prix *m* de lancement

intro-ident *n TV etc* identification *f* d'intro

introit ['ɪntrɔɪt] *n Rel* introït *m*

introspection [ɪntrə'spekʃən] *n* introspection *f*

introspective [ɪntrə'spektɪv] *adj* introspectif

introversion [ɪntrə'vɜ:ʃən] *n Psy* introversion *f*

introvert ['ɪntrəvɜ:t] *adj, n* introverti, -ie

introverted ['ɪntrəvɜ:tɪd] *adj* introverti; **she's become very i. since the accident** elle est devenue très renfermée depuis l'accident

intrude [ɪn'tru:d] **1** *vi* **I hope I'm not intruding** j'espère que je ne vous dérange pas *ou* que je ne suis pas importun; **to i. on sb's privacy** s'ingérer dans la vie privée de qn; **she didn't want her work to i. on her family life** elle ne voulait pas que son travail empiète sur sa vie de famille; **a supermarket would i. on the character of the village** un supermarché gâcherait le caractère pittoresque du village **2** *vt* (*opinion*) imposer; **to i. a note of caution into the discussion** introduire une note de prudence dans la discussion

intruder [ɪn'tru:dər] *n* (*on other people*) intrus, -use, importun, -une; (*burglar*), *Comptr* intrus *m*; **she felt like an i.** elle se sentait de trop; *Comptr* **i. detection** détection *f* des intrus

intrusion [ɪn'tru:ʒən] *n* intrusion *f*; **I hope I am not guilty of an i.** j'espère que je ne suis pas indiscret *ou* que je ne dérange pas

intrusive [ɪn'tru:sɪv] *adj* (*person*) importun, indiscret; (*noise, presence*) gênant; *Ling* intrusif

intubate ['ɪntjʊbeɪt] *vt Med* intuber

intuit [ɪn'tju:ɪt] *vt Fml* deviner intuitivement *ou* par intuition

intuition [ɪntju:'ɪʃən] *n* intuition *f*; **I have an i. that ...** j'ai l'intuition que ..., mon intuition me dit que ...

intuitive [ɪn'tju:ɪtɪv] *adj* intuitif

intuitively [ɪn'tju:ɪtɪvlɪ] *adv* intuitivement, par intuition

Inuit ['ɪnju:ɪt] **1** *n* Inuit *m inv* **2** *adj* inuit *inv*

inundate ['ɪnʌndeɪt] *vt* inonder (**with** de); *Fig* **to be inundated with letters** être submergé de lettres; **to be inundated with phone calls** recevoir une quantité énorme de coups de téléphone

inundation [ɪnʌn'deɪʃən] *n* inondation *f*

inure [ɪ'njʊər] *vt* habituer (**to** à)

invade [ɪn'veɪd] **1** *vt* (*country, Fb pitch etc*) envahir; **to i. sb's privacy** violer l'intimité de qn **2** *vi* envahir

invader [ɪn'veɪdər] *n* envahisseur *m*

invading [ɪn'veɪdɪŋ] *adj* (*army*) d'invasion

invalid[1] [ɪn'vælɪd] *adj* (*argument, objection, ticket etc*) non valable; *Jur* (*marriage*) invalide, non valide; (*decision*) nul et non avenu; *Comptr* invalide; **your position is morally i.** d'un point de vue moral votre position ne tient pas; *Comptr* **i. character** caractère *m* invalide; *Comptr* **i. file name** nom *m* de fichier invalide

invalid² [ˈɪnvəlɪd] **1** *n* (*ill person*) malade *mf*; (*disabled person*) invalide *mf*, infirme *mf*; **I'm not an i.!** je ne suis pas infirme! **2** *adj* (*chronically ill*) malade; (*disabled*) invalide, infirme; **she has an i. sister** (*disabled*) elle a une sœur infirme; (*in poor health*) elle a une sœur d'une santé délicate

▶ **invalid out** *vtsep esp Br Mil* **to be invalided out (of the army)** être réformé pour raisons médicales

invalidate [ɪnˈvælɪdeɪt] *vt* **(a)** (*theory, hypothesis etc*) infirmer **(b)** *Jur* (*will*) invalider, rendre nul; (*document, contract*) vicier; (*verdict*) casser, infirmer

invalidation [ɪnvælɪˈdeɪʃən] *n* (*of theory etc, Jur of document, contract*) invalidation *f*; *Jur* (*of verdict*) infirmation *f*, cassation *f*

invalid car *n* voiture *f* d'infirme

invalid carriage *n* véhicule *m* spécial pour handicapé

invalid chair *n* fauteuil *m* roulant

invalidity [ɪnvəˈlɪdɪtɪ] *n* **(a)** (*disability*) invalidité *f*; *Admin* **i. benefit** prestation *f* d'invalidité; **i. pension** pension *f* d'invalidité **(b)** (*of passport, contract etc*) invalidité *f*; (*of argument*) manque *m* de fondement

invaluable [ɪnˈvæljʊəb(ə)l] *adj* extrêmement utile; (*help, assistance*) inestimable; **her help was i. (to us)** elle nous a été d'une aide inestimable *ou* très précieuse

invariable [ɪnˈveərɪəb(ə)l] *adj* invariable; (*routine*) immuable

invariably [ɪnˈveərɪəblɪ] *adv* invariablement; **he would i. arrive late** il arrivait immanquablement en retard

invariant [ɪnˈveərɪənt] *adj Fml* constant

invasion [ɪnˈverʒən] *n* **(a)** *Mil, Fig* (*by army, by tourists*) invasion *f*; **these invasions of my privacy** ces intrusions *fpl* dans mon intimité **(b) i. of sb's rights** violation *f* des droits de qn

invasive [ɪnˈveɪsɪv] *adj Med* invasif; **i. surgery** chirurgie *f* invasive *ou* effractoire

invective [ɪnˈvektɪv] *n* invective *f*; **a torrent of invective** un flot d'invectives *ou* d'injures *fpl*

inveigh [ɪnˈveɪ] *vi* invectiver (**against** contre)

inveigle [ɪnˈveɪg(ə)l, -viː] *vt* (*sb*) entortiller; **to i. sb into doing sth** entortiller qn pour qu'il fasse qch

invent [ɪnˈvent] *vt* (*machine, story etc*) inventer; *Fig* **he invented a movie-star mother** il s'est inventé une mère star de cinéma; **recently invented** d'invention récente

invention [ɪnˈvenʃən] *n* **(a)** (*something invented*) invention *f*; (*lie*) invention, mensonge *m*; **this is pure i.** c'est une pure invention **(b)** (*ability to invent*) esprit *m* inventif, inventivité *f* **(c)** (*act of inventing*) (*of machine etc*) invention *f*; **a story of his own i.** une histoire de son cru

inventive [ɪnˈventɪv] *adj* inventif

inventiveness [ɪnˈventɪvnɪs] *n* esprit *m* inventif, inventivité *f*

inventor [ɪnˈventər] *n* inventeur, -trice

inventory¹ [ˈɪnvənt(ə)rɪ] *n* **(a)** (*list*) inventaire *m*; **to draw up** *or* **take an i.** dresser *ou* faire un inventaire; **i. of fixtures** état *m* des lieux; **i. balance** balance *f* d'inventaire; **i. management** gestion *f* de l'inventaire **(b)** (*stock*) stock(s) *m(pl)*; **i. account** compte *m* de stock; **i. control** gestion *f ou* contrôle *m* des stocks; **i. level** niveau *m* des stocks; **i. turnover rate** vitesse *f* de rotation des stocks

inventory² *vt* (*property, stock*) inventorier, dresser l'inventaire de

inverse [ɪnˈvɜːs] **1** *adj* inverse; **in i. order** en sens inverse; *Math* **i. function** fonction *f* inverse; **in i. ratio/proportion** en raison/proportion inverse (**to** de) **2** *n* inverse *m*, contraire *m* (**of** de)

inversely [ɪnˈvɜːslɪ] *adv* inversement

inversion [ɪnˈvɜːʃən] *n* **(a)** (*of image*) renversement *m*; *Mus* **i. of a chord** (*action*) renversement d'un accord; (*result*) accord *m* dérivé **(b)** [ⓘA72-3,17] *Gram* (*of words in phrase, Math of integral*) inversion *f* **(c)** *Ch* (*of sugar etc*) inversion *f* **(d)** *Psy* (**sexual**) **i.** inversion *f* sexuelle

invert¹ [ˈɪnvɜːt] **1** *adj* (*sugar*) inverti **2** *n Psy* inverti, -ie

invert² [ɪnˈvɜːt] *vt* **(a)** (*object*) (*turn upside down*) renverser, retourner; *Mus* (*chord*) renverser **(b)** (*reverse*) (*order, positions*) invertir, intervertir, renverser; *Gram* (*subject etc*) inverser **(c)** *Ch* (*sugar*) invertir

invertebrate [ɪnˈvɜːtɪbrɪt] *adj, n Zool* invertébré *m*

inverted [ɪnˈvɜːtɪd] *adj* **(a)** (*upside down, Mus chord*) renversé; **i. snobbery** snobisme *m* à l'envers; **i. snob** personne *f* qui fait preuve de snobisme à l'envers **(b)** (*reversed*) (*word order etc*) *Opt* (*image*) renversé; *Sewing* **i. pleat** pli *m* inverti *ou* creux **(c)** *Psy* (*instinct*) inverti

inverted commas *npl* guillemets *mpl*; **in i.** entre guillemets

invest [ɪnˈvest] **1** *vt* **(a)** *Fin* (*money*) placer, investir; (*capital, Fig time etc*) investir; **to i. money in real estate** faire des placements dans l'immobilier; **capital invested** mise *f* de fonds, capital *m* engagé *ou* investi

(b) *Lit* (*install*) (*bishop, Pope*) introniser; (*president*) installer

(c) *Lit* (*provide*) (*sb*) investir (**with authority/***etc* de l'autorité/*etc*); **to i. a subject with interest** rendre un sujet intéressant; **his novels i. criminality with too much glamour** ses romans donnent une image trop séduisante du monde du crime

2 *vi* investir, faire des placements, placer son argent; **to i. in property** faire des placements dans l'immobilier; **we're going to i. in three new machines** nous allons investir dans trois nouvelles machines; *F* **you should i. in a good dictionary** tu devrais t'offrir *ou* te payer un bon dictionnaire

investigate [ɪnˈvestɪgeɪt] **1** *vt* (*question*) examiner, étudier; (*crime*) faire une enquête sur, enquêter sur **2** *vi* **I'll go and i.** je vais voir ce qui se passe

investigating [ɪnˈvestɪgeɪtɪŋ] *adj* **i. committee** commission *f* d'enquête; **i. officer** officier *m* chargé de l'enquête

investigation [ɪnvestɪˈgeɪʃən] *n* investigation *f*; (*by police, tax authority etc*) enquête *f* (**of** sur); **to conduct** *or* **carry out an i.** conduire *ou* effectuer une enquête; **the question is under i.** la question est à l'étude; **on further i.** en poursuivant les recherches; **on further i., the ruins turned out to be ...** des recherches plus approfondies ont révélé que les ruines étaient ...; **to make investigations** faire des investigations; (*of police*) procéder à une enquête

investigative [ɪnˈvestɪgətɪv] *adj* **i. journalism** journalisme *m* d'investigation; **i. journalist** journaliste *mf* d'investigation; *Journ, TV* **i. team** équipe *f* d'investigation

investigator [ɪnˈvestɪgeɪtər] *n* enquêteur, -euse; **(private) i.** détective *m* privé

investiture [ɪnˈvestɪtʃər] *n* (*installation in office*) investiture *f*; (*of bishop etc*) intronisation *f*

investment [ɪnˈvestmənt] *n Fin* placement *m*, investissement *m*; (*money invested*) investissement, mise *f* de fonds; **good** *or* **safe i.** placement sûr; **long-/short-term i.** placement à long/court terme; **i. analyst** analyste *mf* en placements; **i. income** revenu *m* provenant d'investissements; **i. portfolio** portefeuille *m* d'investissements

investment account *n* compte *m* d'investissement

investment bank *n* banque *f* d'affaires

investment capital *n* capital-investissement *m*

investment company *n* société *f* de portefeuille *ou* d'investissement

investment consultancy *n* société *f* de conseil en investissement

investment management *n* gestion *f* de portefeuille

investment plan *n* plan *m* d'investissement

investment trust *n* trust *m ou* société *f* de placement, fonds *m* commun de placement

investor [ɪnˈvestər] *n* investisseur *m*; **investors in the company** les personnes qui ont investi dans l'entreprise

inveterate [ɪnˈvetərɪt] *adj* (*drunkard, gambler, smoker*) invétéré; (*opponent*) acharné; (*liar*) incorrigible, impénitent

invidious [ɪnˈvɪdɪəs] *adj* **(a)** (*unpleasant*) pénible; (*task*) ingrat, peu agréable; **to be in an i. position** être dans une position peu enviable **(b)** (*comparison*) inéquitable

invigilate [ɪnˈvɪdʒɪleɪt] *Br Sch, Univ* **1** *vi* surveiller les candidats (*à un examen*) **2** *vt* (*exam*) surveiller

invigilator [ɪnˈvɪdʒɪleɪtər] *n Br Sch, Univ* surveillant, -ante (*des candidats à un examen*)

invigorate [ɪnˈvɪgəreɪt] *vt* (*of air, walk, holiday etc*) vivifier; **she invigorates an otherwise lifeless production of Hamlet** elle donne un souffle de vie à un Hamlet plutôt morne

invigorating [ɪnˈvɪgəreɪtɪŋ] *adj* vivifiant

invincibility [ɪnvɪnsɪˈbɪlɪtɪ] *n* invincibilité *f*; (*of belief, faith*) caractère *m* inébranlable

invincible [ɪnˈvɪnsɪb(ə)l] *adj* (*army*) invincible; (*faith, conviction*) inébranlable

inviolability [ɪnvaɪələˈbɪlɪtɪ] *n* inviolabilité *f*

inviolable [ɪnˈvaɪələb(ə)l] *adj* inviolable

inviolably [ɪnˈvaɪələblɪ] *adv* inviolablement

inviolate [ɪnˈvaɪəlɪt] *adj Fml* inviolé

invisibility [ɪnvɪzɪˈbɪlɪtɪ] *n* invisibilité *f*

invisible [ɪnˈvɪzɪb(ə)l] *adj* invisible; **i. to the naked eye** invisible à l'œil nu; *Econ* **i. earnings** gains *mpl* invisibles; **i. exports/imports** exportations *fpl*/importations *fpl* invisibles; **i. ink** encre *f* sympathique; **i. mending** stoppage *m*

invisibly [ɪnˈvɪzɪblɪ] *adv* invisiblement; **he had it i. mended** (*hole, garment*) il l'avait fait stopper

invitation [ɪnvɪˈteɪʃən] *n* invitation *f* (**to do sth** à faire qch); **at sb's i.** sur l'invitation de qn; **an i. to lunch** une invitation à déjeuner; **by i. only** uniquement sur invitation; *Fig* **the speech was an i. to criticism** ce discours ne pouvait pas manquer de provoquer la critique; **that's an i. to burglars** c'est une invitation aux cambrioleurs; **i. (card)** carte *f* d'invitation

invite[1] [ɪn'vaɪt] *vt* **(a)** (*ask to come*) inviter (**to** à); **to i. sb in** inviter qn à entrer; **to i. oneself** s'inviter soi-même; **the invited guests** les invités *mpl* **(b)** (*request*) inviter (**sb to do sth** qn à faire qch); **applications are invited for the position** toute personne intéressée est invitée à déposer un dossier de candidature **(c)** (*arouse*) (*danger, criticism*) (*of person*) s'exposer à; (*of action*) provoquer; **to i. trouble** aller au-devant des ennuis

invite[2] ['ɪnvaɪt] *n F* invitation *f*

▶ **invite back, invite in, invite round** *etc* = **ask back, ask in, ask round** *etc*

inviting [ɪn'vaɪtɪŋ] *adj* attrayant; (*dish*) appétissant; **her eyes were dark and i.** ses yeux étaient sombres et attirants; **not very i.** peu attrayant; **the water looks i.** l'eau donne envie de se baigner

invitingly [ɪn'vaɪtɪŋlɪ] *adv* (*arranged, displayed*) d'une manière attrayante; (*to smile, beckon*) en guise d'invitation

in vitro [ɪn'viːtrəʊ] *adj* **i. fertilization** fertilisation *f* in vitro

invocation [ɪnvə'keɪʃən] *n* invocation *f*

invoice[1] ['ɪnvɔɪs] *n Com* facture *f*; **to make out an i.** établir une facture; **as per i.** conformément à la facture; **within 30 days of i.** dans les 30 jours après la facturation; **payable against i.** à payer à réception de la facture; **i. clerk** facturier, -ière; **i. date** date *f* de facturation; **i. price** prix *m* facturé

invoice[2] *vt* (*goods, person*) facturer; **who do I i.?** à qui dois-je adresser la facture?; **to i. sb for sth** facturer qch à qn; **invoiced sales** ventes *fpl* facturées

invoiceable ['ɪnvɔɪsəb(ə)l] *adj* facturable

invoicing ['ɪnvɔɪsɪŋ] *n* (*of goods etc*) facturation *f*; **i. address** adresse *f* de facturation; **i. instructions** instructions *fpl* de facturation; **i. software** logiciel *m* de facturation

invoke [ɪn'vəʊk] *vt* **(a)** (*God, sb's memory, law etc*) invoquer; **to i. sb's aid** appeler qn à son secours; **to i. a blessing on an undertaking** demander à Dieu de bénir une entreprise **(b)** (*summon up*) (*spirit*) évoquer

involuntarily [ɪn'vɒlənt(ə)rɪlɪ] *adv* involontairement

involuntary [ɪn'vɒləntərɪ] *adj* involontaire

involve [ɪn'vɒlv] *vt* **(a)** (*in crime, scandal etc*) impliquer (**in** dans); (*in quarrel*) mêler (**in** dans); **he is involved in the plot** il est compromis dans le complot; **over 200 people were involved in planning the event** plus de 200 personnes ont participé à la préparation de l'événement; **he's involved in high finance/language teaching** il est dans la haute finance/l'enseignement des langues; **when I first became involved in teaching** quand j'ai commencé à enseigner; **he's getting involved with the school orchestra** il commence à prendre part aux activités de l'orchestre de l'école; **I'm getting really involved in this job** je commence à trouver ce travail vraiment intéressant; **the novel doesn't really i. the reader** le lecteur ne se sent pas impliqué dans ce roman; **they didn't want to get involved in another war** ils ne voulaient pas s'engager dans un autre conflit; **the police became involved** la police est intervenue; **no one wanted to get involved** personne n'a voulu s'en mêler; **he doesn't want to get involved** il ne veut pas s'engager; **don't get involved!** (*in other people's problems, argument etc*) ne t'en mêle pas!; **I'm too emotionally involved** cela me concerne de trop près *ou* me touche trop; **he got involved with his friend's wife** il a eu une liaison avec la femme de son ami

(b) (*include, entail etc*) impliquer, entraîner; **my job involves a lot of travel** je dois beaucoup voyager dans mon travail; **it involves learning new techniques** cela implique l'apprentissage de nouvelles techniques; **what exactly is involved in carrying out a project like this?** qu'est-ce que ça implique exactement la réalisation d'un tel projet?; **it involves getting to London by 5.30 in the morning** ça veut dire qu'il faut arriver à Londres à 5h 30 le matin; **all it involves is sitting by the phone** tout ce qu'il y a à faire, c'est de rester assis à côté du téléphone

(c) (*have to do with*) concerner; **this discussion doesn't i. you** cette discussion ne vous concerne pas; **there's been a theft – how much money is involved?** il y a eu un vol – de combien d'argent s'agit-il?

involved [ɪn'vɒlvd] *adj* (*complicated*) (*style, discours*) compliqué; (*story, plot*) complexe, compliqué

involvement [ɪn'vɒlvmənt] *n* **(a)** (*participation*) participation *f* (**in** à); (*in crime*) implication *f* (**in** dans); **his i. of his sister in the fraud is unforgivable** il est impardonnable qu'il ait impliqué sa sœur dans cette fraude; **I've had no further i. with him since** je n'ai plus jamais eu affaire à lui depuis; **her i. with this man** sa liaison avec cet homme; **our country's i. in this war** la participation de notre pays à cette guerre **(b)** (*complexity*) complexité *f*

invulnerability [ɪnvʌlnərə'bɪlɪtɪ] *n* invulnérabilité *f*

invulnerable [ɪn'vʌlnərəb(ə)l] *adj* (*person*) invulnérable; (*position etc*) inattaquable

inward ['ɪnwəd] **1** *adj* **(a)** (*intimate*) (*thoughts, feelings etc*) intérieur **(b)** (*directed to the inside*) (orienté *ou* se dirigeant) vers l'intérieur; **i. customs clearance** entrée *f* en douane; **i. investment** investissements *mpl* étrangers; *Acct* **i. payment** paiement *m* reçu **2** *adv* = **inwards**; **i. opening door** porte *f* qui s'ouvre vers l'intérieur

inward-looking ['ɪnwədlʊkɪŋ] *adj* introspectif

inwardly ['ɪnwədlɪ] *adv* intérieurement; **I was i. pleased** dans mon for intérieur j'étais content

inwards ['ɪnwədz] *adv* vers l'intérieur; *Com, Naut* pour l'importation

I/O ['aɪ'əʊ] *n Comptr* (*abbr* **input/output**) E/S; **I/O port** port *m* d'E/S

IOC [aɪəʊ'siː] *n* (*abbr* **International Olympic Committee**) CIO *m*

iodine [*Br* 'aɪədiːn, *Am* -daɪn] *n Ch* iode *m*; *Pharm* **(tincture of) i.** teinture *f* d'iode

iodize ['aɪədaɪz] *vt Med, Phot* ioder

iodoform [aɪ'ɒdəfɔːm] *n Ch, Pharm* iodoforme *m*

ion ['aɪən] *n Phys, Ch, El* ion *m*; **hydrogen i.** ion d'hydrogène; **i. beam** faisceau *m* ionique

Ionic [aɪ'ɒnɪk] *adj Archit, Liter* (*order, verse*) ionique; *Ling, Mus* (*dialect, mode*) ionien

ionic [aɪ'ɒnɪk] *adj Phys, Ch, El* ionique

ionization [aɪənaɪ'zeɪʃən] *n* **(a)** *Phys, El* ionisation *f* **(b)** *Med* (traitement *m* par) ionisation *f*

ionize ['aɪənaɪz] *Phys, El* **1** *vt* (*air, gas*) ioniser **2** *vi* (*of acid etc*) s'ioniser

ionosphere [aɪ'ɒnəsfɪər] *n* ionosphère *f*

iota [aɪ'əʊtə] *n* **(a)** (*in Greek alphabet*) iota *m* **(b)** (*tiny amount*) iota *m*; **she hadn't changed an** *or* **one i.** (*looked the same*) elle n'avait pas changé d'un iota; **not an i. of truth** pas un brin de vérité

IOU, *pl* **IOUs** [aɪəʊ'juː, -'juːz] *n* (= **I owe you**) reconnaissance *f* (de dette)

IPA [aɪpiː'eɪ] *n* (*abbr* **International Phonetic Alphabet**) API *m*

ipso facto ['ɪpsəʊ'fæktəʊ] *adv* ipso facto

IQ [aɪ'kjuː] *n* (*abbr* **intelligence quotient**) QI *m*; **to have an IQ of ...** avoir un QI de ...

IRA [aɪɑː'reɪ] *n* (*abbr* **Irish Republican Army**) IRA *f*

Iran [ɪ'rɑːn, ɪ'ræn] *n* Iran *m*

Iranian [ɪ'reɪnɪən] **1** *adj* iranien **2** *n* **(a)** Iranien, -ienne **(b)** *Ling* iranien *m*

Iraq [ɪ'rɑːk, ɪ'ræk] *n* Irak *m*

Iraqi [ɪ'rɑːkɪ] **1** *adj* irakien, iraquien **2** *n* Irakien, -ienne, Iraquien, -ienne

irascibility [ɪræsɪ'bɪlɪtɪ] *n* irascibilité *f*

irascible [ɪ'ræsɪb(ə)l] *adj* (*person*) irascible, coléreux; (*temperament*) colérique

irascibly [ɪ'ræsɪblɪ] *adv* (*to say etc*) sur un ton irrité

irate [aɪ'reɪt] *adj* (*person, telephone call*) furieux

ire ['aɪər] *n Lit* courroux *m*, colère *f*

Ireland ['aɪələnd] *n* Irlande *f*; **Northern I.** l'Irlande du Nord; **the Republic of I.** la République d'Irlande

iridescence [ɪrɪ'desəns] *n Lit* (*of plumage, fabric etc*) irisation *f*, chatoiement *m*

iridescent [ɪrɪ'desənt] *adj Lit* iridescent, chatoyant

iris ['aɪrɪs] *n* **(a)** *pl* **irides** ['aɪrɪdiːz] *Anat* iris *m* (de l'œil) **(b)** *pl* **irises** ['aɪrɪsɪz] (*flower*) iris *m*; **yellow i.** iris jaune *ou* des marais **(c)** *Myth* **I.** Iris *f*

Irish ['aɪərɪʃ] **1** *adj* **(a)** (*people, government, butter etc*) irlandais, d'Irlande; **an I. American** un(e) Américain, -aine d'origine irlandaise; **I. joke** histoire *f* drôle aux dépens des Irlandais, ≈ histoire belge **(b)** *F* (*stupid, illogical*) stupide; **that's a bit I.** c'est un peu bête; **I. bull** proposition *f* absurde car contradictoire **2** *n* **(a)** *Ling* irlandais *m* **(b) the I.** (*pl*) les Irlandais *mpl*

Irish coffee *n* Irish coffee *m*, = café *m* noir au whiskey irlandais couronné de crème fraîche

Irishism ['aɪərɪʃɪz(ə)m] *n* expression *f* irlandaise

Irishman, *pl* **Irishmen** ['aɪərɪʃmən] *n* Irlandais *m*

Irish Sea *n Geog* mer *f* d'Irlande

Irish setter *n* setter *m* irlandais

Irish stew *n* ragoût *m* à l'irlandaise

Irishwoman, *pl* **Irishwomen** ['aɪərɪʃwʊmən, -wɪmɪn] *n* Irlandaise *f*

irk [ɜːk] *vt* agacer

irksome ['ɜːksəm] *adj* agaçant

iron[1] ['aɪən] *n* **(a)** (*metal*) fer *m*; **(made of) i.** de *ou* en fer; **he has an i. constitution** il a une santé de fer; **man of i.** homme

dur *ou* sans pitié; **will of i., i. will** volonté *f* de fer; **i. bar** barre *f* de fer; **i. bridge** pont *m* en fer; *Fig* **i. discipline** discipline *f* de fer; **i. filings** limaille *f* de fer; **an i. fist** *or* **hand in a velvet glove** une main de fer dans un gant de velours; *Metal* **i. foundry** fonderie *f* de fonte; *US Hist* **the i. horse** = la locomotive; **the i. and steel industry** l'industrie *f* sidérurgique, la sidérurgie; *Br Pol* **the I. Lady** la Dame de Fer; *Med* **i. lung** poumon *m* d'acier; *Ch* **i. nitride** nitride *m* de fer; *Miner, Ch* **i. ore** minerai *m* de fer
(b) (*in diet*) fer *m*; **i. deficiency** manque *m* de fer
(c) (*device, implement*) (*for laundry*) fer *m* à repasser; **electric/steam i.** fer (à repasser) électrique/à vapeur; *Fig* **to have several irons in the fire** avoir plusieurs affaires en route; *Fig* **to have too many irons in the fire** courir trop de lièvres à la fois
(d) *Horseriding* (*of stirrup*) étrier *m*
(e) *Golf* (crosse *f* en) fer *m*; **i. shot** coup *m* de fer
(f) *Arch* (*for prisoner*) **irons** fers *mpl*, chaînes *fpl*
(g) *Med* **irons** (*supports*) attelles *fpl*

iron² *vti* (*clothes*) repasser; **I've been ironing all morning** j'ai repassé *ou* fait du repassage toute la matinée

▶ **iron out** *vtsep* (*crease*) faire disparaître au fer (chaud); *Fig* (*resolve*) (*problem*) résoudre; **to i. out the difficulties** aplanir les difficultés; **have you ironed out your differences?** est-ce que vous avez résolu vos différends?

Iron Age *n* l'âge *m* de fer

ironclad ['aɪənklæd] **1** *adj* **(a)** *Arch* (*ship*) cuirassé **(b)** *Fig* (*alibi, assurance, guarantee*) à toute épreuve **2** *n Naut, Hist* cuirassé *m*

Iron Curtain *n* le rideau de fer

iron-grey *adj* gris (de) fer

ironic(al) [aɪ'rɒnɪk, -ɪk(ə)l] *adj* ironique

ironically [aɪ'rɒnɪklɪ] *adv* ironiquement; (*to talk*) avec ironie; **i., the box was empty** l'ironie, c'est que la boîte était vide

ironing ['aɪənɪŋ] *n* repassage *m*; **I've got a lot of i. to do** j'ai beaucoup de repassage à faire; **i. board** planche *f ou* table *f* à repasser

ironmonger ['aɪənmʌŋgər] *n Br* quincaillier *m*; **i.'s (shop)** quincaillerie *f*

ironmongery ['aɪənmʌŋgərɪ] *n Br* (*goods, shop, Hum medals*) quincaillerie *f*

ironstone ['aɪənstəʊn] *n* **(clay) i.** minerai *m* de fer (argileux)

ironware ['aɪənweər] *n* ferronnerie *f*

ironwork ['aɪənwɜːk] *n* **(a)** (*work in wrought iron*) ferronnerie *f*; (*parts made of iron*) ferrure(s) *f(pl)* **(b)** (*often with sing verb*) **ironworks** (*for smelting*) fonderie *f* de fonte; (*for casting*) usine *f* sidérurgique, forges *fpl*

irony ['aɪrənɪ] *n* ironie *f*; **the i. is that …** l'ironie c'est que …; **i. of fate** ironie du sort; **in one of life's little ironies** par une ironie du sort

irradiate [ɪ'reɪdɪeɪt] *vt* **(a)** (*of light, heat*) (*the earth etc*) irradier; (*of light, rays*) (*surface*) illuminer **(b)** (*subject to radiation*) (*substance etc*) irradier; *Med* (*patient*) traiter par irradiation; **irradiated food** aliments *mpl* irradiés

irradiation [ɪreɪdɪ'eɪʃən] *n* **(a)** *Phys, Opt etc* irradiation *f*; (*of surface by light*) illumination *f* **(b)** *Nucl Phys* irradiation *f*; *Med* (traitement *m* par) irradiation, radiothérapie *f*

irrational [ɪ'ræʃən(ə)l] **1** *adj* **(a)** (*person, behaviour, fear*) irrationnel; **don't be so i.!** soyez un peu plus rationnel! **(b)** *Math* (*number*) irrationnel **2** *n* **the i.** l'irrationnel *m*

irrationally [ɪ'ræʃən(ə)lɪ] *adv* (*to behave*) de façon irrationnelle

irreconcilable [ɪrekən'saɪləb(ə)l] *adj* **(a)** (*enemy*) irréconciliable; (*hatred*) implacable **(b)** (*belief, idea*) incompatible, inconciliable (**with** avec)

irrecoverable [ɪrɪ'kʌvərəb(ə)l] *adj* (*debt*) irrécouvrable; (*loss*) irrémédiable; (*object*) irrécupérable

irrecoverably [ɪrɪ'kʌvərəblɪ] *adv* (*lost*) pour toujours

irredeemable [ɪrɪ'diːməb(ə)l] *adj* **(a)** (*fault*) irréparable; (*disaster etc*) irrémédiable; *Rel* **no sinner is i.** on peut tous se racheter **(b)** *Fin* (*funds*) irremboursable; (*bill*) non convertible

irredeemably [ɪrɪ'diːməblɪ] *adv* irrémédiablement

irreducible [ɪrɪ'djuːsɪb(ə)l] *adj* irréductible

irrefutable [ɪrɪ'fjuːtəb(ə)l] *adj* (*evidence*) irréfutable, irrécusable; (*statement*) irréfutable

irregular [ɪ'regjʊlər] **1** *adj* **(a)** (*not conforming to rule*) (*behaviour, attendance etc, Gram plural, verb*) irrégulier; (*life*) déréglé; **this is highly i.** c'est contraire aux règles **(b)** (*uneven*) (*outline, shape etc*) irrégulier; (*surface*) irrégulier, inégal, -aux; **i. features** traits *mpl* irréguliers **(c)** (*pulse, breathing*) irrégulier **(d)** *Mil* **i. troops** troupes *fpl* irrégulières, irréguliers *mpl* **2** *n* (*usu pl*) *Mil* **irregulars** troupes *fpl* irrégulières, irréguliers *mpl*

irregularity [ɪregjʊ'lærɪtɪ] *n* irrégularité *f*; *Admin etc* **irregularities** (*in accounts etc*) irrégularités

irregularly [ɪ'regjʊləlɪ] *adv* irrégulièrement, de façon irrégulière

irrelevance [ɪ'reləvəns], **irrelevancy** [ɪ'reləvənsɪ] *n* **(a)** (*state of being inapplicable*) inapplicabilité *f* (**to** à); (*inappropriateness*) manque *m* d'à-propos **(b)** (*remark, action etc*) remarque *f*/action *f*/*etc* sans rapport avec la question; **the defence of the frontier has become an i.** la défense de la frontière n'a plus de raison d'être; **irrelevancies** points *mpl* qui n'ont rien à voir avec la question

irrelevant [ɪ'reləvənt] *adj* non pertinent; (*remark etc*) hors de propos; **that is i.** cela n'a aucun rapport *ou* n'a rien à voir avec la question; **the monarchy had become i.** la monarchie n'avait plus de raison d'être, la monarchie avait perdu sa raison d'être; **it's i. now whether he changes his mind or not** maintenant ça ne fait plus rien qu'il change d'avis ou non

irreligious [ɪrɪ'lɪdʒəs] *adj* irréligieux

irremediable [ɪrɪ'miːdɪəb(ə)l] *adj* (*evil, loss etc*) irrémédiable; (*fault*) incorrigible

irremediably [ɪrɪ'miːdɪəblɪ] *adv* irrémédiablement

irremovable [ɪrɪ'muːvəb(ə)l] *adj* (*stain*) indélébile; (*official*) inamovible

irreparable [ɪ'repərəb(ə)l] *adj* (*damage*) irréparable; (*loss*) irrémédiable, irrécupérable

irreparably [ɪ'repərəblɪ] *adv* (*damaged*) irréparablement; (*lost*) irrémédiablement

irreplaceable [ɪrɪ'pleɪsəb(ə)l] *adj* irremplaçable

irrepressible [ɪrɪ'presɪb(ə)l] *adj* (*urge*) irrésistible, irrépressible; (*yawn*) irrépressible; (*good humour*) que rien n'entame, à toute épreuve; **i. laughter** fou rire *m*; **he's i.** rien ne peut l'abattre

irrepressibly [ɪrɪ'presɪblɪ] *adv* **i. optimistic/enthusiastic/good humoured** d'un optimisme/un enthousiasme/une bonne humeur à toute épreuve

irreproachable [ɪrɪ'prəʊtʃəb(ə)l] *adj* irréprochable

irreproachably [ɪrɪ'prəʊtʃəblɪ] *adv* irréprochablement, de façon irréprochable

irresistible [ɪrɪ'zɪstɪb(ə)l] *adj* irrésistible

irresistibly [ɪrɪ'zɪstɪblɪ] *adv* irrésistiblement

irresolute [ɪ'rezəluːt] *adj* indécis, irrésolu

irresolutely [ɪ'rezəluːtlɪ] *adv* d'un air irrésolu

irresoluteness [ɪ'rezəluːtnɪs], **irresolution** [ɪrezə'luːʃən] *n* indécision *f*, irrésolution *f*

irrespective [ɪrɪ'spektɪv] *adv* **i. of sth** indépendamment *ou* sans tenir compte de qch; **we'll go ahead i. of whether you agree or not** nous allons le faire que tu sois d'accord ou non

irresponsibility [ɪrɪspɒnsɪ'bɪlɪtɪ] *n* irresponsabilité *f*

irresponsible [ɪrɪ'spɒnsɪb(ə)l] *adj* irresponsable; **he was behaving like an i. idiot** il se comportait en irresponsable

irresponsibly [ɪrɪ'spɒnsɪblɪ] *adv* de façon irresponsable

irretrievable [ɪrɪ'triːvəb(ə)l] *adj* (*loss*) irrémédiable; (*money*) irrécupérable; (*mistake, situation*) irréparable; **because of the i. breakdown of their marriage** parce que leur mariage était irrémédiablement brisé

irretrievably [ɪrɪ'triːvəblɪ] *adv* (*lost*) irrémédiablement, à tout jamais; **to break down i.** (*of marriage*) se briser irrémédiablement

irreverence [ɪ'revərəns] *n* irrévérence *f* (**towards** envers, pour)

irreverent [ɪ'revərənt] *adj* irrévérencieux

irreverently [ɪ'revərəntlɪ] *adv* irrévérencieusement

irreversible [ɪrɪ'vɜːsɪb(ə)l] *adj* **(a)** (*decision, step etc*) irrévocable **(b)** (*process*) irréversible

irrevocable [ɪ'revəkəb(ə)l] *adj* irrévocable; **i. letter of credit** lettre *f* de crédit irrévocable, crédit *m* documentaire irrévocable

irrevocably [ɪ'revəkəblɪ] *adv* irrévocablement

irrigable ['ɪrɪgəb(ə)l] *adj* (*land*) irrigable

irrigate ['ɪrɪgeɪt] *vt Agr, Med* (*fields, wound*) irriguer

irrigation [ɪrɪ'geɪʃən] *n Agr, Med* (*of fields, wound*) irrigation *f*; *Agr* **i. canal** *or* **ditch** canal *m* d'irrigation

irritability [ɪrɪtə'bɪlɪtɪ] *n* irritabilité *f*

irritable ['ɪrɪtəb(ə)l] *adj* irritable; **i. bowel syndrome** colite *f*

irritably ['ɪrɪtəblɪ] *adv* (*to say, answer*) d'un ton irrité, avec humeur

irritant ['ɪrɪtənt] *adj, n Med* irritant *m*; *Fig* **at least we can be an i.** au moins nous pouvons jouer les empêcheurs de tourner en rond

irritate ['ɪrɪteɪt] *vt* **(a)** (*sb*) irriter, agacer; (*animal*) exciter, agacer **(b)** *Med* irriter

irritating ['ɪrɪteɪtɪŋ] *adj* **(a)** irritant, agaçant; **i. little habits** des petites manies agaçantes **(b)** *Med* irritant

irritatingly ['ɪrɪteɪtɪŋlɪ] *adv* (*to say, behave*) de façon agaçante; **i. slow/jolly** d'une lenteur/bonne humeur exaspérante

irritation [ɪrɪ'teɪʃən] *n* **(a)** irritation *f*; **state of nervous i.** état *m* d'énervement **(b)** *Med* (*of throat etc*) irritation *f*

is [ɪz] *see* **be**

ISBN [aɪesbiːˈen] *n* (*abbr* **International Standard Book Number**) ISBN *m*

ISDN [aɪesdiːˈen] *n Comptr* (*abbr* **integrated services digital network**) RNIS *m*

-ish [ɪʃ] *suff* **(a)** (*with adjective*) **blueish** bleuâtre; **shortish** plutôt petit **(b)** (*with noun*) **girlish** de petite fille; **wolfish** de loup **(c)** (*with time, numbers etc*) **around eightish** vers huit heures, aux environs de huit heures; **he's fortyish** il a la quarantaine

isinglass [ˈaɪzɪŋglɑːs] *n* (*in wine-making*) ichtyocolle *f*; *Culin* gélatine *f*

Islam [ˈɪzlɑːm] *n* (*religion*) islam *m*; (*people*) l'Islam, le monde musulman; **to go over to I.** se convertir à l'islam

Islamic [ɪzˈlæmɪk] *adj* islamique

island [ˈaɪlənd] *n* **(a)** *Geog* île *f*; (*small*) îlot *m*; **the Pacific Islands** les îles du Pacifique **(b)** *Fig* (*in road*) îlot *m*; (*for pedestrians*) refuge *m*; (*of houses etc*) groupe *m*; (*in supermarket*) gondole *f*; **i. of resistance** îlot *m* de résistance; **an i. of calm** un havre de paix; *Rail* **i. platform** quai *m* d'entre-voie, quai entre voies

islander [ˈaɪləndər] *n* (*in general*) insulaire *mf*; (*of specific island*) habitant, -ante de l'île

isle [aɪl] *n* (*poetic except in certain proper names*) île *f*; **the I. of Man** l'île de Man

islet [ˈaɪlɪt] *n* îlot *m*

ism [ˈɪz(ə)m] *n F usu Pej* doctrine *f*, idéologie *f*

isn't [ˈɪz(ə)nt] = **is not** *see* **be**

ISO [aɪesˈəʊ] *n* (*abbr* **International Standards Organization**) ISO *f*

isobar [ˈaɪsəʊbɑːr] *n Met, Phys* isobare *f*

isolate [ˈaɪsəleɪt] *vt Med, Pol etc* (*person*), *Ch* (*substance*), *Biol* (*culture*) isoler (**from** de, d'avec); **she isolated herself from other people** elle s'est isolée des autres gens

isolated [ˈaɪsəleɪtɪd] *adj* isolé; **i. case** *or* **instance** cas *m* isolé; *Fin* **i. post allowance** prime *f* d'éloignement

isolation [aɪsəˈleɪʃən] *n* **(a)** (*state, action*) isolement *m*; *F* **these problems do not exist in i. (from one another)** ces problèmes n'existent pas isolément; **to look at sth in i.** considérer qch isolément **(b)** *Med* (*of patient*) isolement *m*; **i. hospital** hôpital *m* d'isolement (de contagieux); **i. ward** salle *f* des contagieux

isolationism [aɪsəˈleɪʃənɪz(ə)m] *n* isolationnisme *m*

isolationist [aɪsəˈleɪʃənɪst] *adj, n* isolationniste *mf*

isosceles [aɪˈsɒsɪliːz] *adj Geom* (*triangle*) isocèle

isotherm [ˈaɪsəʊθɜːm] *n Met* isotherme *f*

isotonic [aɪsəʊˈtɒnɪk] *adj* isotonique

isotope [ˈaɪsəʊtəʊp] *n Ch, Phys* isotope *m*

I-spy *n Br* = jeu *m* pour enfants où un des joueurs donne la première lettre d'un mot et où les autres doivent deviner l'objet auquel il pense

Israel [ˈɪzreɪ(ə)l] *n* Israël *m*

Israeli [ɪzˈreɪlɪ] **1** *adj* israélien **2** *n* Israélien, -ienne

Israelite [ˈɪzr(ɪ)əlaɪt] **1** *adj* israélite **2** *n* Israélite *mf*

issue¹ [ˈɪʃ(j)uː] *n* **(a)** (*subject*) problème *m*, question *f*; **an important i.** une question importante; **the issues of the day** les questions du jour; **I don't want to make an i. of it** je ne veux pas en faire toute une affaire; **to join i. with sb** discuter l'opinion de qn (**about sth** au sujet de qch); **the point at i. is the effect it has on the environment** le problème est l'effet que cela a sur l'environnement; **to be at i. with sb** être en désaccord avec qn; **I would like to take i. with you on that point** je voudrais débattre ce point avec vous; **I would take i. with that** je ne suis pas d'accord là-dessus; **that's not the i.** ce n'est pas (là) le problème; **to evade** *or* **avoid the i.** prendre la tangente; **to confuse the i.** compliquer les choses; *Jur* **i. (of fact/of law)** (*matter*) question *ou* point *m* de fait/de droit; (*conclusion*) conclusion *f*

(b) (*act of issuing*) *Admin, Fin* (*of banknotes, money orders, stamps etc*) émission *f*; *Admin, Mil etc* (*of equipment etc*) distribution *f*; (*of book*) parution *f*, publication *f*; *Rail etc* (*of tickets etc*) délivrance *f*; (*in library*) (*of books*) prêt *m*; *Fin* **i. price** taux *m* d'émission; *Mil etc* **i. boots/shirts** bottes *fpl*/chemises *fpl* réglementaires; *Mil* **i. of orders** publication *f* des ordres

(c) (*copy*) (*of magazine*) numéro *m*; **the November i.** le numéro de novembre

(d) *Med* (*of blood, pus*) décharge *f*

(e) *Fml* (*offspring*) descendance *f*; **to die without i.** mourir sans (laisser de) descendance

issue² **1** *vi* **(a)** (*of blood, water*) s'écouler (**from** de); (*of smoke*) s'échapper (**from** de); (*of smell*) se dégager (**from** de)

(b) *Fml* (*of children*) provenir (**from** de); **the children issuing from this marriage** les enfants issus de ce mariage

2 *vt* (*banknotes etc*) émettre; (*bill*) créer; (*new edition, prospectus etc*) publier; *Fin* (*letter of credit*) fournir; *Mil* (*order*) publier, donner; *Jur* (*judgement*) rendre; (*provisions etc*) distribuer; (*train tickets etc*) délivrer; (*of library*) (*books*) prêter; **to i. sb with sth** délivrer qch à qn; **each man will be issued with two uniforms** chaque homme recevra deux uniformes; **no books will be issued after 8 pm** le service de prêt se termine à huit heures; **to i. a statement** faire une déclaration; *Jur* **to i. a summons** décerner *ou* lancer une citation

issued securities [ˈɪʃ(j)uːd] *npl Fin* titres *mpl* émis

issued (share) capital *n* capital-action *m* émis

issueless [ˈɪʃ(j)uːlɪs] *adv Fml* **to die i.** mourir sans laisser de descendance

issuer [ˈɪʃ(j)uːər] *n Fin* **i. of a draft** émetteur *m* d'une traite

issuing [ˈɪʃ(j)uːɪŋ] **1** *adj esp Fin* émetteur, -trice; **i. bank** banque *f* émettrice **2** *n* (*of loan, banknotes*) émission *f*; (*of provisions*) distribution *f*; (*in library*) (*of books*) prêt *m*

Istanbul [ɪstænˈbuːl] *n* Istanbul *m*

isthmus, *pl* **isthmuses** [ˈɪsməs, -məsɪz] *n Geog* isthme *m*

IT [aɪˈtiː] *n* (*abbr* **information technology**) informatique *f*

it [ɪt] **1** *pers pron* [①A26-7,a-d; B17,1,c] (*referring to inanimate objects, animals and children, but in French taking the gender of the noun for which* **it** *stands*) **(a)** [①B63,2] (*subject*) il, elle; **the house is small but it's my own** c'est une petite maison mais elle est à moi; **where is your hat? – it's in the cupboard** où est votre chapeau? – il est dans l'armoire

(b) [①A28,i] (*direct object*) le, la; (*before vowel*) l'; **I don't believe it** je ne le crois pas

(c) (*indirect object*) lui *mf*; **fetch the dog and give it something to eat** allez chercher le chien et donnez-lui à manger

(d) *F* (*stressed*) **he thinks he's it** il se croit sorti de la cuisse de Jupiter; **this book is absolutely it!** c'est un livre épatant!; **this is it — it's now or never!** cette fois-ci c'est la bonne — c'est maintenant ou jamais!; **this is it, the moment we've all been waiting for!** nous y voilà, c'est le moment que nous attendons tous!; **that's it, we're in for it now!** ça y est, on est foutu; **that's it for today** (*we have no more time etc*) c'est fini pour aujourd'hui

(e) (*as unspecified object of a verb*) **to face it** faire front; **blast it!** zut!

(f) (*as unspecified object of a preposition*) **now for it!** et maintenant allons-y!; **there is nothing for it but to run** il n'y a qu'une chose à faire, c'est de filer; *F* **he's (in) for it!** qu'est-ce qu'il va prendre!; **to have a bad time of it** en voir de dures

(g) (*as complement*) **who is it?** qui est-ce?; **that's it** c'est bien ça; (*as encouragement*) c'est bien

(h) [①B27-28,E] (*as subject of impersonal verb*) **it frightens me** cela me fait peur; **it doesn't matter** cela ne fait rien; **it's raining** il pleut; **it's ten o'clock** il est dix heures; **it's Monday** c'est lundi

(i) [①B63,2] **it's nonsense talking like that** c'est *ou* il est absurde de dire ça; **it's impossible to work in this heat** c'est *ou* il est impossible de travailler par cette chaleur; **it says in …** on lit dans …; **the fog made it difficult to see** le brouillard réduisait beaucoup la visibilité; **I find it hard to understand why** je trouve difficile de comprendre pourquoi; **you may rely upon it that he will do his best** vous pouvez être sûr qu'il fera de son mieux

(j) (*with prepositions*) **to consent to it** y consentir; **above it, over it** au-dessus, dessus; **below it, under(neath) it** au-dessous, dessous; **as we walked away from it** tandis que nous nous en éloignions; **he's not bad, far from it** il n'est pas méchant, loin de là; **give me half of it** donnez-m'en la moitié; **think of it** pensez-y; **don't tread on it** ne marchez pas dessus; **the Committee has devoted much care to the task before it** le comité a accordé beaucoup d'attention à la tâche qui lui incombait; **I cracked his head with it** je lui ai fendu la tête avec

2 *n* (*in children's games*) **you're it!** c'est toi qui y es *ou* qui t'y colles!

Italian [ɪˈtæljən] **1** *adj* italien; (*embassy, ambassador, history*) d'Italie; (*teacher, lesson, dictionary*) d'italien; **I. Switzerland** Suisse *f* italienne **2** *n* **(a)** Italien, -ienne **(b)** *Ling* italien *m*

italic [ɪˈtælɪk] *Typ* **1** *adj* (*character*) italique **2** *n* **italic(s)** italique *m*; **to print in italic(s)** imprimer en italique; **the italics are mine** les italiques sont de moi

italicization [ɪtælɪsaɪˈzeɪʃən] *n* (*putting into italics*) mise *f* en italique(s)

italicize [ɪˈtælɪsaɪz] *vt Typ* imprimer *ou* mettre en italique; **italicized words** mots *mpl* en italique

Italo- [ɪˈtæləʊ] *pref* italo-; **I. -American** italo-américain

Italy [ˈɪtəlɪ] *n* Italie *f*

ITC [aɪtiːˈsiː] *n* (*abbr* **Independent Television Commission**) commission *f* de surveillance des télévisions britanniques privées

itch¹ [ɪtʃ] *n* démangeaison *f*; **I've got an awful i. on my back** mon dos me démange horriblement; *Fig* **to have an i. for sth/to do sth** avoir envie de qch/de faire qch; *Fig F* **if you've got an i., scratch it** si ça te dit, vas-y

itch² *vi* (a) (*of person*) éprouver des démangeaisons; **my hand itches** la main me démange; **where does it i.?** où est-ce que cela vous démange?; **these bites really i.** ce que ces piqûres me démangent!; *Fig* **to have an itching palm** être cupide (b) *F* **to be itching to do sth** brûler d'envie de faire qch; **I was itching to speak** la langue me démangeait; **she is itching to be off** ça la démange de partir

itching ['ɪtʃɪŋ] *n* démangeaison *f*; **i. powder** poil *m* à gratter

itchy ['ɪtʃɪ] *adj* **I've got an i. hand** la main me démange; *Fig* **to have i. feet** brûler d'envie de partir; **I've always had i. feet** j'ai toujours eu la bougeotte

it'd ['ɪt(ə)d] (a) = **it would**, *see* **would** (b) = **it had**, *see* **have²**

item ['aɪtəm] **1** *n Com* article *m*; (*in bookkeeping*) écriture *f*, article, poste *m*; *Journ* (*very brief*) entrefilet *m*; (*longer*) article; **i. of expenditure** article *ou* chef *m* de dépense; **the second i. of the contract** l'article deux du contrat; **the items on the agenda** les questions *fpl* à l'ordre du jour; *Th etc* **the last i. on the programme** le dernier numéro du programme; *Journ* **news items** nouvelles *fpl*; **there was an i. on the news about it yesterday** ils en ont parlé aux informations hier; *F* **they're an i.** ils sortent ensemble **2** *adv Old-fashioned* (*when listing*) item

itemize ['aɪtəmaɪz] *vt* (*bill etc*) détailler

iterate ['ɪtəreɪt] *vt* réitérer, répéter (constamment); *Comptr, Math* itérer

iteration [ɪtə'reɪʃən] *n* itération *f*

iterative ['ɪt(ə)rətɪv] *adj Comptr* itératif

itinerant [ɪ'tɪnərənt, aɪ-] *adj* (*salesman, comedian, musician*) ambulant; (*preacher, worker*) itinérant

itinerary [aɪ'tɪnərərɪ] *n* itinéraire *m*

it'll ['ɪt(ə)l] = **it will**

its [ɪts] [①A30,8; B19-20,E] **1** *poss adj* son, sa, *pl* ses; (*in the f before a vowel sound*) son; **i. nose, mouth, and eyes** (*of animal*) son nez, sa bouche, et ses yeux; **i. extent** (*of forest etc*) son étendue *f*; **a charm of i. own** un charme qui n'appartient qu'à lui/à elle **2** *poss pron* le sien, la sienne, *pl* les sien(ne)s

it's (a) = **it is**, *see* **be** (b) = **it has**, *see* **have²**

itself [ɪt'self] *pers pron* [①A29] (a) (*emphatic*) lui-même, elle-même, soi-même; **it is simplicity i.** c'est tout ce qu'il y a de plus simple; **she is kindness i.** elle est la bonté même (b) [①B26,D] (*reflexive*) **the dog hurt i.** le chien s'est fait mal (c) (*after prepositions*) **the child was left by i.** l'enfant était laissé(e) tout(e) seul(e); **the thing in i.** la chose en elle-même; **in i. it's not a bad idea** en soi l'idée n'est pas mauvaise

ITV [aɪti:'vi:] *n Br* (*abbr* **Independent Television**) = une des chaînes de télévision privées britanniques

IUD [aɪju:'di:] *n Med* (*abbr* **intra-uterine device**) stérilet *m*

IV [aɪ'vi:] *Med* (*abbr* **intravenous**) IV

I've [aɪv] = **I have**

ivory ['aɪvərɪ] **1** *n* (a) (*substance*) ivoire *m*; (*object*) (objet *m* d')ivoire; **a collection of ivories** une collection d'ivoires; *Fig F* **ivories** (*teeth*) dents *fpl*; (*piano keys*) touches *fpl*; **i. trade** commerce *m* de l'ivoire (b) (*colour*) ivoire *m* **2** *adj* (*made of ivory*) d'ivoire, en ivoire; *Fig* **i. tower** tour *f* d'ivoire

Ivory Coast *n* la Côte d'Ivoire

ivory-white ['aɪvərɪ'waɪt] *adj* (*teeth*) d'une blancheur d'ivoire

ivy ['aɪvɪ] *n* (*plant*) lierre *m*

Ivy League *n US* ensemble *m* des huit universités les plus prestigieuses du nord-est des États-Unis

IYHF [aɪwaɪeɪtʃ'ef] *n* (*abbr* **International Youth Hostel Federation**) FIAJ *f*

J

J, j [dʒeɪ] *n* (*letter*) J, j *m*; **two J's** *or* **Js** deux J
jab¹ [dʒæb] *n* **(a)** (*with sharp object*) coup *m* (sec); **a j. with an elbow/a knife** un coup de coude/de couteau; **she gave him a sharp j. in the ribs (with her elbow)** elle lui a mis un coup de coude dans les côtes **(b)** *Br F* (*injection*) injection *f*, piqûre *f*; **to give sb a j.** faire une injection *ou* une piqûre à qn; (*for TB, malaria etc*) vacciner qn; **have you had all the necessary jabs?** est-ce qu'on t'a fait tous les vaccins nécessaires? **(c)** *Boxing* coup *m* droit, direct *m*
jab² (-bb-) **1** *vt* **(a)** (*poke, prick*) **to j. sb/sth** piquer qn/qch (**with sth** avec qch, du bout de qch); **to j. sb with one's elbow/a knife** donner un coup de coude/couteau à qn; **she jabbed him in the eyes with her fingers** elle lui a planté ses doigts dans les yeux
(b) (*thrust*) enfoncer, planter (d'un coup sec) (**into** dans); **she jabbed a finger at him to emphasize her point** elle a pointé le doigt dans sa direction pour appuyer ses propos
2 *vi* **(a)** (*poke, prick*) **to j. at sb/sth** piquer qn/qch (**with sth** avec qch, du bout de qch); **to j. at sb with a knife/an umbrella** donner un coup de couteau/de parapluie à qn
(b) *Boxing* envoyer un coup droit *ou* un direct (**at** à)
jabber¹ [ˈdʒæbər] *n F* **(a)** (*noise*) brouhaha *m* **(b)** (*chat*) conversation *f*, *Pej* jacasseries *fpl*; **to have a j.** bavarder, tailler une bavette
jabber² *F* **1** *vi* **(a)** (*talk fast, unclearly*) baragouiner; **what are you jabbering about?** qu'est-ce que tu baragouines? **(b)** (*chatter*) bavarder, tailler une bavette, *Pej* jacasser **2** *vt* (*excuse, explanation*) bafouiller, bredouiller; **to j. a few words in French/***etc* baragouiner quelques mots de français/*etc*
▶ **jabber away, jabber on** *vi* = **jabber² 1**
▶ **jabber out** *vtsep* (*excuse, explanation etc*) bafouiller, bredouiller
jabbering [ˈdʒæbərɪŋ] *n* **(a)** (*incomprehensible*) baragouinage *m* **(b)** (*chattering*) bavardage *m*, *Pej* jacasseries *fpl*
jacaranda [dʒækəˈrændə] *n* (*shrub*) jacaranda *m*
Jack [dʒæk] *n* **before you could say J. Robinson** sans qu'on ait eu le temps de dire ouf; *Br F* **I'm all right, J.** ça marche très bien pour moi (et les autres, je m'en fiche); *F* **an 'I'm all right, J.' attitude** une attitude je-m'en-foutiste
jack [dʒæk] *n* **(a)** (*person*) **every man j. (of them/us/you)** absolument tout le monde; **j. of all trades** touche-à-tout *m*; *Prov* **j. of all trades, master of none** propre à tout, propre à rien **(b)** (*lifting device*) *Aut* cric *m*; *Tech* vérin *m* **(c)** *Cards* valet *m*; **the j. of spades** le valet de pique **(d) jacks** (*game*) (jeu *m* d')osselets *mpl* **(e)** (*in bowling*) cochonnet *m* **(f)** *Tel* prise *f*; *El* **j. (socket)** prise *ou* fiche *f* femelle; **j. plug** (*connector*) prise *ou* fiche mâle; **microphone/headphone j.** prise de microphone/de casque
▶ **jack in** *vtsep Br Sl* (*job, project, girlfriend*) plaquer, laisser tomber
▶ **jack up** *vtsep Aut, Tech* soulever (avec un cric/un vérin); *Fig F* (*increase*) (*price, salaries*) relever
jackal [ˈdʒækɔːl, -k(ə)l] *n* (*animal*) chacal *m*
jackass [ˈdʒækæs] *n* **(a)** (*male donkey*) âne *m*, *F* baudet *m* **(b)** *F* (*person*) idiot, -ote, imbécile *mf* **(c) laughing j.** (*bird*) dacélo *m*
jackboot [ˈdʒækbuːt] *n Mil* botte *f* de cavalier; *Fig* **life under the j. of a military dictatorship** la vie sous la botte de la dictature militaire
jackdaw [ˈdʒækdɔː] *n* (*bird*) choucas *m*
jacket¹ [ˈdʒækɪt] *n* **(a)** (*man's coat*) veste *f*, veston *m*; (*woman's*) veste, jaquette *f* **(b)** *Culin* **j. potatoes, potatoes cooked in their jackets** pommes *fpl* de terre en robe des champs *ou* en robe de chambre **(c)** (*of record, computer diskette*) pochette *f*; (*for documents*) chemise *f*; *Tech* (*of boiler, pipe*) chemise, enveloppe *f*; **(dust) j.** (*of book*) jaquette *f*
jacket² *vt Tech* (*cylinder, boiler etc*) garnir *ou* envelopper d'une chemise, chemiser
Jack Frost *n* le Bonhomme Hiver
jackhammer [ˈdʒækhæmər] *n* marteau-piqueur *m*
jacking point *n* point *m* de levage, emplacement *m* prévu pour le cric
jack-in-the-box, *pl* **jack-in-the-boxes** *n* diable *m* à ressort, boîte *f* à surprise(s); *F* **to jump up and down like a j.** ne pas tenir en place; **stop jumping up and down like a j.** arrête de sauter dans tous les sens comme ça
jackknife¹, *pl* **-knives** [ˈdʒæknaɪf, -naɪvz] *n* **(a)** couteau *m* de poche, canif *m* **(b)** *Swimming* **j. (dive)** saut *m* de carpe
jackknife² *vi* **(a)** *Aut* (*of articulated vehicle*) se mettre en portefeuille **(b)** *Swimming* faire un saut de carpe
jackpot [ˈdʒækpɒt] *n* **(a)** *Cards* (*in poker etc*) pot *m* **(b)** (*in competition*) gros lot *m*; **to hit** *or* **win the j.** gagner le gros lot; *Fig* **to hit the j.** (*be successful*) (*of person*) gagner le gros lot, décrocher la timbale; (*of book, record etc*) faire un malheur *ou* un tabac
jack rabbit *n Zool* (*North American hare*) gros lièvre *m* américain
Jack Tar *n Old-fashioned, F* matelot *m*
Jacobean [dʒækəˈbɪən] *adj* de l'époque de Jacques 1er (*1603–1625*); **the J. period** l'époque *f* de Jacques 1er
Jacobite [ˈdʒækəbaɪt] *adj, n Hist* jacobite *m*
jacuzzi® [dʒəˈkuːzɪ] *n* (*bath, pool*) jacuzzi® *m*
jade [dʒeɪd] **1** *n* **(a)** *Miner* jade *m* **(b)** (*colour*) **j. (green)** vert *m* (de) jade **2** *adj* (*colour*) **j.(-green)** couleur *inv* de jade, vert *inv* (de) jade
jaded [ˈdʒeɪdɪd] *adj* (*person*) (*tired*) las, fatigué; (*performance, piece of writing, cliché*) faiblard; **to be** *or* **feel j. with sth** être las de qch; **to become j. with sth** se lasser de qch; **I was served a rather j. piece of beef** on m'a servi un morceau de bœuf tout flétri; **j. palate** palais *m* blasé; *Fig* appétit *m* fatigué
Jag [dʒæg] *n F* (*Jaguar® car*) Jag *f*
jag [dʒæg] *n* **(a)** *Sl* (*drinking bout*) soûlerie *f*; **to go on a (drinking) j.** se soûler, prendre une cuite **(b)** *Sl* **to have a crying j.** avoir une crise de larmes **(c)** *Br F* (*injection*) piquouze *f*
jagged [ˈdʒægɪd] *adj* (*coastline, mountain top*) déchiqueté, découpé; (*edge*) déchiqueté, découpé, dentelé; (*line, tear*) irrégulier; (*knife, blade*) entaillé, ébréché; (*rock*) pointu, dentelé; **the j. outline of the coast** les dentelures *fpl ou* découpures *fpl* de la côte
jaggy [ˈdʒægɪ] *n* (*on printed character*) courbe *f* en escalier
jaguar [*Br* ˈdʒægjʊər, *Am* ˈdʒægwɑːr] *n* (*animal*) jaguar *m*
jail¹ [dʒeɪl] *n* (*place, imprisonment*) prison *f*; **to be in j.** être en prison; **to put in j., to send to j.** mettre en prison; **to go to j.** aller en prison, faire de la prison; **he was sent to j.** *or* **he went to j. for ten years** il a été condamné à dix ans de prison; **she was in j. for ten years, she went to j. for ten years** elle a fait dix ans de prison; **to break out of j.** s'évader de prison; **open j.** prison ouverte
jail² *vt* mettre en prison, emprisonner; **to j. sb for theft** condamner qn à la prison pour vol; **he was jailed for ten years** il a été condamné à dix ans de prison
jailbait [ˈdʒeɪlbeɪt] *n Am Sl* (*girl*) mineure *f* (*avec qui les relations sexuelles sont interdites*)
jailbird [ˈdʒeɪlbɜːd] *n F* (*actually in prison*) taulard, -arde; (*constantly going to prison*) cheval *m* de retour
jailbreak [ˈdʒeɪlbreɪk] *n* évasion *f* de prison; **to do a j.** s'évader; **to attempt a j.** essayer de s'évader
jailbreaker [ˈdʒeɪlbreɪkər] *n* évadé, -ée
jailer [ˈdʒeɪlər] *n* geôlier, -ière
jailhouse, *pl* **-houses** [ˈdʒeɪlhaʊs, -haʊzɪz] *n Am* prison *f*
jailor [ˈdʒeɪlər] *n* = **jailer**
jalop(p)y [dʒəˈlɒpɪ] *n F* (vieille) bagnole *f*, (vieux) tacot *m*, (vieille) guimbarde *f*
jam¹ [dʒæm] *n* **(a)** *Aut* (*congestion*) bouchon *m*, embouteillage *m*, encombrement *m* **(b)** (*crowd of people*) **there was a great j. of people outside the theatre** il y avait une foule énorme devant le théâtre **(c)** (*in pipe, machine etc*) engorgement *m*; (*in printer*) bourrage *m* **(d)** *F* (*difficult situation*) **to be in/get into a (bit of a) j.** être/se mettre dans le pétrin; **to get out of/get sb out of a j.** se tirer/tirer qn du pétrin **(e)** *Mus* = **jam session**

jam² (-mm-) **1** *vt* (**a**) (*pack, cram*) (en)tasser (**into** dans); (*thrust, put forcefully*) enfoncer, fourrer (**into** dans); **it had been jammed with goodies** il avait été rempli à ras bords de bonnes choses; **to j. one's foot on the brake(s)** écraser le frein *ou* la pédale de frein
(**b**) (*squeeze, wedge*) coincer; **she got her hand jammed** *or* **she jammed her hand in the drawer** elle s'est coincé la main dans le tiroir; **to j. a door open with a book** maintenir une porte ouverte à l'aide d'un livre
(**c**) (*immobilize, stop from working*) (*window, shutter etc*) coincer, bloquer; (*weapon, mechanism*) enrayer, bloquer; (*pipe*) boucher; **the drawer is jammed** le tiroir est coincé *ou* bloqué; **to be jammed in the ice** être bloqué par les glaces
(**d**) (*of people, vehicles*) (*street, corridor etc*) encombrer, bloquer; (*building, town*) envahir; **the hall was jammed (with people), people jammed the hall** la salle était pleine à craquer *ou* bondée
(**e**) *Rad* (*broadcast, station*) brouiller
(**f**) *Tel* (*of calls etc*) (*lines*) encombrer; (*switchboard*) faire sauter; **the switchboard was jammed** le standard était saturé
2 *vi* (**a**) (*of drawer, window, lift etc*) se coincer, se bloquer; (*of gun, machine*) s'enrayer, se bloquer; (*of brake, wheel, paper in printer*) se bloquer
(**b**) (*crowd*) s'entasser (**into** dans)

jam³ *n Culin* confiture *f*; **strawberry j.** confiture de fraises; *Br Fig* **what do you want, j. on it?** ça ne te suffit pas?, que veux-tu de plus?; **j. jar** *or* **pot** pot *m* à confiture; **jar** *or* **pot of j.** pot *m* de confiture(s); **j. tart** tarte *f* à la confiture

▶ **jam in 1** *vtsep* (**a**) (*wedge in*) coincer; **the crowd were jamming him in** il était coincé par la foule; **her car was being jammed in by a large truck** un gros camion était en train de la coincer (**b**) (*pack or press tightly in*) (*passengers etc*) (en)tasser; (*objects*) bourrer; **he had jammed as many quotations as he could find into the essay** il avait farci sa dissertation de toutes les citations qu'il avait trouvées **2** *vi* (*crowd in*) s'entasser; **they all jammed in** (*into train*) ils s'y entassèrent tous; **we won't all be able to j. in at once** nous n'allons jamais tous tenir à la fois

▶ **jam on** *vtsep* (**a**) *Aut* **to j. on the brakes** écraser le frein *ou* la pédale de frein (**b**) (*put on forcefully or solidly*) (*lid, hat etc*) enfoncer

Jamaica [dʒəˈmeɪkə] *n* Jamaïque *f*

Jamaican [dʒəˈmeɪkən] **1** *adj* jamaïquain, jamaïcain, de la Jamaïque **2** *n* Jamaïquain, -aine, Jamaïcain, -aine

jamb [dʒæm] *n* (*side post*) (*of door, window, chimney*) chambranle *m*, jambage *m*, montant *m*

jamboree [dʒæmbəˈriː] *n* (**a**) (*scouts' meeting*) jamboree *m* (**b**) *F* (*celebration, party*) fête *f*, réunion *f*; (*festivities*) réjouissances *fpl* (tapageuses); **village j.** fête *f* de village

jammies [ˈdʒæmɪz] *npl* (*in children's language*) pyjama *m*

jamming [ˈdʒæmɪŋ] *n* (**a**) *Rad* brouillage *m* (délibéré) (**b**) *Tel* (*of lines*) encombrement *m*

jammy [ˈdʒæmɪ] *adj* (**a**) (*covered with jam*) plein de confiture (**b**) *Br F* (*lucky*) veinard, verni; **he's a j. devil** quel veinard, celui-là!, il est verni, celui-là! (**c**) *Br F* (*easy*) facile; **j. job** filon *m*, bonne planque *f*

jam-packed [ˈdʒæmˈpækt] *adj* (*suitcase, bag etc*) plein à craquer, bourré (**with** de); **j. (with people)** (*hall, bus etc*) plein à craquer, bondé; (*street*) noir de monde, bondé; **this magazine is j. with interesting articles** ce magazine est truffé *ou* regorge d'articles intéressants

jam session *n Mus* bœuf *m*, séance *f* de jazz improvisé; **to have a j.** faire un bœuf

Jane [dʒeɪn] *n* (**a**) Jeanne *f* (**b**) *US Sl* (*woman*) nana *f*; **J. Doe** (*unidentified woman*) (*under arrest*) inconnue *f*; (*corpse*) morte *f* non identifiée

jangle¹ [ˈdʒæŋg(ə)l] *n* (*of metal objects, keys etc*) cliquetis *m*; (*of bell*) bruit *m* discordant

jangle² **1** *vi* (*of metal objects, keys etc*) cliqueter; (*of bells*) retentir d'un bruit discordant; **it jangled on my nerves** cela me mettait les nerfs en pelote **2** *vt* (**a**) (*keys etc*) faire cliqueter; (*bells*) faire retentir d'un bruit discordant (**b**) (*upset*) **jangled nerves** nerfs en pelote

jangling [ˈdʒæŋg(ə)lɪŋ] *n* = **jangle¹**

janitor [ˈdʒænɪtər] *n Am, Scot* (*caretaker*) concierge *mf*

January [ˈdʒænjʊərɪ] *n* [ⓘ**A75-6**,B-C; **B58-9**,B-C] janvier *m*; **in J.** au mois de janvier, en janvier; (**on**) **the third of J.** le trois janvier

Jap [dʒæp] *Offensive F* **1** *n* Japonais, -aise **2** *adj* japonais

Japan [dʒəˈpæn] *n* Japon *m*

Japanese [dʒæpəˈniːz] **1** *adj* japonais; (*embassy, ambassador, history*) du Japon; (*teacher, lesson, dictionary*) de japonais; **J. lantern** lanterne *f* vénitienne **2** *n* (**a**) Japonais, -aise; **the J.** (*pl*) les Japonais *mpl* (**b**) *Ling* japonais *m*

jape [dʒeɪp] *n Old-fashioned* tour *m*, blague *f*; **to play japes on sb** jouer des tours à qn, faire des blagues à qn

japonica [dʒəˈpɒnɪkə] *n Bot* cognassier *m* du Japon

jar¹ [dʒɑːr] *n* (*jolt, shock*), *Fig* choc *m*, secousse *f*; **his fall/the news gave him a nasty j.** sa chute/la nouvelle l'a fortement ébranlé *ou* beaucoup secoué; **he gave his wrist a j. when he fell** il s'est cogné le poignet en tombant

jar² (-rr-) **1** *vi* (**a**) (*make an unpleasant sound*) rendre un son discordant; *Mus* (*of note*) détonner (**b**) (*of colours, furniture*) détonner, jurer (**with** avec); (*of ideas, styles, remarks*) détonner, être incompatible, ne pas s'accorder (**with** avec); **to j.** (**with each other**) (*of colours, ideas*) se heurter, détonner; **to j. on sb's feelings** froisser qn **2** *vt* (*window pane, building*) ébranler; (*table, microphone*) faire bouger; (*wrist, ankle etc*) se cogner; (*of news*) ébranler, secouer; **someone jarred my elbow** quelqu'un m'a cogné le coude

jar³ *n* (**a**) (*container*) pot *m*; (*for storing oil etc*) jarre *f*; (**glass**) **j.** pot *m*; (*large*) bocal *m* (**b**) *Br F* (*beer*) pot *m*; **to have a j.** prendre un pot; **we had a few jars** on a pris un pot ou deux

▶ **jar on, jar upon** *vipo* (*of noise*) (*the ears*) écorcher; **his voice jars (up)on my nerves** sa voix me tape sur les nerfs *ou* me crispe

jargon [ˈdʒɑːgən] *n Pej* (*specialized language*) jargon *m*; **legal j.** jargon juridique, langage *m* du Palais; **to talk (in) j.** parler en jargon, jargonner

jarring [ˈdʒɑːrɪŋ] *adj* (**a**) (*noise, voice etc*) discordant; *Mus* (*note*) qui détonne; *Fig* (*incident, behaviour*) qui produit une sensation désagréable (**b**) (*blow*) qui ébranle tout le corps

jasmine [ˈdʒæzmɪn, ˈdʒæs-] *n* (*shrub*) (**common** *or* **white**) **j.** jasmin *m* (commun *ou* blanc); **winter j.** jasmin d'hiver; **j. perfume** (essence *f* de) jasmin; **j. tea** thé *m* au jasmin

jaundice [ˈdʒɔːndɪs] *n* (**a**) *Med* jaunisse *f*, ictère *m* (**b**) *Fig* (*bitterness*) amertume *f*

jaundiced [ˈdʒɔːndɪst] *adj* (**a**) *Med* ictérique, bilieux (**b**) *Fig* (*bitter*) aigri, amer; (*jealous*) jaloux; **to look on the world** *or* **on things with a j. eye** (*bitterly*) voir tout en noir; (*jealously*) tout regarder d'un œil jaloux; **to take a j. view of a situation** voir une situation d'un mauvais œil

jaunt [dʒɔːnt] *n* (petite) excursion *f*, balade *f*, sortie *f*; **on a j.** en excursion, en balade; **to go on** *or* **for a j.** faire une (petite) excursion *ou* une balade

jauntily [ˈdʒɔːntɪlɪ] *adv* (*to remark*) (*casually*) d'une manière désinvolte, avec désinvolture; (*cheerfully*) gaiement, avec entrain, d'un air enjoué; (*to walk*) d'un pas guilleret; (*to wear one's hat*) d'une façon désinvolte; (*of woman, stylishly*) coquettement

jauntiness [ˈdʒɔːntɪnɪs] *n* (*carefreeness*) désinvolture *f*, insouciance *f*; (*cheerfulness*) enjouement *m*, vivacité *f*; **the j. of his step** son pas guilleret

jaunty [ˈdʒɔːntɪ] *adj* (*carefree*) désinvolte, insouciant, dégagé; (*cheerful, lively*) enjoué; **with a j. air** d'un air dégagé; **j. step** pas *m* guilleret; **he wore his cap at a j. angle** sa casquette était négligemment posée sur sa tête

Java [ˈdʒɑːvə] *n* (île *f* de) Java *f*

Javanese [dʒɑːvəˈniːz] **1** *adj* javanais **2** *n* (**a**) Javanais, -aise; **the J.** (*pl*) les Javanais *mpl* (**b**) *Ling* javanais *m*

javelin [ˈdʒævlɪn] *n* (*weapon*), *Sp* javelot *m*; **j. thrower** lanceur, -euse de javelot; **j. throwing** lancer *m* du javelot; *Sp* **the j.** (*event*) l'épreuve *f* de javelot

jaw¹ [dʒɔː] *n* (**a**) *Anat* mâchoire *f*; **the lion opened its jaws** le lion a ouvert la gueule; *Fig* **her j. dropped** (*in surprise*) elle en est restée bouche bée, les bras lui en sont tombés; *Fig* **to set one's j.** (*show determination*) décider de s'accrocher (**b**) *Fig* **the jaws of a valley/cave** l'entrée *f* d'une vallée/grotte; **the jaws of a volcano** la bouche d'un volcan; **the jaws of hell** les portes *fpl* de l'enfer; **to snatch sb from the jaws of death/the enemy** arracher qn des griffes de la mort/de l'ennemi (**c**) (*of pincer, wrench etc*) mâchoire *f*, mors *m*

jaw² *n F* (*moralizing talk*) sermon *m*; **to have a** (**good**) **j.** tailler une bavette, bavarder; **he's all j. and no action** il parle beaucoup, mais au moment d'agir …

jaw³ *F vi* (*chat*) bavarder (**about** de); (*moralize*) prêcher, moraliser; **she's been jawing away on the phone all morning** elle n'a pas arrêté de papoter au téléphone de toute la matinée

jawbone [ˈdʒɔːbəʊn] *n* (os *m*) maxillaire *m*, mâchoire *f*

jawbreaker [ˈdʒɔːbreɪkər] *n* (**a**) *F* (*word*) mot *m* imprononçable; (*name*) nom *m* à coucher dehors (**b**) (*sweet*) bonbon *m* (très dur)

-jawed [dʒɔːd] *suff* **round/long/***etc***-j.** à la mâchoire ronde/allongée/*etc*; *Boxing etc F* **glass-j.** à la mâchoire fragile

jay [dʒeɪ] *n* (*bird*) geai *m* (des chênes); **blue j.** geai bleu

jaywalk [ˈdʒeɪwɔːk] *vi* traverser la rue d'une manière imprudente *ou* en dehors des passages pour piétons

jaywalker [ˈdʒeɪwɔːkər] *n* piéton *m* imprudent (*qui traverse en dehors des passages pour piétons*)

jaywalking [ˈdʒeɪwɔːkɪŋ] *n* imprudence *f* (*de la part d'un piéton*)

jazz [dʒæz] *n* **(a)** *Mus* jazz *m*; **j. band/music** orchestre *m*/musique *f* de jazz **(b)** *Am Sl* (*talk*) baratin *m*; **she gave me a lot of j. about it** elle m'a fait tout un baratin là-dessus; **what's (all) this j. about your leaving?** qu'est-ce que c'est que cette histoire comme quoi tu t'en vas? **(c)** *Sl* **and all that j.** et tout le tremblement *ou* bazar

▸ **jazz up** *vtsep F* **(a)** *Mus* adapter pour le jazz **(b)** *Fig* (*enliven*) (*clothes, room, style*) égayer; (*party*) animer, mettre de l'entrain dans; (*taste*) relever; (*building*) retaper

jazzy [ˈdʒæzɪ] *adj F* (*tune*) aux rythmes jazz; *Fig* (*flashy*) tapageur, voyant; (*non-pejorative sense*) sympa

JCB® [dʒeɪsiːˈbiː] *n Br* = pelle *f* hydraulique automotrice

jealous [ˈdʒeləs] *adj* **(a)** (*fearful of rivals*) jaloux, *f* -ouse; **a j. woman** une femme jalouse, une jalouse; **I don't see why you're getting so j.** je ne sais pas pourquoi tu fais une telle crise de jalousie **(b)** (*envious*) jaloux **(of** de); **to be j. of sb** être jaloux de qn, jalouser qn **(c)** (*vigilant, possessive*) jaloux **(of** de); **with a j. eye** d'un œil jaloux; **j. of one's good name** jaloux de sa réputation

jealously [ˈdʒeləslɪ] *adv* **(a)** (*enviously*) jalousement, avec jalousie **(b)** (*vigilantly*) avec un soin jaloux; **a j. guarded secret** un secret jalousement gardé

jealousy [ˈdʒeləsɪ] *n* jalousie *f*

jeans [dʒiːnz] *npl* **(pair of) j.** jean(s) *m(pl)*; **blue j.** blue-jean *m*

jeep [dʒiːp] *n Aut* jeep *f*

jeepers (creepers) [ˈdʒiːpəz(ˈkriːpəz)] *int Old-fashioned Am F* ça alors!

jeer¹ [dʒɪər] *n* raillerie *f*, moquerie *f*; **the jeers of the crowd** (*boos*) les huées *fpl* de la foule

jeer² **1** *vi* (*boo*) huer, conspuer; (*mock*) railler **2** *vt* **to j. sb** (*boo*) huer qn, conspuer qn; (*mock*) se moquer de qn, railler qn

▸ **jeer at** *vipo* = **jeer² 2**

jeering [ˈdʒɪərɪŋ] **1** *adj* railleur, moqueur; (*laughter*) moqueur **2** *n* railleries *fpl*, moqueries *fpl*; (*shouts*) cris *mpl* railleurs *ou* moqueurs; (*of crowd*) huées *fpl*

jeez [dʒiːz] *int F* mon Dieu!

Jehovah [dʒɪˈhəʊvə] *n Bible* Jéhovah; *Rel* **J.'s Witness** témoin *m* de Jéhovah

jejune [dʒɪˈdʒuːn] *adj Lit* naïf, *f* naïve

jejunum [dʒɪˈdʒuːnəm] *n Anat* jéjunum *m*

Jekyll and Hyde [dʒekələndˈhaɪd] *n* **he's a (real) J.** c'est un vrai docteur Jekyll; **to have a J. personality** faire un dédoublement de la personnalité

jell [dʒel] *vi* **(a)** (*of liquid*) se gélifier, prendre (en gelée) **(b)** *Fig* (*of ideas*) prendre corps *ou* forme; (*of plans*) prendre tournure *ou* forme *ou* corps; (*of team, cabinet*) parvenir à la cohésion; **they have jelled very well** ils sont parvenus à une excellente cohésion

jellied [ˈdʒelɪd] *adj Culin* (*eel etc*) en gelée

jello® [ˈdʒeləʊ] *n Am Culin* gelée *f*

jelly¹ [ˈdʒelɪ] *n* **(a)** (*preserve*) gelée *f*; **redcurrant j.** gelée de groseille(s) **(b)** *Br* (*dessert*) gelée *f*; **my knees were like j.** j'avais les jambes en coton **(c)** (*gel-like substance*) gelée *f*; *Culin* (*aspic*) gelée (de viande); **petroleum j.** vaseline *f* **(d)** *Br Sl* (*gelignite*) dynamite *f*

jelly² *vt Culin* gélifier, mettre en gelée

jelly baby *n Br* bonbon *m* gélifié (*en forme de petit bonhomme*)

jellybean [ˈdʒelɪbiːn] *n* bonbon mou (*couvert de sucre dur et en forme de haricot*)

jellyfish, *pl* **-fish** *or* **-fishes** [ˈdʒelɪfɪʃ] *n* méduse *f*

jelly roll *n Am* (*cake*) roulé *m* (à la gelée/à la confiture)

jemmy¹ [ˈdʒemɪ] *n Br* **(burglar's) j.** pince-monseigneur *f*, *pl* pinces-monseigneur

jemmy² *vt Br* **to j. a door (open)** forcer une porte à la pince-monseigneur

jenny [ˈdʒenɪ] *n* (*female donkey*) ânesse *f*; **j. wren/robin** troglodyte *m ou* roitelet *m*/rouge-gorge *m* femelle

jeopardize [ˈdʒepədaɪz] *vt* (*health, future, sb's life*) compromettre, mettre en danger *ou* en péril; (*chances, career*) compromettre; (*one's business*) laisser péricliter

jeopardy [ˈdʒepədɪ] *n* danger *m*, péril *m*; **to be in j.** (*of person, one's life*) être en danger *ou* en péril; (*of one's happiness, career, future etc*) être menacé *ou* compromis; **his business is in j.** son affaire périclite; **to put in j.** = **jeopardize**; **to put sb in j.** mettre qn en danger *ou* en péril

jerbil [ˈdʒɜːbɪl] *n* (*rodent*) gerbille *f*

jerk¹ [dʒɜːk] *n* **(a)** (*sudden pull, push etc*) secousse *f*, saccade *f*, coup *m* sec; **she gave the rope a j.** elle a donné une secousse à la corde, elle a tiré d'un coup sec sur la corde; **to move by jerks** *or* **in jerks** *or* **in a series of jerks** (*of vehicle etc*) avancer par saccades *ou* par à-coups, cahoter **(b)** (*sudden start, jump*) sursaut *m*; **to wake up with a j.** se réveiller en sursaut **(c)** *Sp* (*in weightlifting*) jeté *m*

jerk² **1** *vt* (*pull, push etc suddenly*) donner une secousse *ou* une saccade à; (*repeatedly*) donner des secousses *ou* des saccades à, secouer; (*pull*) tirer d'un coup sec; **they jerked the washing machine across the floor** ils ont déplacé la machine à laver à travers la pièce par à-coups; **to j. sth out of sb's hands** arracher qch (d'un coup sec) des mains de qn; **to j. forward/back** (*of collision etc*) (*sb's head, body*) rejeter en avant/en arrière; **she jerked her head** (*in car crash etc*) sa tête a été rejetée en arrière

2 *vi* **(a)** (*shake*) secouer; **to j. (along** *or* **forward)** (*of vehicle*) avancer par saccades *ou* par à-coups, cahoter; **to j. forward/back** (*of head, body*) être rejeté en avant/en arrière; **she jerked forward then slid back** elle se jeta en avant puis se glissa vers l'arrière; **to j. to a halt** (*of vehicle, train*) s'arrêter brusquement (avec des secousses)

(b) (*start, jump*) sursauter

(c) (*of muscle*) se contracter, avoir un spasme/des spasmes; *Anat* avoir un réflexe *ou* des réflexes

jerk³ *n F Pej* (*fool*) crétin, -ine, abruti, -ie; (*obnoxious person*) con(n)ard *m*; **don't be a j.** ne fais pas le con

▸ **jerk off** *vi Vulg* (*masturbate*) se branler

▸ **jerk out** *vtsep* (*words, excuses etc*) balbutier, dire d'une façon saccadée

jerkily [ˈdʒɜːkɪlɪ] *adv* (*to move*) par saccades, par à-coups; (*to walk*) d'un pas saccadé; (*to write, speak*) d'une manière saccadée *ou* hâchée

jerky [ˈdʒɜːkɪ] *adj* (*movement*) saccadé; (*voice, style, speech etc*) saccadé, heurté, hâché; **he took his first j. steps at the age of ten months** il a fait ses premiers pas un peu saccadés à l'âge de dix mois; **in j. French** dans un français heurté *ou* hâché

jerrican [ˈdʒerɪkæn] *n* jerrycan *m*, bidon *m*

Jerry [ˈdʒerɪ] *n* (*dimin of* **German**) *Old-fashioned F Pej* (*soldier*) Boche *m*, Fritz *m*; (*the Germans*) les Boches

jerry-built [ˈdʒerɪbɪlt] *adj Pej* (*house*) en carton-pâte, bon marché, construit comme une cabane à lapins

jerry can *n* = **jerrican**

Jersey [ˈdʒɜːzɪ] *n* **(a)** (*island*) Jersey *f* **(b)** **J. (cow)** vache *f* de Jersey *ou* jersiaise

jersey [ˈdʒɜːzɪ] *n* **(a)** (*garment*) tricot *m* (de laine); *Sp* maillot *m* **(b)** (*material*) jersey *m*; **j. wool/silk, wool/silk j.** jersey de laine/de soie

Jerusalem [dʒəˈruːsələm] *n* **(a)** Jérusalem *mf* **(b)** **J. artichoke** topinambour *m*

jest¹ [dʒest] *n* (*joke*) plaisanterie *f*; (*witty remark*) mot *m* d'esprit; **in j.** (*to say, speak etc*) en plaisantant, pour rire, par plaisanterie; **(only) half in j.** en ne plaisantant qu'à moitié; **to act in j.** plaisanter; *Prov* **(there is) many a true word spoken in j.** on dit souvent la vérité sous le couvert d'une plaisanterie

jest² *vi* (*joke*) plaisanter **(about** sur); (*make witty remarks*) faire des mots d'esprit; **he's not a person to j. with** on ne plaisante pas *ou* on ne badine pas avec lui

jester [ˈdʒestər] *n* (*joker*) farceur, -euse; *Hist* **(court) j.** bouffon *m ou* fou *m* (du roi)

jesting [ˈdʒestɪŋ] **1** *adj* (*remark etc*) fait pour plaisanter *ou* pour rire **2** *n* (*jokes*) plaisanteries *fpl*; (*witty remarks*) mots *mpl* d'esprit

jestingly [ˈdʒestɪŋlɪ] *adv* en plaisantant; **j. known as ...** désigné par le terme farceur de ...

Jesuit [ˈdʒezjʊɪt] **1** *n Rel, Fig Pej* jésuite *m* **2** *adj Rel* (*missionary, theologian*) jésuite; (*college, seminary*) de jésuites

Jesuitical [dʒezjʊˈɪtɪk(ə)l] *adj Fig Pej* jésuitique

Jesus [ˈdʒiːzəs] **1** *n* Jésus *m*; **J. Christ** Jésus-Christ *m*; *F* **J. freak** fou/folle de Jésus **2** *int Sl* **J. (Christ)!, J. wept!** nom de Dieu!

jet¹ [dʒet] *n* **j. (aircraft)** avion *m* à réaction, jet *m*; **to travel by j.** voyager en jet *ou* en avion à réaction; **j. engine** réacteur *m*, moteur *m* à réaction; *Mil* **j. fighter, fighter j.** chasseur *m* à réaction; **j. fuel** kérosène *m*, carburéacteur *m*; **j. propulsion** propulsion *f* par réaction

jet² *n* **(a)** (*of liquid, steam etc*) jet *m* **(b)** (*nozzle*) jet *m*, ajutage *m*, buse *f*; (*on printer*) buse; (*of stove*) brûleur *m*; *Aut* gicleur *m*; **(water) j.** (*in whirlpool, bath etc*) gicleur

jet³ *vi* **(-tt-)** **(a)** (*of liquid*) sortir en jet, gicler **(b)** *Av F* voyager en jet *ou* en avion à réaction; **she jets round the world** elle parcourt le monde en jet

jet⁴ **1** *n Miner* jais *m*; **j. earrings/necklace** boucles d'oreille (noires)/collier (noir) de *ou* en jais; **j. black** noir *m* de jais **2** *adj* noir comme (du) jais, (noir) de jais

▸ **jet in** *vi* arriver par avion

▸ **jet off** *vi* s'envoler **(to** pour)

jetfoil [ˈdʒetfɔɪl] *n* hydroglisseur *m*

jet lag *n* fatigue *f* due au décalage horaire; **I'm suffering from j.** je suis fatigué à cause du décalage horaire

jet-lagged [ˈdʒetlægd] *adj* fatigué à cause du décalage horaire; **in my current j. state** fatigué comme je le suis (à cause du décalage horaire)

jet-powered [dʒet'paʊəd], **jet-propelled** [dʒetprə'peld] *adj (engine, aircraft)* à réaction

jetsam ['dʒetsəm] *n (no pl) Naut, Fig* épaves *fpl*

jet set *n* jet set *m ou f*

jetsetter ['dʒetsetər] *n* membre *m* du *ou* de la jet set

jet-skiing *n* jet-ski *m*

jet stream *n Met* courant-jet *m*, jet *m*, jet-stream *m*

jettison ['dʒetɪs(ə)n] *vt Naut (cargo)* jeter à la mer *ou* par-dessus bord, se délester de; *Av (bombs, fuel etc)* larguer; *Fig (hope, plan, tradition etc)* abandonner, renoncer à

jetty ['dʒetɪ] *n* **(a)** *(breakwater)* jetée *f*, môle *m* **(b)** *(for landing)* embarcadère *m*, débarcadère *m*, appontement *m*

Jew [dʒu:] *n* Juif *m*, Juive *f*; *Mus* **J.'s harp** guimbarde *f*

Jew-baiting ['dʒu:beɪtɪŋ] *n* persécution *f* des Juifs

jewel ['dʒu:əl] *n* **(a)** *(piece of jewellery)* bijou *m*, joyau *m*; *(gem)* pierre *f* précieuse; *Fig (person)* perle *f*; *(thing of value)* perle, bijou; **j. case** coffret *m ou* écrin *m* à bijoux **(b)** *(of watch)* rubis *m*

jewelled, *US* **jeweled** ['dʒu:əld] *adj (tiara, brooch)* orné de pierres précieuses; *(watch)* monté sur rubis

jeweller, *US* **jeweler** ['dʒu:ələr] *n* bijoutier, -ière, joaillier, -ière; **j.'s (shop)** bijouterie *f*, bijouterie-joaillerie *f*

jewellery, *US* **jewelry** ['dʒu:əlrɪ] *n* bijoux *mpl*, joyaux *mpl*; **a piece of j.** un bijou

Jewess ['dʒu:es, -ɪs] *n* Juive *f*

Jewish ['dʒu:ɪʃ] *adj* juif, *f* juive

Jewry ['dʒu:ərɪ] *n* la communauté juive, les Juifs *mpl*

JFK [dʒeɪef'keɪ] *n* **(a)** *US abbr* **John F. Kennedy (b)** = aéroport *m* de New York

jib[1] [dʒɪb] *n* **(a)** *Naut (sail)* foc *m* **(b)** *Tech (of crane, derrick)* flèche *f*, bras *m* **(c)** *Old-fashioned Fig* **I don't like the cut of his j.** son allure ne me plaît guère

jib[2] *vi* **(-bb-) (a)** *(of person)* se rebiffer, regimber, rechigner **(at sth** devant qch); **to j. at doing** rechigner à faire **(b)** *(of horse)* regimber, se dérober

jibe[1] [dʒaɪb] *n, vi* = **gibe**

jibe[2] *vi Am (agree)* s'accorder **(with** avec)

jiffy ['dʒɪfɪ] *n F* **in (half) a j.** en un instant, en moins de rien, en un clin d'œil; **I'll be back/there in a j.!** je reviens/j'arrive tout de suite *ou* dans un instant!

Jiffy bag® ['dʒɪfɪbæg] *n* enveloppe *f ou* pochette *f* matelassée

jig[1] [dʒɪg] *n (dance, music)* gigue *f*

jig[2] *vi* **(-gg-) (a)** *(dance)* danser la gigue **(b)** *(shake)* **to j. (up and down), to j. about** *or* **around** se trémousser (en dansant), sautiller

jigger[1] ['dʒɪgər] *n (measure for whisky)* = 42 ml

jigger[2] *vt F (damage)* esquinter

jiggered ['dʒɪgəd] *adj Br* **(a)** *Old-fashioned F (surprised)* étonné; **well I'm j.!, well, I'll be j.!** zut alors!; **I'm** *or* **I'll be j. if ...** *(confounded)* que le diable m'emporte si ... **(b)** *Old-fashioned Sl (tired)* crevé, claqué **(c)** *F (broken) (TV etc)* naze, déglingué, foutu; **my ankle/back is j.** je me suis niqué la cheville/le dos

jiggery-pokery ['dʒɪgərɪ'pəʊkərɪ] *n Br F* manigances *fpl*, micmacs *mpl*; **there was some sort of j. going on** il y avait des manigances *ou* des micmacs dans l'air

jiggle ['dʒɪg(ə)l] **1** *vt* **to j. (about** *or* **around)** remuer légèrement **2** *vi* **to j. (about** *or* **around)** être légèrement secoué; *(of earrings)* se balancer; **try not to let it j. about** fais en sorte qu'il ne soit pas trop secoué; **I can feel something jiggling about** je sens quelque chose qui remue; **her breasts j. when she runs** ses seins ballottent quand elle court; **stop jiggling about!** arrête de gigoter!

jigsaw ['dʒɪgsɔ:] *n* **(a)** *Carp* scie *f* à chantourner **(b)** *(game)* **j. (puzzle)** puzzle *m*

jihad [dʒɪ'hæd] *n (Muslim holy war)* djihad *m*

jilt [dʒɪlt] *vt (lover, girlfriend etc)* laisser tomber, *F* plaquer

jimjams ['dʒɪmdʒæmz] *npl* **(a)** *F* pyjama *m* **(b)** *F Hum* **to have the j.** *(fear)* avoir les chocottes; *(revulsion)* avoir la chair de poule; *(anxiety)* avoir les nerfs en pelote

jimmy ['dʒɪmɪ] *n, vt Am* = **jemmy**

jingle[1] ['dʒɪŋg(ə)l] *n* **(a)** *(of bells)* tintement *m*; *(of keys etc)* tintement, cliquetis *m*; *(of spurs)* cliquetis **(b)** *(catchy tune)* ritournelle *f*; *(for children)* comptine *f*; *Rad, TV (in advertisement)* jingle *m*

jingle[2] **1** *vi (of bells)* tinter, tintinnabuler; *(of keys, coins etc)* tinter, cliqueter **2** *vt (coins, keys etc)* faire tinter *ou* cliqueter; *(bells)* faire tinter *ou* tintinnabuler

jingling ['dʒɪŋglɪŋ] **1** *n* = **jingle**[1] **(a) 2** *adj* **j. sound** *(of bells)* tintement *m*; *(of keys)* cliquetis *m*

jingo ['dʒɪŋgəʊ] *n Old-fashioned F* chauvin, -ine; **by j.!** nom d'une pipe!

jingoism ['dʒɪŋgəʊɪz(ə)m] *n Pej* chauvinisme *m*

jingoistic [dʒɪŋgəʊ'ɪstɪk] *adj Pej* chauvin

jinks [dʒɪŋks] *npl F* **high j.** la rigolade; **we had high j.** on a eu une séance de rigolade, on s'est bien marrés; **stop the high j.!** trêve de rigolade!; **that's enough high j. for today** assez rigolé pour aujourd'hui; *Iron* **there'll be high j. when my parents find out** ça va barder *ou* chauffer quand mes parents l'apprendront

jinx[1] [dʒɪŋks] *n F (person, object)* porte-malheur *m inv*, porte-guigne *m inv*; *(spell, curse)* maléfice *m*, (mauvais) sort *m*; *(bad luck)* guigne *f*; **to have a j.** avoir la guigne; **to put a j. on** porter la guigne à; **to break the j.** échapper à la guigne

jinx[2] *vt F (usually passive) (person, project etc)* porter la guigne à; **to be jinxed** avoir la guigne

JIT [dʒeɪaɪ'ti:] *Mktg (abbr* **just in time)** juste à temps, JAT; **J. production** production *f* JAT, production juste à temps

jitterbug[1] ['dʒɪtəbʌg] *n (dance)* jitterbug *m*

jitterbug[2] *vi* (-gg-) danser le jitterbug

jitters ['dʒɪtəz] *npl F* **the j.** *(anxiety)* la frousse, la trouille; **to have** *or* **get the j.** avoir la frousse **(about** de); **she's got the j. about her exam** elle a la trouille à cause de son examen; **it gives me the j.** ça me fiche la trouille *ou* la frousse

jittery ['dʒɪtərɪ] *adj F (anxious)* (très) nerveux; **to be j., to get j.** avoir la frousse, être (très) nerveux

jiujitsu [dʒu:'dʒɪtsu:] *n* jiu-jitsu *m*

jive[1] [dʒaɪv] *n* **(a)** *(music, dance)* = swing *m*, rock *m* **(b)** *Am Sl (deceiving talk)* baratin *m*; *(foolish talk)* foutaises *fpl*; **j. (talk)** = argot *m* des musiciens de jazz noirs américains de Harlem dans les années trente

jive[2] **1** *vi* **(a)** *(dance)* = danser le swing *ou* le rock **(b)** *Am Sl (talk nonsense)* déconner **2** *vt Am Sl (mislead)* baratiner

Jnr *(abbr* **junior)** Jr

Joan [dʒəʊn] *n* Jeanne *f*; **J. of Arc** Jeanne d'Arc

Job [dʒəʊb] *n* Job *m*; **to have the patience of J.** avoir la patience d'un ange; **you're a J.'s comforter** vous n'êtes pas d'un grand réconfort

job[1] [dʒɒb] *n* **(a)** *(piece of work, task)* travail *m*, tâche *f*; **to do its j.** *(of medicine, alcohol etc)* faire son effet; **to do the j.** faire l'affaire; **if that ointment doesn't do the j.** si cette pommade n'a pas d'effet; **the garage/hairdresser did a good j. on her** le garage/coiffeur a fait un bon travail; **to make a good** *or* **successful j. of sth** bien réussir qch; **it's quite a (difficult) j.** c'est tout un travail **(to do** sth que de faire qch); *Fig* **to lie down** *or* **fall down on the j.** *(avoid working)* tirer au flanc; **on a j.** en déplacement; *F* **to be on the j.** *(sexually)* faire une partie de jambes en l'air; **this shelf isn't strong** *or* **good enough for the j.** cette étagère ne tiendra pas le coup; **to do odd jobs** faire des petits travaux, bricoler à droite et à gauche; *Ind* **it's a precision j.** c'est un travail de précision; *F* **the car has had a paint j.** la bagnole a été repeinte; **he's done a good j. of work** il a fait du bon boulot; *Com* **j. lot** lot *m* (de marchandises); **a j. lot of books/etc** des livres/*etc* en vrac, un lot de livres/*etc*; **to buy/sell sth as a j. lot** acheter/vendre qch en lot *ou* en vrac

(b) *(responsibility, duty)* travail *m*; **they are only doing their j.** ils ne font que leur travail; **I was given the j. of breaking the bad news** c'est à moi que la tâche est revenue *ou* c'est moi qui ai été chargé d'annoncer la mauvaise nouvelle; **it's my j. to ...** je suis chargé de ..., c'est mon travail de ...; **it's my j. to remind her** c'est à moi de le lui rappeler; **that's not your j.** ce n'est pas votre travail, ce n'est pas à vous de faire ça; **I make it my j. to ...** je me charge de ...; **I'll have the j. of clearing it all up later** c'est moi qui serai obligé de ranger *ou* qui devrai ranger tout ça plus tard; **this muscle has the j. of ...** le rôle de ce muscle est de ...; **that's not part of his j.** ça n'entre pas dans ses fonctions, ça ne fait pas partie de son travail *ou* de ses attributions

(c) *(employment, post)* emploi *m*, travail *m*, *F* boulot *m*, *F* job *m*; **to create (new) jobs** créer des emplois, créer de nouveaux emplois; **she knows her j.** elle connaît son travail *ou* son affaire *ou* son métier *ou F* son boulot; **to give up one's j., to resign from one's j.** démissionner; *Ind etc* **500 jobs were lost** *or* **axed** il y a eu 500 suppressions d'emplois, 500 emplois *ou* postes ont été supprimés; **it's more than my j. is worth** ça serait risquer de perdre mon emploi, ça ne vaut pas la peine de perdre mon emploi pour ça; **on-the-j. training** formation *f* sur le tas; **to be out of a j.** être sans travail; *Br F* **to give jobs to the boys** placer ses copains; **it's jobs for the boys** les boulots vont directement aux copains

(d) *(difficulty, trouble)* **to have (quite) a j.** *or* **a difficult j. doing** *or* **to do sth** avoir du mal à faire qch; **it was quite a j. getting her to come at all** ça a déjà été difficile de la convaincre de venir; *F* **she had the devil** *or Sl* **a hell of a j. doing it** elle a eu tout le mal du monde *ou* un mal de tous les diables *ou* un mal fou à faire cela; *F* **they've got a real j. on their hands with that baby** ils ont du pain sur la planche avec ce bébé; **it's a j. and a half** c'est un sacré boulot (**doing** pour faire)

(**e**) *Sl* (*crime*) coup *m*; **to do a j.** monter un coup; **they did that bank j.** ils ont monté le coup de la banque

(**f**) *Comptr* travail *m*; **j. control** gestion *f* des travaux

(**g**) *F* (*manufactured object*) **that TV is a really nice j.** cette télé, c'est du beau travail; **his car is the red j. parked on the corner** sa voiture, c'est le bel engin rouge qui est garé au coin; **a souped-up j.** (*car or motorcycle*) une bagnole/une moto au moteur gonflé

(**h**) *Fig* (*phrases*) *Br* **it's** *or* **what a good j. (that) ...!** heureusement que ... + *ind*, c'est heureux que ... + *sub*; *Br F* **he got what he deserved, (and) a good j. too!** il a eu ce qu'il méritait, et c'est tant mieux *ou* c'est bien fait pour lui *ou* j'en suis très heureux!; **that's just the j.** c'est exactement ce qu'il faut; *Br F* **the baby has done a big j.** le bébé a fait un gros caca; *F* **to do a j. on a car** (*wreck*) bousiller une voiture; *F* **to do a j. on sb** (*beat up*) tabasser qn; **that journalist did a real j. on him** ce journaliste l'a descendu en flammes *ou* vraiment soigné; **the makeup department did a good j. (on him)** les maquilleurs se sont surpassés

job² *vi* (**-bb-**) (**a**) (*do small jobs*) faire des petits travaux, bricoler (**b**) (*do piecework*) travailler à la tâche *ou* à la pièce

jobbery [ˈdʒɒbərɪ] *n Br F* micmacs *mpl*, trafics *mpl*

jobbing [ˈdʒɒbɪŋ] *Br* **1** *adj* (*worker*) (qui travaille) à la tâche *ou* à la pièce; **j. gardener** jardinier, -ière à la journée **2** *n* (**a**) (*piecework*) travail *m* à la tâche *ou* à la pièce (**b**) (*odd jobs*) bricolage *m*

Jobcentre [ˈdʒɒbsentər] *n Br* = agence *f* nationale pour l'emploi, ANPE *f*

job creation *n* création *f* d'emplois; **j. scheme** programme *m* de création d'emplois

job description *n* profil *m ou* description *f* de poste; **that's not in my j.** ça ne fait pas partie de mon travail

job hunter *n* demandeur, -euse d'emploi

job hunting *n* chasse *f* à l'emploi; **to go j.** aller à la recherche d'un emploi

jobless [ˈdʒɒblɪs] **1** *adj* sans travail, au chômage **2** *npl* **the j.** les chômeurs *mpl*, les demandeurs *mpl* d'emploi; **the j. figures** le nombre des chômeurs *ou* des demandeurs d'emploi

job losses *npl* suppressions *fpl* d'emplois

job offers *npl* offres *fpl* d'emplois

job opportunities *npl* perspectives *fpl* d'emploi, débouchés *mpl*

job satisfaction *n* satisfaction *f* dans le travail

job security *n* sécurité *f* de l'emploi

job seeker *n* demandeur, -euse d'emploi

job-share¹ *n* partage *m* du travail; **we could do it as a j.** nous pourrions nous partager le travail; **they applied for the post as a j.** ils se sont presentés pour le poste en proposant de se partager le travail

job-share² *vi* partager le travail; **we could apply to j.** nous pourrions nous présenter en proposant de nous partager le travail

job sharing *n* partage *m* des emplois *ou* des fonctions

job-shop specialist *n Mktg* spécialiste *m* de production à la commande

jobsworth [ˈdʒɒbzwɜːθ] *n* petit chef *m* qui ne veut pas se mouiller ni se fatiguer

job title *n* titre *m* (de fonction)

Jock [dʒɒk] *n Sl* (*Scot*) Écossais, -aise; **hello, J.!** salut, l'Écossais!

jock [dʒɒk] *n Am Univ F* (*sportsman*) sportif *m*

jockey¹ [ˈdʒɒkɪ] *n Horseracing* (*man*) jockey *m*; (*woman*) femme *f* jockey; **amateur j.** jockey amateur, gentleman(-rider) *m*; **j. cap** casquette *f* de jockey; **J. ® shorts** caleçon *m*

jockey² **1** *vi* (*scheme*) manœuvrer, intriguer (**for a job**/*etc* pour obtenir *ou* se faire donner un poste/*etc*); **to j. for position** manœuvrer *ou* intriguer pour se placer avantageusement **2** *vt* (*persuade forcefully, deceive*) **to j. sb into doing sth** emberlificoter qn pour qu'il fasse qch; **to j. sb out of a job** évincer *ou* chasser qn d'un poste

jockstrap [ˈdʒɒkstræp] *n* slip *m* à coquille

jocose [dʒəˈkəʊs] *adj* facétieux

jocular [ˈdʒɒkjʊlər] *adj* (*humorous*) facétieux, amusant, jovial; (*jolly*) enjoué; **in (a) j. vein** (*to say, reply etc*) d'un ton facétieux *ou* amusant *ou* rieur

jocularity [dʒɒkjʊˈlærɪtɪ] *n* (*humour*) humour *m*; (*jollity*) jovialité *f*; **an atmosphere of j.** une atmosphère joviale

jocularly [ˈdʒɒkjʊləlɪ] *adv* (*humorously*) facétieusement; (*with jollity*) jovialement; **he was j. known as 'the Walrus' by his pupils** ses élèves lui donnaient le surnom facétieux du 'Morse'

jocund [ˈdʒɒkənd] *adj Lit* jovial, enjoué

jodhpurs [ˈdʒɒdpəz] *npl* pantalon *m ou* culotte *f* de cheval, jodhpurs *mpl*

Joe [dʒəʊ] *n Am F* (*man, fellow*) mec *m*, type *m*; **he's an ordinary J.** c'est un mec comme les autres; **J. Public, J. Blow,** *Sl* **J. Schmo,** *Br* **J. Bloggs** Monsieur *m* Tout-le-monde, ≈ Monsieur Dupont

joey [ˈdʒəʊɪ] *n Austr F* (*kangaroo*) petit kangourou *m*

jog¹ [dʒɒg] *n* (**a**) (*push*) poussée *f*, coup *m* sec; (*shake*) secousse *f*; (*with elbow*) coup de coude; *Fig* **to give sb's memory a j.** rafraîchir la mémoire de *ou* à qn (**b**) (*run*) **j.** (**trot**) petit trot *m*; **at a j. (trot)** au petit trot; **to break into a j.** (*of person, horse*) se mettre à trotter (**c**) *Sp* **to go for a j.** aller faire un jogging

jog² (**-gg-**) **1** *vt* (*push*) pousser (d'un coup sec); (*shake*) secouer; **she jogged my elbow** elle m'a poussé le coude; *Fig* **to j. sb's memory** rafraîchir la mémoire de *ou* à qn; *Fig* **to j. sb into action** inciter qn à l'action; **to j. sb out of it** secouer qn; **to j. sb out of their complacency** tirer qn de sa complaisance **2** *vi Sp* faire du jogging; **to go jogging** aller faire un jogging

▶ **jog along** *vi* (*of vehicle etc*) cahoter; (*of person*) trotter; *Fig* (*of person, factory, country etc*) aller tant bien que mal; *Fig* **I'm jogging along quite happily** je vais mon petit bonhomme de chemin

jogger [ˈdʒɒgər] *n Sp* (**a**) (*person*) jogger *m*, joggeur, -euse; *Med F* **j.'s nipple** irritation *f* des tétons due au frottement contre les vêtements (**b**) (*shoe*) chaussure *f* de jogging

jogging [ˈdʒɒgɪŋ] *n Sp* jogging *m*; **to like j.** aimer faire du jogging, aimer le jogging; **j. bottoms** pantalon *m* de jogging *ou F* de survêt; **j. outfit** *or* **suit** tenue *f* de jogging, jogging *m*; **j. shoes** chaussures *fpl* de jogging

joggle¹ [ˈdʒɒg(ə)l] *n* légère secousse *f*

joggle² **1** *vt* secouer légèrement; **to j. sth around** remuer qch; **he joggled his daughter on his knee** il faisait sauter sa fille sur ses genoux **2** *vi* (*shake*) être secoué; **they joggled up and down in the back** ils étaient secoués *ou* bringuebalés à l'arrière

jog-trot *vi* (**-tt-**) (*of horse, Fig of person*) aller au petit trot

John [dʒɒn] *n* (**a**) Jean *m*; **J. Bull** John Bull *m*, l'Anglais *m* typique; (*the English*) les Anglais *mpl*; (*England*) l'Angleterre *f*; *Am* **J. Doe** (*average person*) l'Américain *m* moyen, ≈ Monsieur Dupont; *F* (*unidentified man*) (*under arrest*) inconnu *m*; (*corpse*) mort *m* non identifié; *Am F* **one's J. Hancock** *or* **J. Henry** sa signature, son gribouillis; *Am* **J. Q. Public** Monsieur *m* Tout-le-monde; **(Saint) J. the Baptist** saint *m* Jean-Baptiste; *F* **J. Thomas** (*penis*) zob *m*, popol *m* (**b**) **J. Dory** (*fish*) dorée *f*, saint-pierre *m inv*

john [dʒɒn] *n* (**a**) *Am F* **the j.** (*lavatory*) le petit coin, les cabinets *mpl* (**b**) *Am Sl* (*prostitute's client*) micheton *m*

Johnny [ˈdʒɒnɪ] *n F Old-fashioned* (*man*) gars *m*; *F* (**rubber**) **j., j. bag** (*condom*) capote *f*; *F* **J.-come-lately** (*new arrival*) nouveau venu *m*; *US Hist F* **J. Reb** soldat *m* confédéré

join¹ [dʒɔɪn] *n* (*in wallpaper, masonry, tape etc*) raccord *m*; *Tech* (*junction between elements*) joint *m*; (*in fabric*) couture *f*

join² **1** *vt* (**a**) (*unite*) (*planks, pieces of material etc*) joindre, unir; (*connect, link*) (*towns, words, points etc*) relier; (*edges of a wound etc*) rapprocher, réunir; (*pipes, electric wires*) raccorder; **to j. two things end to end** joindre deux choses bout à bout; **the Siamese twins are joined at the thigh** les frères siamois sont rattachés (l'un à l'autre) par la cuisse; **to j. in marriage** *or* **in matrimony** unir par le mariage; *Mil, Fig* **to j. battle** engager le combat (**with** avec); *Fig* **we shall j. forces** nous unirons nos forces; *Fig* **to j. forces** *or* **hands (with sb) to do** *or* **in doing** se joindre *ou* s'unir (à qn) pour faire; **we joined hands** nous nous sommes pris par la main, nous nous sommes donné la main

(**b**) (*catch up with, meet*) (*person*) rejoindre, retrouver; (*associate oneself with*) (*person*) se joindre à (**in doing** pour faire); (*take part in*) (*game*) prendre part à; **to j. a discussion** se joindre à *ou* prendre part à une discussion; **to j. sb in** *or* **for a drink** prendre un verre avec qn, se joindre à qn pour prendre un verre; **will you j. us?** voulez-vous vous joindre à nous?; **may I j. you?** puis-je me joindre à vous?; **why don't you j. (us at) our table?** venez donc vous asseoir à notre table!; **we are joined in the studio by ...** ... vient nous rejoindre *ou* vient se joindre à nous dans notre studio

(**c**) (*go to, return to*) rejoindre; *Mil, Naut* **to j. one's regiment/ship** rejoindre son régiment/son bâtiment; **we shall soon j. the motorway** nous rejoindrons bientôt l'autoroute

(**d**) (*intersect with, flow into*) rejoindre; **to j. the sea** (*of river*) rejoindre la mer, se jeter dans la mer

(**e**) (*become a member of*) (*club, political party*) s'inscrire à, entrer dans, adhérer à; (*class, course*) s'inscrire pour *ou* à; (*company, group, religious order*) entrer dans; (*the army, navy, police*) s'engager dans, s'enrôler dans, entrer dans; **to**

j. a religious order/the newspaper entrer dans les ordres/au journal; **to j. the queue** se mettre à la queue; **I'm looking for a well-paid and interesting job – j. the queue!** je cherche un travail bien payé et intéressant – bienvenue au club!

2 *vi* **(a)** *(of pieces of fabric, planks etc)* se toucher, se joindre; *(of pipes, wires)* se raccorder

(b) to j. with sb *(associate oneself with)* se joindre à qn, s'associer à qn (**in doing** pour faire); **we j. with you in your sorrow** nous compatissons à votre douleur

(c) *(of roads, lines, rivers)* se rejoindre

(d) *(enrol in club, political party etc)* s'inscrire, devenir membre

▶ **join in 1** *vi (take part)* se mettre de la partie, participer, prendre part; **I'll sing first and then you (all) j. in** je chanterai d'abord et ensuite vous vous joindrez à moi **2** *vipo (take part in) (game, activity)* prendre part à, participer à; *(discussion)* prendre part à, se joindre à, participer à; **to j. in the protest(s)** s'associer aux protestations, joindre sa voix aux protestations; **to j. in the singing** chanter; **you'll all j. in the chorus** vous chanterez tous le refrain en chœur

▶ **join on 1** *vtsep (fasten)* attacher (**to** à); *(add)* ajouter (**to** à) **2** *vi (fasten)* s'attacher (**to** à); **the paragraph joins on here** le paragraphe vient s'ajouter ici; **they joined on at the end of the parade** ils se sont mis à la queue du défilé

▶ **join together 1** *vtsep* = **join² 1 (a) 2** *vi* = **join² 2 (a)**, **(b)**

▶ **join up 1** *vi* **(a)** *Mil* s'engager; *(for class etc)* s'inscrire **(b)** *(of pieces of fabric etc)* se toucher, se joindre; *(of pipes, wires)* se raccorder **(c) to j. up with sb** *(catch up with, meet)* rejoindre qn, retrouver qn; **the three friends always j. up over Christmas** les trois amis se retrouvent toujours à Noël; **to j. up with the motorway** rejoindre l'autoroute **2** *vtsep (planks, pieces of material etc)* joindre, assembler; *(pipes, electric cables)* raccorder; *(two machines)* accoupler

joiner ['dʒɔɪnər] *n* **(a)** *Br (carpenter)* menuisier *m* **(b)** *F (person who likes joining clubs etc)* personne *f* qui aime participer à des activités et s'inscrire à des clubs

joinery ['dʒɔɪnərɪ] *n Br* menuiserie *f*; **piece of j.** article *m ou* pièce *f* de menuiserie

joint¹ [dʒɔɪnt] *n* **(a)** *Anat* articulation *f*, jointure *f*; **out of j.** déboîté; **to put one's arm/shoulder out of j.** se démettre *ou* se disloquer *ou* se déboîter le bras/l'épaule; *Br Fig* **to put sb's nose out of j.** *(make envious)* dépiter qn

(b) *Tech* joint *m*, jointure *f*; *Carp* assemblage *m*; (**soldered** *or* **welded**) **j.** soudure *f*

(c) *Br Culin* rôti *m*; **j. of beef** rôti de bœuf; **j. of lamb** *(leg)* gigot *m* d'agneau; *(shoulder)* épaule *f* d'agneau

(d) *F Pej (nightclub)* boîte *f*; *(restaurant)* restau *m*, gargote *f*; *(place)* endroit *m*; (**gambling**) **j.** tripot *m*

(e) *Sl (cannabis cigarette)* joint *m*

joint² *vt Culin (chicken etc)* découper (aux jointures)

joint³ *adj (statement, decision, agreement, responsibility)* commun; *(contract etc) (between two parties)* bilatéral; *(between more than two parties)* collectif; *(in partnership with others)* co-; *(legacy)* conjoint; *Banking* **j. account** compte *m* joint *ou* commun; **j. author** coauteur *m*; *Admin* **j. commission** commission *f* mixte; *Admin* **j. committee** comité *m* mixte; *Jur* **j. custody** garde *f* conjointe; *Fin* **j. debtor** codébiteur *m*; **j. efforts** efforts *mpl* conjugués *ou* communs *ou* réunis; **j. fare** tarif *m* commun; *Fin* **j. financing** financement *m* conjoint; **j. heir** cohéritier, -ière; **j. holder** *(of record, trophy etc)* codétenteur, -trice; **j. management** cogestion *f*; **j. owner** *(of property)* copropriétaire *mf*; **to be j. owners of** *(car, shares etc)* posséder *ou* détenir en commun; **j. ownership** copropriété *f*; **j. passport** passeport *m* conjoint; **we have a j. passport** nous sommes sur le même passeport; *Cin* **j. production** coproduction *f*; **j. purchaser** coacquéreur *m*; *Com* **j. report** rapport *m* collectif; **j. signature** *(of husband and wife etc)* signature *f* conjointe; **j. undertaking** *or* **venture** entreprise *f* commune; *(company)* coentreprise *f*, société *f* en participation; **j. venture agreement** accord *m* de partenariat

joint and several *adj Fin* **j. debtor** débiteur *m* solidaire; **j. guarantor** garant *m* solidaire; **j. liability** responsabilité *f* solidaire et indivise

Joint Chiefs of Staff *npl US Mil* chefs *mpl* d'état-major des armées

jointed ['dʒɔɪntɪd] *adj (puppet, limb etc)* articulé; **a j. chicken** un poulet découpé

jointing tape ['dʒɜɪntɪŋ] *n TV etc* bande *f* de collure

jointly ['dʒɔɪntlɪ] *adv* conjointement (**with** avec); *Jur* **j. liable** *or* **responsible** *(debtors etc)* solidaire; *Jur* **to act j.** *(of several parties)* agir solidairement; **j. and severally** conjointement et solidairement; **to own/manage j.** coposséder/cogérer

joint-stock company *n Br Fin* société *f* (anonyme) par actions, société *f* en commandite

joist [dʒɔɪst] *n Constr* solive *f*

jojoba [həʊ'həʊbə] *n Bot* jojoba *m*

joke¹ [dʒəʊk] *n* **(a)** *(remark)* plaisanterie *f*, *F* blague *f*; **to make** *or* **tell** *or* **crack a j.** faire une plaisanterie (**about sth** de qch, à propos de qch); **a dirty j.** une histoire cochonne; **to say/do sth for a j.** dire/faire qch histoire de rire *ou* pour rire; **he's always ready with a j.** il a toujours le mot pour rire; **the j. is on me** je suis le dindon de la farce; **she can't take a j.** elle ne comprend pas la plaisanterie; **he didn't see the j.** *(didn't appreciate something funny)* il n'a pas trouvé ça drôle; *(didn't understand somebody's joke)* il n'a pas compris la plaisanterie; **to make a j. about** *(laugh at)* se moquer de; **to make a j. of everything** prendre tout à la plaisanterie *ou F* à la blague *ou* à la rigolade; **he tried to make a j. of it** il a essayé d'en rire; **to make jokes about sth** faire des blagues sur *ou* à propos de qch; **the j. is that ...** le comique de l'histoire, c'est que ...; **what a j.!** *(how ridiculous)* quelle blague!; *(how funny)* ce que c'est amusant *ou* drôle!; *F* **that's** *or* **it's no j.!** *(not easy)* ce n'est pas de la tarte!; *(serious)* ce n'est pas de la blague!; **it's no j. waiting for hours** ce n'est pas amusant *ou* drôle d'attendre des heures; **it's getting beyond a j.** ça commence à ne plus être drôle, ça dépasse le stade de la plaisanterie

(b) *(prank, trick)* (**practical**) **j.** farce *f*, plaisanterie *f*, tour *m*, *F* blague *f*; **to play a (practical) j. on sb** faire une farce *ou* une plaisanterie *ou F* une blague à qn, jouer un tour à qn

(c) *F (person or thing inspiring ridicule)* plaisanterie *f*; **to be a j.** *(of novel, so-called planning, festival etc)* être lamentable; **their economic policy is nothing more than a j.** leur politique économique n'est qu'une vaste plaisanterie; **to regard sb as a j.** considérer qn comme un objet de risée; **he treats the rules as a j.** il se moque du règlement; **this is turning into a j.** *(is getting annoying)* c'est en train de tourner à la farce

joke² *vi* plaisanter, *F* blaguer (**about** sur, à propos de); **to j. about** *(laugh at)* se moquer de; **we were able to j. about it afterwards** après nous avons pu en rire; **to j. with sb** plaisanter avec qn; **I was only joking** ce n'était qu'une plaisanterie, je plaisantais; **you're joking!, you must be** *or* **you've got to be joking!** vous voulez rire!, sans blague!; **I'm not joking!** je ne plaisante pas!

joker ['dʒəʊkər] *n* **(a)** *(making or playing jokes)* farceur, -euse, *F* blagueur, -euse, *Pej* plaisantin *m* **(b)** *F Pej (person)* type *m*, individu *m*; *(stupid person)* abruti *m* **(c)** *Cards* joker *m*; *Fig* **that's the j. in the pack** c'est la grande inconnue; *Fig* **she's the j. in the pack** avec elle, c'est la grande inconnue

jokey ['dʒəʊkɪ] *adj* = **joky**

jokily ['dʒəʊkɪlɪ] *adv* en plaisantant

joking ['dʒəʊkɪŋ] **1** *adj (tone)* moqueur, de plaisanterie; *(comment, response)* moqueur **2** *n (no pl)* plaisanteries *fpl*, *F* blagues *fpl*; **the j. must stop** assez plaisanté *ou F* blagué; **j. apart** *or* **aside** toute plaisanterie mise à part, *F* blague à part

jokingly ['dʒəʊkɪŋlɪ] *adv* en plaisantant

joky ['dʒəʊkɪ] *adj (person)* qui aime raconter des plaisanteries; *(mood, conversation etc)* jovial; *(remark)* moqueur; *(present etc)* farfelu

jollies ['dʒɒlɪz] *npl Am F* **to get one's j. (from) doing sth** *(get pleasure from)* prendre son pied à faire qch

jollification [dʒɒlɪfɪ'keɪʃən] *n F (merrymaking)* réjouissances *fpl*

jolliness ['dʒɒlɪnɪs], **jollity** ['dʒɒlɪtɪ] *n (cheerfulness)* jovialité *f*, gaieté *f*; *(merrymaking)* réjouissances *fpl*

jolly¹ ['dʒɒlɪ] **1** *adj F (cheerful)* jovial, gai, joyeux; *(pleasant)* agréable; **j. hockey sticks** *(expression qui se réfère à une jeune fille ou à une femme éduquée dans le privé, adorant le sport, terriblement boute-en-train mais peu intellectuelle. Utilisée aussi bien comme interjection que comme adjectif par ex.* I'm afraid she's a bit too j. hockey sticks for me) **2** *adv Br F (very)* drôlement, rudement; **it serves him j. well right!** c'est drôlement *ou* rudement bien fait pour lui!; **yes, I j. well <u>did</u> do it!** oui, je l'ai bel et bien fait!; **j. good!** formidable!; **and a j. good job too!** et c'est tant mieux!

jolly² *vt F* amadouer, enjôler; **I jollied him into accepting** je l'ai amadoué *ou* enjôlé tant et si bien qu'il a fini par accepter

▶ **jolly along** *vtsep* = **jolly²**

Jolly Roger *n Naut* pavillon *m* noir (des pirates)

jolt¹ [dʒɒlt] *n* **(a)** *(shake)* secousse *f*; *(of vehicle)* cahot *m*, secousse, à-coup *m*, *pl* à-coups; *(of engine)* à-coup, secousse; **to wake up with a j.** se réveiller en sursaut **(b)** *Fig (shock, surprise)* choc *m*; **it gave me a bit of a j.** ça m'a fait un choc *ou* un coup

jolt² **1** *vi (shake)* secouer; **to j. along** *(of vehicle)* cahoter, tressauter, avancer en cahotant *ou* par à-coups; **to j. forward** *(of vehicle, train)* s'ébranler avec une secousse; **his head jolted forward/back** *(on impact)* sa tête a été rejetée en avant/en arrière; **to j. to a stop** (*of vehicle, train*) s'arrêter en cahotant *ou* avec des à-coups

2 *vt* **(a)** (*shake*) secouer; (*of vehicle*) (*passengers*) cahoter, secouer; **to j. forward/back** (*of collision etc*) (*sb's head*) rejeter en avant/en arrière; (*passenger, suitcase*) projeter en avant/en arrière; **to j. sth off the roof** faire tomber qch du toit

(b) *Fig* (*shock, surprise*) secouer, donner un choc à; *Fig* **to j. sb into action** secouer (les puces à) qn; *Fig* **the nation was jolted into action by the news** cette nouvelle a poussé le pays à entrer en action; *Fig* **to j. sb out of a depression** faire sortir qn d'une dépression tout d'un coup; *Fig* **that jolted him out of his smugness!** ça lui a fait perdre sa belle suffisance d'un seul coup!

jolting ['dʒɒltɪŋ] *n* (*no pl*) (*of vehicle*) cahots *mpl*; (*of plane*) secousses *fpl*

Jonah ['dʒəʊnə] *n Bible* Jonas; *Fig* (*jinx*) porte-malheur *m inv*

jonquil ['dʒɒŋkwɪl] *n* (*flower*) jonquille *f*

Jordan ['dʒɔːd(ə)n] *n* (*country*) Jordanie *f*; **the J.** (*river*) le Jourdain

Jordanian [dʒɔː'deɪnɪən] **1** *adj* jordanien; (*embassy, ambassador*) de Jordanie **2** *n* Jordanien, -ienne

josh[1] [dʒɒʃ] *n F* (*joke*) blague *f*

josh[2] *F* **1** *vt* (*tease*) chambrer, vanner (**about** sur), mettre en boîte (**about** à cause de) **2** *vi* (*joke*) blaguer; **only joshing!** je blaguais!

joss [dʒɒs] *n* **j. stick** bâton *m* d'encens

jostle[1] ['dʒɒs(ə)l] *n* (*push*) bousculade *f*

jostle[2] **1** *vi* (*push each other*) se bousculer; (*use one's elbows*) jouer des coudes (**for sth** pour obtenir qch); **to j. against sb** bousculer qn; *Fig* **to j. for jobs** se bousculer *ou* jouer des coudes pour décrocher un emploi; *Fig* **to j. for position** essayer de bien se placer **2** *vt* bousculer; **to be jostled, to get (oneself) jostled** se faire bousculer (**by** par); **to j. sb out of the way** écarter qn à coups de coudes *ou* en jouant des coudes; **to j. one's way (through)** se frayer un chemin à coups de coude

jostling ['dʒɒs(ə)lɪŋ] *n* (*of crowd*) bousculade(s) *f(pl)*

jot[1] [dʒɒt] *n* (*used in negatives*) **he doesn't care a j.** il n'en a rien à faire, il ne s'en soucie pas du tout; **there isn't a j. of truth in what you say** il n'y a pas la moindre parcelle *ou* part de vérité dans ce que vous dites

jot[2] *vt* (-tt-) = **jot down**

▶ **jot down** *vtsep* noter, prendre note de, prendre en note; **to j. down (some) notes** prendre des notes

jotter ['dʒɒtər] *n* (*notepad*) bloc-notes *m, pl* blocs-notes; *Sch* (*exercise book*) cahier *m*

jottings ['dʒɒtɪŋz] *npl* notes *fpl* (prises à la hâte); **she made a few j. of ideas** elle a noté quelques idées à la hâte

joule [dʒuːl] *n Phys* joule *m*; **J. effect** effet *m* Joule

journal ['dʒɜːn(ə)l] *n* **(a)** (*periodical*) revue *f*, journal *m* **(b)** (*record of events*) journal *m*; *Com* (*for transactions*) livre *m* de comptes; *Acct* **j. entry** contre-passation *f*, passation *f* d'écriture **(c)** *Tech* **j. bearing** palier *m*

journalese [dʒɜːnə'liːz] *n Pej F* style *m ou* jargon *m* journalistique

journalism ['dʒɜːnəlɪz(ə)m] *n* journalisme *m*

journalist ['dʒɜːnəlɪst] *n* journaliste *mf*

journalistic [dʒɜːnə'lɪstɪk] *adj* journalistique

journey[1] ['dʒɜːnɪ] *n* voyage *m*; (*of short distance*) trajet *m*; **it was quite a j. to get here** ça a été toute une épopée pour arriver jusqu'ici; **it is a two-day j. by car** c'est à deux journées de route en voiture; **Falkirk is only a short j. away (from here)** Falkirk est tout près d'ici; **to make a j.** faire un voyage; **to set off** *or* **out on a j.** partir en voyage; **it's not wise to set out on such a j. at this time of year** ce n'est pas prudent d'entreprendre un tel voyage en cette période de l'année; **to go (away) on a j.** partir en voyage; **to get to** *or* **reach the end of one's j.** arriver à destination, arriver à la fin de son voyage *ou* trajet; **have a good j.!** bon voyage!; **to have an hour's j. to work** avoir une heure de trajet pour se rendre à son travail; **to go on a train j.** prendre le train, voyager par le train; **the return j., the j. home** *or* **back** le voyage de retour, le retour; (*from work*) le trajet de retour; **the outward j.** le voyage d'aller, l'aller *m*; **j. time** durée *f* du voyage/trajet

journey[2] *vi Lit* voyager; **to j. on** continuer son voyage

journeyman, *pl* **-men** ['dʒɜːnɪmən] *n* (*craftsman*) compagnon *m*, ouvrier *m*; **j. baker** ouvrier boulanger; **j. carpenter** compagnon charpentier

journo ['dʒɜːnəʊ] *n Am F* journaliste *mf*

joust[1] [dʒaʊst] *n Hist, Fig* joute *f*

joust[2] *vi Hist* jouter (**with** contre); *Fig* batailler

jousting ['dʒaʊstɪŋ] *n Hist, Fig* joutes *fpl*; **a j. match** une bataille

jovial ['dʒəʊvɪəl] *adj* jovial, enjoué; **she's in a j. mood** elle est d'humeur joviale; **to feel j.** être enjoué

joviality [dʒəʊvɪ'ælɪtɪ] *n* jovialité *f*, enjouement *m*

jovially ['dʒəʊvɪəlɪ] *adv* jovialement

jowl [dʒaʊl] *n* **(a)** (*jaw*) mâchoire *f* **(b)** (*hanging flesh on cheek*) bajoue *f*; **he had heavy jowls** il avait de grosses bajoues

-jowled [dʒaʊld] *suff* **long/square/***etc***-j.** à la mâchoire allongée/carrée/*etc*; **a heavy-j. face** un visage aux grosses bajoues

joy [dʒɔɪ] *n* **(a)** (*happiness*) joie *f*; **to jump** *or* **leap/weep** *or* **cry for j.** sauter *ou* bondir/pleurer de joie; **wild with j., beside oneself with j.** fou *ou* ivre de joie; **to our great j.** à notre grande joie; **I wish you (great) j.** je vous souhaite beaucoup de bonheur; *Iron* **I wish you j. (of it)!** je vous souhaite bien du plaisir!, vous m'en voyez fort aise!

(b) (*pleasure*) plaisir *m*; **the joys of marriage/of spring** les joies *ou* plaisirs du mariage/du printemps; **full of the joys of spring** au comble du bonheur; **the joys of having children** les joies qu'apportent les enfants; **the joys of having a car** les joies d'avoir une voiture; **her style is a j. to watch** son style est un plaisir pour les yeux; **he's a j. to work for** c'est un plaisir de travailler pour lui; **our new car is a j. to drive** avec notre nouveau modèle la conduite est un plaisir; **she's a j. to be with, it's a j. to be with her** c'est un plaisir que d'être à ses côtés; **our grandchildren are an absolute j.** nos petits-enfants sont très mignons

(c) *Br F* (*no pl*) (*success*) succès *m*; **(did you have** *or* **get) any j.?** ça a marché?, tu as réussi?; **no j.!** ça n'a rien donné!, ça n'a pas marché!; **you won't get any j. from him** tu n'arriveras à rien avec lui

joyful ['dʒɔɪfʊl] *adj* (*person, face, news etc*) joyeux

joyfully ['dʒɔɪfəlɪ] *adv* joyeusement, avec joie; (*to celebrate, be reunited*) dans la joie; **to be j. happy** être plein d'un bonheur joyeux *ou* allègre

joyfulness ['dʒɔɪfʊlnɪs] *n* (grande) joie *f*, allégresse *f*

joyless ['dʒɔɪlɪs] *adj* triste, sans joie; (*face, grin*) triste

joylessly ['dʒɔɪlɪslɪ] *adv* tristement, sans joie

joyous ['dʒɔɪəs] *adj esp Lit* (*occasion, person etc*) joyeux; (*news*) heureux

joyously ['dʒɔɪəslɪ] *adv esp Lit* joyeusement, avec joie; (*to celebrate*) dans la joie; **to be j. happy** être plein d'un bonheur joyeux *ou* allègre

joypad ['dʒɔɪpæd] *n Comptr* joypad *m*

joyride[1] ['dʒɔɪraɪd] *n F* (*in stolen car*) virée *f* (dans une voiture volée); **to go for a** *or* **on a j.** faire une virée (dans une voiture volée); *Fig* **it's no j. working with him** travailler avec lui, ce n'est pas une partie de plaisir

joyride[2] *vi* (*pt* **joyrode** [-rəʊd]; *pp* **joyridden** [-rɪd(ə)n]) *F* faire une virée (dans une voiture volée); **to go joyriding** faire une virée (dans une voiture volée)

joyrider ['dʒɔɪraɪdər] *n* voleur, -euse (qui prend une voiture pour faire une virée)

joystick ['dʒɔɪstɪk] *n Av* manche *m* à balai; *Comptr* manette *f* (de jeu), manche à balai

JP [dʒeɪ'piː] *n Br Jur* (*abbr* **justice of the peace**) juge *m* de paix

jubilant ['dʒuːbɪlənt] *adj* (*shouts*) de joie; (*expression*) épanoui, radieux; (*crowd*) exultant; (*party, celebration*) joyeux; **to be j.** (*of person*) déborder de joie, jubiler, exulter; **to be j. at** *or* **about** *or* **over the news** être transporté de joie par la nouvelle

jubilantly ['dʒuːbɪləntlɪ] *adv* avec jubilation

jubilation [dʒuːbɪ'leɪʃən] *n* (*of person*) (grande) joie *f*, exultation *f*, jubilation *f*; **to be a cause for (great) j.** être l'occasion de (grandes) réjouissances; **scenes of j.** scènes de réjouissances

jubilee ['dʒuːbɪliː] *n* **(golden) j.** jubilé *m*, (fête *f* du) cinquantième anniversaire *m* (*de mariage etc*); **silver/diamond j.** (fête du) vingt-cinquième/soixantième anniversaire

Judaea [dʒuː'diːə] *n Hist* Judée *f*

Judaic [dʒuː'deɪɪk] *adj* judaïque

Judaism ['dʒuːdeɪɪz(ə)m] *n Rel* judaïsme *m*

Judas ['dʒuːdəs] *n* (*traitor*), *Bible* Judas *m*; *Bible* **J. Iscariot** Judas Iscariote; **J. kiss** baiser *m* de Judas

judas ['dʒuːdəs] *n* **j. (hole** *or* **window)** (*in door*) judas *m*

judder[1] ['dʒʌdər] *n Br* vibrations *fpl*; (*of brakes*) trépidation *f*; (*of clutch, tool*) broutage *m*, broutement *m*

judder[2] *vi Br* vibrer; (*of brakes*) trépider; (*of clutch, tool*) brouter; **to j. to a halt** (*of train, vehicle*) s'arrêter avec de violentes secousses

judge[1] [dʒʌdʒ] *n* **(a)** *Jur, Sp etc* juge *m*; (*of contest*) juge, membre *m* du jury; *Jur* **the judges** (*the bench*) la magistrature assise; *Bible* **(the Book of) Judges** le livre des Juges

(b) *Fig* juge *m*, connaisseur *m*; **good j.** (*of cars, horses, wine*) spécialiste *mf* (**of** en); **she fancies herself as a good j. of men** elle croit savoir juger les hommes; **I'm not sure he's the best j. of such things** je ne suis pas sûr qu'il soit très bon juge en la matière; **to be a good** *or* **keen j. of character** être bon *ou* fin psychologue; **I'll let you be the j. of that** je vous en fais juge, je vous laisse juge; **I will be the j. of that** c'est moi qui jugerai de cela

judge² **1** *vt* **(a)** *Jur, Sp etc* (*try, give decision about*) juger; *Jur* **to j. a case** juger une affaire

(b) (*assess critically*) (*person, situation, text etc*) juger; (*estimate, evaluate*) (*distance, speed, weight, price etc*) estimer, évaluer; **her latest novel has been judged a failure by the critics** les critiques ont estimé que son dernier roman était mauvais; **to j. sb by** *or* **on sth** juger qn sur *ou* d'après qch; **to j. people by appearances** juger d'après les apparences; **to j. sth at its true** *or* **proper value/on its merits** juger *ou* apprécier qch à sa juste valeur/selon ses mérites

(c) (*think, consider*) juger (**that** que; **if, whether** si); **to j. it necessary to ...** juger nécessaire de ...

2 vi (*assess, estimate, pass judgement*), *Jur, Rel* juger; **to j. by appearances** juger d'après les apparences; **as far as I can j.** autant que je puisse en juger; **to j. for oneself** (en) juger par soi-même; **judging by** *or* **from his letter/my first impressions** à en juger par *ou* d'après sa lettre/mes premières impressions; **who will be judging?** (*in competition*) qui va faire fonction de juge?

judg(e)ment, *Am* judgment [ˈdʒʌdʒmənt] *n* **(a)** *Jur, Rel, Fig* jugement *m*; *Jur* **to pass** *or* **give** *or* **deliver j.** prononcer *ou* rendre un jugement (**on** sur); *Jur* **to sit in j.** (*of court*) siéger; *Fig* **to sit in j. on** *or* **over sb, to pass j. on sb** porter un jugement sur qn, juger qn; *Fig* **to sit in j., to pass j.** porter des jugements, juger (les gens); *Rel* **the Last J., J. Day** le Jugement dernier

(b) (*no pl*) (*discernment*) jugement *m*; **political/financial j.** discernement *m* en matière de politique/finances; **to have/lack (good** *or* **sound) j.** avoir du/manquer de jugement; **to have very sound j.** avoir une grande sûreté de jugement, avoir un jugement très sûr; **this decision shows good j.** cette décision montre du discernement; **to trust sb's j.** s'en remettre au jugement de qn

(c) (*opinion*) jugement *m*; **to give one's j. on** exprimer *ou* formuler son jugement sur, donner *ou* exprimer son avis sur; **to form a j.** se faire une opinion, se former un jugement; **in my j.** à mon sens; **against my better j.** tout en sachant que je me trompe/trompais sans doute

judg(e)mental, *Am* judgmental [dʒʌdʒˈment(ə)l] *adj* (*person, book etc*) critique; **I don't want to seem j. but ...** je ne veux pas avoir l'air de critiquer mais ...; *Mktg* **j. forecasting** prévision *f* par estimation; *Mktg* **j. method** méthode *f* estimative

judicature [ˈdʒuːdɪkətʃər] *n Jur* (*administration of justice*) justice *f*; (*system*) organisation *f* judiciaire; (*judges*) magistrature *f*

judicial [dʒuːˈdɪʃ(ə)l] *adj Jur* (*inquiry, power, proceedings*) judiciaire; **j. murder** assassinat *m* légal *ou* juridique; *US* **j. review** = examen *m* de la conformité d'une loi à la constitution; **j. separation** séparation *f* de corps

judicially [dʒuːˈdɪʃəlɪ] *adv Jur* judiciairement

judiciary [dʒuːˈdɪʃɪərɪ] *Jur* **1** *adj* judiciaire **2** *n* (*judges*) magistrature *f*; (*branch of government*) pouvoir *m* judiciaire; (*system of courts*) organisation *f* judiciaire

judicious [dʒuːˈdɪʃəs] *adj* (*person, mind, thought etc*) judicieux

judiciously [dʒuːˈdɪʃəslɪ] *adv* judicieusement

judiciousness [dʒuːˈdɪʃəsnɪs] *n* (*of person, mind*) discernement *m*, bon sens *m*; (*of thought, remark*) bon sens

judo [ˈdʒuːdəʊ] *n* judo *m*

judy, Judy [ˈdʒuːdɪ] *n Br Sl* (*girl, woman*) nana *f*

jug¹ [dʒʌg] *n* **(a)** *Br* (*for cream, milk, water*) pot *m*; (*for wine*) pichet *m*; **coffee j.** (*of electric percolator*) verseuse *f*; *Sl* **his ears are like j. handles** il a les oreilles en contrevent *ou* comme des esgourdes; **j. kettle** = bouilloire *f* (électrique) haute; *Am* **j. wine** vin *m* ordinaire **(b)** *Old-fashioned Sl* (*prison*) taule *f*, tôle *f*; **in (the) j.** au trou, en taule *ou* tôle

jugful [ˈdʒʌgfʊl] *n* (*of cream, milk, water*) (plein) pot *m*; (*of wine*) (plein) pichet *m*

jugged [dʒʌgd] *adj Culin* **j. hare** civet *m* de lièvre

juggernaut [ˈdʒʌgənɔːt] *n* **(a)** *Br* (*lorry*) (gros) poids *m* lourd, *F* mastodonte *m* **(b)** *Fig* (*destructive force*) vague *f* de fond, vague déferlante, raz-de-marée *m inv*

juggins [ˈdʒʌgɪnz] *n Old-fashioned Br F* (*simpleton*) nigaud, -aude, cruche *f*

juggle [ˈdʒʌg(ə)l] **1** *vi* (*with balls, figures*) jongler **2** *vt* (*balls, figures*) jongler avec

juggler [ˈdʒʌglər] *n* jongleur, -euse

juggling [ˈdʒʌglɪŋ] *n* jonglerie *f*, art *m* du jongleur; (*trickery*) fourberie *f*

Jugoslav [ˈjuːgəʊslɑːv] *adj, n* = **Yugoslav**

Jugoslavia [juːgəʊˈslɑːvɪə] *n* = **Yugoslavia**

Jugoslavian [juːgəʊˈslɑːvɪən] *adj, n* = **Yugoslavian**

jugular [ˈdʒʌgjʊlər] *Anat* **1** *adj* jugulaire **2** *n* (veine *f*) jugulaire *f*; *Fig* **to go for the j.** attaquer toutes griffes dehors *ou* tous azimuts

juice¹ [dʒuːs] *n* **(a)** (*of fruit, vegetables, meat*) jus *m*; (*of plant*) suc *m*; *Br* **j. extractor** centrifugeuse *f* (électrique); *Physiol* **gastric** *or* **digestive juices** sucs gastriques *ou* digestifs **(b)** *F* (*electricity*) jus *m*, courant *m*; (*gas*) gaz *m*; (*petrol*) essence *f*

juice² *vt* (*apple, orange etc*) extraire le jus de

▶ **juice up** *vtsep Am Sl* **(a)** (*liven up*) (*party*) mettre de l'animation *ou* de l'ambiance dans; (*add power to*) (*engine*) gonfler **(b) to get juiced up** (*drunk*) se soûler

juicer [ˈdʒuːsər] *n Am* centrifugeuse *f* (électrique)

juiciness [ˈdʒuːsɪnɪs] *n* (*of meat*) juteux *m*; *Fig* (*of story, detail*) piquant *m*, (côté *m*) croustillant *m*; **the j. of these melons** ces melons bien juteux

juicy [ˈdʒuːsɪ] *adj* (*fruit*) juteux; (*meat*) plein de jus, qui rend du jus; *Fig* (*story, detail*) croustillant, piquant; **the j. part of the story** le plus croustillant de l'histoire; *F* **a j. deal** (*lucrative*) une affaire juteuse; **a nice j. morsel** (*of meat etc*) un morceau de choix bien succulent; **a nice j. scandal** un scandale bien juteux; *Br Sl* **she's a j. bit** (*sexy*) elle est très excitante, c'est une sacrée allumeuse

jujitsu [dʒuːˈdʒɪtsuː] *n* jiu-jitsu *m*

juju [ˈdʒuːdʒuː] *n* (*charm, fetish*) gri(s)-gri(s) *m*

jukebox [ˈdʒuːkbɒks] *n* juke-box *m*

julep [ˈdʒuːlɪp] *n Am* (*drink*) **(mint) j.** bourbon *m* frappé à la menthe

Julian [ˈdʒuːlɪən] *adj* (*calendar etc*) julien

Julius Caesar [ˈdʒuːljəs] *n* Jules César

July [dʒuːˈlaɪ, dʒʊˈlaɪ] *n* [①**A75-6**,B-C; **B58-9**,B-C] juillet *m*; **in J.** au mois de juillet, en juillet; **(on) the fifth of J.** le cinq juillet

jumble¹ [ˈdʒʌmb(ə)l] *n* **(a)** (*disorder*) fouillis *m*, pagaïe *f*, méli-mélo *m*, *pl* mélis-mélos; *Fig* (*of ideas etc*) méli-mélo, fouillis, fatras *m*; (*of words*) fatras; **in a j.** (*papers etc*) en pagaïe, en fouillis; *Fig* (*ideas etc*) (em)brouillé **(b)** *Br* (*unwanted articles*) bric-à-brac *m inv*

jumble² *vt* (*documents, toys, books etc*) mélanger, mettre la pagaïe dans; (*clothes, shoes etc*) mélanger; *Fig* (*ideas, details, words etc*) (em)brouiller, mélanger; **the pages got all jumbled** les pages se sont complètement mélangées; **the clothes lay jumbled on the floor** les vêtements gisaient pêle-mêle sur le sol; **everything was jumbled** tout était mélangé; **he jumbled the details** il s'est emmêlé *ou* embrouillé dans les détails

▶ **jumble together, jumble up** *vtsep* = **jumble²**

jumble sale *n Br* vente *f* de charité

jumbo [ˈdʒʌmbəʊ] *F* **1** *adj* **j.(-sized)** (*bag, portion*) géant, énorme; (*feet, pants*) énorme, de géant; *St Exch* **j. trade** opération *f* jumbo **2** *n* (*pl* **-os**) **(a)** (*person, animal, thing*) mastodonte *m*; *Av* avion *m* géant, jumbo-jet *m*, *pl* jumbo-jets, (avion) gros porteur *m* **(b) J.** (*elephant*) = surnom *m* de l'éléphant

jumbo jet *n Av* avion *m* géant, jumbo-jet *m*, *pl* jumbo-jets, (avion) gros porteur *m*

jump¹ [dʒʌmp] *n* **(a)** (*leap*) saut *m*, bond *m*; (*by parachute*) saut (en parachute); **to take** *or* **make a j.** faire un saut *ou* un bond, sauter; **in** *or* **at one j.** d'un (seul) bond; *F* **go take a j.!** va te faire voir (ailleurs)!, va te faire cuire un œuf!; *Fig* **to be one j. ahead of** avoir une longueur d'avance sur; *F* **to have the j. on sb** (*have a head start*) avoir pris une longueur d'avance sur qn dès le départ; *Cin* **j. cut** (*abrupt scene change*) faux *m* raccord, saut *m* de montage

(b) (*on racecourse etc*) obstacle *m*; **to put a horse over a j.** faire sauter un obstacle à un cheval

(c) (*in temperature, unemployment etc*) hausse *f* (soudaine) (**in** de); **the j. in prices** la flambée des prix, la hausse (soudaine) des prix; **to take a (sudden) j.** faire un bond

(d) (*sudden movement, start*) sursaut *m*; **that gave me a j.** cela m'a fait sursauter *ou* tressauter

(e) *Comptr* saut *m*, branchement *m*

jump² **1** *vi* **(a)** (*leap*) (*of person, animal etc*) sauter; (*from aircraft*) sauter (en parachute); **j.!** (*to child, dog*) allez, hop!, saute!; **to j. to one's feet** se (re)lever d'un bond; **to j. to the ground** sauter à terre; **to j. for joy** (*feel elated, leap in the air*) sauter de joie; **to j. (down) from a wall/tree** sauter (du haut) d'un mur/arbre; **to j. from a train/vehicle** sauter d'un train/d'un véhicule; **to j. across a ditch** franchir un fossé d'un bond, sauter un fossé

(b) (*go directly*) sauter; **to j. from one subject to another** *or* **to the next** sauter d'un sujet à l'autre; **I jumped to the third chapter** je suis passé directement au troisième chapitre; **the film then jumps to the present** puis le film fait un saut jusqu'au présent; **to j. from the bottom to the top of the list** remonter toute la liste d'un seul coup (**c**) (*of profit, temperature etc*) faire un bond; (*of price*) flamber, faire un bond

(**d**) (*make a sudden movement*) (*of person*) sursauter, tressauter; (*of heart*) faire un bond, bondir; (*of record player needle, chisel, drill*) sauter; **we nearly jumped out of our skins** (*from surprise*) nous avons failli sauter au plafond; (*from fear, shock*) ça nous a fait *ou F* fichu un de ces coups; **the sight of her** (**nearly**) **made me j. out of my skin** ça m'a fait *ou F* fichu un de ces coups de la voir

(**e**) *Fig* (*phrases*) **to j. at an offer/a chance/a suggestion** sauter sur une offre/une occasion/une proposition; **you should j. at it** vous devriez sauter dessus; **to j. to conclusions** tirer des conclusions prématurées *ou* hâtives; **to j. to the conclusion that …** conclure prématurément que …; **and j. to it!** et que ça saute!; **let's wait and see which way she jumps** attendons de voir sa réaction, attendons de voir comment elle va réagir; *F* **to j. down sb's throat** (*reply sharply to*) rabrouer qn, rembarrer qn, envoyer qn paître *ou* promener; (*criticize*) engueuler qn; *Am F* **to j. all over sb** (*scold, criticize*) passer un savon à qn, engueuler qn

(**f**) *F* **to be** (**really**) **jumping** (*of party, nightclub*) être très animé

2 *vt* (**a**) (*hedge, ditch etc*) franchir d'un bond, sauter (par-dessus); *Fig* (*skip*) (*paragraph, word, page etc*) sauter; *Sch* **to j. a class** sauter une classe; **to j. a** *or* **the groove** (*of record player needle*) sauter

(**b**) (*cause to jump*) (*horse*) faire sauter; *Sp* **to j. a horse over a hurdle** faire sauter une haie à un cheval

(**c**) *Am* **to j. rope** sauter à la corde

(**d**) (*escape from, pass, leave illegally etc*) *Jur* **to j. bail** se dérober à la justice (*alors qu'on jouit de la liberté provisoire*); *Aut* **to j. the lights** griller *ou* brûler le feu rouge *ou* les feux; *Br* **to j. the queue** passer avant son tour, resquiller; **to j. the rails** (*of train*) dérailler; *Naut* **to j. ship** (*of sailor*) déserter (le navire)

(**e**) *Rail F* (*get on*) **to j. a train** sauter dans un train (**to** à destination de); (*without paying*) prendre un train sans billet

(**f**) *F* (*attack, ambush, take over*) **to j. sb** sauter *ou* tomber sur (le paletot de) qn; **to j. a train** (*of bandits etc*) attaquer un train; *Am* **to j. a claim** s'emparer illégalement d'une concession

▶ **jump about, jump around** *vi* sautiller; *Fig* (*of story, film etc*) partir dans toutes les directions

▶ **jump back** *vi* (*of person, vehicle*) faire un bond en arrière, reculer d'un bond; **the story then jumps back twenty years** à ce moment-là l'histoire fait un saut de vingt ans en arrière

▶ **jump down** *vi* (*from wall etc*) sauter (à terre); **to j. down from a wall/tree** sauter (du haut) d'un mur/arbre

▶ **jump forward** *vi* (*of person, vehicle*) faire un bond en avant; **at this point the film jumps forward two years** à ce moment-là le film fait un saut de deux années en avant; **if I can briefly j. forward to …** si je peux anticiper brièvement sur …

▶ **jump in 1** *vi* (*into pool, river etc*) sauter (dedans); (*into vehicle, train*) monter (vite); (*into conversation*) intervenir; *Aut* **j. in!** montez!; *Fig* **to j. in at the deep end** se jeter tête baissée dans les problèmes **2** *vipo* = **jump into**

▶ **jump into** *vipo* (*river, ditch etc*) sauter dans; (*car etc*) sauter *ou* monter dans; **to j. into bed with sb** coucher avec qn

▶ **jump off 1** *vi* (**a**) (*from wall, train etc*) sauter (**from** de) (**b**) *Horseriding* faire un barrage **2** *vipo* (*bicycle, train etc*) sauter de; **to j. off a wall/***etc* sauter (du haut) d'un mur/*etc*

▶ **jump on 1** *vi* (*on to vehicle, train*) monter; (*on to bicycle*) sauter dessus **2** *vipo* (**a**) (*bus, train etc*) monter *ou* sauter dans; (*bicycle*) sauter sur (**b**) *F* **to j. on sb** (*reprimand*) passer un savon à qn; **you should j. on that kind of thing at once** tu devrais couper court à ce genre de choses

▶ **jump out** *vi* (*from vehicle, train etc*) sauter (**of, from** de); **I'll j. out at the traffic lights** je vais descendre au feu rouge; **to j. out of bed** sauter (à bas) du lit; **to j. out of the window** sauter par la fenêtre; **to j. out of the bushes/one's hiding place** bondir d'entre les buissons/de sa cachette; *Fig* **to j. out at sb** (*of mistake etc*) sauter aux yeux de qn

▶ **jump over 1** *vipo* (*hedge, ditch etc*) franchir d'un bond, sauter (par-dessus) **2** *vi* sauter (par-dessus)

▶ **jump up** *vi* (**a**) (*to one's feet*) se (re)lever d'un bond; **up she jumped** d'un bond, elle se (re)leva *ou* elle fut debout; **to j. up and down** sautiller (**b**) *F* (*increase suddenly*) = **jump² 1** (**c**)

jumped-up [dʒʌmp'tʌp] *adj Br F Pej* (*recently promoted, arrogant*) récemment promu (et qui a la grosse tête); (*upstart*) parvenu; **some j. little salesman/civil servant** un petit péteux de vendeur/fonctionnaire

jumper¹ ['dʒʌmpər] *n* (**a**) *Br* (*sweater*) pull(-over) *m* (**b**) *Am* (*sleeveless dress*) robe-chasuble *f*

jumper² *n* (**a**) (*horse, athlete*) sauteur, -euse; **to be a good j.** être bon sauteur, bien sauter (**b**) *Am Aut* **jumpers, j. cables** câbles *mpl* de démarrage (**c**) *Comptr* **j.** (**wire**) cavalier *m*

jumpily ['dʒʌmpɪlɪ] *adv* (*nervously*) nerveusement

jumpiness ['dʒʌmpɪnɪs] *n* (*of person*) nervosité *f*; *St Exch* (*of markets*) nervosité, fébrilité *f*

jumping ['dʒʌmpɪŋ] **1** *adj* (*insect*) sauteur **2** *n* (*leaps*) sauts *mpl*; *Horseriding* (*show jumping*) jumping *m*, concours *m* hippique

jumping bean *n Bot* haricot *m* sauteur

jumping jack *n* (*toy figure*) pantin *m*; *Br* (*firework*) pétard *m* à répétition

jumping-off *n* **j. place** *or* **point** (*for journey*) point *m* de départ (**for** pour); *Fig* (*for talks, in one's career*) tremplin *m*, point de départ

jump jet *n Av* avion *m* à décollage vertical

jump leads *npl Br Aut* câbles *mpl* de démarrage

jumpmaster ['dʒʌmpmæstər] *n Am Mil* moniteur, -trice de parachutisme

jump-off *n Horseriding* barrage *m*

jump rope *n Am* corde *f* à sauter

jump seat *n* strapontin *m*

jump-start¹ *n* **to give a j. to** = **jump-start²**

jump-start² *vt* (*car*) *Br* (*push*) faire démarrer en poussant; *Am* (*with jumper cables*) faire démarrer au moyen de câbles de démarrage; *Fig* **to j. the economy** relancer l'économie

jump suit *n Clothing* combinaison-pantalon *f*; (*for baby*) grenouillère *f*

jumpy ['dʒʌmpɪ] *adj* (**a**) (*nervous*) (*person, gestures etc*) nerveux; *St Exch* (*market*) nerveux, fébrile (**b**) (*fitful, jerky*) (*style, gestures etc*) saccadé

junction ['dʒʌŋkʃən] *n* (**a**) (*in roads, railway lines*) embranchement *m*, bifurcation *f*, jonction *f*; (*between two roads*) jonction; (*in rivers*) confluent *m*; (*in pipes*) embranchement, jonction, raccordement *m*; (*crossroads*) carrefour *m*; (*station*) gare *f* de jonction *ou* de raccordement; (*weld*) soudure *f*; *El* connexion *f*; *El* (*of wires*) branchement *m*; *El* **j. box** boîte *f* de dérivation; *Br* **j. 5** (*on motorway*) (*exit*) la sortie 5; (*entrance*) l'entrée *f* 5 (**b**) *Fml* (*no pl*) (*joining*) jonction *f*

juncture ['dʒʌŋktʃər] *n esp Fml* (**a**) (*critical point in time*) **at this j.** en ce moment même, dans ces circonstances; (*in past*) à ce moment même; **we have reached a critical j.** nous sommes dans une situation critique (**b**) *Anat* jonction *f*

June [dʒu:n] *n* (①**A75-6**,**B-C**; **B58-9**,**B-C**) juin *m*; **in J.** au mois de juin, en juin; (**on**) **the ninth of J.** le neuf juin

June beetle *n* hanneton *m*

June bug *n* hanneton *m*

jungle ['dʒʌŋg(ə)l] *n* (*forest, Fig competitive environment*) jungle *f*; **a j. animal/plant/***etc* une bête/plante/*etc* de la jungle; *Fig* **a j. of red tape** une montagne de paperasseries; *US Offensive Sl* **j. bunny** négro *m*; **j. fever** paludisme *m*; **j. gym** (*climbing frame*) cage *f* à l'écureuil; *Sl* **j. juice** (*alcohol*) tord-boyaux *m* (artisanal); **j. warfare** combat *m* de jungle

junior ['dʒu:njər] **1** *adj* (**a**) (*in age*) **to be j. to sb** être plus jeune que qn; **she's three years j. to me, she's j. to me by three years** elle est plus jeune que moi de trois ans; **j. orchestra/club** orchestre *m*/club *m* de jeunes; **Hudson J.** *or* **Jnr** *or* **Jr** *or* **Jun** (*the son*) Hudson fils *ou* junior *ou* Jr; (*one of two or more brothers*) Hudson junior *ou* Jr; *Sp* **j. event/team** épreuve *f*/équipe *f* de minimes/de cadets/de juniors

(**b**) (*in rank*) subalterne; **to be j. to sb** être au-dessous de qn; **j. teacher/executive** jeune professeur *m*/cadre *m*; **j. clerk** commis *m* ordinaire, jeune employé, -ée, employé, -ée subalterne; *Br Univ* **j. common room** salle *f* des étudiants de licence; *Br Jur* **j. counsel** jeune avocat *m*, jeune avocate *f*; *Br Parl* **j. minister** secrétaire *mf* d'État (**in** à); *Com* **j. partner** jeune associé, -ée

(**c**) (*small*) petit; *Clothing* **j. miss** (*for clothes' size*) fillette *f*; **j. portions available** (*in restaurant*) menu enfant; *Com* **j. sizes** petites tailles

2 *n* (**a**) (*younger person*) cadet, -ette; *esp Am F* **where's j.?** où est le petit/la petite?; **to be sb's j.** être le cadet de qn, être plus jeune que qn; **she's three years my j., she's my j. by three years** elle est ma cadette de trois ans, elle est plus jeune que moi de trois ans

(**b**) (*subordinate*) (employé, -ée) subalterne *mf*, *F Pej* sous-fifre *m*; **he's our office j.** (*performing general duties*) c'est notre factotum

(**c**) *Br Sch* (*between 7 and 11*) élève *mf* du cours élémentaire *ou* du cours moyen; *Am Sch, Univ* élève/étudiant, -ante d'avant-dernière année; *Br* **to go to the juniors, to attend the juniors** (*junior school*) aller à l'école primaire

(**d**) *Sp* (*between 13 and 15*) minime *mf*; (*between 15 and 17*) cadet, -ette; (*between 17 and 21*) junior *mf*

junior classes *npl Br Sch* petites classes *fpl*
junior college *n Am Univ* = institut *m* universitaire du premier cycle
junior high school *n Am Sch* (*between 11 and 15*) = collège *m* d'enseignement secondaire
junior school *n Br Sch* (*between 7 and 11*) école *f* primaire
junior year *n Am Sch, Univ* avant-dernière année *f*
juniper ['dʒu:nɪpə*r*] *n* **j. (tree)** genévrier *m*, genièvre *m*; **j. berries** baies *fpl ou* grains *mpl* de genièvre; *Pharm* **j. oil** essence *f* de genièvre
junk¹ [dʒʌŋk] *n* (*no pl*) **(a)** (*unwanted objects*) bric-à-brac *m inv*; (*outdated objects*) vieilleries *fpl*; (*old iron*) ferraille *f*; (*inferior goods*) camelote *f*, pacotille *f*, *F* cochonnerie(s) *f* (*pl*) saleté(s) *f*(*pl*); **clear your j. off the table** retire tout ton bazar de la table; **j. dealer** brocanteur, -euse; **j. heap** (*public*) dépotoir *m*; (*in garden etc*) tas *m* de détritus; (*old car*) tas *m* de ferraille; *Fig* **to throw sth/sb on the j. heap** mettre qch/qn au rebut; *Fig* **young people who end up on the j. heap** les jeunes qui finissent sous les ponts; *Am* **j. jewelry** bijoux *mpl* (de) fantaisie; **j. room** pièce *f* de débarras *m*
(b) *Fig F* (*bad-quality book, play etc*) navet *m*, foutaise *f*; *Sl* (*nonsense*) foutaises *fpl*, conneries *fpl*
(c) *Sl* (*heroin etc*) came *f*; **to be on j.** se camer
junk² *vt F* (*get rid of, discard*) (*old furniture, documents etc*) balancer, mettre à la poubelle; (*ideas, plan*) laisser tomber, balancer
junk³ *n* (*Chinese boat*) jonque *f*
junk bond *n Fin* obligation *f* de pacotille, junk bond *m*
junket¹ ['dʒʌŋkɪt] *n* **(a)** *Culin* lait *m* caillé (*souvent parfumé*) **(b)** *F* (*feast*) festin *m*, banquet *m* **(c)** (*pleasure trip*) plaisir *m*, voyage *m* d'agrément; *Pej* (*by public official*) voyage (d'agrément) aux frais de la princesse *ou* du contribuable
junket² *vi* **(a)** (*feast*) banqueter, festoyer **(b)** *Am* (*travel*) faire un voyage d'agrément; *Pej* (*of public official*) voyager aux frais de la princesse *ou* du contribuable
junketing ['dʒʌŋkɪtɪŋ] *n* voyages *mpl* faits aux frais de la princesse *ou* du contribuable
junk food *n* aliment *m* peu nutritif, *F* cochonneries *fpl*; **to eat j.** manger n'importe quoi, *F* manger des cochonneries
junkie ['dʒʌŋkɪ] *n Sl* (*drug addict*) drogué, -ée, camé, -ée; *Fig* **a chocolate/sugar j.** un fou/une folle de chocolat/sucre, un(e) accro du chocolat/sucre; *Fig* **a football/chess j.** un(e) fana de football/d'échecs
junk mail *n Pej* courrier *m* publicitaire, prospectus *mpl*, *F* pub *f*
junkman, *pl* **-men** ['dʒʌŋkmæn, -men] *n Am* chiffonnier *m*, brocanteur *m*
junk shop *n* boutique *f* de brocanteur
junky ['dʒʌŋkɪ] **1** *adj F* (*goods*) de camelote; (*novel, film etc*) nul, à la manque **2** *n Sl* = **junkie**
junkyard ['dʒʌŋkjɑ:d] *n* (*for metal*) dépôt *m* de ferrailleur; (*for rags, discarded objects*) dépôt de chiffonnier; *Fig* **their garden is a real j.** leur jardin est un véritable dépotoir
Juno ['dʒu:nəʊ] *n Myth, Astron* Junon *f*; *Fig* déesse *f*
Junoesque [dʒu:nəʊ'esk] *adj* d'une grâce souveraine
junta ['dʒʌntə] *n Mil, Pol usu Pej* junte *f*
Jupiter ['dʒu:pɪtə*r*] *n Myth* Jupiter *m; Astron* Jupiter *f*
Jurassic [dʒu:'ræsɪk] *adj, n Geol* jurassique *m*
juridical [dʒʊ'rɪdɪk(ə)l] *adj* juridique
jurisdiction [dʒʊərɪs'dɪkʃən] *n* **(a)** *Jur* juridiction *f*; **area within** *or* **under the j. of ...** territoire soumis à l'autorité judiciaire *ou* à la juridiction de ...; **to come** *or* **fall within** *or* **under the j. of a court** (*of question etc*) tomber sous *ou* relever de *ou* rentrer dans la juridiction d'une cour; **to recognize the j. of the Court** reconnaître l'autorité judiciaire du tribunal
(b) (*general authority*) autorité *f*; **to have j. over sb** avoir autorité sur qn; **he has no j. over his brother's activities** il n'a aucune emprise *ou* aucun pouvoir sur ce que fait son frère
(c) *Fig* (*field of activity*) compétence *f*, ressort *m*; **this matter does not come within** *or* **is not in** *or* **falls outside our j.** cette affaire ne relève pas de notre compétence, cette affaire n'est pas de notre compétence *ou* de notre ressort
jurisprudence [dʒʊərɪs'pru:dəns] *n* jurisprudence *f*
jurist ['dʒʊərɪst] *n Fml* (*expert*) juriste *mf*, légiste *m*; (*writer*) juriste; *US* (*lawyer*) avocat, -ate; (*student*) étudiant, -ante en droit
juror ['dʒʊərə*r*] *n* **(a)** *Jur* juré *m*; **woman j.** femme *f* juré, jurée *f* **(b)** (*in competition etc*) membre *m* du jury
jury ['dʒʊərɪ] *n* [①A11,g,i] **(a)** *Jur* jury *m*; **to be** *or* **serve** *or* **sit on the j.** faire partie *ou* être membre du jury, *F* être de jury; **to pack** *or* **rig** *or* **stack a** *or* **the j.** composer un jury partisan; **foreman of the j.** président *m* du jury; **ladies and gentlemen of the j.! members of the j.!** mesdames et messieurs les jurés!; **the j. is out** le jury est en délibération; *Fig F* **the j. is still out on that (one)** (*final decision has not been made*) rien de définitif n'a été décidé; *US Jur* **(federal) grand j.** = tribunal *m* (fédéral) se prononçant sur la mise en accusation; **special j.** jury spécial; **j. fixing,** *Br Sl* **j. nobbling** corruption *f* de jurés; **j. packing** *or* **rigging** *or* **stacking** = composition *f* d'un jury partisan
(b) (*for examination, competition*) jury *m*
jury box *n* banc *m* des jurés
jury duty *n* devoir *m* de participation au jury; **to do one's j.** s'acquitter de son devoir de participation au jury; **to be called (up) for j.** être convoqué comme juré
juryman, *pl* **-men** ['dʒʊərɪmən] *n* juré *m*
jury service *n* devoir *m* de participation au jury; **to do one's j.** s'acquitter de son devoir de participation au jury; **to be called (up) for j.** être convoqué comme juré
jurywoman, *pl* **-women** ['dʒʊərɪwʊmən, -wɪmɪn] *n* femme *f* juré, jurée *f*
just¹ [dʒʌst] **1** *adj* **(a)** (*fair*) (*person, criticism etc*) juste **(to, towards** envers, à l'égard de**)** **(b)** (*legitimate*) (*cause, anger, claim*) juste, légitime; (*reward, punishment, law, peace*) juste; **to get one's j. deserts** avoir ce qu'on mérite; **it's only j. that ...** ce n'est que justice que ... + *sub*; **it's only j. to ask such questions** il est bien normal de poser de telles questions; **as (it) is only j.** comme de juste; **to show j. cause for concern, to have j. cause to be concerned** avoir de bonnes raisons de s'inquiéter **(c)** (*observation, account etc*) juste **2** *npl* **the j.** les justes *mpl*; *Lit* **to sleep the sleep of the j.** dormir du sommeil du juste
just² *adv* **(a)** (*exactly, precisely*) juste, justement, exactement, précisément; **he's j. the man you are looking for** c'est juste *ou* exactement *ou* tout à fait l'homme qu'il vous faut; **that's j. what happened** c'est justement *ou* exactement *ou* bien ce qui est arrivé; **j. how many are there?** combien y en a-t-il au juste *ou* exactement?; **j. why does she do it?** pour quelles raisons exactement le fait-elle?, pourquoi exactement le fait-elle?; **that's j. why she did it** c'est précisément *ou* exactement pour cela qu'elle l'a fait, c'est justement pourquoi elle l'a fait; **j. as you wish** (c'est) comme tu veux; **I left the books j. as they were** *or* **j. the way they were** j'ai laissé les livres exactement comme *ou* tels que je les ai trouvés, j'ai laissé les livres tels quels; **that's j. it** *or* **j. the point!** précisément!, justement!, voilà!; **j. so** (*like this*) exactement comme ça!; *Br* (*that's right*) exactement!, précisément!, voilà!; **he set the vase down j. so** (*carefully*) il a posé le vase avec soin; *F usu Pej* **her house is always j. so** sa maison est toujours archi-impeccable; **it's** *or* **that's j. like him!** (*typical of him*) c'est bien de lui!; **isn't that j. my luck!** c'est bien ma chance!; **I have j. the same problem** j'ai exactement le même problème; **j. the same** (*nevertheless*) cela n'empêche, tout de même
(b) (*with place*) juste; **j. here** juste ici, ici même
(c) (*with time: exactly*) juste; **j. then, j. at that moment** juste à ce moment, à ce moment précis; **it's j. ten o'clock** *or Br* **j. on ten o'clock** il est dix heures juste(s) *ou* pile, il est tout juste dix heures; **j. when** *or* **as the door was opening** au moment même où la porte s'ouvrait; **j. as** *or* **when I was leaving** juste comme *ou* juste quand *ou* au moment même où je partais; **she's j. in time for a drink** elle arrive pile pour *ou* elle arrive juste à temps pour prendre un verre
(d) (*with time: at this moment*) **he's busy j. now** il est occupé en ce moment *ou* pour l'instant; **I'm not ready j. now** *or* **j. yet** je ne suis pas encore prêt, je ne suis pas prêt pour le moment; **she's j. leaving, she's leaving j. now** elle part (tout de suite *ou* à l'instant); **she's not leaving j. now** *or* **j. yet** elle ne part pas encore, elle ne part pas tout de suite; **to be j. about to do sth** être sur le point de faire qch; **(I'm) j. coming!, I'm coming j. now!** j'arrive!; **my hair is j. turning grey** *or* **is j. beginning to turn grey** mes cheveux commencent juste à grisonner
(e) [①B29,10] (*with time: a short while ago, recently*) **to have j. arrived/woken up/written a letter** venir d'arriver/de se réveiller/d'écrire une lettre; **I've only j. seen him and I haven't had time yet to ...** je viens seulement de le voir et je n'ai pas encore eu le temps de ...; **I've (only) j. seen him going downstairs** je viens de le voir à l'instant qui descendait; **I saw him j. now, I've j. (now) seen him** je l'ai vu à l'instant, je viens de le voir; **I've only j. this minute seen him** je viens de le voir à l'instant, je l'ai vu à l'instant; **I saw him j. yesterday, I j. saw him yesterday** je l'ai vu pas plus tard qu'hier; **he has j. (now) left school** il sort du lycée; **'j. picked/cooked'** (*newly*) 'cueilli/cuit du jour'; **'j. arrived'** 'fraîchement arrivé'
(f) (*only, no more than*) seulement, juste; **I have come j. to see you** je viens seulement *ou* juste *ou* uniquement pour

vous voir; **we have j. a few copies left** il nous (en) reste quelques exemplaires seulement *ou* juste quelques exemplaires; **I've got j. one left** il ne m'en reste qu'un; **she's j. a baby** ce n'est qu'un bébé; **it costs j. ten dollars** ça ne coûte que dix dollars, ça coûte dix dollars seulement; **it's j. ten o'clock** il est seulement dix heures, il n'est que dix heures; **(wait) j. a moment!** (attendez) un petit instant!, un instant!; **j. a minute, aren't you supposed to be somewhere else?** une seconde, tu n'es pas censé être ailleurs?; **give me j. a tiny bit** donnez-m'en (juste) un petit peu *ou* rien qu'un petit peu

(g) (*only a little, slightly*) juste, (un) peu; **j. a little more/ less/better** juste un peu plus/moins/mieux; **j. in front/ behind/above/below** juste devant/derrière/au-dessus/au-dessous; **j. over/under fifty pounds** un tout petit peu plus de/moins de cinquante livres; **it's j. before ten (o'clock)** il est presque dix heures; **we go to bed j. before ten (o'clock)** nous nous couchons juste avant *ou* peu avant dix heures; **j. after my birthday** juste après *ou* peu après mon anniversaire

(h) (*merely, simply*) simplement; **tell him j. to wait** dites-lui qu'il n'a qu'à attendre; *F* **I'll j. pop in** je ne ferai qu'entrer et sortir; **j. ask if you need money** vous n'avez qu'à demander si vous avez besoin d'argent; **they won't accept j. to please <u>me</u>** ils n'accepteront pas uniquement pour *ou* rien que pour me faire plaisir à moi; **we j. can't understand it** nous n'arrivons vraiment pas à comprendre; **why not? – because I j. don't** pourquoi pas? – parce que c'est comme ça; **I j. don't want to** je ne veux pas, un point c'est tout

(i) (*easily*) **I can j. see him as a doctor** je le vois très bien médecin; **I can j. smell the sea air, looking at these photos** rien qu'en regardant ces photos je sens l'air de la mer

(j) (*by a narrow margin, barely*) **(only) j.** de justesse; **he (only) j. (about) managed to catch the train** il a eu le train de justesse, c'est tout juste s'il a eu le train; **they (only) j. missed the train** ils ont manqué le train de peu; **I have (only) j. enough** *or* **j. about enough to live on** j'ai tout juste de quoi vivre; **she caught the train but (only) j.** elle a eu le train mais c'était juste *ou* c'était de justesse; **you're (only) j. in time** vous arrivez à temps, mais c'est de justesse

(k) (*utterly, completely*) absolument; **it was j. splendid!** c'était absolument merveilleux!, c'était merveilleux, ni plus ni moins!; **it was j. a nightmare** c'était un véritable cauchemar; *Br* **do you remember? – don't I j.!** vous vous en souvenez? – et comment (que je m'en souviens) *ou* vous pensez (si je m'en souviens)!

(l) (*in comparisons*) **j. as, j. about as** tout aussi; **that's j. (about) as good** c'est tout aussi bien, c'est tout comme; **that will do j. as well** ça fera aussi bien l'affaire

(m) (*in threats, orders, exhortations*) **j. (you) try!** essaie donc un peu!; **j. (you) wait!** tu n'as qu'à attendre!; (*threat*) attends, tu vas voir!, tu ne perds rien pour attendre!; **j. (you) read this!** lisez donc cela!; **j. think** réfléchis donc un peu; **j. look!** regardez-moi ça!; **j. be quiet, will you!** veux-tu bien te taire!; **j. who do you think you are?** pour qui vous prenez-vous, au juste?

(n) **j. about** (*approximately*) plus ou moins, à peu près; (*almost*) quasiment; **it's j. about ten (o'clock)** il est plus ou moins *ou* à peu près dix heures; **j. about!** plus ou moins!, à peu près!; *F* **that j. about does it** (*I'm leaving*) ça suffit comme ça *ou* amplement *ou* largement; **I've j. about had enough of this** j'en ai vraiment par dessus la tête de ça

(o) (*indicating preference*) **I would j. as soon stay here** j'aimerais tout autant rester ici; **he would j. as soon that ...** il aimerait tout autant que ... + *sub*

(p) **it's j. as well (that)** ... (*fortunate*) heureusement que ...; **and (it was) j. as well** et c'était une chance, et tant mieux; **I might j. as well have remained silent** j'aurais (tout) aussi bien fait de garder le silence; **they could j. as well do without it** ils feraient (tout) aussi bien de s'en passer

justice [ˈdʒʌstɪs] *n* **(a)** (*no pl*) (*power of law*) justice *f*; **to administer** *or* **dispense/exercise j.** rendre/exercer la justice; **to demand/obtain j.** demander/obtenir justice; **to bring sb to j.** traduire qn en justice

(b) (*no pl*) (*fairness*) (*of cause, claim, decision etc*) légitimité *f*; (*of reward, punishment*) justice *f*; **in all j.** en toute justice; **in (all) j. to her, we should say ...** pour être juste envers elle *ou* pour lui rendre justice, on devrait dire ...; **to do sb j., to do j. to sb** (*of photo, garment, hairstyle etc*) avantager qn, mettre qn en valeur; **to do j. to a meal** faire honneur à un repas; **to do oneself j.** se mettre en valeur, se montrer sous son meilleur jour; *Fml* **with j.** (*with good reason*) avec juste raison, à juste titre

(c) (*judge in Supreme Court*) juge *m*; **Mr J. Long** (*title*) Monsieur le juge Long; **Mrs J. Long** Madame le juge Long

Justice Department *n US* Ministère *m* de la Justice

justice of the peace *n* juge *m* de paix

justifiable [ˈdʒʌstɪfaɪəb(ə)l] *adj* justifié, légitime; *Jur* **j. homicide** homicide *m* justifiable

justifiably [ˈdʒʌstɪfaɪəblɪ] *adv* légitimement, à juste titre; **they acted quite j.** ils ont agi en toute légitimité

justification [dʒʌstɪfɪˈkeɪʃən] *n* **(a)** justification *f* **(for** de, pour); **in j. of** comme justification de; **there's no j. for behaviour like that!** rien ne peut justifier un tel comportement!; **what's her j. for this?** comment justifie-t-elle ceci?; **with some j., I might add** à juste titre, ajouterais-je; **that's no j.!** ce n'est pas une raison! **(b)** *Typ, Comptr* justification *f*; **left/right j.** justification à gauche/droite

justify [ˈdʒʌstɪfaɪ] *vt* **(a)** (*person, decision, action, sb's behaviour etc*) justifier; **to j. oneself in the eyes of sb** se justifier aux yeux de qn; **that does not j. your voting for my rival** cela n'est pas une raison suffisante pour que vous votiez pour mon rival; **to be justified in doing sth** (*have a good reason to*) avoir de bonnes raisons pour faire qch, être fondé à faire qch; **a fully justified decison/fear** une décision/ une crainte bien fondée *ou* qui se justifie; **am I justified in thinking that ...?** ai-je raison de croire que ...?

(b) *Typ, Comptr* justifier; **left/right justified** justifié à gauche/droite

just-in-time production *n Mktg* production *f* juste à temps

just-in-time purchasing *n Mktg* achat *m* juste à temps

justly [ˈdʒʌstlɪ] *adv* (*fairly, rightly*) avec justice, justement; **j. famous** (*deservedly*) célèbre à juste titre

justness [ˈdʒʌstnɪs] *n* **(a)** (*of cause, demand*) légitimité *f* **(b)** (*accuracy*) (*of idea, remark etc*) justesse *f*

► **jut out** [dʒʌt] **(-tt-) 1** *vi* (*of balcony, rock etc*) faire saillie, être en saillie; **to j. out over sth** (*overhang*) surplomber qch, avancer sur qch; **the headland juts (out) into the sea** le cap avance (en saillie) dans la mer; **something is jutting out of your pocket** quelque chose dépasse de votre poche; **his chin juts out** il a un menton en galoche **2** *vtsep* (*chin*) avancer

jute [dʒuːt] *n* (*plant, fibre*) jute *m*

juvenile [ˈdʒuːvɪnaɪl, *Am* -ˈn(ə)l] **1** *adj* **(a)** *Pej* (*childish*) (*behaviour, ideas etc*) puéril; **don't be so j.!** ne sois pas si puéril *ou* gamin! **(b)** (*for young people*) (*books, games etc*) pour enfants, pour la jeunesse; (*hobbies, activities*) d'enfant(s); *Fml* (*youthful*) juvénile **2** *n Fml* jeune *mf*, adolescent, -ente

juvenile court *n Jur* tribunal *m* pour enfants

juvenile delinquency *n* délinquance *f* juvénile

juvenile delinquent *n* jeune délinquant, -ante

juvenile offender *n* accusé, -ée mineur(e)

juvenilia [dʒuːvɪˈnɪlɪə] *npl* œuvres *fpl* de jeunesse; **a piece of Mozart j.** une œuvre de jeunesse de Mozart

juxtapose [dʒʌkstəˈpəʊz] *vt* juxtaposer

juxtaposition [dʒʌkstəpəˈzɪʃən] *n* juxtaposition *f*; **to be in j.** se juxtaposer

K

K[1], k [keɪ] *n* **(a)** (*letter*) K, k *m* **(b)** (*abbr* **kilo**) k.

K[2] *n* **(a)** (*thousand (pounds)*) **he earns 30K** il gagne 30KF **(b)** *Comptr* (*abbr* **kilobyte**) Ko *m*; **how many k are left?** combien de Ko reste-t-il?; **720k diskette** disquette *f* de 720 Ko

kaffeeklatsch [ˈkæfeɪklætʃ] *n Am* = réunion *f* de femmes qui bavardent en prenant le café

Kaffir [ˈkæfər] *Offensive Sl* **1** *adj* caf(f)re **2** *n* Caf(f)re *mf*

Kafkaesque [kæfkəˈesk] *adj* kafkaïen

kaftan [ˈkæftæn] *n* kaftan *m*

kale, kail [keɪl] *n* (*cabbage*) **(curly) k.** chou *m* frisé

kaleidoscope [kəˈlaɪdəskəʊp] *n* kaléidoscope *m*

kaleidoscopic [kəlaɪdəˈskɒpɪk] *adj* kaléidoscopique

kamikaze [kæmɪˈkɑːzɪ] *adj, n* kamikaze *m*

kangaroo [kæŋgəˈruː] *n* **(a)** (*animal*) kangourou *m* **(b)** **k. court** tribunal *m* irrégulier

Kan(s) *abbr* **Kansas**

kaolin [ˈkeɪəlɪn] *n* kaolin *m*

kapok [ˈkeɪpɒk] *n* kapok *m*; *Bot* **k. tree** kapokier *m*

Kaposi's sarcoma [kæˈpəʊsɪzsɑːˈkəʊmə] *n Med* sarcome de Kaposi *m*

kaput [kəˈpʊt] *adj F* fichu, foutu

karakul [ˈkærəkʊl] *n* (*sheep, fur*) karakul *m*, caracul *m*

karaoke [kæræˈəʊkeɪ] *n Mus* karaoké *m*; **k. machine** karaoké *m*

karate [kəˈrɑːtɪ] *n Sp* karaté *m*; **k. chop** coup *m* de karaté

karma [ˈkɑːmə] *n Hindu Rel* karma *m*

kart [kɑːt] *n* kart *m*; **k. racing** karting *m*

karting [ˈkɑːtɪŋ] *n* karting *m*

Kashmir [kæʃˈmɪər] **1** *n Geog* Cachemire *m*; *Tex* cachemire *m* **2** *adj* **k.** en cachemire; **k. wool** cachemire *m*

kayak [ˈkaɪæk] *n* (*canoe*) kayac *m*, kayak *m*

KB [keɪˈbiː] *n Comptr* (*abbr* **kilobyte**) Ko *m*

KBE [keɪbiːˈiː] *n Br* (*abbr* **Knight (Commander of the Order) of the British Empire**) Chevalier *m* de l'Ordre de l'Empire britannique

KCB [keɪsiːˈbiː] *n Br* (*abbr* **Knight Commander (of the Order) of the Bath**) Chevalier *m* Commandeur de l'Ordre du Bain

kebab [kəˈbæb] *n Culin* kébab *m*

kedge[1] [kedʒ] *n Naut* **k. (anchor)** ancre *f* à jet

kedge[2] *Naut* **1** *vt* (*boat*) haler, touer sur une ancre à jet **2** *vi* se touer sur une ancre à jet

kedgeree [kedʒəˈriː] *n Culin* = mets *m* de riz accommodé avec du beurre, des œufs et du poisson

keel[1] [kiːl] *n* **(a)** *Naut, Av* quille *f*; **on an even k.** *Naut* sans différence de tirant d'eau *ou* de calaison; *Fig* stable; **to be back on an even k.** (*of situation etc*) être de nouveau stable, s'être stabilisé; (*of person*) avoir retrouvé son égalité d'âme; **to put a company/the economy (back) on an even k.** (re)mettre une entreprise/l'économie d'aplomb **(b)** *Bot* (*of leaf, petal etc*) carène *f*

keel[2] *vt* (*boat*) mettre en carène

▶ **keel over 1** *vi* (*of boat*) chavirer; *F* (*of person*) (*unconscious*) tomber dans les pommes; (*dead*) tomber raide mort; (*of structure, hut etc*) se renverser; **to k. over backwards** tomber à la renverse **2** *vtsep* (*boat*) faire chavirer

keelhaul [ˈkiːlhɔːl] *vt* **(a)** *Naut, Hist* (*sailor*) faire passer sous la quille **(b)** (*rebuke*) réprimander sévèrement, *F* passer un savon à

keen[1] [kiːn] *adj* **(a)** (*enthusiastic*) (*yachtsman, follower*) ardent, assidu; (*reader*) passionné; (*at school, work*) zélé; **as a k. reader of your articles, I ...** lecteur assidu de vos articles, je ...; **I'll come with you, but I'm not k.** j'y vais avec toi, mais je n'en brûle pas d'envie; **look, I'm really not k.** écoute, je n'en ai vraiment pas envie *ou* je n'y tiens vraiment pas; **she's very k. for us to do it** elle tient beaucoup à ce que nous le fassions; **he seemed very k. at first** (*on idea, proposal etc*) au départ il avait l'air très enthousiaste; **to be as k. as mustard** déborder d'enthousiasme, brûler d'ardeur; **to be k. on doing sth** avoir très envie de faire qch; **to be k. on sth** (*on golf, politics, novel*) adorer qch; (*idea, proposal*) être plein d'enthousiasme pour qch; **he wasn't k. on the idea** l'idée ne l'emballait pas; **she's k. on him** il lui plaît; **she's k. on sport** le sport la passionne, elle adore le sport; **to take a k. interest in sth** suivre qch avec un intérêt vif; **a k. desire for peace** un ardent désir de paix; **k. competition** concurrence *f* acharnée *ou* âpre; **there is a k. demand for these stocks** ces fonds sont activement recherchés; *Br Com* **k. prices** prix *mpl* au plus bas, prix étudiés; **k. golfer** enragé *m* de golf; **k. sportsman** ardent sportif *m*; **a k. advocate of ...** un partisan fervent de ...

(b) (*perceptive*) (*eye, look*) perçant, pénétrant, vif; (*mind*) fin, pénétrant, vif; **to have a k. eye for a bargain** être prompt à reconnaître une bonne affaire; **to have a k. ear** avoir l'oreille *ou* l'ouïe fine; **to have a k. ear for a tune/for accents** reconnaître facilement les mélodies/les accents; **a k. sense of smell** un odorat très développé; **to have a k. awareness of a problem** être profondément conscient d'un problème

(c) (*intense*) (*sorrow*) aigu, *f* aiguë; (*regret*) poignant; (*remorse*) cuisant; **k. appetite** rude appétit *m*; **to have a k. appetite for success** avoir un appétit de succès dévorant; **k. pleasure** vif plaisir *m*

(d) (*cold*) (*wind, air*) vif, piquant

(e) (*sharp*) (*knife, blade*) affilé, aiguisé; *Fig* (*sound*) aigu; **k. edge** fil *m* tranchant; **k. edged** bien affilé, aiguisé, tranchant

(f) *US Sl* (*very good*) génial

keen[2] *vi* (*at funeral*) chanter une mélopée (*en veillant un corps*)

keenly [ˈkiːnlɪ] *adv* **(a)** (*enthusiastically*) avec enthousiasme; **to be k. interested in ...** s'intéresser vivement à ...; **a k. contested competition/election/***etc* une compétition/des élections/*etc* âprement disputée(s) **(b)** (*intensely*) profondément; (*to regret*) amèrement; **to feel sth k.** être profondément affecté par qch **(c)** **the wind was blowing k.** il faisait un vent âpre

keenness [ˈkiːnnɪs] *n* **(a)** (*of person*) enthousiasme *m*; (*at school, work*) zèle *m*; (*of troops*) mordant *m*; **k. on doing sth** grand désir *m* de faire qch **(b)** (*of sight*) acuité *f*; (*of hearing, sense of smell*) finesse *f*; (*of mind*) pénétration *f*, finesse *f* **(c)** (*of feeling, emotion etc*) intensité *f*; (*of grief, sense of remorse*) acuité *f* **(d)** (*of blade*) tranchant *m* **(e)** (*of the cold*) âpreté *f*, rigueur *f*

keep[1] [kiːp] *n* **(a)** (*food*) nourriture *f*; (*money*) frais *mpl* de subsistance; **to pay for one's k.** payer sa pension; **do you give your parents any money for your k.?** est-ce que tu donnes de l'argent à tes parents pour payer ta pension?; **she can only just afford to pay for her k.** elle arrive tout juste à se nourrir et à se loger; **to earn one's k.** (*earn a living*) subvenir à ses besoins; (*pay one's way*) (*of employee*) mériter son salaire; (*of lodger etc*) rendre de menus services pour payer sa pension; **to earn its k.** (*of equipment*) être rentable; **the van may be old but it still earns its k.** la camionnette est vieille mais elle nous rend encore bien service

(b) (*of castle*) donjon *m*

(c) *F* **for keeps** pour de bon

keep[2] (*pt & pp* **kept** [kept]) **1** *vt* **(a)** (*retain*) (*sth*) garder; (*sb's attention*) retenir; **you can k. the book I lent you** vous pouvez garder le livre que je vous ai prêté; **to k. sth for sb** garder qch pour qn; **I asked them to k. it for me** je leur ai demandé de me le garder; **to k. from sb sth** (*not inform of*) ne pas révéler qch à qn; **to k. sth for later** garder *ou* conserver *ou* réserver qch pour plus tard; **to k. the best for** *or* **until last** garder le meilleur pour la fin; **to k. sth in reserve** *or* **in store** tenir qch en réserve; **to k. a seat for sb** garder une place à qn; **to k. one's figure** garder la ligne; **to k. its shape/colour** (*of garment*) conserver sa forme/couleur; **to k. one's job** garder *ou* conserver son emploi

(b) (*store*) (*provisions, letters etc*) garder; **the cupboard where I k. the crockery** l'armoire où je mets la vaisselle; **k. medicines out of the reach of children** ranger les médicaments hors de la portée des enfants

(c) (*maintain*) (*order*) maintenir; (*silence, secret*) garder; **to k. one's composure** garder son sang-froid; **to k. one's course** continuer *ou* poursuivre son chemin; **he keeps**

himself to himself il est très réservé; **he prefers to k. himself to himself** il évite les contacts; **they k. themselves to themselves** ils font bande à part

(**d**) (*maintain in a condition*) **to k. sth clean/secret** tenir qch propre/secret; **k. dry** craint l'humidité; *F* **k. it clean!** (*no vulgarity*) pas de grossièretés!; **to k. oneself warm** (*by staying in the warmth*) se tenir au chaud; (*by dressing warmly*) s'habiller chaudement; **to k. the door open/shut** garder *ou* laisser la porte ouverte/fermée; **the noise kept me awake** le bruit m'a empêché de dormir; **to k. sb wondering** laisser qn se poser des questions; **to k. sb waiting** faire attendre qn; **troops were kept on the alert** les soldats ont été maintenus en état d'alerte; **to k. one's hands in one's pockets** garder les mains dans ses poches

(**e**) (*look after, tend*) (*sheep, herds*) garder; (*garden etc*) entretenir; (*person*) subvenir aux besoins de; (*mistress*) entretenir; **well/badly kept road** route bien/mal entretenue; **he doesn't earn enough to k. himself** il ne gagne pas de quoi vivre; **he has his parents to k.** il a ses parents à (sa) charge; **I've got a family to k.** j'ai une famille à nourrir

(**f**) (*possess*) (*bees, poultry etc*) élever; (*shop*) tenir

(**g**) (*detain*) (*at home, in hospital, prison*) garder; **the doctor kept him in bed** le médecin l'a obligé à garder le lit; **there was nothing to k. me in England/with that firm** rien ne me retenait en Angleterre/dans cette entreprise; **what kept you?** qu'est-ce qui t'a retardé?; *Iron* comment tu as fait pour aller si vite?; **don't let me k. you** (*from your work etc*) je ne veux pas te retenir

(**h**) (*observe*) (*the law, a rule*) observer, suivre; (*promise*) tenir, remplir; (*vow*) rester fidèle à; (*treaty*) tenir, respecter, observer; (*date, appointment*) ne pas manquer à; **to k. late hours** se coucher tard; **to k. one's word** tenir (sa) parole; *Rel* **to k. the commandments** observer les commandements; **if you cannot k. the appointment** si vous ne pouvez pas être présent au rendez-vous

(**i**) (*diary, accounts, Com the books*) tenir; **to k. a record of events** prendre les événements en note; **to k. a note of sth** noter qch

(**j**) (*protect*) préserver (**sb from evil** qn du mal); **God k. (you)!** Dieu vous garde!; **God k. his soul!** (que) Dieu ait son âme!; *Sp* **to k. goal** être gardien de but; *Cr* **to k. wicket** garder le guichet

(**k**) (*celebrate*) (*festival, feast day*) célébrer

2 *vi* (**a**) (*remain, stay*) rester, se tenir; **to k. well** (*stay*) rester en bonne santé; **are you keeping well?** vous vous portez bien?; **she doesn't k. well** elle ne jouit pas d'une bonne santé; **how are you keeping?** comment allez-vous?; **to k. quiet** se tenir *ou* rester tranquille; **to k. awake/calm** rester éveillé/calme; **the weather is keeping cool/fine** le temps reste frais/se maintient au beau

(**b**) (*continue*) continuer; **to k. straight on** continuer tout droit; **k. (to the) left/right** serrez à gauche/droite; **to k. doing sth** ne pas cesser *ou* ne pas arrêter de faire qch; **to k. working** continuer de travailler; **to k. smiling** garder le sourire; **don't k. asking questions** ne posez pas tout le temps des questions; **I wish you wouldn't k. saying that** j'aimerais bien que tu arrêtes de répéter cela; **I don't know how she keeps going on so little sleep** je ne sais pas comment elle arrive à tenir le coup en dormant si peu; **it's amazing the firm has kept going for so long** c'est incroyable que l'entreprise soit parvenue à se maintenir aussi longtemps

(**c**) (*of food etc*) se garder, se conserver; **the story will k.** (*you can tell it to me later*) l'histoire n'y perdra rien; **what I've got to tell you won't k. till tomorrow** ce que j'ai à te dire n'attendra pas jusqu'à demain; **will it k. till later?** (*news etc*) est-ce que ça peut attendre?

▶ **keep at 1** *vipo* (**a**) (*continue to work at*) (*one's homework etc*) travailler; **to k. hard at it** travailler sans relâche (**b**) (*nag*) **to k. at sb to do sth** harceler qn *ou F* être toujours sur le dos de qn pour qu'il fasse qch **2** *vtaspo* **to k. sb at it** (*working*) faire travailler qn

▶ **keep away 1** *vi* ne pas approcher (**from** de); **she told the children to k. away from the river** elle a dit aux enfants de ne pas s'approcher de la rivière; **k. away (from me)!** n'approchez pas!; **I can't k. away from chocolates** je ne peux pas résister quand je vois des chocolats; **to k. away from drugs/alcohol** ne pas toucher à la drogue/à l'alcool

2 *vtas* **k. that dog away (from me)!** tenez ce chien loin de moi!; **the wind will k. the rain away** le vent empêchera la pluie; **to k. matches away from the children** tenir les allumettes hors de la portée des enfants; **the rain kept a lot of spectators away** la pluie a dissuadé bien des spectateurs de venir

▶ **keep back 1** *vi* ne pas approcher; **k. back!** n'approche pas! **2** *vtsep* (**a**) (*crowd*) contenir, retenir; (*tears*) refouler, retenir; **he tried desperately to k. back his laughter** il s'efforça désespérément de se retenir *ou* s'empêcher de rire (**b**) (*withhold*) **to k. a sum back from sb's wages** retenir une somme sur le salaire de qn; **you're keeping something back from me** tu me caches quelque chose (**c**) *Sch* (*pupil*) garder en retenue; (*oblige to repeat a year*) faire redoubler; **to be kept back a year** redoubler (**d**) (*delay*) retenir; (*of strong wind etc*) retarder (**e**) (*prevent from making progress*) (*of lack of qualifications etc*) handicaper

▶ **keep down 1** *vi* se baisser **2** *vtas* (*head, voice*) baisser; **to k. the noise (level) down** faire moins de bruit; *Fig* **to k. one's head down** garder un profil bas; **I can't k. my food down** je rejette tout ce que je mange **3** *vtsep* (*repress*) garder le contrôle sur, avoir la mainmise sur; (*prices*) empêcher d'augmenter; **they were kept down by a repressive government** ils étaient contrôlés par un gouvernement répressif; *prov* **you can't k. a good man down** les hommes de bien sont toujours récompensés

▶ **keep from 1** *vtaspo* (**a**) (*conceal*) **to k. sth from sb** cacher qch à qn (**b**) (*prevent*) **to k. sb from doing sth** empêcher qn de faire qch (**c**) (*distract*) **to k. sb from his/her work** retenir qn de son travail **2** *vipo* (*refrain*) **to k. from doing sth** se retenir de faire qch

▶ **keep in 1** *vtsep* (*person*) empêcher de sortir; *Sch* (*pupil*) garder en retenue; (*fire*) entretenir; **the police/the doctor kept him in overnight** la police/le docteur l'a gardé pour la nuit; *Fig* **to k. one's hand in** garder la main

2 *vtaspo* (*keep supplied with*) **to k. sb in sth** (*of person*) approvisionner qn en qch; **to k. sb in clothes/food** fournir de l'habillement/de la nourriture à qn; **to k. sb in beer/cigarettes** payer sa bière/ses cigarettes à qn; **to k. sb in luxury** permettre à qn de vivre dans le luxe; **his pocket money just about kept him in beer** son argent de poche lui servait tout juste à payer sa bière; **the grant barely keeps me in food** ma bourse me permet tout juste de me payer de quoi manger

▶ **keep in with** *vipo F* **to k. in with sb** cultiver qn, rester en bons termes avec qn

▶ **keep off 1** *vi* (*stay away*) ne pas approcher **2** *vipo* **k. off the grass!** défense de marcher sur le gazon!; **would you please k. off those flower beds** s'il vous plaît, ne marchez pas sur ces parterres de fleurs; **if you don't k. off my property ...** si vous pénétrez dans ma propriété ... **3** *vtaspo* **to k. your hands off that!** n'y touchez pas!; **k. your hands off me** bas les mains *ou F* les pattes! **4** *vtas* **to k. one's coat off** rester sans (son) manteau; **the wind will k. the rain off** le vent empêchera la pluie

▶ **keep on 1** *vi* (**a**) continuer; **to k. on doing sth** continuer à faire qch, ne pas cesser de faire qch; **don't k. on asking questions** ne posez pas tout le temps des questions

(**b**) (*annoyingly, naggingly*) **don't k. on so!** arrête!; **I can't stand the way he keeps on about it** je ne supporte pas qu'il insiste tout le temps là-dessus; **he just keeps on and on about it** il n'arrête pas d'en parler

2 *vtsep* (**a**) (*continue to wear*) (*coat etc*) garder

(**b**) (*not turn off*) **to k. the central heating on** maintenir le chauffage central; **to k. the lights/TV on** laisser les lumières/la télé allumée(s)

(**c**) (*continue to employ*) garder; **he was kept on by the firm** l'entreprise l'a gardé

▶ **keep on at** *vipo F* **to k. on at sb (to do sth)** harceler qn *ou F* être toujours sur le dos de qn (pour qu'il fasse qch)

▶ **keep out 1** *vi* (*avoid, stay away from*) ne pas entrer (**of** dans); **to k. out of danger** rester à l'abri du danger; **try to k. out of trouble** essaie de ne pas t'attirer d'ennuis; **to k. out of an argument** rester en dehors d'une dispute; **k. out** (*sign*) défense d'entrer; **k. out of this!** mêlez-vous de ce qui vous regarde! **2** *vtsep* (*prevent from entering*) empêcher d'entrer

▶ **keep to 1** *vipo* (**a**) (*adhere to*) (*promise*) tenir; **to k. to a subject** s'en tenir à un sujet; **to k. to the script** (*of actors*) s'en tenir au script

(**b**) (*remain in, on*) rester dans; (*the left, the right*) tenir; **to k. to one's bed** garder le lit; **to k. to main roads** rester sur les grandes routes

2 *vtaspo* (**a**) (*hold*) **to k. sb to a promise** faire tenir une promesse à qn; **to k. delays/costs to a minimum** minimiser les délais/les coûts

(**b**) (*not reveal*) **to k. sth to oneself** garder qch pour soi, taire qch; **to k. one's impressions/opinions to oneself** garder ses impressions/opinions pour soi; **you can k. your remarks to yourself!** tes remarques, tu peux te les garder!; **k. your hands to yourself!** bas les mains *ou F* les pattes!

▶ **keep up 1** *vi* (**a**) (*of rain, snow etc*) continuer

(**b**) (*remain level, go at same speed*) tenir le rythme

2 *vtsep* (**a**) (*maintain*) (*building, road etc*) entretenir

(b) (*continue*) (*custom*) conserver; (*correspondence, one's French etc*) entretenir; **we must k. it up** il nous faut continuer nos efforts; **k. it up!** continuez!; **k. up the good work!** continuez à bien travailler!

(c) (*stop from falling or waning*) (*building, interest etc*) soutenir; (*courage*) soutenir, maintenir; **to k. up appearances** garder *ou* sauver les apparences

(d) (*stop from going to bed*) empêcher d'aller se coucher; (*stop from sleeping*) empêcher de dormir; **worry had kept her up all night** l'inquiétude l'avait tenue éveillée toute la nuit

▶ **keep up with** *vipo* (a) (*remain level with, go at same speed as*) **to k. up with sb** aller à la même allure que qn; **I can't k. up with you** vous marchez/parlez/*etc* trop vite pour moi; **he couldn't k. up with the rest of the children in his class** il n'arrivait pas à suivre dans sa classe; **I can barely k. up with her** (*she changes so much*) ça change tellement vite avec elle que j'ai du mal à suivre; *F* **to k. up with the Joneses** rivaliser de standing avec ses voisins; **to k. up with events** suivre les événements; **to k. up with the times** être à la page

(b) (*remain in contact*) **to k. up with sb** rester en contact avec qn

keeper ['ki:pər] *n* (*person*) garde *m*; (*in zoo, of park, lighthouse*) gardien, -ienne; (*of museum etc*) conservateur *m*; (*of herds*) gardien, -ienne, gardeur, -euse; (*gamekeeper*) garde-chasse *m*, *pl* gardes-chasse(s); *Fb F* goal *m*, gardien de but; **I'm not my brother's k.** je ne suis pas responsable de mon frère

keep-fit *n* **to do k.** faire de la gymnastique; **k. class** cours *m* de gymnastique

keeping ['ki:pɪŋ] *n* (*of rule, promise*) observation *f*; (*of feast day*) célébration *f*; **to have sb/sth in one's k.** avoir qn/qch en garde *ou* sous sa garde; **in God's k.** à la garde de Dieu; **in k. with ...** en accord avec ...; **in k. with their commitment** conformément à leur engagement; **it is in k. with his principles** c'est conforme à *ou* en accord avec ses principes; **it's in k. with everything I have been told about her** cela concorde avec tout ce qu'on m'a dit sur elle; **out of k. with ...** en désaccord avec ...; **it was rather out of k. with the spirit of the occasion** cela détonnait avec l'esprit de l'occasion; **good k. qualities** (*of food*) bonnes qualités à la conservation

keepsake ['ki:pseɪk] *n* souvenir *m*; **as a k. of his visit** en souvenir de sa visite

keg [keg] *n* (*of beer*) barillet *m*; (*of water*) tonnelet *m*; (*of herring*) caque *f*

keg beer *n Br Culin* bière *f* pression

kelp [kelp] *n* (*seaweed*) varech *m*

Ken *abbr* **Kentucky**

ken¹ [ken] *n Lit* **within sb's k.** dans les connaissances *ou* la compétence de qn; **beyond sb's k.** hors de la compétence de qn

ken² *vt Scot, Dial* = **know²**

kennel ['ken(ə)l] *n* (a) (*of guard dog etc*) niche *f*; (*of hunting dog*) chenil *m*; **kennels** établissement *m* d'élevage de chiens; **to put a dog into kennels** mettre un chien en pension (b) **the k.** (*hounds*) la meute (c) (*of fox*) terrier *m*

kennelmaid ['ken(ə)lmeɪd] *n* employée *f* d'éleveur de chiens *ou* de chenil

Kenya ['ki:njə, 'ken-] *n* Kenya *m*

Kenyan ['kenjən] **1** *adj* kenyan **2** *n* Kenyan, -ane

kept¹ [kept] *adj Old-fashioned, Hum* **k. woman** femme *f* entretenue

kept² *pt, pp see* **keep²**

kerb [kɜ:b] *n Br* bordure *f ou* bord *m* de trottoir; **to draw up at the k.** s'arrêter le long du trottoir; *St Exch F* **business done on the k.** opérations effectuées en coulisse, après clôture de Bourse; *Aut* **k. weight** poids *m* à vide, poids en ordre de marche

kerb broker *n St Exch F* coulissier *m*, courtier *m* en valeurs mobilières

kerbcrawl ['kɜ:bkrɔ:l] *vi* accoster les prostitué(e)s en voiture

kerbcrawler ['kɜ:bkrɔ:lər] *n* personne *f* qui accoste les prostitué(e)s en voiture

kerbcrawling ['kɜ:bkrɔ:lɪŋ] *n* accostage *m* de prostitué(e)s en voiture

kerb drill *n Aut* précautions *fpl* pour traverser la rue

kerbstone ['kɜ:bstəʊn] *n Br* (*of pavement*) pierre *f* de parement

kerbstone market *n St Exch F* coulisse *f*

kerchief ['kɜ:tʃɪf] *n Old-fashioned* (*for head*) mouchoir *m* de tête; (*for neck*) fichu *m*

kerfuffle [kə'fʌf(ə)l] *n esp Br F* remue-ménage *m*, tohu-bohu *m*

kern [kɜ:n] *vt Typ* créner, rapprocher

kernel ['kɜ:n(ə)l] *n* (a) (*of nut*) intérieur *m*; (*in stone*) amande *f* (*of pine cone*) pignon *m*; (*of cereal*) grain *m* (b) *Fig* (*of problem etc*) fond *m*, essentiel *m*; **a k. of truth** un fond de vérité

kerning ['kɜ:nɪŋ] *n Typ* crénage *m*, rapprochement *m* de caractères

kerosene ['kerəsi:n] *n* (a) *Av* kérosène *m* (b) *Am* (*paraffin*) pétrole *m* lampant; **k. lamp** lampe *f* à pétrole

kestrel ['kestrəl] *n* (*bird*) (faucon *m*) crécerelle *f*

ketch [ketʃ] *n Naut* ketch *m*, dundee *m*, dindet *m*

ketchup ['ketʃəp] *n* (**tomato**) **k.** ketchup *m*

kettle [ket(ə)l] *n* (*for boiling water*) bouilloire *f*; (*for cooking*) chaudron *m*; **to boil a k. of water** mettre une bouilloire d'eau à bouillir; **has the k. boiled?** est-ce que l'eau a bouilli?; **I'll put the k. on** je mets l'eau à chauffer pour le thé *etc*; *F* **here's a pretty** *or* **a fine k. of fish!** nous voilà dans de beaux draps!; *F* **that's quite a different k. of fish** ça c'est une autre affaire

kettledrum ['ket(ə)ldrʌm] *n Mus* timbale *f*

key¹ [ki:] **1** *n* (a) (*of lock, door etc*) clef *f*, clé *f*; **to turn the k.** (**in the door**) donner un tour de clef (à la porte); *Old-fashioned Fig* **to have the k. of the door** (*have reached one's majority*) avoir atteint sa majorité; **k. card** (*for hotel room*) carte-clé *f*, *pl* cartes-clés

(b) *Fig* **the k. to happiness/economic success** la clé du bonheur/de la réussite économique; **the k. to good health** les secrets *mpl* d'une bonne santé; *Fig* **it was the k. to his success** cela lui a ouvert les portes du succès; *Fig* **the k. to understanding sth** la clé permettant de comprendre qch; *Fig* **education is the k. to the nation's progress** l'éducation est la clé du progrès de la nation

(c) (*answers*) (*to mystery, code etc*) clef *f*; (*of map etc*) légende *f*; *Sch* corrigé *m*; (*to exercises*) solutions *fpl*; *Comptr* (*of sort, identification etc*) indicatif *m*, critère *m*

(d) *Mus* ton *m*; **major/minor k.** ton majeur/mineur; **the k. of C** le ton d'ut; **to be off** *or* **out of k.** chanter/jouer faux; **k. signature** armature *f*

(e) *Art etc* (*of painting*) caractéristique *f* de luminosité; **picture painted in a low k.** tableau peint dans des tons sombres

(f) (*button etc*) (*of piano, organ, typewriter, computer, telephone etc*) touche *f*; *El* manette *f*; *Mus* (*of wind instrument*) clef *f*; *Comptr* **k. combination** combinaison *f* de touches

(g) (*turning device*) clef *f*, carotte *f*; (*of clock, mechanical toy etc*) remontoir *m*

(h) *Constr* (*roughness of surface*) rappointis *m*

2 *adj attrib* (*most important*) **k. factor/post/industry** facteur *m*/poste *m*/industrie *f* clef; **k. person** (*in organization*) cheville *f* ouvrière, pilier *m*, pivot *m* (**in** de)

key² *vt Comptr* taper; (*data, text*) taper, saisir; **to k. to disk** saisir

▶ **key in** *vtsep Comptr etc* = **key²**

▶ **key up** *vtsep* (a) (*usu passive*) (*make tense*) **the crowd were keyed up for the match** la foule était tendue dans l'attente du match; **to be all keyed up** être crispé *ou* tendu (b) *Comptr* = **key²**

key-account *n Mktg* compte-clé *m*; **k. management** gestion *f* de comptes-clés; **k. sales** ventes *fpl* aux comptes-clés

key bar *n Com* (*in store*) stand *m* de clef-minute

keyboard¹ ['ki:bɔ:d] *n* (*of piano, typewriter, computer*) clavier *m*; *Comptr* **k. buffer** mémoire *f* tampon de clavier; *Mus* **k. instrument** instrument *m* à clavier; *Comptr* **k. layout** disposition *f* de clavier; *Comptr* **k. map** schéma *m* de clavier; *Comptr* **k. operator** claviste *mf*, opérateur, -trice de saisie; *Mus* **k. player** joueur, -euse de synthétiseur; **k. skills** compétences *fpl* de claviste; *Comptr* **k. template** réglette *f* de clavier

keyboard² *vt Comptr* (*text, data*) taper, saisir

keyboarder ['ki:bɔ:dər] *n Comptr* claviste *mf*, opérateur, -trice de saisie

keyboarding ['ki:bɔ:dɪŋ] *n Comptr* (*of data*) frappe *f*, saisie *f*; **k. accuracy** précision *f* de frappe; **k. error** faute *f* de frappe; **k. problems** problèmes *mpl* au niveau de la frappe; **k. skills** compétences *fpl* de claviste; **k. speed** vitesse *f* de frappe

keyboardless computer ['ki:bɔ:dlɪs] *n* ordinateur *m* sans clavier

keyboards ['ki:bɔ:dz] *npl Mus* claviers *mpl*; **on k.** aux claviers

key club *n US* club *m* privé dont les membres possèdent chacun une clef

keyhole ['ki:həʊl] *n* trou *m* de serrure; **to look through the k.** regarder par le trou de la serrure; *Carp* **k. saw** scie *f* à guichet

keyhole surgery *n* chirurgie *f* à incision minimale

keying ['ki:ɪŋ] *n* (a) *Comptr* = **keyboarding** (b) *Mus* (*of piano*) accordage *m*

keying in *n Comptr* = **keyboarding**
keyless entry ['kiːlɪs] *n* (*to room*) ouverture *f* sans clé
key money *n* arrhes *fpl*, *F* pas *m* de porte
Keynesian ['keɪnzɪən] *adj* keynésien
keynote ['kiːnəʊt] **1** *n Mus* tonique *f*; (*of speech, approach*) idée *f* dominante; (*of policy*) mot *m* d'ordre; **k. speech** discours *m* d'ouverture; **k. speaker** = **keynoter 2** *vt* mettre l'accent sur
keynoter ['kiːnəʊtər] *n US* orateur *m* qui prononce le discours d'ouverture
key numbers *npl* (*on squared map*) numéros *mpl* de repérage
keypad ['kiːpæd] *n Comptr* pavé *m*
key punch *n Comptr* perforatrice *f* à clavier
key rack *n* (*in hotel etc*) tableau *m* (des clefs)
key ring *n* porte-clefs *m inv*, étui *m* porte-clefs
keystone ['kiːstəʊn] *n Archit* clef *f* de voûte; *Fig* (*of policy*) clef de voûte, pivot *m*
keystroke ['kiːstrəʊk] *n Comptr* frappe *f* (de touche); **keystrokes per minute/hour** vitesse *f* de frappe à la minute/à l'heure
keyword ['kiːwɜːd] *n* mot-clé *m*, *pl* mot-clés, mot-clef *m*, *pl* mots-clefs
KG [keɪ'dʒiː] *n Br abbr* **Knight of the Order of the Garter**
kg (*abbr* **kilogram**) kg
KGB [keɪdʒiː'biː] *n* KGB *m*; **KGB agent/officer** agent *m*/officier *m* du KGB
khaki ['kɑːkɪ] **1** *n* (*colour, fabric*) kaki *m* **2** *adj* kaki *inv*
kHz (*abbr* **kilohertz**) kHz
kibbutz, *pl* **-zim** [kɪ'bʊts, kɪ'bʊtsiːm] *n Agr* kibboutz *m*, *pl* kibboutzim
kibitz ['kɪbɪts] *vi Am F* donner des conseils non sollicités, ramener son grain de sel
kibitzer ['kɪbɪtsər] *n Am F Cards etc* celui/celle qui donne des conseils non sollicités, donneur, -euse d'avis; (*meddler*) mouche *f* du coche
kibosh ['kaɪbɒʃ] *n Sl* **to put the k. on** (*hopes, plans*) réduire en poussière; (*holidays, new car etc*) faire tomber à l'eau
kick[1] [kɪk] *n* **(a)** (*with foot*) coup *m* de pied; (*of horse etc*) ruade *f*; **to give sb/sth a k.** donner un coup de pied à qn/qch; **to have a powerful k.** (*of footballer, horse*) avoir un coup de pied puissant; (*of swimmer*) avoir un battement de pied puissant; *F* **she just needs a k. up the backside** *or* **in the pants** elle a juste besoin d'un coup de pied au derrière; **k. pleat** (*in skirt*) pli *m* d'aisance
(b) *F* (*vigour*) vigueur *f*, énergie *f*; **a drink with a k. in it** une boisson qui donne un coup de fouet; **to get a k. out of sth/doing sth** prendre plaisir à qch/à faire qch; **to do sth for kicks** faire qch pour s'amuser; **to get one's kicks doing sth** prendre son pied à faire qch; *Sl* **he's on a jazz/tennis k. at the moment** son truc en ce moment c'est le jazz/tennis
(c) (*recoil*) (*of gun*) recul *m*, réaction *f*; (*of mechanism etc*) cahot *m*, secousse *f*
(d) (*of engine*) retour *m* en arrière
kick[2] **1** *vi* (*once*) donner un coup de pied; (*several times*) donner des coups de pied; (*of animal*) ruer; *Sp* (*of athlete*) démarrer; (*of gun*) reculer, repousser
2 *vt* (*once*) donner un coup de pied à; (*several times*) donner des coups de pied à; (*push with foot*) pousser du pied; (*of horse etc*) détacher un coup de pied à; *Fb* (*ball*) botter; (*goal*) marquer; **to get kicked** (*once*) recevoir un coup de pied; (*several times*) recevoir des coups de pied; *Fig F* **to get kicked in the teeth** recevoir un coup en vache; *F* **to k. sb's behind** flanquer à qn un coup de pied au derrière; *Sl* **to k. the bucket** casser sa pipe, crever; *Fig* **to k. a man when he's down** donner le coup de pied de l'âne à qn; *Fig* **to k. sb upstairs** promouvoir qn pour le mettre hors d'état de nuire; **I could have kicked myself** je me serais donné des gifles; **I could k. myself!** quel imbécile je fais!; **to k. a bad habit** se défaire d'une mauvaise habitude; **to k. the habit** (*of smoker*) arrêter (de fumer); (*of drug addict*) décrocher, arrêter (la drogue)
▶ **kick about, kick around 1** *vi F* (*of person, thing*) (*hang around, be somewhere*) traîner; (*travel around*) rouler sa bosse; **there are plenty of people like that kicking around** des gens comme ça, ce n'est pas ça qui manque; **you don't find many of these kicking around nowadays** des comme ça, ça ne court pas les rues de nos jours **2** *vtas* **(a)** (*play with*) (*ball*) taper dans; *F* (*idea etc*) tester **(b)** (*mistreat*) traiter sans ménagements; **you shouldn't let yourself be kicked around like that** tu ne devrais pas te laisser traiter comme ça
▶ **kick against** *vipo F* (*rebel against*) regimber contre; *Fig* **to k. against the pricks** (*against fate*) s'en prendre au destin
▶ **kick aside** *vtsep* (*ball, piece of paper*) écarter d'un coup de pied; (*pieces of paper*) écarter à coups de pied
▶ **kick away** *vtsep* repousser du pied
▶ **kick away at** *vipo* (*door*) mettre des coups de pied dans
▶ **kick back 1** *vi* (*recoil*) (*of engine*) donner des retours en arrière; (*of gun*) reculer, repousser **2** *vtsep* (*return by kicking*) (*ball*) relancer, **3** *vtas* (*person*) rendre un coup de pied à; **I immediately kicked him back** je lui ai tout de suite rendu son coup de pied
▶ **kick in** *vtsep* (*break open*) (*door etc*) enfoncer à coups de pied; *F* **to get one's head kicked in** se faire casser la tête
▶ **kick off 1** *vtsep* (*shoes*) enlever d'un coup de pied **2** *vi Fb* donner le coup d'envoi; *Fig F* (*start*) démarrer, débuter
▶ **kick out 1** *vtsep* (*person*) chasser à coups de pied; *F* (*of job, house, pub etc*) mettre à la porte; *Fb* (*ball*) renvoyer; **to be kicked out** (*of job, house, pub etc*) être mis à la porte **2** *vi* **(a)** (*of horse etc*) ruer; (*of person*) (*once*) donner un coup de pied; (*several times*) donner des coups de pied; **she would k. out at anyone who came near** elle donnait des coups de pied à tous ceux qui s'approchaient **(b)** (*swim vigorously*) s'élancer avec des battements vigoureux
▶ **kick over** *vtsep* (*overturn*) renverser d'un coup de pied; **to k. over the traces** secouer le joug
▶ **kick up** *vtsep F* (*cause*) **to k. up a fuss** faire des histoires; **to k. up a row** *or* **a racket** faire du tapage *ou* du boucan
kickback ['kɪkbæk] *n F Pej* (*payment*) dessous-de-table *m inv*, pot-de-vin *m*
kick boxer *n* tireur, -euse, personne *f* pratiquant la boxe française
kick boxing *n Sp* boxe *f* française
kicker ['kɪkər] *n* **(a)** *Rugby* botteur *m* **(b)** (*horse, mule*) cheval *m*/mulet *m* qui rue **(c)** *TV* **k. (light)** projecteur *m* de décrochement, contre-jour *m*, *pl* contre-jours
kickoff ['kɪkɒf] *n Fb* coup *m* d'envoi; *Fig F* démarrage *m*; *Fb* **k. at two o'clock** la partie commence *ou* le coup d'envoi sera donné à deux heures; *F* **for a k.** pour commencer
kickstand ['kɪkstænd] *n* (*of bicycle*) béquille *f*
kick-start[1] *n* = **kick-starter**
kick-start[2] *vt* (*motorbike, engine*) démarrer au kick; *Fig* (*economy*) relancer, donner un sérieux coup de pouce à
kick-starter *n* (*on motorbike*) démarreur *m* au pied, kick *m*
kick turn *n Ski* conversion *f*
kid[1] [kɪd] *n* **(a)** *F* (*child*) gamin, -ine, gosse *mf*, mioche *mf*; *US* **say k.!** dis-moi, mon petit/ma petite; **my k. brother** mon petit frère; **it's k.'s stuff** (*easy*) c'est facile à faire; (*childish*) c'est (bon) pour les gosses **(b)** (*animal*) chevreau *m*, chevrette *f*; (*skin*) (peau *f* de) chevreau, cabron *m*
kid[2] *F* **1** *vt* en conter à, faire marcher; **you're kidding us** tout ça c'est des blagues, tu veux nous faire marcher; **who do you think you're trying to k.?** et tu crois que je vais avaler ça?; **to k. sb that …** faire croire à qn que …; **to k. oneself** se faire des illusions; **I k. you not** je ne plaisante pas; **she's just kidding that she's hurt** elle fait semblant d'avoir mal **2** *vi* **(I was) only kidding** je plaisantais; **daddy's not really hurt, he's just kidding** papa n'est pas blessé pour de vrai, il fait semblant; **no kidding!** sans blague!; **are you kidding?** (*that's a ridiculous suggestion*) tu plaisantes?
▶ **kid on** *vtsep, vi* = **kid**[2]
kiddie, kiddy ['kɪdɪ] *n F* petit(e) gosse *mf*
kiddo ['kɪdəʊ] *n F* **are you ready, k.?** tu es prêt(e), mon grand/ma grande?
kidglove ['kɪdglʌv] *adj* **to give sb the k. treatment** ménager qn, traiter qn avec ménagement
kid gloves *npl* gants *mpl* (en peau) de chevreau; *Fig* **to handle with k.** (*person*) ménager, prendre des gants avec; (*situation*) traiter avec délicatesse
kidnap ['kɪdnæp] *vt* **(-pp-)** kidnapper
kidnapper ['kɪdnæpər] *n* kidnappeur, -euse, ravisseur, -euse
kidnapping ['kɪdnæpɪŋ] *n Jur* kidnapping *m*, enlèvement *m*, rapt *m*
kidney ['kɪdnɪ] *n* **(a)** *Anat* rein *m*; **k. failure** insuffisance *f* rénale; *Med* **k. tray** cuvette *f* à pansements réniforme, *F* haricot *m*; *Old-fashioned* **people of that k.** les gens de cette espèce **(b)** *Culin* rognon *m* **(c)** *Geol* rognon *m* de silex *etc*
kidney bean *n* (*French bean*) haricot *m* nain; (*scarlet runner*) haricot d'Espagne *ou* à grappes
kidney donor *n* donneur, -euse de rein
kidney machine *n* rein *m* artificiel
kidney-shaped *adj* (*bean etc*) en forme de haricot, réniforme
kidney stone *n Med* calcul *m* rénal
kidney vetch *n Bot* (*plant*) (anthyllide *f*) vulnéraire *f*, trèfle *m* jaune
kidology [kɪ'dɒlədʒɪ] *n Br F* **it's all k.** ce ne sont que des histoires
kill[1] [kɪl] *n* **(a)** (*in hunting*) (*of fox, deer etc*) mise *f* à mort; (*animals killed*) gibier *m* tué, tableau *m* de chasse; **to be in at the k.** assister à la mise à mort; *Fig* assister au

dénouement de qch (et en tirer profit) **(b)** *Mil* (*of enemy aircraft*) descente *f*; (*of enemy warship*) coulée *f*

kill[2] **1** *vt* **(a)** (*person, animal, microbes*) tuer; (*plant*) faire mourir; *Mil* (*enemy*) détruire; (*partridge*) tuer, descendre; (*of butcher*) (*cow etc*) abattre, tuer; (*nerve of tooth*) tuer; (*in hunting*) (*animal*) servir; **to be killed by gunshots/in an accident** être tué à coups de fusil/dans un accident; **to be killed by the radiation/a mysterious illness** mourir des radiations/d'une maladie mystérieuse; **to k. oneself** se suicider; *F* (*overexert oneself*) se tuer (**doing** à faire); *F* (*with laughing*) être mort de rire; *Iron* **don't k. yourself, will you** ne te fais pas trop mal, surtout; **to k. oneself with work** se tuer à (force de) travailler; **the shock would k. her** le choc la tuerait; *F* **I'll k. you!** (*if you do that again etc*) je t'étrangle!; *F* **this one'll k. you** (*of joke*) ça va te faire mourir de rire; **this superstition will be hard to k.** cette superstition aura la vie dure; *Prov* **to k. two birds with one stone** faire d'une pierre deux coups, faire coup double; **to k. sb with kindness** faire du mal à qn par excès de bonté; *F* **my feet/these shoes are killing me** mes pieds/ces chaussures me font atrocement souffrir; *F* **the heat is killing me!** j'étouffe!, je meurs de chaud!

(b) *Fig* (*time*) tuer; (*ambition*) éteindre; (*love, sense of humanity etc*) détruire, étouffer; *Pol* (*bill*) couler; *Journ etc* (*passage, story*) supprimer; (*file*) effacer; (*printer*) arrêter; (*pain*) atténuer; (*smells*) neutraliser; *Tech* (*sound*) amortir; **to k. time** tuer le temps; **k. that light!** éteignez-moi ça tout de suite!

(c) *Fb* (*ball*) bloquer; *Tennis* (*balle*) tuer, massacrer

2 *vi* tuer; **k. or cure remedy** remède *m* de cheval; **k. or be killed** tuer ou se faire tuer

► **kill off** *vtsep* tuer; (*whole population*) exterminer; (*hope*) anéantir; (*small businesses*) faire disparaître; **to k. off a character** (*of author etc*) faire mourir un personnage

killer [ˈkɪlər] *n* **(a)** (*person*) tueur, -euse; (*murderer*) meurtrier, -ière; **k. disease** maladie *f* meurtrière; **k. instinct** instinct *m* meurtrier; *Fig* agressivité *f* **(b)** *F* (*difficult question*) colle *f*; **the exam was a real k.** cet examen n'était pas piqué des hannetons; **that dance was a k.!** cette danse m'a tué!; **this hill's a real k.** (*is very difficult*) cette côte est vraiment mortelle; (*people die on it*) cette côte est meurtrière; **the real k. is that …** le comble c'est que …; **this one's a k.** (*joke*) celle-là est à mourir de rire

killer whale *n Zool* épaulard *m*

killing [ˈkɪlɪŋ] **1** *adj* **(a)** (*blow*) meurtrier, assassin **(b)** *F* (*exhausting*) (*work, dance*) tuant, crevant **(c)** *F* (*very amusing*) crevant; **it's too k. for words** c'est à mourir de rire, c'est à se tordre **2** *n* (*of animal for meat*) abattage *m*; (*of person*) meurtre *m*; *Mil* (*of enemy*) destruction *f*; **the k. of 500 seal pups** le massacre de 500 bébés phoques; *F* **to make a k.** (*on Stock Exchange etc*) faire un bénéfice énorme *ou* une affaire à tout casser

-killing [ˈkɪlɪŋ] *suff* -icide; **germ-k.** bactéricide

killingly [ˈkɪlɪŋlɪ] *adv* **it's k. funny** c'est à mourir de rire

killjoy [ˈkɪldʒɔɪ] *n* rabat-joie *m inv*

kiln [kɪln] *n* four *m* (céramique); (*for drying*) séchoir *m*, sécherie *f*, étuve *f*; **k. drying** *or* **seasoning** séchage *m* au four, étuvage *m*; (*in brewing*) touraillage *m*

kilo [ˈkiːləʊ] *n* kilo *m*

kilobaud [ˈkɪləbɔːd] *n* kilobaud *m*

kilobyte [ˈkɪləbaɪt] *n Comptr* kilo-octet *m*

kilocalorie [ˈkɪləʊkælərɪ] *n Phys* kilocalorie *f*

kilocycle [ˈkɪləsaɪk(ə)l] *n Phys, El* kilocycle *m*

kilogram(me) [ˈkɪləgræm] *n* kilogramme *m*

kilohertz [ˈkɪləʊhɜːts] *n* kilohertz *m*

kilometre, *US* **kilometer** [ˈkɪləmiːtər, *esp Am* kɪˈlɒmɪtər] *n* kilomètre *m*; **distance in kilometres** distance *f* kilométrique

kilometric [kɪləˈmetrɪk] *adj* kilométrique

kilovolt [ˈkɪləvəʊlt] *n El* kilovolt *m*

kilowatt [ˈkɪləwɒt] *n El* kilowatt *m*

kilowatt-hour *n El* kilowatt-heure *m*, *pl* kilowatt-heures

kilt [kɪlt] *n* kilt *m* (écossais)

kilted [ˈkɪltɪd] *adj* (*figure, soldier*) en kilt; **k. skirt** kilt *m*

kilter [ˈkɪltər] *n F* **out of k.** (*of machine part*) détraqué; (*out of balance*) (*of schedule, budget etc*) déséquilibré; **this is running out of k. with the rest of the machine** c'est en décalage par rapport au reste de la machine

kimono [kɪˈməʊnəʊ] *n* kimono *m*

kin [kɪn] *n Fml* parents *mpl*; **his k.** ses parents, sa parenté; **to be k. to sb** être parent de qn, être apparenté avec qn; **he's no k. of mine** il n'est pas de ma famille

kind[1] [kaɪnd] *n* **(a)** (①A13,3,a) (*class, sort*) genre *m*, espèce *f*, sorte *f*; **what k. is it?** de quelle sorte *ou* de quel genre (est-ce)?; **what k. of tree is this?** quelle sorte *ou* quel genre d'arbre est-ce?; **what k. of woman is she?** quel genre *ou* quelle sorte de femme est-ce?; **people of all kinds** des gens de toutes sortes; **the worst k. of people** des gens de la pire espèce; **it's a k. of fish** c'est une espèce de poisson; **they have so many different kinds of bread** ils ont tellement de sortes de pain différentes; **they did have some flour, but it wasn't the right k.** ils avaient bien de la farine, mais ce n'était pas la bonne; **something of the k.** quelque chose de ce genre; **nothing of the k.** rien de la sorte; **she's terribly boring – she's nothing of the k.!** elle est terriblement ennuyeuse – pas du tout! loin de là!; **in a k. of a way** en quelque façon; **this k. of woman,** *F* **these k. of women** ce genre de femmes; **he's not the understanding k.** il n'est pas du genre compréhensif; **I know your k.!** je connais les gens de ton espèce!; **she's more the stay-at-home k.** elle est plus du genre à rester à la maison; **well, it's beer of a k., I suppose** oui, on peut appeler ça de la bière, je suppose; **he speaks French — of a k.** il parle français — plus ou moins; **we're two of a k.** nous sommes de la même espèce *ou* race; **it's the only one of its k.** c'est le seul en son genre; **what k. of person do you think I am!** pour quel genre de personne me prends-tu?; **he's that k. of person** il est comme ça; **this is my k. of party** c'est le genre de soirée que j'aime; **you're my k. of girl** tu es mon type de femme, tu es le type de femme que j'aime; **I'm not that k. of girl** ce n'est pas mon genre; **is this the k. of thing you're looking for?** est-ce que c'est quelque chose de ce genre que vous cherchez?; **that's not the k. of thing I meant** ce n'est pas exactement ce que je voulais; **this is not the k. of thing you can do overnight** ce n'est pas le genre de chose qu'on fait du jour au lendemain; *F* **it was a k. of saucer-shaped thing** c'était une espèce de truc en forme de soucoupe; *F* **there's a k. of bump just here** il y a comme une bosse ici; *F* **I heard a k. of thump** j'ai entendu une espèce de cognement *ou* comme un cognement

(b) (*nature, character*) **difference in k.** différence *f* spécifique; **payment in k.** paiement *m* en nature; **to repay sb in k.** (*as opposed to cash*) rembourser qn en nature; (*for an injury, disservice*) rendre à qn la monnaie de sa pièce

(c) *F* **k. of** (*with adjectives and verbs*) un peu, plutôt; **you look k. of tired** tu as l'air un peu *ou* plutôt fatigué; **it's k. of late** il est un peu tard; **I'm k. of worried** je suis un peu inquiet; **I've k. of changed my mind** je crois bien que j'ai changé d'avis; **I k. of expected it** je m'y attendais un peu; **I k. of like it** (*like it a little*) j'aime plus ou moins ça; (*quite a bit*) j'aime bien ça; **do you like it? – k. of** tu aimes ça? – plus ou moins, ça va, couci-couça; **do you agree? – k. of** tu es d'accord? – plus ou moins

kind[2] *adj* gentil; **to be k. to sb** se montrer gentil avec qn, se montrer bon pour *ou* envers qn; **it's very k. of you to …** c'est bien aimable de votre part *ou* à vous de …; *Fml* **(would you) be k. enough to** *or* **so k. as to …** ayez la bonté de …, veuillez (bien) …; **you are really too k.** vous êtes vraiment trop aimable; **k. to the skin** (*of detergents etc*) qui n'irrite pas la peau; **by k. permission of …** avec l'aimable autorisation de …; **give him my k. regards** faites-lui mes amitiés; **k. words** paroles *fpl* bienveillantes

kinda [ˈkaɪndə] *F* = **kind of,** *see* **kind[1]** **(c)**

kindergarten [ˈkɪndəgɑːt(ə)n] *n Sch* jardin *m* d'enfants, école *f* maternelle

kind-hearted [ˈkaɪndˈhɑːtɪd] *adj* (*person*) qui a bon cœur; (*action, response*) bienveillant; **that was very k. of you** c'était très gentil de votre part; **he's very k.** il a très bon cœur, il a le cœur sur la main

kindle [ˈkɪnd(ə)l] **1** *vt* **(a)** (*flame, fire*) allumer; (*coal, wood*) enflammer, embraser **(b)** (*hatred*) allumer; (*emotions, passions*) faire naître, susciter; (*desires*) enflammer; (*suspicions, sorrow*) aviver; (*enthusiasm*) exciter **2** *vi* (*of fire, wood, passions etc*) s'allumer, s'enflammer

kindliness [ˈkaɪndlɪnɪs] *n* gentillesse *f*, bonté *f*

kindling [ˈkɪndlɪŋ] *n* **k. (wood)** bois *m* d'allumage, petit bois

kindly [ˈkaɪndlɪ] **1** *adv* gentiment, avec bonté; **she spoke very k. of you** elle a dit des choses très aimables *ou* gentilles à votre égard; **to be k. disposed towards sb/sth** être bien disposé envers qn/qch; **the council k. agreed to let us use the town hall** le conseil nous a aimablement autorisés à utiliser l'hôtel de ville; **(will you) k. close the window** voudriez-vous avoir la bonté *ou* la gentillesse de fermer la fenêtre?; *Com* **k. remit by cheque** prière de nous couvrir par chèque; **not to take k. to sb/sth** ne pas aimer qn/qch **2** *adj* (*person*) gentil, bon; (*tone, advice*) bienveillant

kindness [ˈkaɪndnɪs] *n* **(a)** gentillesse *f*, amabilité *f* **(towards sb** envers qn), bonté *f* **(towards sb** pour qn); **thanks for your k.** merci de votre gentillesse *ou* amabilité; **to repay sb's k.** payer qn de sa gentillesse; **to show k. to sb** témoigner de la bonté à qn; *Fml* **would you have the k. to …?** voulez-vous avoir la bonté *ou* gentillesse de …?; **to do sth out of the k. of**

one's heart faire qch par gentillesse; *Iron* **and I suppose it was out of the k. of your heart that you did that?** et je suppose que c'est ton bon cœur qui t'a poussé à faire ça?

(**b**) **a k.** un service (rendu); **to do sb a k.** rendre service à qn; **would you at least do me the k. of listening to my proposal?** me ferez-vous au moins l'amabilité d'écouter ma proposition?

kindred ['kındrıd] **1** *n Old-fashioned* (*relatives*) parents *mpl*; (*family*) famille *f* **2** *adj* de la même nature, du même genre; **k. spirits** âmes *fpl* sœurs

kinematic [kınə'mætık, kaın-] *adj Phys* cinématique

kinematics [kınə'mætıks, kaın-] *n* [①**A10**,c] *Phys* cinématique *f*

kinetic [kı'netık, kaı-] *adj Phys, Art* cinétique

kinetics [kı'netıks] *n* [①**A10**,c] *Phys* cinétique *f*

kinfolk ['kınfəʊk] *npl Am* parents *mpl* et alliés *mpl*

king [kıŋ] *n* (**a**) *also Fig* roi *m*; *Ind etc* magnat *m*; **the kings and queens of England** les souverains *mpl* d'Angleterre; *Bible* **K. of Kings** Roi des rois; *Bible* **the three Kings** les Rois *mpl* Mages; *Bible* (**the Book of**) **Kings** le livre des Rois; **a k.'s ransom** une fortune (**b**) *Chess, Cards* roi *m*; (*in draughts*) dame *f*

king cobra *n Zool* cobra *m* royal

king crab *n Zool* limule *m*, crabe *m* des Moluques

kingcup ['kıŋkʌp] *n* (**a**) (*buttercup*) bouton *m* d'or (**b**) (*marsh marigold*) populage *m*, souci *m* d'eau

kingdom ['kıŋdəm] *n* (**a**) royaume *m*; **the k. of heaven** le royaume des cieux (**b**) (*animal*) règne *m*; **in the animal k.** chez les animaux (**c**) *Rel* règne *m*; **Thy k. come** que Ton règne vienne; *F* **k. come** le paradis; *F* **to send sb to k. come** expédier qn dans l'autre monde; *F* **until k. come** jusqu'à l'éternité

kingfisher ['kıŋfıʃər] *n* martin-pêcheur *m*, *pl* martins-pêcheurs

kingly ['kıŋlı] *adj Lit* de roi; (*royal*) royal

king penguin *n Zool* manchot *m* royal

kingpin ['kıŋpın] *n* (**a**) *Aut* axe *m* de rotule *ou* de fusée, pivot *m* de fusée; *Fig* (*of organization, company*) cheville *f* ouvrière (**b**) (*in tenpin bowling*) quille *f* du milieu

king prawn *n Zool, Culin* grosse crevette *f*

kingship ['kıŋʃıp] *n* royauté *f*

king-size(d) ['kıŋ'saız, -d] *adj Com* géant; (*cigarette*) long; **k. bed** lit *m* king size; **a k. headache** un mal de crâne atroce; **a k. problem** un problème de poids

kink[1] [kıŋk] *n* (**a**) vrillage *m*; (*in felt*) grigne *f*; (*of hair*) crêpelure *f*; *Tex* vrille *f*, boucle *f*; **the rope's got a k. in it** il y a un vrillage dans la corde (**b**) (*in character*) déséquilibre *m*, aberration *f*; **it's one of her little kinks** c'est l'une de ses petites manies

kink[2] *vi* (*of rope*) se nouer, se tortiller, vrillonner; (*of thread*) vriller

kinkiness ['kıŋkınıs] *n* (*sexual*) (*tastes*) goûts *mpl* bizarres; **no k.!** pas de trucs bizarres!

kinky ['kıŋkı] *adj* (**a**) (*hair*) crêpelé, crépu (**b**) *Sl* (*person*) (*sexually*) qui a des goûts sexuels excentriques; *F* (*eccentric*) extravagant; *F* (*clothes etc*) (*strange*) bizarre, extravagant; (*erotic, pornographic*) pervers

kinsfolk ['kınzfəʊk] *npl* = **kinfolk**

kinship ['kınʃıp] *n* parenté *f*

kinsman, *pl* **-men** ['kınzmən] *n Lit* parent *m*

kinswoman, *pl* **-women** ['kınzwʊmən, -wımın] *n Lit* parente *f*

kiosk ['kiːɒsk] *n* kiosque *m*

kip[1] [kıp] *n Br F* (**a**) (*sleep*) **to have a k.** piquer un roupillon; **to get some k.** roupiller; **an hour's k.** un roupillon d'une heure (**b**) (*bed*) pieu *m*, plumard *m*; **to be still in one's k.** être encore au plumard

kip[2] *vi* (**-pp-**) *Br F* (*sleep*) roupiller

▶ **kip down** *vi Br F* pieuter

kipper[1] ['kıpər] *n Culin* hareng *m* légèrement salé et fumé, kipper *m*

kipper[2] *vt* (*herring*) saler et fumer; **kippered herring** = **kipper**[1]; *Fig F* **to k. one's lungs** s'enfumer les poumons

kir [kıər] *n* (*drink*) kir *m*; **k. royale** kir royal

kirk [kɜːk] *n Scot* église *f*; **the K.** l'Église (presbytérienne) d'Écosse

kiss[1] [kıs] *n* baiser *m*; **to give/blow sb a k.** donner/envoyer un baiser à qn; **give mummy a kiss!** (*to child*) fais une bise à maman!; *Med* **to give sb the k. of life** faire le bouche-à-bouche à qn; *Fig* **to be the k. of death for sb/sth** (*of act, decision*) être fatal pour qn/qch; **k. curl** accroche-cœur *m*, *pl* accroche-cœurs

kiss[2] **1** *vt* (**a**) (*person*) donner un baiser à, embrasser; (*forehead or hand, holy object*) baiser; (*ceremonially*) (*person*) donner l'accolade à; **to k. sb on the cheek/lips** embrasser qn sur la joue/les lèvres; **they kissed each other** ils se sont embrassés; **mummy will k. it better** maman va te faire un bisou et tu n'auras plus mal; **to k. the book** baiser la Bible (pour prêter serment); *Lit* **to k. the dust** mordre la poussière; **to k. sb goodbye** dire au revoir à qn en l'embrassant; *F* **you can k. that promotion goodbye** tu peux dire au revoir à cet avancement; *Vulg* (**you can**) **k. my arse!** va te faire foutre!

(**b**) (*touch lightly*) frôler; *Billiards* (*of ball*) frapper par contrecoup

2 *vi* (**a**) (*of two people*) s'embrasser; **to k. and make up** se réconcilier; **he's the k. and tell type** il est du genre à aller le crier sur tous les toits quand il a une aventure; **how much did you get for your k. and tell story?** combien on t'a payé(e) pour raconter les détails de ton aventure avec elle/lui?

(**b**) (*of two objects*) se frôler; *Billiards* (*of balls*) se frapper par contrecoup

▶ **kiss away** *vtsep* **to k. away sb's tears** sécher les larmes de qn en l'embrassant

kisser ['kısər] *n* (**a**) (*person*) embrasseur, -euse; **to be a great k.** bien embrasser (**b**) *Sl* (*mouth*) gueule *f*

kiss-off ['kısɒf] *n Am F* **to give sb the k.** (*of girlfriend etc*) plaquer qn; (*of employer*) virer qn

kissogram ['kısəgræm] *n* = message *m* délivré par une personne déguisée et accompagné d'un baiser; **a k. girl** une fille qui délivre des messages et est chargée d'embrasser le destinataire

kit[1] [kıt] *n* (**a**) (*equipment*) matériel *m*, équipement *m*; *Mil etc* petit équipement; *Mil etc* **k. inspection** revue *f* de détail *ou* d'inspection (**b**) *Sp* (*clothes*) tenue *f*; *F* **to get one's k. off** se déshabiller (**c**) (*set of parts*) **to buy sth in k. form** acheter qch en prêt-à-monter *ou* en pièces détachées; **to make sth from a k.** faire qch à partir de pièces détachées

kit[2] *vt* (**-tt-**) = **kit out, kit up**

▶ **kit out, kit up** *vtsep esp Br* (*soldier etc*) équiper, fournir son équipement à; (**all**) **kitted out** complètement équipé; *Mil* **to be kitted out** toucher son paquetage

kitbag ['kıtbæg] *n* sac *m* (de) marin; *Mil* sac à paquetage, sac de grande monture

kitchen ['kıtʃın] *n* cuisine *f*; *Pol F* **k. cabinet** conseillers *mpl* particuliers; **k. hand** aide *mf* de cuisine; **k. knife** couteau *m* de cuisine; **k. stove** cuisinière *f*; **k. unit** élément *m* de cuisine; **k. utensils** batterie *f* de cuisine

kitchenette [kıtʃı'net] *n* coin-cuisine *m*, *pl* coins-cuisines, cuisinette *f*

kitchen foil *n Culin* papier *m* d'aluminium

kitchen paper *n* essuie-tout *m inv*

kitchen roll *n* essuie-tout *m inv*

kitchen sink *n* évier *m*; *Th* **k. drama** = théâtre *m* réaliste qui prend surtout pour sujet la vie quotidienne des ouvriers; *Fig F* **to take everything but the k.** (*on holiday etc*) emporter toute la maison; (*of thief, husband moving out etc*) ne laisser que les murs

kitchen table *n* table de cuisine; **it's on the k.** il est sur la table de la cuisine

kitchenware ['kıtʃınweər] *n* vaisselle *f* de cuisine

kite [kaıt] *n* (**a**) (*toy*) cerf-volant *m*, *pl* cerfs-volants; *Fin F* traite *f* en l'air, billet *m* de complaisance; **k. balloon** ballon *m* observateur, *F* saucisse *f*; *F* **as high as a k.** (*drunk*) ivre, soûl; (*drugged*) drogué, camé; (*very excited*) tout fou, *f* toute folle (**b**) *Br F* (*aeroplane*) avion *m*, taxi *m* (**c**) (*bird*) milan *m*

kith [kıθ] *n Arch* (*still used in*) **our k. and kin** nos parents et amis; **to have neither k. nor kin** être seul sur la terre

kitsch [kıtʃ] **1** *n* kitsch *m*; **a piece of k.** du kitsch **2** *adj* kitsch *inv*

kitschy ['kıtʃı] *adj* kitsch *inv*; **it's k.** c'est du kitsch

kitten ['kıt(ə)n] *n* (*young cat*) chaton *m*, petit(e) chat(te); (*term of endearment*) ma petite, ma mignonne; **a cat and her kittens** une chatte et ses petits; *Br F* **he'll have kittens** (*of person*) il va se mettre dans tous ses états; **to be having kittens** (*of person*) être dans tous ses états

kittenish ['kıtənıʃ] *adj* (*playful*) enjoué; (*flirtatious*) coquet

kittiwake ['kıtıweık] *n* (*bird*) mouette *f* tridactyle

kitty[1] ['kıtı] *n F* (*cat*) minou *m*, minet *m*; (*kitten*) chaton *m*; **here k., k.** minou, minou, viens

kitty[2] *n* (**a**) *Cards etc* cagnotte *f*; (*of group*) cagnotte, caisse *f* commune (**b**) (*at bowls*) cochonnet *m*

kiwi ['kiːwiː] *n* (**a**) (*bird*) aptéryx *m*, kiwi *m* (**b**) *F* (*New Zealander*) **K.** Néo-Zélandais, -aise (**c**) *Culin* **k.** (**fruit**) kiwi *m*

KKK [keıkeı'keı] *n US abbr* **Ku Klux Klan**

kleptomania [kleptə'meınıə] *n* kleptomanie *f*

kleptomaniac [kleptə'meınıæk] *adj, n* kleptomane *mf*

klutz [klʌts] *n Am F* brise-tout *m inv*

km (*abbr* **kilometre**) km

km/h (*abbr* **kilometres per hour**) km/h

knack [næk] *n* talent *m*, chic *m*; (*esp physical*) tour *m* de main; **to have the k. of** *or* **a k. for doing sth** avoir le talent de *ou* le chic pour faire qch; (*esp physically*) avoir le coup *ou* le tour de main pour faire qch; **to have lost the k. of sth** n'avoir plus l'habitude de qch; **there's a k. to it** il y a un truc; **there's a k. to opening this door** il y a un truc pour ouvrir la porte; **you have a k. for telephoning me at exactly the wrong moment** tu as le chic pour me téléphoner précisément au mauvais moment

knacker¹ ['nækər] *n Br* (**a**) (*of horses*) équarrisseur *m*; **k.'s yard** chantier *m* d'équarrissage, équarrissoir *m* (**b**) (*of buildings*) entrepreneur *m* de démolitions; (*of ships*) démolisseur *m* de vieux navires

knacker² *vt Br F* (*person*) crever, tuer; (*machine etc*) bousiller

knackered ['nækəd] *adj Br F* (*tired*) (*person*) crevé, mort; (*broken*) (*machine etc*) foutu, naze

knapsack ['næpsæk] *n Old-fashioned* havresac *m*, sac *m* à dos; *Mil* sac d'ordonnance, havresac

knave [neɪv] *n* (**a**) *Cards* valet *m*; **k. of clubs** valet de trèfle (**b**) *Old-fashioned* (*scoundrel*) fripon *m*, coquin *m*

knavery ['neɪvərɪ] *n Old-fashioned* friponnerie *f*, coquinerie *f*

knead [ni:d] *vt* (**a**) (*dough, clay*) pétrir, malaxer, travailler (**b**) *Med* (*muscles*) masser, pétrir

knee¹ [ni:] *n* (**a**) genou *m*, -oux; **these trousers are out at the k.** ce pantalon est troué au genou; **to sit on sb's k.** *or* **knees** s'asseoir sur les genoux de qn; **to put sb over one's k.** (*spank*) donner une fessée à qn; **she put him over her k. and spanked him** elle l'a attrapé sur ses genoux et lui a donné une fessée; **he learnt the song at his mother's k.** il a appris la chanson sur les genoux de sa mère; **to fall** *or* **drop to one's knees** tomber à genoux; **on your knees!** à genoux!; **to go down on one's knees** s'agenouiller; *Fig* se mettre à genoux; *Lit* **to bend** *or* **bow the k. to** *or* **before sb** fléchir le genou devant qn, s'incliner devant qn; *Fig* **to ask for sth on one's (bended) knees** *or* **on bended k.** demander qch à genoux; *Fig* **to bring sb to his knees** obliger qn à capituler; *Fig* **the crisis brought the government to its knees** la crise a mis le gouvernement à genoux; **the famine has brought the country to its knees** la famine a entraîné le pays au bord de la ruine; *Vet* **broken knees** (*of horse*) couronnement *m*; *Anat* **k. reflex, k. jerk** réflexe *m* patellaire *ou* rotulien

(**b**) *MecE, Constr* raccord *m* coudé, coude *m*; (*in naval architecture*) courbe *f* (de consolidation); **k. bracket** console-équerre *f*, *pl* consoles-équerres; **k. (plate)** gousset *m* (de charpente); *Carp etc* **k. timber** bois *m* courbant *ou* coudé

knee² *vt* (*hit*) donner un coup de genou à; **she kneed him in the groin** elle lui a donné un coup de genou dans les parties; **she kneed the door open** (*push*) elle poussa la porte du genou; **he kneed the box out of the way** il écarta la boîte du genou

kneecap¹ ['ni:kæp] *n Anat* rotule *f*

kneecap² *vt* **to k. sb** tirer dans les rotules de qn

kneecapping ['ni:kæpɪŋ] *n* **it was the third k. that week** c'était la troisième fois de la semaine que quelqu'un se faisait tirer dans les rotules

knee-deep *adj* (*mud, water*) jusqu'aux genoux; **to be k. in mud** être enfoncé dans la boue jusqu'aux genoux; *Fig* **to be k. in paperwork** être dans la paperasse jusqu'au cou

knee-high *adj, adv* à hauteur du genou; **the snow/water was k.** la neige/l'eau arrivait à hauteur du genou; **to go k. into the water** entrer dans l'eau jusqu'aux genoux; *F* **when I was k. to a grasshopper** quand j'étais haut comme trois pommes

kneejerk ['ni:dʒɜ:k] *adj* (*reaction*) instinctif, épidermique; *Pol* (*conservatism, radicalism*) enraciné; **k. conservative/radical** conservateur *m*/radical *m* primaire

kneel [ni:l] *vi* (*pt, pp* **knelt** [nelt], *occ* **kneeled**) s'agenouiller, se mettre à genoux; *Fig Lit,* **to k. to sb** se mettre à genoux devant qn

knee-length *adj* (*dress*) qui descend jusqu'aux genoux; (*boot, socks*) qui monte jusqu'aux genoux

kneeler ['ni:lər] *n* (*cushion*) (*in church*) agenouilloir *m*

kneeling ['ni:lɪŋ] **1** *adj* agenouillé, à genoux **2** *n* agenouillement *m*

kneepad ['ni:pæd] *n* genouillère *f*

kneeroom ['ni:rʊm] *n* espace *m* aux genoux

knees-up ['ni:zʌp] *n Br F* java *f*; **to have a k.** faire la java; **there was a bit of a k. in the pub** on a un peu fait la java au pub

knell [nel] *n* glas *m*; **to toll the (death) k.** sonner le glas; *Fig* **this news/refusal rang the death k. of her hopes** cette nouvelle/ce refus sonnait le glas de ses espérances

knelt *see* **kneel**

knickerbocker ['nɪkəbɒkər] *n Culin* **k. glory** coupe *f* glacée géante

knickerbockers ['nɪkəbɒkəz] *npl* culotte *f* (bouffante), knickerbockers *mpl*

knickers ['nɪkəz] *npl* [①A10,e] (**a**) (petite) culotte *f* (*de femme*); *Old-fashioned F* **k.!** (*nonsense*) balivernes!; *Vulg* **to get into sb's k.** s'envoyer qn, culbuter qn; *Br F* **to get one's k. in a twist** paniquer (**about** à cause de) (**b**) *US* (*breeches*) = **knickerbockers**

knick-knack ['nɪknæk] *n F* colifichet *m*, babiole *f*, bibelot *m*

knife¹, *pl* **knives** [naɪf, naɪvz] *n* (**a**) couteau *m*; *Surg* (*with narrow blade*) bistouri *m*; **k. and fork** couverts *mpl*; *Old-fashioned F* **before you could say k.** en un rien de temps, en moins de rien; **to go through sth like a k. through butter** entrer dans qch comme dans du beurre; **this k. wouldn't cut butter** ce couteau ne coupe que ce qu'il voit *or* ne coupe rien; *Fig* **it was an atmosphere you could have cut with a k.** l'atmosphère était extrêmement tendue; *Fig* **to get** *or* **have one's k. into sb** en vouloir à qn; *Fig* **the knives are out for him** on ne donne pas cher de sa peau; **it was war to the k. between them** ils étaient à couteaux tirés; *Med F* **to go under the k.** passer sur le billard; *Med F* **he was under the k. for two hours** (*in operation*) il a passé deux heures sur le billard; **k. attack** attaque *f* au couteau; **k. grinder** (*person*) rémouleur *m*, repasseur *m* de couteaux; (*instrument*) meule *f* à aiguiser; *Tech* **k. sharpener** aiguisoir *m* (pour couteaux); **k. wound** blessure *f* provoquée par un coup de couteau

(**b**) (*blade*) (*on machine*) lame *f*; (*of guillotine*) couperet *m*

knife² *vt* (*stab*) donner un coup de couteau à, poignarder; **he's been knifed** il a recu un coup de couteau, il a été poignardé

knife-edge **1** *n Fig* **he had been on a k. all day** (*nervous*) il avait été sur les nerfs toute la journée; *Fig* **the situation/game/***etc* **was balanced on a k.** la situation/la partie/*etc* ne tenait qu'à un fil **2** *adj* **trousers with a k. crease** pantalon au pli cassant

knife-point *n* pointe *f* de couteau; **to be robbed at k.** se faire voler sous la menace d'un couteau

knife-rest *n* porte-couteau *m*, *pl* porte-couteaux

knifing ['naɪfɪŋ] *n* attaque *f* au couteau

knight¹ [naɪt] *n* (**a**) chevalier *m*; *Liter* **the Knights of the Round Table** les Chevaliers de la Table Ronde; *Br* **K. of (the Order of) the Garter** chevalier de l'Ordre de la Jarretière; **k. errant** (*pl* **knights errant**) chevalier errant, paladin *m*; *Hist* **k. service** service *m* de haubert (**b**) *Chess* cavalier *m*

knight² *vt* faire *ou* créer chevalier

knighthood ['naɪthʊd] *n* (*title*) **he has just been given a k.** il vient d'être fait *ou* créé chevalier

knightly ['naɪtlɪ] *adj* (*conduct etc*) chevaleresque, de chevalier

knit [nɪt] (*pt, pp* **knitted** *or* **knit**) **1** *vt* (**a**) (*sweater etc*) tricoter; **k. two, purl two** deux à l'endroit, deux à l'envers (**b**) **to k. one's brows** froncer les sourcils **2** *vi* (**a**) tricoter, faire du tricot; (*as opposed to purl*) tricoter à l'endroit (**b**) *Med* (*of bones*) se souder

► **knit together** **1** *vi Med* (*of bones*) se souder **2** *vt* (*join*) **their experience k. them together more tightly than ever** l'expérience qu'ils ont vécue les a liés plus que jamais

► **knit up** *vtsep* assembler (en le tricotant)

knitted ['nɪtɪd] *adj* (**a**) tricoté, de *ou* en tricot; (*lace*) au tricot; **a k. jumper** un tricot; **k. fabric** tricot *m*; **k. goods** tricots, articles *mpl* en tricot (**b**) **k. eyebrows** sourcils *mpl* froncés

knitter ['nɪtər] *n* tricoteur, -euse

knitting ['nɪtɪŋ] *n* (**a**) (*activity*) tricotage *m*; (*work*) tricot *m*; **to do some k.** tricoter; **I've brought my k.** j'ai apporté mon tricot; **k. needle** aiguille *f* à tricoter; **k. machine** machine *f* à tricoter, tricoteuse *f*; **k. pattern** modèle *m* de tricot; **k. wool** laine *f* à tricoter (**b**) (*of bones*) soudure *f*

knob¹ [nɒb] *n* (**a**) (*on cane, bannisters*) pomme *f*; (*on door, drawer etc*) bouton *m*, poignée *f*; (*on radio etc*) bouton; (*on surface, forehead etc*) bosse *f*, protubérance *f*; *Br F* **it comes with all the knobs on** (*with all refinements etc*) il est équipé de tous les accessoires possibles et imaginables; *Br F* **the same to you with knobs on!** c'est celui qui le dit qui l'est! (**b**) (*piece*) **a k. of butter** une noix de beurre (**c**) *Br Vulg* (*penis*) bite *f*

knobbed [nɒbd] *adj* (*stick*) à pommeau

knobbly ['nɒblɪ] *adj* couvert de bosses; (*tree*) noueux; **k. knees** genoux *mpl* bossués

knock¹ [nɒk] *n* (**a**) (*blow*) coup *m*; **to give sb a k. on the head** porter à qn un coup à la tête; (*and make unconscious*) assommer qn d'un coup sur la tête; **to get a nasty k.** prendre un vilain coup; *F* **his pride took a bit of a k.** sa fierté en a pris un coup; **to give sb's chances/hopes a k.** miner les chances/espoirs de qn; **to be brought up in the school of hard knocks** être élevé à la dure; *F* **he's had a few knocks** (*in business, life*) il en a vu de dures; **k.-for-k. insurance** = assurance *f* entraînant le remboursement séparé des clients par leurs compagnies respectives

(**b**) **k. at the door** coup *m* à la porte; **to hear a k.** entendre frapper; **to give a loud k.** frapper très fort; **k., k.!** toc, toc!; **a k., k. joke** = blague *f* dont la première ligne du dialogue est 'toc, toc!'

(c) *MecE etc* (*sound*) cognement *m*, cliquetis *m*; (*of fuel in engine*) détonation *f*

knock² 1 *vt* (a) (*hit*) frapper, heurter, cogner; **to k. sb on the head** frapper qn sur la tête; **to k. sb unconscious** assommer qn; **to k. sb flying** envoyer valdinguer qn; **to k. one's head against sth** se cogner la tête contre qch; **to k. a nail into a wall** enfoncer un clou dans un mur; **to k. a hole in** *or* **through sth** faire un trou dans qch

(b) (*Fig phrases*) **to k. holes in an argument** démolir un argument; **to k. an idea/a scheme on the head** abandonner *ou* laisser tomber une idée/un projet; **our plans have been knocked on the head** nos projets sont tombés à l'eau; **to k. some sense into sb** apprendre à vivre à qn; **that'll k. a bit of sense into her!** ça lui apprendra!; **to k. sb into shape** mettre qn au pas; **the army soon knocked his enthusiasm out of him** l'armée a eu tôt fait de tuer en lui toute trace d'enthousiasme; **to k. sb sideways** *or* **for six** (*amaze*) abasourdir *ou* stupéfier qn

(c) *F* (*criticize*) débiner; **don't k. it until you've tried it** ne crache pas dessus avant d'avoir essayé

2 *vi* (a) frapper (**at** à); **to k. at the door** frapper à la porte; **to k. against sth** se donner un coup *ou* se cogner contre qch; **she knocked against him** elle s'est cognée contre lui; **he felt his foot k. against a hard object** il a senti son pied cogner contre *ou* rencontrer quelque chose de dur; **his knees were knocking** ses genous s'entrechoquaient

(b) (*of engine*) cogner, cliqueter; (*of bearings*) tambouriner

▶ **knock about, knock around** 1 *vtsep* (a) (*mistreat*) (*person*) bousculer, maltraiter, malmener; **he knocks his wife about** il bat sa femme; **the furniture has been badly knocked about** les meubles ont été fort maltraités

(b) *F* (*discuss*) (*idea, suggestion*) débattre

2 *vi F* (a) **to k. about with sb** fréquenter qn; **they knocked about together at school** ils se fréquentaient à l'école

(b) (*hang around*) traîner; **has anyone seen my keys knocking about?** quelqu'un a vu traîner mes clés dans un coin?; **that's what I wear to k. about in** ce sont mes vêtements d'intérieur; **he's knocked about quite a bit** il a pas mal roulé sa bosse

3 *vipo F* **to k. about the world/countryside** rouler sa bosse; **she's been knocking about Glasgow for years** ça fait des années qu'elle traîne à Glasgow; **your keys are knocking about the kitchen somewhere** tes clés traînent dans un coin de la cuisine

▶ **knock back** *vtsep F* (a) (*drink*) **to k. back a drink** s'enfiler *ou* s'envoyer un verre (b) (*cost*) coûter; **it knocked me back £200** ça m'a coûté 200 livres (c) (*reject*) (*idea, proposal*) rejeter; (*candidate*) refuser (d) (*surprise*) abasourdir, sidérer

▶ **knock down** *vtsep* (a) renverser; (*person*) mettre à terre; (*wall, building etc*) abattre; **he was knocked down by a car** il a été renversé par une voiture (b) (*at auction*) adjuger, vendre; **to k. sth down to sb** adjuger qch à qn (c) *F* (*reduce*) (*price*) baisser; (*reduce price of*) solder; **it's been knocked down to £50** ça a été soldé à 50 livres; **she wanted £15 but I knocked her down to 10** elle demandait 15 livres mais j'ai réussi à la faire descendre jusqu'à 10

▶ **knock off** 1 *vtsep* (a) (*cause to fall off*) faire tomber; **he was knocked off his bike by a car** une voiture l'a fait tomber de son vélo; **to k. a book off the table** faire tomber un livre de la table; *F* **to k. sb's head** *or* **block off** casser la tête à qn; *Fig* **to k. sb off their pedestal** *or* **perch** faire tomber qn de son piédestal; *Fig* **I managed to get something knocked off the price** j'ai réussi à faire rabattre quelque chose du prix

(b) *F* (*steal*) piquer, faucher; **to k. off a bank** se faire une banque

(c) *F* (*kill*) zigouiller

(d) *F* **k. it off!** (*stop it*) arrêtez!, ça suffit!

(e) *F* (*produce quickly*) (*letter, report, song etc*) expédier

2 *vi* (*at end of day*) finir; **let's k. off for a coffee** arrêtons-nous pour prendre un café

▶ **knock out** *vtsep* (a) (*remove*) retirer, enlever; *F* **to k. sb's brains/teeth out** casser la tête/les dents à qn (b) (*make unconscious*) assommer raide; *Boxing* mettre knock-out (c) *Sp* (*in tournament etc*) **to be knocked out** être éliminé (d) *Mil* (*tank etc*) détruire

▶ **knock over** *vtsep* (*cause to fall*) faire tomber; (*overturn*) renverser

▶ **knock together** 1 *vtsep* (a) (*make hastily*) (*shelter, raft etc*) assembler en vitesse; **we knocked together a rough shelter** on s'est fabriqué une espèce d'abri (b) (*hit together*) entrechoquer; *Fig* **they should have their heads knocked together** il faudrait les secouer un bon coup 2 *vi* (*of knees, two objects*) s'entrechoquer

▶ **knock up** 1 *vtsep* (a) (*make hastily*) (*shed etc*) construire en vitesse; (*meal*) improviser; **I'll k. us up some spaghetti** je vais nous préparer des spaghetti en vitesse (b) *Br* (*wake*) réveiller (c) *Cr* **to k. up a century** faire cent points (d) *Sl* (*make pregnant*) mettre en cloque; **to get knocked up** se faire mettre en cloque 2 *vi Tennis* faire des balles (*avant la partie, pour se faire la main*)

knockabout ['nɒkəbaʊt] 1 *adj* (*game etc*) pour rire; **k. comedian** bateleur *m*, bouffon *m*; **k. comedy** (grosse) farce *f* 2 *n* (a) (*game*) partie *f* pour rire (b) *Naut* petit voilier *m*

knockdown ['nɒkdaʊn] *adj* (a) **k. blow** coup *m* d'assommoir; *Fig F* **a k. argument** un argument de choc (b) *Br F* **k. price** (*at auction*) prix *m* minimum; (*very low price*) prix très bas (c) (*machine, furniture etc*) démontable

knocker ['nɒkər] *n* (a) (**door**) **k.** marteau *m* (de porte), heurtoir *m* (b) *Sl* **knockers** (*breasts*) nichons *mpl* (c) *F* (*critic*) critiqueur *m*

knocking ['nɒkɪŋ] 1 *n* (a) (*at door*) coups *mpl* (*à la porte etc*) (b) (*of engine*) cognement *m* 2 *adj Com* **k. copy** publicité *f* comparative dénigrante

knocking-off time *n F* heure *f* de sortie

knocking-shop *n Br Sl* bordel *m*

knock-kneed [nɒk'niːd] *adj* (*person*) cagneux

knock-knees *npl* genoux *mpl* cagneux

knock-on *adj* **k. effect** répercussions *fpl*

knockout ['nɒkaʊt] 1 *adj* (a) **k. blow** coup *m* qui provoque un K.-O; *Fig* coup de grâce; **to deliver the k. blow** *Boxing* mettre K.-O; *Fig* donner le coup de grâce; *F* **k. drops** soporifique *m* (*esp ajouté à une boisson*)

(b) *Sp* **a k. competition** une compétition avec (épreuves) éliminatoires; *Sp* **the k. stage of a competition** les (épreuves) éliminatoires d'une compétition

(c) *Fig F* (*stunning*) magnifique, fantastique

2 *n* (a) *Boxing* knock-out *m*, *pl* knock-outs; *Fig* coup *m* de grâce

(b) *F* (*impressive person or thing*) merveille *f*; **he's/she's a k.** (*attractive*) ce qu'il/elle est beau/belle

(c) (*at auction*) entente *f* (*entre concurrents pour baisser les prix*)

knock-up *n Tennis* **to have a k.** faire quelques balles (*avant la partie, pour se faire la main*)

knoll [nəʊl] *n* tertre *m*, monticule *m*, butte *f*, mamelon *m*

knot¹ [nɒt] *n* (a) (*with rope, string*) nœud *m*; **to tie/untie a k.** faire/défaire un nœud; **k. of hair** chignon *m*; *Fig F* **to tie the k.** (*get married*) se marier (b) (*in wood*) nœud *m* (c) *Naut* (*unit of speed*) nœud *m*; **to make 10 knots** (*of ship*) filer 10 nœuds; *F* **at a rate of knots** à toute vitesse; *Fig F* **she was spending her money at a rate of knots** elle jetait l'argent par les fenêtres (d) (*group*) (*of people*) groupe *m*; (*of trees*) bouquet *m* (e) (*in muscle*) raideur *f*; **to have a k. in one's stomach** avoir l'estomac noué

knot² (-tt-) 1 *vt* (*piece of string*) (*make one knot*) faire un nœud à; (*make several knots*) faire des nœuds à; **k. the end of the string around the door handle** nouez le bout de la corde à la poignée de la porte; *Br F* **get knotted!** va te faire voir! 2 *vi* (*of string*) se nouer, faire des nœuds; **her stomach knotted with fear** la peur lui nouait l'estomac

▶ **knot together** *vtsep* **k. them together** noue-les ensemble

knotty ['nɒtɪ] *adj* (a) (*rope, hair etc*) plein de nœuds (b) (*problem etc*) épineux, embrouillé; (*question*) difficile, épineux (c) (*wood etc*) noueux, raboteux; (*hands*) noueux

know¹ [nəʊ] *n F* **to be in the k.** être au courant (de l'affaire); *Sp etc* (*have inside information*) avoir des tuyaux; **those in the k.** les initiés *mpl*

know² (*pt* **knew** [njuː]; *pp* **known** [nəʊn]) 1 *vt* (a) (*be acquainted with*) (*person, place*) connaître; (*poverty, happiness etc*) savoir ce que c'est que; **to get** *or* **come to k. sb** faire la connaissance de qn; **when I first knew her** quand j'ai fait sa connaissance; **to have known happiness/poverty** avoir connu le bonheur/la pauvreté; **I've never known anything like it** je n'ai jamais rien vu de semblable; **I don't k. her to speak to** je ne la connais que de vue; **I k. him to say hello to** nous nous saluons; **I'd like to get to k. him better** j'aimerais bien le connaître mieux; **knowing him, he'll probably want to** tel que je le connais, il voudra certainement; **he is well known to the police** il est bien connu de la police

(b) (*to have knowledge of*) (*sth*) savoir; **I k. that** ça je le sais; **to get to k. sth** apprendre qch; **to k. sth by heart** savoir qch par cœur; **how was I to k. you were saving it?** comment est-ce que je pouvais savoir que tu l'avais mis de côté?; **to k. more than one is telling** en savoir plus long qu'on n'en dit; **the end of civilisation as we k. it** la fin de la civilisation en tant que telle; **well, what do you k.!** sans blague!, tiens, tiens!; **she thinks she knows all the answers** elle croit tout savoir; *Fig F* **to k. a thing or two, to k. one's way about** *or* **around** être malin *ou* roublard; **he knows his own mind** il sait ce qu'il veut; **I'll have you k. that ...** sachez que ...; **everyone knows that ...** personne n'ignore que ...; **I**

knew (that) she had talent je lui connaissais du talent; **how do you k. (that) he will come?** qui vous dit qu'il viendra?; **do you k. when .../why ...?** savez-vous quand .../pourquoi ...?; **heaven** *or* **God (only) knows when I shall get back** Dieu (seul) sait quand je serai de retour; **she didn't quite k. what to say** elle ne savait trop que dire; **I don't k. that I do** (*agree etc*) je n'en suis pas sûr; **I k. him to be a liar** je sais que c'est un menteur; **she is known to be a keen photographer** on sait qu'elle aime beaucoup la photographie; **please let us k. whether ...** veuillez nous faire savoir si ...; **I don't want it known/widely known** je ne veux pas que cela se sache/que tout le monde l'apprenne; **he let it be known that he was available** il a fait savoir qu'il était disponible; **it has been known (to happen)** c'est une chose qu'on a vue se produire, ça c'est vu; **I have never known him tell a lie** à ce que je sache, il n'a jamais menti; **I've never known him (to) be this late** je ne l'ai jamais vu être aussi en retard; **she doesn't k. what fear is** elle ne sait pas ce que c'est que d'avoir peur; **to k. what it's like to be happy/poor** savoir ce que c'est que d'être heureux/pauvre; **nobody knows anything about it** personne n'en sait rien; **to k. all about cars** être très calé sur les voitures; **we k. all about her!** si nous la connaissons? et comment!; **we knew nothing about** *or* **of it** nous l'ignorions; **I'll be back before you k. it** je serai bientôt de retour; **it'll be Christmas before we k. it** le temps va passer vite jusqu'à Noël

(c) (*recognize*) reconnaître; (*distinguish*) distinguer (**from** de, d'avec); *F* **he doesn't k. one end of a car from another** il n'y connaît absolument rien en voitures; **don't you k. me?** vous ne me reconnaissez pas?; **I'd k. him anywhere** je le reconnaîtrais n'importe où; **I knew her by her walk** je l'ai reconnue à son allure *ou* à sa démarche; **I knew him for a troublemaker** j'ai deviné que c'était un agitateur; **to k. good from evil** distinguer le bien du mal; **I didn't k. the one from the other** je ne pouvais pas les distinguer l'un de l'autre

(d) (*understand*) savoir; (*subject*) connaître; **I don't k. much about it** je ne sais pas grand-chose là-dessus; **she knows German** elle sait parler allemand; **do you k. anything about physics?** est-ce que tu connais quelque chose en physique?; **what do you k.?** qu'est-ce que tu en sais?; **to k. what one is talking about** savoir de quoi on parle; **to k. how to read/swim/do sth** savoir lire/nager/faire qch; **to k. how to behave** savoir se conduire

(e) *F* **don't I k. it!** à qui le dites-vous!; **wouldn't you k. it!** comme par hasard!; **not if I k. Jean-Luc!** tel que je connais Jean-Luc, sûrement pas!; **she is pretty and doesn't she k. it!** elle est jolie et elle le sait bien!

(f) **to k. better than to ...** bien se garder de ...; **I k. better (than that)** je m'y connais mieux que ça; (*I won't be caught out*) on ne m'y prendra pas, *F* pas si bête!; **he is old enough to k. better** à son âge il devrait être plus raisonnable; **you can't blame him, he doesn't k. any better** on ne peut pas lui en vouloir, il ne se rend pas compte; **you k. best** vous en êtes le meilleur juge; **you k. best what should be done** vous savez mieux que personne ce qu'il faut faire

(g) *Bible* (*sexually*) connaître

2 *vi* savoir; **had I known** si j'avais su; **as far as I k., for all I k.** autant que je sache; **I don't want to k.** je ne veux pas le savoir; **when I mentioned that he just didn't want to k.** quand j'ai mentionné ça il n'a rien voulu savoir; *F* **I wouldn't k.** (*I don't know*) je ne saurais dire; *F* **you k.** (*sentence filler*) vous voyez; **k. what I mean?** tu vois ce que je veux dire?; **as everyone knows** comme tout le monde le sait; **who knows?** qui sait?; **to k. about sth** être informé de qch, être au courant de qch; **I don't k. about that** (*I'm not certain*) je n'en suis pas sûr; **to k. of sb** avoir entendu parler de qn; **to get to k. of sth** apprendre qch; *F* **not that I k. of, not as far as I k.** pas que je sache

know-all *n F* je-sais-tout *mf*; **he's/she's a bit of a k.** c'est un peu monsieur/madame je-sais-tout

know-how *n F* savoir-faire *m*; (*technical*) connaissances *fpl* techniques

knowing ['nəʊɪŋ] **1** *adj* (*intelligent, educated*) intelligent, instruit; (*cunning*) fin, malin, rusé; (*smile*) entendu **2** *n* **there's no k.** c'est impossible à dire; **there's no k. what will happen** on ne peut pas savoir ce qui va se passer

knowingly ['nəʊɪŋlɪ] *adv* (*with knowledge of the facts*) sciemment, en connaissance de cause; (*cunningly*) finement, d'un air rusé; (*to smile*) d'un air entendu; *Com* **never k. undersold** si vous trouvez moins cher, avertissez-nous

know-it-all *n esp Am F* je-sais-tout *mf*

knowledge ['nɒlɪdʒ] *n* **(a)** (*of fact*) connaissance *f*; **it has come to my k. that ...** il est venu *ou* parvenu à ma connaissance que ..., j'ai appris que ...; **I had no k. of it** je ne le savais pas, je l'ignorais; **lack of k.** ignorance *f* (**of** de); **it is (a matter of) common k. that ...** c'est un fait notoire que ...; **to (the best of) my k.** à ma connaissance, (autant) que je sache; **not to my k.** pas que je sache; **without my k.** à mon insu; **to speak with full k. (of the facts)** parler en connaissance de cause *ou* en pleine connaissance des faits

(b) (*learning*) savoir *m*, connaissance(s) *f(pl)*; **to have a k. of several languages** savoir parler plusieurs langues; **he has a little k.** *or* **a working k. of Latin** il a quelques connaissances en latin; **her k. is immense** ses connaissances sont très étendues; **k. of the world** connaissance du monde; *prov* **k. is power** savoir c'est pouvoir; **to show off one's k.** étaler sa science

(c) **carnal k.** connaissance *f* charnelle

knowledgeable ['nɒlɪdʒəb(ə)l] *adj* (*about situation*) bien informé; **she's very k. about cars** elle s'y connaît en voitures

knowledge base *n Comptr* base *f* de connaissances

knowledge-based system *n Comptr* système *m* basé sur les connaissances

knowledge engineer *n Comptr* (*in artificial intelligence*) cogniticien, -ienne

known [nəʊn] *adj* connu; (*thief, enemy, supporter*) notoire; **a k. fact** un fait bien connu; *Petr* **k. reserves** réserves *fpl* prouvées

knuckle ['nʌk(ə)l] *n* **(a)** (*joint*) articulation *f ou* jointure *f* (du doigt); *F* **that was a bit near the k.** c'était assez limite; *F Hum* **k. sandwich** coup *m* de poing; **he'll get a k. sandwich if he's not careful** il va se prendre un coup de poing dans la tronche s'il ne fait pas gaffe **(b)** *Culin* (*of leg of lamb*) (*meat*) souris *f*; (*bone*) manche *m*; **k. of veal/pork** jarret *m* de veau/porc; **k. of ham** jambonneau *m*; **k. end** (*of pork*) jambonneau *m*

▶ **knuckle down** *vi F* (*begin working hard*) s'y mettre sérieusement; **to k. down to sth** se mettre à qch

▶ **knuckle under** *vi F* (*give in*) mettre les pouces

knuckle-duster *n* coup-de-poing *m* (américain), *pl* coups-de-poing

knurl[1] [nɜːl] *n* **(a)** (*in wood*) nœud *m* **(b)** (*in metalworking*) moletage *m*; (*tool*) molette *f*, godronnoir *m*

knurl[2] *vt* (*in metalworking*) molet(t)er, godronner

KO[1], *pl* **KO's** ['keɪ'əʊ, 'keɪ'əʊz] *n Boxing etc Sl* K.-O. *m*

KO[2] *vt* (*3rd person pr* **KO's** ['keɪ'əʊz]; *prp* **KO'ing**; *pp, pt* **KO'd**) *Boxing etc F* mettre K.-O.

koala [kəʊ'ɑːlə] *n* **k. (bear)** koala *m*

Koch's bacillus [kɒxsbə'sɪləs] *n Med* bacille de Koch *m*

kohlrabi [kəʊl'rɑːbɪ] *n* chou-rave *m*, *pl* choux-raves, turnep(s) *m*

kola ['kəʊlə] *n* (*plant*) cola *m*, kola *m*; **k. (tree)** kolatier *m*; **k. nut** noix *f* de cola *ou* de kola

kook [kʊk] *n Am F* drôle *m* d'oiseau, énergumène *mf*

kookaburra ['kʊkəbʌrə] *n* dacélo *m*

Koran (the) [ðəkɔː'rɑːn] *n Rel* le Koran, le Coran

Koranic [kɔː'rænɪk] *adj* coranique

Korea [kə'rɪə] *n* Corée *f*; **North/South K.** Corée du Nord/du Sud

Korean [kə'rɪən] **1** *adj* coréen **2** *n* **(a)** Coréen, -enne **(b)** *Ling* coréen *m*

korma ['kɔːmə] *n Culin* **chicken/prawn k.** = poulet/crevettes à la sauce indienne au yaourt ou à la crème

kosher ['kəʊʃər] *adj Jewish Rel* cascher *inv*, kascher *inv*; *F* (*legitimate*) légitime, comme il faut, impec

kowtow [kaʊ'taʊ] *vi* **(a)** *F* (*act obsequiously*) **to k. to sb** faire des courbettes devant qn **(b)** (*bow*) se prosterner (**to** devant)

KP ['keɪ'piː] *n US Mil Sl* (*abbr* **kitchen police**) **to do KP (duty)** être de corvée de patates

kph [keɪpiː'eɪtʃ] (*abbr* **kilometres per hour**) km/h

kraft [krɑːft] *n* papier *m* d'emballage fort, papier Kraft

Krakow ['krɑːkɒf] *n* Cracovie *f*

Kraut [kraʊt] *n Offensive Sl* boche *mf*

Kremlin (the) [ðə'kremlɪn] *n* le Kremlin; *F* **K. watcher** spécialiste *mf* du Kremlin, kremlinologiste *mf*

Kremlinologist [kremlɪ'nɒlədʒɪst] *n* kremlinologiste *mf*

krill [krɪl] *n* krill *m*

krona ['krəʊnə] *n Fin* couronne *f*

Kt *abbr* **knight**

kudos ['kjuːdɒs] *n* (*prestige*) prestige *m*; (*fame*) célébrité *f*; **to get the k. for sth** recevoir toute la gloire pour qch; **to receive k.** être acclamé

Ku Klux Klan ['kuː'klʌks'klæn] *n* Ku Klux Klan *m*

kumquat ['kʊmkwɒt] *n* kumquat *m*

kung fu ['kʌŋ'fuː] *n* kung-fu *m*; **a k. expert** un expert en kung-fu

Kurd [kɜːd] **1** *adj* kurde **2** *n* Kurde *mf*

Kurdish ['kɜːdɪʃ] **1** *adj* kurde **2** *n Ling* kurde *m*

Kurdistan [kɜːdɪ'stɑːn] *n* Kurdistan *m*

Kuwait [kʊ'weɪt, kjuː-] *n* Koweït *m*

Kuwaiti [kʊ'weɪtɪ, kjuː-] **1** *adj* koweïtien **2** *n* Koweïtien, -ienne

kV (*abbr* **kilovolt**) kV

kvetch [kvetʃ] *vi US F* geindre, se plaindre

kW (*abbr* **kilowatt**) kW

kWh (*abbr* **kilowatt-hour**) kWh

Ky *abbr* **Kentucky**

Kyrie ['kɪrɪeɪ] *n Rel* **K. (eleison** [ɪ'leɪsɒn]**)** kyrie *m*

L

L, l [el] *n* **(a)** (*letter*) L, l *mf* **(b) L-plate** plaque *f* d'auto-école; **L-shaped room** pièce *f* en forme de L.
l [el] **(a)** (*abbr* **litre**) l. **(b)** (*abbr* **length**) longueur, long. **(c)** (*abbr* **line**) ligne **(d)** (*abbr* **left**) gauche
LA [el'eɪ] *n US abbr* **Los Angeles**
La *abbr* **Louisiana**
la [lɑː] *n Mus* la *m*; **sing it to 'la'** chante-le en la
laager ['lɑːgər] *n Pol* (*esp in South Africa*) camp *m*
Lab *Br Pol* (*abbr* **Labour**) *see* = **labour¹**
lab [læb] *n F* (*abbr* **laboratory**) labo *m*
labcoat ['læbkəʊt] *n* blouse *f* de laboratoire
label¹ ['leɪb(ə)l] *n* **(a)** (*on parcel, bottle etc*) étiquette *f*; **sticky l.** étiquette gommée **(b)** *Com* (*indication of brand*) label *m*, étiquette *f*; **to record on the Motown l.** (*of singer, musician etc*) enregistrer sous le label Motown; **designer l.** (*on clothes*) marque *f*, griffe *f* **(c)** *Comptr* (*of tape, file*) label *m* **(d)** *Fig* (*of person*) étiquette *f*; **the l. 'reactionary' stayed with him all his life** l'étiquette de réactionnaire lui est restée toute sa vie **(e)** *Ch* marque *f*
label² *vt* **(-ll-,** *US* **-l-)** **(a)** (*tie label to*) étiqueter; (*stick label on*) coller une étiquette sur; **a bottle labelled poison** une bouteille marquée poison; **all luggage must be clearly labelled** tous les bagages doivent être clairement étiquetés **(b) to l. sb a liar** *etc* qualifier qn de menteur *etc* **(c)** *Ch* marquer
labelling ['leɪb(ə)lɪŋ] *n* étiquetage *m*
labellum, *pl* **-bella** [lə'beləm, -ə] *n Bot* labelle *m*
labial ['leɪbɪəl] **1** *adj* labial; *Ling* **l. consonant** consonne *f* labiale **2** *n Ling* labiale *f*
labialize ['leɪbɪəlaɪz] *vt Ling* labialiser
labiate ['leɪbɪeɪt] *Bot* **1** *adj* labié **2** *n* labiée *f*
labiodental [leɪbɪəʊ'dent(ə)l] *adj Ling* labiodental
labium, *pl* **-a** ['leɪbɪəm, -ə] *n Anat* **labia** (*of vulva*) labia *mpl*, lèvres *fpl*
labor, labored *etc US* = **labour, laboured** *etc*
laboratory [lə'bɒrətrɪ, *esp Am* 'læbrətɔːrɪ] *n* laboratoire *m*; **dental l.** laboratoire de prothèse dentaire; **l. assistant** laborantin, -ine; **l. equipment** matériel *m* de laboratoire; **l. experiment** expérience *f* en laboratoire
laboratory-tested *adj* testé en laboratoire
laborious [lə'bɔːrɪəs] *adj* **(a)** pénible, fatigant; (*task*) laborieux **(b)** (*style*) laborieux
laboriously [lə'bɔːrɪəslɪ] *adv* péniblement
laboriousness [lə'bɔːrɪəsnɪs] *n* **(a)** (*of task, ascent etc*) pénibilité *f* **(b)** (*of literary style*) caractère *m* laborieux
labour¹, *US* **labor** ['leɪbər] *n* **(a)** (*work*) travail *m*, labeur *m*; **manual l.** travail manuel; **division of l.** division *f* du travail

(b) (*workers*) main-d'œuvre *f*; **male/female l.** main-d'œuvre masculine/féminine; **cost of l.** prix *m* de la main-d'œuvre; **capital and l.** le capital et la main-d'œuvre; *Br Hist* **Minister of L.** ministre *m* du travail; **l. dispute** conflit *m* du travail; *Br formerly* **l. exchange** bureau *m* de placement; **l. force** main-d'œuvre *f*; **l. laws** législation *f* du travail; **l. relations** relations *fpl* dans l'entreprise, relations de travail; **l. shortage** pénurie *f* *ou* crise *f* de main-d'œuvre; **l. supply** main-d'œuvre disponible; *US* **l. union** syndicat *m* (ouvrier); **l. unrest** agitation *f* ouvrière

(c) *Pol* **L.** les travaillistes *mpl*; **the L. party** le parti travailliste; **L. Member (of Parliament)** député *m* travailliste; **L. leader** dirigeant, -ante (du parti) travailliste

(d) (*task*) **the twelve labours of Hercules** les douze travaux *mpl* d'Hercule; **I'm not doing this as a l. of love** je ne fais pas ça pour le plaisir

(e) *Obst* travail *m*; **premature l.** accouchement *m* avant terme; **woman in l.** femme en couches; **to be in l.** être en train d'accoucher; **she went into l. at 3 o'clock** le travail a commencé à 3 heures; **to induce l.** provoquer l'accouchement; **it was a difficult l.** ça a été un accouchement difficile; **l. pains** douleurs *fpl* de l'accouchement; **l. ward** salle *f* d'accouchement
labour², *US* **labor** **1** *vi* **(a)** (*of person*) travailler, peiner; **to l. for sth** se donner de la peine pour obtenir qch; **he laboured all his life for peace** il a travaillé toute sa vie pour la paix; **to l. at** *or* **over sth** peiner *ou* trimer sur qch; **to l. up a hill** gravir péniblement une côte; **to l. under great difficulties** être aux prises avec de grandes difficultés; **to l. under a sense of injustice** nourrir un sentiment d'injustice; **to l. under a misapprehension** être dans l'erreur, être (la) victime d'une erreur

(b) (*of engine*) fatiguer, peiner; (*of ship*) bourlinguer, fatiguer; **to l. uphill** (*of car*) peiner dans les côtes

2 *vt* **I won't l. the point** je ne m'étendrai pas là-dessus
labour camp *n* camp *m* de travail
Labour Day *n Am* fête *f* du travail
laboured, *US* **labored** ['leɪbəd] *adj* **(a)** (*breathing*) pénible **(b)** (*style etc*) trop travaillé, trop élaboré; (*joke*) laborieux
labourer, *US* **laborer** ['leɪbərər] *n* travailleur *m*; *Ind* manœuvre *m*; *Prov* **the l. is worthy of his hire** toute peine *ou* tout travail mérite salaire; **unskilled l.** ouvrier *m* non spécialisé; **agricultural l.** ouvrier agricole
labouring, *US* **laboring** ['leɪbərɪŋ] *adj* **the l. class** la classe ouvrière; **a l. job** un travail manuel
labour intensive *adj* qui demande une main-d'œuvre importante
Labourite, *US* **Laborite** ['leɪbəraɪt] *n Pol* travailliste *mf*
labour market *n* marché *m* du travail
labour-saving, *US* **labor-** *adj* (*device, invention*) qui simplifie la tâche; **l. device** (*in household*) appareil *m* ménager; **computers are not always l. devices** les ordinateurs ne font pas toujours gagner du temps
Labrador ['læbrədɔːr] *n* **(a)** *Geog* Labrador *m* **(b)** (*dog*) labrador *m*
laburnum [lə'bɜːnəm] *n* (*tree*) cytise *m* (à grappes)
labyrinth ['læbərɪnθ] *n* **(a)** *Archit etc* labyrinthe *m*, dédale *m* **(b)** *Anat* (*of the ear*) labyrinthe *m*
labyrinthine [læbə'rɪnθaɪn] *adj Archit* en labyrinthe; *Fig* (*procedures, structure*) extrêmement compliqué, labyrinthique
lac [læk] *n* gomme *f* laque, laque *f*
lace¹ [leɪs] *n* **(a)** *Tex* dentelle *f*; **bobbin** *or* **pillow l.** dentelle aux fuseaux *ou* au coussin; **l. curtain** rideau *m* en *ou* de dentelle **(b)** (*of shoe*) lacet *m* **(c)** (*braid*) **gold/silver l.** galon *m* d'or/d'argent
lace² **1** *vt* **(a)** (*shoes*) lacer; **to l. sth with sth** entrelacer qch de *ou* avec qch **(b)** *F* **to l. a drink** ajouter de l'alcool à une boisson; **milk laced with rum** lait au rhum; **she laced his cup of tea with poison** elle ajouta du poison à sa tasse de thé; *Fig* **he laced his story with salacious details** il ajoutait des détails salaces à son histoire; **her account was laced with scandalous lies** son récit était plein de mensonges effrontés **2** *vi* (*of boots etc*) se lacer
▶ **lace into** *vipo F* (*attack*) s'en prendre à; (*physically*) rosser, s'en prendre à
▶ **lace up** **1** *vtsep* (*shoes*) lacer **2** *vi* **shoes that l. up** chaussures à lacets; **they l. up at the sides** elles se lacent *ou* s'attachent sur le côté
lacemaker ['leɪsmeɪkər] *n* fabricant, -ante de dentelles; (*woman only*) dentellière *f*
lacemaking ['leɪsmeɪkɪŋ] *n* dentellerie *f*
lacerate ['læsəreɪt] *vt* lacérer, déchirer
lacerated ['læsəreɪtəd] *adj* (*hand, skin*) lacéré; **to be l. by pain** être transpercé par la douleur; **l. feelings** sentiments profondément blessés
laceration [læsə'reɪʃən] *n* **(a)** (*action*) lacération *f*, déchirement *m* **(b)** (*tear*) déchirure *f*
lace-up **1** *n* (*shoe*) chaussure *f* à lacets **2** *adj* (*shoe*) à lacets
lacewing ['leɪswɪŋ] *n Ent* **l. (fly)** hémérobe *m*
lacework ['leɪswɜːk] *n* (*art*) dentellerie *f*; **l. objects** objets en dentelle
lachrymal ['lækrɪm(ə)l] *adj Anat* lacrymal; **l. gland** glande *f* lacrymale; **l. duct** conduit *m* lacrymal
lachrymose ['lækrɪməʊs] *adj* larmoyant
lacing ['leɪsɪŋ] *n* **(a)** **milk with a l. of rum** lait avec un petit goût de rhum **(b)** (*on uniform*) galon *m*
lack¹ [læk] *n* manque *m* (**of** de); **l. of judgment/time** manque

de jugement/temps; **l. of money** pénurie *f* d'argent; **she was tired from l. of sleep** elle était fatiguée de n'avoir pas assez dormi; **for l. of ...** faute de ...

lack² **1** *vt* (*experience, skill, humour etc*) manquer de; **what the country lacks in modern tourist amenities it more than makes up for in natural beauty** la beauté naturelle du paysage compense largement le manque de structures touristiques; **we l. nothing** nous ne manquons de rien, il ne nous manque rien **2** *vi* (*of time*) manquer; **time was lacking** on manquait de temps; **he's lacking in purpose** il lui manque un but; **to be lacking in confidence/experience** manquer de confiance/d'expérience; **they l. for nothing** ils ne manquent de rien; *F* **to be lacking** (*mentally*) être (un peu) simplet

lackadaisical [lækə'deɪzɪk(ə)l] *adj* (*person, manner etc*) apathique, *F* je-m'en-foutiste; **to take a l. approach to one's work** prendre son travail avec désinvolture

lackey ['lækɪ] *n Pej* larbin *m*

lacklustre, *US* **lackluster** ['læklʌstər] *adj* (*eyes, gaze*) terne, sans brillant; (*performance*) médiocre

laconic [lə'kɒnɪk] *adj* (*person, answer etc*) laconique

laconically [lə'kɒnɪklɪ] *adv* laconiquement

lacquer¹ ['lækər] *n* (*for wood, hair etc*) laque *f*; (*coloured*) peinture *f* laquée; **a red l. screen** un écran recouvert de laque rouge

lacquer² *vt* laquer; **a lacquered box** une boîte en laque

lacquerwork ['lækəwɜːk] *n* laque(s) *m(pl)*

lacrimal ['lækrɪm(ə)l] *adj* = **lachrymal**

lacrosse [lə'krɒs] *n Sp* lacrosse *m*

lacrymal ['lækrɪm(ə)l] *adj* = **lachrymal**

lactate [læk'teɪt] *vi* produire du lait

lactation [læk'teɪʃən] *n* lactation *f*

lacteal ['læktɪəl] *adj* lactaire

lactic ['læktɪk] *adj Ch* lactique; **l. acid** acide *m* lactique

lactose ['læktəʊz] *n Ch* lactose *m*

lacuna, *pl* **-ae, -as** [læ'kjuːnə, -iː, -əz] *n* (*in knowledge, manuscript*) lacune *f*

lacustrine [lə'kʌstraɪn] *adj* (*plant etc*) lacustre

lacy ['leɪsɪ] *adj* (*made of lace*) de dentelle; (*resembling lace*) fin comme de la dentelle

lad [læd] *n* **(a)** *F* (*young man*) jeune homme *m*; (*boy*) garçon *m*; **he's only a l.** ce n'est qu'un gosse; **the doctor's l.** (*son*) le fils du docteur; **come on, lads!** allons, les gars!; **he's a bit of a l.** *or* **quite a l.** c'est un gaillard; **one of the lads** un des gars; **listen, my l.** écoute, mon petit gars **(b)** *Br Horseracing* **(stable) l.** lad *m*

ladder¹ ['lædər] *n* **(a)** échelle *f*; **it's unlucky to walk under a l.** ça porte malheur de passer sous une échelle; *Fig* **the social l.** l'échelle sociale; *Fig* **to get one's foot on the l.** mettre un pied dans le circuit; *Fig* **to reach the top of the l.** atteindre le sommet de l'échelle; **fish** *or* **salmon l.** échelle à saumons **(b)** *esp Br* (*in stocking*) échelle *f*; **I've got a l.** j'ai une échelle à mon collant, mon collant est filé

ladder² *esp Br* **1** *vt* (*stocking*) filer **2** *vi* (*of stocking*) se démailler, filer

ladder-proof *adj esp Br* (*stockings*) qui ne filent pas

laddie ['lædɪ] *n Scot F* garçon *m*; (*term of endearment*) mon petit gars

laden ['leɪd(ə)n] *adj* chargé (**with** de); **I was l. with shopping** j'avais les bras chargés de commissions; **fully l. ship** navire en pleine charge; **heavily l. tree** arbre chargé de fruits

la-di-da, la-de-da ['lɑːdɪ'dɑː] *adj F* (*air, voice*) affecté, maniéré

ladies ['leɪdɪz] *n* toilettes *fpl* (des dames); (*as sign*) dames; **can you tell me where the l. is?** pouvez-vous m'indiquer où sont les toilettes?

lading ['leɪdɪŋ] *n* **(a)** (*action*) (*of ship*) chargement *m*; (*of merchandise*) mise *f* à bord **(b)** (*cargo*) chargement *m*

ladle¹ ['leɪd(ə)l] *n* **(a) (soup) l.** louche *f* **(b)** *Ind* puisoir *m*; *Metal* **foundry l.** poche *f* de fonderie

ladle² *vt* **to l. (out) the soup** servir le potage (avec une louche); *F* **to l. out advice** prodiguer des conseils

ladleful ['leɪd(ə)lfʊl] *n* pleine louche *f* (**of** de)

lady, *pl* **-ies** ['leɪdɪ, -ɪz] *n* **(a)** dame *f*; **l. doctor** femme *f* médecin; **l. of the bedchamber** (*at court*) dame d'atours; **she's a real l.** c'est une femme très comme il faut; **she's no l.** ce n'est pas une femme comme il faut; **a l. and a gentleman** une dame et un monsieur; **a young l.** une jeune fille; (*married*) une jeune dame; **an old l.** une vieille dame; **how are you, young l.?** (*to child*) comment allez-vous, jeune fille?; **listen to me, young l.** écoute un peu, jeune fille; **ladies and gentlemen!** (*at meeting etc*) mesdames, mesdemoiselles, messieurs!; **come in, ladies!** entrez donc, mesdames!; **he's a ladies' man** c'est un homme à femmes; **the l. of the house** la maîtresse de maison; **painted l.** (*butterfly*) belle-dame *f*, *pl* belles-dames; **ladies' fingers** (*vegetable*) gombo(s) *m(pl)*; **l.'s maid** femme de chambre; *Am* **ladies' room** toilettes *fpl* des dames; **ladies' tailor** tailleur *m* pour dames; **l.'s watch** montre pour dames

(b) *Rel* **Our L.** Notre-Dame *f*, la sainte Vierge; **L. chapel** chapelle *f* de la Vierge; **L. Day** la fête de l'Annonciation (*le 25 mars*)

(c) (*title*) **L. Browne** (*no Fr equivalent*) lady Browne (*femme de Sir David Browne*); **the l. of the manor** la châtelaine; *Pej* **L. Bountiful** = dame *f* patronnesse; *F* **stop behaving like L. Muck** arrête de jouer les grandes dames

(d) *Old-fashioned* (*wife*) femme *f*, épouse *f*; **how's your good l.?** comment va votre dame?; **this is my l. wife** voici mon épouse; **my young l.** (*fiancée*) ma fiancée, ma future

ladybird, *Am* **ladybug** ['leɪdɪbɜːd, -bʌg] *n* coccinelle *f*, *F* bête *f* à bon Dieu

ladyfinger ['leɪdɪfɪŋgər] *n Culin* boudoir *m*

lady-in-waiting *n* (*at court*) dame *f* d'honneur

lady-killer *n F* bourreau *m* des cœurs, don Juan *m*

ladylike ['leɪdɪlaɪk] *adj* (*woman*) comme il faut, bien élevée; (*air, behaviour*) distingué; **climbing trees isn't very l.** les vraies demoiselles ne grimpent pas aux arbres; **it's not a l. thing to say** ce n'est pas beau dans la bouche d'une jeune fille

ladyship ['leɪdɪʃɪp] *n* **her l., your l.** madame (la comtesse *etc*); *Iron* **her l. doesn't feel like it** madame n'en a pas envie

lady's-slipper [leɪdɪz'slɪpər] *n* (*orchid*) sabot *m* de Vénus

lag¹ [læg] *n* (*delay*), *El* retard *m*; *Ind etc* **time l.** décalage *m*

lag² *vi* (**-gg-**) être à la traîne

▶ **lag behind** **1** *vi* (*of people, walkers, company industry*) être à la traîne; **don't l. behind** ne reste pas à la traîne; **salaries are still lagging behind** les salaires sont restés à un niveau inférieur; **she always lags behind on the way to school** sur le chemin de l'école elle est toujours à la traîne **2** *vipo* **to l. behind the others** être à la traîne par rapport aux autres

lag³ *n esp Br Sl* **an old l.** (*jailbird*) un repris de justice, un récidiviste

lag⁴ *vt* (*boiler etc*) calorifuger, isoler

lager ['lɑːgər] *n* bière *f* blonde; *Br F* **l. lout** voyou *m*; (*drunk*) voyou imbibé de bière

laggard ['lægəd] *n* (*in race*) traînard, -arde; **the laggards in the class** ceux qui apprennent plus lentement que les autres

lagging ['lægɪŋ] *n* **(a)** (*action*) (*of boiler*) garnissage *m*, calorifugeage *m* **(b)** (*material*) (*for boiler*) revêtement *m* calorifuge

lagoon [lə'guːn] *n Geog* **(a)** (*of atoll*) lagon *m* **(b)** (*with sand, shingle etc*) lagune *f*

lah [lɑː] *n Mus* = **la**

lah-di-dah ['lɑːdɪ'dɑː] *adj* = **la-di-da**

laid *see* **lay²**

laid-back [leɪd'bæk] *adj F* (*person, atmosphere*) relax, décontracté

lain *see* **lie⁴**

lair [leər] *n* (*of big cat*) tanière *f*, repaire *m*, *esp Litt* antre *m*; *Fig* (*room etc*) antre; **brigands' l.** repaire de brigands

laird [leəd] *n Scot* propriétaire *m* (foncier)

laisser-faire, laissez-faire [leser'feər] *n esp Econ* laisser-faire *m*; **l. policy** politique *f* de laisser-faire

laity ['leɪɪtɪ] *n* **the l.** les laïques *mpl*

lake¹ [leɪk] *n* lac *m*; **salt l.** lac salé; **ornamental l.** bassin *m*, pièce *f* d'eau décorative; **the Great Lakes** les Grands Lacs; **the Lakes** la région des lacs (*au nord-ouest de l'Angleterre*); **the L. poets** les (poètes *mpl*) lakistes *mpl*; *Fig* **the Common Market's wine l.** = le surplus de vin du Marché Commun; *Sl* **go jump in the l.** va te faire voir; **l. dwelling** habitation *f* lacustre; **l. front** *or* **shore** *or* **side** bord *m* de lac; **they live on the l. front** *or* **shore** ils habitent au bord du lac; **a l.-side picnic** un pique-nique au bord du lac

lake² *n* (*pigment*) laque *f*; **crimson l.** laque carminée

Lake District *n* la région des lacs (*au nord-ouest de l'Angleterre*)

Lake Geneva *n* le lac Léman, le lac de Genève

Lakeland ['leɪklənd] *n* la région des lacs (*au nord-ouest de l'Angleterre*)

lam¹ [læm] *n Am Sl* (*flight*) fuite *f*; **to be on the l.** être en cavale; **to take it on the l.** partir en cavale

lam² *vi* (**-mm-**) *F* **to l. into sb** (*hit*) rosser qn, étriller qn; (*verbally*) étriller qn

lama ['lɑːmə] *n Rel* lama *m*; **the Dalai** *or* **Grand L.** le dalaï-lama

lamb¹ [læm] *n* agneau *m*; **ewe l.** agnelle *f*; **ewe with l.** brebis *f* pleine; *Rel* **L. (of God)** Agneau (de Dieu); *F* **to be a l.** (*of person*) être gentil comme tout; **she accepted my decision like a l.** elle a accepté ma décision sans broncher; *F* **my l.** (*term of endearment*) mon petit; **poor l.** (*person*) pauvre petit(e); *prov* **like a l. to the slaughter** comme une vache que l'on emmène à l'abattoir; **the miners refused to go like lambs to the slaughter and decided to fight the closures** les mineurs ont refusé d'aller à l'abattoir et ont décidé de s'opposer à la fermeture des puits; *Culin* **l. cutlet** *or* **chop** côtelette *f* d'agneau; *Bot* **l.'s lettuce** mâche *f*; *F* **l.'s tails** (*of hazel tree*) chatons *mpl*; **l.'s wool** laine *f* d'agneau; **a l.'s wool sweater** un pull en laine d'agneau

lamb² *vi* (*of ewe*) agneler, mettre bas

lambast [læm'bæst], **lambaste** [læm'beɪst] *vt* (*person*) réprimander, *Lit* fustiger

lambing ['læmɪŋ] *n* agnelage *m*; **the l. season** l'agnelage

lambskin ['læmskɪn] *n* peau *f* d'agneau; (*fur*) agnelin *m*

lame¹ [leɪm] *adj* (*person, horse*) boiteux; (*through accident etc*) estropié; **l. leg** jambe boiteuse; **to be l.** boiter; **to be l. in one leg** boiter d'une jambe; **to be completely l.** être handicapé des deux jambes; **to go l.** se mettre à boiter; *Fig* **l. excuse** excuse boiteuse; **l. argument** argument boiteux *ou* qui ne tient pas debout; *Liter* **l. verses** vers boiteux *ou* qui boitent

lame² *vt* (*person, horse*) estropier; **to be lamed by an accident/illness** rester boiteux à la suite d'un accident/d'une maladie; **she had been lamed by polio** elle est restée boiteuse à cause de la polio

lamé ['lɑːmeɪ] *n Tex* lamé *m*; **gold/silver l.** lamé d'or/d'argent; **a gold l. dress** une robe en lamé d'or

lamebrain ['leɪmbreɪn] *n F* idiot, -e, abruti, -e

lamely ['leɪmlɪ] *adv* (*to apologize*) faiblement

lameness ['leɪmnɪs] *n* claudication *f*; (*of horse*) boiterie *f*; *Fig* (*of excuse etc*) faiblesse *f*

lament¹ [lə'ment] *n* **(a)** lamentation *f* **(b)** *Mus* complainte *f*

lament² **1** *vt* se lamenter sur, pleurer; (*person*) pleurer; **I was lamenting my lost youth** je pleurais ma jeunesse perdue; **the nation did not l. the death of the dictator** le pays n'a pas pleuré la mort du dictateur; **it's to be lamented** c'est à regretter **2** *vi* se lamenter (**over sth** sur qch); pleurer (**over sb/sth** qn/qch)

lamentable [lə'məntəb(ə)l] *adj* (*loss, failure*) déplorable; (*pathetic*) (*performance etc*) lamentable; **it's l.!** c'est déplorable!

lamentably [lə'məntəblɪ] *adj* déplorablement; (*pathetically*) lamentablement

lamentation [læmən'teɪʃən] *n* lamentation *f*; *Bible* **the Lamentations of Jeremiah** les Lamentations de Jérémie

lamented [lə'mentɪd] *adj* **the late l. Mr Jones** le regretté M. Jones

laminate¹ ['læmɪnert] *n* stratifié *m*

laminate² **1** *vt* **(a)** (*bond*) laminer, lamifier; (*glass*) feuilleter; (*plastic*) stratifier; (*wood*) contreplaquer **(b)** (*split*) diviser en lamelles **(c)** (*cover*) (*paper etc*) plastifier **2** *vi* **(a)** (*bond*) se laminer **(b)** (*split*) se diviser en lamelles

laminated ['læmɪneɪtəd] *adj* **(a)** (*glass*) feuilleté; (*wood*) contreplaqué; **l. plate glass** verre *m* (de sécurité) feuilleté; *Ind* **l. plastics** plastique *m* stratifié; *MecE* **l. spring** ressort *m* à lames (superposées) **(b)** (*paper etc*) plastifié; **l. jacket** (*of book*) jaquette *f* plastifiée

Lammas ['læməs] *n* **L. (Day)** le premier août

lammergeier ['læməgaɪər] *n* (*bird*) gypaète *m* barbu

lamp [læmp] *n* **(a)** lampe *f*; **bicycle l.** (*fixed*) phare *m* de bicyclette; (*detachable*) lampe de bicyclette; **portable l., inspection l.** (*in garage etc*) baladeuse *f*; **street l.** réverbère *m*; **hanging l.** suspension *f* **(b)** **neon l.** lampe au néon; **ultraviolet l.** lampe à ultra-violets

lampblack ['læmpblæk] *n* noir *m* de fumée

lamplight ['læmplaɪt] *n* lumière *f* de la lampe; **to work by l.** travailler à la lampe

lamplit ['læmplɪt] *adj* éclairé

lampoon¹ [læm'puːn] *n* pamphlet *m*, libelle *m*

lampoon² *vt* (*person*) brocarder, railler

lampoonist [læm'puːnɪst] *n* satiriste *m*, pamphlétaire *m*

lamppost ['læmppəʊst] *n* (*in street*) réverbère *m*

lamprey, *pl* **-eys** ['læmprɪ, -ɪz] *n* (*eel*) lamproie *f*

lampshade ['læmpʃeɪd] *n* abat-jour *m inv*

lampstand ['læmpstænd] *n* pied *m* de lampe

LAN [læn] *n Comptr abbr* **local area network**

lance¹ [lɑːns] *n* (*weapon*) lance *f*; *Arch, Lit* **to break a l. with sb** rompre une lance avec qn

lance² *vt Med* (*abscess*) percer, inciser

lance corporal *n Br Mil* soldat *m* de première classe

lanceolate(d) ['lɑːnsɪəleɪt, -ɪd] *adj Bot* lancéolé

lancer ['lɑːnsər] *n* **(a)** *Mil* lancier *m* **(b)** (*dance*) **lancers** (quadrille *m* des) lanciers *mpl*

lancet ['lɑːnsɪt] *n* **(a)** *Med* lancette *f* **(b)** *Archit* **l. (arch)** lancette *f*; **l. window** fenêtre *f* en ogive

Lancs *abbr* **Lancashire**

land¹ [lænd] *n* **(a)** (*as opposed to sea*) terre *f*; **on l.** sur terre; **to travel by l.** voyager par voie de terre; **l. breeze** brise *f* de terre; **l. route** voie *f* de terre; *Naut* **to make l.** reconnaître la terre; *Fig* **to see how the l. lies** tâter le terrain; *Mil etc* **(to attack) by l., sea and air** (attaquer) par terre, par mer et par air; **l. warfare** guerre *f* sur terre; **l. army, l. forces** armée *f* de terre

(b) (*earth, soil*) terre *f*, sol *m*; **arable l.** terre arable; **man lives off the l.** c'est la terre qui nourrit les hommes; **to live off the l.** (*of farmers*) vivre en autarcie; (*of army*) subsister sans ravitaillement

(c) (*country*) pays *m*, terre *f*; **the best in the l.** le meilleur du pays; **the l. of the midnight sun** le pays du soleil de minuit; **to be still in the l. of the living** être encore de ce monde; **a l. fit for heroes** (*expression attribuée à Lloyd George qui exprimait par là sa vision de l'Angleterre victorieuse au sortir de la Grande Guerre*; *souvent utilisée ironiquement, par ex.* if the returning veterans hoped for a l. fit for heroes, they were to be sadly disappointed); *prov* **a l. flowing with milk and honey** un pays où coulent le lait et le miel; **a l. of opportunity** un pays où tout est possible; **the l. of dreams/Nod** le pays des rêves/de Morphée

(d) (*property*) terre(s) *f(pl)*; **private l.** terrain privé; **a piece of l.** un terrain; **the farmer wouldn't allow campers on his l.** le fermier n'acceptait pas de campeurs sur ses terres; **to buy l.** acheter des terres

land² **1** *vt* **(a)** (*put on land*) (*from ship, plane*) débarquer; *Com* (*merchandise*) décharger

(b) *Av* (*bring down to land*) (*plane*) faire atterrir; **they landed him on the deck of the ferry** ils l'ont fait atterrir sur le pont du ferry; **to l. a man on the moon** faire alunir un homme

(c) *Zool* (*fish*) amener à terre

(d) *F* (*win, obtain*) se dégoter; **they landed all the prizes** ils ont raflé tous les prix; **he's just landed a good job** il vient juste de dégoter un bon boulot

(e) *F* (*in phrases*) **that will l. you in prison** tu vas te retrouver en prison; **you've landed us in a nice mess!** vous nous avez mis dans de beaux draps!; **to be landed with sth** rester avec qch sur les bras; **I've been landed with the job of telling him** c'est à moi qu'il est revenu de le lui dire

2 *vi* **(a)** (*from ship, plane*) débarquer; (*of aircraft, pilot*) atterrir; (*on deck of aircraft carrier*) apponter; **to l. on the moon** alunir; **to l. on the sea** amerrir; *Av* **when do we l.?** quand est-ce que nous atterrissons?

(b) (*jumping off wall etc*) se recevoir; (*from great height, parachutist*) atterrir; **he slipped and landed in a puddle** il a glissé et a atterri dans une flaque d'eau; **to l. flat on one's back** se retrouver les quatre fers en l'air; **to l. on one's feet** retomber sur ses pieds; (*of cat*) retomber sur ses pattes; *Fig F* **he always manages to l. on his feet** il arrive toujours à retomber sur ses pattes

(c) *Sp* (*after jumping*) (*of gymnast, ski-jumper, horse*) se réceptionner

▶ **land up** *vi F* (*in a ditch, hospital, jail etc*) se retrouver; **I landed up having to dance with him** il a fallu que je danse avec lui; **I always landed up with the worst jobs** je me retrouvais toujours avec les tâches les plus ingrates à faire

land act *n Jur* loi *f* agraire

land agent *n* régisseur *m*

landau ['lændɔː] *n* (*carriage*) landau *m*, *pl* landaus

land bank *n* crédit *m* foncier

land bridge *n* isthme *m*

land charge *n Acct* dette *f* foncière

landed ['lændɪd] *adj attrib* **(a)** (*owning land*) **the l. gentry** la petite noblesse; *Acct* **l. costs** coûts *mpl* fonciers; **l. estate** propriété *f* foncière; **l. property** propriété foncière *ou* territoriale; **l. proprietor** propriétaire *m* terrien **(b)** *Can Admin* **l. immigrant** immigrant *m* reçu

landfall ['lændfɔːl] *n Naut* (*arrival*) atterrissage *m*; (*sight of land*) arrivée *f* en vue de terre; **to make (a) l.** (*arrive*) atterrir; (*sight land*) arriver en vue de terre

landfill ['lændfɪl] *n* remblai *m*; **to use sth as l.** utiliser qch pour remblayer *ou* comme remblai; **l. site** décharge publique

land girl *n Br Hist* fille *f* de ferme (pendant la deuxième guerre mondiale)

landing ['lændɪŋ] *n* **(a)** *Naut* débarquement *m*; *Com* déchargement *m*; **l. and port charges** *Com* frais *mpl* de débarquement et de port; **l. operation** opération *f* de débarquement

(b) *Av* (*of aircraft*) (*on land*) atterrissage *m*; (*on sea*) amerrissage *m*; (*on deck of ship*) appontage *m*; *Av* **blind/instrument l.** atterrissage sans visibilité/aux instruments; **visual l.** atterrissage à vue; **forced** *or* **emergency l.** atterrissage forcé

(**c**) *Constr* (*of staircase*) palier *m*; (*corridor*) couloir *m*
(**d**) (*of fish*) prise *f*; **l. net** épuisette *f*
(**e**) (*of gymnast, ski-jumper*) réception *f*

landing card *n Naut* (*of passenger*) carte *f* de débarquement
landing craft *n* chaland *m ou* engin *m* de débarquement
landing field *n* terrain *m* d'atterrissage
landing flap *n* volet *m* d'atterrissage
landing force *n Mil, Naut* troupes *fpl* de débarquement
landing gear *n Av* train *m* (d'atterrissage); **to retract the l.** relever *ou* rentrer le train d'atterrissage
landing lights *npl* feux *mpl ou* rampe *f* d'atterrissage
landing party *n Mil, Naut* compagnie *f* de débarquement
landing stage *n* débarcadère *m*, embarcadère *m*
landing strip *n* piste *f* (d'atterrissage)
landing wheels *npl* train *m* d'atterrissage
landing zone *n Mil, Av* zone *f* d'atterrissage (*des troupes aéroportées*)
landlady ['lændleɪdɪ] *n* (**a**) (*from whom one rents accommodation*) (*owner*) propriétaire *f*; (*living on premises*) logeuse *f* (**b**) *Br* (*of pub*) (*owner*) propriétaire *f*; (*manageress*) gérante *f* (**c**) (*of small hotel*) aubergiste *f*, hôtelière *f*; **seaside l.** propriétaire *f* d'une auberge au bord de la mer
landlegs ['lændlegz] *npl F* (*of sailor*) **to get one's l.** se familiariser de nouveau avec la terre
landless ['lændlɪs] *adj* sans terre; **l. peasants** paysans qui ne sont pas propriétaires
landlocked ['lændlɒkt] *adj* (*country*) sans accès à la mer; (*port etc*) entouré de terre; **l. sea** mer *f* intérieure
landlord ['lændlɔːd] *n* (**a**) (*of property*) bailleur *m*; (*from whom one rents accommodation*) (*owner*) propriétaire *m*; (*living on premises*) logeur *m* (**b**) *Br* (*of pub*) (*owner*) propriétaire *m*; (*manager*) gérant *m*; (*form of address*) patron (**c**) (*landowner*) propriétaire *m* (foncier)
landlubber ['lændlʌbər] *n Naut F Hum* marin *m* d'eau douce
landmark ['lændmɑːk] *n* (**a**) (point *m* de) repère *m*; *Av* repère, point *m* de repérage (au sol); *Naut* amer *m*, indice *m* (à terre), point à terre; **that clump of trees is a natural l.** ce groupe d'arbres est un repère naturel (**b**) (*important event*) point *m* décisif, événement *m* marquant; **to be a l.** (*of event*) faire époque *ou* date; **l. decision** décision qui fait époque *ou* date (**c**) (*boundary marker*) borne *f* limite
landmass ['lændmæs] *n Geog* masse *f* de terre
land mine *n* mine *f* terrestre
landowner ['lændəʊnər] *n* propriétaire *m* foncier
landowning ['lændəʊnɪŋ] *adj* **the l. classes** les classes qui possèdent des terres
land reform *n* réforme *f* agraire
land register *n* cadastre *m*
landscape[1] ['lændskeɪp] **1** *n* (*land, painting*) paysage *m*; *Comptr* **l. mode** mode *m* paysage **2** *adv* (*to print*) à l'italienne
landscape[2] *vt* (*area*) aménager en parc; **they had their garden landscaped** ils ont employé un jardinier paysagiste pour aménager leur propriété
landscape architect *n Am* paysagiste *mf*
landscape architecture *n Am* architecture *f* de paysage
landscape design *n* architecture *f* de paysage
landscape designer *n* paysagiste *mf*
landscape gardener *n* jardinier *m* paysagiste
landscape gardening *n* paysagisme *m*
landscape painter *n Art* paysagiste *mf*
landscaping ['lændskeɪpɪŋ] *n* paysagisme *m*
Land's End *n* la pointe de Cornouaille
landslide ['lændslaɪd] *n* (**a**) éboulement *m*, affaissement *m*, glissement *m* (de terrain) (**b**) *Pol* raz-de-marée *m inv* électoral; **to win the elections by a l.** gagner les élections avec une écrasante majorité; **l. victory** victoire *f* écrasante; **l. majority** majorité *f* écrasante
landslip ['lændslɪp] *n* = **landslide**
land tax *n* contributions *fpl* foncières (*sur les propriétés non bâties*)
landward ['lændwəd] **1** *adv* (**to**) **l.** du côté de la terre, vers la terre **2** *adj* **on the l. side** vers l'intérieur, du côté de la terre
lane [leɪn] *n* (**a**) (*in country*) petite route *f* de campagne; (*in town*) ruelle *f*, passage *m* (**b**) *Naut* route *f* de navigation (**c**) *Aut etc* (**traffic**) **l.** voie *f*; **l. markings** bandes *fpl* délimitant les voies; **four-l. road** route à quatre voies (de circulation); **don't change lanes** ne change pas de voie; **traffic is reduced to two lanes** la circulation ne se fait plus que sur deux files; **stay in l.** restez dans votre file; **get in(to) l.** mettez-vous sur la bonne file (**d**) *Sp* (*for runner, swimmer*) couloir *m*
langlauf ['læŋlaʊf] *n* ski *m* de fond; **l. skier** skieur, -euse de fond
language ['læŋgwɪdʒ] *n* (**a**) [①A7,d,xi; B4,3,d] (*of a people*) langue *f*; **the English l.** la langue anglaise; **foreign languages** langues étrangères; **I never learned to speak the l.** je n'ai jamais appris à parler la langue; *Fig* **we don't talk the same l.** nous ne parlons pas le même langage
(**b**) (*vocabulary*) langage *m*; **the l. of flowers** le langage des fleurs; **bad l.** langage grossier, grossièretés *fpl*; **to use bad/foul l.** parler grossièrement; (**mind your**) **l.!** surveillez votre langage!; **code l.** langage convenu, code *m*; **business l.** langage *ou* langue *f* des affaires; *Comptr* **computer l., machine l.** langage machine; **l. teaching/learning/course** enseignement *m*/apprentissage *m*/cours *m* de langues; **l. exchange holiday** échange *m* linguistique
language laboratory *n* laboratoire *m* de langues
language studies *npl* études *fpl* de langues
languid ['læŋgwɪd] *adj* languissant, langoureux
languidly ['læŋgwɪdlɪ] *adv* (*to move*) languissamment, langoureusement; (*to say*) d'une voix langoureuse
languidness ['læŋgwɪdnɪs] *n* langueur *f*
languish ['læŋgwɪʃ] *vi* languir; (*of plant*) dépérir; **to l. for sb/sth** languir après *ou* pour qn/qch; *F* **it languished in my in-tray for a week** c'est resté dans ma corbeille à courrier pendant une semaine; **to l. in prison** moisir en prison; **she spends her day languishing on the sofa** elle passe ses journées langoureusement allongée sur le canapé
languishing ['læŋgwɪʃɪŋ] *adj* languissant, langoureux
languor ['læŋgər] *n* langueur *f*
languorous ['læŋgərəs] *adj* langoureux
languorously ['læŋgərəslɪ] *adv* langoureusement
lank [læŋk] *adj* **l. hair** cheveux plats
lankness ['læŋknɪs] *n* (*of hair*) aspect *m* terne et sans vigueur
lanky ['læŋkɪ] *adj* (*person*) grand et filiforme
lanolin(e) ['lænəlɪn] *n Ch, Pharm* lanoline *f*; **l. shampoo** shampooing *m* à la lanoline
lantern ['læntən] *n* (**a**) lanterne *f*, falot *m*; *Naut* fanal *m*, -aux; **Chinese l.** lanterne vénitienne; *Hist* **magic l.** lanterne magique; **l. slides** plaques *fpl* de lanterne magique (**b**) *Archit* (*of dome*) lanterne *f*, lanternau *m* (**c**) **l. jaws** joues *fpl* creuses
lantern-jawed [læntən'dʒɔːd] *adj* aux joues creuses
lanyard ['lænjɑːd, -jəd] *n Naut* aiguillette *f*; (*for rigging*) ride *f*; (*of knife etc*) amarrage *m*
Laos [laʊs] *n* Laos *m*
Laotian ['laʊʃɪən] **1** *adj* laotien **2** *n* Laotien, -ienne
lap[1] [læp] *n* (*of seated person*) genoux *mpl*, *Lit* giron *m*; **to sit on sb's l.** s'asseoir sur les genoux de qn; **it's in the l. of the gods** Dieu seul le sait; **it's not going to fall into your l.** (*you'll have to work for it*) ça ne va pas te tomber tout cuit (dans le bec); **it dropped in(to) my l.** c'est tombé du ciel; **to live in the l. of luxury** vivre dans le luxe; *Fig* **to drop sth in sb's l.** coller qch à qn; *Aut* **l. belt** ceinture *f* ventrale; **l. and shoulder belt** ceinture trois points
lap[2] *n* (**a**) *Sp* (*of track, circuit*) tour *m*; **to do three laps** faire trois tours de circuit; **they're on the third l.** ils en sont au troisième tour; *Fig* **to be on the last l.** en être à la dernière étape; **l. of honour** tour d'honneur (**b**) *MecE* recouvrement *m*; *Constr* (*of tiles, slates*) chevauchement *m*, recouvrement; *Metal* **l. joint** ourlet *m*; **l. weld(ing)** soudure *f* à recouvrement (**c**) (*of wire around cylinder etc*) tour *m*
lap[3] (**-pp-**) **1** *vt* (**a**) *Sp* **to l. an opponent** prendre un tour d'avance sur un concurrent; **runners being lapped should move to the outside** les coureurs qui ont un tour de retard doivent s'écarter; **to l. the course** faire un tour de circuit
(**b**) (*wrap*) **to l. sth round sth** enrouler qch autour de qch
(**c**) *Constr* (*planks*) enchevaucher, poser à recouvrement; (*tiles*) donner du recouvrement à; **to l. a joint with sheet metal** chaperonner un assemblage
2 *vi* (**a**) *Sp* (*of runner*) faire le tour du stade; (*of car*) faire le tour du circuit
(**b**) **to l. over sth** dépasser *ou* recouvrir qch; (*of tiles etc*) chevaucher qch
lap[4] *n* (*of waves*) clapotement *m*, clapotis *m*
lap[5] **1** *vt* (*of animal*) (*milk*) laper **2** *vi* (*of waves*) clapoter
► **lap up** *vtsep* (**a**) (*milk*) laper (**b**) *Fig F* (*book*) dévorer; **he laps up everything she says** il boit toutes ses paroles; **it was sheer flattery but he lapped it all up** c'était de la flatterie pure et simple mais il a tout gobé *ou* avalé
laparoscope ['læpərəskəʊp] *n Med* laparoscope *m*
laparoscopy [læpə'rɒskəpɪ] *n Med* laparoscopie *f*
laparotomy [læpə'rɒtəmɪ] *n Surg* laparotomie *f*
lapdog ['læpdɒg] *n* chien *m* d'appartement; *Fig* marionnette *f*
lapel [lə'pel] *n* (*on jacket*) revers *m*
lapidary ['læpɪd(ə)rɪ] *adj, n* lapidaire *m*
lapis lazuli ['læpɪs'læzʊlɪ] *n* (*stone, colour*) lapis(-lazuli) *m inv*
Lapland ['læplænd] *n* Laponie *f*
Laplander ['læplændər] *n* Lapon, -one
Lapp [læp] **1** *adj* lapon **2** *n* (**a**) Lapon, -one (**b**) *Ling* lapon *m*
lapping ['læpɪŋ] *n* (*of waves*) clapotement *m*, clapotis *m*
lapse[1] [læps] *n* (**a**) (*mistake*) erreur *f*, faute *f*; (*fault*) faute,

défaillance *f*; (*in behaviour*) écart *m* de conduite; (*in standards etc*) baisse *f* (**in** de); (*in security*) défaillance; **l. of memory** défaillance *ou* absence *f* de mémoire, oubli *m*; **it was a l. in good manners** il/elle/*etc* a temporairement oublié ses bonnes manières; **a l. in (good) taste** une faute de goût; **a l. in concentration/vigilance** un écart de concentration/vigilance; **it was just a temporary l.** ce n'était qu'une défaillance temporaire; **moral l.** faux pas *m*; (*sexual infidelity*) écart *m*

(b) (*passage*) (*of time*) cours *m*, marche *f*; **a time l.** un laps de temps; **after a l. of three months** après un laps de temps de trois mois

(c) (*expiry*) expiration *f*

lapse² *vi* **(a)** (*make mistake, err*) **he only lapsed once** il n'a fait qu'une seule erreur; **his concentration lapsed for a split second** il a relâché sa concentration pendant une fraction de seconde; **if standards of education are allowed to l.** si on laisse baisser les niveaux scolaires

(b) (*fall, go*) **to l. into silence** se taire; **to l. into unconsciousness** sombrer dans l'inconscience; **he's lapsing back into his old ways** il retombe dans ses vieilles habitudes; **it's too easy to l. back into English** c'est trop facile de revenir à l'anglais

(c) (*morally*) être coupable d'un écart de conduite; (*more serious*) manquer à ses devoirs; **he tried to give up drinking but he would all too often l.** il essayait d'arrêter de boire mais trop souvent retombait dans son travers

(d) *Jur* (*of right, passport etc*) périmer, se périmer; (*of estate*) devenir disponible; (*of legacy*) devenir caduc; (*of law*) tomber en désuétude; (*of insurance policy etc*) cesser d'être en vigueur; *Rel* (*of person*) cesser de pratiquer; **to allow a right to l.** laisser périmer *ou* laisser tomber un droit; **my club membership has lapsed** ma carte de membre du club a expiré

lapsed [læpst] *adj* **(a)** *Rel* déchu **(b)** (*postal order etc, right*) périmé; (*inheritance*) tombé en dévolu; (*contract, inheritance*) caduc, *f* caduque; (*insurance policy, membership*) expiré

laptop ['læptɒp] *n Comptr* portable *m*

lapwing ['læpwɪŋ] *n* (*bird*) vanneau *m* (huppé)

larceny ['lɑːsənɪ] *n Jur* vol *m*; **petty l.** vol simple, vol minime; *US* **grand l.** vol qualifié

larch [lɑːtʃ] *n* mélèze *m*

lard¹ [lɑːd] *n Culin* saindoux *m*; *esp Am F* **he's a tub of l.** c'est un sac de graisse

lard² *vt Culin* (*meat*) larder, barder; *F Pej* **to l. one's writings with quotations** larder ses écrits de citations

larder ['lɑːdər] *n* garde-manger *m inv*

large [lɑːdʒ] **1** *adj* **(a)** (*physical size*) grand; (*bulky*) (*package, meal, portion*) gros; (*person*) (*tall*) grand; (*fat*) gros; **l. audience** public *m* nombreux; **a l. company** une grosse entreprise; **to grow** *or* **get larger** (*of town, deficit*) s'agrandir; (*of person, amount*) grossir; **to make sth larger** agrandir qch; **there she is, as l. as life** la voilà, en chair et en os; **larger than life** hors pair; **the l. size** (*packet etc*) la grande taille; **have you this dress in a l. size?** avez-vous cette robe en grande taille?; **to have a l. following** avoir un public nombreux; **a l. family** une famille nombreuse; **the l. intestine** le gros intestin; **a l. parcel** un gros paquet, un paquet volumineux; **a l. sum** une grosse *ou* forte somme; *Fin* **l. denominations** grosses coupures *fpl*; **l. town** grande ville; **l. whisky** double whisky *m*

(b) (*extensive, significant*) **to a l. extent, in l. part** en grande partie; **a l. part of my time/job/day** une grande partie de mon temps/mon travail/ma journée; **in l. measure** dans une large mesure; **to take a larger part in sth** prendre une plus grande part à qch; **to trade on a l. scale** faire les affaires en grand; **l. powers** (*comprehensive*) pouvoirs larges *ou* étendus; **l. views** (*liberal*) idées larges

2 *adv* **by and l.** en gros; **by and l. they vote Conservative** ils votent conservateur pour la plupart

3 *n* **to set a prisoner at l.** élargir *ou* relaxer un prisonnier; **to be at l.** être libre *ou* en liberté; **the murderer is still at l.** l'assassin court toujours; **he was acting as the UN's ambassador at l.** il a joué le rôle de médiateur auprès des Nations Unies; **people at l.** (*in general*) le grand public, la grande masse du public; **teachers at l.** la masse des professeurs; **at l.** (*in detail*) tout au long, en détail; **to talk at l.** parler au hasard

large-handed [lɑːdʒ'hændɪd] *adj* généreux

large-hearted [lɑːdʒ'hɑːtɪd] *adj* au grand cœur

largely ['lɑːdʒlɪ] *adv* en grande partie, pour une grande part; **his job is l. administrative** son travail est surtout administratif; **it's l. the case that people ...** dans la plupart des cas les gens ...; **it's l. a case of finding the right people** il s'agit surtout de trouver les gens qu'il faut

large-minded *adj* aux idées larges, à l'esprit large

largeness ['lɑːdʒnɪs] *n* (*of body*) grosseur *f*; (*of profits, majority etc*) grandeur *f*, importance *f*; (*of power*) étendue *f*; (*of ideas*) largeur *f*; (*of soul*) grandeur

large-print *adj* **l. book** livre en gros caractères

large-scale *adj* (*undertaking, farmer*) gros; (*map*) à grande échelle; **l. disaster** grande catastrophe *f*; *Comptr* **l. integration** intégration *f* à grande échelle

largess(e) [lɑː'ʒes] *n* largesse *f*

largish ['lɑːdʒɪʃ] *adj* assez grand, assez gros

largo, *pl* **-s** ['lɑːgəʊ, -z] *adv, n Mus* largo *m inv*

lariat ['lærɪət] *n* **(a)** *Am* lasso *m* **(b)** (*for tethering animals*) corde *f* à piquet

lark¹ [lɑːk] *n* (*bird*) alouette *f*; **to rise** *or* **get up** *or* **be up with the l.** se lever au chant du coq; **she sings like a l.** elle chante comme un rossignol

lark² *n F* (*joke etc*) farce *f*, rigolade *f*, blague *f*; **to do sth for a l.** faire qch histoire de rire *ou* de rigoler; **what a l.!** quelle farce!; **I'd like to know what his little l. is** je me demande ce qu'il mijote; **I don't want any more of the 'I lost my homework' l.** ne me faites plus le coup du 'j'ai perdu mes devoirs'; **I don't like this fancy dress l.** je n'aime pas du tout cette histoire de bal masqué; **are you still at the teaching l.?** tu fais toujours ce foutu métier de prof?

▶ **lark about, lark around** *vi F* (*play jokes*) faire des farces; (*have good time*) rigoler; **some children were larking around with an old tyre** des enfants s'amusaient avec un vieux pneu

larkspur ['lɑːkspɜːr] *n* (*plant*) pied-d'alouette *m*, *pl* pieds-d'alouette

larva, *pl* **-vae** ['lɑːvə, -viː] *n Ent* larve *f*

larval ['lɑːv(ə)l] *adj Ent* larvaire

laryngitis [lærɪn'dʒaɪtɪs] *n Med* laryngite *f*; **to have l.** avoir une laryngite

laryngoscope [lə'rɪŋgəskəʊp] *n* laryngoscope *m*

larynx ['lærɪŋks] *n Anat* larynx *m*

lasagne [lə'sænjə] *n Culin* lasagnes *fpl*

lascivious [lə'sɪvɪəs] *adj* lascif

lasciviously [lə'sɪvɪəslɪ] *adv* lascivement

lasciviousness [lə'sɪvɪəsnɪs] *n* lascivité *f*

laser ['leɪzər] *n* laser *m*; **l. beam** rayon *m* laser; **l. checkout** (*in supermarket*) caisse *f* munie de lecteurs laser; **l. printer** imprimante *f* (à) laser; **l. printing** impression *f* laser; **l. printout** imprimé *m* laser, copie *f* laser; **l. quality** qualité *f* laser; **l. surgery** chirurgie *f* au laser

laser-guided *adj* guidé au laser

lash¹ [læʃ] *n* **(a)** (*blow with whip*) coup *m* de fouet; (*end of whip*) lanière *f* (de fouet); **the l.** (*punishment*) le (supplice du) fouet; **to receive ten lashes** recevoir dix coups de fouet; **he felt the l. of the Prime Minister's tongue** il a été durement critiqué par le Premier ministre **(b)** *Anat* cil *m*

lash² **1** *vt* **(a)** (*with whip*) (*horse etc*) fouetter, cingler; (*person*) fouetter, flageller; (*of rain*) (*windows, sb's face*) fouetter; (*of waves*) (*shore*) battre, fouetter; **the wind/storm lashed the sea into a fury** le vent/l'orage s'abattit sur la mer qui se déchaîna; **he lashed the crowd into a frenzy** il a soulevé la foule jusqu'à l'hystérie

(b) (*verbally*) cingler; **to l. sb with one's tongue** adresser à qn des paroles cinglantes

(c) (*move from side to side*) **to l. its tail** (*of cat, lion etc*) fouetter l'air de la queue

2 *vi* **to l. against the windows** (*of rain*) fouetter les vitres; **the rain** *or* **it was lashing down** il pleuvait dru; **to l. against the shore** (*of waves*) battre *ou* fouetter le rivage; **the rain lashed down on the tent** la pluie fouettait la tente

lash³ *vt* (*tie*) lier, attacher; *Naut* amarrer; **to l. down a load on a trailer** lier une charge sur une remorque

▶ **lash about** *vi* (*in pain*) se débattre (de douleur)

▶ **lash back** *vi* (*reply strongly*) répondre violemment

▶ **lash out 1** *vi* **(a) to l. out at sb** (*physically*) envoyer un coup à qn; (*verbally*) s'en prendre agressivement à qn; **he lashed out at me with his fists/feet** il m'a envoyé des coups de poing/coups de pied **(b)** *F* (*spend extravagantly*) faire une folie *ou* des folies; **I'm going to l. out on a new coat** je vais faire des folies et me payer un nouveau manteau; **they really lashed out on their daughter's wedding** ils ont dépensé une fortune pour le mariage de leur fille **2** *vtsep F* **I lashed out £10 on a bottle of wine** j'ai claqué 10 livres sur une bouteille de vin

lashing¹ ['læʃɪŋ] **1** *adj* (*rain*) cinglant **2** *n* **(a)** (*with whip*) coups *mpl* de fouet **(b)** *Old-fashioned* **(tongue) l.** verte réprimande *f*; **to give sb a tongue l.** réprimander qn sévèrement **(c)** *Br F* **lashings of sth** des tas de qch; **apple-pie with lashings of cream** de la tarte aux pommes avec une tonne de crème

lashing² *n* (*rope*) câble *m*

lass [læs] *n esp Scot, North Eng* jeune fille *f*; **country l.** jeune campagnarde *f*
Lassa ['lɑːsə] *n Med* **L. fever** fièvre *f* de Lhassa
lassie ['læsɪ] *n esp Scot* fillette *f*; **a wee l.** une petite fille
lassitude ['læsɪtjuːd] *n* lassitude *f*
lasso[1] [læ'suː] *n* lasso *m*
lasso[2] *vt* prendre au lasso
last[1] [lɑːst] **1** *adj* **(a)** [①A19,g,ii] (*final*) dernier; **the l. guest to arrive** le dernier des invités à arriver; **the l. but one** l'avant-dernier, *pl* les avant-derniers; **the l. syllable but one** l'avant-dernière syllabe; **the l. but three** le troisième à partir de la fin; **this is your l. chance** c'est votre dernière chance; **in the l. resort, as a l. resort** en dernière ressource, en dernier recours; **you are my l. hope** vous êtes mon dernier espoir; **in the l. place** enfin, pour finir; **in the l. analysis** au bout du compte; **to have the l. word** (*come after other speakers*) parler le dernier; (*in argument*) avoir le dernier mot; **the l. word in comfort/luxury** (*hotel etc*) le summum du confort/luxe; **this model is the l. word in car design** ce modèle est le dernier cri de la conception automobile; **I'm down to my l. pound** il ne me reste plus qu'une livre; **every l. scrap of bread had been eaten** on avait mangé jusqu'à la dernière miette; **at the l. moment** *or* **minute** au dernier moment; **the l. day of the month** le dernier jour du mois; **to do sth l. thing at night** faire qch juste avant d'aller se coucher
(b) (*most recent*) **l. Tuesday, Tuesday l.** mardi dernier; **l. January** en janvier dernier; **the l. time I saw him** la dernière fois que je l'ai vu; **l. week** la semaine dernière, la semaine passée; **l. night** (*during the night*) la nuit dernière; (*in the evening*) hier (au) soir; **I slept badly l. night** j'ai mal dormi cette nuit; **I haven't been to church for the l. few weeks** je ne suis pas allé à l'église ces dernières semaines; **in the l. fifty years** pendant les cinquante dernières années; **this day l. week** il y a huit jours aujourd'hui; **this day l. year** l'an dernier à la même date; **l. financial year** exercice *m* écoulé
(c) (*least likely*) **you're the l. one to critisize** tu es vraiment mal placé pour critiquer; **you're the l. person I expected to see here** tu es bien la dernière personne que je pensais rencontrer ici; **he's the l. person I'd ask to help me** c'est (bien) la dernière personne à qui je demanderais de l'aide; **that's the l. thing that's worrying me** ça c'est le cadet de mes soucis; **that's the l. thing I'd do in your position** c'est (bien) la dernière chose que je ferais si j'étais à ta place
2 *n* **(a)** (*person*) **the l.** le dernier, la dernière; **am I the l.?** (*to arrive*) suis-je le dernier?; *Ind* **l. in, first out** dernier entré, premier sorti; *Bible* **the l. shall be first** les derniers seront les premiers
(b) (*end*) **we'll never hear the l. of it** on n'a pas fini d'en entendre parler; **we haven't heard the l. of this problem** tôt ou tard ce problème va refaire surface; **I think we've heard the l. of him** je pense qu'on n'en entendra plus parler; **that's the l. I saw of him** je ne l'ai pas revu depuis; **that's the l. of the wine** (*that's all there is left*) c'est tout ce qui reste comme vin; (*that's the last drop gone*) il n'y a plus de vin maintenant; **to** *or* **till the l.** jusqu'au bout, jusqu'à la fin; **faithful to the l.** fidèle jusqu'au bout; **at l., at long l.** enfin; **now at l. I understand** enfin, je comprends; *Lit* **to look one's l. on sth** voir qch pour la dernière fois; *Lit* **to breathe one's l.** rendre le dernier soupir; *Lit* **to be near one's l.** (*death*) être proche de sa fin; **towards the l.** vers la fin de sa vie
3 *adv* **(a)** (*in time*) **when I l. saw him, when I saw him l.** la dernière fois que je l'ai vu; **I can't remember when I l. ate** je ne sais pas depuis quand je n'ai pas mangé
(b) (*in order*) **he spoke l.** il a parlé le dernier; **she came** *or* **finished l.** (*in the exam*) elle a été dernière (*à l'examen*); **she came** *or* **finished l.** (*in the race*) elle est arrivée dernière (*de la course*)
(c) l., I would like to say ... et pour finir, je voudrais dire ...; **l. but not least** enfin et surtout; **l. but not least on the list we have Mr ...** et enfin sur la liste, je ne voudrais pas oublier M ...
last[2] **1** *vi* durer, se maintenir; **it's too good to l.** c'est trop beau pour durer; **if the good weather lasts** si le beau temps se maintient; **cream doesn't l. long** (*deteriorates quickly*) la crème fraîche ne se conserve pas longtemps; **cakes never l. long in this house** (*they get eaten quickly*) les gâteaux ne durent jamais très longtemps *ou F* ne font jamais long feu dans cette maison; **the supplies will not l. two months** les vivres ne feront pas deux mois; **their friendship won't l. long** leur amitié ne durera pas; **he won't l. long in that job** il ne tiendra pas très longtemps à ce poste, *F* il ne fera pas long feu à ce poste
2 *vt* **it will l. me a lifetime** j'en ai pour la vie; **it has lasted him well** ça lui a fait du profit; **she couldn't l. the pace** elle n'a pas pu tenir le rythme
last[3] *n* (*for shoe*) forme *f* (à chaussure)
▶ **last out 1** *vtsep* **to l. sb out** (*of person*) survivre à qn; **he'll l. us all out** il nous survivra tous; **to l. the year out** (*of person*) survivre jusqu'à la fin de l'année; (*of supplies etc*) suffire pour l'année; **my overcoat will l. the winter out** mon pardessus fera encore l'hiver; **I don't know if I'll be able to l. out the afternoon without any coffee** je ne sais pas si j'arriverai à tenir tout l'après-midi sans café; **the doctor doubted whether she would l. out the night** le docteur n'était pas sûr qu'elle passerait la nuit **2** *vi* (*of person*) tenir le coup
last-ditch *adj* ultime; **a l. effort** un ultime effort
lasting ['lɑːstɪŋ] *adj* durable; (*material etc*) résistant; **l. peace** paix durable
Last Judgment *n Rel* Jugement *m* Dernier
lastly ['lɑːstlɪ] *adv* pour finir, en dernier lieu
last-minute *adj* (*decision*) de dernière minute
last name *n* nom *m* de famille
last rites *npl Cathol* derniers sacrements *mpl*
lat (*abbr* **latitude**) latitude, lat.
latch[1] [lætʃ] *n* **(a)** loquet *m*; (*small, for shutters etc*) loqueteau *m*; (*of vehicle door etc*) pêne *m*, gâche *f*; **to leave the door on the l.** fermer la porte sans la verrouiller **(b)** *MecE* (*of lever, moving mechanical part*) verrou *m*
latch[2] *vt* **(a)** (*door*) fermer au loquet **(b)** *MecE* (*lever, moving part*) verrouiller, bloquer
▶ **latch on** *vi F* **(a)** (*attach oneself*) **to l. on to sb/sth** s'accrocher à qn/qch **(b)** (*understand*) piger; **to l. on to sth** piger qch; **it took him a while to l. on** il a mis un moment pour piger
latchkey ['lætʃkiː] *n* clef *f* de maison, clef de porte d'entrée; **l. child** *or F* **kid** = enfant *mf* dont les parents travaillent et qui doit rentrer seul après l'école
late [leɪt] **1** *adj* **(a)** (*after the appointed time*) en retard; (*delayed*) retardé; **to be l. (for sth)** être en retard (pour qch); **she was too l. to help** elle est arrivée trop tard pour apporter son aide; **it was too l. to do anything about it** il était trop tard pour faire quoi que ce soit; **am I too l. to register?** est-il trop tard pour que je m'inscrive?; **it's never too l.** il n'est jamais trop tard; **the train is l./is ten minutes l.** le train a du retard/a dix minutes de retard; **we apologize for the l. running of the train** veuillez nous excuser pour ce retard; **her baby was five days l.** son bébé est né avec cinq jours de retard; **l. payment penalty** indemnité *f* de retard; *Rugby* **l. tackle** plaquage *m* à retardement
(b) (*far on in the day etc*) tard; **it is l.** il est tard; **it is getting l.** il se fait tard; **it is too l.** il est trop tard; **I was l. going to bed** je me suis couché tard; **to keep l. hours** être un couche-tard; **at this l. hour** à l'heure qu'il est
(c) (*towards the end of a period of time*) **why have they left it to this l. hour before informing us?** pourquoi ont-ils attendu la dernière minute pour nous en informer?; **in the l. afternoon** tard dans l'après-midi; **in l. summer** vers la fin de l'été; *Fig* **it's a bit l. in the day (to start making changes)** il est un peu tard (pour commencer à faire des modifications); **to be in one's l. thirties** avoir entre trente-cinq et quarante ans, *F* avoir la trentaine bien tassée; **in the l. (nineteen) eighties** vers la fin des années 1980; **l. edition** (*of a newspaper*) dernière édition *f*; **a l. marriage** un mariage sur le tard; **l. arrival** (*at hotel*) arrivée *f* tardive; **he will be a l. arrival** il arrivera tard; **l. availability** (*of holiday, seat*) disponibilité *f* de dernière minute; **l. cancellation** (*of flight*) annulation *f* de dernière minute; *Mktg* **l. entrant** concurrent *m* tardif; **l. entry** (*in competition*) inscription de dernière minute; *Mktg* lancement *m* tardif; **Denmark only came into the tournament as a l. entry** le Danemark s'est inscrit au tournoi en toute dernière minute; *Journ* **l. story** nouvelle *f* de dernière minute
(d) (*fruit etc*) tardif; **l. frosts** gelées tardives *ou* printanières
(e) *Fml* (*deceased*) feu, défunt, décédé; **my l. father** feu mon père; **the l. queen** feu la reine, la feue reine
2 *adv* **(a)** (*after the appointed time*) en retard; **to arrive too l.** arriver trop tard; *Prov* **better l. than never** mieux vaut tard que jamais
(b) (*far on in the day etc*) tard; **he came home very l.** il est rentré fort tard; **to work l.** travailler tard; **to go to bed l.** se coucher tard; **to sleep** *or* **stay in bed l.** faire la grasse matinée; **l. into the night** jusqu'à une heure avancée de la nuit; **l. in the year** vers la fin de l'année; **l. in life** sur le tard; **to marry l. in life** se marier tard *ou* sur le tard

(c) (*recently*) **as l. as last week** pas plus tard que la semaine dernière

(d) (*formerly*) *esp Fml* **l. of this address** dernièrement domicilié à cette adresse; **Sir Geoffrey, l. of the Diplomatic Corps** Sir Geoffrey, qui fut anciennement membre du Corps diplomatique

(e) *Lit* = **lately**

3 *n* **of l.** récemment; **as events of l. have shown ...** comme les récents événements l'ont montré ...

late adopter *n Mktg* utilisateur *m* tardif

latecomer ['leɪtkʌmər] *n* retardataire *mf*; *Fig* **to be a l. to business/politics** arriver tardivement dans les affaires/en politique

lately ['leɪtlɪ] *adv* dernièrement, récemment, ces derniers temps; **what have you been doing l.?** qu'avez-vous fait ces derniers temps?; **it is only l. that the matter has become known** la chose n'a été sue que ces jours-ci

latency ['leɪtənsɪ] *n* latence *f*, état *m* latent; **l. period** temps *m* de latence

lateness ['leɪtnɪs] *n* (a) (*of fruit etc*) tardiveté *f*; (*of person*) retard *m*; **I will not tolerate l.** je ne tolérerai aucun retard (b) **the l. of the hour** l'heure avancée

late-night *adj* **a l. bar/disco** un bar/une discothèque qui ferme très tard; **a l. party** une soirée qui commence tard; **l. showing** (*of film*) séance *f* de minuit

latent ['leɪtənt] *adj* (*disease, homosexuality, possibility*) latent; *Bot* **l. bud** œil *m* dormant; *Com* **l. defect** vice *m* caché; *Phys* **l. heat** chaleur *f* latente; **l. period** temps *m* de latence

later ['leɪtər] (*comp of* **late**) **1** *adj* [①A19,g,ii] ultérieur; (*of two variants*) (*edition, version, model etc*) dernier; **I caught a l. train** j'ai pris un autre train plus tard; **l. events proved that ...** la suite des événements a démontré que ...; **at a l. meeting** dans une séance ultérieure; **l. investigations revealed that ...** les enquêtes ultérieures *ou* qui ont suivi ont révélé que ...; **his l. novels** (*of dead person*) les romans qu'il a écrit vers la fin de sa carrière; (*of living person*) ses romans les plus récents; **in l. life she ...** plus tard dans sa vie, elle ...

2 *adv* plus tard; **l. (on) we went to the cinema** plus tard nous sommes allés au cinéma; **sooner or l.** tôt ou tard; **no l. than tomorrow** demain au plus tard; **a moment l.** l'instant d'après; **this happened l. (on)** cela est arrivé après *ou* plus tard *ou* ultérieurement; **a few days l.** quelques jours plus tard, *Lit* à quelques jours de là; **three pages l.** trois pages plus loin; **as we shall see l.** comme nous le verrons plus tard *ou* par la suite; *F* **see you l.!** à plus tard!

lateral ['læt(ə)rəl] *adj* latéral; *MecE* **l. motion/play** mouvement *m*/jeu *m* latéral; **he's good at l. thinking** il sait trouver des approches originales

laterally ['læt(ə)rəlɪ] *adv* latéralement

latest ['leɪtɪst] **1** *adj* [①A19,g,ii] (*superl of* **late**) dernier; **this author's l. work** le dernier ouvrage de cet auteur; **his l. views on the subject** ses vues les plus récentes sur ce sujet; **the very l. improvements** les tout derniers perfectionnements; **the very l. news** les informations de toute dernière heure; **the l. edition** la dernière édition; **l. date** (*deadline*) date *f* limite; *Com, Jur* terme *m* de rigueur, délai *m* de rigueur; **the l. fashions** la dernière mode; *Com* **l. novelties** dernières nouveautés *fpl*

2 *n* **have you heard the l.?** savez-vous la dernière?; **the l. I can come would be four o'clock** je ne pourrai pas venir après quatre heures; **the l. she could leave the decision until was this evening** elle ne pouvait pas remettre la décision à plus tard que ce soir; **at the l.** au plus tard; **Wednesday at the l.** mercredi au plus tard

latex ['leɪteks] *n* latex *m*

lath [læθ] *n* (a) *Constr* latte *f*; **l. -and-plaster partition** cloison lattée et plâtrée (b) (*of Venetian blind*) lame *f*

lathe [leɪð] *n* tour *m*; **precision l.** tour de précision; **l. bed** banc *m ou* bâti *m* de tour; **capstan** *or* **turret l.** tour (à) revolver; **polishing l.** touret *m* à polir *ou* de polisseur

lather[1] ['lɑːðər] *n* (a) mousse *f* de savon; **to make a l.** (*of soap*) mousser (b) (*on horse*) écume *f*; **horse all in a l.** cheval couvert d'écume; *F* **to work oneself** *or* **get into a l.** se mettre dans tous ses états (**about sth** à propos de qch); **don't get into such a l.** ce n'est pas la peine de te mettre dans tous tes états

lather[2] **1** *vt* (a) savonner (**sb's chin** le menton à qn); **to l. one's face** se savonner le visage; (*in order to shave*) se mettre du savon à barbe sur le visage (b) *Old-fashioned F* (*thrash*) rosser **2** *vi* (*of soap*) mousser

lathe-turned ['leɪðtɜːnd] *adj* fait au tour, tourné

Latin ['lætɪn] **1** *adj* latin; **the L. races** les races latines **2** *n* (a) (*Southern European*) Latin, -ine (b) *Ling* latin *m*; **written in L.** écrit en latin

Latin America *n* Amérique *f* latine

Latin American *adj* latino-américain, *pl* latino-américains

latinize ['lætɪnaɪz] *vt* latiniser

Latino [læ'tiːnəʊ] *n US* latino *mf*

Latin Quarter *n* (*in Paris*) le Quartier latin

latish ['leɪtɪʃ] **1** *adj* (a) (*after the appointed time*) un peu en retard (b) (*far on in the day etc*) un peu tardif; **at a l. hour** à une heure assez avancée **2** *adv* (*see adj*) (a) un peu en retard (b) un peu tard

latitude ['lætɪtjuːd] *n* (a) *Geog* latitude *f*; **in northern/southern latitudes** dans les latitudes boréales/australes; **at a l. of 30° north** par 30° (de) latitude nord; **in these latitudes** sous ces latitudes (b) (*freedom*) **to allow sb the greatest l.** laisser à qn la plus grande latitude *ou* la plus grande liberté d'action; **it doesn't give us much l.** (*of deadline, budget etc*) cela ne nous donne pas une grande marge de manœuvre; **they are given a lot of l.** on leur donne beaucoup de liberté

latrine [lə'triːn] *n esp Mil* latrines *fpl*

latter ['lætər] **1** *adj* (a) [①A72,9] (*of two*) dernier (b) [①A19,g,ii] (*belonging to the end*) dernier; **the l. years of her life** les dernières années de sa vie; **the l. half** *or* **part of June** la deuxième moitié de juin **2** *n* [①A72,9] **the l.** (*of two*) le dernier, la dernière, *pl* les derniers, les dernières

latter-day *adj* (a) moderne, d'aujourd'hui (b) *Rel* **the L. Saints** les Mormons *mpl*

latterly ['lætəlɪ] *adv* (a) (*recently*) récemment (b) (*towards the end of a period*) vers la fin

lattice ['lætɪs] *n* treillis *m*, treillage *m*; *Constr etc* **l. beam** *or* **girder** poutre *f* en treillis *ou* à croisillons; **l. window** fenêtre *f* à losanges *ou* à vitraux sertis de plomb

latticed ['lætɪst] *adj* treillissé, treillagé; *Fig* (*branches*) entrecroisé

latticework ['lætɪswɜːk] *n* treillage *m*, treillis *m*

Latvia ['lætvɪə] *n* Lettonie *f*

Latvian ['lætvɪən] **1** *adj* letton **2** *n* (a) Letton, -one (b) *Ling* letton *m*

laud [lɔːd] *vt Lit* louer

laudable ['lɔːdəb(ə)l] *adj* louable, digne de louanges

laudably ['lɔːdəblɪ] *adv* louablement; **she was l. restrained** sa retenue était digne de louanges

laudanum ['lɔːd(ə)nəm] *n Pharm* laudanum *m*

laudatory ['lɔːdət(ə)rɪ] *adj* (*speech, remarks etc*) élogieux, louangeur, -euse

laugh[1] [lɑːf] *n* rire *m*; **to burst into a (loud) l.** éclater de rire, partir d'un éclat de rire; **to give a short l.** avoir un petit rire; **with a l.** en riant; **he likes a (good) l.** il aime bien rire; **to have the last l.** avoir sa vengeance; **to raise a l.** faire rire; **look outside if you want a l.** regarde dehors si tu veux rigoler; *F* **to do sth for a l.** faire qch pour rire; **what a l.!** quelle rigolade!; *Iron* **that's a l.!** quelle blague!, la bonne blague!; **the l.'s on us** on a été refait; **these old films are usually good for a l.** ces vieux films sont généralement drôles

laugh[2] **1** *vi* rire; **to l. at** *or* **over** *or* **about sth** rire de qch; **there's nothing to l. about** il n'y a pas de quoi rire; **to l. at sb** se moquer de qn; **to l. to oneself** rire tout seul; **to l. and cry at the same time** pleurer et rire en même temps; **I didn't know whether to l. or cry** je ne savais pas si je devais rire ou pleurer; **to l. till one cries** *or* **till the tears come** rire (jusqu')aux larmes; **to l. up one's sleeve** rire dans sa barbe; **to l. in sb's face** rire au nez de qn; *F* **if I get that job I'll be laughing** si j'obtenais ce travail ça serait génial; *F* **if you've already done this before, you're laughing** si tu as déjà fait ça c'est un jeu d'enfant; *F* **when his granny dies, he'll be laughing** quand sa grand-mère mourra, il vivra comme un prince *ou* il pourra mettre les doigts de pied en éventail; *F* **you've already got your visa, you're laughing** toi, tu as déjà ton visa, tu n'as pas de problèmes; *F* **don't make me l.** laissez-moi rire!; *F* **I soon made him l. on the other side of his face** je lui ai bientôt fait passer son envie de rire; *F* **you'll l. on the other side of your face one of these days** un de ces jours tu vas rire jaune; *F* **to l. all the way to the bank** se frotter les mains; *Prov* **he who laughs last laughs longest, he laughs best who laughs last** rira bien qui rira le dernier

2 *vt* **he laughed a bitter l.** il eut un rire amer; **to l. oneself silly** rire comme un bossu *ou* une baleine; **his suggestion was laughed out of court** sa suggestion fut rejetée catégoriquement; **I'd be laughed out of court** je me couvrirais de ridicule

▶ **laugh down** *vtsep* (*proposal*) tourner en ridicule

▶ **laugh off** *vtsep* **he laughed the matter off** il tourna la chose en plaisanterie; *F* **to l. one's head off** être mort de rire

laughable ['lɑːfəb(ə)l] *adj* risible, ridicule

laughably ['lɑːfəblɪ] *adv* risiblement; (*easy*) ridiculement

laughing ['lɑːfɪŋ] **1** *adj* (*face*) riant; (*eyes, expression*) rieur;

it's no l. matter il n'y a pas de quoi rire; **I'm in no l. mood** je n'ai pas envie de rire **2** *n* rires *mpl*; **we could hear the sound of l.** nous entendions des rires
laughing gas *n* gaz *m* hilarant
laughing hyena *n* hyène *f* rieuse
laughing jackass *n* (*bird*) dacélo *m*
laughingly ['lɑːfɪŋlɪ] *adv* **(a)** (*to say*) en riant **(b)** **that's l. called art** on a le culot d'appeler ça de l'art
laughing stock *n* (objet *m* de) risée *f*; **to make a l. of oneself** se couvrir de ridicule; **to be a l.** être la risée de tous; **to make sb a l.** couvrir qn de ridicule; **to make sb the l. of the village** faire de qn la risée du village
laughter ['lɑːftər] *n* rire(s) *m(pl)*; **to cause l.** provoquer les rires *ou* l'hilarité; **there was l. at her words** ce qu'elle dit provoqua des rires; **to receive a proposal with l.** accueillir une proposition par des rires; **everything I say is received with l.** on rit de tout ce que je dis
launch[1] [lɔːntʃ] *n* (*boat, of warship*) chaloupe *f*; **(motor) l.** vedette *f*
launch[2] *n* (*of ship, rocket, missile, new product etc*) lancement *m*; **l. pad** (*for rockets, missiles*) plate-forme *f* de lancement; **l. party** réception *f* (*pour le lancement d'un produit*); **l. site** (*centre*) base *f* de lancement; **l. vehicle** (*for rocket*) véhicule *m* de lancement, lanceur *m*
launch[3] *vt* (*ship, torpedo, rocket*) lancer; (*ship's boats*) mettre à l'eau; (*person, business, enquiry, new product*) lancer; *Mil* (*offensive*) déclencher; **to l. sb on a career** lancer qn dans une carrière; **once he is launched on the subject** une fois lancé sur le sujet
▶ **launch into** *vi po* **to l. into abuse of sb** se répandre en invectives contre qn; **to l. into a story** se lancer dans une histoire; **to l. into a complaint** se mettre à se plaindre
▶ **launch out** *vi* **to l. out into a new market** se lancer sur un nouveau marché; **to l. out on one's own** (*in business*) faire cavalier seul
launcher ['lɔːntʃər] *n* (*vehicle*) lanceur *m*; (*launching pad*) rampe *f* *ou* plate-forme *f* de lancement; (*for planes*) catapulte *f* de lancement; *Mil* **grenade l.** lance-grenades *m inv* (à fusil)
launching ['lɔːntʃɪŋ] *n* (*of ship*) lancement *m*; (*of small boat, ship's barge etc*) mise *f* à l'eau; (*of torpedo, projectile, rocket*) lancement; *Com, Fin* (*of product, loan*) lancement; *Mil* (*of attack, offensive*) déclenchement *m*, lancement; *Av* **l. catapult** catapulte *f* de lancement; *Mil, Astronaut* **l. pad** *or* **platform** (*for rockets, missiles*) plate-forme *f* de lancement; *Av* **l. ramp** rampe *f* de lancement; **l. site** (*centre*) base *f* de lancement
launder ['lɔːndər] *vt* (*clothes*) blanchir; *Fig* **to l. money** blanchir de l'argent
launderette [lɔːndə'ret] *n Br* laverie *f* automatique
laundering ['lɔːndərɪŋ] *n* (*of clothes*) blanchissage *m*; *Fig* (*of money*) blanchiment *m*
laundress ['lɔːndres] *n* blanchisseuse *f*
laundrette [lɔːn'dret] *n Br* laverie *f* automatique
laundromat ['lɔːndrəʊmæt] *n Am* laverie *f* automatique
laundry ['lɔːndrɪ] *n* **(a)** (*place*) blanchisserie *f*; (*in house*) buanderie *f*; **to send sth to the l.** envoyer qch à la blanchisserie **(b)** (*clothes*) lessive *f*; (*clean*) linge *m* propre; (*dirty*) linge sale; **to do the l.** faire la lessive; **l. bag** sac *m* de blanchisserie; **l. basket** panier *m* à linge; **l. list** liste *f* de blanchissage; **l. room** (*in house, apartment block*) buanderie *f*; **l. service** service *m* de blanchissage
laureate ['lɔːrɪət] **1** *adj* lauréat; *Br* **Poet L.**, *pl* **Poets Laureate** poète *m* lauréat (*dignité conférée par la Couronne*) **2** *n* lauréat, -ate
laurel ['lɒrəl] *n* (*tree*) laurier *m*; **l. wreath** couronne *f* de lauriers; *Fig* **to win laurels** se couvrir de lauriers; *Fig* **to rest on one's laurels** se reposer sur ses lauriers; *Fig* **he must look to his laurels** il est en passe d'être éclipsé
lav [læv] *n Br F* (*abbr* **lavatory**) petit coin *m*, cabinets *mpl*
lava ['lɑːvə] *n* lave *f*; **l. stream** *or* **flow** coulée *f* de lave
lavabo *pl* **-os** [lə'veɪbəʊ, -əʊz] *n Rel* lavabo *m*
lavalier [læ'væljе] *n* (*clip mike*) micro *m* cravate
lavatorial [lævə'tɔːrɪəl] *adj* (*humour*) scatologique
lavatory ['lævətrɪ] *n* (*room, object*) W.-C. *mpl*, toilettes *fpl*; **public l.** W.-C. publics, toilettes publiques; *Br* **l. humour** humour *m* scatologique; **l. pan** cuvette *f* de W.-C.; **l. paper** papier *m* hygiénique
lavender ['lævɪndər] **1** *n* (*shrub*) lavande *f*; **l. water** eau *f* de lavande **2** *adj* (*colour*) lavande *inv*
lavish[1] ['lævɪʃ] *adj* **(a)** (*person*) prodigue; **to be l. with one's money** dépenser sans compter; **to be l. with the cream/sugar** ne pas pleurer la crème/le sucre; **to be l. in one's praise** être prodigue d'éloges **(b)** (*gift, house etc*) somptueux; (*praise*) dithyrambique; (*meal*) plantureux; (*spending*) extravagant; **to live in a l. style** mener la grande vie
lavish[2] *vt* **to l. money on sb** dépenser des fortunes pour qn; **to l. praise on sb** se répandre en éloges sur qn; **to l. care on sb** prodiguer des soins à qn; **to l. care on sth** être extrêmement soigneux avec qch
lavishly ['lævɪʃlɪ] *adv* **(a)** avec prodigalité; **to spend l.** dépenser de l'argent sans compter; **to praise sb l.** se répandre en éloges sur qn; **we were l. entertained by them** ils se sont royalement occupés de nous **(b)** (*to furnish*) somptueusement
lavishness ['lævɪʃnɪs] *n* **(a)** (*of person*) prodigalité *f* **(b)** (*of furnishings etc*) somptuosité *f*
law [lɔː] *n* **(a)** (*rule*) loi *f*; *Phil* principe *m*; *Parl* **to pass/repeal a l.** voter/abroger une loi; **there's no l. against it** aucune loi ne l'interdit; *Phys* **the laws of gravity** les lois de la pesanteur; *Econ* **l. of diminishing returns** loi des rendements décroissants; **l. of supply and demand** loi de l'offre et de la demande; **by the l. of averages** par la loi des probabilités
(b) (*set of rules*) **the l.** la loi; *Sp* **the off-side l.** les règles *ou* le règlement du hors-jeu; **it's the l.** c'est la loi; **it's against the l.** c'est contre la loi (**to do sth** de faire qch); **to carry out the l.** appliquer la loi; **to keep/break the l.** respecter *ou* observer/enfreindre la loi; **l. and order** ordre *m* public; **to have the force of l.** avoir force de loi; **his word is l.** sa parole a force de loi; **he thinks he's above the l.** il se croit tout permis; **no-one is above the l.** personne n'est au-dessus des lois; **to be a l. unto oneself** n'en faire qu'à sa tête; **there's one l. for the rich and another for the poor** il y a une loi pour les riches et une pour les pauvres; *Rel Hist* **the L., the l. of Moses** la loi mosaïque
(c) *Jur* (*system of justice*) droit *m*; **civil l.** = droit civil; **common l.** (*as opposed to statute law*) droit coutumier; (*of general application*) droit civil; **criminal l.** droit pénal *ou* criminel, législation *f* criminelle; **l. of contract** = droit des obligations; **Roman l.** droit romain; **judgment quashed on a point of l.** arrêt cassé pour vice de forme; **Bachelor/Doctor of Laws** = licencié(e)/docteur en droit; **to read** *or* **study l.** étudier le droit, faire son droit; **to practise l.** exercer la profession d'avocat, être avocat; **l. reports** rubrique *f* juridique (*donnant des détails juridiques sur des procès d'un intérêt particulier*)
(d) (*justice*) **to go to l.** avoir recours à *ou* recourir à la justice; **to hand sb over to the l.** remettre qn à la justice; **to be at l.** être en procès; **to take the l. into one's own hands** faire justice soi-même; **l. costs** frais *mpl* de procédure; *F* **the l.** (*police*) la police; *F* **run! here's the l.** barre-toi! voilà les flics; *F* **I'll have the l. on you if you don't stop that!** si vous n'arrêtez pas tout de suite, j'appelle les flics; *prov* **the long arm of the l.** le bras de la justice
law-abiding *adj* respectueux des lois, qui observe la loi; **l. people** gens qui respectent les lois
lawbreaker ['lɔːbreɪkər] *n* transgresseur *m* de la loi
lawbreaking ['lɔːbreɪkɪŋ] *n* infraction *f* à la loi
lawcourt ['lɔːkɔːt] *n* cour *f* de justice, tribunal *m*
law enforcement *n* application *f* de la loi; **l. agency** organisme *m* chargé de faire respecter la loi; **l. officer** agent *m* de police
law firm *n* cabinet *m* d'avocats, cabinet juridique
lawful ['lɔːfʊl] *adj* (*owner, activities*) légal; (*right, wife, child etc*) légitime; (*contract*) valide; (*claim etc*) juste; **to go about one's l. business** vaquer à ses occupations; **l. trade** commerce *m* licite
lawfully ['lɔːfʊlɪ] *adv* légalement, légitimement
lawgiver ['lɔːgɪvər] *n Lit* législateur *m*
lawless ['lɔːlɪs] *adj* (*country, society*) sans loi; (*times*) d'anarchie; **l. behaviour** comportement débridé
lawlessness ['lɔːlɪsnɪs] *n* (*of times*) anarchie *f*; (*of conduct*) caractère *m* débridé; **the town was in a state of utter l.** la ville était plongée dans l'anarchie la plus totale
law lord *n Br* membre *m* juriste de la Chambre des Lords
lawmaker ['lɔːmeɪkər] *n* législateur *m*
lawn[1] [lɔːn] *n Tex* linon *m*
lawn[2] *n* (*grass*) pelouse *f*, (parterre *m* de) gazon *m*; **do not walk on the l.** ne pas marcher sur la pelouse; **to mow** *or* **cut the l.** tondre le gazon; **l. fertilizer** *or* **food** engrais *m* à gazon; **l. sprinkler** arrosoir *m* de pelouse; (*spinning*) tourniquet *m* arroseur; **l. tennis** tennis *m*
lawnmower ['lɔːnməʊər] *n* tondeuse *f* (à gazon)
law officer *n* conseiller *m* juridique
Lawrence of Arabia ['lɒrəns] *n* Lawrence d'Arabie
law school *n* faculté *f* de droit
law student *n* étudiant, -ante en droit
lawsuit ['lɔːs(j)uːt] *n* procès *m*, action *f* judiciaire; **to bring a l. against sb** intenter un procès à qn
lawyer ['lɔːjər] *n* (*provides advice, appears in court*) avocat *m*; (*authenticates documents*) notaire *m*; (*in company*)

conseiller *m* juridique; **we'll have to see a l.** il nous faudra consulter un avocat

lax [læks] *adj* **(a)** (*conduct, principles*) relâché; (*person*) laxiste; (*discipline*) lâche; **l. morals** morale laxiste; **to be l. in (carrying out) one's duties** ne pas toujours observer ses devoirs **(b)** (*vague, imprecise*) vague; **l. use of the term 'paranoid'** emploi peu précis du mot 'paranoïaque' **(c)** *Med* **l. bowels** intestins relâchés

laxative ['læksətɪv] *adj, n Med* laxatif *m*

laxity ['læksɪtɪ], **laxness** ['læksnɪs] *n* (*of morals, security*) relâchement *m*; (*of discipline*) laxisme *m*; **l. in performing one's duties** laxisme dans l'accomplissement de ses devoirs

lay[1] [leɪ] *n* **(a)** **l. of the land** configuration *f* du pays *ou* du terrain; *Fig* **to find out the l. of the land** tâter le terrain **(b)** *Sl* **she's an easy l.** c'est une fille facile; **he's a good l.** il baise bien

lay[2] (*pt, pp* **laid** [leɪd]) **1** *vt* **(a)** (*make horizontal*) coucher; (*of wind, rain*) (*corn*) coucher, abattre; **to l. sb/sth flat** coucher *ou* étendre qn/qch (par terre); **to l. sb flat** (*with punch*) terrasser qn, abattre qn; **laid low by sickness** terrassé par la maladie

(b) (*place*) mettre, placer, poser (**sth on sth** qch sur qch); **to l. a book on the table** poser un livre sur la table; **to l. one's hand on sb's shoulder** mettre la main sur l'épaule de qn; **to l. the blame (for sth) on sb** faire porter la responsabilité (de qch) à qn; **he laid particular emphasis** *or* **stress on the importance of security** il a particulièrement insisté sur la sécurité; **if you l. a finger on her** si tu touches à un cheveu de sa tête; **to have nowhere to l. one's head** ne pas avoir où reposer la tête; *F* **to l. eyes on sb/sth** voir qn/qch; *F* **to l. one on sb** en mettre une à qn; **to l. sb to rest** enterrer qn; **to l. sth bare** (*one's feelings, sb's motives*) mettre qch à nu; **to l. oneself open to criticism/the charge that ...** s'exposer à la critique/l'accusation selon laquelle ...

(c) (*cause to subside*) (*dust etc*) fixer; (*ghost*) exorciser, conjurer; **to l. sb's fears to rest** ôter toutes les inquiétudes de qn

(d) (*of hen etc*) (*egg*) pondre; *Fig* **he nearly laid an egg** (*in surprise*) il a failli en faire une jaunisse

(e) *Sp* (*bet*) faire; (*sum of money*) parier, miser

(f) *esp Fml* (*present*) (*question, request*) soumettre (**before sb** devant qn); **he laid all the facts before me** il me présenta tous les faits; *Jur* **to l. a complaint** déposer une plainte, porter plainte; **to l. a matter before the court** saisir le tribunal d'une affaire; *Jur* **to l. information** présenter une information; **to l. claim to sth** prétendre à qch; **the town lays claim to being the place where golf was invented** les gens de cette ville prétendent que c'est ici que le golf fut inventé

(g) (*impose*) (*penalty*) imposer (**upon sb** à qn); (*fine etc*) infliger (**on sb** à qn); **to l. a curse on sb/sth** jeter un sort à qn/qch

(h) (*dispose, arrange*) (*foundations*) poser, jeter, asseoir; (*bricks*) ranger; (*railway, cable*) poser; (*concrete*) couler; (*carpet*) poser, tendre; (*fire*) préparer; *Naut* (*mine*) poser, mouiller; (*trap*) dresser, tendre; (*ambush*) tendre; **they laid plans to evacuate the city** ils ont prévu un plan d'évacuation de la ville; **they had laid plans to send their money abroad** ils avaient pris toutes les dispositions nécessaires pour envoyer leur argent à l'étranger; *Br* **to l. the table** mettre *ou* dresser la table; **to l. the table for three** mettre la table pour trois personnes, mettre trois couverts

(i) *Sl* (*have sex with*) **to l. a girl** s'envoyer une fille; **to get laid** s'envoyer en l'air

2 *vi* **(a)** *Sl* (*incorrectly used for* **lie**) **to l. in bed** rester couché

(b) (*of bird*) pondre

(c) *Sl* **to l. about one** (*hit out*) frapper de tous côtés

lay[3] *adj* **(a)** laïque; *Rel* **l. brother** frère lai, frère convers; **l. sister** sœur laie, sœur converse; **l. preacher** *or* **reader** prédicateur *m* laïque; **to the l. mind it seems complicated** aux yeux du profane cela semble compliqué **(b)** *Art* **l. figure** mannequin *m*

lay[4] *n Arch* (*song, poem*) lai *m*

lay[5] *pt see* = **lie[4]**

▶ **lay aside** *vtsep* (*prejudices, reservation*) mettre de côté, oublier; (*work, document, money*) mettre de côté; **it's best to have something laid aside for emergencies** il est préférable d'avoir de l'argent de côté en cas de pépins

▶ **lay away** *vtsep* (*money etc*) mettre de côté

▶ **lay back** *vtsep* (*of horse*) (*ears*) rabattre, coucher

▶ **lay by** *vtsep* mettre de côté

▶ **lay down 1** *vtsep* **(a)** (*deposit*) déposer, poser; **to l. down one's arms** rendre *ou* déposer les armes

(b) (*place horizontally*) (*person*) coucher, étendre; **to l. oneself down** se coucher

(c) (*abandon*) (*one's duties, one's responsibilities for sth*) quitter, se démettre de; **to l. down one's life** sacrifier sa vie, faire le sacrifice de sa vie (**for** pour)

(d) *Naut* (*ship*) mettre en chantier *ou* sur cale

(e) (*establish*) (*principle, rule*) poser, imposer, établir; (*conditions*) fixer; (*duties*) spécifier; (*rule of behaviour*) indiquer, prescrire; **to l. down that ...** stipuler que ...; **to l. down the law** dicter sa loi (**to sb** à qn; **about** sur)

(f) (*store*) (*wine*) mettre en cave *ou* sur chantier

2 *vi Sl* = **lie down**

▶ **lay in** *vtsep* faire provision de, s'approvisionner en; **to l. in provisions** faire des provisions; **we've laid in plenty of food for the weekend** nous avons prévu beaucoup de nourriture pour le week-end; *Com* **to l. in goods** *or* **stock** faire provision de marchandises

▶ **lay into** *vipo F* **to l. into sb** (*hit*) rosser qn; (*verbally*) passer un savon à qn

▶ **lay off 1** *vtsep* **(a)** (*workers*) licencier; (*temporarily*) mettre en chômage technique **(b)** (*in insurance*) **to l. off a risk** effectuer une réassurance; *Horseracing etc* **to l. off a bet** faire la contrepartie d'un pari **(c)** *Sp* **to l. the ball off for sb** placer le ballon en bonne position pour qn **2** *vipo* **(a)** *F* (*abstain from*) s'abstenir de; **to l. off drink** arrêter de boire **(b)** *Sl* **to l. off sb** (*leave alone*) foutre la paix à qn **3** *vi Sl* **l. off!** (*leave me alone*) fous-moi la paix!

▶ **lay on** *vtsep* **(a)** *Br* (*install*) (*gas, electricity, water*) installer **(b)** *F* (*organize*) (*party, entertainment etc*) organiser; **I'll l. on the drinks/food** je m'occuperai de la boisson/la nourriture; **I'll l. on a car for you at the station** j'enverrai une voiture vous chercher à la gare **(c)** (*apply*) (*coat of plaster etc*) étendre, coucher, appliquer; *Art* **to l. on the paint** peindre dans la pâte *ou* en pleine pâte; *F* **to l. it on (thick)** *or* **with a trowel** (*flatter*) flatter grossièrement; (*exaggerate*) exagérer, y aller un peu fort

▶ **lay out** *vtsep* **(a)** (*arrange, display*) (*objects*) arranger, disposer; (*merchandise*) étaler, déployer; (*meal*) servir; **to l. out one's reasons** exposer ses raisons

(b) (*dead body*) faire la toilette de

(c) *F* (*knock down*) (*person*) étendre d'un coup, coucher par terre *ou* sur le carreau; *Boxing* envoyer au tapis

(d) **to l. out money** dépenser *ou* débourser de l'argent; **to l. oneself out to help sb** se mettre en quatre pour aider qn; **he's not going to l. himself out** il ne fera pas d'effort, *F* il ne va pas se fouler

(e) (*plan, design*) (*gardens etc*) tracer; (*physically*) disposer; *Typ* (*text*) mettre en page

▶ **lay over** *vi Am* (*during journey*) faire (une) halte

▶ **lay up** *vtsep* **(a)** (*store*) mettre en réserve; (*supplies*) accumuler, amasser; **you're laying up a lot of trouble for yourself** tu vas t'attirer beaucoup d'ennuis **(b)** (*take out of service*) (*ship*) désarmer, déséquiper, mettre en rade; (*car*) mettre sur cales **(c)** **to be laid up** (*with illness*) être alité, être obligé de garder le lit

layabout ['leɪəbaʊt] *n F* paresseux *m*

lay-by *n Br* (*on road*) espace *m* de stationnement (*sur le bas-côté de la route*); (*on motorway*) = aire *f* de stationnement

lay day *n Com* jour *m* de planche; **l. days** jours *mpl* de planche, estarie *f*

layer[1] ['leɪər] *n* **(a)** (*of paint, chocolate, clouds, clothes etc*) couche *f*; (*of dung*) lit *m*; *Constr* (*of cement, bricks etc*) assise *f*, lit; *Geol* (*of rocks etc*) couche, strate *f*; **the upper layers of the atmosphere** les couches supérieures de l'atmosphère; *Culin* **l. cake** gâteau *m* fourré (*à la crème*) **(b)** (*hen etc*) **good l.** bonne pondeuse *f* **(c)** (*of plant*) marcotte *f*

layer[2] *vt* **(a)** poser *ou* disposer en couches; (*hair*) dégrader; **I'd like my hair layered** j'aimerais un dégradé; **a layer(ed) cut** une coupe en dégradé **(b)** (*rosebush etc*) marcotter

layette [leɪ'et] *n* layette *f*

laying ['leɪɪŋ] **1** *adj* **l. hen** poule *f* pondeuse **2** *n* **(a)** (*of rails, pipes, cables, carpet etc*) pose *f*; (*of foundations*) assise *f*; (*of underwater cable*) immersion *f*; (*of mines*) mouillage *m* **(b)** (*of eggs*) ponte *f*

laying down *n* **(a)** (*of principle etc*) établissement *m* **(b)** (*of sewage system, cable*) pose *f*; (*of ship*) mise *f* en chantier *ou* sur cale **(c)** (*of arms*) dépôt *m*

laying off *n* (*of workers*) licenciement *m*

laying on *n Rel* **l. on of hands** imposition *f* des mains

laying out *n* (*of dead body*) toilette *f*

layman, *pl* **-men** ['leɪmən] *n* **(a)** *Rel* laïque *m* **(b)** *Fig* personne *f* non initiée, profane *m*

lay-off *n* **(a)** *Ind* (*action*) licenciement *m*; (*temporary*) mise *f* en chômage *m* technique **(b)** *Ftbl* petite passe *f* de côté

layout ['leɪaʊt] *n* **(a)** (*plan*) (*of building, town*) tracé *m*; (*of* *gardens*) dessin *m* **(b)** (*arrangement*) (*of house, building etc*) plan *m*, agencement *m*; (*of piece of machinery*) agencement *ou* disposition *f* des pièces **(c)** *Typ* (*of text etc*) mise *f* en page, disposition *f*; *Journ* **l. card** (*for pages*) plan *m* de maquette; **l. compositor** maquettiste *mf*; **l. sheet** (*for pages*) maquette *f*, trame *f* de maquette

layover [ˈleɪəʊvər] *n Am* escale *f*

layperson [ˈleɪpɜːsən] = **layman, laywoman**

laywoman, *pl* **-women** [ˈleɪwʊmən, -wɪmɪn] *n* **(a)** *Rel* laïque *f* **(b)** *Fig* personne *f* non initiée, profane *f*

Lazarus [ˈlæzərəs] *n Bible* Lazare *m*

laze [leɪz] *vi* **to l. (about** *or* **around)** paresser, fainéanter; **you've spent the whole morning lazing around** tu as passé la matinée entière à traînasser; **to l. on the beach** faire le lézard sur la plage; **to l. in bed** traînasser au lit, faire la grasse matinée; **to l. away a couple of hours in the sun** passer quelques heures à paresser au soleil

lazily [ˈleɪzɪlɪ] *adv* paresseusement

laziness [ˈleɪzɪnɪs] *n* paresse *f*, fainéantise *f*

lazy [ˈleɪzɪ] *adj* **(a)** (*person*) paresseux, fainéant; **a l. person** un paresseux, une paresseuse; **a l. smile** un sourire nonchalant; **I feel too l. to do it** je n'ai pas l'énergie de le faire; *Am* **l. Susan** plateau *m* tournant; **to have a l. eye** avoir un œil paresseux **(b)** (*moments*) de paresse; **we spent a l. afternoon in the garden** nous avons passé l'après-midi à paresser dans le jardin; **these l. summer days** ces journées d'été où l'on ne fait rien; **to go for a l. sail around the islands** faire une croisière relax autour des îles

lazybones [ˈleɪzɪbəʊnz] *n F* paresseux, -euse, fainéant, -ante

lb (*abbr* **libra**) livre, lb

LBO [elbiːˈəʊ] *n Fin* (*abbr* **leveraged buy-out**) OPA *f* à crédit

lbw [elbiːˈdʌb(ə)ljuː] *Cr* (*abbr* **leg before wicket**) *see* = **leg**

L/C *n, Com* (*abbr* **letter of credit**) l/c *f*

LCD [elsiːˈdiː] *n Comptr* (*abbr* **liquid crystal display**) affichage *m* à cristaux liquides, LCD *m*; **LCD screen** écran *m* LCD

LCL *Com* (*abbr* **less than container load**) conteneur *m* chargé en partie

LEA [eliːˈeɪ] *n Br Admin* (*abbr* **Local Education Authority**) = organisme *m* chargé de l'enseignement au niveau régional

lea [liː] *n Lit* prairie *f*, pâturage *m*

leach [liːtʃ] **1** *vt* (*liquid*) filtrer; (*ore*) lessiver; **to l. away** *or* **out salts** extraire des sels par lessivage **2** *vi* (*of liquid*) filtrer **(through** à travers); **fertilizers have been leaching into the water supply** des engrais ont infiltré la réserve d'eau

lead¹ [liːd] *n* **(a) to take the l., to go** *or* **move into the l.** prendre la tête, prendre la première place; **to take the l. over sb** prendre le pas *ou* les devants sur qn; **to have a l. of 10 metres** avoir une avance de 10 mètres; **she's hanging on to the l.** (*in race*) elle conserve la tête de la course; (*in points table etc*) elle conserve la tête du classement; **she's hanging on to her l.** (*in race*) elle conserve son avance; (*in points table etc*) elle conserve son avance au classement; **he's opened up a tremendous l.** il a pris une avance considérable; **to be in the l.** être en tête; **to lose one's l.** ne plus être en tête; **the company has lost its l. in portables** la société n'est plus le premier producteur de portables

(b) (*example*) **to follow sb's l.** suivre l'exemple de qn; **to give a l. (to sb)** donner l'exemple (à qn); *Mktg* **l. user** utilisateur *m* pilote

(c) (*clue*) indice *m*; **the police have no leads** la police n'a aucune piste; **to give sb a l.** mettre qn sur la voie; **to be following up an important l.** être sur une piste importante

(d) *Cards* **to have the l.** jouer le premier; **your l.!** à vous de jouer!; **is it my l.?** c'est mon tour?, c'est à moi de jouer?; **to follow the l. in clubs** fournir à trèfle

(e) *Th, Cin* premier rôle *m*; **juvenile l.** jeune premier, jeune première; **male l.** premier rôle masculin; **to sing the l.** chanter le rôle principal; **to play the l.** jouer le premier rôle

(f) (*for dog etc*) laisse *f*; **dogs must be kept on a l.** les chiens doivent être tenus en laisse; **l. reins** (*of horse*) grandes guides *fpl*

(g) *El* câble *m ou* branchement *m* de canalisation, amenée *f* de courant, fil *m* électrique

(h) *Journ* (*main story*) **it'll be the l. in tomorrow's papers** ce sera à la une des journaux demain

lead² (*pt, pp* **led** [led]) **1** *vt* **(a)** (*guide*) mener, conduire, guider **(sb to a place** qn à un endroit); (*blind person etc*) conduire, guider par la main; **to l. the conversation round to the subject of ...** amener la conversation sur le sujet de ...; **to l. sb into error** induire qn en erreur; **that leads me to another point I wanted to make** ceci m'amène à un autre point que je voulais soulever; (*horse*) mener par la bride; (*dog*) tenir en laisse; *Prov* **you can l. a horse to water (but you cannot make it drink)** on ne fait pas boire un âne qui n'a pas soif; *Jur* **to l. a witness** poser des questions tendancieuses à un témoin; **to l. the way** marcher le premier *ou* en tête; **to l. a team to victory** mener une équipe à la victoire; **to l. the conversation back to a subject** ramener la conversation sur un sujet; *Fig* **he is easily led** il est très influençable; **she led them to safety** elle les a conduits en lieu sûr; *Rel* **l. us not into temptation** ne nous soumets pas à la tentation

(b) (*cause*) amener, porter **(sb to do sth** qn à faire qch); **that leads me to believe that ...** cela m'amène à croire que ...; **I was led to the conclusion that ...** je fus amené à la conclusion que ...; **what led you to apply for this job?** qu'est-ce qui vous a conduit *ou* amené à postuler?

(c) (*happy life, sad life*) mener; **to l. sb a dog's life** faire une vie de chien à qn

(d) (*be leader of*) (*team, dance, attack*) mener; (*army*) commander; **leading his troops** à la tête de ses troupes; **to l. a party** être chef de parti; **to l. an orchestra** conduire un orchestre; **to l. the congregation in prayer** conduire la congrégation à la prière

(e) (*be ahead of*) **to l. the field** mener; *Fig* **to l. the field in ...** être au premier rang en matière de ...; **to l. sb by eight points** avoir une avance sur qn de huit points; **she leads the class in maths** elle est la première de sa classe en maths; **we l. the world in ...** nous sommes les leaders mondiaux de ...

(f) *Cards* **to l. a card** entamer *ou* attaquer d'une carte; **to l. clubs** jouer *ou* attaquer trèfle

(g) *Tech* (*water to a place*) amener; (*actually install*) installer; (*rope through a pulley*) faire passer

2 *vi* **(a)** (*of road*) mener, conduire **(to** à); **road that leads to the town** route qui mène *ou* va à la ville; **door that leads into the garden** porte qui communique avec le jardin *ou* qui donne accès au jardin; **to l. to a good result** aboutir à un bon résultat, produire un heureux effet; **to l. to a discovery** conduire *ou* aboutir à une découverte; **drinking too much can l. to violence** l'excès d'alcool peut conduire à la violence; **one thing leads to another** une chose en amène une autre; **to l. to nothing** n'aboutir *ou* ne mener à rien; **to l. to a misunderstanding** conduire à un malentendu; **action which led to criticism** action qui a motivé des critiques; **this led to several of them losing their jobs** à cause de cela, plusieurs d'entre eux ont perdu leur emploi

(b) (*go first*) (*in competition, race, dance etc*) mener; **you l. and I'll follow** vas-y, je te suis; *Boxing, Cards* ouvrir le jeu, jouer le premier, entamer; **he leads with the left** il est gaucher; **he led with a left** il a donné un coup du gauche; **to l. with** (*of newspaper*) titrer en première page, faire ses gros titres *ou* sa première page sur

(c) (*of barrister*) être l'avocat principal; **he led for the prosecution** avocat principal, il dirigea l'accusation

lead³ [led] *n* **(a)** (*metal*) plomb *m*; *f* **to go down like a l. balloon** tomber à plat; *Sl* **they pumped him full of l.** ils l'ont truffé *ou* farci de plomb; **l. ore** minerai *m* de plomb; **l. paint** peinture *f* à base de plomb; **l. pipe** tuyau *m* de plomb **(b)** *Br Constr* **roof leads** plombs *mpl* de couverture; **window leads** plombs de vitrail *ou* de vitraux **(c)** (*for pencil*) mine *f* **(d)** *Naut* (plomb *m* de) sonde *f*; *F* **to swing the l.** tirer au flanc **(e)** *Fishing* plomb *m*

lead⁴ *vt* **(leaded** [ˈledɪd]; **leading** [ˈledɪŋ]) **(a)** *Constr* (*roof*) plomber; (*windows*) enchâsser dans les plombs **(b)** *Fishing* (*line, net*) plomber **(c)** *Typ* (*lines of type*) interligner

▶ **lead away** [liːd] *vtsep* (*prisoner etc*) emmener

▶ **lead back 1** *vtsep* ramener **2** *vi* ramener

▶ **lead off 1** *vi* **(a)** (*begin*) commencer, débuter **(with** par); (*in debate*) entamer les débats; (*in game*) jouer le premier; *Billiards* donner l'acquit; (*at dance*) ouvrir le bal **(b) several doors/corridors l. off the hall** il y a plusieurs portes/couloirs qui donnent dans le hall **2** *vtsep* **(a)** (*discussion*) amorcer; (*attack*) lancer **(b)** (*prisoner etc*) emmener

▶ **lead on 1** *vtas* **to l. sb on to talk (about ...)** encourager qn à parler (de ...); **try and l. him on to the subject of football** essaie de l'aiguiller sur le sujet du football *ou F* le brancher sur le football; *F* **to l. sb on** (*deceive*) tromper qn, duper qn **2** *vi* **l. on!** en avant!

▶ **lead out** [led] *vtsep Typ* (*lines of text*) augmenter l'interlignage de

▶ **lead up** [liːd] **1** *vi* **to l. up to a subject** amener un sujet; **I was just leading up to that** j'allais justement y venir; **I couldn't see what he was leading up to** je ne voyais pas où il voulait en venir; **the chords that l. up to the final movement** les accords qui introduisent le dernier mouvement; **the period leading up to the war** la période précédant la guerre; **there's a path leading up to the ski lift** il y a un chemin qui mène au téléski **2** *vtsep* (*troops, class etc*) faire avancer; **he led us up (a staircase)** il nous a fait monter (un escalier)

lead content [led] *n* (*of fuel*) indice *m* de plomb
lead crystal *n* verre *m* de *ou* au plomb
leaded ['ledɪd] *adj* **l. window** vitre *f* plombée; **l. petrol** essence *f* au plomb
leaden ['led(ə)n] *adj* (*made of lead*) de plomb; (*complexion*) plombé; **l.-eyed** aux yeux ternes; **l.-footed** à la démarche pesante; **l. limbs** membres inertes; **a l. sky** un ciel *m* de plomb; **the l. calm of the sea** la mer grise et immobile
leader ['li:dər] *n* **(a)** (*of expedition, group, organization etc*) chef *m*; *Mil* (*of unit*) commandant *m*; (*of riot*) meneur *m*; *Br Mus* premier violon *m*; *US Mus* chef *m* d'orchestre; *Br Jur* avocat *m* principal; **to be a born l.** être fait pour donner des ordres *ou* commander; *Br* **L. of the House of Commons** chef de la majorité à la Chambre des Communes; *Sp* **team l.** chef d'équipe; **a major group, a l. in its field** un groupe important, un leader dans sa branche
(b) (*in race*) **he's still the l.** il mène toujours; **the three leaders** les trois premiers
(c) (*in horse team*) cheval *m* de tête; (*in dog team*) chien *m* de tête; **the leaders** l'attelage *m* de devant
(d) (*of tape, film*) (bande) amorce *f*
(e) *Journ* (*main item*) article *m* principal; (*article*) article de fond; *Br* (*editorial*) éditorial *m*, -aux; **l. writer** éditorialiste *mf*
(f) *Am Com* (*loss leader*) produit *m* d'appel
(g) *Mktg* (*product*) numéro un *m* (sur le marché); (*company*) chef *m* de file, leader *m*
leadership ['li:dəʃɪp] *n* **(a)** (*qualities shown*) qualités *fpl* de chef; **no one showed any l.** personne n'a montré des qualités de chef; **the organization lacks l.** l'organisation manque d'un vrai chef; **to be under sb's l.** être sous la conduite de qn; **l. potential** qualités de chef **(b)** (*position*) (*of party, union etc*) direction *f*; (*duties as leader*) fonctions *fpl* de chef; *Mil* commandement *m*; **l. battle/contest** bataille *f* pour la direction **(c)** (*leaders*) dirigeants *mpl*
lead-free [led'fri:] **1** *adj* (*petrol, paint*) sans plomb **2** *n* (*petrol*) essence *f* sans plomb
lead-in ['li:dɪn] *n* **(a)** (*introduction*), *Mus* introduction *f*; *El, Tel etc* (*of cable*) entrée *f* **(b)** *Rad etc* (*to aerial*) descente *f* d'antenne; **l. groove** (*on record*) sillon *m* initial
leading¹ ['li:dɪŋ] **1** *adj* **(a)** (*chief*) premier, principal; **a l. authority in the field** un grand spécialiste du domaine; **the l. statesmen of Europe** les hommes d'État dirigeants de l'Europe; **a l. shareholder** un des principaux actionnaires; **he's one of Britain's l. novelists** c'est l'un des plus grands romanciers contemporains de Grande Bretagne; **she's a l. light in local politics** c'est une personnalité très influente de la politique locale; **to play a l. role in a matter** jouer un rôle prépondérant dans une affaire
(b) (*in front*) (*car*) de tête; *Mil* **l. patrol** patrouille *f* de tête; **l. axle** *or* **wheels** (*of vehicle*) essieu *m* porteur d'avant; *Cards* **l. card** première carte *f*; *El* **l. current** courant *m* déphasé en avant; *Av* **l. edge** (*of wing*) bord *m* d'attaque; **to be on the l. edge of technology** être à la pointe de la technologie; **l. edge technology** technologie *f* de pointe; **l. shoot** (*of plant*) pousse *f* principale *ou* terminale; *Comptr* **l. zeroes** zéros *mpl* à gauche
(c) l. question question *f* tendancieuse; *Jur* question posée au témoin de manière à suggérer la réponse
2 *n* (*of horses etc*) conduite *f*, menage *m*; **l. rein** (*for horse*) longe *f*
leading² ['ledɪŋ] *n Typ* interligne *f*
leading article ['li:dɪŋ] *n Journ Br* (*editorial*) éditorial *m*; *Am* (*main item*) article *m* principal
leading lady *n Cin, Th* premier rôle *m*
leading man *n Cin, Th* premier rôle *m*; **who's going to be your l.?** qui sera ton partenaire masculin *ou* ta co-vedette masculine?
leading part *n Cin, Th* premier rôle *m*
leading reins *n* (*for child*) harnais *m*
leading role *n Cin, Th* premier rôle *m*
leading strings *n Am* (*for child*) harnais *m*
lead manager *n* chef *m* de file
lead-out *n El, Tel* (*of wire etc*) sortie *f*; **l. groove** (*of record*) sillon *m* de sortie
lead pencil [led] *n* crayon *m* à mine de plomb
lead poisoning *n Med* intoxication *f* saturnine *ou* par le plomb
lead shot *n* grenaille *f* de plomb, petit plomb *m*
lead time [li:d] *n Com* (*for production*) délai *m* de réalisation *ou* de production; (*for delivery*) délai de livraison
lead-up *n* veille *f*; **in the l. to independence** dans la période qui a précédé l'indépendance
leadwork ['ledwɜ:k] *n Archit* (*of window*) plombs *mpl*
leaf, *pl* **leaves** [li:f, li:vz] *n* **(a)** (*of plant, tree*) feuille *f*; **to put out leaves, to come into l.** feuiller; **the trees have already started coming into l.** les arbres commencent déjà à avoir des feuilles; **in l.** couvert de feuilles, en feuilles; **to shake like a l.** trembler comme une feuille; **l. bud** bourgeon *m* à feuille; **l. green** vert prairie *m inv*; *Ent* **l. insect** phyllie *f*; **l. mould** terreau *m* de feuilles; **l. tobacco** tabac *m* en feuilles; **outer l. of a cigar** robe *f* d'un cigare
(b) (*of book*) feuillet *m*; **single l.** (*in bookbinding*) carton *m* de deux pages; *Fig* **to turn over a new l.** (*of person*) changer de conduite; *Fig* **to take a l. out of sb's book** prendre exemple *ou* modèle sur qn
(c) (*of gold, silver etc*) feuille *f*
(d) (*of door*) battant *m*, vantail, -aux *m*; (*of shutter*) battant; (*of spring*) lame *f*, feuille *f*, feuillet *m*; (*of table*) (*inserted*) rallonge *f* (*de table*); (*hinged*) battant
▶ **leaf through** *vipo* (*book*) feuilleter
leaflet¹ ['li:flɪt] *n Com etc* prospectus *m*; *Pol* tract *m*; **instruction l.** mode *m* d'emploi; **l. drop** distribution *f* de prospectus
leaflet² *vt* **to l. an area** distribuer des prospectus dans un quartier
leafstalk ['li:fstɔ:k] *n Bot* pétiole *m*
leafy ['li:fɪ] *adj* (*tree*) feuillu; **a l. lane** *or* **street** une rue bordée d'arbres; **a l. suburb** une banlieue verte; **a l. canopy** un dais de feuillage *ou* de verdure
league¹ [li:g] *n* **(a)** (*association*) ligue *f*; **everyone is in l. against them** tout le monde est ligué contre eux; **to be in l. with sb** être de connivence avec qn; *F* être de mêche avec qn **(b)** *Fig* **I'm not in your l., I'm not in the same l. as you** je ne suis pas de votre niveau; **they're not in the same l.** ils ne sont pas du même niveau; **I thought I was good but he's in another l.** je pensais que j'étais bon mais il est bien meilleur que moi
league² *n Hist* (*measurement*) lieue *f*
▶ **league together** *vi* faire alliance (**with** avec); **to l. together against sb/sth** se liguer contre qn/qch
league champions *n Fb* vainqueurs *mpl* du championnat, équipe *f* en tête du championnat
league leaders *npl Fb* leader *m* du championnat
league match *n Fb* match *m* de championnat
League of Nations *n Hist* la Société des Nations
league table *n Fb* classement *m* du championnat; *Fig* **a l. of statistics** un classement statistique
leak¹ [li:k] *n* **(a)** (*of liquid, gas, secrets*) fuite *f* **(b)** (*entry*) (*of water etc*) infiltration *f*, rentrée *f*; *Naut* voie *f* d'eau; **to spring a l.** (*of ship*) faire eau, avoir une voie d'eau; (*of shoes*) prendre l'eau **(c)** *Sl* **to take** *or* **have a l.** (*urinate*) pisser un coup
leak² **1** *vi* **(a)** (*of tank etc*) avoir une fuite, fuir; (*of ship etc*) faire eau, avoir une voie d'eau; **roof that leaks** toit qui laisse entrer la pluie; **my shoes l.** mes chaussures prennent l'eau **(b)** (*of liquid*) fuir, couler; (*of gas*) fuir; (*of truth, news etc*) s'ébruiter, transpirer **2** *vt* **(a) the bucket/pipe was leaking water** l'eau coulait du seau/du tuyau; **the pipe had been leaking gas** le tuyau de gaz avait une fuite; **the radiator had been leaking water everywhere** le radiateur avait fui et il y avait de l'eau partout **(b)** *F* (*information etc*) divulguer
▶ **leak out** *vi* (*of water, gas etc*) fuir; *Fig* (*of truth, information etc*) filtrer; **the acid was leaking out of the battery** de l'acide fuyait de la batterie
leakage ['li:kɪdʒ] *n* **(a)** (*of water, gas, official secrets*) fuites *fpl* **(b)** (*loss of stock*) (*in a business*) coulage *m*
leaky ['li:kɪ] *adj* (*barrel*) qui coule, qui fuit; (*boat*) qui fait eau; (*shoes*) qui prennent l'eau; (*tap, roof*) qui fuit; *Fig F* **this department is very l.** il y a plein de fuites dans ce service
lean¹ [li:n] **1** *adj* **(a)** (*person, dog*) svelte; (*face*) mince; (*too thin*) (*animal*) efflanqué; *Fig* **the company is now fitter and leaner than it was before** l'entreprise se porte mieux depuis que sa structure a été allégée **(b)** (*meat*) maigre **(c) a l. year/period** une année/une période de vaches maigres; **we had a l. time** nous avons eu une période de vaches maigres; **a l. harvest** une mauvaise *ou* maigre récolte **(d)** (*fuel, mixture*) pauvre **2** *n* (*on meat*) maigre *m*
lean² *n* (*inclined position*) inclinaison *f*
lean³ (*pt, pp* **leaned** [li:nd]; **leant** [lent]) **1** *vi* (*of person*) s'appuyer (**against** contre, à; **on** sur, à); **to l. on one's elbow(s)** s'accouder; **leaning against a wall** appuyé à *ou* contre un mur; **to l. back in one's chair** s'appuyer contre le dossier de sa chaise; *Fig* **to l. on sb** (*for support*) se reposer sur qn; *F* (*to pay money etc*) faire pression sur qn; **she still leans on her father for advice** elle a toujours recours aux conseils de son père; **to l. forward/out of the window** se pencher en avant/à la fenêtre; **to l. over/towards sth** se pencher sur/vers qch; **that wall is leaning towards the right** ce mur penche vers la droite; **to l. towards a theory** être plutôt partisan d'une théorie; **I think I'm leaning towards the opinion that you were right after all** je

commence à penser qu'en fin de compte tu avais raison; **to l. towards socialism** pencher vers le socialisme; *F* **to l. over backwards to do sth** se mettre en quatre pour faire qch

2 *vt* (*ladder etc*) appuyer (**against** contre); **to l. sth against sth** adosser qch à *ou* contre qch

lean-burn engine *n* moteur *m* Lean Burn

leaning ['li:nɪŋ] **1** *adj* penché; (*wall*) qui penche **2** *n* (*tendency*) inclination *f* (**towards** pour), penchant *m* (**towards** pour, vers), tendance *f* (**towards** à); **to have leanings towards communism** être de tendance communiste, pencher vers le communisme; **to have artistic leanings** avoir des dispositions artistiques

Leaning Tower of Pisa *n* la tour (penchée) de Pise

leanness ['li:nnɪs] *n* maigreur *f*

leant *see* **lean³**

lean-to 1 *adj* **l. roof** comble *m* en appentis; **l. garage** garage *m* attenant à la maison, avec un toit incliné **2** *n* appentis *m*

leap¹ [li:p] *n* (*jump*) saut *m*, bond *m*; *Fig* **to take a l. in the dark** faire un saut dans l'inconnu; **a l. of faith** un acte de foi; **his heart gave a l.** son cœur bondit, son cœur fit un bond; *Fig* **to advance by leaps and bounds** avancer à pas de géant; **his French had improved by leaps and bounds** il avait fait des progrès phénoménaux en français; **with one l. she cleared the ditch** d'un saut *ou* d'un bond elle franchit le fossé; **the company has taken a great l. forward** la société a fait un grand bond en avant

leap² (*pt, pp* **leaped** [li:pt]; *or* **leapt** [lept]) **1** *vi* (**a**) sauter, bondir; **to l. to one's feet** se lever brusquement; **to l. over a ditch** sauter un fossé; **to l. at the opportunity** sauter sur l'occasion; **to l. for joy** sauter *ou* bondir de joie; **her heart leapt for joy** elle bondit de joie; **she nearly leapt out of her skin** elle a sauté au plafond (**b**) (*of flame etc*) jaillir **2** *vt* (**a**) (*ditch*) sauter, franchir d'un saut (**b**) (*cause to leap*) **to l. a horse over a ditch** faire sauter *ou* faire franchir un fossé à un cheval

▶ **leap up** *vi* (**a**) (*of person*) bondir (**to do** pour faire); (*get to one's feet*) se lever brusquement; **their dog leapt up at me** leur chien m'a sauté dessus (**b**) (*of flame*) jaillir

leap day *n* jour *m* intercalaire, le 29 février

leapfrog¹ ['li:pfrɒg] *n* **to play l.** jouer à saute-mouton

leapfrog² *vt* (**-gg-**) (**a**) **to l. sth** sauter par-dessus qch à saute-mouton (**b**) *Fig* (*stage in process*) sauter; **he leapfrogged several of his more senior colleagues to get the post** il a obtenu le poste en passant devant plusieurs de ses collègues d'un échelon supérieur

leapt *see* **leap²**

leap year *n* année *f* bissextile

learn [lɜ:n] (*pt, pp* **learnt** [lɜ:nt]; *occ* **learned**) **1** *vt* (**a**) (*French, maths etc*) apprendre; **to l. to read/drive** apprendre à lire/conduire; **she's learning the violin** elle apprend à jouer du violon, elle étudie le violon; *Fig* **he has learnt his lesson** ça lui servira de leçon; **when will she l. her lesson?** quand est-ce qu'elle comprendra?

(**b**) (*hear about*) (*news, test results etc*) apprendre; **we are sorry to l. that ...** nous sommes désolés d'apprendre que ...

(**c**) *Arch, Sl* (*teach*) **to l. sb sth** apprendre qch à qn; *Sl* **that'll l. him!** ça lui apprendra!

2 *vi* apprendre; **they're learning about Victorian times** ils étudient l'époque Victorienne; **to l. from one's mistakes** tirer un enseignement de ses erreurs; **it is never too late to l.** on apprend à tout âge

▶ **learn of** *vipo* apprendre

learned ['lɜ:nɪd] *adj* (*person*) savant, érudit; (*style*) savant; *Jur* **my l. friend** mon éminent confrère; **l. journal** journal savant; **l. profession** profession intellectuelle; **l. treatise** traité savant

learner ['lɜ:nə(r)] *n* (**a**) apprenant, -ante; **learners of English** les apprenants d'anglais, les gens qui apprennent l'anglais; **advanced l.** personne *f* d'un bon niveau; **intermediate l.** personne d'un niveau intermédiaire; **to be a quick/good l.** apprendre vite/facilement; **she's a slow/bad l.** elle n'apprend pas vite/facilement (**b**) (*beginner*) élève *mf*, débutant, -ante; *Aut* **l. (driver)** apprenti *m* conducteur

learning ['lɜ:nɪŋ] *n* (**a**) (*act of learning*) apprentissage *m*; **l. capacity** capacités *fpl* d'apprentissage; **l. disability** difficulté *f* d'apprentissage (**b**) (*knowledge*) instruction *f*, savoir *m*, connaissances *fpl*; **seat** *or* **centre of l.** centre *m* intellectuel; **a man of great l.** un homme de grand savoir

learning curve *n* courbe *f* d'expérience *ou* d'apprentissage, courbe d'assimilation; **to have a fast l.** avoir des facultés d'assimilation rapide; **we're back on the l.** il nous faut tout réapprendre

learnt *see* **learn**

lease¹ [li:s] *n Jur* bail *m*, *pl* baux; (*of equipment*) location *f*; (*of house to let*) bail (à loyer); (*of farming land*) bail à ferme; (*document*) (contrat *m* de) bail; **to sign a l.** signer un bail; **long l.** bail à long terme *ou* à longue échéance; **to take on a new l., to renew the l. of a house** renouveler le bail d'une maison; *Fig* **to take on a new l. of life** (*of person*) renaître à la vie; (*of industry, town, football club*) retrouver un nouveau souffle; **meeting Sarah has given him a new l. of life** sa rencontre avec Sarah lui a redonné goût à la vie; **it's like a new l. of life** on se sent renaître; **cleaning the engine will give the car a new l. of life** ça va retaper la voiture de nettoyer le moteur; **l. contract** (*for property*) contrat *m* de bail; (*for equipment*) contrat *m* en location; *Acct* **l. charges** charges *fpl* locatives; *Acct* **l. revenue** loyers *mpl*

lease² *vt* (**a**) (*of owner*) **to l. (out)** (*house*) louer, donner à bail; (*land*) affermer (**b**) (*of tenant*) (*house*) louer, prendre à bail; (*of person*) (*equipment, vehicle*) louer; (*land*) affermer

leaseback ['li:sbæk] *n* cession-bail *f*

leasehold ['li:shəʊld] **1** *n* (**a**) tenure *f* à bail (*esp tenure en vertu d'un bail emphytéotique*) (**b**) (*property*) propriété *f ou* immeuble *m* loué(e) à bail **2** *adj* tenu à bail

leaseholder ['li:shəʊldə(r)] *n* locataire *mf*

lease-purchase *n* crédit-bail *m*; **l. contract** contrat *m* de crédit-bail

leash¹ [li:ʃ] *n* laisse *f*; **to put a dog on the l.** mettre une laisse à un chien; *Fig* **to keep sb on a tight l.** tenir qn étroitement en laisse; **to keep one's emotions on a tight l.** avoir étroitement en mains les rênes de ses émotions

leasing ['li:sɪŋ] *n* (*of house*) location *f* à bail; (*of land*) affermage *m*; *Ind, Com* (*of equipment etc*) location; (*on lease-purchase*) location-bail *f*; (*system*) location avec option d'achat, LOA *f*, crédit-bail *m*

least [li:st] **1** *adj* (*smallest*) **(the) l.** (le *ou* la) moindre, (le *ou* la) plus petit(e); **to get upset at the l. thing** se fâcher pour un rien; **the government clamps down on the l. sign of opposition** le gouvernement serre la vis au moindre signe d'opposition; **the l. mention of religion was absolutely forbidden** la moindre référence à la religion était interdite; **I'm not the l. bit musical** je ne suis pas musicien pour un sou; **I'm not the l. bit tired** je ne suis pas du tout fatigué

2 *n* (**a**) **(the) l.** (le) moins; **to say the l. (of it)** le moins qu'on puisse dire; **she was not very polite, to say the l.** le moins qu'on puisse dire, c'est qu'elle n'a pas été très polie; **it's the l. I can do** c'est la moindre des choses; **that's the l. of my worries** c'est le dernier de mes soucis

(**b**) **at l.** (tout) au moins; **at l. as old/expensive as ...** au moins aussi vieux/cher que ...; **I can at l. try** je peux toujours essayer; **it cost at l. £1,000** cela lui a coûté 1 000 livres au bas mot; **she's at l. seventy** elle a au moins soixante-dix ans; **at the very l. they should pay your expenses** ce serait vraiment la moindre des choses qu'ils remboursent tes dépenses

(**c**) **not in the l.** pas du tout, *Fml* aucunement, nullement; **it doesn't matter in the l.** cela n'a pas la moindre importance; **I'm not in the l. upset** je ne suis fâché en aucune manière

3 *adv* **(the) l.** (le) moins; **the l. unhappy** le moins malheureux; **he deserves it l. of all** il le mérite moins que personne; **we didn't expect to win any prizes, l. of all this one** nous ne nous attendions pas à gagner un prix, et en tout cas, certainement pas celui-là; **it always happens when you are l. expecting it** ça arrive toujours au moment où tu t'y attends le moins

leastways, *Am* **leastwise** ['li:stweɪz, -waɪz] *adv F* ou (tout) du moins ...

leather¹ ['leðə(r)] *n* (**a**) cuir *m*; **l. shoes** chaussures *fpl* en cuir; **fancy l. goods** maroquinerie *f* (**b**) *Br F* (*clothes*) **leathers** cuir *m* (**c**) (*of pump, valve etc*) cuir *m*; **stirrup l.** étrivière *f*

leather² *vt F* (*person*) tanner le cuir à

leather-bound *adj* (*book*) relié (en) cuir

leathercloth ['leðəklɒθ] *n* toile *f* cuir

leatherette [leðə'ret] *n Old-fashioned* similicuir *m*

leathering ['leðərɪŋ] *n F* **to give sb a l.** tanner le cuir à qn

leatherjacket ['leðədʒækɪt] *n Ent* larve *f* de la tipule

leatherneck ['leðənek] *n US F* soldat *m* de l'infanterie de marine

leatherwork ['leðəwɜ:k] *n* (**a**) (*activity*) travail *m* du cuir (**b**) (*products*) articles *mpl* de cuir; **fancy l.** maroquinerie *f*

leathery ['leðərɪ] *adj* (*skin*) tanné; (*food*) coriace

leave¹ [li:v] *n* (**a**) (*permission*) permission *f*, autorisation *f*; **to ask l. to do sth** demander la permission de faire qch; **to grant** *or* **give sb l. to do sth** donner *ou* accorder à qn la permission de faire qch; *Arch, Fml* **by** *or* **with your l.** avec votre permission; **without so much as a by your l.** sans même en demander la permission

(**b**) *Admin, Mil etc* (*holiday*) congé *m*; **l. of absence** (*in army*) permission *f* exceptionnelle; (*in civil service etc*) congé *m* exceptionnel; **to be on l.** être en congé; **to take two weeks' l.** prendre deux semaines de congé

(c) (*farewell*) adieux *mpl*, congé *m*; **to take one's l.** prendre congé; **to take (one's) l. of sb** faire ses adieux à qn; **to take l. of one's senses** perdre l'esprit

leave[2] (*pt, pp* **left** [left]) **1** *vt* (a) (*depart from*) (*place, person*) quitter; (*room*) quitter, sortir de; **he has left London** il est parti de Londres, il a quitté Londres; **he left Oxford without finishing his studies** il a quitté Oxford sans avoir terminé ses études; **she left school at 16** elle a quitté l'école à 16 ans; **she never leaves the house** elle ne sort jamais de la maison; *Sch* **may I l. the room?** puis-je sortir?; **his eyes never left her** il ne la quittait pas des yeux; **to l. the table** se lever de table; **to l. one's job** quitter son emploi; *Mil etc* **to l. the service** quitter le service; *Naut* **to l. harbour** sortir du port; **to l. one's wife** quitter sa femme; **to be left behind** *or* **standing** être dépassé *ou* distancé (par ses concurrents); **to l. the rails** (*of train*) dérailler; **the car left the road** la voiture a quitté la route

(b) (*put, deposit*) **to l. sth somewhere** (*deliberately*) laisser qch quelque part; (*by mistake*) oublier *ou* laisser qch quelque part; **to l. things (lying) about** laisser traîner des choses; *F* **take it or l. it** c'est à prendre ou à laisser; **to l. a message for sb** laisser un mot *ou* un message *ou* un billet pour qn

(c) (*allow to remain*) laisser; **to l. the door open** laisser la porte ouverte; **to l. sth unfinished** laisser qch inachevé; **he left his supper untouched** il ne toucha pas à son dîner; **to l. a page blank** laisser une page en blanc; **l. me alone!** laissez-moi tranquille!; **left to oneself** livré à soi-même; **his work/attitude leaves much to be desired** son travail/attitude laisse beaucoup à désirer; **it leaves me cold** ça me laisse froid; **nothing was left to chance** on avait paré à toutes les éventualités; **to l. hold** *or* **go of sth** lâcher qch; **to l. sb for dead** laisser qn pour mort; *Fig* (*in race etc*) clouer qn sur place; **to l. sb to do sth** laisser qn faire qch, laisser à qn le soin de faire qch; **to l. sb in charge of sth** confier la responsabilité de qch à qn; **he was left in charge of cooking the food** c'est lui qui s'est occupé de faire à manger; **let's l. it at that, we'll l. it at that** (*not do any more work*) arrêtons-nous là; (*not argue any more*) n'en parlons plus; **to l. sth with sb** confier qch à qn; *Fig* **I'll l. it with you** (*let you make decision etc*) je te laisse t'en occuper; **l. it with me** laisse-moi m'en occuper; **I'll l. it to you** je m'en remets à vous; **I l. it to you to decide** je vous laisse le soin de décider; **l. it to me** laisse-moi faire, je m'en occupe

(d) (*after dying*) **to l. a wife and three children** laisser une femme et trois enfants; **to l. one's money to sb** laisser *ou* léguer sa fortune à qn; **she had been left a widow at thirty** elle s'était retrouvée veuve à l'âge de trente ans

(e) **to be left** (*remain*) rester; **there are no strawberries left** il ne reste plus de fraises; **how many are there left?** combien est-ce qu'il en reste?

(f) *Math* **three from seven leaves four** sept moins trois égale quatre

2 *vi* partir; **we l. tomorrow** nous partons demain; **we are leaving for Paris** nous partons pour Paris; **I was just leaving when ...** j'étais sur le point de partir lorsque ...

▶ **leave behind** *vtas* (a) (*forget*) (*one's hat etc*) oublier (b) (*leave in a place*) laisser; **he left his family behind in Manchester and ...** il a laissé sa famille à Manchester et ...; **they left me behind** ils sont partis sans moi (c) (*in race etc*) **he's left the other runners (well) behind** il a pris beaucoup d'avance sur les autres concurrents, *F* il a largué tous les autres concurrents; **she left the other pupils behind** elle est passée première devant tous les autres élèves

▶ **leave in** *vtsep* (*section of text etc*) inclure, retenir

▶ **leave off 1** *vipo F* **to l. off doing sth** cesser de faire qch; **to l. off work** cesser le travail; **why can't you l. off the subject for a day?** et si tu arrêtais de parler de ça pendant une journée?; *F* **l. off pestering me!** arrête de m'embêter!

2 *vtsep* (a) (*not replace*) (*lid etc*) ne pas (re)mettre; **to l. sb off a list** (*accidentally*) oublier qn dans une liste; (*deliberately*) exclure qn d'une liste

(b) **l. the light off** n'allume pas; **l. the telly off for a bit** éteins la télé un petit moment; **I left the heating off** je n'ai pas mis le chauffage

3 *vi* s'arrêter; **where did we l. off?** (*in reading etc*) où en sommes-nous restés?; *Sl* **l. off!** ça suffit comme ça!, arrête!

▶ **leave on** *vtsep* (*coat, gloves etc*) garder; **to l. the light/TV on** laisser la lumière/la télé allumée

▶ **leave out** *vtsep* (a) (*omit*) (*a line etc*) omettre

(b) (*not involve*) **l. her out of this!** laissez-la en dehors de ça!; **to l. sb out of one's plans** exclure qn de ses projets; **to feel left out** se sentir de trop

(c) (*leave ready, available*) **I'll l. your dinner out on the table for you** je te laisse ton dîner sur la table; **l. the disks out where I can see them** laisse les disquettes en évidence

(d) (*not put away*) **we l. the car out on the street** nous laissons la voiture dehors dans la rue; **who left the milk out overnight?** qui a oublié de mettre le lait au frigo hier soir?

(e) *Sl* **l. it out!** (*stop it*) arrête!

▶ **leave over** *vtas* (a) **what's left over?** qu'est-ce qui reste?; **you can keep what is left over** vous pouvez garder le surplus (b) (*postpone*) remettre à plus tard

leaved [liːvd] *adj* feuillé, feuillu

-leaved [liːvd] *suff* **three-l.** (*screen etc*) à trois panneaux; **broad-l. tree** arbre à larges feuilles; **ivy-l.** à feuilles de lierre

leaven[1] [ˈlev(ə)n] *n Culin; Fig* levain *m*

leaven[2] *vt* (*bread, dough*) faire lever; *Fig* **her account is leavened with interesting anecdotes** elle a agrémenté son récit d'anecdotes intéressantes

leavening [ˈlevənɪŋ] *n* = **leaven**

leaver [ˈliːvər] *n* **(school) leavers** élèves *mpl* sortants

leave-taking *n* adieux *mpl*

leaving [ˈliːvɪŋ] *n* départ *m*

leavings [ˈliːvɪŋz] *npl* (*from meal*) restes *mpl*

Lebanese [lebəˈniːz] **1** *adj* libanais **2** *n* Libanais, -aise

Lebanon [ˈlebənən] *n* Liban *m*

▶ **lech after** [letʃ] *vipo F* reluquer

lecher [ˈletʃər] *n* débauché *m*, *F* coureur *m* de jupons

lecherous [ˈletʃərəs] *adj* (*person*) lubrique, débauché; (*look, smile*) lubrique

lecherously [ˈletʃərəslɪ] *adv* lubriquement

lechery [ˈletʃərɪ] *n* lubricité *f*

lectern [ˈlektən] *n* (*in church etc*) lutrin *m*; (*in library*) pupitre *m*

lector [ˈlektɔːr] *n Univ* (*for foreign languages*) lecteur, -trice

lecture[1] [ˈlektʃər] *n* (a) conférence *f*; *Univ* cours *m* magistral **(on** sur); **to give/attend a l.** (*public*) donner/assister à une conférence; (*university*) donner/assister à un cours magistral; **history l.** cours *m* d'histoire; **l. on Napoleon** cours sur Napoléon (b) *F* (*reprimand*) sermon *m*, semonce *f*; **to give** *or* **read sb a l.** faire la morale à qn; (*for wrongdoing*) semoncer qn, sermonner qn

lecture[2] **1** *vi* donner une conférence *ou* des conférences; *Univ* donner un cours magistral **(on** sur); **he lectured on Eastern affairs** il a donné une conférence sur l'Orient; **she lectures in Economics** elle donne des cours d'économie à l'université, elle est maître-assistant en économie; **he lectures at Stirling** il est maître-assistant à l'université de Stirling **2** *vt F* (*person*) faire la morale à; (*for wrongdoing*) sermonner, semoncer

lecture hall *n* salle *f* de conférences

lecturer [ˈlektʃərər] *n* (a) conférencier, -ière (b) *Univ* **(junior** *or* **assistant) l.** = maître-assistant *m*; **(senior) l.** = maître *m* de conférences; **to be a maths l.** être assistant *m* en maths; **is she a good l.?** est-ce qu'elle est bon professeur?

lectureship [ˈlektʃəʃɪp] *n Univ* poste *m* de maître-assistant; **she got a l.** elle a été nommée maître-assistante

lecture theatre *n* amphithéâtre *m*

LED [eliːˈdiː] *n Comptr* (*abbr* **light-emitting diode**) DEL *f*

led *see* **lead**[2]

ledge [ledʒ] *n* (a) rebord *m*, saillie *f*; (*on wall, building*) corniche *f* (b) *Geol* **l. of rock** plate-forme *f* rocheuse; (*awash or under water*) banc *m* de rochers

ledger [ˈledʒər] *n* (a) (*in bookkeeping*) grand livre *m* (b) *Mus* **l. line** ligne *f* supplémentaire (*à la portée*)

lee [liː] *n* (a) *Naut* (*side*) côté *m* sous le vent; **l. shore** terre *f* sous le vent (b) (*shelter*) **in** *or* **under the l. of a rock** abrité par un rocher

leeboard [ˈliːbɔːd] *n Naut* aile *f ou* semelle *f* de dérive

leech [liːtʃ] *n* (a) (*animal*) sangsue *f* (b) *F Pej* (*person*) sangsue *f*, crampon *m*; **to cling** *or* **stick to sb like a l.** se cramponner à qn comme une sangsue

▶ **leech onto** *vipo F* se cramponner à

leek [liːk] *n* (*vegetable*) poireau *m*

leer[1] [lɪər] *n* (*sexual*) regard *m* lubrique; (*cruel*) regard sadique

leer[2] *vi* **to l. at sb** (*sexually*) regarder *ou F* reluquer qn d'un air lubrique; (*cruelly*) regarder qn d'un air sadique

leering [ˈlɪərɪŋ] *adj* (*sexual*) concupiscent, lubrique; (*cruel*) sadique

leery [ˈlɪərɪ] *adj F* **to be l. of sb/sth** se méfier de qn/qch; **why are you so l. of showing your emotions?** pourquoi as-tu si peur de montrer tes émotions?

lees [liːz] *npl* (*in wine*) lie *f*

leeward [ˈliːwəd] *Naut* **1** *adj, adv* sous le vent **2** *n* côté *m* sous le vent; **to pass to l. of a ship** passer sous le vent d'un navire

Leeward Islands *npl* (*in South Pacific or West Indies*) les îles *fpl* sous le Vent

leeway [ˈliːweɪ] *n* (a) (*freedom*) liberté *f* d'action; (*safety margin*) marge *f* de sécurité (b) *Naut* dérive *f*; **to make l.**

dériver (à la voile); *Fig, F* **he has a lot of l. to make up** il a un fort retard à rattraper

left[1] ['left] **1** *adj* gauche; **on my l. hand** à ma gauche; *F* **to have two l. feet** s'emmêler les pinceaux; *Am F* **l. field candidate** candidat *m* inattendu; *Am* **to come out of l. field** surgir de l'ombre; *Comptr* **l. arrow** flèche *f* vers la gauche; **l. arrow key** touche *f* de déplacement à gauche; *Typ* **l. justified** justifié à gauche; **l. margin** marge *f* de gauche; *TV, Cin* **l. pan** panoramique *m* horizontal DG

2 *adv* (*to turn etc*) à gauche; *Mil* **l. turn!** à gauche, gauche!; **eyes l.!** tête (à) gauche!

3 *n* gauche *f*; *Boxing* gauche *m*; **on the l., to the l.** à gauche; *Aut etc* **to keep (to the) l.** tenir la gauche; *Pol* **the L.** la gauche; *Pol* **l. wing** (*of party, group*) aile *f* gauche; *Mil* gauche *f*; *Sp* **to play on the l. wing** être ailier gauche

left[2] *pt, pp see* = **leave[2]**

left-hand *adj* **(a)** (*pocket etc*) de gauche; **on the l. side** à gauche; **l. turn** virage *m* à gauche; *Aut* **to have l. drive** avoir le volant à gauche **(b)** *Tech* (*lock, screw, drill*) à gauche; **l. thread** filetage *m* à gauche

left-handed ['left'hændɪd] **1** *adj* **(a)** (*person*) gaucher, -ère; (*golf club etc*) pour gaucher; **l. blow** coup *m* de la main gauche **(b)** *F* **l. compliment** compliment *m* peu flatteur **(c)** *Tech* = **left-hand (b) 2** *adv* **to play tennis l.** jouer au tennis de la main gauche

left-hander ['left'hændər] *n* (*person*) gaucher, -ère; *Boxing* coup *m* du gauche

leftie ['leftɪ] *n Pol F* gauchiste *mf*

leftist ['leftɪst] *Pol* **1** *n* gauchiste *mf* **2** *adj* gauchiste; (*person*) de gauche

left luggage *n Br* bagages *mpl* déposés à la consigne; **l. (office)** consigne *f*; **l. lockers** consigne automatique

leftover ['leftəʊvər] **1** *adj* **there was some l. chicken** il restait du poulet; **I made a curry with the l. chicken** j'ai fait un curry avec le reste du poulet; **you could use the l. paint/wallpaper** tu pourrais utiliser la peinture/le papier peint qu'il reste; *Com* **l. stock** restes *mpl* **2** *n* **(a)** *Com, Culin* **leftovers** restes *mpl* **(b)** (*from the past*) survivance *f* **(from** de)

left-wing *adj Pol* de gauche; **they are very l.** ils sont très à gauche; **he has slightly l. ideas** il a des idées gauchisantes

left-winger *n* **(a)** *Pol* (*in party, union*) homme/femme de gauche; (*in Parliament*) député *m* de la gauche; **the left-wingers** la gauche **(b)** *Sp* ailier *m* gauche

leg[1] [leg] *n* **(a)** (*of person, horse*) jambe *f*; (*of dog, bird, insect, reptile*) patte *f*; **wooden l.** jambe *f* de bois; *Fig* **you don't have a l. to stand on** vos arguments ne tiennent pas debout; **you won't have a l. to stand on if they find this letter** s'ils trouvent cette lettre, vous êtes fichu; *Fig* **to be on one's last legs** (*to be tired*) ne plus pouvoir mettre un pied devant l'autre; (*to be dying*) avoir un pied dans la tombe; **the business is on its last legs** la société est au bord de la faillite *ou* mal en point; **after 10 miles we were on our last legs** après 10 mil(l)es nous n'en pouvions plus; **the government is on its last legs** le gouvernement est mal en point; **the car/TV is on its last legs** la voiture/la télé a fait son temps; **to give sb a l. up** (*over a wall, fence etc*) faire la courte échelle à qn; (*into the saddle*) aider qn à monter en selle; *F* (*in job etc*) donner un coup de pouce à qn; *F* **to pull sb's l.** faire marcher qn; *F* **show** *or* **shake a l.!** (*it's time to get up*) debout!; *Sl* **to get one's l. over** (*have sex*) s'envoyer en l'air; *F* **l. show** revue *f*; **l. rest** appui-jambes *m inv*; *Med* étrier *m*; *Med* **l. iron** prothèse *f* orthopédique

(b) *Culin* (*of chicken*) cuisse *f*; (*of veal*) cuisseau *m*; **roast l. of pork** cuissot *m* de porc rôti; **l. of lamb** gigot *m*; **frogs' legs** cuisses de grenouille

(c) (*of trousers*) jambe *f*; (*of stocking etc*) tige *f*; **these trousers are a bit short in the l.** ce pantalon est un peu court au niveau des jambes

(d) (*of table, chair*) pied *m*; (*of tripod etc*) jambe *f*; (*of trestle*) montant *m*

(e) *Cr* = le terrain à gauche et en arrière du joueur qui est au guichet; *Cr* **l. before wicket** (mis hors jeu) à pied obstructif; **l. drive** coup *m* arrière à gauche

(f) (*of journey, race*) étape *f*; (*in relay race*) relais *m*

leg[2] *vt* **(-gg-)** *F* **to l. it** (*walk*) faire la route à pied; (*hurry*) marcher *ou* courir vite

legacy ['legəsɪ] *n Jur* legs *m*; **to come into a l.** faire un héritage; **to leave sb a l.** laisser un héritage *ou* quelque chose en héritage à qn; *Fig* **this desk is a l. from my predecessor** j'ai hérité ce bureau de mon prédécesseur; **the l. of the war was a divided Europe** l'héritage de la guerre fut une Europe divisée; **the crisis left a l. of bitterness** la crise a créé un climat d'amertume

legal ['li:g(ə)l] *adj* **(a)** (*lawful*) légal; (*commerce*) licite; **to be l. currency** *or* **tender** avoir cours

(b) (*error*) judiciaire; (*mind, affairs*) juridique; **by l. process** par voies légales, par voies de droit; **to go into the l. profession** faire une carrière juridique; **l. action** action *f* (en justice); **to take l. action against sb** intenter une action contre qn; **l. adviser** conseiller, -ère juridique; **to take l. advice** = consulter un avocat; **to have a l. claim to sth** avoir légalement droit à qch; **l. dispute** litige *m*; **l. entity** personne *f* morale; **l. limit** (*of alcohol*) taux *m* d'alcoolémie autorisé; **l. manager** responsable *mf* juridique; **l. owner** propriétaire *m* légitime; **l. proceedings** poursuites *fpl* judiciaires; **to initiate l. proceedings against sb** engager des poursuites judiciaires contre qn; **l. recourse** recours *m* contentieux; **l. redress** recours *m* à la justice; **l. reserve** réserve *f* légale; **l. security** caution *f* judiciaire; *esp US* **l. separation** séparation *f* judiciaire; **l. status** statut *m* légal, statut juridique; **l. technicality** vice *m* de forme; **l. year** année *f* civile; *Comptr* (*character etc*) autorisé; *Am* (*paper format*) légal

legal aid *n* assistance *f* juridique

legal charges *npl* frais *mpl* judiciaires

legal department *n* (*of bank etc*) (service *m ou* bureau *m* du) contentieux *m*

legal document *n* acte *m* authentique

legalese [li:gə'li:z] *n F* jargon *m* juridique

legal expert *n* expert *m* juridique, avocat *m* conseil

legal holiday *n US* jour *m* férié

legalism ['li:gəlɪz(ə)m] *n* légalisme *m*

legalistic [li:gə'lɪstɪk] *adj* formaliste

legality [lɪ'gælɪtɪ] *n* légalité *f*

legalization [li:gəlaɪ'zeɪʃən] *n* légalisation *f*

legalize ['li:gəlaɪz] *vt* (*drug, document*) légaliser; (*deed*) rendre légal, autoriser

legally ['li:gəlɪ] *adv* légalement; **l. responsible** responsable en droit; **l. binding contract** contrat qui engage les personnes devant la loi

legate ['legɪt] *n Rel, Antiq* légat *m*

legatee [legə'ti:] *n* légataire *mf*

legation [lɪ'geɪʃən] *n* légation *f*

legato [lɪ'gɑ:təʊ] *adv Mus* legato

legend ['ledʒənd] *n* (*story, inscription etc*) légende *f*; **to be/become a l. in one's own lifetime** être/devenir une légende vivante

legendary ['ledʒənd(ə)rɪ] *adj* légendaire

legerdemain [ledʒədə'meɪn] *n Lit Fig* tour *m* de passe-passe

-legged ['legɪd, legd] *suff* **short/bare** *etc***-l.** aux jambes courtes/nues *etc*; **two-l.** (*person*) à deux jambes; (*animal*) à deux pattes

leggings ['legɪŋz] *npl* (*for dancers*) jambières *fpl*; (*for women*) caleçon *m*

leggy ['legɪ] *adj* (*person*) aux longues jambes; (*plant*) étiolé; **a l. girl** une fille tout en jambes

Leghorn ['leghɔ:n] *n Geog* Livourne

legibility [ledʒɪ'bɪlɪtɪ] *n* (*of handwriting*) lisibilité *f*

legible ['ledʒɪb(ə)l] *adj* (*handwriting*) lisible, net

legibly ['ledʒɪblɪ] *adv* (*to write*) lisiblement

legion ['li:dʒ(ə)n] **1** *n* légion *f*; **the Foreign L.** la Légion étrangère; **the L. of honour** la Légion d'honneur **2** *adj Lit* (*many*) **their name is l.** ils sont légion; **the difficulties were l.** les difficultés étaient innombrables

legionary ['li:dʒənərɪ] **1** *adj* de la légion **2** *n* légionnaire *m*

legionnaire [li:dʒə'neər] *n* légionnaire *m*; **l.'s disease** maladie *f* du légionnaire

legislate ['ledʒɪsleɪt] *vi* faire des *ou* les lois, légiférer; **we can't l. for all possible situations** nous ne pouvons pas prévoir des lois pour tous les cas de figure possibles; **to l. against sth** instaurer une loi contre qch; **child labour had been legislated out of existence by 1900** grâce à la législation, le travail des enfants fut interdit à partir de 1900

legislation [ledʒɪs'leɪʃən] *n* (*laws*) législation *f*; (*action*) élaboration *f* des lois; **further l. may be needed** il faudrait renforcer la législation; **to bring in l. to …** créer une loi *ou* des lois pour …; **piece of l.** loi *f*

legislative ['ledʒɪslətɪv] *adj* législatif; **the L. Assembly** l'Assemblée *f* législative; **l. power** pouvoir *m* législatif

legislator ['ledʒɪsleɪtər] *n* législateur, -trice

legislature ['ledʒɪslətjər] *n* corps *m* législatif

legit [lɪ'dʒɪt] *adj F* réglo; **this deal is strictly l.** cette affaire est parfaitement réglementaire

legitimacy [lɪ'dʒɪtɪməsɪ] *n* (*of child, opinion etc*) légitimité *f*

legitimate[1] [lɪ'dʒɪtɪmət] *adj* (*child, authority, reason etc*) légitime; **l. expenditure** dépenses *fpl* justifiées; **it's l. to assume that …** on peut légitimement penser que …, il est légitime de penser que …; **the l. stage** le théâtre traditionnel

legitimate[2] [lɪ'dʒɪtɪmeɪt] *vt* (*child*) légitimer

legitimately [lɪ'dʒɪtɪmətlɪ] *adv* légitimement
legitimatize [lɪ'dʒɪtɪmɪtaɪz], **legitimize** [lɪ'dʒɪtɪmaɪz] *vt* légitimer
legless ['leglɪs] *adj* **l. cripple** cul-de-jatte *m*, *pl* culs-de-jatte; *Fig F* **to be l.** (*drunk*) être soûl
legman, *pl* **-men** ['legmæn, -mən] *n Am* (**a**) *Journ* = reporter *m* qui fait la chronique des chiens écrasés (**b**) (*errand boy etc*) garçon *m* de courses, coursier *m*
leg-of-mutton *adj* **l. sleeves** manches *fpl* gigot
leg-pull *n F* blague *f*
leg-puller [-pʊlər] *n F* blagueur, -euse, farceur, -euse
legroom ['legrʊm] *n* place *f* pour les jambes; **these little cars don't give you any l.** dans ces petites voitures, on n'a aucune place pour les jambes
legume ['legju:m] *n* (*vegetable*) légumineuse *f*; **legumes** (*plants*) légumineuses *fpl*
leguminous [lɪ'gju:mɪnəs] *adj Bot* légumineux; **l. plant** légumineuse *f*
legwarmer ['legwɔ:mər] *n* (*usu pl*) **legwarmers** jambières *fpl*
legwork ['legwɜ:k] *n F* **there's a lot of l. in this job** c'est un travail où l'on marche beaucoup; **I'm the one that gets all the l.** c'est toujours moi qui me déplace ici
Leics *abbr* **Leicestershire**
leisure ['leʒər, *US* 'li:ʒər] *n* loisir(s) *m*(*pl*); **to have enough l. for reading** avoir le loisir *ou* le temps de lire; **to do sth at one's l.** faire qch à loisir *ou* dans ses moments de loisir; **l. activities** activités *fpl* de loisir; **l. break** court séjour *m* de détente; **l. club** club *m* de loisirs; **l. industry** industrie *f* des loisirs; **l. market** marché *m* des loisirs; **l. tourism** tourisme *m* de loisir, tourisme ludique
leisure centre *n* centre *m* de loisirs
leisured ['leʒəd] *adj* (**a**) (*life etc*) de loisir (**b**) (*person*) qui a des loisirs; **the l. classes** les rentiers *mpl*
leisure hours *npl* heures *fpl* de loisir
leisureliness ['leʒəlɪnɪs] *n* (*of pace*) caractère *m* mesuré; (*of weekend*) caractère détendu; **the l. of sea travel** la détente apportée par une croisière
leisurely ['leʒəlɪ] **1** *adj* (*person*) qui n'est jamais pressé; (*pace*) tranquille; (*weekend*) détendu, relax; (*journey*) par petites étapes; **progress had been all too l.** nous progressions/ils progressaient beaucoup trop lentement; **they moved with a l. grace** ils se déplaçaient avec grâce et lenteur; **to go for a l. stroll** aller se promener tranquillement; **we had a l. time of it at the beach** nous nous sommes bien reposés à la plage; **to do sth in a l. fashion** faire qch sans se presser **2** *adv* (*without haste*) sans se presser
leisure time *n* temps *m* libre
leisure wear *n* vêtements *mpl* sport
lemming ['lemɪŋ] *n* lemming *m*; **to follow sb like lemmings** suivre qn comme des moutons (de Panurge)
lemon ['lemən] **1** *n* (**a**) (*fruit, colour*) citron *m*; *F* **they squeezed him like a l.** ils l'ont pressé comme un citron; **fresh l. juice** (*drink*) citron pressé; *Culin* **l. curd** pâte *f* à tartiner au citron; **l. balm** (*plant*) mélisse *f* officinale, citronnelle *f*; **l. grass** citronnelle; **l. meringue pie** tarte *f* au citron meringuée; **l. sole** (*fish*) limande-sole *f*; **l. squeezer** presse-citrons *m inv*; **l. tea** thé *m* au citron; **l. tree** citronnier *m*; **l. verbena** verveine *f* citronnelle
(**b**) *F* (*worthless person*) personne *f* qui ne vaut rien; (*thing*) chose *f* qui ne vaut rien; **what a l.!** quelle cruche!; *F* **I felt like a real l.** j'ai eu l'air vraiment malin
2 *adj* **l. (coloured)** (jaune) citron *inv*
lemonade [lemə'neɪd] *n* (*carbonated*) limonade *f*; (*freshly sqeezed*) citronnade *f*
lemony ['lemənɪ] *adj* (*smell, taste*) citronné
lemur ['li:mər] *n* maki *m*
lend [lend] (*pt, pp* **lent** [lent]) **1** *vt* (**a**) prêter (**sth to sb, sb sth** qch à qn); **to l. money at interest** prêter de l'argent à intérêt
(**b**) (*give*) **to l. sb a (helping) hand** donner un coup de main à qn; **to l. an ear** *or* **one's ear to …** prêter l'oreille à …; **to l. one's name to a project** donner son nom à un projet; **to l. dignity to an occasion** rehausser le prestige d'un événement; **to l. weight to an argument** donner du poids à un argument; **to l. credibility/drama to a story** rendre une histoire crédible/dramatique; **the bloodstains on his trousers lent support to his story** les taches de sang sur son pantalon accréditèrent son histoire; **distance lends enchantment to the view** tout paraît beau (vu) de loin; **to l. oneself** *or* **itself to sth** se prêter à qch; **the story doesn't l. itself to dramatization** l'histoire ne se prête pas à une dramatisation
2 *vi* **to l. against securities** prêter sur titres
▶ **lend out** *vtsep* prêter
lender ['lendər] *n* (*person*) prêteur, -euse; *Fin* (*institution*) organisme *m* de crédit
lending ['lendɪŋ] *n* (*of money, item*) prêt *m*; **l. bank** (*in specific deal, loan etc*) banquier *m* prêteur; **l. country** pays *m* créancier; **l. library** bibliothèque *f* de prêt; **l. policy** (*of bank, country*) politique *f* de prêt; **l. rate** taux *m* d'intérêt consenti pour un prêt
lend-lease *n* (*no pl*) *Econ Hist* prêt-bail *m*
length [leŋθ] *n* (**a**) (*in space*), *Swimming* longueur *f*; **to swim a few lengths** faire quelques longueurs; **it's 4.50m in length** ça fait 4 50m de long; **to win by a l./half a l.** (*in race*) gagner d'une longueur/d'une demi-longueur; **to wander the l. and breadth of the country** errer dans tout le pays; **I fell full l. on the ground** je suis tombé de tout mon long
(**b**) (*in time*) durée *f*; (*of book, journey etc*) longueur *f*; **about 300 pages/30,000 words in l.** (*book*) d'une longueur d'environ 300 pages/30 000 mots; **his essay was a bit under l.** sa dissertation était un peu trop courte; **l. of service** (*in post*) ancienneté *f*; **the l. of time required to do sth** le temps qu'il faut pour faire qch; **at (great) l.** (*to talk*) longuement; (*to explain sth*) en détail
(**c**) **to go to the l. of doing sth** aller jusqu'à faire qch; **to go to great lengths to do sth** se donner beaucoup de mal à *ou* pour faire qch; **he would go to any lengths (to do sth)** il ne reculerait devant rien (pour faire qch); **I never dreamed that they would go to such lengths** je n'aurais jamais imaginé qu'ils iraient si loin
(**d**) (*of vowel, syllable*) longueur *f*
(**e**) *Tennis, Cr* longueur *f* de balle
(**f**) (*of string etc*) morceau *m*, bout *m*; (*of material*) pièce *f*, coupon *m*; (*of wood*) morceau; (*of pipe*) tronçon *m*; *Sewing* **dress/trouser l.** coupon de robe/pantalon; *Sewing* **what l. do I need for …?** quel métrage faut-il pour …?
lengthen ['leŋθən] **1** *vt* (*skirt, chain etc*) allonger, rallonger; (*interval*) prolonger; (*vowel, account*) allonger **2** *vi* (*of days etc*) allonger, rallonger; (*of intervals etc*) augmenter; (*of shadows*) s'allonger
lengthening ['leŋθənɪŋ] *n* allongement *m*
lengthily ['leŋθɪlɪ] *adv* longuement
lengthways, *Am* **lengthwise** ['leŋθweɪz, -waɪz] *adv* dans le sens de la longueur, longitudinalement
lengthy ['leŋθɪ] *adj* (*speech, report*) long, *f* longue, plein de longueurs; (*process, description*) long
leniency ['li:nɪənsɪ] *n* indulgence *f* (**to, towards** envers)
lenient ['li:nɪənt] *adj* indulgent (**to, towards** envers); (*punishment*) peu sévère; *Jur* **a l. sentence** un jugement clément
leniently ['li:nɪəntlɪ] *adv* (*to judge*) avec clémence; (*to mark, treat etc*) avec indulgence
Lenin ['lenɪn] *n* Lénine *m*
Leningrad ['lenɪngræd] *n Hist* Léningrad *m*
Leninism ['lenɪnɪz(ə)m] *n Pol* léninisme *m*
Leninist ['lenɪnɪst] *adj, n Pol* léniniste *mf*
lenitive ['lenɪtɪv] *adj, n Med* lénitif *m*
lens [lenz] *n* (**a**) *Opt* lentille *f*; (*of spectacles*) verre *m*; **converging/diverging l.** lentille *f* convergente/divergente; **concave/convex l.** lentille concave/convexe (**b**) *Phot* objectif *m* (photographique); *Electron* **electron l.** lentille *f* électronique; **mirror l.** objectif à lentille spéculaire; **l. attachment** accessoire *m* d'objectif; **l. cleaning fluid** produit *m* de nettoyage pour lentilles; **l. cap** capuchon *m ou* bouchon *m* d'objectif; **l. holder** étui *m* à objectif; **l. hood** parasoleil *m* (**c**) *Anat* **(crystalline) l.** (*of the eye*) cristallin *m*
Lent [lent] *n Rel* Carême *m*; **to keep L.** faire carême; **to give up sth for L.** renoncer à qch pour le Carême
lentil ['lentɪl] *n Bot, Culin* lentille *f*; **l. soup** soupe *f* aux lentilles
Leo ['li:əʊ] *n Astron* Lion; **to be (a) L.** être Lion
leonine ['li:ənaɪn] *adj Lit* léonin
leopard ['lepəd] *n* léopard *m*; *Fig F* **a l. cannot change its spots** on ne se refait pas; **l. skin** peau *f* de léopard; **a l.-skin coat** un manteau en léopard
leotard ['li:ətɑ:d] *n* maillot *m* (de danseur), justaucorps *m*
leper ['lepər] *n Med, Fig* lépreux, -euse; **l. hospital** *or* **colony** léproserie *f*
lepidopteran [lepɪ'dɒptərən] *adj, n Ent* lépidoptère *m*
leprechaun ['leprəkɔ:n, -hɔ:n] *n Myth* farfadet *m*, lutin *m*
leprosy ['leprəsɪ] *n Med* lèpre *f*; **to have l.** avoir la lèpre
leprous ['leprəs] *adj Med* lépreux
lesbian ['lezbɪən] **1** *adj* lesbien **2** *n* lesbienne *f*
lesbianism ['lezbɪənɪz(ə)m] *n* lesb(ian)isme *m*
lesion ['li:ʒən] *n Jur, Med* lésion *f*
less [les] **1** *adj* (*comp* **lesser**) (**a**) [①**A10**,b,iii; **A19**,g,iii] (*not so much*) moins de; **we have l. time/money than we thought** nous avons moins de temps/d'argent que nous ne pensions; **l. trouble/difficulty** moins de peine/difficulté; **it's l. than a week's work** cela représente moins d'une semaine de travail; **he has even l. idea about cars than I do** il s'y connaît encore moins que moi en matière de voiture; **he is l.**

than thirty il a moins de trente ans; **l. than (sign)** (signe *m*) inférieur à, signe plus petit que

(b) (*smaller*) **the distance is l. than I thought** la distance est moindre que je ne le pensais

2 *prep* moins; **a year l. two days** une année moins deux jours; **I've £50, l. what I spent on records** j'ai 50 livres, moins ce que j'ai dépensé en disques

3 *pron* moins; **the l. you know the better** le moins tu en sais, le mieux c'est; **I don't think any (the) l. of you** tu n'as pas baissé dans mon estime; **I see l. of her nowadays** je la vois moins ces temps-ci; **in l. than an hour** en moins d'une heure; **in l. than no time** en un rien de temps; **I can't sell it at l. than cost price** je ne peux pas le vendre à moins du prix de revient; **the l. said about it the better** moins on en parle mieux cela vaut; *F* **l. of that!** ça suffit!

4 *adv* [①A70,d; B10,E,1] (a) moins; **l. (well) known** moins (bien) connu; **she is l. musical than her sister** elle est moins musicienne que sa sœur; **I'm l. happy with that** ça me satisfait *ou* plaît moins; **one person l.** une personne de moins; **one mouth l. to feed** une bouche de moins à nourrir; **not a penny l.** pas un sou de moins; **l. and l.** de moins en moins; **no more, no l.** ni plus ni moins; **still l., even l.** encore moins

(b) (*in negative constructions*) **nothing l. than** (*at the very least*) rien (de) moins que; **I want nothing l.** je ne veux rien de moins; **there's nothing I want l. than to hurt him** je ne veux surtout pas le blesser; **he was nothing l. than overjoyed at the news** il fut absolument ravi de la nouvelle; **it's nothing l. than monstrous!** c'est absolument monstrueux!; **this wall is no l. than a metre thick** ce mur n'a pas moins d'un mètre d'épaisseur; **no l. a person than the headmistress** (*came to see me etc*) la directrice en personne; (*had signed the letter etc*) la directrice elle-même; **they have no l. than six cars** ils ont six voitures, pas moins; **the letter was signed by Vincent, no l.** la lettre était signée de Vincent, lui-même et en personne; **she was driving a Rolls, no l.** elle conduisait une Rolls, tu te rends compte!; **I expected no l. from you** je n'en attendais pas moins de vous; **they don't own a fridge, much l. a freezer** ils n'ont pas de réfrigérateur, et encore moins de congélateur; **the news of his death came as no l. of a shock for being expected** on avait beau s'y attendre, la nouvelle de sa mort n'en fut pas moins un choc

-less [lɪs] *suff* sans; **roofless** sans toit; **penniless** sans le sou; **sleeveless** sans manches

lessee [le'siː] *n Jur* (*of premises etc*) locataire *mf* (à bail); (*of casino etc*) tenancier, -ière; (*of farm*) fermier *m*

lessen ['les(ə)n] 1 *vi* s'amoindrir, diminuer; (*of symptoms etc*) s'atténuer 2 *vt* (*costs etc*) diminuer; (*importance, severity of sth*) amoindrir; (*noise*) atténuer; (*activity*) ralentir; (*fervour, enthusiasm*) calmer

lessening ['les(ə)nɪŋ] *n* amoindrissement *m*, diminution *f*

lesser ['lesər] *adj* [①A19,g,iii] (a) (*in size*) petit (b) (*in importance*) moindre; *prov* **to choose the l. of two evils** de deux maux choisir le moindre; **to a l. extent** *or* **degree** dans une moindre mesure, à un degré moindre

lesson ['les(ə)n] *n* (a) leçon *f*; *Sch* cours *m*; (*in primary school*) leçon; **Spanish l.** cours d'espagnol; **swimming l.** cours de natation; **to be an object l. to sb** servir d'exemple à qn; **to learn a l. from sth** tirer une leçon de qch; **he has learnt his lesson** il a compris; **let that be a l. to you!** que cela vous serve de leçon!; **it'll teach him a l.** ça lui servira de leçon (b) *Rel* (*reading from Bible*) lecture *f* de l'Écriture sainte

lessor [le'sɔːr] *n Jur* bailleur, -eresse

lest [lest] *conj* (a) [①A69,b,vii] *esp Lit* de peur *ou* de crainte que ... (ne) + *sub*; **l. we forget** pour ne pas oublier (b) *Arch* (*after verbs of fearing*) **I feared l. he should fall** je craignais qu'il (ne) tombât

let¹ [let] *n Tennis* **l. (ball)** balle *f* de filet, balle let; **l.!** filet!; **to play a l.** remettre une balle let *ou* de filet en jeu

let² *n Br* (*of property*) location *f*; **short l.** location de courte durée

let³ *n Jur* **without l. or hindrance** en toute liberté

let⁴ (*pt, pp* **let**; *prp* **letting**) 1 *vt* (a) [①A40,C,1,a; B33,2,b,i] (*allow*) permettre, laisser; **to l. sb do sth** laisser qn faire qch, permettre à qn de faire qch; **the police would not l. anyone pass** la police ne laissait passer personne *ou* ne permettait à personne de passer; **to l. oneself be guided** se laisser guider; **l. me tell you that ...** permettez-moi de vous dire que ...; **it wasn't easy, l. me tell you!** ça n'a pas été facile, crois-moi!; **to l. sth fall** laisser échapper qch; **l. me go with them** laissez-moi partir avec eux; **he l. go the rope** il a lâché la corde; **someone has l. the dog loose** quelqu'un a lâché le chien; **to l. sb know sth** faire savoir qch à qn, faire part de qch à qn; **l. me know when ...** faites-moi savoir quand ...; **l. me know if ...** préviens-moi si ...; **I will l. him know you are here** je vais le prévenir que vous êtes ici; **l. me hear the story** racontez-moi l'histoire; **to l. sth pass** passer sur qch; **we couldn't l. it pass any longer** nous n'avons pas pu laisser passer ça; **to l. sth get one down** se laisser abattre à cause de qch; **to l. sth get to one** se laisser affecter par qch; **to l. things get on top of you** se laisser submerger

(b) *Br* (*house etc*) louer; **(house) to l.** maison à louer

(c) *Arch Med* **to l. blood** pratiquer une saignée

2 *v aux* [①A39,8; B32,4] (*supplying 1st & 3rd person of imperative*) **let's hurry!** dépêchons-nous!; **let's not have an argument about it!** on ne va pas se disputer pour ça!; **why don't we go to the beach on Saturday? — oh yes, let's!** et si on allait à la plage samedi? — oh oui! oui!; **l. us pray** prions; **l. there be light** que la lumière soit; **don't let's leave yet** ne partons pas tout de suite; **now, don't let's have any nonsense!** allons, pas de bêtises!; *Fml* **l. him do it at once!** qu'il le fasse tout de suite!; *Math* **l. AB be equal to CD** supposons que AB soit égal à CD; **l. me see!** voyons un peu!; **l. them all come!** qu'ils viennent tous!; **don't l. me see you here again!** que je ne vous retrouve plus ici!

let⁵ *conj* **l. alone** sans parler de, moins encore; **we haven't been to England, l. alone Scotland** nous n'avons pas été en Angleterre, moins encore en Écosse

▶ **let by** *vtas* **to l. sb by** laisser passer qn

▶ **let down** *vtsep* (a) (*blinds etc*) baisser; **to l. one's hair down** laisser tomber ses cheveux; *Fig* se détendre, se laisser aller

(b) *Sewing* (*dress etc*) rallonger

(c) *F* (*disappoint*) (*person*) décevoir; **to l. sb down gently** ménager qn; **I won't l. you down** vous pouvez compter sur moi; **he has been badly let down** il a été gravement déçu; **the car let us down again** la voiture nous a encore lâchés; **you've let everyone down, most of all yourself** tu as fait du tort à tout le monde, à commencer par toi-même; **I've been let down by the babysitter** la baby-sitter m'a laissé tomber; **to l. the side down** manquer à ses obligations

(d) (*tyre etc*) dégonfler

▶ **let in** *vtsep* (a) (*person*) laisser entrer; (*air, rain, draught*) laisser entrer; **to l. in the light** laisser entrer *ou* passer la lumière; **he's got a key, so he can l. himself in** puisqu'il a une clef, il peut entrer; **my shoes l. in water** mes chaussures prennent l'eau

(b) **to l. sb in on a secret** dire un secret à qn; **to l. sb in on a plan** mettre qn au courant d'un projet

(c) *Sewing etc* (*section*) ajouter, introduire

(d) *F* **I didn't know what I was letting myself in for** je ne savais pas à quoi je m'exposais; **we're letting ourselves in for a lot of work** nous allons avoir beaucoup de travail; **to l. oneself in for a lot of problems** s'exposer à beaucoup de problèmes

▶ **let into** *vtaspo* (a) (*person to house etc*) laisser *ou* faire entrer dans (b) **to l. sb into a secret** dévoiler un secret à qn, mettre qn dans le secret (c) *Sewing etc* **to l. a piece into a skirt** mettre *ou* ajouter une pièce à une jupe

▶ **let off 1** *vtsep* (a) (*explode, fire*) (*explosive device*) faire partir; (*firework*) tirer, faire partir

(b) (*release*) (*steam*) lâcher, laisser échapper; *Fig* **to l. off steam** se défouler

(c) (*excuse*) **to l. sb off from sth/doing sth** dispenser qn de faire qch; **I'll l. you off this time** pour cette fois, je ne dirai rien; **to l. sb off lightly** ne pas être sévère avec qn; **you let him off too easily** vous n'avez pas été assez sévère avec lui; **I'll let you off you off this time** je vous pardonne (pour) cette fois-ci; **to be let off with a fine** en être quitte pour une amende

(d) (*permit to leave*) (*from school, work*) laisser partir

(e) (*from vehicle*) laisser (descendre)

2 *vi F* (*fart*) péter

▶ **let on** *vi F* (a) (*tell*) dire; **don't let on that I was there** n'allez pas dire que j'y étais; **he didn't let on that he saw her** (*didn't tell anyone*) il n'a pas dit qu'il l'avait vue; (*didn't acknowledge her*) il a fait semblant de ne pas la voir; **don't let on!** pas un mot! (b) (*claim*) **he wasn't as ill as he let on** il n'était pas aussi malade qu'il voulait bien le faire croire

▶ **let out** *vtsep* (a) (*release*) (*person*) laisser sortir; (*bird*) laisser échapper; (*prisoner*) élargir; (*secret*) révéler, divulguer; **the porter let me out** le gardien m'a ouvert la porte; **I'll l. myself out** ce n'est pas la peine de me raccompagner; **can you l. yourself out?** faut-il vous raccompagner *ou* reconduire?; *Fig* **that lets me out** (*it couldn't have been me*) me voilà soulagé; (*I can't do it*) je suis tranquille; **to l. out the air from** laisser échapper l'air de; (*balloon etc*) dégonfler; **to l. out the bath water** vider la baignoire; **to l. out a yell** laisser échapper un cri (**b**) (*expand*) (*jacket, trousers etc*) élargir, agrandir; (*sail*) larguer

(**c**) (*fire etc*) **who let the fire out?** qui a laissé le feu s'éteindre?

(**d**) *Br* (*rent out*) louer

▶ **let through** *vtas* (*person, water, light*) laisser passer

▶ **let up 1** *vi* (*of rain, pressure of business etc*) se calmer; **once he's started he never lets up** une fois lancé il ne s'arrête plus; **the noise/arguing never lets up** le bruit/les disputes ne s'arrêtent jamais **2** *vtsep* **l. him up** (*from the ground*) laisse-le se relever

let-down *n F* déception *f*

lethal ['li:θ(ə)l] *adj* mortel; *F* **that vodka's l.!** cette vodka est mortelle!; **l. dose** dose *f* mortelle *ou* létale; **l. injury** blessure *f* mortelle; **l. weapon** arme *f* meurtrière

lethally ['li:θəlɪ] *adv* **the knife glinted l. in the sun** la lame assassine brillait au soleil; **a l. effective sub-machinegun** une mitraillette d'une efficacité redoutable; **a l. effective debater** un argumentateur d'une efficacité redoutable; **a l. biting wit** un humour mordant redoutable

lethargic [lɪ'θɑ:dʒɪk] *adj* (*person*) léthargique; (*movement, attempt, voice*) mou, *f* molle

lethargically [lɪ'θɑ:dʒɪklɪ] *adv* d'une manière léthargique; **to move l.** se déplacer mollement

lethargy ['leθədʒɪ] *n* léthargie *f*

let-out *n F* (*excuse*) excuse *f*; **l. clause** échappatoire *f*

letter¹ [letər] *n* (**a**) (*communication*) lettre *f*; **I've had a l. from him** j'ai reçu une lettre de lui; **are there any letters for me?** y a-t-il du courrier pour moi?; **to notify sb by l.** informer qn par lettre; **your letter of ...** votre lettre en date du ...; *Banking, Com* **l. of credit/exchange** lettre de crédit/change; **l. of advice** lettre d'avis; **l. of acknowledgement** accusé *m* de réception; **l. of apology** lettre *f* d'excuse; **l. of complaint** lettre *f* de réclamation; **l. of confirmation** lettre *f* de confirmation; **l. of dismissal** lettre *f* de licenciement; **l. of guarantee** lettre *f* de garantie; **business l.** lettre d'affaires; **rejection l.** lettre de refus; **l. card** carte-lettre *f*, *pl* cartes-lettres; **l. rate** tarif *m* lettres; **l. scales** pèse-lettre *m*; **l. tray** corbeille *f ou* panier *m* à courrier; **letters column** rubrique *f* courrier des lecteurs; **letters patent** lettres *fpl* patentes; **letters to the editor** courrier *m* des lecteurs

(**b**) (*of alphabet*) lettre *f*; *Typ* lettre, caractère *m*; **to have letters after one's name** avoir des titres; **according to the l. of the law** selon la lettre de la loi; **to obey to the l.** obéir à la lettre

(**c**) *Lit* **letters** (belles-)lettres *fpl*, littérature *f*; **man of letters** homme *m* de lettres

letter² *vt* marquer avec des lettres; (*engrave*) graver des lettres sur

letter bomb *n* lettre *f* piégée

letter box *n* boîte *f* à *ou* aux lettres

lettered ['letəd] *adj* (**a**) *Fml* (*person*) lettré (**b**) (*object*) marqué avec des lettres; **a briefcase lettered with my initials** une mallette gravée à mes initiales

letterhead ['letəhed] *n* en-tête *m inv*; (*paper*) papier *m* à en-tête

lettering ['letərɪŋ] *n* (**a**) (*action*) lettrage *m* (**b**) (*result*) caractères *mpl*

letter opener *n* coupe-papier *m inv*

letterpress ['letəpres] *n* (**a**) *Typ* (*method*) impression *f* typographique; **l. printing** typographie *f* (**b**) (*text*) texte *m* (*accompagnant une illustration*)

letter-quality *Comptr* **1** *adj* **l. printer** imprimante *f* qualité courrier **2** *n* qualité *f* courrier

letting ['letɪŋ] *n Br* (*renting out*) (*of house etc*) location *f*

lettuce ['letɪs] *n* laitue *f*

let-up *n F* (*in conflict etc*) trêve *f*; (*in pressure*) diminution *f* (**in** de); (*in weather*) accalmie *f*; (*in efforts, fighting*) relâchement *m*; **to work fifteen hours without a l.** travailler quinze heures d'affilée; **there's been no l. in the rain since this morning** il n'a pas arrêté de pleuvoir depuis ce matin

leucocyte ['lu:kəsaɪt] *n Med* leucocyte *m*

leukaemia, *US* **leukemia** [lu:'ki:mɪə] *n Med* leucémie *f*; **to have l.** avoir la leucémie

leukaemic, *US* **leukemic** [lu:'ki:mɪk] *adj Med* leucémique

leukocyte ['lu:kəsaɪt] *n Med* leucocyte *m*

Levant [lɪ'vænt] *n* **the L.** le Levant

Levantine [lə'væntaɪn] **1** *adj* levantin **2** *n* Levantin, -ine

levee ['levɪ] *n US Constr* (*of river*) levée *f*, digue *f*

level¹ ['lev(ə)l] **1** *n* (**a**) (*height*) (*of prices, the sea etc*) niveau *m*; (*in surveying*), *Geog* altitude *f*, niveau; (*quantity*) (*of alcohol etc*) taux *m*; **at eye l.** à (la) hauteur des yeux; **to maintain prices at a high l.** maintenir les prix à un niveau élevé; **to be on a l. with sb** être du même niveau que qn, être sur un pied d'égalité avec qn; **on a l. with sth** au niveau *ou* à la hauteur de qch, de niveau avec qch; **her ambition is on a l. with mine** son ambition est du même ordre que la mienne; **to come down to sb's l.** se mettre au niveau *ou* à la portée de qn; **to sink to** *or* **be brought down to sb's l.** tomber au niveau de qn; *Comptr* **l. of access** niveau *m* d'accès; *Phys etc* **energy l.** niveau *m* énergétique; **at ministerial l.** à l'échelon *m* ministériel; **noise l.** (*of engine etc*) niveau de bruit; *MecE* **oil l.** niveau d'huile; **radiation l.** niveau de radiation

(**b**) (*flat ground*) terrain *m* de niveau; **to be dead l.** être parfaitement de niveau; **on the l.** (*built etc*) sur un terrain plat; *F* (*person*) honnête; *F* **is he on the l.?** est-ce qu'on peut lui faire confiance?; *F* **it's completely on the l.** c'est tout à fait légal

(**c**) *Carp* (*tool*) niveau *m*; **l.** (**rule**) latte *f ou* règle *f* de niveau

2 *adj* (**a**) (*not sloping*) horizontal; (*ground*) de niveau, à niveau; (*road, pitch etc*) (*flat*) plat; *Av* **l. flight** vol horizontal; *Fig* **to create a l. playing field** créer une situation qui soit juste pour tout le monde *ou* qui ne défavorise personne

(**b**) **l. with ...** au niveau de ..., à (la) hauteur de ...; **l. with the ground** au ras du sol, à ras de terre; **they are about l. in ability** leurs compétences se valent; **to do one's l. best** faire tout son possible, faire de son mieux; **it's l. pegging** (*between the two*) il y a égalité; **they're l. pegging** ils sont à égalité; **a l. spoonful** une cuillerée rase

(**c**) (*steady*) (*tone etc*) égal; **to keep a l. head** garder son sang-froid

3 *adv* **hold the tray l.** tiens le plateau droit; *Av* **to fly l.** voler en palier; *Sp, Fig* **to draw l. with ...** arriver à la hauteur de ...; (*in rowing*) venir bord à bord avec ...

level² (**-ll-**, *US* **-l-**) **1** *vt* (**a**) (*surface*) niveler, égaliser; (*land etc*) araser; **to l. a town (to the ground)** raser une ville

(**b**) (*aim*) (*rifle*) pointer; (*canon*) braquer; (*telescope*) diriger (**at** sur); **to l. one's gun at sb** ajuster *ou* viser qn avec son fusil, mettre qn en joue; **to l. criticism at sb** émettre des critiques sur qn; **to l. accusations at sb** lancer des accusations contre qn; **to l. a blow at sb** porter un coup à qn

(**c**) (*in surveying*) (*region*) effectuer des opérations de nivellement dans, niveler

2 *vi F* **to l. with sb** parler franchement à qn

▶ **level down** *vtsep esp Pol* niveler par le bas

▶ **level off, level out 1** *vtsep* (*ground, surface*) aplanir **2** *vi* (**a**) (*of prices etc*) se stabiliser, plafonner; **demand levels off at this time of year** la demande se stabilise à cette époque de l'année (**b**) *Av* attaquer le palier, voler en palier

▶ **level up** *vtsep esp Pol* accroître le niveau moyen

level crossing *n Br Rail* passage *m* à niveau

level-headed *adj* pondéré

leveller, *US* **leveler** ['lev(ə)lər] *n Pol* égalitaire *mf*; *Lit* **death is a great l.** tous les hommes sont égaux devant la mort

lever¹ ['li:vər, *Am* 'levər] *n* levier *m*; *MecE* levier, manette *f*

lever² *vt* **to l. a box open** ouvrir une caisse avec un levier; **he levered the box open with a piece of wood** il a ouvert la caisse avec un morceau de bois; *Fig* **he has levered himself into a very strong position** il s'est hissé à un poste très important

▶ **lever off** *vtsep* (*lid, top, tyre*) enlever (avec un levier); (*padlock*) faire sauter

▶ **lever out** *vtsep* (*object*) extraire; *Fig* (*person*) évincer; **he has been levered out of his job** on l'a évincé de son emploi

▶ **lever up** *vtsep* (*lid etc*) soulever (avec un levier); **he levered himself up onto his elbow** il s'est soulevé en s'aidant de son coude

leverage ['li:vərɪdʒ] *n* (**a**) *MecE* (*power*) force *f ou* puissance *f ou* effet *m* de levier; **to bring l. to bear on sth** (*on door etc*) faire pression sur qch (**b**) *Fig* influence *f*; (*through manœuvre*) effet *m* de levier; **to exert some l. on sb** exercer de l'influence sur qn; **we have no l. we could bring to bear on him** nous n'avons pas de prise sur lui

leveraged ['li:vərɪdʒd] *adj Com* **l. buy-out** OPA *f* à crédit

lever-arch file *n* classeur *m* à levier

leveret ['levərɪt] *n* levraut *m*

leviathan [lɪ'vaɪəθ(ə)n] *n* (**a**) *Bible* léviathan *m* (**b**) *esp Lit* (*something huge*) monstre *m*

Levis® ['li:vaɪz] *npl* Levis® *m*; **a pair of L.** un Levis

levitate ['levɪteɪt] **1** *vi* se soulever (par lévitation) **2** *vt* soulever (par lévitation)

levitation [levɪ'teɪʃən] *n* lévitation *f*

levity ['levɪtɪ] *n* légèreté *f*

levy¹ ['levɪ] *n* (**a**) (*tax*) impôt *m*, contribution *f*; **capital l.** prélèvement *m* sur le capital; **import l.** taxe *f* à l'importation (**b**) (*action*) (*of tax, troops*) levée *f*

levy² *vt* (**a**) (*tax*) lever, percevoir; (*fine*) infliger; **to l. a duty on goods** imposer des marchandises; **to l. a fine on sb** frapper qn d'une amende (**b**) *Mil* (*troops*) lever

levying of taxes ['levɪɪŋ] *n* levée *f* des impôts

lewd [lu:d] *adj (behaviour, gesture, joke)* obscène; *(smile, look)* lubrique
lewdly ['lu:dlɪ] *adv* de façon obscène, lubriquement
lewdness ['lu:dnɪs] *n (of joke, behaviour, gesture)* obscénité *f*; *(of smile, look)* lubricité *f*
lexical ['leksɪk(ə)l] *adj* lexical
lexicalize ['leksɪkəlaɪz] *vt* lexicaliser
lexicographer [leksɪ'kɒgrəfər] *n* lexicographe *mf*
lexicographical [leksɪkə'græfɪk(ə)l] *adj* lexicographique
lexicography [leksɪ'kɒgrəfɪ] *n* lexicographie *f*
lexicology [leksɪ'kɒlədʒɪ] *n* lexicologie *f*
lexicon ['leksɪkən] *n* lexique *m*
lexis ['leksɪs] *n* lexique *m*
lh [el'eɪtʃ] *Mus etc (abbr* **left hand***)* main gauche
liabilities [laɪə'bɪlɪtɪz] *npl Com, Fin* passif *m*; *(in bankruptcy)* masse *f* passive; **assets and l.** actif *m* et passif; **to meet one's l.** faire face à ses engagements
liability [laɪə'bɪlɪtɪ] *n* **(a)** *Jur (responsibility)* responsabilité *f*; **employer's l.** *(for accidents at work)* responsabilité patronale; **civil l.** responsabilité civile; **limited l. company** société *f* à responsabilité limitée; **her firm wouldn't accept l. for the accident** son entreprise refusa d'endosser la responsabilité de l'accident
(b) *(disadvantage)* désavantage *m*, handicap *m*; **your brother is a l. to us** ton frère ne nous attire que des problèmes
(c) *(likelihood)* disposition *f*, tendance *f* **(to sth** à qch; **to do sth** à faire qch); **l. to a fine** risque *m* d'amende; **l. for military service** obligations *fpl* militaires; **l. to explode** *(of product etc)* danger *m* d'explosion
(d) *Acct* dette *f*
(e) *Com (on bills of exchange)* encours *m*
liable ['laɪəb(ə)l] *adj* **(a)** *Jur (responsible)* responsable **(for** de); **you are l. for the damage** vous êtes responsable du dommage; **l. party** responsable *mf*
(b) *(subject)* assujetti, tenu, astreint **(to** à); **l. to a tax** assujetti à un impôt, redevable d'un impôt; **l. to tax** passible de taxe *ou* d'impôts; **person l. to tax** assujetti *m*; **l. to a fine** passible d'une amende; **l. to customs duty** passible de droits de douane; **l. to military service** astreint au service militaire
(c) *(likely)* **to be l. to do sth** *(of person, thing)* risquer de faire qch; **she's l. to make mistakes** elle est susceptible de faire des fautes; **when he gets angry he is l. to do anything** quand il se met en colère, il est capable de tout
liaise [li:'eɪz] *vi* **to l. with sb about sth** *(be in contact with)* être en contact avec qn à propos de qch; *(work together with)* collaborer avec qn; **the two parties have agreed to l.** les deux parties ont accepté de collaborer; **the successful applicant will be required to l. with head office** le candidat retenu sera en contact direct avec le siège
liaison [lɪ'eɪzɒn] *n* **(a)** *(cooperation)* coopération *f*; *Mil etc* **l. agent/officer** agent *m*/officier *m* de liaison **(b)** *(love affair)* liaison *f* (amoureuse)
liana [lɪ'ɑ:nə] *n Bot* liane *f*
liar ['laɪər] *n* menteur, -euse; **you l.!** espèce de menteur!
Lib [lɪb] *Pol (abbr* **Liberal***)* libéral
lib [lɪb] *n F* = **liberation**;= **women's l.** MLF *m*
libation [laɪ'beɪʃən] *n* libation *f*
libel[1] ['laɪb(ə)l] *n* diffamation *f*; *Jur* diffamation (par écrit), écrit *m* diffamatoire; **to utter a l. against sb** publier un article *ou* un écrit diffamant qn; **action for l., l. action** procès *m* en diffamation; **to sue sb for l.** poursuivre qn en justice pour diffamation; **that's l.!** c'est une calomnie *ou* de la diffamation!; **l. case** procès *m* en diffamation; **l. laws** lois *fpl* contre la diffamation
libel[2] *vt* **(-ll-**, *US* **-l-)** *(person)* calomnier; *Jur* diffamer par écrit
libellous, *US* **libelous** ['laɪbələs] *adj (document etc)* diffamatoire
liberal ['lɪb(ə)rəl] **1** *adj* **(a)** *(idea etc)* libéral; *(person)* d'esprit large; **a l. education** une éducation libérale; **l. minded** large d'esprit **(b)** *(generous)* libéral, généreux; **l. with one's money** prodigue de son argent **(c)** *(abundant)* ample; **a l. supply of food** une nourriture abondante; **a l. helping** une portion généreuse **(d)** *Pol* **L.** libéral **2** *n Pol* **L.** libéral, -ale
liberalism ['lɪb(ə)rəlɪz(ə)m] *n* libéralisme *m*
liberality [lɪbə'rælɪtɪ] *n* **(a)** *(of views)* libéralisme *m* **(b)** *(with money etc)* libéralité *f*, générosité *f*
liberalize ['lɪb(ə)rəlaɪz] *vt* libéraliser
liberally ['lɪb(ə)rəlɪ] *adv* libéralement, généreusement
liberate ['lɪbəreɪt] *vt* **(a)** libérer **(b)** *Ch (gas)* libérer, dégager **(c)** *Fin* **to l. capital** libérer des capitaux
liberated ['lɪbəreɪtɪd] *adj (person)* libéré; *(ideas, views, opinions)* progressiste; **a l. woman** une femme libérée; **these are l. times** on vit à une époque libérée; **her ideas aren't l.** elle n'est pas libérée
liberation [lɪbə'reɪʃən] *n* **(a)** libération *f*; *Fr Hist* **after the l.** après la Libération; **l. movement** mouvement *m* de libération; **she doesn't believe in women's l.** elle ne croit pas à la libération de la femme **(b)** *Ch, Phys (of gas, heat)* dégagement *m* **(c)** *Fin* **l. of capital** mobilisation *f* de capitaux
liberator ['lɪbəreɪtər] *n* libérateur, -trice
Liberia [laɪ'bɪərɪə] *n* Libéria *m*
Liberian [laɪ'bɪərɪən] **1** *adj* libérien **2** *n* Libérien, -ienne
libertarian [lɪbə'teərɪən] **1** *n* libertaire *mf* **2** *adj (philosophy, idea, tendency etc)* libertaire
libertine ['lɪbəti:n] *adj, n* libertin, -ine
liberty ['lɪbətɪ] *n* liberté *f*; **l. of conscience** liberté de conscience; **at l.** *(free)* libre; **to be at l. to do sth** être libre de faire qch; **Statue of L.** statue *f* de la Liberté; *Naut* **l. ticket** permission *f* de terre *ou* d'aller à terre; **to take the l. of doing** *or* **to do sth** se permettre *ou* prendre la liberté de faire qch; *F* **what a l.!** quel culot!; **civil liberties** libertés civiques; **to take liberties with sb** prendre *ou* se permettre des libertés avec qn; **the government is taking liberties** le gouvernement se fiche du monde; **to take liberties with a translation** se permettre des libertés dans une traduction
libidinous [lɪ'bɪdɪnəs] *adj* libidineux
libido [lɪ'bi:dəʊ, -'baɪ-] *n Psy* libido *f*
LIBOR ['laɪbɔ:r] *n Br Fin (abbr* **London Inter-Bank Offer Rate***)* ≈ TIOP *m*
Libra ['li:brə] *n Astron* (la) Balance; **to be (a) L.** être Balance
librarian [laɪ'breərɪən] *n* bibliothécaire *mf*
librarianship [laɪ'breərɪənʃɪp] *n (subject)* bibliothéconomie *f*
library ['laɪbrərɪ] *n (of books, Comptr of programs)* bibliothèque *f*; *(of tapes, CDs)* discothèque *f*; *Br* **mobile l.** bibliobus *m*; **photographic l.** photothèque *f*; **film l.** cinémathèque *f*; **music l.** discothèque *f*; **record l.** discothèque *f*; *F* **he's a walking l.** c'est une encyclopédie vivante; **l. book** livre *m* de bibliothèque; **l. card** *or* **ticket** carte *f* de bibliothèque; **l. film** film *m* d'archives; **l. footage** images *fpl* d'archives
library science *n* bibliothéconomie *f*
librettist [lɪ'bretɪst] *n Th* librettiste *mf*
libretto, *pl* **-i, -os** [lɪ'bretəʊ, -i:, -əʊz] *n* libretto *m*, *pl* librettos, livret *m (d'opéra)*
Libya ['lɪbɪə] *n* Libye *f*
Libyan ['lɪbɪən] **1** *adj* libyen; **the L. Desert** le désert de Libye **2** *n* Libyen, -yenne
lice *see* **louse**
licence, *US* **license** ['laɪsəns] *n* **(a)** permis *m*, autorisation *f*; *Com (to manufacture, sell)* licence *f*; **under l. from the inventor** avec l'autorisation de l'inventeur; **l. to sell alcohol** licence des débits de boissons; **made/manufactured under l.** construit/fabriqué sous licence; **dog l.** taxe *f* sur les chiens; *Br* **(driving) l.** *Am* **driver's l.** permis de conduire; **gun l.** permis de port d'arme(s); **import/export l.** licence d'importation/d'exportation; *Am* **liquor l.** licence des débits de boissons; **manufacturing l.** brevet *m* *ou* licence de fabrication; **marriage l.** *Br* **special l.** = dispense *f* de bans; *Br* **they were married by special l.** ils se sont mariés avec dispense de bans; *Av* **pilot's l.** brevet de pilote; **shooting l.** permis de chasse; *Br* **television l.** *(fee)* redevance *f* télévisuelle; **trading l.** carte *f* de commerce; **l. agreement** contrat *m* de concession; **l. holder** licencié *m*
(b) *esp Pej (freedom)* licence *f*
licence fee *n Br* redevance *f* télévisuelle
licence number *n* numéro *m* d'immatriculation
licence plate *n Am* plaque *f* d'immatriculation
license[1] ['laɪsəns] *vt* **to l. sth to sb** accorder une licence à qn pour qch; **to l. sb to sell drink/practise medicine** autoriser qn à tenir un débit de boissons/exercer la médecine; *Com* **to l. sb to manufacture/sell** accorder une licence à qn pour fabriquer/vendre; **to l. a car** *(of owner)* acheter une vignette pour une voiture; **licensed to sell beer, wines and spirits** autorisé à vendre de l'alcool, *Can* licencié à vendre des boissons alcooliques; **to be licensed to carry a gun** avoir un permis de port d'arme(s)
license[2] *n US* = **licence**
licensed ['laɪsənst] *adj (produit)* sous licence; *Admin* autorisé, patenté; *Av (pilot)* breveté; **l. brand name** nom *m* de marque sous licence; **l. house** *or* **premises** débit *m* de boissons; **l. restaurant/hotel** restaurant *m*/hôtel *m* ayant la licence des débits de boissons; *Br Old-fashioned Fml* **l. victualler** patron *m* de bar
licensee [laɪs(ə)n'si:] *n* concessionnaire *mf*, détenteur, -trice d'une patente *ou* d'un permis; *(for manufacturing)* détenteur d'une licence; *(of pub etc)* gérant, -ante, propriétaire *mf*
licensing ['laɪsənsɪŋ] *n* **l. agreement** accord *m* de licence; *Br* **l. hours** *(of pub)* heures *fpl* d'ouverture; *Br* **l. laws** lois *fpl* relatives aux débits de boissons alcoolisées
licensor *n* concédant *m*

licentiate [laɪ'senʃɪət] *n Univ* diplômé, -ée
licentious [laɪ'senʃəs] *adj* licencieux
licentiousness [laɪ'senʃəsnɪs] *n* licence *f*
lichen ['laɪkən, 'lɪtʃən] *n* lichen *m*
lichgate ['lɪtʃgeɪt] *n* = porche *m* d'entrée de cimetière surmonté d'un petit toit
licit ['lɪsɪt] *adj* licite
licitly ['lɪsɪtlɪ] *adv* licitement
lick[1] [lɪk] *n* **(a)** coup *m* de langue; **to give sth/sb a l.** lécher qch/qn; **give me a l. of your ice cream** laisse-moi goûter ta glace; *Old-fashioned F* **a l. and a promise** (*wash*) un brin de toilette **(b)** *F* (*small amount*) **a l. of paint** un petit coup de peinture; **a few licks of paint** deux ou trois coups de pinceau; **l. (of hair)** mèche *f* **(c)** *F* (*speed*) **at (a) great l., at full l.** à toute allure, à toute vitesse **(d) salt l.** (*provided for cattle*) pain *m* de sel; (*place*) terrain *m* salifère (*où les bêtes viennent lécher le sol*)
lick[2] *vt* **(a)** lécher; *Fig* **to l. one's lips** *or F* **one's chops** se lécher *ou* se pourlécher les babines; *Fig* **to l. one's wounds** panser ses blessures; *F* **to l. sb's boots** lécher les bottes à qn; *Vulg* **to l. sb's arse** lécher le cul de qn; *F* **to l. sb into shape** dresser qn; **to l. sth up** (*of animal*) laper qch; *Fig F* **to l. the plate clean** ne pas laisser une miette dans son assiette

(b) *F* (*defeat*) (*opponent*) mettre une raclée à; (*beat physically*) (*person*) battre, rosser; **he's got them licked** (*is certain to beat*) il va les écraser; **when it comes to marketing, they've got us licked** pour ce qui est du marketing, on ne leur arrive pas à la cheville; **I've got the problem licked** j'ai surmonté le problème; **this one has got me licked** (*of problem*) ça me dépasse
lickety-split ['lɪkɪtɪ'splɪt] *adv Am F* à toute vitesse, *F* à toute berzingue
licking ['lɪkɪŋ] *n F* (*of opponent*) raclée *f*; (*physical beating*) raclée *f*, rossée *f*; **they gave the other team a l.** ils ont mis une raclée à l'autre équipe
lickspittle ['lɪkspɪt(ə)l] *n Old-fashioned* lèche-bottes *m inv*
licorice ['lɪkərɪs] *n Am* = **liquorice**
lid [lɪd] *n* **(a)** (*of box, pan etc*) couvercle *m*; *Br Fig* **that puts the (tin) l. on it!** ça c'est le comble!; **this put the l. on her hopes of winning** cela a anéanti ses espoirs de gagner; **to take the l. off sth** ôter le couvercle de qch; *Fig* mettre qch au grand jour; *F* **to keep the l. on a piece of information** garder une information pour soi **(b)** (*eyelid*) paupière *f*
lidded ['lɪdɪd] *adj* (*box etc*) à couvercle
lidless ['lɪdlɪs] *adj* (*eyes*) sans paupières
lido ['li:dəʊ] *n Br* (*swimming pool*) piscine *f* en plein air
lie[1] [laɪ] *n* (*untruth*) mensonge *m*; **it's all lies** *or* **a pack of lies!** c'est un tissu de mensonges!; **to tell a l.** dire un mensonge; *F* **in 1986, no, I tell a l., it was 1987** en 1986, non, je dis une bêtise, c'était en 1987; *prov* **there are lies, damned lies and statistics** on fait dire ce que l'on veut aux chiffres; **to give the l. to sb** donner tort à qn; **to give the l. to an argument** démentir un argument
lie[2] (*pt, pp* **lied** [laɪd]; *prp* **lying** ['laɪɪŋ]) **1** *vi* (*tell untruth*) mentir **(to sb** à qn); **to l. about one's age** mentir sur son âge; **to l. through one's teeth** mentir effrontément **2** *vt* **she lied her way into the building** elle a pénétré dans l'immeuble grâce à quelques mensonges; **he always lies his way out of difficulties** il se sort toujours des difficultés en mentant
lie[3] *n* **(a)** (*of land*) disposition *f*; **l. of the land** configuration *f ou* disposition du terrain, topographie *f*; *Fig* **to find out the l. of the land** tâter le terrain **(b)** *Golf* (*of ball*) position *f*, assiette *f*
lie[4] *vi* (*pt* **lay** [leɪ]; *pp* **lain** [leɪn]; *prp* **lying** ['laɪɪŋ]) **(a)** (*of person, animal*) (*be in lying position*) être couché (à plat); (*go into lying position*) s'allonger; **he was lying down on the floor** il était allongé *ou* couché par terre; **to l. on one's back/side** être couché sur le dos/côté; **to be lying ill in bed** être (malade et) alité; **we found him lying dead** nous l'avons trouvé mort; **here lies ...** (*on gravestone*) ci-gît ...; **to l. in bed** rester au lit; **I lay awake all night** je n'ai pas pu dormir de la nuit; **I lay awake until 5. 30** je suis resté sans pouvoir dormir jusqu'à 5h30; **to l. hidden** rester caché; **to l. in wait for sb** guetter l'arrivée de qn; **the gamekeeper lay in wait all night for the poacher** le garde-chasse est resté tapi toute la nuit à attendre le braconnier

(b) (*of object*) être, se trouver; **the papers lay on the table** les papiers étaient sur la table; **all her clothes were lying on the floor** tous ses vêtements étaient étalés par terre; **town lying in a valley** ville située dans une vallée; **a vast plain lay before us** une vaste plaine s'étendait devant nous; **our way lies through the woods** notre chemin passe par les bois; **to l. in ruins** (*of building*) être en ruines; (*of career etc*) être détruit; **the obstacles that l. in our way** les obstacles qui bloquent notre chemin; **these hills l. between us and the sea** ces collines sont entre nous et la mer; *Naut* **ship lying at her berth** navire mouillé *ou* amarré à son poste; **the money is just lying in the bank doing nothing** l'argent dort à la banque; **the snow did not l.** la neige n'a pas tenu; **to l. dormant** (*of volcano*) être en sommeil *ou* au repos; **to l. (heavy) on one's stomach** (*of food*) peser sur l'estomac

(c) (*of abstract thing*) **sins that l. heavy on the conscience** péchés qui pèsent sur la conscience; **the onus of proof lies with them** c'est à eux qu'incombe la charge de la preuve; **the responsibility lies with the author** la responsabilité incombe à l'auteur; **to know where one's interests l.** savoir où se trouvent ses intérêts; **the difference lies in this, that ...** la différence réside dans le fait que ...; **the fault lies with you** c'est de votre faute; **a brilliant future lies before her** un brillant avenir s'ouvre devant elle; **what lies behind this uncharacteristic generosity?** qu'y a-t-il derrière cette générosité inhabituelle?; **my talents do not l. in that direction** je n'ai pas de dispositions *ou* de talent pour cela

(d) *Jur* (*of action, appeal*) être recevable
▶ **lie about** *vi* (*of thing, person*) traîner; **to leave one's papers lying about** laisser traîner ses papiers
▶ **lie back** *vi* se coucher sur le dos; (*in armchair*) se renverser; **just l. back and relax** (*literally*) allongez-vous et détendez-vous; **when you've finished you can l. back and take things easy** quand tu auras fini tu pourras te reposer
▶ **lie down** *vi* se coucher, s'étendre; **go and l. down** va t'allonger; **to l. down on one's bed** s'allonger sur son lit; **to l. down on the ground** se coucher *ou* s'allonger par terre; **l. down!** (*to dog*) couché!; *Fig* **to take an insult lying down** ne pas relever une insulte; *Fig* **he won't take it lying down** il ne se laissera pas faire
▶ **lie in** *vi* faire la grasse matinée
▶ **lie off** *vi* (*of ship*) rester au large
▶ **lie over** *vi* (*of thing*) être remis à plus tard; **to let a bill l. over** différer l'échéance d'un effet
▶ **lie to** *vi* (*of ship*) être à la cape, tenir la cape
▶ **lie up** *vi* **(a)** (*because of illness*) garder le lit, garder la chambre; (*hide*) se cacher **(b)** (*of car*) être en panne; (*of ship*) désarmer
lie detector *n* détecteur *m* de mensonges; **to take a l. test** passer au détecteur de mensonges
lie-down *n* **to have a l.** faire une sieste *ou* un petit somme
lief [li:f] *adv Arch* **I would as l. ...** j'aimerais autant ...
liege [li:dʒ] *n Hist* suzerain *m*; **my l.!** sire!
lie-in *n* **to have a l.** faire la grasse matinée
lien [li:(ə)n] *n Jur* (*on property*) privilège *m*, droit *m* de rétention; **to have a l. (up)on a cargo** avoir un recours sur un chargement
lieu [lju:, lu:] *n Fml* **in l. of ...** au lieu de ...; **to stand in l. of ...** tenir lieu de ...; **I'll take something else in l.** je prendrai quelque chose d'autre à la place; **two weeks salary in l. of notice** deux semaines de salaire en guise de préavis; **time off in l.** repos *m* compensateur
Lieut *Mil* (*abbr* **Lieutenant**) Lieut, Lt.
Lieut-Col *Mil* (*abbr* **Lieutenant-Colonel**) Lieut. -Col.
lieutenant [lef'tenənt] *esp US* [lu:'tenənt] *n Mil, Fig* lieutenant *m*; *Naut* lieutenant de vaisseau; *Mil* **l. colonel** (*pl* **lieutenant colonels**) lieutenant-colonel *m*, *pl* lieutenants-colonels; *Mil* **l. general** (*pl* **lieutenant generals**) général *m* de corps d'armée; *Naut* **l. commander** (*pl* **lieutenant commanders**) capitaine *m* de corvette; *Can* **L. Governor** Lieutenant-Gouverneur *m*
life *pl* **lives** [laɪf, laɪvz] *n* **(a)** (*existence*) vie *f*; **to take sb's l.** tuer qn; **to take one's own l.** se suicider; **to give l. to sb** donner la vie à qn; **to come to l. again** revenir à la vie; **it is a matter of l. and death** c'est une question de vie ou de mort; **to be hovering between l. and death** être entre la vie et la mort; **to believe in l. after death** croire à la vie après la mort; **to risk one's l., to risk l. and limb** risquer sa peau; **to escape with one's l.** avoir la vie sauve; **to lose one's l.** perdre la vie, périr; **no lives were lost** il n'y a eu aucune victime, on ne déplore aucune victime; **100 lives were lost** il y a eu 100 morts; **run for your lives!** sauve qui peut!; **a cat has nine lives** un chat a neuf vies; *F* **not on your l.!** jamais de la vie!; **he was rowing for dear l.** il ramait de toutes ses forces; **she can't sing to save her l.** elle est totalement incapable de chanter; *F* **I couldn't for the l. of me think what he wanted** je ne pouvais absolument pas imaginer ce qu'il voulait; *Art* **to draw from l.** dessiner d'après nature; **characters taken from l.** caractères pris sur le vif; **that's her to the l.** (*in that portrait, play etc*) c'est elle toute crachée; **animal/vegetable l.** la vie animale/végétale; **bird l.** la vie des oiseaux

(b) (*period of existence*) (*of person*) vie *f*; **a l. of Tolstoy** une biographie de Tolstoï; **(useful) l.** (*of machine*) vie *ou* durée *f* utile; **to work all one's l.** travailler durant toute sa vie; **never in (all) my l.** jamais de la vie; **in his early l.** quand il était jeune; **to be given a l. sentence,** *F* **to get l.** être condamné à vie; **appointed for l.** nommé à vie; *F* **to be in for l.** (*in prison*) en avoir pris pour la vie; **to mate for l.** (*of animal, bird*) s'unir pour la vie; *Nucl, Phys* **average** *or* **mean l.** (*of atom, isotope*) vie moyenne; **l. annuity/pension** pension *f*/rente *f* viagère; **l. interest** usufruit *m*; (*of possession*) viager *m*; **l. story** biographie *f*

(c) (*mode of existence*) vie *f*; *F* **to live** *or* **lead the l. of Riley** se la couler douce; **to make a new l. for oneself** refaire sa vie; **to depart this l.** quitter ce monde; **the man/woman in one's l.** l'homme/la femme de sa vie; **way of l.** manière *f* de vivre, (train *m* de) vie; **the American way of l.** le style de vie américain; **dieting has become a way of l. with some people** certaines personnes passent leur vie à faire des régimes; **to see l.** se frotter à la vie, partir à l'aventure; **he has seen l.** il sait ce que c'est que la vie; **you really see l. as a cop** quand on est flic, on en voit de toutes les couleurs; **he makes her l. a misery** il lui rend la vie impossible; **to make l. worth living** (*of sth*) donner un sens à l'existence; **l. is worth living when I'm with her** avec elle la vie vaut la peine d'être vécu; *F* **how's l.?** comment ça va?; **what a l.!** quelle vie!; **such is** *or* **that's l.!** c'est la vie!; **this is the l.!** voilà ce que j'appelle vivre!; **the good l.** la belle vie; **he led** *or* **lived a good l.** il a eu une vie exemplaire

(d) (*liveliness*) **to come to l.** (*of person, place, play etc*) s'animer; **to bring a party to l.** (*of person*) animer une fête; **to bring sb to l.** (*of play, book etc*) faire vivre qn; **full of l.** (*person*) plein de vie *ou* d'entrain; (*street etc*) plein de mouvement *ou* d'animation; **to put new l. into** (*person, company etc*) ranimer; **the l. and soul of the party** le boute-en-train de la soirée; **there's no l. in this place** ça manque d'entrain ici; **he may be 80 but there's l. in the old dog yet** il a peut-être 80 ans mais il est encore vif; **the critics say I'm finished but there's l. in the old dog yet** les critiques disent que je suis fini mais je n'ai pas dit mon dernier mot; **there's l. in the old car yet** elle marche toujours, la vieille bagnole

life-and-death *adj* **a l. situation** une affaire de vie ou de mort; **a l. struggle** une lutte désespérée; (*literally*) une guerre à mort

life assurance *n* assurance-vie *f*, *pl* assurances-vie

life belt *n* ceinture *f* de sauvetage

lifeblood ['laɪfblʌd] *n* (*of company etc*) âme *f*; *Lit* (*of person*) sang *m*; **the government are draining the l. from small businesses** le gouvernement est en train de saigner les petites entreprises; **the l. of the economy** le pivot de l'économie

lifeboat ['laɪfbəʊt] *n* **(a)** (*launched from coast*) canot *m* de sauvetage; **l. station** poste *m* de sauvetage **(b)** (**ship's**) **l.** embarcation *f* de sauvetage

lifeboatman, *pl* **-men** ['laɪfbəʊtmən] *n* sauveteur *m*

life buoy *n* bouée *f* de sauvetage

life capitalization *n Fin* capitalisation *f* viagère

life class *n Art* cours *m* de dessin avec modèle nu

life cycle *n* (*of animal, product*) cycle *m* de vie

life-cycle chart *n Mktg* (*of product*) courbe *f* du cycle de vie

life expectancy *n* espérance *f* de vie

life force *n* élan *m* vital

life form *n Zool etc* forme *f* de vie

life-giving *adj* vivifiant; (*sun, water*) nourricier

lifeguard ['laɪfgɑːd] *n* (*at the seaside*) surveillant *m* de baignade; (*at swimming pool*) maître *m* nageur; **to be on l. duty** surveiller la baignade

Life Guards *npl Br Mil* le corps de cavaliers appartenant à la maison du roi, les Gardes du corps

life imprisonment *n* emprisonnement *m* à perpétuité *ou* vie

life insurance *n* assurance-vie *f*, *pl* assurances-vie

life jacket *n* gilet *m* de sauvetage

lifeless ['laɪflɪs] *adj* sans vie; (*style, gestures, acting etc*) mou, *f* molle; (*expression*) vide; (*performance*) mort; **she fell l. to the floor** elle est tombée raide sur le sol

lifelessly ['laɪflɪslɪ] *adv* sans vie

lifelessness ['laɪflɪsnɪs] *n* (*of party etc*) manque *m* d'animation; (*of gestures*) mollesse *f*; (*of paintings*) froideur *f*

lifelike ['laɪflaɪk] *adj* (*portrait etc*) vivant, qui a de la vie; **it's very l.** c'est très réaliste

lifeline ['laɪflaɪn] *n* **(a)** *Naut* ligne *f* de sauvetage; (*aboard ship*) garde-corps *m inv*, attrape *f*, sauvegarde *f*; (*of diver*) corde *f* de communication; *Fig* **to throw sb a l.** venir à l'aide de qn; *Fig* **for us it was a financial l.** cet argent a permis notre survie **(b)** (*in palmistry*) ligne *f* de vie

lifelong ['laɪflɒŋ] *adj, attrib* (*friendship etc*) de toute la vie; **a l. friend** un ami de toujours; **a l. ambition** une ambition de toujours

life member *n* membre *m* à vie

life membership *n* adhésion *f* à vie

life peer *n Br* pair *m* à vie

life preserver *n Am* (*life belt*) ceinture *f* de sauvetage

lifer ['laɪfər] *n F* condamné, -ée à perpétuité

life raft *n* canot *m* (pneumatique) de sauvetage

life-saver *n* **(a)** (*person*) sauveteur *m* **(b)** *Fig* planche *f* de salut; **that cup of tea was a l.!** cette tasse de thé m'a redonné vie; **you're a l.** tu me sauves la vie!

life-saving *n* **l. apparatus** appareils *mpl ou* engins *mpl* de sauvetage; **l. vaccine** vaccin *m* qui sauve la vie

life sciences *npl* sciences *fpl* de la vie

life-size(d) *adj* (*portrait etc*) grandeur nature

life span *n* (*of person, animal etc*) espérance *f* de vie; (*of machine*) durée *f* de vie

lifestyle ['laɪfstaɪl] *n* style *m* de vie, mode *m* de vie; *Mktg* **l. analysis** analyse *f* du style de vie; *Mktg* **l. segmentation** segmentation *f* par styles de vie

life subscription *n* abonnement *m* à vie

life-support *adj Med* **l. system** *or* **machine** respirateur *m*; *Astron* **l. system** équipement *m* de survie; *Med* **to be on a l. system** *or* **machine** être sous assistance respiratoire; **to switch off the l. system** *or* **machine** arrêter le respirateur *ou* la respiration artificielle

life-threatening *adj* (*disease*) qui peut être mortel; **it's not l.** ce n'est pas mortel; **in a l. situation, the fish** ... quand il se sent en danger de mort, le poisson ...

lifetime ['laɪftaɪm] *n* (*of person*) vie *f*; (*of lamp, machine, fin of option*) durée *f*, vie; *Nucl Phys* (*of atom, isotope*) durée de vie, longévité *f*; *St Exch* (*of an option*) durée de vie; **in** *or* **during one's l.** de son vivant; **such a bill is unlikely within the l. of this parliament** un tel projet de loi est peu probable tant que ce parlement est en place; **a l. of happiness** toute une vie de bonheur; **it's the chance** *or* **opportunity of a l.** cette chance n'arrive qu'une fois dans la vie; **the holiday of a l.** des vacances sensationnelles; **a l. supply** une réserve pour la vie; **he's bought enough envelopes to last him a l.** il a acheté suffisamment d'enveloppes pour tenir jusqu'à la fin de ses jours

LIFO ['lɪːfəʊ] *Com* (*abbr* **last in, first out**) DEPS

lift¹ [lɪft] *n* **(a)** (*raising device*) *Br* ascenseur *m*; *Br* (**goods**) **l.** monte-charge *m inv*, élévateur *m*; **ski l.** (re)monte-pente *m*, *pl* remonte-pentes; **l. attendant** garçon *m* d'ascenseur; *Ski* **l. pass** forfait *m* de remontées mécaniques; *Br* **l. shaft** cage *f* d'ascenseur

(b) *esp Br* (*car ride*) **to give sb a l.** prendre *ou* emmener qn en voiture; **could you give me a l. to the station?** (*it's on your way*) est-ce que tu peux me déposer à la gare?; (*make special trip*) est-ce que tu peux m'emmener à la gare?; **can I give you a l.?** est-ce que je peux vous conduire *ou* déposer quelque part?; **I'll try to arrange a l. for anyone who hasn't got a car** je ferai en sorte que tout le monde ait une place dans une voiture; **we've been waiting over two hours for a l.** cela fait deux heures que nous attendons que quelqu'un veuille bien nous prendre; **we got a great l. yesterday, all the way to Lyons** on a eu de la chance hier, il y a quelqu'un qui nous a emmenés jusqu'à Lyon

(c) *F* **to give sb a l.** (*cheer up*) remonter le moral à qn

(d) (*extent of rise*) (*of crane etc*) hauteur *f* de levage; (*of pump*) hauteur d'élévation; *MecE* (*of valve, cam*) levée *f*; (*of millrace*) (hauteur de) chute *f*; (*between bearings etc*) différence *f* de niveau

(e) (*raising power*) (*of balloon, gas*) force *f* ascensionnelle; *Av* portance *f*, poussée *f* (aérodynamique), sustentation *f*

lift² **1** *vt* **(a)** (*weight*) lever, soulever; (*one's head*) lever, dresser; (*one's eyes, arm*) lever; **to l. weights** (*as exercise*) faire des haltères; **he never lifts a finger to help** il ne lève *ou* bouge jamais le petit doigt pour aider; **she has only to l. a finger and everyone comes running** elle n'a qu'à lever le petit doigt et tout le monde accourt; **to l. sth (up) again** soulever qch, relever qch; **to l. sb (up)** (*who has fallen*) aider qn à se relever; **to l. a child up** (*take in one's arms*) prendre un enfant dans ses bras; *Lit* **to l. (up) one's voice in prayer** adresser une prière au ciel; **to l. sth down** (*from a shelf etc*) descendre qch; **the wind lifted him off his feet** il a été soulevé par le vent

(b) (*potatoes, bulbs etc*) arracher; *Com* (*goods*) enlever

(c) *Cr, Golf* (*ball*) donner de l'essor à; *Tennis* (*shot*) lifter

(d) *F* (*take, steal*) voler, *F* piquer; **he had his wallet lifted** il s'est fait piquer son portefeuille; **to l. a passage from an author/a book** piquer un passage chez un auteur/dans un livre; **you'll get lifted (by the police) if you do that in public** tu vas te faire choper par les flics si tu fais ça en public (**e**) (*remove*) (*embargo*) lever; (*mortgage*) déshypothéquer

2 *vi* (**a**) (*of valve etc*) se lever, se soulever; (*of floor*) (*as a result of damp etc*) se soulever

(**b**) (*disperse*) (*of fog*) se lever, se dissiper; *US* (*of rain*) cesser

(**c**) *Naut* (*of vessel*) s'élever à la lame

▶ **lift off 1** *vi* (*of aircraft, rocket*) décoller **2** *vtsep* (*lid etc*) soulever

▶ **lift out** *vtsep* (*from box etc*) sortir (**from** de); *Mil* (*troops*) évacuer (par avion *ou* hélicoptère)

▶ **lift up** *vtsep* = **lift²**

liftboy ['lɪftbɔɪ] *n Br* liftier *m*

liftgate ['lɪftgeɪt] *n US Aut* hayon *m* arrière

lifting ['lɪftɪŋ] *n* (**a**) *Aut* **l. ramp** *or* **platform** pont *m* élévateur; **l. capacity** puissance *f* de levage; *Av* **l. force** *or* **power** force *f* de sustentation, puissance ascensionnelle (**b**) (*of potatoes, bulbs*) arrachage *m* (**c**) (*of embargo*) levée *f*; (*of mortgage, ban*) mainlevée *f*

liftoff ['lɪftɒf] *n* (*of rocket*) décollage *m*; **we have l.** lancement réussi

lift-operator *n Br* liftier *m*

ligament ['lɪgəmənt] *n Anat* ligament *m*; **to tear a l.** se déchirer un ligament

ligature¹ ['lɪgətjər] *n* (**a**) *Surg* ligature *f* (**b**) *Typ* ligature *f* (**c**) *Mus* liaison *f*

ligature² *vt* (**a**) *Surg* (*vein*) ligaturer, barrer (**b**) *Typ* (*two vowels*) ligaturer; **o e ligatured** e dans l'o

light¹ [laɪt] *n* (**a**) lumière *f*; **artificial/electric l.** lumière artificielle/électrique; **by the l. of the moon** au clair *ou* à la clarté de la lune; **the l. of day** la lumière du jour, le jour; **things will look different in the cold l. of day** demain tu verras les choses sous un autre aspect; **it's getting l.** le jour se lève; **to bring sth to l.** (*of investigations*) mettre qch en évidence, révéler qch; **to come to l.** (*of crime etc*) être découvert; **to see the l.** (*realise the truth*) être convaincu *ou* converti; **to (first) see the l. of day** (*of person*) naître, voir le jour; **to be in sb's l.** faire de l'ombre à qn; *Phys* **infrared/ultraviolet l.** lumière infrarouge/ultraviolette; **source of l., l. source** source *f* lumineuse; **against the l., with one's back to the l.** à contre-jour; *Comptr* **l. pen** crayon *m* lumineux *ou* optique, photostyle *m*; **good/bad l.** bon/mauvais éclairage *m*; **to act according to one's lights** agir conformément à ses idées

(**b**) (*figurative senses*) **in a bad l.** sous un mauvais angle; **in a positive/favourable l.** sous un angle positif/favorable; **in a poor l. he could pass for 40** dans la pénombre on pourrait penser qu'il a 40 ans; **in a good l. he could pass for 40** avec un bon éclairage on pourrait penser qu'il a 40 ans; **to throw** *or* **shed** *or* **cast l. on sth** faire la lumière sur qch, éclaircir qch; **to see sb/sth in a new l. /in their/its true l.** voir qn/qch sous un jour nouveau/sous son vrai jour; **to see sth in a different l.** voir qch sous un jour différent *ou* sous un autre angle; **the question should be considered in the l. of these facts** on devrait considérer la question à la lumière de ces faits; **in the l. of …** (*considering*) prenant en considération *ou* en compte …

(**c**) (*object*) (*in room etc*) lumière *f*; (*on car, train, ship etc*) feu *m*; **lights out** l'extinction *f* des feux; **to put** *or* **turn on the l.** allumer; **to put** *or* **turn off the l.** éteindre (la lumière); *F* **to go out like a l.** (*fall asleep quickly*) s'endormir aussitôt couché; (*faint, become unconscious*) s'évanouir; **(traffic) lights** feux *mpl* de circulation *ou* de signalisation routière, *F* feu rouge; **turn right at the (traffic) lights** tournez à droite au feu rouge; *Aut* **dip your lights** roulez en code; *Aut* **lights-on warning buzzer** alarme *f* d'oubli des feux; **she was showing no lights** (*of ship*) il naviguait *ou* faisait route tous feux éteints; *Tech* **control** *or* **warning l.** voyant lumineux

(**d**) (*lighthouse*) phare *m*

(**e**) (*fire*) (*in eyes*) éclat *m*; **to set l. to sth** mettre le feu à qch; **could I have a l.?** est-ce que tu peux me donner du feu?; **have you got a l.?** vous avez du feu, s'il vous plaît?

(**f**) *Archit* (*window*) fenêtre *f*; (*small round*) lucarne *f*; (*of mullioned window*) jour *m*; (*of greenhouse*) carreau *m*

(**g**) *Art, Phot* lumière *f*, clair *m*; **l. effects** effets *mpl ou* jeux *mpl* de lumière; **l. and shade** les ombres et la lumière

light² *vt* (*pt, pp* **lit** [lɪt]; *occ* **lighted**) (**a**) (*lamp, fire etc*) allumer; **to l. a fire** allumer un feu; *Fig* **to l. sb's fire** exciter qn (**b**) (*room, street*) éclairer, illuminer; **to l. the way for sb** éclairer qn

light³ *adj* (**a**) (*room etc*) clair, (bien) éclairé; **it is/will soon be l.** il fait/fera bientôt jour (**b**) (*hair, complexion*) blond; (*colour*) clair; **painted in l. tones** peint en tons clairs *ou* lumineux; **l. blue** bleu clair *inv*

light⁴ 1 *adj* (**a**) (*load, blow etc*) léger; (*soil*) meuble; (*deficient*) (*weight*) faible; **with a l. step** d'un pas léger; **l. touch** (*of painter, author, film director*) finesse *f*; **she's got a very l. touch with pastry** les pâtisseries qu'elle fait sont très légères; **to be l. on one's feet** avoir le pas léger; **as l. as a feather** léger comme une plume; **to have a l. meal** prendre un repas léger; **to be a l. sleeper** avoir le sommeil léger; **l. beer** bière légère; **l. breeze** brise faible *ou* légère; **l. showers** ondées *fpl*; *Mktg* **l. user** faible utilisateur *m*

(**b**) (*not of full weight, size etc*) (*aircraft, engine*) léger; (*not fully loaded*) (*ship*) lège; **l. aircraft** avion *m* petit porteur; *Mil* **l. artillery** artillerie *f* légère *ou* de petit calibre; **l. infantry** infanterie *f* légère; *Metal* **l. castings** petites pièces *fpl* de fonderie; **l. crop** faible récolte *f*; **l. van** fourgonnette *f*

(**c**) (*not strenuous*) (*job*) facile; **a little l. housework** un petit peu de ménage mais sans vous forcer; *Mil* **l. duty** service *m* réduit; **l. punishment** peine *f* légère; **l. work** petits travaux *mpl*, travail peu fatigant

(**d**) (*not serious*) (*comedy, style, music etc*) léger; **to make l. of sth** traiter qch à la légère; (*of accusation*) attacher peu d'importance à qch; **l. reading** lecture(s) *f(pl)* récréative(s) *ou* délassante(s); **l. talk** propos *mpl* frivoles *ou* légers; **l. verse** poésie *f* facile

2 *adv* légèrement; **to travel l.** voyager léger *inv*

▶ **light into** *vipo F* (*attack verbally or physically*) tomber dessus, rentrer dedans; **she really lit into him** elle lui est carrément tombée dessus *ou* rentrée dedans

▶ **light on** *vipo* (*find*) (*solution, correct method, cure etc*) trouver; **his eyes lighted on the picture** ses yeux se posèrent sur le tableau

▶ **light out** *vi Am F* décamper

▶ **light up 1** *vi* (*put lights on*) allumer, mettre la lumière; *F* (*of smoker*) allumer sa cigarette/sa pipe/*etc*; **his eyes lit up** ses yeux se sont animés; **the whole sky lit up** le ciel entier s'illumina **2** *vtsep* (*room*) éclairer; (*cigarette, pipe*) allumer; **the house was lit up** la maison était illuminée; **a smile lit up her face** un sourire a illuminé son visage

light beam *n* faisceau *m* lumineux

light bulb *n* ampoule *f*

light-coloured *adj* clair

light cue *n TV etc* signal *m* lumineux

light-emitting [laɪtɪmɪtɪŋ] *adj* **l. diode** diode *f* électroluminescente

lighten¹ ['laɪt(ə)n] **1** *vt* (**a**) (*light up*) (*darkness, face*) éclairer; (*house etc*) rendre plus clair (**b**) (*colour, sky*) éclaircir **2** *vi* s'éclairer, s'illuminer; **her face lightened** son visage s'éclaira

lighten² 1 *vt* (*reduce weight of*) alléger; (*ship*) délester; *Fig* **to l. sb's load** (*make work or life easier*) décharger qn **2** *vi* **my heart lightened** j'ai été soulagé

▶ **lighten up** *vi esp Am F* se dérider; **come on, l. up!** tu ne peux pas parler de choses moins sérieuses?

light entertainment *n* divertissement *m*; **it's not exactly l.** (*of job*) ce n'est pas ce qu'on fait de plus divertissant; (*of music, play etc*) ce n'est pas ce qu'il y a de plus léger

lighter¹ ['laɪtər] *n* allume-gaz *m inv*; (*for cigarettes*) briquet *m*; (*in car*) allume-cigare *m*; **l. flint** pierre *f* à briquet; **l. fluid/fuel** essence *f* à briquet

lighter² *n Naut* allège *f*, gabare *f*

lighterage ['laɪtərɪdʒ] *n Naut* (*unloading*) déchargement *m* par allèges *ou* par gabares, gabarage *m*; (*fee*) droits *mpl* ou frais *mpl* d'allège *ou* de gabarage

lighter-than-air *adj* (*aircraft*) plus léger que l'air

light-fingered [laɪt'fɪŋgəd] *adj F* **he's l.** c'est un voleur; *F* il a la main leste

light flare *n* fusée *f* éclairante

light-footed *adj* agile, leste, au pied léger

light-headed *adj* (**a**) (*dizzy*) **to feel l.** (*through lack of food etc*) se sentir un peu étourdi (**b**) (*frivolous*) écervelé; (*excited*) excité; **the realization that she had won made her feel quite l.** elle était tout excitée de réaliser qu'elle avait gagné

light-hearted ['laɪthɑːtɪd] *adj* (*person*) allègre; (*remark, discussion*) léger

lighthouse ['laɪthaʊs] *n* phare *m*; **l. keeper** gardien *m* de phare

lighting ['laɪtɪŋ] *n* (**a**) (*of stage set etc*) éclairage *m*; (*lights themselves*) lumières *fpl*; **l. angle** angle *m* d'éclairage; **l. board** pupitre *m* d'éclairage; **l. cameraman** directeur *m* de la photographie, chef-opérateur *m* cadreur; **l. effects** effets *mpl* d'éclairage *ou* de lumière; **l. engineer** (ingénieur *m*) éclairagiste *m*; **l. technician** éclairagiste *m*, éclairo *m*; *Br Admin* **l. up time** heure *f* d'éclairage (**b**) (*of painting*) éclairage *m*, exposition *f*

lightly ['laɪtlɪ] *adv* (**a**) légèrement; (*to walk*) d'un pas léger; **to sleep l.** (*generally*) avoir le sommeil léger; (*on one occasion*) dormir d'un sommeil léger; **to cook sth l.** faire cuire qch légèrement; **her responsibilities sit l. on her** ses responsabilités ne lui pèsent pas; **to get off l.** s'en tirer à bon compte (**b**) (*to say*) d'un ton léger; **to speak l. of sth** parler de qch à la légère; **to take a decision l.** prendre une décision à la légère

lightness[1] ['laɪtnɪs] *n* (*brightness*) clarté *f*

lightness[2] *n* (*in weight etc*) légèreté *f*; **l. of foot** agilité *f*; **l. of heart** gaieté *f* de cœur; **l. of touch** (*of pianist, tennis player*) légèreté; (*of artist*) légèreté de pinceau; (*of writer*) légèreté de style

lightning ['laɪtnɪŋ] *n* éclairs *mpl*, foudre *f*; **a flash of l.** un éclair; **struck by l.** frappé par la foudre; **as quick as l., with l. speed,** *F* **like greased l.** rapide comme l'éclair; *Prov* **l. never strikes twice in the same place** la foudre ne frappe jamais deux fois au même endroit; **l. attack** attaque *f* éclair; **l. strike** grève *f* surprise; **l. visit** visite *f* éclair

lightning bug *n Am* (*firefly*) luciole *f*

lightning conductor *or Am* **rod** *n* paratonnerre *m*

lightproof ['laɪtpruːf] *adj* opaque

light ray *n* rayon *m* lumineux

lights [laɪts] *npl Culin* (*of cow etc*) mou *m*

light-sensitive *adj Phys* photosensible

lightship ['laɪtʃɪp] *n Naut* bateau-feu *m*, *pl* bateaux-feux, bateau-phare *m*, *pl* bateaux-phares

light table *n* (*for artwork, page makeup*) table *f* de montage

light wave *n* onde *f* lumineuse

lightweight ['laɪtweɪt] **1** *n Boxing* poids *m* léger; *Pej* (*unimpressive person*) personne *f* qui manque d'envergure; **intellectual/political l.** personne qui manque d'envergure intellectuelle/politique **2** *adj* (*garment etc*) léger

light year *n Astron* année-lumière *f*, *pl* années-lumière, année de lumière *Fig* **they are light years ahead** ils ont des années-lumières d'avance

lignite ['lɪgnaɪt] *n Miner* lignite *m*

likable ['laɪkəb(ə)l] = **likeable**

like[1] [laɪk] **1** *adj* semblable, pareil; **they are of l. temperament** ils ont le même tempérament; **they are as l. as two peas (in a pod)** ils se ressemblent comme deux gouttes d'eau; *El* **l. poles** pôles *mpl* semblables *ou* de même nom; *Math* **l. terms/quantities** termes *mpl*/quantités *fpl* semblables

2 *prep* (**a**) (*similar to*) **to be l. sb/sth** être semblable à qn/à qch, ressembler à qn/à qch; **we're l. sisters** nous sommes comme des sœurs; **to taste l. sth** avoir le même goût que qch; **to look l. sth/sb** ressembler à qch/qn; **I want to find one l. it** je veux trouver le/la même; **people l. you** des gens comme vous; **what's the weather l.?** quel temps fait-il?; **you know what she's l.** vous savez comme elle est; **he was l. a father to me** il a été comme un père pour moi; **when I hear things l. that** quand j'entends des choses pareilles; **I know plenty of people l. that** je connais pas mal de gens comme ça; **something very much l. it** quelque chose qui y ressemble beaucoup; **it costs something l. £10** cela coûte environ 10 livres; **it will cost more l. £20** ça coûtera plutôt dans les 20 livres; **that's more l. it** voilà qui est mieux; **we don't have anything l. as many people as we need** on est loin d'avoir tout le monde qu'il nous faut; **it's just l. (at) home** c'est comme à la maison; *F* **that's something l. it!** voilà qui est réussi!; **there's nothing l. it** il n'y a rien de mieux; **she is nothing l. as intelligent as you** elle est loin d'être aussi intelligente que vous; **that's not l. him** (*not his way of behaving etc*) ça ne lui ressemble pas; **that's just l. him!** c'est bien de lui!; **that's just l. a woman/a man!** c'est typiquement féminin/masculin!; **l. father l. son** tel père, tel fils

(**b**) (*in the manner of*) comme; **I think l. you** je pense comme vous; **just l. anybody else** comme tout le monde; **to speak French l. a native** parler français comme un natif; *F* **to run l. blazes** *or* **hell** *or* **mad** courir comme un dératé; *F* **be l. that then!** puisque c'est ça, fais comme tu veux!; **don't be l. that about it, he didn't mean what he said** ne le prends pas mal, ce n'est pas ce qu'il voulait dire; **l. this?** (*am I doing it correctly?*) comme ça?; **whisk the egg whites gently, l. this** battez les blancs délicatement, comme ceci; **don't talk l. that** ne parlez pas comme ça; **I'm sorry to keep bothering you l. this** je suis désolé de vous déranger continuellement comme ça

(**c**) (*such as*) tel que; **take more exercise, l. jogging** fais plus d'exercice, du jogging par exemple

3 *adv F* **l. enough, (as) l. as not** probablement, vraisemblablement; *Sl* **he looked angry, l.** il était comme en colère; *Sl* **he just came up behind me, l.** il est arrivé derrière moi, comme ça

4 *conj F* (**a**) (**= as**) comme; **do l. I do** faites comme moi; **l. I said** comme je l'ai dit

(**b**) (**= as if**) **he behaved l. he was scared** il s'est conduit comme s'il avait peur; **he looked l. he'd seen a ghost** on aurait dit qu'il avait vu un fantôme

5 *n* (*person*) semblable *mf*, pareil, -eille; **he and his l.** lui et ses semblables; **it's too good for the likes of me** c'est trop bien pour des gens comme moi; **the likes of you** des gens comme toi, *Pej* des gens de ton acabit; **music, painting and the l.** la musique, la peinture, et autres choses du même genre; **musicians, painters and the l.** musiciens, peintres et compagnie; **I've never seen the l. (of it)** *or* **its l.** je n'ai jamais vu une chose pareille; **it was music, the l. of which I had never heard** c'était de la musique comme je n'en avais jamais entendue

like[2] *n* (*usu pl*) **likes** (*tastes*) goûts *mpl*, préférences *fpl*; **likes and dislikes** préférences *fpl*; **I don't think she has any very strong likes or dislikes** je ne pense pas qu'elle ait des préférences très marquées

like[3] *vt* (**a**) (*person*) aimer bien; **I l. him** je l'aime bien, il me plaît bien; **I don't l. him** je ne l'aime pas, il ne me plaît pas; **how do you l. him?** comment le trouvez-vous?; **she is well liked** elle est très appréciée

(**b**) (*enjoy*) aimer (bien); **he likes school** il aime l'école; **do you l. tea?** aimez-vous le thé?; **I don't l. it at all** (*situation etc*) cela ne me plaît pas du tout; **if he doesn't l. it he can go elsewhere** si ça ne lui plaît pas il peut aller ailleurs; **whether she likes it or not** que cela lui plaise ou non; **these plants don't l. the damp** ces plantes craignent l'humidité; **I l. to see them now and again** j'aime les voir de temps à autre; *F Iron* **(well) I l. that!** en voilà une bonne!, elle est bien bonne, celle-là!

(**c**) (*to want*) aimer (**to do (à)** faire); **he doesn't l. people to talk about it** il n'aime pas qu'on en parle; **I would very much l. to go** j'aimerais beaucoup y aller; **would you l. me to go with you?** voulez-vous que je vous accompagne?; **I would l. to know whether ...** je voudrais bien savoir si ...; **I would l. time to consider it** j'aimerais avoir le temps d'y réfléchir; **I would l. some tea** je prendrais bien une tasse de thé; **would you l. a cigarette?** voulez-vous une cigarette?; **I would l. nothing better** je ne demande pas mieux; **I would l. nothing better than a hot bath** il n'y a rien qui me ferait autant plaisir qu'un bon bain chaud; **as you l.** comme vous voudrez; **to do just as one likes** n'en faire qu'à sa tête; **I can do as I l. with it** j'en fais ce que je veux; **he thinks he can do anything he likes** il se croit tout permis; **she is free to do as she likes** elle est libre d'agir à sa guise *ou* de faire comme il lui plaira; **if you l.** si vous voulez; **when you l.** quand il vous plaira; **as much as you l.** tant que vous voudrez; **I didn't l. to mention it** j'ai préféré ne pas le mentionner; **I wanted to ring you but I didn't l. to** (*I would have disturbed you, upset you etc*) je voulais te téléphoner mais j'ai préféré ne pas le faire

likeable ['laɪkəb(ə)l] *adj* (*person*) agréable, sympathique

likeableness ['laɪkəb(ə)lnɪs] *n* (*of person*) amabilité *f*

likelihood ['laɪklɪhʊd] *n* vraisemblance *f*, probabilité *f*, apparence *f*; **there is little l. of his succeeding** il y a peu de chances qu'il réussisse; **there's a strong l. that ...** il y a une forte probabilité pour que ... + *sub*; **there is every l. that ...** il y a toutes les chances que ... + *sub*; **in all l.** selon toute probabilité, selon toute vraisemblance

likely ['laɪklɪ] **1** *adj* (**a**) (*probable*) vraisemblable, probable; **it's not a very l. scenario** ce scénario n'est pas très vraisemblable; **the pub is a l. place to find him** le pub est probablement l'endroit où le trouver; *F Iron* **that's a l. story!** la belle histoire!, en voilà une bonne!; **it's more than l.** c'est plus que probable; **it's not very l.** c'est peu probable; **it's l. to rain** il y a des chances pour qu'il pleuve; **she is quite l. to do it** il y a des chances qu'elle le fasse; **books l. to interest young people** ouvrages susceptibles d'intéresser les jeunes; **this plan is most l. to succeed** ce projet a beaucoup de chances de réussir; **are the neighbours l. to object?** y a-t-il des chances que les voisins s'y opposent?

(**b**) (*promising*) prometteur; *Br Dial* **a l. lad** un gars qui promet; **a l. candidate/horse** un candidat/cheval susceptible *ou* qui a des chances de gagner; **this looked a l. spot to find what they were looking for** l'endroit semblait tout indiqué pour trouver ce qu'ils cherchaient

2 *adv* **most l., very l.,** *US F* **l.** vraisemblablement, très probablement; **as l. as not** vraisemblablement; *F* **not l.!** jamais de la vie!

like-minded *adj* du même avis; (*having same tastes*) qui ont les mêmes goûts

liken ['laɪk(ə)n] *vt* comparer (**to** à)

likeness ['laɪknɪs] *n* (**a**) (*similarity*) ressemblance *f* (**between** entre; **to** à); **God created man in his own l.** Dieu a créé l'homme à son image; **a close l.** une ressemblance étroite;

family l. air *m* de famille **(b)** (*image*) portrait *m*, image *f*; **the portrait is a good l.** le portrait est très ressemblant

likewise ['laɪkwaɪz] *adv* (*similarly*) de même, aussi; **to do l.** faire de même, en faire autant; **pleased to meet you – l.!** ravi de vous rencontrer – moi de même!

liking ['laɪkɪŋ] *n* goût *m*, penchant *m*; **to one's l.** au goût de qn; **is it to your l.?** cela est-il à votre goût?, est-ce que cela vous plaît?; **to have a l. for sth** avoir du goût pour qch, aimer qch; **I have taken a l. to her** elle m'est devenue sympathique; **to acquire a l. for sth** se mettre à aimer qch

lilac ['laɪlək] **1** *n* (*flower, tree, colour*) lilas *m* **2** *adj* **l. (-coloured)** lilas *inv*

Lilliputian [lɪlɪ'pjuːʃən] *adj Lit* lilliputien

Lilo® ['laɪləʊ] *n* = matelas *m* pneumatique

lilt [lɪlt] *n* **(a)** (*of verse*) rythme *m*, cadence *f*; **a song with a l.** une chanson au rythme entraînant; **to speak with a Welsh l.** parler avec des intonations galloises **(b)** *Arch, Scot* chant *m*, air *m*

lilting ['lɪltɪŋ] *adj* (*rythme*) musical; (*tune*) cadencé, scandé

lily ['lɪlɪ] *n* (*flower*) lis *m*; **l. of the valley** muguet *m*; **l. pad** feuille *f* de nénuphar

lily-livered ['lɪlɪlɪvəd] *adj* couard

lily-white *adj* blanc/*f* blanche comme le lis, d'une blancheur de lis; *F* (*character*) blanc comme neige

limb [lɪm] *n* **(a)** (*of body*) membre *m*; **the lower limbs** les membres inférieurs; **to tear an animal l. from l.** mettre un animal en pièces **(b)** (*of tree*) (grosse) branche *f*; (*of cross*) bras *m*; *F* **to be out on a l.** (*be alone*) être en plan; (*be in dangerous position*) être dans une situation délicate; *F* **his refusal to compromise left him out on a l.** son refus d'accepter un compromis l'a mis dans une situation délicate; *F* **to go out on a l.** prendre des risques

-limbed [lɪmd] *suff* **loose-l.** souple; **strong-l.** aux membres solides, solide

limber[1] ['lɪmbər] *n Mil* (*of gun carriage*) avant-train *m*, *pl* avant-trains

limber[2] *vt Mil* **to l. a gun** attacher une pièce de canon à l'avant-train

limber[3] *adj* souple

▶ **limber up 1** *vi Sp* s'échauffer **2** *vtsep Sp* (*muscles*) se chauffer; **to l. up one's fingers** (*of pianist etc*) s'échauffer les doigts

limbering-up exercises [lɪmbərɪŋ'ʌp] *npl* exercices *mpl* d'assouplissement

limbless ['lɪmlɪs] *adj* (*person*) à qui il manque un membre/plusieurs membres; (*with no arms or legs*) sans membres; **l. ex-servicemen** grands mutilés *mpl* de guerre

limbo ['lɪmbəʊ] *n* **(a)** *Rel* les limbes *mpl*; *Rel; Fig* **to be in l.** être dans les limbes **(b)** (*dance*) limbo *m*; **l. dancer** danseur, -euse de limbo

lime[1] [laɪm] *n* (*fruit*) lime *f*, citron *m* vert; (*tree*) limettier *m*; **l. juice** jus *m* de citron vert; **l. green** (*colour*) vert vif; **a l.-green coat** un manteau vert vif

lime[2] *n* (*linden tree*) tilleul *m*

lime[3] *n* **(a)** (*substance*) chaux *f*; **l. pit** carrière *f* de pierre à chaux **(b)** (*for catching birds*) glu *f*; **l. twig** gluau *m*

lime[4] *vt* **(a)** *Agr* (*soil*) chauler **(b)** (*twigs*) **to l. birds** prendre des oiseaux à la glu *ou* au gluau

limeade ['laɪmeɪd] *n* = jus *m* de citron vert additionné de sucre et d'eau gazeuse

limekiln ['laɪmkɪln] *n* four *m* à chaux

limelight ['laɪmlaɪt] *n* **in the l.** sous les feux de la rampe, très en vue; **she doesn't like the l.** elle n'aime pas sentir les projecteurs braqués sur elle; **an actor who's never out of the l.** un acteur très en vue; **to seek the l.** rechercher la vedette; **to steal the l.** voler la vedette

limerick ['lɪmərɪk] *n* limerick *m*, = poème *m* en cinq vers, burlesque et grivois

limestone ['laɪmstəʊn] *n Geol* calcaire *m*

limey ['laɪmɪ] *Am, Austr Sl* **1** *n* Anglais *m* **2** *adj* anglais

limit[1] ['lɪmɪt] *n* **(a)** (*boundary*) limite *f*, borne *f*; *MecE* (*of elasticity etc*) limite; (*in insurance*) plein *m*; **to fix** *or* **set a l.** *or* **limits** fixer *ou* mettre une limite *ou* des limites (**to** à); **within a ten kilometre l.** dans un rayon de dix kilomètres; **within limits** dans une certaine mesure; **I like jazz but within limits** j'aime le jazz mais jusqu'à un certain point; **the limits of decency** les limites de la décence; **time l.** (*for speaker etc*) limite de temps; (*for payment etc*) délai *m*; (*on special privilege etc*) durée *f*; **to be over the (legal) l.** (*of drunken driver*) avoir bu plus qu'il n'est permis au volant; *Fin* **credit l.** limite *ou* plafond *m* du crédit; **what is the l. on this road?** (*speed*) quelle est la limitation de vitesse sur cette route?; **to fix a l.** (*in insurance*) fixer les pleins; **there's a l. to everything!** il y a une limite à tout!; **there's no l. to her ambition** son ambition est sans limites; **to know no limits** ne connaître aucune limite; **his arrogance knows no limits** son arrogance ne connaît pas de limites; **that's the l.!** ça c'est le comble!; **he's the l.!** il est impossible!; **off limits** (*place*) inaccessible; *Mil* consigné à la troupe; **to be off limits to sb** (*of place*) être inaccessible à qn; *Mil* **to put a bar off limits** consigner un bar

(b) *MecE* (*tolerance*) tolérance *f*; **l. gauge** (*device*) calibre *m* de tolérance; (*external*) bague *f* à tolérance; (*internal*) bouchon *m* à tolérance

limit[2] *vt* (*sb, sth*) limiter, borner, restreindre; **I have to l. my calorie intake** je dois limiter ma consommation de calories; **to l. oneself to …** (*in speaking*) se borner à …; **to l. oneself to the bare necessities** se restreindre au strict nécessaire; **to l. oneself to two whiskies** se limiter à deux whiskies; **I will l. myself to observing that …** je me bornerai à observer que …

limitation [lɪmɪ'teɪʃən] *n* limitation *f*; **to know one's limitations** connaître ses limites

limited ['lɪmɪtəd] *adj* (*number, intelligence, skills etc*) limité, restreint; *Com* (*market*) étroit, restreint; **l. circulation** circulation restreinte

limited company *n Com* société *f* à responsabilité limitée

limited edition *n* (*of book*) édition *f* à tirage limité

limited liability *n Jur* responsabilité *f* limitée

limited stop bus *n* bus *m* à nombre d'arrêts limité

limited stop train *n* train *m* à nombre d'arrêts limité

limiter ['lɪmɪtər] *n Rad, TV* limiteur *m*

limitless ['lɪmɪtlɪs] *adj* sans bornes, illimité

limousine [lɪmʊ'ziːn], *F* **limo** ['lɪməʊ] *n Aut* limousine *f*

limp[1] [lɪmp] *n* boitement *m*, *Lit* claudication *f*; **to walk with a l., to have a l.** boiter

limp[2] *vi* boiter, *Lit* claudiquer; **to l. home** *Sp* terminer la course tant bien que mal; *Fig* rentrer tant bien que mal; **to l. along** aller en boitant *ou F* clopin-clopant; (*of ship etc*) avancer péniblement; **she limped along the corridor** elle remonta le couloir en boitant

limp[3] *adj* mou, *f* molle, flasque; **l. binding** (*of book*) cartonnage *m* souple; **to go l.** (*of person*) s'affaisser; **let your arm go l.** relâche ton bras; **to feel l.** (*of person*) se sentir mou *ou* sans énergie; **l. with the heat** abattu par la chaleur; **the heat makes me feel l.** je suis abattu par la chaleur

limpet ['lɪmpɪt] *n* patelle *f*, arapède *m*; *F* (*person*) crampon *m*; **to stick to sb like a l.** ne pas lâcher *ou* cramponner qn; *Mktg* **l. method** (*small pack on bigger one*) méthode *f* du 'mini produit gratuit en plus'; *Mil* **l. mine** mine *f* magnétique

limp-home mode *n Aut* mode *m* dégradé

limpid ['lɪmpɪd] *adj Fml* (*water, style*) limpide

limply ['lɪmplɪ] *adv* (*without firmness*) mollement, flasquement; (*without energy*) mollement, sans énergie

limpness ['lɪmpnɪs] *n* mollesse *f*, manque *m* d'énergie

limp-wristed ['lɪmp'rɪstəd] *adj F* efféminé

linchpin ['lɪntʃpɪn] *n* esse *f*, cheville *f* d'essieu; *Fig* (*of organization etc*) cheville ouvrière

Lincs *Br abbr* **Lincolnshire**

linctus ['lɪŋktəs] *n Pharm* sirop *m*

linden ['lɪndən] *n* **l. (tree)** tilleul *m*

line[1] [laɪn] *n* **(a)** (*mark*) ligne *f*, trait *m*; (*of shore, face*) contours *mpl*; (*of car etc*) lignes; *Geog F* **the L.** (*equator*) la Ligne (de l'Équateur); **straight l.** (ligne) droite *f*; **broken/wavy l.** trait discontinu; **to put a l. through sth** barrer qch; *Tennis* **on the l.** sur la ligne; *Aut* **white l.,** *US* **yellow l.** (*in centre of road*) ≈ ligne blanche, bande *f* médiane; **the lines of the hand** les lignes de la main; **the lines on one's forehead** les rides *fpl* de son front; **his face was covered with lines** son visage était plein de rides; **the hard lines of his face** ses traits durs; **to draw a l. under sth** (*underline it*) souligner qch; *Fig* **you have to draw the l. somewhere** il y a une limite à tout; **he doesn't know where to draw the l.** il ne sait pas où s'arrêter; **that's where I draw the l.** pour moi c'est la limite à ne pas dépasser; (*warning another person etc*) ça va trop loin; **I draw the l. at lying** je refuse de mentir; (*referring to other people*) je ne tolère pas le mensonge

(b) (*row of people or things*) (*side by side*) ligne *f*, rangée *f*; (*one behind the other*) file *f*; *Am* (*queue*) queue *f*; **twenty cars in a l.** (*one behind the other*) vingt voitures à la file; **l. of traffic** colonne *f* de véhicules; **to put objects in a l.** aligner des objets; **to stand in a l.** (*of person in a queue*) faire la queue; (*of children*) être en rang; *Am* **to stand in l.** faire la queue; **to fall** *or* **get into l., to form a l.** (*of people*) se mettre en ligne; (*of children*) se mettre en rang; (*of soldiers*) former les rangs; **out of l.** désaligné; **to be out of l. with sb** (*in opinions*) être en désaccord avec qn; **to be out of l. with** (*policy etc*) ne pas être conforme avec; *Fig* **to be out of l.** (*in what one does, says*) dépasser les bornes; **to get out of l.** se désaligner; *Fig* (*of political group*) se désolidariser; (*of* *individual*) faire cavalier seul; **your decision is not in l.** *or* **is out of l. with government policy** votre décision n'est pas conforme à *ou* n'est pas en accord avec la politique du gouvernement; **in l. with my decision** conformément à ma décision; **he's in l. for promotion** il est sur la liste des promotions (futures); **to overstep the l.** dépasser la mesure; **to fall into l. with sb's ideas** se conformer aux idées de qn; **to be on the l.** (*of one's job, reputation etc*) être en jeu; **to put one's job/reputation on the l.** mettre son travail/sa réputation en jeu; **to lay one's reputation/life on the l.** (**for sb/sth**) mettre sa réputation/vie en jeu (pour qn/qch); **to lay it on the l.** mettre les choses au point; **to lay it on the l. to sb** parler franchement à qn

(**c**) *Ind* (**assembly**) **l.** chaîne *f* de montage; (**production**) **l.** chaîne de production

(**d**) (*cord etc*), *Naut* ligne *f*, corde *f*, cordage *m*; (*for mooring*) amarre *f*; (*for clothes*) corde *ou* fil *m* à linge; *Fishing* ligne (de pêche); (*in surveying*), *Constr* cordeau *m*; *El* **high-tension l.** ligne à haute tension; *El, Tel* **overhead/underground l.** ligne aérienne/souterraine; **your clothes are out on the l.** tes vêtements sont sur le fil

(**e**) *Tel* ligne *f*; **shared** *or* **party l.** ligne partagée; **hold the l. please** restez en ligne s'il vous plaît, ne quittez pas; **the line's very bad** la communication est mauvaise; **I have Bill on the l.** j'ai Bill en ligne *ou F* au bout du fil; **she's on the other l.** elle est sur l'autre ligne; **all the lines to London are busy** toutes les lignes pour Londres sont occupées; *TV, Rad* **the lines are open from 8 o'clock** (*for viewers and listeners to express their views*) les standards sont ouverts à partir de 8 heures

(**f**) *Mil etc* ligne *f*; **lines** lignes (*de fortification etc*); **the front/rear lines** le front/l'arrière *m*; **to be in the front l.** *Mil* être au front; *Fig* être en première ligne; *Mil etc* **fighting l., l. of battle** ligne de combat *ou* de bataille; **l. of conduct** ligne de conduite; **to be killed in the l. of duty** (*of policeman*) mourir dans l'exercice de ses fonctions; (*of soldier*) mourir au champ d'honneur; *Fig* **to win all along the l.** gagner sur toute la ligne

(**g**) (*direction*) (*of march, communication, route*) ligne *f*; (*of communication, Rail track*) voie *f*; *Mil etc* **l. of advance** direction *f* de marche; **l. of argument** raisonnement *m*; **l. of attack** ligne d'attaque; **l. of fire** (*of gun*) ligne de tir; **l. of sight** ligne de visée; (*on rifle*) ligne de mire; **l. of thought** raisonnement; **l. of vision** ligne de mire; **to work on the same lines as sb** travailler dans la même direction que qn; **to be working on the right lines** être en bonne voie; **what l. are you going to take?** quel parti allez-vous prendre?; **we must take a firm l. with such people** il nous faut être ferme avec des gens comme ça; **along the lines of** dans le genre *ou* style de

(**h**) (*of text*) ligne *f*; (*of poetry*) vers *m*; **first l. of a paragraph** alinéa *m*; **new l.** (*in dictating*) à la ligne; **opening/closing lines of a play** premières/dernières répliques d'une pièce; *Th* **not to know one's lines** ne pas savoir son rôle; **to learn one's lines** apprendre son rôle; **to forget one's lines** oublier son texte, *F* avoir un trou; *F* **just a l. to tell you ...** deux mots pour vous dire ...; *F* **I'll drop you a l.** je vous enverrai un petit mot; **to read between the lines** lire entre les lignes; *Th* **l. rehearsal** lecture *f* collective; *Typ etc* **l. width** longueur *f* de ligne

(**i**) (*information*) *F* **to get a l. on sb** se renseigner sur qn; **I wish I could get a l. on him** j'aimerais avoir des renseignements sur lui; *F* **to get a l. on sth** obtenir des tuyaux sur qch; *F* **to give sb a l. on sth** tuyauter qn sur qch; *F* **don't hand me that l.!** à d'autres!

(**j**) (*family*) lignée *f*, ligne *f*; **male/female l.** ligne masculine/féminine; **long l. of ancestors** longue suite d'ancêtres; **he comes from a long l. of politicians** il descend d'une longue lignée d'hommes politiques; **in (a) direct l.** en ligne directe; **to be descended in (a) direct l. from sb** descendre en droite ligne de qn

(**k**) *F* (*job etc*) métier *m*; **l. of business** genre *m* d'affaires, branche *f*; **what l. (of business) are you in?** dans quelle branche est-ce que tu travailles?; **that's not my l.** ce n'est pas mon rayon; **that's more (in) my l.** (*what I'm good at*) cela est plus dans mes compétences *ou F* mes cordes; (*what I like*) je préfère cela, *F* c'est plus mon truc

(**l**) *Com* (*of goods*) ligne *f*; **a new l. in menswear** une nouvelle ligne pour hommes; **they've brought out a new l. in perfume** ils ont sorti une nouvelle ligne de parfum; *F* **a rice pudding or something in that l.** un gâteau de riz ou quelque chose dans ce genre(-là); *Mktg* **l. addition** ajout *m* à la ligne; *Mktg* **l. extension** extension *f* de ligne; *Mktg* **l. filling** consolidation *f* de ligne; **l. management** (*of l. of products*) gestion *f* de ligne

(**m**) *Fin* **l. of credit** ligne *f* de crédit

(**n**) (*company*) (*of steamers etc*) ligne *f*, compagnie *f*

line² *vt* (**a**) (*piece of paper*) faire des lignes sur; **to become lined** (*of forehead, face*) se rider (**b**) (*border*) border; **to l. the roads with troops** aligner des troupes sur les routes; **the crowd lined the street** la foule s'alignait le long du trottoir; **lined with trees** bordé d'arbres

line³ *vt* (**a**) *Sewing etc* (*coat, jacket etc*) doubler (**with** de); **fur-lined gloves** gants fourrés; *Fig F* **to l. one's own pockets** se servir, se remplir les poches; **to l. a box with paper** tapisser une boîte de papier; **you need something to l. your stomach** tu dois avaler quelque chose avant; *Culin* **to l. a tin with pastry** foncer un moule de pâte; **nest lined with moss** nid garni de mousse; **the walls were lined with books** les murs étaient couverts de livres (**b**) *Tech* (*bearing*) garnir, recouvrir; (*wall, furnace*) revêtir, incruster (**with** de); (*well*) cuveler; **to l. a shaft with metal** blinder un puits

▶ **line up 1** *vtsep* (**a**) (*people, objects*) aligner, mettre en ligne (**b**) *F* (*plan*) prévoir, avoir en vue; **have you got anyone lined up for the job?** avez-vous quelqu'un en vue pour le poste?; **what have you got lined up for us?** qu'est-ce que vous nous préparez? **2** *vi* (*of people*) s'aligner, se mettre en ligne, se ranger; (*form queue*) faire la queue

lineage¹ [ˈlɪnɪɪdʒ] *n* lignée *f*, lignage *m*; **to boast an ancient l.** se vanter d'une longue généalogie; **to trace one's l.** retracer sa généalogie

lineage² [ˈlaɪnɪdʒ] *n* (*for newspaper ad*) lignage *m*

lineal [ˈlɪnɪəl] *adj* linéal; (*descendant, succession*) en ligne directe

lineaments [ˈlɪnɪəmənts] *npl Lit* traits *mpl*, linéaments *mpl*

linear [ˈlɪnɪər] *adj* linéaire; *Math* **l. equation** équation *f* linéaire; **l. measure** mesure *f* linéaire, mesure de longueur; *Phys* **l. expansion** dilatation *f* linéaire

line caption *n* légende *f*

line command *n Comptr* ligne *f* de commande

lined¹ [laɪnd] *adj* (*paper*) réglé, rayé; **deeply l. forehead** front creusé de rides

lined² *adj* (**a**) (*coat*) doublé; (*glove*) fourré; *Fig F* **well l. purse** bourse bien garnie (**b**) *Aut* (*brake*) garni; **steel-l.** (*cylinder*) chemisé d'acier

line drawing *n* dessin *m* au trait

line end hyphen *n* tiret *m* de fin de ligne

line engraving *n* gravure *f* au trait

line feed *n Comptr* changement *m* de ligne; **to do a l.** aller à la ligne

line fishing *n* pêche *f* à la ligne

line manager *n Com* chef *m* hiérarchique

linen [ˈlɪnɪn] *n* (**a**) linge *m*; *Old-fashioned* (*underwear*) petit linge; **dirty l.** linge sale; *Fig F* **don't wash your dirty l. in public** il faut laver son linge sale en famille; **l. basket** panier *m* à linge; **l. cupboard** armoire *f* à linge; **l. room** *or* **store** lingerie *f* (**b**) *Tex* toile *f* (de lin); **l. dress** robe en lin; **the l. industry** l'industrie *f* linière *ou* toilière; **l. paper** papier toilé; **l. sheets** draps fil

line-oriented *adj Comptr* orienté ligne

line-out *n Rugby* touche *f*, remise *f* en jeu

line printer *n Comptr* imprimante *f* par lignes, imprimante ligne

line printout *n Comptr* imprimé *m* ligne à ligne

liner¹ [ˈlaɪnər] *n Naut* (paquebot *m*) transatlantique *m*

liner² *n* (*of cylinder*) fourreau *m*

linesman, *pl* **-men** [ˈlaɪnzmən] *n Tennis* juge *m* de lignes; *Fb* juge *m* de touche

line space *n* interligne *m*

line spacing *n Comptr* interlignage *m*, espacement *m* de lignes

line-up *n* (**a**) *Am* (*queue*) queue *f* (de personnes); (*for identity parade*) rangée *f* de personnes (*assemblées par la police pour l'identification d'un suspect*) (**b**) *Sp* formation *f* (*d'une équipe sur le terrain*); *Rad, TV etc* **this evening's l.** (*of guests, stars*) nos invités ce soir

linework [ˈlaɪnwɜːk] *n Art* dessin *m* au trait

ling¹ [lɪŋ] *n* (*fish*) lingue *f*

ling² *n Bot* bruyère *f* commune

linger [ˈlɪŋgər] *vi* (**a**) (*of person*) s'attarder, traîner (**over** sur); (*of custom, memory*) subsister; **to l. over a meal** s'attarder sur un repas; **a doubt still lingered** un doute subsistait encore dans mon *ou* son *etc* esprit (**b**) (*of invalid*) **to l. (on)** languir, traîner

lingerie [ˈlænʒəri] *n* lingerie *f*

lingering [ˈlɪŋgərɪŋ] *adj* (**a**) (*look*) prolongé; (*doubt*) qui subsiste encore; **I had l. doubts/regrets** je gardais un doute/des regrets; **there was a l. hope that ...** on conservait un vague espoir que ... (**b**) (*illness*) qui traîne, chronique; (*death*) lent; **she died a l. death** la mort l'a emportée lentement

lingo, *pl* **-oes** ['lɪŋgəʊ, -əʊz] *n F* **the l. of the country** (*its language*) la langue du pays; **technical/scientific l.** jargon *m* technique/scientifique
lingua franca ['lɪŋgwə'fræŋkə] *n* langue *f* de communication, langue véhiculaire
linguist ['lɪŋgwɪst] *n* (*student of linguistics*) linguiste *mf*; **to be a good/no l.** être/ne pas être doué pour les langues
linguistic [lɪŋ'gwɪstɪk] *adj* linguistique; **l. atlas** atlas *m* linguistique
linguistically [lɪŋ'gwɪstɪklɪ] *adv* linguistiquement
linguistics [lɪŋ'gwɪstɪks] *n* [ⓘA10,c] linguistique *f*
liniment ['lɪnɪmənt] *n* liniment *m*
lining ['laɪnɪŋ] (*of coat, jacket, dress*) doublure *f*; (*of hat*) coiffe *f*; *Tech* (*of brakes, bearing*) garniture *f*, fourrure *f*; (*of furnace, pump*) chemise *f*; (*of well*) cuvelage *m*; (*of tunnel*) paroi *f*; (*of stomach*) paroi; **l. paper** (*for drawer*) papier *m* pour tiroirs; (*for shelves*) papier pour recouvrir les étagères
link[1] [lɪŋk] *n* **(a)** (*of chain*) chaînon *m*, maillon *m*, maille *f*; *Naut* (*of chain*) paillon *m*
(b) *Fig* (*connection*) lien *m*, liaison *f* (**between** entre); **there's a l. between your health and your job** il y a un lien entre votre santé et votre travail; **air/radio l.** liaison *f* aérienne/radiophonique; **he is a l. between the old world and the new** il sert de trait d'union entre le vieux monde et le nouveau; **he was an unwitting l. in a chain of events which ...** sans le savoir, il était le maillon d'une chaîne d'événements qui ...; **this l. in the chain of events** cet épisode de la série d'événements; **the weak l.** le maillon faible; *TV etc* **l. man** speaker *m*; *Comptr* **l. program** programme *m* éditeur de liens; **l. road** bretelle *f* d'autoroute, bretelle d'accès
(c) *MecE etc* pièce *f* de liaison, tige *f* d'assemblage
link[2] **1** *vt* (*two machines, two cities, two river banks etc*) relier; **a tunnel linking Britain and France** un tunnel reliant la Grande-Bretagne à la France; **the two companies are in no way linked** il n'y a aucun lien entre les deux sociétés; **closely linked** (*of companies, theories etc*) étroitement lié; **to l. negotiations to a discussion of Palestine** lier des négociations à une discussion sur la Palestine; **I always l. him with my stay in ...** je l'associe toujours dans mon esprit à mon séjour à ...; **his name has been linked with several well-known actresses** son nom a été associé à plusieurs actrices bien connues; **it's all linked together** tout cela se tient; **wages linked to the cost of living** salaires indexés sur le coût de la vie; **to l. hands/arms** se donner la main/le bras
2 *vi* **to l. on to sth** s'attacher à qch
▶ **link up 1** *vi* (*of motorways, spaceships, travellers*) se rejoindre (**with** à); (*of cables*) se raccorder (**with** à); (*of TV stations*) établir une liaison; (*of two companies*) s'associer; (*of climbers*) (*with rope*) s'attacher (**with** à); **we'll l. up with you in Paris** nous vous rejoindrons à Paris; **that links up with what we were saying earlier about ...** cela rejoint ce que nous disions précédemment à propos de ...; **the space rocket will l. up with the orbiting satellite** la navette spatiale rencontrera le satellite en orbite; *TV* **we'll be linking up with Germany at 10 o'clock** nous serons en liaison directe avec l'Allemagne à 10 heures; **we'll be linking up with a French company for this project** nous serons associés à une entreprise française pour ce projet
2 *vtsep* (*to network, cabling system etc*) rattacher (**to** à); (*two computers, broadcasting stations*) relier; **the computers are all linked up** les ordinateurs sont tous rattachés les uns aux autres; **they haven't been linked up to the network yet** ils n'ont pas encore été reliés au réseau; **it's all linked up with what's happening at ...** ça a un lien avec ce qui se passe à ...
linkage ['lɪŋkɪdʒ] *n* lien *m*
linked [lɪŋkt] *adj* lié
linking ['lɪŋkɪŋ] *n* enchaînement *m*, liaison *f*; *Astronaut* **l. up** (*of two spaceships*) jonction *f*
links [lɪŋks] *npl* (*usu with sing verb*) (**golf**) **l.** terrain *m ou* parcours *m* de golf
link(-)up *n* lien *m*, liaison *f* (**between** entre); **a satellite l.** une liaison satellite
linnet ['lɪnɪt] *n* linotte *f* (mélodieuse)
linoleum [lɪ'nəʊlɪəm], *F* **lino** ['laɪnəʊ] *n* linoléum *m*
linseed ['lɪnsi:d] *n* graine *f* de lin; **l. oil** huile *f* de lin
lint [lɪnt] *n* **(a)** *Med* pansement *m* ouatiné **(b)** (*of cotton, duster*) peluche *f*
lintel ['lɪnt(ə)l] *n Constr* (*of door, window*) linteau *m*
lint-free *adj* (*cloth*) sans peluches
lion ['laɪən] *n* **(a)** (*animal*) lion *m*; **l.'s** *or* **lions' den** antre *m* du lion; *Fig* **the l.'s share** la part du lion; *Fig* **to put one's head into the l.'s mouth** se fourrer dans la gueule du loup; **l. cub** lionceau *m*; **l. house** fauverie *f*; **l. hunter** chasseur *m* de lion; **l. tamer** dresseur *m* de lion **(b)** *Old-fashioned* (*famous person*) personnage *m* en vue; **a literary l.** sommité *f* littéraire; **the l. of the day** la célébrité du jour
lioness ['laɪənes] *n* (*animal*) lionne *f*
lionheart ['laɪənhɑ:t] *n Hist* (**Richard**) **the L.** Richard Cœur de Lion
lion-hearted ['laɪənhɑ:tɪd] *adj* au cœur de lion
lionize ['laɪənaɪz] *vt* (*person*) porter aux nues
lip [lɪp] *n* **(a)** (*of person*) lèvre *f*; (*of animal*) babine *f*; **to do** *or* **pay l. service to sth** faire semblant de s'intéresser à qch; **the company is paying l. service to the need for a crèche** l'entreprise prétend s'intéresser à la nécessité d'une crèche; *F* **to keep one's l. buttoned (up)** ne pas souffler mot; **button your l.!** pas un mot!; **to smack** *or* **lick one's lips** se lécher les babines; **no complaint ever passes his lips** il ne se plaint jamais; **to read sb's lips** lire sur les lèvres de qn; *F* **read my lips** (*believe what I say*) écoutez-moi bien; **l. synchronization** *or F* **sync** synchronisation *f* labiale
(b) *F* (*impudence*) effronterie *f*, insolence *f*; **none of your l.!, don't give me any of your l.!** ne te fiche pas de moi!
(c) *Med* (*of wound*), *Bot* lèvre *f*; (*of orchid*) labelle *m*
(d) (*rim*) (*of cup, cavity*) bord *m*, rebord *m*; (*of well*) margelle *f*; (*of crater*) bord; (*projection*) rebord, saillie *f*; **pouring l.** (*of jug*) bec *m*
lip-flap *n* (*in dubbing*) lèvres *fpl* non-synchro
lip gloss *n* brillant *m* à lèvres
lipid ['lɪpɪd] *n Med* lipide *m*
liposuction ['laɪpəʊsʌkʃən] *n* liposuccion *f*
-lipped [lɪpt] *suff* **red-l.** aux lèvres rouges
lippy ['lɪpɪ] *adj Am Sl* effronté
lip-read 1 *vi* lire sur les lèvres **2** *vt* **she can l. what you're saying** elle peut lire sur vos lèvres
lip-reader *n* **to be a good l.** bien savoir lire sur les lèvres
lip-reading *n* lecture *f* sur les lèvres
lip salve *n* baume *m* pour les lèvres
lipstick ['lɪpstɪk] *n* rouge *m* à lèvres
lip-synch ['lɪpsɪŋk] *vi* faire une interprétation mimée
liquefaction [lɪkwɪ'fækʃən] *n* liquéfaction *f*
liquefied ['lɪkwɪfaɪd] *adj* **l. natural/petroleum gas** gaz *m* naturel/de pétrole liquéfié
liquefy ['lɪkwɪfaɪ] **1** *vt* (*gas etc*) liquéfier **2** *vi* (*of gas etc*) se liquéfier
liqueur [li:'kɜ:r, lɪ'kjʊər] *n* **(a)** liqueur *f* (de dessert); **l. brandy** fine *f*; **l. chocolates** bonbons *mpl* à la liqueur; **l. glass** verre *m* à liqueur **(b)** (*in winemaking*) liqueur *f* d'expédition
liquid ['lɪkwɪd] **1** *adj* **(a)** liquide; (*sound*) doux, *f* douce, clair; *Hum* **to have a l. lunch** boire de l'alcool en guise de déjeuner **(b)** *Fin* liquide, disponible **(c)** *Ling* (*consonant*) liquide **2** *n* **(a)** liquide *m* **(b)** *Ling* (consonne *f*) liquide *f*
liquid assets *npl Acct* actif *m* liquide, disponibilités *fpl*, liquidités *fpl*
liquidate ['lɪkwɪdeɪt] *vt* **(a)** *Fin* (*company, debt*) liquider; (*capital*) mobiliser; *St Exch* **to l. a position** liquider une position **(b)** (*kill*) liquider
liquidation [lɪkwɪ'deɪʃən] *n Fin* (*of company, debt*) liquidation *f*; (*of capital*) mobilisation *f*; **to go into l.** (*of company*) entrer en liquidation
liquidator ['lɪkwɪdeɪtər] *n* (*of company in liquidation*) liquidateur, -trice
liquid crystal *n Comptr* cristal *m* liquide; **l. display** affichage *m* à cristaux liquides
liquid diet *n* régime *m* ne comprenant que des liquides, *Spec* diète *f* hydrique
liquidity [lɪ'kwɪdɪtɪ] *n* **(a)** (*of substance*) liquidité *f* **(b)** *Fin* liquidité *f*; **l. ratio** ratio *m* de liquidité
liquidize ['lɪkwɪdaɪz] *vt* **(a)** liquéfier **(b)** *Culin* passer au mixeur
liquidizer ['lɪkwɪdaɪzər] *n Culin* mixeur *m*
liquid measure *n* mesure *f* de capacité pour les liquides
liquid oxygen *n* oxygène *m* liquide
Liquid paper® *n* correcteur *m* liquide
liquid paraffin *n* huile *f* de paraffine
liquor ['lɪkər] *n* **(a)** *Am* alcool *m*; **he can't hold** *or* **take his l.** il ne supporte pas l'alcool; **l. store** marchand *m* de vins et spiritueux; **to be the worse for l.** être ivre **(b)** *Old-fashioned Culin* (*of roast*) jus *m*; (*of oysters*) eau *f*
▶ **liquor up** *Am Sl* **1** *vi* se soûler **2** *vtsep* soûler; **to be all liquored up** être soûl
liquorice, *Am* **licorice** ['lɪkərɪs] *n* réglisse *f*
Lisbon ['lɪzbən] *n* Lisbonne *f*
lisle [laɪl] *n Tex* **l. (thread)** fil *m* d'Écosse; **l. stockings** bas *mpl* de fil
lisp[1] [lɪsp] *n* zézaiement *m*, chuintement *m*; **to have a l., to speak with a l.** zézayer, chuinter
lisp[2] *vti* zézayer, chuinter

lissom [ˈlɪsəm] *adj Lit* souple, agile, leste

list¹ [lɪst] *n* liste *f*; *Admin etc* bordereau *m*; **l. of names** liste nominative; *St Exch* **l. of quotations** bulletin *m* de cours; *Fin etc* **l. of investments** (bordereau *m* de) portefeuille *m*; *Fig* **it's (at the) top of my l.** (*I'll do it first*) c'est la première chose que je doive faire; **a fridge is top of my l.** (*to buy*) la première chose que je doive acheter, c'est un frigidaire; **a diamond necklace is top of my l.** (*as gift*) le cadeau que je préférerais avoir est un collier de diamants; **top of the l. for the government is the appointment of …** ce qui figure en tête des priorités du gouvernement c'est de nommer …; *Fig* **it's (at the) bottom of the l.** (*least important*) ce n'est pas à faire en priorité; **you're/your name's not on the l.** vous ne figurez pas sur la liste; **to make out** *or* **draw up a l.** établir *ou* dresser une liste; **to enter sth on a l.** porter qch sur une liste; *Com* **l. price** prix *m* catalogue

list² *vt* **(a)** (*enter in list*) enregistrer; (*names etc*) inscrire *ou* porter sur une liste; **his phone number isn't listed (in the directory)** son numéro de téléphone ne figure pas dans l'annuaire; **to l. on the Stock Exchange** introduire en Bourse **(b)** (*display as list*) **to l. names in alphabetical order** faire une liste des noms par ordre alphabétique; **you can l. the data in various ways** on peut faire apparaître les données de différentes manières **(c)** (*recite, enumerate*) énumérer; **the striking workers listed their demands** les ouvriers en grève énumérèrent leurs revendications

list³ *n Naut* (*leaning*) bande *f*, gîte *f*; **to have a l.** donner de la bande, prendre de la gîte; **l. to starboard** gîte à tribord

list⁴ *vi Naut* donner de la bande **(to starboard** à tribord**)**, prendre de la gîte

list⁵ *n Hist* **lists** (*for tournament*) lice *f*; *Fig* **to enter the lists** entrer en lice (**against sb** contre qn)

listed [ˈlɪstɪd] *adj* **(a)** *St Exch* **l. securities** *or* **stock** valeurs *fpl* admises *ou* inscrites à la cote (officielle); **l. on the Stock Exchange** coté en Bourse; **l. company** société *f* cotée en Bourse **(b)** *Br* **l. monument** monument *m* classé

listed building *n Br Archit* immeuble *m* classé

listen [ˈlɪs(ə)n] *vi* **(a)** écouter; **to l. to sb/sth** écouter qn/qch; **to l. with half an ear** n'écouter que d'une oreille; **you're not listening to a word I'm saying!** tu n'écoutes pas un traître mot de ce que je dis!; **we listened to their daughter singing** nous avons écouté chanter leur fille; **I listened to her singing** je l'ai écoutée chanter

(b) (*pay attention*) faire attention, écouter; **he wouldn't l.** il n'a rien voulu savoir; **to l. to reason** écouter la voix de la raison; **don't l. to him, make up your own mind** n'écoute pas ce qu'il te dit, prends la décision toi-même; **l.! I've got an idea** écoutez, j'ai une idée

(c) will you l. (out) for the phone? peux-tu surveiller le téléphone?; **to l. out for the postman/doctor** tendre l'oreille pour entendre l'arrivée du facteur/docteur; **will you l. out for the baby?** si le bébé pleure est-ce que tu peux aller voir?; **he listened for the sound of the car driving off** il tendit l'oreille pour être sûr d'entendre la voiture quand elle partirait; **she tapped on the wall, listening for a hollow sound** elle cherchait à quel endroit le mur était creux en tapant avec ses doigts

▶ **listen in** *vi Rad* écouter la radio; **to l. in to other people's conversations** écouter les conversations d'autrui; **I'd like to l. in on the discussion** j'aimerais assister à cette discussion

listener [ˈlɪsnər] *n* **(a) to be a good l.** savoir écouter **(b)** *Rad* auditeur, -trice

listening [ˈlɪsnɪŋ] *n* écoute *f*; (*in language learning*) compréhension *f* orale; **l. post** poste *m* d'écoute; **l. time** heure *f* d'écoute; (*length of time*) durée *f* d'écoute

listing [ˈlɪstɪŋ] *n* (*action*) listage *m*; (*position*) classement *m*; *Comptr* listing *m*; **l. paper** papier *m* continu, (papier) listing *m*; **the listings** (*in newspapers*) la rubrique des spectacles; *TV* le programme télévisé; **listings magazine** magazine *m* de spectacles; *Am Tel* **do you have a l. for J. Smith?** est-ce que vous avez un J. Smith dans vos fichiers?

listless [ˈlɪstlɪs] *adj* apathique, sans énergie

listlessly [ˈlɪstlɪslɪ] *adv* sans énergie; **to stare l. into space** regarder dans le vague; **he watched l. as they took away his furniture** il assistait à la saisie de ses meubles le regard vide

listlessness [ˈlɪstlɪsnɪs] *n* apathie *f*

lit [lɪt] *see* = **light²**

litany [ˈlɪtənɪ] *n Rel* litanies *fpl*; *Fig* (*of complaints etc*) litanie

litchi [ˈliːtʃiː, ˈlaɪ-] *n* = **lychee**

liter [ˈliːtər] *n US* = **litre**

literacy [ˈlɪtərəsɪ] *n* alphabétisation *f*; **there's a l. problem in this country** il y a dans ce pays un problème d'alphabétisation; **we want to achieve 90% l. before …** nous nous fixons comme objectif un taux d'alphabétisation de 90% avant …; **l. level** degré *m* d'instruction *ou* d'alphabétisation; **adult l. classes** cours *m* d'alphabétisation pour adultes; **l. campaign** campagne *f* d'alphabétisation; **l. test** test *m* pour mesurer le niveau d'alphabétisation

literal [ˈlɪtərəl] **1** *adj* **(a)** (*translation*) littéral, mot à mot; **he's very l.-minded** il prend tout au pied de la lettre; **in the l. sense of the word** au sens propre du mot; **to take sth in a l. sense** prendre qch au pied de la lettre; **it meant l. starvation for thousands of farmers** cela signifiait que des milliers de fermiers allaient littéralement mourir de faim **(b)** *Math* (*coefficient*) littéral; *Typ* **l. error** coquille *f* **2** *n Typ* coquille *f*

literally [ˈlɪtərəlɪ] *adv* **(a)** (*to translate*) littéralement, mot à mot; **l. speaking** à proprement parler; **to take sth l.** prendre qch au pied de la lettre **(b)** *F* (*as intensifier*) littéralement

literary [ˈlɪtərərɪ] *adj* (*work, agent, criticism etc*) littéraire; **l. man** homme *m* de lettres

literate [ˈlɪtərɪt] *adj* **(a)** qui sait lire et écrire; **computer l.** qui sait utiliser l'informatique **(b)** (*educated*) lettré

literature [ˈlɪtərɪtʃər] *n* **(a)** littérature *f*; **French l.** la littérature française **(b)** (*giving information*) documentation *f*; *Com etc* prospectus *mpl*, brochures *fpl*; **the l. of a subject** la littérature publiée sur une question

lithe [laɪð] *adj* agile

lithium [ˈlɪθɪəm] *n Ch* lithium *m*

lithograph [ˈlɪθəgrɑːf] *n* lithographie *f*

lithographic [lɪθəˈgræfɪk] *adj* lithographique

lithography [lɪˈθɒgrəfɪ] *n* lithographie *f*, procédés *mpl* lithographiques

Lithuania [lɪθjʊˈeɪnɪə] *n* Lituanie *f*

Lithuanian [lɪθjʊˈeɪnɪən] **1** *adj* lituanien **2** *n* **(a)** Lituanien, -ienne **(b)** *Ling* lituanien *m*

litigant [ˈlɪtɪgənt] *Jur* **1** *adj* **l. parties** parties *fpl* plaidantes *ou* en litige **2** *n* plaideur, -euse

litigate [ˈlɪtɪgeɪt] *Jur* **1** *vi* plaider **2** *vt* (*matter, property*) contester, mettre en litige

litigation [lɪtɪˈgeɪʃən] *n Jur* litige *m*; **in l.** en litige; **to go to l.** (*of person*) aller en justice; (*of matter*) être porté en justice

litigious [lɪˈtɪdʒəs] *adj* **(a)** *Jur* litigieux **(b)** *Fml Pej* (*person*) chicaneur

litmus [ˈlɪtməs] *n Ch* tournesol *m*; **l. paper** papier *m* (de) tournesol; **l. test** essai *m* de réaction au papier tournesol; *Fig* test *m* décisif; **this will be a l. test of the government's will** ce sera un test décisif pour juger de la détermination du gouvernement

litre, ***US*** **liter** [ˈliːtər] *n* litre *m*

litter¹ [ˈlɪtər] *n* **(a)** (*in public place*) détritus *mpl*, immondices *fpl*; (*from people eating*) papiers *mpl* gras; **please clear up your l.** (*in park*) veuillez nettoyer vos ordures; **dropping l. is forbidden, no l.** (*on sign*) défense de déposer des ordures **(b)** (*of animal*) portée *f*; **five young at a l.** *or* **in one l.** cinq petits d'une portée **(c)** (*for carrying wounded*) civière *f*; *Hist* (*conveyance*) litière *f*; **to be carried in a l.** être porté en litière **(d)** *Agr* (*of straw etc*) litière *f*; (*of stable etc*) fumier *m*; (*for cat*) litière

litter² **1** *vt* **(a)** (*of person*) (*streets etc*) couvrir de détritus *ou* d'immondices; (*room etc*) mettre en désordre; (*of objects*) couvrir, joncher; **he litters his room with dirty socks** il parsème sa chambre de chaussettes sales; **the streets were littered with bottles** les rues étaient couvertes *ou* pleines de bouteilles; **table littered with papers** table encombrée de papiers; **her works are littered with allusions to the classics** ses écrits sont encombrés d'allusions aux auteurs classiques; **the pages of the book are littered with obscenities** le livre est un tissu d'obscénités; *Fig* **beaches littered with tourists** des plages jonchées de touristes

(b) to l. (down) a horse faire la litière à un cheval; **to l. (down) a stable** étendre de la paille dans une écurie

2 *vi* (*of animal*) mettre bas, avoir une portée

litter basket *n* (*in street*) poubelle *f*, boîte *f* à ordures

litter bin *n* (*in street*) poubelle *f*, boîte *f* à ordures; **throw it in the l.** jette-le à la poubelle

litterbug [ˈlɪtəbʌg] *n F* personne *f* qui jette des détritus n'importe où

litter lout *n Br F* personne *f* qui jette des détritus n'importe où

little [ˈlɪt(ə)l] **1** *adj* **(a)** [①A17,3,a] (*comp* **smaller,** *F* **littler**, *superl* **smallest,** *F* **littlest**) (*small*) petit; **l. girl** petite fille *f*, fillette *f*; **l. ones** (*children*) enfants *mpl*, *F* mioches *mpl*; (*of animal*) petits *mpl*; **l. things like that matter** les petits détails comme cela ont leur importance; *Br Hum* **the l. woman** ma/sa bourgeoise; **I'm fed up with the l. woman role** j'en ai marre d'être la petite femme soumise; **poor l. girl!** pauvre petite!; *F* **a tiny l. house** une toute petite maison; **wait a l. while!** attendez un petit moment!; **a l. something** (*gift*) une babiole;

(*to eat*) un petit quelque chose; **the l. man** (*the average person*) les petites gens *fpl*; *F esp Irish* **the l. people** les lutins *mpl*; **L. Englander** isolationniste *mf*; **the l. finger/toe** le petit doigt/orteil *ou* doigt de pied; *F* **he has you (twisted) round his l. finger** il fait ce qu'il veut de toi; **l. hand** (*of clock*) petite aiguille *f*

(b) (*comp* **less,** *superl* **least**) (*not much*) peu de; **l. money** peu d'argent; **a l. money** un peu d'argent; **I could do with a l. lunch** je mangerais bien un petit quelque chose pour déjeuner; **to gain l. advantage from sth** ne tirer que peu d'avantages de qch; **there is l. point in complaining** ça ne vaut pas vraiment la peine de porter plainte; **it makes l. sense** ça n'a pas beaucoup de sens; **we're only a l. way into the discussion** nous venons juste d'entamer la discussion; *F* **be it ever so l.** si peu que ce soit; **with what l. French I knew** avec le peu de français que je connaissais

(c) *Pej* (*mind*) mesquin; *prov* **l. things please l. minds** à petits esprits, peu n'en faut

2 *n* **(a)** (*comp* **less**; *superl* **least**) peu *m*; **to eat l. or nothing** manger peu ou pas du tout; **he knows very l.** il ne sait pas grand-chose; **he has done l. for us** il n'a pas fait grand-chose pour nous; **I see very l. of her** je ne la vois guère; **given the l. that I know about this subject** étant donné le peu de connaissances que j'ai dans ce domaine; **to think l. of sb** ne pas avoir une haute opinion de qn; **to make** *or* **think l. of sth** faire peu de cas de qch; *prov* **every l. helps** les petits ruisseaux font les grandes rivières; **I can only give you half an hour – every little helps** je ne peux t'accorder qu'une demi-heure – c'est mieux que rien; **l. by l.** peu à peu, petit à petit

(b) a l. more encore un peu; **a l. more and he would have died** il est passé à deux doigts de la mort; **a l. hot** un peu chaud; **for/after a l.** (*time*) pendant/après un certain temps; **he helped him a l.** il l'a aidé un peu; **I was not a l. afraid** j'avais très peur; *Prov* **a l. of what you fancy does you good** il n'y a pas de mal à se faire du bien; **wait a l.!** attendez un peu!

3 *adv* **(a)** (*comp* **less**; *superl* **least**) (*hardly*) peu; **l. known** peu connu; **l. more than an hour ago** il y a à peine une heure; **that's l. less than bribery** ça frise la corruption; **l. short of disgusting/outrageous** quand même un peu dégoûtant/scandaleux; **he studied too l.** il a étudié trop peu, il n'a pas assez étudié; **l. as it matters ...** même si ça n'a pas l'air important ...; **I realized how l. I knew him** je me suis rendu compte à quel point je le connaissais peu; **if you think how l. money they actually have** quand on pense au peu d'argent dont ils disposent; **how l. it really matters in the end!** tout cela est tellement peu important au bout du compte

(b) [①**A72,a,iv**] **he l. knows** *or* **thinks** *or* **suspects ...** il ne se doute guère ...; **l. did I think that ...** je ne pensais pas du tout que ...; **I l. expected him to come** je ne m'attendais guère à ce qu'il vienne

(c) l. enough assez peu; **you eat l. enough as it is** tu manges déjà assez peu comme ça

littoral ['lɪtərəl] *Geog* **1** *adj* littoral **2** *n* littoral *m*

lit up *adj Br Sl* (*drunk*) éméché

liturgical [lɪ'tɜːdʒɪk(ə)l] *adj* liturgique

liturgy ['lɪtədʒɪ] *n* liturgie *f*

livable ['lɪvəb(ə)l] *adj* = **liveable**

live¹ [laɪv] **1** *adj* **(a)** (*animal, person*) vivant, en vie; (*coal*) ardent; **a l. issue** un sujet brûlant; **a restaurant where you order your fish l.** un restaurant où on choisit son poisson vivant; *F* **a real l. filmstar** une vedette de cinéma en chair et en os; **l. bait** appât *m* vivant, vif *m*; **l. birth** enfant *m* né vivant; **l. weight** (*of animal for slaughter*) poids *m* vif *ou* vivant

(b) *TV, Rad* (*broadcast*) en direct; *TV* **recorded before a l. audience** enregistré en public; **a l. performance** un spectacle (en direct); **I never saw a l. performance by the Beatles** je n'ai jamais vu les Beatles en concert; **l. broadcast** retransmission *f* en direct, direct *m*, émission *f* en direct; **l. end** (*of studio*) salle *f* de direct; **l. music** musique *f* live

(c) *Mil* (*ammunition*) actif; (*bomb*) actif, amorcé, armé; (*cartridge*) à balle, réel; *El* **l. wire** câble *m ou* fil *m* sous tension *ou* en charge *ou* chargé; *F* **she's a l. wire** elle est très énergique, *F* elle pète la forme

(d) *Tech* (*load*) roulant, mobile; **l. axle** essieu *m* moteur, pont *m*

2 *adv TV, Rad* **to be broadcast l.** être diffusé en direct; **to play/perform l.** (*of band, comedian*) faire de la scène; **the band hasn't performed l. for nearly ten years** le groupe n'a pas fait de scène depuis presque dix ans; **the show comes l. from New York City** le spectacle nous arrive en direct de New York; **an astronaut speaking l. from Skylab** un astronaute parlant en direct de Skylab

live² [lɪv] **1** *vi* **(a)** (*exist, be alive*) vivre; **as long as my father lived there was no question of selling** tant que mon père était vivant il n'était pas question de vendre; **she lived in the 19th century** elle vécut au 19ème siècle; **we l. in interesting times** nous vivons une époque intéressante; **she'll l. to be 100** elle vivra jusqu'à 100 ans, elle sera centenaire; **she has only a few months to l.** il ne lui reste plus que quelques mois à vivre; **long l. the king!** vive le roi!; **as long** *or* **so long as I l.** tant que je vivrai; *F* **you'll l.!** tu survivras!; *Prov* **you l. and learn** on apprend à tout âge; *prov* **l. and let l.** il faut que tout le monde vive; **this is what I call living!** c'est ce que j'appelle vivre!; **if you've never been to Venice, you haven't lived** si tu n'es jamais allé à Venise tu n'as pas vraiment vécu; **I want to l. a little** je veux profiter de la vie; **his name will l.** son nom restera *ou* sera immortalisé; **this day will l. in history** ce jour fera date dans l'histoire; **he lives by his writing** il vit de sa plume; **he lives by buying and selling antiques** il vit en faisant du commerce d'antiquités; **to l. by one's wits** (*of smuggler etc*) vivre d'expédients; (*of people in hardship*) se débrouiller pour survivre; **to l. by one's beliefs** vivre selon ses croyances; **to l. well** vivre bien; **to l. like a king** *or* **a lord** vivre comme un prince; **to l. in style** mener grand train; **to l. in poverty/fear** vivre dans la pauvreté/peur; **she lived only for her husband** elle n'a vécu que pour son mari; **we're living for the day we emigrate** nous vivons dans l'attente du jour où ous émigrerons; **she was living for the chance of revenge** la perspective de vengeance était sa raison de vivre; **you'll always l. with the guilt** la culpabilité vous poursuivra toute la vie; **you'll just have to l. with the idea!** il faudra que tu te fasses à cette idée!, il faudra que tu t'y fasses; **it's not ideal but I can l. with it** ce n'est pas l'idéal mais je m'y ferai

(b) (*reside*) habiter, vivre; **to l. in Paris** habiter (à) Paris, vivre à Paris; **to l. in France** vivre en France; **to l. in a flat/house** vivre en appartement/dans une maison; **she lives in a fifth floor flat** elle vit dans un appartement au cinquième étage; **to l. at Number 10** habiter au numéro 10; **to l. in the country** habiter *ou* vivre à la campagne; **where do you l.?** où est-ce que vous habitez?; **fish l. in water** les poissons vivent dans l'eau; **the house doesn't seem to be lived in** la maison ne paraît pas habitée; **to l. with** (*boyfriend, parents*) vivre avec; (*friend, parents*) habiter avec; **he lives with his wife and daughter** il vit avec sa femme et sa fille; **he's difficult/easy to l. with** il est difficile/facile à vivre

2 *vt* **to l. a happy life** mener une vie heureuse; **to l. a life of luxury** mener la grande vie; **life is not worth living** la vie ne vaut pas d'être vécue; **it makes life worth living** cela donne une raison de vivre; **to l. a lie** vivre sur un mensonge; *Th* **to l. a part** entrer dans la peau d'un personnage

▶ **live down** *vtsep* **to l. down one's past** faire oublier son passé; **this is awful, I'll never l. it down!** c'est terrible, je n'arriverai jamais à faire oublier

▶ **live in** *vi* **(a)** (*of student*) **I'll be living in next year** je serai interne l'année prochaine **(b)** (*of housekeeper etc*) habiter sur place

▶ **live off** *vipo* **to l. off sth** vivre de qch; **to l. off sb** vivre aux crochets de qn

▶ **live on 1** *vi* (*continue to live*) continuer à vivre; **he lived on for another three years** il vécut encore trois ans; **his memory will l. on** sa mémoire lui survivra **2** *vipo* (*depend on*) **to l. on vegetables** se nourrir de légumes; **to l. on one's capital** vivre sur son capital; **it's not enough to l. on** ce n'est pas suffisant pour vivre; **to earn enough to l. on** gagner de quoi vivre; **they lived on her salary** ils ont vécu sur son salaire

▶ **live out 1** *vi* (*of student*) être externe; (*of servant*) ne pas coucher au domicile de ses patrons **2** *vtsep* (*period, one's life*) passer; **they lived out their lives in poverty** ils vécurent toute leur vie dans la pauvreté; **he won't l. out the year** il ne passera pas l'année; **to l. out one's dreams/fantasies** vivre ses rêves/fantasmes

▶ **live through** *vipo* (*war, hard times etc*) vivre; (*survive*) (*war, drought*) survivre à; **anyone who has lived through times like these will know that ...** quiconque a vécu cette époque sait que ...; **he's unlikely to l. through the winter** il est peu vraisemblable qu'il passe l'hiver

▶ **live together** *vi* vivre ensemble, être en ménage

▶ **live up** *vtas F* **to l. it up** faire la fête

▶ **live up to** *vipo* **to l. up to expectations** (*of person, party, film etc*) tenir ses promesses; **his brother has given him a lot to l. up to** son frère a placé la barre très haut; **it's too much for me to l. up to** on m'en demande trop; **to l. up to one's principles** vivre selon ses principes; **to l. up to one's**

reputation ne pas faillir à sa réputation; **to l. up to one's promise** tenir sa promesse

liveable ['lɪvəb(ə)l] *adj* **(a)** (*life*) supportable **(b) l. in** (*house, room*) (*habitable*) habitable; (*acceptable*) vivable **(c) l. with** (*person*) avec qui on peut vivre; **he's l. with** c'est quelqu'un avec qui on peut vivre

lived-in ['lɪvdɪn] *adj* (*house, flat*) accueillant; *F* (*face*) mûr; **to have a l. feel (to it)** être accueillant

live entertainment *n* spectacle *m*; (*broadcast*) spectacles *mpl* en direct; **nobody goes to see l. any more** plus personne ne va au spectacle de nos jours; **the theatre and other forms of l.** le théâtre et autres formes de divertissement

live-in *adj* (*chauffeur, nanny etc*) logé et nourri; **l. accommodation** (*for staff*) logement *m* à demeure; *Hum* **l. lover** compagnon *m*/compagne *f* (avec qui l'on vit)

livelihood ['laɪvlɪhʊd] *n* moyens *mpl* d'existence, gagne-pain *m inv*; **to earn** *or* **gain one's l.** gagner sa vie *ou* son pain; **tourism is our l.** le tourisme est notre gagne-pain; **to lose one's l.** perdre ses moyens de subsistance

liveliness ['laɪvlɪnɪs] *n* vivacité *f*; *Fin* (*of market*) animation *f*

livelong ['lɪvlɒŋ] *adj Lit* **the l. day** toute la journée, tout le long du jour; **the l. night** toute la nuit

lively ['laɪvlɪ] **1** *adj* **(a)** (*person*) vivant, plein de vie; (*cheerful*) gai; (*colour*) vif; (*music*) gai; (*performance*) vivant; (*imagination*) fertile; (*town, description, party, conversation*) animé; **you're very l. today** tu es en forme aujourd'hui; *F* **to make it** *or* **things l. for sb** rendre la vie dure à qn; **things are getting l.** (*in discussion, meeting etc*) ça chauffe; **to take a l. interest in sth** s'intéresser vivement à qch **(b)** (*car, engine*) nerveux; (*horse*) fougueux; (*boat*) rapide; **that's quite a l. clutch** c'est un embrayage plutôt sensible **2** *adv F* **look l.!** grouille-toi!

▶ **liven up** ['laɪv(ə)n] **1** *vtsep* (*person, meeting etc*) animer, égayer; (*proceedings*) activer; **to l. up the conversation** ranimer la conversation; **you need to l. up your style** vous devriez mettre plus de mouvement dans votre style; **some pictures would l. up the text a bit** quelques photos égaieraient un peu le texte **2** *vi* s'animer, s'activer, *F* se décoincer

liver¹ ['lɪvə*r*] *n Anat, Culin* foie *m*; *Culin* **l. pâté** pâté *m* de foie

liver² *n* (*person*) **fast l.** viveur, -euse, noceur, -euse; **loose l.** libertin *m*, débauché *m*

liveried ['lɪvərɪd] *adj* en livrée

liverish ['lɪvərɪʃ] *adj Fig F* (*irritable*) irritable; **to be** *or* **feel l.** avoir une crise de foie

Liverpudlian [lɪvə'pʌdlɪən] **1** *adj* de Liverpool **2** *n* personne *f* originaire de Liverpool; (*inhabitant*) habitant, -ante de Liverpool

liverwurst ['lɪvəwɜːst] *n Am* saucisse *f* de foie

livery ['lɪvərɪ] *n* **(a)** (*uniform*) livrée *f*; **full l.** grande livrée; **in l.** en livrée; *Br* **l. company** corporation *f* d'un corps de métier (de la cité de Londres) **(b) l. horse** cheval *m* de louage; **l. stables** écuries *fpl* de chevaux de louage

livestock ['laɪvstɒk] [①**A11**,f,ii] *n* bétail *m*

livid ['lɪvɪd] *adj* **(a)** (*angry*) furieux; **to be l. with anger,** *F* **to be absolutely l.** être fou de rage; **it makes me l.!** ça me met en rage! **(b)** (*complexion*) livide, blême; (*sky*) plombé; **a l. bruise** un bleu très marqué

living ['lɪvɪŋ] **1** *adj* (*person*) vivant; **did she have any l. relatives?** avait-elle encore de la famille?; **she is our finest l. artist** c'est notre meilleure artiste contemporaine; **while she was l.** de son vivant; **there is not a l. soul to be seen** on ne rencontre pas âme qui vive *ou F* pas un chat; **he has done more for them than any man l.** il a fait plus pour eux que n'importe qui; **a l. death** une vie pire que la mort; **l. fossil** espèce *f* fossile; *Fig* (*person*) vieux fossile *m*; **to make sb's life a l. hell** faire de la vie de qn un enfer; **l. language** langue *f* vivante; **within l. memory** dans la mémoire des vivants; **l. proof** preuve *f* vivante; **the sculpture had been carved out of the l. rock** la sculpture avait été taillée à même le roc

2 *n* **(a)** (*way of life*) vie *f*; **l. in the country** la vie à la campagne; **to be fond of good l.** être un bon vivant; **fast l. will do him no good** ça ne lui vaut rien de mener une vie débridée

(b) (*livelihood*) vie *f*; **to earn one's l.** gagner sa vie; **to work for one's** *or* **a l.** travailler pour gagner sa vie; **to write for a l.** vivre de sa plume; **what does he do for a l.?** qu'est-ce qu'il fait?, quel est son métier?; **to make a l.** gagner sa vie; **she makes a l. out of it** elle en vit; **l. wage** minimum *m* vital

(c) the l. (*pl*) les vivants *mpl*; **still in the land of the l.** encore vivant *ou* de ce monde

(d) *Br Rel* bénéfice *m*, cure *f*

living conditions *npl* conditions *fpl* de vie

living quarters *npl* (*of person*) logement *m*; (*in ship*) emménagements *mpl*

living room *n* (salle *f* de) séjour *m*

living space *n* espace *m* vital

living standards *npl* niveau *m* de vie

Livy ['lɪvɪ] *n* Tite-Live *m*

lizard ['lɪzəd] *n* lézard *m*; **l. (skin) handbag** sac *m* à main en lézard

llama ['lɑːmə] *n* lama *m*

LLB [elel'biː] *n* (*abbr* **Legum Baccalaureus**) ≈ Bachelier en Droit

LLD [elel'diː] *n* (*abbr* **Legum Doctor**) ≈ Docteur en Droit

LNG [elen'dʒiː] *n* (*abbr* **liquefied natural gas**) GNL *m*

lo [ləʊ] *int Arch, Lit* voici, voilà; *Hum* **lo and behold, there he was** et voilà qu'il était là

loach [ləʊtʃ] *n* loche *f*

load¹ [ləʊd] *n* **(a)** (*burden*) fardeau *m*; (*of lorry, ship etc*) charge *f*, chargement *m*; (*contents of vehicle*) (*of gravel etc*) camion *m*, tombereau *m*; (*of wood*) charge; **useful l.** charge utile; **that's a l. off my mind!** cela m'enlève un poids!; **to share** *or* **spread the l.** (*the work*) répartir le travail; **to shed its l. on the motorway** (*of lorry*) répandre son chargement sur l'autoroute; **l. factor** (*number on plane*) coefficient *m* de remplissage; **l. restraint mesh** filet *m* de retenu de charge; **l. space** coffre *m*; (*of lorry*) plancher *m* de chargement; **l. unit** unité *f* de chargement

(b) *F* (*a lot*) **it's a l. of rubbish** *or* **nonsense** (*novel, theory etc*) c'est n'importe quoi; *Sl* **it's a l. of crap** *or* **bullshit** c'est des conneries; *F* **get a l. of that!** (*look*) vise un peu!; (*listen*) écoute un peu ça!; *F* **he's got loads of them** il en a des quantités *ou* des tas; **loads of money** plein de fric; *F* **we've done it loads of times** on l'a fait plein de fois; *F* **we've got loads of time** nous avons largement le temps

(c) *MecE, El* charge *f*; **safe l.** charge de sécurité; **machine working at full l.** machine qui fonctionne *ou* travaille à pleine charge; **under l.** en charge; *El* **to shed the l.** délester; *El* **l. shedding** délestage *m*

load² **1** *vt* **(a)** (*lorry, ship, camera, gun, film, shell, program*) charger; **to l. passengers** (*of bus*) prendre des voyageurs; **to l. a washing machine/dishwasher** mettre du linge dans le lave-linge/de la vaisselle dans le lave-vaisselle, remplir le lave-linge/lave-vaisselle; **to l. a program into a computer** entrer un programme dans un ordinateur; **he was loaded with shopping** il avait les bras chargés de courses; **loaded with cares** accablé de soucis; **I'm going to l. some more work onto you** je vais vous confier encore un peu de travail; **I don't think it's fair to l. all the work onto one person** je trouve que ce n'est pas juste de donner tout le travail à une seule personne; *MecE* (*spring*) serrer, bander

(b) (*dice*) piper; *Fig* **the dice were loaded in our favour** la situation nous a été favorable

(c) (*in insurance*) (*premium*) majorer

2 *vi Comptr* (*of software etc*) se charger; (*of lorry*) prendre un chargement; (*of ship*) prendre une cargaison; *Aut* **no loading or unloading between 9am and 4pm** (*on sign*) chargement ou déchargement interdits entre 9h et 16h

▶ **load down** *vtsep* **to l. sb down with** (*packages, work, responsability*) surcharger qn de; **to be loaded down with worry** être accablé de soucis; **to be loaded down with anxiety** être rongé d'anxiété

▶ **load up** **1** *vtsep* (*lorry etc*), *Comptr* charger **2** *vi* (*of ship*) prendre une cargaison; (*of lorry etc*) prendre un chargement

loadable ['ləʊdəb(ə)l] *adj* (*software etc*) qui peut se charger, chargeable

load bed *n* (*of truck*) plateau *m* de chargement

load box *n* (*on vehicle*) soute *f*

loaded ['ləʊdɪd] *adj* **(a)** (*lorry, ship, camera, gun etc*) chargé **(b)** (*dice*) pipé; **the situation was loaded against me** la situation m'a été défavorable; **a l. question** une question insidieuse; **a l. word** un mot trop connoté **(c)** *Sl* (*person*) (*wealthy*) richissime; (*drunk*) soûl; *esp Am* (*on drugs*) drogué, camé; **to get l.** (*drunk*) se soûler; (*on drugs*) se shooter

loader ['ləʊdə*r*] *n* **(a)** (*person*) chargeur *m* **(b)** (*device*) chargeuse *f*; *Constr* chargeur *m*

loading ['ləʊdɪŋ] *n* (*of lorry, ship, plane, camera, gun*) chargement *m*; **l. bay** aire *f ou* quai de chargement; **l. charges** coût *m* d'affrètement; **l. procedure** procédure *f* de chargement; **l. ramp** rampe *f* de chargement; **l. time** délai *m* de chargement; (*on ship*) délai d'embarquement

load line *n Naut* ligne *f* de charge

loaf¹, *pl* **loaves** [ləʊf, ləʊvz] *n* **(a)** *Culin* pain *m*; **a l. of bread** un pain; *Prov* **half a l. is better than none** *or* **than no bread** faute de grives on mange des merles **(b)** *F* (*head*) **to use one's l.** faire marcher son ciboulot; **use your l.** fais un peu marcher ton ciboulot

▶ **loaf about, loaf around** *vi* traîner

loafer ['ləʊfər] *n* (**a**) (*person*) fainéant, -ante (**b**) (*shoe*) mocassin *m*
loam [ləʊm] *n Agr, Geol* terreau *m*
loamy ['ləʊmɪ] *adj* (*soil*) riche en terreau
loan[1] [ləʊn] *n* (*money, object*) (*from borrower's point of view*) emprunt *m*; (*from lender's point of view*) prêt *m*; **l. of money** prêt *ou* avance *f* d'argent; **it was very generous of you to give me a l. of that money** c'était très généreux de ta part de me prêter cet argent; **it's a l., you can have it as a l.** je vous le prête; **can I have the l. of ...?** puis-je emprunter ...?; **to give sb a l. of sth** prêter qch à qn; **on l. from the Louvre** prêt du Louvre; **to have sth on permanent l.** disposer de qch en prêt permanent; **she's on l. from Head Office** elle est détachée du bureau central; **the video you want is out on l.** la vidéo que vous voulez est sortie; **to raise a l. on an estate** emprunter de l'argent sur une terre; **to take out a l.** faire un emprunt; **long/short-term l.** prêt/emprunt à long/court terme; **secured l.** prêt/emprunt gagé *ou* garanti; **unsecured l., l. without security** prêt/emprunt à découvert; **l. against securities** prêt *m* sur titres; **l. at interest** prêt *m* à intérêts; **l. to value** rapport *m* entre le capital restant dû et la valeur du bien financé; *Acct* **loans and advances to customers** créances *fpl* clients; **l. agreement** contrat *m* de prêt; *Acct* **l. capital** capital *m* sur prêt; **l. insurance** assurance *f* crédit; **l. maturity** échéance *f* emprunt; *Fin* **l. note** titre *m* d'obligation, titre de créance; **l. risk cover** couverture *f* du risque de crédit; **l. stock** emprunt *m* obligataire; *Acct* **loans outstanding** encours *m*; **l.-back facility** (*in insurance*) possibilité *f* d'emprunt sur le montant de son assurance-vie
loan[2] *vt* prêter (**sth to sb** qch à qn); **loaned by the Louvre** prêt *m* du Louvre
loan account *n Banking* compte *m* de prêt
loan shark *n F* usurier *m*
loan word *n Ling* mot *m* d'emprunt
loath [ləʊθ] *adj* **to be l. to do sth** hésiter à faire qch; *esp Lit* **nothing l.** sans hésiter
loathe [ləʊð] *vt* détester, exécrer; **I l. milk** j'ai horreur du lait, je déteste le lait; **to l. doing sth** détester faire qch
loathing ['ləʊðɪŋ] *n* dégoût *m*, répugnance *f* (**for** pour); **to feel l. for sb** éprouver du dégoût pour qn; **to fill sb with l.** remplir qn de dégoût, dégoûter qn; **to have a l. for milk** avoir horreur du lait
loathsome ['ləʊðsəm] *adj* (*person*) répugnant; (*habit*) détestable; (*smell*) nauséabond; **that was a l. thing to do/say!** c'était vraiment dégoûtant de faire/dire ça!
loathsomeness ['ləʊðsəmnɪs] *n* nature *f* repoussante *ou* dégoûtante
lob[1] [lɒb] *n Sp* lob *m*, chandelle *f*
lob[2] *vt* (**a**) *Tennis, Fb* lober (**b**) *F* (*throw*) balancer; **l. that over!** balance-moi ça!
lobby[1] ['lɒbɪ] *n* (**a**) (*corridor*) couloir *m*, antichambre *f*, vestibule *m*; (*of court*) promenoir *m*; (*of theatre*) entrée *f*; (*of hotel*) hall *m* (**b**) **the l. of the House** (*in Parliament*) = la salle des pas perdus; *Parl* **division lobbies** = vestibules où passent les députés lorsqu'ils se divisent pour voter (**c**) *Pol etc* (*pressure group*) lobby *m*, groupe *m* de pression; **the anti-abortion l.** le groupe de pression contre l'avortement
lobby[2] **1** *vi* (*of pressure group*) faire pression (**in favour of/against** en faveur de/contre); **they're lobbying for tax reform** ils font pression pour obtenir une réforme fiscale **2** *vt esp Pol* (*person*) faire pression sur
lobby correspondent *n Journ* correspondant, -ante de l'assemblée, couloiriste *m*
lobbyist ['lɒbɪɪst] *n Pol etc* lobbyiste *mf*, membre *m* d'un groupe de pression
lobe [ləʊb] *n* (**a**) *Anat* (*of ear etc*) lobe *m* (**b**) *Bot* lobe *m*
lobelia [ləʊ'biːlɪə] *n Bot* lobélie *f*
lobotomize [ləʊ'bɒtəmaɪz] *vt Surg* lobotomiser
lobotomy [ləʊ'bɒtəmɪ] *n Surg* lobotomie *f*
lobster ['lɒbstər] *n* homard *m*; **spiny l.** langouste *f*; **l. boat** homardier *m*; (*for spiny lobster*) langoustier *m*; **l. pot** casier *m* à homards; (*for spiny lobster*) casier à langoustes
local ['ləʊk(ə)l] **1** *adj* local; **the l. doctor** le médecin du quartier; **a matter of l. politics** une question de politique locale; **they voted for the l. man** ils ont voté pour le candidat local; *Fin, Com* **l. bill** effet *m* sur place; *Tel* **l. call** communication *f* locale; **l. channel** canal *m* local, chaîne *f* locale; **l. colour** couleur *f* locale; **l. edition** édition *f* locale; **l. radio** radio *f* locale; **l. radio station** station *f* de radio locale; **l. showers** averses *fpl* éparses; **l. television** télévision *f* locale; **l. train** (train *m*) omnibus *m*; **l. wine** vin *m* du pays

2 *n* (**a**) **the locals** (*people*) les gens *mpl ou* les habitants *mpl* du coin

(**b**) *Surg F* (*anaesthetic*) anesthésie *f* locale

(**c**) *F* **the l.** (*pub*) le pub du coin; (*in France*) le café du coin; **this is my l.** c'est le pub où je vais régulièrement
local anaesthetic *n Surg* anesthésie *f* locale; **to give sb a l.** faire une anesthésie locale à qn
local area network *n Comptr* réseau *m* local
local authorities *npl Pol* autorités *fpl* locales *ou* régionales
local bus *n Comptr* bus *m* local; **l. card** carte *f* de bus local; **l. disk** disque *m* connecté au bus local
locale [ləʊ'kɑːl] *n* (*of events*) lieu *m*; **the l. for a film** le lieu de tournage d'un film
local government *n Pol* (*in county*) ≈ l'administration *f* départementale; (*in town*) ≈ l'administration communale
locality [ləʊ'kælɪtɪ] *n* (*neighbourhood*) endroit *m*, lieu *m*; **in our l.** (*part of town*) dans notre quartier; (*out of town*) dans notre région; **in the general l. of the incident** sur les lieux de l'incident; **a man was seen in the l. at around 8 o'clock** un homme a été vu dans les environs vers 8 heures
localize ['ləʊkəlaɪz] *vt* (*epidemic etc*) localiser; **to become localized** (*of disease, pain*) se localiser (**in** dans)
localized ['ləʊkəlaɪzd] *adj* localisé
locally ['ləʊkəlɪ] *adv* localement; (*to live, be well known, work etc*) dans le quartier; **l. produced wine** vin du pays; **we get them printed l.** nous les faisons imprimer sur place; **I prefer to shop l.** je préfère faire mes courses dans le quartier; **he set up in business l.** il a monté une affaire sur place
local news *n* informations *fpl* régionales
local paper *n* journal *m* local
local time *n* heure *f* locale; **6am l.** 6 heures du matin heure locale
locate [ləʊ'keɪt] **1** *vt* (**a**) (*to find*) localiser, situer; *El* (*fault etc*) repérer, localiser; **to l. sth on a map** situer qch sur une carte; *Naut* **to l. a ship** déterminer la position d'un navire (en mer) (**b**) (*to situate*) situer; **the new shopping centre is located in the old market square** le nouveau centre commercial est situé sur la place du vieux marché **2** *vi* (*of company etc*) s'installer
location [ləʊ'keɪʃən] *n* (**a**) (*site, place*) emplacement *m*; *Mktg* **l. pricing** fixation *f* des prix selon l'endroit (**b**) *Cin* **to be on l.** tourner en extérieur; **filmed on l.** filmé en extérieur; **l. marks** (*in studio*) points *mpl* de repère au sol; **l. shot** plan *m* en extérieur; **l. shots** extérieurs *mpl* (**c**) (*finding*) localisation *f*; *El* (*of fault etc*) repérage *m*
locative ['lɒkətɪv] *adj, n Gram* locatif *m*
loch [lɒx] *n Scot* lac *m*; **sea l.** bras *m* de mer, fjord *m*
lock[1] [lɒk] *n* (**a**) (*on door etc*) serrure *f*; (*padlock*) cadenas *m*; **under l. and key** sous clef; (*of person*) sous les verrous; *Comptr* (*in network*) verrouillage *m*, blockage *m*; *Comptr* **l. inhibit** contre-verrou *m*

(**b**) *MecE* verrou *m*, *pl* -ous

(**c**) (*on gun*) platine *f*; **we sold it l. stock and barrel** nous avons tout vendu sans exception; **we bought the whole estate l. stock and barrel** nous avons acheté toute la propriété; **he swallowed the story l. stock and barrel** il a tout avalé; **the motion was rejected l. stock and barrel** la motion a été rejetée en bloc

(**d**) (*in wrestling*) étreinte *f*, clef *f*; **arm l.** clef de bras

(**e**) *Aut etc* angle *m* de braquage; **on full l.** braqué au maximum; **l. ring** jonc d'arrêt *m*; **l. turns** tours *mpl* de volant

(**f**) (*on canal*) écluse *f*; **l. chamber** sas *m* (d'écluse); **l. gate** porte *f* d'écluse

(**g**) *Rugby* **l.** (**forward**) avant *m* de deuxième ligne
lock[2] **1** *vt* (**a**) fermer à clef, verrouiller; **behind locked doors** à huis clos; **to l. sb in a room** enfermer qn dans une chambre; **to l. sth (away) in a drawer** enfermer qch dans un tiroir; **to l. valuables (away) in a safe** mettre des objets de valeur dans un coffre

(**b**) (*steering wheel*) (*disable*) bloquer; (*put on full lock*) braquer à fond; (*machine parts*) enclencher; (*computer, keyboard, files*) verrouiller; **his jaws were tightly locked** il avait les dents serrées; **to be locked in each other's arms** se tenir étroitement enlacés; **to be locked in a passionate embrace** être passionnément enlacés; *Fig* **to be locked in sb's deadly embrace** être pris dans les griffes de qn; **to be locked (together) in a struggle** (*of people*) être engagés corps à corps dans une lutte; **to be locked in negotiation/dispute** être enfermé dans une négociation/un conflit; *Fig* **to l. horns with the enemy** livrer bataille avec l'ennemi; *Fig* **they have locked horns** (*of people*) ils sont en désaccord

2 *vi* (**a**) (*of wheels etc*) se bloquer; **the door locks on the inside** la porte se ferme de l'intérieur; **the door locks automatically** la porte se verrouille automatiquement; **the parts l. into each other** les parties s'enclenchent l'une dans l'autre

(**b**) *Aut* **to l. left/right** braquer à gauche/à droite

lock³ *n* (*of hair*) mèche *f*, boucle *f*; *Arch, Lit* **locks** cheveux *mpl*, chevelure *f*

▶ **lock in** *vtsep* **(a)** (*person*) enfermer à clef, mettre sous clef; **to get locked in** se faire enfermer; **to l. oneself in** s'enfermer **(b) to be locked in** (*to pension scheme etc*) ne pas avoir la possibilité de changer; (*to contract*) être lié; **to be locked into a company** (*as a source of supply etc*) être totalement dépendant d'une société; *St Exch, Fin* **to l. in a hedge** immobiliser une couverture

▶ **lock off** *vtsep Typ, Comptr* débloquer; (*bad sector*) interdire l'accès à; **this key locks the caps on and off** cette touche bloque et débloque les majuscules

▶ **lock on** *vtsep Typ, Comptr* bloquer, verrouiller; **l. the caps on before you start typing** bloque les majuscules avant de commencer à taper

▶ **lock on to** *vipo* (*of radar etc*); *Fig* s'accrocher à

▶ **lock out** *vtsep* **(a) to l. sb out** enfermer qn dehors; **I found myself locked out** en rentrant j'ai trouvé la porte fermée (à clef); **I've locked myself out (of my room)** je me suis enfermé dehors **(b)** *Ind* (*workforce*) lock-outer

▶ **lock up 1** *vtsep* **(a)** (*sth*) mettre sous clef; (*sb, sth*) enfermer; (*in jail*) mettre sous les verrous; (*house*) fermer à clef; **to l. a house up for the winter** barricader une maison pour l'hiver; **he should be locked up!** il faudrait l'enfermer! **(b)** *Fin* (*capital*) immobiliser, bloquer, engager **2** *vi* **it's time to l. up** c'est l'heure de fermer; **to l. up for the night** fermer le soir jusqu'au lendemain

locker ['lɒkər] *n* (*for luggage, in school*) casier *m*; *Naut* coffre *m*; *Av* **overhead l.** coffre à bagage; **l. room** (*in factory, sports pavilion etc*) vestiaire *m*; **l.-room jokes/language** plaisanteries grossières/langage grossier

locket ['lɒkɪt] *n* médaillon *m*

locking ['lɒkɪŋ] *adj attrib* **(a)** *Aut* **l. bar** barre *f* antivol; *MecE etc* **l. device/mechanism** dispositif *m*/mécanisme *m* de verrouillage; **a car with central l.** une voiture avec fermeture centralisée des portes **(b)** *Comptr* **l. connector** connecteur *m* autobloquant; **l. device** dispositif *m* de verrouillage

locking on *n Electron* (*of radar etc*) accrochage *m* (**to a target** d'un objectif)

locking up *n* mise *f* sous clef; (*of house etc*) fermeture *f*; *Fin* (*of capital*) immobilisation *f*

lockjaw ['lɒkdʒɔː] *n* tétanos *m*; **to have l.** avoir le tétanos

lock-keeper *n* (*on canal*) gardien *m* d'écluse, éclusier *m*

locknut ['lɒknʌt] *n* contre-écrou *m*, *pl* contre-écrous

lock-out *n* lock-out *m inv*

locksmith ['lɒksmɪθ] *n* serrurier *m*

lock-to-lock *adv Aut* de butée à butée

lockup ['lɒkʌp] *n* **(a)** *Br* (*for storage*) remise *f*; **l. (garage)** box *m* **(b)** *F* (*police cells*) violon *m*, bloc *m* **(c)** *Aut* (*of wheel*) lock-up *m*; (*gear*) rapport *m* bloqué; **l. clutch** embrayage *m* de prise directe

loco¹ ['ləʊkəʊ] *n F* (*train*) loco *f*

loco² *adj US F* (*mad*) fou, *f* folle, *F* dingue

locomotion [ləʊkə'məʊʃən] *n* locomotion *f*

locomotive [ləʊkə'məʊtɪv] **1** *adj* locomotif, -ive; *Anat* locomoteur, -trice **2** *n Rail* locomotive *f*

locum ['ləʊkəm] *n Br* **l. (tenens)** ['tenenz] (*for doctor, cleric*) remplaçant, -ante; **to take a l. job** faire un remplacement, prendre un emploi de remplaçant; **she's working as a l. in a hospital in London** elle fait un remplacement dans un hôpital de Londres

locus, *pl* **loci** ['ləʊkəs, 'ləʊsaɪ, 'ləʊsiː] *n* **(a)** *Math* lieu *m* géométrique **(b)** *Biol* (*of gene*) locus *m*

locust ['ləʊkəst] *n* **(a)** *Ent* locuste *f*, sauterelle *f* **(b)** *Bot* **l. bean** caroube *f*; **l. (tree)** (*carob tree*) caroubier *m*; (*false acacia*) robinier *m*

locution [ləʊ'kjuːʃən] *n* locution *f*

lode [ləʊd] *n Geol, Min* filon *m*, veine *f*

lodestar ['ləʊdstɑːr] *n* **(a)** étoile *f* directrice; **the l.** l'étoile polaire **(b)** *Fig* référence *f*

lodestone ['ləʊdstəʊn] *n Miner* aimant *m* naturel

lodge¹ [lɒdʒ] *n* **(a)** (*for concierge etc*) loge *f*; **keeper's l.** maison *f* de garde-chasse; **(gate) l.** (*to estate*) pavillon *m* d'entrée, pavillon du garde; *Univ* **master's l.** résidence *f* du directeur du collège; **shooting l.** pavillon *m* de chasse; **l. keeper** portier *m* **(b)** (*free masons'*) loge *f*, atelier *m*; **the Grand L. of France** le Grand Orient (de France); **l. (meeting)** tenue *f* **(c)** (*of otter*) terrier *m*; (*of beaver*) hutte *f* **(d)** (*of Native Americans*) hutte *f*, wigwam *m*

lodge² 1 *vt* **(a)** (*accommodate*) loger, héberger

(b) (*deposit*) déposer, remettre; (*money*) consigner, déposer (**with sb** chez qn); (*bonds*) déposer (**with a bank** dans une banque); **securities lodged as collateral** titres déposés *ou* remis en nantissement; *Jur* **to l. an appeal** interjeter appel, faire appel; **to l. a complaint** déposer une plainte; **to l. a complaint against sb** porter plainte contre qn

2 *vi* **(a)** (*of person*) loger; **to l. with sb** (*rent room from*) louer une chambre *ou* des chambres chez qn; (*have meals provided*) être en pension chez qn

(b) (*of thing*) rester, se loger; **a fishbone lodged in his throat** il s'est coincé une arête dans le gosier; **a bullet lodged close to his spine** il a reçu une balle qui est allée se loger près de sa colonne vertébrale; **the words had lodged in her memory** les mots étaient gravés dans sa mémoire

lodger ['lɒdʒər] *n* locataire *mf* (*en meublé*); (*who has meals provided*) pensionnaire *mf*; **to take (in) lodgers** louer des chambres; (*provide meals too*) prendre des pensionnaires

lodging ['lɒdʒɪŋ] *n* **(a)** (*room etc*) logement *m*; **to find a night's l.** trouver où coucher pour la nuit; *Am* **l. industry** industrie *f* hôtelière **(b)** (*usu pl*) **lodgings** logement *m*, appartement *m* meublé, *Arch* logis *m*; **to live** *or* **be in lodgings** loger *ou* habiter en garni *ou* en (hôtel) meublé; **l. house** hôtel *m* garni **(c)** (*of money, securities etc*) dépôt *m*, consignation *f*, remise *f*; *Jur* (*of complaint*) déposition *f*; (*of appeal*) interjection *f*

loft¹ [lɒft] *n* (*attic*) grenier *m*, soupente *f*; (*in church, hall etc*) galerie *f*, tribune *f*; **l. conversion** aménagement *m* d'un grenier; **we're thinking of doing a l. conversion** nous avons l'intention d'aménager le grenier

loft² *vt* (*ball*) donner de la hauteur à

loftily ['lɒftɪlɪ] *adv* **(a)** (*situated*) en hauteur **(b)** *Pej* (*to reply*) de manière hautaine

loftiness ['lɒftɪnɪs] *n* **(a)** (*of mountain etc*) hauteur *f* **(b)** *Pej* (*of person*) arrogance *f*, hauteur *f*

lofty ['lɒftɪ] **1** *adj* **(a)** (*mountain, tree, building etc*) haut, élevé **(b)** *Pej* (*person, manner*) hautain **(c)** (*aim, desire etc*) noble; (*style*) relevé, soutenu; **the l. words in which the argument is expressed** le style relevé de l'argumentation **2** *n F* (*tall person*) **hello, l.!** salut, mon grand!

log¹ [lɒg] *n* **(a)** (*of wood*) bûche *f*; (*esp for building*) rondin *m*; *Fig* **to sleep like a l.** dormir comme une souche; **l. jam** embâcle *m* de bûches; *Fig* (*in talks etc*) impasse *f* **(b)** (*record*) carnet *m* de route *ou* de bord; *Naut* journal *m*, *pl* -aux; *Av* carnet de vol; **ship's l.** journal de bord; **to write up the l.** noter les détails du voyage **(c)** *Naut* (*for measuring speed*) loch *m*

log² *vt* **(a)** (*order, in accounts*) enregistrer; *Naut etc* porter au journal; (*results etc*) noter sur un registre; (*of computer*) enregistrer; **the ship's arrival at Southampton was logged at 0800 hours** l'arrivée du bateau à Southampton a été portée au journal à 0800 heures; *Av* **to l. (up) 1,000 hours** inscrire 1 000 heures de vol **(b)** (*wood*) tronçonner, débiter en bûches **(c) the ship logged 15 knots** le navire filait à 15 nœuds

log³ *n Math F* logarithme *m*; **l. tables** tables *fpl* de logarithmes

▶ **log in** *vi, vtsep Comptr* = **log on**

▶ **log off** *Comptr* **1** *vi* (*of user*) sortir, terminer *ou* clore une session **2** *vtsep* faire sortir

▶ **log on** *Comptr* **1** *vi* (*of user*) entrer, ouvrir une session; (*to remote system*) entrer en communication; **to l. to a system** se connecter à un système; **to l. on to a data base** entrer dans une base de données **2** *vtsep* faire entrer

▶ **log out** *vi, vtsep Comptr* = **log off**

loganberry ['ləʊgənberɪ] *n* (*fruit*) ronce-framboise *f*, *pl* ronces-framboises

logarithm ['lɒgərɪθ(ə)m] *n* logarithme *m*

logarithmic [lɒgə'rɪθmɪk] *adj* **(a)** (*curve*) logarithmique; (*paper*) à divisions logarithmiques **(b) l. table** table *f* des logarithmes

logbook ['lɒgbʊk] *n* **(a)** (*record*) registre *m*; *Av* carnet *m* de vol; *Aut* (*personal record*) carnet de route; *Naut* journal *m* de bord; (*of machine*) journal de travail; *Rad* carnet d'écoute **(b)** *Br Aut* (*official documents*) ≈ carte *f* grise

log cabin *n* hutte *f* en rondins, cabane *f* en bois

log fire *n* feu *m* de bois

logger ['lɒgər] *n* bûcheron *m*

loggerheads ['lɒgəhedz] *n F* **to be at l. with sb** avoir un différend avec qn (**about** au sujet de); **they were constantly at l.** ils se disputaient tout le temps; **his views were at l. with …** ses opinions étaient en contradiction avec …

loggia ['lɒdʒɪə] *n Archit* loge *f*, loggia *f*

logging ['lɒgɪŋ] *n* **(a)** (*of details, events*) inscription *f* dans un journal; *Comptr* enregistrement *m*; **l. of an order** enregistrement *m* d'une commande **(b)** (*felling timber etc*) exploitation *f* forestière; **l. camp** camp *m* forestier

log hut *n* hutte *f* en rondins, cabane *f* en bois

logic ['lɒdʒɪk] *n* **(a)** logique *f*; **I don't see the l. of it** je ne vois pas la logique (dans tout cela) **(b)** *Comptr* **l. analyser** analyseur *m* logique; **l. card** carte *f* logique; **l. chip** puce *f* logique; **l. circuit** circuit *m* logique; **l. gate** porte *f* logique; **l. seeking** recherche *f* logique

logical [ˈlɒdʒɪk(ə)l] *adj* (*conclusion, person*), *Comptr* logique; **do be l.!** essaie d'être logique!; **l. access control** contrôle *m* d'accès logique; **l. access protection** protection *f* d'accès logique; **l. drive** unité *f* logique; **l. file** fichier *m* logique; **l. log** journal *m* logique; **l. operator** opérateur *m* logique
logically [ˈlɒdʒɪklɪ] *adv* logiquement
logic-chopper *n* ergoteur, -euse
logic-chopping *n* ergotage *m*
logistic [lɒˈdʒɪstɪk], **logistical** [lɒˈdʒɪstɪk(ə)l] *adj* logistique
logistics [lɒˈdʒɪstɪks] *n* [①A10,c] *Mil* logistique *f*; **the l. of the situation** les données logistiques de la situation
log line *n Naut* ligne *f* de loch
logo [ˈləʊgəʊ] *n* sigle *m*, logo *m*; **l. page/screen** (*of software package*) page *f*/écran *m* d'accueil
logoff [ˈlɒgɒf] *n* **l. timed at ...** fin de session enregistrée à ...
logon [ˈlɒgɒn] *n* ouverture *f* de session; **l. timed at ...** ouverture de session prévue à ...
logrolling [ˈlɒgrəʊlɪŋ] *n* **(a)** transport *m* des billes à la rivière **(b)** *US Pol* alliance *f* politique dans un but intéressé
log running *n* flottage *m* du bois
log transporter *n* fardier *m*
logwood [ˈlɒgwʊd] *n* (*wood*) (bois *m* de) campêche *m*; (*tree*) campêcher *m*
loin [lɔɪn] *n* **(a)** *Anat Lit* **loins** reins *mpl*; *Lit* **sprung from the loins of ...** sorti des reins de ... **(b)** *Culin* (*of mutton, veal*) filet *m*; (*of veal*) longe *f*; (*of mutton*) carré *m*; (*of beef*) aloyau *m* et faux-filet; (*of pork*) échine *f*, filet; **l. chop** côtes *fpl* premières
loincloth [ˈlɔɪnklɒθ] *n* pagne *m*
loiter [ˈlɔɪtər] *vi* (*suspiciously*) rôder; (*delay*) s'attarder (en route); **stop loitering and hurry up** arrête de flâner, dépêche-toi; *Jur* **to l. (with intent)** rôder (d'une manière suspecte dans un endroit fréquenté)
loitering [ˈlɔɪtərɪŋ] *n Jur* **l. with intent** délit *m* d'intention
loll [lɒl] *vi* **(a)** (*of person*) être étendu (paresseusement); **lolling back in an armchair** affalé dans un fauteuil **(b)** (*of tongue*) **to l. (out)** pendre
▶ **loll about, loll around** *vi* (*of person*) paresser, fainéanter
lollipop [ˈlɒlɪpɒp] *n* (*candy*) sucette *f*; (*ice*) glace *f* à l'eau; (*chocolate*) esquimau® *m*; *Br F* **l. man/lady** = contractuel, -elle qui aide les écoliers à traverser la rue
lollop [ˈlɒləp] *vi esp Br F* **to l. along** courir lourdement; **the rabbit lolloped off** le lapin s'éloigna en bondissant
lolly [ˈlɒlɪ] *n* **(a)** *F* (*candy*) sucette *f*; (*ice*) glace *f* à l'eau; (*chocolate*) esquimau® *m* **(b)** *Austr F* (*sweet*) bonbon *m* **(c)** *Br Sl* (*money*) fric *m*, flouze *m*
Lombard rate [ˈlɒmbaːd] *n Banking* taux *m* Lombard
London [ˈlʌndən] *n* Londres; **a L. street** une rue de Londres; **a L. bus/taxi** un bus/taxi londonien
Londoner [ˈlʌndənər] *n* Londonien, -ienne; **a L. born and bred** un Londonien pure souche
London pride *n Bot* saxifrage *f* ombreuse
lone [ləʊn] *adj esp Lit* (*person, thing*) solitaire, seul; (*place*) isolé, désert; **a l. parent** un parent isolé; *Fig* **to play a l. hand** agir tout seul, être seul contre tous
loneliness [ˈləʊnlɪnɪs] *n* (*of house, person, village, political position*) isolement *m*; (*feeling*) solitude *f*; **with only the l. of old age to look forward to** avec la seule perspective de vieillir dans la solitude
lonely [ˈləʊnlɪ] *adj* (*person,*) seul; (*life, job*) solitaire; (*place, farmhouse*) isolé; **a l. figure** une silhouette; *Fig* (*politician etc*) une figure isolée; *Fig* **to travel a l. road** avoir un parcours solitaire; **to feel very l.** se sentir bien seul; **are you feeling l.?** vous vous sentez seul?; **life is very l. since the children left home** la vie est bien morne depuis que les enfants ont quitté la maison
lonely hearts club *n* club *m* des cœurs solitaires
lonely hearts column *n* rubrique *f* des cœurs solitaires, rubrique rencontre
loner [ˈləʊnər] *n* solitaire *mf*
lonesome [ˈləʊnsəm] **1** *adj Am* solitaire, seul; **to feel l.** se sentir seul **2** *n F* **to be on one's l.** être seul avec soi-même; **to do sth all on one's l.** faire qch tout seul
Lone Star State *n US* Texas *m*
lone wolf *n Fig* solitaire *m*; **to be a bit of a l.** être un peu solitaire
long[1] [lɒŋ] (**longer** [ˈlɒŋgər]; **longest** [ˈlɒŋgɪst]) **1** *adj* **(a)** (*in size*) long, *f* longue; **how l. is the table?** quelle est la longueur de la table?; **to make sth longer** allonger qch, rallonger qch; **to be six metres l.** faire six mètres de long; **a 20 foot l. swimming pool** une piscine de 6 mètres de long; *F* **to be l. on charm/good ideas** *etc* être plein de charme/bonnes idées *etc*; **l. in the leg** aux longues jambes; *F* **l. in the tooth** (*old*) vieux, *f* vieille; **to go the l. way round** (*to a place*) prendre le chemin le plus long; *Fig* **the best by a l. way** de loin le meilleur; *Typ* **l. dash** trait *m*; **a l. face** un visage allongé; *Fig* **to have a l. face, to pull a l. face** faire la tête, faire une tête de six pieds de long; **l. lease** bail *m* emphytéotique; **l. service award** prime *f* d'ancienneté; **patience is not my l. suit** la patience n'est pas mon fort; **l. trousers** (*for boy*) pantalon *m* long

(b) (*in time*) long, *f* longue; **it will take a l. time** cela prendra longtemps, ce sera long; **a l. time ago** il y a (bien) longtemps; **it's a l. time since I was (last) in Paris** ça fait longtemps que je ne suis pas allé à Paris; **I've been wanting to go for a l. time** ça fait longtemps que j'ai envie d'y aller; **to wait for a l. time** attendre longtemps; **it's been a l. night** la nuit a été longue; **we've all had a l. day** nous avons tous eu une longue journée; **we're going away for a l. weekend** nous partons pour un week-end prolongé *ou* long *ou* grand week-end; **the days are getting longer** les jours rallongent; **three days at the longest** trois jours (tout) au plus; **it was a l. haul** (*of journey*) le voyage a été long; *Fig* (*to complete this project, make a full recovery from illness etc*) c'était un travail de longue haleine; **it looks like being a l. job** cela va prendre du temps; **to take the l. view of sth** voir qch à long terme; **in the l. term** *or* **run** à long terme, à longue échéance; **it'll all be all right in the l. run** tout s'arrangera avec le temps; **to have a l. memory** avoir (une) bonne mémoire; **to have a l. talk with sb** parler longuement avec qn; **he took a l. drink from the flask** il but une longue gorgée à la bouteille; **to take a l. hard look at sth** fixer longuement qch; **l. player** (*record*) longue durée *f*; *Med* **l. stay** (lit *m* de) long séjour *m*; *Mil* **l.-service men** engagés *mpl* à long terme; *Univ* **the l. vacation** les grandes vacances

(c) *Com* **l. hundred** cent vingt; **l. dozen** treize; *St Exch* **l. position** position *f* acheteur *ou* longue

2 *n* **(a) the l. and the short of the matter is that ...** le fin mot de l'affaire c'est que ...; **that's the l. and the short of it!** un point c'est tout!; **(b)** *St Exch* (*bill*) effet *m* à longue échéance

3 *adv* **(a)** [①B29-30,11] (*for a long period*) longtemps; **I didn't wait l.** je n'ai pas attendu longtemps; **l. live the King/Queen!** vive le roi/la reine!; **as l. as** (*for the same length of time as*) aussi longtemps que; (*during the time that*) tant que; (*provided that*) du moment que; (*since, seeing that*) puisque; **I followed him for as l. as I could** je l'ai suivi aussi longtemps que j'ai pu; **as l. as I am alive** tant que je vivrai; **I'll never forget that day for as l. as I live** jamais de ma vie je n'oublierai ce jour; **as l. as you're happy** (*provided that*) du moment que tu es heureux; **you can take my car so l. as you're careful** tu peux prendre ma voiture du moment que tu es prudent; **to look at sb/sth l. and hard** fixer qn/qch longuement; *Fig* **to look at sth l. and hard** se pencher longuement sur qch; **I've thought l. and hard about this and ...** j'y ai longuement réfléchi et ...; **he was not l. in coming** il n'a pas tardé à venir; **before l.** avant peu, sous peu; **for l.** pendant longtemps; **I won't stay for l.** je ne resterai pas longtemps; **it won't take l.** cela ne prendra pas longtemps, cela ne sera pas long; **she won't be l.** (*will be here soon*) elle ne tardera pas; (*will soon have finished*) elle a bientôt fini; **is he going to be l.?** (*in arriving, finishing*) il en a pour longtemps?; **are you going to be much longer?** tu en as encore pour longtemps?; *F* **so l.!** au revoir!, à bientôt!

(b) (*since sometime in the past*) depuis longtemps; **I have l. been convinced of it** j'en suis convaincu depuis longtemps; **they have l. since left England** ça fait longtemps qu'ils ont quitté l'Angleterre

(c) how l.? combien de temps?; **how much longer will he be?** (*until ready etc*) il en a encore pour longtemps?; (*until he arrives*) dans combien de temps sera-t-il là?; **how l. have you known her?** depuis combien de temps est-ce que tu la connais?

(d) l. before/after longtemps avant/après; **not l. before/after** peu de temps avant/après; **l. before I met you** longtemps avant que je te rencontre; **l. ago** il y a longtemps; **not (very) l. ago** il n'y a pas longtemps; **in the days of l. ago** autrefois, *Lit* jadis

(e) (*for the duration of*) **all day/night l.** tout le long du jour/de la nuit, pendant toute la journée/la nuit; **all winter l.** tout au long de l'hiver

(f) I could no longer hear him je ne l'entendais plus; **she no longer lives here** elle n'habite plus ici; **I couldn't wait any longer** je ne pouvais plus attendre; **five minutes longer** cinq minutes de plus; **I'll wait five minutes but no longer** je veux bien attendre cinq minutes mais pas plus
long[2] *vi* **to l. to do sth** avoir bien envie de faire qch, être impatient de faire qch, rêver de faire qch; **to l. for sth** désirer qch fortement *ou* ardemment; **he longed to be free** il avait hâte d'être libre; **I'm longing for the weekend/the**

holidays j'ai hâte d'être en week-end/vacances; **I l. for you** tu me manques beaucoup; **I'm longing for home** (*native land*) mon pays me manque; (*my house*) ma maison me manque; **to l. for sb's return** attendre impatiemment le retour de qn; **we're longing for them to leave** nous avons hâte qu'ils partent; **a much longed-for baby** un bébé très désiré; **a longed-for holiday** des vacances très attendues

long³ [lɒndʒ] *Geog* (*abbr* **longitude**) long

long-awaited ['lɒŋəweɪtɪd] *adj* (*event, birth etc*) très attendu

longboat ['lɒŋbəʊt] *n Naut* chaloupe *f*; (*of Vikings*) drakkar *m*

longbow ['lɒŋbəʊ] *n Mil, Hist* arc *m* (d'homme d'armes)

long-dated *adj Fin* à longue échéance

long-distance 1 *adj Tel* longue distance; *Tel F* **is it l.?** est-ce que c'est un appel longue distance?; *Tel* **l. call** communication *f* hors circonscription; **l. footpath** sentier *m* de grande randonnée; *Br* **l. lorry driver** conducteur, -trice de poids lourd, *F* routier *m*; *Sp* **l. race** course *f* de fond; *Sp* **l. runner** coureur, -euse de fond **2** *adv* **to telephone l.** faire un appel longue distance

long division *n Math* division *f* à rallonge(s)

long-drawn-out *adj* (*sigh etc*) prolongé; (*story, explanation etc*) interminable; **l. tale** récit *m* prologée *ou* à n'en plus finir; **a l. scream** un cri prolongée

long drink *n* long drink *m*

long-established *adj* établi depuis longtemps

longevity [lɒn'dʒevɪtɪ] *n* longévité *f*

long-forgotten *adj* oublié depuis longtemps

longhair ['lɒŋheər] *Am* **1** *adj* **(a)** (*cat, dog*) à poil(s) long(s) **(b)** *Old-fashioned F* (*for intellectuals*) pour les intellos; **l. music** musique *f* classique **2** *n F* **(a)** *Old-fashioned* (*intellectual*) intello *mf* **(b)** (*hippie*) chevelu *m*

longhaired ['lɒŋheəd] *adj* **(a)** (*cat, dog etc*) à poil(s) long(s); (*person*) aux cheveux longs **(b)** *Am F* = **longhair**

longhand ['lɒŋhænd] *n* écriture *f* ordinaire *ou* courante *ou* non abrégée; **in l.** (*written*) en clair, écrit à la main

long-haul *adj Av* long-courrier, *pl* longs-courriers; **a l. carrier** un long-courrier

longing ['lɒŋɪŋ] **1** *n* désir *m*, grande envie *f* (**for** de); **to be filled with l. to do sth** être plein d'un ardent désir de faire qch **2** *adj* **to cast l. looks at sth** jeter des regards pleins d'envie à qch

longingly ['lɒŋɪŋlɪ] *adv* avec envie; **to look l. at sth** couver qch des yeux; **she was looking l. out of the window** elle regardait languissamment par la fenêtre

longish ['lɒŋɪʃ] *adj* assez long, plutôt long

longitude ['lɒndʒɪtju:d] *n Geog* longitude *f*

longitudinal [lɒndʒɪ'tju:dɪn(ə)l] *adj* longitudinal; *Constr* **l. beam** longeron *m*

longitudinally [lɒndʒɪ'tju:dɪn(ə)lɪ] *adv* longitudinalement

long johns *n F* (*underwear*) caleçon *m* long

long jump *n Br Sp* saut *m* en longueur

long jumper *n Br Sp* sauteur, -euse en longueur

long-legged ['lɒŋ'legɪd] *adj* (*person*) aux jambes longues; (*horse*) haut sur pattes; (*bird*) à longues pattes

long-life *adj* (*battery*) longue durée; (*milk, juice*) longue conservation

long-lived ['lɒŋ'lɪvd] *adj* (*person*) qui vit longtemps; **we're a very l. family** dans la famille on vit très vieux

long-lost *adj* (*manuscript, painting etc*) perdu depuis longtemps; **she has been reunited with her l. brother** elle a retrouvé son frère dont elle avait été séparée depuis très longtemps; **I'm seeking some l. cousins** je suis à la recherche de cousins que j'ai perdu de vue depuis longtemps; **he welcomed me like a l. friend** il m'a accueilli comme si on avait été des amis qui ne s'étaient pas vus depuis des années

long-playing *adj* **l. record** disque *m* (de) longue durée, (disque) microsillon *m*

long-range *adj* (*plane*) long-courrier; (*gun, radar*) à longue portée; **l. camera** appareil *m* de photo longue portée; *Mil* **l. missile** missile *m* longue portée; *Met* **l. forecast** prévisions *fpl* météorologiques à long terme

long-running *adj* (*film, play*) qui tient l'affiche; (*TV/radio programme*) qui est diffusé depuis longtemps

longship ['lɒŋʃɪp] *n* (*of Vikings*) drakkar *m*

longshoreman, *pl* **-men** ['lɒŋʃɔ:mən] *n Am Naut* débardeur *m*

long shot *n* (*competitor, racehorse etc*) outsider *m*; **it's a l. but …** il n'y a pas de grandes chances que ça marche mais …; *Cin* plan *m* général; **not by a l.** loin de là

long-sighted *adj* **(a)** *Opt* hypermétrope; (*in old age*) presbyte **(b)** *Fig* (*policy, decision*) prévoyant

long-sightedness [lɒŋ'saɪtɪdnɪs] *n* **(a)** hypermétropie *f*; (*in old age*) presbytie *f* **(b)** *Fig* (*of policy, decision*) prévoyance *f*

long-sleeved *adj* (*dress, pullover*) à manches longues

long-standing *adj* (*arrangement, friendship etc*) de longue date; **l. accounts** vieux comptes *mpl*

long-stay bed *n Med* lit *m* (de) long séjour

long-stay car park *n* parking *m* longue durée

long-suffering *adj* patient, endurant; (*tolerant*) indulgent

long-term *adj* **(a)** (*detainee, prisoner*) qui subit un emprisonnement de longue durée; **the l. unemployed** les chômeurs de longue durée; **l. unemployment** chômage *m* de longue durée **(b)** *Fin* (*loan, policy etc*) à long terme; *Acct* **l. borrowings** emprunts *mpl* à long terme; *Acct* **l. capital** capitaux *mpl* permanents; *Acct* **l. investments** (*on balance sheet*) immobilisations *fpl* financières; **l. planning** planification *f* à long terme

longways ['lɒŋweɪz] *adv* = **lengthways**

long-winded [lɒŋ'wɪndɪd] *adj Pej* (*story*) interminable; (*speaker, speech*) verbeux

loo [lu:] *n Br F* **the l.** les toilettes *fpl*, les cabinets *mpl*; **to go to the l.** aller aux toilettes; **in the l.** aux toilettes, aux cabinets; **l. paper** papier *m* hygiénique *ou* toilette; **l. seat** siège *m* des toilettes *ou* des WC

loofah ['lu:fə] *n* (*for washing*), *Bot* loofa(h) *m*, luffa *m*

look¹ [lʊk] *n* **(a) to have** *or* **take a l. at sth** regarder qch; (*quickly*) jeter un coup d'œil sur qch; *F* **let's have a l.** (*show me*) fais voir; **to take a good l. at sb/sth** bien examiner qn/qch; **I didn't get a good l. at him** je n'ai pas bien vu comment il était; **did you get a good l. at him?** vous l'avez vu clairement?; **to have a l. round the town** faire un tour dans la ville; **to have a l. through some magazines** jeter un coup d'œil à des magazines

(b) (*with eyes*) regard *m*; **a suspicious/nasty/angry l.** un regard soupçonneux/mauvais/méchant; **he shot me a poisonous l.** il m'a lancé un regard foudroyant; **he has a strange l. in his eyes** il a un drôle de regard dans les yeux; **we were getting some very odd looks** nous attirions des regards très étonnés; *prov* **if looks could kill …** si ses yeux étaient des revolvers …

(c) (*search*) **to have a l. for sth** chercher qch; **have you had a good l. for it?** est-ce que tu as bien cherché?; **let's have a quick l. for it** on va jeter un coup d'œil pour essayer de le trouver

(d) (*appearance*) (*of object*) aspect *m*, air *m*, apparence *f*; (*of person*) tête *f*; **she has the l. of a troublemaker** elle a une tête à faire des histoires; **it has the l. of a successful marriage** cela a l'air d'un mariage heureux; **I don't like the l. of this at all!** cela ne me plaît pas du tout; **the business has a suspicious l. about it** l'affaire paraît suspecte *ou* louche; **I like the l. of him** il me plaît; **I don't like the l. of him** (*he seems suspicious*) sa tête ne me revient pas; **I don't like the l. of the weather** le temps a l'air inquiétant; **she has the l. of her grandfather about her** elle a des airs de son grand-père; **the New L.** (*fashion*) le new-look; **this year's new l.** la nouvelle mode de cette année; **the new-l. format/Ford Fiesta®** le format/la Ford Fiesta® nouvelle version

(e) good looks beauté *f*; **to lose one's looks** perdre ses charmes; **looks don't matter** l'apparence ne compte pas; **she's got her mother's looks** elle a la beauté de sa mère

look² 1 *vi* **(a)** regarder; **to l. through** *or* **out of the window** regarder par la fenêtre; **to l. down a list** parcourir une liste du regard; **to l. the other way** (*avert one's gaze*) détourner les yeux; *Fig* fermer les yeux; **to l. into sb's eyes** regarder qn dans les yeux; **I'm just looking, thank you** (*to shop assistant*) je ne fais que regarder, merci; *Prov* **l. before you leap** il faut réfléchir avant d'agir; **to l. on the bright side** voir les choses du bon côté; **the house looks south** la maison est exposée au sud; **to l. to** *or* **towards the future** penser à l'avenir

(b) (*search*) chercher; **we've looked everywhere** nous avons cherché partout

(c) (*seem, appear*) avoir l'air, paraître, sembler; **to l. old** avoir l'air *ou* faire vieux; **to l. ill** avoir l'air malade, avoir mauvaise mine; **to l. well** (*of person*) avoir bonne mine; **that dress looks well on you** cette robe vous va bien; **she looks tired** elle a l'air fatigué(e); **she's not as stupid as she looks** elle est moins bête qu'elle n'en a l'air; **he doesn't l. his age** on ne lui donnerait pas son âge; **to l. like sb** ressembler à qn; **what does she l. like?** comment est-elle?; **it looks like an elephant** on dirait un éléphant; **things are looking bad** *or* **black** les choses prennent une mauvaise tournure; **things are looking good** ça a l'air d'aller *ou* de bien se passer; **the crops l. promising** la récolte s'annonce bien; **you l. as if you've slept badly** vous avez l'air d'avoir mal dormi; **it looks as if he didn't want to go** il semble qu'il ne veuille pas y aller; **he looks the part** il est fait pour ce rôle; **she looks like winning, it looks like she'll win** on dirait qu'elle va gagner; **it looks like rain** on dirait qu'il va pleuvoir (**d**) (*expressing annoyance, desiring attention etc*) **l. here!** écoutez donc!, dites donc!; (**now**) **l.** écoute; *F* **l. sharp!** fais gaffe!

(**e**) (*envisage*) **I'm not looking to cause any trouble** je ne veux pas causer de problème; **they're looking to appoint a new headmaster** ils envisagent d'engager un nouveau directeur

2 *vt* **to l. sb (full** *or* **straight) in the face** regarder qn (bien) en face *ou* dans les yeux; **I can never l. her in the face again** je ne pourrai plus jamais la regarder en face; **to l. sb up and down** regarder qn de haut en bas, toiser qn; **l. what you've done!** regarde ce que tu as fait!; **l. where you're going!** fais attention où tu vas!

▶ **look about** = **look around**

▶ **look after** *vipo* (*a sick person etc*) veiller sur, soigner; (*possessions, an object*) faire attention à; (*one's health, teeth etc*) surveiller, faire attention à; (*one's interests*) prendre soin de; **can you l. after the house for us?** peux-tu garder *ou* faire attention à la maison?; **could you l. after my things while I go to ...?** pourriez-vous surveiller mes affaires pendant que je vais à ...?; **granny's looking after the children this weekend** mamie garde les enfants ce week-end; **he needs a lot of looking after** il a bien besoin qu'on s'occupe de lui; **l. after yourself!** prends bien soin de toi!; **you're well looked after** on s'occupe bien de vous; **he can l. after himself** (*at home etc*) il peut se débrouiller (tout seul); (*in fight etc*) il sait se débrouiller (tout seul); **the garden needs a lot of looking after** c'est un jardin qui a besoin d'être entretenu; **the car has been well looked after** la voiture est bien entretenue

▶ **look around 1** *vi* (**a**) (*turn head around*) regarder derrière soi

(**b**) (*have a look*) regarder autour de soi; (*in town, museum etc*) faire un tour; **can I just l. around?** (*in shop*) puis-je jeter un coup d'œil?

(**c**) (*search*) regarder partout; **to l. around for sth** chercher qch; **I'll go upstairs and l. around** je monte jeter un coup d'œil

2 *vipo* **to l. around the house** (*out of interest*) jeter un coup d'œil dans la maison; (*search*) chercher partout dans la maison; **to l. around town** (*have a look*) faire un tour en ville; **to l. around the shops** faire le tour des boutiques

▶ **look at** *vipo* (**a**) regarder; **what are you looking at?** qu'est-ce que vous regardez?; **just l. at that!** regardez-moi ça!; *F* **she won't l. at a man** les hommes, elle ne leur jette même pas un regard; **I haven't looked at another woman in the last forty years** en quarante ans, je n'ai pas regardé une autre femme; **they won't l. at our offer** ils ne font aucun cas de notre offre; **what's he like to l. at?** de quoi a-t-il l'air?; **she's not much to l. at** ce n'est pas une beauté; **he's not much to l. at** il n'est pas très beau; **if you l. at the result** si vous considérez le résultat; **I don't like his way of looking at things** je n'aime pas la manière dont il voit les choses; **I don't l. at it that way at all** je ne le vois pas de cet œil-là; **just l. at the mess we're in!** regarde les ennuis qu'on a!; **just l. at you!** (*you look awful, a mess etc*) mais regarde-toi donc!

(**b**) (*examine*) (*brakes, tooth etc*) regarder, jeter un coup d'œil sur

▶ **look away** *vi* tourner la tête

▶ **look back** *vi* regarder en arrière; **to l. back on the past** se retourner sur le passé; *Fig* **he has never looked back since that day** depuis ce jour sa situation n'a cessé de s'améliorer

▶ **look down** *vi* (*from a height*) regarder en *ou* vers le bas; (*lower one's eyes*) baisser les yeux; **don't l. down!** ne regarde pas en bas!; **she looked down on the town below her** elle regarda la ville en bas; **the chalet looks down on the valley** le chalet donne sur la vallée

▶ **look down on** *vipo* (*think little of, despise*) mépriser

▶ **look for** *vipo* chercher; **go and l. for him** allez le chercher; **he's looking for trouble** il cherche les ennuis

▶ **look forward** *vi* (*to the future*) regarder vers l'avenir

▶ **look forward to** *vipo* attendre avec plaisir; **I'm looking forward to seeing her again** il me tarde de la revoir; **I'm looking forward to the weekend** vivement le week-end!; **he hasn't got much to l. forward to in life** il n'a pas grand-chose à attendre de la vie; **they don't exactly l. forward to a visit to the dentist** ils appréhendent d'aller chez le dentiste; **I'm not exactly looking forward to going** je n'ai pas vraiment envie d'y aller; **I'm so looking forward to seeing you all again** j'aimerais tant vous revoir, ça me ferait tellement plaisir de vous revoir; **I'm not looking forward to it at all** je n'y tiens pas du tout; **I l. forward to hearing from you** (*at end of letter*) dans l'attente de vous lire

▶ **look in** *vi* (**a**) (*at window etc*) regarder (à l'intérieur), jeter un coup d'œil (à l'intérieur) (**b**) (*visit*) entrer en passant; **I'll l. in again tomorrow** je repasserai demain; **to l. in on sb** aller *ou* passer voir qn

▶ **look into** *vipo* (*investigate*) examiner, étudier; (*allegations*) prendre en considération; **it needs a bit of looking into** il faut étudier la question

▶ **look on 1** *vi* regarder, être spectateur; **while a crowd looked on** sous les regards de la foule **2** *vipo* (*consider*) considérer, envisager; **I l. on him as a friend** je le considère comme un ami

▶ **look onto** *vipo* (*of room*) (*garden, street etc*) donner sur

▶ **look out 1** *vi* (**a**) (*through window etc*) regarder (à l'extérieur), jeter un coup d'œil (à l'extérieur) (**b**) (*be careful*) prendre garde, être sur ses gardes; **l. out!** attention!, prenez garde! **2** *vtsep* trouver, *F* dénicher

▶ **look out for** *vipo* (**a**) (*look for*) guetter (l'arrivée de) (**b**) (*be on guard for*) (*person, pickpockets, errors etc*) faire attention à (**c**) *esp Am* (*take care of*) prendre soin de

▶ **look out onto** *vipo* (*of room*) (*garden, street etc*) donner sur

▶ **look over** *vipo* (*have a look at*) jeter un coup d'œil sur; (*papers*) parcourir; (*house for sale*) visiter

▶ **look round** *vi, vipo* = **look around**

▶ **look through 1** *vt* (**a**) (*papers etc*) parcourir, examiner rapidement (**b**) (*not see*) **she just looked straight through me** (*deliberately*) elle m'a ignoré; (*not deliberately*) elle m'a regardé sans me voir **2** *vi* (*at window, lock etc*) regarder par la fenêtre/la serrure *etc*

▶ **look to** *vipo* (**a**) (*rely on*) compter sur; **we're looking to you to help us** *or* **for help** nous comptons sur vous pour nous aider; **you can't always l. to your parents for money** on ne peut pas toujours s'en remettre à ses parents pour l'argent (**b**) (*ensure*) **l. to it that you ...** faites en sorte de ...; **l. to it that he ...** faites en sorte qu'il ... + *sub*; *Old-fashioned* **l. to your daughter** faites attention à *ou* surveillez votre fille

▶ **look up 1** *vtsep* (**a**) (*word in a dictionary etc*) chercher (**b**) (*go to visit*) (*person*) aller voir, passer chez; **l. me up** venez me voir **2** *vi* (**a**) (*from below*) regarder en haut; (*raise one's eyes*) lever les yeux; **if you could all l. up at this picture here** si vous regardez tous le tableau du haut (**b**) *Fig* **to be looking up** (*of business*) reprendre; (*of shares*) remonter; **things are looking up** la situation s'améliore; **things are looking up for her** sa situation s'améliore

▶ **look upon** *vipo* = **look on²**

▶ **look up to** *vipo* (*respect*) respecter, estimer

lookalike ['lʊkəlaɪk] *n* (*person*) sosie *m*; **she's a Princess Diana l.** c'est un sosie de la Princesse Diana; **it's just another Renault l.** c'est la copie conforme de la Renault

looker ['lʊkər] *n F* (**good**) **l.** (*of a woman*) belle femme *f*; (*younger*) beau brin *m* de fille; (*of a man*) bel homme *m*

looker-on *pl* **lookers-on**, *n* spectateur, -trice (**at** de), *Pej* badaud *m*

look-in *n F* (*chance*) **he won't have** *or* **get a l.** il n'a pas la moindre chance; **everyone gets a l.** tout le monde a sa chance

looking-glass ['lʊkɪŋglɑːs] *n Old-fashioned* miroir *m*, glace *f*

looking room *n TV* salle *f* de visionnage

lookout ['lʊkaʊt] *n* (**a**) **l.** (**post**) poste *m* d'observation *ou* de vigie (**b**) (*person*), *Mil* guetteur *m*; *Naut* homme *m* de veille *ou* de vigie (**c**) (*action*) surveillance *f*, observation *f*; *Naut* veille *f*; **to keep a l.** être aux aguets; *Naut* veiller, être en *ou* de vigie; **to be on the l. for** (*person*) guetter; (*sth*) être à la recherche de; **to be on l. duty** être de guet (**d**) *F* **that's a poor l. for him** c'est de mauvais augure pour lui; **that's your l.!** ça c'est ton affaire *ou F* tes oignons!

lookover ['lʊkəʊvər] *n* **to give sth a (quick) l.** jeter un coup d'œil sur qch

look-see *n F* **to go and have** *or* **take a l.** aller jeter un coup d'œil

look-up table *n Comptr* table *f* de recherche *ou* de référence

loom¹ [luːm] *n Tex* métier *m* à tisser

loom² *vi* apparaître indistinctement (*comme une menace*); **dangers looming ahead** dangers qui menacent; **to l. (large)** (*of event etc*) paraître imminent, être tout proche; **it looms large in his view of things** cela joue un rôle important dans sa manière de voir les choses

▶ **loom up** *vi* (*of ship, person in authority etc*) surgir

loon [luːn] *n* (**a**) (*bird*) *Am* plongeon *m*, *Can* huart *m* (**b**) *F* (*fool*) imbécile *mf*; (*crazy*) fada *m*

loony ['luːnɪ] *F* **1** *n* dingue *mf*; *also Fig* **l. bin** maison *f* de fous **2** *adj* dingue, timbré; *Br Pej* **the l. left** les gauchos

loop¹ [luːp] *n* (**a**) (*of ribbon, film etc*) boucle *f*; (*of fingerprint*) anse *f*; (*of river*) méandre *m*, boucle; (*in skating*) croisé *m*; (*of spiral, spool*) tour *m*; (*contraceptive coil*) stérilet *m*; *Av* boucle, looping *m*; *Am F* **to knock** *or* **throw sb for a l.**

abasourdir qn; *Sewing* **l. stitch** picot *m*; *Rail* **l.** **(line)** voie *f* d'évitement, voie de raccordement; (*at terminus*) boucle d'évitement

(b) *El* boucle *f*, bouclage *m*; *Nucl, Phys* (*of reactor*) boucle, circuit *m*; *Comptr* boucle d'itération; *Tel* circuit (branché), ligne *f* dérivée; *Electron* **l. antenna** *or* **aerial** cadre *m* d'antenne; **l. circuit** circuit bouclé; **l. current** courant *m* circulant dans un circuit bouclé

loop² **1** *vt* **(a)** (*piece of string etc*) faire une boucle *ou* des boucles à; **to l. sth around sth** enrouler qch autour de qch **(b)** *Av* **to l. the loop** faire un looping, boucler la boucle **(c)** *El* boucler **2** *vi* **(a)** faire une boucle **(b)** *Comptr* tourner sur une boucle

▶ **loop back** **1** *vi* (*of river etc*) faire une boucle; *Comptr* (*of program*) faire une boucle pour retourner **(to** à**)** **2** *vtsep* (*curtain*) retenir avec une embrasse

loophole ['lu:phəʊl] *n* **(a)** (*in law etc*) point *m* faible; **to find a l.** trouver une échappatoire **(b)** (*gap*) trou *m*, ouverture *f*; (*in fortified wall*) meurtrière *f*

looping ['lu:pɪŋ] *n Av* **l. the loop** looping *m*

loopy ['lu:pɪ] *adj F* (*crazy*) toqué, timbré, maboul

loose¹ [lu:s] *adj* **(a)** (*not fastened or attached*) (*screw, nail, brick, part*) qui se détache *ou* se défait; (*page*) détaché; (*knot*) défait, délié; (*floorboard*) désajusté; (*tooth*) qui bouge; *El* (*connection*) desserré; (*cable*) volant; **to come l., to get l.** se dégager, se détacher; (*of knot*) se défaire, se délier; (*of screw*) se desserrer; (*of iron bar etc*) se desceller; **to work l.** (*of machine parts*) se desserrer, prendre du jeu; (*of tooth*) se déchausser; (*of hair in bun etc*) se dénouer; **to let the riot police l. on the crowd** lâcher les CRS sur la foule; **I'm dying to be let l. on the garden** je crève d'envie de pouvoir m'en donner à cœur joie dans le jardin; **to let a dog l.** lâcher un chien; **they let their dog run l. in the fields** ils ont laissé leur chien courir en liberté dans les champs; **to let l. a torrent of abuse** lâcher un torrent d'injures; *Com* (*goods*) en vrac; **l. cash** *or* **change** menue monnaie *f*; *Br* **l. cover** (*on furniture*) housse *f*; **l. end** (*of a rope*) bout *m* qui pend; *Fig* **to be at a l. end** se trouver désœuvré, n'avoir rien à faire; *Fig* **to tie up the l. ends** régler les derniers détails; **l. ball** *Cr* balle *f* mal lancée; *Tennis* balle qui traîne; *Sp* **l. horse** cheval *m* sauvage

(b) (*slack*) détendu; (*cable*) mou, f molle; (*knot*) lâche; (*skin*) flasque; (*piece of clothing*) ample; (*coat*) flottant; **this skirt is much too l. at the waist** cette jupe est bien trop large à la taille; **to have l. bowels** avoir la diarrhée; *Med* **l. cough** toux *f* grasse

(c) (*in structure, arrangement*) *Tex* (*weave*) lâche, à claire-voie; *Mil* (*order*) dispersé; **l. chippings** gravillons *mpl*

(d) (*imprecise*) vague, peu exact; (*style*) lâche, décousu; (*translation*) approximatif

(e) (*immoral*) dissolu, débauché; (*woman*) de mauvaise vie; **l. living** mauvaise vie *f*, inconduite *f*; **l. morals** mœurs *fpl* relâchées

(f) (*irresponsible*) **l. talk** propos *mpl* irréfléchis

loose² *n* **to be on the l.** (*of prisoner*) être en cavale; (*of escaped tiger etc*) être en liberté; **there's a horde of louts on the l. in town** il y a une horde de voyous lâchés dans la ville; *Hum* **her husband's on the l. tonight** son mari est en vadrouille ce soir

loose³ *adv* **to hang l.** (*of rope etc*) pendre, flotter; *esp US Fig F* (*relax*) se relaxer, se détendre; (*not panic*) rester calme

loose⁴ *vt* **(a)** (*set free*) délier, détacher; **to l. one's hold** lâcher prise **(b)** (*untie*) (*knot etc*) délier, dénouer, défaire; (*hair*) dénouer, détacher; *Naut* (*mooring rope*) larguer; (*sail*) déferler **(c)** (*fire*) (*arrow*) décocher

▶ **loose off** **1** *vi Mil F* (*with machine gun etc*) tirer **(at** sur**)**; *Fig F* **to l. off at sb** (*tell off*) engueuler qn **2** *vtsep* (*fire*) (*a few rounds*) tirer, lâcher

loose-fitting *adj* (*item of clothing*) ample, large

loose-leaf *adj* (*album*) à feuilles mobiles, à feuillets rechargeables; **l. binder** classeur *m*, grébiche *f*; **l. paper** feuillet *m* mobile

loose-limbed *adj* souple

loosely ['lu:slɪ] *adv* **(a)** (*to hold sth*) sans serrer; **to be l. fixed** être mal serré *ou* mal ajusté, avoir du jeu; **her dress hung l. on her body** elle flottait dans sa robe **(b)** (*to speak*) sans précision; **l. translated** traduit approximativement; **the word is often used l.** le mot est souvent employé de façon imprécise; **l. connected** *or* **related** vaguement lié

loosen ['lu:s(ə)n] **1** *vt* (*slacken*) (*knot*) défaire, délier, relâcher; (*nut*) desserrer, dégager, décoller; (*rope*) relâcher, détendre; (*necktie, item of clothing*) desserrer; (*restrictions*) assouplir; **to l. sb's bonds** desserrer les liens de qn; **to l. one's grip** relâcher son étreinte; **to l. sb's tongue** délier *ou* dénouer la langue à qn; *Med* **to l. the bowels** relâcher le ventre **2** *vi* (*of knot etc*) se délier, se défaire; (*of screw etc*) se desserrer; (*of rope*) se relâcher

▶ **loosen up** **1** *vi* (*of person*) (*relax*) se mettre à l'aise; (*of athlete etc*) s'assouplir; **he always loosens up after a few drinks** il est toujours plus décontracté après un verre ou deux; **she loosens up once you get to know her** elle perd de sa froideur une fois qu'on la connaît **2** *vtsep* (*muscles*) relâcher

looseness ['lu:snɪs] *n* **(a)** (*of tooth, stone etc*) déchaussement *m*; (*of pin, bolt etc*) jeu *m*; (*of skin*) flaccidité *f*; (*of rope*) relâchement *m*; (*of piece of clothing*) ampleur *f* **(b)** (*of terminology*) imprécision *f* **(c)** (*of discipline, morals etc*) relâchement *m*

loosestrife ['lu:sstraɪf] *n* (*plant*) **(purple) l.** salicaire *f* commune

loot¹ [lu:t] *n* **(a)** (*goods*) butin *m*; **soldiers on the l.** soldats qui se livrent à des pillages **(b)** *F* (*money*) flouze *m*, fric *m*

loot² **1** *vt* (*city etc*) piller, mettre à sac; (*shops*) piller; (*goods*) voler **2** *vi* se livrer au pillage

looter ['lu:tər] *n* pilleur, -euse, pillard, -arde

looting ['lu:tɪŋ] *n* pillage *m*

lop [lɒp] *vt* **(-pp-)** (*tree*) élaguer, ébrancher

▶ **lop off** *vtsep* (*branch*) couper, élaguer

▶ **lope along** [ləʊp] *vi* (*of person*) avancer à grandes enjambées; (*of leopard etc*) courir tout en puissance; (*of hare*) avancer en bondissant

▶ **lope off** *vi* (*of person*) partir d'une démarche élastique; **the tiger loped off into the jungle** le tigre pénétra dans la jungle de sa démarche souple

lop-eared ['lɒpɪəd] *adj* (*rabbit, dog etc*) aux oreilles pendantes

lopsided [lɒp'saɪdɪd] *adj* qui manque de symétrie, asymétrique; (*picture*) de guingois, de travers; **a l. grin** un sourire en coin; **a l. group with twice as many women as men** un groupe déséquilibré comptant deux fois plus de femmes que d'hommes; **a l. account of the conflict** une description partiale du conflit

loquacious [lɒ'kweɪʃəs] *adj* loquace

loquaciousness [lɒ'kweɪʃəsnɪs], **loquacity** [lɒ'kwæsɪtɪ] *n* loquacité *f*

lord¹ [lɔ:d] *n* **(a)** seigneur *m*; **l. of the manor** châtelain *m*; **our sovereign l. the king** notre seigneur souverain, le roi; (*in Middle Ages etc*), *Hum* **her l. and master** son seigneur et maître

(b) *Rel* **L. God Almighty** Seigneur Dieu Tout-puissant; **the L.** le Seigneur; **in the year of our L. ...** en l'an de grâce ...; **the L.'s Prayer** le Pater; **L.'s Day Observance Society** = Société *f* pour l'Observance du Jour du Seigneur; *F* **(good) L.!, O L.!** mon Dieu!; *F* **L. knows if ...** Dieu sait si ...

(c) *Br* (*title*) lord *m*; **L. Hailsham said that ...** Lord Hailsham a dit que ...; *Pol* **the House of Lords, the Lords** la Chambre des Lords; **the L. Mayor** le Lord Maire

(d) (*flower*) **lords and ladies** arum *m* maculé, pied-de-veau *m*, *pl* pieds-de-veau

lord² *vi F* **to l. it** mener la grande vie; **to l. it over sb** traiter qn de haut

lordly ['lɔ:dlɪ] *adj* **(a)** noble, de grand seigneur **(b)** *Pej* (*arrogant*) hautain; **his l. airs** ses airs de grand seigneur; **in a l. manner** avec hauteur

lordship ['lɔ:dʃɪp] *n* **(a)** (*authority*) suzeraineté *f* **(b)** **Your L.** *also Hum* votre Seigneurie; (*to nobleman*) monsieur le comte *etc*; (*to judge*) votre honneur

lordy ['lɔ:dɪ] *int esp Am F* Seigneur!

lore [lɔ:r] *n* science *f*, savoir *m*; **country l.** connaissance *f* des choses de la campagne

lorgnette [lɔ:'njet] *n* (*spectacles*) face-à-main *m*, *pl* faces-à-main; (*opera glasses*) jumelles *fpl* (de théâtre) à manche

lorry ['lɒrɪ] *n Br* camion *m*; **l. driver** conducteur *m* de camion, conducteur de poids lourd, routier *m*; *Euph Hum* **it fell off the back of a l.** (*is stolen*) je l'ai trouvé

lose [lu:z] (*pt, pp* **lost** [lɒst]; *prp* **losing** ['lu:zɪŋ]) **1** *vt* **(a)** (*money, right etc*) perdre; (*mislay*) perdre, égarer; (*through death, injury*) (*one's father, baby, arm, voice etc*) perdre; **you will l. nothing by waiting** vous ne perdrez rien à attendre; **to have nothing to l.** n'avoir rien à perdre; **the expression loses something in translation** l'expression perd quelque chose à la traduction; **to l. one's heart to sb** tomber amoureux de qn; **to l. one's reason** perdre la raison; **to l. one's reputation** se perdre de réputation; **to l. one's nerve** ne pas avoir le courage; **he had lost interest in his work** son travail ne l'intéressait plus; **the patient is losing strength** le malade s'affaiblit; **many lives were lost in the disaster** la catastrophe a coûté la vie à de nombreuses personnes; **to be lost at sea** périr en mer; **to l. one's way, to get lost** perdre son chemin, se perdre, s'égarer; *Sl* **get lost!** fiche-moi le camp!; **to l. one's balance** perdre l'équilibre; **to l. share** (*of* *market*) perdre des parts de marché; **to l. sight of sb** perdre qn de vue; **to l. sight of the reason for doing sth** perdre de vue la raison pour laquelle on fait/a fait qch; *Fig F* **I'm lost!, you've lost me!** je suis largué, je ne vous suis plus; *Fig F* **you lost me when you started using technical terms** j'ai perdu le fil quand tu as commencé à employer des termes techniques

(b) (*deliberately*) **to l. weight** perdre du poids; **I've lost 10 kilos** j'ai perdu 10 kilos, j'ai maigri de 10 kilos; **to l. oneself in the crowd** se perdre dans/se mêler à la foule; **to l. one's pursuers** (*of sb being chased*) larguer ses poursuivants; **to l. oneself in a book** se plonger dans un livre

(c) (*fail to win*) (*match, race, battle, trial*) perdre; **the motion was lost** (*in debate*) la motion a été rejetée

(d) (*waste*) (*time*) gaspiller, perdre; **the joke was lost on him** la plaisanterie lui est passée au-dessus de la tête; **American humour is lost on us** nous ne comprenons rien à l'humour américain

(e) clock that loses five minutes a day pendule qui retarde de cinq minutes par jour

(f) (*bring about loss of*) **the decision will l. us our jobs** la décision nous coûtera nos emplois; **that mistake lost him the match** cette faute lui coûta la partie

2 *vi* **(a)** perdre; **to l. heavily** (*in betting*) perdre une grosse somme; (*by a large margin*) se faire écraser; **both armies lost heavily** les deux armées ont subi de lourdes pertes; **to l. in value** perdre de sa valeur; **our team was losing at half-time** notre équipe perdait à la mi-temps; **we've lost on the sale of the house** nous avons perdu sur la vente de la maison; **it loses in translation** on perd un peu à la traduction

(b) (*of clock, watch*) retarder

▶ **lose out** *vi* être (le/la) perdant(e); **British industry is losing out to the Japanese** les Britanniques sont victimes de la concurrence japonnaise

▶ **lose out on** *vipo F* **to l. out on a deal** faire les frais d'une affaire; **to l. out on a contract** (*not get*) laisser échapper un contrat; **they lost out on it** ils ont été perdants

loser [ˈluːzər] *n Sp etc* perdant, -ante; **the winners and the losers** les gagnants et les perdants, les vainqueurs et les vaincus; **to be a good/bad l.** être bon/mauvais joueur; **to back a l.** miser sur un perdant; **<u>you'll</u> be the l.** c'est toi qui y perdras; **he's a born l.** il est toujours perdant, il n'arrive jamais à rien

losing [ˈluːzɪŋ] *adj* perdant; **to fight a l. battle** se livrer à une bataille perdue d'avance; **the l. side** les vaincus *mpl*; *Sp* l'équipe *f* perdante

loss [lɒs] *n* **(a)** perte *f*; **there have been heavy government losses in the Midlands** (*in election*) le gouvernement a perdu beaucoup de sièges dans les Midlands; **the catastrophe resulted in great l. of life** la catastrophe a fait beaucoup de victimes; *Mil etc* **to sustain** *or* **suffer heavy losses** subir de grosses pertes; **she has never recovered from the l. of her mother** elle ne s'est jamais remise d'avoir perdu sa mère; **he is a great l. to the British theatre** c'est une grande perte pour le théâtre britannique; **it's no great l. that they're leaving** leur départ n'est pas une grosse perte; **to feel a sense of l.** ressentir un vide; *Jur* **l. of civil rights** perte des droits civiques, dégradation *f* civique; **without l. of face** sans perdre la face; *Rel* **l. of grace** amission *f* de la grâce; **l. of sight** perte de la vue

(b) *Fin, Com* (*in insurance*) sinistre *m*; (*of product being manufactured or transported*) freinte *f*, déperdition *f*; **l. of earnings** manque *m* à gagner; **l. in transit** freinte *ou* déchet *m* de route; **to sell at a l.** vendre à perte; **to run at a l.** (*of business*) tourner à perte; **to cut one's losses** faire la part du feu; **total l.** perte *f* totale

(c) *Fig* **to be at a l.** ne savoir que faire; (*not know what to say*) ne savoir que dire; (*not know what to answer*) ne savoir que répondre; **to be at a (total) l. to explain ...** être (totalement) incapable d'expliquer ...; **to be at a l. (to know) what to do/say** ne savoir que faire/dire; **she's never at a l. for an answer** elle a *ou* trouve toujours réponse à tout; **he's never at a l. for something to say** il n'est jamais à court (de mots)

loss adjuster *n* expert-répartiteur *m*

loss leader *n* article *m ou* produit *m* d'appel; *Mktg* **l. pricing** fixation *f* d'un prix d'appel

loss-making *adj Com* qui tourne à perte, déficitaire

lost [lɒst] **1** *pt, pp see* **lose²**

2 *adj* perdu; **the child was l.** l'enfant s'était perdu; **to give sb/sth up for l.** abandonner tout espoir de retrouver qn/qch; **30 people were reported l. at sea** 30 personnes auraient péri en mer; **to seem** *or* **look l.** avoir l'air dépaysé; (*at party, in lesson*) avoir l'air perdu; **she's l. to the world** le monde n'existe plus pour elle; **she's completely l. in her book** elle est complètement absorbée dans sa lecture; **to be l. in thought** être perdu dans ses pensées; **the joke was l. on them** ils n'ont rien compris à la plaisanterie; **it's l. on me** ça me passe au dessus de la tête, je n'y comprends rien; *F* **when they talk shop I'm quite l.** quand ils parlent boutique, je suis complètement largué; **l. soul** âme *f* perdue, âme damnée; **to wander (about) like a l. soul** errer comme une âme en peine; **he looks like a l. sheep without his wife** sans sa femme, il a l'air complètement perdu; **l. cause** cause *f* perdue; *US* **l. river** rivière *f* souterraine

lost and found *n* objets *mpl* trouvés; *US* **l. department** (bureau *m* des) objets trouvés

lost property *n* objets *mpl* trouvés; **l. office** (bureau *m* des) objets trouvés

lot [lɒt] **1** *n* **(a) a l. (of)** beaucoup (de); **what a l. of people!** que de monde!; **such a l. of people** tant de monde; **quite a l. (of sth)** une quantité considérable (de qch), *F* pas mal (de qch); **I saw quite a l. of her in Paris** je l'ai vue assez souvent pendant mon séjour à Paris; **not a l.** pas beaucoup; **what did you think of his speech? – not a l.!** qu'as-tu pensé de son discours? – pas grand-chose!; **a l. of explaining to do** beaucoup d'explications à donner; **we had a l. of fun** nous nous sommes bien amusés; **I would have given a l. to ...** j'aurais donné gros pour ...; **I've got a l. to do before bedtime** j'ai beaucoup à faire avant ce soir; **I've got a whole l. of things to do** j'ai un tas de choses à faire

(b) (*selection*) sort *m*, tirage *m* au sort; **drawn by l.** tiré au sort; **to draw** *or* **cast lots for sth** tirer qch au sort, tirer au sort pour qch

(c) (*destiny*) sort *m*, part *f*, partage *m*, destin *m*, destinée *f*; **to be happy/content with one's l.** être content de son sort; **it fell to my l. to decide** c'était à moi de décider; **the poor man's l.** la condition du pauvre; **to throw** *or* **cast in one's l. with sb** partager le sort *ou* la fortune de qn

(d) (*land*) (lot *m* de) terrain *m*; *Cin* **(studio) l.** terrain (de studio); *Am* **parking l.** parking *m*

(e) (*at auction*) (*of merchandise*) lot *m*; *Fin* (*of bonds, shares*) paquet *m*; **in lots** par lots; **to buy/sell in one l.** acheter/vendre en bloc; *St Exch* **l. size** unité *f* de transaction

(f) (*referring to person/people*) **a bad l.** un mauvais sujet, un vaurien; **a nice l. of people** des gens très agréables; *Iron* **you're a nice l., you are!** vous êtes incroyables, vous!; *F Pej* **that l. next door** la bande d'à côté; *F* **listen, you l.!** écoutez tous; *F* **you arrange to get your l. there in time** arrangez-vous pour que votre groupe soit là à l'heure; **the l.** tous, tout le monde; **the whole l. of you** vous tous; **you rotten l.!** espèces de voyous!; **the whole l. of them** toute la bande

(g) the l. (*everything*) tout; **I bought the l.** j'ai acheté le tout; *F* **the whole damn l.** tout le bazar

2 *adv* **a l.** beaucoup; **a l. bigger** beaucoup *ou* bien plus gros; **such a l.** tellement; **times have changed a l.** les temps ont bien changé; **he thought a l. before deciding** il a beaucoup réfléchi avant de se décider; **thanks a l.** merci beaucoup

loth [ləʊθ] *adj* = **loath**

lotion [ˈləʊʃən] *n* lotion *f*

lots [lɒts] *F* **1** *npl* **l. (of)** beaucoup (de); **I've got l. of things to do** j'ai beaucoup de *ou* un tas de choses à faire; **he has l. and l. of money** il a énormément d'argent; **he's l. of fun to be with** il est très amusant **2** *adv F* beaucoup

lottery [ˈlɒtərɪ] *n* loterie *f*; *Fig* **it's a bit of a l.** c'est une loterie

lotto [ˈlɒtəʊ] *n* (*game*) loto *m*

lotus, *pl* **-uses** [ˈləʊtəs, -əsɪz] *n* lotus *m*; **l. position** (*in yoga*) (position *f* du) lotus

lotus-eater *n Myth* mangeur *m* de lotus, lotophage *m*

loud [laʊd] **1** *adj* **(a)** bruyant, retentissant; (*noise, shout*) grand; (*explosion*) violent; (*laugh*) gros; (*voice*) fort; (*person, behaviour*) bruyant; **to be l. in one's praise of sb/sth** se répandre en louanges sur qn/qch; **to be l. in one's condemnation of sb/sth** condamner qn/qch avec force; **you're too l.!** tu fais trop de bruit!; **in a l. voice** à haute voix; **l. applause** applaudissements vifs; **l. protests** protestations vives; **l. sobs** gros sanglots

(b) (*colour etc*) criard, voyant; (*clothes*) voyant; **he wore a l. checked suit** il portait un costume voyant à carreaux

2 *adv* (*to speak*) haut, à haute voix; (*to shout*) fort; **to talk out l.** parler à haute voix; (*in loud voice*) parler (très) fort; **to think out l.** penser tout haut; **to turn the radio/TV up l.** mettre la radio/TV plus fort; **louder!** parlez plus fort!; *Rad* **I hear you l. and clear** je te reçois cinq sur cinq; *F* (*I understand*) j'ai compris

loud-hailer [ˈlaʊdˈheɪlər] *n Br* porte-voix *m inv*

loudly [ˈlaʊdlɪ] *adv* (*to shout*) haut, fort, à voix haute; (*to laugh*) bruyamment; (*to knock at the door*) rudement; **you're**

not speaking l. enough vous ne parlez pas assez fort; **he has always dressed rather l.** il a toujours porté des vêtements assez voyants

loudmouth ['laʊdmaʊθ] *n F Pej* **to be a l.** être *ou* avoir une grande gueule; (*not be discreet*) avoir une grande langue

loudmouthed ['laʊdmaʊðd] *adj F Pej* (*who speaks loudly*) gueulard; (*who can't keep a secret*) qui ne sait pas tenir sa langue

loudness ['laʊdnɪs] *n* **(a)** (*of engine, traffic, radio etc*) bruit *m*; **the l. of her voice** sa voix forte **(b) the l. of his ties** ses cravates voyantes; **the l. of his behaviour** sa conduite tapageuse

loudspeaker [laʊd'spiːkər] *n* haut-parleur *m*, *pl* haut-parleurs; **l. van** camionnette *f* munie d'un haut-parleur

lough [lɒx] *n* (*in Ireland*) lac *m*

Louis ['luːɪ] *n* **L. the Fourteenth** Louis XIV

Louisiana [luːiːzɪ'ænə] *n* Louisiane *f*

lounge¹ [laʊndʒ] *n* **(a)** (*in house, hotel*) salon *m*; **l. lizard** = gigolo *m* qui traîne dans les bars des hôtels; **l. suit** complet veston *m* **(b)** *Am* (*sofa*) canapé *m*; **l. chair** fauteuil *m*; *Rail* **l. car** voiture-salon *f*, *pl* voitures-salons

lounge² *vi* (*on sofa etc*) s'étendre paresseusement; **I've been lounging in an armchair all afternoon** j'ai passé l'après-midi affalé dans un fauteuil

▶ **lounge about, lounge around** *vi usu Pej* flâner

▶ **lounge away** *vtsep* **to l. away the time** passer le temps à flâner

lounge bar *n Br* (*dans un 'pub' qui contient deux bars séparés, l'expression désigne le plus confortable des deux dont les prix sont un peu plus élevés que ceux du 'public bar'*) *m* bar ≈ select

lounger ['laʊndʒər] *n* **(a)** (*person*) flemmard, -arde **(b) (sun) l.** chaise *f* longue **(c)** *Am* (*settee*) canapé *m*

louse [laʊs] *n* **(a)** (*insect*) (*pl* **lice**) pou *m*, poux **(b)** *Sl* (*person*) (*pl* **louses**) fripouille *f*, salaud *m*

▶ **louse up** *vtsep Sl* (*ruin, spoil*) bousiller, ficher en l'air

lousewort ['laʊswɜːt] *n* (*plant*) herbe *f* aux poux

lousiness ['laʊzɪnɪs] *n F* (*of weather etc*) caractère *m* horrible; (*of service in restaurant etc*) mauvaise qualité *f*

lousy ['laʊzɪ] *adj* **(a)** (*full of lice*) pouilleux, plein de poux; *Fig, F* **this place is l. with ...** ça grouille de ...; *F* **to be l. with money** être un gros richard

(b) *F* affreux; (*headache, cold, day, week*) sale, mauvais; (*weather*) sale, de chien; (*hotel, colour etc*) moche; (*holiday, party, meal, book, essay*) minable, nul; (*quality, workmanship*) mauvais; (*computer, car*) qui ne vaut rien, nul; (*raincoat, pen*) qui ne vaut rien; **that's a l. thing to do** *or* **say** c'est dégueulasse *ou* moche de faire *ou* dire une chose pareille; **he's l. to his wife** il est dégueulasse avec sa femme; **a l. trick** un sale tour; **don't buy them, they're l.** n'achetez pas ça, c'est de la camelote *ou Vulg* de la merde; **they made a l. job of it** ils se sont plantés; **he's in a l. mood** il est d'une humeur de chien; **we had a l. time on holiday** nous avons passé des vacances nulles *ou* dégueulasses; **all for a l. £5** tout ça à cause de 5 malheureuses livres; **to feel/look l.** se sentir horriblement mal/avoir l'air horrible; **I'm l. at science** je suis nul en sciences

lout [laʊt] *n* (*oaf*) lourdaud *m*, rustre *m*; (*hooligan*) voyou *m*; **you clumsy l.!** espèce de lourdaud!

loutish ['laʊtɪʃ] *adj* rustre, lourdaud; **l. manners** des manières de rustre

louv(e)red ['luːvəd] *adj* (*door*) à persiennes; *Naut* muni d'un louvre *ou* de louvres; *Aut, Av* (*car bonnet, air inlet*) à persiennes, à volet; *Archit* (*belfry*) à abat-sons

louvre, *US* **louver** ['luːvər] *n* **(a)** *Archit* **l. (board)** abat-vent *m inv*, abat-son *m*, *pl* abat-sons *de clocher* **(b)** (*in door, window*) persienne *f*; *Naut* louvre *m*; *Aut, Av* (*of ventilation inlet, car bonnet*) persienne, volet *m*; *MecE* (*of air intake*) ouïe *f*

lovable ['lʌvəb(ə)l] *adj* (*character, person*) sympathique; (*baby*) adorable; **l. rogue** petit coquin *m*

lovage ['lʌvɪdʒ] *n Bot, Culin* ache *f* de(s) montagne(s)

love¹ [lʌv] *n* **(a)** amour *m*; **l. of** *or* **for sb** amour de *ou* pour *ou* envers qn; **l. of** *or* **for sth** amour de qch; **he has a great l. for Scotland** il a beaucoup d'amour pour l'Écosse; **there's no l. lost between them** ils ne peuvent pas se sentir; **a teacher with little l. for his pupils** un professeur qui n'a pas beaucoup de sympathie pour ses élèves; **for the l. of God** pour l'amour de Dieu; **give my l. to your parents** faites mes amitiés *fpl* à vos parents; **with l. from ...** (*at end of letter*) affectueuses pensées *fpl* de ...; **Bill sends his l.** Bill vous fait ses amitiés; **give my l. to ...** faites mes amitiés à ...; **I wouldn't do it for l. or money** je ne le ferais pour rien au monde; **to do sth for l.** faire qch pour le plaisir

(b) (*between lovers*) amour *m* (*the pl is f in Lit use*); **to be/fall in l. with sb** être/tomber amoureux de qn; **head over heels in l.** amoureux fou, éperdument amoureux; **to make l. to sb** faire l'amour avec qn; *Old-fashioned* (*to court*) faire la cour à qn; **to marry for l.** faire un mariage d'amour; **she's the l. of my life** c'est la femme *ou* l'amour de ma vie; **it was l. at first sight** ce fut le coup de foudre; **his first l.** son premier amour; **l.-hate relationship** relation *f* qui va de l'amour à la haine; **l. affair** aventure *f*; **l. letter** billet *m* doux; **l. life** vie *f* amoureuse; **l. match** mariage *m* d'amour; **l. song** chanson *f* d'amour; **l. story** histoire *f ou* roman *m* d'amour

(c) (*term of endearment*) **(my) l.** mon amour; *esp Eng F* **more coffee, l.?** tu prends encore du café, mon petit/ma petite?; *esp Eng F* **there you are, l.!** voilà, ma petite dame/mon (petit) gars/mon petit monsieur!

(d) *Tennis etc* zéro *m*, rien *m*; **l. fifteen/fifteen l.** rien à quinze/quinze à rien; **l. game** jeu *m* blanc; **two sets to l.** deux sets à rien *ou* à zéro

love² *vt* **(a)** (*person*) aimer; **to l. one another** s'aimer; *prov* **l. me, l. my dog** qui m'aime aime mon chien **(b)** (*sth*) aimer (passionnément); (*music etc*) adorer; **they l. animals** ils aiment les animaux; **to l. to do sth, to l. doing sth** aimer (à) faire qch; **will you come with me? – I'd l. to** voulez-vous m'accompagner? – avec (le plus grand) plaisir; **she'd l. to see you again** elle serait enchantée *ou* ravie de vous revoir; **I'd l. to come** j'aimerais beaucoup venir

lovebird ['lʌvbɜːd] *n* (*bird*) perruche *f* inséparable; *F Hum* **lovebirds** (*people*) tourtereaux *mpl*

lovebite ['lʌvbaɪt] *n* suçon *m*

love child *n Euph* enfant *m* naturel *ou* illégitime, enfant de l'amour

love-in-a-mist *n* (*plant*) nigelle *f* (de Damas), cheveux *mpl* de Vénus

loveless ['lʌvlɪs] *adj* sans amour

love-lies-bleeding ['lʌvlaɪz'bliːdɪŋ] *n* (*plant*) amarante *f* à fleurs en queue

loveliness ['lʌvlɪnɪs] *n* beauté *f*; (*of woman, countryside etc*) charme *m*

lovelorn ['lʌvlɔːn] *adj* languissant

lovely ['lʌvlɪ] *adj* **(a)** (*attractive, fine*) beau, *f* belle; (*food, smell, idea*) bon, *f* bonne; (*day, weather etc*) beau; **what a l. woman!** quelle femme charmante!; **have a l. time** amusez-vous bien; **it's been l. seeing you again** ça a été charmant de vous revoir; *F* **it's l. and warm** il fait une chaleur agréable; **I've made a copy for you – oh! l.!** j'en ai fait une copie pour vous – comme c'est gentil! **(b)** (*kind, friendly*) très aimable

lovemaking ['lʌvmeɪkɪŋ] *n* rapports *mpl* sexuels; *Old-fashioned* (*courting*) cour *f* (amoureuse); **his l.** la façon dont il fait l'amour

love nest *n* nid *m* d'amour

lover ['lʌvər] *n* **(a)** amant *m*; *Old-fashioned* (*suitor*) amoureux *m*, prétendant *m*; **they were lovers** ils étaient amants; **to take a l.** (*of woman*) prendre un amant; (*of man*) prendre une maîtresse **(b)** (*of nature etc*) amoureux, -euse, fou, *f* folle

loverboy ['lʌvəbɔɪ] *n F Iron* **(a)** grand séducteur *m*, le chéri de ces dames; **morning, l.!** (*said by a woman*) bonjour, chéri! **(b)** (*non-romantic sense*) **we're still waiting for l.!** on attend toujours le petit coco!

love seat *n* canapé *m* deux places, causeuse *f*

lovesick ['lʌvsɪk] *adj* qui languit d'amour

lovesickness ['lʌvsɪknɪs] *n* mal *m* d'amour

lovey-dovey ['lʌvɪdʌvɪ] *adj Sl* (*talk*) mièvre, à la guimauve; **to get l.** (*of person*) (*get sexy*) s'exciter; **they've gone all l.** ils sont comme deux tourtereaux

loving ['lʌvɪŋ] *adj* **(a)** affectueux; **a l. husband and father** un mari et un père aimant; *Lit* **l. kindness** bonté *f*; **your l. mother** (*at end of letter*) ta mère qui t'aime **(b) l. cup** coupe *f* de l'amitié

-loving ['lʌvɪŋ] *suff* **adventure/danger-l.** qui aime l'aventure/le danger; **home-l.** casanier, -ière; **fun-l.** qui aime s'amuser

lovingly ['lʌvɪŋlɪ] *adv* affectueusement, tendrement

low¹ [ləʊ] **1** *adj* **(a)** (*not high*) bas, *f* basse; **to cook sth over a l. heat** *or* **a l. fire** faire cuire qch à feu doux; **my stocks are rather l.** mes stocks sont un peu dégarnis; **our water supply is getting l.** notre réserve d'eau baisse; **a dress with a l. neckline** une robe décolletée; **to make sb a l. bow** saluer qn très bas; *Cards* **the l. cards** les basses cartes *fpl*; **a l. spade** un petit pique; **a l. blow** un coup bas; **lower-case** minuscule; **lower case** en minuscules; **l. (gear)** rapport *m* inférieur; (*on automatic gearbox*) conduite *f* lente; **l. price** bas prix; **the lowest price** le prix le plus bas; **l. sales** ventes *fpl* faibles; **l. temperature** basse température *f*; **l. tension** basse tension *f*; **l. wages** salaires *mpl* peu élevés; **l. wage economy** économie *f* où les salaires sont bas; **l. fuel level warning light** témoin *m* de niveau de carburant; **lower part** (*of ladder etc*) bas *m*; **the lower Alps** les basses Alpes *fpl*; **lower**

back reins *mpl*; **lower back pain** mal *m* de reins; **lower jaw** mâchoire *f* inférieure; *Med* **lower leg** jambe *f*

(**b**) (*inferior*) bas, *f* basse, peu élevé; **l. birth** basse naissance *f*; **all the people, high and l.** tous, du haut comme du bas de l'échelle sociale; **the lower classes** le bas peuple; **the lower ranks** (*in army etc*) les rangs inférieurs; **the lower school, the lower forms** les petites classes; **the lower animals** les animaux inférieurs; **to have a l. opinion of sb** avoir une mauvaise opinion de qn; **the lowest of the l.** le dernier des derniers; **that's a l. trick!** ça, c'est un sale coup!; **that was rather a l. thing to do** ce n'était pas très joli de faire une chose pareille; **l. company** mauvaise compagnie; **l. cunning** ruse *f* et bassesse *f*

(**c**) **to be very l.** *or* **in a very l. state** (*of invalid*) être bien bas; **to feel l., to be in l. spirits** (*depressed*) se sentir déprimé, *F* avoir le cafard; *Med* **l. physical condition** mauvaise condition *f* physique

(**d**) (*not loud*) bas, *f* basse; *Mus* **l. note** note *f* basse; **l. murmur** faible murmure *m*; **in a l. voice** à voix basse, à mi-voix

(**e**) *Rel* **l. Mass** messe *f* basse; **L. Sunday** Pâques *fpl* closes, dimanche *m* de Quasimodo

2 *adv* (**a**) (*to hang, aim*) bas; **to bow l.** saluer très bas; **dress cut l. in the back** robe *f* décolletée dans le dos; *Boxing* **to hit l.** frapper bas; **to fly l.** (*of bird, aircraft*) voler bas; **to bring sb l.** humilier qn, abaisser qn; **to lie l.** se tapir, rester tapi

(**b**) **the lowest paid employees** les employés les moins payés

(**c**) (*to speak*) à voix basse; **turn the music down l.** baisse la musique; *Mus* **to set lower** (*song etc*) baisser d'une *ou* de deux octaves; **I can't sing that l.** je ne peux pas chanter aussi bas; **we're (running) l. on fuel/food** nous n'avons presque plus de carburant/nourriture; **the fire is burning l.** le feu baisse; **light turned l.** lumière en veilleuse

3 *n* (**a**) *Met* zone *f* de basse pression

(**b**) **to reach a new l.** descendre encore plus bas; **a record l.** le point le plus bas jamais atteint; **sterling has reached an all-time l.** la livre a atteint son niveau le plus bas, la livre n'avait jamais atteint un niveau aussi bas

low² *vi* (*of cattle*) meugler

low-alcohol *adj* (*drink*) peu alcoolisé

low-angle shot *n TV, Cin* contre-plongée *f*

lowboy ['ləʊbɔɪ] *n Am* commode *f*

lowbrow ['ləʊbraʊ] *Pej* **1** *adj* peu intellectuel **2** *n* personne *f* peu intellectuelle

low-budget *adj* (*film, holiday etc*) à petit budget

low-calorie *adj* (*diet*) hypocalorique; **l. menu** menu *m* basses calories

low-class *adj* (*lower-class*) populaire

low-cost *adj* à bas prix; (*housing, accommodation*) à loyer modéré

Low Countries *npl* Pays-Bas *mpl*

low-cut *adj* (*dress*) décolleté

low density housing *n* zones *fpl* d'habitation peu peuplées

low-down *F* **1** *adj esp Am* (*mean*) ignoble; **that's a l. trick** ça, c'est un coup rosse **2** *n* **to give sb the l.** tuyauter qn (**on** sur); **to get the l.** se rencarder (**on** sur)

low-end *adj Mktg* bas de gamme

lower¹ ['ləʊər] *adj* inférieur; (*shelves, rungs*) du bas; **l. ASCII** ASCII *m* inférieur

lower² *vt* (**a**) (*head, eyes, window, blinds*) baisser; (*veil*) abaisser, rabattre; *Th* **to l. the curtain** baisser le rideau; *Aut* **to l. the hood** décapoter

(**b**) (*reduce*) (*light, one's voice, key*) baisser; (*pressure*) réduire; (*price*) baisser, rabaisser; (*temperature*) abaisser; (*enemy's morale*) déprimer; **to l. one's expectations** viser plus bas; **to l. the quality of sth** nuire à la qualité de qch; *Med* **to l. sb's resistance** (*of tiredness etc*) diminuer la résistance de qn; **to l. standards** devenir moins exigeant; **to l. oneself** (*degrade*) s'abaisser, se ravaler (**to** à)

(**c**) (*reduce in height*) (*object*) diminuer la hauteur de; (*ceiling*) abaisser

(**d**) (*let down*) (*trunk from attic, stretcher into boat*) descendre; **to l. oneself (into/onto sth)** se laisser tomber (dans/sur qch); *Naut* (*mast*) amener, caler; (*ship's boat*) mettre à la mer; **l. away!** laissez aller!; **to l. sb on a rope** (faire) descendre qn au bout d'une corde; *Boxing* **to l. one's guard** baisser sa garde; *Fig* relâcher son attention

lower³ ['laʊər] *vi* (**a**) (*of person*) se renfrogner; **to l. at sb** regarder qn d'un mauvais œil, menacer qn du regard (**b**) (*of sky*) se couvrir; (*of storm*) menacer

lower case letter ['ləʊər] *n* minuscule *f*

lower-class *adj* (*accent*) populaire; **l. people** prolétaires *mpl*

lowering¹ ['ləʊərɪŋ] *n* (**a**) abaissement *m* (**b**) (*of prices*) abaissement *m*, diminution *f*; (*of pressure*) réduction *f* (**c**) (*reducing in height*) diminution *f* de la hauteur; (*of ceiling*) abaissement *m* (**d**) (*letting down*) (*of ladder etc*) descente *f*; *Naut* (*of mast*) calage *m*; (*of ship's boat*) mise *f* à la mer

lowering² ['laʊərɪŋ] *adj* (*look, sky*) menaçant

lowest bidder ['ləʊɪst] *n* moins-disant *m*

lowest common denominator *n* plus petit dénominateur *m* commun

low-flying *adj* (*airplane*) volant à basse altitude

low front *n* front *m* de basses pressions

low German *n Ling* bas allemand *m*

low-grade *adj* (**a**) (*coal etc*) de qualité inférieure (**b**) (*official*) de grade inférieur

low-heeled ['ləʊhiːld] *adj* (*shoe*) à talon plat

low income families *npl* familles *fpl* à faible revenu

lowing ['ləʊɪŋ] *n* meuglement *m*

low-involvement *adj Mktg* (*purchasing*) à faible participation des consommateurs

low-key *adj* (*approach, debate, discussion*) modéré; (*film*) au style dépouillé; (*person*) réservé; **to keep sth l.** contenir qch, modérer qch

lowland ['ləʊlənd] *n* plaine *f* (basse); **the Lowlands** (*in Scotland*) les Lowlands *fpl*

low-level *adj* (**a**) (*radioactivity*) faible; *Med* **l. infection** infection *f* bénigne (**b**) (*discussion*) à la base (**c**) *Comptr* **l. language** langage *m* de bas niveau

lowlife ['ləʊlaɪf] *n Sl* crapule *f*; **his l. friends** ses amis pas très recommandables

lowliness ['ləʊlɪnɪs] *n* humilité *f*, modestie *f*

low-loader *n* camion *m* à plate-forme surbaissée

lowly ['ləʊlɪ] *adj* humble, modeste

low-lying *adj* situé à basse altitude; (*land*) bas, enfoncé

low-maintenance battery *n* batterie *f* à entretien réduit

low-necked ['ləʊnekt] *adj* (*dress*) décolleté

lowness ['ləʊnɪs] *n* (**a**) (*of wall etc*) faible hauteur *f*; (*of island, hills*) faible altitude *f* (**b**) (*of note*) gravité *f* (**c**) (*of behaviour*) bassesse *f* (**d**) **l. (of spirits)** abattement *m*, découragement *m*

low-octane fuel *n* carburant *m* à faible indice d'octane

low-pitched ['ləʊpɪtʃt] *adj* (**a**) (*sound, voice*) grave; (*piano*) accordé à un diapason bas (**b**) (*roof*) à faible pente

low-pressure *adj* (**a**) *Met* (*zone*) de basse pression (**b**) (*cylinder, machine*) à basse pression *ou* tension

low-profile *adj* (*politician, company etc*) discret, qui adopte *ou* garde un profil bas; **l. tyre** pneu *m* taille basse

low-radiation monitor *n* moniteur *m* basse radiation

low relief *n* bas-relief *m*

low-rise **1** *adj* **l. building** immeuble *m* peu élevé *ou* bas **2** *n* immeuble *m* bas

low-speed *adj* (*machine*) à petite vitesse

low-spirited *adj* abattu, déprimé

low tar *adj* (*cigarette*) à taux de goudron faible

low-tech ['ləʊtek] *adj* rudimentaire, *F* pas très évolué; **as regards text-processing they're very l.** en matière de traitement de texte, ils ne sont pas très à la page

low technology *n* technologie *f* de base

low-tension circuit *n* circuit *m* basse tension

low tide *n* marée *f* basse

low-voltage *adj* à faible voltage, à faible tension

loyal ['lɔɪəl] *adj* (**a**) (*friend etc*) fidèle, dévoué (**to** à), loyal (**to** envers); *Mktg* **l. -customer discount** remise *f* de fidelité au client fidèle (**b**) (*to sovereign*) fidèle au souverain; **to drink the l. toast** porter le toast au souverain

loyalist ['lɔɪəlɪst] *adj, n* loyaliste *mf*

loyally ['lɔɪəlɪ] *adv* fidèlement, loyalement

loyalty ['lɔɪəltɪ] *n* loyalisme *m*; (*to friends, employer etc*) loyauté *f* (**to** envers); **you'll have to decide where your loyalties lie** il faudra que tu décides de quel côté tu es; **to have divided loyalties** être partagé; **to create customer l.** fidéliser la clientèle; *Mktg* **l. discount** remise *f* de fidélité

lozenge ['lɒzɪndʒ] *n* (**a**) *Pharm* pastille *f* (**b**) *Math, Her* losange *m*

LP [el'piː] *n* (*abbr* **long player**) 33 tours *m*

LQ [el'kjuː] (*abbr* **letter quality**) qualité *f* courrier; **LQ printer** imprimante *f* de qualité courrier

LSD [eles'diː] *n* (**a**) (*abbr* **lysergic acid diethylamide**) LSD *m* (**b**) *Br Old-fashioned abbr* **pounds, shillings and pence**

LSE [eles'iː] *n Br Univ abbr* **London School of Economics**

LSI [ele'saɪ] *n Comptr abbr* **large-scale integration**

Lt *Mil* (*abbr* **Lieutenant**) Lt

lt *abbr* **low tension**

LTA [eltiː'eɪ] *abbr* **Lawn Tennis Association**

Ltd *Br Com abbr* **limited**

lubricant ['luːbrɪkənt] **1** *adj* lubrifiant **2** *n* lubrifiant *m*

lubricate ['luːbrɪkeɪt] *vt* lubrifier, graisser; **lubricated condom** préservatif *m* lubrifié; *Fig F* **we were all well lubricated** (*drunk*) nous étions tous bien imbibés

lubricating ['lu:brɪkeɪtɪŋ] *n* lubrification *f*; **l. oil** huile *f* de graissage
lubrication [lu:brɪ'keɪʃən] *n* lubrification *f*, graissage *m*; *F Hum (alcohol)* gnôle *f*; **l. nipple** graisseur *m*; **l. oil** huile *f* de lubrification; **l. system** circuit *m* de lubrification
lubricator ['lu:brɪkeɪtər] *n (device)* graisseur *m*, appareil *m* de graissage; **gravity-feed l.** graisseur par gravité
lubricity [lu:'brɪsɪtɪ] *n Lit (lewdness)* lubricité *f*
Lucerne [lu:'sɜ:n] *n Geog* Lucerne *f*; **(the) Lake (of) L.** le lac des Quatre-Cantons
lucerne [lu:'sɜ:n] *n Br Bot, Agr* luzerne *f*
lucid ['lu:sɪd] *adj (mind, style)* lucide; *(explanation)* clair; *Med* **l. interval** intervalle *m* lucide *ou* de lucidité
lucidity [lu:'sɪdɪtɪ] *n* lucidité *f*
lucidly ['lu:sɪdlɪ] *adv* lucidement; *(explained, outlined etc)* avec clarté
Lucifer ['lu:sɪfər] *n* Lucifer *m*
luck [lʌk] *n (chance)* chance *f*; **good l.** bonne chance, bonheur *m*; **bad l.** malchance *f*, mauvaise fortune *f*, *F* déveine *f*; **piece** *or* **stroke of l.** coup *m* de chance, aubaine *f*, *F* coup de bol; **to bring sb bad/good l.** porter malheur/bonheur à qn; **to keep sth for l.** garder qch comme porte-bonheur; **good l. (to you)!** bonne chance!; **good l. with the exams/for Friday** bonne chance pour les examens/pour vendredi; *Iron* **good l. to him!** qu'il le fasse si ça lui chante!; **to wish sb l.** souhaiter bonne chance à qn; **better l. next time** ça ira mieux la prochaine fois; **to be in l.** avoir de la chance *ou F* de la veine; **to be out of l.** ne pas avoir de chance; **to be down on one's l.** avoir la guigne; **to try one's l.** tenter sa chance; **don't trust to l.** n'y compte pas trop; *(when you can do something about it)* ne laisse rien au hasard; **her l. has changed** sa chance a tourné; **he has all the l.** *F* c'est un veinard; **to have the l. of the devil** avoir une chance de tous les diables; **just my l.!** c'est bien ma chance!; **with my l. it won't work** avec ma chance habituelle, ça ne marchera pas; **no such l.!** je n'ai pas (eu) cette chance!, *F* tu parles!; **hard l.!** pas de chance!; **I've got to work, worst l.** il faut que je travaille, pas de chance!; **by good l.** par bonheur; **as l. would have it** par bonheur; **as l. would have it, I was there** le hasard a voulu que je sois là; **it's the l. of the draw** c'est le hasard
▶ **luck out** *vi Am F* avoir du pot
luckily ['lʌkɪlɪ] *adv* heureusement, par bonheur; **l. for her** par chance pour elle
luckless ['lʌklɪs] *adj Fml* **(a)** *(person)* malheureux, malchanceux **(b)** *(day)* de malchance
lucky ['lʌkɪ] *adj (person)* chanceux; *(time, moment)* propice; **to be l.** *(of person)* avoir de la chance; **you're a very l. person** vous avez beaucoup de chance; **who's the l. man?** *(she's going to marry)* qui est l'heureux élu?; *F* **(you) l. devil!, l. beggar!** veinard!; *Iron* **you'll be l.!** tu peux toujours courir!; **to be born l.** être né coiffé; **to have a l. break** avoir un coup de chance *ou* de pot; **l. in love/at cards** heureux en amour/au jeu; **it's l. you came when you did** c'est une chance que tu sois arrrivé à ce moment-là; **she's l. to be alive** elle a de la chance d'être en vie; **l. shot** coup de bol *ou* de veine; **my l. number** mon chiffre porte-bonheur; **to make a l. guess** tomber juste; **it's not my l. day** ce n'est pas mon jour de chance; **that was l.** ça a été un coup de chance; **it's l.** *(of thing)* ça porte bonheur
lucky charm *n* porte-bonheur *m inv*
lucky dip *n Br* = baquet *m* rempli de sciure etc où l'on plonge la main pour en retirer une surprise
lucrative ['lu:krətɪv] *adj* lucratif
lucre ['lu:kər] *n Pej Hum* lucre *m*; **to do sth for (filthy) l.** agir par amour du gain *ou* du lucre
ludicrous ['lu:dɪkrəs] *adj* risible, comique, ridicule; **it's l. to ...** c'est ridicule de ...; **he looked faintly l.** il avait l'air assez grotesque
ludicrously ['lu:dɪkrəslɪ] *adv* ridiculement
ludo ['lu:dəʊ] *n Br (game)* jeu *m* des petits chevaux
luff[1] [lʌf] *n Naut* **(a)** *(of sail)* lof *m*, ralingue *f* du vent, chute *f* avant **(b)** *(of bow)* épaule *f*
luff[2] *Naut* **1** *vi* lof(f)er, faire une aulof(f)ée **2** *vt* **to l. the boat (up)** faire loffer la barque
lug[1] [lʌg] **(-gg-)** *vt (sth heavy)* traîner, tirer; **to l. sth along** *or* **away** entraîner qch; **to l. sth about with one** promener *ou* trimbaler qch avec soi
lug[2] *n* **(a)** *Tech* oreille *f* **(b)** *F (ear)* esgourde *f*
lug[3] *n Naut* = **lugsail**
lug[4] *n Zool* = **lugworm**
luge [lu:ʒ] *n Sp* luge *f*
luggable ['lʌgab(ə)l] *n Comptr* portable *m* (lourd)
luggage ['lʌgɪdʒ] *n* bagage(s) *m(pl)*; **a piece of l.** un bagage; *Av* **l. bay** *or* **compartment** soute *f* à bagages; **l. label** étiquette *f* à bagages; **l. locker** consigne *f* automatique; **l. rack** *Rail* porte-bagages *m inv*; *Aut* galerie *f*; *Naut* **l. room** *or* **hold** soute *f* à bagages; **l. trolley** chariot *m* (à bagages); *Rail* **l. van** fourgon *m* à bagages
lugger ['lʌgər] *n Naut* lougre *m*
lughole ['lʌghəʊl] *n Br F* oreille *f*, *F* esgourde *f*; **are your lugholes blocked?** est-ce que tu as les portugaises ensablées?
lugsail ['lʌgseɪl, 'lʌgs(ə)l] *n Naut* voile *f* à bourcet
lugubrious [lu:'gu:brɪəs] *adj* lugubre
lugubriously [lu:'gu:brɪəslɪ] *adv* lugubrement
lugworm ['lʌgwɜ:m] *n Zool* ariénicole *f*
Luke [lu:k] *n* Luc *m*; **Saint L.** saint Luc
lukewarm ['lu:kwɔ:m] *adj (water, friendship etc)* tiède; **the critics gave the play a l. reception** les critiques ont accueilli la pièce avec tiédeur; **to become l.** tiédir
lull[1] [lʌl] *n* moment *m* de calme; *(in fighting)* répit *m*; *Naut* accalmie *f*; **the l. before the storm** le calme avant la tempête; **there was a l. in the conversation** la conversation tomba
lull[2] *vt (person) (send to sleep)* bercer, endormir; *(fears)* endormir; **to l. a child to sleep** endormir un enfant en le berçant; **to l. sb into a false sense of security** endormir la vigilance de qn
lullaby ['lʌləbaɪ] *n Mus* berceuse *f*
lumbago [lʌm'beɪgəʊ] *n Med* lumbago *m*; **to have l.** avoir un lumbago
lumbar ['lʌmbər] *adj Anat* lombaire; **l. adjustable seat** siège *m* à réglage lombaire; *Med* **l. puncture** ponction *f* lombaire, rachicentèse
lumber[1] ['lʌmbər] *n* **(a)** *Br (useless objects)* objets *mpl* encombrants; **l. room** (pièce *f* de) débarras *m* **(b)** *Am (wood)* bois *m* de charpente *ou* de construction
lumber[2] **1** *vt* **(a)** *(place)* encombrer, embarrasser; **to l. a room with furniture** encombrer une pièce de meubles; *F* **to get lumbered with a task** se taper *ou* se coltiner un travail; **to l. sb with sth** flanquer qch à qn; **they've lumbered me with the cooking** c'est moi qui me suis tapé tous les repas; **I was lumbered with him for the whole evening** je l'ai eu sur le dos pendant toute la soirée **(b)** *Am (trees)* abattre; *(wood)* débiter **2** *vi* avancer d'un pas pesant
▶ **lumber about** *vi* se trimbaler çà et là
▶ **lumber along** *vi (of person)* avancer à pas pesants *ou* d'un pas lourd
▶ **lumber up** *vtsep* = **lumber**[2]
lumbering ['lʌmbərɪŋ] *adj* lourd, pesant
lumberjack ['lʌmbədʒæk] *n esp Am* bûcheron *m*
lumberjacket ['lʌmbədʒækɪt] *n* blouson *m*; *(longer)* canadienne *f*
lumberman, *pl* -men ['lʌmbəmən] *n Am* bûcheron *m*
lumberyard ['lʌmbəjɑ:d] *n Am* chantier *m* de bois
luminary ['lu:mɪnərɪ] *n (person)* lumière *f*; *(of science etc)* sommité *f*
luminescence [lu:mɪ'nesəns] *n Phys* luminescence *f*
luminescent [lu:mɪ'nesənt] *adj Phys* luminescent
luminosity [lu:mɪ'nɒsɪtɪ] *n* luminosité *f*
luminous ['lu:mɪnəs] *adj* lumineux; *(socks, strip on clothing, roadsign, colours)* fluorescent
lumme, lummy ['lʌmɪ] *int Br Old-fashioned F* nom de Dieu!, mince alors!
lummox ['lʌməks] *n Old-fashioned F* lourdaud, -e
lump[1] [lʌmp] *n* **(a)** *(of stone)* gros morceau *m*, bloc *m*; *(of earth, clay)* motte *f*; *(of sugar, cheese etc)* morceau; *(of lead etc)* masse *f*; *(in porridge etc)* grumeau *m*; *Med (internal)* grosseur *f*; *(external)* excroissance *f*; *(caused by knock etc)* bosse *f*; *Fig* **to have a l. in one's throat** avoir la gorge serrée; **to pay in a l.** payer tout ensemble; **l. sum** somme *f* globale, forfait *m*; **in a l. sum** forfaitairement; **l.-sum** forfaitaire; *(fixed price for contract etc)* prix *m* forfaitaire; **Parisians, taken in the l., are ...** en général, les Parisiens sont ...
(b) *F Pej (person)* empoté *m*; **great l. of a girl** grosse dondon *f*
(c) *Br F* **the l.** *(casual workers)* ouvriers *mpl* indépendants (non déclarés)
lump[2] *vt* mettre en bloc *ou* en masse *ou* en tas
lump[3] *vt F* **if he doesn't like it, he can l. it, he can like it or l. it** que ça lui plaise ou pas, c'est le même prix; **you'll have to l. it!** il faudra que tu fasses avec!, il faudra en passer par là!
▶ **lump together** *vtsep (things)* rassembler, mettre ensemble; **to l. people together** considérer des personnes en bloc, *Pej* mettre tout le monde dans le même sac
lumpectomy [lʌm'pektəmɪ] *n Surg* ablation *f* de tumeur mammaire
lumpen ['lʌmpən] *adj* grossier; **the l. proletariat** le sous-prolétariat
lumpfish ['lʌmpfɪʃ] *n* lompe *m*, lump *m*

lumpish [ˈlʌmpɪʃ] *adj* **(a)** (*clumsy*) balourd, pataud; **great l. man** lourdaud *m* **(b)** (*stupid*) stupide
lumpy [ˈlʌmpɪ] *adj* (*sauce*) grumeleux; (*surface, mattress*) bosselé; (*forehead etc*) couvert de bosses
lunacy [ˈluːnəsɪ] *n* **(a)** *F* (*action, idea*) action *f*/idée *f* folle; **it's sheer l.** c'est de la folie (pure et simple) **(b)** *Med* aliénation *f* mentale, folie *f*; *Jur* démence *f*
lunar [ˈluːnər] *adj* (*cycle, module, orbit etc*) lunaire; **l. eclipse** éclipse *f* de lune; **l. landing** alunissage *m*, atterrissage *m* sur la lune
lunaria [luːˈneərɪə] *n Bot* lunaire *f*
lunatic [ˈluːnətɪk] **1** *adj* fou, *f* folle; **l. asylum** maison *f* de fous; **the l. fringe** les extrémistes *mpl*, les cinglés *mpl* **2** *n* fou, *f* folle; *Old-fashioned Med* aliéné, -ée
lunch¹ [lʌntʃ] *n* [①A6,d,iii] déjeuner *m*, *Can, Belg* dîner *m*, *US* (*snack*) (*eaten at any time*) petit repas *m*, casse-croûte *m inv*; **to have l.** prendre son déjeuner, déjeuner; **they have l. at one o'clock** ils déjeunent à une heure; **what time** *or* **when is l.?** à quelle heure déjeune-t-on?; **what's for l.?** qu'y a-t-il pour le déjeuner?; **we're having trout for l.** il y a de la truite au déjeuner; **let's go out for l.** allons déjeuner dehors; **how long do you get for l.?** combien de temps tu as pour déjeuner?; **what are you doing for l.?** que fais-tu à midi?; **we're having people to l.** nous avons du monde à déjeuner; **she's at l.** *or* **has gone to l.** elle est sortie déjeuner; *esp Am Sl* **to be out to l.** (*be crazy*) débloquer un peu, avoir une case de vide; *Mktg* **l. marketing** mercatique *f* qui consiste à inviter les clients à déjeuner; **l. menu** menu *m* déjeuner
lunch² **1** *vi Fml* déjeuner, *Can, Belg* dîner; **we lunched on sandwiches** nous avons déjeuné de sandwichs **2** *vt Fml* (*entertain to lunch*) inviter à déjeuner
lunchbox [ˈlʌntʃbɒks], *Am* **lunchbucket** [ˈlʌntʃbʌkɪt] *n* panier-repas *m*, *pl* paniers-repas
lunch break *n* (*in course of working day*) pause *f* du déjeuner
lunch counter *n Am* (*in store*) bar *m* de restauration rapide
luncheon [ˈlʌntʃ(ə)n] *n Fml* déjeuner *m*; **l. meat** pâté *m* de viande; *Br Com etc* **l. voucher** ticket-repas *m*, *pl* tickets-repas, chèque-restaurant *m*, *pl* chèques-restaurant
luncheonette [ˈlʌnʃəˈnet] *n Am* petit restaurant *m*, café-restaurant *m*
lunch hour *n* heure *f* du déjeuner; **to go shopping during one's l.** aller faire des courses à l'heure du déjeuner
lunchpail [ˈlʌntʃpeɪl] *n Am* panier-repas *m*, *pl* paniers-repas
lunchroom [ˈlʌntʃrʊm] *n Am* = pièce *f* où l'on peut manger ses sandwichs etc à l'heure du déjeuner
lunch time *n* (*noon, one o'clock etc*) moment *m* du déjeuner
lung [lʌŋ] *n* poumon *m*; **to shout at the top of one's lungs** crier à tue-tête; **l. cancer** cancer *m* du poumon; **l. transplant** greffe *f* du poumon
lunge¹ [lʌndʒ] *n* **(a)** mouvement *m* (brusque) en avant; **she made a l. for the ball** elle s'est jetée sur la balle **(b)** *Fencing* botte *f*
lunge² *vi Fencing* se fendre; **to l. at sb** se jeter sur qn; *Fencing* porter *ou* pousser une botte à l'adversaire
▶ **lunge forward** *vi* se jeter en avant
lupin, *US* **lupine** [ˈluːpɪn] *n* (*plant*) lupin *m*
lupine [ˈluːpaɪn] *adj* de loup
lurch¹ [lɜːtʃ] *n* **to leave sb in the l.** (*in danger, difficulty etc*) laisser qn dans le pétrin; (*to desert*) planter là qn
lurch² *n* (*of ship*) embardée *f*, coup *m* de roulis; (*of car*) embardée; **with a drunken l.** (*to stagger etc*) en titubant; (*to reach out*) d'un geste d'homme/de femme ivre; **to give a l.** (*of ship, car etc*) faire une embardée; **with a l., the train was off again** le train est reparti avec un à-coup; **a l. to the left/right** un virage à gauche/droite
lurch³ *vi* **(a)** (*of ship, car etc*) faire une embardée **(b)** (*of person*) tituber
▶ **lurch along** *vi* (*of person*) marcher en titubant; (*of economy*) progresser tant bien que mal
lurcher [ˈlɜːtʃər] *n* (*dog*) lévrier *m* bâtard
lure¹ [ˈlʊər] *n* **(a)** (*attraction*) attrait *m*; **the l. of the sea** l'attrait de la mer **(b)** (*in hunting*) (*decoy*) leurre *m*; *Fig* appât *m*; (*wooden duck*) appât factice
lure² *vt* **(a)** (*person*) attirer, séduire; **to be lured into a trap** être attiré dans un piège; **he was lured into it by his friends** il s'y est laissé entraîner par ses amis **(b)** (*fish, falcon etc*) leurrer
lurid [ˈlʊərɪd] *adj* **(a)** (*sensational*) (*account, language*) corsé, à sensation; **she gave us a l. description of her operation** elle nous a fait une description atroce de son opération; **l. details** détails *mpl* effroyables **(b)** (*fiery*) cuivré; (*flames*) rougeoyant; *Pej* (*colour*) criard; **a l. sunset** un coucher de soleil flamboyant **(c)** *Lit* (*pale*) (*light*) blafard; (*complexion*) livide
luridly [ˈlʊərɪdlɪ] *adv* **(a)** (*to describe*) de façon sensationnelle **(b)** (*to glow*) en rougeoyant **(c)** *Lit* (*with a pale light*) avec une lueur blafarde
lurk [lɜːk] *vi* se cacher; **there's a man lurking in the alleyway** il y a un homme qui se cache dans la ruelle; **I'll just l. in the background** je me fondrai dans les décors
lurking [ˈlɜːkɪŋ] *adj* (*feeling, suspicion etc*) vague; **I have one l. doubt** j'ai encore un léger doute; **if you have any l. doubts** s'il vous reste des doutes; **l. errors in the text** des erreurs qui sont passées inaperçues dans le texte
luscious [ˈlʌʃəs] *adj* succulent; (*fruit*) fondant, succulent; **a l. blonde** une blonde appétissante
lush¹ [lʌʃ] *adj* **(a)** (*grass, plant*) plein de sève, luxuriant **(b)** (*luxurious*) **l. surroundings** environnement *m* luxueux; **a l. sound** un son riche
lush² *n esp Am Sl* (*alcoholic*) poivrot, -ote
lushness [ˈlʌʃnɪs] *n* (*of grass etc*) luxuriance *f*
lust [lʌst] *n* (*sexual*) désir *m* (charnel *ou* sexuel), *Pej* luxure *f*; **l. for power** soif *f* de pouvoir
▶ **lust after** *vipo* (*person*) désirer; (*thing*) convoiter
▶ **lust for** *vipo* (*object*) convoiter; **to l. for power/revenge** avoir soif de pouvoir/de revanche
luster, lusterless *etc US* = **lustre, lustreless** *etc*
lustful [ˈlʌstfʊl] *adj* lascif, libidineux
lustfully [ˈlʌstfʊlɪ] *adv* lascivement
lustily [ˈlʌstɪlɪ] *adv* (*to sing, shout*) à pleine gorge
lustre, *US* **luster** [ˈlʌstər] *n* **(a)** (*shine*) éclat *m*, lustre *m*; (*of cloth*) cati *m*, lustre **(b)** (*of chandelier*) pendeloque *f* **(c)** (*fabric*) **(cotton) l.** lustrine *f*
lustreless, *US* **lusterless** [ˈlʌstəlɪs] *adj* terne; (*eyes, hair*) sans éclat
lustreware, *US* **lusterware** [ˈlʌstəweər] *n Cer* poterie *f* à reflets métalliques, poterie lustrée
lustrous [ˈlʌstrəs] *adj* (*hair, eyes*) brillant; (*fabric*) lustré
lusty [ˈlʌstɪ] *adj* vigoureux, fort, robuste; **l. voices** voix puissantes
lute [luːt] *n Mus* luth *m*; **l. maker** luthier *m*; **l. player** joueur, -euse de luth, luthiste *mf*
Lutheran [ˈluːθərən] *adj, n Rel, Hist* luthérien, -ienne
luv [lʌv] *n F* = **love¹**
luvvie [ˈlʌvɪ] *n F* (*actor, actress*) comédien, -ienne
luxation [lʌkˈseɪʃən] *n Med* luxation *f*
Luxemb(o)urg [ˈlʌksəmbɜːg] *n* **the Grand Duchy of L.** le Grand-duché de Luxembourg
luxuriance [lʌgˈzjʊərɪəns, lʌkˈs-] *n* (*of vegetation, style etc*) exubérance *f*, luxuriance *f*
luxuriant [lʌgˈzjʊərɪənt, lʌkˈs-] *adj* exubérant, luxuriant; **l. (growth of) hair** chevelure *f* abondante; **l. beard** barbe *f* drue
luxuriantly [lʌgˈzjʊərɪəntlɪ, lʌkˈs-] *adv* avec exubérance, en abondance
luxuriate [lʌgˈzjʊərɪeɪt, lʌkˈs-] *vi* **to l. in a hot bath** se prélasser dans un bain chaud
luxurious [lʌgˈzjʊərɪəs, lʌkˈs-] *adj* (*apartment, lifestyle*) luxueux, somptueux; (*tastes*) de luxe
luxuriously [lʌgˈzjʊərɪəslɪ, lʌkˈs-] *adv* **(a)** (*furnished*) luxueusement, avec luxe **(b)** (*to stretch*) avec volupté
luxuriousness [lʌgˈzjʊərɪəsnɪs, lʌkˈs-] *n* luxe *m*
luxury [ˈlʌkʃərɪ] **1** *n* **(a)** luxe *m*; **to live in (the lap of) l.** vivre dans le luxe; **l. tax** taxe *f* sur les produits de luxe **(b)** (*object*) objet *m* de luxe; **one of life's little luxuries** un des petits plaisirs de l'existence; **to indulge in the l. of a cigar** se payer le luxe d'un cigare; **it's a l. not to have to cook** c'est un luxe de ne pas avoir à faire la cuisine **2** *adj attrib* (*car, apartment etc*) de luxe; **l. brand** marque *f* de luxe; **l. goods** articles *mpl* de luxe; **l. liner** paquebot *m* de luxe; **l. market** marché *m* du luxe
LV [elˈviː] *Br abbr* **luncheon voucher**
LW [elˈdʌb(ə)ljuː] *abbr Rad* **(long wave)** LW
lychee [laɪˈtʃiː] *n* (*fruit*) litchi *m*
lychgate [ˈlɪtʃgeɪt] *n* = **lichgate**
lye [laɪ] *n* (*of soda, potassium*) lessive *f*
lying² [ˈlaɪɪŋ] **1** *adj* (*false*) (*person*) menteur, -euse; (*account*) mensonger **2** *n* (*falsehoods*) mensonges *mpl*
lying-in *n Old-fashioned Med* couches *fpl*
lymph [lɪmf] *n Physiol* lymphe *f*; **l. node** *or* *Old-fashioned* **gland** glande *f ou* ganglion *m* lymphatique
lymphatic [lɪmˈfætɪk] *Physiol* **1** *adj* lymphatique; **l. node** *or* *Old-fashioned* **gland** glande *f ou* ganglion *m* lymphatique **2** *n* (*vessel*) lymphatique *m*
lymphocyte [ˈlɪmfəʊsaɪt] *n Med* lymphocyte *m*
lynch¹ [lɪntʃ] *vt* lyncher
lynch² *adj attrib* **l. law** loi *f* de lynch; **l. mob** foule *f* responsable d'un lynchage; (*about to lynch*) foule prête à un lynchage
lynching [ˈlɪntʃɪŋ] *n* lynchage *m*

lynx [lɪŋks] *n* (*animal*) lynx *m*
lynx-eyed *adj* aux yeux de lynx
lyre ['laɪər] *n Mus* lyre *f*
lyrebird ['laɪəbɜːd] *n* oiseau-lyre *m*, *pl* oiseaux-lyres, ménure *m*
lyric ['lɪrɪk] **1** *adj* (*poet, drama*) lyrique **2** *n* **(a)** (*poem*) poème *m* lyrique **(b) lyrics** (*of song*) paroles *fpl*; **l. writer** parolier *m*
lyrical ['lɪrɪk(ə)l] *adj* **(a)** (*poetry etc*) lyrique **(b)** (*expressively formulated*) dit *ou* écrit sur un ton lyrique; *F* **she got positively l. about it** elle y a montré un enthousiasme fou; **to wax l. about sth** déborder d'enthousiasme pour qch
lyrically ['lɪrɪklɪ] *adv* **(a)** *Liter* avec lyrisme, lyriquement **(b)** (*to speak*) avec enthousiasme
lyricism ['lɪrɪsɪz(ə)m] *n* lyrisme *m*
lyricist ['lɪrɪsɪst] *n* **(a)** (*of musical etc*) parolier *m* **(b)** (*poet*) poète *m* lyrique
lysergic [lɪ'sɜːdʒɪk, laɪ-] *adj* (*acid*) lysergique

M

M, m [em] *n* (*letter*) M, m *mf*; **two Ms** *or* **M's** deux M
m (*abbr* **metre(s)**) m
MA [e'meɪ] *n abbr* **(a)** *Univ* **Master of Arts** (*degree*) *Eng* maîtrise *f* de *ou* ès lettres; *Scot* licence *f* de *ou* ès lettres; (*person*) titulaire *mf* d'une maîtrise/licence de *ou* ès lettres; **to have an MA in Russian** avoir une maîtrise/licence de russe; **Susan Long, MA** Susan Long, Maîtrise de lettres/licenciée ès lettres **(b) Massachusetts**
ma [mɑː] *n F* maman *f*
ma'am [mɑːm] *n* madame *f*
mac[1] [mæk] *n Br F* (*raincoat*) imper *m*
mac[2] *n US F* **hey, m.!** hé, mon vieux *ou* mon pote!
macabre [mə'kɑːbrə] *adj* macabre; **a taste for the m.** le goût du macabre
macadam [mə'kædəm] *n Constr* macadam *m*
macadamize [mə'kædəmaɪz] *vt Constr* (*road*) macadamiser
macaroni [mækə'rəʊnɪ] *n* [①A13,7] *Culin* macaroni(s) *m(pl)*; **m. cheese** macaroni(s) au gratin
macaroon [mækə'ruːn] *n Culin* macaron *m*
macaw [mə'kɔː] *n* (*bird*) ara *m*
Mace[1]® [meɪs] *n* (*gas*) gaz *m* lacrymogène *ou* incapacitant
Mace[2]® *vt* **to m. sb** asperger qn de gaz lacrymogène *ou* incapacitant
mace[1] [meɪs] *n* (*weapon, symbol of office*) masse *f*
mace[2] *n Bot, Culin* macis *m*
macebearer ['meɪsbeərər] *n* massier *m*
Macedonia [mæsɪ'dəʊnɪə] *n* Macédoine *f*
Macedonian [mæsɪ'dəʊnɪən] **1** *adj* macédonien **2** *n* **(a)** (*person*) Macédonien, -ienne **(b)** *Ling* macédonien *m*
macerate ['mæsəreɪt] *vti* macérer
Mach [mæk] *n Phys* **M. (number)** (nombre *m* de) Mach *m*; **at M. 3** à Mach 3
machete [mə'tʃetɪ, -'tʃeɪtɪ] *n* machette *f*
Machiavellian [mækɪə'velɪən] *adj* machiavélique
machination [mækɪ'neɪʃən] *n* machination *f*, manœuvre *f*
machine[1] [mə'ʃiːn] *n* **(a)** machine *f*; **(vending) m.** distributeur *m* (automatique); **m. made** fait à la machine; **m. shop** atelier *m* d'usinage; **m. tool** machine-outil *m*, *pl* machines-outils **(b)** *Fig Pej* (*person*) automate *m*, robot *m*, machine *f* **(c)** *Fig* (*organization*) **propaganda m.** appareil *m* de propagande; **the organization runs like a m.** l'organisation fonctionne très efficacement
machine[2] *vt* **(a)** *Ind* (*part*) usiner, façonner, travailler à la machine **(b)** *Sewing* coudre *ou* piquer à la machine
▶ **machine down** *vtsep Ind* (*metal*) amincir
machine code *n Comptr* code *m* machine; **m. instruction** instruction *f* de code machine
machine gun *n Mil* mitrailleuse *f*
machine-gun *vt* mitrailler
machine gunner *n Mil* mitrailleur *m*
machine gunning *n Mil* mitraillage *m*
machine-hour *n* heure-machine *f*, *pl* heures-machine
machine language *n Comptr* langage *m* machine
machine-readable *adj Comptr* (*data*) lisible par ordinateur; **in m. format** dans un format lisible par ordinateur
machinery [mə'ʃiːnərɪ] *n* **(a)** (*parts*) mécanisme(s) *m(pl)*; (*machines*) machines *fpl*, machinerie *f* **(b)** (*of organization*) **the m. of government** les rouages *mpl* du gouvernement; **administrative m.** appareil *m* administratif
machine time *n* temps-machine *m*
machine-time intensive *adj* qui nécessite beaucoup de temps-machine
machine translation *n Comptr* traduction *f* automatique
machinist [mə'ʃiːnɪst] *n* **(a)** *Ind* (*operator*) opérateur, -trice **(b)** *Sewing* mécanicien, -ienne
machismo [mæ'kɪzməʊ, -'tʃɪz-] *n F* machisme *m*; **I'm getting a bit tired of his m.** il commence à m'agacer avec son côté macho
macho ['mætʃəʊ] *adj F* macho *inv*; **m. type** macho *m*
macintosh ['mækɪntɒʃ] *n* = **mackintosh**
mackerel ['mækrəl] *n* (*pl* **-rel** *or occ* **-rels**) (*fish*) maquereau *m*; **m. sky** ciel pommelé *ou* moutonné
mackintosh ['mækɪntɒʃ] *n* imperméable *m*
macramé [mə'krɑːmɪ] *n* macramé *m*
macro ['mækrəʊ] *n Comptr* macro *m*, macrocommande *f*; **m. command** macrocommande *f*; **m. language** macrolangage *m*
macrobiotics [mækrəʊbaɪ'ɒtɪks] *n* [①A10,c] macrobiotique *f*
macrocomputing ['mækrəʊkəm'pjuːtɪŋ] *n Comptr* macroinformatique *f*
macrocosm ['mækrəkɒzəm] *n* macrocosme *m*
macro-economic *adj* macro-économique
macroeconomics [mækrəʊiːkə'nɒmɪks] *n* [①A10,c] macro-économie *f*
macromarketing [mækrəʊ'mɑːkɪtɪŋ] *n* macromercatique *f*, macromarketing *m*
macron ['mækrɒn] *n Typ* macron *m*
macroscopic [mækrə'skɒpɪk] *adj* macroscopique
mad [mæd] **1** *adj* **(madder, maddest) (a)** (*insane*) fou, *f* folle, *m before vowel or h mute* fol, dément; *Med* aliéné; (*idea, plan*) insensé; *F* **as m. as a hatter** *or* **as a March hare** fou à lier; **she's very nice but as m. as a hatter!** elle est très gentille mais elle a un grain!; **it is enough to drive you m.** il y a de quoi devenir fou, c'est à vous rendre fou; **to go m.** devenir fou; **nationalism gone m.** nationalisme forcené; **m. with fear** mort de peur; **m. with desire/envy/***etc* fou de désir/jalousie/*etc*

(b) (*enthusiastic*) **to be m. about sb/sth** (*like very much*) être fou de qn/qch; **I'm not m. on Indian food** je ne raffole pas de la cuisine indienne; **to be m. about** *or* **on sport/climbing** être un passionné *ou* mordu de sport/d'escalade, avoir la passion du sport/de l'escalade; **I'm not m. about the idea** ce n'est pas une idée qui m'emballe; **m. for revenge** assoiffé de revanche

(c) *F* (*angry*) furieux, furibond; **that kind of attitude makes me m.** ce genre d'attitude me met hors de moi; **to be m. with** *or* **at sb** être furieux contre qn; **m. bull** taureau furieux *ou* enragé; *Vet* **m. dog** chien *m* enragé

(d) (*frantic*) **there was a m. rush for the door** on s'est précipité à la porte; *F* **to run/shout/work like m.** courir/crier/travailler comme un fou

2 *adv F* **m. keen on sb/sth** fou de qn/qch; **to be m. keen on an idea** être emballé par une idée; **I'm not m. keen on Indian food/reggae** je raffole pas de la cuisine indienne/de reggae
Madagascan [mædə'gæskən] **1** *adj* malgache **2** *n* Malgache *mf*
Madagascar [mædə'gæskər] *n* Madagascar *m*; **they live in M.** ils vivent à Madagascar; **M. is an island** Madagascar est une île
madam ['mædəm] *n* **(a)** (*as form of address*) madame *f*; **M. Chairman** Madame la Présidente; **Dear M.** (*in letter*) Madame **(b)** (*pl* **madams**) (*in brothel*) tenancière *f* de bordel, maquerelle *f* **(c)** *Br F Pej* **she's a bit of a m.** elle est un peu pimbêche; **she's a proper little m.** c'est une vraie petite pimbêche
madcap ['mædkæp] **1** *adj* (*scheme, idea*) insensé **2** *n* insensé, -ée
mad cow disease *n F* maladie *f* de la vache folle
madden ['mæd(ə)n] *vt* (*make angry*) exaspérer, rendre fou
maddening ['mæd(ə)nɪŋ] *adj* (*exasperating*) exaspérant; **the really m. thing is that we could so easily have won** ce qui est rageant c'est qu'on aurait facilement pu gagner
maddeningly ['mæd(ə)nɪŋlɪ] *adv* **a m. long wait** une attente interminable; **he's m. slow/stupid** il est d'une lenteur/bêtise exaspérante; **he was m. calm about the whole thing** il est resté d'un calme horripilant
madder ['mædər] *n* **(a)** *Bot* garance *f*; **m. root** alizari *m* **(b)** (*in dyeing*) teinture *f* de garance
madding ['mædɪŋ] *adj Arch, Lit* furieux, déchaîné; **far from the m. crowd** loin de la foule et du bruit
made [meɪd] **1** *pt, pp see* **make**[2] **2** *adj* fait, fabriqué; **m. in France** fabriqué en France; *F* **he's a m. man** son avenir est assuré, sa fortune est faite; **she's m., she's got it m.** son avenir est assuré

Madeira [mə'dɪərə] *n* **(a)** *Geog* Madère *f*; **to go to M.** aller à Madère **(b)** *(wine)* vin *m* de Madère, madère *m* **(c)** *Culin* **M. cake** gâteau *m* de Savoie

made-up *adj* **(a)** *(not true)* faux, *f* fausse; *(intended to deceive)* inventé de toutes pièces **(b)** *Sewing (garment)* tout fait **(c)** *(wearing make-up)* maquillé; **heavily m.** très maquillée

madhouse ['mædhaʊs] *n Arch (lunatic asylum)* maison *f* de fous; *Fig* **this place is a m.!** c'est une véritable maison de fous ici!

madly ['mædlɪ] *adv* **(a)** *(to behave)* comme un fou/une folle **(b)** *F (very)* follement; *(to love)* à la folie, éperdument, follement; **m. in love** follement *ou* éperdument amoureux; **I can't say I'm m. interested in it** je ne peux pas dire que ça m'intéresse follement **(c)** *(desperately) (to work, rush, struggle etc)* comme un fou/une folle; **people rushed m. in every direction** les gens couraient comme des fous dans tous les sens

madman, *pl* **-men** ['mædmən] *n* fou *m*, aliéné *m*, dément *m*; **he's a complete m.!** il est complètement fou!; **like a m.** *(to fight)* comme un forcené, désespérément; *(to shout)* comme un perdu; *(to drive)* comme un fou

madness ['mædnɪs] *n* folie *f*, démence *f*; **in a fit of m.** dans un accès *ou* dans un moment de folie; **it's sheer m.** c'est insensé, c'est de la folie; **it would be m. to ...** ce serait de la folie de ...

Madonna [mə'dɒnə] *n Rel (Mary)* Madonne; **M.** *or* **m.** *(statue, picture)* madone *f*

madrigal ['mædrɪg(ə)l] *n Mus* madrigal *m*

madwoman, *pl* **-women** ['mædwʊmən, -wɪmɪn] *n* folle *f*, aliénée *f*, démente *f*

maelstrom ['meɪlstrəʊm] *n (whirlpool)* tourbillon *m*; *Fig* **the m. of modern life** le tourbillon de la vie moderne

maestro, *pl* **-tros, -tri** ['maɪstrəʊ, -trəʊz, -triː] *n Mus* maestro *m*, *pl* maestros

Mae West ['meɪ'west] *n Old-fashioned F (lifejacket)* gilet *m* de sauvetage

mafia ['mæfɪə] *n* mafia *f*

mafioso [mæfɪ'əʊsəʊ] *n* mafioso *m*

mag [mæg] *n F* = **magazine (a)**

magazine [mægə'ziːn] *n* **(a)** *(publication)* magazine *m*, revue *f*; **illustrated m.** revue illustrée, magazine; **sports m.** magazine sportif; *Rad, TV* **m. (programme)** magazine *m* (télévisé), émission *f* magazine **(b)** *(for cartridges)* chargeur *m*, magasin *m*; *Phot* magasin; **m. rifle** fusil *m* à répétition *ou* à chargeur **(c)** *Mil (store) (of arms etc)* magasin *m*, dépôt *m*; **powder m.** *Mil* magasin à poudre, poudrière *f*, dépôt d'explosifs; *Naut* soute *f* aux poudres *ou* à poudre

magenta [mə'dʒentə] *n, adj (colour)* magenta *m inv*

maggot ['mægət] *n* ver *m*, asticot *m*

maggoty ['mægətɪ] *adj* véreux, plein de vers *ou* d'asticots

Magi ['meɪdʒaɪ] *npl Bible* **the (Three) M.** les (trois) rois mages *mpl*

magic ['mædʒɪk] **1** *n* magie *f*, enchantement *m*; **like m., as if by m.** comme par enchantement; *Fig* **the m. had gone out of their marriage** leur vie conjugale avait perdu tout son charme; **black/white m.** magie noire/blanche **2** *adj* **(a)** magique; **m. carpet** tapis *m* volant; **m. lantern** lanterne *f* magique; **m. wand** baguette *f* magique; **to say the m. word** *(say please)* dire s'il vous plaît **(b)** *Br Sl (excellent)* génial, super

▶ **magic away** *vtsep (pt, pp* **magicked***)* faire disparaître comme par magie *ou* par enchantement

magical ['mædʒɪkəl] *adj* magique

magically ['mædʒɪklɪ] *adv* magiquement; *Fig (to disappear)* (comme) par magie *ou* par enchantement

magician [mə'dʒɪʃən] *n* magicien, -ienne

magic square *n Math* carré *m* magique

magisterial [mædʒɪs'tɪərɪəl] *adj* **(a)** *(tone, air)* magistral; *Pej* doctoral **(b)** *Jur* de magistrat

magistrate ['mædʒɪstreɪt] *n* magistrat *m*, juge *m*; *Eng* **magistrates' court** ≈ tribunal *m* d'instance

magma ['mægmə] *n Geol* magma *m*

Magna Carta ['mægnə'kɑːtə] *n Eng Hist* la Grande Charte (de l'année 1215)

magnanimity [mægnə'nɪmɪtɪ] *n* magnanimité *f*; *(nobility)* grandeur *f* d'âme

magnanimous [mæg'nænɪməs] *adj* magnanime; **to be m.** se montrer magnanime

magnanimously [mæg'nænɪməslɪ] *adv* magnanimement, avec magnanimité

magnate ['mægneɪt] *n (of industry etc)* magnat *m*

magnesia [mæg'niːʃə] *n* **(a)** *Ch* magnésie *f* **(b)** *Pharm* magnésie *f* blanche

magnesium [mæg'niːzɪəm] *n Ch* magnésium *m*

magnet ['mægnɪt] *n* **(a)** aimant *m* **(b)** *Fig (for tourists etc)* pôle *m* d'attraction

magnetic [mæg'netɪk] *adj* **(a)** *(attraction, field, pole etc)* magnétique; *Comptr* **m. card** carte *f* magnétique; **m. card/character reader** lecteur *m* de cartes/caractères magnétiques; **m. lock** serrure *f* magnétique; **m. needle** aiguille *f* aimantée; *Comptr* **m. tape** bande *f* magnétique; *Comptr* **m. tape unit** *or* **drive** dérouleur *m* de bande magnétique, unité *f* de bande magnétique **(b)** *Fig (personality)* magnétique

magnetically [mæg'netɪklɪ] *adv* magnétiquement

magnetic north *n* nord *m* magnétique

magnetic resonance imaging *n Med* imagerie *f* par résonance magnétique

magnetic stripe *n* piste *f* magnétique; **m. card** carte *f* à piste magnétique; **m. reader** lecteur *m* de pistes magnétiques

magnetism ['mægnɪtɪz(ə)m] *n Phys, Fig,* magnétisme *m*

magnetization [mægnɪtaɪ'zeɪʃən] *n* aimantation *f*, magnétisation *f*

magnetize ['mægnɪtaɪz] **1** *vt* **(a)** *(needle etc)* aimanter **(b)** *Fig (person)* magnétiser, attirer *(par magnétisme personnel)*; **he was magnetized by her good looks** il était fasciné par sa beauté **2** *vi (of iron etc)* s'aimanter

magnetizing ['mægnɪtaɪzɪŋ] *adj (current, field etc)* magnétisant

magneto [mæg'niːtəʊ] *n El* magnéto *f*

magneto-electric *adj Phys* magnéto-électrique

magnificat [mæg'nɪfɪkæt] *n Rel* magnificat *m inv*

magnification [mægnɪfɪ'keɪʃən] *n Opt etc* grossissement *m*; *(of sound)* amplification *f*; *Opt* **high m.** fort grossissement

magnificence [mæg'nɪfɪsəns] *n* magnificence *f*

magnificent [mæg'nɪfɪsənt] *adj* magnifique; *(meal, wine)* excellent

magnificently [mæg'nɪfɪsəntlɪ] *adv* magnifiquement

magnifier ['mægnɪfaɪər] *n* verre *m* grossissant

magnify ['mægnɪfaɪ] *vt* **(a)** *(image)* grossir, agrandir; *(sound)* amplifier; *Fig (importance)* grossir, exagérer; **to m. sth out of all proportion** beaucoup exagérer l'importance de qch **(b)** *Rel, Arch (the Lord)* magnifier

magnifying ['mægnɪfaɪɪŋ] *n* **m. glass** loupe *f*; *Opt* **m. power** *(of lens, microscope)* grossissement *m*

magnitude ['mægnɪtjuːd] *n* importance *f*; *Astron* magnitude *f*; *Math* grandeur *f*, valeur *f*; *Astron* **star of the first m.** étoile *f* de première magnitude; *Fig* **of the first m.** de premier ordre; *(mistake)* gravissime

magnolia [mæg'nəʊlɪə] *n Bot* magnolia *m*, magnolier *m*; *(colour)* rose *m* pâle; **m. tree** magnolia *m*, magnolier *m*

magnum, *pl* **-ums** ['mægnəm, -əmz] *n (of champagne etc)* magnum *m*

magnum opus *n Liter etc* chef-d'œuvre *m*, *pl* chefs-d'œuvre

magpie ['mægpaɪ] *n (bird)* pie *f*; *F, Fig (hoarder)* thésauriseur, -euse

mag tape *n* bande *f* magnétique; **m. cassette** cassette *f* à bande magnétique; **m. reader** lecteur *m* de bandes magnétiques

Magyar ['mægjɑːr] **1** *adj* magyar **2** *n* Magyar, -are

maharajah [mɑːhə'rɑːdʒə] *n* maharajah *m*

maharani [mɑːhə'rɑːniː] *n* maharani *f*

maharishi [mɑːhə'riːʃɪ] *n Hindu Rel* maharishi *m*

mahogany [mə'hɒgənɪ] *n (tree, wood, colour)* acajou *m*; **m. table** table *f* en acajou

Mahometan [mə'hɒmətən] *adj, n Old-fashioned* mahométan, -ane

maid [meɪd] *n* **(a)** *(servant)* bonne *f*, domestique *f*; **lady's m.** femme *f* de chambre; **m. of all work** bonne à tout faire; **m. of honour** *(to queen)* demoiselle *f* d'honneur; *Am (at wedding)* première demoiselle d'honneur **(b)** *Arch, Lit (girl)* jeune fille *f*; *(virgin)* vierge *f*

maiden ['meɪd(ə)n] **1** *n* **(a)** *Lit (girl)* jeune fille *f*; *(virgin)* vierge *f* **(b)** *Cr* **m. (over)** = série *f* de six balles pendant laquelle aucun point n'est marqué **2** *adj attrib (first)* premier, -ère; **m. aunt** tante *f* non mariée; **m. flight** premier vol *m*, vol inaugural; **m. name** nom *m* de jeune fille; **m. speech** premier discours *m*; **m. voyage** première traversée *f*, traversée inaugurale

maidenhair ['meɪd(ə)nheər] *n* **m. (fern)** adiante *m*, cheveu *m* de Vénus

Maid of Orleans [ɔː'lɪənз] *n Hist* **the M.** la Pucelle (d'Orléans)

maidservant ['meɪdsɜːvənt] *n Arch* domestique *f*

maid service *n (at self-catering apartment)* service *m* de femme de ménage

mail[1] [meɪl] *n* **(a)** *(letters, parcels)* courrier *m*; **it came in the m.** c'est arrivé au courrier; **was there anything in the m. for me?** est-ce qu'il y avait du courrier pour moi?; **has the m. been yet?** est-ce que le facteur est passé?; *Am* **m. drop** boîte *f* aux lettres; **m. room** service *m* du courrier **(b)** *(postal service)* poste *f*, courrier *m*; **m. train** train *m* postal, train-poste *m*, *pl* trains-poste; **m. van** *Rail* wagon-poste *m*, *pl* wagons-poste; *Aut* voiture *f ou* fourgon *m* des postes **(c)** *Arch* (*coach*) malle *f*, malle-poste *f*, *pl* malles-poste(s); **m. coach** malle-poste

mail[2] *vt* (*letters, parcels*) (*send*) envoyer par la poste, expédier; (*put in mailbox*) mettre à la poste, poster

mail[3] *n* (*armour*) mailles *fpl*; **coat of m.** cotte *f* de mailles

mailbag ['meɪlbæg] *n* sac *m* postal

mailbox ['meɪlbɒks] *n Am* boîte *f* aux lettres; *Comptr* **electronic m.** boîte *f* aux lettres électronique

mailing ['meɪlɪŋ] *n* (*mailshot*) publipostage *m*, mailing *m*; **m. list** liste *f* d'adresses

mailman, *pl* **-men** ['meɪlmæn, -men] *n Am* facteur *m*, préposé *m*

mailmerge ['meɪlmɜːdʒ] *n Comptr* publipostage *m*; **m. letter** lettre *f* envoyée par publipostage; **m. program** programme *m* de publipostage

mail order *n Com* commande *f* par correspondance; **m. (selling)** vente *f* par correspondance, VPC *f*; **m. catalogue** catalogue *m* de vente par correspondance; **m. company** société *f* de vente par correspondance; **m. firm** maison *f* de vente par correspondance; **m. specialist** vépéciste *m*

mailshot[1] ['meɪlʃɒt] *n* mailing *m*, publipostage *m*

mailshot[2] *vt* envoyer un mailing *ou* un publipostage à

mail transfer *n* virement *m* par courrier

maim [meɪm] *vt* (*person*) estropier, mutiler

main[1] [meɪn] *n* **(a)** (*pipe*) canalisation *f ou* conduite *f* maîtresse *ou* principale; *El* câble *m* de distribution **(b) in the m.** (*on the whole*) en général, en gros, en somme, généralement (parlant) **(c)** *Arch, Lit* **the m.** (*ocean*) le grand large, l'océan *m*

main[2] *adj* principal; **the m. body of ...** le gros de ...; **our m. concern** notre préoccupation majeure; **m. line of business** activité *f* principale exercée, APE *f*; *Comptr* **m. board** carte *f* principale; *Agr* **m. crop** culture *f* principale; **m. entrance** entrée *f* principale; **the m. point** *or* **thing** l'essentiel, le principal; **m. idea** (*of book, film etc*) idée *f* mère *ou* maîtresse *ou* directrice; *Gram* **m. clause** proposition *f* principale; *Culin* **m. course** *or* **dish** plat *m* principal *ou* de résistance; **m. road** grande route *f*; **m. street,** *Am F* **m. drag** rue *f* principale; **m. sewer** grand collecteur *m*; *Rail etc* **m. line** voie *f* principale, grande ligne *f*; *Naut* **m. masts** mâts *mpl* majeurs; **m. deck** pont *m* principal, premier pont

mainbrace ['meɪnbreɪs] *n Naut* grand bras *m* de vergue

mainframe ['meɪnfreɪm] *n Comptr* **m. (computer)** ordinateur *m* central

mainland ['meɪnlænd] *n* (*continental land mass*) continent *m*; **you can see the Scottish m.** on voit la côte écossaise; **we live on the m.** (*not on island*) nous n'habitons pas dans les îles; **the French m., the m. of France** la France continentale

mainline ['meɪnlaɪn] *Sl* **1** *vi* (*of drug user*) se piquer **2** *vt* **to m. heroin** s'injecter de l'héroïne dans les veines

mainliner ['meɪnlaɪnər] *n Sl* (*drug addict*) = drogué, -ée qui se pique

mainly ['meɪnlɪ] *adv* principalement, surtout; **the passengers were m. old men** la plupart des passagers étaient des vieux messieurs; **a m. Spanish-speaking population** une population à majorité *ou* principalement *ou* surtout hispanophone; **their diet consists m. of insects** ils se nourrissent essentiellement *ou* principalement *ou* surtout d'insectes; **she was m. to blame** c'est elle la principale responsable, c'est surtout de sa faute

mainmast ['meɪnmɑːst, -məst] *n Naut* grand mât *m*

mains [meɪnz] *npl* secteur *m*; **the house hasn't been connected to the m.** la maison n'a pas été raccordée au secteur; **electric m.** (*cables*) canalisations *fpl* d'électricité; **gas m.** conduites *fpl* de gaz; **water m.** canalisations *ou* conduites d'eau; **m. adaptor** adaptateur *m* secteur; **m. electricity** courant *m* secteur; *Rad* **m. set** poste *m* secteur; **m. water** eau *f* de ville

mainsail ['meɪnseɪl, 'meɪns(ə)l] *n Naut* grand-voile *f*, *pl* grand(s)-voiles

mainsheet ['meɪnʃiːt] *n Naut* grand-écoute *f*, *pl* grand-écoutes

mains-powered *adj* fonctionnant sur secteur

mainspring ['meɪnsprɪŋ] *n* **(a)** *MecE* grand ressort *m*; (*of clock etc*) ressort moteur **(b)** *Fig* (*force behind sth*) moteur *m*

mainstay ['meɪnsteɪ] *n* **(a)** *Naut* étai *m* de grand mât **(b)** (*of economy, philosophy, policy*) base *f*, pilier *m*; (*of family*) soutien *m* principal

mainstream ['meɪnstriːm] **1** *n* courant *m* principal; **he belongs to the m. of French tradition** il fait partie de la grande tradition française; **a writer who has moved away from the m.** un auteur qui est sorti des sentiers battus **2** *adj* **m. Hollywood movies** films *mpl* dans la grande tradition hollywoodienne; *Mus* **m. jazz** = style *m* de jazz qui se situe entre le traditionnel et le moderne; **m. politics** courants *mpl* politiques dominants

maintain [meɪn'teɪn] *vt* **(a)** (*keep in good condition*) (*road, machine, car*) entretenir **(b)** (*support*) (*family etc*) entretenir, subvenir aux besoins de, nourrir; (*army*) entretenir **(c)** (*order, discipline*) maintenir; (*conversation etc*) soutenir; (*relations etc*) entretenir; (*health, advantage, lead*) garder, conserver; (*attitude, one's silence*) garder, observer; (*one's rights*) défendre; **to m. speed** conserver l'allure **(d)** (*assert*) (*opinion, fact*) soutenir; **to m. that ...** maintenir *ou* soutenir que ... + *ind*

maintenance ['meɪntɪnəns] *n* **(a)** (*of car, Rail Tel of lines*) entretien *m*; (*of equipment, roads etc*) entretien, maintenance *f*; **m. contract** contrat *m* de maintenance; **m. costs** coûts *mpl* de maintenance, frais *mpl* d'entretien; **m. department** service *m* de maintenance *ou* d'entretien; **m. engineer** téchnicien *m* de maintenance; **m. handbook** manuel *m* d'entretien; **m. kit** trousse *f* d'entretien; **m. man** ouvrier *m* d'entretien; **m. manual** manuel *m* d'entretien; **m. staff** personnel *m* d'entretien; **m. vehicle** camion-atelier *m*, *pl* camions-ateliers

(b) (*of law and order*) maintien *m*

(c) (*of family, troops etc*) entretien *m*

(d) *Jur* (*alimony*) pension *f* alimentaire; *Sch* **m. grant** bourse *f* d'entretien; *Jur* **m. order** obligation *f* alimentaire

(e) (*of one's rights*) défense *f*

maintenance-free *adj* qui ne nécessite aucun entretien; **m. battery** batterie *f* sans entretien

maison(n)ette [meɪzə'net] *n* (appartement *m*) duplex *m*

maître d' [metrə'diː] *n esp Am* maître *m* d'hôtel

maize [meɪz] *n esp Br* maïs *m*

Maj *Mil abbr* **major**

majestic [mə'dʒestɪk] *adj* majestueux; (*bearing*) majestueux, plein de majesté; (*scenery*) grandiose

majestically [mə'dʒestɪklɪ] *adv* majestueusement

majesty ['mædʒəstɪ] *n* majesté *f*; **God in all His m.** Dieu dans toute sa majesté; **His M. (the King)** Sa Majesté le Roi; **Her M. (the Queen)** Sa Majesté la Reine; **Your M.** Votre Majesté; *Br* **on His/Her M.'s Service** (pour le) service de Sa Majesté (≈ service de l'État); (*on envelope*) ≈ en franchise

Maj Gen *Mil abbr* **major general**

major[1] ['meɪdʒər] *n Mil* (*in infantry*) chef *m* de bataillon; (*in cavalry etc*) chef d'escadron; **m. general** général *m* de division

major[2] **1** *adj* **(a)** (*big*) grand; (*main*) le plus grand; (*company*) de première importance, de premier ordre; (*distinction, improvement, changes, difficulties*) de taille, grand; (*problem, cause, concern, interest, new novel, discovery*), *Mus* majeur; (*accident, disaster*) grand; **the m. brands** les marques les plus importantes; **it's a m. brand** c'est une des marques les plus importantes; **the m. teams** les plus grandes équipes; **it's of m. importance** c'est de la plus haute importance; **the significance of this event is quite m.** c'est un événement de toute première importance; **the party was a m. disaster** la fête a été une catastrophe absolue; **any problems? – nothing m.** des problèmes? – rien d'important; **he's our m. programmer** c'est notre programmeur principal; **we invested in a m. way** nous avons investi de manière considérable; **he's taken up Spanish in a m. way** il s'est mis à fond à l'espagnol; **he's fallen for Susie in a m. way** il est tombé follement amoureux de Susie; **the m. portion** la majeure partie, la plus grande partie; **m. decision** décision *f* capitale; **m. illness** maladie *f* grave; *Mus* **m. key** ton *m ou* mode *m* majeur; *Am Sp* **m. league** première division *f*; *Mil* **m. offensive** vaste offensive *f*; *Med etc* **m. operation** grosse opération *f*; *Phil* **m. premise** prémisse *f* majeure; **m. prophets** grands prophètes *mpl*; **m. repairs** grosses réparations *fpl*; *Aut* **m. road** route *f* principale *ou* à priorité; **to undergo m. surgery** subir une intervention chirurgicale importante

(b) *Old-fashioned Br Sch* **Martin m.** Martin aîné, l'aîné des deux Martin

2 *n* **(a)** *Jur* (*person*) majeur, -eure

(b) *US Univ* (*area of study*) matière *f* principale; **physics m.** (*student*) étudiant, -ante en physique

major[3] *vi US Univ* **to m. in a subject** se spécialiser dans une matière

Majorca [mə'jɔːkə] *n* Majorque *f*

Majorcan [mə'jɔːkən] **1** *adj* majorquin **2** *n* Majorquin, -ine

major-domo, *pl* **-os** [meɪdʒə'dəʊməʊ, -əʊz] *n* majordome *m*

majorette [meɪdʒə'ret] *n Am* **(drum) m.** majorette *f*

majority [mə'dʒɒrɪtɪ] *n* **(a)** [①**A11,g,i**] (*of votes*) majorité *f*; **the m.** (*of people etc*) la plus grande partie, le plus grand nombre; **a two-thirds m.** une majorité des deux tiers; **to**

have a m. avoir la majorité; **to be in a** *or* **the m.** être majoritaire; **elected by a m.** élu à la majorité; **in the m. of cases** dans la majorité des cas; **m. decision** décision *f* prise à la majorité; **m. government** (*having majority*) gouvernement *m* disposant de la majorité; **system of m. government** gouvernement à la majorité absolue, système *m* majoritaire; *Fin* **m. holding** participation *f* majoritaire; **m. party** parti *m* majoritaire; **m. rule** gouvernement à la majorité absolue, système majoritaire; *Jur* **m. verdict** verdict *m* de la majorité; **m. vote** majorité

(b) *Jur* (*age*) majorité *f*; **to attain** *or* **reach one's m.** atteindre sa majorité, devenir majeur

make¹ [meɪk] *n* **(a)** *Com, Ind* (*of product*) marque *f*; **cars of all makes** voitures de toutes marques; **what m. is it?** c'est quelle marque? **(b)** (*construction*) façon *f*, fabrication *f*, construction *f*; **of French m.** de fabrication française **(c)** *F* **to be on the m.** (*financially*) chercher à s'enrichir; (*sexually*) draguer

make² (*pt, pp* **made** [meɪd]) **1** *vt* **(a)** (*construct, produce, prepare etc*) (*bread, tea, meal, bed, hole etc*) faire; (*machine etc*) construire, fabriquer; (*paper, box, chair etc*) fabriquer, faire; (*payment, transaction*) effectuer, faire; (*a change*) opérer, faire, effectuer; (*mistake*) commettre, faire; (*speech, excuses, promise etc*) faire; **bread is made (out) of flour** on fait le pain avec de la farine **the chair is made (out) of wood** la chaise est en bois; **what is it made (out) of?** en quoi est-ce fait?, *F* c'est en quoi?; **to show what one is made of** donner sa mesure, montrer de quoi on est capable; **just let them try to cause trouble and we'll show them what we're made of!** qu'ils essaient de faire des histoires et ils verront de quel bois on se chauffe!; **I'm not made of money** je ne suis pas millionnaire; **do you want to m. something of it?** ça te dérange?; **to m. something of oneself** faire quelque chose de sa vie; **the army will m. a man of him** l'armée fera de lui un homme; **God made man** Dieu a créé l'homme; **the water had made a hole in the rock** l'eau avait percé la roche; **they seem made for each other** ils semblent faits l'un pour l'autre; **to m. trouble** provoquer le désordre; (*cause problems*) causer des ennuis (**for sb** à qn); **they made room for one more on the sofa** ils se sont poussés pour (lui) faire une place sur le canapé; **could you m. room for some pudding?** est-ce que tu as encore une petite place pour le dessert?; **to m. time to do sth** trouver le temps de faire qch; **to m. a noise** faire du bruit; **I m. the rules around here** ici, c'est moi qui dirige; **to m. an attempt to do sth** essayer de faire qch; **it makes all the difference** ça change tout; **to m. love/war** faire l'amour/la guerre; **to m. one's escape** s'échapper, se sauver; *Knitting* **to m. one/two** faire un jeté simple/double

(b) (*form*) établir, assurer (**a connection between** ... le raccordement de ...); *El* (*of contact points*) (*circuit*) fermer; **two and two m. four** deux et deux font quatre; **that makes (it) the third time he's been late** c'est *ou* ça fait la troisième fois qu'il arrive en retard; **they m. a handsome couple** ils font un beau couple

(c) (*gain*) (*money*) faire; **to m. £400 a week** gagner *ou F* se faire 400 livres par semaine; **to m. one's fortune** faire fortune; **to m. a fortune** (*on a sale etc*) gagner une fortune; *F* **to m. a bit on the side** faire de la gratte; **to m. a name for oneself** se faire un nom; **to make an enemy of sb** se faire un ennemi de qn

(d) (*cause to be successful*) (*person*) faire la fortune de; **this book made her** *or* **her name** ce livre l'a rendue célèbre; **this will m. him or break him** cela sera ou son succès ou sa ruine; **it made my day** ça m'a fait très plaisir; *Iron* **you've made my day** tu m'as fait gagner ma journée

(e) (*cause to be*) **to m. sb happy/rich/sad** rendre qn heureux/riche/triste; **to m. sb hungry/sleepy** donner faim/ sommeil à qn; **to m. sb angry** mettre qn en colère, fâcher qn; **he made her a star** il a fait d'elle une star; **to m. sb one's heir** constituer qn son héritier; **to m. sth known** faire connaître qch; **to m. oneself heard** se faire entendre; **to m. oneself ill** se rendre malade; **to m. oneself tired** se fatiguer; **to m. oneself useful** se rendre utile; **to m. oneself comfortable** se mettre à l'aise

(f) [ⓘA40,B,1,a] (*cause or compel to do*) **to m. sb speak/ sleep** faire parler/dormir qn; (*stronger*) forcer *ou* obliger *ou* contraindre qn à parler/dormir; **what makes you say/ believe that?** qu'est-ce qui te fait dire/croire ça?; **I made him stop** je l'ai forcé à s'arrêter; **don't m. me laugh!** tu me fais rire!; **her remarks made me feel more cheerful** ses remarques m'ont remonté le moral; **m. them see how important it is** montrez-leur combien c'est important; **he makes playing the violin look easy** à le regarder, on dirait qu'il est facile de jouer du violon; **to m. sb look stupid** faire passer qn pour un idiot; **what made you say that?** qu'est-ce qui vous a fait dire cela?; **you can't m. me!** tu ne peux pas me forcer!; **you made me!** tu m'y as obligé *ou* forcé!; **it makes my eyes water** ça me fait pleurer

(g) (*estimate, calculate*) **what time do you m. it?** quelle heure avez-vous?; **I m. it five kilometres** je pense que ça fait cinq kilomètres

(h) (*reach*) (*station, port etc*) arriver à; (*catch*) (*train, flight*) avoir; **will we m. the airport in time?** est-ce que nous arriverons à temps à l'aéroport?; **we'll m. Newport before lunch** nous serons à Newport avant le déjeuner; **he'll be lucky to m. 50** il a de la chance s'il atteint 50 ans; **to m. twenty knots** (*of ship*) faire vingt nœuds

(i) *F* (*manage to attend on, at*) (*show, meeting etc*) assister à; **I can m. 2 o'clock** je peux être là à deux heures; **can you m. Friday?** est-ce que tu es libre vendredi?; **can you m. lunch on Friday?** peux-tu te libérer pour le déjeuner vendredi?

(j) *F* (*establish as*) **let's m. it a day everyone can come** autant s'arranger pour que ce soit un jour où tout le monde puisse venir; **if we made it a Wednesday** ... si on faisait ça un mercredi ...; **can we m. it your place?** est-ce qu'on peut faire ça chez toi?; **better m. it** *or* **that two whiskies** mettez-moi un deuxième whisky

(k) (*become, be*) être; **she'd m. a good diver/singer** elle ferait une bonne plongeuse/chanteuse; **to m. sb a present of sth** faire cadeau de qch à qn; **you'll never m. a diver/singer** tu ne seras jamais plongeur/chanteur

(l) *Sl* (*have sexual intercourse with*) se faire

(m) *F* **to m. it** (*arrive in time*) arriver à temps; (*finish in time*) finir à temps; (*manage to attend*) se libérer; (*be successful*) réussir; **you've got it made** tu n'as plus de soucis à te faire pour ton avenir; **to m. it with sb** (*have sexual intercourse*) se faire qn; **we'll never m. it** (*by that time*) nous n'y arriverons jamais; **I made it home for lunch** je suis arrivé à la maison (à temps) pour le déjeuner; **to m. it in politics** réussir en politique

2 *vi* **(a) to m. as if** *or* **as though to do sth** (*get ready to*) s'apprêter à faire qch; (*pretend*) faire semblant *ou* mine de faire qch; **he made as if to speak** il a eu l'air de vouloir parler; **she made (as if) to get up** elle a fait mine de se lever

(b) to m. do (*cope*) se débrouiller; **we'll just have to m. do** (*with what we have*) il va falloir faire avec; **we could m. do with ten** (*though we should have more*) nous pourrions nous débrouiller avec dix; **we'll have to m. the milk do** il faut nous contenter du peu de lait que nous avons; **I'll just have to m. that do** il va falloir que je fasse avec

(c) they're just making believe (*in playing*) ils font comme si; **let's m. believe that** ... (*in playing*) on dirait que ...

(d) to m. sure *or* **certain of sth** s'assurer de qch; **have you made sure?** tu t'en es assuré?

(e) *F* **to m. like** (*pretend*) faire semblant *ou* mine de; **he makes like he's the boss** il se conduit comme si c'était lui le patron

▶ **make after** *vipo* se lancer à la poursuite de

▶ **make away** *vi* = **make off**

▶ **make away with** *vipo F* **(a)** (*steal*) partir avec, voler **(b)** (*kill*) tuer, supprimer; **to m. away with oneself** se suicider

▶ **make for** *vipo* **(a)** (*head towards*) (*place, the door*) se diriger vers; *Naut* faire route sur, mettre le cap sur; **where are you making for?** où allez-vous?; **ship making for Hull** navire à destination de Hull **(b)** (*contribute to*) (*happiness, well-being etc*) contribuer à; **these agreements m. for peace** ces accords favorisent la paix; **it doesn't m. for easy reading** c'est difficile à lire

▶ **make into** *vtaspo* **you could m. this room into an office** tu pourrais transformer cette pièce en bureau, tu pourrais faire de cette pièce un bureau

▶ **make of** *vtaspo* **(a)** (*understand*) **I don't know what to m. of that remark** je ne sais pas comment interpréter cette remarque; **what do you m. of her?** qu'est-ce que tu penses d'elle?; **we couldn't m. much of what he said** nous n'avons pas compris grand-chose à ce qu'il a dit

(b) (*attach importance to*) attacher de l'importance à; **you're making too much of this** tu y attaches trop d'importance; **the press has made a lot of this visit** la presse a fait beaucoup de bruit autour de cette visite; **the prosecution made much of this fact** l'accusation a fait grand cas de ce fait; **to m. much** *or* **a lot of** (*be attentive to*) (*person*) être aux petits soins pour; (*child etc*) câliner, choyer; (*flatter*) flatter

▶ **make off** *vi F* (*leave*) prendre la fuite, s'enfuir, décamper, filer; **the thieves made off in a van** les bandits se sont enfuis dans une camionnette

▶ **make off with** *vipo F* (*steal*) **to m. off with the cash** filer avec l'argent; **somebody's made off with my overcoat** on m'a volé *ou* chipé mon pardessus

▶ **make out 1** *vtsep* **(a)** *(write) (list etc)* faire, établir, dresser; *(bill)* établir, dresser, relever; *(cheque)* faire, établir **(to sb** à l'ordre de qn); **to m. out an invoice** libeller une facture; **who do I m. it out to?** *(the cheque)* je le mets à quel ordre?

(b) *F (claim)* **she made out she knew them personally** elle a fait croire qu'elle les connaissait personnellement; **to m. sb out to be richer than he is** faire qn plus riche qu'il ne l'est; **she's not such a fool as people m. out** elle n'est pas aussi bête qu'on le dit; **he made me out to be a miser** il m'a fait passer pour un avare

(c) *(usu with neg) (understand, decipher) (riddle, problem)* comprendre; *(person's reasons, meaning of sth)* démêler; *(handwriting)* déchiffrer; *(business, matter)* débrouiller; **I can't m. out the address** je n'arrive pas à lire *ou* déchiffrer l'adresse; **I can't m. this guy out** ce type est une énigme pour moi; **I can't m. it out** *(situation, mystery)* je ne m'y retrouve pas, je n'y comprends rien

(d) *(discern)* distinguer, discerner; **I can never m. out whether she's being serious or not** je n'arrive jamais à savoir si elle est sérieuse ou non

(e) *(conclude)* **how do you m. that out?** comment arrivez-vous à ce résultat *ou* à cette conclusion?

2 *vi* **(a)** *F (succeed)* se débrouiller; **how is she making out at her new school?** comment ça marche dans sa nouvelle école?; **he's making out very well** ça marche très bien pour lui

(b) *Am Sl (kiss, fondle)* se peloter; *(have sexual intercourse)* faire l'amour

▶ **make over** *vtsep (transfer)* céder, transférer **(sth to sb** qch à qn); **she has made the estate over to her granddaughter** elle a cédé la propriété à sa petite-fille

▶ **make towards** *vipo (head for)* se diriger vers; **he made towards the bar** il s'est dirigé vers le bar

▶ **make up 1** *vtsep* **(a)** *(invent) (story, excuses)* inventer; **he's making the whole thing up** ce qu'il dit est inventé de toutes pièces, il raconte des histoires; **I'm making it up as I go along** j'improvise au fur et à mesure

(b) *(compensate for) (deficit, loss)* combler; **we made up the time** nous avons rattrapé notre retard; **to m. up lost ground** rattraper; **we've got a lot of ground to m. up** on a beaucoup à rattraper; **I'll m. it up to you** *(for forgetting your birthday etc)* je me rattraperai, je me ferai pardonner; *(for helping me)* je te rendrai ça

(c) *(complete) (amount)* compléter; **we need two more players to m. up the team** il nous faut deux joueurs de plus pour compléter l'équipe; **another two players would m. it up to 11** avec deux joueurs de plus, on arriverait à onze; **I was only invited to m. up the numbers** *(in team, for meal etc)* je n'ai été invité que pour compléter l'équipe/la table/*etc*; **to m. up the difference** parfaire la somme; **I'll make your savings up to the price of a new bike** je compléterai tes économies pour que tu puisses acheter un nouveau vélo

(d) *(form)* constituer; **all the elements that go to m. up a happy marriage** tout ce qui contribue à faire un bon mariage; **the community is made up primarily of old people** cette communauté est constituée essentiellement de personnes âgées

(e) *(prepare, put together) (list)* dresser; *(parcel, bed)* faire; *Com (clothes)* faire, confectionner; *Com* **to m. up orders** préparer des commandes; **customer's own material made up** on travaille à façon; *Pharm* **to m. up a prescription** préparer les médicaments prescrits sur une ordonnance; **to m. up the fire** préparer le feu; *(add fuel)* alimenter le feu

(f) *(in bookkeeping) (account)* régler, établir, arrêter; *(the books)* régler, balancer; **to m. up one's accounts** faire ses comptes

(g) *(apply make-up to)* maquiller; **to m. one's face** *or* **oneself up** se maquiller; **the actors are being made up** les acteurs se font maquiller

(h) to m. it up *(settle quarrel)* se réconcilier **(with sb** avec qn)

2 *vi* **(a)** *(end quarrel)* se réconcilier

(b) *(catch up)* **he's making up on the leaders** il rattrape ceux qui sont en tête

(c) *(apply make-up)* se maquiller

▶ **make up for** *vipo (losses)* compenser; *(lost time)* rattraper; **that makes up for it** c'est une compensation; **to m. up for the lack of sth** suppléer au manque de qch; **how can I m. up for forgetting your birthday?** comment puis-je me faire pardonner d'avoir oublié ton anniversaire?; **what she lacks in skill she makes up for in enthusiasm** son manque de savoir-faire est compensé par son enthousiasme

▶ **make up to** *vipo (ingratiate oneself with)* **to m. up to sb** essayer de se faire bien voir de qn

▶ **make with** *vipo Am F* **(a)** *(produce)* faire; **to m. with the music** faire de la musique; **m. with the French fries** *(to waiter etc)* dépêche-toi de servir les frites; *(to cook)* dépêche-toi de faire les frites **(b)** *(use)* se servir de; **he made with the food mixer** il s'est servi du mixeur

make-believe 1 *n* **you shouldn't indulge in m.** tu ne devrais pas te complaire dans des chimères; **what is real and what is m.?** qu'est-ce qui est du domaine du réel et qu'est-ce qui est du domaine de l'invention?; **that's all m.** tout cela est (de la) pure fantaisie; **to live in the land of m.** se faire des illusions, ne pas avoir le sens des réalités **2** *adj* **a m. world** un monde imaginaire

make-or-break *adj attrib* **it's m. time!** maintenant, ça passe ou ça casse!; **it was one of those m. moments** c'était un moment décisif

makeover ['meɪkəʊvər] *n* transformation *f*

maker ['meɪkər] *n* **(a)** *(person)* faiseur, -euse; *Com, Ind* fabricant *m*; *(of machinery, planes, cars etc)* constructeur *m* **(b)** *Rel* **our M.** le Créateur; **he's gone to meet his M.** il est monté au ciel; **that's between you and your M.** c'est entre toi et le Seigneur

make-ready *n Typ* mise *f* en train

makeshift ['meɪkʃɪft] **1** *adj* de fortune; **a m. clotheshorse** un séchoir artisanal; **m. equipment** installation *f* de fortune; **it looks a bit m.** ça a l'air un peu rudimentaire; **it's only meant to be m.** ce n'est qu'une solution temporaire **2** *n* *(solution etc)* pis-aller *m inv*, expédient *m*; *(object)* pis-aller, moyen *m* de fortune

make-up *n* **(a)** *(cosmetics)* maquillage *m*; *Th* maquillage, fard *m*; *TV etc* **m. (department)** (service *m*) maquillage; **she wears far too much m.** elle se maquille beaucoup trop; **she wears m.** elle se maquille; **I'm not wearing any m.** je ne suis pas maquillée; **to put m. on** se maquiller; **m. artist** maquilleur, -euse; **m. bag** trousse *f* à maquillage; *Th etc* **m. box** boîte *f* à maquillage; **m. girl** maquilleuse *f*; *Th etc* **m. man** maquilleur *m*; **m. remover** démaquillant *m*; *TV etc* **m. room** salle *f* de maquillage, loge *f*

(b) *(composition)* composition *f*; *(of person)* caractère *m*; **it's not in his m. to apologize** ce n'est pas dans son caractère de s'excuser

(c) *Typ* mise *f* en pages, imposition *f*

(d) *US Sch (exam)* examen *m* de rattrapage; **m. classes** cours *mpl* de rattrapage

(e) *(putting together, assembly)* fabrication *f*; *(of clothes)* confection *f*

(f) *Banking* **m. date** date *f* de situation

makeweight ['meɪkweɪt] *n* complément *m*; *(stopgap)* bouche-trou *m*, *pl* bouche-trous; **they only asked me to join the team as a m.** ils ne m'ont demandé d'entrer dans l'équipe que pour leur servir de bouche-trou

making ['meɪkɪŋ] *n* fabrication *f*; *(of clothes)* confection *f*, façon *f*; *(of bridge, machine)* construction *f*; *(of film)* tournage *m*; **this ordeal was the m. of him** cette épreuve lui a forgé le caractère; **history in the m.** l'histoire en train de se faire; **a musician/poet in the m.** un musicien/poète en herbe; **the film was three years in the m.** le tournage du film a duré trois ans; **problems of one's own m.** des problèmes qu'on s'est créé soi-même; *El* **m. and breaking** *(of circuit)* fermeture *f* et ouverture *f*

makings ['meɪkɪŋz] *npl* **to have the m. of ...** avoir tout ce qu'il faut pour devenir ...; **it has the m. of a good film, but it'll need a lot of work** avec beaucoup de travail, ça pourrait faire un bon film; **he has the m. of a statesman** il a l'étoffe d'un homme d'État

malachite ['mæləkaɪt] *n Miner* malachite *f*

maladjusted [mælə'dʒʌstɪd] *adj Psy* inadapté, -ée

maladjustment [mælə'dʒʌstmənt] *n Psy* inadaptation *f*; **emotional m.** déséquilibre *m* émotif

maladministration [mælədmɪnɪs'treɪʃən] *n* mauvaise administration *f*, mauvaise gestion *f*

maladroit [mælə'drɔɪt] *adj* maladroit

maladroitly [mælə'drɔɪtlɪ] *adv* maladroitement

malady ['mælədɪ] *n Fml* mal *m*, maladie *f*

Malagasy [mælə'gɑːzɪ] **1** *n (person)* Malgache *mf*; *Ling* malgache *m* **2** *adj* malgache

malaise [mæ'leɪz] *n* malaise *m*

malapropism ['mæləprɒpɪz(ə)m] *n* pataquès *m*

malaria [mə'leərɪə] *n Med* malaria *f*, paludisme *m*; **to have m.** avoir la malaria *ou* le paludisme

malarial [mə'leərɪəl] *adj* paludéen, palustre; **m. fever** fièvre *f* paludéenne

malark(e)y [mə'lɑːkɪ] *n F* ânerie *f*

Malawi [mə'lɑːwɪ] *n* Malawi *m*

Malay [mə'leɪ] **1** *adj* malais; **the M. Peninsula** la presqu'île malaise **2** *n* **(a)** Malais, -aise **(b)** *Ling* malais *m*
Malaya [mə'leɪə] *n* Malaisie *f*
Malayan [mə'leɪən] **1** *adj* malais **2** *n* Malais, -aise
Malaysia [mə'leɪzɪə] *n* Malaisie *f*, Malaysia *f*
malcontent ['mælkəntent] *adj, n* mécontent, -ente
male [meɪl] **1** *adj* (*child, hormone, flower, plug*) mâle; (*sex, attitude, public*) masculin; **m. chauvinism** machisme *m*; **m. chauvinist** phallocrate *m*, macho *m*; *F* **m. chauvinist pig** phallocrate *m*; **a m. friend** un ami; **m. nurse** infirmier *m*; **m. line (of descent)** ligne *f* masculine; *usu Hum* **m. menopause** andropause *f*; **m. plug** fiche *f*, prise *f* mâle; **m. socket** prise *f* mâle; *Comptr* **m. to female adaptor** adaptateur mâle/femelle *m* **2** *n Biol, Bot* mâle *m*; *esp F* (*man*) homme *m*, *F* mec *m*; **the average French m.** le Français moyen
male bonding *n* amitié *f* virile
malediction [mælɪ'dɪkʃən] *n Fml* malédiction *f*
malefactor ['mælɪfæktər] *n Fml* malfaiteur, -trice
malevolence [mə'levələns] *n* malveillance *f* (**towards** envers)
malevolent [mə'levələnt] *adj* malveillant
malevolently [mə'levələntlɪ] *adv* avec malveillance; (*to look at sb*) d'un œil malveillant
malformation [mælfɔː'meɪʃən] *n Med etc* malformation *f*, difformité *f*
malformed [mæl'fɔːmd] *adj* difforme
malfunction[1] [mæl'fʌŋkʃən] *n* fonctionnement *m* défectueux, mauvais fonctionnement; *Med* (*of organ*) dysfonctionnement *m*
malfunction[2] *vi* mal fonctionner
Mali ['mɑːlɪ] *n* Mali *m*
Malian ['mɑːlɪən] **1** *adj* malien **2** *n* Malien, -ienne
malice ['mælɪs] *n* **(a)** méchanceté *f*, malveillance *f*; **out of m.** par méchanceté *ou* malveillance; **to bear m. to** *or* **towards sb, to bear sb m.** en vouloir à qn **(b)** *Jur* intention *f* criminelle *ou* délictueuse; **with m. aforethought** avec intention criminelle, avec préméditation
malicious [mə'lɪʃəs] *adj* **(a)** méchant, malveillant **(b)** *Jur* fait avec intention criminelle *ou* délictueuse, criminel; **m. intent** intention de nuire *ou* criminelle
maliciously [mə'lɪʃəslɪ] *adv* **(a)** (*to say, do*) méchamment, avec malveillance **(b)** *Jur* avec intention criminelle, avec préméditation
malign[1] [mə'laɪn] *adj* pernicieux, nuisible
malign[2] *vt* calomnier, diffamer; **much maligned man** homme calomnié
malignancy [mə'lɪgnənsɪ] *n* **(a)** (*of person*) malignité *f*, méchanceté *f* **(b)** *Med* (*of disease*) malignité *f*, virulence *f*; (*of tumour*) malignité
malignant [mə'lɪgnənt] *adj* **(a)** (*person*) malveillant, méchant **(b)** *Med* (*tumour etc*) malin, *f* maligne
malignantly [mə'lɪgnəntlɪ] *adv* avec malveillance, méchamment
malinger [mə'lɪŋgər] *vi* faire semblant d'être malade, *F* tirer au flanc
malingerer [mə'lɪŋgərər] *n* simulateur, -trice, faux malade, *f* fausse malade; **she's just a m.** c'est une tire-au-flanc
malingering [mə'lɪŋgərɪŋ] *n* simulation *f* (de maladie)
mall [mɔːl] *n esp Am Com* **(shopping) m.** centre *m* commercial
mallard ['mælɑːd] *n* (*duck*) colvert *m*
malleability [mælɪə'bɪlɪtɪ] *n* (*of person, metal*) malléabilité *f*
malleable ['mælɪəb(ə)l] *adj* (*person, metal*) malléable
mallet ['mælɪt] *n* **(a)** (*hammer*) (*small*) maillet *m*; (*large*) mailloche *f* **(b)** *Sp* (*in croquet, polo*) maillet *m*
mallow ['mæləʊ] *n* (*plant*) mauve *f*
malnutrition [mælnjuː'trɪʃən] *n* malnutrition *f*; (*lack of food*) sous-alimentation *f*
malodorous [mæ'ləʊdərəs] *adj Fml* malodorant
malpractice [mæl'præktɪs] *n* (*in professional life*) faute *f* professionnelle; (*of doctor*) négligence *f*, incurie *f*; *esp Am Jur* **m. suit** poursuites *fpl* judiciaires pour négligence; *esp Am Jur* **m. insurance** = assurance *f* souscrite pour parer à des poursuites judiciaires pour négligence
malt[1] [mɔːlt] *n* malt *m*; **m. extract** extrait *m* de malt; *Am* **m. liquor** bière *f*; **m. vinegar** vinaigre *m* de malt; **m. (whisky)** whisky *m* de malt
malt[2] *vt* (*in brewing*) (*barley*) malter; **malted milk** lait *m* malté
Malta ['mɔːltə] *n* Malte *f*
Maltese [mɔːl'tiːz] **1** *adj* maltais; **M. cross** croix *f* de Malte **2** *n* **(a)** (*person*) Maltais, -aise **(b)** *Ling* maltais *m*
maltreat [mæl'triːt] *vt* (*person, animal*) maltraiter, malmener
maltreatment [mæl'triːtmənt] *n* mauvais traitement(s) *m(pl)*
mam [mæm] *n Dial* maman *f*
mam(m)a *n* **(a)** ['mæmə, *Old-fashioned* mə'mɑː] (*mother*) maman *f* **(b)** ['mæmə] *Am Sl* (*young woman*) nana *f*

mammal ['mæməl] *n* mammifère *m*
mammalian [mæ'meɪlɪən] *adj, n* mammifère *m*
mammary ['mæmərɪ] *adj Anat* mammaire; **m. glands** glandes *fpl* mammaires
mammography [mæ'mɒgrəfɪ] *n Med* mammographie *f*
Mammon ['mæmən] *n Bible* Mammon *m*; *Fig* **the worship of M.** l'adoration *f* de l'argent
mammoth ['mæməθ] **1** *n* mammouth *m* **2** *adj* énorme, gigantesque, colossal
mammy ['mæmɪ] *n* **(a)** *F* (*mother*) maman *f* **(b)** *Old-fashioned US* (*black nurse*) bonne *f* d'enfants noire
Man [mæn] *n* **the Isle of M.** l'île *f* de Man
man[1], *pl* **men** [mæn, men] *n* **(a)** [①A14,12,c] (*adult male*) homme *m*; **men and women** les hommes et les femmes; **m. and wife** mari et femme; **to live as m. and wife** vivre maritalement; **men** (*on public convenience*) hommes; **an old m.** un vieillard, un vieil homme; **an ambitious m.** un ambitieux; **a dead m.** un mort; **good m.!** bravo, mon gars!; **I've known him m. and boy** je le connais depuis toujours; **a m.'s jacket/bicycle** une veste/bicyclette d'homme; **men's clothes/trousers** vêtements/pantalon pour homme; *Com* **men's department** rayon *m* hommes; **soap for men** savon pour homme; **to make a m. of sb** faire un homme de qn; **the army made a m. of him** l'armée a fait de lui un homme; **he took it like a m.** il a pris ça courageusement; **a game that sorts the men from the boys** un jeu qui distingue les hommes des gamins; **he isn't m. enough to tell me** il n'est pas assez courageux pour me le dire; **to talk to sb m. to m.** parler à qn d'homme à homme; **tell me, m. to m.** dis-moi, entre nous; **he's just the m. for me** c'est l'homme qu'il me faut; **he's just the m. for the job** c'est l'homme de la situation; **to be one's own m.** être son maître, ne dépendre de personne; **he's a m.'s m.** il préfère la compagnie des hommes; **a m. about town** un mondain; **the m. in the street** l'homme de la rue; **what does the m. in the street think?** que pense l'homme de la rue?; **the m. in the moon** = visage *m* que l'on peut s'imaginer distinguer lors de la pleine lune; **m. of God** homme *m* d'église; **a m. of learning** un érudit; **a m. of peace** un homme de paix; *Sp* **the m. of the match** le héros du match; **our m. in Rome** *Journ* notre correspondant *m* à Rome; *Com* notre représentant *m* à Rome; (*spy*) notre agent *m* à Rome; (*diplomat*) notre envoyé *m* à Rome; **they took on 200 men** ils ont embauché 200 ouvriers; *Mil* **officers and men** officiers *mpl* et hommes de troupe; *Hum* **a m.'s got to do what a m.'s got to do** (il) faut ce qu'il faut!

(b) (*individual, person*) homme *m*; **any m.** n'importe qui; **few men** peu de gens; **they replied as one m.** ils répondirent d'une seule voix; **they rose as one m.** ils se levèrent comme un seul homme; **they were patriots/communists to a m.** ils étaient tous patriotes/communistes; **every m. jack** tous sans exception

(c) (*humanity*) l'homme *m*; **iron age m.** l'homme de l'âge de fer; *Prov* **m. proposes, God disposes** l'homme propose et Dieu dispose; **m. does not** *or* **cannot live by bread alone** on ne se nourrit pas que de pain

(d) (*type of person*), *Univ* **an Oxford/a Cambridge m.** un diplômé d'Oxford/de Cambridge; **I'm a whisky m. myself** moi, c'est le whisky que je préfère; **he's a six-pints-a-day m.** il boit ses six pintes par jour

(e) *Old-fashioned* (*manservant*) domestique *m*, valet *m*; *Hist* (*vassal*) homme *m*

(f) *Sp* (*player*) joueur *m*

(g) (*in chess*) pièce *f*; (*in draughts*) pion *m*

(h) *esp US Sl* **hey m.!** (*hello*) salut mon pote!; (*as interjection*) eh! mec!; **m., am I tired!** bon sang, qu'est-ce que je suis crevé!; **you should have seen it, m.!** bon sang tu aurais dû voir ça!

(i) (*black American slang*) **the M.** (*whites*) les Blancs *mpl*; (*police*) les flics *mpl*; (*drug peddler*) le dealer

man[2] *vt* (**-nn-**) **(a)** (*work at*) **who's manning reception today?** qui assure la réception aujourd'hui?; **reception wasn't manned at the time** personne n'assurait *ou* n'était à la réception à ce moment-là; **someone has to be there to m. the phone** quelqu'un doit être là pour répondre au téléphone; **the campaign office was manned by volunteers** la permanence de la campagne était assurée par des volontaires

(b) (*operate*) (*machine*) assurer le fonctionnement de; (*plane, boat etc*) être membre de l'équipage de; *Mil* **to m. a gun** servir *ou* manœuvrer une pièce d'artillerie; **to m. the barricades** défendre les barricades; **the fort was manned by a handful of legionnaires** le fort était tenu par une poignée de légionnaires; **m. the pumps!** armez les pompes!; **m. the boats!** mettez les canots (de sauvetage) à la mer!; **the bomber was manned by a crew of five men** le bombardier avait un équipage de cinq hommes; **the plane is manned by a pilot and a navigator** l'équipage de l'avion consiste en un pilote et un navigateur; **was the spaceship manned?** y avait-il des hommes à bord du vaisseau spatial?; **the machines had to be manned all the time** il fallait quelqu'un continuellement pour assurer le fonctionnement des machines

-man [mæn] *suff* **two-m. toboggan** luge *f* à deux places; **five-m. crew** équipage *m* de cinq hommes

manacle[1] ['mænək(ə)l] *n* (*usu pl*) **manacles** menottes *fpl*

manacle[2] *vt* mettre *ou* passer les menottes à; **manacled to the wall** attaché au mur par des menottes

manage ['mænɪdʒ] **1** *vt* **(a)** (*run*) (*company, factory, project, bank etc*) diriger; (*estate*) diriger, gérer; (*the economy, one's money, resources, account*) gérer; **to m. sb's affairs** gérer les affaires de qn; **to m. a pop singer/football team** être (le) manager d'un chanteur de pop/d'une équipe de football

(b) (*deal with*) (*situation*) gérer; **to know how to m. sb** savoir prendre qn; **she finds it difficult to m. her pupils** elle a du mal à tenir ses élèves

(c) (*be able to*) **to m. to do sth** (*succeed*) réussir *ou* arriver *ou* parvenir à faire qch; *Iron* (*contrive*) s'arranger pour faire qch, réussir à faire qch; **we managed to persuade her** nous avons réussi à la persuader; **I think I can m. it** je crois que je peux le faire *ou* que je peux y arriver; **I shall never m. to learn it** jamais je n'arriverai à l'apprendre; **how do you m. not to dirty your hands?** comment faites-vous pour ne pas vous salir les mains?; **I hope she'll m. to be there** j'espère qu'elle pourra venir

(d) (*be able to produce, consume, carry etc*) **£100 is the most that I can m.** je ne peux pas aller au-delà de 100 livres; **can you m. some more pudding?** vous reprendnez bien encore du dessert?; **I can't m. Friday** (*I'm not free*) je ne peux pas me libérer vendredi; **can you m. dinner on Thursday?** est-ce que vous pouvez venir dîner jeudi?; **I can't m. three suitcases** je ne peux pas porter trois valises; **can you m. the stairs?** (*carrying so much, being elderly etc*) est-ce que tu arrives à monter les escaliers?

2 *vi* se débrouiller; **she manages well** elle se débrouille bien; **can you m.?** (*with all those suitcases etc*) tu y arriveras?; **we shall m. better next time** nous nous débrouillerons mieux la prochaine fois; **he'll m. all right** il se débrouillera; **we could just m.** (*financially*) on avait juste de quoi vivre; **I don't know how I would have managed without you** je ne sais pas comment j'aurais fait sans toi

manageable ['mænɪdʒəb(ə)l] *adj* **(a)** (*thing, vehicle*) maniable; (*hair*) facile à coiffer; **the smaller suitcase is a more m. size** la plus petite valise est plus maniable **(b)** (*person, child*) facile, docile **(c)** (*undertaking*) faisable **(d)** (*company*) gérable

managed fund ['mænɪdʒd] *n Fin* (*in insurance*) fonds *m* géré

management ['mænɪdʒmənt] *n* **(a)** (*action*) (*of company, factory, project etc*) gestion *f*, direction *f*; (*of economy, money, resources*) gestion; **business m.** gestion des affaires; **bad m.** mauvaise gestion; *Com* **under new m.** (*change of ownership*) changement *m* de propriétaire; (*change of manager*) nouvelle direction; **m. by objectives** gestion par objectifs; **m. committee** comité *m* de direction; **m. contract** contrat *m* de gestion; **m. fee** honoraires *mpl* consultant; **m. function** fonction *f* d'encadrement; **m. report** rapport *m* de gestion; (*accounts statistics*) tableau *m* de bord; **m. skills** qualités *fpl* de gestionnaire; **m. style** mode *m* de gestion; **m. summary** résumé *m* managérial; **m. technique** méthode *f* de gestion; **m. tool** outil *m* de gestion

(b) (*with sing or pl verb*) (*managers, employers*) administration *f*, direction *f*; **senior m.** les cadres *mpl* supérieurs, la Direction; **representatives of m. and unions** des représentants du patronat et des syndicats; **m. buy-out** = rachat *m* d'une société par la direction; **m. team** équipe *f* dirigeante

management accounts *npl* comptes *mpl* de gestion

management consultancy *n Com* (*activity*) conseils *mpl* pour la gestion; (*firm*) cabinet *m* (de) conseils

management consultant *n Com* conseil *m* en gestion

management information system *n Com* système *m* intégré de gestion

management studies ['stʌdɪz] *npl Univ* études *fpl* de gestion

manager ['mænɪdʒər] *n* **(a)** (*of bank, company, factory, project*) directeur *m*; (*of café, bar, store*) gérant *m*, patron *m*; (*of department in large store*) chef *m*; (*of funds, money*) gestionnaire *m*; (*of assets*) administrateur *m*; (*of estate*) régisseur *m*; (*of entertainer, rock band, football team etc*) manager *m*; *Pol* (*of political party*) chef, dirigeant *m*; **I want to see the m.!** je veux voir le responsable!; **she's a good m.** (*of home etc*) elle est bonne ménagère **(b)** *Comptr* (*of disk etc*) gestionnaire *m*

manageress [mænɪdʒə'res] *n* (*of bank, company, factory, project*) directrice *f*; (*of café, bar, shop*) gérante *f*, patronne *f*

managerial [mænɪ'dʒɪərɪəl] *adj* directorial; (*position*) de commande; **m. experience** expérience *f* de la direction; **at m. level** au niveau de la direction; **m. skills** qualités *fpl* de gestionnaire; **m. staff** cadres *mpl*

managing ['mænɪdʒɪŋ] *adj* directeur, -trice; **m. director** président-directeur *m* général; **m. editor** directeur de rédaction

manatee [mænə'tiː] *n Zool* lamantin *m*

man-bites-dog story [mænbaɪts'dɒg] *n Journ* article-paru dans la rubrique des chiens écrasés

Manchuria [mæn'tʃʊərɪə] *n* Mandchourie *f*

Manchurian [mæn'tʃʊərɪən] **1** *adj* mandchou **2** *n* Mandchou, -oue

Mancunian [mæŋ'kjuːnɪən] **1** *n* habitant, -ante de Manchester; (*by birth*) originaire *mf* de Manchester **2** *adj* de Manchester

Mandarin ['mændərɪn] *Ling* **1** *n* mandarin *m* **2** *adj* **M. Chinese** mandarin *m*

mandarin[1] ['mændərɪn] *n* **(a)** *Chinese Hist; Fig* mandarin *m*; **m. collar** col *m* chinois, col officier **(b)** (*fruit*) mandarine *f*; (*tree*) mandarinier *m* **(c)** (*colour*) mandarine *f inv*

mandarin duck *n Orn* mandarin *m*

mandate ['mændeɪt] *n* **(a)** (*instructions*), *Pol* mandat *m*; **the government has a m. to ...** le gouvernement est mandaté pour ...; **his superior had given him a m. to ...** son supérieur lui a donné mandat pour ... **(b)** (*territory*) pays *m* sous mandat *m*

mandatory ['mændətərɪ] *adj* (*obligatory*) obligatoire; *Jur* mandataire; **m. writ** mandement *m*

mandible ['mændɪb(ə)l] *n* **(a)** (*of insect*) mandibule *f* **(b)** (*of vertebrate*) mâchoire *f* inférieure

mandolin(e) [mændə'lɪn] *n Mus* mandoline *f*

mandrake ['mændreɪk] *n* (*plant*) mandragore *f*

mandrel, mandril ['mændrəl] *n MecE* mandrin *m*, arbre *m* (de tour)

mandrill ['mændrɪl] *n* (*ape*) mandrill *m*

mane [meɪn] *n* (*of horse, lion etc*), *Fig* crinière *f*

man-eater *pl* **man-eaters** *n* **(a)** (*animal*) mangeur *m* d'hommes **(b)** *Fig* (*woman*) mangeuse *f* d'hommes

man-eating *adj* **(a)** (*animal*) mangeur d'hommes; **m. shark** requin *m* mangeur d'hommes **(b)** (*tribe etc*) anthropophage, cannibale

maneuver, maneuverable *etc US* = **manoeuvre, manoeuvrable** *etc*

man Friday *n Liter* Vendredi *m*; *Fig* homme *m* à tout faire

manful ['mænfʊl] *adj* vaillant, courageux

manfully ['mænfʊlɪ] *adv* vaillamment, courageusement; **he was struggling m. with the suitcases/his second steak** il se démenait vaillamment avec les valises/son deuxième steak

manganese [mæŋgə'niːz] *n Miner, Ch* manganèse *m*; **m. steel** acier *m* au manganèse

mange [meɪndʒ] *n Vet* gale *f*

mangel-wurzel ['mæŋg(ə)l'wɜːz(ə)l] *n* betterave *f* fourragère

manger ['meɪndʒər] *n Agr* mangeoire *f*, auge *f* d'écurie; *Bible* crèche *f*

mangle[1] ['mæŋg(ə)l] *n* (*for clothes*) essoreuse *f* (à rouleaux)

mangle[2] *vt* (*clothes*) essorer (*dans une essoreuse à rouleaux*)

mangle[3] *vt* **(a)** (*mutilate*) (*person, body*) mutiler; (*piece of meat*) charcuter, massacrer; **their bodies were horribly mangled** leurs corps ont été atrocement mutilés **(b)** *Fig* (*quotation*) estropier; (*text*) mutiler, dénaturer

mango, *pl* **-oes** ['mæŋgəʊ, -əʊz] *n* (*fruit*) mangue *f*, (*tree*) manguier *m*; **m. chutney** condiment *m* à la mangue

mangrove ['mæŋgrəʊv] *n* **m. (tree)** manglier *m*, palétuvier *m*; **m. swamp** mangrove *f*

mangy ['meɪndʒɪ] *adj* **(a)** (*dog*) galeux **(b)** *F* (*furniture etc*) minable, miteux

manhandle ['mænhænd(ə)l] *vt* **(a)** (*treat roughly*) (*person*) brutaliser, malmener **(b)** (*move by hand*) (*sth*) transporter à la force des bras; (*goods etc*) manutentionner; **they manhandled the piano into position** ils ont poussé le piano pour le mettre à sa place

manhole ['mænhəʊl] *n* (*for drain*) trou *m* de visite, regard *m*; (*for boiler*) trou d'homme; **m. cover** *or* **lid** plaque *f* d'égout

manhood ['mænhʊd] *n* **(a)** (*maturity*) âge *m* d'homme, âge viril; **to reach m.** devenir un homme; **he had barely reached m.** il avait à peine atteint l'âge adulte **(b)** (*masculinity*) virilité *f*; **he felt he had to prove his m.** il pensait devoir prouver sa virilité **(c)** (*men*) les hommes *mpl*; **British m.** les hommes britanniques **(d)** *Hum F* (*genitals*) bijoux *mpl* de famille

man-hour *n Ind etc* heure *f* de travail, *Spec* heure-homme *f*, *pl* heures-hommes

manhunt ['mænhʌnt] *n* chasse *f* à l'homme
mania ['meɪnɪə] *n* **(a)** (*passion*) passion *f*, folie *f*, *Pej* manie *f* **(for sth** de qch); **to have a m. for sth** avoir une passion pour qch, avoir la passion *ou* la folie/la manie de qch; **to have a m. for stamp-collecting** avoir la folie des timbres **(b)** *Psy* manie *f*; **suicidal m.** folie *f* du suicide
maniac ['meɪnɪæk] *n Psy* maniaque *mf*; *F* (*wild person*) fou *m*, folle *f*, cinglé, -ée; *F* **a m. driver** un fou du volant; **to drive like a m.** conduire comme un fou; *F* **a soccer m.** un fou de football
maniacal [mə'naɪək(ə)l] *adj* (*laughter etc*) dément
manic ['mænɪk] *adj Psy* (*wish etc*) qui tient de la folie; *Fig* **she made m. gestures** elle faisait des gestes désordonnés; **at a m. speed** à une vitesse folle
manic depression *n Psy* psychose *f* maniaco-dépressive
manic-depressive *adj, n Psy* maniaco-dépressif, -ive
manicure¹ ['mænɪkjʊər] *n* soin *m* des mains; **to have a m.** se faire faire les mains et les ongles; **to give sb a m.** faire les mains et les ongles de qn; **how much is a m.?** combien coûte un soin des mains et des ongles?; **m. set** trousse *f* de manucure
manicure² *vt* (*person*) soigner les mains de, faire les mains et les ongles à; **to m. one's nails** se faire les ongles; **manicured hands** des mains très soignées
manicurist ['mænɪkjʊərɪst] *n* manucure *mf*
manifest¹ ['mænɪfest] *adj* manifeste, évident; **to make sth m.** rendre qch évident; **this makes it m. that ...** cela prouve que ...
manifest² *n Naut, Av* (*document*) manifeste *m*
manifest³ *vt* **(a)** (*display*) manifester, témoigner; **to m. itself** (*of symptom, talent etc*) se manifester, se révéler **(b)** *Naut* (*goods*) faire figurer sur le manifeste
manifestation [mænɪfes'teɪʃən] *n* manifestation *f*
manifestly ['mænɪfestlɪ] *adv* manifestement
manifesto [mænɪ'festəʊ] *n Pol etc* manifeste *m*
manifold ['mænɪfəʊld] **1** *adj* (*numerous*) multiple, nombreux **2** *n Tech* tubulure *f*, collecteur *m*
manikin ['mænɪkɪn] *n* = **mannikin**
manil(l)a [mə'nɪlə] *n* **m. envelope** enveloppe *f* en papier kraft; **m. paper** papier *m* kraft; **m. rope** (cordage *m* en) manille *f*
manioc ['mænɪɒk] *n* **(a)** *Bot* manioc *m* **(b)** *Culin* cassave *f*
manipulate [mə'nɪpjʊleɪt] *vt* **(a)** (*handle, operate etc*) (*object*) manipuler; (*mechanical device*) manœuvrer, actionner; (*lever, pedal*) actionner; *Med* **to m. bones** faire des manipulations **(b)** *Pej* (*person*) manipuler; (*accounts*) truquer
manipulation [mənɪpjʊ'leɪʃən] *n* **(a)** (*of object*) manipulation *f* **(b)** *Pej* (*of person*) manipulation *f*; (*of accounts*) trucage *m*
manipulative [mə'nɪpjʊlətɪv] *adj* manipulateur, -trice
manipulator [mə'nɪpjʊleɪtər] *n* **(a)** *Pej* tripoteur, -teuse, manipulateur, -trice **(b)** (*of machine etc*) manipulateur, -trice
Man(it) *abbr* **Manitoba**
Manitoba [mænɪ'təʊbə] *n* Manitoba *m*
mankind [mæn'kaɪnd] *n* **(a)** (*the human race*) le genre humain, l'humanité *f*, l'espèce *f* humaine **(b)** (*men*) les hommes *mpl*
manlike ['mænlaɪk] *adj* (*resembling a human*) humain; (*resembling a man*) masculin; (*of woman*) masculin, *Pej* hommasse
manliness ['mænlɪnɪs] *n* virilité *f*, caractère *m* viril
manly ['mænlɪ] *adj* (*sport, activity*) d'homme, masculin; (*behaviour, character*) mâle, viril
man-made *adj* (*fibre, fabric, product*) synthétique; (*lake, beach*) artificiel; **m. attraction** (*in tourism*) centre *m* d'intérêt 'non-naturel'; **m. desert** désert *m* créé par l'homme; **m. laws** lois *fpl* faites par l'homme
manna ['mænə] *n* **(a)** *Bible etc* manne *f*; *prov* **it was m. from heaven** c'était un don du ciel **(b)** *Bot, Pharm etc* manne *f* du frêne
manned [mænd] *adj* (*spacecraft, flight*) habité; *see also* **man²**
mannequin ['mænɪkɪn] *n* (*person, dummy*), *Art* mannequin *m*
manner ['mænər] *n* **(a)** [①**A23-4**,3,c; **B11-2**,5,A] (*way, method, style*) manière *f*, façon *f* **(of doing sth** de faire qch); **the m. in which ...** la manière dont ...; **in a m. of speaking** en quelque sorte, dans un certain sens; *Gram* **adverb of m.** adverbe *m* de manière; **he does it (as if** *or* **as) to the m. born** il le fait comme s'il avait fait ça toute sa vie

(b) (*etiquette*) **manners** manières *fpl*; **(good) manners** bonnes manières, savoir-vivre *m*, politesse *f*; **bad manners** mauvaises manières, manque *m* de savoir-vivre, manque d'éducation; **it is bad manners to stare** il est mal élevé de dévisager les gens; **she has bad table manners** elle ne sait pas se tenir à table; *Fig* **I'll teach you some manners, young man!** (*punish for rudeness*) je vais vous apprendre la politesse, jeune homme!; **where are your manners?** (*to child*) en voilà des manières!; **he's got no manners** il est très mal élevé; **I'm forgetting my manners, would you like some tea?** mais où avais-je la tête?, je ne vous ai pas proposé de thé!

(c) (*variety*) espèce *f*, sorte *f*; **all m. of people/things** toutes sortes de gens/choses; *Lit* **what m. of person is she?** quel genre de femme est-ce?; **by no m. of means, not by any m. of means** absolument pas; **they're not rich by any m. of means** ils ne sont absolument pas riches

(d) (*attitude, behaviour*) façon *f* d'être; **I do not like his m.** je n'aime pas sa façon d'être; **she's got a very abrasive m.** elle est très acerbe

(e) *Lit* **manners** (*customs of a people*) mœurs *fpl*, usages *mpl*
mannered ['mænəd] *adj Art, Liter* maniéré; *Pej* (*person*) maniéré, affecté; (*style*) recherché, précieux
mannerism ['mænərɪz(ə)m] *n Pej* (*of person*) maniérisme *m*, affectation *f*; (*habit*) (*of writer etc*) particularité *f*; *Art, Liter* maniérisme
mannerly ['mænəlɪ] *adj* poli, courtois
mannikin ['mænɪkɪn] *n* **(a)** (*small man*) petit homme *m*; (*dwarf*) nabot *m* **(b)** *Art, Med, Surg* mannequin *m*
mannish ['mænɪʃ] *adj* (*woman*) hommasse; **she has a m. voice** elle a une voix d'homme; **she looks m.** on dirait un homme
manoeuvrability, *US* **maneuverability** [mənu:vrə'bɪlɪtɪ] *n* maniabilité *f*
manoeuvrable, *US* **maneuverable** [mə'nu:vrəb(ə)l] *adj* (*plane, car etc*) manœuvrable, maniable
manoeuvre¹, *US* **maneuver** [mə'nu:vər] *n* **(a)** *Mil, Naut etc* (*action*) manœuvre *f*; **manoeuvres** (*exercise*) manœuvres *fpl*; **troops on manoeuvres** troupes en manœuvres **(b)** (*action, remark*) manœuvre *f*; **a clever m.** une manœuvre habile; **there wasn't much room for m.** (*between cars etc*) il n'y avait pas beaucoup de place pour manœuvrer *ou* faire une manœuvre; *Fig* il y avait peu de marge de manœuvre; *Pej* **manoeuvres** (*plotting*) menées *fpl*, intrigues *fpl*
manoeuvre², *US* **maneuver 1** *vt Mil, Naut* (*army, fleet of ships*) manœuvrer, faire manœuvrer; **we manoeuvred the piano through the door** nous avons fait passer le piano par la porte; **she manoeuvred her car into the space** elle a garé sa voiture dans l'emplacement (en manœuvrant); *Fig* **to m. sb into a corner** prendre qn au piège, *F* coincer qn **2** *vi Mil, Fig* (*of troops, politician etc*) manœuvrer; *Naut* (*of ship*) évoluer
manoeuvring, *US* **maneuvering** [mə'nu:vrɪŋ] *n Mil* manœuvres *fpl*; *Pej* (*plotting*) menées *fpl*, intrigues *fpl*
man-of-war, *pl* **men-of-war** *n* **(a)** *Naut Arch* vaisseau *m ou* bâtiment *m* de guerre **(b) (Portuguese) m.** (*jellyfish*) physalie *f*, galère *f*
manometer [mæ'nɒmɪtər] *n* manomètre *m*
manor ['mænər] *n* **(a)** *Hist* (*estate*) seigneurie *f*; **m. (house)** manoir *m*; **the lord/lady of the m.** le châtelain/la châtelaine **(b)** *Br Sl* (*police district*) fief *m*
manorial [mə'nɔ:rɪəl] *adj Hist* seigneurial
manpower ['mænpaʊər] *n Ind etc* (*labour*) main-d'œuvre *f*; *Mil* effectifs *mpl*; **m. planning** planification *f* de la main-d'œuvre; **m. shortage** manque *m* de main-d'œuvre
manqué ['mɒŋkeɪ] *adj* (*placed after noun*) manqué
mansard ['mænsɑ:d] *n Archit* **m. (roof)** toit *m* en mansarde
manse [mæns] *n esp Scot Rel* presbytère *m*
manservant, *pl* **menservants** ['mænsɜ:vənt, 'mensɜ:vənts] *n* domestique *m*; (*personal*) valet *m* (de chambre)
mansion ['mænʃən] *n* (*in country*) château *m*; (*in town*) hôtel *m* (particulier); **m. (house)** manoir *m*, château *m*
Mansion House *n* = résidence *f* du Lord Mayor of London
mansize(d) ['mænsaɪz(d)] *adj* de la grandeur d'un homme; *Fig* (*handkerchief etc*) pour homme; (*helping of food*) gros, copieux
manslaughter ['mænslɔ:tər] *n Jur* (*through negligence*) homicide *m* involontaire *ou* par imprudence
mantel ['mænt(ə)l] *n* = **mantelpiece**
mantelpiece ['mænt(ə)lpi:s] *n* (*shelf*) dessus *m ou* tablette *f* de cheminée; **on the m.** sur la cheminée
mantilla [mæn'tɪlə] *n Clothing* mantille *f*
mantis ['mæntɪs] *n* (*insect*) mante *f*
mantle ['mænt(ə)l] *n* (*covering*) (*of lava, snow*) manteau *m*; (*of gas lamp*) manchon *m*; *Arch* (*cloak*) (*of woman*) mante *f*, pèlerine *f*; *Fig* **to take on the m. of office** assumer les responsabilités qui incombent au poste
man-to-man *adj, adv* (*talk*) d'homme à homme; *Fb etc* **m. marking** marquage *m* individuel
mantrap ['mæntræp] *n* piège *m* à hommes
manual ['mænjʊəl] **1** *adj* (*work, worker etc*) manuel; **m. dexterity** dextérité *f*; *Aut* **m. gears** *or* **gearbox** boîte *f* de vitesses mécanique, boîte manuelle *ou* mécanique; *Aut* **m. transmission** transmission *f* mécanique; **m. typewriter**

machine *f* à écrire mécanique **2** *n* **(a)** (*handbook*) manuel *m* **(b)** (*car*) voiture *f* à embrayage manuel **(c)** (*mode of operation*) **to be on m.** être sur commande manuelle **(d)** *Mus* (*of organ*) clavier *m*

manually ['mænjʊəlɪ] *adv* manuellement, à la main

manufacture¹ [mænjʊ'fæktʃər] *n* **(a)** (*of industrial product*) fabrication *f*; (*of cars, computers*) construction *f*; (*of clothing*) confection *f*; **of Italian m.** de fabrication italienne **(b) manufactures** (*products*) produits *mpl* manufacturés

manufacture² *vt* **(a)** (*industrial product*) fabriquer; (*car, aircraft, computer*) construire; (*clothing etc*) confectionner; **manufactured product** produit *m* manufacturé **(b)** *Fig* (*invent*) inventer (de toutes pièces); **to m. an opportunity to do sth** inventer une occasion de faire qch

manufacturer [mænjʊ'fæktʃərər] *n* fabricant, -ante; (*of cars, aircraft, computers*) constructeur *m*; **send it back to the manufacturers** renvoyez-le au fabricant; **m.'s recommended price** prix conseillé par le fabricant; **m.'s instructions** notice *f* du constructeur; **m.'s liability** responsabilité *f* du fabricant; *Mktg* **m. brand** marque *f* de fabricant

manufacturing [mænjʊ'fæktʃərɪŋ] **1** *adj* industriel; **the country's m. industry** le secteur industriel du pays **2** *n* fabrication *f*; **the decline of m.** le déclin de l'industrie manufacturière; **m. company** entreprise *f* industrielle; **m. costs** frais *mpl* de fabrication; **m. defect** vice *m* *ou* défaut *m* de fabrication; **m. licence** licence *f* de fabrication; **m. plant** usine *f* de fabrication

manure¹ [mə'njʊər] *n Agr* engrais *m*; **farmyard m.** fumier *m* (d'étable); **chemical m.** engrais chimique; **liquid m.** purin *m*; **m. heap** tas *m* de fumier

manure² *vt Agr* (*soil*) engraisser; (*with farmyard manure*) fumer

manuscript ['mænjʊskrɪpt] **1** *n* manuscrit *m*; **in m.** (*book*) sous forme de manuscrit **2** *adj* manuscrit, écrit à la main

Manx [mæŋks] **1** *adj* de l'île de Man; **M. cat** chat *m* sans queue de l'île de Man **2** *n* **(a)** *Ling* mannois *m* **(b)** (*pl*) **the M.** (*people*) les habitants *mpl* de l'île de Man

many ['menɪ] **1** *adj* [①**A5,B**] (*comp* **more**, *superl* **most**) un grand nombre de, beaucoup de, de nombreux, bien des; **m. people** beaucoup *ou* un grand nombre de gens; **m. times** bien des fois, de nombreuses fois; **in m. cases** dans bien des cas, dans de nombreux cas; **in m. ways** de bien des façons; **for m. years** pendant de longues années *ou* de nombreuses années; **m. and varied** nombreux et très variés; **one of his m. acquaintances** une de ses nombreuses relations; **like so m. others** comme tant d'autres; **he told me in so m. words that …** il m'a fait comprendre que …; **too m. people** trop de monde; **a few (drinks) too m.** quelques verres de trop; **how m. times?** combien de fois?; **I have as m. books as you** j'ai autant de livres que vous; **four accidents in as m. days** quatre accidents en quatre jours; **a good m. things** pas mal de choses; **m. a night** *or* **m.'s the night I've done that** j'ai fait ça maintes nuits; **there are only so m. ways you can cook chicken** il n'y a pas une infinité de façons de préparer le poulet; *Prov* **m. hands make light work** à plusieurs, l'ouvrage avance vite

2 *pron* beaucoup, un grand nombre; **not (very) m.** pas beaucoup; **m. of us** beaucoup *ou* un grand nombre d'entre nous; **how m.?** combien?; **as m. as you like** autant que vous voulez; **they tried to bring back as m. as possible** ils ont essayé d'en rapporter le plus possible; **as m. again, as m. more, twice as m.** deux fois plus; **too m.** trop; **there are too m.** il y en a trop; **so m.** tant

3 *npl* **the m.** la foule, la masse; **the sacrifices made by the few for the m.** les sacrifices faits par la minorité pour la masse

many-coloured *adj* multicolore

man-year *n* année-personne *f*, *pl* années-personnes

many-sided *adj* **(a)** (*figure*) à plusieurs côtés **(b)** (*problem*) complexe, compliqué **(c)** (*person*) aux talents variés

Maoist ['maʊɪst] *adj, n Pol* maoïste *mf*

Maori ['maʊrɪ] **1** *adj* maori **2** *n* **(a)** Maori, -ie **(b)** *Ling* maori *m*

map¹ [mæp] *n* carte *f* (géographique); (*of town, underground, building*) plan *m*; (*of keyboard*) schéma *m*; *Fig* **it's off the m.** c'est à l'autre bout du monde; *Fig* **to put a town on the m.** mettre une ville en vedette, faire parler d'une ville; **this will put us on the m.** ça va nous faire de la publicité; **the village was wiped off the m.** le village a été rayé de la carte; **he's a good m. reader** il sait bien lire les cartes *ou* les plans; **m. maker** cartographe *mf*; *Aut* **m. pocket** vide-poche *m*, bac *m* à cartes; **m. reading** lecture *f* des cartes; *Aut* **m. reading lamp** lecteur *m* de carte, spot *m* de lecture; **m. reference** référence *f* topographique, coordonnées *fpl*

map² *vt* **(-pp-)** **(a)** (*region etc*) dresser une carte de **(b)** *Math* faire un graphique de **(c)** *Fig* (*plot*) (*progress etc*) consigner

► **map out** *vtsep* (*route*) tracer; (*programme*) dresser, élaborer; **his life had already been mapped out for him** sa vie était déjà toute tracée

maple ['meɪp(ə)l] *n* **(a) m. (tree)** érable *m*; **m. leaf** feuille *f* d'érable; **m. sugar** sucre *m* d'érable; **m. syrup** sirop *m* (de sucre) d'érable **(b)** (*wood*) (bois *m* d')érable *m*

mapping ['mæpɪŋ] *n* **(a)** (*of region*) établissement *m* d'une carte **(b)** *Comptr* (*in network*) unité *f* logique

mar [mɑːr] *vt* **(-rr-)** (*pleasure, performance*) gâter, gâcher; (*joy*) troubler; (*beauty of landscape, scenery*) gâcher, gâter, déparer; (*person's beauty*) déparer, gâcher; **to make or m. sb** faire la fortune ou la ruine de qn

marabou ['mærəbuː] *n* (*bird*) marabout *m*

maraca [mə'rækə] *n Mus* maraca *f*

maraschino [mærəs'kiːnəʊ] *n* marasquin *m*; **m. cherries** cerises *fpl* au marasquin

marathon ['mærəθən] *n Sp etc* **m. (race)** marathon *m*; **m. meeting** conférence-marathon *f*; **m. runner** marathonien, -ienne; **m. speech** marathon oratoire

maraud [mə'rɔːd] *vi* marauder, être en maraude; **to go marauding** partir en maraude

marauder [mə'rɔːdər] *n* maraudeur, -euse

marauding [mə'rɔːdɪŋ] *adj* maraudeur, -euse; **m. hordes of looters** des hordes de pillards qui maraudent

marble¹ ['mɑːb(ə)l] *n* **(a)** (*rock*) marbre *m*; **m. cake** gâteau *m* marbré; **m. cutter** (*person*) marbrier *m*; **m. floor** sol *m* de *ou* en marbre; **m. quarry** marbrière *f*; **m. statue** statue *f* de marbre **(b)** (*glass ball*) bille *f*; **to play marbles** jouer aux billes; *Fig F* **she's still got all her marbles** elle a encore toute sa tête; *Fig F* **to lose one's marbles** perdre la boule **(c)** *Art* (*object*) marbre *m*

marble² *vt Tech* (*in bookbinding*) marbrer, raciner

marbled ['mɑːb(ə)ld] *adj* marbré

marbling ['mɑːblɪŋ] *n* marbrure(s) *f(pl)*

March [mɑːtʃ] *n* [①**A75-6,B-C; B58-9,B-C**] mars *m*; **in M.** en mars, au mois de mars; **(on) the first/the seventh of M.** le premier/le sept mars

march¹ [mɑːtʃ] *n* **(a)** (*by soldiers etc*) marche *f*; **m. in step** marche au pas; **on the m.** en marche; *Fig* **the middle classes are on the m.** la classe moyenne s'est mobilisée; **it is two days' m. from here** c'est à deux jours de marche d'ici; **m. past** défilé *m* **(b)** (*pace*) pas *m*, allure *f*; **quick m.** pas cadencé; **slow m.** pas de parade **(c)** (*demonstration*) marche *f*, manifestation *f*; **to go on a m.** participer à une marche **(d)** (*progress*) (*of time etc*) marche *f*, progrès *m*; **to be overtaken by the m. of events** être dépassé par les événements **(e)** *Mus* marche *f*

march² **1** *vi Mil etc* marcher; **to m. off** se mettre en marche; **he marched off in a rage** il est parti, fou de rage; **to m. by** *or* **past (sb)** défiler (devant qn); **quick m.!** en avant, marche!; **they marched to the town hall to protest** ils ont manifesté jusqu'à la mairie; **time marches on** (*I ought to go*) l'heure tourne; **she marched into his office** elle est entrée dans son bureau d'un pas décidé **2** *vt* (*troops*) faire marcher au pas; **he was marched off to prison** il a été emmené en prison

marcher ['mɑːtʃər] *n* (*demonstrator*) manifestant, -ante; **peace m.** manifestant, -ante pour la paix

marching ['mɑːtʃɪŋ] *n Mil etc* marche *f*; **in m. order** en tenue de campagne; (*in formation*) en formation de marche; **m. orders** feuille *f* de route; *Fig F* **to give sb his/her m. orders** mettre qn à la porte

marchioness ['mɑːʃənes] *n* marquise *f*

mare [meər] *n* jument *f*

mare's nest ['meəznest] *n* illusion *f*

margarine [mɑːdʒə'riːn] *n* margarine *f*

margarita [mɑːgə'riːtə] *n* (*drink*) margarita *f*

marge [mɑːdʒ] *n Br F* margarine *f*

margin ['mɑːdʒɪn] *n* **(a)** (*on paper, page etc*) marge *f*; **to write sth in the m.** écrire qch dans la marge; **there were some notes in the m.** il y avait quelques notes dans la marge; **m. release** (*on typewriter*) déclenche-marge *m inv*; **m. setting** marge *f*; (*action*) pose *f* de marges; **m. stop** margeur *m*

(b) (*edge*) bord *m*; (*of forest*) lisière *f*; (*of lake etc*) bord, rive *f*; **on the margin(s) of society** en marge de la société

(c) *Com, Fin* marge *f*; *St Exch* acompte *m* (*versé à un courtier*); *Com* **the margins are very tight** les marges sont très réduites; **to win by a narrow m.** (*in race etc*) gagner de justesse; **to beat sb by a m. of 20 seconds** battre qn de 20 secondes; **to win by an enormous m.** gagner haut la main; **the election was won by a wide m.** ils ont remporté les élections avec une majorité confortable; **she won the election by a m. of 26 votes** elle a gagné les élections à 26 voix près; **a m. of error** une marge d'erreur; **there is little m. for error** la marge d'erreur est très faible; *St Exch* **m. call** appel *m* de couverture *ou* de marge *ou* de garantie; *St Exch* **m. default** défaut *m* de couverture; *St Exch* **m. requirement** niveau *m* de dépôt requis

marginal ['mɑːdʒɪn(ə)l] **1** *adj* **(a)** *(role, activity)* marginal; **m. case** cas *m* limite; **m. land(s)** terre(s) *f(pl)* pauvre(s) **(b)** *(note)* marginal, en marge **(c)** *(slight)* *(improvement, increase etc)* léger; **of m. interest/importance** d'un intérêt/d'une importance limité(e); **of m. use** d'un usage restreint **(d)** *Br Pol* *(seat, constituency)* à majorité précaire **2** *n Br Pol* siège *m ou* circonscription *f* à majorité précaire

marginalization [mɑːdʒɪnəlaɪ'zeɪʃən] *n* marginalisation *f*

marginalize ['mɑːdʒɪnəlaɪz] *vt* marginaliser

marginally ['mɑːdʒɪn(ə)lɪ] *adv* *(slightly)* légèrement

marguerite [mɑːgə'riːt] *n* *(plant)* grande marguerite *f*, marguerite des champs

marigold ['mærɪgəʊld] *n* *(plant)* souci *m*; **African m.** rose *f* d'Inde; **French m.** œillet *m* d'Inde

marihuana, marijuana [mærɪ'hwɑːnə] *n* marijuana *f*

marina [mə'riːnə] *n* port *m* de plaisance, marina *f*

marinade[1] [mærɪ'neɪd] *n Culin* marinade *f*

marinade[2], **marinate** ['mærɪneɪd, -eɪt] *vt Culin* (faire) mariner

marine [mə'riːn] **1** *adj* *(life, biology)* marin; *Com* **m. bill of lading** connaissement *m* maritime; **m. artist** peintre *m* de marines; **m. insurance/risk** assurance *f*/risque *m* maritime; **m. insurance policy** police *f* d'assurance maritime **2** *n* **(a)** *Mil, Naut* *(soldier)* ≈ fusilier *m* marin; *Br* **the Royal Marines**, *US* **the US M. Corps** ≈ les fusiliers marins; *F* **(go) tell it to the marines!** allez raconter ça ailleurs *ou* à d'autres! **(b)** **merchant** *or* **mercantile m.** marine *f* marchande

marine architect *n* ingénieur *m* des constructions navales

marine engineering *n* génie *m* maritime

mariner ['mærɪnər] *n Old-fashioned, Lit, Naut* marin *m*

marionette [mærɪə'net] *n* marionnette *f* à fils

marital ['mærɪt(ə)l] *adj* *(relating to marriage)* conjugal, matrimonial; *Admin* **m. obligations** obligations *fpl* conjugales; **m. status** situation *f* de famille

maritime ['mærɪtaɪm] *adj* *(nation, law)* maritime; **m. climate** climat *m* océanique

marjoram ['mɑːdʒərəm] *n Bot, Culin* marjolaine *f*

Mark [mɑːk] *n* Marc *m*

mark[1] [mɑːk] *n* **(a)** *(scratch, stain etc)* marque *f*, trace *f*

(b) *(trace)* *(of suffering etc)* trace *f*, marque *f*; **to make one's m.** *(succeed)* se faire un nom *ou* une réputation; **he made his m.** *(because he couldn't write)* il a fait une croix; **years of imprisonment had left their m. on him** ses années de captivité avaient laissé des traces

(c) *(sign, proof)* signe *m*; **as a m. of respect** en signe de respect

(d) *(reference on instrument etc)* marque *f*, repère *m*; *F* **he's not up to the m.** *(good enough)* il n'est pas à la hauteur; *Br F* **I'm not feeling up to the m.** je ne suis pas dans mon assiette

(e) *(target for shooting etc)* cible *f*; *(objective)* but *m*; **unemployment has passed the three million m.** le nombre des chômeurs a passé la barre des trois millions; *F* **an easy m.** *(person)* une dupe; *Fig* **to hit the m.** toucher en plein dans le mille; *Fig* **to miss the m.** mettre à côté

(f) *Sch* *(out of twenty etc)* point *m*; *(overall grade)* note *f*; **to give sb/sth marks out of ten/twenty** noter qn/qch sur dix/vingt; **to get good marks** avoir de bonnes notes; **she got the highest m.** *or* **marks in the class** c'est elle qui a eu la *ou* les meilleure(s) note(s) de la classe; **full marks** *(in a specific subject)* note maximale; **full marks for effort!** bravo d'avoir essayé!; **bad m.** *or* **marks** mauvais point; **(you get) no marks for guessing who did it** tu n'auras aucun mal à deviner qui a fait ça

(g) *Sp* *(starting line)* ligne *f* de départ; **on your marks! get set! go!** à vos marques! prêts! partez!; **to be quick off the m.** *(in race)* démarrer vite; *(to understand)* avoir l'esprit vif; **you were quick off the m.** *(in doing sth)* tu n'as pas perdu de temps; **to be slow off the m.** *(in race)* prendre un mauvais départ; *(to understand)* être long à la détente; **you were too slow off the m.** *(in doing sth)* tu as mis trop de temps

(h) *Ind, Mil* *(of machine etc)* série *f*; **m. II/III** série II/III

(i) **(assay) m.** *(on gold, silver)* poinçon *m* de garantie

(j) *Culin* **(gas) m. 4** thermostat *m* 4

mark[2] *vt* **(a)** *(put mark on)* *(linen, silverware, cards etc)* marquer; *(goods)* estampiller; *Tech* *(jewellery etc)* signer; **her towels were marked with her initials** ses serviettes de bain portaient ses initiales; **face marked by** *or* **with smallpox** visage marqué par la petite vérole; **his face was marked with suffering** son visage était marqué par la souffrance

(b) *Com* **to m. (the price of) an article** mettre le prix à un article; *St Exch* **to m. stock** coter des valeurs; *St Exch* **to m. to market** comptabiliser au prix de marché

(c) *Sch* *(homework)* corriger, noter; **to m. sth right/wrong** compter qch comme juste/faux; **to m. exam papers** noter *ou* corriger des copies (d'examen); **marked out of 10** noté sur 10

(d) *(indicate)* marquer, indiquer; **to m. a place on the map** indiquer un lieu sur la carte; **stream that marks the boundary of the estate** ruisseau qui marque la limite de la propriété; **X marks the spot** X indique l'endroit; **this decision marks a change in policy** cette décision marque un changement de politique

(e) *(show)* *(one's approval, dissatisfaction)* témoigner, montrer; *(the beat)* accentuer; **to m. time** *Mil* marquer le pas; *Fig* piétiner, faire du sur place, ne pas avancer; **to m. an era** faire époque; **to m. an anniversary** célébrer un anniversaire

(f) *Sp, Fb etc* *(opponent)* marquer

(g) *(characterize)* caractériser

(h) *(pay attention to)* *(sb, sth)* faire attention à; **…, m. you** …, remarque; **m. what I say** faites bien attention à ce que je dis; **m. my words** c'est moi qui vous le dis

mark[3] *n* *(coin)* mark *m*

▶ **mark down** *vtsep* **(a)** *(write down)* relever **(b)** **they had marked him down as a troublemaker** ils l'avaient catalogué comme fauteur de troubles; **he was marked down for the post of …** il avait été pressenti pour le poste de … **(c)** *Com* *(goods)* baisser le prix de, *Spec* démarquer; **everything has been marked down to half price** tout a été réduit à moitié prix **(d)** *Sch* *(homework)* baisser la note de

▶ **mark in** *vtsep* noter; *(area on map etc)* hachurer

▶ **mark off** *vtsep* **(a)** *(in surveying)* *(line, road)* jalonner; **to m. off a distance on the map** *(measure)* indiquer une distance sur la carte; **the route was marked off in 1 km sections** le trajet était divisé en tronçons d'un kilomètre **(b)** *(separate with fence etc)* *(area)* délimiter **(c)** *(distinguish)* **to m. sb off from sb** distinguer qn de qn **(d)** *(with a tick etc)* cocher

▶ **mark out 1** *vtas* *(distinguish)* distinguer **(from** de**)**; **he was marked out for promotion from …** il était destiné à occuper un poste important dès … **2** *vtsep* *(mark with lines)* *(cricket ground etc)* tracer les lignes de

▶ **mark up** *vtsep* **(a)** *(write up)* noter, inscrire **(b)** *Com* *(goods)* augmenter le prix de, *Spec* majorer **(c)** *Sch* *(essay)* majorer la note de **(d)** *Publishing* *(text)* préparer, corriger

markdown ['mɑːkdaʊn] *n Com* réduction *f*

marked [mɑːkt] *adj* **(a)** **badly m. face** *(after accident)* visage balafré; **m. cards** cartes *fpl* marquées; **m. man** homme *m* marqué; **he's a m. man** il est repéré; *(he's going to be killed)* c'est un homme mort **(b)** *(difference, improvement etc)* marqué, (très) net, (très) sensible; *(accent)* prononcé; **the change is becoming more m.** le changement s'accentue

marked-down *adj Com* démarqué

markedly ['mɑːkɪdlɪ] *adv* de façon marquée *ou* très nette *ou* très sensible; **m. better** nettement meilleur; **m. different** nettement *ou* sensiblement différent

marked-up *adj Com* majoré

marker ['mɑːkər] *n* **(a)** *Sch* correcteur, -trice; **he's a hard m.** il note sévèrement **(b)** *Ind, MecE* *(marking device)* marqueur *m*; *(tool)* marquoir *m*; **m. (pen)** marqueur *m* **(c)** *(indicator)* jalon *m*, repère *m*; *(flag)* fanion *m*; *(stick)* piquet *m* d'alignement *ou* de jalonnement; *(for debt)* reconnaissance *f* de dettes; *(biological, genetic)* marqueur *m*; *Av etc* (radio)phare *m*, (radio)balise *f*; *Av* **m. beacon** radiobalise; *Naut* **m. buoy** bouée *f* de balisage **(d)** *Fb etc* marqueur, -euse

market[1] ['mɑːkɪt] *n* **(a)** *(collection of stalls)* marché *m*; *(large)* foire *f*; **cattle/fish m.** marché aux bestiaux/poissons; **m. stall** étalage *m*

(b) *Com, Econ, St Exch* marché *m*; **cotton m.** marché du coton; **to put one's flat on the m.** mettre son appartement en vente; **the most economical car on the m.** la voiture la plus économique du marché; **to come onto the m.** arriver sur le marché; **to take sth off the m.** retirer qch du marché; **to be in the m. for sth** *(of person)* être acheteur de qch; **to find a m. for sth** trouver un débouché *ou* des acheteurs pour qch; **there's no m. for these products** il n'y a pas de marché *ou* de demande pour ces produits, ces produits ne se vendent pas; **m. analyst** analyste *mf* du marché; **m. challenger** challengeur *m*; **m. choice** choix *m* sur le marché; *(product preferred by market)* choix du marché; *St Exch* **m. commentator** chroniquier *m* boursier; **m. competition** concurrence *f* du marché; **m. conditions** conditions *fpl* du marché; *St Exch* **m. crisis** choc *m* boursier; **m. development** développement *m* de marché; **m. entry** lancement *m* sur le marché; **m. exposure** exposition *f* sur le marché; **m. follower** suiveur *m* (sur le marché); **m. gap** manque *m* sur le marché; **m. growth** croissance *f* du marché; **m. intelligence**

intelligence *f* mercatique; *St Exch* **m. maker** mainteneur *m ou* teneur *m* du marché; **m. minimum** (*base sales*) ventes *fpl* de base; *St Exch* **m. order** ordre *m* au mieux; **m. penetration** pénétration *f* du marché; **m. pioneer** pionnier *m*; **m. player** acteur *m* de marché; **m. potential** (*of product*) potentiel *m* sur le marché; (*of market*) potentiel *m* du marché; *St Exch* **m. price list** mercuriale *f*; **m. report** étude *f* de marché, rapport *m ou* bilan *m* commercial; **m. rollout** élargissement *m* du marché; **m. segment** segment *m* de marché; **m. size** (*of product*) part *f* de marché; (*of market*) taille *f* du marché; *St Exch* taille boursière; **m. survey** étude *f* de marché; **m. test** marché-test *m*, test *m* de marché; *St Exch* **m. trend** conjoncture *f* boursière

market² *vt* (-t-) commercialiser

marketability [mɑːkɪtəˈbɪlɪtɪ] *n* possibilité *f* d'être commercialisé; **we are doubtful about the m. of these machines** nous doutons que ces machines soient commercialisables

marketable [ˈmɑːkɪtəb(ə)l] *adj* (*goods*) vendable, commercialisable

marketable securities [sɪˈkjʊərɪtɪz] *npl Fin* valeurs *fpl* de placement, valeurs réalisables

market analysis *n* analyse *f* de marché

market behaviour *n* comportement *m* du marché

market day *n* jour *m* de marché

market-driven *adj* déterminé par les contraintes du marché; **m. economy** économie *f* de marché

market economy *n* économie *f* de marché

marketeer [mɑːkɪˈtɪər] *n* (**a**) *Br Pol* (**pro-**)**M.** partisan, -ane du Marché Commun (**b**) *Mktg* mercaticien, -ienne

marketer [ˈmɑːkɪtər] *n Mktg* mercaticien, -ienne

market forces [ˈfɔːsɪz] *npl* forces *fpl* du marché

market garden *n esp Br* jardin *m* maraîcher

market-garden *adj esp Br* **m. produce** produits *mpl* maraîchers

market gardener *n* maraîcher, -ère

market gardening *n* culture *f* maraîchère

marketing [ˈmɑːkɪtɪŋ] *n* (**a**) (*of new product*) commercialisation *f*, marketing *m*

(**b**) (*study*) marketing *m*, mercatique *f*; **m. analyst** analyste *mf* mercaticien(ne); **m. audit** audit *m* mercatique; **m. campaign** campagne *f* de marketing; **m. channel** circuit *m* de commercialisation *ou* distribution; **m. consultancy** (*service, activity*) conseil *m* en mercatique; **m. consultancy firm** société *f* de conseil en mercatique; **m. consultant** conseiller, -ère en mercatique, conseiller, -ère commercial; **m. department** service *m* (de) marketing; **m. director** directeur, -trice du marketing, dirco *m*, directeur, -trice commercial(e); **m. engineering** mercatique *f* informatisée; **m. executive** responsable *mf* du marketing, cadre *m* en mercatique; **m. expert** mercaticien, -ienne; **m. intelligence** intelligence *f* mercatique, intelligence d'entreprise; **m. manager** directeur *m* du marketing, responsable *mf* mercatique, responsable marketing; **m. mix** (plan *m* de) marchéage *m*, marketing-mix *m*; **m. network** réseau *m ou* circuit *m* de commercialisation; **m. plan** plan *m* marketing *ou* mercatique; **m. planner** responsable *mf* de planification mercatique; **m. planning** planification *f* mercatique; **m. policy** politique *f* de mercatique, politique commerciale; **m. questionnaire** questionnaire *f* d'étude de marché; **m. strategy** stratégie *f* marketing; **m. subsidiary** filiale *f* de distribution; **m. team** équipe *f* commerciale; **m. technique** technique *f* commerciale

marketization [mɑːkɪtaɪˈʒeɪʃən] *n* marchéisation *f*

market leader *n* (*company*) leader *m* du marché, chef *m* de file; (*product*) numéro un *m* sur le marché, produit *m* qui domine le marché

market place *n* (**a**) (*market square*) place *f* du marché (**b**) *Econ* marché *m*; **the products in the m.** les produits sur le marché

market price *n* prix *m* courant

market research *n* étude *f* de marché; **m. company** société *f* d'études mercatiques

market share *n* part *f* du marché; **to lose m.** voir sa part du marché diminuer

market square *n* place *f* du marché

market town *n* ville *f* de marché

market trader *n Br* vendeur, -euse qui fait les marchés

market value *n* valeur *f* marchande

marking [ˈmɑːkɪŋ] *n* (**a**) (*of linen, cattle etc*) marquage *m*; **m. ink** encre *f* à marquer (**b**) **markings** (*distinctive marks*) marques *fpl*; (*on animal*) (*spots*) taches *fpl*; (*stripes*) rayures *fpl*; *Av* insignes *mpl* (**c**) *Sch* (*of homework*) correction *f*; (*work to be marked*) copies *fpl* (à corriger); **m. scheme** barème *m* (**d**) *Fb etc* marquage *m* (**e**) *St Exch* **m. to market** comptabilisation *f* au prix de marché

marksman, *pl* **-men** [ˈmɑːksmən] *n* tireur *m* d'élite

marksmanship [ˈmɑːksmənʃɪp] *n* adresse *f ou* habileté *f* au tir

markswoman, *pl* **-women** [ˈmɑːkswʊmən, -wɪmɪn] *n* tireuse *f* d'élite

mark-up *n Com* majoration *f*

marl [mɑːl] *n Agr* marne *f*; **m. pit** marnière *f*

marlin [ˈmɑːlɪn] *n* (*fish*) poisson *m* épieu

marlin(e)spike [ˈmɑːlɪnspaɪk] *n Naut* épissoir *m*

marly [ˈmɑːlɪ] *adj* (*soil*) marneux

marmalade [ˈmɑːməleɪd] *n Culin* (**orange**) **m.** confiture *f* d'oranges

marmoset [ˈmɑːməzet] *n* (*animal*) ouistiti *m*, marmouset *m*

marmot [ˈmɑːmɒt] *n* (*animal*) marmotte *f*

maroon¹ [məˈruːn] *n* (**a**) (*colour*) rouge *m inv* foncé, bordeaux *m inv* (**b**) (*firework*) fusée *f* de détresse

maroon² *vt* abandonner (*sur une île déserte*)

marooned [məˈruːnd] *adj Fig* isolé

marquee [mɑːˈkiː] *n* (*tent*) grande tente *f*

marquess, marquis [ˈmɑːkwɪs] *n* marquis *m*

marquetry [ˈmɑːkɪtrɪ] *n* marqueterie *f*

marram [ˈmærəm] *n Bot* **m. grass** oyat *m*

marriage [ˈmærɪdʒ] *n* (**a**) mariage *m*; **a happy m.** un ménage heureux; *Fml* **to take/give sb in m.** prendre/donner qn en mariage; **m. of convenience** mariage de convenance; **uncle by m.** oncle par alliance; **m. bed** lit *m* conjugal; **m. broker** personne *f* qui arrange des mariages; **m. bureau** agence *f* matrimoniale; **m. ceremony** cérémonie *f* de mariage; **m. settlement** contrat *m* de mariage; (*in favour of daughter*) dot *f*; (*in favour of wife*) douaire *m*; **m. vows** vœux *mpl* du mariage (**b**) *Fig* mariage *m*, alliance *f* (*entre les choses*); **a m. of minds** une union des esprits

marriageable [ˈmærɪdʒəb(ə)l] *adj* (*daughter*) mariable, à marier; **of m. age** enâge de se marier

marriage certificate *n* acte *m* du *ou* de mariage

marriage guidance *n* conseil *m* conjugal; **m. counsellor** conseiller, -ière conjugal(e)

marriage lines [laɪnz] *npl F* acte *m* du/de mariage

married [ˈmærɪd] *adj* marié; **a m. couple** un couple marié; **the young/newly m. couple** les jeunes/nouveaux mariés *mpl*; **m. life** vie *f* conjugale; **m. name** nom *m* de femme mariée; **m. quarters** logements *mpl* pour familles

marrow [ˈmærəʊ] *n* (**a**) (*in bone*) moelle *f*; **to be frozen to the m.** être transi de froid, être glacé jusqu'à la moelle (**b**) *Lit* (*essence*) essence *f* (**c**) *Br* (**vegetable**) **m.** courge *f*; (*small*) courgette *f*

marrowbone [ˈmærəʊbəʊn] *n* os *m* à moelle

marrowfat [ˈmærəʊfæt] *n* **m.** (**pea**) pois *m* carré

marry [ˈmærɪ] (*pt, pp* **married** [ˈmærɪd]) **1** *vt* (**a**) (*get married to*) se marier avec, épouser; **they've been married for nearly twenty years** cela fait presque vingt ans qu'ils sont mariés; **they're happily married** ils forment un ménage heureux; **will you m. me?** veux-tu m'épouser?; **to get married** se marier; *Fig* **he's married to his job** son travail passe avant tout, il n'y a que son travail qui compte

(**b**) (*of priest, parent*) marier, unir

(**c**) *Fig* (*combine*) allier, marier

2 *vi* se marier; **she never married** elle ne s'est jamais mariée; **to m. beneath oneself** se mésallier; **to m. for money** faire un mariage d'argent; **to m. into money** épouser quelqu'un issu d'une famille riche; **she married into the Smith family/the aristocracy** elle a épousé un membre de la famille Smith/de l'aristocratie; **to m. again** *or* **a second time** se remarier; **he isn't the marrying kind** il n'est pas du genre à se marier; **it was a case of 'm. in haste, repent at leisure'** c'était un de ces cas où l'on se marie en vitesse et où l'on passe sa vie à le regretter; *Fig* **the flavours m. well** les parfums se marient bien

▶ **marry off** *vtsep* (*dispose of by marriage*) marier; **they were desperate to m. her off** ils voulaient à tout prix la marier

▶ **marry up 1** *vtsep* (*bring together*) (*two parts*) joindre; (*colours*) marier **2** *vi* (*line up, fit*) coïncider, concorder; (*of colours*) aller bien ensemble, se marier; **check that the two parts m. up** vérifier que les deux parties coïncident

Mars [mɑːz] *n Astron* Mars *f*; *Myth* Mars *m*

marsh [mɑːʃ] *n* marais *m*, marécage *m*; *Old-Fashioned* **m. fever** malaria *f*; **m. gas** gaz *m* des marais; **m. marigold** (*plant*) souci *m* d'eau, populage *m*

marshal¹ [ˈmɑːʃəl] *n* (**a**) *Br Mil, Av* **M. of the RAF** ≈ Commandant *m* en Chef des Forces aériennes; **Air Chief M.** = général *m* d'armée aérienne; **M. of the Diplomatic Corps** ≈ Chef *m* du Protocole (**b**) (*at race, demonstration, march*) membre *m* du service d'ordre (**c**) *US Jur* = fonctionnaire *m* ayant les attributions d'un shérif; (*police officer*) officier *m* de la police fédérale

marshal² *vt* (**-ll-**, *US* **-l-**) (*people, troops*) rassembler (et placer en ordre/en rang); (*arguments*) passer en revue; (*thoughts*) rassembler; *Rail* (*trucks, wagons*) trier, manœuvrer; **the children were marshalled into a line** on a fait mettre les enfants en ligne; **he marshalled the children out of the room** il a dirigé les enfants vers la sortie; **to m. facts** rassembler des faits et les mettre en ordre; **we need to m. more support for the project** il nous faut mobiliser plus de monde pour le projet

marshalling yard [ˈmɑːʃəlɪŋ] *n Rail* gare *f* de triage

marshland [ˈmɑːʃlænd] *n* terres *fpl* marécageuses, marécages *mpl*

marshmallow [mɑːʃˈmæləʊ] *n* (**a**) *Culin* (pâte *f* de) guimauve *f* (**b**) (*plant*) guimauve *f*, althée *f*

marshy [ˈmɑːʃɪ] *adj* (*ground*) marécageux

marsupial [mɑːˈsuːpɪəl] *adj, n* marsupial *m*, -aux

mart [mɑːt] *n* centre *m* commercial, marché *m*; (**auction**) **m.** salle *f* des ventes

marten [ˈmɑːtɪn] *n* (*animal*) mart(r)e *f*

martial [ˈmɑːʃəl] *adj* martial, guerrier; **m. arts** arts *mpl* martiaux; **m. law** loi *f* martiale; **to declare m. law** proclamer l'état de siège

Martian [ˈmɑːʃən] *n* Martien, -ienne

martin [ˈmɑːtɪn] *n* (*bird*) (**house**) **m.** martinet *m*

martinet [ˈmɑːtɪnet] *n Mil* officier *m* à cheval sur la discipline; **to be a m.** être autoritaire

martingale [ˈmɑːtɪŋgeɪl] *n* (**a**) (*part of harness*) martingale *f* (**b**) *Naut* **m.** (**guy** *or* **stay**) martingale *f* du beaupré

martini [mɑːˈtiːnɪ] *n* martini *m*

Martinican [mɑːtɪˈniːkən] **1** *adj* martiniquais **2** *n* Martiniquais, -aise

Martinmas [ˈmɑːtɪnməs] *n* la Saint-Martin

martyr¹ [ˈmɑːtər] *n* martyr, -yre; **to die a m. in** *or* **to a cause** mourir martyr d'une cause; **he is a m. to rheumatism** ses rhumatismes lui font souffrir le martyre; *F* **my brother's such a m.** mon frère se prend pour un vrai martyr; *F* **stop making such a m. of yourself!** arrête de jouer les martyrs!

martyr² *vt* (*person*) martyriser; **a martyred people** un peuple martyr

martyrdom [ˈmɑːtədəm] *n Rel, Fig* martyre *m*

martyrize [ˈmɑːtəraɪz] *vt* martyriser

marvel¹ [ˈmɑːv(ə)l] *n* merveille *f*; **the marvels of science/the world** les merveilles de la science/du monde; **it would be a m. if she won** ce serait un miracle *ou* un prodige si elle gagnait; **to work marvels** faire des merveilles; (*of treatment etc*) faire merveille; **we're not expecting anybody to work marvels** nous n'attendons de miracle de personne; *F* **you're a bloody m.!** tu es un as!; *Iron* (*you idiot*) espèce d'andouille!

marvel² (**-ll-**, *US* **-l-**) **1** *vi* (*at splendour, beauty*) s'émerveiller (**at** de); (*at cost*) s'étonner (**at** de) **2** *vt* **I m. that you are always so calm** ton calme m'impressionne; **I m. that you can be so calm at a time like this** je me demande comment tu peux être aussi calme à un moment pareil; **she marvelled that he had agreed** elle s'est étonnée qu'il ait consenti

marvellous, *US* **marvelous** [ˈmɑːv(ə)ləs] *adj* merveilleux; **it would be m. if …** ce serait merveilleux si …; *Iron* **isn't it m.!** ça c'est le bouquet *ou* le comble!

marvellously, *US* **marvelously** [ˈmɑːv(ə)ləslɪ] *adv* merveilleusement

Marxian [ˈmɑːksɪən] *adj Phil* marxien, -ienne

Marxism [ˈmɑːksɪz(ə)m] *n Pol* marxisme *m*

Marxism-Leninism *n Pol* marxisme-léninisme *m*

Marxist [ˈmɑːksɪst] *adj, n Pol* marxiste *mf*

Marxist-Leninist *adj, n Pol* marxiste-léniniste *mf*

Mary Magdalene [meərɪˈmægdəliːn] *n* Marie-Madeleine *f*

Mary Queen of Scots *n* Marie Stuart *f*

Mary Stuart [ˈstjʊət] *n* Marie Stuart *f*

marzipan [ˈmɑːzɪpæn] *n Culin* massepain *m*, pâte *f* d'amandes; **m. fruits** fruits *mpl* en pâte d'amandes

mascara¹ [mæsˈkɑːrə] *n* mascara *m*

mascara² *vt* **she had heavily mascara'd eyes** elle avait les cils très maquillés

mascot [ˈmæskət] *n* mascotte *f*; (*on car bonnet*) enjoliveur *m* de capot

masculine [ˈmæskjʊlɪn] **1** *adj* (**a**) masculin, mâle; (*woman*) masculine; *F Pej* hommasse (**b**) *Gram* masculin **2** *n* [①**B5-6,A**] *Gram* masculin *m*; **in the m.** au masculin

masculinity [mæskjʊˈlɪnɪtɪ] *n* masculinité *f*

maser [ˈmeɪzər] *n Nucl Phys* maser *m*

MASH [mæʃ] *n US Mil* (*abbr* **Mobile Army Surgical Hospital**) hôpital *m* de campagne

mash¹ [mæʃ] *n* (**a**) (*pulp*) **to reduce to a m.** (*paper etc*) réduire en pâte *ou* en bouillie (**b**) *Br F* (*mashed potato*) purée *f* de pommes de terre (**c**) *Agr* (*for pigs, poultry*) pâtée *f* (**d**) (*in brewing*) fardeau *m* (*de malt et d'eau chaude*)

mash² *vt* (**a**) **to m.** (**up**) broyer, écraser; *Culin* faire une purée de (**b**) (*in brewing*) brasser, mélanger

mashed [mæʃt] *adj* **m. potato(es)** purée *f* (de pommes de terre)

masher [ˈmæʃər] *n Tech* (*device*) broyeur *m*, écraseur *m*, mélangeur *m*; *Culin* (**potato**) **m.** presse-purée *m inv*

mashie, mashy [ˈmæʃɪ] *n Golf* mashie *m*

mask¹ [mɑːsk] *n* (**a**) masque *m*; (*silk or velvet, for eyes*) loup *m*; **to put on a m.** mettre un masque, se masquer; **with the m. off** à visage découvert; *Fig* **a m. of happiness/confidence** une apparence de bonheur/confiance trompeuse; *Fig* **the m. had slipped** le masque était tombé; *Fig* **to throw off** *or* **drop the m.** lever le masque, se démasquer (**b**) (*moulded likeness*) (*of face*) moulage *m*, masque *m*

mask² *vt* (**a**) (*person*) masquer (**b**) (*conceal*) (*one's feelings, thoughts*) cacher, dissimuler, déguiser; (*taste, smell*) dissimuler, masquer; **an apparent cheerfulness masked her deep pessimism** une gaieté apparente masquait son profond pessimisme (**c**) *Mil etc* (*battery, beam of light etc*) masquer

masked [mɑːskt] *adj* (*man, robber, ball*) masqué; *Mil* **m. battery** batterie *f* masquée; *Comptr* **m. ROM** mémoire *f* morte masquée

masking [ˈmɑːskɪŋ] *n* **m. tape** bande *f* de papier-cache

masochism [ˈmæsəkɪz(ə)m] *n* masochisme *m*

masochist [ˈmæsəkɪst] *n, adj* masochiste *mf*

masochistic [mæsəˈkɪstɪk] *adj* masochiste

mason [ˈmeɪs(ə)n] *n* (**a**) maçon *m* (**b**) **M.** (*freemason*) franc-maçon *m*, *pl* francs-maçons

masonic [məˈsɒnɪk] *adj* (franc-)maçonnique, des francs-maçons, de la franc-maçonnerie; **m. lodge** loge *m* maçonnique

masonry [ˈmeɪsənrɪ] *n* (**a**) maçonnerie *f*; **m. drill** foret *m* de maçon (**b**) **M.** (*freemasonry*) franc-maçonnerie *f*

masquerade¹ [mæskəˈreɪd] *n* mascarade *f*

masquerade² *vi* **to m. as sb** se faire passer pour qn; **dictatorship masquerading as democracy** dictature qui essaie de se faire passer pour une démocratie

Mass¹ [mæs] *n Rel, Mus* messe *f*; **M. for the dead** messe de requiem, messe des morts; **to celebrate/say M.** célébrer/dire la messe; **to go to M.** aller à la messe

Mass² *abbr* **Massachusetts**

mass¹ [mæs] *n* (**a**) (*large number*) (*of people*) foule *f*, multitude *f*, *F* masse *f*; (*of objects, letters*) grande quantité *f*, multitude, *F* masse; *F* **I've masses (of things) to do** j'ai un tas *ou* des masses de choses à faire; **we've masses of room** nous avons beaucoup de place; **he was a m. of bruises** il était entièrement couvert de bleus; **the (great) m. of the people** la plus grande partie *ou* la majorité de la population; **the masses** les masses *fpl*, le grand public; **m. circulation** grande diffusion *f*, diffusion de masse; **m. communication** communication *f* de masse; **m. consumption** consommation *f* de masse; **m. distribution** distribution *f* de masse, grande distribution; **m. hysteria** hystérie *f* collective; **m. meeting** grand rassemblement *m*; **m. protest** protestation *f* en masse; *Comptr* **m. storage** mémoire *f* de masse; **m. tourism** tourisme *m* de masse
(**b**) (*body*) *Phys* masse *f*

mass² **1** *vt* (*troops etc*) masser **2** *vi* (*of troops*) se masser; (*of clouds*) s'amonceler

massacre¹ [ˈmæsəkər] *n* massacre *m*, tuerie *f*; *Sp etc F* **it was a m.** cela a été un massacre *ou* une hécatombe

massacre² *vt also Fig* massacrer; *Sp etc F* **they were massacred** ils ont été massacrés *ou* démolis

massage¹ [ˈmæsɑːʒ] *n* massage *m*; **m. oil** huile *f* de massage; *also Euph* **m. parlour** salon *m* de massage

massage² *vt* (**a**) (*body, scalp*) masser (**b**) *Fig* (*manipulate*) **to m. the figures** manipuler *ou* trafiquer les chiffres

masseur [mæˈsɜːr] *n* masseur *m*

masseuse [mæˈsɜːz] *n* masseuse *f*

mass grave *n* fosse *f* commune, *Pej* charnier *m*

massif [ˈmæsiːf] *n Geog* massif *m*

massive [ˈmæsɪv] *adj* énorme; (*heart attack, stroke*) foudroyant; **invasion on a m. scale** invasion massive; **the m. scale of the Mafia's operations** l'échelle massive sur laquelle la Mafia opère; *Pharm etc* **m. dose** dose massive

massively [ˈmæsɪvlɪ] *adv* massivement; (*strong, fat*) extrêmement; **to invest m. in sth** investir massivement dans qch

mass market *n* marché *m* de (la) grande consommation

mass-market *adj* (*products*) de grande consommation

mass media *npl TV* (mass) médias *mpl*

mass murder *n Jur* meurtre *m ou* tuerie *f* en masse, boucherie *f*

mass murderer *n* tueur *m* fou, boucher *m*

mass number *n Nucl Phys* nombre *m* de masse

mass-produce *vt Ind* fabriquer en série
mass-produced [mæsprə'dju:st] *adj Ind* produit en série
mass production *n Ind* fabrication *f ou* production *f* en série; **it goes into m. next week** la production en série commence la semaine prochaine
mast [mɑ:st] *n* **(a)** *Naut* mât *m*; **the masts** les mâts, la mâture; **to sail before the m.** servir comme simple matelot **(b)** *Rad, TV* pylône *m*
mastectomy [mæs'tektəmɪ] *n Surg* mastectomie *f*
-masted ['mɑ:stɪd] *suff Naut* **three/four/***etc***-m.** à trois/quatre/*etc* mâts
master¹ ['mɑ:stər] *n* **(a)** (*man in charge, employer, owner of pet*) maître *m*; *Naut* (*of merchant ship*) capitaine *m*, commandant *m*; *Univ* (*esp at Oxford and Cambridge*) directeur *m*, principal *m* (*de certains collèges universitaires*); **the m. of the house** le maître de (la) maison; **to be m. in one's own house** être maître chez soi; **to be one's own m.** être son (propre) maître; **to be m. of the situation** être maître de la situation; *Prov* **like m. like man** tel maître, tel valet; **m. bedroom** chambre *f* principale; **m. copy** original *m*; **m. disk** disque *m*/disquette *f* maître; *Comptr* **m. file** fichier *m* maître, master *m*; **m. key** passe-partout *m inv*; *TV* **m. monitor** récepteur *m* de contrôle final; **m. plan** plan *m* d'ensemble; *Mus* **m. (record)** (disque *m*) original *m*; **m. soundtrack** mixage *m* magnétique final; *El* **m. switch** commutateur *m ou* disjoncteur *m* principal; **m. tape** bande *f* mère *ou* maîtresse; *TV* cassette *f* prête à diffuser
(b) (*skilled person*) maître *m*; **to be a m. of one's art** posséder son art en maître; **she was a m. of the epigrammatic phrase** elle était un génie du style épigrammatique; **to be a m. of one's brief** connaître son sujet à fond; *Art* **old m.** (*painter*) maître *m*; (*painting*) tableau *m* de maître; **m. carpenter/mason** maître *m* charpentier/maçon
(c) (*instructor*) maître *m*; **fencing/dancing m.** maître d'escrime/de danse
(d) *esp Br Sch* (*in primary school*) maître *m*, instituteur *m*; (*in secondary school*) professeur *m*; **French/Geography m.** professeur de français/géographie
(e) *Old-fashioned* (*form of address to small boys*) **M. David Thomas** Monsieur David Thomas; **M. David** (*said by servant*) Monsieur David
master² *vt* (*person*) se rendre maître/maîtresse de; (*horse, emotions, situation, subject*) maîtriser; (*difficulty*) surmonter, triompher de; **to have mastered a subject** posséder un sujet à fond; **I never really mastered the language** je n'ai jamais eu une maîtrise parfaite de la langue; **to have mastered the violin** être un/une violoniste accompli(e); **to m. one's brief** dominer son sujet
-master ['mɑ:stər] *suff Naut* **three/four/***etc***-m.** trois-mâts/quatre-mâts/*etc m inv*, navire *m* à trois/quatre/*etc* mâts
Mastercard® ['mɑ:stəkɑ:d] *n* carte *f* Eurocard Mastercard
master class *n Mus, Th* (*given by opera singer, actor etc*) cours *m* de maître
masterful ['mɑ:stəfʊl] *adj* (*tone, voice, performance*) magistral; **she was wrapped in his m. arms** il l'enveloppait de ses bras puissants; **you're so m.!** quel homme/quelle femme!
masterfully ['mɑ:stəfʊlɪ] *adv* (*to perform*) magistralement; **he said m.** dit-il d'un ton magistral
masterly ['mɑ:stəlɪ] *adj* magistral, de maître; **m. stroke** coup *m* de maître; **in a m. manner** de main de maître
master mariner *n Naut* capitaine *m* marchand
mastermind¹ ['mɑ:stəmaɪnd] *n* esprit *m* supérieur; (*of undertaking etc*) cerveau *m*; **she was the m. behind the robbery** c'était elle le cerveau du vol
mastermind² *vt* (*project etc*) diriger, organiser; (*plot etc*) tramer
Master of Arts [ɑ:ts] *n Univ* ≈ maître *m* ès lettres; (*diploma*) ≈ maîtrise *f* ès lettres
master of ceremonies ['serɪmənɪz] *n* (*at formal event*) maître *m* des cérémonies; *TV etc* animateur *m*, présentateur *m*
Master of (fox)hounds [('fɒks)haʊndz] *n* maître *m* d'équipage, grand veneur *m*
Master of Science *n Univ* ≈ maître *m* ès sciences; (*diploma*) ≈ maîtrise *f* ès sciences
master of works [wɜ:ks] *n Com* maître *m* d'œuvre
masterpiece ['mɑ:stəpi:s] *n* chef-d'œuvre *m*, *pl* chefs-d'œuvre
master race *n* race *f* supérieure
master sergeant *n US Mil* sergent-chef *m*, *pl* sergents-chefs
master/slave system *n* système *m* maître/esclave
masterstroke ['mɑ:stəstrəʊk] *n* coup *m* de maître
mastery ['mɑ:stərɪ] *n* **(a)** (*control*) contrôle *m* **(of** de), domination *f* **(over** sur) **(b)** (*knowledge*) (*of subject*) maîtrise *f*
masthead ['mɑ:sthed] *n Naut* tête *f ou* ton *m* de mât, haut *m* du mât; (*of newspaper*) ours *m*; *Naut* **m. light** feu *m* de tête de mât
mastic ['mæstɪk] *n* (*resin, cement*) mastic *m*
masticate ['mæstɪkeɪt] *vt* **(a)** (*food*) mâcher, mastiquer **(b)** *Ind* (*rubber etc*) triturer, malaxer
mastiff ['mæstɪf] *n* (*dog*) mastiff *m*
mastitis [mæs'taɪtɪs] *n Med* mastite *f*
mastodon ['mæstədɒn] *n* mastodonte *m*
mastoid ['mæstɔɪd] *adj, n Anat* **m. (process)** (apophyse *f*) mastoïde *f*; *Med F* **mastoids** mastoïdite *f*
masturbate ['mæstəbeɪt] **1** *vi* se masturber **2** *vt* masturber
masturbation [mæstə'beɪʃən] *n* masturbation *f*, *esp Med* onanisme *m*
masturbatory [mæstə'beɪtərɪ] *adj* masturbatoire, onaniste
mat¹ [mæt] *n* (*on floor etc*) (*of straw, rushes*) natte *f*; (*of wool etc*) (petit) tapis *m*, carpette *f*; (*at entrance*) paillasson *m*, essuie-pieds *m inv*; *Sp* (*in wrestling*) tapis; **(table) m.** (*for hot dish*) dessous *m* de plat; (*for vase, ornament*) napperon *m*; **(table** *or* **place) m.** (*for plates*) set *m* de table; *Fig F* **to be on the m.** (*be in trouble*) être sur la sellette
mat² **(-tt-) 1** *vt* (*hair etc*) emmêler **2** *vi* (*of hair, fibres etc*) s'emmêler, se coller ensemble
mat³ *adj* (*colour, paint, paper*) mat
matador ['mætədɔ:r] *n* matador *m*
match¹ [mætʃ] *n* **(a)** (*of person*) égal, -ale; **to meet one's m.** trouver son maître; **to be more than a m. for sb** être trop fort pour qn; **they were no m. for the other team** ils n'étaient pas à la hauteur de l'autre équipe; **you're no m. for her** tu n'es pas à sa hauteur; **to be a bad/good m.** (*of things*) aller mal/bien ensemble, être mal/bien assortis; **to find a m. for a wallpaper** (*find curtains etc in suitable colour*) assortir un papier peint; (*find the same*) réassortir un papier peint; **perfect m. of colours** assortiment parfait de couleurs
(b) *Sp* (*of football, rugby, cricket, baseball*) match *m*; (*of golf*) partie *f*; (*of tennis*) match, partie; (*swimming*) compétition *f*; *Golf* **m. play** partie par trous; *Tennis* **m. point** balle *f* de match
(c) (*marriage*) mariage *m*; **to make a good m.** faire un bon mariage; **he's a good m.** c'est un bon *ou* un excellent parti
match² **1** *vt* (*person*) égaler, être l'égal de, rivaliser avec; (*colours, gloves, stockings*) assortir; **his jacket doesn't m. his trousers** sa veste ne va pas avec son pantalon; **the music didn't m. her mood** la musique ne correspondait pas à son humeur; **we can't m. their prices** nous ne pouvons pas rivaliser avec leurs prix; **will their deeds m. their words?** est-ce que leurs actes seront à la hauteur de leurs paroles?; **there's nobody to m. him** il n'a pas son pareil; **to m. sb against sb** opposer qn à qn; *Sp* **Scotland has been matched against Brazil** l'Écosse rencontrera le Brésil; **evenly matched** de force égale, bien assortis; **we will try to m. this material for you** (*find something similar to*) nous essayerons de trouver un tissu assorti; **a well-matched couple** un couple bien assorti; **I need a new hat to m. my suit** j'ai besoin d'un nouveau chapeau qui aille avec mon tailleur; **m. the names to the faces** (*in competition*) trouvez les noms correspondant aux visages
2 *vi* (*of colours etc*) (*go well together*) aller (bien) ensemble, être bien assortis; (*be exactly the same*) être exactement les mêmes; (*of fingerprints, descriptions etc*) correspondre; **the carpet doesn't m.** la moquette n'est pas assortie au reste; **I need some shoes to m.** il me faut des chaussures assorties *ou* pour aller avec
match³ *n* (*for lighting*) allumette *f*; **to put a m. to sth** mettre (le) feu à qch
▶ **match up** **1** *vtsep* (*combine*) faire correspondre; **to m. up the names with the faces** faire correspondre les noms et les visages; **to m. up two colours** harmoniser *ou* assortir deux couleurs; **I want to m. up this colour** (*find exact match*) j'aimerais trouver exactement la même couleur **2** *vi* (*of fingerprints etc*) correspondre; (*of colours etc*) (*go well together*) aller (bien) ensemble, être bien assortis; (*be exactly the same*) être exactement les mêmes; **the descriptions didn't m. up** les descriptions ne correspondaient pas; **the suit jacket and trousers don't m. up** la veste et le pantalon ne vont pas ensemble
▶ **match up to** *vipo* **to m. up to sb's expectations** répondre aux espérances *ou* à l'attente de qn
matchbox ['mætʃbɒks] *n* boîte *f* d'allumettes
matching ['mætʃɪŋ] *adj* (*hat, colours etc*) assorti; **these pictures are a m. pair** ces tableaux se font pendant
matchless ['mætʃlɪs] *adj* incomparable, sans égal, sans pareil
matchmaker ['mætʃmeɪkər] *n* faiseur, -euse de mariages, marieur, -euse
matchmaking ['mætʃmeɪkɪŋ] *n* entremise *f*

matchstick ['mætʃstɪk] *n* allumette *f*; **to have m. legs** avoir des jambes comme des allumettes; **m. man** *or* **figure** (*drawing*) bonhomme *m* dessiné avec des bâtons

matchwood ['mætʃwʊd] *n* bois *m* d'allumettes; **smashed** *or* **reduced to m.** réduit en miettes

mate¹ [meɪt] *n* **(a)** (*sexual partner*) (*animal*) mâle *m*, femelle *f*; *F Hum* (*spouse*) mari *m*, femme *f* **(b)** *Br F* (*friend*) copain *m*, copine *f*, pote *m*; **thanks, m.** (*to friend*) merci, mon pote; (*to stranger*) merci, m'sieur; **watch where you're going, m.!** eh mec, regarde où tu vas! **(c)** (*assistant*) assistant, -ante, aide *mf*; **plumber's m.** aide plombier **(d)** *Naut* (*on merchant vessel*) officier *m*; **first** *or* **chief m.** second *m*; **second m.** lieutenant *m* **(e)** *MecE* (*part*) pièce *f* qui s'accouple (*avec une autre*); pièce qui s'emboîte (*dans une autre*)

mate² **1** *vt* (*animals, birds*) accoupler; *Old-fashioned* marier, unir (**sb with sb** qn à qn) **2** *vi* (*of birds, animals*) s'accoupler

mate³ *n Chess* mat *m*

mate⁴ *vt Chess* (*king*) mettre échec et mat, mater

mater ['meɪtər] *n Old-fashioned Br F* **(the) m.** ma mère, maman *f*

material [mə'tɪərɪəl] **1** *n* **(a)** (*substance*) matière *f*, substance *f*; (*for building*) matériau *m*; **raw material(s)** matière(s) première(s); **glass is a brittle m.** le verre est un matériau cassant; **he isn't officer m.** il n'a pas l'étoffe *ou* l'envergure d'un officier

(b) (*equipment for specific activity*) matériel *m*; **photographic materials** matériel de photographie

(c) (*cloth*) tissu *m*, étoffe *f*; **dress m.** tissu pour robes

(d) (*information for a book etc*) matériaux *mpl*; **the m. for a play** les matériaux d'une pièce

(e) (*produced by writer, singer etc*) **this singer writes her own m.** cette chanteuse écrit ses propres textes

2 *adj* **(a)** (*point of view etc*) matérialiste; (*comfort, interests*), *Phil, Phys, Rel* matériel; **m. possessions** des biens matériels; **to have enough for one's m. comfort** *or* **needs** avoir de quoi vivre matériellement

(b) (*important*) important, essentiel (**to** pour)

(c) *Jur* (*fact, testimony*) pertinent; **m. witnesses** témoins *mpl* de fait

materialism [mə'tɪərɪəlɪz(ə)m] *n* matérialisme *m*

materialist [mə'tɪərɪəlɪst] *adj, n* matérialiste *mf*

materialistic [mətɪərɪə'lɪstɪk] *adj* matérialiste; (*pleasures, mind etc*) matériel

materialize [mə'tɪərɪəlaɪz] *vi* (*of event*) se réaliser; (*of plans*) aboutir, se réaliser; (*of psychic ectoplasm*) apparaître, prendre forme; **the promised computers never materialized** les ordinateurs promis ne se sont jamais matérialisés; **the job he promised me never materialized** le travail qu'il m'avait promis ne s'est jamais matérialisé; **the project failed to m.** le projet n'a jamais abouti; **she promised to lend me a thousand pounds but the money never materialized** elle avait promis de me prêter mille livres mais je n'en ai jamais vu la couleur

materially [mə'tɪərɪəlɪ] *adv* **(a)** *Phil, Phys, Rel* matériellement; **to benefit m. from sth** bénéficier matériellement de qch **(b)** (*appreciably*) sensiblement, d'une manière appréciable; **m. different/better** sensiblement différent/meilleur

materiel, matériel [mətɪərɪ'el] *n Mil* matériel *m*

maternal [mə'tɜːn(ə)l] *adj* maternel

maternally [mə'tɜːn(ə)lɪ] *adv* maternellement

maternity [mə'tɜːnɪtɪ] *n* maternité *f*; *Br* **m. benefit** ≈ allocation *f* de maternité; **m. dress** robe *f* de grossesse; **m. hospital** maternité; **m. leave** congé *m* de maternité; **m. ward** maternité

matey ['meɪtɪ] *adj Br F* copain-copain; **to be m.** (*of people*) être à tu et à toi, être copains; **she's very m. all of a sudden** elle est bien aimable tout d'un coup

math [mæθ] *n Am F* = **maths**

mathematical [mæθ(ə)'mætɪk(ə)l] *adj* (*science, calculation*) mathématique; (*knowledge*) en mathématiques; **he's a m. genius** c'est un mathématicien de génie; **victory for the party is now a m. impossibility** mathématiquement, le parti ne peut pas gagner; **I haven't got a m. mind** je n'ai pas l'esprit mathématique

mathematically [mæθ(ə)'mætɪklɪ] *adv* mathématiquement

mathematician [mæθ(ə)mə'tɪʃən] *n* mathématicien, -ienne

mathematics [mæθ(ə)'mætɪks] *n* [①A10,c] **(a)** (*subject*) mathématiques *fpl*; **pure/applied m.** mathématiques pures/appliquées; **m. lesson/teacher** cours *m*/professeur *m* de mathématiques **(b)** (*calculations*) calculs *mpl*

maths [mæθs] *npl Br F* math(s) *fpl*; **m. lesson/teacher** cours *m*/professeur *m* de maths; *Comptr* **m. co-processor** coprocesseur *m* mathématique *ou* arithmétique

matinée ['mætɪneɪ] *n* **(a)** *Th, Cin* **m. (performance)** matinée *f*; *Old-fashioned Cin* **m. idol** = acteur *m* idolâtré par les femmes surtout dans les années 30 ou 40 **(b)** *Br* **m. coat** veste *f* (de bébé)

matiness ['meɪtɪnɪs] *n Br F* camaraderie *f*

mating ['meɪtɪŋ] *n* (*of animals, birds*) accouplement *m*; **the m. season** la saison des amours; **m. call** appel *m* du mâle; **m. instinct** instinct *m* de reproduction; **m. ritual** parade *f* nuptiale

matins ['mætɪnz] *npl Cathol* matines *fpl*; *Church of Eng* office *m* du matin

matriarch ['meɪtrɪɑːk] *n* femme *f* chef de tribu *ou* de famille

matriarchal [meɪtrɪ'ɑːk(ə)l] *adj* matriarcal

matriarchy ['meɪtrɪɑːkɪ] *n* matriarcat *m*

matric [mə'trɪk] *n Arch Br F* = **matriculation (b)**

matricide ['meɪtrɪsaɪd, 'mæ-] *n* **(a)** (*person*) matricide *mf* **(b)** (*crime*) matricide *m*

matriculate [mə'trɪkjʊleɪt] *vi* **(a)** (*of student*) s'inscrire, se faire inscrire **(b)** *Br Arch* (*pass exam etc*) être reçu à l'examen d'entrée à l'université

matriculation [mətrɪkjʊ'leɪʃən] *n Sch* **(a)** (*enrolment*) inscription *f* (*comme étudiant*); **m. fee** frais *mpl* d'inscription **(b)** *Br Arch* (*exam*) examen *m* de fin d'études (*pour entrer à l'université*)

matrimonial [mætrɪ'məʊnɪəl] *adj esp Fml* matrimonial

matrimony ['mætrɪmənɪ] *n esp Fml* mariage *m*; *Rel* **joined in holy m.** unis par les saints nœuds du mariage

matrix, *pl* **-ixes, -ices** ['meɪtrɪks, -ɪksɪz, -ɪsiːz] *n* **(a)** *Math etc* matrice *f*; *Fig* (*of forces, relations etc*) configuration *f* **(b)** *Geol, Miner* matrice *f*, gangue *f*, gaine *f* **(c)** *Metal, Typ etc* matrice *f*, moule *m*; *Art, Cer* (*of plaster moulds etc*) mère *f* **(d)** *Comptr* **m. printer** imprimante *f* matricielle

matron ['meɪtrən] *n* **(a)** (*woman*) matrone *f*; **m. of honour** (*at wedding*) dame *f* d'honneur **(b)** (*of institution, boarding school*) intendante *f*; *Old-fashioned* (*of hospital*) infirmière *f* en chef

matronly ['meɪtrənlɪ] *adj* de matrone

matt [mæt] *adj* = **mat³**

matte [mæt] *n TV* cache *m*

matted ['mætɪd] *adj* (*cloth*) feutré; (*hair*) emmêlé; **his hair was m. with blood** il avait du sang séché dans les cheveux

matter¹ ['mætər] *n* **(a)** (*substance*) matière *f*; *Phil etc* **form and m.** la forme et la matière; **organic/inorganic m.** la matière organique/inorganique

(b) (*affair*) affaire *f*, chose *f*; **it's a m. of the utmost importance** c'est une affaire de la plus haute importance; **the m. is closed** le dossier est clos; **let's come back to the m. in hand** revenons à ce qui nous occupe *ou F* à nos moutons; **it's an easy/no easy m.** c'est/ce n'est pas facile; **it's no great m.** ce n'est pas grand-chose; **it's no laughing m.** il n'y a pas de quoi rire; **it is a m. for regret** c'est regrettable; **it's a m. for congratulations** cela mérite des félicitations; **that's quite another m.** cela, c'est tout autre chose; **to do sth as a m. of course** faire qch systématiquement; **that's a m. of opinion/taste** c'est une question d'opinion/de goût; **that is a m. for the courts to decide** sur ce point, c'est à la justice de trancher; **it's simply a m. of time** (*is inevitable*) cela arrivera tôt ou tard; (*is a question of time only*) c'est une simple question de temps; **it'll only be a m. of days before they find out** ce n'est qu'une question de jours avant qu'ils découvrent la vérité; **it's just a m. of knowing which button to press** il s'agit juste de savoir sur quel bouton appuyer; **it's just a m. of replacing a few worn-out parts** il suffit de remplacer quelques pièces usées; **it's just a m. of £100** c'est l'affaire de 100 livres; *Iron* **there's the small m. of that money you owe me** il y a cette question de la petite somme que vous me devez; **within a m. of hours** en quelques heures; **for that m.** d'ailleurs; **and so am I for that m.** moi aussi d'ailleurs; **he isn't very well known in London or anywhere else for that m.** il n'est pas très connu à Londres, et nulle part ailleurs en fait; **it's a m. of fact** c'est un fait; **as a m. of fact** en fait

(c) **as matters stand** au point où en sont les choses; **her remarks made matters worse** ses remarques n'ont fait qu'aggraver les choses; **to make matters worse, it had started to rain** pour tout arranger, il s'était mis à pleuvoir; **matters of the heart** affaires *fpl* de cœur *ou* sentimentales; **in matters of religion** en ce qui concerne la religion; **business matters** affaires; **money matters** affaires d'argent

(d) (*problem*) **what's the m.?** qu'est-ce qu'il y a?, qu'y a-t-il?; **what's the m. with you?** qu'est-ce que vous avez?, qu'avez-vous?; **what's the m. with my hat?** qu'est-ce qu'il a, mon chapeau?; **what's the m. with asking her out to the movies?** je ne vois pas ce qu'il y a de mal à lui demander si elle veut aller au cinéma; **I don't know what's the m. with me** je ne sais pas ce que j'ai; **there's something the m.** il y a quelque chose (qui ne va pas), il se passe quelque chose; **there's something the m. with his throat** il a quelque chose à la gorge; **there's nothing the m. with you/the television** tu n'as/la télé n'a rien; **he went on talking as if nothing was the m.** il continua de parler comme si de rien n'était

(e) no m.! n'importe!, peu importe!; **no m. what he does/says** quoi qu'il fasse/dise; **no m. how** par n'importe quel moyen; **no m. how hard I pushed against the door, it wouldn't open** j'avais beau pousser la porte de toutes mes forces, elle ne s'ouvrait pas; **no m. what** quoi qu'il arrive; **no m. when** à n'importe quel moment; **no m. when you ...** peu importe quand tu ...; **no m. who** qui que ce soit; **no m. who gave it to you** peu importe qui te l'a donné; **no m. where** où que ce soit

(f) *Med* (*pus*) pus *m*

(g) *Typ* matière *f*, copie *f*

matter[2] *vi* avoir de l'importance, être important (**to** pour), *Fml* importer (**to** à); **nothing matters much to him any more since his wife died** plus rien n'a d'importance pour lui depuis la mort de sa femme; **what really matters is that ...** ce qui est vraiment important, c'est que ...; **that is what matters most** c'est le plus important; **it doesn't m.** ce n'est pas important, cela ne fait rien, peu importe; **it doesn't m. how much it costs** peu importe le prix; **it doesn't m. – perhaps not to you, but it matters to <u>me</u>** ce n'est pas important – pour toi, peut-être, mais pour moi c'est important; **it doesn't m. a bit** cela n'a pas la moindre importance; **it doesn't m. to her what people think** elle se moque de ce que pensent les gens; **what does it m. to you?** qu'est-ce que cela peut bien vous faire?; **nothing else matters** tout le reste est sans importance; **these things m.** ces choses-là comptent; **you need to identify the people who m. in the company** il faut que tu identifies qui compte dans l'entreprise

Matterhorn (the) [ðə'mætəhɔːn] *n* le (Mont) Cervin

matter-of-fact *adj* (*person, manner, statement etc*) terre-à-terre, prosaïque; **to say sth in a m. tone** dire qch sur un ton neutre

Matthew ['mæθjuː] *n* Mat(t)hieu *m*

matting ['mætɪŋ] *n* (*material*) natte(s) *f(pl)*, paillassons *mpl*

mattins ['mætɪnz] *npl* = **matins**

mattock ['mætək] *n Agr* (*tool*) hoyau *m*, pioche *f*

mattress ['mætrɪs] *n* matelas *m*; **inflatable** *or* **air m.** matelas pneumatique

maturation [mætjʊ'reɪʃən] *n* (*of fruit, abscess etc*) maturation *f*; (*of wine, whisky*) vieillissement *m*; (*of intelligence etc*) développement *m*

mature[1] [mə'tjʊər] *adj* **(a)** (*person, fruit*) mûr; (*animal*) adulte; *Psy* (*intelligence*) qui dénote beaucoup de maturité; **the more m. trees are slower to come into leaf** les arbres les plus vieux ont des feuilles plus tard que les autres; **to be m. for one's age** *or* **years** être mûr pour son âge; **of m. years** (*person*) d'âge mûr; *Br* **would suit a m. person** (*in job advertisement*) conviendrait à une personne d'âge mûr; **after m. consideration** après mûre réflexion; **m. cheese** fromage *m* fait; *Br Univ* **m. student** = étudiant, -ante plus âgé(e) que la moyenne *ou* qui entreprend des études sur le tard **(b)** *Fin* (*bill*) échu

mature[2] **1** *vt* **the cheese/wine is matured for five years before it's sold** le fromage/vin vieillit pendant cinq ans avant d'être vendu **2** *vi* **(a)** (*of plant*) mûrir; (*of wine*) vieillir; (*of person*) devenir plus mûr, acquérir de la maturité; **she had matured into a sophisticated young woman** elle était devenue une jeune femme sophistiquée; **to let a plan m.** laisser mûrir un projet; **his plans had not yet matured** ses projets n'étaient pas encore mûris *ou* mûrs **(b)** *Fin* (*of bill*) échoir, arriver à échéance

maturely [mə'tjʊəlɪ] *adv* (*to decide*) de façon raisonnable; **to behave m.** se comporter en adulte

maturity [mə'tjʊərɪtɪ] *n* **(a)** (*of fruit, wine, cheese etc*) maturité *f*; **to come to** *or* **reach m.** arriver à maturité; **the years of m.** (*of person*) l'âge *m* mûr; **the novels of her m.** les romans qu'elle a écrits à l'âge mûr **(b)** *Fin* **(date of) m.** (*of bill*) échéance *f*; **payable at m.** payable à l'échéance; **m. date** terme *m ou* date *f* d'échéance; **m. value** valeur *f* à l'échéance

maudlin ['mɔːdlɪn] *adj* larmoyant, pleurard; (*drunk*) dans un état d'ivresse larmoyante; **m. sentimentality** sentimentalité larmoyante; **to become m.** se mettre à larmoyer *ou* à pleurnicher

maul[1] [mɔːl] *n Rugby* maul *m*

maul[2] *vt* **(a)** (*of tiger etc*) blesser; (*more seriously*) mutiler; *Fig* (*author, book, play*) éreinter, tailler en pièces **(b)** (*grope*) (*woman*) tripoter

mauling ['mɔːlɪŋ] *n* **to get a m.** (*from a lion*) être blessé; (*more seriously*) être mutilé; *F* (*by enemy troops, opposing team*) être battu à plates coutures, recevoir une raclée; (*from critics*) se faire éreinter

maunder ['mɔːndər] *vi* **(a)** (*in speech*) **to m. (on)** radoter, rabâcher **(b)** (*dawdle*) **to m. (along)** traîner, errer

maundy ['mɔːndɪ] *n Rel* **M. Thursday** le jeudi saint; *Br* **m. money** = pièces *fpl* frappées pour l'aumône royale du jeudi saint

Mauritania [mɒrɪ'teɪnɪə] *n* Mauritanie *f*

Mauritian [mə'rɪʃən] **1** *adj* mauricien **2** *n* Mauricien, -ienne

Mauritius [mə'rɪʃəs] *n* l'île *f* Maurice

mausoleum [mɔːsə'liːəm] *n* mausolée *m*

mauve [məʊv] *adj, n* (*colour*) mauve *m*

maverick ['mævərɪk] *n* **(a)** (*unorthodox person*) non-conformiste *mf*, franc-tireur *m*, *pl* francs-tireurs; **m. MP/salesman** député/vendeur qui fait les choses à sa façon **(b)** *Am* (*stray steer*) bouvillon *m* errant sans marque de propriétaire

maw [mɔː] *n* **(a)** (*stomach*) (*of ruminant*) quatrième poche *f* de l'estomac; (*of bird*) jabot *m*; *F* (*of person*) panse *f* **(b)** (*mouth*) (*of animal, fish*) gueule *f*

mawkish ['mɔːkɪʃ] *adj Pej* (*person*) d'une sensiblerie outrée, mièvre; (*novel etc*) d'une sentimentalité exagérée, mièvre

mawkishness ['mɔːkɪʃnɪs] *n Pej* (*of person*) sensiblerie *f* outrée, mièvrerie *f*; (*of novel etc*) sentimentalité *f* exagérée, mièvrerie

max [mæks] *adj, n* (*abbr* **maximum**) max *m*

maxi ['mæksɪ] *F* **1** *adj* (*skirt, coat*) maxi (*no feminine ending*) **2** *n* (*skirt*) maxi *f*; (*coat*) maxi *m*

maxim ['mæksɪm] *n* maxime *f*

maximal ['mæksɪməl] *adj Fml* maximal

maximization [mæksɪmaɪ'zeɪʃən] *n* maximalisation *f*, maximisation *f*

maximize ['mæksɪmaɪz] *vt* maximiser, maximaliser

maximum, *pl* **-a** ['mæksɪməm, -ə] **1** *n* maximum *m*, *pl* -ums, -a; **to the m.** au maximum; **at the m.** au (grand) maximum; **to reach one's m.** plafonner **2** *adj* maximum, maximal; **m. load** charge *f* limite; **we guarantee m. security** nous garantissons une sécurité maximum; **m. security prison** prison *f* de haute sécurité; **m. security unit** quartier *m* de haute sécurité; **m. speed** (*highest possible*) vitesse *f* maximale *ou* maximum; (*highest permitted*) vitesse limite; **m. temperatures** températures *fpl* maximales

May [meɪ] *n* [①A75-6,B-C; B58-9,B-C] mai *m*; **in (the month of) M.** en mai, au mois de mai; **(on) the first/the seventh of M.** le premier/le sept mai

may[1] [meɪ] *v aux* [①A57-58,d; B37,K,2] (*3rd person sing* **may**; *pt, cond* **might** [maɪt]; *no pres or past participle*) **(a)** (*expressing possibility*) **he m.** *or* **might return at any moment** il peut *ou* pourrait revenir d'un moment à l'autre; **she m.** *or* **might not be hungry** elle n'a peut-être pas faim, il se peut qu'elle n'ait pas faim; **we m. remind ourselves at this point that ...** il n'est pas inutile de rappeler ici que ...; **that m. or m. not be true** cela est peut-être vrai ou peut-être pas; **he m.** *or* **might have lost it** peut-être qu'il l'a perdu, il se peut qu'il l'ait perdu; **Queen Anne m. have stayed here** il se peut que la reine Anne ait séjourné ici; **you m.** *or* **might see her if you stay another hour** vous la verrez peut-être si vous restez encore une heure; **something I said m.** *or* **might have offended him** j'ai peut-être dit quelque chose qui l'a blessé; **it m.** *or* **might not be the fastest car in the world, but ...** ce n'est peut-être pas la voiture la plus rapide du monde, mais ...; **it m.** *or* **might be that ...** il se peut *ou* se pourrait bien que + *sub* ...; **you m.** *or* **might be wondering why I'm doing that** vous vous demandez peut-être pourquoi je fais cela; **you m.** *or* **might well ask!** je me le demande!; **you m. find it funny now, but wait till it's your turn!** tu trouves peut-être ça drôle maintenant mais tu verras quand ce sera ton tour!; **be that as it m.** quoi qu'il en soit; **that's as m. be, but we can't afford it** peut-être, mais nous ne pouvons pas nous le permettre; **but that's as m. be, it's all history now** enfin, tout ça, c'est du passé; **whatever faults he m.** *or* **might have he is never dull** quels que soient ses défauts, il n'est jamais ennuyeux; **we m.** *or* **might as well stay where we are** autant rester où nous sommes

(b) (*asking or giving permission*) **m. I come in?** est-ce que je peux entrer?; **m. I write to you? – of course you m.** pourrais-je vous écrire? – bien sûr, je vous en prie; **you m. go** vous pouvez partir; (*at end of interview*) vous pouvez disposer; **if I m.** *or* **might be allowed to express an opinion** si je puis me permettre; **if I m.** *or* **might say so** si j'ose dire; **m. I?** vous permettez?

(c) *esp Fml* (*be allowed to*) **passengers m. take only one item of hand luggage** les passagers ne peuvent prendre *ou* ne sont autorisés à prendre qu'un bagage à main; **candidates m. consult a dictionary** l'utilisation d'un dictionnaire est autorisée pendant l'examen

(d) *Fml* (*in clauses expressing purpose, fear etc*) **I only**

hope it m. last! pourvu que cela *ou* ça dure!; **I fear you m. be right** j'ai bien peur que tu aies raison; **I pray that you m. be mistaken** j'espère que tu te trompes; **so that others m. sleep in peace** pour que les autres puissent dormir en paix

(e) (*expressing a wish*) **m. she rest in peace!** qu'elle repose en paix!; **m. the best man win!** que le meilleur gagne!; **much good m. it do you!** grand bien vous fasse!

may² *n* **m. (blossom)** fleurs *fpl* d'aubépine; **m. tree** aubépine *f*

Maya ['maɪə] *n* **(a)** Maya *mf* **(b)** *Ling* maya *m*

Mayan ['maɪən] **1** *adj* maya **2** *n* **(a)** Maya *mf* **(b)** *Ling* maya *m*

maybe ['meɪbiː] **1** *adv* peut-être; **m. so, but ...** peut-être mais ...; **m. not, but ...** peut-être (pas) mais ...; **m. yes, m. no** peut-être bien que oui, peut-être bien que non; **m. she won't accept** peut-être qu'elle n'acceptera pas, elle n'acceptera peut-être pas **2** *n F* **I don't want any maybes** c'est oui ou non!

May beetle *or* **bug** *n Ent* hanneton *m*

Mayday ['meɪdeɪ] **1** *n* **M. (signal)** mayday *m*, SOS *m* **2** *int* (*distress signal*) mayday!

May Day *n* le premier mai; **M. parade** défilé *m* du premier mai

mayfly ['meɪflaɪ] *n Ent* éphémère *m* vulgaire

mayhem ['meɪhem] *n* **(a)** (*chaos*) confusion *f* totale, chaos *m*; (*violent behaviour*) grabuge *m*; **it was m.** c'était le chaos; **to create** *or* **cause m.** (*to cause chaos*) semer la pagaille; (*to behave violently*) faire du grabuge **(b)** *Jur* (*maiming*) mutilation *f*; *Am* **to commit m. on sb** se livrer à des voies de fait contre qn

mayn't ['meɪənt] = **may not**, *see* **may¹**

mayo ['meɪəʊ] *n Am F* mayo *f*

mayonnaise [meɪə'neɪz] *n Culin* mayonnaise *f*

mayor [meər] *n* maire *m*

mayoress ['meəres] *n* **(a)** (*mayor*) maire *m*, *Old-fashioned* mairesse *f* **(b)** *esp Br* (*mayor's wife*) mairesse *f*

maypole ['meɪpəʊl] *n* mât *m*

May queen *n* = reine *f* d'un carnaval ayant lieu au mois de mai

maze [meɪz] *n* labyrinthe *m*, dédale *m*; *Fig* (*of streets, regulations etc*) dédale

Mb *Comptr* (*abbr* **megabyte**) Mo

MBA [embiː'eɪ] *n Univ* (*abbr* **Master's in Business Administration**) MBA *m*

MBE [embiː'iː] *n Br* (*abbr* **Member of the Order of the British Empire**) (*award*) Ordre *m* de l'Empire Britannique; (*person*) membre *m* de l'Ordre de l'Empire Britannique

MBO [embiː'əʊ] *n Com* **(a)** (*abbr* **management buy-out**) rachat *m* d'une entreprise par la direction **(b)** (*abbr* **management by objectives**) gestion *f* selon objectifs

MC [em'siː] *n* (*abbr* **Master of Ceremonies**) (*at formal event*) maître *m* des cérémonies; *TV etc* animateur *m*, présentateur *m*

MCP [emsiː'piː] *n F* (*abbr* **male chauvinist pig**) phallocrate *m*, macho *m*

MD [em'diː] *n* **(a)** *Med* (*abbr* **Doctor of Medicine**) docteur *m* en médecine **(b)** *Com* (*abbr* **Managing Director**) P-DG *m*

Md *abbr* **Maryland**

ME [em'iː] *n, Med* (*abbr* **myalgic encephalomyelitis**) encéphalomyélite *f* myalgique

Me *abbr* **Maine**

me [*unstressed* mɪ, *stressed* miː] *pers pron* [①**A26**,a; **B17**,2,a-c] **(a)** [①**A42**,3] (*unstressed*) me; (*before vowel sound*) m'; (*with preposition*) moi; **he knows me** il me connaît; **he told me so** il me l'a dit; **listen to me** écoutez-moi; **lend it (to) me** prêtez-le-moi; **she wrote me a letter** elle m'a écrit une lettre; **I'll take it with me** je le prendrai avec moi; **he's younger than me** il est plus jeune que moi; **no-one knows the real me** personne ne sait vraiment qui je suis

(b) [①**B19**,5,a-b] (*stressed*) moi; **you and me** vous et moi; **he was thinking of me** il pensait à moi; **that's for me** ça c'est pour moi

(c) (*complement of verb* **to be**) **it's me!** c'est moi!; **is it just me or is there a smell of gas in here?** est-ce que je me fais des idées ou est-ce que ça sent le gaz?; **this jacket isn't really me** cette veste n'est pas vraiment mon style

(d) (*in int*) **silly me! I've forgotten the address** ce que je peux être bête! j'ai oublié l'adresse; **clumsy me! I've spilled my drink!** ce que je peux être maladroit! j'ai renversé mon verre!

mead [miːd] *n* (*drink*) hydromel *m*

meadow ['medəʊ] *n* pré *m*, prairie *f*; **m. grass** pâturin *m*, herbe *f* des prés; **m. saffron** (*plant*) colchique *m* d'automne, safran *m* des prés; **m. pipit** (*bird*) pipit *m* des prés, farlouse *f*

meadowland ['medəʊlænd] *n* prairie(s) *f(pl)*

meadowsweet ['medəʊswiːt] *n* (*plant*) (spirée *f*) ulmaire *f*, reine *f* des prés

meagre, *US* **meager** ['miːgər] *adj* maigre

meagrely, *US* **meagerly** ['miːgəlɪ] *adv* maigrement, piètrement; **they exist m.** ils arrivent tout juste à subsister

meal¹ [miːl] *n* repas *m*; **I've had a huge m.** j'ai mangé comme quatre; **to eat between meals** manger entre les repas; **would you like some wine with your m.?** est-ce que vous prendrez du vin (avec votre repas)?; **in Spain the evening m. is later** en Espagne, on dîne plus tard; **to invite sb round for a m.** inviter qn à dîner; **enjoy your m.!** (*waiter etc to customers*) bon appétit!; *Fig F* **don't make a m. of it!** n'en fais pas toute une histoire!; **she always makes a m. of everything** il faut toujours qu'elle complique tout; *F* **the job is just a m. ticket** ce travail n'est qu'un gagne-pain; *F* **he's just a m. ticket to her** elle n'est avec lui que pour son argent; **m. tray** plateau *m* repas

meal² *n* (*of oats, rye, corn etc*) farine *f*

meals-on-wheels [miːlzɒn'wiːlz] *n Br Admin* = (service *m* de) repas *mpl* (servis) à domicile pour personnes âgées ou handicapées; **she gets m.** on lui livre ses repas à domicile

mealtime ['miːltaɪm] *n* heure *f* du repas; **they only see each other at mealtimes** ils ne se voient qu'aux heures des repas

mealworm ['miːlwɜːm] *n Ent* ver *m* de farine

mealy ['miːlɪ] *adj* **(a)** (*in consistency*) farineux **(b)** (*covered in meal*) saupoudré de farine, poudreux **(c) m. complexion** teint *m* blême

mealy-mouthed [miːlɪ'maʊðd] *adj Pej* doucereux, mielleux, patelin

mean¹ [miːn] *n* **(a)** (*middle*) (juste) milieu *m*, moyen terme *m*; **the golden** *or* **happy m.** le juste milieu **(b)** *Math* moyenne *f*

mean² *adj* (*medium, average*) moyen; **m. time between failures** moyenne *f* de temps entre deux pannes

mean³ *adj* **(a)** *esp Br* (*with money*) avare, *F* radin; **to be m. with one's praise** *or* **compliments** être avare de compliments; **he's very m. about tipping** il n'aime pas donner de pourboires

(b) (*low, ignoble*) (*person, character, action*) bas, méprisable, mesquin; (*wretched*) misérable, pauvre; **even to the meanest intelligence** même pour les esprits les plus obtus; **he has a m. streak** il peut être méchant quand il veut; **a m. trick** un vilain tour, *F* un sale coup; **that's m. of her** ce n'est pas chic de sa part; *F* **I feel very m. about not going** j'ai honte de ne pas y aller

(c) *esp Am F* (*vicious, tough*) méchant, vicieux

(d) (*with* **no**) **no m. ...** un très bon .../une très bonne ...; **he's no m. scholar** c'est un grand érudit; **it was no m. feat** ce n'était pas une mince affaire; **it is no m. task (to do sth)** ce n'est pas une mince affaire *ou* ce n'est pas rien (de faire qch)

(e) *esp Am F* (*excellent*) formidable; **he plays a m. guitar** c'est un guitariste formidable

(f) *Am F* (*poorly*) **to feel m.** se sentir mal en train

mean⁴ *vt* (*pt, pp* **meant** [ment]) **(a)** (*have intention*) **to m. to do sth** avoir (bien) l'intention de faire qch, (bien) compter faire qch, vouloir faire qch; **what do you m. to do?** que comptez-vous faire?, qu'est-ce que vous avez l'intention de faire?; **I never meant to go** je n'ai jamais eu l'intention d'y aller; **I m. him no harm** je ne lui veux pas de mal; **she didn't m. (to do) it** elle ne l'a pas fait exprès; **without meaning it** sans le vouloir; **I meant to!** (*do what I did*) c'était bien mon intention!; **to m. well by sb** avoir de bonnes intentions à l'égard de qn; **she means well** elle a de bonnes intentions; **I m. to be obeyed** j'entends qu'on m'obéisse; **I m. to succeed** je veux réussir; **I m. to see justice done** je veux que justice soit faite

(b) (*intend*) **I meant this book for you** je vous destinais ce livre; **the remark was meant for you** la remarque s'adressait à vous *ou* vous était destinée; **the remark wasn't meant to be overheard** cette remarque n'était pas censée être entendue; **it was meant as a joke/compliment/insult** c'était censé être une blague/un compliment/une insulte; **you weren't meant to open the presents until tomorrow** tu n'étais pas censé ouvrir les cadeaux avant demain; **I have a feeling this was meant to be** *or* **happen** j'ai le sentiment que ça devait arriver; **do you m. him?** est-ce de lui que vous parlez?, est-ce lui à qui vous faites allusion?; **this portrait is meant to be the duke** ce portrait est censé représenter le duc; **we were meant for each other** nous sommes faits l'un pour l'autre

(c) (*signify*) (*of person*) vouloir dire; (*of word, phrase, event etc*) vouloir dire, signifier; **what does that word m.?** que signifie ce mot?; **the name means nothing to me** ce nom ne me dit rien; **what is meant by ...?** que veut dire ...?; **all this means nothing** tout cela ne rime à rien; **it doesn't m. anything** (*what you saw, heard*) cela ne prouve rien; **this means war/the end of our relationship** c'est la guerre/la fin de notre amitié; **what do you m.?** que voulez-vous dire?;

what do you m. by that? qu'entendez-vous par là?; **I know what you m.!** (*I quite agree*) et comment!; **what, me?, I don't know what you m.!** qui moi?, je ne vois pas ce que vous voulez dire!; **she knew what it meant to be hungry** elle savait ce que c'était que d'avoir faim

(d) (*speak sincerely*) **do you think he meant what he said?** pensez-vous qu'il l'ait dit sérieusement?, est-ce que tu crois qu'il parlait sérieusement?; **I didn't m. that** ce n'est pas ce que je voulais dire; **you don't m. it!** vous voulez rire!, vous plaisantez!; **I m. it** je parle sérieusement; **you're my best friend – do you m. that?** tu es mon meilleur ami – tu le penses vraiment?; **when I say no, I m. no** quand je dis non, c'est non; **do you m. to tell me ...?** est-ce que tu es en train de me dire que ...?; **I m. (to say)!** je veux dire!

(e) (*be of importance*) **the price means nothing to him** le prix importe peu pour lui; **doesn't your daughter's education m. anything to you?** est-ce que l'éducation de ta fille ne t'intéresse pas?; **I cannot tell you what he has meant to me** je ne saurais vous dire tout ce qu'il a été pour moi; **my Sundays m. /independence means a lot to me** le dimanche/mon indépendance est sacré(e) pour moi

(f) (*imply, involve*) signifier, impliquer; **it would m. the children having to change school again** cela signifierait que les enfants devraient changer d'école une fois de plus; **just because you've been to university doesn't m. you know everything** ce n'est pas parce que tu es allé à l'université que tu sais tout; **it doesn't m. we have to stop seeing each other** ça ne veut pas dire que nous devons cesser de nous voir

meander¹ [mɪ'ændər] *n Geog* méandre *m*

meander² *vi* **(a)** (*of person*) errer çà et là, flâner; (*in speaking*) divaguer **(b)** (*of river*) serpenter, faire des méandres

meandering [mɪ'ændərɪŋ] *adj* **(a)** (*speech etc*) sans plan, sans suite **(b)** (*river*) qui serpente *ou* fait des méandres

meanie ['mi:nɪ] *n F* **(a)** *esp Br* (*miserly person*) rapiat, -ate, pingre *mf* **(b)** *esp US* (*nasty person*) **what a m.!** quel chameau!, qu'il est vache!

meaning ['mi:nɪŋ] **1** *n* signification *f*, sens *m*; *Ling* (*of term etc*) acception *f*; **what is the m. of this word?** que signifie *ou* que veut dire ce mot?; **what's the m. of this?** (*expressing indignation*) qu'est-ce que cela signifie?; *Fig F* **loyalty? you don't know the m. of the word!** tu ne sais pas ce que c'est que la loyauté!; **life had no m. for him** la vie n'avait plus aucun sens pour lui; **to understand sb's m.** comprendre ce que qn veut dire; *F* **if you get my m.** si tu vois ce que je veux dire; **a look full of m.** un regard significatif **2** *adj* (*look, smile*) significatif, qui en dit long

meaningful ['mi:nɪŋfʊl] *adj* (*full of meaning*) significatif, éloquent; (*expressive*) (*look, smile*) significatif, qui en dit long; *esp Pol* **m. talks** conversations *fpl* constructives; **a m. relationship** une relation sérieuse

meaningfully ['mi:nɪŋfʊlɪ] *adv* (*to sing*) de façon expressive; **he smiled m. at her** le sourire qu'il lui fit en disait long

meaningless ['mi:nɪŋlɪs] *adj* dénué *ou* vide de sens, qui ne signifie rien; **a m. act/remark** un non-sens

meanly ['mi:nlɪ] *adv* **(a)** *esp Br* (*in miserly fashion*) en lésinant, chichement **(b)** (*ignobly*) (*to act, behave*) peu loyalement, indignement **(c)** (*wretchedly*) misérablement, pauvrement

meanness ['mi:nnɪs] *n* **(a)** *esp Br* (*with money*) avarice *f*; *F* radinerie *f* **(b)** (*nastiness*) mesquinerie *f*, méchanceté *f* **(c)** (*baseness*) bassesse *f*, petitesse *f*; **the m. of vision expressed in his speech ...** l'étroitesse d'esprit que reflétait son discours ... **(d)** (*poor quality, poverty*) médiocrité *f*, pauvreté *f*

means [mi:nz] *npl* (*often with sing verb*) **(a)** (*method*) moyen(s) *m(pl)*; **to use every possible m. to do sth** employer tous les moyens pour faire qch; **there is no m. of escape** il n'y a pas d'issue; **by all m.** (*by every possible method*) par tous les moyens (possibles); (*certainly*) mais certainement!, mais oui!; **may I come in? – by all m.!** puis-je entrer? – je vous en prie!; **by no m.** en aucune façon, nullement; **she is not stupid by any (manner of) m.** elle est loin d'être stupide; **by some m. or other** d'une manière ou d'une autre; **by m. of sth** au moyen *ou* à l'aide de qch; **they escaped by m. of a secret passage** il se sont enfuis par un passage secret; **she succeeded by m. of her own hard work** elle a réussi grâce à son travail acharné; **a m. to an end** un moyen d'arriver à ses fins

(b) (*income*) moyens *mpl*, ressources *fpl*; (*wealth*) fortune *f*; **according to our m.** selon nos moyens; **to live beyond/within one's m.** vivre au-dessus de/selon ses moyens; **private m.** ressources personnelles; **a man of m.** un homme dont les revenus sont élevés; **to be without m.** (*without resources*) être sans ressources; (*without wealth*) être sans fortune; **they are without the m. to deal with the problem** ils n'ont pas les moyens de résoudre le problème

means of production *n pl Econ* moyens *m pl* de production

means of transport *n* moyen *m* de transport

means test *n Admin* = enquête *f* sur la situation (de fortune)

means-test *vt Admin* **to m. sb** = faire une enquête sur les ressources de qn avant de lui accorder une aide sociale

meant *see* **mean⁴**

meantime, meanwhile ['mi:ntaɪm, -waɪl] *n, adv* **in the meantime, (in the) meanwhile** dans l'intervalle, pendant ce temps-là, en attendant

measles ['mi:z(ə)lz] *npl* (*usu with sing verb*) *Med* rougeole *f*; **to have (the) m.** avoir la rougeole; **German m.** rubéole *f*

measly ['mi:zlɪ] *adj F* insignifiant, minable; **he gave her a m. present** il lui a offert une bricole; **keep your m. money!** garde ton sale argent!; **they pay her a m. sum of money** ils la payent une misère

measurable ['meʒərəb(ə)l] *adj* **(a)** mesurable; **a m. difference** (*m in sb's performance etc*) une différence sensible **(b)** *Ch etc* (*constituent*) dosable

measure¹ ['meʒər] *n* **(a)** (*measurement*) mesure *f*; *Fig* **to get the m. of sb** prendre la mesure de qn, jauger qn; **to have the m. of sb** savoir comment s'y prendre avec qn

(b) (*instrument*) (*for grain, milk etc*) mesure *f*

(c) (*quantity*) dose *f*, mesure *f*; **a m. of whisky** une dose de whisky; **to give sb short m.** donner moins que la mesure à qn; **half m.** demi-mesure *f*, *pl* demi-mesures; *Fig* **there are no half measures with her** avec elle, il n'y a pas de demi-mesure; *Fig* **then she insulted the other man for good m.** elle a aussi insulté l'autre pour ne pas faire de jaloux; **he gave him a couple of kicks for good m.** il lui a donné quelques coups de pied en prime

(d) (*degree*) **in some m.** dans une certaine mesure; **she was in great m. to blame for what happened** elle est en grande partie responsable de ce qui s'est passé; **a m. of independence** une certaine indépendance

(e) (*limit*) mesure *f*, limite *f*; **beyond m.** outre mesure

(f) (*action, step*) mesure *f*, démarche *f*; **to take measures** prendre des mesures; **to take extreme measures** employer les grands moyens

(g) *Parl* (*bill*) projet *m* de loi

(h) (*in poetry*) mesure *f*

(i) *esp Am Mus* mesure *f*

measure² **1** *vt* (*distance, time, person etc*) mesurer; (*wall etc*) métrer, mesurer; (*piece of land*) arpenter; (*person for clothes*) mesurer, prendre les mesures de; *Fig* **to m. one's length (on the ground)** (*fall*) s'étaler par terre, tomber de tout de son long; *Fig* **to m. one's strength** *or* **oneself with sb** mesurer ses forces avec qn, se mesurer avec *ou* contre qn; *Fig* **to m. one's words** mesurer *ou* peser ses paroles **2** *vi* mesurer; **column measuring 10 metres** colonne qui mesure 10 mètres

▶ **measure off** *vtsep* (*material etc*) mesurer

▶ **measure out** *vtsep* (*corn etc*) mesurer; (*distribute*) répartir, attribuer; **the barman measured out a double whisky** le barman versa un double whisky; **m. out two cups of flour** préparez deux mesures de farine

▶ **measure up 1** *vtsep* (*wood*) mesurer; **to m. sb up for a suit** prendre les mesures de qn pour un costume; **to get measured up for a new suit** se faire prendre ses mesures pour un nouveau costume; *Fig* **they measured each other up** (*before fight etc*) ils se sont jaugés **2** *vi* (*of employee etc*) faire le poids, être à la hauteur

▶ **measure up to** *vipo* **to m. up to one's job** se montrer à la hauteur de sa tâche; **to m. up to sb/sth** être à la mesure de qn/qch; **to m. up to sb's expectations** répondre aux attentes de qn; **the holiday didn't m. up to their expectations** leurs vacances n'ont pas été à la mesure de leurs espérances **the meal didn't m. up to her usual standards** le repas qu'elle nous a préparé n'était pas aussi bon que d'habitude

measured ['meʒəd] *adj* **(a)** (*time, distance etc*) mesuré, déterminé **(b)** (*deliberate*) (*movement, step*) cadencé; **with m. steps** à pas mesurés *ou* comptés; **m. tread** marche *f* scandée **(c)** (*language*) modéré; **to speak in m. tones** parler sur un ton modéré **(d)** (*in poetry*) (*verse etc*) mesuré

measurement ['meʒəmənt] *n* (①B56-7,D,1) (*quantity, length etc*) mesure *f*; (*action*) mesure, mesurage *m*; **the measurements of a room/an object** les dimensions *fpl* d'une pièce/d'un objet; **bust/waist/hip m.** (*of person*) tour *m* de poitrine/taille/hanches; **to take a customer's measurements** prendre les mesures d'un client

measurement ton *n* tonne *f* d'arrimage *ou* d'encombrement

measuring ['meʒərɪŋ] *n* **m. chain** (*in surveying*) chaîne *f* d'arpenteur *ou* d'arpentage; **m. cup/jug** mesure *f*; **m. glass** verre *m* gradué; **m. spoon** cuillère *f* à doser; **m. tape** mètre *m* à ruban

meat [miːt] *n* (a) viande *f*; *Old-fashioned* **m. and drink** le manger et le boire; *Fig* **it was m. and drink to them** c'était une véritable aubaine pour eux; *Prov* **one man's m. is another man's poison** on ne discute pas des goûts et des couleurs, ce qui guérit l'un tue l'autre; **m. broth** bouillon *m* gras; **m. diet** régime *m* carné; **m. hook** croc *m ou* crochet *m* de boucherie; *Culin* **m. loaf** = hachis *m* de bœuf (b) *Fig* (*substantial content*) (*of book, film, article etc*) substance *f*

meatball ['miːtbɔːl] *n Culin* boulette *f* (de viande)

meathead ['miːthed] *n US F* crétin, -ine, imbécile *mf*

meatpacking ['miːtpækɪŋ] *n Am* abattage *m* et boucherie *f*

meaty ['miːtɪ] *adj* (a) (*sausage etc*) riche en viande; (*smell etc*) de viande; *Fig* (*book etc*) riche (b) (*fleshy*) charnu

Mecca ['mekə] *n* la Mecque; *Fig* **a M. for antique lovers** un paradis pour les passionnés d'objets anciens

mechanic [mɪ'kænɪk] *n* mécanicien *m*; **I'm not much of a m.** je ne suis pas très mécanicien

mechanical [mɪ'kænɪk(ə)l] *adj* (a) *Tech* mécanique; **m. breakdown insurance** assurance *f* panne mécanique; **m. digger** pelleteuse *f* mécanique; **m. drawing** dessin *m* industriel; **m. efficiency** rendement *m* mécanique; **m. engineer** ingénieur *m* mécanicien; **m. engineering** génie *m* mécanique; **m. failure** défaillance *f* mécanique; **he has no m. skill** il n'a aucune compétence en mécanique; **m. wear** usure *f* mécanique

(b) *Fig* (*reply, smile etc*) machinal, automatique, mécanique; **to give a m. response** répondre machinalement; **a m. gesture** un geste machinal; **her playing is very m.** (*of pianist etc*) elle joue d'une façon très mécanique

mechanically [mɪ'kænɪklɪ] *adv* (a) *Tech* mécaniquement; **m. driven** actionné mécaniquement; **I'm not very m. minded** je ne suis pas très doué pour tout ce qui est mécanique (b) *Fig* (*to reply, smile etc*) machinalement

mechanics [mɪ'kænɪks] *n* [①A10,c] (a) (*science*) mécanique *f* (b) (*working parts*) mécanisme *m*

mechanism ['mekənɪz(ə)m] *n* (*device, working parts*), *Phil, Psy etc* mécanisme *m*

mechanistic [mekə'nɪstɪk] *adj* (*view of universe, explanation*) mécaniste

mechanization [mekənaɪ'zeɪʃən] *n* mécanisation *f*

mechanize ['mekənaɪz] *vt* mécaniser; (*troops*) motoriser

mechanized ['mekənaɪzd] *adj* **m. industry** industrie mécanisée; *Mil* **m. troops** troupes motorisées

Med (the) [ðə'med] *n F* la Méditerranée

M. Ed [e'med] *n* (*abbr* **Master of Education**) ≈ CAPES *m*

medal ['med(ə)l] *n* médaille *f*; **to award a m. to sb** décerner une médaille *ou* une décoration à qn; **to be awarded a m. for bravery** être décoré pour sa bravoure; *US Mil* **M. of Honor** = la plus haute distinction américaine donnée en récompense à un soldat

medallion [mɪ'dæljən] *n* médaillon *m*; **m. man** macho *m*

medallist, *US* **medalist** ['medəlɪst] *n Sp etc* médaillé, -ée; **gold/silver m.** titulaire *mf* d'une *ou* de la médaille d'or/d'argent

meddle ['med(ə)l] *vi* (*interfere*) se mêler (**in** de); (*tamper*) toucher (**with** à); **to m. in other people's affairs** se mêler des affaires d'autrui

meddler ['medlər] *n* **he's a terrible m.** il met son nez partout

meddlesome ['med(ə)lsəm] *adj* qui se mêle de tout

meddling ['medlɪŋ] **1** *adj* = **meddlesome 2** *n* (*action*) ingérence *f* (**in** dans)

media ['miːdɪə] *npl* [①A13,3,a] **the (mass) m.** les médias *mpl*; **the m. were waiting for her when she flew in** les journalistes l'attendaient à sa descente d'avion; **m. advertising** publicité-média *f*; **m. analysis** analyse *f* de médias; **m. analyst** critique *mf* des médias; **m. buyer** acheteur *m* d'espaces dans les médias, acheteur d'espaces publicitaires; **m. coverage** couverture *f* par les médias; **m. event** événement *m* médiatique; **m. exposure** (*coverage*) couverture *f* médiatique; (*of product*) exposition *f* dans les médias; **m. hype** battage *m* médiatique; **m. mogul** magnat *m* (de presse), magnat des médias; **m. person** professionnel -elle des médias; **m. studies** études *fpl* de communication

media-conscious *adj* (*politician etc*) médiatique

mediaeval, mediaevalist = **medieval, medievalist**

medial ['miːdɪəl] **1** *adj* intermédiaire (**to** entre); (*letter*) médial **2** *n Ling* médiale *f*

median ['miːdɪən] **1** *adj* médian; *Am Aut* **m. strip** terre-plein *m* central, *Can* médiane *f* **2** *n* (a) *Anat* (*nerve*) nerf *m* médian; (*vein*) veine *f* médiane (b) (*in statistics*), *Math* médiane *f*

mediant ['miːdɪənt] *n Mus* médiante *f*

mediate ['miːdɪeɪt] **1** *vi* (*of person*) agir en *ou* servir de médiateur (**between** entre) **2** *vt* **to m. a peace** intervenir en qualité de médiateur pour amener la paix

mediation [miːdɪ'eɪʃən] *n* médiation *f*; **to go to m.** recourir à une médiation

mediator ['miːdɪeɪtər] *n* médiateur, -trice

medic ['medɪk] *n F* (*student*) étudiant, -ante en médecine, carabin *m*; (*doctor*) toubib *m*

Medicaid ['medɪkeɪd] *n US* = assistance *f* médicale pour les défavorisés

medical ['medɪk(ə)l] **1** *adj* médical; (*book etc*) de médecine; (*student*) en médecine; **you need m. attention** il faut vous faire soigner par un médecin; **m. certificate** certificat *m* médical; *Admin* **m. officer of health** = médecin *m* départemental; **m. examination** visite *f* médicale; *esp US* **m. examiner** médecin *m* légiste; **m. history** antécédents *mpl* médicaux; **m. jurisprudence** médecine *f* légale; **m. practitioner** médecin *m*, membre *m* du corps médical; **the m. profession** (*people*) le corps médical; (*activity*) la profession médicale; **m. record** dossier *m* médical

2 *n* visite *f* médicale; **to have a m.** passer une visite médicale; **he failed the m.** il n'a pas été accepté pour raisons de santé

medically ['medɪklɪ] *adv* médicalement; **to be m. examined** subir un examen médical

medicament [me'dɪkəmənt] *n* médicament *m*

Medicare ['medɪkeər] *n* (a) *US* = assistance *f* médicale pour les personnes âgées et les handicapés (b) *Can* assurance-maladie *f*

medicate ['medɪkeɪt] *vt* (*patient*) faire suivre un traitement à

medicated ['medɪkeɪtɪd] *adj* (*shampoo*) médical, traitant; (*soap*) médical

medication [medɪ'keɪʃən] *n* (*medicine, drugs*) médicaments *mpl*; **to take one's m.** prendre ses médicaments; **to be on m.** suivre un traitement

medicinal [me'dɪsɪn(ə)l] *adj* médicinal, médicamenteux; **m. plants** plantes *fpl* médicinales; **m. properties** vertus *fpl* curatives; *Hum* **it's just for m. purposes** (*having a whisky etc*) c'est mon médicament

medicinally [me'dɪsɪn(ə)lɪ] *adv* (*to use a herb, substance*) médicalement, comme médicament; (*to treat*) médicalement

medicine ['medsɪn] *n* (a) (*practice, science*) médecine *f*; **to practise m.** exercer la médecine; **to study m.** faire des études de médecine, étudier la médecine (b) (*remedy*) médicament *m*; *Fig* **to give sb a taste of his/her own m.** rendre la pareille à qn; *Fig* **to take one's m.** avaler la pilule, supporter les conséquences (de son action); *Sp* **m. ball** medecine-ball *m*; **m. chest** *or* **cabinet** (armoire *f* à) pharmacie *f*; **m. man** (sorcier *m*) guérisseur *m*

medico ['medɪkəʊ] *n F* = **medic**

medieval [medɪ'iːvəl] *adj* du moyen âge, médiéval; *Fig* (*attitudes, person*) rétrograde; **it's m. here** c'est le moyen âge ici

medievalist [medɪ'iːvəlɪst] *n* médiéviste *mf*

mediocre [miːdɪ'əʊkər] *adj* médiocre

mediocrity [miːdɪ'ɒkrɪtɪ] *n* (*quality*) médiocrité *f*; **a m.** (*person*) un/une médiocre

meditate ['medɪteɪt] **1** *vi* (a) (*reflect*) méditer (**on, upon** sur), réfléchir (**on, upon** sur, à) (b) (*be in or enter into a state of meditation*) méditer; *esp Rel* se recueillir **2** *vt* (*project, undertaking*) méditer

meditation [medɪ'teɪʃən] *n* (a) (*thinking*) méditation *f* (**upon** sur) (b) (*state*) recueillement *m* (c) *Liter* **meditations** méditations *fpl*

meditative ['medɪtətɪv] *adj* méditatif, recueilli

meditatively ['medɪtətɪvlɪ] *adv* d'un air méditatif

Mediterranean [medɪtə'reɪnɪən] **1** *adj* méditerranéen; **the M. Sea** la mer Méditerranée **2** *n* **the M.** la Méditerranée

medium[1], *pl* **-a, -ums** ['miːdɪəm, -ə, -əmz] *n* [①A13,3] (a) (*mid-point*) milieu *m*, moyen terme *m* (**between** entre)

(b) *Art* (*for working in*) matériau *m*; (*for advertising*) support *m*, médium *m*; **marble is her favourite m.** elle préfère travailler le marbre; **opera is his preferred m.** l'opéra est son moyen d'expression favori; **television is a powerful m.** la télévision est un média *ou* un moyen de communication *ou* un moyen de diffusion puissant; **through the m. of the press** par l'intermédiaire de la presse, par voie de presse; **French was the m. through which they communicated** ils communiquaient en français, le français était la langue dans laquelle ils communiquaient; **advertising m.** support publicitaire

(c) *Phys* milieu *m*, véhicule *m*; *Biol* culture *f*, bouillon *m* de culture

(d) (*in spiritualism*) médium *mf*

medium[2] **1** *adj* moyen; **of m. height** de taille moyenne; **cook in a m. oven** cuire à four moyen; **m. sized** de grandeur moyenne, de taille moyenne; **in the m. term** à moyen terme; *TV, Cin* **m. close-up** plan *m* rapproché *ou* moyen; **m. dry**

wine vin *m* demi-sec, *pl* vins demi-secs; *Rad* **m. wave** onde *f* moyenne **2** *n* (*something of medium size*) **this teeshirt's a m.** ce tee-shirt est une taille moyenne *ou* un deux; **available in small, m. and large** disponible en petit, moyen et grand
medium-haul *adj* (*flight, route*) moyen-courrier
medium-range *n* **m. ballistic missile** missile *m* balistique de moyenne portée
medium-rare *adj* à point
medium-term *adj* (*financing, forecast*) à moyen terme
medlar ['medlər] *n* (*fruit*) nèfle *f*; **m. (-tree)** néflier *m*
medley ['medlɪ] *n* (*of people, objects*) mélange *m*, méli-mélo *m*, *pl* mélis-mélos; *Mus* pot-pourri *m*, *pl* pots-pourris; *Swimming* **400 metres m. (race)** 4 x 100 mètres quatre nages
medulla [me'dʌlə] *n* **(a)** *Bot* médulle *f*, moelle *f* **(b)** *Anat* (*of bone*) moelle *f*
meek [mi:k] *adj* doux, *f* douce, docile; **m. and mild** doux comme un agneau
meekly ['mi:klɪ] *adv* avec soumission, docilement
meekness ['mi:knɪs] *n* douceur *f* de caractère, soumission *f*, docilité *f*
meerschaum ['mɪəʃəm] *n Miner* écume *f* (de mer); **m. (pipe)** pipe *f* en écume (de mer)
meet[1] [mi:t] *n* **(a)** (*in hunting*) rassemblement *m* de la meute **(b)** *esp Am* (*meeting*) réunion *f*
meet[2] (*pt, pp* **met** [met]) **1** *vt* **(a)** (*by accident*) (*person*) rencontrer; **to m. sb on the stairs** croiser qn dans l'escalier; **to m. another car** croiser une autre voiture

(b) (*by arrangement*) (*person*) rejoindre, retrouver; **to go to m. sb** aller au-devant de qn, aller à la rencontre de qn; **to m. sb at the station** aller chercher qn à la gare; **the bus meets the train** il y a une correspondance entre le train et l'autobus; **I arranged to m. him at three o'clock** j'ai pris rendez-vous avec lui pour trois heures; **I'll m. you at the crossroads** je te retrouve au croisement

(c) (*become acquainted with*) rencontrer, faire la connaissance de; **I met her at the Martins'** je l'ai rencontrée chez les Martin; **pleased to m. you** ravi de faire votre connaissance; **have you met my husband?** vous connaissez mon mari?; **I get to m. a lot of people in my job** mon travail m'amène à rencontrer beaucoup de gens; **I like meeting people** j'aime rencontrer des gens; **she's the nicest person I've ever met** c'est la personne la plus gentille que j'ai jamais rencontrée; **m. Mr Thomas** je vous présente M. Thomas

(d) (*join*) **the stream meets the river** le ruisseau se jette dans la rivière; **where East meets West** où l'est et l'ouest se rencontrent; **here the road meets the railway** c'est ici que la route rejoint *ou* croise le chemin de fer

(e) (*come into contact with*) **his eyes met mine** nos regards se sont croisés; **he was afraid to m. her eye** il avait peur de croiser son regard; **her mouth met his** leurs bouches se rencontrèrent; **her car met an oncoming lorry and ...** sa voiture a percuté un camion qui arrivait en sens inverse et ...

(f) (*be perceived by*) **a strange sound met our ears** nous avons entendu un bruit étrange; **a remarkable sight met our eyes** nous avons été témoins d'un spectacle incroyable; **there's more to this than meets the eye** on ne connaît pas les dessous de cette affaire; **there's more to him than meets the eye** c'est quelqu'un de plus complexe qu'il n'y paraît au premier abord

(g) (*satisfy*) (*a need*) satisfaire, répondre à; (*demands*) satisfaire; (*condition, requirement*) satisfaire à; (*objection, criticism*) répondre à; (*cheque*) honorer; *Com* (*order*) satisfaire, assurer; *Com* (*bill of exchange*) honorer, faire honneur à; **to m. sb's wishes** combler les désirs de qn; **to m. sb's expectations** répondre à l'attente de qn; **to m. one's commitments** remplir ses engagements; *Com* **to m. demand** répondre à la demande; **to m. expenses** supporter les dépenses, subvenir aux frais; **the cost will be met by the company** les frais seront pris en charge par la compagnie

(h) (*face*) (*danger*) affronter; (*the enemy*) rencontrer, affronter; (*difficulty*) se heurter à; **she met her death in an air crash** elle a trouvé la mort *ou* péri dans un accident d'avion; *Sp* **he will m. the champion in June** il rencontrera *ou* affrontera le champion en juin

2 *vi* **(a)** (*by accident*) (*of people*) se rencontrer (par hasard)

(b) (*by arrangement*) (*of people*) se retrouver; **let's m. for lunch** on se retrouve pour le déjeuner?; **where shall we m.?** où se retrouve-t-on?; **when shall we m. again?** quand nous reverrons-nous?; **we should m. more often** on devrait se voir plus souvent

(c) (*become acquainted*) se rencontrer, se connaître; **they met in 1980** ils se sont rencontrés *ou* connus en 1980

(d) (*of society, assembly*) se réunir; **the club meets every other Tuesday** le cercle se réunit un mardi sur deux

(e) (*join*) se rencontrer, se rejoindre; (*of rivers*) confluer, se rejoindre; **a country where East and West m.** un pays où se rencontrent l'est et l'ouest; **his eyebrows m.** ses sourcils se touchent

(f) (*come into contact*) se rencontrer; **the two cars met head on** les deux voitures se sont heurtées de plein fouet; **our eyes met** nos regards se sont croisés; **their hands met** leurs mains se rencontrèrent
meet[3] *adj Arch, Lit* convenable, séant; **it is m. that ...** il convient que ...
▶ **meet up** *vi* se rencontrer; **we'll have to m. up next time I'm in Paris** il faudra qu'on se voie la prochaine fois que je passerai à Paris; **we met up with an Australian** nous avons rencontré un Australien
▶ **meet with** *vipo* **(a) to m. with a refusal** essuyer un refus; **to m. with difficulties** rencontrer des difficultés; **to m. with failure** échouer; **the proposal has met with fierce opposition** la proposition s'est heurtée à une opposition très vive; **the expedition met with disaster** l'expédition a tourné au désastre; **he has met with an accident** il lui est arrivé un accident; **the plan didn't m. with her approval** le projet n'a pas reçu son accord **(b)** *esp Am* (*meet*) (*for discussion*) rencontrer, retrouver; (*for lunch etc*) retrouver
meeting ['mi:tɪŋ] *n* **(a)** (*encounter*) rencontre *f*; **during my first m. with him** lors de notre première rencontre; *Lit* **m. of minds** communion *f* de pensée; **m. place** (*inside*) lieu *m* de réunion; (*outside*) rendez-vous *m*; **m. point** (*of lines, things*) point *m* de jonction; *Math* point de rencontre; (*for people*) lieu *m* de rendez-vous

(b) (*of society, assembly etc*) réunion *f*, séance *f*; (*in business, discussion*) réunion, conférence *f*; **he's in a m.** il est en conférence *ou* réunion; **at our last m.** lors de notre dernière réunion; **to hold a m.** tenir une réunion; **to call a m. of the shareholders** convoquer les actionnaires; **to open the m.** déclarer la séance ouverte; **to address the m.** prendre la parole; **meetings secretary** secrétaire *mf* de séance

(c) *Sp* meeting *m*; *Horseracing* (réunion *f* de) courses *fpl*

(d) *Rel* (*of Quakers*) **to go to m.** aller au temple; **m. house** temple *m*
meg [meg] *n Comptr Sl* méga *m*
mega ['megə] *adj F* (*tremendous*) super, génial; (*big*) énorme
mega- ['megə] *pref F* **m. -rich/famous/intelligent** hyper riche/célèbre/intelligent
megabuck ['megəbʌk] *n esp Am Sl* **megabucks** une fortune; **m. project** projet *m* qui coûte une fortune
megabyte ['megəbaɪt] *n Comptr* méga-octet *m*, *F* méga *m*; **20 m. memory** mémoire *f* de 20 méga-octets
megacycle ['megəsaɪk(ə)l] *n El* mégacycle *m*
megadeath ['megədeθ] *n* mort *f* d'un million de personnes
megagroup ['megəgru:p] *n Mus* supergroupe *m*
megahertz ['megəhɜ:ts] *n El* mégahertz *m*
megalith ['megəlɪθ] *n* mégalithe *m*
megalithic [megə'lɪθɪk] *adj* mégalithique
megalomania [megələʊ'meɪnɪə] *n* mégalomanie *f*
megalomaniac [megələʊ'meɪnɪæk] *adj, n* mégalomane *mf*
megaphone ['megəfəʊn] *n* mégaphone *m*
mega-resort *n* mégastation *f*, station *f* très importante
megastar ['megəstɑ:r] *n* superstar *f*
megaton ['megətʌn] *n* mégatonne *f*
megavolt ['megəvɒlt] *n El* mégavolt *m*
megawatt ['megəwɒt] *n El* mégawatt *m*
meiosis [maɪ'əʊsɪs] *n* **(a)** (*in rhetoric*) litote *f* **(b)** *Biol* méiose *f*
melaena [me'li:nə] *n Med* mélna *m*, méléna *m*
melancholia [melən'kəʊlɪə] *n* mélancolie *f*
melancholic [melən'kɒlɪk] *adj* mélancolique
melancholy ['melənkəlɪ] **1** *n* mélancolie *f*, **a bout of m.** un accès de mélancolie **2** *adj* (*person*) mélancolique; (*news*) triste, attristant
melee ['meleɪ] *n* mêlée *f*
mellifluous [me'lɪfluəs] *adj* (*words etc*) mélodieux
mellow[1] ['meləʊ] *adj* **(a)** (*flavour, taste*) doux, *f* douce; (*wine*) moelleux, velouté; (*fruit*) fondant, mûr; (*voice, sound*) moelleux, doux; (*colour, light*) chaud, doux, velouté; **m. tobacco** tabac doux **(b)** (*person*) détendu; *F* (*pleasantly drunk*) un peu gris; **to grow m.** (*of person*) s'adoucir
mellow[2] **1** *vi* **(a)** (*of flavour, taste, light*) s'adoucir; (*of wine*) mûrir, prendre du moelleux *ou* du velouté; (*of voice, sound*) devenir plus chaud *ou* riche *ou* moelleux, s'adoucir **(b)** (*of character*) s'adoucir; **to m. with age** s'adoucir *ou* devenir plus accommodant *ou* plus tolérant avec l'âge **2** *vt* **(a)**

(*flavour, taste*) rendre plus doux; (*wine*) donner du moelleux *ou* du velouté à **(b)** (*person's character*) adoucir; **age has mellowed her** l'âge a adouci son caractère

▶ **mellow out** *vi F* s'adoucir; **why don't you m. out a bit?** pourquoi est-ce que tu n'essayes pas de te détendre un peu?

mellowing ['meləʊɪŋ] *n* (*of wine*) maturation *f*; (*of character*) adoucissement *m*

mellowness ['meləʊnɪs] *n* (*of flavour, light, colour, character*) douceur *f*; (*of wine*) moelleux *m*, velouté *m*; (*of voice, sound*) velouté, moelleux

melodic [mɪ'lɒdɪk] *adj Mus* mélodique

melodious [mɪ'ləʊdɪəs] *adj* mélodieux

melodiously [mɪ'ləʊdɪəslɪ] *adv* mélodieusement

melodrama ['melədrɑːmə] *n* mélodrame *m*

melodramatic [melədrə'mætɪk] *adj* mélodramatique

melodramatically [melədrə'mætɪklɪ] *adv* d'un air *ou* d'une manière mélodramatique

melody ['melədɪ] *n* mélodie *f*

melon ['melən] *n* **(a)** (*fruit*) melon *m*; **m. seeds** pépins *mpl* de melon **(b)** *Am F* (*profits, money*) gros bénéfices *mpl* (à distribuer); **to carve** *or* **cut up the m.** distribuer les bénéfices

melt [melt] (*pt, pp* **melted**; *pp adj* **molten** ['məʊlt(ə)n]) **1** *vi* fondre; (*of solid in liquid*) fondre, se dissoudre; **to m. in the mouth** fondre dans la bouche; **to m. into ...** (*of colour etc*) se fondre dans ...; *Fig* **my heart** *or* **I melted** j'ai été attendri; **she melted (inside) at his touch** elle fondait sous ses caresses; **to m. into thin air** disparaître

2 *vt* (*ice, metal*) (faire) fondre; (*salt etc*) (faire) fondre, (faire) dissoudre; **to m. sb's heart** attendrir qn; **m. the butter in a pan** faire fondre le beurre dans une casserole; *Fig F* **I'm absolutely melted** (*very hot*) je cuis; **melted snow** neige fondue

▶ **melt away** *vi* **(a)** (*of snow*) fondre complètement **(b)** (*of clouds, vapour*) se dissiper; (*of crowd*) se disperser; (*of anger, objections, resistance etc*) se dissiper, s'évanouir

▶ **melt down** *vtsep* (*scrap metal etc*) fondre

meltdown ['meltdaʊn] *n Nucl, Phys* fusion *f*

melting ['meltɪŋ] **1** *adj* (*wax, neige*) qui fond; *Fig* (*voice, words etc*) attendrissant **2** *n* (*act of melting*) (*of metal*) fonte *f*, fusion *f*; (*of snow*) fonte; **m. point/temperature** point *m*/température *f* de fusion; *Fig* **everything's in the m. pot** tout est à refaire; *Fig* **the United States is a m. pot** les États-Unis sont un creuset *ou* un melting-pot

member ['membər] **1** *n* **(a)** (*of family, club etc*) membre *m*; (*of party*) adhérent, -ente; **to be a m. of the family** faire partie de la famille; **a m. of the audience** un spectateur, une spectatrice; **a m. of the opposite sex** une personne du sexe opposé **(b)** (*limb*) membre *m*; **(male) m.** membre (viril) **(c)** *Math* élément *m* **2** *adj* **m. country/state** pays/état membre

Member of Congress *n US Pol* député *m*

Member of Parliament *n Br Can Pol* député *m*; *Br* **the M. (of Parliament) for Newcastle** le député de Newcastle

membership ['membəʃɪp] *n* **(a)** (*state of being a member*) appartenance *f*; **m. of any political party is incompatible with this post** le titulaire de ce poste ne peut adhérer à aucun parti politique; **she resigned her m. of the party** elle a rendu sa carte du parti; **to pay one's m. (fee)** payer sa cotisation; **to renew one's m.** se réinscrire; **m. card** carte *f* de membre *ou* d'adhérent; **m. list** liste *f* des membres; **m. number** numéro *m* d'adhérent

(b) (*members*) membres *mpl*, adhérents *mpl*; (*number of members*) (*of society etc*) nombre *m* des membres *ou* des adhérents, effectif *m*; **club with a m. of a thousand** club de mille membres; **the majority of our m.** la majorité de nos membres

membrane ['membreɪn] *n Biol etc* membrane *f*

membranous ['membrənəs] *adj* membraneux

memento, *pl* **-oes, -os** [mɪ'mentəʊ, -əʊz] *n* souvenir *m*

memo ['meməʊ] *n* note *f* de service; *Comptr* **m. field** champ *m* mémo; **m. pad** bloc-notes *m*, *pl* blocs-notes

memoir ['memwɑːr] *n* (*essay*) (*scientific etc*) étude *f*, monographie *f*; (*biography*) notice *f* biographique; **memoirs** mémoires *fpl*

memorable ['memərəb(ə)l] *adj* (*speech, occasion*) mémorable; **a film m. largely for its sex and violence** un film surtout remarqué pour ses scènes de sexe et de violence

memorably ['memərəblɪ] *adv* mémorablement, de façon mémorable

memorandum, *pl* **-da, -dums** [memə'rændəm, -də, -dəmz] *n* **(a)** *Admin* (*within office etc*) note *f* de service **(b)** (*reminder*) note *f* **(c)** (*in diplomacy*) mémorandum *m* **(d)** *Jur* (*of sale etc*) mémoire *m*; (*of contract*) mémoire, sommaire *m* des articles; **m. of association** charte *f* constitutive d'une société à responsabilité limitée, acte *m* de société; **m. and articles of association** statuts *mpl* de société **(e)** *Com* **m. book** carnet *m*, calepin *m*, agenda *m*

memorial [mɪ'mɔːrɪəl] **1** *adj* (*statue, festival, tablet, plaque etc*) commémoratif; *Rel* **m. service** cérémonie *f* du souvenir **2** *n* **(a)** (*monument*) monument *m* (commémoratif) **(b)** (*prize etc*) prix *m* commémoratif

memorize ['meməraɪz] *vt* apprendre par cœur

memory ['memərɪ] *n* **(a)** (*faculty*) mémoire *f*; **to have a good/bad m.** avoir (une) bonne/mauvaise mémoire; **to have a good m. for faces/names** avoir la mémoire des visages/des noms; **to have a bad m. for faces/names** ne pas avoir la mémoire des visages/des noms; *F* **m. like a sieve** mémoire de lièvre, très mauvaise mémoire; **m. loss, loss of m.** perte *f* de mémoire; **if my m. serves me right** si j'ai bonne mémoire; **in** *or* **within living m.** de mémoire d'homme; **from m.** (*to play, recite, paint sth*) de mémoire; **to commit sth to m.** apprendre qch par cœur

(b) (*something remembered*) (*of sb, sth*) souvenir *m*; **I have no m. of you saying any such thing** je ne me souviens pas que tu aies dit cela; **childhood memories** souvenirs d'enfance; **I have very pleasant memories of your friend** je garde un excellent souvenir de votre ami; **her earliest memories are of music** ses plus anciens souvenirs sont des airs de musique; **to take a trip down m. lane** (*visit place*) aller sur les lieux de son passé; **it's a real trip down m. lane hearing that song** cette chanson me rappelle ma jeunesse; **this television programme will take viewers on a trip down m. lane** cette émission rappellera de vieux souvenirs aux téléspectateurs; **to keep sb's m. alive** garder le souvenir de qn; **in m. of ...** à la mémoire de ..., en souvenir de ...

(c) *Comptr* mémoire *f*; **m. address** adresse *f* de mémoire; **m. buffer** zone *f* de mémoire tampon; **m. capacity** capacité *f* de mémoire; **m. card** carte *f* mémoire; **m. cell** cellule *f* mémoire; **m. chip** puce *f* mémoire; **m. management** gestion *f* de mémoire; *Aut* **m. seat** siège *m* à positions mémorisables; **m. typewriter** machine *f* à écrire à mémoire

memory bank *n* bloc *m* de mémoire

memory expansion card *n* carte *f* d'extension de mémoire

memory-intensive *adj Comptr* (*application*) qui prend beaucoup de place en mémoire

memory-loadable *adj Comptr* chargeable en résident

memory-resident *adj Comptr* résident en mémoire

men [men] *see* **man**[1]

menace[1] ['menɪs] *n* **(a)** menace *f*; **there was m. in his voice** il parlait d'un ton menaçant; **to demand money with menaces** réclamer de l'argent en usant de menaces **(b)** *F* **that kid's a m.** cet enfant est une véritable plaie; **he's a m. behind the wheel of a car** c'est un vrai danger au volant; **that carpet's a m.** ce tapis est dangereux

menace[2] *vt* menacer

menacing ['menəsɪŋ] *adj* menaçant; **in a m. voice** d'une voix menaçante

menacingly ['menəsɪŋlɪ] *adv* (*to look*) d'un air menaçant; (*to say*) d'un ton menaçant

menagerie [mɪ'nædʒərɪ] *n* ménagerie *f*

mend[1] [mend] *n* **(a)** (*improvement*) *F* **to be on the m.** (*of person*) être en voie de guérison; (*of situation*) s'arranger, s'améliorer **(b)** (*in fabric etc*) raccommodage *m*; (*darn*) reprise *f*; **the socks have a m. in the heel** les chaussettes ont été raccommodées au talon

mend[2] **1** *vt* **(a)** (*repair*) (*item of clothing etc*) raccommoder; (*darn*) (*item of clothing, socks*) repriser; (*fishing net*) rem(m)ailler; (*tool, road, shoes etc*) réparer **(b)** (*put right*) rectifier, corriger; **to m. one's ways** s'amender, se corriger; **to m. one's manners** s'amender; *Prov* **least said soonest mended** moins on parle, mieux cela vaut **2** *vi* (*of broken bones*) se ressouder; *F* **you'll/it'll soon m.** tu t'en remettras; **we'll have to make do and m.** il va falloir faire avec

mendacious [men'deɪʃəs] *adj Fml* (*person*) menteur, -euse; (*report*) mensonger

mendacity [men'dæsɪtɪ] *n Fml* (*characteristic*) propension *f* au mensonge

Mendelian [men'diːlɪən] *adj Biol* mendélien

mendicant ['mendɪkənt] **1** *adj* **(a)** *Lit* mendiant, de mendiant **(b)** *Rel* **m. friar** moine *m* mendiant; **m. order** ordre *m* mendiant **2** *n* **(a)** *Lit* mendiant, -ante **(b)** *Rel* moine *m* mendiant

mending ['mendɪŋ] *n* **(a)** (*of clothes etc*) raccommodage *m* **(b)** (*clothes*) vêtements *mpl* à raccommoder

menfolk ['menfəʊk] *npl* **the m.** (*in contrast to women*) les hommes *mpl*; **the women worked alongside their** *or* **the m.** les femmes travaillaient aux côtés des hommes

menial ['miːnɪəl] **1** *adj* (*task*) ingrat; (*job*) subalterne **2** *n usu Pej* laquais *m*; (*in household*) domestique *mf*

meningitis [menɪn'dʒaɪtɪs] *n Med* méningite *f*; **to have m.** avoir *ou* faire une méningite

meniscus, *pl* **-ci, -scuses** [mɪ'nɪskəs, -saɪ, -skəsəz] *n* ménisque *m*

menopausal ['menəpɔːzəl] *adj* ménopausique; (*woman*) à la ménopause

menopause ['menəpɔːz] *n Physiol* ménopause *f*; **to be going through the m.** être en ménopause

menses ['mensiːz] *npl Physiol* menstrues *fpl*

menstrual ['menstrʊəl] *adj Physiol* (*cycle*) menstruel

menstruate ['menstrʊeɪt] *vi Physiol* avoir ses règles

menstruation [menstrʊ'eɪʃən] *n Physiol* menstruation *f*

mensuration [menʃə'reɪʃən] *n* **(a)** *Fml* (*act of measuring*) mesurage *m*, mesure *f* **(b)** *Math* mensuration *f*

menswear ['menzweər] *n Com* vêtements *mpl* pour hommes; **m. (department)** rayon *m* homme

mental ['ment(ə)l] *adj* **(a)** (*state, age etc*) mental; **I made a m. note to speak to her about it** je me suis dit qu'il ne fallait pas oublier de lui en parler; **I've made a m. note of it** j'y pense; **m. arithmetic** calcul *m* mental; **m. block** blocage *m*; **m. breakdown** dépression *f*; *Jur* **m. cruelty** cruauté *f* mentale; **m. deficiency** déficience *f ou* débilité *f* mentale; **m. defective** arriéé, -ée; **m. health** santé *f* mentale; **m. hospital** *or* **home** hôpital *m ou* clinique *f* psychiatrique; **m. illness** maladie *f* mentale; **m. reservation** doute *m* **(b)** *Sl* (*mad*) cinglé, dingue

mentality [men'tælɪtɪ] *n* (*of person*) mentalité *f*

mentally ['ment(ə)lɪ] *adv* mentalement; **m. deficient** *or* **defective** débile mental; **m. ill/handicapped** malade/handicapé mental; **to be m. ill** être un malade mental; **the m. ill/handicapped** les malades/handicapés mentaux

menthol ['menθɒl] *n* menthol *m*; **m. cigarettes** cigarettes *fpl* au menthol

mentholated ['menθəleɪtɪd] *adj Pharm* mentholé

mention[1] ['menʃən] *n* (*reference*) référence *f*, mention *f*; **m. was made of ...** on a parlé de ..., on a fait allusion à ...; **I never heard m. of her name again** je n'entendis plus jamais prononcer son nom; **to make no m. of sth** passer qch sous silence, ne pas faire mention de qch; **there is no m. of this extra charge in the brochure** la brochure ne mentionne pas ce supplément; **at the m. of food** quand on parle/a parlé de manger; **at the m. of her name he turned white** quand il entendit, son nom il pâlit; **he gets a brief m. in her autobiography** elle le mentionne brièvement dans son autobiographie; *Mil* **m. in dispatches** citation *f* à l'ordre du jour

mention[2] *vt* (*sb, sth*) parler de; (*fact, detail*) relever, mentionner; **the sum mentioned** la somme indiquée; **I had forgotten to m. that ...** j'avais oublié de vous dire que ...; **she mentioned that she had lived in Bristol** elle mentionna qu'elle avait vécu à Bristol; **I shall m. it to him** je lui en parlerai, je lui en toucherai un mot; **too numerous to m.** trop nombreux pour les citer; **I have no money worth mentioning** je n'ai pour ainsi dire pas d'argent; **I didn't think it was worth mentioning** je ne pensais pas que c'était la peine d'en parler; **as mentioned above** comme mentionné ci-dessus; **not to m. ...** sans parler de ...; **I heard my name mentioned** j'ai entendu prononcer mon nom; **did she m. my name?** est-ce qu'elle a parlé de moi?; **to m. sb in one's will** coucher qn sur son testament; *F* **don't m. it!** (*after being thanked*) il n'y a pas de quoi!; (*drop the subject*) ne m'en parlez pas!, n'en parlez pas!; *Mil* **to be mentioned in dispatches** être cité à l'ordre du jour

mentor ['mentɔːr] *n* mentor *m*, guide *m*

menu ['menjuː] *n* **(a)** *Culin* menu *m*; **today's m.** la carte du jour **(b)** *Comptr* menu *m*; **m. bar** barre *f* de menu; **m. builder** générateur *m* de menus; **m. item** élément *m* de menu; **m. option** option *f* de menu

menu-controlled *adj Comptr* contrôlé par menu

menu-driven *adj Comptr* contrôlé *ou* piloté par menu(s)

MEP [emiː'piː] *n Br* (*abbr* **Member of the European Parliament**) membre *m* du Parlement européen

mercantile ['mɜːkəntaɪl] *adj* commercial, commerçant; **m. nation** nation *f* commerçante; **m. marine** marine *f* marchande; **m. law** droit *m* commercial

mercantilism ['mɜːkəntɪlɪz(ə)m] *n* mercantilisme *m*

mercantilist ['mɜːkəntɪlɪst] *adj, n* mercantiliste *m*

mercenary ['mɜːsɪn(ə)rɪ] **1** *adj Pej* (*person*) intéressé; **for purely m. reasons** uniquement pour l'argent; **must you be so m.?** tu ne penses qu'à l'argent! **2** *n* (*soldier*) mercenaire *m*

mercerized ['mɜːsəraɪzd] *adj Ind* (*cotton*) mercerisé

merchandise[1] ['mɜːtʃəndaɪz] *n* marchandise(s) *f(pl)*

merchandise[2] *vi* faire du commerce *ou* du négoce

merchandiser ['mɜːtʃəndaɪzər] *n* marchandiseur *m*

merchandising ['mɜːtʃəndaɪzɪŋ] *n* marchandisage *m*

merchant ['mɜːtʃənt] **1** *n* **(a)** *Com esp Old-fashioned* (*dealer*) négociant, -ante, marchand, -ande; **wine m.** négociant en vins **(b)** *F* **speed m.** chauffard *m*; **gloom m.** pessimiste *mf* **(c)** *Am Com* (*shopkeeper*) marchand, -ande, boutiquier, -ière **2** *adj* marchand, de commerce; **m. bank** banque *f* d'affaires; **m. navy** *or* **marine** marine *f* marchande; **m. seaman** marin *m* à bord d'un navire marchand; **m. ship** *or* **vessel** navire *m* marchand

merchant banker *n* banquier *m* d'affaires

merchantman, *pl* **-men** ['mɜːtʃəntmən] *n* (*ship*) navire *m* marchand, navire de commerce

merciful ['mɜːsɪfʊl] *adj* (*God*) miséricordieux (**to** pour); (*judge*) clément (**to** envers); **m. heavens!** grands Dieux!; **death was a m. release from his suffering** la mort fut une délivrance pour lui

mercifully ['mɜːsɪfʊlɪ] *adv* **(a)** (*showing mercy*) avec clémence **(b)** (*fortunately*) heureusement

merciless ['mɜːsɪlɪs] *adj* impitoyable, sans pitié, sans merci

mercilessly ['mɜːsɪlɪslɪ] *adv* impitoyablement, sans pitié; **the rain beat down m.** la pluie tombait sans répit

mercurial [mɜː'kjʊərɪəl] *adj* **(a)** (*lively*) (*temperament, character, person*) vif, éveillé **(b)** (*changeable*) inconstant, d'humeur changeante **(c)** *Med, Pharm* (*product*) mercuriel

Mercury ['mɜːkjʊrɪ] *n Myth* Mercure *m*; *Astron* Mercure *f*

mercury ['mɜːkjʊrɪ] *n Ch* mercure *m*; **m. poisoning** empoisonnement *m* au mercure

mercy ['mɜːsɪ] *n* pitié *f*; *Rel* miséricorde *f*; *Rel* **Lord have m.!** Seigneur prends pitié!; **to show m. to sb** faire preuve de pitié envers qn; **to have m. on sb** avoir *ou* prendre pitié de qn; **to be without m.** être impitoyable *ou* sans pitié; **to call** *or* **beg for m.** demander grâce; **to throw oneself on sb's m.** s'abandonner à la merci de qn; *Old-fashioned* **m.!** grâce!; **at the m. of sb/sth** à la merci de qn/qch; **to be thankful** *or* **grateful for small mercies** être reconnaissant des moindres bienfaits; **what a m.!** quel bonheur!, quelle chance!; **works of m.** œuvres *fpl* de charité; **m. flight** vol *m* de secours (*pour transporter un malade à l'hôpital*); **m. killing** euthanasie *f*

mere [mɪər] *adj* simple; **a m. coincidence** une coïncidence pure et simple; **it's a m. formality** ce n'est qu'une simple formalité; **it was only by the merest chance that ...** ce n'est que par le plus grand des hasards que ...; **I shudder at the m. thought of it** je frissonne rien que d'y penser; **he's a m. child** ce n'est qu'un enfant; **he clearly hadn't the merest notion of who I was** il était clair qu'il n'avait pas la moindre idée de mon identité

merely ['mɪəlɪ] *adv* simplement, seulement; **he m. smiled** il se contenta de sourire; **I mention this m. to draw attention to ...** je n'ai dit cela que pour attirer l'attention sur ...

meretricious [merɪ'trɪʃəs] *adj Fml* (*style etc*) factice

merge [mɜːdʒ] **1** *vt* (*two systems, classes*) fusionner, amalgamer; *Comptr* (*files*) fusionner; **to m. sth in** *or* **into sth** fondre qch dans qch, amalgamer qch avec qch; **the two regiments were merged (into one)** les deux régiments ont été regroupés

2 *vi Com, Fin* (*of companies, banks etc*) s'amalgamer, fusionner; *Aut* (*of lanes, roads etc*) se rencontrer; **the sea and sky merged** le ciel et la mer se confondaient; **the colours/shapes/voices merged (into each other)** les couleurs/formes/voix se mêlaient; **to m. into the background** (*of building*; *Fig Pej of person*) se fondre dans le décor; **to m. into the shadows** disparaître dans l'ombre

merger ['mɜːdʒər] *n Com, Fin* (*of several companies*) fusion *f*, fusionnement *m*; **m. talks** discussions *fpl* en vue d'une fusion

meridian [mə'rɪdɪən] **1** *n* **(a)** *Geog* méridien *m* **(b)** *Astron* (*of star*) méridien *m*, point *m* culminant **2** *adj Astron* (*altitude, angle etc*) méridien; **m. line** (ligne *f*) méridienne *f*

meridional [mə'rɪdɪən(ə)l] **1** *adj* méridional **2** *n* Méridional, -ale

meringue [mə'ræŋ] *n Culin* meringue *f*

merino [mə'riːnəʊ] *n* (*sheep, wool*) mérinos *m*

merit[1] ['merɪt] *n* **(a)** (*deserving aspect*) mérite *m*; **according to one's merits** (*to be rewarded*) selon ses mérites; *Jur* **the merits of a case** le bien-fondé d'une cause; **to judge a proposal on its merits** juger une proposition pour ce qu'elle vaut; **to stand on its own merits** avoir une valeur en soi; *Rel* **to acquire m.** gagner du mérite; **her remarks at least had the m. of being frank** au moins, ses remarques avaient le mérite d'être franches

(b) (*worth*) valeur *f*, mérite *m*; **in order of m.** par ordre de mérite; **these paintings have no m. at all** ces tableaux n'ont aucune valeur artistique; *Am* **m. system** régime *m* du mérite; *Am* **m. increase** augmentation *f* au mérite

merit[2] *vt* (*reward, punishment etc*) mériter

meritocracy [merɪ'tɒkrəsɪ] *n* méritocratie *f*

meritorious [merɪ'tɔːrɪəs] *adj Fml (deed, conduct)* méritoire, louable
merlin ['mɜːlɪn] *n (bird)* (faucon *m*) émerillon *m*
mermaid ['mɜːmeɪd] *n Myth* sirène *f*
merman, *pl* **-men** ['mɜːmæn, -men] *n Myth* triton *m*
Merovingian [merəʊ'vɪndʒɪən] *Hist* **1** *adj* mérovingien **2** *n* Mérovingien, -ienne
merrily ['merɪlɪ] *adv* gaiement, gaîment, joyeusement
merriment ['merɪmənt] *n* gaieté *f*, gaîté *f*; **there was much m. at the thought of this** l'idée fit beaucoup rire; **sounds of m.** des rires
merry ['merɪ] *adj (comp* **merrier**; *superl* **merriest**) **(a)** *(happy)* joyeux, gai; **to make m.** se divertir, s'amuser, s'égayer; **M. Christmas!** joyeux Noël!; *F* **the weather is playing m. hell with the rail timetables** le mauvais temps a complètement chamboulé l'horaire des trains; *F* **my back is giving me m. hell** mon dos me fait souffrir atrocement; *prov* **the more the merrier** plus on est de fous, plus on rit; *Arch, Lit* **M. England** l'aimable Angleterre; **the m. month of May** le gentil mois de mai; **Robin Hood and his m. men** Robin des Bois et ses joyeux *ou* gais lurons
  (b) *F (slightly drunk)* gai, éméché, un peu gris
merry-go-round *n* manège *m*, *Belg* carrousel *m*
merrymaking ['merɪmeɪkɪŋ] *n* réjouissances *fpl*
mescalin(e) ['meskəlɪn] *n Pharm* mescaline *f*
mesh¹ [meʃ] *n* **(a)** *(of net, sieve etc)* maille *f*; **m. stockings** bas *mpl* filet **(b)** *MecE* prise *f*, engrènement *m*, engrenage *m*; **in m.** en prise
mesh² **1** *vi* **(a)** *(coordinate)* concorder **(b)** *MecE (of teeth, wheels)* engrener, s'engrener; *(be in mesh)* être en prise (**with** avec); *(engage)* se mettre en prise (**with** avec) **2** *vt MecE (of cogwheels)* endenter, engrener
mesmeric [mez'merɪk] *adj Fml* magnétique, hypnotique
mesmerize ['mezməraɪz] *vt Old-fashioned* hypnotiser; *Fig* fasciner
mesmerizing ['mezməraɪzɪŋ] *adj* fascinant
meson ['miːzɒn] *n Nucl, Phys* méson *m*
Mesopotamia [mesəpə'teɪmɪə] *n* Mésopotamie *f*
mess¹ [mes] *n* **(a)** *(disorder)* désordre *m*; *F* pagaïe *f*, pagaille *f*; *(bungled job etc)* gâchis *m*; **the kitchen's a m.** la cuisine est en désordre, *F* la cuisine est un vrai foutoir; **you're** *or* **you look a m.!** tu es dans un triste état!; **my hair's a m.** mes cheveux sont dans un triste état; **to be in a m.** *(of person)* être dans le pétrin *ou* dans de beaux draps; **everything's in a m.** tout est en désordre; **to make a m. of** *(job, translation, repair etc)* gâcher, saboter, *F* saloper; **the dentist made a real m. of it** le dentiste a vraiment salopé le travail; **to make a m. of things** tout gâcher; *F* **after the fight his face was a terrible m.** après la bagarre il avait le visage tout amoché; *F* **he's a m.** *(has complexes)* il est bourré de complexes; *(because of drugs etc)* il est dans un piteux état
  (b) *(dirt)* saleté *f*; **to make a m. of the tablecloth** salir la nappe; **dog's m.** crotte *f* de chien; **the dog's done a m. on the carpet** le chien a fait ses besoins sur le tapis
  (c) *Mil (food) (for officers)* popote *f*; *(for men)* ordinaire *m*; *(room) (for officers)* mess *m*; *(for men)* réfectoire *m*; *Naut* **m. deck** poste *m* d'équipage; **m. jacket** spencer *m*; **m. kit** ustensiles *mpl* ou matériel *m* d'ordinaire *ou* de campement; **m. tin** gamelle *f* (individuelle)
  (d) *Bible (food)* **m. of pottage** plat *m* de lentilles
mess² **1** *vt (make dirty)* salir, souiller **2** *vi* **(a)** *Mil etc* manger en commun; **to m. together** manger à la même table **(b)** *Sl (exaggerate)* **no messing!** sans blagues!; **there were two hundred of them, no messing!** ils étaient deux cents et je n'exagère pas! **(c)** *F (defecate) (of dog, cat)* faire des *ou* ses saletés
▶ **mess about, mess around** **1** *vi* **(a)** *(play the fool)* faire l'imbécile; *(waste time)* traîner, glandouiller **(b)** *(tinker)* tripoter; **don't m. around with something that doesn't belong to you** ne touche pas à ce qui ne t'appartient pas **(c)** *(sexually)* **to m. around with sb** s'amuser avec qn; **stop messing around with my sister!** laisse ma sœur tranquille! **2** *vtsep* **(a)** *(treat badly)* traiter de façon inconsidérée; **I wish you'd stop messing me about and make up your mind** j'aimerais bien que tu arrêtes de te moquer de moi et que tu te décides **(b)** *(alter)* chambouler
▶ **mess up** **1** *vtsep* **(a)** *(put in disorder) (room, clothes etc)* mettre en désordre, semer la pagaïe dans; **you'll m. up my hair!** tu vas me décoiffer! **(b)** *(ruin) (job)* gâcher, *F* saloper; **he's messed everything up** il a tout gâché; **you've messed up all our plans** tu as chamboulé tous nos projets **2** *vi Am F (at work, university etc)* tout rater; **to m. up on an exam** merdouiller dans *ou* à un examen
▶ **mess with** *vipo F (meddle with)* **don't m. with me!** ne me cherche pas!; **you shouldn't m. with people like that** *(get involved with)* tu ne devrais pas fréquenter des gens comme ça; *(get on wrong side of)* tu ne devrais pas mécontenter ces gens-là; **that's what happens when you m. with drugs!** voilà ce qui arrive quand on touche à la drogue!
message ['mesɪdʒ] *n* **(a)** message *m*; **to send a m. to sb** envoyer un message à qn; **to leave a m. for sb** laisser un message *ou* un mot pour qn; *(when telephoning)* laisser un message pour qn; **m. form** fiche-message *f*, *pl* fiches-messages; *F* **have you got the m.?, is the m. getting across?** tu as bien compris?, tu as pigé?; *F* **people seem to be getting the m., the m. seems to be getting across** les gens ont l'air de commencer à comprendre; **you get the screen m. ...** l'écran affiche ... **(b)** *(meaning) (of a book etc)* message *m*; **the film's m. is clear** le message qui ressort du film est clair **(c)** *Scot (errand)* commission *f*, course *f*
message boy *n* garçon *m* de courses
message switching ['swɪtʃɪŋ] *n Telecom* commutation *f* des messages
messenger ['mesɪndʒər] *n* messager, -ère; *(in large offices etc)* coursier, -ière; *Mil* coureur *m*; *Admin (in diplomacy)* courrier *m* (diplomatique); *Com* commissionnaire *m*; *Br* **King's/Queen's m.** ≈ courrier *m* d'État; **by m.** par porteur; **m. boy** garçon *m* de courses
Messiah [mɪ'saɪə] *n Rel, Mus, Fig* Messie *m*
messianic [mesɪ'ænɪk] *adj* messianique
messily ['mesɪlɪ] *adv (to eat)* salement; *Fig* **his first marriage ended rather m.** son premier mariage s'est mal terminé
messmate ['mesmeɪt] *n Mil etc* camarade *mf* de table; *Naut* camarade de plat
Messrs ['mesəz] *npl (abbr* **Messieurs**) MM
mess-up *n F* gâchis *m*, pagaïe *f*
messy ['mesɪ] *adj* **(a)** *(dirty)* sale; *(untidy) (room, hair, appearance)* en désordre; *(handwriting)* illisible; **to have a m. appearance** avoir l'air peu soigné; **m. eater** personne qui mange salement, cochon *m*; **oranges are a m. fruit (to eat)** les oranges sont difficiles à manger proprement; **it's a m. job** c'est salissant; **this room's so m.** cette pièce est dans un tel désordre!
  (b) *(unpleasantly complex)* confus, embrouillé; **a m. business** *(criminal etc)* une sale histoire; **the official story is getting messier and messier** l'histoire officielle s'embrouille de plus en plus; **it's a rather m. solution** c'est une solution assez compliquée; **his m. private life** sa vie privée troublée
mestiza [me'stiːzə] *n* métisse *f*
mestizo, *pl* **-os** [me'stiːzəʊ, -əʊz] *n* métis *m*
met¹ [met] *pt, pp see* **meet²**
met² *adj Br F (abbr* **meteorological**) météo; **the m. office** la météo
metabolic [metə'bɒlɪk] *adj Biol* métabolique; **m. rate** taux *m* métabolique
metabolism [mɪ'tæbəlɪz(ə)m] *n Biol* métabolisme *m*
metabolize [mɪ'tæbəlaɪz] *vt* transformer par métabolisme
metacarpal [metə'kɑːp(ə)l] *adj, n Anat* métacarpien *m*
metacarpus [metə'kɑːpəs] *n Anat* métacarpe *m*
metal¹ ['met(ə)l] **1** *n* **(a)** métal *m*; **m. detector** détecteur *m* de métal; **m. engraver** graveur *m* sur métaux; **m. polish** produit *m* pour faire briller les métaux **(b)** *Typ* caractères *mpl*, métal *m*, plomb *m* **(c)** *(stones) Rail* ballast *m* (de voie ferrée); **(road) m.** cailloutis *m*, pierraille *f* **(d)** *(in glassmaking)* verre *m* en fusion **2** *adj (made of metal)* métallique, en métal
metal² *vt* (**-ll-**, *US* **-l-**) *Br Constr (road)* empierrer; **metalled road** route *f* empierrée
metalanguage ['metəlæŋgwɪdʒ] *n* métalangage *m*
metallic [mɪ'tælɪk] *adj (sound, voice), Ch, El etc* métallique; *(taste)* de métal; **m. paint** peinture *f* métallisée; **m. sheen** éclat *m* métallique; **a m. blue/green** un bleu/vert métallique
metallurgical [metə'lɜːdʒɪk(ə)l] *adj* métallurgique
metallurgy [me'tælədʒɪ] *n* métallurgie *f*
metalwork ['met(ə)lwɜːk] *n* **(a)** *(practice, technique)* travail *m* des métaux; *Br Sch* **m. teacher/lesson** professeur *m*/cours *m* de travail des métaux **(b)** *(articles)* métal *m* ouvré; *Art* ferronnerie *f*; **piece of m.** pièce *f* en métal ouvré; *Art* objet *m* en ferronnerie
metalworker ['met(ə)lwɜːkər] *n Ind* (ouvrier *m*) métallurgiste *m*, *F* métallo *m*; **art m.** ferronnier *m ou* serrurier *m* d'art
metamorphic [metə'mɔːfɪk] *adj Geol* métamorphique; *Biol* métamorphosique
metamorphose [metə'mɔːfəʊz] **1** *vt* métamorphoser, transformer (**into** en) **2** *vi* se métamorphoser (**into** en)
metamorphosis, *pl* **-oses** [metə'mɔːfəsɪs, -əsiːz] *n* métamorphose *f*
metaphor ['metəfər] *n* métaphore *f*, image *f* (**for** symbolisant); **mixed m.** métaphore multiple

metaphoric(al) [metə'fɒrɪk, -ɪk(ə)l] *adj* métaphorique
metaphorically [metə'fɒrɪklɪ] *adv* métaphoriquement
metaphysical [metə'fɪzɪk(ə)l] *adj* métaphysique
metaphysics [metə'fɪzɪks] *n* [①**A10,c**] métaphysique *f*
metatarsal [metə'tɑːs(ə)l] *adj, n Anat* métatarsien *m*
metatarsus [metə'tɑːsəs] *n Anat* métatarse *m*
▶ **mete out** [miːt] *vtsep* (*punishment*) distribuer, infliger; (*reward*) distribuer, décerner; **to m. out justice** faire justice
meteor ['miːtɪər] *n* météore *m*; **m. shower** pluie *f* d'étoiles filantes
meteoric [miːtɪ'ɒrɪk] *adj Astron* météorique; *Fig* **m. rise** ascension *f* fulgurante
meteorite ['miːtɪəraɪt] *n* météorite *m ou f*, aérolit(h)e *m*
meteorological [miːtɪərə'lɒdʒɪk(ə)l] *adj* météorologique
meteorologist [miːtɪə'rɒlədʒɪst] *n* météorologiste *mf*, météorologue *mf*
meteorology [miːtɪə'rɒlədʒɪ] *n* météorologie *f*
meter[1] ['miːtər] *n* (*device*) compteur *m*; *Aut* parcmètre *m*, *Can* compteur de stationnement; *Aut F* **I'm on a m.** je suis garé à un parcmètre; *Aut F* **m. maid** contractuelle *f*; **m. reading** relevé *m* (de(s) compteur(s)); **m. reader** (*person*) releveur, -euse de(s) compteur(s)
meter[2] *n US* = **metre**
methadone ['meθədəʊn] *n Med* méthadone *f*; **to be on m.** (*of drug addict*) prendre de la méthadone
methane ['miːθeɪn] *n Ch* méthane *m*
methinks [mɪ'θɪŋks] *v impers* (*pt* **methought** [mɪ'θɔːt]) *Arch, Lit, Hum* il me semble; **you are sad, m.** il me semble que vous êtes triste
method ['meθəd] *n* (*in research, science*) méthode *f*; **the m. of doing sth** la manière de faire qch; *Admin* **methods of payment** modalités *fpl* de paiement; **to work without m.** travailler sans méthode; **to lack m.** manquer de méthode, ne pas être méthodique; *prov* **there's m. in his madness** il n'est pas aussi fou qu'il en a l'air; *Th, Cin* **M. acting** jeu *m* selon la méthode de Stanislavski; **M. actor/actress** acteur *m*/actrice *f* adepte de la méthode de Stanislavski; *Ind* **methods engineer** ingénieur *m* des méthodes; **methods engineering** étude *f* des méthodes
methodical [mɪ'θɒdɪk(ə)l] *adj* méthodique
methodically [mɪ'θɒdɪklɪ] *adv* méthodiquement, avec méthode
Methodism ['meθədɪz(ə)m] *n Rel* méthodisme *m*
Methodist ['meθədɪst] *adj, n Rel* méthodiste *mf*
methodology [meθə'dɒlədʒɪ] *n* méthodologie *f*
meths [meθs] *n Br F* alcool *m* à brûler; **m. drinker** buveur, -euse d'alcool à brûler
Methuselah [mə'θjuːzələ] *n Bible* Mathusalem *m*; *Fig* **as old as M.** vieux comme Hérode
methyl ['meθɪl] *n Ch* méthyle *m*; **m. alcohol** alcool *m* méthylique
methylated ['meθɪleɪtɪd] *adj* **m. spirits** alcool *m* dénaturé, alcool à brûler
methylene ['meθɪliːn] *n Ch* méthylène *m*
meticulous [mɪ'tɪkjʊləs] *adj* méticuleux, minutieux; **with m. attention to detail** avec une attention méticuleuse *ou* minutieuse pour les détails
meticulously [mɪ'tɪkjʊləslɪ] *adv* méticuleusement, minutieusement; (*to describe*) dans le détail; **to be m. dressed** être tiré à quatre épingles
meticulousness [mɪ'tɪkjʊləsnɪs] *n* méticulosité *f*, minutie *f*
me-too product *n Mktg* produit *m* tactique
metre[1], *US* **meter** ['miːtər] *n Liter* (*in poetry*) mètre *m*, mesure *f*; **in m.** en vers
metre[2], *US* **meter** *n* (*measurement*) mètre *m*
metric ['metrɪk] *adj* (*system*) métrique; **to go m.** adopter le système métrique; **m. area/volume** métrage *m*; **m. ton** tonne *f* (métrique)
metrical ['metrɪk(ə)l] *adj* métrique
metrication [metrɪ'keɪʃən] *n* adoption *f ou* introduction *f* du système métrique
metrics ['metrɪks] *n* [①**A10,c**] (*in poetry*) métrique *f*
metro ['metrəʊ] *n* métro *m*
metronome ['metrənəʊm] *n Mus* métronome *m*
metropolis [mɪ'trɒpəlɪs] *n* (*city*) métropole *f*
metropolitan [metrə'pɒlɪtən] **1** *adj* (*area etc*) urbain; **M. France** France *f* métropolitaine; *Br* **M. Police** police *f* de Londres **2** *n* (*inhabitant*) habitant, -ante de la métropole *ou* de la capitale; *Rel* (*bishop*) métropolitain *m*
mettle ['met(ə)l] *n* (*courage*) (*of person*) courage *m*, force *f* d'âme; (*of horse*) fougue *f*; **to be on one's m.** être prêt à donner le meilleur de soi-même; **to show one's m.** montrer de quoi on est capable
mettlesome ['met(ə)lsəm] *adj Old-fashioned* (*person*) plein de courage; (*horse*) fougueux
mew[1] [mjuː] *n* (*of cat*) miaulement *m*
mew[2] *vi* (*of cat*) miauler
mewing ['mjuːɪŋ] *n* miaulement *m*
mews [mjuːz] *npl* (*with sing or pl verb*) *Br* **(a)** (*street*) ruelle *f* (*sur laquelle donnaient des écuries*); **m. cottage, m. house** = maison *f* assez luxueuse aménagée dans une ancienne écurie **(b)** *Arch* (*stables*) écuries *fpl*
Mexican ['meksɪkən] **1** *adj* mexicain **2** *n* Mexicain, -aine
Mexico ['meksɪkəʊ] *n* Mexique *m*; **M. City** Mexico *f*
mezzanine ['metsəniːn] *n* **(a)** *Archit* **m. (floor)** mezzanine *f*, entresol *m* **(b)** *Th Am* corbeille *f*, *Br* premier dessous *m* (*de la scène*)
mezzo ['metsəʊ] *Mus* **1** *adv* mezzo; **m. forte** mezzo forte **2** *n* = **mezzo-soprano**
mezzo-soprano *n Mus* (*voice*) mezzo-soprano *m*, *pl* mezzo-sopranos, -ni; (*singer*) mezzo-soprano *f*
mezzotint ['metsəʊtɪnt] *n* mezzo-tinto *m inv*
mfd *Com* (*abbr* **manufactured**) fabriqué
mg (*abbr* **milligram(s)**) mg
Mgr *Rel* (*abbr* **monsignor**) Mgr
Mhz *El* (*abbr* **megahertz**) Mhz
MI [e'maɪ] *n Comptr* (*abbr* **machine intelligence**) IA *f*
mi [miː] *n Mus* mi *m*
MI5 [emaɪ'faɪv] *n Br* (*abbr* **Military Intelligence Section 5**) MI5 *m*, ≈ DST *f* (*contre-espionnage*)
MI6 [emaɪ'sɪks] *n Br* (*abbr* **Military Intelligence Section 6**) MI6 *m*, ≈ DGSE *f* (*espionnage*)
MIA [emaɪ'eɪ] *adj, n Am Mil* (*abbr* **missing in action**) porté disparu
miaow[1] [mɪ'aʊ] **1** *n* (*of cat*) miaulement *m*, miaou *m* **2** *int* miaou
miaow[2] *vi* (*of cat*) miauler
mic [mɪk] *n TV, Rad* micro *m*
mica ['maɪkə] *n Miner* mica *m*
mice *see* **mouse**
Mich *abbr* **Michigan**
Michael ['maɪk(ə)l] *n* Michel *m*; *Br Sl* **to take the M.** *see* **mickey (b)**
Michaelmas ['mɪkəlməs] *n* la Saint-Michel; *Br* **M. term** *Univ* premier trimestre *m* (*de l'année scolaire dans certaines universités*); *Jur* session *f* de la Saint-Michel; *Bot* **M. daisy** aster *m* d'automne
Michelangelo [maɪkə'læn(d)ʒələʊ] *n Art* Michel-Ange *m*
Mick [mɪk] *n* (*dimin of* **Michael**) Michel *m*; *Offensive Sl* (*Irishman*) Irlandais *m*
mickey ['mɪkɪ] *n F* **(a)** **m. (finn)** boisson *f* droguée (secrètement) **(b)** *Br* **to take the m. out of sb** se payer la tête de qn; **are you taking the m.?** tu te payes ma/sa tête?
Mickey Mouse **1** *n* Mickey *m* **2** *adj F Pej* (*car*) à la noix; (*job, course, firm*) bidon, pas sérieux; (*degree*) bidon, sans aucune valeur; (*watch etc*) de pacotille
micro ['maɪkrəʊ] *n Comptr* micro *m*
micro- ['maɪkrəʊ] *pref* micro-
microanalysis [maɪkrəʊə'næləsɪs] *n Ch* microanalyse *f*
microbe ['maɪkrəʊb] *n* microbe *m*
microbial [maɪ'krəʊbɪəl], **microbic** [maɪ'krəʊbɪk] *adj* microbien
microbiology [maɪkrəʊbaɪ'ɒlədʒɪ] *n* microbiologie *f*
microcamera [maɪkrəʊ'kæmərə] *n* appareil *m* de microphotographie
microchannel architecture [maɪkrəʊ'tʃæn(ə)l] *n Comptr* architecture *f* à micro-canaux
microchip ['maɪkrəʊtʃɪp] *n Comptr* puce *f* (électronique)
microcircuit ['maɪkrəʊsɜːkɪt] *n Comptr* microcircuit *m*
microcircuitry ['maɪkrəʊsɜːkɪtrɪ] *n Comptr* microcircuits *mpl*
microclimate ['maɪkrəʊklaɪmɪt] *n Met* microclimat *m*
micrococcus [maɪkrəʊ'kɒkəs] *n Biol* microcoque *m*, micrococcus *m*
microcode [maɪkrəʊ'kəʊd] *n Comptr* microcode *m*
microcomputer ['maɪkrəʊkəm'pjuːtər] *n* micro-ordinateur *m*, *pl* micro-ordinateurs
microcosm ['maɪkrəʊkɒz(ə)m] *n* microcosme *m*
microdot ['maɪkrəʊdɒt] *n* micropoint *m*
microeconomic [maɪkrəʊiːkə'nɒmɪk] *adj* microéconomique
microeconomics [maɪkrəʊiːkə'nɒmɪks] *n* [①**A10,c**] microéconomie *f*
microelectronics [maɪkrəʊelek'trɒnɪks] *n* [①**A10,c**] microélectronique *f*
microfiche ['maɪkrəʊfiːʃ] *n* microfiche *f*
microfilm[1] ['maɪkrəʊfɪlm] *n* microfilm *m*
microfilm[2] *vt* microfilmer
microfloppy ['maɪkrəʊ'flɒpɪ] *n* microdisquette *f*
microgroove ['maɪkrəʊgruːv] *n* microsillon *m*
microlight ['maɪkrəʊlaɪt] *n Av* U. L. M. *m*
micromarketing [maɪkrəʊ'mɑːkɪtɪŋ] *n* micromercatique *f*
micromesh ['maɪkrəʊmeʃ] *adj* (*stocking*) à mailles très fines
micrometer [maɪ'krɒmɪtər] *n* micromètre *m*

micron ['maɪkrɒn] *n* (*measurement*) micron *m*
Micronesia [maɪkrəʊ'ni:zɪə] *n* Micronésie *f*
microorganism [maɪkrəʊ'ɔ:gənɪz(ə)m] *n* micro-organisme *m*, *pl* micro-organismes
microphone ['maɪkrəfəʊn] *n* microphone *m*, micro *m*; **speak into the m.** parlez dans le micro; **a good m. voice** une voix qui passe bien à la radio/à l'enregistrement
microphysics [maɪkrəʊ'fɪsɪks] *n* [①A10,c] microphysique *f*
microprocessor ['maɪkrəʊ'prəʊsesər] *n Comptr* microprocesseur *m*
microreader ['maɪkrəʊri:dər] *n* microliseuse *f*
microscope ['maɪkrəskəʊp] *n* microscope *m*; **under the m.** au microscope; *Fig* **to put sth under the m.** examiner qch à la loupe
microscopic [maɪkrə'skɒpɪk] *adj* **(a)** (*very small*) microscopique **(b)** (*examination etc*) au microscope, microscopique
microscopy [maɪ'krɒskəpɪ] *n* microscopie *f*
microsecond ['maɪkrəʊsekənd] *n* microseconde *f*
microspacing ['maɪkrəʊspeɪsɪŋ] *n Comptr* micro-espacement *m*
microsurgery [maɪkrəʊ'sɜ:dʒərɪ] *n* microchirurgie *f*
microtechnology [maɪkrəʊtek'nɒlədʒɪ] *n* microtechnologie *f*
microwave[1] ['maɪkrəʊweɪv] *n Electron, Rad* micro-onde *f*, *pl* micro-ondes; **m. (oven)** (four *m* à) micro-ondes *m inv*
microwave[2] *vt* **to m. sth** faire cuire qch au (four à) micro-ondes; **microwaved food** nourriture *f* cuite au (four à) micro-ondes
micturition [mɪktjʊ'rɪʃən] *n Med* miction *f*
mid [mɪd] *adj* **in m. ocean** en plein océan, en pleine mer; **from m. June to m. August** de la mi-juin à la mi-août; **m. season** demi-saison *f*, *pl* demi-saisons; **he stopped in m. sentence** il s'est interrompu au milieu de sa phrase; **m. Wales** le centre du pays de Galles; **the m. 1960s** le milieu des années soixante
midafternoon [mɪdɑ:ftə'nu:n] *n* milieu *m* de l'après-midi; **in m.** au milieu de l'après-midi
midair [mɪd'eər] **1** *adj* (*collision*) en plein ciel **2** *n* **in m.** en plein ciel
Midas ['maɪdəs] *n* Midas *m*; *prov* **to have the M. touch** transformer tout ce qu'on touche en or; *Hum* **to have the M. touch in reverse** tout faire rater
mid-Atlantic *adj* **m. accent** accent mi-américain mi-britannique
midday ['mɪd'deɪ] *n* midi *m*; **at m.** à midi; **m. meal** repas *m* de midi, déjeuner *m*
midden ['mɪd(ə)n] *n Br* (*dunghill*) (tas *m* de) fumier *m*; *F* **this room is like a m.** cette pièce est une vraie porcherie
middle ['mɪd(ə)l] **1** *adj* du milieu; (*in between*) intermédiaire; **the m. house/sister** la maison/la sœur du milieu; *Mus* **m. C** do *m* de serrure *ou* du milieu du piano; *Fig* **to steer a m. course** adopter une solution intermédiaire; **in the m. distance** au second plan; *Anat* **m. ear** oreille *f* moyenne; **m. finger** médius *m*, majeur *m*; *Art* **m. ground** second plan *m*; *Fig* **to occupy the m. ground** (*in political spectrum*) adopter une position intermédiaire; **m. name** second prénom *m*; *Fig* **procrastination is your m. name!** tu remets toujours tout au lendemain; **honesty is her m. name** c'est l'honnêteté même; **laziness is his m. name** c'est un incorrigible paresseux; **generosity isn't exactly his m. name!** on ne peut pas dire qu'il soit particulièrement généreux; **m. neck** (*of beef*) côtes *fpl* découvertes
2 *n* **(a)** milieu *m*; **in the m. of …** au milieu de …; **in the m. of nowhere** dans un coin perdu; **in the m. of the summer** en plein été; **about the m. of August** à la mi-août; **in the m. of the night** en pleine nuit; **I was in the m. of reading/of watching a programme** j'étais en train de lire/de regarder une émission; **he was driving down the m. of the road** il roulait au (beau) milieu de la route; *F* **they split the money down the m.** ils ont partagé l'argent en deux parties égales
(b) *F* (*waist*) taille *f*, ceinture *f*; **round one's m.** autour de sa taille; **the water came up to his m.** l'eau lui arrivait à la taille
middle age *n* âge *m* mûr; **man of m. age** homme d'âge mûr; **in m. age** à l'âge mûr; **in early m. age he …** quand il a atteint l'âge mûr, il …; **to be past m. age** être sur le retour
middle-aged [mɪd(ə)l'eɪdʒd] *adj* (*person*) entre deux âges, d'un certain âge; **m. spread** bourrelets *mpl* (qui viennent avec l'âge)
Middle Ages ['eɪdʒɪz] *n* moyen âge *m*
Middle America *n* (*sector of society*) l'Amérique *f* moyenne
middlebrow ['mɪd(ə)lbraʊ] *adj* qui ne demande pas trop d'efforts intellectuels
middle-class *adj* bourgeois
middle classes *npl* bourgeoisie *f*
Middle East *n Geog* Moyen-Orient *m*
Middle Eastern *adj* du Moyen-Orient
Middle England *n* l'Angleterre *f* moyenne
Middle English *n Ling* moyen anglais *m*
middleman, *pl* **-men** ['mɪd(ə)lmæn, -men] *n Com* intermédiaire *m*; **m.'s market** marché *m* des intermédiaires
middle management *n* cadres *mpl* moyens
middle manager *n* cadre *m* moyen
middlemost ['mɪd(ə)lməʊst] *adj* le plus proche du milieu
middle-of-the-road *adj* (*policy*) modéré; *Mus Pej* grand public
middle-roader [mɪd(ə)l'rəʊdər] *n US Pol* modéré, -ée
middle school *n Br Sch* = école *f* pour les élèves de 9 à 13 ans
middle-sized *adj* de taille moyenne
middleweight ['mɪd(ə)lweɪt] *n* (*boxer*) poids moyen *m*; **m. champion** champion *m* poids moyen
Middle West *n Geog* Midwest *m*
middling ['mɪdlɪŋ] *adj* (*mediocre*) médiocre; (*fairly good*) passable, assez bon; *F* **how are you? – m.** comment allez-vous? – comme ci comme ça
middy ['mɪdɪ] *n Naut F* midship *m*
Mideast [mɪd'i:st] *n esp US* (= **Middle East**) **the M.** le Moyen-Orient
midfield [mɪd'fi:ld] *n Fb etc* milieu *m* de terrain; **to play in m.** jouer au milieu du terrain; **m. player** (joueur, -euse de) milieu de terrain
midfielder [mɪd'fi:ldər] *n Fb etc* milieu *m* de terrain
midge [mɪdʒ] *n* (*insect*) moucheron *m*
midget ['mɪdʒɪt] **1** *n* (*small person*) nain, *f* naine, nabot, -ote **2** *adj* miniature
midi ['mɪdɪ] **1** *adj* **(a)** (*skirt, coat etc*) de longueur moyenne, midi *inv* **(b) m. system** (*stereo*) chaîne *f* midi **2** *n* (*skirt, coat etc*) jupe *f*/manteau *m*/*etc* de longueur moyenne
midland ['mɪdlənd] *adj* (*plain etc*) du centre (*d'un pays*)
Midlands (the) [ðə'mɪdləndz] *npl* les Midlands *fpl* (*comtés du centre de l'Angleterre*); **a M. accent** un accent des Midlands
midlife ['mɪdlaɪf] *n* quarantaine *f*; **m. crisis** (*in professional etc life*) crise *f* à l'abord de la quarantaine; (*in sex life also*) démon *m* de midi; **to be going through a m. crisis** traverser la crise de la quarantaine
midmorning [mɪd'mɔ:nɪŋ] *n* milieu *m* de la matinée; **m. coffee break** pause-café *f* au milieu de la matinée
midnight ['mɪdnaɪt] *n* minuit *m*; **at m.** à minuit; **m. blue** bleu *m* nuit; **m. feast** festin *m* nocturne; **m. Mass** messe *f* de minuit; **to burn the m. oil** travailler tard dans la nuit; **a m. snack** un casse-croûte en plein milieu de la nuit; **m. sun** soleil *m* de minuit; **the land of the m. sun** le pays du soleil de minuit
midriff ['mɪdrɪf] *n Anat* (*diaphragm*) diaphragme *m*; (*stomach*) estomac *m*; **bare m.** ventre *m* nu, taille *f* nue
midshipman, *pl* **-men** ['mɪdʃɪpmən] *n Naut* aspirant *m* (*de marine*), *F* midship *m*
midships ['mɪdʃɪps] *adv Naut* au milieu du navire, par le travers
midst [mɪdst] *n* **in the m. of sth** au milieu de qch; **in the m. of winter** au milieu *ou* au cœur de l'hiver, en plein hiver; **in the m. of all this** (*these events*) sur ces entrefaites; **in the m. of the celebration** en plein milieu de la fête; **in our/your/their m.** parmi nous/vous/eux; **there are traitors in our m.** il y a des traîtres parmi nous
midstream [mɪd'stri:m] *n* **in m.** au milieu du courant; *Fig* **she stopped in m.** (*of speaker*) elle s'est arrêtée en plein milieu de son récit
midsummer ['mɪdsʌmər] *n* (*middle of summer*) milieu *m* de l'été, cœur *m* de l'été; (*solstice*) solstice *m* d'été; **in m.** au milieu *ou* au cœur de l'été, en plein été; **m. madness** folie *f*
Midsummer Day *n* la Saint-Jean
Midsummer Night's Dream (A) *n Liter* le Songe d'une Nuit d'Été
midterm ['mɪd'tɜ:m] *n* **(a)** *Pol US* milieu *m* du mandat présidentiel, *Br* milieu du mandat du Premier Ministre; *US* **m. elections** élections *fpl* au milieu du mandat présidentiel **(b)** *Sch, Univ* milieu *m* du trimestre; **m. break** vacances *fpl* de milieu de trimestre; **m. exams** examens *mpl* de milieu de trimestre
midway ['mɪdweɪ] *adv* à mi-chemin, à mi-distance; **m. up the hill** à mi-côte; **m. between … and …** à mi-distance *ou* à mi-chemin entre … et …; **a style m. between John's and Paul's** un style intermédiaire entre celui de John et celui de Paul
midweek [mɪd'wi:k] *n* milieu *m* de la semaine; **I'll see you m.** je te verrai vers le milieu de la semaine; **m. show** spectacle *m* de milieu de semaine
Midwest [mɪd'west] *n* Midwest *m*
midwife, *pl* **-wives** ['mɪdwaɪf, -waɪvz] *n* sage-femme *f*, *pl* sages-femmes, accoucheuse *f*

midwifery ['mɪdwɪfərɪ] *n* **(a)** (*profession*) profession *f* de sage-femme **(b)** (*obstetrics*) obstétrique *f*
midwinter ['mɪd'wɪntər] *n* (*middle of winter*) milieu *m* de l'hiver, cœur *m* de l'hiver; (*solstice*) solstice *m* d'hiver
mien [mi:n] *n Lit* mine *f*, air *m*, contenance *f*
miffed [mɪft] *adj F* froissé, piqué, fâché
might[1] [maɪt] *n* (*strength*) puissance *f*, force(s) *f(pl)*; **with all one's m.** (*to work, push etc*) de toute sa force, de toutes ses forces; *Lit* **with m. and main** de toutes mes/ses/*etc* forces; **she strove with m. and main to prevent it** elle a fait tout ce qu'elle a pu pour empêcher cela; *Prov* **m. is right** la raison du plus fort est toujours la meilleure
might[2] *v, aux* [①A57-8,d] *see* **may[1]**; **are you coming? – I m.** tu viens? – peut-être; **she refused, as well she m.** rien d'étonnant à ce qu'elle ait refusé; **when I mentioned his name she blushed, as well she m.** quand j'ai prononcé son nom, elle a rougi, et cela n'a rien d'étonnant; **and who m. you be?** qui êtes-vous, sans indiscrétion?; **and what m. you be doing here?** peut-on savoir ce que vous faites là?; **I wonder what I m. have done to offend him** je me demande ce que j'ai bien pu faire pour le fâcher; **he m. have arrived in time if ...** il aurait pu arriver à temps si ...; **you m. shut the door** vous pourriez fermer la porte!; **all the same, you m. have made less noise!** tout de même vous auriez pu faire moins de bruit!; **I was afraid he m. have done it** j'avais peur qu'il ne l'ait *ou Fml* l'eût fait
might-have-been *n F* (*person*) raté, -ée
mightily ['maɪtɪlɪ] *adv* **(a)** (*powerfully*) puissamment, fortement **(b)** *F* (*extremely*) extrêmement; **to be m. relieved** être vraiment soulagé
mighty ['maɪtɪ] **1** *adj* (*comp* **mightier**; *superl* **mightiest**) **(a)** (*powerful*) (*nation, army etc*) puissant; (*blow*) grand **(b)** (*large, imposing*) grandiose, majestueux **(c)** *esp Am F* (*considerable*) grand; **you're in a m. hurry** vous êtes diablement pressé **2** *adv esp Am F* rudement; **you're making a m. big mistake** vous commettez là une erreur colossale; **she looked m. pleased with herself** elle avait l'air très contente d'elle
mignonette [mɪnjə'net] *n* (*plant*) réséda *m*
migraine ['mi:greɪn, 'maɪ-] *n Med* migraine *f*; **to suffer from m.** souffrir de migraines; **a bad m.** une forte migraine; **m. sufferer** migraineux, -euse
migrant ['maɪgrənt] **1** *adj* = **migratory**; **m. worker** travailleur *m* itinérant **2** *n* (*person, bird etc*) migrateur, -trice
migrate [maɪ'greɪt] *vi* (*of bird*) migrer; (*of person*) émigrer; **to m. south** migrer vers le sud; **people who had migrated from eastern Europe** les gens qui avaient émigré d'Europe de l'est
migration [maɪ'greɪʃən] *n* (*of birds*) migration *f*; (*of people*) émigration *f*
migratory ['maɪgrətrɪ, maɪ'greɪtərɪ] *adj* (*bird*) migrateur; (*movement*) migratoire
Mike [maɪk] *n* (*dimin of* **Michael**) = Michel *m*; *F* **for the love of M.** pour l'amour du ciel
mike [maɪk] *n F abbr* micro *m*
milch [mɪltʃ] *adj Old-fashioned* **m. cow** *Agr* vache *f* laitière; *Fig* vache à lait
mild [maɪld] **1** *adj* **(a)** (*person, remark*) doux, *f* douce; (*answer*) conciliant; (*criticism*) léger, anodin
(b) (*punishment*) peu sévère, léger
(c) (*climate*) doux, *f* douce, tempéré; (*winter*) doux, clément; **the weather is getting milder** le temps s'adoucit
(d) (*dish*) peu épicé; (*cigar, tobacco, soap*) doux, *f* douce; (*sedative, medicine*) léger; **m. cheddar** cheddar *m* doux; **a m. curry** un curry peu épicé
(e) *Med* (*illness, infection*) bénin, *f* bénigne; **a m. form of measles** une forme bénigne de rougeole
(f) (*slight*) (*astonishment*) léger; **the joke caused some m. amusement** la plaisanterie a fait sourire; **the play caused a m. sensation** la pièce a fait un peu de bruit; **the play was a m. success** la pièce a obtenu un succès modéré
(g) *Tech* **m. steel** acier *m* doux
2 *n Br* (*beer*) bière *f* brune
mildew ['mɪldju:] *n* **(a)** (*fungus*) (*on wheat etc*) rouille *f*; (*on vines etc*) mildiou *m* **(b)** (*stains*) (*on fabric, leather etc*) moisissure *f*, moisi *m*, piqûres *fpl*
mildewy ['mɪldju:ɪ] *adj* (*bread*) moisi; (*wallpaper etc*) piqué par l'humidité, moisi; **m. smell** odeur de moisi; **to go m.** (*of plant*) se rouiller, (*of bread*) moisir; (*of vine*) être atteint par le mildiou; (*of paper etc*) se piquer
mildly ['maɪldlɪ] *adv* **(a)** (*to say*) doucement, avec douceur **(b)** (*moderately*) modérément; **it has a m. laxative effect** ça a un léger effet laxatif; **to be m. successful** (*of play*) obtenir un succès modéré; **to put it m.** pour ne pas dire plus; **he's a bastard, and that's putting it m.!** c'est un salaud, et c'est peu dire
mild-mannered *adj* placide, imperturbable
mildness ['maɪldnɪs] *n* **(a)** (*of person, weather*) douceur *f*; (*of criticism*) caractère *m* anodin; (*of punishment*) légèreté *f* **(b)** *Med* (*of disease*) bénignité *f*
mile [maɪl] *n* (*distance*) mil(l)e *m*; **five miles** cinq mil(l)es; *Sp* **four-minute m.** mil(l)e couru en quatre minutes; **a 200-m. journey** un voyage de 200 mil(l)es; **miles per hour** mil(l)es par heure; **smaller cars do more miles to the** *or* **per gallon** les petites voitures consomment moins; **you don't see anyone for miles and miles** on parcourt des kilomètres sans voir personne; **m. after m. of sandy beaches** des plages de sable sur des kilomètres et des kilomètres; **people came from miles around** les gens sont venus de kilomètres à la ronde; **it's miles from anywhere** c'est à des kilomètres de tout; **he lives miles away** il habite très loin d'ici; **you'll recognize him a m. off** tu ne risques pas de le rater; **you can smell the factory a m. off** on sent les fumées de l'usine à des kilomètres; **you can tell she's Italian a m. off** elle a vraiment le type italien; *F* **to be miles away** (*be daydreaming*) être dans la lune; **someone not a thousand** *or* **million miles from us** une certaine personne qui ne se trouve pas très loin de nous; *F* **I feel miles better** je me sens beaucoup mieux; *F* **he's miles better than the others** il est bien meilleur que les autres; *F* **it sticks out a m.** ça vous crève les yeux, ça se voit comme le nez au milieu de la figure; *F* **I can see you coming a m. off!** (*I know what you want*) je te vois venir (avec tes gros sabots)!; *F* **he'd run a m.** (*if that happened*) il prendrait ses jambes à son cou; *Fig* **to go the extra m.** faire un petit effort supplémentaire
mileage ['maɪlɪdʒ] *n* **(a)** (*distance travelled*) distance *f* en mil(l)es, *Can* millage *m*, ≈ kilométrage *m*; **car with a very low** *or* **small m.** voiture qui a très peu roulé; *Admin, Com etc* **m. (allowance)** indemnité *f* de déplacement
(b) (*per gallon*) = consommation *f* aux cent kilomètres; **how much m. do you get?** combien est-ce que la voiture consomme aux cent?; **you can improve the m. by keeping the engine clean** on consomme moins avec un moteur propre; *Fig F* **the opposition got a lot of m. out of the scandal** l'opposition a largement profité de ce scandale, ce scandale a largement profité à l'opposition; *Fig F* **there's no m. in it** (*in idea etc*) ça ne nous mènera nulle part, on ne peut rien en tirer
milestone ['maɪlstəʊn] *n* borne *f* routière, ≈ borne kilométrique; *Fig* événement *m* important; **this discovery is a m. in medical research** cette découverte marque une étape importante dans la recherche médicale
milieu ['mi:ljɜ:] *n Fml* milieu *m*
militancy ['mɪlɪtənsɪ] *n* militantisme *m*
militant ['mɪlɪtənt] **1** *adj* militant; *Old-fashioned* **the Church m.** l'Église *f* militante **2** *n Pol etc* militant, -ante
militarily ['mɪlɪtərɪlɪ] *adv* militairement
militarism ['mɪlɪtərɪz(ə)m] *n* militarisme *m*
militarist ['mɪlɪtərɪst] *n* militariste *mf*
militaristic [mɪlɪtə'rɪstɪk] *adj* militariste
militarize ['mɪlɪtəraɪz] *vt* militariser
military ['mɪlɪtərɪ] **1** *adj* (*aircraft, base, service etc*) militaire; **a strong m. presence** une forte présence militaire; **the m.-industrial complex** le complexe militaro-industriel; **m. academy** école *f* militaire; **m. attaché** attaché *m* militaire; *Jur* **m. court** *or* **tribunal** tribunal *m* militaire; **m. man** militaire *m*; **m. police** police *f* militaire; **m. service** service *m* militaire **2** *npl* **the m.** les militaires *mpl*, l'armée *f*; **the m. were called in** on a fait venir l'armée
militate ['mɪlɪteɪt] *vi* (*of fact, reason etc*) militer (**against** contre)
militia [mɪ'lɪʃə] *n* milice *f*, *US* ≈ garde *f* nationale
militiaman, *pl* **-men** [mɪ'lɪʃəmən] *n* milicien *m*, soldat *m* de la milice, *US* ≈ garde *m* national
milk[1] [mɪlk] *n* **(a)** lait *m*; *Culin* **with m.** au lait; *Lit* **land of m. and honey** pays *m* de cocagne; *prov* **to be full of the m. of human kindness** être la bonté même; **he's not exactly overflowing with the m. of human kindness** (*kind-hearted*) ce n'est pas un tendre; (*generous*) ce n'est pas quelqu'un de particulièrement généreux; **m.-and-water** insipide; **m. bar** milk-bar *m*, *pl* milk-bars; **m. bottle** bouteille *f* de lait; **m. chocolate** chocolat *m* au lait; **m. churn** bidon *m* à lait; **m. diet** régime *m* lacté; **m. duct** canal *m* galactophore; **m. gland** glande *f* galactogène; **m. jug** pot *m* à *ou* au lait; **m. powder** lait *m* en poudre; *Culin* **m. pudding** entremets *m* sucré au lait; **m. run** *Av F* vol *m* sans problèmes; *Fig* (*routine*) parcours *m* de routine; **m. train** premier train *m* du matin
(b) (*in plant, coconut*) lait *m*; *Prov* **there's no point in crying over spilt m.** ce qui est fait est fait
milk[2] *vt* **(a)** (*cow etc*) traire **(b)** *F Pej* (*exploit*) (*person*)

dépouiller; (*country, colony*) exploiter; **the newspapers milked the story for all it was worth** les journaux ont tiré tout ce qu'ils ont pu de l'histoire; **they just milked all his ideas** ils se sont approprié toutes ses idées
milk cap *n Bot* (*fungus*) lactaire *m*
milker ['mɪlkər] *n* (*cow etc*) **good/bad m.** bonne/mauvaise laitière *f*
milk float *n* voiture *f* de livraison du lait
milkiness ['mɪlkɪnɪs] *n* (*of liquid etc*) couleur *f* laiteuse, aspect *m* laiteux
milking ['mɪlkɪŋ] *n* (*of cow*) traite *f*; **m. machine** trayeuse *f* mécanique; **m. pail** seau *m* à traire; **m. parlour** salle *f* de traite
milkmaid ['mɪlkmeɪd] *n* trayeuse *f*, fille *f* de laiterie
milkman, *pl* -men ['mɪlkmən] *n* (*delivery man*) livreur *m* de lait
milk of magnesia *n Pharm* magnésie *f* hydratée
milk round *n* tournée *f* du *ou* de laitier; *Br Univ F* = tournée *f* de recrutement des entreprises à la recherche de nouveaux diplômés dans les universités
milk-shake *n* milk-shake *m*, *pl* milk-shakes
milksop ['mɪlksɒp] *n Old-fashioned F Pej* poule *f* mouillée
milk tooth *n Anat* dent *f* de lait
milkweed ['mɪlkwi:d] *n Bot* laiteron *m*, lait *m* d'âne
milk-white *adj* d'une blancheur laiteuse
milky ['mɪlkɪ] *adj* **(a)** (*containing milk*) qui contient du lait; **I like my coffee m.** (*with lots of milk*) j'aime mon café avec beaucoup de lait **(b)** (*colour*) laiteux, *Lit* lactescent; (*gem*) laiteux; **m. white** blanc laiteux
Milky Way *n Astron* Voie *f* lactée
mill[1] [mɪl] *n* **(a)** **(flour) m.** moulin *m* (à farine); (*large*) minoterie *f*; *F* **he's been through the m.** il en a bavé; **to put sb through the m.** en faire baver à qn; **coffee/pepper m.** moulin à café/à poivre; **(crushing) m.** broyeur *m*, concasseur *m* **(b)** *Metal* **(rolling) m.** laminoir *m*, train *m* (de laminage) **(c)** (*factory*) usine *f*; **cotton m.** filature *f* de coton; **steel m.** aciérie *f*; *Old-fashioned* **m. hand** ouvrier, -ière textile; **m. owner** industriel *m* du textile
mill[2] *vt* (*wheat, flour*) moudre; *Tech* (*crush*) broyer; *MecE* (*gears*) fraiser, tailler; (*screw*) moleter; (*coin*) créneler
▶ **mill about, mill around** *vi* (*of crowd*) grouiller
millboard ['mɪlbɔ:d] *n* carton-pâte *m inv*
milled [mɪld] *adj* **(a)** (*grain etc*) moulu **(b)** **m. edge** (*on coin*) crénelage *m*, grènetis *m*
millenium [mɪ'lenɪəm] *n* **(a)** (*thousand years*) millénaire *m*, mille ans *mpl* **(b)** *Rel, Hist* millénium *m*
millepede ['mɪlɪpi:d] *n* mille-pattes *m inv*
miller ['mɪlər] *n* meunier *m*; (*on large scale*) minotier *m*
millet ['mɪlɪt] *n Bot, Culin* millet *m*, mil *m*; **Indian m.** sorgho *m*, millet d'Inde
millibar ['mɪlɪbɑ:r] *n Met* millibar *m*
milligram(me) ['mɪlɪgræm] *n* milligramme *m*
millilitre, *US* milliliter ['mɪlɪli:tər] *n* millilitre *m*
millimetre, *US* millimeter ['mɪlɪmi:tər] *n* millimètre *m*; **a 10-m. gap** un espace de 10 millimètres
milliner ['mɪlɪnər] *n* modiste *f*, chapelier, -ière
millinery ['mɪlɪnərɪ] *n Old-fashioned* (articles *mpl* de) modes *fpl*; **m. department** (*in shop*) rayon *m* des chapeaux
milling ['mɪlɪŋ] *n* **(a)** (*grinding*) (*of grain*) mouture *f*, moulage *m* **(b)** *Metal* fraisage *m*; (*of screw etc*) moletage *m*; (*of coin*) cordonnage *m*; **m. cutter** fraise *f*, fraiseuse *f*; **m. machine** fraiseuse **(c)** (*on coin*) cordon *m*, grènetis *m*, tranche *f* cannelée
million ['mɪljən] *n* [①A12,1,h,i] million *m*; **two m. men** deux millions d'hommes; **half a m.** un demi-million; **worth millions** (*person*) riche à millions; **an actor who gave pleasure to millions** un acteur qui a diverti des millions de gens; *F* **I've told him a m. times** je le lui ai dit mille fois; *F* **she's one in a m.** elle est unique; *F* **thanks a m.!** merci mille fois!; *Iron* eh bien, merci!; *F* **I feel like a m. dollars** je me sens en pleine forme
millionaire [mɪljə'neər] *n* millionnaire *mf*, milliardaire *mf*; **to be a m. twice/three times over** être deux/trois fois millionnaire; **I've got a m. uncle** j'ai un oncle millionnaire *ou* milliardaire
millionairess [mɪljə'neəres] *n* millionnaire *f*
millionth ['mɪljənθ] **1** *adj* millionième **2** *n* **(a)** (*person, thing*) millionième *mf* **(b)** (*fraction*) millionième *m*
millipede ['mɪlɪpi:d] *n* mille-pattes *m inv*
millisecond ['mɪlɪsekənd] *n* milliseconde *f*
millpond ['mɪlpɒnd] *n* réservoir *m ou* retenue *f* de moulin; **sea as calm *or* smooth as a m.** mer *f* d'huile
millrace ['mɪlreɪs] *n* (*channel*) bief *m* de moulin; (*water*) courant *m* du bief
millstone ['mɪlstəʊn] *n* meule *f* (de moulin); *Fig* **a m. round my neck** un boulet que je traîne
millstream ['mɪlstri:m] *n* courant *m* du bief
millwheel ['mɪlwi:l] *n* roue *f* de moulin
millwright ['mɪlraɪt] *n* constructeur *m* de moulins
milometer [maɪ'lɒmɪtər] *n Aut etc* compteur *m* de mil(l)es, ≈ compteur kilométrique
milt [mɪlt] *n* (*of fish*) laitance *f*, laite *f*
mime[1] [maɪm] *n Th* (*performance*) mime *m*; (*actor*) mime *mf*; **a version of Hamlet in m.** une version d'Hamlet en mime; **m. artist** mime *mf*
mime[2] *Th* **1** *vt* (*scene*) mimer **2** *vi* mimer; (*of singer*) faire du play-back; **to m. to a song** chanter en playback
mimeo(graph)[1] ® ['mɪmɪəʊgrɑ:f] *n* **(a)** (*machine*) machine *f* à ronéotyper **(b)** (*document*) polycopie *f*
mimeo(graph)[2] ® *vt* ronéotyper
mimic[1] ['mɪmɪk] *n* imitateur, -trice
mimic[2] *vt* (*pt, pp* **mimicked** [mɪmɪkt]) (*imitate*) (*person*) imiter, mimer, *F* singer; (*voice, walk, behaviour, nature etc*) imiter
mimicry ['mɪmɪkrɪ] *n* **(a)** imitation *f* **(b)** *Biol* mimétisme *m*
mimosa [mɪ'məʊzə] *n* (*shrub*) mimosa *m*
min **(a)** (*abbr* **minute(s)**) min. **(b)** (*abbr* **minimum**) min
minaret [mɪnə'ret] *n* minaret *m*
mince[1] [mɪns] *n Br Culin* viande *f* hachée; **m. pie** = tartelette *f* fourrée aux raisins secs
mince[2] **1** *vt* **(a)** (*chop up*) (*meat etc*) hacher; **minced meat** viande *f* hachée **(b)** (*always in negative*) (*speak plainly*) **not to m. one's words** ne pas mâcher ses mots, parler net; **not to m. matters** pour parler net **2** *vi* **(a)** (*walk in affected manner*) marcher à petits pas affectés *ou* efféminés **(b)** (*talk in affected manner*) parler avec une élégance affectée *ou* minaudière
mincemeat ['mɪnsmi:t] *n Culin* = préparation *f* de raisins secs, écorce d'oranges et graisse de bœuf pour tartelettes; *F* **to make m. of sb** (*in fist fight, boxing match*) réduire qn en bouillie, démolir qn; (*in football, tennis match*) écraser qn; (*in debate, argument*) démolir qn; **the lawyer made m. of his testimony** l'avocat a démoli son témoignage
mincer ['mɪnsər] *n Culin* (*device*) hachoir *m*
mincing ['mɪnsɪŋ] *adj* (*manner, tone*) affecté, minaudier; (*steps, gait*) efféminé
mind[1] [maɪnd] *n* **(a)** (*thoughts*) esprit *m*; **such a thought had never entered his m.** une telle pensée ne lui était jamais venue à l'esprit; **to have sth on one's m.** avoir qch qui vous préoccupe; **it's all in your m.!** tu te fais des idées!; **it's all in the m.** tout ça, c'est dans la tête; **in the m.'s eye** dans l'imagination; **in her m.'s eye she could see them staring at her** elle se les imaginait la fixant; **to put *or* set sb's m. at rest** rassurer qn; **to be easy/uneasy in one's m.** avoir/ne pas avoir l'esprit tranquille; **I couldn't get it off my m.** je ne pouvais pas m'empêcher d'y penser; **a walk will take my m. off it** une promenade me changera les idées; **it's a problem that is always on my m.** c'est un problème auquel je n'arrête pas de penser; **she couldn't get their faces out of her m.** elle ne pouvait oublier leurs visages; **put it out of your m.** n'y pensez plus

(b) (*memory*) mémoire *f*; **to have a m. like a sieve** avoir (une) très mauvaise mémoire; **to bear *or* keep sth in m.** (*think about*) songer à qch; (*take into account*) tenir compte de qch; (*not forget*) ne pas oublier qch, garder qch à l'esprit; **we must bear in m. that she is only a child** il ne faut pas oublier que ce n'est qu'une enfant; **I'll bear it in m.** (*what you suggested*) je m'en souviendrai; **to call sth to m.** se rappeler qch, se souvenir de qch; **it brings *or* calls to m. Beethoven's Fifth** cela rappelle la cinquième de Beethoven; **to put sb in m. of sb/sth** rappeler qn/qch à qn; **it went (completely *or* clean) out of my m.** cela m'est (complètement) sorti de l'esprit

(c) (*opinion*) avis *m*, idée *f*; **to change one's m.** changer d'avis *ou* d'idée, se raviser; **I've changed my m. about him** j'ai changé d'avis *ou* d'idée à son égard; **I've changed my m. about moving to London** (*don't want to*) j'ai changé d'avis, je ne veux plus aller vivre à Londres; (*want to*) j'ai changé d'avis, je veux maintenant aller vivre à Londres; *F* **I gave him a piece of my m.** je lui ai dit son fait *ou* ses quatre vérités; **to be of one m., to be of the same m.** être du même avis, être d'accord; **to my m.** selon moi, à mon avis; **to speak one's m.** dire ce qu'on pense; **to keep an open m. about sth** réserver son opinion sur qch

(d) (*will, wants*) **to know one's own m.** savoir ce qu'on veut; **you've got a m. of your own** tu peux décider toi-même; **the car seemed to have a m. of its own** la voiture semblait faire ce que bon lui semblait; **make up your m.!** décidez-vous!; **to make up one's m.** se décider; **I can't make up your m. for you** je ne peux pas décider à ta place; **to be in two minds about sth** être indécis sur qch; **I'm in two**

minds about going je ne sais pas si je vais y aller; **I've a good m. to do it** je suis bien tenté de le faire; **I've half a m. to tell his parents** j'ai presqu'envie de le dire à ses parents; **to set one's m. on sth** vouloir absolument avoir qch, se mettre la tête d'avoir qch; **to set one's m. on doing sth** vouloir absolument faire qch, se mettre en tête de faire qch; **to have sth in m.** avoir qch en vue; **what kind of party did you have in m.?** à quelle sorte de soirée est-ce que tu pensais?; **I had in m. something smaller** je pensais à quelque chose de plus petit; **the person I have in m.** la personne à laquelle je pense; **who did you have in m. for the job?** à qui pensiez-vous pour le poste?

(e) (*attention*) **to give one's whole m. to sth** accorder toute son attention à qch; **to keep one's m. on sth** se concentrer sur qch; **your m. is not on the job** tu n'as pas la tête à ce que tu fais; **I'm sure if you put your m. to it you could do it** je suis sûr que si tu essayais vraiment, tu pourrais le faire

(f) (*way of thinking*) **attitude of m.** manière *f* de penser; **to have a good m.** être intelligent, avoir la tête bien faite; **to have the m. of a three-year-old** avoir l'esprit *ou* l'intelligence d'un enfant de trois ans; **I haven't got a scientific m.** je n'ai pas l'esprit scientifique; **you've got a dirty m.!** tu as l'esprit mal placé!; **you've got a nasty m.** tu vois le mal partout; **it's probably just my suspicious m. but I don't trust him** c'est probablement que je suis trop suspicieux, mais je n'ai pas confiance en lui

(g) (*reason*) raison *f*; **to be out of one's m.** avoir perdu la raison *ou* la tête; *F* (*drunk, from drugs*) être parti; **are you out of your m.?, you must be out of your m.!** est-ce que tu as perdu la tête?; *F* **he was out of his m. with boredom** *or* **bored out of his m.** il s'ennuyait à mourir; **to be in one's right m.** avoir toute sa raison *ou* toutes ses facultés

(h) (*person*) esprit *m*; **one of the most brilliant minds of this century** l'un des esprits les plus brillants de ce siècle; *Prov* **great minds think alike (, fools seldom differ)** les grands esprits se rencontrent; *Hum* **how about a drink? – great minds think alike!** si on prenait une verre? – les grands esprits se rencontrent!

mind² **1** *vt* **(a)** (*pay attention to*) (*sb, sth*) faire attention à, prêter attention à; (*concern oneself with*) (*sth*) s'occuper de; **never m. the car** ne t'en fais pas *ou* ne t'inquiète pas pour la voiture; **don't m. him, he's always like that** ne fais pas attention à lui, il est toujours comme ça; *Iron* **don't m. me, I only live here!** je t'en prie, fais comme chez toi!; **don't m. them** ne faites pas attention à eux; **m. you, I've always thought that ...** remarquez, j'ai toujours pensé que ...; **but, m. you, it was late** mais, voyez-vous, il était tard; **m. what you're doing!** faites attention à ce que vous faites!

(b) (*take care*) **m. you're not late!** faites en sorte de ne pas être en retard!; **m. you write to him!** n'oubliez pas de lui écrire!; **m. you don't fall!** faites attention de ne pas tomber!; **m. the step!** attention à la marche!; **would you m. where you're putting your feet, please?** est-ce que tu peux faire attention où tu mets les pieds, s'il te plaît?; **m. your backs (please)!** attention devant!; **to m. one's language** surveiller son langage; *Br F* **m. how you go!** fais attention à toi!; *F* **don't be late, m.!** surtout, ne sois pas en retard!

(c) (*object to*) **what I m. is ...** ce qui me gêne, c'est que ...; **I don't m. the cold** le froid ne me gêne pas; **I don't m. trying** je veux bien essayer; **do you m. my asking ...?** puis-je vous demander sans indiscrétion ...?; **how much do you earn, if you don't m. my** *or* **me asking?** combien est-ce que vous gagnez, sans indiscrétion?; **I wouldn't m. a cup of tea** je prendrais volontiers une tasse de thé; **I wouldn't m. having his salary** ça ne me dérangerait pas de gagner autant que lui

(d) (*look after*) (*children*) garder, surveiller; (*animals etc*) garder; (*house*) garder, veiller sur; **to m. the shop** s'occuper du magasin

(e) *Arch, Dial* (*remember*) se souvenir de, se rappeler

2 *vi* **(a)** (*object*) **would you m. if ...?** est-ce que cela vous gênerait *ou* dérangerait si ...?; **do you m.!** (*how dare you*) dites donc!; **if you don't m.** si cela ne vous dérange pas; **I don't m.** (*it doesn't matter to me*) cela m'est égal; (*go ahead*) je veux bien; **if nobody minds** si personne n'y voit d'inconvénient; **do you m. if I smoke?** cela ne vous dérange *ou* gêne pas que je fume?; *F* **another drop of wine? – I don't m. if I do** encore un peu de vin? – ce n'est pas de refus

(b) (*trouble oneself*) **never m.!** (*it doesn't matter*) ça ne fait rien!, tant pis!; (*don't worry*) ne vous inquiétez pas!; *F* **never you m.!** (*don't be nosy*) ça, c'est mon affaire!, ça ne te regarde pas; (*don't get upset*) ne t'en fais pas

▶ **mind out** *vi Br* faire attention **(for** à)

mind-blowing *adj Sl* (*drug*) hallucinant; (*experience*) ahurissant, époustouflant

mind-boggling ['maɪndbɒglɪŋ] *adj F* époustouflant

minded ['maɪndɪd] *adj* disposé, enclin **(to do sth** à faire qch); **if you were so m.** si vous le vouliez; **commercially m.** qui a le sens du commerce, commerçant; **to be mechanically m.** être bon mécanicien; **she isn't very money-m.** (*money isn't important to her*) elle n'est pas très préoccupée par les questions d'argent

minder ['maɪndər] *n* (*bodyguard*) garde *m*; **(child** *or* **baby) m.** gardienne *f*, *F* nounou *f*; *Ind* **(machine) m.** surveillant *m*

mindful ['maɪndfʊl] *adj esp Fml* (*keeping in mind*) **to be m. of sth** se souvenir de qch, ne pas oublier qch; **m. of this warning ...** se souvenant de cet avertissement ...; **m. of the danger to her health** soucieuse de sa santé; **he is always m. of others** il pense toujours aux autres

mindless ['maɪndlɪs] *adj* (*senseless*) (*destruction, violence*) gratuit; (*task, job*) stupide, abrutissant

mind-reader *n* voyant, -ante; **I'm not a m.!** je ne peux pas lire dans *ou* deviner tes/ses/*etc* pensées, je ne suis pas devin

mind share *n Mktg* part *f* de notoriété

mine¹ [maɪn] *n* **(a)** (*for coal etc*) mine *f*; **he went down the m. at 16** il est descendu dans la mine à 16 ans; *Fig* **a m. of information** une mine d'informations; **m. shaft** puits *m* de mine; **m. workings** chantiers *mpl* d'exploitation minière **(b)** *Mil, Naut* mine *f*; **(land) m.** mine terrestre; **to lay a m.** (*on land*) poser une mine; (*at sea*) mouiller une mine; **m. detector** détecteur *m* de mines

mine² **1** *vt* **(a)** (*coal seam*) exploiter; (*coal, gold*) extraire **(b)** *Mil, Naut* miner; **mined area** zone *f* minée **2** *vi Min* **to m. for coal/gold** extraire du charbon/de l'or

mine³ **1** *poss pron* [①**A**30,8; **B**20,E,2] le mien, la mienne, *pl* les miens, les miennes; **this letter is m.** cette lettre est à moi; **this signature is not m.** cette signature n'est pas de moi; **I took her hands in m.** je pris ses mains dans les miennes; **a friend of m.** un(e) de mes ami(e)s, un(e) ami(e) à moi; **it is no business of m.** ce n'est pas mon affaire, ça ne me regarde pas; **everything of m. had been ripped to shreds** toutes mes affaires avaient été réduites en lambeaux; *Fml* **m. was a difficult/thankless task** c'était une tâche difficile/ingrate que la mienne; **what's yours is m.** ce qui est à toi est à moi; **so much money and it's (m.,) all m.!** tant d'argent, et c'est à moi, rien qu'à moi!; *F* **m.'s a beer** (*in pub*) pour moi, ce sera une bière

2 *poss adj Arch, Lit* mon, ma, *pl* mes; *Hum* **m. host** l'aubergiste *m*

minefield ['maɪnfiːld] *n Mil, Naut* champ *m* de mines; *Fig* terrain *m* miné

minehunter ['maɪnhʌntər] *n Naut* chasseur *m* de mines

minelayer ['maɪnleɪər] *n Naut* mouilleur *m* de mines

minelaying ['maɪnleɪɪŋ] *n Mil* pose *f* de mines; *Naut* mouillage *m* de mines

miner ['maɪnər] *n Min* mineur *m*; **m.'s lamp** lampe *f* de mineur

mineral ['mɪn(ə)rəl] **1** *adj* (*oil etc*) minéral; **the m. kingdom** le monde minéral; **m. spring** source *f* d'eau minérale; **m. water** eau *f* minérale **2** *n* **(a)** minéral *m*; *Min* **m. deposits** gisements *mpl* miniers *ou* minéraux; **the m. resources of a country** les ressources *fpl* minières d'un pays **(b)** *Old-fashioned Br* **minerals** (*drinks*) boissons *fpl* gazeuses

mineralogist [mɪnə'rælədʒɪst] *n* minéralogiste *mf*

mineralogy [mɪnə'rælədʒɪ] *n* minéralogie *f*

minestrone [mɪnə'strəʊnɪ] *n* minestrone *m*

minesweeper ['maɪnswiːpər] *n Naut* dragueur *m* de mines

minesweeping ['maɪnswiːpɪŋ] *n Naut* dragage *m* des mines

mingle ['mɪŋg(ə)l] **1** *vt* (*usu passive*) mélanger **(with** avec); **her tears were mingled with laughter** elle pleurait et riait à la fois; **joy mingled with sadness** joie mêlée de tristesse **2** *vi* (*of things*) se mélanger; (*of person*) (*at party*) circuler; **to m. with the crowd** se mêler à la foule

▶ **mingle together** *vi* se mélanger

mingy ['mɪndʒɪ] *adj Br F* (*mean*) (*person*) mesquin, *F* radin; (*salary, gift*) minable; (*amount of money*) ridicule; **a m. helping** une portion minuscule; **a m. five pounds** cinq malheureuses livres

mini ['mɪnɪ] *n F* (*dress etc*) mini *f*; (*style*) mini *m*

mini- ['mɪnɪ] *pref* mini(-); **minibiography** mini-biographie *f*; **minirecording studio** mini-studio *m* d'enregistrement

miniature ['mɪnɪtʃər] **1** *n* (*figure, bottle, painting*) miniature *f*; **to paint in m.** peindre en miniature; **Paris in m.** (*model*) Paris en miniature; **m. painter** miniaturiste *mf* **2** *adj* en miniature; (*garden, bottle etc*) miniature; (*book etc*) minuscule; *Phot* (*camera*) (de) petit format; **m. golf** mini-golf *m*; **m. poodle** caniche *m* nain

miniaturist ['mɪnɪtʃərɪst] *n Art* miniaturiste *mf*

miniaturize ['mɪnɪtʃəraɪz] *vt* miniaturiser

minibar ['mɪnɪbɑːr] *n* minibar *m*

mini-break *n* (*holiday*) mini-séjour *m*

minibudget ['mɪnɪbʌdʒɪt] *n* budget *m* auxiliaire *ou* exceptionnel
minibus ['mɪnɪbʌs] *n* minibus *m*; **m. service** service *m* de minibus
minicab ['mɪnɪkæb] *n Br* radio-taxi *m*, *pl* radio-taxis; **m. firm** société *f* de radio-taxis
minicomputer [mɪnɪkəm'pju:tər] *n* mini-ordinateur *m*
mini-cruise *n* mini-croisière *f*
minidisk ['mɪnɪdɪsk] *n* mini-disquette *f*
mini-floppy *n* mini-disquette *f*
minim ['mɪnɪm] *n Br Mus* blanche *f*; **m. rest** demi-pause *f*, *pl* demi-pauses
minimal ['mɪnɪm(ə)l] *adj* **(a)** (*very small*) minime **(b)** (*minimum*) minimal, minimum; **m. value** valeur minimale *ou* minimum
minimalism ['mɪnɪməlɪz(ə)m] *n* minimalisme *m*
minimalist ['mɪnɪməlɪst] *n, adj* minimaliste *mf*
minimization [mɪnɪmaɪ'zeɪʃən] *n* minimisation *f*
minimize ['mɪnɪmaɪz] *vt* (*sth, importance of sth*) minimiser; (*noise, friction etc*) réduire *ou* limiter au minimum
minimum, *pl* **-a** ['mɪnɪməm, -ə] **1** *n* minimum *m*, *pl* minimums, minima; **a m. of two years' experience** un minimum de deux ans d'expérience; **as a m.** au minimum; **to reduce sth to a m.** réduire qch au minimum; **keep the questions to a m.** essayez de poser le moins de questions possible; **in order to keep mistakes to a m.** de façon à avoir le minimum d'erreurs; **in order to reduce delays to a m.** de façon à réduire l'attente au maximum
2 *adj* minimum, minimal; *Br Fin* **m. lending rate** taux *m* de crédit minimum; **m. rates** taux *mpl* minima; **m. speed** vitesse *f* minimum *ou* minimale; **m. wage** salaire *m* minimum; **m. charge** charge *f* minimum; **m. connecting time** (*in travelling*) temps *m* minimal de correspondance; *Com* **m. stock level** stock *m* d'alerte
mining ['maɪnɪŋ] *n* **(a)** *Min* exploitation *f* minière; **m. area/town** région *f*/ville *f* minière; **m. engineer** ingénieur *m* des mines; **the m. industry** l'industrie *f* minière **(b)** *Mil, Naut* pose *f* de mines (**of an area** dans une zone), minage *m*
minion ['mɪnjən] *n Pej* (*lackey*) larbin *m*; *F Iron* (*subordinate*) subordonné, -ée; **the minions of the law** les laquais *mpl* de l'ordre établi
minipill ['mɪnɪpɪl] *n* mini-pilule *f*
mini-roundabout *n* mini rond-point *m*
miniseries ['mɪnɪsɪəri:z] *n TV* minifeuilleton *m*, mini-série *f*
miniskirt ['mɪnɪskɜ:t] *n* minijupe *f*
minister[1] ['mɪnɪstər] *n* **(a)** *Pol* ministre *m* (d'État); *Br* **M. of State** ministre d'État; *Br* **M. of Defence** ministre de la Défense; **M. for Tourism** ministre du Tourisme **(b)** *Rel* (*Protestant*) pasteur *m*, ministre *m*; (*Jesuit*) ministre; **m. general** ministre général
minister[2] *vi* **to m. to sb** soigner qn, s'occuper de qn; **to m. to sb's needs** pourvoir *ou* subvenir aux besoins de qn; *Rel* **to m. to a parish** desservir une paroisse
ministerial [mɪnɪ'stɪərɪəl] *adj* **(a)** *Pol* ministériel **(b)** *Rel* sacerdotal **(c)** *Jur* exécutif; **m. functions** fonctions *fpl* exécutives
ministering ['mɪnɪstərɪŋ] *adj* **m. angel** ange *m* de bonté
ministration [mɪnɪ'streɪʃən] *n* **(a)** *Fml* (*assistance*) soins *mpl* **(b)** *Rel* sacerdoce *m*; **to receive the ministrations of a priest** être administré par un prêtre
ministry ['mɪnɪstrɪ] *n* **(a)** *Pol* (*department*) ministère *m*; (*government*) ministère, gouvernement *m*; *Br* **the M. of Defence** le Ministère de la Défense; **M. of Transport** ministère des Transports **(b)** *Rel* **the m.** le sacerdoce; **he was intended for the m.** il fut destiné à l'Église
mini tower *n Comptr* mini-tour *f*
mink [mɪŋk] *n* (*animal*) **(American)** **m.** vison *m*; **m. farm** *or* **ranch** visonnière *f* **(b)** (*fur*) vison *m*; **a m. (coat)** un manteau de vison, un vison; **m. oil** huile *f* de vison
Minn *abbr* **Minnesota**
minnow ['mɪnəʊ] *n* (*fish*) vairon *m*; (*any small fish*) fretin *m*; *Fig* menu fretin
Minoan [mɪ'nəʊən] *adj* minoen
minor[1] ['maɪnər] **1** *adj* (*lesser*) secondaire, mineur; (*unimportant*) petit, peu important; (*detail, repair*) mineur, petit; **the film is a m. classic** le film est un classique de moindre importance; **of m. importance** sans grande importance; *Mus* **m. key** ton *m* mineur; *Fig* **in a m. key** plutôt triste; **to play a m. part** *or* **role** *Cin, Th etc* avoir un petit rôle; *Fig* jouer un rôle mineur *ou* accessoire; *Med* **m. operation** petite opération *f*, opération sans gravité; *Rel* **m. orders** ordres *mpl* mineurs; **m. road** route *f* secondaire; *Old-fashioned Br Sch* **Martin m.** Martin junior
2 *n* **(a)** *Jur* mineur, -eure
(b) *US Univ* matière *f* secondaire
minor[2] *vi US Univ* **to m. in physics** étudier la physique comme matière secondaire
Minorca [mɪ'nɔ:kə] *n* Minorque *f*
Minorcan [mɪ'nɔ:kən] **1** *adj* minorquin **2** *n* Minorquin, -ine
minority [mɪ'nɒrɪtɪ, maɪ-] *n* **(a)** [①**A11,g,i**] (*of total number*) minorité *f*; **to be in a** *or* **the m.** être en minorité; **to be in a m. of one** être seul de son opinion; *Fin* **m. holding** participation *f* minoritaire; **m. opinion** opinion *f* d'une minorité; **m. opinion must be respected** on doit respecter l'opinion de la minorité; *Pol* **m. party/government** parti *m*/gouvernement *m* minoritaire; *Parl* **m. report** rapport *m* exprimant l'opinion d'une minorité **(b)** *Jur* (*age*) minorité *f*
Minotaur ['maɪnətɔ:r] *n Myth* **the M.** le Minotaure
minster ['mɪnstər] *n Br* cathédrale *f*; (*attached to abbey*) église *f* abbatiale; **York M.** la cathédrale d'York
minstrel ['mɪnstrəl] *n* **(a)** (*in Middle Ages*) ménestrel *m* **(b)** *Lit* (*poet*) poète *m*; (*musician*) musicien *m*; (*singer*) chanteur *m* **(c)** (*actor, singer with blackened face*) acteur/musicien blanc maquillé en noir; *Th* **m. show** = spectacle *m* de music-hall avec des acteurs blancs imitant des noirs
mint[1] [mɪnt] *n* (*plant*) menthe *f*; (*sweet*) bonbon *m* à la menthe; **m. chocolate** chocolat *m* à la menthe; *esp US* **m. julep** bourbon *m* à la menthe; **m. sauce** sauce *f* à la menthe; **m. tea** (*tea with mint*) thé *m* à la menthe; (*herbal tea*) infusion *f* de menthe
mint[2] *n Fin* **the (Royal) M.** ≈ (l'hôtel *m* de) la Monnaie; *F* **to be worth a m.** (*of person*) rouler sur l'or; (*of thing*) valoir une somme fabuleuse *ou* une fortune; *F* **to make a m.** gagner une fortune; **to be in m. condition** être comme neuf *ou* à l'état neuf; *Philat* **m. stamp** timbre non oblitéré *ou* neuf
mint[3] *vt* **(a)** (*coins*) frapper; *Fig F* **he must be minting it** il doit rouler sur l'or; **the company was minting it with their latest model** l'entreprise ramassait l'argent à la pelle grâce au nouveau modèle **(b)** *Lit* (*word, expression*) inventer, forger, créer
minuet [mɪnjʊ'et] *n Mus* menuet *m*
minus ['maɪnəs] **1** *prep* moins; **ten m. eight leaves two** dix moins huit égale(nt) deux; **he managed to escape, but m. his luggage** il a réussi à s'échapper, mais sans (ses) bagages; **it's m. twelve degrees** il fait moins douze degrés **2** *adj Math* (*quantity, number*) négatif; *Sch* **B m.** B moins; **but, on the m. side, the pay is low** mais le revers de la médaille, c'est que c'est mal payé; **the m. side of a situation** les désavantages d'une situation; **m. sign** moins *m* **3** *n Math* (*sign*) moins *m*
minuscule ['mɪnəskju:l] *adj* miniscule; *F* (*salary*) dérisoire
minute[1] ['mɪnɪt] *n* **(a)** [①**A75,A,d; B58,A,d**] (*measurement of time*) minute *f*; **it's ten minutes to** *or* *Am* **of three** il est trois heures moins dix; **ten minutes past** *or* *Am* **after three** trois heures dix; **to observe a one-m. silence** observer une minute de silence; **at five-m. intervals, at intervals of five minutes** toutes les cinq minutes; **it's five minutes from here** c'est à cinq minutes d'ici; **the town centre is a ten-m. walk/drive from here** le centre-ville est à dix minutes d'ici à pied/en voiture; **a m.'s rest** un moment de repos; **wait a m.!** attendez une minute *ou* un instant!; **go downstairs this m.!** descends immédiatement!; **just a m.** (attendez) un instant *ou* une minute; **he's come in this (very) m.** il vient de rentrer à l'instant, il vient juste de rentrer; **the m. my back was turned she ...** j'avais à peine le dos tourné qu'elle ...; **he'll be here any m.** il va arriver d'une minute à l'autre; **it'll be ready in a m.** ça sera prêt dans une minute *ou* un instant; **in a few minutes** dans quelques minutes; **I've just popped in for a m.** je ne fais qu'entrer et sortir, je ne fais que passer; **until the last m.** jusqu'à la dernière minute; **at the last m.** à la dernière minute
(b) *Math, Astron* minute *f*
(c) (*note*) note *f* (de service); cette; **minutes** (*of meeting*) compte rendu *m*, procès-verbal *m*; **to take the minutes of a meeting** faire le compte rendu d'une réunion
minute[2] *vt* (*facts, remarks etc*) prendre note de; (*meeting*) dresser le procès-verbal *ou* le compte rendu de
minute[3] [maɪ'nju:t] *adj* **(a)** (*small*) tout petit, minuscule; **the minutest details** les moindres détails; **he told us about his holiday in m. detail** il nous a raconté ses vacances par le menu **(b)** (*detailed*) (*examination etc*) minutieux
minute hand *n* (*of watch etc*) grande aiguille *f*
minutely [maɪ'nju:tlɪ] *adv* (*to examine etc*) minutieusement, en détail
minutes book ['mɪnɪts] *n* registre *m* des procès-verbaux
minute steak *n Culin* steak *m* minute
minute timer *n* minuterie *f*
minutiae [maɪ'nju:ʃɪi:] *npl* petits détails *mpl* infimes
minx [mɪŋks] *n F* friponne *f*, coquine *f*; **you little m.!** petite espiègle!, petite polissonne!
MIPS [mɪps] *n Comptr* (*abbr* **million instructions per second**) MIPS *m*

miracle [ˈmɪrək(ə)l] *n Rel* miracle *m*; *Fig* miracle, prodige *m*; **by a m.** par miracle; **I can't perform miracles** je ne peux pas faire de miracles; **it sounds like a m.** cela tient du miracle; **it's a m. that ...** c'est (un) miracle que ... + *sub*; *F* **thanks, you're a m.** merci, tu es fantastique; *Med; Fig* **m. cure** remède *m* miracle; *Pharm* **m. drug** remède *m* miracle; *Th* **m. play** miracle *m*; **m. worker** faiseur, -euse de miracles

miraculous [mɪˈrækjʊləs] *adj Rel, Fig* miraculeux; **to have a m. escape** s'en sortir indemne comme par miracle; *Iron* **she made a m. recovery as soon as the weekend arrived** comme par miracle, son état de santé s'est amélioré juste avant le week-end

miraculously [mɪˈrækjʊləslɪ] *adv* miraculeusement, (comme) par miracle; **m. low prices** des prix incroyablement bas

mirage [ˈmɪrɑːʒ] *n* mirage *m*

mire [ˈmaɪər] *n (bog)* bourbier *m*; *(mud)* boue *f*, bourbe *f*, *Lit* fange *f*; *Fig* **to drag sb through the m.** traîner qn dans la boue

mirror¹ [ˈmɪrər] *n* glace *f*, miroir *m*; *Aut* **in my/the m.** dans mon/le rétroviseur; *Fig* **to hold a m. to society** refléter l'image d'une société; *Fig* **the press is the m. of public opinion** la presse est le miroir de l'opinion publique; **m. finish/polish** fini *m*/polissage *m* spéculaire; **m. image** *(seen in mirror)* reflet *m*; *(inverted)* image *f* inversée; *(exact copy)* réplique *f*, copie *f* conforme; **m. writing** écriture *f* spéculaire *ou* en miroir

mirror² *vt also Fig* refléter; **the steeple is mirrored in the lake** le clocher se reflète *ou* se mire dans le lac; *Fig* **his experience exactly mirrors my own** nous avons eu des expériences identiques

mirth [mɜːθ] *n* gaieté *f*, allégresse *f*

mirthful [ˈmɜːθfʊl] *adj (amused)* gai, joyeux; *(amusing)* amusant

mirthless [ˈmɜːθlɪs] *adj* sans gaieté, peu réjouissant; *(laugh)* forcé, sans joie

MIRV [mɜːv] *n Mil (abbr* **multiple independently targeted re-entry vehicle***)* MIRV *m*

miry [ˈmaɪərɪ] *adj* fangeux, bourbeux

misadventure [mɪsədˈventʃər] *n* mésaventure *f*; *(less serious)* contretemps *m*; *Jur* **a verdict of death by m.** un verdict de mort accidentelle

misalliance [mɪsəˈlaɪəns] *n* mésalliance *f*

misanthrope [ˈmɪzənθrəʊp] *n* misanthrope *mf*

misanthropic [mɪzənˈθrɒpɪk] *adj (person)* misanthrope; *(mood etc)* misanthropique

misanthropist [mɪˈzænθrəpɪst] *n* misanthrope *mf*

misanthropy [mɪˈzænθrəpɪ] *n* misanthropie *f*

misapply [mɪsəˈplaɪ] *vt* **(a)** mal employer **(b)** *Fin* = **misappropriate**

misapprehend [mɪsæprɪˈhend] *vt Fml (sb, sth)* mal comprendre; *(person's words)* mal comprendre, se méprendre sur

misapprehension [mɪsæprɪˈhenʃən] *n* malentendu *m*, méprise *f*; **to be** *or* **to labour under a m.** se méprendre, se tromper; **the Government appears to be (labouring) under the m. that ...** le gouvernement semble s'imaginer que ...

misappropriate [mɪsəˈprəʊprɪeɪt] *vt (funds)* détourner

misappropriation [ˈmɪsəprəʊprɪˈeɪʃən] *n (of funds)* détournement *m*

misbegotten [mɪsbɪˈgɒt(ə)n] *adj* **(a)** *Old-fashioned F (badly thought out)* mal conçu, *F* biscornu **(b)** *Arch (child)* illégitime, bâtard

misbehave [mɪsbɪˈheɪv] *vi* se conduire mal; *(of child)* se tenir mal; **he has been misbehaving at school** il n'a pas été sage à l'école

misbehaviour, *US* **misbehavior** [mɪsbɪˈheɪvjər] *n (bad behaviour)* mauvaise conduite *f*; *(more serious)* inconduite *f*

misc *(abbr* **miscellaneous***)* divers

miscalculate [mɪsˈkælkjʊleɪt] **1** *vt (amount, distance etc)* mal calculer; *(sb's response etc)* se tromper sur **2** *vi* mal calculer; *Fig* se tromper

miscalculation [mɪskælkjʊˈleɪʃən] *n* erreur *f* de calcul; *Fig* mauvais calcul *m*

miscarriage [mɪsˈkærɪdʒ] *n* **(a)** *Obst* fausse couche *f*, *Spec* interruption *f* de grossesse spontanée; **to have a m.** faire une fausse couche **(b)** *(failure) (of project)* échec *m*, insuccès *m*; *Jur* **m. of justice** erreur *f* judiciaire **(c)** *(in post) (of letter, package)* égarement *m*, perte *f*

miscarry [mɪsˈkærɪ] *vi* **(a)** *Obst* faire une fausse couche, *Spec* avorter **(b)** *(of scheme, enterprise)* échouer, avorter, ne pas réussir **(c)** *(of letter, parcel)* s'égarer, se perdre; *(reach wrong address)* parvenir à une fausse adresse

miscast [mɪsˈkɑːst] *vt (pt, pp* **miscast***) Th, Cin etc* **to m. an actor/actress** donner à un acteur/une actrice un rôle qui ne lui convient pas; **he was miscast in the part** ce n'était pas un rôle qui lui convenait

miscegenation [mɪsɪdʒɪˈneɪʃ(ə)n] *n Fml* métissage *m*

miscellaneous [mɪsəˈleɪnɪəs] *adj* varié, divers; **the file marked 'm.'** le dossier 'divers'; *Journ* **m. news** faits *mpl* divers

miscellany [mɪˈselənɪ] *n* **(a)** *(of objects etc)* mélange *m*, collection *f* **(b)** *Liter* recueil *m*, anthologie *f*

mischance [mɪsˈtʃɑːns] *n* mésaventure *f*; **by m.** par malchance

mischief [ˈmɪstʃɪf] *n* **(a)** *(naughtiness)* bêtises *fpl*; *(esp of very small children)* bêtises, sottises *fpl*; **out of sheer m.** par pure espièglerie; **he's full of m.** il est très espiègle; **to keep sb out of m.** empêcher qn de faire des sottises *ou* des bêtises; **that'll keep her out of m.** ça l'occupera, pendant ce temps-là elle ne fera pas de bêtises; **I wonder what m. he's up to** je me demande ce qu'il trame *ou* fricote

(b) *(trouble)* **to make m. (for sb)** créer des problèmes (à qn), faire du tort (à qn); **to make m. between people** semer la discorde entre les gens

(c) *F (child)* fripon, -onne; **little m.** petit(e) espiègle, petit(e) coquin(e)

(d) *F (injury)* **to do oneself a m.** se faire mal, s'esquinter

mischiefmaker [ˈmɪstʃɪfmeɪkər] *n* brandon *m* de discorde; *(gossip)* mauvaise langue *f*

mischievous [ˈmɪstʃɪvəs] *adj* **(a)** *(naughty) (child)* espiègle, malicieux, coquin; **m. trick** *or* **prank** espièglerie *f*; **to play a m. trick on sb** jouer un tour *ou* faire une farce à qn; **as m. as a monkey** malin comme un singe; **a m. grin/wink** un sourire/clin d'œil malicieux **(b)** *(malicious) (person)* méchant, malveillant, malfaisant; *(remarque)* malveillant

mischievously [ˈmɪstʃɪvəslɪ] *adv* **(a)** *(naughtily)* par espièglerie; *(to grin, wink, smile)* malicieusement **(b)** *(maliciously)* méchamment

mischievousness [ˈmɪstʃɪvəsnɪs] *n* **(a)** *(naughtiness) (of child)* malice *f*, espièglerie *f* **(b)** *(malice)* méchanceté *f*

misconceive [mɪskənˈsiːv] *vt Fml* se méprendre sur

misconceived [mɪskənˈsiːvd] *adj (idea, scheme)* mal conçu

misconception [mɪskənˈsepʃən] *n (false idea)* conception *f* erronée, idée *f* fausse; **a popular** *or* **common m.** une idée fausse très répandue

misconduct¹ [mɪsˈkɒndʌkt] *n* mauvaise conduite *f*; *Jur (sexual)* adultère *m*; **professional m.** faute *f* professionnelle

misconduct² [mɪskənˈdʌkt] *vt (matter, business)* mal diriger, mal gérer; **to m. oneself** mal se conduire

misconstruction [mɪskənˈstrʌkʃən] *n Fml* fausse interprétation *f*

misconstrue [mɪskənˈstruː] *vt* mal interpréter

miscount¹ [ˈmɪskaʊnt] *n (miscalculation)* erreur *f* de calcul; *(mistake in addition)* erreur d'addition; *Pol (of votes)* erreur dans le dépouillement du scrutin

miscount² [mɪsˈkaʊnt] *vti* mal compter

miscreant [ˈmɪskrɪənt] *adj, n Lit* scélérat, -ate, misérable *mf*

misdeal¹ [mɪsˈdiːl] *n Cards* maldonne *f*

misdeal² *vti (pt, pp* **misdealt** [mɪsˈdelt]) *Cards* **to m. (the cards)** faire maldonne

misdeed [mɪsˈdiːd] *n* méfait *m*, mauvaise action *f*; *Jur* crime *m*, délit *m*

misdemeanour, *US* **misdemeanor** [mɪsdɪˈmiːnər] *n* **(a)** *Jur* délit *m* **(b)** *(minor act of misbehaviour)* écart *m* de conduite; *(more serious)* méfait *m*

misdiagnose [mɪsˈdaɪəgnəʊz] *vt Med* **to m. the symptoms/illness/***etc* faire une erreur de diagnostic; *Fig* **to m. the situation** faire une mauvaise analyse de la situation

misdiagnosis [mɪsdaɪəgˈnəʊsɪs] *n Med* erreur *f* de diagnostic; *Fig* **his m. of the situation** sa mauvaise analyse de la situation

misdirect [mɪsdɪˈrekt] *vt* **(a)** *(person)* envoyer au mauvais endroit **(b)** *(letter)* envoyer à la mauvaise adresse **(c)** *(blow)* mal diriger **(d)** **to m. the jury** mal instruire le jury

misdirected [mɪsdɪˈrektɪd] *adj* **(a)** *(letter, parcel etc)* envoyé à la mauvaise adresse **(b)** *(blow)* frappé à faux **(c)** *(zeal)* mal employé

misdirection [mɪsdɪˈrekʃən] *n* **(a)** *(on letter)* erreur *f* d'adresse **(b)** *(of resources, talents)* mauvais emploi *m*, mauvais usage *m*

miser [ˈmaɪzər] *n* avare *mf*

miserable [ˈmɪzər(ə)b(ə)l] *adj* **(a)** *(unhappy)* malheureux, triste; **I feel m.** j'ai le cafard; **don't look so m.!** remetstoi! **to make sb's life m.** rendre la vie impossible à qn

(b) *(unpleasant) (condition)* misérable, déplorable; *(journey)* pénible, affreux; **if only I didn't have this m. cold!** si je n'avais pas cet affreux rhume!; **what a m. day** quelle journée épouvantable; **what m. weather!** quel temps épouvantable!

(c) *(poor, wretched)* misérable, pitoyable; *(wage, amount)* dérisoire; **I've only got a m. £70** je n'ai que 70 malheureuses livres; **a m. failure** *(plan etc)* un ratage complet *ou* lamentable; *(person)* un raté

miserably ['mɪz(ə)rəblɪ] *adv* **(a)** *(unhappily) (to look)* d'un air malheureux; *(to say)* d'un ton malheureux **(b)** *(in poverty)* pauvrement; **to live m.** vivre dans la misère **(c)** *(very badly) (to perform)* lamentablement; **to be m. paid** avoir un salaire de misère; **to fail m.** échouer lamentablement

Miserere [mɪzə'rɪərɪ] *n Rel* **(a)** *(psalm)* miséréré *m*, miserere *m* **(b) m. (seat) = misericord (b)**

misericord [mɪ'zerɪkɔːd] *n Rel* **(a)** *(in monastery)* miséricorde *f* **(b)** *(seat)* miséricorde *f*, patience *f* (de stalle)

miserliness ['maɪzəlɪnɪs] *n* avarice *f*, pingrerie *f*

miserly ['maɪzəlɪ] *adj (person)* avare, pingre

misery ['mɪzərɪ] *n* **(a)** *(unhappiness)* détresse *f*, tristesse *f*; *(suffering)* souffrance(s) *f(pl)*; *(stronger)* supplice *m*; **to make sb's life a m.** rendre la vie impossible à qn; **to put an animal out of its m.** donner le coup de grâce à un animal; *Hum* **to put sb out of their m.** mettre fin aux souffrances *ou* au supplice de qn **(b)** *Br F (person)* geignard, -arde, grincheux, -euse

misery-guts ['mɪzərɪgʌts] *n F* rabat-joie *m inv*, empêcheur, -euse de tourner en rond

misfire¹ [mɪs'faɪər] *n (of rifle)* raté *m* (de percussion); *(of missile, car)* raté d'allumage

misfire² *vi (of firearm)* rater, faire long feu; *(of rocket)* avoir un raté d'allumage; *(of engine)* avoir un raté/des ratés; *Fig (of joke)* manquer son effet, *F* foirer; *(of plan)* rater, *F* foirer

misfit ['mɪsfɪt] *n (person)* inadapté, -ée; **a social m.** un inadapté social

misfortune [mɪs'fɔːtʃən] *n* malheur *m*, malchance *f*; **I had the m. to …** j'ai eu le malheur *ou* la malchance de …

misgiving [mɪs'gɪvɪŋ] *n* doute *m* **(about sth** sur qch); **not without misgivings** non sans hésitation; **to have misgivings** avoir des doutes **(about sb** à l'égard de qn; **about sth** au sujet de qch); **to be filled with m.** être en proie au doute; **she had misgivings about allowing them to go** elle hésitait à les laisser y aller

misgovern [mɪs'gʌvən] *vt* mal gouverner

misgovernment [mɪs'gʌvənmənt] *n* mauvais gouvernement *m*, mauvaise administration *f*

misguided [mɪs'gaɪdɪd] *adj (person)* malavisé; *(missionary, reformer, politician)* mal inspiré; *(attempt)* malencontreux; *(energy, idealism)* mal placé; **you would be m. to trust him** vous seriez mal avisé *ou* inspiré de lui faire confiance; **in the m. belief that …** croyant à tort que …

misguidedly [mɪs'gaɪdɪdlɪ] *adv* de façon peu judicieuse, malencontreusement

mishandle [mɪs'hænd(ə)l] *vt* **(a)** *(machine, appliance)* mal se servir de; *(substance, product)* manipuler sans prendre les précautions nécessaires **(b)** *(manage badly) (situation etc)* mal gérer; *(person)* mécontenter; **if you m. the staff** si vous ne traitez pas le personnel avec considération

mishandling [mɪs'hændlɪŋ] *n (of situation, staff etc)* mauvaise gestion *f*

mishap ['mɪshæp] *n* incident *m*, mésaventure *f*; **after many mishaps** après bien des incidents *ou* des mésaventures *ou* des péripéties

mishear [mɪs'hɪər] *vti (pt, pp* **misheard** [mɪs'hɜːd]) mal entendre

mishmash ['mɪʃmæʃ] *n F* méli-mélo *m*

misinform [mɪsɪn'fɔːm] *vt* mal informer; **to be misinformed** être mal informé

misinformation [mɪsɪnfə'meɪʃən] *n* fausse information *f*

misinterpret [mɪsɪn'tɜːprɪt] *vt (person's words)* mal interpréter; *(person)* mal interpréter les paroles de; **this decision should not be misinterpreted as …** cette décision ne doit pas être interprétée comme …

misinterpretation [mɪsɪntɜːprɪ'teɪʃən] *n* mauvaise *ou* fausse interprétation *f*; **open to m.** *(of rules, statement etc)* susceptible d'être mal interprété

misjudge [mɪs'dʒʌdʒ] *vt (sb)* mal juger, se tromper sur le compte de; *(sth)* mal juger (de), se méprendre sur; *(distance)* mal évaluer; **it appears I misjudged you** il semblerait que je vous aie mal jugé

misjudg(e)ment [mɪs'dʒʌdʒmənt] *n* jugement *m* erroné, erreur *f* de jugement; *(of distance)* mauvaise évaluation *f ou* estimation *f*

miskey¹ ['mɪskiː] *n* faute *f* de frappe

miskey² [mɪs'kiː] *vt* ne pas taper correctement

mislay [mɪs'leɪ] *vt (pt, pp* **mislaid** [mɪs'leɪd]) *(one's umbrella etc)* égarer; **I've just mislaid it somewhere** je l'ai juste mis quelque part, mais je ne me souviens plus où

mislead [mɪs'liːd] *vt (pt, pp* **misled** [mɪs'led]) *(deceive) (person)* induire en erreur, tromper **(as to** quant à); **to m. sb into thinking sth** faire croire qch à qn; **her behaviour misled him into thinking her feelings were stronger** sa conduite lui a laissé croire que ses sentiments étaient plus profonds, mais il n'en était rien

misleading [mɪs'liːdɪŋ] *adj (advertisement etc)* trompeur; **the description she gave was deliberately m.** elle a fait exprès de donner une fausse description

mismanage [mɪs'mænɪdʒ] *vt (matter, business)* mal administrer, mal diriger, mal gérer

mismanagement [mɪs'mænɪdʒmənt] *n* mauvaise administration *f*, mauvaise gestion *f*

mismatch ['mɪsmætʃ] *n Comptr* différence *f*; *(between two sets of data)* décalage *m*; **they're a m.** *(of two people)* ils sont mal assortis

misnomer [mɪs'nəʊmər] *n* terme *m* qui ne convient pas, terme mal approprié; **changes which, by a great m., are called progress** changements auxquels on donne fort mal à propos le nom de progrès

misogynist [mɪ'sɒdʒɪnɪst, maɪ-] *n* misogyne *mf*

misogynistic [mɪsɒdʒɪ'nɪstɪk, maɪ-] *adj* misogyne

misogyny [mɪ'sɒdʒɪnɪ, maɪ-] *n* misogynie *f*

misplace [mɪs'pleɪs] *vt* **(a)** *(one's affections etc)* mal placer; **misplaced remark** remarque déplacée *ou* hors de propos; **misplaced trust** confiance mal placée **(b)** *(lose temporarily) (book etc)* égarer **(c)** *Ling (tonic accent etc)* placer à faux

misprint¹ ['mɪsprɪnt] *n Typ* erreur *f* typographique, faute *f* d'impression, *F* coquille *f*

misprint² [mɪs'prɪnt] *vt* imprimer incorrectement

mispronounce [mɪsprə'naʊns] *vt* mal prononcer

mispronunciation [mɪsprənʌnsɪ'eɪʃən] *n (act)* prononciation *f* incorrecte; *(instance)* faute *f* de prononciation

misquotation [mɪskwəʊ'teɪʃən] *n* citation *f* inexacte

misquote [mɪs'kwəʊt] *vt (sth, author)* citer incorrectement *ou* inexactement; **I've been misquoted** *(by the press etc)* on a déformé mes propos

misread [mɪs'riːd] *vt (pt, pp* **misread** [mɪs'red]) *(text etc)* mal lire, mal interpréter; *Comptr* ne pas lire correctement; *Fig* **to m. the situation** mal interpréter la situation; **I misread her remarks** j'ai mal interprété ses remarques

misrepresent [mɪsreprɪ'zent] *vt (the facts)* dénaturer, présenter sous un faux jour; **I have been misrepresented in the press as …** j'ai été représenté à tort dans la presse comme …

misrepresentation [mɪsreprɪzen'teɪʃən] *n (of the facts etc)* présentation *f* erronée, dénaturation *f*, travestissement *m*; *Jur* fausse déclaration *f*

misrule [mɪs'ruːl] *n* **(a)** *(inefficient rule)* mauvais gouvernement *m*, mauvaise administration *f* **(b)** *(disorder)* désordre *m*, confusion *f*

Miss *abbr* **Mississippi**

miss¹ [mɪs] *n (shot, stroke etc)* coup *m* manqué; *Billiards* manque *m* de touche; *F* **I think I'll give that film/the party a m.** je ne pense pas que j'irai voir ce film/que j'irai à cette soirée; **I'll give the soup a m.** je ne prendrai pas de soupe; **thanks, but I think I'll give it a m.** merci, pas cette fois; *Prov* **a m. is as good as a mile** rater de près ou de loin, c'est toujours rater

miss² **1** *vt* **(a)** *(fail to hit, find, attend, catch etc)* manquer, rater; *(opportunity)* manquer, laisser échapper, rater; *(appointment)* manquer; *(meal) (accidentally)* rater; *(skip)* sauter; **to m. one's entrance** *(of actor)* rater son entrée; **to m. one's cue** *(of actor)* manquer sa réplique; **to m. one's way** s'égarer; *Fig F* **to m. the boat** *or* **the bus** rater le coche; **I missed him (by two minutes)** je l'ai manqué *ou* raté (de deux minutes); **an opportunity not to be missed** une occasion à ne pas manquer *ou* laisser passer; **a life of missed opportunities** une vie d'occasions manquées; **I've missed my turn** j'ai perdu mon tour; **I missed the first five minutes of the programme** j'ai raté les cinq premières minutes de l'émission; *F* **you haven't missed much!** vous n'avez pas perdu *ou* raté grand-chose!; **you don't m. much!** rien ne t'échappe!; *F* **you don't know what you're missing** tu ne sais pas ce que tu rates; **he never misses a chance to put other people down** il ne manque jamais une occasion de rabaisser les autres; **he narrowly** *or* **just missed being killed** il a failli se faire tuer; **the boss doesn't m. a thing** rien n'échappe au patron; **you can't m. the house** vous ne pouvez pas manquer de reconnaître la maison, vous ne pouvez pas rater la maison

(b) *(not hear) (question, remark etc)* ne pas entendre; *(not understand) (joke)* ne pas saisir; **you m. a lot if you read this novel in translation** on perd beaucoup à ne pas lire ce roman dans le texte; **you've missed the point** vous n'avez pas compris; *(in your answer)* vous avez répondu à côté

(c) *(omit) (word, line)* omettre, sauter; **to m. one's stop** *(of passenger etc)* rater son arrêt

(d) *(notice absence of)* **I missed him at the meeting** j'ai remarqué qu'il n'était pas à la réunion; **we are sure to be missed** on va sûrement remarquer notre absence; **they**

won't m. a few biscuits quelques biscuits de plus ou de moins, quelle est la différence?

(**e**) (*feel lack of*) **I m. you** tu me manques; **don't you m. your family?** est-ce que ta famille ne te manque pas?; **I m. the countryside/my piano** la campagne/mon piano me manque; **I m. being able to do what I like** ça me manque de ne pas pouvoir faire ce que je veux; **I missed my umbrella** mon parapluie m'aurait été bien utile; **I m. the older version** j'aimais mieux l'ancien modèle; **you can't m. what you've never had** ce que l'on n'a jamais eu ne nous manque pas; **I am not allowed cigarettes, but I don't m. them** on me défend de fumer, mais ça ne me manque pas

(**f**) (*lack*) (*always in continuous form*) **the table's missing one of its legs** il manque un pied à la table

2 *vi* (**a**) (*miss target*) manquer *ou* rater son coup; **missed!** manqué!, *F* raté!

(**b**) (*be absent*) (*always in continuous form*) manquer; **how many members are missing tonight?** combien avons-nous de membres absents *ou* d'absents ce soir?, combien y a-t-il d'absents ce soir?; **nothing is missing** il ne manque rien

miss[3] *n* (**a**) **M. Martin** Mademoiselle *f* Martin; (*on envelope*) Mademoiselle *ou* Mlle Martin; *Old-fashioned* **the M. Martins, the Misses Martin** les demoiselles *fpl* Martin; **thank you, M. Martin** merci Mademoiselle; **M. World** Miss *f* Monde; **M.!** (*to waitress etc*) Mademoiselle!, s'il vous plaît!; (*to older woman*) Madame!, s'il vous plaît! (**b**) *Br Sch F* la maîtresse; (*in secondary school*) la prof; **yes M.** (*to woman teacher*) oui, madame (**c**) *F Hum* (*girl*) (**young**) **m.** jeune demoiselle *f*

▶ **miss out 1** *vi* (*not benefit*) **you missed out there** vous avez raté quelque chose **2** *vtsep* (*omit*) (*accidentally*) oublier; (*page, paragraph, passage*) sauter, oublier; (*intentionally*) omettre; **this film/book misses out ...** il manque ... à ce film/livre; **they decided to m. out the pudding** ils ont préféré de se passer de dessert

▶ **miss out on** *vipo* (*good film, great party etc*) rater; **a lot of people are missing out on state benefits they are entitled to** bien des gens ne profitent pas des allocations auxquelles ils ont droit

missal ['mɪs(ə)l] *n Rel* missel *m*

misshapen [mɪs'ʃeɪpən] *adj* (*person, limb etc*) difforme; (*hat*) déformé

missile ['mɪsaɪl, *Am* 'mɪs(ə)l] *n* (**a**) (*projectile*) projectile *m* (**b**) *Mil* missile *m*; **m. base** base *f* de lancement de missiles; **m. launcher** lance-missiles *m inv*

missing ['mɪsɪŋ] *adj* (*person etc*) (*not present*) absent; (*object*) égaré, disparu; (*money*) (*stolen*) disparu; (*lacking*) qui manque; **there are two cups m.** il manque deux tasses, il y a deux tasses qui manquent; **here's the m. part** voilà la pièce qui manquait *ou* qui était perdue *ou* qui avait disparu; **one climber is m.** on est sans nouvelles d'un des alpinistes; *Mil etc* **to report sb m.** porter qn disparu; *Mil* **m. in action** porté disparu au combat; **to go m.** disparaître

missing link *n* (*in anthropology, piece of information*) maillon *m ou* chaînon *m* manquant

missing person *n* personne *f* disparue, disparu, -ue; *Admin* **missing persons bureau** service *m* qui s'occupe des personnes disparues

mission ['mɪʃən] *n* (**a**) (*task*) mission *f*; **to charge** *or* **entrust sb with a m.** charger qn d'une mission, confier une mission à qn; **m. accomplished** mission accomplie; **minister on a special m.** ministre en mission spéciale; **she thinks her m. is to ...** elle croit avoir pour mission de ...; **reconnaissance m.** mission de reconnaissance (**b**) (*body of persons*) mission *f*; *US* (*permanent*) représentation *f* diplomatique; **military/trade m.** mission *f* militaire/commerciale (**c**) *Rel* **foreign/home missions** missions *fpl* étrangères/métropolitaines (**d**) *Rel* (*place*) **m.** (**station**) mission *f*

missionary ['mɪʃənərɪ] **1** *n* missionnaire *mf* **2** *adj* (*priest, work*) missionnaire; (*vocation*) de missionnaire; *also Fig* **m. zeal** prosélytisme *m*; *F* **m. position** position *f* du missionnaire; *Mktg* **m. selling** ventes *fpl* de prospection

mission control *n Astronaut* centre *m* de contrôle des vols spatiaux

missis ['mɪsɪz] *n Sl* = **missus**

missive ['mɪsɪv] *n Fml* missive *f*

misspell ['mɪs'spel] *vt* (*pt, pp* **misspelt** ['mɪs'spelt]) mal orthographier

misspelling ['mɪs'spelɪŋ] *n* faute *f* d'orthographe **the frequent m. of this word** le fait que ce mot soit fréquemment mal orthographié

misspend ['mɪs'spend] *vt* (*pt, pp* **misspent** ['mɪs'spent]) (*money, time*) mal employer, gaspiller; **a misspent youth** une jeunesse dissipée

missus ['mɪsɪs, 'mɪsɪz] *n F* (**a**) (*wife*) **the** *or* **my/his/your m.** la patronne (**b**) (*woman*) **m.!** M'dame!

mist [mɪst] *n Met* brume *f*; (*on mirror etc*) buée *f*; **to see things through a m.** voir trouble; *Fig* **lost in the mists of time** perdu dans la nuit des temps

▶ **mist over** *vi* (**a**) (*of landscape*) disparaître dans la brume (**b**) (*of mirror*) se couvrir de buée, s'embuer; (*of eyes*) se voiler, s'embuer

▶ **mist up** *vti* = **mist over** (**b**) **misted-up windscreen** pare-brise *m* embué

mistakable [mɪs'teɪkəb(ə)l] *adj* **easily m.** facile à confondre (**for** avec)

mistake[1] [mɪs'teɪk] *n* erreur *f*, faute *f*; **m. in calculation/in the date** erreur de calcul/de date; **grammatical mistakes** fautes de grammaire; **it would be a m. to imagine that ...** ce serait une erreur d'imaginer que ...; **to make a m.** faire *ou* commettre une faute *ou* une erreur, se tromper (**about, over** sur, au sujet de, quant à); **you're making a big m.** tu es en train de commettre une grosse erreur; **to make the m. of doing sth** faire *ou* commettre l'erreur de faire qch; **it's an easy m. to make** c'est une erreur qu'il est facile de faire; **make no m.** que l'on ne s'y trompe pas; **by m.** (*to do sth*) par erreur, par méprise; **there is** *or* **can be no m. about that** il n'y a pas à s'y tromper; **there must be some m.** il doit y avoir une erreur; *F* **this is hard work and no m.!** c'est vraiment très dur très; (**sorry,**) **my m.!** je suis désolé, je me suis trompé *ou* j'ai fait erreur!; **my m.** c'est moi qui me suis trompé

mistake[2] *vt* (*pt* **mistook** [mɪs'tʊk]; *pp* **mistaken** [mɪs'teɪkən]) (*person's words, intentions*) se méprendre sur; (*confuse*) (*person, object*) confondre (**for sb/sth** avec qn/qch); (*house etc*) se tromper de; **there's no mistaking it** il n'y a pas à s'y méprendre; **I mistook him for someone else** je l'ai pris pour quelqu'un d'autre, je l'ai confondu avec quelqu'un d'autre

mistaken [mɪs'teɪkən] **1** *pp see* **mistake**[2] **2** *adj* (*opinion*) erroné; (*idea*) faux, *f* fausse; **I must be m.** je dois faire erreur; **if I'm not m.** si je ne me trompe (pas); **in the m. belief that ..., under the m. impression that ...** croyant, à tort, que ...; **it was** (**a case of**) **m. identity** il y a eu erreur sur la personne

mistakenly [mɪs'teɪkənlɪ] *adv* par erreur, par méprise; **it was m. believed to be ...** on croyait à tort que c'était ...

mister ['mɪstər] *n F* m'sieur *m*

mistime [mɪs'taɪm] *vt* (*counterattack, announcement*) faire au mauvais moment; (*entrance on stage*) rater; **to m. a punch/smash/pass** ne pas frapper/smasher/faire une passe au moment opportun; **the launch of the new product had been badly mistimed** le nouveau produit n'avait pas été lancé au moment propice; **to m. a joke** raconter une blague trop vite/trop lentement; **I mistimed the potatoes** j'ai mis les pommes de terre en route trop tôt/trop tard; **he badly mistimed it** il a vraiment choisi le mauvais moment il a fait une grosse erreur de timing; **she mistimed her entrance/intervention/***etc* elle est entrée/intervenue/*etc* au mauvais moment, elle a mal choisi son moment pour entrer/intervenir/*etc*

mistimed [mɪs'taɪmd] *adj* (*remark, intervention etc*) inopportun, mal à propos; (*blow*) mal calculé

mistiness ['mɪstɪnɪs] *n* (*mist*) brouillard *m*, brume *f*

mistlethrush ['mɪs(ə)lθrʌʃ] *n* (*bird*) (*grive f*) draine *f*

mistletoe ['mɪs(ə)ltəʊ] *n Bot* gui *m*

mistook *see* **mistake**[2]

mistranslate [mɪstræns'leɪt] *vt* mal traduire; **it's often mistranslated as ...** c'est souvent traduit à tort par ...

mistranslation [mɪstræns'leɪʃən] *n* mauvaise traduction *f*; (*mistake in translation*) erreur *f* de traduction

mistreat [mɪs'triːt] *vt* (*sb, sth*) maltraiter

mistreatment [mɪs'triːtmənt] *n* mauvais traitement *m*

mistress ['mɪstrɪs] *n* (**a**) (*woman in charge*) maîtresse *f*; **to be one's own m.** être indépendante, être sa propre maîtresse; **to be m. of oneself** *or* **of one's emotions** être maîtresse de soi(-même); **she was the m. of the situation** elle était maîtresse de la situation; *Old-fashioned* **the m. of the house** la maîtresse de maison (**b**) (*owner of pet*) maîtresse *f* (**c**) *esp Br Sch* (*woman teacher*) (*in primary school*) maîtresse *f* (d'école), institutrice *f*; (*in secondary school*) professeur *m*; **the French m.** le professeur de français (**d**) (*lover*) maîtresse *f* (**e**) *Arch* **M.** (*in titles*) Madame *f*

mistrial [mɪs'traɪəl] *n Jur* jugement *m* entaché d'un vice de procédure; *US* (*because jury cannot agree*) procès *m* ajourné, l'unanimité n'ayant pas été atteinte parmi le jury

mistrust[1] [mɪs'trʌst] *n* méfiance *f* (**of** à l'égard de), défiance *f* (**of** à l'égard de), manque *m* de confiance (**of** en)

mistrust² *vt* se méfier de, se défier de, ne pas avoir confiance en
mistrustful [mɪs'trʌstfʊl] *adj* méfiant, défiant (**of sth** à l'égard de qch; **of sb** à l'égard de qn, envers qn)
mistrustfully [mɪs'trʌstfʊlɪ] *adv* avec méfiance, avec défiance
misty ['mɪstɪ] *adj* (*place etc*) brumeux, embrumé; (*weather*) brumeux; (*form*) flou, voilé, estompé; (*memory*) vague, confus; **m. eyes** yeux embués; **m. blue** bleu gris; **it's m.** le temps est brumeux; **the windscreen is all m.** le pare-brise est tout couvert de buée
misunderstand [mɪsʌndə'stænd] (*pt, pp* **misunderstood** [mɪsʌndə'stʊd]) **1** *vt* (*misinterpret*) (*sb, sth*) mal comprendre; (*misjudge*) (*sb*) méconnaître, se méprendre sur le compte de; (*action etc*) mal comprendre, mal interpréter, se méprendre sur; **we misunderstood each other** il y a eu un malentendu entre nous; **don't m. me, I'm as opposed to this plan as you are** comprends-moi bien, je suis aussi opposé à ce projet que toi **2** *vi* mal comprendre; **if I have not misunderstood** si j'ai bien compris
misunderstanding [mɪsʌndə'stændɪŋ] *n* **(a)** (*misconception*) erreur *f*; (*mistake*) malentendu *m*, méprise *f*; (*confusion of two objects*) quiproquo *m*; **I think there's been a m.** je crois qu'il y a eu un malentendu *ou* (une) méprise **(b)** (*disagreement*) malentendu *m*, désaccord *m*, différend *m*
misuse¹ [mɪs'ju:s] *n* (*of sth*) mauvais usage *m ou* emploi *m*; (*of authority*) abus *m*; (*of word*) emploi abusif; *Jur* **fraudulent m. of funds** détournement *m* de fonds
misuse² [mɪs'ju:z] *vt* (*sth*) faire (un) mauvais usage *ou* (un) mauvais emploi de; (*one's authority*) abuser de; (*word*) employer à tort *ou* abusivement
mite [maɪt] *n* **(a)** *Arch, Lit* (*sum of money*) **the widow's m.** le denier de la veuve **(b)** (*small amount*) *F* **it's a m. expensive** c'est un peu cher **(c)** *F* (*child*) petit gosse *m*, petite gosse *f*, mioche *mf*; (*animal*) petite bête *f*; **poor little m.!** pauvre petit! **(d)** *Ent* acarien *m*
miter ['maɪtər] *n, v US* = **mitre**
mitigate ['mɪtɪgeɪt] *vt* (*sb's anger*) adoucir; (*suffering, grief etc*) adoucir, atténuer; (*pain*) apaiser; (*punishment, effects, Jur crime*) atténuer
mitigating ['mɪtɪgeɪtɪŋ] *adj esp Jur* **m. circumstances** circonstances *fpl* atténuantes
mitigation [mɪtɪ'geɪʃən] *n Fml* (*of pain*) adoucissement *m*; (*of punishment*) atténuation *f*; **if you have anything to say in m. of this offence** si vous avez quelque chose à dire pour votre défense; **in m. of this, it should be noted that ...** il faut noter que ... et ceci constitue une circonstance atténuante; **in m. of the accused's crime ...** à la décharge de l'accusé ...
mitral ['maɪtrəl] *adj Anat* **m. valve** valvule *f* mitrale
mitre¹, *US* **miter** ['maɪtər] *n* (*headdress*) mitre *f*
mitre², *US* **miter** *n Carp* **m. (joint)** (assemblage *m* à) onglet *m*; **m. box** boîte *f* à onglet(s); **m. square** équerre *f* (à) onglet
mitre³, *US* **miter** *vt Carp etc* **(a)** (*shape*) (*part*) tailler à onglet **(b)** (*join*) (*two parts*) assembler à onglet
mitt [mɪt] *n* **(a)** = **mitten**; *Baseball* gant *m* **(b)** *F* (*hand*) patte *f*
mitten ['mɪt(ə)n] *n* (*glove without separate fingers*) moufle *f*, *Can* mitaine *f*; (*glove with no fingers*) mitaine; *Boxing F* **mittens** gants *mpl*
mix¹ [mɪks] *n* **(a)** (*of mortar, plaster*) mélange *m*; **(cake) m.** préparation *f* pour gâteaux; **there was a good m. of people at the party** il y avait un mélange intéressant de personnes à la soirée; *Com* **product m.** assortiment *m* de produits, *Spec* mix *m* **(b)** (*in recording*) mixage *m*; **the 12-inch m.** (*record*) le trente centimètres
mix² **1** *vt* mêler, mélanger (**several things together** plusieurs choses ensemble; **sth with sth** qch à *ou* avec qch); (*drink*) préparer; (*mortar, plaster*) gâcher; *Culin* (*salad*) retourner; *US* (*cards*) battre, mélanger; **to m. business with pleasure** mélanger le travail et les loisirs; **you should never m. your drinks** il ne faut jamais mélanger les alcools; **to m. one's metaphors** confondre deux expressions; *F* **to m. it (with sb)** (*fight*) se bagarrer (avec qn); **do you want to m. it?** tu veux te battre?

2 *vi* (*of things*) se mélanger (**with** avec, à); **sport and drug-taking don't m.** le sport et l'utilisation de drogue ne font pas bon ménage; **to m. with people** (*of person*) fréquenter des gens; **I don't m. much** je ne fréquente pas beaucoup de gens; **to m. with the crowd** se mêler à la foule; **to m. with the guests** circuler parmi les invités
▶ **mix up** *vtsep* **(a)** (*prepare*) (*drink, medication*) préparer **(b)** (*put in disorder*) (*one's papers etc*) mettre le désordre dans; **everything got mixed up** tout avait été mélangé **(c)** (*confuse*) confondre (**with** avec); **I was mixing you up with your brother** je vous confondais avec votre frère; **I was getting all mixed up** je ne savais plus où j'en étais **(d)** (*involve*) **to be mixed up in an affair** être mêlé à une affaire, être compromis *ou* impliqué dans une affaire; **mixed up in something dishonest** impliqué dans quelque chose de malhonnête **(e)** *esp US Sl* **to m. it up** (*fight*) en venir aux coups
mix-down *n TV etc* mixage *m* avec réduction de pistes
mixed ['mɪkst] *adj* mélangé; **person of m. blood/race** sang-mêlé *mf inv*; *F* **they were a m. bag** (*of people or things*) il y avait de tout; **her resignation was a m. blessing** sa démission avait du bon et du mauvais; **to meet with a m. reception** recevoir un accueil mitigé; **in m. company** en présence de personnes des deux sexes; *Tennis* **m. doubles** double *m* mixte; *Econ* **m. economy** économie *f* mixte; **m. farming** élevage *m* et culture *f*; **m. feelings** sentiments *mpl* contradictoires; **it was with m. feelings that I took up the position** c'est sans grand enthousiasme que j'ai accepté le poste *Culin* **m. grill** mixed-grill *m, pl* mixed-grills; **m. marriage** mariage *m* mixte; **m. metaphor** métaphore *m* multiple; **m. school** école *f* mixte; **m. vegetables** jardinière *f ou* macédoine *f* de légumes
mixed-ability *adj usu attrib* (*classes*) qui regroupe des élèves de niveaux différents
mixed-up *adj F* (*person*) déboussolé, qui ne sait plus où il en est; **a crazy m. kid** un pauvre gosse un peu paumé
mixer ['mɪksər] *n* **(a)** (*machine*), *Ind etc* mélangeuse *f*, agitateur *m*; *TV etc* mixeur *m*, mélangeur *m*; *Culin* **(food) m.** mixeur *m*, mixer *m*; *Br* **m. (tap)** mélangeur *m*; (*with single control*) mitigeur *m* **(b) to be a good m.** (*socially*) être très sociable **(c)** (*drink*) = boisson *f* non-alcoolisée que l'on utilise pour allonger certains alcools **(d)** *esp US Univ F* (*party*) = soirée *f* pour permettre aux étudiants de faire connaissance
mixing ['mɪksɪŋ] *n* **(a)** mélange *m*; **m. bowl** bol *m* mélangeur; **m. chamber** (*in engine*) chambre *f* de mélange *ou* de carburation; **m. drum** mélangeur *m* (à tambour) **(b)** *TV etc* mixage *m*, mélange *m* sonore; **m. console** table *f* de mixage; **m. desk** pupitre *m* de mixage
mixture ['mɪkstʃər] *n* **(a)** (*of objects, people, styles, fuel*) mélange *m*; **their music is a m. of traditional and modern** leur musique est un mélange de moderne et de traditionnel; **(cake) m.** préparation *f* pour gâteaux; **he's an odd m.** c'est un type difficile à cerner, c'est un drôle de type; *Aut* **m. adjusting screw** vis *f* de richesse **(b)** *Pharm* mixtion *f*, mixture *f*
mix-up *n* (*confusion*) confusion *f*; (*misunderstanding*) malentendu *m*; *F* (*mess*) pagaïe *f*, pagaille *f*; **there's been a m. with the reservations** ils se sont embrouillés dans les réservations
mizzen ['mɪz(ə)n] *n Naut* **m. (sail)** artimon *m*
mizzenmast ['mɪz(ə)nmɑ:st] *n Naut* mât *m* d'artimon
ml (*abbr* **millilitre(s)**) ml
MLR [eme'lɑ:r] *n Br Fin* (*abbr* **minimum lending rate**) taux *m* de crédit minimum
mm (*abbr* **millimetre(s)**) mm
MMFs [eme'mefs] *npl St Exch* (*abbr* **money market funds**) = sicav *fpl* monétaires
MNA [eme'neɪ] *n Can* (*in Quebec*) (*abbr* **Member of the National Assembly**) MAN *m*
mnemonic [nɪ'mɒnɪk] **1** *adj* mnémonique **2** *n* moyen *m* mnémotechnique
MO [e'məʊ] *n* **(a)** *Mil etc abbr* **medical officer** **(b)** (*abbr* **modus operandi**) (*of criminal*) façon *f* d'agir **(c)** (*abbr* **money order**) mandat-poste *m*
mo [məʊ] *n Br F* instant *m*, minute *f*; **half a mo!** une petite seconde!
moan¹ [məʊn] *n* **(a)** (*sound*) gémissement *m*, plainte *f* **(b)** *F* (*complaint*) plainte *f*, jérémiades *fpl*; **to have a (good) m.** râler un bon coup
moan² **1** *vi* **(a)** (*make sound*) gémir, pousser des gémissements; (*of wind*) mugir, gémir **(b)** *F* (*complain*) geindre, gémir, *F* râler, ronchonner; **to m. about sth** se plaindre de qch; **he's always moaning (and groaning)** il est toujours à gémir *ou* à geindre *ou F* à ronchonner; **he's a real m. Minnie** c'est un vrai geignard; **what are they moaning about now?** de quoi se plaignent-ils maintenant? **2** *vt* (*sth*) dire en gémissant
moaner ['məʊnər] *n F* ronchonneur, -euse, râleur, -euse
moaning ['məʊnɪŋ] *n* **(a)** (*sound*) gémissement(s) *m(pl)* **(b)** *F* (*complaining*) jérémiades *fpl*
moat [məʊt] *n* fossé(s) *m(pl)*, douves *fpl*
mob¹ [mɒb] *n* **(a)** *Pej* **the m.** (*the masses*) la populace, *F* le populo; **m. rule** voyoucratie *f* **(b)** (*crowd*) foule *f* (agitée); (*gang*) bande *f*, troupe *f*; (*of reporters etc*) meute *f*; **mobs of drunken hooligans** des hordes de hooligans ivres **(c)** *F* (*gang*) bande *f*, clique *f*; **the M.** (*Mafia*) la mafia; **which m. were you in?** (*in forces*) dans quel régiment étais-tu?

mob² *vt* **(-bb-)** (*of angry crowd*) (*person*) assaillir, attaquer; (*of fans, reporters etc*) (*person*) assiéger, se presser autour de; (*place*) prendre d'assaut, assiéger; **the crowds mobbing the entrance** la foule qui se pressait à l'entrée

mobbed [mɒbd] *adj F* (*crowded*) bondé

mobile¹ ['məʊbaɪl] *adj* mobile; **the patient is m.** le patient peut se déplacer; *F* **are you m.?** (*do you have a car with you?*) vous êtes motorisé?; **he wants to stay professionally m.** il veut être libre de ses mouvements dans son métier; *TV etc* **m. control room** régie *f* mobile; *Mil* **m. defence** troupes *fpl* mobiles; **m. features** physionomie *f* changeante; *TV* **m. studio** studio *m* mobile; **m. warfare** guerre *f* de mouvement

mobile² *n* **(a)** *Art* mobile *m* **(b)** (*phone*) téléphone *m* mobile, radio-téléphone *m*, *pl* radio-téléphones

mobile home *n Aut* (*caravan*) camping-car *m*, *pl* camping-cars; (*house*) = maison *f* sans fondations qui peut être déplacée

mobile kitchen *n Mil* cuisine *f* roulante

mobile library *n Br* bibliothèque *f* itinérante, bibliobus *m*

mobile phone *n Tel* téléphone *m* mobile, radio-téléphone *m*, *pl* radio-téléphones

mobile shop *n* camion-magasin *m*, *pl* camions-magasins

mobility [məʊ'bɪlɪtɪ] *n* mobilité *f*; **she has very little m. in her right arm** elle peut à peine bouger son bras droit; **he values his professional m.** il tient à conserver sa liberté de mouvement dans son métier; *Br Admin* **m. allowance** allocation *f* de déplacement (*versée aux personnes handicapées*)

mobilization [məʊbɪlaɪ'zeɪʃən] *n* (*of troops, capital, support etc*) mobilisation *f*; *Mil* **m. order** (*general*) appel *m* de mobilisation; (*to individual recruit*) ordre *m* de mobilisation

mobilize ['məʊbɪlaɪz] **1** *vt* (*troops, capital, public opinion*) mobiliser **2** *vi Mil, Fig* se mobiliser

mobster ['mɒbstər] *n esp Am* gangster *m*

moccasin ['mɒkəsɪn] *n* (*footwear*) mocassin *m*

mocha ['mɒkə] *n* **(a) m. (coffee)** (café *m*) moka *m* **(b)** (*coffee and chocolate flavour*) parfum *m* chocolat-café

mock¹ [mɒk] *n Br Sch* examen *m* blanc; **to make a m. of sb/sth** se moquer de qn/qch

mock² *adj* (*imitation*) simulé; *Br Sch* **m. examination** examen *m* blanc; **m. fight** simulacre *m* de combat; **to indulge in m. heroics** jouer au *ou* se prendre pour un héros; **m. tortoiseshell** (*rims, frame etc*) en imitation écaille; **m. trial/elections** simulacre *m* de procès/d'élections

mock³ **1** *vt* (*ridicule*) (*person*) se moquer de, *Lit* railler; (*imitate*) (*person*) imiter en se moquant, ridiculiser **2** *vi* **to m. at** se moquer de, *Lit* railler

mocker ['mɒkər] *n* **(a)** (*person*) moqueur, -euse, railleur, -euse **(b)** *Br F* **to put the mockers on sth** (*spoil*) foutre qch en l'air

mockery ['mɒkərɪ] *n* **(a)** (*action*) moquerie *f*, raillerie *f* **(b)** (*person, thing*) sujet *m ou* objet *m* de moquerie *ou* de raillerie, objet de risée; **to make a m. of sb** ridiculiser qn; **to make a m. of oneself** se ridiculiser; **to make a m. of sth** faire perdre toute crédibilité à qch **(c)** (*pretence*) parodie *f*, simulacre *m* **(of** de); **the trial was a mere m.** le procès n'a été qu'un simulacre

mocking ['mɒkɪŋ] **1** *adj* moqueur, railleur **2** *n* moquerie *f*, raillerie *f*; **she couldn't put up with their m. any more** elle ne pouvait plus supporter leurs railleries

mockingbird ['mɒkɪŋbɜːd] *n* moqueur *m*

mockingly ['mɒkɪŋlɪ] *adv* (*to say*) d'un ton moqueur *ou* railleur; (*to smile*) d'un air moqueur

mock orange *n Bot* seringa(t) *m*

mock turtle soup *n Culin* consommé *m* à la tête de veau

mock-up *n* maquette *f*

MOD [eməʊ'diː] *n Br* (*abbr* **Ministry of Defence**) Ministère *m* de la Défense; **MOD property** propriété *f* du Ministère de la Défense

Mod [mɒd] *n Scot Mus* festival *m* de musique et de littérature dans les Highlands

mod [mɒd] *F* **1** *adj* **m. cons** confort *m* moderne; **the car comes equipped with the latest m. cons** la voiture dispose de toutes les options **2** *n Br* **mods** = adolescents *mpl* à l'apparence soignée opposés aux rockers pendant les années soixante

modal ['məʊd(ə)l] [①**A55-9,18; B36-37,K**] *Gram* **1** *adj* modal **2** *n* verbe *m* modal

modality [məʊ'dælɪtɪ] *n* modalité *f*

mode [məʊd] *n* **(a)** (*manner*) mode *m*, façon *f* **(of** de); **m. of transport** mode de transport **(b)** (*fashion*) mode *f* **(c)** *Mus, Phil, Comptr* mode *m*

model¹ ['mɒd(ə)l] *n* **(a)** (*small version*) (*built as a hobby*) modèle *m* (réduit), maquette *f*; *Com, Ind* maquette *f*; (*in naval architecture etc*) gabarit *m*; (*in surveying*) plan *m* en relief; **m. aircraft** (*toy*) modèle (réduit) *ou* maquette d'avion; *Ind* maquette d'avion; **m. kit** modèle en pièces détachées; **m. maker** (*as hobby*) modéliste *mf*; *Ind* maquettiste *mf*

(b) (*example*), *Com* modèle *m*; **this is our latest m.** c'est notre dernier modèle; *Com, Ind* **there are several different models** il y a plusieurs modèles différents; **Paris models** (*clothing*) modèles de la haute couture parisienne

(c) *Econ etc* modèle *m*

(d) (*perfect example*) **to take sb as one's m.** prendre modèle sur qn, prendre qn pour modèle; **to be a m. of virtue** être un modèle *ou* un exemple de vertu; **m. pupil** écolier, -ière modèle

(e) (*person*), *Art* modèle *m*; **(fashion) m.** mannequin *m*, modèle *m*

model² **(-ll-**, *US* **-l-) 1** *vt* **(a)** *Art* (*figure, group*) modeler **(after, (up)on** sur); *Fig* **to m. oneself on sb** prendre exemple sur qn, se modeler sur qn **(b)** (*of fashion model*) (*dress etc*) présenter **2** *vi* (*of artist's model*) poser (comme modèle); (*of fashion model*) travailler comme mannequin *ou* modèle

modeller, *US* **modeler** ['mɒdələr] *n* modeleur, -euse

modelling, *US* **modeling** ['mɒdəlɪŋ] *n* **(a)** (*occupation*) métier *m* de mannequin; **to get a career in m.** faire une carrière de mannequin **(b)** (*of dress etc*) présentation *f* **(c)** *Art* modelage *m*; **m. clay** pâte *f* à modeler

modem¹ ['məʊdem] *n Comptr* modem *m*; **m. card** carte *f* modem; **m. link** liaison *f* par modem; **m. transmission** transmission *f* par modem

modem² *vt* envoyer par modem; **to m. sth to sb** envoyer qch à qn par modem

moderate¹ ['mɒdərɪt] **1** *adj* modéré; (*drinker*) tempéré; (*language*) mesuré; (*price*) modéré, modique, moyen; (*income, size*) moyen; **to express oneself in m. language** s'exprimer en termes modérés; **a m. breeze** une légère brise **2** *n Pol etc* (*person*) modéré, -ée

moderate² ['mɒdəreɪt] **1** *vt* **(a)** (*one's demands, wishes, one's zeal*) modérer; **to be a moderating influence on sb** exercer une influence modératrice sur qn **(b)** *Fml* (*meeting*) présider; (*discussion*) arbitrer **2** *vi* **(a)** (*of storm*) s'apaiser, se calmer **(b)** *Fml* (*at meeting*) présider

moderately ['mɒdərɪtlɪ] *adv* (*to eat, drink, like*) modérément; (*fast, well-off*) assez, moyennement; **m. priced** à prix moyen

moderation [mɒdə'reɪʃən] *n* **(a)** modération *f*, mesure *f*; (*of language*) sobriété *f*; **in m.** avec modération, modérément; **taken in m. alcohol is not harmful** consommé avec modération, l'alcool n'est pas nocif **(b)** *Univ* (*at Oxford University*) **Moderations** = premier examen *m* pour le grade de *Bachelor of Arts*

moderator ['mɒdəreɪtər] *n* **(a)** (*at meeting*) président, -ente **(b)** *Univ* (*of exam*) examinateur, -trice qui assure l'harmonisation de la notation **(c)** *Phys* (*of reactor etc*) modérateur *m*, ralentisseur *m*

Moderator of the General Assembly *n Scot Rel* modérateur *m ou* président *m* du synode (de l'Église d'Écosse)

modern ['mɒdən] **1** *adj* moderne; **m. times** les temps *mpl* modernes; **m. languages** langues *fpl* vivantes; **m. Greek** grec *m* moderne **2** *n* moderne *mf*

modernism ['mɒdənɪz(ə)m] *n* **(a)** modernisme *m* **(b)** *Ling* néologisme *m*

modernist ['mɒdənɪst] *n, adj* moderniste *mf*

modernity [mɒ'dɜːnɪtɪ] *n* modernité *f*

modernization [mɒdənaɪ'zeɪʃən] *n* modernisation *f*

modernize ['mɒdənaɪz] **1** *vt* moderniser **2** *vi* se moderniser

modest ['mɒdɪst] *adj* **(a)** (*not boastful*) modeste; **to be m. about one's achievements** ne pas se vanter de ses réussites **(b)** (*moderate*) (*request*) modeste, modéré; (*fortune*) modeste; **to be m. in one's requirements** être peu exigeant; **a m. house** une maison sans prétentions *ou* à l'aspect modeste **(c)** *Old-fashioned* (*chaste*) pudique

modestly ['mɒdɪstlɪ] *adv* **(a)** (*not boastfully*) modestement, avec modestie **(b)** (*moderately*) modérément **(c)** (*in sexual sense*) modestement, pudiquement

modesty ['mɒdɪstɪ] *n* **(a)** (*of person*) modestie *f*; **in all m.** en toute modestie **(b)** (*of request*) modération *f*; (*of expense*) modicité *f* **(c)** *Old-fashioned* (*chasteness*) pudeur *f*

modicum ['mɒdɪkəm] *n* **a m. of …** un minimum de …, un petit peu de …, un brin de …; **a m. of truth** une petite part de vérité; **she doesn't have even a m. of taste** elle n'a aucun goût

modification [mɒdɪfɪ'keɪʃən] *n* modification *f*; **to make modifications to sth** apporter des modifications à qch

modify ['mɒdɪfaɪ] *vt* **(a)** (*alter*) modifier; (*reduce*) (*punishment*) mitiger, atténuer; **she modified her opinion of him in the light of this information** elle a changé d'avis à son égard lorsqu'elle a appris cela **(b)** *Gram, Ling* (*verb, vowel etc*) modifier

modish ['məʊdɪʃ] *adj* (*hat etc*) à la mode

modishly ['məʊdɪʃlɪ] *adv* (*dressed*) à la mode
modiste [məʊ'diːst] *n* modiste *f*
Mods [mɒdz] *npl F* (*at Oxford University*) = premier examen *m* pour le grade de *Bachelor of Arts*
modular ['mɒdjʊlər] *adj Archit, Math etc* modulaire; (*furniture*) modulaire, à éléments (composables)
modulate ['mɒdjʊleɪt] **1** *vt* (*one's voice, sound, Phys amplitude etc*) moduler; **modulating frequency** fréquence *f* de modulation **2** *vi Mus* moduler
modulation [mɒdjʊ'leɪʃən] *n* (*of voice*) modulation *f*, inflexion *f*; *Mus, El, Electron* modulation
modulator ['mɒdjʊleɪtər] *n El, Electron* modulateur *m*
module ['mɒdjuːl] *n Archit, Astronaut Constr etc* module *m*; *Univ* module, unité *f* de valeur; (*of RAM chips*) barrette *f*
modulus, *pl* **-i** ['mɒdjʊləs, -aɪ] *n Math, Phys* module *m*, coefficient *m*
modus operandi ['məʊdəsɒpə'rændaɪ, -diː] *n* façon *f* de procéder
modus vivendi ['məʊdəsvɪ'vendaɪ, -diː] *n* modus *m* vivendi
moggy ['mɒgɪ] *n Br F* (*cat*) minou *m*; (*esp male*) matou *m*
Mogul ['məʊgəl] *n Hist* mogol *m*
mogul[1] ['məʊgəl] *n F* (*powerful person*) gros bonnet *m*, grand manitou *m*, nabab *m*; **movie m.** grand manitou du cinéma
mogul[2] *n Ski* bosse *f*
mohair ['məʊheər] *n* mohair *m*; **m. sweater** pull *m* en mohair
Mohammed [məʊ'hæmɪd] *n Rel* Mahomet *m*, Mohammed *m*
Mohammedan [məʊ'hæmɪd(ə)n] *adj, n* mahométan, -ane
Mohawk ['məʊhɔːk] *n* (*native American*) Mohawk *mf*
mohawk ['məʊhɔːk] *n Am* (*hairstyle*) iroquois *m*
Mohican [məʊ'hiːkən] *n* (*native American*) Mohican *mf*
mohican [məʊ'hiːkən] *n Br* (*hairstyle*) iroquois *m*
moiré ['mwɑːreɪ] *adj, n Tex* moiré *m*
moist [mɔɪst] *adj* humide; (*skin, hand*) moite; (*heat*) moite, humide; (*cake*) moelleux; **eyes m. with tears** yeux mouillés de larmes, yeux embués; **to grow m.** se mouiller, s'humecter
moisten ['mɔɪs(ə)n] **1** *vt* mouiller, humecter; **to m. a cloth with ...** imbiber un chiffon de ... **2** *vi* (*of eyes*) se mouiller
moistness ['mɔɪstnɪs] *n* humidité *f*; (*of skin, palms*) moiteur *f*
moisture ['mɔɪstʃər] *n* humidité *f*; (*on mirror etc*) buée *f*
moisturize ['mɔɪstʃəraɪz] *vt* humidifier; (*skin*) hydrater
moisturizer ['mɔɪstʃəraɪzər] *n* (*for skin*) crème *f ou* lotion *f* hydratante, (lait *m*) hydratant *m*
molar ['məʊlər] **1** *n* molaire *f* **2** *adj* molaire
molasses [mə'læsɪz] *npl* (*with sing verb*) mélasse *f*; *Am F* **to be as slow as m. (in winter)** être d'une lenteur de limace *ou* d'escargot *ou* de tortue
mold, molder *etc US* = **mould, moulder** *etc*
mole[1] [məʊl] *n* (*birthmark*) grain *m* de beauté
mole[2] *n* **(a)** (*animal*) taupe *f*; **m. catcher** taupier *m*; **m. trap** taupière *f* **(b)** *Fig* (*spy*) espion *m*, taupe *f*
mole[3] *n* (*breakwater*) môle *m*, digue *f*
molecular [mə'lekjʊlər] *adj Phys* (*mass etc*) moléculaire
molecule ['mɒlɪkjuːl] *n Ch, Phys* molécule *f*
molehill ['məʊlhɪl] *n* taupinière *f*
moleskin ['məʊlskɪn] *n* **(a)** (peau *f* de) taupe *f*; **m. coat** manteau *m* en taupe **(b)** (*material*) velours *m* de coton
molest [mə'lest] *vt* (*pester*) importuner; (*physically*) (*of person*) molester, agresser, attaquer; (*of dog*) attaquer; (*sexually*) commettre un attentat à la pudeur sur la personne de
molestation [məʊles'teɪʃən] *n* (*physical*) agression *f*; (*sexual*) attentat *m* à la pudeur
molester [mə'lestər] *n* (**child**) **m.** coupable *mf* d'attentat à la pudeur sur un/des enfant(s)
moll [mɒl] *n Sl* (**gangster's**) **m.** poule *f ou* môme *f* (d'un gangster)
mollify ['mɒlɪfaɪ] *vt* (*sb, sb's anger*) calmer, apaiser
mollusc, *US* **mollusk** ['mɒləsk] *n* mollusque *m*
mollycoddle ['mɒlɪkɒd(ə)l] *vt F* (*child*) dorloter, élever dans du coton
Molotov ['mɒlətɒf] *n* **M. cocktail** cocktail *m* Molotov
molt, molting *US* = **moult, moulting**
molten ['məʊltən] *adj Metal* fondu, en fusion; **m. metal** métal en fusion
molybdenum [mɒ'lɪbdɪnəm] *n* molybdène *m*
mom [mɒm] *n Am F* maman *f*
moment ['məʊmənt] *n* **(a)** moment *m*, instant *m*; **at the (present) m.** actuellement, en ce moment; **at this m.** (*presently, now*) en ce moment; **it was at this m. that ...** c'est à cet instant que ...; **just at that m.** à ce moment *ou* cet instant précis; **I have just** *or* **only this m. heard about it** je viens de l'apprendre, je l'apprends à l'instant; **at the last m.** à la dernière minute, au dernier moment; **I haven't a m. to spare** je n'ai pas un instant *ou* une minute de libre; **wait a m.!, just a m.!, one m.!** une seconde!, une minute!, un instant!; **he may return at any m.** il peut revenir d'un instant à l'autre; **I saw her a m. ago** je l'ai vue il y a un instant *ou* une seconde; **the m. he arrives** dès qu'il arrivera, dès son arrivée; **the m. she saw him** dès l'instant où elle le vit; **I'll be with you in a m.** je suis à vous dans une minute *ou* dans un instant; **nothing else for the m.** rien de plus pour le moment *ou* l'instant; **I don't for one m. believe that this will happen** je ne crois pas un instant que ça va se produire; **not a m.'s hesitation** pas une seconde d'hésitation; **without a m.'s hesitation** sans hésiter une seconde; **the man of the m.** l'homme du jour *ou* du moment; **to live for the m.** profiter du moment présent; **the m. of truth** la minute *ou* l'heure de vérité; **the film had its moments** il y avait quelques bons moments *ou* passages dans le film; **she has her moments of being quite pleasant** il y a des moments où elle est assez agréable; **I have my moments, you know** ça m' arrive, des fois!
(b) *Phys, Math etc* moment *m*; **m. of inertia** moment d'inertie
(c) (*importance*) **of great m.** d'une importance considérable, de grande *ou* haute importance; **of little m.** de peu d'importance; **to be of no m.** n'avoir aucune importance
momentarily ['məʊməntərɪlɪ] *adv* **(a)** (*very briefly*) momentanément **(b)** *esp Am* (*very soon*) très bientôt, d'un moment à l'autre
momentary ['məʊməntərɪ] *adj* momentané, passager
momentous [məʊ'mentəs] *adj* (*decision*) capital, très important; **on this m. occasion** en cette occasion mémorable
momentousness [məʊ'mentəsnɪs] *n* importance *f* capitale; (*of an occasion*) importance
momentum, *pl* **-ta** [məʊ'mentəm, -tə] *n* **(a)** *Phys* force *f* vive, force d'impulsion; *Nucl, Phys* (*of particle*) impulsion *f* **(b)** (*impetus*) vitesse *f* (acquise), élan *m*; *Fig* (*of attack etc*) force *f*; *Fig* **carried away by my own m.** emporté par mon (propre) élan; **to gather m.** (*of moving object*) acquérir de la force (vive) *ou* de la vitesse; (*of political movement etc*) prendre de l'ampleur, s'amplifier; *Fig* **to lose one's m.** être en perte de vitesse; *Fig* **we'll never get that m. back again** on ne retrouvera jamais ce rythme
Mon (*abbr* **Monday**) lun
Monaco ['mɒnəkəʊ, mə'nɑːkəʊ] *n* (**principality of**) **M.** (principauté *f* de) Monaco *m ou f*
monad ['mɒnæd] *n Phil, Biol, Ch* monade *f*
Mona Lisa ['məʊnə'liːzə] *n Art* **the M.** la Joconde
monarch ['mɒnək] *n* monarque *m*
monarchic(al) [mɒ'nɑːkɪk, -ɪk(ə)l] *adj* monarchique
monarchist ['mɒnəkɪst] *adj, n* monarchiste *mf*
monarchy ['mɒnəkɪ] *n* monarchie *f*
monastery ['mɒnəstrɪ] *n* monastère *m*
monastic [mə'næstɪk] *adj Rel, Fig* monastique, monacal; (*attitude*) monacal; **he's a m. sort of person** il mène une vie monacale *ou* de moine
monasticism [mə'næstɪsɪz(ə)m] *n* **(a)** (*way of life*) vie *f* monastique **(b)** (*system*) système *m* monastique, monachisme *m*
monaural [mɒ'nɔːrəl] *adj* monaural
Monday ['mʌndɪ] *n* [①A75-6,B-C; B58-9,B-C] lundi *m*; **every M.** tous les lundis; *F* **that M. morning feeling** le cafard du lundi matin *ou* de l'après-weekend
MONEP ['məʊnep] *n St Exch* MONEP *m*
monetarism ['mʌnɪtərɪz(ə)m] *n Econ* monétarisme *m*
monetarist ['mʌnɪtərɪst] *adj, n Econ* monétariste *mf*
monetary ['mʌnɪt(ə)rɪ] *adj* (*unit etc*) monétaire; **m. area** zone *f* monétaire
money ['mʌnɪ] *n* **(a)** (*no pl*) argent *m*; **to do sth for m.** faire qch pour l'argent; **to earn** *or* **make m.** gagner de l'argent; **to earn good m.** bien gagner; **the job's boring but the m.'s good** le travail est ennuyeux mais ça paye bien *ou* c'est bien payé; **to throw good m. after bad** s'enfoncer davantage dans une mauvaise affaire; **it's throwing m. away, it's m. down the drain** c'est de l'argent gaspillé *ou* jeté par la fenêtre; **to be worth a lot of m.** (*of thing*) valoir cher, avoir beaucoup de valeur; (*of person*) être riche; *F* **to be made of m.** être plein aux as, rouler sur l'or; **I'm not made of m.** je ne suis pas cousu d'or, je ne suis pas riche comme Crésus; *F* **to be in the m.** être en fonds; *St Exch* être dans les cours; *St Exch* **at the m.** à parité; *St Exch* **out of the m.** hors des cours; **there's m. to be made in this business** il y a de l'argent à gagner dans ce métier; **there's no m. in it** ça ne paye pas; **to have m. to burn** avoir de l'argent à jeter par les fenêtres; **your m. or your life!** la bourse ou la vie!; *Fig* **it was m. for old rope** *or* **for jam** c'était de l'argent facilement gagné; **you've had your m.'s worth** vous en avez eu pour votre argent; **to put m. on a horse** mettre de l'argent sur un cheval; **to put one's m. where one's mouth is** passer aux

actes; **for my m. Jackson is the better player** à mon avis, Jackson est le meilleur joueur; *Prov* **m. is the root of all evil** l'argent est la source de tous les maux; *Prov* **m. makes m.** l'argent va à l'argent; *prov* **m. talks** c'est l'argent qui décide de tout; **m. of account** monnaie *f* de compte; **m.-back guarantee** garantie *f* de remboursement intégral; **'m.-back guarantee'** 'satisfait ou remboursé'; **m. -back offer** offre *f* de remboursement; **m. belt** ceinture *f* porte-monnaie *inv ou* porte-billets *inv*; **m. market** marché *m* monétaire *ou* financier; **m. market funds** = sicav *fpl* monétaires; **m. matters** affaires *fpl* d'argent, questions *fpl* financières; **m.-off deal** réduction *f* de prix; **m.-off voucher** bon *m* de remboursement; **m. order** mandat-poste *m, pl* mandats-poste; **international m. order** mandat *m* international; **m. spider** petite araignée *f* rouge; **m. supply** masse *f* monétaire; **m. trader** cambiste *m*

(b) (*pl* **moneys**, *occ* **monies** ['mʌnɪz]) (*currency*) monnaie *f*; *Arch, Jur* **moneys, monies** (*sums*) argent *m*, fonds *mpl*, sommes *fpl* (d'argent); **public moneys** deniers *mpl* publics

moneybag ['mʌnɪbæg] *n* **(a)** sac *m* à argent; (*of bus conductor etc*) sacoche *f* **(b)** *Old-fashioned F* (*person*) **moneybags** richard, -arde, rupin, -ine

moneybox ['mʌnɪbɒks] *n Br* (*child's*) tirelire *f*

moneychanger ['mʌnɪtʃeɪndʒər] *n* **(a)** (*person*) courtier, -ière de change **(b)** (*machine*) = distributeur *m* de monnaie

moneyed ['mʌnɪd] *adj* riche, qui a de l'argent, fortuné, nanti; **the m. classes** les classes *fpl* possédantes

money-grubber *n F* grippe-sou *m, pl* grippe-sous, pingre *m*

money-grubbing ['mʌnɪgrʌbɪŋ] *adj F* grippe-sou *inv*

moneylender ['mʌnɪlendər] *n* (*person*) prêteur, -euse (à intérêt); (*establishment*) maison *f* de prêt

moneymaker ['mʌnɪmeɪkər] *n* (*shop, business, product*) magasin *m*/affaire *f*/produit *m* qui rapporte

moneymaking ['mʌnɪmeɪkɪŋ] **1** *adj* (*business etc*) qui rapporte **2** *n* acquisition *f* d'argent

Mongol ['mɒŋgəl] **1** *adj Geog* mongol **2** *n* **(a)** Mongol, -ole **(b)** *Ling* mongol *m*

mongol ['mɒŋgəl] *adj, n Old-fashioned Med* mongolien, -ienne

Mongolia [mɒŋ'gəʊlɪə] *n* Mongolie *f*

Mongolian [mɒŋ'gəʊlɪən] **1** *adj* mongol **2** *n* **(a)** Mongol, -ole **(b)** *Ling* mongol *m*

mongolism ['mɒŋgəlɪz(ə)m] *n Old-fashioned Med* mongolisme *m*

mongoloid ['mɒŋgəlɔɪd] *adj* (*features etc*) de mongolien

mongoose, *pl* **-ses** ['mɒŋguːs, -sɪz] *n* mangouste *f*

mongrel ['mʌŋgrəl] **1** *n* (*dog*) bâtard, -arde; (*other animal*) métis, -isse **2** *adj* (*dog*) bâtard; (*other animal, F Pej race*) métis, -isse

moni(c)ker ['mɒnɪkər] *n Sl* (*name*) nom *m*; (*nickname*) surnom *m*

monies ['mʌnɪz] *npl* **see money (b)**

monitor[1] ['mɒnɪtər] *n* **(a)** (*person*) surveillant, -ante, contrôleur, -euse; *Tel* opérateur *m* d'interception; *esp Br Old-fashioned Sch* = élève *mf* qui a une fonction de surveillant **(b)** (*device*), *Rad* appareil *m* de contrôle *ou* de surveillance, moniteur *m*; *TV* **m. (screen)** écran *m* de contrôle; **m. (speaker)** (*on stage*) = enceinte *f* qui permet aux musiciens de s'entendre jouer **(c)** *Comptr* moniteur *m*

monitor[2] *vt Rad, Med etc* (*broadcasts, patient's condition etc*) surveiller; *Tel* (*conversation*) écouter, être à l'écoute de; *Cin* (*sound recording*) contrôler; (*level of pollution*) examiner, surveiller, contrôler

monitoring ['mɒnɪtərɪŋ] *n* (*of broadcasts, phonecalls*) écoute *f*; (*of conversation*) surveillance *f*; (*of patient*) surveillance continue, monitorage *m*; *Rad* **m. station** station *f ou* centre *m* d'écoute

monk [mʌŋk] *n* moine *m*

monkey ['mʌŋkɪ] *n* **(a)** (*animal*) singe *m*; **female m., she-m.** guenon *f*; **m. house** pavillon *m* des singes; *Fig* **you little m.!** (*child*) petit(e) polisson(ne)!, petit(e) espiègle!; **little m. face** petite frimousse espiègle; *Sl* **to make a m. (out) of sb** se payer la tête de qn; *Sl* **I don't give a m.'s (fart)** je m'en fous complètement; *Am Sl* **to have a m. on one's back** être toxicomane; *Am* **m. bars** cage *f* à écureuil; *F* **m. business** (*dishonest behaviour*) magouilles *fpl*, combines *fpl*; (*mischief*) bêtises *fpl*; **m. jacket** spencer *m* (*de garçon de café etc*); *US Sl* **m. suit** smoking *m*; *Fig* F **m. tricks** espiègleries *fpl*

(b) *Constr etc* (*of pile-driver*) mouton *m*

(c) *Am Sl* (billet *m ou* fafiot *m* de) cinq cents dollars *mpl*

▶ **monkey about, monkey around** *vi F* (*fool around*) faire des bêtises, faire l'imbécile; **to m. about with sth** (*play with*) tripoter qch, jouer avec qch; **somebody's been monkeying about with the lock** quelqu'un a essayé de forcer la serrure; **to m. about with the brakes on sb's car** saboter les freins de la voiture de qn

monkey nut *n Br Culin* cacah(o)uète *f*

monkey puzzle tree *n Bot* désespoir *m* des singes, *Spec* araucaria *m*

monkey wrench *n Tech* clef *f* anglaise *ou* à crémaillière *ou* à griffes

monkfish ['mʌŋkfɪʃ] *n* lotte *f*, baudroie *f*

monkish ['mʌŋkɪʃ] *adj* de moine, monacal

monkshood ['mʌŋkshʊd] *n* (*plant*) (aconit *m*) napel *m*

mono ['mɒnəʊ] **1** *adj* mono *inv* **2** *n* **recorded in m.** enregistré en mono

monochrome ['mɒnəkrəʊm] **1** *adj Phot* monochrome; *Art* monochrome, en camaïeu; *Comptr* **m. monitor** moniteur *m* monochrome; **m. screen** écran *m* monochrome **2** *n Art* camaïeu *m*, (peinture *f*) monochrome *m*

monocle ['mɒnək(ə)l] *n* monocle *m*

monoclonal [mɒnəʊ'kləʊnəl] *adj Biol* **m. antibody** anticorps *m* monoclonal

monocoque ['mɒnəkɒk] *n Aut* monocoque *m*

monoculture ['mɒnəʊkʌltʃər] *n Agr* monoculture *f*

monogamous [mɒ'nɒgəməs] *adj* monogame

monogamy [mɒ'nɒgəmɪ] *n* monogamie *f*

monogram ['mɒnəgræm] *n* monogramme *m*

monogrammed ['mɒnəgræmd] *adj* (*handkerchief*) brodé à mes/ses/*etc* initiales

monograph ['mɒnəgræf] *n* monographie *f*

monolingual [mɒnəʊ'lɪŋgwəl] *adj* monolingue

monolith ['mɒnəlɪθ] *n* monolithe *m*

monolithic [mɒnə'lɪθɪk] *adj* **(a)** (*monument*) monolithe **(b)** *Pol etc* monolithique

monologue ['mɒnəlɒg] *n* monologue *m*

monomania [mɒnəʊ'meɪnɪə] *n* monomanie *f*

monometallism [mɒnjəʊ'metəlɪz(ə)m] *n Fin* monométallisme *m*

mononucleosis [mɒnəʊnjuːklɪ'əʊsɪs] *n Med* mononucléose *f*

monophonic [mɒnəʊ'fɒnɪk] *adj* monophonique

monoplane ['mɒnəʊpleɪn] *n Av* monoplan *m*

monopolist [mə'nɒpəlɪst] *n* monopoliste *mf*

monopolization [mənɒpəlaɪ'zeɪʃən] *n* monopolisation *f*

monopolize [mə'nɒpəlaɪz] *vt Com, Fig* monopoliser, accaparer

monopoly [mə'nɒpəlɪ] *n Com, Fig* monopole *m*; **to have a m. of sth** *or* **on sth** avoir *ou* détenir le monopole de qch, monopoliser qch; **no political party has a m. of morality** aucun parti politique ne détient le monopole de la moralité; **to form a m.** truster; **m. market** marché *m* monopolistique

monorail ['mɒnəʊreɪl] *n Rail etc* monorail *m*

monosodium glutamate [mɒnəʊ'səʊdɪəm 'gluːtəmeɪt] *n* glutamate *m* de sodium

monosyllabic [mɒnəʊsɪ'læbɪk] *adj* monosyllabe, monosyllabique; **he's rather m.** il ne s'exprime que par monosyllabes

monosyllable [mɒnəʊ'sɪləb(ə)l] *n* monosyllabe *m*; **he replied in monosyllables** il a répondu par monosyllabes

monotheism ['mɒnəʊθiːɪz(ə)m] *n* monothéisme *m*

monotheistic [mɒnəʊθiː'ɪstɪk] *adj* monothéiste

monotone ['mɒnətəʊn] **1** *adj* monotone **2** *n* (*in speaking*) débit *m* monotone; **to speak in a m.** parler d'une voix uniforme *ou* monotone

monotonous [mə'nɒtənəs] *adj* **(a)** (*job etc*) monotone **(b)** (*sound*) monotone, monocorde

monotonously [mə'nɒtənəslɪ] *adv* de *ou* d'une manière *ou* façon monotone

monotony [mə'nɒtənɪ] *n* monotonie *f*; **to relieve** *or* **break the m.** rompre la monotonie

Monotype® ['mɒnətaɪp] *n Typ* (*machine*) Monotype® *f*; *Art* monotype *m*

mono-unsaturated [mɒnəʊʌn'sætʃəreɪtɪd] *adj* (*fat*) mono-insaturé

monoxide [mɒ'nɒksaɪd] *n Ch* **carbon m.** oxyde *m* de carbone

Monsignor [mɒn'siːnjər] *n Cathol* monseigneur *m*

monsoon [mɒn'suːn] *n Met* mousson *f*; **the m. season** la mousson

monster ['mɒnstər] **1** *n* **(a)** monstre *m*; *Fig* **a m. of cruelty** un monstre de cruauté **(b)** (*large person*) colosse *m*, géant, -ante; **his last novel was a m.** son dernier roman est un pavé **2** *adj F* (*enormous*) monstre, colossal, énorme

monstrance ['mɒnstrəns] *n Rel* ostensoir *m*

monstrosity [mɒn'strɒsɪtɪ] *n* monstruosité *f*, horreur *f*

monstrous ['mɒnstrəs] *adj* **(a)** (*repugnant*) monstrueux; *Old-fashioned* **it is perfectly m. that …** c'est monstrueux que … + *sub* **(b)** (*enormous*) énorme, monstrueux

monstrously ['mɒnstrəslɪ] *adv* monstrueusement

mons veneris [mɒnz'venərɪs] *n* mont *m* de Vénus

Mont *abbr* **Montana**

montage [mɒn'tɑːʒ] *n Cin, Phot* montage *m*

Monte Carlo [mɒntɪ'kɑːləʊ] *n* Monte-Carlo

Montezuma [mɒntɪ'zu:mə] *n* Moctezuma *m*, Montezuma *m*; *F Hum* **M.'s revenge** turista *f*

month [mʌnθ] *n* [①A75,B,1,a; B58,B,1,a] mois *m*; **in the m. of August** au mois d'août; **in the summer/winter months** pendant les mois d'été/d'hiver; **a m. ago today** il y a aujourd'hui un mois; **a thirteen-m.-old baby, a thirteen months' old baby** un bébé de treize mois; **from m. to m.** de mois en mois; **once a m.** une fois par mois; *F* **never in a m. of Sundays** jamais de la vie; *F* **to see sb once in a m. of Sundays** voir qn une fois tous les trente-six du mois; *Euph* **it's that time of the m.** (*menstruation*) je suis/elle est indisposée

monthly ['mʌnθlɪ] **1** *adj* mensuel; *Com* **m. payment** *or* **instalment** mensualité *f*, mensualisation *f*, paiement *m* mensuel; *Physiol* **m. periods** règles *fpl*; *Rail etc* **m. season ticket** (billet *m* d')abonnement *m* mensuel **2** *adv* mensuellement, tous les mois; **it happens once or twice m.** ça arrive une ou deux fois par mois; **to make payments m.** mensualiser les paiements **3** *n* **(a)** (*publication*) revue *f ou* publication *f* mensuelle **(b)** *Old-fashioned F* **monthlies** (*menstruation*) règles *fpl*

Montreal [mɒntrɪ'ɔ:l] *n* Montréal

monument ['mɒnjʊmənt] *n* monument *m* **(to** à); **ancient monuments** monuments historiques

monumental [mɒnjʊ'ment(ə)l] *adj* **(a)** (*statue, literary work, error, stupidity etc*) monumental; (*ignorance*) prodigieux **(b) m. mason** marbrier *m*

monumentally [mɒnjʊ'mentəlɪ] *adv* (*important, stupid, conceited etc*) extrêmement

moo[1] [mu:] **1** *n* **(a)** (*of cow*) meuglement *m*, beuglement *m* **(b)** *F* **silly** *or* **stupid old m.**! vieille bique! **2** *int* **m.**! meuh!

moo[2] *vi* **(mooed)** (*of cow*) meugler, beugler

mooch [mu:tʃ] *vt Am F* (*cadge*) emprunter **(from sb** à qn); **he's always mooching cigarettes (from me)** il est toujours en train de (me) taper des cigarettes

▸ **mooch about, mooch around** *vi F* traîner, flemmarder

moocow ['mu:kaʊ] *n F* (*in children's language*) vache *f*, meumeu *f*

mood[1] [mu:d] *n* **(a)** [①A39,8; B30-32,G] (*in logic*), *Gram* mode *m* **(b)** *esp US Mus* mode *m*

mood[2] *n* (*state of mind*) humeur *f*, disposition *f*; **as the m. takes her** selon son humeur; **to be in a (bad) m.** être de mauvaise humeur; **to be in a good m.** être de bonne humeur; **to be in a generous m.** être en veine de générosité; **to be in the m. for reading** avoir envie de lire; **he's in no m. for jokes** il n'est pas d'humeur à rire; **I'm not in the m.** ça ne me dit rien; **I wasn't in the m. (for it)** je n'étais pas d'humeur à ça; **m. music** musique *f* d'ambiance

moodily ['mu:dɪlɪ] *adv* (*to look*) d'un air morose; (*to say*) d'un ton morose *ou* maussade, maussadement; (*to behave*) avec morosité

moodiness ['mu:dɪnɪs] *n* morosité *f*, maussaderie *f*

moody ['mu:dɪ] *adj* **(a)** (*sulky*) chagrin, morose, maussade **(b)** (*changeable*) d'humeur changeante, lunatique

moon[1] [mu:n] *n* lune *f*; **to land on the m.** alunir; *Fig* **to ask for the m.** demander la lune; **to promise sb the m.** promettre la lune à qn; *F Hum* **many moons ago** il y a bien longtemps; *F* **to be over the m.** être enchanté *ou* ravi **(about** de)

moon[2] *Sl* **1** *vi* (*bare one's buttocks*) montrer ses fesses **2** *vt* (*sb*) montrer ses fesses à

▸ **moon about, moon around** *vi* musarder, flâner

▸ **moon over** *vipo* (*person*) languir pour; (*photograph*) regarder amoureusement

moonbeam ['mu:nbi:m] *n* rayon *m* de lune

moon buggy *n* jeep *f* lunaire

moonfaced ['mu:nfeɪst] *adj* à la figure toute ronde

moon landing *n* alunissage *m*, atterrissage *m* sur la lune

moonless ['mu:nlɪs] *adj* (*night etc*) sans lune

moonlight[1] ['mu:nlaɪt] *n* clair *m* de lune; **in the m., by m.** au clair de lune, à la clarté *ou* la lumière de la lune; *Br F* **m. flit** déménagement *m* à la cloche de bois; *Br F* **to do a m. flit** déménager à la cloche de bois

moonlight[2] *vi F* (*work illegally*) faire du travail au noir, travailler au noir

moonlighter ['mu:nlaɪtər] *n F* (*illegal worker*) travailleur, -euse au noir

moonlighting ['mu:nlaɪtɪŋ] *n F* (*illegal work*) travail *m* (au) noir

moonlit ['mu:nlɪt] *adj* éclairé par la lune

moonrise ['mu:nraɪz] *n* lever *m* de (la) lune

moonshine ['mu:nʃaɪn] *n* **(a)** *Am F* (*illegal alcohol*) alcool *m* illicitement distillé **(b)** *F* (*nonsense*) balivernes *fpl*, fariboles *fpl* **(c)** (*moonlight*) clair *m* de lune

moonshot ['mu:nʃɒt] *n Astronaut* tir *m* lunaire

moonstone ['mu:nstəʊn] *n* (*gem*) adulaire *f*, feldspath *m* nacré, pierre *f* de lune

moonstruck ['mu:nstrʌk] *adj* dérangé, *F* toqué

moon walk *n* marche *f* sur la lune

moony ['mu:nɪ] *adj F* (*dreamy*) rêveur; **what are you looking so m. about?** pourquoi est-ce que tu as l'air si rêveur?

Moor [mʊər] *n* Maure *m*, Mauresque *f*, More *m*, Moresque *f*

moor[1] [mʊər] *n* lande *f*

moor[2] *Naut* **1** *vt* (*ship*) amarrer; (*buoy, mine*) mouiller **2** *vi* s'amarrer

moorcock ['mʊəkɒk] *n* (*bird*) lagopède *m* rouge d'Écosse

moorhen ['mʊəhen] *n* **(a)** (*water bird*) poule *f* d'eau **(b)** (*red grouse*) lagopède *m* rouge d'Écosse (femelle)

mooring ['mʊərɪŋ] *n Naut* **(a) m. buoy** (bouée *f* de) corps-mort *m*, *pl* corps-morts, coffre *m* d'amarrage; **m. line** câble *m* d'amarrage **(b)** (*place*) poste *m* d'amarrage; **ship at her moorings** navire sur ses amarres

Moorish ['mʊərɪʃ] *adj* maure, *f* mauresque, more, *f* moresque

moorland ['mʊələnd] *n* lande *f*

moose [mu:s] *pl* **moose**, *n* **(a) (American) m.** orignal *m*, élan *m* du Canada **(b)** (*in Europe*) élan *m*

moot[1] [mu:t] *adj* (*question etc*) sujet à controverse, discutable; **it is a m. point** c'est discutable

moot[2] *vt* (*always in passive*) *Fml* **to be mooted** (*of question*) être soulevé; (*of solution*) être suggéré

mop[1] [mɒp] *n* (*for floor*) balai *m* à franges; (*sponge mop*) balai-éponge *m*, *pl* balais-éponges; (*for dishes*) lavette *f* (à vaisselle); *Fig* **m. of hair** tignasse *f*

mop[2] *vt* (-pp-) **to m. the floor** passer un coup de serpillière, laver par terre; **to m. one's brow** s'éponger le front

▸ **mop up 1** *vtsep* **(a)** (*clean up*) (*water etc*) éponger; **to use a piece of bread to m. up the sauce** saucer son assiette avec un morceau de pain **(b)** *Mil etc* (*last remnants*) liquider **2** *vi* (*clean floor*) passer un coup de serpillière, laver par terre; *Mil etc* nettoyer, faire une opération de nettoyage

mope [məʊp] *vi* être triste *ou* mélancolique, broyer du noir

▸ **mope about, mope around** *vi* broyer du noir

moped ['məʊped] *n Br* mobylette® *f*, *F* mob *f*

moppet ['mɒpɪt] *n F* (*child*) gamin, -ine, gosse *mf*

mopping ['mɒpɪŋ] *n* (*of floor etc*) nettoyage *m*

mopping up *n* **(a)** = **mopping (b)** *Mil etc* **m. operations** opérations *fpl* de nettoyage

moquette [mɒ'ket] *n Tex* moquette *f*

MOR [eməʊ'ɑ:r] *adj esp Mus abbr* **middle-of-the-road**

moraine [mɒ'reɪn] *n Geol* moraine *f*

moral ['mɒrəl] **1** *adj* (*person, certainty, victory etc*) moral; **to give sb m. support** soutenir qn moralement; **young people today have no m. fibre** les jeunes d'aujourd'hui n'ont ni caractère ni moralité; **m. obligation** obligation *f* morale; **m. philosophy** morale *f*, éthique *f*; **m. standard** valeur *f* morale; **m. standards** sens *m* moral, valeurs morales; **m. tale** conte *m* moral; **m. values** valeurs morales

2 *n* **(a)** (*lesson*) (*of a story*) morale *f*, moralité *f*; **to draw the m. from a story** tirer la morale d'une histoire; **there's a m. to that story** cette histoire a une morale; **story with a m.** conte moral

(b) (*usu pl*) **morals** moralité *f*, principes *mpl* moraux; **man of loose morals** homme de mœurs relâchés

morale [mɒ'rɑ:l] *n* (*no pl*) moral *m*; **m. is very low/high** le moral est très bas *ou* mauvais/bon; **good for m.** bon pour le moral; **to undermine the m. of the army** saper le moral des troupes, démoraliser les troupes

moralist ['mɒrəlɪst] *n* moraliste *mf*

moralistic [mɒrə'lɪstɪk] *adj usu Pej* moraliste

morality [mə'rælɪtɪ] *n* **(a)** (*of person, decision, principles*) moralité *f*; **moralities** principes *mpl* moraux **(b)** *Th* **m. (play)** moralité *f*

moralize ['mɒrəlaɪz] *vi* moraliser

moralizing ['mɒrəlaɪzɪŋ] **1** *adj* moralisant, moralisateur, -trice **2** *n* **I'm tired of your incessant m.!** j'en ai assez que tu me fasses la morale!

morally ['mɒrəlɪ] *adv* moralement; **m. bound to do sth** moralement obligé de faire qch

Moral Majority *n US Pol* = ultra-conservateurs *mpl* aux États-Unis prônant un retour aux valeurs morales

morass [mə'ræs] *n* marais *m*; *Fig* (*of figures etc*) bourbier *m*

moratorium [mɒrə'tɔ:rɪəm] *n* moratoire *m*, moratorium *m* **(on** sur); **to hold a m. on sth** procéder à un moratoire sur qch

morbid ['mɔ:bɪd] *adj* **(a)** (*idea, curiosity etc*) morbide, malsain **(b)** *Med* (*anatomy*) pathologique; (*symptom*) morbide, pathologique

morbidity [mɔ:'bɪdɪtɪ] *n* morbidité *f*; **m. (rate)** morbidité *f*

morbidly ['mɔ:bɪdlɪ] *adv* d'une façon morbide *ou* malsaine

morbidness ['mɔ:bɪdnɪs] *n* (*of idea, curiosity etc*) caractère *m* morbide *ou* malsain, morbidité *f*

mordant ['mɔːd(ə)nt] *adj (wit)* mordant, caustique

more [mɔːr] **1** *adj (cars, people, water, time etc)* plus de, davantage de; **he has m. patience than I (have)** il a plus de patience que moi; **one m.** un de plus, encore un; **one or m.** un ou plusieurs; **one m. hour** une heure de plus, encore une heure; **there's only one m. problem to solve** il n'y a plus qu'un problème à résoudre; **(some) m. bread, please!** encore du pain, s'il vous plaît!; **is there any m. bread?** est-ce qu'il reste du pain?; **to have some m. wine** reprendre du vin; **have you (got) any m. books?** avez-vous d'autres livres?; **that's m. than enough** c'est plus qu'il n'en faut; **he is m. than 30** il a plus de 30 ans, il a 30 ans passés; **she's m. of an artist than her sister** elle est plus artiste que sa sœur; **I have no m. money** je n'ai plus d'argent; **no m. soup, thank you** plus de potage, merci

2 *n, indef pron* **do you want (any** *or* **some) m.?** en voulez-vous encore?, est-ce que vous en revoulez?; **what m. can I say?** que puis-je dire de plus?; **there is nothing m. to be said** il n'y a plus rien à dire, il n'y a rien à ajouter; **I need still m.** il m'en faut encore davantage; **I needn't say m.** pas besoin d'en dire davantage; **m. than that I can't say** je ne peux pas en dire plus; **he knows m. about it than you (do)** il en sait plus (long) que vous; **she doesn't know any m. about it** elle n'en sait pas davantage; **we should see m. of each other** nous devrions nous voir plus *ou* davantage; **the latest budget is just m. of the same** il n'y a rien de nouveau dans le dernier budget; **... and there's (plenty) m. where that came from** ... et ce n'est pas fini! **what is m.** (et) qui plus est, de plus; **neither m. nor less** ni plus ni moins; **I have no m.** je n'en ai plus; **I can do no m.** je ne peux pas faire plus; **let us say no m. about it** n'en parlons plus; *F* **say no m.!** cela suffit!, n'en dites pas plus!; **he's just a good friend, nothing m.** c'est un bon ami, rien de plus; **the m. you have the m. you want** plus on a, plus on en veut; **the m. I read, the m. I learn** plus je lis, plus j'apprends

3 *adv* **(a)** [①**A18**,4,a-b; **B10**,E,1; **B12**,F] *(to form comp)* plus; **m. interesting** plus intéressant; **he became m. and m. drunk** il est devenu de plus en plus ivre; **m. easily** plus facilement; **this is far m. serious** c'est bien *ou* beaucoup plus grave

(b) *(with verbs) (to eat, exercise etc)* plus, davantage; **this word is used m.** ce mot s'emploie plus *ou* davantage; **it's used m. than that one** il s'emploie plus que celui-là; **I would think m. of her if ...** j'aurais une plus haute opinion d'elle si ...; **(the) m.'s the pity** c'est d'autant plus malheureux *ou* plus regrettable; **he is no m. a lord than I am** il n'est pas plus lord que moi; **no m. can I (ni)** moi non plus; **I would no m. have suspected him than I would my own mother** je ne l'aurais pas soupçonné davantage que ma propre mère; **it's m. a question of luck** c'est plus une question de chance; **this m. than makes up for it** ça fait plus que compenser

(c) *(with adjectives etc)* plus; **he was m. surprised than annoyed** il était plus surpris que fâché; **m. than satisfied** plus que satisfait; **that's m. like it!** ça, c'est mieux!; **m. or less** plus ou moins; **I am all the m. surprised as ...** je suis d'autant plus étonné que ...; **this made things all the m. difficult** ça a rendu les choses d'autant plus difficiles; **it makes me all the m. proud** je n'en suis que plus fier

(d) *(in time)* **once m.** encore une fois, une fois de plus; **I can't see her any m.** je ne peux plus la voir; **he doesn't drink any m.** il ne boit plus; *Lit* **he is no m.** il n'est plus, il est mort

(e) (the) m. fool you! que tu es bête!; **all the m. reason for going/telling her** raison de plus pour y aller/le lui dire

moreish ['mɔːrɪʃ] *adj F* **this cake is very m.** ce gâteau a un petit goût de revenez-y

morel [mɒ'rel] *n (fungus)* morille *f*

morello [mə'reləʊ] *n* **m. (cherry)** griotte *f*

moreover [mɔː'rəʊvər] *adv* de plus, et qui plus est

mores ['mɔːreɪz] *npl Fml* mœurs *fpl*

morganatic [mɔːgə'nætɪk] *adj* **m. marriage** mariage *m* morganatique

morgue [mɔːg] *n* **(a)** morgue *f*; **it's like a m. here** c'est complètement mort ici **(b)** *Journ Sl* archives *fpl*

MORI ['mɔːrɪ] *n (abbr* **Market and Opinion Research Institute)** = institut *m* de sondage, ≈ IPSOS *m*

moribund ['mɒrɪbʌnd] *adj Fml* moribond

morish ['mɔːrɪʃ] *adj F* = **moreish**

Mormon ['mɔːmən] *adj, n Rel* mormon, -one

morn [mɔːn] *n Lit* matin *m*

morning ['mɔːnɪŋ] *n* [①**B58**,B,3] matin *m*; *(whole period)* matinée *f*; **to work from m. till night, to work m., noon and night** travailler du matin au soir; **this m.** ce matin; **tomorrow m.** demain matin; **the next m., the m. after** le lendemain matin; **the m. before** la veille au matin; *F* **the m. after (the night before)** *(after drinking bout)* un lendemain de cuite; **you look a bit the m. after the night before** tu as fait la fête hier soir?; **I had that m. after feeling** j'avais la gueule de bois; **four o'clock in the m.** quatre heures du matin; **early in the m.** de bon *ou* grand matin; **on Wednesday m.** mercredi matin; **on the m. of Sunday 1st April** le dimanche 1er avril au matin; *F* **to be a m. person** être du matin; **good m.!** *F* **m.!** bonjour!; **in the course of the m.** dans la matinée; **a m.'s work** une matinée de travail; **m. coffee** café *m* (servi le matin); **m. off** matinée *f* de congé; **m. paper** journal *m* du matin

morning-after pill *n* pilule *f* du lendemain

morning coat *n* queue-de-pied *m*

morning dress *n* habit *m*

morning-glory *n (plant)* belle-de-jour *f*, liseron *m*

morning room *n* = petit salon *m*

morning sickness *n Med* nausées *fpl* matinales

morning star *n Astron* étoile *f* du berger

Moroccan [mə'rɒkən] **1** *adj* marocain **2** *n* Marocain, -aine

Morocco [mə'rɒkəʊ] *n* Maroc *m*

morocco [mə'rɒkəʊ] *n (leather)* maroquin *m*; **m. -bound** relié en maroquin

moron ['mɔːrɒn] *n* **(a)** *F (idiot)* idiot, -ote, crétin, -ine **(b)** *Med* faible *mf* d'esprit

moronic [mə'rɒnɪk] *adj F (stupid)* idiot, crétin

morose [mə'rəʊs] *adj (person, disposition)* chagrin, morose

morosely [mə'rəʊslɪ] *adv* d'un air chagrin *ou* morose

moroseness [mə'rəʊsnɪs] *n* morosité *f*, humeur *f* chagrine *ou* morose

morpheme ['mɔːfiːm] *n Ling* morphème *m*

Morpheus ['mɔːfɪəs] *n Myth* Morphée *m*; *Hum* **in the arms of M.** dans les bras de Morphée

morphine ['mɔːfiːn], **morphia** ['mɔːfɪə] *n* morphine *f*; **m. addict** morphinomane *mf*; **m. addiction** morphinomanie *f*

morphological [mɔːfə'lɒdʒɪk(ə)l] *adj* morphologique

morphology [mɔː'fɒlədʒɪ] *n* morphologie *f*

morris dance ['mɒrɪs] *n* danse *f* folklorique anglaise

morrow ['mɒrəʊ] *n Arch, Lit (next day)* lendemain *m*; **on the m.** le lendemain

Morse [mɔːs] *n Telecom* **M. (alphabet/code)** (alphabet *m*/code *m*) morse *m*

morsel ['mɔːs(ə)l] *n* (petit) morceau *m*; **choice** *or* **dainty m.** morceau de choix

mortadella [mɔːtə'delə] *n* **m. (sausage)** mortadelle *f*

mortal ['mɔːt(ə)l] **1** *adj* **(a)** mortel; **all men are m.** tous les hommes sont mortels; **m. remains** dépouille *f* mortelle **(b)** *(fatal)* mortel, fatal, -als **(to** à); **m. blow** coup *m* mortel; **m. sin** péché *m* mortel **(c)** *(until death)* **m. enemy** ennemi *m* mortel; **m. combat** combat *m* à mort **(d)** *(very great)* **to be in m. fear of sth** avoir très peur de qch, craindre qch par-dessus tout **(e)** *F (conceivable)* **it's no m. use** ça ne sert absolument à rien **2** *n* mortel, -elle; **ordinary mortals like us** des gens comme nous

mortality [mɔː'tælɪtɪ] *n* **(a)** *(of person etc)* condition *f* mortelle **(b)** *(death rate)* mortalité *f*

mortally ['mɔːt(ə)lɪ] *adv* mortellement; **m. wounded** blessé à mort; **to be m. afraid (of sb)** être mort de peur (devant qn); **they are m. afraid that ...** ils craignent par-dessus tout que ...; **m. offended** très offusqué

mortar[1] ['mɔːtər] *n* **(a)** *Constr* mortier *m* **(b)** *Pharm, Culin etc* mortier *m*; **m. and pestle** pilon *m* et mortier **(c)** *Mil* mortier *m*; **m. attack** attaque *f* au mortier; **m. shell** obus *m* de mortier

mortar[2] *vt Constr (stones)* cimenter avec du mortier

mortarboard ['mɔːtəbɔːd] *n Univ* = coiffure *f* traditionnelle portée par les universitaires en Angleterre et dans d'autres pays anglo-saxons

mortgage[1] ['mɔːgɪdʒ] *n Fin (for house purchase)* crédit *m* immobilier; *(raised on property)* hypothèque *f*; **to raise a m.** prendre un crédit immobilier/une hypothèque; **to buy a house on a m.** prendre un crédit immobilier *ou* emprunt-logement pour acheter une maison; **m. deed** acte *m* hypothécaire; **m. loan** emprunt *m* hypothécaire; **m. rate** taux *m* d'emprunt hypothécaire; **m. (re)payments** remboursements *mpl* d'un emprunt-logement

mortgage[2] *vt Fin (land, house etc)* hypothéquer; *(title deeds)* engager, mettre en gage; *F* **we're mortgaged up to the eyeballs** *or* **up to the hilt** on a des crédits jusqu'au cou; *Fig* **to m. one's future** hypothéquer l'avenir

mortgagee [mɔːgɪ'dʒiː] *n* créancier, -ière hypothécaire

mortgager, mortgagor ['mɔːgɪdʒər] *n* débiteur, -trice hypothécaire

mortice ['mɔːtɪs] *n, vt* = **mortise**

mortician [mɔː'tɪʃən] *n US* entrepreneur *m* de pompes funèbres

mortification [mɔːtɪfɪ'keɪʃən] *n* **(a)** *(humiliation)* humiliation *f, Lit* mortification *f*; **to my (eternal) m.** à ma (grande) honte **(b)** *Rel (of the flesh)* mortification *f* **(c)** *Med* nécrose *f*

mortify ['mɔːtɪfaɪ] **1** *vt* **(a)** *(humiliate)* humilier, *Lit* mortifier; *F* **I was mortified** j'étais mort de honte **(b)** *Rel (the flesh)* mortifier **2** *vi Med* se gangrener, se nécroser

mortifying ['mɔːtɪfaɪɪŋ] *adj (experience etc)* humiliant, *Lit* mortifiant

mortise¹ ['mɔːtɪs] *n Carp* mortaise *f*; **m. lock** serrure *f* encastrée

mortise² *vt Carp (cut mortise in)* mortaiser; **to m. two beams (together)** emmortaiser *ou* emboîter deux poutres

mortuary ['mɔːtjʊərɪ] **1** *n* morgue *f* **2** *adj* mortuaire

Mosaic [məʊ'zeɪɪk] *adj Bible (law etc)* mosaïque, de Moïse

mosaic [məʊ'zeɪɪk] *n Art etc* mosaïque *f*; **m. floor** dallage *m* en mosaïque

Moscow ['mɒskəʊ] *n* Moscou

Moses ['məʊzɪz] **1** *n Bible* Moïse *m*; **M. basket** moïse *m* **2** *int Old-fashioned F* **Holy M.!** grand Dieu!

▶ **mosey along** ['məʊzɪ] *vi esp Am F* flâner, se promener sans se presser; **I'll just m. along to the bar** je vais faire un tour au bar; **I'll be moseying along now** *(leaving)* je vais y aller

Moslem ['mɒzləm] *adj, n* musulman, -ane

mosque [mɒsk] *n* mosquée *f*

mosquito, *pl* **-oes** [məs'kiːtəʊ, -əʊz] *n* moustique *m*; **m. bite** piqûre *f* de moustique; **m. net** moustiquaire *f*; **m. repellent** produit *m* antimoustique

moss [mɒs] *n* **(a)** *Bot* mousse *f*; **m. rose** rose *f* moussue, *F* rose mousseuse **(b)** *Miner* **m. agate** agate *f* mousseuse **(c)** *Knitting* **m. stitch** point *m* de riz

mossy ['mɒsɪ] *adj* moussu

most [məʊst] *(superl of* **many, much***)* **1** *adj (cows, milk etc)* le plus de; **you have made (the) m. mistakes** c'est vous qui avez fait le plus de fautes; **m. women** la plupart des femmes; **in m. cases** dans la majorité *ou* la plupart des cas; **for the m. part** *(in greatest number of cases)* pour la plupart; *(most often)* le plus souvent *ou* la plupart du temps

2 *n, indef pron* **(a)** *(greatest amount)* **the m.** le plus, le maximum; **do the m. you can** faites le plus que vous pourrez; **at the (very) m.** au (grand) maximum, (tout) au plus; **to make the m. of a situation** tirer le meilleur parti d'une situation; **to make the m. of one's talents** tirer le meilleur parti de ses capacités; **she made the m. of her time in Mexico** elle a profité au maximum du temps qu'elle a passé au Mexique; **the opposition made the m. of the scandal** l'opposition a tiré tout ce qu'elle pouvait du scandale; **make the m. of it** profitez-en au maximum

(b) *(majority)* **m. of the women/cars** la plupart *ou* la majorité des femmes/des voitures; **m. of the work** la plus grande *ou* la majeure partie du travail; **m. of the time** la plupart du temps; **he is more reliable than m.** on peut compter sur lui plus que sur bien des gens

3 *adv* **(a)** [①**A18-19**,a-f; **B10-11**,E,2] *(to form superl)* le plus; **the m. beautiful woman** la plus belle femme; **they bought the m. expensive (ones)** ils ont acheté les plus chers/chères; **those who have answered m. accurately** ceux qui ont répondu le plus exactement

(b) [①**A19**,f] *(very)* très, bien; **m. unhappy** bien malheureux; **m. likely** *or* **probably** très probablement; **he has been m. rude** il a été on ne peut plus impoli

(c) *(to drink, talk etc)* le plus; **what I want m.** ce que je désire par-dessus tout; **that's what worries me (the) m.** c'est ce qui m'inquiète le plus

mostly ['məʊstlɪ] *adv* **(a)** *(in the main)* surtout, principalement; **they come m. from Scotland** ils viennent surtout d'Écosse; **a m. young audience** un public composé pour une large part de jeunes, un public composé en majorité de jeunes; **they're m. working-class** ils sont issus de la classe ouvrière pour la plupart **(b)** *(most often)* le plus souvent, la plupart du temps

MOT [eməʊ'tiː] *n Br Admin* **(a)** *abbr* **Ministry of Transport (b)** *Aut (test)* = contrôle *m* technique **(c)** *Aut (certificate)* = certificat *m* de contrôle technique; **6 months' MOT** *(in advertisement)* = certificat *m* de contrôle technique valable pendant six mois

mote [məʊt] *n Lit* grain *m* de poussière; *Bible* **the m. in thy brother's eye** la paille dans l'œil du voisin

motel [məʊ'tel] *n* motel *m*

motet [məʊ'tet] *n Mus* motet *m*

moth [mɒθ] *n (insect)* papillon *m* nocturne *ou* de nuit; **(clothes) m.** mite *f*; *F* **the moths have been at my fur coat** mon manteau de fourrure est tout mangé par les mites

mothball¹ ['mɒθbɔːl] *n* boule *f* de naphtaline; *Fig* **to put a project in mothballs** remettre un projet à plus tard; **to take a project out of mothballs** déterrer un projet; *Fig* **to put a ship in mothballs** retirer un navire du service actif et le couvrir de bâches

mothball² *vt Fig (ship)* retirer du service actif et couvrir de bâches; *(plan)* remettre à plus tard; *(piece of equipment)* entretenir en vue d'une utilisation future

moth-eaten *adj* **(a)** mangé des *ou* par les mites, mité **(b)** *F (in poor condition)* miteux, misérable; *(hotel)* miteux

mother¹ ['mʌðər] *n* **(a)** mère *f*; *Admin, Jur* mère de famille; **yes, m.!** oui, maman!; **m. -to-be** future maman *f*; **m. of six** mère de six enfants; *Br F* **shall I be m.?** *(pour out tea)* je fais le service?; *Fig F* **I've got the m. and father of all headaches** j'ai un mal de tête épouvantable; *Fig F* **we had the m. and father of a row** nous avons eu une de ces empoignades!; **every m.'s son was there!** tout le monde était là, il ne manquait personne; *Rel* **reverend m.** (sœur *f*) supérieure *f*; *(form of address)* ma mère; **m.'s boy** garçon *m* à sa maman; **m.'s little helper** *(helpful child)* enfant qui aide sa mère dans les tâches ménagères; *Fig Hum* = alcool *m* ou médicament *m* consommé pour oublier ses soucis; *Fig Hum* **m.'s ruin** *(gin)* gin *m*; **m. church** église *f* mère; **m. country** mère-patrie *f, pl* mères-patries; *(of colony)* métropole *f*; **m. hen** mère *f* poule; *Geol etc* **m. rock** roche *f* mère; **m. ship** ravitailleur *m*; **m. wit** bon sens *m* inné

(b) *US Vulg* salaud *m*, fumier *m*, ordure *f*

mother² *vt* materner, dorloter

motherboard ['mʌðəbɔːd] *n Comptr* carte *f* mère

motherfucker ['mʌðəfʌkər] *n US Vulg* salaud *m*, fumier *m*, ordure *f*

motherfucking ['mʌðəfʌkɪŋ] *adj attrib US Vulg* putain de

motherhood ['mʌðəhʊd] *n* maternité *f*

mothering ['mʌðərɪŋ] *n* soins *mpl* maternels; **m. skills** capacité *f* à s'occuper d'un petit

Mothering Sunday *n Br* fête *f* des Mères

mother-in-law, *pl* **mothers-in-law** *n* belle-mère *f, pl* belles-mères; *F* **m.'s tongue** *(plant)* sansevière *f*

motherland ['mʌðəlænd] *n* patrie *f*, pays *m* natal

motherless ['mʌðəlɪs] *adj* sans mère, orphelin (de mère)

motherly ['mʌðəlɪ] *adj* maternel, de mère

Mother Nature *n* la Nature

mother-of-pearl *n* nacre *f*; **m. decoration** décoration *f* en nacre

mother of vinegar *n Ch* mère *f* de vinaigre

Mother's Day ['mʌðəz] *n* fête *f* des Mères

Mother Superior *n Rel* Mère *f* supérieure

mother tongue *n Ling* langue *f* maternelle

moth-hole *n* trou *m* de mite

mothproof¹ ['mɒθpruːf] *adj* traité à l'antimite

mothproof² *vt* traiter à l'antimite

motif [məʊ'tiːf] *n Art, Mus etc* motif *m*

motion¹ ['məʊʃən] *n* **(a)** *Phys etc* mouvement *m*; *(of vehicle, apparatus)* marche *f*, mouvement; *Phys* **body in m.** corps *m* en mouvement; **car in m.** voiture en marche; **to put** *or* **set a machine in m.** mettre une machine en marche; *Fig* **to put** *or* **set a process in m.** mettre un processus en branle; *Fig* **I'll set things** *or* **the wheels in m.** je vais mettre les choses en route; *esp Am Cin* **m. picture** film *m*; *MecE* **m. study** analyse *f* du mouvement, chronophotographie *f*

(b) *(of arm etc)* mouvement *m*; *(sign)* geste *m*; **to go through the motions** agir machinalement; **he's just going through the motions** il fait juste semblant; **you could at least go through the motions** tu devrais au moins le faire pour la forme

(c) *(in meeting, debate)* motion *f*, proposition *f*; **to propose a m.** faire une proposition; **to put the m.** mettre la motion *ou* la proposition aux voix; **the m. was carried** la motion fut adoptée

(d) *Jur (application)* demande *f*, requête *f*

(e) *Br (bowel evacuation)* évacuation *f*; **motion(s)** *(faeces)* selles *fpl*

motion² **1** *vt* **to m. sb to do sth** faire signe à qn de faire qch; **to m. sb away/in** faire signe à qn de s'éloigner/d'entrer **2** *vi* **to m. to sb to do sth** faire signe à qn de faire qch

motionless ['məʊʃənlɪs] *adj* immobile; **to remain m.** ne pas bouger, rester immobile

motivate ['məʊtɪveɪt] *vt (decision, employees)* motiver; **to m. sb to do sth** pousser *ou* inciter qn à faire qch; **they were motivated by a desire to help others** ils étaient poussés par un désir d'aider les autres

motivated ['məʊtɪveɪtɪd] *adj* motivé; **to be highly m.** être très motivé

motivation [məʊtɪ'veɪʃən] *n* motivation *f*; **he lacked the m. to succeed** il n'était pas assez motivé pour réussir; *Mktg* **m. research** recherche *f* sur la motivation

motivator ['məʊtɪveɪtər] *n* **he's a good m.** il sait motiver les gens

motive ['məʊtɪv] **1** *n* **(a)** (*reason*) motif *m*, raison *f*; (*for a crime*) mobile *m*; **interest is a powerful m.** l'intérêt est un puissant ressort; **I wonder what his m. is** je me demande pourquoi *ou* pour quelle raison il fait cela; **I don't understand what her m. is for refusing to …** je ne comprends pas pourquoi *ou* pour quelle raison elle refuse de … **(b)** *Art* (*of painting etc*) motif *m* **2** *adj* moteur, -trice

motive power *n* force *f* motrice

motley ['mɒtlɪ] **1** *adj* **(a)** (*diverse*) varié, hétéroclite; **m. crew** *or* **crowd** bande *f ou* mélange *m* hétéroclite **(b)** (*of different colours*) bariolé, bigarré **2** *n* **(a)** (*mixture*) mélange *m* hétéroclite **(b)** *Hist* (*jester's costume*) costume *m* de bouffon de cour

motocross ['məʊtəʊkrɒs] *n Sp* moto-cross *m*

motor[1] ['məʊtər] **1** *n* **(a)** (*engine*) moteur *m*; *Rail* **(electric) m. carriage** (voiture *f*) motrice *f*; **m. manufacturer** constructeur *m* automobile; **m. mechanic** mécanicien *m* garagiste; **m. scooter** scooter *m*; **m. show** salon *m* de l'auto(mobile); **m. vehicle** voiture *f* automobile; *Naut* **m. vessel** bateau *m* à moteur **(b)** *Br* (*car*) auto(mobile) *f*, voiture *f*; **m. industry** industrie *f* automobile; **m. insurance** assurance *f* automobile; **the m. trade** l'automobile *f* **2** *adj Anat* (*muscle, nerve*) moteur, -trice; *Med* **m. paralysis** paralysie *f* des centres moteurs; *MecE* **m. torque** couple *m* moteur

motor[2] *vi* voyager en auto *ou* en voiture; **we motored across France** nous avons traversé la France en voiture

motorail ['məʊtəreɪl] *n Rail* **m. (service)** train(s) *m(pl)* auto-couchettes

motor-assisted ['məʊtərə'sɪstɪd] *adj* **m. bicycle** cyclomoteur *m*

motorbike ['məʊtəbaɪk] *n* moto *f*

motorboat ['məʊtəbəʊt] *n* canot *m* à moteur; (*fast*) vedette *f*

motorcade ['məʊtəkeɪd] *n* cortège *m* de voitures

motorcar ['məʊtəkɑːr] *n Br* automobile *f*, voiture *f*

motor caravan *n* camping-car *m*, *pl* camping-cars

motorcycle ['məʊtəsaɪk(ə)l] *n* motocyclette *f*, moto *f*; **m. accident** accident *m* de moto; **m. combination** moto et sidecar; **m. courier** coursier *m*, porteur *m*; **m. gang** bande *f* de motards; **m. policeman** agent *m* motocycliste, motard; **m. rider** motocycliste *mf*, motard; **m. wheel** roue *f* de moto

motorcycling ['məʊtəsaɪklɪŋ] *n* motocyclisme *m*

motorcyclist ['məʊtəsaɪklɪst] *n* motocycliste *mf*

motor-driven *adj* à moteur; (*device*) actionné *ou* commandé par un moteur

motor engineer *n* ingénieur *m* en automobile, motoriste *m*

motor fuel *n* carburant *m*

motor-home *n Am* auto-caravane *f*, *pl* auto-caravanes, camping-car *m*, *pl* camping-cars

motoring ['məʊtərɪŋ] *n* conduite *f* (automobile); **school of m.** auto-école *f*, *pl* auto-écoles; **m. correspondent** chroniqueur *m* automobile; **m. holiday** virée *f* en voiture; **m. offence** infraction *f* au code de la route; **m. organization** association *f* d'automobilistes

motorist ['məʊtərɪst] *n* automobiliste *mf*

motorization [məʊtəraɪ'zeɪʃən] *n* motorisation *f*

motorize ['məʊtəraɪz] *vt* motoriser; **motorized** motorisé; **motorized bicycle** vélomoteur *m*

motor launch *n* vedette *f*

motor lodge *n* motel *m*

motorman, *pl* **-men** ['məʊtəmæn, -men] *n US* (*on tram*) wattman *m*; (*on subway*) conducteur *m*

motor neurone disease *n Med* maladie *f* de Charcot, sclérose *f* latérale amyotrophique

motor race *n* course *f* automobile

motor racing *n* course *f* automobile

motor rally *n* rallye *m* automobile

motor sport *n* sport *m* automobile

motorway ['məʊtəweɪ] *n Br* autoroute *f*; **m. accident** accident *m* sur autoroute; **m. driving** conduite *f* sur autoroute; **m. exit** sortie *f* d'autoroute; **m. madness** conduite dangereuse sur autoroute; **m. network** réseau *m* autoroutier; **m. police** police *f* de l'autoroute; **m. restaurant** restoroute *m*; **m. services** services *mpl* autoroutiers

Motown ['məʊtaʊn] *n* **(a)** *US F* = surnom *m* de la ville de Détroit **(b)** *Mus* style *m* Motown

mottled ['mɒt(ə)ld] *adj* (*fabric*) tacheté, moucheté; (*skin*) marbré; (*wood*) madré

motto, *pl* **-oes** ['mɒtəʊ, -əʊz] *n* **(a)** devise *f*; **that's my m.** voilà ma devise **(b)** *Her* devise *f* **(c)** *Typ* épigraphe *f* **(d)** *Mus* motif *m* **(e)** *Br* (*in Christmas cracker*) (*riddle*) devinette *f*; (*funny saying*) phrase *f* amusante

mould[1], *US* **mold** [məʊld] *n* (*fungus*) moisi *m*, moisissure *f*

mould[2], *US* **mold** *n* **(a)** *Art, Cer etc* moule *m*; *Typ* (*of character*) matrice *f*; *Culin* **(jelly) m.** moule *m* à gelée; *Lit* **to be cast in a heroic m.** être de la trempe des héros; **he is cast in his father's m.** il est fait dans le même moule que son père; **people cast in the same m.** des gens sortis du même moule; **a star in the John Wayne m.** une star du style John Wayne; *Fig* **to break the m.** rompre avec la tradition **(b)** (*template*), *Constr etc* calibre *m*, profil *m*; *Naut, Av* gabarit *m* **(c)** *Culin* **rice m.** gâteau *m* de riz **(d)** *Archit* moulure *f*

mould[3], *US* **mold** *vt* **(a)** (*make from a mould*) mouler; **the bucket is moulded in plastic** le seau est moulé dans du plastique **(b)** (*shape*) mouler; (*person's character*) façonner, former; **to m. clay/etc into sth** façonner l'argile/*etc* pour en faire qch; *Fig* **she moulded them into a team** elle a fait d'eux une équipe; *Fig* **public opinion has been moulded by the media** l'opinion publique a été façonnée par les médias **(c)** (*adhere closely to*) **the dress moulded her figure** la robe moulait ses formes

mould[4], *US* **mold** *n* (*earth*) terre *f* meuble; **vegetable m.** terreau *m*, humus *m*

moulded, *US* **molded** ['məʊldɪd] *adj* (*plastic*) moulé

moulder, *US* **molder** ['məʊldər] *vi* (*of wood*) tomber en poussière, s'effriter; (*of food*) moisir; (*of building etc*) se désagréger; *Fig* (*of person*) moisir

▶ **moulder away**, *US* **molder away** *vi* = **moulder**

moulding, *US* **molding** ['məʊldɪŋ] *n* **(a)** *Metal etc* moulage *m* **(b)** *Fig* (*of character, public opinion*) formation *f*, façonnement *m* **(c)** *Archit* (*ornament*) moulure *f*; (*edging strip*) baguette *f*; **drip** *or* **weather m.** (*on window, door*) jet *m* d'eau; (*on wall*) larmier *m*; **plain m.** listeau *m*, listel *m*; **grooved m.** moulure *f* à gorge

mouldy, *US* **moldy** ['məʊldɪ] *adj* moisi; **to smell m.** sentir le moisi

moult[1], *US* **molt** [məʊlt] *n* mue *f*

moult[2], *US* **molt** *vi* (*of cat, dog*) perdre ses poils; (*of bird, reptile*) muer; **I must be moulting!** je perds mes poils!

moulting, *US* **molting** ['məʊltɪŋ] **1** *adj* en mue **2** *n* mue *f*

mound [maʊnd] *n* (*artificial*) tertre *m*, monticule *m*, butte *f*; *Constr etc* remblai *m*; (*of stones etc*) monceau *m*, tas *m*; (*natural*) monticule

mount[1] [maʊnt] *n* **(a)** (*mountain*) mont *m*; **M. Sinai** le mont Sinaï **(b)** (*in palmistry*) mont *m*

mount[2] *n* **(a)** (*support*), *Tech* montage *m*, support *m*; *Mil etc* affût *m*, trépied *m*; (*of lens, prism*) monture *f* **(b)** *Art etc* (*of painting etc*) carton *m* de montage **(c)** (*horse*) cheval *m*, monture *f*; *Horseracing* (*ride*) monte *f*

mount[3] **1** *vt* **(a)** (*climb onto*) (*bicycle, horse*) monter sur, enfourcher; **to m. the scaffold** monter sur l'échafaud; **to m. the throne** monter sur le trône; **to m. the pavement** (*of car etc*) monter sur le trottoir

(b) (*mate with*) couvrir, monter

(c) (*climb*) (*stairs, hill*) monter, gravir; (*ladder*) monter à

(d) (*set on*) **to m. sb (on a horse)** hisser qn sur un cheval; **to m. a squadron of cavalry** monter un escadron de cavalerie; **they were mounted on grey horses** ils chevauchaient des chevaux gris

(e) *Tech* installer; (*precious stone*) monter, sertir; *Art, Phot* (*painting, photograph*) monter; *Mil etc* (*cannon*) mettre sur (son) affût; (*machine, engine etc*) monter, installer

(f) (*prepare*) **to m. a play/an exhibition** monter une pièce/une exposition; *Mil* **to m. an offensive** lancer une offensive; *Mil* **to m. guard** monter la garde

2 *vi* **(a)** *Horseriding* se mettre en selle

(b) (*rise, climb*) monter; **the blood mounted to his head** le sang lui est monté à la tête; **the cost was mounting** le coût augmentait

▶ **mount up** *vi* monter, augmenter; **the bill was mounting up** la facture augmentait; **her savings soon mounted up** ses économies augmentèrent rapidement; **it all mounts up** ça finit par chiffrer

mountain ['maʊntɪn] *n* montagne *f*; **range of mountains, m. range** chaîne *f* de montagnes; **to spend one's holidays in the mountains** passer ses vacances à la montagne; *Fig* **a m. of work** un travail monstre; *Fig* **a m. of evidence** des quantités de preuves; *Fig* **mountains of essays to mark** des tas de rédactions à corriger; **butter/beef m.** (*surplus*) montagne de beurre/bœuf; *Fig* **to make a m. out of a molehill** faire une montagne d'un rien; **m. ash** (*tree*) sorbier *m* commun *ou* sauvage; **m. bike** vélo *m* tout-terrain, VTT *m*; **m. biking** vélo *m* tout-terrain, VTT *m*, randonnée *f* en VTT; *Geog* **m. chain** chaîne *f* de montagnes; **m. climbing** alpinisme *m*; **m. lion** puma *m*, couguar *m*; **m. pass** col *m*; **m. pine** pin *m* de montagne; **m. rescue** secours *mpl* en montagne; **m. rescue service** service *m* de secours en montagne; **m. resort** station *f* de montagne, station montagnarde; **m. scenery/stream** paysage *m*/ruisseau *m* de montagne; **m. sickness** mal *m* des montagnes; **m. side/top** flanc *m ou* versant *m*/sommet *m* de montagne; **m. tribe** tribu *f* montagnarde; *Mil* **m. troops** chasseurs *mpl* alpins

mountaineer[1] [maʊntɪ'nɪər] *n* alpiniste *mf*
mountaineer[2] *vi* faire de l'alpinisme
mountaineering [maʊntɪ'nɪərɪŋ] *n* alpinisme *m*
mountainous ['maʊntɪnəs] *adj* (*country etc*) montagneux; *Fig* **m. seas** vagues gigantesques
Mountain Standard Time *n Am* heure *f* normale des Montagnes Rocheuses
mountebank ['maʊntɪbæŋk] *n Lit* charlatan *m*
mounted ['maʊntɪd] *adj* **the m. police** la police montée; **m. policeman** policier *m* à cheval
Mountie ['maʊntɪ] *n F* = membre *m* de la Gendarmerie Royale du Canada
mounting ['maʊntɪŋ] **1** *n* (*support*), *Tech* support *m*; *MecE* (*of machine, engine*) bâti *m*, socle *m*; (*of rifle etc*) monture *f*, garniture *f*; (*of precious stone*) monture, sertissage *m*; *Mil* (*of machine gun*) affût *m*, trépied *m*; *MecE* **engine mountings** pièces *fpl* d'assemblage de moteur; **m. bracket** support de montage; **m. point** (*for seatbelt*) point *m* d'ancrage **2** *adj* **m. costs/death toll** coût/nombre des morts en augmentation; **there is m. evidence against her** il y a de plus en plus de preuves contre elle
mounting-block *n Horseriding* montoir *m*
mourn [mɔːn] **1** *vt* (*sb, sth, sb's death*) pleurer; **there's no point mourning what might have been** cela ne sert à rien de se lamenter sur ce qui aurait pu se passer **2** *vi* être en deuil
▶ **mourn for** *vipo* **to m. for sb** pleurer (la mort de) qn; **to m. for sth** pleurer qch, déplorer qch
▶ **mourn over** *vipo* = **mourn for**
mourner ['mɔːnər] *n* **(a)** (*at funeral*) personne *f* qui suit le cortège funèbre; **the mourners** le convoi, le cortège funèbre **(b)** (*person grieving*) personne *f* endeuillée, personne qui porte le deuil
mournful ['mɔːnfʊl] *adj* triste, mélancolique
mournfully ['mɔːnfʊlɪ] *adv* tristement
mourning ['mɔːnɪŋ] *n* deuil *m*; (*clothing*) (vêtements *mpl ou* habits *mpl* de) deuil; **to be in m.** être en deuil; **to wear m.** porter le deuil; **to go into m.** se mettre en deuil, prendre le deuil; **house of m.** maison *f* endeuillée
mouse[1], *pl* **mice** [maʊs, maɪs] *n* **(a)** (*animal*) souris *f*; **young m.** souriceau *m*; **m. grey, m. colour(ed)** gris *m* souris; **m. hole** trou *m* de souris **(b)** *F* (*timid person*) timide *mf*; **are you a man or a m.?** t'es un homme ou quoi? **(c)** *Comptr* souris *f*; **m. button** bouton *m* de souris; **m. driver** programme *m* de commande de la souris; **m. keys** touches *fpl* souris; **m. mat** tapis *m* de souris
mouse[2] [maʊz] *vi* (*of cat etc*) chasser les souris
mouser ['maʊzər] *n* (*cat etc*) souricier *m*; **she's a good m.** elle attrape bien les souris
mousetrap ['maʊstræp] *n* souricière *f*, tapette *f*; *F* **m. (cheese)** fromage *m* ordinaire, *Can* fromage à souris
moussaka [mʊ'sɑːkə] *n* moussaka *f*
mousse [muːs] *n* (*for hair*), *Culin* mousse *f*; **chocolate m.** mousse au chocolat
moustache [məs'tɑːʃ], *US* **mustache** ['mʌstæʃ] *n* moustache(s) *f(pl)*; **short m., clipped m.** moustache courte *ou* en brosse
mousy ['maʊsɪ] *adj* **(a)** (*colour*) gris sale; *F* (*hair*) châtain terne *inv* **(b)** (*timid*) timide **(c)** (*smell etc*) de souris
mouth[1] [maʊθ] *n* (*pl* **mouths** [maʊðz]) **(a)** (*of person, horse, cow etc*) bouche *f*; (*of dog, carnivore etc*) gueule *f*; **to have one's m. full** avoir la bouche pleine; **don't speak with your m. full** ne parle pas (avec) la bouche pleine; **to have seven mouths to feed** avoir sept bouches à nourrir; *Fig* **big m.** (*person*) gueulard *m*, grande gueule *f*; **to be** *or* **have a big m.** être *ou* avoir une grande gueule; **you had to open your big m., didn't you!** il a fallu que tu ouvres ta grande gueule!; **me and my big m.!** pourquoi faut-il toujours que je l'ouvre!; *F* **he's all m.** parler, c'est tout ce qu'il sait faire; *F* **keep your m. shut about this** garde ça pour toi; **to put words into sb's m.** (*misquote*) faire dire à qn ce qu'il ne dit pas; **I don't want to put words into your m. but …** dites -moi si je me trompe mais … *Mus* **m. organ** harmonica *m*
(b) (*opening etc*) (*of tunnel, cave*) ouverture *f*, entrée *f*; (*of river*) embouchure *f*
mouth[2] **1** *vt* **(a)** (*say without sincerity*) dire de façon mécanique, dire mécaniquement **(b)** (*say silently*) (*words*) former; **she mouthed something to me** elle a essayé de me dire quelque chose en remuant les lèvres silencieusement **2** *vi esp Am* (*grimace*) grimacer, faire des grimaces
mouthful ['maʊθfʊl] *n* **(a)** bouchée *f*; (*of soup, wine etc*) gorgée *f*; **to swallow sth in** *or* **at one m., to make one m. of sth** ne faire qu'une bouchée de qch; (*soup, wine*) avaler qch d'une seule gorgée; **I swallowed** *or* **got a m. (of water)** (*when swimming etc*) j'ai bu la *ou* une tasse; *esp Am F* **you said a m.** (*were right*) tu as bien parlé; *Br F* **to give sb a m.** (*insult*) lancer une bordée d'injures à qn; (*say exactly what one thinks*) dire quelque chose à qn sans détour
(b) *F* (*long word, phrase*) mot *m*/phrase *f* difficile à prononcer; (*person's name*) nom *m* à coucher dehors; **cerebral thrombosis is quite a m.** thrombose cérébrale est vraiment difficile à prononcer
mouthpiece ['maʊθpiːs] *n* **(a)** (*of loudhailer*) embout *m*; (*of pipe*) tuyau *m*, bout *m*; *Mus* (*of clarinet etc*) bec *m*; *Mus* (*of horn etc*) embouchure *f*; *Tel* microphone *m* **(b)** (*person, magazine*) (*of party etc*) porte-parole *m inv*; *US Sl* (*lawyer*) avocat *m* (au criminel)
mouth-to-mouth *adj Med* **m. resuscitation** bouche-à-bouche *m*; **to give sb m. resuscitation** faire du bouche-à-bouche à qn
mouthwash ['maʊθwɒʃ] *n Pharm* bain *m* de bouche; (*for teeth*) eau *f* dentifrice
mouthwatering ['maʊθwɔːtərɪŋ] *adj* alléchant, qui fait venir l'eau à la bouche
mouthy ['maʊðɪ] *adj F* gueulard, grande gueule
movable ['muːvəb(ə)l] **1** *adj* **(a)** mobile; *Rel* **m. feast** fête *f* mobile **(b)** *Jur* mobilier, meuble; **m. property** biens *mpl* meubles **2** *npl Jur* **movables** biens *mpl* meubles
move[1] [muːv] *n* **(a)** (*motion*) mouvement *m*; **to make a m. towards sth** faire un mouvement vers qch; **there was a general m. towards** *or* **for the door** tout le monde s'est dirigé vers la porte; **we must make a m.** il faut partir; **don't make a m.!** (*or I'll shoot, they'll see us etc*) ne bouge pas!; **the police were watching her every m.** la police surveillait ses moindres gestes; **on the m.** en marche; **to be always on the m.** ne jamais rester en place; *F* **to get a m. on** se grouiller, se manier *ou* magner (le train)
(b) *Fig* (*action, step*) démarche *f*, action *f*, manœuvre *f*; **smart m.** manœuvre habile; **at one time there was a m. to …** à un moment, on avait envisagé de …; **what's the next m.?** qu'est-ce qu'il faut faire maintenant?; **to make the first m.** faire le premier pas; **don't make a m. without contacting me** (*don't do anything*) ne fais rien sans me contacter; **when would the enemy make his m.?** quand l'ennemi allait-il se décider à agir?; **the Government has made moves towards resolving …** le gouvernement a pris des mesures pour résoudre …
(c) (*from home, office etc*) déménagement *m*; **after ten years in the job she needed a m.** après dix ans passés à faire le même travail, elle avait besoin de changement
(d) *Chess etc* coup *m*; **mate in four moves** (échec et) mat en quatre coups; **to have first m.** commencer la partie; **to make a m.** jouer; **(it's) your m.** à vous de jouer, c'est votre tour; **to learn the moves** apprendre comment les pièces se déplacent
(e) *Comptr* (*of text block etc*) déplacement *m*
move[2] **1** *vt* **(a)** (*shift*) (*furniture, troops etc*) déplacer, changer de place; (*employee*) muter (**to** à); (*drive*) (*wheels etc*) entraîner; *Chess etc* (*piece*) jouer; *Comptr* (*text block etc*) déplacer; *Com* vendre; **to m. sth from its place** changer qch de place; **could you m. your feet/bag (out of the way) please?** est-ce que tu peux pousser tes pieds/ton sac s'il te plaît?; **to m. one's position** changer de place; **to m. one's chair near the fire** approcher son fauteuil du feu; **he was moved to London** on l'a muté à Londres; **to m. house/ premises** déménager; **to m. heaven and earth** remuer ciel et terre; **come on, m. yourself! we're going to be late!** allez, remue-toi! on va être en retard!
(b) (*stir*) (*one's head etc*) remuer, bouger; (*of wind etc*) (*branches etc*) agiter, remuer; (*set in motion*) mouvoir, animer, mettre en mouvement; *Med* **to m. one's bowels** aller à la selle
(c) *Fig* (*sway*) ébranler la résolution de; **you won't m. me** tu ne me feras pas changer d'avis; **I won't be moved** je ne changerai pas d'avis; **nothing will m. him** il est inflexible; **to m. sb to do sth** pousser *ou* inciter qn à faire qch
(d) (*affect emotionally*) (*sb*) émouvoir, toucher; **easily moved** émotif; **to m. sb to anger** provoquer la colère de qn; **to m. sb to tears** émouvoir qn (jusqu')aux larmes; **to m. sb to pity** exciter la pitié de qn
(e) (*in debate etc*) (*resolution*) proposer; **to m. that …** proposer que … + *sub*
2 *vi* **(a)** (*stir*) bouger; (*change one's position*) se déplacer; **they won't m. on the question of compensation** ils ne fléchiront pas sur la question des compensations; **to m. to another seat** changer de place; **to m. in high society** fréquenter la haute société; **don't m.!** ne bougez pas!; **I'm stuck, I can't m.** je suis coincé, je ne peux pas bouger; **I can't get it to m.** je n'arrive pas à le/la faire bouger; **could you m. so that we can get in?** pourriez-vous vous pousser que nous puissions entrer?; **the way the dancers m.** la façon de se mouvoir *ou* de bouger des danseurs; **she moves like a**

model elle marche comme un mannequin; **I saw the curtains m.** j'ai vu les rideaux bouger; **something moved in the bushes** quelque chose a bougé dans les buissons; *F* **come on, m.!** (*hurry*) allez, magne-toi le train *ou* remue-toi!; **wait till the car stops moving** attends que la voiture soit arrêtée; *Com* **this product's not moving** (*not selling*) ce produit ne se vend pas

(**b**) (*of machine parts etc*) bouger; **this part is meant to m.** cette partie est censée bouger; **what makes it m.?** qu'est-ce qui le fait tourner/avancer/descendre/*etc*?; **it moves upwards and downwards in the ...** ça monte et ça descend dans le ...; **to m. freely** (*of part*) jouer librement; (*of dissident, prisoner*) se déplacer librement

(**c**) (*progress, advance*) avancer; **the earth moves round the sun** la terre tourne autour du soleil; **it moves in an elliptical orbit** il/elle décrit une ellipse; **to m. towards a place** se diriger *ou* s'avancer vers un endroit; **the traffic was only just moving** les voitures avançaient à peine; **things are moving slowly** les choses avancent lentement; **that's really moving!** (*that's fast*) ça fonce!; (*referring to work*) ça avance!, ça progresse!; **it's time we were moving, we must be moving** il est temps de partir

(**d**) (*act*) agir; **it is for him to m. first in the matter** c'est à lui d'agir le premier dans cette affaire

(**e**) (*to new home, office etc*) déménager; **we have moved to new premises** nous avons déménagé dans de nouveaux locaux; **to m. to the country** aller s'installer à la campagne

(**f**) *Chess etc* jouer

▶ **move about, move around 1** *vi* bouger, remuer; (*travel and move house*) bouger; **I heard someone moving about** j'ai entendu quelqu'un se déplacer; **he finds it difficult to m. about** il a du mal à se déplacer; **he moves around a lot** (*in job etc*) il est toujours en déplacement **2** *vtsep* (*furniture etc*) déplacer, changer de place; **they keep moving her around from one department to another** ils n'arrêtent pas de la faire passer d'un service à l'autre

▶ **move along 1** *vtsep* (*of police officer*) (*onlookers, beggars etc*) faire circuler **2** *vi* (**a**) (*to make room*) se déplacer, se pousser; **m. along and let the old lady sit down** poussez-vous un peu pour laisser la vieille dame s'asseoir (**b**) (*leave*) partir, s'en aller; **I ought to be moving along** il faut que je m'en aille; **the policeman told us to m. along** le policier nous a dit de circuler; **m. along (please)!** circulez, s'il vous plaît! (**c**) (*continue*) **moving along to my next question** pour passer à ma question suivante

▶ **move away 1** *vtsep* (*sth*) écarter, éloigner (**from** de) **2** *vi* (**a**) (*go away*) s'éloigner, s'écarter, s'en aller (**b**) (*go to new home etc*) déménager; **they've moved away from here** ils ont déménagé

▶ **move back 1** *vtsep* (**a**) (*to more distant position*) (*people*) (faire) reculer; (*things*) mettre en retrait; **could you m. your car back?** pourriez-vous reculer? (**b**) (*to former position*) remettre en place **2** *vi* (**a**) (*retreat*) (se) reculer (**b**) (*to former position*) retourner, revenir (**c**) (*to former home etc*) retourner; **they have moved back to London** (*come*) ils sont revenus habiter à Londres; (*gone*) ils sont repartis habiter à Londres; **to m. back to one's old job** reprendre son ancien travail

▶ **move down 1** *vtsep* (**a**) (*change position of*) (*sth*) descendre; *Typ etc* **m. this section down** mettez cette section plus bas (**b**) (*demote*) rétrograder; **to m. sb down three places** rétrograder qn de trois places; *Sch* **to be moved down (a class)** descendre de classe **2** *vi* (*be demoted*) descendre; **the team moved down to the fourth division** l'équipe est descendue en quatrième division

▶ **move forward 1** *vtsep* (*object, date etc*) avancer; (*troops*) faire avancer **2** *vi* (s')avancer

▶ **move in 1** *vtsep* (**a**) (*send*) (*troops*) envoyer; **troops were moved in by helicopter** les troupes ont été transportées par hélicoptère (**b**) (*install*) (*furniture*) installer **2** *vi* (**a**) (*take up residence*) emménager; **he has moved in with his girlfriend** il est allé s'installer chez sa petite amie (**b**) (*enter situation*) entrer en scène, faire son apparition; **the market changed when the multinationals moved in** le marché a changé quand les multinationales ont fait leur apparition (**c**) (*advance*) s'avancer; **troops moved in to quell the riots** les troupes sont intervenues pour réprimer les émeutes

▶ **move into** *vipo* (*diversify into*) se reconvertir dans

▶ **move off** *vi* (**a**) (*go away*) s'éloigner, s'en aller, partir (**b**) (*start journey*) (*of train, army etc*) se mettre en marche; (*of car etc*) démarrer

▶ **move on 1** *vtsep* (*crowd etc*) faire circuler **2** *vi* (**a**) (*go further on journey etc*) avancer, continuer son chemin; **can we m. on to the next item on the agenda?** pouvons-nous passer à la question suivante de l'ordre du jour?; **time's moving on** il se fait tard; **it's time we were moving on** il est temps que nous partions (**b**) (*make progress*) (*of science*) faire des progrès, évoluer; **women have moved on** les femmes ont évolué *ou* changé

▶ **move out 1** *vtsep* (*remove*) (*sth*) sortir; (*sb*) faire sortir; **the troops will be moved out** les troupes se retireront; **people were moved out (of their homes) to make way for the new road** les gens ont dû quitter leur maison pour permettre la construction de la nouvelle route **2** *vi* (**a**) (*leave home etc*) déménager (**b**) *Mil* (*withdraw*) se retirer

▶ **move over** *vi* se ranger, se pousser; **m. over!** pousse-toi!; **they moved over to a market economy** ils sont passés à une économie de marché

▶ **move up 1** *vtsep* (**a**) (*change position of*) (*object*) monter; *Typ etc* **m. this section up** mettez cette section plus haut; **the regiment was moved up to the front** on a envoyé le régiment au front

(**b**) (*promote*) promouvoir; **they've moved her up to be assistant manager** ils l'ont promue directrice-adjointe; *Sch* **to be moved up (a class)** passer dans la classe supérieure

2 *vi* (**a**) (*advance*) s'avancer, avancer

(**b**) (*be promoted*) être promu; *Sch* passer dans la classe supérieure; *St Exch* (*of shares*) se relever; **he has moved up in my estimation** il est monté dans mon estime

(**c**) (*to make room*) se pousser; **m. up so I can sit down** pousse-toi (un peu) que je m'assoie

moveable ['mu:vəb(ə)l] *adj* = **movable**

movement ['mu:vmənt] *n* (**a**) (*change of place*) mouvement *m*; (*on stock exchange*) activité *f*; (*of vehicles, goods, capital*) mouvement, circulation *f*; *Mil etc* mouvement, manœuvre *f*; (*of prices etc*) mouvement; **there was a general m. towards the door** tout le monde s'est dirigé vers la porte; **to watch sb's movements** (*of police etc*) surveiller les faits et gestes *ou* les allées et venues de qn; *Fig* **there had been little m. in the negotiations** les négociations n'avaient pas beaucoup avancé; **free m. of labour** libre circulation de la main-d'œuvre

(**b**) (*motion*) (*of one's arm etc*) mouvement *m*, geste *m*

(**c**) (*group, tendency*) (*political, literary, artistic etc*) mouvement *m*

(**d**) (*mechanism of clock*) mouvement *m*

(**e**) *Mus* (*of symphony etc*) mouvement *m*

(**f**) *Physiol* **to have a (bowel) m.** aller à la selle

mover ['mu:vər] *n* (**a**) (*in debate*) auteur *m* d'une motion, motionnaire *mf* (**b**) *Am* (*removal firm, person*) déménageur *m* (**c**) **he's a beautiful** *or* **lovely m.** (*footballer etc*) il a une démarche superbe; (*dancer*) il est superbe quand il danse (**d**) *F* **movers and shakers** les grands pontes *mpl*

movie ['mu:vɪ] *n esp Am* film *m*; **the movies** le cinéma; **m. actor/actress** acteur/actrice de cinéma; **m. camera** caméra *f*; **m. channel** chaîne *f* de cinéma; **m. house** cinéma; **m. industry** industrie *f* cinématographique; **m. star** vedette *f*; **m. theater** cinéma

moviegoer ['mu:vɪgəʊər] *n esp Am* cinéphile *mf*, amateur *m* de cinéma

moving ['mu:vɪŋ] **1** *adj* (**a**) (*in motion*) en mouvement, mouvant; (*train, vehicle*) en marche; (*part etc*) mobile; *Phys* **m. body** corps *m* en mouvement; **m. pavement,** *US* **sidewalk** trottoir *m* roulant; *Am Cin Old-fashioned* **m. picture** film *m*; **m. staircase** escalier *m* mécanique; *Mil* **m. target** cible *f* mobile

(**b**) (*force etc*) moteur, -trice; **the m. spirit** (*in a venture*) l'âme *f*

(**c**) (*touching*) (*scene, story etc*) émouvant, touchant

2 *n* mouvement *m*; (*being moved*) déplacement *m*; **m. (out)** (*from house etc*) déménagement *m*; **m. in** (*into house etc*) emménagement *m*; *US* **m. van** camion *m* de déménagement

movingly ['mu:vɪŋlɪ] *adv* d'une manière émouvante *ou* touchante

mow [məʊ] *vti* (*pt* **mowed** [məʊd], *pp* **mown** [məʊn]) (**a**) (*lawn*) tondre (**b**) *Agr* (*corn, field*) faucher

▶ **mow down** *vtsep* (*slaughter*) faucher

mower ['məʊər] *n* (**a**) (*machine*), *Agr* faucheuse *f*; (**lawn**) **m.** tondeuse *f* (à gazon) (**b**) *Agr* (*person*) faucheur, -euse

mowing ['məʊɪŋ] *n* (**a**) (*of lawn*) tonte *f* (**b**) *Agr* (*of hay etc*) fauchage *m*

mown *see* = **mow**

MP [em'pi:] *n* (**a**) *Br Parl* (*abbr* **Member of Parliament**) député *m* (**b**) *Mil* (*abbr* **Military Police**) police *f* militaire; (*abbr* **Military Policeman**) membre *m* de la police militaire

mpg [empi:'dʒi:] *n* (*abbr* **miles per gallon**) mil(l)es au gallon; **what sort of m. do you get?** combien faites-vous au cent?

mph [empi:'eɪtʃ] *n* (*abbr* **miles per hour**) mil(l)es à l'heure, ≈ kilomètres à l'heure

MPhil [em'fɪl] *n* (*abbr* **Master of Philosophy**) = DEA *m*

MPV [empiː'viː] *n Aut* (*abbr* **multi-purpose vehicle**) véhicule *m* multifonction, véhicule à usages multiples

Mr ['mɪstər] *n* (*form of address, not used without name*) **Mr Thomas** Monsieur *m* Thomas; (*on envelope*) Monsieur *ou* M. Thomas; **Mr President** Monsieur le Président; *F* **Mr Big** le cerveau de l'affaire; *F* **Mr Right** l'homme *m* idéal

MRC [emɑː'siː] *n Br* (*abbr* **Medical Research Council**) Comité *m* pour la recherche médicale

MRI [emɑː'raɪ] *n Med* (*abbr* **magnetic resonance imaging**) IRM *f*

Mrs ['mɪsɪz] *n* (*form of address, not used without name*) **Mrs Long** Madame Long; (*on envelope*) Madame *ou* Mme Long

MS[1], **ms**, *pl* **MSS, mss** (*abbr* **manuscript**) manuscrit *m*

MS[2] [em'es] *n* (*abbr* **multiple sclerosis**) sclérose *f* en plaques

Ms [mɪz] *n* (*form of address, not used without name*) **Ms Martin** (*unmarried*) Mademoiselle *f* Martin; (*married*) Madame *f* Martin; (*on envelope*) Madame *ou* Mme Martin

MSc [emes'siː] *n* (*abbr* **Master of Science**) (*degree*) maîtrise *f* de *ou* ès sciences; (*person*) titulaire *mf* d'une maîtrise

MSG [emes'dʒiː] *n* (*abbr* **monosodium glutamate**) glutamate *m* de sodium

MST [emes'tiː] *n, abbr* **Mountain Standard Time**

Mt (*abbr* **Mount**) Mt

MTBF [emtiːbiː'ef] *n Comptr* (*abbr* **mean time between failures**) moyenne *f* de temps entre deux pannes

much [mʌtʃ] **1** *adj* (*usu only with neg and interr*) beaucoup de; *Fml* **m. care** beaucoup de soin; *Iron* **m. good may it do you!** grand bien vous fasse!; **how m. money?** combien d'argent?; **too m. money** trop d'argent; **so m. money** tellement *ou* tant d'argent; **as m. money as** autant d'argent que

2 *adv* [①**A24-5**,d,iv] beaucoup; **I don't like them m., I don't m. like them** je ne les aime pas beaucoup; **m. as I'd like to** (*I can't accept, be there etc*) bien que je le veuille; **m. as I'd like to, I can't come** je voudrais bien, mais je ne peux pas venir; (**very**) **m. better** beaucoup mieux; **m. worse** bien pire; **it doesn't matter m.** cela n'a pas beaucoup d'importance; **m. more/less pleasant** beaucoup plus/moins agréable; **m. the largest** de beaucoup le plus grand, le plus grand de beaucoup; **m. too small** beaucoup trop petit; **we are m. obliged to you for …** nous vous sommes très obligés de *ou* pour …; **thank you very m.** (**for …**) merci beaucoup (de *ou* pour …); **it's (pretty** *or* **very) m. the same thing** c'est à peu près la même chose; **he's m. the same** (*of sb ill*) son état n'a pas changé; **that's m. how I felt** c'est à peu près ce que j'ai ressenti, moi aussi; **m. to my astonishment** à mon grand étonnement; *F Iron* **he doesn't like beer, does he? – not m. he doesn't!** il n'aime pas la bière, non? – et comment, il aime ça!

3 *pron* (**a**) beaucoup; **m. remains to be done** il reste beaucoup à faire; **m. has happened while you have been away** il s'est passé bien des choses pendant votre absence; **there is not m. of it** il n'y en a pas beaucoup; **it's not worth m.** *or F* **not up to m.** cela ne vaut pas grand-chose; **to make m. of sth** accorder beaucoup d'importance à qch; **I'll say this m. for him** je dirai ceci en sa faveur; **there's not (all) that m.** il n'y en a pas tellement *ou* tant que ça; **I don't think m. of it** je n'aime pas beaucoup ça; **it wasn't m. of a surprise** ce n'était pas une grande surprise; **she isn't m. of a singer** comme chanteuse, elle n'est pas terrible; **it wasn't m. of a joke** ce n'était pas terrible comme plaisanterie

(**b**) (*phrases*) **m. as I like him** quelle que soit mon affection pour lui; **m. as I try, I can't succeed** j'ai beau essayer, je n'y arrive pas; **the result was m. as I expected** le résultat correspondait bien à ce que j'attendais; **as m.** autant; **as m. again** encore autant; **twice as m.** deux fois autant; **I expected as m.** je m'y attendais; **I suspected** *or* **guessed** *or* **thought as m.** je m'en doutais; **as m. as** autant que; **as m. as possible** autant que possible; **quite as m. as …** tout autant que …; **not quite as m. as …** pas tout à fait autant que …; **it is as m. your fault as (it is) mine** c'est autant de votre faute que de la mienne; **it is as m. as he can do to read** c'est tout juste s'il sait lire; **it was as m. as we could do to stand upright** nous avions le plus grand mal à nous tenir debout; **he looked at me as m. as to say …** il me regarda avec l'air de (vouloir) dire …; **as m. as that?** (au)tant que cela?; **do you love her as m. as that?** vous l'aimez donc tant *ou* à ce point-là?; **he went away without so m. as saying goodbye** il est parti sans même dire au revoir; **I would not so m. as raise a finger to help him** je ne lèverais pas même le petit doigt pour l'aider; **so m.** tant, tellement; **he has drunk so m. that …** il a tellement bu que …; **so m. the better** tant mieux; **so m. so that …** au point que …, à tel point que …; **not so m. a …, more a …** pas vraiment un …, mais plutôt un …; **so m. for his friendship!** et voilà ce qu'il appelle l'amitié!; **so m. per cent** tant pour cent; **so m. a kilo** tant le kilo; **too m.** trop; **m. too m.** beaucoup trop; **£10 too m.** 10 livres de trop; **to cost too m.** coûter trop cher; **this is (really) too m.!** c'est vraiment trop fort!; *F* **that's a bit m.!** c'est un peu fort!; **you can't have too m. of a good thing** abondance de biens ne nuit pas

muchness ['mʌtʃnɪs] *n F* **they're much of a m.** (*of pictures, books, people etc*) ils se ressemblent beaucoup; (*of two candidates*) ils se valent; **it's (all) much of a m.** (*doesn't really matter*) ça revient au même

muck [mʌk] *n* (**a**) (*dung*) fumier *m*; *Agr* **m. spreader** épandeur *m* (**b**) (*dirt*) saleté *f*; (*from the streets*) saletés (**c**) *Br F* (*rubbish, unhealthy food, obscene book etc*) cochonnerie *f*; (*unappetizing food*) saloperie *f*; (*worthless objects*) camelote *f* (**d**) *Br F* (*mess*) **to make a m. of sth** saloper qch

▶ **muck about, muck around** *Br F* = **mess about, mess around**

▶ **muck in** *vi Br F* **to m. in with sb** (*share room*) crécher avec qn; (*join in*) partager le boulot avec qn; **everyone mucked in** (*helped out*) tout le monde s'y est mis

▶ **muck out 1** *vtsep* (*stables etc*) nettoyer **2** *vi* nettoyer l'écurie/les écuries/*etc*

▶ **muck up** *vtsep Br F* (**a**) (*make dirty*) saloper (**b**) (*make a mess of*) ficher en l'air; (*job*) bousiller; (*plans*) flanquer par terre

muckheap ['mʌkhiːp] *n* tas *m* de fumier *ou* d'ordures

muckraker ['mʌkreɪkər] *n F* journaliste *mf* à l'affût des scandales, *Sl* fouille-merde *m inv*

muckraking ['mʌkreɪkɪŋ] *n F* révélation *f* de scandales

mucky ['mʌkɪ] *adj Br F* sale; **m. books** (*obscene*) des livres cochons; **you're a m. pup!** que tu es sale!

mucous ['mjuːkəs] *adj* muqueux; **m. membrane** muqueuse *f*

mucus ['mjuːkəs] *n* (**a**) *Physiol* mucus *m*, mucosité *f* (**b**) *Bot* mucosité *f*

mud [mʌd] *n* boue *f*, gadoue *f*; (*in swamp*) bourbe *f*; (**river**) **m.** vase *f*; **to get stuck** *or* **to sink in the m.** s'embourber; (*of ship*) s'envaser; *Fig* **to drag sb's name in the m.** traîner qn dans la boue; *Fig* **to fling** *or* **sling** *or* **throw m. at sb** couvrir qn de boue; *F* **his name is m.** il est mal vu; *Old-fashioned F* **here's m. in your eye!** à votre santé!, à la vôtre!; *F* **as clear as m.** clair comme du jus de boudin; *Med* **m. bath** bain *m* de boue; *Geog etc* **m. flat** banc *m* de boue; **m. hut** hutte *f* de terre; **m. pie** (*made by child*) pâté *m* de sable *ou* de boue; *Am Culin* = sorte *f* de flan au chocolat

mudbank ['mʌdbæŋk] *n* (*in river*) banc *m* de vase

muddle[1] ['mʌd(ə)l] *n* confusion *f*, *F* embrouillamini *m*; **to be in a m.** (*of things*) être en désordre *ou* en pagaille *ou* en pagaïe; (*of person*) ne plus savoir où l'on est; **to get into a m. (about sth)** s'embrouiller (au sujet de qch); **to make a m. of sth** faire qch de travers

muddle[2] *vt* (**a**) (*put in disorder*) (*sth, story*) embrouiller, brouiller; (*matter, affair*) gâcher (**b**) (*bewilder*) (*person*) embrouiller; **to get muddled** s'embrouiller

▶ **muddle along** *vi* (*cope haphazardly*) faire son chemin *ou* se débrouiller tant bien que mal

▶ **muddle through 1** *vi* (*get through haphazardly*) se débrouiller *ou F* se dépatouiller *ou* s'en tirer tant bien que mal **2** *vipo* **to m. through a crisis** traverser une crise tant bien que mal; **to m. through an exam** passer un examen tant bien que mal

▶ **muddle up** *vtsep* (**a**) (*mix up*) mélanger; **I've muddled the dates up** j'ai mélangé les dates (**b**) (*bewilder*) (*sb*) embrouiller

muddled ['mʌd(ə)ld] *adj* (**a**) (*objects*) en désordre, *F* en pagaille *ou* pagaïe (**b**) (*person, ideas*) confus, embrouillé

muddleheaded [mʌd(ə)l'hedɪd] *adj* (*person*) à l'esprit confus, brouillon, -onne; **m. ideas** idées confuses *ou* embrouillées

muddler ['mʌdlər] *n* brouillon, -onne, esprit *m* brouillon

muddy[1] ['mʌdɪ] *adj* (**a**) (*path*) boueux, bourbeux; (*stream*) bourbeux, vaseux; (*jacket etc*) crotté, couvert de boue; **to taste m.** avoir un goût de vase (**b**) (*liquid, wine etc*) trouble; (*colour*) sale; (*complexion*) brouillé, terreux; **m. brown** couleur (de) terre

muddy[2] *vt* (**a**) (*one's clothes etc*) crotter (**b**) (*water*) troubler; *Fig* **to m. the waters** semer la confusion

mudflap ['mʌdflæp] *n* pare-boue *m inv*

mudguard ['mʌdgɑːd] *n Br* garde-boue *m inv*

mudlark ['mʌdlɑːk] *n Old-fashioned F* gamin, -ine des rues

mudpack ['mʌdpæk] *n* masque *m* à l'argile

mudskipper ['mʌdskɪpər] *n* (*fish*) gobie *m* des marais

mudslinger ['mʌdslɪŋər] *n F* calomniateur, -trice

mudslinging ['mʌdslɪŋɪŋ] *F* **1** *n* calomnies *fpl* **2** *adj* diffamatoire

mud-stained *adj* taché de boue

muesli ['mjuːzlɪ] *n* müesli *m*, musli *m*

muezzin [muːˈezɪn] *n* muezzin *m*
muff¹ [mʌf] *vt Br Old-fashioned F (bungle)* rater, louper; *Golf etc (stroke)* manquer, rater
muff² *n* **(a)** *(for hands)* manchon *m* **(b)** *Vulg (female sex organs)* minette *f*; **m. -diver** lécheur *m* de minette
muffin [ˈmʌfɪn] *n Br Culin* muffin *m*
muffle [ˈmʌf(ə)l] *vt* **(a)** *(deaden sound of) (oars, bell etc)* assourdir, étouffer; *Mus (drum)* assourdir **(b)** *(wrap)* emmitoufler; **to m. oneself up** s'emmitoufler
muffled [ˈmʌf(ə)ld] *adj* **(a)** *(sound, footstep)* étouffé, assourdi; *(oar)* assourdi; *(voice)* étouffé; *Mus* **m. drums** tambours voilés **(b)** *(wrapped)* **m. (up)** emmitouflé
muffler [ˈmʌflər] *n* **(a)** *(scarf)* cache-nez *m inv*, cache-col *m*, *pl* cache-col(s) **(b)** *Am Aut* silencieux *m*; *MecE* **(exhaust) m.** gueule-de-loup *f*, *pl* gueules-de-loup **(c)** *Mus (on piano)* étouffoir *m*
Mufti [ˈmʌftɪ] *n Muslim Rel* mufti *m*, muphti *m*
mufti [ˈmʌftɪ] *n Mil etc Sl* tenue *f* civile; **in m.** en civil
mug¹ [mʌg] *n* **(a)** *(for beer)* chope *f*, pot *m*; *(for tea etc)* grande tasse *f*; *(made of metal)* quart *m* **(b)** *F (face)* gueule *f*, trombine *f*, bouille *f*; **ugly m.** sale gueule, gueule d'empeigne; *esp Am* **m. (shot)** photo *f (d'un criminel)*; **shut your (ugly) m.!** ferme ta sale gueule! **(c)** *Br F (gullible person)* poire *f*, andouille *f*; **it's a m.'s game** c'est bon pour les poires
mug² *vt F (attack) (person)* attaquer, agresser
mug³ *vi* faire des grimaces
► **mug up** *Br Sch F* **1** *vi (study, revise)* plancher, bûcher; **to m. up on sth** plancher sur qch **2** *vtsep (subject)* potasser
mugful [ˈmʌgfʊl] *n (of beer)* chope *f*, pot *m*; *(of coffee, tea)* grande tasse *f*
mugger [ˈmʌgər] *n F* agresseur *m*
mugging [ˈmʌgɪŋ] *n F* agression *f*
muggins [ˈmʌgɪnz] *n Br F* idiot, -ote, nouille *f*; *(oneself)* ma pomme; **I suppose m. will have to do it!** je suppose que c'est ma pomme qui va s'y coller!
muggy [ˈmʌgɪ] *adj (weather)* lourd
mugwump [ˈmʌgwʌmp] *n Am Pol F (independent)* non-inscrit, -ite; *(neutral)* neutre *mf*
mulatto [mjuːˈlætəʊ] *Old-fashioned* **1** *adj* mulâtre **2** *n* mulâtre *mf*, mulâtresse *f*
mulberry [ˈmʌlbərɪ] *n (fruit)* mûre *f*; **m. (bush** *or* **tree)** mûrier *m*
mulch¹ [mʌltʃ] *n* paillis *m*
mulch² *vt* pailler
mulct [mʌlkt] *vt* **(a)** *Jur* frapper d'une amende **(b)** *Old-fashioned, or Lit (cheat)* **to m. sb of sth** extorquer qch à qn
mule¹ [mjuːl] *n* **(a) (he) m.** mulet *m*; **(she) m., m. mare** mule *f*; **as stubborn as a m.** têtu comme une mule; **m. driver,** *Am F* **m. skinner** muletier *m*; **m. path** chemin *m ou* sentier *m* muletier; **m. train** caravane *f* de mules **(b)** *F (stubborn person)* tête *f* de mule **(c)** *Tex* **m. (jenny)** renvideur *m*
mule² *n (slipper)* mule *f*
muleteer [mjuːlɪˈtɪər] *n* muletier *m*
mulish [ˈmjuːlɪʃ] *adj* entêté, têtu (comme une mule)
mulishness [ˈmjuːlɪʃnɪs] *n* entêtement *m*
mull [mʌl] *vt (wine, beer)* chauffer avec des épices
► **mull over** *vtsep (consider) (idea)* ruminer, retourner dans sa tête; **I've been mulling it over and ...** j'y ai réfléchi et ...
mulled [mʌld] *adj* **m. wine** vin *m* chaud épicé
mullet [ˈmʌlɪt] *n (fish)* **grey m.** muge *m* (capiton), mulet *m*; **red m.** rouget(-barbet) *m*
mulligatawny [mʌlɪgəˈtɔːnɪ] *n* **m. (soup)** potage *m* au curry
mullion [ˈmʌlɪən] *n Archit* meneau *m* (vertical)
mullioned [ˈmʌlɪənd] *adj Archit (window)* à meneau(x)
multi- [ˈmʌltɪ] *pref* multi-
multi-access *adj Comptr* à accès multiple
multibrand [ˈmʌltɪbrænd] *n Mktg* marque *f* multiple, multimarque *f*
multi-centre holiday *n* vacances *fpl* en circuit
multicoloured [ˈmʌltɪkʌləd] *adj* multicolore
multicriterion sorting [mʌltɪkraɪˈtɪərɪən] *n Comptr* classement *m* multicritère
multicultural [mʌltɪˈkʌltʃər(ə)l] *adj* multiculturel
multicurrency [mʌltɪˈkʌrənsɪ] *adj* multidevise
multidirectional [mʌltɪdɪˈrekʃən(ə)l] *adj* multidirectionnel
multifaceted [mʌltɪˈfæsɪtɪd] *adj* qui a plusieurs facettes
multifarious [mʌltɪˈfeərɪəs] *adj Fml* varié, divers
multiform [ˈmʌltɪfɔːm] *adj* multiforme
multi-fuel engine *n* moteur *m* polycarburant
multi-functional *adj Comptr* multi-fonction; **m. keyboard** clavier *m* multi-fonction
multi-function display *n* affichage *m* multifonction
multi-grade oil *n* huile *f* multigrade
multilateral [mʌltɪˈlæt(ə)rəl] *adj* multilatéral
multilingual [mʌltɪˈlɪŋgwəl] *adj (person)* polyglotte; *(country)* plurilingue
multimedia [mʌltɪˈmiːdɪə] **1** *adj* multimédia; **m. group** groupe *m* multimédia **2** *n* multimédia *m*
multimillionaire [mʌltɪmɪlɪəˈneər] *adj, n* multi-millionnaire *mf*
multimodal operator [mʌltɪˈməʊd(ə)l] *n* opérateur *m* de transport multimodal, OTM *m*
multinational [mʌltɪˈnæʃən(ə)l] **1** *adj* multinational; **m. company** multinationale *f* **2** *n* multinationale *f*
multi-ownership *n* multipropriété *f*
multi-part stationery *n* papier *m* multiple
multiparty [mʌltɪˈpɑːtɪ] *adj Pol (state)* pluripartite
multi-plate clutch *n* embrayage *m* à disques multiples
multiple [ˈmʌltɪp(ə)l] **1** *adj* multiple; *El* **batteries in m.** accumulateurs *mpl* en parallèle; *Tel* **m. circuit** circuit *m* multiple; **m. injuries** blessures *fpl* multiples; **m. ownership** multipropriété *f*; *Psy* **m. personality** personnalité *f* multiple; *El, Rad etc* **m. reception** réception *f* multiple; **m. store** magasin *m* à succursales (multiples); **m. switchboard** multiple *m* (téléphonique) **2** *n* **(a)** *Math* multiple *m*; **lowest** *or* **least common m.** plus petit commun multiple **(b)** *Tel* multiplage *m* **(c)** *Com (chain store)* magasin *m* à succursales (multiples)
multiple-choice *adj (question, exam)* à choix multiple
multiple sclerosis *n Med* sclérose *f* en plaques
multiplex¹ [ˈmʌltɪpleks] *n (cinema)* complexe *m* multisalles
multiplex² *vt* multiplexer
multiplexer [ˈmʌltɪpleksər] *n* multiplexeur *m*
multiplication [mʌltɪplɪˈkeɪʃən] *n* [ⓘA71,7; B56,B,4] *Math etc* multiplication *f*; **m. table** table *f* de multiplication
multiplicity [mʌltɪˈplɪsɪtɪ] *n* multiplicité *f*
multiplier [ˈmʌltɪplaɪər] *n Math, Comptr, El* multiplicateur *m*
multiply [ˈmʌltɪplaɪ] **1** *vt Math, Fig* multiplier; **to m. 2 by 6** multiplier 2 par 6 **2** *vi* **(a)** *(of species, difficulties etc)* se multiplier **(b)** *Math* multiplier, faire une/des multiplication(s)
multi-point fuel-injected engine *n* moteur *m* à injection multipoint
multiprocessor [mʌltɪˈprəʊsesər] *n* multiprocesseur *m*
multipurpose [mʌltɪˈpɜːpəs] *adj (tool, vehicle)* à usages multiples, polyvalent
multiracial [mʌltɪˈreɪʃəl] *adj* multiracial
multiscan monitor [ˈmʌltɪskæn] *n* moniteur *m* à balayage multiple
multiscreen [ˈmʌltɪskriːn] *n* **(a) m. (cinema)** complexe *m* multisalles, cinéma *m* multisalle **(b)** *TV* écran-mosaïque *m*, multi-écran *m*; **m. channel** canal *m* mosaïque
multisector [ˈmʌltɪsektər] *adj* multisectoriel; **m. journey** voyage *m* multi-secteur; **m. ticketing** délivrance *f* de billets multi-secteurs
multi-spreadsheet *n* multifeuille *f*
multistage [ˈmʌltɪsteɪdʒ] *adj El, MecE (amplifier, compressor)* à plusieurs étages; *Aut* **m. converter** convertisseur *m* multi-étagé; *Astronaut* **m. rocket** fusée *f* composite à étages multiples
multistorey, *US* **multistory** [mʌltɪˈstɔːrɪ] *adj (building)* à plusieurs étages; **m. (carpark)** parking *m* à plusieurs niveaux, parc *m* de stationnement à plusieurs niveaux
multisyllabic [mʌltɪsɪˈlæbɪk] *adj* polysyllabique
multitasking [mʌltɪˈtɑːskɪŋ] *n Comptr* multitâche *m*
multitrack [mʌltɪˈtræk] *adj (recording)* multipiste
multitracking [mʌltɪˈtrækɪŋ] *n (in recording)* enregistrement *m* multipiste
multitude [ˈmʌltɪtjuːd] *n* **(a)** *(large number) (of reasons etc)* multitude *f*, multiplicité *f*; *Fig* **to cover** *or* **hide a m. of sins** *(of carpet, woodwork etc)* ça cache des horreurs invraisemblables; *esp Hum (of job title, definition)* ça englobe des tas de choses **(b)** *Fml, Lit (crowd)* multitude *f*, foule *f*
multitudinous [mʌltɪˈtjuːdɪnəs] *adj Fml* nombreux, innombrable
multi-user *adj Comptr* pour utilisateurs multiples; **m. software** logiciel *m* multi-utilisateur; **m. system** système *m* multi-utilisateur
multi-valve *adj* multisoupape
multivision [ˈmʌltɪvɪʒən] *n* multivision *f*
mum¹ [mʌm] *n Br F (mother)* maman *f*
mum² *F* **1** *n* **m.'s the word!** motus (et bouche cousue)! **2** *adj* **to keep m. (about sth)** ne pas souffler mot (de qch)
mumble¹ [ˈmʌmb(ə)l] *n* marmonnement *m*, marmottement *m*; **to say in a m.** dire en marmonnant
mumble² **1** *vt* marmonner, marmotter; **he mumbled a few words** il a marmonné quelques mots **2** *vi* marmonner, parler entre ses dents *ou* dans sa barbe, manger ses mots
mumbo jumbo [ˈmʌmbəʊˈdʒʌmbəʊ] *n F (nonsense)* âneries *fpl*; *(words etc)* charabia *m*; *(ritual phrases etc)* bla-bla *m*; **astrology is just a load of m.** l'astrologie, c'est du pipeau
mummer [ˈmʌmər] *n Th* mime *mf*

mummery ['mʌmərɪ] *n Th* momerie *f*
mummification [mʌmɪfɪ'keɪʃən] *n* momification *f*
mummify ['mʌmɪfaɪ] **1** *vt* momifier **2** *vi* se momifier
mummy[1] ['mʌmɪ] *n (embalmed body)* momie *f*
mummy[2] *n Br F (mother)* maman *f*
mumps [mʌmps] *npl (usu with sing verb) Med* oreillons *mpl*; **to have m.** avoir les oreillons
munch [mʌntʃ] *vt* mâcher, mâchonner
▶ **munch at** *vipo* mastiquer
▶ **munch away** *vi* mastiquer; **he was munching away at an apple** il mastiquait (bruyamment) une pomme
▶ **munch on** *vipo* = **munch at**
munchies ['mʌntʃɪz] *npl F (snacks)* petites choses *fpl* à grignoter; **to have the m., to have an attack of the m.** *(desire to eat)* avoir la fringale
mundane [mʌn'deɪn] *adj* banal, ordinaire
municipal [mju:'nɪsɪp(ə)l] *adj* municipal; **m. buildings** = mairie *f*; *(in large town)* hôtel *m* de ville; *Can, Austr* **m. district** = municipalité *f*
municipality [mju:nɪsɪ'pælɪtɪ] *n* municipalité *f*
munificence [mju:'nɪfɪsəns] *n* munificence *f*
munificent [mju:'nɪfɪsənt] *adj* munificent, généreux
munitions [mju:'nɪʃənz] *npl* munitions *fpl*; **m. dump** dépôt *m* de munitions; **m. factory** fabrique *f ou* usine *f* de munitions; **m. worker** personne *f* qui travaille dans une usine de munitions
mural ['mjʊərəl] *Art* **1** *adj* mural; **m. paintings** peintures *mpl* murales **2** *n* peinture *f* murale
murder[1] ['mɜ:dər] *n* meurtre *m*; *Jur* homicide *m* volontaire; *Jur* **premeditated m.,** *US* **m. in the first degree** assassinat *m*; **to commit (a) m.** commettre un meurtre/assassinat; **m. case** affaire *f* de meurtre; **m. trial** procès *m* pour meurtre; **the m. weapon** l'arme *f* du crime; *Fig* **it's (sheer** *or* **downright) m. in the rush hour** c'est (absolument) cauchemardesque *ou* infernal aux heures de pointe; **it's m. trying to park in the town centre** c'est cauchemardesque *ou* infernal d'essayer de se garer dans le centre-ville; *Fig* **he gets away with m.** il peut tout se permettre, personne ne lui dit quoi que ce soit; **their kids get away with m.** leurs gosses font absolument tout ce qu'ils veulent
murder[2] **1** *vt* **(a)** *(kill)* assassiner; *Fig F* **I'll m. you (for that)!** je vais te tuer! **(b)** *Fig F (destroy) (song, tune etc)* massacrer, saboter **(c)** *Fig F (defeat heavily)* battre à plates coutures **(d)** *Br Fig, F (drink, eat)* **I could m. a beer/pizza** je me taperais bien une bière/une pizza **2** *vi* commettre un meurtre
murderer ['mɜ:dərər] *n* meurtrier *m*, assassin *m*
murderess ['mɜ:dəres] *n* meurtrière *f*
murderous ['mɜ:dərəs] *adj* meurtrier, assassin; **with m. intent** dans une intention homicide; **a m.-looking knife** un couteau à l'apparence particulièrement menaçante; **to give sb a m. look** lancer un regard meurtrier à qn
murk [mɜ:k] *n* obscurité *f*, ténèbres *fpl*
murky ['mɜ:kɪ] *adj* obscur, ténébreux; *(sky)* brouillé; *(details)* sordide; **m. past** passé *m* obscur *ou* ténébreux
murmur[1] ['mɜ:mər] *n* **(a)** *(of voices, waves)* murmure *m*; *Med* **heart m.** souffle *m* (au cœur) **(b)** *(of approval, discontent etc)* murmure *m*; **without a m.** *(to do sth)* sans murmurer, sans broncher; **in a m.** à voix basse
murmur[2] **1** *vi* murmurer, susurrer; *(complain)* murmurer **(against** contre) **2** *vt (sth)* murmurer, dire à voix basse
murmuring ['mɜ:mərɪŋ] *n* murmure *m*; **murmurings** *(complaints)* murmures **(against** contre)
Murphy ['mɜ:fɪ] *n Am* **M. bed** lit *m* escamotable; *F* **M.'s Law** loi *f* de l'emmerdement maximum
muscatel [mʌskə'tel] *n* muscat *m*
muscle ['mʌs(ə)l] *n* **(a)** *Anat* muscle *m*; **she didn't move a m.** elle n'a pas bronché; **he has plenty of m.** il est bien musclé; **m. fibre** fibres *fpl* musculaires **(b)** *Fig (political, financial)* pouvoir *m*; **it would give our campaign more m.** cela donnerait plus de force à notre campagne
▶ **muscle in** *vi F (force one's way in)* s'immiscer, s'imposer **(on sth** dans qch); **a lot of big companies are muscling in** de nombreuses grosses sociétés arrivent en force; **to m. in on sb's territory** marcher sur les plates-bandes de qn; **we don't want them muscling in** nous ne voulons pas qu'ils marchent sur nos plates-bandes
musclebound ['mʌs(ə)lbaʊnd] *adj* très musclé
muscleman, *pl* **-men** ['mʌs(ə)lmæn, -men] *n (strongman)* Monsieur *m* Muscle
Muscovite ['mʌskəvaɪt] **1** *adj* moscovite **2** *n* Moscovite *mf*
muscular ['mʌskjʊlər] *adj* **(a)** *Anat (system, tissue, action)* musculaire **(b)** *(man)* musclé
muscular dystrophy *n Med* myopathie *f*
musculature ['mʌskjʊlətʃər] *n Anat* musculature *f*
Muse [mju:z] *n* **(a)** *Myth* Muse *f*; **the (nine) Muses** les Muses **(b)** *(of poet)* **the m.** les muses *fpl*
muse [mju:z] **1** *vi* songer, rêver **2** *vt* **that's queer, he mused** voilà qui est bien étrange, songea-t-il
▶ **muse on** *vipo* songer à
museum [mju:'zɪəm] *n* musée *m*; **m. piece** pièce *f* de musée; *Fig Hum* **his car's a m. piece** sa voiture est une pièce de musée
mush [mʌʃ] *n* **(a)** *F (pulp)* bouillie *f*, purée *f* **(b)** *esp US Culin* bouillie *f* de farine de maïs **(c)** *F (sentimentality)* sentimentalité *f* (à l'eau de rose)
mushroom[1] ['mʌʃrʊm] *n* **(a)** *(fungus)* champignon *m*; **cultivated** *or* **button mushrooms** champignons de couche *ou* de Paris; **m. cloud** champignon (atomique); **m. farm** champignonnière *f*; **m. grower** champignonniste *mf*; **m. soup** potage *m* aux champignons; **m. town** ville *f* champignon **(b)** *Sewing* boule *f* à repriser
mushroom[2] *vi* **(a)** *(gather mushrooms)* faire la cueillette des champignons; **to go mushrooming** aller aux champignons **(b)** *(grow rapidly)* pousser comme un champignon/des champignons; *(proliferate)* se multiplier, proliférer; **profits/costs have mushroomed in the past year** les profits/coûts ont considérablement augmenté durant l'année passée
mushrooming ['mʌʃrʊmɪŋ] *n* **(a)** *(gathering of mushrooms)* cueillette *f* des champignons **(b)** *(rapid growth)* croissance *f* rapide; *(proliferation)* multiplication *f* rapide, prolifération *f*
mushy ['mʌʃɪ] *adj* **(a)** *(food etc)* en bouillie; *(ground etc)* détrempé; *(pear etc)* blet, *f* blette; **m. peas** purée *f* de pois **(b)** *F (sentimental)* sentimental, à l'eau de rose, à la guimauve; **m. sentimentality** sentimentalité *f* à l'eau de rose *ou* à la guimauve
music ['mju:zɪk] *n* musique *f*; **to set words to m.** mettre des paroles en musique; **(sheet) m.** partition *f*; **I can't play without m.** je ne peux pas jouer sans partition; *Fig* **those words were m. to his ears** il était ravi d'entendre ces mots, ces mots le remplirent d'aise; **m. and effects track** bande *f* musique et effets (sonores), version *f* internationale; **m. box** boîte *f* à musique; **m. case** porte-musique *m inv*; **m. centre** *(stereo unit)* combiné *m* stéréophonique; *esp Br* **m. hall** music-hall *m*, *pl* music-halls; **m. lover** mélomane *mf*; **m. paper** papier *m* à musique; **m. press** presse *f* musicale; **m. stand** pupitre *m* à musique; **m. station** station *f* musicale; **m. video** clip *m*
musical ['mju:zɪk(ə)l] **1** *adj* **(a)** musical; *(instrument)* de musique; **to be m.** *(of person)* être (bon) musicien/(bonne) musicienne; **m. box** boîte *f* à musique; **m. chairs** chaises *fpl* musicales; *also Fig* **to play m. chairs** jouer aux chaises musicales; *Cin, Th* **m. comedy** comédie *f* musicale; **m. evening** soirée *f* musicale **(b)** *(sound, voice)* harmonieux, mélodieux **2** *n Cin, Th* comédie *f* musicale
musician [mju:'zɪʃən] *n* musicien, -ienne
musicianship [mju:'zɪʃənʃɪp] *n* qualités *fpl* de musicien/musicienne
musicologist [mju:zɪ'kɒlədʒɪst] *n* musicologue *mf*
musicology [mju:zɪ'kɒlədʒɪ] *n* musicologie *f*
musing ['mju:zɪŋ] **1** *adj* songeur, pensif, rêveur **2** *n* **musings** rêverie(s) *f(pl)*
musk [mʌsk] *n (substance, smell)* musc *m*; **m. cat** civette *f*; **m. deer** porte-musc *m inv*, musc *m*; **m. ox** bœuf *m* musqué; **m. (plant)** musc *m*; **m. rose** *(flower)* rose *f* musquée; *(bush)* rosier *m* musqué
musket ['mʌskɪt] *n Mil, Hist* mousquet *m*
musketeer [mʌskɪ'tɪər] *n Mil, Hist* mousquetaire *m*; **the Three Musketeers** Les Trois Mousquetaires
musketry ['mʌskɪtrɪ] *n Mil* tir *m* au fusil
muskrat ['mʌskræt] *n* **(a)** *(North American)* rat *m* musqué, ondatra *m* **(b)** *(European)* desman *m* musqué
musky ['mʌskɪ] *adj* musqué, de musc
Muslim ['mʌzlɪm] *adj, n* = **Moslem**
muslin ['mʌzlɪn] *n Tex* mousseline *f*, *Am* calicot *m*
musquash ['mʌskwɒʃ] *n* **(a)** *(animal)* rat *m* musqué, ondatra *m* **(b)** *(fur)* rat *m* musqué
muss [mʌs] *vt Am F* = **muss up**
▶ **muss up** *vtsep Am F (hair)* déranger; *(dress)* froisser, chiffonner
mussel ['mʌs(ə)l] *n* moule *f*; **m. bank** *or* **bed** banc *m* de moules; *(man-made)* moulière *f*
must[1] [mʌst] *n F* **(a)** *(necessity)* nécessité *f*, chose *f* indispensable; **the ability to speak Russian is a m.** il est indispensable de savoir parler russe, une bonne connaissance du russe est un must; **sunglasses are a m.** les lunettes de soleil sont indispensables **(b)** *(thing not to be missed, that must be done)* chose *f* à ne pas manquer/à faire à tout prix; **this film's a m.** c'est un film à ne pas manquer
must[2] *modal, aux v inv* [①**A58,e; B36-7,K,1**] **(must not** *is often contracted into* **mustn't) (a)** *(expressing obligation)* **you m. be ready at four o'clock** vous devez *ou* devrez être prêt à

quatre heures, il faut *ou* faudra que vous soyez prêt à quatre heures; **you m. hurry up** il faut vous dépêcher; **you mustn't tell anyone** vous ne devez le dire à personne, il ne faut le dire à personne; **you mustn't touch it!** il ne faut pas y toucher!; **we mustn't be late** il ne faut pas que nous soyons en retard; **they mustn't find out** il ne faut pas qu'ils le sachent; **plant that m. have continual attention** plante qui demande des soins continuels; **I simply m. see him** il faut absolument que je le voie; **he is stupid, I m. say** il est stupide, je dois l'avouer; **I m. say I thought it was rather good** je dois dire que c'était très bien; *Iron* **very clever, I m. say!** je dois dire que c'est très astucieux!; **if you m.** si c'est vraiment nécessaire; **m. you be so silly?** qu'est-ce que tu peux être bête!; **why m. you always be so unhelpful?** pourquoi faut-il toujours que tu sois si peu serviable?; **if you m. drink so much, what do you expect?** si tu t'entêtes à boire autant, il ne faut pas t'étonner!

(**b**) (*suggesting, inviting*) **you m. come and visit us** il faut que vous veniez nous voir; **we m. go out for a drink** il faut que nous allions boire un verre

(**c**) (*expressing probability*) **you m. be hungry after your walk** vous devez avoir faim après votre promenade; **it m. be interesting working there** ça doit être intéressant de travailler là; **you m. be joking** tu plaisantes!; *F* **she mustn't be very happy** elle ne doit pas être très heureuse; **I m. have made a mistake** j'ai dû me tromper; **she m. have been talking about somebody else** elle devait parler de quelqu'un d'autre; **if he says so it m. be true** s'il le dit c'est que c'est vrai; **was it her? – it m. have been** est-ce que c'était elle? – oui, je pense; **I saw that he m. have suspected something** j'ai bien vu qu'il avait dû se douter de quelque chose

must[3] *n* (*in winemaking*) moût *m*

must[4] *n* (*mould*) moisi *m*, moisissure *f*

mustache ['mʌstæʃ] *n US* = **moustache**

mustang ['mʌstæŋ] *n* (*horse*) mustang *m*

mustard ['mʌstəd] *n Bot, Culin* moutarde *f*; **m. and cress** moutarde blanche et cresson *m* alénois; **French m.** = sorte *f* de moutarde aux condiments; *Am Fig Sl* **to cut the m.** se montrer à la hauteur; *Mil* **m. gas** gaz *m* moutarde; *Med* **m. plaster** cataplasme *m* sinapisé *ou* à la moutarde; **m. pot** moutardier *m*, pot *m* à moutarde; **m. powder** farine *f* de moutarde; **m. seed** graine *f* de moutarde

muster[1] ['mʌstər] *n* (*action of gathering*) rassemblement *m*; (*meeting*) assemblée *f*, réunion *f*; (*roll call*), *Naut etc* appel *m*; *Mil* contrôles *mpl*; *Fig* **to pass m.** passer, être passable, être acceptable; **m. roll** feuille *f* d'appel

muster[2] **1** *vt* (**a**) (*supporters, funds*) rassembler; **society that musters a hundred members** association qui compte cent membres; **she mustered all her strength** elle a rassemblé toutes ses forces; **to m. one's courage** rassembler son courage, prendre son courage à deux mains; **we need all the help we can m.** nous avons besoin de toute l'aide que nous pouvons trouver (**b**) *Naut* (*men*) faire l'appel de; (*crew*) assembler **2** *vi* s'assembler, se rassembler

▶ **muster up** *vtsep* = **muster**[2](**a**)

musty ['mʌstɪ] *adj* (*taste, smell*) de moisi; (*books, room*) qui sent le moisi; **to smell m.** sentir le moisi; (*of room etc*) sentir le renfermé

mutability [mjuːtə'bɪlɪtɪ] *n* mutabilité *f*

mutable ['mjuːtəb(ə)l] *adj* (**a**) variable, mutable (**b**) *Ling* sujet à mutation

mutant ['mjuːtənt] *adj, n* mutant *m*

mutate [mjuː'teɪt] **1** *vi* subir une mutation; **to m. into sth** se transformer en qch **2** *vt* faire subir une mutation à

mutation [mjuː'teɪʃən] *n* altération *f*, changement *m*; *Biol* mutation *f*; **m. of type** métatypie *f*

mute[1] [mjuːt] **1** *adj* (**a**) (*person, appeal etc*) muet; **she stood m. with wonder** elle restait muette d'étonnement (**b**) *Ling* muet; (*consonant*) sourd **2** *n* (**a**) (*dumb person*) muet, -ette (**b**) *Mus* sourdine *f*

mute[2] *vt* (**a**) (*muffle*) amortir, étouffer, assourdir (**b**) *Mus* mettre une sourdine à, assourdir

muted ['mjuːtɪd] *adj* (*sound, voice etc*) assourdi, sourd; (*colour*) sourd; (*protest, criticism etc*) voilé; *Mus* (*trumpet etc*) en sourdine; **to discuss in m. tones** discuter à voix basse

mutely ['mjuːtlɪ] *adv* silencieusement, en silence

mutilate ['mjuːtɪleɪt] *vt* (*person*) mutiler, estropier; (*statue, play*) mutiler; *Fig* (*passage, quotation*) tronquer

mutilation [mjuːtɪ'leɪʃən] *n* mutilation *f*

mutineer [mjuːtɪ'nɪər] *n* mutiné *m*, mutin *m*

mutinous ['mjuːtɪnəs] *adj* rebelle, mutiné, mutin; (*crew*) mutiné, insurgé

mutiny[1] ['mjuːtɪnɪ] *n* révolte *f*, mutinerie *f*

mutiny[2] *vi* se révolter, se mutiner (**against** contre)

mutism ['mjuːtɪz(ə)m] *n* mutisme *m*

mutt [mʌt] *n F* (**a**) (*dog*) clebs *m*, clébard *m* (**b**) (*idiot*) idiot, -ote, andouille *f*; **poor m.!** pauvre mec!

mutter[1] ['mʌtər] *n* murmure *m*; **a m. of discontent** un murmure de mécontentement

mutter[2] **1** *vt* marmonner, marmotter; (*say unclearly*) dire dans sa barbe; **a muttered protest** un marmottement de protestation; **he muttered something to himself** (*angrily*) il a murmuré quelque chose entre ses dents **2** *vi* marmonner, marmotter; (*speak unclearly*) parler dans sa barbe; (*complain*) murmurer

muttering ['mʌtərɪŋ] *n* marmottement *m*, grommellement *m*; **mutterings** (*complaints*) murmures *mpl* de mécontentement

mutton ['mʌt(ə)n] *n Culin* mouton *m*; **leg of m.** gigot *m*; **m. chop** *or* **cutlet** côtelette *f* de mouton; *F* **m.-chop whiskers** favoris *mpl* en côtelette; *Fig* **m. dressed (up) as lamb** femme *f* qui essaie de faire plus jeune que son âge

muttonchops ['mʌt(ə)ntʃɒps] *npl* (*whiskers*) favoris *mpl* en côtelette

muttonhead ['mʌt(ə)nhed] *n F* andouille *f*, cornichon *m*

mutual ['mjuːtʃʊəl] *adj* (**a**) (*reciprocal*) (*feelings etc*) mutuel, réciproque; *El* (*attraction*) mutuel; **the feeling is m.** c'est réciproque; **m. benefit society** société *f* de secours mutuel; **m. (investment) fund** fonds *m* commun de placement, FCP *m*; *Fin* **m. insurance** assurance *f* mutuelle; **m. insurance company** mutuelle *f* (**b**) (*shared*) commun; **a m. friend** un ami commun

mutually ['mjuːtʃʊəlɪ] *adv* mutuellement, réciproquement; **to be m. exclusive** s'exclure l'un(e) l'autre

Muzak® ['mjuːzæk] *n* musiqueette *f*

muzzle[1] ['mʌz(ə)l] *n* (**a**) (*mouth of animal*) museau *m* (**b**) (*device*) (*for dog etc*) muselière *f*; (*for horse*) bâillon *m* (**c**) (*of gun*) bouche *f*, gueule *f*; **m. velocity** vitesse *f* initiale

muzzle[2] *vt* (*dog*) museler; *Fig* (*press etc*) museler, bâillonner

muzzle-loader *n Mil* pièce *f* se chargeant par la bouche

muzzy ['mʌzɪ] *adj F* (*ideas*) confus; (*outline, picture*) flou, estompé; **I feel m.** (*slightly unwell*) je me sens tout drôle; **my head feels a bit m.** j'ai la tête qui tourne; **she was m. about what it really meant** elle ne comprenait pas bien ce que tout cela signifiait

MV [em'viː] (**a**) *El* (*abbr* **megavolt(s)**) MV (**b**) *Naut* (*abbr* **motor vessel**) bateau *m* à moteur

MW [em'dʌb(ə)ljuː] (**a**) *Rad* (*abbr* **Medium Wave**) P. O. *fpl* (**b**) *El* (*abbr* **megawatt(s)**) MW

my [maɪ] **1** *poss adj* [ⓘ**A30**,8; **A42-3**; **B19-20**,E,1] mon, ma, *pl* mes; (*in the f sing before a vowel sound*) mon; **my hat and gloves** mon chapeau et mes gants; **in my opinion** à mon avis; **one of my friends** un de mes amis, un ami à moi; **my own son** mon propre fils; **my hair is grey** j'ai les cheveux gris; **if you don't mind my asking** si je peux me permettre de vous le demander; **my idea would be to …** mon idée à moi serait de …; **my turn!** à moi! **2** *int F* **my! how you've changed!** mon Dieu, comme vous avez changé!; **my! my! aren't we touchy!** oh là là! que vous êtes susceptible!; **(oh) my!** ça par exemple!

myalgic encephalomyelitis [maɪ'ældʒɪkensefələʊmaɪə'laɪtɪs] *n Med* encéphalomyélite *f* myalgique

mycology [maɪ'kɒlədʒɪ] *n Bot* mycologie *f*

myelitis [maɪə'laɪtɪs] *n Med* myélite *f*

myeloma [maɪə'ləʊmə] *n Med* myélome *m*

myna(h) ['maɪnə] *n* **m. (bird)** mainate *m*

myocardial [maɪəʊ'kɑːdɪəl] *n Med* **m. infarct(ion)** infarctus *m* du myocarde

myopia [maɪ'əʊpɪə] *n* myopie *f*; *Fig* manque *m* de perspicacité

myopic [maɪ'ɒpɪk] *adj* (*person, eyes, look*) myope; *Fig* qui manque de perspicacité

myriad ['mɪrɪəd] **1** *n* myriade *f* **2** *adj Lit* innombrable

myriapod ['mɪrɪəpɒd] *adj, n Biol* myriapode *m*

myrmidon ['mɜːmɪd(ə)n] *n Pej Hum* homme *m* de main

myrrh [mɜːr] *n* myrrhe *f*

myrtle ['mɜːt(ə)l] *n* (*shrub*) myrte *m*; *Am* (*periwinkle*) pervenche *f* grimpante

myself [maɪ'self] *pers pron* [ⓘ**A29**] (**a**) (*emphatic*) moi(-même); **I did it m.** je l'ai fait moi-même; *F* **I'm not quite m.** je ne suis pas dans mon assiette; **I m. believe that …** (quant à) moi *ou* pour ma part, je crois que … (**b**) [ⓘ**B26**,D] (*reflexive*) me; (*before vowel sound*) m'; **I've hurt m.** je me suis fait mal; **I was enjoying m. very much** je m'amusais beaucoup (**c**) (*after preposition*) **I live by m.** je vis tout seul; **I was laughing to m.** je riais tout seul; **I'll keep it for m.** je le garderai pour moi

mysterious [mɪs'tɪərɪəs] **1** *adj* mystérieux **2** *n* (*no pl*) **the m.** le mystérieux

mysteriously [mɪs'tɪərɪəslɪ] *adv* mystérieusement, de façon mystérieuse

mysteriousness [mɪs'tɪərɪəsnɪs] *n* caractère *m* mystérieux, mystère *m* (**of** de)

mystery ['mɪstərɪ] **1** *n* mystère *m*; **to make a m. of sth** faire (un) mystère de qch; **why make such a m. out of it?** pourquoi (faire) tant de mystères?; **it's a m. to me** pour moi, c'est un mystère; **there's no great m. about it** ça n'a rien de mystérieux; (*it's not a secret*) ce n'est un secret pour personne; **the key to the m.** la clef du mystère; **m. novel** roman *m* à énigmes; *Th* **m. (play)** mystère; **m. tour** voyage *m* surprise **2** *adj* (*guest, prize*) surprise; **m. man** mystérieux individu *m*; **who was the m. benefactor?** qui était le mystérieux bienfaiteur?

mystic ['mɪstɪk] **1** *adj Rel* mystique; (*rites, arts*) ésotérique; (*power*) occulte **2** *n* mystique *mf*

mystical ['mɪstɪk(ə)l] *adj* mystique

mysticism ['mɪstɪsɪz(ə)m] *n* mysticisme *m*

mystification [mɪstɪfɪ'keɪʃən] *n* (*action, result*) mystification *f*; **to our (great) m.** à notre grande perplexité

mystify ['mɪstɪfaɪ] *vt* (*bewilder*) (*person*) laisser perplexe, déconcerter; **mystified by …** intrigué par …; **I was mystified** j'étais perplexe

mystique [mɪs'tiːk] *n* mystique *f*

myth [mɪθ] *n* mythe *m*

mythical ['mɪθɪk(ə)l] *adj* mythique

mythological [mɪθə'lɒdʒɪk(ə)l] *adj* mythologique

mythology [mɪ'θɒlədʒɪ] *n* mythologie *f*

myxomatosis [mɪksəmə'təʊsɪs] *n* myxomatose *f*

N

N, n [en] **1** *n* (*letter*) N, n *m*; **two N's** *or* **Ns** deux N **2** *abbr* **(a)** **(North)** N. **(b)** *Phys* **(Newton)** N.

n/a, N/A *Admin abbr* **not applicable**

NAACP [eneɪeɪsiːˈpiː] *n US* (*abbr* **National Association for the Advancement of Colored People**) = association *f* nationale pour la promotion des personnes de couleur

NAAFI [ˈnæfɪ] *n Br Mil* (*abbr* **Navy, Army and Air Force Institutes**) (*organization, canteen, shop*) = coopérative *f* militaire

nab [næb] *vt* **(-bb-)** *Sl* **(a)** (*steal*) faucher **(b)** (*catch doing sth, arrest*) pincer, choper; **to get nabbed** se faire pincer *ou* choper

nabob [ˈneɪbɒb] *n* nabab *m*

nacelle [næˈsel] *n* **(a)** (*of aircraft*) carlingue *f*, habitacle *m*; **(engine) n.** fuseau-moteur *m*, *pl* fuseaux-moteur **(b)** (*of airship, balloon*) nacelle *f*

nacre [ˈneɪkər] *n* nacre *f*

nadir [ˈneɪdɪər] *n* nadir *m*; *Fig* point *m* le plus bas

naevus, *US* **nevus,** *pl* **-i** [ˈniːvəs, -aɪ] *n Med* nævus *m*, *pl* nævi

naff [næf] *adj Br Sl* **(a)** (*tasteless*) ringard; **(b)** (*stupid*) nul; **it was pretty n. of me to do that** j'ai été carrément nul d'avoir fait ça

▶ **naff off** *vi Br Sl* **n. off!** casse-toi!

NAFTA [ˈnæftə] *n* (*abbr* **North American Free Trade Agreement**) ALENA *m*

nag[1] [næg] *n F* (*horse*) bidet *m*, bourrin *m*

nag[2] *n* (*person*) enquiquineur, -euse; (*woman also*) chipie *f*; **she's a terrible n.** elle n'arrête pas de nous/le/*etc* harceler

nag[3] **(-gg-)** **1** *vi* **he's always nagging** il n'arrête pas de me/te/*etc* casser les pieds *ou* harceler **2** *vt* (*person*) casser les pieds à, harceler; (*of doubt*) harceler; (*of conscience*) ne pas laisser en paix, tourmenter; **she's always nagging (at) him to get it fixed** elle n'arrête pas de lui casser les pieds *ou F* de l'asticoter pour qu'il le fasse réparer; **he nags her to death** il la harcèle sans pitié; **why do I always have to n. you into doing everything?** pourquoi faut-il que je sois toujours après toi pour que tu fasses quoi que ce soit?

▶ **nag at** *vipo* = **nag[3] 2; her conscience was nagging at her to go to the police** sa conscience l'exhortait sans répit à se rendre à la police

nagger [ˈnægər] *n* = **nag[2]**

nagging [ˈnægɪŋ] **1** *adj* (*pain*) tenace; (*worry, fear, uncertainty*) tenace, qui persiste; **I've got a n. doubt that …** je n'arrête pas de me demander si …; **I've still got this n. doubt about him** je n'arrête pas de me poser des questions à son sujet; **I've got this n. feeling that …** j'ai cette impression persistante que …; **he has a n. wife** sa femme est une enquiquineuse **2** *n* harcèlement *m*; **I've had enough of your n.!** j'en ai assez que tu me harcèles *ou F* m'enquiquines!

naiad *pl* **-ads, -ades** [ˈnaɪæd, -ædz, -ədiːz] *n Myth* naïade *f*

nail[1] [neɪl] *n* **(a)** (*for fixing*) clou *m*; *Fig* **another n. in sb's coffin/the coffin of sth** un autre coup funeste à qn/qch; *Fig, F* **to hit the n. (right) on the head** mettre le doigt dessus **(b)** (*of person*) ongle *m*; **n. varnish** *or* **polish** *or esp US* **enamel** vernis *m* à ongles **(c)** *F* **to pay on the n.** payer rubis sur l'ongle; **she demanded cash on the n.** elle a exigé qu'on la paie en argent comptant

nail[2] *vt* **(a)** clouer **(onto** à**)**; **to n. sth shut** clouer qch; **she nailed the plank into place** elle a fixé la planche à l'aide de clous; *Fig* **he stood nailed to the spot** il est resté cloué au sol **(in fear/astonishment** de peur/surprise**)** **(b)** (*shoes, door etc*) clouter **(c)** *F* (*catch*) (*person*) attraper, coincer; *F* **to n. a lie** exposer un mensonge; **we should n. the lie that unemployment is falling** nous devrions démontrer que la soi-disant baisse du chômage n'est qu'un tissu de mensonges

▶ **nail down** *vtsep* **(a)** (*fasten*) (*lid of a box*) clouer; (*furniture*) fixer à l'aide de clous; *Fig F* **you'd better n. that table down or it'll walk** tu ferais bien de cadenasser cette table au sol sinon elle va disparaître **(b)** *F* **we couldn't n. him down to anything definite** nous n'avons pu obtenir aucun engagement précis de sa part; **to n. sb down on a date** obtenir de qn qu'il fixe une date

▶ **nail up** *vtsep* (*crate, box*) clouer; (*door, window*) condamner

nail-biting **1** *adj F* (*finish, excitement etc*) palpitant; (*film, story*) à suspense **2** *n* habitude *f* de se ronger les ongles

nailbrush [ˈneɪlbrʌʃ] *n* brosse *f* à ongles

nailfile [ˈneɪlfaɪl] *n* lime *f* à ongles

nail punch *n Tech* chasse-clou *m*, *pl* chasse-clous, chasse-pointe *m*, *pl* chasse-pointes

nail scissors *n* ciseaux *mpl* à ongles

nail set *n Tech* chasse-clou *m*, *pl* chasse-clous, chasse-pointe *m*, *pl* chasse-pointes

naïve, naive [naɪˈiːv] *adj* (*person, manner etc*) naïf; (*ingenuous*) ingénu; *Art* **n. art** l'art *m* naïf

naïvely, naively [naɪˈiːvlɪ] *adv* naïvement

naïveté, naivety [naɪˈiːvtɪ] *n* naïveté *f*

naked [ˈneɪkɪd] *adj* **(a)** (*person*) nu, *F* à poil; (*arm, back etc*) découvert, nu; (*wall etc*) nu, dégarni; (*countryside, tree*) dénudé, nu; *Biol* (*stalk, tail etc*) nu; **stark n.** tout nu, *F* nu comme un ver; **to strip (oneself) n.** se mettre nu *ou F* à poil **(b)** *Fig* (*sword, flame, eye, lightbulb*) nu; (*aggression, exploitation*) (*not concealed*) non dissimulé; (*outright*) flagrant; **n. facts** faits bruts; **visible to the n. eye** visible à l'œil nu; *St Exch* **n. sale** vente *f* nue; **the n. truth** la pure vérité, la vérité toute nue

nakedness [ˈneɪkɪdnɪs] *n* nudité *f*

NALGO [ˈnælgəʊ] *n Br* (*abbr* **National and Local Government Officers' Association**) = association *f* des fonctionnaires nationaux et régionaux

namby-pamby [ˈnæmbɪˈpæmbɪ] **1** *n* (*ineffectual person*) gnangnan *mf*, gnian-gnian *mf*, *pl* gnian-gnians, mollasson, -onne **2** *adj* (*spineless*) (*person*) ramolli, gnangnan *inv*, gnian-gnian *inv*; (*remark, attitude*) faiblard

name[1] [neɪm] *n* **(a)** (*of person, object, plant etc*) nom *m*; (*of ship*) devise *f*, nom; *Com* (*of company, business*) raison *f* sociale; (*of account*) intitulé *m*; (*of play, novel etc*) titre *m*; **full n.** nom et prénoms *mpl*; **what's your n.?** quel est votre nom?, comment vous appelez-vous?; **my n. is …** je m'appelle …; **a man by the n. of Blenkinsop** un homme du nom de Blenkinsop; **to go by** *or* **under the n. of …** être connu sous le nom de …; **he answers to his n.** (*of dog etc*) il répond quand on l'appelle; **to know sb by n.** connaître qn de nom; **to know sb by another** *or* **a different n.** connaître qn sous un autre nom; **to mention sb/sth by n.** nommer qn/qch; **you were mentioned by n.** on a cité votre nom, on vous a nommé; **to put a n. to sth** donner un nom à qch, mettre un nom sur qch; **to put a n. to a face** mettre un nom sur un visage; **to take sb's n.** (*of police etc*) prendre le nom de qn; *Fb* donner un carton jaune à qn; *Fb* **to have one's n. taken** recevoir un carton jaune; **he took his idol's n.** il a pris le nom de son idole; **I'm sorry, I didn't catch** *or* **get your n.** désolé, je n'ai pas bien entendu votre nom; **what n. shall I say?** (*to caller*) qui dois-je annoncer?; **famous n.** (*person*) célébrité *f*; **a big n. in the theatre** un nom bien connu dans le monde du théâtre; **to send in one's n.** (*for competition etc*) se faire inscrire; (*have oneself announced*) se faire annoncer; **to put one's n. down** (*in election*) poser sa candidature; (*on list*) s'inscrire **(for sth** pour qch**)**; **list of names** liste nominative; **in the n. of …** au nom de …; **in the n. of the law/the king** au nom de la loi/du roi; **in the n. of God** *or* **Heaven, in God's** *or* **Heaven's n.** pour l'amour de Dieu; *F* **what in the n. of God** *or* **Heaven** *or* **goodness are you doing?** que diable faites-vous là?; **to be master/prime minister in n. only** n'être maître/premier ministre que de nom; **they are married in n. only** (*marriage hasn't been consummated*) leur mariage est un mariage blanc; (*without love*) ils ne sont mariés que pour la forme; **the PSF is a socialist party in n. only** le PSF n'a de socialiste que le nom; **she was President in all but n.** elle avait tout du Président sauf le nom; **they are married in all but n.** c'est comme s'ils étaient mariés; **insulting n.** appellation injurieuse; **to call sb names** insulter qn; **she called me a rude n.** elle m'a insulté;

that's the n. of the game c'est ce qui compte; **not to have a penny/a decent pair of shoes to one's n.** ne pas avoir un centime/une paire de chaussures convenable à soi; **to have several books to one's n.** être l'auteur de plusieurs livres; **to have several victories/trophies to one's n.** avoir remporté plusieurs victoires/trophées; *Com* **n. brand** *or* **product** marque *f*; **n. label** étiquette *f* de nom; *Mktg* **n. licensing** cession *f* de licence de nom

(**b**) (*reputation*) réputation *f*, renommée *f*; **she has a good/bad n.** elle a (une) bonne/(une) mauvaise réputation; **to get a bad n.** se faire une mauvaise réputation; **she has a n. for honesty** elle est connue *ou* réputée pour son honnêteté; **the firm has established a n. for quality** l'entreprise s'est bâtie une réputation de qualité; **to have a n. for prompt and efficient service** être réputé pour ses services rapides et efficaces; **to make a n. for oneself** se faire un nom *ou* une réputation (**as** de)

name² *vt* (**a**) (*give name to*) (*person, thing*) nommer, donner un nom à; (*ship*) baptiser; **he was named Peter** on lui a donné le nom de Peter, on l'a appelé *ou* nommé Peter; **someone named Thompson** un nommé Thompson; **to n. sb after sb** *or US* **for sb** donner à qn le nom de qn; **they named her Cathy after the heroine of Wuthering Heights** ils l'ont appelée Cathy, comme l'héroïne des Hauts du Hurlevent

(**b**) (*appoint*) nommer; **he was named (as) President** il a été nommé président; **she was named (as) best supporting actress** elle a été élue pour le meilleur second rôle féminin

(**c**) (*designate, identify by name*) désigner (par son nom); (*example, fact*) citer; (*reveal name of*) révéler le nom de, nommer; **n. the kings of England/these species of birds** donnez les noms des rois d'Angleterre/de ces espèces d'oiseaux; *Jur* **to n. sb as a beneficiary** (*in one's will etc*) désigner qn comme bénéficiaire; *Jur* **to n. sb as a witness** citer qn comme témoin; *Br Parl* **to n. a member** (*of the Speaker, in House of Commons*) signaler à la Chambre l'indiscipline d'un membre; **to n. names** donner des noms; **naming no names** sans nommer personne; *F* **you n. it, she's done it/got it** tout ce qu'on peut imaginer, elle l'a fait/le possède

(**d**) (*set*) (*day, amount*) fixer; **n. your price** donnez-moi un prix

name-calling *n* insultes *fpl*

named [neɪmd] *adj* nommé; **on the n. day** le jour fixé

name day *n* fête *f*

name-dropper *n* **she's a terrible n.** elle ne manque jamais de glisser des noms de personnalités (supposées connues d'elle) dans la conversation

name-dropping *n* **there was a lot of n. in his speech** il n'a pas arrêté de glisser des noms de personnalités (supposées connues de lui) dans son discours

nameless ['neɪmlɪs] *adj* (**a**) (*unknown*) (*person*) inconnu, obscur; (*anonymous*) (*writer, grave etc*) anonyme; **someone who shall be** *or* **remain n.** quelqu'un dont je tairai le nom (**b**) (*dread, grief etc*) indéfinissable, indicible, inexprimable; (*vice etc*) abominable

namely ['neɪmlɪ] *adv* c'est-à-dire, à savoir

name part *n Th, Cin* vrai rôle *m*; (*title role*) rôle qui donne son titre au film/à la pièce

nameplate ['neɪmpleɪt] *n* écusson *m*, médaillon *m* (*portant un nom*); (*on door etc*) plaque *f*; **manufacturer's n.** (*on machine etc*) plaque du constructeur

namesake ['neɪmseɪk] *n* homonyme *mf*; **my famous n.** la célébrité qui porte le même nom que moi

nametape ['neɪmteɪp] *n* marque *f* à linge

naming ['neɪmɪŋ] *n* (**a**) (*giving name*) attribution *f* d'un nom; (*of ship*) baptême *m*; **n. of a product** attribution *f* d'un nom à un produit (**b**) (*choosing*) (*of official*) nomination *f* (**c**) (*fixing*) (*of day, amount*) fixation *f*

nan¹, nana ['næn, 'nænə] *n F* (*grandmother*) mamie *f*, grand-maman *f*, mémé *f*

nan² *n Culin* **n. (bread)** pain *m* nan

nancy ['nænsɪ] *Old-fashioned Pej Sl* **1** *n* **n. (boy)** (*homosexual*) tapette *f*; (*effeminate man*) homme *m* efféminé, chochotte *f* **2** *adj* (*behaviour, ways etc*) de chochotte, de tapette

nanny ['nænɪ] *n* (**a**) (*nursemaid*) bonne *f* d'enfant, nurse *f*; (*in children's language*) nounou *f* (**b**) *F* (*grandmother*) mamie *f*, mémé *f* (**c**) **n. (goat)** chèvre *f*, *F* biquette *f*

nanosecond ['nænəʊsekənd] *n* nanoseconde *f*

nap¹ [næp] *n* (*sleep*) petit somme *m*; **afternoon n.** sieste *f*; **to take** *or* **have a n.** faire un petit somme; (*after lunch*) faire la sieste

nap² *vi* (**-pp-**) faire un petit somme; (*doze*) sommeiller; *Fig* **to be caught napping** (*off guard*) être pris au dépourvu

nap³ *n Tex* (*of cloth, velvet, felt*) poil *m*; **cloth with raised n.** étoffe molletonnée *ou* tirée à poil *ou* garnie; **against the n.** à rebrousse-poil, à rebours

nap⁴ *vt Tex* (*cloth*) garnir, gratter, lainer; (*wool, cotton*) molletonner

nap⁵ *n* (**a**) *Cards* **to go n.** demander les cinq levées; *Old-fashioned Fig* **to go n. on sth** être sûr et certain de qch; *Old-fashioned Fig* **to hold a n. hand** avoir en main toutes les cartes pour réussir (**b**) *Horseracing* tuyau *m* sûr

nap⁶ *vt Horseracing F* **to n. a winner** donner un tuyau sûr

napalm¹ ['neɪpɑːm] *n* napalm *m*; **n. bomb** bombe *f* au napalm

napalm² *vt* bombarder au napalm

nape [neɪp] *n* **n. (of the neck)** nuque *f*

naphtha ['næfθə] *n Ind* naphte *m*

naphthalene ['næfθəliːn] *n Ch, Com* naphtaline *f*, naphtalène *m*

napkin ['næpkɪn] *n* (**a**) **(table) n.** serviette *f* (de table) (**b**) *Br Fml* **(baby's) n.** couche *f* (de bébé) (**c**) *US* **(sanitary) n.** serviette *f* hygiénique

napkin ring *n* rond *m* de serviette

Napoleon [nə'pəʊlɪən] *n* Napoléon *m*

Napoleonic [nəpəʊlɪ'ɒnɪk] *adj* napoléonien

nappy ['næpɪ] *n Br* couche *f* (de bébé)

nappy rash *n* rougeurs *fpl* aux fesses, *Med* érythème *m* fessier

narc [nɑːk] *n US Sl* = agent *m* de la brigade des stups

narcissism ['nɑːsɪsɪz(ə)m] *n* narcissisme *m*

narcissistic [nɑːsɪ'sɪstɪk] *adj* narcissique

narcissus [nɑː'sɪsəs] *n, pl* **narcissi, narcissuses** [nɑː'sɪsaɪ, -'sɪsəsɪz] (*plant*) narcisse *m*

narcosis [nɑː'kəʊsɪs] *n Med* narcose *f*

narcotic [nɑː'kɒtɪk] **1** *adj* narcotique, stupéfiant **2** *n* narcotique *m*, stupéfiant *m*; *US* **narcotics agent** agent *m* de la brigade des stupéfiants; *US* **narcotics (branch)** (*of police force*) brigade *f* des stupéfiants

nark¹ [nɑːk] *n Br Sl* **(copper's) n.** indic *m*, mouchard *m*

nark² *vt Br F* (*annoy*) taper sur les nerfs de, énerver; **to get narked** s'énerver, s'exciter; **she's really narked about it** ça l'énerve vraiment

narky ['nɑːki] *adj Br F* de mauvais poil; **to get n.** se mettre en pétard

narrate [nə'reɪt] *vt* (*of person*) narrer, raconter, relater; (*of story, book*) raconter, relater; *TV, Cin* (*film, documentary*) lire *ou* dire le commentaire de; *Rad* (*play*) narrer

narration [nə'reɪʃən] *n* (**a**) (*of story etc*) narration *f*; *TV, Cin* (*of film, documentary*) (lecture *f* du) commentaire *m*; *Rad* (*of play*) narration (**b**) (*account*) récit *m*, narration *f*

narrative ['nærətɪv] **1** *n* (**a**) (*story*) récit *m*; *Liter* **the n.** le récit (**b**) (*art*) (l'art *m* de) la narration **2** *adj* (*style, poem*) narratif; **n. writer** narrateur, -trice

narrator [nə'reɪtər] *n* narrateur, -trice; *Mus* récitant, -ante

narrow¹ ['nærəʊ] **1** *adj* (*path etc*) étroit; (*body, waist, face*) mince; (*valley etc*) resserré; (*passage, channel*) étranglé; *Ling* (*vowel*) tendu; (*mind*) étroit, borné; (*existence*) limité, circonscrit; **to grow** *or* **become n.** se rétrécir; **to have n. shoulders** ne pas être large d'épaules, avoir des épaules étroites; **within n. bounds** dans des limites étroites; **to have a n. escape** *or F* **squeak** l'échapper belle; **n. bodied aircraft** avion *m* petit porteur; *Rail* **n. gauge (railway)** (chemin *m* de fer à) voie *f* étroite; **a n. interpretation** (*of rules etc*) une interprétation au pied de la lettre; **a n. majority** une faible majorité; **by a n. margin** (*to win, lose*) de peu; **they won by the n. margin of two points** ils ont gagné de deux petits points; **to win/lose by the narrowest of margins** gagner/perdre de très peu; **in the narrowest sense** dans le sens le plus strict; *Sp* **n. victory** victoire *f* remportée de justesse; **to suffer a n. defeat** être vaincu de peu; **to take a n. view of sth** adopter un point de vue étroit sur qch

2 *npl* **narrows** (*of river*) étranglement *m*

narrow² **1** *vt* (*road etc*) resserrer, rétrécir; (*space, choice, possibilities, chances*) restreindre, limiter; (*gap*) réduire, resserrer; (*ideas*) rétrécir; **to n. a margin of victory/defeat** réduire l'ampleur d'une victoire/défaite; **narrowed eyelids** paupières mi-closes **2** *vi* (*of road, path*) devenir plus étroit, se rétrécir; **the gap between rich and poor has narrowed** l'écart entre les riches et les pauvres s'est resserré

▶ **narrow down** *vtsep* (*limit*) limiter; (*possibilities*) restreindre, réduire; (*candidates*) réduire le nombre de; **that narrows it down to two suspects** cela nous laisse avec *ou* nous ramène à deux suspects

narrow-boat *n* péniche *f*

narrowing ['nærəʊɪŋ] *n Med* (*of artery etc*) rétrécissement *m*

narrowly ['nærəʊlɪ] *adv* (**a**) (*to interpret*) étroitement, strictement, au pied de la lettre (**b**) (*only just*) de peu; **he n. missed being run over** il a failli se faire écraser; **they n. escaped being caught** ils ont failli se faire prendre; **the missile just n. missed them** le missile les a ratés de peu

narrow-minded *adj* (*person*) (d'un esprit) borné, à l'esprit étroit; (*views, opinions*) borné; (*approach, outlook*) étroit, limité; **to be n. about politics/sex** être borné en ce qui concerne la politique/le sexe

narrow-mindedness [nærəʊ'maɪndɪdnɪs] *n* (*of person*) étroitesse *f* ou petitesse *f* d'esprit; (*of views, outlook*) caractère *m* borné

narrowness ['nærəʊnɪs] *n* (*of path, shoulders, passage etc*) étroitesse *f*; (*of sb's waist*) minceur *f*; (*of space etc*) petitesse *f*, exiguïté *f*; (*of gap, difference*) caractère *m* limité; (*of existence, intelligence etc*) limitations *fpl*; **n. of mind** étroitesse d'esprit

narw(h)al, narwhale ['nɑːwəl] *n* narval *m*, *pl* narvals

NASA ['næsə] *n US Astronaut* (*abbr* **National Aeronautics and Space Administration**) NASA *f*

nasal ['neɪz(ə)l] **1** *adj Anat, Ling etc* nasal; **the n. cavities** les fosses *fpl* nasales; **to have a n. voice** parler du nez **2** *n Ling* nasale *f*

nasalize ['neɪzəlaɪz] *vt* (*syllable etc*) nasaliser

nasally ['neɪzəlɪ] *adv* par le nez; **to speak n.** parler du nez, nasiller

nascent ['neɪsənt, 'næs-] *adj Fml* (*talent, discontent, suspicion etc*) naissant; *Ch* (*body, element*) à l'état naissant

nastily ['nɑːstɪlɪ] *adv* **(a)** (*unpleasantly*) désagréablement **(b)** (*maliciously*) méchamment **(c)** (*indecently*) indécemment

nastiness ['nɑːstɪnɪs] *n* **(a)** (*of smell, taste*) caractère *m* désagréable; (*of surroundings, building*) caractère répugnant; **the n. of the weather** le mauvais temps **(b)** (*of person*) méchanceté *f*; (*of remark*) méchanceté, malveillance *f*; **the n. of his behaviour** son comportement malveillant **(c)** (*of book, film etc*) ignominie *f*, bassesse *f*; (*of crime, rape*) atrocité *f*, abjection *f*

nasturtium [nə'stɜːʃ(ə)m] *n* (*plant*) capucine *f*

nasty ['nɑːstɪ] *adj* **(a)** (*unpleasant, bad*) désagréable; **his behaviour left (me with) a n. taste in the mouth** sa conduite m'a laissé un arrière-goût désagréable; **to give sb a n. fright** faire une sale peur à qn; **he had a n. surprise** il a eu une mauvaise surprise; **it gave her a n. shock** ça lui a donné un sale coup; **n. accident** accident *m* grave; **n. cold/rash** méchant(e) rhume/éruption; **n. corner** tournant dangereux; **n. wound** vilaine blessure; **she's had a n. attack of bronchitis** elle a fait une mauvaise bronchite; **he's had quite a n. blow to the head** il a pris un mauvais coup sur la tête; **n. weather** sale ou mauvais temps; **the weather turned n.** le temps s'est dégradé

(b) (*malicious*) (*person*) méchant, mauvais, déplaisant, *F* rosse; **to turn n.** devenir méchant; **to be n. to sb** être méchant envers qn; **that was a really n. thing to do** c'est vraiment méchant d'avoir fait ça; **n. trick** vilain tour, *F* sale tour; **what a n. little mind you've got!** que tu es méchant ou horrible!; *F* **he's a n. piece of work** c'est un sale individu ou un sale type

(c) (*indecent*) (*book, film etc*) ignoble; (*crime, rape*) ignoble, atroce; **n. word** vilain mot

natal ['neɪt(ə)l] *adj* natal, -als, de naissance

natality [nə'tælɪtɪ] *n esp US* (*birth rate*) natalité *f*

natch [nætʃ] *int F* sûr

nation ['neɪʃən] *n* **(a)** (*state*) nation *f*; *Pol* **United Nations (Organization)** (Organisation *f* des) Nations *fpl* Unies **(b)** (*people*) pays *m*; **the whole n. rose in arms** tout le pays se souleva; **the Prime Minister addressed the n.** le Premier Ministre s'est adressé à la nation; **to serve the n.** servir l'État

national ['næʃən(ə)l] **1** *adj* national; (*custom*) du pays; *Journ* **the n. dailies** les quotidiens nationaux; **n. newspaper** journal *m* à diffusion nationale; **n. readership survey** étude *f* nationale du lectorat; **n. scenic area** zone *f* protégée pour la beauté de son paysage **2** *n* **(a)** ressortissant, -ante (d'un pays); **a French n.** un(e) Français(e); **foreign nationals** ressortissants de pays étrangers **(b)** (*newspaper*) journal *m* ou quotidien *m* national

national anthem *n* hymne *m* national

national debt *n Econ* dette *f* publique

national grid *n El* réseau *m* national

National Health Service *n Br* ≈ Sécurité *f* Sociale; **to get treatment on the National Health** se faire soigner sous le régime de la Sécurité Sociale

national hunt (racing) *n Horseracing* courses *fpl* d'obstacles

national insurance *n Br Admin* = cotisation *f* déduite du salaire qui alimente la Sécurité; **n. contributions** cotisations *fpl* à la Sécurité sociale

nationalism ['næʃənəlɪz(ə)m] *n* nationalisme *m*

nationalist ['næʃənəlɪst] **1** *n* nationaliste *mf* **2** *adj* nationaliste; **N. China** la Chine nationaliste

nationalistic [næʃənə'lɪstɪk] *adj* nationaliste

nationality [næʃə'nælɪtɪ] *n* [①**A20-21**,d; **B10**,D] nationalité *f* **what n. are you?** de quelle nationalité êtes-vous?, quelle est votre nationalité?; **to take** *or* **adopt British n.** prendre la nationalité britannique

nationalization [næʃənəlaɪ'zeɪʃən] *n* **(a)** (*of industry etc*) nationalisation *f* **(b)** (*of foreigner*) naturalisation *f*

nationalize ['næʃənəlaɪz] *vt* **(a)** (*industry etc*) nationaliser **(b)** (*foreigner*) naturaliser

nationally ['næʃənəlɪ] *adv* nationalement; **to be n. renowned** avoir une renommée nationale

national park *n* parc *m* national

national service *n esp Br Mil* service *m* militaire

National Trust *n Br Admin* organisme *m* pour la protection du patrimoine historique

nation-state *n Pol* état-nation *m*

nationwide ['neɪʃənwaɪd] **1** *adj* (*opinion*) répandu dans tout le pays; (*campaign, survey*) au niveau national **2** *adv* (*to advertise etc*) au niveau national; (*to be known*) dans tout le pays

native ['neɪtɪv] **1** *n* **(a)** (*person*) (*of country, town*) originaire *mf*; (*in colonial sense*) indigène *mf*; **she was a n. of Scotland** elle était originaire d'Écosse; **n. of Australia** Australien, -ienne de naissance; **she speaks English like a n.** elle parle anglais comme un Anglais; **to go n.** adopter la manière de vivre des habitants, *Hum* adopter les mœurs des indigènes

(b) (*plant, animal*) indigène *mf*; **the koala is a n. of Australia** le koala est originaire d'Australie

2 *adj* **(a)** (*country etc*) natal, -als, de naissance; **n. costume** costume *m* national; **n. land** pays *m* natal, terre *f* natale, patrie *f*; **n. language** langue *f* maternelle; **he returned to his n. London** il est revenu à Londres, sa ville natale

(b) (*plant, inhabitant etc*) indigène **(to** de, à); **n. American** (*indigenous inhabitant*) Indien, -ienne d'Amérique; **n. labour** main d'œuvre *f* indigène

(c) (*qualities etc*) naturel, inné; **n. wit** esprit *m* naturel

(d) (*metals, minerals*) (à l'état) natif

native-born *adj* indigène, natif; **a n. German** un(e) Allemand(e) de naissance

native speaker *n Ling* locuteur *m* natif; **a French n. speaker** une personne de langue maternelle française, une personne dont la langue maternelle est le français; **I'm not a n. speaker** ce n'est pas ma langue maternelle

Nativity [nə'tɪvɪtɪ] *n Rel* nativité *f*; **the (festival of the) N.** la Nativité; *Th* **N. play** mystère *m* de la Nativité; **N. scene** crèche *f*

Nato, NATO ['neɪtəʊ] *n* (*abbr* **North Atlantic Treaty Organisation**) Otan *m*; **N. forces** les forces *fpl* de l'Otan

natter[1] ['nætər] *n esp Br F* causerie *f*, causette *f*; **to have a n.** bavarder, jacter

natter[2] *vi esp Br F* bavarder, jacter; **what were you two nattering about?** de quoi étiez-vous en train de bavarder, tous les deux?

natty ['nætɪ] *adj F* **(a)** (*person, dress etc*) chic *inv* **(b)** (*gadget etc*) astucieux

natural ['nætʃərəl] **1** *adj* **(a)** (*colour, taste*) naturel; **the n. world** le monde physique; **the n. order (of things)** l'ordre *m* des choses; **death from n. causes** mort *f* naturelle; **a n. blonde** une vraie blonde; **in the n. state** à l'état naturel ou primitif; **for the rest of one's n. life** *or F* **one's n.** pour le reste de sa vie; **n. gift** *or* **talent (for sth/doing sth)** don *m* naturel (pour qch/faire qch); *TV, Rad etc* **and that brings us to a n. break** et ceci nous amène tout naturellement à une pause; *Phys* **n. frequency** fréquence *f* propre; **n. justice** loi *f* naturelle; **n. mother** mère *f* naturelle; *Mus* **n. note** (note *f*) naturelle *f*; *Mus* **n. scale** gamme *f* naturelle; **n. size** grandeur *f* nature; **n. wavelength** longueur *f* d'onde propre

(b) (*normal, to be expected*) naturel, normal; **it is n. for a woman to ...** il est dans ou de la nature de la femme de ...; **it's n. (enough) (that) ...** il est (bien) naturel que ... + *sub*; **it's only n. that ...** il est ou c'est tout à fait normal que ... + *sub*; **as is (only) n.** comme de raison; **n. consequence** conséquence *f* naturelle; **n. inclination** penchant *m* naturel, inclination *f* naturelle; **my n. inclination would be to ...** j'inclinerais naturellement à ...; **one's** *or* **the n. reaction is to ...** la réaction instinctive est de ...; **I'm sure there's a perfectly n. explanation for it** je suis sûr qu'on peut l'expliquer de façon tout à fait naturelle; **to be a n. dancer/orator/leader** être un danseur/orateur/dirigeant né

(c) (*unaffected*) naturel; **be** *or* **act n.!** soyez naturel!; **that'll look more n.** ça fera plus naturel

(d) *Arch* (*illegitimate*) (*child*) naturel

2 *n* **(a) as an actor, he's a n.** c'est un acteur né; **she's a n. for the part** elle est faite pour ce rôle

(b) *Mus* (*note*) (note *f*) naturelle *f*; (*sign*) bécarre *m*

natural-born *adj* (*singer, leader etc*) né; **n. Frenchwoman** Française de naissance
natural childbirth *n Med* accouchement *m* naturel
natural disaster *n Geog, Geol* catastrophe *f* naturelle
natural gas *n* gaz *m* naturel
natural history *n* histoire *f* naturelle
naturalism ['nætʃərəlɪz(ə)m] *n Liter, Phil* naturalisme *m*
naturalist ['nætʃərəlɪst] *adj, n Bot, Zool* naturaliste *mf*
naturalistic [nætʃərə'lɪstɪk] *adj Liter etc* naturaliste
naturalization [nætʃərəlaɪ'zeɪʃən] *n* **(a)** (*of alien, foreign word*) naturalisation *f* **(b)** (*of plant, animal*) acclimatation *f*
naturalize ['nætʃərəlaɪz] **1** *vt* **(a)** (*alien, word*) naturaliser; **to become naturalized** (*of person*) se faire naturaliser **(b)** (*plant, animal*) acclimater **2** *vi* (*of plant etc*) s'acclimater
natural language *n Ling* langue *f* naturelle
natural law *n* loi *f* naturelle *ou* de la nature
naturally ['nætʃərəlɪ] *adv* **(a)** naturellement; (*to speak*) naturellement, sans affectation; (*to behave*) avec naturel; (*to die*) de mort naturelle; **n. occurring** naturel; **n. curly hair** cheveux qui frisent naturellement; **he's n. shy/funny/cheerful** il est timide/drôle/enjoué de nature; **she has a n. optimistic disposition** elle est d'un naturel optimiste; **it comes n. to him** c'est un don chez lui; **it comes n. to him to** ... il a une facilité innée pour ...; **although it didn't come n., he forced himself to ask questions** bien que cela ne lui vienne pas naturellement, il se forçait à poser des questions
(b) **n. (enough)** (*of course*) naturellement, bien entendu
natural medicine *n* médecine *f* douce *ou* naturelle, physiothérapie *f*
naturalness ['nætʃərəlnɪs] *n* **(a)** (*of acting*) caractère *m* naturel **(b)** (*of person*) naturel *m*
natural philosophy *n Old-fashioned Phys* physique *f*
natural resources *npl* ressources *fpl* naturelles
natural sciences *npl Phys, Ch etc* sciences *fpl* naturelles
natural selection *n Biol* sélection *f* naturelle
natural wastage *n Econ, Ind* départs *mpl* volontaires et en retraite
nature ['neɪtʃər] *n* **(a)** (*character*) (*of thing*) nature *f*, caractère *m*; (*of person*) nature, naturel *m*, tempérament *m*; **it is in the n. of things that** ... il est dans l'ordre *ou* la nature des choses que ...; **a jealous n.** un naturel *ou* caractère jaloux; **to have a** *or* **to be of a happy n.** être d'un heureux naturel; **it's not in her n.** ce n'est pas dans sa nature (**to do** de faire); **by n.** par tempérament, de (sa) nature, naturellement; **shy by n.** timide de nature, d'un naturel timide
(b) (*sort*) genre *m*, sorte *f*; **things of this n.** les choses de ce genre; **something in the n. of a** ... une espèce *ou* une sorte de ...; **something of that n., anyway** quelque chose dans le genre *ou* de cette espèce, en tout cas; **that was in the n. of being a compliment, coming from him** c'était plutôt un compliment, venant de lui; *Fml* **what is the n. of your complaint?** quelle est la nature de votre réclamation?; *Admin* **n. of contents** désignation *f* du contenu
(c) (*the natural world*) nature *f*; **to let n. take its course** laisser faire la nature; **the n. versus nurture debate** le débat nature/culture; *Hum F* **to answer a call of n.** satisfaire un besoin naturel; **to draw/paint from n.** dessiner/peindre d'après nature; **to go against n.** aller contre la nature; **return to n.** retour à l'état de nature
nature lover *n* amoureux, -euse de la nature
nature reserve *n Zool* réserve *f* naturelle
nature study *n Sch* histoire *f* naturelle
nature trail *n* sentier *m* aménagé dans la nature
naturism ['neɪtʃərɪz(ə)m] *n* naturisme *m*
naturist ['neɪtʃərɪst] *n* naturiste *mf*
naught [nɔːt] *n* **(a)** *Arch, Lit* (*nothing*) rien *m*; **to come to n.** (*of plans etc*) échouer, n'aboutir à rien; **to bring to n., to set at n.** anéantir **(b)** *US Math* zéro *m*
naughtily ['nɔːtɪlɪ] *adv* **to behave n.** se conduire mal, ne pas être sage, être vilain; **rather n., I spread rumours about her private life** j'ai fait courir des rumeurs sur sa vie privée, ce qui est un peu vilain
naughtiness ['nɔːtɪnɪs] *n* **(a)** (*of child etc*) mauvaise conduite *f* **(b)** (*mild indecency*) grivoiserie(s) *f(pl)*
naughty ['nɔːtɪ] *adj* **(a)** (*child*) vilain, méchant; **it was very n. of you** c'était très vilain de ta part; **you n. child!** petit vilain!; **he's been a n. boy** *or* **n.** il a été vilain *ou* méchant, il n'a pas été sage **(b)** *F* (*indecent*) (*story*) grivois, cochon; (*song*) gaillard, paillard; (*book, picture, person*) cochon; **n. words** gros mots *mpl* *Iron* **n. n.!** (*with sexual connotation*) petit coquin *ou* cochon!
nausea ['nɔːsɪə] *n* **(a)** *Med* nausée *f*, envie *f* de vomir; **to be overcome with n.** avoir mal au cœur, avoir des nausées **(b)** (*disgust*) dégoût *m*, nausée *f*, écœurement *m*
nauseate ['nɔːsɪeɪt] *vt* **(a)** *Med* donner des nausées à, donner mal au cœur à **(b)** (*disgust*) donner la nausée à, écœurer, dégoûter
nauseating ['nɔːsɪeɪtɪŋ] *adj* **(a)** *Med* nauséeux **(b)** (*disgusting*) dégoûtant, écœurant; **I find him n.** il m'écœure, il me dégoûte; **in n. detail** avec des détails écœurants *ou* à donner la nausée
nauseatingly ['nɔːsɪeɪtɪŋlɪ] *adv* d'une façon dégoûtante *ou* écœurante; **he made it look so n. easy** il l'a fait avec une facilité écœurante; **he's n. clever/good-looking** il est tellement intelligent/beau que c'en est écœurant
nauseous ['nɔːsɪəs] *adj* **(a)** *Med* nauséeux; *Am* **to feel n.** ['nɔːʃəs] avoir mal au cœur, avoir des nausées **(b)** (*disgusting*) nauséabond, écœurant
nautical ['nɔːtɪk(ə)l] *adj* nautique, marin; (*term, expression*) de navigation, de marine; **he had a n. air/bearing** il avait l'air/l'allure d'un marin; **he comes from a n. background** il vient d'une famille de marins; **n. almanac** éphémérides *fpl* nautiques; **n. club** club *m* nautique; **n. mile** mil(l)e *m* marin
nautilus, *pl* **-uses, -i** ['nɔːtɪləs, -əsɪz, -aɪ] *n* (*mollusc*) nautile *m*
naval ['neɪv(ə)l] *adj* (*attaché, base, battle etc*) naval, -als; (*power*) maritime; **the N. College** l'École *f* navale; **n. dockyard** arsenal *m* maritime; **n. officer** officier *m* de marine; **n. stores** (*depot*) entrepôts *mpl* maritimes; (*supplies*) approvisionnements *mpl* *ou* matériel *m* *ou* fournitures *fpl* de navires
naval architect architecte *m* naval
naval architecture *n* architecture *f* navale
nave[1] [neɪv] *n* (*of wheel*) moyeu *m*
nave[2] *n Archit* (*of church*) nef *f*
navel ['neɪv(ə)l] *n* *Anat* nombril *m*, ombilic *m*; *Fig* **to contemplate one's n.** se regarder le nombril, faire du nombrilisme
navel orange *n Culin* orange *f* navel *inv*
navigability [nævɪgə'bɪlɪtɪ] *n* (*of river, vessel*) navigabilité *f*; (*of balloon*) dirigeabilité *f*
navigable ['nævɪgəb(ə)l] *adj* (*river, vessel*) navigable; (*balloon*) dirigeable; **ship in n. condition** vaisseau en état de prendre la mer *ou* de naviguer
navigate ['nævɪgeɪt] **1** *vi* naviguer; *Aut* **I'll drive if you n.** je conduis si vous me dirigez **2** *vt* (*seas*) naviguer dans *ou* sur; **this river is difficult to n.** la navigation est difficile sur ce fleuve; **to n. a ship** (*steer*) gouverner *ou* diriger un navire; (*plot path of*) naviguer; *F* **to n. one's way to the door** (*through crowd*) se frayer un chemin jusqu'à la porte; **the drunk navigated his way to the door** le soûlard a réussi à trouver son chemin jusqu'à la porte
navigating officer ['nævɪgeɪtɪŋ] *n* officier *m* de navigation, officier navigateur
navigation [nævɪ'geɪʃən] *n* navigation *f*; (*of ship, balloon*) conduite *f*
navigation aids *npl* aides *fpl* à la navigation
navigational [nævɪ'geɪʃənəl] *adj* (*instrument etc*) de navigation; (*aids*) à la navigation
navigation lights *npl* feux *mpl* de navigation
navigation officer *n* officier *m* de navigation, officier navigateur
navigator ['nævɪgeɪtər] *n* **(a)** *Naut, Av* (officier *m*) navigateur *m*; *Aut* navigateur **(b)** *Hist* (*explorer*) navigateur *m*
navvy ['nævɪ] *n Br* (*worker*) terrassier *m*
navy ['neɪvɪ] *n* **(a)** marine *f*, marine de guerre, marine militaire; **to serve in the n.** servir dans la marine *ou* sur mer; **Minister** *or US* **Secretary for the N.** ≈ ministre *m* de la Marine **(b)** *Com* **n. cut** carotte *f* de tabac hachée
navy (blue) **1** *n* bleu *m* marine *inv* **2** *adj* bleu marine *inv*; **n. (blue) socks** chaussettes *fpl* bleu marine
nay [neɪ] **1** *adv Arch, Lit, Dial* non; *Lit* (*introducing a more emphatic statement*) (et) même, qui plus est, voire; **I am astounded, n., disgusted** j'en suis ahuri, voire révolté **2** *n* *Arch, Lit* non *m*; **ayes and nays** (*in voting*) voix *fpl* pour et contre; **I was one of the n.-sayers** j'étais un de ceux qui ont voté contre
Nazarene ['næzəriːn] *adj, n Bible* nazaréen, -éenne; **the N.** le Nazaréen
Nazi ['nɑːtsɪ] **1** *adj* nazi; (*persecution, seizure of power*) par les nazis **2** *n* nazi, -ie
Nazism ['nɑːtsɪz(ə)m] *n* nazisme *m*
NB [en'biː] **(a)** (*abbr* **nota bene**) NB **(b)** (*abbr* **New Brunswick**) N-B
NBG, nbg [enbiː'dʒiː] *adj F* (*abbr* **no bloody good**) (*person*) nul, bon à rien; (*book etc*) nul
NC *abbr* **North Carolina**
NCB [ensiː'biː] *n Br* (*abbr* **National Coal Board**) = direction *f* des charbonnages britanniques
NCO [ensiː'əʊ] *n Mil* (*abbr* **noncommissioned officer**) sous-officier *m*, *pl* sous-officiers
ND *abbr* **North Dakota**

Neandert(h)al [nɪ'ændətɑːl] **1** *adj* **(a)** *Geol* du Néanderthal; **(b)** *F* (*attitude etc*) qui tient de la préhistoire **2** *n F* (*uncultured person*) homme *m* des cavernes

Neandert(h)al man *n* (*in anthropology*) l'homme *m* de Néanderthal

neap [niːp] **1** *adj* **n. tide** marée *f* de morte-eau; **n. tides** (marées de) mortes-eaux *fpl* **2** *n* marée *f* de morte-eau

Neapolitan [nɪə'pɒlɪt(ə)n] **1** *adj* napolitain; **N. ice cream** tranche *f* napolitaine **2** *n* Napolitain, -aine

near¹ [nɪər] **1** *adv* **(a)** (*in space or time*) près; (*closely-connected by kinship or intimacy*) proche; **she lives quite n.** elle habite tout près; **to come** *or* **draw n.** (s')approcher **(to sb/sth** de qn/qch**)**; **come nearer** venez plus près, approchez-vous; **the time is drawing n.** l'heure approche; **to bring sth nearer** rapprocher qch **(to** de**)**; **nearer and nearer** de plus en plus près; **n. at hand** (*of thing*) tout près, à proximité; (*of event*) tout proche; **keep** *or* **stay n. to me** restez près de moi; **he was standing n. to the table** il se tenait près de la table; **those n. and dear to him** ceux qui le touchent de près, ses proches; **no, it took nearer to three days** non, ça a pris plutôt trois jours

(b) (*in extent*) **as n. as I can remember** autant que je puisse m'en souvenir; **they came n. to blows/to splitting up** ils en sont presque venus aux coups/à se séparer; **they were n. to giving up** ils étaient sur le point d'abandonner; **n. to tears/despair** au bord des larmes/du désespoir; **I came n. to crying** j'ai été sur le point de pleurer; **he's nowhere n. so** *or* **as strong as you** il est loin d'être aussi fort que vous; **she's nowhere n. finished** elle est loin d'avoir fini; **as n. as makes no difference** à peu de chose près; **50 or n. enough, 50 or as n. as makes no difference** 50 ou peu s'en faut, à peu de chose près 50; **a n. total failure** un échec presque total

(c) *Arch, Lit* (= **nearly**) presque, à peu près

2 *prep* **(a)** (*in space*) près de; **n. the village** près du village; **bring your chair near(er) the fire** (r)approchez votre chaise du feu; **to come** *or* **draw n. (to) sb/sth** (s')approcher de qn/qch

(b) (*in time*) **it is n. Christmas** Noël approche, on approche de Noël; **we're getting n. that stage** on approche *ou* se rapproche de cette phase; **it was n. the time when he had his accident** c'était à l'époque de son accident

(c) (*in extent*) près de, sur le point de; **n. death** sur le point de mourir; **he came n. (to) being run over** il a failli être écrasé

(d) (*in resemblance*) **to be** *or* **to come n. sb/sth** ressembler à qn/qch; **language that is nearer Latin than Italian** langue qui est plus près *ou* proche du latin que de l'italien; **nobody can come anywhere n. her** il n'y a personne à son niveau; **he's nowhere n. it!** (*with guess etc*) il n'y est pas du tout!; **perhaps your definition comes n. it** *or* **the mark** votre définition s'approche peut-être de la vérité

3 *adj* **(a)** (*relative*) proche; **I felt very n. to her when she said that** je me suis senti très proche d'elle quand elle a dit cela; **we grew n. to one another** nous sommes devenus intimes; **our n. relations** nos proches (parents)

(b) (*referring to side*) **n. foreleg** (*of horse etc*) pied *m* du montoir

(c) (*place, time, event*) proche; **go to the nearest chemist's** allez à la pharmacie la plus proche; **in the n. future** dans un proche avenir; **give the measurements to the nearest metre** donnez les mesures au *ou* à un mètre près; *St Exch* **n. month** échéance *f* proche

(d) it was a n. miss (*of attempt*) cela a raté de peu *ou* de justesse; **it was a n. thing** (*we only just escaped, attempt nearly succeeded*) il s'en est fallu de peu; (*nearly hit target*) il ne manquait pas grand-chose; **this is the nearest thing we have to a conference room** c'est ce que nous avons qui ressemble le plus à une salle de conférence; **it's the nearest you'll get to fresh cheese/a bookshop in these parts** c'est ce que vous trouverez de mieux en matière de fromage/librairie par ici; **the nearest equivalent** l'équivalent le plus proche; **it's quite n. the original** (*of translation*) c'est assez proche de l'original

4 *npl often Hum* **one's nearest and dearest** ses plus proches parents

near² *vt* (s')approcher de; **as we were nearing Oxford** comme nous approchions d'Oxford; **the road is nearing completion** la route est près d'être achevée; **we are nearing our goal** nous touchons au but; **he seemed to be nearing a breakdown/a crisis/a turning point** il semblait au bord de la dépression/d'une crise/d'un tournant; *Lit* **he's nearing his end** il approche de la fin

near- [nɪər] *pref* **n.-perfect** presque parfait; **a n.-disaster** un désastre évité de peu

nearby 1 [nɪə'baɪ] *adv* tout près; **is it n.?** est-ce que c'est près d'ici?; **to live n.** habiter dans les parages; **in a house n.** dans une maison voisine; **they stood n., watching** ils se tenaient à proximité et regardaient **2** ['nɪəbaɪ] *adj* proche; **a n. house** une maison voisine *ou* avoisinante

near-death experience expérience *f* aux frontières de la mort

Near East *n* Proche-Orient *m*

near letter quality *n Comptr* qualité *f* courrier; **n. printer** imprimante *f* de qualité courrier

nearly ['nɪəlɪ] *adv* **(a)** (*almost*) presque; **it's n. midnight** il est presque *ou* bientôt minuit; **we're n. there** nous y sommes presque; **I've got n. all of them** je les ai presque *ou* à peu près tous; **I'm n. forty** j'ai près de *ou* presque quarante ans; **it cost n. ten pounds** cela a coûté près de *ou* presque dix livres; **very n.** peu s'en faut; **I very n. resigned on the spot** il s'en est fallu de peu pour que je ne démissionne sur le champ; **I very n. fell/burst out laughing** j'ai bien failli tomber/éclater de rire; **he very n. died** il a frôlé la mort; **she's not n. as old as me** elle est loin d'être aussi âgée que moi

(b) (*closely*) (de) près; *Biol* **n. allied species** espèces *fpl* voisines

nearly man *n F* espoir *m* raté

nearly-new *adj* presque neuf

near miss *n Aut, Av* collision *f* évitée de justesse

nearness ['nɪənɪs] *n* (*of time, place*) proximité *f*; (*of place*) voisinage *m*; (*of friends*) intimité *f*; **their growing n. to one another** leur intimité grandissante

nearside ['nɪəsaɪd] *Br* **1** *n* (*of horse*) côté *m* gauche; *Aut* (*in Britain*) (*of road*) gauche *f*; (*of vehicle*) côté gauche; (*in France, US etc*) (*of road*) droite *f*; (*of vehicle*) côté droit **2** *adj Aut* (*in Britain*) gauche; (*in France, US etc*) droit; **keep to the n. lane** serrez (*in Britain*) à gauche *ou* (*in France, US etc*) à droite

near-sighted *adj* myope; *Fig* (*policy, government etc*) obtus

near-sightedness [nɪə'saɪtɪdnɪs] *n* myopie *f*; *Fig* imprévoyance *f*

neat [niːt] *adj* **(a)** (*tidy*) (*person*) ordonné, qui a de l'ordre; (*in one's appearance*) soigné, net; (*room, drawer etc*) bien rangé, en ordre; (*exercise book etc*) bien tenu, propre; (*garden*) bien tenu, *F* propret; (*way of dressing, handwriting*) soigné; **he's a n. worker** son travail est très soigné; **his clothes are always very n.** ses vêtements sont toujours très nets

(b) (*elegant, well-formed*) (*turn of phrase, answer etc*) bien tourné, adroit; (*idea, solution*) ingénieux; **she is small and n.** elle est petite et bien faite; *esp Am* **a n. plan** un plan bien pensé; **a n. little gadget** un petit gadget bien conçu; **that's a n. trick** c'est malin; **a n. manoeuvre** une manœuvre adroite; **a n. piece of work** un ouvrage bien exécuté; **she made a n. job of it** elle a fait du bon travail; **the surgeon made a n. job of those stitches** le chirurgien a bien soigné ces points de suture

(c) (*tight*) étroit; **it's rather n. across the shoulders/around the waist** c'est un peu étroit au niveau des épaules/à la taille

(d) (*undiluted*) pur, sans eau; **to take** *or* **drink one's whisky n.** boire son whisky sec

(e) *Am F* (*good*) super

neaten ['niːt(ə)n] *vt* = **neaten up**

▶ **neaten up** *vtsep* (*clothes*) ajuster; (*hair, garden*) arranger; (*hair, by trimming etc*) rafraîchir; (*room*) ranger; (*presentation*) fignoler, peaufiner; **go and n. yourself up a bit** va t'arranger un peu

neatly ['niːtlɪ] *adv* **(a)** (*to put away etc*) d'une manière soignée *ou* ordonnée, avec ordre; **n. set out** disposé avec soin; **n. written** écrit soigneusement; **everything is n. in its place** tout est soigneusement rangé à sa place **(b)** (*cleverly etc*) adroitement; **n. phrased** bien tourné; **that is n. put** c'est joliment dit; **that brings us n. back to my opening question** cela nous ramène justement à ma question de départ

neatness ['niːtnɪs] *n* **(a)** (*of handwriting, clothes*) netteté *f*; (*of garden*) apparence *f* soignée; (*of room etc*) bon ordre *m*; (*of exercise book etc*) propreté *f*; **the n. of her appearance** son allure *ou* apparence soignée; **personal n. is essential** il est essentiel d'avoir une apparence soignée **(b)** (*skill, cleverness*) adresse *f*, habileté *f*; (*of solution, idea*) ingéniosité *f*; (*of phrase*) tournure *f* adroite

nebula *pl* -æ *or* -s ['nebjʊlə, -iː] *n Astron* nébuleuse *f*

nebulous ['nebjʊləs] *adj* (*vague*), *Astron* nébuleux

necessaries ['nesɪsərɪz] *npl* **the n.** (*food, money etc*) ce qu'il faut pour vivre; *Jur* (*means to live*) le nécessaire; **we haven't got enough for the n.** nous n'avons pas assez pour nous payer le strict nécessaire

necessarily [nesɪ'serəlɪ] *adv* **(a)** nécessairement; **it's not n. the case** ce n'est pas nécessairement *ou* forcément vrai **(b)** *(inevitably)* inévitablement, forcément

necessary ['nesɪsərɪ] **1** *adj* **(a)** *(indispensable)* nécessaire **(to** *or* **for sb/sth** à qn/qch); **the time/space/resources n.** le temps/l'espace/les ressources nécessaire(s); **everything n.** tout ce qui est nécessaire; **it is n. to do something** il est nécessaire de faire quelque chose, il faut faire quelque chose; **it is n. for him to return** il faut qu'il revienne; **I find it n. to ...** je juge nécessaire de ...; **it is n. that ...** il est nécessaire *ou* il faut que ... + *sub*; **it's not n. to be rude** ce n'est pas la peine d'être impoli; **to make all n. arrangements** prendre toutes les dispositions utiles *ou* nécessaires; **to make it n. for sb to do sth** mettre qn dans l'obligation de faire qch; **if n.** si cela est nécessaire, s'il le faut, le cas échéant, au besoin; **whenever n.** chaque fois qu'il le faudra; **as and when n.** quand c'est/ce sera nécessaire; **to do what is n.** faire le nécessaire; **not to do more than is absolutely n.** ne faire que le strict nécessaire *ou* l'essentiel

(b) *(inevitable)* *(result, conclusion, etc)* nécessaire, inévitable; **a n. evil** un mal nécessaire

2 *n F* **the n.** *(things, action required)* le nécessaire; *(money)* les fonds *mpl*; **his father will provide the n.** *(money)* son père fournira les fonds; **to do the n.** faire le nécessaire

necessitate [nɪ'sesɪteɪt] *vt* nécessiter, rendre nécessaire

necessitous [nɪ'sesɪtəs] *adj Fml* nécessiteux, dans le besoin; **their present n. state** leur indigence actuelle

necessity [nɪ'sesɪtɪ] *n* **(a)** *(abstract need)* nécessité *f*; **by** *or* **from** *or* **out of n.** par nécessité, par la force des choses; **of n.** nécessairement, forcément; *Prov* **n. is the mother of invention** en cas de besoin on trouve toujours une solution

(b) *(specific need)* nécessité *f*, besoin *m* **(of doing sth** de faire qch); **the n. for sth** le besoin de qch; **if the n. arose** *or* **should arise** si le besoin s'en faisait sentir; **in case of n.** au besoin, en cas de besoin; **case of absolute n.** cas *m* de force majeure; **there's no n. to be rude** ce n'est pas la peine d'être impoli; **is there any real n. for such haste?** une telle hâte est-elle nécessaire *ou* indispensable?

(c) *(usu pl)* **necessities** *(things needed)* le nécessaire; **the bare necessities** le strict nécessaire; **the necessities of life** les nécessités *fpl* de la vie; **a car is not one of life's necessities** une voiture n'est pas indispensable; **a washing machine is a n.** une machine à laver est indispensable

(d) *Fml* *(poverty)* dénuement *m*; **the family live in dire n.** la famille vit dans le dénuement le plus complet

neck¹ [nek] *n* **(a)** *(of person, animal)* cou *m*; **to throw** *or* **fling one's arms round sb's n.** sauter *ou* se jeter au cou de qn; **n. microphone** micro *m* cravate; *Fig* **to be up to one's n. in work** avoir du travail par-dessus la tête, être débordé de travail; *Fig F* **he's in it up to his n.** il y est jusqu'au cou; *Fig* **to stick one's n. out** prendre des risques; *(and say sb will win etc)* s'engager; *Fig F* **to risk/save one's n.** risquer/sauver sa peau; *F* **to get it in the n.** avoir des ennuis; *Horseracing* **to win by a n.** gagner d'une encolure; **to finish n. and n.** arriver à égalité; **it's n. or nothing** il faut risquer *ou* jouer le tout pour le tout; *F* **what are you doing in this n. of the woods?** qu'est-ce que tu fais dans le coin?

(b) *Br Sl* *(cheek)* culot *m*; **to have a (brass) n.** avoir du culot; **to have the (brass) n. to do sth** avoir le culot de faire qch

(c) *(of dress, shirt)* encolure *f*; **square/round n.** encolure carrée/ronde; **V-n.** encolure en pointe *ou* en V; **high n.** col *m* montant; **low n.** décolleté *m*

(d) *Culin* *(of lamb)* collier *m*, collet *m*; *(of beef)* collier

(e) *(of bottle)* goulot *m*, col *m*; *(of vase)* col; *(of pipe)* rétrécissement *m*, étranglement *m*; *Anat* *(of uterus, bone)* col; *(of land)* langue *f*; *(of string instrument)* manche *m*, collet *m*

(f) *Sl* **to have a n.** *(kiss etc)* = **neck²**

neck² *vi Sl* *(of couple)* se bécoter; **he was necking with her** ils se bécotaient

neckband ['nekbænd] *n* *(ribbon etc)* tour *m* de cou; *(on shirt)* col *m*

neckerchief ['nekətʃɪf] *n Old-fashioned* foulard *m*, tour *m* de cou

necklace ['neklɪs] *n* collier *m*

necklet ['neklɪt] *n* collier *m* *(de fourrure etc)*

neckline ['neklaɪn] *n* encolure *f*; **dress with a plunging n.** robe au décolleté plongeant

necktie ['nektaɪ] *n US* cravate *f*

neckwear ['nekweər] *n Com* cols *mpl*, cravates *fpl* et foulards *mpl*

necrology [ne'krɒlədʒɪ] *n Fml* **(a)** *(list of deaths)* nécrologie *f*; *Rel* nécrologe *m* **(b)** *(obituary)* nécrologie *f*

necromancer ['nekrəʊmænsər] *n* nécromancien, -ienne

necromancy ['nekrəʊmænsɪ] *n* nécromancie *f*

necrophilia [nekrəʊ'fɪlɪə] *n* nécrophilie *f*

necrophobia [nekrəʊ'fəʊbɪə] *n* nécrophobie *f*

necropolis [ne'krɒpəlɪs] *n* nécropole *f*

necrosis [ne'krəʊsɪs] *n Med* nécrose *f*

nectar ['nektər] *n* **(a)** *Myth, Bot* nectar *m* **(b)** *esp US* *(fruit juice)* nectar *m*

nectarine ['nektərɪːn] *n* brugnon *m*, nectarine *f*; **n. (tree)** brugnonier *m*

ned [ned] *n esp Scot F* casseur *m*; **he's a bit of a n.** il est du genre casseur

NEDC [eniːdiː'siː] *n Br Admin* *(abbr* **National Economic Development Council)** = Agence *f* nationale pour le développement économique

Neddy ['nedɪ] *n Br Admin F* = **NEDC**

née [neɪ] *adj* née; **Mrs Thomas, n. Long** Mme Thomas, née Long

need¹ [niːd] *n* **(a)** *(requirement)* besoin *m*; **to feel/satisfy a n.** éprouver/satisfaire un besoin; **if need(s) be, in case of n.** en cas de besoin, au besoin, s'il (en) est besoin, si besoin (en) est; **n. for sth/sb** besoin de qch/qn; **there is no n. to ...** il n'est pas nécessaire de ..., ce n'est pas la peine de ...; **(there's) no n. to wait** (il est) inutile d'attendre, ce n'est pas la peine d'attendre; **without the n. for sth** sans nécessiter qch; **the information will be made available on a n.-to-know basis** les informations ne seront fournies qu'à ceux qui en ont besoin; **the boss works on a n.-to-know basis** le patron ne dit que ce qu'on a besoin de savoir; **to be in n.** *or* **have n. of sth** avoir besoin de qch; **to be badly in n. of repair** avoir bien *ou* grand besoin d'être réparé; **she is in n. of a rest** elle a besoin de se reposer *ou* de repos; **to attend to sb's needs** pourvoir aux besoins de qn; **that will meet my needs** cela fera mon affaire; **my most pressing n. is (for) a ...** ce dont j'ai le plus besoin dans l'immédiat est de ...; **whenever/wherever there's a n. for it** chaque fois que/partout où c'est nécessaire

(b) *(difficulty)* adversité *f*, difficulté *f*; *(financial difficulty)* besoin *m*, indigence *f*; **in times** *or* **in the hour of n.** dans les moments difficiles; **in my hour of n.** au moment où j'en ai eu besoin; **to be in n.** être dans la nécessité *ou* dans le besoin; **their n. is greater than mine** ils en ont plus besoin que moi

(c) *Mktg* **n. identification** identification *f* des besoins; **n. level** niveau *m* des besoins; **n. market** marché *m* des besoins; **n. recognition** reconnaissance *f* des besoins; **n. set** ensemble *m* de besoins; **needs analysis** analyse *f* des besoins; **needs assessment** estimation *f* des besoins; **needs-based market** marché *m* fondé sur les besoins; **needs-based segmentation** segmentation *f* fondée sur les besoins; **needs study** étude *f* des besoins; **needs-and-wants exploration** exploration *f* des besoins et des désirs

need² [①A59,19] **1** *vt* *(3rd person sing pr ind* **needs**; *pt, pp* **needed)** **(a)** *(of person)* avoir besoin de; *(of thing)* exiger, nécessiter, demander; **my bike needs a few repairs** mon vélo a besoin de quelques réparations; **his hair needs cutting** il a besoin de se faire couper les cheveux; **they n. to be oiled/covered in plastic** il faut les graisser/couvrir d'un plastique; **this soup needs more salt/pepper** cette soupe manque de sel/poivre; **to n. rest** avoir besoin de repos; **I work because I n. the money** je travaille par besoin d'argent; **these facts n. no (further) comment** ces faits se passent de commentaire; **a much needed lesson** une leçon dont on avait grand besoin; **what he needs is a thrashing** ce dont il a besoin, c'est d'une bonne raclée, ce qu'il lui faudrait c'est une bonne raclée; **you'll n. to take more money** il va falloir que tu prennes plus d'argent; **the baby needs changing** il faut changer le bébé; **he needs to do more work on it/to see a doctor** il faut qu'il y travaille davantage/qu'il voie un docteur; **they n. to be told everything** il faut qu'on leur dise tout; **I didn't n. to be reminded of it** je n'avais pas besoin qu'on me le rappelle; **he didn't n. to be told twice** il ne se l'est pas fait dire deux fois; **you only needed to ask** vous n'aviez qu'à demander; *Iron* **that's all I n.!** j'avais bien besoin de ça!; **the last thing we n. is someone like him snooping about the place** la dernière chose qu'il nous faut c'est bien que quelqu'un comme lui vienne fouiner par ici; **who needs two cars anyway?** comme si on avait besoin d'avoir deux voitures!

(b) *impers* **it needs a great deal of skill to do it properly** il faut beaucoup d'habileté pour le faire correctement; **it needs more patience than I have** cela exige *ou* requiert plus de patience que je n'en ai

2 *modal aux v* [①A40C; B,1,a] *(3rd person sing pr ind* **need**; *pt* **need**; *no prp*; *no pp)* **adults only n. apply** les adultes seuls peuvent postuler; **you needn't trouble yourself** (vous n'avez) pas besoin de vous déranger; **we needn't have bothered after all** nous n'aurions pas dû nous déranger après tout; **you needn't bother!** ne prends pas cette peine!; **n. you go yet?** est-ce qu'il faut que tu partes déjà?; **n. I go on?** faut-il que je continue?; **you needn't wait** il est inutile que vous attendiez, inutile (pour vous) d'attendre; **I n. hardly tell you how grateful I am** il n'est pas besoin de vous dire combien je vous suis reconnaissant; **it n. not necessarily be true** ce n'est pas nécessairement vrai

needful ['ni:dfʊl] **1** *adj Old-fashioned* nécessaire (**to** à; **for** pour) **2** *n F* **to do the n.** faire le nécessaire; (*pay, provide money*) casquer

neediness ['ni:dɪnɪs] *n* indigence *f*

needle¹ ['ni:d(ə)l] *n* **(a)** (*for sewing etc*) aiguille *f*; *Bot* (**pine**) **n.** aiguille *f* de pin; **it's like looking for a n. in a haystack** c'est comme chercher une aiguille dans une botte de foin; **hypodermic n.** aiguille pour injections hypodermiques; *F* **I hate needles** j'ai horreur des piqûres!; *Sl* **to be on the n.** (*take drugs*) se piquer

(**b**) *Br F* **to give sb the n.** (*irritate*) taper sur les nerfs à qn, agacer qn; (*deliberately*) faire enrager qn; (*anger*) mettre qn en rogne; **she's got the n.** elle est en rogne (**with** contre)

(**c**) *Tech* (*of record player, compass, speedometer etc*) aiguille *f*; *Aut* (*in float*) pointeau *m*; (*of scales*) aiguille, langue *f*, languette *f*; **compass n.** aiguille aimantée; *Art* **engraving n.** pointe *f* pour taille douce, pointe sèche; **n. noise** *or* **scratch** (*on record player*) bruit *m* d'aiguille

(**d**) *Archit* obélisque *m*; *Geol, Geog* aiguille *f* (rocheuse); *Ch, Miner* **crystalline needles** aiguilles cristallines

needle² *vt F* (*irritate*) agacer, taper sur les nerfs à; (*deliberately*) faire enrager; (*anger*) mettre en rogne; **to n. sb about not having a girlfriend** narguer qn parce qu'il n'a pas de petite amie; **to n. sb about his/her exam results** narguer qn à propos de ses résultats à un examen

needlecord ['ni:d(ə)lkɔ:d] *n Tex* velours *m* mille-raies

needlecraft ['ni:d(ə)lkrɑ:ft] *n* travail *m* à l'aiguille, travaux d'aiguille

needle match *n Sp F* match *m* acharné

needle-nosed pliers *n* pince *f* à bec fin

needlepoint ['ni:d(ə)lpɔɪnt] *n* (*embroidery*) tapisserie *f* à l'aiguille

needless ['ni:dlɪs] *adj* inutile; (*remark*) déplacé; **n. to say, we shall refund the money** il va de soi que nous rembourserons l'argent

needlessly ['ni:dlɪslɪ] *adv* (*to be rude, pedantic, to worry*) inutilement; (*to die, suffer, work*) pour rien

needle threader *n Sewing* filifère *m*, enfile-aiguilles *m inv*

needletime *n* (*for broadcasting records*) durée *f* de passage à l'antenne

needle valve *n MecE* soupape *f* à pointeau *ou* à aiguille

needlewoman, *pl* **-women** ['ni:d(ə)lwʊmən, -wɪmɪn] *n* (*seamstress*) couturière *f*; **I'm no n.** je ne sais pas coudre

needlework ['ni:d(ə)lwɜ:k] *n* travaux *mpl* d'aiguille; (*school subject*) couture *f*; **she's good at n.** elle coud bien

needs [ni:dz] *adv Old-fashioned* (*used only with* **must**) de toute nécessité; **if n. must ...** s'il le faut absolument...; **ah well! n. must!** ah! il le faut bien; *Prov* **n. must when the devil drives** nécessité fait loi

needy ['ni:dɪ] **1** *adj* (*person*) nécessiteux, indigent; **to be emotionally n.** manquer d'affection **2** *npl* **the n.** les nécessiteux *mpl*

ne'er [neər] *adv Lit* (= **never**) (ne ...) jamais; **n. the less** néanmoins

ne'er-do-well *n, adj* propre *mf* à rien

nefarious [nɪ'feərɪəs] *adj* (*person, purpose etc*) infâme, scélérat

nefariously [nɪ'feərɪəslɪ] *adv* d'une manière infâme

nefariousness [nɪ'feərɪəsnɪs] *n* (*of deed, crime, behaviour*) infâmie *f*; (*of person*) scélératesse *f*

neg [neg] *n, adj* (*abbr* **negative**) négatif *m*

negate [nɪ'geɪt] *vt* **(a)** *esp Fml* (*deny*) nier **(b)** (*nullify*) (*effect*) annuler; (*efforts, work*) anéantir; (*law etc*) annuler **(c)** *Gram* mettre au négatif

negation [nɪ'geɪʃən] *n* **(a)** (*denial*) (*of fact, proposition etc*) négation *f* **(b)** (*nullification*) (*of sb's work, efforts*) anéantissement *m*

negative¹ ['negətɪv] **1** *adj* (*reply, result, virtue etc*), *Math, El, Phot* négatif; **don't be so n.** ne sois pas aussi négatif; **he's a very n. sort of person** il est très négatif; *Math* **n. sign** (signe *m*) moins *m*; **n. (income) tax** impôt *m* négatif

2 *n* **(a)** [①A46-47,9; B60,B] (*reply*) négative *f*; *Gram* négation *f*; *Math* valeur *f ou* quantité *f* négative; **to answer in the n.** répondre négativement *ou* par la négative; *Math* **two negatives make a positive** moins moins égale plus; *Gram* **to put a statement into the n.** mettre une affirmation à la forme négative

(**b**) *Phot* (cliché *m*) négatif *m*; *El* (*of battery*) plaque *f* négative

3 *adv* (*in answer to a question*) non

negative² *vt* **(a)** (*plan, project*) s'opposer à, rejeter **(b)** (*hypothesis, theory*) réfuter; (*report*) contredire, nier

negative equity *n Fin* **to suffer from n.** souffrir des conséquences de la dévalorisation de sa propriété, dont la valeur est devenue inférieure à celle du prêt contracté pour son achat

negatively ['negətɪvlɪ] *adv* négativement

negativism ['negətɪvɪz(ə)m] *n* négativisme *m*

negativity [negə'tɪvɪtɪ] *n* négativité *f*; **because of the n. of his attitude** à cause de son attitude négative; **to feel a lot of n. towards sb** avoir beaucoup de sentiments négatifs contre qn

neglect¹ [nɪ'glekt] *n* (*of person*) négligence *f*; (*of machine, property etc*) mauvais entretien *m*; **n. of one's duties/responsibilities** manquement *m* à ses devoirs/responsabilités; **out of** *or* **from** *or* **through n.** par négligence; **his n. of his children led to a court case** le fait qu'il néglige ses enfants a donné lieu à un procès; **to die in total n.** mourir complètement abandonné *ou* dans l'abandon le plus total; **to die of n.** mourir à cause d'un manque de soins; **to suffer n.** souffrir d'un manque de soins; **the equipment was allowed to fall into n.** le matériel n'a pas été entretenu

neglect² *vt* **(a)** (*not look after*) (*children, health etc*) négliger; **to n. oneself** négliger sa personne, se négliger; **the garden looks neglected** le jardin est mal tenu *ou* à l'abandon; **are you feeling neglected?** est-ce que vous avez l'impression qu'on vous néglige? **(b)** (*ignore*) (*duties*) négliger, oublier; (*one's responsibilities*) manquer à; (*one's post*) délaisser, abandonner; **to n. to do sth** omettre de faire qch; **he chooses to n. my advice** il choisit de ne pas tenir compte de mon conseil

neglectful [nɪ'glektfʊl] *adj* négligent; **to be n. of sth/sb** négliger qch/qn; **n. of one's duty** oublieux de son devoir; **to be n. of one's responsibilities/obligations** manquer à ses responsabilités/obligations

negligé(e) ['neglɪʒeɪ] *n* négligé *m*, déshabillé *m*

negligence ['neglɪdʒəns] *n* (*lack of care*), *Jur* négligence *f*; **through n.** par négligence; **n. of one's duties/responsibilities** manquement *m* à ses devoirs/responsabilités

negligent ['neglɪdʒənt] *adj* **(a)** (*neglectful*) négligent; **to be n. of sth** négliger qch; (*of one's duties, responsibilities etc*) être oublieux de qch, manquer à qch **(b)** (*casual*) (*air, tone*) nonchalant, insouciant

negligently ['neglɪdʒəntlɪ] *adv* **(a)** (*neglectfully*) avec négligence; **to fail n. to do sth** avoir la négligence de faire qch **(b)** (*casually*) négligemment, nonchalamment

negligible ['neglɪdʒɪb(ə)l] *adj* (*amount*) négligeable

negotiability [nɪgəʊʃə'bɪlɪtɪ] *adj Fin* négociabilité *f*

negotiable [nɪ'gəʊʃəb(ə)l] *adj* **(a)** *Fin etc* (*bill, document, demands, fee etc*) négociable; **not n.** non-négociable **(b)** (*barrier, obstacle etc*) franchissable; (*path etc*) praticable; **the path was not easily n.** le chemin n'était guère praticable

negotiate [nɪ'gəʊʃɪeɪt] **1** *vt* **(a)** (*business deal, marriage*) négocier, traiter; (*loan, treaty, fee*) négocier; (*peace*) traiter; *Fin* (*bill*) négocier, trafiquer; **price to be negotiated** prix *m* à débattre **(b)** (*obstacle etc*) franchir; *Fig* (*difficulty*) surmonter; *Aut* (*bend*) négocier, prendre; (*minefield*) traverser; (*rapids*) passer **2** *vi* négocier; **to be negotiating with sb for ...** être en traité *ou* en marché avec qn pour ...; **to n. for peace** entreprendre des pourparlers de paix; **to n. about sth** négocier qch

negotiation [nɪgəʊʃɪ'eɪʃən] *n* **(a)** (*of treaty, loan etc*) négociation *f*; **under n.** en négociation; **to be in n. with sb** être en pourparler(s) avec qn; **to break off/resume negotiations** rompre/reprendre les négociations; **pay/redundancy negotiations** négociations sur les salaires/les licenciements; **peace negotiations** pourparlers *mpl* de paix **(b)** (*of obstacle*) franchissement *m*; (*of corner*) prise *f*

negotiator [nɪ'gəʊʃɪeɪtər] *n* négociateur, -trice

Negress ['ni:grɪs] *n* Noire *f*; (*in anthropology*), *Pej* négresse *f*

Negro, *pl* **-oes** ['ni:grəʊ, -z] **1** *adj* noir, nègre; **the N. race** la race noire *ou* nègre; *Mus* **N. spiritual** Négro Spiritual *m* **2** *n* Noir *m*; (*in anthropology*), *Pej* nègre *m*

Negroid ['ni:grɔɪd] *adj, n* (*in anthropology*) négroïde *mf*

neigh¹ [neɪ] *n* hennissement *m*

neigh² *vi* hennir

neighbour, *US* **neighbor** ['neɪbər] *n* **(a)** (*person, country*) voisin, -ine; **to be a good n.** être bon voisin **(b)** *Bible etc* (*fellow human being*) prochain *m*; **love thy n. as thyself** aime ton prochain comme toi-même

▶ **neighbour on,** *US* **neighbor on** *vipo* (*adjoin*) être contigu à; (*of country*) être limitrophe à

neighbourhood, *US* **neighborhood** [ˈneɪbəhʊd] *n* **(a)** (*vicinity*) **in the n. of** (*place*) aux alentours de, dans les environs de; **to live in the (immediate) n. of …** demeurer à proximité de …; **anyone in the n. of the crime should contact the police** quiconque se trouvait à proximité du lieu du crime doit contacter la police; **in the n. of 10** environ 10, dans les 10; **a figure in the n. of £2000** un chiffre avoisinant les 2 000 livres

(b) (*district*) voisinage *m*, quartier *m*; **I was in the n.** j'étais dans le coin *ou* dans le quartier *ou* dans le voisinage; **the whole n. is talking about it** tout le voisinage *ou* le quartier en parle; **a very friendly n.** un quartier très sympa; **a good/bad n.** un bon/mauvais quartier; **she's the n. gossip** c'est la commère du quartier *ou* du voisinage

neighbourhood watch *n Br* = système *m* de surveillance mis en œuvre par les habitants d'un quartier

neighbouring, *US* **neighboring** [ˈneɪbərɪŋ] *adj* avoisinant, voisin

neighbourliness, *US* **neighborliness** [ˈneɪbəlɪnɪs] *n* (relations *fpl* de) bon voisinage *m*, bons rapports *mpl* entre voisins; **an act of n.** un acte de bon voisinage; **to show a little n.** se montrer bon voisin; **the n. of the family next door** l'obligeance *f* de la famille d'à-côté

neighbourly, *US* **neighborly** [ˈneɪbəlɪ] *adj* (*person*) obligeant, bon voisin; (*action, behaviour etc*) de bon voisin; (*visit*) de bon voisinage; **it was very n. of them** c'était très obligeant de leur part; **to be n. with sb** entretenir des rapports de bons voisinage avec qn; **people used to be more n.** autrefois les gens entretenaient de meilleurs rapports avec leurs voisins

neighing [ˈneɪɪŋ] *n* hennissement(s) *m(pl)*

neither [ˈnaɪðər, ˈniːðər] [ⓘA37,f] **1** *adv* **n. … nor …** ni … ni …; **he will n. eat nor drink** il ne veut ni manger ni boire; **n. (the) one nor the other** ni l'un ni l'autre; **that's n. here nor there** (*irrelevant*) ça n'a rien à voir

2 *conj* [ⓘA68,1,a,iv; A72,a,iv] non plus; **n. do I** (ni) moi non plus; **if you don't go n. will I** si vous n'y allez pas je n'irai pas non plus; **I haven't read it, n. do I intend to** je ne l'ai pas lu et d'ailleurs je n'en ai pas l'intention; **the funding wasn't available and n. was the necessary expertise** ni les fonds ni les compétences nécessaires n'étaient disponibles

3 *adj* **n. driver was injured** ni l'un ni l'autre des conducteurs n'a été blessé; **on n. side** ni d'un côté ni de l'autre

4 *pron* **which do you want? – n.** lequel voulez-vous? – ni l'un(e) ni l'autre; **n. of my two brothers can come** aucun de mes deux frères ne peut venir; **n. of us is satisfied** nous ne sommes satisfaits ni l'un ni l'autre

nelly [ˈnelɪ] *n Br Sl* **not on your n.!** jamais de la vie!

nelson [ˈnels(ə)n] *n* (*in wrestling*) nelson *m*; **double** *or* **full n.** double nelson

nematode [ˈnemətəʊd] *n* nématode *m*

Nemesis [ˈnemɪsɪs] *n Myth* Némesis *f*; *Fig* **this/he was my N.** *or* **n.** cela/il a été ma ruine

neo- [ˈniːəʊ] *pref* néo-

neoclassic(al) [niːəʊˈklæsɪk, -ɪk(ə)l] *adj* néo-classique, *pl* néo-classiques

neoclassicism [niːəʊˈklæsɪsɪz(ə)m] *n* néo-classicisme *m*

neocolonialism [niːəʊkəˈləʊnɪəlɪz(ə)m] *n* néo-colonialisme *m*

neofascism [niːəʊˈfæʃɪz(ə)m] *n* néo-fascisme *m*

neofascist [niːəʊˈfæʃɪst] *adj, n* néo-fasciste *mf*, *pl* néo-fascistes

neogothic [niːəʊˈgɒθɪk] *adj, n Archit* néo-gothique *m*, *pl* néo-gothiques

neolithic [niːəʊˈlɪθɪk] *adj* néolithique; **the N. age** l'âge *m* de la pierre polie, le néolithique

neologism [nɪˈɒlədʒɪz(ə)m] *n* néologisme *m*

neon [ˈniːɒn] *n Ch* néon *m*; *El* **n. light** lumière *f* au néon; **n. sign** enseigne *f* au néon; **n. tube** tube *m* fluorescent *ou* au néon

neonatal [niːəʊˈneɪt(ə)l] *adj* néo-natal, *pl* néo-natals

neonazi [niːəʊˈnɑːtsɪ] *adj, n* néo-nazi, -ie, *pl* néo-nazis, -ies

neophyte [ˈniːəʊfaɪt] *n Rel etc* néophyte *mf*

neoplasm [ˈniːəʊplæz(ə)m] *n Med* néoplasme *m*

Nepal [nɪˈpɔːl] *n* Népal *m*

Nepalese [nepəˈliːz], **Nepali** [neˈpɔːlɪ] **1** *adj* népalais **2** *n* **(a)** Népalais, -aise **(b)** *Ling* népalais *m*

nephew [ˈnefjuː] *n* neveu *m*

nephrite [ˈnefraɪt] *n Miner* néphrite *f*

nephritic [neˈfrɪtɪk] *adj Med* néphrétique

nephritis [neˈfraɪtɪs] *n Med* néphrite *f*; **to have n.** avoir une néphrite

nephron [ˈnefrɒn] *n Anat* néphron *m*

nepotism [ˈnepətɪz(ə)m, ˈniː-] *n* népotisme *m*

Neptune [ˈneptjuːn] *n Astron* Neptune *f*; *Myth* Neptune *m*

nerd [nɜːd] *n Pej F* nullard, -arde, nul, *f* nulle

Nereid [ˈnɪərɪɪd] *n Myth* Néréide *f*

Nero [ˈnɪərəʊ] *n Antiq* Néron *m*

nerve[1] [nɜːv] *n* **(a)** *Anat* nerf *m*; **to take the n. out of a tooth** (*of dentist*) dévitaliser une dent; **to be in a state of nerves** être sur les nerfs; **we're living on our nerves** nous vivons sur les nerfs; **it's her nerves** c'est les nerfs; **my nerves won't stand it** mes nerfs vont lâcher; **to get on sb's nerves** taper sur les nerfs à qn, énerver qn; **she's got nerves of steel** elle a des nerfs d'acier; **war of nerves** guerre des nerfs

(b) (*courage*) courage *m*; (*coolness*) sang-froid *m*; **his n. failed him, he lost his n.** le courage lui a manqué; **a pilot who has lost his n.** un pilote qui n'est plus mentalement en état de voler; **he never regained his n.** il n'a jamais retrouvé son courage

(c) *F* (*cheek*) culot *m*; **to have the n. to do sth** avoir le toupet *ou* le culot de faire qch; **what a n.!** quel culot!; **you've got a n.!** tu es gonflé!

(d) *Bot, Ent, Archit* nervure *f*

nerve[2] *vt* **to n. oneself to do sth** s'armer de courage pour faire qch; **to n. sb for sth** encourager qn pour qch, donner du courage à qn pour qch

nerve cell *n Anat* neurone *f*

nerve centre *n Anat* centre *m* nerveux; *Fig* centre *m* névralgique

nerve ending *n Anat* terminaison *f* nerveuse

nerve fibre *n Anat* fibre *f* nerveuse

nerve gas *n Mil etc* gaz *m* neurotoxique

nerveless [ˈnɜːvlɪs] *adj* **(a)** (*calm*) (*person*) calme, plein de sang-froid; (*courage, bravery*) imperturbable **(b)** (*lacking strength*) (*person, limb etc*) inerte; (*style etc*) sans vigueur, languissant; **the cup fell from her n. fingers** la tasse a échappé à ses doigts engourdis

nerve specialist *n Med* neurologue *mf*

nerve-(w)racking [ˈnɜːvrækɪŋ] *adj* (*experience*) éprouvant; (*wait, suspense*) angoissant

nerviness [ˈnɜːvɪnɪs] *n* **(a)** *Br F* (*tension*) nervosité *f* **(b)** *Am F* (*cheek*) culot *m*

nervous [ˈnɜːvəs] *adj* **(a)** nerveux; (*timid*) craintif; **to be n.** (*before a performance, an exam etc*) avoir le trac; (*before going to the dentist etc*) avoir peur; **to be n. about sth** s'inquiéter à propos de qch; **are you n. about the exams?** est-ce que tu appréhendes les examens?; **he's n. about flying** il appréhende *ou* a peur de voyager en avion; **to be n. about doing sth** avoir peur *ou* appréhender de faire qch; **I was a bit n. about lending him the car** j'avais un peu d'appréhension à l'idée de lui prêter ma voiture; **the bank was n. about making the loan** la banque hésitait à accorder le prêt; **I'm still a little n. about taking on this contract** j'hésite encore un peu à accepter ce contrat; **if you're n. about offering him the job** (*are worried*) si vous craignez de lui proposer l'emploi; (*are uncertain*) si vous hésitez à lui proposer l'emploi; **he gets terribly n. every time he has to make a speech** chaque fois qu'il doit faire un discours il a un trac terrible *ou* il devient terriblement nerveux *ou* anxieux; **I feel** *or* **am n. in his presence** sa présence me rend nerveux; **airports make me n.** les aéroports me rendent nerveux; **he makes me n.** (*is intimidating*) il m'intimide; **don't hold your glass like that, you're making me n.** ne tiens pas ton verre comme ça, tu me rends nerveux *ou* tu me fais peur

(b) *Anat* (*exhaustion etc*) nerveux; **n. complaint** maladie *f* de nerfs

nervous breakdown *n Med* dépression *f* nerveuse; **to have a n.** faire une dépression nerveuse

nervous energy *n* énergie *f* nerveuse

nervously [ˈnɜːvəslɪ] *adv* nerveusement; **he wondered n. if …** il se demanda, avec une certaine nervosité, si …

nervousness [ˈnɜːvəsnɪs] *n* **(a)** (*timidity*) timidité *f*; (*before performance*) trac *m* **(b)** (*tension, anxiety*) nervosité *f*

nervous system *n* système *m* nerveux

nervy [ˈnɜːvɪ] *adj* **(a)** *Br F* (*tense*) nerveux; **to feel n.** avoir les nerfs en pelote **(b)** *Am F* (*cheeky*) qui a du culot

nest[1] [nest] *n* (*of bird, wasps etc*) nid *m*; (*nestful*) (*of fledgelings*) nichée *f*, couvée *f*; (*of eggs*) couvée; *Fig* (*of bandits, machine guns etc*) repaire *m*, nid; *Fig* **the children have all left** *or* **flown the n.** les enfants ont tous quitté le nid; **n. of tables** table *f* gigogne

nest[2] **1** *vi* (*of bird etc*) (se) nicher, faire son nid; (*of tables etc*) s'emboîter **2** *vt* **(a)** (*pipes etc*) emboîter **(b)** *Comptr, Typ* imbriquer

nest box *n* (*for hens*) pondoir *m*; (*for wild birds*) nichoir *m*

nested [ˈnestɪd] *adj Comptr, Typ* imbriqué

nest egg *n* (*money*) pécule *m*

nestful ['nestfʊl] *n* (*of fledgelings*) nichée *f*, couvée *f*; (*of eggs*) couvée

nesting ['nestɪŋ] **1** *adj* (*bird*) nicheur **2** *n* **(a) to go (bird) n.** aller dénicher des œufs/des oisillons; **n. time** saison *f* de la ponte **(b)** *Comptr, Typ* imbrication *f*

nesting box *n* (*for hens*) pondoir *m*; (*for wild birds*) nichoir *m*

nestle ['nes(ə)l] **1** *vi* se pelotonner, se blottir; (*of house, tree*) être blotti; **to n. (up) close to sb** se pelotonner *ou* se blottir *ou* se serrer contre qn; **to n. (up) against sb's shoulder** se blottir contre l'épaule de qn; **village nestling in a valley** village blotti *ou* tapi dans une vallée **2** *vt* **to n. one's face against sb's shoulder** se blottir contre l'épaule de qn

nestling ['neslɪŋ] *n* oisillon *m*

net[1] [net] *n* **(a)** filet *m*; **to haul in a n.** relever un filet; *Fig* **to be caught in the n.** être pris au piège *ou* au filet; *Fig* **to slip through the n.** passer à travers les mailles du filet; *Fb* **to put the ball in the n.** envoyer la balle dans le filet **(b)** *Tex* tulle *m*

net[2] **(-tt-)** *vt* **(a)** (*capture*) (*fish, hares, Fig criminals etc*) prendre au filet; *Fig* (*tax evaders, drugs*) mettre la main sur; *Fig* **the charity appeal netted several large donations** l'appel caritatif a rapporté plusieurs dons importants **(b)** (*river*) tendre des filets dans **(c)** *Fb* **he netted the ball twice** (*scored two goals*) il a marqué deux buts **(d)** (*in gardening*) (*peas etc*) protéger avec un filet

net[3] **1** *adj* (*weight, price*) net, *f* nette; **n. proceeds of a sale** (produit *m*) net *m* d'une vente; **terms strictly n.** sans déduction; **n. amount** somme *f* nette; **n. total** montant *m* net; **n. assets** actif *m* net; *Acct* **n. book value** valeur *f* comptable nette; *Acct* **n. current assets** actif circulant net; **n. dividend** dividende *m* net; **n. earnings** (*of company*) bénéfices *mpl* nets; (*of worker*) salaire *m* net; *Acct* **n. income** (*in accounts*) produit net; (*of individual*) revenu *m* net; *Acct* **n. interest income** net financier; **n. loss** perte *f* nette; **n. operating profit** rentabilité *f* nette d'exploitation; *Acct* **n. present value rate** taux *m* d'actualisation; **n. profit** bénéfice net, net commercial; **n. receipts** recette *f* nette; **n. result** résultat *m* final; **n. return** retour *m* net, montant du retour net; *Comptr* **n. storage capacity** capacité *f* nette de stockage; **n. tonnage** (*of ship*) tonnage *m* net; *Acct* **n. variance** écart *m* net; **n. worth** actif *m* net, situation *f* nette

2 *n* prix *m*/poids *m*/bénéfice *m*/*etc* net; **n. payable** net *m* à payer

3 *adv* **n. of tax** net d'impôt; **n. of VAT** hors TVA

net[4] *vt Fin* (*sum of money*) (*of person*) toucher net, gagner net; (*of enterprise etc*) rapporter net

netball ['netbɔːl] *n Sp* netball *m*

net curtain *n* rideau *m* de tulle

nether ['neðər] *adj* inférieur, bas; **the n. regions** *Lit* l'enfer *m*, les régions *mpl* infernales; *Hum* (*of body*) les parties *fpl* basses; **the n. regions of the rue St. Denis** le bas de la rue St. Denis

Netherlands ['neðələndz] *npl* **the N.** les Pays-Bas *mpl*; **in the N.** dans les *ou* aux Pays-Bas

net play *n Tennis* jeu *m* au filet

nett [net] *adj, n, adv, vt* = **net**[3,4]

netting ['netɪŋ] *n* (*nets*) (*for protection, camouflage*) filet(s) *m(pl)*; (*around tennis court etc*) grillage *m*; *Tex* tulle *m*

nettle[1] ['net(ə)l] *n* (*weed*) ortie *f*; *Med* **n. rash** urticaire *f*; *Fig* **to grasp the n.** y aller carrément; **to grasp the n. of reorganisation** s'attaquer au problème épineux de la réorganisation

nettle[2] *vt* (*irritate*) irriter, énerver

netware loadable module ['netweər] *n Comptr* module *m* logiciel téléchargeable

network[1] ['netwɜːk] *n* **(a)** (*of canals, streets, contacts, users etc*) réseau *m*; **electricity n.** réseau électrique

(b) *Comptr, TV, Rad* réseau *m*; **n. access costs** coûts *mpl* d'accès au réseau; **n. adaptor card** carte-adaptateur *f* réseau; **n. administrator** administrateur *m* de réseau; **n. architecture** architecture *f ou* topologie *f* de réseau; **n. card** carte *f* réseau; *TV* **n. controller** contrôleur *m* de réseau, directeur *m* d'antenne *ou* de chaîne; **n. driver** gestionnaire *m* de réseau; **n. management** administration *f* de réseau; **n. manager** gestionnaire *m* de réseau; **n. operating system** système *m* d'exploitation réseau; **n. server** serveur *m* de réseau; **n. software** logiciel *m* de réseau; **n. station** station *f* réseau; **n. supervisor** superviseur *m* de réseau; **n. television** télévision *f* nationale, *US* télévision diffusée par les grands réseaux américains; **n. traffic** trafic *m* de réseau

network[2] **1** *vt* **(a)** (*to cover*) parcourir; **the country was networked with canals** le pays était parcouru de canaux; **to n. the country with railway lines/motorways** construire un réseau ferroviaire/autoroutier à travers le pays **(b)** *TV, Rad* diffuser sur l'ensemble du réseau; **networked programmes** programmes *mpl* diffusés en réseau **(c)** *Comptr* mettre en réseau; **networked systems** systèmes *mpl* en réseau **2** *vi esp Am* (*establish contacts*) établir un réseau de contacts

networking ['netwɜːkɪŋ] *n* **(a)** *Comptr* travail *m* en réseau; (*connecting as network*) mise *f* en réseau; **to have n. capabilities** (*of terminal*) offrir la possibilité d'intégration à un réseau **(b)** *esp Am* (*establishing contacts*) établissement *m* d'un réseau de contacts

neural ['njʊərəl] *adj Anat* neural; *Comptr* **n. network** réseau *m* neuronal

neuralgia [njʊ'rældʒə] *n Med* névralgie *f*; **to have n.** avoir une névralgie

neuralgic [njʊ'rældʒɪk] *adj Med* névralgique

neurasthenia [njʊərəs'θiːnɪə] *n Med* neurasthénie *f*

neurasthenic [njʊərəs'θenɪk] *adj, n Med* neurasthénique *mf*

neuritis [njʊ'raɪtɪs] *n Med* névrite *f*

neurological [njʊərə'lɒdʒɪk(ə)l] *adj* neurologique

neurologist [njʊə'rɒlədʒɪst] *n* neurologue *mf*

neurology [njʊə'rɒlədʒɪ] *n* neurologie *f*

neuromuscular [njʊərəʊ'mʌskjuːlər] *adj* neuromusculaire

neuron ['njʊərɒn] *n Physiol* neurone *m*

neurone ['njʊərəʊn] *n Biol* neurone *m*

neuropathology [njʊərəʊpə'θɒlədʒɪ] *n* neuropathologie *f*

neurosis, *pl* **neuroses** [njʊ'rəʊsɪs, -siːz] *n* névrose *f*

neurosurgeon [njʊərəʊ'sɜːdʒən] *n* neurochirurgien, -ienne

neurosurgery [njʊərəʊ'sɜːdʒərɪ] *n* neurochirurgie *f*

neurosurgical [njʊərəʊ'sɜːdʒɪk(ə)l] *adj* neurochirurgical

neurotic [njʊ'rɒtɪk] **1** *adj* **(a)** (*person*) névrosé; *Fig F* **he's positively n. about it** c'est une obsession chez lui; **to be n. about losing one's keys** avoir une peur obsessionnelle de perdre ses clés; **she gets very n. if everything isn't exactly as she left it** elle pique des crises folles si elle ne trouve pas tout exactement comme elle l'a laissé; **I think I'm getting a bit n. about it** je crois que je suis en train d'en faire une obsession **(b)** (*relating to a neurosis*) névrotique **2** *n* névrosé, -ée

neurotically [njʊ'rɒtɪklɪ] *adv* de façon obsessionnelle; **to be n. obsessed with sth** avoir une obsession névrotique de qch

neuroticism [njʊ'rɒtɪsɪz(ə)m] *n* névrose *f*

neurotransmitter [njʊərəʊtrænz'mɪtər] *n Biol* neurotransmetteur *m*

neuter[1] ['njuːtər] **1** *adj* **(a)** *Gram* neutre **(b)** *Biol* neutre, asexué **2** *n* **(a)** *Gram* neutre *m*; **in the n.** au neutre **(b)** (*animal*) animal *m* châtré; (*bee*) abeille *f* asexuée *ou* ouvrière

neuter[2] *vt Vet* (*cat etc*) châtrer

neutral ['njuːtr(ə)l] **1** *adj* (*colour*), *Pol etc* neutre; **to remain n.** rester neutre; *Pol* rester neutre, garder la neutralité **2** *n* **(a)** (*nation*) (État *m ou* pays *m*) neutre *m*; (*person*) ressortissant, -ante d'un État neutre **(b)** (*person*) (*in an argument, politics etc*) personne *f* neutre **(c)** *Aut* point *m* mort; **in n.** au point mort

neutralism ['njuːtrəlɪz(ə)m] *n* neutralisme *m*

neutralist ['njuːtrəlɪst] *adj, n* neutraliste *mf*

neutrality [njuː'trælɪtɪ] *n Pol etc* neutralité *f*; *Ch* (*of salt*) neutralité, indifférence *f*

neutralization [njuːtrəlaɪ'zeɪʃən] *n* neutralisation *f*

neutralize ['njuːtrəlaɪz] *vt* (*opposition, country*) neutraliser; **to n. one another** (*of chemical agents*) se neutraliser; (*of forces*) se neutraliser, s'annuler

neutrino [njʊ'triːnəʊ] *n Phys* neutrino *m*

neutron ['njuːtrɒn] *n Nucl Phys* neutron *m*; **n. bomb** bombe *f* à neutrons; **n. star** étoile *f* à neutrons

Nev *abbr* **Nevada**

never ['nevər] **1** *adv* **(a)** [①A72,a,iv; A23,3,a,ii] (ne …) jamais; **I n. go there** je n'y vais jamais; **n. again!** plus jamais!; **I'll n. go there again, n. again will I go there** je n'irai plus jamais; **he n. came back** il n'est jamais revenu; **he's n. yet been beaten** il n'a encore jamais été battu; **I've n. yet understood why** je n'ai jamais compris pourquoi; **n. in (all) my life, n. in all my born days** jamais de la vie; **that n.-to-be-forgotten day** ce jour inoubliable; **n. say die!** accroche-toi!; **n. fear!** n'aie pas peur!, ne t'en fais pas!

(b) (*emphatic neg*) **I n. expected him to come** je ne m'attendais pas du tout à ce qu'il vienne; **she n. said a word** elle n'a pas dit un mot; **this will n. do!** c'est inacceptable!; **n. ever do that again!** ne refais jamais cela!; **they n. even wrote back** ils n'ont jamais répondu; **n. a one** pas un seul; *F* **you (surely) n. left him all alone!** ne me dites pas que vous l'avez laissé tout seul!

(c) *Lit* **be he n. so brave** quelque courageux qu'il soit, si courageux soit-il

2 *int Br F* **n.!** (*incredulity*) pas possible!; **he n. did!** ça alors! *esp Old-fashioned,* **well I n.!** ça par exemple!

never-ending *adj* perpétuel, éternel, sans fin; (*complaints,* *noise*) incessant; (*job, sermon, evening*) interminable; **my problems seem to be n.** mes problèmes semblent ne pas en finir; **a n. supply of funny stories** un stock inépuisable d'histoires drôles; **housework is n.** le ménage n'est jamais fini

never-failing *adj* inépuisable, intarissable

nevermore [nevə'mɔːr] *adv Lit* (ne ...) plus jamais, (ne ...) jamais plus; **n.!** jamais plus!, plus jamais!

never-never 1 *n Br F* **to buy sth on the n.** acheter qch à crédit *ou* à tempérament **2** *adj* **n. land** pays *m* imaginaire; **you're living in n. land if you believe that ...** tu rêves si tu crois que ...

nevertheless [nevəðə'les] *adv* néanmoins, cependant; **I love him n.** je l'aime quand même *ou* malgré tout

nevus ['niːvəs] *n US* = **naevus**

new [njuː] **1** *adj* nouveau, -elle; (*before masculine noun beginning with vowel or silent h*) nouvel; (*not used*) neuf, *f* neuve; **I need a n. car** (*different*) il me faut une nouvelle voiture; **I'd prefer a new car** *or* **a car that's n.** (*which has not been used*) je préférerais une voiture neuve *ou* qui soit neuve; **we visited a n. country** (*one we did not know*) nous avons visité un nouveau pays; **America was a n. country** (*just developing*) l'Amérique était un pays neuf; **I felt a n. man** je me sentais un homme nouveau *ou* neuf; **she's got a n. man** elle a un nouveau mec; **it's made a n. man of him** cela a fait de lui un autre homme *ou* un homme neuf *ou* un nouvel homme; **would you like a n. glass?** (*for a different wine*) désirez-vous un autre verre?; **what's n.?** quoi de neuf *ou* de nouveau?; **that's nothing n.!** rien de nouveau à cela!; **it's quite n. to me** c'est tout nouveau *ou* neuf pour moi; *F* **that's a n. one on me!** c'est la première fois que j'entends/je vois cela; **she's n. to this work** elle débute dans ce travail; **I'm n. to this town** je suis nouveau venu dans cette ville; **to be dressed in n. clothes** être habillé de neuf; *Com* **in n. condition, as n.** à l'état (de) neuf; **to do sth up like n.** remettre qch à neuf; **n. ideas** (*modern ideas*) idées neuves; **a completely n. idea** une idée tout à fait nouvelle *ou* neuve; **the subject is quite n.** le sujet n'a pas encore été traité; *Sch* **the n. boys** les nouveaux; *Mil* **the n. guard** la garde montante; *Pol* **the N. Left/Right** la nouvelle gauche/droite; **n. account manager** responsable *mf* des nouveaux comptes-clients; *Mktg* **n. and improved** nouveau et meilleur; *Fig* **n. blood** du sang neuf; **n. business** nouvelles affaires *fpl*; (*new company*) nouvelle entreprise *f*; **to look for n. business** faire de la prospection; *Mktg* **n. buy situation** situation *f* de nouvel achat; *St Exch* **n. issue** nouvelle émission *f*; *St Exch* **n. issue market** marché *m* des nouvelles émissions; **n. moon** nouvelle lune *f*; **n. potatoes** pommes *fpl* de terre nouvelles; **n. students** nouveaux étudiants, nouvelles étudiantes; **n. technology** nouvelle technologie *f*; **n. wine** vin *m* primeur

2 *adv* (*used to form compound adj*) nouvellement; **n. blown** (*flower*) fraîchement *ou Lit* frais épanoui; **n.-cut grass** herbe fraîchement coupée; **n.-found** (*confidence, happiness*) tout neuf; (*friend etc*) nouveau; **n.-laid egg** œuf fraîchement pondu; **n.-made** *or* **n.-baked bread** pain frais; **n. mown hay** foin fraîchement *ou Lit* frais coupé

New Age *n* new age *m*, nouvel âge *m*

newborn ['njuːbɔːn] *adj* nouveau-né, *f* nouveau-née; **n. baby** nouveau-né, -née, *pl* nouveau-nés, -nées

New Brunswick ['brʌnzwɪk] *n* Nouveau-Brunswick *m*

New Caledonia *n* Nouvelle-Calédonie *f*

newcomer ['njuːkʌmər] *n* nouveau venu *m*, nouvelle venue *f* (**to** dans)

newel ['njuːəl] *n Constr etc* **(a)** (*of spiral staircase*) noyau *m* **(b)** (*of bannister*) **n. (post)** pilastre *m*

New England *n* Nouvelle-Angleterre *f*

newfangled ['njuːfæŋg(ə)ld] *adj Pej* nouveau genre *inv*; (*word, idea etc*) moderne; **n. gadgets** gadgets *mpl* à la dernière mode

Newfie ['njuːfɪ] *n Can F* Terre-Neuvien, -ienne; **N. joke** = plaisanterie *f* sur les Terre-Neuviens, ≈ histoire *f* belge

Newfoundland ['njuːfəndlænd, -lənd, -'faʊndlənd] **1** *n* **(a)** Terre-Neuve *f* **(b) N. (dog)** terre-neuve *m inv* **2** *adj* terre-neuvien

Newfoundlander ['njuːfəndlændər, njuː'faʊndləndər] *n* (*native*) Terre-Neuvien, -ienne; (*inhabitant*) habitant, -ante de Terre-Neuve

New Guinea *n* Nouvelle-Guinée *f*

newish ['njuːɪʃ] *adj F* (*car, dress etc*) assez neuf, *f* assez neuve

newly ['njuːlɪ] *adv* (*usu hyphenated in conjunction with attributive adj before n*) récemment, nouvellement, fraîchement; **n.-dug** fraîchement creusé; **n.-formed** récemment formé; **n.-discovered/returned** qui vient d'être découvert/de rentrer; **n.-elected MP's** députés nouvellement élus; **n.-painted wall** mur qui vient d'être peint; **n.-industrialized country** nouveau pays *m* industrialisé; **n.-industrializing country** pays en voie d'industrialisation

newlyweds ['njuːlɪwedz] *npl* nouveaux mariés *mpl*, jeunes mariés

New Man *n* nouvel homme *m*

new maths *n* maths *fpl* modernes

New Mexico *n* Nouveau-Mexique *m*

newness ['njuːnɪs] *n* (*of idea etc*) nouveauté *f*; (*of piece of clothing etc*) état *m* neuf; (*of bread etc*) fraîcheur *f*; (*of wine*) jeunesse *f*; **her n. to** *or* **in the job** le fait qu'elle soit nouvelle à ce poste

New Orleans *n* Nouvelle-Orléans *f*

new product *n Mktg* nouveau produit *m*; **n. department/director** service *m*/directeur *m* des produits nouveaux; **n. marketing** marketing *m* de nouveau produit

news [njuːz] *npl* (*usu with sing verb*) **(a)** nouvelle(s) *f(pl)*; **what's the n.?** quelles nouvelles?, quoi de nouveau *ou* de neuf?; **there's been no n. so far** on n'a pas encore de nouvelles; **I've got some n. for you** j'ai une nouvelle à vous annoncer; **have you heard the n.?** est-ce que vous avez appris la nouvelle?; **a sad piece of n., sad n.** une triste nouvelle; **good/bad n.** bonne/mauvaise nouvelle; *Prov* **no n. is good n.** pas de nouvelles, bonnes nouvelles; *Prov* **bad n. travels fast** les mauvaises nouvelles vont vite; **I've got some good n., and some bad n.** j'ai deux nouvelles, une bonne et une mauvaise; **have I got n. for you!** j'ai quelque chose à vous annoncer!; **that's n. to me!** première nouvelle!

(b) the n. *Rad, TV* les informations *fpl*; *TV* le (télé)journal; **to be in the n.** faire parler de soi dans la presse, *esp Pej* défrayer la chronique; **a city that is in the n. a lot these days** une ville dont on parle beaucoup ces jours-ci; **he's always in the n.** on parle toujours de lui dans la presse; **financial n.** chronique financière; **sports n.** chronique des sports; **local/national/world n.** informations locales/nationales/internationales; **n. in brief** faits *mpl* divers; **the n. headlines** les principaux titres de l'actualité; **n. analyst** commentateur, -trice; **n. blackout** blackout *m* sur l'actualité, censure *f* de l'actualité; **to impose a n. blackout on sth** empêcher la divulgation de qch; **the government has imposed a n. blackout** le gouvernement a fait le blackout; **n. broadcasting** diffusion *f* des informations; *TV* **n. centre** salle *f* de rédaction télévision; **n. channel** chaîne *f* d'information continue; **n. content** contenu *m* d'informations; **n. coverage** reportage *m* d'actualités; **n. editor** rédacteur *m* en chef des actualités; **n. item** nouvelle *f*, information *f*; **n. page** page *f* d'actualités; **n. programme** nouvelles *fpl*; *TV* journal *m* télévisé; **n. reporter** reporter *m*; **n. satellite** satellite *m* d'informations; **n. sheet** bulletin *m* d'information; **n. story** sujet *m*, affaire *f*; **n. value** intérêt *m* médiatique; **n. vendor** marchand, -ande de journaux; **n. writer** rédacteur *m* d'actualités

(c) (*person, event etc*) sujet *m* propre au reportage; **to make n.** faire sensation; **she's no longer n.** on ne parle plus d'elle; **the fact that she's leaving is bad n. for the company** son départ est mauvais pour la société; **dog bites man is not n.** les faits divers, ça n'a pas d'intérêt; *F* **it's bad n.** (*poor quality*) c'est de la camelote; *F* **he's bad n.** (*is unpopular etc*) c'est un enquiquineur

news agency *n* agence *f* de presse; **n. journalist** agencier *m*

newsagent ['njuːzeɪdʒənt] *n Br* marchand, -ande de journaux; (*shopkeeper also selling papers*) dépositaire *mf* de journaux

news bulletin *n* bulletin *m ou* flash *m* d'information(s)

newscast ['njuːzkɑːst] *n TV* informations *fpl*

newscaster ['njuːzkɑːstər] *n TV* présentateur, -trice du journal télévisé

news conference *n* conférence *f* de presse

newsdealer ['njuːzdiːlər] *n US* = **newsagent**

news desk *n* service *m* des informations, bureau *m* du rédacteur en chef des actualités

newsfilm ['njuːzfɪlm] *n* film *m* d'actualités

newsflash ['njuːzflæʃ] *n Rad, TV* flash *m* d'information(s)

newshawk, newshound ['njuːzhɔːk, -haʊnd] *n F* reporter *m*, chasseur *m* de copie

newsletter ['njuːzletər] *n* bulletin *m* (d'informations), circulaire *f*

news magazine *n Rad, TV, Journ* magazine *m* d'information

newspaper ['njuːzpeɪpər] *n* journal *m*; **daily n.** (journal) quotidien *m*; **weekly n.** (journal) hebdomadaire *m*; **to work for** *or* **on a n.** travailler dans *ou* pour un journal; **to wrap sth in/line a drawer with n.** emballer qch dans/tapisser un tiroir de (papier) journal; **n. ads** petites annonces *fpl* des journaux; **n. advertisement** annonce-presse *f*, *pl* annonces-presses; **n. advertising** publicité *f* dans la presse; **n. article** article *m* de presse *ou* journal; **n. artist** (*for layout*) maquettiste *mf*; **n. clippings** *or* **cuttings** coupures *fpl* de journaux; **n. editor** rédacteur *m* de journal; **n. group** groupe *m* de presse; **n. office** bureau *m* de la presse; **n. photographer** photographe *mf* de presse; **n. publisher** éditeur *m* de presse; **n. rack** porte-journaux *m inv*; **n. report** reportage *m*

newspaperman, newspaperwoman ['nju:zpeɪpəmæn, 'nju:zpeɪpəwʊmən] *n* **(a)** *Journ* (*reporter*) journaliste *mf*; (*proprietor*) propriétaire *mf* de journal **(b)** *Br* (*vendor*) marchand, -ande de journaux

newsprint ['nju:zprɪnt] *n* papier *m* (de) journal; **I got my hands covered in n.** (*ink*) je me suis mis de l'encre plein les mains

newsreader ['nju:zri:dər] *n Rad, TV* présentateur, -trice du journal

newsreel ['nju:zri:l] *n Cin* actualités *fpl*

newsroom ['nju:zru:m] *n Journ, TV* salle *f* de rédaction des informations

news service *n* agence *f* de presse

news stand *n* kiosque *m* à journaux

newsworthiness ['nju:zwɜ:ðɪnɪs] *n* intérêt *m* médiatique

newsworthy ['nju:zwɜ:ðɪ] *adj* d'un intérêt médiatique

newsy ['nju:zɪ] *adj F* (*letter*) plein de nouvelles

newt [nju:t] *n* triton *m*; *Br Sl* **pissed as a n.** soûl comme une bourrique, beurré comme un petit lu

New Testament *n Rel* Nouveau Testament *m*

new-to-the-company product *n Mktg* produit *m* nouveau dans la compagnie

new-to-the-world product *n Mktg* produit *m* nouveau dans le monde

new town *n* (*newly built*) ville *f* nouvelle; (*new part of town*) ville *f* neuve

new wave *n Cin* nouvelle vague *f*; *Mus* new wave *f*

New World *n* nouveau monde *m*

New Year *n* Nouvel An *m*

New Year's Day *n* jour *m* de l'an

New Year's Eve *n* Saint Sylvestre *f*

New York [jɔ:k] *n* New York *m*

New Yorker ['jɔ:kər] *n* New-yorkais, -aise

New Zealand ['zi:lənd] *n* Nouvelle-Zélande *f*

New Zealander ['zi:ləndər] *n* Néo-Zélandais, -aise

next [nekst] **1** *adj* **(a)** (*in location*) d'à côté; **the n. room** la pièce voisine *ou* d'à côté; **it's the n. house** c'est la maison voisine *ou* d'à côté; **the girl (from) n. door** la jeune fille d'à côté; **he lives n. door (to us)** il habite à côté (de chez nous); **he's the boy-n.-door type** c'est un bon petit gars; **n.-door neighbours** voisins *mpl* d'à côté *ou* immédiats; **we are n.-door neighbours** nous sommes voisins; *Fig* **it's n. door to madness** cela confine à la folie; **this has left us n. door to the poorhouse** cela nous a mis quasiment sur la paille

(b) (*in time*) (*in future*) prochain; (*in past or in listing events*) suivant; **I leave n. month** je pars le mois prochain; *F* **see you n. week** à la semaine prochaine; **the n. thing I remember is ...** la première chose dont je me rappelle après ça c'est ...; **the n. week it rained** la semaine d'après *ou* suivante il a plu; **the n. month was awful** le mois suivant fut terrible; **in the n. few weeks we will discover ...** dans les semaines à venir *ou* qui vont venir nous allons découvrir ...; **in the n. four weeks we were to discover that ...** dans les quatre semaines suivantes *ou* qui suivirent nous devions découvrir que ...; **this time n. year** d'ici un an; **n. Friday, (on) Friday n.** vendredi prochain; **the n. day** le lendemain, le jour d'après; **the n. day but one** le surlendemain; **(the) n. morning** le lendemain matin; **the week/year after n.** dans deux semaines/ans; **n. Easter/summer** à Pâques prochain/ l'été prochain; **from one moment to the n.** d'un instant à l'autre

(c) (*in order*) prochain; **it's the n. station** c'est la prochaine gare; **the n. turning on the right** le prochain tournant à droite; **the n. chapter/page** le chapitre/la page suivant(e); **(the) n. time I see him** la prochaine fois que je le verrai; **ask the n. person you meet** demandez à la première personne que vous rencontrerez; **the n. thing is to ...** maintenant il s'agit de ...; **your name is n. on the list** votre nom est le suivant *ou* prochain sur la liste; **n. (person) please** au suivant, s'il vous plaît; **who's n.?, whose turn is it n.?** à qui le tour?, c'est à qui?; **you're n.** après c'est ton tour; **(the) n. to speak is ...** la parole est maintenant à ...; **(the) n. to arrive was Penelope** Pénélope est arrivée à la suite; **your train is the n. but one** ton train n'est pas le prochain, mais celui d'après; **the n. size up/down** la taille au-dessus/au-dessous

2 *adv* **(a)** (*afterwards*) ensuite, après; **what shall we do n.?** qu'est-ce que nous allons faire maintenant?; **what did you do n.?** qu'avez-vous fait après *ou* ensuite?; *F* **you'll be asking me to give up my job (for you) n.!** tu n'as qu'à me demander de laisser tomber mon travail pendant que tu y es!; *F* **whatever n.!** par exemple!, et quoi encore!; *F* **what (ever) will they think of n.!** que ne vont-ils pas inventer!; *F* **what will he do n.!** qu'est-ce qu'il va bien pouvoir faire maintenant?

(b) (*again*) la prochaine fois; **when I n. saw him, when n. I saw him** quand je l'ai revu; **when shall we meet n.?** quand nous reverrons-nous?; **we had no idea when we would n. meet** nous ignorions complètement quand nous allions nous revoir

(c) n. to à côté de; **her room is n. to mine** sa chambre est à côté de la mienne; **I can't bear wool n. to my skin** je ne supporte pas la laine à même la peau; **I got the n. to last loaf** j'ai eu l'avant-dernière baguette; **n. to my dog I like my sister best** après mon chien, c'est ma sœur que je préfère; **I got it for n. to nothing** je l'ai eu pour presque rien *ou* pour une bouchée de pain; **there's n. to nothing left** il ne reste presque rien; **there is n. to no evidence** il n'y a pour ainsi dire pas de preuves; **in n. to no time** en un rien de temps; *US F* **to get n. to sb** (*friendly with*) se mettre bien avec qn

(d) (*with superlatives*) **the n. best thing would be to ...** à défaut, le mieux serait de ...; **the n. fastest after the Ferrari was ...** la voiture la plus rapide après la Ferrari était ...; **the n. highest building in the world is ...** le deuxième immeuble dans le monde pour la hauteur, c'est ...; **Mark is the n. oldest/youngest** (*second oldest/youngest of all of them*) Mark est le second par ordre d'âge; **who is the n. oldest/youngest after Mark?** qui est le suivant *ou* le prochain par ordre d'âge après Mark?

next-of-kin *n* (*relative*) parent *m* le plus proche; (*used as pl*) famille *f*; **to inform the n.** prévenir la famille

NG take [en'dʒi:] *n TV, Cin* mauvaise prise *f*

NH *abbr* **New Hampshire**

NHI [eneɪtʃ'aɪ] *n Br* (*abbr* **National Health Insurance**) ≈ S. S. *f*

NHS [eneɪtʃ'es] *n Br* (*abbr* **National Health Service**) ≈ S. S. *f*

NI [e'naɪ] *n Br* (*abbr* **National Insurance**) ≈ S. S. *f*

Niagara [naɪ'æg(ə)rə] *n* Niagara *m*; **(the) N. Falls** les chutes *fpl* du Niagara

nib [nɪb] *n* **(a)** (*of fountain pen*) (bec *m* de) plume *f*; **broad n.** grosse plume, plume à gros bec; **fine n.** plume fine, plume à bec fin **(b)** *Tech* (*of tool etc*) pointe *f*

nibble¹ ['nɪb(ə)l] *n* **(a)** (*action*) grignotement *m*; **to have a n. at the cake** grignoter le gâteau **(b)** *Fishing* touche *f*; **I didn't get** *or* **have a n. all day** le poisson n'a pas mordu *ou* je n'ai pas fait une seule touche de toute la journée **(c)** (*food*) juste de quoi grignoter; (*of biscuit etc*) petit morceau *m*; **I feel like a n. of something** j'ai envie de grignoter un petit morceau; *F* **nibbles** amuse-gueules *mpl*

nibble² **1** *vt* grignoter; **to n. sb's ear** mordiller l'oreille à qn **2** *vi* (*of fish, F of person*) mordre à l'hameçon

▶ **nibble at** *vipo* (*biscuit etc*) grignoter; **she was nibbling at his ear** elle lui mordillait l'oreille; **to n. at the bait** (*of fish, F of person*) mordre à l'hameçon; **they're nibbling at our offer** notre offre les séduit

▶ **nibble away** *vtsep* (*remove*) grignoter entièrement

▶ **nibble away at** *vipo* (*biscuit, carrot*) grignoter; *Fig* (*value of money etc*) écorner, entamer

▶ **nibble on** *vipo* (*biscuit etc*) grignoter

nibbler ['nɪblər] *n* grignoteur, -euse; **he's a compulsive n.** il n'arrête pas de grignoter

nibs [nɪbz] *n F Iron* **his n.** Sa Majesté

NIC [enaɪ'si:] *n* **(a)** (*abbr* **newly-industrializing country**) pays *m* en voie d'industrialisation **(b)** (*abbr* **national insurance contribution**) cotisation *f* à la Sécurité sociale

NiCad battery [nɪ'kæd] *n* accumulateur *m* au cadmium nickel

Nicaragua [nɪkə'rægjʊə] *n* Nicaragua *m*

Nicaraguan [nɪkə'rægjʊən] **1** *adj* nicaraguayen **2** *n* Nicaraguayen, -enne

nice [naɪs] *adj* **(a)** (*pleasant*) (*person*) gentil, *f* gentille, agréable, aimable; (*car, house, shirt, park, trip etc*) joli, beau, *f* belle; (*meal, idea, hotel etc*) bon, *f* bonne; (*view*) beau; (*evening, smell, taste*) bon, agréable; (*place*) agréable; **it's n. here** c'est bien, ici; **to have a n. time** bien s'amuser; **sending flowers was a n. gesture** c'était gentil d'envoyer des fleurs; **to be n. to sb** se montrer gentil *ou* aimable envers qn; **it is n. of you to ...** c'est gentil de votre part de ..., vous êtes bien aimable de ...; **it's not n. of you to make fun of him** ce n'est pas gentil *ou* bien de vous moquer de lui; **it's not a n. thing to happen to anyone** ce n'est pas agréable quand ça arrive; **he's a n. chap** il est gentil, c'est un gentil garçon; **have a n. day!** bonne journée!; **it's turned out n. again** il fait encore beau; **the garden is beginning to look n.** le jardin commence à être joli; *F* **n. one!** bien joué!, bravo!

(b) (*intensive*) **n. and handy** bien commode; **it's n. and cool** il fait bien frais; **it's n. and easy** c'est très facile; **a n. cold drink** une boisson bien fraîche; **to have a n. long chat** faire une bonne petite causette

(c) (*respectable*) **n. people** des gens bien; **he's such a n. boy** il est tellement bien, ce garçon; **it's not n.** ce n'est pas bien; **it's not a n. story** c'est une histoire peu édifiante

(d) *Iron* **we are in a n. mess!** nous voilà dans de beaux draps!; **that's a n. way to behave!** en voilà des manières!; **that's a n. way to talk to your mother/father/sister!** en voilà une manière de parler à ta mère/ton père/ta sœur!; **you're a n. one to talk about being punctual!** tu peux bien parler d'être ponctuel!

(e) *Fml* (*delicate, subtle*) (*question etc*) délicat; (*taste etc*) subtil, fin, recherché; (*distinction*) subtil; **it's a n. point** c'est délicat

(f) *Old-fashioned* (*scrupulous*) scrupuleux

nice-looking ['naɪslʊkɪŋ] *adj* beau, *f* belle, joli

nicely ['naɪslɪ] *adv* (a) (*pleasantly, kindly*) gentiment; (*well*) bien; **ask n.!** demande poliment!; **sit n., Jessica!** tiens-toi bien, Jessica!; **to be coming along** *or* **doing n.** (*of roast, cake etc*) être bien en train de cuire; (*of garden*) commencer à prendre tournure; (*of investments*) bien se porter; (*of invalid, pupil*) faire de bons progrès; **to do n. (for oneself)** bien s'en sortir; **everything was n. done** tout était bien fait; **those will do (very) n.** ceux-là feront très bien l'affaire; **he spoke very n. about you** il m'a parlé de vous en très bons termes

(b) (*accurately*) (*judged*) exactement, avec justesse; (*scrupulously*) minutieusement, scrupuleusement; **a n. turned phrase** une phrase bien tournée; **that's n. put** voilà qui est bien dit

(c) (*respectably*) **n. brought up** bien élevé

niceness ['naɪsnɪs] *n* (a) (*pleasantness*) (*of person*) gentillesse *f*, amabilité *f*; (*of house, hotel etc*) caractère *m* agréable; **the n. of the weather** le temps agréable (b) *Fml* (*delicacy, subtlety*) (*of question*) délicatesse *f*; (*of taste, distinction*) subtilité *f*

nicety ['naɪsɪtɪ] *n* (a) (*of calculation etc*) exactitude *f*, précision *f*; (*of judgement*) finesse *f*; (*of question*) subtilité *f*, délicatesse *f*; **to a n.** exactement, à la perfection (b) **niceties** (*subtleties*) subtilités *fpl*; **social niceties** règles *fpl* de la politesse

niche [niːʃ] *n* (*for statue etc*) niche *f*; (*in market*) créneau *m*; **to carve out** *or* **make a n. for oneself** (trouver à) se caser; **n. market** niche, créneau spécialisé; **n. marketing** mercatique *f* ciblée; *Mktg* **n. player** acteur *m* sur un segment de marché; *Mktg* **n. product** produit *m* ciblé

nicher ['niːʃər] *n Mktg* spécialiste *mf* dans une niche

niching ['niːʃɪŋ] *n Mktg* segmentation *f* en niches

Nick [nɪk] *n F* **Old N.** le diable

nick¹ [nɪk] *n* (a) (*in wood*) entaille *f*, encoche *f*; (*in blade*) brèche *f*; (*on chin, in finger etc*) entaille, coupure *f*; **to give oneself a n.** se couper (b) **in the n. of time** juste à temps; **you've come just in the n. of time** vous tombez bien (c) *Br F* (*condition*) état *m*; **in good/bad n.** en bon/mauvais état; **he's in pretty good n. for his age** il est en bonne forme pour son âge (d) *Br Sl* (*prison*) taule *f*; **to take sb to the (local) n.** (*police station*) emmener qn au poste

nick² *vt* (a) (*stick etc*) entailler, encocher; (*blade*) ébrécher; (*cards*) biseauter; **to n. oneself** se couper; **to n. one's finger/chin** s'entailler *ou* se couper le doigt/le menton (b) *esp Br Sl* (*arrest*) pincer, choper, épingler; **to get nicked** se faire pincer *ou* choper *ou* épingler; **you're nicked!** tu es fait! (c) *esp Br Sl* (*steal*) piquer, faucher; **it was nicked last week** quelqu'un l'a piqué *ou* fauché la semaine dernière (d) *Am Sl* (*overcharge*) **they've nicked me for 50 dollars** je me suis fait avoir de 50 dollars; **how much did they n. you for that?** combien ils t'ont fait payer ça?

nickel¹ ['nɪk(ə)l] *n* (a) *Metal* nickel *m*; **n. plating** nickelage *m* (b) *Am* (*coin*) pièce *f* de cinq cents

nickel² *vt* (**-ll-**, *US* **-l-**), nickeler

nickel-and-dime *adj esp US* (*business operation*) de quatre sous

nickel-cadmium battery *n* batterie *f* au nickel-cadmium

nickel-plate *vt* nickeler

nicker ['nɪkər] *n* (*no pl*) *Br Sl* livre *f* sterling; **five n.** cinq livres sterling

nickname¹ ['nɪkneɪm] *n* surnom *m*

nickname² *vt* surnommer

nicotine ['nɪkətiːn] *n* nicotine *f*; **n. addict** accro *mf* à la nicotine; **n. poisoning** nicotinisme *m*, tabagisme *m*; **n.-stained** (*fingers, teeth*) jaune de nicotine

nicotinism ['nɪkətiːnɪz(ə)m] *n Med* nicotinisme *m*, tabagisme *m*

niece [niːs] *n* nièce *f*

Nielsen ['niːlsən] *n Am TV* **N. rating** ≈ Audimat *m*

niff¹ [nɪf] *n Br Sl* puanteur *f*; **there's a bit of a n. in here** ça pue là-dedans

niff² *vi Br Sl* puer

niffy ['nɪfɪ] *adj Br Sl* puant, qui pue; **it's a bit n. in here** ça pue là-dedans

nifty ['nɪftɪ] *adj F* (a) (*clever*) (*person*) adroit, débrouillard; (*thing*) commode; **he's pretty n.** il se débrouille bien; **that was a n. piece of driving** ça c'est de la conduite!; **a n. piece of footwork** un beau jeu de jambes; **a n. idea** une idée géniale; **it's a very n. little car** c'est une petite voiture très commode *ou* pratique (b) *Am* (*attractive*) (*dress etc*) coquet, pimpant

Niger ['naɪdʒər] *n* (a) (*river*) Niger *m* (b) (*country*) (République *f* du) Niger *m*

Nigeria [naɪ'dʒɪərɪə] *n* Nigeria *m*

Nigerian [naɪ'dʒɪərɪən] **1** *adj* nigérian **2** *n* Nigérian, -ane

niggard ['nɪgəd] *n Old-fashioned* pingre *mf*, avare *mf*

niggardliness ['nɪgədlɪnɪs] *n* (*of person*) avarice *f*, pingrerie *f*; (*of sum, salary*) maigreur *f*

niggardly ['nɪgədlɪ] *adj* (*person*) avare, pingre, mesquin; (*sum, portion*) maigre; (*budget*) étroit; (*acknowledgement*) mesquin; **don't be so n. with the wine/caviare!** ne sois pas aussi regardant sur le vin/caviar!; **she's quite n. with her compliments/thanks** elle est assez avare de compliments/de remerciements

nigger ['nɪgər] *n Offensive Sl* nègre *m*, négresse *f*; *Old-fashioned F* **there's a n. in the woodpile** il y a anguille sous roche; *Old-fashioned F*, **he's the n. in the woodpile** le problème, c'est lui

niggle¹ ['nɪg(ə)l] **1** *vi* (*be overfussy*) couper les cheveux en quatre; **he always has something to n. about** (*complain*) il a toujours quelque chose à redire; **don't n. about details** ne chipote pas sur les détails; **he's been niggling on at** *or* **away at me all week** il m'a cassé les pieds toute la semaine (**about** à propos de) **2** *vt* (*of doubt etc*) triturer l'esprit à, tracasser; (*annoy*) embêter; **he keeps niggling me to get it done** il n'arrête pas de m'embêter *ou* de me casser les pieds pour que je le fasse

niggle² *n* (a) (*minor criticism*) petit reproche *m*; **I've just one or two little niggles about ...** il y a juste une ou deux petites choses à revoir au niveau de ... (b) (*worry*) tracasserie *f*, doute *m* (c) (*complaint*) protestation *f*; **to have a little n. about sth** ronchonner à propos de qch

niggler ['nɪglər] *n* (*who annoys people*) enquiquineur, -euse; (*who worries about details*) coupeur, -euse de cheveux en quatre

niggling ['nɪg(ə)lɪŋ] *adj* (*details etc*) insignifiant; (*pain*) persistant; (*doubt, worry*) insinuant; **I've got a n. feeling that I left the light on** je n'arrête pas de me demander si je n'ai pas laissé la lumière allumée

nigh [naɪ] *Arch, Lit, Dial* **1** *adv* près, proche; **n. unto death** près de mourir; **the end is n.!** la fin est proche! **2** *prep* près de

night [naɪt] *n* (a) (*hours of darkness*) nuit *f*; (*evening*) soir *m*; **at n.** (à) la nuit; (*in the evening*) le soir; **in the n.** (pendant) la nuit; **last n.** la nuit dernière; (*in the evening*) hier soir; **the n. before** la veille (au soir); **I saw him on Thursday n.** je l'ai vu jeudi soir; **ten o'clock at n.** dix heures du soir; **it was a warm n.** la nuit était douce; **all n. long** toute la nuit; **good n.!** (*when going to bed*) bonne nuit!; (*when leaving*) bonsoir!; **to have a good/bad n.** bien/mal dormir; **to have a late/early n.** se coucher tard/tôt; **too many late nights can be bad for you** se coucher tard trop souvent peut nuire à la santé; **to work day and n.** *or* **n. and day** travailler nuit et jour; **to have a n. off** avoir une soirée libre; **to travel by n.** *or* **at n.** voyager de nuit *ou* la nuit; **we stayed the n. (there)** nous y avons passé la nuit; **to spend the n. together/with sb** passer la nuit ensemble/avec qn; **the n. sky, the sky at n.** le ciel nocturne; **n. is falling** la nuit tombe, il commence à faire nuit; **n. boat/train/flight** bateau *m*/train *m*/vol *m* de nuit; **n. clerk** (*in hotel*) réceptionniste *mf* de nuit; **n. clothes** vêtements *mpl* de nuit; **n. driving** conduite *f* de nuit; *Journ* **n. editor** rédacteur *m* en chef de nuit; *Mil Av* **n. fighter** chasseur *m* de nuit; *Cin* **n. filter** filtre *m* pour effet de nuit; *Naut* **n. lights** feux *mpl* de position; **n. manager** (*of hotel*) directeur *m* de nuit; **n. porter** concierge *m* de nuit; **n. safe** (*outside bank*) coffre *m* de nuit; *Old-fashioned* **n. soil** excréments *mpl* humains; *Am* **n. table** table *f* de chevet; **n. watch** (*period, guards*) garde *f* de nuit; *Naut* quart *m* de nuit; **n. watchman** veilleur *m* de nuit, garde *m ou* gardien *m* de nuit; **n. work** travail *m* de nuit

(b) (*evening's entertainment*) soirée *f*; **to have a n. out** sortir; **that was a great n. last n.** on a passé une super soirée hier; **to make a n. of it** faire la fête toute la nuit; *Th etc* **first n.** première *f*; **Wagner n.** soirée Wagner

night bird *n Orn* oiseau *m* de nuit *ou* nocturne; *Fig* noctambule *mf*, *Hum* oiseau de nuit
night blindness *n Med* héméralopie *f*
nightcap ['naɪtkæp] *n* (a) (*drink*) = boisson *f* prise avant de se coucher; **would you like a n.?** prendrez-vous quelque chose avant de vous coucher? (b) (*hat*) bonnet *m* de nuit
nightclub ['naɪtklʌb] *n* boîte *f* de nuit
nightclubbing ['naɪtklʌbɪŋ] *n* **to go n.** sortir en boîte
nightdress ['naɪtdres] *n* chemise *f* de nuit
nightfall ['naɪtfɔːl] *n* tombée *f* du jour *ou* de la nuit; **at n.** à la nuit tombante
nightgown ['naɪtgaʊn] *n* chemise *f* de nuit
nighthawk ['naɪthɔːk] *n Am F* (*person*) noctambule *mf*, *Hum* oiseau *m* de nuit
nightie ['naɪtɪ] *n F* = **nightdress**
nightingale ['naɪtɪŋgeɪl] *n* rossignol *m*
nightjar ['naɪtdʒɑːr] *n* (*bird*) engoulevent *m* (d'Europe)
nightlife ['naɪtlaɪf] *n* vie *f* nocturne; **what's the n. like?** qu'est-ce qu'on peut faire le soir?; **there's not much n.** il n'y a pas grand-chose à faire le soir
night-light *n* veilleuse *f*
nightlong ['naɪtlɒŋ] *adj* (*party, wake etc*) qui dure toute la nuit
nightly ['naɪtlɪ] **1** *adj* de toutes les nuits; (*in the evening*) de tous les soirs; **n. performance** représentation *f* tous les soirs; **it's a n. occurrence** c'est comme ça toutes les nuits/tous les soirs; **there are n. flights** il y a des vols toutes les nuits; **he would take his n. stroll** il faisait sa promenade nocturne **2** *adv* toutes les nuits; (*in the evening*) tous les soirs; **performances n.** représentations tous les soirs
nightmare ['naɪtmeər] *n* cauchemar *m*; **to give sb nightmares** donner des cauchemars à qn; **getting to work was an absolute n.** se rendre au travail était un véritable cauchemar; **the journey/experience was a n.** ça a été un voyage/une expérience cauchemardesque; **the prospect was a n. to me** cette perspective me donnait des cauchemars
nightmarish ['naɪtmeərɪʃ] *adj* cauchemardesque
night-night *int F* bonne nuit
night nurse *n Med* infirmier, -ière de nuit *ou* de garde
night owl *n F* (*person*) noctambule *mf*, *Hum* oiseau *m* de nuit
nights [naɪts] *adv* (*to work*) de nuit
night school *n* cours *mpl* du soir
nightshade ['naɪtʃeɪd] *n* (*plant*) (**black**) **n.** morelle *f* noire
night shift *n* équipe *f* de nuit; **to be on (the) n.** être de nuit
nightshirt ['naɪtʃɜːt] *n* chemise *f* de nuit
night stick *n Am* (*of policeman*) matraque *f*
night-time **1** *n* nuit *f*; **at n.** la nuit **2** *adj* nocturne; **n. television** télévision *f* de nuit
nightwear ['naɪtweər] *n* vêtements *mpl* de nuit
nihilism ['naɪ(h)ɪlɪz(ə)m] *n* nihilisme *m*
nihilist ['naɪ(h)ɪlɪst] *n* nihiliste *mf*
nihilistic [naɪ(h)ɪ'lɪstɪk] *adj* nihiliste
Nikkei index ['nɪkeɪ] *n* indice *m* Nikkei
nil [nɪl] *n* [①A71,3,a] rien *m*; (*on report sheet etc*) néant *m*; *Sp* zéro *m*; **they won three n.** ils ont gagné par trois à zéro
Nile [naɪl] *n* Nil *m*
nimble ['nɪmb(ə)l] *adj* (*person, fingers etc*) agile, souple; (*leap, movement*) leste, agile; (*mind, thinking etc*) vif; **n.-fingered** aux doigts agiles *ou* souples *ou* de fée; **n.-footed** aux pieds agiles *ou* légers
nimbleness ['nɪmb(ə)lnɪs] *n* (*of person, limbs etc*) agilité *f*, souplesse *f*; (*of movement, leap*) agilité; (*of mind etc*) vivacité *f*
nimbly ['nɪmb(ə)lɪ] *adv* (*to move, leap*) agilement, avec légèreté; **she n. unpicked the knot** elle a défait le nœud de ses doigts agiles *ou* souples
nimbus, *pl* **-i, -uses** ['nɪmbəs, -aɪ, -əsɪz] *n* (a) *Met* nimbus *m* (b) (*of saint*) (*cloud*) nuage *m* lumineux; (*halo*) halo *m* (c) *Art* nimbe *m*, auréole *f*
NIMBY, nimby ['nɪmbɪ] *n F* (*abbr* **not in my back yard**) = personne *f* qui est favorable à un projet (construction d'autoroute, offre d'asile etc) à condition qu'il ne soit pas mis en œuvre près de chez elle
nincompoop ['nɪŋkəmpuːp] *n F* nigaud, -aude, andouille *f*; **you stupid n.!** bougre d'andouille!
nine [naɪn] *adj, n* neuf *m*; **n. times out of ten** neuf fois sur dix; **to have n. lives** (*of cat*) avoir neuf vies; (*of person*) avoir l'âme chevillée au corps; *Cards* **the n. of diamonds** le neuf de carreau; **to dial** *Br* **999** *or US* **911** appeler les urgences; *F* **dressed up to the nines** sur son trente et un; **to work n. to five** travailler de 9 à 5; **I couldn't stand a n.-to-five job** je ne supporterais pas de travailler de 9 à 5
ninefold ['naɪnfəʊld] **1** *adj* **there's been a n. increase in ...** ... a été multiplié par neuf **2** *adv* **to increase n.** (se) multiplier par neuf
ninepin ['naɪnpɪn] *n* (a) **ninepins** (*game*) (jeu *m* de) quilles *fpl* (b) (*pin*) quille *f*; *F* **to go down like ninepins** tomber comme des mouches
nineteen [naɪn'tiːn] *adj, n* dix-neuf *m*; **she is n.** elle a dix-neuf ans; *Br F* **to talk n. to the dozen** bavarder comme une pie
nineteenth [naɪn'tiːnθ] **1** *adj* dix-neuvième; *Hum* **the n. hole** (*of golf course*) le bar du golf **2** *n* (a) (*person, thing*) dix-neuvième *mf* (b) (*fraction*) dix-neuvième *m*
ninetieth ['naɪntɪɪθ] **1** *adj* quatre-vingt-dixième **2** *n* (a) (*person, thing*) quatre-vingt-dixième *mf* (b) (*fraction*) quatre-vingt-dixième *m*
ninety ['naɪntɪ] *adj, n* quatre-vingt-dix *m*, *Belg Swiss* nonante; **n.-one/n.-nine** quatre-vingt-onze/quatre-vingt-dix-neuf, *Belg Swiss* nonante-un/nonante-neuf; **the nineties** (*decade*) les années quatre-vingt-dix; **temperatures in the nineties** des températures autour de trente-cinq degrés; **she's in her nineties** elle est nonagénaire; *Jur* **n.-nine years' lease** bail *m* emphytéotique de quatre-vingt-dix-neuf ans
ninny ['nɪnɪ] *n Old-fashioned F* niais, -aise, nigaud, -aude
ninth [naɪnθ] **1** *adj* neuvième **2** *n* (a) (*person, thing*) neuvième *mf* (b) (*fraction*) neuvième *m* (c) *Mus* neuvième *f*
Nip [nɪp] *n Br Offensive Sl* (*Japanese*) jap *mf*
nip[1] [nɪp] *n* (a) (*pinch*) pincement *m*; **to give sb a n.** pincer qn (b) (*of frost, cold*) morsure *f*; (*frost*) coup *m* de gelée; **the n. of the early morning air** le froid *ou* le piquant du petit jour; *F* **there's a n. in the air** ça pince, l'air est piquant
nip[2] **(-pp-)** **1** *vt* (a) (*pinch*) pincer; **to n. one's finger** se pincer le doigt
(b) (*remove*) (*buds etc*) pincer, éborgner; *Fig F* **to n. sth in the bud** écraser *ou* étouffer qch dans l'œuf
(c) (*of cold, frost*) (*face, fingers etc*) pincer, piquer; (*buds etc*) brûler; *Bot* **nipped by the frost** brûlé par la gelée
2 *vi Br F* (*go quickly*) **just n. across** *or* **along** *or* **down to the baker's** cours vite chez le boulanger, fais donc un saut chez le boulanger; **he nipped back to see if she was alright** il est repassé pour voir si elle allait bien; **to n. in and out of the traffic** se faufiler adroitement parmi les voitures; **I'll n. through to Glasgow next week** je ferai un saut à Glasgow la semaine prochaine
nip[3] *n F* (*drink*) (*of brandy etc*) goutte *f*, petit verre *m*, doigt *m*; **to have** *or* **take a n.** boire *ou* prendre une goutte
► **nip in** *vi Br F* **I just nipped in to see him** je suis entré juste un instant pour le voir; **if you're passing, do n. in and see us** si vous passez par ici, rendez-nous donc une petite visite; **she saw a parking place and quickly nipped in** elle a vu une place libre et elle s'est empressée de la prendre; **could I just n. in in front of you?** (*in queue etc*) pourrais-je passer devant vous?; **he always nips into the pub on the way home** il fait toujours un petit détour par le pub en rentrant chez lui; **he nipped into the doorway** il s'engouffra dans l'entrée
► **nip off** **1** *vi Br F* filer; (*to avoid sb/sth*) s'esquiver **2** *vtsep* **to n. sth off** enlever *ou* couper qch (en le pinçant)
► **nip out** *vi Br F* sortir; **he's just nipped out for a second** (*from house, office etc*) il est sorti un instant; **I'll n. out and buy a paper** je sors acheter un journal
nipper ['nɪpər] *n* (a) *Br F* (*child*) gamin, -ine, gosse *mf*; **I've lived here since I was a n.** j'habite ici depuis que je suis tout(e) gamin(e) *ou* gosse (b) (*of lobster etc*) pince *f* (c) **(pair of) nippers** (*tool*) pince(s) *f(pl)* (de serrage), tenaille(s) *f(pl)*
nipple ['nɪp(ə)l] *n* (a) *Anat* mamelon *m*, bout *m* de sein; (*of feeding bottle*) tétine *f* (b) *Geog* mamelon *m* (c) (**grease**) **n.** graisseur *m*
nippy ['nɪpɪ] *adj F* (a) *Br* (*nimble*) vif; (*quick*) rapide; **look n.!** grouille-toi!; **a n. little car** une petite voiture nerveuse (b) (*wind etc*) froid, piquant; **it's a bit n. today** il fait un froid/un vent vif *ou* mordant aujourd'hui (c) (*flavour*) fort
nirvana [nɪə'vɑːnə] *n Rel* nirvana *m*
nisi ['naɪsaɪ] *adj Jur* (*decree, order*) provisoire; (*decision*) rendu sous condition
Nissen ['nɪs(ə)n] *n* **N. hut** hutte préfabriquée (en tôle)
nit [nɪt] *n* (a) *Ent* lente *f*; **to have nits** avoir des poux (b) *Br F* (*person*) nigaud, -aude, andouille *f*; **you silly n.!** andouille!; **don't be such a n.!** ne sois pas aussi bête!
niter ['naɪtər] *n US* = **nitre**
nitery ['naɪtərɪ] *n US F* boîte *f* de nuit
nit-pick *vi F* chercher la petite bête, ergoter, chinoiser
nit-picker *n F* chipoteur, -euse
nit-picking *F* **1** *n* chipotage *m*, chinoiserie *f* **2** *adj* (*attitude etc*) chipoteur, chicanier; **I'm tired of his n. criticisms of everything I do** j'en ai assez qu'il critique tout ce que je fais avec autant de chicanerie
nitrate ['naɪtreɪt] *n Ch* (*of silver etc*) nitrate *m*; **potassium n.** nitrate de potassium, salpêtre *m*; *Agr* **n. fertilizers, nitrates** engrais *mpl* azotés
nitre ['naɪtər] *n* salpêtre *m*
nitric ['naɪtrɪk] *adj Ch* (*oxide etc*) nitrique; **n. acid** acide *m* (trioxo)nitrique; *Com* eau-forte *f*, *pl* eaux-fortes

nitro [ˈnaɪtrəʊ] *n Sl* = **nitroglycerin(e)**

nitrogen [ˈnaɪtrədʒən] *n Ch* azote *m*; **to fix n.** (*of plant*) fixer l'azote; **n. dioxide** dioxyde *m* d'azote

nitroglycerin(e) [naɪtrəʊˈglɪsəriːn] *n* nitroglycérine *f*

nitrous [ˈnaɪtrəs] *adj* (*oxide etc*) nitreux, d'azote

nitty-gritty [ˈnɪtɪˈgrɪtɪ] *n F* (*of a matter*) aspects *mpl* pratiques; **when you get down to the n.** quand on considère les aspects pratiques de la chose

nitwit [ˈnɪtwɪt] *n F* idiot, -ote, imbécile *mf*; **don't be such a n.!** arrête de faire l'idiot *ou* l'imbécile!

nix[1] [nɪks] *Am F* **1** *n* (*nothing*) rien *m* (du tout), *Sl* que dalle **2** *int* rien à faire!

nix[2] *vt Am F* (*project, proposal*) refuser, rejeter

NJ *abbr* **New Jersey**

NLM [enelˈem] *n Comptr* (*abbr* **netware loadable module**) module *m* logiciel téléchargeable

NLQ *n Comptr* (*abbr* **near letter quality**) qualité *f* courrier

NM *abbr* **New Mexico**

NMR [eneˈmɑːr] *n Med* (*abbr* **nuclear magnetic resonance**) RMN *f*

no [nəʊ] **1** *adj* [①A35,b,i] **(a)** (*not any*) pas de, aucun (*with* **ne** *expressed or understood*), -une; **he has no bread** il n'a pas de pain; **this fact is of no importance whatever** ce fait n'a aucune importance; **I have no intention of doing it** je n'ai aucune intention de le faire; **it's no distance** ce n'est pas loin; **I am in no way surprised** je n'en suis aucunement étonné; **no nonsense!** pas de bêtises!; **no smoking** défense de fumer; *esp Lit* **no father was ever more indulgent** jamais père ne fut plus indulgent

(b) (*not at all*) ne ... pas (du tout); **it's no easy job** ce n'est pas une tâche facile; **he's no artist** ce n'est pas un artiste, il n'est pas artiste; **he's no friend of mine** il ne fait pas de mes amis, tant s'en faut; *Cr* **no ball** balle nulle; *F* **no way!** pas question!; *F* **no way am I going to work on Saturday** il n'est pas question que je travaille samedi; **no way can I get him to admit he was wrong** il n'y a pas moyen de lui faire admettre qu'il a eu tort

(c) (*with gerund*) **there's no pleasing him** il n'y a pas moyen de le satisfaire; **there's no getting out of it** impossible de s'en tirer

2 *adv* **(a)** (*with comparatives*) ne ... plus, ne ... pas; **I'm no taller than he (is)** je ne suis pas plus grand que lui; **how is she? – no better** comment va-t-elle? – pas mieux; **no less than £100** pas moins de 100 livres; **he's no longer here** il n'est plus ici

(b) [①B61,D,1] (*answer*) non; **no, no, you're wrong!** mais non, mais non, vous vous trompez!; **to say no** dire non; (*deny*) dire que non

(c) *Arch, Lit, Scot* (*not*) **pleasant or no, it's true** agréable ou non *ou* pas, c'est vrai; **whether or no** que cela soit ou non

3 *n* (*pl* **noes**) non *m inv*; **she won't take no for an answer** elle n'acceptera pas de refus; **ayes and noes** (*in voting*) voix *fpl* pour et contre; **the noes have it** c'est le non qui l'emporte

No., no (*abbr* **number**) No, N°, n°

Noah [ˈnəʊə] *n Bible* Noé *m*; **N.'s ark** *Bible* l'arche *f* de Noé; (*toy*) arche de Noé

nob[1] [nɒb] *n Sl* (*head*) caboche *f*

nob[2] *n esp Br Sl* (*upper-class person*) aristo *mf*; **the nobs** les rupins *mpl*, les aristos *mpl*

nobble [ˈnɒb(ə)l] *vt Br F* **(a)** *Horseracing* doper (avant la course); *Fig* **to n. sb's chances of doing sth** bousiller *ou* saboter les chances que qn a de faire qch **(b)** (*bribe*) (*witness etc*) soudoyer, acheter **(c)** (*steal*) faucher, piquer **(d)** (*grab*) (*thief*) pincer, choper, épingler; (*person*) attraper (au passage); **a journalist nobbled him in the corridor** un journaliste l'a coincé dans le couloir

Nobel [nəʊˈbel] **the N. prize** le prix Nobel; **N. prize for Literature** prix Nobel de littérature; **N. Peace Prize** prix Nobel de la Paix; **N. prizewinner** *or US* **laureate** prix Nobel

nobility [nəʊˈbɪlɪtɪ] *n* **(a)** (*of rank, heart etc*) noblesse *f* **(b) the n.** (*nobles*) la noblesse

noble [ˈnəʊb(ə)l] **1** *adj* **(a)** (*birth, person*) noble; **to be of n. descent** *or* **birth** être de naissance noble **(b)** (*sentiment etc*) noble; *F Hum* **I'll be n. and let you have the last piece of cake** je vais me montrer grand seigneur et te laisser le dernier morceau de gâteau; *F Hum* **that's very n. of you** c'est très généreux *ou* charitable de ta part; **n. soul** grande âme *f*; **to have a n. soul** avoir de la grandeur d'âme **(c)** (*building, proportions, sight etc*) majestueux; (*mountain*) altier, imposant; **n. wine** vin *m* noble, grand vin **(d)** (*metal*) noble **2** *n* noble *mf*, aristocrate *mf*

noble art *n* (*boxing*) noble art *m*

noble gas *n Ch* gaz *m* rare

nobleman, *pl* **-men** [ˈnəʊb(ə)lmən] *n* noble *m*, aristocrate *m*

nobleminded [nəʊb(ə)lˈmaɪndɪd] *adj* (*person*) magnanime, aux nobles sentiments; (*sentiment, action, commitment*) noble

nobleness [ˈnəʊb(ə)lnɪs] *n* **(a)** (*of birth etc*) noblesse *f* **(b)** (*of mind, action etc*) noblesse *f*; (*of soul*) grandeur *f* **(c)** (*of statue, horse etc*) proportions *fpl* superbes *ou* magnifiques; (*of building etc*) aspect *m* majestueux

noblewoman, *pl* **-women** [ˈnəʊb(ə)lwʊmən, -wɪmɪn] *n* (femme *f*) noble *f*, aristocrate *f*

nobly [ˈnəʊb(ə)lɪ] *adv* **(a)** noblement; **n. born** noble de naissance; *F Hum* **he n. gave up his weekends** il a magnanimement renoncé à ses week-ends; **she n. offered him the last piece of cake** elle s'est montré grand seigneur et lui a offert le dernier morceau de gâteau **(b)** (*splendidly*) (*proportioned etc*) magnifiquement, superbement

nobody [ˈnəʊbədɪ] **1** *pron* [①B60,B] personne (*with* **ne** *expressed or understood*); **n. spoke to me** personne ne m'a parlé; **who's there? – n.** qui est là? – personne; **n. knows it** personne ne le sait; **n. is perfect** nul *ou* personne n'est parfait; **n. was more surprised than me** *or* **than I (was)** personne n'a été plus étonné que moi; **n. who was there heard anything** aucun de ceux *ou* personne parmi tous ceux qui étaient là n'a entendu quoi que ce soit; **there was n. there** *or* **about** il n'y avait personne; **n. else** personne d'autre; *F* **like n.'s business** comme personne, comme pas un; *F* **the dogs were barking like n.'s business** les chiens aboyaient à vous rompre les tympans; **she's n.'s fool** elle n'est pas folle; **when he was n.** alors qu'il était encore inconnu; **as far as they're concerned, if you don't have money, you're n.** pour eux si tu n'as pas d'argent tu es un zéro *ou* un moins que rien

2 *n* (*person*) nullité *f*, zéro *m*; **they're (mere) nobodies** ce sont des gens de rien; **some n. of a journalist** un journaliste à la manque

no-claim(s) *adj* **n. bonus** (*in car insurance*) bonus *m*; **loss of n. bonus** malus *m*

nocturnal [nɒkˈtɜːn(ə)l] *adj* nocturne

nocturne [ˈnɒktɜːn] *n* **(a)** *Mus* nocturne *m* **(b)** *Art* effet *m* de nuit

nod[1] [nɒd] *n* **(a)** inclination *f* de la tête; (*of consent*) signe *m* d'assentiment, signe de tête affirmatif; (*greeting*) signe de la tête; **to answer with a n.** répondre d'un signe de tête; **she gave me a n.** elle m'a fait un petit signe de la tête; *Fig* **to give sb the n.** donner le feu vert à qn; *F* **on the n.** sans débats; **a n. in sb's direction** un signe de tête à l'intention de qn; **these terms are a n. in the direction of Marxist scholars** ces termes sont des renvois *ou* références aux intellectuels marxistes; *Prov* **a n. is as good as a wink** pas besoin d'en dire davantage *ou* plus(, on a compris)

(b) the land of N. le pays des songes; *Hum* **to be in the land of N.** être dans les bras de Morphée

nod[2] **(-dd-) 1** *vt* **to n. one's head** faire un signe de tête (de haut en bas); **she nodded her head in agreement** elle a fait un signe de tête affirmatif; **he nodded his head in agreement at the proposal** il accepta la proposition d'un signe de tête; **to n. one's agreement/approval** consentir/approuver d'un signe de tête **2** *vi* **(a) to n. (in agreement/approval)** consentir/approuver d'un signe de tête; **to n. to sb** (*in greeting*) faire un signe de tête à qn **(b)** (*in sleep*) dodeliner (de) la tête **(c)** (*of plumes etc*) ballotter, danser

▶ **nod off** *vi F* s'endormir

nodal [ˈnəʊd(ə)l] *adj Opt, Phys* nodal

nodding [ˈnɒdɪŋ] *n* **I'm on n. terms with my neighbours** mes voisins et moi nous nous saluons; **we are on n. terms, we have a n. acquaintance** nous nous saluons; **we still only have a n. acquaintance** nous nous saluons et c'est tout; *Fig* **she had only a n. acquaintance with the town's history** elle n'avait qu'une vague connaissance de l'histoire de la ville

noddle [ˈnɒd(ə)l] *n esp Br F* (*head, intelligence*) caboche *f*; **use your n.!** fais marcher ta caboche *ou* ton ciboulot!

node [nəʊd] *n Astron, Math, Phys* (*of orbit, curve etc*) nœud *m*, point *m* nodal; *Bot* (*of tree trunk etc*) nœud; *Med* nœud, nodosité *f*; *Comptr* noyau *m*

nodular [ˈnɒdjʊlər] *adj Geol, Med etc* nodulaire

nodule [ˈnɒdjuːl] *n Geol, Med, Bot* nodule *m*

Noël [nəʊˈel] *n* **(a)** (*Christmas*) Noël *m* **(b)** *Arch* (*carol*) Noël *m*

no-frills *adj* (*airline, travel*) sans prestation de services; (*insurance policy etc*) de base; (*car, bicycle etc*) sans gadgets; (*service, wedding*) sans chichis, tout simple

noggin [ˈnɒgɪn] *n* **(a)** (*container*) (petit) pot *m*; **to have a n.** (*drink*) prendre un verre **(b)** *F* (*head*) caboche *f*

no-go *adj Mil etc* **n. areas** = régions *fpl* où l'autorité du gouvernement est impuissante ou n'est pas reconnue; **this is a n. area** (*forbidden*) c'est une zone défendue (**for** à); (*dangerous*) c'est une zone dangereuse (**for** pour)

no-good *esp Am F* **1** *adj* bon à rien **2** *n* bon *m* à rien, bonne *f* à rien
no-hoper [nəʊ'həʊpər] *n* tocard *m*
nohow ['nəʊhaʊ] *adv Am Sl* pas question
noise [nɔɪz] *n* **(a)** bruit *m*; **a loud n.** un gros bruit; **to make a n.** faire du bruit; *Fig (complain, make a fuss)* protester (**about sth** au sujet de qch); **he made a lot of n. about improving working conditions** *(talked about it)* il a fait beaucoup de bruit au sujet d'une éventuelle amélioration des conditions de travail; *F* **the big n.** *(in company etc)* le grand manitou; *F* **she's a big n. in publishing** c'est quelqu'un d'important dans le monde de l'édition; *F* **shut** *or* **hold your n.!** fermela!; **n. insulation** insonorisation *f*; **n. reduction hood** capot *m* d'insonorisation
(b) *(sound)* bruit *m*, son *m*; *Rad, Electron etc* bruit, parasite(s) *m(pl)*; **she's making noises about retiring** elle donne à entendre qu'elle va prendre sa retraite; **to make encouraging noises** dire des choses encourageantes; **to make the right noises** se montrer compréhensif; **clicking n.** cliquetis *m*; **tinkling n.** tintement *m*
noise abatement campaign *n* campagne *f ou* lutte *f* contre le bruit
noise-absorbing *adj* insonorisé
noiseless ['nɔɪzlɪs] *adj (machine, movement etc)* silencieux; **with n. tread** à pas feutrés
noiselessly ['nɔɪzlɪslɪ] *adv* sans bruit, silencieusement
noiselessness ['nɔɪzlɪsnɪs] *n* silence *f*
noise level *n* niveau *m* de bruit
noisily ['nɔɪzɪlɪ] *adv* bruyamment, à grand bruit
noisiness ['nɔɪzɪnɪs] *n* caractère *m* bruyant; **because of the n. of the street** à cause du bruit qu'il y a dans la rue; **I can't stand their n.** je ne peux pas supporter le bruit qu'ils font
noisome ['nɔɪsəm] *adj Fml* **(a)** *(offensive) (smell)* fétide; *(sight, behaviour, person)* répugnant **(b)** *(harmful) (plant, germ)* nocif, nuisible
noisy ['nɔɪzɪ] *adj* bruyant; **to be n.** *(of person)* faire du bruit; **the TV is a bit n.** la télé est un peu forte
nomad ['nəʊmæd] *adj, n* nomade *mf*
nomadic [nəʊ'mædɪk] *adj* nomade
no-maintenance battery *n* batterie *f* sans entretien
no man's land *n* terrains *mpl* vagues; *Mil, Fig* no man's land *m*, zone *f* neutre; *Fig (intellectual, psychological etc)* zone floue
nom de plume, *pl* **noms de plume** ['nɒmdə'plu:m] *n* pseudonyme *m (d'un auteur)*
nomenclature [nəʊ'menklətʃər] *n* nomenclature *f*
nominal ['nɒmɪn(ə)l] *adj (in name only)* nominal; **to be the n. head** n'être chef que de nom; *Acct* **n. capital** capital *m* nominal; *Jur* **n. damages** dommages-intérêts *mpl* symboliques; *Acct* **n. ledger** grand livre *m* général; **n. price** prix *m* fictif; **n. rent** loyer *m* insignifiant; **n. value** valeur *f* nominale
nominally ['nɒmɪn(ə)lɪ] *adv (in name)* nominalement
nominate ['nɒmɪneɪt] *vt (appoint)* nommer, désigner; *(propose)* proposer, présenter la candidature de; **to n. sb to a post** nommer *ou* désigner qn à un poste; **to n. sb for a post** proposer qn pour un poste; **to n. sb as president** nommer qn président
nomination [nɒmɪ'neɪʃən] *n* **(a)** *(proposal) (of candidate etc)* proposition *f*; *Cin (for an award)* nomination *f*; **the three nominations for best ...** les trois nominés pour le prix du meilleur ...; *Pol* **n. papers** dossier *m* de candidature **(b)** *(appointment) (of candidate)* nomination *f*; *(of president, judge etc)* investiture *f*
nominative ['nɒmɪnətɪv] *Gram* **1** *n* nominatif *m*; **in the n.** au nominatif **2** *adj* nominatif
nominator ['nɒmɪneɪtər] *n* **his nominators** ceux qui ont proposé sa nomination
nominee [nɒmɪ'ni:] *n* candidat, -ate, personne *f* désignée; **n. company** prête-nom *m*, *pl* prête-noms
non- [nɒn] *pref* non-
nonabsorbent [nɒnəb'zɔ:bənt] *adj* non absorbant
nonacceptance [nɒnək'septəns] *n (of bill, treaty)* refus *m* d'acceptation
nonagenarian [nəʊnədʒɪ'neərɪən] *adj, n* nonagénaire *mf*
nonaggression [nɒnə'greʃən] *n Pol* non-agression *f*; **n. pact** pacte *m* de non-agression
nonalcoholic [nɒnælkə'hɒlɪk] *adj (drink)* non alcoolisé
nonaligned [nɒnə'laɪnd] *adj Pol (country)* non aligné
nonalignment [nɒnə'laɪnmənt] *n Pol* non-alignement *m*
no-name product *n Mktg* produit *m* sans nom
nonappearance [nɒnə'pɪərəns] *n (of person) Jur* noncomparution *f*; **I put his n. down to the fact that ...** j'ai pensé qu'il n'était pas venu parce que ...
nonarrival [nɒnə'raɪv(ə)l] *n* non-arrivée *f*
non-ASCII character *n Comptr* caractère *m* non ASCII
nonattendance [nɒnə'tendəns] *n* absence *f* (**at** à)
non-bank *adj* non-banque
non-business marketing *n* mercatique *f* non-commerciale
nonce[1] [nɒns] *n Old-fashioned* **for the n.** pour la circonstance, pour l'occasion; **n. word** mot *m* créé pour l'occasion, mot de circonstance
nonce[2] *n Br Prison Sl (sex offender)* délinquant *m* sexuel *(s'attaquant en particulier aux enfants)*
nonchalance ['nɒnʃələns] *n* nonchalance *f*
nonchalant ['nɒnʃələnt] *adj* nonchalant
nonchalantly ['nɒnʃələntlɪ] *adv* nonchalamment
noncombatant [nɒn'kɒmbətənt] *adj, n Mil* non-combattant *m*
noncommissioned ['nɒnkə'mɪʃənd] *adj Mil* sans brevet; **n. officer** sous-officier *m*
noncommittal [nɒnkə'mɪt(ə)l] *adj (answer etc)* qui n'engage à rien; **to be n.** *(when answering)* ne pas s'engager; **why are you being so n.?** pourquoi est-ce que tu ne veux pas t'engager?
non-competition clause *n* clause *f* de non-concurrence
noncompletion [nɒnkəm'pli:ʃən] *n (of job)* non-achèvement *m*; *(of contract)* non-exécution *f*
noncompliance [nɒnkəm'plaɪəns] *n* refus *m* (de consentement); **n. with an order** refus d'obéissance à un ordre
nonconductor [nɒnkən'dʌktər] *n Phys* non-conducteur *m*, mauvais conducteur *m*; *El* isolant *m*
nonconformism [nɒnkən'fɔ:mɪz(ə)m] *n* non-conformisme *m*
nonconformist [nɒnkən'fɔ:mɪst] *adj, n* non-conformiste *mf*
nonconformity [nɒnkən'fɔ:mɪtɪ] *n* non-conformité *f*
noncontributory [nɒnkən'trɪbjʊt(ə)rɪ] *adj (pension scheme)* sans versements de la part des bénéficiaires
nonconvertible [nɒnkən'vɜ:təb(ə)l] *adj* inconvertible
nondescript ['nɒndɪskrɪpt] *adj (person, object)* quelconque; *(colour)* neutre, *Pej* fade; **a very n. looking person** une personne d'apparence très quelconque
nondestructive [nɒndɪ'strʌktɪv] *adj (test)* non destructif
nondetachable [nɒndɪ'tætʃəb(ə)l] *adj* inamovible
nondirectional [nɒndə'rekʃən(ə)l, -dɪ-] *adj Electron, Rad* non directionnel
non-DOS disk *n Comptr* disque *m* à format incompatible avec DOS
non-drip *adj (paint)* qui ne coule pas
non-dutiable *n Com* exempt de droits de douane
none [nʌn] **1** *pron* [①**A35**,b; **B15**,2,a-b] **(a)** *(not any)* aucun, -une; **n. of you can tell me** aucun d'entre vous *ou* personne ne peut me le dire; **n. of this concerns me** rien de ceci ne me regarde; **no news today? – n.** pas de nouvelles aujourd'hui? – aucune(s); **n. at all** pas un(e) seul(e); **n. of these vegetables are** *or esp Fml* **is worth keeping** tous ces légumes sont bons à jeter; **n. of the milk was fresh** tout le lait avait tourné; **how much of the wood did you use? – n. of it** quelle quantité du bois avez-vous utilisée? – pas un seul morceau; **n. of the money/the water was left** il ne restait rien de l'argent/de l'eau; **n. of your impudence!** pas d'insolences de votre part!; *F* **n. of that!** pas de ça!; *Arch, Hum* **answer came there n.** de réponse il n'en arriva point
(b) *(no-one)* personne, nul; **the visitor was n. other than the king** le visiteur n'était (nul) autre que le roi; **she is aware, n. better, that ...** elle sait mieux que personne que ...
(c) *Admin* **n.** *(in schedules etc)* néant
2 *adv* **(a) I like him n. the better/worse for that** je ne l'en aime pas plus/moins
(b) he was n. too soon il est arrivé juste à temps; **she was n. too happy about it** elle n'en était pas trop contente; **his position is n. too secure** sa position est loin d'être assurée
non-EC country *n* pays *m* hors communauté
nonentity [nɒ'nentɪtɪ] *n (person)* personne *f* insignifiante; **she's a bit of a n.** elle est plutôt insignifiante
non-erasable memory *n Comptr* mémoire *f* non-effaçable
nonessential [nɒnɪ'senʃəl] **1** *adj* non essentiel **2** *n (usu pl)* **nonessentials** superflu *m*, accessoire *m*; **if you're travelling light forget the nonessentials** si tu voyages avec peu de bagages, n'emporte rien de superflu
nonetheless [nʌnðə'les] *adv* = **nevertheless**
nonevent [nɒnɪ'vent] *n F* bide *m*; **the press conference was pretty much a n.** la conférence de presse ne valait pas le déplacement
nonexecutive [nɒnɪg'zekjʊtɪv] *n* **n. director** = administrateur *m* à temps partiel à titre consultatif
nonexistence [nɒnɪg'zɪstəns] *n* non-existence *f*
nonexistent [nɒnɪg'zɪstənt] *adj* non existant, inexistant
nonferrous [nɒn'ferəs] *adj* non ferreux
non-fiction *n* **n. (books)** ouvrages *mpl* généraux
non-fulfilment *n (of contract)* non-exécution *f*
non-impact printer *n* imprimante *f* sans impact
non(in)flammable [nɒn(ɪn)'flæməb(ə)l] *adj* ininflammable

non-interlaced display *n Comptr* affichage *m* non entrelacé
nonintervention [nɒnɪntə'venʃən] *n Pol* non-intervention *f*
noninterventionist [nɒnɪntə'venʃənɪst] *Pol* **1** *n* non-interventionniste *mf* **2** *adj* (*policy*) non-interventionniste, de non-intervention
non-iron *adj* lavé-repassé *inv*
non-judgmental *adj* objectif; **to try to be n.** s'efforcer de ne pas porter de jugements
non-linear *adj* non linéaire
nonmalignant [nɒnmə'lɪgnənt] *adj Med* bénin, *f* bénigne
non-member *n* (*at club etc*) invité, -ée; **open to non-members** ouvert au public; **non-members of the EC** pays *mpl* non membres de la CE
non-negotiable *adj* (*bill, demands etc*) non négociable
non-nuclear *adj* (*country*) non nucléarisé; (*war, defence, policy*) non nucléaire
no-no *n F* **that's a n.** c'est défendu; **criticizing his cooking is a n.** critiquer sa cuisine est fortement déconseillé
non-observance *n* (*of laws, Lent etc*) inobservance *f*
no-nonsense *adj* (*approach*) direct; **she's a very n. kind of person** c'est quelqu'un qui ne plaisante pas; **she told him so in her usual n. way** elle le lui a dit très directement, comme à son habitude; **his n. handling of the unrest** la fermeté avec laquelle il a fait face aux troubles
nonpareil ['nɒnpəreɪl] *Old-fashioned, Lit* **1** *n* (*person*) prodige *m*; (*object*) chose *f* sans pareille **2** *adj* incomparable, sans égal
non-participating *adj St Exch* (*share*) sans droit de participation
non-partisan *adj* neutre, impartial
non-payment *n* non-paiement *m*; **for n.** faute de paiement
non-performance *n* (*of contract*) non-exécution *f*, inexécution *f*
non-performing loan *n Banking* prêt *m* en souffrance
non-person *n Pol* proscrit, -ite; *F* **I felt like a n.** je me suis senti une non-valeur
nonplus [nɒn'plʌs] *vt* (**-ss-**) interloquer
non-poisonous *adj* non toxique; (*snake*) non venimeux; (*mushroom*) non vénéneux
non-printable character *n* caractère *m* non imprimable
non-probability method *n Mktg* (*of sampling*) méthode *f* non probabiliste
non-probability sampling *n Mktg* échantillonnage *m* non probabiliste
non-procedural language *n Comptr* langage *m* non procédural
non-productive *n* (*capital*) improductif
non-profit-making, *Am* **nonprofit** [nɒn'prɒfɪt] *adj* (*association*) sans but lucratif; **on a n. basis** sur une base non lucrative
non-proliferation *n Mil* non-prolifération *f*; **n. treaty** traité *m* de non-prolifération
non-racist *adj* non raciste
non-recoverable *n Comptr* (*file, data*) non récupérable
nonrecurring [nɒnrɪ'kɜːrɪŋ] *adj* exceptionnel, extraordinaire; **n. expenditure** frais *mpl ou* dépenses *fpl* extraordinaires
non-reflecting *adj* anti-reflet
non-refundable packaging *n Com* emballage *m* perdu
nonresident [nɒn'rezɪdənt] **1** *n* non-résident, -ente; *Sch* externe *mf*; (*in hotel*) client, -ente de passage; **open to nonresidents** (*hotel*) ouvert aux hôtes de passage **2** *adj* non résident
nonreturnable [nɒnrɪ'tɜːnəb(ə)l] *adj* (*bottle*) non consigné; (*deposit for holiday etc*) non remboursable; *Com* sans réserve de retour
non-return valve *n MecE* clapet *m* anti-retour
nonscheduled [nɒn'ʃedjuːld] *adj* (*flight*) spécial; **n. stop** étape *f* non-prévue
nonsectarian [nɒnsek'teərɪən] *adj* non sectaire
nonsense ['nɒns(ə)ns] **1** *n* bêtises *fpl*, idioties *fpl*; **a piece of n.** une bêtise, une absurdité; **to talk (a lot of) n.** dire des bêtises *ou* des idioties; **I don't think we'll get any more n. from them** je pense qu'ils vont arrêter leurs bêtises; **I've translated all the words, but the result is just n.** j'ai traduit tous les mots, mais le résultat est complètement absurde; **it's n. to think that …** il est absurde de penser que …; **to make a n. of sth** (*undo, go against etc*) ôter tout sens à qch; **I won't stand for any n.** je ne supporterai aucune imbécillité; **there's no n. about her** elle ne plaisante pas; **n. verse** vers *mpl* comiques et absurdes
2 *int* **n.!** n'importe quoi!
nonsensical [nɒn'sensɪk(ə)l] *adj* (*speech, reason etc*) absurde, qui n'a pas de sens
nonsensically [nɒn'sensɪklɪ] *adv* absurdement
non sequitur [nɒn'sekwɪtər] *n* **his conversation was full of non sequiturs** il n'y avait pas de suite dans sa conversation; **that's a n.** ça manque de suite
non-sexist **1** *adj* non sexiste **2** *n* personne *f* non sexiste
nonshrink [nɒn'ʃrɪŋk] *adj* irrétrécissable
nonskid [nɒn'skɪd] *adj* antidérapant; **n. tyre** (pneu *m*) antidérapant *m*
non-smoker *n* **(a)** non-fumeur, -euse; **she's been a n. all her life** elle n'a jamais fumé de sa vie **(b)** *Rail* (*compartment*) compartiment *m* non-fumeurs
non-smoking *adj* (*carriage, area*) non-fumeurs; (*seat*) non-fumeur
non-specialist **1** *n* non-spécialiste *mf* **2** *adj* non spécialisé
nonstandard [nɒn'stændəd] *adj* (*size etc*) spécial; *Ling* d'usage non général; **it's a n. usage** ce n'est pas un usage général
nonstarter [nɒn'stɑːtər] *n Sp, Horseracing etc* non-partant *m*; *F* **the project's a n.** le projet est fichu d'avance
nonstick ['nɒn'stɪk] *adj* (*frying pan etc*) avec revêtement anti-adhésif, qui n'attache pas; (*surface*) anti-adhésif
non-stop **1** *adj Rail* (*train*) direct; (*journey*) sans arrêt; *Av* (*flight*) sans escale; *Cin* (*show*) permanent; (*films, cartoons*) en continu; **n. music programme** programme *m* musical en continu **2** *adv* (*to talk*) sans arrêt; (*to work*) sans interruption; **we flew to Sydney n.** nous avons fait un vol sans escale jusqu'à Sydney
nontaxable [nɒn'tæksəb(ə)l] *adj* non imposable
nontransferability [nɒntrænsfərə'bɪlɪtɪ] *n* (*of property, right*) incessibilité *f*
nontransferable [nɒn'trænsfərəb(ə)l] *adj* (*property, right*) incessible; (*share*) nominatif
non-U *adj Br Old-fashioned F* = pas classe
non-union *adj* (*labour*) non syndiqué; (*company, firm*) qui ne reconnaît pas de syndicat en son sein; **n. worker** non-syndiqué *m*
non-user *n* non utilisateur *m*
nonverbal [nɒn'vɜːb(ə)l] *adj* non verbal
nonvintage [nɒn'vɪntɪdʒ] *adj* (*wine*) non millésimé
nonviolence [nɒn'vaɪələns] *n* non-violence *f*
nonviolent [nɒn'vaɪələnt] *adj* non violent
nonvoting [nɒn'vəʊtɪŋ] *adj Fin* (*share*) sans droit de vote
non-wasting *adj* (*asset*) indéfectible
non-White **1** *adj* (*in South Africa*) de couleur **2** *n* personne *f* de couleur
noodle ['nuːd(ə)l] *n* **(a)** *Culin* (*usu pl*) **noodles** nouilles *fpl* **(b)** *Old-fashioned F* (*simpleton*) nouille *f*, nigaud, -aude **(c)** *F* (*head*) caboche *f*
nook [nʊk] *n* (*corner*) coin *m*, recoin *m*; (*in room*) renfoncement *m*; (*retreat*) refuge *m*; **nooks and crannies** coins et recoins
nooky, nookie ['nʊkɪ] *n Sl Hum* (*sex*) crac-crac *m*; **he wants his n.** il veut s'envoyer en l'air
noon [nuːn] *n* midi *m*; **it is twelve n.** il est midi; **about n.** vers midi; **the n. train** le train de midi
noonday ['nuːndeɪ], *Old-fashioned* **noontide** ['nuːntaɪd] *n Lit* midi *m*; **the n. sun** le soleil de midi
no-one ['nəʊwʌn] *pron* = **nobody 1**
noose [nuːs] *n* nœud *m* coulant; (*for trapping animals*) lacet *m*, lacs *m*, collet *m*; (*lasso*) lasso *m*; *Fig* **to put one's head in a n.** signer son arrêt de mort; **(hangman's) n.** corde *f* (de potence)
nope [nəʊp] *adv F* non
nor [nɔːr] *conj* [①**A68,a,iii**] **(a)** (*continuing the force of a neg*) ni; **he has neither father n. mother** il n'a ni père ni mère, il n'a pas de père ni de mère; **he neither drinks n. smokes** il ne boit ni ne fume; **neither she n. her mother is at home** ni sa mère ni elle ne sont chez elles
(b) [①**A72,a,iv**] (*and not*) **I do not know, n. can I guess** je n'en sais rien et je ne peux pas le deviner; **n. was this all** et ce n'était pas tout; **I haven't read it, n. do I intend to** je ne l'ai pas lu et d'ailleurs je n'en ai pas l'intention; **he hasn't any, n. have I** il n'en a pas, ni moi non plus *ou* et moi non plus; **n. do I/does his wife** moi/sa femme non plus
Nordic ['nɔːdɪk] *Geog* **1** *adj* nordique, scandinave **2** *n* Nordique *mf*, Scandinave *mf*
nordic ['nɔːdɪk] *adj Ski* nordique
nor'east [nɔː'riːst] *Naut* = **northeast**
nor'easterly [nɔː'riːstəlɪ] *Naut* = **northeasterly**
nor'eastern [nɔː'riːstən] *Naut* = **northeastern**
norm [nɔːm] *n* norme *f*; **according to the n.** selon la norme; **to deviate from the n.** sortir de la norme; **it's the n.** c'est la règle
normal ['nɔːm(ə)l] **1** *adj* (*person, situation, behaviour, development, result*) normal; *Math* (*line etc*) normal (**to** à); *Ch* (*solution etc*) normal, titré; **it's n. to react/feel like that** c'est normal de réagir/se sentir comme ça; **he arrived at the**

n. time il est arrivé à l'heure habituelle; **any n. person would have ...** toute personne normalement constituée aurait ...; **n. salt** sel *m* neutre; **n. temperature** température *f* moyenne *ou* normale; **n. working** *or* **running** (*of engine etc*) régime *m* normal

2 *n* état *m* normal, condition *f* normale; *Math* normale *f*, perpendiculaire *f*; **temperature above n.** température *f* au-dessus de la normale; **things quickly got back to n. after the strike** les choses rentrèrent rapidement dans l'ordre après la grève; **he'll soon be back to n.** tout rentrera bientôt dans l'ordre

normality [nɔːˈmælɪtɪ], *US* **normalcy** [ˈnɔːməlsɪ] *n* normalité *f*; **a return to n.** un retour à la normale; **to return to n.** redevenir normal

normalization [nɔːməlaɪˈzeɪʃən] *n* normalisation *f*

normalize [ˈnɔːməlaɪz] **1** *vt* normaliser **2** *vi* se normaliser, redevenir normal

normally [ˈnɔːməlɪ] *adv* normalement; **n. I would have offered you a lift, but ...** je vous aurais bien proposé de vous emmener, mais ...; **I wouldn't n. ask you, but everyone else is away** cela m'ennuie de vous le demander, mais tous les autres sont partis

Norman [ˈnɔːmən] **1** *adj* normand; **N. architecture** l'architecture *f* normande; (*in Britain*) l'architecture romane (anglaise); *Hist* **the N. Conquest** la conquête normande; *Ling, Hist* **N. French** normand *m* **2** *n* Normand, -ande

Normandy [ˈnɔːməndɪ] *n* Normandie *f*; *Hist* **the N. landings** le débarquement

nor'nor'east [nɔːnɔːˈriːst] *Naut* = **north-north-east**

nor'nor'west [nɔːnɔːˈwest] *Naut* = **north-north-west**

Norse [nɔːs] **1** *adj* nordique; (*Norwegian*) norvégien; **N. mythology** mythologie *f* scandinave **2** *n Ling* nordique *m*, norrois *m*; **Old N.** vieux norrois

Norseman, *pl* **-men** [ˈnɔːsmən] *n Hist* Scandinave *m*

north [nɔːθ] **1** *n* nord *m*; **true n.** nord vrai *ou* géographique; **magnetic n.** nord magnétique; **house facing n.** maison exposée au nord; **to the n. of** au nord de; **in the n.** au nord, dans le nord; **to live in the n. of England** habiter dans le nord de l'Angleterre; **the N.** *US Hist* les États *mpl* du nord (des États-Unis); (*affluent countries*) l'hémisphère *m* nord; **the N.-South divide** la division nord-sud; **the (Canadian) Far N.** le Grand Nord Canadien

2 *adv* au nord; (*to travel*) vers le nord; **it's n. of here** c'est au nord d'ici; **I'm going up n.** je vais dans le nord; **n. by east/by west** nord-quart-nord-est/nord-quart-nord-ouest

3 *adj* nord *inv*; (*country, wind*) du nord; (*wall etc*) exposé au nord; **n.-facing** exposé au nord; **on the n. side** du côté nord; **n. transept** (*in church*) transept septentrional

North Africa *n* Afrique *f* du Nord

North African **1** *adj* nord-africain **2** *n* (*person*) Nord-Africain, -aine

North America *n* Amérique *f* du Nord

North American **1** *adj* nord-américain; **N. Free Trade Agreement** Accord *m* de libre-échange nord-américain **2** *n* (*person*) Nord-Américain, -aine

Northants *abbr* **Northamptonshire**

northbound [ˈnɔːθbaʊnd] *adj* (*train, traffic etc*) en direction du nord; *Aut* **the n. carriageway** la voie nord (de l'autoroute)

North Carolina *n* Caroline *f* du Nord

North Country *n* le Nord (de l'Angleterre); **he has a strong north-country accent** il a un accent du nord prononcé

northeast [nɔːθˈiːst] **1** *n* nord-est *m*; *Naut* nordé *m* **2** *adj* (du) nord-est *inv*; **n. wind** vent *m* du nord-est **3** *adv* au nord-est; (*to travel*) vers le nord-est; **n. by east** nord-est-quart-est; **n. by north** nord-est-quart-nord

northeaster [nɔːθˈiːstər] *n* (*wind*) vent *m* du nord-est

northeasterly [nɔːθˈiːstəlɪ] **1** *adj* (*wind etc*) du nord-est *inv*; (*district etc*) (au *ou* du) nord-est; (*direction*) vers le nord-est **2** *adv* vers le nord-est **3** *n* = **northeaster**

northeastern [nɔːθˈiːstən] *adj* (du) nord-est *inv*

northerly [ˈnɔːðəlɪ] **1** *adj* (*wind etc*) du nord; (*district etc*) (du *ou* au) nord *inv*; (*direction*) vers le nord; **n. aspect** (*of house*) exposition *f* au nord **2** *adv* vers le nord

northern [ˈnɔːðən] *adj* **(a)** (du) nord *inv*, septentrional; **n. hemisphere** hémisphère *m* nord; **n. lights** aurore *f* boréale **(b)** *Br* (*of north of England*) du nord (de l'Angletere); (*manner*) typique des gens du nord (de l'Angleterre)

northerner [ˈnɔːðənər] *n* **(a)** habitant, -ante du Nord (*de l'Angleterre etc*); **the Northerners** les gens *mpl* du Nord; **he's a typical n.** on voit bien qu'il est du Nord **(b)** *US Hist* nordiste *mf*

Northern Ireland *n* Irlande *f* du Nord

North Island *n* île *f* du Nord

North Korea *n* Corée *f* du Nord

north-northeast **1** *adj, n* nord-nord-est *m inv* **2** *adv* au nord-nord-est; (*to travel*) vers le nord-nord-est

north-northwest **1** *adj, n* nord-nord-ouest *m inv* **2** *adv* au nord-nord-ouest; (*to travel*) vers le nord-nord-ouest

North Pole *n* pôle *m* Nord

North Sea *n* mer *f* du Nord

North-Sea gas *n* gaz *m* de la mer du Nord

North Star *n* étoile *f* polaire

Northumb *abbr* **Northumberland**

northward [ˈnɔːθwəd] **1** *adj* (*journey*) au nord, du côté du nord **2** *n* nord *m* **3** *adv* = **northwards**

northwards [ˈnɔːθwədz] *adv* vers le nord

northwest [nɔːθˈwest] **1** *n* nord-ouest *m* **2** *adj* (du) nord-ouest *inv*; **n. wind** vent *m* du nord-ouest **3** *adv* au nord-ouest; (*to travel*) vers le nord-ouest; **n. by west** nord-ouest-quart-ouest; **n. by north** nord-ouest-quart-nord

northwester [nɔːθˈwestər] *n* (*wind*) vent *m* du nord-ouest

northwesterly [nɔːθˈwestəlɪ] **1** *adj* (*wind etc*) du nord-ouest; (*district etc*) (au *ou* du) nord-ouest *inv*; (*direction*) vers le nord-ouest **2** *adv* vers le nord-ouest **3** *n* = **northwester**

northwestern [nɔːθˈwestən] *adj* (du) nord-ouest *inv*

Norway [ˈnɔːweɪ] *n* Norvège *f*

Norway lobster *n Zool* langoustine *f*

Norwegian [nɔːˈwiːdʒən] **1** *adj* norvégien **2** *n* **(a)** Norvégien, -ienne **(b)** *Ling* norvégien *m*

nor'west [nɔːˈwest] *Naut* = **north-west**

nor'westerly [nɔːˈwestəlɪ] *Naut* = **northwesterly**

nor'western [nɔːˈwestən] *Naut* = **northwestern**

nose[1] [nəʊz] *n* **(a)** (*of person, animal*) nez *m*; **her n. is bleeding** elle saigne du nez; **to blow one's n.** se moucher; **to hold one's n.** se boucher le nez; **to speak through one's n.** parler du nez, nasiller; **to have one's n. in a book** avoir le nez dans un livre; **the parson's** *or* **pope's n.** (*of fowl*) le croupion; *Fig* **he can't see any further than the end of his n.** il ne voit pas plus loin que le bout de son nez; **it's under your n.** vous l'avez sous le nez; **I did it under his very n.** *or* **right under his n.** je l'ai fait sous son nez; **to poke one's n. into other people's business** fourrer *ou* mettre son nez dans les affaires des autres; **to turn up one's n. at sth** dédaigner qch; **to look down one's n. at sb** regarder qn de haut en bas; *Fig* (*despise*) mépriser qn; **she walked by with her n. in the air** elle passa avec un air dédaigneux *ou* supérieur; *Prov* **to cut off one's n. to spite one's face** se punir soi-même; **that's cutting off your n. to spite your face** c'est toi le perdant; **to lead sb by the n.** mener qn par le bout du nez; *F* **to pay through the n. for sth** payer qch une fortune *ou* les yeux de la tête; **to win by a n.** gagner d'un nez; *F* **to rub sb's n. in it** retourner le couteau dans la plaie; *F* **to have a n. (a)round** faire un tour d'inspection; **to get up sb's n.** (*of person*) taper sur les nerfs de qn; **it really gets up my n. that ...** ça me met en boule que ...; *Fig* **to keep one's n. clean** se tenir à carreau; **n. drops** gouttes *fpl* pour le nez; **to have a n. job** (*cosmetic surgery*) se faire refaire le nez; **he specializes in n. jobs** il est spécialisé dans la chirurgie du nez; **n. ring** (*of bull etc*) anneau *m* nasal, nasière *f*; (*of person*) anneau porté au nez

(b) (*of wine etc*) bouquet *m*; **to have a good n.** (*of person*) avoir bon nez *ou* le nez fin *ou* l'odorat fin; *Fig* **to have a n. for sth** (*of person*) avoir du flair pour qch

(c) *Tech* (*of vehicle, plane etc*) nez *m*, avant *m*; (*of engine*) nez; (*of tool*) bec *m*, nez; (*of bullet, missile*) pointe *f*, ogive *f*; *Naut* (*of torpedo*) cône *m* de choc

nose[2] **1** *vt* **the ship nosed her way through the fog** le navire avançait à l'aveuglette à travers le brouillard; **the car nosed its way forward/out of the garage** la voiture avança prudemment/sortit prudemment du garage **2** *vi* **the ship nosed through the fog** le navire avançait à l'aveuglette à travers le brouillard

▶ **nose about, nose around** **1** *vi* fureter, fouiner; **what are you nosing around here for?** pourquoi est-ce que tu fouines par ici? **2** *vipo* (*office, room, garden*) fureter dans, fouiner dans; **a policeman was nosing around the car/dustbin** un agent de police fouinait *ou* furetait autour de la voiture/poubelle

▶ **nose out** **1** *vtsep* **(a)** (*of dog*) (*game*) flairer **(b)** *F* (*secret*) découvrir, éventer; (*person*) dépister, dénicher; (*good restaurant, bargain*) dénicher **2** *vi* (*of car, driver*) sortir prudemment; **the car nosed out into the traffic** la voiture s'est prudemment faufilée entre les autres; **the van nosed through the crowds/up the ramp** la camionnette a traversé la foule/monté la rampe prudemment *ou* tout doucement

▶ **nose through** *vipo* (*papers etc*) fouiller dans

nosebag [ˈnəʊzbæg] *n* musette *f* (mangeoire)

noseband [ˈnəʊzbænd] *n* (*on harness*) muserolle *f*

nosebleed ['nəʊzbliːd] *n* saignement *m* de nez; **to have a n.** saigner du nez
nose cone *n* (*of plane*) cône *m* de nez; (*of rocket*) ogive *f*
nose dive *n Av* (vol *m*) piqué *m*; *F* **to take a n.** (*of prices*) faire un plongeon, piquer du nez
nose-dive *vi Av* piquer du nez, descendre en piqué; *F* (*of prices*) faire un plongeon, piquer du nez
nosegay ['nəʊzgeɪ] *n* petit bouquet *m* (de fleurs)
nose-to-tail *adj* (*traffic*) pare-choc(s) contre pare-choc(s)
nosey ['nəʊzɪ] *adj F* = **nosy**
nosh[1] [nɒʃ] *n Sl* (*food*) bouffe *f*; **time for some n.!** c'est l'heure de bouffer *ou* de la bouffe!
nosh[2] *vi Sl* (*eat*) bouffer
no-show *n* (*at airport, for travel*) désistement *m*, défection *f*, no-show *m*
nosh-up *n Br Sl* (*meal*) boustifaille *f*
nosily ['nəʊzɪlɪ] *adv F* indiscrètement
nosiness ['nəʊzɪnəs] *n F* indiscrétion *f*, curiosité *f*
no-smoking *adj* (*carriage, area*) non-fumeurs; (*seat*) non-fumeur
nostalgia [nɒs'tældʒɪə] *n* nostalgie *f*
nostalgic [nɒs'tældʒɪk] *adj* nostalgique; **a n. moment** un moment de nostalgie
nostalgically [nɒs'tældʒɪklɪ] *adv* avec nostalgie, nostalgiquement
nostril ['nɒstrɪl] *n* (*of person*) narine *f*; (*of horse, ox etc*) naseau *m*
nostrum ['nɒstrəm] *n Old-fashioned usu Pej, Fig* panacée *f*; (*quack medicine*) remède *m* de charlatan
nosy ['nəʊzɪ] *adj F* curieux, fouinard; (*questions*) indiscret; **don't be so n.!** ne soyez pas si curieux!; **I don't mean to be n. but ...** je ne veux pas me mêler de ce qui ne me regarde pas mais ...
nosy parker *n Br F* fouinard, -arde, fureteur, -euse
not [nɒt] **1** *adv* [①**A25**,f] **(a)** [①**A46**,9,a] (*following the aux verb informally affixed as* **n't**) ne ... pas; **I don't** *or* **do n. know** je ne sais pas; **he won't** *or* **will n. come** il ne viendra pas; **is she coming? – no, she isn't** *or* **she's n.** est-ce qu'elle vient? – non(, elle ne vient pas); **don't move** ne bougez pas; **I'm n. in the least surprised** je ne suis nullement étonné; **you understand, don't you?** vous comprenez, n'est-ce pas?; **she would n. wear a hat!** (*stressed*) un chapeau, elle n'en porterait pas!
(b) (*elliptically in answers etc*) **n. at all, n. a bit (of it)** pas du tout; **n. in any way, n. in the least** pas le moins du monde; **thank you so much! – n. at all!** merci beaucoup! – je vous en prie; **n. if I've got anything to do with it** pas si j'ai mon mot à dire; **n. likely!** jamais de la vie!; **whether he likes it or n.** que cela lui plaise ou non; **little or n. at all** peu ou pas, peu ou point; **I think/hope n.** je crois/j'espère que non; **n. always** pas toujours; **n. any more** *or* **longer** plus maintenant; **n. even in France** (non) pas même en France; **n. just** *or* **simply** pas seulement; **n. so** pas du tout; **n. yet** pas encore
(c) [①**A46**-7,9,b] (*with a non-finite verb*) **n. wishing to be seen, I drew the curtain** comme je ne désirais pas être vu, j'ai tiré le rideau; **n. including ...** sans compter ...; **n. to mention ...** pour ne pas parler de ...; *F* **n. to worry!** ne vous en faites pas!; **she asked me n. to do it** elle m'a demandé de ne pas le faire
(d) (*in contrasts*) **she's n. my mother but my aunt** ce n'est pas ma mère, c'est ma tante; **he is respected but n. loved** il est respecté mais (non) pas aimé; **n. only ... but also ...** non seulement ... mais encore ...
(e) (*with pronoun or noun*) **n. I** pas moi; **n. one replied** pas un(e) n'a répondu; *Old-fashioned* **he'll never pay, n. he!** il ne paiera jamais, c'est sûr!; **n. everyone was so enthusiastic** tout le monde n'était pas aussi enthousiaste; **n. a word was spoken** on n'a pas dit un mot; **who will believe it? – n. a soul** qui le croira? – personne
(f) (*understatement*) **I wasn't sorry to go** j'étais bien content de partir; **a n. inconsiderable sum of money** une somme non négligeable; **n. without reason/regret** non sans raison/regrets; **they were annoyed, n. to say furious** ils étaient ennuyés, pour ne pas dire furieux; *F* **n. half!** et comment!, tu parles!
(g) (*with adverb or adjective*) non; **n. far from the town** non loin de la ville; **n. negotiable** non négociable; **n. guilty** non coupable
(h) *Arch, Lit* (*following the verb*) **I know n.** je ne sais point; **fear n.!** n'ayez crainte!
(i) *esp Am Sl* **the party was fantastic, n.!** la fête ne cassait rien du tout
2 *conj* **n. that ...** ce n'est pas que ... + *sub*, non (pas) que ... + *sub*; **n. that I can remember** pas autant que je m'en souvienne

notability [nəʊtə'bɪlɪtɪ] *n Old-fashioned* (*person*) notabilité *f*, notable *m*; (*state*) prééminence *f*
notable ['nəʊtəb(ə)l] **1** *adj* (*person, thing*) notable, insigne, remarquable; (*person*) éminent; **with a few n. exceptions** avec quelques exceptions et non des moindres; **in a speech n. only for its length** dans un discours qui n'avait de remarquable que sa longueur; **the town is chiefly n. for ...** la ville se distingue essentiellement par ... **2** *n Fml* notable *m*
notably ['nəʊtəblɪ] *adv* (*particularly*) notamment, particulièrement
notarize ['nəʊtəraɪz] *vt* authentifier; **notarized contract/deed** contrat *m*/acte *m* notarié
notary ['nəʊtərɪ] *n Jur* **n. (public)** notaire *m*
notation [nəʊ'teɪʃən] *n Mus etc* notation *f*; *Math* numération *f*
notch[1] [nɒtʃ] *n* **(a)** (*in wood*) entaille *f*, encoche *f*; (*in belt, rack*) cran *m*; (*of toothed wheel*) cran, dent *f*; (*in blade etc*) brèche *f*; *Sewing* cran; (*in diskette*) encoche; **to cut a n.** faire une entaille *ou* une encoche; **to take one's belt in a n.** resserrer sa ceinture d'un cran; *Fig* se serrer la ceinture; *Fig* **a n. on the bedpost** une conquête
(b) *Fig* (*grade, level*) **to be a n. above the rest** être dans la catégorie supérieure; **it raised their spirits a n. or two but ...** cela leur a quelque peu remonté le moral mais ...
(c) *Am* (*in mountain*) défilé *m*, gorge *f*
notch[2] *vt* (*stick etc*) entailler, encocher; (*wheel*) denteler, créneler; (*blade*) ébrécher
► **notch up** *vtsep* (*point*) marquer; (*victory*) remporter
note[1] [nəʊt] *n* **(a)** (*in writing*) note *f*; (*on a text*) note, annotation *f*, remarque *f*; (*letter*) mot *m*; *Univ* **lecture notes** notes (de cours); **to make notes, to take (down) notes** prendre des notes; **to take** *or* **make a n. of sth** prendre note de qch; **I must make a n. of it** il faut que je m'en souvienne; **they have no n. of any such meeting** ils n'ont aucune trace de cette réunion; **without notes** (*to speak, lecture*) sans notes; **to speak from notes** parler d'après des notes; **to write** *or* **make notes on a text** annoter un texte; **diplomatic n.** note *f* diplomatique, mémorandum *m*; *Acct* **notes to the accounts** annexes *fpl*
(b) *Mus* note *f*; (*of piano etc*) touche *f*; **to sing** *or* **play a false n.** faire une fausse note; **there was a n. of impatience in her voice** il y avait une pointe d'impatience dans sa voix; **to introduce a n. of discord/optimism** introduire une note discordante/optimiste; **speech that strikes the right n.** discours dans la note voulue; **to end on a more serious/a lighter n. ...** pour conclure sur une note plus sérieuse/gaie, ...
(c) *Fin, Com* billet *m*; (*money*) billet (de banque); **n. of hand** reconnaissance *f* (de dette), billet simple; **credit/debit n.** note *f ou* bordereau *m* de crédit/de débit; **hundred-franc notes** billets *ou* coupures *fpl* de cent francs
(d) (*distinction*) distinction *f*, marque *f*, renom *m*; **a man of n.** un homme de qualité *ou* de marque; **nothing of n.** rien d'extraordinaire *ou* de spécial
(e) to take n. of sth noter qch
note[2] *vt* (*notice*) noter, remarquer; (*error*) relever; (*fact*) constater; **it should be noted that ...** il est à noter que ...; **we duly n. that ...** nous prenons bonne note (de ce) que ...; *Jur* **which fact is hereby duly noted** dont acte
► **note down** *vtsep* prendre note de
notebook ['nəʊtbʊk] *n* carnet *m*, calepin *m*; (*larger*) cahier *m*; (*for shorthand etc*) bloc-notes *m*, *pl* blocs-notes, notebook *m*; **n. (computer)** notebook *m*, ordinateur *m* bloc-notes
notecase ['nəʊtkeɪs] *n Br Old-fashioned* portefeuille *m*
noted ['nəʊtɪd] *adj* (*person*) distingué, éminent; (*thing*) fameux (**for sth** pour qch), remarquable (**for sth** par qch); **the area is n. for its cheese** la région est célèbre *ou* fameuse pour son fromage
notelet ['nəʊtlət] *n* carte-lettre *f*, *pl* cartes-lettres
notepad ['nəʊtpæd] *n* (*also on screen*) bloc-notes *m*, *pl* blocs-notes; **n. computer** ardoise *f* électronique
notepaper ['nəʊtpeɪpər] *n* papier *m* à lettres
not equals sign *n* signe *m* différent de
note-taking *n* prise *f* de notes
noteworthy ['nəʊtwɜːðɪ] *adj* (*fact etc*) remarquable; **it is n. that ...** il convient de noter que ...
not-for-profit *adj Am* = **nonprofit**
nothing ['nʌθɪŋ] **1** *pron* [①**B60**,B] rien **n. at all** rien du tout; **he does n.** il ne fait rien; **I saw n.** je n'ai rien vu; **what are you doing? – n.** que faites-vous? – rien; **it's better than n.** c'est mieux que rien; **n. can beat French cooking** il n'y a rien de mieux que la cuisine française; **a cheese sandwich is better than n.** un sandwich au fromage, c'est mieux que rien *ou* c'est toujours ça; **n. could be simpler** rien de plus simple, c'est tout ce qu'il y a de plus simple; **you can't live on n.** on ne peut pas vivre de rien; **he let me have it for almost** *or*

next to n. il me l'a cédé pour presque rien *ou* pour une bouchée de pain; **they pay him next to n.** ils le paient trois fois rien; **it looks like n. on earth** c'est ridicule; **as if n. had happened** comme si de rien n'était; **say n. about it** n'en dites rien; **to say n. of …** sans parler de …; **she gets angry about n.** elle se fâche pour un rien; **there's n. in these rumours** ces bruits sont sans fondement; *F* **there's n. to it** (*it's easy*) c'est simple comme bonjour; **there's n. in it** (*no difference*) il n'y a aucune différence; (*in choosing between two candidates etc*) ils se valent, il n'y a aucune différence entre eux; (*in race*) ils sont à égalité; **he was n. if not discreet** il était surtout discret, il était discret avant tout; **n. new/remarkable** rien de nouveau/de remarquable; **that's n. new** ce n'est pas nouveau; **that's n. unusual** cela n'a rien d'anormal; **n. much** pas grand-chose; **there is n. more to be said** il n'y a plus rien à dire; **I have n. to do** je n'ai rien à faire; **to have n. to do with sb/sth** n'avoir rien à voir avec qn/qch; **that's n. to do with you** ce n'est pas votre affaire, cela ne vous regarde pas; **these people will stop at n.** ces gens ne reculent devant rien; **there's n. to cry/worry about** il n'y a pas de quoi pleurer/s'inquiéter; **to have n. on** (*no engagement*) être libre; (*no clothes*) être tout nu; **as a pianist he has n. on his brother** comme pianiste il n'arrive pas à la cheville de son frère; **he has n. of his father in him** il n'a rien de son père; **n. but …** rien que …; **n. but the best will satisfy her** seul ce qu'il y a de meilleur la satisfait; **n. but the truth** rien que la vérité; **n. else** rien d'autre; **n. else matters** tout le reste n'est rien, rien d'autre n'a d'importance; **there's n. else for it** c'est inévitable; **there's n. like a cold bath in the mornings** il n'y a rien de tel qu'un bain froid le matin; **to do sth for n.** (*in vain*) faire qch pour rien; (*free of charge*) faire qch gratuitement; **it's not for n. that …** ce n'est pas pour rien *ou* sans raison que …; **to come to n.** ne pas aboutir; (*of hopes etc*) s'anéantir; (*of scheme etc*) s'effondrer; **all my efforts came to n.** tous mes efforts se sont révélés inutiles; **to count for n.** ne compter pour rien; **he is n. to her** (*she doesn't care for him*) il lui est indifférent; (*she is much better than he is*) elle est bien meilleure que lui; **£1 000 is n. to her** 1 000 livres ne sont rien pour elle; **that's n. to what mum will say** ce n'est rien par rapport à ce que Maman va dire; **in those days it was n. to see …** en ce temps-là on voyait facilement …; **it's n. to me either way** cela m'est égal; **to think n. of doing sth** (*not hesitate to do*) ne pas hésiter à faire qch; **she thinks n. of walking 10 km** pour elle 10 km à pied, ce n'est rien; **to think n. of sb** avoir peu d'estime pour qn; **I can make n. of it** je n'y comprends rien du tout; *F* **n. doing** rien à faire, pas question; *F* **to do sth in n. flat** faire qch en deux temps trois mouvements; *Prov* **n. ventured, n. gained** qui ne risque rien n'a rien

2 *n* **(a)** (*nonexistence*) néant *m*, rien *m*

(b) (*trifle*) bagatelle *f*, rien *m*; (*person*) zéro *m*, nullité *f*; **a hundred francs? – a mere n.!** cent francs? – une bagatelle!; **to whisper sweet nothings to sb/in sb's ear** chuchoter des mots doux à qn/à l'oreille de qn

(c) *Math* zéro *m*

3 *adv* **n. like** *or* **near so** *or* **as big** loin d'être aussi grand; **London is n. like as near as that** Londres est bien plus loin que ça; **she looks n. like her sister** elle ne ressemble pas du tout *ou* en rien à sa sœur; **it's n. less than** *or* **short of madness** c'est de la folie ni plus ni moins; **it's n. less than scandalous that …** c'est ni plus ni moins un scandale que …

nothingness ['nʌθɪŋnɪs] *n* néant *m*; **a feeling** *or* **sense of n.** un sentiment de vide

notice[1] ['nəʊtɪs] *n* **(a)** (*notification*) avis *m*, notification *f*; (*warning*) préavis *m*, avertissement *m*; (*served by bailiff*) exploit *m* (d'huissier); **to give sb n. of sth** prévenir *ou* avertir qn de qch; **to give official n. that …** donner acte que …; **n. is hereby given that …** le public est avisé que …; **without (prior) n.** sans préavis; **until further n.** jusqu'à nouvel ordre *ou* nouvel avis; **public n.** avis au public; **important n.** avis important; *Rel* **the weekly notices** les annonces *fpl* de la semaine; *Jur* **n. of appeal** intimation *f* d'appel; *Com* **n. of claim** déclaration *f* de sinistre; **n. of receipt** accusé *m* de réception; **n. of a/the meeting** convocation *f*; **n. to pay** avertissement; **at short n.** dans un bref délai; **to give sb short n.** prendre qn de court; **that's rather short n.** c'est un peu court comme délai; **at a moment's** *or* **a minute's n.** sur-le-champ; **without a moment's n.** sans crier gare; **to require three months' n.** exiger un préavis de trois mois; **next time give me a bit more n.** la prochaine fois prévenez-moi un peu plus à l'avance; **n. (to quit)** (avis de) congé *m*; **to be under n. to quit** avoir reçu son congé; **what n. do you require?** quel est le terme du congé?; **to give sb n.** (*of landlord, employer*) congédier qn, donner son congé à qn; (*of employer*) licencier qn; **to give sb a week's n.** donner ses huit jours à qn; **to give n., to give** *or* **hand in one's n.** (*of tenant, employee*) donner *ou* demander (son) congé; (*of employee*) donner sa démission, démissionner; **n. period** (*in employment*) terme *m* de préavis

(b) (*poster*) affiche *f*, placard *m*; (*sign, card etc*) écriteau *m*, pancarte *f*

(c) (*in newspaper etc*) annonce *f*; (*review*) (*of play, work etc*) critique *f*; **they put a birth n. in the local paper** ils ont passé un faire-part de naissance dans le quotidien régional; **the play got good notices** la pièce a eu de bonnes critiques

(d) (*attention*) **to take n. of** faire attention *ou* prêter attention à; (*warning*) tenir compte de; **to take not the slightest n. of sth** ne pas prêter la moindre attention à qch; **nobody took any n. of me** personne n'a fait attention à moi; **I warned him but he took no n. (of me)** je l'ai prévenu mais il n'a pas prêté la moindre attention à ce que je lui ai dit; **I should take no n.** *or* **I shouldn't take any n. of it if I were you** je n'y ferais pas attention à ta place; **it has come to my n. that …** il est venu à ma connaissance que …; **to attract n.** (*of author etc*) commencer à être connu *ou* à percer; (*of performance, publication etc*) être remarqué; **to avoid n.** se dérober aux regards; **the fact escaped everyone's n.** ce fait a échappé à tout le monde; **to bring** *or* **call sth/sb to sb's n.** appeler *ou* porter *ou* attirer l'attention de qn sur qch/qn; **the baby is beginning to take n.** le bébé commence à avoir conscience des choses

notice[2] **1** *vt* remarquer, s'apercevoir de; (*errors*) relever; **didn't anybody n. him leaving?** est-ce que personne n'a remarqué qu'il partait?; **without his noticing it** sans qu'il s'en aperçoive; **she's beginning to get herself noticed** elle commence à être connu *ou* à percer; **to be noticed** *or* **to get oneself noticed by sb** attirer l'attention de qn (sur soi) **2** *vi* remarquer; **nobody will ever n.** personne ne s'en apercevra *ou* ne le remarquera jamais; **what happened? – I don't know, I didn't n.** qu'est-ce qui s'est passé? – je ne sais pas, je ne m'en suis pas rendu compte

noticeable ['nəʊtɪsəb(ə)l] *adj* (*perceptible*) perceptible; (*difference, improvement, change*) sensible; **it was very n. that she didn't speak to her husband** on ne pouvait pas ne pas remarquer qu'elle ne parlait pas à son mari

noticeably ['nəʊtɪsəblɪ] *adv* sensiblement

noticeboard ['nəʊtɪsbɔːd] *n* panneau *m* d'affichage; (*in schools, clubs etc*) tableau *m* d'affichage; (*on house for sale etc*) écriteau *m*

notifiable [nəʊtɪ'faɪəb(ə)l] *adj* (*disease*) dont la déclaration aux autorités est obligatoire

notification [nəʊtɪfɪ'keɪʃən] *n* (*of fact etc*) avis *m*, notification *f*; (*of birth etc*) déclaration *f*; **letter of n.** lettre *f* notificative

notify ['nəʊtɪfaɪ] *vt* annoncer, notifier; (*birth*) déclarer; **to n. sb of sth** avertir *ou* aviser qn de qch; **to n. the authorities of a fact** saisir l'administration d'un fait; **to n. the police of sth** signaler qch à la police; **have you notified the police?** avez vous prévenu la police?; **to be notified of sth** recevoir notification de qch, être avisé de qch; *Com* **to send sth n.** expédier qch 'notify'

notion ['nəʊʃən] *n* **(a)** (*idea*) notion *f*, idée *f*; **to have no n. of sth** ne pas avoir la moindre notion de qch; **to have no n. of time** n'avoir pas la notion *ou* le sens de l'heure; **I haven't the first n. about it** je n'en ai pas la moindre idée; **I haven't the first n. about physics/French** je n'y connais absolument rien en physique/français; **I have a n. that …** j'ai dans l'idée que …; **she has some pretty strange notions** elle a de drôles d'idées

(b) (*whim*) caprice *m*; **as the n. takes him** comme il en a envie; **to have a n. to do sth** avoir envie de faire qch

(c) *Phil* (*concept*) notion *f*, concept *m*

(d) *Am* **notions** (*ribbons, needles etc*) (articles *mpl* de) mercerie *f*

notional ['nəʊʃən(ə)l] *adj* (*abstract*) hypothétique; *Phil* spéculatif; (*imaginary*) (*things, relations etc*) imaginaire

notoriety [nəʊtə'raɪətɪ] *n* notoriété *f*; **to seek n.** chercher à se faire remarquer; **this action gained** *or* **earned him some n.** cette action lui a valu une certaine notoriété

notorious [nəʊ'tɔːrɪəs] *adj* d'une triste notoriété; (*criminal, thief*) notoire; (*place*) mal famé; (*liar*) fieffé; **Mexico City is n. for being one of the world's most polluted cities** Mexico est réputée pour être *ou* a la triste notoriété d'être l'une des villes les plus polluées au monde; **to be n. for being late/one's lack of tact** être réputé pour arriver en retard/son manque de tact

notoriously [nəʊ'tɔːrɪəslɪ] *adv* notoirement; **n. cruel** connu pour sa cruauté; **to be n. difficult/dangerous** être bien connu pour sa difficulté/ses dangers

Notts *abbr* **Nottinghamshire**

notwithstanding [nɒtwɪθ'stændɪŋ] **1** *prep* malgré, en dépit de, *Fml* nonobstant **2** *adv* quand même, tout de même, néanmoins
nougat ['nuːgɑː] *n* nougat *m*
nought [nɔːt] *n* **(a)** [①A71,3,a] *Math* zéro *m* **(b)** = **naught (a)**
noughts and crosses *n Br (game)* ≈ morpion *m*
noun [naʊn] *n* [①A8-16,3; B5-8,3] *Gram* substantif *m*, nom *m*; **proper n.** [①A8,3,2; B8,10] nom propre; **n. clause** proposition *f*; **n. phrase** [①B64,7] proposition nominale, syntagme *m* nominal
nourish ['nʌrɪʃ] *vt* **(a)** *(person, plant, wood, leather)* nourrir; **to n. sb on** *or* **with sth** nourrir qn de qch; **to be well nourished** être bien nourri **(b)** *Old-fashioned (feeling, hope etc)* nourrir, entretenir
nourishing ['nʌrɪʃɪŋ] *adj* nourrissant, nutritif
nourishment ['nʌrɪʃmənt] *n* **(a)** *(food)* nourriture *f*, aliments *mpl*; *(nourishing quality)* richesse *f* nutritive; **to take (some) n.** se nourrir, s'alimenter; **you're not getting enough n.** tu ne t'alimentes pas bien; **to receive n.** être nourri; *(of plants)* trouver sa nourriture; **it's full of n.** c'est très nourrissant *ou* nutritif **(b)** *(action)* alimentation *f*
nous [naʊs] *n Br Sl* bon sens *m*; *(know-how)* savoir-faire *m*; **she's got a lot of n.** elle a beaucoup de bon sens, elle est très sensée; **anyone with any n.** n'importe qui doté d'un minimum de bon sens
nova, *pl* **-ae** *or* **-s** ['nəʊvə, -iː] *n Astron* nova *f*, *pl* novae
Nova Scotia ['nəʊvə'skəʊʃə] *n* Nouvelle-Écosse *f*
novel[1] ['nɒv(ə)l] *n* roman *m*
novel[2] *adj* nouveau, *f* nouvelle, original; **that's a n. idea!** voilà qui est original!
novelette [nɒvə'let] *n (short novel)* nouvelle *f*; *(sentimental story)* petit roman *m* à l'eau de rose
novelist ['nɒvəlɪst] *n* romancier, -ière
novella [nəʊ'velə] *n* nouvelle *f*
novelty ['nɒvəltɪ] *n* **(a)** *(quality)* nouveauté *f*; **the n. will soon wear off** l'attrait de la nouveauté ne tardera pas à s'estomper; **there was no n. in it any more** cela n'avait plus rien de nouveau; **the n. of this scheme is that …** ce que ce programme a de nouveau *ou* d'innovateur c'est que … **(b)** *(thing)* nouveauté *f*; *Com* (article *m* de) nouveauté, fantaisie *f*; **such ideas are a n.** ces idées sont complètement nouvelles; **as the only Chinese child, he was something of a n.** seul enfant chinois, il faisait figure de nouveauté; **to have n. value** avoir l'attrait de la nouveauté
November [nəʊ'vembər] *n* [①A75-6,B-C; B58-9, B-C] novembre *m*; **in N.** au mois de novembre, en novembre; **(on) the first/the fifth of N.** le premier/le cinq novembre
novena [nəʊ'viːnə] *n Cathol* neuvaine *f*
novice ['nɒvɪs] *n* apprenti, -ie, débutant, -ante; *Rel* novice *mf*; **to be a n. in** *or* **at sth** être novice en qch; **I'm still a bit of a n. at this** je suis encore un peu novice; **he was something of a sexual n.** il était pour ainsi dire novice en matière de sexe
noviciate, novitiate [nəʊ'vɪʃɪət] *n Rel* **(a)** *(state, period)* noviciat *m* **(b)** *(living quarters)* noviciat *m*, maison *f* des novices
now [naʊ] **1** *adv* **(a)** [①A23,3,a,i] *(this instant)* maintenant *(at present)* maintenant, à présent; *(nowadays)* actuellement, à l'heure actuelle; *(in narrative)* alors, à ce moment-là; **what shall we do n.?** qu'est-ce que nous allons faire maintenant?; *F* **it's (a case of) n. or never** c'est le moment ou jamais; **n. or never!, n. for it!** allons-y!; **goodbye for n.!** à bientôt!; **that'll do for n.** ça suffit pour le moment; **it's two years n. since his mother died** ça fait maintenant deux ans que sa mère est morte; **he won't be long n.** il ne va plus tarder; **even n., I don't understand** même maintenant je ne comprends pas; **and n. I must go** sur ce je vous quitte; **n. is the time to …** c'est le bon moment pour …; **right n.** *(immediately)* tout de suite; **I'm not in a position right n. to decide** je ne peux rien décider pour le moment; **all was n. ready** dès lors tout était prêt; **he was even n. on his way** il était déjà en route; **just n.** *(past)* il y a un instant; *(present)* en ce moment; **she left just n.** elle vient de partir; **(every) n. and then, (every) n. and again** de temps en temps, de temps à autre; **n. one thing, n.** *or* **then another** tantôt une chose, tantôt l'autre; **n. here n. there** tantôt ici tantôt là; **up to n.** jusqu'ici; **from n. on** à partir de maintenant, dorénavant; **it should be finished in three days from n.** cela devrait être fini d'ici trois jours; **I'm leaving in three days from n.** je pars dans trois jours; **he ought to be here by n., he ought to have been here before n.** il devrait déjà être arrivé; **until n.** jusqu'ici; **and n. for some music** et maintenant, un peu de musique
(b) *(without temporal significance) (explanatory or in development of an argument)* or; **n. to come back to what we were saying** pour revenir à ce que nous disions; **n. it happened that …** *(in story)* or il advint que …; **n. what's the matter with you!** qu'avez-vous donc?; **come n.!** voyons!; **n., n.! stop quarrelling!** voyons, voyons! assez de querelles!; **well n.!** eh bien!; **n. then, stop fighting** allons, arrêtez de vous battre; **n. then, listen to what I have to say!** allons *ou* bon, écoutez ce que j'ai à vous dire!; **n. then, what's all the noise about?** eh bien alors, qu'est-ce que c'est que tout ce bruit?
2 *conj* maintenant que, à présent que; **n. (that) I'm older I think differently** maintenant que je suis plus âgé je pense autrement
3 *adj esp Am F (look, people)* actuel
nowadays ['naʊədeɪz] *adv* aujourd'hui, de nos jours, à l'heure actuelle; **where's she working n.?** où travaille-t-elle actuellement?
nowhere ['nəʊweər] **1** *adv* [①B60,B] nulle part; **she was n. to be found** on ne la trouvait nulle part, elle était introuvable; **we're getting n. fast** nous n'avançons pas d'un poil; **that kind of attitude will get you n. fast** ce genre d'attitude ne t'avancera *ou* ne te servira à rien du tout; **qualifications alone will get you n.** les diplômes seuls ne suffisent pas; **it's n. near the shopping centre** ce n'est pas du tout dans les parages du centre commercial; **it's n. near enough** c'est loin d'être suffisant; **he's n. near as intelligent as his sister** il est loin d'être aussi intelligent que sa sœur; **we're n. near ready** on est loin d'être prêt; **the rest are n.** *(in race, sales etc)* les autres ne sont plus dans le coup; **she finished n.** elle a fini loin derrière
2 *n* **a small place in the middle of n.** un petit trou perdu; **he seemed to come from n.** il est apparu tout d'un coup; **the money won't just come from n.** l'argent ne va pas tomber du ciel; **he came from n. to win the race** il a fait une remontée spectaculaire et a gagné la course; **the Greens came from n. to win nearly 15% of the vote** les Verts sont partis de rien et ont remporté près de 15% des votes
nowt [naʊt] *pron, n N Eng Dial* (ne …) rien *m*; **I don't do owt for n.** je ne fais rien pour rien
noxious ['nɒkʃəs] *adj* nocif; *(gas, fumes)* délétère, nocif
nozzle ['nɒz(ə)l] *n Tech (of pipe)* ajutage *m*, jet *m*; *(of fire hose etc)* lance *f*; *(of syringe)* canule *f*; *(of bellows)* bec *m*, tuyau *m*, buse *f*; *(of vacuum cleaner)* suceur *m*; *(of injector, turbine)* tuyère *f*, ajutage; *(for icing)* douille *f*; *(of petrol pump)* pistolet *m*
NPV [enpiː'viː] *n Acct (abbr* **net present value)** VAN *f*, valeur *f* actuelle nette; **N. rate** taux *m* d'actualisation
NRS [enaːr'es] *n (abbr* **national readership survey)** étude *f* nationale sur le lectorat
NS *abbr* **Nova Scotia**
ns *(abbr* **nanosecond)** ns
NSPCC [enespiːsiː'siː] *n Br (abbr* **National Society for the Prevention of Cruelty to Children)** = comité *m* national pour la prévention des mauvais traitements envers les enfants
nth [enθ] *adj* **(a)** *F* énième; **to the n. degree** au énième degré; **for the n. time** pour la énième fois **(b)** *Math* **to the n. power** à la puissance n
nuance ['njuːɒns] *n* nuance *f*; **a n. of meaning** une nuance; **I detected a n. of uncertainty in his voice** j'ai décelé une note d'incertitude dans sa voix
nuanced ['njuːɒnst] *adj* nuancé; **finely n.** subtilement nuancé
nub [nʌb] *n* **(a)** *(protuberance)* bosse *f*, protubérance *f* **(b) the n. of the matter** *or* **issue** le cœur du sujet
nubile ['njuːbaɪl] *adj* **(a)** *(sexually attractive)* désirable **(b)** *fml (marriageable)* nubile
nuclear ['njuːklɪər] *adj* **(a)** *Phys, Mil* nucléaire; **n. energy** énergie *f* nucléaire *ou* atomique; **n. fission** fission *f* nucléaire; **n. fusion** fusion *f* nucléaire; *Med* **n. magnetic resonance** résonance *f* magnétique nucléaire; *Med* **n. magnetic resonance scanner** scanner *m* de résonance magnétique nucléaire; **n. physics** physique *f* nucléaire; **n. power** électricité *f* d'origine nucléaire; **n. power station** *or* **plant** centrale *f* (d'énergie) nucléaire; **n. war(fare)** guerre *f* nucléaire; *Mil* **n. weapon** arme *f* nucléaire; **n. winter** hiver *m* nucléaire; *Pol* **the N. Powers** les puissances *fpl* nucléaires **(b)** *(family)* nucléaire
nuclear-free *adj* **n. zone** zone *f* anti-nucléaire
nucleic [njuː'kliːɪk] *adj Ch (acid)* nucléique
nucleus, *pl* **-ei** ['njuːklɪəs, -ɪaɪ] *n* **(a)** *Phys, Biol, Astron* noyau *m* **(b)** *Fig (of organization etc)* noyau *m*; *(of argument etc)* cœur *m*; **the n. of a library** *(beginnings)* un commencement de bibliothèque; **the n. of a fine sales team** les premiers éléments d'une bonne équipe de vente
nuddy ['nʌdɪ] *n Br F Hum* **in the n.** tout nu, à poil
nude [njuːd] **1** *adj (person)* nu; *Art* **n. figure** nu *m*, nudité *f* **2** *n* **(a)** *Art* **a n.** un nu; **the n.** *(genre)* le nu; **to draw/paint from the n.** dessiner/peindre des nus *ou* des académies **(b) in the n.** tout nu
nudge[1] [nʌdʒ] *n* coup *m* de coude; *F* **n. n. humour** humour *m* à allusions scabreuses; *Aut* **n. bar** barre *f* de calandre

nudge[2] *vt* pousser du coude, donner un coup de coude à; **to n. one's way through a crowd** jouer des coudes pour se frayer un chemin à travers la foule; **we nudged the sofa forward a few inches** nous avons avancé le sofa de quelques centimètres

nudism ['nju:dɪz(ə)m] *n* nudisme *m*, naturisme *m*

nudist ['nju:dɪst] *n* nudiste *mf*, naturiste *mf*; **n. camp** *or* **colony** camp *m* de nudistes

nudity ['nju:dɪtɪ] *n* nudité *f*

nugatory ['nju:gətərɪ] *adj Lit, Fml* sans valeur

nugget ['nʌgɪt] *n* (*of gold*) pépite *f*; *Fig* **a n. (of useful information)** une information très utile; **a n. (of wisdom)** une perle; **chicken nuggets, nuggets of chicken** morceaux *mpl* de poulet

nuisance ['nju:səns] *n* **(a)** (*person*) casse-pieds *mf inv*; **go away, you('re a) n.!** va-t'en, tu m'embêtes *ou* tu me casses les pieds!; **she's a bit of a n.** elle est un peu casse-pieds; **he's being a n.** (*of child, drunk*) il m'embête/l'embête/*etc*; **to make a n. of oneself** embêter le monde; **the TV won't work – it's a real n.** la télé ne marche pas – c'est vraiment embêtant; **long skirts are a n.** les jupes longues sont gênantes; **this keyboard/pen is a n.** ce clavier/stylo est embêtant; **it's a n. for me to have to ...** cela me gêne *ou F* m'embête de devoir ...; **what a n.!, that's a n.!** que c'est embêtant *ou* agaçant!; **at least we won't have the n. of going through customs** au moins nous ne serons pas embêtés à devoir passer à la douane; **to have n. value** être un élément gênant

(b) *Jur* dommage *m*; (*to public at large*) atteinte *f* portée aux droits du public; (*to individual*) atteinte portée aux droits privés des voisins

nuisance call *n Tel* appel *m* anonyme

nuisance caller *n* auteur *m* d'appels anonymes

NUJ [enju:'dʒeɪ] *n Br* (*abbr* **National Union of Journalists**) = syndicat *m* national des journalistes

nuke[1] [nju:k] *n esp US F* (*bomb*) bombe *f* nucléaire

nuke[2] *vt esp US F* atomiser

null [nʌl] *adj Jur etc* (*decree, act etc*) nul, *f* nulle; (*legacy*) caduc, *f* caduque; **to render n.** (*decree, will*) annuler, infirmer, invalider

null and void *adj* nul et non avenu

nullification [nʌlɪfɪ'keɪʃən] *n* annulation *f*, invalidation *f*

nullify ['nʌlɪfaɪ] *vt* (*contract, result*) annuler, rendre nul; (*act*) infirmer; (*decree*) invalider; **his marriage was nullified** son mariage a été déclaré nul

nullity ['nʌlɪtɪ] *n Jur* (*of marriage*) nullité *f*, invalidité *f*; (*of inheritance*) caducité *f*; **n. suit** demande *f* en nullité de mariage

null modem cable *n Comptr* câble *m* de connexion sans modem

NUM [enju:'em] *n Br* (*abbr* **National Union of Mineworkers**) = syndicat *m* national des mineurs

numb[1] [nʌm] *adj* (*limb*) engourdi, gourd; (*mind*) engourdi; **to go n.** s'engourdir; **hands n. with cold** mains engourdies par le froid; **to be n. with shock/grief** être hébété par le choc/la douleur; **n. with terror** glacé d'horreur; **to become n. to sth** devenir insensible à qch

numb[2] *vt* (*limbs, mind etc*) engourdir; **she was numbed by her father's death** elle était sous le choc après la mort de son père, la mort de son père l'a laissée sous le choc

number[1] ['nʌmbər] *n* **(a)** [①**A70-2,16; B56-57**] (*quantity*), *Math* nombre *m*; **three-figure n.** nombre de trois chiffres; **even/odd/prime n.** nombre pair/impair/premier; **the n. of people present** le nombre des présents; **we were in equal numbers** *or* **equal in n.** nous étions en nombre égal; **they are few in n.** ils sont peu nombreux; *Fml* **without n.** sans nombre, innombrable; **a n. of ...** un certain nombre de ...; **she is one of a n. of people who ...** elle figure parmi les personnes qui ...; **a large n. of men were killed** un grand nombre d'hommes a éte tué *ou* ont été tués; **any n. of ...** un grand nombre de ..., bon nombre de ...; **to be present in small numbers/in (great) numbers** être présents en petit nombre/en grand nombre; **they are coming in ever-increasing numbers** ils sont de plus en plus nombreux à venir; **one of their n.** (l')un d'entre eux; *Bible* **(the Book of) Numbers** le Livre des Nombres, les Nombres

(b) (*symbol*) chiffre *m*; **the n. eight** le chiffre huit; *Comptr* **n. key** touche *f* numérique

(c) [①**A71,5**] (*of house, page, telephone etc*) numéro *m*; (*of soldier etc*) (numéro) matricule *m*; **I live at n. 40** j'habite au (numéro) 40; *F* **to do n. one** (*in children's language*) faire pipi, faire la petite commission; *F* **to do n. two** (*in children's language*) faire la grosse commission; *F* **to look after n. one** tirer la couverture à soi; **he's only interested in n. one** tout ce qui l'intéresse c'est sa pomme; **my n. one priority** la première de mes priorités; *F* **to be at n. one** (*of record*) être (le) numéro un; *F* **he's my n. two** c'est mon adjoint; *Aut* **registration n.** numéro d'immatriculation; *Fig F* **I've got your n.!** je sais ce que tu as en tête; **to draw a lucky n.** (*at lottery etc*) tirer un bon numéro; *F* **his n.'s up** il a son compte, il est fichu

(d) *Gram* nombre *m*

(e) *Th* numéro *m*; **for my next n. I'd like to sing ...** j'aimerais vous chanter maintenant ...; **instrumental n.** morceau *m* instrumental

(f) *Journ* (*of newspaper etc*) numéro *m*; (*of work appearing in editions*) livraison *f*, fascicule *m*; **current n.** numéro du jour/de la semaine/du mois, dernier numéro; **back n.** vieux numéro

(g) *Sl* (*woman*) nana *f*, nénette *f*; **she's a good-looking n.** c'est une jolie nénette

(h) *F* **that car/dress is a nice little n.** elle est pas mal, cette voiture/robe

(i) *F* **a cushy n.** (*job*) une bonne planque; **she's got a nice little n. there** (*situation*) elle s'est dégoté un bon plan

number[2] *vt* **(a)** (*give number to houses on a street, pages etc*) numéroter **(b)** (*count*) compter; **his days are numbered** ses jours sont comptés; **to n. sb among one's friends** compter qn au nombre de *ou* parmi ses amis **(c)** (*amount to*) **they numbered no more than twenty** ils n'étaient pas plus de vingt; **the town/the army numbers thirty thousand** la ville/l'armée compte trente mille habitants/trente mille hommes

▶ **number off** *vi Mil* se numéroter

number-coded *adj* codé en chiffres

number-crunch *vt Comptr F* faire subir des calculs rapides à

number-cruncher ['nʌmbəkrʌntʃər] *n Comptr* super-ordinateur *m*

number crunching *n Comptr* calculs *mpl* (rapides)

numbering ['nʌmbərɪŋ] *n* (*of houses, pages etc*) numérotage *m*; **n. machine** numéroteur *m*; **n. system** système *m* de numérotation

numberless ['nʌmbəlɪs] *adj* innombrable, sans nombre

number-one *adj* numéro un; **n. brand** marque numéro un

numberplate ['nʌmbəpleɪt] *n Br Aut* plaque *f* minéralogique *ou* d'immatriculation

numbers lock *n Comptr* verrouillage *m* du clavier numérique; **n. key** touche *f* de verrouillage du clavier numérique

Number Ten *n Br* = Downing Street

numbly ['nʌmlɪ] *adv* (*to react, say*) mollement; (*to look, stare*) d'un air engourdi

numbness ['nʌmnɪs] *n* (*of fingers etc*) engourdissement *m*; (*of emotions etc*) torpeur *f*

numbskull ['nʌmskʌl] *n F* nigaud, -aude, bêta, -asse; **stop behaving like such a n.!** arrête de faire le nigaud comme ça!

numeracy ['nju:m(ə)rəsɪ] *n* degré *m* d'aptitude en calcul

numeral ['nju:m(ə)r(ə)l] **1** *n* chiffre *m*, nombre *m*; **Roman numerals** chiffres romains; **the cardinal numerals** les numéraux *mpl* cardinaux **2** *adj* (*word, letter etc*) numéral

numerate ['nju:mərət] *adj* qui a le sens de l'arithmétique; **applicants should be highly n.** les candidats doivent avoir des compétences élevées en calcul; **to be barely n.** savoir à peine compter

numeration [nju:mə'reɪʃən] *n Math* numération *f*; **binary n.** numération binaire

numerator ['nju:məreɪtər] *n Math* numérateur *m*

numeric [nju:'merɪk] *Comptr* **1** *adj* numérique; **n. coding** codage *m* numérique; **n. pad** pavé *m* numérique **2** *npl* **numerics** chiffres *mpl ou* caractères *mpl* numériques

numerical [nju:'merɪk(ə)l] *adj* (*value, superiority, order etc*) numérique; **n. control** (*of machine, tools*) contrôle *m* numérique; *Comptr* **n. keypad** clavier *m ou* pavé *m* numérique

numerically [nju:'merɪklɪ] *adv* numériquement

numerous ['nju:m(ə)rəs] *adj* nombreux; **to grow more n.** devenir de plus en plus nombreux

numismatic [nju:mɪz'mætɪk] *adj* numismatique

numismatics [nju:mɪz'mætɪks] *n* [①**A10,c**] numismatique *f*

numismatist [nju:'mɪz(ə)mətɪst] *n* numismate *mf*

num lock *Comptr* (*abbr* **numbers lock**) verr num

numskull ['nʌmskʌl] *n F* = **numbskull**

nun [nʌn] *n Rel* religieuse *f*, *F* bonne sœur; **to become a n.** se faire religieuse, prendre le voile, entrer en religion

nuncio, *pl* **-s** ['nʌnʃɪəʊ, -z] *n Rel* nonce *m*

nunnery ['nʌnərɪ] *n Old-fashioned* couvent *m* de religieuses

nuptial ['nʌpʃəl] *Lit* **1** *adj* nuptial; **their n. day** le jour de leurs noces **2** *npl* **nuptials** noces *fpl*

NUR [enju:'ɑ:r] *n Br abbr* (**National Union of Railwaymen**) = syndicat *m* national des employés des chemins de fer

nurse[1] [nɜ:s] *n* **(a)** (*in hospital*) infirmier, -ière; (*privately employed*) infirmier, -ière, garde-malade *mf*, *pl* gardes-malades; **thank you, n.** merci mademoiselle/madame; **n. will take out the stitches** l'infirmière retirera les points de suture; **(male) n.** infirmier *m* **(b)** (*looking after children*) nurse *f*, bonne *f* d'enfant; **(wet) n.** nourrice *f* **(c)** *Ent* (*of bees, ants*) ouvrière *f*

nurse² **1** *vt* **(a)** (*sick person, F a cold*) soigner; **she nursed him back to health** elle lui a fait recouvrer la santé grâce à ses soins

(b) (*suckle*) (*baby*) nourrir (de son lait), allaiter

(c) *Fig* (*plants etc*) soigner; (*horse, team etc*) ménager en vue du dernier effort à donner; (*feeling, hope etc*) nourrir, entretenir; (*project*) mitonner, mijoter; **he nursed the damaged plane back to base** il a réussi à ramener l'avion endommagé jusqu'à la base; **they nursed the family business through the worst of the recession** ils ont maintenu l'entreprise familiale sur pied au pire de la récession; *Br Pol* **to n. one's constituency** chauffer ses électeurs; **to n. an old grievance** entretenir un grief

(d) (*clasp*) (*child*) bercer, dorloter; (*whisky, drink*) siroter; **to n. one's knee** tenir son genou dans ses mains

2 *vi* **(a) she wants to n.** elle voudrait être infirmière

(b) (*of baby*) téter

nursemaid ['nɜːsmeɪd] *n* bonne *f* d'enfants, nurse *f*; *Fig* **I'm not your n.!** je ne suis pas votre bonne!

nursery ['nɜːs(ə)rɪ] *n* **(a)** (*room*) (*in house*) chambre *f* des enfants *ou* d'enfants; (*in hospital*) pouponnière *f* **(b)** (*establishment*) (*school*) maternelle *f*; **(day) n.** crèche *f*, garderie *f*; **n. education** enseignement *m* de maternelle; **n. provision** service *m* de garderie **(c) n. (garden)** pépinière *f*; **n. gardener** pépiniériste *mf*

nurseryman, *pl* **-men** ['nɜːs(ə)rɪmən] *n* pépiniériste *m*

nursery nurse *n* puéricultrice *f*

nursery rhyme *n* comptine *f*

nursery school *n* maternelle *f*; **n. teacher** maîtresse *f*/maître *m* d'école maternelle

nursery slopes *npl Ski* pentes *fpl* pour débutants

nursing ['nɜːsɪŋ] **1** *adj* **n. mother** mère *f* qui allaite **2** *n* **(a)** (*suckling*) (*of baby*) allaitement *m* **(b)** (*care given by a nurse*) soins *mpl* **(c)** (*profession*) profession *f* d'infirmier/d'infirmière; **to go into n.** devenir infirmier/infirmière

nursing auxiliary *n* aide *mf* soignant(e)

nursing home *n* (*hospital*) clinique *f*; (*for the mentally ill*) maison *f* de santé; (*for elderly people*) maison de retraite

nursing officer *n Br* infirmier/infirmière en chef

nursing staff *n* (*in hospital*) personnel *m* soignant, infirmiers, -ières

nurture¹ ['nɜːtʃər] *n* éducation *f*; (*of plant*) soins *mpl*

nurture² *vt* **(a)** (*feed*) (*children, plants etc*) nourrir; (*feelings etc*) nourrir, entretenir; (*plan, scheme*) préparer, élaborer **(b)** (*bring up*) élever, faire l'éducation de

NUS [enjuː'es] *n Br* (*abbr* **National Union of Students**) ≈ UNEF *f*

NUT [enjuː'tiː] *n Br* (*abbr* **National Union of Teachers**) ≈ F. E. N. *f*

nut [nʌt] *n* **(a)** (*walnut*) noix *f*; (*peanut*) cacahuète *f*; (*hazelnut*) noisette *f*; (*almond*) amande *f*; (*Brazil nut*) noix du Brésil; **a bag of nuts and raisins** un sachet de fruits secs mélangés; **fruit and n. (chocolate)** chocolat *m* aux fruits et aux noisettes/amandes/*etc*; *F* **tough** *or* **hard n. to crack** (*problem*) problème *m* difficile à résoudre; **a hard** *or* **tough n.** (*person*) personne *f* difficile *ou* peu commode; **n. cutlet** côtelette *f* végétarienne (*à base de noix, noisettes etc*); **n. roast** rôti *m* végétarien (*à base de noix, noisettes etc*)

(b) *F* (*head*) caboche *f*; **to be off one's n.** être timbré *ou* toqué, avoir perdu la boule; **to go off one's n.** (*go mad*) perdre la boule; (*become angry*) piquer une crise; *Br Sl* **to do one's n.** voir rouge

(c) *F* (*mad person*) dingue *mf*, barjo *mf*; **don't be a n.** arrête de dérailler *ou* débloquer; **a jazz/tennis n.** un(e) dingue *ou* fana de jazz/de tennis

(d) *MecE* écrou *m*; **butterfly** *or* **wing n.** écrou à oreilles, écrou (à) papillon; *Fig* **the nuts and bolts of the problem** les détails pratiques du problème; *Fig* **the nuts and bolts of a language** les éléments de base d'une langue

(e) *Br Com, Min* **n. coal, nuts** gailletin *m*, têtes *fpl* de moineau

(f) *esp Am Sl* **nuts** (*testicles*) couilles *fpl*

nut-brown *adj* (couleur) noisette *inv*; (*hair*) châtain; (*skin*) brun

nutcase ['nʌtkeɪs] *n F* dingue *mf*, cinglé, -ée; **he's a complete n.** il est complètement dingue *ou* cinglé *ou* timbré

nutcracker ['nʌtkrækər] *n* **(pair of) nutcrackers** casse-noisette(s) *m inv*, casse-noix *m inv*

nuthatch ['nʌthætʃ] *n* (*bird*) sittelle *f*

nuthouse ['nʌthaʊs] *n F* maison *f* de fous

nutmeg ['nʌtmeg] *n* (noix *f* de) muscade *f*; **n. (tree)** muscadier *m*; **n. grater** râpe *f* à muscade

nutrient ['njuːtrɪənt] **1** *adj* nutritif **2** *n* substance *f* nutritive

nutriment ['njuːtrɪmənt] *n Fml* nourriture *f*

nutrition [njuː'trɪʃən] *n* nutrition *f*

nutritional [njuː'trɪʃənəl] *adj* nutritionnel; (*value*) nutritif; *Com* **n. labelling** étiquetage *m* de l'apport nutritionnel

nutritionist [njuː'trɪʃənɪst] *n* nutritionniste *mf*

nutritious [njuː'trɪʃəs] *adj* nutritif, nourrissant

nutritive ['njuːtrɪtɪv] *adj* = **nutritional**

nuts [nʌts] *F* **1** *adj* **(a)** (*mad*) cinglé; **to go n.** perdre la boule **(b) to be n. about sb/sth** (*very fond of*) être fou/folle de qn/qch, raffoler de qn/qch **2** *int esp Am* (*damn*) zut!

nutshell ['nʌtʃel] *n* coquille *f* de noix/de noisette/*etc*; *Fig* **that's the whole thing in a n.** voilà toute l'affaire (résumée) en un mot *ou* en deux mots; *Fig* **(to put it) in a n. ...** pour résumer ..., bref ...

nutter ['nʌtər] *n Br F* dingue *mf*, toqué, -ée

nutty ['nʌtɪ] *adj* **(a)** (*in taste*) au goût de noisette; (*taste, flavour*) de noisette; (*containing nuts*) aux noisettes/noix/*etc* **(b)** *F* (*mad*) dingue; **as n. as a fruitcake** complètement dingue; **to be n. about sb/sth** raffoler de qn/qch

nuzzle ['nʌz(ə)l] *vti* **to n. (against) sb's shoulder** (*of dog, horse*) fourrer son nez sur l'épaule de qn; (*of person*) se blottir dans le creux de l'épaule de qn; **to n. sb's hand** fourrer son nez dans la paume de la main de qn; **he nuzzled her neck** il lui caressait le cou de ses lèvres; **the dog nuzzled up to my leg** le chien me reniflait la jambe

NY *abbr* **New York**

NYC *abbr* **New York City**

nylon ['naɪlɒn] *n Tex* nylon *m*; **n. sheets** draps *mpl* en nylon; **n. stockings** nylons, bas *mpl* nylon; **n. thread** fil *m* de nylon

nymph [nɪmf] *n* **(a)** *Myth* nymphe *f*; **tree** *or* **wood n.** hamadryade *f*; **sea n.** néréide *f*; **water n.** naïade *f* **(b)** *Ent* nymphe *f*

nymphet ['nɪmfɪt] *n* nymphette *f*

nympho, *pl* **-s** ['nɪmfəʊ, -z] *adj, n F* = **nymphomaniac**

nymphomania [nɪmfəʊ'meɪnɪə] *n Med* nymphomanie *f*

nymphomaniac [nɪmfəʊ'meɪnɪæk] *adj, n* nymphomane *f*

NYSE [enwaɪes'iː] *n abbr* **New York Stock Exchange**

NZ *abbr* **New Zealand**

O

O[1], o [əʊ] *n* **(a)** (*letter*) O, o *m*; **two Os** *or* **O's** deux O; *Sch, Hist Eng* **O-level (exam)**, *Scot* **O-grade (exam)** ≈ BEPC *m* (brevet élémentaire du premier cycle) **(b)** [①A71,3,a,5] *Tel etc* zéro *m*
O[2] *int* (*vocative*) O, ô
O[3] *abbr* **Ohio**
oaf, *pl* **-s** [əʊf, -s] *n* rustre *m*; **you clumsy o.!** espèce de gros empoté!
oafish ['əʊfɪʃ] *adj* rustre
oak [əʊk] *n* **(a) o. (tree)** chêne *m*; **o. apple** noix *f* de galle; **o. grove** chênaie *f*; **o. leaf** feuille *f* de chêne; **o. wood** (*forest*) bois *m* de chênes **(b) o. (wood)** (*material*) (bois de) chêne; **o. furniture** meubles *mpl* de *ou* en chêne; **dark o. (colour)** couleur *f* vieux chêne **(c)** *Old-fashioned Br Univ* = porte *f* extérieure d'un appartement dans les universités d'Oxford et Cambridge; **to sport one's o.** fermer sa porte aux visiteurs
oaken ['əʊk(ə)n] *adj* de *ou* en chêne
oakum ['əʊkəm] *n* étoupe *f* (noire), filasse *f*; **to pick o.** démêler *ou* tirer l'étoupe
OAP [əʊeɪ'piː] *n Br* (*abbr* **old age pensioner**) retraité, -ée
oar [ɔːr] *n* aviron *m*, rame *f*; (*as opposed to scull*) aviron de nage; *Fig F* **to put** *or* **stick one's o. in** mettre son grain de sel; **good o.** (*rower*) bon rameur, bonne rameuse
oarlock ['ɔːlɒk] *n Am* tolet *m*
oarsman, *pl* **-men** ['ɔːzmən] *n* rameur *m*
oarswoman, *pl* **-women** ['ɔːzwʊmən, -wɪmɪn] *n* rameuse *f*
OAS [əʊeɪ'es] *n* (*abbr* **Organization of American States**) OEA *f*
oasis, *pl* **oases** [əʊ'eɪsɪs, -iːz] *n* oasis *f*; *Fig* **an o. of calm** une oasis de calme
oast [əʊst] *n* séchoir *m* (à houblon)
oasthouse ['əʊsthaʊs] *n* sécherie *f* (de houblon)
oat [əʊt] *n* (*plant*) avoine *f* (commune); **oats** (*food*) avoine; **(porridge) oats** flocons *mpl* d'avoine; *Br Sl* **to get one's oats** (*have sex*) baiser, prendre son pied; *F* **to sow one's wild oats** faire des fredaines, jeter sa gourme; *F* **to be off one's oats** avoir perdu l'appétit; (*be off form*) être patraque; *F* **to be feeling one's oats** (*be self-important*) ne plus se sentir; (*be cheerful*) avoir la pêche
oatcake ['əʊtkeɪk] *n Culin* galette *f* d'avoine
oath, *pl* **oaths** [əʊθ, əʊðz] *n* **(a)** (*pledge*) serment *m*; **o. of allegiance** serment d'allégeance; **to take an o.**, *Jur* **to take the o.** prêter serment; **he took** *or* **swore an o. to avenge his father's death** il a juré de venger la mort de son père; *Jur* **to be on** *or* **under o.** être sous serment, être assermenté; *Jur* **to put sb on** *or* **under o.** faire prêter serment à qn; **she swore on her o. that ...** elle a juré sous serment que ... **(b)** (*swearword*) juron *m*, gros mot *m*
oatmeal ['əʊtmiːl] *n* farine *f* d'avoine; (*colour*) beige *m*; *Culin* **o. porridge**, *Am* **o.** bouillie *f* d'avoine, porridge *m*
OAU [əʊeɪ'juː] *n* (*abbr* **Organization of African Unity**) OUA *f*
OB [əʊ'biː] *n Br TV* (*abbr* **outside broadcast**) émission *f* en extérieur; **OB unit** car *m* régie, unité *f* mobile; **OB van** car *m* de reportage
obduracy ['ɒbdjʊrəsɪ] *n* entêtement *m*, obstination *f*
obdurate ['ɒbdjʊrɪt] *adj* (*stubborn*) (*person*) entêté, obstiné, têtu; (*refusal, attitude etc*) inflexible; **to remain o.** ne pas fléchir, rester inflexible; **to be o. in the face of pressure** ne pas fléchir sous la pression; **an o. sinner** un pécheur impénitent
obdurately ['ɒbdjʊrɪtlɪ] *adv* (*stubbornly*) avec entêtement; (*to resist*) inflexiblement; **to remain o. silent** garder un silence obstiné *ou* têtu; **to refuse o.** refuser obstinément, s'entêter à refuser
OBE [əʊbiː'iː] *n Br abbr* **Officer of the Order of the British Empire**
obedience [ə'biːdɪəns] *n* **(a)** obéissance *f* (**to sb** à qn; **to the law** à la loi); **to show o. to sb** se montrer obéissant envers qn **(b)** *Rel* **the Roman o.** l'obédience *f* de Rome
obedient [ə'biːdɪənt] *adj* obéissant; (*animal, child*) obéissant, docile; **to be o. to sb** être obéissant envers qn; *Arch* **Your o. servant** (*in letter*) votre serviteur dévoué
obediently [ə'biːdɪəntlɪ] *adv* docilement; **she had o. done everything which had been asked of her** elle s'était docilement exécutée
obelisk ['ɒbəlɪsk] *n* **(a)** *Archit* obélisque *m* **(b)** *Typ* croix *f*, obèle *m*; **double o.** diésis *m*
obese [əʊ'biːs] *adj* obèse
obeseness [əʊ'biːsnɪs] *n* obésité *f*
obesity [əʊ'biːsɪtɪ] *n* obésité *f*
obey [ə'beɪ] **1** *vt* (*person, order*) obéir à; **to o. the law** obéir à la loi; **his legs refused to o. him** ses jambes refusaient d'obéir **2** *vi* obéir
obfuscate ['ɒbfʌskeɪt] *vt* obscurcir
obfuscation [ɒbfə'skeɪʃən] *n* obscurcissement *m*
obituary [ə'bɪtjʊərɪ] *n* nécrologie *f*, notice *f* nécrologique; **o. (list)** registre *m* des morts, nécrologe *m*; *Journ* **the o. column, the obituaries** la nécrologie, la rubrique nécrologique; **o. notice** notice nécrologique
object[1] ['ɒbdʒɪkt] *n* **(a)** (*thing*) objet *m*; *Comptr* **o. code** code *m* objet; **o. finder** (*of microscope*) chercheur *m* d'objet; *Comptr* **o. linking and embedding** incorporation *f* d'objets liés

(b) (*subject etc*) objet *m*; **o. of pity/contempt** objet de pitié/mépris; **to be an o. of ridicule** être en butte au ridicule; **she was the o. of his desires** elle était l'objet de ses désirs; **o. of a contract** objet d'un contrat

(c) (*purpose*) but *m*, objectif *m*, fin *f*; **to have sth for** *or* **as an o.** avoir qch pour objectif *ou* pour but; **with this o. (in view)** dans cette intention, à cette fin; **with the sole o. of doing sth** à seule fin de faire qch; **what's the o. of the exercise** *or* **all this?** ça sert à quoi?, quel est le but de tout ceci?; **what is the o. of all this noise?** pourquoi tout ce bruit?; **to defeat one's o.** manquer son but; **the o. of the exercise** le but de l'exercice; **to succeed in** *or* **attain one's o.** atteindre son but

(d) (*obstacle*) **expense is no o.** peu importe le prix, le prix n'est pas un obstacle; **distance is no o.** la distance importe peu

(e) [①A73,b; B49-50,2] *Gram* **direct/indirect o.** complément *m* d'objet direct/indirect
object[2] [əb'dʒekt] *vi* faire une/des objection(s); **to o. to sth** faire objection à qch; (*of demonstrators etc*) protester contre qch; **he objected to being asked to help** il a protesté parce qu'on lui a demandé d'aider; **I o. to being treated like a child** je n'aime pas qu'on me prenne pour un gamin; **to o. to doing sth** se refuser à faire qch; **I o. to the fact that ...** ce qui me dérange (vraiment), c'est que ...; **to o. to sb** avoir des objections à faire contre qn; **I don't o. to his** *or* **him coming here but ...** je ne vois pas d'objection à ce qu'il vienne ici mais ...; **he objects (to it)** il s'y oppose; **I o.!** je ne suis pas d'accord!, je proteste!; **if no one objects** si personne n'y voit d'objection(s); *Jur* **to o. to a witness** récuser un témoin
objection [əb'dʒekʃən] *n* **(a)** (*protest*) objection *f*; **no objections were raised at the time** cela n'avait soulevé aucune objection à l'époque; **to make no o. to** *or* **against sth** ne pas voir d'objection à qch; **I have no o. to her doing so** je n'ai pas d'objection à ce qu'elle le fasse; **I have no o. to him** je n'ai rien contre lui; **if you have no o.** si vous n'y voyez pas d'inconvénient; **to raise an o.** soulever une objection; *Jur* **o. to a witness** récusation *f* de témoin; **does anyone have any objection(s)?** est-ce que quelqu'un a une objection *ou F* quelque chose contre?; **does anyone have any objections if I open the window?** est-ce que quelqu'un verrait un inconvénient à ce que j'ouvre la fenêtre?

(b) (*reason for objecting*) inconvénient *m*; **the chief o. to your plan is its cost** le plus grand inconvénient de votre projet, c'est son coût; **I see no o. (to it)** je n'y vois pas d'inconvénient
objectionable [əb'dʒekʃənəb(ə)l] *adj* (*unpleasant*) désagréable; (*person*) insupportable; (*view, state of affairs*) inacceptable; (*language etc*) choquant
objective [əb'dʒektɪv] **1** *adj* **(a)** objectif; **let's be o.** soyons objectifs; **it is an o. fact that ...** le fait est que ... **(b)** *Gram* (*case*) accusatif **2** *n* **(a)** (*aim, goal*) objectif *m*, but *m*; **to**

achieve one's objectives atteindre ses objectifs; **the committee has set out its objectives** le comité a fixé ses objectifs **(b)** *Opt* objectif *m* **(c)** *Gram* cas *m* régime, cas accusatif
objectively [əb'dʒektɪvlɪ] *adv* objectivement, d'une manière objective
objectivism [əb'dʒektɪvɪz(ə)m] *n* objectivisme *m*
objectivity [ɒbdʒek'tɪvɪtɪ] *n* objectivité *f*
object lesson *n* bon exemple *m* **(in diplomacy** *etc* de diplomatie *etc*); **an o. lesson in how to be successful in business** une parfaite illustration de la manière de réussir dans les affaires; **an o. lesson in what not to do** l'exemple par excellence de ce qu'il ne faut pas faire
objector [əb'dʒektər] *n Pol etc* opposant *m*, personne *f* qui émet des objections; **the objectors to the plan** les personnes qui s'opposent au projet
object-orientated ['ɒbdʒɪkt'ɔ:rɪənteɪtɪd] *adj Comptr* orienté objet; **o. language** langage *m* à objets; **o. programming** programmation *f* par objets
oblate ['ɒbleɪt] *adj Math etc* aplati (aux pôles), raccourci
obligate ['ɒblɪgeɪt] *vt* **to o. sb to do sth** mettre qn dans l'obligation de faire qch; **to feel obligated to help** se sentir dans l'obligation d'aider; **to be obligated to do sth** avoir l'obligation de faire qch; **to feel obligated to sb** se sentir redevable envers qn
obligation [ɒblɪ'geɪʃən] *n* [①**A58-9**,e,f; **B36**,K,1,a] obligation *f*; **to put sb/to feel under an o. to ...** mettre qn/se sentir dans l'obligation de ...; **moral o.** obligation morale; **to be under an o. to do sth** être dans l'obligation de faire qch; **I am under no o. to go with them** rien ne m'oblige à les accompagner; *Com* **without o.** sans engagement; **to do sth out of (a sense of) o.** faire qch parce que l'on s'y sent obligé; **to be under an o. to sb** avoir une dette de reconnaissance envers qn; **I am under a great o. to him** je lui suis redevable de beaucoup; *Com* **to meet one's obligations** faire face à ses engagements
obligatory [ɒ'blɪgət(ə)rɪ] *adj* obligatoire; **after the o. exchange of greetings** après les salutations de rigueur; **ties are o.** la cravate est obligatoire
oblige [ə'blaɪdʒ] **1** *vt* **(a)** (*compel*) obliger, astreindre **(sb to do sth** qn à faire qch); **to be obliged to do sth** être obligé *ou* tenu de faire qch; *Admin* être astreint à faire qch; **I feel obliged to tell him** je me vois contraint de lui dire
(b) (*do a favour for*) rendre service à, *Fml* obliger; **he did it to o. us** il l'a fait pour nous rendre service *ou* par complaisance
(c) (*make indebted*) (*usu passive*) **to be obliged to sb** être reconnaissant à qn **(for sth** pour qch); *F* **much obliged** merci beaucoup; **I would be obliged if you would ...** je vous serais reconnaissant de bien vouloir ...
2 *vi* **he did it to o.** il l'a fait pour rendre service *ou* par complaisance; **to be always willing to o.** etre très obligeant *ou* toujours prêt à rendre service; **anything to o.** tout ce que vous voudrez pour vous faire plaisir; **I'm sorry, I can't o.** je suis désolé, je ne peux pas
obliging [ə'blaɪdʒɪŋ] *adj* obligeant, serviable; **that's very o. of you** c'est très aimable de votre part
obligingly [ə'blaɪdʒɪŋlɪ] *adv* obligeamment, complaisamment, complaisamment; *also Iron* **they had very o. left the door open** ils avaient été assez aimables pour laisser la porte ouverte
oblique [ə'bli:k] **1** *adj* (*line, angle*) oblique **(to** à); (*indirect*) (*reference, hint etc*) indirect; **o. glance** regard *m* en biais; *Gram* **o. case** cas *m* indirect *ou* oblique **2** *n* (*line*) (ligne *f*) oblique *f*; *Geom* (*figure*) figure *f* oblique; *Anat* (muscle *m*) oblique *m*; *Typ* barre *f* transversale *ou* oblique
obliquely [ə'bli:klɪ] *adv* obliquement, de biais, obliquement; (*indirectly*) (*to refer*) d'une façon indirecte; (*to glance*) de *ou* en biais
obliqueness [ə'bli:knɪs], **obliquity** [ə'blɪkwɪtɪ] *n also Geom* obliquité *f*; (*indirectness*) caractère *m* indirect
obliterate [ə'blɪtəreɪt] *vt* (*erase*) (*figures, footprints, traces etc*) effacer; (*the past, a culture*) annihiler; (*a stamp*) oblitérer; (*destroy*) (*buildings etc*) détruire; **the town had been all but obliterated during the war** la ville avait été quasiment rayée de la carte pendant la guerre
obliteration [əblɪtə'reɪʃən] *n* (*erasing*) effacement *m*; (*of past, culture etc*) anéantissement *m*; (*destruction*) (*of buildings, town, evidence etc*) destruction *f*
oblivion [ə'blɪvɪən] *n* oubli *m*; **to fall** *or* **sink into o.** tomber dans l'oubli; **to consign to o.** condamner à l'oubli
oblivious [ə'blɪvɪəs] *adj* oublieux **(of, to** de); **I was o. of** *or* **to what was going on** je n'étais pas conscient *ou* je n'avais pas conscience de ce qui se passait; **he was o. to danger** il était inconscient du danger
obliviously [ə'blɪvɪəslɪ] *adv* (*to carry on etc*) en toute inconscience
oblong ['ɒblɒŋ] **1** *adj* oblong, -ongue; (*face etc*) allongé **2** *n* rectangle *m*
obloquy ['ɒbləkwɪ] *n Fml* opprobre *m*
obnoxious [əb'nɒkʃəs] *adj* (*person, action etc*) odieux; (*smell etc*) repoussant
oboe ['əubəu] *n Mus* hautbois *m*; **o. (player)** hautboïste *mf*
oboist ['əubəuɪst] *n Mus* hautboïste *mf*
obscene [əb'si:n] *adj* (*indecent*) (*song, telephone call, word etc*) obscène; *Fig* (*profits, prices, demands etc*) scandaleux; **it's o. that they are so rich when people are starving** il est scandaleux *ou* révoltant qu'ils soient aussi riches alors qu'il y a des gens qui meurent de faim
obscenely [əb'si:nlɪ] *adv* d'une manière obscène; **o. rich** scandaleusement riche
obscenity [əb'senɪtɪ] *n* obscénité *f*; **disgusted by the o. of such profits/salaries** dégoûté par ces bénéfices/salaires scandaleux; **the o. of people earning millions while others starve** le caractère scandaleux *ou* révoltant d'une situation où certains gagnent des millions tandis que d'autres meurent de faim; **o. laws** lois *fpl* concernant les outrages à la pudeur
obscurantism [ɒbskjʊ'ræntɪz(ə)m] *n* obscurantisme *m*
obscurantist [ɒbskjʊ'ræntɪst] *adj, n* obscurantiste *mf*
obscure[1] [əb'skjʊər] *adj* **(a)** (*unclear*) (*speech, book etc*) obscur; **for some o. reason he thought it would help** il pensait, pour d'obscures raisons, que ça serait utile **(b)** (*little known*) (*birth, background*) obscur; (*author, book*) inconnu, peu connu, obscur; (*village etc*) inconnu, ignoré **(c)** (*vague*) (*feeling*) vague, obscur **(d)** (*dark*) obscur, sombre, ténébreux; **to grow** *or* **become o.** s'obscurcir, s'assombrir
obscure[2] *vt* **(a)** (*hide from view*) cacher; **to o. sth from sb's view** cacher qch à qn **(b)** (*make unclear*) (*argument, facts, truth*) obscurcir **(c)** (*overshadow*) éclipser, voiler **(d)** (*darken*) obscurcir, assombrir
obscurely [əb'skjʊəlɪ] *adv* **(a)** (*to speak*) de façon obscure *ou* mystérieuse **(b)** (*to feel, see*) vaguement, obscurément
obscurity [əb'skjʊərɪtɪ] *n* obscurité *f*; *Fig* **to sink back into o.** retomber dans l'oubli
obsequies ['ɒbsɪkwɪz] *npl* obsèques *fpl*, funérailles *fpl*
obsequious [əb'si:kwɪəs] *adj* obséquieux
obsequiously [əb'si:kwɪəslɪ] *adv* obséquieusement
obsequiousness [əb'si:kwɪəsnɪs] *n* obséquiosité *f*
observable [əb'zɜ:vəb(ə)l] *adj* observable; (*change, difference, improvement*) perceptible; **it was o. that ...** on a pu observer que ...
observance [əb'zɜ:vəns] *n* **(a)** (*of law, custom etc*) observation *f*, observance *f* **(b)** (*practice*) **religious observances** pratiques *fpl* religieuses
observant [əb'zɜ:vənt] *adj* observateur, -trice **(of** de); **that's very o. of you** tu es bien observateur
observation [ɒbzə'veɪʃən] *n* **(a)** observation *f*; *Mil* (*of terrain, enemy*) surveillance *f*; **to put/keep under o.** (*house, premises*) mettre/tenir en observation; (*person*) mettre/tenir sous surveillance; **this fact has not escaped his o.** ce fait n'a pas échappé à sa vigilance; *Med* **to keep sb in hospital for o.** garder qn en observation à l'hôpital; **to take an o.** (*in surveying*), *Astron* faire une observation; *Naut* faire le point; **o. aircraft** avion *m* de reconnaissance; *Rail* **o. coach** *or* **car** voiture *f* panoramique
(b) (*remark*) observation *f*, remarque *f*; **to make an o.** faire une observation *ou* une remarque **(about sb/sth** sur qn/qch)
observational research [ɒbzə'veɪʃən(ə)l] *n* étude *f* par observation
observation point *n* point *m* d'observation
observation post *n Mil* poste *m* d'observation
observation satellite *n Astronaut* satellite *m* d'observation
observation ward *n Med* salle *f* d'observation
observatory [əb'zɜ:vət(ə)rɪ] *n* observatoire *m*
observe [əb'zɜ:v] *vt* **(a)** (*stars etc*) observer; **to o. the enemy's movements** surveiller les mouvements ennemis **(b)** (*notice*) (*fact etc*) remarquer, noter; **he didn't o. her leaving** il ne l'a pas vue partir **(c)** (*say*) **to o. that ...** observer *ou* faire remarquer que ... **(d)** (*respect, follow*) (*the law, the proprieties, a fast*) observer; (*the Sabbath*) respecter, observer; (*order*) se conformer à; **to o. silence** observer le silence; **a two minutes' silence was observed** on observa/ ils observèrent/*etc* deux minutes de silence
observer [əb'zɜ:vər] *n* **(a)** (*watcher*) observateur, -trice; **to be a close o. of sth** observer qch de près; **to be a keen o. of sth** suivre qch attentivement **(b) a strict o. of protocol** une personne qui respecte *ou* observe le protocole à la lettre **(c)** (*expert*) expert *m*, spécialiste *mf* **(of** de); **political observers** experts *ou* spécialistes en politique

obsess [əb'ses] *vt* obséder; **to be obsessed with** *or* **by an idea** être obsédé *ou* hanté par une idée; **to be obsessed with sb** être obsédé par qn

obsession [əb'seʃən] *n* obsession *f* **(with** de); **to have an o. with sb/an idea** être obsédé par qn/une idée; **it's becoming a bit of an o.** ça tourne à l'obsession; **cleanliness is an o. with her** c'est une maniaque de la propreté

obsessional [əb'seʃən(ə)l] *adj* obsessionel; **to be o. about sth/sb** être obsédé par qch/qn

obsessive [əb'sesɪv] **1** *adj* (*person*) à tendances obsessionnelles; (*behaviour, hatred, fear*) obsessionnel; (*idea, image*) obsédant; **he was becoming quite o. about it** ça devenait une obsession chez lui; **she never struck me as the o. type** elle ne m'a jamais semblé être du genre obsessionnel **2** *n* **he's a bit of an o.** il est du genre obsessionnel; **our boss is a real o. when it comes to punctuality** la ponctualité est une véritable obsession chez notre patron; **you're turning into an o.** ça tourne à l'obsession chez toi

obsessively [əb'sesɪvlɪ] *adv* de manière obsessionnelle; **he's o. concerned with his appearance** il est obsédé par son apparence; **to be o. afraid of sth** avoir une peur maladive de qch; **he is o. tidy** c'est un maniaque de la propreté; **she is almost o. interested in birds/politics** son intérêt pour les oiseaux/la politique frise l'obsession

obsolescence [ɒbsə'les(ə)ns] *n* (*of law, ideas*) caractère *m* désuet; (*of word, term*) vieillissement *m*; *Ind etc* (*of equipment*) obsolescence *f*; **to fall into o.** tomber en désuétude; *Ind* **planned o.** obsolescence prévue; *Ind, Com* **built-in o.** obsolescence programmée

obsolescent [ɒbsə'les(ə)nt] *adj* (*equipment*) obsolescent; (*falling into disuse*) qui tombe en désuétude; (*word, term*) qui vieillit, qui a vieilli

obsolete ['ɒbsəliːt] *adj* (*word, idea, law*) désuet, -ète, tombé en désuétude; (*design etc*) démodé, dépassé; (*technique, equipment*) obsolète, périmé; (*ship*) déclassé; (*institution*) caduc, -que

obstacle ['ɒbstək(ə)l] *n* obstacle *m*; **to be an o. to sth** faire obstacle à qch; **to put obstacles in sb's way** faire obstacle à qn; **o. course** *Mil* parcours *m ou* piste *f* d'obstacles; *Fig* parcours du combattant; **it's only one part of the o. course of finding a job** ce n'est qu'un bout du parcours du combattant qu'il faut suivre pour trouver un emploi; *Sp* **o. race** course *f* d'obstacles

obstetric(al) [ɒb'stetrɪk, -ɪk(ə)l] *adj* obstétrical

obstetrician [ɒbste'trɪʃən] *n* médecin *m* accoucheur, obstétricien, -ienne

obstetrics [ɒb'stetrɪks] *n* (①**A10**, c) obstétrique *f*

obstinacy ['ɒbstɪnəsɪ] *n* (*of person*) obstination *f*, entêtement *m*; (*of resistance*) ténacité *f*; *Med* (*of disease*) persistance *f*

obstinate ['ɒbstɪnɪt] *adj* **(a)** (*person, refusal*) obstiné **(in doing sth** à faire qch); (*resistance etc*) tenace; **to be o.** s'entêter, s'obstiner **(b)** (*illness, cold, spot*) tenace, coriace; (*stain, grease*) rebelle

obstinately ['ɒbstɪnɪtlɪ] *adv* obstinément; (*to resist*) avec acharnement; **to behave o.** se montrer obstiné

obstreperous [əb'strepərəs] *adj* (*rebellious*) rebelle; (*noisy*) bruyant, tapageur; **don't get o. with me!** ne me faites pas d'histoires!; **to get o. about sth** faire un scandale de qch

obstreperously [əb'strepərəslɪ] *adv* (*rebelliously*) *F* en rouspétant; (*noisily*) bruyamment, tapageusement; **to behave o.** faire des histoires

obstreperousness [əb'strepərəsnɪs] *n* (*of crowd, children*) caractère *m* tapageur; (*of sb's tone*) agressivité *f*; **I won't put up with your o. any longer** j'en ai assez de tes caprices et de ton agressivité

obstruct [əb'strʌkt] **1** *vt* **(a)** (*block*) (*road etc*) obstruer, encombrer; (*pipe etc*) boucher; *Med* (*intestine*) oblitérer, obstruer; (*view*) boucher, cacher; **her view was obstructed by a tall man** un homme de haute taille lui bouchait *ou* cachait la vue

(b) (*hinder progress*) (*person's movements, attempts*) gêner, entraver; (*traffic, shipping*) entraver; (*reforms, inquiry, investigation*) faire obstruction à; **to o. sb's path** barrer le chemin à qn; *Jur* **to o. the course of justice** entraver le cours de la justice; **to o. sb in the execution of his duty** gêner qn dans l'exercice de ses fonctions; *Sp* **to o. another player** faire obstruction; *Parl* **to o. a bill** faire obstruction

2 *vi Sp* faire obstruction

obstruction [əb'strʌkʃən] *n* **(a)** (*action*) (*of street*) obstruction *f*; (*of pipe etc*) engorgement *m*; *Med* (*of intestine*) obstruction, oblitération *f*; (*of traffic, person in their affairs etc*) entravement *m*; *Sp, Pol* obstruction **(b)** (*blockage*) (*in road*) encombrement *m*; (*to shipping*) entrave *f*; (*in pipe*) engorgement *m*; **to cause an o.** (*on road*) entraver la circulation; *Rail* **an o. on the line** un obstacle sur la voie

obstructionism [əb'strʌkʃənɪz(ə)m] *n Pol* obstructionnisme *m*

obstructionist [əb'strʌkʃənɪst] *adj, n Pol* obstructionniste *mf*

obstructive [əb'strʌktɪv] *adj* (*person*) qui fait de l'obstruction, qui met des bâtons dans les roues; (*tactic, attitude*) d'obstruction; *Med* obstructif, obstruant; *Parl etc* **to be o.** faire de l'obstruction, être obstructionniste

obtain [əb'teɪn] **1** *vt* (*information, money etc*) obtenir; **to o. sugar from beet** extraire du sucre de la betterave; **I obtained permission to see him** j'ai obtenu la permission de le voir **2** *vi Fml* (*of practice etc*) avoir cours; (*of rules*) être en vigueur

obtainable [əb'teɪnəb(ə)l] *adj* **easily o.** facile à obtenir; **this model is only o. in America** on ne peut se procurer ce modèle qu'en Amérique

obtrude [əb'truːd] *Fml* **1** *vt* mettre en avant; **to o. one's opinions on others** imposer ses opinions à autrui; **to o. oneself** s'imposer **2** *vi* **(a)** (*of person*) s'imposer **(b)** (*of object*) dépasser **(from** de)

obtrusion [əb'truːʒən] *n* intrusion *f*

obtrusive [əb'truːsɪv] *adj* **(a)** (*person, behaviour, question*) importun, indiscret **(b)** (*smell etc*) pénétrant

obtrusively [əb'truːsɪvlɪ] *adv* importunément; (*to behave*) indiscrètement; **the lights were o. bright** l'éclairage ôtait tout sentiment d'intimité

obtrusiveness [əb'truːsɪvnɪs] *n* **(a)** (*of behaviour, presence*) importunité *f* **(b)** (*of smell*) caractère *m* pénétrant

obtuse [əb'tjuːs] *adj* **(a)** (*person, mind*) obtus; (*behaviour, remark*) stupide; **you're being deliberately o.** tu fais exprès de ne pas comprendre **(b)** (*blunt-ended*) obtus, émoussé; *Geom* **o. angle** angle obtus

obtuseness [əb'tjuːsnɪs] *n* (*of person, behaviour, remark*) stupidité *f*

obverse ['ɒbvɜːs] **1** *adj* **o. side** (*of medal*) avers *m*, face *f* **2** *n* (*of medal*) avers *m*, face *f*; (*of truth etc*) opposé *m*

obviate ['ɒbvɪeɪt] *vt* (*difficulty etc*) parer à, obvier à; (*objection*) répondre à; **this obviates the need to ...** ceci pare à la nécessité de ...

obvious ['ɒbvɪəs] **1** *adj* évident, clair, manifeste; (*lie, displeasure*) manifeste; (*feature*) frappant; **it's quite o. that she is lying** il est évident *ou* clair *ou* manifeste qu'elle ment, elle ment, cela saute aux yeux; **you were too o.** (*unsubtle*) tu n'as pas été très subtil; **it was the o. thing to do** c'était tout indiqué, cela s'imposait; **an o. comparison would be with the French Revolution** la première comparaison qui vient à l'esprit est la révolution française; **his patriotism is a little (too) o.** son patriotisme sonne faux; **there was a very o. stain in the middle** il y avait une tache bien visible en plein milieu; **there are several o. objections to the plan** ce projet présente plusieurs inconvénients on ne peut plus évidents; *Com* **o. defect** vice *m* apparent

2 *n* **to state the o.** enfoncer une porte ouverte; **it would be stating the o. to say that we were surprised by the news** il va sans dire que ces nouvelles nous ont surpris; **to miss the o.** passer à côté de l'essentiel

obviously ['ɒbvɪəslɪ] *adv* **(a)** (*in an obvious way*) manifestement; **he's so o. English** il est si manifestement anglais; **he did it so o.** il l'a fait si ostensiblement; **they are different, but not o.** ils sont différents, mais ça ne saute pas aux yeux; **he wasn't o. the right choice but ...** au premier abord il n'était pas évident que c'était le bon choix mais ...

(b) (*of course*) évidemment; **do you prefer this? – o.** préférez-vous cela? – bien sûr *ou* (*in exasperation*) évidemment; **o. not!** bien sûr que non!, évidemment non!; **I'll o. have to turn the offer down** il va sans dire que je vais devoir refuser l'offre

obviousness ['ɒbvɪəsnɪs] *n* évidence *f*, clarté *f*; (*of lie*) caractère *m* manifeste; **the o. of his displeasure** son mécontentement manifeste

OC [əʊ'siː] *n Mil* (*abbr* **Officer Commanding**) chef *m* de corps

ocarina [ɒkə'riːnə] *n Mus* ocarina *m*

occasion[1] [ə'keɪʒən] *n* **(a)** (*time*) occasion *f*; **on this o.** en cette occasion; **this is not the o. to discuss such matters** les circonstances sont peu appropriées pour parler de ces choses; *Fml* **on the o. of his daughter's marriage** à l'occasion du mariage de sa fille; **I am prepared to overlook it on this o., but ...** je veux bien fermer les yeux cette fois-ci, mais ...; **on one o.** une fois; **on another o.** une autre fois; **on several occasions** à plusieurs reprises; **on rare occasions** rarement; **on such an o.** en pareille occasion; **on great occasions** dans les grandes occasions; **words appropriate to the o.** paroles de circonstance; **to dress to suit the o.** mettre la tenue appropriée; **she could have dressed to suit the o.** elle aurait pu faire l'effort de s'habiller un peu mieux

(b) **on o.** (*occasionally*) parfois, de temps en temps

(c) (*event*) événement *m*; **her wedding was quite an o.** son mariage a été un grand événement *ou* n'a pas été une petite affaire; **an o. to remember** un événement mémorable; **we'll make this an o. to remember** nous allons fêter ça dans les règles; **there was a real sense of o.** il y avait une vraie atmosphère de célébration; **he has no sense of o.** (*for celebration*) il n'a pas le sens de la fête; (*for serious event*) il n'a pas le sens des convenances

(d) (*opportunity*) occasion *f*; **I'll speak to him on the first o.** je lui parlerai à la première occasion; **should the o. arise** si l'occasion se présente, s'il y a lieu, le cas échéant

(e) *Fml* (*cause*) sujet *m*, cause *f*; **to have o. to suspect sb/to be angry** avoir lieu de soupçonner qn/d'être en colère; **there's** *or* **you have no o. to be alarmed** il n'y a pas lieu de vous inquiéter; **this action was the o. of great suffering** cette action a donné lieu à de grandes souffrances

occasion[2] *vt Fml* (*fear, inconvenience, surprise etc*) causer; (*response*) susciter, provoquer

occasional [ə'keɪʒ(ə)nəl] *adj* (a) (*visit*) espacé, occasionnel; (*incident*) qui se produit de temps en temps, occasionnel; **I still get the o. twinge in my back** mon dos m'élance toujours un peu de temps en temps; **o. showers** averses *fpl* éparses *ou* occasionnelles; **I have the o. cigarette/glass of wine** il m'arrive de fumer une cigarette/de boire un verre de vin; **he is an o. smoker** il ne fume qu'occasionnellement (b) (*play, verse etc*) de circonstance; **o. chair** chaise *f* volante; **o. table** table *f* volante, guéridon *m*

occasionally [ə'keɪʒən(ə)lɪ] *adv* de temps en temps, parfois, occasionnellement; **we only see them very o. nowadays** nous ne les voyons que très occasionnellement *ou* de loin en loin ces temps-ci

occident ['ɒksɪdənt] *n* occident *m*, couchant *m*; *Pol etc* **the O.** l'Occident

occidental [ɒksɪ'dent(ə)l] *adj* occidental

occipital [ɒk'sɪpɪt(ə)l] *adj, n Anat* occipital *m*

occiput ['ɒksɪpʌt] *n Anat* occiput *m*

occlude [ə'klu:d] *vt Fml* (*opening etc*) occlure, fermer, boucher; (*eyelids, Ch gas*) occlure

occlusion [ə'klu:ʒən] *n* (a) (*of pipe etc, Ch of gas*) occlusion *f* (b) (*of tooth*) occlusion *f* (molaire/*etc*)

occlusive [ə'klu:sɪv] *Ling* **1** *adj* **o. consonant** consonne *f* occlusive **2** *n* (consonne *f*) occlusive *f*

occult [ɒ'kʌlt, 'ɒkʌlt] **1** *adj* occulte, secret, -ète; **the o. sciences** les sciences *fpl* occultes **2** *n* **the o.** l'occulte *m*

occultism ['ɒkʌltɪz(ə)m] *n* occultisme *m*

occupancy ['ɒkjʊpənsɪ] *n* (a) *Jur* possession *f* à titre de premier occupant (b) (*of building*) occupation *f*, habitation *f*; **o. forecast** (*in hotels*) prévision *f* du taux d'occupation; **o. levels** (*in hotels*) niveaux *mpl* d'occupation

occupant ['ɒkjʊpənt] *n* (*of house etc*) occupant, -ante; *Jur* premier occupant; (*of car etc*) occupant *m*; (*of job*) titulaire *mf*; (*of seat on board, of position*) détenteur, -trice

occupation [ɒkjʊ'peɪʃən] *n* (a) [①B4,B,2,b] (*activity*) occupation *f*; (*profession*) métier *m*, profession *f*; (*on form*) qualité *f*; **a leisure o.** un loisir (b) (*of house, land*) occupation *f*; **to be in o. of a house** occuper une maison; **how long have they been in o.?** cela fait combien de temps qu'ils occupent les lieux?; **fit for o.** (*house*) habitable; **army/troops of o.** armée *f*/troupes *fpl* d'occupation; **they decided to organize an o. of the Embassy** ils ont décidé d'organiser l'occupation de l'Ambassade; *Hist* **the Roman o. of Britain** l'occupation de la Grande-Bretagne par les Romains; *Hist* **the O.** (*of France*) l'Occupation *f*

occupational [ɒkjʊ'peɪʃən(ə)l] *adj* **o. disease** maladie *f* professionnelle; **o. hazard** risque *m* du métier; **o. illness** maladie professionnelle; *Med* **o. medicine** médecine *f* du travail; **o. therapist** ergothérapeute *mf*; **o. therapy** thérapeutique *f* occupationnelle, ergothérapie *f*

occupied ['ɒkjʊpaɪd] *adj* (a) (*house, Mil territory*) occupé; **this seat is o.** cette place est prise; **in o. France** dans la France occupée *ou* de l'Occupation (b) (*busy*) **to be o. in** *or* **with doing sth** être occupé à faire qch; **he was o. with thoughts of ...** il était occupé à penser à ...; **to keep sb o.** occuper qn; **to keep one's mind o.** s'occuper l'esprit

occupier ['ɒkjʊpaɪər] *n* (*tenant*) locataire *mf*; (*of house*) occupant, -ante, habitant, -ante; **to the o.** (*on letter*) à l'attention de l'occupant

occupy ['ɒkjʊpaɪ] *vt* (a) (*house etc*) occuper, habiter; (*land*) occuper; (*position*) occuper, remplir; *Mil* (*enemy country*) occuper; (*strategic point*) s'emparer de; **the workers have occupied the building** les ouvriers ont occupé le bâtiment (b) (*room, space, attention*) occuper; **to o. one's time (in** *or* **with) doing sth** occuper son temps à faire qch; **her work occupies all her time** son travail occupe tout son temps; **it occupied two hours of the afternoon** cela a pris deux heures dans l'après-midi; **to o. one's mind** s'occuper l'esprit

occur [ə'kɜ:r] *vi* (**-rr-**) (a) (*happen*) (*of event etc*) avoir lieu, arriver, se produire; (*of opportunity, vacancy*) se présenter; (*of accident*) avoir lieu, se produire; **this seldom occurs** cela arrive rarement; **I hope it will not o. again** j'espère que cela ne se répétera pas

(b) (*be present*) (*of objects, types etc*) se rencontrer, se trouver, se présenter; **this word occurs twice in the letter** on trouve *ou* on rencontre ce mot deux fois dans la lettre

(c) (*of idea etc*) venir à l'esprit; **this thought has occurred to me** cela m'est déjà venu à l'esprit; **it didn't o. to them that she might be lying** il ne leur est pas venu à l'esprit que peut-être elle mentait

occurrence [ə'kʌrəns] *n* (a) **two hours before its o.** deux heures avant que cela eût lieu; *Fml* **to be of frequent o.** arriver *ou* se produire fréquemment; **the o. of two murders on the same day** le fait que deux meurtres aient été commis le même jour; **the o. of leukemia in this community is twice ...** le nombre des cas de leucémie dans cette communauté est le double de ...; **the o. of storms** (*frequency*) la fréquence des tempêtes; **to prevent the o. of violence** combattre (le phénomène de) la violence

(b) (*event*) fait *m*, événement *m*; **an everyday o.** un fait quotidien; **a singular o.** un fait étrange; **this was the first o. of its kind** c'était la première fois qu'un événement de cette espèce se produisait

ocean ['əʊʃən] *n* océan *m*; **the Atlantic O.** l'océan Atlantique; *Fig* **an o. of sand** une mer de sable; *Fig* **we've got oceans of time** nous avons énormément de temps; **o. current** courant *m* océanique; **o. floor** fond *m* sous-marin; **o. freight** fret *m* maritime

ocean-going *adj* (*ship*) au long cours, de haute mer

Oceania [əʊʃɪ'eɪnɪə] *n* Océanie *f*

oceanic [əʊʃɪ'ænɪk] *adj* (*voyage, climate*) océanique

oceanographer [əʊʃə'nɒgrəfər] *n* océanographe *mf*

oceanography [əʊʃə'nɒgrəfɪ] *n* océanographie *f*

ocelot ['ɒsəlɒt] *n* ocelot *m*

ochre, *US* **ocher** ['əʊkər] **1** *n Miner* ocre *f*; **red o.** ocre rouge; **yellow o.** jaune *m* d'ocre, ocre jaune **2** *adj* **o.(-coloured)** ocre *inv*

o'clock [ə'klɒk] *adv* [①A75,A; B58,A] **one o.** une heure; **two/three o.** deux/trois heures; **at four o.** à quatre heures; **the seven o. train** le train de sept heures

OCR [əʊsi:'ɑ:r] *n Comptr* (a) (*abbr* **optical character reader**) lecteur *m* (à reconnaissance) optique de caractères, lecteur OCR (b) (*abbr* **optical character recognition**) reconnaissance *f* optique des caractères; **O. font** fonte *f* reconnue optiquement; **O. software** logiciel *m* de reconnaissance de caractères, logiciel d'OCR

octagon ['ɒktəgən] *n Geom* octogone *m*

octagonal [ɒk'tægən(ə)l] *adj Geom* octogonal

octahedral [ɒktə'hi:drəl, -'hed-] *adj Geom* octaédrique

octahedron, *pl* **-ons, -a** ['ɒktə'hi:drən, -'hed-, -ənz, -ə] *n Geom* octaèdre *m*

octane ['ɒkteɪn] *n Ch* octane *m*; **o. number** *or* **rating** indice *m* d'octane

octave ['ɒktɪv] *n Rel, Mus, Fencing* octave *f*; (*in poetry*) huitain *m*; *Mus* **an o. apart** à une octave de différence

octavo [ɒk'teɪvəʊ] *adj, n Typ* in-octavo *m inv*

octet [ɒk'tet] *n* (a) *Mus* octuor *m* (b) (*in poetry*) huitain *m* (c) *Ch* octet *m*

October [ɒk'təʊbər] *n* [①A75-6,B-C; B58-9,B-C] octobre *m*; **in O.** au mois d'octobre, en octobre; **(on) the first/seventh of O.** le premier/sept octobre; **an O. morning** un matin d'octobre

octogenarian [ɒktədʒɪ'neərɪən] *adj, n* octogénaire *mf*

octopod ['ɒktəpɒd] *adj, n* octopode *m*

octopus ['ɒktəpəs] *n* poulpe *m*, pieuvre *f*

octosyllabic [ɒktəsɪ'læbɪk] *adj* (*verse, word*) octosyllabe, octosyllabique

octuple ['ɒktju:p(ə)l] *adj, n* octuple *m*

ocular ['ɒkjʊlər] **1** *adj* (*nerve etc*) oculaire **2** *n Opt* (*of microscope etc*) oculaire *m*

oculist ['ɒkjʊlɪst] *n* oculiste *mf*

OD[1] [əʊ'di:] *n F* (*abbr* **overdose**) overdose *f*

OD[2] (*pt, pp* **OD'd**) *vi F* (*abbr* **overdose**) prendre une overdose (**on** de); *Fig Sl* **I think I've rather OD'd on pizzas** je crois que j'ai un peu forcé sur les pizzas; **they OD'd on soap-operas** ils se sont pris une overdose de séries télévisées

odalisk, odalisque ['əʊdəlɪsk] *n* odalisque *f*

odd [ɒd] *adj* (a) (*strange*) bizarre; *Com* **o. size** taille *f* peu courante; **the o. thing about it is that ...** le curieux de l'affaire *ou* ce qui est bizarre c'est que ...; **it's o. your not knowing about it** c'est drôle *ou* bizarre que vous n'en sachiez rien; **it would look o. to refuse** ça ferait drôle si tu refusais/on refusait/*etc*; **how o. that he should have forgotten it!** comme c'est drôle *ou* bizarre qu'il l'ait oublié!; **(well,) that's o.!** voilà qui est bizarre *ou* singulier!, c'est curieux!; **an o. way of saying sorry** une drôle de manière *ou* une curieuse manière de s'excuser

(b) *Math etc* (*number*) impair; *Comptr* **o. parity** parité *f* impaire

(c) (*one of a set*) dépareillé; (*one of a pair*) déparié, dépareillé; **o. socks** chaussettes dépareillées; **o. lot** *Com* articles *mpl* dépareillés; *St Exch* = nombre *m* d'actions ne correspondant pas à l'unité habituelle; **to be the o. man (out)** être en trop; *Fig* être à part; **to play at o. man out** jouer à qui sera éliminé; **she was the o. woman out, not being German** n'étant pas allemande, elle faisait figure d'exception; **which of these books is the o. one out?** lequel de ces livres n'a rien à voir avec les autres?, trouvez l'intrus

(d) (*occasional*) **they got the o. tin of food** on leur servait des boîtes de conserve de temps en temps *ou* par-ci par-là; **he scores the o. goal** il marque un but de temps en temps *ou* par-ci par-là; **at o. times** par-ci par-là; **at o. moments** dans mes/ses/*etc* moments perdus; **we get the o. visitor** nous avons de la visite de temps en temps

(e) (*odd uses*) **a hundred o. sheep** cent et quelques moutons; **twenty o. pounds** un peu plus de vingt livres; **a few o. things to do** quelques petites choses à faire; **nobody, apart from the o. anthropologist, ...** personne, à part quelques (rares) anthropologues, ...; **an** *or* **any o. piece of cloth** un bout d'étoffe quelconque; **o. jobs about the house** petits travaux dans la maison

oddball ['ɒdbɔːl] *F* **1** *n* excentrique *mf* **2** *adj* (*ideas, friends*) excentrique

oddbod ['ɒdbɒd] *n F* original, -ale

oddity ['ɒdɪtɪ] *n* **(a)** (*strangeness*) singularité *f*, bizarrerie *f*; **he has some little oddities** il a quelques petits travers **(b)** (*thing*) chose *f* bizarre, curiosité *f*; **she's a bit of an o.** (*odd*) elle est un peu bizarre; (*sticks out*) c'est un cas à part; **I'm sick of people treating me like an o.** j'en ai marre qu'on me traite comme si j'étais anormal; **this movie is an o.** (*weird*) c'est un film bizarre; (*unusual*) c'est un film à part

odd-jobman, odd-jobber ['ɒd'dʒɒbmæn, -ɒbər] *n* homme *m* à tout faire

odd-looking *adj* (à l'apparence) bizarre

oddly ['ɒdlɪ] *adv* bizarrement, étrangement; **o. enough nobody knew anything about it** chose curieuse, personne n'en savait rien; **an o. shaped face** un visage aux contours bizarrement irréguliers; **I find her o. attractive** je la trouve étrangement attirante

oddment ['ɒdmənt] *n* (*one of a set*) article *m* dépareillé; (*sale item*) fin *f* de série; (*piece of material*) coupon *m* d'étoffe; **remnants and oddments** soldes *mpl* et occasions *fpl*

oddness ['ɒdnɪs] *n* étrangeté *f*, bizarrerie *f*

odds [ɒdz] *npl* **(a)** (*probability*) chances *fpl*; **what are the o. on his getting the job?** quelles chances a-t-il d'avoir le poste?; **the o. are that she was lying** il y a de grandes chances pour qu'elle ait menti; **the o. are against him/in his favour** il y a peu de chance(s)/de grosses chances qu'il réussisse; **the o. are that he'll succeed** il y a gros à parier qu'il réussira; **it's against all the o.** c'est fort peu probable; **they fought** *or* **struggled against great o. to win the election** bien que les chances de succès étaient extrêmement minces, ils ont réussi à remporter l'élection; **we're always fighting against enormous o.** nous nous battons toujours contre des montagnes; **what are the o. that she'll remember?** quelles chances y a-t-il qu'elle s'en souvienne?; *Br F* **what's the o.?** (*what does it matter?*) qu'est-ce que ça fait?; *Br F* **it makes no o.** ça ne fait rien, cela n'a pas d'importance; **it makes no o. what she says** ce qu'elle dit n'a pas d'importance

(b) *Horseracing etc* cote *f*; **o. on** *or* **against a horse** cote d'un cheval; **short/long o.** faible/forte cote; **the o. are (at) ten to one** la cote est à dix contre un; *Sp* **to give sb o. of ten to one** proposer à qn un pari à dix contre un

(c) to be at o. with sb (*be in disagreement*) ne pas être d'accord avec qn; (*be on bad terms*) être brouillé avec qn (**over** à propos de); **his latest statement is at o. with his earlier account** sa dernière déposition ne concorde pas avec son premier récit des faits

(d) o. and ends *or* *Br F* **sods** (*miscellaneous articles*) bricoles *fpl*; (*of cloth*) bouts *mpl*; **I've still a few o. and ends to do** j'ai encore quelques bricoles *ou* petites choses à faire

odds-on *adj* **o. bet** pari *m* inégal; **o. favourite** grand favori *m*; **it's o. that he won't notice** il y a gros à parier qu'il ne le remarquera pas

ode [əʊd] *n Liter* ode *f*

odious ['əʊdɪəs] *adj* odieux (**to** à)

odiously ['əʊdɪəslɪ] *adv* odieusement

odiousness ['əʊdɪəsnɪs] *n* caractère *m* odieux, abjection *f*

odium ['əʊdɪəm] *n* haine *f*; **to bring** *or* **cast o. upon sb** rendre qn odieux (aux yeux des autres)

odometer [əʊ'dɒmɪtər] *n US* compteur *m* (kilométrique)

odontology [ɒdɒn'tɒlədʒɪ] *n* odontologie *f*

odor ['əʊdər] *n US* = **odour**

odorless ['əʊdəlɪs] *adj US* = **odourless**

odorous ['əʊdərəs] *adj* **(a)** odorant, qui exhale une odeur (agréable) **(b)** *F* (*bad-smelling*) malodorant

odour, *US* **odor** ['əʊdər] *n* odeur *f*; (*pleasant smell*) odeur (agréable), parfum *m*; *F* (*bad smell*) mauvaise odeur; *Fig Fml* **to be in good/bad o. with sb** être bien/mal vu de qn; **you're not in good o. with the boss** tu n'es pas en odeur de sainteté auprès du patron; *Rel* **o. of sanctity** odeur de sainteté

odourless, *US* **odorless** ['əʊdəlɪs] *adj* inodore, sans odeur

Odyssey ['ɒdɪsɪ] *n Myth* **the O.** l'Odyssée *f*; *Fig* **a spiritual o.** une odyssée spirituelle

OECD [əʊiːsiː'diː] *n* (*abbr* **Organization for Economic Cooperation and Development**) OCDE *f*

oedema, *US* **edema** [ɪ'diːmə] *n* œdème *m*

Oedipal ['iːdɪpəl] *adj Psy* œdipien, -ienne

Oedipus ['iːdɪpəs] *n Myth* œdipe *m*; *Psy* **O. complex** complexe *m* d'œdipe

OEM [əʊiː'em] *n Comptr* (*abbr* **original equipment manufacturer**) constructeur *m* de systèmes originaux; **O. sale** vente *f* OEM

o'er [ɔːr, 'əʊər] *prep, adv Lit* = **over**

oesophagus, *US* **esophagus**, *pl* **-gi, -guses** [iː'sɒfəgəs, -gaɪ, -gəsɪz] *n Anat* œsophage *m*

oestrogen, *US* **estrogen** ['iːstrədʒən] *n Biol, Ch* œstrogène *m*

oestrous, *US* **estrous** ['iːstrəs] *adj Biol* (*cycle etc*) œstral

oestrus, *US* **estrus** ['iːstrəs] *n Biol* œstrus *m*

of [ɒv, *unstressed* əv] *prep* **(a)** [①**A16**,3,b] (*belonging to*) de; **the name of the country/city** le nom du pays/de la ville; **the names of the districts** le nom des régions; **citizen of London** citoyen, -enne de Londres; **he is a friend of mine** c'est un de mes amis

(b) (*indicating separation, origin, cause*) de; **south of** au sud de; **within a mile of** à moins d'un mil(l)e de; **free of** libre de; **of noble birth** de naissance noble; **works of Shakespeare** œuvres de Shakespeare; **to ask a favour of sb** demander une faveur à qn; **of my own choice** de mon propre choix; **she died of grief** elle mourut de chagrin; **proud of sth** fier de qch; **I'm sick of it** j'en ai assez

(c) (*indicating agency*) de; **it is very good** *or* **kind of you** c'est bien aimable de votre part, c'est très gentil à vous; **how clever of her** comme c'est intelligent de sa part; *Arch* **beloved of all** aimé de tout le monde

(d) (*indicating material*) de, en; **made of wood** fait de *ou* en bois; **wall of stone** mur en *ou* de pierre; **full of water** plein d'eau

(e) (*concerning, in respect of*) **to think of sb** penser à qn; **what do you think of him?** que pensez-vous de lui?; **to warn sb of sth** avertir qn de qch; **of President Taylor it was said that ...** il a été dit du Président Taylor que ...; **guilty of** coupable de; **doctor of medicine** docteur en médecine; **well, what of it?** et bien?, et après?

(f) (*in description*) **the city of Rome** la ville de Rome; **man of genius** homme de génie; **people of foreign appearance** gens à l'air étranger; **child of ten** enfant (âgé(e)) de dix ans; **his wife of twenty years** la femme avec qui il est marié depuis vingt ans; **that fool of a sergeant** cet imbécile de sergent; **all of a tremble** tout tremblant

(g) (*with grammatical subject*) de; **the love of a mother** l'amour d'une mère

(h) (*with grammatical object*) de; **the fear of God** la crainte de Dieu; **great drinker of whisky** grand buveur de whisky

(i) (*partitive*) **three quarters of the crowd** trois quarts de la foule; *F* **no more of that!** plus de ça!; **how much of it do you want?** combien en voulez-vous?; **many/several of us** beaucoup/plusieurs d'entre nous; **there were two/several of us** nous étions deux/plusieurs; **she is one of us** elle est des nôtres; **one of the best** un des meilleurs; **the best of men** le meilleur des hommes; **the bravest of the brave** le brave des braves; **he, of all men** *or* **people** lui entre tous; **this day of all days** ce jour entre tous; **you, of all people, should know ...** toi, plus que tout le monde, devrais savoir que ...

(j) (*with expressions of time*) **of late years** (pendant) ces dernières années; **of late** dernièrement, récemment; *F* **of an evening** le soir

off¹ [ɒf] **1** *adv* **(a)** *(away)* **house a mile o.** maison à un mil(l)e de distance; **some way o.** à quelque distance; **far o.** au loin, dans le lointain; **to go** *or* **be o.** *(leave)* s'en aller, partir; **isn't it time you were o. to bed?** n'est-il pas l'heure que tu ailles te coucher?; **I'm o. to London** je pars pour Londres; **I must be o.** (il faut que) je me sauve, il faut que je m'en aille; **be o. with you!** sauve-toi!, va-t-en!; **o. you go, you'll be late!** sauve-toi *ou* vas-y, tu vas être en retard!; **they're o.!** *(of racers, racehorses etc)* ils sont partis!, ils ont pris le départ!; **to go o.** (**to sleep**) s'endormir; *Th* **to speak o.** parler depuis les coulisses; **he's o. again!** *(complaining etc)* le voilà qui remet ça!; **o. we go again!** nous voilà repartis!

(b) *(indicating separation, removal)* **to take o. one's coat** retirer *ou* ôter son manteau; **with his jacket/trousers o.** sans sa veste/son pantalon; **a button has come o.** un bouton a sauté; **could you take two centimetres o.?** *(off sleeves etc)* est-ce que vous pourriez enlever deux centimètres?; **to cut sb's head o.** couper *ou* trancher la tête à qn, décapiter qn; **o. with her head!** qu'on lui coupe la tête!; **o. with those wet clothes!** retire(-moi) *ou* enlève(-moi) ces vêtements humides!; **hands o.!** bas les pattes!

(c) *(not functioning, turned off)* **the light/radio is o.** la lumière/radio est éteinte; **the gas/electricity/water is o.** le gaz/l'électricité/l'eau est coupé(e); **the ignition is o.** l'allumage est coupé

(d) *(in price)* **20%/£5 o.** 20%/5 livres de réduction *ou* de remise, réduction *f ou* remise *f* de 20%/5 livres

(e) *(indicating completion)* **to finish o. a piece of work** finir *ou* terminer un travail

(f) *(away from work etc)* **have you any time o. during the week?** avez-vous des heures libres pendant la semaine?; **he's o. today** il ne travaille pas aujourd'hui; **to take some time o.** se libérer; **day o.** jour de congé; **to give the staff a day o.** donner un jour de congé à son personnel; **to arrange to take two days o.** prendre deux jours de congé; **I get two hours o. for lunch** j'ai deux heures de libres pour le déjeuner

(g) *(in phrases)* **o. and on, on and o.** par intervalles; *(from time to time)* de temps en temps; *F* **right** *or* **straight o.** immédiatement, sur-le-champ, tout de suite

2 *prep* **(a)** *(from)* de; **to fall o. sth** tomber de qch; **to take a ring o. one's finger** ôter une bague de son doigt; **to cut a slice o. sth** couper une tranche de qch; **we dined o. a leg of lamb** nous avons dîné d'une tranche de gigot; *El* **to work o. the mains** se brancher sur secteur; **get that knife o. him!** prends-lui son couteau!; *F* **to borrow money/buy sth o. sb** emprunter de l'argent/acheter qch à qn; *F* **I caught a cold o. my brother** mon frère m'a passé son rhume; **o. the top of one's head** *(to say, answer etc)* comme ça; **o. the cuff** *(to make a speech)* au pied levé; **(get) o.!** enlevez-vous de là!; **o. the sofa!** *(don't stand on it)* descends du canapé!; *(don't sit on it)* lève-toi du canapé!

(b) *(indicating reduction in price etc)* **a third o. everything** rabais d'un tiers sur toute la marchandise; *Com* **10%/£20 o. a price** 10%/20 livres de réduction *ou* de remise sur un prix; **that's 2 seconds o. the record** c'est 2 secondes de moins que le record

(c) *(away from, outside of)* écarté de, éloigné de; **village o. the beaten track** village dans un coin reculé; **street o. the main road** rue qui donne sur la grande route; **it's just o. Regent Street** c'est tout près de Regent Street

(d) *(on vacation)* **to have time o. work** avoir du temps (de) libre; *see also* **1(f)**

(e) *(not liking)* **to be o. one's food** ne pas avoir d'appétit; **I'm o. coffee at the moment** ces temps-ci je n'ai pas envie de boire de café; *(because of doctor's orders)* en ce moment, je n'ai plus le droit au café; **he's o. drugs/drink** il ne se drogue/boit plus; *F* **I'm o. her** je ne l'aime plus

(f) *Naut* **o. the Cape** au large du Cap; *(at latitude of)* à la hauteur du Cap; **o. the coast of Spain** au large de la côte espagnole; **to sail o. the wind** naviguer vent largue

3 *adj* **(a)** *(not functioning)* **o. position** position *f* arrêt; *(of lever)* position de repos; *(on scale)* position 'zéro'; *(of brakes)* position de desserrage; **o. switch** bouton *m* d'arrêt

(b) *(referring to side)*, *Horseriding* **o. leg** jambe *f* de dehors; *Cr* **o. drive** coup *m* en avant à droite

(c) *(on vacation, not working)* en congé, en vacances; **to be o. sick** être absent parce qu'on est malade, être malade; **o. day** jour de congé; **he's o. today** il n'est pas là aujourd'hui; **are you o. tomorrow?** tu travailles demain?; *(no school)* tu (n')as (pas d')école demain?; *(no college)* tu (n')as (pas) cours demain?; **when are you o. this afternoon?** à quelle heure tu finis cet après-midi?; **I'm o. from 3 to 5** je ne travaille pas entre 3 et 5 heures

(d) *(cancelled, finished)* *(marriage, trip, meeting)* annulé; *(engagement)* rompu; **it's all** *or* **the whole thing is o.** *(of relationship)* tout est fini; *(of deal)* la transaction est annulée *ou* ne se fera pas, *F* l'affaire est tombée à l'eau; **the lamb is o.** *(in restaurant)* il n'y a plus d'agneau

(e) *(not fresh)* **to be o.** *(of food)* ne plus être frais; *(of meat)* être avarié; *(of milk, orange juice etc)* être tourné; **this beer's o.** cette bière est éventée

(f) *(inaccurate, unsuccessful)* **his timing was a bit o.** *(when he asked for a rise etc)* il n'a pas choisi un très bon moment; **an o. day** un jour où l'on n'est pas en forme *ou* en train; *(with bad luck)* un jour sans

(g) *F* **that's a bit o.!** *(improper, unfair)* c'est pas un truc à faire!; *(not nice)* ça c'est pas sympa!

(h) **to be well/badly o.** *(financially)* être à l'aise/dans le besoin *ou* la gêne; **to be badly o. for sth** être à court de qch; **how are we o. for money/time?** combien d'argent/de temps avons-nous?; **how are we o. for coffee/bread?** est-ce qu'il y a encore du café/pain?; **he is better o. where he is** il est bien mieux où il est; **you'd be better o. accepting their offer** tu ferais mieux d'accepter leur offre

off² *n Horseracing* **the o.** le départ; **to be ready for the o.** être prêt pour le départ

off³ *vt Sl* *(kill)* descendre, zigouiller

off-air *adj, adv* hors antenne

offal ['ɒf(ə)l] *n* *(of animal)* *(edible)* abats *mpl*

off-balance sheet *adj* hors bilan; **o. transactions** opérations *fpl* de hors bilan

offbeat ['ɒfbiːt] **1** *n Mus* temps *m* faible **2** *adj F* *(person, clothes, music)* original, excentrique

off-Broadway ['ɒfbrɔːdweɪ] *adj US Th* *(production)* en dehors de Broadway

off-camera *adj, adv* hors caméra

off-centre, off-centred, *US* **-center, -centered** [ɒf'sentər, -təd] *adj* décentré, décalé; *Fig* *(analysis, description)* légèrement inexact, pas tout à fait exact; *(humour, style)* excentrique, saugrenu

off-chance *n* **on the o.** à tout hasard; **I went on the o. that they would be there** j'y suis allé au cas peu probable où ils y seraient; **they had waited for hours on the o. of meeting their hero** ils avaient attendu pendant des heures dans l'espoir de rencontrer leur héros

off-colour, *US* **off-color** *adj* **(a)** *Br* *(unwell)* **to be** *or* **feel o.** ne pas se sentir dans son assiette; **to look o.** ne pas avoir l'air dans son assiette **(b)** *Old-fashioned* *(joke)* d'un goût douteux

off-course *adj* *(bet)* effectué hors des champs de course

offcut ['ɒfkʌt] *n* *(from wooden plank, cloth, carpet)* chute *f*; *(for animals)* rognures *fpl*; **offcuts** *(of meat)* restes *mpl* du découpage

off-duty *adj* qui n'est pas de service

offence, *US* **offense** [ə'fens] *n* **(a)** *Jur etc* *(minor)* infraction *f*; *(more serious)* délit *m*; **petty** *or* **minor o.** contravention *f* (de simple police); **second o.** récidive *f*

(b) *(no pl)* *(annoyance, displeasure)* blessure *f* faite à la susceptibilité de qn; **to take o.** s'offenser, se froisser **(at sth** de qch); **to take o. at the slightest thing** s'offenser d'un rien; **to cause** *or* **to give o. to sb** *(of person, personal remarks)* offenser *ou* blesser *ou* froisser qn; *(of film, book, programme)* heurter la sensibilité de qn; **I meant no o., I didn't mean to cause o.** je ne voulais offenser personne; **his speech caused a great deal of o. to the Catholic church** son discours a profondément déplu à l'église catholique; **it's an o. to the eye** cela choque la vue *ou* les regards

(c) *Mil* *(attack)* attaque *f*, agression *f*

(d) ['ɒfens] *US Sp* attaque *f*

offend [ə'fend] **1** *vt* *(person)* offenser, blesser, froisser; *(the Lord, Islam etc)* offenser; **to be offended at** *or* **by sth** se froisser *ou* s'offenser de qch; **to be easily offended** être très susceptible, se froisser facilement; **I hope you won't be offended if I ...** j'espère que vous ne vous froisserez pas si je ...; **to o. the eye** choquer les regards *ou* la vue; **harsh sound that offends the ear** son dur qui écorche *ou* heurte l'oreille

2 *vi* **(a)** *(cause offence)* **I didn't mean to o.** *(give offence to the general public)* je ne voulais offenser personne; *(give offence to you)* je ne voulais pas t'offenser *ou* te froisser

(b) *Jur* commettre une infraction *ou* *(more serious)* un délit; **to o. a second time** récidiver

▶ **offend against** *vipo* *(law, principle)* violer, enfreindre; *(common sense)* choquer; *(good taste)* heurter; **his behaviour offends against good manners** son comportement est un outrage aux bonnes manières

offended [ə'fendɪd] *adj* **(a)** *(insulted)* blessé, offensé, froissé; **in an o. tone of voice** d'une voix offensée **(b)** *Jur* **the o. party** l'offensé, -ée

offender [ə'fendər] *n* malfaiteur *m*; *Jur* délinquant, -ante; *Jur* **first o.** délinquant, -ante primaire

offending [ə'fendɪŋ] *adj* fautif
offense [ə'fens] *n US* = **offence**
offensive [ə'fensɪv] **1** *adj* **(a)** (*word, action*) blessant, offensant, choquant; (*spectacle*) choquant, repoussant; (*smell*) repoussant, nauséabond; **morally o. book** livre moralement choquant; **these remarks were o. to many people** ces remarques ont choqué de nombreuses personnes; **to be o. to sb** (*of person*) se montrer blessant envers qn; **in an o. tone** d'un ton injurieux **(b)** *Mil etc* offensif; **o. marketing** mercatique *f* offensive **2** *n Mil, Sp, Fig* offensive *f*; **to take the o.** prendre l'offensive; **to be on the o.** être sur l'offensive
offensively [ə'fensɪvlɪ] *adv* **(a)** (*shockingly*) d'une manière blessante *ou* choquante; (*to say*) d'un ton injurieux **(b)** *Mil, Sp* offensivement
offensiveness [ə'fensɪvnɪs] *n* (*of sight, behaviour*) nature *f* offensante *ou* choquante; (*of smell*) nature nauséabonde; (*of remark etc*) nature injurieuse; **the o. of her tone** son ton injurieux
offer¹ ['ɒfər] *n* offre *f*, proposition *f*; **I had several offers of help** plusieurs personnes m'ont proposé de m'aider; **we need somebody to help, any offers?** nous avons besoin de quelqu'un pour nous aider, est-ce qu'il y a des volontaires?; **I've had the o. of a job** on m'a fait une offre d'emploi, on m'a offert un emploi; **I've had the o. of a car for the weeekend** on m'a proposé une voiture pour le week-end; *Com* **to make an o. for sth** faire une offre pour qch; *Com* **on o.** (*on sale*) en vente; **what is on o. in the negotiations?** qu'est-ce qui est proposé dans les négociations?; **£500 or nearest o.** = prix à débattre autour de 500 livres; *Com* **special o.** promotion *f*; **on special o.** en promotion; **job offers** offres d'emploi; **o. of marriage** demande *f* en mariage; **to make sb an o.** faire une offre *ou* une proposition à qn; *esp Hum* **to make sb an o. they can't refuse** faire à qn une proposition à laquelle il est impossible de dire non; *St Exch* **o. price** cours *m ou* prix *m* vendeur
offer² **1** *vt* (*sth, one's services*) offrir; (*excuses*) présenter; (*one's hand*) tendre; (*remark, criticism, description*) faire; (*opinion*) avancer; (*advice, chance, explanation*) donner; (*definition*) proposer; (*of scheme etc*) (*difficulties, advantages*) présenter; **to o. sb sth** offrir qch à qn; **he was offered a job** on lui a offert un emploi; **he offered her his car for the weekend** il lui a proposé (de lui prêter) sa voiture pour le week-end; **house offered for sale** maison mise en vente; **the conditions that we are able to o. you** les conditions que nous sommes à même de vous faire; **they're offering two weeks' skiing for £200** ils proposent deux semaines aux sports d'hiver pour 200 livres; **to o. to do sth** offrir de faire qch; **this offers a glimpse of things to come** ceci donne une petite idée de ce qui va suivre; *Jur* **to o. a plea** exciper d'une excuse; **to o. resistance** offrir de la résistance
2 *vi* **if occasion offers** si une belle occasion se présente
▶ **offer up** *vtsep* (*prayers, thanks to God*) offrir
offering ['ɒfərɪŋ] *n* **(a)** (*thing offered*) offre *f*; *Rel* offrande *f*; **this year's offerings from Hollywood** ce qu'Hollywood nous propose cette année; **his latest o. is a poem entitled ...** sa dernière production est un poème intitulé ...; **let's hope this essay is better than your last o.** espérons que cette dissertation sera meilleure que votre dernier chef-d'œuvre; **and this, I believe, was your o., Smith** et voici votre torchon, Smith **(b)** (*action*) offre *f*; **the o. of thanks/ congratulations** les remerciements/congratulations
offertory ['ɒfət(ə)rɪ] *n Rel* **(a)** (*of mass*) offertoire *m* **(b)** (*of collection*) quête *f*; (*amount collected*) montant *m* de la quête; **o. box** tronc *m*
offhand [ɒf'hænd] **1** *adv* (*immediately*) **I don't know o.** comme ça de but en blanc, je ne le sais pas; **nonsense! o. I can think of six** n'importe quoi! je peux en nommer six sur-le-champ **2** *adj* (*casual*) cavalier, désinvolte; (*brusque*) brusque; **to be o. with sb** se montrer désinvolte *ou* cavalier à l'égard de qn; **to treat sb in an o. manner** traiter qn cavalièrement *ou* avec désinvolture
offhanded [ɒf'hændɪd] *adj* = **offhand 2**
offhandedly [ɒf'hændɪdlɪ] *adv* (*casually*) avec désinvolture; **I didn't like the way she o. assumed that ...** je n'ai pas aimé la désinvolture avec laquelle elle a supposé que ...
offhandedness [ɒf'hændɪdnɪs] *n* (*casualness*) désinvolture *f*; (*brusqueness*) brusquerie *f*
off-highway *adj, adv* tout-terrain, hors-route
office ['ɒfɪs] *n* **(a)** bureau *m*; (*of lawyer*) étude *f*; *Am* (*of doctor, dentist*) cabinet *m* (de consultation); **to work in an o., to have an o. job** avoir un emploi de bureau; **to stay late at the o.** rester tard au bureau; **the whole o. knows** tout le monde le sait au bureau, tout le bureau le sait; **o. address** adresse *f* au bureau; **o. automation** bureautique *f*; **o. building** *or* **block** immeuble *m* de bureaux; **o. equipment** matériel *m* de bureau; **o. expenses** frais *mpl* de bureau; **o. furniture** mobilier *m* de bureau; **o. manager** chef *m* de bureau; **o. party** soirée *f* entre collègues de bureau; **for o. use only** (*on form*) (cadre) réservé à l'administration; **o. politics** = jeux *mpl* d'alliances, antipathies etc au sein d'une entreprise; **o. romance** liaison *f* au bureau
(b) *Pol etc* (*position*) charge *f*, fonctions *fpl*; **the o. of Prime Minister** la fonction de premier ministre; **high o.** fonctions hautes; **public o.** fonction publique; **to be in o., to hold o.** être en fonction; (*of government, politician*) être au pouvoir; **he has never held high o.** il n'a jamais occupé de poste élevé; **to be out of o.** ne plus être au pouvoir; **to take o., to come into o.** entrer en fonctions; (*of government*) arriver au pouvoir; **to seek o.** chercher à se faire élire
(c) *Fml* (*service*) **through** *or* **owing to the good offices of a friend** grâce aux bons offices *ou* par les bons soins d'un ami; **to offer one's good offices to sb** proposer ses bons offices à qn
(d) *Rel* **o. of the day** office *m* du jour; **o. for the dead** office des morts; **last offices** (*for the dead*) derniers devoirs *mpl*; (*funeral*) obsèques *fpl*
(e) *Fml* **offices** (*of a house*) communs *mpl* et dépendances *fpl*
office boy *n* garçon *m* de bureau
officeholder ['ɒfɪshəʊldər] *n* employé, -ée de l'État, fonctionnaire *mf*
office hours *npl* heures *fpl* de bureau
Office of Fair Trading *n Br* = organisme *m* de défense des consommateurs et de régulation des pratiques commerciales
officer ['ɒfɪsər] *n* **(a)** (*official*) fonctionnaire *mf*; **municipal o.** officier *m* municipal; *Admin* **clerical o.** secrétaire *mf* d'administration; **administrative o.** ≈ administrateur, -trice civil(e); **customs o.** douanier, -ière; **police o.**, *US* **o.** agent *m ou* officier de police; *Am* **O. Smith** officier Smith; **yes, o.** oui, monsieur/madame l'agent **(b)** *Mil etc* officier *m*; (*in Salvation Army*) officier, -ière; **o. of the day** officier de jour **(c) high o.** (*of an order*) grand dignitaire *m*
office staff *n* personnel *m* de bureau
office work *n* travail *m* de bureau
office worker *n* employé, -ée de bureau
official [ə'fɪʃəl] **1** *adj* (*statement, visit, strike etc*) officiel; (*language*) (*officially recognized*) officiel; (*bureaucratic*) administratif; **to act in one's o. capacity** agir dans l'exercice de ses fonctions; **she was speaking in her o. capacity as General Secretary** elle parlait en sa qualité de Secrétaire général; **o. letter** pli *m* officiel *ou* de service; *St Exch* **o. market** marché *m* officiel; **o. opening** (*of new factory etc*) inauguration *f*; **the o. organist** le/la titulaire de l'orgue; *Fin* **o. quotation** cote *f* officielle; **o. rate** taux *m* officiel; *Fin* **o. receiver** administrateur, -trice judiciaire, syndic *m* de faillite; **o. receivership** liquidation *f* judiciaire; *Sp* **o. record** record *m* homologué
2 *n* responsable *mf*; (*of government*) fonctionnaire *mf*, *Pej* bureaucrate *mf*; (*at sports meeting etc*) commissaire *mf*; *US Sp* (*referee*) arbitre *m*; **minor officials** petits fonctionnaires; **the o. at the entrance** le préposé à l'entrée
officialdom [ə'fɪʃəldəm] *n* (*no pl*) (*officials*) administration *f*; *Pej* (*bureaucracy*) bureaucratie *f*, fonctionnarisme *m*
officialese [əfɪʃə'liːz] *n F* jargon *m* administratif
officially [ə'fɪʃəlɪ] *adv* officiellement
officiate [ə'fɪʃɪeɪt] *vi Rel* **to o. at a service** officier à un office; **to o. at a church** desservir une église; **officiating minister** (pasteur *m*) officiant *m*
officious [ə'fɪʃəs] *adj* trop zélé
officiously [ə'fɪʃəslɪ] *adv* avec trop de zèle; **to behave o. towards sb** faire l'empressé auprès de qn
offing ['ɒfɪŋ] *n* **in the o.** en perspective, en vue; **there is an election in the o.** une élection est en perspective *ou* en vue; **there could be some changes in the o.** il se pourrait qu'il y ait des changements en perspective; **there's a dispute in the o.** il y a de la dispute dans l'air; **Christmas is in the o.** Noël se profile à l'horizon
off-key **1** *adv Mus* faux **2** *adj* **(a)** *Mus* **he/the lead trumpet was o.** il/la première trompette n'était pas dans le ton **(b)** *Fig* (*remark, comment etc*) inopportun, déplacé
off-licence *n Br* **(a)** (*premises*) = magasin *m* de vins et spiritueux **(b)** (*licence*) = licence *f* permettant la vente de boissons alcoolisées à emporter
off-line *adj* **(a)** *Comptr* non connecté; (*processing*) en différé; (*printer*) déconnecté; **to be o.** ne pas être connecté; **to go o.** se déconnecter; **o. backup** sauvegarde *f* externe; *TV* **o. editing** montage *m* 'off-line'; *TV* **o. editor** monteur *m* 'off-line'; **o. mode** mode *m* autonome; **o. operation** opération *f*

autonome *ou* indépendante (**b**) **o. connection** (*changing plane with different airline*) correspondance *f* avec changement de compagnie aérienne

off-load *vt* (**a**) (*unload*) décharger; (*from boat*) débarquer (**b**) *Fig* (*get rid of*) fourguer (**onto** à); **he off-loads most of his work on(to) his colleagues** il se décharge de la plus grande partie de son travail sur ses collègues; **we off-loaded the kids onto my parents for the weekend** nous avons fourgué les gosses à mes parents pour le week-end; **to o. the blame/responsibility onto sb** rejeter le blâme/la responsabilité sur qn; **he tried to o. the blame for these decisions onto his civil servants** il a essayé de mettre ces décisions sur le dos de ses fonctionnaires

off-loading *n* (*unloading*) déchargement *m*

off-peak *adj* (*holidays, accommodation etc*) en basse saison; *Mktg* **o. buying** achats *mpl* aux heures creuses; **o. electricity** électricité *f* consommée pendant les heures creuses; *Rail etc* **o. fare** = billet *m* à prix réduit avec lequel on peut voyager en dehors des heures de pointe; **o. hours** heures *fpl* creuses *ou* hors pointe; *El* **o. rate** tarif *m* de nuit

off-piste *adj, adv Ski* hors-piste

offprint ['ɒfprɪnt] *n* tirage *m* à part, tiré *m* à part

off-putting *adj Br F* (*person*) peu engageant; (*smell*) répugnant; (*appearance, manner, prospect*) rébarbatif; (*experience*) démoralisant

off-ramp *n* (*from motorway*) bretelle *f* de sortie

off-road *adj Aut* **o. vehicle** véhicule *m* tout terrain *inv*

off-roader [ɒf'rəʊdər] *n Aut* tout-terrain *m*

off-sales *npl Br* = vente *f* de boissons alcoolisées à emporter

offscreen ['ɒfskriːn] *Cin* **1** *adv* **o., he's really charming** dans la vie de tous les jours c'est un homme tout à fait charmant **2** *adj* (*life*) privé

off-season *adj* (*rate etc*) hors-saison *inv*, de basse saison; **to go on an o. holiday** partir en vacances hors saison *ou* en basse saison

offset¹ ['ɒfset] *n* (**a**) *Fin* (*compensation*) compensation *f* **o. agreement** accord *m* de compensation (**b**) *MecE* (*of wheel*) désaxage *m*, décentrement *m*, déport *m* (**c**) *Typ* (*process*) offset *m*; **printed in o.** tiré en offset; **o. lithography** lithographie *f* offset; **o. plate** plaque *f* offset (**d**) *Bot* (*of plant*) rejeton *m*

offset² *vt* (*pt, pp* **offset**; *prp* **-setting**) (**a**) *Fin* (*compensate for*) (*losses, increasing cost etc*) compenser; **to o. one thing against another** compenser quelque chose par quelque chose d'autre; **to o. losses against tax** déduire le montant de ses pertes de ses impôts (**b**) *MecE* (*wheel*) désaxer, décentrer; (*part*) déporter, décaler (**c**) *Typ* (*print*) (*book*) imprimer en offset

offshoot ['ɒfʃuːt] *n* (*of tree*) rejeton *m*; *Fig* (*of family*) branche *f*; (*of language*) dérivé *m*; (*of political party, artistic movement etc*) ramification *f*

offshore ['ɒfʃɔːr] **1** *adv Petr* (*to live, drill etc*) en mer, au large **2** *adj* (**a**) **o. wind** vent *m* de terre *ou* d'aval (**b**) (*near coast*) côtier, littoral; (*far from coast*) éloigné de la côte; *Petr* (*exploration, drilling*) en mer, off-shore; **o. fishing** pêche *f* côtière; *Petr* **o. installations** installations *fpl* pétrolières marines *ou* off-shore; *Petr* **o. oilfield** champ *m* (pétrolifère) en mer *ou* off-shore (**c**) *Com* (*taking place abroad*) **o. purchases** achats *mpl* à l'étranger; **o. company** compagnie *f* off-shore; **o. investment** placement *m* off-shore

off-shot *adj, adv TV, Cin* hors plan

offside ['ɒf'saɪd] **1** *n Aut* (*in Britain*) côté *m* droit; (*in France, US, Can etc*) côté gauche **2** *adj* (**a**) *Sp* hors jeu; **the o. rule** *or* **law** la règle du hors-jeu (**b**) *Aut* (*in Britain*) du côté droit; (*in France, US, Canada etc*) du côté gauche **3** *adv Sp* hors jeu

offspring ['ɒfsprɪŋ] *n* (*no pl*) (*of animal, Hum children*) progéniture *f*; **none of her o. were there** sa progéniture n'était pas là; **bring the o.** amenez votre progéniture

offstage [ɒf'steɪdʒ] *Th* **1** *adv* (*to hear voices etc*) derrière la toile; **his life o.** (*of actor*) sa vie privée; **o., he is really charming** dans la vie de tous les jours c'est un homme tout à fait charmant **2** *adj* (*life*) privé; (*noises*) derrière la toile

off-street *adj* **o. parking** parking *m* privé

off-the-cuff *adj* (*remark, opinion*) impromptu; (*speech*) improvisé

off-the-peg, *Am* **off-the-rack** *adj* (*clothes*) de prêt-à-porter

off-the-record *adj* (*comment, briefing*) officieux; **on the understanding that it is strictly o.** à titre strictement officieux

off-the-wall *adj F* (*humour*) dément

off-white **1** *adj* blanc cassé *inv* **2** *n* blanc *m* cassé

oft [ɒft] *adv Arch, Lit* souvent; **many a time and o.** maintes et maintes fois

oft- [ɒft] *pref Arch, Lit* **o.-visited/-quoted** souvent visité/cité

often ['ɒf(ə)n, 'ɒft(ə)n] *adv* [①**A23,3,a,ii**] souvent, fréquemment; **I don't see her very o. now** je ne la vois plus très souvent; **how o.?** (*how many times*) combien de fois?; (*at what intervals*) tous les combien?; **how o. have I told you!** combien de fois ne vous l'ai-je pas dit!; **I visited her as o. as I could** je lui rendais visite aussi souvent que je le pouvais; **as o. as not** assez souvent; **more o. than not** le plus souvent; **every so o.** de temps en temps, de temps à autre; **it cannot be repeated too o.** on ne saurait trop le répéter; **once too o.** une fois de trop

ogle ['əʊg(ə)l] *vt* lorgner, guigner, reluquer

ogre ['əʊgər] *n* ogre *m*

ogress ['əʊgrɪs] *n* ogresse *f*

oh [əʊ] *int* oh; (*expressing doubt*) ah?; **oh how tired I am!** ah! que je suis fatigué!; **oh no!** oh non!; **oh yes you will!** mais si!; **oh really?** ah oui?; **oh damn!** et merde!, oh merde!, et zut!

ohc [əʊeɪtʃ'siː] (*abbr* **overhead camshaft**) **o. engine** moteur *m* ACT

ohm [əʊm] *n El* ohm *m*

OHMS [əʊeɪtʃem'es] *Br* (*abbr* **On His/Her Majesty's Service**) = au service de Sa Majesté

oho [əʊ'həʊ] *int* (*expressing triumph*) ah ah!

oik [ɔɪk] *n Br Sl* prolo *mf*

oil¹ [ɔɪl] *n* (**a**) (*edible*), *Art* huile *f*; **to cook in** *or* **with o.** faire la cuisine à l'huile; **fried in o.** frit à l'huile; **to paint in oils** peindre à l'huile; *Fig* **to pour o. on troubled waters** apaiser les esprits; **o. cake** tourteau *m* de lin

(**b**) *Ind* (*petroleum*) pétrole *m*; (*for lubricating etc*) huile *f* (de graissage); *Aut* huile; *Aut* **to check the o.** vérifier le niveau d'huile; *Aut* **o. change** vidange *f*; **to have an o. change** faire faire la vidange; **o. company** compagnie *f* pétrolière; **o. cooling** refroidissement *m* par huile; **o. crisis** choc *m* pétrolier; **o. drain hole** orifice *m* d'écoulement d'huile; **o. drain plug** bouchon *m* de vidange; **o. drum** bidon *m* à pétrole; **o. filter** filtre *m* à huile; **o. gauge** jauge *f* d'huile; **o. heating** chauffage *m* au mazout; **o. industry** industrie *f* pétrolière; **o. pressure** pression *f* d'huile; **o. pressure switch** manocontact *m* d'huile; **o. pressure warning light** témoin *m* d'alerte de pression d'huile moteur; **o. pump** pompe *f* à huile; **o. seal** joint *m* d'huile; **o. slick** nappe *f* de pétrole; *St Exch* **o. shares, oils** valeurs *fpl* pétrolières, pétroles; **o. sump** carter *m* d'huile; **o. tanker** (*ship*) pétrolier *m*; **o. temperature gauge** indicateur *m* de température d'huile; **o. well** puits *m* pétrolifère *ou* de pétrole

(**c**) **essential o.** essence *f*, huile *f* essentielle

oil² *vt* (*machine*) huiler, graisser, lubrifier; **to o. one's skin** s'enduire la peau d'huile; **to o. the wheels** graisser les roues; *Fig* faciliter les choses

oil-bearing *adj Geol* pétrolifère

oilcan ['ɔɪlkæn] *n* (*for applying oil*) burette *f*; (*large container*) bidon *m* à huile

oilcloth ['ɔɪlklɒθ] *n* toile *f* cirée

oil-cooled ['ɔɪlkuːld] *adj* refroidi par huile

oiled [ɔɪld] *adj* huilé; *Fig F* **to be well o.** (*drunk*) être soûl; **to get well o.** se soûler; **o. silk** taffetas *m* imperméable

oiler ['ɔɪlər] *n Naut* (*tanker*) pétrolier *m*

oilfield ['ɔɪlfiːld] *n* gisement *m ou* champ *m* pétrolifère

oilfired ['ɔɪlfaɪəd] *adj* **o. central heating** chauffage *m* central au mazout

oiliness ['ɔɪlɪnɪs] *n* (**a**) (*of clothes, rags etc*) aspect *m* graisseux; (*of dish, sauce*) caractère *m* gras *ou* huileux; **the o. of her cooking** sa cuisine grasse (**b**) *Pej* (*of person*) onctuosité *f*

oil lamp *n* lampe *f* à pétrole

oil paint *n* peinture *f* à l'huile

oil painting *n* peinture *f* à l'huile; *Fig Hum* **he's/she's no o.** ce n'est pas une beauté

oilpaper ['ɔɪlpeɪpər] *n* papier huilé

oil-producing *adj* (**a**) (*shale etc*) pétrolifère; (*country*) producteur, -trice de pétrole (**b**) (*plant*) oléifère; (*substance etc*) oléifiant

oil refinery *n* raffinerie *f* de pétrole

oilrich ['ɔɪlrɪtʃ] *adj* (*countries*) enrichi par le pétrole

oil rig *n* derrick *m*; (*offshore*) plate-forme *f* de forage, *pl* plates-formes de forage

oilskin ['ɔɪlskɪn] *n* (*fabric*) toile *f* cirée; (*garment*) ciré *m*

oilstone ['ɔɪlstəʊn] *n* (*for sharpening*) pierre *f* à huile

oily ['ɔɪlɪ] *adj* (**a**) (*hands, rag*) graisseux; (*food*) gras, huileux (**b**) *Pej* (*manner etc*) onctueux; (*voice*) gras

oink¹ [ɔɪŋk] *vi* (*of pig*) grogner

oink² *n* (*of pig*) grognement *m*

ointment ['ɔɪntmənt] *n* onguent *m*, pommade *f*

OK¹, okay¹ ['əʊ'keɪ] *F* **1** *int* **OK!** OK!, bon!, d'accord!; **OK?** OK?, d'accord?; **OK, if I could have your attention for a moment ...** bon, si je pouvais avoir votre attention pour un instant ...; **OK, it wasn't a great movie but I've seen worse** bon, d'accord, ce n'était pas un film super mais j'ai vu pire

2 *adj* **(a)** (*in order, fine*) correct, exact; **everything's OK** tout est en règle *ou* OK; **to be OK** (*unhurt*) aller bien; **are you OK?, did I hurt you/are you upset?** ça va?, je ne t'ai pas fait mal/tu es fâché?; **I'll be OK when I get home** ça ira une fois que je serai à la maison; **but is the car OK?** mais est-ce que la voiture n'a rien?; **that's OK by** *or* **with me** d'accord!; **is that OK by** *or* **with your mother** est-ce que ta mère est d'accord?; **is it OK to bring my friend?** est-ce que ça vous dérange si je viens avec mon ami?; **no, it is not OK** pas question; **clothes like that are OK for a party** des vêtements comme ça, ça va bien pour aller à une soirée

(b) (*acceptable*) (*meal, film etc*) pas mal; (*candidate, singer etc*) pas mauvais, pas mal; **how are things? – OK** comment ça va? – ça peut aller; **the meal/her performance was more than OK** le repas/sa prestation était au-dessus de la moyenne; **was I OK?** comment j'étais?; *Sl* **an OK computer** un ordinateur pas mal

(c) (*understanding*) **she was OK about it** elle n'a pas fait d'histoires; **are you sure he'll be OK about letting us use the car?** tu es sûr qu'il ne fera pas d'histoires pour nous laisser la voiture?

(d) (*likeable etc*) (*person*) **he's an OK sort of guy** c'est un type plutôt bien; **she's OK but ...** elle est assez sympa mais ...

(e) to be OK for work/money (*have enough of*) avoir assez de travail/d'argent; **is everybody OK for drink?** est-ce que tout le monde a à boire?

3 *n* **to give one's OK to sth** approuver qch; **to give the OK** donner le feu vert; **the doctor's given me the OK to use my arm again** le docteur m'a dit que je pouvais recommencer à me servir de mon bras

OK² *vt* (*pt, pp* **OK'd**), **okay²** *vt F* (*give permission or approval to*) approuver; (*course of action*) donner le feu vert à

okapi [əʊ'kɑːpɪ] *n* (*animal*) okapi *m*

okay ['əʊ'keɪ] *F* = **OK**

okey-doke, okey-dokey [əʊkɪ'dəʊk, -kɪ] *int F* d'accord

Okie ['əʊkɪ] *n Am F Pej* (*inhabitant*) habitant, -ante de l'Oklahoma; *Hist* (*migrant worker from Oklahoma*) = un des nombreux petits fermiers qui ont quitté le Midwest dans les années 30 pour chercher du travail dans d'autres états

Okla *abbr* **Oklahoma**

okra ['ɒkrə] *n* (*vegetable*) okra *m*

old [əʊld] **1** *adj* **(a)** [①**A17,3,a**] (*aged*) (*person*) vieux, *f* vieille, âgé; (*in sing before a qualified noun beginning with a vowel or h mute*) vieil; (*car, furniture, food etc*) vieux; **you're as o. as you feel** on a l'âge de ses artères; **she married a man who was o. enough to be her father** elle s'est mariée avec un homme qui aurait pu être son père; **to grow** *or* **get older** vieillir; **to be growing** *or* **getting o.** vieillir, prendre de l'âge; **an o. man** un homme âgé, un vieillard, *F* un vieux; **an o. woman** une femme âgée, une vieille femme, *F* une vieille; **o. people, o. folk(s)** (*in general*) les personnes âgées, *F* les vieux *mpl*; **the o. people next door** le couple âgé qui habite à côté, *F* les vieux qui habitent à côté; **my o. friend** mon vieil ami; **he's an o. friend of mine** c'est un de mes vieux amis; **an o. debt** une dette de longue date; **that's an o. dodge** c'est un coup classique; **an o. story** une vieille histoire; **that's an o. one!** (*of joke*) c'est une vieille blague; **o. memories** vieux souvenirs; **as o. as the hills** (*of person, joke etc*) vieux comme le monde; **as o. as Methuselah** (*of person*) vieux comme Hérode *ou* Mathusalem; *Sl* **the O. Bill** les flics *mpl*, les poulets *mpl*; *Br* **the o. school tie** = la franc-maçonnerie des écoles privées et des universités; **the O. Country** le pays; **they kept in close touch with events in the O. Country** ils suivaient de près ce qui se passait au pays; **o. gold** (*colour*) vieil or; **to go over o. ground** revenir sur un terrain déjà parcouru; *Pol etc* **the o. guard** la vieille garde; *Fig* **one of the o. guard** un vieux de la vieille; **o. hand** ancien, -ienne; **to be an o. hand at sth** être rompu à faire qch; **to be o. hat** être démodé; **o. money** anciens francs *mpl*; (*in UK*) ancienne monnaie *f*; **it's o. money** (*of old wealthy family*) c'est une vieille fortune; **o. rose** (*colour*) vieux rose; *Fig* **a boss/politician of the o. school** un patron/homme politique de la vieille école; **o. wine** vin vieux; **o. wives' tale** conte *m* de bonne femme; **the O. World** l'ancien monde *m*

(b) (*with specific age*) **how o. are you?** quel âge avez-vous?; **the oldest of the tribe** l'aîné, -ée de la tribu; **to be five years o.** avoir cinq ans, être âgé de cinq ans; **she is older than I am** elle est plus âgée *ou* vieille que moi; **when you're older** (*to child*) quand tu seras plus grand; **at six years o.** à (l'âge de) six ans; **a two-year-o. (child)** un(e) enfant (âgé(e)) de deux ans; **to be o. enough to do sth** être assez grand pour faire qch, être d'âge à faire qch

(c) (*former*) ancien; **my o. house/school** mon ancienne maison/école; **an o. flame** un(e) ancien(ne) amoureux/amoureuse, *F* un ancien flirt; **in the o. days** autrefois

(d) *Ling, Hist* **O. English/French** ancien anglais/français

(e) *F* (*intensifier*) **any o. how** n'importe comment; **any o. thing** n'importe quoi; **it's a strange o. world** c'est un drôle de monde; **we had a fine o. time** nous avons passé un sacré bon moment

(f) [①**A17,3,a**] *F* (*expressing familiarity or affection*) **o. Fred** le Fred; *Old-fashioned* **o. man** *or* **chap** *or* **fellow** *or* **boy** (*addressing sb*) mon vieux, mon pote; *F* **the o. man** (*father*) le paternel; *Old-fashioned* (*boss*) le patron; *Naut* (*captain*) le capitaine; *Mil* (*colonel*) le colonel; *Sl* **my** *or* **the o. man** (*father*) le paternel, mon vieux; (*husband*) mon homme; *Sl* **my** *or* **the o. woman** *or* **lady** (*wife*) la patronne, *Sl* la bourgeoise; (*mother*) ma *ou* la vieille; *Old-fashioned* **come on, o. girl** allons ma vieille; *Fig F* **to be (a bit of) an o. woman** avoir des manies de vieille fille; **he was being a bit of an o. woman about it** il en faisait tout un cinéma

(g) *Lit* **in days of o.** autrefois, au temps jadis; **I know him of o.** je le connais depuis longtemps

2 *npl* **the o.** les vieux *mpl*; **popular with o. and young** apprécié des jeunes et des moins jeunes

old age *n* la vieillesse; **in o. she was still beautiful** dans sa vieillesse elle était encore très belle; **he's saving for his o.** il économise pour ses vieux jours; **o. pension** retraite *f*; **o. pensioner** retraité, -ée

Old Bailey *n Jur* = tribunal *m* criminel de Londres

old boy *n* (*former pupil*) ancien élève *m*; *Br* **the o. network** = la franc-maçonnerie des écoles privées et des universités

olden ['əʊld(ə)n] *adj Lit* **in o. times, in the o. days** au temps jadis

Old English sheepdog *n* bobtail *m*

old-established *adj* ancien, établi depuis longtemps

olde-worlde ['əʊldɪ'wɜːldɪ] *adj Hum, Pej* (*house, village etc*) qui a un aspect vieillot factice

old-fashioned [əʊld'fæʃənd] **1** *adj* (*dress*) (*outdated*) démodé, passé de mode; (*from former times*) d'autrefois, de l'ancien temps; (*person*) démodé, vieux jeu *inv*; (*manners*) de l'ancien temps; (*atmosphere, charm, air*) vieillot; (*ideas*) arriéré, vieillot, vieux jeu; **I like to do things the o. way** j'aime bien faire les choses à l'ancienne; **he's rather o. in his views/attitudes** il a des opinions/attitudes un peu vieillottes *ou* vieux jeu; **o. Christmas** Noël à l'ancienne; **you can call me o. but ...** tu vas peut-être me trouver vieux jeu, mais ...; *F* **o. look** (*glance*) regard de travers **2** *n Am* = cocktail *m* composé de whisky, d'amers, de sucre et d'eau de seltz

old girl *n* (*former pupil*) ancienne élève *f*

Old Glory *n US F* la bannière étoilée

oldie ['əʊldɪ] *n F* **(a)** (*old thing*) vieillerie *f*, antiquaille *f*; (*song*) vieux tube *m*; **that's a real o.** (*song, joke etc*) il ne date pas d'aujourd'hui celui-là!; **oldies but goldies** (*songs*) bons vieux tubes; (*jokes*) bonnes vieilles blagues *fpl* **(b)** (*old person*) vieillard, -arde

oldish ['əʊldɪʃ] *adj* assez vieux, *f* assez vieille

old maid *n Old-fashioned* vieille fille *f*; *Fig* **he's a bit of an o.** il a des manies de vieille fille

Old Man River *n US* = le Mississippi

old master *n Art* (*painter*) maître *m*; (*painting*) tableau *m* de maître

Old Nick *n F* Satan *m*

old pupil *n* ancien(ne) élève *mf*

oldster ['əʊldstər] *n Am F* vieillard *m*, vieille *f*

old-style *adj* à l'ancienne (mode); *Hist* **the o. calendar** le calendrier ancien style

Old Testament *n* **the O.** l'Ancien Testament *m*

old-time *adj attrib* du temps jadis; **o. dancing** danses *fpl* du bon vieux temps

old-timer *n F* **(a)** ancien, -ienne; (*experienced person*) vieux *m* de la vieille **(b)** *esp Am* (*form of address*) (*old man*) vieux *m*

old-world *adj* (*of former times*) de l'ancien temps, d'autrefois; *Geog, Hist* de l'ancien monde

OLE [əʊel'iː] *n Comptr* (*abbr* **object linking and embedding**) OLE *m*

ole [əʊl] *adj F* vieux, *f* vieille

oleaginous [əʊlɪ'ædʒɪnəs] *adj* oléagineux; *Fig Lit* mielleux

oleander [əʊlɪ'ændər] *n* (*shrub*) oléandre *m*, laurier-rose *m*, *pl* lauriers-rose(s)

olfactory [ɒl'fæktərɪ] *adj* (*bulb, nerve etc*) olfactif

oligarchic(al) [ɒlɪ'gɑːkɪk, -ɪk(ə)l] *adj* oligarchique

oligarchy ['ɒlɪgɑːkɪ] *n* oligarchie *f*

olive ['ɒlɪv] **1** *n* **(a)** (*fruit*) olive *f*; **o. oil** huile *f* d'olive **(b) o. (tree)** olivier *m*; *Fig* **to hold out the o. branch** proposer la paix (**to sb** à qn); **o. grove** *or* **plantation** oliv(er)aie *f*; **o. grower** oléiculteur, -trice **(c) o. (wood)** (bois *m* d')olivier *m*

(d) *(colour)* **o. (green)** (vert *m*) olive *m inv* **2** *adj* (*complexion etc*) olivâtre; **o. (green)** (*dress, scarf etc*) (vert) olive *inv*; *US Mil* **o. drab** gris vert; **in his o. drabs** dans son treillis

Olympiad [əˈlɪmpɪæd] *n Sp* olympiade *f*

Olympian [əˈlɪmpɪən] **1** *adj* (*air, calm etc*) olympien; (*god*) de l'Olympe **2** *n* Olympien, -ienne

Olympic [əˈlɪmpɪk] **1** *adj Antiq, Sp* (*stadium, record etc*) olympique; **the O. flame** la flamme olympique; **the O. Games** les Jeux *mpl* olympiques **2** *npl* **the Olympics** les Jeux *mpl* olympiques

Olympus [əˈlɪmpəs] *n* l'Olympe *m*

O&M [əʊəndˈem] *n* (*abbr* **organization and methods**) **O. department** bureau *m* des méthodes

Oman [əʊˈmɑːn] *n* Oman *m*

Omani [əʊˈmɑːnɪ] **1** *n* Omanais, -aise **2** *adj* omanais

ombudsman, *pl* **-men** [ˈɒmbʊdzmən] *n* ombudsman *m*, médiateur *m* (*entre individus et instances gouvernementales*), *Can* protecteur *m* du citoyen

omega [ˈəʊmɪgə] *n* (*in Greek alphabet*) oméga *m*

omelette, *US* **omelet** [ˈɒmlɪt] *n Culin* omelette *f*; **ham/cheese/mushroom o.** omelette au jambon/au fromage/aux champignons; *Fig* **you can't make an o. without breaking eggs** on ne fait pas d'omelette sans casser d'œufs

omen [ˈəʊmen] *n* présage *m*, augure *m*, auspice *m*; **to take sth as a good/a bad** *or* **an ill o.** prendre qch comme un bon/mauvais augure; **all the omens seemed good** tous les présages paraissaient favorables

ominous [ˈɒmɪnəs] *adj* (*event*) de mauvais augure; (*look*) lourd de sens; (*sign, lack of enthusiasm, news, silence*) inquiétant; **o.-looking sky** ciel menaçant; **an o. silence** (*implying disaster*) un silence lourd de menaces; **I heard an o. crack** j'entendis un craquement qui ne présageait rien de bon; **an emergency meeting? — that sounds o.** une réunion d'urgence? — ça ne présage rien de bon

ominously [ˈɒmɪnəslɪ] *adv* (*to say sth*) d'une voix qui ne présage rien de bon; **it was o. quiet** il régnait un calme inquiétant; **o., there was no answer when they rang** le téléphone ne répondait pas, ce qui ne présageait rien de bon; **the deadline was drawing o. close** la date limite se rapprochait dangereusement

omission [əʊˈmɪʃən] *n* omission *f*; *Typ* bourdon *m*; *Rel* omission *f*; *Rel* **sin of o.** péché *m ou* faute *f* d'omission; **to sin by o.** pécher par omission

omit [əʊˈmɪt] *vt* **(-tt-)** **(a)** (*details, word etc*) omettre; **to o. any mention of** *or* **reference to sb/sth** omettre toute mention de *ou* référence à qn/qch **(b) to o. to do sth** omettre de faire qch; **not to o. to do sth** ne pas manquer de faire qch

omnibus, *pl* **-uses** [ˈɒmnɪbəs, -bəsɪz] **1** *n* **(a)** (*book*) recueil *m*; **Edgar Allan Poe o.** recueil d'œuvres d'Edgar Allan Poe; **detective o.** recueil de romans policiers **(b)** *Arch* (*vehicle*) **(horse) o.** omnibus *m*; **(motor) o.** autobus *m* **2** *adj* (*in publishing*) **o. volume** *or* **edition** (*of stories, poems etc*) gros recueil *m*; *TV, Rad* **o. edition** = rediffusion *f* hebdomadaire de tous les épisodes d'un feuilleton quotidien; *Mktg* **o. survey** enquête *f* omnibus

omnidirectional [ˈɒmnɪdɪˈrekʃən(ə)l] *adj* (*aerial, microphone*) omnidirectionnel

omnipotence [ɒmˈnɪpətəns] *n* omnipotence *f*, toute-puissance *f*

omnipotent [ɒmˈnɪpətənt] **1** *adj* omnipotent, tout-puissant, *pl* tout-puissants **2** *n Lit* **the O.** le Tout-Puissant

omnipresence [ɒmnɪˈprezəns] *n* omniprésence *f*

omnipresent [ɒmnɪˈprezənt] *adj* omniprésent

omniscience [ɒmˈnɪsɪəns] *n* omniscience *f*

omniscient [ɒmˈnɪsɪənt] *adj* omniscient

omnivore [ˈɒmnɪvɔːr] *n* omnivore *m*

omnivorous [ɒmˈnɪvərəs] *adj* omnivore; *Fig* (*reader*) qui lit de tout

omnivorously [ɒmˈnɪvərəslɪ] *adv* (*to read*) de tout

on [ɒn] **1** *prep* **(a)** (*indicating position*) sur; **on the table** sur la table; **on Arran/the Isle of Wight** sur Arran/l'île de Wight; **on Corsica/Crete** en Corse/Crète; **on Majorca/Minorca** à Majorque/Minorque; **on the other side of the page** de l'autre côté de la page; **on page four** à la quatrième page, à la page quatre; **house on the main road** maison sur la grande route; *Am* **she lives on Sixth Avenue** elle habite dans la Sixième Avenue; **room on the second floor** chambre au second (étage); **on the right/left** à droite/gauche; **on this side** de ce côté; **don't tread on it** ne marchez pas dessus; **the post with the seagull on it** le poteau sur lequel il y a la mouette; **on the high seas** en haute mer; **on the train** dans le train; **on foot/horseback** à pied/cheval; **on a bicycle** à bicyclette; **hanging on the wall** pendu au mur; **on the ceiling** au plafond; **he has a ring on his finger** il a une bague au doigt; **he had his rucksack on his back** il portait son sac sur le dos; **have you any money on you?** avez-vous de l'argent sur vous?; **on (the) television/radio** à la télévision/radio; **what's on the other channel?** qu'est-ce qu'il y a sur l'autre chaîne?

(b) (*indicating direction*) **on(to)** sur; **to fall on(to) sth** tomber sur qch; **to climb on(to) a wall** grimper sur un mur; **to march on London** avancer vers *ou* sur Londres

(c) (*indicating membership*) **to be on the committee** être membre du comité; **to be on a jury** être membre d'un jury; **to be on a newspaper** (*work for*) travailler dans un journal; **he's on the Guardian now** il travaille *ou* il est au Guardian à présent

(d) (*in expressions of time*) **on Sunday** dimanche; **on Sundays** le dimanche; **on the day of my arrival** le jour de mon arrivée; **on the following day** le lendemain; **on April 3rd** le trois avril; **on a fine day in June** par une belle journée de juin; **on and after the fifteenth** à partir du quinze; **on or about the twelfth** vers le douze; **on the hour** à l'heure juste; **on that occasion** à cette occasion; **on the death of his mother** à la mort de sa mère; **on my arrival** à mon arrivée; **on my first/last/***etc* **visit** lors de ma première/dernière/*etc* visite; **on (my) entering the room** quand je suis entré *ou* en entrant dans la pièce, à mon entrée dans la pièce; **on realizing what he had done** quand il s'est rendu compte de ce qu'il avait fait; **on completing the test candidates should ...** quand ils auront fini l'examen les candidats devront ...; **on the count of three** à trois; **on the third stroke** au troisième coup; **on time** ponctuel, à l'heure; **just on a year ago** (*approximately*) il y a près d'un an

(e) (*indicating manner*) **on the cheap** à bon marché; **on the sly** en cachette, *F* en douce

(f) (*indicating state*) en; **on sale** en vente

(g) (*about, concerning*) sur; **a book on France** un livre sur la France; **a lecture on history** une conférence d'histoire; **you should read Watson on toxicology** vous devriez lire les écrits de Watson sur la toxicologie; **what have you got on him?** qu'est-ce que vous avez sur lui?; **the police have nothing on him** la police n'a rien sur lui

(h) (*indicating activity*) **I am here on business/on a mission of mercy** je suis ici pour affaires/pour remplir une mission de charité; **could I speak to you on a matter of some delicacy?** pourrais-je vous parler d'une affaire assez délicate?; **on tour** en tournée; **on holiday** en vacances; **to be working on sth** travailler à qch

(i) (*indicating source of support*) **to live on one's private income/a student grant** vivre de ses rentes/d'une bourse d'études; **to retire on a pension of £5,000 a year** prendre sa retraite avec une pension de 5 000 livres par an; **many live on less than that** beaucoup vivent avec moins que ça; **to be on the dole** toucher le chômage; **this round (of drinks) is on me** c'est moi qui paie cette fois-ci; **he's on insulin/heroin** il prend de l'insuline/de l'héroïne; **to be on drugs** se droguer; **what was he on?** (*drug*) qu'est-ce qu'il avait pris?; **she's on the pill** elle prend la pilule; **it runs** *or* **works on gas/electricity/***etc* ça marche au gaz/à l'électricité/*etc*; **to travel on a British passport** voyager avec un passeport britannique

(j) (*compared with*) **prices are up on last year** les prix ont augmenté par rapport à l'année dernière

(k) *Horseracing etc* **to put money on a horse** parier *ou* miser sur un cheval; **he's got £500 on me going the full ten rounds** il a parié 500 livres que je vais faire les dix tours

2 *adv* **(a)** (*indicating direction, position*) **to put the cloth on** mettre la nappe; **to put the kettle on** mettre la bouilloire à chauffer; **it's not on properly** (*lid, covering etc*) il n'est pas bien mis; **to be on** (*of actor*) être en scène; **we're on in ten minutes** c'est à nous dans dix minutes; **to put on one's clothes** s'habiller; **put something on** (*clothing*) mets quelque chose; **what had she got on?** (*clothes*) qu'est-ce qu'elle portait?, comment était-elle habillée?; **to have nothing on** (*be naked*) être tout nu

(b) (*expressing continuation*) **to go on** continuer **(doing** à faire); **to march/work/battle on** continuer sa marche/son travail/la lutte; **to drive/sail/talk on** continuer à rouler/naviguer/parler; **on, on, we must keep on!** en avant, en avant, il faut continuer!; **the speech/he went on and on** le discours/il n'en finissait plus *ou* pas; *F* **he's always on about the war/teenagers/***etc* il n'arrête pas de déblatérer sur la guerre/les adolescents/*etc*; *F* **what was he on about?** qu'est-ce qu'il racontait *ou* rabâchait?; *F* **he's always on at** *or* **to me** (*nagging*) il s'en prend toujours à moi **(to do** pour que je fasse); *F* **why is he always getting on at them about their hair?** pourquoi est-ce qu'il s'en prend toujours à leur coiffure?; *F* **I've been on at them for months to get it fixed** cela fait des mois que je suis sur leur dos pour qu'ils le fassent réparer; **and so on** et ainsi de suite; **on with the show!** que le spectacle continue!

(c) (*in time*) **later on** plus tard; **from that day on** à partir *ou* dater de ce jour; **well on in years** d'un âge avancé

(d) (*in operation*) (*machine, engine*) en marche; (*light, television, radio*) allumé; (*gas, tap*) ouvert; (*alarm*) enclenché; **the brakes are on** les freins sont serrés; **is the electricity on?** est-ce que l'électricité est mise?

(e) (*taking place*) **the meeting is on right now** la réunion est en train de se dérouler; **the play was on for weeks** la pièce a tenu l'affiche pendant des semaines; **what's on tonight?** (*on TV etc*) qu'est-ce qu'il y a ce soir?; (*what are we doing?*) qu'est-ce qu'on fait ce soir?; *TV, Rad* **there's nothing good on** il n'y a rien de bien; **it's not on today** (*programme*) ça ne passe pas aujourd'hui; **what's on at the cinema?** qu'est-ce qu'on donne *ou* joue au cinéma?; **it's on at the Filmhouse** il passe au Filmhouse; **have you anything on this evening?** est-ce que vous avez quelque chose de prévu *ou* en vue pour ce soir?; **is the party still on?** est-ce que la soirée se fait toujours?; **it's (still) on** (*hasn't been cancelled*) ça tient toujours

(f) *F* (*anxious to take part*) **I'm on!** je suis de la partie!; **you're on!** d'accord!, c'est bon!

(g) *F* (*acceptable*) **that sort of behaviour isn't on** cette sorte de comportement n'est pas admissible; **it's not on, charging £10 a ticket!** faire payer un billet 10 livres ça dépasse les bornes!; **you're not on!** (*I refuse your offer*) rien à faire!

(h) to be on to sth (*understand*) comprendre *ou* saisir *ou F* piger qch; **they were on to him at once** (*saw what he was up to*) ils ont tout de suite vu clair dans son jeu; **to be on to a good thing** être sur une bonne affaire; **the police are on to her** la police est sur sa piste; **I'll put you on to her** (*on phone*) je vais vous la passer

(i) *Horseracing* **to put a bet on** faire un pari; **I have a bet on** j'ai fait un pari

(j) on and off *see* **off[1] 1 (g)**

(k) (*on duty*) (*in hospital, surgery etc*) de garde; (*in shop, administration etc*) de service; **I'm on at three o'clock, then off at nine o'clock** je commence à trois heures et je finis à neuf heures

3 *adj* **(a) on position** position *f* marche; (*of brakes*) position de serrage; **on/off switch** interrupteur *m* marche/arrêt; *Fig* **an on-off romance/relationship** une idylle/relation qui marche par à-coups; **it's a bit of an on-off relationship** ils passent leur temps à casser et à retourner ensemble

(b) *Cr* **drive to the on side, on drive** coup *m* avant à gauche

(c) *F* **it was not one of his on days** il n'était pas dans un de ses meilleurs jours

on-air *adj, adv* à l'antenne; **o. (warning) light** voyant *m* de passage à l'antenne

onanism [ˈəʊnənɪz(ə)m] *n* onanisme *m*

on-board *adj* **(a)** *Com* **o. surcharge** surcharge *f* 'on-board' **(b)** *Comptr* **o. RAM** RAM *f* sur carte

on-camera *adj, adv* à l'image

once [wʌns] **1** *adv* **(a)** (*one time only*) une fois; **not o.** pas une seule fois, jamais; **he's never o. said he was sorry** il ne s'est jamais excusé, il ne s'est pas excusé une seule fois; **o. only** une seule fois; **more than o.** plus d'une fois; **o. a week** une fois par semaine; **o. or twice** une ou deux fois, une fois ou deux; **o. in a while** une fois de temps en temps; **o. more, o. again** une fois de plus, encore une fois; **o. too often** une fois de trop; **o. and for all** une fois pour toutes; **you may do so this o.** *or* **just for (this) o.** je vous le permets pour une fois *ou* pour cette fois(-ci); **for o. you are right** pour une fois tu as raison; **a o.-in-a-lifetime opportunity** une occasion qui ne se présente qu'une fois

(b) (*formerly*) autrefois; **o. upon a time there was a princess, there was o. a princess** il était une fois une princesse; **o. (upon a time) children used to respect their elders** il fut un temps où les enfants respectaient leur aînés; **I knew him o.** je l'ai connu autrefois *ou* dans le temps; **o. it would have all been so easy** il fut un temps où ça aurait été si facile; **a o.-flourishing company** une entreprise autrefois prospère

(c) at o. (*immediately*) tout de suite, immédiatement; (*at the same time*) à la fois, en même temps; **all at o. we were home** tout à coup nous étions arrivés à la maison; **to do several things at o.** faire plusieurs choses à la fois *ou* en même temps; **it all happened at o.** tout est arrivé en même temps

2 *conj* (*when*) **o. he reached home, he collapsed** une fois arrivé chez lui, il s'effondra; **(if) o. you hesitate you're lost** dès que vous *ou* si vous hésitez, vous êtes fichu; **o. you master this, everything will be ...** dès que *ou* quand vous aurez maîtrisé cela, tout sera ...

once-over *n F* **to give sb/sth the o.** jeter un coup d'œil (scrutateur) sur qn/qch; **to give a room a o.** (*with duster*) passer un coup de chiffon dans une chambre

oncology [ɒŋˈkɒlədʒɪ] *n* oncologie *f*

oncoming [ˈɒnkʌmɪŋ] *adj* **(a)** (*approaching*) approchant, qui approche; **the o. traffic** (*for vehicle*) les véhicules venant en sens inverse; (*for pedestrian*) les véhicules qui approchent **(b)** *Ind* **o. shift** poste *m* entrant

oncosts [ˈɒnkɒsts] *npl Com* frais *mpl* généraux

OND [əʊenˈdiː] *n Br* (*abbr* **Ordinary National Diploma**) ≈ diplôme *m* d'études techniques

one [wʌn] **1** *adj* **(a)** un; **twenty-o. apples** vingt et une pommes; **to have a thousand** *or* **a million and o. things to do** avoir des tas de choses à faire; **o. or two people saw it** une ou deux personnes l'ont vu; **o. day out of two, o. day in every two** un jour sur deux; **o. stormy evening in January** par une soirée de janvier où il faisait de l'orage; **o. man in a hundred** un homme entre *ou* sur cent; **for o. thing I'm short of cash** entre autres raisons je suis à court d'argent; **o. thing at a time** chaque chose en son temps; **o. thing you'll need to know is ...** il y a quelque chose qu'il vous faudra savoir: ...; *F* **it was o. hell of a journey** ça a été un voyage épouvantable; **o. way and another** (*on balance*) à tous (les) points de vue; **o. way or another** d'une manière ou d'une autre

(b) (*single*) seul; **my o. and only suit** mon seul et unique complet; **my o. and only daughter** (*only child*) ma fille unique; (*only daughter*) ma seule fille; **the o. and only Marilyn Monroe** la seule et l'unique Marilyn Monroe; **her o. worry** son seul *ou* unique souci; **they were of o. mind on the subject** ils partageaient le même avis sur le sujet; **no o. man can do it** il n'y a pas d'homme qui puisse le faire à lui seul *ou* tout seul; **they cried out with o. voice** *or* **as o. man** ils s'écrièrent d'une seule voix *ou* comme un seul homme; **all in o. direction** tous dans la même direction; **o. and the same thought** une seule et même pensée; *F* **it's all o.** cela revient au même; *F* **it's all o. to me** ça m'est égal

2 *n* **(a)** un *m*; **chapter o.** chapitre un, chapitre premier; *Sp* **o., two, three, go!** un(e), deux, trois, partez!; **o. fifty** (*a hundred and fifty*) cent cinquante; (*one pound and fifty pence*) une livre cinquante (pence); (*one dollar fifty cents*) un dollar cinquante (cents); (*time*) deux heures moins dix, une heure cinquante; **o. (o'clock)** une heure; *Horseracing* **the odds are (at) ten to o.** la cote est à dix contre un; *F* **it's ten to o. that** *or Am* **o. will get you ten that he's at the office** je parie (à) dix contre un qu'il est au bureau

(b) (*individual thing, person*) **there's only o. left** il n'en reste qu'un; **I was the only o. there** j'étais le seul à me trouver là; **she's the only o. you need to worry about** c'est la seule personne de qui *ou* dont tu doives te préoccuper; **the top/bottom stair but o.** l'avant-dernière marche; **to arrive in ones and twos** arriver un par un ou deux par deux; **two for the price of o.** deux pour le prix d'un; **two volumes in o.** deux volumes en un; **chauffeur and gardener in** *or* **rolled into o.** chauffeur et jardinier en un; **to be at o. with sb** être d'accord avec qn; *F* **there's o. born every minute** comment peut-on être aussi stupide!; *F* **I landed him o.** je lui ai flanqué un marron; **o. for the road** le coup de l'étrier; **to have o. too many** (*drink*) boire un verre de trop; *Sp* **to be o. up on an opponent** être en avance d'un point/d'un jeu/d'un but/*etc* sur un concurrent; *F* **to be o. up on sb** (*have advantage*) avoir l'avantage sur qn

(c) *Knitting* **to make o.** faire une augmentation, augmenter d'une maille

(d) *St Exch* unité *f*

3 *dem pron* [①A30,9; B13-14,6] **this o.** celui-ci, celle-ci; *F* **these ones** ceux-ci, celles-ci; **that o.** celui-là, celle-là; *F* **those ones** ceux-là, celles-là; **which o. do you prefer?** lequel/laquelle préférez-vous?; **the o. I spoke of** celui/celle dont j'ai parlé; **to pick the ripe plums and leave the green ones** cueillir les prunes mûres et laisser les vertes; **the big/silly/blonde o.** (*woman*) la grosse/l'imbécile/la blonde; **the right/wrong o.** le bon/mauvais; **the ones with the long sleeves** ceux avec les manches longues; **the scheme was a good o. on paper** le plan était excellent en théorie; **that's a good o.!** (*story, joke*) elle est bonne, celle-là!; **have you heard the o. about ...?** est-ce que tu as déjà entendu celle de ...?; **that's a hard o.** (*a difficult question*) vous me posez une colle; **our loved** *or* **dear ones** ceux qui nous sont chers; (*our dead friends, relatives*) nos chers disparus; **the little ones** (*children*) les petits enfants; **he's a strange o., that boy** il est bizarre ce garçon

4 *indef pron* **(a)** [①A20,b; A37-38,h; B15,2] (*pl* **some, any**) **I haven't a pencil, have you got o.?** je n'ai pas de crayon, en avez-vous un?; **this question is o. of extreme delicacy** ce problème est délicat entre tous; **o. of them** l'un d'entre eux, l'un d'eux; **give me o. of them** donnez m'en un; *Old-fashioned F* **I think he's o. of them** (*homosexual*) je crois qu'il en est; **o. of these days** un de ces jours; **she is o. of the family** elle fait partie de la famille, elle est de la famille; **he is o. of us** il est des nôtres; **o. of my friends** un de mes amis, un ami à moi; **any o. of us** n'importe lequel d'entre nous; **o. and all** tous sans exception; **Merry Christmas to o. and all** Joyeux Noël à tous; *prov* **o. for all and all for o.** un pour tous et tous pour un; **(the) o. ... the other** l'un ... l'autre; **you can't have o. without the other** l'un ne va pas sans l'autre; **o. after the other** l'un après l'autre; **o. at a time** un à la fois; **o. by o.** un à un, un par un

(b) (*particular person*) [①A38,iv] **I want the opinion of o. better able to judge** je voudrais avoir l'opinion de quelqu'un qui soit plus capable de juger; **o. Anne Martin** une certaine Anne Martin; **I, for o., do not believe it** pour ma part je n'en crois rien; **I'm not o. to complain** je ne suis pas du genre à me plaindre; **I'm not much of a o. for sweets** je ne suis pas grand amateur de bonbons; **he's a great o. for letting you know exactly what he thinks** il n'a pas son pareil pour vous faire savoir ce qu'il pense; **she's a great o. for foreign travel** elle adore voyager à l'étranger; *Old-fashioned* **you are a o.!** vous êtes fameux *ou* impayable, vous!

(c) [①A28,h; B15,2,c] *esp Fml* (*people in general*) (*subject*) on; (*direct and indirect object*) vous; **o. cannot always be right** on ne peut pas toujours avoir raison; **if o. wanted to do it** si l'on voulait le faire; **it is enough to make o. weep** il y a de quoi vous faire pleurer; **o.'s** son, sa, *pl* ses; (*object*) votre, *pl* vos; **if o. loses o.'s** *or US* **his** ... si on perd son ...

(d) o. another l'un l'autre, l'une l'autre, *pl* les uns les autres, les unes les autres; **to look at o. another** se regarder

one-act *adj attrib* **o. play** pièce *f* en un acte

one-armed *adj* (*person*) manchot; *Br F* **o. bandit** machine *f* à sous

one-eyed *adj* (*person*) borgne; **o. man/woman** borgne *mf*

one-horse *adj F* **o. town** petite ville *f* de rien du tout, trou *m* perdu

one-legged *adj* unijambiste; **o. man/woman** unijambiste *mf*

one-liner *n* bon mot *m*

one-man *adj attrib* (*job etc*) pour un seul homme; **o. band** homme-orchestre *m*, *pl* hommes-orchestres; *Fig* entreprise *f* individuelle; **o. show** *Art* exposition *f* individuelle; *Th* (spectacle *m*) solo *m*; *Fig* entreprise individuelle; *Com* **o. company** société *f* à une seule personne *ou* à personne unique *ou* unipersonnelle

oneness ['wʌnnɪs] *n* (*unity*) unité *f*; (*of opinions*) accord *m*

one-night *adj* **o. stand** *Th* représentation *f* unique; *Mus* unique concert *m*; *F* (*sexual encounter*) histoire *f* *ou* rencontre *f* sans lendemain

one-off *Br* **1** *adj Com* (*item*) spécial, hors série; (*order, job*) unique; (*situation*) exceptionnel; **a o. design** un modèle exclusif **2** *n* (*object*) objet *m*/exemplaire *m* unique; (*order*) commande *f* unique; (*job*) tâche *f* unique; **he was a o.** c'était quelqu'un d'unique; **the mistake was a o.** cette erreur ne se reproduira pas; **her success was a o.** son succès sera sans lendemain; **I promise you, this is a o.** c'est exceptionnel, je vous le promets; **as a o., you can have it for just £50** à titre exceptionnel, je vous le laisse pour 50 livres

one-one, one-on-one *adj, adv Am* = **one-to-one**

one-parent *adj* **o. family** famille *f* monoparentale

one-party *adj attrib* à parti unique

one-piece *adj* d'une seule pièce; *Tech* (*casting*) monobloc *inv*; **o. swimsuit** maillot *m* une pièce

one price *n* prix *m* unique

oner ['wʌnər] *n Br F* **to do sth in a o.** faire qch d'un seul coup; **to down a drink in a o.** faire cul sec; **he got it in a o.** (*understood*) il a tout de suite pigé; (*got answer*) il a tout de suite trouvé la solution

onerous ['ɒnərəs, 'əʊ-] *adj* (*tax, task, responsibility*) lourd; **he's finding all this responsibility rather o.** il trouve que toutes ces responsabilités sont plutôt lourdes à porter

oneself [wʌn'self] *pron* (①A29) **(a)** [①B26,D] (*reflexive*) se; **to wash/feed/flatter o.** se laver/se nourrir/se flatter; **to look after o.** (*when ill*) (*generally*) se soigner, s'occuper de soi; **to speak of o.** parler de soi; **to keep o. to o.** être peu sociable, ne pas se mêler aux autres; **to feel o. again** se sentir complètement rétabli **(b)** (*emphatic*) soi-même; *Fml* **one must do it o.** il faut le faire soi-même; **to do sth all by o.** faire qch tout seul

one-sided *adj* (*unfair*) (*contest*) inégal; (*contract*) inégal, inéquitable; (*judgment*) partial; (*relationship*) à sens unique

one-step *n* (*dance*) one-step *m*

one-stop *adj Com* **o. buying** achats *mpl* regroupés; *Comptr* **o. desktop connection** connexion *f* directe à un ordinateur de bureau; *Com* **o. shop** *or* **store** magasin *m* où l'on trouve de tout; *Com* **o. shopping** achats *mpl* regroupés (dans un seul magasin)

one-time *adj* ancien; **Mr Martin, o. mayor** M. Martin, ancien maire

one-to-one 1 *adj* (*correspondence, connection, relationship between meanings, figures etc*) univoque; (*relationship between people*) exclusif; (*conversation, meeting*) seul à seul, en tête à tête; **the first time I met her in a o. situation** la première fois que je l'ai rencontrée en tête à tête *ou* seul à seul; **o. tuition** cours *mpl* particuliers **2** *adv* (*to talk, meet*) seul à seul, en tête à tête; (*to correspond*) de manière univoque, exclusivement

one-touch *adj* **o. electric windows** lève-vitre *m* électrique à commande tactile

one-track *adj* **to have a o. mind** avoir une idée fixe; (*be obsessed with sex*) ne penser qu'à ça *ou* qu'à une chose; **will you stop going on about work—you're developing a o. mind** vas-tu arrêter de parler de travail—ça devient une idée fixe chez toi

one-upmanship [wʌn'ʌpmənʃɪp] *n F* art *m* de se montrer supérieur aux autres; **this is no time for o.** ce n'est pas le moment d'essayer de démontrer sa supériorité; **that's a nice piece of o.** voilà une belle démonstration de supériorité

one-way *adj* **(a)** (*ticket*) simple; *Com* (*packaging*) perdu **(b)** (*street, traffic*) à *ou* en sens unique; **their relationship was all o.** leurs rapports étaient à sens unique; **o. valve** clapet *m* anti-retour

ongoing ['ɒngəʊɪŋ] *adj* **(a)** (*continuing, permanent*) continuel; **for them it's an o. state of affairs** pour eux c'est une situation courante *ou* habituelle **(b)** (*happening now*) (*research, discussions, restructuring*) en cours, actuel; (*work*) en cours; **is it o. at the moment?** est-ce que c'est en train de se faire?

onion ['ʌnjən] *n* **(a)** oignon *m*; **string of onions** chapelet *m* d'oignons; *Culin* **o. soup** soupe *f* à l'oignon **(b)** *Br Sl* **she knows her onions** elle connaît son affaire, elle s'y connaît

onionskin ['ʌnjənskɪn] *n* (*paper*) pelure *f* d'oignon

oniony ['ʌnjənɪ] *adj* (*in smell*) qui sent l'oignon; (*in taste*) qui a un goût d'oignon

on-line *adj* **(a)** *Comptr* connecté, en ligne; (*with a connection set up*) connecté; **to be o. to sth** être connecté à qch; **to be o. to sb/sth** (*by modem*) être en ligne avec qn/qch; **to go on.** se connecter; **to put the printer o.** connecter l'imprimante; **o. backup** sauvegarde *f* en ligne; **o. cashdesk terminal** terminal *m* de paiement connecté; *TV* **o. editing** montage *m* 'on-line', conformation *f*; *TV* **o. editor** monteur *m* 'on-line'; **o. interviewing** enquête *f* téléphonique 'en ligne'; *Comptr* **o. mode** mode *m* connecté; **o. operation** opération *f* en ligne; **o. programming** programmation *f* en ligne; **o. test** test *m* en ligne; **o. time** durée *f* de connexion

(b) o. area (*area where carrier has right to operate*) zone *f* autorisée

onlooker ['ɒnlʊkər] *n* spectateur, -trice; (*at accident, incident*) badaud *m*

only ['əʊnlɪ] **1** *adj* seul, unique; **o. child** enfant *mf* unique; **o. son/daughter** (*sole child*) fils/fille unique; (*sole son/daughter*) seul(e) fils/fille; **his o. answer was to laugh** pour toute réponse il a ri; **we are the o. people who know it** nous sommes les seuls à le savoir; **you are not the o. one** vous n'êtes pas le seul; **the o. thing is that it's rather expensive** seulement ça coûte cher; **Edinburgh is the o. place to live** Edimbourg est la ville idéale pour vivre

2 *adv* [①A24,d,iii] seulement, ne ... que, ne ... rien que; **she has o. one brother** elle n'a qu'un (seul) frère; **it's o. a scratch** c'est seulement une égratignure, ce n'est (rien) qu'une égratignure; **o. half an hour more** plus qu'une demi-heure; **one man o.** un seul homme; **(entrance for) season ticket holders o.** entrée réservée aux abonnés; **o. an expert could advise us** seul un expert pourrait nous conseiller; **I o. touched it** je n'ai fait que le toucher; **he has o. to ask for it** il n'a qu'à le demander; **I will o. say that I disagree** je me bornerai à dire que je ne suis pas de cet avis; **I shall be o. too pleased to come** je ne serai que trop heureux de venir; **o. if you agree** seulement si tu es d'accord; **o. think what pleasure it gave me** imaginez un peu le plaisir que cela m'a fait; **if o. I knew where he was!** si seulement je savais où il est!; **if o. they knew!, if they o. knew!** si (seulement) ils savaient!; **not o. useful but also decorative** non seulement utile, mais aussi décoratif; **she left o. yesterday** elle n'est partie qu'hier; **o. last week he appeared to be quite happy** la semaine dernière encore, il semblait parfaitement heureux; **I saw her/used it o. yesterday** je l'ai vue/m'en suis servi pas plus tard qu'hier; **o. just** à peine; **it's o. me** (*wanting to come in, speak to you etc*) ce n'est que moi

3 *conj* mais; **the book is interesting, o. rather too long** le livre est intéressant, mais un peu long; **I would do it o. I can't spare the time** je le ferais si j'avais le temps

only-begotten [əʊnlɪbɪˈgɒt(ə)n] *adj, n Rel* **the o. (Son) of the Father** le Fils unique du Père

o.n.o. [əʊenˈəʊ] *adv Com* (*abbr* **or nearest offer**) à débattre

onomatopoeia [ɒnəmætəˈpiːə] *n* onomatopée *f*

onomatopoeic [ɒnəmætəˈpiːɪk] *adj* onomatopéique

on-ramp *n* (*to motorway*) bretelle *f* d'accès

on-road *adj, adv* (*performance*) sur route

onrush [ˈɒnrʌʃ] *n* (*of people*) ruée *f*; (*of water*) torrent *m*; (*of emotions, desire*) flot *m*, vague *f*; (*of pain, grief*) vague

on-screen *adj Comptr* **o. graphics** graphiques *mpl* affichés; **o. help** aide *f* en ligne

onset [ˈɒnset] *n* **(a)** (*beginning*) (*of winter, illness, war*) début *m*, commencement *m*; **the o. of a disease** la première attaque d'une maladie **(b)** (*attack*) assaut *m*, attaque *f*

onshore [ˈɒnʃɔːr] *adj* **(a)** (*wind etc*) du large **(b)** (*oil rig etc*) à terre

on-site *adj, adv* (*supervision, maintenance*) sur site

onslaught [ˈɒnslɔːt] *n* assaut *m*, attaque *f*; (*of policies etc*) attaque

on switch *n* bouton *m* de marche

Ont *abbr* **Ontario**

on-the-job *adj* **o. training** formation *f* sur le tas

on-the-spot fine *n* amende *f* immédiate

onto [ˈɒntʊ, *unstressed* ˈɒntə] *prep* = **on to**, *see* **on**

ontological [ɒntəˈlɒdʒɪk(ə)l] *adj Phil* ontologique

ontology [ɒnˈtɒlədʒɪ] *n Phil* ontologie *f*

onus [ˈəʊnəs] *n* responsabilité *f*, obligation *f*; **the o. is on the government to compensate the victims** il incombe au gouvernement d'indemniser les sinistrés; **the o. is now on United to attack** United se doit maintenant d'attaquer; **the o. is on you to lodge a complaint** il tient à toi de déposer une plainte; *Jur* **o. of proof** charge *f* de la preuve; **the o. of proof lies with you** c'est à vous qu'il incombe d'en apporter la preuve

onward [ˈɒnwəd] **1** *adv* = **onwards 2** *adj* (*motion etc*) en avant; **we wish you a pleasant o. journey** nous vous souhaitons une bonne continuation pour votre voyage; **o. connection** correspondance *f*; **o. flight** continuation *f* en vol

onwards [ˈɒnwədz] *adv* en avant, plus loin; **from tomorrow/then o.** à partir de demain/de ce moment-là; **from this time o.** désormais, dorénavant

onyx [ˈɒnɪks] *n Miner* onyx *m*

oodles [ˈuːd(ə)lz] *npl F* **there's o. of it** il y en a un tas *ou* des tas *ou* une tapée; **to have o. of money** avoir un paquet *ou* une tonne de fric; **o. of cream** des tonnes de crème; **o. of time/space** plein de temps/d'espace

ooh [uː] *int* (*expressing surprise, awe, pleasure*) oh!

oolite [ˈəʊəlaɪt] *n* (*rock*) oolithe *m*

oomph [ʊmf] *n F* **(a)** (*energy*) énergie *f*; **to have plenty of o.** (*person*) avoir la pêche, avoir du punch; (*song, plot etc*) avoir du punch **(b)** (*sex appeal*) sex-appeal *m*

oops [uːps] *int* **(a)** (*to child who has fallen down*) houp-là! **(b)** (*after sb has made a mistake*) oh là là!

oops-a-daisy *int* = **oops**

ooze[1] [uːz] *n* **(a)** (*mud*) vase *f*, limon *m* **(b)** (*flow*) (*of liquid*) suintement *m*

ooze[2] **1** *vi* suinter **(from** de); **the wound was oozing with pus/blood** du pus/sang suintait de la plaie; **water that oozes out from the rock** eau qui sourd du rocher; **the walls were oozing with water** les murs suintaient, l'eau suintait des murs; **the mud oozed up between her toes** la boue sourdait lentement entre ses orteils; *Fig* **to o. with confidence** déborder d'assurance **2** *vt* **the wound was oozing pus/blood** du pus/sang suintait de la plaie; *Fig* **to o. confidence** déborder d'assurance; **to o. charm** exsuder un charme mielleux; *Fig* **this place just oozes wealth** cet endroit sue l'opulence

op[1] [ɒp] *n Surg, Mil F* (*abbr* **operation**) opération *f*

op[2] *adj Art* **op art** op art *m*

opacity [əʊˈpæsɪtɪ] *n* opacité *f*; *Fig* (*of writing etc*) caractère *m* obscur, obscurité *f*

opal [ˈəʊp(ə)l] *n* **(a)** (*mineral*) opale *f*; **o. necklace** collier *m* d'opale **(b)** (*colour*) opale *m inv* **(c) o. (glass)** verre *f* opale, opaline *f*

opalescence [əʊpəˈlesəns] *n* opalescence *f*

opalescent [əʊpəˈlesənt] *adj* opalescent; (*hue*) opale *inv*; (*haze etc*) opalisé

opaline [ˈəʊpəlaɪn] **1** *adj* opalin **2** *n* (*glass*) opaline *f*

opaque [əʊˈpeɪk] *adj* **(a)** opaque; **to become o.** s'opacifier **(b)** *Fig* (*words, comments, style*) obscur

opaqueness [əʊˈpeɪknɪs] *n* = **opacity**

OPEC [ˈəʊpek] *n Petr* (*abbr* **Organization of Petroleum-Exporting Countries**) OPEP *f*; **O. countries/prices** pays/prix de l'OPEP

op-ed [ˈɒped] *n Journ* (*leaders page*) page *f* face éditorial

open[1] [ˈəʊp(ə)n] **1** *adj* **(a)** (*box, door, book, shop etc*) ouvert; *Fig* **my door is always o.** ma porte t'est/vous est/*etc* toujours ouverte; **half o.** (*door, window*) entrouvert, entrebâillé; **o. to the public** (*museum etc*) ouvert *ou* accessible au public; **o. all night** ouvert (toute) la nuit; **o. late** ouvert en nocturne; *Jur* **in o. court** en plein tribunal; **career o. to very few** carrière accessible à très peu de gens *ou* très fermée; *Golf, Tennis* **o. championship** championnat open *inv ou* ouvert; *Sp* **o. tournament** tournoi ouvert; **o. invitation** invitation permanente; **it's an o. invitation to tax-dodgers/thieves** c'est une invitation à la fraude fiscale/aux voleurs; **o.** *Br* **day** *or Am* **house** journée *f* porte(s) ouverte(s); **to keep o. house** tenir table ouverte

(b) (*not enclosed*) découvert, non couvert; (*coast, position*) exposé **(to** à); **in the o. countryside** en pleine campagne, en rase campagne; **there's a lot of o. countryside** c'est la pleine campagne; **o. country** (*not offering protection*) terrain découvert; **in (the) o. country** (*not wooded*) en pleine *ou* rase campagne; **to work in the o. fields** travailler en pleins champs; **in the o. air** au grand air, à ciel ouvert; **to sleep in the o. air** coucher à la belle étoile; **the o. sea** la haute mer, le large; **o. space** (*park*) espace *m* vert; **the city was designed with lots of o. spaces** la ville a été conçue de manière très aérée; **the wide o. spaces** les grands espaces; **o. to the elements/to the winds** exposé aux intempéries/aux quatre vents; **o. to doubt** douteux; **o. to ridicule** qui prête au ridicule; **o. to criticism** critiquable; **o. to question** contestable; **she is still o. to persuasion on the issue** on peut encore lui faire changer d'avis sur la question; **the Government has left itself o. to the criticism that ...** le gouvernement a prêté le flanc à la critique de ...; **o. to any reasonable offer** disposé à considérer toute offre raisonnable; **to be o. to suggestions** être ouvert à toute suggestion; *Fb* **to leave the goal o.** dégarnir ses buts; **o. carriage** voiture découverte

(c) (*frank*) (*person, personality*) ouvert, franc, *f* franche; (*conflict, disagreement*) ouvert; (*preference, favouritism*) manifeste, public, *f* -ique; **to be o. in one's affection** témoigner ouvertement son affection; **to be o. with sb** parler franchement à qn, être franc avec qn; **he is o. about his homosexuality** il ne cache pas son homosexualité; **her o. dislike** son aversion déclarée; **they are in o. revolt** ils sont en révolte ouverte; **o. enemy** ennemi déclaré; **o. hostilities** guerre ouverte; **o. inquiry** enquête publique; **o. letter** (*in newspaper*) lettre ouverte; **o. secret** secret *m* de Polichinelle

(d) (*flower, lips, hand*) ouvert; **o. at the neck** (*of dress*) échancré; **his shirt was o. at the neck** le col de sa chemise était ouvert; **with eyes o. wide** les yeux écarquillés; **to welcome with o. arms** (*person*) accueillir à bras ouverts; (*proposal, development etc*) accueillir avec enthousiasme; *Ling* **o. vowel** voyelle ouverte; **o. wound** (*gaping*) plaie *f* béante; (*not healed*) plaie non cicatrisée

(e) (*clear, unobstructed*) libre, non obstrué; **road o. to traffic** route ouverte à la circulation; **to keep one's bowels o.** aller à la selle régulièrement; (*of diet*) faciliter le transit intestinal; **to keep a day o. for sb** réserver un jour pour qn; **the job is still o.** la place est toujours vacante; **membership o. to anyone over 18** inscription ouverte à toute personne de plus de 18 ans; **two courses/choices are o. to us** deux moyens/choix s'offrent à nous; **an o. border** une frontière ouverte; *Mus* **o. string** corde *f* à vide; **o. view** vue *f* dégagée

(f) (*unresolved*) non résolu; (*question, case*) pendant; **to keep an o. mind on sth** réserver son opinion sur qch; **to leave the matter o.** ne pas prendre de décision *ou* ne pas trancher sur la question; **I want to leave the return date o.** (*on ticket*) je ne veux pas réserver le retour tout de suite

(g) *Fin* **o. cheque** chèque *m* en blanc; **o. credit** crédit *m* à découvert, crédit en blanc

(h) *Fb etc* (*play*) (*free-flowing*) ouvert, dégagé

2 *n* **(a) in the o.** (*outdoors*) dehors; (*to go for a stroll, work etc*) au grand air, dehors; (*not hidden*) au grand jour; **to sleep in the o.** dormir à la belle étoile; *Fig* **to bring sth out into the o.** mettre qch au grand jour; **their mutual dislike was out in the o.** ils affichaient ouvertement l'antipathie qu'ils avaient l'un pour l'autre; *Fig* **let's get all this out in the o.** jouons cartes sur table; **to come out into the o. about sth** révéler qch

(b) *Sp* open *m*

3 *adv* **to fling the door wide o.** ouvrir la porte toute grande; **the door flew o.** la porte s'ouvrit brusquement; **to**

cut o. couper, ouvrir; **to force sth o.** forcer qch; **to smash/ lever sth o.** ouvrir qch en le fracassant/à l'aide d'un levier

open² **1** *vt* **(a)** (*door, book, parcel, hand, eyes etc*) ouvrir; (*bottle*) ouvrir, déboucher; (*letter*) ouvrir, décacheter; (*post*) ouvrir, dépouiller; (*institution, establishment*) inaugurer; (*legs etc*) écarter; **to o. the door wide** ouvrir la porte toute grande; *Med* **to o. the bowels** aller à la selle; **to o. one's shop** (*in morning etc*) ouvrir son magasin; **to o. a new shop** ouvrir *ou* monter un nouveau magasin; **to o. a park to the public/a road (to traffic)** ouvrir un parc au public/une route à la circulation; **to o. one's heart** ouvrir son cœur, s'ouvrir **(to sb** à qn); **that opens new prospects for me** cela m'ouvre de nouveaux horizons; **to o. Parliament** ouvrir la session du Parlement

(b) (*make*) (*tunnel*) creuser; (*hole*) faire

(c) (*begin*) commencer; (*negotiations, conversation, debate*) entamer, engager; (*performance*) ouvrir; (*fire, hostilities*) ouvrir; **to o. an account in sb's name** ouvrir un compte à qn; *Jur* **to o. the case** exposer les faits

2 *vi* **(a)** s'ouvrir; **to half o.** (*of door etc*) s'entrebâiller, s'entrouvrir; **door that opens into the garden** porte qui donne sur le jardin; **o. wide!** (*said by doctor, dentist etc*) ouvrez grand la bouche!

(b) (*of shop, museum*) ouvrir; **to o. late** (*of shop*) ouvrir en nocturne; **as soon as the season opens** dès l'ouverture de la saison

(c) (*of view, prospects*) s'étendre; (*of flower*) s'épanouir, s'ouvrir

(d) (*begin*) commencer; **the play opens with a death scene** la pièce s'ouvre sur une scène de mort; *Cin* **the film opens next week** le film sort la semaine prochaine; *St Exch* **the FTSE opened at 1083** l'indice FT a ouvert à 1083

▶ **open out 1** *vi* **(a)** (*of flower*) s'ouvrir; (*of wings*) se déployer; (*of view, prospects*) s'ouvrir, s'étendre **(b)** (*become wider*) s'élargir **(into** pour donner dans) **(c)** *Fig* (*of person*) s'ouvrir **2** *vtsep* **(a)** (*unfold*) (*sheet of paper, map*) ouvrir, déplier **(b)** (*develop*) (*company*) développer **(c)** (*widen*) (*hole*) élargir, agrandir; (*mouth of pipe*) évaser

▶ **open up 1** *vi* **(a)** (*of flower*) s'ouvrir

(b) (*of view, prospects*) s'ouvrir, s'étendre; **new markets are opening up** de nouveaux marchés sont en train de s'ouvrir

(c) (*of shopkeeper etc*) ouvrir; **this is the police, o. up!** police! ouvrez!

(d) (*of new shop etc*) ouvrir

(e) *Fig* (*of person*) s'ouvrir **(to sb** à qn)

(f) *Mil* ouvrir le feu

2 *vtsep* **(a)** (*letter, parcel, box, newspaper*) ouvrir

(b) (*make accessible*) (*a country to trade, mine*) ouvrir; (*path*) ouvrir, frayer, rendre praticable; **this remote area is being opened up for development** cette région reculée commence à être exploitée

(c) (*possibility of sth*) ouvrir; **to o. up opportunities** donner des chances

(d) (*start*) **to o. up a business** ouvrir *ou* monter une affaire; **to o. up shop** (*in the morning etc*) ouvrir la boutique

open-air *adj* (*restaurant, market, life etc*) en plein air; (*swimming pool*) découvert; **she's an o. girl** elle aime la vie *ou* les occupations en plein air

open-and-shut *adj* **it was an o. case** tout était clair comme de l'eau de roche; **this may not be such an o. case as it first appears** ce n'est peut-être pas aussi simple que cela paraît au premier abord

opencast ['əʊpənkɑːst] *adj Br* (*mining*) à ciel ouvert, au jour

open-date ticket *n* billet *m* open *inv ou* ouvert

open-door *adj* **o. policy** (*for immigrants*) politique *f* d'ouverture des frontières; (*of university etc*) politique d'ouverture

open-ended ['əʊpən'endɪd] *adj* **o. credit/contract** crédit/ contrat *m* à durée indéterminée; **o. discussion** libre discussion *f*; **it's a bit too o.** c'est un peu trop vague; **can we leave it o. for the time being?** est-ce nous pouvons ne pas tout fixer tout de suite?; **avoid o. commitments** évite de t'engager sans fixer de limites; **could we keep the arrangement o.?** pourrions-nous garder une certaine flexibilité au niveau de notre arrangement?; **o. question** question *f* ouverte; **o. spanner** clé *f* ouverte

opener ['əʊpənər] *n* **(a)** *Th* (*item on programme*) premier numéro *m*; *F* **for openers** pour commencer **(b)** (*device*) **(bottle) o.** décapsuleur *m*; **(can** *or* **tin) o.** ouvre-boîtes *m inv* **(c)** *Cr* premier batteur *m*

open-eyed *adj* qui a les yeux ouverts; **to look at sb in o. astonishment** regarder qn les yeux écarquillés de surprise

open-handed [əʊpən'hændɪd] *adj* généreux; **to be o.** être généreux, avoir la main sur le cœur

open-heart *adj* (*surgery*) à cœur ouvert

open-hearted [əʊpən'hɑːtɪd] *adj* (*kind*) charitable

open-hearth *adj Metal* **o. furnace** four *m* à sole, four Martin

opening ['əʊpənɪŋ] **1** *n* **(a)** (*of door, shop, account, one's heart etc*) ouverture *f*; **formal o.** inauguration *f*; **the o. of Parliament** l'ouverture du Parlement; *Com* **late o. Friday** ≈ nocturne le vendredi

(b) (*beginning*) (*of play, new era*) commencement *m*, début *m*; (*of negotiations*) ouverture *f*; (*start of letter*) formule *f* de début; *Jur* (*speech by lawyer*) exposition *f* des faits

(c) (*open space*) (*in wall*) ouverture *f*, trou *m*; (*for door, window*) embrasure *f*, baie *f*; (*in forest*) clairière *f*; (*man-made also*) percée *f*; (*between the trees*) échappée *f*

(d) (*mouth, entrance*) (*of cave, tunnel*) entrée *f*; (*of sack*) ouverture *f*

(e) (*opportunity*) occasion *f* favorable; (*job*) poste *m*, place *f* **(as** de); *Com* (*for merchandise*) débouché *m*; **this could be your big o.** ça pourrait être la chance de ta vie; **I didn't get an o.** (*to mention it*) je n'ai pas eu l'occasion

2 *adj* **o. address** *or* **speech** discours *m* d'ouverture; **o. balance sheet** bilan *m* d'ouverture; *Cr* **o. batsman** premier batteur *m*; *Cards* **o. bid** annonce *f* d'entrée *ou* d'indication; **o. bracket** parenthèse *f* ouvrante; **o. ceremony** cérémonie *f* d'inauguration; *Th* **o. day** jour *m* d'ouverture; *Th* **the o. lines** les premières lignes; **o. price** cours *m* d'ouverture; **o. quotation marks** guillemets *mpl* ouvrants; *Th* **the o. scene** la scène d'ouverture; **o. stock** stock *m* initial

opening hours *npl* heures *fpl* d'ouverture

opening night *n Th* première *f*

opening time *n* heure *f* d'ouverture

openly ['əʊpənlɪ] *adv* ouvertement; (*publicly*) publiquement; (*in front of everyone*) au vu (et au su) de tous; (*to speak*) sans réticence; **to be o. critical of sb** critiquer qn ouvertement; **to act o.** agir à découvert *ou* cartes sur table, jouer franc jeu

open market *n* marché *m* libre

open-minded *adj* qui a l'esprit ouvert; **to be o. on** *or* **about sth** ne pas avoir de parti pris *ou* d'idée préconçue sur qch; **her parents are very o.** ses parents sont des gens très ouverts

open-mouthed [əʊpən'maʊðd] *adj* **to stand o.** *or* **in o. astonishment** rester bouche bée

openness ['əʊpənnɪs] *n* **(a)** (*frankness*) franchise *f*; **I was surprised by the o. with which they expressed their criticism** cela m'a surpris qu'ils expriment leurs critiques aussi ouvertement **(b)** (*of mind*) largeur *f*, ouverture *f* **(c)** (*of coastline etc*) situation *f* exposée; (*of terrain*) aspect *m* découvert; **the o. of the countryside** les grands horizons

open outcry system *n St Exch* système *m* de criée

open-plan *adj* (*office*) paysager; (*flat*) sans cloison; **we've gone o.** nous avons maintenant un bureau paysager

open prison *n* prison *f* ouverte

open sandwich *n Culin* canapé *m*

open season *n Hunting* chasse *f* ouverte; *Fig* **to declare o. on sb/sth** partir en guerre contre qn/qch

open shop *n Ind* atelier *m* qui admet les ouvriers non-syndiqués

open ticket *n* billet *m* open *inv*

open-top *adj* décapotable

open-topped bus *n* autobus *m* à impériale

Open University *n Br* = enseignement *m* universitaire par correspondance doublé d'émissions de télévision ou de radio

open verdict *n Jur* verdict *m* de décès sans cause déterminée

openwork ['əʊpənwɜːk] *n* (*piece of embroidery*) ouvrage *m* ajouré *ou* à jour; (*holes*) jours *mpl*, ajours *mpl*; **o. stockings** bas ajourés *ou* à jour

opera ['ɒp(ə)rə] *n* opéra *m*; **comic o., o. bouffe** opéra bouffe *ou* comique; **o. (company)** (compagnie *f* d')opéra; **o. glasses** jumelles *fpl* de théâtre; **o. goer** amateur *m* d'opéra; **o. (house)** opéra; **o. singer** chanteur, -euse d'opéra

operable ['ɒp(ə)rəb(ə)l] *adj* **(a)** *Surg* (*disease, tumour*) opérable **(b)** (*system etc*) utilisable

operand ['ɒpərænd] *n* opérande *m*

operate ['ɒpəreɪt] **1** *vi* **(a)** (*of machine*) fonctionner; (*of burglar, company etc*) opérer, travailler; **the wage increase will o. from the first of January** l'augmentation des salaires prendra effet à partir du premier janvier **(b)** *Surg* opérer; **to o. (on sb) for appendicitis** opérer (qn) de l'appendicite; **to be operated on** subir une opération *ou* une intervention chirurgicale, se faire opérer

2 *vt* **(a)** (*of person*) (*machine*) manœuvrer; (*brakes*) actionner; (*of part of machine*) commander, actionner; **operated by electricity** actionné par l'électricité

(b) *Com* (*rail or bus service, business*) exploiter

operatic [ɒpəˈrætɪk] **1** *adj* d'opéra; **o. society** groupe *m* d'opéra d'amateurs **2** *npl* **operatics** (*amateur*) opéra *m* d'amateurs

operating [ˈɒpəreɪtɪŋ] *adj attrib* **(a)** *Acct* **income from o. activities** produits *mpl* d'exploitation; **o. cost** charge *f* opérationnelle; **o. costs** frais *mpl ou* coûts *mpl* d'exploitation; **o. expenses** frais d'exploitation; **o. income** produits d'exploitation; **o. loss** perte *f* d'exploitation; **o. margin** marge *f* d'exploitation; **o. profit** bénéfice *m* d'exploitation; **o. profit or loss** résultat *m* d'exploitation; **o. ratio** coefficient *m* d'exploitation

(b) o. instructions instructions *fpl ou* règlements *mpl* de service; *Comptr* **o. speed** vitesse *f* d'exécution; *Comptr* **o. system** système *m* d'exploitation; **o. system command** commande *f* du système d'exploitation

(c) *Surg* **o. table** table *f* d'opération; **o.** *Br* **theatre** *or US* **room** salle *f* d'opération, bloc *m* opératoire

operation [ɒpəˈreɪʃən] *n* **(a)** (*functioning*) (*of appliance, machine*) fonctionnement *m*, marche *f*; (*of mechanism*) jeu *m*; **in o.** (*machine*) en marche, en fonctionnement; (*law*) en application, en vigueur; **to come into o.** (*of machine*) commencer à fonctionner; (*of law*) entrer en application *ou* en vigueur; (*of curfew, rationing*) être imposé

(b) (*controlling*) (*of machine etc*) manœuvre *f*, commande *f*; (*of reactor, ship, transport system, business*) exploitation *f*

(c) (*process*) opération *f*; (*element*) (*of manufacture etc*) unité *f*; **it's a tricky o.** c'est une opération délicate; **(mathematical) o.** opération (mathématique); *Comptr* **(computer) o.** opération (machine); **operations research** recherche *f* opérationnelle; **a firm's operations** les activités *fpl* d'une entreprise; **the company is moving its soft drinks o.** la société déménage sa branche de boissons non alcoolisées; **operations manager** directeur *m* des exploitations

(d) *Mil etc* opération *f*; **operations room** salle *f* d'opérations (*d'un état-major*); **O. Snow** opération Neige

(e) *Surg* opération *f*, intervention *f* (chirurgicale); **an o. to have one's appendix out** une opération de l'appendicite; **to perform an o. on sb** opérer qn **(for** de); **to undergo** *or* **have an o.** se faire opérer, subir une opération *ou* une intervention chirurgicale **(for** de); **a throat o.** une opération de la gorge

operational [ɒpəˈreɪʃən(ə)l] *adj* **(a)** *Mil etc* opérationnel; **o. training** instruction *f* tactique, entraînement *m* de guerre *ou* au combat **(b)** (*machine*) opérationnel, en état de marche *ou* de fonctionnement; **the new power station should be o. next year** la nouvelle centrale électrique devrait être opérationnelle l'an prochain **(c)** *Com* (*costs, requirements*) d'exploitation; *Acct* **o. cost accounting** comptes *mpl* analytiques d'exploitation; *Acct* **o. cost centre** centre *m* d'analyse opérationnel; **o. marketing** mercatique *f* opérationnelle; **o. planning** planification *f* des opérations

operative [ˈɒpərətɪv] **1** *adj* **(a)** (*law, rule etc*) en vigueur; **to become o.** (*of law*) entrer en vigueur, prendre effet; **the o. word** le mot clé **(b)** *Surg* (*method*) opératoire **2** *n* **(a)** (*worker*) ouvrier, -ière; (*of machine etc*) opérateur, -trice **(b)** *US* (*detective*) détective *m* **(c)** (*secret agent*) agent *m* secret

operator [ˈɒpəreɪtər] *n* **(a)** (*person*) (*of machine*) opérateur, -trice; (*of business*) exploitant, -ante; **the o. of the service, British Airways, ...** la compagnie qui assure le service, British Airways, ...; **(tour) o.** tour opérateur *m*, voyagiste *m*; *F* **he's a pretty slick o.** c'est un petit débrouillard, il se débrouille plutôt bien; **he's a pretty quick o.** il va vite en besogne **(b)** *Tel* téléphoniste *mf*; *Com* (*in hotel etc*) standardiste *mf*; **radio** *or* **wireless o.** (opérateur, -trice de) radio *m*; *Tel* **switchboard o.** standardiste *mf* **(c)** *Math* (*of logarithm, logical*) opérateur *m*

operetta [ɒpəˈretə] *n Mus* opérette *f*

ophthalmic [ɒfˈθælmɪk] *adj* (*nerve, complaint*) ophtalmique; (*hospital*) ophtalmologique; **o. optician** opticien, -ienne optométriste

ophthalmologist [ɒfθælˈmɒlədʒɪst] *n Med* ophtalmologiste *mf*, ophtalmologue *mf*

ophthalmology [ɒfθælˈmɒlədʒɪ] *n Med* ophtalmologie *f*

opiate [ˈəʊpɪɪt] *n Pharm* opiacé *m*; *Fig Pej* **the o. of television** la télévision, cette drogue abrutissante

opine [əʊˈpaɪn] *vt Old-fashioned, Lit, Am* (*be of opinion*) être d'avis **(that** que + *sub*); (*state opinion*) exprimer l'avis **(that** que + *ind*)

opinion [əˈpɪnjən] *n* opinion *f*; **in my o.** à mon avis; **in the o. of experts** de l'avis *ou* au dire des experts, suivant *ou* selon l'opinion des experts; **to be of the o. that ...** être d'avis *ou* estimer que ...; **to be of the same o. as sb** être du même avis que qn, avoir la même opinion que qn; **to have a high/low o. of sb** avoir une bonne/mauvaise opinion de qn; **to express** *or* **put forward an o.** exprimer une opinion; **to ask sb's o.** demander l'avis de qn, consulter qn; **I'd like your o.** j'aimerais avoir ton opinion *ou* savoir ce que tu en penses; **that's my o., for what it's worth** c'est mon humble avis; **to form an o. of sb/sth** se faire une opinion sur *ou* de qn/qch; **I have no strong opinion(s) on the matter** je n'ai pas d'opinion très arrêtée sur la question; **what is your o. of him/on the situation?** que pensez-vous de lui/de la situation?; **opinions differ** les avis sont partagés; **o. is divided on the subject** les avis divergent sur le sujet; **that's a matter of o.** chacun ses opinions; **it's a matter of o.** c'est discutable; **it is the o. of the court that ...** la cour est d'avis que ...; **you ought to have a second o.** *Med* vous devriez consulter un autre médecin; (*generally*) vous devriez consulter quelqu'un d'autre; *Mktg* **o. former** *or* **leader** leader *m* d'opinion; **o. measurement technique** technique *f* de sondage de l'opinion

opinionated [əˈpɪnjəneɪtɪd] *adj Pej* (*tone*) dogmatique; (*person*) qui a des idées très arrêtées; **he can be quite o. on the subject** il a tendance à beaucoup dogmatiser sur le sujet

opinion poll *n* sondage *m* d'opinion (publique)

opinion pollster *n* sondeur, -euse (d'opinion)

opinion survey *n* sondage *m* d'opinion (publique)

opium [ˈəʊpɪəm] *n* opium *m*; **o. addict** opiomane *mf*; **o. den** fumerie *f* d'opium; **o. poppy** pavot *m* somnifère

Oporto [əˈpɔːtəʊ] *n* Porto *m*

opossum [əˈpɒsəm] *n* (*animal*) opossum *m*

opp (*abbr* **opposite**) en face

opponent [əˈpəʊnənt] *n* (*of reform, deregulation, in argument, match*) adversaire *mf*; (*of government*) opposant, -ante **(of** à)

opportune [ˈɒpətjuːn] *adj* (*time*) opportun; (*action*) à propos; **you have come at an o. moment** vous arrivez à propos, vous tombez bien

opportunely [ɒpəˈtjuːnlɪ] *adv* opportunément; (*to arrive*) opportunément, en temps opportun

opportunism [ɒpəˈtjuːnɪz(ə)m] *n* opportunisme *m*

opportunist [ɒpəˈtjuːnɪst] *adj, n* opportuniste *mf*

opportunistic [ɒpətjuːˈnɪstɪk] *adj* (*person, policy, disease*) opportuniste

opportunity [ɒpəˈtjuːnɪtɪ] *n* occasion *f* **(for** *or* **of doing sth, to do sth** de faire qch); **at every o.** à la moindre occasion; **at the first** *or* **earliest o.** à la première occasion; **I would go if I were you, it's the o. of a lifetime** à ta place j'irais, c'est la chance de ta vie; **if I get an o.** si l'occasion se présente, si j'en ai l'occasion; **to miss an o.** laisser passer *ou* perdre une occasion; **I'd like to take this o. to thank everyone** j'aimerais profiter de cette occasion pour remercier tout le monde; **a job with opportunities** un emploi qui offre des perspectives; *Mktg* **o. and issue analysis** analyse *f* des attraits et des atouts; *Mktg* **o. and threat analysis** analyse *f* des opportunités et des menaces; *Mktg* **o. to hear** occasion *f* d'entendre; *Mktg* **o. to see** occasion *f* de voir

oppose [əˈpəʊz] *vt* **(a)** (*resist*) (*person*) s'opposer à, résister à; (*reform, act etc*) faire obstacle *ou* opposition à; **to be opposed to sth** être opposé à qch; *Jur* **to o. an action/a marriage** s'opposer à un acte/un mariage **(b)** (*contrast*) opposer; (*two colours etc*) mettre en opposition *ou* en contraste

opposed [əˈpəʊzd] *adj* opposé; **as opposed to** par opposition à; **I'd say he was 'robust' as o. to simply 'fat'** je dirais qu'il était 'costaud' plutôt que simplement 'gros'

opposing [əˈpəʊzɪŋ] *adj* (*armies, characters, viewpoints*) opposé; (*party*) opposant; **o. team** équipe *f* adverse

opposite [ˈɒpəzɪt] **1** *adj* (*characters*) opposé; (*opinion*) contraire; (*end of room etc*) autre; (*wall*) d'en face, opposé; **to be of the o. opinion** être d'opinion contraire *ou* d'un avis contraire; **the o. sex** l'autre sexe; **in the o. direction** en sens inverse, dans le sens opposé; **they went in o. directions** ils prirent des directions opposées; **the diagram on the o. page** la figure ci-contre; *Aut* **o. lock** contre-braquage *m*; **to apply o. lock** contre-braquer; **o. number** (*of politician etc*) homologue *mf*

2 *n* contraire *m*; **the exact o.** exactement le contraire

3 *adv* en face; **the house o.** la maison (d')en face; **the page o.** la page ci-contre

4 *prep* en face de, vis-à-vis (de); **to stand/sit o. sb** être (debout)/être assis en face de qn, faire vis-à-vis à qn; **house o. the church** maison en face de l'église *ou* qui fait face à l'église; **we live o. them** nous habitons en face de chez eux; *Th, Cin* **she played o. many famous stars** elle a eu beaucoup de grandes vedettes comme partenaires

opposition [ɒpəˈzɪʃən] *n* opposition *f*, résistance *f*; *Com* (*competitors*) concurrence *f*; **to act in o. to public opinion** agir contrairement à l'opinion publique; **to meet with fierce o.** rencontrer une farouche opposition; **to break down all o.** vaincre toutes les résistances; *Pol* **to be in o.** être dans l'opposition; **the o.** le camp adverse; *Br Pol* **the O.** l'opposition; *Astron* **in o.** en opposition

oppress [ə'pres] *vt* (*conquered race, poor etc*) opprimer; (*the mind*) oppresser, opprimer

oppressed [ə'prest] **1** *adj* (*people*) opprimé **2** *npl* **the o.** les opprimés *mpl*

oppression [ə'preʃən] *n* oppression *f*

oppressive [ə'presɪv] *adj* **(a)** (*law, régime*) oppressif, opprimant **(b)** (*atmosphere*) lourd, étouffant; (*heat*) oppressant, accablant, étouffant **(c)** (*mental burden, excessive attentiveness, affection*) oppressant

oppressively [ə'presɪvlɪ] *adv* **(a)** (*to rule*) d'une manière oppressive **(b) it was o. hot** il faisait une chaleur accablante *ou* étouffante **(c)** (*with excessive affection*) d'une manière oppressante *ou* étouffante

oppressiveness [ə'presɪvnɪs] *n* **(a)** (*of law, regime*) caractère *m* oppressif **(b)** (*of weather*) lourdeur *f*; **the o. of the heat** la chaleur accablante *ou* étouffante **(c)** (*emotional*) caractère *m* oppressant

oppressor [ə'presər] *n* oppresseur *m*

opprobrious [ə'prəʊbrɪəs] *adj Fml* injurieux, outrageant

opprobrium [ə'prəʊbrɪəm] *n Fml* opprobre *m*; **to incur sb's o.** s'attirer le mépris de qn

opt [ɒpt] *vi* opter (**for** pour; **between** entre); **to o. to do sth** choisir de faire qch

▶ **opt in** *vi* (*join*) choisir de participer

▶ **opt into** *vipo* (*join*) **to o. into an association/the Common Market/***etc* entrer dans une association/le Marché Commun/*etc*

▶ **opt out** *vi* choisir de ne plus participer (**of** à); **to o. out of one's responsibilities/an agreement** se désengager de ses responsabilités/d'un accord; *Br* **to o. out** (**of local authority control**) (*of school, hospital etc*) devenir autonome; **to o. out of society** se mettre en marge de la société; **I'm opting out** pour moi, c'est terminé

optative ['ɒptətɪv] *adj, n Gram* optatif *m*

optic ['ɒptɪk] **1** *adj* optique; **o. drive** lecteur *m* optique; *Anat* **o. nerve** nerf *m* optique; **o. scanner** scanneur *m* optique **2** *n Br* **o.** ® = mesure *f* transparente (*utilisée dans les bars*)

optical ['ɒptɪk(ə)l] *adj* optique; (*instrument*) d'optique; **o. axis/centre** (*of lens*) axe *m*/centre *m* optique; *Comptr* **o. drive** lecteur *m* optique; **o. illusion** illusion *f* d'optique

optical character reader *n Comptr* lecteur *m* optique de caractères

optical character recognition *n Comptr* reconnaissance *f* optique des caractères

optical disk *n Comptr* disque *m* optique

optical fibre *n* fibre *f* optique; **o. cable** câble *m* à fibre optique; **o. technology** fibre *f* optique

optician [ɒp'tɪʃən] *n* opticien, -ienne

optics ['ɒptɪks] *n* [①**A10**,c] optique *f*

optimal ['ɒptɪm(ə)l] *adj* optimal; **o. price** prix *m* optimum; **o. pricing** fixation *f* du prix optimal; *Mktg* **o. psychological price** prix *m* psychologique optimum

optimism ['ɒptɪmɪz(ə)m] *n* optimisme *m*

optimist ['ɒptɪmɪst] *n* optimiste *mf*; **ever the o.** l'éternel optimiste

optimistic [ɒptɪ'mɪstɪk] *adj* optimiste; **things are looking quite o.** les choses se présentent plutôt bien

optimistically [ɒptɪ'mɪstɪklɪ] *adv* d'une manière optimiste, avec optimisme; **they o. predicted record profits** ils se sont montrés optimistes et ont prédit des bénéfices record

optimizer ['ɒptɪmaɪzər] *n Comptr* optimiseur *m*

optimum, *pl* **-ima** ['ɒptɪməm, -ɪmə] **1** *n* optimum *m* **2** *adj* **o. conditions** conditions optimums *ou* optima

option ['ɒpʃən] *n* **(a)** (*choice*) option *f*, choix *m*; **I can see no other o.** je ne vois pas d'autre solution; **the military o.** l'option militaire; **to have the o. of doing sth** avoir la possibilité *ou* le choix de faire qch; **we have the o. of staying here** nous avons la possibilité de rester ici; **to give** *or* **allow sb the o. of doing sth** donner à qn la possibilité de faire qch; **he didn't give me much o.** il ne m'a pas vraiment donné le choix; **we have no o. but to agree** nous ne pouvons rien faire d'autre que donner notre accord; **I haven't got any o., I've got no o.** je n'ai pas le choix; **do I have any o.?** est-ce que j'ai le choix?; **you leave me no o. but to phone the police** vous ne me laissez pas d'autre choix que celui d'appeler la police; *Jur* **imprisonment without the o. of a fine** emprisonnement sans substitution d'amende; **which of them is the best o.?** lequel est le meilleur choix?; **there was no soft o.** il n'y avait pas de solution facile; **it's no soft o.** ce n'est pas une partie de plaisir; **they always go for the soft o.** ils choisissent toujours la solution de facilité; **it's best to leave** *or* **keep your options open** il est préférable d'envisager toutes les possibilités; **to consider** *or* **review one's options** considérer toutes les lignes d'action possibles; **o. to buy** option *f* d'achat; **o. to sell** option *f* de vente; *Comptr* **o. box** case *f* d'option; *Comptr* **o. button** case *f* d'option
(b) *Com, St Exch etc* option *f*, (marché *m* à) prime *f*; **o. on shares** option *f* sur actions; **to take an o. on sth** prendre une option sur qch; *St Exch* **buyer's/seller's o.** prime acheteur/vendeur; *St Exch* **to take up an o.** lever une prime; *St Exch* **o. deal** opération *f* à prime; **options desk** desk *m* d'options; **options trading** négociations *fpl* à prime

optional ['ɒpʃən(ə)l] *adj* facultatif; **evening dress is o.** la tenue de soirée n'est pas de rigueur; **o. extras** accessoires *mpl* en option; *Mktg* **o.-feature pricing** fixation *f* du prix en fonction des options; **o. retirement at sixty** pré-retraite *f* à soixante ans; *Sch* **o. subjects** (*one must be chosen*) matières *fpl* à option *ou* optionnelles; (*possible to choose none*) matières facultatives

optomagnetic [ɒptəmæg'netɪk] *adj* magnéto-optique

optometrist [ɒp'tɒmɪtrɪst] *n* optométriste *mf*

opt-out 1 *adj attrib* (*clause, provisions*) de désengagement **2** *n* désengagement *m*

opulence ['ɒpjʊləns] *n* (*wealth*) opulence *f*, richesse *f*

opulent ['ɒpjʊlənt] *adj* **(a)** (*wealthy*) opulent **(b)** (*plentiful*) généreux, opulent

opulently ['ɒpjʊləntlɪ] *adv* (*to dress, decorate, dine etc*) avec opulence; (*to live*) dans l'opulence

opus, *pl* **opuses** *or* **opera** ['əʊpəs, 'ɒp-, -əsɪz, 'ɒpərə] *n* opus *m*

or [ɔːr, *unstressed* ər] *conj* [①**A68**,1,a,c] ou; (*with neg*) ni; **do you want beef or ham?** voulez-vous du bœuf ou du jambon?; **either one or the other** soit l'un soit l'autre, l'un ou l'autre; **either come in or (else) go out** entrez ou (bien) sortez; **don't move or (else) I'll shoot** pas un geste ou je tire; **either you or he has done it** c'est vous ou (c'est) lui qui l'a fait; **without money or luggage** sans argent ni bagages; **in a day or two** dans un ou deux jours; **a mile or so** environ un mil(l)e; **did she do it or not?** est-ce qu'elle l'a fait ou pas?; **we could go to the beach or we could go to the zoo** nous pourrions aller soit à la plage soit au zoo; *F* **do it now or else** fais-le tout de suite ou sinon ... (ça va aller mal)

oracle ['ɒrək(ə)l] *n* oracle *m*; (*priest, priestess*) oracle; **the Delphic o.** l'oracle de Delphes; **to consult the o.** consulter les oracles

oracular [ɒ'rækjʊlər] *adj* (*style etc*) d'oracle, oraculaire; (*réponse etc*) équivoque, obscur

oracy ['ɒrəsɪ] *n Fml* facultés *fpl* orales

oral ['ɔːrəl] **1** *adj* (*agreement, tradition, contraceptive*) oral; (*vaccine*) buccal; (*administration of medication*) par la bouche, par voie orale; *Anat* **o. cavity** cavité *f* orale *ou* buccale; **o. sex** rapports *mpl* bucco-génitaux; *Sch* **o. examination** (examen *m*) oral *m* **2** *n Sch* (examen *m*) oral *m*

orally ['ɔːrəlɪ] *adv* oralement, de vive voix; *Pharm* par la bouche, par voie orale

Orange ['ɒrɪndʒ] *n* **(a)** *Geog* **the O. (River)** l'Orange *m* **(b)** *Hist* **the Prince of O.** le prince d'Orange; **William of O.** Guillaume d'Orange

orange ['ɒrɪndʒ] **1** *n* **(a)** (*fruit*) orange *f*; **o. juice** jus *m* d'orange; **o. marmalade** confiture *f* d'orange(s); **o. peel** peau *f ou* écorce *f ou Culin* zeste *m* d'orange; **o. segment** quartier *m* d'orange; **o. squash** boisson *f* à l'orange **(b) o. (tree)** oranger *m*; **o. blossom** fleurs *fpl* d'oranger; **o. flower water** eau *f* de fleur d'oranger; **o. grove** orangeraie *f*; **o. stick** (*for fingernails*) bâtonnet *m* **(c)** (*colour*) orange *m*, orangé *m* **2** *adj* (*colour*) orangé, orange *inv*; **o. red** rouge orangé

orangeade [ɒrɪn'dʒeɪd] *n* (*fizzy*) soda *m* (à l')orange, boisson *f* gazeuse à l'orange

Orange Free State *n* État *m* libre d'Orange

Orangeman, *pl* **-men** ['ɒrɪndʒmən] *n Br* = orangiste *m* (*du parti protestant de l'Irlande du Nord*)

Orange Order *n* Ordre *m* des Orangistes

orangery ['ɒrɪndʒərɪ] *n* orangerie *f*

Orange Walk *n* = défilé *m* des Orangistes, le 12 juillet

orang-outang, -utan [ɔːræŋuː'tæŋ, -'tæn] *n* (*ape*) orang-outan(g) *m*, *pl* orangs-outan(g)s

oration [ɔː'reɪʃən] *n* allocution *f*, discours *m*; **funeral o.** oraison *f* funèbre

orator ['ɒrətər] *n* orateur, -trice

oratorical [ɒrə'tɒrɪk(ə)l] *adj* (*style, talent*) oratoire; **o. emphasis** accent *m* oratoire

oratorio [ɒrə'tɔːrɪəʊ] *n Mus* oratorio *m*

oratory[1] ['ɒrət(ə)rɪ] *n* (*art*) art *m* oratoire; (*speaking skill*) éloquence *f*; **powers of o.** facultés *fpl* oratoires; **a brilliant piece of o.** un brillant spécimen d'art oratoire; **flight of o.** envolée *f* éloquente

oratory[2] *n Rel* oratoire *m*

orb [ɔːb] *n* globe *m*, sphère *f*; (*of regalia*) globe; *Arch, Lit* (*planet etc*) orbe *m*; **the o. of the sun** le globe du soleil; **the o. and the sceptre** l'orbe et le sceptre

orbit[1] [ˈɔːbɪt] *n* **(a)** (*of planet, space vehicle, Fig of country*) orbite *f*; **in o.** en orbite; **to enter** *or* **go into o.** se mettre *ou* se placer en orbite; **to send a satellite into o.** lancer un satellite en orbite, mettre un satellite sur orbite; *Fig* **the family o.** le cercle familial; *F* **to go into o.** (*get angry*) entrer en furie **(b)** *Anat* (*of eye*) orbite *f* **(c)** *Fig* (*scope*) domaine *m*; **such matters don't come within the o. of my department** ces affaires-là ne sont pas du domaine de mon service *ou* ne relèvent pas de mon service

orbit[2] **1** *vt* **to o. the sun** décrire une orbite *ou* orbiter autour du soleil **2** *vi* (*of satellite etc*) être en orbite, décrire une orbite

orbital [ˈɔːbɪt(ə)l] **1** *adj* **(a)** *Astron etc* orbital; *Br* **o. road** périphérique *m* **(b)** *Anat* (*cavity etc*) orbitaire **2** *n Br* (*road*) périphérique *m*

Orcadian [ɔːˈkeɪdɪən] **1** *n* habitant, -ante des îles Orcades; (*native*) originaire *mf* des îles Orcades **2** *adj* des îles Orcades

orchard [ˈɔːtʃəd] *n* verger *m*; **apple o.** pommeraie *f*

orchestra [ˈɔːkɪstrə] *n* [①**A11**,g,i] *Mus* orchestre *m*; *Th* **o. pit** fosse *f* d'orchestre *ou* de l'orchestre; *Th* **the o. stalls,** *Am* **the o.** les fauteuils *mpl* d'orchestre

orchestral [ɔːˈkestr(ə)l] *adj* orchestral

orchestrate [ˈɔːkɪstreɪt] *vt* (*symphony etc, Fig press campaign etc*) orchestrer

orchestration [ɔːkɪsˈtreɪʃən] *n* orchestration *f*

orchid [ˈɔːkɪd] *n* (*plant*) orchidée *f*; (*wild*) orchis *m*; **o. grower** cultivateur, -trice d'orchidées

orchis [ˈɔːkɪs] *n* (*plant*) orchis *m*

ordain [ɔːˈdeɪn] *vt* **(a)** (*decree*) ordonner, fixer; (*measure*) décréter; **fate ordained** *or* **it was ordained that we should meet** il était écrit que nous nous rencontrerions, le sort a voulu que nous nous rencontrions **(b)** *Rel* (*priest*) ordonner; **to be ordained** être ordonné, recevoir les ordres

ordeal [ɔːˈdiːl] *n* **(a)** épreuve *f*; **to go through a terrible o.** subir *ou* passer par une terrible épreuve; **it is an o. for me to make a speech** je suis au supplice quand je dois faire un discours; **they spoke of their o.** ils ont évoqué le supplice *ou* l'épreuve qu'ils ont vécu(e) **(b)** *Jur, Hist* épreuve *f* judiciaire, ordalie *f*; **o. by fire** épreuve du feu

order[1] [ˈɔːdər] *n* **(a)** (*instruction*) ordre *m*; *Mil* ordre, consigne *f*; **I have orders to remain here** j'ai ordre de rester ici; **to give orders/an o.** donner des ordres/un ordre; **he gave orders for the trunks to be packed** il donna l'ordre de boucler les malles; **to obey** *or* **follow orders** obéir aux ordres, suivre la consigne; **our orders are to ...** nous avons l'ordre de ...; **to be under orders from the President** tenir ses ordres du Président; **and that's an o.!** c'est un ordre!; **orders are orders** les ordres sont les ordres; *Fig* **I don't take (my) orders from him** je ne suis pas à ses ordres; **until further orders** jusqu'à nouvel avis *ou* ordre; **by o. of the King** par ordre du roi, de par le roi; *Mil* **o. of the day** ordre du jour

(b) (*in restaurant*), *Com* commande *f*; **to place an o. with sb, to give sb an o.** passer une commande à qn, commander qch à qn; **to deliver an o.** livrer une commande; **another firm got the o.** ils ont passé la commande auprès d'une autre compagnie; **it's on o.** c'est commandé; **made to o.** fabriqué sur commande; (*suit*) fait sur mesure; **I can't do it to o.** ça ne se commande pas; **have you given your o.?** (*in restaurant*) est-ce que vous avez commandé?; **have they taken your o.?** est-ce qu'on a pris votre commande?; *Am* **an o. of French fries** une portion de frites; **o. cycle time** durée *f* du cycle de commande; **o. department** service *m* des commandes; **o. number** numéro *m* de commande *ou* d'ordre; **o. processing** traitement *m* des commandes; **o. taking** prise *f* de commande; *Com* **o. to remittance cycle** cycle *m* commande-livraison-facturation

(c) (*document*) ordre *m*; *Com, Admin* bon *m*; *Fin* mandat *m*; **o. in council** = décret *m* du gouvernement, arrêté *m* ministériel; (*statutory order*) décret-loi *m*, *pl* décrets-lois; **o. to pay** *or* **for payment** ordonnance *f* de paiement; **o. to sell** ordre *m* de vente; **o. to view** permis *m* de visiter (*une maison à vendre*); *Jur* **o. of the court** injonction *f* de la cour; **deportation o.** arrêté *m* d'expulsion; *Fin* **pay to the o. of J. Martin** payez à l'ordre de J. Martin; **pay J. Martin or o.** payez à J. Martin ou à son ordre; **cheque to o.** chèque *m* à ordre

(d) (*peace, harmony*) ordre *m*; **to keep** *or* **maintain o. in a town** assurer *ou* maintenir l'ordre dans une ville; *Sch* **to keep o. in class** maintenir la discipline dans une classe; **to establish/restore o.** mettre de/rétablir l'ordre

(e) (*condition*) **machine in (good) working o.** machine *f* en (bon) état de fonctionnement *ou* de marche; **out of o.** (*mechanism*) détraqué, dérangé; (*telephone*) en dérangement; (*lift, machine*) en panne

(f) (*in meeting etc*) **o. of the day** ordre *m* du jour; *Fig* **simplicity/optimism was the o. of the day** la simplicité/l'optimisme était de rigueur; **promiscuity/extravagance was the o. of the day in Ancient Rome** la promiscuité sexuelle/un faste somptuaire était monnaie courante dans la Rome antique; **to rule a question out of o.** statuer qu'une interpellation n'est pas dans les règles; *Br F* **you're out of o.!** tu as dépassé les bornes!; **to call sb to o.** rappeler qn à l'ordre; *Parl* **o.! o.!** de l'ordre!; *Jur* **o. in court!** silence dans la salle!; *Rel* **o. of service** office *m*; *Parl* **o. paper** copie *f* de l'ordre du jour

(g) (*tidiness, organization*) ordre *m*; **in o.** (*as it should be*) en ordre; (*document*) en règle, conforme à la règle; **to put things in o.** mettre les choses en ordre; **to put** *or* **set one's affairs in o.** mettre ses affaires en ordre, régler ses affaires; *Fig* **to set one's house in o.** remettre de l'ordre dans ses affaires

(h) (*system*) ordre *m*; **the old o. is changing** l'ancien ordre des choses devient caduc; **it's not in the natural o. of things** ce n'est pas dans l'ordre des choses; **I think a celebration is in o.** je pense que ça mérite d'être fêté; **it's perfectly in o. for them to ask for your papers** ils ont parfaitement le droit de vous demander vos papiers

(i) (*sequence*) ordre *m*; **in the correct** *or* **right/wrong o.** dans le bon ordre/le désordre; **in alphabetical/chronological o.** en *ou* par ordre alphabétique/chronologique; **in o. of age** par rang d'âge; *Th, Cin* **in o. of appearance** par ordre d'apparition; **o. of battle** ordre de bataille

(j) (*class*) classe *f*; *Biol* ordre *m*; **the higher/lower orders (of society)** les classes supérieures/inférieures; **workmanship of the highest o.** travail *m* de premier ordre; **population of** *or* **in** *or Am* **on the o. of 100, 000** population *f* de l'ordre de 100 000 habitants; **o. of magnitude** ordre de grandeur; **a disaster/a project/investment of this o. (of magnitude)** un désastre/un projet/des investissements de cette envergure; *Archit* **Ionic/Doric o.** ordre ionique/dorique; *Rel* **to take holy orders** entrer dans les ordres; **to be in (holy) orders** être prêtre/moine/religieuse; **monastic o.** ordre monastique; **o. of knighthood** ordre de chevalerie

(k) [①**A69**,b,vii] **in o. to do sth** afin de *ou* pour faire qch; **in o. that they understand** afin *ou* pour qu'ils comprennent

order[2] **1** *vt* **(a) to o. sb to do sth** ordonner à qn de faire qch; **she ordered them into her office/off the premises** elle leur a ordonné d'entrer dans son bureau/de quitter les lieux; **he's been ordered to report tomorrow** il a reçu l'ordre de se présenter demain; **he ordered them into battle** il leur a donné l'ordre de livrer bataille; *Jur* **to be ordered to pay costs** être condamné aux dépens

(b) (*in restaurant*), *Com* commander; **to o. goods from Paris** commander des marchandises à Paris; **we can o. it for you** nous pouvons vous le commander; **to o. a taxi** (faire) appeler un taxi; **what have you ordered for dessert?** qu'est-ce que vous avez commandé comme dessert?

(c) (*arrange*) (*furniture etc*) arranger; (*papers, books etc*) classer, ranger; (*one's life*) ordonner, agencer; (*one's thoughts*) mettre de l'ordre dans; **to o. sth according to author/size** classer *ou* ranger qch par auteur/taille; **to o. one's affairs** mettre ses affaires en ordre; *Mil* **o. arms!** reposez armes!

(d) *Med* (*treatment*) prescrire, ordonner; *Fig* **that's just what the doctor ordered** c'est exactement ce qu'il me fallait

2 *vi* (*in restaurant*) commander

▶ **order about, order around** *vtsep* (*person*) commander; **he likes ordering people about** il aime commander les autres; **you can't o. me about!** je n'ai pas d'ordres à recevoir de toi

▶ **order in** *vtsep* (*supplies, food*) commander; (*police, troops*) faire venir

▶ **order off** *vtsep Sp* (*player*) expulser (du terrain)

▶ **order out** *vtsep* (*from room etc*) mettre dehors

▶ **order up** *vtsep* **(a)** (*troops, air support etc*) faire monter **(b)** (*stationery supplies, round of drinks etc*) commander

order book *n* carnet *m* de commandes; **the order books are full** les carnets de commandes sont pleins

ordered [ˈɔːdəd] *adj* ordonné; (*in good order*) en bon ordre; **an o. life** une vie régulière *ou* réglée

orderer [ˈɔːdərər] *n* acheteur *m*

order form *n* bon *m ou* bulletin *m* de commande

orderliness [ˈɔːdəlɪnɪs] *n* **(a)** (*methodical nature*) méthode *f*; (*of existence*) caractère *m* rangé *ou* réglé; **the o. of her records/room/papers/***etc* le bon ordre dans lequel se trouvaient ses disques/sa chambre/ses papiers/*etc* **(b)**

(*discipline*) (*of crowd, football supporters etc*) discipline *f*; (*of pupils*) bonne conduite *f*

orderly ['ɔːdəlɪ] **1** *adj* **(a)** (*arrangement*) ordonné, méthodique; (*room etc*) en ordre, ordonné, rangé; (*life*) réglé, rangé, régulier; (*mind*) méthodique; **to be very o.** (*of person*) avoir beaucoup de méthode; **to do sth in an o. way** *or* **manner** faire qch avec beaucoup de méthode

(b) (*crowd*) discipliné; **leave the building in an o. fashion** quittez l'immeuble dans l'ordre et avec calme; **an o. retreat/withdrawal** une retraite/un repli ordonné(e)

2 *n* **(a)** *Mil* planton *m*; **to be on o. duty** être de planton; **o. room** salle *f* des rapports; **o. officer** officier *m* de service

(b) hospital o., medical o. aide-infirmier, -ière; *Mil* infirmier *m*, ambulancier *m*

Order of Merit *n Br* ≈ Ordre *m* du Mérite

Order of the Garter *n Br* Ordre *m* de la Jarretière

ordinal ['ɔːdɪn(ə)l] **1** *adj* [①A70,16,1; B56,B] (*number*) ordinal **2** *n* (*number*) nombre *m* ordinal

ordinance ['ɔːdɪnəns] *n Fml* (*decree*) ordonnance *f*, règlement *m*

ordinand ['ɔːdɪnænd] *n Rel* ordinand *m*

ordinarily ['ɔːdɪn(ə)rɪlɪ, *Am* ɔːdɪ'nerɪlɪ] *adv* **(a)** (*in an everyday manner*) normalement; **he was quite o. dressed** il était habillé de façon tout à fait banale; **a more than o. gifted/stupid child** un enfant d'une intelligence/stupidité supérieure à la normale; **a more than o. attractive woman** une femme d'une beauté exceptionnelle **(b)** (*usually*) d'habitude, ordinairement, d'ordinaire; **did he seem nervous? – not more than he o. is** est-ce qu'il avait l'air nerveux? – pas plus que d'habitude *ou* qu'à l'ordinaire

ordinary ['ɔːdɪn(ə)rɪ] **1** *adj* ordinaire; **o. Englishman** Anglais moyen *ou* typique; **she was just an o. tourist** c'était une touriste comme une autre; **this is no o. house/car** ce n'est pas une maison/voiture ordinaire; **in the o. course of events, in the o. run of things** d'ordinaire; *Pej* **a very o. kind of man** un homme tout à fait ordinaire *ou* quelconque; *Com* **o. activities** activités *fpl* ordinaires; (*balance sheet item*) opérations *fpl* courantes; *Fin* **o. creditor** créancier *m* ordinaire; *Sch Formerly Br* **O.-level,** *Scot* **O.-grade** ≈ BEPC *m* (brevet élémentaire du premier cycle); *Br Naut* **o. seaman** matelot *m*; *Br Fin* **o. share** action *f* ordinaire

2 *n* **(a)** ordinaire *m*; **out of the o.** exceptionnel, qui sort de l'ordinaire; **nothing out of the o. happened** il n'est rien arrivé d'inhabituel *ou* d'exceptionnel

(b) *Rel* **the O. (of the Mass)** l'Ordinaire *m* (de la messe)

ordinate ['ɔːdɪnɪt] *n Math* ordonnée *f*

ordination [ɔːdɪ'neɪʃən] *n Rel* ordination *f*

ordnance ['ɔːdnəns] *n* **(a)** *Mil* (*unit*) (service *m* du) matériel *m*; *Br* **Royal Army O. Corps,** *US* **O. Service** Service *m* du Matériel; **o. and supplies** les ravitaillements *mpl* **(b)** *Mil* (*artillery*) artillerie *f*; **piece of o.** bouche *f* à feu, pièce *f* d'artillerie; **o. factory** manufacture *f* d'artillerie

Ordnance Survey *n Br* ≈ Institut *m* Géographique National; *Br* **ordnance(-survey) map** ≈ carte *f* de l'Institut Géographique National

ordure ['ɔːdjʊər] *n Lit* ordure *f*

ore [ɔːr] *n* minerai *m*; **iron/aluminium o.** minerai de fer/d'aluminium; **rich** *or* **high-grade o.** minerai à *ou* de haute teneur; **o. deposit** gisement *m* de minerai

Ore(g) *abbr* **Oregon**

oregano [ɒrɪ'gɑːnəʊ] *n Bot, Culin* origan *m*

organ ['ɔːgən] *n* **(a)** *Mus* orgue *m*; *Rel* orgues *fpl*; **grand o.** grand orgue, grandes orgues; **choir o.** orgue du chœur; **American o.** orgue de salon; **street o.** orgue de Barbarie; **o. builder** facteur *m* d'orgues; **o. loft** *or* **gallery** tribune *f* d'orgue; **o. pipe** tuyau *m* d'orgue; **o. stop** jeu *m* d'orgue

(b) *Anat* (*of human body, plant*) organe *m*; *Euph* (*penis*) membre *m*; **o. of hearing** organe de l'ouïe; **the vocal organs** l'appareil vocal; **o. transplant** transplantation *f* d'organe

(c) *Fig* (*instrument*) (*of government*) organe *m*; (*newspaper*) (*of government, party*) organe, porte-parole *m inv*; **an efficient o. of propaganda** un organe de propagande efficace; **the official o.** l'organe officiel

organdie ['ɔːgəndɪ] *n Tex* organdi *m*; **o. dress** robe *f* d'organdi

organ-grinder *n* joueur, -euse d'orgue de Barbarie; *Fig* **I want to speak to the o. not his monkey** je veux parler au responsable, pas au sous-fifre

organic [ɔː'gænɪk] *adj* **(a)** organique; (*fertilizer*) organique, biologique; *Ecol* (*food, farming, gardening etc*) biologique; **o. chemistry** chimie *f* organique; **o. chemist** organicien, -ienne **(b) an o. whole** un ensemble systématique, un tout intégré; **an o. part** une partie intégrante; **o. growth/change** croissance/changement naturel(le) *ou* spontané(e)

organically [ɔː'gænɪklɪ] *adv* **(a)** organiquement; (*to farm, garden*) avec un engrais organique; **o. grown foods** produits biologiques **(b)** *Fig* **to change/grow o.** changer/grandir naturellement *ou* spontanément; *Fig* **to be o. linked** être fondamentalement lié

organism ['ɔːgənɪz(ə)m] *n* organisme *m*

organist ['ɔːgənɪst] *n* organiste *mf*

organization [ɔːgənaɪ'zeɪʃən] *n* **(a)** (*action*) organisation *f* **(b)** (*association*) organisation *f*, organisme *m*; **charity o.** organisation charitable, œuvre *f* de charité; **youth o.** mouvement *m* de jeunesse **(c)** *Ind* (*of labour*) syndicalisation *f*

organizational [ɔːgənaɪ'zeɪʃən(ə)l] *adj* (*defect, skills etc*) d'organisation, de structure, organisationnel; **o. buyer** acheteur *m* (pour une organisation); **o. marketer** mercaticien *m* au sein d'une organisation

organizationally [ɔːgənaɪ'zeɪʃən(ə)lɪ] *adv* du point de vue de l'organisation; **he doesn't get involved o. in the project** il n'est pas impliqué au niveau de l'organisation du projet

organization and methods *npl Ind* organisation *f* scientifique du travail; **o. department** bureau *m* des méthodes

organization chart *n* (*of company*) organigramme *m*

organization tree *n* organigramme *m* en arborescence

organize ['ɔːgənaɪz] **1** *vt* **(a)** (*sort out, put into groups etc*) organiser; **to o. people into work groups** répartir les gens dans des groupes de travail

(b) (*arrange, bring about*) (*concert, party etc*) organiser; (*transport, food, accommodation*) s'occuper de; (*money*) s'occuper de trouver; (*one's time*) organiser, aménager; *F* (*a day off etc*) se faire accorder; **she organized it so that we got in free** elle s'est arrangée pour que nous puissions entrer sans payer; **I'll just go and o. something to eat** (*do it myself*) je vais préparer quelque chose à manger; **don't worry, it's all organized** ne t'inquiète pas, tout est organisé

(c) *Ind* (*workers*) syndiquer

2 *vi* **(a)** s'organiser

(b) *Ind* (*of workers*) se syndiquer

organized ['ɔːgənaɪzd] *adj* (*society, crime, person, files*) organisé; *Sch* **o. games** jeux *mpl* dirigés; **o. labour** = les organisations *fpl* ouvrières

organizer ['ɔːgənaɪzər] *n* (*person*) organisateur, -trice; (*diary etc*) organiseur *m*; (*electronic*) agenda *m* (électronique); **she's a born o.** elle a le sens de l'organisation, c'est une organisatrice née

organizing ['ɔːgənaɪzɪŋ] *adj attrib* (*ability, committee*) d'organisation

orgasm ['ɔːgæz(ə)m] *n Physiol* orgasme *m*; **to have an o.** avoir un orgasme, jouir; *Fig Sl* **they were having orgasms** ça les faisait bander, ils ont trouvé ça jouissif *ou* bandant

orgasmic [ɔː'gæzmɪk] *adj Physiol* orgastique; *Sl* (*pleasure, experience etc*) jouissif

orgiastic [ɔːdʒɪ'æstɪk] *adj* orgiaque

orgy ['ɔːdʒɪ] *n* (*sexual, Fig of colour*) orgie *f*; (*of violence*) déchaînement *m*; **orgies** (*in ancient Greece, Rome*) orgies, bacchanales *fpl*; **drunken o.** beuverie *f*, *F* soûlerie *f*

oriel ['ɔːrɪəl] *n Archit* **o. (window)** oriel *m*

orient[1] ['ɔːrɪənt] *n* orient *m*; **the O.** l'Orient

orient[2] ['ɔːrɪent] *vt* = **orientate**

oriental [ɔːrɪ'ent(ə)l] **1** *adj* oriental; **o. rug** tapis *m* d'Orient **2** *n* **O.** (*person*) Oriental, -ale

orientalist [ɔːrɪ'entəlɪst] *n* orientaliste *mf*

orientate ['ɔːrɪənteɪt] *vt* (*map*) orienter; **to o. oneself** (*physically, psychologically*) s'orienter

orientation [ɔːrɪən'teɪʃən] *n* orientation *f*; *esp Am* **o. course** cours *m* d'introduction

oriented ['ɔːrɪentɪd] *adj* orienté

-oriented ['ɔːrɪentɪd] *suff* **profit-o.** axé sur le profit; **youth-o.** qui s'adresse à la jeunesse; *Comptr* **computer-o. language** langage orienté machine; **export-o.** (*company, industry*) tourné vers l'exportation

orienteering [ɔːrɪən'tɪərɪŋ] *n Sp* course *f* d'orientation

orifice ['ɒrɪfɪs] *n* orifice *m*

origami [ɒrɪ'gɑːmɪ] *n* (art *m* du) pliage *m*, origami *m*

origin ['ɒrɪdʒɪn] *n* **(a)** origine *f*; **to trace an event back to its o.** remonter à l'origine d'un événement; **to have its origins in** … tirer son origine de …; **the custom has its o.** *or* **origins in** … l'origine de cette coutume est …; *Archit* **point of o.** (*of curve etc*) point *m* d'origine; **word/woman of Greek o.** mot *m*/femme *f* d'origine grecque; **a man of humble o.** un homme d'humble origine *ou* extraction; *Com* **country of o.** pays *m* d'origine; *Com* **certificate of o.** certificat *m* d'origine; *Com* **o. of goods label** marque *f* d'origine **(b)** *Anat* (*of muscle*) attache *f*

original [ə'rɪdʒɪn(ə)l] **1** *adj* **(a)** (*first*) (*suggestion, idea etc*) premier, initial; (*manuscript, painting*) original; **the o. colour** la couleur d'origine; *Rel* **o. sin** péché *m* originel; **the o. members of the band** les premiers membres du groupe; *TV etc* **based on an o. idea by** … d'après une idée originale de …; **o. meaning of a word** sens premier d'un mot; **in the o. Chinese** dans le texte original en chinois/dans le texte chinois d'origine; **to translate from the o. German** traduire d'après le texte allemand original; **o. defect** vice *m* originaire; **o. edition** édition *f* princeps *ou* originale; **o. guarantee** garantie *f* d'origine; *Fin, Com* **o. invoice** facture *f* originale; *Com* **o. packaging** *or* **packing** emballage *m* d'origine; **o. value** valeur *f* d'origine; *Cin* **o. version** version *f* originale, VO *f*

(b) (*innovative*) (*writer, style, idea, approach etc*) original **2** *n* **(a)** (*of painting, invoice etc*) original *m*; *Fin* (*of bill of exchange*) primata *m*; **to copy sth from the o.** copier qch sur l'original; **to read the classics in the o.** lire les classiques dans le texte

(b) *F* (*person*) original, -ale

originality [ərɪdʒɪ'nælɪtɪ] *n* originalité *f*

originally [ə'rɪdʒɪn(ə)lɪ] *adv* **(a)** (*initially, to begin with*) à l'origine, au départ; **the building was o. used as a warehouse** à l'origine *ou* au départ, l'immeuble servait d'entrepôt; **o. we come from Hampshire** nous sommes originaires du Hampshire; **where do you come from o.?** d'où êtes-vous originaire?; **that's what I o. thought** c'est ce que je pensais au début *ou* au départ; **I o. heard about it in Spain** c'est en Espagne que j'en ai entendu parler pour la première fois

(b) (*in an innovative way*) d'une façon originale, avec originalité

originate [ə'rɪdʒɪneɪt] **1** *vi* (*of person*) être originaire (**from** de); (*of language*) dériver, provenir (**from** de); (*of river*) prendre sa source (**in** dans); **the fire originated under the floor** le feu a pris naissance sous le plancher; **the scheme originated with me** je suis à l'origine de ce projet, je suis l'auteur *ou* l'initiateur de ce projet; **the custom originated in France** cette coutume est née en France; **originating airline** compagnie *f* aérienne de départ **2** *vt* donner naissance à, être l'auteur de; (*proposal*) être l'auteur de; (*reform, project etc*) être à l'origine de, être l'auteur *ou* l'initiateur, -trice de

originator [ə'rɪdʒɪneɪtər] *n* créateur, -trice; (*of proposal*) auteur *m*; (*of scheme*) auteur, initiateur, -trice

oriole ['ɔːrɪəʊl] *n* (*bird*) loriot *m*, *Can* oriole *m*; **golden o.** loriot (jaune d'Europe)

Orkneys (the) [ðɪ'ɔːknɪz] *npl* les Orcades *fpl*

ormolu ['ɔːməluː] *n* similor *m*

ornament[1] ['ɔːnəmənt] *n* **(a)** (*vase etc*) ornement *m* **(b)** (*no pl*) (*decoration*) (*of style, architecture etc*) ornements *mpl*; (*on dress etc*) garniture *f*; **by way of o.** pour ornement **(c)** *Mus* ornement *m*

ornament[2] ['ɔːnəment] *vt* (*room etc*) orner, ornementer (**with** de); (*dress etc*) agrémenter, embellir (**with** de); (*one's style*) orner (**with** de)

ornamental [ɔːnə'ment(ə)l] *adj* décoratif, ornemental; **o. tree/plant** arbre *m*/plante *f* d'ornement; **o. lake** *or* **pond** pièce *f* d'eau

ornamentation [ɔːnəmen'teɪʃən] *n* ornementation *f*

ornate [ɔː'neɪt] *adj* orné, ornementé, *Pej* chargé; **o. style** style imagé *ou* fleuri

ornately [ɔː'neɪtlɪ] *adv* de façon très ornementée, *Pej* avec une surabondance d'ornements; (*written*) dans un style très fleuri

ornery ['ɔːnərɪ] *adj Am F* (*unpleasant*) désagréable; (*bad-tempered*) rouspéteur, -teuse; (*stubborn*) têtu

ornithological [ɔːnɪθə'lɒdʒɪk(ə)l] *adj* ornithologique

ornithologist [ɔːnɪ'θɒlədʒɪst] *n* ornithologue *mf*, ornithologiste *mf*

ornithology [ɔːnɪ'θɒlədʒɪ] *n* ornithologie *f*

orotund ['ɒrəʊtʌnd] *adj esp Lit* (*sound*) plein, riche; (*writing*) (*pompous*) emphatique, pompeux

orphan[1] ['ɔːfən] **1** *n* **(a)** orphelin, -ine; **to be left an o.** devenir orphelin, -ine; **war o.** pupille *mf* de la Nation **(b)** *Typ* orpheline *f* **2** *adj* **an o. child** un orphelin, une orpheline; *Pharm* **o. drug** médicament *m* orphelin

orphan[2] *vt* **he had been orphaned at the age of six** il est devenu orphelin à l'âge de six ans; **they were orphaned by the war** ils ont perdu leurs parents pendant la guerre

orphanage ['ɔːf(ə)nɪdʒ] *n* orphelinat *m*

Orpheus ['ɔːfjuːs] *n Myth* Orphée *m*

orthodontics [ɔːθəʊ'dɒntɪks] *n* [①A10,c] orthodontie *f*

orthodontist [ɔːθəʊ'dɒntɪst] *n* orthodontiste *mf*

orthodox ['ɔːθədɒks] **1** *adj* **(a)** *Rel* orthodoxe; **the O. Church** l'Église *f* orthodoxe **(b)** (*historian etc*) traditionaliste, orthodoxe; (*method, opinion etc*) orthodoxe **2** *npl Rel* **the o.** (*people*) les orthodoxes *mpl*

orthodoxy ['ɔːθədɒksɪ] *n* **(a)** (*of doctrine, person's opinions*) orthodoxie *f* **(b)** (*in Jewish religion*) judaïsme *m* rabbinique

orthogonal [ɔː'θɒgən(ə)l] *adj Math* orthogonal

orthographic(al) [ɔːθə'græfɪk, -ɪk(ə)l] *adj* orthographique

orthographically [ɔːθə'græfɪklɪ] *adv* orthographiquement

orthography [ɔː'θɒgrəfɪ] *n* **(a)** (*spelling*) orthographe *f* **(b)** *Math* projection *f* orthogonale

orthopaedic, *US* **orthopedic** [ɔːθə'piːdɪk] *adj Med* (*treatment, device*) orthopédique; **o. surgeon** (chirurgien, -ienne) orthopédiste *mf* **o. surgery** chirurgie *f* des os

orthopaedics, *US* **orthopedics** [ɔːθə'piːdɪks] *n* [①A10,c] *Med* orthopédie *f*

orthopaedist, *US* **orthopedist** [ɔːθə'piːdɪst] *n Med* orthopédiste *mf*

orthoptist [ɔː'θɒptɪst] *n* orthoptiste *mf*

ortolan ['ɔːtələn] *n* (*bird*) **o. (bunting)** ortolan *m*

Orwellian [ɔː'welɪən] *adj* orwellien

oryx ['ɒrɪks] *n* (*antelope*) oryx *m*

OS [əʊ'es] *n Comptr* (*abbr* **operating system**) système *m* d'exploitation

Oscar ['ɒskər] *n Cin* oscar *m*; **O.-winning picture** film primé aux oscars; **in her O.-winning role** dans le rôle qui lui a valu l'oscar

oscillate ['ɒsɪleɪt] *vi Phys, Rad* osciller; *Fig* **to o. between two opinions** osciller *ou* balancer *ou* hésiter entre deux opinions

oscillating ['ɒsɪleɪtɪŋ] *adj* (*electron*) oscillateur

oscillation [ɒsɪ'leɪʃən] *n* (*of pendulum etc*) oscillation *f*

oscillator ['ɒsɪleɪtər] *n* oscillateur *m*; **o. valve** *or* **tube** lampe *f* oscillatrice

oscillatory ['ɒsɪleɪt(ə)rɪ] *adj* oscillant, oscillatoire

oscillogram [ɒ'sɪləgræm] *n* oscillogramme *m*

oscillograph [ɒ'sɪləgræf] *n* oscillographe *m*

oscilloscope [ɒ'sɪləskəʊp] *n El* oscilloscope *m*

osculate ['ɒskjʊleɪt] *vi* **(a)** *Fml, Hum* (*kiss*) s'embrasser **(b)** *Geom* **curve that osculates with a line** courbe osculatrice à une ligne (**at a point** en un point)

osculation [ɒskjʊ'leɪʃən] *n Geom* osculation *f*; **point of o.** point *m* d'attouchement

osier ['əʊzɪər, 'əʊʒər] *n* osier *m*; **o. basket** panier *m* d'osier; **o. bed** oseraie *f*

osmosis [ɒz'məʊsɪs] *n Ch, Physiol, Fig* osmose *f*

osmotic [ɒz'mɒtɪk] *adj Ch, Physiol* osmotique

osprey ['ɒspreɪ] *n* **(a)** (*bird*) balbuzard *m* pêcheur *ou* fluviatile, *Can* aigle *m* pêcheur **(b)** (*feather*) aigrette *f*

ossicle ['ɒsɪk(ə)l] *n Anat* (*of ear*) osselet *m*

ossification [ɒsɪfɪ'keɪʃən] *n* ossification *f*

ossified ['ɒsɪfaɪd] *adj* (*cartilage*) ossifié; *Fig* (*mind, ideas, social system*) sclérosé; (*person*) à l'esprit sclérosé; **the o. old fools who run this country** les vieux fossiles abrutis qui dirigent ce pays

ossify ['ɒsɪfaɪ] **1** *vi* (*of cartilage*) s'ossifier; *Fig* (*of person*) se fossiliser; (*of government, mind*) se scléroser **2** *vt* (*cartilage*) ossifier; *Fig* amener *ou* entraîner la sclérose de

ossuary ['ɒsjʊərɪ] *n* ossuaire *m*

Ostend [ɒs'tend] *n* Ostende *mf*

ostensible [ɒs'tensɪb(ə)l] *adj* allégué; **the o. justification for their action was …** la raison qu'ils ont alléguée pour justifier leur acte était …

ostensibly [ɒ'stensɪblɪ] *adv* en apparence; **while the Confederation is o. a single state, …** alors qu'en apparence *ou* qu'officiellement la Confédération est un état unique, …; **he went out o. to buy some tobacco** il sortit sous prétexte d'acheter du tabac *ou* soi-disant pour acheter du tabac; **he married her o. for love** il l'a soi-disant épousée par amour

ostentation [ɒsten'teɪʃən] *n* ostentation *f*

ostentatious [ɒsten'teɪʃəs] *adj* plein d'ostentation; (*person, attitude*) prétentieux, ostentatoire

ostentatiously [ɒsten'teɪʃəslɪ] *adv* avec ostentation, d'une manière ostentatoire; **to display sth o.** faire ostentation de qch; **to be o. rich** faire ostentation de sa richesse

ostentatiousness [ɒsten'teɪʃəsnɪs] *n* = **ostentation**

osteoarthritis [ɒstɪəʊɑː'θraɪtɪs] *n Med* arthrose *f*; **to have o.** avoir de l'arthrose

osteomyelitis [ɒstɪəʊmaɪ'laɪtɪs] *n Med* ostéomyélite *f*

osteopath ['ɒstɪəpæθ], *US also* **osteopathist** [ɒstɪ'ɒpəθɪst] *n Med* (médecin *m*) ostéopathe *mf*

osteopathy [ɒstɪ'ɒpəθɪ] *n Med* ostéopathie *f*

osteoporosis [ɒstɪəʊpɔː'rəʊsɪs] *n Med* ostéoporose *f*

ostler ['ɒslər] *n Br Hist* valet *m* d'écurie, garçon *m* d'écurie

ostracism ['ɒstrəsɪz(ə)m] *n* ostracisme *m*; **to suffer the o. of the press** être frappé d'ostracisme par la presse

ostracize ['ɒstrəsaɪz] *vt* frapper d'ostracisme, mettre au ban de la société; (*country, company*) frapper d'ostracisme; **she's been ostracized at work** on l'a mise en quarantaine au travail

ostrich ['ɒstrɪtʃ] *n* autruche *f*; *Fig* **o. policy** politique *f* de l'autruche

OT [əʊ'ti:] **(a)** (*abbr* **Old Testament**) AT *m* **(b)** *abbr* **occupational therapy; occupational therapist**

OTC [əʊti:'si:] *n* **(a)** *Br Sch* (*abbr* **Officers' Training Corps**) corps *m* de formation des officiers **(b)** *St Exch* (*abbr* **over-the-counter**) **O. market** marché hors cote

OTH [əʊti:'eɪtʃ] *Mktg* (*abbr* **opportunity to hear**) ODE *f*

other ['ʌðər] **1** *adj* [①A36-37,e; B14,B,1,b] autre **the o. one** l'autre *mf*; **every o. day/week** un jour/une semaine sur deux, tous les deux jours/toutes les deux semaines; **the o. day** l'autre jour; **the o. four** les quatre autres; **potatoes and o. vegetables** pommes de terre et autres légumes; **o. people have seen it** d'autres l'ont vu; **o. people's property** le bien d'autrui; **any o. book** tout autre livre; **no one o. than he knows it** nul autre que lui ne le sait, il n'y a que lui qui le sache; **somebody o. than me/you/her/***etc* quelqu'un d'autre; **all verbs o. than those in -er** tous les verbes autres que ceux en -er; **some woman or o.** une femme quelconque; *Acct* **o. debtors** (*item on balance sheet*) créances *fpl* diverses; *Br Mil* **o. ranks** = ensemble des militaires non gradés; **the o. woman/man** (*in relationship*) l'autre

2 *pron* [①A36-37,e; B15,2,a-b] autre *mf*; **one after the o.** l'un après l'autre; **the others** les autres; **all the others are there** tous les autres sont là; **some ... others ...** les uns ... les autres ...; **have you got any others?** (*any more*) en avez-vous encore?; (*any different ones*) en avez-vous d'autres?; **I have no o.** je n'en ai pas d'autre; **for this reason, if for no o.** pour cette raison, à défaut d'une autre; **no** *or* **none o. than the great actress Greta Garbo** nulle autre que la grande Greta Garbo; **one or o. of us will see to it** l'un de nous y veillera; **others** (*other people*) les autres; (*not as grammatical subject*) autrui *m*; **to see oneself as others see one** se voir comme les autres vous voient; **they prefer you to all others** ils vous préfèrent à tout autre; **the property of others** le bien d'autrui; **someone or o. said ...** quelqu'un a dit ...; **something or o. I said** quelque chose que j'ai dû dire; **somehow or o.** d'une façon ou d'une autre; **to be somewhere or o.** être dans les parages

3 *adv* autrement; **to see things o. than as they are** voir les choses autrement qu'elles ne le sont; **o. than that everything is fine** à part ça *ou* autrement, tout va bien; **she never speaks of them o. than admiringly** c'est toujours avec admiration qu'elle parle d'eux

4 *n Am Hum* **your significant o.** l'homme/la femme de ta vie; **to talk about this, that and the o.** parler de ci et ça; *F Hum* **to have a bit of the o.** (*sex*) prendre un peu son pied

otherwise ['ʌðəwaɪz] **1** *adv* **(a)** (*differently*) autrement (**than** que); **he could not do o.** il n'a pas pu faire autrement; **to think o.** penser différemment *ou* autrement; **if she's not o. engaged** si elle n'est pas occupée à autre chose; (*socially*) si elle n'a pas d'autres obligations; **except where o. stated** sauf indication contraire; **all people rich or o.** tout le monde, riches et pauvres

(b) (*apart from that*) à part cela *ou* ça, autrement; **o. he is quite sane** à part cela il est complètement sain d'esprit

2 *adj* **the facts were o.** les faits étaient différents *ou* autres; *Fml* **should it be o.** s'il en était autrement

3 *conj* autrement, sans quoi, sans cela; **do what I tell you, o. everything will go wrong** faites ce que je vous dis, autrement *ou* sans quoi *ou* sans cela tout ira de travers

otherworldly [ʌðə'wɜ:ldlɪ] *adj* détaché de ce monde

otic ['əʊtɪk] *adj Anat* otique

otitis [əʊ'taɪtɪs] *n Med* otite *f*

OTS [əʊti:'es] *Mktg* (*abbr* **opportunity to see**) ODV *f*

OTT [əʊ'ti:ti:] *adj esp Br Sl* (*abbr* **over the top**) exagéré; **there was no need to be quite so O. about it** ce n'était pas la peine d'en faire toute une histoire

otter ['ɒtər] *n* (*animal*) loutre *f*; **sea o.** loutre de mer *ou* marine; **o. hound** chien *m* pour la chasse aux loutres

Ottoman ['ɒtəmən] *Hist* **1** *adj* ottoman **2** *n* Ottoman, -ane

ottoman *n* (*furniture*) ottomane *f*

ouch [aʊtʃ] *int* (*expressing pain*) aïe!, ouille!

ought¹ [ɔ:t] *v aux* [①A59,f; B36-7,K,1] (*with present and past meaning*; *inv*; **o. not** *is frequently abbreviated to* **oughtn't**) **(a)** (*obligation*) **this o. to have been done before** on aurait dû *ou* il aurait fallu le faire avant; **to behave as one o.** se conduire comme il convient; **to drink more than one o.** boire plus que de raison; **I thought I o. to let you know about it** j'ai cru devoir vous en faire part; **one o. never to be unkind** il ne faut *ou* on ne doit jamais être malveillant

(b) (*desirability*) **you o. to go and see it** vous devriez aller le voir; **you o. not to have waited** vous n'auriez pas dû attendre; **I o. to be going** il me faut partir; **you o. to have seen it!** tu aurais dû *ou* il fallait voir ça!

(c) (*probability*) **they o. to be in Paris by now** ils doivent être à Paris maintenant; **you o. to be able to get £50 for it** tu devrais pouvoir en tirer 50 livres; **your horse o. to win** votre cheval devrait gagner; **you o. to know** vous êtes bien placé pour le savoir, vous devriez le savoir

ought² *n Arch, Lit* = **aught**

Ouija® ['wi:dʒə] *n* **O. (board)** oui-ja *m*

ounce¹ [aʊns] *n* (*measurement*) once *f*, = 28, 35g. ; (**troy**) **o.** (*of gold, silver*) = 31,1035g.; *Fig* **an o. of intelligence/humanity/***etc* une once *ou* un tant soit peu d'intelligence/d'humanité/*etc*; **if you had an o. of sense** si tu avais un gramme de bon sens; *Fig* **he hasn't an o. of courage** il n'a pas un sou de courage, il n'est pas courageux pour deux sous

ounce² *n* (*animal*) once *f*, panthère *f* des neiges

our ['aʊər] *poss adj* [①A30,8; A42,3; B19-20,E,1] notre, *pl* nos **o. friends** nos ami(e)s; **o. father and mother** notre père et notre mère, nos père et mère; **o. two** les deux nôtres; *Com* **o. Mr Martin** M. Martin de notre maison

ours ['aʊəz] *poss pron* [①A30,8; B20,E,2] le nôtre, la nôtre, *pl* les nôtres; **your house is larger than o.** votre maison est plus grande que la nôtre; **this is o.** ceci est à nous, ceci nous appartient; **o. is a nation of travellers** nous sommes une nation de voyageurs; **a friend of o.** un(e) de nos ami(e)s, un(e) ami(e) à nous; **it's no business of o.** cela ne nous regarde pas

ourself [aʊə'self] *pers pron* (*said by monarch, editor etc*) nous-même

ourselves [aʊə'selvz] *pers pron pl* [①A29] **(a)** (*emphatic*) nous-mêmes; **we o. do not believe it** nous, pour notre part, ne le croyons pas **(b)** [①B26,D] (*reflexive*) nous; **we are enjoying o. very much** nous nous amusons bien **(c)** (*after preposition*) nous, nous-mêmes; **we say to o.** nous nous disons; **we shouldn't talk about o.** on ne doit pas parler de soi; **instead of fighting among o.** au lieu de nous battre entre nous

ousel ['u:z(ə)l] *n* = **ouzel**

oust [aʊst] *vt* **(a)** évincer; **the ousted ruler** le dirigeant évincé; **to o. sb from his post** déloger qn de son poste **(b)** *Jur* (*deprive*) déposséder, évincer (**of** de)

out¹ [aʊt] **1** *adv* **(a)** (*outside*) dehors; **to go** *or* **walk o.** sortir; **to run/stagger o.** sortir en courant/chancelant; **it's colder inside than o.** il fait plus froid à l'intérieur qu'à l'extérieur; **what's it** *or* **the weather like o.?** quel temps fait-il dehors?; **where are you going?—o.** où allez-vous?—dehors; **o. you go!** sortez!, hors d'ici!, allez, hop!; **voyage o.** voyage *m* d'aller

(b) (*not in, not at home, released*) **I was only o. for a minute** je ne suis sorti qu'une minute; **my father is o.** mon père est sorti; **she's o. a lot in the daytime** elle est souvent absente pendant la journée; **we've been o. a lot recently** (*to theatres, restaurants etc*) nous sommes beaucoup sortis ces temps-ci; (*not been at home*) nous avons été beaucoup absents ces temps-ci; **he's o. in September** (*of prisoner*) il sort en septembre; **he is o. and about again** il est de nouveau sur pied; **she loves getting o. and about in her pushchair** elle aime beaucoup qu'on la promène en poussette; **she's o. picking mushrooms** elle est sortie (pour aller) cueillir des champignons; **the men are o.** (*on strike*) les ouvriers sont en grève; **to bring the workforce o.** appeler le personnel à la grève; **you'll have everybody o. if you're not careful** tu vas provoquer une grève générale si tu ne fais pas attention; **the jury was o. for two hours** le jury s'est retiré pendant deux heures pour délibérer; **the tide is o.** la marée est basse

(c) (*distant*) **a long way o.** loin, éloigné; **o. at sea** en mer, au large; **four days o. from Rio** à quatre jours de Rio; **o. there** là-bas; **she does not live far o. (of the town)** elle n'habite pas loin de la ville; **o. in the country** dans la campagne

(d) (*uncovered, in the open*) découvert, exposé; (*secret*) connu; (*flower*) épanoui; **he's been o. for years** (*openly homosexual*) cela fait des années qu'il ne cache plus son homosexualité; **he's not o.** il n'a pas révélé son homosexualité; **the tulips are o. early this year** les tulipes ont fleuri de bonne heure cette année; **the cherry tree is o.** le cerisier est en fleur; **the sun is o.** il fait soleil; **the moon is/the stars are o.** on voit la lune/les étoiles; *F* **the best game o.** le meilleur jeu qui soit; **the book is o.** (*published*) le livre est paru; (*borrowed*) le livre est en prêt; **to be o. at the elbows** (*of garment*) être troué *ou* percé aux coudes; **to whip o. a revolver** tirer *ou* sortir vivement un revolver; **o. loud** tout haut, à haute voix; **to say sth straight** *or* **right o.** dire qch carrément *ou* sans détours; *F* **o. with it!** allons, dites-le!, expliquez-vous!; **truth will o.** tôt ou tard la vérité se saura

(e) (*indicating aim*) **he's simply o. for money** tout ce qui l'intéresse c'est l'argent; **she was o. for a good time** elle cherchait à s'amuser; **he's only o. for what he can get** il ne cherche qu'à servir ses propres intérêts; (*sexually*) tout ce qu'il veut, c'est s'envoyer en l'air; **to be o. to get sb** en avoir après qn; **I am not o. to reform the world** je n'ai pas entrepris de réformer le monde; **I'm o. for big results** je vise (à) de grands résultats

(**f**) (*not in place*) **I've put my shoulder o. (of joint)** je me suis luxé l'épaule; *Pol* **the party that's o. (of power)** le parti qui n'est pas au pouvoir; **long skirts are o. this year** les jupes longues ne sont plus à la mode cette année; **the players who are o. (of the game)** les joueurs qui sont hors jeu *ou* ont été éliminés; *Cr* **not o.** = encore au guichet (*à la fin de l'innings, de la journée*); **to be o. for ten** avoir marqué dix

(**g**) (*inaccurate*) **to be o.** être dans l'erreur; **I was £25 o.** je m'étais trompé de 25 livres; **to be o. in one's calculations** s'être trompé dans ses calculs; **I was not far o.** je ne me trompais pas de beaucoup; **the shot was only a centimetre o.** le coup n'a manqué le but que d'un centimètre; *F* **he was miles o.** il était totalement à côté

(**h**) (*not functioning*) **the fire/gas is o.** le feu/gaz est éteint; **the light was o.** la lumière était éteinte

(**i**) (*indicating completion*) **before the week is o.** avant la fin de la semaine; *Rad* **o.!** terminé!

(**j**) (*unconscious*) **to be o. cold** être K.-O. ; **to be o. for seven seconds** (*of boxer*) rester au plancher pendant sept secondes; *F* **to be o. on one's feet** tomber de fatigue; **I went** *or* **was o. like a light** (*fell asleep*) je me suis endormi comme une bûche

(**k**) **o. of** (*outside*) hors de, en dehors de; **o. of danger** hors de danger; **o. of sight** hors de vue; **to be o. of the country** être à l'étranger; **o. of doors = outdoors 1**; **hardly were the words o. of my mouth** à peine avais-je prononcé ces mots; **I'm glad I'm o. of the whole business** je suis content de ne plus rien avoir à faire avec ça; **to feel o. of it** se sentir de trop; **to go o. of the house** sortir de la maison; **is there a way o. of it?** y a-t-il (un) moyen d'en sortir?; **to throw sth/ to jump o. of the window** jeter qch/sauter par la fenêtre; **from o. of the open window came bursts of laughter** par la fenêtre ouverte arrivaient des éclats de rire; **Gladiator by Monarch o. of Gladia** (*in breeding*) Gladiateur par *ou* issu de Monarch et Gladia; **to drink o. of a glass** boire dans un verre; **to drink o. of the bottle** boire à (même) la bouteille; **to copy sth o. of a book** copier qch dans un livre; **the firemen are paid o. of the rates** on paie les pompiers sur le budget de la ville; **she paid them o. of her own pocket** elle les a payés de sa poche; **choose one o. of these ten** choisissez-en un parmi les dix; **three days o. of four** trois jours sur quatre; **one o. of every three** un sur trois; **hut made o. of a few old planks** cabane faite de quelques vieilles planches; **o. of friendship/curiosity** par amitié/ curiosité; **to act o. of fear** (*habitually*) agir sous l'emprise de la peur; (*on precise occasion*) agir sous le coup de la peur; **to be o. of tea/ideas** être à court de thé/d'idées; **o. of cash** démuni d'argent; *Com* **I am o. of this item** je n'ai plus cet article pour le moment

2 *int* (**a**) **o. (with you)!** sortez!, hors d'ici!

(**b**) *Tennis* out!

3 *adj* (*outward*) **the o. door** la (porte de) sortie; *Com* **o. tray** corbeille *f* de courrier à envoyer

4 *n* (**a**) *esp US F* (*from difficult situation*) échappatoire *f*; **always leave yourself an o.** garde-toi toujours une porte de sortie *ou* une échappatoire

(**b**) *Tennis* balle *f* (qui tombe) en dehors des limites

(**c**) *TV, Cin* (*point where clip ends*) sortie *f*

5 *prep* **to go o. the door** sortir par la porte; **to look o. the window** regarder par la fenêtre

out² *vt* **to o. sb** (*reveal to be homosexual*) révéler que qn est homosexuel

out- *pref* (*généralement accolé à un verbe mais aussi à un substantif, ce préfixe est utilisé pour surenchérir sur l'expression d'origine; semblable à l'expression 'être plus royaliste que le roi'*) **the Opposition are attempting to out-Tory the Tories** l'opposition essaie d'être plus conservatrice que les conservateurs eux-mêmes

outage ['aʊtɪdʒ] *n* (**a**) *Com* (*amount lost*) perte(s) *f(pl)*, quantité *f* perdue; **stock o.** rupture *f* de stock (**b**) *El* coupure *f*; (*of machine*) panne *f*

out-and-out *adj* (*liar, villain*) fieffé, achevé; (*republican etc*) convaincu; (*disaster, failure*) total; (*scandal, disgrace*) véritable; (*success, triumph*) éclatant

outasight [aʊtə'saɪt] *adj, int esp Am Sl* fantastique

outback *Austr* **1**['aʊtbæk] *n* **the o.** l'intérieur *m* **2**[aut'bæk] *adv* à l'intérieur

outbid [aʊt'bɪd] *vt* (*pt* **outbid**; *pp* **outbid, -bidden** ['bɪdən]) (*at auction*) **to o. sb** enchérir sur qn et emporter la vente; **they were easily outbid by the Getty Museum** le musée Getty n'a eu aucun mal à surenchérir et emporter la vente

outboard ['aʊtbɔːd] *Naut* **1** *adj* **o. motor** moteur *m* hors bord **2** *n* (*motor*) moteur *m* hors bord

outbound ['aʊtbaʊnd] *adj* en partance; **o. tourism** tourisme *m* émetteur

outbox ['aʊtbɒks] *vt* boxer mieux que; **he was completely outboxed** il a été complètement dominé

outbreak ['aʊtbreɪk] *n* (*of hostilities*) déclenchement *m*, début *m*, commencement *m*; (*of violence*) déclenchement; **there's been an o. of flu** il y a eu de nombreux cas de grippe; **there has been another o. of cholera** de nouveaux cas de choléra ont été enregistrés; **precautions against an o. of typhus** précautions contre une épidémie de typhus; **in order to prevent another o.** (*epidemic*) pour empêcher une autre épidémie; **o. of fire** incendie *m*; **at the o. of war** quand la guerre a éclaté

outbuilding ['aʊtbɪldɪŋ] *n* bâtiment *m* extérieur; **outbuildings** dépendances *fpl*

outburst ['aʊtbɜːst] *n* éclat *m*; (*of generosity*) élan *m*; (*of hatred etc*) déchaînement *m*, éruption *f*; (*of energy*) accès *m*; (*of activity, enthusiasm*) débordement *m*; (*of violence, gunfire*) explosion *f*; **an o. of laughter** un grand éclat de rire; **o. of temper** accès *ou* éclat de colère; **she apologized for her o.** elle s'est excusée de l'éclat qu'elle venait de faire

outcast ['aʊtkɑːst] *n* banni, -ie, proscrit, -ite; **an o. of society, a social o.** un paria

outclass [aʊt'klɑːs] *vt* (*competitor*) surclasser

outcome ['aʊtkʌm] *n* résultat *m*, issue *f*; **the o. of our labours** le fruit de nos travaux; **I don't know what the o. will be** je ne sais pas ce qui en résultera

outcrop ['aʊtkrɒp] *n* (**a**) *Geol* affleurement *m*, pointement *m* (**b**) (*projecting part*) saillie *f*

outcry ['aʊtkraɪ] *n* (*protest*) protestations *fpl*, tollé *m*; **there was a public o. when the hospital was closed** un tollé général s'est élevé contre la fermeture de l'hôpital; **to raise an o. against sb/sth** crier haro sur qn/qch; *St Exch* **by open o.** à la criée

out-cue *n TV, Cin* signal *m* de sortie; (*video*) point *m* de sortie

outdated [aʊt'deɪtɪd] *adj* (*clothes, furniture*) démodé; (*custom, beliefs*) désuet, -uète, démodé; (*word, expression*) vieilli, démodé; (*textbook, theory*) démodé, périmé

outdistance [aʊt'dɪstəns] *vt* distancer, dépasser

outdo [aʊt'duː] *vt* (*pt* **outdid** [aʊt'dɪd]; *pp* **outdone** [aʊt'dʌn]) l'emporter *ou* renchérir sur, surpasser (**sb in sth** qn en qch); **we don't want to be outdone when it comes to quality** nous ne voulons surtout pas être surpassés en ce qui concerne la qualité; **they are all anxious to o. each other** c'est à qui fera le mieux; **not to be outdone** pour ne pas être en reste (**in** de)

outdoor ['aʊtdɔːr] *adj* (*life*) au grand air, en plein air, de plein air; (*swimming pool*) en plein air, découvert; (*games, activities*) de plein air; **she's an o. person** c'est une personne qui aime le grand air *ou* qui aime être dehors; **he's/she's not an o. person** il est casanier *ou F* pantouflard/ elle est casanière *ou F* pantouflarde; **o. advertising** publicité *f* extérieure; **o. aerial** antenne *f* extérieure; **o. clothes** (*warm*) vêtements *mpl* chauds; (*waterproof*) vêtements de pluie; **o. shoes** chaussures *fpl*; (*big*) grosses chaussures; **leave your o. shoes at the door** laissez vos chaussures à la porte; *Cin, TV* **o. scenes** *or* **shots** extérieurs *mpl*; *Cin* **o. set** décor *m* en extérieur; **o. work** travail *m* (à l')extérieur *ou* en plein air

outdoors [aʊt'dɔːz] **1** *adv* dehors; (*in open air*) en plein air; **to sleep o.** coucher à la belle étoile; **to sow o.** (*in gardening*) semer en pleine terre **2** *n* **the o.** la vie au grand air *ou* en plein air; **the great o.** la nature à l'état sauvage; **she's an o. person** c'est une personne qui aime le grand air *ou* qui aime être dehors

outer ['aʊtər] *adj attrib* (*walls, covering*) extérieur; (*surface*) externe, extérieur; **the secretary in the o. office** la secrétaire qui se trouve dans le bureau à l'extérieur; **just within the o. limits of what is acceptable** tout juste à la limite de l'acceptable; *Archit* **o. door** avant-portail *m*, *pl* avant-portails; **o. garments** vêtements *mpl* de dessus; **o. space** espace *m* intersidéral

Outer Mongolia *n* Mongolie-Extérieure *f*

outermost ['aʊtəməʊst] *adj* (**a**) (*closest to outside*) le plus à l'extérieur; **the o. layer was waterproofed** la première couche était imperméable; **make sure the coloured side is o.** assure-toi que le côté coloré se trouve à l'extérieur (**b**) (*most remote*) le plus reculé *ou* écarté; **to the o. parts of the earth** jusqu'aux extrémités de la terre

outfall ['aʊtfɔːl] *n* (*of pipe*) embouchure *f*
outfit¹ ['aʊtfɪt] *n* **(a)** (*clothes*) ensemble *m*; *Mil* tenue *f*; (*for child to play with*) panoplie *f* **(b)** (*equipment*) équipement *m* **(c)** *F* (*organization, company etc*) boîte *f*; (*of workers*) équipe *f* d'ouvriers; *Mil* (*unit*) unité *f*; (*rock band etc*) groupe *m*
outfit² *vt* (*person, thing*) équiper (**with** de)
outfitter ['aʊtfɪtər] *n* **(a)** *esp Br* (*for clothes*) spécialiste *mf* de la confection **(b)** *Am* (*for hunting etc equipment*) fournisseur *m*
outflank [aʊt'flæŋk] *vt* **(a)** *Mil* (*enemy position*) déborder, tourner; **outflanking movement** mouvement débordant *ou* tournant **(b)** *Fig* (*person*) circonvenir
outflow ['aʊtfləʊ] *n* (*of liquid*) écoulement *m*; (*of lava*) coulée *f*; (*from sewer*) décharge *f*; *Fin* (*of gold, currency*) sortie *f*
outfox [aʊt'fɒks] *vt* (*person*) se montrer plus rusé que; (*security system*) déjouer
outgoing ['aʊtgəʊɪŋ] **1** *adj* **(a)** (*departing*) (*tenant, official*) sortant; (*minister*) sortant; (*resigning*) démissionnaire; (*train, boat, plane*) en partance; *Tel* (*call*) sortant; **o. mail** courrier *m* à expédier; *Ind* **o. shift** équipe *f* sortante *ou* relevée; **o. tide** marée *f* descendante **(b)** (*sociable*) sociable; (*extrovert*) extraverti **2** *npl Fin* **outgoings** dépenses *fpl*, débours *mpl*, sorties *fpl* de fonds
outgrow [aʊt'grəʊ] *vt* (*pt* **outgrew** [aʊt'gruː]; *pp* **outgrown** [aʊt'grəʊn]) **(a)** (*one's clothes etc*) devenir trop grand pour **(b)** (*habit*) perdre avec le temps *ou* en vieillissant; **I would have thought he'd have outgrown all that by now** j'aurais pensé qu'il aurait dépassé tout ça à présent; **to have outgrown one's friends** ne plus avoir grand-chose en commun avec ses amis **(c)** (*grow larger than*) (*person, thing*) croître plus vite que, devenir plus grand que
outgrowth ['aʊtgrəʊθ] *n* excroissance *f*
outguess [aʊt'ges] *vt* (*person*) déjouer les intentions de
outgun [aʊt'gʌn] *vt* avoir une puissance de feu supérieure à
out-Herod *vt Lit* **to o. Herod** se montrer plus cruel qu'Hérode
outhouse ['aʊthaʊs] *n* bâtiment *m* extérieur, dépendance *f*; *Am* (*outside lavatory*) toilettes *fpl* extérieures
outing ['aʊtɪŋ] *n* **(a)** (*excursion*) excursion *f*, sortie *f*; (*drive*) sortie, excursion, promenade *f* en voiture; (*walk*) promenade; *Sp* (*of footballer etc*) match *m*; **his first o. this season** (*of horse*) son premier concours de la saison; **day's o.** (*in a car etc*) sortie pour la journée; **school o.** sortie scolaire **(b)** (*of homosexual person*) révélation *f* de l'homosexualité
outlandish [aʊt'lændɪʃ] *adj* incongru, bizarre
outlast [aʊt'lɑːst] *vt* (*object*) durer plus longtemps que; (*person*) survivre à; **it has outlasted ten centuries of war, weather and vandalism** cela a résisté à dix siècles de guerres, d'intempéries et de vandalisme; **the theory has outlasted all its critics** cette théorie a résisté à l'assaut de tous les critiques
outlaw¹ ['aʊtlɔː] *n* hors-la-loi *m inv*; **to declare sb an o.** déclarer qn hors la loi
outlaw² *vt* **(a)** *Hist* (*person*) mettre hors la loi, proscrire **(b)** (*custom etc*) proscrire, bannir
outlay ['aʊtleɪ] *n* frais *mpl*, dépenses *fpl*, débours *mpl*; **to get back** *or* **recover one's o.** rentrer dans ses fonds; **without any great o.** (*by company*) sans grande mise de fonds; (*by individual*) à peu de frais
outlet ['aʊtlet] *n* **(a)** *Tech* orifice *m* (d'émission); (*for air, gas*) sortie *f*; (*for steam*) échappement *m*; (*of pipe*) débouché *m*; *HydE* **o. pipe** *or* **drain** tuyau *m* d'écoulement **(b)** *Fig* exutoire *m*; **an o. for one's energy** un exutoire pour son trop-plein d'énergie **(c)** *Com* (*for goods*) débouché *m*; **(retail) o.** point *m* de vente **(d)** *esp Am El* prise *f* de courant
outline¹ ['aʊtlaɪn] *n* **(a)** (*form*) **outline(s)** (*of hill, building, boat etc*) contour(s) *m(pl)*, profil *m*; (*of person, building*) silhouette *f*; (*of car*) ligne *f*
(b) (*drawing*) dessin *m* au trait, tracé *m*; (*in text processing*) plan *m* de document; *Fig* (*of play, novel*) argument *m*, canevas *m*; (*of plan, policy etc*) grandes lignes *fpl*, grands traits *mpl*; **drawn in o.** dessiné au trait; **in o.** en gros, dans les grandes lignes; **rough o.** premier jet *m*; **main** *or* **general** *or* **broad outlines** (*of project*) ébauche *f*; **a fairly detailed o. of the plan** une description assez détaillée du projet; **could you give us a quick o. of your plans?** pourriez-vous nous décrire les grandes lignes de votre projet?; **an o. of French history** un résumé de l'histoire de France; **outlines of astronomy** éléments *mpl* d'astronomie; **o. agreement** protocole *m* d'accord; **o. drawing** dessin *m* au trait; *Comptr* **o. font** police *f* vectorielle; **o. plan** plan *m* schématique *ou* d'ensemble; **o. script** scénario *m* indicatif
outline² *vt* **(a)** (*the shape of sth*) silhouetter **(b)** (*plot of a novel etc*) esquisser; (*plan, project*) esquisser, tracer les grandes lignes de; (*plan of action*) ébaucher, indiquer; **I briefly outlined my objections/what needed to be done** j'ai donné un bref aperçu de mes objections/de ce qui devait être fait
outliner ['aʊtlaɪnər] *n Comptr* outliner *m*
outlive [aʊt'lɪv] *vt* (*person*) survivre à; **he will o. us all** il nous enterrera tous; **to have outlived its usefulness** (*of machine, theory etc*) ne plus servir (à rien); **he had outlived the era which had need of him** l'époque qui avait besoin de lui était maintenant révolue
outlook ['aʊtlʊk] *n* **(a)** (*view*) vue *f*, perspective *f*; **the political/economic o.** l'horizon *m* politique/économique; **the o. is gloomy** (*for industry, economy, weather etc*) les perspectives ne sont pas réjouissantes **(b)** (*attitude*) façon *f* de voir les choses; **we need a fresh o. on the matter** nous avons besoin d'un nouveau regard sur le sujet; **o. on life** conception *f* de la vie **(c)** **to be on the o. for sth** être à l'affût de qch
outlying ['aʊtlaɪɪŋ] *adj attrib* éloigné, isolé; **o. areas** régions *fpl* périphériques
outmanoeuvre, *US* **outmaneuver** [aʊtmə'nuːvər] *vt Mil* (*the enemy*) l'emporter sur en tactique; *Fig* (*person*) déjouer les tactiques de; **we've been outmanoeuvred** nos tactiques ont été déjouées
outmatch [aʊt'mætʃ] *vt* surclasser, dominer
outmoded [aʊt'məʊdɪd] *adj* (*custom, beliefs*) désuet, -uète, démodé; (*furniture, theory, word*) démodé
outnumber [aʊt'nʌmbər] *vt* (*the enemy etc*) l'emporter en nombre sur; **we were heavily outnumbered** nous étions très minoritaires; **they outnumbered us three to one** ils étaient en majorité de trois à un par rapport à nous
out-of-court *adj* (*settlement*) à l'amiable
out-of-doors *adv* = **outdoors 1**
out-of-focus *adj* flou
out-of-phase *adj TV, Cin* déphasé
out-of-pocket *adj* **o. expenses** menues dépenses *fpl*, frais *mpl*
out-of-shot *adj TV, Cin* en dehors du champ
out-of-sync *adj* désynchronisé, hors synchronisation
out-of-the-way *adj* **(a)** (*place etc*) écarté, loin de tout et de tous **(b)** (*unusual*) peu ordinaire, peu commun, insolite; **it was nothing o.** cela n'avait rien d'extraordinaire
out-of-town *adj Am* (*store*) situé en dehors du centre-ville
out-of-towner [aʊtəv'taʊnər] *n Am F* étranger, -ère à la ville; **he's an o.** il n'est pas d'ici
outpace [aʊt'peɪs] *vt* (*competitor etc*) dépasser, distancer; **demand has outpaced production** la demande a dépassé la production
outpatient ['aʊtpeɪʃənt] *n* malade *mf* qui vient consulter à l'hôpital; **he was being treated as an o.** il était traité en consultation externe; **outpatients' department** service *m* des consultations externes; **o. treatment** traitement *m* ambulatoire
outplacement ['aʊtpleɪsmənt] *n esp US* = licenciement *m* accompagné d'aide et de conseils fournis par l'employeur pour trouver un autre emploi
outplay [aʊt'pleɪ] *vt* (*person*) jouer mieux que; **she was outplayed** son adversaire a joué mieux qu'elle
outpoint ['aʊtpɔɪnt] *n* (*on tape, film*) point *m* de sortie
outpost ['aʊtpəʊst] *n Mil* poste *m* avancé; **the last o. of civilization** le dernier bastion de la civilisation
outpouring ['aʊtpɔːrɪŋ] *n* (*of feelings*) épanchement *m*, effusion *f*; (*of ideas, literary creativity*) déluge *m*, flux *m*; **outpourings of the heart** épanchements, effusions
output¹ ['aʊtpʊt] *n* **(a)** (*of factory, worker*) production *f*, rendement *m*; (*of machine*) débit *m*, rendement; **o. of an author** production littéraire d'un auteur; **he kept up a phenomenal o. throughout his writing career** il a produit à un rythme phénoménal tout au long de sa carrière littéraire; *Acct* **o. tax** TVA *f* encaissée
(b) *MecE etc* (*of engine*) puissance *f*, rendement *m*; *El* (*of generator*) débit *m*; *El* **power o.** puissance débitée *ou* de sortie; *MecE* **o. shaft** arbre *m* de sortie; *MecE* **o. torque** couple *m* en sortie; **o. voltage** tension *f* de sortie
(c) *Comptr* (*of data, information*) sortie *f*; (*of data processing operation*) résultat(s) *m(pl)*; **o. buffer** mémoire *f* tampon de sortie; **o. card** carte *f* sortie, carte résultat; **o. device** dispositif *m ou* périphérique *m* de sortie; **o. file** fichier *m* de sortie; **o. formatting** mise *f* en forme de sortie; **o. port** port *m* de sortie
output² *vt* (*pt, pp* **output**) **(a)** (*of factory etc*) produire **(b)** *Comptr* sortir (**to** sur)
outrage¹ ['aʊtreɪdʒ] *n* **(a)** (*vicious act*) atrocité *f*; (*violation of decency*) scandale *m*; **to commit an o. on** *or* **against sb** commettre une atrocité sur qn; **$200 a ticket?!, it's an o.!** 200 dollars un billet?!, c'est un scandale!; **o. against humanity/society** crime *m* contre l'humanité/la société *ou*

de lèse-humanité/de lèse-société; **bomb o.** (*in headline*) attentat *m* à la bombe **(b)** (*indignation*) indignation *f* **(at** contre)

outrage² *vt* **(a)** (*public decency, feelings etc*) outrager, faire outrage à **(b)** (*make indignant*) (*person*) scandaliser, outrer; **she's easy to o.** elle se scandalise facilement; **I am outraged** je suis scandalisé *ou* outré

outrageous [aʊt'reɪdʒəs] *adj* (*cruelty*) atroce; (*price, conduct*) scandaleux; (*statement, accusation*) outrageant; **it's/he's o.!** cela/il dépasse toutes les bornes!; **he enjoys being o.** il aime scandaliser; *F* **an o. get-up** une tenue extravagante

outrageously [aʊt'reɪdʒəslɪ] *adv* (*cruel*) atrocement; (*expensive*) scandaleusement; (*to behave*) d'une façon scandaleuse; (*to dress*) de façon extravagante

outrageousness [aʊt'reɪdʒəsnɪs] *n* (*of behaviour*) caractère *m* scandaleux; (*of clothes, hairstyle*) extravagance *f*; **the o. of the prices** les prix scandaleux

outrank [aʊt'ræŋk] *vt* **(a)** (*be of higher rank than*) être supérieur en grade à; **he was outranked by most of those present** la plupart des personnes présentes avaient un grade supérieur au sien **(b)** (*take precedence over*) avoir *ou* prendre le pas sur; **to be outranked by** donner *ou* céder le pas à

outreach ['aʊtriːtʃ] *n Admin* = activité *f* visant à encourager les gens à profiter des avantages sociaux

outrider ['aʊtraɪdər] *n* (*on horseback*) cavalier *m* d'escorte; **(motor-cycle) o.** motard *m* d'escorte

outrigger ['aʊtrɪgər] *n* **(a)** (*in rowing*) porte-nage *m inv* en dehors; (*boat*) outrigger *m* **(b)** (*on canoe*) balancier *m*

outright [aʊt'raɪt] **1** *adv* **(a)** (*completely*) complètement; (*immediately*) du premier coup, sur le coup; **to buy sth o.** acheter qch (au) comptant; **he was killed o.** il fut tué sur le coup *ou* net **(b)** (*bluntly*) sans ménagement; (*frankly*) franchement, carrément; (*to deny*) carrément; **to refuse o.** refuser tout net **2** ['aʊtraɪt] *adj attrib* (*failure*) total; (*refusal*) net; **it's o. wickedness** c'est de la pure méchanceté; **an o. disaster** un vrai désastre; **o. payment** somme *f* forfaitaire; **o. sale** vente *f* au comptant; **o. gift** don *m* pur et simple; **the o. winner** le vainqueur incontesté

outrival [aʊt'raɪv(ə)l] *vt* **(-ll-**, *US* **-l-)** (*person*) surpasser, l'emporter sur

outrun [aʊt'rʌn] *vt* (*pt* **outran** [aʊt'ræn]; *pp* **outrun**; *prp* **outrunning) (a)** (*go faster than*) **to o. sb** gagner qn de vitesse; **he can o. the rest of the team** il court plus vite que le reste de l'équipe **(b)** (*exceed*) **his zeal outruns his discretion** son ardeur l'emporte sur son jugement

outs [aʊts] *npl Am F* **to be on the o. with sb** être brouillé avec qn; **they're on the o.** ils sont brouillés

outsell [aʊt'sel] *vt* (*pt, pp* **outsold** [aʊt'səʊld]) (*object*) se vendre mieux que; (*competitors*) vendre plus que; **we are being outsold by the competition** nos concurrents vendent plus que nous

outset ['aʊtset] *n* commencement *m*; **at the o.** au départ, au début; **from the o.** dès le début

outshine [aʊt'ʃaɪn] *vt* (*pt, pp* **outshone** [aʊt'ʃɒn]) **(a)** (*shine brighter than*) briller plus que **(b)** *Fig* (*surpass*) surpasser, éclipser; **I don't like being outshone** je n'aime pas qu'on m'éclipse *ou* me surpasse

outside **1** [aʊt'saɪd] *n* (*of book, building etc*) extérieur *m*; **on the o. of sth** à l'extérieur de qch; **from the o.** de l'extérieur, du dehors; **the fruit is yellow on the o.** le fruit est jaune à l'extérieur; **friends on the o.** (*of prisoner*) des amis dehors; **to open a door from the o.** ouvrir une porte du dehors *ou* de l'extérieur; **at the o.** (*at most*) tout au plus, au maximum; **to come up on the o.** (*in race*) arriver sur l'extérieur

2 ['aʊtsaɪd] *adj* **(a)** (*influence*) extérieur; (*help*) de l'extérieur; **o. aerial** antenne *f* extérieure; **o. diameter** diamètre *m* extérieur; **o. interests** intérêts *mpl* en dehors de son travail/de sa famille; *Constr* **o. measurements** dimensions *fpl* hors d'œuvre; **o. work** travail *m* extérieur *ou* à l'extérieur *ou* (*in open air*) au grand air *ou* en plein air; **o. worker** (*at home*) ouvrier, -ière à domicile; **the o. world** le monde extérieur

(b) (*price, odds, amount etc*) maximum; **there's an o. chance** (*remote*) ce n'est pas exclu **(of** ... que ... + *sub*); **I think we have an o. possibility** je pense que nous avons une toute petite chance

(c) *Sp* **o. left/right** ailier *m* gauche/droit; *Rugby* **o. half** demi *m* d'ouverture; *Rugby* **o. centre** deuxième centre *m*

3 [aʊt'saɪd] *adv* dehors, à l'extérieur, au dehors; **to go o.** sortir, aller dehors; **to run/dash/***etc* **o.** sortir en courant/à toute vitesse/*etc*; **the taxi is o.** le taxi vous attend dehors; **seen from o.** vu de dehors *ou* de l'extérieur; **vase that is black o. and in** vase qui est noir à l'extérieur et à l'intérieur; *F* **o. of** à l'extérieur de, en dehors de; *F* **o. of a few friends nobody knows anything about it** sauf *ou* à part quelques amis, personne n'en sait rien

4 [aʊt'saɪd] *prep* **(a)** (*in space*) en dehors de, hors de, à l'extérieur de; **o. my bedroom** (*at the door*) à la porte de ma chambre; (*below the windows*) sous les fenêtres de ma chambre; **I'll meet you o. the cinema** je vous rencontrerai devant le cinéma; **o. the town** en dehors de la ville

(b) (*not part of*) **o. working hours** en dehors des heures de travail; **he's o. the family** il n'appartient pas à la famille; **that's o. our agreement** ça ne fait pas partie de notre accord; **that's o. our terms of reference** cela n'entre pas dans nos attributions; **it's o. our range** (*of gun, tank etc*) c'est hors de (notre) portée; (*of aircraft*) ce n'est pas dans notre rayon d'action; (*too expensive*) ce n'est pas dans nos prix

(c) (*apart from*) en dehors de; **o. a few friends** en dehors de quelques amis

outside broadcast *n* production *f* extérieure, émission *f* en extérieur; **o. van** car *m* de reportage

outside broadcasting *n* émissions *fpl* diffusées de l'extérieur des studios; **o. vehicle** car *m* régie, unité *f* mobile de tournage

outside lane *n Aut* (*in Britain*) voie *f* de droite; (*in France, US etc*) voie de gauche; (*on athletic track*) couloir *m* extérieur

outside line *n Tel* ligne *f* extérieure

outside market *n St Exch* coulisse *f*

outsider [aʊt'saɪdər] *n* **(a)** (*socially*) étranger, -ère; **he had always been a bit of an o.** il avait toujours été un peu à l'écart **(b)** (*in election*), *Horseracing, Sp etc* outsider *m* **(c)** *St Exch* coulissier *m*

outsize ['aʊtsaɪz] *n Com* (*large size*) très grande taille *f*; (*in men's clothes*) très grand patron *m*

outsize(d) ['aʊtsaɪz(d)] *adj usu attrib* **(a) o. dress** robe en très grande taille **(b)** (*packet etc*) géant; (*appetite, ego*) démesuré

outskirts ['aʊtskɜːts] *npl* limites *fpl*, (a)bords *mpl*; (*of forest*) orée *f*, lisière *f*; (*of town*) faubourgs *mpl*; (*of city*) banlieue *f*, périphérie *f*

outsmart [aʊt'smɑːt] *vt F* (*person*) surpasser en finesse; **they had been outsmarted once again** une fois de plus ils avaient trouvé plus malin qu'eux

outsourcing ['aʊtsɔːsɪŋ] *n Ind* (*of supplies, parts etc*) achat *m* à l'étranger

outspend [aʊt'spend] *vt* dépenser plus que

outspoken [aʊt'spəʊkən] *adj* (*person*) franc, *f* franche, carré; **to be o.** parler franc, ne pas mâcher ses mots; **o. criticism** critique franche

outspokenly [aʊt'spəʊkənlɪ] *adv* franchement, carrément, rondement

outspokenness [aʊt'spəʊkənnɪs] *n* franchise *f*, franc-parler *m*

outspread [aʊt'spred] *adj* étendu, étalé, déployé; **with wings o., with o.** ['aʊtspred] **wings** les ailes déployées; **with o. arms, with arms o.** les bras grand ouverts

outstanding [aʊt'stændɪŋ] *adj* **(a)** (*remarkable*) remarquable, exceptionnel, hors du commun; **man of o. talents/merits/intelligence** homme aux talents/mérites exceptionnels/à l'intelligence exceptionnelle; **matter of o. importance** affaire de première importance; **she plays o. tennis** c'est une joueuse de tennis exceptionnelle *ou* remarquable

(b) (*main, prominent*) (*feature*) marquant

(c) (*unresolved*) (*business*) en suspens, en cours de règlement; (*problem*) pas encore résolu

(d) *Fin* (*amount, account*) impayé, à recouvrer, à percevoir; (*payment*) arriéré, en retard; (*invoice, amount*) en souffrance; (*interest*) échu, arriéré; **o. account** compte *m* en souffrance; *Banking* **o. cheques** chèques *mpl* en circulation; **o. debts (due to us)** créances *fpl* à recouvrer, recouvrements *mpl*

outstandingly [aʊt'stændɪŋlɪ] *adv* éminemment, exceptionnellement

outstay [aʊt'steɪ] *vt* (*person*) rester plus longtemps que; **I hope I haven't outstayed my welcome** j'espère ne pas avoir abusé de votre hospitalité

outstretched ['aʊtstretʃt] *adj* (*wing*) déployé; (*leg, arm*) tendu; **with arms o., with o. arms** (*to welcome sb*) les bras grand ouverts; **to lie o.** être allongé de tout son long

outstrip [aʊt'strɪp] *vt* **(-pp-)** (*person when running*) devancer, dépasser; *Sp* (*competitor*) distancer; *Fig* (*expectations, budget*) dépasser; (*surpass*) surpasser **(sb in sth** qn en qch)

out-supplier *n Com* fournisseur *m* potentiel

outtake ['aʊtteɪk] *n Cin, TV* coupure *f*, prise *f* non-utilisée, coupe *f*

outvote [aʊt'vəʊt] *vt* (*usu in pass*) (*person, government*) mettre en minorité; (*proposal*) rejeter à la majorité des voix; **we were outvoted** nous avons été mis en minorité, la majorité des voix a été contre nous

outward [ˈaʊtwəd] **1** *adj* **(a)** **in an o. direction** vers l'extérieur; **o. half** (*of ticket*) billet *m* aller; **o. trip** voyage *m* aller; *Econ* **o. investment** investissement *m* à l'étranger **(b)** (*appearance*) extérieur; **o. form** extérieur *m*, dehors *m* **2** *adv* = **outwards**; *Naut* **o.-bound** (*ship*) en partance; (*for foreign destination*) en route pour l'étranger; *Sch* **o.-bound course** école *f* d'endurance (en plein air)

outwardly [ˈaʊtwədlɪ] *adv* en apparence; **she was o. calm** en apparence elle était calme

outwards [ˈaʊtwədz] *adv* vers l'extérieur; **to turn one's feet o.** tourner les pieds en dehors

outwear [aʊtˈweər] *vt* (*pt* **outwore** [aʊtˈwɔːr]; *pp* **outworn** [aʊtˈwɔːn]) **the system has outworn its usefulness** le système est désormais périmé

outweigh [aʊtˈweɪ] *vt* **(a)** (*be more important than*) l'emporter sur; **these arguments were outweighed by considerations of security** les questions de sécurité l'ont emporté sur ces arguments **(b)** (*weigh more than*) peser plus que

outwit [aʊtˈwɪt] *vt* **(-tt-)** (*person*) se montrer plus malin que; (*thwart plans of*) déjouer les intentions *ou* les menées de; **once again he had been outwitted** une fois de plus il avait trouvé plus malin que lui

outwith [aʊtˈwɪθ] *prep Scot* = **outside**

out words *npl TV, Rad* mots *mpl* en trop (dans une séquence)

outworn [ˈaʊtˈwɔːn] *adj* (*custom, idea*) périmé

ouzel [ˈuːz(ə)l] *n* (*bird*) **ring o.** merle *m* à plastron *ou* à collier; **water o.** cincle *m* plongeur, merle d'eau

oval [ˈəʊv(ə)l] **1** *adj* (en) ovale; *US Pol* **the O. Office** = le bureau du Président des États-Unis **2** *n* ovale *m*

ovarian [əʊˈveərɪən] *adj Anat, Bot* ovarien

ovariectomy [əʊvərɪˈektəmɪ] *n Surg* ovariectomie *f*

ovary [ˈəʊvərɪ] *n Anat, Bot* ovaire *m*

ovate [ˈəʊveɪt] *adj Biol* ové, ovale

ovation [əʊˈveɪʃən] *n* ovation *f*; **to give sb an o.** faire une ovation *ou* un triomphe à qn; **to give sb a standing o.** se lever pour applaudir qn; **the performers received a standing o.** tout le monde s'est levé pour applaudir les acteurs

oven [ˈʌv(ə)n] *n* four *m*; *Ind* four, étuve *f*; **electric/gas o.** four électrique/à gaz; **to put sth in the o.** mettre qch au four; **to cook sth in a slow/quick o.** cuire qch à four doux/vif; **it's like an o. in here** on se croirait dans un four ici; **to put one's head in the o.** se suicider (au gaz); **o. gloves** *or* **mitts** gants *mpl* isolants

oven-proof *adj* (*dish*) allant au four

oven-ready *adj* (*meal, dish*) prêt à mettre au four; (*chicken, meat*) prêt à rôtir

ovenware [ˈʌv(ə)nweər] *n* vaisselle *f* allant au four

over [ˈəʊvər] **1** *prep* **(a)** (*on surface of, on top of*) sur; **to spill ink o. the table** répandre de l'encre sur la table; **to spread a cloth o. sth** étendre une toile sur *ou* par-dessus qch; **all o. the north of England** sur tout le nord de l'Angleterre; **to search all o. Paris** chercher dans tout Paris; **famous all o. the world** célèbre dans le monde entier; **to glance o. sth** parcourir qch des yeux *ou* du regard; **length o. all** longueur totale *ou* hors tout; *F* **to be all o. sb** (*be excessively polite*) faire l'empressé auprès de qn; (*be excessively physical*) être collé aux basques de qn; **o. (the top of) sth** par-dessus qch; **to throw sth o. the wall** jeter qch par-dessus le mur; **to read o. sb's shoulder** lire par-dessus l'épaule de qn; **with his coat o. his shoulder** le manteau sur l'épaule; **he wore an old coat o. his uniform** il portait un vieux manteau par-dessus son uniforme; **to stumble** *or* **trip o. sth** buter contre qch

(b) [①A67] (*above*) **directly o. our heads** juste au-dessus de nos têtes; **bending o. his work** courbé sur son travail; **to have a chat o. a glass of wine** bavarder tout en prenant un verre de vin; **to discuss sth o. lunch** discuter de qch pendant le déjeuner; **I couldn't hear her o. the noise of the machine** je ne pouvais pas l'entendre à cause du bruit de la machine; **with his hat o. his eyes** le chapeau enfoncé jusqu'aux yeux; *Math* **12 o. 3** 12 divisé par 3; **to have an advantage o. sb** avoir un avantage sur qn; **to reign/govern o. a country** régner sur/gouverner un pays

(c) (*about*) à propos de; **to laugh o. sth** rire (à propos) de qch; **to cry o. sb/sth** pleurer qn/qch; **we had trouble o. the tickets** nous avons eu des ennuis à propos de *ou* au sujet des billets; **to fight o. sth** se battre à cause de *ou* au sujet de qch; (*in order to obtain it*) se battre pour (obtenir) qch

(d) [①A67] (*across*) **to cross o. the road** traverser la rue; **the house o. the way** la maison d'en face; **o. the border** de l'autre côté *ou* au-delà de la frontière; **to live o. the river** habiter de l'autre côté de la rivière; **from o. the seas** de par delà les mers; **the bridge o. the river** le pont qui enjambe la rivière

(e) (*in excess of*) **numbers o. a hundred** numéros au-dessus de cent; **o. ten pounds** plus de dix livres; **not o. 250 grams** (*in post office*) jusqu'à 250 grammes; **to be o. the limit** dépasser la limite; (*of drunk driver*) avoir dépassé le taux légal d'alcoolémie; **children o. five (years of age), the o. fives** les enfants au-dessus de *ou* de plus de cinq ans; **he's o. fifty** il a (dé)passé la cinquantaine; **he spoke for o. an hour** il a parlé pendant plus d'une heure; **he receives tips o. and above his wages** il reçoit des pourboires en sus de son salaire

(f) (*in the course of*) **o. the last three years** au cours des trois dernières années; **o. Christmas** pendant la période de Noël *ou* des fêtes; **I'll do it o. the weekend** je le ferai pendant le week-end; **o. a period of several weeks** pendant plusieurs semaines; **let's spread it o. a period of weeks** étalons-le sur une période de plusieurs semaines

(g) (*recovered from the effects of*) **I'm/you're/she's/***etc* **o. the worst** le plus mauvais moment est passé; **to be o. a cold** être guéri d'un rhume; **she's o. the disappointment** elle est remise de sa déception; **don't worry, you'll be o. her soon** ne t'en fais pas, bientôt tu n'y penseras plus

2 *adv* **(a)** (*everywhere*) **famous the world o.** célèbre dans le monde entier; **to ache all o.** avoir mal partout; **that's him all o.** c'est tout lui

(b) (*indicating repetition*) **I've had to do it all o. again** j'ai dû tout refaire, j'ai dû le faire de *ou* à nouveau; **ten times o.** dix fois de suite; **twice o.** à deux reprises; **o. and o. (again)** à de nombreuses reprises, *esp Lit* maintes et maintes fois, *esp Lit* à maintes reprises; **he did it o. and o. (again) until ...** il a recommencé des dizaines de fois jusqu'à ce que ...

(c) (*over the top of sth*) par-dessus, dessus; **throw it o.!** (*over the wall etc*) lance-le par-dessus!; *F* (*throw it to me*) lance-le moi!; **Concorde flew o.** le Concorde est passé

(d) (*down*) **to knock sth o.** renverser qch; **and o. I went** et me voilà par terre

(e) (*to other side*) **please turn o.!** voir au dos!, tournez s'il vous plaît!; **to turn sth o. and o.** tourner et retourner qch; **to bend sth o.** plier qch

(f) (*across*) **he led me o. to the window** il m'a conduit à la fenêtre; **to cross o.** (*street etc*) traverser; (*the Channel etc*) faire la traversée; **o. there** là-bas; **o. here** ici, de ce côté; **ask him o.** demandez-lui de venir (chez nous); **our friends are coming o. tomorrow** nos amis vont venir nous voir demain; **to deliver sth o. to sb** remettre qch à qn; **to hand sth o. to sb** remettre qch entre les mains de qn; *Rad* **o.** à vous; *Rad* **o. and out** à vous, terminé; **o. to you** (*it's your turn*) c'est votre tour, c'est à vous; **now o. to our Cardiff studio** nous passons maintenant l'antenne à nos studios de Cardiff

(g) (*in excess*) en plus, en excès; **allow five minutes o.** ajoutez-y cinq minutes; **children of fourteen and o.** les enfants de quatorze ans et plus; **three into seven goes twice and one o.** sept divisé par trois donne deux, et il reste un; **you will keep what is (left) o.** vous garderez l'excédent *ou* le surplus; **I have one card left o.** il me reste une carte

(h) (*excessively*) (*easy, difficult, expensive*) trop; **we're not o. busy** nous n'avons pas trop à faire; **he didn't look o. cheerful** il n'était pas d'une gaieté folle

(i) (*until later*) **to hold o.** (*decision*) remettre (à plus tard)

3 *adj* (*finished*) fini, terminé; **the danger is o.** le danger est passé; **the rain is o.** la pluie s'est arrêtée *ou* a cessé; **the game is o.** la partie est finie; **the war was just o.** la guerre venait de finir *ou* de s'achever; **when the strike is o.** quand la grève sera finie; **it is (all) o.** c'est fini; **it is all o. with me** c'en est fait de moi; **it's all o. between us** tout est fini entre nous; **that's o. and done with** voilà qui est fini et bien fini

4 *n* **(a)** *Com* **shorts and overs** déficits *mpl* et excédents *mpl*; **overs** (*in publishing*) exemplaires *mpl* de passe

(b) *Cr* série *f* de six balles

overabundance [əʊvərəˈbʌndəns] *n* surabondance *f*

overabundant [əʊvərəˈbʌndənt] *adj* surabondant

overachieve [əʊvərəˈtʃiːv] *vi* (*exceed expectations*) faire mieux que prévu; **parents shouldn't push their children to o.** les parents ne devraient pas pousser leurs enfants à en faire trop

overachiever [əʊvərəˈtʃiːvər] *n esp Sch* personne *f* qui en fait trop; (*successful person*) surdoué, -ée

overact [əʊvəˈrækt] *vi* (*of actor*) forcer son jeu

overactive [əʊvərˈæktɪv] *adj* trop actif; *Med* **to have an o. thyroid** faire de l'hyperthyroïdie

over-age *adj* au-dessus de l'âge limite

overall[1] [ˈəʊvərɔːl] **1** *adj* **(a)** (*from one end to the other*) total, hors tout **(b)** (*taken as a whole*) général; **o. efficiency** (*total efficiency*) rendement *m* total; (*efficiency in general*) rendement global; **o. plan** plan *m* d'ensemble **2** *adv* dans l'ensemble, globalement; **England came third o.** au classement général l'Angleterre a fini troisième; **yacht measuring ... o.** yacht dont la longueur totale *ou* hors tout est de ...

overall[2] *n* *(garment)* blouse *f*; *(child's)* tablier *m*, blouse; **overalls** combinaison *f* (de travail), salopette *f*, *F* bleus *mpl* (de travail)

overanxious [əʊvər'æŋkʃəs] *adj* **(a)** *(excessively worried)* trop inquiet; **you're being o. about her** tu t'inquiètes beaucoup trop pour elle; **he is o. about getting us to follow the regulations** sa grande préoccupation c'est de nous faire suivre le règlement **(b)** *(excessively eager)* **o. to please** trop soucieux de plaire

overarm ['əʊvərɑːm] **1** *adj Cr* **o. bowling,** *Tennis* **o. service** service *m* au-dessus de la tête; *Swimming* **o. stroke** brasse *f* indienne, nage *f* (à l')indienne **2** *adv Tennis* **to serve o.**, *Cr* **to bowl o.** servir par en dessus

overawe [əʊvə'rɔː] *vt* intimider; *(of prospect, difficulty, surroundings)* impressionner; **don't be overawed by him** ne te laisse pas intimider par lui, ne sois pas intimidé par lui

overbalance [əʊvə'bæləns] **1** *vi* *(of person)* perdre l'équilibre; *(of thing)* se renverser **2** *vt* *(knock over)* renverser

overbearing [əʊvə'beərɪŋ] *adj* autoritaire; **in an o. manner** autoritairement

overblown [əʊvə'bləʊn] *adj* *(flower)* trop épanoui *ou* ouvert; *(style, book)* ampoulé; *(praise)* excessif

overboard ['əʊvəbɔːd] *adv Naut* par-dessus bord; **to be washed o.** être enlevé par une lame; **to throw sb/sth o.** *(into water)* jeter qn/qch par-dessus bord *ou* à la mer; *Fig* **to throw sb/sth o.** se débarrasser de qn/abandonner qch; **to fall o.** tomber à la mer; **man o.!** un homme à la mer!; *F* **to go o.** *(be enthusiastic)* s'emballer **(for sb/sth** pour qn/qch)

overbook [əʊvə'bʊk] *vti* *(of airline etc)* surréserver, surbooker; **this flight was overbooked** il y a eu surréservation sur ce vol

overbooking [əʊvə'bʊkɪŋ] *n* surréservation *f*, surbook(ing) *m*, surlocation *f*

overboot ['əʊvəbuːt] *n* couvre-chaussure *m*, *pl* couvre-chaussures

overburden [əʊvə'bɜːd(ə)n] *vt* *(with work, responsibility)* surcharger, accabler **(with** de); **he is not overburdened with principles** ce ne sont pas les principes qui l'étouffent

overcapitalization [əʊvəkæpɪtəlaɪ'zeɪʃən] *n Fin* surcapitalisation *f*

overcapitalize [əʊvə'kæpɪtəlaɪz] *vt Fin* surcapitaliser

overcast ['əʊvəkɑːst] *adj* *(sky, weather)* couvert, nuageux; *(day)* nuageux; *Fig* *(face)* assombri; *(expression, look)* sombre; **it will become o. later** cela se couvrira plus tard; **it's looking a bit o.** ça a l'air un peu couvert

overcautious [əʊvə'kɔːʃəs] *adj* trop prudent **(about** à propos de)

overcautiously [əʊvə'kɔːʃəslɪ] *adv* avec trop de prudence, avec une prudence excessive

overcharge [əʊvə'tʃɑːdʒ] **1** *vt* **(a)** *Com* faire payer trop cher à; **to o. sb for** *or* **on sth** faire payer qch trop cher à qn; **he overcharged me by a pound** il m'a fait payer une livre en trop **(b)** *Fig* *(overload)* *(battery)* surcharger **2** *vi* *(of shopkeeper etc)* faire payer trop cher

overcoat ['əʊvəkəʊt] *n* pardessus *m*

overcome [əʊvə'kʌm] *vt* *(pt* **overcame** [əʊvə'keɪm]; *pp* **overcome)** **(a)** *(one's opponents etc)* triompher de, vaincre; *(difficulty, problem)* venir à bout de, avoir raison de; *(one's reluctance, fears etc)* dominer, maîtriser; *(obstacle)* surmonter, vaincre; **to o. a disability** surmonter un handicap **(b)** **to be o. with** *or* **by** *(grief)* être accablé de; *(sleep, tears)* être gagné par; *(emotion, heat)* succomber à; *(fumes)* être asphyxié par; **I was quite overcome** j'ai été bouleversé

overcompensate [əʊvə'kɒmpenseɪt] *vi* surcompenser; **to o. for sth** surcompenser qch

overconfidence [əʊvə'kɒnfɪdəns] *n* confiance *f* exagérée **(in** en); **to be guilty of o.** faire preuve d'une confiance exagérée

overconfident [əʊvə'kɒnfɪdənt] *adj* **(a)** *(about winning, finding a job etc)* trop confiant; **you're being o. about her reaction/the exam** tu présumes un peu trop de sa réaction/de ta réussite à l'examen **(b)** *(self-important)* présomptueux

overcook [əʊvə'kʊk] *vt* (faire) trop cuire

over-correction *n* *(of air/fuel ratio etc)* sur-correction *f*

overcritical [əʊvə'krɪtɪk(ə)l] *adj* trop critique

overcrowd [əʊvə'kraʊd] *vt* *(bus etc)* trop remplir, surcharger; *(city, region etc)* surpeupler

overcrowded [əʊvə'kraʊdɪd] *adj* trop rempli **(with** de); *(with people)* surchargé, bondé; *(city, region etc)* surpeuplé; *(classroom)* surchargé

overcrowding [əʊvə'kraʊdɪŋ] *n* *(of bus)* remplissage *m* excessif; *(of room etc)* encombrement *m*; *(of city)* surpeuplement *m*; **o. is a problem in our schools** les sureffectifs sont un problème dans nos écoles

overdemand [əʊvədɪ'mɑːnd] *n* demande *f* excédentaire

overdeveloped [əʊvədɪ'veləpt] *adj Phot etc* trop développé

overdo [əʊvə'duː] *vt* *(pt* **overdid** [əʊvə'dɪd]; *pp* **overdone** [əʊvə'dʌn]) **(a)** *(exaggerate)* *(welcome, praise)* exagérer; **to o. one's enthusiasm** manifester un enthousiasme un peu forcé; **he overdoes the charm** il fait un peu trop le charmeur
(b) *(do or have too much of)* forcer *ou* exagérer sur; **don't o. the chocolates** ne te gave pas de chocolats; **you've overdone the salt/cream** tu as un peu forcé sur le sel/la crème; **she overdoes the jogging** elle force un peu trop sur le jogging; **to o. the telly-watching** trop regarder la télé; *F* **to o. it** *or* **things** *(work too hard)* en faire trop, se surmener; **you've been overdoing it** *or* **things** *(you need a rest)* tu en as trop fait; *Iron* **don't o. it!** surtout ne te surmènes pas!
(c) *Culin* trop cuire

overdose[1] ['əʊvədəʊs] *n* dose *f* excessive, surdose *f*, overdose *f*; **to take an o.** prendre une dose excessive *ou* une surdose *ou* une overdose de drogue; *(commit suicide)* prendre une dose massive de barbituriques/*etc*; **to die of an o.** mourir d'overdose

overdose[2] *vi* **he overdosed on heroin** *(took too much)* il a pris une overdose *ou* surdose d'héroïne; *(died)* il est mort d'une overdose *ou* surdose d'héroïne; *Fig* **to o. on chocolate** exagérer sur le chocolat; **to o. on TV** se prendre une overdose de télé

overdraft ['əʊvədrɑːft] *n Banking* découvert *m*, solde *m* débiteur; **to have an o.** avoir un découvert; **to pay off an/one's o.** rembourser un/son découvert; **o. facility** autorisation *f* de découvert, facilités *fpl* de caisse; **o. limit** plafond *m* de découvert; **o. loan** prêt *m* à découvert

overdraw [əʊvə'drɔː] *(pt* **overdrew** [əʊvə'druː]; *pp* **overdrawn** [əʊvə'drɔːn]) *Banking* **1** *vt* **to o. one's account** mettre son compte à découvert; **overdrawn account** compte *m* à découvert *ou* désapprovisionné, compte débiteur; **to be overdrawn** être à découvert; **your account is overdrawn** votre compte est débiteur; **to be £100 overdrawn** avoir un découvert de 100 livres; **to go overdrawn** passer en découvert **2** *vi* tirer à découvert

overdress [əʊvə'dres] *vi* *(dress too elegantly)* s'habiller de façon trop élégante; *(wear too many clothes)* trop se couvrir; **to be overdressed** être habillé de façon trop élégante/être trop couvert

overdrive ['əʊvədraɪv] *n Aut* vitesse *f* surmultipliée, overdrive *m*; **in o.** en surmultipliée; *Fig* **to go into/be in o.** passer/être passé (à) la vitesse supérieure

overdub [əʊvə'dʌb] *vt* *(sound)* doubler

overdubbing [əʊvə'dʌbɪŋ] *n* doublage *m*, voice over *m*

overdue [əʊvə'djuː] *adj* *(amount, account)* en souffrance; *(interest)* qui n'a pas été payé à l'échéance; *(person, train, library book)* en retard; *(reform, law, improvement etc)* qui fait défaut; **to be long o.** *(of law, reform etc)* faire défaut depuis longtemps; **changes to the law on divorce were long o.** ça faisait longtemps qu'on aurait dû apporter des modifications à la loi sur les divorces; **the baby was two weeks o.** le bébé avait deux semaines de retard; **she's o.** *(of pregnant woman)* elle a dépassé le terme

overeat [əʊvə'riːt] *vi* *(pt* **overate** [əʊvə'ret]; *pp* **overeaten** [əʊvə'riːt(ə)n]) trop manger, manger avec excès

overeating [əʊvə'riːtɪŋ] *n* excès *mpl* alimentaires *ou* de table

overelaborate [əʊvərɪ'læbərət] *adj* *(style, ideas, design)* trop recherché; *(proposal)* trop compliqué

overemphasis [əʊvə'remfəsɪs] *n* accentuation *f* excessive

overemphasize [əʊvər'emfəsaɪz] *vt* trop accentuer; **it would be impossible to o. it** on ne saurait trop l'accentuer

overemployment [əʊvərɪm'plɔɪmənt] *n* suremploi *m*

overenthusiastic [əʊvərɪnθjuːzɪ'æstɪk] *adj* (par) trop enthousiaste

overestimate [əʊvə'restɪmeɪt] *vt* *(cost, person's talent, difficulty)* surestimer, surévaluer; *(danger)* exagérer; *(one's strength)* trop présumer de; *Com* *(assets)* majorer; **to o. one's own importance** surestimer sa propre importance

overexcite [əʊvərek'saɪt] *vt* surexciter

overexcited [əʊvəre'ksaɪtɪd] *adj* surexcité

overexcitement [əʊvərek'saɪtmənt] *n* surexcitation *f*

overexert [əʊvəreg'zɜːt] *vt* **to o. oneself** trop se fatiguer, se surmener

overexertion [əʊvəreg'zɜːʃən] *n* surmenage *m*

overexpose [əʊvəreks'pəʊz] *vt Phot* surexposer

overexposure [əʊvəreks'pəʊʒər] *n Phot* surexposition *f*; *Fig* *(on the media)* surmédiatisation *f*; **to suffer from o.** faire trop parler de soi; **because of people's o. to advertising** parce que les gens sont bombardés de publicité

overfamiliar [əʊvəfə'mɪlɪər] *adj* **to be o. with sb** *(too friendly etc)* se montrer trop familier *ou* prendre des libertés excessives avec qn; **I'm not o. with the rules** les règlements ne me sont pas tellement familiers; **I'm not o. with what's**

been going on here je ne suis pas très au courant de ce qui s'est passé ici

overfeed [əʊvə'fiːd] **1** *vt* suralimenter; **to be overfed** être suralimenté **2** *vi* se suralimenter, trop manger

overflow¹ ['əʊvəfləʊ] *n* **(a)** *(action)* débordement *m* **(b)** *(excess liquid)* débordement *m*; *Comptr* dépassement *m* de capacité; *Fig (of population)* surplus *m*; **o. meeting** réunion *f* supplémentaire *(pour ceux qui ont trouvé salle comble)* **(c)** *(outlet)* trop-plein *m inv*; **o. pipe** (tuyau *m* de) trop-plein; *(in cistern)* déversoir *m*

overflow² [əʊvə'fləʊ] **1** *vi* *(of liquid, cup, heart)* déborder; *(of gutter, stream)* déborder, dégorger; **room overflowing with people** salle qui regorge de monde; **the guests overflowed into the other rooms** les invités se sont répandus dans les autres pièces; *Fig esp Lit* **her heart overflowed with joy** son cœur débordait de joie **2** *vt* **to o. its banks** *(of river)* sortir de son lit

overflowing [əʊvə'fləʊɪŋ] **1** *adj (water, river etc)* qui déborde; *(container)* plein à déborder; *(joy, gratitude)* débordant **2** *n* **full to o.** plein à déborder

overfly [əʊvə'flaɪ] *vt* (*pt* **overflew** [əʊvə'fluː]; *pp* **overflown** [əʊvə'fləʊn]) survoler

overfond ['əʊvəfɒnd] *adj* trop attaché **(of** à); **I'm not o. of oranges** je ne raffole pas des oranges

overfull [əʊvə'fʊl] *adj* trop plein **(of, with** de); **to be o.** *(after eating too much)* être gavé

overgearing [əʊvə'gɪərɪŋ] *n Fin* surendettement *m*

overgrown [əʊvə'grəʊn] *adj* **(a)** (re)couvert **(with sth** de qch); **o. with weeds** (re)couvert de *ou* envahi par les mauvaises herbes; **o. with ivy** (re)couvert de *ou* tapissé de *ou* envahi de lierre **(b) he's like an o. schoolboy** il est resté très écolier; **you great big o. baby you!** espèce de grand bébé!

overhang¹ ['əʊvəhæŋ] *n* surplomb *m*; *Constr* **to have an o.** porter à faux; **a balcony with an o. of three feet** un balcon avec une saillie d'un mètre

overhang² [əʊvə'hæŋ] (*pt, pp* **overhung** [əʊvə'hʌŋ]) **1** *vt (of balcony, rocks etc)* surplomber, faire saillie au-dessus de **2** *vi (of balcony, rocks etc)* surplomber, être en surplomb, faire saillie; *(of wall)* être en surplomb, déverser

overhanging [əʊvə'hæŋɪŋ] *adj (rocks, balcony)* en surplomb; *(wall)* en surplomb, déversé

overhaul¹ ['əʊvəhɔːl] *n* **(a)** *(examination) (of machine etc)* révision *f*, vérification *f*; **complete o.** révision complète **(b)** *(repairs) (of vehicle, machine)* révision *f*, remise *f* en état; *Fig (of organization, theory, schedule)* remaniement *m*

overhaul² [əʊvə'hɔːl] *vt* **(a)** *(examine) (machine)* réviser, vérifier **(b)** *(repair) (machine)* remettre en état; *Fig (organization, theory, schedule)* remanier **(c)** *(overtake)* dépasser

overhead [əʊvə'hed] **1** *adv* au-dessus; **the stars o.** les étoiles dans le ciel **2** ['əʊvəhed] *adj (cable etc)* aérien; **o. camshaft** arbre *m* à cames en tête; *Constr, Rail* **o. crossing** croisement *m* supérieur; *Com* **o. expenses** *or* **charges** frais *mpl* généraux; *Art, Phot, MecE* **o. lighting** éclairage *f* vertical; **o. railway** chemin *m* de fer aérien; **o. projector** rétroprojecteur *m*; *TV, Cin* **o. shot** plan *m* en plongée; **o. valves** soupapes *fpl* en dessus *ou* en tête; *Tennis* **o. volley** volée *f* rattrapée au-dessus de la tête **3** ['əʊvəhed] *n Com* charge *f* opérationnelle; *Am* **o.,** *Br* **overheads** frais *mpl* généraux; **o. budget** budget *m* des charges

overhead-valve engine *n* moteur *m* à soupapes en tête

overhear [əʊvə'hɪər] (*pt, pp* **overheard** [əʊvə'hɜːd]) **1** *vt (conversation etc)* surprendre, entendre (par hasard); **they were overheard discussing it** ils ont été surpris en train d'en parler; **I couldn't help overhearing what you were saying** je n'ai pas pu m'empêcher d'entendre ce que vous disiez **2** *vi* **I couldn't help overhearing** je n'ai pas pu m'empêcher d'entendre ce que vous disiez/ce qu'il disait/*etc*

overheat [əʊvə'hiːt] **1** *vt (oven etc)* surchauffer, trop chauffer; *(economy)* provoquer la surchauffe de **2** *vi (of engine etc)* chauffer; *(of economy)* entrer en surchauffe

overheated [əʊvə'hiːtɪd] *adj (engine, room)* surchauffé; *(economy)* en surchauffe; **to get o.** *(of engine, brakes etc)* chauffer; *(of economy)* entrer en surchauffe; *Fig (of person) (become agitated)* (trop) s'échauffer

overheating [əʊvə'hiːtɪŋ] *n* surchauffe *f*; *MecE* échauffement *m* (anormal)

overhype [əʊvə'haɪp] *vt* faire tout un tabac sur; *(counterproductively)* faire trop de battage sur

overindulge [əʊvərɪn'dʌldʒ] **1** *vt (person)* montrer trop d'indulgence envers; *(spoil)* gâter; *(own predilections etc)* accorder une place excessive à; **to o. oneself** se faire plaisir; *(eating, drinking)* exagérer (sur la nourriture/la boisson), faire des excès (de table); **she tends to o. her taste for fine food** elle aime la bonne chère et elle ne se prive pas **2** *vi (to eat, drink too much)* faire des excès (de table); **to o. in chocolate/champagne** forcer sur le chocolat/le champagne

overindulgence [əʊvərɪn'dʌldʒəns] *n* **(a)** indulgence *f* excessive **(of sb** envers qn) **(b)** *(in food, drink)* excès *mpl*, abus *m*

overjoyed [əʊvə'dʒɔɪd] *adj* ravi, enchanté **(at** de), transporté de joie **(at** par); **he was o. to meet her** il était ravi *ou* enchanté de la rencontrer

overkeen [əʊvə'kiːn] *adj* empressé **(to do** de faire); **he wasn't o. on her/the idea** elle/l'idée ne lui plaisait pas outre mesure

overkill ['əʊvəkɪl] *n Mil* surcapacité *f* de tuer; *Fig* **it's o.** c'est exagéré, c'est trop; **don't you think we could be accused of o.?** ne croyez-vous pas qu'on pourrait nous accuser d'exagérer?; **so many police for such a demonstration was o.** le nombre d'agents de police était complètement disproportionné face à une telle manifestation; **media o.** médiatisation *f* excessive, surmédiatisation *f*

overladen [əʊvə'leɪd(ə)n] *adj* surchargé **(with** de)

overland 1 [əʊvə'lænd] *adv* par voie de terre **2** ['əʊvəlænd] *adj* **o. journey** voyage *m* par voie de terre; **o. route** voie *f* de terre; *Av* trajet *m* survolant la terre

overlap¹ ['əʊvəlæp] *n* **(a)** *(act, state of overlapping)* recouvrement *m*; *Constr (of tiles etc)* chevauchement *m*; **an o. of two inches** un chevauchement de 5 cm; **there is some o. between philosophy and religion** il y a des points communs entre la philosophie et la religion; **the o. between two departments** les activités communes à deux départements **(b)** *(overlapping part)* partie *f* chevauchante

overlap² [əʊvə'læp] *vti* (**-pp-**) recouvrir (partiellement); *(of categories etc)* avoir un domaine commun; *(in time)* coïncider; *(of theories, evidence)* avoir des points communs; **to o. (one another)** *(of tiles, slates)* se chevaucher; **our holidays will o. by a week** nos vacances vont coïncider pendant une semaine

overlapping [əʊvə'læpɪŋ] *adj (tiles, planks etc)* qui se chevauchent; *(responsibilities)* qui se recoupent; *(holidays)* qui coïncident

overlay¹ ['əʊvəleɪ] *n* **(a)** *(of paint, varnish)* couche *f* **(b)** *Comptr* recouvrement *m*; **o. program** programme *m* en recouvrement

overlay² [əʊvə'leɪ] *vt* (*pt, pp* **overlaid** [əʊvə'leɪd]) **(a)** recouvrir, couvrir **(with** de) **(b)** *TV, Cin* incruster, superposer

overleaf [əʊvə'liːf] *adv* au dos (de la page); **see o.** voir au verso *ou* au dos

overlie [əʊvə'laɪ] *vt* (*pt* **overlay** [əʊvə'leɪ]; *pp* **overlain** [əʊvə'leɪn]) recouvrir, couvrir

overload¹ ['əʊvələʊd] *n* **(a)** *El* surcharge *f*, surélévation *f* d'intensité; *(of engine)* excès *m* d'injection; **o. running** marche *f* en surcharge **(b)** *(of vehicle) (excess weight)* (poids *m* en) surcharge *f*

overload² [əʊvə'ləʊd] *vt (lorry, machine)* surcharger; *(person)* surmener; **to o. sb with work/responsibility** surcharger qn de travail/responsabilités

overlong [əʊvə'lɒŋ] **1** *adv* trop longtemps **2** *adj* trop long, *f* trop longue

overlook [əʊvə'lʊk] *vt* **(a)** *(look out over)* avoir vue sur, donner sur; **the castle/hill overlooks the town** le château/la colline surplombe la ville; **the window overlooks the street** la fenêtre donne sur la rue; **we are overlooked by our neighbours** nos voisins ont vue sur nous

(b) *(fail to notice) (detail, fact)* négliger; *(opportunity)* négliger, laisser échapper; **I overlooked the fact** ce fait m'a échappé

(c) *(disregard) (contribution, project)* ne pas prendre en compte; *(breaches of procedure)* fermer les yeux sur; *(mistake)* laisser passer; **I cannot o. this insolence** je ne peux pas laisser passer cette insolence; **he had been overlooked for promotion once again** une fois de plus quelqu'un d'autre avait été promu à sa place

overlord ['əʊvəlɔːd] *n Hist* suzerain *m*

overly ['əʊvəlɪ] *adv* trop, excessivement; **not o.** pas trop

overlying [əʊvə'laɪɪŋ] *adj* superposé; *(stratum)* surjacent

overmanned [əʊvə'mænd] *adj* **to be o.** avoir un personnel trop nombreux; *Ind* avoir un surplus de main-d'œuvre

overmanning [əʊvə'mænɪŋ] *n* surplus *m* de personnel *ou Ind* de main-d'œuvre

overmuch [əʊvə'mʌtʃ] *adv* (par) trop, outre mesure; **she didn't seem to mind o.** ça ne semblait pas trop la déranger, ça ne semblait pas la déranger outre mesure

overnight 1 [əʊvə'naɪt] *adv* (pendant) la nuit; *(to change etc)* du jour au lendemain; *Fin* au jour le jour, J.J.; **to stay o.** passer la nuit; **leave to soak o.** laisser tremper toute la nuit; **he became famous/rich o.** il est devenu célèbre/riche du jour au lendemain **2** ['əʊvənaɪt] *adj* d'une nuit; **to be an o.**

success devenir célèbre du jour au lendemain; **o. guest** ami, -ie qui passe la nuit (*chez qn*); (*in hotel*) client, -ente qui passe la nuit; **o. stay** séjour *m* d'une nuit; (*in hotel*) nuitée *f*; *Sp* **o. leader** leader *m* du jour; *Fin* **o. rate** taux *m* de l'argent au jour le jour; **o. stop** arrêt *m* pour la nuit

overnight bag *n* petit sac *m* de voyage; (*suitcase*) petite valise *f*

overnight case *n* mallette *f*

overoptimism [əʊvə'rɒptɪmɪz(ə)m] *n* optimisme *m* exagéré; **to suffer from** *or* **be guilty of o.** être excessivement *ou* par trop optimiste

overoptimistic [əʊvərɒptɪ'mɪstɪk] *adj* excessivement *ou* par trop optimiste (**about** quant à); **I am not o. about their chances** je ne crois pas qu'ils aient de grandes chances

over-packaging *n Mktg* suremballage *m*

overpaid [əʊvə'peɪd] *adj* surpayé, trop payé

overparticular [əʊvəpə'tɪkjʊlər] *adj* (par) trop exigeant; **he's not o. about these things** il se moque un peu de ces choses-là

overpass ['əʊvəpɑːs] *n* (*for pedestrians*) passerelle *f* surélevée; (*road*) autopont *m*, pont *m* autoroutier

overpay [əʊvə'peɪ] *vt* (*pt, pp* **overpaid** [əʊvə'peɪd]) (*person*) surpayer, trop payer

overpayment [əʊvə'peɪmənt] *n* **(a)** (*of taxes, on bill*) trop-perçu *m*, *pl* trop-perçus **(b)** (*of employee*) rémunération *f* excessive

overplay [əʊvə'pleɪ] *vt* **to o. one's hand** *Cards* annoncer au-dessus de ses moyens; *Fig* présumer de ses chances (de réussite)

overpolite [əʊvəpə'laɪt] *adj* trop poli

overpopulated [əʊvə'pɒpjʊleɪtɪd] *adj* surpeuplé

overpopulation [əʊvəpɒpjʊ'leɪʃən] *n* surpeuplement *m*, surpopulation *f*

over-positioning *n Mktg* surpositionnement *m*

overpower [əʊvə'paʊər] *vt* (*person*) maîtriser; **to be overpowered by superior numbers** succomber sous *ou* être écrasé par le nombre

overpowering [əʊvə'paʊərɪŋ] *adj* (*grief, heat etc*) accablant; (*smell, taste*) (*unpleasant*) effroyable; (*much stronger than others*) prédominant; (*desire etc*) irrésistible; **I find him o.** je le trouve par trop imposant

overprice [əʊvə'praɪs] *vt* demander un prix excessif pour

overpriced [əʊvə'praɪst] *adj* trop cher, d'un prix excessif

overpricing [əʊvə'praɪsɪŋ] *n* fixation *f* d'un prix trop élevé

overprint[1] ['əʊvəprɪnt] *n* **(a)** *Typ* impression *f* en surcharge; (*on postage stamp etc*) surcharge *f*; *Phot* surimpression *f* **(b)** (*postage stamp*) timbre-poste surchargé, *pl* timbres-poste surchargés

overprint[2] [əʊvə'prɪnt] **1** *vt Typ* (*correction*) imprimer en surcharge; *Comptr* surimprimer; (*postage stamp*) surcharger; *Phot* tirer en surimpression **2** *vi Comptr* surimprimer

overprinting [əʊvə'prɪntɪŋ] *n Typ* impression *f* en surcharge; *Comptr* surimpression *f*; *Phot* (tirage *m* en) surimpression

overproduce [əʊvəprə'djuːs] *vti* surproduire

overproduction [əʊvəprə'dʌkʃən] *n* surproduction *f*

overrate [əʊvə'reɪt] *vt* (*person's abilities, person*) surévaluer, surestimer; (*restaurant, film*) surfaire; **I think he's overrated as an actor** j'estime que sa réputation en tant qu'acteur est surfaite; **sex is overrated** le sexe, ce n'est pas aussi formidable qu'on le dit

overrated [əʊvə'reɪtɪd] *adj* (*film, book*) surfait; (*actor*) à la réputation surfaite

overreach [əʊvə'riːtʃ] **1** *vt* **to o. oneself** trop présumer de ses forces **2** *vi* (*of horse*) (s')attraper

overreact [əʊvərɪ'ækt] *vi* réagir de façon excessive (**to** à; **against** contre); **I don't want to o. but I do think something has to be done** sans vouloir dramatiser je crois vraiment qu'on devrait faire quelque chose

overreaction [əʊvərɪ'ækʃən] *n* réaction *f* trop forte *ou* excessive; **to accuse sb of o.** accuser qn de réagir de façon excessive

override[1] [əʊvə'raɪd] *n Tech* forçage *m* en mode manuel; **manual o.** (*on automatic camera, lift etc*) commande *f* de passage en mode manuel

override[2] (*pt* **overrode** [əʊvə'rəʊd]; *pp* **overridden** [əʊvə'rɪd(ə)n]) *vt* **(a)** (*disregard*) (*objections, protest, rules, decision*) passer outre à **(b)** (*take precedence over*) avoir plus d'importance que, avoir la priorité sur; **decision that overrides a former decision** décision qui annule une décision antérieure; **this duty overrode all her other commitments** cette tâche a pris la priorité sur tous ses autres engagements **(c)** (*automated process*) annuler **(d)** (*horse*) surmener

overriding [əʊvə'raɪdɪŋ] *adj* (*ambition, factor*) principal; (*importance*) capital; (*objection*) majeur; (*principle*) premier; **it was not an o. factor** ce n'a pas été un facteur décisif; **to have an o. desire to do sth** être en proie à un irrésistible désir de faire qch; **but there are o. reasons** mais il y a des raisons d'ordre majeur

overripe [əʊvə'raɪp] *adj* trop mûr; (*cheese*) trop fait

overrule [əʊvə'ruːl] *vt* (*proposal, advice*) rejeter; *Jur* (*decision*) annuler, casser; *Jur* (*claim, objection*) rejeter; **she was overruled by her boss** son patron a rejeté ce qu'elle avait proposé; *US Jur* **objection overruled** objection rejetée

overrun[1] ['əʊvərʌn] *n* **(a)** *Typ* (*at end of line*) chasse *f*; (*at end of page*) report *m*, ligne(s) *f(pl)* à reporter; *Comptr* **o. error** perte *f* d'informations par engorgement; *Aut* **o. valve** limiteur *m* de régime **(b)** *Com* **(cost) overruns** dépassement *m* du coût estimé

overrun[2] [əʊvə'rʌn] (*pt* **overran** [əʊvə'ræn]; *pp* **overrun**; *prp* **overrunning**) **1** *vt* **(a)** (*of invaders*) (*country*) envahir; **garden overrun with weeds** jardin envahi par les mauvaises herbes; **house overrun with mice** maison infestée de souris

(b) (*allotted time*) dépasser; *Rail* (*signal*) brûler; **to o. a budget** dépasser un budget

(c) *Typ* (*word*) reporter à la ligne/à la page suivante; **words that o. the line** mots qui chassent

2 *vi TV, Rad* déborder; **words that o. (into the margin)** mots qui chassent; **the TV programme/the speech overran** le programme télévisé/le discours a duré plus longtemps que prévu; **you mustn't o.** vous ne devez pas dépasser le temps qui vous est imparti; **the project has overrun by three weeks** le projet a dépassé la date limite de trois mois

oversale ['əʊvəseɪl] *n Am* surlocation *f*

overseas **1** ['əʊvəsiːz] *adj* (*colony, trade*) d'outre-mer; (*branch, office of business*) à l'étranger **2** [əʊvə'siːz] *adv* à l'étranger, *Lit* par delà les mers; **from o.** d'outre-mer

oversee [əʊvə'siː] *vt* (*pt* **oversaw** [əʊvə'sɔː]; *pp* **overseen** [əʊvə'siːn]) (*workshop, site etc*) surveiller

overseer ['əʊvəsɪər] *n* surveillant, -ante; *Ind* contremaître, -tresse; *Constr* chef *m* de chantier

oversell ['əʊvəsel] *vt* (*pt, pp* **oversold** [əʊvə'səʊld]) **(a)** (*praise too highly*) exagérer les mérites de **(b)** *Com* (*sell too much of*) vendre trop de; **the flight/concert had been oversold** trop de billets avaient été vendus par rapport au nombre de places pour le vol/concert

oversensitive [əʊvə'sensɪtɪv] *adj* hypersensible; **you're just being o.** tu fais de l'hypersensibilité; **to be a bit o. about criticism** être un peu trop sensible aux critiques

oversew ['əʊvəsəʊ] *vt* (*pt* **oversewed** ['əʊvəsəʊd]; *pp* **oversewn** ['əʊvəsəʊn]) *Sewing* surjeter; (*edge*) surfiler

oversexed [əʊvə'sekst] *adj* qui a une libido démesurée; **you're o.** tu es un obsédé sexuel, tu ne penses qu'à ça

overshadow [əʊvə'ʃædəʊ] *vt* **(a)** (*spread shadow over*) ombrager, couvrir de son ombre **(b)** *Fig* (*of atmosphere*) planer sur; **the negotiations were overshadowed by gloom** une atmosphère morose planait sur les négociations; **his success had been overshadowed by his father's death** sa réussite avait été assombrie par la mort de son père **(c)** *Fig* (*eclipse*) éclipser; **he had always been overshadowed by his brother** son frère l'avait toujours éclipsé

overshoe ['əʊvəʃuː] *n* couvre-chaussure *m*, *pl* couvre-chaussures; (*with wooden soles*) galoche *f*; **rubber overshoes** caoutchoucs *mpl*

overshoot [əʊvə'ʃuːt] (*pr, pp* **overshot** [əʊvə'ʃɒt]) **1** *vt* dépasser; (*of shot, gun*) porter au delà de; **to o. the mark** dépasser le but; *Fig* dépasser les bornes; *Av* **to o. the runway** dépasser la piste; (*deliberately*) survoler la piste; **to o. a production target** dépasser *ou* excéder un objectif de production **2** *vi* (*of plane, pilot*) dépasser la piste

overshot ['əʊvəʃɒt] *adj HydE* (*wheel*) mû par en dessus

oversight ['əʊvəsaɪt] *n* **(a)** (*omission*) oubli *m*, omission *f*; **through** *or* **by an o.** par mégarde, par inadvertance, par oubli **(b)** (*supervision*) surveillance *f*

oversimplification [əʊvəsɪmplɪfɪ'keɪʃən] *n* simplification *f* excessive

oversimplify [əʊvə'sɪmplɪfaɪ] *vti* simplifier à outrance

oversized ['əʊvəsaɪzd] *adj* trop grand; (*class*) surchargé; *F* (*very big*) énorme; **you great o. oaf!** espèce de grosse brute!

oversleep [əʊvə'sliːp] *vi* (*pt, pp* **overslept** [əʊvə'slept]) ne pas se réveiller à temps, *F* avoir une panne d'oreiller; **in order to stop him from oversleeping** pour qu'il se réveille à temps, *F* pour qu'il n'ait plus de pannes d'oreiller

oversleeve ['əʊvəsliːv] *n* manchette *f*

overspend [əʊvə'spend] (*pt, pp* **overspent** [əʊvə'spent]) **1** *vi* dépenser trop; **to o. by …** dépenser … de trop **2** *vt* (*budget*) dépasser

overspending [əʊvə'spendɪŋ] *n* dépense *f* excessive

overspill [ˈəʊvəspɪl] *n* **o.** **(population)** surplus *m ou* déversement *m* de population; **o. town** = ville *f* servant à décongestionner une agglomération surpeuplée

overstaffed [əʊvəˈstɑːft] *adj* qui a un excédent de personnel

overstaffing [əʊvəˈstɑːfɪŋ] *n* excédents *mpl* de personnel, sureffectifs *mpl*

overstate [əʊvəˈsteɪt] *vt* (*facts etc*) exagérer; **I am neither overstating nor understating the case** je n'exagère ni dans un sens ni dans l'autre; **it would not be overstating the problem to say that ...** on pourrait dire sans exagérer que ...

overstay [əʊvəˈsteɪ] *vt* **to o. one's welcome** abuser de l'hospitalité de ses hôtes; *Mil* **to o. one's leave** dépasser la durée de sa permission

oversteer[1] [ˈəʊvəstɪər] *n Aut* comportement *m* survireur, survirage *m*

oversteer[2] [əʊvəˈstɪər] *vi Aut* survirer; **a car which oversteers** une voiture survireuse

overstep [əʊvəˈstep] *vt* **(-pp-)** (*limit, boundary, one's powers*) outrepasser; *Fig* **to o. the mark** dépasser les bornes

overstock [əʊvəˈstɒk] *vt* (*outlet*) munir de stocks excessifs; (*farm*) mettre trop de bétail dans; (*pond*) mettre trop de poissons dans; **to be overstocked** (*of shop*) avoir des stocks excessifs

overstocking [əʊvəˈstɒkɪŋ] *n Com* stockage *m* excessif

overstrike [ˈəʊvəstraɪk] *n* (*in printing*) surimpression *f*

oversubscribe [əʊvəsəbˈskraɪb] *vt Fin* (*share issue*) sursouscrire

overt [əʊˈvɜːt] *adj* évident, manifeste; **do you have to be quite so o. about it?** dois-tu absolument le montrer aussi clairement?; *Jur* **o. act** acte *m* manifeste

overtake [əʊvəˈteɪk] *vt* (*pt* **overtook** [əʊvəˈtʊk]; *pp* **overtaken** [əʊvəˈteɪk(ə)n]) **(a)** *esp Br* (*go past*) (*competitor, car*) doubler, dépasser; (*previous level*) dépasser; **demand has overtaken supply** la demande a dépassé l'offre **(b)** (*of fate etc*) s'abattre sur; **their plans/we were overtaken by fate** le sort s'est joué de leurs projets/nous; **overtaken by events** dépassé *ou* devancé par les événements; **darkness overtook us** la nuit nous surprit

overtaking [əʊvəˈteɪkɪŋ] *n esp Br Aut* dépassement *m*; **o. lane** voie *f* de dépassement; **no o.** défense de doubler

overtax [əʊvəˈtæks] *vt* **(a)** *Fin* (*nation*) accabler sous les impôts; (*individual*) surtaxer, surimposer **(b)** (*overburden*) (*person*) surmener; (*resources*) peser lourdement sur; **to o. one's strength** se surmener, abuser de ses forces; **to o. sb's patience** abuser de la patience de qn

over-the-counter *adj* (*sales*) au comptant; (*medication*) vendu sans ordonnance; *Fin* **o. market** marché *m* hors cote

overthrow[1] [ˈəʊvəθrəʊ] *n* (*of empire, government*) renversement *m*; (*of person*) chute *f*

overthrow[2] [əʊvəˈθrəʊ] *vt* (*pt* **overthrew** [əʊvəˈθruː]; *pp* **overthrown** [əʊvəˈθrəʊn]) (*person*) défaire, vaincre; (*empire*) renverser, abattre; (*government, established order*) renverser

overtime [ˈəʊvətaɪm] **1** *n* **(a)** *Ind* heures *fpl* supplémentaires; **to do o.** faire des heures supplémentaires; **o. ban** refus *m* de faire des heures supplémentaires; **o. pay/rate** paiement *m*/ tarif *m* des heures supplémentaires; **to get o. (pay)** être payé pour les heures supplémentaires que l'on fait **(b)** *US Sp* temps *m* supplémentaire **2** *adv Ind* **to work o.** faire des heures supplémentaires; *Fig* **my imagination was working o.** mon imagination galopait *ou* s'emballait

overtire [əʊvəˈtaɪər] *vt* (*person*) surmener; **to o. oneself, to get overtired** se surmener, trop se fatiguer; **to be overtired** (*of child*) être trop fatigué

overtiredness [əʊvəˈtaɪədnɪs] *n Med* surmenage *m*

overtly [əʊˈvɜːtlɪ] *adv* ouvertement

overtness [əʊˈvɜːtnɪs] *n* franchise *f*

overtone [ˈəʊvətəʊn] *n* **(a)** (*suggestion*) (*of sadness, bitterness*) nuance *f*, soupçon *m*; **there are overtones of racism in her books** il y a des relents de racisme dans ses livres; **the phrase has an o. of disparagement** l'expression comporte un soupçon *ou* un rien de dénigrement; **an o. of criticism** une note critique **(b)** *Mus* harmonique *m*

overtrade [əʊvəˈtreɪd] *vi* avoir une marge d'exploitation trop étroite

overture [ˈəʊvətjʊər] *n Mus* ouverture *f*; *Fig* **to make overtures/sexual overtures to sb** faire des avances à qn; **peace overtures** propositions de paix

overturn [əʊvəˈtɜːn] **1** *vt* (*table, government, status quo*) renverser; (*car*) faire verser; (*boat*) faire chavirer; (*theory*) démonter; **the bill was overturned in the Senate** le projet de loi a été rejeté par le Sénat **2** *vi* se renverser; (*of vehicle*) verser, capoter; (*of boat*) chavirer; (*of plane*) capoter

overuse[1] [əʊvəˈjuːs] *n* emploi excessif **(of** de**)**; **the phrase has been made meaningless by o.** l'expression a perdu tout son sens à force d'être trop employée

overuse[2] [əʊvəˈjuːz] *vt* trop employer

overvaluation [əʊvəvæljuːˈeɪʃən] *n* surévaluation *f*

overvalue [əʊvəˈvæljuː] *vt* **(a)** *Com* (*assets*) surestimer, majorer; (*object*) surestimer, surévaluer **(b)** *Fig* (*person's abilities etc*) surestimer, surévaluer, exagérer

overview [ˈəʊvəvjuː] *n* (*of situation etc*) vue *f* d'ensemble

overvoltage protection [ˈəʊvəvəʊltɪdʒ] *n* protection *f* contre la surtension

overwater [əʊvəˈwɔːtər] *vt* (*plant*) trop arroser

overwatering [əʊvəˈwɔːtərɪŋ] *n* (*of plant*) arrosage *m* excessif

overweening [əʊvəˈwiːnɪŋ] *adj* (*person, attitude*) outrecuidant, présomptueux; (*ambition, vanity*) sans bornes

overweight **1** [əʊvəˈweɪt] *adj* (*person*) trop gros; (*luggage*) en excédent; **he's a few kilos o.** il a quelques kilos en trop **2** [ˈəʊvəweɪt] *n* (*excess weight*) surpoids *m*, poids *m* en excès

overwhelm [əʊvəˈwelm] *vt* (*the enemy*) écraser, accabler; (*with kindness*) combler; (*with shame*) confondre; **overwhelmed with work** débordé de travail; **overwhelmed with phone calls** submergé d'appels; **I am overwhelmed (by your kindness)** je suis confus (de votre gentillesse); **overwhelmed with joy/grief/despair** au comble de la joie/ du malheur/du désespoir; **to be overwhelmed with relief** être profondément soulagé

overwhelming [əʊvəˈwelmɪŋ] *adj* (*need, desire etc*) irrésistible; (*joy, happiness*) débordant; (*grief, sense of guilt*) accablant; (*heat, pressure*) écrasant, accablant; (*defeat, majority*) écrasant; **to have an o. desire to do sth** éprouver le besoin irrésistible de faire qch

overwhelmingly [əʊvəˈwelmɪŋlɪ] *adv* (*beaten, defeated*) d'une manière écrasante; **it is o. sad** c'est affreusement triste

overwind [əʊvəˈwaɪnd] *vt* (*pt, pp* **overwound** [əʊvəˈwaʊnd]) (*watch etc*) trop remonter

overwork [əʊvəˈwɜːk] *n* surmenage *m*; **suffering from o.** surmené

overwork[2] **1** *vt* (*person*) surmener, surcharger de travail; (*muscle, heart*) surmener; (*idea, metaphor etc*) utiliser à outrance; **to o. oneself** se surmener **2** *vi* se surmener

overworking [əʊvəˈwɜːkɪŋ] *n* surmenage *m*

overwrite[1] [ˈəʊvəraɪt] *n Comptr* **o. mode** mode *m* de superposition

overwrite[2] [əʊvəˈraɪt] *vt Comptr* (*data*) superposer

overwrought [əʊvəˈrɔːt] *adj* (*with grief*) accablé; **to be o.** (*nervous and upset*) avoir les nerfs à vif, être angoissé; **the child was o.** l'enfant était à bout; **to become o.** s'affliger, se tourmenter

overzealous [əʊvəˈzeləs] *adj* trop zélé

Ovid [ˈɒvɪd] *n* Ovide *m*

oviduct [ˈəʊvɪdʌkt] *n Biol* oviducte *m*

ovine [ˈəʊvaɪn] *adj* (*animal etc*) ovin

oviparous [əʊˈvɪpərəs] *adj Biol* ovipare

ovoid [ˈəʊvɔɪd] **1** *adj* ovoïde **2** *n* figure *f* ovoïde

ovulate [ˈɒvjʊleɪt] *vi Biol* ovuler

ovulation [ɒvjʊˈleɪʃən] *n Biol* ovulation *f*

ovule [ˈɒvjuːl] *n Biol* ovule *m*

ovum, *pl* **ova** [ˈəʊvəm, ˈəʊvə] *n Biol* ovule *m*

ow [aʊ] *int* aïe!, ouille!

owe [əʊ] (*pp, pt* **owed** [əʊd]) *vt* **(a)** (*money*) devoir; **to o. sb sth, to o. sth to sb** devoir qch à qn; **the sum owed (to) her by her brother** la somme que son frère lui doit *ou* qui lui est due par son frère; **I still o. you for the petrol** je vous dois encore l'essence; **what** *or* **how much do I o. you?** qu'est-ce que je te dois?, combien est-ce que je te dois?

(b) *Fig* (*respect, obedience etc*) devoir; **I o. you an apology/an explanation** je vous dois des excuses/une explication; **you o. it to yourself to do your best** vous vous devez à vous-même de faire de votre mieux; **I o. my life to you** je vous dois la vie; **to o. sb a favour** être redevable d'un service à qn; **to what do I o. this honour?** qu'est-ce qui me vaut cet honneur?; **he owes his success to his parents' influence** il doit son succès à l'influence de ses parents

owing [ˈəʊɪŋ] *adj* **(a) there is £5 o.** 5 livres restent dues; **all the money o. to me** tout l'argent qui m'est dû **(b) o. to** (*because of*) en raison de, à cause de; **o. to a recent bereavement** en raison d'un deuil récent; **o. to the force of circumstances** par la force des choses

owl [aʊl] *n* hibou *m*, *pl* -oux, chouette *f*; *Fig* **a wise old o.** (*person*) un vieux sage; *F* **o. glasses** lunettes *fpl* (parfaitement) rondes

owlet [ˈaʊlɪt] *n* jeune hibou *m*, jeune chouette *f*

owlish [ˈaʊlɪʃ] *adj* de hibou; **o. look** air *m* de faux sage

own[1] [əʊn] **1** *vt* **(a)** (*land, house, car etc*) posséder, être propriétaire de; (*washing machine, stereo, dog etc*) avoir, posséder; **who owns this land?** qui est le propriétaire de cette terre?; **who owns this stereo?** à qui appartient cette chaîne stéréo?; **he behaves as if he owned the place** il se conduit comme en pays conquis; **you don't o. me!** je ne t'appartiens pas!; **company owned by the state** compagnie qui appartient à l'État

(b) *Fml* (*admit*) **I o. that I was wrong** je reconnais que j'ai eu tort, j'ai eu tort, je l'avoue *ou* je le reconnais; **to o. oneself beaten** s'avouer vaincu; *esp Jur* **to o. a child** (*recognize as one's own*) reconnaître un enfant; *F* **I won't o. you!** je ne te connais plus!

2 *vi* **to o. to a mistake** reconnaître *ou* avouer une erreur; **he owns to being forty** (*admits he is*) il admet qu'il a quarante ans

own² **1** *adj* propre; **her o. money** son propre argent; **I saw it with my o. eyes** je l'ai vu de mes propres yeux; **I had my o. table** j'avais ma table à moi; **I do my o. cooking** je fais la cuisine moi-même, je fais ma propre cuisine; **the supermarket does its o. baking** le supermarché cuit son propre pain; **to roll one's o. cigarettes** rouler ses cigarettes; **to score an o. goal** *Fb* marquer un but pour l'équipe adverse; *Fig* apporter de l'eau au moulin de l'adversaire; **to be one's o. man/woman** vivre à sa façon *ou* à son idée

2 *pron* **(a) my/his/***etc* **o.** le mien/le sien/*etc*; **one's o.** le sien; **they are my o.** ce sont les miens, ils sont à moi, ils m'appartiennent; **to look after one's o.** (*property*) soigner son bien; (*friends, relatives*) s'occuper des siens; **I have money of my o.** j'ai de l'argent à moi; **a child of his o.** un enfant à lui; **the house is my o.** la maison est à moi *ou* m'appartient; **to make sth one's o.** s'approprier qch; **she took the song and made it her o.** elle s'est approprié la chanson; **she has a copy of her o.** elle a un exemplaire à elle *ou* en propre; **for reasons of his o.** pour des raisons qui le regardent; **his ideas are his o.** ses idées lui sont propres; **a style of one's o.** *or* **all one's o.** un style original *ou* propre *ou* spécifique; *F* **to roll one's o.** rouler ses cigarettes; **the landscape has a wild beauty of its o.** le paysage a une beauté sauvage qui lui est propre; **may I have it for my (very) o.?** est-ce que je peux l'avoir pour moi seul?; **there's not a thing here that I can call my o.** il n'y a pas ici un objet qui m'appartienne en propre; **my time is my o.** mon temps est à moi *ou* m'appartient, je suis libre de mon temps

(b) to do sth on one's o. (*without company*) faire qch tout seul; (*on one's own initiative*) faire qch de sa propre initiative *ou* de son propre chef; **to be** *or* **work on one's o.** travailler tout seul; (*be in business alone*) être établi à son propre compte; **I am (all) on my o.** je suis seul; **you're on your o.!** c'est à toi de te débrouiller!

(c) to come into one's o. (*develop fully*) s'épanouir; **to get one's o. back** se venger; **to hold one's o.** (*of patient, in argument, fight etc*) se maintenir

▶ **own up** *vi* (*confess*) avouer; **to o. up to a crime/to having done sth** avouer un crime/avoir fait qch

own-brand *Mktg* **1** *adj* **our o. butter** du beurre sous notre propre marque; **o. product** produit *m* à marque de distributeur **2** *n* marque *f* de distributeur

own-branding *n Mktg* apposition *f* de sa propre marque

owner ['əʊnər] *n* (*of house, land, car*) propriétaire *mf*; (*of business*) patron, -onne, propriétaire; (*of dog etc*) propriétaire, maître, -esse; **the o. of this stereo** la personne à qui cette chaîne stéréo appartient; **cars parked here at (the) owners' risk** les voitures garées ici le sont aux risques de leurs propriétaires; *Naut* **the owners** (*of ship*) les armateurs *mpl*, l'armement *m*; *Acct* **o.'s capital account** compte *m* de l'exploitant; *Aut* **o. driver** conducteur, -trice propriétaire

ownerless ['əʊnəlɪs] *adj* sans propriétaire; (*dog*) sans maître

owner-occupancy *n* fait *m* d'être propriétaire du logement qu'on occupe; **o. has increased** de plus en plus de gens sont propriétaires de leurs logements

owner-occupier *n* propriétaire-occupant *m*, *pl* propriétaires-occupants

ownership ['əʊnəʃɪp] *n* possession *f*; (*right*) (droit *m* de) propriété *f*; **to have o. of sth** être en possession de qch; **she wants o. of the car** elle veut être propriétaire de la voiture; **the o. of the house is contested** les droits de propriété sont contestés; **change of o.** *Com* changement *m* de propriétaire; *Jur* mutation *f*; **under new o.** (*notice in shop, restaurant etc*) nouveau propriétaire; **during her o. of the property** pendant qu'elle possédait la propriété; **the bus company is now in private o.** la compagnie de bus est maintenant aux mains du secteur privé

own-label *adj* = **own-brand**

owt [aʊt] *pron Eng Dial* = **anything**

ox, *pl* **oxen** [ɒks, 'ɒks(ə)n] *n* bœuf *m*; **ox cart** char *m* à bœufs; *Culin* **ox heart/tongue** cœur *m*/langue *f* de bœuf

oxalic [ɒk'sælɪk] *adj Ch* oxalique

oxblood ['ɒksblʌd] *adj, n* (*colour*) rouge sang *m inv*

oxbow ['ɒksbəʊ] *n Geog* **o. (lake)** bras *m* mort (*d'un cours d'eau*)

Oxbridge ['ɒksbrɪdʒ] **1** *n* les universités d'Oxford et de Cambridge **2** *adj* (*graduate etc*) de l'université d'Oxford ou de Cambridge

oxen *see* **ox**

oxeye ['ɒksaɪ] *n* **o. daisy, white o.** (*flower*) marguerite *f* des champs

Oxfam ['ɒksfæm] *n Br* = œuvre *f* de bienfaisance travaillant pour le Tiers Monde; **O. shop** = magasin *m* où l'œuvre de bienfaisance Oxfam vend des articles d'occasion et d'artisanat au profit du Tiers Monde

Oxford ['ɒksfəd] *n* **O. bags** (*trousers*) pantalon *m* très large; **O. blue** (*colour*) bleu foncé *m inv*; *Univ, Sp* = sportif *m* qui a concouru pour l'Université d'Oxford; **O. shoes** oxfords *mpl*, souliers *mpl* richelieu

oxherd ['ɒkshɜːd] *n* bouvier, -ière

oxhide ['ɒkshaɪd] *n* cuir *m* de bœuf

oxidation [ɒksɪ'deɪʃən] *n Ch* oxydation *f*

oxide ['ɒksaɪd] *n Ch* oxyde *m*

oxidization [ɒksɪdaɪ'zeɪʃən] *n Ch* oxydation *f*

oxidize ['ɒksɪdaɪz] *Ch* **1** *vt* oxyder **2** *vi* s'oxyder

Oxonian [ɒk'səʊnɪən] **1** *adj* oxfordien, -ienne, oxonien, -ienne **2** *n Univ* membre *m* de l'Université d'Oxford

oxtail ['ɒksteɪl] *n Culin* queue *f* de bœuf; **o. soup** soupe *f* de queue de bœuf

oxyacetylene [ɒksɪə'setɪliːn] *n* **o. burner** *or* **torch** chalumeau *m* oxyacétylénique de découpage; **o. cutting** découpage *m* au chalumeau

oxygen ['ɒksɪdʒən] *n Ch* oxygène *m*; **o. bottle** *or* **cylinder** bouteille *f* d'oxygène; **o. mask/tent** masque *m*/tente *f* à oxygène

oxygenate ['ɒksɪdʒɪneɪt, ɒk'sɪ-] *vt* oxygéner

oxygenation [ɒksɪdʒɪ'neɪʃən] *n* oxygénation *f*

oxygenize ['ɒksɪdʒɪnaɪz] *vt* oxygéner

oyez [əʊ'jeɪ, əʊ'jez] *int* **o.! o.!** oyez!

oyster ['ɔɪstər] *n* huître *f*; **pearl o.** (huître) perlière *f*; *Fig* **the world is your o.** le monde t'appartient; **o. bed** *or* **bank** huîtrière *f*, banc *m* d'huîtres; **o. breeder** *or* **farmer** ostréiculteur, -trice; **o. farm** *or* **park** parc *m* à huîtres; **o. knife** couteau *m* à huîtres; **o. mushroom** pleurote *f*; **o. shell** écaille *f* d'huître

oystercatcher ['ɔɪstəkætʃər] *n* (*bird*) huîtrier *m*

Oz [ɒz] *n Sl* Australie *f*

oz *abbr* **ounce(s)**

ozone ['əʊzəʊn] *n Ch* ozone *m*; (*bracing air*) bon air *m* frais; **o. depletion** appauvrissement *m* en ozone; **o. layer** couche *f* d'ozone; *Met* ozonosphère *f*

ozone-friendly *adj* (*product, spraycan*) qui préserve la couche d'ozone

P

P, p [piː] *n* **(a)** *(letter)* P, p *m*; *F* **to mind one's P's and Q's** *(be polite)* se surveiller **(b)** *Br* *(abbr* **penny, pence)** penny *m*, *pl* pence; **a 20p stamp** un timbre à 20 pence

p. *(abbr* **page)** p.

PA [piː'eɪ] *n* **(a)** *(abbr* **public address) PA (system)** (système *m* de) sonorisation *f*, système *m* de haut-parleurs, *F* sono *f*; **an announcement over the PA** une annonce par haut-parleurs **(b)** *(abbr* **personal assistant)** *(of executive)* assistant, -ante; *(with secretarial duties)* secrétaire *mf* (de direction) **(c)** *(abbr* **Press Association)** agence *f* de presse britannique **(d)** *(abbr* **production assistant)** assistant *m* de production

Pa *abbr* **Pennsylvania**

pa [pɑː] *n F* papa *m*

p.a. *(abbr* **per annum)** par an; **£16,000 p.a.** 16 000 livres par an

pace¹ [peɪs] *n* **(a)** *(step)* pas *m*; **ten paces off** à dix pas de distance; *Mil etc* **one p. forward!** un pas en avant!

(b) *(gait)* allure *f*; *(of horse etc)* amble *m*; **to put a horse through its paces** faire passer un cheval à la montre; **to put a car/machine through its paces** mettre une voiture/une machine à l'épreuve; **to put sb through his/her paces** mettre qn à l'épreuve

(c) *(speed)* vitesse *f*, train *m*, allure *f*; **there was a lot of p. on the ball** la balle filait à toute allure; **at a smart p.** à vive allure; **at a slow p.** à petite allure; **at walking p.** au pas; **to keep p. with sb** marcher du même pas que qn, aller à la même allure que qn; *Fig* *(in activity)* suivre le rythme de qn; **I can't keep p. with today's teenagers** avec les adolescents d'aujourd'hui, je n'arrive pas à suivre; **supply is keeping p. with demand** l'offre suit la demande; **our incomes haven't kept p. with inflation** nos revenus n'ont pas augmenté au même rythme que l'inflation; **the company did not keep p. with developments in the industry** la société n'a pas suivi le rythme des développements dans l'industrie; **it's all happened so fast I can barely keep p. with it** tout est arrivé si vite que j'ai du mal à suivre le rythme; **to force the p.** forcer le pas *ou* l'allure; **the p. has slackened** l'allure s'est ralentie; **to set the p.** donner le pas; *Sp* donner *ou* régler l'allure; *(of company etc)* mener le train; **to stand the p.** tenir le rythme; **he can't stand the p.** il ne tient pas le rythme; *Cr* **p. bowler** lanceur *m* rapide

pace² **1** *vi* marcher à pas mesurés; *(of horse etc)* aller l'amble; **to p. about** *or* **up and down** faire les cent pas **2** *vt* *(room, street)* arpenter; *Sp* *(runner)* tirer; **to p. oneself** *(when running, drinking)* trouver son rythme; *(when eating)* garder de la place pour la suite

pace³ ['pɑːtʃeɪ] *prep Fml* n'en déplaise à

▸ **pace off, pace out** *vtsep* *(distance)* mesurer au pas

pacemaker ['peɪsmeɪkər] *n* **(a)** *Sp* *(of runner)* meneur, -euse de train **(b)** *Med* *(device)* stimulateur *m* (cardiaque), pacemaker *m* **(c)** *Anat* nœud *m* sinusal cardiaque

pacesetter ['peɪssetər] *n Sp* meneur, -euse de train; *Fig* **to be a p.** mener le train

pacey ['peɪsɪ] *adj* = **pacy**

pachyderm ['pækɪdɜːm] *n* *(animal)* pachyderme *m*

pacific [pə'sɪfɪk] *adj* **(a)** *Geog* **the P. (Ocean)** l'océan *m* Pacifique, le Pacifique **(b)** *Fml* *(not aggressive)* pacifique; *(peaceful)* paisible

pacifically [pə'sɪfɪklɪ] *adv* pacifiquement

pacification [pæsɪfɪ'keɪʃən] *n Pol* *(of country etc)* pacification *f*; *(of person)* apaisement *m*

pacifier ['pæsɪfaɪər] *n* **(a)** *esp Am* *(for babies)* sucette *f*, tétine *f* **(b)** *(person)* pacificateur, -trice

pacifism ['pæsɪfɪz(ə)m] *n* pacifisme *m*

pacifist ['pæsɪfɪst] *n, adj* pacifiste *mf*

pacify ['pæsɪfaɪ] *vt* *(crowd, country etc)* pacifier; *(person, sb's anger)* apaiser, calmer; *(sb's demands)* apaiser; **she refused to be pacified** elle n'a jamais voulu se calmer

pack¹ [pæk] *n* **(a)** *(bundle etc)* *(of goods)* paquet *m*, ballot *m*; *(backpack)* sac *m* à dos; *(of beast of burden)* bât *m*; *esp Am* *(of cigarettes)* paquet; **an economy p. of washing powder** un paquet de lessive de taille économique; **a four-/six-p. of beer** un pack de quatre/six; **a p. of lies** un tissu de mensonges; *Med* **wet/cold p.** enveloppement *m* humide/froid

(b) *(group)* *(of people, thieves)* groupe *m*, bande *f*; *(of wolves, foxhounds)* meute *f*; *(of staghounds)* équipage *m*; *(of cub scouts, Brownies)* meute; **wolves hunt in packs** les loups chassent en meutes; **p. of fools** bande *ou* tas *m* d'imbéciles; *Rugby* **the p.** le pack; *TV, Cin* **p. shot** pack shot *m*

(c) *(set)* *(of playing cards)* jeu *m*

(d) *Geog* **(ice) p.** banquise *f*

pack² **1** *vt* **(a)** *(put into box, carton etc)* emballer, empaqueter; *(put into suitcase etc)* mettre dans sa valise/son sac/sa malle/etc; *(in cotton wool, newspaper etc)* emballer, envelopper; *Com* emballer, conditionner; **did you p. any towels?** est-ce que tu as mis des serviettes dans les bagages?; *esp Am* **shall I p. these for you?** *(in supermarket)* je vous emballe vos achats?

(b) *(cram)* *(passengers into a train etc)* entasser; *(earth into a hole etc)* tasser; **we were packed in like sardines** nous étions serrés comme des harengs (en caque) *ou* comme des sardines; *Naut* **to p. on all sail** mettre toutes voiles dehors

(c) *(fill)* remplir, bourrer **(sth with sth** qch de qch); *Constr, Min etc* *(trench)* remblayer; **to p. one's case/one's bags** faire sa valise/ses bagages; *Fig* **to p. one's bags** *(leave)* plier bagages; **we're not packed** nous n'avons pas fait nos bagages; *Th* **the show packed the house** le spectacle a fait salle comble, le spectacle s'est joué à guichets fermés

(d) *esp Am* *(carry in a backpack)* transporter dans un sac à dos; **to p. a pistol** porter un revolver; *F* **to p. a punch** *(of person)* cogner dur; *(of drink)* donner un coup de fouet

(e) *MecE* *(packing box)* garnir, étouper

(f) *(rig)* **to p. a jury** se composer un jury favorable; **to p. a meeting** s'assurer un nombre prépondérant de partisans à une réunion; *Cards* **to p. the cards** apprêter les cartes

(g) *Comptr* *(database)* condenser, compacter

2 *vi* **(a)** *(prepare luggage)* faire sa/ses valise(s) *ou* ses bagages; **a tent that packs easily** une tente facile à emballer; *F* **to send sb packing** envoyer promener qn

(b) *(crush)* *(of person, animal)* s'entasser **(into** dans)

(c) *Rugby* former le pack

▸ **pack away** **1** *vtsep* **(a)** *(store)* ranger; *(bed)* replier **(b)** *F* **I've never seen anyone p. it away like him/p. away the beer like he does** je n'ai jamais vu personne engouffrer de la nourriture comme lui/avaler autant de bière que lui; **she can really p. away the food when she gets going** ce qu'elle peut engouffrer quand elle s'y met **2** *vi* *(of bed)* se replier; **this tent packs away easily** cette tente se replie *ou* se range facilement

▸ **pack down** **1** *vtsep* *(earth, snow etc)* tasser **2** *vi* **(a)** *(be compacted)* **to p. down hard** *(of snow etc)* se tasser **(b)** *Rugby* former la mêlée

▸ **pack in** **1** *vtsep* **(a)** *(cram in)* entasser; **I couldn't p. anything more in** je ne pouvais pas en faire rentrer plus; **they packed a lot of sightseeing into their short trip** ils ont visité énormément d'endroits pendant leur bref séjour; **one more thing to be packed into the Christmas period** une chose de plus pour laquelle il va falloir trouver du temps pendant la période de Noël; *F* **this movie is packing them in** ce film attire les foules; **we were packed in like sardines** nous étions serrés comme des harengs (en caque) *ou* comme des sardines

(b) *Br F* *(stop, give up)* arrêter; *(job)* laisser tomber, plaquer; **to p. in smoking** arrêter de fumer; **to p. in jogging** laisser tomber le jogging; **p. it in!** arrête!, ça suffit!

(c) *(finish relationship with)* **he's packed her in** il l'a larguée *ou* plaquée

(d) *Am* *(bring in)* **if you p. it in, p. it out** = remmenez vos ordures

2 *vi* **(a)** *(crowd in)* entrer en foule *ou* en masse

(b) *F* *(stop working)* *(of machine etc)* tomber en panne; *(of person)* arrêter; **the photocopier's just packed in on me** la photocopieuse vient de me lâcher

▶ **pack off** *vtsep F* (*send*) expédier; **to p. the kids off to school/bed** expédier *ou* envoyer les enfants à l'école/au lit; **his father packed him off to America/to boarding school** son père l'a expédié en Amérique/en pension

▶ **pack out** *vtsep F* (*fill completely*) (*room*) remplir à craquer; **the hall/pub was packed out** la salle/le bar était plein(e) à craquer *ou* comble *ou* bondé(e); **the theatre had been packed out for weeks** le théâtre faisait salle comble depuis des semaines; **the event was completely packed out** il n'y avait plus un seul billet pour ce spectacle

▶ **pack up 1** *vtsep* (*suitcase*) faire; (*belongings*) emballer; (*at end of class, work etc*) (*books, tools*) ranger **2** *vi* **(a)** (*before moving house*) emballer ses affaires **(b)** (*store things away at end of class, work etc*) ranger ses affaires, *F* remballer **(c)** *F* (*stop working*) (*of machine etc*) tomber en panne; **my car's packed up** ma voiture m'a lâché; **her heart has packed up** son cœur a lâché *ou* cédé

package[1] ['pækɪdʒ] *n* **(a)** (*parcel*) paquet *m*, colis *m* **(b)** *Comptr* (*software*) logiciel *m* **(c)** *Com* (*offer*) offre *f*; **the employment p. includes ...** les avantages accompagnant ce poste sont ...; **the p. includes a company car** l'offre comprend une voiture de société; **I didn't know this would be extra, I thought we were buying a p.** je ne savais pas que ce serait en supplément, je pensais que tout était compris; **you get all these services in a complete p.** vous obtenez tous ces services selon un marché global **(d)** *US* **p. store** = magasin *m* qui vend des boissons alcoolisées (à emporter)

package[2] *vt Com etc* emballer, conditionner; *F* **to p. sb** (*pop star, candidate etc*) créer l'image de marque de qn; **she has packaged herself as a sex symbol** elle s'est créé *ou* fabriqué une image de sex-symbol

package deal *n Com* contrat *m* global, forfait *m*

package holiday *n* vacances *fpl* à prix forfaitaire

packager ['pækɪdʒər] *n* (*in publishing*) packager *m*

package tour *n* voyage *m* à prix forfaitaire

package tourism *n* tourisme *m* organisé

packaging ['pækɪdʒɪŋ] *n* (*action*) emballage *m*, conditionnement *m*; (*materials*) emballage; *F* (*of pop star, candidate etc*) image *f* (*fabriquée autour d'une personnalité publique*); **the p. of the project is all wrong** la façon dont on a présenté le projet ne marche pas du tout

pack animal *n* animal *m* de bât *ou* de charge, bête *f* de somme

pack drill *n Mil* exercice *m* en tenue de campagne (à titre de punition), *Sl* bal *m*

packed [pækt] *adj* **p. (with people)** (*bus, train etc*) bondé; (*hall etc*) plein à craquer, comble, bondé; **p. with tourists** plein de touristes; **the book was p. with information** le livre était truffé *ou* bourré de renseignements; *Th etc* **to play to a p. house** faire salle comble

packed lunch *n* panier-repas *m*, *pl* paniers-repas

packer ['pækər] *n* **(a)** *Com etc* (*person*) emballeur, -euse, empaqueteur, -euse; **fruit p.** emballeur, -euse de fruits **(b)** (*device*) machine *f* à emballer *ou* à empaqueter; (*for tamping down*) bourroir *m*

packet ['pækɪt] *n* **(a)** (*of tea, cigarettes etc*) paquet *m*; *Comptr* (*of data*) paquet; **I made the sauce from a p.** j'ai fait la sauce à partir d'un sachet; **pay p.** (*envelope*) enveloppe *f* de paie; (*money*) paie *f*; **wage p.** (*envelope*) enveloppe de salaire; (*money*) salaire *m*; **(postal) p.** colis *m* (postal), paquet poste; *Sl* **to make** *or* **earn a p.** gagner un fric fou; *Sl* **that'll cost a p.** ça va coûter les yeux de la tête; **p. soup** bouillon *m ou* potage *m* en sachet; *Comptr* **p. switching** commutation *f* par paquets; *Comptr* **p.-switching network** réseau *m* à commutation de paquets

(b) *Old-fashioned* **p. (boat)** paquebot *m*

(c) *Sl* (*male genitals*) = contour *m* des parties génitales masculines moulées dans un pantalon; **what a p.!** quel entrejambe!

packhorse ['pækhɔːs] *n* cheval *m* de somme; *F* **I'm not your p.!** je ne suis pas ton porteur

pack ice *n* (glace *f* de) banquise *f*, pack *m*

packing ['pækɪŋ] *n* **(a)** *Com etc* (*material, act*) emballage *m*; **postage and p.** frais *mpl* d'emballage et d'envoi; **p. costs** frais d'emballage; **p. list** liste *f* de colisage; **p. materials** matériaux *mpl* d'emballage; **p. paper** papier *m* d'emballage

(b) (*for holiday etc*) **to do one's p.** faire sa/ses valise(s), faire ses bagages; **there isn't much p. (to do)** il n'y a pas beaucoup de bagages à faire

(c) (*material, object added or inserted, Constr etc for trench etc*) remblai *m*; **p. box** presse-étoupe *m*; *MecE* **p. ring** (*of cylinder*) rondelle *f ou* bague *f* de garniture; (*of piston*) segment *m*, bague, garniture *f*

packing case *n* caisse *f* d'emballage

packsaddle ['pæksæd(ə)l] *n* bât *m*

pack train *n* convoi *m* de bêtes de somme

pact [pækt] *n* pacte *m*; **to make a p. with sb** faire un pacte avec qn, pactiser avec qn (**to do sth** pour faire qch)

pacy ['peɪsɪ] *adj* (*film, novel*) qui a un rythme d'enfer, musclé; (*sportsperson*) rapide

pad[1] [pæd] *n* **(a)** (*for protection, to prevent chafing etc*) coussinet *m*; (*for brake*) plaquette *f*; (*keypad*) bloc *m*; *Sp* **shin pads**, *Cr* **pads** jambières *fpl*; **shoulder p.** (*in dress, jacket*) épaulette *f*

(b) *Med* tampon *m*, compresse *f*; (*for feminine hygiene*) serviette *f* hygiénique

(c) (*on body*) (*of finger, toe*) pulpe *f*; (*of dog, fox, hare etc*) coussinet *m*

(d) (*writing paper*) bloc *m*; (*on desktop*) sous-main *m inv*; **(inking) p.** tampon *m* encreur

(e) *Av etc* (*for helicopters*) aire *f* de décollage et d'atterrissage; **launching p.** aire *ou* plate-forme *f* de lancement

(f) *Sl* (*home*) appart *m*; **we went to his p.** on a été chez lui

pad[2] *vt* **(-dd-) (a)** (*armchair, door, wall*) capitonner **(b)** = **pad out**

pad[3] *n* (*sound*) (*of animal*) pas *mpl* sourds; (*of person*) pas feutrés; **the p. of his footsteps** ses pas feutrés; **she heard the p. of feet in the corridor** elle a entendu quelqu'un qui marchait à pas feutrés dans le couloir

pad[4] *vi* **(-dd-) to p. (along)** (*of dog etc*) trotter; **to p. about** (*of person*) aller et venir à pas feutrés; **stop padding about in your bare feet** ne marche pas pieds nus

▶ **pad out** *vtsep* (*fill out*) (*speech, essay etc*) étoffer; **they included two old songs to p. the album out** ils ont inclu deux vieilles chansons pour étoffer l'album; **they padded out the meal with some rice** ils ont complété le repas avec du riz

padded ['pædɪd] *adj* (*door, wall etc*) capitonné; (*garment*) matelassé, ouatiné; (*envelope*) rembourré; **p. bra** soutien-gorge *m* à bonnets renforcés; **p. cell** cabanon *m*; **p. shoulders** (*of dress etc*) épaulettes *fpl*

padding ['pædɪŋ] *n* **(a)** (*material*) (*for cushion etc*) bourre *f*, rembourrage *m*; (*for seat, jacket etc*) rembourrage; (*on walls, door*) capitonnage *m* **(b)** (*in speech, essay etc*) délayage *m*

paddle[1] ['pæd(ə)l] *n* **(a)** (*for canoe*) pagaie *f*; **double p.** pagaie à double pale **(b)** (*blade*) (*of paddleboat, waterwheel*) aube *f*, pale *f*, palette *f*; **p. wheel** roue *f* à aubes *ou* à palettes **(c)** (*of turtle, penguin, cetacean*) nageoire *f*; (*of duck*) patte *f* **(d)** (*table-tennis bat*) raquette *f* de ping-pong **(e)** (*walk in water*) **to go for a p.** aller patauger dans l'eau

paddle[2] 1 *vt* **(a) to p. a/the/one's canoe** pagayer; *prov* **to p. one's own canoe** (*get by on one's own*) se débrouiller (tout seul), arriver par soi-même **(b)** *Am F* (*hit*) donner une fessée à **2** *vi* **(a)** (*in canoe*) pagayer; (*in rowing boat*) tirer en douce; (*of duck*) nager **(b)** (*walk in water*) patauger; (*in mud etc*) patauger, patouiller; **paddling pool** pataugeoire *f*

paddle boat *n* bateau *m* à aubes *ou* à roues

paddle steamer *n* vapeur *m* à aubes *ou* à roues

paddock ['pædək] *n* (*field for horse*), *Horseracing* paddock *m*; *Austr* (*field*) champ *m*

Paddy ['pædɪ] *n F* (*Irishman*) Irlandais *m*; **hey, P.!** hé, l'Irlandais

paddy[1] ['pædɪ] *n* **(a)** *Br F* **to be/get in a p.** être/se mettre en rogne (**about** pour) **(b)** *US F* **p. wagon** panier *m* à salade

paddy[2] *n* **(a) p. field** rizière *f* **(b)** *Com* (*rice*) paddy *m*

padlock[1] ['pædlɒk] *n* cadenas *m*

padlock[2] *vt* (*door*) cadenasser, fermer au cadenas; **he padlocked his bike to the fence** il a cadenassé son vélo à la grille

padre ['pɑːdreɪ] *n Rel* prêtre *m*; *Mil* aumônier *m* (militaire)

paean ['piːən] *n Fml* péan *m*, pæan *m*

paediatric, *US* **pediatric** [piːdɪ'ætrɪk] *adj* (*hospital, care etc*) de pédiatrie; (*specialist*) en pédiatrie; **p. surgery** chirurgie *f* pédiatrique

paediatrician, *US* **pediatrician** [piːdɪə'trɪʃən] *n* pédiatre *mf*

paediatrics, *US* **pediatrics** [piːdɪ'ætrɪks] *n* (①A10,c) pédiatrie *f*

paedology, *US* **pedology** [piː'dɒlədʒɪ] *n* pédologie *f*

paedophile, *US* **pedophile** ['piːdəʊfaɪl] *n* pédophile *mf*

paedophilia, *US* **pedophilia** [piːdəʊ'fɪlɪə] *n* pédophilie *f*

pagan ['peɪgən] *adj, n* païen, -ïenne

paganism ['peɪgənɪz(ə)m] *n* paganisme *m*

page[1] [peɪdʒ] *n* page *f*; **on p. 6** à la page 6; **continued on p. 6/on back p.** suite *f* (en) page 6/en dernière page; **the sports/business pages** (*in newspaper*) la section sport/économie; *Fig* **a glorious p. in our history** une page glorieuse de l'histoire de notre pays; **p. break** coupure *f* de page; **p. break character** caractère *m* de changement de page; **p. bromide** bromure *m* de page; **p. depth** hauteur *f* de page; *Comptr* **p.**

description language langage *m* de description de page; **p. design** mise *f* en page; *Comptr* **p. down** page suivante; *Comptr* **p. down key** touche *f* page suivante; **p. format** format *m* de page; **p. length** longueur *f* de page; *Typ* **p. make-up** mise *f* en pages; *Journ* **p. one** Une *f*; *Journ* **p. plan** plan *m* de mise en page; *Comptr* **p. preview** visualisation *f* de la page complète sur l'écran; *Comptr* **p. scanner** lecteur *m* de pages; *Journ* **p. three** = page sur laquelle une femme pose seins nus dans certains quotidiens britanniques; **p. three girl** = femme *f* posant seins nus dans certains quotidiens britanniques; *Comptr* **p. up** page précédente; *Comptr* **p. up key** touche *f* page précédente

page² *vt* (*book*) paginer

page³ *n* (*at hotel*) jeune chasseur *m*; (*at wedding*) page *m* (d'honneur); (*attending person of rank*) page

page⁴ *vt* (*call*) **to p. sb** (*of pageboy*) appeler qn; (*by loudspeaker*) appeler qn par haut-parleur; (*by sending messenger*) envoyer chercher qn par un chasseur; (*by paging device*) appeler qn par radio portative; **I'm having her paged** je la fais appeler; **paging Mr Wilson** on demande M. Wilson

▶ **page down** *vi Comptr* feuilleter en avant

▶ **page off** *vtsep Typ* paginer

▶ **page up** *vi Comptr* feuilleter en arrière

pageant [ˈpædʒənt] *n* (*display*) spectacle *m* grandiose *ou* majestueux; (*of historical events*) cortège *m* historique; *Fig* **the rich p. of our country's history** la riche galerie de tableaux de l'histoire de notre pays

pageantry [ˈpædʒəntrɪ] *n* apparat *m*, pompe *f*

pageboy [ˈpeɪdʒbɔɪ] *n* **(a) p. (style)** (*hairstyle*) coiffure *f* à la page **(b)** = **page³**

page number *n* numéro *m* de page

page numbering *n* numérotage *m* des pages, pagination *f*

page printer *n Comptr* imprimante *f* page par page, imprimante par pages; **p. language** langage *m* d'imprimante par pages

page proofs *npl Typ* épreuves *fpl* en pages

pager [ˈpeɪdʒər] *n Telecom* récepteur *m* d'appel *ou* de poche

page-turner *n F* (*book*) livre *m* passionnant *ou* captivant

paginate [ˈpædʒɪneɪt] *vt* (*make into pages*) mettre en pages; (*number pages in*) paginer

pagination [pædʒɪˈneɪʃən] *n* (*page makeup*) mise *f* en pages; (*numbering*) pagination *f*

pagoda [pəˈgəʊdə] *n Archit* pagode *f*

pah [pɑː] *int* pouah!

paid [peɪd] **1** *pt, pp see* **pay² 2** *adj* **(a)** (*person, work*) rétribué, rémunéré; **p. holidays** congés *mpl* payés; **to get p. sick/maternity leave** avoir droit aux congés de maladie/de maternité **(b)** *Com* (*goods, bill*) payé **(c) to put p. to sb's chances/hopes** réduire les chances/espoirs de qn en poussière; **well, that's put p. to that!** et voilà, tout tombe à l'eau!

paid-out *adj attrib* **p. form** bon *m* de décaissement; **p. voucher** bon *m* de débours

paid-up *adj* **(a) (fully) p. member** (*of party*) membre *m* qui a payé sa cotisation **(b)** *Fin* (*capital*) versé; (*shares*) libéré; **fully p. policy** police *f* d'assurance dont les primes sont à jour; **to make a life assurance policy p.** cesser de cotiser à une assurance-vie (sans l'annuler); **p. share capital** capital *m* appelé et libéré

pail [peɪl] *n* (*bucket*) seau *m*

pailful [ˈpeɪlfʊl] *n* plein seau *m*

pain¹ [peɪn] *n* **(a)** (*physical*) douleur *f*; (*mental*) peine *f*, douleur; **I have a p. in my leg** j'ai une douleur à la jambe; **there was a lot of p. in his right arm** son bras droit lui faisait très mal *ou* le faisait terriblement souffrir; **to cause sb p.** (*physical*) faire mal à qn, faire souffrir qn; (*mental*) faire de la peine à qn; **to be in great p.** souffrir beaucoup; **he was carried from the field in great p.** il souffrait beaucoup quand on l'a transporté hors du terrain; **the p. was unbearable** la douleur était insupportable; **to put a wounded animal out of its p.** achever un animal blessé; **shooting pains** élancements *mpl*, douleurs lancinantes; **labour pains** douleurs de l'accouchement

(b) *F* (*nuisance*) **he's a p. (in the neck** *or Vulg* **arse)** il est casse-pieds *ou* emmerdant *ou* chiant; **working can be a p. sometimes** il y a des fois où c'est vraiment casse-pieds d'avoir à travailler

(c) (*trouble*) (*usu pl*) **pains** peine *f*; **to take pains** *or* **be at great pains** *or* **go to great pains to do sth** se donner de la peine *ou* du mal pour faire qch; **as she was at pains to explain** ce qu'elle se donnait du mal à expliquer; **to take pains over sth** se donner du mal pour qch; **to have nothing for one's pains** en être pour sa peine

(d) *Fml* **on** *or* **under p. of death** sous peine de mort

pain² *vt* **(a)** (*mentally*) faire de la peine à, peiner, attrister; **it pained her to see them quarrel** ça lui faisait de la peine *ou* ça la peinait de les voir se disputer; **it pains me to have to tell you that …** je regrette infiniment d'avoir à vous dire que … **(b)** *Old-fashioned* (*physically*) faire souffrir, faire mal à; **the wound still pained her** la blessure la faisait encore souffrir *ou* lui faisait encore mal

pained [peɪnd] *adj* **p. expression** air *m* affligé *ou* peiné; **to look p.** avoir l'air affligé *ou* peiné

painful [ˈpeɪnfʊl] *adj* **(a)** (*wound, part of the body*) douloureux; **I find walking p.** j'ai mal quand je marche; **to become p.** (*of limb etc*) devenir douloureux, s'endolorir; **that looked p.!** ça a dû faire mal! **(b)** (*unpleasant*) (*spectacle, effort, subject*) pénible; **a p. memory** un souvenir désagréable; **it was p. to see (it)** c'était pénible à voir; **the expensive shops were a p. reminder of their poverty** les boutiques chères leur rappelaient péniblement leur pauvreté **(c)** (*difficult*) (*task*) laborieux, pénible **(d)** *F* (*bad*) (*performance, singing*) atroce

painfully [ˈpeɪnfʊlɪ] *adv* **(a)** (*with physical pain*) douloureusement; **her head throbbed p.** elle sentait une douleur lancinante à la tête; **she fell p.** elle s'est fait mal en tombant **(b)** (*shy, embarrassing*) atrocement, péniblement; **it was p. obvious** c'était tellement évident que c'en était embarrassant **(c)** (*with difficulty*) (*to climb etc*) laborieusement

painkiller [ˈpeɪnkɪlər] *n* calmant *m*, analgésique *m*

painkilling [ˈpeɪnkɪlɪŋ] *adj* calmant, analgésique

painless [ˈpeɪnlɪs] *adj* indolore, sans douleur; *Fig F* **replacing the fan belt was fairly p.** remplacer la courroie de ventilateur n'a pas posé trop de problèmes; **the p. way to pay your bills** la manière commode de payer vos factures

painlessly [ˈpeɪnlɪslɪ] *adv* (*without pain*) sans douleur; *Fig F* (*effortlessly*) sans effort, sans problème

painstaking [ˈpeɪnzteɪkɪŋ] *adj* (*person*) soigneux, appliqué, assidu; (*labour*) soigné; (*investigation*) poussé; (*accuracy, attention to detail*) extrême

painstakingly [ˈpeɪnzteɪkɪŋlɪ] *adv* avec (grand) soin; **to be p. accurate/detailed in one's work** faire preuve d'une extrême précision/attention aux détails dans son travail

paint¹ [peɪnt] *n* peinture *f*; *Art* couleur *f*; *Med* badigeon *m*; *F* (*face make-up*) fard *m*; **wet p.!** (*on sign*) attention, peinture fraîche!; **box of paints** boîte *f* de couleurs; **tube of p.** tube *m* de peinture *ou* de couleur; **p. gun/roller** pistolet *m*/rouleau *m* à peinture; **p. pot** pot *m* à peinture; *Comptr* **p. program** programme *m* de dessin; **p. shop** magasin *m* de couleurs; *Ind* (*in factory etc*) atelier *m* de peinture

paint² **1** *vt* **(a)** *Art* peindre; **to p. a portrait in oils** peindre un portrait à l'huile; **to p. a picture** peindre un tableau; **to p. (a picture of) sb** faire le portrait de qn

(b) (*coat with paint*) (*room, door etc*) peindre (**green** en vert); *Med* (*throat*) badigeonner; **the kitchen needs painting** la cuisine a besoin d'être repeinte; *Th* **to p. the scenery for a play** brosser les décors d'une pièce; **to p. one's nails** se vernir les ongles; *F* **to p. one's face** (*put on make-up*) se maquiller, se farder; *Fig* **to p. the town red** faire la noce *ou* la bringue

(c) (*depict*) dépeindre; **to p. a favourable/an unfavourable picture of a situation** brosser un tableau favorable/défavorable de la situation; **to p. everything in rosy colours** peindre tout en rose

2 *vi Art* faire de la peinture; **to p. in watercolours/in oils** faire de l'aquarelle/de la peinture à l'huile; **I've always wanted to p.** j'ai toujours voulu faire de la peinture; **I wish I could p. like that!** si seulement je pouvais peindre comme cela!

paintbox [ˈpeɪntbɒks] *n* boîte *f* de couleurs

paintbrush [ˈpeɪntbrʌʃ] *n* pinceau *m*

painter¹ [ˈpeɪntər] *n* **(a)** *Art* peintre *m*; (*of toys etc*) coloriste *mf*; **landscape/portrait p.** paysagiste *mf*/portraitiste *mf* **(b) (house) p.** peintre *m* (en bâtiments); **J. Smith, painters and decorators** J. Smith, peintre et décorateur

painter² *n Naut* (*rope*) bosse *f*; **to cut the p.** couper l'amarre

painting [ˈpeɪntɪŋ] *n* **(a)** (*picture*) tableau *m*, peinture *f* **(b)** (*of house, picture etc*) peinture *f*; **to study p.** étudier la peinture; **landscape/portrait p.** peinture de paysages/portraits; **(house) p.** peinture en bâtiment

paintwork [ˈpeɪntwɜːk] *n* peinture(s) *f(pl)*; (*on car etc*) peinture *f*

pair¹ [peər] *n* **(a)** [①A10,e] (*of shoes, scissors, vases, legs etc*) paire *f*; (*of horses*) attelage *m*; (*man and woman, male and female animal*) couple *m*; (*in rowing*) deux *m*; **in pairs** deux par deux; **the p. of you** vous deux; **they can go to bed without their supper, the p. of them!** qu'ils aillent au lit sans manger tous les deux!; **what a p.!** (*of two people*) quelle paire!; **a p. of trousers** un pantalon; *Old-fashioned* **a p. of scales** une balance; **p. of step(ladder)s** escabeau *m*; **these**

two pictures are a p. (*match*) ces deux tableaux se font pendant; **socks that are not a p.** chaussettes dépareillées; **where is the p. of this glove?** où se trouve l'autre gant de cette paire?; *Cards* **p. royal** brelan *m*; **a p. of aces/tens** une paire d'as/de dix

(**b**) *Br Parl* (*two MPs from opposing parties*) = deux membres *mpl* de partis adverses qui se sont associés (pour un vote); (*MP from opposing party*) = membre du parti adverse avec qui on peut s'associer

pair[2] **1** *vi* faire la paire (**with sb/sth** avec qn/qch); (*of birds etc*) s'accoupler, s'apparier (**with** avec); *Br Parl* s'associer (**with sb** avec qn) **2** *vt* (*socks etc*) appareiller, assortir; (*birds etc*) accoupler, apparier; *Mktg* **paired comparison** comparaison *f* par paire

▶ **pair off 1** *vi* (*of people*) former un/des couple(s) **2** *vtsep* (*objects*) arranger deux par deux; (*people*) mettre deux par deux; **they were paired off by their hostess** leur hôtesse les a mis ensemble; **he's trying to get them paired off** (*in a relationship*) il essaie de les mettre ensemble

▶ **pair up** *vi* s'associer, se mettre ensemble; **to p. up with sb** s'associer avec qn, se mettre avec qn

paisley ['peɪzlɪ] *n Tex* **p. pattern** (dessin *m*) cachemire *m*; **p. scarf** foulard à dessin cachemire

pajamas [pə'dʒɑːməz] *npl* [①A10,e] *US* = **pyjamas**

Paki ['pækɪ] *n, adj Br Offensive Sl* pakistanais, -aise *mf*; (*corner shop*) épicerie *f* tenue par un/des Pakistanais; (*restaurant*) restaurant *m* pakistanais; **fancy a P.?** (*meal*) ça te dit de manger pakistanais?

Paki-basher ['pækɪbæʃər] *n Br Offensive Sl* = raciste *mf* qui attaque les Pakistanais, les Indiens et les Bengalais

Paki-bashing *n Br Offensive Sl* = persécution *f* des Pakistanais, des Indiens et des Bengalais

Pakistan [pɑːkɪ'stɑːn] *n* Pakistan *m*

Pakistani [pɑːkɪ'stɑːnɪ] **1** *adj* pakistanais **2** *n* Pakistanais, -aise

pakora [pə'kɔːrə] *npl Culin* = beignets *mpl* de légumes/poisson/*etc*

pal [pæl] *n F* copain *m*, copine *f*; **be a p. and make me a coffee!** sois gentil, tu voudrais bien me faire un café?; **watch where you're going p.!** regarde où tu vas mon vieux *ou* (*more aggressively*) mon coco!

▶ **pal up** *vi F* (*become friends*) (*of two people*) devenir copains/copines; **to p. up with sb** devenir copain/copine avec qn

palace ['pælɪs] *n* (**a**) palais *m*; **bishop's/archbishop's p.** palais épiscopal/archiépiscopal; **p. guard** (*person*) garde *m* du palais; (*all guards*) garde *f* du palais; *Pol* **p. revolution** révolution *f* de palais (**b**) *Br* **the P., Buckingham P.** (*royal entourage*) Buckingham *m*; **the P. raised no objections to the visit** Buckingham n'a élevé aucune objection concernant la visite; **a P. spokesperson** un porte-parole de Buckingham

paladin ['pælədɪn] *n Lit, Hist* paladin *m*

palaeographer [pælɪ'ɒgrəfər] *n* paléographe *mf*

palaeography [pælɪ'ɒgrəfɪ] *n* paléographie *f*

Palaeolithic [pælɪəʊ'lɪθɪk] *adj* paléolithique; **the P. age** le paléolithique, l'âge *m* de la pierre taillée

palaeontologist [pælɪɒn'tɒlədʒɪst] *n* paléontologiste *mf*, paléontologue *mf*

palaeontology [pælɪɒn'tɒlədʒɪ] *n* paléontologie *f*

palatable ['pælətəb(ə)l] *adj* (*meal*) d'un goût agréable, agréable au palais; (*wine*) qui se laisse boire; *Fig* (*doctrine, suggestion etc*) acceptable (**to** aux yeux de)

palatal ['pælət(ə)l] **1** *adj Anat, Ling* palatal **2** *n Ling* palatale *f*

palatalize ['pælətəlaɪz] *vt Ling* palataliser, mouiller

palate ['pælɪt] *n Anat* palais *m*; **hard p.** palais (dur), voûte *f* du palais, voûte palatine; **soft p.** voile *m* du palais; **to have a good p.** avoir le palais fin

palatial [pə'leɪʃəl] *adj* (*building*) magnifique, grandiose; (*dimensions, scale*) monumental

palatinate [pə'lætɪnɪt] *n Hist* palatinat *m*; **the Rhineland p.** le palatinat du Rhin

palaver [pə'lɑːvər] *n* (**a**) *F* (*fuss*) histoires *fpl*; **what's all the p. about?** qu'est-ce qui cloche? (**b**) *Old-fashioned* (*discussion*) palabre *m ou f*; **after a long p.** après de longs *ou* longues palabres

pale[1] [peɪl] *adj* pâle; (*because ill, angry, afraid etc*) blême, pâle; (*colour*) pâle, clair; **a p. blue dress** une robe bleu pâle; **p. as death, deathly p.** pâle comme un mort, d'une pâleur mortelle; **to grow** *or* **become p.** pâlir; **to turn p. with fright** pâlir de terreur; **by the p. light of the moon** à la lumière blafarde de la lune; *Fig* **a p. reflection/imitation of sth** un pâle reflet/une pâle copie de qch; *Br* **p. ale** pale-ale *m*

pale[2] *vi* (*of person*) pâlir, blêmir; *Fig* **my adventures p. beside yours** mes aventures semblent bien pâles auprès des vôtres; *Fig* **to p. into insignificance** devenir insignifiant

pale[3] *n* (**a**) (*of fence*) pieu *m* (**b**) **beyond the p.** (*behaviour, remarks*) inacceptable; (*of person*) pas fréquentable

paleface ['peɪlfeɪs] *n* visage *m* pâle

pale-faced ['peɪlfeɪst] *adj* au visage *ou* au teint pâle; **they looked p.** leurs visages étaient pâles

paleness ['peɪlnɪs] *n* pâleur *f*

Palestine ['pælɪstaɪn] *n* Palestine *f*; **the P. Liberation Organization** l'Organisation *f* de Libération de la Palestine

Palestinian [pælɪ'stɪnɪən] **1** *adj* palestinien **2** *n* Palestinien, -ienne

palette ['pælɪt] *n Art* palette *f*; **p. knife** couteau *m* à palette; *Culin* spatule *f*

palimony ['pælɪmənɪ] *n F* = pension *f* alimentaire versée au concubin/à la concubine

palimpsest ['pælɪmpsest] *adj, n* palimpseste *m*

palindrome ['pælɪndrəʊm] *n* palindrome *m*

paling ['peɪlɪŋ] *n* (*fence*) palissade *f*, palis *m*; (*stake*) pieu *m*

palisade [pælɪ'seɪd] *n* (**a**) palissade *f* (**b**) *Am* **palisades** (*cliffs*) falaises *fpl* abruptes

pall[1] [pɔːl] *n* (**a**) (*over coffin*) poêle *m* (**b**) *Fig* (*of smoke etc*) voile *m*; (*of snow, darkness, gloom etc*) manteau *m*

pall[2] *vi* (*become uninteresting*) perdre son attrait (**on sb** pour qn); **it never palls** on ne s'en lasse pas

pallbearer ['pɔːlbeərər] *n* porteur *m* (*du cercueil*)

pallet[1] ['pælɪt] *n* (*straw mattress*) paillasse *f*; *Lit* (*poor bed*) grabat *m*

pallet[2] *n* (**a**) *Com* palette *f*; **p. truck** transpalette *f* (**b**) *Art* = **palette**

palletizable [pælɪ'taɪzɪb(ə)l] *adj Com* palettisable

palletization [pælɪtaɪ'zeɪʃən] *n Com* palettisation *f*

palletize ['pælɪtaɪz] *vt Com* palettiser

palletizer ['pælɪtaɪzər] *n Com* palettiseur *m*

palliasse ['pælɪæs] *n* paillasse *f*

palliate ['pælɪeɪt] *vt Fml* (*make less severe*) pallier; (*illness*) lénifier; (*fears*) apaiser; (*offence*) pallier, atténuer; **her words had a palliating effect** ses paroles ont eu un effet lénifiant

palliative ['pælɪətɪv] *adj, n* palliatif *m*; **to have a p. effect** (*of medicine*) avoir un effet palliatif *ou* lénifiant; (*of words*) avoir un effet lénifiant

pallid ['pælɪd] *adj* (*person, face, complexion etc*) pâle, blême, blafard; (*skin, hands*) pâle; (*light, moon*) blafard; *Fig* (*performance*) fade, insipide; **a p. reflection/imitation of sth** un pâle reflet/une pâle copie de qch

pallidness ['pælɪdnɪs], **pallor** ['pælər] *n* pâleur *f*

pally ['pælɪ] *adj F* **to be p. with sb** être copain/*f* copine avec qn

palm[1] [pɑːm] *n* (**a**) **p. (tree)** palmier *m*; *Br* **p. court orchestra** = petit orchestre *m* jouant dans le salon d'un hôtel (décoré de palmiers); **p. grove** *or* **plantation** palmeraie *f*; **p. leaf** feuille *f* de palmier; **p. oil** huile *f* de palme *ou* de palmier; **p. wine** vin *m* de palme (**b**) (*branch*) palme *f*; *Rel* rameau *m*, buis *m* (bénit); *Fig* **to bear** *or* **win** *or* **carry off the p.** remporter la palme

palm[2] *n* (*of hand*) paume *f*; (*of glove*) empaumure *f*; **to read sb's p.** lire les lignes de la main à qn; *F* **to grease sb's p.** graisser la patte à qn; *F* **to have** *or* **hold sb in the p. of one's hand** avoir qn dans sa poche

palm[3] *vt* (*conceal*) (*coin, brooch, card etc*) escamoter; **to p. a card** (*in conjuring*) filer une carte

▶ **palm off** *vtsep* (**a**) (*dispose of something unwanted*) faire passer, *F* refiler (**sth on sb** qch à qn); **they're palming the children off on us for the weekend** ils vont nous refiler les enfants pour le week-end (**b**) (*give something worthless to*) **when I complained, they palmed me off with a standard letter** quand je me suis plaint, ils m'ont refilé une lettre toute faite; **she tried to p. me off with some ridiculous excuse** elle a essayé de me faire avaler une excuse ridicule

palmist ['pɑːmɪst] *n* chiromancien, -ienne

palmistry ['pɑːmɪstrɪ] *n* chiromancie *f*

Palm Sunday *n* Dimanche *m* des Rameaux

palmtop ['pɑːmtɒp] *n* **p. (computer)** ordinateur *m* de poche

palmy ['pɑːmɪ] *adj* **p. days** (*of country etc*) époque *f* florissante; **in his p. days** dans ses beaux jours

palpable ['pælpəb(ə)l] *adj* (*tangible*) palpable, que l'on peut toucher; *Fig* (*obvious*) (*lack of enthusiasm, interest*) manifeste; (*lie*) évident; (*difference*) sensible, manifeste

palpably ['pælpəblɪ] *adv* manifestement

palpate ['pælpeɪt] *vt Med* palper

palpation [pæl'peɪʃən] *n Med* palpation *f*, palper *m*

palpitate ['pælpɪteɪt] *vi* palpiter

palpitating ['pælpɪteɪtɪŋ] *adj* palpitant

palpitation [pælpɪ'teɪʃən] *n* palpitation *f*; **to get** *or* **have palpitations** avoir des palpitations

palsied ['pɔːlzɪd] *adj Med* paralysé; *Lit* (*step, grip*) tremblant

palsy ['pɔːlzɪ] *n Old-fashioned Med* paralysie *f*

paltry ['pɔːltrɪ] *adj* (*amount, sum*) misérable, dérisoire; **p. excuses** piètres excuses *fpl*

pampas [ˈpæmpəz] *n Geog* **the P.** la Pampa; **p. grass** herbe *f* des pampas
pamper [ˈpæmpər] *vt* (*person*) choyer, dorloter; **a hotel where you will be pampered** un hôtel où l'on sera à vos petits soins; **to p. oneself** se faire plaisir; **pampered tastes** goûts *mpl* difficiles
pamphlet [ˈpæmflɪt] *n* brochure *f*; (*literary, scientific*) opuscule *m*; (*libellous, scurrilous*) pamphlet *m*
pamphleteer [pæmflɪˈtɪər] *n* auteur *m* de brochures; (*scurrilous*) pamphlétaire *mf*
Pan [pæn] *n Myth* Pan *m*
pan¹ [pæn] *n* **(a)** (*for cooking*) casserole *f*; *Scot* **p. loaf** pain *m* de mie; **p. scourer** éponge *f* à récurer les casseroles **(b)** (*of scales*) plateau *m*; *Min* (*for gold*) batée *f*; **(lavatory) p.** cuvette *f* (de W.C.); *F* **to go down the p.** s'en aller en fumée; **that's six months' work down the p.!** voilà six mois de travail qui s'en vont en fumée! **(c)** *Geol etc* cuvette *f*, bassin *m* de déposition *ou* de sédimentation; **salt p.** marais *m* salant, saline *f*, salin *m* **(d)** *TV, Cin* **p. down** panoramique *m* vers le bas; **p. up** panoramique verticale
pan² (**-nn-**) **1** *vt Min* (*gravel etc*) laver à la batée **2** *vi* laver le gravier/*etc* à la batée; **to p. for gold** laver le gravier/*etc* à la batée pour en extraire l'or
pan³ *vt* (**-nn-**) *F* (*criticize adversely*) (*film, play etc*) éreinter, esquinter
pan⁴ (**-nn-**) *TV, Cin* **1** *vt* **to p. the camera** faire un panoramique, panoramiquer; **to p. the camera across the room** prendre la salle en panoramique, faire un panoramique de la salle **2** *vi* panoramiquer; **the camera pans around the bay** la caméra prend la baie en panoramique *ou* fait un panoramique de la baie; **to p. across the room** prendre la salle en panoramique, faire un panoramique de la salle; **a panning shot** une prise panoramique, un panoramique
▶ **pan down** *vi TV, Cin* faire un panoramique vers le bas
▶ **pan out 1** *vi F* (*turn out*) **it didn't p. out (well)** cela n'a pas marché; **it depends how things p. out** ça dépend de comment les choses vont s'arranger **2** *vtsep Min* (*wash*) laver à la batée
▶ **pan up** *vi TV, Cin* faire un panoramique vers le haut
panacea [pænəˈsɪə] *n* panacée *f*
panache [pəˈnæʃ] *n* (*style*) panache *m*
Pan-African *adj* panafricain
Pan-Africanism [pænˈæfrɪkənɪz(ə)m] *n* panafricanisme *m*
Panama [ˈpænəmɑː] *n* **(a)** (*country*) Panama *m*; **the P. Canal** le canal de Panama **(b) p. (hat)** panama *m*
Panamanian [pænəˈmeɪnɪən] **1** *adj* panaméen **2** *n* Panaméen, -éenne
Pan-American *adj* panaméricain; **the P. Highway** la route panaméricaine
Pan-Americanism *n* panaméricanisme *m*
panatella [pænəˈtelə] *n* **p. (cigar)** panatel(l)a *m*
panavision [ˈpænəvɪʒən] *n* panavision *f*
pancake¹ [ˈpænkeɪk] *n* **(a)** *Culin* crêpe *f* **(b)** *Av* **p. (landing)** atterrissage *m* brutal **(c) p. (make-up)** fond *m* de teint
pancake² *vi Av* faire un atterrissage brutal
Pancake Day *n Culin* mardi gras *m*
Pancake Tuesday *n Culin* mardi gras *m*
panchromatic [pænkrəʊˈmætɪk] *adj Phot* panchromatique
pancreas [ˈpæŋkrɪəs] *n Anat* pancréas *m*
pancreatic [pæŋkrɪˈætɪk] *adj* pancréatique
panda [ˈpændə] *n* panda *m*; **giant p.** panda géant; *Br* **p. car** voiture *f* pie
pandemic [pænˈdemɪk] *Med* **1** *adj* pandémique **2** *n* pandémie *f*
pandemonium [pændɪˈməʊnɪəm] *n* **it's p.** c'est la confusion la plus totale, c'est un désordre indescriptible; **their entire household was in p.** c'était un véritable cirque chez eux quand je suis arrivé
pander [ˈpændər] *vi* **these films p. to our worst instincts** ces films font appel à nos pires instincts; **to p. to sb** encourager bassement qn; **to p. to a vice** encourager un vice; **to p. to sb's whims** se prêter aux exigences de qn
Pandora [pænˈdɔːrə] *n Myth* Pandore *f*; **P.'s box** boîte *f* de Pandore
pane [peɪn] *n* (*of window*) vitre *f*, carreau *m*; **a p. of glass** un carreau, une vitre
panegyric [pænɪˈdʒaɪrɪk] *adj, n Fml* panégyrique *m*
panel¹ [ˈpæn(ə)l] *n* **(a)** (*on wall, of door*) panneau *m*; (*in ceiling*) caisson *m*; (*of altarpiece*) panneau; (*of cartoon strip*) case *f*; *Sewing* panneau; *Archit, Constr* entre-deux *m inv*; **p. light** lampe *f ou* éclairage *m* de tableau de bord
(b) (*list of jury members*) tableau *m ou* liste *f* du jury; (*of committee members*) liste des membres d'un comité *ou* d'une commission; (*group*) (*of enquiry etc*) comité *m*, commission *f*; (*working party*) groupe *m* de travail; (*round table*) table *f* ronde; **the p.** *Jur, Rad, TV* le jury; *Scot Jur* (*the accused*) l'accusé(e), *pl* les accusé(e)s; **p. of experts** comité *ou* commission d'experts; *Mktg* (*for market research*) panel *m*; *Mktg* **p. of expert opinion** panel de spécialistes; **p. discussion** table ronde, *Mktg* débat *m*; *Mktg* **p. member** panéliste *m*; *Mktg* **p. research** recherches *fpl* par panel
panel² *vt* (**-ll-**, *US* **-l-**) recouvrir de panneaux; (*wall*) lambrisser; (*surface*) plaquer
panel beater *n Aut etc* tôlier *m*
panel game *n Rad, TV* jeu *m* télévisé/radiophonique par équipes
panelled, *US* **paneled** [ˈpæn(ə)ld] *adj* (*room, wall*) recouvert *ou* revêtu de boiseries, lambrissé
panelling, *US* **paneling** [ˈpæn(ə)lɪŋ] *n* **(a)** (*wall covering*) lambris *m*, boiseries *fpl*, placage *m*; **oak p.** lambris *mpl* de chêne **(b)** (*material*) panneaux *mpl*
panellist, *US* **panelist** [ˈpæn(ə)lɪst] *n Jur, Rad, TV* membre *m* du jury; (*of committee*) membre du comité; (*of working party*) membre du groupe de travail
panel pin *n Carp* pointe *f* à tête d'homme
panel truck *n Am Aut* camionnette *f*, fourgonnette *f*
pang [pæŋ] *n* **pangs of jealousy** tourments *mpl* de la jalousie; **to feel a p.** sentir un pincement au cœur; **a p. of conscience** un soubresaut de conscience; **to feel** *or* **have pangs of remorse** être tiraillé par les remords; **pangs of hunger** tiraillements *mpl* d'estomac
panhandle¹ [ˈpænhænd(ə)l] *Am F* **1** *vi* mendier **2** *vt* essayer de taper
panhandle² *n* **(a)** *Geog* langue *f* de terre; **the Texas p.** = langue de terre correspondant à la partie nord-ouest du Texas **(b)** *TV, Cin* manche *m* (de tête de caméra)
panhandler [ˈpænhændlər] *n Am F* mendiant, -ante
panic¹ [ˈpænɪk] *n* panique *f*; *F* **there's no p.** il n'y a pas le feu; **to create** *or* **cause (a) p.** causer un mouvement de panique; **to throw the crowd/the stockmarkets into a p.** affoler la foule/les marchés; **in a p.** paniqué, affolé; **to get into a p. over** *or* **about sth** s'affoler à cause de qch; *F* **it was p. stations** c'était la panique totale *ou* l'affolement général; *Fin* **p. buying/selling** achat *m*/vente *f* sous le coup de la panique; **p. measures** mesures *fpl* dictées par la panique; **p. reaction** réaction *f* de panique
panic² (*pt, pp* **panicked**) **1** *vt* (*person, crowd etc*) remplir de panique, paniquer, affoler; (*horse*) affoler; **the news panicked the government into action** la panique provoquée par cette nouvelle a poussé le gouvernement à l'action; **she was panicked into resigning** sous le coup de la panique, elle a démissionné **2** *vi* être pris de panique, s'affoler, paniquer (**about** à propos de); **don't p.!** ne t'affole pas!, ne panique pas!
panic³ *n Bot* **p. (grass)** panic *m* (d'Italie)
panic attack *n* crise *f* de panique
panic button *n* bouton *m* déclencheur du signal d'alarme; *Fig F* **to hit the p.** paniquer
panicky [ˈpænɪkɪ] *adj F* (*feelings*) panique; (*person*) sujet à la panique; (*reaction, response*) affolé; (*market etc*) enclin à la panique; **a p. decision** une décision prise sous le coup de la panique; **don't get p.!** ne paniquez pas!, ne vous affolez pas!
panic-stricken *adj* pris de panique, affolé; (*reaction, response, look*) affolé
panjandrum [pænˈdʒændrəm] *n Lit* gros bonnet *m*
pannier [ˈpænɪər] *n* (*basket*) panier *m*; (*on motorbike or bicycle*) sacoche *f*; (*of beast of burden*) panier de bât
panning [ˈpænɪŋ] *n TV, Cin* panoramique *m*; **p. handle** poignée *f* de panoramique; **p. shot** prise *f* panoramique
panoply [ˈpænəplɪ] *n* panoplie *f*
panorama [pænəˈrɑːmə] *n* panorama *m*
panoramic [pænəˈræmɪk] *adj* (*view etc*) panoramique
panpipes [ˈpænpaɪps] *npl Mus* flûte *f* de Pan
pansy [ˈpænzɪ] *n* **(a)** (*flower*) pensée *f* **(b)** *Offensive Sl* (*male homosexual*) pédale *f*, tante *f*
pant¹ [pænt] *n* souffle *m* pantelant *ou* haletant
pant² **1** *vi* **(a)** (*gasp*) haleter; (*of animal*) battre du flanc; **to p. for breath** chercher à reprendre haleine; **she panted up the hill** elle a monté la côte en haletant *ou* soufflant **(b)** *F* (*be eager*) **he's panting to do it** il a tellement envie de le faire **2** *vt* **listen to me, she panted** écoute-moi, a-t-elle haleté
▶ **pant out** *vtsep* (*say*) dire en haletant
pantechnicon [pænˈteknɪkən] *n Old-fashioned Br* (*van*) camion *m* de déménagement
pantheism [ˈpænθiːɪz(ə)m] *n* panthéisme *m*
pantheist [ˈpænθiːɪst] *adj, n* panthéiste *mf*
pantheistic [pænθiːˈɪstɪk] *adj* panthéiste
pantheon [ˈpænθɪən] *n* panthéon *m*
panther [ˈpænθər] *n* panthère *f*; *Am* (*puma*) couguar *m*, puma *m*; *US Pol* **Black P.** Panthère *f* noire; **the (Black) Panthers** =

mouvement *m* politique fondé par des militants noirs américains dans les années soixante
panties ['pæntɪz] *npl* culotte *f*, slip *m* (*de femme*)
pantihose ['pæntɪhəʊz] *npl esp Am* collant *m*
panting ['pæntɪŋ] *n* halètement *m*
panto ['pæntəʊ] *n Br Th F* = **pantomime (a)**
pantograph ['pæntəgrɑːf] *n* **(a)** *Art* pantographe *m*, singe *m* **(b)** *El* (*of electric train*) pantographe *m*
pantomime ['pæntəmaɪm] *n* **(a)** *Br Th* (*traditional winter show*) = revue-féerie *f* à grand spectacle (présentée aux environs de Noël) **(b)** (*dumb show*) pantomime *f* **(c)** *Br F* (*ridiculous situation*) cirque *m*, sérénade *f*; **there was a bit of a p. over who should pay** ça a été une sérénade *ou* une pantomime pour savoir qui devait payer
pantry ['pæntrɪ] *n* (*cupboard*) (grand) placard *m* à provisions, dépense *f*
pants [pænts] *npl* [①A10,e] **(a)** *Br* (*underwear*) slip *m*; (*boxer shorts*) caleçon *m* **(b)** *esp Am* (*trousers*) pantalon *m*; *F* **to give sb a kick in the p.** donner un coup de pied au derrière à qn; *F* **to beat the p. off sb** mettre une sacrée volée à qn; *F* **to scare the p. off sb** faire une peur *ou* trouille bleue à qn; *F* **to bore the p. off sb** barber qn comme ce n'est pas permis; *F* **to be caught with one's p. down** être pris dans une situation des plus embarrassantes; *F* **it's clear who wears the p. around here** il n'y a pas de doute sur qui porte le pantalon ici
panty ['pæntɪ] *n* **p. girdle** gaine-culotte *f*, *pl* gaines-culottes; **p. liner** protège-slip *m*, *pl* protège-slips
pantyhose ['pæntɪhəʊz] *npl Am* collant *m*
panzer ['pænzər] *n* panzer *m*; **a p. division** une division blindée
Pap [pæp] *n Med* **P. test** *or* **smear** frottis *m* vaginal
pap [pæp] *n* (*baby food*) bouillie *f*; *Pej* (*nonsense*) idioties *fpl*, stupidités *fpl*
papa [pə'pɑː] *n Old-fashioned* papa *m*
papacy ['peɪpəsɪ] *n* papauté *f*
papadum ['pæpədəm] *n* = **poppadom**
papal ['peɪp(ə)l] *adj* papal; **p. bull** bulle *f* papale; **p. interdict** interdit *m* papal; **p. nuncio** nonce *m* du Pape; **p. throne** trône *m* pontifical
paparazzi [pæpə'rætsɪ] *npl Journ, Phot Pej* paparazzi *mpl*
papaw [pə'pɔː] *n Bot* **(a)** (*asimina triloba*) (*fruit*) asimine *f*; (*tree*) asiminier *m* **(b)** = **papaya**
papaya [pə'paɪə] *n* (*carica papaya*) papaye *f*; (*tree*) papayer *m*
paper¹ ['peɪpər] *n* **(a)** papier *m*; (*for wall*) papier peint; **a sheet/a piece of p.** une feuille/un morceau de papier; **a pile of p.** une pile de papier; **to put sth down on p.** mettre qch par écrit; **on p. it is an army of 300,000** sur le papier *ou* en théorie, c'est une armée de 300 000 hommes; **it's a good plan on p.** ce projet est excellent en théorie; **the p. industry** l'industrie *f* papetière, la papeterie; **p. aeroplane** *or* **dart** avion *m* en papier; **p. bag** sac *m* en papier; **p. cup** (*for drinking*) gobelet *m* en carton; (*for small cake*) caissette *f*; **p. folding machine** machine *f* à plier les documents; *Comptr* **p. format** format *m* de papier; **p. handkerchief** *or* **tissue** *or F* **hankie** mouchoir *m* en papier; **p. profits** profits *mpl* fictifs; **p. tape** bande *f* de papier; **p. tape reader** lecteur *m* de bandes de papier; **p. tiger** tigre *m* de papier; **p. towel** serviette *f* en papier
(b) (*document*) écrit *m*, document *m*; *Fin etc* papier *m* valeur; (*banknotes*) billets *mpl* de banque; **private** *or* **personal papers** papiers personnels; **(identity) papers** papiers (d'identité); *Fin* **long/short p.** papier à long/court terme; **p. securities** papiers valeurs, titres *mpl* fiduciaires
(c) *Sch* **(examination) p.** épreuve *f* écrite; (*questions*) questions *fpl* d'examen; (*answer*) copie *f*; **the Shakespeare/history p.** l'épreuve (écrite) sur Shakespeare/d'histoire
(d) (*scholarly study, report*) article *m*; **to read** *or* **give a p.** faire un exposé, *F* lire un papier
(e) (*newspaper*) journal *m*, -aux
(f) (*of printer*) **p. advance** avancement *m* du papier; **p. bin** bac *m* à papier; **p. blockage** bourrage *m* de papier; **p. feed** entraînement *m ou* alimentation *f* du papier; **p. feed device** dispositif *m* d'avancement du papier; **p. guide** guide-papier *m*; **p. handling** gestion *f* du papier; **p. input** entrée *f* de papier; **p. jam** bourrage de papier; **p. out indicator** indicateur *m* de fin du papier; **p. out light** voyant *m* de fin du papier; **p. out warning** avertissement *m* de fin du papier; **p. park function** fonction *f* de parcage de l'imprimante; **p. path** chemin *m* du papier; **p. release arm** levier *m* de dégagement du papier; **p. tray** bac *m* à feuilles
paper² *vt* (*room*) tapisser
▶ **paper over** *vtsep* **to p. sth over** (*with wallpaper*) masquer qch en le tapissant; *Fig* **to p. over the cracks** (*disguise faults*) masquer les défauts; (*disguise disagreements*) masquer les mésententes
paperback ['peɪpəbæk] **1** *n* livre *m* de poche; **available in p.** disponible en livre de poche; **p. sales** ventes *fpl* de livres de poche **2** *adj* **p. book/edition** livre *m*/édition *f* de poche
paperboard ['peɪpəbɔːd] *n* carton *m*
paperboy ['peɪpəbɔɪ] *n* (*deliverer*) livreur *m* de journaux; (*seller*) vendeur *m* de journaux
paper chase *n Sch, Sp* jeu *m* de piste; *Fig* **education has become an academic p.** l'éducation est devenue une véritable course aux diplômes
paperclip ['peɪpəklɪp] *n* trombone *m*
paper currency *n* papier-monnaie *m*, *pl* papiers-monnaie
papergirl ['peɪpəgɜːl] *n* (*deliverer*) livreuse *f* de journaux; (*seller*) vendeuse *f* de journaux
paperhanger ['peɪpəhæŋər] *n* **(a)** (*decorator*) peintre *m* décorateur **(b)** *US Sl* (*counterfeiter*) faux-monnayeur *m*, *pl* faux-monnayeurs
paperknife ['peɪpənaɪf] *n* coupe-papier *m inv*
paperless ['peɪpəlɪs] *adj* **the p. office** = le bureau dans lequel on n'utilize pas de papier, tout étant informatisé
paper mill *n* usine *f* à papier; (*on small scale*) fabrique *f* de papier
paper money *n* papier-monnaie *m*, *pl* papiers-monnaie, monnaie *f* de papier
paper round *n* tournée *f* de distribution des journaux; **to have** *or* **do a p.** distribuer les journaux
paper shop *n Br F* marchand *m* de journaux
paperweight ['peɪpəweɪt] *n* presse-papiers *m inv*
paperwork ['peɪpəwɜːk] *n* paperasseries *fpl*; (*official documents*) papiers *mpl*; **to do the p.** s'occuper du travail de bureau; **I'm drowning in p.** je suis dans la paperasserie jusqu'au cou
papery ['peɪpərɪ] *adj* qui ressemble à du papier; (*thin*) mince comme du papier; **p. skin** peau *f* parcheminée
papier-mâché [pæpjeɪ'mæʃeɪ] *n* carton-pâte *m*
papilloma [pæpɪ'ləʊmə] *n Med* papilloma *m*
papist ['peɪpɪst] *n, adj Pej* papiste *mf*
papistry ['peɪpɪstrɪ] *n Pej* papisme *m*
paprika [pə'priːkə] *n* paprika *m*
Papua ['pæpjʊə] *n* **(a)** *Hist* Papouasie *f* **(b) P. New Guinea** Papouasie-Nouvelle-Guinée *f*
Papuan ['pæpjʊən] **1** *adj* papou **2** *n* Papou, -oue
papyrus, *pl* **-ri** [pə'paɪrəs, -raɪ] *n* papyrus *m*
par [pɑːr] *n* **(a)** (*equality*) pair *m*, égalité *f*; **to be on a p. with sb/sth** être au niveau de qn/qch; **they're on a p.** ils sont au même niveau
(b) *Fin* **p. of exchange** pair *m* du change; **above/below p.** au-dessus/au-dessous du pair; **at p.** au pair; **close to p.** au voisinage de la parité; **p. value** nominal *m*, valeur *f* nominale
(c) (*average*) moyenne *f*; **above/below p.** au-dessus/au-dessous de la moyenne; *F* **to feel below p.**, **not to feel up to p.** ne pas être dans son assiette; **the film wasn't really up to p.** le film n'est pas aussi bon qu'on aurait pu s'y attendre
(d) *Golf* par *m*; **to be under/over p.** être en dessous/au-dessus du par; **a p.-three (hole)** un par trois; *Fig F* **that's about p. for the course** c'est ce à quoi il faut s'attendre; **his behaviour was about p. for the course** son comportement n'a rien eu de vraiment surprenant
para ['pærə] *n* **(a)** (*abbr* **paragraph**) par. **(b)** *Mil F* (*abbr* **paratrooper**) para *m*
parable ['pærəb(ə)l] *n* parabole *f*; **teaching in parables** enseignement en paraboles
parabola [pə'ræbələ] *n Math* parabole *f*
parabolic [pærə'bɒlɪk] *adj Math etc* (*curve, mirror*) parabolique; *TV* **p. dish** antenne *f* parabolique, parabole *f*
paracetamol [pærə'siːtəmɒl] *n* paracétamol *m*; **take two p.** *or* **paracetamols** prenez deux cachets de paracétamol
parachute¹ ['pærəʃuːt] *n* parachute *m*; **to drop sb/sth by p.** larguer qn/qch par parachute, parachuter qn/qch; **brake** *or* **tail p.** parachute de freinage (à l'atterrissage); **p. flare** fusée *f* (éclairante) à parachute; **p. harness** ceinture *f ou* harnais *m* de parachute; **p. jump/descent** saut *m*/descente *f* en parachute; **to make a p. jump** sauter en parachute; **p. pack** (*parachute*) parachute (plié et prêt à servir); (*container*) enveloppe *f ou* sac *m* de parachute
parachute² **1** *vi* sauter en parachute **2** *vt* (*person, supplies*) parachuter, larguer par parachute
▶ **parachute in 1** *vtsep* (*send*) (*troops, supplies etc*) parachuter, envoyer par parachute **2** *vi* être parachuté; **I'll p. in** je vais me faire parachuter, je vais descendre en parachute
parachuting ['pærəʃuːtɪŋ] *n* (*activity*) parachutisme *m*; (*of person, supplies*) parachutage *m*
parachutist ['pærəʃuːtɪst] *n* parachutiste *mf*
parade¹ [pə'reɪd] *n* **(a)** *Mil* (*exercise*) exercice *m*; **church p.** (*of battalion etc*) rassemblement *m* pour assister à l'office du

dimanche; **on p.** à l'exercice; **p. ground** terrain *m* d'exercices *ou* de manœuvres
(b) (*procession*) défilé *m*; *Rel* procession *f*; **fashion p.** défilé de mannequins; *Mil* **to go on p.** défiler
(c) (*display*) parade *f*; *Pej* **to make a p. of one's knowledge/feelings** étaler sa culture/ses sentiments; **a street where you'll see all the new fashions on p.** une rue où l'on arbore toutes les dernières créations de la mode; **all the world leaders were on p.** il y avait tout une panoplie de chefs d'états
(d) (*along beach*) boulevard *m*; **a p. of shops** une rangée de magasins
(e) *Fencing* parade *f*
parade[2] **1** *vt* (a) *Mil* (*troops*) faire parader, faire défiler; (*assemble*) (*battalion*) rassembler (b) (*riches*) faire parade *ou* étalage de; (*knowledge, feelings, opinions*) afficher, faire étalage de; **to p. one's dislike of sb** montrer clairement son antipathie à l'égard de qn **2** *vi* (a) *Mil* (*for exercise, inspection*) parader; **to p. through the streets** défiler dans les rues (b) *Fig* (*show off*) se pavaner; **young people parading up and down the beach with next to nothing on!** des jeunes gens qui se pavanent sur la plage avec presque rien sur le dos!
paradigm ['pærədaɪm] *n* paradigme *m*
paradigmatic [pærədɪg'mætɪk] paradigmatique
paradise ['pærədaɪs] *n Rel; Fig* paradis *m*; **an earthly p.** un paradis sur terre; **to go to p.** aller au paradis; **bird of p.** paradisier *m*, oiseau *m* de paradis
paradisiac [pærə'dɪzɪæk,], **paradisiacal** [pærədɪ'zaɪək(ə)l] *adj* paradisiaque
paradox ['pærədɒks] *n* paradoxe *m*
paradoxical [pærə'dɒksɪk(ə)l] *adj* paradoxal
paradoxically [pærə'dɒksɪklɪ] *adv* paradoxalement
paraffin ['pærəfɪn] *n* paraffine *f*; **p. (oil)** (*fuel*) pétrole *m* (lampant), kérosène *m*; *Pharm* **liquid p.** huile *f* de paraffine; **to coat with p.** paraffiner; **p. lamp** lampe *f* à pétrole; **p. wax** paraffine solide
paragliding ['pærəglaɪdɪŋ] *n Sp* parapente *m*
paragon ['pærəgən] *n* (*of virtue, beauty*) modèle *m*
paragraph[1] ['pærəgrɑːf] *n* paragraphe *m*, alinéa *m*; *Journ* (*short article*) entrefilet *m*; **new p.** (*when dictating*) à la ligne; **to start a new p.** aller à la ligne; **p. indent** alinéa *m*; *Typ* **p. (mark)** pied *m* de mouche
paragraph[2] *vt* (*piece of writing*) diviser en paragraphes
Paraguay ['pærəgwaɪ] *n* Paraguay *m*
Paraguayan [pærə'gwaɪən] **1** *adj* paraguayen **2** *n* Paraguayen, -enne
parakeet ['pærəkiːt] *n* (*bird*) perruche *f*
parallel[1] ['pærəlel] **1** *adj* (a) *Math etc* parallèle (**to** *or* **with sth** à qch); **to be** *or* **run p. to sth** être parallèle à qch; *Gym* **p. bars** barres *fpl* parallèles; *El* **p. circuits** circuits *mpl* parallèles; *El* **p. connection** couplage *m ou* montage *m* en parallèle *ou* en dérivation; *Comptr* **p. input/output** entrée/sortie *f* parallèle; *Comptr* **p. interface** interface *f* parallèle; *Math etc* **p. lines** lignes *fpl* parallèles; *Aut* **p. parking** stationnement *m* en créneau; *Comptr* **p. port** port *m* parallèle; *Comptr* **p. printer** imprimante *f* (en) parallèle; **p. printer cable** câble *m* d'imprimante parallèle; **p. printer port** port *m* d'imprimante parallèle; *Comptr* **p. processing** traitement *m* en simultanéité; **p. rule(r)** règle *f* à (tracer des) parallèles, parallèle *m*; *Mktg* **p. selling** vente *f* parallèle; *Ski* **p. turn** virage *m* en parallèle
(b) (*analogous*) pareil, semblable; (*case, situation*) analogue (**to** *or* **with sth** à qch); **the two cases are exactly p.** les deux cas sont analogues
2 *n* (a) *Math* (ligne *f*) parallèle *f*; *Geog, Astron* parallèle *m*; *Mil* (*trench*) (tranchée *f*) parallèle *f*; *Typ* **parallels** barres *fpl*
(b) *El* **in parallel** (*connected*) en parallèle, en dérivation; **out of p.** (*of dynamo*) déphasé, hors de phase, hors de synchronisme; *Comptr* **p.-to-serial converter** convertisseur *m* parallèle-série
(c) (*analogy*) parallèle *m*, comparaison *f*; **to draw a p. between two things** établir un parallèle *ou* une comparaison entre deux choses; **without p.** sans pareil
parallel[2] *vt* (**-l-**) (a) (*be similar to*) être analogue à (b) (*be equal to*) égaler; **the victory has not been paralleled** cette victoire est restée sans égal
parallelism ['pærəlelɪz(ə)m] *n* parallélisme *m*
parallelogram [pærə'leləgræm] *n* parallélogramme *m*
paralyse, *US* **paralyze** ['pærəlaɪz] *vt Med, Fig* paralyser; **paralysed in one leg** paralysé d'une jambe; *Fig* **laws that p. industry** lois qui paralysent l'industrie; **paralysed with fear** paralysé par l'effroi, glacé d'effroi
paralysing, *US* **paralyzing** ['pærəlaɪzɪŋ] *adj Med, Fig* (*poison, fear etc*) paralysant
paralysis [pə'ræləsɪs] *n Med, Fig* paralysie *f*
paralytic [pærə'lɪtɪk] **1** *adj* (a) *Med* paralytique; **p. stroke** attaque *f* de paralysie (b) *Br F* (*very drunk*) **he's p.** il est ivre mort **2** *n Med* paralytique *mf*
paralytically [pærə'lɪtɪklɪ] *adv Br F* **p. drunk** ivre mort
paralyze, paralyzing *US* = **paralyse, paralysing**
paramedic [pærə'medɪk] **1** *n* auxiliaire *mf* médical(e) **2** *adj* (*skills, qualification*) paramédical
parameter [pə'ræmɪtər] *n Math Comptr etc* paramètre *m*; **to set the parameters of** paramétrer; *Fig* **within the parameters of the enquiry** dans les limites fixées par les paramètres de l'enquête
paramilitary [pærə'mɪlɪtrɪ] **1** *adj* paramilitaire **2** *n* membre *m* d'une formation paramilitaire
paramount ['pærəmaʊnt] *adj* (*chief, leader*) suprême; (*necessity, consideration, interest*) primordial; **it is of p. importance** c'est d'une importance primordiale; **it is p. that we do this** il est primordial que nous fassions ceci
paramour ['pærəmʊər] *n Old-fashioned, Lit* amant *m*, amante *f*
paranoia [pærə'nɔɪə] *n* paranoïa *f*; *Fig F* **you're suffering from p.** tu es parano
paranoiac [pærə'nɔɪɪk] *adj, n* paranoïaque *mf*; **he's an absolute p.** il est complètement paranoïaque
paranoid ['pærənɔɪd] *adj* paranoïaque; (*delirium, madness*) paranoïde; *Fig* **he's p. about being cheated** il est obsédé par l'idée qu'on cherche à l'avoir; **you're being p.** tu es parano; **I know it'll sound p., but ...** je suis sûr que tu vas me trouver parano mais ...
paranormal [pærə'nɔːməl] **1** *adj* (*experience, phenomenon etc*) paranormal **2** *n* **the p.** le paranormal
parapet ['pærəpet] *n* (a) *Mil* (*in fortress*) parapet *m*; (*of trench*) berge *f* (b) (*wall*) parapet *m*; (*railing*) garde-fou *m*, *pl* garde-fous; (*of bridge*) garde-corps *m inv*
paraphernalia [pærəfə'neɪlɪə] *npl* (*things*) affaires *fpl*; (*equipment*) attirail *m*; **and all the other p.** et tout le bazar
paraphrase[1] ['pærəfreɪz] *n* paraphrase *f*
paraphrase[2] *vt* paraphraser
paraplegia [pærə'pliːdʒə] *n Med* paraplégie *f*
paraplegic [pærə'pliːdʒɪk] *adj, n Med* paraplégique *mf*
parapsychology [pærəsaɪ'kɒlədʒɪ] *n* parapsychologie *f*, métapsychique *f*
parasite ['pærəsaɪt] *n* (*animal, plant*), *Fig* parasite *m*; **to be a p. on society** (*of person*) parasiter la société
parasitic [pærə'sɪtɪk] *adj* (*insect, plant, person*) parasite (**on** de); (*existence*) de parasite; **to be p. on an organism/on society** parasiter un organisme/la société; *Electron etc* **p. noise** (bruit *m*) parasite *m*
parasitism ['pærəsaɪtɪz(ə)m] *n* parasitisme *m*
parasitize ['pærəsɪtaɪz] *vt* parasiter
parasitology [pærəsaɪ'tɒlədʒɪ] *n* parasitologie *f*
parasol ['pærəsɒl] *n* (*over table etc*) parasol *m*; (*ladies'*) ombrelle *f*; **p. pine** pin *m* parasol; **p. mushroom** coulemelle *f*
paratrooper ['pærətruːpər] *n Mil* parachutiste *m*
paratroops ['pærətruːps] *npl Mil* parachutistes *mpl*
paratyphoid [pærə'taɪfɔɪd] *n* paratyphoïde *f*
parboil ['pɑːbɔɪl] *vt Culin* faire cuire à demi (dans l'eau)
parcel[1] ['pɑːs(ə)l] *n* (a) (*bundle, packet*) paquet *m*, colis *m*; **parcel(s) office** bureau *m* des messageries, messageries *fpl*; **parcels service** (*courier*) messagerie *f*; **p. post** colis postal; *Aut* **p. shelf** tablette *f* (b) (*of land*) parcelle *f* (c) *St Exch* (*of bonds*) paquet *m*; *Com* (*batch*) lot *m*
parcel[2] *vt* (**-ll-**, *US* **-l-**) emballer, empaqueter
▶ **parcel out** *vtsep* (*distribute*) (*inheritance*) parceller, partager; (*land*) lotir, morceler; (*provisions, books*) répartir
▶ **parcel up** *vtsep* (*wrap*) empaqueter, emballer
parch [pɑːtʃ] *vt* (*of sun*) (*grass, earth etc*) dessécher; (*cereal crops*) rôtir, griller, sécher
parched [pɑːtʃt] *adj* (*earth, grass etc*) desséché; (*lips, throat etc*) sec; *F* **to be** *or* **feel p.** (*be thirsty*) mourir de soif
parchment ['pɑːtʃmənt] *n* parchemin *m*; **p. paper** papier *m* parchemin *ou* parcheminé
pardon[1] ['pɑːd(ə)n] *n* (a) **(I beg your) p.?** (*asking sb to repeat sth*) pardon?, comment?; **I beg your p.!** (*in disapproval, shock etc*) je vous demande pardon!, *F* pardon?, hein? (b) *Jur* grâce *f*; (*document*) lettre *f* de grâce; **free p.** grâce; **to grant sb a free p.** (*of monarch*) faire grâce à qn; **to receive the King's/Queen's p.** être gracié; **general p.** amnistie *f*
pardon[2] *vt* (a) (*fault etc*) pardonner, excuser; **p. my contradicting you, p. me for contradicting you** pardonnez(-moi) si je vous contredis (b) **to p. sb** pardonner à qn; **to p. sb for sth** pardonner qch à qn; **you could be pardoned for thinking so** il est facile de croire cela; **p. me!** (*in apology*) je vous demande pardon!; *Am* **p. me?** (*asking sb to repeat sth*) pardon?; *Iron* **p. me for speaking!** hou là là,

excuse-moi d'avoir osé m'exprimer!; **p. me for breathing!** hou là là, excuse-moi d'exister! **(c)** *Jur* gracier, amnistier; *Rel* **to p. sb sth** absoudre qn de qch

pardonable ['pɑːdənəb(ə)l] *adj* **(a)** pardonnable, excusable **(b)** *Jur* graciable

pardonably ['pɑːdənəblɪ] *adv* de façon bien pardonnable *ou* excusable; **he was p. late** il est bien pardonnable *ou* excusable qu'il soit arrivé en retard

pare [peər] *vt* (*vegetable etc*) éplucher; (*finger nails*) rogner; (*horseshoe*) parer; **expenses have been pared to the bone** les frais généraux ont été réduits *ou* ramenés au strict minimum

▶ **pare down** *vtsep* (*expenditure etc*) réduire; **the budget has been pared down to the bone** le budget a été réduit *ou* ramené au strict minimum

parent ['peərənt] **1** *n* père *m*, mère *f*, *pl* parents *mpl*; **when you first become a p.** quand on devient père/mère; **the p.-child relationship** la relation parents-enfant; **each p. should …** le père et la mère devraient …; **if neither p. can …** si ni le père ni la mère ne peuvent …; *Sch* **p. power** pouvoir *m* de décision des parents d'élèves; *Sch* **p.-teacher association** association *f* de parents d'élèves **2** *adj* **the p. plant** la plante mère; **the p. tree** l'arbre d'origine; **the p. birds feed their young** les parents nourrissent leurs oisillons

parentage ['peərəntɪdʒ] *n* origine *f*; **of unknown p.** de parents inconnus

parental [pə'rent(ə)l] *adj* (*authority etc*) des parents, parental

parent company *n Com* société *f ou* maison *f* mère

parenthesis, *pl* **-theses** [pə'renθəsɪs, -iːz] *n* parenthèse *f*; **in parentheses** entre parenthèses

parenthesize [pə'renθəsaɪz] *vt* (*words*) mettre entre parenthèses

parenthetical [pærən'θetɪk(ə)l] *adj* entre parenthèses; *Gram* **p. clause** incidente *f*

parenthetically [pærən'θetɪklɪ] *adv* entre parenthèses, par parenthèse; **could I just say p. …** je voudrais dire entre parenthèses que …

parenthood ['peərənthʊd] *n* (*fatherhood*) paternité *f*; (*motherhood*) maternité *f*

parenting ['peərəntɪŋ] *n* (*art*) art *m* d'être parent; (*activity*) métier *m* de parent; **to benefit from good p.** bénéficier d'une bonne éducation parentale; **p. skills** capacités *fpl* à élever des enfants

pariah [pə'raɪə] *n* paria *m*; **p. dog** chien *m* paria, chien métis des Indes

paring ['peərɪŋ] *n* **(a)** *Culin* **p. knife** couteau *m* à légumes **(b)** (*usu pl*) **parings** (*of vegetables etc*) épluchures *fpl*; (*of nails*) rognures *fpl*; (*of metal*) cisaille *f*

pari passu [pærɪ'pæsʊ] *adv Lit* **to go p. with …** marcher de pair avec …

Paris ['pærɪs] *n* Paris *m*; **the P. basin** le bassin parisien

parish ['pærɪʃ] *n Rel* paroisse *f*; **p. boundary** limites *fpl* de la paroisse; **p. church** église *f* paroissiale; *Br Admin* **(civil) p.** commune *f*; **p. council** = conseil *m* municipal (*d'une petite commune*); **p. hall** salle *f* paroissiale; **p. priest** prêtre *m* de la paroisse; **p.-pump issue** histoire *f* de clocher; **p.-pump politics** politique *f* d'intérêts de clocher; **p. register** registre *m* paroissial; **p. school** école *f* communale

parishioner [pə'rɪʃənər] *n* paroissien, -ienne

Parisian [pə'rɪzɪən] **1** *adj* parisien **2** *n* Parisien, -ienne

parity ['pærɪtɪ] *n* **(a)** (*equality*) (*of status, rank etc*) égalité *f*; (*of pay*) égalité, parité *f*; **to achieve p. of productivity with Japan** atteindre le niveau de productivité du Japon; **ambulance staff want p. with firemen** les ambulanciers veulent obtenir l'égalité de statut avec les pompiers

(b) *Fin* parité *f*; **franc-dollar p.** parité franc-dollar; **p. of exchange** parité de change; **p. value** valeur *f* au pair

(c) *Comptr* parité *f*; **odd p./even p./no p.** parité impaire/parité paire/pas de parité; **p. bit** bit *m* de parité; **p. error** erreur *f* de parité

(d) p. of reasoning raisonnement *m* analogue

park[1] [pɑːk] *n* **(a)** parc *m*; (*in hunting*) réserve *f*; **(public) p.** jardin *m* public, parc; **deer p.** parc (clôturé) réservé aux cerfs; **national p.** parc national; *Ind, Com* **business/industrial p.** zone *f* commerciale/industrielle; *Br* **car p.** parc de stationnement, parking *m* **(b)** *Aut* (*gear*) stationnement *m*

park[2] **1** *vt* **(a)** (*car*) garer, parquer; **to be double parked** (*of car, driver*) être garé en double file; *F* **to p. oneself** (*in a chair etc*) s'installer **(b)** (*sheep*) parquer **(c)** *Mil* (*artillery etc*) mettre en parc **(d)** *Comptr* (*hard disk*) parquer; **to be parked** être en parquage **2** *vi* (*of car, driver, aircraft etc*) stationner, se garer

parka ['pɑːkə] *n* (*coat*) parka *m ou f*

park-and-ride *n* = système *m* consistant à garer sa voiture près d'une gare et à continuer son trajet en train/en métro/*etc*

parked [pɑːkt] *adj* (*car, plane etc*) en stationnement, garé

parker ['pɑːkər] *n* **she's a good p.** elle sait très bien faire les créneaux

parking ['pɑːkɪŋ] *n* (*of cars, planes etc*) stationnement *m*; **p. is a problem in town** il est difficile de se garer *ou* de stationner en ville; **no p.** défense de stationner; **p. prohibited** stationnement interdit; **double p.** stationnement en double file; *Am Aut* **p. brake** frein *m* à main, frein de stationnement; **p. fees** tarif *m* de stationnement; **p. fine** amende *f* de stationnement; *Aut* **p. lights** feux *mpl* de position; **p. lock** (*on automatic gearbox*) position *f* parking; *Astronaut* **p. orbit** orbite *f* d'attente; **to get a p. ticket** avoir une contravention pour stationnement illégal

parking area *n* aire *f* de stationnement, parking *m*

parking attendant *n* gardien, -ienne de parking

parking bay *n* place *f* de stationnement

parking lot *n Am* parking *m*, parc *m* de stationnement

parking meter *n* parcmètre *m*, *Can* compteur *m* de stationnement

parking place *n* (*for one vehicle*) (*in street, car park*) place *f* de parking

parking space *n* (*for one vehicle*) (*in street, car park*) place *f* de parking; **there's more p. (space) behind the restaurant** il y a encore des places de parking derrière le restaurant

Parkinson ['pɑːkɪnsən] *n* **(a)** *Med* **P.'s disease** maladie *f* de Parkinson; **to have P.'s disease** avoir la maladie de Parkinson *ou* un parkinson **(b)** *Hum* **P.'s law** = plus on a de temps pour accomplir une tâche plus on prend de temps pour l'accomplir

park keeper *n* gardien, -ienne de parc

parkland ['pɑːklænd] *n* espace *m* vert

park officer *n* gardien, -ienne de parc

parkway ['pɑːkweɪ] *n Am Aut* = grande voie *f* de communication

parky ['pɑːkɪ] *adj Br F* (*weather*) frisquet

parlance ['pɑːləns] *n* langage *m*, parler *m*; **in common p.** dans la langue de tous les jours, en langage courant; **in legal/civil service/football p.** en termes juridiques *ou* de pratique/administratifs/de football; **in the p. of the EC** dans le langage de la CE, selon les termes de la CE

parley[1] ['pɑːlɪ] *n* conférence *f*; *Mil* (*with enemy*) pourparlers *mpl*; **to hold a p.** parlementer **(with** avec)

parley[2] *vi* être en pourparlers, parlementer **(with the enemy** avec l'ennemi); (*begin discussions*) entrer en pourparlers, parlementer

parliament ['pɑːləmənt] *n* [①A11,g,i] parlement *m*; **P.** le Parlement; **in P.** au Parlement

parliamentarian [pɑːləmen'teərɪən] *n* (*member of parliament*) parlementaire *mf*, membre *m* du Parlement; (*expert in parliamentary procedures*) expert *m* en procédures parlementaires

parliamentary [pɑːlə'ment(ə)rɪ] *adj* (*government, rule*) parlementaire; **p. candidate** *Br* candidat, -ate à la Chambre des communes; (*in France*) candidat, -ate à la députation; **p. election** élection *f* législative; **p. privilege** immunité *f* parlementaire; *Br* **p. private secretary** = député *m* détaché auprès d'un ministre pour l'aider dans ses devoirs parlementaires; **p. reporter** journaliste *mf* parlementaire; *Br* **p. secretary** ≈ ministre *m* d'État

parlour, *US* **parlor** ['pɑːlər] *n Old-fashioned, Am* (*living room*) salon *m*; (*of convent*) parloir *m*; **beauty p.** salon de beauté; *Am* **beer p.** bar *m* (où l'on sert de la bière); *Am* **funeral p.** entreprise *f* de pompes funèbres; *Am* **ice-cream p.** salon de dégustation de glaces; **to go to the ice-cream p.** aller chez le glacier; **p. games** petits jeux *mpl* de salon *ou* de société

parlourmaid ['pɑːləmeɪd] *n* bonne *f* (*affectée au service de table*)

parlous ['pɑːləs] *adj Lit, Hum* (*state*) précaire; (*situation*) périlleux

Parma ['pɑːmə] *n* Parme *m*; **P. ham** jambon *m* de Parme

Parmesan [pɑːmɪ'zæn] *n* **P. (cheese)** parmesan *m*

Parnassus [pɑː'næsəs] *n* Parnasse *m*

parochial [pə'rəʊkɪəl] *adj Rel* paroissial; *Fig Pej* provincial; **p. outlook** esprit *m* de clocher; *Am* **p. school** école *f* religieuse

parochialism [pə'rəʊkɪəlɪz(ə)m] *n Pej* esprit *m* de clocher; (*of approach, attitude*) provincialisme *m*

parodist ['pærədɪst] *n* parodiste *mf*

parody[1] ['pærədɪ] *n* parodie *f*, pastiche *m*; (*of justice*) parodie; (*of truth*) travestissement *m*

parody[2] *vt* parodier, pasticher

parole[1] [pə'rəʊl] *n Jur* (*from jail*) libération *f* conditionnelle; **prisoner on p.** prisonnier, -ière (*de droit commun*) libéré(e) conditionnellement; *Mil* prisonnier *m* sur parole; **to be put on p.** être mis en liberté conditionnelle, être libéré conditionnellement; **to break one's p.** manquer à sa parole; **day p.** libération conditionnelle de jour; **p. supervisor** surveillant, -ante de liberté conditionnelle

parole² *vt Mil* libérer sur parole; *Jur* libérer conditionnellement, mettre en liberté conditionnelle; **paroled inmate** prisonnier, -ière libéré(e) conditionnellement, libéré, -ée conditionnel(le)
paroxysm ['pærəksɪz(ə)m] *n Med* (*of fever*) paroxysme *m*; (*of anger, guilt*) accès *m*; (*of jealousy, grief*) crise *f*; **to be in paroxysms of laughter** avoir le fou rire; **to send sb into paroxysms of laughter** donner le fou rire à qn; **to be in a p. of delight** être absolument ravi
parquet ['pɑːkeɪ] *n* **(a) p. (floor)** parquet *m*; **p. flooring** parquet **(b)** *US Th* premiers rangs *mpl* du parterre
parricide ['pærɪsaɪd] *n* **(a)** (*person*) parricide *mf* **(b)** (*crime*) parricide *m*
parrot¹ ['pærət] *n* (*bird, Fig person*) perroquet *m*; *F* **I was as sick as a p.** ça m'a rendu malade
parrot² *vt* répéter comme un perroquet
parrot-fashion *adv F* **to repeat sth p.** répéter qch comme un perroquet; **to learn sth p.** (*by repetition*) apprendre qch en le répétant; **he learnt it p.** (*by mimicking sounds*) il est capable de le répéter comme un perroquet
parrotfish ['pærətfɪʃ] *n* perroquet *m* de mer
parry¹ ['pærɪ] *n Fencing, Boxing* parade *f*
parry² **1** *vt Fencing, Boxing etc* (*blow*) parer; *Fig* (*question*) se dérober à, éluder **2** *vi Fencing* **to p. and thrust** parer et tirer
parse [pɑːz] *vt* **(a)** *Gram* (*word*) faire l'analyse (grammaticale) de; (*sentence*) faire l'analyse logique de **(b)** *Comptr* analyser
Parsee ['pɑːsiː, pɑː'siː] *adj, n* parsi, -ie
parse error *n Comptr* erreur *f* d'analyse (syntaxique)
parser ['pɑːzər] *n Comptr* analyseur *m* syntaxique
parsimonious [pɑːsɪ'məʊnɪəs] *adj* parcimonieux; **to be p. with one's money** dépenser son argent avec parcimonie
parsimoniously [pɑːsɪ'məʊnɪəslɪ] *adv* parcimonieusement
parsimony ['pɑːsɪmənɪ] *n esp Fml* parcimonie *f*; **this is not a time for p.** ce n'est guère l'occasion de se montrer parcimonieux
parsing ['pɑːzɪŋ] *n* **(a)** *Gram* (*of word*) analyse *f* grammaticale; (*of sentence*) analyse logique **(b)** *Comptr* analyse *f* syntaxique
parsley ['pɑːslɪ] *n Bot, Culin* persil *m*; **p. sauce** sauce *f* au persil
parsnip ['pɑːsnɪp] *n Bot, Culin* panais *m*
parson ['pɑːs(ə)n] *n* (*clergyman*) ecclésiastique *m*; (*Protestant priest*) pasteur *m*; **the p.'s nose** (*of chicken etc*) le croupion
parsonage ['pɑːsənɪdʒ] *n Old-fashioned* ≈ presbytère *m*, cure *f*
part¹ [pɑːt] **1** *n* **(a)** (*portion, component*) partie *f*; *Ind etc* pièce *f*; **(a) p. of the house is to let** une partie de la maison est à louer; **good in parts** bon en partie; **it's not bad in parts** il y a des parties qui ne sont pas mal; **the funny/odd p. about it is that ...** ce qu'il y a de comique/d'étrange c'est que ...; **the best/worst p. was when he started laughing** le mieux/le pire ça a été quand il s'est mis à rire; **the hard p. is remembering** le plus dur c'est de se souvenir; **that was the easy p.** ça c'était le plus facile; **in the early p. of the week** au début *ou* dans les premiers jours de la semaine; **for the best** *or* **greater p. of five years** (*to wait, last etc*) presque cinq ans; **the greater p. of the population** la plus grande partie de la population; **(one) p. of her wanted to agree with them** une partie d'elle-même voulait être d'accord avec eux; **to be** *or* **form p. of sth** faire partie de qch; **it's become (a) p. of our daily routine** ça fait maintenant partie de notre routine quotidienne; **it's all p. of growing up** c'est ce qui se passe quand on grandit; **it is p. and parcel of ...** c'est une partie intégrante *ou* essentielle de ...; **to contribute in p. to the expenses** contribuer pour partie aux frais; **this is due in p. to inflation** c'est en partie dû à l'inflation; **for the most p.** pour la plupart; *Culin etc* **ten parts of water to one of milk** dix mesures d'eau pour une mesure de lait; [ⓘB20,1,b,iv] **the parts of the body** les parties du corps; *Gram* **parts of speech** parties du discours; **(spare) parts** pièces détachées *ou* de rechange; **parts and labour warranty** garantie *f* pièces et main-d'œuvre; **parts list** nomenclature *f*

(b) (*active role*) part *f*; *Th, Cin etc* rôle *m*; **to play a p.** *Th* avoir un rôle; *Fig* (*act, pretend*) jouer la comédie; *Th etc* **small p.** petit rôle; *Th* **she took** *or* **played the p. of Esmeralda** elle a joué le rôle d'Esmeralda; **to play a p. in sth** (*be involved in, contribute to*) jouer un rôle dans qch; **to have** *or* **play a large/small p. in sth** avoir *ou* jouer un rôle important/peu important dans qch; **she played a large p. in persuading the company to relocate** c'est surtout elle qui a persuadé l'entreprise de se relocaliser; **to take p. in sth** prendre part à qch, participer à qch; **to take p. in the conversation** prendre part à *ou* se mêler à la conversation; **she takes an active p. in decision-making** elle participe activement au processus de prise de décision; *TV etc* **those taking p. were ...** avec le concours de ...; **to take no p. in sth** ne pas prendre part à qch, ne pas participer à qch; **I had no p. in it** je n'y suis pour rien; **I want no p. of** *or* **in it** (*I don't want to be involved*) je ne veux rien avoir à faire là-dedans; **to dress/look the p.** mettre une tenue de circonstance/avoir la tête de l'emploi

(c) *Mus* (*for specific instrument or voice*) partie *f*; (*of song, fugue*) voix *f*; (*written score*) partition *f*; **a two-p. song** une mélodie à deux voix

(d) (*side*) parti *m*; **to take sb's p.** prendre parti pour qn, prendre fait et cause pour qn; **an indiscretion on the p. of ...** une indiscrétion de la part de ...; **for my p.** pour ma part; **to keep one's p. of the agreement** respecter sa part de l'accord

(e) (*region*) **in that p. of the world** dans cette partie du monde; **in those parts** dans cette région-là, *F* dans ce coin-là; **they are not from our p. of the world** ils ne sont pas de chez nous; **in these parts** par ici; **what are you doing in these parts?** qu'est-ce que vous faites ici *ou* dans ces parages?

(f) (*in publishing, of part work*) fascicule *m*, livraison *f*; **p. two** (*of book, TV programme*) deuxième partie *f*; *Rad, TV* **a serial in four parts** un feuilleton en quatre épisodes

(g) to take sth in good/bad p. prendre qch en bonne/mauvaise part, prendre qch du bon/mauvais côté

(h) *Fml* (*usu pl*) **parts** (*abilities*) moyens *mpl*, facultés *fpl*; **man of many parts** homme à facettes

(i) *Am* (*parting in hair*) raie *f*

2 *adv* partiellement, en partie; **I'm p. Spanish** je suis en partie espagnol; **p. silk, p. cotton** mi-soie mi-coton; **a mythical creature, p. woman, p. fish** une créature mythique mi-femme, mi-poisson; **p. one and p. the other** moitié l'un moitié l'autre; **will you take it in p. exchange?** voulez-vous le reprendre?; *Com* **p. consignment** expédition *f* partielle; *Com* **p. load** chargement *m* partiel; **p. owner** copropriétaire *mf*; *Com* **p. shipment** expédition partielle
part² **1** *vt* séparer (**sth from sth** qch de qch); (*rock etc*) séparer en deux; (*curtains*) entrouvrir; (*two people*) séparer; (*of bodyguard*) (*crowd*) ouvrir un passage dans; **to p. one's hair** se faire une raie (dans les cheveux); **to p. one's hair in the middle/at the side** se faire la raie au milieu/sur le côté; **his hair was parted on the left/in the middle** il avait la raie à gauche/au milieu; **they can't bear to be parted** ils ne supportent pas d'être séparés; **to p. company** (*of associates, friends*) se séparer; (*become detached*) (*of one object from another*) se détacher (**from** de); *Hum* **to p. company with one's horse/bike** (*fall off*) tomber de son cheval/vélo; **this is where we p. company** (*I'm going in the opposite direction*) c'est ici que nous nous quittons; (*where I begin to disagree with you*) c'est là que nos points de vue divergent, c'est là que je ne suis plus d'accord

2 *vi* (*of crowd etc*) se diviser; (*of two people*) se quitter, se séparer; (*of roads*) diverger; (*of cable etc*) rompre, céder; **her lips parted in a smile** ses lèvres s'entrouvrirent dans un sourire; **the curtains parted** les rideaux s'entrouvrirent; **to p. good friends** se quitter bons amis; **let us part (as) friends** séparons-nous (en) bons amis; **to p. from sb** quitter qn; (*separate*) se séparer de *ou* d'avec qn; **to p. with sth** (*get rid of*) se débarrasser *ou* se défaire de qch; (*give up*) céder qch; *Jur* (*right, possession*) aliéner qch; **he hates to p. with (his) money** il n'aime pas débourser
partake [pɑː'teɪk] *vi* (*pt* **partook** [pɑː'tʊk]; *pp* **partaken** [pɑː'teɪkən]) *Fml* **to p. in sth** participer à qch (**with sb** avec qn); **to p. of the nature of sth** relever de qch; **it partakes of a certain grandeur** c'est empreint d'une certaine grandeur; *Old-fashioned* **to p. of a meal** prendre un repas; *Old-fashioned, Hum* **do you p.?** (*would you like a drink?*) vous prendrez bien un petit verre?; **I no longer p.** (*don't drink*) je ne bois plus; *Rel* **to p. of the Sacrament** s'approcher des sacrements
parthenogenesis [pɑːθənəʊ'dʒenɪsɪs] *n Biol* parthénogénèse *f*
Parthian ['pɑːθɪən] *adj* **P. shot** flèche *f* du Parthe
partial ['pɑːʃəl] *adj* **(a)** (*biassed*) partial (**towards sb** envers qn); (*unjust*) injuste **(b)** *F* **to be p. to sb/sth** (*like*) avoir un faible *ou* une prédilection pour qn/qch, avoir un penchant pour qn/qch; **I am rather p. to a spot of whisky after dinner** je bois volontiers un petit verre de whisky après dîner **(c)** (*in part*) partiel; **p. disability** incapacité partielle; **p. eclipse** éclipse partielle
partiality [pɑːʃɪ'ælɪtɪ] *n* **(a)** (*bias*) partialité *f* (**towards** envers, en faveur de); (*favouritism*) favoritisme *m* **(b)** (*liking*) prédilection *f*, penchant *m*, faible *m* (**for** pour)
partially ['pɑːʃəlɪ] *adv* **(a)** (*with bias*) avec partialité **(b)** (*partly, in part*) partiellement, en partie; **p. sighted** malvoyant; **the p. sighted** (*npl*) les malvoyants *mpl*
participant [pɑː'tɪsɪpənt] *adj, n* participant, -ante (**in** à)

participate [pɑːˈtɪsɪpeɪt] *vi* (*of person*) prendre part, participer (**in sth** à qch); *Lit* **to p. in sb's joy** s'associer à la joie de qn
participating [pɑːˈtɪsɪpeɪtɪŋ] *adj* participant
participation [pɑːtɪsɪˈpeɪʃən] *n* participation *f* (**in sth** à qch); **thank you for your p.** merci d'avoir participé
participial [pɑːtɪˈsɪpɪəl] *adj Gram* participial
participle [ˈpɑːtɪsɪp(ə)l] *n* [①**A44-45; B35-36,**I] *Gram* participe *m*; **present/past p.** participe présent/passé
particle [ˈpɑːtɪk(ə)l] *n* (**a**) (*of matter*) particule *f*; (*of metal*) paillette *f*; (*of sand*) grain *m*; *Nucl Phys* particule, corpuscule *m*; **p. physics** physique *f* des particules; *Nucl Phys* **p. accelerator** accélérateur *m* de particules; *Constr* **p. board** panneau *m* d'aggloméré; **there's not a p. of truth in the story** il n'y a pas une ombre de vérité dans ce récit (**b**) *Gram* particule *f*
parti-coloured, *US* **-colored** [ˈpɑːtɪkʌled] *adj esp Lit* bigarré, bariolé
particular [pəˈtɪkjʊlər] **1** *adj* (**a**) (*specific*) particulier; **that p. book** ce livre-là, ce livre en particulier; **is there any p. time you'd like to come?** y a-t-il une heure qui vous convienne en particulier?; **they didn't have this p. brand** ils n'avaient pas cette marque-là; **which p. thing/person did you have in mind?** à quoi/qui pensiez-vous en particulier?; **this one is a p. favourite of mine** j'affectionne tout particulièrement celui-ci; **he is a p. friend of mine** c'est l'un de mes meilleurs amis; **why did you insist on this p. one?** pourquoi as-tu insisté sur celui-là en particulier?; **in my p. field (of study/research)** dans ma spécialité; **my own p. feelings** mes sentiments personnels; **to take p. care over doing sth** faire qch avec un soin (tout) particulier; **to take p. care to do sth** mettre un soin (tout) particulier à faire qch; **to do sth for no p. reason** faire qch sans raison précise; **I didn't notice anything (in) p.** je n'ai rien remarqué de particulier; **in p.** en particulier

(**b**) *Old-fashioned, Fml* (*detailed*) (*account etc*) détaillé, circonstancié

(**c**) (*person*) (*exacting*) méticuleux, minutieux, soigneux; (*about rules etc*) pointilleux; (*about choice of friends, methods used etc*) difficile, exigeant; **I have to be quite p. about what I eat** je dois faire très attention à ce que je mange; **it had to be pure silk, he was most p. about it** il fallait que ce soit de la soie pure, il a insisté; **to be p. about one's food** (*demanding*) être exigeant pour la nourriture; (*difficult*) être difficile pour la nourriture; **to be p. about one's dress** soigner sa mise *ou* sa tenue; *F* **I'm not p. (about it)** (*I don't care*) je n'y tiens pas plus que ça; **he's not p. about where the goods come from** l'origine des marchandises lui importe peu

2 *n* détail *m*; **alike in every p.** semblables en tout point; **they differ in several particulars** ils diffèrent en plusieurs points; **to go into particulars** entrer dans les détails; **to give particulars of sth** donner les détails de qch; **to ask for fuller particulars about sth** demander des précisions *ou* des détails supplémentaires sur qch; **to take down sb's particulars** prendre les coordonnées de qn; **for further particulars apply to …** pour plus amples détails *ou* renseignements s'adresser à …
particularity [pətɪkjʊˈlærɪtɪ] *n* (**a**) (*special quality*) particularité *f* (**b**) (*exacting nature*) méticulosité *f*; (*detailed nature*) (*of description etc*) minutie *f*
particularize [pəˈtɪkjʊləraɪz] *Fml* **1** *vt* spécifier **2** *vi* entrer dans les détails, préciser
particularly [pəˈtɪkjʊləlɪ] *adv* particulièrement, en particulier; **it's cold here, p. at night** il fait froid ici, particulièrement *ou* spécialement la nuit; **note p. that …** notez en particulier que …; **be p. careful** faites particulièrement attention; **not p.** pas particulièrement *ou* spécialement; **she's not p. rich** elle n'est pas tellement riche
particulate emissions [pɑːˈtɪkjʊlɪt] *npl* émission *f* de particules
parting [ˈpɑːtɪŋ] *n* (**a**) (*division*) séparation *f*; (*of the waters*) partage *m*; *Fig* **to be at** *or* **to have come to the p. of the ways** être à la croisée des chemins (**b**) (*leave-taking*) séparation *f*; **it was a painful p.** la séparation a été douloureuse; **p. kiss** baiser *m* d'adieu; **p. shot** remarque *f* (faite en partant); **p. words** mots *mpl* d'adieu (**c**) *Br* (*in hair*) raie *f*; **centre/side p.** raie au milieu/sur le côté
partisan [pɑːtɪˈzæn] **1** *n* (*supporter, resistance fighter*) partisan -ane **2** *adj* (**a**) partisan; **to act in a p. spirit** (*of politician etc*) faire preuve d'esprit de parti; (*be prejudiced*) faire preuve de parti pris (**b**) *Mil* partisan
partisanship [pɑːtɪˈzænʃɪp] *n* partialité *f*; (*of politician etc*) esprit *m* de parti
partition¹ [pɑːˈtɪʃən] *n* (**a**) (*dividing*) division *f*, découpage *m*; (*of conquered country, inheritance etc*) (*division*) partition *f*; (*sharing out*) partage *m* (**b**) (*screen*) séparation *f*, cloisonnage *m*; (*wall*) cloison *f*; (*of ship's hold etc*) compartiment *m*; *Constr* **internal p.**, **p. wall** cloison (**c**) *Comptr* partition *f*
partition² *vt* (**a**) (*divide*) diviser; (*inheritance etc*) partager; (*conquered country*) démembrer, partager (**b**) = **partition off** (**c**) *Comptr* (*hard disk*) découper
▶ **partition off** *vtsep* (*room*) cloisonner; (*part of a room*) séparer par une cloison
partitive [ˈpɑːtɪtɪv] *adj, n* [①**B4-5,**C] *Gram* partitif *m*
partly [ˈpɑːtlɪ] *adv* partiellement, en partie; **wholly or p.** en tout ou en partie; **p. by force, p. by persuasion** moitié par la force, moitié par la persuasion; **a p. eaten sandwich** un sandwich à moitié mangé; **she was only p. convinced** elle n'était qu'à moitié convaincue
part music *n* musique *f* d'ensemble
partner¹ [ˈpɑːtnər] *n Com etc* associé, -ée (**with sb in sth** de qn dans qch); (*in tennis, driving etc*) partenaire *mf*; (*in dancing*) cavalier, -ière, partenaire; (*of cowboy, bank robber etc*) acolyte *m*; (*person one lives with*) compagnon *m*, compagne *f*; (*boyfriend, girlfriend*) ami *m*, amie *f*; **our European partners** nos partenaires européens; **partners should consider each other's moods** chacun au sein du couple doit prendre les humeurs de l'autre en considération; **they became partners** ils se sont associés; **to be sb's p. in a crime** être associé à qn dans un crime; *Cards* **to cut** *or* **draw for partners** = faire les rois
partner² *vt Com etc* (*be partner of*) être associé à *ou* avec; (*become partner of*) s'associer à *ou* avec; (*in games*) être le/la partenaire de; (*in dancing*) être le cavalier/la cavalière de
partnership [ˈpɑːtnəʃɪp] *n* (**a**) association *f* (**in sth with sb** avec qn dans qch); **p. in crime** association dans le crime; *Com etc* **to enter** *or* **go into p. with sb** s'associer avec qn; **to take sb into p.** prendre qn comme associé(e); **p. marketing** mercatique *f* de partenariat; **p. sponsoring** parrainage-partenariat *m* (**b**) *Com etc* (*company*) société *f* de personnes
partridge [ˈpɑːtrɪdʒ] *n* (*pl* **partridges, partridge**) perdrix *f*; *Culin* perdreau *m*
part singing *n* chant *m* à plusieurs voix
part song *n* mélodie *f* à plusieurs voix
part-time **1** *adj* (*job, work*) à temps partiel, à mi-temps; **on a p. basis** à temps partiel, à mi-temps; **p. worker/employee** ouvrier, -ière/employé, -ée qui travaille à temps partiel *ou* à mi-temps; **p. contract** contrat *m* à temps partiel **2** *adv* (*to work*) à temps partiel, à mi-temps
part-timer *n F* = **part-time worker/employee**
parturition [pɑːtjʊˈrɪʃən] *n Med* parturition *f*
partway [ˈpɑːtweɪ] *adv* **they were p. through the rehearsal** ils avaient commencé à répéter depuis déjà un moment; **I'm only p. through it** (*the book, the task*) je ne l'ai pas encore fini; **they had gone p. towards an agreement** ils s'acheminaient vers un accord; **we were p. there** (*in project etc*) nous en avions fait une bonne partie; **this will go p. towards covering the costs** cela couvrira une bonne partie des coûts
part work *n* (*in publishing*) ouvrage *m* à fascicules
party¹ [ˈpɑːtɪ] *n* (**a**) *Pol* parti *m*; **a p. member, a member of the p.** un membre du parti; **p. quarrels** querelles *fpl* partisanes; *TV, Rad* **p. political broadcast** émission *f* reservée à un parti politique; **that was a p. political broadcast on behalf of the Liberal Party** vous venez de voir/d'entendre une émission du parti libéral; **p. politics/spirit** politique *f*/esprit *m* de parti; **he's just making a p. political point** son argument ne relève que de la politique politicienne; **to follow** *or* **toe the p. line** obéir aux directives du parti

(**b**) (*gathering*) fête *f*; (*evening celebration*) soirée *f*; (*reception*) réception *f*; **dinner p.** dîner *m*; *F* **he's caught the p. spirit** il s'est abandonné aux joies de la fête; **p. dress** belle robe *f*; **p. games** = jeux *mpl* auxquels on joue dans les soirées/les fêtes; *F* **p. pooper** trouble-fête *mf inv*

(**c**) (*group*) (*of tourists etc*) groupe *m*, bande *f*; *Min Ind* (*of miners, workers etc*) brigade *f*, équipe *f*, groupe; *Mil etc* détachement *m*; **the official p.** le groupe des officiels, les officiels *mpl*; **will you join our p.?** voulez-vous être des nôtres?; **we're a small p.** nous sommes peu nombreux; **I was one of the p.** j'étais de la partie; **the wedding/funeral p.** les invités au mariage/le cortège funéraire; *Constr* **p. wall** mur *m* mitoyen

(**d**) (*participant, Jur to a suit, to a dispute*) partie *f*; **the parties to the case** les parties en cause; **to be p. to a suit** être en cause; *Com etc* **parties to a bill of exchange** intéressé(e)s à une lettre de change; **to be/become (a) p. to a crime** être/se rendre complice d'un crime; **I would never be (a) p. to such a thing** je ne me ferais jamais complice d'une chose pareille, je ne m'associerais jamais à une chose pareille

(**e**) *F* (*person*) individu *m*, type *m*

party² *vi F* faire la bringue, faire la fête; **let's p.!** faisons la bringue *ou* la fête!; **to p. the night away** faire la bringue *ou* la fête toute la nuit

partygoer ['pɑːtɪgəʊər] *n* habitué, -ée des soirées; (*on one occasion*) invité, -ée; **the streets were full of partygoers** les rues étaient pleines de gens se rendant à des soirées

party leader *n* chef *m* de parti

party line *n Tel* ligne *f* partagée

party machine *n* machine *f* du parti

party man *n* homme *m* de parti

party piece *n* = chanson *f*/poème *m*/*etc* que l'on récite à l'occasion d'une fête; *Iron* **that's his p.** c'est son numéro habituel

PASCAL [pæ'skæl] *n Comptr* PASCAL *m*

paschal ['pæsk(ə)l] *adj* pascal

pass¹ [pɑːs] *n* (*in mountains*) col *m*

pass² *n* **(a)** (*permit*) permis *m*, laissez-passer *m inv*; *Mil* permission *f*; **(free) p.** *Rail etc* titre *m ou* carte *f* de circulation; *Th etc* (*free ticket*) billet *m* gratuit *ou* de faveur

(b) (*in examination*) **to obtain** *or* **get a p.** être reçu; **p. mark** moyenne *f*; **to get a p. mark** avoir la moyenne

(c) (*movement*) (*of footballer, magician etc*) passe *f*; *Fencing* passe, passade *f*, botte *f*; **the aircraft made two low passes over the village** l'avion a effectué deux passages à basse altitude au-dessus du village; *F* **to make a p. at sb** draguer qn, faire des propositions à qn

(d) (*in data analysis*) examen *m* (**through** de); (*of read head*) passage *m*; **to make a p. over sth** passer sur qch

(e) *Old-fashioned F* (*situation*) **things have come to a pretty p.!** voilà donc où en sont les choses!; **things came to such a p. that ...** les choses en vinrent à ce point *ou* à tel point que ...

pass³ 1 *vi* **(a)** (*go past*) passer; *Aut* (*overtake*) doubler, dépasser; *Cards* passer, renoncer, passer parole; (*at dominoes*) bouder; **we p. on the stairs every morning** nous nous croisons tous les matins dans l'escalier; **the tourists passed into the dining hall** les touristes sont passés dans le réfectoire; **words passed between them** ils ont eu une altercation; **to p. along a street** passer par une rue; **the procession passed slowly** le cortège passa *ou* défila lentement; **everyone smiles as he passes** tout le monde sourit à son passage; **the motorway passes close to the village** l'autoroute passe tout près du village; **to let sb p.** *or* **allow sb to p.** laisser passer qn; **they shall not p.!** ils ne passeront pas!; *Rail etc* **p. along** *or* **down the car!** avancez!, dégagez la portière!; **to p. unobserved** passer inaperçu; **I can't allow such a mistake to p. unremarked** je ne peux pas permettre qu'une telle erreur ne soit pas relevée; **let it p.!** passe pour cela!, *F* laisse courir!; **I'd like to say in passing** soit dit en passant; *Aut* **no passing** défense de doubler; *Cards, Fig* **p.!** je passe!; *Fig* **I think I'll p. on the onions** je le voudrais sans les oignons; **can I p. on the mountain climbing this afternoon?** est-ce que je peux être dispensé d'escalade cet après-midi?

(b) (*of time*) (se) passer, s'écouler; **when five minutes had passed** au bout de cinq minutes; **it seemed like no time at all had passed since I had last seen her** on aurait dit que pas une minute ne s'était écoulée depuis la dernière fois que je l'avais vue; **how time passes!** comme le temps passe (vite)!; **to let the opportunity p.** laisser passer l'occasion

(c) (*be transferred*) **water passes from a liquid to a solid state when it freezes** l'eau passe de l'état de liquide à celui de solide quand il gèle; **the expression has passed into the language** l'expression est passée dans la langue; **his fortune passed to his brother** sa fortune est revenue à son frère

(d) (*go away*) passer; (*of clouds etc*) s'en aller; **I was about to say something witty, but the moment passed** j'allais dire quelque chose de spirituel, mais j'ai laissé passer l'occasion

(e) *Old-fashioned* (*take place*) avoir lieu, se passer; **I don't know what passed between them** je ne sais pas ce qui s'est passé entre eux; *Arch, Lit* **to come to p.** arriver, avoir lieu; *Arch, Lit* **it came to p. that ...** or il arriva *ou* advint que ...

(f) (*be accepted*) **it would p. in certain circles** cela passerait dans certains milieux; *F* **you'd p. in a crowd!** tu n'es pas si mal que ça!; **she could p. for an Italian** elle pourrait passer pour une Italienne

(g) (*succeed in examination*) être reçu

2 *vt* **(a)** (*go past*) (*window, building etc*) passer devant; (*person*) croiser; (*destination*) dépasser; (*frontier*) passer, franchir; *Naut* (*headland*) dépasser, doubler; (*overtake*) (*person, another ship*) dépasser, rattraper; (*another car, runner*) doubler, dépasser; (*in league table*) passer devant; **not a word about it had passed her lips** elle n'en avait pas dit un mot; *Lit* **to p. understanding** dépasser l'entendement

(b) (*succeed in*) (*exam*) être reçu *ou* admis à; **to p. a test** (*of vehicle, product*) subir une épreuve avec succès; (*of person*) réussir une épreuve, subir une épreuve avec succès

(c) (*be accepted by*) **bill that has passed the House of Commons** projet de loi qui a été voté par la Chambre des Communes; **to p. the censor/the customs** être accepté par la censure/la douane

(d) (*approve*) (*invoice*) approuver, admettre, apurer; (*expenditure*) allouer; *Parl etc* (*bill, resolution*) passer, voter, adopter; **to p. a dividend of 5%** (*of company*) approuver un dividende de 5%; **the censor has passed the play/the film** le censeur a accordé le visa; **to p. for press** donner le bon à tirer; *Sch* **to p. a candidate** recevoir un candidat, admettre un candidat; *Mil etc* **to be passed fit** être reconnu apte

(e) (*give, transfer*) (faire) passer; (*counterfeit banknote etc*) (faire) passer, écouler, *F* refiler; **to p. sth from hand to hand** passer qch de main en main; **p. me the salt, please** passez-moi le sel, s'il vous plaît; *Fb etc* **to p. the ball** passer le ballon

(f) (*put*) passer; **to p. one's hand between the bars** passer *ou* glisser sa main à travers les barreaux; **to p. a rope round sth** passer une corde autour de qch; **to p. a sponge over sth** passer l'éponge sur qch; **to p. one's hand over one's brow** se passer la main sur le front

(g) *Mil* **to p. troops in review** passer des troupes en revue

(h) **to p. the time** (*of person*) passer le temps; **it passes the time** cela fait passer le temps

(i) (*utter*) **to p. criticism on sth** faire la critique de qch; **to p. remarks** faire des commentaires *ou* des observations (**on sth** sur qch); *Jur* **to p. sentence** prononcer le jugement; **to p. judgement on sb** porter un jugement sur qn, juger qn

(j) *Physiol* **to p. water** uriner; *Med* **to p. blood** avoir du sang dans les urines; **has he passed anything?** est-ce qu'il a uriné ou été à la selle?

▶ **pass away** *vi* **(a)** *Euph* (*die*) s'éteindre **(b)** (*disappear*) disparaître

▶ **pass by 1** *vi* **(a)** (*go past*) passer; (*carry on without stopping*) continuer son chemin; **luckily a taxi was passing by** heureusement un taxi passait par là **(b)** (*of time*) passer **2** *vipo* (*go past*) (*house etc*) passer devant **3** *vtas* (*ignore*) ignorer; **life is passing me by** je n'ai pas l'impression de vivre; **life has passed her by** elle n'a pas vraiment vécu; **whenever a chance comes, don't let it p. you by** quand une occasion se présente, ne la laissez pas échapper

▶ **pass down** *vtsep* **(a)** (*hand down*) passer; **p. me down that cup** passez-moi cette tasse **(b)** (*knowledge, story etc*) transmettre; (*clothing etc*) passer (**from ... to** de ... en)

▶ **pass off 1** *vi* **(a)** (*take place*) **everything passed off well** tout s'est bien passé **(b)** (*end*) (*of pain*) passer, disparaître; **is the nausea passing off?** est-ce que la nausée se passe? **2** *vtsep* **(a)** (*pretend to be*) **to p. oneself off as an artist** se faire passer pour (un) artiste; **she passed him off as a duke** elle l'a fait passer pour un duc; **to p. sth off as sth** faire passer qch pour qch **(b)** (*dismiss*) **to p. sth off as a joke** (*accept as a joke*) prendre qch en riant *ou* comme une plaisanterie; (*claim to be a joke*) dire qu'on a fait/dit qch pour rire

▶ **pass on 1** *vi* **(a)** *Euph* (*die*) décéder, s'éteindre

(b) (*proceed*) (*on journey*) continuer son chemin *ou* sa route; **to p. on to another subject** passer à un autre sujet; **passing on to the question of cost, ...** si nous passons maintenant à la question du coût, ...

2 *vtsep* (*tell or give to other people*) faire circuler; (*give to other people*) (faire) passer; **read this and p. it on** lisez ceci et faites circuler; **these price increases have been passed on to the consumer** ces hausses des coûts ont été répercutées sur le consommateur; **these cost reductions have been passed on to the consumer** le consommateur a bénéficié de ces réductions des coûts

▶ **pass out 1** *vi* **(a)** (*faint*) s'évanouir **(b)** (*leave*) sortir (**of** de); **don't let this document p. out of your hands** gardez soigneusement ce document **(c)** *Sch etc* (*after final examination*) sortir; **cadets passing out** élèves sortants; **passing-out list** classement *m* de sortie **2** *vtsep* (*distribute*) distribuer

▶ **pass over 1** *vtsep* **to p. sb over** (*for promotion*) passer par-dessus le dos à qn; **he's been passed over again** on lui a encore passé par-dessus le dos **2** *vtaspo* **to p. one's eye over sth** jeter un coup d'œil à qch **3** *vipo* **(a)** (*cross*) (*river etc*) traverser, franchir; (*obstacle*) franchir, passer sur **(b)** (*ignore*) passer sous silence; (*difficulty etc*) passer sur, glisser sur; **they passed over the subject in silence** ils ont passé la question sous silence **4** *vi* **(a)** (*end*) (*of storm*) se dissiper, finir **(b)** **to p. over to the enemy** passer à l'ennemi

▸ **pass round** *vtsep* faire passer; **p. the cakes round** faites passer les gâteaux; *Fig* **to p. round the hat** faire une quête

▸ **pass through 1** *vi* (*travel through*) passer; **I was just passing through** je ne faisais que passer; **the bullet passed right through** la balle a traversé; **the bus doesn't stop in Hull, it just passes through** le bus ne s'arrête pas à Hull, il ne fait que traverser la ville **2** *vipo* **(a)** (*travel through*) (*country etc*) traverser; **he was only passing through Paris** il n'était que de passage à Paris **(b)** (*experience*) (*crisis*) traverser

▸ **pass up** *vtsep* **(a)** *F* (*not take*) (*offer of a job etc*) refuser; (*chance*) laisser passer **(b)** (*hand up*) passer; **p. (me) up that hammer** passe-moi ce marteau

passable ['pɑːsəb(ə)l] *adj* **(a)** (*of acceptable quality*) passable, assez bon; **it's p.** ce n'est pas trop mal; **a very p. soufflé** un soufflé plutôt bien réussi **(b)** (*river, forest etc*) traversable, franchissable; (*road*) praticable

passably ['pɑːsəblɪ] *adv* passablement, assez; **to perform p.** offrir une performance passable

passage ['pæsɪdʒ] *n* **(a)** (*act of passing*) (*journey*) passage *m*; *esp Naut* traversée *f*; *Pol* (*of bill*) adoption *f*; **with the p. of time** avec le temps; **bird of p.** oiseau *m* de passage; *Naut* **to have a bad** *or* **rough p.** avoir *ou* faire une mauvaise traversée; *Naut* **to work one's p.** gagner son passage (en travaillant à bord); **to force a p.** se forcer un passage; *Jur* **right of p.** droit *m* de passage

(b) (*corridor*) couloir *m*, corridor *m*; (*alley, at end of street*) passage *m*, ruelle *f*; **underground p.** passage souterrain; *Geog* **the North-West/North-East p.** le passage Nord-Ouest/Nord-Est

(c) *MecE* canalisation *f*, conduit *m*, conduite *f*; **air p.** conduit d'aérage, conduit(e) d'air; *Anat* **air passages** voies *fpl* aérifères; *Anat* **the back p.** le rectum

(d) (*from book, piece of music etc*) passage *m*; **selected passages** morceaux *mpl* choisis

passageway ['pæsɪdʒweɪ] *n* **(a)** (*space*) passage *m*; **to leave a p.** laisser le passage libre **(b)** (*alley*) passage *m*, ruelle *f*; (*corridor*) couloir *m*, corridor *m*

pass book *n Banking* livret de dépôts *m*

passé ['pæseɪ] *adj* (*outdated*) qui n'est plus à la mode, dépassé

passel ['pæs(ə)l] *n US F* (*of people etc*) tas *m*

passenger ['pæsəndʒər] *n* **(a)** (*on train*) voyageur, -euse; (*on ship, aircraft, in car*) passager, -ère; **p. and cargo plane** avion *m* mixte; **p. and cargo ship** bateau *m* mixte; *Rail* **p. carriage** *or* **car** voiture *f ou* wagon *m* de voyageurs; **p. compartment** (*of car*) habitacle *m*; **p. kilometre** kilomètre-passager *m*; **p. load factor** (*in transport*) taux *m* d'occupation des places; *Aut* **p. safety cage** habitacle de sécurité; *Aut* **p. survival cell** cellule *f* de survie

(b) *esp Br F* (*non-contributing member*) non-valeur *f*, *pl* non-valeurs, poids *m* mort; **we can't carry passengers** on ne peut pas traîner de poids morts

passenger wagon *n Aut* voiture *f* familiale

passe-partout [pæspɑː'tuː] *n* **(a)** (*key*) (clef *f*) passe-partout *m inv* **(b)** *Art, Phot* (*method of framing*) encadrement *m* sous verre; (*gummed paper*) bande *f* de papier de bordure

passer-by ['pɑːsəbaɪ] *n* (*pl* **passers-by**) passant, -ante

passim ['pæsɪm] *adv* passim

passing ['pɑːsɪŋ] **1** *adj* (*hour, minute etc*) qui passe/passait; (*remark*) en passant; (*whim, fancy*) passager, éphémère; **he is growing stronger with each p. day** il devient de plus en plus fort avec chaque jour qui passe; **flag down a p. car** fais signe à une voiture de s'arrêter; **she flagged down a p. car** elle a fait signe à une voiture qui passait de s'arrêter; *Lit* **the p. hour** l'heure *f* fugitive; *Tennis* **p. shot** passing-shot *m*, *pl* passing-shots; *Com* **p. trade** clients *mpl ou* clientèle *f* de passage

2 *n* **(a)** (*going past*) (*of train, birds etc*) passage *m*; (*overtaking*) (*of another car*) dépassement *m*, doublement *m*; *Com* (*of dividend*) passation *f*; **in p.** (*incidentally*) en passant; **p. place** (*on road*) = emplacement *m* ménagé pour laisser passer un véhicule venant en sens inverse; *Rail* voie *f* d'évitement *ou* de dédoublement

(b) (*of time*) écoulement *m*; (*of sb's beauty*) disparition *f*; *esp Fml* (*death*) mort *f*; *Lit* **p. bell** glas *m*

(c) (*approval*) *Pol etc* (*of resolution*) adoption *f*; (*of law*) vote *m*; *Fin, Com* (*of accounts*) approbation *f*

(d) (*giving*) (*of message etc*) transmission *f*; *Jur* (*of judgement*) prononcé *m*; *Fb etc* (*of the ball*) passes *fpl*

3 *adv Arch, Lit* **p. fair** de toute beauté

passion ['pæʃən] *n* **(a)** passion *f*; **to have a p. for sb** aimer qn passionnément; *Fig* **to have a p. for music/painting/cars** avoir la passion de la musique/de la peinture/des voitures; **to have a p. for Chinese cooking** adorer la cuisine chinoise; *Jur* **crime of p.** crime *m* passionnel

(b) (*anger*) colère *f*, emportement *m*; **a fit of p.** un accès de colère; **to be in a p. about sth** être fou de colère à cause de qch; **to fly into a p.** s'emporter

(c) (*strong emotion*) passion *f*; **passions are running high on this issue** ce sujet déchaîne les passions; **to sing/speak with great p.** chanter/parler avec passion; **imagine getting into such a p. about a football match!** se mettre dans un tel état à propos d'un match de foot!; **to hate sb/sth with a p.** avoir horreur de qn/qch

(d) *Rel* **the P.** (**of Christ**) la Passion (de Jésus-Christ); **P. Sunday/week** le dimanche/la semaine de la Passion; **p. play** mystère *m* de la Passion

passionate ['pæʃənɪt] *adj* **(a)** (*speech*) véhément; (*advocate, believer*) fervent, ardent; **a p. plea for justice** un véhément appel à la justice **(b)** (*love, lover*) passionné, ardent; (*embrace, kiss*) passionné; (*relationship*) passionnel; **to make p. love** faire l'amour avec passion; **a p. weekend** un week-end de passion

passionately ['pæʃənɪtlɪ] *adv* (*to love, defend sth*) passionnément, ardemment, avec passion; (*to believe, be committed to*) ardemment, avec ferveur; (*to speak*) avec passion, avec véhémence; (*to sing*) avec passion; **to be p. in love with sb** aimer qn passionnément; **to be p. fond of sth/doing sth** adorer qch/faire qch

passionflower ['pæʃənflaʊər] *n* (*plant*) passiflore *f*

passion fruit *n Bot, Culin* fruit *m* de la passion

passionless ['pæʃənlɪs] *adj* sans passion

passive ['pæsɪv] [①**A53-4**,16; **B36**,J] **1** *adj* **(a)** passif; *Metal, El* (*iron, electrode etc*) passif; *Comptr* **p. matrix screen** écran *m* à matrice passive; *Pol* **p. resistance** résistance *f* passive; **p. smoking** tabagisme *m* passif **(b)** *Gram* passif; **the p. voice** la voix passive **(c)** *Com* (*debts*) ne portant pas d'intérêt **2** *n Gram* **the p.** la voix passive, le passif; **verb in the p.** verbe *m* au passif

passively ['pæsɪvlɪ] *adv* **(a)** passivement **(b)** *Gram* au passif, à la forme passive

passiveness ['pæsɪvnɪs], **passivity** [pæ'sɪvɪtɪ] *n* (*of mind, metal etc*) passivité *f*

passkey ['pɑːskiː] *n* (clef *f*) passe-partout *m inv*

pass laws *npl* = lois *fpl* qui anciennement restreignaient la liberté de mouvement de la population noire en Afrique du Sud

Passover ['pɑːsəʊvər] *n Jewish Rel* la Pâque

passport ['pɑːspɔːt] *n* passeport *m*; **ship's p.** permis *m* de navigation; *Fig* **this job was her p. to fame** ce travail a été son passeport pour la célébrité; **money is a p. to anything** l'argent ouvre toutes les portes; **p. control** contrôle *m* des passeports; **p. number** numéro *m* de passeport

passport-sized photograph *n* photo *f* d'identité

password ['pɑːswɜːd] *n Mil, Comptr etc* mot *m* de passe; *Comptr* **p. protection** protection *f* par mot de passe

password-protected *adj Comptr* protégé par mot de passe

past[1] [pɑːst] **1** *adj* passé; **the time for negotiating is p.** l'heure n'est plus à la négociation; **those days are p.** ces temps sont révolus; **in p. times., in times p.** autrefois, *Lit* au temps jadis; **p. chairmen** (*former chairmen*) anciens présidents; **she's a p. master at it** elle est experte en la matière; **she's a p. master at doing it** elle est passée maître dans l'art de le faire; **the p. week** la semaine dernière *ou* passée; **the p. two months** les deux derniers mois; **for some time p.** depuis quelque temps; *Gram* **in the p. tense** au passé

2 *n* **(a) the p.** le passé; **in the p.** autrefois; **it is a thing of the p.** (*no longer exists*) (*of institution, custom*) ça n'existe plus; (*of relationship*) c'est du passé; (*is old-fashioned*) c'est périmé; **those days are a thing of the p.** cette époque est révolue; **to live in the p.** vivre dans le passé

(b) (*background*) (*of person*) passé *m*; **woman with a p.** femme *f* qui a vécu *ou* qui a un passé; **town with a p.** ville *f* historique; **our country's glorious p.** le glorieux passé de notre pays

(c) [①**A48-9**,11; **B28**,**F3-4**] *Gram* passé *m*; **in the p.** au passé

past[2] **1** *prep* (*beyond*) au delà de; **a little p. the bridge** un peu plus loin que le pont, un peu au delà du pont; **to walk p. the house** passer devant la maison; **it is p. four (o'clock)** il est quatre heures passées; **half/a quarter p. four** quatre heures et demie/et quart; *Br* **ten (minutes) p. four** quatre heures dix; **it is half p.** il est la demie; **this bread is p. its sell-by date** ce pain a dépassé sa date limite de vente; **to be p. all understanding** dépasser toute compréhension; **p. endurance** insupportable; **that's p. all belief** c'est incroyable; **I'm p. work** (*too old*) je ne suis plus d'âge à travailler; (*too ill*) je ne peux plus travailler; **I'm p. caring** (*what happens, what you or they have done etc*) je n'en ai plus rien à faire; *F* **to be p. it** (*of person*) être trop vieux (*pour travailler, pour jouer au tennis etc*); (*of car, machine*) avoir son compte; *F* **I wouldn't put it p. her** elle en est bien capable; **I wouldn't put anything p. this government** ce gouvernement est capable de tout *ou* du pire

2 *adv* **to walk/go p.** passer; **to run p.** passer en courant

pasta ['pæstə] *n Culin* pâtes *fpl* (alimentaires)

paste¹ [peɪst] *n* **(a)** (*malleable substance*) pâte *f*; *Cer* **hard/soft p.** pâte dure/tendre **(b)** (*glue*) colle *f*; **p. pot** pot *m* de colle **(c)** *Culin* (*for pastry*) pâte *f* (à pâtisserie); **fish p.** = mousse *f* de poisson; **liver p.** = sorte de pâté de foie; **meat p.** = sorte de pâté **(d)** (*jewellery*) stras(s) *m*; **it's only p.** ce n'est que du stras(s); **p. jewellery** bijoux *mpl* en stras(s)

paste² *vt* **(a)** (*glue*) (*poster, picture etc*) coller (**on** sur; **in** dans); (*wallpaper*) encoller; *Comptr* coller **(b)** *F* (*beat up*) rosser, casser la figure à; (*defeat heavily*) mettre la pâtée à

▶ **paste up** *vtsep* (*notice*) afficher; (*bill, advert*) coller, monter

pasteboard ['peɪstbɔːd] *n* carton *m*

pastel ['pæst(ə)l] *n Art* (*crayon*) (crayon *m*) pastel *m*; (*drawing*) pastel; **p. drawing, drawing in p.** (dessin *m* au) pastel; **p. blue** bleu pastel *m inv*; **p. shades** tons *mpl* pastel

pastern ['pæstən] *n* pâturon *m*, paturon *m*

paste-up *n* (*in publishing*) maquette *f*

pasteurization [pæstʃəraɪ'zeɪʃən] *n* pasteurisation *f*

pasteurize ['pæstʃəraɪz] *vt* pasteuriser; **pasteurized milk** lait *m* pasteurisé

past historic *n* [①B28,F,4] *Gram* passé *m* simple

pastiche [pæ'stiːʃ] *n* pastiche *m*

pastille ['pæstɪl] *n* **(a)** pastille *f*; **fruit pastilles** = pâtes *fpl* de fruits **(b)** (*for fumigating the air*) pastille *f* à brûler

pastime ['pɑːstaɪm] *n* passe-temps *m inv*

pastiness ['peɪstɪnɪs] *n* **(a)** (*of face*) teint *m* terreux **(b)** (*of bread etc*) consistance *f* pâteuse

pasting ['peɪstɪŋ] *n* **(a)** (*gluing*) (*of poster etc*) collage *m*; (*of wallpaper*) encollage *m* **(b)** *F* (*beating*) rossée *f*, raclée *f*; **to give sb a p.** mettre une raclée à qn, rosser qn; *Sp* **to get a p.** être battu à plate(s) couture(s); *Sp* **to give sb a p.** mettre la pâtée à qn

pastor ['pɑːstər] *n Rel* pasteur *m*

pastoral ['pɑːstərəl] **1** *adj* **(a)** (*rural*) pastoral; **p. land** (terre *f* en) pâturages *mpl*; **a p. people** un peuple de bergers **(b)** *Rel* pastoral; **p. letter** (lettre *f*) pastorale *f* **(c)** *Sch* (*care*) qui concerne la santé physique et spirituelle des élèves **2** *n* **(a)** *Liter, Mus, Art, Th* pastorale *f* **(b)** *Rel* (lettre *f*) pastorale *f*

past participle *n* [①A45,7; B35-6, I,2] *Gram* participe *m* passé

past perfect *n* [①A49,11,e; B28-9,F,5] *Gram* plus-que-parfait *m*

pastrami [pə'strɑːmɪ] *n Culin* = bœuf *m* fumé et épicé

pastry ['peɪstrɪ] *n* pâte *f*; (*cake*) pâtisserie *f*; **short(-crust) p.** pâte brisée; **flaky** *or* **puff p.** pâte feuilletée; **p. board** planche *f* à pâtisserie; **p. brush** pinceau *m* à pâtisserie; **p. case** fond *m* de tarte; **p. cutter** emporte-pièce *m inv*

pastrycook ['peɪstrɪkʊk] *n* pâtissier, -ière

pasturage¹ ['pɑːstʃərɪdʒ] *n* **(a)** (*right*) (droit *m* de) pâturage *m ou* pacage *m* **(b)** (*land*) = **pasture¹**

pasture¹ ['pɑːstʃər] *n* **p. (land)** (lieu *m* de) pâture *f*, pâturage *m*, herbage *m*; **to be put out to p.** *Agr* être mis au pré *ou* au pâturage; *Fig* être mis à la retraite *ou* au vert; *Fig* **to move on to pastures new** *or* **greener pastures** aller vers de nouveaux horizons

pasture² **1** *vi* paître, pâturer, pacager **2** *vt* (*of shepherd*) (*animals*) (faire) paître; (*of animals*) (*field*) pâturer

pasty¹ ['peɪstɪ] *adj* **(a)** (*face, complexion*) terreux; (*person*) qui a le teint terreux; **p.-faced** au teint terreux **(b)** (*texture*) pâteux

pasty² ['pæstɪ] *n Br Culin* = (petit) pâté *m* en croûte (*cuit sans moule*); **Cornish p.** = pâté (en croûte) qui contient du bœuf, des pommes de terre et autres légumes

pat¹ [pæt] *n* **(a)** (*tap*) petite tape *f*; (*on animal*) petite tape, caresse *f*; **to give sb a p. on the back** donner une tape dans le dos à qn; *Fig* (*congratulate*) féliciter qn; *Fig* **to give oneself a p. on the back** se féliciter **(b)** (*lump*) (*of butter*) rondelle *f*, médaillon *m*; **cow p.** bouse *f* de vache

pat² *vt* **(-tt-)** (*tap*) tapoter; (*animal*) caresser, flatter (de la main); **to p. one's hair** se tapoter les cheveux; **she patted the little boy's head** elle a tapoté la tête du petit garçon; **to p. sb on the back** donner une tape dans le dos à qn; *Fig* (*congratulate*) féliciter qn; *Fig* **to p. oneself on the back** se féliciter

pat³ **1** *adv* **his answer came p.** il a répondu du tac au tac; **to know** *or* **have sth off p.** savoir qch par cœur; **he had his explanation off p.** il avait une explication toute prête; **to stand p.** *Cards* jouer d'autorité; *esp Am* (*not give in*) refuser de bouger **2** *adj* (*answer, solution*) facile; (*explanation*) simple

pat⁴ **(a)** (*abbr* **patent**) brev. **(b)** (*abbr* **patented**) breveté

▶ **pat down** *vtsep* (*soil, cement etc*) tasser (doucement)

patch¹ [pætʃ] *n* **(a)** (*of cloth*) pièce *f* (*pour raccommoder un vêtement*); (*on garment*) pièce (rapportée); (*on sail*) placard *m*; (*for bromide corrections*) cache *m*; *Med* (*nicotine, drug treatment*) timbre *m*, patch *m*; *Comptr* (*correction*) correction *f*; *Aut etc* (**rubber**) **p.** (*for inner tube*) rustine *f*; **to put a p. on a garment** mettre une pièce à *ou* rapiécer un vêtement; *F* **his last novel isn't a p. on the others** son dernier roman est loin de valoir les autres; **(eye) p.** couvre-œil *m*, *pl* couvre-œils; *El, Tel* **p. board** tableau *m* de commutation (à cordon); *El, Tel* **p. cord** cordon *m* de commutation; **p. pocket** poche *f* rapportée *ou* appliquée

(b) (*of colour, light*) tache *f*; (*of fog, mist*) nappe *f*; (*of oil*) flaque *f*; (*of ice*) plaque *f*; **p. of blue sky** pan *m ou* coin *m ou* échappée *f* de ciel bleu; **rough patches** (*on wood, metal etc*) aspérités *fpl*; **the book was good in patches** le livre contient de bons passages; *F* **to be going through** *or* **to have struck a bad p.** traverser une mauvaise période

(c) (*of land*) lopin *m*, parcelle *f*; (*of vegetables*) carré *m*; *F* (*of police*) secteur *m*; *F* **keep off my p.!** (*territory*) ne mets pas les pieds sur mon territoire!

patch² *vt* (*piece of clothing*) mettre une pièce à, rapiécer; (*inner tube*) poser une rustine à; *Naut* (*sail*) placarder

▶ **patch together** *vtsep F* (*temporary shelter, something broken*) assembler; (*business plan, team, government*) mettre sur pied; **they patched together a documentary** ils ont monté un documentaire tant bien que mal; **we are beginning to p. together an understanding of …** petit à petit nous commençons à nous faire une idée de …; *Pej* **the whole thing is a bit patched together** tout est un peu mal fichu

▶ **patch up** *vtsep F* (*repair temporarily*) (*object, Fig marriage*) rafistoler; *Med F* (*person*) retaper; **I managed to p. the car up** j'ai réussi à retaper la voiture; **we've patched things up** (*after quarrel, argument*) nous avons réussi à arranger les choses; **they patched up their differences** ils ont réglé leurs différends

patchboard ['pætʃbɔːd] *n* (*for electrical connections*) tableau *m* de raccordement

patching ['pætʃɪŋ] *n* (*of piece of clothing*) rapiéçage *m*, rapiècement *m*; **we can use that old jacket for p.** nous pouvons utiliser cette vieille veste pour faire du rapiècement *ou* rapiéçage

patchwork ['pætʃwɜːk] *n Sewing, Fig* patchwork *m*; **p. quilt** couverture *f* en patchwork; *Fig* **a p. team** une équipe disparate *ou* hétéroclite; **a p. of measures** un assemblage disparate *ou* hétéroclite de mesures; *Fig* **a p. of fields** une campagne bigarrée

patchy ['pætʃɪ] *adj* (*paintwork etc, Fig novel etc*) inégal

pate [peɪt] *n Arch, Hum* (*head*) caboche *f*; **bald p.** crâne *m* chauve

pâté ['pæteɪ] *n Culin* pâté *m*; **liver p.** pâté de foie; **p. sandwich** sandwich *m* au pâté

patella, *pl* **-ae, -as** [pə'telə, -iː, -əz] *n Anat* rotule *f*

paten ['pæt(ə)n] *n Rel* patène *f*

patent¹ ['peɪtənt, 'pætənt] **1** *adj* **(a)** (*protected by patent*) breveté; **p. medicine** spécialité *f* pharmaceutique *ou* médicale

(b) *Jur* **letters p.** lettres *fpl* patentes *ou* de noblesse; (*of inventor*) lettres patentes, brevet *m* d'invention *ou* d'inventeur

(c) **p. leather** cuir *m* verni; **p.-leather shoes** chaussures *fpl* vernies

(d) (*evident*) (*lack of concern, disrespect*) manifeste; (*fact*) évident; **that's a p. lie!** c'est un mensonge éhonté!

2 *n* **(a)** (*right*) brevet *m* d'invention; (*invention*) invention *f*/fabrication *f* brevetée; **to take out a p. for an invention** faire breveter une invention; **p. applied for, p. pending** demande de brevet déposée; **infringement of a p.** contrefaçon *f*; **p. application** demande *f ou* dépôt *m* de brevet

(b) (*grant of nobility*) lettres *fpl* patentes; **p. of nobility** lettres d'anoblissement *ou* de noblesse

patent² *vt* (*invention*) (*of authorities*) protéger par un brevet, breveter; (*of inventor*) faire breveter, prendre un brevet pour; **patented** breveté

patentable ['peɪtəntəb(ə)l] *adj* brevetable

patent agent *n* agent *m* en brevets (d'invention)

patent attorney *n US* conseil *m* en matière de brevets

patentee [peɪtən'tiː] *n* détenteur, -trice d'un/du brevet

patently ['peɪtəntlɪ] *adv* manifestement; **he was p. lying** il était manifeste qu'il mentait; **it was p. obvious that …** il était absolument évident que …

Patent Office *n* = Institut *m* national de la propriété industrielle

patentor ['peɪtəntər] *n* organisme *m* délivrant un brevet

patent rights *npl* propriété *f* industrielle

pater ['peɪtər] *n Old-fashioned Br F* (**the**) **p.** le paternel

paterfamilias [peɪtəfə'mɪlɪæs] *n Fml* chef *m* de famille

paternal [pəˈtɜːnəl] *adj* (*love, attention*) paternel; (*role, responsibilities*) de père; *Lit* **under the p. roof** dans la maison paternelle; **p. grandparents** grands-parents *mpl* paternels
paternalism [pəˈtɜːnəlɪz(ə)m] *n* paternalisme *m*
paternalist [pəˈtɜːnəlɪst] **1** *adj* paternaliste **2** *n* personne *f* à tendances paternalistes
paternalistic [pətɜːnəˈlɪstɪk] *adj* paternaliste
paternalistically [pətɜːnəˈlɪstɪklɪ] *adv* (*to govern*) avec paternalisme; (*to say*) d'un ton paternaliste; (*to smile*) d'un air paternaliste
paternally [pəˈtɜːnəlɪ] *adv* paternellement
paternity [pəˈtɜːnɪtɪ] *n* paternité *f*; **there are doubts about his p.** on n'est pas sûr de l'identité de son père; **p. leave** congé *m* de paternité; *Jur* **p. suit** procès *m* en paternité
path, *pl* **paths** [pɑːθ, pɑːðz] *n* **(a)** (*through forest etc*) chemin *m*, sentier *m*; (*in garden*) allée *f*; *Fig* (*in research etc*) voie *f*; (*of inquiry, investigation*) ligne *f*; *Comptr* (*of paper in printer*) chemin; *Comptr* (*of directory structure*) chemin (d'accès); *Fig* **the p. of glory** le chemin de la gloire; **this was a certain p. to disaster** cela menait tout droit au désastre
(b) (*course*) (*of moving body*) trajet *m*, course *f*; (*of projectile, particle, planet*) trajectoire *f*; (*of ray of light*) passage *m*, trajet; (*of sun*) route *f*; **p. of a bullet** (*through the air*) trajectoire d'une balle; (*through the body*) trajet *ou* sillon *m* d'une balle; **he killed everyone in his p.** il a tué tout le monde sur son chemin *ou* passage; **in the p. of a vehicle** sur le chemin *ou* passage d'un véhicule; **a tree blocked his p.** un arbre lui bloquait le passage *ou* chemin; **their paths had crossed before** leurs chemins s'étaient déjà croisés
pathetic [pəˈθetɪk] *adj* **(a)** (*touching*) (*sight etc*) touchant, attendrissant; **she looked rather p.** elle était touchante **(b)** *F* (*weak, poor, useless*) (*excuse, game, person etc*) lamentable, pitoyable; **you're p.!** tu es lamentable!; **how p.!, it's p.!, isn't it p.?** c'est (vraiment) lamentable! **(c)** *Liter* **the p. fallacy** l'attribution *f* des caractéristiques humaines à la nature
pathetically [pəˈθetɪklɪ] *adv* **(a)** (*touchingly*) pitoyablement; **they wept p.** ils pleuraient d'une façon pitoyable; **she looked at him p.** elle lui jeta un regard pitoyable **(b)** *F* (*atrociously*) lamentablement; **p. bad** (*performance, speech etc*) lamentable; **p. easy** si facile que c'en est ridicule; **that's a p. weak excuse** c'est une excuse lamentable; **they performed p.** ils ont offert une performance lamentable *ou* pitoyable; **he's so p. arrogant** il est si arrogant que c'en est ridicule
pathfinder [ˈpɑːθfaɪndər] *n* **(a)** (*scout*) éclaireur, -euse; (*pioneer*) pionnier, -ière **(b)** (*aircraft*) avion *m* éclaireur
pathological [pæθəˈlɒdʒɪk(ə)l] *adj* (*hatred, liar etc*) pathologique
pathologically [pæθəˈlɒdʒɪklɪ] *adv* pathologiquement; **to be p. afraid of sth** avoir une peur pathologique de qch
pathologist [pəˈθɒlədʒɪst] *n* pathologiste *mf*; **(forensic) p.** médecin *m* légiste
pathology [pəˈθɒlədʒɪ] *n* pathologie *f*
pathos [ˈpeɪθɒs] *n* pathétique *m*
pathway [ˈpɑːθweɪ] *n* sentier *m*
patience [ˈpeɪʃəns] *n* **(a)** patience *f*; **to try** *or* **tax sb's p.** éprouver la patience de qn; **my p. is exhausted** *or* **is at an end** ma patience est à bout, je suis à bout de patience; **you've exhausted my p.** tu as abusé de ma patience; **(have) p.!** (prenez) patience!; **to lose p.** perdre patience; **I've no p. with him** il m'énerve, il m'agace **(b)** *Br Cards* réussite *f*; **to play p.** faire des réussites
patient [ˈpeɪʃənt] **1** *adj* patient; **to be p.** (*naturally*) être patient, avoir de la patience; (*on specific occasion*) être patient, patienter, prendre patience; **you will have to be p.** il vous faudra être patient **2** *n* malade *mf*, patient, -ente; (*after operation*) opéré, -ée; **a doctor and his patients** un médecin et ses clients *ou* patients; **p. care** soins *mpl* administrés aux patients
patiently [ˈpeɪʃəntlɪ] *adv* patiemment; **a long illness, p. borne** une longue maladie, endurée avec patience
patina [ˈpætɪnə] *n* patine *f*; **to take on a p.** (*of bronze*) se patiner
patio [ˈpætɪəʊ] *n* patio *m*; **p. doors** porte-fenêtre *f*, *pl* portes-fenêtres
patriarch [ˈpeɪtrɪɑːk] *n Rel etc* patriarche *m*
patriarchal [peɪtrɪˈɑːk(ə)l] *adj* patriarcal
patriarchy [ˈpeɪtrɪɑːkɪ] *n* patriarcat *m*, système *m* patriarcal
patrician [pəˈtrɪʃən] *adj, n Antiq etc* patricien, -ienne
patricide [ˈpætrɪsaɪd] *n* **(a)** (*person*) parricide *mf* **(b)** (*crime*) parricide *m*
patrimony [ˈpætrɪmənɪ] **(a)** (*inheritance*) patrimoine *m* **(b)** (*of church*) biens-fonds *mpl*, revenu *m*
patriot [ˈpeɪtrɪət, ˈpæ-] *n* patriote *mf*
patriotic [peɪtrɪˈɒtɪk, pæ-] *adj* (*person*) patriote; (*speech, feeling etc*) patriotique
patriotically [peɪtrɪˈɒtɪklɪ, pæ-] *adv* patriotiquement, avec patriotisme
patriotism [ˈpeɪtrɪətɪz(ə)m, ˈpæ-] *n* patriotisme *m*
patrol¹ [pəˈtrəʊl] *n* patrouille *f*; (*of police*) patrouille (de surveillance); (*of nightwatchman, police officer on foot*) ronde *f*; **to be on p.** être en patrouille, patrouiller; **p. bomber** patrouilleur *m* de bombardement, bombardier *m* patrouilleur; **p. car** voiture *f* de reconnaissance *ou* de liaison policière; *Naut* **p. craft** *or* **vessel** patrouilleur, vedette *f* de surveillance; **p. leader** (*in scouts*) chef *m* de patrouille
patrol² (-ll-) **1** *vi* patrouiller, être en patrouille **2** *vt* (*area etc*) patrouiller dans, faire une patrouille dans; (*border*) patrouiller à; **the border is heavily patrolled** de nombreuses patrouilles surveillent la frontière
patrolman, *pl* **-men** [pəˈtrəʊlmən] *n* **(a)** *Br* (*employee of AA, RAC etc*) patrouilleur *m* **(b)** *US* (*policeman*) agent *m* de police (en service de ronde)
patrolwoman, *pl* **-women** [pəˈtrəʊlwʊmən, -wɪmɪn] *n US* femme *f* agent de police (en service de ronde)
patron [ˈpeɪtrən] *n* **(a)** (*of artists, the arts etc*) protecteur, -trice, mécène *m*; (*of charity*) patron, -onne; *Rel, Hist* (*of living*) patron *m*, collateur *m*; *Rel* **p. saint** (saint) patron, (sainte) patronne **(b)** *Com* (*of shop*) client, -ente; (*regular*) habitué, -ée
patronage [ˈpætrənɪdʒ] *n* **(a)** (*support etc*) patronage *m*, protection *f*; (*of art*) mécénat *m*; (*of charity*) patronage; *Pej* (*condescension*) (*towards sb*) attitude *f* condescendante **(of** envers); **concert under the p. of ...** concert patronné par ... **(b)** (*of hotel etc*) clientèle *f* **(c)** *Church of Eng* droit *m* de présentation (à un bénéfice) **(d)** *Pol* népotisme *m*; **yet another p. appointment** encore une nomination qui tient du népotisme
patroness [ˈpeɪtrənɪs] *n Old-fashioned* (*of the arts etc*) protectrice *f*; (*of charity*) (dame *f*) patronnesse *f*
patronize [ˈpætrənaɪz] *vt* **(a)** (*artist etc*) patronner; (*art*) encourager; (*hospital etc*) subventionner; (*charitable institution*) souscrire à **(b)** *Pej* (*treat in a patronizing way*) traiter avec condescendance; **don't p. me!** je n'ai pas besoin de ta condescendance! **(c)** *Com* (*company, shop*) accorder sa clientèle à; (*cinema, restaurant etc*) être un(e) habitué(e) de, fréquenter; **a restaurant patronized by the famous** un restaurant fréquenté par des gens célèbres
patronizing [ˈpætrənaɪzɪŋ] *adj* (*person, tone etc*) condescendant; **to be p. towards sb** se montrer condescendant envers qn, traiter qn avec condescendance
patronizingly [ˈpætrənaɪzɪŋlɪ] *adv* (*to look*) d'un air condescendant; (*to say*) d'un ton condescendant; (*to treat sb*) avec condescendance
patronymic [pætrəˈnɪmɪk] **1** *adj* patronymique **2** *n* patronyme *m*, nom *m* patronymique
patsy [ˈpætsɪ] *n Am Sl* (*dupe*) gobeur *m*, jobard *m*
patten [ˈpæt(ə)n] *n* socque *m* (*pour protéger les chaussures de la boue*)
patter¹ [ˈpætər] *n* (*of footsteps*) petit bruit *m*; (*of mice*) trottinement *m*; (*of rain*) crépitement *m*; (*gentler*) tambourinement *m*; *Hum* **soon we'll be hearing the p. of tiny feet** la famille s'élargira bientôt
patter² *vi* (*walk*) trottiner, marcher à petits pas rapides; (*of rain*) crépiter; (*more gently*) tambouriner
patter³ *n* (*of sales person*) baratin *m*, boniment *m*; (*of comedian*) bagout *m*; (*chatter*) bavardage *m*; *F* **p. merchant** baratineur *m*
patter⁴ *vi* (*chatter*) bavarder sans arrêt, caqueter
▶ **patter about** *vi* (*walk, run*) trottiner çà et là
pattern¹ [ˈpæt(ə)n] *n* **(a)** (*design*) (*on wallpaper, fabric etc*) motif *m*; (*of hit marks on a target, on the ground etc*) groupement *m*; *Comptr* (*of perforations*) combinaison *f*; **streets arranged in an orderly p.** rues établies suivant un plan ordonné; *Mil, Av* **p. bombing** bombardement *m* systématique; *Comptr* **p. recognition** reconnaissance *f* de formes
(b) (*of events, behaviour etc*) **the normal p. of trade** la tendance normale du marché; **some clear patterns emerge from the statistics** des tendances nettes ressortent des statistiques; **the evening followed the usual p.** la soirée s'est déroulée selon le schéma habituel; **a typical p. of events** une suite d'événements type; **patterns of behaviour** comportements *mpl* types; **there was a certain p. in his behaviour** son comportement suivait un certain schéma
(c) (*model*) modèle *m*, dessin *m*; *Sewing etc* (*paper cutout*) patron *m*; *Knitting* modèle; *Metal* modèle, gabarit *m*, calibre *m*; **machines all built to one p.** machines construites *ou* fabriquées toutes sur le même modèle; *Sewing* **to cut out a**

shirt from a p. tailler une chemise sur un patron; *Ind* **p. designer** dessinateur, -trice de modèles; **p. maker** modeleur, -euse; *Sch* **p. drill** exercice *m* d'apprentissage des structures grammaticales

(**d**) (*example*) modèle *m*, exemple *m*; **to set a p.** créer un modèle; **this opening debate set the p. for ...** ce débat d'ouverture a donné le ton *ou* la note de ...

(**e**) *Com* (*sample*) échantillon *m*; **p. book/card** livre *m*/carte *f* d'échantillons

pattern² *vt* (**a**) (*draw patterns on*) tracer des motifs sur; (*decorate with patterns*) orner de motifs (**b**) (*model*) **to p. sth after** *or* **(up)on sth** modeler qch sur qch

patterned ['pætənd] *adj* à dessins, à motifs

patty ['pætɪ] *n Culin* pâté *m* (en croûte)

paucity ['pɔːsɪtɪ] *n* (*of information, proof etc*) manque *m*; (*of money, food, materials, talent etc*) manque, pénurie *f*

paunch [pɔːntʃ] *n* (*of person*) ventre *m*, *F* bide *m*, bedaine *f*; (*of ruminant*) panse *f*, rumen *m*; **to develop a p.** prendre du ventre *ou F* du bide

paunchy ['pɔːntʃɪ] *adj F* ventru, pansu

pauper ['pɔːpər] *n* indigent, -ente; **to die a p.** mourir dans l'indigence; **p.'s grave** fosse *f* commune

pause¹ [pɔːz] *n* (**a**) pause *f*, arrêt *m*; (*on recording*) blanc *m* sonore; (*in conversation etc*) silence *m*; **to have a p.** faire une pause; *Comptr* **p. key** touche *f* pause (**b**) (*in poetry*) repos *m*; (*caesura*) césure *f* (**c**) *Mus* point *m* d'orgue; (*over a rest*) point d'arrêt (**d**) *esp Lit* **to give sb p.** faire hésiter qn; (*make sb think*) donner à réfléchir à qn

pause² *vi* (**a**) (*stop*) (*when working*) faire une pause; (*when speaking*) s'interrompre, faire une pause; (*when leaving etc*) marquer un temps d'arrêt, s'arrêter; **to p. for breath/thought** faire une pause pour reprendre son souffle/réfléchir (**b**) (*hesitate*) hésiter; **to make sb p.** faire hésiter qn; (*make sb think*) donner à réfléchir à qn (**c**) **to p. on a word** s'arrêter sur un mot; *Mus* **to p. on a note** tenir une note

pave [peɪv] *vt* (*road etc*) paver; *Fig* **to p. the way** préparer le terrain (**for sth** pour qch); **the streets here aren't paved with gold** on ne roule pas sur l'or ici

pavement ['peɪvmənt] *n* (**a**) *esp Br* (*path beside street*) trottoir *m* (**b**) *Am* (*roadway*) chaussée *f* (**c**) (*material*) pavé *m*

pavement artist *n* artiste *mf* des rues (qui dessine sur les trottoirs)

pavement café *n* café *m* en terrasse

pavilion [pə'vɪlɪən] *n Br Sp, Archit etc* pavillon *m*

paving ['peɪvɪŋ] *n* (**a**) (*action*) pavage *m*; (*with tiles*) carrelage *m*; (*with slabs*) dallage *m*; **p. stone** pierre *f* à paver, pavé *m*; **p. tile** carreau *m ou* (*bigger*) dalle *f* (de pavage) (**b**) (*surface*) pavé *m*; (*made of bigger slabs*) dalles *fpl*

Pavlova [pæv'ləʊvə] *n Culin* vacherin *m*; **raspberry P.** vacherin à la framboise

Pavlovian [pæv'ləʊvɪən] *adj Psy* (*treatment, reaction, response*) pavlovien

paw¹ [pɔː] *n* (*of animal, F of person*) patte *f*; *F* **paws off!** bas les pattes!; *F* **you're not getting your dirty** *or* **sweaty paws on my new bike!** il n'est pas question que tu touches à mon nouveau vélo!

paw² *vt* (**a**) (*of animal*) donner un/des coup(s) de patte à; **to p. the ground** (*of horse*) gratter (la terre) du pied (**b**) *F* (*of person*) tripoter, peloter

pawky ['pɔːkɪ] *adj Scot* (*witty*) pince-sans-rire

pawl [pɔːl] *n MecE etc* (*of catch*) cliquet *m*; **p. and ratchet wheel** roue *f ou* encliquetage *m* à rochet

pawn¹ [pɔːn] *n* (**a**) (*object pawned*) gage *m*, nantissement *m* (**b**) **in p.** en gage; **to put one's watch in p.** mettre sa montre en gage *ou* au mont-de-piété *ou F* au clou; **to get sth out of p.** dégager qch (du mont-de-piété); **p. ticket** reconnaissance *f* (de dépôt de gage)

pawn² *vt* mettre en gage *ou* au mont-de-piété *ou F* au clou, engager; *Fig* (*one's life, honour*) engager

pawn³ *n Chess* pion *m*; *Fig* **to be sb's p.** être le jouet de qn

pawnbroker ['pɔːnbrəʊkər] *n* prêteur, -euse sur gage(s)

pawnbroking ['pɔːnbrəʊkɪŋ] *n* prêt *m* sur gage(s)

pawnshop ['pɔːnʃɒp] *n* bureau *m* de prêt sur gage(s), mont-de-piété *m*, *pl* monts-de-piété

pawpaw ['pɔːpɔː] *n* = **papaw**

pax [pæks] *int Br Sl* (*truce*) pouce!

pay¹ [peɪ] *n* (**a**) salaire *m*, paie *f*, paye *f*; (*of domestic staff*) gages *mpl*; (*of civil servant*) traitement *m*, salaire; (*of member of parliament*) indemnité *f*; *Mil* solde *f*; **to get an extra £10 a week in one's p.** toucher 10 livres de salaire en plus par semaine; **the p.'s good/terrible** ça paie bien/mal; *Pej* **to be in sb's p.** être à la solde *ou* aux gages de qn; *Mil* **p. book** livret *m* de solde; **p. deductions** retenues *fpl* salariales; **p. dirt** gisement *m*; *Fig* **to hit p. dirt** commencer à rapporter; **p. dispute** conflit *m* salarial; *Acct* **p. ledger** livre *m* de paie

(**b**) (*payment*) **p. bed** lit *m* pour malade payant (*dans un hôpital*); *TV* **p. channel** chaîne *f* à péage *ou* payante; **p. desk** caisse *f*; **p. television** télévision *f* à péage, télévision payante

pay² (*pt, pp* **paid** [peɪd]) **1** *vt* (**a**) (*account, invoice*) payer, régler; (*fine*) payer; (*dividend*) distribuer; (*debt*) payer, liquider, régler, acquitter; (*creditor*) rembourser; (*money*) verser; (*premium*) verser, acquitter; **to p. sb £100** payer 100 livres à qn; **how much do you p. for tea?** combien est-ce que vous payez le thé?; **I paid £5 for it** je l'ai payé cinq livres; **I expect to p. my way** je m'attends à payer mon écot; **to be paid in four instalments** payable en quatre versements; **to p. cash (down)** *or* **ready money** payer (argent) comptant, payer au comptant; **p. self, p. cash** (*on cheque*) payez (à l'ordre de) moi-même; **to p. money into an account** alimenter un compte, approvisionner un compte; **to p. money into sb's account** verser de l'argent au compte de qn; **to p. something on account** verser une somme à titre de provision; *F* **to make sb p. through the nose** écorcher qn; *Fig* **they paid a heavy price for this mistake** cette erreur leur a coûté cher

(**b**) (*employees*) payer; **to be paid by the hour/the week** être payé à l'heure/la semaine; **badly paid job** travail *m* mal payé; **to p. sb to do sth** payer qn pour faire qch; **I wouldn't do it if you paid me** je ne le ferais pas même si on me payait

(**c**) (*give*) **to p. tribute** *or* **homage to sb** rendre hommage à qn; **to p. one's respects to sb** présenter ses respects à qn; **to p. one's (last) respects to sb** rendre les derniers devoirs à qn; **to p. a visit to sb** rendre visite à qn; **we paid a visit to the Louvre** nous avons visité le Louvre; **p. attention to what you are doing** faites attention à ce que vous faites

(**d**) (*profit*) **it will p. you to do it** c'est dans votre intérêt de le faire

2 *vi* (**a**) payer; **who's paying?** qui paie?; **p. at the gate** *or* **door** entrée payante; *Admin Br* **p. as you earn**, *Am* **p. as you go** retenue *f* (de l'impôt sur le revenu) à la base *ou* à la source; **how would you like to p.?** comment souhaitez-vous régler?; **to p. by cheque** payer *ou* régler par chèque

(**b**) *Com, Fin etc* **to p. on demand** payer à vue *ou* à présentation; **p. to the order of ...** payez à l'ordre de ...; *Fin* **p. to bearer** payez au porteur

(**c**) (*be profitable*) **business that doesn't p.** affaire qui ne rapporte pas *ou* qui n'est pas rentable; **it wouldn't p.** cela ne serait pas rentable; **it pays to advertise** la publicité rapporte; **it pays to be honest** l'honnêteté est toujours récompensée; **it doesn't always p. to tell the truth** on n'a pas toujours intérêt à dire la vérité

► **pay back** *vtsep* (**a**) (*loan, person*) rembourser (**b**) *Fig* (*have revenge on*) **to p. sb back in his own coin** rendre la pareille à qn, rendre la monnaie de sa pièce à qn; **I'll p. you back for this!** je te le revaudrai!, tu me le paieras!

► **pay for** *vipo* (*sth*) payer; **his uncle paid for his schooling** son oncle a payé ses études; *Fig F* **he'll p. for this!, I'll make him p. for this!** il me le payera!; *Fig F* **you'll p. for this tomorrow** (*for drinking too much etc*) tu vas en subir les conséquences demain; **it's all paid for** (*someone has paid for everything*) tout a été réglé; (*I've paid for everything*) c'est à mes frais; **a free holiday with everything paid for** des vacances gratuites tout compris

► **pay in 1** *vtsep* (*cheque, money*) verser sur son compte; **to p. in a cheque** déposer un chèque, *esp Fml* remettre un chèque à l'encaissement **2** *vi* faire un versement

► **pay off 1** *vtsep* (**a**) (*finish paying*) (*debt etc*) liquider, régler; (*creditor*) rembourser; (*mortgage*) purger; **to p. sth off over three years** acheter *ou* payer qch en trois ans; **I'm still paying it off** je n'ai pas encore fini de le payer

(**b**) (*dismiss*) (*worker, troops*) licencier; (*sailors*) débarquer; (*servant*) congédier

(**c**) *F* (*bribe*) soudoyer, donner des pots de vin à

2 *vi* (*of deal etc*) être payant *ou* rentable *ou* fructueux; (*of efforts etc*) porter ses *ou* des fruits; **all these years of work have paid off at last** nous sommes enfin récompensés après toutes ces années de travail; **it paid off** ça a valu la peine

► **pay out 1** *vtsep* (**a**) (*spend*) payer, débourser; **I've had to p. out a lot on car repairs this year** j'ai eu beaucoup à débourser pour les réparations de voiture cette année (**b**) (*salaries*) payer (**c**) (*pt, pp* **payed**) *Naut* (*cable*) (laisser) filer **2** *vi* payer

► **pay up 1** *vi* (*pay debt*) payer, *F* s'exécuter; **I finally made him p. up** j'ai finalement réussi à le faire payer *ou* débourser; **p. up!** allez, l'argent!, *Sl* aboule! **2** *vtsep* (*pay*) payer

payable ['peɪəb(ə)l] **1** *adj* (**a**) payable; **rates p. by the tenant** = impôts à la charge du locataire; *Com* **p. at sight/to order/to bearer** payable à vue/à ordre/au porteur; *Com* **p. at thirty**

days exigible: trente jours; **p. in cash** payable comptant; **p. on delivery** payable à la livraison; **to make a bill p. to sb** faire un billet à l'ordre de qn; **cheque p. to bearer** chèque *m* au porteur; **please make your cheque p. to Miss Johnston** veuillez libeller votre chèque à l'ordre de Miss Johnston; **bonds made p. in francs** bons libellés en francs **(b)** *Min* (*seam etc*) exploitable **2** *npl US* **payables** factures *fpl* à payer

pay and display *n* (*car park*) parking *m* à horodateur

pay-as-you-view TV *n* télé *f* à péage à la consommation

pay award *n* augmentation *f* de salaire

payback ['peɪbæk] *n Fin* récupération *f* du capital investi; **p. period** délai *m* de récupération du capital investi

pay cheque, *US* **pay check** *n* chèque *m* de règlement de traitement *ou* de salaire, *F* chèque de fin de mois

payday ['peɪdeɪ] *n* jour *m* de paie, paie *f*; *Mil* jour de solde; *St Exch* jour de liquidation *ou* de règlement

PAYE [pi:eɪwaɪ'i:] *n Br* (*abbr* **pay as you earn**) retenue *f* (de l'impôt sur le revenu) à la base *ou* à la source; **P. and NIC return** déclaration *f* sociale

payee [peɪ'i:] *n* (*of postal order, cheque etc*) bénéficiaire *mf*; *Com* (*of bill*) porteur *m*, preneur *m*

payer ['peɪər] *n* payeur, -euse; **they're slow payers** ils ne payent pas vite

pay formula *n* formule *f* de paie

pay freeze *n* gel *m ou* blocage *m* des salaires

pay increase *n* augmentation *f* de salaire

paying ['peɪɪŋ] *adj* **(a)** (*student etc*) payant; *Com* **p. agent** domiciliataire *m*; **p. agent for commercial bills** domiciliation *f* d'effets de commerce; *Com* **p. bank** domiciliataire *m*, établissement *m* payeur, domiciliation *f* bancaire; **p. guest** pensionnaire *mf* **(b)** (*business etc*) rémunérateur, -trice, profitable, qui rapporte; **it's not a p. proposition** cette proposition n'est pas avantageuse *ou* profitable

paying back *n* (*of loan*) remboursement *m*

paying in *n* (*of money, cheque etc*) (*into one's account*) versement *m*, encaissement *m*; **p. book** carnet *m* de versements; **p. date** date *f* d'encaissement; **p. slip** bordereau *m* de versement *ou* de remise

paying off *n* **(a)** (*of debt*) liquidation *f*, règlement *m* **(b)** (*dismissal*) (*of workers*) licenciement *m*; *Naut* (*of sailors*) débarquement *m*; (*of servants*) congédiement *m*

paying up *n Fin* **p. of a share** libération *f* d'une action

payload ['peɪləʊd] *n* (*of vehicle*) charge *f* payante *ou* utile; (*of missile*) charge utile; *Av* poids *m* utile

paymaster ['peɪmɑ:stər] *n* intendant *m*, caissier *m*, payeur *m*; *Mil* trésorier *m*; *Naut* commissaire *m*; **the terrorists' p.** le commanditaire des terroristes

Paymaster General *n Br* Trésorier-payeur *m* général

payment ['peɪmənt] *n* **(a)** (*act or fact of paying*) (*of money*) paiement *m*, versement *m*; (*of debt*) paiement, liquidation *f*, règlement *m*, acquittement *m*; (*of fine*) paiement; (*of invoice*) paiement, règlement; (*of creditor*) remboursement *m*; **to stop p. on a cheque** faire opposition sur un chèque; (**hire purchase**) **p.** paiement par traites; **I'm behind on the payments** j'ai du retard dans les paiements; **non p.** défaut *m* de paiement; **to present a bill for p.** présenter un effet au paiement *ou* à l'encaissement; **on p. of £100** contre paiement de 100 livres; **p. against documents** paiement contre documents; **p. at maturity** paiement à échéance; **p. at sight** paiement à vue; **p. by cheque** paiement par chèque; **p. by electronic transfer** paiement électronique; **p. by instalments** paiement par acomptes; **p. in advance** paiement anticipé *ou* par anticipation *ou* d'avance; **p. in arrears** paiement arriéré; **p. in cash** paiement comptant, règlement au comptant; **p. in full** paiement intégral; **p. of a dividend** passation *f ou* distribution *f* d'un dividende; **p. advice** avis *m* de paiement; **p. card** carte *f* de paiement; **p. day** jour *m* fixé comme échéance de paiement; **p. facilities** facilités *fpl* de paiement; **p. method** mode *m* de paiement; **p. on account** acompte *m*; **to make a p. on account** donner un acompte; **p. order** ordre *m* de paiement; **p. period** délai *m* de paiement; **p. schedule** échéancier *m ou* délais de paiement; **p. term** délai de paiement

(b) (*remuneration*) paiement *m*, rémunération *f*; **as (a) p. for your services** en rémunération de vos services; **she would not accept p.** elle n'a pas voulu accepter de paiement; **you can expect little but gratitude in p. for your efforts** ne vous attendez pas à beaucoup plus que de la gratitude en retour de vos efforts; **p. received** (*stamped on invoice*) pour acquit

payoff ['peɪɒf] *n* **(a)** (*final payment*) règlement *m*; *Fin* rentabilité *f* **(b)** *F* (*bribe*) pot-de-vin *m*, *pl* pots-de-vin **(c)** *F* (*ending*) dénouement *m* **(d)** (*reward*) récompense *f*

payola [peɪ'əʊlə] *n F* (*bribe*) pot-de-vin *m*, *pl* pots-de-vin

pay packet *n* (*envelope containing pay*) enveloppe *f* de paie; (*pay itself*) paie *f*, salaire *m*

pay phone *n* téléphone *m* public; (*enclosed*) cabine *f* téléphonique

pay rise *n* augmentation *f* de salaire

payroll ['peɪrəʊl] *n* **(a)** (*list of employees*) liste *f* du personnel; *Mil* feuille *f ou* état *m* de solde; **to be on the p.** être salarié; **how many do you have on the p.?** combien d'employés avez-vous?; **she's been on our p. for over twenty years** elle fait partie de notre personnel depuis plus de vingt ans; *Pej* **he's on our p.** (*we're bribing him*) on l'a acheté; *Acct* **p. ledger** journal *m ou* livre *m* de paie **(b)** (*money paid*) masse *f* salariale

pay slip *n* bulletin *m ou* feuille *f* de paie

PBX [pi:bi:'eks] *n Telecom* (*abbr* **private branch exchange**) autocommutateur *m* privé

PC ['pi:'si:] **1** *n* **(a)** *Br* (*abbr* **Police Constable**) = agent *m* de police **(b)** (*abbr* **personal computer**) O.I. *m* **2** *adj* (*abbr* **politically correct**) politiquement correct

pc ['pi:'si:] *n* (*abbr* **postcard**) carte *f* postale

PCB [pi:si:'bi:] *n* **(a)** *Ch* (*abbr* **polychlorinated biphenyl**) PCB *m* **(b)** *Electron* (*abbr* **printed circuit board**) carte *f* à *ou* de circuits imprimés

PCMCIA [pi:si:'emsi:aɪ'eɪ] *Comptr* (*abbr* **PC memory card international association**) PCMCIA

PD ['pi:'di:] *US* (*abbr* **Police Department**) service *m* de police

pdq [pi:di:'kju:] **1** *adv F* (*abbr* **pretty damn(ed) quick**) illico presto, rapido **2** *n* (*abbr* **processes data quickly**) (*machine*) terminal *m* électronique de paiement, TEP *m*

PDSA [pi:di:e'seɪ] *n Br* (*abbr* **People's Dispensary for Sick Animals**) ≈ SPA *f*

PE ['pi:'i:] *n Sch* (*abbr* **physical education**) EPS *f*; **PE lesson/teacher** cours *m* /professeur *m* d'EPS

pea [pi:] *n* pois *m*; *Culin* (**green** *or* **garden**) **peas** petits pois; **p. green** vert feuille *m inv*; *Naut* **p. jacket** caban *m*; **p. pod** cosse *f* de pois; **like two peas in a pod** comme deux gouttes d'eau; **p. soup** soupe *f* aux pois (cassés); (*thick*) purée *f* de pois (cassés)

peace [pi:s] *n* **(a)** (*absence of war, conflict*) paix *f*; (*treaty*) traité *m* de paix; **at p.** en paix (**with** avec); **to live in p. with one's neighbours** (*of person, tribe, country*) vivre en paix *ou* en harmonie avec ses voisins; **in time of p.** en temps de paix; **to make (one's) p. with sb** faire la paix *ou* se réconcilier avec qn; **we come in p.** nous venons en amis; *Hist* **the P. of Amiens** la Paix d'Amiens

(b) (*public order*) **to keep the p.** (*of citizen*) ne pas troubler l'ordre public; (*of police, troops*) veiller à l'ordre public; **to break** *or* **disturb the p.** troubler *ou* violer l'ordre public; (*at night*) faire du tapage nocturne

(c) (*tranquillity*) (*of soul, night etc*) tranquillité *f*; **for the sake of p. and quiet** pour avoir la paix; **to leave sb in p.** laisser qn tranquille *ou* en paix; **he gave me no p. until I agreed** il ne m'a pas laissé tranquille *ou* en paix tant que je n'ai pas accepté; *esp Rel* **go in p.!** allez en paix!; **p. of mind** tranquillité d'esprit; **it will give you p. of mind** ça te tranquillisera; **to be at p.** (*of dead person*) reposer en paix; **to hold** *or* **keep one's p.** se taire

peaceable ['pi:səb(ə)l] *adj* pacifique, qui aime la paix; **p. man** homme de paix; **p. means** moyens pacifiques

peaceably ['pi:səblɪ] *adv* pacifiquement

peace campaigner *n* militant, -ante pour la paix

Peace Corps *n US* = organisme *m* américain de coopération qui envoie des volontaires dans le Tiers-Monde

peace dividends *npl* dividendes *mpl* de la paix

peace formula *n* formule *f* de paix

peaceful ['pi:sfʊl] *adj* **(a)** (*calm*) paisible, calme, tranquille; (*death*) paisible; (*colour*) doux, *f* douce **(b)** (*not warlike or aggressive*) pacifique; **p. settlement of a dispute** règlement *m* pacifique d'un litige

peacefully ['pi:sfʊlɪ] *adv* (*to sleep, die*) paisiblement, tranquillement; (*to demonstrate, resolve differences*) pacifiquement; **p. situated** situé dans un lieu paisible; **p., at home** (*in death notice*) mort dans son lit

peacefulness ['pi:sfʊlnɪs] *n* tranquillité *f*, paix *f*; **the organizers have guaranteed the p. of the demonstration** les organisateurs ont garanti que la manifestation se déroulerait dans le calme

peace initiative *n* initiative *f* de paix

peacekeeping ['pi:ski:pɪŋ] *n* maintien *m* de la paix; *Mil* **p. force** force *f* de maintien de la paix

peace-loving *adj* pacifique

peace movement *n* mouvement *m* pour la paix

peace negotiations *npl* négociations *fpl* pour la paix

peace offering *n* cadeau *m* de réconciliation

peace pipe *n* calumet *m* de la paix

peace plan *n* plan *m* de paix
peace process *n* processus *m* de paix
peace studies *npl* études *fpl* sur la paix
peace talks *npl* pourparlers *mpl* de paix
peacetime ['pi:staɪm] *n* temps *m* de paix; **in p.** en temps de paix
peace treaty *n* traité *m* de paix
peach¹ [pi:tʃ] *n* pêche *f*; **p. (tree)** pêcher *m*; **p. (colour)** pêche *f inv*; **p. melba** pêche melba; **a peaches and cream complexion** un teint de pêche; *F* **she's a p.** c'est une jolie fille; *F* **it's a p.** c'est magnifique
peach² *vi Old-fashioned Sl* **to p. on sb** (*inform on*) moucharder qn
peacock ['pi:kɒk] *n* (*bird*) paon *m*; **p. (blue)** bleu paon *m inv*; **p. butterfly** paon (du jour)
peahen ['pi:hen] *n* paonne *f*
peak¹ [pi:k] *n* **(a)** (*of mountain*) pic *m*, cime *f*, sommet *m*; (*mountain*) pic; **the highest peaks** les plus hauts sommets; *Culin* **whisk the egg white until it forms stiff peaks** battre les blancs en neige jusqu'à ce qu'ils forment des becs
(b) (*maximum point*) maximum *m*; (*of graph, load*) pointe *f*; *Med* (*of fever*) pointe, poussée *f*; *Phys* (*of wave*) crête *f*; **prosperity was at its p.** la prospérité était à son apogée *ou* à son maximum; **in p. condition** dans une forme excellente; **p. demand** forte demande *f*; **p. load** charge *f* maximum; (*of generator*) débit *m* maximum; **p. rate** taux *m* fort; **p. sales** ventes *fpl* maximales
(c) (*of cap*) visière *f*; (*of bicycle saddle, anchor etc*) bec *m*; (*of roof*) pointe *f*
peak² *vi* (*of curve etc*) passer par son apogée; **inflation peaked at 10%** l'inflation a fait une pointe à 10%; *Sp* **she peaked in time for the Olympics** (*of athlete*) elle a atteint le maximum de sa forme juste à temps pour les Jeux olympiques
▶ **peak out** *vi* (*reach top limit*) atteindre son maximum
peaked [pi:kt] *adj* (*cap*) à visière
peak hours *npl* (*for traffic*) heures *fpl* de pointe; (*in shop etc*) heures d'affluence
peak period *n* (*for traffic*) heures *fpl* de pointe; (*in shop etc*) heures d'affluence
peak viewing hours *npl TV* heures *fpl* de grande écoute
peak viewing time *n TV* heure *f* de grande écoute
peaky ['pi:kɪ] *adj F* **to look p.** ne pas avoir l'air dans son assiette; **to feel p.** ne pas se sentir dans son assiette
peal¹ [pi:l] *n* (*bells*) carillon *m*; (*noise*) carillon, carillonnement *m*; (*of organ*) grondement *m*; (*of thunder*) coup *m*, grondement; **to ring a p.** sonner un carillon, carillonner; **peals of laughter** éclats *mpl* de rire; **to go** *or* **break into peals of laughter** lancer de grands éclats de rire
peal² **1** *vi* (*of bells*) (*chime*) carillonner; (*ring out loudly*) sonner à toute volée; (*of thunder, of the organ*) retentir, gronder; (*of laughter*) résonner; **to p. with laughter** éclater de rire **2** *vt* (*bells*) sonner à toute volée; (*tune*) carillonner
▶ **peal out** *vi* = **peal² 1**
peanut ['pi:nʌt] *n* cacahuète *f*; **p. butter** beurre *m* de cacahuète; **p. oil** huile *m* d'arachide; *F* **they pay us peanuts** (*small sum of money*) ils nous paient deux fois rien; **that's peanuts to him** pour lui, c'est deux fois rien
pear [peər] *n* poire *f*; **p. (tree)** poirier *m*
peardrop ['peədrɒp] *n* bonbon *m* parfumé à la poire
pearl¹ [pɜ:l] *n* perle *f*; (*cultured*) perle de culture; *Prov* **to cast pearls before swine** jeter des perles aux cochons *ou* aux pourceaux; **he comes out with some real pearls** (*amusing comments etc*) il sort de vraies perles; **pearls of dew** perles de rosée; **pearls of wisdom** perles de sagesse; *Iron* inepties *fpl*; **p. button** bouton *m* de nacre; **p. grey** gris perle *m inv*; *El* **p. lightbulb** ampoule *f* opale; **p. necklace** collier *m* de perles
pearl² *vi* **(a)** (*of moisture etc*) perler, former des gouttelettes **(b)** (*dive for pearls*) pêcher des perles
pearl³ *n, vt Knitting* = **purl**
pearl barley *n* orge *m* perlé
pearl diver *n* pêcheur, -euse de perles
pearl oyster *n* huître *f* perlière
pearly ['pɜ:lɪ] *adj* perlé; **p. (white) teeth** dents *fpl* perlées *ou* de perle; **p. nautilus** (*mollusc*) nautile *m*, nautilus *m*
Pearly Gates *npl F* portes *fpl* du Paradis
pearly king/queen *n Br* = marchand, -ande des quatre saisons de Londres portant(e) une tenue traditionnelle couverte de boutons de nacre
pear-shaped *adj* en forme de poire; (*female figure*) qui s'épaissit au niveau des hanches
peasant ['pezənt] *n* paysan, -anne, *Pej* péquenaud, -aude rustre *mf*; **p. ways** mœurs *fpl* paysannes
peasantry ['pezəntrɪ] *n* (*people*) paysannerie *f*, paysans *mpl*
pease [pi:z] *n* **p. pudding** purée *f* de pois (cassés)
peashooter ['pi:ʃu:tər] *n* petite sarbacane *f*
peasouper [pi:'su:pər] *n esp Br F* (*fog*) purée *f* de pois
peat [pi:t] *n* tourbe *f*; **turf** *or* **sod** *or* **block of p.** motte *f* de tourbe; **to cut** *or* **dig p.** tourber; **p. bog** tourbière *f*; **p. cutter** tourbier, -ière; **p. cutting** *or* **digging** tourbage *m*; **p. moss** (*for garden*) tourbe horticole
peaty ['pi:tɪ] *adj* (*soil*) tourbeux; (*taste*) de fumée de tourbe
pebble ['peb(ə)l] *n* **(a)** caillou *m*, -oux; (*big, smooth and rounded*) galet *m*; *F* **you're not the only p. on the beach** il n'y a pas que toi au monde; **p. beach** plage *f* de galets; *Constr* **p. dash** crépi *m* (moucheté); **p.-dash finish** crépi **(b)** *Opt* (*crystal*) cristal *m* de roche; (*lens*) lentille *f* en cristal de roche
pebble-dash *vt Constr* (*wall*) crépir
pebbly ['peblɪ] *adj* caillouteux; (*beach*) de galets
pecan ['pi:kən, pɪ'kæn] *n* **p. (nut)** noix *f* de pecan, *Can* pacane *f*; **p. (tree)** pacanier *m*; *Culin* **p. pie** tourte *f* aux noix de pecans *ou Can* aux pacanes
peccadillo [pekə'dɪləʊ] *n* peccadille *f*
peccary ['pekərɪ] *n* (*animal*) pécari *m*
peck¹ [pek] *n* **(a)** (*of bird*) coup *m* de bec; **to have a p. at sth** picoter qch **(b)** *F* (*kiss*) bise *f*, bécot *m*; **to give sb a p.** faire une bise à qn
peck² **1** *vt* **(a)** (*of bird*) (*sth*) picoter, becqueter; (*person*) donner un coup de bec à **(b)** *F* (*to kiss*) faire une bise à **2** *vi* **to p. (at sth)** (*of bird*) picoter (qch), donner des coups de bec (à qch); **to p. at one's food** pignocher
peck³ *n* (*measure*) (*of oats etc*) picotin *m*
pecker ['pekər] *n* **(a)** *F* (*bird*) pic *m* vert **(b)** *Br Sl* **keep your p. up!** (du) courage! **(c)** *esp Am Vulg* (*penis*) bite *f*
pecking ['pekɪŋ] *n* **p. order** (*among birds*) hiérarchie *f* du becquetage; *Fig* hiérarchie sociale; (*in business etc*) hiérarchie
peckish ['pekɪʃ] *adj F* **to be** *or* **feel p.** avoir un creux
pectin ['pektɪn] *n Ch* pectine *f*
pectoral ['pektər(ə)l] **1** *adj Anat, Med etc* pectoral; **p. cross** (*of bishop*) croix *f* pectorale; **p. fin** (*of fish*) nageoire *f* pectorale **2** *n* **(a)** *Rel, Hist* pectoral *m* **(b)** *Anat* (muscle *m*) pectoral *m*
peculate ['pekjʊleɪt] **1** *vi* détourner des fonds **2** *vt* (*funds*) détourner
peculation [pekjʊ'leɪʃən] *n* malversation *f*
peculiar [pɪ'kju:lɪər] *adj* **(a)** (*strange*) bizarre, curieux; (*eccentric*) original; **well, that's p.** tiens, c'est bizarre *ou* curieux!, voilà qui est singulier!; **he/she is a little p.** il/elle est un peu bizarre **(b)** (*characteristic*) particulier; **her singing style is p. to her** son style de chant lui est particulier; **this species is p. to Scandinavia** cette espèce n'existe qu'en Scandinavie **(c)** (*special*) spécial, particulier; **of p. interest** d'un intérêt tout particulier
peculiarity [pɪkju:lɪ'ærɪtɪ] *n* **(a)** (*strangeness*) bizarrerie *f*, singularité *f*; (*eccentricity*) originalité *f*; **one of her little peculiarities** une de ses petites manies **(b)** (*distinctive feature*) particularité *f*
peculiarly [pɪ'kju:lɪəlɪ] *adv* **(a)** (*strangely*) singulièrement **(b)** (*specially*) particulièrement
pecuniary [pɪ'kju:nɪərɪ] *adj Fml* pécuniaire; **p. difficulties** embarras *mpl* pécuniaires *ou* financiers, ennuis *mpl* d'argent
▶ **ped down** [ped] *vi TV* abaisser, baisser
▶ **ped up** *vi TV* monter, élever
pedagogic(al) [pedə'gɒdʒɪk, -ɪk(ə)l] *adj* pédagogique
pedagogue ['pedəgɒg] *n* pédagogue *m*, *Pej* pédant, -ante
pedagogy ['pedəgɒdʒɪ] *n* pédagogie *f*
pedal¹ ['ped(ə)l] *n* (*of bicycle, car, machine, musical instrument etc*) pédale *f*; **soft p.** (*of piano*) pédale douce, sourdine *f*; **loud p.** pédale forte; **p. keyboard** (*of organ*) pédalier *m*; *Mus* **p. (note)** (note *f* de) pédale; *Aut* **p. pressure** pression *f* sur la pédale; **p. pushers** (*trousers*) (pantalon *m*) corsaire *m*
pedal² (-ll-, *US* -l-) **1** *vi* **(a)** *Cycling etc* pédaler; **she had pedalled around France when she was a teenager** adolescente, elle avait parcouru la France à vélo; **he pedalled off** il est parti (à vélo) **(b)** *Mus* (*in playing organ*) jouer sur le pédalier; (*in playing piano*) mettre la pédale **2** *vt* (*bicycle*) appuyer sur les pédales de; **to p. a bicycle around Europe** parcourir l'Europe à vélo *ou* à bicyclette; **he pedalled his bike up the hill** il a pédalé jusqu'en haut de la côte sur son vélo
pedal³ *adj Anat* (*relating to foot*) pédieux
pedal bin *n* poubelle *f* à pédale
pedal boat *n* pédalo *m*
pedal car *n* voiture *f* à pédales
pedal-operated ['ped(ə)lɒpəreɪtɪd] *adj MecE etc* commandé par pédale(s)
pedant ['pedənt] *n Pej* pédant, -ante; **don't be such a p.!** ne sois pas aussi pédant!

pedantic [pɪˈdæntɪk] *adj* pédant
pedantically [pɪˈdæntɪklɪ] *adv* avec pédantisme; (*to say*) d'un ton pédant
pedantry [ˈpedəntrɪ] *n* pédantisme *m*, pédanterie *f*
peddle [ˈped(ə)l] **1** *vi* faire du colportage; (*with drugs*) faire du trafic de drogues **2** *vt* (*goods, Fig ideas, theories*) colporter; **to p. drugs** faire du trafic de drogues
peddler [ˈpedlər] *n* **(a)** **(drug) p.** trafiquant, -ante de drogues **(b)** *US* = **pedlar**
pederast [ˈpedəræst, ˈpiː-] *n* pédéraste *m*
pederasty [ˈpedəræstɪ, ˈpiː-] *n* pédérastie *f*
pedestal [ˈpedɪst(ə)l] *n Archit, Art etc* piédestal *m*, *pl* -aux; *Fig* **to put sb on a p.** mettre qn sur un piédestal; **p. table** guéridon *m*; **p. washbasin** lavabo-colonne *m*
pedestrian [pɪˈdestrɪən] **1** *adj* (*on foot*) pédestre; *Fig* (*style etc*) prosaïque, terre à terre *inv*; (*pace, rhythm*) lourd **2** *n* piéton *m*; *Br* **p. crossing** passage *m* pour piétons, passage clouté; **p. precinct** zone *f* piétonnière
pedestrian-controlled crossing *n* passage *m* piéton à bouton d'appel
pedestrianization [pɪdestrɪənaɪˈzeɪʃən] *n* (*of area*) aménagement *m* en zone piétonnière; **in favour of p.** en faveur de l'aménagement de zones piétonnières
pedestrianize [pɪˈdestrɪənaɪz] *vt* (*road*) aménager en zone piétonnière
pediatric, pediatrician *etc US* = **paediatric, paediatrician** *etc*
pedicure[1] [ˈpedɪkjʊər] *n* **(a)** (*activity*) soins *mpl* des pieds, *Spec* pédicurie *f*; **to have a p.** se faire soigner les pieds, aller chez le/la pédicure **(b)** (*person*) pédicure *mf*
pedicure[2] *vt* (*feet*) soigner
pedigree [ˈpedɪgriː] **1** *n* **(a)** (*of dog etc*) pedigree *m*; **to have a p.** (*of dog*) être un chien de race, avoir un pedigree **(b)** (*background*) passé *m*, antécédents *mpl*; **she had an impeccable political p.** ses antécédents politiques étaient irréprochables **(c)** (*person's ancestry*) ascendance *f*, généalogie *f* **(d)** (*genealogical table*) arbre *m* généalogique **2** *adj* (*dog etc*) de (pure) race; (*person*) de bonne lignée
pediment [ˈpedɪmənt] *n Archit* fronton *m*
pedlar [ˈpedlər] *n* colporteur *m*, marchand *m* ambulant
pedology *US* = **paedology**
pedometer [pɪˈdɒmɪtər] *n* podomètre *m*
pedophile, pedophilia *US* = **paedophile, paedophilia**
pee[1] [piː] *n F* pipi *m*, *Sl* pisse *f*; **to go and have a p.** aller faire pipi, *Sl* aller pisser; **he was desperate for a p.** il avait énormément envie de faire pipi *ou Sl* de pisser; **cat's p.** pipi *ou Sl* pisse de chat
pee[2] *vi F* faire pipi, *Sl* pisser
peek[1] [piːk] *n* regard *m* furtif, coup *m* d'œil (furtif); **to take** *or* **have a p. (at sth/sb)** jeter un coup d'œil (furtif) (à *ou* sur qch/qn)
peek[2] *vi* jeter un regard *ou* un coup d'œil furtif **(at** sur), risquer un coup d'œil; **no peeking!** on ne regarde pas!
peekaboo [ˈpiːkəbuː] **1** *int* coucou! **2** *adj US* (*blouse etc*) (*see-through*) transparent; (*with holes*) avec *ou* en broderie(s) ajourée(s)
peel[1] [piːl] *n* (*of apple etc*) pelure *f*, épluchure *f*; (*of potato etc*) épluchure; (*of orange, lemon*) écorce *f*; *Culin* zeste *m*
peel[2] **1** *vt* (*fruit*) peler, éplucher; (*potatoes etc*) éplucher; (*oak, almonds*) décortiquer; **to p. the bark/skin** enlever l'écorce/la peau; **to keep one's eyes peeled** ouvrir l'œil; **we were all keeping our eyes peeled for a pub** nous guettions tous un pub, nous étions tous à l'affût d'un pub **2** *vi* (*of paint etc*) s'écailler; (*of nose, back etc*) peler; *Med* se desquamer; (*of bark*) se détacher; (*of wall*) se décrépir; **you're peeling** tu pèles; **the skin on his back was starting to p.** son dos commençait à peler
▶ **peel off 1** *vtsep* (*rind, skin, shirt, vest*) enlever; **to p. off one's clothes** se déshabiller **2** *vi* **(a)** (*become detached*) (*of paint, nail varnish etc*) s'écailler; (*of skin*) se détacher; *Med* se desquamer; *Av* se détacher de la formation; **the skin on my nose is peeling off** mon nez pèle **(b)** *F* (*undress*) se déshabiller
peeler [ˈpiːlər] *n* **(a)** *Culin* (*device*) éplucheur *m*; **potato p.** économe *m* **(b)** *Br Arch* (*policeman*) agent *m* de police
peeling [ˈpiːlɪŋ] **1** *n* **(a)** *Med* (*of skin*) desquamation *f* **(b)** **peelings** (*of potato etc*) épluchures *fpl* **2** *adj* (*nose, back etc*) qui pèle/pelait
peep[1] [piːp] *n* **(a)** (*furtive glance*) coup *m* d'œil furtif; **to have** *or* **take a p. at sth** jeter un regard furtif sur qch; **to get a p. at sth** entrevoir qch **(b)** (*of light*) rayon *m*
peep[2] *vi* (*glance furtively*) jeter un coup d'œil; **to p. at sb/sth** regarder qn/qch à la dérobée, jeter un coup d'œil furtif sur qn/qch; **to p. through the door** jeter un coup d'œil (furtif) par la porte; **I saw you peeping through the keyhole** je vous ai vu regarder par le trou de la serrure; **someone was peeping at her from behind the curtains** quelqu'un l'observait, caché derrière les rideaux; **no peeping!** on ne regarde pas!; **a Peeping Tom** un voyeur
peep[3] *n* (*sound*) (*of bird*) pépiement *m*, piaulement *m*; (*of mouse*) cri *m*; *F* **if I hear so much as a p. out of you** si tu fais le moindre bruit; *F* **we haven't heard a p. from him for months** ça fait des mois qu'il n'a pas donné le moindre signe de vie
peep[4] *vi* (*of bird*) pépier, piauler; (*of mouse*) crier
▶ **peep out** *vi* (*be visible*) se laisser entrevoir, se montrer; (*of flower*) percer, pointer; **his feet were peeping out from beneath the curtains** ses pieds dépassaient de derrière les rideaux; **her big toe was peeping out through a hole in her sock** son gros doigt de pied pointait par un trou de sa chaussette
peep-bo [ˈpiːpbəʊ] **1** *int* coucou! **2** *n* **to play (at) p.** jouer à cache-cache (*avec un enfant*)
peepers [ˈpiːpəz] *n Sl* (*eyes*) mirettes *fpl*
peephole [ˈpiːphəʊl] *n* **(a)** (*in door*) judas *m* **(b)** *MecE etc* (trou *m* de) regard *m*
peepshow [ˈpiːpʃəʊ] *n* (*pictures*) vues *fpl* stéréoscopiques; (*erotic, with live model*) peepshow *m*
peer[1] [pɪər] *n* **(a)** (*equal*) pair *m*; **you will not find his p.** vous ne trouverez pas son pareil; **he is without p.** il n'a pas son pareil; **she does not have many peers** peu l'égalent; *Jur* **a jury of one's peers** un jury de ses pairs **(b)** (*noble*) pair *m*; *Br* **p. of the realm** pair du Royaume-Uni; *Br* **life p.** pair à vie
peer[2] *vi* **to p. at sb/sth** scruter qn/qch du regard; **he peered at the writing** il fixa son regard sur ce qui était écrit; **he peered (out) into the night** il cherchait à percer l'obscurité; **to p. round the corner** risquer un coup d'œil au coin de la rue; **he was peering through the curtains** il guettait entre les rideaux; **he was peering into the bottom of his glass** il scrutait le fond de son verre; **several pairs of eyes were peering at her** plusieurs paires d'yeux étaient braquées sur elle
peerage [ˈpɪərɪdʒ] *n* **(a)** (*noble title, rank*) pairie *f*; **life p.** pairie à vie; **to confer a p. on sb, to raise sb to the p.** élever qn à la pairie **(b)** (*no pl*) **the p.** (*peers*) les pairs *mpl* **(c)** (*book*) (almanach *m*) nobiliaire *m*
peeress [ˈpɪərɪs] *n* pairesse *f*
peer group *n* pairs *mpl*
peerless [ˈpɪəlɪs] *adj Lit* sans pareil, sans égal, hors pair
peer pressure *n* influence *f* des pairs
peeve [piːv] *vt F* mettre en boule, irriter; **to be peeved** être fâché *ou* irrité; **to be peeved at sb for not doing sth** être fâché contre qn parce qu'il n'a pas fait qch; **I was peeved at his behaviour/the decision** son comportement/cette décision m'a mis en boule *ou* m'a irrité
peevish [ˈpiːvɪʃ] *adj* maussade, irritable; (*response*) maussade; (*child*) grognon
peevishly [ˈpiːvɪʃlɪ] *adv* (*to say*) avec mauvaise humeur, d'un ton irrité; (*to respond*) d'un air maussade
peevishness [ˈpiːvɪʃnɪs] *n* (*of person*) maussaderie *f*, mauvaise humeur *f*; (*of response, behaviour*) maussaderie
peewit [ˈpiːwɪt] *n* (*bird*) vanneau *m* (huppé)
peg[1] [peg] *n* **(a)** (*pin, bolt*) (*wooden*) cheville *f*; (*metal*) fiche *f*; (*of barrel*) fausset *m*, fosset *m*; *MecE* clavette *f*, goupille *f*; (*for tent*) piquet *m*; *Mus* (*on violin*) cheville; *Br* **(clothes) p.** pince *f* à linge; **(hat** *or* **coat) p.** patère *f*; *esp Br Com* **a suit off the p.** un costume de confection; **off the p. clothing** prêt-à-porter *m*; *Fig* **to take sb down a p. (or two)** remettre qn à sa place; **that's a p. to hang a grievance on** voilà un prétexte de plainte; **we can use this as a p. to hang our story on** nous pouvons centrer notre article là-dessus; *F* **p. leg** (*wooden leg*) jambe *f* de bois, pilon *m*; (*person*) = personne *f* qui a une jambe de bois
(b) *Br* (*of whisky etc*) doigt *m*
peg[2] *vt* **(-gg-)** **(a)** (*structure, joint*) cheviller; **to p. sth in place** cheviller qch; **to p. clothes on the line** accrocher du linge sur la corde (*avec des pinces à linge*) **(b)** *St Exch, Fin* (*prices*) (*fix*) fixer; (*stabilize*) stabiliser; **to p. sth to the rate of inflation** indexer qch sur le taux de l'inflation
▶ **peg away** *vi F* (*work hard*) bosser **(at sth** à qch); **to p. away at one's algebra** piocher *ou* bûcher son algèbre
▶ **peg down** *vtsep* (*fix*) (*net etc*) fixer avec des piquets; *Fig* **to p. sb down to a price** obliger qn à s'engager sur un prix
▶ **peg out 1** *vtsep* **(a)** (*mark with pegs*) (*plot of land*) piqueter, jalonner, borner; (*line*) jalonner **(b)** (*hang*) **to p. out clothes on the line** accrocher du linge sur la corde (*avec des pinces à linge*) **2** *vi* **(a)** *Sl* (*die*) casser sa pipe **(b)** (*in croquet*) toucher le piquet final (et se retirer de la partie)
pegboard [ˈpegbɔːd] *n* **(a)** (*for hanging things*) panneau *m* alvéolé **(b)** (*for game*) table *f* à trous

pegging [ˈpegɪŋ] *n* **(a)** *St Exch, Fin* (*of prices etc*) (*fixing*) fixation *f*; (*stabilizing*) stabilisation *f*; (*to rate of inflation etc*) indexation *f* **(b)** *Br Sp, Fig* **it's level p.** ils sont à égalité
PEI [pi:i:ˈaɪ] *n Geog* (*abbr* **Prince Edward Island**) IPE *f*
pejorative [pɪˈdʒɒrətɪv] **1** *adj* péjoratif **2** *n* (mot *m*) péjoratif *m*
pejoratively [pɪˈdʒɒrətɪvlɪ] *adv* péjorativement
peke [pi:k] *n F* (chien *m*) pékinois *m*
Pekinese [pi:kɪˈni:z] **1** *adj* pékinois **2** *n* **(a)** (*person*) Pékinois, -oise **(b)** (*dog*) (chien *m*) pékinois *m*
Peking [pi:ˈkɪŋ] *n* Pékin *m*
Pekingese [pi:kɪŋˈi:z] *adj, n* = **Pekinese**
pelagic [pɪˈlædʒɪk] *adj* pélagique
pelargonium [peləˈgəʊnɪəm] *n* (*plant*) pélargonium *m*
pelican [ˈpelɪkən] *n* (*bird*) pélican *m*
pelican crossing *n Br* passage *m* clouté avec feux opérés par les piétons
pellagra [peˈlægrə, -ˈleɪ-] *n Med* pellagre *f*
pellet [ˈpelɪt] *n* (*of paper, bread, clay etc*) boulette *f*; (*of dung*) bille *f*; (*in shotgun cartridge*) grain *m* de plomb; *Pharm* pilule *f*, grain; *Orn* (*regurgitated food of owl etc*) boulette (d'aliments regurgités), bol *m* alimentaire; *Metal, Ch* boulette
pell-mell [ˈpelˈmel] *adv* pêle-mêle; (*to run*) à la débandade
pellucid [peˈlu:sɪd] *adj Lit* pellucide, transparent; *Fig* (*mind etc*) lucide; (*style*) clair, limpide
pelmet [ˈpelmɪt] *n* lambrequin *m*
Peloponnese (the) [ðəpeləpəˈni:s] *n* le Péloponnèse
Peloponnesian [peləpəˈni:sɪən] *adj* péloponnésien, du Péloponnèse
pelota [pəˈlɒtə] *n* (*game*) pelote *f* basque
pelt[1] [pelt] *n* **(a)** (*skin*) (*of sheep, goat*) peau *f*, fourrure *f* **(b)** (*in tanning*) (*with hair on*) peau *f* verte; (*without hair*) peau en tripe
pelt[2] *n* **(at) full p.** (*to run, flee*) à toute vitesse, ventre à terre
pelt[3] **1** *vt* **to p. sb with stones/snowballs** bombarder qn de pierres/boules de neige; **he pelted abuse at them** il les a criblés d'injures; **to p. sb with criticism** mitrailler *ou* accabler qn de critiques

2 *vi* **(a)** (*of rain etc*) tomber à verse; **it was pelting with rain** la pluie tombait à verse, il pleuvait à verse; **pelting rain** pluie battante

(b) (*go fast*) aller à toute vitesse *ou* à toute allure, *F* foncer; **he came pelting round the corner** il a débouché du coin à toute allure; **the kids pelted off down the street** les gosses ont descendu la rue à toute allure *ou* ventre à terre; **he pelted upstairs** il est monté comme une flèche *ou* ventre à terre; **she's really pelting through her work** elle abat son travail à toute allure; **he pelted through the exam** il a fait l'examen à toute allure *ou* à toute vitesse
▶ **pelt down** *vi* (*of rain etc*) tomber à verse; **the rain** *or* **it was pelting down** la pluie tombait à verse, il pleuvait à verse
pelvic [ˈpelvɪk] *adj Anat* pelvien; **p. bone** os *m* du bassin; **p. fins** pelviennes *fpl*; **p. floor** plancher *m* pelvien; **p. girdle** ceinture *f* pelvienne; **p. inflammatory disease** salpingite *f* aiguë *ou* chronique
pelvis [ˈpelvɪs] *n Anat* **(a)** bassin *m*, pelvis *m* **(b)** (*of kidney*) bassinet *m*
pen[1] [pen] *n* stylo *m*; **fountain p.** stylo à plume, stylo-plume *m*; **ball(point) p.** stylo à bille, stylo-bille *m*; **felt(-tip) p.** (crayon *m ou* stylo) feutre *m*; **drawing** *or* **mapping p.** plume *f* à dessin; **p.(-and-ink) drawing** dessin *m* à la plume *ou* à l'encre; **stroke of the p.** trait *m* de plume; **to put p. to paper** prendre la plume; **to live by one's p.** vivre de sa plume; *Prov* **the p. is mightier than the sword** la plume blesse souvent plus que l'épée; *Comptr* **p. plotter** traceur *m* à plumes
pen[2] *vt* (**-nn-**) (*letter, article etc*) écrire, rédiger
pen[3] *n* **(a)** (*for sheep etc*) parc *m*, enclos *m*; (*for bulls*) toril *m*; (*for pigs*) porcherie *f* **(b)** *Naut* (*for submarine*) abri *m* **(c)** *Am Sl* (*penitentiary*) tôle *f*, taule *f*, trou *m*; **in the p.** en tôle *ou* taule, au trou; **ten years in the p.** dix ans de tôle *ou* taule
pen[4] *vt* (**-nn-**, *Lit* **pent**) (*sheep etc*) parquer
pen[5] *n* (*female swan*) cygne *m* femelle
▶ **pen in, pen up** *vtsep* (*sheep etc*) parquer; **we were penned up in the room for weeks** nous sommes restés parqués dans la pièce pendant des semaines; **we spent the week penned up in a caravan** nous avons passé toute la semaine enfermés dans une caravane
penal [ˈpi:n(ə)l] *adj Jur* (*laws, code*) pénal; (*offence*) qui comporte *ou* entraîne une pénalité; **p. colony** *or* **settlement** colonie *f* pénitentiaire; **p. servitude** travaux *mpl* forcés
penalization [pi:nəlaɪˈzeɪʃən] *n* infliction *f* d'une peine (**of sb** à qn); *Sp* pénalisation *f*
penalize [ˈpi:nəlaɪz] *vt* **(a)** (*impose a penalty on*) (*person*) sanctionner; *Sp* (*competitor, player*) pénaliser **(b)** (*attach a penalty to*) (*crime*) attacher une peine à **(c)** (*disadvantage*) désavantager, pénaliser; **to p. sb for doing sth** désavantager *ou* pénaliser qn parce qu'il a fait qch; **this penalizes those living in the country** ceci défavorise *ou* désavantage les gens qui habitent à la campagne
penalty [ˈpenəltɪ] *n* **(a)** (*punishment*) peine *f*, pénalité *f*; *Com* (*for late delivery etc*) amende *f*; *Admin* sanction *f* (pénale); **to impose penalties** prendre des sanctions; **on** *or* **upon** *or* **under p. of death** sous peine de mort; **the p. for this is death/excommunication** la peine encourue pour ce crime est la mort/l'excommunication; **to pay the p. of one's foolishness** subir les conséquences *ou* être puni de sa sottise; **one of the penalties of fame/wealth** un des désavantages dont la gloire/la richesse s'accompagne; **to pay the p. of fame** payer la rançon de la gloire; **p. interest** pénalité de retard, intérêts *mpl* moratoires

(b) *Sp* pénalisation *f*, pénalité *f*
penalty area *n Fb* surface *f* de réparation
penalty box *n* **(a)** *Fb* surface *f* de réparation **(b)** (*in ice hockey*) banc *m* de pénalité
penalty clause *n* clause *f* pénale
penalty kick *n Fb* penalty *m*, *pl* penalties; *Rugby* coup *m* de pied de pénalité
penalty shootout *n Fb* épreuve *f* des penalties
penalty spot *n Fb* point *m* de réparation
penalty stroke *n Golf* coup *m* d'amende
penalty throw *n* penalty *m*, *pl* penalties
penance [ˈpenəns] *n Rel* pénitence *f*; **to do p.** faire pénitence (**for** de, pour); **to do sth as a p.** faire qch par pénitence
pence [pens] *see* **penny**
pencil [ˈpens(ə)l] *n* **(a)** crayon *m*; **to mark/write sth in p.** *or* **with a p.** marquer/écrire qch au crayon; **drawing in p., p. drawing** (dessin *m* au) crayon, crayonnage *m*; **p. lead** mine *f* de crayon; **p. mark** trait *m ou* marque *f* de *ou* au crayon; **p. sketch** croquis *m* (au crayon) **(b)** *Geom* (*of curves etc*) faisceau *m*; *Opt* **p. of light rays** faisceau de lumière
pencil[2] *vt* (**-ll-**, *US* **-l-**) (*mark with a pencil*) marquer au crayon; (*draw, sketch in pencil*) dessiner/esquisser au crayon, crayonner; (*write*) (*note*) écrire au crayon, crayonner; **to p. one's eyebrows** se faire les sourcils (au crayon); **pencilled eyebrows** sourcils *mpl* dessinés au crayon
▶ **pencil in** *vtsep* (*write*) écrire au crayon; **the date has been pencilled in** on a fixé provisoirement la date; **p. me in for Friday** inscrivez-moi provisoirement pour vendredi; *Fig* en principe, vous pouvez compter sur moi vendredi
pencil case *n* plumier *m*
pencil sharpener *n* taille-crayon(s) *m inv*
pendant [ˈpendənt] *n* **(a)** (*necklace*) pendentif *m* **(b)** (*ornamental piece*) (*of necklace*) pendentif *m*; (*on bracelet*) breloque *f*; (*of chandelier*) pendeloque *f*
pending [ˈpendɪŋ] **1** *adj* (*trial*) pendant, en instance; (*negotiations*) en cours; *Admin, Com* (*documents*) en souffrance, en attente; **p. tray** corbeille *f* pour les documents en attente **2** *prep* en attendant
pendulous [ˈpendjʊləs] *adj* (*breasts, lip, ear etc*) pendant
pendulum [ˈpendjʊləm] *n Phys* pendule *m*; (*in clockmaking*) balancier *m*, pendule; **p. ball** *or* **bob** lentille *f* de pendule *ou* de balancier; **p. clock** horloge *f* à pendule *ou* à balancier
penetrable [ˈpenɪtrəb(ə)l] *adj* **(a)** (*material, defences*) pénétrable; **easily p.** facile à pénétrer **(b)** (*prose etc*) **barely p.** difficilement compréhensible
penetrate [ˈpenɪtreɪt] **1** *vt* pénétrer; **darkness that the eye could not p.** ténèbres que l'œil ne pouvait percer; **to p. sb's mind** voir clair dans l'esprit de qn **2** *vi* pénétrer; (*of ideas, beliefs*) s'implanter; **the water is penetrating everywhere** l'eau pénètre *ou* s'introduit partout; **to p. through sth** passer à travers qch; **to p. into a forest** pénétrer dans une forêt; **the custom has not penetrated to this part of the country** cette coutume n'est pas parvenue jusqu'à cette partie du pays; **it hasn't penetrated** (*hasn't been understood*) ça n'a pas fait le tour, ça n'est pas rentré
penetrating [ˈpenɪtreɪtɪŋ] *adj* (*wind, cold*) pénétrant; (*sound, voice, scream*) perçant; (*bullet, shell*) perforant; (*mind, analysis*) pénétrant; **to have a p. eye** avoir des yeux perçants; **a p. stare** un regard pénétrant *ou* perçant; **p. oil** dégrippant *m*
penetration [penɪˈtreɪʃən] *n* pénétration *f*; (*of ideas, customs*) implantation *f*
penetrative [ˈpenɪtrətɪv] *adj* (*sex*) avec pénétration; (*questioning*) approfondi
pen friend *n* correspondant, -ante
penguin [ˈpeŋgwɪn] *n* manchot *m*, gorfou *m*, *F* pingouin *m*; *F Hum* **p. suit** queue *f* de pie
penholder [ˈpenhəʊldər] *n* porte-plume *m inv*
penicillin [penɪˈsɪlɪn] *n* pénicilline *f*
peninsula [pɪˈnɪnsjʊlə] *n* péninsule *f*, presqu'île *f*
peninsular [pɪˈnɪnsjʊlər] *adj* péninsulaire

penis, *pl* **-nes** ['pi:nɪs, -ni:z] *n Anat* pénis *m*, verge *f*; *Psy* **p. envy** envie *f* du pénis
penitence ['penɪtəns] *n* pénitence *f*, repentir *m*; **to perform p.** faire pénitence; **to show (one's) p. for one's actions** se repentir *ou* faire pénitence de ses actions; **to be without p.** ne pas se repentir
penitent ['penɪtənt] **1** *adj* pénitent, repentant; **to be** *or* **feel p.** se repentir, faire pénitence **2** *n* pénitent, -ente
penitential [penɪ'tenʃəl] **1** *adj* pénitentiel **2** *n* (*book*) pénitentiel *m*
penitentiary [penɪ'tenʃərɪ] **1** *n* **(a)** *Am* (*prison*) pénitencier *m* **(b)** *Cathol* (*person*) pénitencier *m*; (*tribunal*) pénitencerie *f* **2** *adj Am* (*crime*) puni de réclusion dans un pénitencier *ou* une centrale
penitently ['penɪtəntlɪ] *adv* d'un air contrit; (*to say etc*) d'un ton contrit; (*to act, behave*) avec contrition
penknife ['pennaɪf] *n* canif *m*
penmanship ['penmənʃɪp] *n* (*calligraphy*) calligraphie *f*
Penn(a) *abbr* **Pennsylvania**
pen name *n* nom *m* de plume; (*of journalist*) nom de guerre
pennant ['penənt] *n* flamme *f*, banderole *f*; *Naut* flamme, guidon *m*
penniless ['penɪlɪs] *adj* sans le sou; **to be p.** être sans le sou, ne pas avoir le sou; **to leave sb p.** laisser qn sans le sou
Pennines (the) [ðə'penaɪnz] *npl* la chaîne Pennine, les Pennines *fpl*
pennon ['penən] *n* flamme *f*, banderole *f*
Pennsylvania [pensɪl'veɪmɪə] *n* Pennsylvanie *f*
penny ['penɪ] *n* [ⓘA13,3,c] **(a)** *Br* (*coin*) (*pl usu* **pennies**) penny *m*, *pl* pennies; **they haven't a p.** (**to their name** *or Old-fashioned* **to bless themselves with**) ils sont sans le sou *ou* sans un sou vaillant; **pennies from heaven** une aubaine; *Prov* **take care of the pennies and the pounds will take care of themselves** les petits ruisseaux font les grandes rivières; **to count every p.** compter ses sous; **it was worth every p.** je n'ai/nous n'avons/*etc* pas regretté le prix que je l'ai/nous l'avons/*etc* payé; **you'd better start saving (up) your pennies** tu ferais mieux de commencer à mettre de l'argent de côté; **not a p. more** pas un sou de plus; *F* **the p.'s dropped** (*I understand now*) j'y suis, ça y est; (*he's understood*) il y est, ça y est
(b) *Br* (*value*) (*pl* **pence** [pens]) penny *m*, *pl* pence; **I paid 60 pence for it** je l'ai payé 60 pence; **a ten/fifty pence piece** une pièce de dix/cinquante pence; **to buy ten pence worth of sweets** acheter pour dix pence de bonbons; **(new) p.** = nouveau penny; **(old) p.** (*before 1971*) = ancien penny; *Fig* **they're two** *or* **ten a p. nowadays** c'est monnaie courante à l'heure actuelle; **a p. for your thoughts** *or* **for them** à quoi rêvez-vous *ou* pensez-vous?; *Prov* **in for a p. in for a pound** quand le vin est tiré il faut le boire; *esp Br F* **a bad p.** (*rogue, worthless person*) bon *m* à rien, bonne *f* à rien; **it didn't cost them a p.** ça ne leur a pas coûté un centime; **that'll cost a p. or two** cela va coûter de l'argent; **to earn** *or* **turn an honest p.** gagner honnêtement sa vie
(c) *US, Can* (*cent*) cent *m*
penny black *n Philat* = premier timbre-poste *m* britannique
penny-dreadful *n Old-fashioned F* roman *m* à deux sous *ou* à sensation
penny farthing *n* (*bicycle*) vélocipède *m*
penny-in-the-slot *adj Old-fashioned* (*machine*) à sous
penny-pincher ['penɪpɪntʃər] *n* pingre *mf*, radin *m*
penny-pinching ['penɪpɪntʃɪŋ] **1** *adj* (*person*) radin, pingre, qui fait des économies de bouts de chandelle; (*action, step*) mesquin; (*lifestyle, measures*) de lésine, d'économie de bouts de chandelle **2** *n* pingrerie *f* (**with, on** sur)
penny whistle *n Mus* flûtiau *m*
penny-wise *adj Prov* **to be p. and pound-foolish** faire des économies de bouts de chandelle d'un côté et avoir les poches trouées de l'autre
pennyworth ['penɪwɜ:θ] *n* **to buy a p. of sweets** acheter pour un penny de bonbons; *Fig* **not a p.** rien du tout
penology [pi:'nɒlədʒɪ] *n* pénologie *f*
pen pal *n F* correspondant, -ante
penpusher ['penpʊʃər] *n F Pej* gratte-papier *m inv*, scribouillard, -arde
penpushing ['penpʊʃɪŋ] *F Pej* **1** *adj* (*job etc*) de gratte-papier **2** *n* paperasse *f*, paperasserie *f*
pension¹ *n* **(a)** ['penʃən] (*payment*) retraite *f*, pension *f*; **government** *or Br* **state p.** pension sur l'État; **to be on a p.** (*of elderly person*) vivre de sa retraite *ou* d'une pension; **to retire on a p.** prendre sa retraite; (**retirement** *or* **old age**) **p.** (pension de) retraite; **p. contribution** cotisation *f* vieillesse **(b)** ['pɒnsɪɒn] (*hotel*) pension *f* de famille; **en p.** (*at hotel*) en pension
▸ **pension off** *vtsep* mettre à la retraite; *F* (*sth*) mettre au rebut
pensionable ['penʃənəb(ə)l] *adj* (*person*) qui a droit à une pension *ou* à sa retraite; (*injury, job etc*) qui donne droit à une pension; **p. age** âge *m* de départ en retraite
pension book *n* livret *m* de retraite (*permettant de toucher sa pension*)
pensioner ['penʃənər] *n* pensionné, -ée; (**old-age**) **p.** retraité, -ée
pension fund *n* (*money*) capital *m* retraite; (*company*) caisse *f* de retraite
pension plan *n* régime *m* de retraite
pension scheme *n* caisse *f* de retraite
pensive ['pensɪv] *adj* pensif; (*music, silence*) méditatif
pensively ['pensɪvlɪ] *adv* pensivement, d'un air pensif
pent [pent] *see* **pen⁴**
pentagon ['pentəgən] *n Geom* pentagone *m*; *US Mil* **the P.** le Pentagone
pentagonal [pen'tægən(ə)l] *adj* pentagonal
pentameter [pen'tæmɪtər] *n* (*in poetry*) pentamètre *m*
Pentateuch (the) [ðə'pentətju:k] *n Bible* le Pentateuque
pentathlete [pen'tæθli:t] *n Sp* pentathlonien, -ienne
pentathlon [pen'tæθlən] *n Sp* pentathlon *m*
Pentecost ['pentɪkɒst] *n Rel* Pentecôte *f*
pentecostal [pentɪ'kɒst(ə)l] *adj Rel* de la Pentecôte; **the P. Church** l'église pentecôtiste
penthouse ['penthaʊs] *n* **(a)** (*apartment*) = appartement *m* de standing au dernier étage d'un immeuble; **p. suite** (*apartment*) = suite *f* grand luxe au dernier étage d'un hôtel **(b)** (*shed*) appentis *m*
pent-up *adj* (*emotion, frustation, desire*) refoulé; (*energy, rage*) contenu
penultimate [pe'nʌltɪmɪt] *adj* pénultième, avant-dernier
penumbra [pe'nʌmbrə] *n* pénombre *f*
penurious [pe'njʊərɪəs] *adj Fml* (*poor*) indigent; **reduced to a p. condition** réduit à l'indigence
penury ['penjʊrɪ] *n* **(a)** (*poverty*) indigence *f* **(b)** (*dearth*) manque *m* (**of** de)
peony ['pi:ənɪ] *n* (*plant*) pivoine *f*
people¹ ['pi:p(ə)l] *n* [ⓘA11,g,iii] (*with pl verb*) **(a)** gens *mpl*; **there were five p. in the room** il y avait cinq personnes dans la pièce; **young p.** les jeunes gens; **old p.** les personnes *fpl* agées, *F* les vieux *mpl*; **old p.'s home** maison *f* de retraite pour personnes âgées; **there were not many p.** il n'y avait pas beaucoup de gens *ou* de monde; **most p.** la plupart des gens; **rich p.** les (gens) riches; **homeless p.** les sans-abris *mpl*; **blind/deaf p.** les aveugles *mpl*/les sourds *mpl*; **stop annoying p.** arrête d'embêter le monde; **he's one of those p. who …** il est de ceux qui …, c'est un homme qui …; **you of all p. should know better!** tu devrais bien être le dernier/la dernière à faire pareille erreur!; **I met Janet of all p. at the theatre** Janet était bien la dernière personne que je m'attendais à rencontrer au théâtre; **it's a question of knowing the right p.** il faut avoir des relations; **we're having p. to dinner tonight** nous avons des invités *ou* du monde à dîner ce soir; **p. don't like being told they're wrong** les gens n'aiment pas qu'on leur dise qu'ils ont tort; **p. say that …** on dit que …; **she's a p. person** elle est très sociable; **p. meter** (*for viewing figures*) audimètre *m*
(b) (*nation*) peuple *m*, nation *f*; **the French p.** les Français *mpl*; **the Sikhs/Russians are a proud p.** les Sikhs/les Russes sont un peuple fier; **English-speaking peoples** peuples *ou* nations de langue anglaise
(c) (*citizens*) peuple *m*, citoyens *mpl* (*d'un État*); **the common p.** le peuple, *Pej* la populace; **a man of the p.** un homme sorti du peuple; **a king and his p.** un roi et ses sujets *ou* son peuple
(d) (*population*) peuple *m*, habitants *mpl*; **the p. of Paris** les habitants de Paris; **town p.** gens *mpl* de la ville, citadins *mpl*; **country p.** gens de la campagne, campagnards *mpl*
(e) (*employees*) employés, -ées; (*workers*) ouvriers, -ières; **I'll get one of my p. to do it** un de mes employés/ouvriers le fera; **our p. in Moscow** (*representatives*) nos représentants à Moscou; (*compatriots*) nos compatriotes installés à Moscou; **the p. in accounts** les gens de la comptabilité
(f) *Old-fashioned F* (*family*) famille *f*; **how are your p.?** comment va votre famille?
people² *vt* peupler (**with** de); **a country peopled by many different races** un pays multiracial
people carrier *n Aut* monospace *m*
people power *n* pouvoir *m* populaire
people's republic *n* république *f* populaire
PEP [pep] *n* (*abbr* **personal equity plan**) PEA *m*
pep [pep] *n F* entrain *m*, allant *m*, fougue *f*; **full of p.** plein d'entrain *ou* d'allant; **p. pill** excitant *m*, stimulant *m*; **p. talk** petit discours *m* d'encouragement
▸ **pep up** *vtsep* (**-pp-**) *F* (*person*) ragaillardir, revigorer; (*dish,*

punch etc) relever; (*presentation, style*) égayer; (*plant*) revigorer; **to p. up a business** remonter une affaire

pepper¹ ['pepər] *n* **(a)** (*spice*) poivre *m*; **p. (plant)** poivrier *m*; **black/white p.** poivre noir *ou* gris/blanc; **p. mill** moulin *m* à poivre; **p. pot** poivrière *f*; **p. steak** steak *m* au poivre **(b)** (*vegetable*) **(sweet) p.** piment *m* doux, poivron *m*; **green/red/yellow p.** poivron vert/rouge/jaune

pepper² *vt* **(a)** (*meat etc*) poivrer **(b)** *Fig* **to p. with bullets** cribler de balles; **peppered with swearwords** pimentée de jurons; **peppered with spelling mistakes** parsemé de fautes d'orthographe

pepper-and-salt *adj* (*hair*) poivre et sel; (*jacket etc*) marengo

peppercorn ['pepəkɔːn] *n* **(a)** grain *m* de poivre **(b)** *Jur* **p. rent** loyer *m* nominal *ou* insignifiant

peppermint ['pepəmɪnt] *n* **(a)** (*plant*) menthe *f* poivrée; (*flavour*) menthe poivrée, peppermint *m* **(b)** (*sweet*) bonbon *m* à la menthe, pastille *f* de menthe

peppery ['pepərɪ] *adj* **(a)** (*dish etc*) poivré **(b)** (*person*) irascible, coléreux, colérique

peppy ['pepɪ] *adj F* (*person*) plein d'entrain *ou* d'allant

pepsin ['pepsɪn] *n Ch, Physiol* pepsine *f*

peptic ['peptɪk] *adj Physiol* peptique; **p. ulcer** ulcère *m* gastro-duodénal

peptone ['peptəʊn] *n Biol, Ch* peptone *f*

Péquiste [peɪ'kiːst] *n Can* (*member, supporter of Parti québécois*) péquiste *mf*

per [pɜːr] *prep Com etc* par; **p. annum** par an; **p. capita** par personne; **the highest p. capita income in Europe** le revenu par habitant le plus élevé d'Europe; **sent p. carrier** envoyé par messagerie; **p. day** par jour; **100 km p. hour** cent kilomètres à l'heure; **ten francs p. kilo** dix francs le kilo; **p. pro signature** signature *f* par procuration; **as p. invoice** suivant facture; **as p. your instructions** conformément à vos instructions; **as p. sample** conformément à l'échantillon; *F* **as p. usual** comme d'habitude

peradventure [pɜːrəd'ventʃər] *adv Arch* (*by chance*) par aventure, par hasard

perambulate [pə'ræmbjʊleɪt] *vt Fml* (*one's garden etc*) parcourir, se promener dans

perambulator [pə'ræmbjʊleɪtər] *n Arch, Fml* landau *m*

p/e ratio [piː'iː] *n Acct* (*abbr* **price/earnings ratio**) ratio *m* cours-bénéfice

perceive [pə'siːv] *vt* **(a)** (*notice*) (*sound, light, smell*) percevoir; (*person*) apercevoir; (*difference*) percevoir, distinguer; (*become aware of*) s'apercevoir de; **he perceived that he was being watched** il s'aperçut qu'on l'observait **(b)** (*understand*) (*the truth etc*) percevoir

perceived [pə'siːvd] *adj Mktg* **p. performance** résultats *mpl* perçus; **p. quality** qualité *f* perçue; **p. risk** risque *m* perçu; **p. service** service *m* perçu; **p. value** valeur *f* perçue; **p. value pricing** tarification *f* en fonction de la valeur perçue

per cent, percent [pə'sent] **1** *n* **10 p.** 10 pour cent; **what p. of people ...?** combien de personnes ...?; (*speaking statistically*) quel pourcentage de personnes ...?; **50 p. of the staff** la moitié du personnel; (*speaking statistically*) 50 pour cent du personnel; **p. sign** signe *m* pour cent **2** *adj* **a 5 p. increase** une augmentation de 5 pour cent; **thirty p. solution** solution à trente pour cent **3** *adv* **a hundred p. efficient** cent pour cent efficace; **I'm ninety p. sure** je suis sûr à quatre-vingt dix pour cent

percentage [pə'sentɪdʒ] *n* **(a)** (*proportion*) pourcentage *m*; **p. of acid/alcohol** teneur *f* en acide/en alcool; **to express sth as a p.** exprimer qch en pourcentage; **what p. of tenants own a car?** combien de locataires ont une voiture?; (*speaking statistically*) quelle est la proportion de locataires qui ont une voiture?; **in a high/tiny p. of cases** dans une vaste/petite proportion des cas **(b)** *Com* pourcentage *m*; **to allow a p. on all transactions** allouer un pourcentage *ou* un tantième sur toutes les opérations; *F* **what's my p.?** quel pourcentage est-ce que je touche?; *Fig F* **there's no p. in it** il n'y a rien à gagner

percentile [pə'sentaɪl] *n* centile *m*

perceptibility [pəseptɪ'bɪlɪtɪ] *n* perceptibilité *f*

perceptible [pə'septɪb(ə)l] *adj* perceptible; *Phil* cognoscible; (*difference*) sensible; **p. to the eye** visible; **p. to the ear** perceptible à l'oreille, audible

perceptibly [pə'septɪblɪ] *adv* sensiblement

perception [pə'sepʃən] *n* **(a)** (*act of perceiving*) perception *f*; **organs of p.** organes *mpl* percepteurs **(b)** (*ability to perceive*) sensibilité *f*; **powers of p.** facultés *fpl* perceptives **(c)** (*understanding*) perception *f*; **the public's p. of the government's role** la façon dont l'opinion publique perçoit le rôle de l'État; **to have different perceptions of a situation** percevoir une situation différemment

perceptive [pə'septɪv] *adj* **(a)** (*perspicacious*) (*person, remark*) perspicace; (*analysis, article*) qui témoigne de clairvoyance **(b)** (*able to perceive*) perceptif; **p. faculties** facultés *mpl* perceptives

perceptively [pə'septɪvlɪ] *adv* (*to write, comment*) avec perspicacité

perceptiveness [pə'septɪvnɪs] *n* (*perspicacity*) perspicacité *f*

perceptoscope [pə'septəskəʊp] *n Mktg* perceptoscope *m*

perch¹ [pɜːtʃ] *n* **(a)** (*for bird*) perchoir *m*; *F* **to knock sb off his/her p.** (*depose*) détrôner qn; (*force to abandon pretensions*) rabattre son caquet à qn **(b)** *Arch* (*measurement*) perche *f*

perch² **1** *vi* (*of bird*) se percher (**on** sur); (*of person*) se percher, se jucher; *Orn* **perching bird** oiseau *m* percheur **2** *vt* **castle perched on a hill** château perché sur (le sommet d')une colline; **with his glasses perched on the end of his nose** avec ses lunettes perchées sur le bout du nez; **to p. oneself on sth** se percher *ou* se jucher sur qch

perch³ *n* (*fish*) perche *f*

perchance [pə'tʃɑːns] *adv Arch, Lit* (*perhaps*) peut-être

percipient [pə'sɪpɪənt] *adj Fml* (*faculty*) percepteur, -trice; (*person*) perspicace

percolate ['pɜːkəleɪt] **1** *vi* (*of liquid*) s'infiltrer; (*of coffee etc*) filtrer, passer; *Fig* (*of information, news*) filtrer **2** *vt* (*of liquid*) (*sand etc*) filtrer à travers, s'infiltrer dans; (*of person, with filter etc*) (*liquid*) filtrer; (*coffee*) passer

percolator ['pɜːkəleɪtər] *n* cafetière *f* à pression; (*for large quantities*) percolateur *m*

percussion [pə'kʌʃən] *n* **(a)** *Mus* **p. instruments** instruments *mpl* de *ou* à percussion; **p. player** percussionniste *mf*; **p. (section)** percussions *fpl* **(b)** (*in firearm*) percussion *f*; **p. gun** fusil *m* à percussion; *Mil* **p. pin** rugueux *m* (de fusée) **(c) p. drill** perceuse *f* à percussion

percussionist [pə'kʌʃənɪst] *n* percussionniste *mf*

percussive [pə'kʌsɪv] *adj* percutant

perdition [pə'dɪʃən] *n Lit* perte *f*, ruine *f*; *Rel* perdition *f*

peregrination [perɪgrɪ'neɪʃən] *n Lit* pérégrination *f*

peregrine falcon ['perɪgrɪn] *n* faucon *m* pèlerin

peremptorily [pə'remptərɪlɪ] *adv* (*to order etc*) péremptoirement, de façon péremptoire

peremptory [pə'remptərɪ] *adj* péremptoire; (*refusal*) absolu, sans appel; (*tone, person*) péremptoire, impérieux; *Jur* **p. writ** mandat *m* de comparaître en personne

perennial [pə'renɪəl] **1** *adj* (*problems, worries*) continuel, perpétuel; (*beauty, hope*) perpétuel, éternel; (*interest*) continuel; (*plant*) vivace **2** *n* plante *f* vivace

perennially [pə'renɪəlɪ] *adv* (*worried, dissatisfied etc*) continuellement, perpétuellement; (*beautiful*) éternellement

perestroika [perə'strɔɪkə] *n* perestroïka *f*

perfect¹ ['pɜːfɪkt] **1** *adj* **(a)** parfait; **a p. example of ...** un exemple parfait de ...; **a p. piece of work** un travail impeccable *ou* parfait; **her behaviour was far from p.** son comportement a beaucoup laissé à désirer; **to be in p. condition** (*of thing*) être impeccable; (*of person*) être en excellente forme; **her English is p.** son anglais est impeccable *ou* parfait; **no one's p.** personne n'est parfait; **p.!** parfait!; **the p. gift** le cadeau idéal; **the p. opportunity** l'occasion idéale *ou* rêvée; **a wine that is the p. accompaniment for fish** un vin qui accompagne parfaitement le poisson; **it was a p. day** (*weather*) il faisait un temps magnifique; (*activities*) nous avons passé une excellente journée

(b) (*complete*) **he's a p. stranger to me** il m'est tout à fait inconnu; **I have a p. right to be here** j'ai parfaitement le droit d'être ici; **it makes p. sense (to me)** cela me semble être une excellente idée; *F* **he's a p. idiot** c'est un parfait imbécile; **he's being a p. nuisance** il est carrément empoisonnant

(c) *Math* (*number, square*) parfait; *Mus* (*intervalle*) juste; (*chord*) parfait; **p. binding** (*in bookbinding*) reliure *f* sans couture; *Mus* **p. cadence** cadence *f* parfaite; **to have p. pitch** avoir l'oreille absolue

(d) *Gram* **the p. tense** le passé composé, le parfait

2 [①**A48-9**,d-e; **B28**,F,3] *n Gram* **the p.** le passé composé, le parfait; **verb in the p.** verbe au passé composé *ou* au parfait

perfect² [pə'fekt] *vt* (*make perfect*) (*method*) perfectionner, parfaire; (*invention, design*) mettre au point

perfectibility [pəfektɪ'bɪlɪtɪ] *n* perfectibilité *f*

perfectible [pə'fektɪb(ə)l] *adj* perfectible

perfection [pə'fekʃən] *n* **(a)** (*state*) perfection *f*; **it was sheer p.** c'était absolument parfait; **p. itself** la perfection même; **to attain p.** toucher *ou* arriver à la perfection; **to do sth to p.** faire qch à la perfection **(b)** (*action*) (*of job etc*) perfectionnement *m*

perfectionism [pə'fekʃənɪz(ə)m] *n* perfectionnisme *m*

perfectionist [pəˈfekʃənɪst] **1** *n* perfectionniste *mf*; **she's such a p.** elle est tellement perfectionniste **2** *adj* perfectionniste

perfective [pəˈfektɪv] *Gram* **1** *adj* perfectif **2** *n* aspect *m* perfectif

perfectly [ˈpɜːfɪktlɪ] *adv* (*symmetrical, flat, harmless*) parfaitement; (*idiotic, meaningless, useless*) complètement; (*to know sth*) à fond; (*to do sth*) à la perfection; **she's p. right** elle a parfaitement raison; **to be p. honest/frank with you** pour être tout à fait honnête/franc avec vous; **I'm p. capable of doing it** je suis tout à fait *ou* parfaitement capable de le faire; **you know p. well** (*what I mean*) tu le sais parfaitement bien *ou* très bien; **it would be p. pointless** cela ne servirait à rien du tout

perfidious [pəˈfɪdɪəs] *adj Lit* perfide; **p. Albion** la perfide Albion

perfidiously [pəˈfɪdɪəslɪ] *adv Lit* perfidement

perfidiousness [pəˈfɪdɪəsnɪs], **perfidy** [ˈpɜːfɪdɪ] *n Lit* perfidie *f*

perforate [ˈpɜːfəreɪt] **1** *vt* (*pierce*) perforer, percer, transpercer; (*metal sheet, ticket*) poinçonner; *Tech* (*paper*) (*with line of holes*) perforer en pointillé **2** *vi Med* (*of ulcer*) déterminer une perforation

perforated [ˈpɜːfəreɪtɪd] *adj* perforé; (*stamps*) dentelé; *Med* (*eardrum*) crevé; **p. ulcer** perforation *f* ulcéreuse; **tear along the p. line** détachez suivant le(s) pointillé(s)

perforation [pɜːfəˈreɪʃən] *n* **(a)** (*action*) perforage *m*, perçage *m*; (*of stamps*) perforage **(b)** (*hole*) perforation *f*, (petit) trou *m*; *Med* perforation; (*for counterfoils etc*) (perforation(s) en) pointillé *m*; (*of postage stamp*) dentelure *f*; **tear along the perforations** déchirer selon le(s) pointillé(s); *Philat* **p. gauge** adontomètre *m*; *Comptr* **p. skip** saut *m* de perforation

perforce [pəˈfɔːs] *adv Lit* forcément

perform [pəˈfɔːm] **1** *vt* **(a)** (*ritual*) célébrer; (*miracle*) faire; (*one's duty*) remplir; (*actions*) effectuer, réaliser; (*task*) accomplir; **to p. a contract** exécuter un contrat; *Surg* **to p. an operation on sb** opérer qn

(b) *Th etc* (*play*) jouer, représenter; (*dance*) exécuter; (*piece of music*) exécuter, jouer; *Fig* (*rôle*) tenir, remplir

2 *vi* **(a)** (*of machine*) marcher, fonctionner; **it performs well in all conditions** (*of vehicle, machine etc*) elle donne de bonnes performances en toutes conditions; **to p. well/badly** (*of student etc*) avoir de bons/mauvais résultats; **how are your shares performing?** comment vos actions se tiennent-elle?; **how does he p. in bed?** comment est-il au lit?; **I couldn't p.** (*sexually*) je n'ai pas pu

(b) *Th etc* (*of theatre company*) donner une/des représentation(s), jouer; (*of actor, instrumentalist, orchestra*) jouer; (*of singer*) chanter; (*of dancer*) danser; (*of mime artist etc*) exécuter un/des numéro(s); **to p. in a play** tenir un rôle *ou* jouer dans une pièce; **he performed well in the role of Claudius** il a bien joué *ou* interprété le rôle de Claudius; **to p. on the flute** jouer de la flûte

performance [pəˈfɔːməns] *n* **(a)** (*action*) (*of contract*) exécution *f*; (*of task, duty*) accomplissement *m*; (*of rite*) célébration *f*

(b) (*quality, ability*), *Sp etc* performance *f*; (*of actor*) interprétation *f*; (*of musician*) exécution *f*, interprétation; (*of dancer*) exécution; (*of pupil, economy, exports*) résultats *mpl*, performances; (*in bed*) performance sexuelle; (*of employee, plane, engine, piece of equipment*) rendement *m*, performance; (*of shares*) rendement; (*at work*) productivité *f*; *Ind* cadence *f* (de travail); *MecE* (*of machine*) fonctionnement *m*, marche *f*; (*of material*) comportement *m*, tenue *f*; **to put up a good p.** (*of team etc*) accomplir une bonne performance; (*in exam, interview, court case*) bien s'en tirer; **a good/poor p. in exams** de bons/mauvais résultats à des examens; *Th, Mus* **she gave a superb p.** son interprétation était fantastique; **p. bonus** prime *f* de rendement *ou* de performance; **p. statistics** statistiques *fpl* de performance

(c) (*event*), *Th etc* (*of play etc*) représentation *f*; (*at cinema*) séance *f*; **first p.** première *f*; **there is no p. tonight** il y a relâche ce soir; *Fig* **he made such a p. about having to wash his hair** il a fait toute une histoire parce qu'il devait se laver les cheveux; *Fig* **what a p.!** quel spectacle!; *Fig* **it's such a p. cooking Christmas dinner!** que c'est compliqué de préparer un dîner de Noël!

performance appraisal *n* (*of employee*) appréciation *f*, évaluation *f*

performance car *n Aut* voiture *f* puissante, voiture haute performance

performance indicator *n* indice *m* de performance

performance-related *adj* (*pay*) calculé en fonction de productivité

performative [pəˈfɔːmətɪv] *adj, n Ling* performatif *m*

performer [pəˈfɔːmər] *n Mus* exécutant, -ante, artiste *mf*, interprète *mf*; *Th* acteur, -trice, artiste *mf*; **he has been a consistent p.** (*in sport*) il a toujours été régulier; **an accomplished p. on the flute** un joueur de flûte accompli; **a good/bad p.** (*student*) un bon/mauvais élève; (*car*) une voiture performante/peu performante

performing [pəˈfɔːmɪŋ] **1** *adj* (*dog, seal*) savant **2** *n* (*of symphony etc*) exécution *f*, interprétation *f*

performing arts *npl* arts *mpl* du spectacle

performing rights *npl Th* droits *mpl* de représentation; *Mus* droits d'exécution

perfume[1] [ˈpɜːfjuːm, *Am* pəˈfjuːm] *n* parfum *m*; **p. counter** (*in shop*) rayon *m* parfumerie

perfume[2] [pəˈfjuːm] *vt* parfumer; **to p. the air** embaumer l'air

perfumed [ˈpɜːfjuːmd] *adj* (*soap etc*) parfumé

perfumery [pəˈfjuːmərɪ] *n* parfumerie *f*

perfunctorily [pəˈfʌŋktrɪlɪ] *adv* (*to examine*) superficiellement; (*to order, instruct*) sommairement; (*to read*) mécaniquement; (*to greet sb*) négligemment

perfunctory [pəˈfʌŋkt(ə)rɪ] *adj* (*examination, glance*) rapide; (*smile*) mécanique; (*letter, style, instructions*) sommaire; **it was just a p. enquiry** il/elle/*etc* m'a juste demandé pour la forme; **her p. manner** ses manières négligentes; **he greeted me with a p. nod** il m'a salué d'un petit signe négligent de la tête

pergola [ˈpɜːgələ] *n* pergola *f*

perhaps [pəˈhæps, præps] *adv* peut-être; **p. (so)/not** peut-être (bien) que oui/que non; **p. he's forgotten** peut-être qu'il a oublié; **p. we shall come back tomorrow** peut-être reviendrons-nous demain; **p. you would like to try it on** voulez-vous l'essayer?

perigee [ˈperɪdʒiː] *n Astron* périgée *m*

perihelion [perɪˈhiːlɪən] *n Astron* périhélie *m*

peril [ˈperɪl] *n* péril *m*, danger *m*; **in p.** en danger, en péril; **in p. of one's life** en danger de mort; **to do sth at one's (own) p.** faire qch à ses risques et périls; **peril(s) of the sea** (*in marine insurance*) fortune(s) *f(pl)* de mer

perilous [ˈperɪləs] *adj* périlleux, dangereux

perilously [ˈperɪləslɪ] *adv* dangereusement; **p. close to the edge of the cliff** dangereusement proche du bord de la falaise; **he came p. close to getting himself sacked** il a bien failli se faire mettre à la porte

perimeter [pəˈrɪmɪtər] *n* périmètre *m*; **p. alarm** alarme *f* périmétrique; **p. fence** clôture *f*

perinatal [perɪˈneɪt(ə)l] *adj Med* (*treatment, care, death*) périnatal

perineum [perɪˈniːəm] *n Anat* périnée *m*

period [ˈpɪərɪəd] *n* **(a)** période *f*; (*stage*) moment *m*, époque *f*, stade *m*; *Astron* cycle *m*, période; *Phys* période; **for a p. of three months** pendant une période de trois mois; **during** *or* **for the p. of their stay here** pendant (la durée de) leur séjour ici; **a long p. of illness** de longs ennuis de santé; *Com* **p. of grace** délai *m* de grâce; **p. of notice** délai-congé *m*; **within the agreed p.** dans les délais convenus; *Banking* **deposit for a fixed p.** dépôt *m* à terme fixe; *Met* **clear periods** éclaircies *fpl*; **sunny periods** intervalles *mpl* ensoleillés; *Banking* **p. money** dépôts à terme

(b) *Sch* heure *f* de cours; **a French/maths p.** un cours de français/maths; **a free p.** une heure de libre

(c) (*menstruation*) **(monthly) period(s)** règles *fpl*; **I've got my p.** j'ai mes règles; **when you have your first p.** la première fois que tu auras tes règles; **p. pains** douleurs *fpl* des règles

(d) (*age*) époque *f*; (*era*) ère *f*; **p. costume** toilette *f* d'époque; **p. detail** détail *m* historique; **p. dress** (*costume*) costume(s) *m(pl)* de l'époque; (*woman's garment*) robe *f* de style; **p. furniture** meubles *mpl* de style *ou* d'époque; **p. piece** curiosité *f*; **p. play/novel/drama** comédie *f*/roman *m*/drame *m* historique

(e) *esp Am Gram, Typ* (*full stop*) point *m*; *Am F* **he's no good at math! – he's no good, p.!** il est nul en math! – il est nul tout court!; *Am F* **you're not going to the party, p.!** tu n'iras pas à cette soirée, un point c'est tout!

(f) *Liter* (*sentence*) phrase *f*; *Mus* phrase complète

periodic [pɪərɪˈɒdɪk] *adj* périodique; *Ch* **p. table** classification *f* périodique

periodical [pɪərɪˈɒdɪk(ə)l] **1** *adj* périodique **2** *n* (publication *f*) périodique *m*; **the p. room** la salle des périodiques

periodically [pɪərɪˈɒdɪklɪ] *adv* périodiquement

peripatetic [perɪpəˈtetɪk] *adj* ambulant, itinérant; (*teacher*) en poste sur plusieurs établissements

peripheral [pəˈrɪfərəl] **1** *adj* **(a)** (*area, vision etc*) périphérique; **of purely p. importance** d'une importance purement accessoire; **this issue is p. to the central debate** ce problème est accessoire au débat principal **(b)** *Comptr* périphérique; **p. device** *or* **unit** unité *f* périphérique; **p.**

equipment matériel *m* périphérique, périphériques *mpl*; **p. interchange program** logiciel *m* de commutation de périphérique **2** *n Comptr* périphérique *m*

periphery [pəˈrɪfərɪ] *n* périphérie *f*; **on the p. of one's vision** à la périphérie de son champ de vision; **on the p. of the crowd** en bordure de la foule; **on the p. of society** en marge de la société

periphrasis, *pl* **-es** [pəˈrɪfrəsɪs, -iːz] *n Liter* périphrase *f*

periphrastic [perɪˈfræstɪk] *adj Liter* périphrastique

periscope [ˈperɪskəʊp] *n* périscope *m*; *TV, Cin* **p. shot** plan *m* en contre-plongée

perish [ˈperɪʃ] **1** *vi* **(a)** (*of person*) périr; *F* **p. the thought!** loin de moi cette pensée!; **if, p. the thought, you should die ...** si, Dieu nous en préserve, vous deviez mourir ... **(b)** (*of rubber, leather*) se détériorer; (*of fresh food*) s'avarier **2** *vt* (*rubber, leather*) détériorer; (*fresh food*) avarier

perishability [periʃəˈbɪlɪtɪ] *n Com* périssabilité *f*

perishable [ˈperɪʃəb(ə)l] **1** *adj* périssable **2** *npl* **perishables** marchandises *fpl* périssables

perished [ˈperɪʃt] *adj* détérioré, usé; *F* **I'm p.** (*very cold*) je meurs de froid

perisher [ˈperɪʃər] *n Br Sl* (*pest*) saligaud *m*; **little p.** petit coquin *m*

perishing [ˈperɪʃɪŋ] *adj* **(a)** *F* (*very cold*) très froid; **it's p.** il fait un froid de canard; **I'm p.** je meurs de froid **(b)** *Br Sl* (*intensifier*) sacré; (*car, machine*) satané; **p. idiot** sacré idiot; **it's a p. nuisance** c'est sacrément ennuyeux

peristalsis [perɪˈstælsɪs] *n* péristaltisme *m*

peristyle [ˈperɪstaɪl] *n Archit* péristyle *m*

peritoneum [perɪtəˈniːəm] *n Anat* péritoine *m*

peritonitis [perɪtəˈnaɪtɪs] *n Med* péritonite *f*; **to have p.** avoir une péritonite

periwig [ˈperɪwɪg] *n Hist* perruque *f*

periwinkle¹ [ˈperɪwɪŋk(ə)l] *n* (*plant*) (petite) pervenche *f*; **p. (blue)** bleu pervenche *m inv*

periwinkle² *n* (*mollusc*) bigorneau *m*

perjure [ˈpɜːdʒər] *vt Jur* **to p. oneself** faire un faux témoignage

perjurer [ˈpɜːdʒərər] *n Jur* faux témoin *m*

perjury [ˈpɜːdʒərɪ] *n Jur* faux témoignage *m*; **to commit p.** faire un faux témoignage; **the penalty for p.** la peine encourue quand on fait un faux témoignage

perk¹ [pɜːk] *n Br F* à-côté *m*, *pl* à-côtés, avantage *m*; **perks include ...** les avantages acquis comprennent ...; **free tickets are one of the perks of the job** un des avantages de ce travail est que l'on peut obtenir des billets gratuits; **clean air is a p. of working in the country** l'air pur est un des avantages du travail à la campagne

perk² *F* **1** *vi* (*of coffee*) passer **2** *vt* (*coffee*) faire

▶ **perk up 1** *vi* (*become more cheerful, after illness*) se requinquer; (*of party*) s'animer; **I don't know what to do to make him p. up** je ne sais pas quoi faire pour lui remonter le moral **2** *vtsep* **(a)** (*revive*) (*person*) requinquer, ragaillardir; (*cheer up*) remonter le moral à; **the coffee perked her up** le café l'a requinquée *ou* ravigotée **(b)** (*raise*) **to p. up its ears** (*of dog*) dresser les oreilles

perkily [ˈpɜːkɪlɪ] *adv* d'un air animé; (*to answer, say*) d'un ton dégagé *ou* désinvolte

perky [ˈpɜːkɪ] *adj* (*lively*) plein d'entrain, animé; (*cheerful*) guilleret; (*tone*) dégagé, désinvolte; (*remark*) désinvolte

perm¹ [pɜːm] *n* (*in hair*) permanente *f*; **to have a p.** se faire faire une permanente

perm² *vt* **to p. sb's hair** faire une permanente à qn; **to have one's hair permed** se faire faire une permanente

perm³ *n Br* (*in football pools*) permutation *f*

permafrost [ˈpɜːməfrɒst] *n Geol* permafrost *m*

permanence [ˈpɜːmənəns] *n* permanence *f*

permanency [ˈpɜːmənənsɪ] *n* permanence *f*

permanent [ˈpɜːmənənt] **1** *adj* permanent; (*residence, address*) fixe; (*ink, stain*) indélébile; **p. hearing loss** perte définitive de l'ouïe; *Com* **p. inventory** stock *m* de sécurité, stock stratégique, inventaire *m* permanent; **p. press** (*for clothes*) plissé *m* permanent; **she was in a p. state of depression** elle était dans un état de dépression permanent; **p. site** (*caravan site*) terrain *m* de caravaning permanent; **p. wave** (*in hair*) permanente *f*; *Br Rail* **p. way** voie *f* (ferrée) **2** *n* (*in hair*) permanente *f*

permanganate [pəˈmæŋgəneɪt] *n Ch* permanganate *m*

permeability [pɜːmɪəˈbɪlɪtɪ] *n* perméabilité *f*

permeable [ˈpɜːmɪəb(ə)l] *adj* perméable

permeate [ˈpɜːmɪeɪt] **1** *vt* **(a)** (*penetrate*) filtrer *ou* passer à travers; **the soil was permeated with water** le sol était saturé d'eau; **a smell of flowers permeated the room** des fleurs embaumaient la pièce; **his clothes were permeated by a smell of napthalene** ses vêtements étaient imprégnés d'une odeur de naphtaline; **the house was permeated by damp** la maison était imprégnée d'humidité

(b) *Fig* (*of feeling, idea etc*) imprégner; **this attitude permeated 18th-century thought** la pensée du 18e siècle a été imprégnée par cette attitude; **the country was permeated with fear** le pays était plongé dans la peur; **doubt had permeated the organisation** le doute s'était infiltré dans l'organisation

2 *vi* passer; **to p. through sth** filtrer *ou* passer à travers qch; **water permeates everywhere** l'eau s'infiltre partout

Permian [ˈpɜːmɪən] *adj Geol* permien

permissible [pəˈmɪsɪb(ə)l] *adj* admissible, acceptable

permission [pəˈmɪʃən] *n* [ⓘA57,c-d; B37,K,2] permission *f*, autorisation *f*; **to ask/give/refuse sb p. to do sth** demander/donner/refuser à qn la permission *ou* l'autorisation de faire qch; **with your p.** avec votre permission *ou* autorisation; **you have my p.** je te donne la permission, je t'y autorise; **published by kind p. of ...** publié avec l'aimable autorisation de ...

permissive [pəˈmɪsɪv] *adj* (*tolerant*) permissif; **p. society** société *f* permissive

permissively [pəˈmɪsɪvlɪ] *adv* de manière permissive

permissiveness [pəˈmɪsɪvnɪs] *n* permissivité *f*

permit¹ [ˈpɜːmɪt] *n* permis *m*; (*allowing entry*) laissez-passer *m inv*; (*at Customs*) acquit-à-caution *m*, *pl* acquits-à-caution, passavant *m*; **export p.** autorisation *f* d'exporter; **work p.** permis de travail; **p. holders only** (*on sign*) réservé aux personnes autorisées

permit² [pəˈmɪt] (**-tt-**) **1** *vt* permettre; **to p. sb to do sth** permettre à qn de faire qch, autoriser qn à faire qch; **larger telescopes p. us to ...** des télescopes plus performants nous permettent de ...; **if I may be permitted** si vous me le permettez; **p. me to tell you ...!** (*angrily*) laissez-moi vous dire que ...!; *Br Admin* **permitted hours** (*for selling alcohol*) = heures *fpl* légales de vente des boissons alcoolisées **2** *vi* **if time permits** si j'ai/nous avons/*etc* le temps; **weather permitting** si le temps le permet

▶ **permit of** *vipo Fml* (*admit possibility of*) admettre; **this permits of only one explanation** ceci n'admet qu'une explication

permutation [pɜːmjʊˈteɪʃən] *n* permutation *f*

permute [pəˈmjuːt] *vt Ling, Math* permuter

pernicious [pəˈnɪʃəs] *adj* pernicieux; *Med* **p. anaemia** anémie *f* pernicieuse

perniciously [pəˈnɪʃəslɪ] *adv* pernicieusement

pernickety [pəˈnɪkɪtɪ] *adj F* (*person*) tatillon, pointilleux; (*job*) délicat, minutieux; **to be p. about one's food** être difficile sur la nourriture; **soufflé can be rather a p. thing to make** le soufflé est un plat assez délicat à préparer

perorate [ˈperəreɪt] *vi Fml* **(a)** (*conclude speech*) faire la péroraison **(b)** (*speak at length*) discourir longuement

peroration [perəˈreɪʃən] *n Fml* **(a)** (*conclusion*) péroraison *f* **(b)** (*long speech*) long discours *m*, discours de longue haleine

peroxide¹ [pəˈrɒksaɪd] *n Ch* peroxyde *m*; *F* **p. blonde** blonde *f* oxygénée, fausse blonde *f*

peroxide² *vt* (*hair*) (faire) blondir à l'eau oxygénée

perpendicular [pɜːpənˈdɪkjʊlər] **1** *adj* perpendiculaire (**to** à); (*wall etc*) vertical; (*upright, straight*) à plomb; (*cliff*) à pic; **line p. to another** ligne perpendiculaire à une autre; *Archit* **p. style** style *m* (gothique) perpendiculaire **2** *n* **(a)** (*plumb line*) fil *m* à plomb; **out of (the) p.** hors d'aplomb, hors d'équerre **(b)** *Geom* perpendiculaire *f*

perpendicularly [pɜːpənˈdɪkjʊləlɪ] *adv* perpendiculairement; (*to rise, fall, drop*) verticalement, à la verticale; (*to be built*) d'aplomb; **the cliff rose p.** la falaise s'élevait tout droit

perpetrate [ˈpɜːpɪtreɪt] *vt* (*crime*) commettre, perpétrer; (*fraud, error*) commettre

perpetration [pɜːpɪˈtreɪʃən] *n* (*of crime*) perpétration *f*; (*of fraud, deception*) accomplissement *m*

perpetrator [ˈpɜːpɪtreɪtər] *n* (*of crime*) auteur *m*; **the p.** l'auteur du délit

perpetual [pəˈpetjʊəl] *adj* (*eternal*) perpétuel, éternel; (*incessant*) sans fin, continuel, incessant; *Chess* **p. check** échec *m* perpétuel; *Com* **p. inventory** inventaire *m* permanent, stock *m* de sécurité; *Phys* **p. motion** mouvement *m* perpétuel; **p. snow** neiges *fpl* éternelles

perpetually [pəˈpetjʊəlɪ] *adv* (*eternally*) perpétuellement, éternellement; (*ceaselessly*) sans cesse; (*continually*) continuellement, perpétuellement

perpetuate [pəˈpetjʊeɪt] *vt* perpétuer; **to p. the species** perpétuer l'espèce

perpetuation [pəpetjʊˈeɪʃən] *n* perpétuation *f*

perpetuity [pɜːpɪˈtjuːɪtɪ] *n* **(a)** perpétuité *f*; **in** *or* **for p.** à perpétuité **(b)** *Jur* (*of property*) jouissance *f* à perpétuité; **(annuity in) p.** rente *f* perpétuelle

perplex [pə'pleks] *vt* laisser *ou* rendre perplexe; **she was perplexed by his lack of enthusiasm** son manque d'enthousiasme la laissait *ou* rendait perplexe
perplexed [pə'plekst] *adj* perplexe
perplexing [pə'pleksɪŋ] *adj* (*problem etc*) troublant; (*book, play etc*) difficile (à comprendre); (*person*) déconcertant; **it's very p.** on n'y comprend rien; **I find his attitude most p.** son attitude me laisse totalement perplexe
perplexity [pə'pleksɪtɪ] *n* perplexité *f*
perquisite ['pɜːkwɪzɪt] *n Br Fml* = **perk**[1]
perry ['perɪ] *n* (*drink*) poiré *m*
per se ['pɜː'seɪ] *adj* en soi; **it is not a bad idea p.** en soi, ce n'est pas une mauvaise idée
persecute ['pɜːsɪkjuːt] *vt* persécuter; **to be persecuted in the press** faire l'objet d'attaques répétées dans la presse
persecution [pɜːsɪ'kjuːʃən] *n* persécution *f*; *Psy* **p. complex** *or* **mania** complexe *m* de persécution
persecutor ['pɜːsɪkjuːtər] *n* persécuteur, -trice
perseverance [pɜːsɪ'vɪərəns] *n* persévérance *f*
persevere [pɜːsɪ'vɪər] *vi* persévérer (**with** *or* **in sth** dans qch; **with sb** avec qn); **to p. in one's belief that …** persister à croire que …; **to p. in doing sth** persister à faire qch
persevering [pɜːsɪ'vɪərɪŋ] *adj* persévérant; **thanks to our p. staff** grâce à la persévérance de notre personnel
Persia ['pɜːʃə] *n* Perse *f*
Persian ['pɜːʃən] **1** *adj* persan; *Antiq* perse; (*cat, horse*) persan; (*carpet*) de Perse **2** *n* **(a)** (*person*) Persan, -ane; *Antiq* Perse *mf* **(b)** (*cat*) chat *m* persan **(c)** *Ling* perse *m*
Persian Gulf (the) *n* le Golfe persique
persimmon [pɜː'sɪmən] *n* **(a)** (*fruit*) plaquemine *f*; (*from Japan*) kaki *m* **(b) p. (tree)** plaqueminier *m*
persist [pə'sɪst] *vi* **(a)** persister, s'obstiner (**in doing sth** à faire qch); **to p. in one's opinion** persister *ou* s'obstiner dans son opinion; **to p. in one's belief that …** persister à croire que … **(b)** (*of fog, fever etc*) persister, continuer; (*of belief*) persister
persistence [pə'sɪstəns] *n* **(a)** persistance *f*, ténacité *f*, obstination *f* (**in doing sth** à faire qch) **(b)** (*of fog, fever, belief etc*) persistance *f*
persistent [pə'sɪstənt] *adj* (*person*) persistant, opiniâtre, tenace; (*doubts, problems, pain etc*) continuel, incessant; (*rumours*) persistant; (*rain*) continuel, qui s'obstine; **p. offender** récidiviste *mf*; **to be in p. pain** souffrir continuellement; **to have a p. belief in sth** persister à croire à qch; *Com* **p. demand for …** demande suivie *ou* soutenue pour …
persistently [pə'sɪstəntlɪ] *adv* avec persistance; (*to fail, refuse, warn*) à plusieurs reprises; (*to be late, short of funds*) continuellement; **she p. offended** elle récidivait sans cesse
persnickety [pə'snɪkɪtɪ] *adj US F* = **pernickety**
person ['pɜːs(ə)n] *n* **(a)** personne *f*, *Pej* individu *m*, type *m*; **what's he/she like as a p.?** il/elle est comment sur le plan personnel?; **I like her as a p.** je l'aime bien en tant que personne; **he/she is a kind/strange p.** c'est une personne gentille/étrange, c'est quelqu'un de gentil/d'étrange; **a coffee/football p.** un amateur de café/de foot; **are you a cat p. or a dog p.?** est-ce que tu préfères les chats ou chiens?; **there is no p. of that name here** il n'y a personne de ce nom ici; *Jur* **some p. or persons unknown** un certain quidam; **in p.** en propre, en personne; **he came in p.** il est venu en personne; **to deliver sth in p.** remettre qch en main(s) propre(s); **help came, in the p. of Amanda** on a trouvé de l'aide, en la personne d'Amanda; **to carry weapons on one's p.** porter des armes sur soi; **to be one's own p.** vivre à sa façon *ou* à son idée; *Tel* **p. to p. call** appel *m* avec préavis *ou* de personne à personne

(b) *Gram* **verb in the first p.** verbe à la première personne; **the second p. plural** la deuxième personne du pluriel; **the story is told in the first p.** l'histoire est racontée à la première personne

(c) *Rel* **(one) God in three Persons** la Trinité
-person ['pɜːs(ə)n] *suff* **chairp.** directeur, -trice; **spokesp.** porte-parole *m inv*; **salesp.** vendeur, -euse
persona [pə'səʊnə] *n also Psy* personnage *m*; **p. grata/non grata** persona grata/non grata; *Fig* **you'll be p. non grata unless you bring a present** tu ne seras pas bien vu si tu n'apportes pas de cadeau; **to be p. non grata with sb** ne pas être dans les petits papiers de qn
personable ['pɜːsənəb(ə)l] *adj* bien (fait) de sa personne; **he's a very p. young man** c'est un jeune homme qui présente très bien
personage ['pɜːsənɪdʒ] *n* personnage *m*
personal ['pɜːsən(ə)l] *adj* personnel; **to be careless about one's p. appearance** négliger sa tenue; **to make a p. appearance** venir *ou* paraître en personne; **for p. reasons** pour des raisons personnelles; **don't be p., don't make p. remarks** ne faites pas d'allusions personnelles; **it's nothing p. but …** ça n'a rien de personnel mais …; **to do sb a p. favour** rendre un service à qn à titre personnel; **it's a p. matter** c'est une affaire privée *ou* personnelle; **my p. opinion** *or* **view is that …** à mon avis …; **this is not my p. opinion** ce n'est pas mon opinion personnelle; **to give a p. touch to sth** donner une touche personnelle à qch; **I want it for my p. use** j'en ai besoin pour mon usage personnel; **articles for p. use** (*at customs*) objets à usage personnel; **p. accident insurance** assurance *f* pour les personnes transportées; **have you got any p. accident insurance?** est-ce que vous avez une assurance contre les accidents?; *Jur* **p. action** (*relating to property*) action *f* mobilière; **personal assets** patrimoine *m*; *Banking* **p. assets profile** profil *m* patrimonial; *Sp etc* **p. best** record *m* personnel; **3 mins 22 secs is my p. best** mon record (personnel) est 3 min 22; **p. data** données *fpl* nominatives; *Fin* **p. equity plan** plan *m* d'épargne en actions; **p. financial statement** état *m* de fortune; **p. friend** ami(e) personnel(le); *Admin* **p. income** revenu *m* des personnes physiques; **p. liberty** liberté *f* individuelle; **p. organizer** (*electronic*) organiseur *m*, agenda *m* électronique; (*book form*) agenda; *Mktg* **p. observation** observation *f* en situation; **p. property insurance** assurance sur les objets personnels; *Mktg* **p. selling** ventes *fpl* personnelles; *Acct* **p. wealth statement** état *m* de fortune
personal assistant *n* (*of executive etc*) assistant, -ante; (*with secretarial duties*) secrétaire *mf* de direction
personal column *n Journ* petites annonces *fpl*
personal computer *n* ordinateur *m* individuel
personal effects *npl* effets *mpl* personnels
personal estate *n* biens *mpl* personnels *ou* meubles *ou* mobiliers
personal hygiene *n* hygiène *f* intime
personal identification number *n Banking* code *m* confidentiel (*d'une carte bancaire*)
personality [pɜːsə'nælɪtɪ] *n* **(a)** (*character*) personnalité *f*; **he's got no p.** il n'a aucune personnalité **(b)** (*well-known person*) personnalité *f*; *Mktg* **p. promotion** (*of product by personality*) promotion *f* par une personnalité; **TV/sports p.** personnalité célèbre de la télévision/du monde du sport **(c)** *Old-fashioned* (*personal remark*) **to indulge in personalities** faire des remarques personnelles
personality cult *n* culte *m* de la personnalité
personality disorder *n Psy* trouble *m* de la personnalité
personality test *n Psy* test *m* de personnalité
personalize ['pɜːsənəlaɪz] *vt* personnaliser; **a personalized shirt** une chemise personnalisée; **personalized letter** lettre *f* personnelle; **I don't want to p. the issue** je ne veux pas donner un tour personnel à ce problème
personal loan *n Banking* prêt *m ou* crédit *m* personnel
personally ['pɜːsən(ə)lɪ] *adv* personnellement; (*to intervene, see sb*) en personne; **to attend to sth p.** s'occuper de qch en personne *ou* personnellement; **p. I think …** pour ma part je pense …; **that belongs to me p.** cela m'appartient en propre; **to deliver sth to sb p.** remettre qch à qn en main(s) propre(s); **don't take it p.** (*what was said, done*) n'en faites pas une affaire personnelle, ne le prenez pas personnellement; **I didn't mean it p.** ma remarque n'avait rien de personnel
personal pronoun *n* [①**A26-28**; **B16-19**,**D**] *Gram* pronom *m* personnel
personal property *n* biens *mpl* personnels *ou* meubles *ou* mobiliers
personal stereo *n* baladeur *m*
personalty ['pɜːsənəltɪ] *n Jur* biens *mpl* meubles, biens mobiliers
personification [pɜːsɒnɪfɪ'keɪʃən] *n* personnification *f*; **to be the p. of meanness** être l'avarice même *ou* l'avarice personnifiée *ou* l'avarice en personne; **he is the p. of this new trend in English fiction** il incarne cette nouvelle tendance de la fiction anglaise
personify [pɜː'sɒnɪfaɪ] *vt* personnifier; **he's meanness personified** il est *ou* c'est l'avarice même *ou* l'avarice personnifiée *ou* l'avarice en personne
personnel [pɜːsə'nel] *n* personnel *m*; **I work in p.** (*the department*) je travaille au service du personnel; (*the field*) je suis dans la branche du personnel; *Mil* **p. carrier** véhicule *m* de transport de personnel; (*aircraft*) avion *m* de transport de personnel; **p. consultant** conseiller *m* du travail; **p. department** service *m* du personnel; **p. director** directeur *m* du personnel; **p. file card** fiche *f* signalétique; **p. files** fichiers *mpl* des salariés; **p. management** direction *f ou* administration *f* du personnel; **p. manager** directeur du personnel; **p. representative** délégué *m* du personnel
perspective [pə'spektɪv] **1** *n* **(a)** *Math, Art* perspective *f*; **to**

draw an object in/out of p. dessiner un objet en perspective/en faussant la perspective

(**b**) *Fig* (*relative importance*) **to see a matter in its true p.** voir une affaire sous son vrai jour; **to put sth in(to) p.** remettre qch à sa (vraie) place; **let's keep things in p.** n'exagérons rien; **to see events in a historical p.** voir des événements dans une perspective *ou* optique historique

(**c**) *Fml* (*view, Fig prospect*) perspective *f*; **a fine p. opened out before his eyes** une belle perspective s'ouvrit devant ses yeux

2 *adj Art* (*drawing etc*) en perspective, perspectif; **p. lines of a picture** fuyants *mpl* d'un tableau

perspex® [ˈpɜːspeks] *n* plexiglas(s)® *m*

perspicacious [pɜːspɪˈkeɪʃəs] *adj Fml* (*person*) perspicace; (*comment, analysis etc*) clairvoyant, lucide, fin

perspicaciously [pɜːspɪˈkeɪʃəslɪ] *adv Fml* avec perspicacité *ou* clairvoyance *ou* discernement

perspicacity [pɜːspɪˈkæsɪtɪ] *n Fml* perspicacité *f*

perspicuity [pɜːspɪˈkjuːɪtɪ] *n Fml* (*of person*) perspicacité *f*; (*of style etc*) clarté *f*, netteté *f*, lucidité *f*

perspicuous [pəˈspɪkjʊəs] *adj Fml* clair, net, *f* nette, lucide

perspicuously [pəˈspɪkjʊəslɪ] *adv Fml* clairement, nettement

perspiration [pɜːspəˈreɪʃən] *n* (**a**) (*sweat*) transpiration *f*, sueur *f*; **beads of p.** gouttes *fpl* de sueur; **bathed in** *or* **dripping with p.** trempé de sueur, en nage (**b**) (*act*) transpiration *f*, perspiration *f*

perspire [pəˈspaɪər] *vi* transpirer

persuadable [pəˈsweɪdəb(ə)l] *adj* **easily p.** facile à persuader

persuade [pəˈsweɪd] **1** *vt* persuader, convaincre (**to do** de faire); **to p. sb not to do sth** dissuader qn de faire qch; **to p. sb that …** persuader qn que … + *ind*; **nothing could p. her** aucun argument n'a pu la convaincre; **she persuaded herself that everything would work out** elle s'est persuadée *ou* convaincue elle-même que tout marcherait bien **2** *vi Fml* **the argument fails to p.** cet argument n'est pas très convaincant

persuasion [pəˈsweɪʒən] *n* (**a**) (*act of persuading, ability to persuade*) persuasion *f*; **powers of p.** force *f ou* pouvoir *m* de persuasion; **the art of p.** l'art *m* de la persuasion (**b**) (*beliefs*) (**religious**) **p.** (*religion*) religion *f*, confession *f*; **political p.** opinions *fpl* politiques; **he was of a different political p. altogether** ses opinions politiques étaient complètement différentes; **to be of the Catholic p.** être de religion catholique; *Hum* **a person of the male/female p.** un homme/une femme; *Old-fashioned* **it's my p. that …** je suis persuadé *ou* convaincu que …

persuasive [pəˈsweɪzɪv, -sɪv] *adj* (*person*) persuasif; (*argument*) convaincant

persuasively [pəˈsweɪzɪvlɪ, -sɪvlɪ] *adv* (*to say*) d'un ton persuasif; (*to argue, write*) de façon convaincante

persuasiveness [pəˈsweɪzɪvnɪs, -sɪv-] *n* (*of person*) force *f* persuasive *ou* de persuasion; (*of argument*) caractère *m* convaincant; **the p. of her tone** son ton persuasif

pert [pɜːt] *adj* (**a**) (*cheeky*) effronté (**b**) (*of clothing*) (*stylishly neat*) pimpant (**c**) (*nose, breasts*) pointu; (*bottom*) petit et ferme

pertain [pəˈteɪn] *vi Fml* (**a**) (*belong*) appartenir (**to sth** à qch); **the house and the land pertaining to it** la maison et le terrain qui font partie de la propriété (**b**) (*have reference*) **to p. to sth** se rapporter à qch, avoir un rapport avec qch, avoir rapport à qch

pertinacious [pɜːtɪˈneɪʃəs] *adj Fml* obstiné, opiniâtre

pertinaciously [pɜːtɪˈneɪʃəslɪ] *adv Fml* obstinément, opiniâtrement

pertinence [ˈpɜːtɪnəns] *n* (*of question, criticism*) pertinence *f*, à-propos *m*; (*of remark*) pertinence, à-propos, justesse *f*

pertinent [ˈpɜːtɪnənt] *adj* (*question, criticism*) pertinent; (*remark*) pertinent, juste; **to be p. to** (*question*) avoir un rapport avec, avoir rapport à

pertinently [ˈpɜːtɪnəntlɪ] *adv* d'une manière pertinente, avec à-propos

pertly [ˈpɜːtlɪ] *adv* (**a**) (*cheekily*) avec effronterie (**b**) (*in a lively way*) d'un air guilleret

pertness [ˈpɜːtnɪs] *n* (**a**) (*cheekiness*) effronterie *f* (**b**) (*liveliness*) air *m* guilleret (**c**) **the p. of her breasts** ses petits seins bien fermes

perturb [pəˈtɜːb] *vt* (**a**) (*worry*) troubler, inquiéter; **to be perturbed** être troublé *ou* inquiet; **if you are perturbed by this idea** si cette idée vous inquiète (**b**) *Lit* (*put into confusion*) (*kingdom etc*) jeter le désordre *ou* la perturbation dans (**c**) *Astron* (*star*) dévier; *Phys* (*compass needle*) affoler

perturbation [pɜːtəˈbeɪʃən] *n* (**a**) *Fml* (*of mind*) agitation *f*, inquiétude *f*, trouble *m* (**b**) *Phys* (*of magnetic needle*) affolement *m*

perturbed [pəˈtɜːbd] *adj* troublé, inquiet

Peru [pəˈruː] *n* Pérou *m*

perusal [pəˈruːz(ə)l] *n Fml* lecture *f*; **for your p. and approval** pour que vous l'étudiez et l'approuviez; **for your p. when you have time** pour que vous y jetiez un coup d'œil, quand vous en aurez le temps

peruse [pəˈruːz] *vt* (**a**) (*read carefully*) lire attentivement, prendre connaissance de (**b**) (*read quickly*) (*magazine, newspaper*) feuilleter; (*letter, article*) survoler

Peruvian [pəˈruːvɪən] **1** *adj* péruvien **2** *n* Péruvien, -ienne

perv [pɜːv] *n F* = **pervert**[1]

pervade [pɜːˈveɪd] *vt* s'infiltrer dans, se répandre dans; **the scent of pine trees pervaded the air** l'air était embaumé de l'odeur des pins; **the novel is pervaded by a sense of gloom** le roman est imprégné d'une atmosphère lugubre; **minor errors p. the entire dictionary** le dictionnaire est parsemé de petites erreurs; **such attitudes p. British business** ces attitudes sont omniprésentes dans *ou* se retrouvent à tous les niveaux de l'entreprenariat britannique

pervading [pɜːˈveɪdɪŋ] *adj* (*smell*) pénétrant; (**all-**)**p.** qui se répand partout; (*influence, feeling etc*) dominant; **the p. nostalgia of his work** la nostalgie qui est omniprésente dans son œuvre

pervasive [pɜːˈveɪsɪv] *adj* qui se répand partout; (*gloom, smell*) envahissant

perverse [pəˈvɜːs] *adj* (**a**) (*wicked*) pervers, perverti; (*stubborn*) entêté; (*contrary*) contrariant; **to take a p. pleasure in doing** prendre un malin plaisir à faire; **then it would be p. to deny that …** (*illogical*) alors ce serait illogique de nier que … (**b**) (*sexually deviant*) pervers

perversely [pəˈvɜːslɪ] *adv* (*wickedly*) perversement, avec perversité; (*contrarily*) d'une manière contrariante; **to p. believe that …** s'entêter à croire que …

perverseness [pəˈvɜːsnɪs] *n* (*wickedness*) perversité *f*; (*contrariness*) esprit *m* contraire *ou* contrariant; (*cantankerousness*) caractère *m* revêche *ou* acariâtre

perversion [pəˈvɜːʃən] *n* (**a**) (*act of corrupting*) pervertissement *m*; (*perverted action, form*) perversion *f*; **a p. of the truth** un travestissement de la vérité (**b**) (**sexual**) **perversions** perversions *fpl* sexuelles

perversity [pəˈvɜːsɪtɪ] *n* = **perverseness**

pervert[1] [ˈpɜːvɜːt] *n Psy* (**sexual**) **p.** pervers(e) (sexuel(le)); *F* **your brother is such a p.!** ton frère est un véritable obsédé!

pervert[2] [pəˈvɜːt] *vt* (*corrupt morally*) (*person*) pervertir; (*distort*) (*facts*) altérer, dénaturer; *Jur* **to p. the course of justice** entraver le bon fonctionnement de la justice; **to p. the truth** déformer la vérité

perverted [pəˈvɜːtɪd] *adj* pervers

pervious [ˈpɜːvɪəs] *adj* perméable (*à l'eau etc*)

pesky [ˈpeskɪ] *adj esp Am F* embêtant, empoisonnant; **what are those p. kids up to now?** que font ces maudits *ou* sacrés gosses maintenant?

pessary [ˈpesərɪ] *n Med* ovule *m*

pessimism [ˈpesɪmɪz(ə)m] *n* pessimisme *m*; **there is growing p. about the prospects for peace** on est de plus en plus pessimiste quant aux chances de paix

pessimist [ˈpesɪmɪst] *n* pessimiste *mf*; **don't be such a p.!** ne sois pas si pessimiste!

pessimistic [pesɪˈmɪstɪk] *adj* pessimiste

pessimistically [pesɪˈmɪstɪklɪ] *adv* avec pessimisme

pest [pest] *n* (**a**) (*animal, insect, plant*) animal *m*/insecte *m*/plante *f* nuisible; **rabbits are a p. here** ici les lapins sont un fléau; **p. control** (*activity*) (*for rats*) dératisation *f*; (*for insects*) désinsectisation *f*; (*department*) (*for rats*) service *m* de dératisation; (*for insects*) service de désinsectisation (**b**) *F* (*nuisance*) **stop being a p.!** arrête d'embêter le monde!; **he's a perfect p.!** c'est un vrai poison!; **having to take the dog for a walk is a real p.** c'est vraiment empoisonnant *ou* embêtant d'avoir à promener le chien

pester [ˈpestər] *vt* tourmenter, importuner; **to p. sb to do sth** harceler qn pour qu'il fasse qch; **to p. sb with questions** importuner *ou* assommer *ou* harceler qn de (ses) questions; **to p. sb for money** harceler qn pour obtenir de l'argent

pesticide [ˈpestɪsaɪd] *n* pesticide *m*

pestiferous [peˈstɪfərəs] *adj Lit* (*air*) pestilentiel; (*doctrine*) pernicieux

pestilence [ˈpestɪləns] *n Lit* peste *f*

pestilential [pestɪˈlenʃəl] *adj Med* (*disease*) pestilentiel; (*smell*) pestilentiel, infect; *F* (*irritating*) assommant, empoisonnant

pestle [ˈpes(ə)l] *n Culin* pilon *m*

pet[1] [pet] *n* (**a**) (*animal*) animal *m* domestique *ou* familier *ou* de compagnie; **do you have any pets?** est-ce que tu as un animal?; **a p. monkey/budgerigar** un singe/une perruche apprivoisé(e); **sorry, no pets** les animaux ne sont pas admis (**b**) (*favourite child*) enfant *mf* gâté(e); **mother's/teacher's p.** le chouchou de sa maman/du professeur; **my p.!** mon chéri!, mon petit chou!; **my p. hate** ma bête noire; **p. subject** sujet *m* de prédilection

pet² (-tt-) **1** *vt* (**a**) (*make a pet of*) (*person*) choyer, chouchouter (**b**) (*stroke, pat*) (*person, dog etc*) caresser, câliner **2** *vi F* (*sexually*) se caresser, *F* se peloter

pet³ *n Old-fashioned F* **to be in a p.** (*to sulk*) faire la tête, être de mauvaise humeur (**about** à cause de); **to go in a p.** faire la tête

petal ['pet(ə)l] *n* (**a**) (*of flower*) pétale *m* (**b**) *F* (*term of affection*) **thanks p.** merci mon chou

petard [pe'tɑːd] *n* **to be hoist with one's own p.** être pris à son propre piège

Pete [piːt] *n F* **for P.'s sake!** pour l'amour du ciel!

Peter ['piːtər] *n* **he's a real P. Pan** c'est un vrai gosse; **P. Pan collar** col *m* Claudine

peter ['piːtər] *n Sl* (*safe*) coffre-fort *m*, *pl* coffres-forts

▶ **peter out** *vi F* (*of conversation, interest, enthusiasm etc*) tarir; (*of scheme, plan*) n'aboutir à rien; (*of path, stream*) disparaître; (*of flame etc*) mourir; **the party gradually petered out** les gens ont quitté la fête peu à peu

peterman ['piːtəmæn] *n Sl* (*safe-breaker*) casseur *m* de coffres-forts

petersham ['piːtəʃəm] *n Tex* gros-grain *m*, *pl* gros-grains

pet food *n* nourriture *f* pour animaux de compagnie

petite [pə'tiːt] *adj* (*woman*) menu

petition¹ [pɪ'tɪʃən] *n* (**a**) (*request*) requête *f*, supplique *f*; (*document*) pétition *f*; **to grant a p.** faire droit à une pétition; **to hand in/sign a p.** remettre/signer une pétition; **to get up a p.** faire signer une pétition (**b**) *Jur* **p. for mercy** recours *m* en grâce; **p. for a divorce** demande *f* en divorce; **p. in bankruptcy** (*made by creditors*) requête *f* des créanciers; (*made by bankrupt*) requête du négociant insolvable (**c**) (*to God*) prière *f*

petition² **1** *vt* (*court, sovereign etc*) adresser *ou* présenter une pétition à **2** *vi* (*with document*) pétitionner; **to p. for sth** (*collect signatures*) faire signer une pétition pour qch; (*present petition*) adresser une pétition pour qch; *Fml* **to p. for mercy** se pourvoir *ou* recourir en grâce; *Jur* **to p. for divorce** faire une demande de divorce

petitioner [pɪ'tɪʃənər] *n* pétitionnaire *mf*; *Jur* requérant, -ante

pet name *n* (*diminutive*) surnom *m*

petrel ['petrəl] *n* (*bird*) pétrel *m*

petrifaction [petrɪ'fækʃən], **petrification** [petrɪfɪ'keɪʃən] *n* pétrification *f*

petrified ['petrɪfaɪd] *adj* (*wood etc*) pétrifié; *F* **p. with fear** pétrifié *ou* paralysé de terreur; *F* **I was p. he would shoot me** j'étais mort de peur à l'idée qu'il me tire dessus

petrify ['petrɪfaɪ] **1** *vt* (*wood etc*) pétrifier; *F* (*with fear*) pétrifier, paralyser **2** *vi* se pétrifier

petrifying ['petrɪfaɪɪŋ] *adj F* (*frightening*) paralysant

petrochemical [petrəʊ'kemɪk(ə)l] **1** *adj* (*industry etc*) pétrochimique **2** *npl* **petrochemicals** produits *mpl* pétrochimiques

petrodollar ['petrəʊdɒlər] *n* pétrodollar *m*

petrol ['petrəl] *n Br Aut* essence *f*, *Swiss* benzine *f*; **to fill up with p.** faire le plein d'essence; **to run out of p.** tomber en panne d'essence; **high-grade** *or* **four-star p.** = supercarburant *m*, *F* super *m*; **p. company** compagnie *f* pétrolière; **p. filler cap** bouchon *m* d'essence; **p. filler pipe** tuyau *m* de remplissage d'essence; **p. gauge** jauge *f* à essence

petrol bomb *n* cocktail *m* Molotov

petrol-bomb *vt* jeter des cocktails Molotov sur

petrol can *n* bidon *m* à essence

petrol cap *n* bouchon *m* de réservoir

petroleum [pə'trəʊlɪəm] *n* pétrole *m*; **p. industry** industrie *f* pétrolière; **p. jelly** vaseline *f*

petrology [pe'trɒlədʒɪ] *n* pétrologie *f*

petrol pump *n* (*at petrol station, in car*) pompe *f* à essence

petrol station *n* station-service *f*, *pl* stations-services

petrol tank *n* réservoir *m* à essence

petrol tanker *n* pétrolier *m*

pet shop *n* animalerie *f*

petticoat ['petɪkəʊt] *n* (*skirt length*) jupon *m*; (*full length*) combinaison *f*; *F* **p. government** gouvernement *m* en jupon

pettifogging ['petɪfɒgɪŋ] *adj Old-fashioned* (*detail*) insignifiant; (*objection*) de pure chicane; (*person*) chicanier; **p. lawyer** avocassier *m*

pettiness ['petɪnɪs] *n* (*insignificance*) insignifiance *f*; (*small-mindedness*) mesquinerie *f*

petting ['petɪŋ] *n F* pelotage *m*; **heavy p.** attouchements *mpl*

pettish ['petɪʃ] *adj* (*person*) de mauvaise humeur, maussade, irritable; (*behaviour, reaction*) maussade, morose

pettishly ['petɪʃlɪ] *adv* avec mauvaise humeur

petty ['petɪ] *adj* (**a**) (*insignificant, minor*) petit, insignifiant; **p. annoyances** tracasseries *fpl*, petits ennuis *mpl* (**b**) **p.(-minded)** mesquin

petty cash *n Com* petite caisse *f*; **p. box** petite caisse; **p. management** tenue *f* de caisse; **p. voucher** bon *m* de (petite) caisse

petty crime *n* actes *mpl* délictueux

petty larceny *n Jur* vol *m* simple

petty-mindedness [petɪ'maɪndɪdnɪs] *n* mesquinerie *f*

petty offences *npl* contraventions *fpl*

petty officer *n Naut* second maître *m*; **chief p. officer** maître *m*

petulance ['petjʊləns] *n* irascibilité *f*, mauvaise humeur *f*; **an outburst of p.** un accès de mauvaise humeur

petulant ['petjʊlənt] *adj* irritable, susceptible; (*frown*) irrité; **he became quite p.** il s'est montré vraiment susceptible; **you're in a p. mood today!** tu es vraiment susceptible aujourd'hui!

petulantly ['petjʊləntlɪ] *adv* (*to look at*) d'un air irrité; (*to say*) d'un ton irrité; (*to react*) avec humeur

petunia [pɪ'tjuːnɪə] *n* (*plant*) pétunia *m*

pew [pjuː] *n* banc *m* d'église; *F* **take** *or* **have a p.!** assieds-toi!

pewter ['pjuːtər] *n* étain *m*; **p. (ware)** étains *mpl*, vaisselle *f* d'étain; **I like p. (ware)** j'aime les étains

PG [piː'dʒiː] *adj Br Cin* (*abbr* **parental guidance**) (*film*) = qui exige une autorisation parentale

PGCE [piːdʒiːsiː'iː] *n Br Sch* (*abbr* **postgraduate certificate in education**) = diplôme *m* d'enseignement

PgDn *Comptr* (*abbr* **page down**) PgSv

PgUp *Comptr* (*abbr* **page up**) PgPr

pH [piː'eɪtʃ] *n Ch* pH *m*; **a pH of 9** un pH de 9

phalanx ['fælæŋks] *n* (**a**) (*pl usu* **phalanxes** ['fælæŋksɪz]) (*in ancient armies*), *Fig* armée *f* (**b**) *Anat, Bot* (*pl usu* **phalanges** [fə'lændʒiːz]) phalange *f*

phallic ['fælɪk] *adj* phallique; **p. symbol** symbole *m* phallique

phallus ['fæləs] *n* phallus *m*

phantasm ['fæntæz(ə)m] *n Lit* (*illusion*) illusion *f*; (*ghost*) apparition *f*

phantasmagoria [fæntæzmæ'gɒrɪə] *n Lit* fantasmagorie *f*

phantasy ['fæntəsɪ] *n* = **fantasy**

phantom ['fæntəm] *n* fantôme *m*, spectre *m*; *Tel* **p. circuit** circuit *m* fantôme; *Med* **p. limb** membre *m* fantôme; **p. pregnancy** grossesse *f* nerveuse; **p. ship** vaisseau *m* fantôme

Pharaoh ['feərəʊ] *n Antiq* pharaon *m*

Pharisee ['færɪsiː] *n Antiq, Fig* pharisien, -ienne

pharmaceutical [fɑːmə'sjuːtɪk(ə)l] **1** *adj* pharmaceutique; **p. rep(resentative)** visiteur, -euse médical(e) **2** *npl* **pharmaceuticals** (*medicines*) produits *mpl* pharmaceutiques; (*industry*) industrie *f* pharmaceutique; **I'm in pharmaceuticals** je suis dans la pharmaceutique; **pharmaceuticals company** société *f* pharmaceutique

pharmacist ['fɑːməsɪst] *n* pharmacien, -ienne

pharmacological [fɑːməkə'lɒdʒɪk(ə)l] *adj* pharmacologique

pharmacologist [fɑːmə'kɒlədʒɪst] *n* pharmacologiste *mf*, pharmacologue *mf*

pharmacology [fɑːmə'kɒlədʒɪ] *n* pharmacologie *f*

pharmacopoeia [fɑːməkəʊ'piːə] *n* (*book*) pharmacopée *f*; (*collection of drugs*) pharmacopée, pharmacie *f*

pharmacy ['fɑːməsɪ] *n* pharmacie *f*

pharyngitis [færɪn'dʒaɪtɪs] *n Med* pharyngite *f*

pharynx ['færɪŋks] *n Anat* pharynx *m*

phase¹ [feɪz] *n* (*of phenomenon, process, moon etc*) phase *f*; **it's still in the development p.** c'est encore en cours de développement; **initial/final p.** phase initiale/finale; *Rugby* **second p.** deuxième temps *m*; **to enter upon a new p.** entrer dans une nouvelle phase; **it's just a p. (he's/she's going through)** ça lui passera; *Phys, MecE* **in p.** en phase (**with sth** avec qch); **out of p.** *Phys, MecE* hors de phase, déphasé; *Fig* déphasé; *El* **single/two/three-p. current** courant *m* monophasé/diphasé/triphasé; *TV* **p. distortion** déphasage *m*

phase² *vt* (**a**) (*changes, new methods*) introduire progressivement; (*project*) développer en phases successives; (*schedule, introduction of technology etc*) échelonner; **the negotiations have to be properly phased** les diverses phases des négociations doivent être correctement planifiées (**b**) *El etc* mettre en phases, caler en phase

▶ **phase in** *vtsep* (*changes, new methods etc*) introduire progressivement; (*new systems, equipment etc*) mettre en place progressivement

▶ **phase out** *vtsep* (**a**) (*get rid of gradually*) (*methods, equipment, jobs etc*) éliminer progressivement; *Hum* (*boyfriend*) faire sortir de sa vie; **the system is being phased out** ce système est en cours d'abandon (**b**) (*get rid of*) éliminer; **that's all been phased out now** ça n'existe plus maintenant

phased [feɪzd] *adj* (**a**) par phases, progressif; (*evacuation*) progressif (**b**) *El* phasé; (*light*) cohérent

phasing ['feɪzɪŋ] *n* (**a**) (*planning*) planification *f* par phases; (*of manufacturing schedule etc*) échelonnement *m*; (*phasing in*)

(*of measures, new methods*) introduction *f* progressive (**b**) *El etc* mise *f* en phase, calage *m* en phase
phasing in *n* (*of new methods etc*) adoption *f ou* introduction *f* progressive; (*of new systems, new equipment etc*) mise *f* en place progressive
phasing out *n* (*of old methods, equipment etc*) élimination *f* progressive
PhD [piːeɪtʃ'diː] *n Univ* (*abbr* **Doctor of Philosophy**) (*diploma*) = doctorat *m*; (*person*) docteur *m*, titulaire *mf* d'un doctorat; **to have a P. in Maths** avoir un doctorat en maths
pheasant ['fez(ə)nt] *n* faisan *m*; **cock p.** (coq *m*) faisan; **hen p.** (poule *f*) faisane *f*; **young p., p. poult** faisandeau *m*; **p. shoot** faisanderie *f*; **p. shooting** chasse *f* au faisan
phenix ['fiːnɪks] *n US Myth* = **phoenix**
phenobarbitone [fiːnəʊ'bɑːbɪtəʊn] *n Pharm* phénobarbital *m*
phenol ['fiːnɒl] *n Ch* phénol *m*
phenomenal [fɪ'nɒmɪn(ə)l] *adj* (*very great*) phénoménal, prodigieux; *Phil* phénoménal
phenomenally [fɪ'nɒmɪn(ə)lɪ] *adv* prodigieusement; **he's p. rich/stupid** il est phénoménalement riche/d'une insondable bêtise
phenomenological [fənɒmənə'lɒdʒɪk(ə)l] *adj* phénoménologique
phenomenologist [fənɒmə'nɒlədʒɪst] *n* phénoménologue *mf*
phenomenology [fənɒmə'nɒlədʒɪ] *n* phénoménologie *f*
phenomenon, *pl* **-mena** [fɪ'nɒmɪnən, -mɪnə] *n* phénomène *m*
pheromone ['ferəməʊn] *n* phérormone *f*, phéromone *f*
phew [fjuː] *int* (*when hot*) pfff!; (*disgust*) pouah!; (*relief*) ouf!
phial ['faɪəl] *n* fiole *f*, flacon *m*, ampoule *f*
Phil *abbr* **Philadelphia**
philander [fɪ'lændər] *vi Lit Pej* courir le jupon
philanderer [fɪ'lændərər] *n Pej* coureur *m* de jupons
philandering [fɪ'lændərɪŋ] *Pej* **1** *n* **she had had enough of his p.** elle en avait assez qu'il coure le jupon **2** *adj* (*ways, habits*) de coureur de jupon; **her p. husband** son coureur de jupon de mari
philanthropic [fɪlən'θrɒpɪk] *adj* philanthropique; (*person*) philanthrope
philanthropist [fɪ'lænθrəpɪst] *n* philanthrope *mf*
philanthropy [fɪ'lænθrəpɪ] *n* philanthropie *f*
philatelic [fɪlə'telɪk] *adj* philatélique
philatelist [fɪ'lætəlɪst] *n* philatéliste *mf*
philately [fɪ'lætəlɪ] *n* philatélie *f*
-phile [faɪl] *suff* -phile; **Anglop.** anglophile *mf*; **Francop.** francophile *mf*
philharmonic [fɪlə'mɒnɪk] **1** *adj* philharmonique **2** *n* philharmonie *f*, société *f* philharmonique
-philia ['fɪlɪə] *suff* -philie; **necrophilia** nécrophilie *f*; **anglophilia** anglophilie *f*
Philippine ['fɪlɪpiːn] **1** *adj* philippin **2** *n* [①A11,g,ii] **the Philippines** les (îles *fpl*) Philippines *fpl*
philistine ['fɪlɪstaɪn] **1** *n Art, Liter* béotien, -ienne, philistin *m*; *Bible* **P.** Philistin *m* **2** *adj Art, Liter* béotien, philistin
philistinism ['fɪlɪstɪnɪz(ə)m] *n* philistinisme *m*
Phillips ® ['fɪlɪps] *adj* **P. screw/screwdriver** vis *f*/tournevis *m* à empreinte cruciforme
philodendron [fɪlə'dendrən] *n* (*plant*) philodendron *m*
philological [fɪlə'lɒdʒɪk(ə)l] *adj* philologique
philologist [fɪ'lɒlədʒɪst] *n* philologue *mf*
philology [fɪ'lɒlədʒɪ] *n* philologie *f*
philosopher [fɪ'lɒsəfər] *n* philosophe *mf*; **the p.'s stone** la pierre philosophale
philosophic(al) [fɪlə'sɒfɪk, -ɪk(ə)l] *adj Phil* philosophique; *Fig* (*person, attitude*) philosophe; **she was p. about her defeat** elle a pris sa défaite en philosophe *ou* avec philosophie
philosophically [fɪlə'sɒfɪklɪ] *adv Phil* philosophiquement; *Fig* (*to react etc*) en philosophe, avec philosophie
philosophize [fɪ'lɒsəfaɪz] *vi* philosopher
philosophy [fɪ'lɒsəfɪ] *n* philosophie *f*; **a personal p.** une philosophie personnelle; **one's own p. about sth** sa conception personnelle de qch; **my p. is ...** ma philosophie c'est ...; **with p.** (*to endure hardship*) avec philosophie, en philosophe
philtre, *US* **philter** ['fɪltər] *n* philtre *m*
phiz [fɪz], **phizog** ['fɪzɒg] *n esp Br Old-fashioned Sl* (*face*) binette *f*, tronche *f*
phlebitis [flɪ'baɪtɪs] *n Med* phlébite *f*; **to have p.** avoir une phlébite
phlegm [flem] *n* (**a**) (*mucus*) flegme *m*, pituite *f* (bronchiale); **to cough up p.** tousser gras (**b**) *Fml* (*composure*) flegme *m*, calme *m*
phlegmatic [fleg'mætɪk] *adj* flegmatique
phlegmatically [fleg'mætɪklɪ] *adv* flegmatiquement
phlox [flɒks] *n* (*plant*) phlox *m*
-phobe [fəʊb] *suff* -phobe *mf*
phobia ['fəʊbɪə] *n* phobie *f*; **to have a p. about sth** avoir une phobie pour qch
-phobia ['fəʊbɪə] *suff* -phobie *f*
phobic ['fəʊbɪk] *adj, n Med* phobique *mf*; *Fig* **he's really p. about tidiness** c'est un vrai maniaque du rangement
-phobic ['fəʊbɪk] *suff* -phobe
Phoenician [fɪ'niːʃən] *Antiq* **1** *adj* phénicien **2** *n* (**a**) Phénicien, -ienne (**b**) *Ling* phénicien *m*
phoenix, *US* **phenix** ['fiːnɪks] *n Myth* phénix *m*; **to rise, p.-like, from ...** renaître, tel un phénix, de ...
phone[1] [fəʊn] *n* téléphone *m*; **to be on the p.** (*talking*) être au téléphone; (*have a telephone*) avoir le téléphone; *F* **to give sb a p.** donner un coup de téléphone *ou* de fil à qn; **he was on the p. for an hour** il a passé une heure au téléphone; **he's on the p.** (*in office*) il est en ligne; **quiet, Mummy's on the p.** tais-toi, maman a quelqu'un au bout du fil; **I've got Mummy on the p.** j'ai Mama au bout du fil; **to get on the p. to sb** téléphoner à qn; **I couldn't get her on the p.** je n'ai pas réussi à l'avoir au téléphone *ou* à la joindre; **could you get Maria on the p. for me?** est-ce que tu pourrais m'appeler Maria (au téléphone)?; **get off the p.!** raccroche!; **to speak to sb on** *or* **over the p.** parler à qn au téléphone
phone[2] **1** *vt* (**a**) **to p. sb** téléphoner à qn, appeler qn au téléphone, donner un coup de téléphone *ou F* de fil à qn; **to p. the office/police** téléphoner au bureau/à la police (**b**) **to p. a piece of news** téléphoner une nouvelle **2** *vi* téléphoner; **to p. home** téléphoner à la maison
phone[3] *n Ling* phonème *m*
-phone [fəʊn] *suff* -phone; **Anglop./Francop.** anglophone/ francophone
▶ **phone in** *vi* téléphoner; **to p. in sick** téléphoner pour dire qu'on est malade
▶ **phone up** *vtsep* = **phone**[2] **1**
phone bill *n* facture *f* de téléphone
phone book *n* annuaire *m* (du téléphone)
phone booth *n* cabine *f* téléphonique
phone box *n* cabine *f* téléphonique
phone call *n* coup *m* de téléphone
phonecard ['fəʊnkɑːd] *n Br Tel* télécarte *f*
phone-in *n, adj* **p.** (**programme**) émission *f* à ligne ouverte, émission au cours de laquelle les téléspectateurs/auditeurs peuvent intervenir par téléphone
phoneme ['fəʊniːm] *n Ling* phonème *m*
phonemic [fə'niːmɪk] *adj* phonémique
phone number *n* numéro *m* de téléphone
phone tap *n* écoute *f* téléphonique
phone tapping *n* écoutes *fpl* téléphoniques
phonetic [fə'netɪk] *adj* phonétique; **p. alphabet** alphabet *m* phonétique
phonetically [fə'netɪklɪ] *adv* phonétiquement
phonetician [fəʊnə'tɪʃən] *n* phonéticien, -ienne
phonetics [fə'netɪks] *n* [①A10,c] (**a**) (*science*) phonétique *f* (**b**) (*symbols*) phonétique *f*
phoney, *esp US* **phony** ['fəʊnɪ] *F* **1** *adj* (*comp* **phonier**; *superl* **phoniest**) faux, *f* fausse; (*story, excuse etc*) bidon; **he's p.** (*US* **as a two-dollar bill**) il est faux comme un jeton, il est faux jeton; *Hist* **p. war** drôle *f* de guerre **2** *n* (*impostor*) imposteur *m*; (*insincere person*) faux jeton *m*; (*fake object*) faux *m*
phonic ['fɒnɪk, 'fəʊnɪk] *adj* phonique
phonograph ['fəʊnəgræf] *n Am* phonographe *m*
phonology [fə'nɒlədʒɪ] *n* phonologie *f*
phony ['fəʊnɪ] *adj, n esp US F* = **phoney**
phooey ['fuːɪ] *int* peuh!
phosgene ['fɒzdʒiːn] *n Ch* phosgène *m*
phosphate[1] ['fɒsfeɪt] *n Ch* phosphate *m*; **p. of lime, calcium p.** phosphate de chaux; **p. mine** *or* **works** phosphaterie *f*
phosphide ['fɒsfaɪd] *n Ch* phosphure *m*
phosphite ['fɒsfaɪt] *n Ch* phosphite *m*
phosphoresce [fɒsfə'res] *vi* être phosphorescent, luire par phosphorescence
phosphorescence [fɒsfə'resəns] *n* phosphorescence *f*
phosphorescent [fɒsfə'resənt] *adj* phosphorescent
phosphoric [fɒs'fɒrɪk] *adj Ch* phosphorique
phosphorous ['fɒsfərəs] *adj Ch* phosphoreux
phosphorus ['fɒsfərəs] *n Ch* phosphore *m*
photo ['fəʊtəʊ] *n* photo *f*; **to take good photos** prendre de bonnes photos; **to take a good p.** (*be photogenic*) être photogénique; **p. album** album *m* (de) photos
photo- ['fəʊtəʊ] *pref* photo-
photo call *n Cin, TV* séance *f* de photos
photocard ['fəʊtəʊkɑːd] *n* carte *f* portant une photo d'identité du titulaire
photocell ['fəʊtəʊsel] *n* photocellule *f*

photocomposition [fəʊtəʊkɒmpə'zɪʃən] *n* photocomposition *f*; **p. machine** photocomposeuse *f*
photocompositor [fəʊtəʊkəm'pɒzɪtər] *n* (*machine*) photocomposeuse *f*
photocopier ['fəʊtəʊkɒpɪər] *n* photocopieur *m*, photocopieuse *f*
photocopy¹ ['fəʊtəʊkɒpɪ] *n* photocopie *f*; **to take** *or* **make a p. of sth** faire une photocopie de qch, photocopier qch
photocopy² **1** *vt* photocopier **2** *vi* **these pictures won't p. very well** ces dessins ne donneront pas de bonnes photocopies; **to do some photocopying** faire des photocopies
photoelectric [fəʊtəʊɪ'lektrɪk] *adj* photoélectrique; **p. cell** cellule *f* photoélectrique, photocellule *f*
photoelectron [fəʊtəʊɪ'lektrɒn] *n Phys* photoélectron *m*
photoengraving [fəʊtəʊɪn'greɪvɪŋ] *n* photogravure *f*
photo finish *n Sp* photo-finish *f inv*
Photofit® ['fəʊtəʊfɪt] *n* **P. (picture)** portrait-robot *m*, *pl* portraits-robots
photogenic [fəʊtə'dʒenɪk] *adj* photogénique
photograph¹ ['fəʊtəgrɑːf] *n* photo *f*, photographie *f*; **in the p.** sur la photo; **to have a p. of sth** avoir qch en photo; **to take sb's p.** prendre une photo de qn; **he had his p. taken** il s'est fait photographier; **she takes a good p.** (*is photogenic*) elle est photogénique; **p. album** album *m* de photos *ou* de photographies
photograph² **1** *vt* photographier, prendre en photo **2** *vi* **to p. well** (*be photogenic*) être photogénique; **it won't p. well in this light** cela ne fera pas une bonne photo dans cette lumière
photographer [fə'tɒgrəfər] *n* photographe *mf*; **she's a good/bad p.** elle prend de bonnes/mauvaises photos
photographic [fəʊtə'græfɪk] *adj* (*process, paper, description etc*) photographique; **to have a p. memory** avoir une mémoire photographique; **p. agency** agence *f* photographique; **p. library** photothèque *f*, archives *fpl* photographiques
photographically [fəʊtə'græfɪklɪ] *adv* photographiquement
photography [fə'tɒgrəfɪ] *n* photographie *f*
photogravure [fəʊtəʊgrə'vjʊər] *n* photogravure *f*
photojournalism [fəʊtəʊ'dʒɜːnəlɪz(ə)m] *n* photoreportage *m*
photojournalist [fəʊtəʊ'dʒɜːnəlɪst] *n* reporter *m* photographe, photojournaliste *mf*
photolithography [fəʊtəʊlɪ'θɒgrəfɪ] *n* photolithographie *f*
photoluminescence [fəʊtəʊluːmɪ'nesəns] *n* photoluminescence *f*
photometer [fəʊ'tɒmɪtər] *n Phys* photomètre *m*
photometry [fəʊ'tɒmɪtrɪ] *n Phys* photométrie *f*
photomontage ['fəʊtəʊmɒn'tɑːʒ] *n* photomontage *m*
photon ['fəʊtɒn] *n Phys* photon *m*
photo opportunity *n* séance *f* de photo
photosensitive [fəʊtəʊ'sensɪtɪv] *adj* photosensible
photosetter ['fəʊtəʊsetər] *n Br* photocomposeuse *f*, photocompositeur *m*
photosetting ['fəʊtəʊsetɪŋ] *n Br* photocomposition *f*; **p. machine** photocomposeuse *f*
Photostat®**¹** ['fəʊtəʊstæt] *n* photostat *m*
Photostat®**²** **1** *vt* faire un photostat de **2** *vi* faire des photostats
photo-story *n* roman-photo *m*, *pl* romans-photos
photosynthesis [fəʊtəʊ'sɪnθɪsɪs] *n* photosynthèse *f*
photosynthesize [fəʊtəʊ'sɪnθɪsaɪz] *vt* photosynthétiser
phototropism [fəʊtəʊ'trəʊpɪz(ə)m] *n Biol* phototropisme *m*
phototypesetter [fəʊtəʊ'taɪpsetər] *n Br* photocompositeur *m*
phototypesetting [fəʊtəʊ'taɪpsetɪŋ] *n Br* photocomposition *f*
photovoltaic [fəʊtəʊvɒl'teɪɪk] *adj* photovoltaïque; **p. cell** cellule *f* photovoltaïque, photopile *f*; **p. effect** effet *m* photovoltaïque
phrasal ['freɪzəl] *adj* [①**A59-61**; **B62,3,a**] *Gram* **p. verb** verbe *m* à particule, verbe composé
phrase¹ [freɪz] *n* expression *f*; *Mus* phrase *f*; *Gram* locution *f* (adverbiale *etc*), membre *m* de phrase; **noun p.** syntagme *m* nominal; **could you describe it for us in a p. or two?** est-ce que vous pourriez nous le décrire en quelques phrases?; **in Voltaire's p.** comme dirait Voltaire
phrase² *vt* **(a)** (*verbally*) exprimer, donner un tour à; (*letter, invitation, question, answer*) tourner; **that is how he phrased it** voilà comment il s'est exprimé, voilà comment il a tourné cela **(b)** *Mus* phraser
phrase book *n* manuel *m ou* guide *m* de conversation
phraseology [freɪzɪ'ɒlədʒɪ] *n* phraséologie *f*
phrasing ['freɪzɪŋ] *n* **(a)** (*of text*) phraséologie *f*; (*of thought*) expression *f*; (*of answer, notice etc*) tournure *f* **(b)** *Mus* phrasé *m*
phrenic nerve ['frenɪk] *n Med* nerf *m* phrénique
phrenology [frɪ'nɒlədʒɪ] *n* phrénologie *f*
phthisis ['θaɪsɪs] *n Med* phtisie *f*
phut [fʌt] *adv F* **to go p.** (*of business, engine etc*) claquer; **the light went p.** la lumière s'est éteinte
phylactery [fɪ'læktərɪ] *n Jewish Rel* phylactère *m*
phylloxera [fɪlɒk'sɪərə] *n* (*insect*) phylloxéra *m*
phylum, *pl* **-la** ['faɪləm, -lə] *n Biol* phylum *m*
physic ['fɪzɪk] *n Arch* remède *m*
physical ['fɪzɪk(ə)l] **1** *adj* **(a)** (*relating to the body*) physique; *Med* (*symptoms*) somatique; **rugby is a very p. sport** le rugby est un sport dans lequel il y a beaucoup de contacts physiques; **the game got very p.** le jeu est devenu très physique; **p. contact** contact *m* physique; **p. exercises** *or* **training** *or Br F* **jerks** (exercices *mpl* de) gymnastique *f*; **p. fitness** (bonne) forme *f* physique; **p. handicap** handicap *m* physique; **p. strength** force *f* physique; **it left him a p. wreck** ça lui a détruit la santé
(b) (*concrete, material*) physique; **p. access control** contrôle *m* d'accès physique; *Comptr* **p. disk cache** cache *m* disque physique; *Mktg* **p. distribution** distribution *f* physique; *Mktg* **p. distribution management** gestion *f* de la distribution physique; *Geog* **p. features** topographie *f*; **p. impossibility** impossibilité *f* matérielle *ou* physique; *Com* **p. inventory** inventaire *m* effectif; **p. presence** présence *f* physique; **p. property** propriété *f* physique
2 *n Med F* visite *f* médicale; **to have a p.** passer une visite médicale
physical chemistry *n* chimie *f* physique
physical education *n* culture *f ou* éducation *f* physique
physical examination *n Med* visite *f* médicale
physical geography *n* géographie *f* physique
physically ['fɪzɪklɪ] *adv* **(a)** physiquement; **p. attractive** attirant sur le plan physique; **p. fit** en bonne forme physique; **to be p. handicapped** être handicapé physique **(b)** (*materially*) physiquement, matériellement; **seeing it on TV isn't the same as being p. there** le voir à la télévision ce n'est pas la même chose que d'y assister en personne
physical sciences *npl* sciences *fpl* physiques
physician [fɪ'zɪʃən] *n* médecin *m*
physicist ['fɪzɪsɪst] *n* physicien, -ienne
physics ['fɪzɪks] *n* [①**A10,c**] physique *f*
physio ['fɪzɪəʊ] *n Med F* **(a)** (*abbr* **physiotherapist**) kiné *mf* **(b)** (*abbr* **physiotherapy**) kiné *f*
physiognomy [fɪzɪ'ɒnəmɪ] *n Fml* (*of person*) physionomie *f*; *Geog* (*of region*) configuration *f*
physiological [fɪzɪə'lɒdʒɪk(ə)l] *adj* physiologique
physiologically [fɪzɪə'lɒdʒɪklɪ] *adv* physiologiquement
physiologist [fɪzɪ'ɒlədʒɪst] *n* physiologiste *mf*, physiologue *mf*
physiology [fɪzɪ'ɒlədʒɪ] *n* physiologie *f*
physiopathology [fɪzɪəʊpə'θɒlədʒɪ] *n Med* physiopathologie *f*
physiotherapist [fɪzɪəʊ'θerəpɪst] *n* kinésithérapeute *mf*
physiotherapy [fɪzɪəʊ'θerəpɪ] *n* kinésithérapie *f*, rééducation *f*; **to have p.** faire de la rééducation
physique [fɪ'ziːk] *n* physique *m*; **fine p.** beau physique; **poor p.** physique ingrat; **he hasn't the p. for it** il n'a pas le physique de l'emploi
pi [paɪ] *n* (*in Greek alphabet*), *Math* pi *m*
pianissimo [pɪə'nɪsɪməʊ] *adv, n* pianissimo *m*
pianist ['pɪənɪst] *n* pianiste *mf*
piano¹ [pɪ'ænəʊ], *Fml* **pianoforte** [pɪænəʊ'fɔːrtɪ] *n* piano *m*; **sonata for p. and violin** sonate pour piano et violon; **p. accordion** accordéon *m*; **p. concerto** concerto *m* pour piano; **p. duet** duo *m* pour piano; **p. key** touche *f* de piano; **p. player** pianiste *mf*; **p. stool** tabouret *m* de piano; **p. tuner** accordeur *m* de pianos
piano² [pɪ'ɑːnəʊ] *adj, adv Mus* piano
piastre [pɪ'æstər] *n* (*currency*) piastre *f*
piazza [pɪ'ætsə] *n* (*esp in Italy*) place *f* (publique); *Br* (*covered*) galerie *f*
PIBOR ['paɪbɔːr] *n* (*abbr* **Paris interbank offered rate**) TIOP *m*, PIBOR *m*
pic [pɪk] *n F* **(a)** (*picture*) image *f*; (*photograph*) photo *f* **(b)** *Br Cin* **the pics** le ciné, le cinoche
pica ['paɪkə] *n Typ* pica *m*
picador ['pɪkədɔːr] *n* picador *m*
Picardy ['pɪkədɪ] *n* Picardie *f*
picaresque [pɪkə'resk] *adj* (*novel*) picaresque
piccalilli [pɪkə'lɪlɪ] *n Culin* pickles *mpl* à la moutarde
piccaninny [pɪkə'nɪnɪ] *n Old-fashioned Offensive Sl* (*negro child*) négrillon, -onne
piccolo ['pɪkələʊ] *n Mus* piccolo *m*
pick¹ [pɪk] *n* **(a)** (*tool*) pic *m*, pioche *f*; **(miner's) p.** pic à main **(b)** *Mus* (*plectrum*) plectre *m*, médiator *m*
pick² *n* **the p.** (*best*) (*of people*) l'élite *f*, la crème; (*of apples, new films etc*) le meilleur, *pl* les meilleurs; **the p. of the bunch** le meilleur de tous *ou F* du lot; (*several people*) le dessus du panier, *F* le gratin; **we had first p.** nous avons été les premiers à choisir; **take your p.** choisissez

pick³ 1 *vt* **(a)** *(choose)* choisir, sélectionner; **to p. one's words (carefully)** (bien) choisir ses mots; *Horseracing etc* **to p. a winner** choisir *ou* désigner un gagnant; *Fig* **we've certainly picked a winner in Paul Rodger** nous avons vraiment tiré le bon numéro avec Paul Rodger; **he was picked for Scotland** il a été choisi pour représenter l'Écosse; **to p. one's way through a field** traverser un champ en regardant où on met les pieds; **you picked a fine time to tell me** tu as bien choisi ton moment pour me le dire; **to p. a fight** chercher la bagarre (**with sb** à qn)

(b) *(gather)* *(flowers, fruit etc)* cueillir

(c) *(lock)* crocheter; **to p. rags** détisser *ou* effilocher des chiffons; **to p. sb's pocket** faire les poches à qn; **she picked a hole in her jumper** elle a fait un trou à son pull en tirant sur la laine; *Fig* **to p. holes in sth** *(in argument, theory, book etc)* trouver des failles dans qch; *F* **she's constantly picking holes (in everything)** elle n'arrête pas de chercher la petite bête; **to p. sb's brains** tirer parti de l'intelligence *ou* des connaissances de qn; **can I p. your brains a minute?** est-ce que je peux faire appel à tes connaissances une minute?; **to p. a bone** décortiquer un os; *Fig* **to have a bone to p. with sb** avoir un compte à régler avec qn; **to p. one's nose/teeth** se curer le nez/les dents; **to p. a spot/scab** gratter un bouton/une croûte

(d) *(of birds)* *(corn etc)* picoter, becqueter

(e) *Mus* **to p. a guitar** pincer la guitare

2 *vi* *(choose)* choisir; **you p. first** choisis d'abord; **to p. and choose** faire le/la difficile

▶ **pick at** *vipo* **to p. at one's food** picorer; **to p. at a scab** gratter une croûte

▶ **pick off** *vtsep* **(a)** *(remove)* *(flowers, leaves etc)* enlever, ôter; **p. those papers off the ground** ramassez ces papiers qui sont par terre; **to p. the meat off a bone** décortiquer un os; **she picked herself off the floor** elle s'est relevée **(b)** *(of gunman, sniper)* descendre, abattre; *(several people)* descendre *ou* abattre un à un; *Fig* *(opponent etc)* éliminer; *(several opponents)* éliminer les uns après les autres

▶ **pick on** *vipo* **(a)** *(victimize)* s'en prendre à; **stop picking on her** arrête de t'en prendre à elle; **why p. on me?** pourquoi s'en prendre à moi?; **p. on sb your own size!** ne t'attaque pas à qn de plus faible que toi! **(b)** *(choose)* *(person, thing)* choisir; **I always get picked on for the worst jobs** c'est toujours à moi que reviennent les tâches les plus ingrates

▶ **pick out** *vtsep* **(a)** *(remove)* *(sth)* extirper, enlever **(b)** *(select)* *(sth)* choisir; **he picked out the best peaches** il a choisi les meilleures pêches; **to p. out a criminal** *(in identification parade)* identifier un criminel **(c)** *(recognize)* repérer; **she was easy to p. out in her orange coat** elle était facilement reconnaissable *ou* facile à repérer avec son manteau orange **(d)** *(highlight)* **picked out in gold** rehaussé d'or **(e)** *Mus* **to p. out a tune** essayer de retrouver un air

▶ **pick over** *vipo* *(fruit etc)* trier; *Fig* *(performance, exam, details)* débattre de

▶ **pick up 1** *vtsep* **(a)** *(lift up)* prendre; *(sth from the ground)* ramasser; *(sth that has fallen over)* relever; *(telephone)* décrocher; *Knitting* *(stitch)* relever; **to p. up survivors** *(of ship, helicopter)* recueillir des survivants; **to p. up the odd pound here or there** *(earn)* gagner un peu d'argent par ci par là; **to p. up a child** *(in one's arms)* prendre un enfant dans ses bras; *(after falling)* relever un enfant; **to p. oneself up** *(after falling)* se relever; *Fig* *(recover from crisis)* se remettre; **to p. up the pieces** *(after breaking sth)*, *Fig* ramasser les morceaux; **we were left to p. up the bill** c'est nous qui avons dû casquer; **let me p. up the bill** laisse-moi payer

(b) *(collect)* aller prendre *ou* chercher; **I'll p. you up at the station** je viendrai vous chercher *ou* vous prendre à la gare; **the train stops to p. up passengers** le train s'arrête pour prendre des voyageurs

(c) *(catch)* **to p. up a cold** ramasser *ou* attraper un rhume

(d) *(acquire)* **to p. sth up cheap** acheter qch bon marché; **she's good at picking up bargains** elle a du flair pour les bonnes affaires; **to p. up a parking ticket** attraper un PV

(e) *F* *(initiate casual sexual relationship with)* **to p. up a man/woman** lever *ou* emballer un homme/une femme; **he tried to p. her up** il l'a draguée; **to p. up a customer** *(of prostitute)* racoler *ou* raccrocher un client

(f) *(arrest)* *(person)* arrêter

(g) *(message)* capter, recevoir; *Rad* *(station)* capter; *El* *(current)* prendre, capter; *(of searchlight)* *(plane etc)* repérer; **the police have picked up a trail** la police a trouvé une piste

(h) *(learn)* *(trick, language, fact)* apprendre; *(news, information)* recueillir; **to p. up a habit** prendre une habitude; **I don't know where he's picking up these funny ideas from** je ne sais pas où il va chercher ces idées bizarres; **she seems to have picked up the idea that ...** elle a l'air de s'être mis dans la tête que ...

(i) *(notice)* *(error)* relever

(j) *(continue)* *(discussion)* reprendre; **we soon picked up the road again** nous avons vite retrouvé notre chemin

(k) *(reprimand)* **to p. sb up sharply** reprendre qn vertement; **I'd like to p. Chris Jones up on that (point)** *(in debate)* j'aimerais reprendre Chris Jones sur ce point; **to p. sb up for a mistake** réprimander qn pour avoir fait une erreur

(l) *Aut etc* **to p. up speed** reprendre de la vitesse; **to p. up strength** *(of person)* reprendre des forces

2 *vtas* *(make better)* *(person)* remonter; **that will p. you up** voilà qui vous remontera

3 *vi* **(a)** *(improve)* s'améliorer; *(after illness)* retrouver la santé *ou* ses forces, se rétablir; **business is picking up** les affaires reprennent; **the weather looks like picking up** le temps a l'air de se remettre; **the game certainly picked up in the second half** la partie s'est animée pendant la deuxième mi-temps

(b) *(continue)* *(of conversation, negotiations etc)* reprendre; *(in relationship)* recommencer; **let's p. up where we left off** reprenons là où nous nous étions arrêtés

(c) *Sp etc* **to p. up on sb** rattraper qn; **this engine picks up well** ce moteur a de bonnes reprises

pick-a-back *adv, adj, n* = **piggyback**

pickaninny [pɪkəˈnɪnɪ] *n Old-fashioned Offensive Sl* = **piccaninny**

pickaxe¹, *US* **pickax** [ˈpɪkæks] *n (tool)* pioche *f*, pic *m*

pickaxe², *US* **pickax** *vt* piocher

picker [ˈpɪkər] *n* **(a)** *(of fruit etc)* cueilleur, -euse **(b)** *(of cotton etc)* démêleur, -euse

pickerel [ˈpɪkərəl] *n (fish)* doré *m*

picket¹ [ˈpɪkɪt] *n* **(a)** *Ind etc* *(of strikers)* piquet *m* de grève; *(one person)* gréviste *mf* en faction **(b)** *Mil etc* *(detachment)* piquet *m* *(d'hommes)*; *(one soldier)* factionnaire *m*; **to be on p.** être de piquet **(c)** *(stake)* *(of fence etc)* piquet *m*, pieu *m*; *(for horses etc)* piquet d'attache

picket² (-t-) **1** *vt* **(a)** *Ind etc* **to p. a factory** mettre un piquet de grève aux portes d'une usine **(b)** *(fence)* *(area)* entourer de piquets *ou* de pieux **(c)** *(fasten)* *(horses)* mettre au(x) piquet(s) **2** *vi Ind etc* faire le piquet de grève

picket duty *n* piquet *m*

picket fence *n* palis *m*, palissade *f*

picketing [ˈpɪkɪtɪŋ] *n Ind etc* blocage *m* par des piquets de grève

picket line *n* piquet *m* de grève

picking [ˈpɪkɪŋ] *n* **(a)** *(choosing)* choix *m* **(b)** *(of fruit, flowers etc)* cueillette *f*; **p. season** cueillette **(c)** *(of lock)* crochetage *m*

pickings [ˈpɪkɪŋz] *npl (money etc)* bénéfices *mpl*; **to make rich p. from a scheme** tirer de gros bénéfices d'une affaire

pickle¹ [ˈpɪk(ə)l] *n* **(a)** **pickles** pickles *mpl*, conserves *fpl* au vinaigre; **mixed pickles** mélange *m* de pickles **(b)** *(marinade)* saumure *f* **(c)** *F* *(predicament)* **to be in a bit of a p.** être dans de beaux draps *ou* dans le pétrin

pickle² *vt* saumurer, conserver (au vinaigre *ou* à la saumure)

pickled [ˈpɪk(ə)ld] *adj* **(a)** saumuré, en saumure; **p. cabbage/onions** chou *m* rouge/oignons *mpl* au vinaigre **(b)** *F (drunk)* gris, pompette

pickling [ˈpɪk(ə)lɪŋ] *n* saumurage *m*, conservation *f* au vinaigre; **p. onions** petits oignons *mpl*

picklock [ˈpɪklɒk] *n* **(a)** *(person)* crocheteur *m* *(de serrures)* **(b)** *(key)* crochet *m*, rossignol *m*

pick-me-up *n F* remontant *m*

pickpocket [ˈpɪkpɒkɪt] *n* voleur, -euse à la tire, pickpocket *m*

pick-up *n* **(a)** *(collection)* ramassage *m*; *Electron, Rad* *(of signal)* captage *m*; **a p. point** *(for passengers on coach journey, goods etc)* point *m* de ramassage **(b)** *(device)* *(on record player)* lecteur *m* (phonographique), pick-up *m inv*; *Electron etc* *(of waves, vibrations)* capteur *m*, détecteur *m*; **p. arm** bras *m* de pick-up **(c)** *(vehicle)* **p. (truck)** pick-up *m inv*, camionnette *f* à plateau **(d)** *F* *(man, woman)* conquête *f* **(e)** *F* *(improvement)* amélioration *f*; *(of business etc)* reprise *f*; *(of optimism)* regain *m*

picky [ˈpɪkɪ] *adj F* difficile; **to be p. about one's food** être difficile sur la nourriture

picnic¹ [ˈpɪknɪk] *n* pique-nique *m*, *pl* pique-niques; **to go on a p.** aller faire un pique-nique, aller pique-niquer; *Fig F* **it was no p.** cela n'a pas été une partie de plaisir; **p. area** *or* **site** aire *f* de pique-nique; **p. basket** *or* **hamper** panier *m* à pique-nique; *(filled)* panier garni; **we had a p. lunch** nous avons pique-niqué à midi; **we'll take a p. lunch with us** nous emporterons un pique-nique (pour le déjeuner)

picnic² *vi* (*pt, pp* **picnicked**) pique-niquer, faire un pique-nique
picnicker ['pɪknɪkər] *n* pique-niqueur, -euse
Pict [pɪkt] *n Hist* Picte *mf*
Pictish ['pɪktɪʃ] *adj Hist* picte, pictique
pictogram ['pɪktəgræm] *n* pictogramme *m*
pictograph ['pɪktəgrɑːf] *n* pictographe *m*
pictorial [pɪk'tɔːrɪəl] **1** *adj* (*magazine etc*) illustré; (*representation*) en images; **p. dictionary** dictionnaire *m* en images **2** *n* périodique *m* illustré, journal *m* illustré
pictorially [pɪk'tɔːrɪəlɪ] *adv* en images
picture¹ ['pɪktʃər] *n* **(a)** (*image*) (*painting*) tableau *m*, peinture *f*; (*drawing*) dessin *m*; (*in picture book etc*), *TV* image *f*; (*illustrating text*) illustration *f*; (*photograph*) photo *f*; **to paint a p.** faire *ou* peindre un tableau; **to draw a p.** faire un dessin; **to get one's p. in the paper** avoir sa photo dans le journal; **p. cheque** image-chèque *f*; **p. completion** (*in assessing, testing etc*) images à compléter; **p. dealer** marchand, -ande de tableaux; *Journ* **p. desk** bureau *m* des illustrations; **p. editor** illustrateur *m*; **p. hat** chapeau *m* gainsborough; *Comptr* **p. memory** mémoire *f* d'images; *Old-fashioned* **p. palace** cinéma *m*; *TV* **p. quality** qualité *f* des images; **p. story** roman-photo *m*; **p. tube** tube *m* image; **p. window** baie *f* vitrée
(b) *Cin F* (*film*) film *m*; **to make a p.** faire un film; *Br* **to go to the pictures** aller au cinéma
(c) *Fig* **the political/economic p.** la situation politique/économique; *Med* **we don't know the clinical p.** nous ne savons pas quelle est la situation clinique; **to get a mental p. of sth** se représenter qch; **to paint a bleak p. of the future** présenter une triste image de l'avenir; **this book gives a more accurate p. of the General** ce livre offre un portrait plus fidèle du général; **a clearer p. is emerging of what is taking place in the city** une image plus nette de ce qui se passe dans la ville est en train de se dessiner
(d) (*phrases*) **she's a p., she looks a p.** elle est à peindre; **he's no p.!** ce n'est pas une beauté!; **she looked an absolute p. in her new dress** elle était à croquer avec sa nouvelle robe; **he's the p. of health** il respire la santé; **she looked a p. of misery** elle faisait pitié; **his face was a p.** il a fait une tête à mourir de rire; **to be in the p.** être au courant *ou* au fait; **put/keep me in the p.** mets/tiens-moi au courant; **I get the p.** je vois; **to be out of the p.** être dépassé, être en dehors du coup; **it doesn't come into the p.** cela n'entre pas en ligne de compte; **when did he come into the p.?** quand a-t-il commencé à être question de lui?
picture² *vt* **(a)** (*imagine*) **to p. (to oneself)** s'imaginer, se figurer, se représenter; **I can't p. him as a teacher** je ne me l'imagine *ou* le figure pas professeur; **p. yourself as leader/at 80** imagine-toi dirigeant/à 80 ans **(b)** (*represent, portray*) représenter; (*in words*) dépeindre, décrire; *Fig* **Orwell pictures a world where …** Orwell décrit *ou* dépeint un monde où …
picture book *n* livre *m* d'images; (*travel book etc*) livre illustré
picture card *n Cards* figure *f*
picture dictionary *n* dictionnaire *m* en images
picture frame *n* cadre *m*
picture framer *n* encadreur *m*
picture gallery *n* musée *m* de peinture
picture library *n* banque *f* d'images, photothèque *f*, archives *fpl* photos
picture postcard *n* carte *f* postale illustrée
picture puzzle *n* rébus *m*
picture research *n* documentation *f* iconographique
picture researcher *n* documentaliste *mf* iconographique
picturesque [pɪktʃə'resk] *adj* pittoresque; (*descriptions etc*) imagé; *Euph* **she told him in p. language to leave** elle lui a ordonné de partir dans un langage assez cru
picturesquely [pɪktʃə'resklɪ] *adv* pittoresquement; (*to describe, write*) de façon imagée
picturesqueness [pɪktʃə'resknɪs] *n* pittoresque *m*
picture writing *n* pictographie *f*
piddle¹ ['pɪd(ə)l] *vi F* faire pipi
piddle² *n F* pipi *m*; **to have a p.** faire pipi
piddling ['pɪdlɪŋ] *adj F* insignifiant, ridicule
pidgin ['pɪdʒɪn] *n Ling* pidgin *m*; **p. English** *etc* ≈ petit nègre *m*
pie [paɪ] *n* (*with meat*) = pâté *m* en croûte; (**apple** *etc*) **p.** = tourte *f* (aux pommes *etc*); *esp Am* (*without top*) tarte *f* (aux pommes *etc*); **chicken p.** = croustade *f* de volaille; **cottage** *or* **shepherd's p.** hachis *m* parmentier; **fish p.** = timbale *f* de poissons; *F* **p. in the sky** des châteaux en Espagne; **p. dish** (*for fruit pies*) tourtière *f*; (*for meat pies*) terrine *f*; **easy as p.** simple comme bonjour
piebald ['paɪbɔːld] **1** *adj* (*horse*) pie **2** *n* (cheval *m*) pie *m*
piece [piːs] *n* **(a)** (*of paper, bread etc*) morceau *m*, bout *m*; (*of string, ribbon*) bout; (*of land*) parcelle *f*; (*of cloth*) morceau, coupon *m*; (*of glass etc*) morceau, fragment *m*, éclat *m*; (*of machine etc*) partie *f*, pièce; (*of music, poetry*) morceau; (*in book*) passage *m*; *Journ* article *m*, papier *m*; **a p. of clothing** un vêtement; **a p. of furniture** un meuble; **a p. of luggage** (*suitcase*) une valise; (*bag*) un sac; **how many pieces of luggage do you have?** combien de bagages avez-vous?; **one p. of hand-luggage** un bagage à main; **to do a p. of work** faire un travail; **to show sb a p. of one's work** montrer un échantillon de son travail à qn; **he's a nasty p. of work** c'est un sale type; **a p. of advice** un conseil; **p. of bravery/folly** acte *m* de bravoure/folie; **a p. of carelessness** une étourderie; **a p. of cruelty** une cruauté; **p. of (good) luck** coup *m* de chance; **what a p. of luck!** quelle chance!; **a p. of news** une nouvelle; *Fig F* **it was a p. of cake** c'était de la tarte; *Fig* **everyone wants a p. of the cake** tout le monde veut sa part du gâteau; *Tex* **p. goods** marchandises *fpl* ou tissus *mpl* à la pièce
(b) (*in games*) (*in backgammon*) dame *f*; (*in dominoes*) domino *m*; *Draughts* pion *m*; *Chess* pièce *f*; (*of jigsaw puzzle*) pièce
(c) *esp Br* (*coin*) **five-/fifty-pence p.** pièce *f* de cinq/cinquante pence
(d) (*weapon*) (*of artillery*) pièce *f*; (*firearm*) arme *f*; *F* **to be carrying a p.** porter une arme, être armé
(e) *Sl* (*girl*) nana *f*; **she's a nice** *or* **tasty p.** c'est une belle nana *ou* nénette
(f) *Metal* **punched/shaped p.** pièce *f* estampée/profilée; **to cast cylinders in one p.** couler des cylindres d'un seul jet *ou* en bloc; **cast** *or* **pressed** *or* **made in one p.** monobloc *inv*
(g) *esp Am* (*short distance*) **he lives down the road a p.** il n'habite pas loin d'ici; **I'll walk with you down the road a p.** je vais faire un petit bout de chemin avec toi
(h) (*in phrases*) **they are all of a p.** (*of people*) ils sont tous du même genre *ou* acabit; **it's all of a p. to me** pour moi c'est la même chose *ou* ça revient au même; **to be still in one p.** (*of person, car etc after accident*) être encore entier; **all in one p.** (*made, constructed*) tout d'une pièce, d'un seul morceau, d'un seul tenant; **to give sb a p. of one's mind** dire ses quatre vérités à qn; **to say one's p.** dire ce qu'on a à dire; **p. by p.** morceau par morceau; *Com* **to sell sth by the p.** vendre qch à la pièce; *F* **to go to pieces** (*of person*) s'effondrer (complètement), *F* craquer; *Sp* (*of team etc*) s'effondrer; **to fall to pieces** (*of bicycle, furniture, plans etc*) tomber en morceaux; (*of house etc*) se délabrer, crouler; **my coat is falling to pieces** mon manteau part en morceaux; **her life was falling to pieces** toute sa vie s'effondrait; **to take a machine to pieces** démonter une machine; **to break sth in** *or* **to pieces** briser qch, mettre qch en morceaux
▶ **piece together** *vtsep* (*assemble*) (*model, jigsaw etc*) joindre, assembler les morceaux de; (*broken vase, chair, torn letter*) recoller les morceaux de; (*facts etc*) coordonner; **to p. together what happened** reconstituer ce qui s'est passé; **detectives are piecing together a picture of the events** les enquêteurs sont en train de se faire une idée des événements
-piece [piːs] *suff* **one-p. overall** combinaison *f*; **a three-p. suite** un salon trois pièces; **two-/three-p. suit** costume *m* deux/trois pièces; **a twenty-four-p. dinner service** un service de table vingt-quatre pièces; **three-p. ensemble** trio *m*; **a four-p. band** un groupe de quatre éléments; **a twenty-p. orchestra** un orchestre de vingt musiciens *ou* éléments
piecemeal ['piːsmiːl] **1** *adv* par morceaux; (*gradually*) petit à petit, peu à peu; **the collection was sold p.** les pièces de la collection ont été vendues séparément **2** *adj* fragmentaire, parcellaire; (*work*) fait petit à petit; (*funding, transformation*) morcelé, fragmenté
piece rate *n Ind* salaire *m* à la tâche *ou* à la pièce
piecework ['piːswɜːk] *n Ind* travail *m* à la tâche *ou* à la pièce
pie chart *n* graphique *m* à secteurs, camembert *m*
piecrust ['paɪkrʌst] *n* croûte *f* de pâté
pied [paɪd] *adj* bigarré, panaché; **the P. Piper of Hamelin** le Joueur de flûte d'Hamelin
pied-à-terre, *pl* **pieds-à-terre** [pjeɪdɑː'teər] *n* pied-à-terre *m inv*
Piedmont ['piːdmɒnt] *n* Piémont *m*
pie-eyed *adj Sl* (*drunk*) rond, bourré; **to get p.** se saouler
pier [pɪər] *n* **(a)** (*at seaside resort*) jetée *f*; (*of stone*) jetée, môle *m*, digue *f*; (*on piles*) estacade *f* **(b)** *Constr* (*of stonework*) pilier *m*
pierce [pɪəs] **1** *vt* percer, transpercer; **to p. a hole in sth** faire *ou* percer un trou dans qch; **to have one's ears pierced** se faire percer les oreilles; **to p. the darkness** (*of light*) trouer

l'obscurité; **to p. the air with one's cries** percer l'air de ses cris **2** *vi* **to p. through the enemy's lines** pénétrer les lignes de l'ennemi

piercing ['pɪəsɪŋ] *adj* (*tool, cry*) aigu, perçant; (*look*) perçant, pénétrant; (*cold, wind*) pénétrant

pierhead ['pɪəhed] *n* musoir *m*

pierrot ['pɪərəʊ] *n Th* pierrot *m*

piety ['paɪətɪ] *n* piété *f*

piffle ['pɪf(ə)l] *n F* futilités *fpl*, bêtises *fpl*, niaiseries *fpl*; **to talk p.** dire des futilités *ou* des bêtises

piffling ['pɪflɪŋ] *adj F* (*objection, mistake*) insignifiant; (*sum, wage*) ridicule, insignifiant; (*occupation, activity*) futile; (*speech etc*) creux; **some p. little assistant** un petit assistant insignifiant

pig¹ [pɪg] *n* **(a)** (*animal*) porc *m*, cochon *m*; *Am* (*young pig*) cochonnet *m*, porcelet *m*; *F* (*glutton*) goinfre *m*, glouton, -onne; *F* (*unpleasant person*) salaud *m*, salope *f*, sale type *m*; *Sl Pej* (*police officer*) flic *m*; **to eat like a p., to make a p. of oneself** manger comme un cochon *ou* un goinfre, s'empiffrer, se goinfrer; *F* **you dirty little p.!** petit cochon!; *F* **he's a greedy p.** c'est un goinfre; *F* **what a selfish p.!** quel sale égoïste!; *Sl* **the filing cabinet was a p. to move** ça a été vachement difficile de déplacer le classeur; *Fig F* **to buy a p. in a poke** acheter chat en poche; *Fig F* **when pigs fly** quand les poules auront des dents; *Br F* **to make a p.'s ear of sth** saloper qch; **wild p.** sanglier *m*; *Am* (*piglet*) marcassin *m*, jeune sanglier

(b) *Metal* (*of casting*) gueuse *f*; (*of lead, tin etc*) saumon *m*

pig² (-gg-) **1** *vi* (*of sow*) mettre bas, cochonner **2** *vt F* **(a) to p. oneself** (*eat excessively*) s'empiffrer, se goinfrer (**on sth** de qch) **(b) to p. it** (*be untidy, dirty*) vivre comme des cochons

▶ **pig out** *vi F* (*eat excessively*) s'empiffrer, se goinfrer (**on sth** de qch)

pigeon ['pɪdʒɪn] *n* **(a)** (*bird*) pigeon *m*; **p. fancier** colombophile *mf*; **p. loft** pigeonnier *m*; **p. post** transport *m* de dépêches par pigeons voyageurs **(b)** *Br F* **that's not my p.** (*concern*) ce n'est pas mon truc

pigeon-breasted [pɪdʒɪn'brestɪd], **pigeon-chested** [pɪdʒɪn'tʃestɪd] *adj* à la poitrine saillante

pigeonhole¹ ['pɪdʒɪnhəʊl] *n* **(a)** (*in desk*) case *f*, casier *m*; *Fig* **to put sb in a p.** cataloguer qn, étiqueter qn **(b)** (*in dovecote*) boulin *m*

pigeonhole² *vt* **(a)** (*classify*) (*papers etc*) caser, classer; (*complaint etc*) classer; (*file away in memory*) reléguer dans sa mémoire **(b)** (*defer*) remettre à plus tard; **the scheme had been pigeonholed until further notice** le projet avait été remis jusqu'à nouvel ordre **(c)** (*person*) étiqueter, cataloguer, mettre une étiquette à; **I don't like being pigeonholed** je n'aime pas qu'on me catalogue

pigeon-toed *adj* qui marche les pieds tournés en dedans

pig farm *n* porcherie *f*, élevage *m* de porcs

piggery ['pɪgərɪ] *n* porcherie *f*; *F* (*gluttony*) goinfrerie *f*

piggish ['pɪgɪʃ] *adj F* (*person*) (*dirty*) sale, malpropre; (*gluttonous*) goinfre

piggy ['pɪgɪ] *F* **1** *n* (*in children's language*) cochonnet *m*, petit cochon *m*; **p. in the middle** (*children's game*) = jeu *m* d'enfants dans lequel l'un des participants doit attraper la balle que les autres s'envoient; *Fig* **I've had enough of being p. in the middle** j'en avais assez d'être pris entre deux feux **2** *adj* (*gluttonous*) goinfre; (*behaviour*) de goinfre; (*eyes*) porcin; **that was p. of you!** tu t'es goinfré!

piggyback ['pɪgɪbæk] **1** *adv* **(a)** (*on one's back*) sur le dos; **to ride p. on sb** monter sur le dos de qn **(b)** *Comptr* **to mount sth p. on sth** superposer qch sur qch **2** *adj Comptr* **p. board** carte *f* fille **3** *n* **to give sb a p.** porter qn sur son dos; **can I have a p.?** est-ce que je peux monter sur ton dos?

piggybacking ['pɪgɪbækɪŋ] *n* **(a)** *Com* exportation *f* kangourou **(b)** *Banking* portage *m*

piggy bank *n* tirelire *f*

pig-headed *adj* obstiné, entêté

pigheadedly [pɪg'hedɪdlɪ] *adv* obstinément

pigheadedness [pɪg'hedɪdnɪs] *n* obstination *f*, entêtement *m*

pig iron *n* fer *m* de première coulée, fonte *f* brute *ou* en gueuses

Pig Latin *n* = argot *m* codé utilisé en milieu scolaire

piglet ['pɪglɪt], *n* cochonnet *m*, porcelet *m*

pigment ['pɪgmənt] *n* **(a)** *Art etc* couleur *f*, colorant *m*, pigment *m* **(b)** *Physiol* pigment *m*; **p. cell** cellule *f* pigmentaire

pigmentation [pɪgmən'teɪʃən] *n* pigmentation *f*

pigmented [pɪg'mentɪd] *adj* pigmenté

pigmy ['pɪgmɪ] *n, adj* = **pygmy**

pigpen ['pɪgpen] *n Am* = **pigsty**

pigskin ['pɪgskɪn] *n* (*leather*) peau *f* de porc; **p. purse** bourse *f* en peau de porc

pigsty ['pɪgstaɪ] *n* **(a)** porcherie *f* **(b)** *Fig F* (*house, room*) porcherie *f*; **your room is a p.** ta chambre est une vraie porcherie

pigswill ['pɪgswɪl] *n* pâtée *f* pour les porcs; *F* (*food*) pâtée pour chiens

pigtail ['pɪgteɪl] *n* natte *f*

pike¹ [paɪk] *n* **(a)** (*weapon*) pique *f*; **p. bearer** piquier *m* **(b)** *Br Dial* (*peak in the Lake District*) pic *m*

pike² *n* (*fish*) brochet *m*

pike³ *n esp Am* = **turnpike**

pikestaff ['paɪkstɑːf] *n* **(a)** (*weapon*) bois *m ou* hampe *f* de pique **(b)** (*for walking*) bâton *m* à pointe de fer

pilaf(f) ['piːlæf] *n Culin* pilaf *m*, pilau *m*

pilaster [pɪ'læstər] *n Archit* pilastre *m*

pilau, pilaw ['piːlaʊ, -ləʊ, -lɔː] *n* = **pilaf**

pilchard ['pɪltʃəd] *n* (*fish*) pilchard *m*

pile¹ [paɪl] *n* **(a)** (*heap*) (*of wood, stones, rubbish etc*) tas *m*; (*of objects, goods etc*) tas, amas *m*, amoncellement *m*; (*of gold*) monceau *m*; (*of plates, laundry etc*) pile *f*; **to put in(to) a p., to make a p. of** mettre en tas, empiler; *F* **he made his p. in the fur trade** (*fortune*) il a fait fortune dans le commerce de fourrure; *F* **she must have made a p. out of that deal** elle a dû gagner une fortune dans ce contrat; *F* **to have piles** *or* **a p. of ironing/work to do** avoir un tas de repassage/travail à faire; *Fig F* **to be at the top/bottom of the p.** être favorisé/défavorisé

(b) *El* (**electric**) **p.** pile *f* (électrique); *Nucl Phys* (**atomic**) **p.** pile, réacteur *m* (atomique)

(c) (*building*) édifice *m*; *F Hum* **the family p.** la cabane familiale

pile² **1** *vt* (*earth etc*) entasser, amonceler; (*objects*) mettre en tas; (*wood, books etc*) empiler; **they piled food onto my plate** ils ont amoncelé de la nourriture dans mon assiette; **the table was piled high with dishes** des assiettes s'empilaient sur la table **2** *vi F* **seven of them piled into the car** sept d'entre eux se sont entassés dans la voiture

pile³ *n Tex* (*of carpet etc*) poil *m*; **p. fabrics** tissus *mpl* à poil

pile⁴ *n Constr* pieu *m*; **to drive piles** enfoncer des pieux; **built on piles** bâti sur pilotis; **p. dwelling** (*in prehistoric times*) habitation *f* lacustre

▶ **pile in** *F* **1** *vi* (*of people*) entrer en masse; **p. in everybody!** (*into car etc*) allez-y, montez tout le monde! **2** *vtsep* (*cause to enter in large numbers, quantity*) entasser

▶ **pile off** *vi F* descendre en masse

▶ **pile on** *vtsep* (*give in large numbers, quantity*) amonceler; **my plate was full, but they piled on more** mon assiette était pleine mais ils m'ont resservi une platée; **to p. on the pressure** faire monter la pression; **to p. on the agony** dramatiser; **to p. on the runs** marquer un grand nombre de points; *F* **to p. it on** exagérer, en rajouter

▶ **pile out** *vi F* (*of people*) partir en masse; (*from vehicle*) sortir en masse; **fifteen piled out of the compartment** quinze personnes ont quitté le compartiment en masse

▶ **pile up** **1** *vi* (*form into pile(s)*) s'amonceler, s'entasser, s'empiler; (*of cars*) se caramboler; **dirty dishes were piling up** la vaisselle sale s'empilait *ou* s'amoncelait; **work was piling up on her desk** le travail s'amoncelait sur son bureau; **the clouds are piling up** les nuages s'amoncellent **2** *vtsep* **(a)** (*form into pile(s)*) entasser, empiler; **p. the leaves up here** entasse les feuilles ici; **to p. up money** amasser de l'argent **(b)** *F* (*crash, wreck*) **to p. up one's plane/a car** bousiller son appareil/une voiture; **ship piled up on the rocks** navire échoué sur les rochers

pile-driver *n Constr* sonnette *f*; *F* (*blow*) coup *m* d'assommoir; *Fb* shoot *m* vigoureux

piles [paɪlz] *npl Med* hémorroïdes *fpl*; **to have p.** avoir des hémorroïdes

pile-up *n Ant* carambolage *m*, téléscopage *m* en série

pilfer ['pɪlfər] *vti* chaparder (**sth from sb** qch à qn)

pilferage ['pɪlfərɪdʒ] *n* = **pilfering**

pilferer ['pɪlfərər] *n* chapardeur, -euse

pilfering ['pɪlfərɪŋ] *n* petits vols *mpl*, larcins *mpl*; **the percentage lost through p.** le pourcentage perdu imputable aux petits vols

pilgrim ['pɪlgrɪm] *n* pèlerin, -ine; **pilgrims to Lourdes/Mecca** les pèlerins de Lourdes/de la Mecque

pilgrimage ['pɪlgrɪmɪdʒ] *n Rel, Fig* pèlerinage *m*; **to go on a p., to make a p.** aller en pèlerinage, faire un pèlerinage

Pilgrim Fathers *npl Hist* (pères *mpl*) Pèlerins *mpl*

Pilgrim's Progress *n Liter* le voyage du pèlerin

pill [pɪl] *n Pharm* pilule *f*; **the p.** (*contraceptive*) la pilule; **she's on the p.** elle prend la pilule; (**sugar-coated**) **p.** dragée *f*; *F* **to be a p. popper** se bourrer de médicaments

pillage¹ ['pɪlɪdʒ] *n Lit* pillage *m*

pillage² *Lit* **1** *vt* (*town*) piller, saccager, mettre à sac **2** *vi* se livrer au pillage, piller

pillager [ˈpɪlɪdʒər] *n* pilleur, -euse, pillard, -arde

pillar [ˈpɪlər] *n Archit* pilier *m*; (*of table, pedestal table*) pied *m* central; *Fig* **a p. of the Church/of society** un pilier de l'Église/de la société; **to be a p. of strength** être d'un grand appui; **I've been rushing around from p. to post** je n'ai pas arrêté de courir d'un endroit à l'autre *ou* de droite à gauche; **p. of fire/smoke** colonne de feu/fumée; **p. of rock** colonne rocheuse; **p. of salt** statue *f* de sel; *Aut* **door p.** montant *m* de porte

pillar box *n Br* boîte *f* aux lettres; **p. red** ≈ rouge drapeau *inv*

pillared [ˈpɪləd] *adj Archit* à piliers

pillbox [ˈpɪlbɒks] *n* **(a)** (*for pills*) boîte *f* à pilules **(b) p. (hat)** petit chapeau *m* rond sans bord **(c)** *Mil* blockhaus *m*

pillion [ˈpɪljən] *n* (*on motorcycle*) **p. (seat)** siège *m* arrière, selle *f* tandem, tan-sad *m*, *pl* tan-sads; **to ride p.** monter derrière; **p. rider** *or* **passenger** passager, -ère (de derrière)

pillock [ˈpɪlək] *n Br Sl* (*fool*) abruti *m*, con *m*

pillory¹ [ˈpɪlərɪ] *n* pilori *m*

pillory² *vt Hist, Fig* (*person*) mettre au pilori; *Fig* (*evil, corrupt practice*) dénoncer

pillow¹ [ˈpɪləʊ] *n* oreiller *m*; **p. fight** bataille *f* d'oreillers *ou* de polochon(s); **p. talk** conversation *f* sur l'oreiller

pillow² *vt* **to p. one's head on one's arms** poser sa tête sur ses bras; **her head was pillowed on a mound of leaves** sa tête reposait sur un oreiller de feuilles

pillowcase, pillowslip [ˈpɪləʊkeɪs, -slɪp] *n* taie *f* d'oreiller

pilot¹ [ˈpaɪlət] **1** *n* **(a)** *Av, Naut* pilote *m* **(b)** *TV* émission *f* pilote **2** *adj attrib* **p. factory** *or* **plant** usine-pilote *f*, *pl* usines-pilotes; **p. questionnaire** questionnaire-pilote *m*, *pl* questionnaires-pilotes; **p. scheme** projet-pilote *m*, *pl* projets-pilotes; *Ind, Com* **p. series** présérie *f*; **p. study** enquête-pilote *f*, *pl* enquêtes-pilotes; **p. survey** enquête-pilote *f*, *pl* enquêtes-pilotes, étude-pilote *f*, *pl* études-pilotes

pilot² *vt* (*ship, plane etc*) piloter; (*person through obstacles*) mener, conduire; **to p. the country through difficult times** aider le pays à traverser une mauvaise passe

pilot balloon *n Met* ballon-sonde *m*, *pl* ballons-sondes

pilot boat *n* bateau-pilote *m*, *pl* bateaux-pilotes

pilot burner *n* (*on gas cooker etc*) veilleuse *f*

pilot cutter *n* bateau-pilote *m*, *pl* bateaux-pilotes

pilot fish *n* poisson *m* pilote

pilot flame *n* (*on gas cooker etc*) veilleuse *f*

pilot house *n* (kiosque *m* de) timonerie *f*

pilot jet *n* (*on gas cooker etc*) veilleuse *f*

pilot lamp *n El etc* (lampe *f*) témoin *m*

pilot light *n* (*on gas cooker etc*) veilleuse *f*; *El etc* (lampe *f*) témoin *m*

pilot officer *n* sous-lieutenant *m* (aviateur)

pilot run *n Ind, Com* présérie *f*

pilot waters *npl* zone *f* de pilotage

pimento [pɪˈmentəʊ] *n* (*plant*), *Culin* piment *m*

pimp¹ [pɪmp] *n* souteneur *m*, proxénète *m*, *Sl* maquereau *m*

pimp² **1** *vi* être proxénète *ou* souteneur; **to p. for sb** maquer qn **2** *vt* maquer

pimpernel [ˈpɪmpənel] *n* (*flower*) mouron *m*; **scarlet p.** mouron rouge

pimple [ˈpɪmp(ə)l] *n* (*on skin*) bouton *m*; **to come out in pimples** boutonner, bourgeonner

pimply [ˈpɪmplɪ] *adj* boutonneux, couvert de boutons

PIMS [pɪmz] *n Mktg* (*abbr* **profit impact of marketing strategy**) IRSM *m*

PIN [pɪn] *n* (*abbr* **Personal Identification Number**) **P. (number)** code *m* confidentiel (*d'une carte bancaire*)

pin¹ [pɪn] *n* **(a)** épingle *f*; (*for hair*) épingle (à cheveux); (*brooch*) broche *f*; **(safety) p.** épingle de *ou* à nourrice; **you could have heard a p. drop** on aurait entendu voler une mouche; **as bright** *or* **clean as a new p.** propre comme un sou neuf; **for two pins I'd punch his face** pour un rien je lui casserais la figure; **pins and needles** (*tingling*) fourmillements *mpl*; **I've got pins and needles in my foot** j'ai des fourmis dans le pied; *Sewing* **p. tuck** nervure *f*

(b) *MecE* axe *m*; (*de fixation etc*) goupille *f*, clavette *f*; (*of hinge*) gond *m*; *El* (*of plug, on connector*) broche *f*; (*of printhead*) aiguille *f*; *Surg* (*for fracture*) broche, clou *m*; **(firing) p.** percuteur *m*; **(safety) p.** (*of grenade*) goupille; **p. wheel** (*on printer*) roue *f* à picots

(c) *Golf* drapeau *m* de trou; (*at ninepins*) quille *f*; **p. table** billard *m* chinois *ou* japonais

(d) *F* **pins** (*legs*) quilles *fpl*, cannes *fpl*; **to feel a bit shaky on one's pins** (*after illness etc*) ne pas se sentir très sûr sur ses quilles *ou* cannes

pin² *vt* **(-nn-)** **(a)** (*fasten with pin*) épingler, attacher avec une/des épingle(s) (**to** à); (*notice to noticeboard, map to wall*) attacher *ou* fixer avec une/des punaise(s), punaiser (**to** à); **to p. papers together** épingler des papiers ensemble

(b) *MecE etc* cheviller, goupiller, mettre une goupille à

(c) (*hold still*) fixer, clouer; **to p. sb against** *or* **to a wall** clouer *ou* plaquer qn contre un mur; **to p. sb's arms to his sides** coller *ou* plaquer les bras de qn au corps; **to be pinned under a fallen tree** se trouver pris *ou* coincé sous un arbre déraciné; *Fig* **to p. the blame on sb** rejeter la responsabilité sur qn; **you can't p. this on me** tu ne peux pas me mettre ça sur le dos; **to p. one's hopes on sb/sth** mettre tous ses espoirs en qn/dans qch

(d) *Constr* (*wall etc*) étayer, étançonner

▶ **pin back** *vtsep Surg* recoller; *Fig F* **to p. back one's ears** tendre l'oreille; *Fig F* **p. back your ears** ouvrez bien vos oreilles

▶ **pin down** *vtsep* **(a)** (*trap*) coincer; **he pinned me down** (*in fight etc*) il m'a coincé; **they were pinned down by the wreckage** ils ont été coincés dans les décombres; *Mil* **to p. down the enemy** coincer l'ennemi; **pinned down by enemy fire** coincé par le feu de l'ennemi

(b) (*force to be definite*) obliger à s'engager; **I tried to p. her down to a time** j'ai essayé de l'obliger à donner une heure précise; **to p. sb down to do sth** obliger *ou* contraindre qn à faire qch; **without pinning himself down to anything** sans s'engager à rien

(c) (*identify*) identifier; **we couldn't p. down the source of the noise** nous ne pouvions pas identifier la source du bruit; **a feeling that's difficult to p. down** un sentiment qu'il est difficile d'isoler *ou* d'identifier; **it's difficult to p. it down** c'est difficile de mettre le doigt dessus

▶ **pin up** *vtsep* **(a)** (*fasten to wall etc*) (*photo etc*) fixer au mur *etc*, punaiser **(b)** (*fasten*) **to p. up one's hair** relever ses cheveux; **to p. up a hem** rabattre un ourlet avec des épingles

pinafore [ˈpɪnəfɔːr] *n esp Br* (*apron*) tablier *m*; **p. (dress)** robe *f* à bretelles, robe-chasuble *f*, *pl* robes-chasubles

pinball [ˈpɪnbɔːl] *n* (*machine, game*) flipper *m*; **p. machine** flipper, billard *m* électrique

pincer [ˈpɪnsər] *n* (*of crab, insect etc*) pince *f*; *Mil* **p. movement** mouvement *m ou* manœuvre *f* en tenailles

pincers [ˈpɪnsəz] *npl* [①A10,e] (*tool*) **(pair of) p.** pince *f*, tenaille(s) *f(pl)*

pinch¹ [pɪntʃ] *n* **(a)** (*action*) pincement *m*; **to give sb a p.** pincer qn; **the p. of hunger** les tiraillements *mpl* de la faim; *F* **to feel the p.** être gêné; **at** *or Am* **in a p.** à la rigueur **(b)** (*of salt etc*) pincée *f*; (*of snuff*) prise *f*; *Fig* **to take sth with a p. of salt** ne pas prendre qch pour argent comptant

pinch² **1** *vt* **(a)** (*nip*) (*sb, sb's cheek etc*) pincer; **these shoes are pinching my feet** ces chaussures me font mal aux pieds *ou* me blessent; **I had to p. myself** (*I thought I was dreaming*) je me suis pincé

(b) *F* (*steal*) piquer, faucher (**from sb** à qn); (*arrest*) (*thief etc*) épingler, pincer, choper; **I've had my purse pinched** on m'a piqué *ou* fauché mon porte-monnaie; **who's pinched my pen?** qui est-ce qui m'a chipé *ou* piqué mon stylo?; **to get pinched** (*of thief etc*) se faire pincer *ou* épingler *ou* choper

2 *vi* **(a)** (*nip*) blesser; **shoe that pinches** chaussure qui blesse *ou* qui serre; *Fig* **that's where the shoe pinches** c'est là que le bât blesse

(b) to p. and scrape *or* **save** faire des économies de bouts de chandelle

▶ **pinch off** *vtsep* (*remove*) enlever en pinçant; **to p. off a bud** épincer un bourgeon

▶ **pinch out** *vtsep* épincer

pinchbeck [ˈpɪntʃbek] *Lit* **1** *n* toc *m* **2** *adj* (*sham*) simili, en toc

pinched [pɪntʃt] *adj* **(a)** (*face*) tiré, hâve; (*features*) tiré; **to be p. with hunger** être tenaillé par la faim **(b)** (*restricted*) étroit; **to be (a bit) p. for money/time** être à court d'argent/de temps; **to be (a bit) p. for space** être un peu à l'étroit

pinch-hit *vi Am* **to p. for sb** *Baseball* frapper à la place de qn; *Fig* remplacer qn

pinch-hitter *n Am Baseball* frappeur *m* d'urgence *ou* suppléant

pinch-runner *n Am Baseball* coureur *m* d'urgence *ou* suppléant

pincushion [ˈpɪnkʊʃən] *n* pelote *f* à épingles

pine¹ [paɪn] *n* **(a) p. (tree)** pin *m* **(b)** (*wood*) (bois *m* de) pin *m*; **p. furniture** meubles *mpl* en pin

pine² *vi* languir; **to p. with grief** languir de tristesse

▶ **pine away** *vi* = **pine²**

▶ **pine for** *vipo* languir pour *ou* après; **to p. for home/the good old days** avoir la nostalgie du foyer/du bon vieux temps; **he's pining for a good plate of sauerkraut** il meurt d'envie de manger une bonne assiette de choucroute

pineapple [ˈpaɪnæp(ə)l] *n* ananas *m*; **p. juice** jus *m* d'ananas

pine cone *n* pomme *f ou* cône *m* de pin, pigne *f*

pine forest *n* forêt *f* de pins, pinède *f*
pine kernel *n* pignon *m* (de pin)
pine marten *n* martre *f*
pine needle *n* aiguille *f* de pin
pine nut *n* pignon *m* (de pin)
ping¹ [pɪŋ] *n* (*of sth hitting wine glass, small bell etc*) tintement *m*, petit bruit *m* clair; (*of bullet etc*) cinglement *m*
ping² *vi* (*of sth hitting wine glass, small bell etc*) tinter, faire un petit bruit clair; (*of bullet etc*) cingler
pinger [ˈpɪŋər] *n* (*timer*) minuteur *m*
ping-pong *n* ping-pong *m*; **p. table/ball** table *f*/balle *f* de ping-pong
pinhead [ˈpɪnhed] *n* **(a)** tête *f* d'épingle **(b)** *F* (*stupid person*) idiot, -ote, abruti, -ie
pinhole [ˈpɪnhəʊl] *n* **(a)** trou *m* d'épingle; *Opt* (*in screen etc*) ouverture *f* minuscule; *Phot* sténopé *m*; **p. camera** sténoscope *m*; **p. source of light** source *f* de lumière punctiforme *ou* ponctuelle **(b)** *Tech* trou *m* de cheville *ou* de goujon
pining [ˈpaɪnɪŋ] *n* langueur *f*, languissement *m*; (*strong desire*) désir *m* ardent (**for sth** de qch); (*for home*) nostalgie *f*
pinion¹ [ˈpɪnjən] *n Orn* (*flight feathers*) penne *f*, rémige *f*
pinion² *vt* **(a)** (*hold*) **to p. sb to the ground/against a wall** clouer qn au sol/contre un mur; **to p. sb's arms** (*tie*) attacher *ou* lier les bras de qn; (*hold*) tenir les bras de qn **(b)** (*bird*) rogner les ailes à
pinion³ *n MecE* pignon *m*; **p. wheel** roue *f* à pignon
pink¹ [pɪŋk] **1** *n* **(a)** (*colour*) rose *m*; **in the p. of condition** *or* **health** en excellente *ou* parfaite santé; (*of racehorse etc*) entraîné à fond; **to be in the p.** (*of person*) se porter à merveille **(b)** (*flower*) œillet *m*; **garden p.** (œillet) mignardise *f* **2** *adj* **(a)** (*colour*) rose; **to turn** *or* **go p.** (*with embarrassment etc*) rosir; **to see p. elephants** voir double; **p. champagne** champagne *m* rosé; *Am F* **p. collar job** = emploi *m* typiquement féminin; *Am F* **p. collar workers** employées *fpl* de bureau; **p. eyes** (*of albino*) yeux *mpl* rouges; **the p. pound** = le pouvoir d'achat de la communauté homosexuelle **(b)** *F* = **pinko**
pink² *vt Sewing etc* (*with pinking shears*) denteler, cranter; (*leather etc*) travailler à jour, évider
pink³ *vi* (*of engine*) cliqueter
pinkeye [ˈpɪŋkaɪ] *n Med* conjonctivite *f* aiguë contagieuse
pink gin *n* = cocktail *m* à base de gin et d'angustura
pinkie [ˈpɪŋkɪ] *n Am, Scot F* petit doigt *m*, auriculaire *m*
pinking¹ [ˈpɪŋkɪŋ] *n Sewing etc* découpage *m*, découpure *f*; **p. shears** *or* **scissors** ciseaux *mpl* à cranter *ou* à denteler
pinking² *n* (*of engine*) cliquetis *m* (*produit par les auto-allumages*)
pinkish [ˈpɪŋkɪʃ] *adj* rosé, rosâtre
pink lady *n* = cocktail *m* à base de gin et de grenadine
pinko [ˈpɪŋkəʊ] *n, adj esp Am Pol F* gauchisant, -ante
pink slip *n US F* avis *m* de licenciement; **to get one's p.** être licencié
pinky¹ [ˈpɪŋkɪ] *n Am, Scot F* = **pinkie**
pinky² *adj F* rosé, rosâtre; **p. grey** gris *m inv* rosâtre *ou* rosé
pin money *n* (*for small purchases*) argent *m* de poche; *Arch* (*given to wife*) argent pour le ménage
pinnace [ˈpɪnɪs] *n Naut* chaloupe *f*, grand canot *m*
pinnacle [ˈpɪnək(ə)l] *n* **(a)** (*of mountain*) cime *f*; **a p. of rock** un piton rocheux; *Fig* **on the highest p. of fame** à l'apogée *ou* au sommet de la gloire **(b)** *Archit* pinacle *m*, clocheton *m*; (*of ridge*) couronnement *m*
pinny [ˈpɪnɪ] *n esp Br F* tablier *m*
pinout [ˈpɪnaut] *n Comptr* broche *f* de sortie
pinpoint¹ [ˈpɪnpɔɪnt] *n* (*tip of a pin*) pointe *f* d'épingle; (*very small point*) point *m* infime *ou* infinitésimal; **p. accuracy** haute précision *f*; *Mil* **p. bombing** bombardement *m* de précision
pinpoint² *vt* (*point out*) indiquer exactement; (*locate*) (*place, fact, argument, consideration*) localiser *ou* repérer exactement; (*source of rumour, cause of problem*) déterminer, identifier; *Mil* (*aim at*) viser avec précision; (*fire on, bomb*) effectuer un tir/un bombardement de précision sur; **to p. a problem** isoler un problème, mettre le doigt sur un problème
pinprick [ˈpɪnprɪk] *n* piqûre *f* d'aiguille; *F* **pinpricks** (*annoying things*) tracasseries *fpl*
pinstripe [ˈpɪnstraɪp] *n Tex* rayures *fpl* fines; **p. suit, pinstripes** costume *m* rayé
pint [paɪnt] *n* **(a)** (*measurement*) pinte *f* (= 0,568 litre; *US* = 0,473 litre) **(b)** *Br F* **a p.** (*beer*) une pinte de bière; **I'm going for a p.** je vais prendre une bière; **p. mug** *or* **pot** chope *f* d'une pinte
pinta [ˈpaɪntə] *n Br F* pinte *f* de lait
pintail [ˈpɪnteɪl] *n* **(a)** (*wild duck*) pilet *m* **(b)** (*grouse*) tétras *m* à longue queue, *Can* gelinotte *f* à queue fine
pinto [ˈpɪntəʊ] *adj, n Am* **p.** (**horse**) (cheval *m*) pie *m*; *Culin* **p. beans** haricots *mpl* pinto
pint-size(d) *adj F* minuscule
pin-up *n F* (*woman, picture of woman*) pin-up *f inv*; **he's a real p.** c'est un vrai canon
Pinyin [ˈpɪnˈjɪn] *n Ling* pinyin *m*
pioneer¹ [paɪəˈnɪər] *n* pionnier, -ière; **a p. researcher in the field of …** un chercheur qui est à l'avant-garde des travaux dans le domaine de …; **her p. work in the study of radioactivity** ses travaux innovateurs dans le domaine de la radioactivité
pioneer² *vt* **to p. a new method** être le premier/l'un des premiers à développer une nouvelle méthode; **to p. research into …** être à l'avant-garde de la recherche dans …
pioneering [paɪəˈnɪərɪŋ] *adj* (*work*) innovateur, -trice; (*scientist etc*) qui fait œuvre de pionnier; **to do p. work in a science** faire œuvre de pionnier dans une science, ouvrir la voie dans une science; **in p. days** au temps des pionniers; **p. company** entreprise *f* innovatrice
pious [ˈpaɪəs] *adj* pieux; **p. fraud** pieux mensonge *m*; *F* (*person*) hypocrite *mf*; **p. hope** espoir *m* vain; **these p. hopes** ces vains espoirs
piously [ˈpaɪəslɪ] *adv* pieusement, avec piété
piousness [ˈpaɪəsnɪs] *n* piété *f*
PIP [pɪp] *n Comptr* (*abbr* **peripheral interchange program**) logiciel *m* de commutation de périphérique
pip¹ [pɪp] *n* (*of fruit*) pépin *m*
pip² *n* **(a)** (*on card, die etc*) point *m* **(b)** *Br Mil F* **to get one's third p.** ≈ recevoir sa troisième ficelle **(c)** *Rad* (*sound*) top *m*; (*on radar*) top d'écho; **the pips** *Rad* = les bips *mpl* sonores; *Tel* la tonalité de crédit épuisé
pip³ *vt* **(-pp-)** *F* **to be pipped at the post** se faire coiffer *ou* battre sur le poteau
pip⁴ *n Br Old-fashioned F* **to give sb the p.** embêter qn
pipe¹ [paɪp] *n* **(a)** (*tube*) tuyau *m*, conduit *m*, conduite *f*, canalisation *f*; **pipes and fittings** tuyauterie *f* et accessoires *mpl* de tuyauterie **(b)** *Mus* chalumeau *m*; *Naut* (*of boatswain*) sifflet *m*; (*of bird*) chant *m*; **the pipes** (*bagpipes*) la cornemuse **(c)** (*for smoking*) pipe *f*; **to smoke a p.** fumer une pipe; *F* **put that in your p. and smoke it!** mettez ça dans votre poche et votre mouchoir par-dessus!
pipe² **1** *vi Mus* jouer du chalumeau; (*play the bagpipes*) jouer de la cornemuse; (*of bird etc*) siffler; (*speak shrilly*) parler d'une voix flûtée; *Naut* donner un coup de sifflet

2 *vt* **(a)** (*house etc*) installer *ou* poser des canalisations dans; (*water, oil etc*) canaliser; **piped water** eau *f* courante; **to p. oil to a refinery** amener le pétrole à une raffinerie par oléduc *ou* par pipeline; *F* **piped music** musique *f* de fond

(b) *Mus* (*tune*) jouer au chalumeau; (*on bagpipes*) jouer à la cornemuse; (*sing*) chanter d'une voix flûtée; *Naut* (*order*) siffler; *Naut* **to p. sb aboard** rendre les honneurs du sifflet à qn

(c) *Sewing etc* (*cushion etc*) passepoiler

(d) *Culin* (*cake*) décorer avec une (poche à) douille

(e) *Comptr* (*commands*) chaîner

▶ **pipe down** *vi F* **(a)** (*make less noise*) faire moins de bruit; **p. down!** moins de bruit! **(b)** (*not talk so much*) rabattre son caquet; **p. down!** boucle-la!; **he piped down when he realized she knew a lot more about it** il a rabattu son caquet quand il s'est rendu compte qu'elle en savait bien plus que lui
▶ **pipe in** *vtsep* **to p. in the guests** (*in Scotland*) jouer de la cornemuse en tête de la procession (lors de l'entrée solennelle des invités)
▶ **pipe up** *vi* (*start to speak*) commencer à parler; **a little voice piped up** une petite voix s'est fait entendre
pipe band *n* orchestre *m* de cornemuses
pipeclay [ˈpaɪpkleɪ] *n* terre *f* de pipe
pipe cleaner *n* cure-pipe *m*, *pl* cure-pipes
pipe dream *n* rêve *m* (chimérique), projet *m* illusoire
pipeline [ˈpaɪplaɪn] *n* **(a)** (*large pipe*) canalisation *f*, conduite *f*; (*for gas*) conduite de gaz naturel, gazoduc *m*; (*for petrol*) oléoduc *m*, pipeline *m* **(b)** *Fig* (*for news, technology etc*) canal *m ou* voie *f* d'acheminement; **it's in the p.** c'est en route; **there's a pay rise in the p.** il y a une augmentation de salaire en perspective
pipe major *n Mil* cornemuse-chef *m*
pipe of peace *n* calumet *m* de la paix
piper [ˈpaɪpər] *n Mus* joueur, -euse de chalumeau; (*of bagpipes*) joueur, -euse de cornemuse, cornemuseur *m*, cornemuseux *m*; *Prov* **he who pays the p. calls the tune** qui paye a bien le droit de choisir
pipe rack *n* porte-pipes *m inv*
pipe tobacco *n* tabac *m* à pipe
pipette [pɪˈpet] *n Ch etc* pipette *f*, compte-gouttes *m inv*

piping ['paɪpɪŋ] **1** *adj* (*sound*) flûté, aigu, *f* aiguë; (*voice*) flûté **2** *adv* **p. hot** tout chaud, bouillant **3** *n* **(a)** (*system*) canalisations *fpl*; (*pipes collectively*) conduites *fpl*, tuyaux *mpl*, tuyauterie *f*, canalisations **(b)** *Mus etc* (*sound of pipe*) son *m* du chalumeau; (*sound of bagpipes*) son de la cornemuse; (*of birds*) gazouillement *m*, gazouillis *m*; *Naut* coups *mpl* de sifflet **(c)** *Sewing etc* (*material*) passepoil *m* **(d)** *Culin* (*of cake*) décoration *f* faite à la (poche à) douille; **p. bag** poche *f* à douille **(e)** *Comptr* (*of commands*) chaînage *m*

pipistrelle [pɪpɪ'strel] *n* **p. (bat)** pipistrelle *f*

pipit ['pɪpɪt] *n* (*bird*) pipit *m*

pippin ['pɪpɪn] *n* (*apple*) (pomme *f*) reinette *f*

pipsqueak ['pɪpskwiːk] *n F* (*person*) petit bonhomme *m* de rien du tout, gringalet *m*

piquancy ['piːkənsɪ] *n* **(a)** (*of food*) goût *m* piquant **(b)** *Fig* (*of tale, affair etc*) sel *m*, piquant *m*

piquant ['piːkənt] *adj* (*flavour, story*) piquant

piquantly ['piːkəntlɪ] *adv* d'une manière piquante, avec du piquant

pique¹ [piːk] *n* dépit *m*, ressentiment *m*; **in a fit of p.** dans un accès de dépit

pique² *vt* **(a)** (*offend*) (*person*) piquer, dépiter; **to feel piqued by sth** être dépité par qch; **to p. sb's pride** piquer *ou* blesser qn dans son orgueil **(b)** (*arouse*) (*sb's curiosity, interest*) piquer, exciter

piquet [pɪ'ket] *n Cards* piquet *m*

piracy ['paɪrəsɪ] *n* **(a)** *Naut etc* piraterie *f*; **an act of p.** un acte de piraterie; **air p.** piraterie de l'air **(b)** (*of copyright*) atteinte *f* au droit d'auteur; (*of ideas etc*) pillage *m*, vol *m*; (*of software etc*) piratage *m*; **film p.** piratage de films

piranha [pɪ'rɑːnə] *n* (*fish*) piranha *m*, piraya *m*

pirate¹ ['paɪrɪt] *n* **(a)** *Naut* (*person*) pirate *m*; (*ship*) navire *m* pirate **(b)** *Rad* (*person*) pirate *m* **(c)** (*of literary work etc*) contrefacteur *m*; (*of ideas etc*) voleur, -euse; **p. cassettes/videos** cassettes *fpl*/vidéos *fpl* pirates; **p. program** programme *m* pirate; **p. software** logiciel *m* pirate

pirate² *vt* **(a)** *Naut* (*ship*) s'emparer de **(b)** (*invention, ideas etc*) s'approprier, voler; (*brand*) contrefaire; (*cassette, film etc*) pirater; **to p. a book** (*republish without permission*) republier un livre sans autorisation; (*copy*) contrefaire *ou* démarquer un livre

pirated ['paɪrɪtɪd] *adj* pirate; **a p. edition** une édition pirate

pirate radio *n* radio *f* pirate

pirate station *n* poste *m ou* émetteur *m* pirate

piratical [paɪ'rætɪk(ə)l] *adj* **(a)** *Naut* de pirate **(b)** *Com* (*reproduction etc*) de contrefacteur, de contrefaçon

pirating ['paɪrɪtɪŋ] *n* (*of software etc*) piratage *m*

pirouette¹ [pɪrʊ'et] *n* pirouette *f*

pirouette² *vi* pirouetter, faire une/des pirouette(s)

Pisa ['piːzə] *n* Pise *f*

piscatorial [pɪskə'tɔːrɪəl] *adj Fml* halieutique

Piscean ['paɪsɪən] *Astrol* **1** *n* **to be a P.** être Poissons **2** *adj* **the P. male** l'homme Poissons; **P. characteristics** caractéristiques des Poissons

Pisces ['paɪsiːz] *n Astrol* les Poissons *mpl*; **I'm a P.** je suis (des) Poissons

piss¹ [pɪs] *n Sl* pisse *f*; **to have a p.** pisser; **to take the p. out of sb** se foutre (de la gueule) de qn; **to take the p. out of sth** se foutre de qch; **you're taking the p.!** tu te fous de moi!, tu déconnes!; **the artist is taking the p.** cet artiste se fout de la gueule du monde; *Br* **p. artist** (*bungler*) propre *mf* à rien, savate *f*; (*braggart, phoney*) grande gueule *f*; (*drunk*) soûlard, -arde; **it was p. easy** c'était de la tarte; **p. poor** (*very bad*) complètement nul

piss² *Sl* **1** *vi* pisser; **it's pissing with rain** il pleut comme vache qui pisse **2** *vt* (*blood etc*) pisser; **to p. oneself, to p. one's pants** pisser dans son froc; **to p. the bed** pisser au lit; **I almost pissed myself laughing** j'ai tellement rigolé que j'ai failli en pisser dans mon froc

▶ **piss about, piss around** *Sl* **1** *vi* (*behave foolishly*) faire le con, déconner; (*waste time*) glandouiller **2** *vtas* (*waste time of*) **to p. sb about** *or* **around** faire perdre son temps à qn

▶ **piss down** *vi Sl* (*rain*) **it's pissing down** il pleut à vache qui pisse

▶ **piss off** *Sl* **1** *vi* (*go away*) foutre le camp; **p. off!** fous le camp! **2** *vtsep* (*annoy*) faire chier; **that really pisses me off** ça me fait vraiment chier; **to be pissed off** en avoir ras le cul

pissed [pɪst] *adj* **(a)** *Br Sl* (*drunk*) soûl, bourré, plein; **to get p.** se soûler la gueule; **as p. as a newt, p. out of one's mind** rond comme une queue de pelle **(b)** *US Sl* (*angry*) en rogne, en boule; **to be p. at sb** être en rogne contre qn

pisshead ['pɪshed] *n Br Sl* (*drunkard*) soûlard, -arde

piss-take *n Br Sl* (*joke*) blague *f*; (*parody*) parodie *f*

piss-taker *n Br Sl* (*mocker*) personne *f* qui se fout du monde; **he's a real p.** il se fout vraiment de la gueule du monde

piss-up *n Br Sl* (*drinking spree*) **to go on** *or* **have a p.** (aller) se soûler la gueule; **they couldn't organize a p. in a brewery** ils ne sont pas foutus d'organizer quoi que ce soit correctement

pistachio [pɪ'stɑːʃɪəʊ] *n* **p. (nut)** pistache *f*; **p. (tree)** pistachier *m*

piste [piːst] *n Ski* piste *f*

pistil ['pɪstɪl] *n Bot* pistil *m*

pistol ['pɪst(ə)l] *n* **(a)** (*gun*) pistolet *m*; **to hold a p. to sb's head** tenir un pistolet braqué contre la tempe de qn; *Fig* mettre le couteau sous la gorge à qn; *Fig* **to make a decision with a p. to one's head** prendre une décision avec le couteau sous la gorge; **p. shot** coup *m* de pistolet **(b)** *Tech* (*of pneumatic tool*) pistolet *m*; **p. grip** (*of tool, camera*) poignée *f* pistolet

pistol-whip *vt* (**-pp-**) frapper avec un pistolet

piston ['pɪstən] *n MecE, Mus* (*of brass instrument*) piston *m*; *Aut* **p. dwell** temps *m* d'immobilité du piston; **p. engine** moteur *m* à pistons; **p. head** tête *f ou* fond *m* du piston; **p. ring** segment *m* (de piston); **p. walls** parois *fpl* du piston

pit¹ [pɪt] *n* **(a)** (*hole in ground*) fosse *f*; *Min* puits *m*; (*coal mine*) mine *f*; **to dig a p.** creuser une fosse; *Aut etc* **inspection p.** fosse de visite; *Lit* **the (bottomless) p.** (*hell*) l'enfer *m*, les enfers; *Min* **to work in the pits** travailler à la mine; **he went down the pits when he was 16** il est descendu à la mine à 16 ans

(b) *Fig Sl* (*awful*) **it's/he's the pits** c'est/il est nul

(c) *Th* (*seating, spectators*) parterre *m*; *Am* (*at Stock Exchange*) marché *m*; (*for cock fight*) arène *f*; (*for bears*) fosse *f*; **(orchestra) p.** fosse d'orchestre; *Sp* **the pits** les stands *mpl* de ravitaillement

(d) (*mark*) (*on metal, glass etc*) piqûre *f*, alvéole *m*

(e) *Med* (*from smallpox etc*) cicatrice *f*, marque *f*; *Anat* **the p. of the stomach** le creux de l'estomac; *Fig* **her rejection hit him in the p. of his stomach** son rejet lui a fait l'effet d'un coup de poing dans l'estomac

(f) *Br Sl* (*bed*) pieu *m*; **in one's p.** au pieu

(g) (*stone*) (*of cherry etc*) noyau *m*

pit² *vt* (**-tt-**) (*cherries etc*) dénoyauter

pit³ *vt* (**-tt-**) **(a) to p. sb against sb** mettre qn aux prises avec qn, opposer qn à qn; **to p. oneself against sb** se mesurer à qn; **to p. one's wits against sb** se mesurer avec qn **(b)** (*of acids etc*) (*metal etc*) piquer, trouer; *Med* (*of smallpox etc*) (*sb's face*) grêler, marquer

pita ['pɪtə] *n* = **pitta**

pit-a-pat **1** *adv* **to go p.** (*of rain etc*) crépiter; (*of feet*) trottiner; (*of the heart*) faire toc-toc **2** *n* (*of rain*) crépitement *m*; (*of feet*) trottinement *m*; (*of heart*) battement *m*

pitch¹ [pɪtʃ] *n* **(a)** (*act of throwing*) (*of stone, ball etc*) lancement *m*

(b) *Br* (*place*) (*in market*) place *f*, emplacement *m*; (*of stallholder, beggar etc*) place habituelle

(c) *Sp* (*for football etc*) terrain *m*; *Cr* terrain entre les guichets

(d) *Mus* (*of note*) hauteur *f*; **to have perfect p.** avoir l'oreille absolue; **to give the orchestra the p.** donner le ton à l'orchestre; **to rise in p.** monter de ton; **p. pipe** diapason *m* à bouche

(e) (*degree*) **to such a p. that ...** à tel point que ...; **expectation had reached fever p.** l'attente était fébrile

(f) (*talk*) **(sales) p.** baratin *m*, boniment *m* publicitaire; (*of advertising agency*) spéculative *f*; *Am Sl* **to make a p. for** (*express support for*) vanter les mérites de

(g) *Constr* (*slope*) (*of staircase*) pente *f*, rampant *m*; (*of roof*) pente, inclinaison *f*; *Tech* (*of plane*) inclinaison, basile *f*

(h) *Archit* (*of ceiling*) hauteur *f*

(i) (*of ship, aircraft*) (*type of movement*) tangage *m*; (*instance*) coup *m* de tangage; **angle of p., p. angle** angle *m* de tangage

(j) *Tech* (*spacing*) (*of rivets, holes*) espacement *m*, écartement *m*; (*of cogwheel, screw, propeller etc, Typ of characters*) pas *m*; **p. circle** cercle *m* primitif; (*of wheel*) ligne *f* d'engrènement

pitch² **1** *vt* **(a)** (*throw*) (*ball, stone etc*) jeter, lancer; (*in baseball*) lancer; **to p. the hay onto the cart** jeter le foin sur la charrette

(b) (*set up*) (*tent*) dresser, monter; (*camp*) établir; *Cr* **to p. wickets** planter *ou* dresser les guichets

(c) *Mus* jouer dans une clef donnée; **to p. one's voice higher/lower** hausser/baisser le ton de sa voix

(d) (*aim*) **to p. an estimate too low** arrêter un devis trop bas; **to p. one's aspirations too high** viser trop haut; **stories pitched at older children** histoires écrites pour des enfants plus âgés

(e) *F* **to p. a yarn** raconter des histoires

2 *vi* **(a)** (*in baseball*) lancer

(**b**) (*fall*) tomber; **to p. forward** (*be thrown*) être projeté en avant; (*fall*) piquer du nez; **he pitched into the water** il est tombé dans l'eau; **the ball pitched on a stone** le ballon a rebondi sur une pierre

(**c**) (*of ship, aircraft*) tanguer

pitch[3] *n* (*substance*) poix *f*; (*from coal tar*) brai *m*; **black** *or* **dark as p.** (*hair, eyes*) noir comme le jais; (*room, night*) noir comme dans un four

pitch[4] *vt* (*coat with pitch*) brayer, enduire de poix *ou* de brai

▶ **pitch in** *vi* (*contribute to a task*) s'y mettre; (*contribute money etc*) payer son écot; **they all pitched in to help** ils ont tous donné un coup de main

▶ **pitch into** *vipo F* (*attack*) (*physically*) attaquer, se lancer sur; (*verbally*) dire son fait à; **to p. into a task** se mettre à une tâche

▶ **pitch on** *vipo* (*choose*) choisir

▶ **pitch out** *vtsep* (*person*) (*from house*) expulser; (*from competition*) éliminer; (*rubbish*) balancer, jeter; **to p. sb out of office** démettre qn de ses fonctions

pitch-black *adj* noir comme le jais; **her p. hair** ses cheveux noirs de jais; **it's p.** (*I can't see*) il fait noir comme dans un four

pitch-dark *adj* **it's p.** (*outside*) il fait nuit noire; (*in cellar etc*) il fait noir comme dans un four

pitched [pɪtʃt] *adj* **p. battle** bataille *f* rangée

pitcher[1] ['pɪtʃər] *n* (*jug*) cruche *f*, pichet *m*; (*large*) broc *m*; *esp Am* (*small jug*) pot *m*; *prov* **little pitchers have big ears** = pas devant les enfants

pitcher[2] *n Baseball* lanceur *m*

pitchfork[1] ['pɪtʃfɔːk] *n Agr* fourche *f*; (*two-pronged*) bident *m*

pitchfork[2] *vt* (*hay*) lancer avec une fourche; *Fig F* (*force*) (*person*) parachuter (**into a job** à un poste)

pitching ['pɪtʃɪŋ] *n Naut, Av* (*of ship, plane*) tangage *m*

pitch pine *n Bot* pitchpin *m*

piteous ['pɪtɪəs] *adj* pitoyable, piteux; **he was a p. sight** il faisait pitié

piteously ['pɪtɪəslɪ] *adv* pitoyablement, piteusement

pitfall ['pɪtfɔːl] *n* (*pit*) trappe *f*, fosse *f*; *Fig* (*trap*) piège *m*; **the pitfalls of English** les pièges de l'anglais

pith [pɪθ] *n* (**a**) (*of orange etc*) peau *f* blanche; *Bot* (*medulla*) mœlle *f*; **p. helmet** casque *m* (colonial) en sola (**b**) *Fig* (*of argument, idea etc*) essence *f*; (*piquancy*) (*of story*) piquant *m*

pithead ['pɪthed] *n Min* bouche *f* de puits; **p. ballot** vote *m* des mineurs; **p. baths** bains *mpl*/douches *fpl* de la mine

pithiness ['pɪθɪnɪs] *n* (*of style etc*) concision *f*

pithy ['pɪθɪ] *adj* (**a**) (*orange etc*) couvert de peau blanche; (*stem etc*) moelleux (**b**) (*style etc*) concis; **p. phrase** phrase *f* lapidaire

pitiable ['pɪtɪəb(ə)l] *adj* pitoyable, piteux; (*appearance, object*) minable, lamentable; **she was in a p. state** elle était dans un état à faire pitié, elle était dans un état pitoyable *ou* dans un piteux état

pitiful ['pɪtɪful] *adj* (**a**) (*arousing pity*) pitoyable; **it's p. to see him like this** ça fait pitié de le voir comme ça (**b**) *Pej* (*deplorable*) lamentable, pitoyable

pitifully ['pɪtɪfʊlɪ] *adv* (**a**) (*arousing pity*) pitoyablement; **she was p. thin** elle était d'une maigreur pitoyable (**b**) *Pej* (*deplorably*) lamentablement, pitoyablement; **he was p. bad at drawing** il était lamentable en dessin; **she sings p.** elle chante lamentablement mal; **p. small** (*salary*) de misère; (*house etc*) si petit que c'en est lamentable

pitiless ['pɪtɪlɪs] *adj* impitoyable; (*wind, cold*) cruel

pitilessly ['pɪtɪlɪslɪ] *adv* impitoyablement, sans pitié; **p. cruel** d'une cruauté impitoyable; **to behave p. towards sb** se montrer impitoyable envers qn

piton ['piːtɒn] *n* (*in mountaineering*) piton *m*

pit pony *n Min* cheval *m* de mine

pit prop *n Min* poteau *m ou* étai *m* de mine

pitta ['pɪtə] *n* **p. bread** pita *m*

pittance ['pɪtəns] *n* (*wages*) salaire *m* de misère; (*income*) maigre revenu *m*, revenu misérable; **his pension is a p.** sa retraite est dérisoire

pitted ['pɪtɪd] *adj* (**a**) (*metal etc*) piqué, alvéolé; (*surface of moon*) alvéolé; (*skin*) (*by smallpox*) grêlé; (*by acne*) couvert de marques (**b**) (*olives*) dénoyauté

pitter-patter ['pɪtəpætər] *n, vi* = **patter**[1,2]

pitting ['pɪtɪŋ] *n* (*on metal surface*) piquage *m*

pituitary [pɪ'tjuːɪt(ə)rɪ] *Anat* **1** *n* **p. (gland)** hypophyse *f*, glande *f* pituitaire **2** *adj* pituitaire

pity[1] ['pɪtɪ] *n* (**a**) (*compassion*) pitié *f*; **to have** *or* **take p. on sb** avoir pitié de qn, prendre qn en pitié; **to take p. on sb** (*be moved to pity*) s'apitoyer sur qn; **she deserves no p.** elle ne mérite pas qu'on s'apitoie sur elle; **are you entirely without p.?** es-tu incapable du moindre sentiment de pitié?; **to show no p.** ne manifester aucune pitié; **the thought moved him to p.** cette pensée lui inspira de la pitié; **to do sth out of p. for sb** faire qch par pitié pour qn; **for p.'s sake** par pitié

(**b**) (*misfortune*) **what a p.!** quel dommage!; **it's a great p. that ...** il est bien malheureux *ou* dommage que ... + *sub*; **it's no great p. that ...** ce n'est pas si grave que ... + *sub*; (*quite a good thing*) encore heureux que ... + *sub*; **more's the p.** c'est bien dommage

pity[2] *vt* (*person*) plaindre, avoir pitié de; **he is to be pitied** il est à plaindre

pitying ['pɪtɪɪŋ] *adj* compatissant; (*look*) compatissant, de pitié

pityingly ['pɪtɪɪŋlɪ] *adv* (*to look*) avec pitié, d'un air compatissant; (*to say*) d'un ton compatissant

Pius ['paɪəs] *n* Pie *m*

pivot[1] ['pɪvət] *n* (**a**) *MecE etc* pivot *m*, axe *m*; (*of crane*) pivot; (*of axle etc*) tourillon *m* (**b**) *Fig* (*person in company etc*) pivot *m*, cheville *f* ouvrière; *Mil* **p. (man)** pivot, guide *m*, homme *m* de base

pivot[2] (**-t-**) **1** *vi* pivoter, tourner (**on sth** sur qch); **she pivoted on her left leg** elle pivota sur sa jambe gauche; *Fig* **their plans pivoted around her** leurs projets reposaient sur elle **2** *vt* (*turn*) (*sth*) faire pivoter; (*set on a pivot*) (*gun*) monter sur pivot

pivotal ['pɪvət(ə)l] *adj* (*point*) cardinal; *Fig* (*position etc*) clef *inv*; (*importance*) capital; **she is p. in their plans** elle joue un rôle central dans leurs projets

pix [pɪks] *npl F* = **pics**, *see* **pic**

pixel ['pɪksəl] *n Comptr* pixel *m*; **p. density** densité *f* en pixels

pixie ['pɪksɪ] *n* (*elf*) lutin *m*; (*fairy*) fée *f*

pixil(l)ated ['pɪksɪleɪtəd] *adj US Sl* (*drunk*) bourré, plein

pixy ['pɪksɪ] *n* = **pixie**

pizza ['piːtsə] *n Culin* pizza *f*; **p. base** pâte *f* à pizza; **p. parlour** pizzeria *f*

pizzazz [pə'zæz] *n F* = **pzazz**

pizzeria [piːtsə'riːə] *n* pizzeria *f*

pkg *n abbr* **package**

pkt *n abbr* **packet**

Pl (*abbr* **Place**) = rue

pl *Gram* (*abbr* **plural**) pl

P & L [piːə'nel] *n Com, Fin* (*abbr* **profit and loss**) pertes *fpl* et profits *mpl*

placard[1] ['plækɑːd] *n* (*written notice*) écriteau *m*; (*poster*) affiche *f*; (*carried by protester*) pancarte *f*

placard[2] *vt* (*wall*) placarder

placate [plə'keɪt] *vt* apaiser, calmer

place[1] [pleɪs] *n* (**a**) (*location*) endroit *m*, lieu *m*; (*in street names*) rue *f*; **an ideal p. for a picnic** un endroit idéal pour pique-niquer; **a good p. to meet people** un bon endroit pour rencontrer des gens; **this is the p.!** (*here we are*) nous voilà arrivés!; **to move from one p. to another** se déplacer d'un endroit à un autre; **the village/museum was an interesting p.** le village/musée était intéressant; **I'm looking for a p. to stay** je cherche un logement; **can you recommend a p. to eat?** pouvez-vous me recommander un restaurant?; **this is no p. for you** ce n'est pas un endroit pour vous; **I've broken my arm in two places** je me suis cassé le bras en deux endroits; **I can't be in two places at once** je ne peux pas être à deux endroits à la fois; **the book was good in places** le livre était bon par endroits; **all over the p.** (*in many different places*) partout; *Fig* (*in disorder*) dans tous les sens; *Fig F* **the team were all over the p.** l'équipe a joué n'importe comment; *Fig F* **these figures are all over the p.** (*are inaccurate*) ces chiffres ont été calculés n'importe comment; *Fig F* **at the interview he was all over the p.** (*panicking, unclear*) il a raconté n'importe quoi à l'entretien; *Fig F* **this paragraph is all over the p.** ce paragraphe a été écrit n'importe comment; *Fig F* **to go places** (*succeed*) réussir (dans la vie); *Rugby, Fb* **p. kick** coup *m* de pied placé; **p. name** nom *m* de lieu; **the other p.** *Br Univ F* (*at Oxford*) Cambridge; (*at Cambridge*) Oxford; *Br Parl* (*in House of Commons*) la Chambre des Lords; (*in House of Lords*) la Chambre des Communes; **Belmont P.** rue Belmont

(**b**) (*assigned to sb, sth*) place *f*; **everything in its p.** chaque chose à sa place; **in its proper time and p.** en temps et lieu; **to find a p. for sth** trouver une place pour qch; **this town has a special p. in my affections** j'ai une tendresse particulière pour cette ville; **to hold sth in p.** tenir qch en place; **to lose/find one's p.** (*in a book*) perdre/retrouver sa page; **his anger gave p. to pity** sa colère a fait place à un sentiment de pitié; **to take sb's p.** remplacer qn; (*oust*) prendre la place de qn; **a woman's p. is in the home** la place d'une femme est à la maison

(**c**) (*for specific purpose*) **p. of birth/death/amusement** lieu *m* de naissance/de décès/de divertissement; **p. of**

business lieu de travail; *Fin* **p. of issue** lieu d'émission; **p. of payment** lieu de paiement; **p. of refuge** lieu de refuge; **p. of residence** résidence *f*, domicile *m* (réel); *Br Jur* **p. of safety order** (*for child*) = décision *f* de mise en sûreté; **at my p. of work** à mon travail; **p. of worship** édifice *m* consacré au culte

(d) to take p. (*happen*) avoir lieu; **the marriage will not take p.** le mariage n'aura pas lieu *ou* ne se fera pas; **many changes have taken p.** il y a eu beaucoup de changements; **while this was taking p.** tandis que cela se passait

(e) (*residence*) **a little p. in the country** une petite maison à la campagne; *F* **nice p. you've got here** c'est bien chez vous!; *F* **come round to my p.** venez chez moi; *F* **your p. or mine?** on va chez toi ou chez moi?

(f) (*seat etc*) **is this p. taken?** est-ce que cette place est prise?; **to book a p.** réserver une place; **to change places with sb** changer de place avec qn; **to give up** *or* **offer one's p. to sb** laisser sa place à qn; **if I get there first I'll keep a p. for you** si j'arrive le premier je te garderai une place; **to keep sb's p. in a queue** garder la place de qn dans une file d'attente; **to set** *or* **lay an extra p. at table** mettre une assiette de plus à table

(g) (*vacancy etc*) **to get a p. at university** être admis à l'université; **the school still has five places left** cette école a encore cinq places de libres

(h) this remark is out of p. (*inappropriate*) cette observation est déplacée *ou* hors de propos; **to look out of p.** (*of person*) ne pas être à sa place *ou* dans son élément; (*of thing*) ne pas être à sa place; **he didn't look out of p.** il ne déparait pas; **it's not my p. to do it** ce n'est pas à moi de le faire

(i) (*situation*) **put yourself in my p.** mettez-vous à ma place; **if I were in your p. I'd go** à votre place, j'irais

(j) (*in society, competition etc*) place *f*, rang *m*; **to keep sb in his p.** montrer à qn où est sa place; **to know one's p.** savoir où est sa place; *Iron* **I know my p.** je sais où est ma place; *Fig* **to put sb in his p.** remettre qn à sa place; **in first/second p.** en premier/second lieu; *Sp* **to finish in second/last p.** finir à la deuxième/dernière place *ou* en deuxième/dernière position; *Horseracing* **to back a horse for a p.** jouer un cheval placé; *Math* **to three decimal places** à trois décimales

(k) (*parts of an argument etc*) **in the first p. ..., in the second p. ...** en premier lieu ..., en second lieu ...; **I don't know why they gave him the job in the first p.** d'ailleurs je ne sais même pas pourquoi ils l'ont embauché

place² **1** *vt* **(a)** (*put*) placer, mettre; **to p. a book back on a shelf** remettre un livre (en place) sur un rayon; **to p. a book with a publisher** confier un livre à un éditeur; **to p. a matter in sb's hands** mettre une affaire dans les mains de qn; **I p. myself at your disposal** je me mets à votre disposition; **to p. a child in sb's care** confier un enfant à la garde de qn; **to p. a child in care/with foster parents** placer *ou* mettre un enfant à la D.D.A.S.S/dans une famille d'acceuil

(b) the house is well placed (*situated*) la maison est bien située; **how are we placed for time?** combien de temps avons-nous?; **how are you placed for money?** comment ça va côté finances?; **you're better placed than I am to answer that** tu es mieux placé que moi pour répondre à cela; **British industry is well placed to ...** l'industrie britannique est à même de ...; **strategically placed airfields** des terrains d'aviation stratégiquement situés

(c) *Com, Fin etc* (*goods, shares*) placer, vendre; (*loan*) placer, négocier; (*invest*) (*funds*) placer; (*contract*) adjuger, concéder; **to p. an order** passer une commande; **to p. an order for sth** passer commande de qch; **to p. an order with sb** passer commande à qn; **to p. a bet** faire un pari; **to p. a bet on sb/sth** parier sur qn/qch

(d) (*find a job for*) placer

(e) (*class*), *Sch, Sp etc* **to be placed third** se classer troisième; **I would p. him among the outstanding biographers of the century** je le classerais parmi les meilleurs biographes du siècle; *Horseracing* **was your horse placed?** est-ce que votre cheval s'est classé dans les trois premiers?

(f) (*identify*) (*sound*) localiser; **I know his face but I can't p. him** je l'ai déjà vu mais je n'arrive pas à le remettre

2 *vi Am esp Horseracing* se classer entre les trois premiers

placebo [plə'siːbəʊ] *n Med, Fig* placebo *m*; **the p. effect** l'effet *m* placebo

place card *n* carte *f* portant le nom du convive

place mat *n* set *m* de table

placement ['pleɪsmənt] *n* **(a)** (*putting in place*) placement *m*, mise *f* en place; (*siting*) localisation *f*; (*of funds, bet*) placement; (*of contract*) adjudication *f*; (*of order*) passage *m*; (*finding job*) placement; **the p. of children in care/with foster parents** le placement d'enfants à la D.D.A.S.S./dans des familles d'accueil **(b)** (*of trainee etc*) stage *m*; **to get a p.** (*of trainee*) trouver un stage

placenta [plə'sentə] *n Anat, Bot* placenta *m*

place setting *n* (*at table*) couvert *m*

placid ['plæsɪd] *adj* placide, calme, tranquille

placidity [plə'sɪdɪtɪ], **placidness** ['plæsɪdnɪs] *n* placidité *f*, calme *m*, tranquillité *f*

placidly ['plæsɪdlɪ] *adv* placidement, calmement, tranquillement

placing ['pleɪsɪŋ] *n* **(a)** = **placement** (*a*) **(b) p. of an order** passation *f* de commande **(c)** *Sp etc* (*ranking*) classement *m*

placket ['plækɪt] *n Sewing* patte *f*

plagiarism ['pleɪdʒərɪz(ə)m] *n* plagiat *m*; **student accused of p.** étudiant accusé d'avoir copié

plagiarist ['pleɪdʒərɪst] *n* plagiaire *mf*

plagiarize ['pleɪdʒəraɪz] **1** *vt* (*author*) plagier; (*work*) plagier, faire un plagiat de, contrefaire; (*student's essay*) copier (**from** dans) **2** *vi* se livrer à des plagiats

plague¹ [pleɪg] *n Med* peste *f*; *Bible, Fig* (*scourge*) fléau *m*, plaie *f*; **to avoid sb/sth like the p.** éviter qn/qch comme la peste; *Arch* **a p. on both your houses!** allez tous au diable!; *Arch* **a p. on you and your statistics!** allez au diable, toi et tes statistiques!; **p. ridden** *or* **stricken** infesté par la peste

plague² *vt* (*person*) tourmenter, harceler; **she was plagued by illness** la maladie la poursuivait sans relâche; **to p. sb's life** empoisonner l'existence de qn; **to p. sb with questions** harceler qn de questions; **our journey was plagued by minor problems** nous avons été accablés de petits ennuis pendant notre voyage; **the team was plagued by injury** l'équipe a collectionné les blessures

plaice [pleɪs] *n* (*fish*) carrelet *m*, plie *f* (franche)

plaid [plæd, *Scot* pleɪd] *n* **(a)** (*material*) tartan *m*, tissu *m* écossais **(b)** (*part of Highland costume, travelling rug*) plaid *m*

plain¹ [pleɪn] **1** *adj* **(a)** (*clear, unambiguous*) clair, évident; **to make sth p. to sb** faire comprendre qch à qn; **to make one's feelings p.** exprimer clairement ses sentiments; **they made their contempt for him p.** ils n'ont pas caché leur mépris pour lui; **it's as p. as (p.) can be** *or* **as p. as a pikestaff** *or* **as the nose on your face** c'est on ne peut plus clair, c'est clair comme le jour; **it's p. (to see) that you don't like me** il est évident que vous ne m'aimez pas; **I'll be quite p. with you** je vais être franc avec toi; **in p. English** clairement; **what is that in p. English?** = qu'est-ce que ça veut dire en bon français?; **p. answer** réponse *f* carrée; **p. speaking** franc parler *m*; **the p. truth** la pure *ou* simple vérité

(b) (*simple*) (*style, furniture, dress, sewing*) simple, sans recherche; (*cigarettes*) sans filtre; (*unadorned*) (*rice, yoghurt etc*) nature; **that's just p. foolishness/ignorance** c'est de la pure bêtise/ignorance; *Knitting* **one p. one purl** une maille à l'endroit, une maille à l'envers; **p. country people** de simples campagnards; **in p. clothes** en civil; **p.-clothes policeman** agent *m* en civil; **p. cooking** cuisine *f* simple; **p. knitting** tricot *m* à l'endroit; **p. living** vie *f* simple; *Tex* **p. material** tissu *m* uni; **p. paper fax** télécopieur *m ou* fax *m* sur papier ordinaire

(c) (*uniformly coloured*) (*wallpaper, carpet, material etc*) uni; (*paper*) non réglé

(d) (*unattractive*) (*woman*) pas particulièrement belle, plutôt quelconque; **she's rather a p. Jane** c'est une jeune fille plutôt quelconque

2 *adv F* **(a)** (*simply*) simplement; **he's just p. ignorant** il est tout simplement ignorant

(b) (*frankly*) franchement; **to speak p.** parler franc *ou* sans détours; **she told him p. what she thought about him** elle lui a dit franchement *ou* sans détours ce qu'elle pensait de lui

plain² *n Geog* plaine *f*; **alluvial p.** plaine alluviale; **the Great Plains** la Prairie (américaine)

plainchant ['pleɪntʃɑːnt] *n* = **plainsong**

plain chocolate *n* chocolat *m* à croquer

plain flour *n* farine *f*

plainly ['pleɪnlɪ] *adv* **(a)** (*clearly*) (*to see*) clairement, nettement; **to speak p.** (*be frank*) parler franchement *ou* sans détours; **I can p. see that I am not welcome here** je vois bien que je ne suis pas le bienvenu ici; **p. visible/audible** qui se voit/s'entend clairement; **p. I was not wanted** il était clair que j'étais de trop; **they were p. exhausted** ils étaient de toute évidence épuisés **(b)** (*simply*) (*to live*) simplement; (*to dress*) simplement, sans recherche

plainness ['pleɪnnɪs] *n* **(a)** (*clarity*) (*of concise language*) clarté *f*, simplicité *f*; (*of frank language*) franchise *f*, rondeur *f* **(b)** (*simplicity*) (*of lifestyle etc*) simplicité *f* **(c)** (*lack of beauty*) manque *m* de beauté

plainsong ['pleɪnsɒŋ] *n Mus* plain-chant *m*
plain-spoken *adj* franc, *f* franche
plaint [pleɪnt] *n Jur* plainte *f*
plaintiff ['pleɪntɪf] *n Jur* demandeur, -eresse, plaignant, -ante
plaintive ['pleɪntɪv] *adj* plaintif
plaintively ['pleɪntɪvlɪ] *adv* plaintivement
plaintiveness ['pleɪntɪvnɪs] *n* ton *m* plaintif
plait¹ [plæt] *n* (*of hair*) natte *f*, tresse *f*; **she had her hair in plaits** elle avait des nattes
plait² *vt* (*hair etc*) natter, tresser
plan¹ [plæn] *n* **(a)** (*proposal, intention*) projet *m*, plan *m*; (*timetable*) planning *m*; (*for the future*) projet; **p. of battle** plan de bataille; **p. of campaign** plan d'action; *Fin* **investment p.** plan d'investissement; *Econ* **five-year p.** plan quinquennal; *Av* **flight p.** plan de vol; **to change one's plans** changer ses projets; **to have no fixed plan(s)** ne pas avoir de projet bien déterminé; **everything went according to p.** tout a marché comme prévu; **the best p. would be to ...** la meilleure solution serait de ...; **it would be a good p. to ...** ce serait une bonne idée de ...; **what are your plans for the summer?** quels sont vos projets pour cet été?; **I've thought of a p.** j'ai imaginé un plan; **to have other plans** avoir d'autres projets; **they had other plans for us** ils avaient autre chose en vue en ce qui nous concernait
(b) (*drawing etc*) (*of building, town*) plan *m*; (*in surveying*) (*of area*) plan, levé *m*; (*outline*) (*of novel etc*) plan; **ground p.** plan géométral
plan² (-nn-) **1** *vt* **(a)** (*arrange*) (*trip*) projeter; (*attack etc*) combiner; (*crime*) comploter, tramer; **everything had been planned down to the last detail** tout avait été planifié dans les moindres détails; **to p. to do sth** projeter de faire qch; **we don't have anything planned tomorrow afternoon** nous n'avons rien de prévu demain après-midi; **things did not go as planned** les choses ne se sont pas passées comme prévu; **this had been planned** cela avait été prévu
(b) (*make a plan of*) faire *ou* dessiner le plan de; *Econ* (*production etc*) planifier; (*new novel etc*) faire *ou* établir *ou* élaborer le plan de; **to p. one's lessons** (*of teacher*) préparer ses cours; **the school was planned for 500 pupils** l'école a été prévue pour 500 élèves
2 *vi* faire des projets; **to p. for the future** faire des projets d'avenir; **they had planned for six** ils avaient tout prévu pour six personnes
▶ **plan ahead** *vi* faire des projets; (*for lunch, party*) s'y prendre à l'avance
▶ **plan on** *vipo* (*have intention of*) (*sth*) prévoir; **to p. on doing sth** prévoir *ou* projeter *ou* avoir l'intention de faire qch; **we're planning on going to Brazil** *or* **on a trip to Brazil** nous projetons *ou* nous avons l'intention de partir au Brésil, nous projetons un voyage au Brésil; **don't p. on being able to persuade him** ne compte pas arriver à le persuader; **we hadn't planned on staying long** nous n'avions pas prévu de *ou* ne comptions pas rester longtemps
▶ **plan out** *vtsep* (*make detailed plans for*) prévoir (en détail); **he had planned it all out** il avait tout prévu, il en avait établi tous les détails
plane¹ [pleɪn] **1** *adj* (*angle, geometry etc*) plan; **p. surface** surface *f* plane; *Math* **p. trigonometry** trigonométrie *f* rectiligne **2** *n* **(a)** *Geom* plan *m*; **horizontal/vertical p.** plan horizontal/vertical; *Opt* **focal p.** plan focal; *Geol* **fault p.** plan de faille **(b)** *Fig* plan *m*, niveau *m*; **on the economic p.** sur le plan économique; **a higher p. of intelligence** un niveau intellectuel supérieur **(c)** *Av* **tail p.** plan *m* fixe horizontal
plane² *n* (*aeroplane*) avion *m*; **by p.** en avion; **it's just a short p. ride** c'est un court voyage en avion; **p. ticket** billet *m* d'avion
plane³ *vi* (*of bird, aircraft*) planer; **to p. down** descendre en vol plané *ou* en planant; **to p. along the water** (*of hydroplane*) glisser à la surface de l'eau
plane⁴ *n* (*tool*) rabot *m*
plane⁵ *vt Carp etc* (*wood*) raboter, aplanir, planer; (*metal*) aplanir, planer; **to p. a surface smooth** aplanir une surface; (*also wood*) raboter une surface
plane⁶ *n* **p. (tree)** platane *m*
planet ['plænɪt] *n Astron* planète *f*; **the biggest country on the p.** le plus grand pays de la planète
planetarium [plænɪ'teərɪəm] *n* planétarium *m*
planetary ['plænɪt(ə)rɪ] *adj Astron* (*system, time, movement*) planétaire
plangent ['plændʒənt] *adj Lit* élégiaque
planing ['pleɪnɪŋ] *n Carp etc* (*of wood*) rabotage *m*, planage *m*, aplanissage *m*; (*of metal*) planage, aplanissage; **p. machine** raboteuse *f*
planisphere ['plænɪsfɪər] *n* planisphère *m* céleste
plank¹ [plæŋk] *n* **(a)** *Carp, Constr etc* planche *f* (épaisse), madrier *m*; *Naut* **to walk the p.** passer à la planche **(b)** *Fig Pol* **this was a main p. in the party platform** c'était un des principaux articles du programme du parti
plank² *vt Constr* (*floor*) planchéier
▶ **plank down** *vtsep* (*put down heavily*) poser brusquement
planking ['plæŋkɪŋ] *n* (*planks*) planches *fpl*, madriers *mpl*
plankton ['plæŋktən] *n* plancton *m*
planned ['plænd] *adj* **(a)** prévu, projeté; **the p. meeting never took place** la réunion qui avait été prévue n'a jamais eu lieu; **well/badly p.** bien/mal conçu; (*plot, crime*) bien/mal concerté *ou* organisé; **was it a p. parenthood?** c'était vraiment votre/leur intention d'avoir un enfant? **(b)** *Econ etc* planifié; **p. economy** économie *f* planifiée *ou* dirigée; **p. takeover of** projet *m* d'OPA sur
planner ['plænər] *n* **(a)** (*person*) planificateur, -trice; **(town) p.** urbaniste *mf* **(b)** (*on wall of office etc*) planning *m*; (*chart*) chronogramme *m*; (*diary*) agenda *m*
planning ['plænɪŋ] *n* **(a)** (*of project, plot etc*) conception *f*, élaboration *f*; (*of menus*) élaboration; **the expedition will require careful p.** il faudra une organisation minutieuse pour mener à bien cette expédition; **it's still at the p. stage** c'est encore à l'état de projet; **the project was halted at the p. stage** le projet n'a pas dépassé le stade de la planification **(b)** *Econ* planification *f*, *F* planning *m*; *Admin* **to get p. permission to build sth** *or* **for sth** obtenir le permis de construire qch; **town p.** urbanisme *m*; **family p.** planning familial
plant¹ [plɑːnt] *n* **(a)** plante *f*; **flowering p.** plante à fleurs; **pot p., house p.** plante d'appartement; **bedding p.** plant *m* à repiquer; *Agr* **p. breeder** phytogénéticien, -ienne; **p. physiology** physiologie *f* végétale
(b) *Ind* (*equipment*) équipement *m*, matériel *m* (industriel); (*facility*) installation *f* (industrielle); (*factory*) usine *f*; **cooling p.** appareil *m* de refroidissement; **(electric) power p., generating p.** centrale *f* électrique
(c) *Sl* (*spy*) taupe *f*; (*from police*) mouchard *m*; (*of magician, memory man*) compère *m*; (*something planted in order to incriminate*) coup *m* monté; **the drugs were a p.** la drogue avait été placée là pour me/le/*etc* mettre en cause
plant² *vt* **(a)** (*tree etc*) planter; **to p. a field with wheat** mettre un champ en blé **(b)** (*insert, place*) (*stake in the ground etc*) planter; *Mil etc* (*bomb*) poser; *F* (*spy*) planter; **to p. an idea in sb's mind** implanter une idée dans l'esprit de qn; *F* **a well planted blow** un coup bien asséné *ou* bien appliqué; *F* **he planted a big kiss on her cheek** il lui planta un gros baiser sur la joue; *F* **to p. oneself in front of sb** se planter devant qn; **to p. incriminating evidence on sb** fabriquer de fausses preuves contre qn
▶ **plant out** *vtsep Agr, Gardening* (*seedling*) repiquer
plantain¹ ['plæntɪn] *n* (*plant*) plantain *m*
plantain² *n* **(a)** (*fruit*) banane *f* des Antilles **(b) p. (tree)** bananier *m* du paradis
plantar ['plæntər] *adj Anat* plantaire
plantation [plæn'teɪʃən] *n* (*of trees, cotton etc*) plantation *f*
plant biology *n* phytobiologie *f*
planter ['plɑːntər] *n* **(a)** (*plantation owner, worker*) planteur, -euse; **coffee/sugar/cotton p.** planteur, -euse de café/de sucre/de coton **(b)** (*tool*) planteuse *f* **(c)** (*pot for house plant*) cache-pot *m inv*; (*for outside*) jardinière *f*
plant hire *n* location *f* de matériel industriel
plant life *n* (*life of plants*) vie *f* végétale
plaque [plæk] *n* **(a)** (*bronze, marble etc*) plaque *f* (commémorative) **(b)** (*on teeth*) plaque *f* dentaire
plash¹ [plæʃ] *n* (*of waves, stream etc*) clapotement *m*, clapotis *m*; (*of object falling into water*) flac *m*
plash² *vi* (*of liquids*) clapoter, faire un clapotis; (*of falling object etc*) faire flac (*sur l'eau etc*)
plasm ['plæz(ə)m] *n Biol* protoplasme *m*
plasma ['plæzmə] *n* plasma *m*; **(blood) p.** plasma (sanguin); *Comptr* **p. display** affichage *m* à plasma; *Comptr* **p. screen** écran *m* (à) plasma
plasmapheresis [plæzmə'ferəsɪs] *n Med* plasmaphérèse *f*, échange *m* plasmatique
plaster¹ ['plɑːstər] *n* **(a)** *Constr etc* plâtre *m*; **to put a leg in p.** plâtrer une jambe, mettre une jambe dans le plâtre **(b)** *Br Med* **(sticking) p.** pansement *m* adhésif, sparadrap *m*; **corn p.** pansement coricide
plaster² *vt* **(a)** *Constr etc* (*wall*) plâtrer, enduire de plâtre **(b)** *Fig* **the wall was plastered with advertisements** le mur était tapissé d'affiches; **plastered with mud** (*person, shoes, car etc*) couvert de boue; **her face was plastered with make-up** elle avait un peu forcé sur le maquillage; **he plastered his hair down** il aplatit ses cheveux; **her name was plastered over the front pages** son nom s'étalait en première page; *Sl* **to get plastered** (*drunk*) se beurrer, se

pinter; *Sl* **he's plastered** il est beurré *ou* pinté **(c)** *Med* (*leg etc*) plâtrer

plasterboard ['plɑːstəbɔːd] *n Constr* Placoplâtre® *m*

plaster cast *n Surg* plâtre *m*; *Art* (*object cast*) moulage *m* en plâtre

plasterer ['plɑːstərər] *n* plâtrier *m*

plaster of Paris *n* plâtre *m* de Paris, plâtre de moulage

plasterwork ['plɑːstəwɜːk] *n Constr* plâtres *mpl*

plastic ['plæstɪk] **1** *n* **(a)** plastique *m*; **laminated p.** (plastique) stratifié *m*, lamifié *m*; **moulded p.** plastique moulé; **wrapped in p.** emballé dans du plastique; **the plastics industry** l'industrie *f* des plastiques

(b) *F* **p. (money)** monnaie *f* électronique; **he paid for it with p.** il l'a payé avec une carte de crédit

2 *adj* **(a)** (*made of plastic*) (*bag, cup*) en plastique; **p. bomb** (bombe *f* au) plastic *m*; **to blow up a house with a p. bomb** plastiquer une maison; **p. bullet** balle *f* de plastique; **p. explosive** plastic *m*

(b) *Art etc* plastique; **the p. arts** les arts *mpl* plastiques

(c) (*artificial*) synthétique, artificiel; **p. smile** sourire *m* artificiel

Plasticine® ['plæstɪsiːn] *n* pâte *f* à modeler

plasticity [plæs'tɪsɪtɪ] *n* plasticité *f*; *Art, Cin* effet *m* plastique

plastic surgeon *n* spécialiste *mf* de chirurgie esthétique, plasticien, -ienne

plastic surgery *n* (*cosmetic*) chirurgie *f* esthétique; (*after accident etc*) chirurgie réparatrice

plate[1] [pleɪt] *n* **(a)** (*for food*) assiette *f*; **dinner/soup p.** assiette plate/creuse; *Fig F* **to have a lot on one's p.** avoir du pain sur la planche; *Fig F* **I've already got far too much on my p.** j'ai déjà largement à faire; *Fig F* **I've got enough on my p. without him causing problems** j'ai déjà assez à faire sans qu'il ne crée des problèmes; *Fig F* **to hand sth to sb on a p.** apporter qch à qn sur un plateau; *Fig F* **he got it handed to him on a p.** on le lui a apporté sur un plateau; *Rel etc* **(collection) p.** plateau *m* de quête; *Rel etc* **to pass round the p.** faire la quête; **p. rack** égouttoir *m*; **p. service** (*in restaurant*) service *m* à l'assiette; **p. warmer** chauffe-assiettes *m inv*

(b) (*small piece*) (*of metal, glass, plastic etc*) petite plaque *f*, lamelle *f*; *Geol, Med* plaque; **(dental) p.** (*for straightening teeth*) appareil *m* (dentaire); (*dentures*) dentier *m*; *Geol* **p. tectonics** tectonique *f* des plaques

(c) *Metal* (*large piece*) plaque *f*; *Ind* (grande) feuille *f*; (*of armour*) plaque, plate *f*; (*of door hinge*) paumelle *f*; *Aut* **p. clutch** embrayage *m* à disque *ou* à plateau; **hot p.** (*on cooker*) plaque chauffante; (*single plate*) réchaud *m*; (*plate warmer*) chauffe-assiettes *m inv*; **name p.** (*on door*) plaque de porte; (*of street*) plaque de rue; (*of machine*) plaque d'identification *ou* de série; *Br Aut etc* **number p.** plaque d'immatriculation

(d) *El* (*of battery etc*) plaque *f*, lame *f*; *Electron* (*of electron tube*) plaque, anode *f*

(e) (*in engraving*), *Typ* plaque *f*; (*in engraving*), *Phot etc* cliché *m*; (*engraving*) planche *f*, gravure *f*, estampe *f*; *Phot* **(photographic) p.** plaque (photographique); *Typ* **p. cylinder** cylindre *m* porte-plaque; **p. 12 (a)** (*in book*) planche 12 (a)

(f) *Constr* **(wall) p.** (*of beam*) plaque *f* d'assise

(g) (*plated metal*) (*gold*) orfèvrerie *f*; **silver p.** argenterie *f*; **it's (only) p.** c'est du plaqué

(h) *Sp* coupe *f* (*d'or, d'argent donnée en prix*)

plate[2] *vt* **(a)** (*protect with plates of metal*) blinder, recouvrir *ou* garnir de plaques **(b)** (*add layer of metal to*) métalliser; (*with gold*) plaquer en or; (*with silver*) plaquer en argent

plate armour *n Mil, Naut* blindage *m*

plateau, *pl* **-eaux, -eaus** ['plætəʊ, -əʊz] *n Geog* plateau *m*; *Fig* **to reach a p.** atteindre un palier

plated ['pleɪtɪd] *adj* **(a)** (*protected with metal plates*) recouvert *ou* garni de plaques; **armour p.** blindé **(b)** (*coated with metal*) plaqué; **gold p.** plaqué or; **silver p.** argenté; **chromium p.** chromé

plateful ['pleɪtfʊl] *n* assiettée *f*, (pleine) assiette *f*

plate glass *n Tech* glace *f* de vitrage très épais; **p. window** (*of shop*) vitrine *f*; (*of house*) baie *f* vitrée

platelayer ['pleɪtleɪər] *n Br Rail* poseur *m* de rails

plateless printing ['pleɪtlɪs] *n* impression *f* sans presse

platelet ['pleɪtlɪt] *n* (*in blood*) plaquette *f*

plate-making *n Typ* préparation *f* des plaques offset

platen ['plæt(ə)n] *n* rouleau *m*

plate-room manager *n Typ* conducteur *m* de presse

platform ['plætfɔːm] *n* **(a)** (*raised flat surface*) plate-forme *f*, *pl* plates-formes; *Rail* (*where passengers stand*) quai *m*; (*where train stops*) voie *f*; (*of weighing machine*) tablier *m*; (*of crane*) passerelle *f*; *Petr* **drilling p.** plate-forme de forage; **launching/firing p.** plate-forme de lancement/de tir (de missiles); *Rail* **the train waiting at p. one** le train au départ voie no 1; *Rail* **to wait on the p.** (*of person*) attendre sur le quai; *Rail* **what p. is it for London?** quel quai est-ce pour Londres?; *Am Rail* **p. car** (wagon *m*) plate-forme; *Rail* **p. ticket** ticket *m* de quai; **arrival/departure p.** quai d'arrivée/de départ

(b) (*at public meeting*) estrade *f*, tribune *f*; *Pol Fig* (*of party*) plate-forme *f*, *pl* plates-formes, programme *m*; **he used his programme on TV as a p. for promoting his political views** son émision télévisée lui servait de tribune pour promouvoir ses opinions politiques

(c) platforms (*shoes*) chaussures *fpl* à semelles compensées

platform shoes *npl* chaussures *fpl* à semelles compensées

platform soles *npl* semelles *fpl* compensées

plating ['pleɪtɪŋ] *n* **(a)** (*protective*) blindage *m*; **steel** *or* **armour p.** blindage **(b)** (*coating with metal*) placage *m*; (*copper*) cuivrage *m*; (*gold*) dorage *m*, dorure *f*; (*silver*) argentage *m*, argenture *f*

platinum ['plætɪnəm] **1** *n* platine *m*; **p. blond hair** cheveux blond platiné *ou* blond platine *ou* platinés; **she's a p. blonde** c'est une blonde platinée; **p. disc** disque *m* de platine **2** *adv* **to go p.** (*of record*) devenir disque de platine

platitude ['plætɪtjuːd] *n* (*remark*) platitude *f*, banalité *f*, lieu *m* commun

platitudinous [plætɪ'tjuːdɪnəs] *adj* (*style, speech*) plat, banal

Plato ['pleɪtəʊ] *n* Platon *m*

Platonic [plə'tɒnɪk] *adj* (*philosophy etc*) platonicien; (*love*) platonique; **he wanted to keep things p.** il voulait que leur relation reste platonique

platoon [plə'tuːn] *n Mil* (*in infantry*) section *f*; (*in tanks*) peloton *m*; *Fig* (*of assistants, students*) armée *f*; **p. commander** chef *m* de section *ou* de peloton

platter ['plætər] *n* **(a)** (*plate*) plat *m* **(b)** *esp Am F* (*record*) disque *m*

platypus ['plætɪpəs] *n* (*animal*) ornithorynque *m*

plaudits ['plɔːdɪts] *npl esp Lit* (salve *f* d')applaudissements *mpl*; **the new menus on trains have won the p. of passengers** les nouveaux menus servis dans les trains ont été accueillis avec enthousiasme par les passagers

plausibility [plɔːzə'bɪlɪtɪ] *n* (*of argument, excuse etc*) plausibilité *f*; **the plot is lacking in p.** l'intrigue n'est guère plausible; **I would question the p. of someone doing …** il ne me semble guère plausible que quelqu'un fasse …; **she argued, with some p., that …** elle a avancé, de façon assez convaincante, que …

plausible ['plɔːzəb(ə)l] *adj* **(a)** (*excuse etc*) plausible, vraisemblable; (*pretext etc*) spécieux **(b)** (*person, argument*) convaincant

plausibly ['plɔːzəblɪ] *adv* plausiblement; (*to argue etc*) de façon convaincante

play[1] [pleɪ] *n* **(a)** *Th* pièce *f* de théâtre; **Shakespeare's plays** les pièces *ou* le théâtre de Shakespeare; **(radio) p.** pièce radiophonique; **(television) p.** dramatique *f*

(b) (*movement*) (*of mechanical part*) course *f*; (*unwanted slack*) jeu *m*; (*of light*) jeu, reflets *mpl*; **a complex p. of forces** un rapport de forces complexe; **there's still too much p. in the brakes** il y a encore trop de jeu dans les freins; **to come into p.** entrer en jeu, intervenir; **to bring** *or* **call** *or* **put sth into p.** mettre qch en jeu *ou* en œuvre; (*one's faculties*) exercer qch; *F* **to make a p. for sth** jouer le grand jeu pour obtenir qch; *F* **to make a p. for sb** (*try to seduce*) jouer le grand jeu à qn, faire des avances à qn; **to give** *or* **allow full p. to one's imagination** donner libre cours à son imagination; **to make great p. of sth** beaucoup insister sur qch

(c) (*of children etc*) jeu *m* **I didn't want to interrupt the children's p.** je ne voulais pas interrompre les enfants alors qu'ils étaient en train de jouer; **at p.** en train de jouer; **the aristocracy at p.** l'aristocratie en train de se détendre; **to say sth in p.** dire qch en plaisantant *ou* pour rire; **p. on words** calembour *m*, jeu *m* de mots

(d) *Sp* **p. began at one o'clock** la partie a commencé à une heure; **after some very boring p. in the first half …** après une première mi-temps très ennuyeuse …; *Tennis* **there was some incredibly fast p. in the final set** il y a eu des échanges très rapides au dernier set; **what a good piece of p.!** quel beau coup!, bien joué!; *Cr* **rain stopped p.** la partie a été interrompue par la pluie; **in p.** (*of ball*) en jeu; **out of p.** hors jeu

(e) (*gambling*) jeu *m* (de hasard); **to lose at p.** perdre au jeu

play[2] **1** *vi* **(a)** (*have fun*) jouer; (*of animals*) folâtrer, gambader

(b) (*participate in game*) jouer; **to p. against sb/a team** jouer contre qn/une équipe; **to p. in goal** être goal; **who**

plays first? à qui de commencer?; (*at bowling*) à qui la boule?; *Golf* à qui l'honneur?; **to p. fair** jouer franc jeu; **to p. hard to get** se faire désirer; **to p. for money** (*in gambling*) jouer pour de l'argent; **to p. high** *or* **for high stakes** (*in gambling*) jouer gros (jeu); *Cards* **to p. high/low** jouer une forte/basse carte; **do you p.?** est-ce que tu sais jouer?

(**c**) (*move*) (*of light, colour, fountain*) jouer, chatoyer; **the sun is playing on the water** le soleil joue sur l'eau

(**d**) *Th etc* (*act*) jouer; **to p. on the stage** (*of actor*) jouer *ou* se produire sur la scène; **production/film now playing at ...** pièce/film qui passe actuellement à ...; **to p. to packed houses** jouer *ou* se produire à guichets fermés

(**e**) *Mus* (*of instrument, musician, band*) jouer; **they always have music playing full blast** ils mettent toujours leur musique plein pot; **I could hear the radio playing in the next room** j'entendais (le son de) la radio dans la pièce à côté

2 *vt* (**a**) *Sp etc* (*game of tennis etc*) faire, jouer; (*match*) jouer, disputer; (*include on one's team*) inclure dans son équipe; **to p. football/tennis** jouer au football/tennis; **to p. cards/chess** jouer aux cartes/échecs; **to p. sb at chess** faire une partie d'échecs avec qn; **Real Madrid played Dynamo Kiev** le Real de Madrid a affronté *ou* a joué contre le Dynamo de Kiev; *Fb etc* **to p. left back** jouer arrière gauche; **the team was playing two substitutes** l'équipe jouait avec deux remplaçant(e)s; *Sp* **to p. a shot/ball** jouer un coup/une balle; *Cards* **to p. a card** jouer une carte; **to p. clubs/spades** jouer trèfle/pique; *Chess etc* **to p. a move** jouer; *F* **to p. a hunch** jouer *ou* agir sur une intuition; **I'll p. you for the drinks** je vous joue les consommations

(**b**) *Th, Cin* (*part*) jouer; (*tragedy*) jouer, représenter; **to p. Macbeth** jouer *ou* tenir le rôle de Macbeth; *Fig* **to p. an important part** jouer un rôle important; *F* **to p. the fool** faire l'idiot(e) *ou* l'imbécile; *F* **don't p. the innocent with me!** ne fais pas l'innocent avec moi!

(**c**) *Mus* **to p. the piano/the flute** jouer du piano/de la flûte; **to p. a piece** jouer un morceau; **to p. a record-player** faire marcher un tourne-disques; **to p. a record/a tape** passer *ou* mettre un disque/une cassette; **can you p. some Pink Floyd?** tu peux mettre quelque chose des Pink Floyd?; **the neighbours were playing loud music** les voisins avaient mis la musique à fond

(**d**) **to p. a joke** *or* **a trick on sb** jouer un tour à qn

(**e**) *esp Lit* **to p. sb false** trahir qn

(**f**) (*direct*) diriger (**upon, over** sur); **to p. the hose on the fire** diriger la lance sur le feu

▶ **play about** *or* **around** *vi* (**a**) (*play*) jouer, s'amuser; **stop playing around with that gun!** arrête de jouer avec ce revolver!

(**b**) (*not be serious*) s'amuser; **it's time he stopped playing about and settled down** il est temps qu'il arrête de s'amuser et qu'il se fixe

(**c**) (*consider possibilities*) **to p. around with an idea** retourner une idée dans sa tête; **to play around with a tune** expérimenter avec un air; **they played around with the words to find a good slogan** ils jonglaient avec les mots pour trouver un bon slogan; **they played around with various names** ils ont considéré plusieurs noms

(**d**) (*sexually*) avoir des aventures; **to p. around with sb** avoir une aventure avec qn; **you're just playing around (with me)** tu joues avec moi

▶ **play along 1** *vi* (**a**) (*accompany*) **I played the fiddle while he played along on the accordeon** je jouais du violon tandis qu'il m'accompagnait à l'accordéon (**b**) (*cooperate*) coopérer (**with** avec) **2** *vtas* (*manipulate*) (*person*) manipuler

▶ **play at** *vipo* (**a**) **to p. at soldiers** jouer aux soldats; **to p. at keeping shop** jouer au marchand/à la marchande (**b**) (*dabble in*) **to p. at doing sth** faire qch en amateur; **they played at being revolutionaries** ils jouaient aux petits révolutionnaires; **they're just playing at being married** ils voient le mariage comme un jeu; *F* **what do you think you're playing at?** à quoi tu joues?

▶ **play back** *vtsep* (*tape*) écouter, passer

▶ **play down** *vtsep* (*importance of sth*) minimiser; (*problem*) dédramatiser; **the government is trying to p. down its role** le gouvernement tente de minimiser l'importance de son rôle

▶ **play in** *vtsep* (**a**) *Sp* **to p. oneself in** (*become accustomed*) se faire au jeu (**b**) (*with music*) accueillir en musique

▶ **play into** *vipo* **to p. into sb's hands** faire le jeu de qn

▶ **play off 1** *vtsep* (*oppose*) **to p. sb off against sb** opposer qn à qn; **they played their enemies off against each other** ils ont dressé leurs ennemis les uns contre les autres **2** *vi Sp* (*attempt to break tie*) faire *ou* jouer la belle

▶ **play on 1** *vi* (*continue to play*) continuer à jouer **2** *vipo* (**a**) (*exploit*) **to p. on sb's feelings** jouer sur les sentiments de qn (**b**) (*pun on*) **to p. on words** jouer sur les mots; **the title plays on a line from Shakespeare** le titre est un jeu de mots sur une phrase de Shakespeare

▶ **play out** *vtsep* (**a**) (*act*) **the events being played out on the world's stage** les événements qui se déroulent dans le monde (**b**) *F* (*usu passive*) (*exhaust*) **to be played out** (*of person, horse etc*) être vanné *ou* éreinté; (*of idea etc*) être vieux jeu *ou* démodé; (*of story*) avoir perdu tout intérêt (**c**) (*with music*) **they were played out to the strains of ...** leur départ a été accompagné par l'air de ...

▶ **play up 1** *vi* (**a**) *Br F* (*of car, child, horse etc*) faire des siennes; **my back/war wound is playing up again** mon dos/ma blessure de guerre recommence à me faire souffrir (**b**) *F* (*flatter*) **to p. up to sb** flatter qn **2** *vtas Br F* (*cause difficulties to*) énerver, *F* taper sur le système de; **my rheumatism is playing me up** mes rhumatismes me font souffrir **3** *vtsep* (*emphasize*) faire ressortir; (*incident, scandal*) exploiter

▶ **play upon** *vipo* = **play on 2**

▶ **play with** *vipo* (**a**) (*to amuse oneself with*) **to p. with a doll/dolls** jouer *ou* s'amuser avec une poupée/jouer à la poupée; **to p. with one's glasses** jouer (distraitement) avec ses lunettes; **to be playing with fire** jouer avec le feu; **to p. with sb's affections** jouer avec l'affection de qn; **to p. with words** jouer sur les mots (**b**) (*to have at one's disposal*) **we've got plenty of time to p. with** nous avons beaucoup de temps à nous; **we don't have a lot of money to p. with** nous n'avons pas beaucoup d'argent à notre disposition (**c**) *F* **to p. with oneself** (*masturbate*) se toucher

playable ['pleɪəb(ə)l] *adj* (*football pitch etc*) praticable; (*shot, ball, music*) jouable

play-act *vi* (*pretend*) jouer la comédie; (*clown around*) faire le clown

play-acting *n* **it's just p.** (*pretence*) c'est de la comédie; (*clowning around*) c'est pour rire

play area *n* aire *f* de jeux

playback ['pleɪbæk] *n* réécoute *f*; *TV etc* présonorisation *f*, play-back *m*, présono *f*

playbill ['pleɪbɪl] *n Th* (*poster*) affiche *f* (de théâtre); *Am* (*programme*) programme *m*

playboy ['pleɪbɔɪ] *n* playboy *m*

player ['pleɪər] *n* (**a**) *Sp* joueur, -euse; (*team member*) équipier, -ière, joueur, -euse; **card/billiards p.** joueur, -euse de cartes/billard (**b**) *Mus* musicien, -ienne; (*of instrument*) joueur, -euse; **a good guitar p.** un(e) bon(ne) guitariste; **the band's piano p.** le pianiste du groupe; **p. piano** piano *m* mécanique (**c**) (*machine*) **record p.** tourne-disque *m, pl* tourne-disques; **cassette p.** lecteur *m* de cassettes, magnétophone *m* (à cassettes) (**d**) *Th* acteur, -trice; (*of part*) interprète *mf* (**e**) *Com, Mktg* acteur *m*

playfellow ['pleɪfeləʊ] *n Old-fashioned* = **playmate**

playful ['pleɪfʊl] *adj* (*person, cat*) espiègle; (*mood*) enjoué, badin; (*remark*) espiègle, enjoué; **she gave him a p. push** elle l'a poussé pour jouer *ou* par espièglerie

playfully ['pleɪfʊlɪ] *adv* (*to say, remark*) en badinant, d'un ton enjoué; (*to smile*) d'un air enjoué; (*to push sb etc*) pour jouer, par espièglerie

playfulness ['pleɪfʊlnɪs] *n* (*of remark*) caractère *m* badin; (*of person, cat*) espièglerie *f*

playgoer ['pleɪgəʊər] *n* habitué, -ée du théâtre

playground ['pleɪgraʊnd] *n Sch* cour *f* (de récréation); (*outside of school*) parc *m* de jeu; *Fig* **St Tropez is the p. of the rich** St Tropez est le lieu de villégiature des riches

playgroup ['pleɪgruːp] *n* ≈ (école *f*) maternelle *f*

playhouse ['pleɪhaʊs] *n* (**a**) *Th* théâtre *m* (**b**) (*for children*) maison *f*

playing ['pleɪɪŋ] *n* (**a**) (*by children etc*) jeu *m*; **I'm not in the mood for p.** je ne suis pas d'humeur à jouer (**b**) *Sp* jeu *m*; **the team's p.** le jeu de l'équipe; **p. is more important than winning** il est plus important de jouer que de gagner (**c**) *Mus* jeu *m*; **his p. is superb** son jeu est magnifique; **her p. of the sonata was superb** elle a joué la sonate de façon magnifique

playing card *n* carte *f* à jouer

playing field *n* terrain *m* de jeux *ou* de sports

playlist ['pleɪlɪst] *n TV etc* liste *f* de disques à programmer

playmate ['pleɪmeɪt] *n* camarade *mf* (de jeu); (*friend*) copain *m*, copine *f*

play-off *n Sp* belle *f*

playout music ['pleɪaʊt] *n* musique *f* (de générique) de fin

playpen ['pleɪpen] *n* parc *m* (pour bébé)

playroom ['pleɪruːm] *n* salle *f* de jeux

playschool ['pleɪskuːl] *n* ≈ (école *f*) maternelle *f*

plaything ['pleɪθɪŋ] *n* jouet *m*; *F* **she's just his p.** il se sert d'elle comme d'un jouet

playtime [ˈpleɪtaɪm] *n Sch* récréation *f*, *F* récré *f*
playwright [ˈpleɪraɪt] *n* auteur *m* dramatique, dramaturge *m*
plaza [ˈplɑːzə] *n US* **(a)** *(square)* place *f* **(b)** *(shopping center)* centre *m* commercial **(c)** *Aut (service area)* aire *f* de service
plc, PLC [piːelˈsiː] *n* **(a)** *Br Com (abbr* **public limited company***)* ≈ SARL *f*; **Smith p.** Smith SARL **(b)** *Mktg (abbr* **product life-cycle***)* cycle *m* de vie du produit
plea [pliː] *n* **(a)** *(appeal)* appel *m*; **p. for mercy** appel à la clémence; **to make a p. for tolerance** en appeler à *ou* implorer la tolérance **(b)** *(excuse)* excuse *f*, prétexte *m* **(for doing sth** pour faire qch); **on the p. that he had a prior engagement** sous prétexte d'un autre engagement; **they did not accept his p. that he had simply forgotten** il a allégué qu'il avait simplement oublié mais ils n'ont pas accepté cette excuse **(c)** *Jur* défense *f*; **special p.** exception *f* péremptoire; **to enter a p. of guilty/not guilty** plaider coupable/non coupable; **to put forward a p. of insanity** *(of counsel)* plaider la folie
plea bargaining *n Am* = accord *m* entre le juge et l'accusé qui permet à l'accusé de voir ses charges réduites en échange de sa coopération
plead [pliːd] *(pt, pp* **pleaded,** *occ Am* **pled** [pled]) **1** *vi* **(a) to p. with sb for sb/sth** intervenir *ou* intercéder *ou* plaider auprès de qn pour qn/qch; **to p. for mercy** implorer la clémence, en appeler à la clémence; **to p. for justice** demander que justice soit faite; **they were pleading with him to stop** ils le suppliaient de s'arrêter

(b) *Jur* plaider **(for** pour; **against** contre); **to p. guilty/not guilty** plaider coupable/non coupable; **how do you p.?** plaidez-vous coupable ou non coupable?

2 *vt* **(a)** *Jur, Fig (case)* plaider; *Fig* **to p. sb's cause with sb** intercéder pour qn auprès de qn, plaider la cause de qn auprès de qn; **to p. insanity** *(of counsel)* plaider la folie

(b) *(claim) (ignorance etc)* prétexter; *(excuse)* invoquer, alléguer
pleading [ˈpliːdɪŋ] **1** *adj* suppliant, implorant **2** *n* **(a)** prières *fpl* **(for sb** en faveur de qn) **(b)** *Jur (speech)* plaidoyer *m*; *(action)* plaidoirie *f*; *(art)* l'art *m* de plaider
pleadingly [ˈpliːdɪŋlɪ] *adv (to say)* d'un ton suppliant *ou* implorant; *(to look)* d'un regard suppliant *ou* implorant
pleasant [ˈplezənt] *adj* agréable; *(person)* agréable, affable, aimable; **p. breeze** brise *f* douce *ou* agréable; **it's a p. day** il fait bon aujourd'hui; **to have a p. day** *(relaxing etc)* passer agréablement la journée; **I had a p. day at the office** tout s'est bien passé au bureau; **to make oneself p.** *or* **to be p. (to sb)** se rendre agréable (auprès de qn); **he was very p.** il s'est montré très affable *ou* très gentil; **the account of the trial does not make p. reading** le récit du procès n'est pas une lecture des plus agréables; **p. dreams!** fais de beaux rêves!
pleasantly [ˈplezəntlɪ] *adv* agréablement, d'une manière agréable; **she smiled p. at him** elle lui sourit d'un air affable; **p. situated** agréablement situé, d'une situation agréable; **to be p. surprised** être agréablement surpris
pleasantness [ˈplezəntnɪs] *n (of place etc)* agrément *m*, charme *m*; *(of person, manner etc)* affabilité *f*
pleasantry [ˈplezəntrɪ] *n* **(a)** *(joke)* plaisanterie *f* **(b) pleasantries** *(polite remarks)* civilités *fpl*
please¹ [pliːz] **1** *int* s'il vous plaît/s'il te plaît; **come in, p.** entrez, s'il vous plaît, entrez, je vous prie; **p. don't cry** ne pleurez pas, je vous en supplie; **p., daddy, p.** s'il te plaît, papa; **p. tell me ...** voudriez-vous bien me dire ...; **may I? – p. do!** vous permettez? – je vous en prie!; **p. sit down** *or* **take a seat** veuillez vous asseoir; **p. don't interrupt!** veuillez bien ne pas m'/nous interrompre; **p. do not walk on the grass** *(on sign)* prière de ne pas marcher sur le gazon; **would you like some cake/to come with me? – yes, p.** est-ce que vous voulez un peu de gâteau/venir avec moi? – oh, oui, avec plaisir; **p. let me win the lottery!** Mon Dieu, j'aimerais tant gagner au loto!; *Sch* **p., sir!** pardon, monsieur!; **(oh) p.!** *(in indignation, disgust etc)* c'est pas vrai!

2 *vt (give pleasure to)* plaire à, faire plaisir à; *(make content)* contenter, satisfaire; **the news pleased her immensely** cette nouvelle lui a fait immensément plaisir; **to try to p. sb** chercher à faire plaisir à qn; **you can't p. everybody** on ne peut plaire à tout le monde; *prov* **you can't p. all of the people all of the time** on ne peut pas faire plaisir à tout le monde; **he's hard to p.** il est difficile (à contenter); **she's easy to p., she's easily pleased** elle n'est pas difficile; **music that pleases the ear** musique qui flatte l'oreille; **p. yourself!** faites comme il vous plaira *ou* comme vous voudrez; *Fml* **His Majesty has been graciously pleased to ...** il a plu à sa gracieuse Majesté de ...

3 *vi* **(a)** *(like)* **to do as one pleases** agir à sa guise *ou* à son gré; **do as you p.** faites comme vous voudrez; **he will only do as he pleases** il n'en fait jamais qu'à sa tête; **just as you p.** comme vous voudrez; **if you p.** s'il vous/te plaît; **and then, if you p., he blamed me for it!** et le comble c'est qu'il a dit que c'était de ma faute!

(b) *(give pleasure)* faire plaisir; **he tries hard to p.** il fait tout pour me/te/*etc* faire plaisir

4 *v impers Arch, Lit* **may it p. your Majesty** plaise *ou* n'en déplaise à votre Majesté; **p. God!** plaise à Dieu!, Dieu le veuille!
please² *n* **without so much as a p. or thank you** sans même dire merci
pleased [pliːzd] *adj (satisfied)* satisfait, content; *(happy)* heureux; *(smile)* de satisfaction; **to be p. with sth/sb** être content de qch/qn; **to be p. to do sth** faire qch avec plaisir; **he's very p. with himself** il est très content *ou* fort satisfait de lui-même *ou Pej* de sa petite personne; **I'm very p. (that) she's coming** cela me fait énormément plaisir qu'elle vienne, je suis ravi *ou* très content qu'elle vienne; **I'll be p. to come** je viendrai avec plaisir; **p. to meet you** enchanté de faire votre connaissance; **I'm so p. to see you** je suis très content *ou* cela me fait grand plaisir de vous voir; **she didn't exactly look p. to see me** elle n'avait pas vraiment l'air contente de me voir; **I'm p. to say that ...** je suis heureux de pouvoir vous dire que ...; *Fml* **I am p. to inform you that ...** j'ai le plaisir de vous aviser que ...; **to be p. for sb** être content pour qn; *F* **he's as p. as Punch** il est heureux comme un roi
pleasing [ˈpliːzɪŋ] *adj (news, result)* qui fait plaisir; *(meal, film, conversation etc)* agréable; *(person, manner)* agréable, plaisant
pleasingly [ˈpliːzɪŋlɪ] *adv* agréablement
pleasurable [ˈpleʒərəb(ə)l] *adj* agréable
pleasurably [ˈpleʒərəblɪ] *adv* agréablement
pleasure¹ [ˈpleʒər] *n* **(a)** *(contentment)* plaisir *m*; **to take** *or* **find p. in doing sth** éprouver du plaisir à faire qch, prendre *ou* avoir (du) plaisir à faire qch; **it gave me great p.** cela m'a fait énormément plaisir; **her books gave p. to many people** beaucoup de gens ont pris du plaisir à lire ses livres; *Fml* **I have p. in informing you that ...** j'ai le plaisir *ou* je suis heureux de vous apprendre que ...; **it gives me no p. to inform you that ...** j'ai la triste tâche de vous apprendre que ...; **it's a real p. to see you looking so cheerful** cela me fait vraiment plaisir de vous voir si gai; **it is a p. to listen to him** on a plaisir à l'écouter; **thank you very much – (it was) a p.** merci beaucoup – de rien; **the p. was all mine** tout le plaisir était pour moi; **I haven't the p. of knowing her** *or* **of her acquaintance** je n'ai pas le plaisir de la connaître; **with p.** avec plaisir, volontiers; **with the greatest (of) p.** avec le plus grand plaisir; *Fml* **Mr Stevens requests the p. of the company of Miss Miller at ...** *(invitation)* M. Stevens prie Mlle Miller de lui faire le plaisir d'assister à ...

(b) *(enjoyment)* plaisir(s) *m(pl)*; **life given up to p., life of p.** vie adonnée au plaisir; **to take one's p.** s'amuser, se divertir; **to travel for p.** voyager pour son plaisir; **p. cruising** navigation *f* de plaisance; **p. trip** partie *f* de plaisir

(c) *Old-fashioned (will)* volonté *f*, bon plaisir *m*; **at sb's p.** au gré de qn, au bon plaisir de qn; **during the King's p.** pendant le bon plaisir du roi
pleasure² *Arch* **1** *vt* faire plaisir à **2** *vi* se plaire, prendre plaisir **(in sth** à qch; **in doing sth** à faire qch)
pleasure boat *n* bateau *m* de plaisance
pleasure principle *n Psy* (principe *m* de la) recherche *f* du plaisir
pleasure seeker *n* jouisseur, -euse
pleasure seeking [ˈsiːkɪŋ] *n* recherche *f* des plaisirs
pleat¹ [pliːt] *n Sewing etc* pli *m*
pleat² *vt (skirt etc)* plisser, faire des plis à
pleated [ˈpliːtɪd] *adj (skirt etc)* plissé
pleating [ˈpliːtɪŋ] *n (no pl) (pleats)* plis *mpl*, plissé(s) *m(pl)*
pleb [pleb] *n F* prolo *mf*
plebby [ˈplebɪ] *adj F* prolo
plebeian [pləˈbiːən] *adj, n* plébéien, -ienne
plebiscite [ˈplebɪsɪt] *n* plébiscite *m*; **to hold a p.** organiser un plébiscite; **to vote for sb/sth by p.** plébisciter qn/qch
plectrum [ˈplektrəm] *n Mus (for guitar etc)* médiator *m*
pledge¹ [pledʒ] *n* **(a)** *(oath)* promesse *f*, vœu *m*; **a p. of loyalty/support** une promesse *ou* un serment de loyauté/soutien; **the Opposition has given a p. to repeal this law** l'opposition a fait le serment d'abroger cette loi; *Old-fashioned* **to take** *or* **sign the p.** *(of abstainer)* promettre de s'abstenir d'alcool **(b)** *(object of value)* gage *m*, nantissement *m*; **to hold in p.** (dé)tenir en gage *ou* en nantissement; **to redeem a p.** retirer un gage; *Fin* **p. over property** gage *m* immobilier; **p. holder** détenteur, -trice de gage(s), (créancier *m*) gagiste *m* **(c)** *(sign)* **p. of good faith** garantie *f* de bonne foi

pledge² *vt* **(a)** (*promise*) (*one's word etc*) engager; **to p. oneself** *or* **one's word to do sth** s'engager à faire qch; **to be pledged to do sth** avoir pris l'engagement de faire qch; **to p. one's loyalty/support** accorder sa loyauté/son soutien; **to p. one's honour** donner sa parole d'honneur, s'engager sur l'honneur (**to do sth** à faire qch); **to p. one's allegiance to the king** vouer obéissance au roi; **to p. money** (*in radio, television appeal*) promettre un don **(b)** (*give as pledge or security*) donner *ou* mettre en gage, déposer en gage *ou* en nantissement, engager

pledgee [ple'dʒiː] *n Fin* gagiste *mf*

pledgor ['pledʒər] *n Fin* gageur *m*

pleiad, *pl* **-ads, -ades** ['plaɪəd, -ædz, -ədiːz] *n* **(a)** *Liter* pléiade *f* **(b)** *Myth, Astron* **the Pleiads, the Pleiades** les Pléiades *fpl*

plenary ['pliːnərɪ] *adj* complet, -ète, entier; **p. power** (*of dictator*) pouvoir *m* absolu; (*of president*) pleins pouvoirs; **p. assembly** assemblée *f* plénière; **p. session** (*at conference*) séance *f* plénière

plenipotentiary [plenɪpə'tenʃ(ə)rɪ] *adj, n* plénipotentiaire *m*

plenitude ['plenɪtjuːd] *n* plénitude *f*

plentiful ['plentɪfʊl] *adj* abondant, copieux; **to be p.** abonder

plentifully ['plentɪfʊlɪ] *adv* abondamment, copieusement

plenty ['plentɪ] **1** *n* abondance *f*; **p. of ...** beaucoup de ..., *F* plein de ...; **you've got p. of time** vous avez largement le temps; **to arrive in p. of time** arriver de bonne heure; **to have p. to live on** avoir largement de quoi vivre; **that's p.** (*when being served food, drink*) ça suffit; *F* **there's p. more where that came from!** (*food etc*) quand il y en a plus, il y en a encore; **take as much as you like, there's p. more** prenez-en autant que vous voulez, il en reste beaucoup; **land of p.** pays *m* de cocagne; **year of p.** année *f* d'abondance **2** *adv F* **it's p. big enough** c'est bien assez gros **3** *adj Arch, US* abondant; **money is p.** l'argent ne manque pas *ou* abonde

pleonasm ['pliːənæz(ə)m] *n* pléonasme *m*

pleonastic [pliːə'næstɪk] *adj* pléonastique, redondant; **to be p.** (*of word*) être un pléonasme

plethora ['pleθərə] *n* pléthore *f*, surabondance *f*

pleural ['plʊər(ə)l] *adj Med* pleural; **p. membrane** plèvre *f*

pleurisy ['plʊərɪsɪ] *n Med* pleurésie *f*; **to have p.** avoir *ou* faire une pleurésie

plexus ['pleksəs] *n* **(a)** *Anat* plexus *m* **(b)** *Fig* (*maze*) enchevêtrement *m*

pliability [plaɪə'bɪlɪtɪ] *n* (*of stem etc*) flexibilité *f*, souplesse *f*; (*of character*) docilité *f*, souplesse

pliable ['plaɪəb(ə)l] *adj* pliable, pliant, flexible; (*leather*) souple; *Fig* (*character etc*) docile, malléable, souple

pliers ['plaɪəz] *npl* [①A10,e] (*tool*) pince(s) *f(pl)*, tenaille(s) *f(pl)*; **a pair of p.** des tenailles

plight¹ [plaɪt] *n* condition *f ou* état *m* critique; **to be in a sorry** *or* **sad p.** (*of person, country, economy*) être dans une mauvaise passe; **she saw my p. and helped me get up** elle a vu que ça n'allait pas et m'a aidé à me relever; **what a p. you're in!** comme vous voilà fait!

plight² *vt* **to p. one's troth to sb** *Arch* donner sa foi à qn; (*promise to marry*) se fiancer à qn

Plimsoll ['plɪmsəl] *n Naut* **P. line** *or* **mark** ligne *f* de Plimsoll

plimsolls ['plɪmsəlz] *npl Br* (chaussures *fpl* de) tennis *mpl*

plinth [plɪnθ] *n Archit* plinthe *f*; (*of statue, column*) socle *m*

Pliny ['plɪnɪ] *n* **P. the Elder/the Younger** Pline *m* l'Ancien/le Jeune

plip key [plɪp] *n Aut* plip *m*

PLO [piːel'əʊ] *n* (*abbr* **Palestine Liberation Organization**) OLP *f*; **P. representatives** représentants de l'OLP

plod¹ [plɒd] *n* **(a)** (*walking*) démarche *f* lourde *ou* lente; **it's a long p.** il faut marcher longtemps **(b)** (*heavy work*) travail *m* pénible

plod² (**-dd-**) **1** *vi* **(a)** (*walk*) marcher lourdement *ou* péniblement; **to p. on** continuer sa marche pénible; **he plodded home alone** (*dejected*) seul et malheureux, il est rentré chez lui **(b)** (*work*) = **plod away 2** *vt* **to p. one's way** avancer *ou* marcher d'un pas lent

plod³ *n Sl* (*policeman*) flic *m*, poulet *m*

▶ **plod along** *vi* **(a)** (*walk slowly*) avancer *ou* marcher d'un pas lent **(b)** (*work slowly*) travailler laborieusement (**with** à)

▶ **plod away** *vi* (*work slowly*) travailler laborieusement (**at** à), peiner, trimer (**at** sur)

▶ **plod on** *vi* = **plod along**

▶ **plod through** *vipo* (*work slowly at*) travailler laborieusement à; **I'm plodding through a rather boring book just now** j'avance péniblement dans un livre plutôt barbant en ce moment

plodder ['plɒdər] *n Pej* besogneux, -euse

plodding ['plɒdɪŋ] *adj* (*steps*) pesant, lourd

plonk¹ [plɒŋk] *n* (*sound*) bruit *m* sourd

plonk² *vt* = **plonk down**

plonk³ *n Br F* (*wine*) pinard *m*; (*poor quality wine*) piquette *f*

▶ **plonk away** *vi F* **to p. away on one's guitar** gratouiller sa guitare; **to p. away on the piano** pianoter

▶ **plonk down** *vtsep* poser lourdement; **just p. it down there** pose-le par là; **to p. oneself down in an armchair** se laisser tomber dans un fauteuil

▶ **plonk out** *vtsep F* **to p. out a tune on a guitar/piano** jouer maladroitement un air à la guitare/au piano

plonker ['plɒŋkər] *n Br Sl* **(a)** (*penis*) bite *f*, *Hum* zizi *m* **(b)** (*fool*) branleur *m*

plook [plʊk] *n Scot, North Eng F* (*pimple*) bouton *m*

plop¹ [plɒp] **1** *n* **(a)** (*splash*) flac *m*, plouf *m* **(b)** (*soft sound*) pouf *m* **2** *adv* **to go p.** (*of sth falling into water etc*) faire plouf; (*of sth landing softly*) faire pouf

plop² *vi* (**-pp-**) **(a)** (*splash*) faire flac *ou* plouf, tomber en faisant flac *ou* plouf **(b)** (*land softly*) tomber; **she plopped exhausted onto the bed** épuisée, elle s'est laissée tomber sur le lit

plosive ['pləʊsɪv] *Ling* **1** *adj* (*consonant*) explosif **2** *n* explosive *f*

plot¹ [plɒt] *n* **(a)** (*conspiracy*) complot *m*, conspiration *f*; **a p. on sb's life** un complot pour tuer qn; **to hatch a p.** tramer *ou* ourdir un complot **(b)** *Liter, Th, Cin* (*of play, novel etc*) intrigue *f*, action *f*; *Fig* **the p. thickens** l'affaire se corse **(c)** *Math etc* tracé *m*; (*graph*) graphe *m*, graphique *m*; *Av, Naut* (*of ship's or plane's route*) tracé, graphe; (*on radar*) pointé *m* **(d)** (*land*) (parcelle *f ou* lot *m* de) terrain *m*; (*small*) lopin *m* de terre; **building p.** terrain à bâtir; **(vegetable) p.** (*in garden*) potager *m*

plot² (**-tt-**) **1** *vt* **(a)** (*plan*) (*person's downfall*) machiner, combiner; **to p. sb's murder** comploter de tuer qn, combiner le meurtre de qn

(b) *Liter, Cin etc* **a well plotted novel/film** un roman/film qui a une bonne intrigue

(c) *Math, Phys* (*curve, diagram, graph*) tracer; (*in surveying etc*) (*area of land*) dresser *ou* lever le plan de, faire le levé de; (*geometric figure*) tracer, rapporter; (*point on map*) marquer, tracer, repérer; (*on radar*) marquer, relever; *Comptr* tracer; *Fig* (*progress, development*) suivre; **to p. a course** (*for plane, ship*) relever *ou* tracer une route; *Av, Naut* **to p. the position** faire le point

2 *vi* (*conspire*) comploter, conspirer (**against sb** contre qn)

plotter ['plɒtər] *n* **(a)** (*conspirator*) conspirateur, -trice, comploteur *m* **(b)** (*on radar*) marqueur, -euse, plotteur *m*; *Comptr* (*device*) traceur *m*

plotting ['plɒtɪŋ] *n* **(a)** (*conspiring*) complot(s) *m(pl)*, conspiration(s) *f(pl)* **(b)** *Comptr* **p. board** *or* **table** table *f* traçante, traceur *m* de courbes

plough¹, *US* **plow** [plaʊ] *n* **(a)** charrue *f*; **under the p.** (*of land*) cultivé; *Fig* **to put one's hand to the p.** mettre la main à la pâte **(b)** *Astron* **the P.** la Grande Ourse

plough², *US* **plow 1** *vt* **(a)** (*field*) labourer; (*furrow*) tracer, creuser; (*of ship*) (*waves*) fendre, sillonner; **to p. the soil** labourer la terre, retourner la terre (à la charrue); **ploughed land** terres *fpl* labourées **(b)** *Old-fashioned Br Sch F* **to p. an exam** se planter à un examen; **to be** *or* **get ploughed in an exam** être recalé *ou* collé à un examen **2** *vi Agr* labourer la terre

▶ **plough back,** *US* **plow back** *vtsep Com, Fin* réinvestir (**into** dans); **profits ploughed back into the business** bénéfices réinvestis dans l'affaire

▶ **plough in,** *US* **plow in** *vtsep* (*manure etc*) enterrer *ou* enfouir dans le sol en labourant; *Com, Fin etc* (*money etc*) investir

▶ **plough into,** *US* **plow into 1** *vipo* **(a)** (*of vehicle*) rentrer dans, foncer dans **(b)** (*attack*) (*physically*) se jeter sur; (*verbally*) s'en prendre à **2** *vtaspo* (*money etc*) investir dans

▶ **plough on,** *US* **plow on** *vi* (*continue laboriously*) **to p. on with one's work/a book** poursuivre laborieusement son travail/sa lecture; **let's p. on another fifteen minutes** encore un petit effort d'un quart d'heure; **as negotiations p. on** tandis que les négociations se poursuivent laborieusement

▶ **plough through,** *US* **plow through 1** *vipo* (*move laboriously*) **to p. through the snow** avancer péniblement dans la neige; *Fig* **to p. through a book** lire laborieusement un livre; **to p. through some work** faire un travail laborieusement; **they were ploughing through their work** ils avançaient laborieusement dans leur travail; **I've got all this to p. through** j'ai tout ça à me taper

2 *vtaspo* **to p. one's way through the snow** avancer péniblement dans la neige; **to p. one's way through a book** lire un livre à grand peine; **I'm ploughing my way through this** (*book*) je suis en train de lire ce pavé; **he was ploughing his way through a huge plate of spaghetti** il s'efforçait de finir une énorme assiette de spaghettis

▶ **plough up,** *US* **plow up** *vtsep* **(a)** (*turn over, Fig churn up*) (*field etc*) labourer **(b)** (*remove*) (*weeds etc*) déraciner *ou* arracher à la charrue

ploughing, *US* **plowing** [ˈplaʊɪŋ] *n* labourage *m*, labour *m*

ploughing back, *US* **plowing back** *n* **p. of profits** réinvestissement *m* des bénéfices

ploughland, *US* **plowland** [ˈplaʊlænd] *n* (*cultivated land*) terres *fpl* cultivées; (*ploughed land*) terres labourées; (*arable land*) terre arable *ou* labourable

ploughman, *US* **plowman,** *pl* **-men** [ˈplaʊmən] *n* laboureur *m*; *Br* **p.'s lunch** = snack *m* à base de pain, de fromage et de pickles

ploughshare, *US* **plowshare** [ˈplaʊʃeər] *n* soc *m* de charrue

plover [ˈplʌvər] *n* (*bird*) pluvier *m*; **golden p.** pluvier doré; *Culin* **p.'s eggs** œufs *mpl* de vanneau

plow, plowland *etc US* = **plough, ploughland** *etc*

ploy [plɔɪ] *n* stratagème *m*, *F* truc *m*

pluck¹ [plʌk] *n* (*courage*) cran *m*, courage *m*; **she's got plenty of p.** elle a du cran *ou* du courage, elle a du cœur au ventre

pluck² *n* (*pull*) (*at guitar string etc*) pincement *m*

pluck³ **1** *vt* **(a)** (*pull out*) (*hair, feathers etc*) arracher; (*flower*) cueillir; *Fig* **they were plucked from danger by a helicopter** un hélicoptère les a arrachés au danger; *Fig* **to p. sb from obscurity** arracher qn à l'obscurité; *Fig* **these figures have been plucked from the air** ces chiffres ne reposent sur rien de concret **(b)** (*pull*) **to p. sb's sleeve** tirer qn par la manche; *Mus* **to p. a guitar** pincer les cordes d'une guitare **(c)** (*remove feathers from*) (*poultry*) plumer; **to p. one's eyebrows** s'épiler les sourcils **2** *vi* **to p. at sb's sleeve** tirer qn par la manche

▶ **pluck up** *vtsep* **to p. up (one's) courage to do sth** rassembler son courage pour faire qch

pluckily [ˈplʌkɪlɪ] *adv* courageusement, avec cran *ou* courage

pluckiness [ˈplʌkɪnɪs] *n* cran *m*, courage *m*

plucky [ˈplʌkɪ] *adj* courageux; **to be p.** être courageux, avoir du courage *ou* du cran

plug¹ [plʌg] *n* **(a)** (*for sink, bath, tank etc*) bonde *f*; (*stopper*) bouchon *m*, tampon *m*; (*dentistry*), *Surg* tampon (*d'ouate, de coton*); *Geol* culot *m* volcanique; **to pull the p. out** (*of sink etc*) enlever la bonde

(b) *El* fiche *f*, prise *f* de courant, prise mâle; *Tech* (*for nail, screw in wall*) fiche *f*; **(spark) p.** bougie *f*; *El* **two-/three-pin p.** fiche à deux/trois broches; **to pull the p. out** (*disconnect electrical appliance*) débrancher; *Fig F* **to pull the p. on sb** couper tous ses moyens à qn; **to pull the p. on a project** enrayer un projet; *Comptr* **p. compatible** compatible au niveau du matériel; **p. socket** prise de courant, prise femelle; *Aut* **p. spanner** clé *f* à bougies

(c) *US* **(fire) p.** bouche *f* d'incendie

(d) (*of toilet*) chasse *f* d'eau; **to pull the p.** tirer la chasse

(e) **p. of tobacco** chique *f* de tabac

(f) *Com F* (*publicity*) pub *f*; **the DJ gave the album a p.** l'animateur a fait de la pub pour l'album

plug² **(-gg-)** *vt* **(a)** (*block*) (*opening, pipe*) boucher, obturer; (*wound*) tamponner; (*of dentist*) (*cavity*) obturer; **to p. a leak** arrêter une fuite **(b)** *Com F* (*promote*) (*product*) faire du battage *ou* de la pub pour **(c)** *esp Am Sl* (*shoot*) (*person*) fusiller, flinguer

▶ **plug away** *vi F* (*persevere*) persévérer (**at sth** dans qch), s'acharner (**at sth** sur qch)

▶ **plug in** *El* **1** *vtsep* (*lamp etc*) brancher; (*printer to computer etc*) connecter **2** *vi* (*insert plug*) brancher

▶ **plug into** **1** *vtaspo El* (*connect*) **to p. sth into sth** brancher qch sur qch **2** *vipo El* (*connect*) **the TV plugs into that socket** la télé se branche sur cette prise; *Fig* **to p. into a computer network** avoir accès à un réseau informatique; **to p. into public opinion** se mettre à l'écoute de l'opinion publique

▶ **plug up** *vtsep* = **plug² (a)**

plughole [ˈplʌghəʊl] *n* (*in sink, bathtub*) bonde *f*, trou *m* d'écoulement; *F* **that's £300 down the p.!** voilà 300 livres par la fenêtre!; *F* **his company's going down the p.** sa société se casse la figure

plug-in-and-go *adj Comptr* prêt à brancher

plug-ugly *adj F* (*person*) affreux

plum [plʌm] **1** *n* **(a)** (*fruit*) prune *f*; **p. (tree)** prunier *m*; **p. brandy** (eau *f* de vie de) prune; **p. cake** cake *m*; **p. jam** confiture *f* de prunes; **p. pudding** pudding *m* de Noël **(b)** *F* (*job*) boulot *m* en or; (*part in play etc*) rôle *m* en or **2** *adj* (*colour*) prune *inv*

plumage [ˈpluːmɪdʒ] *n* plumage *m*

plumb¹ [plʌm] *n* (*perpendicular*) aplomb *m*; **out of p.** hors d'aplomb; **p. (bob)** (*of plumb line*) plomb *m*

plumb² *vt* **(a)** (*in surveying*) vérifier l'aplomb de; (*wall*) vérifier l'aplomb de, plomber **(b)** *Naut, Fig* sonder; *Fig* **to p. the depths** toucher le fond

plumb³ **1** *adj* droit, vertical, d'aplomb **2** *adv* perpendiculairement (**with sth** à qch), à la verticale, à l'aplomb (**with sth** de qch); *F* **p. in the centre** en plein milieu, au beau milieu; (*of target*) en plein dans le mille; *Am F* **p. crazy** complètement fou

▶ **plumb in** *vtsep* (*install*) (*washing machine etc*) raccorder

plumbago [plʌmˈbeɪgəʊ] *n* **(a)** *Bot* plumbago *m* **(b)** *Miner* plombagine *f*

plumber [ˈplʌmər] *n* plombier *m*; **p.'s mate** aide *m* plombier

plumbing [ˈplʌmɪŋ] *n* **(a)** (*action, job*) plomberie *f* **(b)** (*pipes*) plomberie *f*, tuyauterie *f*, tuyaux *mpl*; (*toilets, washbasins etc*) installations *fpl* sanitaires; *F Hum* **to inspect the p.** (*urinate*) aller faire pipi

plumb line *n* (*weighted string*) fil *m* à plomb; (*vertical line*) verticale *f*; *Naut* (ligne *f* de) sonde *f*

plume¹ [pluːm] *n* **(a)** *Arch, Lit* (*feather*) plume *f*; **a p. of smoke** une volute de fumée; **a p. of spray** un jet d'eau; *Fig Lit* **in borrowed plumes** paré des plumes du paon **(b)** (*ornament*) panache *m*, aigrette *f*; (*on helmet*) plumet *m*, panache

plume² *vt* **(a)** (*ornament*) orner *ou* garnir de plumes; **black-plumed** aux plumes noires; **plumed helmet** casque *m* empanaché **(b)** (*preen*) **to p. itself** (*of bird*) se lisser les plumes; **to p. oneself on sth** (*of person*) se glorifier de qch

plummet¹ [ˈplʌmɪt] *n* (*weight*) (*of plumb line, fishing line, sounding line*) plomb *m*

plummet² *vi* plonger, tomber à la verticale; (*of morale, popularity, standards*) chuter; (*of prices etc*) s'effondrer; (*of blood pressure etc*) tomber soudainement; **the aircraft plummeted to the ground** l'avion s'est écrasé au sol

plummy [ˈplʌmɪ] *adj Br F* **(a)** *usu Pej* (*voice*) de la haute, snobinard **(b)** *Old-fashioned* (*job*) agréable, bien payé

plump¹ [plʌmp] *adj* (*person*) grassouillet, dodu, boulot, bien en chair; (*baby, chicken, cheeks*) dodu; (*hands*) potelé

plump² *vt* **to p. oneself into an armchair** s'affaler dans un fauteuil

▶ **plump down** *vtsep* (*suitcase etc*) laisser tomber lourdement; **she plumped herself down on the sofa** elle s'est affalée sur le sofa

▶ **plump for** *vipo F* (*choose*) choisir

▶ **plump out** *vi* = **plump up 2**

▶ **plump up** **1** *vtsep* (*shake*) (*pillow*) secouer **2** *vi* (*become fat*) devenir dodu

plumpness [ˈplʌmpnɪs] *n* embonpoint *m*, rondeur *f*; **to be inclined to p.** avoir tendance à prendre de l'embonpoint; **the p. of the baby's arms** les bras potelés du bébé

plunder¹ [ˈplʌndər] *n* (*booty*) butin *m*; (*act*) pillage *m*

plunder² **1** *vt* (*country etc*) piller, mettre à sac; *Fig* (*bookshelves, fridge*) faire une descente dans **2** *vi* piller

plundering [ˈplʌndərɪŋ] **1** *adj* pillard **2** *n* pillage *m*

plunge¹ [plʌndʒ] *n* plongeon *m*; *Fig* baisse *f* radicale, chute *f* (**in** de); **to take a p.** faire un plongeon, plonger (**into** dans); *Fig* (*of profits etc*) s'effondrer; *F* **to take the p.** (*resolve to do sth*) prendre le taureau par les cornes; (*get married*) se marier

plunge² **1** *vt* (*into water*) plonger, immerger; **to p. a dagger into sb's back** plonger un poignard dans le dos de qn; **plunged in darkness** plongé dans l'obscurité; **to p. sb into despair** plonger qn dans le désespoir

2 *vi* (*of person*) (*into water*) plonger, se jeter (la tête la première); (*into forest etc*) s'enfoncer; (*into affair etc*) se jeter à corps perdu; (*into conversation*) se lancer; (*in gambling*) jouer sans compter *ou* gros jeu; (*of ship*) tanguer, piquer du nez; (*of profits*) s'effondrer; **the lorry plunged over the cliff** le camion plongea par-dessus la falaise; **the aircraft plunged to the ground** l'avion s'est écrasé au sol; **the aircraft was plunging to the ground** l'avion tombait en chute libre vers le sol; **she plunged to her death** elle fit une chute mortelle; **necklines have plunged this year** cette année les décolletés sont plus profonds; **to p. forward** s'élancer en avant; **he plunged on regardless** il a continué quand même

plunger [ˈplʌndʒər] *n* **(a)** (*device*) (*on pump, in coffee-maker, syringe*) piston *m*; *Aut* piston plongeur; (*in lock*) bonhomme *m* de verrouillage; (*of detonator*) manette *f*; **(rubber) p.** (*for clearing sink etc*) ventouse *f* **(b)** *F* (*gambler*) flambeur, -euse

plunging [ˈplʌndʒɪŋ] **1** *adj* (*prices*) en chute libre; **p. neckline** décolleté *m* plongeant **2** *n* (*of boat*) tangage *m*

plunk [plʌŋk] *vt* **(a)** (*banjo etc*) pincer les cordes de **(b)** (*drop heavily*) laisser tomber lourdement

▶ **plunk down** *vtsep* laisser tomber lourdement

pluperfect [ˈpluːpɜːfɪkt] [①**A49**,e; **B28-29**,5] *Gram* **1** *adj* plus-que-parfait; **p. subjunctive** plus-que-parfait *m* du subjonctif **2** *n* plus-que-parfait *m*; **in the p.** au plus-que-parfait

plural [ˈplʊər(ə)l] **1** *adj* **(a)** *Gram* pluriel **(b)** *Pol* **p. vote** vote *m* plural **2** *n* [①**A9-15**; **B7-8**,C] *Gram* pluriel *m*; **in the p.** au pluriel

pluralism ['plʊərəlɪz(ə)m] *n* **(a)** *Phil etc* pluralisme *m* **(b)** (*holding of several posts*) cumul *m* de(s) fonctions
plurality [plʊə'rælɪtɪ] *n* **(a)** pluralité *f* **(b)** (*of functions*) cumul *m* **(c)** *Am Pol* (*relative majority*) majorité *f* relative *ou* simple
plus [plʌs] **1** *prep* plus; **seven p. nine** sept plus neuf; **two floors p. an attic** deux étages plus un grenier; **remember this, p. what she told you** rappelle-toi de ça, en plus de ce qu'elle t'a dit
2 *adj* **on the p. side of the account** à l'actif du compte; **on the p. side, the bicycle is very light** la légèreté est l'un des avantages de cette bicyclette; **fifteen p.** (*quantity*) plus de cinquante; (*age*) au-dessus de quinze ans
3 *n* (*pl* **plusses** ['plʌsɪz]) *Math* (*symbol*) plus *m*; (*positive quantity*) quantité *f* positive; *Fig* (*advantage*) avantage *m*, atout *m*; **it's a p.** c'est un plus *ou* avantage *ou* atout; *Comptr* **p. key** touche *f* plus
plus fours *npl* culotte *f* (bouffante) de golf
plush[1] [plʌʃ] *n Tex* peluche *f*
plush[2] *adj* **(a)** *Tex* en peluche **(b)** *F* (*apartment etc*) somptueux, luxueux; (*restaurant, hotel*) de luxe
plushy ['plʌʃɪ] *adj F* = **plush**[2] **(b)**
plus sign *n Math* (*symbol*) signe *m* plus; (*in formula*) signe positif
Plutarch ['plu:tɑ:k] *n* Plutarque *m*
Pluto ['plu:təʊ] *n* **(a)** *Myth* Pluton *m* **(b)** *Astron* Pluton *f*
plutocracy [plu:'tɒkrəsɪ] *n* ploutocratie *f*
plutocrat ['plu:təkræt] *n often Pej* ploutocrate *mf*
plutocratic [plu:tə'krætɪk] *adj* ploutocratique
plutonium [plu:'təʊnɪəm] *n Ch* plutonium *m*
pluviometer [plu:vɪ'ɒmɪtər] *n* pluviomètre *m*
ply[1] [plaɪ] *n* **(a)** (*of plywood*) placage *m*, épaisseur *f*; (*of tyre*) pli *m*; **two-p. paper handkerchief** mouchoir *m* en papier double épaisseur **(b)** (*strand*) (*of wool, rope*) fil *m*, brin *m*; **three-p. wool** laine *f* trois fils; **what p. is it?** c'est de la laine à combien de fils? **(c)** *F* (*plywood*) contre-plaqué *m*; **three-p.** contre-plaqué à trois plis
ply[2] **1** *vt* **(a)** (*use*) (*tool*) manier vigoureusement; (*needle*) faire courir; (*trade*) exercer **(b)** (*supply*) **to p. sb with questions** presser qn de questions; **to p. sb with drink** ne pas arrêter de verser à boire à qn, verser force rasades à qn; **to p. sb with food** donner abondamment à manger à qn **(c) to p. an ocean** (*of ship*) faire la traversée; **to p. a route** (*of ship, bus etc*) assurer une liaison **2** *vi* (*of ship, bus etc*) faire le service *ou* la navette (**between ... and ...** entre ... et ...); **to p. for hire** (*of taxi etc*) prendre des clients
plywood ['plaɪwʊd] *n* contre-plaqué *m*
PM [pi:'em] *n Br, Can Pol* (*abbr* **Prime Minister**) Premier Ministre *m*
pm ['pi:em] *adv* [①**A75**,A,e; **B58**,A,e] (*abbr* **post meridiem**) **6 pm** 18h; **10 am or pm?** 10 heures du matin ou du soir?
PMS [pi:e'mes] *n Med* (*abbr* **premenstrual syndrome**) syndrome *m* prémenstruel
PMT [pi:em'ti:] *n Med* (*abbr* **premenstrual tension**) syndrome *m* prémenstruel
pneumatic [nju:'mætɪk] *adj* pneumatique; *F* (*bosom*) plantureux, généreux; **p. brakes** freins *mpl* pneumatiques; **p. drill** marteau-piqueur *m*, *pl* marteaux-piqueurs; *Br* **p. tyre** pneu(matique) *m*
pneumatically [nju:'mætɪklɪ] *adv* **p. operated** (*machine*) à air comprimé
pneumatics [nju:'mætɪks] *n* [①**A10**,c] *Phys* pneumatique *f*
pneumonia [nju:'məʊnɪə] *n Med* pneumonie *f*; **to have p.** avoir une pneumonie
PO [pi:'eʊ] *n* **(a)** (*abbr* **Post Office**) **PO Box** B.P. **(b)** (*abbr* **postal order**) mandat *m* postal **(c)** *Naut* (*abbr* **petty officer**) second maître *m*
po [pəʊ] *n Br Old-fashioned F* pot *m* de chambre, Jules *m*
poach[1] [pəʊtʃ] *vt Culin* (*eggs etc*) pocher; **poached egg** œuf *m* poché
poach[2] **1** *vt* (*steal*) (*game etc*) braconner; (*steal from*) (*woods etc*) braconner dans; *Fig* (*employee*) débaucher **2** *vi* braconner; *Fb etc* rester près des buts de l'équipe adverse; **to p. on sb's preserves** braconner sur la chasse réservée de qn; *Fig* empiéter sur le domaine de qn
poacher[1] ['pəʊtʃər] *n* (**egg**) **p.** pocheuse *f* (à œufs)
poacher[2] *n* (*thief*) braconnier *m*
poaching ['pəʊtʃɪŋ] *n* (*thieving*) braconnage *m*
pock [pɒk] *n Med* pustule *f* (*de la petite vérole*)
pocket[1] ['pɒkɪt] *n* **(a)** (*of jacket etc*) poche *f*; **waistcoat p.** gousset *m*; **to put one's hands in one's pockets** mettre les mains dans ses poches; **to go through sb's pockets** faire les poches à qn; *F* **to have sb in one's p.** avoir qn dans sa poche; *F* **to live in each other's** *or* **one another's pockets** ne pas se lâcher d'une semelle; **prices to suit every p.** des prix à la portée de tout le monde; *Fig F* **to line one's pockets** se remplir les poches; *Fig* **he's always got his hand in his p.** il a toujours la main sur le portefeuille, il est toujours à débourser; **to be in p.** y gagner; **to be out of p.** (*over a transaction*) y être de sa poche, ne pas rentrer dans ses fonds; **how much are you out of p.?** combien est-ce que vous avez dépensé?; **to pay for sth out of one's own p.** payer qch de sa poche; **p. modem** modem *m* de poche; **p. size** (*in bookbinding*) format *m* de poche
(b) (*bag*) (*for hops wool*) sac *m*; *Billiards* blouse *f*
(c) *Min* (*of ore, water, gas*) poche *f*; (*of firedamp*) nid *m*
(d) (*small area*) (*of resistance, rebellion etc*) poche *f*
pocket[2] *vt* (**-t-**) **(a)** (*put in pocket*) empocher, mettre dans sa poche; *Pej* (*steal*) *F* chiper **(b)** (*insult*) avaler, encaisser **(c)** (*one's feelings*) faire taire; **to p. one's pride** faire taire son amour-propre **(d)** *Billiards* (*ball*) blouser
pocket battleship *n Naut* cuirassé *m* de poche
pocket billiards *n* billard *m* américain; *Fig Sl* **to play p.** jouer avec ses cacahuètes
pocketbook ['pɒkɪtbʊk] *n Am* **(a)** (*handbag*) sac *m* à main **(b)** (*small book*) livre *m* de poche
pocket calculator *n* calculette *f*, calculatrice *f* de poche
pocket comb *n* peigne *m* de poche
pocket computer *n* ordinateur *m* de poche
pocket dictionary *n* dictionnaire *m* de poche
pocketful ['pɒkɪtfʊl] *n* pleine poche *f*; **pocketfuls of sweets** de pleines poches *ou* des poches pleines de bonbons
pocket handkerchief *n* mouchoir *m* de poche
pocketknife ['pɒkɪtnaɪf] *n* couteau *m* de poche, canif *m*
pocket money *n* argent *m* de poche
pocket notebook *n* carnet *m*
pockmark ['pɒkmɑ:k] *n* marque *f* de la petite vérole
pockmarked ['pɒkmɑ:kt] *adj* (*face*) grêlé; (*surface of the moon etc*) plein de trous
pod[1] [pɒd] *n* **(a)** (*of beans, peas etc*) cosse *f*, gousse *f* **(b)** (*of silkworm*) cocon *m* **(c)** *Av* (*of jet engine*) nacelle *f*; **engine p.** nacelle-moteur *f*, *pl* nacelles-moteur
pod[2] (**-dd-**) *vt* (*peas*) écosser
podgy ['pɒdʒɪ] *adj* (*person*) boulot, -otte; (*finger*) boudiné, rondelet; (*knees*) grassouillet; **to get p.** engraisser
podium, *pl* **-ia** ['pəʊdɪəm, -ɪə] *n* estrade *f*; (*for medallist*) podium *m*
poem ['pəʊəm] *n* poème *m*, poésie *f*
poet ['pəʊɪt] *n* poète *m*; *Br* **p. laureate** poète lauréat
poetaster [pəʊɪ'tæstər] *n Pej* mauvais poète *m*, rimailleur *m*
poetess ['pəʊɪtɪs] *n Old-fashioned* femme *f* poète, poétesse *f*
poetic(al) [pəʊ'etɪk, -ɪk(ə)l] *adj* poétique; **poetic justice** justice *f* divine; **poetic licence** licence *f* poétique
poetically [pəʊ'etɪklɪ] *adv* poétiquement; **p. gifted** doué pour la poésie
poetics [pəʊ'etɪks] *n* [①**A10**,c] poétique *f*
poetry ['pəʊɪtrɪ] *n* poésie *f*; **to write p.** écrire des poèmes; **the art of p.** l'art *m* poétique; **it was p. in motion** c'était un vrai plaisir pour les yeux; **p. reading** *or* **recital** lecture *f* de poèmes
po-faced ['pəʊfeɪst] *adj F Pej* avec une tête d'enterrement; **why are you looking so p.** pourquoi fais-tu une telle tête d'enterrement?; **the p. old cow!** sale gueule de vache!
pogo[1] ['pəʊgəʊ] *n* **p. stick** = échasse *f* à ressort
pogo[2] *vi* danser le pogo
pogrom ['pɒgrəm] *n* pogrom(e) *m*
poignancy ['pɔɪnjənsɪ] *n* (*of an emotion etc*) caractère *m* poignant; **a moment of great p.** un moment très poignant
poignant ['pɔɪnjənt] *adj* (*feeling*) poignant, vif; (*regret etc*) amer, -ère
poignantly ['pɔɪnjəntlɪ] *adv* d'une façon poignante
poinsettia [pɔɪn'setɪə] *n* (*plant*) poinsettia *m*
point[1] [pɔɪnt] *n* **(a)** (*in space*) point *m*; **p. of arrival/departure** point d'arrivée/de départ; **at that p. on the road** à cet endroit de la route; **the train goes to Taunton and all points west** le train dessert Taunton et toutes les gares dans cette direction; **p. of contact** point de contact; *Com* **p. of sale** point de vente; **p. of view** point de vue; **to consider sth from all points of view** considérer qch sous tous ses aspects
(b) (*precise moment*) **at this p. in time** en ce moment même; **at this p. the phone rang** c'est alors que le téléphone a sonné, à ce moment-là le téléphone a sonné; **at one p. I thought we would all be killed** à un certain moment, j'ai cru que nous allions tous être tués; **to be on the p. of doing sth** être sur le point de faire qch; **on** *or* **at the p. of death** sur le point de mourir, à l'article de la mort; **to be on the p. of departure** être sur le point de partir; **p. of no return** point de non-retour; **a high/low p. in sb's life** un moment fort/difficile de la vie de qn; **when it came to the p.** quand le moment critique est arrivé; **there comes a p. in everyone's life when ...** dans la vie de chacun il arrive un moment où

...; **up to a (certain) p.** jusqu'à un certain point; **she had reached the p. where she was no longer interested** elle en était arrivée à perdre tout intérêt; **severe to the p. of cruelty** sévère jusqu'à la cruauté

(c) (*of argumentation etc*) point *m*; **the chief p. of an argument** le point essentiel d'un raisonnement; **figures that give p. to his argument** chiffres qui ajoutent du poids à sa thèse; **on that p. we disagree** là-dessus nous ne sommes pas d'accord; **I take your p.** je vois ce que vous voulez dire; **p. taken!** (*agreeing*) très juste!; **OK, OK p. taken!** ça va, ça va, j'ai compris!; **she has a p.** elle a raison; **to make a p.** faire une remarque; **to make a p. of doing sth** ne pas manquer de faire qch; **my p.** *or* **the p. I'm making is that ...** là où je veux en venir c'est que ...; **you've made your p.!** ça va, j'ai compris!; **the teacher went through the essay p. by p.** le professeur a repris la dissertation point par point; **in p. of fact** en fait, à vrai dire; **p. of grammar/of law** question *f* de grammaire/de droit; **p. of honour** point d'honneur; **p. of order** point de réglementation; **the p.** (*subject*) le sujet, la question; **the p. at issue** le sujet dont il est question; **the p. is (that) ...** c'est que ...; **get** *or* **come to the p.!** (venons-en) au fait!; **that's the p.** c'est bien de cela qu'il s'agit; **that's not the p.** il ne s'agit pas de cela; **that's beside the p.!** ce n'est pas le problème *ou* la question!; **you're missing the p.** tu n'as pas compris ce que je voulais dire; **on this p.** à cet égard, à ce propos; **this is very much to the p.** c'est bien parlé *ou* bien dit

(d) (*purpose*) **what would be the p. (of doing that)?** à quoi bon (faire cela)?; **there is no p. in (doing) it** cela ne servirait à rien; **I can't see the p.** (*of doing it*) je ne vois pas l'intérêt

(e) (*characteristic*) **a p. of interest** un détail intéressant; **a p. of similarity/difference** une similarité/différence; **to have its good points** avoir ses bons côtés; **tact has never been one of your strong points** la délicatesse n'a jamais été ton fort; **its price is a p. in its favour** son prix est un de ses atouts

(f) *Gram* **(full) p.** point *m*; *Math* **(decimal) p.** virgule *f* (décimale); **three p. five (3.5)** trois virgule cinq (3,5)

(g) (*in game, exam etc*) point *m*; **to score so many points** marquer *ou* obtenir tant de points; **you get three points for a correct answer** une bonne réponse vaut trois points; *Cards etc* **to play ten pence a p.** jouer à dix pence le point; *Boxing* **to win on points** gagner aux points; *Boxing* **beaten on points** battu aux points; *Boxing* **a points decision** une décision aux points; **p. system** (*at school etc*) barème *m*, système *m* de notation *f*; (*in game etc*) système d'attribution des points; *Cycling* **points competition** classement *m* par points

(h) *Typ etc* (*measure*) point *m*; **the thermometer went up/down two points** le thermomètre a monté/a baissé de deux degrés; *St Exch* **rise/fall of one p.** (*of price*) hausse *f*/ baisse *f* d'un point

(i) (*sharp end*) (*of needle, nail, sword, tool etc*) pointe *f*; (*of drill*) mouche *f*; (*of quill pen*) bec *m*; *Geog* pointe, promontoire *m*; **to dance on points** faire des pointes; **on (full) p.** (*of dancer*) sur la pointe; **on demi-p.** (*of dancer*) sur la demi-pointe; **to end in a p.** aller *ou* se terminer en pointe; **to give a p. to a pencil** tailler un crayon; **p. of a joke** piquant *m ou* sel *m* d'une plaisanterie; **points** (*of horse etc*) extrémités *fpl*; (*in hunting*) (*of deer*) cors *mpl*; *Fig* **not to put too fine a p. on it ...** pour dire les choses clairement ...

(j) *Br El* (*off mains*) prise *f* de courant; **eight-p. distributor** (*in engine*) distributeur *m* (d'allumage) à huit plots

(k) *Aut* **points** contacts *mpl* de rupteur

(l) *Br Rail* **points** aiguillage *m*; **p. lever** levier *m* d'aiguille

(m) the points of the compass les aires *fpl* du vent; **to alter course 16 points** venir de 16 quarts

(n) (*in backgammon*) flèche *f*, pointe *f*, case *f*

point² **1** *vt* **(a)** (*aim*) (*gun*) pointer, braquer; (*telescope*) diriger, orienter, braquer (**at** sur); (*finger*) pointer; **to p. one's finger at sb** montrer qu du doigt; *Fig* **to p. the finger at sb** montrer qn du doigt; **to p. a gun at sb** braquer *ou* pointer une arme sur qn; **to p. a camera at sth/sb** braquer un appareil photo sur qch/qn; *F* **just p. me in the right direction** dites-moi simplement quelle direction je dois prendre; **she pointed the car/the boat towards home** elle a pris la direction de la maison

(b) (*indicate*) **to p. the way** indiquer *ou* montrer le chemin (**to sb** à qn, **to a place** vers un endroit); *Fig* indiquer la direction à suivre (**towards sth** pour parvenir à qch); **the ship/car was pointing the wrong way** le navire/la voiture était tourné(e) du mauvais côté

(c) (*in ballet*) **to p. the toe** *or* **the foot** pointer le pied

(d) *Constr* (*wall*) jointoyer

(e) (*of hunting dog*) (*game*) arrêter

2 *vi* **(a)** (*indicate*) **the magnetic needle always points north** l'aiguille aimantée est toujours tournée vers le nord; **the hour hand is pointing to 10** la petite aiguille indique 10 heures; **the arrow points in the direction of the entrance** la flèche indique la direction de l'entrée; **this points to the fact that ...** ceci montre *ou* indique que ...; **everything seems to p. to success** tout semble indiquer le succès; **everything points to suicide** tout indique un suicide

(b) (*with finger etc*) **to p. at sb/sth** montrer *ou* désigner qn/qch du doigt *etc*; **don't p., it's rude** ne montre pas du doigt, ce n'est pas poli

(c) (*of hunting dog*) tomber en arrêt

▶ **point off** *vtsep Math* (*decimals*) séparer par une virgule

▶ **point out** *vtsep* **(a) to p. sb/sth out to sb** montrer qn/qch à qn; (*with one's finger*) montrer *ou* désigner qn/qch du doigt à qn

(b) (*indicate, show*) (*error etc*) signaler, relever; (*fact*) faire remarquer; **to p. out sth to sb** attirer l'attention de qn sur qch, signaler *ou* faire remarquer qch à qn; **to p. out to sb that he is wrong** faire remarquer à qn qu'il a tort; **to p. out to sb the advantages of sth** montrer à qn les avantages de qch; **might I p. out that ...?** permettez-moi de vous faire observer *ou* remarquer que ...; **he has been pointed out to me as a capable man** on me l'a signalé comme un homme capable

▶ **point up** *vtsep* (*highlight*) mettre en évidence

point-blank **1** *adj Mil etc* (*firing*) direct, à bout portant; (*refusal, denial*) catégorique; **to fire at p. range** tirer à bout portant; **he was shot at p. range** on lui a tiré dessus à bout portant **2** *adv* **to fire p. at sb** tirer sur qn à bout portant; **he asked me p. whether ...** il m'a demandé de but en blanc si ...; **to deny sth p.** nier qch catégoriquement; **to refuse p.** refuser catégoriquement *ou* (tout) net (**to do sth** de faire qch)

point-by-point *adj* **p. analysis** analyse *f* point par point

point duty *n* (*of police officer*) service *m* de la circulation; **policeman on p.** agent *m* de circulation; **to be on p.** être à la circulation

pointed ['pɔɪntɪd] *adj* **(a)** (*having a sharp point*) pointu; (*beard*) (taillé) en pointe; **p.-nose pliers** pince *f* à bec pointu **(b)** (*remark*) sarcastique, mordant; (*allusion, look*) peu équivoque, peu voilé

pointedly ['pɔɪntɪdlɪ] *adv* (*to say*) d'un ton sarcastique *ou* mordant; (*to refer*) explicitement, nettement; **not too p.** sans appuyer; **she stared p. at the ceiling during the speech** elle fixa ostensiblement son regard au plafond pendant le discours

pointedness ['pɔɪntɪdnɪs] *n* (*of remark*) mordant *m*; (*of allusion*) caractère *m* explicite

pointer ['pɔɪntər] *n* **(a)** (*of clock*) aiguille *f*; (*of scales*) aiguille, languette *f*; *Sch* (*at blackboard*) baguette *f*; *Comptr* pointeur *m*; **optical** *or* **illuminated p.** (*for slides*) flèche *f* lumineuse **(b)** *F* (*advice*) tuyau *m*; **to give sb a few pointers on sth** donner à qn quelques indications *ou* tuyaux à propos de qch; **a p. to the future** une indication des choses à venir **(c)** (*dog*) pointer *m* **(d)** *Constr* (*bricklayer's tool*) pointe *f*

pointillism ['pwæntɪlɪz(ə)m] *n Art* pointillisme *m*

pointing ['pɔɪntɪŋ] *n Constr* (*of wall*) jointoiement *m*

pointing device *n Comptr* pointeur *m*

pointless ['pɔɪntlɪs] *adj* (*story etc*) qui ne rime à rien; (*joke*) fade, sans sel; (*remark etc*) qui n'a rien à voir avec la question; (*action, suffering*) inutile; (*violence*) gratuite; (*existence*) sans but; **it would be p.** ce serait inutile, cela ne servirait à rien (**to do** de faire); **it is a p. exercise** ça ne sert à rien

pointlessly ['pɔɪntlɪslɪ] *adv* (*to argue, work, die etc*) inutilement, vainement

pointlessness ['pɔɪntlɪsnɪs] *n* (*of joke etc*) fadeur *f*; (*of remark etc*) manque *m* d'à-propos; (*of action, changes*) inutilité *f*; (*of violence*) gratuité *f*; (*of existence*) futilité *f*

point-of-purchase promotion *n* promotion *f* sur point d'achat

point-of-sale *n* point *m* de vente; **p. competition** concurrence *f* entre points de vente; **p. display** exposition *f* sur le lieu de vente; **p. information** information *f* sur le lieu de vente, ILV *f*; **points-of-sale network** réseau *m* de points de vente; **p. promotion** communication *f ou* promotion *f ou* publicité *f* sur le lieu de vente, CLV *f*, PLV *f*; **p. terminal** terminal *m* point de vente, TPV *m*

pointsman ['pɔɪntsmən] *n Br Rail* aiguilleur *m*

point source *n* source *f* ponctuelle

point-to-point *adj* **(a)** *Br Sp* **p. (race)** cross *m* à cheval **(b)** *Telecom* **p. audioconference** audioconférence *f* point à point

point work *n* (*of ballet dancer*) pointes *fpl*

pointy-headed [pɔɪntɪ'hedɪd] *adj US Pej* intello

poise¹ [pɔɪz] *n* **(a)** (*balance*) équilibre *m*; (*state of composure*) aplomb *m*; **to recover one's p.** retrouver son aplomb; **to have p.** (*of person*) avoir de la prestance; **a man of p.** un homme pondéré **(b)** (*of head, body*) port *m*

poise² *vt* équilibrer; (*in hand*) tenir en équilibre; **to be poised** être en équilibre; (*of person*) être équilibré; **her hand was poised over the telephone** sa main était suspendue au-dessus du téléphone; **she poised herself on the edge of the desk** elle s'assit délicatement sur le bord du bureau; **the cat was poised ready to spring** le chat se tenait prêt à bondir; **Rome was poised to conquer the known world** Rome se tenait prête à conquérir le monde connu; **to be poised on the brink of sth** être à deux doigts de qch

poised [pɔɪzd] *adj* posé; **she's very p. for one so young** elle a beaucoup de prestance *ou* est très posée pour quelqu'un d'aussi jeune

poison¹ [ˈpɔɪzən] *n* poison *m*; **to take p.** s'empoisonner; *F* **what's your p.?** (*drink*) qu'est-ce que tu veux boire?; **p. gas** gaz *m* toxique; **p. gland** (*of animal*) glande *f* à venin; **p. pen letter** lettre *f* anonyme venimeuse

poison² *vt* (*of person*) (*sb, sth*) empoisonner; (*of substance*) (*sb*) intoxiquer; *Fig* (*the mind*) corrompre, pervertir; (*sb's life*) empoisonner; **to p. sb's mind against sb** monter qn contre qn; **poisoned arrow** flèche *f* empoisonnée; *Fig* **poisoned chalice** cadeau *m* empoisonné; **poisoned food** nourriture *f* empoisonnée

poisoner [ˈpɔɪzənər] *n* empoisonneur, -euse

poisoning [ˈpɔɪzənɪŋ] *n* (*by person*) (*of person, food*) empoisonnement *m*; (*by substance*) (*of person*) intoxication *f*; (*of mind*) corruption *f*

poison ivy *n* (*plant*) sumac *m* vénéneux, *Can* herbe *f* à la puce

poisonous [ˈpɔɪzənəs] *adj* (*substance*) toxique, intoxicant; (*gas*) asphyxiant, toxique; (*animal*) venimeux; (*plant*) vénéneux; *Fig* (*doctrine*) pernicieux; (*remark, allegation*) vénéneux; (*atmosphere*) malfaisant; (*coffee, liquid*) répugnant

poke¹ [pəʊk] *n* **(a)** (*push*) poussée *f*; (*with elbow*) coup *m* de coude; **to give sth a p. with one's finger/a stick** pousser qch du doigt/du bout d'un bâton; **to give sb a p. in the eye** (*with finger*) mettre le doigt dans l'œil à qn; (*with umbrella*) mettre un coup de parapluie dans l'œil à qn; **to give sb a (friendly) p. in the ribs** donner une bourrade (amicale) à qn **(b)** *Sl* (*act of sexual intercourse*) partie *f* de jambes en l'air; **to give sb a p.** sauter qn, tirer un coup avec qn

poke² **1** *vt* **(a) to p. one's finger in sb's eye** mettre le doigt dans l'œil à qn; **he poked his finger at the map** il a pointé le doigt vers la carte; **to p. one's umbrella in sb's eye** mettre un coup de parapluie dans l'œil à qn; **he poked the ice with a stick** il a tâté la glace du bout d'un bâton; **to p. sb in the ribs** (*friendly gesture*) donner une bourrade (amicale) à qn; **to p. a hole in sth** faire un trou dans qch, crever qch

(b) (*insert*) (*finger in cake, thermometer in mouth*) enfoncer, planter; (*finger up nose*) fourrer **(in(to)** dans); **to p. one's head through the window** passer la tête par la fenêtre; *F* **to p. one's nose into other people's business** fourrer son nez dans les affaires des autres

(c) (*fire*) tisonner, attiser

(d) to p. fun at sb/sth se moquer de qn/qch

(e) *Sl* (*have sexual intercourse with*) sauter, tirer un coup avec

2 *vi* **to p. at sth (with one's finger/a stick)** tâter qch du bout du doigt/d'un bâton; *F* **to p. into other people's business** fourrer son nez dans les affaires des autres

poke³ *n Dial esp Scot* (*bag*) sac *m*, sachet *m*

▶ **poke about, poke around** **1** *vi* **(a)** (*search*) fouiller, fureter; **a dog was poking about in the bushes** un chien fouinait *ou* furetait dans les buissons; **she was poking about in the wardrobe for something to wear** elle fouillait dans l'armoire pour trouver quelque chose à mettre **(b)** (*make unwanted enquiries*) fourrer son nez partout, fouiner; **that social worker is always poking about** cette assistante sociale est toujours en train de fourrer son nez partout **2** *vipo* (*search in*) (*antique shop etc*) fouiller dans

▶ **poke out** **1** *vi* (*protrude*) sortir, dépasser **(of, from** de); **her umbrella was poking out (of her bag)** son parapluie sortait *ou* dépassait de son sac; **his stomach was poking out** son ventre dépassait **2** *vtsep* **(a)** (*push out*) **to p. one's head out (of the window)** passer *ou* sortir la tête par la fenêtre; **to p. one's tongue out** tirer la langue **(at sb** à qn) **(b) to p. sb's eye out** éborgner qn

poker¹ [ˈpəʊkər] *n* (*for fire*) tisonnier *m*; **p. work** pyrogravure *f*

poker² *n Cards* poker *m*; **p. dice** dés *mpl* pour jouer au poker d'as; (*game*) poker *m* d'as; *F* **p. face** visage *m* impassible; *F* **p.-faced** (*person*) au visage impassible; (*reply, response*) qui ne trahit aucune émotion; **p. game** partie *f* de poker

poky [ˈpəʊkɪ] *adj* (*room*) exigu, -uë; **to live in a p. little place** être logé à l'étroit

Polack [ˈpəʊlæk] *n Offensive Sl* Polaque *mf*

Poland [ˈpəʊlənd] *n* Pologne *f*

polar [ˈpəʊlər] *adj Geog, Math, Phys* polaire; **p. bear** ours *m* polaire *ou* blanc

polarity [pəʊˈlærɪtɪ] *n Phys* polarité *f*

polarization [pəʊləraɪˈzeɪʃən] *n Phys* polarisation *f*; *Fig esp Pol* radicalisation *f*

polarize [ˈpəʊləraɪz] **1** *vt* **(a)** *Phys* (*light, iron bar etc*) polariser **(b)** (*make extreme*) (*opinions*) radicaliser **2** *vi* **(a)** *Phys* se polariser **(b)** (*of opinions ec*) se radicaliser

polarizing filter [ˈpəʊləraɪzɪŋ] *n TV, Cin* filtre *m* polarisant

Polaroid® [ˈpəʊlərɔɪd] *n* **(a)** *Phot* (*camera*) Polaroïd *m*; (*photograph*) photographie *f* instantanée **(b)** *Opt* Polaroïd *m*; **Polaroids** (*sunglasses*) lunettes *fpl* de soleil (à verre) polaroïd

Pole [pəʊl] *n* [①A20,d] (*person*) Polonais, -aise

pole¹ [pəʊl] *n* **(a)** (*stick, rod*) perche *f*; (*fixed in ground*) poteau *m*; (*for plants*) échalas *m*, rame *f*; (*of scaffolding*) mât *m*; (*for flag*) hampe *f*; (*of stretcher*) bras *m*; *Naut* (*of mast*) flèche *f*; (*of tent*) piquet *m*; (*of circus tent*) mât; *Br F* **to be up the p.** (*mad*) être timbré *ou* toqué **(b)** *Arch* (*measurement*) perche *f*

pole² *n El, Geog* pôle *m*; **North P.** Pôle Nord, pôle arctique *ou* boréal; **South P.** Pôle Sud, pôle antarctique *ou* austral; **magnetic/true p.** pôle magnétique/géographique; *Fig* **to be poles apart** (*of people*) être aux antipodes l'un de l'autre; (*of views etc*) être diamétralement opposés; **opposite poles** (*of magnet*) pôles contraires; **p. Star** étoile *f* polaire

poleaxe¹, *US* **poleax** [ˈpəʊlæks] *n* merlin *m*

poleaxe², *US* **poleax** *vt* (*hit*) (*person*) assommer; (*animal*) abattre avec un merlin; *Fig* **she was poleaxed by the news** la nouvelle l'a abasourdie *ou* assommée

polecat [ˈpəʊlkæt] *n* (*animal*) putois *m*

polemic [pəˈlemɪk] **1** *n* polémique *f* **2** *adj Fml* polémique

polemical [pəˈlemɪk(ə)l] *adj* polémique

polemicist [pəˈlemɪsɪst] *n* polémiste *mf*

polemics [pəˈlemɪks] *n* [①A10,c] polémique *f*

pole-vault¹ *vi Sp* sauter à la perche

pole-vault², pole-vaulting *n Sp* saut *m* à la perche

pole-vaulter *n Sp* sauteur, -euse à la perche, perchiste *mf*

police¹ [pəˈliːs] *n inv* [①A11,f,ii] (*with pl verb*) **the p. (force)** la police; **twenty p. were on duty** vingt agents *mpl* (de police) étaient de service; **to be a member of the p. (force), to be in the p.** être de *ou* dans la police; *US* **p. captain** ≈ commissaire *m* de police; **p. car** voiture *f* de police; *Br* **p. constable** agent *m* de police; *US* **the p. department** la Police; **p. dog** chien *m* policier; *Br* **the P. Federation** = syndicat *m* de la police britannique; **p. informer** indicateur, -trice; *Br* **p. inspector** inspecteur *m* de police; (*in the CID*) commissaire *m* de police; **p. officer** policier *m*; **p. state** état *m* policier; **p. station** poste *m* de police; (*bigger*) commissariat *m*; **p. van** (*for transporting prisoners*) voiture *f* cellulaire; (*for transporting police*) car *m* de police; **hours of careful p. work** des heures d'un travail poussé de la part de la police

police² *vt* **(a)** (*the country*) maintenir l'ordre dans; **to p. a football match/demonstration** assurer l'ordre à un match de football/une manifestation; **the area is heavily policed** la zone est sous haute surveillance **(b)** *Fig* (*institution etc*) surveiller, contrôler; (*measures etc*) veiller au respect de; **should the Press p. itself?** la presse doit-elle être autorisée à s'auto-réglementer?

policeman, *pl* **-men** [pəˈliːsmən] *n* agent *m* (de police)

policewoman, *pl* **-women** [pəˈliːswʊmən, -wɪmɪn] *n* femme *f* agent (de police)

policing [pəˈliːsɪŋ] *n* **(a)** (*by police*) maintien *m* de l'ordre; **the p. of the match/demonstration was inadequate** le service d'ordre du match/de la manifestation était inadéquat; **p. policy** politique *f* de maintien de l'ordre **(b)** *Fig* **the p. of these regulations** la responsabilité de veiller au respect de cette réglementation

policy¹ [ˈpɒlɪsɪ] *n* politique *f*; (*measure*) mesure *f*; **foreign p.** politique étrangère *ou* extérieure; **economic/agricultural p.** politique économique/agricole; **we have the right policies** nous avons les mesures adéquates; **my p. is not to tell him anything** ma politique, c'est de ne rien lui dire; **sales p.** politique de vente; **p. changes, changes of p.** changements *mpl* de politique; **p. meeting** séance *f* de concertation; **p. position** position *f* de principe

policy² *n* (*in insurance*) police *f* (d'assurance); **(fully) comprehensive** *or* **all-risks p.** police tous risques; **to take out a p.** souscrire à une police d'assurance

policyholder [ˈpɒlɪsɪhəʊldər] *n* assuré, -ée

policy paper *n* = document *m* énonçant une position de principe

policy statement *n* déclaration *f* de principe
polio ['pəʊlɪəʊ] *n Med* polio *f*; **to have p.** avoir la polio
poliomyelitis [pəʊlɪəʊmaɪə'laɪtɪs] *n Med* poliomyélite *f*
Polish ['pəʊlɪʃ] [①A20,d] **1** *adj* polonais **2** *n Ling* polonais *m*
polish[1] ['pɒlɪʃ] *n* **(a)** (*finish of surface etc*) poli *m*, brillant *m*, lustre *m*; (*of metals*) poli, brunissure *f*; **high p.** poli brillant; **to lose its p.** se dépolir, se ternir; **to take the p. off sth** dépolir qch, ternir qch; **to give the table a p.** cirer la table
(b) (*substance*) crème *f ou* pâte *f* à polir; **boot** *or* **shoe p.** cirage *m*, crème pour chaussures; **floor p.** encaustique *f ou* cire *f* à parquet; **metal p.** produit *m* pour faire briller les métaux; **nail p.** vernis *m* à ongles
(c) *Fig* (*refinement*) (*of person*) belles manières *fpl*, savoir-vivre *m inv*; (*of novel, style, performance*) élégance *f*; **to have a certain p.** (*of person*) avoir un certain savoir-vivre; (*of novel, style etc*) avoir une certaine élégance; **to lack p.** (*of person*) manquer d'éducation *ou* de savoir-vivre; (*of novel, style etc*) manquer d'élégance; **to give sth a final p.** mettre la dernière main à qch
polish[2] *vt* **(a)** (*wood, metal etc*) polir; (*gold, silver*) brunir; (*shoes*) cirer; (*brass*) astiquer, faire briller; (*stone etc*) lisser; (*parquet floor, tiles*) cirer, encaustiquer; (*rice*) glacer, polir **(b)** *Fig* (*make more refined*) (*person, manners*) polir, dégrossir; (*style, interpretation*) polir, perfectionner; **to p. one's French** perfectionner son français
▶ **polish off** *vtsep F* (*course, dish*) finir; (*meal, bottle, job*) expédier; (*put finishing touch to*) (*job*) mettre la dernière main à; (*get rid of, defeat*) (*rebels, competitor etc*) liquider, régler son compte à; **to p. off one's drink** vider son verre; **such hard work at his age polished him off** un travail aussi dur à son âge l'a achevé
▶ **polish up** *vtsep* **(a)** faire reluire; (*brass objects*) astiquer, brunir, lustrer **(b)** (*improve*) (*one's French*) perfectionner; (*style*) polir
polished ['pɒlɪʃt] *adj* **(a)** poli; (*wood, floor, shoes*) ciré **(b)** (*manners etc*) poli, distingué **(c)** (*style etc*) châtié, raffiné
polisher ['pɒlɪʃər] *n* **(a)** (*person*) (*of metals etc*) polisseur, -euse, brunisseur, -euse; (*of brass*) astiqueur, -euse **(b)** (*tool*) instrument *m* à polir, polissoir *m*; (*for metal*) brunissoir *m*; **electric floor p.** cireuse *f* électrique à parquet
Politburo ['pɒlɪtbjʊərəʊ] *n Pol* Politburo *m*
polite [pə'laɪt] *adj* **(a)** (*courteous*) poli (**to sb** envers *ou* avec qn); **I was just being p.** j'ai fait/dit ça par politesse; **p. refusal** refus *m* poli **(b) p. society** (*well-mannered people*) les gens bien élevés; **this word is not used in p. society** ce mot ne s'utilise pas chez les gens bien élevés
politely [pə'laɪtlɪ] *adv* poliment
politeness [pə'laɪtnɪs] *n* politesse *f*
politic ['pɒlɪtɪk] *adj* **(a)** *Fml* (*person, conduct*) politique, avisé, *Pej* rusé, astucieux; **it would not be p. to ...** ce ne serait pas prudent de ... **(b) the body p.** le corps politique; (*the state*) l'État *m*
political [pə'lɪtɪk(ə)l] *adj* **(a)** *Pol* (*party etc*) politique; **he isn't very p.** il n'a pas une forte conscience politique; **p. beliefs** opinions *fpl* politiques; **p. editor** rédacteur *m* en chef politique **(b)** *Fig* **she's a p. animal** elle ne pense qu'en termes de politique; **things are getting far too p. in the office** ça devient vraiment intenable au bureau avec toutes ces manigances *ou F* magouilles; **it was a p. decision** c'était une décision qui relevait de la politique interne de l'entreprise/du service/*etc*; **p. correctness** le politiquement correct
political asylum *n* asile *m* politique; **to request/be granted p.** demander/se voir accorder l'asile politique
politically [pə'lɪtɪklɪ] *adv* **(a)** politiquement; **p. informed** au courant des choses de la politique; **to be p. aware** avoir une conscience politique, être politisé; **p. radical** radical sur le plan politique **(b)** *Fig* **p. that wouldn't be a wise thing to say** du point de vue tactique, ce ne serait pas une chose à dire; **p. correct** politiquement correct
political prisoner *n* prisonnier, -ière politique
political science *n* sciences *fpl* politiques
politician [pɒlɪ'tɪʃən] *n* **(a)** homme *m*/femme *f* politique; *esp Pej* politicien, -ienne **(b)** *esp Am Pej* (*self-interested*) politicard, -arde
politicize [pə'lɪtɪsaɪz] *vt* (*debate, problem, person etc*) politiser
politicking ['pɒlɪtɪkɪŋ] *n* activité *f* électorale menée pour obtenir des suffrages
politico [pə'lɪtɪkəʊ] *n esp Am Pej* politicord *m*,
politico-economical *adj* politico-économique
politics ['pɒlɪtɪks] *n* [①A10,c] politique *f*; **to be interested in p.** s'intéresser à la politique; **to talk p.** parler politique; **his p. are right of centre** (politiquement parlant) il se situe à droite; **what are her p.?** de quel bord est-elle?, politiquement, où est-ce qu'elle se situe?; **foreign p.** politique étrangère; *Fig* **office p.** intrigues *fpl* de bureau
polity ['pɒlɪtɪ] *n Pol* **(a)** (*constitution*) constitution *f* politique; (*form of government*) régime *m*; (*state*) État *m* **(b)** (*management*) administration *f* politique
polka ['pɒlkə] *n Mus* polka *f*; *Tex* **p. dots** pois *mpl*; **blue p. dot tie** cravate bleue à pois (blancs)
poll[1] [pəʊl] *n* **(a)** (*voting*) vote *m* (par bulletins), scrutin *m*; **to go to the polls** aller aux urnes; **to head the p.** arriver en tête de scrutin; **heavy/light p.** forte/faible participation électorale; **a 76% p.** un taux de participation de 76%; **to get a large share of the p.** remporter *ou* réunir une grande proportion des voix *ou* suffrages **(b)** (*survey*) sondage *m*; **(public) opinion p.** sondage d'opinion; **to carry out a p.** faire un sondage
poll[2] **1** *vt* **(a)** (*of polling clerk*) (*person*) recueillir le bulletin de vote de; (*of candidate*) (*votes*) réunir; **the Conservatives polled 41% nationally** les conservateurs ont remporté 41% des voix *ou* suffrages au niveau national; **to p. a vote for sb** donner sa voix à qn, voter pour qn **(b)** (*in opinion poll*) sonder **(c)** (*tree*) étêter, écimer; (*bull*) décorner **(d)** *Comptr* interroger **2** *vi* **the party polled well** le parti a remporté une bonne proportion des suffrages *ou* des voix
poll[3] *n* (*animal*) vache *f etc* sans cornes
pollard[1] ['pɒlɑːd] *n* (*tree*) arbre *m* étêté; (*animal*) animal *m* sans cornes
pollard[2] *vt* (*tree*) étêter, écimer
pollen ['pɒlən] *n Bot* pollen *m*; **p. count** taux *m* de pollen; **p. sac** sac *m* pollinique
pollinate ['pɒlɪneɪt] *vt Bot* polliniser
pollination [pɒlɪ'neɪʃən] *n Bot* pollinisation *f*, fécondation *f*; **self-p.** pollinisation directe; **cross-p.** pollinisation croisée
polling ['pəʊlɪŋ] *n* **(a)** scrutin *m*, élections *fpl*; **p. day** jour *m* des élections *ou* du scrutin; **p. booth** isoloir *m*; **p. station** bureau *m* de vote **(b)** *Comptr* (*querying*) interrogation *f*
polliwog ['pɒlɪwɒg] *n Am* (*tadpole*) têtard *m*
pollster ['pəʊlstər] *n* enquêteur, -euse; **according to the pollsters** selon les sondages
poll tax *n Br Fin* capitation *f*; *Br formerly* (*local tax*) = impôt *m* local (*forfaitaire pour chaque habitant*)
pollutant [pə'luːtənt] *n* polluant *m*
pollute [pə'luːt] *vt* (*river, atmosphere etc*) polluer; (*language, mind*) contaminer
polluter [pə'luːtər] *n* pollueur, -euse
pollution [pə'luːʃən] *n* **(a)** (*contamination*) (*of river, atmosphere*) pollution *f*; (*of language, mind*) contamination *f*; **p. policy** politique *f* anti-pollution; **atmospheric p., p. of the atmosphere** pollution atmosphérique *ou* de l'air **(b)** (*pollutants*) polluants *mpl*; **the river is full of p.** la rivière est très polluée
pollution-free *adj* non pollué
Polly ['pɒlɪ] *n F* (*parrot*) **(pretty) P.** Jacquot *m*
Pollyanna [pɒlɪ'ænə] *n esp Am* optimiste *mf*
pollywog ['pɒlɪwɒg] *n Am* (*tadpole*) têtard *m*
polo ['pəʊləʊ] *n Sp* polo *m*; **to play p.** jouer au polo; **p. neck** (*collar*) col *m* roulé; **p. neck (sweater)** pullover *m* à col roulé; *Sp* **p. pony** poney *m* de polo; **p. shirt** polo *m*, chemise *f* polo; *Sp* **p. stick** maillet *m*
polonaise [pɒlə'neɪz] *n Mus* polonaise *f*
poltergeist ['pɒltəgaɪst] *n* esprit *m* frappeur
poly ['pɒlɪ] **1** *n Br F* = **polytechnic 2** *adj F* **p. bag** sac *m* (en) plastique
poly- ['pɒlɪ] *pref* poly-
polyandrous [pɒlɪ'ændrəs] *adj* polyandre
polyandry ['pɒlɪændrɪ] *n* polyandrie *f*
polyanthus [pɒlɪ'ænθəs] *n* primevère *f* des jardins
polychromatic [pɒlɪkrəʊ'mætɪk] *adj* polychrome
polychrome ['pɒlɪkrəʊm] **1** *adj* polychrome **2** *n* (*statue*) statue *f* polychrome; (*colouring*) polychromie *f*
polyclinic [pɒlɪ'klɪnɪk] *n Med* polyclinique *f*
polyester [pɒlɪ'estər] *n Ch* polyester *m*
polyethylene [pɒlɪ'eθɪliːn] *n esp Am Ch* polyéthylène *m*, polythène *m*
polygamist [pə'lɪgəmɪst] *n* polygame *mf*
polygamous [pə'lɪgəməs] *adj* polygame
polygamy [pə'lɪgəmɪ] *n* polygamie *f*
polyglot ['pɒlɪglɒt] *adj, n* polyglotte *mf*
polygon ['pɒlɪgən] *n Geom* polygone *m*
polygonal [pə'lɪgən(ə)l] *adj Geom* polygonal
polygraph ['pɒlɪgrɑːf] *n* détecteur *m* de mensonges; **to take a p. test** subir un test au détecteur de mensonges
polyhedron [pɒlɪ'hiːdrən] *n Geom* polyèdre *m*
polymath ['pɒlɪmæθ] *n* esprit *m* universel
polymer ['pɒlɪmər] *n Ch* polymère *m*
polymerization [pɒlɪmərаɪ'zeɪʃən] *n Ch* polymérisation *f*
polymorphic [pɒlɪ'mɔːfɪk] *adj Biol, Ch* polymorphe, polymorphique

polymorphism [pɒlɪ'mɔ:fɪz(ə)m] *n Biol, Ch* polymorphisme *m*, polymorphie *f*

polymorphous [pɒlɪ'mɔ:fəs] *adj* = **polymorphic**

Polynesia [pɒlɪ'ni:zɪə] *n* Polynésie *f*

Polynesian [pɒlɪ'ni:zɪən] **1** *adj* polynésien **2** *n* Polynésien, -ienne

polyneuritis [pɒlɪnjʊ'raɪtɪs] *n Med* polynévrite *f*

polynomial [pɒlɪ'nəʊmɪəl] *n Math* polynôme *m*

polyp ['pɒlɪp] *n Zool, Med* polype *m*

polyphase ['pɒlɪfeɪz] *adj El* polyphasé

polyphonic [pɒlɪ'fɒnɪk] *adj Mus, Ling* polyphonique

polyphony [pə'lɪfənɪ] *n Mus, Ling* polyphonie *f*

polypropylene [pɒlɪ'prəʊpɪli:n] *n Ch* polypropène *m*, polypropylène *m*

polypus ['pɒlɪpəs] *n Med* polype *m*

polysaccharide [pɒlɪ'sækəraɪd] *n Ch* polysaccharide *m*, polyoside *m*

polystyrene [pɒlɪ'staɪri:n] *n Ch* polystyrène *m*; **p. packaging** emballage *m* en polystyrène

polysyllabic [pɒlɪsɪ'læbɪk] *adj* polysyllabe, polysyllabique

polysyllable ['pɒlɪsɪləb(ə)l] *n* polysyllabe *m*

polytechnic [pɒlɪ'teknɪk] **1** *adj* polytechnique **2** *n Br Univ* ≈ Institut *m* universitaire de technologie

polytheism ['pɒlɪθi:ɪz(ə)m] *n* polythéisme *m*

polytheistic [pɒlɪθi:'ɪstɪk] *adj* polythéiste

polythene ['pɒlɪθi:n] *n esp Br* polyéthylène *m*, polythène *m*; **p. bag** sac *m* en plastique

polyunsaturated [pɒlɪʌn'sætjʊreɪtɪd] *adj Ch* polyinsaturé; **p. fats** graisses *fpl* polyinsaturées

polyurethane [pɒlɪ'jʊərɪθeɪn] *n Ch etc* polyuréthane *m*

polyvalent [pɒlɪ'veɪlənt] *adj Ch* polyvalent

polyvinyl [pɒlɪ'vaɪnɪl] *n Ch* polyvinyle *m*; **p. chloride** chlorure *m* de polyvinyle

pom [pɒm] *n Austr F* Anglais, -aise

pomegranate ['pɒmɪgrænɪt] *n* **(a)** (*fruit*) grenade *f* **(b) p. (tree)** grenadier *m*

Pomerania [pɒmə'reɪnɪə] *n* Poméranie *f*

Pomeranian [pɒmə'reɪnɪən] **1** *n* (*dog*) loulou *m* (de Poméranie) **2** *adj* de Poméranie; **P. dog** loulou *m* (de Poméranie)

pommel¹ ['pɒm(ə)l] *n* (*of sword, saddle*) pommeau *m*; *Gym* **p. horse** cheval *m* d'arçons

pommel² *vt* (**-ll-**, *US* **-l-**) = **pummel²**

pommie, pommy ['pɒmɪ] *n Austr F* Anglais, -aise; **p. bastard** salaud *m* d'Anglais, sale Anglaise *f*

pomp [pɒmp] *n* pompe *f*, éclat *m*, faste *m*; **p. and circumstance** (grand) apparat *m*

Pompeii [pɒm'peii:] *n* Pompéi *f*

pompom, pompon ['pɒmpɒm, -pɒn] *n* (*tuft*) pompon *m*

pom-pom *n Mil* canon-mitrailleuse *m*, *pl* canons-mitrailleuses (*système Maxim*)

pomposity [pɒm'pɒsɪtɪ] *n Pej* (*of person*) suffisance *f*; (*of remark, style*) emphase *f*

pompous ['pɒmpəs] *adj Pej* (*person*) plein de suffisance; (*style, remark*) emphatique, pompeux

pompously ['pɒmpəslɪ] *adv Pej* (*to behave, talk etc*) avec suffisance; (*to write*) avec emphase

pompousness ['pɒmpəsnɪs] *n Pej* (*of person*) suffisance *f*; (*of style, remark*) emphase *f*

ponce¹ [pɒns] *n esp Br Sl* **(a)** (*effeminate man*) gonzesse *f*, pédé *m* **(b)** (*pimp*) = homme *m* vivant aux crochets d'une prostituée

ponce² *vi esp Br Sl* (*live off earnings*) vivre aux crochets d'une prostituée

▶ **ponce about, ponce around** *vi Br Sl* **(a)** (*waste time*) glandouiller **(b)** (*of effeminate man*) se pavaner

▶ **ponce up** *vtsep Sl* (*dress up*) **to get all ponced up** se mettre sur son trente-et-un

poncey ['pɒnsɪ] *adj esp Br Sl* = **poncy**

poncho, *pl* **-os** ['pɒntʃəʊ, -əʊz] *n* poncho *m*

poncy ['pɒnsɪ] *adj esp Br Sl* (*effeminate*) (*manner etc*) efféminé, de gonzesse

pond [pɒnd] *n* étang *m*; (*in park*) bassin *m*, pièce *f* d'eau; (*in village*) mare *f*; (*for fish*) vivier *m*, réservoir *m*; (*of mill*) réservoir; *F* **the P.** (*the Atlantic*) l'Atlantique *m*; **p. life** = vie *f* animale des eaux stagnantes

ponder ['pɒndər] **1** *vt* (*question*) réfléchir sur; (*opinion, proposal*) considérer, peser; (*situation*) méditer (sur), réfléchir à; (*idea*) considérer; **to p. whether ...** se demander si ... **2** *vi* réfléchir, méditer; **to p. over** *or* **on sth** réfléchir à *ou* méditer sur qch

ponderable ['pɒndərəb(ə)l] *adj* pondérable

ponderous ['pɒndərəs] *adj* **(a)** (*large*) massif, énorme; (*movements, person*) lourd **(b)** (*task, work*) laborieux **(c)** (*style*) lourd, pesant; (*joke, remark*) lourd

ponderously ['pɒndərəslɪ] *adv* (*to move*) lourdement; (*to make progress*) laborieusement

pondweed ['pɒndwi:d] *n* (*plant*) épi *m* d'eau

pone [pəʊn] *n US* (**corn**) **p., p. bread** pain *m* de maïs

pong¹ [pɒŋ] *n Br F* (*smell*) puanteur *f*; **what a p.!** ça pue!, ça schlingue!; **there's a terrible p. of fish!** ça pue le poisson à plein nez!

pong² *vi Br F* (*smell*) puer, schlinguer; **the room still pongs of cigarettes** la pièce pue encore la cigarette

pongy ['pɒŋɪ] *adj Br F* (*smelly*) **it's a bit p. in here** ça pue *ou* schlingue là-dedans

pontiff ['pɒntɪf] *n Rel* pontife *m*; **the sovereign p.** le souverain pontife

pontifical [pɒn'tɪfɪk(ə)l] **1** *adj Rel* pontifical **2** *n Rel* (*book*) pontifical *m*

pontificate¹ [pɒn'tɪfɪkeɪt] *n Rel* pontificat *m*

pontificate² [pɒn'tɪfɪkeɪt] *vi Rel, Fig Pej* pontifier; **to p. about sth** pontifier à propos de *ou* sur qch

Pontius Pilate ['pɒnʃəs'paɪlət] *n Bible* Ponce Pilate

pontoon¹ [pɒn'tu:n] *n* (*float*) ponton *m*; *Av* (*on aeroplane*) flotteur *m*; **p. bridge** pont *m* de bateaux, pont flottant

pontoon² *n Br Cards* vingt-et-un *m*

pony ['pəʊnɪ] *n* **(a)** (*animal*) poney *m*; *US* (*small horse*) petit cheval *m*; *US* **cow p.** cheval de ranch; **p. trekking** randonnées *fpl* à dos de poney **(b)** *Br Sl* (*25 pounds*) vingt-cinq livres *fpl* sterling **(c)** *US Sch F* (*in exam*) traduction *f* (juxtalinéaire) **(d)** (*drinking glass*) petit verre *m* (sans pied)

ponytail ['pəʊnɪteɪl] *n* (*hairstyle*) queue *f* de cheval; **to wear one's hair in a p.** avoir une queue de cheval

pooch [pu:tʃ] *n Sl* (*dog*) cabot *m*, clebs *m*

poodle ['pu:d(ə)l] *n* caniche *mf*; *Fig* (*servile follower*) larbin *m*

poof¹ [pʊf] *n Br Offensive Sl* pédé *m*, tante *f*

poof² *int* pouf; **and then suddenly, p., it disappeared!** et puis pouf! il a disparu!

poofter ['pʊftər] *n Br Offensive Sl* pédé *m*, tante *f*

poofy ['pʊfɪ] *adj Br Offensive Sl* de gonzesse, de pédé; **some p. guy** une espèce de pédé; **it's p. to ...** c'est bon pour les gonzesses *ou* les pédés de ...; **to look p.** avoir l'air d'un pédé

pooh [pu:] **1** *int* bah!, peuh! **2** *n* (*in children's language*) (*faeces*) caca *m*

pooh-pooh¹ *n* = **pooh 2**

pooh-pooh² *vt* (*idea, warning, piece of advice*) se moquer de, faire peu de cas de

pool¹ [pu:l] *n* (*pond*) mare *f*; (*puddle*) flaque *f* d'eau; (*ornamental*) pièce *f* d'eau; (*left on beach by tide*) bâche *f*; (*in river*) clame *m*; (**swimming**) **p.** piscine *f*; **lying in a p. of blood** étendu dans une mare de sang; **a p. of light** une flaque de lumière

pool² *n* **(a)** (*group etc*) groupe *m*; *Com* (*of companies*) groupement *m*, pool *m*; *Econ* fonds *m* commun; (*of company cars, computers etc*) parc *m*; *Fig* (*of ideas, talent etc*) réservoir *m*; **a p. of experience** une mine d'expériences bigarrées; **a p. of experts/advisers** un groupe *ou* une équipe d'experts/de conseillers; **a p. of funds** un fonds commun; **typing p.** central *m* dactylographique, pool de dactylos

(b) (*in games*) (*kitty*) cagnotte *f*; *Billiards* poule *f*

(c) *Br* **football pools,** *F* **pools** = concours *m* de pronostics de matchs de football; **to do the pools** faire des concours de pronostics (sur des matchs de football)

pool³ *vt* (*capital, profits, ideas*) mettre en commun; (*resources*) grouper, mettre en commun; *Com etc* (*orders*) grouper; **pooled services** services *mpl* en commun

pool⁴ *n* (*game*) billard *m* américain; **p. cue** queue *f* de billard; **p. hall** salle *f* de billard; **p. table** (table *f* de) billard

poolroom ['pu:lrʊm] *n Am* salle *f* de billard

poop [pu:p] *n Naut* **(a) p. (deck)** (pont *m* de) dunette *f*, gaillard *m* d'arrière **(b)** (*raised part*) poupe *f*

pooped [pu:pt] *adj esp Am F* (*exhausted*) claqué, vanné

pooper-scooper ['pu:pə'sku:pər] *n F* ramasse-crottes *m inv*

poor [pɔ:r] **1** *adj* **(a)** (*having little wealth*) pauvre; **a p. man/woman** un pauvre/une pauvre; **as p. as a church mouse** pauvre comme Job; **I'm poorer by a thousand francs, I'm a thousand francs poorer** j'en suis pour mille francs; **the p. man's champagne** le champagne du pauvre; **p. relation** parent *m* pauvre; **p. white** blanc/blanche des classes défavorisées

(b) (*inferior*) mauvais, médiocre; (*quality*) inférieur; (*health*) fragile; (*soil*) maigre, peu fertile; (*weather*) mauvais; **I've a p. memory** je n'ai pas une bonne mémoire; **to have p. sight** avoir une mauvaise vue; **her hearing is very p.** elle entend très mal, elle est très dure d'oreille; **to be p. at maths** être faible en math(s); **his French is very p.** son français est très faible; **to cut a p. figure** faire piètre figure; **the patient had a p. night** le malade a passé une mauvaise nuit; **to be a p. sailor** ne pas avoir le pied marin; **he gave a p. account of himself** il ne s'en est pas très bien tiré; **in p. condition** en mauvaise condition; **p. excuse** piètre excuse;

p. harvest mauvaise récolte; **p. light** mauvais éclairage; **p. loser** mauvais perdant; **p. performance** (*of company*) contre-performance *f*; **p. reception** (*unwelcoming*) mauvais accueil; *Rad etc* mauvaise transmission; *Com* **p. sales (figures)** mauvais chiffre de ventes; **to come a p. second** (*in race*) se classer deuxième, loin derrière le vainqueur; **in terms of exports, Britain comes a p. second to Japan** en matière d'exportations, la Grande-Bretagne est en deuxième position, loin derrière le Japon; **I come a very p. second in his affections** je n'ai qu'une misérable deuxième place dans son cœur; **it's a p. substitute for the real thing** c'est loin de valoir l'original; **in p. taste** de mauvais goût; **there was a p. turnout** peu de gens sont venus

(**c**) (*to be pitied*) pauvre; **p. creature!, p. thing!** pauvre petit!, pauvre petite!; **the p. soul!** le pauvre!, la pauvre!; **p. Philippe!** pauvre Philippe!; **I'm so sorry for the p. man** comme je le plains, le pauvre homme; **when p. Alice was alive** du vivant de la pauvre Alice; **p. you, you p. thing** (*to man*) mon pauvre vieux; (*to woman*) ma pauvre vieille

2 *npl* **the p.** les pauvres *mpl*

poor box *n Rel* tronc *m* pour les pauvres

poorhouse ['pɔːhaʊs] *n Hist* asile *m* des pauvres

poor law *n Hist* = loi *f* sociale dictant les conditions dans lesquelles les pauvres étaient pris en charge par les communes

poorly ['pɔːlɪ] **1** *adv* pauvrement; **p. dressed** pauvrement vêtu; **to be p. off** (*financially*) avoir des problèmes d'argent; **p. lit** mal éclairé; **he did p. in his exams** il a eu de mauvais résultats à ses examens; **p. suited to these conditions** mal adapté à ces conditions; **to perform p. at low temperatures** donner de mauvais résultats en basses températures **2** *adj pred F* (*person*) souffrant, indisposé; **she's looking p.** elle n'a pas l'air bien, elle a mauvaise mine; **I'm feeling p.** je ne suis pas dans mon assiette

poorness ['pɔːnɪs] *n* (**a**) (*of person*) pauvreté *f* (**b**) (*inferiority*) médiocrité *f*

pop[1] [pɒp] **1** *int* crac!, pan!; **to go p.** éclater, crever; **p. goes the cork!** paf! le bouchon saute **2** *n* (**a**) (*sound of cork etc*) bruit *m* sec (**b**) *F* (*fizzy drink*) boisson *f* gazeuse

pop[2] (**-pp-**) **1** *vi* (**a**) éclater, péter; (*of cork*) sauter, péter; (*of balloon, corn*) éclater; (*of ears*) se déboucher tout d'un coup

(**b**) *F* (*go quickly*) **to p. over** *or* **across** *or* **down to the grocers** faire un saut (jusque) chez l'épicier; **they popped by** *or* **round to see us** ils sont passés nous voir; **I'm going to p. into town** je vais faire un saut en ville; **to p. into bed** se mettre vite au lit

2 *vt* (**a**) (*balloon*) crever; (*cork*) faire sauter; **to p. corn** faire du pop-corn

(**b**) (*put quickly*) mettre; **to p. sth into a drawer** mettre *ou* glisser qch dans un tiroir; **to p. one's head out of the window** passer la tête par la fenêtre

(**c**) *F* **then he popped the question** alors il lui a/m'a demandé de l'épouser

(**d**) *F* **to p. pills** se bourrer de comprimés

(**e**) *Old-fashioned Br Sl* (*pawn*) mettre en gage *ou* au clou

pop[3] *n Am F* (*father*) papa *m*

pop[4] **1** *adj* pop; **p. art** pop'art *m*, pop *m*; **p. music** musique *f* pop; **p. singer** chanteur, -euse de pop; **p. song** chanson *f* pop **2** *n Mus* (musique *f*) pop *m ou f*

pop[5] (*abbr* **population**) pop

▶ **pop in 1** *vi F* entrer en passant *ou* un instant (**at sb's** chez qn); **I've just popped in** je ne fais que passer; **he popped in to say hullo** il est passé (me/nous/*etc*) dire bonjour **2** *vtas* porter; **could you p. these trousers in at the dry cleaners?** est-ce que tu peux porter ce pantalon au pressing?

▶ **pop off** *vi* (**a**) *F* (*leave abruptly*) filer, partir (**b**) *Br Sl* (*die*) claquer

▶ **pop out** *vi F* (*go out*) sortir; **I only popped out for five minutes** je ne suis sorti que cinq minutes; **his eyes were popping out of his head** les yeux lui sortaient de la tête

▶ **pop up** *vi F* (**a**) (*rise suddenly*) surgir; **a head popped up through the trap door** une tête a surgi de la trappe (**b**) **this question has popped up again** cette question est revenue sur le tapis; **he popped up again some years later in Miami** il est réapparu quelques années après à Miami

popcorn ['pɒpkɔːn] *n* pop-corn *m*

pope [pəʊp] *n* (*in Catholic Church*) pape *m*; (*in Eastern Orthodox Church*) pope *m*; *Culin* **the p.'s nose** le croupion

popemobile ['pəʊpməbiːl] *n F* papamobile *f*

popery ['pəʊpərɪ] *n Pej* papisme *m*

popeyed ['pɒpaɪd] *adj F* (*having protuberant eyes*) aux yeux exorbités; (*with surprise*) aux yeux écarquillés

popgun ['pɒpgʌn] *n* (*toy*) (*rifle*) fusil *m* à bouchon; (*handgun*) pistolet *m* à bouchon

popinjay ['pɒpɪndʒeɪ] *n Old-fashioned* fat *m*, freluquet *m*

popish ['pəʊpɪʃ] *adj Pej* papiste

poplar ['pɒplər] *n* (*tree*) peuplier *m*

poplin ['pɒplɪn] *n Tex* popeline *f*

popover ['pɒpəʊvər] *n Culin* beignet *m*

poppadom, poppadum ['pɒpədəm] *n Culin* poppadum *m*

popper ['pɒpər] *n* (**a**) *Br F* (*on clothing, bag etc*) bouton-pression *m*, *pl* boutons-pression (**b**) *F* (*drug*) **poppers** poppers *mpl*

poppet ['pɒpɪt] *n Old-fashioned F* **she's a p.** elle est charmante; **my p.** (*to boy, man*) mon chéri; (*to girl, woman*) ma chérie; (*to boy or girl*) mon (petit) chou

poppet valve *n* soupape *f* en champignon

popping ['pɒpɪŋ] *n* (*of microphone*) saturation *f* acoustique

poppy ['pɒpɪ] *n* (*plant*) pavot *m*; (*flower*) coquelicot *m*; (*worn on Armistice Day*) = coquelicot en papier porté le jour de l'Armistice; **p. (coloured), p. red** rouge coquelicot *inv*; **p. seed** graine(s) *f(pl)* de pavot

poppycock ['pɒpɪkɒk] *n F* bêtises *fpl*, inepties *fpl*

Poppy Day *n Br* anniversaire *m* (du jour) de l'Armistice

Popsicle® ['pɒpsɪk(ə)l] *n Am Culin* ≈ Esquimau® *m*

popsy ['pɒpsɪ] *n Old-Fashioned Br F* pépée *f*, nana *f*

populace ['pɒpjʊləs] *n Fml* **the p.** le peuple, *Pej* la populace

popular ['pɒpjʊlər] *adj* (**a**) (*generally liked*) (*person, action etc*) populaire; (*in vogue*) à la mode, en vogue; (*music, song*) populaire; **to make oneself p.** se rendre populaire (**with** auprès de); **his views have not made him p. with the authorities** à cause de ses opinions, il est mal vu des autorités; **she is p. with her colleagues** elle est très populaire auprès de ses collègues, elle est très appréciée par ses collègues; **this was not a p. decision** cette décision n'était pas populaire

(**b**) (*of or for the people*) populaire, du peuple; **with p. appeal** qui plaît au grand public; **by p. demand** à la demande générale; **contrary to p. belief** contrairement à ce que les gens croient; **p. misconception** idée *f* fausse et très répandue; **p. prices** prix *mpl* à la portée de tous; **to be chosen by p. vote** rencontrer l'adhésion du public; **p. work** *or* **treatise** ouvrage *m* de vulgarisation

Popular Front *n Hist* Front *m* populaire

popularity [pɒpjʊ'lærɪtɪ] *n* popularité *f*; *Com* (*of product etc*) succès *m* auprès du (grand) public; **the president's p. has fallen** *or* **diminished** la popularité du président a baissé; **to experience a rise/fall in p.** voir sa popularité augmenter/baisser; **to grow/decline in p.** devenir plus/moins populaire (**among** parmi); **the sport has gained in p.** le sport est de plus en plus populaire; **p. rating** taux *m* de popularité

popularization [pɒpjʊlərаɪ'zeɪʃən] *n* popularisation *f*; (*of science etc*) vulgarisation *f*

popularize ['pɒpjʊlәraɪz] *vt* (*game, activity, form of music*) populariser; (*knowledge, idea, science etc*) vulgariser; (*method*) propager; (*fashion*) mettre en vogue

popularizer ['pɒpjʊləraɪzər] *n* (*of science, ideas*) vulgarisateur, -trie

popularly ['pɒpjʊləlɪ] *adv* communément, généralement; **p. known as ...** (*of plant etc*) dont le nom vulgaire est ...; (*of person*) familièrement appelé ...; **it is p. believed that ...** les gens croient que ..., il est communément admis que ...

populate ['pɒpjʊleɪt] *vt* peupler; **densely** *or* **thickly populated country** pays très peuplé; **sparsely populated** (*region*) peu densément peuplé

population [pɒpjʊ'leɪʃən] *n* population *f*; **the town has a p. of 85,000** la ville compte 85 000 habitants; **p. census** recensement *m* démographique *ou* de la population; **p. control** contrôle *m* démographique; **p. explosion** explosion *f* démographique; **world p. figures are rising** la population mondiale augmente; **p. statistics** statistique(s) *f(pl)* démographique(s)

populism ['pɒpjʊlɪz(ə)m] *n Pol* populisme *m*

populist ['pɒpjʊlɪst] *Pol* **1** *n* populiste *mf* **2** *adj* populiste

populous ['pɒpjʊləs] *adj* populeux, très peuplé

pop-up *adj* (*toaster*) automatique; **p. book** livre *m* en relief; *Comptr* **p. menu** menu *m* local, menu apparaissant à l'écran sur demande; **p. sunroof** toit *m* ouvrant dépliant

porcelain ['pɔːs(ə)lɪn] *n* porcelaine *f*; **a p. collection** une collection d'objets en porcelaine; **p. manufacturer** porcelainier *m*; **p. plate** assiette *f* en porcelaine; **p. ware** porcelaine

porch [pɔːtʃ] *n* (**a**) (*over door*) porche *m*; (**glass**) **p.** (*of hotel etc*) marquise *f*; **p. roof** auvent *m* (**b**) *Am* (*veranda*) véranda *f*

porcine ['pɔːsaɪn] *adj* porcin, de porc

porcupine ['pɔːkjʊpaɪn] (**a**) (*animal*) porc-épic *m*, *pl* porcs-épics (**b**) **p. fish** poisson-globe *m*, *pl* poissons-globes

pore [pɔːr] *n Anat, Bot etc* pore *m*

▶ **pore over** *vipo* (*examine closely*) (*book*) être plongé dans; (*map, contract*) étudier soigneusement; (*problem*) méditer longuement

pork [pɔːk] *n* (**a**) *Culin* porc *m*; **p. chop** côtelette *f* de porc; **p. pie** pâté *m* de porc en croûte; *Sl* **to tell p. pies** (*tell lies*) raconter des bobards; **p.-pie hat** chapeau *m* de feutre rond à forme aplatie; p. **scratchings** grattons *mpl* (b) *US Pol F* **the p. barrel** = fonds *mpl* alloués par le gouvernement à une circonscription destinés à s'attirer les bonnes grâces des électeurs

porker ['pɔːkər] *n* = jeune porc *m* engraissé, destiné à la boucherie

porky¹ ['pɔːkɪ] *adj F* gras, gros

porky² *n Sl* (*lie*) bobard *m*

porn [pɔːn] *F* **1** *n* pornographie *f*; **soft/hard p.** pornographie soft/hard; **p. dealer** vendeur *m* de matériel pornographique; **p. shop** sex-shop *m*; *Br F* **p. squad** = branche *f* de la police chargée de réprimer la production et la distribution illégales de matériel pornographique **2** *adj* porno *inv*

porno ['pɔːnəʊ] *adj* porno *inv*

pornographer [pɔː'nɒgrəfər] *n* pornographe *mf*

pornographic [pɔːnə'græfɪk] *adj* pornographique; *Fig* indécent

pornography [pɔː'nɒgrəfɪ] *n* pornographie *f*; **p. shop** sex-shop *m*; **p. dealer** vendeur *m* de matériel pornographique

porosity [pɔː'rɒsɪtɪ] *n* porosité *f*

porous ['pɔːrəs] *adj* poreux

porousness ['pɔːrəsnɪs] *n* porosité *f*

porphyry ['pɔːfɪrɪ] *n Miner* porphyre *m*

porpoise ['pɔːpəs] *n* (*animal*) marsouin *m*

porridge ['pɒrɪdʒ] *n* (a) *Culin* bouillie *f* d'avoine, porridge *m*; **p. oats** flocons *mpl* d'avoine (b) *Br Sl* **to do p.** purger sa peine en prison

porringer ['pɒrɪndʒər] *n* écuelle *f*

port¹ [pɔːt] *n* (*harbour, town*) port *m*; **the p. of London** le port de Londres; **in p.** au port; **to put into p.** relâcher; **to call at a p.** faire escale à un port; *prov* **any p. in a storm** (*any place will do*) à la guerre comme à la guerre; **p. to p. shipment** expédition *f* port à port; **p. of arrival** port d'arrivée; **p. of call** port d'escale; *Fig* arrêt *m*; **p. of departure** port de départ; **p. of discharge** port d'arrivée; **p. of entry/embarkation** port de débarquement/d'embarquement; **p. of loading** port d'embarquement; **p. of registry** port d'attache; **p. of refuge** port de refuge; **p. authorities** autorités *fpl* portuaires, administration *f* portuaire; **p. charges** *or* **dues** droits *mpl* de port, frais *mpl* portuaires

port² *n* (a) *Naut* (*opening*) sabord *m*; **p.(-lid)** mantelet *m ou* panneau *m ou* volet *m* de sabord, contre-sabord *m*, *pl* contre-sabords; **air** *or* **ventilation p.** sabord d'aération (b) *Tech* (*of cylinder etc*) orifice *m*, lumière *f*; **admission** *or* **inlet p.** orifice *ou* pipe *f* d'admission (c) *Comptr* port *m*; **input/output p.** port entrée/sortie

port³ *n Naut* **p. (side)** bâbord *m*; **land to p.!** la terre par bâbord!; **on the p. bow** par bâbord devant

port⁴ *n* (*wine*) porto *m*; *Old-fashioned* **p. wine stain** tache *f* de vin

port⁵ *vt Comptr* transférer, transporter

portability [pɔːtə'bɪlɪtɪ] *n* portabilité *f*

portable ['pɔːtəb(ə)l] **1** *adj* portatif, portable; *Fin* (*pension, mortgage*) transférable **2** *n* (*television etc*) téléviseur *m etc* portatif *ou* portable; *Comptr* (ordinateur *m*) portable *m ou* portatif *m*

portage ['pɔːtɪdʒ] *n Fml* (a) (*transport*) (*of goods*) transport *m*, port *m*; (*of canoe etc between waterways*) portage *m* (b) (*costs*) frais *mpl* de port *ou* de transport

Portakabin® ['pɔːtəkæbɪn] *n* = baraquement *m* préfabriqué

portal ['pɔːt(ə)l] *n Archit* (*of cathedral*) portail *m*; *Anat* **p. vein** veine *f* porte

Portaloo® ['pɔːtəluː] *n* toilettes *fpl* provisoires

portcullis [pɔːt'kʌlɪs] *n* (*of castle*) herse *f*, sarrasine *f*

portend [pɔː'tend] *vt Fml* présager, faire pressentir

portent ['pɔːtent] *n Fml* (a) (*sign*) présage *m* (b) (*importance*) portée *f*

portentous [pɔː'tentəs] *adj* (a) (*highly significant*) (*event, happening*) prodigieux; (*ominously so*) de mauvais présage *ou* augure (b) (*solemn*) solennel; *Pej* (*over-serious*) pompeux, pontifiant

portentously [pɔː'tentəslɪ] *adv* solennellement; *Pej* pompeusement

porter¹ ['pɔːtər] *n* (a) *Rail* porteur *m*; (*at hotel*) chasseur *m*, garçon *m*; *Am Rail* (*of sleeper*) garçon (b) *esp Br* (*doorkeeper*) (*of museum etc*) portier *m*, concierge *m*; (*of building*) concierge; **p.'s desk** comptoir *m* du concierge; **p.'s lodge** loge *f* de concierge; (*at entrance to large estate*) maisonnette *f* du portier

porter² *n Br Old-fashioned* (*beer*) bière *f* brune (anglaise), porter *m*

porterage ['pɔːtərɪdʒ] *n* (a) (*carrying*) transport *m*, factage *m* (b) (*cost*) prix *m* de transport, factage *m*

porterhouse ['pɔːtəhaʊs] *n Culin* **p. steak** = châteaubriand *m*

portfolio [pɔːt'fəʊlɪəʊ] *n* (a) (*for documents etc*) serviette *f*; (*for drawings, prints*) carton *m*; **candidates are asked to bring a p. of their recent work** on a demandé aux candidats d'apporter un dossier contenant leurs travaux récents; **minister's p.** portefeuille *m* de ministre; **minister without p.** ministre sans portefeuille (b) *Fin* (*of shares*) portefeuille *m*; **securities in p.** valeurs en portefeuille; **p. management** gestion *f* de portefeuille; *Mktg* **p. mix** portefeuille *m* d'activités

porthole ['pɔːthəʊl] *n Naut* hublot *m*

portico, *pl* **-o(e)s** ['pɔːtɪkəʊ, -əʊz] *n Archit* portique *m*

portion¹ ['pɔːʃən] *n* (a) (*part*) partie *f*; (*of inheritance*) part *f*; *Culin* (*of meat etc*) portion *f*; **this p. to be given up** (*on ticket*) côté *m* à détacher; *Jur* **p. (of inheritance)** part d'héritage; **(marriage) p.** dot *f* (b) *Lit* (*destiny*) destinée *f*, sort *m*

portion² *vt* = **portion out**

▶ **portion out** *vtsep* (*property, sum*) partager, répartir

portliness ['pɔːtlɪnɪs] *n* corpulence *f*

portly ['pɔːtlɪ] *adj* corpulent

portmanteau, *pl* **-eaus, -eaux** [pɔːt'mæntəʊ, -əʊz] *n Old-fashioned* valise *f*; **p. word** mot-valise *m*, *pl* mots-valises

portrait ['pɔːtreɪt] **1** *n Art, Fig* portrait *m*; **to have one's p. painted, to sit for one's p.** se faire peindre; **p. bust** (portrait en) buste *m*; *Typ* **p. format** format *m* portrait; **p. gallery** galerie *f* de portraits; **p. lens** objectif *m* pour portraits; *Typ* **p. mode** mode *m* portrait; **p. painter** portraitiste *mf* **2** *adv* (*to print*) en mode portrait, à la française

portraitist ['pɔːtrətɪst] *n* portraitiste *mf*

portraiture ['pɔːtrətjər] *n* (*art*) (art *m* du) portrait *m*

portray [pɔː'treɪ] *vt* (a) (*depict*) dépeindre, décrire; **in the film the soldiers are portrayed as monsters** dans le film les soldats sont dépeints comme des monstres (b) *Arch, Lit* (*paint portrait of*) faire le portrait de

portrayal [pɔː'treɪəl] *n* (a) (*depiction*) description *f*, peinture *f*; *Th, Cin* (*by actor, actress*) interprétation *f* (b) *Arch, Lit* (*portrait*) portrait *m*

Portugal ['pɔːtjʊg(ə)l] *n* Portugal *m*

Portuguese [pɔːtjʊ'giːz] **1** *adj* portugais; **P. man-of-war** (*jellyfish*) physalie *f*, galère *f* **2** *n* (a) Portugais, -aise (b) *Ling* portugais *m*

POS [piːəʊ'es] *n* (*abbr* **point of sale**) PDV *m*

pose¹ [pəʊz] *n* (a) (*of body*) pose *f*, attitude *f*; (*of model*) pose; **to strike a p.** (*of model*) prendre une pose (b) (*affectation*) pose *f*, affectation *f*; **it's just a p.** c'est juste un air qu'il/elle/*etc* se donne

pose² **1** *vt* (a) *Art* (*model*) faire poser; **to p. sb** faire prendre une pose à qn pour son portrait (b) (*problem*) poser, soulever; (*question, difficulty*) soulever; (*danger*) présenter (**to** pour); **to p. a threat to sth** menacer qch **2** *vi* (*for one's portrait, as model*) poser; (*behave affectedly*) poser, se donner des airs (affectés); **to p. for sb** (*as a model*) poser pour qn; **young men posing in biker jackets** (*affectedly*) des jeunes gens se donnant des airs avec leurs blousons de moto; **to p. as a Frenchman/a socialist** se faire passer pour un Français/un socialiste

poser ['pəʊzər] *n F* (a) *Pej* (*person*) poseur, -euse (b) (*difficult question*) colle *f*; **to give sb a p.** poser une colle à qn

poseur [pəʊ'zɜːr] *n Pej* = **poser (a)**

posh [pɒʃ] *Br F* **1** *adj* (*upper-class*) très comme il faut, *Pej* snob; (*hotel, restaurant*) chic, de luxe; **a p. accent** un accent snob; **a p. area** un quartier chic *ou* bourgeois; **you do look p.!** comme tu fais chic!; **it looks p.** ça fait bien **2** *adv* **to talk p.** parler comme un snob

posit ['pɒzɪt] *vt Phil etc, Fml* (*proposition*) avancer, poser en principe (**that** ... que ... + *ind*)

position¹ [pə'zɪʃən] *n* (a) (*of body*) (*posture etc*) position *f*, posture *f*; **in a horizontal/vertical** *or* **upright p.** en position horizontale/verticale; **in the off/on p.** dans la position arrêt/marche

(b) (*mental attitude*) position *f*, point *m* de vue; **to take up an uncompromising p.** adopter une attitude intransigeante (**about sth** à l'égard de qch); **I have no p. on the matter** je n'ai pas d'idée bien arrêtée sur le sujet; **what is the American p. on this issue?** quelle est la position des Américains sur ce problème?; **her p. is that** ... ce qu'elle pense c'est que ..., son point de vue est que ...; *Pol* **p. paper** déclaration *f* de principe

(c) (*place*) position *f*; (*of object*) place *f*; (*of town etc*) situation *f*; *Banking etc* (*window*) guichet *m*; *Av, Naut* (*of plane, ship*) position; *Mil* emplacement *m*, position; **in p.** en place; **out of p.** déplacé; **to put** *or* **get sth into p.** mettre qch en place; *Av, Naut* **to fix** *or* **work out one's p.** faire le point; **to change the p. of sth** changer qch de position; *Fb* **what p. do you play?** en quelle position jouez-vous?, quelle est votre position sur le terrain?; *Naut* **to take up p. ahead/astern** prendre poste en tête/derrière; *Mil* **to move into p.** se mettre en place *ou* en position; **to bring guns into p.** mettre des pièces en batterie *ou* en position; **p. closed** (*in bank etc*) guichet fermé; **p. finding** orientation *f*; *Mil* goniométrie *f*

(**d**) (*situation*) situation *f*; *Old-fashioned* (*social status*) rang *m* social, condition *f*, état *m*; **to be in an awkward p.** se trouver dans une situation difficile *ou* délicate; **to be in a strong p.** être bien placé; **put yourself in my p.** mettez-vous à ma place; **try to see this from my/their/our p.** essayez de voir ceci de mon/leur/notre point de vue; **to be in a p. to do sth** être à même *ou* en mesure de faire qch; **you're in no p. to criticize** tu es vraiment mal placé pour faire des critiques; **what is the financial p. of the firm?** quelle est la situation financière de la maison?; **to keep up one's p.** (*in society*) tenir son rang; **to be in seventh p.** (*in race etc*) être en septième position; *St Exch* **p. limit** limite *f* de position; *St Exch* **p. taking** prise *f* de position

(**e**) *esp Fml* (*job*) poste *m*, emploi *m*, situation *f*; **to work one's way up to a good p.** se faire une belle situation; **p. of trust** poste *m* de confiance

position² *vt* (**a**) (*place*) (*objects*) mettre en place, placer; (*troops*) mettre en position, poster; **to p. oneself** (*of troops, military observer, police etc*) se poster; (*of spectators*) se placer; **the town is positioned on the top of a basalt rock** la ville est située au-dessus d'un rocher de basalte; **we are well positioned to take advantage of this opportunity** nous sommes bien placés pour tirer parti de cette opportunité (**b**) (*locate*) déterminer la position de (**c**) *Mktg* (*product*) positionner

positioning [pə'zɪʃənɪŋ] *n Mktg* positionnement *m*; *Comptr* **p. macro** macro-commande *f* de position; *Mktg* **p. study** étude *f* de positionnement

positive ['pɒzɪtɪv] **1** *adj* (**a**) (*affirmative*) positif; *Med* **the test was p.** le test était positif; **p. answer** (*yes*) réponse *f* affirmative; (*indicating willingness to do sth*) réponse positive *ou* favorable; **p. proof, proof p.** preuve *f* positive *ou* manifeste; *Med etc* **p. reaction** réaction *f* positive; **there was a tremendously p. response to this idea** cette idée a été extrêmement bien accueillie *ou* reçue; **p. vetting** enquête *f* de sécurité

(**b**) *F* (*for emphasis*) **a p. miracle** un véritable miracle; **it's a p. shame** c'est une véritable honte

(**c**) (*certain*) certain, sûr (**of** de); **I'm p. on that point** je n'ai aucun doute à ce sujet; **I'm p. (that) I saw him** je suis certain *ou* sûr de l'avoir vu; **are you sure? – p.!** tu es sûr? – absolument!

(**d**) (*constructive*) (*person, philosophy*) positif; (*proposition, help*) constructif; **he described the talks as 'p.'** il a décrit les discussions comme 'positives'; **p. thinking** pensée *f* positive; **but on the p. side, ...** mais d'un autre côté, ...

(**e**) *Math, El* positif; *Phot* **p. print** positif *m*, épreuve *f* positive

(**f**) *Gram* **p. degree** (*of adjective, adverb*) degré *m* positif

2 *n* (**a**) **to accentuate the p.** mettre l'accent sur le côté positif des choses

(**b**) *Phot* positif *m*, épreuve *f* positive

(**c**) *Gram* degré *m* positif; **in the p.** à la forme affirmative

positive action *or* **discrimination** *n* = mesures *fpl* anti-discriminatoires en faveur de l'égalité des races et des sexes, *Can* action *f* positive

positively ['pɒzɪtɪvlɪ] *adv* (**a**) (*affirmatively*) positivement; **try to think p. about the situation** essaie de voir la situation d'une manière constructive; **people have responded quite p. to our suggestions** nos suggestions ont été fort bien accueillies; **he had been p. vetted on three occasions** il avait fait l'objet de trois enquêtes de sécurité qui s'étaient avérées satisfaisantes; **the body has been p. identified** le corps a été identifié de façon certaine

(**b**) (*for emphasis*) assurément, certainement, sûrement; **I'm p. convinced it was him** je suis absolument convaincu que c'était lui; *F* **p. not** absolument pas; **smiling? — she was p. beaming!** souriante? — elle était littéralement radieuse!

(**c**) *El* **p. charged** à charge positive; *MecE* **p. driven** à commande directe

positivism ['pɒzɪtɪvɪz(ə)m] *n Phil* positivisme *m*

positivist ['pɒzɪtɪvɪst] *adj, n Phil* positiviste *mf*

posology [pə'sɒlədʒɪ] *n Med* posologie *f*

poss *abbr* **possible**

posse ['pɒsɪ] *n* (*of people*) troupe *f*, bande *f*; *US Hist* (*under sheriff*) = détachement *m* d'hommes aux ordres du shériff

possess [pə'zes] *vt* (**a**) (*property etc*) posséder; (*quality, faculty*) avoir, posséder; **all I p.** tout ce que je possède; *Lit* **to be possessed of a property** posséder un bien (**b**) (*of evil spirit*) posséder; **possessed by fear/rage** pris de terreur/de rage; **what possessed you to do that?** qu'est-ce qui vous a pris de faire cela?; **to be possessed with an idea** être obsédé par une idée; **to scream like one possessed** crier comme un possédé (**c**) *Lit* **to p. oneself in patience** se munir de patience

possession [pə'zeʃən] *n* (**a**) (*ownership*) possession *f*, jouissance *f* (**of** de); **to have sth in one's p.** avoir qch en sa possession; **to be in p. of sth** être en possession de qch; **how did the car come into your p.?** comment la voiture est-elle entrée en votre possession?; **to take p. of an estate, to come** *or* **enter into p. of an estate** entrer en possession *ou* en jouissance d'un bien; **to take** *or* **get p. of sth** (*forcefully*) s'emparer de qch; **the information in my p.** les renseignements dont je dispose; **in full p. of one's faculties** en pleine possession de ses facultés; **he's been arrested for p.** (*of drugs*) il a été arrêté pour détention de drogue; **sorry, p. is nine points** *or* **tenths of the law!** la possession vaut titre; *Fb* **to lose p. of the ball** perdre le ballon; *Sp* **to have p.** être en possession du ballon

(**b**) (*object possessed*) possession *f*; **possessions** possessions, biens *mpl*; (*colonies*) possessions, colonies *fpl*

(**c**) (*by demon*) possession *f*

possessive [pə'zesɪv] **1** *adj* (**a**) (*parent etc*) possessif (**about** avec); **she's very p. about her children** c'est une mère très possessive (**b**) [①A30,8; B19-20,E] *Gram* **p. adjective/pronoun** adjectif *m*/pronom *m* possessif; **the p. case** le cas possessif **2** *n Gram* adjectif *m*/pronom *m* possessif; **the p.** (*case*) le possessif

possessiveness [pə'zesɪvnɪs] *n* possessivité *f* (**about** avec)

possessor [pə'zesər] *n* possesseur *m*

possibility [pɒsɪ'bɪlɪtɪ] *n* (**a**) [①A57-8,c-d; B37,K,2] (*of event*) possibilité *f*, éventualité *f*; **have you considered the p. of his being dead?** avez-vous envisagé la possibilité qu'il soit mort?; **within the range** *or* **the bounds of p.** dans la limite du possible; **there's a p. that it will rain** il est possible qu'il pleuve; **there's a definite** *or* **a strong p. that he'll say yes** il est fort probable qu'il dise oui; **there is little p. that he will win** il n'a guère de chances de gagner, il est peu probable qu'il gagne

(**b**) (*possible event, outcome*) éventualité *f*; **that is a distinct p.** c'est bien possible; **to allow for all possibilities** parer à toute éventualité; **the possibilities are endless!** les possibilités sont innombrables!

(**c**) (*potential*) (*usu pl*) **the plan has possibilities** ce projet offre des chances de succès; **the flat has possibilities** l'appartement a un bon potentiel

possible ['pɒsɪb(ə)l] **1** *adj* possible; **it's p.** c'est possible; **that's quite p.** c'est très *ou* fort possible; **it's just p. that ...** il y a des chances pour que ... + *sub*; **anything's p.** tout est possible; **it is p. that he will come** il est possible *ou* il se peut qu'il vienne; **is it p. to see her?** y a-t-il moyen *ou* est-il possible de la voir?; **as cheap/soon as p.** aussi bon marché/tôt que possible; **the best p.** le meilleur possible; **the shortest p. route** l'itinéraire le plus court possible; **to give as many details as p.** donner le plus de détails possible *ou* tous les détails possibles; **what p. interest can you have in it?** mais quel intérêt cela peut-il donc avoir pour vous?; **there's no p. reason why he should have done it** il n'avait absolument aucune raison de le faire; **if p.** (*I will do it*) si possible; **if it's p. to ...** si c'est possible de ...; **whenever/wherever p.** toutes les fois que/partout où c'est possible; **as far as p.** dans la mesure du possible; **the p. nomination of ...** la nomination éventuelle de ...; **to insure against p. accidents** s'assurer contre les accidents éventuels

2 *n* (**a**) **it's in the realms of the p.** c'est dans le domaine du possible

(**b**) *F* (*candidate*) candidat, -ate possible *ou* acceptable; **only two of the jobs/flats are possibles** seuls deux des emplois/appartements sont à considérer

possibly ['pɒsɪblɪ] *adv* (**a**) **I can't p. do it** je ne peux vraiment pas le faire, il ne m'est vraiment pas possible de le faire; **I'll do all I p. can** je ferai tout mon possible; **you can't p. mean that!** vous ne pouvez pas dire ça sérieusement!; **I can't p. allow you to do that!** je ne peux vraiment pas vous permettre de faire cela!; **they can't p. have left yet!** il est tout à fait impossible qu'ils soient déjà partis!; **it can't p. cost that much!** c'est absolument impossible que ça coûte aussi cher que ça!

(**b**) (*perhaps*) peut-être (bien); **he has p. heard of you** il se peut qu'il ait entendu parler de vous; **p.!** c'est possible, cela se peut; **p. not** peut-être pas

possum ['pɒsəm] *n F* (*animal*) opossum *m*; **to play p.** faire le mort; (*keep low profile*) se tenir coi

post¹ [pəʊst] *n* (**a**) (*of fence*) pieu *m*; (*of frame*) montant *m*; *Constr etc* poteau *m*, pilier *m*; (*of door, window*) montant, jambage *m*; *Fb* poteau; (**bed**) **p.** colonne *f* de lit; (**telegraph**) **p.** poteau télégraphique (**b**) (**starting**) **p.** (poteau *m* de) départ *m*; (**winning**) **p.** (poteau d')arrivée *f*; *Sp, Fig* **to be left**

at the p. rater le départ; *Sp. Fig* **to be beaten** *or F* **pipped at the p.** se faire coiffer *ou* battre sur le poteau

post² *vt* **(a)** (*on wall etc*) (*bills, notice etc*) afficher, placarder, coller; **p. no bills** (*on sign*) défense d'afficher; **to p. prices** afficher des prix **(b)** (*on list*) (*person*) inscrire *ou* porter sur une liste; (*in marine insurance*) (*ship*) porter disparu; **to be posted for night duty** être sur la liste (du personnel) de service de nuit; **to be posted missing** être porté disparu *ou* manquant; *St Exch* **to p. security** déposer des garanties

post³ *n Br* **(a)** (*mail*) courrier *m*; (*service*) poste *f*; **by return of p.** par retour du courrier; **when does the next p. go?** à quelle heure est la prochaine levée?; **to miss the p.** manquer la levée; (*in office*) manquer le courrier; **the first p.** la première distribution; **to catch the p.** poster une lettre/un paquet/*etc* à temps (*pour une levée déterminée*); **there's no p. today** (*no letters for you, no delivery service*) il n'y a pas de courrier aujourd'hui; **to put sth in the p.** mettre qch à la poste; **to send sth by p.** envoyer qch par la poste; **has the p. been yet?** est-ce que le facteur est passé?; **was there any p. for me?** est-ce que j'ai du courrier?
(b) *Hist* **p. (coach)** (malle-)poste *f*, *pl* malles-poste(s)

post⁴ *vt* **(a)** *Br* (*letter*) (*put in the post*) mettre à la poste *ou* à la boîte, poster; (*send*) envoyer par la poste, poster; **I'll p. it to you** je vous l'enverrai par la poste, je vous le posterai **(b)** *Acct* (*in bookkeeping*) passer écriture de; (*in computerized accounts*) valider; **to p. an amount** passer un montant **(c)** *F* **I'll keep you posted** (*informed*) je vous tiendrai au courant

post⁵ *n Mil etc* poste *m*; *US* (*permanent station*) camp *m*, fort *m*; (*garrison*) garnison *f*; **to be/die at one's p.** être/mourir à son poste; **advanced** *or* **outlying p.** (*place, group of men*) poste avancé; **lookout p.** poste de guet *ou* d'observation; **frontier p.** poste frontière

post⁶ *vt* **(a)** (*assign*), *Mil etc* désigner *ou* affecter à un commandement; *Com etc* **to be posted to a different branch** être muté dans une autre succursale; *Mil* **to be posted to a unit/a ship** être affecté à une unité/un navire **(b)** *Mil etc* (*position*) poster, placer; (*guard*) poster, placer, mettre en faction; *Fig* **she posted herself at the window** elle s'est postée à la fenêtre

post⁷ *n Fml* (*job*) poste *m*, emploi *m*; **to take up a p.** commencer un travail, débuter dans un poste, *Fml* entrer en fonction

post⁸ *n Br Mil* (*bugle call*) **first p.** première partie *f* de la sonnerie de la retraite; **last p.** dernière partie (de la sonnerie); (*for the dead*) sonnerie *f* aux morts; **to sound the last p. (over the grave)** jouer la sonnerie aux morts

▶ **post on** *vtsep* (*forward*) faire suivre; **I'll p. your mail on to you** je te ferai suivre ton courrier

postage ['pəʊstɪdʒ] *n* (*for mail*) affranchissement *m*, port *m*; **add 10% (for) p. and packing** ajouter 10% pour les frais d'emballage et d'expédition; **additional p.** (*on insufficiently stamped letter*) surtaxe *f* (postale); **p. paid** port payé; **p. rates** tarifs *mpl* postaux; **p. stamp** timbre(-poste) *m*, *pl* timbres-poste

postal ['pəʊst(ə)l] *adj* postal; *US* **p. card** carte *f* postale; **p. charges, p. rates** (*system of charges*) tarifs *mpl* postaux; **p. charges** (*actually charged*) frais *mpl* d'envoi, port *m*; **p. services** services *mpl* postaux

postal order *n* mandat *m* postal

postbag ['pəʊstbæg] *n esp Br* sac *m* postal; *Rad, TV etc* **our p. has been heavy this week** vous avez été nombreux à nous écrire cette semaine

postbox ['pəʊstbɒks] *n esp Br* boîte *f* aux *ou* à lettres

postcard ['pəʊstkɑːd] *n* carte *f* postale

post chaise [ʃeɪz] *n* chaise *f* de poste

postcode ['pəʊstkəʊd] *n Br* code *m* postal

postdate [pəʊst'deɪt] *vt* postdater

postedit [pəʊst'edɪt] *vt* (*in machine translation*) post-éditer

posted price ['pəʊstɪd] *n* prix *m* affiché

poster ['pəʊstər] *n* affiche *f*; (*decorative*) poster *m*; *Mktg* **p. campaign** campagne *f* d'affichage; *Art* **p. paint** gouache *f*

poste restante ['pəʊstres'tɒnt] *n, adv Br* poste *f* restante

posterior [pɒ'stɪərɪər] **1** *adj Fml* postérieur **(to** à); *Anat* (*towards back of body*) dorsal **2** *n F Hum* (*person's bottom*) postérieur *m*, derrière *m*

posterity [pɒ'sterɪtɪ] *n* postérité *f*; **to preserve sth for p.** garder qch pour la postérité; **p. will remember her as …** elle entrera dans la postérité comme …

postern ['pəʊstɜːn] *n* poterne *f*

postgrad [pəʊst'græd] *n F* = **postgraduate 2**

postgraduate [pəʊst'grædjʊɪt] **1** *adj* (*degree, student, qualifications*) de troisième cycle; (*club*) pour les étudiants de troisième cycle; **p. studies** = (études *fpl* de) troisième cycle *m* **2** *n* (*student*) étudiant, -ante de troisième cycle

posthaste ['pəʊst'heɪst] *adv* en toute hâte

posthumous ['pɒstjʊməs] *adj* (*works*) posthume

posthumously ['pɒstjʊməslɪ] *adv* (*to be awarded a medal*) à titre posthume; (*to publish a book, piece of music etc*) après la mort de l'auteur/du compositeur/*etc*

post-ignition *n* auto-allumage *m*

postil(l)ion [pɒ'stɪlɪən] *n* postillon *m*

postimpressionism [pəʊstɪm'preʃənɪz(ə)m] *n Art* post-impressionnisme *m*

postimpressionist [pəʊstɪm'preʃənɪst] *adj, n Art* post-impressionniste *mf*

postindustrial [pəʊstɪn'dʌstrɪəl] *adj* post-industriel

posting¹ ['pəʊstɪŋ] *n* **(a)** (*in diplomatic service, army*) affectation *f* (*à un poste*); **he had been given a p. as sales manager in Eastern Europe** on l'avait envoyé en Europe de l'Est comme directeur des ventes **(b)** *Com* (*in bookkeeping*) passation *f* (*d'écritures*) **(c)** *Mil* (*of guards*) mise *f* en faction

posting² *n Br* (*putting in the post*) mise *f* à la boîte *ou* à la poste; (*sending by mail*) envoi *m* par la poste; **p. date** date *f* de la poste

Post-it® *n* Post-it® *m*

postman, *pl* **-men** ['pəʊstmən] *n* facteur *m*; **p.'s knock** (*game*) ≈ mariage *m* chinois

postmark¹ ['pəʊstmɑːk] *n* cachet *m* de la poste, (cachet d')oblitération *f*; **date as p.** cachet de la poste faisant foi

postmark² *vt* oblitérer; **the letter was postmarked London** la lettre était timbrée (au départ) de Londres

postmaster ['pəʊstmɑːstər] *n* receveur *m* (des postes); **P. General** *Br Hist* = ministre *m* des Postes et Télécommunications; *Can* Ministre des Postes

post meridiem [mə'rɪdɪəm] *adv Fml* (*in the afternoon*) de l'après-midi; (*in the evening*) du soir

postmistress ['pəʊstmɪstrɪs] *n* receveuse *f* des postes

postmodern [pəʊst'mɒdən] *adj Archit, Art etc* post-moderne

postmodernism [pəʊst'mɒd(ə)nɪz(ə)m] *n Archit, Art etc* post-modernisme *m*

postmodernist [pəʊst'mɒd(ə)nɪst] *adj, n Archit, Art etc* postmoderniste *mf*

postmortem [pəʊst'mɔːtəm] **1** *adj* **p. examination** autopsie *f*; **to hold a p. examination** faire une autopsie **(on** sur) **2** *n* autopsie *f*; *Fig* analyse *f* rétrospective *ou* après coup; *Fig* **please, no postmortems** inutile de revenir sur ce qui est terminé

postnatal [pəʊst'neɪt(ə)l] *adj* post-natal, -als; **p. depression** dépression *f* post-natale *ou* post-partum *f*

post office *n* (bureau *m* de) poste *f*; **The Post Office** (*government department*) ≈ les Postes *fpl* et Télécommunications; **p. account** compte *m* postal; **p. box** boîte *f* postale; **p. cheque** chèque *m* postal; **p. van** ≈ camionnette *f* des PTT

postoperative [pəʊst'ɒpərətɪv] *adj Med* postopératoire

post-paid *adj* port payé

postpartum [pəʊst'pɑːtəm] *n Med* postpartum *m*

postpone [pəʊst'pəʊn] *vt* (*departure, project, decision etc*) remettre, reporter, renvoyer à plus tard; (*deadline*) reculer; *Sp* (*match*) différer, ajourner, remettre; (*payment*) différer; **to p. a matter for a week** remettre *ou* renvoyer une affaire à huitaine; **the meeting is postponed until next week** la réunion a été remise à *ou* ajournée jusqu'à la semaine prochaine

postponement [pəʊst'pəʊnmənt] *n* (*of meeting, decision etc*) report *m*; (*of match, trial*) ajournement *m*

postposition [pəʊstpə'zɪʃən] *n Gram* postposition *f*

postprandial [pəʊst'prændɪəl] *adj usu Hum* après le repas; **to go for a p. stroll** faire une promenade digestive

postproduction [pəʊstprə'dʌkʃən] *n TV* post-production *f*; **p. editing** montage *m* de post-production; **p. mixer** (*video*) mélangeur *m* de post-production; **p. studio** studio *m* de post-production

post-purchase *adj Mktg* post-achat; **p. behaviour** comportement *m* post-achat; **p. dissonance** discordance *f* post-achat

postscript ['pəʊsskrɪpt] *n* **(a)** (*in letter*) post-scriptum *m inv*; **by way of p.** en post-scriptum **(b)** (*in book*) postface *f*; *Fig* (*additional events*) suite *f*

Postscript® **printer** *n* imprimante *f* Postscript

post-sync(h)ing ['pəʊstsɪŋkɪŋ] *n TV etc* post-synchro *f*

post-synchronization *n TV etc* post-sonorisation *f*, post-synchronisation *f*

post-test *n Mktg* post-test *m*

post-traumatic stress disorder *n Med* névrose *f* post-traumatique

postulant ['pɒstjʊlənt] *n Rel* postulant, -ante

postulate¹ ['pɒstjʊlɪt] *n* (*in logic*), *Math* postulat *m*

postulate² ['pɒstjʊleɪt] *vt* **(a)** (*in logic*), *Math* postuler, poser en postulat **(b)** (*put forward existence of*) postuler

posture¹ [ˈpɒstʃər] *n* **(a)** posture *f*, pose *f*, attitude *f*; **to have good p.** avoir une bonne posture, bien se tenir **(b)** *Fig* (*attitude*) attitude *f*, position *f* (**on** en ce qui concerne)
posture² *vi* (*physically*) poser; (*in behaviour, attitude*) (*show off*) se donner des airs; (*adopt position*) (*in negotiations, making threat etc*) user de roublardise
posturing [ˈpɒstʃərɪŋ] *n* (*physical*) poses *fpl*; (*in behaviour, attitude*) (*showing off*) affectation *f*, airs *mpl*; (*of politician, negotiator etc*) roublardise *f*
postwar [ˈpəʊstˈwɔːr] *adj* d'après-guerre; **the p. period** l'après-guerre *m inv*
posy [ˈpəʊzɪ] *n* petit bouquet *m*
pot¹ [pɒt] *n* **(a)** (*receptacle*) pot *m*; (*for cooking*) marmite *f*; (*saucepan*) casserole *f*; *Sp Sl* (*trophy*) coupe *f*; **pots and pans** batterie *f* de cuisine; **a p. of tea** un thé (servi dans une théière); *Prov* **it's (a case of) the p. calling the kettle black** c'est la paille et la poutre; *F* **to go to p.** (*of country, economy*) aller à la ruine; (*of hopes, chances*) tomber en poussière; **his health has gone to p.** sa santé s'est délabrée; **her marriage has gone to p.** ça ne va plus du tout avec son mari; *F* **to take a p. shot at sb/sth** (*fire at*) tirer à l'aveuglette sur qn/qch; *Fig* **I'll take a p. shot at it** je vais tenter ma chance; **he took a p. shot at the answer** il a répondu au petit bonheur (la chance) *ou* au pif; **taking a p. shot, I'd say …** au pif, je dirais …
(b) *F* **pots of…** (*a lot of*) des tas de …; **to have pots of money** rouler sur l'or; **we have pots of time** nous avons tout le temps
(c) *Sl* (*marijuana*) herbe *f*; (*hashish*) hasch *m*
(d) (*kitty*) cagnotte *f*
(e) *F* (*potbelly*) bedon *m*
(f) (*potentiometer*) potentiomètre *m*
pot² **(-tt-) 1** *vt* **(a)** (*butter, salted meat etc*) mettre en pot; (*plant*) mettre en pot, empoter; (*baby*) mettre sur son pot; *Billiards* (*ball*) blouser **(b)** (*shoot*) (*rabbit, pheasant etc*) abattre **2** *vi* (*shoot*) **to p. at** (*rabbit, pheasant etc*) lâcher un coup de fusil à
► **pot on** *vtsep* (*plant*) rempoter
► **pot up** *vtsep* (*plant*) mettre en pot, empoter
potable [ˈpəʊtəb(ə)l] *adj Fml, Hum* potable, buvable
potash [ˈpɒtæʃ] *n* potasse *f*
potassium [pəˈtæsɪəm] *n Ch* potassium *m*; **p. chloride** chlorure *m* de potassium
potato, *pl* **-oes** [pəˈteɪtəʊ, -əʊz] *n* pomme *f* de terre; **to dig up** *or* **lift potatoes** arracher des pommes de terre; *Br* **p. crisps,** *Am* **p. chips** (pommes) chips *fpl*; **p. masher** presse-purée *m inv*; **p. peeler** économe *m*, épluche-légumes *m inv*; **p. salad** salade *f* de pommes de terre
potbellied [pɒtˈbelɪd] *adj F* ventru, bedonnant
potbelly [ˈpɒtbelɪ] *n F* gros ventre *m*, bedaine *f*, bedon *m*
potboiler [ˈpɒtbɔɪlər] *n F* œuvre *f* alimentaire
poteen [pɒˈtiːn] *n* = whisky *m* irlandais distillé en fraude
potency [ˈpəʊtənsɪ] *n* (*of argument*) force *f*, puissance *f*; (*of medicine*) efficacité *f*, puissance; (*of alcoholic drink*) force; **sexual p.** puissance sexuelle
potent [ˈpəʊtənt] *adj* (*drug etc*) efficace, puissant; (*motive etc*) convaincant, décisif; (*argument*) fort, puissant; (*drink*) très fort; (*poison*) violent; (*sexually*) viril
potentate [ˈpəʊtənteɪt] *n* potentat *m*
potential [pəˈtenʃəl] **1** *adj Math etc* potentiel; (*danger*) possible, latent; (*enemy, criminal*) en puissance; (*client*) éventuel; **p. market** marché *m* potentiel; *Gram* **the p. mood** le potentiel; **p. user** utilisateur *m* potentiel
2 *n Phys, El* potentiel *m*; *Gram* **the p.** le potentiel; **human p.** potentiel humain; **to reach** *or* **fulfil one's p.** atteindre son maximum; **to have p.** avoir du potentiel; **the building has a lot of** *or* **considerable p.** le bâtiment offre de grandes possibilités d'aménagement; **this idea has great p.** cette idée ouvre de grandes possibilités; **there is the p. for a major accident** tous les risques d'un grave accident sont réunis
potential energy *n Phys* énergie *f* potentielle
potentiality [pətenʃɪˈælɪtɪ] *n* potentialité *f*
potentially [pəˈtenʃəlɪ] *adv* potentiellement
potentiometer [pətenʃɪˈɒmɪtər] *n* potentiomètre *m*
pother [ˈpɒðər] *n Dial* (*confusion*) agitation *f*, confusion *f*; (*din*) tapage *m*, vacarme *m*
pothole [ˈpɒthəʊl] *n Geol* marmite *f* torrentielle *ou* de géants; (*in road*) nid *m* de poule, fondrière *f*
potholer [ˈpɒthəʊlər] *n* spéléologue *mf*
potholing [ˈpɒthəʊlɪŋ] *n* spéléologie *f*; **to go p.** faire de la spéléologie
pothook [ˈpɒthʊk] *n Culin* crémaillère *f*
pothunter [ˈpɒthʌntər] *n Sp F* coureur, -euse de prix
potion [ˈpəʊʃən] *n* potion *f*; **love p.** philtre *m* d'amour
potluck [pɒtˈlʌk] *n F* **to take p.** choisir au hasard; **it was just p.** c'était un pur hasard; **come round for a meal, but you'll have to take p.** venez manger à la maison, mais ça sera à la fortune du pot
pot plant *n* plante *f* en pot
potpourri [pəʊˈpʊərɪ, -pəˈriː] *n* (*dried flowers*) fleurs *fpl* séchées; *Mus, Liter* pot-pourri *m*, *pl* pots-pourris
pot-roast 1 *n* morceau *m* de viande cuit à l'étouffée **2** *vt* cuire à l'étouffée
potsherd [ˈpɒtʃɜːd] *n Archeol* fragment *m* de poterie
pottage [ˈpɒtɪdʒ] *n Arch* potage *m* (épais); (*with meat and vegetables*) potée *f*; *Bible* **mess of p.** = plat *m* de lentilles
potted [ˈpɒtɪd] *adj Culin* (conservé) en pot, en terrine; *F* (*biography etc*) abrégé, condensé; *Culin* **p. meat** terrine *f* de porc *etc*; **p. palm** palmier *m* en pot; **p. plant** plante *f* verte; *Culin* **p. shrimps** = crevettes *fpl* en conserve cuites dans du beurre
potter¹ [ˈpɒtər] *n Art* potier *m*; **p.'s clay** terre *f* de potier *ou* à potier; **p.'s wheel** tour *m* de potier
potter² *vi Br* **(a)** (*do odd jobs*) bricoler **(b)** (*walk about slowly*) traîner, traînasser; **to p. down to the shops** aller faire un tour dans les magasins
► **potter about, potter around** *vi Br* **(a)** (*do odd jobs*) bricoler; **to p. about at odd jobs** bricoler, faire des petits travaux; **to p. about the house** faire des petits travaux *ou* bricoler dans la maison **(b)** (*move about slowly*) traîner, traînasser; **pottering about in country lanes in her car** en se baladant dans les chemins de campagne au volant de sa voiture
► **potter along** *vi* (*move slowly, work slowly*) (*of person*) aller sans se presser; (*of car*) aller doucement; **he's just pottering along** (*in life*) il va son petit bonhomme de chemin; **he just potters along** (*in job*) il avance tranquillement; **I think I'll p. along to the pub** je crois que je vais aller faire un petit tour au pub
pottery [ˈpɒtərɪ] *n* (*art, place*) poterie *f*; **a piece of p.** une poterie; **some p.** des poteries; **a p. vase** un vase en terre *ou* en poterie
potting shed [ˈpɒtɪŋ] *n* cabane *f* de jardin
potty¹ [ˈpɒtɪ] *adj Br F* (*crazy*) toqué, timbré, dingue; **to go p.** devenir timbré *ou* dingue; **to be p. about sb/sth** être toqué de qn/qch; **you're driving me p.** tu me rends dingue, tu me fais tourner en bourrique
potty² *n* (*in children's language*) pot *m* (de chambre) (*d'enfant*); **to p. train one's child** apprendre à son enfant à être propre *ou* à aller sur le pot; **is she p. trained?** est-ce qu'elle est propre?; **p. training** apprentissage *m* de la propreté
pouch [paʊtʃ] *n* **(a)** (*small bag*) (petit) sac *m*; (*for money*) bourse *f*; (*of dispatch rider, courier*) sacoche *f*; (*for ammunition*) étui *m*; **tobacco p.** blague *f* à tabac **(b)** (*of marsupial*) poche *f* ventrale
pouf(fe) [puːf] *n* (*furniture*) pouf *m*
poult [pəʊlt] *n* (*young chicken*) (jeune) poulet *m*; (*young turkey*) dindonneau *m*; (*young pheasant, partridge*) pouillard *m*
poulterer [ˈpəʊltərər] *n* marchand, -ande de volaille, volailler *m*
poultice [ˈpəʊltɪs] *n Med* cataplasme *m*
poultry [ˈpəʊltrɪ] *n* (*no pl*) volaille *f*; **p. dealer** marchand, -ande de volaille, volailler *m*; **p. farm** élevage *m* de volaille, établissement *m* avicole; **p. farmer** aviculteur, -trice, éleveur, -euse de volaille; **p. farming** aviculture *f*
pounce¹ [paʊns] *n* bond *m*; **to make a p. on** (*of bird, animal*) fondre *ou* s'abattre *ou* bondir sur; *F* (*of person*) se précipiter *ou* se jeter sur
pounce² *vi* **(a)** (*of bird, animal*) bondir, attaquer; **to p. on the prey** fondre *ou* s'abattre *ou* bondir sur la proie **(b)** *F* (*of person*) se précipiter, se jeter (**on** sur); (*of police etc*) faire une descente (**on** sur); *Fig* **he pounced on her mistake** il a sauté sur son erreur; **to p. on an opportunity** saisir une chance à la volée; **when the shares are low, we'll p.** quand les actions auront baissé, nous attaquerons
pound¹ [paʊnd] *n* [①A12,1,h,ii] **(a)** (*measurement of weight*) livre *f* (= 453, 6 grammes); **to sell sth by the p.** vendre qch à la livre; **40 pence a p.** quarante pence la livre; *Fig* **to demand one's p. of flesh from sb** exiger son dû de qn; *Culin* **p. cake** quatre-quarts *m inv* **(b)** (*currency unit*) **p. (sterling)** livre *f* (sterling); **p. coin** pièce *f* d'une livre; **p. note** billet *m* d'une livre; **p. sign** signe *m* de la livre (sterling), signe livre
pound² *n* (*for stray animals, cars*) fourrière *f*
pound³ *vt Jur* saisir
pound⁴ 1 *vt* (*crush etc*) (*stones etc*) broyer, piler, concasser; (*salt, sugar, drug*) piler, broyer; (*lumps of earth*) casser, briser; (*earth*) pilonner; (*person*) (*with fists*) battre, rosser; (*in competition*) mettre la pâtée à; *Mil* (*position*) pilonner, marteler; **to p. sth to pieces** réduire qch en miettes *ou* en

morceaux; **to p. sb into submission** s'acharner sur qn jusqu'à ce qu'il se soumette; **to p. the beat** (*of policeman*) patrouiller; **you'll be back to pounding the beat** (*demoted*) on vous remettra à la circulation; **to p. the streets** battre le trottoir

2 *vi* frapper *ou* taper dur; (*of heart*) battre à grands coups; (*of drum, music*) résonner; **to p. at** *or* **on sth** cogner dur sur qch; **to p. on the door** donner de grands coups sur la porte; **the waves pounded against the shore** les vagues s'abattaient *ou* se brisaient sur le rivage; **feet were heard pounding on the stairs** on entendait des pas résonner lourdement dans l'escalier; **she pounded down the road after them** elle s'élança derrière eux sur la route

▶ **pound along** *vi* **they're really pounding along** ils vont à fond de train; **he was pounding along after them** ils les poursuivait à toute allure

▶ **pound away** *vi* (*of waves*) se briser (**at, against** sur); **we heard the guns pounding away** nous entendions le bruit incessant des canons; **the guns pounded away at their position** les canons pilonnaient sans relâche leur position; **he sat pounding away at the piano** il martelait le piano, il jouait du piano comme un forcené; **he was pounding away at the typewriter** il tapait comme un fou sur la machine à écrire

poundage ['paʊndɪdʒ] *n* (**a**) (*weight*) poids *m* en livres (**b**) (*tax, commission*) taxe *f*/commission *f* proportionnelle au poids/à la valeur

-pounder ['paʊndər] *suff* **two/three-p.** (*fish*) poisson de deux/de trois livres (de poids); *Mil* **thirty-p.** canon *m ou* pièce *f* de trente

pounding ['paʊndɪŋ] *n* (*of heart*) battement *m* frénétique; (*of drums*) battement; **the p. of the waves** le martellement des vagues; **to take a p.** (*of boat*) être fortement secoué; (*of troops, city etc*) être pilonné; *Fig* (*of team etc*) être battu à plate(s) couture(s); *Fig* **the economy has taken quite a p.** l'économie a subi des coups de boutoir; *Fig* **the franc took a p.** le franc a été attaqué

pour [pɔːr] **1** *vt* verser (**into** dans); *Metal* couler; **to p. sb a drink** verser un verre à qn; **p. the water down the sink** versez l'eau dans l'évier; *Fig* **the government poured money into the industry** le gouvernement a investi des sommes énormes dans l'industrie; *Fig* **she looked as if she'd been poured into her jeans** elle portait un jean extrêmement moulant

2 *vi* (**a**) **it's pouring (with rain), the rain's pouring down** il pleut à verse, la pluie tombe à torrents; **there were tears pouring down her cheeks** son visage était baigné de larmes; **blood was pouring from the cut on her forehead** le sang s'écoulait en abondance de l'entaille qu'elle avait au front; **the sunlight poured into the room** les rayons du soleil inondaient la pièce; **water was pouring into the cellar** l'eau entrait à flots dans la cave; **sweat was pouring off him** il ruisselait de sueur; **reinforcements poured in to the area** des renforts sont arrivés en masse dans la région; **tourists were pouring into the palace** les touristes entraient en foule dans le palais

(**b**) **this jug doesn't pour well** ce broc ne verse pas bien; **shall I p.?** puis-je faire le service?

▶ **pour down** *vi* (*of rain*) tomber à verse; **it's been pouring down for days** il pleut à verse depuis des jours et des jours

▶ **pour in 1** *vi* (*of water*) se déverser, entrer à flots; **the crowd came pouring in** on entrait à flots *ou* en foule; **invitations came pouring in** ça a été une avalanche d'invitations **2** *vtsep* (*liquid*) verser; *Fig* **the government poured money in** le gouvernement a investi des sommes énormes

▶ **pour off** *vtsep* vider

▶ **pour out 1** *vi* (*of water*) se déverser, sortir à flots; (*of people*) sortir en foule; **smoke was pouring out of the window** des nuages de fumée s'échappaient de la fenêtre; **the words just poured out** les mots sont sortis en flots; **all his feelings came pouring out** il a laissé libre cours à ses émotions

2 *vtsep* (*tea, coffee etc*) verser; (*anger, feelings*) donner libre cours à; (*of chimney*) (*clouds of smoke*) cracher, vomir; *Fig* **he poured out all his frustrations to me** il m'a déballé toutes ses frustrations; **to p. out a torrent of abuse at sb** déverser un torrent d'injures sur qn; **she poured out her feelings to me** elle m'a ouvert son cœur; **Japanese products are being poured out onto the market** les produits japonais arrivent sur le marché à flots continus

pouring ['pɔːrɪŋ] *adj* (*rain*) torrentiel

pout¹ [paʊt] *n* moue *f*

pout² *vi* faire la moue; (*sulk*) bouder; **her pouting lips** ses lèvres boudeuses

pouter ['paʊtər] *n* **p. (pigeon)** pigeon *m* boulant

POV [piːəʊ'viː] *n TV, Cin* (*abbr* **point of view**) angle *m* du regard

poverty ['pɒvətɪ] *n* (**a**) pauvreté *f*; **extreme** *or* **abject p.** misère *f*; **to live in p.** vivre dans la gêne *ou* (*stronger*) la misère; **to be caught in the p. trap** = perdre des avantages sociaux à cause d'une augmentation de revenus (**b**) (*lack*) (*of food etc*) disette *f*, manque *m*, pénurie *f*; (*poor quality*) (*of soil*) pauvreté *f*; **p. of ideas** pénurie *f* d'idées

poverty line *n* seuil *m* de pauvreté; **to live below the p.** vivre en-dessous du seuil de pauvreté

poverty-stricken *adj* (*person*) indigent, réduit à la misère; (*dwelling, area etc*) misérable; **a. p. country** un pays souffrant de la misère

POW [piːəʊ'dʌb(ə)ljuː] *n* (*abbr* **prisoner of war**) P.G. *m*

powder¹ ['paʊdər] *n* poudre *f*; (*gunpowder*) poudre, explosif *m*; **to reduce sth to p.** réduire qch en poudre, pulvériser qch; *Fig* (*destroy*) réduire qch en poussière *ou* en miettes; (**face**) **p.** poudre (de riz); *Am Sl* **to take a p.** (*disappear*) ficher le camp; **p. blue** (*colour*) bleu clair *inv*

powder² *vt* (**a**) (*cake etc*) saupoudrer (**with** de); **landscape powdered with snow** paysage saupoudré de neige; **to p. one's face** se poudrer (le visage); *F Euph* **to go and p. one's nose** aller se laver les mains (**b**) (*convert to powder*) (*milk etc*) réduire en poudre

powder compact *n* poudrier *m*

powdered ['paʊdəd] *adj* (**a**) (*milk etc*) en poudre; (*coal etc*) pulvérisé; **in p. form** sous forme de poudre (**b**) (*face*) poudré

powder keg *n* baril *m* de poudre; *Fig* poudrière *f*

powder puff *n* houppe *f*, houppette *f*

powder room *n Euph* (*in hotel etc*) toilettes *fpl* pour dames

powdery ['paʊd(ə)rɪ] *adj* poudreux; (*crumbly*) friable

power¹ ['paʊər] *n* (**a**) *Pol etc* (*authority, control*) pouvoir *m*, autorité *f*; **to come (in)to p.** arriver au pouvoir; **to be in/out of p.** être/ne pas être au pouvoir; **to lose p.** perdre le pouvoir; **the party in p.** le parti au pouvoir; **to be voted into/out of p.** être nommé au pouvoir/chassé du pouvoir par un vote; **to be in sb's p.** être à la merci de qn; *also Fig* **to be the real p. behind the throne** tirer les ficelles; *also Hum* **the powers that be** les autorités *fpl*; *Rel* **the powers of darkness** les puissances des ténèbres; **to have sb in one's p.** avoir qn à sa merci; **absolute/executive/legislative p.** pouvoir absolu/exécutif/législatif; **they constitute Le Pen's p. base** ils constituent le groupe d'où Le Pen tire son pouvoir; **p. structure** structure *f* du pouvoir; **p. struggle** lutte *f* de pouvoir

(**b**) (*capacity*) pouvoir *m*; **to have the p. to do sth** avoir le pouvoir *ou* la faculté de faire qch; **I'll do everything in my p.** je ferai tout ce qui est en mon pouvoir *ou* tout mon possible; **it is beyond my p.** ce n'est pas en mon pouvoir; **to be at the height** *or* **peak of one's powers** être à l'apogée de sa puissance; **her powers were failing her** les forces lui manquaient; **mental** *or* **intellectual powers** facultés *fpl* intellectuelles; **man of great mental** *or* **intellectual powers** homme doté de grandes facultés intellectuelles; *Phys, Ch* **p. of absorption** capacité *f* d'absorption; **p. of observation** facultés d'observation; **the p. of reason** (*faculty*) la raison; (*strength, force*) la puissance de la raison; **the p. of speech** (*faculty*) la parole; (*force*) le pouvoir de la parole; **powers of concentration** facultés de concentration; **powers of persuasion** dons *mpl* de persuasion

(**c**) (*physical strength*) force *f*, puissance *f*; *F* **more p. to your elbow!** allez-y!

(**d**) (*nation etc*) puissance *f*; **sea/air/industrial/nuclear/world p.** (*country*) puissance maritime/aérienne/industrielle/nucléaire/mondiale; **the great powers** (*countries*) les grandes puissances

(**e**) *F* **that'll do you a p. of good** ça vous fera énormément de bien

(**f**) *Jur* procuration *f*, mandat *m*, pouvoir *m*; *Jur* **p. of attorney** procuration; **to give sb p. of attorney** donner procuration à qn; **p. of life and death** droit *m* de vie et de mort; *Jur* **delegation of powers** délégation *f* de pouvoirs; *Jur* **to furnish sb with full powers** donner pleins pouvoirs à qn; **to act with full powers** agir de pleine autorité; **the police have been given greater powers** la police a reçu des pouvoirs plus importants

(**g**) (*electricity*) courant *m*; **nuclear/wind/hydroelectric p.** énergie *f* nucléaire/éolienne/hydroélectrique; **to shut off/turn on the p.** couper/mettre le courant

(**h**) *Tech* (*of machine etc*) puissance *f*; (*of magnet*) force *f*; *MecE etc* **full p.** puissance maximale; *Aut* **p. box** (*for airbag*) boîtier *m* d'alimentation; *Aut* **p. brakes** freins *mpl* assistés; *MecE* **p. driven** à propulsion mécanique; *Aut* **p. stroke** temps *m* explosion *ou* détente; **p. unit** ensemble *m* moteur-boîte, groupe *m* propulseur, dispositif *m* d'alimentation *ou* de puissance

(i) *Math* (*of a number*) puissance *f*; **three to the p. of ten** trois (à la) puissance dix

power² **1** *vt* (*provide with power*) (*machine*) actionner, faire marcher; (*propel*) propulser; **powered by two engines** actionné par deux moteurs **2** *vi F* (*move fast*) **he powered round the bend** il avala la courbe à toute allure; **she powered into the lead** elle accélèra et prit la tête de la course; **the rocket powered up into the sky** la fusée filait de toute sa puissance vers les étoiles

▶ **power down** **1** *vtsep* mettre hors tension **2** *vi* (*of computer, machine*) se mettre hors tension

▶ **power up** **1** *vtsep* mettre sous tension **2** *vi* (*of computer, machine*) se mettre sous tension

power-assisted [ˈpaʊərəsɪstɪd] *adj Aut* (*steering*) assisté

power cut *n* panne *f* de courant

power-down *n Comptr* mise *f* hors tension

power dressing *n* **she goes in for p.** elle s'habille pour donner une image imposante

-powered [ˈpaʊəd] *suff* **nuclear-p.** à propulsion atomique *ou* nucléaire

power failure *n* panne *f* de courant

powerful [ˈpaʊəfʊl] **1** *adj* **(a)** puissant; (*blow*) grand; (*argument, incentive*) puissant, de poids; (*language, prose style*) vigoureux, qui a de l'impact; (*music, passage*) puissant, plein de vigueur; (*speaker, actor*) qui a de la présence, qui en impose; **to become more p.** (*of State, ruler*) devenir plus puissant; (*of hurricane etc*) augmenter en puissance; **p. dose** (*of drug*) forte dose; **a p. new novel/film** un nouveau roman/film très puissant *ou* fort; **a p. image** une image chargée de force, une image-choc; **there's a p. smell of cats in here** ça pue les chats ici

(b) *Old-fashioned F* **a p. lot of ...** un tas de ...

2 *adv esp US F* **I was p. tired** j'étais rudement fatigué

powerfully [ˈpaʊəfʊlɪ] *adv* puissamment; (*influenced, affected*) fortement; (*to argue*) vigoureusement; **p. built** (*man*) à forte carrure; **it smells p. of cabbage** ça sent le chou à plein nez

powerhouse [ˈpaʊəhaʊs] *n El* centrale *f* électrique; *F* (*person*) personne *f* vigoureuse et dynamique; **she's the p. of the organization** c'est le moteur de l'organisation; **he's a p. of new ideas** il ne tarit pas d'idées nouvelles

powerless [ˈpaʊəlɪs] *adj* impuissant; **in a p. state** dans un état d'impuissance totale; **p. to act** impuissant à agir; **I am p. to help you** je ne peux *ou Fml* puis rien faire pour vous aider

power line *n* ligne *f* électrique

power lunch *n* déjeuner *m* d'affaires où l'on parle gros sous

power outage *n US* rupture *f* de l'alimentation

power pack *n* bloc *m* d'alimentation

power plant *n* centrale *f* électrique; *Aut* (*engine*) groupe *m* moteur

power point *n* prise *f* de courant

power station *n* centrale *f* électrique

power steering *n Aut* direction *f* assistée

power strike *n* grève *f* des employés de l'électricité

power supply *n* alimentation *f* (électrique)

power tool *n* outil *m* électrique

powertrain [ˈpaʊətreɪn] *n Aut* groupe *m* motopropulseur

power-up *n* (*of computer, machine*) mise *f* sous tension; **on p.** à la mise sous tension

power user *n* gros utilisateur *m*

powwow¹ [ˈpaʊwaʊ] *n* (*of American Indians*) assemblée *f*; *F* (*talk, discussion*) palabre *f*, discussion *f*

powwow² *vi* (*of American Indians*) tenir une assemblée; *F* (*talk*) palabrer; *F* **to p. about sth** discuter de qch

pox [pɒks] *n Med F* **the p.** la vérole; *Arch* **a p. on ...!** maudit soit ...!/maudits soient ...!

poxy [ˈpɒksɪ] *adj Sl* (*worthless*) merdique; (*unpleasant*) dégueulasse

pp¹ [piːˈpiː] (*abbr* **per procurationem**) **1** *adv* **pp Jane Smith** p.p. Jane Smith **2** *vt* **shall I pp it?** est-ce que je signe à votre/sa place?

pp² (*abbr* **pages**) pp.; **see pp. 44–47** voir pp. 44 à 47

p & p [piːənˈpiː] *n Br Com* (*abbr* **postage and packing**) port *m* et emballage

PPD [piːpiːˈdiː] *Com* (*abbr* **prepaid**) port payé par le destinataire

PPE [piːpiːˈiː] *n Univ* (*abbr* **philosophy, politics and economics**) études *fpl* de philosophie, sciences politiques et économie

pps [piːpiːˈes] *n* (*abbr* **post postscriptum**) pps

PQ [piːˈkjuː] *n Can* **(a)** *abbr* **Province of Quebec** **(b)** *abbr* **Parti québécois**

PR [piːˈɑːr] *n* **(a)** (*abbr* **public relations**) relations *fpl* publiques, R.P. *fpl*; **we need better PR** il nous faut améliorer nos relations publiques; **a skilful PR man** un homme qui excelle dans les relations publiques; **PR company** entreprise *f* de relations publiques **(b)** *Pol* (*abbr* **proportional representation**) R.P. *f*

practicability [præktɪkəˈbɪlɪtɪ] *n* faisabilité *f*; (*of road etc*) praticabilité *f*

practicable [ˈpræktɪkəb(ə)l] *adj* **(a)** (*feasible*) faisable, réalisable; **as far as is p.** autant que possible **(b)** (*road, ford*) praticable

practical [ˈpræktɪk(ə)l] **1** *adj* **(a)** (*mind, solution, clothing, appliance*) pratique; (*proposition*) réalisable; **he's very p.** il a l'esprit pratique; **we must be p.** il faut que nous soyons raisonnables; **the p. thing to do would be to ...** il serait raisonnable de ...; **I know it's a very boring and p. question** je sais que c'est une question très ennuyeuse et pragmatique; **for all p. purposes** en fin de compte; **of no p. use** *or* **value** inutilisable dans la pratique; **p. application** (*of theory etc*) mise *f* en pratique; (*of invention etc*) réalisation *f* (pratique); *Sch* **p. work** travaux *mpl* pratiques

(b) (*virtual*) **with p. unanimity** d'un consentement presque unanime; **it's a p. certainty** c'est quasiment certain

2 *n Sch* (*lesson*) travaux *mpl* dirigés *ou* pratiques; (*examination*) épreuve *f* pratique

practicality [præktɪˈkælɪtɪ] *n* **(a)** (*feasibility*) aspect *m* pratique, caractère *m* pratique **(b)** (*of person*) sens *m ou* esprit *m* pratique **(c)** **practicalities** (*details*) détails *mpl ou* aspects *mpl* pratiques

practical joke *n* farce *f*

practical joker *n* farceur, -euse

practically [ˈpræktɪklɪ] *adv* **(a)** (*based*) sur la pratique; (*useful*) dans la pratique, en pratique; **to be p. minded** avoir un esprit pratique, avoir du sens pratique; **p. speaking** en pratique **(b)** (*almost*) pour ainsi dire, pratiquement; **there has been p. no snow** il n'y a presque *ou* pratiquement pas eu de neige; **p. the whole of the audience** la quasi-totalité de l'auditoire; **we're p. there** nous y sommes presque, nous sommes pratiquement arrivés

practice¹ [ˈpræktɪs] *n* **(a)** (*action*) pratique *f*; **to put one's ideas into p.** mettre ses idées en pratique; **in p.** en *ou* dans la pratique

(b) (*of profession etc*) exercice *m*; (*of doctor etc*) (*surgery*) cabinet *m*; (*patients*) clientèle *f*; (*of solicitor*) étude *f*; **to be in p.** (*of doctor etc*) exercer; **to set up in** *or* **go into p.** commencer à exercer

(c) (*custom*) coutume *f*, usage *m*; *Ind etc* technique *f*, méthodes *fpl*; **to make a p. of doing sth** se faire une habitude *ou* une règle de faire qch; **it's the usual p.** c'est l'usage; **in hospitals it's standard p. to throw needles away** dans les hôpitaux, la règle est de jeter les seringues usagées; **it's good/bad p. to do this** il est conseillé *ou* recommandé/déconseillé de faire cela

(d) (*exercise, training*) exercice(s) *m(pl)*; *Sp etc* entraînement *m*; **it takes years of p.** cela demande des années de pratique *ou Sp etc* d'entraînement; **I don't get much p.** (*at driving, playing sport, music etc*) je ne m'exerce pas souvent; **I need more p.** j'ai besoin de plus de pratique *ou Sp etc* de m'entraîner davantage; **to do 2 hours' p. a day** s'entraîner *ou* s'exercer deux heures par jour; **to keep in p.** continuer à s'exercer; *Sp* se maintenir en forme; **I have to get back into p.** il faut que je m'y remette; **to get out of p.** perdre l'habitude *ou* la main, se rouiller; **I'm out of p.** je manque de pratique; *Sp* **Alain Prost did 3.25 in p.** Alain Prost a fait 3 mn. 25 aux essais; **he refuses to do his piano p.** il refuse de travailler son piano; *Prov* **p. makes perfect** c'est en forgeant qu'on devient forgeron; *Sp* **p. match** match *m* d'entraînement

practice² *vti US* = **practise**

practiced, practicing *adj US* = **practised, practising**

practise, *US* **practice** [ˈpræktɪs] **1** *vt* **(a)** (*carry out*) (*witchcraft, self-denial etc*) pratiquer; (*method*) suivre; (*principle etc*) mettre en pratique *ou* en action; **to p. what one preaches** mettre en pratique ce que l'on prêche; **to p. a custom** suivre une coutume

(b) (*work at*) (*profession*) pratiquer, exercer; (*medicine*) exercer; *Jur* **to p. law** exercer le métier de notaire/d'avocat; **he studied law/medicine, but never practised it** il a étudié le droit/la médecine, mais n'a jamais exercé

(c) (*do exercises etc on*) (*the piano, flute etc*) travailler, s'exercer à; *Tennis, Billiards etc* (*shot*) s'exercer à; **to p. one's backhand** travailler son revers; *Mus* **to p. one's scales** faire des gammes; **to p. one's French** pratiquer son français (**on sb** avec qn)

2 *vi* **(a)** (*of doctor, lawyer*) exercer

(b) (*do exercises etc*) s'exercer; *Sp* s'entraîner

practised, *US* **practiced** [ˈpræktɪst] *adj* (*teacher, nurse, speaker etc*) experimenté; (*ear, eye*) exercé; *Pej* (*charm*) étudié, compassé; **with a p. hand** d'une main exercée *ou* habile; **with p. ease** avec une grande aisance; **p. in the arts of seduction/deception** rompu aux arts de la séduction/tromperie

practising, *US* **practicing** ['præktɪsɪŋ] *adj* (*doctor, solicitor etc*) en exercice; (*Christian, Catholic*) pratiquant; **a p. homosexual** un homosexuel actif, une homosexuelle active
practitioner [præk'tɪʃənər] *n Fml* praticien, -ienne; **a skilled p. of acupuncture/osteopathy** un acupuncteur/ostéopathe exercé
praetorian [priː'tɔːrɪən] *adj Hist, Fig* **p. guard** garde *f* prétorienne
pragmatic [præg'mætɪk] *adj* pragmatique
pragmatism ['prægmətɪz(ə)m] *n* pragmatisme *m*
pragmatist ['prægmətɪst] *n* pragmatiste *mf*
prairie ['preərɪ] *n* (*North American*) prairie *f*; **the Prairies** les Prairies; **p. dog** chien *m* de prairie; **p. oyster** œuf *m* cru assaisonné; **p. wolf** coyote *m*
praise[1] [preɪz] *n* (*deserved*) éloge(s) *m(pl)*, louange(s) *f(pl)*; (*adulatory or in worship*) louange(s); **in p. of sb/sth** à la louange de qn/qch; **to be full of p. for sb/sth** ne pas tarir d'éloges sur qn/qch; **to sing the praises of sth/sb** chanter *ou* célébrer les louanges de qch/qn; **to sing one's own praises** chanter ses propres louanges, faire son propre éloge; **I have nothing but p. for him** je n'ai rien pour lui que des éloges *ou* louanges; **she deserves special p.** elle mérite tous les éloges *ou* toutes les louanges; **his conduct is beyond all p.** sa conduite est au-dessus de tout éloge; *Arch* **p. be (to God)!** Dieu soit loué!
praise[2] *vt* louer, faire l'éloge de; **to p. sb to the skies** porter qn aux nues; **to p. God** louer *ou* glorifier Dieu
praiseworthiness ['preɪzwɜːðɪnɪs] *n* mérite *m*, valeur *f*
praiseworthy ['preɪzwɜːðɪ] *adj* digne d'éloges, louable, méritoire; **that was very p. of you** c'est très louable de votre part
praline ['prɑːliːn] *n Culin* **(a)** (*filling*) pralin *m* **(b)** (*sweet*) (*almond*) amande *f* pralinée, praline *f*
pram [præm] *n Br* landau *m*, voiture *f* d'enfant
prance [prɑːns] *vi* **(a)** (*of horse*) caracoler; **prancing horse** cheval fringant **(b)** (*of person*) (*to strut*) se pavaner; (*to skip*) avancer en sautillant; **to p. in/out** entrer/sortir en se pavanant/en sautillant; **she pranced in and calmly announced that ...** elle est entrée d'un pas dégagé et a annoncé calmement que ...
▶ **prance about** *vi* (*of horse*) caracoler; (*of person*) se pavaner
prang[1] [præŋ] *n Br F* **to have a p.** (*in car*) avoir un accrochage
prang[2] *vt Br F* (*aeroplane, car*) amocher
prank [præŋk] *n* (*escapade*) frasque *f*, fredaine *f*; (*practical joke*) tour *m*, farce *f*; **to get up to all sorts of pranks** faire les cent coups; **to play pranks on sb** jouer des tours à qn, faire des farces à qn
prankster ['præŋkstər] *n* farceur, -euse
prat [præt] *n Br Sl* (*idiot*) andouille *f*, imbécile *mf*; **I feel like a right p.** j'ai vraiment l'air d'une andouille *ou* d'un imbécile
prate [preɪt] *vi Pej* (*self-importantly*) débiter des niaiseries *ou* des absurdités; (*chatter*) jaser, bavarder
pratfall[1] ['prætfɔːl] *n Am* **to do a p.** tomber sur les fesses; *Fig* se planter
prattle[1] ['præt(ə)l] *n* (*of children*) babil *m*, babillage *m*; (*of busybodies*) bavardage *m*, papotage *m*
prattle[2] *vi* (*talk nonsense*) (*of child*) babiller; (*of adult*) jacasser; (*converse*) bavarder, papoter **(to** avec**)**; **they never stop prattling to one another about ...** ils n'arrêtent pas de bavarder *ou* de papoter ensemble à propos de ...
prawn [prɔːn] *n* crevette *f* rose; (*bigger*) bouquet *m*; **Dublin Bay p.** langoustine *f*; *Culin* **p. cocktail** crevettes *fpl* à la mayonnaise; **p. crackers** beignets *mpl* de crevettes
pray [preɪ] **1** *vi* **(a)** prier; **to p. to God** prier Dieu; **to p. for sb** prier pour qn; **to p. for** (*peace, person's safety etc*) prier pour; **they're praying for a child** ils prient pour avoir un enfant; **to p. for rain/good weather** prier pour qu'il pleuve/ pour qu'il fasse beau; **to p. for sb's soul** prier pour (le repos de) l'âme de qn; **I've been praying for you to say that** j'espérais de tout mon cœur que tu dises cela; *F* **he's past praying for** il est perdu
(b) *Arch* **p. be seated** veuillez (bien) vous asseoir; *Lit, Iron* **and what, p., would you have me say?** et que voudrais-tu donc que je dise?; *Lit, Iron* **and what, p., would you suggest I do?** et que suggèrerais-tu donc que je fasse?
2 *vt* **I prayed that they wouldn't hear me** j'ai prié pour qu'ils ne m'entendent pas; **I p. we are on time** je prie pour que nous arrivions à l'heure
prayer [preər] *n* prière *f*; **p. for the dead** prière pour les morts; **to say one's prayers** faire *ou* dire *ou* réciter ses prières; *Sch* **prayers** la prière du matin en commun; *Church of Eng* **Morning/Evening P.** office *m* du matin/du soir; **his p. was granted** sa prière a été exaucée; **they knelt in p.** ils se sont agenouillés pour prier; **his head was bowed in p.** sa tête était inclinée dans une prière; *F* **he doesn't have a p.** il n'a aucune chance; **p. beads** chapelet *m*; **p. book** livre *m* de messe, missel *m*; **p. mat/wheel** tapis *m*/moulin *m* à prières; **p. meeting** réunion *f* pour prières en commun
praying ['preɪɪŋ] **1** *adj* en prières **2** *n* prière(s) *f(pl)*
praying mantis *n* mante *f* religieuse
pre- [priː] *pref* pré-
preach [priːtʃ] **1** *vi* prêcher; **to p. to sb** prêcher qn; *Fig* **to p. to the converted** prêcher un converti; **to p. against sb** prêcher contre qn; *Fig F* **he's always preaching at me** il est toujours à me faire la leçon *ou* à me sermonner; **stop preaching!** arrête ton sermon! **2** *vt* (*sermon*) prononcer; **to p. a new doctrine** prêcher une doctrine nouvelle; **she preaches austerity and lives in luxury** elle prêche l'austérité mais elle vit dans le luxe
preacher ['priːtʃər] *n* prédicateur *m*; *US* (*clergyman*) pasteur *m*; *Fig Pej* prêcheur, -euse; **he's a poor p.** il prêche mal
preachify ['priːtʃɪfaɪ] *vi F Pej* faire la morale
preaching ['priːtʃɪŋ] **1** *adj* prêcheur **2** *n* prédication *f*; *Fig Pej* sermons *mpl*
preachy ['priːtʃɪ] *adj F Pej* prêcheur, sermonneur
preamble [priː'æmb(ə)l] *n* **(a)** *Fml* (*to legal text*) préambule *m*; (*of book*) introduction *f*, préface *f*; (*of treaty*) préliminaires *mpl*; (*to speech*) préambule, entrée *f* en matière **(b)** *Jur* (*of bill*) exposé *m*
preamplifier [priː'æmplɪfaɪər] *n* préamplificateur *m*
prearrange [priːə'reɪndʒ] *vt* arranger au préalable *ou* d'avance; **at a prearranged signal** sur un signal convenu
prebend ['prebənd] *n Rel* (*stipend*) prébende *f*; (*person*) prébendier *m*
prebendary ['prebənd(ə)rɪ] *n Rel* prébendier *m*
prebilling [priː'bɪlɪŋ] *n Acct* préfacturation *f*
pre-board *vt* (*unaccompanied children etc*) pré-embarquer
precarious [prɪ'keərɪəs] *adj* précaire; **to make a p. living** gagner sa vie précairement; **a p. life** une vie précaire
precariously [prɪ'keərɪəslɪ] *adv* précairement; **p. balanced** dans un équilibre précaire
precariousness [prɪ'keərɪəsnɪs] *n* précarité *f*
precast ['priːkɑːst] *adj* (*concrete*) prémoulé
precaution [prɪ'kɔːʃən] *n* (*act*) précaution *f*; (*attitude*) prévoyance *f*; **to take precautions** prendre des précautions **(against sth** contre qch**)**; (*use contraceptive*) se protéger; **despite all our precautions** en dépit de toutes les précautions que nous avions prises; **as a p.** par mesure de précaution
precautionary [prɪ'kɔːʃən(ə)rɪ] *adj* (*measure*) préventif **(against** contre**)**
precede [prɪ'siːd] *vt* **(a)** (*in time*) précéder; **the conference was preceded by a reception** une réception a eu lieu avant la conférence; **she preceded me as secretary** elle m'a précédé au poste de secrétaire **(b)** (*in space*) précéder, être devant **(c)** (*take precedence over*) avoir le pas *ou* la préséance sur
precedence ['presɪdəns] *n* (*in rank*) préséance *f*; (*in priority etc*) priorité *f*; **in order of p.** par ordre de préséance; **to have** *or* **take p. over sb** avoir le pas *ou* la préséance sur qn, prendre le pas sur qn; **duty that takes p. over all others** devoir qui prime tout; **this job takes p. over everything else** ce travail est à faire en priorité
precedent ['presɪdənt] *n* **(a)** précédent *m*; **to create** *or* **set a p.** créer un précédent; **to break with p.** rompre avec la tradition; **there's no p. for it** il n'y en a pas d'exemple; **according to p.** conformément à la tradition; **without p.** sans précédent **(b)** *Jur* décision *f* judiciaire faisant jurisprudence; **to set p.** faire jurisprudence
preceding [prɪ'siːdɪŋ] *adj* précédent; **the p. day** la veille; **in the p. article/chapter** dans l'article/le chapitre ci-avant
precentor [prɪ'sentər] *n Rel* maître *m* de chapelle
precept ['priːsept] *n* précepte *m*
pre-check-in *n* pré-inscription *f*
precinct ['priːsɪŋkt] *n* **(a)** (*enclosed area*) enceinte *f*, enclos *m*; **precincts** (*of cathedral etc*) enceinte, enclos; **(shopping) p.** centre *m* commercial (*fermé à la circulation automobile*) **(b)** (*boundary*) **within the precincts of** dans l'enceinte de **(c)** *US* (*electoral district*) circonscription *f* électorale; (*police district*) circonscription administrative
preciosity [preʃɪ'ɒsɪtɪ] *n Fml* préciosité *f*
precious ['preʃəs] **1** *adj* (*metals, stones, Lit Pej style*) précieux; **we wasted a lot of p. time** nous avons perdu un temps précieux; **a few p. drops of water** quelques précieuses gouttes d'eau; **that photo is very p. to me** je tiens beaucoup à cette photo; *F Iron* **you and your p. project!** toi et ton sacré projet!; **p. stones** (*in raw state*) pierres *fpl* précieuses; (*cut*) pierreries *fpl*, pierres précieuses

2 *n* (*term of endearment*) **my p.!** mon trésor!, mon amour! **3** *adv F* **there are p. few of them** il y en a très peu; **there's p. little hope** *or* **chance** il n'y a guère d'espoir (**of that** que cela se produise; **of doing sth**/que je/qu'il/*etc* fasse qch)

precipice ['presɪpɪs] *n* précipice *m*; **to fall over a p.** tomber dans un précipice

precipitance [prɪ'sɪpɪtəns], **precipitancy** [prɪ'sɪpɪtənsɪ] *n Fml* (*suddenness, abruptness*) précipitation *f*; (*haste*) empressement *m*; (*rashness*) irréflexion *f*

precipitant [prɪ'sɪpɪtənt] **1** *adj* = **precipitate**[2] **2** *n Ch* précipitant *m*

precipitate[1] [prɪ'sɪpɪtɪt] *n Ch* précipité *m*; **to form a p.** (se) précipiter

precipitate[2] *adj Fml* (*sudden, abrupt, hasty*) précipité; **let's not be p.** ne précipitons pas les choses

precipitate[3] [prɪ'sɪpɪteɪt] **1** *vt* **(a)** (*hasten*) (*crisis, person's downfall, Ch solid substance*) précipiter; **to p. a war/an argument** faire éclater une guerre/une dispute; **to p. matters** précipiter *ou* hâter les choses **(b)** (*throw*) précipiter **2** *vi Ch* (se) précipiter; *Met* se condenser

precipitately [prɪ'sɪpɪtətlɪ] *adv* précipitamment

precipitation [prɪsɪpɪ'teɪʃən] *n* **(a)** *Ch* précipitation *f*; *Met* précipitations; *Met* **annual p.** précipitations annuelles **(b)** *Fml* (*haste*) **to act with p.** agir avec précipitation *ou* précipitamment

precipitous [prɪ'sɪpɪtəs] *adj* **(a)** (*steep*) escarpé, abrupt; (*sheer*) à pic **(b)** (*hasty*) (*departure etc*) précipité

precipitously [prɪ'sɪpɪtəslɪ] *adv* **(a)** (*steeply*) (*to rise, fall*) à pic **(b)** (*hastily*) précipitamment

précis[1], *pl* **précis** ['preɪsi:, 'preɪsi:z] *n* résumé *m*; *Sch* **p. writing** compte-rendu *m* de lecture

précis[2] *vt* faire un résumé de

precise [prɪ'saɪs] *adj* **(a)** (*exact*) (*orders, movements, ideas, details*) précis; **there were a few people, five to be p.** il y avait quelques personnes, cinq pour être précis; **at the p. moment when ...** au moment précis où ..., juste au moment où ... **(b)** (*person*) (*meticulous*) méticuleux; (*punctilious*) pointilleux, formaliste

precisely [prɪ'saɪslɪ] *adv* (*to cost, number etc*) précisément, exactement; (*to describe, draw etc*) avec précision; **at six (o'clock) p.** à six heures précises; **p.!** précisément!, exactement!; **that's p. why** c'est précisément pour ça

preciseness [prɪ'saɪsnɪs] *n* **(a)** (*of figure, calculation etc*) précision *f* **(b)** (*of person*) (*meticulousness*) méticulosité *f*; (*punctiliousness*) formalisme *m*

precision [prɪ'sɪʒ(ə)n] *n* précision *f*; **with mathematical p.** avec une précision (toute) mathématique; *Mil* **p. bombing** bombardement *m* de précision; **p.-engineered** de haute précision; **p. instruments** instruments *mpl* de précision; **p.-made** de (haute) précision; **p. tools** instruments de précision; **p. work/engineering** travail *m*/mécanique *f* de précision

preclude [prɪ'klu:d] *vt esp Fml* (*objection, misunderstanding*) prévenir, empêcher; **to p. sb from doing sth, to p. sb's doing sth** empêcher qn de faire qch

precocious [prɪ'kəʊʃəs] *adj* précoce

precociously [prɪ'kəʊʃəslɪ] *adv* précocement, avec précocité

precociousness [prɪ'kəʊʃəsnɪs], **precocity** [prɪ'kɒsɪtɪ] *n* précocité *f*

precognition [pri:kɒg'nɪʃən] *n Phil etc* connaissance *f* anticipée *ou* antérieure

precombustion [pri:kəm'bʌstʃən] *n* précombustion *f*

preconceive [pri:kən'si:v] *vt* préconcevoir; **preconceived idea** idée *f* préconçue

preconception [pri:kən'sepʃən] *n* idée *f ou* opinion *f* préconçue; (*prejudice*) préjugé *m*; **to free oneself from all preconceptions** se libérer de toute opinion préconçue

precondition[1] [pri:kən'dɪʃən] *n* condition *f* préalable (**of sth** à qch; **for doing** pour faire)

precondition[2] *vt* conditionner (**to do sth** à faire qch)

pre-configured [pri:kən'fɪgəd] *adj* préconfiguré

pre-contractual negotiations *npl* négociations *fpl* précontractuelles

precooked [pri:'kʊkt] *adj* (*food*) précuit

precursor [pri:'kɜ:sər] *n* (*person*) précurseur *m*; (*sign, event*) avant-coureur *m*, *pl* avant-coureurs; (*of machine, aeroplane etc*) ancêtre *m*

precursory [pri:'kɜ:sərɪ] *adj Fml* précurseur; (*symptom*) avant-coureur, *pl* avant-coureurs; (*observation*) préliminaire

predate [pri:'deɪt] *vt* **(a)** (*precede*) (*historical event etc*) précéder **(b)** (*put earlier date on*) (*document*) antidater

predator ['predətər] *n* prédateur *m*; (*bird*) rapace *m*; *Fig* vautour *m*, rapace

predatory ['predət(ə)rɪ] *adj* (*animal*) prédateur, -trice; *Fig* (*person, attentions etc*) rapace; **p. instincts** instincts de bête de proie, instincts prédateurs; **there was nothing p. in her manner** elle n'avait rien de menaçant; *Mktg* **p. pricing** fixation *f* de prix prédateurs

predecease [pri:dɪ'si:s] *vt* prédécéder

predecessor ['pri:dɪsesər] *n* prédécesseur *m*; (*of dignitary etc*) devancier, -ière; **my (immediate) p. (in the job)** mon prédécesseur (à ce poste); **my new desk is much better than its p.** mon nouveau bureau est bien mieux que le précédent

predestination [pri:destɪ'neɪʃən] *n* prédestination *f*

predestine [pri:'destɪn] *vt* prédestiner (**to** à); **to be predestined to do sth** être prédestiné à faire qch; **the letter was predestined to go astray** la lettre était destinée à se perdre

predetermination [pri:dɪtɜ:mɪ'neɪʃən] *n Rel, Phil* prédétermination *f*

predetermine [pri:dɪ'tɜ:mɪn] *vt Rel, Phil* prédéterminer

predetermined [pri:dɪ'tɜ:mɪnd] *adj* prédéterminé

predicament [prɪ'dɪkəmənt] *n* (*difficult situation*) situation *f* difficile, conjoncture *f* malheureuse; **to be in an awkward p.** être dans une mauvaise passe, être dans le pétrin; **this is quite a p. you've landed us in** tu nous as fourrés dans un beau pétrin

predicate[1] ['predɪkət] *n Phil* prédicat *m*; *Gram* attribut *m*

predicate[2] ['predɪkeɪt] *vt* **(a)** (*affirm*) affirmer **(b) to p. sth on sth** (*base*) baser *ou* fonder qch sur qch; **this view is predicated on ...** ce point de vue est basé *ou* fondé sur ... **(c)** *Phil* (*ascribe as a quality*) **to p. a quality of sth** attribuer une qualité à qch

predicative [prɪ'dɪkətɪv] *adj* (*in logic*), *Gram* prédicatif

predict [prɪ'dɪkt] *vt* (*forecast*) (*on basis of instinct, cards etc*) prédire; (*on basis of data*) prévoir

predictable [prɪ'dɪktəb(ə)l] *adj* prévisible; *F* **the film was too p.** ce film était sans surprise; **you're so p.** j'étais sûr que tu allais dire/faire ça; (*boring*) avec toi, aucun imprévu!; **am I getting p.?** tu me vois venir?; **that was p.!** c'était à prévoir!; **there was the p. standing ovation** comme on pouvait le prévoir, le public s'est levé pour l'ovationner/les ovationner

predictably [prɪ'dɪktəblɪ] *adv* comme on pouvait le prévoir; **to behave p.** se comporter de manière prévisible; **the evening proceeded entirely p.** la soirée s'est déroulée sans surprise aucune

prediction [prɪ'dɪkʃən] *n* (*based on instinct, cards etc*) prédiction *f*; (*based on data*) prévision *f*

predictive [prɪ'dɪktɪv] *adj Fml* prophétique; **to be p. of sth** être annonciateur de qch; **the p. power of the theory** la capacité de la théorie de prévoir des événements

predigested [pri:dɪ'dʒestɪd, pri:daɪ-] *adj* prédigéré; *Fig* (*idea*) tout fait

predilection [pri:dɪ'lekʃən] *n* prédilection *f* (**for** pour)

predispose [pri:dɪs'pəʊz] *vt* prédisposer (**to** à); **to p. sb in sb's favour** prédisposer qn en faveur de qn

predisposition [pri:dɪspə'zɪʃən] *n* prédisposition *f* (**to** à)

predominance [prɪ'dɒmɪnəns] *n* prédominance *f*; **there is a p. of women in the profession** il y a une prédominance de femmes dans ce métier

predominant [prɪ'dɒmɪnənt] *adj* prédominant

predominantly [prɪ'dɒmɪnəntlɪ] *adv* d'une manière prédominante; **cars sold here are p. Italian** la plupart des voitures vendues ici sont italiennes; **a p. Jewish area** un quartier à majorité juive; **to be p. concerned with a particular problem** être essentiellement préoccupé par un problème particulier

predominate [prɪ'dɒmɪneɪt] *vi* **(a)** (*prevail*) prédominer, l'emporter (**over** sur) **(b)** (*be in the majority*) être plus nombreux, prédominer

predominating [prɪ'dɒmɪneɪtɪŋ] *adj* prédominant

pre-election *adj* préélectoral

preemie ['pri:mɪ] *n Am F* (*premature baby*) prématuré, -ée

pre-eminence *n* prééminence *f*; **this country's sporting p.** la prééminence de ce pays sur le plan sportif; **to achieve p. in the field of ecology** obtenir une place prééminente dans le domaine de l'écologie

pre-eminent *adj* prééminent

pre-eminently *adv* essentiellement

pre-empt [pri:'empt] *vt* **(a)** (*prevent, frustrate*) (*person*) devancer; (*plan, decision etc*) anticiper sur, devancer **(b)** *Jur* (*land, property*) préempter; *US* (*occupy*) (*land*) occuper (*afin d'obtenir un droit d'achat préférentiel*)

pre-emption [pri:'empʃən] *n Jur* (droit *m* de) préemption *f*

pre-emptive [pri:'emptɪv] *adj* **(a)** *Jur* (*right*) de préemption **(b)** *Cards* (*at bridge*) **p. bid** ouverture *f* préventive, appel *m* élevé (*pour s'assurer l'enchère*) **(c)** *Mil* (*strike, attack*) préventif; *Mktg* **p. penetration strategy** stratégie *f* de pénétration préventive

preen [pri:n] *vt* (*of bird*) (*feathers*) lisser avec le bec; **to p. itself** (*of bird*) se lisser les plumes; *Fig* **to p. oneself** (*of person*) se faire beau/belle; *Fig* **to p. oneself on one's achievements** s'enorgueillir de ses réussites
pre-establish *vt* préétablir
pre-established *adj* préétabli
pre-exist *vi* préexister
pre-existence *n* préexistence *f*
pre-existent, pre-existing *adj* préexistant
prefab ['pri:fæb] *n F* préfabriqué *m*
prefabricate [pri:'fæbrɪkeɪt] *vt* préfabriquer; **prefabricated house** maison *f* préfabriquée *ou* en préfabriqué
preface¹ ['prefɪs] *n* (*of book*) préface *f*, avant-propos *m inv*; (*to speech*) préambule *m*
preface² *vt* **(a)** (*introduce*) **to p. one's remarks with an anecdote** faire précéder ses remarques d'une anecdote; **the events that prefaced the crisis** les événements qui ont précédé la crise **(b)** (*write preface to*) (*book*) préfacer
prefade ['pri:feɪd] *n TV etc* pré-fondu *m*
pre-faded *adj* (*denims*) délavé
prefatory ['prefətərɪ] *adj Fml* (*remark*) préliminaire, d'introduction
prefect ['pri:fekt] *n* **(a)** *Br Sch* = élève *mf* des grandes classes chargé(e) de la discipline **(b)** *Admin* (*French etc official*) préfet *m*
prefectship ['pri:fektʃɪp] *n Br Sch* = responsabilité *f* de maintenir la discipline, attribuée à un(e) élève des grandes classes
prefecture ['pri:fektjʊər] *n* (*in France etc*) préfecture *f*
prefer [prɪ'fɜ:r] *vt* (**-rr-**) **(a)** (*like better*) préférer, aimer mieux; **to p. sth to sth** préférer qch à qch, aimer mieux qch que qch; **I p. her to her sister** je la préfère à sa sœur; **which would you p., wine or beer?** tu préfères du vin ou de la bière?; **I p. meat well done** je préfère la viande bien cuite; **I much p. his first film** je préfère de loin *ou* de beaucoup son premier film; **I would p. to stay at home** j'aimerais mieux *ou* je préférerais rester à la maison; **I would p. it if you didn't mention it to him** je préférerais que vous ne lui parliez pas de cela; **I would p. that you did not repeat this** je préférerais que tu ne répètes pas ça
(b) *Jur* (*legal action*) intenter; **to p. charges** déposer *ou* porter plainte (**against** contre); (*of police*) porter l'affaire en justice
(c) *Fml esp Rel* (*appoint*) (*person to a position*) nommer, élever
preferable ['prefərəb(ə)l] *adj* préférable (**to** à)
preferably ['prefərəblɪ] *adv* de préférence; **would you like to make the presentations? – p. not** voudriez-vous faire les présentations? – je n'y tiens pas
preference ['prefərəns] *n* **(a)** préférence *f*; **this is my p.** voilà celui que je préfère; **I have no p.** je n'ai pas de préférence; **to give sth p.** donner *ou* accorder la préférence à qch (**over sth** sur qch); **women will be given p.** les femmes auront la préférence; **in p. to …** de préférence à …; **in order of p.** par ordre de préférence; **to express a p.** se prononcer; *Mktg* **p. test** test *m* de préférence
(b) *Econ* tarif *m ou* régime *m* de faveur; (*preferential treatment*) traitement *m* préférentiel *ou* de faveur; **imports entitled to p.** importations bénéficiant d'un régime de faveur
(c) *St Exch* droit *m* de priorité; *Br* **p. shares** actions *fpl* privilégiées *ou* de priorité
preferential [prefə'renʃəl] *adj* **(a)** (*treatment, tariff etc*) préférentiel, de faveur; **to get p. treatment** (*of people*) bénéficier d'un traitement préférentiel *ou* de faveur; *Com* **p. price** prix *m* de faveur; *Fin* **p. rate** tarif *m* préférentiel; **p. voting** vote *m* préférentiel **(b)** *Jur* **p. claim** *or* **right** privilège *m*; **p. creditor** créancier, -ière privilégié(e); **p. dividend** dividende *m* privilégié *ou* de priorité
preferment [prɪ'fɜ:mənt] *n Fml esp Rel* (*promotion*) avancement *m*, promotion *f* (**to an office** à une fonction)
preferred [prɪ'fɜ:d] *adj* préféré; *Fin* **p. creditor** créancier *m* privilégié; *Fin* **p. debt** dette *f ou* créance *f* privilégiée; *Am* **p. share** action *f* privilégiée; *Am Fin* **p. stock** actions *fpl* privilégiées *ou* de priorité
prefiguration [pri:fɪgə'reɪʃən] *n* préfiguration *f*
prefigure [pri:'fɪgər] *vt* préfigurer
pre-financing *n Acct* préfinancement *m*
prefix¹ ['pri:fɪks] *n Gram etc* préfixe *m*; (*before name*) particule *f*; (*title*) titre *m*
prefix² *vt* préfixer, mettre un préfixe à
preflight ['pri:flaɪt] *adj* (*inspection etc*) avant vol
pre-focus *vt* mettre au point préalablement
preformatted [pri:'fɔ:mætɪd] *adj Comptr* pré(-)formaté
prefrontal [pri:'frʌnt(ə)l] *adj Anat* préfrontal
preggers ['pregəz] *adj Br F* enceinte
pregnancy ['pregnənsɪ] *n* (*of woman*) grossesse *f*; (*of animal*) gestation *f*; **p. test** test *m* de grossesse
pregnant ['pregnənt] *adj* **(a)** (*woman*) enceinte; (*animal*) pleine; **she's three months p.** elle est enceinte de trois mois; **to become** *or* **get p.** tomber enceinte (**by sb** de qn); **to get sb p.** mettre qn enceinte **(b)** *Fig* (*fertile*) fécond (**with** en); (*pause, silence*) lourd de signification *ou* de sens; **p. with possibilities** riche de possibilités; **p. with danger** plein de danger; **p. with meaning/tension** chargé de sens/tension
pre-hear circuit *n TV, Radio* circuit *m* de pré-écoute
preheat [pri:'hi:t] *vt* préchauffer
pre-heater *n Aut* dispositif *m* de préchauffage; **p. warning light** indicateur *m* de préchauffage
pre-heating *n Aut* préchauffage *m*
prehensile [prɪ'hensaɪl] *adj* préhensile
prehistoric [pri:hɪs'tɒrɪk] *adj Hist, Fig* préhistorique
prehistory [pri:'hɪst(ə)rɪ] *n* préhistoire *f*
pre-ignition *n* (*in engine*) préallumage *m*
pre-installed [pri:ɪn'stɔ:ld] *adj* pré(-)installé
pre-inventory balance *n Acct* balance *f* avant inventaire
prejudge [pri:'dʒʌdʒ] *vt* (*issue etc*) préjuger de, *Lit* préjuger; (*person*) condamner d'avance
prejudice¹ ['predʒʊdɪs] *n* **(a)** (*preconception*) préjugé *m*, parti pris *m* (**against** contre; **in favour of** en faveur de); **racial p.** préjugés raciaux; **I have a p. about** *or* **against that sort of thing** j'ai des préjugés contre ce genre de choses **(b)** *Fml* (*harm*) préjudice *m*, tort *m*, dommage *m*; **to cause p. to** porter préjudice à; *Jur* **without p. (to my rights)** sans préjudice de mes droits; **without p. to the solution of the question** sans préjuger la solution de la question
prejudice² *vt* **(a)** (*bias*) (*person*) prévenir, prédisposer (**against** contre; **in favour of** en faveur de) **(b)** (*harm*) (*reputation, solution etc*) nuire à, faire du tort à, porter préjudice à; (*interests*) nuire à; **without prejudicing my rights** sans préjudice de mes droits
prejudiced ['predʒʊdɪst] *adj* (*person*) plein de préjugés; (*idea, view*) préconçu; **to be p.** avoir des préjugés (**in favour of** en faveur de; **against** contre); **racially p.** plein de préjugés raciaux
prejudicial [predʒʊ'dɪʃəl] *adj* préjudiciable, nuisible (**to** à); **to be p.** porter préjudice (**to** à)
prelacy ['preləsɪ] *n Rel* **(a)** (*office*) prélature *f* **(b)** (*prelates*) prélats *mpl*
prelate ['prelɪt] *n Rel* prélat *m*
prelim ['pri:lɪm] *n F* **(a)** *Sch* examen *m* blanc **(b)** *Typ* **prelims** pages *fpl* de départ, préliminaires *mpl*
preliminary [prɪ'lɪmɪnərɪ] **1** *adj* (*inquiry, selection, interview, negotiations etc, Med examination*) préliminaire; (*stage*) initial, premier; *Sch* préparatoire; **after a few p. remarks** après quelques avant-propos *ou* remarques préliminaires; *Constr etc* **p. scheme** *or* **plan** avant-projet *m*, *pl* avant-projets
2 *n* **(a)** (*to conversation etc*) prélude *m*; **by way of** *or* **as a p.** préalablement, en guise d'introduction *ou* d'avant-propos; **the measure is seen by many as a p. to …** cette mesure est considérée par beaucoup comme une action préliminaire à …
(b) (*of treaty etc*) **preliminaries** préliminaires *mpl*
preloaded [pri:'ləʊdɪd] *adj* préchargé
prelude¹ ['prelju:d] *n Mus, Fig* prélude *m* (**to** à)
prelude² *vt* préluder à, précéder
premarital [pri:'mærɪt(ə)l] *adj* préconjugal, prénuptial; **p. sex** rapports *mpl* avant le mariage, rapports préconjugaux
pre-marketing *n* pré-commercialisation *f*
premature ['premətjʊər] *adj* (*decision, end, death etc*) prématuré; (*baldness, senility*) précoce; **to be two weeks p.** (*of baby*) être né deux semaines avant terme, être prématuré de deux semaines; *F* **you're being a bit p.!** tu vas trop vite!; **it was a bit p. of him** c'était un peu prématuré de sa part; **p. birth** accouchement *m* prématuré *ou* avant terme; **p. ejaculation** éjaculation *f* précoce
prematurely ['premətjʊəlɪ] *adv* (*to decide, die*) prématurément; (*born*) avant terme; **to be p. senile/bald** souffrir de sénilité/calvitie précoce
premed ['pri:med] *n Med F* prémédication *f*
premedicate [pri:'medɪkeɪt] *vt Med* prémédiquer
premedication [pri:medɪ'keɪʃən] *n Med* prémédication *f*
premeditate [pri:'medɪteɪt] *vt* préméditer
premeditated [pri:'medɪteɪtɪd] *adj* (*crime*) prémédité
premeditation [pri:medɪ'teɪʃən] *n* préméditation *f*
premenstrual [pri:'menstrʊəl] *adj* prémenstruel; **p. tension** *or* **syndrome** syndrome *m* prémenstruel; **I think she's feeling p.** je crois que ses règles ne vont pas tarder à arriver
premier ['premɪər] **1** *adj* (tout) premier **2** *n* (*prime minister*) premier ministre *m*

première¹ ['prəmɪeər, 'prem-, *Am* prɪ'mɪər] *n Th, Cin* première *f*
premièrе² **1** *vt* (*play, film*) donner la première de **2** *vi* **the play premièred in New York** la première de la pièce a eu lieu à New York
premiership ['premɪəʃɪp] *n* (*of prime minister*) fonctions *fpl* de premier ministre; **to be elected to the p.** être élu premier ministre; **during her p.** pendant qu'elle était premier ministre; **he had a successful p.** il a rempli son mandat de premier ministre avec succès
premise¹ ['premɪs] *n* (*in logic*) prémisse *f*; **to argue from different premises** discuter à partir de prémisses différentes
premise² *vt* poser en principe (**that** que); (*in logic*) poser en prémisse (**that** que); **to be premised on sth** être basé *ou* fondé sur qch
premises ['premɪsɪz] *npl* (**a**) (*property*) **the p.** le local, les locaux; **business p.** locaux commerciaux; **drinks to be consumed on/off the p.** boissons à consommer dans/hors de l'établissement; **she's still on the p.** elle est encore dans le bâtiment (**b**) *Jur* (*of document*) intitulé *m*
premiss ['premɪs] *n* = **premise¹**
premium ['priːmɪəm] *n* (**a**) (*for insurance*) prime *f*
(**b**) (*additional sum*) (*on price*) supplément *m*; (*on salary*) prime *f*; *Fin etc* (**exchange**) **p.** agio *m*, prix *m ou* prime du change; *St Exch* **to pay a p.** verser *ou* acquitter un premium; **to issue shares at a p.** émettre des actions au-dessus du pair *ou* de leur valeur nominale; **to sell sth at a p.** vendre qch à prime *ou* à bénéfice; **antiques are at a p.** (*are sought after*) les antiquités sont très recherchées; (*sell at high prices*) les antiquités se vendent à prix d'or; **time is at a p.** le temps presse; **her time is at a p.** son temps est précieux; **good translators are at a p.** les bons traducteurs ne courent pas les rues *ou* sont rares; *Fig* **to put** *or* **place a p. on sth** (*of people, government etc*) accorder beaucoup d'importance à qch; (*of circumstances, nature of work etc*) mettre l'accent sur qch
(**c**) *Aut Br* **p. grade petrol,** *Am* **p. fuel** *or* **gasoline** supercarburant *m*, *F* super *m*; **p. marketing** mercatique *f* de prime; **p. price** prix *m* de prestige; **p. rebate** ristourne *f* de prime; **p. selling** vente *f* à prime; **p. service** service *m* premier
premium bonds *npl Br* obligations *fpl* à primes *ou* à lots
premolar [priː'məʊlər] *adj, n Anat* **p.** (**tooth**) (dent *f*) prémolaire *f*
premonition [premə'nɪʃən, priː-] *n* (*of misfortune etc*) prémonition *f*, pressentiment *m*; **to have a p.** avoir un pressentiment; **to have a p. of disaster** pressentir un désastre; **to have a p. that ...** avoir le pressentiment que ..., pressentir que ...
premonitory [prɪ'mɒnɪtərɪ] *adj* prémonitoire
prenatal [priː'neɪt(ə)l] *adj* prénatal, -als
preoccupation [priːɒkjʊ'peɪʃən] *n* préoccupation *f* (**with** à l'égard de); **to have a p. with sth** être préoccupé par qch
preoccupied [priː'ɒkjʊpaɪd] *adj* préoccupé (**with, by** par); **to be p. with** *or* **by sth** se préoccuper de qch
preoccupy [priː'ɒkjʊpaɪ] *vt* (*person, the mind*) préoccuper
preordain [priːɔː'deɪn] *vt* (*destine*) prédéterminer; **it was preordained** c'était prédestiné
prep¹ [prep] **1** *n Br Sch F* (*esp in private school*) (*period*) étude *f* (du soir); (*homework*) devoirs *mpl* (du soir); **p. period** (heure *f* de) permanence *f*; **p. room** (salle *f* d')étude **2** *adj F* **p. school** *Br* école *f* primaire (privée); *Am* collège *m* privé
prep² *vt* (**-pp-**) *Am F* préparer; *Med* **to p. sb for an operation** préparer qn pour une opération
prepack [priː'pæk] *vt Com* préconditionner, préemballer
prepaid [priː'peɪd] *adj* prépayé; *Acct* payé *ou* constaté d'avance; **p. card** carte *f* prépayée; **p. income** produit *m* constaté d'avance
preparation [prepə'reɪʃən] *n* (**a**) (*action*) (*of food, medication etc*) préparation *f*; (*of plane, car etc*) mise *f* en état; **they broke the news to her without any p.** ils lui ont annoncé la nouvelle sans aucune préparation; **p. of accounting entries** précomptabilisation *f*, pré-imputation *f*; **in p. for the summer holidays** en prévision des vacances d'été
(**b**) **preparations** (*measures*) préparatifs *mpl*; **preparations for war** préparatifs de guerre; **to make** (**one's**) **preparations for sth** prendre ses mesures *ou* ses dispositions en vue de qch, faire des préparatifs en vue de qch; **to make** (**one's**) **preparations for a journey** se préparer à *ou* pour un voyage, faire ses préparatifs de voyage
(**c**) *Br Sch* (*esp in private school*) (*period*) étude *f* (du soir); (*homework*) devoirs *mpl* (du soir)
(**d**) (*substance*) (*pharmaceutical etc*) préparation *f*
preparatory [prɪ'pærətərɪ] *adj* préparatoire; *steps, measures*) préalable; **p. to** (*departure, invasion etc*) en préparation pour; **p. to going abroad/resigning** avant d'aller à l'étranger/de démissionner; **p. school** *Br* école *f* primaire (privée); *Am* collège *m* privé
prepare [prɪ'peər] **1** *vt* (*meal etc*) préparer; (*attack etc*) monter, préparer; (*plane, car etc*) mettre en état; **to p. a surprise for sb** préparer *ou* ménager une surprise à qn; **to p. the way for negotiations** préparer la voie pour des négociations; **to p. sb for an exam** préparer qn à un examen; **to p. sb for bad news** préparer qn à recevoir une mauvaise nouvelle; **to p. oneself for sth** se préparer à qch; **their training had prepared them for most eventualities** leur entraînement les avait préparés à presque toutes les éventualités; **prepared from the finest ingredients** préparé avec les meilleurs ingrédients
2 *vi* se préparer, s'apprêter (**for sth** à qch; **to do sth** à faire qch); **to p. for departure** faire ses préparatifs de départ; **to p. for an examination** préparer un examen
prepared [prɪ'peəd] *adj* (**a**) (*willing*) **I am (quite) p. to ...** je suis prêt *ou* disposé à ...; **he was/was not p. to lie** il était/n'était pas disposé à mentir (**b**) (*ready*) **to be p. for anything** être prêt à tout; **to be p. for bad news** être préparé à recevoir une mauvaise nouvelle; **be p.** (*Scout's motto*) toujours prêt; **I wasn't p. for this reaction** je ne m'attendais pas à cette réaction (**c**) (*made*) préparé; **to have a p. excuse/explanation** avoir une excuse/explication toute prête; **well p. dish** plat bien préparé; **a p. speech** un discours préparé (à l'avance); **p. timber** bois refait
preparedness [prɪ'peərɪdnɪs] *n* état *m* de préparation; **I am unsure of their p. to deal with such an eventuality** je doute qu'ils soient prêts à faire face à une telle éventualité; *Mil* **to be in a state of p.** être en état d'alerte (préventive)
prepay [priː'peɪ] *vt* (*pt, pp* **prepaid**) payer *ou* régler d'avance; (*letter etc*) affranchir; **a prepaid envelope** une enveloppe affranchie
prepayment [priː'peɪmənt] *n* paiement *m* à l'avance, paiement préalable; *Acct* charge *f* constatée d'avance; *Acct* **p. and accrued income** compte *m* de régularisation
preponderance [prɪ'pɒndərəns] *n* prépondérance *f* (**over** sur); **there was a p. of French books on the shelf** il y avait une majorité de livres français sur l'étagère
preponderant [prɪ'pɒndərənt] *adj* prépondérant; **boys tend to be p.** il tend à y avoir une majorité de garçons
preponderantly [prɪ'pɒndərəntlɪ] *adv* à un degré prépondérant; **the guests were p. French** les invités étaient pour la majeure partie français
preponderate [prɪ'pɒndəreɪt] *vi* l'emporter (**over** sur)
preposition [prepə'zɪʃən] *n Gram* préposition *f*
prepositional [prepə'zɪʃən(ə)l] *adj* prépositif
prepositionally [prepə'zɪʃən(ə)lɪ] *adv* (*used*) comme préposition
prepossess [priːpə'zes] *vt Fml* (**a**) (*engross*) préoccuper (**b**) (*influence*) influencer
prepossessing [priːpə'zesɪŋ] *adj* (*face*) agréable, avenant; **p. appearance** aspect *m* engageant; (*of person*) air *m* sympathique *ou* avenant; **he's not the most p. of people** ce n'est pas l'homme le plus avenant du monde
preposterous [prɪ'pɒstərəs] *adj* absurde; **that's a p. lie!** c'est complètement absurde!
preposterously [prɪ'pɒstərəslɪ] *adv* d'une façon absurde; **it was p. easy** ça a été un jeu d'enfant
preposterousness [prɪ'pɒstərəsnɪs] *n* absurdité *f*
preppy [prepɪ] *esp Am F* **1** *adj* (*look, clothes etc*) ≈ bon chic bon genre, B.C.B.G. **2** *n* **to be a p.** être *ou* faire très B.C.B.G.
pre-press *n* pré-impression *f*
pre-printed form *n* pré-imprimé *m*
preproduction [priːprə'dʌkʃən] *n TV etc* pré-production *f*
preprogram [priː'prəʊgræm] *vt Comptr etc* préprogrammer; **humans are preprogrammed to behave in certain ways** les êtres humains sont conditionnés à se comporter d'une certaine façon
preprogrammed [priː'prəʊgræmd] *adj Comptr etc* préprogrammé
prepublication [priːpʌblɪ'keɪʃən] *n* pré-publication *f*
prepuce ['priːpjuːs] *n Anat* prépuce *m*
Pre-Raphaelite [priː'ræfəlaɪt] *adj, n Art* préraphaélite *m*
prerecord [priːrɪ'kɔːd] *vt* préenregistrer; *TV, Rad* **prerecorded broadcast** émission *f* en différé; **prerecorded cassette** cassette *f* préenregistrée; **prerecorded telephone message service** audiphone *m*
prerecording [priːrɪ'kɔːdɪŋ] *n* préenregistrement *m*; *TV, Rad* (émission *f* en) différé *m*
prerelease [priːrɪ'liːs] *Cin* **1** *n* (*of film*) avant-première *f* **2** *adj* **p. publicity** bande-annonce *f*
prerequisite [priː'rekwɪzɪt] **1** *adj* préalablement nécessaire, indispensable **2** *n* condition *f* préalable
prerogative [prɪ'rɒgətɪv] *n* prérogative *f*, privilège *m*; **the royal p.** la prérogative royale; **to exercise the royal p.** faire acte de souverain
Pres *Pol etc abbr* **President**

presage¹ [ˈpresɪdʒ] *n Lit* (*sign*) présage *m*; (*foreboding*) pressentiment *m*; **to be a p. of sth** présager qch, être le présage de qch

presage² [ˈpresɪdʒ, prɪˈseɪdʒ] *vt Lit* (*catastrophe etc*) présager, faire pressentir

pre-sales service *n* service *m* pré-vente

Presbyterian [prezbɪˈtɪərɪən] *adj, n Rel* presbytérien, -ienne

Presbyterianism [prezbɪˈtɪərɪənɪz(ə)m] *n Rel* presbytérianisme *m*

presbytery [ˈprezbɪt(ə)rɪ] *n Rel* **(a)** (*in church*) sanctuaire *m* **(b)** *Cathol* (*residence*) presbytère *m* **(c)** (*in Presbyterian Church*) (*court*) consistoire *m*

preschool [priːˈskuːl] *adj* (*age etc*) préscolaire

prescience [ˈpresɪəns] *n Fml* prescience *f*

prescient [ˈpresɪənt] *adj Fml* prescient

prescoring [priːˈskɔːrɪŋ] *n* (*of sound*) pré-enregistrement *m*

prescribe [prɪˈskraɪb] *vt* **(a)** prescrire; **prescribed task** tâche *f* imposée; **in the prescribed time** dans le délai prescrit **(b)** *Med* **to p. sth for sb** prescrire qch à qn

prescription [prɪˈskrɪpʃən] *n* **(a)** (*order*) prescription *f* **(b)** *Med* ordonnance *f*; **available only on (a doctor's) p.** délivré seulement sur ordonnance; **repeat p.** = ordonnance renouvelable; **p. charges** frais *mpl* de médicaments *ou* pharmaceutiques; **p. drugs** médicaments *mpl* délivrés uniquement sur ordonnance

prescriptive [prɪˈskrɪptɪv] *adj* **(a)** (*prescribing action*) normatif **(b)** (*established by custom*) consacré par l'usage *ou* par la coutume

prescriptivism [prɪˈskrɪptɪvɪz(ə)m] *n Phil* normativisme *m*

pre-selector *n Aut* pré-sélecteur *m*; **p. gearbox** boîte *f* à présélection

presence [ˈprezəns] *n* **(a)** présence *f*; **in the p. of ...** en présence de ...; **say nothing about it in his p.** n'en parlez pas devant lui; *Fml* **to be admitted to the p.** (*to see monarch etc*) être admis en présence; **your p. is requested at ...** vous êtes prié d'assister à ...; **the police maintained a discreet p.** (*at demonstration etc*) la police a assuré une surveillance discrète; **the American military p.** la présence militaire américaine; **to make one's p. felt** se faire remarquer, faire sentir sa présence

(b) p. of mind présence *f* d'esprit; **to keep one's p. of mind** garder son sang-froid; **to have the p. of mind to do sth** avoir la présence d'esprit de faire qch

(c) (*bearing*) présence *f*, prestance *f*; **to have stage p.** avoir de la présence sur scène; **he has p.** il a de la présence *ou* de la prestance, il en impose

present¹ [ˈprezənt] **1** *adj* **(a)** (*in attendance*) présent; **to be p. at a ceremony** être présent *ou* assister à une cérémonie; **he cannot be interviewed without a lawyer being p.** on ne peut pas l'interroger sans la présence d'un avocat; **all (those) p. heard it** toute l'assistance l'a entendu; **some of you p. here** quelques-uns d'entre vous, ici présents; **minerals which are p. in the solution** minéraux qui sont présents dans la solution; **p. company excepted** à l'exception des personnes ici présentes, bien sûr

(b) (*in time*) actuel; (*under discussion*) en question; **the p. king** le roi actuel; **at the p. time** *or* **moment** (*at this very moment*) en ce moment; (*in this period of time*) actuellement, aujourd'hui; **up to the p. time** jusqu'ici; **in the p. case** dans le cas qui nous occupe; *Acct* **p. value** valeur *f* actualisée

2 *n* **(a)** [①**A47-8**,10; **B28**,F,1] (*time*), *Gram* présent *m*; **the p.** le présent; **up to the p.** jusqu'à présent, jusqu'ici; **at p.** (*at this very moment*) en ce moment; (*now*) à présent; (*in this period of time*) actuellement, aujourd'hui; **that's all I can tell you at p.** c'est tout ce que je peux vous dire pour l'instant *ou* pour le moment; **no more at p.** rien de plus pour le moment *ou* pour l'instant; **as things are at p.** (*at the stage things have reached*) au point où en sont les choses; (*nowadays*) par les temps qui courent; **for the p.** pour le moment, pour l'instant

(b) *Jur* **by these presents** par la présente

present² *n* (*gift*) cadeau *m*; **to make sb a p. of sth, to give sth to sb as a p.** faire cadeau de qch à qn, donner qch en cadeau à qn; **it's for a p.** (*when buying*) c'est pour offrir

present³ [prɪˈzent] **1** *vt* **(a)** (*introduce, put forward*) présenter; **to p. sb to sb** présenter qn à qn; *Fml* **allow me to p. Miss Lorna Johnston** permettez-moi de vous présenter Miss Lorna Johnston; **to p. sb at court** présenter qn à la cour; *Th* **to p. a play** (*of company etc*) présenter *ou* donner une pièce; *TV, Rad* **to p. a programme** (*of presenter*) présenter une émission; **to p. oneself at** *or* **for an examination** se présenter à *ou* pour un examen; **a good opportunity presents itself** une bonne occasion se présente **(for doing sth** de faire qch); **to p. sb/sth in a good/bad light** présenter qn/qch sous un jour favorable/défavorable; **his attempts to mount the horse presented a strange spectacle** ses tentatives pour se mettre en selle offraient un curieux spectacle

(b) (*give*) (*gift*) donner; (*award, certificate*) remettre; **to p. sth to sb, to p. sb with sth** donner/remettre qch à qn; **the mayor will be presenting the prizes** le maire distribuera les prix; **to p. one's compliments to sb** présenter ses compliments à qn; **they were presented with an empty goalmouth** ils se trouvèrent devant un but vide; **this presented her with no option but to agree** ceci ne lui a pas laissé d'autre alternative que d'accepter; *Mil, Fig* **to p. sb with an easy target** offrir une bonne cible à qn

(c) *Com* **to p. a bill for acceptance** présenter une traite à l'acceptation; *Jur* **to p. a plea** introduire une instance; *Com* **to p. invoices** présenter des factures

(d) *Parl* (*bill*) présenter, introduire; **to p. a plan to a meeting** soumettre un plan à une assemblée

(e) *Mil* **to p. arms** présenter les armes; **p. arms!** présentez armes!

2 *vi Obst* (*of foetus*) se présenter; *Med* **to p. with sth** avoir qch, présenter qch

presentable [prɪˈzentəb(ə)l] *adj* (*person, thing*) présentable; (*garment*) portable, mettable; **am I p.?** je suis présentable?

presentation [prezənˈteɪʃən] *n* **(a)** (*of person, theory, business plan, sales proposal etc*) présentation *f*; (*of play*) présentation, représentation *f*; (*of thesis, dissertation*) soutenance *f*; **to give a p.** faire un exposé; *Comptr* **p. graphics** graphiques *mpl* de présentation; **p. of accounts for audit** reddition *f* de comptes; **p. slides** diapositives *fpl* de présentation; **p. software** logiciel *m* de présentation *ou* de préAO

(b) (*giving*) (*of gift, medal etc to sb*) remise *f*; (*gift*) cadeau *m* (*offert à qn*); **to make a p. to sb** remettre un cadeau/une médaille/*etc* à qn; **p. ceremony** cérémonie *f* de remise des prix/des médailles/*etc*; **p. copy** (*book*) (*sent by publisher*) = exemplaire *m* envoyé à titre gracieux par l'éditeur; (*given by author*) = exemplaire offert à titre d'hommage par l'auteur; *Banking* **p. date** date *f* de présentation

(c) *Com* **payable on p. of the coupon** payable contre remise du coupon; **on p. of the invoice** au vu de *ou* sur présentation de la facture; **p. for acceptance** présentation *f* à l'acceptation; **p. for payment** présentation au paiement

(d) *Obst* (*of foetus*) présentation *f*

presentation pack *n Mktg* paquet *m* de présentation

present-day *adj attrib* actuel; **p. London/Brazil** le Londres/Brésil d'aujourd'hui

presenter [prɪˈzentər] *n Rad, TV etc* présentateur, -trice

presentiment [prɪˈzentɪmənt] *n esp Fml* pressentiment *m*; **to have a p. of danger** avoir le pressentiment qu'il y a du danger

presently [ˈprezəntlɪ] *adv* **(a)** (*soon*) bientôt; (*in past*) au bout d'un certain temps **(b)** *esp Am* (*now*) actuellement, à présent

presentment [prɪˈzentmənt] *n Com* (*of bill of exchange etc*) présentation *f*

present perfect *n* [①**A48**,11,d; **B28**,F,3] *Gram* passé *m* composé

present subjunctive *n* [①**A51-2**, 14; **B30-1**, G,1] *Gram* présent *m* du subjonctif

present tense *n* [①**A47-8**,10; **B28**,F,1] *Gram* temps *m* présent

preservation [prezəˈveɪʃən] *n* **(a)** (*maintenance*) conservation *f*, préservation *f*; (*of peace, order*) maintien *m*; (*in laboratory*) (*of a flower, specimen*) naturalisation *f*; *Com* (*of goods etc*) traitement *m* avant stockage; **in a good state of p.** en bon état de conservation **(b)** (*protection*) préservation *f* **(from a danger** d'un danger)

preservation order *n Br* classement *m* (à titre de monument historique)

preservation society *n* association *f* pour la sauvegarde du patrimoine historique

preservative [prɪˈzɜːvətɪv] *n* conservateur *m*; (*in foods*) agent *m* de conservation, conservateur *m*, préservateur *m*; **it acts as a p. for the wood** cela conserve le bois

preserve¹ [prɪˈzɜːv] *n* **(a)** **(apricot** *etc*) **preserve(s)** (*jam*) confiture *f* (d'abricots *etc*); **preserves** (*bottled fruit*) conserves *fpl* **(b)** (*area*) **(game) p.** réserve *f*; *Fig* **engineering is no longer a male p.** le métier d'ingénieur n'est plus réservé aux hommes; **the kitchen is his p. entirely** la cuisine c'est son domaine à lui

preserve² *vt* **(a)** (*maintain*) (*custom, sense of humour etc*) conserver, préserver; (*peace etc*) maintenir; (*appearance, illusion*) préserver; (*silence etc*) garder, observer **(b)** (*leather, wood, building etc*) protéger, préserver; *Culin* (*fruit etc*) conserver, mettre en conserve; (*in laboratory*) (*plant, animal*) naturaliser **(c)** (*protect*) (*person*) préserver **(from sth** de qch); **saints p. us!** grands dieux!

preserved [prɪˈzɜːvd] *adj* **(a)** (*fruit*) en conserve; **p. food** conserves *fpl*; *Old-fashioned* **p. meat** conserve de viande **(b)** **well/badly p.** (*building etc*) en bon/mauvais état de conservation; **well p.** (*person*) bien conservé

preserver [prɪˈzɜːvər] *n* (*person*) (*of traditions etc*) conservateur, -trice

preserving [prɪˈzɜːvɪŋ] *n* (a) *Old-fashioned* **p. pan** bassine *f* à confitures (b) = **preservation**

preset [priːˈset] 1 *vt* (*pt, pp* **preset**, *prp* **presetting**) *Tech, Electron* (*machine etc*) prérégler 2 *adj* préréglé; *Comptr* présélectionné

preshrink [priːˈʃrɪŋk] *vt* (*pt* **preshrank,** [-ˈʃræŋk]; *pp* **preshrunk** [-ˈʃrʌŋk]) (*fabric*) rendre irrétrécissable

preshrunk [priːˈʃrʌŋk] *adj* (*fabric*) irrétrécissable

preside [prɪˈzaɪd] *vi* présider; **to p. at** *or* **over a meeting** présider une réunion; **the man who presided over the collapse of the company** l'homme qui était président lors de la chute de l'entreprise; **to p. over events** (*direct*) diriger les événements

presidency [ˈprezɪdənsɪ] *n* présidence *f*; **to assume the p.** assumer la présidence

president [ˈprezɪdənt] *n* président *m*; (*of American company*) président-directeur *m* général, P-D.G. *m*; **P. Clinton** le président Clinton; **Mr P.** Monsieur le président

president-elect *n Pol* président *m* élu

presidential [prezɪˈdenʃəl] *adj* présidentiel; **to nurse p. ambitions** *or* **aspirations** aspirer à *ou* ambitionner la présidence; **p. elections** (élections *fpl*) présidentielles *fpl*; **p. hopeful** présidentiable *mf*

presidium [prɪˈsɪdɪəm, -ˈzɪd-] *n Pol* présidium *m*

press¹ [pres] *n* (a) (*act of pushing*) (*of sth*) pression *f*; (*crowd*) foule *f*; *Lit* (*of battle*) mêlée *f*; **at the p. of a button, it ...** il suffit d'appuyer sur un bouton pour qu'il ...; **give it a slight p.** appuyez légèrement là-dessus; **give your trousers a p.** donne un coup de fer à ton pantalon; **to force one's way through the p.** fendre la foule, se frayer un chemin à travers la foule

(b) (*device*) (*for trousers, tennis racquet, coins etc*) presse *f*; (*for wine, cider, oil*) pressoir *m*; **hydraulic p.** presse hydraulique

(c) *Typ* (**printing**) **p.** presse *f* (d'imprimerie); **to go to p.** être mis sous presse, aller à l'impression; **we go to p. at 5.00**; on est mis sous presse à 5.00; (*copy deadline*) on boucle à 5.00; **at the time of going to p.** au moment d'être mis sous presse; **hot** *or* **straight from the p.** tout frais; **ready for p.** prêt à mettre sous presse; **to pass a proof for p.** donner le bon à tirer; **the Conway P.** (*printing firm*) l'Imprimerie *f* Conway; (*publishing firm*) les Éditions *fpl* Conway; **p. day** jour *m* de tirage

(d) *Journ* **the p.** la presse, les journaux; **p. freedom, freedom of the p.** la liberté de la presse; **to write for the p.** écrire pour les journaux; **to have** *or* **get a good/bad p.** avoir bonne/mauvaise presse; **the story appeared in the p.** on a parlé de cette affaire dans la presse; **they managed to keep her name out of the p.** ils ont réussi à ce que son nom ne paraisse pas dans la presse; **p. advertising** publicité *f* dans la presse; **p. copy** (*of book*) exemplaire *m* de service de presse; **p. hand-out** communiqué *m* de presse; **p. photographer** photographe *mf* de presse; **p. relations** relations *fpl* presse; **p. secretary** porte-parole *m inv*

(e) (*in weightlifting*) développé *m*

(f) *Scot* (*cupboard*) (**linen** *or* **clothes**) **p.** armoire *f* à linge

press² 1 *vt* (a) (*push*) (*sth*) appuyer sur; (*squeeze*) presser, serrer; (*into clay, wet cement etc*) enfoncer; (*grapes*) pressurer; (*with feet*) fouler; **he pressed my hand in his** il a serré ma main dans la sienne; **she pressed the child to her** elle a serré l'enfant contre elle; **she pressed her nose against the window** elle a collé son nez à la vitre; **to p. sth home** enfoncer qch; **to p. sth shut** fermer qch en appuyant dessus; **to p. sth flat** aplatir qch; **to p. sth (back) into shape** rendre sa forme à qch; **to p. a lemon** presser un citron; **to p. flowers** presser des fleurs

(b) *Tech* mettre sous presse; (*metal*) matricer, estamper; (*record*) matricer, presser; (*holes*) percer; (*paper*) calandrer

(c) (*trousers, skirt*) repasser, donner un coup de fer à; *Sewing* **to p. a seam** rabattre une couture

(d) (*put pressure on*) **to p. the enemy hard** *or* **closely** serrer l'ennemi de près, talonner l'ennemi; **to p. sb hard** harceler qn; **pressed by one's creditors** harcelé par ses créanciers; **to be pressed for time/money** être à court de temps/d'argent; **to p. sb for an answer/a decision** presser qn pour qu'il réponde/prenne une décision; **to p. sb to do sth** presser qn de faire qch; **if you p. her she'll tell you** si tu insistes, elle te le dira; **if pressed, he would admit ...** quand on insistait *ou* le poussait, il admettait ...; **to p. sth into service (as sth)** utiliser qch (comme qch)

(e) (*persist with sth*) **to p. an analogy/a comparison too far** pousser une analogie/une comparaison trop loin; **to p. (home) one's advantage** profiter de son avantage; **to p. one's attentions on sb** faire des avances à qn; **to p. a claim** insister sur une demande; **to p. a gift on sb** forcer qn à accepter un cadeau; **can I p. another piece of cake on you?** vous mangerez bien une autre part de gâteau?; **to p. a point** insister sur un point; *Jur* **to p. charges** porter plainte

2 *vi* (a) (*push*) appuyer, exercer une pression; **don't p. too hard** n'appuyez pas trop fort; **the crowd was pressing forward towards the exit** la foule se pressait pour gagner la sortie; **to p. close against sb** se serrer contre qn; **stop pressing!** (*pushing me*) ne poussez pas!

(b) **time is pressing** le temps presse; **nothing presses** rien ne presse; **to p. for an answer** insister pour avoir une réponse immédiate; **to p. for an adjournment/the law to be tightened up** exiger un ajournement/que la loi soit renforcée

▶ **press down** 1 *vtsep* appuyer sur; (*with force*) enfoncer 2 *vi* **to p. down on sb** peser sur qn

▶ **press on** *vi* (*walk faster*) presser *ou* forcer le pas; (*travel faster*) se presser, se dépêcher; (*continue journey*) continuer son chemin; (*persevere with activity*) persévérer, ne pas abandonner; (*continue activity*) continuer; **to p. on** *or* **ahead with one's work** poursuivre son travail; **p. on regardless!** allez-y quand même

▶ **press out** *vtsep* (a) (*juice etc*) exprimer (b) *Tech* (*holes*) percer (**out of** dans); (*shapes, parts*) découper (**out of** dans)

press agent *n* (*for film star, organization etc*) agent *m* de publicité

press attaché *n* attaché, -ée de presse

press badge *n* macaron *m* de presse

press baron *n* magnat *m* de la presse, baron *m* de presse

press box *n* tribune *f* de la presse

press-button *adj Tel* **p. dialling** numérotation *f* à touches

press campaign *n* campagne *f* de presse

press card *n* carte *f* de presse *ou* de journaliste

press clipping *n* coupure *f* de journal *ou* de presse

Press Complaints Commission *n* commission *f* des plaintes contre la presse

press conference *n* conférence *f* de presse

press coverage *n* couverture-presse *f*

press cutting *n* coupure *f* de journal *ou* de presse

pressed [prest] *adj* **p. flowers** fleurs *fpl* pressées; *Old-fashioned* **p. beef** bœuf *m* salé, bouilli et moulé en forme; **p. steel** acier *m* embouti

press gallery *n* tribune *f* de la presse

press gang *n Hist* enrôleurs *mpl*, racoleurs *mpl*

press-gang *vt Hist* **to p. sb into the navy/army** enrôler qn de force dans la marine/l'armée; *Fig F* **to p. sb into doing sth** forcer la main à qn pour qu'il fasse qch

pressing [ˈpresɪŋ] 1 *adj* (*danger, invitation*) pressant; (*work, matters*) urgent, pressant; (*debt*) criard; **the matter is p.** il y a urgence; **there is a p. need for action** il faut agir vite 2 *n* (a) (*act of pressing*) (*on sth*) pression *f*; (*of grapes*) pressurage *m*; (*with feet*) foulage *m*; (*of record, metal*) estampage *m*, matriçage *m*; (*of paper*) calandrage *m*; (*of clothes*) pressing *m* (b) (*pressed metal piece*) pièce *f* matricée

press lord *n* magnat *m* de la presse

pressman, *pl* **-men** [ˈpresmən] *n* (*journalist*) journaliste *m*, reporter *m*

pressmark [ˈpresmɑːk] *n* (*of book in library*) cote *f*

press office *n* service *m* de presse

press officer *n* attaché, -ée de presse

press release *n* communiqué *m* de presse

press report *n* reportage *m*

press stud *n Br* (*on clothing etc*) bouton *m* (à) pression

press-up *n Gym* traction *f*, *F* pompe *f*; **to do press-ups** faire des tractions *ou F* des pompes

pressure¹ [ˈpreʃər] *n* (a) (*on sth, sb*) pression *f*; **I felt the slight p. of his hand on my arm** j'ai senti la légère pression de sa main sur mon bras; *Fig* **to bring p. to bear** *or* **to put p. on sb** exercer une pression sur qn; **to act under p.** agir sous la pression des circonstances; **I can't take all this p.** je ne supporte pas d'être sous une telle pression; **he's been under a lot of p. lately** il est très stressé *ou* vraiment sous pression ces derniers temps; **financial p.** pressions financières; **the p. of business/work/modern life** la pression des affaires/du travail/de la vie moderne; **he pleaded p. of work to excuse his absence** il a excusé son absence en invoquant un excès de travail; **to work at high p.** être débordé; **there's no p., don't come if you don't want to** rien ne t'oblige, si tu ne veux pas venir, ne viens pas

(b) *Phys, MecE etc* pression *f*; (*of fluid, heavy body*) poussée *f*; *El* pression (électrique), tension *f*, voltage *m*; *Met* **high/low-p. area** zone *f* anticyclonique/cyclonique, zone de hautes/basses pressions; **p. pump** pompe *f* à pression; *Med*

p. sore escarre *f*; *Astronaut* **p. suit** combinaison *f* pressurisée; **p. switch** (*for oil pressure*) manocontact *m*
pressure² *vt* (*person*) exercer une pression sur; **stop pressuring me!** arrête de me presser comme ça!; **to p. sb to do** *or* **into doing sth** forcer *ou* obliger qn à faire qch, exercer des pressions sur qn pour qu'il/elle fasse qch
pressure chamber *n MecE* réservoir *m* d'air comprimé
pressure-charged [ˈpreʃətʃɑːdʒd] *adj Aut* suralimenté
pressure-cook *vt Culin* (faire) cuire sous pression *ou* à la cocotte-minute®
pressure cooker *n Culin* cocotte-minute ® *f*, pl cocottes-minute.autocuiseur *m*
pressure gauge *n* manomètre *m*
pressure group *n Pol etc* groupe *m* de pression
pressure point *n Physiol* point *m* de pression; *Med* (*bed sore*) point d'appui
pressurization [preʃəraɪˈzeɪʃən] *n Tech* pressurisation *f*, mise *f*/maintien *m* sous pression
pressurize [ˈpreʃəraɪz] *vt* (a) *Tech* pressuriser; *Av, Astronaut* **pressurized cabin/suit** cabine *f*/combinaison *f* pressurisée; *Nucl Phys* **pressurized water reactor** réacteur *m* à eau sous pression (b) (*put moral pressure on*) (*person*) exercer une pression sur; **to p. sb into doing sth** faire pression sur qn pour qu'il/elle fasse qch; **don't p. me** ne me force pas; **a pressurized environment** un environnement stressant
Prestel® [ˈprestel] *n Br TV* ≈ Minitel® *m*
prestidigitation [prestɪdɪdʒɪˈteɪʃən] *n Fml, Hum* prestidigitation *f*
prestidigitator [prestɪˈdɪdʒɪteɪtər] *n Fml, Hum* prestidigitateur, -trice
prestige [presˈtiːʒ] *n* prestige *m*; **it would mean a loss of p.** ce serait déchoir *ou* déroger; **p. flats** appartements *mpl* de grand standing; **a p. job** un poste prestigieux; **the p. value of the address** le caractère prestigieux de l'adresse, l'adresse prestigieuse; **it has p. value** c'est prestigieux; **p. goods** produits *mpl* prestigieux; **p. model** modèle *m* de prestige; *Mktg* **p. promotion** promotion *f* de prestige
prestigious [presˈtɪdʒəs] *adj* prestigieux
presto¹ [ˈprestəʊ] *adj, adv, n Mus* presto *m*
presto² *int* **hey p.!** et le tour est joué!
prestressed [priːˈstrest] *adj* (*concrete*) précontraint
presumably [prɪˈzjuːməblɪ] *adv* vraisemblablement; **p. she will come** il est probable qu'elle vienne, elle viendra vraisemblablement; **p. you told him that ...** je suppose que vous lui avez dit que ...; **have they left? – p.** ils sont partis? – je pense *ou* vraisemblablement
presume [prɪˈzjuːm] **1** *vt* présumer; **you're presuming rather a lot** tu es bien présomptueux; **to p. sb innocent** présumer qn innocent *ou* que qn est innocent; **he was presumed dead** (*by family etc*) on le croyait mort; (*by authorities*) on a présumé qu'il était mort, on l'a considéré comme décédé; **I p. (that) you've written to him** je suppose que vous lui avez écrit; **I p. so** je suppose, je présume que oui; *Fml* **I wouldn't p. to question her decision** je n'aurais pas la présomption de mettre sa décision en question; *Fml* **I wouldn't p. so far as to ...** je n'aurais pas la présomption de ...
2 *vi Fml* se montrer présomptueux; **to p. on one's friendship with sb** abuser de l'amitié de qn
presumption [prɪˈzʌmpʃən] *n* (a) (*assumption*) présomption *f*; **to make a p. that ...** présumer que ...; **I agreed on the p. that ...** j'ai dit que j'étais d'accord parce que je supposais que ...; **the p. is that she is dead** on présume qu'elle est morte; *Jur* **p. of law** présomption légale; *Jur* **p. of fact** présomption de fait (b) *Fml* (*arrogance*) présomption *f*
presumptive [prɪˈzʌmptɪv] *adj Jur etc* **p. evidence** (preuve *f* par) présomption *f*; **heir p.** héritier *m* présomptif, héritière *f* présomptive
presumptuous [prɪˈzʌmptjʊəs] *adj* présomptueux
presumptuously [prɪˈzʌmptjʊəslɪ] *adv* présomptueusement; **she p. assumed that ...** elle a eu la présomption de croire que ...
presumptuousness [prɪˈzʌmptjʊəsnɪs] *n* présomption *f*; **her p. in assuming that ...** sa présomption à croire que ...
presuppose [priːsəˈpəʊz] *vt* présupposer
presupposition [priːsʌpəˈzɪʃən] *n* présupposition *f*
pre-tax *adj* avant impôt; **p. margin** marge *f* avant impôt; **p. profit** bénéfice *m* avant impôt
pretence, *US* **pretense** [prɪˈtens] *n* (a) (*feigning*) faux-semblant *m*, simulation *f*; **to make a p. of doing sth** faire semblant de faire qch; **under the p. of friendship** sous prétexte d'amitié; **under the p. that ...** sous prétexte que ...; **under** *or* **on the p. of consulting me** sous prétexte de me consulter; **she makes no p. to photographic skills** elle ne prétend pas avoir des dons de photographe; **he made no p. of his boredom/his scepticism** il n'a pas caché son ennui/son scepticisme; **she made no p. of being interested/of feeling anything for him** elle n'a aucunement feint d'être intéressée/de ressentir quoi que ce soit envers lui
(b) (*pretension*) **devoid of all p.** sans aucune prétention
pretend¹ [prɪˈtend] **1** *vt* (a) (*feign*) feindre, simuler; **to p. ignorance** simuler l'ignorance, faire l'ignorant(e); **to p. to be ill** faire semblant d'être malade, faire le/la malade; **to p. to do sth** faire semblant *ou* mine de faire qch; **they pretended that nothing had happened** ils ont fait comme si rien ne s'était passé *ou* comme si de rien n'était; **let's p. that we're astronauts** on dirait qu'on était astronautes; **p. you haven't seen him** fais semblant de ne pas l'avoir vu; **I'll p. I didn't hear that last remark** je vais faire comme si je n'avais pas entendu cette dernière remarque; **it's no use pretending (that) I'm still young** ce n'est pas la peine de prétendre que je suis encore jeune; **he pretends he's 25** il se comporte comme s'il avait 25 ans; **he pretended he was a doctor** (*in order to deceive*) il s'est fait passer pour médecin; **pretending that he had a lot of work to do, he left early** sous prétexte d'avoir beaucoup de travail à faire, il est parti de bonne heure
(b) (*claim*) prétendre; **she does not p. to be artistic** elle ne prétend pas être artiste
2 *vi* (a) (*put on act*) faire semblant, jouer la comédie; **to play at 'let's p.'** jouer à faire semblant; **I can't go on pretending to her like this** je ne peux pas continuer à lui jouer la comédie comme ça; **don't worry, I was only pretending, I still want to do it!** mais non, c'était pour rire, je suis toujours d'accord!; **he appeared interested, but he was just pretending** il s'est montré intéressé mais il faisait semblant *ou* jouait la comédie
(b) *Fml* (*lay claim*) **to p. to sth** prétendre à qch; **I don't p. to great knowledge on the matter/any special expertise** je ne prétends pas savoir grand-chose sur la question/avoir des connaissances particulières; *Arch* **to p. to the throne** prétendre au trône
pretend² *adj F* **it was only p.!** c'était pour rire!; **a p. slap** une claque pour rire; **it's only p. money/a p. gun** ce n'est pas du vrai argent/un vrai pistolet
pretended [prɪˈtendɪd] *adj* (*emotion, interest*) feint, simulé; (*doctor, wealth, ignorance etc*) soi-disant, prétendu
pretender [prɪˈtendər] *n* (a) (*person who puts on act*) simulateur, -trice (b) (*claimant*) prétendant, -ante (**to** à); *Br Hist* **the Old P.** le Prétendant; *Br Hist* **the Young P.** le Jeune Prétendant
pretense [prɪˈtens] *n US* = **pretence**
pretension [prɪˈtenʃən] *n* (a) (*claim, esp a false one*) prétention *f* (**to** à); **man of no pretension(s)** homme sans prétentions; **to have pretensions to literary taste** se piquer de littérature; **to have social pretensions** vouloir arriver; **I make no pretensions to being impartial** je ne prétends pas être impartial (b) = **pretentiousness**
pretentious [prɪˈtenʃəs] *adj* prétentieux
pretentiously [prɪˈtenʃəslɪ] *adv* prétentieusement
pretentiousness [prɪˈtenʃəsnɪs] *n* prétention *f*
preterite [ˈpretərɪt] *n* [①A39,6] *Gram* prétérit *m*, passé *m* simple
preternatural [priːtəˈnætʃərəl] *adj Lit* hors du commun, exceptionnel
pre-test *vt* pré-tester
pre-testing *n* pré-tests *mpl*
pretext [ˈpriːtekst] *n* prétexte *m*; **to give sth as a p.** alléguer qch comme prétexte; **he came under** *or* **on the p. of consulting his sister** il est venu sous prétexte de consulter sa sœur
prettify [ˈprɪtɪfaɪ] *vt esp Pej* enjoliver
prettily [ˈprɪtɪlɪ] *adv* (*decorated, dressed*) joliment; **to smile p.** faire un/des sourire(s) charmeur(s); **she sang very p.** elle a chanté avec beaucoup de charme
prettiness [ˈprɪtɪnɪs] *n* (*of woman*) charmes *mpl*; *Pej* (*of style etc*) mignardise *f*; **the p. of her smile** son joli sourire
pretty [ˈprɪtɪ] **1** *adj* (*woman, child*) joli, mignon; (*thing*) joli; **p. picture/song** joli tableau/jolie chanson; (*with Pej nuance*) joli petit tableau/jolie petite chanson; **as p. as a picture** joli *ou* mignon comme tout; *usu Pej* **his p.-boy good looks** ses charmes de joli garçon; *Pej* **to make p. speeches** dire des gentillesses; *Iron* **(it was) not a p. sight** ce n'était pas beau à voir; *Iron* **a p. state of affairs!, a p. mess!** c'est du joli *ou* du propre!; (*that we're in*) nous voilà dans de beaux draps!; *F* **that'll cost me a p. penny!** ça va me coûter cher!; *F* **to make a p. penny out of sth** tirer une petite fortune de qch; *Hum* **not just a p. face** (*phrase humoristique utilisée pour montrer que l'on est surpris qu'une chose soit bien faite par une personne qui d'ailleurs n'est pas nécessairement jolie, par ex.* I made this table myself – I'm not just a p. face

2 *adv* **(a)** *(fairly)* assez, passablement; **I was p. certain that ...** j'étais à peu près sûr que ...; **I'm p. well** ça ne va pas trop mal; **p. good** *(not bad)* pas mal *ou* mauvais; *(very good)* vraiment bon; **it's p. difficult** c'est plutôt difficile; **p. nearly** *or* **much** *or* **well the same thing** à peu près la même chose

(b) *F* **to be sitting p.** ne pas avoir à s'en faire

▶ **pretty up** *vtsep* enjoliver; **to p. up oneself** se faire beau/belle

pretty-pretty *adj Pej (actor)* insipide, sans caractère; *(paintings, style)* gentillet; *(dress)* cucul la praline; **his p. good looks** son charme presque effeminé

pretzel ['pretz(ə)l] *n Culin* bretzel *m*

prevail [prɪ'veɪl] *vi* **(a)** *(come out strongest)* prévaloir, avoir l'avantage; **let us hope that justice/reason prevails** espérons que la justice/la raison l'emportera; **to p. over** *or* **against sb** prévaloir sur *ou* contre qn, avoir l'avantage *ou* l'emporter sur qn

(b) to p. on sb to do sth *(persuade)* amener *ou* décider qn à faire qch; **he was prevailed (up)on by his friends to ...** il se laissa persuader par ses amis de ...

(c) *(predominate)* prédominer, régner; *(of theory etc)* prédominer, avoir cours; **the conditions prevailing in France** les conditions qui règnent en France

prevailing [prɪ'veɪlɪŋ] *adj* **(a)** *(widespread)* (pré)dominant; **the p. opinion** l'opinion la plus répandue **(b)** *(current)* actuel; **in the then p. moral climate** dans le climat moral qui régnait alors; **the p. cold** le froid qui règne en ce moment; **p. fashions** la mode actuelle; **p. winds** vents *mpl* dominants

prevalence ['prevələns] *n (of opinion etc)* prédominance *f*; *Med* prévalence *f*; **p. of bribery** caractère *m* généralisé de la corruption; **p. of typhus** fréquence *f* des cas de typhus

prevalent ['prevələnt] *adj* **(a)** *(widespread)* (pré)dominant; *(opinion)* le plus répandu; **this opinion is p. among teenagers** cette opinion est très répandue parmi les adolescents; **the disease is p. here** la maladie est très répandue ici **(b)** *(current, prevailing) (conditions)* actuel; *(in the past)* de l'époque

prevaricate [prɪ'værɪkeɪt] *vi* user d'équivoques, tergiverser

prevarication [prɪværɪ'keɪʃən] *n* tergiversation *f*

prevaricator [prɪ'værɪkeɪtər] *n* personne *f* qui tergiverse *ou* qui use d'équivoques

prevent [prɪ'vent] *vt (wedding etc)* empêcher, faire obstacle à; *(accident, misfortune etc)* empêcher, prévenir, parer à; **to p. sb (from) doing sth, to p. sb's doing sth** empêcher qn de faire qch, empêcher que qn ne fasse qch; **to p. a disease from spreading** empêcher une maladie de s'étendre, éviter qu'une maladie ne s'étende; **there is nothing to p. our doing so** il n'y a rien qui nous en empêche; **to be unavoidably prevented from doing sth** être dans l'impossibilité matérielle de faire qch; **I cannot p. him** je ne peux pas l'en empêcher; **to p. any scandal** pour éviter tout scandale; **the police prevented the murderer from being lynched** la police a empêché que l'assassin ne soit lynché

preventable [prɪ'ventəb(ə)l] *adj* évitable; **it would have been easily p.** ç'aurait été facile à éviter; **a p. disease** une maladie que l'on peut prévenir

preventative [prɪ'ventətɪv] *adj, n* = **preventive**

prevention [prɪ'venʃən] *n* prévention *f*; **p. of accidents** prévention des accidents; **p. of disease** prévention de la maladie; **rust/fire/crime p.** protection *f* contre la rouille/les incendies/le crime; **society for the p. of cruelty to children/to animals** société *f* protectrice des enfants/des animaux; *Prov* **p. is better than cure** mieux vaut prévenir que guérir

preventive [prɪ'ventɪv] **1** *adj* **p. medicine** médecine *f* préventive, prophylaxie *f*; **p. measures** mesures *fpl* préventives *ou* de précaution; *Jur* **p. detention** détention *f* préventive **2** *n (measure)* mesure *f* préventive; *(medication)* médicament *m* préventif

preventively [prɪ'ventɪvlɪ] *adv* préventivement; **to act p. against sth** prendre des mesures préventives contre qch

preview¹ ['pri:vju:] *n Cin, Th* avant-première *f*, *pl* avant-premières; *(of art exhibition)* vernissage *m*; *esp US Cin (advertising film)* bande-annonce *f*, *pl* bandes-annonces; **we got a p. of the latest computers** on a eu un aperçu des derniers ordinateurs; *TV etc* **p. monitor** écran *m* de preview

preview² *vt Cin, Th (of person)* voir en avant-première; *(of cinema)* donner *ou* présenter en avant-première; *TV etc* prévisionner; *(film)* passer en avant-première

previous ['pri:vɪəs] **1** *adj* précédent; *(in time)* antérieur **(to** à); *(coming immediately before)* précédent; **they have returned to their p. intransigence** ils sont retournés à leur intransigeance passée; **my p. belief was that ...** mon sentiment était auparavant que ...; **on a p. occasion** une autre fois; **on the p. occasion we had met** la dernière fois que nous nous étions rencontrés; **the p. day** le jour précédent, la veille; **the p. evening** la veille au soir; **in the days/weeks p. to his departure** pendant les jours/semaines qui ont précédé son départ; **in the programme p. to this one** dans l'émission antérieure à celle-ci; **her p. job** son travail précédent; **tell me about your p. jobs** parlez-moi de vos emplois antérieurs; **in a p. existence** dans une vie antérieure; **have you had any p. experience?** avez-vous de l'expérience dans ce domaine?; **p. engagement** engagement *m* antérieur; **p. convictions** condamnations *fpl* antérieures; *(for motoring offences)* contraventions *fpl* antérieures; *Sl* **you're being a bit p.!** vous êtes trop pressé!, vous allez trop vite!

2 *adv* **p. to my departure** avant mon départ

previously ['pri:vɪəslɪ] *adv* auparavant; **three days p.** trois jours auparavant; **I was going to introduce them, but they'd met p.** j'allais les présenter l'un à l'autre, mais ils s'étaient déjà rencontrés

prewar [pri:'wɔ:r] *adj (prices etc)* d'avant-guerre; **the p. period/years** l'avant-guerre *m*/les années *fpl* d'avant-guerre

prey [preɪ] *n* proie *f*; **birds of p.** oiseaux *mpl* de proie, rapaces *mpl*; **beasts of p.** bêtes *fpl* de proie; **to pursue its p.** *(of beast)* poursuivre sa proie; **to be a p. to** être la proie de; *(fear, doubt etc)* être en proie à, être la proie de; **to fall p. to temptation** tomber en proie à la tentation

▶ **prey on, prey upon** *vipo (be predator of) (sth, sb)* faire sa proie de; *Fig* **something is preying on his mind** il y a quelque chose qui le tourmente *ou F* le travaille; **to p. on old people** *(of confidence trickster etc)* abuser des personnes âgées; **to p. on sb's fears/insecurity** exploiter les craintes/l'insécurité de qn

prezzie ['prezɪ] *n Br F* cadeau *m*

price¹ [praɪs] *n* [①B57,D,2] prix *m*; *(of shares)* cours *m*, cote *f*; *Horseracing* cote; **to rise** *or* **increase** *or* **go up in p.** *(of goods)* augmenter; **what p. is that article?** quel est le prix de cet article?; **petrol has come down** *or* **gone down in p.** le prix de l'essence a baissé; **car prices have fallen** le prix des voitures a chuté; **he charges reasonable prices** il pratique des prix raisonnables; **to quote** *or* **name a p.** faire le prix; **his pictures fetch huge prices** ses tableaux atteignent des sommes phénoménales *ou* se vendent à prix d'or; **what p. can you put on good health?** la santé n'a pas de prix; **to be beyond** *or* **without p.** être (d'un prix) inestimable *ou* hors de prix, ne pas avoir de prix; **you can buy it at a p.** vous pouvez l'acheter en y mettant le prix; **this must be done at any p.** il faut que cela se fasse à tout prix *ou* coûte que coûte; **not at any p.** à aucun prix; **I got a good p. for it** j'en ai eu un bon prix; *Fig* **to pay the p. (for sth)** payer le prix (pour qch); *Fig* **the p. paid for progress/fame** la rançon du progrès/de la gloire; *Fig* **to set a high p. on sth** faire grand cas de qch; **it's too high a p. (to pay)** c'est trop cher; *Fig* c'est trop cher payé; **to put** *or* **set a p. on sb's head** mettre la tête de qn à prix; **she's got a p. on her head** sa tête a été mise à prix; **everyone has their p.** il n'y a pas d'homme qu'on ne puisse acheter; *Horseracing* **long/short p.** forte/faible cote; *F* **what p. my chances of being appointed?** quelles sont mes chances d'être nommé?; **what p. glory!** pour ce qu'elle rapporte, la gloire!; **prices and incomes policy** politique *f* des prix et des salaires; *St Exch* **p./earnings ratio** ratio *m* cours-bénéfice; **p. inclusive of tax** prix taxe comprise; **p. agreement** entente *f* sur les prix; **p. break** baisse *f* de prix; **p. ceiling** prix plafond; **p. comparison** comparaison *f* des prix; **p. competitiveness** competitivité-prix *f*; **p. cut** réduction *f* des prix; **p. cutting** baisse de prix; **p. differential** écart *m ou* differential *m* de prix; **p. discount** remise *f* sur les prix; **p. discrimination** discrimination *f* par les prix; **p. elasticity** élasticité *f* des prix; **p. escalation** flambée *f* des prix; **p. ex-works** prix départ usine; **p. floor** prix plancher; **p. hike** hausse *f* de prix; **p. increase** hausse *f* des prix; **p. index** indice *m* des prix; **p. inflation** inflation *f* des prix; **p. label** étiquette *f* porte-prix; **p. labelling** étiquetage *m* des prix; **p. level** niveau *m* de prix; **p. markup** majoration *f* de prix; *Mktg* **p. plan** plan *m* prix; *Mktg* **p. point** point *m* prix; **p. policy** politique *f* des prix; *Mktg* **p. positioning** positionnement *m* de/des prix; **p. reduction** réduction *f* de prix; **p. scale** barème *m* des prix; **p. setting** détermination *f ou* fixation *f* des prix; *St Exch* **p. spreads** écarts *mpl* de cours; **p. stability** stabilité *f* des prix; *Mktg* **p. step** écart *m* de prix; **p. structure** structure *f* des prix; **p. undercutting** gâchage *m* des prix

price² *vt* **(a)** *(indicate cost of)* mettre un prix à; *(decide cost of)* fixer le prix de; **all goods must be clearly priced** le prix des marchandises doit être clairement indiqué; **the book is priced at £10** le livre est vendu (au prix de) dix livres **(b)** *(of customer)* s'informer du prix de **(c)** *Com* **to p. competitors out of the market** éliminer la concurrence en pratiquant des prix déloyaux; **to p. oneself out of the market** perdre sa clientèle en demandant des prix inabordables

▶ **price down** *vtsep Com* baisser le prix de

▶ **price up** *vtsep Com* augmenter le prix de

price-conscious *adj* attentif aux prix

price control *n* contrôle *m ou* régulation *f* des prix

priced [praɪst] *adj* **(a) high-p.** cher, coûteux; **low-p.** bon marché, à bas prix **(b)** (*marked with price*) marqué d'un prix; **everything in the window is p.** tous les prix des articles qui se trouvent dans la vitrine sont indiqués

price-elastic *adj Mktg* au prix élastique

price-fixing *n* (*by companies, cartel*) alignement *m* des prix

price freeze *n* blocage *m* des prix

price-inelastic *adj Mktg* au prix stable

priceless ['praɪslɪs] *n* **(a)** (*invaluable*) inestimable, qui n'a pas de prix **(b)** *F* (*funny*) (*joke, person etc*) impayable

price list *n* tarif *m*, liste *f* de prix

price range *n* écart *m* des prix; **what is your p.?** combien voulez-vous mettre?; **it's not in my p.** ce n'est pas dans mes prix

price rigging *n* alignement *m* des prix

price ring *n* monopole *m* des prix

price-sensitive *adj* sensible au prix

price tag *n* étiquette *f*

price war *n* guerre *f* des prix

pricey ['praɪsɪ] *adj F* cher, coûteux

pricing ['praɪsɪŋ] *n* (*setting price(s)*) fixation *f* du prix (**of sth** de qch); **p. policy** politique *f* des prix; **p. research** recherche *f* sur les prix; **anticipatory p.** fixation *f* des prix par anticipation

prick[1] [prɪk] *n* **(a)** (*of needle etc*) piqûre *f*; **pricks of conscience** remords *mpl* (de conscience), scrupules *mpl*; **to have a p. of conscience** être titillé par sa conscience **(b)** *Vulg* (*penis*) bite *f*, queue *f*; (*man*) connard *m*; **stop making such a p. of yourself!** arrête de faire le con!; **p. teaser** allumeuse *f*

prick[2] **1** *vt* (*make holes in*) (*sausages, potatoes*) piquer; (*balloon*) crever, percer; (*blister*) crever; **to p. one's finger** se piquer au *ou* le doigt; **the nurse pricked my arm with a needle** l'infirmière m'a piqué le bras avec une aiguille; **his conscience is pricking him** sa conscience l'aiguillonne *ou* le tourmente; **to p. a hole in sth** faire un trou dans qch **2** *vi* **his skin was pricking with the heat** sa peau le picotait à cause de la chaleur

▶ **prick out** *vtsep* (*seedlings*) repiquer

▶ **prick up 1** *vtsep* **to p. up one's ears** (*of animal*) dresser les oreilles; (*of person*) tendre *ou* dresser l'oreille **2** *vi* **his ears pricked up** (*of dog*) ses oreilles se sont dressées; (*of person*) il a dressé l'oreille

pricking ['prɪkɪŋ] **1** *adj* piquant; **a p. sensation** un picotement, un fourmillement **2** *n* (*piercing*) piquage *m*; (*sensation*) (*of skin etc*) picotement *m*, fourmillement *m*; **prickings of conscience** remords *mpl* (de conscience)

pricking out *n* (*of seedlings*) repiquage *m*

prickle[1] ['prɪk(ə)l] *n* **(a)** (*of animal*) piquant *m*; (*of plant*) épine *f*, piquant **(b)** (*sensation*) (*of skin etc*) picotement *m*; *Fig* (*of anticipation, excitement*) fourmillement *m*

prickle[2] **1** *vt* piquer, picoter, aiguillonner **2** *vi* (*of skin, parts of body*) fourmiller; *Fig* **to p. with indignation** se hérisser

prickling ['prɪklɪŋ] **1** *adj* (*sensation*) de picotement, de fourmillement **2** *n* picotement *m*

prickly ['prɪklɪ] *adj* **(a)** (*animal*) hérissé de piquants; (*plant*) épineux, piquant; *Fig* (*reply etc*) sec; (*person*) difficile; *Fig* **he's very p. today** il est très susceptible *ou* irritable aujourd'hui **(b)** (*sensation*) de picotement, de fourmillement

prickly heat *n Med* miliaire *f*, sudamina *mpl*

prickly pear *n Bot* (*tree*) figuier *m* de Barbarie; (*fruit*) figue *f* de Barbarie

pride[1] [praɪd] *n* **(a)** (*satisfaction*) fierté *f*, orgueil *m*; (*self-esteem*) amour-propre *m*, orgueil; *Pej* (*vanity*) orgueil, vanité *f*; **her children were a source of great p. to her** elle était très fière de ses enfants, ses enfants étaient sa grande fierté; **the sin of p.** le péché d'orgueil; **puffed up** *or* **blown up** *or* **swollen with p.** bouffi d'orgueil; **I have my p.!** j'ai ma fierté!; **to have too much p. to do sth** être trop fier pour faire qch; **to hurt** *or* **wound sb's p.** blesser l'amour-propre *ou* l'orgueil de qn; **to take (a) p. in sth** être fier de qch; **to take p. in one's work** mettre tout son amour-propre *ou* toute sa fierté dans son travail; **he takes great p. in his daughter's achievements** il est très fier des succès de sa fille; *Prov* **p. comes before a fall** l'arrogance précède la ruine et l'esprit altier la chute

(b) (*person, thing*) fierté *f*; **he is the p. of the family** il est la fierté de la famille; **the p. of my collection** le clou de ma collection; **the p. of the fleet** l'orgueil *m* de la flotte; **she's his p. and joy** elle fait toute sa fierté; **that antique table is her p. and joy** elle est très fière de cette table ancienne

(c) to have p. of place avoir *ou* tenir la place d'honneur

(d) (*of lions*) troupe *f*

pride[2] *vt* **to p. oneself (up)on sth/doing sth** être fier de qch/de faire qch; *Pej* s'enorgueillir *ou* se piquer *ou* se faire gloire de qch/de faire qch; **to p. oneself on one's knowledge of literature** se piquer de littérature

priest [priːst] *n* prêtre *m*; **the priests** (*as a body*) le clergé; *Cathol* **parish p.** = curé *m*; **assistant p.** vicaire *m*; **to become a p.** devenir prêtre

priestess ['priːstes] *n* prêtresse *f*

priesthood ['priːsthʊd] *n* **(a)** (*state*) prêtrise *f*, sacerdoce *m*; **to enter the p.** entrer dans les ordres, se faire prêtre **(b)** (*priests*) **the p.** le clergé

priestly ['priːstlɪ] *adj* sacerdotal, de prêtre; **p. duties** fonctions *fpl* sacerdotales

prig [prɪg] *n* **he's a real little p.** il fait toujours le petit saint; **don't be such a p.!** ne sois pas aussi bégueule!

priggish ['prɪgɪʃ] *adj* (*person*) collet monté *inv*; (*objection, criticism*) pudibond; **she's very p.** elle est très collet monté *ou* très bégueule

priggishness ['prɪgɪʃnɪs] *n* bégueulerie *f*, pudibonderie *f*

prim [prɪm] *adj* **(a)** *usu Pej* (*person*) collet monté *inv*; (*manner*) guindé, compassé; **she's so p. and proper** (*morally*) elle est tellement prude *ou* collet monté; (*in appearance, tidiness etc*) elle est tellement correcte **(b)** (*garden*) méticuleusement entretenu

prima ['priːmə] *adj* **p. ballerina** première danseuse *f* étoile; **p. donna** prima donna *f*, *pl* prime donne *ou* prima donna; *Fig* **he's a real p. donna** il joue à la star; *Fig* **he has a real p. donna mentality** il a *ou* fait des caprices de star

primacy ['praɪməsɪ] *n* **(a)** primauté *f*, prééminence *f* **(b)** *Rel* primatie *f*

primaeval [praɪ'miːv(ə)l] *adj* = **primeval**

prima facie ['praɪmə'feɪʃɪ] **1** *adv* de prime abord **2** *adj Jur* **p. case** = affaire *f* qui d'après les premiers témoignages paraît bien fondée; *Fig* **this is a p. case of ...** à première vue c'est une affaire de ...; *Jur* **p. evidence** commencement *m* de preuve

primal ['praɪm(ə)l] *adj* **(a)** (*first*) primitif, originel; *Psy* **p. scream** cri *m* primal **(b)** (*most important*) (*duty etc*) principal, fondamental

primarily ['praɪmərɪlɪ, praɪ'merɪlɪ] *adv* **(a)** (*principally*) principalement, essentiellement **(b)** (*originally*) à l'origine, originairement

primary ['praɪmərɪ] **1** *adj* (*original*) primitif, originel; (*first*) premier; (*fundamental, main*) premier, principal; *El, Phys etc* (*coil, current, electron etc*) primaire; **p. cause** cause *f* première; *El* **p. cell** élément *m* de pile; *Mktg* **p. demand** demande *f* primaire; *Comptr* **p. file** fichier *m* primaire *ou* principal; *Med* **p. lesion** lésion *f ou* accident *m* primaire; *St Exch* **p. market** marché *m* primaire, marché du neuf; **p. meaning of a word** sens *m* premier d'un mot; *Astron* **p. planet** planète *f* principale *ou* primaire; **p. product** produit *m* de base, matière *f* première, produit brut; *Geol* **p. rocks** roches *fpl* primaires; *Gram* **p. tenses** temps *mpl* primitifs

2 *n* **(a)** *Astron* planète *f* principale, grande planète

(b) *El* bobine *f* primaire

(c) (*colour*) couleur *f* fondamentale

(d) *Orn* (*feather*) rémige *f*

(e) *US Pol* (*election*) (élection *f*) primaire *f*; (*assembly*) assemblée *f* primaire

primary colours *npl* couleurs *fpl* fondamentales

primary education *n Sch* enseignement *m* primaire

primary election *n US Pol* (élection *f*) primaire *f*

primary industries *n Econ* secteur *m* primaire

primary infection *n Med* primo-infection *f*, *pl* primo-infections

primary school *n Sch* école *f* primaire

primate ['praɪmeɪt] *n* **(a)** *Rel* primat *m*; **the P. of All England** l'archevêque *m* de Cantorbéry **(b)** *Zool* primate *m*

prime[1] [praɪm] *adj* **(a)** (*most important*) premier, principal; **of p. importance** d'importance capitale, de (toute) première importance; **p. meridian of Greenwich** méridien *m* (d')origine de Greenwich; **p. motive** principal mobile *m* (**of** de); *Fin* **p. rate** taux *m* préférentiel **(b)** (*excellent*) (*wines etc*) excellent, de qualité supérieure, de première qualité; (*example, condition, building land etc*) excellent; **p. quality meat** viande *f* de premier choix

prime[2] *n* **(a)** (*best time*) **p. of youth** fleur *f* de la jeunesse; **in the p. of life, in one's p.** à *ou* dans la fleur de l'âge; **to be past one's/its p.** ne plus être de la première jeunesse **(b)** *Rel* prime *f*; **to say/sing the p.** dire/chanter prime **(c)** *Math* nombre *m* premier

prime[3] *vt* **(a)** (*warhead, pump, gun etc*) amorcer; **to p. oneself for battle/for a fight** se préparer au combat; *Fig* **to p. the pump** donner son appui (dans un premier temps) **(b**

(*provide with information*) (*person*) renseigner; **to p. sb for a speech** préparer qn à faire son discours; **the witnesses had all been primed by the police** les dépositions des témoins leur avaient été suggérées par la police; **to be well primed (with alcohol)** être bien imbibé **(c)** (*prepare*) (*surface to be painted*) apprêter

prime minister *n* premier ministre *m*

prime ministerial *adj* de/du premier ministre

prime ministership *n* poste *m* de premier ministre; **during her p.** pendant qu'elle était premier ministre

prime mover *n MecE* force *f* motrice; *Fig* (*of plot etc*) âme *f*; *Phil* premier moteur *m*

prime number *n Math* nombre *m* premier

primer[1] ['praɪmər] *n* **(a)** (*of explosive*) amorce *f*; **p. detonator** amorce-détonateur *f*, *pl* amorces-détonateurs **(b)** (*paint*) apprêt *m*

primer[2] *n Old-fashioned* (*reading book*) premier livre *m* de lecture; (*for mathematics etc*) (*junior level*) premier livre; (*more advanced*) introduction *f*

prime time *n TV* heures *fpl* de grande écoute, prime time *m*; **p. advertising** publicité *f* aux heures de grande écoute

primeval [praɪ'miːv(ə)l] *adj* primitif

priming ['praɪmɪŋ] *n* **(a)** (*of pump*) amorçage *m*; **p. (powder)** (*explosive*) amorce *f*; **p. charge** charge *f* d'amorçage **(b)** (*in painting*) (*of wood etc*) apprêtage *m*, apprêt *m*; (*paint*) apprêt

primitive ['prɪmɪtɪv] **1** *adj* primitif; (*manners*) grossier, rude; (*understanding*) rudimentaire; **p. language** langue *f* primitive; **the plumbing is very p.** les installations sanitaires sont plutôt rudimentaires **2** *n Art* (*painter, picture*) primitif *m*; (*in anthropology*) primitif, -ive; *Math* primitive *f*

primitively ['prɪmɪtɪvlɪ] *adv* primitivement; (*constructed, equipped*) de manière rudimentaire

primitiveness ['prɪmɪtɪvnɪs] *n* caractère *m* primitif; (*of plumbing, understanding etc*) caractère rudimentaire; (*of manners*) grossièreté *f*, rudesse *f*

primitivism ['prɪmɪtɪvɪz(ə)m] *n* primitivisme *m*

primly ['prɪmlɪ] *adv* (*to smile, remark*) d'un air collet monté, d'un air guindé; (*to dress, behave*) avec pruderie *ou* pudibonderie, très correctement

primness ['prɪmnɪs] *n* (*of person's behaviour, manner*) pruderie *f*, pudibonderie *f*; (*of person's appearance*) côté *m* très correct, air *m* guindé *ou* compassé; (*of garden*) ordre *m* méticuleux

primogeniture [praɪməʊ'dʒenɪtʃər] *n* primogéniture *f*; **(right of) p.** droit *m* d'aînesse

primordial [praɪ'mɔːdɪəl] *adj* primordial, originel

primordially [praɪ'mɔːdɪəlɪ] *adv* primordialement, originellement

primp [prɪmp] *Old-fashioned F* **1** *vi* (*dress up*) se mettre sur son trente et un; *Pej* s'attifer **2** *vt* **to p. oneself up** se mettre sur son trente et un; *Pej* s'attifer

primrose ['prɪmrəʊz] *n* (*plant*) primevère *f*; **p. (yellow)** jaune pâle *inv*; *Fig Lit* **the p. path** le chemin de la facilité

primula ['prɪmjʊlə] *n* (*plant*) primula *f*, primevère *f*

primus® ['praɪməs] *n* **p. (stove)** réchaud *m* portatif

prince [prɪns] *n* prince *m*; **to live like a p.** vivre comme un prince; **p. of the blood** prince du sang; **P. Charming** prince charmant; **P. Charles** le Prince Charles; *Eng Hist* **the Black P.** le Prince Noir; *Fig* **the P. of Darkness** le prince des ténèbres; **the P. of Wales** le Prince de Galles; **p. consort/regent** prince consort/régent

Prince Edward Island *n* île *f* du Prince-Édouard

princeling ['prɪnslɪŋ] *n* principicule *m*

princely ['prɪnslɪ] *adj* princier; (*gift*) magnifique; **to get a p. salary** être payé princièrement; **a p. sum** une somme princière

princess [prɪn'ses] *n* princesse *f*; **P. Anne** la Princesse Anne; **the P. of Wales** la Princesse de Galles; *Br* **p. royal** Princesse Royale (*titre conféré de temps en temps à la fille aînée du monarque*)

principal[1] ['prɪnsɪp(ə)l] *adj* principal; **p. events in one's life** événements *mpl* capitaux de la vie; **p. boy** (*in pantomime*) = rôle *m* du héros (*joué par une femme*)

principal[2] *n* **(a)** (*person*) (*of college*) principal, -ale; (*of school*) directeur, -trice; *Com, Jur* (*in transaction*) mandant, -ante, commettant *m*; *St Exch* donneur, -euse d'ordre; *Jur* (*of crime*) auteur *m*; *Mus* soliste *mf*; *Th* acteur, -trice qui tient le rôle principal; *Jur* **p. and agent** commettant, -ante et préposé(e); **principals in a duel** adversaires *mpl* dans un duel **(b)** *Fin* (*of debt*) capital *m*, principal *m*; **p. and interest** principal et intérêts

principal clause *n Gram* proposition *f* principale

principality [prɪnsɪ'pælɪtɪ] *n* principauté *f*

principally ['prɪnsɪplɪ] *adv* principalement, surtout

principle ['prɪnsɪp(ə)l] *n* **(a)** (*idea*) principe *m*; **fundamental p.** principe premier *ou* fondamental; **in p.** en principe; **to reach an agreement in p.** aboutir à un accord de principe; **machines that work on the same p.** machines qui fonctionnent sur *ou* d'après le même principe **(b)** (*moral rule*) principe *m*; **to have high principles** avoir des principes; **man of no principles** homme sans principes; **on p.** par principe; **to do sth on p.** faire qch par principe; **to stick to one's principles** rester fidèle à ses principes; **it's the p. of the thing** c'est une question de principe **(c)** *Phil* (*law*) loi *f*; **p. of causality** loi de causalité

principled ['prɪnsɪp(ə)ld] *adj* (*behaviour*) dicté par des principes; (*person*) qui a des principes; **to be p.** (*of person*) avoir des principes; **it was very p. of her to refuse** elle a démontré de hauts principes en refusant; *F* **he doesn't have a p. bone in his body!** il est complètement dépourvu de principes!

print[1] [prɪnt] *n* **(a)** (*imprint*) empreinte *f*; (*of foot*) marque *f*, trace *f*; **thumb p.** empreinte du pouce

(b) (*printed matter*) matière *f* imprimée; **to read several pages of p.** lire plusieurs pages de texte; **to appear in p.** (*of writings*) paraître; (*of author*) se faire imprimer; **to see one's name appear in p.** voir son nom apparaître dans un livre/journal/*etc*; **edition in p.** édition en vente (courante); **out of p.** épuisé; **the p. unions** les syndicats *mpl* des typographes **p. media** la presse écrite et l'édition

(c) (*characters*) caractères *mpl*; **large/small p.** gros/petits caractères; **the p. was so small I could barely read it** il était imprimé en caractères si petits que j'avais du mal à le lire; **always read the small p.** (*of contract, guarantee etc*) il faut toujours lire les petits caractères

(d) (*engraving etc*) estampe *f*

(e) *Phot* épreuve *f*; **to take a p. from a negative** tirer une épreuve d'un cliché; **contact p.** épreuve par contact

(f) (*material*) indienne *f*; **(cotton) p.** imprimé *m*

(g) *Comptr* **p. code** code *m* d'impression; **p. drum** tambour *m* d'impression; **p. file** fichier *m* d'impression; **p. format** format *m* d'impression; **p. head** tête *f* d'impression; **p. job** (*file*) fichier *m* à imprimer; **p. list** liste *f* de fichiers à imprimer; **p. menu** menu *m* d'impression; **p. option** option *f* d'impression; **p. preview** prévisualisation *f*, aperçu *m* avant impression; **p. quality** qualité *f* d'impression; **p. queue** liste *f* de fichiers à imprimer; **p. queuing** mise *f* en attente à l'impression; **p. ribbon** ruban *m* d'impression; **p. screen key** touche *f* d'impression d'écran; **to do a p. screen** imprimer un écran; **p. speed** vitesse *f* d'impression; **p. wheel** roue *f* d'impression

print[2] **1** *vt* **(a)** (*book etc*) imprimer; (*copies*) tirer; (*newspaper*) imprimer, tirer; **printed in France** imprimé en France; **the story was printed in all the national newspapers** la nouvelle a été relatée par tous les grands quotidiens

(b) (*imprint*) imprimer (**sth on sth** qch sur qch); **incidents that p. themselves on the memory** incidents qui se gravent dans la mémoire

(c) (*write*) (*address, name etc*) écrire en lettres d'imprimerie

(d) *Phot* **to p. a negative** tirer une épreuve d'un cliché

(e) *Tex* (*cotton etc*) imprimer

2 *vi* **(a)** (*of printer*) imprimer; *Phot* **the negative hasn't printed very well** le cliché n'a pas donné un très bon résultat au tirage; **the book is now printing** le livre est à l'impression *ou* est actuellement sous presse

(b) (*when writing*) écrire en lettres d'imprimerie; **please p.** (*on form etc*) veuillez écrire en lettres d'imprimerie

▶ **print off** *vtsep* (*book*) imprimer; (*copy*) tirer; (*magazine*) tirer, imprimer

▶ **print out** *vtsep Comptr* imprimer

printable ['prɪntəb(ə)l] *adj* publiable, imprimable

printed ['prɪntɪd] *adj* imprimé; **p. circuit** circuit *m* imprimé; **p. circuit board** carte *f* de *ou* à circuits imprimés; *Tex* **p. cotton** coton *m* imprimé; **p. directory** annuaire *m* papier; **p. form** imprimé *m*, formulaire *m*; **p. matter** (*sent by post*) imprimés *mpl*; **p. paper rate** (*at post office*) tarif *m* imprimés; **such is the power of the p. word** tel est le pouvoir de l'écrit

printer ['prɪntər] *n* **(a)** *Typ etc* (*person*) imprimeur *m*; (*machine*), *Comptr* imprimante *f*; *Telecom* téléscripteur *m*; **p.'s devil** apprenti *m* imprimeur; **p.'s error** faute *f* d'impression, coquille *f*; **p.'s proofs** épreuves *fpl* d'imprimerie; **p.'s reader** correcteur, -trice d'épreuves; *Comptr* **p. buffer** mémoire *f* tampon d'imprimante; **p. cable** câble *m* d'imprimante; *Comptr* **p. code** code *m* d'imprimante; **p. drum** tambour *m* d'impression; **p. engine** mécanique *f* d'impression; **p. font** fonte *f* imprimante; **p. interface** interface *f* d'imprimante; **p. language** langage *m* d'impression; **p. output** sortie *f* d'imprimante; **p. paper** papier *m* d'impression; **p. sharing** partage *m* d'imprimantes;

p. speed vitesse *f* d'impression; **p. spooler** spouleur *m* d'imprimante, pilote *m* de mise en attente des fichiers à imprimer; **p. spooling** mise *f* en attente des fichiers à imprimer; **p. stand** table *f* d'imprimante

(**b**) *Phot* (*person*) tireur, -euse d'épreuves; (*machine*) tireuse *f*

printer driver *n Comptr* programme *f* de commande d'impression, pilote *m* d'imprimante

printer port *n Comptr* port *m* d'imprimante

printing ['prɪntɪŋ] *n* (**a**) (*action*) (*of book*) impression *f*, tirage *m*; (*craft*) imprimerie *f*, typographie *f*; (*writing*) écriture *f* en lettres d'imprimerie; **p. error** erreur *f* typographique; **p. ink** encre *f* d'imprimerie; **p. paper** papier *m* d'impression (**b**) *Phot* tirage *m* (**c**) *Tex* **cotton p.** impression *f* sur coton

printing press *n* presse *f* d'imprimerie

printout ['prɪntaʊt] *n Comptr* impression *f*, sortie *f* (sur) imprimante, copie *f*; (*continuous*) listing *m*, listage *m*

print room *n* cabinet *m* d'estampes

printrun ['prɪntrʌn] *n* tirage *m*; **p. of 5,000** tirage à 5 000 exemplaires

print shop *n* imprimerie *f*

print-through paper *n Comptr* papier *m* à effet d'empreinte, liasse *f* carbonnée

prior[1] ['praɪər] *adj* précédent, antérieur; **p. to** avant; **p. to his winning/appointment** avant qu'il ne gagne/ne soit nommé; **to have a p. claim** avoir des prétentions antérieures; **p. engagement** engagement *m* antérieur; **I have a p. engagement** je suis déjà pris; **to have p. knowledge of sth** être déjà au courant de qch

prior[2] *n Rel* prieur *m*

prioress ['praɪəres] *n Rel* prieure *f*

prioritization [praɪɒrɪtaɪ'zeɪʃən] *n* **the p. of all these jobs** la définition d'un ordre de priorité pour toutes ces tâches; **they opted for a p. of expansion** ils ont décidé de donner la priorité à l'expansion

prioritize [praɪ'ɒrɪtaɪz] **1** *vt* (**a**) (*arrange according to priority*) (*several tasks etc*) donner un ordre de priorité à; **it depends how you p. them** tout dépend de l'ordre de priorité que tu établis; **it was wrongly prioritized** on a mal jugé de son importance (**b**) (*give priority to*) (*one task etc*) donner la priorité à **2** *vi* (*evaluate priorities*) établir un ordre de priorités

priority [praɪ'ɒrɪtɪ] **1** *n* priorité *f*; **to give p. to sb/sth** donner la priorité à qn/qch; **to have p.** (*of job etc*) être prioritaire; (*of person when driving*) avoir la priorité; **to have** *or* **take p. over sb** avoir la préséance *ou* la priorité sur qn; **hygiene has a high p.** l'hygiène est tout à fait prioritaire; **our first p. is to buy the tickets** il faut que nous achetions les billets, c'est une priorité absolue; **p.** (*on message*) urgent; **to have one's priorities right/wrong** savoir/ne pas savoir ce qui est important; **p. of claim** priorité

2 *adj attrib* **p. booking** réservation *f* prioritaire; **p. holder** prioritaire *mf*; *Jur* **p. rights** droits *mpl* de priorité *ou* de préférence; *St Exch* **p. share** action *f* privilégiée; **to get p. treatment** (*of task*) être exécuté *ou* fait en priorité

priory ['praɪərɪ] *n Rel* prieuré *m* (*de couvent*)

prise [praɪz] *vt Br* = **prize**[4]

prism ['prɪz(ə)m] *n* prisme *m*; **p. binoculars** jumelle(s) *f(pl)* prismatiques *ou* à prismes

prismatic [prɪz'mætɪk] *adj* (*shape, colour etc*) prismatique; **p. binoculars** jumelle(s) *f(pl)* prismatiques *ou* à prismes

prison ['prɪz(ə)n] *n* [①**A6,d,i**] *also Fig* prison *f*; **to send sb to p., to put sb in p.** mettre qn en prison; **to throw sb into p.** jeter qn en prison; **he's been in p.** il a fait de la prison; *Fig* **to escape from the p. of one's marriage** mettre fin à un mariage qui était devenu une prison

prison camp *n* camp *m* de prisonniers

prisoner ['prɪz(ə)nər] *n* (**a**) (*captive*) prisonnier, -ière; **to take/hold sb p.** faire/retenir qn prisonnier; **to take prisoners** faire des prisonniers; *Fig* **to take no prisoners** être impitoyable; **p. of conscience** prisonnier, -ière politique *ou* d'opinion; *Fig* **to be a p. of one's past** être prisonnier de son passé (**b**) *Jur* détenu, -ue; (*after sentence*) détenu, -ue, prisonnier, -ière; **p. at the bar** prévenu, -ue; (*for serious crimes*) accusé, -ée

prisoner of war *n* prisonnier *m* de guerre; **p. camp** camp *m* de prisonniers de guerre

prison officer *n* gardien, -ienne de prison

prison visitor *n* visiteur, -euse de prison

prison yard *n* cour *f* de prison

prissy ['prɪsɪ] *adj* (*person*) (*fussy*) pointilleux, maniaque; (*prudish*) collet monté *inv*, bégueule; (*language*) pudibond

pristine ['prɪstaɪn, -iːn] *adj* (*spotless*) impeccable, sans tache; **in p. condition** comme neuf

prithee ['prɪðɪ] *int Arch* je te prie

privacy ['praɪvəsɪ, 'prɪ-] *n* intimité *f*; **the p. of one's home** l'intimité de son foyer; **desire for p.** désir d'échapper aux regards indiscrets; **I like my p.** j'aime avoir un peu d'intimité; **to disturb sb's p.** faire intrusion chez qn; **there is no p. here** on n'est jamais seul ici

Privacy Commissioner *n Can* Commissaire *m* à la protection de la vie privée

private ['praɪvɪt] **1** *adj* (**a**) (*personal*) privé; **can I talk to you about something p.?** puis-je discuter avec vous de quelque chose de personnel?; **can we go somewhere p.?** est-ce que nous pourrions discuter en privé?; **a p. joke** une plaisanterie entre nous/eux/*etc*; **the p. life of an actor** la vie privée d'un acteur; **in p. life** dans la vie privée, dans le privé; **p. individual** particulier *m*; **p. motives** motifs *mpl* personnels; **p. parts** (*genitals*) parties *fpl* (génitales); *Jur* **p. wrong** atteinte *f* aux droits d'un individu

(**b**) (*secret*) secret, -ète; **to keep a matter p.** tenir une affaire secrète; **she is a very p. person** c'est quelqu'un de très discret *ou* réservé; **he is very p. about his affairs** il est très réservé *ou* secret pour ce qui est de ses affaires; **p. and confidential** secret et confidentiel; **to mark a letter p.** marquer sur une lettre 'confidentiel' *ou* 'personnel'; **you stay out of this! — it's p. between John and me** reste en dehors de tout ça! — ça ne regarde que John et moi; **to be received in p. audience** être reçu en audience particulière

(**c**) (*for personal use*) **p. bathroom** salle *f* de bain particulière; *Telecom* **p. branch exchange** autocommutateur *m* privé; **p. bus** bus *m* réservé; **p. car** voiture *f* particulière *ou* privée; **p. house** maison *f* particulière; **p. lessons** cours *mpl* particuliers; **p. office** cabinet *m* particulier; **this is his own p. room** c'est sa pièce à lui; **for my p. use** pour mon usage personnel

(**d**) (*to which public not admitted*) **the funeral will be p.** les obsèques auront lieu dans la plus stricte intimité; **P.** (*on sign*) entrée interdite au public; **p. dance** bal *m* sur invitation; **p. fishing** pêche *f* réservée; **p. function** réception *f* privée; *Tel* **p. line** ligne *f* intérieure; *Th* **p. performance** représentation *f* à bureaux fermés; **p. party** (*gathering*) réunion *f* privée *ou* intime; (*group*) groupe *m* de particuliers; **p. property** propriété *f* privée; **p. road** chemin *m ou* route *f* privé(e); **p. room** (*in hotel etc*) salon *m* réservé; **p. sale** vente *f* à l'amiable

(**e**) **p. company** entreprise *f* privée; **p. nursing home** clinique *f* privée; **p. patient** malade *mf* privé(e); **p. patients** (*of doctor*) clientèle *f* privée; *Br* **p. practice** clientèle privée, cabinet *m* (médical) privé; **p. room** (*in hospital*) chambre *f* particulière

2 *n* (**a**) **in p.** (*in private life*) dans la vie privée; (*with close family*) dans l'intimité; (*with friends etc, not in public*) dans le privé; (*confidentially*) en privé; **married in p.** marié dans l'intimité; **to sit in p.** (*of assembly*) se réunir en séance privée; *Jur* **to hear a case in p.** juger une affaire à huis clos; **to speak to sb in p.** parler à qn en privé; **in p. she admitted she was worried** en privé elle a admis qu'elle était inquiète; (*to herself*) dans son for intérieur elle a admis qu'elle était inquiète

(**b**) *Mil* simple soldat *m*; **the privates and the NCOs** la troupe et les gradés; **p. Jones!** soldat Jones!

(**c**) **privates** (*genitals*) parties *fpl* (génitales)

private bank *n* banque *f* privée

private citizen *n* simple *m* particulier

private detective *n* détective *m* privé

private education *n* (*not state*) enseignement *m* privé

private enterprise *n* entreprise *f* privée; (*principle*) libre entreprise

privateer [praɪvə'tɪər] *n Hist* (*ship*) (bâtiment *m* armé en) corsaire *m*; (*man*) corsaire

private eye *n F* détective *m* privé

private income *n* rentes *fpl*

private industry *n* privé *m*

private investigator *n* détective *m* privé

private-label brand *n Mktg* marque *f* de distributeur

privately ['praɪvɪtlɪ] *adv* (**a**) (*as/by a private individual*) (*to act, speak etc*) en simple particulier; (*to sell*) de gré à gré; **to benefit p. from sth** bénéficier personnellement de qch; **p. owned** qui appartient à un particulier; (*hotel*) familial; (*not state-owned*) du (secteur) privé

(**b**) (*in private*) en privé; **to speak to sb p.** parler à qn en privé *ou* en particulier

(**c**) (*inwardly*) (*to think, suspect etc*) intérieurement

(**d**) (*not through state system*) **I had it done p.** (*of treatment at doctor's, dentist's etc*) je l'ai fait faire à mes frais; **she was p. educated** elle a fait sa scolarité dans le privé; **he had them p. educated** il les a mis dans une école privée

private means *n* rentes *fpl*

private member *n Parl* = simple député *m*; **p.'s bill** = proposition *f* de loi faite par un simple député

private school *n* école *f* privée

private secretary *n* secrétaire *mf* particulier, -ière

private sector *n* (secteur *m*) privé *m*; **p. salaries** salaires *mpl* du secteur privé

private soldier *n* simple soldat *m*, (soldat de) deuxième classe *m*

privation [praɪ'veɪʃən] *n* privation *f* (**of** de); **to live in p.** vivre dans la privation, vivre de privations

privatization [praɪvɪtaɪ'zeɪʃən] *n* privatisation *f*

privatize ['praɪvɪtaɪz] *vt* privatiser

privet ['prɪvɪt] *n* (*plant*) troène *m*; **p. hedge** haie *f* de troènes

privilege¹ ['prɪvɪlɪdʒ] *n* **(a)** *also Comptr* privilège *m*; **to grant sb certain privileges** octroyer certains privilèges *ou* avantages à qn; **to enjoy the p. of doing sth** jouir du privilège *ou* avoir le privilège de faire qch; **it is my p. to introduce ...** j'ai le grand honneur *ou* le privilège de vous présenter ...; **it was a p. to have known her** c'est un privilège de l'avoir connue; **I had the p. of knowing him personally** j'ai eu le privilège de le connaître personnellement **(b)** *Jur* (*of lawyer*) droit *m* de tenir une information secrète; *Parl* immunité *f* parlementaire

privilege² *vt* (*usu passive*) (*person*) privilégier; **I am privileged to be able to present to you ...** j'ai l'honneur *ou* le privilège de vous présenter ...

privileged ['prɪvɪlɪdʒd] **1** *adj* privilégié; **the p. classes** les classes *fpl* privilégiées; **a p. few** quelques privilégiés; **p. information** informations *fpl* confidentielles **2** *npl* **the p.** les privilégiés *mpl*

privily ['prɪvɪlɪ] *adv Arch* en secret

privy ['prɪvɪ] **1** *adj* **(a)** *Fml* **to be p. to sth** (*have knowledge of*) avoir connaissance de qch **(b)** (*private*) *Br* **the P. Council** le Conseil privé (*du souverain*); **the P. Purse** = la cassette du souverain **2** *n Old-fashioned* (*toilet*) cabinets *mpl* (*souvent en dehors de la maison*)

prize¹ [praɪz] *n* **(a)** (*award*) prix *m*; (*what is at stake, to be won*) enjeu *m*; *F* **no prizes for guessing** ce n'est pas difficile à deviner; **to win the p., to carry off the p.** remporter le prix; *Sch* **p. day** jour *m* de la distribution des prix; **p. money** prix; **the p. money is £5000** le prix se monte à 5 000 livres; **what did you do with the p. money?** qu'est-ce que tu as fait avec l'argent du prix? **(b)** (*in a lottery*) lot *m*; **to win first p.** gagner le gros lot; **the first p. is a week in London** le premier prix est une semaine à Londres **(c)** *Naut* (*ship*) prise *f*, capture *f*

prize² *adj attrib* (*example*) excellent, parfait; (*tulips, sheep etc*) primé; **p. bull** taureau *m* primé; *F* **he's a p. idiot** c'est un abruti de première; **it's my p. possession** c'est l'objet que je prise au-dessus de tout

prize³ *vt* (*value*) priser; **to p. sth highly** faire grand cas de qch; **her most prized possession** l'objet qu'elle prise au-dessus de tout

prize⁴ *vt Br* (*force*) **to p. sth up** soulever qch à l'aide d'un levier *etc*; **I managed to p. the plaque off the wall** j'ai réussi à décrocher *ou* détacher la plaque du mur; **to p. a lid open** forcer un couvercle avec un levier *etc*; **they had to p. his hand open to get the key** ils ont dû ouvrir sa main de force pour avoir la clé; **to p. sth out of sb** (*money*) soutirer qch à qn; (*secret, information*) arracher qch à qn; **to p. sth out of sb's grasp** arracher qch à qn

prize draw *n* tombola *f*

prizefight ['praɪzfaɪt] *n* match *m* de boxe professionnel

prizefighter ['praɪzfaɪtər] *n* boxeur *m* professionnel

prizefighting ['praɪzfaɪtɪŋ] *n* boxe *f* professionnelle

prizegiving ['praɪzgɪvɪŋ] *n* distribution *f* des prix

prize list *n* palmarès *m*

prize ring *n Boxing* ring *m* des professionnels

prizewinner ['praɪzwɪnər] *n* (*in game, lottery etc*) gagnant, -ante (du prix); *Sch, Art etc* lauréat, -ate

prizewinning ['praɪzwɪnɪŋ] *adj* (*novel etc*) primé; (*ticket, number*) gagnant

PRO [piːɑː'rəʊ] *n* **(a)** (*abbr* **public relations officer**) responsable *mf* des relations publiques **(b)** *Br* (*abbr* **Public Record Office**) ≈ Archives nationales *fpl*

pro¹ [prəʊ] *n* **(a)** *Sp etc F* (*professional person*) pro *mf inv*; **to turn p.** passer pro; **she was a real p.** (*actress, singer etc*) c'était une vraie pro **(b)** *Sl* (*prostitute*) professionnelle *f*

pro² **1** *adj, prep* pour; **he was very p. (the idea)** il était tout à fait pour (cette idée) **2** *npl* **the pros and cons** le pour et le contre

pro- [prəʊ] *pref* pro-; **to be p.-hanging/-abortion** être partisan de la pendaison/de l'interruption volontaire de grossesse; **a p.-hanging démonstration** une démonstration en faveur de la pendaison; **to be p.-Europe/American** être pro-européen/pro-américain; **the p.-Yeltsin forces** les forces de Yeltsin

proactive [prəʊ'æktɪv] *adj* dynamique, qui prend les devants, plein d'initiative; **you should be more p.** prends plus souvent des initiatives; **p. marketing** mercatique *f* proactive; *esp Am Admin* **p. staffing** dotation *f* par anticipation

pro-am [prəʊ'æm] *adj Golf* (*abbr* **professional-amateur**) **p. tournament** = tournoi *m* opposant des équipes composées chacune d'un professionnel et d'un amateur

probability [prɒbə'bɪlɪtɪ] *n* [①A56-59; B36-37,K] probabilité *f* **in all p.** selon toute probabilité *ou* vraisemblance; **the p. is that it will get hotter** il est probable qu'il fasse encore plus chaud; **there is a strong p./not much p. that ...** il est fort probable/il n'est guère probable que ...; **there would be little p. of our succeeding** nous aurions peu de chances de réussir; **there is every p. that events will prove him right** selon toute probabilité les événements lui donneront raison; *Math* **calculation of probabilities, calculus of p.** calcul *m* des probabilités; **what is the p. of 10% proving defective?** quelle probabilité y a-t-il que 10% s'avèrent défectueux?; **p. laws** lois *fpl* des probabilités; *Mktg* **p. method** (*of sampling*) méthode *f* probabiliste

probable ['prɒbəb(ə)l] **1** *adj* probable; (*story, excuse*) vraisemblable; **it's p. that he'll come** il est probable qu'il viendra; **p. cause of death** cause *f* probable de la mort; *Math* **p. error** erreur *f* probable **2** *n* (*likely candidate, participant*) candidat, -ate/participant, -ante qui a de bonnes chances; *esp Am* (*probable thing, event*) probabilité *f*; **certainties and probables** certitudes *fpl* et probabilités

probably ['prɒbəblɪ] *adv* probablement; **will they come? – p. not** est-ce qu'ils viendront? – probablement pas

probate ['prəʊb(e)ɪt] *n Jur* **(a)** (**grant of**) **p.** (*for will*) validation *f*, homologation *f*; **to grant p. (of a will)** homologuer un testament; *Am* **p. court, court of p.** tribunal *m* des successions et des tutelles **(b)** (*will*) testament *m* revêtu de la formule exécutoire

probation [prə'beɪʃən] *n* **(a)** (*trial period*) (**period of**) **p.** période *f* d'essai; *Rel* (*of novice*) probation *f*; **to be on p.** faire une période d'essai; *Rel* être en probation **(b)** *Jur* (mise *f* en) liberté *f* surveillée; **he'll probably get p.** on lui accordera probablement la liberté surveillée; **p. system** régime *m* de la liberté surveillée; **on p.** en liberté surveillée; **p. officer** = personne *f* chargée de surveiller un délinquant pendant sa période de probation

probationary [prə'beɪʃən(ə)rɪ] *adj* **p. period** période *f* d'essai; *Rel* probation *f*

probationer [prə'beɪʃənər] *n* **(a)** (*person on trial period*) stagiaire *mf*, personne *f* (qui est) à l'essai; *Rel* novice *mf* **(b)** *Jur* délinquant, -ante en liberté surveillée

probe¹ [prəʊb] *n* **(a)** (*instrument*) sonde *f*; (*act*) coup *m* de sonde; **space p.** sonde *f* spatiale **(b)** *F* (*enquiry*) enquête *f* (**into** sur)

probe² **1** *vt Med* (*wound etc*) sonder, explorer; *Fig* (*person*) sonder; (*the past*) fouiller (dans); (*mystery etc*) approfondir, fouiller **2** *vi* **to p. into the past** fouiller dans le passé; **to p. deeply into the human heart** (*of novelist*) sonder le cœur humain; **if you'd probed more deeply** (*to journalist etc*) si vous aviez fait des recherches plus approfondies; **to p. into people's private lives** fouiller dans la vie des gens; **to p. into the circumstances surrounding the accident** analyser *ou* explorer les circonstances dans lesquelles l'accident s'était produit

probing ['prəʊbɪŋ] **1** *adj* (*investigation, enquiry*) approfondi; (*eyes, look*) scrutateur; **she felt the doctor's p. fingers on her arm** elle sentait les doigts du docteur qui sondaient son bras **2** *n Med* (*of wound*) sondage *m*, exploration *f*; (*enquiries, questions*) questions *fpl* (**into** sur); **to do some p.** poser des questions; **I'll do some p. and try to find out why she's so reluctant** je ferai ma petite enquête pour savoir pourquoi elle est si réticente; **no amount of p. will persuade him to reveal the truth** on aura beau insister, rien ne le persuadera à révéler la vérité

probity ['prəʊbɪtɪ] *n Fml* probité *f*, honnêteté *f*

problem ['prɒbləm] *n Math, Fig* problème *m*; **that's your p.** ça, c'est ton problème; **their p. is that they don't have enough time** leur problème c'est qu'ils n'ont pas assez de temps; **money isn't a p.** l'argent n'est pas un problème; **and I thought I had problems!** moi qui pensais que j'avais des problèmes!; **I can't pay until next week – that's not a p.** je ne pourrai pas payer avant la semaine prochaine – ce n'est pas un problème *ou* pas de problème; *F* **I haven't got a car – no p., I'll take you** je n'ai pas de voiture – pas de problème, je t'emmènerai; **social problems** problèmes sociaux; **the housing p.** la crise du logement; **it's a p. to know what to**

do il est bien difficile de savoir quoi faire; **he's a p.** c'est un cas *ou* c'est un problème, celui-là; **I don't want to be a p.** je ne veux pas causer *ou* créer de problème(s); **what seems to be the p.?** qu'est-ce qu'il y a?, où est le problème?; **has anyone got a p. with that?** est-ce que quelqu'un a une objection?, est-ce que ça dérange quelqu'un?; *F* **what's your p.?** tu as un problème ou quoi?; **to have a drink/drug/weight p.** (trop) boire/se droguer/avoir tendance à prendre du poids; **p. area** (*in town*) quartier *m* à problèmes; (*in project*) source *f* de problèmes; **the LX31 always was a p. car** la LX31 nous/leur/*etc* a toujours posé des problèmes; **p. families** familles *fpl* à problèmes; *Journ* **p. page** courrier *m* du cœur; **p. recognition** reconnaissance *f* du problème

problematic(al) [prɒblɪ'mætɪk, -ɪk(ə)l] *adj* (*question, opinion, result etc*) problématique

problematically [prɒblɪ'mætɪklɪ] *adv* problématiquement

problem child *n* **(a)** enfant *mf* à problèmes, enfant difficile **(b)** *Mktg* dilemme *m*

problem-orient(at)ed ['prɒbləmɔːrɪənt(eɪt)ɪd] *adj Comptr* **p. language** langage *m* orienté problème

problem-solving ['prɒbləmsɒlvɪŋ] *n* résolution *f* de problèmes; **p. skills** capacités *fpl* à résoudre les problèmes

proboscis, *pl* **proboscises** [prəʊ'bɒsɪs, prəʊ'bɒsɪsɪz] *n* **(a)** (*of elephant, insect*) trompe *f*; **p. monkey** nasique *m* **(b)** *Hum* (*nose*) appendice *m*

procedural [prə'siːdʒər(ə)l] *adj* de procédure; *Jur* procédural; *Comptr* **p. language** langage *m* de procédures

procedure [prə'siːdʒər] *n* procédure *f*; *Med* (*for administering treatment etc*) protocole *m*; **the correct p.** la marche à suivre, la bonne procédure; **what's the p. for renewing a passport?** quelle est la marche à suivre pour faire renouveler un passeport?; **p. in case of fire** marche à suivre en cas d'incendie; **rules** *or* **order of p.** règles *fpl* de procédure; (*of assembly*) réglement *m* intérieur; **code of criminal p.** code *m* de procédure pénale

procedure-orient(at)ed [prə'siːdʒərɔːrɪənt(eɪt)ɪd] *adj Comptr* orienté procédure; **p. language** langage *m* procédural

proceed [prə'siːd] *vi* **(a)** *esp Fml* (*walk*) marcher; (*drive*) rouler; **in which direction were you proceeding?** dans quelle direction vous dirigiez-vous?; **to p. to a place** (*go to a place*) aller *ou* se rendre à un endroit; (*go towards a place*) se diriger vers un endroit; **to p. with caution** (*go*) avancer prudemment

(b) (*act*) procéder; **how shall we p.?** comment allons-nous procéder?; **how does one p.?** quelle est la marche à suivre?, comment procède-t-on?; **to p. with caution** procéder *ou* agir avec prudence

(c) to p. to do sth (*begin*) se mettre à faire qch, commencer à faire qch; **you may p. to remove the outer casing** vous pouvez maintenant enlever le carter; **to p. to business** (*at meeting etc*) passer aux affaires; **I will now p. to another matter** je passe maintenant à une autre question

(d) (*continue*) se poursuivre, (se) continuer; **to p. (on one's way)** continuer son chemin, poursuivre sa route; **the play proceeded without further interruption** la pièce se poursuivit sans autre interruption; **the project is proceeding well** le projet se déroule bien; **negotiations are now proceeding** des négociations sont en cours; **to pay as the work proceeds** payer au fur et à mesure que l'ouvrage avance; **he immediately proceeded to say the opposite** et le voilà qui se met à dire le contraire; **to p. with sth** poursuivre qch, continuer qch; **before we p. any further** avant d'aller plus loin; **she is proceeding with her complaint** elle persiste *ou* persévère dans sa plainte; **p.!** continuez!

(e) *Jur* **to p. against sb** poursuivre qn (en justice)

(f) (*originate*) **sounds proceeding from a room** bruits qui sortent *ou* proviennent d'une pièce; **the social problems proceeding from lack of education** les problèmes sociaux qui découlent du manque d'éducation

proceeding [prə'siːdɪŋ] *n* **(a)** *Fml* (*way of acting*) manière *f* de procéder, façon *f* d'agir

(b) (*event, operation*) opération *f*; **proceedings** (*of assembly*) débats *mpl*; (*of conference*) actes *fpl*; **proceedings were interrupted by ...** le déroulement des événements a été interrompu par ...; **to co-ordinate proceedings** coordonner les opérations; *Admin* **the entire proceedings were disgraceful** toute l'affaire a été menée d'une façon indigne; *Admin* **to conduct the proceedings** diriger les débats; *Admin* **the proceedings were orderly** la réunion s'est déroulée dans le calme

(c) *Jur* **(legal) proceedings** procès *m*, poursuites *fpl* judiciaires *ou* en justice; **to take** *or* **institute proceedings against sb** intenter une action contre qn, intenter un procès à qn, poursuivre qn en justice; **to order proceedings to be taken against sb** instrumenter contre qn

proceeds ['prəʊsiːdz] *npl* (*from sale etc*) produit *m*, montant *m*; (*of charity*) bénéfices *mpl*; **all the p. of the album will go to charity** tous les bénéfices faits grâce à cet album iront à des œuvres de bienfaisance

process¹ ['prəʊses] *n* **(a)** processus *m*; **it's a slow p.** c'est un processus lent; (*persuading sb, changing over to digital etc*) ça va prendre longtemps; **by a p. of elimination/of trial and error** en procédant par élimination/par tâtonnements *ou* approximations successives; **to be in the p. of doing sth** être en train de faire qch; **he lost most of his friends in the p.** il a perdu presque tous ses amis en faisant cela; **but you ruined the carpet in the p.** mais tu as abîmé la moquette par la même occasion; **during the p. of dismantling** au cours du démontage; **the work is in p.** le travail est en cours; **the building is in the p. of construction/of being repaired** le bâtiment est en cours de construction/de réparation; **the peace p.** le processus de paix

(b) *Tech* (*industrial*) procédé *m*; (*chemical*) réaction *f*; *Typ, Phot* procédés photomécaniques; *Comptr* procédé, opération *f*, traitement *m*; *Metal* **Bessemer p.** procédé Bessemer; **p. engineering** ingénierie *f* de procédé

(c) *Jur* procès *m*, action *f* en justice; (*summons*) sommation *f* de comparaître; **by due p. of law** par voies légales

process² *vt* **(a)** *Ind* (*raw material, product*) traiter, transformer; (*food*) préparer *ou* confectionner industriellement; (*mail*) acheminer; *Comptr* (*information*) traiter; *Admin* (*documents, job applications*) traiter; **to p. an order** donner suite à une commande, traiter une commande; **your request is being processed** votre demande est en cours de traitement; **process(ed) cheese** fromage *m* fondu *ou* à tartiner; (*in slices*) fromage en tranches; **processed food** aliment(s) *m(pl)* conditionné(s); (*precooked*) plat(s) *m(pl)* cuisiné(s) industriellement

(b) *Jur* (*person*) intenter un procès à, poursuivre (en justice)

(c) *Phot* développer

process³ [prə'ses] *vi* (*walk in line*) défiler (en cortège); *Rel* défiler en procession

process camera *n* tireuse *f* optique

processing ['prəʊsesɪŋ] *n* (*of raw material, product*) traitement *m*, transformation *f*; (*of food*) confection *f* *ou* préparation *f* industrielle; *Comptr* (*of data*) traitement; *Phot* (*of film*) développement *m*, traitement; *Admin* (*of application*) traitement; **p. of mail** acheminement *m* du courrier

processing industry *n* industrie *f* de transformation

processing language *n Comptr* langage *m* de traitement

processing plant *n Ind* (*for sewage, waste*) usine *f* de retraitement

processing power *n* puissance *f* de traitement

processing speed *n* vitesse *f* de traitement

processing time *n* temps *m* de traitement

processing unit *n Comptr* unité *f* de traitement

procession [prə'seʃən] *n* (*of people*) cortège *m*, défilé *m*; (*of cars*) file *f*; (*religious*) procession *f*; **to go** *or* **walk in p.** aller en cortège *ou* en procession, défiler; *Fig* **a p. of people came through his office throughout the day** les gens n'ont pas arrêté de défiler dans son bureau de toute la journée

processional [prə'seʃən(ə)l] **1** *adj* processionnel **2** *n Rel* (*book*) processionnal *m*; (*hymn*) hymne *m* processionnel

processor ['prəʊsesər] *n Comptr* processeur *m*; **p. speed** vitesse *f* du processeur

process-server *n Jur* huissier *m* (qui dresse des exploits)

pro-choice *adj* (*pro-abortion*) en faveur de l'intervention volontaire de grossesse

proclaim [prə'kleɪm] *vt* **(a)** (*declare*) (*one's innocence, guilt, despair etc*) proclamer; (*one's love*) déclarer; **to p. that one is innocent** proclamer que l'on est innocent; **to p. sb king** proclamer qn roi; **to have sth proclaimed through the town** faire annoncer *ou* faire crier qch par la ville; **to p. a state of emergency/one's independence** déclarer l'état d'urgence/son indépendance **(b)** *Fig* (*show*) (*one's guilt, anger, joy*) révéler

proclamation [prɒklə'meɪʃən] *n* proclamation *f*, déclaration *f* (publique); (*of banns etc*) publication *f*; **to make** *or* **issue a p.** faire une proclamation

proclivity [prə'klɪvɪtɪ] *n esp Fml* penchant *m* (**for sth** pour *ou* à qch)

proconsul [prəʊ'kɒnsəl] *n Hist* proconsul *m*

procrastinate [prəʊ'kræstɪneɪt] *vi* remettre les choses au lendemain; **stop procrastinating** arrêtez de remettre les choses au lendemain

procrastination [prəʊkræstɪ'neɪʃən] *n* **I've had enough p.** j'en ai assez qu'on remette toujours tout au lendemain; **there's**

too much p. on a trop tendance à remettre les choses au lendemain; *Prov* **p. is the thief of time** il ne faut pas remettre au lendemain ce que l'on peut faire le jour même

procrastinator [prəʊ'kræstɪneɪtər] *n* **she's a terrible p.** il faut toujours qu'elle remette les choses au lendemain

procreate ['prəʊkrɪeɪt] *vi* procréer

procreation [prəʊkrɪ'eɪʃən] *n* procréation *f*

proctor[1] ['prɒktər] *n* **(a)** *Univ* (*at Oxford, Cambridge*) membre *m* exécutif du conseil de discipline; *US* (*invigilator*) = personne *f* chargée de surveiller un/des examen(s) **(b)** *Jur* avoué *m* (*devant une cour ecclésiastique*); **Queen's/King's p.** procureur *m* de la reine/du roi **(c)** *Rel* procureur *m*

proctor[2] *vti US Univ* (*invigilate*) surveiller

procurable [prə'kjʊərəb(ə)l] *adj* que l'on peut se procurer; **they're easily p.** on peut se les procurer facilement; **it is no longer p.** on ne peut plus s'en procurer

procuration [prɒkjʊ'reɪʃən] *n Jur* procuration *f*; **letters of p.** procuration, mandat *m*

procurator ['prɒkjʊreɪtər] *n Jur* fondé *m* de pouvoir(s); *Scot* **p. fiscal** = procureur *m* général

procure [prə'kjʊər] **1** *vt* **(a)** (*obtain*) obtenir, procurer; **to p. sth for sb** procurer qch à qn; **to p. sth (for oneself)** se procurer qch **(b)** (*for prostitution*) (*woman*) offrir les services de **2** *vi* faire du proxénétisme

procurement [prə'kjʊəmənt] *n Fml* acquisition *f* (**of** de); *Ind* achat *m*; **p. (department)** service *m* des achats; **p. officer** agent *m* des achats

procurer [prə'kjʊərər] *n Fml* **(a)** (*of prostitutes*) proxénète *mf* **(b)** (*one who obtains*) personne *f* chargée des acquisitions

procuress [prə'kjʊərɪs] *n Lit* entremetteuse *f*

procuring [prə'kʊərɪŋ] *n* **(a)** (*for prostitution*) proxénétisme *m* **(b)** (*of supplies*) acquisition *f*; *Ind* achat *m*

Prod [prɒd] *n esp Irish, Scot Offensive Sl* protestant, -ante

prod[1] [prɒd] *n* **(a)** (*act*) coup *m* (*donné du bout du doigt etc*); **to give sb a p.** pousser qn (du doigt/avec un baton/*etc*); **she gave him an encouraging p. with her elbow** elle l'a poussé du coude pour l'encourager; *Fig F* **give him a p.** aiguillonnez-le un peu; *Fig F* **he needs an occasional p.** il a besoin qu'on le pousse de temps en temps; **thanks for the p.** (*reminder*) merci de me l'avoir rappelé **(b)** (*object*) aiguillon *m*

prod[2] **(-dd-) 1** *vt* **(a) to p. sb/sth** pousser qn/qch (**with sth** du bout de qch) **(b)** *Fig F* (*person*) aiguillonner, pousser (**into doing sth** à faire qch); **they were finally prodded into action by the news** cette nouvelle les a finalement poussés *ou* incités à entrer en action; **he needs a lot of prodding** il faut toujours le pousser **2** *vi* **to prod at** = **prod**[2] **1(a)**

prodigal ['prɒdɪg(ə)l] **1** *adj* prodigue; *Fml* **to be p. with** *or* **of sth** être prodigue de qch; *Bible* **the P. Son** l'enfant *m* prodigue **2** *n* prodigue *mf*

prodigality [prɒdɪ'gælɪtɪ] *n* prodigalité *f*

prodigally ['prɒdɪg(ə)lɪ] *adv* (*to spend etc*) avec prodigalité

prodigious [prə'dɪdʒəs] *adj* prodigieux

prodigiously [prə'dɪdʒəslɪ] *adv* prodigieusement; (*to eat, drink*) énormément

prodigy ['prɒdɪdʒɪ] *n* prodige *m*, merveille *f*; **child** *or* **infant p.** enfant *mf* prodige

produce[1] ['prɒdju:s] *n* (*no pl*) *Agr* (*products*) produits *mpl*, denrées *fpl*; **p. of Spain** (*on packaging*) produit d'origine espagnole; **agricultural/dairy p.** produits agricoles/laitiers

produce[2] [prə'dju:s] *vt* **(a)** (*manufacture, make*) produire, fabriquer; (*cheese, sausages*) faire; (*wine*) produire; (*sound*) émettre

(b) (*yield*) (*profit*) rapporter; (*milk, apples, steam etc*) produire; *Phys* (*energy*) produire, générer; *El* (*spark*) faire jaillir

(c) (*present*) (*one's ticket, passport*) présenter, montrer; (*reasons*) fournir, donner; (*objection*) émettre; *Jur* (*documents, alibi*) produire, fournir; (*witness*) faire comparaître; **she produced a ten-pound note/a gun** elle a sorti un billet de dix livres/un revolver

(d) (*create*) créer; (*children*) faire; (*reaction*) produire, provoquer, entraîner; (*denial*) entraîner, provoquer; (*anger, despair, uncertainty*) susciter, provoquer, donner lieu à; (*interest*) susciter; (*effect*) provoquer; **to p. a vacuum** produire *ou* faire le vide; **to p. a sensation** (*of book etc*) faire sensation; **the drug produces a sensation of well-being** cette drogue procure une sensation de bien-être; **this writer has produced about thirty novels** cet auteur a écrit *ou* produit une trentaine de romans

(e) *Th* (*play*) (*of person*) (*organize generally*) produire; *Br* (*direct*) mettre en scène; (*of company*) produire, représenter; *Cin, Rad, TV* (*film, radio or TV programme, record*) produire; *Th* **badly produced play** pièce mal montée

producer [prə'dju:sər] *n* **(a)** *Agr, Ind* producteur, -trice; (*of manufactured goods*) producteur, -trice, fabricant *m* (**of** de); **the company/country is an important p. of coffee** *or* **coffee p.** cette entreprise/ce pays est un important producteur de café **(b)** *Th* producteur, -trice; *Br* (*director*) metteur *m* en scène; *Cin, Rad, TV* producteur, -trice

producer goods *npl* biens *mpl* de production *ou* d'équipement

-producing [prə'dju:sɪŋ] *suff* **coffee/oil-p.** producteur, -trice de café/de pétrole; **oil-p. country** pays producteur de pétrole

product ['prɒdʌkt] *n* **(a)** (*result*), *Com* produit *m*; **the p. of ten years' work** le produit de dix années de travail; **the disaster was the p. of bad planning** ce désastre était le résultat d'une mauvaise organisation; **she was a p. of her age** c'était un pur produit de son époque; *Mktg* **p. bundling pricing** fixation *f* des prix par lot; **p. category** catégorie *f* de produit; **p. champion** champion *m* de produit; **p. depth** profondeur *f* de produit; **p. development** développement *m* de produit(s), mise *f* au point de produit(s); **p. development cost** coût *m* de l'élaboration du produit; **p. development programme** programme *m* de mise au point du produit; **p. features** caractéristiques *fpl* du produit; **p. form** type *m* de produit; **p. group manager** directeur *m* de groupe de produits; **p. hierarchy** hiérarchie *f* des produits; **p. information sheet** fiche *f* technique; **p. innovation** innovation *f* de produit; **p. liability insurance** assurance *f* de responsabilité du produit; **p. life-cycle** cycle *m* de vie du produit; **p. life-cycle curve** courbe *f* du cycle *m* de vie d'un produit; **p. line** ligne *f* de produits; **p. line manager** directeur *m* de ligne de produits; **p. manager** chef *m ou* directeur *m* de produit, responsable *mf* produit; **p. management** gestion *f* de produits; **p. mapping** carte *f* perceptuelle de produits; **p. market** marché *m* de produits; **p. marketing** mercatique *f* du produit; **p. mix** assortiment *m ou* mix *m* de produits; **p. mix depth** profondeur *f* de l'assortiment de produits; **p. mix width** largeur *f* de l'assortiment de produits; **p. portfolio** portefeuille *m* de produits; **p. positioning** positionnement *m* du produit; *Mktg* **p. positioning map** carte *f* de positionnement des produits, carte de l'univers des produits; **p. range** gamme *f* de produits; **p. test** test *m* de produit; **p. testing** essais *mpl ou* tests de produit

(b) *Math* produit *m*

product awareness *n Mktg* notoriété *f ou* mémorisation *f* d'un produit; **p. advertising** publicité *f* de sensibilisation au produit; **p. level** degré *m* de mémorisation d'un produit

production [prə'dʌkʃən] *n* **(a)** (*of cars, radios etc*) production *f*, fabrication *f*; (*of milk, apples etc*) production; **to go into p.** (*of car etc model*) entrer en production; **to go out of p.** cesser d'être produit; **to take sth out of p.** cesser de produire qch; **when do we go into p.?** quand est-ce que nous lançons la production?; **is it in p. yet?** est-ce qu'on en a commencé la production?; **to move** *or* **shift p.** relocaliser son unité de production; **drop in p.** chute *f ou* baisse *f* de la production; **p. capacity** capacité *f* de production; **p. control** direction *f* de la production; **p. cost** coût *m* de production; **p. department** service *m* (de) production; **p. editor** rédacteur *m* en chef technique; **p. flowchart** organigramme *m* de production; **p. leadtime** délai *m* de production; **p. meeting** conférence *f* de production; **p. team** équipe *f* de production

(b) (*presentation*) (*of documents*) production *f*, présentation *f*; (*of ticket*) présentation

(c) *Phys* (*of energy*) production *f*, génération *f*

(d) *Cin, Rad, TV, Th* production *f*; *Br* (*directing*) mise *f* en scène; (*finished work*) pièce *f*; **the film goes into p. in the autumn** le tournage du film commence en automne; *F* **to make a p. (number) (out) of sth** (*make fuss*) faire tout un fromage de qch; *Cin* **a film with high/low p. values** un film à gros/petit budget; **p. associate** producteur *m* associé; **p. buyer** responsable *mf* des achats; **p. company** société *f* de production; **p. control room** salle *f* de contrôle de production; **p. director** directeur *m* de production; (*Journ*) directeur *m* de la fabrication; *TV* administrateur *m* de la production; **p. mixer** mélangeur *m* (de production); **p. secretary** secrétaire *mf* de production; **p. switcher** mélangeur *m* (de production); **p. talkback system** réseau *m* d'ordres, intercom *m* de production

production assistant *n* assistant, -ante de production

production car *n* voiture *f* de série

production line *n* chaîne *f* de fabrication; **to work on a p.** travailler à la chaîne

production manager *n* directeur, -trice de la production

production platform *n Petr* plate-forme *f* de production, *pl* plates-formes

productive [prə'dʌktɪv] *adj* **(a)** productif; (*discussions*) positif; (*land etc*) productif, fertile; (*mine etc*) qui rend; **p. period of an author** années *fpl* productives d'un auteur; **the meeting**

wasn't very p. la réunion n'a pas été très productive (b) *Econ* (*work*) productif (c) *Fml* **to be p. of** (*give rise to*) engendrer, produire

productively [prəˈdʌktɪvlɪ] *adv* **to use one's time p.** employer son temps de façon efficace

productivity [prɒdʌkˈtɪvɪtɪ] *n* productivité *f*; **p. agreement** *or* **deal** accord *m* de productivité; **p. bonus** prime *f* de rendement *ou* à la productivité

product/market pair *n Mktg* couple *m* produit/marché

product placement *n Mktg* placement *m* d'un produit

product/price policy *n Mktg* politique *f* de produit/prix

Prof [prɒf] (*abbr* **Professor**) (*in title*) Prof

prof [prɒf] *n F* (*at university*) prof *mf*; (*at hospital*) professeur *m*

profanation [prɒfəˈneɪʃən] *n Rel* profanation *f*

profane[1] [prəˈfeɪn] *adj* (a) (*blasphemous*) (*act*) profane; (*language*) impie, blasphématoire; (*person*) qui blasphème à tout propos (b) *Lit* (*secular*) profane; **things sacred and p.** le sacré et le profane

profane[2] *vt* (*something sacred, one's talent*) profaner

profanity [prəˈfænɪtɪ] *n* (a) (*word, remark*) blasphème *m*, juron *m*; **to utter profanities** blasphémer (b) (*of language*) grossièreté *f*; (*of text*) nature *f* profane; (*of action*) impiété *f*

profess [prəˈfes] *vt* (a) (*declare*) (*one's faith etc*) professer, faire profession de; (*enthusiasm, hatred, disbelief*) professer; **to p. oneself a socialist** se déclarer socialiste, faire profession de socialisme; **to p. oneself satified** se déclarer satisfait; **to p. one's ignorance** avouer son ignorance (b) (*allege, claim*) prétendre; **he professes to be a socialist but ...** il se prétend *ou* se déclare socialiste, mais ...; **I do not p. to be a scholar** je ne prétends pas être savant; **to p. a lack of understanding of sth** prétendre ne pas comprendre qch

professed [prəˈfest] *adj* (a) (*enemy*) déclaré; (*Marxist etc*) déclaré; (*pretended*) prétendu (b) (*monk, nun*) profès, -esse

professedly [prəˈfesɪdlɪ] *adv* (*on one's own admission*) de son propre aveu; (*according to one's claims*) soi-disant

profession [prəˈfeʃən] *n* (a) [①B4,B,2,b,i] (*occupation*) profession *f*; **the p.** (*people*) (les membres *mpl* de) la profession; **the teaching p.** le corps enseignant, les enseignants; **the (learned) professions** les professions libérales; **writer by p.** écrivain professionnel; **she is a doctor by p.** elle est médecin de (sa) profession; *Hum* **the oldest p. (in the world)** le plus vieux métier du monde (b) (*declaration*) profession *f*, déclaration *f*; **p. of faith** profession de foi

professional [prəˈfeʃən(ə)l] **1** *adj* (a) (*paid*) (*dancer, photographer, footballer etc*) professionnel; (*soldier, diplomat*) de carrière; *Fig* **a p. liar/hypochondriac** un menteur/un hypocondriaque professionnel; *Sp etc* **to turn** *or* **go p.** passer *ou* devenir professionnel; **the p. army** l'armée *f* de métier; **p. football** football *m* professionnel; *Fb* **a p. foul** une faute délibérée; **p. man/woman** homme *m*/femme *f* qui exerce une profession libérale

(b) (*relating to job*) professionnel; **p. certificate** certificat *m* d'aptitude professionnelle; **to take a p. interest in sth** s'intéresser professionnellement à qch; **to take p. advice on sth** consulter une personne du métier *ou* un professionnel sur qch; (*on legal, medical matter*) consulter un avocat/un médecin à propos de qch; **conduct that is not p.** (*of doctor etc*) conduite contraire aux usages de la profession; *Euph* **I think she needs p. help** je pense qu'elle a besoin d'aller voir un psychiatre; **p. association** syndicat *m* professionnel; **p. body** organisme *m* professionnel; **p. code of ethics** déontologie *f*; **p. hospitality** industrie *f* de l'hôtellerie; **p. indemnity insurance** assurance *f* d'indemnisation professionnelle; **p. misconduct** faute *f* professionnelle

(c) (*competent*) professionnel; **she is very p.** elle est très professionnelle; **they made a very p. job of the repair** la réparation qu'ils ont faite est digne de professionnels; **his manner was very p.** il s'est comporté en professionnel

2 *n* professionnel, -elle; **it's best to leave such work to the professionals** il vaut mieux laisser ce genre de travail à des professionnels *ou* à des gens du métier; **a golf/rugby p.** un golfeur/rugbyman professionnel

professionalism [prəˈfeʃənəlɪz(ə)m] *n* professionnalisme *m*; **his air of spurious p.** ses airs de faux professionnel

professionally [prəˈfeʃənəlɪ] *adv* (a) (*as a job*) professionnellement; **to sing/dance/play football p.** être un chanteur/danseur/footballeur professionnel (b) (*competently*) comme un professionnel, en professionnel; **it was very p. done** c'est du travail de professionnel

professor [prəˈfesər] *n Univ Br* professeur *m* (de faculté) titulaire d'une chaire; *Am* enseignant, -ante, professeur (de faculté); **she's a p.** elle est professeur; **he's the p. of German** c'est le professeur titulaire de la chaire d'allemand; **P. Martin** le Professeur Martin; (*as address*) Monsieur/Madame Martin, Professeur; (*as address to medical doctor*) Monsieur/Madame le Professeur Martin

professorial [prɒfɪˈsɔːrɪəl] *adj* professoral

professorship [prəˈfesəʃɪp] *n Univ* chaire *f*; **a p. in Modern History** une chaire d'histoire moderne; **to get a p.** obtenir une chaire

proffer [ˈprɒfər] *vt* (**-r-**) *Fml* (*advice*) offrir, présenter; (*opinion, observation*) avancer; (*resignation*) présenter; **to p. one's hand** tendre la main (**to sb** à qn)

proficiency [prəˈfɪʃənsɪ] *n* (*in a subject*) compétence *f*, capacités *fpl* (**in** dans); (*in a language*) maîtrise *f* (**in** de)

proficient [prəˈfɪʃənt] *adj* compétent; (*swimmer*) excellent; **to be p. at German** avoir une bonne maîtrise de l'allemand; **to be a p. liar** avoir le mensonge facile

proficiently [prəˈfɪʃəntlɪ] *adv* avec compétence; (*to speak a language*) couramment; **to swim p.** être un excellent nageur; **to lie p.** avoir le mensonge facile

profile[1] [ˈprəʊfaɪl] *n* (*of person, face, mountain*) profil *m*; *TV, Journ* (*of celebrity*) portrait *m*, profil; (*of company*) profil; *Tech* (*of land, aircraft wing*) profil; (*on graph*) graphique *m*, courbe *f*; **she has the right p. for the job** elle a le profil qui convient pour cet emploi; *Art* **drawn in p.** dessiné de profil; *Fig* **to keep a low p.** (*of person*) garder un profil bas; *Fig* **to have a high p.** (*of person*) être (très) en vue; (*of issue*) être d'actualité; *Fig* **to raise one's p.** se mettre plus en vue; **to raise a party's/sb's p.** promouvoir l'image du parti/de qn; **p. characteristics** (*of tourists*) caractéristiques *fpl*; *TV, Cin* **p. shot** plan *m* de profil; *TV, Cin* **p. spotlight** spot *m* de profil

profile[2] *vt* (*draw in profile*) dessiner *ou* montrer de profil; *TV, Journ* faire le portrait de; **she was profiled in a TV programme** une émission télévisée a présenté son portrait; **the trees are profiled against the horizon** les arbres se profilent sur l'horizon

profit[1] [ˈprɒfɪt] *n Com* bénéfice *m*, profit *m*; *Fig* (*advantage*) avantage *m*; **what p. is there in it for her?** quel avantage cela présente-t-il pour elle?, qu'est-ce que cela peut lui rapporter?; **to make a p.** (*of seller, company*) faire un *ou* des bénéfice(s); (*of goods*) rapporter; **we made a p. on the sale of** *or* **on selling the house** nous avons fait *ou* réalisé un bénéfice sur la vente de la maison; **to turn sth to p.** tirer profit *ou* bénéfice de qch; *Com* **gross/net p.** bénéfice brut/net; **£100 clear p.** 100 livres de bénéfice net; **p. on a transaction** rendement *m* d'une opération; **profits were down/up this year** les bénéfices ont diminué/augmenté cette année; **at a p.** (*to sell sth*) à profit; (*to work a mine*) avec profit; **to derive (a) p. from sth** retirer un bénéfice *ou* un profit de qch; **p. and loss** pertes et profits *mpl*; **p. and loss account** compte *m* de pertes et profits, compte de résultat; **p. or loss** résultat *m*; **p. or loss for the financial year** résultat de l'exercice; **p. centre** centre *m* de profit; *Mktg* **p. impact of marketing strategy** impact *m* sur la rentabilité de la stratégie mercatique; **p. indicator** indice *m* de profit; **p. margin** marge *f* bénéficiaire; **p. opportunity** occasion *f* de profit; **p. optimization** maximisation *f* du profit

profit[2] (**-t-**) **1** *vi* **to p. by** *or* **from sth** bénéficier de qch, tirer profit de qch; **to p. by** *or* **from sb's advice** mettre à profit le conseil de qn; **you could well p. by being more careful** vous avez tout intérêt à faire plus attention **2** *vt Lit* (*person*) rapporter *ou* profiter à

profitability [prɒfɪtəˈbɪlɪtɪ] *n* rentabilité *f*; **p. ratio** ratio *m* de rentabilité

profitable [ˈprɒfɪtəb(ə)l] *adj* (*deal, agreement*) profitable, avantageux; (*speculation, company*) rentable, lucratif; **it will be more p. for us to sell it** ce sera plus avantageux pour nous de le vendre; **it would be a more p. use of your time** ça serait pour vous une meilleure manière d'utiliser votre temps

profitably [ˈprɒfɪtəblɪ] *adv* (*at a profit*) profitablement, avantageusement; (*to invest*) avec bénéfice; **to sell a house p.** vendre une maison à profit; **to use one's time p.** employer utilement son temps

profit-driven *adj* poussé par les profits

profiteer[1] [prɒfɪˈtɪər] *n Pej* affairiste *mf*; **war profiteers** profiteurs *mpl* de guerre

profiteer[2] *vi Pej* faire des bénéfices immoraux

profiteering [prɒfɪˈtɪərɪŋ] *n Pej* mercantilisme *m*, affairisme *m*

profitless [ˈprɒfɪtlɪs] *adj* sans profit; **we spent a p. week investigating the possibilities** nous avons perdu une semaine à étudier les diverses possibilités

profit-making *adj* (*company*) rentable; (*association*) à but lucratif; **this is supposed to be a p. company** cette entreprise est censée être à but lucratif

profit-sharing *n* participation *f* aux bénéfices, intéressement *m*; **p. scheme** plan *m* de participation aux bénéfices, plan d'intéressement

profit-taking *n* prise *f* de bénéfices
profligacy ['prɒflɪgəsɪ] *n* **(a)** (*debauchery*) débauche *f* **(b)** (*extravagance*) prodigalité *f*
profligate ['prɒflɪgət] **1** *adj* **(a)** (*debauched*) débauché **(b)** (*extravagant*) prodigue, dissipateur, -trice **2** *n* **(a)** (*debauchee*) débauché, -ée **(b)** (*extravagant person*) prodigue *mf*
pro forma [prəʊ'fɔːmə] **1** *adv* pour la forme **2** *adj Com* **p. invoice** facture *f* pro forma **3** *n Com* (*invoice*) facture *f* pro forma
profound [prə'faʊnd] *adj* profond
profoundly [prə'faʊndlɪ] *adv* **(a)** (*grateful, deaf, wise*) profondément **(b)** (*to write, express sth*) avec profondeur
profundity [prə'fʌndɪtɪ] *n* profondeur *f*
profuse [prə'fjuːs] *adj* (*copious*) abondant, *Lit* profus; **to offer p. thanks** remercier avec profusion; **to be p. in one's apologies** se confondre en excuses; **to be p. in one's praise** se répandre en compliments; **p. bleeding** hémorragie *f* abondante
profusely [prə'fjuːslɪ] *adv* profusément; **to apologize p.** se confondre en excuses; **to bleed p.** saigner en abondance; **to perspire p.** transpirer abondamment; **to praise sb p.** ne pas tarir d'éloges sur qn; **to thank sb p.** remercier qn avec profusion
profuseness [prə'fjuːsnɪs] *n* profusion *f*
profusion [prə'fjuːʒən] *n* (*abundance*) profusion *f*, abondance *f*; **flowers in p.** des fleurs à profusion
prog [prɒg] *n Old-fashioned TV, Rad F* émission *f*
progenitor [prəʊ'dʒenɪtər] *n* (*ancestor*) ancêtre *m*, aïeul *m*, aïeule *f*, *pl* aïeux; *Fig* (*forerunner*) précurseur *m*; (*founder*) fondateur *m*; *Fml, Hum* (*parent*) géniteur *m*, génitrice *f*
progeny ['prɒdʒɪnɪ] *n Fml* (*offspring*) progéniture *f*; (*descendants*) descendants *mpl*; *Hum* **is this another of your p.?** est-ce que c'est un de tes rejetons?
progesterone [prəʊ'dʒestərəʊn] *n Biol, Ch* progestérone *f*
prognosis, *pl* **-oses** [prɒg'nəʊsɪs, -əʊsiːz] *n* **(a)** *Med* pronostic *m*; (*art*) prognose *f* **(b)** (*forecast*) prévision(s) *f(pl)*, pronostic *m*; **to make a p.** faire un pronostic *ou* des prévisions
prognostic [prɒg'nɒstɪk] **1** *adj* (*test etc*) de pronostic **2** *n Med* signe *m* pronostique
prognostication [prɒgnɒstɪ'keɪʃən] *n* prédiction *f*, présage *m*
program¹ ['prəʊgræm] *n, vt US* = **programme**
program² *n Comptr* programme *m*; **p. card** carte *f* programme; **p. disk** disquette *f* programme; **p. error** erreur *f* de programmation; **p. file** fichier *m* programme; **p. line** ligne *f* de programme
program³ *vti Comptr* programmer; **to p. a computer to do sth** programmer un ordinateur pour qu'il fasse qch; **to be programmed to do sth** être programmé pour faire qch
programmable [prəʊ'græməb(ə)l] *adj* (*computer, oven etc*) programmable; **p. ROM** mémoire *f* morte programmable
programme¹, *US* **program** ['prəʊgræm] *n* **(a)** (*for play, of political party etc*) programme *m*; **what's the p. for today?** quel est le programme aujourd'hui?; **training p.** programme d'instruction *ou* de formation; *Mus* **p. music** musique *f* à programme; *Th* **p. seller** vendeur, -euse de programmes

(b) *TV, Rad* émission *f*, programme *m*; **current affairs p.** émission *ou* programme d'actualités; **p. billing** position *f* d'un programme dans la grille de programmation; **p. bus** tableau *m* de programmation; **p. controller** directeur *m* des programmes *ou* d'antenne; **p. grid** grille *f* de programmes; **p. schedule** grille *f* de programmes; **p. supervisor** chef *m* d'antenne; **p. trail** annonce *f* de programme

(c) *TV* (*channel*) chaîne *f*
programme², *US* **program** *vt* programmer; **to p. sth to do sth** programmer qch pour faire qch; **programmed teaching** *or* **learning** enseignement *m* programmé
programme-maker *n TV etc* réalisateur, -trice
programmer ['prəʊgræmər] *n* **(a)** (*person*) *Comptr* programmeur, -euse; *TV, Rad, Tech* programmateur, -trice **(b)** (*device*) programmateur *m*
programming ['prəʊgræmɪŋ] *n* **(a)** *Comptr* programmation *f*; **p. error** erreur *f* de programmation; **p. language** langage *m* de programmation **(b)** *TV, Rad* programmation *f*
progress¹ ['prəʊgres] *n* (*no pl*) **(a)** (*improvement*) progrès *mpl*; **age of p.** époque *f* *ou* siècle *m* de progrès; **to make p. in one's studies** faire des progrès dans ses études; **he was making slow/rapid p. with the language** il progressait lentement/rapidement dans son apprentissage de la langue; **to make great p.** avancer à pas de géant; (*of industry*) prendre un grand essor; **negotiations are making good p.** les négociations sont en bonne voie; **the patient is making good p.** le patient donne de bons signes de récupération; *Iron* **that's p. for you!** c'est ça le progrès!

(b) (*movement*) (*of time, disease etc*) marche *f*; (*of events*) cours *m*; (*of plan, project*) déroulement *m*; (*of work*) progrès *m*, avancement *m*; *Chess* **the knight's p.** la marche du cavalier; **the work is now in p.** le travail est en cours; **the negotiations in p.** les négociations en cours; **do not enter while a lecture is in p.** défense d'entrer pendant le déroulement d'un cours
progress² [prə'gres] **1** *vi* **(a)** (*improve*) (*of person*) faire des progrès, progresser; (*of project*) progresser, avancer; **her English has progressed a lot** elle a fait de gros progrès en anglais, elle a beaucoup progressé en anglais; **to p. with one's studies** progresser dans ses études; **the patient is progressing satisfactorily** le malade fait des progrès satisfaisants

(b) (*move forwards*) (*in space, time etc*) avancer; **as the inquiry progresses** à mesure que l'enquête avance; **as the year progresses** au fur et à mesure que l'année avance; **to p. towards a place** s'approcher d'un endroit (par étapes successives); **to p. onto more difficult tasks** passer à des tâches plus difficiles; **I never progressed beyond the first lesson** je ne suis jamais allé au-delà de la première leçon

2 *vt esp Com* (*advance*) faire progresser
progress chart *n Ind* diagramme *m* de l'avancement des travaux
progression [prə'greʃən] *n* (*movement*), *Math, Mus* progression *f*; (*of star*) marche *f*; *Mil* avance *f*
progressive [prə'gresɪv] **1** *adj* **(a)** (*movement*) progressif, en avant; *Med* **p. disease** maladie *f* progressive; *Fin* **p. taxation** imposition *f* progressive **(b)** (*forward-looking*) (*ideas, methods*) avancé, progressiste; (*literature, music*) d'avant-garde; **to be p.** (*of person*) avoir des idées avancées *ou* progressistes; *Mus* **p. jazz** jazz *m* progressif; *Pol* **the p. party** le parti progressiste **(c)** *Gram* **the p. form** la forme progressive **2** *n* **(a)** *Pol* progressiste *mf* **(b)** [①A48-50] *Gram* (temps *m*) progressif *m*
progressively [prə'gresɪvlɪ] *adv* progressivement
progressiveness [prə'gresɪvnɪs] *n* progressivité *f*
progress report *n* (*on work*) compte(-)rendu *m* (de l'évolution des travaux), *pl* comptes(-)rendus; (*on patient*) bulletin *m* de santé
prohibit [prə'hɪbɪt] *vt* (*forbid*) défendre, interdire, prohiber; **it is prohibited by law** c'est interdit *ou* défendu par la loi; **smoking prohibited** défense de fumer; **to p. sb from doing sth** (*of person*) défendre *ou* interdire à qn de faire qch; (*of cause, quality etc*) empêcher qn de faire qch; **prohibited goods** marchandises *fpl* prohibées
prohibition [prəʊɪ'bɪʃən] *n* interdiction *f*, prohibition *f* (**from doing sth** de faire qch); *US Hist* **the P.** la Prohibition; *Pol* **p. party** parti *m* prohibitionniste
prohibitionist [prəʊɪ'bɪʃənɪst] *adj, n* prohibitionniste *mf*
prohibitive [prə'hɪbɪtɪv] *adj* prohibitif; **p. price** prix *m* prohibitif *ou* inabordable; **the price of flowers is p.** les fleurs sont hors de prix
project¹ ['prɒdʒekt] *n* projet *m*; *Sch* (*of pupil, group of pupils*) étude *f* pratique; (*for drainage, irrigation etc*) travaux *mpl*; *Am* (**housing**) **p.** lotissement *m*; **p. leader** responsable *mf* de projet; **p. management** gestion *f* de projet; *Comptr* **p. management package** gestionnaire *m* de projets; **p. manager** directeur *m* de projet; **p. milestones** étapes *fpl* principales du projet
project² [prə'dʒekt] **1** *vt* **(a)** (*plan*) projeter; **the Minister's projected visit had to be cancelled** la visite que le Ministre avait prévue a dû être annulée

(b) (*propel*) projeter; (*missile etc*) lancer; **to p. one's voice** projeter sa voix

(c) *Cin etc* (*image, film*) projeter (**onto a screen** sur un écran); *Math* (*line*) projeter; (*plane*) projeter, tracer la projection de; **projected angle** angle *m* projeté; *Art* **projected shadow** ombre *f* portée; **he projected himself as France's saviour** il s'est présenté comme le sauveur de la France; **she projects an image of self-confidence** elle donne d'elle-même l'image d'une personne pleine d'assurance; **the country has successfully projected itself as a stable economy** le pays a réussi à donner de lui l'image d'une économie stable

(d) (*predict*) (*results*) prévoir; **the projected sales figures** le chiffre d'affaires escompté

(e) (*imagine*) **to p. oneself into the past/the future** se transporter dans le passé/l'avenir; *Psy* **to p. one's needs onto other people** projeter ses besoins sur les autres

2 *vi* **(a)** (*protrude*) déborder, dépasser, faire saillie; **the balcony projects over the pavement** le balcon surplombe le trottoir

(b) (*with voice*) projeter sa voix
projected [prə'dʒektɪd] *adj* **(a)** (*motorway, legislation etc*) en projet; **p. growth** croissance *f* prévue **(b)** *TV etc* **p. background** fond *m* projeté, transparence *f*
projectile [prə'dʒektaɪl] **1** *adj* (*force*) impulsif, projectif; **p. weapons** armes *fpl* de jet **2** *n* projectile *m*

projecting [prəˈdʒektɪŋ] *adj Archit* saillant, en saillie; **p. part of a roof** avancée *f* d'un toit
projection [prəˈdʒekʃən] *n* **(a)** (*of one's voice etc*) projection *f*; (*of projectile*) lancement *m*; *Cin* **p. of an image on a screen** projection d'une image sur un écran; *Cin* **p. room** *or* **booth** cabine *f* de projection **(b)** (*in mapmaking*) projection *f* **(c)** (*prediction*) prévision *f*; **demographic projections** projections *fpl* démographiques **(d)** *Psy* projection *f* **(e)** (*protruding part*) saillie *f*; (*of roof etc*) avancée *f*; (*of façade*) avant-corps *m inv*
projectionist [prəˈdʒekʃənɪst] *n Cin* projectionniste *mf*
projective [prəˈdʒektɪv] *adj* **(a)** *Math* (*plane*) de projection; (*geometry*) projectif **(b)** *Psy* **p. test** test *m* projectif
projector [prəˈdʒektər] *n Cin* projecteur *m*
prolapse¹ [ˈprəʊlæps] *n Med* (*of womb etc*) prolapsus *m*
prolapse² *vi Med* (*of organ*) descendre, tomber; **prolapsed** prolabé
prole [prəʊl] *n F Pej* prolo *mf*
proletarian [prəʊlɪˈteərɪən] **1** *adj* prolétarien, prolétaire **2** *n* prolétaire *mf*
proletarianize [prəʊlɪˈteərɪənaɪz] *vt* prolétariser
proletariat [prəʊlɪˈteərɪət] *n* [①A11,g,i] prolétariat *m*
pro-life *adj* **the p. movement** le mouvement pour le respect de la vie (*adversaire de l'interruption volontaire de grossesse*)
pro-lifer *n F* adversaire *mf* de l'interruption volontaire de grossesse
proliferate [prəˈlɪfəreɪt] *vi* proliférer; (*of human beings*) se multiplier
proliferation [prəlɪfəˈreɪʃən] *n* prolifération *f*
prolific [prəˈlɪfɪk] *adj* prolifique, fécond, fertile (**in, of** en); (*writer, composer*) prolifique, fécond; **the country has been a p. producer of inventors** le pays a été fécond en inventeurs; **a p. goalscorer** un gros buteur
prolifically [prəˈlɪfɪklɪ] *adv* (*to write, compose*) abondamment; **she is a p. productive writer** c'est un écrivain prolifique *ou* fécond; **he has been a p. successful goalscorer** il a marqué énormément de buts
prolix [ˈprəʊlɪks] *adj Fml* prolixe, diffus
prolixity [prəʊˈlɪksɪtɪ] *n Fml* prolixité *f*
prologue [ˈprəʊlɒg] *n* prologue *m* (**to** de)
prolong [prəˈlɒŋ] *vt* (*life etc*) prolonger; (*line*) continuer, prolonger; **don't p. the agony** ne me/le/*etc* faites pas souffrir plus longtemps
prolongation [prəʊlɒŋˈgeɪʃən] *n* (*of the time sth lasts*) prolongation *f*; (*of line etc*) prolongement *m*
prolonged [prəʊˈlɒŋgd] *adj* prolongé
PROM [prɒm] *n Comptr* (*abbr* **Programmable Read Only Memory**) mémoire *f* morte programmable
prom [prɒm] *n F* **(a)** *Br* (*at seaside*) front *m* de mer **(b)** *Br Mus* (*concert*) concert-promenade *m*, *pl* concerts-promenades; **the Proms** = série *f* de concerts-promenades, qui a lieu au mois de juillet au Albert Hall de Londres **(c)** *Am Sch* (*dance*) = bal *m* d'étudiants
pro(-)marketeer *n Pol* = partisan *m* de l'appartenance de la Grande-Bretagne au Marché Commun
promenade¹ [ˈprɒmənɑːd] *n* (*place for walking*) promenade *f*; *Br* (*at seaside*) front *m* de mer; *Old-fashioned Th* (*in pit*) promenoir *m*; *Br* **p. concert** concert-promenade *m*, *pl* concerts-promenade; *Naut* **p. deck** pont promenade *m*
promenade² **1** *vi* se promener **2** *vt* exhiber
promenader [ˈprɒmənɑːdər] *n Br Mus F* auditeur, -trice d'un concert-promenade
Promethean [prəˈmiːθɪən] *adj Myth* prométhéen
Prometheus [prəˈmiːθɪəs] *n Myth* Prométhée
prominence [ˈprɒmɪnəns] *n* **(a)** (*of issue, person etc*) éminence *f*; **to bring sth into p., to give sth p.** faire ressortir qch, donner une place importante à qch; **to come** *or* **rise to p.** prendre de l'importance; **she came to international p. with that song** c'est grâce à cette chanson qu'elle a percé au niveau international; **to occupy a position of some p.** (*of politician etc*) occuper une position éminente; (*of house*) être situé sur une éminence **(b)** (*of land, feature etc*) proéminence *f*; (*part sticking up*) saillie *f*, protubérance *f*
prominent [ˈprɒmɪnənt] *adj* **(a)** (*projecting*) saillant, en saillie, proéminent; (*cheekbone*) saillant; (*nose*) proéminent **(b)** (*obvious*) saillant, frappant; (*well-known*) éminent; **p. feature** trait *m* saillant; **in a p. position** dans une position éminente; (*house*) situé sur une éminence; **to hold a p. position** occuper une position éminente; **p. people** personnages *mpl* éminents *ou* en vue
prominently [ˈprɒmɪnentlɪ] *adv* (*to place etc*) bien en vue; **to display sth p.** mettre qch bien en évidence *ou* en vue
promiscuity [prɒmɪˈskjuːɪtɪ] *n* promiscuité *f* sexuelle
promiscuous [prəˈmɪskjʊəs] *adj* **(a)** (*behaviour*) dissolu; (*person*) aux mœurs dissolues; **to be p.** (*of person*) coucher avec n'importe qui *ou* tout le monde; (*of society, group*) être permissif **(b)** *Fml* (*mixed*) confus, mêlé; (*crowd*) hétérogène
promiscuously [prəˈmɪskjʊəslɪ] *adv* **(a) to behave p.** avoir des mœurs dissolues **(b)** *Fml* (*in a random or confused way*) confusément
promise¹ [ˈprɒmɪs] *n* **(a)** (*pledge*) promesse *f*; **to make a p.** faire une promesse; **to keep one's p.** tenir sa promesse; **to break one's p.** manquer à sa parole, ne pas tenir sa promesse; **I'm not making any promises but I'll try my best** je ne promets rien, mais je ferai de mon mieux; **a p. is a p.** chose promise, chose due; **promises, promises!** rien que des promesses!; **empty promises** promesses vaines; **to hold out a p. of sth to sb** laisser espérer qch à qn, faire miroiter qch à qn
(b) (*potential*) (*no pl*) **to show p.** être prometteur, promettre; **child who shows p., child full of p.** enfant qui promet; **young man with every p. of a brilliant future** jeune homme promis à un brillant avenir
promise² **1** *vt* **(a)** (*make a promise of*) promettre; **to p. sb sth** promettre qch à qn; **to p. (sb) to do sth** promettre (à qn) de faire qch; **he promised me he'd do it** il m'a promis qu'il le ferait *ou* de le faire; **they were promised help** on leur a promis de l'aide; **to p. oneself sth** se promettre qch; *F* **you'll be sorry, I p. you** je vous promets que vous le regretterez
(b) (*indicate*) promettre; **it promises to be hot** le temps promet d'être *ou* s'annonce chaud
2 *vi* promettre; **I'll pay you back, I p.** je te rembourserai, je te le promets *ou* c'est promis; **I'll wait for you – (do you) p.?** je t'attendrai – tu le promets? *ou* promis?; **but you promised!** mais tu avais promis!; **the scheme promises well** le projet s'annonce bien
promised [ˈprɒmɪst] *adj* promis; *Bible, Fig* **the P. Land** la Terre promise
promising [ˈprɒmɪsɪŋ] *adj* prometteur, -teuse, qui promet; (*young woman/man*) d'avenir; **she's made a p. start** elle a fait des débuts prometteurs; **the future looks p.** l'avenir promet, l'avenir s'annonce bien
promisingly [ˈprɒmɪsɪŋlɪ] *adv* d'une façon prometteuse *ou* qui promet
promissory [ˈprɒmɪsərɪ] *adj Com* **p. note** billet *m* à ordre
promo [ˈprəʊməʊ] *n Com F* **(a)** (*video*) vidéo *f* promotionnelle; (*for record*) clip *m* **(b)** (*promotion*) promo *f*
promontory [ˈprɒmənt(ə)rɪ] *n* promontoire *m*
promote [prəˈməʊt] *vt* **(a)** (*raise in rank*) promouvoir, donner de l'avancement à; **to be promoted to (the rank of) captain** être promu (au grade de) capitaine, passer capitaine; **to be promoted** être promu, monter en grade; *Fb* (*of team*) passer dans la division supérieure; **to be promoted to the first division** passer *ou* monter en première division
(b) (*encourage*) (*peace, growth, justice, cause*) promouvoir; (*the arts, a project*) encourager; (*success*) favoriser; (*person's interests*) servir; (*result*) amener, contribuer à; *Com* (*product*) promouvoir, faire la promotion de; *Ch* (*reaction*) amorcer, provoquer; *Parl* **to p. a bill** prendre l'initiative d'un projet de loi
promoter [prəˈməʊtər] *n* (*of construction project*) promoteur *m*; *Sp, Th* organisateur, -trice; (*sponsor*) parrain *m*; **to be a p. of** (*theory, idea, cause*) promouvoir; **the main promoters of this idea** les principaux défenseurs de cette idée; **sales p.** promoteur de ventes
promotion [prəˈməʊʃən] *n* **(a)** (*in rank*) promotion *f*, avancement *m*; *Fb* (*of team*) ascension *f*, promotion; **to get p.** être promu, avoir *ou* obtenir de l'avancement; *Fb* (*of team*) passer dans la division supérieure; **to get p. to captain** être promu au grade de capitaine; **to get p. to manager** être promu directeur **(b)** *Com* (*of product*) promotion *f*; **to have a Chanel® p.** avoir des produits Chanel en promotion; **sales p.** promotion des ventes
promotional [prəˈməʊʃən(ə)l] *adj Com* promotionnel; **p. campaign** campagne *f* de promotion; **p. literature** prospectus *mpl* promotionnels; **p. material** matériel *m* de promotion; **p. offer** offre *f* promotionnelle; **p. video** = **promo (a)**
prompt¹ [prɒmpt] **1** *adj* **(a)** (*swift*) rapide, prompt; **the article elicited a p. denial** cet article a été promptement démenti; **to take p. action** prendre des mesures immédiates; **her p. action saved his life** la rapidité de sa réaction lui a sauvé la vie; **to be p. to act** être prompt à agir, agir rapidement; **he was always very p. to understand** il comprenait toujours très vite; **p. payment** paiement *m* dans les plus brefs délais; *Com* **p. reply** (*to letter etc*) prompte réponse *f*, réponse rapide; **p. service** service *m* rapide **(b)** (*on time*) ponctuel **2** *adv* **at three o'clock p.** à trois heures précises
prompt² *n* **(a)** *Th* (*reminder*) **to give an actor a p.** souffler une réplique à un acteur; **p. box** trou *m* du souffleur; *TV* **p. card** aide-mémoire *m*, carton *m* de prompteur; **p. copy**

exemplaire *m ou* manuscrit *m* du souffleur; **p. side** *Br* côté *m* cour; *US* côté jardin; **opposite p. side** *Br* côté jardin; *US* côté cour **(b)** *Comptr* invite *f*, indicatif *m*; (*with wording*) message *m* d'invite; **DOS p.** invite du DOS

prompt[3] *vt* **(a)** (*cause*) (*reaction, reply*) provoquer; **to p. sb to do sth** pousser *ou* porter qn à faire qch; **what prompted you to come?** qu'est-ce qui vous a donné l'idée de venir?; **these events prompted her to …** ces événements l'ont poussée à …; **to be prompted by a feeling of pity** être animé par un sentiment de pitié

(b) (*actor, pupil, speaker*) **to p. sb** *Th* souffler sa réplique à qn; (*provide with correct response, answer*) souffler à qn; **she needed no prompting when asked her opinion on the subject** elle n'avait pas besoin d'encouragement pour donner son opinion sur le sujet; **'where did you go?', the teacher prompted** 'où es-tu allé?' dit le professeur pour l'encourager à parler; **the teacher prompted him with another question** le professeur lui posa une autre question pour le mettre sur la voie

prompter ['prɒmptər] *n Th* souffleur, -euse; **p.'s box** trou *m* du souffleur

prompting ['prɒmptɪŋ] *n* **(a)** (*persuasion, encouragement*) insistance *f*; **they will not do it without the p. of the international community** ils ne le feront pas si la communauté internationale ne les y pousse pas; **I wonder whose p. lies behind these questions** je me demande qui est à l'origine de ces questions; **to do sth at sb's p.** faire qch sur les instances *ou* à l'instigation de qn; **the promptings of conscience** l'aiguillon *m* de la conscience; **he needed no p.** il n'a pas été nécessaire de le pousser

(b) (*of actor, pupil, speaker*) **he needed a lot of p.** (*of actor*) on devait lui souffler tout le temps; **to answer a question without p.** répondre à une question sans que personne ne souffle; *Sch* **no p.!** ne soufflez pas!

promptitude ['prɒmptɪtju:d] *n* = **promptness**

promptly ['prɒmptlɪ] *adv* **(a)** (*rapidly*) promptement, rapidement **(b)** (*punctually*) ponctuellement **(c)** (*immediately*) sur-le-champ, immédiatement

promptness ['prɒmptnɪs] *n* promptitude *f*

promulgate ['prɒməlgeɪt] *vt Fml* **(a)** (*law, edict*) promulguer **(b)** (*idea, doctrine etc*) propager, répandre

promulgation [prɒməl'geɪʃən] *n Fml* **(a)** (*of law, edict*) promulgation *f* **(b)** (*of idea, doctrine*) propagation *f*

prone [prəʊn] *adj* **(a)** (*lying*) (*person, animal etc*) couché sur le ventre, étendu face contre terre; **to be in a p. position** être couché sur le ventre **(b)** (*inclined*) **p. to sth/do sth** enclin *ou* porté à qch/faire qch; **p. to a disease** prédisposé à une maladie

-prone [prəʊn] *suff* **to be accident/disaster-p.** être enclin aux accidents/désastres; **strike-p. industry** industrie sujette aux grèves

proneness ['prəʊnnɪs] *n* propension *f* **(to** à); (*to disease*) prédisposition *f*; **he has a certain p. to accidents/to letting himself be influenced** il est assez enclin aux accidents/à se laisser influencer

prong [prɒŋ] *n* (*of fork*) dent *f*; (*on stag's antler*) pointe *f*

pronged [prɒŋd] *adj* **two-p. fork** fourchette à deux dents; *Mil* **two/three-p. attack** attaque *f* sur deux/trois fronts; **it's a two-p. argument** c'est un argument qui porte sur deux fronts

pronominal [prəʊ'nɒmɪn(ə)l] *adj Gram* pronominal

pronominally [prəʊ'nɒmɪn(ə)lɪ] *adv Gram* pronominalement

pronoun ['prəʊnaʊn] *n* (ⓘ**A26-38; B13-22,6**) *Gram* pronom *m*

pronounce [prə'naʊns] **1** *vt* **(a)** (*word etc*) prononcer; **this letter is not pronounced** cette lettre ne se prononce pas; **is that how you p. it *or* how it's pronounced?** est-ce que c'est comme ça que ça se prononce?

(b) *Fml* (*declare*) déclarer **(that** que); *Jur* (*sentence*) prononcer; (*judgment*) rendre, prononcer; **to p. sb (to be) a genius** déclarer que qn est un génie; **I now p. you man and wife** (*in marriage service*) je vous déclare mari et femme

2 *vi* **to p. on a subject** se prononcer sur un sujet; (*of tribunal*) statuer sur une question; **to p. for *or* in favour of sb/against sb** se prononcer *ou* se déclarer pour/contre qn

pronounceable [prə'naʊnsəb(ə)l] *adj* prononçable; **a barely p. name** un nom tout juste prononçable; **easily p.** facile à prononcer

pronounced [prə'naʊnst] *adj* (*squint, accent, liking*) prononcé, marqué; (*features*) accusé; (*views, opinions*) arrêté; **the change is becoming more p.** le changement s'accentue; **he walks with a p. limp** il boite de façon prononcée

pronouncement [prə'naʊnsmənt] *n esp Fml* déclaration *f*

pronouncing [prə'naʊnsɪŋ] *n Jur* (*of sentence*) prononcé *m*; **p. dictionary** dictionnaire *m* de prononciation

pronto ['prɒntəʊ] *adv F* illico

pronuclear [prəʊ'nju:klɪər] *adj* (*policy, statement etc*) en faveur du nucléaire; **he is p.** il est pour le nucléaire

pronunciation [prənʌnsɪ'eɪʃən] *n* (*of word, language*) prononciation *f*; **his French p. was good** il avait une bonne prononciation en français

proof[1] [pru:f] *n* **(a)** (*evidence*) preuve *f*; **you have no p.** tu n'as pas de preuve; **positive p., p. positive** preuve patente; **clear p. of guilt** preuve évidente de culpabilité; **to give p. of** (*guilt, innocence*) prouver, démontrer; (*commitment, loyalty*) faire preuve de; (*intelligence*) montrer, indiquer; **this is p. that he is lying** cela prouve qu'il ment; **in p. of *or* as a p. of one's good faith** comme preuve *ou* en témoignage de sa bonne foi; **to produce p. to the contrary** fournir la preuve du contraire; *Jur* **the onus *or* the burden of p. lies with …** la charge de la preuve incombe à …; *Com* **p. of debt** affirmation *f* de créance; **p. of one's identity** preuve d'identité; **p. of identity** pièce *f* d'identité; **p. of insurance** attestation *f* d'assurance; **p. of payment** justificatif *m* de paiement; **p. of purchase** (*receipt etc*) preuve d'achat

(b) (*test*) épreuve *f*; **to put sth/sb to the p.** mettre qch/qn à l'épreuve; *Prov* **the p. of the pudding is in the eating** c'est à l'œuvre que l'on connaît l'artisan

(c) *Typ* **(printer's) p.** épreuve *f* (d'imprimerie); **to read proofs** corriger des épreuves; **to pass the proofs** donner le bon à tirer; **at the p. stage** à la correction des épreuves; **p. (correction) marks** signes *mpl* de correction sur épreuve

(d) (*of alcoholic drink*) teneur *f* en alcool

proof[2] *adj* **(a)** (*resistant*) **p. against sth** résistant à qch, à l'épreuve de qch; **p. against damp** imperméable, étanche; *Tech* hydrofuge; **to be p. against danger/disease** être à l'abri du danger/immunisé contre la maladie; **p. against temptation** (*person*) insensible à la tentation **(b) to be 0.9% p.** (*of alcohol*) contenir 0,9% d'alcool

proof[3] *vt* **(a)** *Typ* (*take proof from*) tirer une épreuve de **(b)** (*check proofs of*) corriger **(c)** (*fabric etc*) imperméabiliser; (*against acid etc*) rendre résistant *ou* inattaquable

-proof [pru:f] *suff* **bulletp./heatp.** à l'épreuve des balles/de la chaleur

proofing ['pru:fɪŋ] *n* **(a)** (*action*) (*of fabric etc*) imperméabilisation *f* **(b)** (*coating*) enduit *m* imperméable **(c)** *Typ* (*production*) tirage *m* des épreuves; (*reading*) correction *f* des épreuves

proofread ['pru:fri:d] *Typ* **1** *vi* corriger des épreuves **2** *vt* corriger, relire, corriger les épreuves de; **once it's been proofread** une fois les épreuves corrigées

proofreader ['pru:fri:dər] *n Typ* correcteur, -trice

proofreading ['pru:fri:dɪŋ] *n Typ* correction *f* d'épreuves

prop[1] [prɒp] *n* (*support*) appui *m*, support *m*; (*of wall*) étançon *m*, étai *m*; *Rugby* **p. (forward)** pilier *m*; *Min* **(pit) p.** étai *ou* étançon de mine; *Fig* **he was the p. of his father's old age** c'était lui qui soutenait son père âgé; **this fact serves as a p. to her argument** ce fait étaye son argument; **it is one of the props of his existence** c'est une des choses qui l'aident à vivre

prop[2] *vt* **(-pp-)** (*support*) appuyer, soutenir; **to p. a ladder/a person against a wall** appuyer une échelle/une personne contre un mur; **she propped her chin on her hand** elle posa son menton sur sa main

prop[3] *n Av F* = **propeller**

prop[4] *n Th etc* accessoire *m*; **props** (*person*) accessoiriste *mf*; *Fig* **the rock star's guitar was just a p.** la guitare du chanteur de rock n'était qu'un accessoire; **props department** service *m* des accessoires

prop[5] *Com* (*abbr* **proprietor**) propriétaire *mf*

▶ **prop open** *vtsep* maintenir ouvert; **she propped the door open with a chair** elle a calé *ou* bloqué la porte avec une chaise pour qu'elle reste ouverte

▶ **prop up** *vtsep* (*support*) (*tunnel, building*) appuyer, soutenir; (*wall*) étançonner, étayer; *Fig* (*currency, system etc*) soutenir; **propped up on one's elbows** accoudé; **to p. up a patient on his pillow** redresser un malade sur son oreiller; **to p. a ladder/a person up against a wall** appuyer une échelle/une personne contre un mur; **to p. oneself up against sth** s'appuyer contre qch; **propped up by a pile of books** calé par une pile de livres; *Fig* **the régime is being propped up by the military** le régime est maintenu en place par l'armée; *Hum* **a group of boys propping up a wall** un groupe de jeunes appuyés contre un mur; **are you propping up the wall?** tu as peur que le mur s'écroule?; *Br* **he's always propping up the bar** c'est un vrai pilier de bar; **he'll be out propping up a bar somewhere** il doit être dans un bar quelque part

propaganda [prɒpə'gændə] *n* propagande *f*; **p. film** film *m* de propagande

propagandist [prɒpə'gændɪst] *n, adj* propagandiste *mf*

propagandize [prɒpə'gændaɪz] *Fml* **1** *vi* faire de la propagande

2 *vt* (*one's ideas, theories*) faire de la propagande pour; (*the masses, one's colleagues etc*) faire de la propagande à
propagate ['prɒpəgeɪt] **1** *vt Bot, Phys etc* propager; *Fig* (*ideas etc*) propager, disséminer **2** *vi* (*of animal, plant*) se propager
propagation [prɒpə'geɪʃən] *n Bot, Phys, Fig* propagation *f*
propagator ['prɒpəgeɪtər] *n* (*for seedlings*) = mini-serre *f*, *pl* mini-serres
propane ['prəʊpeɪn] *n Ch* propane *m*
propel [prə'pel] *vt* (**-ll-**) (*sth*) propulser; *Fig* (*urge on*) pousser (**towards** vers); **propelled by ambition** poussé *ou* animé par l'ambition
propellant, propellent [prə'pelənt] **1** *n* (*fuel*) combustible *m*; (*for rocket*) propergol *m*; **liquid/solid (rocket) p.** propergol liquide/solide **2** *adj* propulseur (*no f*), propulsif
propeller [prə'pelər] *n Naut, Av* hélice *f*; **p. blade** pale *f* d'hélice; **p. shaft** *Naut* arbre *m* porte-hélice; *Aut* arbre de transmission
propelling [prə'pelɪŋ] *adj* propulsif; **p. pencil** porte-mine *m inv*
propensity [prə'pensɪtɪ] *n* propension *f* (**to sth** à qch; **to do** *or* **for doing sth** à faire qch)
proper ['prɒpər] **1** *adj* **(a)** (*true, real*) vrai; **it'll be good to sleep in a p. bed** ça va être agréable de dormir dans un vrai lit; **the p. word** le mot juste; **p. meaning of a word** signification *f* propre d'un mot; **what's its p. name?** comment ça s'appelle au juste?; **to get a p. night's sleep** avoir une bonne nuit de sommeil; **it's more a course in design than in architecture p.** c'est plus un cours de design que d'architecture proprement dite; **we're still not in London p. yet** nous ne sommes pas encore arrivés a Londres même
(b) (*most suitable, suited*) convenable; (*behaviour, model etc*) approprié; (*correct in behaviour*) convenable, comme il faut; **is that the p. way to treat your sister?** est-ce que c'est comme ça qu'on traite sa sœur?; **at the p. time** en temps utile, au moment voulu; **to apply to the p. person** s'adresser à qui de droit; **to put sth in the p. place** mettre qch à sa place; **to think it p. to do sth** juger bon *ou* à propos de faire qch; **do as you think p.** faites comme bon vous semblera; *F* **to do the p. thing by sb** faire son devoir, faire ce qu'il faut; **the p. way to do it** la bonne façon de le faire; **the p. use of the subjunctive** l'emploi *m* correct du subjonctif; **paid at the p. rate** payé au taux *ou* au prix convenable; **a very p. old lady** une vieille dame très comme il faut; (*very dignified*) une vieille dame très digne; *F* **a p. little madam** une vraie petite madame; *Old-fashioned* **it's not the p. thing to do** cela ne se fait pas; **it's not p.** ce n'est pas bien; **that's not the p. way to behave!** en voilà des manières!, tiens-toi convenablement!; **she thanked him, as is only p.** elle l'a remercié, comme il se devait
(c) (*characteristic*) **p. use of a drug** emploi *m* rationnel d'un remède; **to put sth to its p. use** utiliser qch correctement *ou* de la bonne façon; *Fml* **p. to sth** propre *ou* particulier à qch
(d) *Br F* (*intensifier*) **we're in a p. mess** nous voilà dans de beaux draps!; **he's a p. fool** c'est un parfait imbécile *ou* une vraie andouille; **we gave him a p. kicking** nous lui avons mis une bonne raclée
2 *adv F* **they got it good and p.** ils ont reçu ce qu'ils méritaient; *F* **to talk p.** parler correctement; *Br Dial* **he was p. angry** il était drôlement en colère
proper fraction *n Math* fraction *f* moindre que l'unité
properly ['prɒpəlɪ] *adv* **(a)** (*correctly*) correctement; **p. speaking** proprement dit, à proprement parler; **speak p.!** tu pourrais t'exprimer convenablement!; **do it p. or not at all** faites-le correctement *ou* comme il faut ou pas du tout; **I haven't been sleeping p.** je dors mal ces temps-ci **(b)** (*suitably*) convenablement; (*correctly in behaviour*) comme il faut; **he very p. refused** il a refusé, comme il le fallait **(c)** *F* (*intensive*) **he was p. fed up** il en avait carrément marre **(d)** *Jur* (*to act*) de bon droit
proper name *n Gram* nom *m* propre
proper noun *n* [①A8,3,2,B8,10] *Gram* nom *m* propre
propertied ['prɒpətɪd] *adj* possédant
property ['prɒpətɪ] *n* **(a)** (*possessions*) propriété *f*, biens *mpl*; (*buildings*) immeuble(s) *m(pl)*; (*land*) propriété (foncière), terrain *m*; (*house*) propriété; **that's my p.** cela m'appartient; **they have p. in Scotland** (*land*) ils ont des terres en Écosse; **personal p.** affaires *fpl ou Lit* effets *mpl* personnel(le)s; **damage to p.** dommages *mpl* matériels; **to be on sb's p.** être sur les terres de qn; **get off my p.!** sortez de ma propriété!; **p. is theft** la propriété, c'est le vol; **this television is stolen p.** cette télévision a été volée; *Acct* **p. improvement cost** impense *f*; **the p. market** le marché immobilier; **p. owner** propriétaire *m* foncier; **p. pages** section *f* immobilier; **p. tax** impôt *m* foncier
(b) *Jur* (*right*) (droit *m* de) propriété *f*; **literary/intellectual p.** propriété littéraire/intellectuelle
(c) (*quality*) (*of thing*) propriété *f*; **(inherent) p.** attribut *m*; **plants with healing properties** plantes qui ont des propriétés *ou* des vertus thérapeutiques
(d) *Th etc* accessoire *m*; **p. man** accessoiriste *m*; **p. mistress** accessoiriste *f*
property developer *n* promoteur *m* (immobilier)
property development *n* promotion *f* immobilière
property speculation *n* spéculation *f* immobilière
prophecy ['prɒfɪsɪ] *n* prophétie *f*
prophesy ['prɒfɪsaɪ] **1** *vi* prophétiser, faire des prophéties; **exactly as she had prophesied** exactement comme elle l'avait prédit **2** *vt* (*event*) prophétiser, prédire
prophet ['prɒfɪt] *n* prophète *m*; *Bible* **the major/minor prophets** les grands/petits prophètes; **the P.** (*in Islam*) le Prophète (Mahomet); *Prov* **no man is a p. in his own country** nul n'est prophète en son pays; *F* **the prophets of doom** les prophètes de malheur
prophetess ['prɒfɪtes] *n* prophétesse *f*
prophetic [prə'fetɪk] *adj* prophétique; **these deeds were p. of his future greatness** ces actions annonçaient sa grandeur future
prophetically [prə'fetɪklɪ] *adv* prophétiquement
prophylactic [prɒfɪ'læktɪk] *Med* **1** *adj* prophylactique **2** *n* prophylactique *m*; (*condom*) préservatif *m*
prophylaxis [prɒfɪ'læksɪs] *n Med* prophylaxie *f*
propinquity [prə'pɪŋkwɪtɪ] *n Fml* **(a)** (*proximity*) proximité *f* (de lieu); **to live in close p. to sb** habiter tout à proximité de qn **(b)** (*of blood relationship*) (proche) parenté *f* **(c)** (*similarity*) affinité *f* (**of ideas** entre les idées)
propitiate [prə'pɪʃɪeɪt] *vt Fml* (*person whom one has offended*) apaiser
propitiation [prəpɪʃɪ'eɪʃən] *n Fml* (*of the gods*) propitiation *f*; *Fig* apaisement *m*
propitiatory [prə'pɪʃɪət(ə)rɪ] *adj Fml* propitiatoire
propitious [prə'pɪʃəs] *adj Fml* (*to person, undertaking*) propice, favorable
propitiously [prə'pɪʃəslɪ] *adv Fml* d'une manière propice
propman ['prɒpmæn] *n Th* accessoiriste *m*
proponent [prə'pəʊnənt] *n* adepte *mf*, partisan *m*
proportion[1] [prə'pɔːʃən] *n* **(a)** [①B56,C] (*relationship*) rapport *m*, proportion *f*; *Math* (*arithmetic, geometric*) proportion; **friction in p. to the load** frottement proportionnel à la charge; **the same ingredients in different proportions** les mêmes ingrédients dans des proportions différentes; **in p. to ...** proportionnellement à ...; **out of all p. to ...** sans commune mesure avec ...; **the payment is out of all p. to the work involved** la rétribution n'est pas du tout proportionnelle au travail requis; **it has grown out of all p. to the original design** cela n'a plus aucune commune mesure avec le plan initial; **in perfect p.** en parfaite harmonie (**to** avec); **out of p.** mal proportionné, disproportionné; **he has no sense of p.** il n'a pas le sens de la mesure; **to lose all sense of p.** ne garder aucune mesure; **let's keep a sense of p.** remettons les choses à leur place; **you're getting this all out of p.** tu as une impression complètement déformée de tout cela; **in direct/inverse p. to sth** en rapport direct/inverse à qch
(b) (*part*) (*of ingredient in mixture*) part *f*, proportion *f*; (*of work, time, money etc*) part, partie *f*; **a large p. of them are students** une grande part *ou* partie d'entre eux sont étudiants; **what p. of the group is French?** quelle est la proportion de Français dans le groupe?
(c) (*dimensions*) **proportions** (*of building, human body, crisis*) proportions *fpl*; (*of machine*) dimensions *fpl*; **a Greek temple of classical proportions** un temple grec de proportions classiques
proportion[2] *vt* proportionner
proportional [prə'pɔːʃən(ə)l] **1** *adj* proportionnel (**to** à), en proportion (**to** de); **inversely/directly p. to ...** inversement/directement proportionnel à ...; *Admin* **p. assessment** coéquation *f*; *Typ* **p. font** police *f* proportionnelle; *Typ* **p. spacing** espacement *m* proportionnel **2** *n Math* proportionnelle *f*
proportionally [prə'pɔːʃən(ə)lɪ] *adv* en proportion, proportionnellement (**to** à); **they spend p. more of their budget on research than does ...** ils accordent à la recherche une proportion de leur budget supérieure à celle que dépense ...
proportional representation *n Pol* représentation *f* proportionnelle
proportionate [prə'pɔːʃənɪt] *adj* proportionné, proportionnel (**to** à); **a p. response** une réponse en conséquence
proportionately [prə'pɔːʃənɪtlɪ] *adv* proportionnellement, en proportion (**to** à)

proportioned [prəˈpɔːʃənd] *adj* **well/badly p.** bien/mal proportionné

proposal [prəˈpəʊz(ə)l] *n* **(a)** (*offer*) proposition *f*, offre *f*; **to make a p.** faire *ou* formuler une proposition; **p. (of marriage)** demande *f* en mariage; **p. of peace, peace p.** proposition de paix **(b)** (*plan*) projet *m*; **the p. to turn the building into a museum** le projet de transformer le bâtiment en musée

propose [prəˈpəʊz] **1** *vt* (*candidate, motion*) proposer; **to p. sb for treasurer** proposer qn pour le poste de trésorier; **he proposed that …** il a proposé que … + *sub*; **to p. a toast** porter un toast; **to p. sb's health** porter un toast à la santé de qn; **to p. to do sth** *or* **doing sth** (*intend*) avoir l'intention de *ou Fml* se proposer de faire qch; **they p. making the street one-way** (*suggest*) ils suggèrent de mettre cette rue en sens unique

2 *vi* **(a)** (*make offer of marriage*) faire une demande en mariage; **he proposed to her** il lui a demandé de l'épouser; **when did he p.?** quand a-t-il fait sa demande en mariage?

(b) *Prov* **man proposes, God disposes** l'homme propose et Dieu dispose

proposed [preˈpəʊzd] *adj* proposé

proposer [prəˈpəʊzər] *n* auteur *m* d'une offre *ou* d'une proposition; (*at club etc*) (*of candidate*) parrain *m*, marraine *f*; **p. of a motion** promoteur *m* d'une motion

proposition[1] [prɒpəˈzɪʃən] *n* **(a)** (*offer*) proposition *f*, offre *f*; (*sexual*) avances *fpl*; *F* (*matter*) affaire *f*; **that's quite a p.!, it's a tough p.!** ce n'est pas une mince affaire!; **I've got a p. (to put to you)** j'ai une proposition (à te faire); *F* **paying p.** affaire rentable *ou* qui rapporte; *F* **that's a very different p.** c'est tout à fait autre chose, c'est une autre histoire; *F* **he's a tough p.** il n'est pas commode **(b)** (*in logic*), *Gram* proposition *f*

proposition[2] *vt* (*sexually*) faire des avances à

propound [prəˈpaʊnd] *vt* (*idea*) émettre; (*programme, theory*) exposer

proprietary [prəˈpraɪɪt(ə)rɪ] *adj* (*right etc*) de propriété, de propriétaire; (*air, attitude*) de propriétaire; *Com* **p. article** article *m* de marque (déposée); **p. brand** marque *f* déposée; **p. medicines** spécialités *fpl* pharmaceutiques; **p. name** nom *m* déposé

proprietor [prəˈpraɪətər] *n* propriétaire *mf*

proprietorial [prəpraɪəˈtɔːrɪəl] *adj* (*attitude, rights*) de propriétaire; **he's very p. about it** il est très possessif avec ça

proprietorship [prəˈpraɪətəʃɪp] *n Fml* **to dispute the p. of sth** disputer la propriété de qch; **under his p.** alors qu'il est/était propriétaire

proprietress [prəˈpraɪətrɪs] *n* propriétaire *f*

propriety [prəˈpraɪətɪ] *n* **(a)** (*correctness*) (*of language, manners, behaviour*) bienséance *f*, correction *f*; (*of action, measure*) opportunité *f* **(b)** (*standard of behaviour*) **to observe the proprieties** observer les convenances

propshaft [ˈprɒpʃɑːft] *n* arbre *m* de transmission

propulsion [prəˈpʌlʃən] *n MecE* propulsion *f*; **means of p.** moyen(s) *m(pl) ou* mode *m* de propulsion

propulsive [prəˈpʌlsɪv] *adj* propulsif; (*movement, effort*) de propulsion; (*force*) moteur, -trice

pro rata [ˈprəʊˈrɑːtə] **1** *adj* proportionnel, au prorata; **p. payment** paiement *m* proportionnel **2** *adv* proportionnellement, au prorata

prorogation [prəʊrəˈgeɪʃən] *n Fml* prorogation *f*

prorogue [prəˈrəʊg] *vt Fml* proroger

prosaic [prəʊˈzeɪɪk] *adj* (*style, mind etc*) prosaïque

prosaically [prəʊˈzeɪɪklɪ] *adv* prosaïquement

proscenium [prəˈsiːnɪəm] *n Th* avant-scène *f*, *pl* avant-scènes; **p. arch** manteau *m* (d'Arlequin)

proscribe [prəʊˈskraɪb] *vt* proscrire

proscription [prəʊˈskrɪpʃən] *n* proscription *f*

prose[1] [prəʊz] *n* **(a)** prose *f*; **p. poem, poem in p.** poème *m* en prose; **p. writer** prosateur *m* **(b)** *Sch, Univ* (*translation*) thème *m*

prose[2] *vi Old-fashioned Pej* tenir des discours ennuyeux

prosecute [ˈprɒsɪkjuːt] **1** *vt* **(a)** *Jur* (*person*) poursuivre (en justice); **the prosecuting counsel** *or US* **attorney** ≈ le Ministère public **(b)** *Fml* (*pursue*) (*claim, activities, war etc*) poursuivre **2** *vi Jur* **to decide to p.** décider d'engager des poursuites judiciaires; **who's prosecuting?** qui plaide pour le Ministère public?

prosecution [prɒsɪˈkjuːʃən] *n* **(a)** *Jur* (*proceedings*) poursuites *fpl* judiciaires, accusation *f*; **the p.** (*lawyers*) les plaignants *mpl*; (*in Crown case*) ≈ le Ministère public; **who's appearing for the p.?** qui plaide pour le Ministère public?; **witness for the p.** témoin *m* à charge; **to bring a p. against sb** engager des poursuites judiciaires contre qn **(b)** *Fml* (*of activity etc*) poursuite *f*

prosecutor [ˈprɒsɪkjuːtər] *n Jur* plaignant *m*; **she was p. in several famous trials** elle a plaidé pour le Ministère public dans plusieurs grands procès

proselyte [ˈprɒsɪlaɪt] *n* prosélyte *mf*

proselytism [ˈprɒsɪlɪtɪz(ə)m] *n* prosélytisme *m*

proselytize [ˈprɒsɪlɪtaɪz] **1** *vt* (*person*) convertir, faire un/une prosélyte de **2** *vi* faire du prosélytisme *ou* des prosélytes

proselytizing [ˈprɒsɪlɪtaɪzɪŋ] *n* prosélytisme *m*

prosodic [prəˈsɒdɪk] *adj* prosodique

prosody [ˈprɒsədɪ] *n* prosodie *f*

prospect[1] [ˈprɒspekt] *n* **(a)** (*expectation, thought*) perspective *f*; **to open up a new p. to sb** ouvrir une nouvelle perspective à qn; **there is very little p. of it** on ne peut guère y compter; **there is every p. that we shall succeed/of his becoming Prime Minister** tout semble indiquer que nous réussirons/qu'il deviendra premier ministre; **no p. of agreement** aucune perspective d'accord; **in p.** en perspective

(b) (*chance, likelihood*) **future prospects** perspectives *fpl* d'avenir; **prospects of success** chances *fpl* de succès; **his prospects are brilliant** un brillant avenir l'attend; **to have prospects** (*of person*) avoir de l'avenir *ou* un avenir prometteur; **a job with prospects** un poste qui offre des perspectives d'avenir

(c) *Com* (*prospective customer*) client *m* éventuel

(d) *Fml* (*view*) vue *f*, perspective *f*

prospect[2] [prəˈspekt] **1** *vi Min, Mktg* prospecter; **to p. for gold** chercher de l'or **2** *vt* (*land, mine*) prospecter

prospecting [prəˈspektɪŋ] *n Min, Mktg* prospection *f*; **oil/gold p.** prospection pétrolière/d'or

prospective [prəˈspektɪv] *adj* (*likely*) en perspective; **my p. son-in-law** mon futur gendre; **p. buyer** acheteur, -euse éventuel(le) *ou* potentiel(le); **the p. sale of the painting at auction** la possibilité d'une vente aux enchères du tableau; **the p. Conservative candidate** l'éventuel candidat des Conservateurs

prospector [prəˈspektər] *n* prospecteur, -trice; **oil p.** chercheur, -euse de pétrole, (géologue *m*) pétrolier *m*; **gold p.** chercheur, -euse d'or

prospectus, *pl* **-tuses** [prəˈspektəs, -təsɪz] *n Com* prospectus *m*, réclame *f*; *Fin* appel *m* à la souscription publique; *Sch, Univ* brochure *f* d'information

prosper [ˈprɒspər] *vi* prospérer, réussir; **how's he doing, still prospering?** comment va-t-il, ça marche toujours bien pour lui?

prosperity [prɒˈsperɪtɪ] *n* prospérité *f*

prosperous [ˈprɒspərəs] *adj* **(a)** (*wealthy*) prospère **(b)** *Lit* (*favourable*) favorable; **p. winds** vents *mpl* favorables

prosperously [ˈprɒspərəslɪ] *adv* d'une manière prospère; **he lives quite p.** il vit dans la prospérité

prosperousness [ˈprɒspərəsnɪs] *n* prospérité *f*

prostaglandin [prɒstəˈglændɪn] *n Physiol* prostaglandine *f*

prostate [ˈprɒsteɪt] *n Anat* **p. (gland)** prostate *f*

prosthesis [ˈprɒsθɪsɪs, prɒsˈθiːsɪs] *n Surg, Gram* prothèse *f*

prosthetics [prɒsˈθetɪks] *n* [①A10,c] prothétique *f*

prostitute[1] [ˈprɒstɪtjuːt] *n* prostituée *f*; **male p.** prostitué *m*

prostitute[2] *vt* (*one's body, talent etc*) prostituer; **to p. oneself** se prostituer

prostitution [prɒstɪˈtjuːʃən] *n* prostitution *f*

prostrate[1] [ˈprɒstreɪt] *adj* **(a)** (*lying down*) couché; (*submissively*) prosterné; **to lie p.** être couché; (*submissively*) être prosterné **(b)** (*exhausted*) abattu, accablé; *Med* prostré; **p. with grief** terrassé par le chagrin

prostrate[2] [ˈprɒstreɪt] *vt* **(a)** (*lay down*) (*on ground*) coucher *ou* étendre par terre; **to p. oneself before sb** se prosterner devant qn **(b)** (*exhaust*) abattre, accabler; *Med* mettre dans un état de prostration; **prostrated by the heat** accablé de chaleur

prostration [prɒˈstreɪʃən] *n* **(a)** (*lying down*) prosternation *f* **(b)** (*exhaustion*) abattement *m*, accablement *m*; *Med* prostration *f*

prosy [ˈprəʊzɪ] *adj F* (*style*) fastidieux; *Old-fashioned* (*person*) verbeux, ennuyeux

protagonist [prəˈtægənɪst] *n* protagoniste *mf*; (*of idea, view*) partisan *m*

protean [prəʊˈtiːən, ˈprəʊtɪən] *adj Lit* protéiforme

protect [prəˈtekt] *vt* **(a)** protéger; (*person's interests etc*) sauvegarder; **to p. sb/sth from** *or* **against** protéger qn/qch de *ou* contre; (*rain etc*) protéger *ou* abriter qn/qch de; **well protected against the cold** bien protégé contre le froid, bien protégé du froid; **to p. sb against sb's anger** soustraire qn à la colère de qn **(b)** *Econ* (*industry*) protéger

protected [prəˈtektɪd] *adj* (*area, species etc*) protégé

protection [prəˈtekʃən] *n* **(a)** protection *f* (**against** contre); (*of person's interests etc*) sauvegarde *f*; **to be under sb's p.** être sous la protection de qn; **under police p.** sous la protection de la police; **to claim the p. of the law** demander la protection de la loi; **p. against attack** protection en cas d'attaque; **society for the p. of birds** société *f* protectrice des oiseaux; **suntan lotion gives** *or* **provides some p. against the sun** le lait solaire protège du *ou* contre le soleil; **p. factor** (*of suntan lotion*) indice *m* de protection; *F* **p. (money)** = argent *m* versé à un racket en échange de sa soi-disant protection; *F* **p. racket** racket *m*

(**b**) *Econ* protectionnisme *m*; (*of industry*) protection *f*

protectionism [prəˈtekʃənɪz(ə)m] *n Econ* protectionnisme *m*

protectionist [prəˈtekʃənɪst] *adj, n Econ* protectionniste *mf*

protective [prəˈtektɪv] *adj* protecteur, -trice; (*clothing, mask etc*) de protection, protecteur; **he is very p. towards his children** il se montre très protecteur envers ses enfants; **to be p. of one's interests** sauvegarder ses intérêts; *Aut* **p. cage** cage *f* de sécurité; *Biol* **p. colouring** *or* **coloration** mimétisme *m* des couleurs; *Econ* **p. duties** droits *mpl* protecteurs

protectively [prəˈtektɪvlɪ] *adv* d'une manière protectrice; (*with protective gesture*) d'un geste protecteur; **he put an arm p. around her shoulder** il entoura son épaule d'un bras protecteur; **to behave p. towards sb** se montrer protecteur envers qn

protector [prəˈtektər] *n* (**a**) (*person*) protecteur, -trice (**b**) (*device*) (*for machine, equipment etc*) dispositif *m* de protection; **ear p.** protège-oreilles *m inv*

protectorate [prəˈtektərɪt] *n Pol* protectorat *m*

protectress [prəˈtektrɪs] *n* protectrice *f*

protégé, -ée [ˈprɒteʒeɪ] *n* protégé, -ée

protein [ˈprəʊtiːn] *n* protéine *f*

proteinaceous [prəʊtiːˈneɪʃəs] *adj Med* protéique

protest¹ [ˈprəʊtest] *n* (**a**) protestation *f*; **to make a p.** protester, élever des protestations (**about sth** à propos de qch); **to register a p.** protester (**with** auprès de); **to raise a strong p.** élever des protestations énergiques; **to give rise to protests** (*of action*) soulever des protestations; **to stage a p.** (*demonstration*) organiser *ou* monter une manifestation; **she has strong grounds for p. at the way she was treated** elle a de bons motifs de protester contre la manière dont elle a été traitée; *Jur* **p. in writing** réserve *f*; **under p.** (*to do sth*) à son corps défendant, en protestant; (*to sign etc*) sous réserve; *Jur* **to act under p.** protester de violence; **she resigned in p. (at this decision)** elle a démissionné en signe de protestation (contre cette décision); **p. march** marche *f* de protestation; **p. meeting** réunion *f* de protestation; **p. song/singer** chanson *f*/chanteur, -euse engagé(e); **p. strike** grève *f* de protestation; *Pol* **p. vote** vote *m* de protestation

(**b**) *Jur, Fin* protêt *m*; **p. for non-acceptance** protêt faute d'acceptation

protest² [prəˈtest] **1** *vt* (**a**) (*one's innocence etc*) protester de; **to p. that ...** protester en disant que ...; *Fin* **to p. a bill** (faire) protester un effet *ou* une lettre de change (**b**) *Am* (*protest against*) (*decision, measure*) protester contre **2** *vi* protester (**against** contre); **the demonstrators protesting against** *or* **about the new tax** les manifestants qui protestent contre le nouvel impôt; **really, I p., that's too much!** non, vraiment, je proteste, c'est trop!

protestable [prəˈtestəb(ə)l] *adj Fin* protestable

Protestant [ˈprɒtɪstənt] *adj, n Rel* protestant, -ante; **the P. Church** = l'église *f* réformée; **P. work ethic** éthique *f* protestante du travail

Protestantism [ˈprɒtɪstəntɪz(ə)m] *n Rel* protestantisme *m*

protestation [prɒtesˈteɪʃən] *n* protestation *f*; **in spite of his protestations of innocence** en dépit de ses protestations d'innocence; **her reaction provoked protestations of love/loyalty from him** sa réaction l'a poussé à protester de son amour/de sa loyauté

protester [prəˈtestər] *n* protestataire *mf*; **anti-nuclear/peace p.** manifestant, -ante contre le nucléaire/pour la paix

protocol [ˈprəʊtəkɒl] *n* (*in diplomacy etc*), *Jur, Comptr* protocole *m*

proton [ˈprəʊtɒn] *n Nucl Phys* proton *m*

protoplasm [ˈprəʊtəplæz(ə)m] *n Biol* protoplasme *m*, protoplasma *m*

prototype [ˈprəʊtətaɪp] *n* prototype *m*; **p. aircraft/car** prototype d'avion/de voiture

protozoa [prəʊtəˈzəʊə] *npl Biol* protozoaires *mpl*

protozoan [prəʊtəˈzəʊən] *n, adj Biol* protozoaire *m*

protract [prəˈtrækt] *vt* prolonger; (*matter, business*) faire traîner en longueur

protracted [prəˈtræktɪd] *adj* prolongé

protraction [prəˈtrækʃən] *n* (**a**) (*of trial etc*) prolongation *f*; (*of procedure etc*) longueur *f* (**b**) *Anat* (*of muscle*) protraction *f*

protractor [prəˈtræktər] *n* (**a**) *Geom* rapporteur *m* (**b**) *Anat* **p. (muscle)** (muscle *m*) protracteur *m*

protrude [prəˈtruːd] **1** *vi* (*of brick, beam etc*) dépasser; (*of shelf, balcony, rock etc*) dépasser, avancer; **his teeth p. (too far)** il a les dents qui avancent; **there was a notebook protruding from her pocket** un carnet dépassait de sa poche **2** *vt* (faire) sortir, pousser en avant, avancer

protruding [prəˈtruːdɪŋ] *adj* en saillie, saillant; (*jaw, teeth*) qui avance; (*eyes*) exorbité, saillant; (*stomach, ribs*) protubérant

protrusion [prəˈtruːʒ(ə)n] *n* (**a**) (*state*) sortie *f*, saillie *f* (**b**) (*thing*) saillie *f*, protubérance *f*; *Anat* protrusion *f*

protuberance [prəˈtjuːbərəns] *n* protubérance *f*

protuberant [prəˈtjuːbərənt] *adj* protubérant

proud [praʊd] **1** *adj* (**a**) (*justifiably*) fier; **to be p. of sth/of having done sth** être fier *ou* s'enorgueillir de qch/d'avoir fait qch; **to be p. of oneself** être fier de soi; *Iron* **I hope you're p. of yourself!** tu peux être fier de toi!; **I'm p. to have known her** je suis fier de l'avoir connue; **it made me feel p. to be Welsh** cela m'a rendu fier d'être gallois; **we're all p. of you** nous sommes tous fiers de toi; **he's the p. owner of ...** il est l'heureux propriétaire de ...; **it was her proudest possession** c'était ce qu'elle avait de plus précieux; **a p. moment** un moment d'intense fierté; **a picture of the p. parents** une photo des parents, débordants de fierté; **as p. as a peacock** *or* **as Punch** fier comme Artaban

(**b**) *Pej* (*arrogant*) orgueilleux, fier; **too p. to apologize** trop fier pour s'excuser; **I'll sit here, I'm not p.** je m'assiérai là, je ne suis pas exigeant

(**c**) (*noble*) fier, digne; (*impressive*) (*city etc*) imposant, magnifique; *Old-fashioned, Hum* **a p. beauty** une beauté orgueilleuse; *Lit* **a p. and noble race** *or* **people** un peuple fier et noble

(**d**) *Tech* (*protruding*) **to stand p. of a surface** dépasser *ou* déborder d'une surface

2 *adv F* **to do sb p.** faire honneur à qn; (*entertain lavishly*) se mettre en frais pour qn; **the caterers did us p.** les traiteurs nous ont fait un festin de rois; **they do you p. at that restaurant** on se régale dans ce restaurant; **to do oneself p.** se dépasser

proudly [ˈpraʊdlɪ] *adv* (**a**) (*with justifiable pride*) fièrement; **we p. present Take That in concert** nous avons le plaisir *ou* nous sommes heureux de vous présenter Take That en concert; **the banners waved p. in the wind** les drapeaux flottaient fièrement dans le vent (**b**) *Pej* (*haughtily*) orgueilleusement

prove [pruːv] (*pp* **proved**, *esp Am, Scot* **proven** [ˈpruːv(ə)n, ˈprəʊ-]) **1** *vt* (**a**) (*demonstrate*) (*the truth of sth*) prouver, démontrer; (*fact*) constater; (*one's identity*) justifier de; (*one's good will*) témoigner de; *Jur* (*a will*) homologuer; **I can't p. it** je ne peux pas le prouver; **to p. that ...** prouver que ...; **the evidence goes to p. that ...** les témoignages concourent à prouver que ...; **she/this assertion was proved wrong** on a prouvé qu'elle avait tort/que cette affirmation était fausse; **subsequent developments proved me right** la suite des événements m'a donné raison; **to p. oneself** faire ses preuves; **what are you trying to p.?** qu'est-ce que tu cherches à prouver?; **to do sth to p. a point** faire qch pour démontrer un point de vue; **that proves my point** ceci confirme ce que je disais; **that doesn't p. anything!** cela ne prouve rien!; *Math* **to p. a sum** faire la preuve d'un calcul

(**b**) *Culin* (*dough*) faire lever

2 *vi* (*of person*) se montrer; **she proved (to be) ideal for the job** elle s'est révélée être la personne idéale pour cet emploi; **if what you say proves (to be) true** si ce que vous dites se confirme; **many of his observations have proved correct** beaucoup de ses observations se sont avérées *ou* révélées justes; **to p. unequal to one's task** se montrer au-dessous de sa tâche

proven [ˈpruːv(ə)n, ˈprəʊ-] **1** *pp esp Am, Scot see* **prove 2** *adj* (*demonstrated*) (*courage, method, remedy etc*) éprouvé; *Scot Jur* **a verdict of p./not p.** un verdict de culpabilité prouvée/non prouvée

provenance [ˈprɒvənəns] *n* provenance *f*, origine *f*

Provençal [prɒvɒnˈsɑːl] **1** *adj* provençal **2** *n* (**a**) Provençal, -ale (**b**) *Ling* provençal *m*

provender [ˈprɒvɪndər] *n Agr* fourrage *m*

proverb [ˈprɒvɜːb] *n* proverbe *m*; *Bible* **(the Book of) Proverbs** le livre des Proverbes

proverbial [prəˈvɜːbɪəl] *adj* proverbial; **as happy as the p. sandboy** gai comme le pinson du proverbe

proverbially [prəˈvɜːbɪəlɪ] *adv* proverbialement

provide [prəˈvaɪd] **1** *vt* (**a**) (*supply*) fournir; **to p. sb with sth, to p. sth for sb** fournir qch à qn, pourvoir qn de qch; **they were well provided with food** ils étaient bien approvisionnés *ou* ravitaillés; **this provided her with an excuse** ça lui a fourni une excuse; **please write your name**

and address in the space provided veuillez écrire vos nom et adresse dans le blanc prévu à cet effet; **to p. an explanation** donner *ou* fournir une explication; **to p. an exit** (*of passage*) offrir une sortie; (*of architect*) ménager une sortie; **to p. a regular bus service** assurer un service d'autobus régulier; **to p. jobs** fournir des emplois; **this factory will p. 500 new jobs** cette usine créera 500 emplois

(**b**) (*stipulate*) stipuler (**that** que); **the law provides that ...** la loi stipule *ou* prévoit que ...

2 *vi* **the Lord will p.** Dieu y pourvoira

▶ **provide against** *vipo* (*attack etc*) se prémunir contre; (*danger*) parer à

▶ **provide for** *vipo* (**a**) (*supply needs of*) pourvoir *ou* subvenir aux besoins de; **to p. for oneself** pourvoir *ou* subvenir à ses propres besoins; **to be well** *or* **amply provided for** avoir grandement de quoi vivre; **he provided for everything** il a subvenu à tout; **he left his family well provided for** il laissa sa famille à l'abri du besoin

(**b**) (*allow for*) **to p. for an eventuality** pourvoir à *ou* parer à une éventualité; **expenses provided for in the budget** dépenses prévues au budget; **this has been provided for** on y a pourvu; **they had failed to p. for that possibility** ils ne s'étaient pas prémunis contre cette possibilité

provided [prə'vaɪdɪd] *conj* **p. (that)** pourvu que + *sub*, à condition que + *sub*; **p. there is enough** pourvu qu'il y en ait assez, à condition qu'il y en ait assez, seulement s'il y en a assez

providence ['prɒvɪdəns] *n* (**a**) *Rel* providence *f* (divine); **by a special p.** par une intervention providentielle; **P. smiled on us** la chance *ou* la fortune nous a souri (**b**) *Old-fashioned* (*foresight*) prévoyance *f*, prudence *f*

provident ['prɒvɪdənt] *adj* prévoyant; *Br* **p. society** société *f* de prévoyance

providential [prɒvɪ'denʃəl] *adj* (*help etc*) providentiel

providentially [prɒvɪ'denʃəlɪ] *adv* providentiellement

providently ['prɒvɪdəntlɪ] *adv* avec prévoyance; **he had p. set aside a considerable sum** il avait eu la prévoyance de mettre une somme considérable de côté

provider [prə'vaɪdər] *n* pourvoyeur, -euse; *Com* fournisseur, -euse; **the region was one of the main providers of unskilled labour** cette région était l'une des principales réserves de main-d'œuvre non qualifiée

providing [prə'vaɪdɪŋ] *conj* = **provided**

province ['prɒvɪns] *n* (**a**) (*of country*) province *f*; **in the provinces** en province (**b**) *Jur* (*of court*) juridiction *f*, ressort *m*, compétence *f*; **that is not (within) my p.** ce n'est pas de mon ressort

provincial [prə'vɪnʃəl] **1** *adj* provincial; (*theatre*) de province **2** *n* provincial, -ale

provincialism [prə'vɪnʃəlɪz(ə)m] *n* provincialisme *m*

proving ['pru:vɪŋ] *n* (*of truth of sth*) preuve *f*, démonstration *f*; (*of fact*) constatation *f*; *Jur* (*of a will*) homologation *f*; **the p. of a theory/a hypothesis** la démonstration d'une théorie/ d'une hypothèse; **p. ground** terrain *m* d'essai

provirus ['prəʊvaɪrəs] *n Med* provirus *m*

provision[1] [prə'vɪʒən] *n* (**a**) (*supply*) provision *f*, réserve *f*; **provisions** (*food*) provisions (de bouche); **to lay in a store of provisions** faire provision de vivres; **wholesale p. business** maison *f* d'alimentation en gros

(**b**) (*act of supplying*) **p. of capital/services** prestation *f* de capitaux/de services; **the p. of free education is under threat** l'éducation gratuite est menacée; **the p. of food to the refugees** l'approvisionnement des réfugiés en nourriture; **the p. of housing to the refugees** le logement des réfugiés; **there was little p. for education in the budget** la part du budget consacrée à l'éducation était faible

(**c**) (*allowance*) **p. for/against sth** (prise *f* des) dispositions *fpl* nécessaires pour assurer qch/pour parer à qch; **to make p. for sth** pourvoir à qch; **the law makes no p. for a case of this kind** la loi ne prévoit pas un cas semblable; **to make p. for one's family** assurer l'avenir de sa famille; **to make p. against sth** prendre des mesures contre qch, se prémunir contre qch; *Acct* **p. for charges** provision *f* pour frais; *Acct* **p. for depreciation** provision pour dépréciation; *Acct* **p. for liabilities** provision pour sommes exigibles

(**d**) (*stipulation*) (*of treaty*) article *m*; (*of contract*) clause *f*, stipulation *f*; **provisions of an act** dispositions *fpl* d'une loi; **to come within the provisions of the law** être prévu par la loi

provision[2] *vt* (*army, ship etc*) approvisionner

provisional [prə'vɪʒən(ə)l] **1** *adj* provisoire; *Jur* provisionnel; (*finding*) par provision; *Br Aut* **p. driving licence** permis *m* de conduire provisoire; **p. government** gouvernement *m* provisoire; **the P. IRA** l'IRA *f* provisoire **2** *n Pol* **the Provisionals** membres *mpl* de l'IRA provisoire

provisionally [prə'vɪʒən(ə)lɪ] *adv* provisoirement; *Jur* provisionnellement; (*to appoint sb*) à titre provisoire

proviso, *pl* **-os** [prə'vaɪzəʊ, -əʊz] *n* (**a**) (*in document*) clause *f* conditionnelle; (*of contract*) condition *f* (**b**) (*stipulation*) stipulation *f*; **with the p. that ...** à condition que ...

provisory [prə'vaɪzərɪ] *adj* conditionnel

Provo ['prəʊvəʊ] *n Pol F* membre *m* de l'IRA provisoire

provocation [prɒvə'keɪʃən] *n* provocation *f*; **at the slightest p.** à la moindre provocation; **to act under p.** agir en réponse à une provocation; **without p.** sans provocation

provocative [prə'vɒkətɪv] *adj* provocateur, -trice, provocant; (*smile, dress etc*) provocant, aguichant; **he's just being p.** il ne fait cela que pour provoquer

provocatively [prə'vɒkətɪvlɪ] *adv* (*to smile, be dressed*) d'une manière *ou* d'un air provocant(e); **..., he said p.** ..., dit-il, provocant; **a p. low-cut dress** une robe au décolleté provocant

provoke [prə'vəʊk] *vt* (**a**) (*person*) provoquer, pousser, inciter (**to do sth** à faire qch); (*irritate*) irriter, agacer, exaspérer; (*dog*) exciter; **to p. sb to anger** mettre qn en colère; **I was provoked** on m'a provoqué *ou F* cherché; **don't p. her** ne la provoque *ou F* cherche pas (**b**) (*arouse*) (*curiosity*) exciter, faire naître; (*gaiety*) provoquer; (*passion, indignation, interest*) soulever; **to p. a reaction** provoquer une réaction

provoking [prə'vəʊkɪŋ] *adj* (*irritating*) irritant, agaçant, exaspérant

provost *n* (**a**) ['prɒvəst] *Sch, Univ* principal *m* (**b**) ['prɒvəst] *Scot Admin* maire *m* (**c**) ['prɒvəʊ] *Mil* **p. marshal** grand prévôt *m*; **p. duty** service *m* prévôtal, prévôté *f*

prow [praʊ] *n* (*of ship*) proue *f*

prowess ['praʊɪs] *n* (**a**) (*skill*) talent *m*, habileté *f*; **her p. at tennis** *or* **as a t. player** son talent au tennis; **she has shown great p.** elle a fait des prouesses; **his sexual/intellectual p.** ses prouesses sexuelles/intellectuelles (**b**) *Lit* (*courage*) vaillance *f*

prowl[1] [praʊl] *n* **to go on the p.** (*of lion etc*), *Fig* partir en chasse; **to be on the p. for sth** être en quête *ou* à la recherche de qch; **let's have a p. around** et si on zyeutait?; *US F* **p. car** (*of police*) voiture *f* de patrouille

prowl[2] **1** *vi* (*of animal, person*) rôder; **to p. about the streets** rôder dans les rues; **to p. about the shops** tourner dans les magasins **2** *vt* **to p. the streets** rôder dans les rues

prowler ['praʊlər] *n* rôdeur, -euse; **there's a p. in the neighbourhood** il y a quelqu'un qui rôde dans le voisinage

prox [prɒks] *adv Old-fashioned Com* (*abbr* **proximo**) (du mois) prochain

proximity [prɒk'sɪmɪtɪ] *n* (*closeness*) proximité *f*; **its p. to London** sa situation à proximité de Londres; **in p. to** à proximité de, près de; **in close p. to** juste à proximité *ou* tout près de; *Fig* **p. of blood** proche parenté *f*; *Mil* **p. fuse** fusée *f* à influence, fusée de proximité

proximo ['prɒksɪməʊ] *adv Old-fashioned Com* (du mois) prochain

proxy ['prɒksɪ] *n* (**a**) (*power*) procuration *f*, délégation *f* de pouvoirs, pouvoir *m*, mandat *m* (**b**) (*person*) mandataire *mf*, fondé *m* de pouvoir(s), délégué, -ée; *Com* agent *m* mandataire; **to make sb one's p.** déléguer ses pouvoirs à qn; **to vote by p.** voter par procuration; **p. bomb** = bombe *f* amenée sur les lieux par une personne agissant sous la contrainte; **p. vote** vote *m* par procuration

prude [pru:d] *n* prude *mf*, bégueule *f*; **don't be such a p.!** ne soyez pas si prude *ou* si bégueule!

prudence ['pru:dəns] *n* prudence *f*; (*common sense*) sagesse *f*

prudent ['pru:dənt] *adj* prudent; (*sensible*) sage

prudential [pru:'denʃəl] *adj US* **p. committee** (*of municipality, company*) = comité *m* de surveillance

prudently ['pru:dəntlɪ] *adv* prudemment

prudery ['pru:dərɪ] *n* pruderie *f*, pudibonderie *f*

prudish ['pru:dɪʃ] *adj* prude, pudibond

prudishness ['pru:dɪʃnɪs] *n* = **prudery**

prune[1] [pru:n] *n* pruneau *m*; *Fig F* **old p.** (*old woman*) vieille bique *f* ratatinée

prune[2] *vt* (**a**) (*rose bush, fruit tree*) tailler; (*tree roots*) rafraîchir; (*tree*) émonder; (*branch*) élaguer (**b**) *Fig* (*article etc*) faire des coupures dans, élaguer; (*list of tasks, demands*) réduire; (*army, bureaucracy*) dégraisser

▶ **prune away, prune off** *vtsep* (*branch*) élaguer

pruning ['pru:nɪŋ] *n* (**a**) (*of rose bush, fruit tree*) taille *f*; (*of tree*) émondage *m*; (*of branch*) élagage *m*; **p. hook** émondoir *m*; **p. knife** serpette *f*; **p. shears** cisailles *fpl* (**b**) *Fig* (*of article etc*) élagage *m*

prurience ['prʊərɪəns], **pruriency** ['prʊərɪənsɪ] *n* lasciveté *f*, lubricité *f*

prurient ['prʊərɪənt] *adj* (à l'esprit) lascif; **to take a p. interest in sth** porter un intérêt lascif à qch

Prussia ['prʌʃə] *n* Prusse *f*

Prussian ['prʌʃən] **1** *adj* prussien; **P. blue** bleu *m* de Prusse **2** *n* Prussien, -ienne

prussic [ˈprʌsɪk] *adj Ch (acid)* prussique, cyanhydrique
pry¹ [praɪ] *vi (pt, pp* **pried***) (into particular matter)* fouiller, fureter (**into sth** dans qch); *(generally)* fourrer son nez partout; **I don't mean to p., but why did you do it?** je sais que ça ne me regarde pas, mais pourquoi est-ce que tu as fait ça?; **to p. into a secret** chercher à pénétrer un secret
pry² *vt (pt, pp* **pried***) Am* = **prize⁴**
▶ **pry loose** *vtsep Am* décoller, détacher
▶ **pry open** *vtsep Am (door, safe etc)* forcer
prying [ˈpraɪɪŋ] *adj* curieux, indiscret, -ète; **safe from p. eyes** à l'abri des regards indiscrets
PS [piːˈes] *n (abbr* **postscript***)* P.S. *m*; **to add a PS to a letter** ajouter un P.S. à une lettre; **PS see you next week** P.S. à la semaine prochaine
psalm [sɑːm] *n* psaume *m*; **p. book** livre *m* de psaumes, psautier *m*; *Bible* **(the Book of) Psalms** (le livre des) Psaumes
psalmist [ˈsɑːmɪst] *n* psalmiste *m*
psalmody [ˈsɑːmədɪ] *n* psalmodie *f*
psalter [ˈsɔːltər] *n* psautier *m*
PSB [piːesˈbiː] *n (abbr* **public service broadcasting***)* émissions *fpl* de service public
PSBR [piːesbiːˈɑːr] *n Br Econ (abbr* **public sector borrowing requirement***)* = besoins *mpl* d'emprunt du secteur public non couverts par les rentrées fiscales
psephological [sefəˈlɒdʒɪk(ə)l] *adj* relatif à l'étude scientifique des élections
psephologist [seˈfɒlədʒɪst] *n* spécialiste *mf* de l'étude des élections
psephology [seˈfɒlədʒɪ] *n* étude *f* scientifique des élections
pseud [sjuːd] *n Br F Pej* crâneur, -euse; **P.'s Corner** *(section de la revue humoristique Private Eye où des articles prétentieux sont publiés pour l'amusement général) par ex.* did you read his article?, absolute P.'s Corner
pseudo [ˈsjuːdəʊ] *adj, pref F* faux, *f* fausse, pseudo-
pseudonym [ˈsjuːdənɪm] *n* pseudonyme *m*; **to write sth under a p.** écrire qch sous un pseudonyme
pseudonymous [sjuːˈdɒnɪməs] *adj (writer)* qui écrit sous un pseudonyme; *(column, article)* écrit sous un pseudonyme
pseudy [ˈsjuːdɪ] *adj F Pej* prétentieux
pshaw [(p)ʃɔː] *int Old-fashioned (indicating disgust)* peuh!
psi [piːeˈsaɪ] *Phys (abbr* **pounds per square inch***)* livres par pouce carré
psittacosis [sɪtəˈkəʊsɪs] *n Med, Vet* psittacose *f*
psoriasis [səˈraɪəsɪs] *n Med* psoriasis *m*
psst [pst] *int (to attract attention)* psitt!, pst!; *(to warn)* chut!
PST [piːeˈstiː] *n Am (abbr* **Pacific Standard Time***)* PST
PSV [piːesˈviː] *n (abbr* **public service vehicle***)* véhicule *m* de transport en commun
▶ **psych out** [saɪk] *vtsep F* = **psyche out**
▶ **psych up** *vtsep F* = **psyche up**
psyche [ˈsaɪkɪ] *n* psychisme *m*; *Phil* psyché *f*, psychè *f*
▶ **psyche out** [saɪk] *vtsep F (unnerve)* déstabiliser; *(guess) (sb's intentions, motives etc)* deviner, percer à jour
▶ **psyche up** *vtsep F (prepare)* **to p. oneself up (for sth)** se préparer mentalement (à faire qch); **to p. sb up for sth** préparer qn mentalement pour qch
psychedelic [saɪkəˈdelɪk] *adj* psychédélique
psyched-up [saɪkˈtʌp] *adj F* gonflé à bloc; **to get oneself p.** se préparer mentalement
psychiatric [saɪkɪˈætrɪk] *adj* psychiatrique; *Br* **p. social worker** assistant, -ante social(e) en psychiatrie
psychiatrist [saɪˈkaɪətrɪst] *n* psychiatre *mf*
psychiatry [saɪˈkaɪətrɪ] *n* psychiatrie *f*
psychic [ˈsaɪkɪk] **1** *adj (also* **psychical** [ˈsaɪkɪk(ə)l]*)* psychique; *(phenomenon etc)* métapsychique; **to have p. powers** avoir des dons *mpl* de voyance, être un peu médium; *F* **I'm not p.!** je ne suis pas devin! **2** *n* médium *m*
psycho [ˈsaɪkəʊ] *adj, n F* psychopathe *mf*
psychoanalyse [saɪkəʊˈænəlaɪz] *vt* psychanalyser
psychoanalysis [saɪkəʊəˈnælɪsɪs] *n* psychanalyse *f*
psychoanalyst [saɪkəʊˈænəlɪst] *n* psychanalyste *mf*
psychoanalytic(al) [saɪkəʊænəˈlɪtɪk, -ɪk(ə)l] *adj* psychanalytique
psychoanalyze [saɪkəʊˈænəlaɪz] *vt* psychoanalyser
psychobabble [ˈsaɪkəʊbæb(ə)l] *n F* jargon *m* de psy
psychodrama [ˈsaɪkəʊdrɑːmə] *n* psychodrame *m*, jeu *m* de rôle
psychographic [saɪkəʊˈgræfɪk] *n* psychographique
psychographics [saɪkəʊˈgræfɪks] *n* [①A10,c] psychographie *f*
psychological [saɪkəˈlɒdʒɪk(ə)l] *adj* psychologique; **the p. moment** le moment psychologique; *Mktg* **p. price** prix *m* psychologique *ou* d'acceptabilité; **p. warfare** guerre *f* psychologique
psychologically [saɪkəˈlɒdʒɪklɪ] *adv* psychologiquement
psychologist [saɪˈkɒlədʒɪst] *n* psychologue *mf*; **child p.** psychologue pour enfants
psychology [saɪˈkɒlədʒɪ] *n* psychologie *f*; **the p. of the football hooligan** la psychologie des hooligans du football; *F* **to use p.** faire preuve de psychologie
psychomotor [ˈsaɪkəʊməʊtər] *adj* psychomoteur, -trice
psychoneurosis [saɪkəʊnjʊˈrəʊsɪs] *n* psychonévrose *f*
psychopath [ˈsaɪkəʊpæθ] *n* psychopathe *mf*
psychopathic [saɪkəʊˈpæθɪk] *adj (person)* psychopathe; *(condition, personality)* psychopathique
psychopathology [saɪkəʊpəˈθɒlədʒɪ] *n* psychopathologie *f*
psychophysiology [saɪkəʊfɪzɪˈɒlədʒɪ] *n* psychophysiologie *f*
psychosis, *pl* **-oses** [saɪˈkəʊsɪs, -əʊsiːz] *n* psychose *f*
psychosomatic [saɪkəʊsəˈmætɪk] *adj* psychosomatique
psychotherapist [saɪkəʊˈθerəpɪst] *n* psychothérapeute *mf*
psychotherapy [saɪkəʊˈθerəpɪ] *n* psychothérapie *f*
psychotic [saɪˈkɒtɪk] *adj, n* psychotique *mf*
psychotropic [saɪkəʊˈtrɒpɪk] *adj Pharm* psychotrope; **p. drug** psychotrope *m*
PT [piːˈtiː] *n (abbr* **physical training***)* E.P.S. *f*
PTA [piːtiːˈeɪ] *n Sch (abbr* **Parent-Teacher Association***)* = association *f* de parents d'élèves et de professeurs
ptarmigan [ˈtɑːmɪgən] *n (bird)* **p.**, *Am* **rock p.** lagopède *m* muet, *Can* lagopède des rochers
Pte *Mil (abbr* **private***)* soldat *m*
pterodactyl [terəʊˈdæktɪl] *n* ptérodactyle *m*
PTO [piːtiːˈəʊ] *(abbr* **please turn over***)* TSVP
ptomaine [ˈtəʊmeɪn] *n Ch* ptomaïne *f*; **p. poisoning** intoxication *f* alimentaire (par les ptomaïnes)
Pty *(abbr* **proprietary company***)* SARL
pub [pʌb] *n Br F* = pub *m*, café *m*, bistro(t) *m*; **p. food** *or F* **grub** = cuisine *f* de pub *ou* de bistrot; **p. lunch** déjeuner *m* simple *(servi dans un pub)*; **to go out for a p. lunch** aller déjeuner dans un pub
pub-crawl¹ *n Br F* tournée *f* des bars; **to go on a p.** faire la tournée des bars, aller de bar en bar, *Can F* partir sur une brosse
pub-crawl² *vi Br F* faire la tournée des bars, aller de bar en bar
puberty [ˈpjuːbətɪ] *n Physiol* puberté *f*; **at p.** à la puberté; **to reach p.** atteindre l'âge de la puberté
pubescence [pjuːˈbesəns] *n* **(a)** *Bot* pubescence *f* **(b)** *Physiol* puberté *f*
pubescent [pjuːˈbesənt] *adj* **(a)** *Bot* pubescent **(b)** *Physiol* pubère
pubic [ˈpjuːbɪk] *adj Anat* pubien; **p. bone** pubis *m*; **p. hair** poils *mpl* pubiens *ou* du pubis; *(single)* poil pubien *ou* du pubis
pubis [ˈpjuːbɪs] *n Anat* pubis *m*
public [ˈpʌblɪk] **1** *adj* public, *f* publique; **to go p.** *(of firm)* émettre *ou* placer des actions dans le public; *(reveal information)* tout dire *ou* raconter; **to go p. with the story** raconter toute l'histoire; **to make sth p.** rendre qch public; *(news etc)* publier qch; **to make a p. appearance** paraître en public; **p. body** corporation *f* de droit public; **p. carrier** transporteur *m* public; **p. corporation** corporation *f* de droit public; **p. data network** réseau *m* public de données; **p. domain** domaine *m* public; **to be p. domain** être dans le domaine public; **in the p. domain** dans le domaine public; **p. domain software** logiciel *m* du domaine public; *F* **p. enemy number 1** ennemi *m* public numéro 1; **p. examination** examen *m* national de l'enseignement public; **p. excursion fare** tarif *m* excursion; **at p. expense** aux frais du contribuable; **to be in the p. eye** être très en vue; **p. figure** personnalité *f* en vue; **p. funds** deniers *mpl* publics; **to work for the p. good** travailler pour le bien public; **p. health official** représentant, -ante de la santé publique; **p. information broadcast** message *m* de grande cause nationale; **to be in the p. interest** servir le bien public; **of p. interest** d'intérêt public; **p. interest in the matter was flagging** l'intérêt du public pour cette affaire faiblissait; **it's p. knowledge** tout le monde sait cela; **p. life** la vie publique; **p. money** deniers *mpl* publics; *St Exch* **p. offering** offre *f* publique; **p. park** jardin *m* public; **in a p. place** dans un lieu public; **to make a p. protest** protester publiquement; **p. sales office** *(of an airline etc)* agence *f* commerciale; **the p. services** les services *mpl* publics; *St Exch* **p. share offer** offre *f* publique de vente; **p. spirit** civisme *m*, sens *m* civique; **p. utility (service)** service *m* public; **p. works** travaux *mpl* publics

2 *n* [①A11,g,i] **the (general) p.** le (grand) public; **book aimed at a wide p.** livre qui s'adresse à un large public; **my p. like the old songs** mon public aime les vieilles chansons; **there isn't much of a p. for that kind of thing** ce genre de choses n'attire pas un grand public; **in p.** en public, publiquement; *Fin* **to issue shares to the p.** placer des actions dans le public
public access channel *n* chaîne *f* ouverte

public address system *n* sonorisation *f*, *F* sono *f*
publican [ˈpʌblɪkən] *n Br* patron, -onne d'un/du pub
public assistance *n* assistance *f* publique
publication [pʌblɪˈkeɪʃən] *n* **(a)** (*of book, news, the banns etc*) publication *f*; (*of order, decree*) promulgation *f*; **my article has been accepted for p.** mon article va être publié; **this is not for p.** ceci n'est pas destiné à la publication; **p. date** (*of book*) date *f* de parution *ou* de publication; **p. day** jour *m* de parution **(b)** (*published work*) publication *f*
public authorities *npl* pouvoirs *mpl* publics
public bar *n Br* (*dans un 'pub' qui contient deux bars séparés, l'expression désigne le plus populaire des deux*) ≈ bistro *m*, café-bar *m*
public call box *n* cabine *f* (téléphonique) publique
public company *n* société *f* anonyme, société *f* cotée en bourse; **p. law** loi *f* sur les sociétés anonymes
public convenience *n* toilettes *fpl* publiques, W.C. *mpl* publics
public defender *n US Jur* = avocat *m* spécialisé dans l'aide judiciaire
public holiday *n* fête *f* légale, jour *m* chômé
public house *n Br Fml* = pub *m*, café *m*, bistrot *m*, *Fml* débit *m* de boissons
public housing *n Am* logements *mpl* sociaux
publicist [ˈpʌblɪsɪst] *n* publicitaire *mf*
publicity [pʌbˈlɪsɪtɪ] *n* (*given to a matter*) publicité *f*, *F* pub *f*; *Com* publicité, réclame *f*; **the football team has received a lot of free p. as a result of this scandal** ce scandale a fait beaucoup de publicité (gratuite) à l'équipe de football; **it's another one of his p.-seeking gimmicks** c'est encore un de ses trucs pour se faire de la publicité; **there's no such thing as bad p.** on ne fait jamais trop parler de soi; **they're very p. conscious** ils sont très conscients de leur image
publicity agent *n* agent *m* publicitaire
publicity campaign *n* campagne *f* de publicité
publicity department *n* publicité *f*
publicity manager *n* chef *m* de publicité
publicity stunt *n* coup *m* de pub
publicize [ˈpʌblɪsaɪz] *vt* (*make known*) faire connaître au public; *Com* (*advertise*) (*product*) faire de la publicité *ou* de la réclame *ou F* de la pub pour; **her resignation was widely publicized** on a fait beaucoup de battage autour de sa démission; **she doesn't p. the fact** elle ne le crie pas sur tous les toits
public lavatory *n* toilettes *fpl* publiques, W.C. *mpl* publics
public lending right *n* = droit *m* d'auteur sur les livres empruntés dans une bibliothèque municipale
public liability insurance *n* assurance *f* responsabilité civile
public limited company *n Br* = société *f* anonyme
publicly [ˈpʌblɪklɪ] *adv* publiquement, en public; *Econ* **p. owned** nationalisé, d'état
public opinion *n* opinion *f* publique; **p. poll** sondage *m* d'opinion publique
Public Record Office *n Br* = Archives *fpl* nationales
public relations *npl* relations *fpl* publiques; **p. consultant** conseiller, -ère en relations publiques; **p. department** service *m* des relations publiques; **p. director** *or* **manager** directeur *m* des relations publiques; **p. officer** agent *m* de(s) relations publiques
public school *n Am* école *f* publique; *Br* école privée; *Br* **a public-school education** une scolarité *ou* des études *fpl* dans le privé; *Br* **he's very public-school** il fait très école privée
public sector *n Econ* secteur *m* public; **p. earnings** revenus *mpl* du secteur public; **p. borrowing requirement** besoins *mpl* d'emprunt du secteur public
public service *n* (*civil service*) fonction *f* publique; **the organisation performs a useful p.** cette organisation offre un service public fort utile; **p. broadcasting** émissions *fpl* de service public; **p. vehicle** véhicule *m* de transport en commun
public speaking *n* art *m* oratoire
public spending *n* dépenses *fpl* publiques
public-spirited *adj* (*person*) qui a le sens civique; (*gesture, response*) dicté par le sens civique; **that was very p. of them** ils ont fait preuve par là d'un grand civisme *ou* sens civique
public transport *n* transports *mpl* en commun; **p. advertising** affichage *m* transport; **p. vehicle** véhicule *m* des transports en commun
publish [ˈpʌblɪʃ] **1** *vt* **(a)** (*of publisher, author*) (*book*) éditer, publier; **we're going to p. it next week** on va le publier la semaine prochaine, ça paraîtra chez nous la semaine prochaine; **who publishes Sartre?** qui édite *ou* publie Sartre?; **just published** (*of book*) vient de paraître; **she's had two novels published** on a publié deux de ses romans **(b)** (*edict, the banns*) publier; (*news*) publier, faire paraître
2 *vi* **they decided not to p.** ils ont décidé de ne pas faire publier la nouvelle/leur ouvrage/cet article/*etc*; **p. and be damned!** publiez si vous voulez et allez au diable!; **we're going to p. and be damned** on publiera, advienne que pourra
publisher [ˈpʌblɪʃər] *n* **(a)** éditeur, -trice **(b)** *Am* (*newspaper owner*) propriétaire *mf* d'un/du journal
publishing [ˈpʌblɪʃɪŋ] *n* **(a)** (*of book, report, accounts etc*) publication *f*; (*profession, business*) édition *f*; **to work** *or* **be in p.** travailler dans l'édition; **p. house** *or* **firm** maison *f* d'édition; **the p. trade** l'édition **(b)** (*of the banns etc*) publication *f*
puce [pjuːs] *adj, n* puce *m inv*
puck[1] [pʌk] *n* (*elf*) lutin *m*, farfadet *m*
puck[2] *n Sp* (*in ice hockey*) palet *m*
pucker[1] [ˈpʌkər] *n* (*in face*) (*wrinkle*) ride *f*; (*fold*) pli *m*; (*in material*) faux pli, godet *m*
pucker[2] **1** *vt* (*one's face*) rider; (*material*) froncer, faire goder *ou* godailler; (*one's brow, forehead etc*) froncer; (*one's lips*) plisser **2** *vi* = **pucker up 1**
▸ **pucker up 1** *vi* (*of garment, material*) faire des faux plis, goder, godailler; **his face puckered up** sa figure s'est crispée; **she puckered up for his kiss** elle tendit les lèvres, se préparant à son baiser **2** *vtsep* (*one's lips*) tendre
puckish [ˈpʌkɪʃ] *adj* malicieux, espiègle
pud [pʊd] *n Br F* pudding *m*; (*dessert*) dessert *m*; **what's for p.?** qu'est-ce qu'il y a comme dessert?; **there's ice-cream for p.** il y a de la glace en dessert
pudding [ˈpʊdɪŋ] *n* **(a)** (*dish*) **(suet) p.** pudding *m*, pouding *m*; **p. basin** *or* **bowl** moule *m* à puddings *ou* à poudings; **p. basin** *or* **bowl haircut** coupe *f* au bol; *Sl Hum* **to be in the p. club** (*be pregnant*) avoir un polichinelle dans le tiroir **(b)** (*dessert*) dessert *m*; **what's for p.?** qu'est-ce qu'il y a comme *ou* pour le dessert? **(c)** *F* (*chubby person*) petit gros *m*, petite grosse *f*; (*baby*) gros bébé *m*
puddingface [ˈpʊdɪŋfeɪs] *n F* visage *m* empâté
puddinghead [ˈpʊdɪŋhed] *n F* idiot, -ote, andouille *f*
puddingstone [ˈpʊdɪŋstəʊn] *n Geol* poudingue *m*
puddle[1] [ˈpʌd(ə)l] *n* (*of water, oil*) flaque *f*; (*small pool*) petite mare *f*; *F* **the dog's made a p. on the carpet** le chien a fait pipi sur le tapis
puddle[2] *vt Metal* (*iron*) puddler
pudenda [pjuːˈdendə] *npl Fml* parties *fpl* génitales
pudgy [ˈpʌdʒɪ] *adj F* (*person*) rondelet, dodu
puerile [ˈpjʊəraɪl] *adj Pej* puéril; **he's being utterly p. about it** il a une attitude complètement puérile à cet égard
puerility [pjʊəˈrɪlɪtɪ] *n Fml* puérilité *f*
puerperal [pjuːˈɜːpərəl] *adj Med* puerpéral
Puerto Rican [pweətəʊˈriːkən, pwɜːtəʊ-] **1** *adj* portoricain **2** *n* Portoricain, -aine
Puerto Rico [pweətəʊˈriːkəʊ, pwɜːtəʊ-] *n* Porto Rico *m*
puff[1] [pʌf] *n* **(a)** (*of breath*) souffle *m*; (*of air*) souffle, bouffée *f*; (*of smoke, steam*) bouffée; **to take a p. at one's pipe** tirer une bouffée de sa pipe; **give me a p.** (*of your cigarette*) passe-moi une bouffée *ou F* une taffe; *F* **out of p.** essoufflé, à bout de souffle; *F* **let me get my p. back** laissez-moi reprendre mon souffle; *Fig F* **our ideas went up** *or* **disappeared in a p. of smoke** nos idées sont parties en fumée
(b) *Sewing* (*of dress*) bouillon *m*; (*of sleeve*) bouffant *m*; *US* (*quilt*) édredon *m*; **p. sleeves** manches *fpl* bouffantes
(c) (*in media*) reportage *m* flatteur; *Old-fashioned F* (*advertisement*) pub *f*, réclame *f* (tapageuse); **I managed to get in a p. about my new book** j'ai réussi à faire de la pub *ou* de la réclame pour mon nouveau livre
(d) *Culin* **cream p.** chou *m* à la crème
puff[2] **1** *vi* (*of person*) souffler; (*of steam engine*) lancer des bouffées de vapeur; **to p. and blow** *or* **pant** haleter; **to p. (away) at one's pipe** tirer sur sa pipe, tirer des bouffées de sa pipe; **the steam engine puffed into view** la fumée indiqua l'arrivée du train; **to p. into the station** entrer en gare dans un nuage de fumée **2** *vt* **(a)** (*smoke, air*) émettre, envoyer; (*pipe etc*) fumer par petites bouffées; (*rice*) (faire) gonfler; **to p. smoke into sb's face** envoyer de la fumée à la figure de qn **(b)** *Old-fashioned F* (*advertise*) (*one's wares*) pousser, vanter
▸ **puff out** *vtsep* **(a)** (*one's cheeks*) gonfler; (*sleeve etc*) faire ballonner *ou* bouffer; **to p. out one's chest** bomber le torse **(b)** (*emit*) (*smoke*) émettre, envoyer **(c)** *F* (*exhaust*) crever; **that walk has puffed me out** cette marche m'a crevé
▸ **puff up** *vtsep* (*one's cheeks*) gonfler; **he was puffed up with pride** il était bouffi d'orgueil
puff adder *n* vipère *f* heurtante
puffball [ˈpʌfbɔːl] *n Bot* vesse-de-loup *f*, *pl* vesses-de-loup
puffed [pʌft] *adj* **(a)** *Sewing* **p. sleeves** manches *fpl*

bouffantes; *Culin* **p. rice** riz *m* gonflé; **p. out** (*of skirt etc*) ballonné; **p. up (with pride)** bouffi d'orgueil **(b)** *F* **p. (out)** (*person*) essoufflé, à bout de souffle; (*tired*) fatigué

puffer [ˈpʌfər] *n F* (*train*) train *m* à vapeur; (*boat*) bateau *m* à vapeur

puffin [ˈpʌfɪn] *n* (*bird*) macareux *m* moine, puffin *m*

puffiness [ˈpʌfɪnɪs] *n* (*of face etc*) aspect *m* bouffi

puff pastry *n Culin* pâte *f* feuilletée

puffy [ˈpʌfɪ] *adj* **(a)** (*swollen*) (*face, clouds*) bouffi, boursouflé; (*eyes*) gonflé, bouffi; **to be p. under the eyes** avoir les yeux bouffis *ou* gonflés **(b)** *F* (*person*) (*short-winded*) à l'haleine courte, poussif; (*out of breath*) hors d'haleine

pug [pʌg] *n* **p. (dog)** carlin *m*; **p. nose** nez *m* écrasé *ou* camus; **p.-nosed** au nez écrasé *ou* camus

pugilism [ˈpju:dʒɪlɪz(ə)m] *n Fml* boxe *f*

pugilist [ˈpju:dʒɪlɪst] *n Fml* pugiliste *m*

pugnacious [pʌgˈneɪʃəs] *adj* querelleur, batailleur, *Lit* pugnace

pugnaciously [pʌgˈneɪʃəslɪ] *adv* d'une manière querelleuse *ou* batailleuse *ou Lit* pugnace; (*to defend sth*) avec pugnacité

pugnacity [pʌgˈnæsɪtɪ], **pugnaciousness** [pʌgˈneɪʃəsnɪs] *n* caractère *m* querelleur *ou* batailleur, *Lit* pugnacité *f*

puke[1] [pju:k] *n F* (*vomit*) dégueulis *m*; **to have a p.** dégobiller, dégueuler

puke[2] *vti F* dégobiller, dégueuler; **it makes me p.!** c'est à gerber!; **you make me p.!** tu es dégueulasse!

pukey [ˈpju:kɪ] *adj Sl* (*disgusting*) merdique

pukka [ˈpʌkə] *adj* **(a)** (*upper-class, posh*) snob **(b)** *Old-fashioned, Hum* (*genuine*) authentique; **a p. Englishman** un vrai Anglais d'Angleterre

pulchritude [ˈpʌlkrɪtju:d] *n Lit* beauté *f*

pull[1] [pʊl] *n* **(a)** (*act of pulling*) tirage *m*, traction *f*; (*of magnet*) force *f* d'attraction; (*in rowing*) coup *m* (d'aviron); *Fig* (*attraction*) (*of foreign places, high salaries etc*) attrait *m*; **give it a hard** *or* **good p.!** tirez fort!; **to give a p. on the rope** tirer sur la corde; **give it one more p.** tire encore un coup; **a few more pulls and I'll be able to reach it** en tirant encore un peu j'arriverai à l'atteindre; **I felt a p. at my sleeve** j'ai senti qu'on me tirait par la manche; *Sl* **to be (out) on the p.** (*looking for sexual partner*) draguer

(b) (*gulp*) (*of beer etc*) gorgée *f*, lampée *f*; **to take a p. at one's pipe** tirer une bouffée de sa pipe

(c) (*influence*) influence *f*; **to have plenty of p.** avoir le bras long

(d) (*climb, effort etc*) **it's a long p. to the top** la montée est rude jusqu'au sommet; **it was a long p. to the shore** (*in rowing boat*) ça a pris du temps pour regagner la rive

(e) (*handle*) poignée *f*; **(bell) p.** cordon *m* de sonnette

(f) *Golf, Cr* coup *m* tiré

(g) *Typ* première épreuve *f*

(h) (*catch*) (*in jumper etc*) accroc *m*; **my cardigan has a p. in it** j'ai fait un accroc à mon cardigan

pull[2] **1** *vt* **(a)** (*rope, person's hair etc*) tirer; (*muscle etc*) se déchirer; (*oar*) manier; **p.** (*notice on door*) tirez, tirer; **pulled muscle** élongation *f*; **he pulled her closer (to him)** il l'a attirée plus près de lui; **he pulled the knot tight(er)** il a resserré le nœud; **she pulled the box from his hands** elle lui a arraché la boîte des mains; **to p. a door/drawer/window open** ouvrir une porte/un tiroir/une fenêtre; **to p. a door shut** *or* **closed** fermer une porte; **to p. the curtains/blinds** tirer les rideaux/stores; **to p. the trigger** presser sur la détente *ou* la gâchette; **p. your chair up to** *or* **nearer the fire** approchez votre fauteuil du feu; **to p. to pieces** déchirer, mettre en morceaux; (*criticize severely*) démolir; **to p. rank on sb** faire valoir son ancienneté sur qn; *Br F* **p. the other one! (it's got bells on!)** laisse-moi rire!; **to p. one's hat (down) over one's eyes** enfoncer *ou* rabattre son chapeau sur les yeux; *TV, Cin* **to p. focus** faire la mise au point

(b) (*haul*) (*cart etc*) traîner, tirer; (*of barge etc*) (*boat*) haler

(c) (*attract*) (*customers, crowd*) attirer; *Sl* (*pick up*) (*man, woman*) lever, emballer

(d) (*extract, remove*) **to p. a cork** déboucher une bouteille; **to p. a plant** arracher une plante; **to p. a tooth** arracher *ou* extraire une dent; **to have a tooth pulled** se faire arracher une dent; **it was like pulling teeth** c'était pénible comme tout; **to p. a pint** tirer une bière; **to p. pints** (*for a living*) travailler comme barman/comme serveuse de bar; **to p. a TV programme** retirer une émission de télé; **to p. sth from the files** (*cancel*) retirer qch des fichiers; *F* **to p. a gun on sb** mettre un pistolet sous le nez de qn

(e) (*do*) *F* **to p. a bank job** se faire une banque; *F* **to p. a fast one on sb** avoir qn, rouler qn; **so you thought you could p. a fast one (on me)?** alors comme ça tu voulais me jouer un tour?; **to p. a trick on sb** jouer un tour à qn; **don't ever p. a stunt like that again** ne me/nous/*etc* refais jamais un tour comme ça; **to p. a face** faire une grimace

(f) *Typ* (*proof*) tirer

(g) *Sp* **to p. the ball** envoyer la balle vers la gauche; *Golf* faire un coup tiré

2 *vi* **(a)** tirer; (*in rowing*) ramer, souquer; **she pulled clear of the pack** elle s'est détachée du peloton; **he pulled clear of the traffic and sped on** il est sorti du flot de la circulation et a accéléré; **he pulled sharply to the left** il a viré brutalement sur la gauche; **the lorry pulled slowly up the hill** le camion gravissait lentement la côte; **to p. on** *or* **at a rope** tirer sur un cordage; **to p. at one's pipe** tirer sur sa pipe; **they're pulling in different directions** (*they disagree*) ils ne s'entendent pas, ils ne sont pas d'accord, *F* ils tirent à hue et à dia

(b) the engine is pulling heavily le moteur fatigue *ou* peine; **the brakes p. to the left/right** les freins tirent à gauche/droite

(c) *Sp* envoyer la balle à gauche; *Golf* faire un coup tiré

▶ **pull about** *vtsep* (*handle roughly*) (*object*) tirer dans tous les sens, tirailler; (*person*) malmener; **stop pulling me about!, she said** ne sois pas aussi brutal!, dit-elle

▶ **pull ahead** *vi* (*in race, election campaign*) prendre la tête; **to p. ahead of one's rival** distancer son rival

▶ **pull along** *vtsep* (*person*) tirer par le bras/par l'épaule/*etc*; (*load etc*) tirer derrière soi

▶ **pull apart 1** *vtsep* **(a)** (*break up*) (*object*) mettre en petits morceaux; (*clothing etc*) déchirer; (*dismantle for storage etc*) démonter; (*body, flesh*) déchiqueter; (*separate*) (*two people fighting*) séparer **(b)** (*criticize*) (*person*) éreinter; (*performance, argument etc*) démolir **2** *vi* **it pulls apart** c'est démontable, ça se démonte

▶ **pull away 1** *vtsep* (*remove forcefully*) **to p. sth away from sth/sb** arracher qch de qch/des mains de qn; **he pulled his hand away** il retira vivement sa main; **they pulled the distraught father away from the burning car** ils ont arraché le père affolé à la voiture en feu **2** *vi* **(a)** (*of train, car*) partir; **the train pulled away from the station** le train a quitté la gare; **as the train began to p. away** alors que le train s'ébranlait; **to p. away from sb** s'écarter de qn; **she's beginning to p. away** (*in race*) elle commence à prendre de l'avance **(b)** (*in rowing*) **p. away!** souquez!

▶ **pull back 1** *vi* (*hesitate*) hésiter; (*not continue with project etc*) se retirer, refuser de continuer; *Mil* décrocher; **they pulled back from committing themselves fully** ils ont renoncé à s'engager complètement **2** *vtsep* (*curtains*) ouvrir; (*covers*) rejeter en arrière; *Mil* retirer; **his father pulled him back from the fire** son père l'a éloigné du feu; **to p. sb/a company back from the brink** faire refaire surface à qn/une entreprise, tirer qn/une entreprise d'affaire

▶ **pull down** *vtsep* **(a)** (*lower*) (*blind, skirt etc*) baisser; **to p. one's hat down over one's eyes** enfoncer *ou* rabattre son chapeau sur ses yeux; **he's pulling the whole team down** il fait baisser le niveau de toute l'équipe; **my marks in the oral exam will p. me down** mes notes à l'oral vont baisser *ou* descendre ma moyenne

(b) (*demolish*) (*house etc*) démolir, abattre

(c) (*of illness, circumstances*) (*person*) abattre

(d) *Comptr* (*menu*) dérouler

(e) *Am F* (*earn*) (*salary*) toucher; (*money*) gagner; **he doesn't p. down much of a salary** il ne gagne pas *ou* touche pas des masses

▶ **pull in 1** *vtsep* **(a)** (*fishing net etc*) rentrer; (*money*) gagner, *F* se faire; **he pulled me in** (*to swimming pool*) il m'a tiré dedans

(b) (*attract*) (*the public*) attirer; **it's really pulling them in** ça attire les foules

(c) *F* (*of police*) (*suspect*) arrêter; **they pulled him in for questioning** ils l'ont arrêté pour l'interroger; **to be pulled in for speeding** être arrêté pour excès de vitesse

(d) *Aut* **to p. one's car in to the kerb** se ranger près du trottoir

(e) to p. oneself *or* **one's stomach in** rentrer son ventre

(f) *Horseriding* (*hold back*) (*horse*) retenir, tirer les rênes de

2 *vi* **(a)** (*stop at side of road*) (*of vehicle, driver*) s'arrêter, se garer; **p. in here** arrête-toi là; **to p. in to the kerb** se ranger près du trottoir; **we'll p. in at** *or* **to the next garage** on s'arrêtera à la prochaine station-service

(b) (*arrive*) (*of train, bus, person*) arriver; **the express pulled in two hours late** l'express est arrivé avec deux heures de retard

▶ **pull into** *vipo* (*arrive at*) (*of train, bus, person etc*) arriver à; **the train was pulling into the station** le train entrait en gare; **the bus pulled into view** le bus apparut; *Sp* **to p. into the lead** prendre la tête

▶ **pull off 1** *vtsep* **(a)** (*remove*) (*clothes, wrapping etc*) enlever; (*detach*) détacher **(from** de); **to p. sth off sth** (*detach from*) détacher qch de qch; **to p. the sheets off the bed** retirer *ou* enlever les draps du lit (**b**) *F* (*win*) (*prize*) décrocher, gagner, remporter; **to p. off a deal** réussir une opération, boucler une affaire; **to p. off a bank raid/a project** réussir un hold-up/un projet; **he pulled it off** il a réussi **2** *vi* **the lid simply pulls off** il suffit de tirer pour enlever le couvercle; **the top pulls off to reveal ...** le dessus se retire et on peut voir ...

▶ **pull on** *vtsep* (*sweater, one's hat etc*) mettre; **to p. sth on over sth else** enfiler qch par-dessus qch d'autre

▶ **pull out 1** *vtsep* (**a**) (*extract*) (*tooth*) arracher, extraire; **to p. a wallet out of one's pocket** tirer *ou* sortir un portefeuille de sa poche; **to p. a nail out of a plank** arracher un clou d'une planche; **to p. a cork out of a bottle** enlever un bouchon d'une bouteille; **to p. a car out of a ditch** sortir une voiture d'un fossé; **to p. the country/economy out of the recession** faire sortir le pays/l'économie de la récession; **p. me out, I'm stuck in the mud!** sors-moi de là, je suis enlisé dans la boue!; **he was pulled out of the burning car** il a été arraché de la voiture en feu; *F* **to p. out all the stops** faire le maximum (**to do sth** pour faire qch)

(**b**) (*withdraw*) (*troops*) retirer

(**c**) (*drawer*) (*open*) ouvrir; (*remove*) enlever, dégager; (*leaf of table, shelf*) tirer

2 *vi* (**a**) *Aut* (*move out to overtake*) déboîter; **to p. out from behind a car** déboîter de derrière une voiture

(**b**) (*leave*) (*of train, bus, person etc*) partir; **when do we p. out?** quand est-ce qu'on part?

(**c**) (*withdraw*) (*of troops*) se retirer; (*of firm from project, buyer*) se désister; (*of firm from place*) quitter une/la région/ville/*etc*

(**d**) (*be extendible or detachable*) (*of drawer*) s'ouvrir; (*of handle*) (*be telescopic*) s'allonger; (*of map*) se déplier; **the table pulls out to seat ten** avec les rallonges c'est une table de dix personnes; **the sofa pulls out so you can sleep on it** on peut déplier le sofa pour dormir dedans

▶ **pull out of** *vipo* (**a**) (*leave*) (*of train, bus, person etc*) partir de; **the train was pulling out of the station** le train sortait de la gare; *Av* **to p. out of a dive** arrêter de piquer; **the country is pulling out of the recession** le pays est en train de sortir de la récession (**b**) (*withdraw from*) (*agreement, deal, country*) se retirer de

▶ **pull over 1** *vtsep* tirer; (*cause to fall*) faire tomber; **careful you don't p. that wardrobe over on top of you!** attention de ne pas te faire tomber l'armoire sur la tête! **2** *vtaspo* **she pulled her sweater over her head** (*putting it on*) elle a enfilé son pull; (*taking it off*) elle a enlevé son pull **3** *vi* **she's pulling over to let the other runners past** elle se met sur le côté pour laisser passer les autres coureurs; *Aut* **to p. over to the kerb** se ranger le long du trottoir

▶ **pull round 1** *vtsep* (*chair, object*) tourner; (*boat*) (*turn*) faire tourner; (*turn through 180 degrees*) faire faire demi-tour à; (*person*) (*help regain consciousness*) ranimer; (*help recover from illness*) remonter, remettre sur pied **2** *vi* (*of ship*) tourner; (*through 180 degrees*) faire demi-tour; (*of person*) (*regain consciousness*) revenir à soi; (*recover from illness*) se remettre

▶ **pull through 1** *vtsep* (**a**) (*of doctor etc*) (*person*) remettre sur pied (**b**) (*help survive difficulty*) (*person*) tirer d'embarras *ou* d'affaire; **he says his faith pulled him through** il dit que c'est sa foi qui lui a permis de s'en sortir **2** *vi* (**a**) (*recover from illness*) s'en tirer (**b**) (*survive difficulty*) se tirer d'affaire, s'en tirer, surmonter ses difficultés

▶ **pull to** *vtsep* (*door*) tirer, fermer

▶ **pull together 1** *vtsep* (*information*) rassembler, réunir; **he pulled them together into a team** il a réussi à faire d'eux une équipe; **to p. oneself together** (*become calm, more organized*) se ressaisir, se reprendre, reprendre ses esprits; **p. yourself together!** ressaisissez-vous! **2** *vi* (*co-operate*) s'entendre; **if we all p. together on this** si nous y mettons tous du nôtre; **p. together!** (*in rowing*) avant partout!

▶ **pull up 1** *vtsep* (**a**) (*raise*) (*blind*) hausser, lever; (*one's skirt*) retrousser, relever; (*plant, weeds*) arracher; **p. up a chair!** prends une chaise!; **to p. one's socks up** tirer *ou* remonter ses chaussettes; *Fig F* se remuer, s'activer; **his good marks in maths pulled him up again** ses bonnes notes en maths ont remonté sa moyenne

(**b**) (*stop*), *Horseriding* (*horse*) arrêter; **to p. oneself up (short)** s'arrêter (*quand on est sur le point de dire ou faire qch d'indiscret*); **to p. sb up (short)** arrêter qn net

(**c**) (*reprimand*) (*person*) rembarrer; **he pulled me up for being late** il m'a rembarré parce que j'étais en retard; *Aut* **to be pulled up (by the police)** se faire arrêter (par un agent)

2 *vi* (**a**) (*stop*) s'arrêter; **the horse pulled up lame** le cheval s'est arrêté en boitant

(**b**) (*close gap*) **to p. up (on another competitor)** réduire la distance (qui vous sépare d'un autre concurrent)

pull-back *n* (*withdrawal*) (*of troops*) retrait *m*

pull-down *adj Comptr* **p. menu** menu *m* déroulant; **p. window** fenêtre *f* déroulante

pullet [ˈpʊlɪt] *n* poulette *f*; (*fattened*) poularde *f*

pulley [ˈpʊlɪ] *n* poulie *f*; **p. block** palan *m*, moufle *mf*; **p. wheel** réa *m*, rouet *m*

pull-in *n Br* (*café*) = restoroute *m*; (*for parking*) parking *m* (*surtout près d'un restaurant*)

Pullman [ˈpʊlmən] *n Rail* **P. (car)** voiture *f* Pullman

pull (marketing) strategy *n Mktg* stratégie *f* (mercatique) 'tirer' *ou* 'tirée'

pull-off *n US Aut* (*rest area*) aire *f* de repos

pull-out 1 *adj attrib* (*section in magazine*) détachable; **p. leaf** (*on desk, table*) rallonge *f* **2** *n Journ* supplément *m* détachable

pullover [ˈpʊləʊvər] *n* pull-over *m*, *pl* pull-overs, *F* pull *m*

pullulate [ˈpʌljʊleɪt] *vi Lit* pulluler (**with life** de vie)

pull-up *n* (**a**) (*of car etc*) arrêt *m* (**b**) (*café*) = restoroute *m* (**c**) *Gym* traction *f*

pulmonary [ˈpʌlmənərɪ] *adj attrib Anat, Med* pulmonaire

pulp¹ [pʌlp] *n* (*of fruit*) pulpe *f*, chair *f*; **dental p.** pulpe dentaire; **paper p.** pâte *f ou* pulpe à papier; **to reduce to (a) p.** (*wood etc*) réduire en pulpe *ou* en pâte; *F* **to beat sb to a p.** mettre qn en bouillie; **p. fiction** romans *mpl* de bas étage *ou* de gare; **p. novels** romans de *ou* à quatre sous

pulp² *vt* (*wood etc*) réduire en pulpe *ou* en pâte; (*fruit*) écraser, réduire en purée; (*books*) mettre au pilon; **pulping machine** (*in papermaking*) pilon *m*

pulpit [ˈpʊlpɪt] *n* (*of minister*) chaire *f*; **condemned from the p.** condamné par l'église

pulpwood [ˈpʌlpwʊd] *n* (*for papermaking*) bois *m* à pâte

pulpy [ˈpʌlpɪ] *adj* pulpeux, charnu

pulsar [ˈpʌlsər] *n Astron* pulsar *m*

pulsate [pʌlˈseɪt] *vi* palpiter; (*vibrate*) vibrer; (*of heart etc*) battre; *Fig* **his novels p. with life** ses romans bouillonnent de vie

pulsation [pʌlˈseɪʃən] *n Physiol, El, Astron* pulsation *f*; (*of heart*) battement *m*, pulsation *f*

pulse¹ [pʌls] *n* (**a**) *Physiol* pouls *m*; **quick p.** pouls fréquent *ou* précipité; **strong/weak p.** pouls fort/faible; **to feel** *or* **take sb's p.** prendre le pouls à qn; **his p. quickened** son pouls s'est accéléré; *Fig* **to have one's finger on the p.** être à la page; *Fig* **to keep one's finger on the p. of ...** se tenir étroitement au courant de ...; **p. rate** fréquence *f* du pouls (**b**) (*of heart*) pulsation *f*, battement *m*; *Phys* (*of light, sound etc*) vibration *f*; *Electron, Rad* impulsion *f*; *Mus* cadence *f*, rythme *m*

pulse² 1 *vi* (**a**) (*of heart*) battre; (*beat hard*) palpiter; **a vein pulsed above his right eye** une veine se gonflait au-dessus de son œil droit; **to p. through the arteries** (*of blood*) circuler dans les artères par pulsations rythmées (**b**) *Fig* vibrer (**with energy** d'énergie); **her novels p. with life** ses romans bouillonnent de vie; **the pulsing music** le rythme saccadé de la musique **2** *vt El etc* (*current*) moduler en impulsions

pulse³ *n* (*plant*) (plante *f*) légumineuse *f*, légume *m* à gousse; (*lentils, beans etc*) légume *m* sec, *Spec* graine *f* de légumes à gousse

pulverization [pʌlvəraɪˈzeɪʃən] *n* pulvérisation *f*

pulverize [ˈpʌlvəraɪz] *vt* pulvériser, réduire en poudre; *F* **to p. sb** (*beat up*) démolir qn; (*defeat heavily*) pulvériser qn; (*criticize severely*) éreinter qn

puma [ˈpjuːmə] *n* (*animal*) puma *m*, couguar *m*

pumice¹ [ˈpʌmɪs] *n* **p. (stone)** (pierre *f*) ponce *f*

pumice² *vt* (*surface*) poncer, passer à la pierre ponce

pummel¹ [ˈpʌm(ə)l] *n* = **pommel¹**

pummel² *vt* (**-ll-**, *US* **-l-**) (*person*) battre, rosser; (*door, sb's chest*) battre; (*mixture into dough*) pétrir; **to be pummelled by the waves** être battu par les vagues; **to be pummelled by artillery** être pilonné par les tirs d'artillerie

pummelling, *US* **pummeling** [ˈpʌm(ə)lɪŋ] *n* volée *f* de coups, raclée *f*; **to give sb a good p.** donner une bonne raclée à qn; **to get a p.** (*of boxer*) se faire taper dessus

pump¹ [pʌmp] *n* (*device*) pompe *f*; **(petrol) p. attendant** pompiste *mf*; **p. room** (*at spa*) pavillon *m* (*où l'on prend les eaux*); **p. water** eau *f* de pompe

pump² 1 *vt* (*water etc*) pomper; **to p. a well dry** assécher *ou* épuiser un puits; **to p. sb's stomach** faire un lavage d'estomac à qn; **to p. air into sb's lungs** insuffler de l'air dans les poumons de qn; **to p. air into a balloon** gonfler un ballon (*à l'aide d'une pompe*); **to p. water into a cavity** amener de l'eau à la pompe dans une cavité; *F* **to p. sb's hand** serrer vigoureusement la main à qn; *F* **to p. sb** (*for information*) tirer les vers du nez à qn; **to p. water into a boiler** refouler de l'eau dans une chaudière; *F* **the athletes were pumped full of drugs** les athlètes étaient complètement dopés; *Sl* **to p. sb full of lead** (*shoot*) trouer la peau à qn; *F* **to p. iron** faire de l'haltérophilie; **he looks as if he pumps iron** on dirait un haltérophile; *Fig* **the government pumped money into the region** le gouvernement a injecté des capitaux dans cette région

2 *vi* **(a)** (*of heart, machine etc*) pomper
(b) *Br Sl* (*pass wind*) péter

pump³ *n* (*shoe*) (*for dancing*) escarpin *m*; (*for sports*) (chaussure *f* de) tennis *f*

▶ **pump in** *vtsep* (*water etc*) faire entrer à l'aide d'une pompe; *Fig* **more money will have to be pumped in** il faudra injecter plus d'argent

▶ **pump out** *vtsep* (*water etc*) pomper; *Naut* **to p. out the holds** assécher les cales; **to p. out sb's stomach** faire un lavage d'estomac à qn

▶ **pump up** *vtsep* (*tyre*) gonfler; (*oil, water*) pomper

pump-action shotgun *n* fusil *m* à pompe

pumping ['pʌmpɪŋ] *n* (*of water etc*) pompage *m*; **p. station** station *f* de pompage

pumpkin ['pʌmpkɪn] *n* potiron *m*, citrouille *f*; **p. pie** tarte *f* au potiron

pun¹ [pʌn] *n* calembour *m*, jeu *m* de mots **(on sth** sur qch); **if you'll forgive** *or* **pardon the p.** pardonnez-moi ce jeu de mots

pun² *vi* **(-nn-)** faire des calembours *ou* des jeux de mots; **..., he punned ...**, plaisanta-t-il

Punch [pʌntʃ] *n* = Polichinelle *m*, Guignol *m*; **P. and Judy show** = (théâtre *m* de) Guignol

punch¹ [pʌntʃ] *n Tech etc* (*tool*) poinçon *m*; (*machine*) poinçonneuse *f*; (*for making holes*) perforatrice *f*; **(ticket) p.** (*of ticket inspector*) poinçon; (*for use by passenger*) composteur *m*; *Comptr* **p. card/tape** carte *f*/bande *f* perforée; **p. card reader** machine *f* interprète de cartes perforées; *Ind* **p. operator** mécanographe *mf*

punch² *vt Tech* (*with tool*) percer, découper à l'emporte-pièce; (*hole*) faire, percer; (*leather etc*) perforer; (*iron sheet*) estamper, étamper; *Comptr* (*card, tape*) perforer; **to p. a ticket** (*of ticket inspector etc*) poinçonner un billet; (*of passenger*) composter un billet; *Comptr* **punched card** carte *f* perforée

punch³ *n* **(a)** (*blow*) coup *m* de poing; **I got quite a p.** je me suis pris un sacré coup de poing; **to pack quite a p.** (*hit hard*) cogner dur; *Boxing* avoir du punch; *Fig* (*of drink*) être corsé; **to pull a p.** retenir un coup; **he didn't pull his punches** (*he hit hard*) il n'y est pas allé de main morte; *Fig* (*he spoke frankly*) il n'a pas mâché ses mots; *Fig* **a documentary that pulls no punches** un documentaire sans complaisance **(b)** *F* (*energy*) punch *m*; **style that has p.** style qui a du punch, style incisif; **p. line** (*of joke*) chute *f*

punch⁴ *vt* (*hit*) (*person*) donner un/des coup(s) de poing à, cogner sur; (*ball, wall etc*) donner un/des coup(s) de poing à, cogner dans; (*typewriter keys, telephone*) taper sur; (*number*) taper, frapper **(into** sur); **to p. a number into a phone** composer un numéro; **to p. sb on the nose** donner un coup de poing sur le nez de qn; **he punched him on the chin** il lui a donné un coup de poing au menton; **the goalie punched the ball clear** le goal a écarté la balle d'un coup de poing; **to p. the air** lever le bras en signe de victoire; *Am* **to p. cattle** être cowboy

punch⁵ *n* (*drink*) punch *m*

▶ **punch away 1** *vtsep* (*ball etc*) détourner d'un coup de poing **2** *vi* donner des coups de poing

▶ **punch in** *vtsep* **(a)** (*box etc*) cabosser (d'un/de coup(s) de poing); *F* **to p. sb's face in** casser la gueule à qn **(b)** (*enter*) (*number, details*) taper; **p. your number in** composez votre numéro

▶ **punch out** *vtsep* **(a)** *Tech* (*pin*) chasser; (*shape, pattern etc*) découper à la matrice **(b) to p. it out with sb** échanger des coups de poing avec qn

punchbag ['pʌntʃbæg] *n Boxing* punching-bag *m*, *pl* punching-bags; *Fig* souffre-douleur *m inv*

punchball ['pʌntʃbɔːl] *n Boxing* punching-ball *m*, *pl* punching-balls

punchbowl ['pʌntʃbəʊl] *n* **(a)** bol *m* à punch **(b)** *Br Geog* (*between two hills*) cuvette *f*

punch-drunk *adj esp Boxing* sonné, abruti (par les coups); *Fig* sonné

puncher¹ ['pʌntʃər] *n Tech* **(a)** (*person*) (*of sheet metal etc*) poinçonneur, -euse, perceur, -euse; *Comptr* (*of cards, tapes*) perforeur, -euse; (*in metalworking*) estampeur, -euse **(b)** (*device*) (*for sheet metal*) poinçonneuse *f*; (*for cardboard, leather etc*) emporte-pièce *m inv*; *Comptr* (*for cards, tapes*) perforatrice *f*

puncher² *n Boxing* puncheur *m*; *Am* **cow p.** cowboy *m*

punching ['pʌntʃɪŋ] *n Tech* (*action*) perçage *m*, poinçonnage *m*; **p. (out)** découpage *m* (à l'emporte-pièce); **p. machine** machine *f* poinçonneuse

punching bag *n Am Boxing* punching-bag *m*, *pl* punching-bags

punchtape reader ['pʌntʃteɪp] *n* lecteur *m* de ruban perforé

punch-up *n Br F* bagarre *f*; **to have a p.** se bagarrer, se battre; **he looked as if he'd been in a p.** on aurait dit qu'il s'était battu *ou* bagarré

punchy ['pʌntʃɪ] *adj F* **(a)** (*slogan etc*) incisif, marquant; (*speech, novel*) plein de punch **(b)** = **punch-drunk**

punctilious [pʌŋk'tɪlɪəs] *adj* pointilleux, méticuleux

punctiliously [pʌŋk'tɪlɪəslɪ] *adv* scrupuleusement, dans les moindres détails

punctiliousness [pʌŋk'tɪlɪəsnɪs] *n* grande attention *f* portée aux détails, méticulosité *f*

punctual ['pʌŋktjʊəl] *adj* (*person*) ponctuel, à l'heure; (*train, bus etc*) à l'heure; **to make a p. start** partir à l'heure

punctuality [pʌŋktjʊ'ælɪtɪ] *n* (*of person*) ponctualité *f*, exactitude *f*; (*of train, bus etc*) exactitude

punctually ['pʌŋktjʊəlɪ] *adv* (*to arrive*) (*of person*) ponctuellement, à l'heure; (*of train, bus etc*) à l'heure; **we intend to leave p. at 7.30** nous comptons partir à 7h30 précises

punctuate ['pʌŋktjʊeɪt] *vt* **(a)** (*sentence etc*) ponctuer **(b)** *Fig* **speech punctuated with anecdotes** discours ponctué *ou* agrémenté d'anecdotes; **speech punctuated with applause** discours entrecoupé d'applaudissements; **a landscape punctuated with clumps of trees** un paysage avec ça et là un bouquet d'arbres

punctuation [pʌŋktjʊ'eɪʃən] *n* ponctuation *f*; **p. mark** signe *m* de ponctuation

puncture¹ ['pʌŋktʃər] *n* **(a)** (*in tyre*) crevaison *f*; (*hole in surface, skin etc*) perforation *f*; **to have a p.** (*action*) crever; (*state*) être crevé; **p. patch** (*for repairing an inner tube*) rustine® *f*; *Cycling* **p. repair kit** trousse *f* à outils, nécessaire *m* de réparation **(b)** *Med* (*action*) (*of abscess*) ponction *f*; **p. wound** trace *f* de piqûre

puncture² 1 *vt* (*tyre*) crever, perforer; *Mil, Sp* (*defence*) percer; *Med* (*blister, abscess*) ponctionner; **a punctured lung** un poumon perforé; *Fig* **to p. sb's pride/self-confidence** entamer la fierté/la confiance en soi de qn; **to p. sb's self-esteem** rabattre le caquet à qn **2** *vi* (*of tyre*) crever

pundit ['pʌndɪt] *n* **(a)** (*expert*) (*political etc*) spécialiste *mf*, expert *m*, *F* pontife *m*, ponte *m*; **according to the pundits** si l'on en croit les spécialistes *ou F* les grands pontes **(b)** (*in India*) pandit *m*

pungency ['pʌndʒənsɪ] *n* **(a)** (*of spice etc*) (*in taste*) saveur *f* piquante; (*in smell*) odeur *f* forte *ou* piquante **(b)** *Fig* (*of words*) âcreté *f*, aigreur *f*; (*of story*) saveur *f*; (*of style etc*) saveur, causticité *f*

pungent ['pʌndʒənt] *adj* **(a)** (*smell etc*) fort, âcre, piquant; (*taste*) piquant; **p. sauce** sauce *f* relevée *ou* épicée **(b)** (*style, wit etc*) mordant, caustique

pungently ['pʌndʒəntlɪ] *adv* d'une manière piquante

Punic ['pjuːnɪk] *adj Hist* punique

puniness ['pjuːnɪnɪs] *n* faiblesse *f*

punish ['pʌnɪʃ] *vt* **(a)** (*child, wrongdoer, mistake*) punir; **to p. sb with imprisonment** punir qn d'une peine d'emprisonnement; **to p. sb for a crime** punir qn pour un crime; **to p. sb for having done sth** *or* **for doing sth** punir qn pour avoir fait qch; *Jur* **to p. sb by** *or* **with a fine** frapper qn d'une amende **(b)** *Sp etc F* (*boxer*) (*hit hard*) taper dur sur; (*opponent's mistake*) ne pas pardonner; (*horse*) malmener; *Aut* (*engine*) fatiguer, forcer; **he really punishes himself in training** il se donne à fond à l'entraînement

punishable ['pʌnɪʃəb(ə)l] *adj* punissable; *Jur* délictueux; **p. by a fine/by death** passible d'amende/d'une peine de mort

punishing ['pʌnɪʃɪŋ] **1** *adj* dur; (*blow*) violent; (*game*) rude; (*work*) épuisant, éreintant; **a p. race** une course épuisante; **a p. schedule** un emploi du temps extrêmement serré **2** *n* punition *f*

punishment ['pʌnɪʃmənt] *n* **(a)** punition *f*, châtiment *m*; *Jur* peine *f*; **as a p. for sth** en punition de qch; **to inflict a p. on sb** donner *ou* infliger une punition à qn; **to escape p.** échapper à la punition; **to make the p. fit the crime** proportionner la punition au crime; **to take one's p. like a man** recevoir sa punition sans broncher

(b) *F* (*blows etc*) **to take a lot of p.** (*of boxer etc*) encaisser; (*of army, warship, tank, car, boat etc*) être malmené; (*of shoes, clothes etc*) être soumis à rude épreuve; **it has to be able to take a lot of p.** (*of footwear, paint etc*) il faut que ça soit résistant; (*of car*) il faut qu'elle soit bien solide; **to inflict severe p. on a team** administrer une cruelle défaite à une équipe

punitive ['pju:nɪtɪv], **punitory** ['pju:nɪt(ə)rɪ] *adj* répressif; (*taxation*) très sévère; *Jur* **p. damages** dommages-intérêts *mpl*; *Mil* **p. expedition** expédition *f* punitive; *Jur* **p. justice** justice *f* répressive

Punjab [ˈpʌndʒɑːb] *n* Pendjab *m*

Punjabi [pʌn'dʒɑ:bɪ] **1** *adj* du Pendjab **2** *n* **(a)** habitant, -ante du Pendjab; (*by birth*) originaire *mf* du Pendjab **(b)** *Ling* pendjabi *m*

punk [pʌŋk] **1** *n* **(a)** (*music fan, rebel etc*) punk *mf*; **p. (rock)** le punk (rock) **(b)** *Am F Pej* (*worthless person*) vaurien *m*, crapule *f* **2** *adj* **(a)** (*music, hairstyle etc*) punk *inv*; **a p. band** un groupe punk **(b)** *Am F* (*worthless*) nul, qui ne vaut rien

punnet ['pʌnɪt] *n esp Br* (*for strawberries etc*) petit carton *m*, barquette *f*

punster ['pʌnstər] *n* faiseur, -euse de calembours *ou* de jeux de mots

punt[1] [pʌnt] *n* (*boat*) bateau *m* à fond plat (*de rivière conduit à la perche*); **p. pole** perche *f* (*pour la conduite d'un bateau à fond plat*)

punt[2] **1** *vt* (*boat*) conduire à la perche; (*person*) transporter dans un bateau à fond plat **2** *vi* **to go punting** faire un tour dans un bateau à fond plat

punt[3] *n Fb, Rugby* coup *m* de volée

punt[4] *Fb, Rugby* **1** *vt* (*ball*) envoyer d'un coup de volée **2** *vi* donner un coup de pied de volée

punt[5] *vi* **(a)** *Cards* ponter; **to p. high** ponter gros **(b)** *Br Horseracing* parier

punt[6] *n* (*Irish currency*) livre *f* irlandaise

punter[1] ['pʌntər] *n Br* **(a)** *Horseracing* parieur, -euse **(b)** *F* (*man*) mec *m*; **the punters** (*the public*) le public, les gens; **the average p.** l'homme de la rue **(c)** *F* (*prostitute's client*) miché *m*, micheton *m* **(d)** *Cards* ponte *m*

punter[2] *n* (*in boat*) canotier *m* (*qui conduit à la perche*)

puny ['pju:nɪ] *adj* (*person*) chétif; (*arms, chest*) frêle, maigre; (*hands*) tout petit; (*effort*) malheureux; (*argument, excuse*) piètre; **a p. little fellow** un petit gringalet; **our p. little guns** nos pauvres *ou* malheureux petits canons; **a p. 50p** cinquante malheureux pence

pup[1] [pʌp] *n* **(a)** (*of dog*) jeune chien, -ienne, chiot *m*; (*of seal*) jeune phoque *m*; (*of wolf*) louveteau *m*; (*of rat*) raton *m*; **a bitch and her pups** une chienne et ses petits; **to be in p.** (*of bitch*) être grosse; *Fig* **to be sold a p.** se faire rouler **(b)** *F* (*young man*) (*self-important*) freluquet *m*; (*impertinent*) petit impertinent *m*

pup[2] *vi* mettre bas

pupa, *pl* **-ae** ['pju:pə, -i:] *n* (*insect*) nymphe *f*

pupate ['pju:peɪt] *vi* (*of insect*) se métamorphoser en nymphe

pupil[1] ['pju:p(ə)l] *n* **(a)** *Sch* élève *mf* **(b)** *Jur* pupille *mf*

pupil[2] *n Anat* (*of eye*) pupille *f*

pupil(l)age ['pju:pɪlɪdʒ] *n Jur* pupillarité *f*; **child in p.** enfant en pupille *ou* en tutelle

pupilometer [pju:pɪ'lɒmɪtər] *n* pupillomètre *m*

puppet ['pʌpɪt] *n* marionnette *f*; *Fig* (*person*) marionnette, fantoche *m*; **glove** *or* **hand p.** marionnette à gaine; *Fig* **p. government** gouvernement *m* fantoche; **p. show** *or* **play** (spectacle *m* de) marionnettes; **p. theatre** (théâtre *m* de) marionnettes

puppeteer [pʌpɪ'tɪər] *n* marionnettiste *mf*

puppetry ['pʌpɪtrɪ] *n* art *m* des marionnettes; (*puppet making*) fabrication *f* de marionnettes

puppy ['pʌpɪ] *n* **(a) p. (dog)** jeune chien, -ienne, chiot *m*; **p. fat** adiposité *f* d'enfance *ou* d'adolescence; **p. love** amour *m* juvénile, amour de jeunesse **(b)** *F* (*young man*) = **pup**[1] **(b)**

purblind ['pɜ:blaɪnd] *adj* **(a)** (*almost blind*) presque aveugle **(b)** *Fml* (*obtuse*) obtus; (*policy, refusal*) aveugle

purchase[1] ['pɜ:tʃɪs] *n* **(a)** (*act of buying, thing bought*) achat *m*; **to make some purchases** faire des achats; *Acct* **p. of debts** rachat *m* des créances; *Mktg* **p. behaviour** comportement *m* d'achat; **p. contract** contrat *m* d'achat; **p. cost** coût *m* d'achat; *Mktg* **p. decision** décision *f* d'achat; *Acct* **p. entry** écriture *f* d'achats; *Mktg* **p. frequency** fréquence *f* d'achat; *Acct* **p. invoice** facture *f* d'achat; *Acct* **p. invoice ledger** journal *m* factures-fournisseurs; *Acct* **p. ledger** (grand) livre *m* d'achats, journal des achats; *Acct* **p. ledger clerk** facturier *m* d'entrée; *Mktg* **p. occasion** occasion *f* d'achat; **p. order** *Com* bon *m* de commande; *St Exch* ordre *m* d'achat; **p. price** prix *m* d'achat; **p. value** valeur *f* d'achat **(b)** (*grip*) prise *f*; **to get** *or* **secure a p. on sth** trouver prise sur qch

purchase[2] **1** *vt* (*object*) acheter, *Fml* acquérir, faire l'acquisition de; *Acct* **to p. a debt** racheter une créance **2** *vi* acheter; **now is the time to p.** c'est maintenant qu'il faut acheter

purchaser ['pɜ:tʃəsər] *n* acheteur, -euse, *Fml* acquéreur, -euse; *Mktg* **p. behaviour** comportement *m* de l'acheteur

purchasing ['pɜ:tʃəsɪŋ] *n* achat *m*; (*of company*) rachat *m*; **p. (department)** service *m* des achats; *Mktg* **p. behaviour** comportement *m* d'achat; **p. co-operative** groupement *m* d'achat; *Econ* **p. power** pouvoir *m* d'achat

purdah ['pɜ:də] *n Muslim Rel* = système *m* qui astreint les femmes à une vie retirée; *Fig* **to go into p.** se retirer, ne voir personne

pure [pjʊər] *adj* (*unadulterated, morally uncorrupted*) pur; **as p. as the driven snow** pur comme l'enfant qui vient de naître; **the p. and simple truth** la vérité pure et simple; *Bible* **the p. in heart** ceux qui ont le cœur pur; **p. Arab (horse)** (cheval *m*) arabe *m* de race pure; **by p. chance** par un pur hasard; **p. English** anglais *m* pur; **p.-minded** pur d'esprit; **p. mathematics** les mathématiques *mpl* pures; *Phil* **p. reason** la raison pure; **p. thoughts** pensées *fpl* pures; **p. silk/wool** pure soie *f*/laine *f*

pure(-)blood 1 *adj* (*horse*) pur sang *inv* **2** *n* (*horse*) pur-sang *m inv*

pure(-)blooded *adj* (*of animal, person*) pur sang *inv*

purebred ['pjʊəbred] **1** *adj* (*dog, bull*) de race (pure), pur sang *inv* **2** *n* animal *m* de race; (*horse*) pur-sang *m inv*

purée[1] ['pjʊəreɪ] *n Culin* purée *f*; **tomato p.** concentré *m* de tomate

purée[2] *vt Culin* (*apples, potatoes etc*) réduire *ou* écraser en purée; **puréed potatoes/spinach** purée *f* de pommes de terre/d'épinards

purely ['pjʊəlɪ] *adv* purement; **he is p. concerned with ...** il est uniquement préoccupé de ...; **p. routine questioning** interrogatoire *m* de simple routine; **it was p. by chance that we met** notre rencontre n'était qu'un pur hasard; **it was p. accidental** c'était un pur hasard; **p. and simply** purement et simplement

pureness ['pjʊənɪs] *n* pureté *f*

purgation [pɜ:'geɪʃən] *n* **(a)** *Med* (*of intestine*) purge *f* **(b)** *Rel* (*in purgatory*) purgation *f* de l'âme

purgative ['pɜ:gətɪv] *adj, n Med* purgatif *m*

purgatory ['pɜ:gət(ə)rɪ] *n Rel* purgatoire *m*; **the souls in p.** les âmes du purgatoire, les âmes en peine; **to live a life of p.** souffrir les peines du purgatoire de son vivant; *Fig* **it was sheer p.** c'était l'enfer, c'était atroce

purge[1] [pɜ:dʒ] *n* **(a)** (*drug etc*) purgatif *m*, purge *f* **(b)** (*action*) *Med* purge *f*; *Pol etc* (*of political party etc*) épuration *f*, nettoyage *m*, purge

purge[2] *vt Med* (*person*) purger; (*political party etc*) nettoyer, épurer; *Rel* **to p. oneself of** *or* **from sin** se laver de ses péchés; *Jur* **to p. oneself of a charge** se disculper, se justifier; *US Jur* **to p. one's contempt** faire amende honorable (*pour outrage aux magistrats*)

purging ['pɜ:dʒɪŋ] *n Med etc* (*of body*) purge *f*, purification *f*; (*of political party etc*) épuration *f*

purification [pjʊərɪfɪ'keɪʃən] *n* purification *f*; (*of gas, oil, water etc*) épuration *f*; *Rel* **the Feast of the P. (of the Virgin Mary)** (la fête de) la Purification

purifier ['pjʊərɪfaɪər] *n* (*for gas, oil etc*) épurateur *m*; (*for air*) assainisseur *m*

purify ['pjʊərɪfaɪ] *vt* (*air etc*) assainir, purifier; (*gas, oil etc*) épurer; (*language*) purifier, épurer; (*blood*) dépurer; (*heart, mind etc*) purifier; **to p. sb of** *or* **from his sins** laver qn de ses péchés

purist ['pjʊərɪst] *n* puriste *mf*; **a linguistic p.** un puriste en matière de linguistique

puritan ['pjʊərɪt(ə)n] *adj, n* **(a)** puritain, -aine **(b)** *Eng Hist* **P.** puritain, -aine

puritanical [pjʊərɪ'tænɪk(ə)l] *adj* puritain

puritanism ['pjʊərɪtənɪz(ə)m] *n* puritanisme *m*

purity ['pjʊərɪtɪ] *n* pureté *f*; **degree of p.** (*of water etc*) (degré *m* de) pureté; (*of gold*) titre *m*; **the p. of sb's motives** la pureté des motifs de qn

purl[1] [pɜ:l] *n Knitting* **p. (stitch)** maille *f* à l'envers

purl[2] *vt Knitting* (*row*) tricoter à l'envers; **knit one, p. one** une maille à l'endroit, une maille à l'envers

purlieus ['pɜ:lju:z] *npl Lit* (*surrounding area*) alentours *mpl*, environs *mpl*; **in the p. of** aux alentours *ou* environs de

purloin [pɜ:'lɔɪn] *vt Fml* voler, dérober

purple ['pɜ:p(ə)l] **1** *adj* violet; **he turned** *or* **went p.** il est devenu cramoisi, son visage s'est empourpré **(with rage** de rage); *Pharm F* **p. heart** = comprimé *m* violet de drinamyl en forme de cœur; *US Mil* **P. Heart** = décoration *f* remise à un blessé de guerre; *Liter* **p. patch** morceau *m* de bravoure; *Liter* **p. prose** prose *f* héroïque **2** *n* (*colour*) violet *m*; (*dye*) pourpre *f*; **born to the p.** né dans la pourpre

purplish ['pɜ:plɪʃ] *adj* violacé, violâtre; (*face*) cramoisi

purport[1] ['pɜ:pɔ:t] *n Fml* (*of document*) (*intention*) esprit *m*; (*of argument*) portée *f*, force *f*

purport[2] [pɜ:'pɔ:t] *vt* **to p. to be sth** (*of person*) prétendre être qch; (*of thing*) être présenté comme étant qch

purpose¹ [ˈpɜːpəs] *n* **(a)** (*object, aim*) but *m*, objectif *m*; **fixed p.** dessein *m ou* objectif bien arrêté; **to gain** *or* **achieve one's p.** atteindre son but *ou* objectif, accomplir son dessein; **for** *or* **with the p. of doing sth** dans l'intention *ou* le but de faire qch; **what is the p. of your visit?** quel est le but *ou* l'objet de votre visite?; **it does not suit her p. to have it widely known** ça ne l'arrangerait pas que ça se sache; **to do sth on p.** faire qch exprès; **to have a sense of p.** être motivé; **his life lacked any real sense of p.** sa vie était dépourvue de but précis; **to give sb a sense of p.** motiver qn; **man of p.** homme *m* résolu *ou* décidé

(b) (*use*) (*of object*) but *m*, objet *m*; **the buildings were not built for this p.** ces bâtiments n'ont pas été construits dans ce but *ou* à cette fin; **I've never understood their p.** je n'ai jamais compris à quoi ils servaient; **does it serve any useful p.?** est-ce que ça sert à quelque chose?; **intended p.** (*of building, amount of money*) destination *f*, affectation *f*; **they were never used for their intended p.** ils n'ont jamais servi à l'usage auquel on les destinait; **to serve no p.** ne servir à rien; **once she had served her p. they abandoned her** une fois qu'elle eut tenu son rôle, ils l'abandonnèrent; **this will suit** *or* **serve your p.** cela fera votre affaire; **made for that very p.** fait tout exprès; **for all purposes** à toutes fins, à tous usages; **intended for practical purposes** destiné à des usages pratiques; **to set up a commission for the p. of investigation** former un comité à des fins d'enquête; **for the p. of this article ...** (*in lease, contract etc*) au sens du présent article ...; **for our purposes we can assume this is true** en ce qui nous concerne, nous pouvons admettre que c'est vrai

(c) to speak to the p. parler à propos; **very much to the p.** fort à propos; **to some p.** utilement, avantageusement, efficacement; **all that will have been to no p.** tout cela n'aura servi à rien; **we're (talking) at cross purposes** il y a malentendu (entre nous), nous ne parlons pas de la même chose/personne; **in order to avoid talking at cross purposes** afin d'éviter tout malentendu

purpose² *vt Fml* **to p. to do sth** *or* **doing sth** se proposer de faire qch

purpose-built *adj* (*conference centre, sports complex*) construit (tout) spécialement; **it's not exactly p. but ...** ce n'est pas exactement fait pour mais ...

purposeful [ˈpɜːpəsfʊl] *adj* (*determined*) résolu, déterminé

purposefully [ˈpɜːpəsfʊlɪ] *adv* (*determinedly*) (*to act*) résolument, avec détermination; (*to walk out etc*) d'un air résolu *ou* déterminé

purposeless [ˈpɜːpəslɪs] *adj* (*existence*) sans but; (*lacking determination*) (*atmosphere*) d'indécision; (*attempts, person*) qui manque de conviction; **the p. air which seems to surround this government** le manque de détermination qui semble caractériser ce gouvernement

purposely [ˈpɜːpəslɪ] *adv* exprès, à dessein, délibérément; **he p. looked the other way** il a regardé exprès de l'autre côté; **I came p. to see her** je suis venu exprès pour la voir

purr¹ [pɜːr] *n* (*of cat*) ronron *m*, ronronnement *m*; (*of machine*) ronflement *m*; (*of car engine etc*) ronronnement; **she's got a very loud p.** (*of cat*) elle ronronne très fort

purr² *vi* (*of cat, car, person*) ronronner

purring [ˈpɜːrɪŋ] **1** *adj* (*cat*) qui ronronne, qui fait ronron **2** *n* = **purr¹**

purse¹ [pɜːs] *n* porte-monnaie *m inv*; *Am* (*handbag*) sac *m* à main; **the public p.** le trésor public; *Old-fashioned* **it is beyond my p.** c'est au-dessus de mes moyens; *Sp* **to put up a p.** offrir un prix; *Sp* **how big is the p.?** à combien se monte le prix?; *F* **she holds the p. strings** c'est elle qui tient les cordons de la bourse; *Fishing* **p. seine** *or* **net** senne *f ou* seine *f* à poche

purse² *vt* **to p. (up) one's lips** *or* **mouth** pincer les lèvres; **she pursed her lips in disapproval** elle pinça les lèvres en signe de désapprobation

purse crab *n Fishing* crabe *m* des cocotiers

purser [ˈpɜːsər] *n Naut* (*in merchant navy*) commissaire *m*; **p.'s mate** cambusier *m*

pursuance [pəˈsjuːəns] *n Fml* exécution *f*; **in p. of one's duty** dans l'exercice de ses fonctions; **in p. of your instructions** conformément à vos instructions

pursuant [pəˈsjuːənt] *adv Fml* **p. to your instructions** conformément à vos instructions

pursue [pəˈsjuː] *vt* **(a)** (*chase*) (*person, animal*) poursuivre; (*pleasure, happiness*) rechercher; (*aim*) chercher à atteindre; **to be pursued by misfortune** être poursuivi par le malheur **(b)** (*continue*) (*one's path, studies*) continuer, poursuivre; (*policy*) poursuivre; (*course of action*) suivre; (*trade, profession*) faire, exercer; (*enquiry, matter*) donner suite à, poursuivre; **the subject was pursued no further** on ne s'attacha pas davantage à débattre ce sujet; **to p. a career in medicine/the law/journalism** faire carrière dans la médecine/le droit/le journalisme

pursuer [pəˈsjuːər] *n* **(a)** poursuivant, -ante **(b)** *Scot Jur* plaignant, -ante

pursuit [pəˈsjuːt] *n* **(a)** (*chase*) poursuite *f*; *Fig* (*of pleasure, knowledge, happiness etc*) recherche *f*, quête *f*; **to be in p. of sb** être à la poursuite de qn; **the dogs were in hot p.** les chiens avaient engagé la chasse; **with two policemen in hot p.** avec deux agents à ses/mes/*etc* trousses; **in p. of his aim** en poursuivant son but; **in p. of happiness** à la poursuite *ou* en quête du bonheur **(b)** (*occupation*) occupation *f*; **(leisure) p.** passe-temps *m inv*; **literary pursuits** travaux *mpl* littéraires

pursuit plane *n Av* chasseur *m*, avion *m* de chasse

pursuit race *n Cycling* poursuite *f*

purulence [ˈpjʊərʊləns] *n Med* **(a)** purulence *f* **(b)** (*pus*) pus *m*

purulent [ˈpjʊərʊlənt] *adj Med* purulent

purvey [pəˈveɪ] *vt Fml Com* (*provisions*) fournir; **we p. a selection of fine wines** nous offrons une sélection de vins fins; **to p. information** diffuser l'information

purveyance [pəˈveɪəns] *n Fml Com* fourniture *f* de provisions, approvisionnement *m*

purveyor [pəˈveɪər] *n Fml Com* fournisseur, -euse (de provisions), approvisionneur, -euse **(of** en; **to** de)

purview [ˈpɜːvjuː] *n* **(a)** *Jur* (*of a law*) corps *m* **(b)** *Fml* (*scope*) (*of inquiry*) limites *fpl*, portée *f*; **it is not within my p. to ...** il n'est pas dans mes compétences de ...

pus [pʌs] *n Med* pus *m*

push¹ [pʊʃ] *n* **(a)** poussée *f*; **to give sth/sb a p.** pousser qch/qn; *Fig* **to give sb a p.** pousser qn; **she just needs a little p.** elle a besoin qu'on la pousse un peu; *F* **to get the p.** (*from job*) se faire virer, être flanqué à la porte; (*from relationship*) se faire plaquer; *F* **to give sb the p.** (*from job*) virer qn, flanquer qn à la porte; (*from relationship*) plaquer qn; **to give a car a p. start** faire démarrer une voiture en la poussant; *Billiards* **p. (stroke)** coup *m* queuté

(b) (*effort*) effort *m*, coup *m* de collier; *Mil* (*attack*) attaque *f* en masse; **to make a p. for change** lutter pour le changement; **the club's p. for promotion** les efforts soutenus du club pour être promu; **the final p. for the summit** le dernier effort pour atteindre le sommet

(c) (*drive*) dynamisme *m*

(d) *F* (*difficult moment*) **at a p.** à la limite; **when it comes to the p., you can always rely on her** aux moments critiques, on peut toujours compter sur elle; **if it comes to the p., he'll choose Sarah not Henry** s'il fallait qu'il choisisse, il prendrait Sarah et pas Henry; **if p. comes to shove** si la situation l'exige

(e) *esp Austr Sl* (*gang*) bande *f*, clique *f* (*de voyous, de pickpockets*)

push² **1** *vt* **(a)** (*person, wheelbarrow etc*) pousser; (*button*) appuyer sur; **to p. sb into the room** pousser qn (pour le faire entrer) dans la pièce; **to p. the door shut/open with one's foot** fermer/ouvrir la porte du pied; **don't p. (me)!** ne (me) poussez pas!, ne (me) bousculez pas!; **did he fall or was he pushed?** il est tombé ou on l'a poussé?; **did he leave or was he pushed?** (*from job*) il est parti de lui-même ou on l'y a poussé?; **to p. sb into a corner** acculer qn; **to p. sb out of the way** écarter qn; **to p. one's way through the crowd** se frayer *ou* s'ouvrir un chemin à travers la foule; **to p. one's way in** (*party, conversation etc*) s'immiscer; **to p. an attack home** pousser à fond une attaque; **to p. home one's advantage** tirer le meilleur parti possible de son avantage; *Fig* **to p. oneself** (*make an effort*) forcer; *Fig* **he needs pushing** il faut toujours le pousser

(b) (*thrust*) (*knife, stick, hands etc*) enfoncer **(into** dans)

(c) *Fig* (*goods*) faire (de) la réclame pour; (*theory, system*) préconiser; (*drugs*) vendre, fournir; **the government is pushing the idea of people setting up small businesses** le gouvernement favorise la création de petites entreprises; **he's pushing himself as a compromise candidate** il se présente comme le candidat du compromis; **to p. one's demands** revendiquer ses droits; *St Exch* **to p. shares** placer des valeurs douteuses; **to p. the line that ...** insister sur le fait que ...

(d) (*force*) **to p. sb into doing sth** pousser qn à faire qch; **don't p. me!** ne me presse pas!; **her parents didn't p. her into the law** ses parents ne l'ont pas poussée à faire du droit; **to p. sb for payment/an answer** harceler qn pour se faire payer/pour qu'il réponde; **don't p. him too far** ne le poussez pas à bout; **I don't want to p. the comparison too far, but ...** je ne veux pas pousser la comparaison trop loin, mais ...; *F* **to p. one's luck** y aller un peu fort; *F* **that's pushing it a bit** tu y vas/il y va/*etc* un peu fort; **I'm terribly**

pushed (for time) je suis très pressé; **to be pushed for money** être à court d'argent

(e) *F* **he's pushing sixty** il frise la soixantaine

2 *vi* **(a)** pousser; (*sign on door*) poussez, pousser; **to p. against sth** pousser qch; *Aut* **we'll have to get out and p.** il va falloir descendre pousser; **stop pushing!** arrêtez de pousser!; *Fig* **you have to p. to get your way** pour réussir il faut savoir se mettre en avant

(b) (*move forward*) avancer (avec difficulté); **the crowd pushed towards the exits** la foule se pressait vers la sortie; **to p. through the crowd** se frayer *ou* s'ouvrir un chemin à travers la foule; **he pushed past me** il m'a bousculé et m'a passé devant

▶ **push about** *or* **around** *vtsep F* (*bully*) (*person*) marcher sur les pieds de, mener par le bout du nez; **we're sick and tired of being pushed about** *or* **around** nous en avons marre d'être menés par le bout du nez *ou* de nous faire marcher sur les pieds

▶ **push ahead** *vi* **(a)** (*continue*) continuer, persévérer; **to p. ahead with the work** poursuivre les travaux **(b)** (*advance*) avancer, progresser (**with** dans); **research is pushing ahead** les recherches avancent

▶ **push along 1** *vtsep* (*move by pushing*) (*pram etc*) pousser **2** *vi F* (*leave*) partir, y aller; **I suppose I should be pushing along soon** il va bientôt falloir que j'y aille

▶ **push around** = **push about**

▶ **push aside** *vtsep* (*shove out of way*) écarter

▶ **push away** *vtsep* (*shove from oneself*) écarter, repousser

▶ **push back** *vtsep* (*shove away*) (*person*) repousser; (*crowd, enemy etc*) faire reculer, refouler; (*attack*) réprimer; (*curtains*) écarter

▶ **push down 1** *vtsep* (*lever, switch*) abaisser; (*prices*) faire baisser; **he pushed down the lid but it wouldn't shut** il a appuyé sur le couvercle mais il ne voulait pas fermer **2** *vi* **(a)** (*of lever etc*) s'abaisser; (*of person*) appuyer **(b)** (*press down*) (*of weight*) peser (**on** sur)

▶ **push for 1** *vipo* faire campagne pour; **the unions are pushing for 10%** les syndicats font pression pour obtenir 10%; **to p. for a decision** exiger qu'une décision soit prise **2** *vtaspo* **to p. sb for an answer** presser qn pour qu'il/elle donne une réponse

▶ **push forward 1** *vtsep* (*cause to move*) pousser en avant, (faire) avancer; **he was pushed forward by the crowd** la foule l'a poussé en avant; *Fig* **to p. oneself forward** se mettre en avant, chercher à s'imposer **2** *vi* (*move forward*) avancer

▶ **push in 1** *vtsep* (*insert*) enfoncer; **the side of the car was pushed in** le flanc de la voiture était enfoncé; **he was standing by the pool and someone pushed him in** il était au bord de la piscine et quelqu'un l'a poussé dedans; **they opened the door and pushed me in** ils ont ouvert la porte et m'ont poussé à l'intérieur; *Sl* **to p. sb's face in** casser la gueule à qn **2** *vi* (*jump queue*) resquiller; **she's always pushing in where she's not wanted** il faut toujours qu'elle s'immisce *ou* s'impose là où on ne veut pas d'elle

▶ **push off 1** *vtsep* **(a)** (*cause to fall*) faire tomber **(b)** (*remove by pushing*) pousser; **p. the lid off** soulève le couvercle **2** *vtaspo* (*cause to fall from*) **he pushed me off the wall** il m'a fait tomber du mur, il m'a poussé du haut du mur; **they tried to p. her (car) off the road** ils ont essayé de faire sortir sa voiture de la route; **to p. sb off a committee** exclure *ou* écarter qn d'un comité **3** *vi* **(a)** *F* (*leave*) partir, se casser; *Naut* pousser au large; *F* **p. off!** fiche le camp!, tire-toi! **(b) the lid pushes off** le couvercle glisse

▶ **push on 1** *vi* (*continue with work, journey etc*) continuer; **to p. on to** *or* **as far as a place** pousser jusqu'à un endroit; **it's time to p. on** (*with journey*) il est temps de nous remettre en route; **to p. on with the work** se remettre au travail **2** *vtsep* **(a)** (*press into place*) (*lid, cover etc*) appuyer sur **(b)** (*encourage*) encourager

▶ **push onto** *vtaspo* **to p. sth onto sb** (*blame, work etc*) mettre qch sur le dos de qn

▶ **push out** *vtsep* **(a)** (*cause to leave*) (*physically*) pousser dehors, faire sortir; **he was pushed out of the group** il a été exclu du groupe; **to p. one's way out** se frayer un chemin vers la sortie **(b)** (*launch*) (*boat*) mettre à l'eau; *Fig F* **to p. the boat out** faire la fête

▶ **push over** *vtsep* (*cause to fall*) faire tomber

▶ **push through 1** *vtsep* **(a)** (*cause to pass through*) faire passer **(b)** *Pol* (*get accepted*) (*bill etc*) faire accepter **(c)** (*bring to completion*) (*work*) mener à bien, parvenir à terminer **2** *vtaspo* (*cause to pass through*) **to p. sth through sth** faire passer qch à travers qch; *Pol* **to p. a bill through Parliament** faire accepter un projet de loi au parlement **3** *vi* (*shove through*) se frayer un chemin **4** *vipo* (*shove through*) se frayer *ou* se faire un chemin à travers; **to p. through a crowd** se frayer un chemin dans la foule

▶ **push to** *vtsep* (*door, shutters*) pousser, fermer

▶ **push up** *vtsep* **(a)** (*lift by pushing*) (*lid etc*) relever, soulever **(b)** (*help climb by pushing*) (*person*) aider à monter (en le poussant) **(c)** (*increase*) (*prices etc*) faire monter

push-bike *n Br F* vélo *m*, bécane *f*

push button *n* (*on machine*) (bouton-)poussoir *m*, *pl* (boutons-)poussoirs; (*of doorbell*) bouton *m* de sonnette *ou* d'appel

push-button *adj* **p. controls** commandes *fpl* automatiques; **p. operation** fonctionnement *m* automatique; **p. telephone** téléphone *m* à touches; **p. war** guerre *f* presse-bouton

pushcart [ˈpʊʃkɑːt] *n* voiture *f* à bras, charrette *f* à bras

pushchair [ˈpʊʃtʃeər] *n Br* (*for baby*) poussette *f*

pusher [ˈpʊʃər] *n* **(a)** *F* (**drug**) **p.** dealer *m* **(b)** (*ambitious person*) ambitieux, -euse, *Pej* arriviste *mf* **(c)** *Br* (**baby's**) **p.** (*utensil*) raclette *f* **(d)** *TV* machiniste *m* chargé du travelling

pushiness [ˈpʊʃɪnɪs] *n F* **they didn't like his p.** ils le trouvaient trop ambitieux; **you need a bit of p.** il faut insister un peu, il faut jouer des coudes

pushing [ˈpʊʃɪŋ] **1** *adj* = **pushy 2** *n* poussée *f*; **no p.!** ne poussez pas!; **there was a lot of p. and shoving** ça poussait et ça se bousculait dans tous les sens

push (marketing) strategy *n Mktg* stratégie *f* mercatique 'pousser', stratégie poussée

pushover [ˈpʊʃəʊvər] *n* **(a)** *F* (*thing*) **it's a p.** c'est un jeu d'enfant, c'est de la tarte **(b)** *F* (*opponent*) adversaire *mf* facile; (*gullible person*) bonne poire *f*; **when it comes to redheads, I'm a p.** quand je rencontre une rousse, je ne peux pas me retenir

pushpin [ˈpʊʃpɪn] *n US* (*for drawing board etc*) punaise *f*

push-pull *n Electron* push-pull *m inv*; **p. circuit/amplifier** circuit *m*/amplificateur *m* push-pull; **p. train** train *m* réversible; *Aut* **p. hand control** (*for disabled driver*) commande *f* manuelle pousser-tirer

pushrod [ˈpʊʃrɒd] *n Aut* (*in engine*) poussoir *m*, tige *f* poussoir *ou* de poussée *ou* de culbuteur

push-start *vt Aut* (*car etc*) faire démarrer en le poussant

push-up *n Gym* traction *f*, *F* pompe *f*; **to do push-ups** faire des tractions *ou F* des pompes

pushy [ˈpʊʃɪ] *adj F* **(a)** (*self-assertive*) **you have to be pretty p. in this work** il faut savoir insister dans ce travail **(b)** (*ambitious*) ambitieux, *Pej* arriviste; **I had very p. parents** mes parents m'ont beaucoup poussé

pusillanimity [pjuːsɪləˈnɪmɪtɪ] *n Fml* pusillanimité *f*

pusillanimous [pjuːsɪˈlænɪməs] *adj Fml* pusillanime

puss [pʊs] *n* **(a)** *F* (*cat*) minet *m*, minette *f*, minou *m*; **P. in Boots** le Chat botté **(b)** *Sl* (*face*) figure *f*

pussy[1] [ˈpʊsɪ] *n* **(a)** *F* **p. (cat)** minet *m*, minette *f*, minou *m* **(b)** *esp Am Vulg* (*female genitals*) chatte *f*; **he hadn't had any p. for months** (*sex*) il n'avait pas baisé depuis des mois; **p. whipped** complètement soumis à sa grognasse

pussy[2] [ˈpʌsɪ] *adj* (*containing pus*) suintant

pussyfoot [ˈpʊsɪfʊt] *vi F* (*avoid committing oneself*) ne pas se mouiller; **stop pussyfooting around!** arrête de tergiverser!; **we could do without all this pussyfooting about** on se passerait bien de toutes ces tergiversations

pussy willow *n* (*tree*) saule *m*

pustule [ˈpʌstjuːl] *n Med, Vet* pustule *f*

put[1] [pʊt] *n* **(a)** *Sp* (*of shot*) lancer *m*, lancement *m* **(b)** *St Exch* **p. (option)** option *f* de vente, put *m*

put[2] (*pt, pp* **put**; *prp* **putting**) **1** *vt* **(a)** (*place*) mettre; **p. it on the table** mettez-le *ou* posez-le sur la table; **to p. one's arms around sb/sth** prendre qn/qch dans ses bras; **she put her head through the window/round the door** elle a passé la tête par la fenêtre/dans l'encoignure de la porte; **to p. a hem on a skirt** faire un ourlet à une jupe; **to p. the telescope to one's eye** porter le télescope à son œil; **to p. a child in a home** placer un enfant dans une maison d'accueil; **to p. sb on the street** (*leave destitute*) mettre qn à la rue; **to p. an advertisement in the paper** mettre *ou* insérer une annonce dans le journal; **to p. a man on the moon** envoyer un homme sur la lune; **to p. a man into orbit** mettre un homme en orbite; **to p. a bowl/a chair into sb's hands** mettre un bol/une chaise entre les mains de qn; **to p. a coin/a letter/a gun into sb's hand** glisser une pièce/une lettre/un revolver dans la main de qn; **to p. a limit/tax on sth** mettre une limite à/une taxe sur qch; **to p. a ban on sth** interdire qch; **to p. a ban on sb doing sth** interdire à qn de faire qch; *F* **p. it there!** (*shake hands*) touchez là!; **to p. oneself into sb's hands** s'en remettre à qn; **to p. a matter into sb's hands** confier une affaire à qn; *Fig* **to p. sb in his/her place** (*reprimand*) remettre qn à sa place; *Fig* **he didn't know where to p. himself** il ne savait plus où se mettre; **p.**

yourself in my position *or* **place** mettez-vous à ma place; **p. it out of your mind** *or* **head** sors-le-toi de la tête; **I had long put this thought out of my mind** ça faisait longtemps que je m'étais sorti cette idée de la tête; **to p. one's signature to sth** apposer sa signature sur *ou* à qch; **to p. one's name to sth** prêter son nom à qch; **to p. honour before riches** préférer l'honneur à l'argent; **to p. a matter right** arranger une affaire, remettre les choses au point; **to p. sb out of suspense** tirer qn du doute; **to p. sb against sb** monter qn contre qn; **to p. an article on the market** mettre un article en vente *ou* sur le marché; **to p. a play on the stage** monter une pièce; **to p. one's thoughts into words** traduire ses pensées par des mots; **to p. money into an undertaking** mettre de l'argent dans une affaire; **to p. money on a horse** miser *ou* parier sur un cheval; **to p. some energy into finishing a job** mettre de l'énergie à achever une tâche; **to p. a lot of work into sth/doing sth** beaucoup travailler à qch/pour faire qch

(b) (*present*) **to p. a question to sb** poser une question à qn; **to p. a case before sb** soumettre un cas à qn; **to p. a resolution to the meeting** présenter une résolution à l'assemblée; *Jur* **I p. it to you that ...** n'est-il pas vrai que ...?; **I put it to him that it would be better to ...** je lui ai suggéré qu'il vaudrait mieux ...; **to p. the case clearly** exposer clairement la situation; **what did you p. for question three?** qu'est-ce que tu as mis à la troisième question?

(c) (*express*) **to p. it bluntly** pour parler franc; **you could have put that better** tu aurais pu tourner cela un peu mieux; **if one may p. it in that way** si l'on peut s'exprimer ainsi; **I wouldn't p. it quite like that** je ne dirais pas cela; **I don't know how to p. it** je ne sais comment dire; **to p. it another way, ...** en d'autres termes, ...; **'to encourage the others', as Voltaire puts it** 'pour encourager les autres' comme dirait Voltaire

(d) (*estimate*) estimer, évaluer; **to p. the population at 10,000** estimer *ou* évaluer la population à 10 000; **I would p. her on a par with** *or* **in the same class as Henry James** je la mettrais dans la même catégorie que Henry James; **I wouldn't have put her age at more than 25** je ne lui aurais pas donné plus de 25 ans; **what would you p. it at?** quelle est votre estimation?

(e) to p. an end to sth mettre fin à qch; **to p. a stop to sth** mettre un terme à qch

(f) (*cause to do, go, be etc*) **to p. sb to do sth** (*to make, have sb do sth*) faire faire qch à qn; (*to designate sb to do sth*) désigner qn pour faire qch; **to p. sb in(to) a good/bad mood** mettre qn de bonne/mauvaise humeur; **to p. a guard on the door** faire surveiller la porte; **to p. a child to bed** mettre un enfant au lit; **to p. sth to (a) good use** faire bon usage de qch, bien employer *ou* utiliser qch; **to p. sb to the test** mettre qn à l'épreuve; **to p. a resolution to the vote** mettre une résolution aux voix; **to p. the enemy to flight** mettre l'ennemi en fuite; **to p. sb to sleep** endormir qn; *Euph* **to have a dog put to sleep** faire piquer un chien; **I'm putting you to a lot of trouble** je vous cause beaucoup d'ennuis; **to p. sb to work** mettre qn au travail (**on sth** sur qch)

(g) (*direct, force*) **to p. a bullet through sb's head** mettre *ou* loger une balle dans la tête de qn; **to p. one's fist through the window** enfoncer la fenêtre d'un coup de poing; *Sp* **to p. the shot** lancer le poids

2 *vi Naut* **to p. (out) to sea** prendre la mer *ou* le large; **to p. into port** faire escale, relâcher, faire relâche

▶ **put about 1** *vtsep* **(a)** (*spread*) (*rumour*) faire circuler; **to p. it about that ...** faire circuler le bruit que ...; **it's being put about by her rivals that ...** ses rivaux font circuler le bruit que ...; **it is being put about that ...** il paraîtrait que ..., le bruit court que ... **(b)** *Naut* **to p. a ship about** virer de bord **(c)** *F* (*be sexually promiscuous*) **to p. oneself about, to p. it about** coucher avec tout le monde **2** *vi Naut* virer de bord

▶ **put across** *vtsep* **(a)** (*communicate*) (*feeling*) communiquer; (*message, idea*) faire passer; **to p. sth across to sb** faire comprendre qch à qn; **she knows how to p. her ideas across** elle sait bien faire passer ses idées; **he's good at putting himself across at interviews** il sait se faire valoir dans les entretiens; **he put himself across badly at the interview** il a donné une mauvaise image de lui-même à l'entretien; **it doesn't p. across the sense of size you get from the place** cela ne restitue pas le sentiment d'immensité qu'on ressent à cet endroit **(b)** *F* **to p. one across on sb** (*trick*) rouler qn, avoir qn

▶ **put around** *vtsep* = **put about 1 (a)**

▶ **put aside** *vtsep* (*place on one side*) (*one's book etc*) poser à côté de soi; (*keep*) mettre de côté; *Fig* (*hope, idea*) renoncer à; *Fig* (*save*) (*money etc*) mettre de côté; **if we p. aside the emotional trauma caused** mis à part le choc émotionnel provoqué; **p. aside all gloomy thoughts** oublie toutes ces pensées maussades; **let's try to p. aside our differences** essayons de laisser nos différends de côté

▶ **put away** *vtsep* **(a)** (*tidy away*) ranger; (*return to its place*) remettre à sa place; (*car*) garer; **p. your money/wallet away** (*I'm paying*) range ton argent/ton portefeuille **(b)** (*save*) mettre de côté; **to p. something away for one's old age** mettre quelque chose de côté pour sa retraite **(c)** *F* (*lock up*) (*in prison*) mettre en taule; (*in asylum etc*) (faire) enfermer **(d)** *F* (*consume*) (*food*) avaler, expédier; (*drink*) siffler; **he can really p. it away** (*drink*) il a une bonne descente; (*food*) il a un appétit d'ogre

▶ **put back 1** *vtsep* **(a)** (*restore to its position*) remettre à sa place; **to p. sth back where one found it** remettre qch là où on l'a trouvé **(b)** (*postpone*) (*meeting etc*) reporter; (*turn back hands of*) (*clock, watch*) retarder; *Fig* **this decision has put the clock back** cette décision nous a ramenés en arrière; *Sch* **his absence has put him back** son absence l'a retardé dans ses études **2** *vi Naut* retourner *ou* revenir *ou* rentrer au port

▶ **put by** *vtsep* (*money*) mettre de côté; (*supplies etc*) mettre en réserve; **to have something put by** (*savings*) avoir des économies

▶ **put down 1** *vtsep* **(a)** (*set down*) poser; **to p. sth down on the ground** poser *ou* déposer qch par terre; *Tel* **to p. down the receiver** *or* **the phone** raccrocher; **p. that gun down!** pose ce revolver!; **to p. down passengers** (*of bus etc*) débarquer *ou* déposer *ou* laisser descendre des voyageurs; **to p. the baby down** (*put to bed*) mettre le bébé au lit, coucher le bébé; **to p. down roots** (*of plant, Fig of person*) s'enraciner; **I couldn't p. it down** (*book*) je l'ai lu d'un trait

(b) (*suppress*) (*revolt, opposition*) réprimer

(c) (*close*) (*umbrella*) fermer

(d) (*write*) noter; **to p. sth down in writing** mettre *ou Fml* coucher qch par écrit; **to p. down one's name** (*enrol*) s'inscrire, se faire inscrire (**for** pour); *F* **p. me down for a ticket/to play** mets-moi sur la liste pour les tickets/des joueurs; **p. me down for £5** inscris-moi pour 5 livres; **p. it down to me** *or* **to my account** inscrivez-le *ou* mettez-le sur mon compte; **we'll have to p. it down to experience** au moins on a appris quelque chose; **to p. sb/sth down as sth** classer qn/qch comme qch; **I should p. her down as thirty** je lui donne trente ans

(e) (*attribute*) **to p. sth down to sb/sth** attribuer *ou* imputer qch à qn/qch; **I p. his success down to luck** j'attribue son succès à la chance

(f) (*pay*) **to p. some money down (as a deposit)** verser *ou* déposer une caution; **how much can you p. down?** combien pouvez-vous verser *ou* déposer en caution?; **I've put £500 down on my new car** j'ai versé 500 livres d'arrhes pour ma nouvelle voiture

(g) (*kill*) (*animal*) abattre; *Vet* **to have a dog put down** faire piquer un chien

(h) (*say negative things about*) dire du mal de; **you're always putting me down** tu n'arrêtes pas de me critiquer; **you shouldn't p. yourself down** tu ne devrais pas te sous-estimer

(i) *esp Parl* **to p. down a motion of censure** déposer une motion de censure

(j) (*wine*) mettre en cave

2 *vi Av* atterrir

▶ **put forward** *vtsep* **(a)** (*suggest*) (*plan, theory etc*) avancer, mettre en avant; (*claim*) émettre; **to p. sb** *or* **sb's name forward (for a post)** suggérer qn *ou* le nom de qn (pour un poste); **to p. oneself forward** (*get oneself noticed*) se mettre en avant; **to p. one's best foot forward** (*walk faster*) presser le pas; *Fig* se mettre en devoir de faire de son mieux **(b)** (*advance*) (*clock, time of meeting etc*) avancer

▶ **put in 1** *vtsep* **(a)** (*place in*) mettre; **to p. one's contact lenses in** mettre ses lentilles de contact; **to p. one's head in at the window** passer la tête par la fenêtre; **you only get out what you p. in** on ne récolte que ce qu'on sème; **and it was before twelve, she put in spitefully** et il n'était pas midi, ajouta-t-elle méchamment; **to p. in a (good) word for sb** dire un mot en faveur de qn

(b) (*install*) installer; **we're having a new telephone put in** on nous installe un nouveau téléphone; **the voters put the Tories in** les électeurs ont mis les conservateurs au pouvoir

(c) (*enter*) présenter; **to p. in a claim/an application** déposer une réclamation/une candidature; **we're putting him in for the 500 metres** nous le présentons pour le 500 mètres; **to p. pupils in for an examination** présenter des élèves à un examen

(d) (*spend time doing*) **to p. in an hour's work** faire une heure de travail; **she's put in a lot of time on this project** elle a passé beaucoup de temps sur ce projet; **they've put in a tremendous amount of work** ils ont fourni une quantité de travail remarquable

2 *vi* **(a)** *Naut* **to p. in at a port** faire escale *ou* relâcher dans un port

(b) *(apply)* **to p. in for an election/for a job** poser sa candidature à une élection/à un poste; **to p. in for two days' leave** demander un congé *ou Mil* une permission de 48 heures

▶ **put off 1** *vtsep* **(a)** *(postpone)* *(meeting, appointment)* remettre *ou* renvoyer à plus tard, ajourner, repousser; *(decision, payment)* remettre à plus tard, différer; *(work)* remettre à plus tard; *(guests)* décommander; **to p. off doing sth** remettre à plus tard de faire qch; **he put off telling her for as long as possible** il a repoussé le plus possible le moment de lui dire; **don't keep putting things off** ne remettez pas toujours à plus tard; *Prov* **never p. off till tomorrow what you can do today** il ne faut jamais remettre au lendemain ce que l'on peut faire le jour même; **let's p. lunch off to another time** nous déjeunerons ensemble une autre fois

(b) *(make excuses to)* **to p. sb off** donner le change à qn, entortiller qn; **to p. sb off with an excuse** se débarrasser de qn *ou* renvoyer qn avec une excuse; **I won't be put off any longer** j'en ai assez qu'on m'entortille

(c) *(allow to get off bus etc)* laisser descendre; *(force to get off)* faire descendre; **could you p. me off at the High Street?** pourriez-vous me laisser descendre *ou* m'arrêter à High Street?

(d) *(switch off)* *(television, radio etc)* éteindre

(e) *(cause dislike in)* *(person)* dégoûter; **there's something about him that puts me off** il y a quelque chose en lui qui me dégoûte; **the mere smell of that cheese puts me off** l'odeur de ce fromage suffit à m'écœurer; **don't be put off by his gruff manner** ne te laisse pas décourager *ou* rebuter par ses manières rébarbatives

2 *vtas* *(disturb)* *(person)* déconcerter, dérouter, troubler; **these interruptions p. me off** ces interruptions me déconcentrent; **the noise was putting her off her tennis** le bruit l'empêchait de bien jouer au tennis; **the worry was putting me off my food** l'inquiétude me coupait l'appétit

3 *vi Naut* déborder du quai, pousser au large; **to p. off from the shore** quitter la côte, prendre le large

▶ **put on** *vtsep* **(a)** *(clothes, shoes)* mettre; **to p. on one's make-up** se maquiller

(b) *(assume)* **to p. on an air of innocence** prendre *ou* se donner un air innocent; **to p. on an act** jouer la comédie; **to p. on an accent** prendre un accent; *F* **you're putting it on!** tout ça c'est du chiqué!

(c) *esp Am F* *(deceive)* **she's putting you on** elle te fait marcher

(d) *(present)* *Th* *(play)* monter; *TV, Rad* *(programme)* diffuser, passer; *TV, Rad* **why can't they p. something decent on for a change?** ils ne pourraient pas passer quelque chose d'intéressant pour une fois?

(e) *(add to weight, price etc)* **to p. on weight** grossir, prendre du poids; **I've put on five kilos** j'ai pris cinq kilos, j'ai grossi de cinq kilos; **they've put 2p on (the price)** on a augmenté le prix de 2 pence

(f) *(switch on)* *(light, gas)* allumer; *(radio, television)* allumer, mettre; **he put on some Vivaldi/the news** il a mis du Vivaldi/les informations; **to p. the kettle on** mettre la bouilloire à chauffer; **to p. the potatoes on** *(to cook)* mettre les pommes de terre à cuire; *(to heat up)* faire chauffer les pommes de terre; **to p. on a record/a tape** passer un disque/une cassette; **to p. on the brake(s)** freiner

(g) *(put into service)* *(train)* mettre en service; **to p. on speed** prendre de la vitesse

(h) *Horseracing etc* *(bet)* **to p. on £1** miser 1 livre

(i) *(advance)* *(clock)* avancer

(j) *(on telephone)* **could you p. him on, please?** pouvez-vous me le passer, s'il vous plaît?

▶ **put on to** *vtaspo* **(a)** *(provide with information about)* **to p. sb on to sth** indiquer qch à qn; **who put you on to it?** *F* qui est-ce qui vous a donné le tuyau?; **who put the police on to me?** qui m'a dénoncé à la police? **(b)** *Tel* **would you p. me on to Mr Lawrence?** voulez-vous me passer M. Lawrence?

▶ **put out 1** *vtsep* **(a)** *(place outside)* mettre dehors; **to p. the cat out** mettre le chat dehors; **to p. the rubbish out** sortir la/les poubelle(s); *Naut* **to p. out a boat** mettre un canot à l'eau; **to p. one's head out of the window** passer la tête par la fenêtre; **the snail put out its horns** l'escargot a sorti ses cornes; **to p. out peace feelers** envoyer des sondages de paix; **to p. sb's eyes out** crever les yeux à qn, éborgner qn

(b) *(arrange for use)* sortir, préparer; **I've put your clothes out** je t'ai sorti *ou* préparé tes vêtements

(c) *(extend)* *(one's hand)* avancer, tendre; *(one's arm)* allonger, tendre; **to p. out one's tongue** tirer la langue; **she put out a foot to trip him up** elle a mis un pied en avant pour le faire trébucher

(d) *(issue)* *(new record, edition, model etc)* sortir; *(appeal, request)* faire; *(statement)* émettre

(e) *(extinguish)* *(candle, fire, light)* éteindre; *(gas)* fermer

(f) *(make unconscious)* *(patient)* endormir

2 *vtas* **(a)** *(make angry)* *(person)* ennuyer, fâcher, contrarier; **to be put out about sth** être mécontent de qch; **she gets terribly put out if you don't agree with her** elle s'énerve si on n'est pas d'accord avec elle

(b) *(inconvenience)* *(person)* déranger, incommoder, gêner; **you mustn't p. yourself out for me** il ne faut pas vous déranger pour moi; **would one more guest p. you out?** est-ce qu'un invité de plus te dérangerait?; **I don't want to p. anyone out** je ne veux déranger personne

(c) *(dislocate)* **to p. one's back/shoulder out** se démettre le dos/l'épaule

(d) **to p. a cow out to grass** mettre une vache en pâture; **to p. money out (to interest)** placer de l'argent (à intérêt); **to p. work out** *(subcontract)* mettre du travail en sous-traitance; **to p. work out to tender** mettre du travail en adjudication

3 *vi* **(a)** *Naut* **to p. out (to sea)** prendre le large *ou* la mer

(b) *Am Sl* **she puts out for anyone** *(is promiscuous)* elle coucherait avec le premier venu

▶ **put over** *vtsep* **(a)** *(communicate)* = **put across** *(a)* **(b)** *US* *(postpone)* remettre à plus tard, différer **(c)** *F* **to p. one over on sb** avoir qn

▶ **put through 1** *vtsep* **(a)** *(carry through)* *(project)* mener à bien, faire aboutir; *(have accepted)* *(deal)* faire accepter

(b) *Tel* *(connect)* **to p. sb through to sb** mettre qn en ligne avec qn, passer qn à qn; **p. him through, please** mettez-le en ligne *ou* passez-le moi, s'il vous plaît; **I'll p. you through to him** je vous le passe

2 *vtaspo* **(a)** *(cause to suffer)* **you've put your mother through a lot of worry** tu as causé beaucoup d'inquiétude à ta mère; **I've put myself through hell for you** j'ai souffert le martyre pour toi; *F* **to p. sb through it** *(at interview etc)* mettre qn à l'épreuve **to p. sb through an ordeal** faire subir une rude épreuve à qn; **have you any idea what you're putting him through?** as-tu la moindre idée de ce que tu lui fais subir?

(b) *(subject to)* **to p. sb/sth through sth** soumettre qn/qch à qch, faire subir qch à qn/qch; **to p. oneself through sth** endurer qch

(c) **she put herself through university** elle s'est payé ses études à l'université

▶ **put to** *vtaspo* *(only in passive)* **to be hard put to it to do sth** avoir beaucoup de mal à faire qch

▶ **put together** *vtsep* **(a)** *(place side by side)* *(two objects)* mettre côte à côte; *(facts)* rapprocher, comparer

(b) *(assemble)* *(parts, components)* assembler, mettre ensemble; *(machine etc)* monter, assembler; *(meal)* préparer, confectionner; *(menu)* élaborer; *(report, story, programme)* mettre sur pied; *(team, show)* monter; *(different elements, contrasting things)* réunir, rassembler; **the programme is nicely put together** ce programme est bien fait; **to p. together a convincing picture of what happened** reconstituer une idée convaincante de ce qui s'est passé; *F* **to p. two and two together** tirer ses conclusions; **I'll just p. a few things together (in my bag)** je vais faire rapidement ma valise; **she's got more brains than the rest of them put together** elle est plus intelligente qu'eux tous mis ensemble

▶ **put up 1** *vtsep* **(a)** *(raise)* *(one's hair, collar of coat etc)* relever; *(umbrella)* ouvrir; *(rocket, distress flare)* envoyer; **could all those going p. up their hands?** que tous ceux qui y vont lèvent la main; **p. up your hands!, p. your hands up!** haut les mains!; *F* **p. them up!** *(in robbery)* haut les mains!; *(before fight)* défends-toi!; **I'm going to p. my feet up for a few minutes** je vais me reposer un peu

(b) *(erect)* *(ladder, tent etc)* dresser; *(house etc)* construire, bâtir; *(monument)* ériger; *(scaffolding)* installer, monter

(c) *(attach to wall)* *(painting)* fixer, accrocher; *(poster)* *(with paste)* coller; *(notice etc)* afficher; *(curtain)* poser, accrocher; *(wallpaper)* poser

(d) *(increase)* *(prices)* augmenter

(e) *(provide accommodation for)* loger, héberger; **I can't p. you up** je ne peux pas vous loger *ou* vous héberger

(f) *(offer)* *(candidate)* proposer **(for the elections** aux élections); **to p. sth up for sale** mettre qch en vente; **to p. a**

picture up for auction mettre un tableau aux enchères; **to p. up resistance** *or* **a fight** *or* **a struggle** (*physically*) opposer une résistance; (*morally*) s'opposer; **to p. up a good case for sth** présenter de bons arguments en faveur de qch

(**g**) (*provide*) (*sum of money*) fournir; **to p. up the money for an undertaking** fournir les fonds d'une entreprise

(**h**) (*sword*) baisser

2 *vi* (**a**) (*stay*) **to p. up at a hotel** descendre dans un hôtel; **I've been putting up at a hotel for three weeks** ça fait trois semaines que je suis à l'hôtel; **where are you putting up?** où est-ce que tu loges?; (*in hotel*) où es-tu descendu?

(**b**) (*of candidate*) **to p. up for the council** poser sa candidature comme conseiller; **to p. up for re-election** se présenter pour être réélu

(**c**) *F* **p. up or shut up!** montrez la couleur de votre argent d'abord!

▶ **put upon** *vipo* **to p. upon sb** (*abuse*) abuser de qn; (*exploit*) exploiter qn; **I won't be put upon** je refuse qu'on abuse de moi

▶ **put up to** *vtaspo* **to p. sb up to doing sth** (*incite*) inciter qn à faire qch; **who put you up to it?** (*put the idea into your head*) qui vous a donné l'idée de faire ça?; (*made you do it*) qui vous a fait faire ça?

▶ **put up with** *vipo* (*tolerate*) supporter, tolérer; **we'll have to p. up with it** il faut l'accepter *ou* nous y résigner; **I don't know how you p. up with the noise** je ne sais pas comment tu peux supporter tout ce bruit; **I'll have to p. up with him** il faudra bien que je le supporte

putative ['pju:tətɪv] *adj attrib Fml* (*father, heir*) putatif

put-down *n F* affront *m*

put-in *n Rugby* introduction *f*

put-on 1 *adj* (*air, smile*) affecté; (*joy*) affecté, feint **2** *n esp Am F* (*deception*) **it's just a p.** c'est du chiqué, c'est de la comédie; **the whole thing was a p. to gain sympathy** toute l'histoire n'était qu'un subterfuge pour s'attirer de la sympathie

put-put[1] ['pʌtpʌt] *n* (*sound*) teuf-teuf *m*

put-put[2] *vi* (*of small engine etc*) faire teuf-teuf

putrefaction [pju:trɪ'fækʃən] *n* putréfaction *f*

putrefy ['pju:trɪfaɪ] **1** *vt* putréfier, pourrir **2** *vi* se putréfier, pourrir, suppurer, s'envenimer; **putrefying corpse** cadavre en état de putréfaction

putrescence [pju:'tresəns] *n Fml* putrescence *f*

putrescent [pju:'tresənt] *adj Fml* putrescent, en putréfaction

putrid ['pju:trɪd] *adj* (**a**) putride (**b**) *F* (*disgusting, horrible*) dégoûtant, dégueulasse

putsch [pʊtʃ] *n* putsch *m*

putt[1] [pʌt] *n Golf* putt *m*; **to hole a long p.** rentrer un long putt

putt[2] *vti Golf* putter

putter[1] ['pʌtər] *n Golf* (*club*) putter *m*; **good/bad p.** (*person*) joueur, -euse qui putte bien

putter[2] *vi US* = **potter**[2]

putting ['pʌtɪŋ] *n* (*game*), *Golf* putting *m*; **to practise p.** s'exercer à putter; **p. green** (putting-)green *m, pl* (putting-)greens; **p. iron** putter *m*

putto, *pl* **putti** ['pʊtəʊ, -ti:] *n Art* putto *m, pl* putti

putty[1] ['pʌtɪ] *n* mastic *m*; **to fill a hole with p.** boucher un trou au mastic, mastiquer un trou; **my legs felt like p.** j'avais les jambes en coton; **p.-coloured** grisâtre; **to be like p. in sb's hands** être comme un petit enfant dans les mains de qn; **p. knife** spatule *f* de vitrier

putty[2] *vt* (*hole*) mastiquer, boucher au mastic

put-up ['pʊtʌp] *adj F* **a p. job** une affaire préparée à l'avance; (*trap*) un coup monté

put-upon *adj* **she was feeling p.** elle avait l'impression qu'on abusait de sa gentillesse; **a p. expression** une tête de martyr

put-you-up *n* canapé-lit *m, pl* canapés-lits

puzzle[1] ['pʌzl] *n* (**a**) (*game*) (*manual*) casse-tête *m inv*; (*mental*) devinette *f*; **p. book** livre *m* de jeux et devinettes (**b**) (*mystery*) énigme *f*

puzzle[2] **1** *vt* (*person*) intriguer, laisser perplexe; **puzzled look** air *m* perplexe; **I was puzzled** j'étais perplexe, je ne savais que penser; **he puzzles me** il m'intrigue, c'est une énigme pour moi; **I am puzzled to know why you have done this** ça m'intrigue de savoir pourquoi tu as fait ça; **to p. one's head over sth** se casser la tête sur qch, chercher à comprendre qch **2** *vi* **to p. about sth** chercher à comprendre qch

▶ **puzzle out** *vtsep* (*problem*) résoudre; (*solution, meaning*) trouver; **I'm still trying to p. out how he did it** je cherche toujours à comprendre comment il l'a fait

▶ **puzzle over** *vipo* (*wonder about*) chercher à comprendre, se casser la tête sur

puzzlement ['pʌzlmənt] *n* perplexité *f*; **to look at sb in p.** regarder qn d'un air perplexe; **an expression of p.** un air perplexe; **much to my p.** à ma grande surprise

puzzler ['pʌzlər] *n F* (*mystery*) énigme *f*; **that's a p.!** (*problem*) voilà une question difficile!

puzzling ['pʌzlɪŋ] *adj* curieux, bizarre

PVC [pi:vi:'si:] *n* (*abbr* **polyvinyl chloride**) PVC *m*; **a P. belt** une ceinture en PVC

PW [pi:'dʌb(ə)lju:] *n* (*abbr* **policewoman**) femme *f* policier

PWR [pi:dʌb(ə)lju:'ɑ:r] *n Nucl Phys* (*abbr* **pressurized-water reactor**) REP *m* (réacteur à eau pressurisée)

PX [pi:'eks] *n US Mil* (*abbr* **post exchange**) foyer *m*

pygmy ['pɪgmɪ] **1** *n* pygmée *m* **2** *adj* pygmée

pyjama [pə'dʒɑ:mə] *n* [①**A10**,e] *esp Br* **(pair of) pyjamas** pyjama *m*; **he's in pyjamas** il est en pyjama; **p. bottoms** *or* **trousers** pantalon *m* de pyjama; **p. jacket** veste *f* de pyjama; **p. party** = fête *f* où tous les invités portent un pyjama; **p. top** (*jacket*) veste de pyjama; (*pull-on type*) haut *m* de pyjama

pylon ['paɪlən] *n* (**a**) (*of metal, reinforced concrete*) pylône *m*; (**electricity**) **p.** pylône (de transformateur électrique) (**b**) *Archit* (*gateway*) pylône *m*

pyorrhea [paɪə'rɪə] *n Med* pyorrhée *f*

pyramid ['pɪrəmɪd] *n Archit, Math* pyramide *f*; **p. selling** vente *f* à la boule de neige, vente pyramidale

pyramidal [pɪ'ræmɪd(ə)l] *adj Fml* pyramidal

pyre ['paɪər] *n* (**funeral**) **p.** bûcher *m* (funéraire)

Pyrenean [pɪrə'ni:ən] *adj* pyrénéen, des Pyrénées; **P. mountain dog** saint-bernard *m inv* des Pyrénées

Pyrenees (the) [ðəpɪrə'ni:z] *npl* les Pyrénées *fpl*

pyrethrum [paɪ'ri:θrəm] *n* (*plant*) pyrèthre *m*

pyretic [paɪ'retɪk] *adj Med* pyrétique

Pyrex® ['paɪreks] *n* Pyrex® *m*; **P. dish** plat *m* en Pyrex

pyrites [paɪ'raɪti:z] *n Miner* pyrite *f*; **iron p.** pyrite de fer, fer *m* sulfuré

pyritic [paɪ'rɪtɪk] *adj Miner* pyriteux

pyromaniac [paɪrəʊ'meɪnɪæk] *n* pyromane *mf*

pyrotechnic [paɪrəʊ'teknɪk] *adj usu attrib* pyrotechnique; **p. display** feu *m* d'artifice

pyrotechnics [paɪrəʊ'teknɪks] *n* [①**A10**,c] pyrotechnie *f*; (*fireworks*) feux *mpl* d'artifice; *Fig* (*of style etc*) fioritures *fpl*

Pyrrhic ['pɪrɪk] *adj Antiq* de Pyrrhus; *Fig* **P. victory** victoire *f* à la Pyrrhus, victoire désastreuse

Pythagoras [paɪ'θægərəs] *n* Pythagore *m*

Pythagorean [paɪθægə'ri:ən] *adj* pythagoricien

python ['paɪθən] *n* python *m*

pyx [pɪks] *n Rel* ciboire *m*

pzazz [pə'zæz] *n F* (*flair*) punch *m*

Q

Q, q [kjuː] *n* (*letter*) Q, q *m*; **two Q's** *or* **Qs** deux Q.
q *Sch etc* (*abbr* **question**) q.
QC [kjuː'siː] *n Br Jur abbr* **Queen's Counsel**
QE2 [kjuːiː'tuː] *n Br Naut* (*abbr* **Queen Elizabeth II**) = le paquebot reine Elizabeth II
QED [kjuːiː'diː] (*abbr* **quod erat demonstrandum**) CQFD (ce qu'il fallait démontrer)
QIP [kjuːaɪ'piː] *n* (*abbr* **quality improvement programme**) programme *m* d'amélioration de la qualité
QM [kjuː'em] *n Mil abbr* **Quartermaster**
QMG [kjuːem'dʒiː] *n Mil* (*abbr* **Quartermaster General**) = Directeur *m* de l'Intendance (militaire)
qt, *pl* **qts** *abbr* **quart,** *pl* **quarts**
q.t. [kjuː'tiː] *n F* (*abbr* **quiet**) **to do sth on the q.t.** faire qch en douce; **to tell sb sth on the q.t.** dire qch à qn discrètement *ou* en confidence; **this is strictly on the q.t.** c'est confidentiel
qty *Com abbr* **quantity**
qua [kwɑː] *prep Fml* **alcohol q. alcohol** l'alcool en tant que tel
quack[1] [kwæk] **1** *int* **q.! q.!** coin-coin! **2** *n* **(a)** (*cry*) coin-coin *m inv* **(b)** (*in children's language*) **q.-q.** (*duck*) canard *m*
quack[2] *vi* **(a)** (*of duck*) cancaner, *F* faire coin-coin **(b)** *F* (*of person*) jacasser
quack[3] *n Pej* **(a) q. (doctor)** (*unqualified*) charlatan *m*; **q. remedy** remède *m* de charlatan; *Fig* fausse solution *f* **(b)** *F* (*doctor*) toubib *m*
quackery ['kwækərɪ] *n* charlatanisme *m*, charlatanerie *f*
quad[1] [kwɒd] *n Sch F* cour *f*
quad[2] *n F* (*child*) quadruplé, -ée
quad[3] *adj Comptr* **q. density** densité *f* quadruple
quadragenarian [kwɒdrədʒə'neərɪən] *adj, n* quadragénaire *mf*
Quadragesima [kwɒdrə'dʒesɪmə] *n Rel* **Q. (Sunday)** (le dimanche de) la Quadragésime
quadrangle ['kwɒdræŋg(ə)l] *n* **(a)** *Geom* figure *f* quadrangulaire, quadrilatère *m* **(b)** (*courtyard*) (*at school, college etc*) cour *f*; *Archit* cour carrée
quadrangular [kwɒ'dræŋgjʊlər] *adj* quadrangulaire
quadrant ['kwɒdrənt] *n Astron, Geom* (*of circle*) quart *m* de cercle; (*of surface*), *Naut* quadrant *m*
quadraphonic [kwɒdrə'fɒnɪk] *adj* quadriphonique, tétraphonique
quadraphonics [kwɒdrə'fɒnɪks] *n sing* [①A10,c] quadriphonie *f*, tétraphonie *f*
quadrasonic [kwɒdrə'sɒnɪk] *adj* tétraphonique
quadratic [kwɒ'drætɪk] *adj Math* (*equation*) quadratique, du second degré
quadrature ['kwɒdrətʃər] *n Math, Astron* quadrature *f*; **q. of the circle** quadrature du cercle
quadrennial [kwɒ'drenɪəl] *adj* quadriennal
quadri- ['kwɒdrɪ] *pref* quadri-
quadrilateral [kwɒdrɪ'lætər(ə)l] *Geom etc* **1** *adj* quadrilatéral **2** *n* quadrilatère *m*
quadrille [kwə'drɪl] *n Mus* quadrille *m*
quadrillion [kwɒ'drɪlɪən] *n Br* quadrillion *m* (10^{24}); *Am* mille billions (10^{15})
quadriplegia [kwɒdrɪ'pliːdʒɪə] *n Med* tétraplégie *f*, quadriplégie *f*
quadriplegic [kwɒdrɪ'pliːdʒɪk] *adj, n Med* tétraplégique *mf*, quadriplégique *mf*
quadroon [kwɒ'druːn] *adj, n* quarteron, -onne
quadruped ['kwɒdrʊped] *adj, n* quadrupède *m*
quadruple[1] [kwɒ'druːp(ə)l] *adj, n* quadruple *m*
quadruple[2] *vti* quadrupler
quadruplet [kwɒ'druːplɪt, 'kwɒdrʊplɪt] *n* **(a)** (*child*) quadruplé, -ée **(b)** *Mus* quartolet *m*
quadruplicate[1] [kwɒ'druːplɪkət] *adj* quadruple; **in q.** en quatre exemplaires
quadruplicate[2] [kwɒ'druːplɪkeɪt] *vt* **(a)** (*multiply by four*) quadrupler, multiplier par quatre **(b)** (*make four copies of*) (*letter etc*) faire *ou* tirer quatre exemplaires de
quaff [kwɒf] *vt Lit* (*wine*) boire à longs traits; (*glass*) vider d'un trait
quagmire ['kwægmaɪər, 'kwɒg-] *n* (*bog*) marécage *m*; *Fig* (*awkward situation*) bourbier *m*
quail[1] [kweɪl] *n inv* (*bird*) caille *f* (des blés), *Can* colin *m*; **q.'s eggs** œufs *mpl* de caille
quail[2] *vi Lit* (*of person*) fléchir, faiblir (**before** devant); **his heart quailed** son cœur défaillit
quaint [kweɪnt] *adj* (*unusual*) curieux; (*attractively old-fashioned*) suranné, vieillot, -otte; (*picturesque*) pittoresque; (*little dog, little hat, wording, little poem*) mignon, -onne; **he has this q. hope that he'll find a permanent job** il croit naïvement qu'il va trouver un emploi permanent; **a q. little cottage** une petite chaumière pittoresque
quaintly ['kweɪntlɪ] *adv* (*unusually*) curieusement; (*picturesquely*) de façon pittoresque; **q. old-fashioned** d'un charme vieillot; **rather q. worded** formulé de façon assez mignonne
quaintness ['kweɪntnɪs] *n* (*unusualness*) étrangeté *f*; (*old-fashioned charm*) pittoresque *m* suranné; **the q. of the wording** la façon assez mignonne dont c'était formulé
quake[1] [kweɪk] *n* **(a)** *F* (*earthquake*) tremblement *m* de terre **(b)** (*shaking*) tremblement *m*
quake[2] *vi* **(a)** (*of person*) trembler, frémir (**with fear** de crainte); **to q. in one's shoes** trembler de peur; **he was quaking with laughter** il était secoué de rires **(b)** (*of thing*) trembler, branler; **quaking grass** brize *f*
Quaker ['kweɪkər] *n Rel* quaker *m*, quakeresse *f*
Quakerism ['kweɪkərɪz(ə)m] *n Rel* quakerisme *m*
qualification [kwɒlɪfɪ'keɪʃən] *n* **(a)** (*diploma etc*) diplôme *m*, qualification *f*; **to have the necessary qualifications for a job** (*skills etc*) avoir les qualités *ou* les compétences requises pour remplir une fonction; (*diplomas*) avoir les diplômes requis *ou* les qualifications requises pour remplir une fonction; **paper** *or* **formal qualifications** diplômes; **professional q.** qualification professionnelle; **what are your qualifications?** quels diplômes avez-vous?; **a q. in translation** un diplôme de traduction; **one of the qualifications for this job is a sense of humour** une des qualités requises pour ce poste est le sens de l'humour

(b) (*successful completion of studies*) obtention *f* d'un diplôme; **on q.** une fois le diplôme obtenu

(c) *Sp* qualification *f*; **on q. for the World Cup** après s'être qualifié pour la Coupe du monde

(d) (*reservation*) réserve *f*, restriction *f*; (*condition*) condition *f*; **to accept without q.** (*without reservation*) accepter sans réserve; (*without conditions*) accepter sans conditions; **to add a few qualifications** (*to a statement, remarks etc*) apporter quelques modifications

(e) *Fml* (*description*) qualification *f*; **the report's q. of them as 'mercenaries'** le fait que le rapport les qualifiait de mercenaires

qualified ['kwɒlɪfaɪd] *adj* **(a)** (*competent*) (*for position etc*) qualifié, compétent, qui a les capacités requises; (*having diploma etc*) qualifié, diplômé; (*for position etc*) qui a les diplômes requis *ou* les qualifications requises; (*pilot etc*) breveté; *Jur* capable (**to do** de faire); **she's very highly q.** elle est très qualifiée; **to be q. to do sth** (*be competent*) avoir les compétences voulues *ou* les capacités requises pour faire qch; (*have diploma etc*) avoir les diplômes requis *ou* les qualifications requises pour faire qch; **I am q. to speak about it** (*I know about it*) je suis bien placé pour en parler; **to be q. to speak** (*at meeting etc*) avoir voix au chapitre; **q. persons** personnes *fpl* compétentes

(b) (*modified*) (*approval, support etc*) modéré; (*praise*) mitigé; **q. success** demi-succès *m inv*

qualifier ['kwɒlɪfaɪər] *n* **(a)** *Sp* (*person, team that qualifies*) qualifié, -ée; (*qualifying round*) série *f* éliminatoire **(b)** *Gram* qualificatif *m* **(c)** (*reservation*) restriction *f*, réserve *f*; (*condition*) condition *f*
qualify ['kwɒlɪfaɪ] **1** *vt* **(a) to q. sb for sth/for doing** *or* **to do sth** (*of course, training etc*) donner à qn les compétences voulues pour qch/pour faire qch, qualifier qn pour qch/pour faire qch; *Jur* donner qualité à qn pour qch/pour faire qch; **my knowledge qualifies me to undertake this work** j'ai les connaissances pour entreprendre cet ouvrage; **what do you**

think qualifies you for this job? en quoi vous considérez-vous comme qualifié pour cet emploi?

(**b**) (*modify*) (*consent etc*) apporter des réserves à; (*statement*) apporter des précisions à, préciser; (*enjoyment*) modérer, diminuer

(**c**) *Fml* (*describe*) **to q. sb/sth as sth** qualifier qn/qch de qch

(**d**) *Gram* qualifier

2 *vi* obtenir son diplôme; *Sp* se qualifier (**for** pour); **to q. for sth** obtenir les diplômes *ou* les qualifications nécessaires pour qch; **to q. as an engineer/a nurse/an accountant** obtenir son diplôme d'ingénieur/d'infirmière/de comptable; **to q. as a doctor** être reçu médecin; **to q. as a pilot** obtenir son brevet de pilote; **you don't q. for a grant** vous ne remplissez pas les conditions requises pour recevoir une bourse; **that doesn't q. as news** (*no-one is interested*) ça n'intéresse personne; (*the information is out of date*) ça n'a rien de nouveau; **it hardly qualifies as a mountain** on ne peut pas vraiment appeler cela une montagne

qualifying ['kwɒlɪfaɪɪŋ] *adj* (**a**) **q. examination** examen *m* pour certificat d'aptitude; (*for acceptance by a particular school*) examen d'entrée; *Sp* **q. round** série *f* éliminatoire (**b**) (*modifying*) modificateur, -trice; **q. statement** déclaration *f* corrective (**c**) *Gram* (*adjective*) qualificatif; (*adverb*) modificatif

qualitative ['kwɒlɪtətɪv] *adj* qualitatif; *Mktg* **q. forecasting** prévisions *fpl* qualitatives; *Mktg* **q. research** études *fpl* qualitatives

qualitatively ['kwɒlɪtətɪvlɪ] *adv* qualitativement

quality ['kwɒlɪtɪ] *n* (**a**) (*degree of excellence*) qualité *f*; **of good q.** de bonne qualité; **of high/poor q.** de qualité supérieure/inférieure; **high/poor q. goods** marchandises *fpl* de bonne/mauvaise qualité; **a q. service/magazine** un service/magazine de qualité; **q. matters more than quantity** la qualité importe plus que la quantité; **the q. of life** la qualité de la vie; *Com* **q. goods** marchandises de qualité; *Com* **q. improvement programme** programme *m* d'amélioration de la qualité; **q. label** label *m* de qualité; **q. newspaper** journal *m* sérieux; **q./price ratio** rapport *m* qualité/prix; *Mktg* **q. positioning** positionnement *m* par la qualité; **q. press** presse *f* de qualité; *esp Am* **to spend q. time together** passer de bons moments ensemble

(**b**) (*characteristic*) (*of person*) qualité *f*, trait *m*; (*of thing*) qualité; (*of sound, voice*) qualité, timbre *m*; **one of the qualities I look for in a friend** une des qualités que je recherche chez un ami; **moral/intellectual qualities** qualités morales/intellectuelles; **he has many (good) qualities** il a beaucoup de qualités

(**c**) *Fml* **to act in the q. of …** agir en qualité de …

(**d**) *Arch* (*high status*) **person of q.** personne *f* de qualité; **the q.** les gens *mpl* de qualité, *Pej* le beau linge

quality assurance *n* assurance *f* qualité

quality-assurance manager *n* directeur *m* de l'assurance-qualité

quality audit *n* audit *m* de qualité

quality circle *n* cercle *m* de qualité

quality control *n* contrôle *m* qualité

quality management *n* gestion *f* qualité

qualm [kwɑːm] *n* (**a**) (*pang of conscience*) scrupule *m*; **to have no qualms about doing sth** n'avoir aucun scrupule à faire qch; **I sometimes have qualms about what I did** j'ai parfois des remords pour ce que j'ai fait (**b**) (*premonition*) pressentiment *m* de malheur; (*anxiety*) inquiétude *f*; **don't you feel any qualms about getting married?** n'éprouves-tu aucune inquiétude à l'idée de te marier?

quandary ['kwɒnd(ə)rɪ] *n* dilemme *m*; **to be in a q.** (*unable to decide what to do*) ne pas trop savoir que faire; **it put him in a q.** il ne savait que faire, il était face à un dilemme

quango ['kwæŋgəʊ] *n Br* (*abbr* **quasi-autonomous non-governmental organization**) = organisation *f* non gouvernementale quasi-autonome

quantifiable [kwɒntɪ'faɪəb(ə)l] *adj* quantifiable

quantifier ['kwɒntɪfaɪər] *n* (*in logic*), *Math, Ling* quantificateur *m*

quantify ['kwɒntɪfaɪ] *vt* (**a**) (*losses, damage*) quantifier, calculer; (*influence, contribution*) quantifier, évaluer; **happiness is hard to q.** le bonheur est difficile à quantifier (**b**) (*in logic*) quantifier

quantitative ['kwɒntɪtətɪv] *adj* quantitatif; *Mktg* **q. forecasting** prévisions *fpl* quantitatives; *Mktg* **q. research** études *fpl* quantitatives

quantitatively ['kwɒntɪtətɪvlɪ] *adv* quantitativement

quantity ['kwɒntɪtɪ] *n* (**a**) [①B57,E] quantité *f*; **a small q. of** une petite quantité de; **to buy sth in large quantities** acheter qch en grande quantité; **they would drink quantities of beer** ils buvaient des litres et des litres de bière; **negligible q.** quantité négligeable; **to produce sth in q.** produire qch en quantité; *Constr* **bill of quantities** devis *m* (**b**) (*in prosody*) quantité *f*; **q. mark** signe *m* de quantité

quantity discount *n Com* escompte *m* sur achat en gros, escompte sur achats groupés, remise *f* pour quantité

quantity surveying *n* métrage *m*

quantity surveyor *n* métreur *m* (vérificateur)

quantity theory *n Econ* théorie *f* quantitative

quantum, *pl* **-a** ['kwɒntəm, -ə] *n Phys* quantum *m*; **q. leap** saut *m* quantique; *Fig* bond *m* en avant; **q. mechanics/optics/physics** mécanique *f*/optique *f*/physique *f* quantique; **q. theory** théorie *f* des quanta

quarantine[1] ['kwɒrəntiːn] *n* quarantaine *f*; **to be in q.** (*of person, animal*) être en quarantaine

quarantine[2] *vt* (*person, ship*) mettre en quarantaine

quark [kwɑːk] *n* (**a**) *Nucl Phys* quark *m* (**b**) (*soft cheese*) ≈ fromage *m* blanc

quarrel[1] ['kwɒr(ə)l] *n* (*dispute*) dispute *f*, querelle *f*; **to pick a q. with sb** faire une scène à qn, se quereller avec qn; **to try to pick a q. with sb** chercher querelle *ou* noise à qn; **they've had a q.** ils se sont disputés *ou Fml* querellés; **what was their q. about?** pourquoi se sont-ils disputés?; **to make up a q.** se réconcilier; **I have no q. with him** je n'ai rien à lui reprocher; **my q. with you is that …** ce que je te reproche c'est que …; **she has no q. with that** elle n'a rien à redire là-dessus

quarrel[2] *vi* (**-ll-**, *US* **-l-**) (**a**) se disputer, *Fml* se quereller (**with sb over** *or* **about sth** avec qn à propos de qch); **they've been quarrelling** ils se sont disputés *ou Fml* querellés; **I don't want to q.** je ne veux pas me disputer *ou F* me bagarrer (**b**) **to q. with sb for doing sth** (*find fault with*) reprocher à qn de faire qch; **to q. with sth** (*take exception to*) ne pas être d'accord avec qch; **I can't q. with that** je n'ai rien à redire à cela; **while I wouldn't q. with your figures …** bien que je ne conteste pas vos chiffres …

quarrelling, *US* **quarreling** ['kwɒr(ə)lɪŋ] **1** *adj* querelleur **2** *n* disputes *fpl*, querelles *fpl*

quarrelsome ['kwɒr(ə)lsəm] *adj* querelleur, batailleur; **in a q. mood** d'humeur batailleuse *ou* querelleuse

quarrier ['kwɒrɪər] *n* = **quarryman**

quarry[1] ['kwɒrɪ] *n* (*animal, bird, Fig person*) proie *f*

quarry[2] *n* (*for stone, slate etc*) carrière *f*; **open q.** carrière à ciel ouvert; **q. stone** moellon *m*; **q. tile** carreau *m* (de céramique)

quarry[3] **1** *vt* (*stone, slate etc*) extraire **2** *vi* exploiter une carrière; **to q. for granite** extraire du granite

▶ **quarry out** *vtsep* (*stone, slate etc*) extraire

quarrying ['kwɒrɪɪŋ] *n* exploitation *f* de carrières

quarryman, *pl* **-men** ['kwɒrɪmən] *n* (ouvrier *m*) carrier *m*; **slate q.** perrayeur *m*, perrier *m*

quart [kwɔːt] *n* (*liquid measurement*) (*in UK*) = 1,136 litres; (*in US*) = 0,946 litre; *Prov* **you can't fit a q. into a pint pot** à l'impossible, nul n'est tenu

quarte [kɑːt] *n Fencing* quarte *f*

quarter[1] ['kwɔːtər] *n* (**a**) (*portion*) (*of apple, circle, century etc*) quart *m*; (*of orange, moon*) quartier *m*; *Culin* (*of beef, lamb*) quartier; **to divide sth in(to) quarters** diviser qch en quatre; **three quarters** trois quarts; **three and a q.** trois et quart; **a q. (of a pound) of coffee** un quart (de livre) de café, = cent grammes de café; **bottle one q.** *or* **a q. full** bouteille au quart pleine; *Culin* **fore/hind q.** quartier de devant/de derrière; **moon at the first q.** lune au premier quartier; **moon in its last q.** lune dans son dernier quartier *ou* sur son décroît; **I can get it for you for a q. of the price** je peux vous l'avoir pour le quart du prix

(**b**) (*of time*) (*three-month period*) trimestre *m*; **to be paid by the q.** être payé par trimestre; **in the first q. of 1990** pendant le premier trimestre de l'année 1990; **in the first q. of the century** pendant le premier quart du siècle; **a q. to six,** *Am* **a q. of six** six heures moins le quart; **it's a q. to** il est moins le quart; **a q. past six,** *Am* **a q. after six** six heures et quart; **it's a q. past** il est le quart; **there's a train at a q. to and a q. past every hour** il y a un train à moins le quart et au quart; **a q. of an hour** un quart d'heure

(**c**) *Naut* (*direction*) aire *f* de vent, quart *m*, côté *m*; **the wind is in the right q.** le vent vient du bon côté

(**d**) (*area*) (*of town*) quartier *m*; **the slum q.** le quartier des taudis; **the residential q.** le quartier résidentiel; **from the four quarters of the globe** des quatre coins du monde; **news from all quarters** nouvelles de partout; **what is he doing in these quarters?** que fait-il dans ces parages?; **an order from high quarters** un ordre d'en haut; **in some quarters there is talk of rebellion** on parle de rébellion dans certains milieux; **you'll get no help from that q.** vous n'obtiendrez aucune aide de ce côté; **it is rumoured in** certain quarters that ... on murmure dans certains milieux que ...

(e) quarters (*lodgings*) *Mil* quartier *m*, cantonnement *m*, logement *m*; (*for servants*) appartements *mpl* (domestiques); *Av* **crew's quarters** locaux *mpl* affectés au personnel de bord

(f) *Naut* **quarters** (*stations*) postes *mpl*; *Naut* **to beat** *or* **pipe to quarters** battre *ou* sonner le branle-bas; *Naut* **general quarters** branle-bas de combat

(g) *esp Lit* (*mercy*) quartier *m*, merci *f*; **to give q.** faire quartier, accorder merci; **to give no q.** ne pas faire de quartier

(h) *Am* (*coin*) pièce *f* de vingt-cinq cents; (*sum*) quart *m* de dollar

quarter² *vt* (a) (*apple etc*) diviser en quatre; (*beef etc*) diviser par quartiers, équarrir; (*time, amount*) réduire des trois quarts; *Hist* (*condemned man*) écarteler; **to q. the ground** (*of hunting dogs*) quêter (b) *Mil* (*lodge*) (*troops*) cantonner, caserner, loger; **to be quartered with sb** loger chez qn

quarterback ['kwɔːtəbæk] *n Am Fb* arrière *m*; *F* **to be a Monday morning q.** être sage a posteriori

quarter binding *n* (*in bookbinding*) demi-reliure *f*

quarter day *n* (jour *m* de) terme *m*

quarterdeck ['kwɔːtədek] *n Naut* (a) plage *f* arrière (b) (*no pl*) **the q.** (*officers*) les officiers *mpl*

quarterfinal [kwɔːtə'faɪnəl] *n Sp* quart *m* de finale; **he's in the quarterfinals** il est en quarts de finale, il dispute les quarts de finale

quarterfinalist [kwɔːtə'faɪnəlɪst] *n* quart-de-finaliste *mf*

quartering ['kwɔːtərɪŋ] *n* (a) (*division*) division *f* en quatre; (*of beef, tree trunk*) équarrissage *m* (b) *Mil* (*lodging*) (*of troops*) logement *m*, cantonnement *m*, stationnement *m*

quarterlight ['kwɔːtəlaɪt] *n Aut* déflecteur *m* de porte avant

quarterly ['kwɔːtəlɪ] **1** *adj* trimestriel; (*subscription*) au trimestre **2** *n* publication *f* trimestrielle **3** *adv* trimestriellement, tous les trimestres, tous les trois mois

quartermaster ['kwɔːtəmɑːstər] *n Naut* maître *m* de timonerie; *Mil* officier *m* chargé des vivres et des fournitures; **Q. General** = Directeur *m* de l'Intendance (militaire); **q.'s store** magasin *m*

quarter note *n esp Am Mus* noire *f*

quarter sessions *npl Br Jur* assises *fpl* trimestrielles, cour *f* trimestrielle de comté

quarterstaff ['kwɔːtəstɑːf] *n Hist* (*weapon*) bâton *m*; **to fence with quarterstaffs** jouer du bâton

quarterwindow ['kwɔːtəwɪndəʊ] *n Aut* glace *f* de custode, custode *f*

quartet(te) [kwɔː'tet] *n* (a) (*players, music, group of four*) quatuor *m*; (*jazz band*) quartette *m*; **string q.** quatuor à cordes (b) *Liter* tétralogie *f*

quartile ['kwɔːtaɪl] *n* quartile *m*

quarto ['kwɔːtəʊ] *adj, n* in-quarto *m inv*

quartz [kwɔːts] *n Miner* quartz *m*; **q. clock** pendule *f* à quartz; **q. crystal** cristal *m* de quartz; **q. lamp** lampe *f* (à vapeur de mercure) à tube de quartz; **q. watch** montre *f* à quartz

quartz-halogen *n* halogène à quartz

quartzite ['kwɔːtsaɪt] *n Miner* quartzite *m*

quasar ['kweɪzɑːr] *n Astron* quasar *m*

quash [kwɒʃ] *vt* (a) (*feeling, plan*) étouffer; (*revolt*) écraser; *F* **to q. sb** écraser qn (b) *Jur* (*verdict, decision*) casser, infirmer, annuler; **to q. proceedings** *or* **an action** arrêter les poursuites

quasi- ['kweɪsaɪ, 'kwɑːzɪ] *pref* quasi-; **q.-contract** quasi-contrat *m*, *pl* quasi-contrats; **q.-scientific** quasi-scientifique, presque scientifique

quatercentenary [kwɒtəsen'tiːnərɪ] *n* quatrième centenaire *m*

quaternary [kwə'tɜːnərɪ] **1** *adj Ch, Geol, Math* quaternaire; *Geol* **the Q. era** l'ère *f* quaternaire **2** *n Geol* **the Q.** le quaternaire

quatrain ['kwɒtreɪn] *n* (*of poem*) quatrain *m*

quaver¹ ['kweɪvər] *n* (a) *Br Mus* (*note*) croche *f* (b) (*trembling*) (*in voice*) tremblement *m*, chevrotement *m*; *Mus* tremolo *m*; **to have a q. in one's voice** parler d'une voix tremblante

quaver² **1** *vi* (*of voice*) chevroter, trembloter; *Mus* faire un tremolo; **quavering voice** voix *f* tremblotante *ou* chevrotante, voix mal assurée **2** *vt* **to q. (out)** (*song*) chevroter

quay [kiː] *n* quai *m*; **alongside the q.** à quai; *Com* **ex-q.** (*goods*) à prendre *ou* livrable à quai

quayside ['kiːsaɪd] *n* quai *m*; **on the q.** sur le quai; **q. worker/crane** ouvrier *m*/grue *f* de quai

queasiness ['kwiːzɪnɪs] *n Med* nausées *fpl*; *Fig* malaise *m*

queasy ['kwiːzɪ] *adj* (*stomach*) délicat; **I feel q.** j'ai la nausée, j'ai mal au cœur; **the drugs make him q.** les médicaments lui donnent des nausées; **the very sight of meat makes her feel q.** la simple vue de la viande lui donne la nausée; **she was looking rather q.** elle avait l'air d'avoir mal au cœur; *Fig* **to feel q. about sth** se sentir mal à l'aise en ce qui concerne qch

Quebec [kwɪ'bek] *n* Québec *m*; **I'm from Q.** je suis Québecois, -oise, je suis du Québec

Quebecer [kɪ'bekər] *n* Québecois, -oise

queen¹ [kwiːn] *n* (a) reine *f*; **Q. Anne** la reine Anne; **a Q. Anne house** une maison de l'époque de la reine Anne; **the kings and queens of England** les souverains *mpl* d'Angleterre; *Br* **the Q.'s (Christmas) message** = discours *m* télévisé et radiodiffusé de la reine le jour de Noël; *Br Parl* **the Q.'s Speech** le discours de la reine marquant le début de l'année parlementaire; **the Q.'s English** l'anglais *m* correct; **don't you understand the Q.'s English?** = tu ne comprends pas le français?; **Q. of heaven** reine du ciel; *esp Iron* **she is the q. of my heart** elle règne sur mon cœur; **the rose is the q. of flowers** la rose est la reine des fleurs; *Bot* **q. of the meadows** reine des prés; **Q. Mother** reine mère

(b) *Cards* dame *f*; *Chess* reine *f*, dame; **Q. of hearts** reine des cœurs

(c) (*insect*) (*of ants etc*) reine *f*; **q. bee** reine des abeilles; *Fig* **she's the q. bee around here** c'est elle qui commande ici, c'est elle la patronne ici

(d) *Offensive Sl* (*male homosexual*) tante *f*, folle *f*

queen² **1** *vt* (a) *F* **to q. it** faire la reine *ou* jouer les personnages importants (**over sb** avec qn) (b) *Chess* (*pawn*) damer **2** *vi Chess* (*of pawn*) aller à dame

queenly ['kwiːnlɪ] *adj* de reine

Queen's Bench *n Br Jur* = section *f* de la Haute Cour Anglaise

Queen's Counsel *n Br Jur* = avocat *m* supérieur

queen-size bed *n* grand lit *m* double

queer¹ ['kwɪər] *n* (a) *Offensive Sl* (*male homosexual*) pédé *m*, pédale *f* (b) *US Sl* (*counterfeit money*) fausse monnaie *f*

queer² *adj* (a) (*strange*) bizarre, étrange, singulier; **she's a q.-looking person** elle a une drôle de tête; **she has a q.-sounding name** elle a un drôle de nom; **q. ideas** idées *fpl* bizarres *ou F* biscornues; *F* **q. in the head** toqué, timbré; *Br F* **to be in Q. Street** être dans une situation (financière) délicate (b) (*suspicious*) suspect, louche; *US Sl* **q. money** fausse monnaie *f* (c) *Offensive Sl* (*homosexual*) pédé, homo (d) *F* (*unwell*) pas bien; **I feel very q.** je me sens tout chose *ou* tout drôle; **to come over** *or* **to be taken q.** avoir un malaise

queer³ *vt F* **to q. the pitch for sb, to q. sb's pitch** bouleverser *ou* faire échouer les plans de qn

queer-bashing *n Br Offensive Sl* (*assaults on homosexuals*) chasse *f* aux pédés

queerly ['kwɪəlɪ] *adv* bizarrement, étrangement

queerness ['kwɪənɪs] *n* étrangeté *f*

quell [kwel] *vt Lit* (*revolt, emotion*) réprimer; (*rioters*) mater; (*person, passion*) dompter

quench [kwentʃ] *vt* (a) **to q. one's thirst** se désaltérer, étancher sa soif (b) (*extinguish*) (*fire, flame*) éteindre (c) (*cool*) (*in metalwork*) (*metal*) tremper; *Fig* (*person's enthusiasm*) atténuer (d) (*suppress*) (*desire*) réprimer, étouffer

querulous ['kwerʊləs] *adj* (*person*) qui se plaint toujours, grognon; (*tone*) plaintif, dolent

querulously ['kwerʊləslɪ] *adv* d'un ton plaintif *ou* dolent

query¹ ['kwiːərɪ] *n* (*question*) question *f*; *Comptr* interrogation *f*; **I have a q.** j'ai une question; **to raise a q.** soulever une question; **to settle a q.** résoudre une question; **there was a note of q. in her voice** il y avait une note d'interrogation dans sa voix; **q.: is this accurate?** (*in margin of document etc*) question: est-ce exact?; *Comptr* **q. language** langage *m* d'interrogation

query² *vt* (a) (*ask*) **to q. if** *or* **whether ...** demander si ...; **how much is that?, he queried** combien est-ce?, demanda-t-il (b) (*put in doubt*) (*question, statement*) mettre en question *ou* en doute; (*mark with question mark*) marquer d'un point d'interrogation; *US* (*question*) (*person*) poser des questions à; **she queried the bill** elle a posé des questions sur la facture; **I would q. it if I were you** à votre place je le vérifierais (c) *Comptr* **to q. a database** interroger une base de données

quest¹ [kwest] *n Lit* quête *f*, recherche *f*; **to go in q. of sb/sth** se mettre *ou* aller *ou* partir à la recherche de qn/qch *ou* en quête de qn/qch; **her q. for justice** sa bataille pour que justice soit faite; **the q. for the Holy Grail** la quête du Graal

quest² *vi Lit* **to q. after** *or* **for sth** être à la recherche de qch

question¹ ['kwestʃən] *n* [①**A45-46,8; B61,C**] (a) (*interrogation*) question *f*, demande *f*; (*in exam*) question; **to ask sb a q. , to ask a q. of sb, to put a q. to sb** poser une question à qn; *Parl* adresser une interpellation à qn; **does anyone have any questions?** quelqu'un a-t-il une question?; **I have a q.** j'ai une question; **the q. is, did she know?** la question est de savoir si elle était au courant; *Gram* **direct/indirect q.** interrogation *f* directe/indirecte; *Sch etc* **list** *or* **set of questions** questionnaire *m*; **a q. and answer session** une séance questions-réponses; *Gram* **q. form** forme *f* interrogative; **q. word** mot *m* interrogatif

(b) (*doubt*) doute *m*; **without q.** sans aucun doute, sans contredit; **to obey without q.** obéir aveuglément; **her courage/dedication is beyond q.** son courage/dévouement est indiscutable; **that is beyond q.** c'est incontestable; **his honesty has never been in q.** son honnêteté n'a jamais été mise en doute; **to call sb's honesty into q.** mettre en question l'honnêteté de qn; **there is no q. about it** il n'y a pas de doute là-dessus; **it's open to q. whether** ... on peut se demander si ...; **the wisdom of this decision is open to q.** le bien-fondé de la décision est discutable

(c) (*matter, issue*) question *f*; **that's the q.** c'est bien là la question; **that's another** *or* **a different q.** c'est une autre histoire; **that is not the q., that is beside the q.** ce n'est pas là la question, il ne s'agit pas de cela; **the q. is whether ...** il s'agit de savoir si ...; **it is out of the q.** c'est hors de question; **it is quite out of the q. for us to ...** il ne saurait être question pour nous de ...; **there's no q. of you(r) going back to work at the moment** il n'est pas question que vous repreniez le travail pour le moment; **there is no q. of going back now** il n'est pas question de revenir en arrière; **it's not a q. of who's right** la question n'est pas de savoir qui a raison; **the Palestinian q.** la question palestinienne; **a q. of life or death** une question de vie ou de mort; **a q. of money/time** une question d'argent/de temps; **it's only a q. of time before it happens** ça arrivera tôt ou tard; **the matter/person in q.** l'affaire/la personne en question; *Jur* **the case in q.** le cas en litige; **there was some q. of ...** il a été question de ...

(d) *Hist* **to put sb to the q.** (*torture*) mettre qn à la question, appliquer la question à qn

question² *vt* (a) (*person*) questionner, interroger (**about** sur, à propos de); **to be questioned** être interrogé; (*of suspect*) subir un interrogatoire; **the people questioned in the survey** les personnes interrogées dans le cadre du sondage; **she was questioned on her views** (*in interview etc*) on l'a interrogée sur ses opinions

(b) (*cast doubt on*) mettre en question *ou* en doute *ou* en cause, contester; **nobody is questioning your ...** personne ne met en doute *ou* en question votre/vos ...; **I q. whether he will come** je doute qu'il vienne; **I q. whether it would not be better to ...** je me demande s'il ne vaudrait pas mieux ...

questionable ['kwestʃənəb(ə)l] *adj* (a) (*doubtful*) contestable, discutable, douteux; **of q. authenticity** (*document etc*) d'une authenticité (fort) douteuse; **this is the most democratic country – that's very q.** c'est le pays le plus démocratique – c'est très discutable (b) *Pej* (*conduct etc*) suspect, équivoque; **in q. taste** d'un goût douteux

questioner ['kwestʃənər] *n* interrogateur, -trice; (*who likes asking questions*) questionneur, -euse; (*calling in to TV programme*) téléspectateur, -trice; (*calling in to radio programme*) auditeur, -trice; (*in studio audience*) spectateur, -trice

questioning ['kwestʃənɪŋ] 1 *adj* (*look etc*) interrogateur, -trice; **to have a q. mind** avoir un esprit curieux 2 *n* questions *fpl*, interrogation *f*; *Mil etc* (*of prisoner*) interrogatoire *m*; **to be held for q.** (*by police*) être détenu pour un interrogatoire

questioningly ['kwestʃənɪŋlɪ] *adv* (*to look at sb*) d'un air interrogateur; (*to say sth*) d'un ton interrogateur

question mark *n* (a) *Gram, Typ* point *m* d'interrogation; *Fig* **a q. hangs over the project** il y a un point d'interrogation quant au projet (b) *Mktg* (*product*) point *m* d'interrogation, dilemme *m*

question master *n Rad, TV* (*of game show*) animateur, -trice, meneur, -euse de jeu

questionnaire [kwestʃə'neər] *n* questionnaire *m*; **q. analysis** dépouillement *m* de questionnaire; **q. construction** construction *f* de questionnaire

question tag *n* [①**A46**,8,b; **B61**,3,b,i] *Gram* queue *f* de phrase interrogative

question time *n Parl* heure *f* consacrée aux questions

quetzal ['ketsəl] *n* (*bird*) quetzal *m*, *pl* quetzals

queue¹ [kjuː] *n* (a) *esp Br* (*line*) (*of people*) queue *f*, file *f*; (*of cars*) file; **is this the q.?** (*for tickets etc*) est-ce que c'est la queue?; **to form a q., to stand in a q.** faire la queue; **there is a q., you know!** il faut faire la queue!; **to join the q.** se mettre à la queue; *Fig* **join the q.!** vous n'êtes pas le seul/la seule; **to jump the q.** passer avant son tour (b) *Comptr* file *f* d'attente (c) *Arch* (*of hair, wig*) queue *f*

queue² 1 *vi* faire la queue; **I spent ages queuing for a bus** j'ai passé des heures à attendre le bus 2 *vt Comptr* (*print jobs*) mettre en file d'attente

▶ **queue up** *vi* faire la queue; **people queued up to shake his hand** les gens faisaient la queue pour lui serrer la main; **people are queuing up for a job like yours** les gens se battent pour décrocher un emploi comme le vôtre

queue-jump *vi* resquiller

queue-jumper *n* resquilleur, -euse

quibble¹ ['kwɪb(ə)l] *n* argutie *f*, chicane *f* sur les mots

quibble² *vi* (*equivocate*) ergoter, chicaner; (*split hairs*) chipoter, couper les cheveux en quatre; **he didn't quibble about the price** il n'a pas chipoté sur le prix

quibbler ['kwɪblər] *n* ergoteur, -euse, chicaneur, -euse

quibbling ['kwɪb(ə)lɪŋ] 1 *n* arguties *fpl*, chicanerie *f*, ergoterie *f* 2 *adj* qui porte sur des vétilles

quiche [kiːʃ] *n Culin* quiche *f*

quick [kwɪk] 1 *adj* (*movement, growth etc*) rapide; *Mus* animé, vif; **that was q.!** ça a été rapide!; **as q. as lightning** *or* **as a flash** aussi vite que l'éclair, en un clin d'œil; **be q. (about it)!** faites vite!, dépêchez-vous!; **he's q.** (*of runner*) il court vite; (*of worker*) il est rapide; (*he understands etc quickly*) il est vif; **q. to act/to anger** prompt à agir/à se fâcher; **she's very q. to take offence** elle se vexe très facilement; **don't be so q. to criticize** ne critique donc pas si vite; **she was q. to realize what had happened** elle s'est vite rendu compte de ce qui s'était passé; **to be q. off the mark** (*in race*) démarrer vite; (*to start sth*) démarrer sans perdre de temps; (*to understand*) avoir l'esprit vif; **he wasn't exactly q. off the mark when it came to ordering drinks** il était plutôt lent à la détente quand il s'agissait de commander les boissons; *F* **let's have a q. one** (*drink*) si on prenait un petit verre?; **they've gone upstairs for a q. one** (*sex*) ils sont montés (pour) tirer un petit coup; **the quickest way there** le chemin le plus court (pour y arriver); **what's the q. way to find a job?** comment trouve-t-on un emploi rapidement?; **I'll just have a q. bath** je vais juste prendre un bain en vitesse; **can I ask you a q. question?** je peux vous poser une petite question?; **q. fix** solution *f* miracle; **q. mind** esprit *m* prompt *ou* vif; **q. recovery (from an illness)** prompt rétablissement *m* (d'une maladie); *Acct* **q. ratio** ratio *m* de liquidité immédiate; **q. reference guide** aide-mémoire *m*; **q. sale** vente *f* rapide; **q. temper** tempérament *m* emporté, irascibilité *f*; **she has a q. temper** elle s'emporte facilement; *Cards* **q. trick** levée *f* assurée

2 *n* (a) (*flesh*) vif *m*; **to bite one's nails to the q.** se ronger les ongles jusqu'au vif; *Fig* **to sting** *or* **cut sb to the q.** blesser *ou* piquer qn au vif

(b) *Rel* **the q. and the dead** (*pl*) les vivants *mpl* et les morts

3 *adv* (a) *F* vite, rapidement; **as q. as possible** aussi vite que possible; **to run quicker** courir plus vite; **he just wants to get rich q.** il ne pense qu'à s'enrichir rapidement; **q.! over here!** vite! par ici!

(b) (*in compounds*) **q.-acting, q.-action** (*mechanism*) à action rapide *ou* immédiate; (*drug, medication*) à action rapide; **q.-drying paint** peinture *f* qui sèche rapidement; **q.-firing rifle** fusil *m* à tir rapide; **q.-growing** (*plant etc*) à croissance rapide; *Constr, Culin* **q.-setting** (*cement, jelly*) à prise rapide

quick-change artiste *n Th* acteur *m* qui change de costume souvent au cours d'un spectacle; *Fig* personne *f* versatile

quicken ['kwɪk(ə)n] 1 *vt* (*step, pace*) hâter, presser, accélérer; *Med* (*pulse*) accélérer; (*stimulate*) (*imagination*) stimuler; (*interest*) exciter; (*appetite*) aiguiser; (*feelings*) provoquer; *Sp* **to q. the pace** accélérer le pas *ou* le rythme 2 *vi* (*of pace, pulse etc*) devenir plus rapide, s'accélérer; *Lit* (*of nature, hope etc*) s'animer, se ranimer; (*of foetus*) bouger

quickening ['kwɪkənɪŋ] 1 *adj* (*pace*) qui s'accélère; *Lit* **her q. hope** ses espoirs grandissants 2 *n* (*of pace, pulse*) accélération *f*; (*of nature etc*) renouveau *m*; *Obst* premiers mouvements *mpl* du foetus

quickfire ['kwɪkfaɪər] *adj attrib* (*questions, repartee*) rapide, au rythme soutenu

quick-freeze *vt Culin* surgeler

quickie ['kwɪkɪ] 1 *n F* (*quick drink*) consommation *f* prise sur le pouce; (*something done quickly*) chose *f* faite à la hâte; **let's have a q.** (*drink*) si on prenait un petit verre?; (*sex*) on fait l'amour en vitesse?; **OK, but make it a q.** si tu veux, mais en vitesse 2 *adj F* **q. divorce** divorce *m* rapide

quicklime ['kwɪklaɪm] *n* chaux *f* vive

quickly ['kwɪklɪ] *adv* vite, rapidement; **q.!** vite!

quickness ['kwɪknɪs] *n* (a) (*rapidity*) vitesse *f*, rapidité *f*; (*of pulse*) rythme *m* rapide (b) (*sharpness*) (*of sight*) acuité *f*; (*of*

hearing) finesse *f*; (*of mind*) vivacité *f*; **q. of temper** caractère *m* emporté *ou* irascible
quicksand ['kwɪksænd] *n* sables mouvants *mpl*; **to get caught** *or* **stuck in q.** *or* **in the quicksands** être pris dans des sables mouvants
quickset ['kwɪkset] *n Br* **q. (hedge)** haie *f* vive
quickshift gearchange ['kwɪkʃɪft] *n* changement *m* de vitesse rapide
quicksilver ['kwɪksɪlvər] *n* vif-argent *m*; **he's/she's just like q.** c'est du vif-argent
quickstep ['kwɪkstep] *n* (*dance*) fox-trot *m* rapide
quick-tempered *adj* emporté, colérique, coléreux, irascible; **to be q.** s'emporter facilement
quick-witted *adj* vif, éveillé, à l'esprit vif
quid[1] [kwɪd] *n Br F* (*inv in pl*) (*pound*) livre *f*; **it cost me 10 q.** ça m'a coûté 100 balles; **to be quids in** être tranquille *ou* peinard
quid[2] *n* (*of tobacco*) chique *f*
quid pro quo [kwɪdprəʊ'kwəʊ] *n* compensation *f*, contrepartie *f*
quiescence [kwɪ'esəns] *n Fml* tranquillité *f*
quiescent [kwɪ'esənt] *adj Fml* inactif, passif
quiet[1] ['kwaɪət] *n* (*calm*) tranquillité *f*, calme *m*; (*silence*) silence *m*; **to enjoy perfect peace and q.** jouir d'une parfaite tranquillité; **the q. of the night** le calme de la nuit; *Br F* **to do sth on the q.** faire qch discrètement, *Pej* faire qch en cachette *ou* à la dérobée
quiet[2] *adj* **(a)** (*with little sound or motion*) (*music*) doux, *f* douce; (*voice*) bas, doux; (*neighbour, neighbourhood*) tranquille, calme; (*sea*) calme; (*engine*) silencieux; **can we go somewhere q.?** est-ce que nous pouvons aller dans un endroit tranquille?; **the wind grew q.** le vent s'est apaisé; **to keep q.** (*make no noise*) rester *ou* se tenir tranquille; (*say nothing*) se taire, ne rien dire, garder le silence; **we must keep q. about it** il ne faut pas en parler; **keep it q.** pas un mot; **she was very q. about her background** elle n'a pas dit grand-chose de ses antécédents; **to keep a child q.** faire taire un enfant; **to keep sb q.** tenir qn tranquille; **be q.!** tais-toi!/taisez-vous!; **q. please!** silence, s'il vous plaît!; **to be as q. as a mouse** (*of person*) être très silencieux; **the house was as q. as the grave** il n'y avait pas un bruit dans la maison; **it's as q. as the grave here on a Saturday** c'est complètement mort ici le samedi; **could I have a q. word (with you)?** est-ce que je peux vous prendre à part pour vous dire deux mots?

(b) (*calm*) doux, *f* douce; **he's a very q. kind of chap** c'est un type très tranquille; **q. disposition** caractère *m* doux *ou* calme; **q. horse** cheval *m* doux *ou* tranquille *ou* sage

(c) (*subdued, discreet*) (*dress, colours etc*) simple, discret, -ète, sobre; **we had a q. laugh over it** nous en avons ri entre nous; **you're very q., is anything wrong?** tu es drôlement silencieux, il y a quelque chose qui ne va pas?; **it's very pretty countryside, in a q. sort of way** c'est un très joli paysage, dans le genre paisible; **q. irony** ironie *f* voilée; **q. optimism** optimisme *m* modéré; **q. wedding** mariage *m* célébré dans l'intimité

(d) (*undisturbed*) calme, tranquille, paisible; **to lead a q. life** mener une vie calme; *F* **anything for a q. life!** n'importe quoi du moment qu'on me fiche la paix!; *Com* **business is very q.** les affaires sont très calmes; **it's very q. in here tonight** (*in the pub, shop etc*) c'est très calme ce soir; **to have a q. drink** boire un coup tranquillement; **to spend a q. evening (in)** passer une soirée tranquille; *F* **all q. on the western front** à l'ouest rien de nouveau
quiet[3] *vt* = **quieten**
▶ **quiet down** = **quieten down**
quieten ['kwaɪət(ə)n] *vt Br* (*uproar etc*) apaiser, calmer; (*person, one's conscience*) tranquilliser; (*child*) faire taire; (*fears, suspicions*) dissiper; (*pain*) calmer
▶ **quieten down** *Br* **1** *vi* **(a)** (*become silent*) se taire **(b)** (*become calm*) (*of person*) se calmer; (*of business*) ralentir **2** *vtsep* **(a)** (*make silent*) faire taire **(b)** (*make calm*) (*person, animal*) calmer
quietly ['kwaɪətlɪ] *adv* **(a)** (*with little sound or motion*) silencieusement, sans bruit **(b)** (*calmly*) tranquillement, doucement; **to be q. determined to do sth** être froidement décidé à faire qch **(c)** (*discreetly*) (*dressed etc*) simplement, discrètement; **to get married q.** se marier sans cérémonie *ou* dans l'intimité **(d)** (*with little excitement*) **we live very q.** nous menons une vie très calme
quietness ['kwaɪətnɪs] *n* **(a)** (*lack of sound*) silence *m* **(b)** (*calmness*) (*of person*) calme *m* **(c)** (*of dress, colour etc*) sobriété *f* **(d)** (*of life*) tranquillité *f*; (*of business*) manque *m* d'activité
quietude ['kwaɪətju:d] *n Lit* quiétude *f*
quietus [kwaɪ'i:təs] *n Lit* (*death*) mort *f*
quiff [kwɪf] *n Br* **q. (of hair)** toupet *m*
quill [kwɪl] *n* **(a)** (*of feather*) tuyau *m*; **q. (feather)** penne *f*; **q. (pen)** plume *f* d'oie (*pour écrire*) **(b)** (*of porcupine etc*) piquant *m*
quilt[1] [kwɪlt] *n* couverture *f* piquée *ou* matelassée; (*eiderdown*) édredon *m* piqué; **(continental) q.** couette *f*, *Swiss* duvet *m*
quilt[2] **1** *vt* **(a)** (*garment etc*) matelasser, ouater, ouatiner et piquer; **quilted jacket** veste *f* matelassée **(b)** (*two pieces of material*) piquer **2** *vi* faire du matelassage
quilting ['kwɪltɪŋ] *n* matelassage *m*
quin [kwɪn] *n Br F* (*child*) quintuplé, -ée
quince [kwɪns] *n* **(a)** (*fruit*) coing *m*; **q. jelly** gelée *f* de coings **(b) q. (tree)** cognassier *m*
quincentenary [kwɪnsen'ti:nərɪ] *n* cinquième centenaire *m*
quinine [kwɪ'ni:n] *n Ch* quinine *f*
quinquagenarian [kwɪŋkwədʒə'neərɪən] *adj, n* quinquagénaire *mf*
Quinquagesima [kwɪŋkwə'dʒesɪmə] *n Rel* **Q. (Sunday)** (le dimanche de) la Quinquagésime
quinsy ['kwɪnzɪ] *n Old-fashioned Med* angine *f* phlegmoneuse
quintal ['kwɪnt(ə)l] *n* (*measurement*) quintal *m* métrique (*de 100 kg*)
quinte [kænt] *n Fencing* quinte *f*
quintessence [kwɪn'tesəns] *n Fml* quintessence *f*
quintessential [kwɪntɪ'senʃəl] *adj Fml* quintessenciel
quintessentially [kwɪntɪ'senʃəlɪ] *adv Fml* fondamentalement
quintet(te) [kwɪn'tet] *n Mus* quintette *m*
quintillion [kwɪn'tɪljən] *n Br* quintillion *m* (10^{30}); *Am* trillion *m* (10^{18})
quintuple[1] [kwɪn'tjʊp(ə)l] *adj, n* quintuple *m*
quintuple[2] *vti* quintupler
quintuplet [kwɪn'tju:plɪt, 'kwɪntjʊplɪt] *n* (*child*) quintuplé, -ée
quip[1] [kwɪp] *n* (*sarcastic remark*) sarcasme *m*, raillerie *f*; (*witty remark*) trait *m ou* mot *m* d'esprit; (*riposte*) repartie *f*
quip[2] (-pp-) **1** *vi* (*make sarcastic remark*) railler; (*be witty*) faire des mots d'esprit **2** *vt* (*say sarcastically*) dire de façon sarcastique; (*say wittily*) dire avec esprit
quire ['kwaɪər] *n* **(a) q. of paper** (*24 sheets*) = main *f* de papier (*25 feuilles*) **(b)** *Typ* **in quires** en feuilles
quirk [kwɜ:k] *n* (*of character*) particularité *f*, bizarrerie *f* de caractère; **he's got a lot of little quirks** il y a plein de choses bizarres chez lui; **a q. of fate** un caprice du sort; **by a q. they both went to Rome** par un effet du hasard, ils sont tous les deux allés à Rome
quirky ['kwɜ:kɪ] *adj* (*sense of humour etc*) bizarre
quisling ['kwɪzlɪŋ] *n Pej* collaborateur, -trice
quit[1] [kwɪt] *adj Fml* quitte, libéré; **to be q. of sb/sth** être débarrassé de qn/qch
quit[2] (*pt, pp* **quitted,** *Dial, US* **quit**; *prp* **quitting) 1** *vi* (*resign*) démissionner; (*in fight*) abandonner; *Comptr* sortir; **you can't fire me, I q.!** vous ne pouvez pas me mettre à la porte, je démissionne!; **to receive notice to q.** (*of tenant*) recevoir son congé

2 *vt* **(a)** (*leave*) (*person, place*) quitter

(b) *Comptr* (*database, programme*) sortir de, quitter

(c) to q. office se démettre de ses fonctions

(d) *F* **to q. one's job** quitter son emploi, démissionner; **to q. doing sth** arrêter *ou* cesser de faire qch; **q. annoying me, will you!** tu vas arrêter de m'ennuyer!; **to q. work** arrêter de travailler, cesser le travail
quite [kwaɪt] *adv* [①A4,B] **(a)** (*entirely*) vraiment; **she's q. happy** elle est tout à fait heureuse; **he's q. happy to let others do the work** ça ne le dérange absolument pas de laisser les autres faire le travail; **q. finished** entièrement *ou* complètement fini; *Iron* **have you q. finished?** c'est pas terminé?; **q. recovered** tout à fait *ou* complètement rétabli; **he was q. obviously drunk** il était manifestement ivre; **q. the best story of its kind** sans aucun doute la meilleure histoire de ce genre; **q. as much** autant; **q. enough** bien assez; **that's q. enough of that!** ça suffit comme ça!; **q. apart from the fact that ...** en dehors du fait que ...; **q. right** (*of sum*) parfaitement juste; (*of clock*) bien à l'heure; **you are q. right** vous avez bien *ou* tout à fait raison; **q. (so)!** parfaitement!, d'accord!; **I'm afraid I'll be a bit late – that's q. all right** je crains d'être un peu en retard – ce n'est pas grave; **not q.** pas tout à fait; **not q. 300** pas tout à fait 300; **it's not q. 2 o'clock** il n'est pas tout à fait 2 heures; **q. the opposite** bien au contraire; **I don't q. know what he will do** je ne sais pas trop ce qu'il fera; **you know q. well what I mean** vous savez très bien ce que je veux dire; **I q. understand** je comprends bien, je me rends parfaitement compte; **I don't q. understand** je ne comprends pas bien; **I can't q. remember when it happened** je ne me souviens pas bien *ou* tout à fait quand ça s'est passé; **in q. another tone**

sur un tout autre ton; **that's q. another matter!** c'est tout autre chose!

(b) *(fairly, rather)* assez; **q. big/small** assez gros/petit; **q. frequently/recently** assez fréquemment/récemment; **this furniture is q. sought after** ces meubles sont assez recherchés; **I q. like him** je l'aime bien; **she is q. happy** elle est assez heureuse; **q. a lot of people/money** un assez grand nombre de gens/une assez grosse somme d'argent; **q. a few people** pas mal de gens

(c) *(really)* **q. a beauty** une vraie beauté; **it was q. a surprise** c'était une véritable surprise; **it's been q. a day** quelle journée!; **she's q. a girl** elle est formidable; **that film was q. something** ce film c'était vraiment quelque chose; **it's q. something when ...** c'est vraiment quelque chose quand ...; **it was q. something (to do sth)** c'était vraiment quelque chose (de faire qch)

quits [kwɪts] *adj* **now we're q.** maintenant nous sommes quittes; **double or q.** quitte ou double; **I'll be q. with him yet** il me le paiera; **let's call it q.** *(agree to end game, dispute)* restons-en là

quittance [ˈkwɪt(ə)ns] *n Fin* quittance *f*, décharge *f*, acquit *m*

quitter [ˈkwɪtər] *n F Pej* personne *f* qui abandonne facilement; **she's not a q.** elle n'est pas du genre à abandonner *ou* à se laisser abattre

quiver[1] [ˈkwɪvər] *n (arrow holder)* carquois *m*; *esp Lit Fig* **to have an arrow** *or* **a shaft left in one's q.** n'être pas à bout de ressources

quiver[2] *n (of person)* tremblement *m*, frisson *m*, frémissement *m*; *(of leaves, lips)* frémissement, tremblement; *(of flesh)* palpitation *f*, frémissement; **with a q. in one's voice** d'une voix frémissante *ou* mal assurée

quiver[3] **1** *vi (of person)* trembler, frémir, frissonner; *(of leaves, lips)* frémir, trembler; *(of voice, light)* trembloter; *(of flesh)* palpiter, frémir; **to q. with fear** trembler de peur; **voice quivering with emotion** voix vibrante d'émotion **2** *vt (of bird)* **to q. its wings** agiter ses ailes

quivering [ˈkwɪvərɪŋ] **1** *adj (person)* tremblant, frissonnant, frémissant; *(leaves, lips)* frémissant, tremblant; *(flesh)* palpitant, frémissant; **the experience had reduced him to a q. mass** *or* **jelly** l'épreuve l'avait réduit à l'état de loque **2** *n (of person)* tremblement *m*, frémissement *m*, frissonnement *m*; *(of leaves, lips)* frémissement, tremblement; *(of flesh)* palpitation *f*, frémissement; *(of eyelashes)* battement *m*

qui vive [kiːˈviːv] *n* **on the q.** sur le qui-vive

Quixote (Don) [dɒnˈkwɪksəʊt, -kiːˈhəʊtɪ] *n Liter* Don Quichotte *m*

quixotic [kwɪkˈsɒtɪk] *adj (person)* chimérique; *(plan, idea, character etc)* donquichottesque; *(behaviour)* chimérique, donquichottesque

quixotically [kwɪkˈsɒtɪklɪ] *adv* en Don Quichotte, à la manière de Don Quichotte

quiz[1] [kwɪz] *n* **(a)** *Rad, TV etc* jeu-concours *m*, *pl* jeux-concours; *(in magazine etc)* questionnaire *m* **(b)** *(questioning)* interrogatoire *m*; *esp Am Sch* examen *m* oral

quiz[2] *vt* **(-zz-)** questionner; *Am Sch (candidate)* faire passer un/l'oral à; **they quizzed me on my political views** ils m'ont interrogé sur mes opinions politiques

quizmaster [ˈkwɪzmɑːstər] *n Rad, TV etc* animateur, -trice, meneur, -euse de jeu

quiz programme *n* jeu *m* télévisé/radiophonique

quiz show *n* jeu *m* télévisé/radiophonique

quizzical [ˈkwɪzɪk(ə)l] *adj (look, air)* interrogateur, -trice; *(mocking)* railleur

quizzically [ˈkwɪzɪk(ə)lɪ] *adv* d'un air interrogateur; *(mockingly)* d'un air railleur

quod [kwɒd] *n Br Sl (prison)* taule *f*; **in q.** en taule

quoin [kɔɪn] *n Constr (cornerstone)* pierre *f* d'angle; *(of wall)* coin *m*; *(internal)* encoignure *f*

quoit [kɔɪt] *n* palet *m*; **to play (at) quoits** jouer au palet

quorate [ˈkwɔːreɪt] *adj Fml, Admin* **to be q.** être en nombre

quorum [ˈkwɔːrəm] *n* quorum *m*; **to have a q.** être en nombre; **to form a q.** constituer un quorum

quota [ˈkwəʊtə] *n (stipulated quantity, number)* quota *m*; *(share)* quote-part *f*, *pl* quotes-parts; *Fin* quotité *f*; **import/export quotas** contingents *mpl ou* quotas d'importation/d'exportation; **to apportion** *or* **fix quotas for import** déterminer les quotas d'importation; **I've had my q. of bad luck** j'ai eu ma dose *ou* part de malchance; **we've had more than our q. of rain recently** nous avons eu plus que notre quota *ou* dose de pluie dernièrement; *Mktg* **q. method** *(of sampling)* méthode *f* des quotas

quotable [ˈkwəʊtəb(ə)l] *adj* **(a)** *(worth quoting)* qui vaut la peine d'être cité, digne d'être cité; *(able to be quoted)* que l'on peut *ou* qu'il est permis de citer; **a very q. phrase** une formule qui vaut la peine d'être citée; **the press find him very q.** les journalistes adorent ses petites phrases **(b)** *St Exch* cotable

quotation [kwəʊˈteɪʃən] *n* **(a)** *(from author etc)* citation *f* **(b)** *Com* prix *m*; *(for repair work etc)* devis *m*; *St Exch* cotation *f*, cote *f*, cours *m*, prix; **to ask for a q.** *(for proposed work)* demander un devis; **they gave me a q. of £500** ils m'ont fait un devis de 500 livres

quotation marks *npl Typ* guillemets *mpl*; **to put a word in q.** mettre un mot entre guillemets

quote[1] [kwəʊt] *n F* **(a)** citation *f*; **a q. from Shakespeare** une citation de Shakespeare **(b) quotes, q. marks** guillemets *mpl*; **in quotes** entre guillemets **(c)** *Com* = **quotation (b)**

quote[2] **1** *vt* **(a)** *(author, passage etc)* citer; *(authority, proof)* alléguer, citer; **he was quoted as saying that ...** il aurait dit que ...; **she said q. ...** et voici exactement ce qu'elle a dit ...; **his q. unquote 'friends'** ses amis entre guillemets; **can I q. you on that?** est-ce que je puis vous citer?; **don't q. me (on this) but ...** ce n'est pas encore officiel *ou* définitif mais ...; **to q. sb as an example** citer qn pour *ou* en exemple; *Admin, Com* **in reply please q. this number** prière de rappeler ce numéro dans toute correspondance ultérieure

(b) *Com (price)* établir, faire; *St Exch (share)* coter; **to q. a price** faire *ou* indiquer un prix; **they quoted me £500 for the work** ils m'ont fait un devis de 500 livres pour ce travail; *St Exch* **stock officially quoted** valeurs *fpl* admises à la cote officielle; **quoted on the Stock Exchange** coté en Bourse; *St Exch* **to q. an expiry** coter une échéance

2 *vi* **(a)** *Com* faire un devis, donner un prix

(b) to q. from a book/an author/memory citer un livre/un auteur/de mémoire

quoth [kwəʊθ] *vt Arch, Hum* **no, q. I** non, dis-je

quotidian [kwəʊˈtɪdɪən] *adj Lit* quotidien, -ienne

quotient [ˈkwəʊʃənt] *n Math* quotient *m*

qv [kjuːˈviː] *(abbr* **quod vide)** cf

qwerty [ˈkwɜːtɪ] *n* **q. keyboard** clavier *m* qwerty

qwertz [kwɜːts] *n* **q. keyboard** clavier *m* qwertz

R

R, r [ɑːr] **1** *n* (*letter*) R, r *m*; **two R's** *or* **Rs** deux R; **the three R's** (*Reading, (w)Riting and (a)Rithmetic*) les bases *fpl* de l'enseignement primaire **2** *adj Am Cin* (*abbr* **Restricted (to persons over 17)**) interdit aux moins de 17 ans
rabbet [ˈræbɪt] *n Carp* feuillure *f*
rabbi [ˈræbaɪ] *n Jewish Rel* rabbin *m*; **chief r.** grand rabbin
rabbinic(al) [rəˈbɪnɪk, -ɪk(ə)l] *adj* rabbinique
rabbit [ˈræbɪt] *n* **(a)** (*animal, fur*) lapin *m*; *Fig* **they breed like rabbits** ils se reproduisent comme des lapins; **to produce a r. out of a hat** (*of conjuror*) faire sortir un lapin d'un chapeau; *Fig* trouver une solution miracle; **to run like a scared r.** courir *ou* détaler comme un lapin; **young r.** lapereau *m*; **wild r.** lapin de garenne; *Am F* **r. ears** (*TV aerial*) antenne *f* portative; *Pej F Hum* **r. food** crudités *fpl*; **I'm fed up with all this r. food** je vais finir par me transformer en lapin avec toutes ces crudités; **r. 's foot** *or* **paw** (*lucky charm*) patte *f* de lapin; **r. hole** terrier *m* de lapin; **r. hutch** (*also Fig Pej*) clapier *m ou* cage *f* à lapin; *Boxing etc* **r. punch** coup *m* du lapin; **r. warren** terrier; *Fig* labyrinthe *m*
(b) *Culin* lapin *m*; **stewed r.** ragoût *m* de lapin
(c) *Old-fashioned Sp* (*poor performer*) nullard, -arde
rabbiting [ˈræbɪtɪŋ] *n* **to go r.** faire la chasse au lapin, chasser le lapin
▶ **rabbit on** *vi Br F* parler sans cesse, ne pas arrêter de parler; **she rabbited on to us about her son-in-law all evening** elle nous a débité toute la soirée des histoires sur son gendre; **do stop rabbiting on** tais-toi un peu; **what is he rabbiting on about?** qu'est-ce qu'il raconte?
rabble [ˈræb(ə)l] *n* **(a)** (*disorderly mob*) foule *f* **(b)** *Old-fashioned Pej* (*lower classes*) **the r.** la populace, *Old-fashioned* la canaille; **r. rouser** agitateur, -trice; **r. rousing** incitation *f* à la révolte; **rabble-rousing speech** discours *m* qui incite à la révolte
Rabelaisian [ræbəˈleɪzɪən] *adj* (*humour etc*) rabelaisien
rabid [ˈræbɪd, ˈreɪ-] *adj Vet* (*dog etc*) enragé; *Fig* (*socialist etc*) enragé, fanatique; (*hatred*) farouche
rabies [ˈreɪbiːz] *n Med, Vet* rage *f*; **the dog is a r. carrier** le chien est porteur de la rage; **r. vaccine** vaccin *m* contre la rage
RAC [ɑːreɪˈsiː] *n Br Aut* (*abbr* **Royal Automobile Club**) ≈ Touring-Club *m*
raccoon [rəˈkuːn] *n* (*animal*) raton *m* laveur; **r. skin hat** toque *f* en raton laveur
race¹ [reɪs] *n* **(a)** *Sp* course *f*; **a hundred metres r.** une course sur cent mètres, un cent mètres; **it's anybody's r.** il n'y a pas de favori; *Sp, Fig* **a r. against time** une course contre la montre; *Horseracing* **the races** les courses; **to go to the races** aller aux courses; **he loves the races** c'est un passionné des courses; *Horseracing* **r. card** programme *m* des courses
(b) (*channel for water*) canal *m*; **mill r.** bief *m* de moulin
(c) (*tide*) raz *m*
race² **1** *vi* **(a)** (*move quickly*) (*of person, animal*) courir à toute vitesse, galoper; **to r. by** (*of time*) filer; **the weekend just raced by** le weekend a passé très vite; **to r. for a bus/train** courir *ou* galoper pour attraper un bus/train; **to r. down the street** dévaler la rue à toute vitesse; **she raced to answer the door** elle se précipita pour ouvrir la porte; **the ambulance raced to the scene of the accident** l'ambulance fonça sur les lieux de l'accident; **the car was racing along** la voiture allait à toute vitesse; **to r. up the stairs** monter les escaliers quatre à quatre; **he raced through his meal** il a avalé son repas à toute vitesse; **the horse raced towards the winning post** le cheval a foncé vers la ligne d'arrivée; **the work is racing ahead** le travail avance très vite; **the clouds are racing across the sky** les nuages filent dans le ciel
(b) *Sp* (*of cyclist, driver*) participer à une épreuve *ou* à des épreuves de vitesse; (*of jockey*) monter; (*of athlete, horse*) courir; *Horseracing* (*of owner*) faire courir des chevaux
(c) (*of engine*) s'emballer
(d) (*of pulse*) être rapide; **my heart is racing** mon cœur bat la chamade
2 *vt* **(a)** (*against person, car etc*) faire la course avec; **I'll r. you home!** le premier arrivé à la maison a gagné!; **come on, r. you!** le premier arrivé là-bas!; **he raced me round the block** il a fait la course avec moi autour du pâté de maisons; **the car raced the bus to the traffic lights** la voiture a fait la course avec le bus pour arriver la première aux feux
(b) (*enter for races*) (*horse*) faire courir; **to r. pigeons** faire des courses de pigeons
(c) (*transport quickly*) **he raced me to the airport** il m'a emmené à l'aéroport à toute vitesse
(d) *Aut* (*engine*) emballer
race³ *n* (*species*) race *f*; **the human r.** la race humaine
racecourse [ˈreɪskɔːs] *n* champ *m* de courses, hippodrome *m*, turf *m*
racegoer [ˈreɪsgəʊər] *n* turfiste *mf*
racehorse [ˈreɪshɔːs] *n* cheval *m* de course
raceme [rəˈsiːm] *n Bot* grappe *f*
race meeting *n Horseracing* courses *fpl*; **there is a r. at Newmarket tomorrow** on court *ou* il y a des courses demain à Newmarket
racer [ˈreɪsər] *n* (*person*) coureur, -euse; (*horse, bicycle, car, motorcycle*) cheval *m*/vélo *m*/voiture *f*/moto *f* de course; (*yacht*) yacht *m* de course, racer *m*
race relations *npl* relations *fpl* interraciales
race riot *n* émeute *f* raciale
racetrack [ˈreɪstræk] *n* (*for cars*) circuit *m*; (*for bikes*) piste *f*; *Horseracing* champ *m* de courses, hippodrome *m*
raceway [ˈreɪsweɪ] *n* **(a)** (*channel for water*) canal *m* **(b)** *esp Am El* conduite *f* pour câbles **(c)** (*car racing*) circuit *m* **(d)** *esp Am Horseracing* champ *m* de courses, hippodrome *m* **(e)** *esp Am Tech* (*for ball bearings*) chemin *m* de roulement à billes
racial [ˈreɪʃəl] *adj* (*discrimination, prejudice*) racial; **r. slur** propos *mpl* racistes
racialism [ˈreɪʃəlɪz(ə)m] *n* racisme *m*
racialist [ˈreɪʃəlɪst] *adj, n* raciste *mf*
racially [ˈreɪʃəlɪ] *adv* **r. biased policy** politique *f* de discrimination raciale; **they were r. discriminated against** ils ont souffert de discrimination raciale; **a r. slanted article** un article à tendance raciste
raciness [ˈreɪsɪnɪs] *n* **(a)** (*liveliness*) (*of writing, style*) verve *f* **(b)** (*suggestiveness*) (*of story, joke*) grivoiserie *f*
racing [ˈreɪsɪŋ] **1** *n Sp* course *f*; *Horseracing* courses *fpl* (de chevaux), hippisme *m*, turf *m*; **motor r.** course automobile **2** *adj* **(a)** *Fig* **it's a r. certainty** c'est certain, c'est une certitude; **if anyone is a r. certainty for divorce, it's them!** s'il y a un couple qui est sûr de divorcer, c'est (bien) eux; **r. man** turfiste *m* **(b)** **r. pulse** pouls *m* élevé; **a r. heart may be a warning sign of a heart attack** avoir des palpitations peut être le signal avant-coureur d'une crise cardiaque
racing bicycle *n* vélo *m* de course
racing car *n* voiture *f* de course
racing colours *n Horseracing* couleurs *fpl* de l'écurie
racing driver *n* coureur *m* automobile, pilote *m* de courses
racing pigeon *n* pigeon *m* voyageur de compétition
racing stable *n* écurie *f* de courses
racism [ˈreɪsɪz(ə)m] *n* racisme *m*
racist [ˈreɪsɪst] *adj, n* raciste *mf*
rack¹ [ræk] *n* **to be going to r. and ruin** (*of country, company*) courir à la ruine; (*of house etc*) se délabrer, tomber en ruines; (*of health, economy, business*) aller de mal en pis; **this country/the economy/this house has gone to r. and ruin** ce pays/l'économie/la maison est dans un état lamentable
rack² *n* **(a)** (*for hay etc*) râtelier *m*; (*sectioned*) casier *m*; (*set of shelves*) étagère *f*; (*bicycle*) support *m ou* râtelier à vélos; **(bottle) r.** casier à bouteilles; **(display) r.** présentoir *m*; **(luggage) r.** porte-bagages *m* **(b)** *Comptr* châssis *m*; *Tech* crémaillère *f* **(c)** *Culin* **r. of lamb** carré *m* d'agneau **(d)** (*in hotel*) **r. rate** plein tarif *m*; **r. slip** fiche *f* de réservation
rack³ *n Hist* (*for torture*) chevalet *m* (*de torture*); *Fig* **to be on the r.** être au supplice; **to keep sb on the r., to have sb on the r.** mettre qn au supplice
rack⁴ *vt* (*person*) (*of disease, pain, guilt etc*) tourmenter,

torturer, faire souffrir le martyre à; **to be racked with pain** être perclus de douleur; **to be racked by doubts** être en proie au doute; **to be racked by guilt** être tourmenté par un sentiment de culpabilité; **her body was racked with sobs** son corps était secoué de sanglots; **to r. one's brains** se creuser la tête *ou F* les méninges

► **rack up** *vtsep Sp etc* (*points*) accumuler

rack and pinion *n* crémaillère *f* (et pignon *m*, *Aut* **r. steering** direction *f* à crémaillère; *Rail* **rack (and pinion) railway** chemin *m* de fer à crémaillère

racket[1] ['rækɪt] *n* (*for tennis etc*) raquette *f*; **r. cover** housse *f* de raquette; **r. press** presse-raquette *m inv*, presse *f*; **rackets** (*game*) jeu *m* de paume

racket[2] *n F* **(a)** (*noise*) vacarme *m*, tintamarre *m*, *F* boucan *m*; **to make a r.** faire du tapage *ou* du vacarme *ou F* du boucan; **will you turn that r. off!** arrêtez ce vacarme! **(b)** (*criminal activity*) escroquerie *f*, racket *m*; **it's a r.** c'est du racket *ou* de l'escroquerie *ou* du vol; **he's involved in some money-laundering r.** il trempe dans des affaires de blanchiment d'argent **(c)** *Hum* (*occupation*) métier *m*; **how did you get into this r.?** comment est-ce que tu es arrivé dans cette branche?; **the teaching r.** le métier d'enseignant

racketeer [rækɪ'tɪər] *n* racketter *m*, racketteur *m*

racketeering [rækɪ'tɪərɪŋ] *n* racket *m*

racking ['rækɪŋ] *adj* (*pain etc*) atroce; (*doubts, guilt*) affreux

rack-rent *n* loyer *m* excessif *ou* exorbitant

racoon [rə'ku:n] *n* = **raccoon**

racquet ['rækɪt] *n* = **racket[1]**

racy ['reɪsɪ] *adj* **(a)** (*lively*) (*description, writing*) piquant **(b)** (*person*) plein de vie, très vivant; (*style*) plein de verve **(c)** (*suggestive*) (*story, joke*) osé

rad **(a)** (*abbr* **radiation**) (*unit*) rd *f* **(b)** *esp Am* (*abbr* **radiator**) radiateur *m*

RADA ['rɑ:də] *n Br* (*abbr* **Royal Academy of Dramatic Art**) = Conservatoire *m* national d'art dramatique

radar ['reɪdɑ:r] *n* radar *m*; **ground r.** radar au sol; **r. detection** détection *f* radar; **r. operator** radariste *mf*, opérateur, -trice radar; **r. screen** écran *m* (de) radar; **r. station** station *f* radar; *Aut* **r. speed check, r. trap** contrôle *m* radar

raddled ['ræd(ə)ld] *adj* (*face*) (*worn-out*) ravagé; (*over made-up*) peinturluré

radial ['reɪdɪəl] **1** *adj* **(a)** *Tech, Math etc* radial; *Aut* **r. engine** moteur *m* en étoile; **r. (ply) tyre** pneu *m* radial; **r. road** radiale *f* **(b)** *Anat* (*artery etc*) radial **2** *n* (*tyre*) pneu *m* radial

radially ['reɪdɪəlɪ] *adv* radialement

radiance ['reɪdɪəns] *n* (*of light, sun*) rayonnement *m*, éclat *m*; (*of beauty, smile*) éclat

radiant ['reɪdɪənt] **1** *adj* **(a)** (*light, sun*) éclatant; **r. heating** chauffage *m* à rayonnement **(b)** (*beauty, smile*) radieux, rayonnant; **a woman of r. beauty** une femme d'une beauté éblouissante; **the bride was r.** la mariée était radieuse *ou* rayonnante; **to be r. with joy** rayonner de joie **2** *n* **(a)** *Phys* point *m* radiant **(b)** (*of heater*) foyer *m* de rayonnement **(c)** *Astron* radiant *m*

radiant energy *n* énergie *f* de rayonnement

radiant heat *n Phys* chaleur *f* radiante

radiantly ['reɪdɪəntlɪ] *adv* radieusement; **to be r. beautiful** être rayonnant de beauté; **she smiled r.** elle eut un sourire radieux; **r. happy** rayonnant de bonheur

radiant point *n* point *m* radiant

radiate ['reɪdɪeɪt] **1** *vi* (*of heat, light*), *Med* (*of pain*) rayonner, irradier **2** *vt* (*heat, light*) émettre; **to r. happiness** rayonner de bonheur

radiation [reɪdɪ'eɪʃən] *n* **(a)** (*radioactivity*) radiation *f*; **to be exposed to r.** être exposé à des radiations **(b)** (*heat*) rayonnement *m* **(c)** (*light*) irradiation *f*; **ultraviolet r.** rayons *mpl* ultraviolets

radiation sickness *n Med* mal *m* des rayons

radiation therapy *n* radiothérapie *f*

radiator ['reɪdɪeɪtər] *n* **(a)** (*for heating*) radiateur *m* **(b)** *Aut* radiateur *m*; **r. cap** bouchon *m* du radiateur; **r. core** faisceau *m* de radiateur; **r. grille** calandre *f*; **r. matrix** faisceau de radiateur

radical ['rædɪk(ə)l] **1** *adj* **(a)** (*opinion, policy etc*) radical; **to make a r. alteration in sth** changer qch radicalement **(b)** *Ling, Math, Bot* radical **2** *n* **(a)** *Pol* radical, -ale **(b)** *Ch, Ling, Math* radical *m*

radicalism ['rædɪkəlɪz(ə)m] *n Pol* radicalisme *m*

radically ['rædɪklɪ] *adv* radicalement

radicle ['rædɪk(ə)l] *n* **(a)** *Bot* (*embryo*) radicule *f*; (*root*) radicelle *f* **(b)** *Ch* radical *m*

radio[1] ['reɪdɪəʊ] *n* **(a)** (*set*) poste *m* (de radio), radio *f*; **to put** *or* **switch** *or* **turn the r. on/off** allumer/éteindre la radio; **she was on the r. last night** elle est passée à la radio hier soir; **R. Moscow** Radio Moscou; **r. advertising** publicité *f* à la radio; **r. announcer** présentateur, -trice de radio; **r. bulletin** bulletin *m* radiophonique; **r. drama** pièce *f* radiophonique; **r. journalism** journalisme *m* de radio; *Telecom* **r. link** liaison *f* radio; **r. listener** auditeur *m*, auditrice *f*; **r. programme** programme *m* radiodiffusé *ou* radiophonique, émission *f* de radio; **r. reporter** reporter *m* radio; **r. set** poste *m* (de radio), radio *f*

(b) (*service, system*) **French r.** radiodiffusion *f* française

(c) *Telecom* radio(télégraphie) *f*; (*in taxi, ship etc*) radio *f*; **to communicate by r.** communiquer par radio; **to send a message by r.** envoyer un message radio; *Phys* **r. astronomy** radioastronomie *f*; **r. car** voiture *f* radio; **r. data system** (*for motorists*) système *m* radio de transmission de données; **r. frequency** radiofréquence *f*; **r. ham** radio-amateur *m*; **r. mast** antenne *f* (radio); **r. message** message *m* radio; **r. microphone** micro-émetteur *m*; **r. receiver** radiorécepteur *m*; **r. satellite** satellite *m* radio; **r. telescope** radiotélescope *m*; **r. vehicle** véhicule *m* radio; **r. waves** ondes *fpl* hertziennes

(d) *Comptr* **r. button** bouton *m* radio

radio[2] **1** *vt* (*information etc*) envoyer par radio; **to r. a person/ship** contacter une personne/un bateau par radio; **to r. one's position** signaler sa position par radio **2** *vi* **to r. for assistance** *or* **help** demander de l'aide par radio

radioactive [reɪdɪəʊ'æktɪv] *adj* (*substance, material etc*) radioactif; **r. dust** poussières *fpl* radioactives; **r. fallout** retombées *fpl* radioactives; **r. waste** déchets *mpl* radioactifs

radioactivity [reɪdɪəʊæk'tɪvɪtɪ] *n* radioactivité *f*

radio alarm *n* radio-réveil *m*, *pl* radio-réveils

radio beacon *n Telecom* radiobalise *f*, radiophare *m*

radio broadcast *n* émission *f* de radio

radiocarbon [reɪdɪəʊ'kɑ:bən] *n* radiocarbone *m*, carbone *m* 14; **r. dating** datation *f* au radiocarbone *ou* carbone 14

radio cassette *n* radiocassette *m*

radio communication *n* contact *m* radio *inv*, liaison *f* radio *inv*, radiocommunications *fpl*

radio-controlled *adj* télécommandé

radio engineer *n* ingénieur *m* radio

radiogram ['reɪdɪəʊgræm] *n* **(a)** *Old-fashioned Br* (*radio and record player*) meuble *m* qui incorpore un poste de radio et un pick-up **(b)** *Rad* (*message*) radiogramme *m*, radiotélégramme *m* **(c)** *Med* = **radiograph**

radiograph ['reɪdɪəʊgrɑ:f] *n Med* radiographie *f*

radiographer [reɪdɪ'ɒgrəfər] *n Med* radiologue *mf*

radiographic [reɪdɪəʊ'græfɪk] *adj Med* radiographique

radiography [reɪdɪ'ɒgrəfɪ] *n Med etc* radiographie *f*

radioisotope [reɪdɪəʊ'aɪsətəʊp] *n* radio-isotope *m*, *pl* radio-isotopes

radiological [reɪdɪəʊ'lɒdʒɪk(ə)l] *adj* radiologique

radiologist [reɪdɪ'ɒlədʒɪst] *n* radiologue *mf*

radiology [reɪdɪ'ɒlədʒɪ] *n* radiologie *f*

radio navigation *n* radionavigation *f*

radio officer *n* radionavigant *m*

radio operator *n* (*on plane*) radio *m*; (*on ship*) radionavigant *m*

radio-pager *n* récepteur *m* d'appel *ou* de poche

radio producer *n* producteur, -trice d'émissions de radio

radio room *n Naut* poste *m* radio de bord

radioscopic [reɪdɪəʊ'skɒpɪk] *adj Med* radioscopique

radioscopy [reɪdɪ'ɒskəpɪ] *n Med* radioscopie *f*

radio spectrum *n* spectre *m* radio *ou* radioélectrique *ou* des fréquences radioélectriques

radio station *n* station *f* de radio, poste *m* radiotélégraphique

radio taxi *n* radio-taxi *m*, *pl* radio-taxis

radiotelegram [reɪdɪəʊ'telɪgræm] *n* radiotélégramme *m*, radiogramme *m*, *F* radio *m*

radiotelephone [reɪdɪəʊ'telɪfəʊn] *n* radiotéléphone *m*

radiotelephony [reɪdɪəʊtɪ'lefənɪ] *n* radiotéléphonie *f*, *Old-fashioned* téléphonie *f* sans fil, T.S.F. *f*

radiotherapist [reɪdɪəʊ'θerəpɪst] *n* radiothérapeute *mf*

radiotherapy [reɪdɪəʊ'θerəpɪ] *n* radiothérapie *f*

radio transmitter *n* (poste *m*) émetteur *m*

radish ['rædɪʃ] *n* radis *m*

radium ['reɪdɪəm] *n Ch* radium *m*; **r. treatment** radiumthérapie *f*

radius, *pl* **-ii** ['reɪdɪəs, -ɪaɪ] *n* **(a)** (*of circle*) rayon *m*; *Av* rayon (d'action), autonomie *f*; **within a r. of ten miles** dans un rayon de seize kilomètres **(b)** (*of crane*) portée *f* **(c)** *Anat* (*bone*) radius *m*

radix, *pl* **-ices** ['reɪdɪks, -ɪsi:z] *n* **(a)** *Math* (*in logarithms etc*) base *f* **(b)** *Ling* radical *m*

RAF [ɑ:reɪ'ef] *n Br Mil* (*abbr* **Royal Air Force**) Armée *f* de l'air britannique

raffia ['ræfɪə] *n Bot* raphia *m*; **r. mat** tapis *m* en raphia

raffish ['ræfɪʃ] *adj* (*look*) canaille; **to have r. friends** avoir des amis qui mènent une vie de patachon

raffle¹ [ˈræf(ə)l] *n* tombola *f*; **I won it in a r.** je l'ai gagné dans une tombola; **r. ticket** billet *m* de tombola

raffle² *vt* **they're raffling (off) a car** un des lots de la tombola est une voiture

raft¹ [rɑːft] *n* **(a)** radeau *m*; **(inflatable) life r.** canot *m* (pneumatique) de sauvetage **(b)** (*in logging*) **timber r.** , *Am* **lumber r.** train *m* de bois *ou* de flottage **(c)** *F* (*large quantity*) **I have a r. of papers on my desk** j'ai une montagne de papiers sur mon bureau; **a r. of new measures** un paquet de nouvelles mesures

raft² **1** *vt* (*wood*) flotter en trains; **they rafted the logs to the paper mill** ils ont flotté les troncs jusqu'à la papeterie **2** *vi* **to r. across the river** traverser le fleuve sur un radeau

rafter [ˈrɑːftər] *n Constr* chevron *m*; **main r.** arbalétrier *m*; **the rafters** le chevronnage

rafting [ˈrɑːftɪŋ] *n Sp* rafting *m*

rag¹ [ræg] *n* **(a)** (*piece of cloth*) chiffon *m*; *Fig* **to feel like a wet r.** être lessivé *ou* ramollo *ou* vidé; *Fig F* **to lose the** *or* **one's r.** sortir de ses gonds; **r. book** livre *m* en tissu; **r. content** (*of paper*) pourcentage *m* de peille; **r. paper** papier *m* à base de peille; **r. picker** chiffonnier, -ière; **r. rug** catalogne *f*

(b) (*old garment*) guenille *f*; **rags** haillons *mpl*, guenilles, loques *fpl*; **to be in rags** être en guenilles *ou* en haillons; **to go from rags to riches** passer de la pauvreté à la richesse; **a rags to riches story** l'histoire d'une réussite sociale fulgurante

(c) *F Pej* (*newspaper*) feuille *f* de chou, torchon *m*; **you don't read that r., do you?** tu ne lis pas ce torchon quand même?; **the local r.** le journal du coin

rag² *n Br Old-fashioned* (*joking etc*) blague *f*, farce *f*; **I did it for** *or* **as a r.** je l'ai fait pour blaguer, c'était une blague; **r. week/day** *semaine ou journée annuelle du calendrier universitaire où les étudiants organisent des kermesses dont les bénéfices vont à des œuvres de charité*

rag³ *vt* **(-gg-)** *Br* (*tease*) taquiner (**about** sur); *Sch* (*teacher etc*) chahuter, asticoter, *F* mettre en boîte; **to r. sb mercilessly** asticoter qn sans arrêt

raga [ˈrɑːgə] *n Mus* raga *m*

ragamuffin [ˈrægəmʌfɪn] *n* (*child*) gamin *m* des rues; **you little r.!** petit polisson!

rag-and-bone *adj Br* **r. man** chiffonnier *m*

ragbag [ˈrægbæg] *n* (*jumble*) (*of things, ideas etc*) fatras *m*, ensemble *m* hétéroclite; **they were a r. team** ils formaient une équipe hétéroclite; **this file's just a r.** ce fichier, c'est un fourre-tout

rag doll *n* poupée *f* de chiffon

rage¹ [reɪdʒ] *n* **(a)** (*of person*) colère *f*, fureur *f*, rage *f*; **to be in a r.** être furieux *ou* fou de rage; **to get** *or* **fly into a r.** se mettre en colère, piquer une colère; **to have a fit of r.** avoir un accès de fureur; **to weep with r.** pleurer de rage **(b)** *F* **to be all the r.** (*of dance, music etc*) faire fureur, être la grande mode

rage² *vi* **(a)** (*of person*) être furieux, rager; **to r. against** *or* **at sb/sth** être furieux *ou* tempêter contre qn/qch **(b)** (*of river, ocean*) être déchaîné *ou* démonté; (*of epidemic, war*) régner, sévir; (*of battle, fire, storm*) faire rage; (*of wind*) souffler en tempête

ragged [ˈrægɪd] *adj* (*garment etc*) en lambeaux, en loques; (*person*) en haillons, en guenilles, déguenillé; **a shirt with r. cuffs** une chemise aux poignets élimés; **she was beginning to look rather r.** elle commençait à avoir l'air dépenaillé; *Mus* **the execution is r.** l'exécution manque d'ensemble; *F* **to run oneself r.** s'éreinter; **she's run r. with those kids** les gosses l'épuisent; *Typ* **r. right/left** non-justifié à droite/à gauche; *Typ* **to print sth r.** imprimer qch sans justification

ragged robin *n Bot* nielle *f* des prés

ragging [ˈrægɪŋ] *n* (*teasing*) taquineries *fpl*; **to give sb a r.** mettre qn en boîte, taquiner qn; **he took a lot of r.** on l'a beaucoup taquiné

raggle-taggle [ræg(ə)lˈtæg(ə)l] *adj* (*army etc*) hétéroclite

raging [ˈreɪdʒɪŋ] **1** *adj* (*person*) furieux, en colère; (*fever*) très fort; (*thirst*) terrible; (*sea*) déchaîné, démonté; (*storm, wind*) déchaîné; **to be in a r. temper** être furieux; **r. toothache** rage *f* de dents **2** *n* (*of person*) colère *f*, fureur *f*, rage *f*; (*of sea, wind*) fureur; **I've listened to his ragings all night** je l'ai écouté rouspéter toute la nuit

raglan [ˈræglən] **1** *n* **r. (coat)** (manteau *m*) raglan *m* **2** *adj* raglan *inv*; **r. sleeves** manches *fpl* raglan; **r. sweater** pull *m* raglan

ragman, *pl* -men [ˈrægmən] *n* chiffonnier *m*

ragout [ˈræguː] *n Culin* ragoût *m*

rag-roll *vt* (*wall etc*) = appliquer de la peinture (sur un mur etc) à l'aide d'un chiffon

ragtag [ˈrægtæg] **1** *n* **the r. and bobtail** la racaille **2** *adj* hétéroclite

ragtime [ˈrægtaɪm] *n Mus* ragtime *m*

rag trade *n F* la confection

ragweed [ˈrægwiːd] *n Bot* herbe *f* à poux

ragwort [ˈrægwɜːt] *n Bot* séneçon *m*, *F* herbe *f* de saint-Jacques

rah-rah [ˈrɑːrɑː] *adj Am* enthousiaste; *Fig* **he's very r. about the President** c'est un fervent admirateur du Président

raid¹ [reɪd] *n* (*on bank etc*) hold-up *m inv*, *F* braquage *m*; (*by police*) descente *f*; *St Exch* raid *m*; *Mil, Av* raid (**on** sur, contre); *Mil, Av* **daylight/night r.** attaque *f* (aérienne) de jour/de nuit

raid² *vt* (*attack*) (*bank, post office*) attaquer, *F* braquer; (*bar, club etc*) (*of police*) faire une descente dans; *Mil* faire un raid *ou* des raids dans; *Av* faire un raid *ou* des raids sur; **the terrorists raided the presidential palace** les terroristes ont fait un raid sur le palais présidentiel; *Fig* **the children raided the fridge** les enfants ont fait une razzia dans le frigo

raider [ˈreɪdər] *n Fin* raider; (*of banks*) voleur *m*, *F* braqueur, -euse de banques; *Mil* (*boat*) raider *m*; (*plane*) bombardier *m*; (*soldier*) membre *m* d'un commando

rail¹ [reɪl] *n* **(a)** (*for protection, support*) (*of escalator, stairway*) main *f* courante; (*of balcony*) balustrade *f*; (*banister*) rampe *f*; *Naut* lisse *f*

(b) (*for hanging things*) **curtain r.** tringle *f* à rideaux; **picture r.** cimaise *f*; **towel r.** porte-serviettes *m inv*

(c) *Rail* (*track*) rail *m*; **to travel by r.** voyager en train; **r. traffic** trafic *m* ferroviaire; **r. pass** carte *f* de train

(d) **rails** *Horseracing* corde *f*; *Naut* bastingage *m*, garde-corps *m inv*, rambarde *f*; **he was pushed to the rails by the other jockeys** il a été forcé de tenir la corde par les autres jockeys; *Rail* **to jump** *or* **leave the rails** dérailler, sortir des rails; *Fig* **to go off the rails** dérailler; (*morally*) s'écarter du droit chemin; **to get the economy back on the rails** remettre l'économie sur les rails; **I did my best to get him back on the rails after his breakdown** j'ai fait de mon mieux pour le remettre sur pieds après sa dépression nerveuse

rail² *n* (*bird*) râle *m*; **water r.** râle d'eau

▶ **rail against, rail at** *vipo Fml* (*person*) s'en prendre à; **to r. against fate** s'en prendre au destin

▶ **rail in** *vtsep* clôturer, entourer d'une clôture

▶ **rail off** *vtsep* fermer avec une clôture *ou* une barrière; **the path down to the beach was railed off after the accident** le chemin qui mène à la plage a été fermé après l'accident

railcar [ˈreɪlkɑːr] *n Am Rail* autorail *m*

railcard [ˈreɪlkɑːd] *n Br* carte *f* de chemin de fer

railfreight [ˈreɪlfreɪt] *n* **to send r.** envoyer par chemin de fer

railhead [ˈreɪlhed] *n Rail etc* tête *f* de ligne

railing¹ [ˈreɪlɪŋ] *n* (*also* **railings**) **(a)** (*barrier*) (*of metal*) grille *f*; (*of wood*) palissade *f*; **iron railings** grille **(b)** (*in dangerous place*) garde-fou *m*, *pl* garde-fous, garde-corps *m inv* **(c)** (*for support*) (*on staircase*) rampe *f*; (*on balcony*) balustrade *f*

railing² *n* (*complaints*) invectives *fpl* (**at, against** contre)

raillery [ˈreɪlərɪ] *n* (*teasing*) raillerie *f*

railman, *pl* -men [ˈreɪlmən] *n* = **railwayman**

rail network *n* réseau *m* ferroviaire

railroad¹ [ˈreɪlrəʊd] *n US* (*system*) chemin *m* de fer; (*track*) voie *f* ferrée; **to travel by r.** voyager en chemin de fer

railroad² *vt* **(a)** *F* (*force acceptance of*) **to r. a bill through Parliament** imposer un projet de loi au Parlement **(b)** *F* (*force into action*) **to r. sb into doing sth** faire pression sur qn pour qu'il fasse qch; **to be railroaded into doing sth** être forcé à faire qch; **I don't want to r. you, but …** je ne voudrais pas te forcer mais …; **she was railroaded into this job** on a fait pression sur elle pour qu'elle prenne ce poste **(c)** *esp Am Jur F* (*convict by false charges*) condamner à l'aide de fausses inculpations; (*hastily*) juger sommairement **(d)** *US* (*transport*) transporter par chemin de fer

railroad car *n* wagon *m*

rail strike *n* grève *f* des chemins de fer

rail transport *n* transport *m* par chemin de fer *ou* train

railway [ˈreɪlweɪ] *n Br, Can* (*system*) chemin *m* de fer; (*track*) voie *f* ferrée; **to travel by r.** voyager en chemin de fer; **to work on the railway(s)** être employé des chemins de fer; **Canadian National Railways** Chemins de fer nationaux du Canada; **r. bridge** pont *m* ferroviaire; **r. company** compagnie *f* des chemins de fer; **r. cutting** traversée *f* en déblai; **r. embankment** remblai *m*; **r. signal** signal *m* ferroviaire; **r. ticket** billet *m* de train; **r. timetable** horaires *mpl* des chemins de fer; (*printed*) fiche *f* horaire; **r. track(s)** voie ferrée

railway carriage *n* voiture *f*, wagon *m*

railway crossing *n* (*over road*) passage *m* à niveau

railway engine *n Br* locomotive *f*

railway engineer *n* ingénieur *m* des chemins de fer

railway guide *n* indicateur *m* des chemins de fer

railway line *n* (*system*) ligne *f* de chemin de fer; (*track*) voie *f* (ferrée)

railwayman, *pl* **-men** ['reɪlweɪmən] *n Br, Can* (*administrative employee*) employé, -ée des chemins de fer; (*technical employee*) cheminot *m*; *Br* (*formerly*) **National Union of Railwaymen** = syndicat *m* des employés de chemins de fer de Grande-Bretagne

railway network *n* réseau *m* ferroviaire *ou* de chemin de fer

railway station *n* gare *f*

railway strike *n* grève *f* des chemins de fer

railway system *n* réseau *m* ferroviaire *ou* de chemin de fer

railway worker *n* employé, -ée des chemins de fer

railway yard *n* dépôt *m* des chemins de fer

rail worker *n* (*general*) employé, -ée des chemins de fer; (*for track, rolling stock*) cheminot *m*

raiment ['reɪmənt] *n Arch, Lit* vêtements *mpl*, habits *mpl*

rain[1] [reɪn] *n* **(a)** pluie *f*; **in the r.** sous la pluie; **it looks like r.** on dirait qu'il va pleuvoir, le temps est à la pluie; *Br* **it's pouring with r.** il pleut à verse, il pleut des cordes; **they had some r. during their holiday** ils ont eu de la pluie pendant leurs vacances; **a river swollen with r., a r-swollen river** une rivière gonflée par les pluies; **the rains** la saison des pluies; **(come) r. or shine** (*whatever the weather*) qu'il pleuve ou qu'il vente; (*whatever the circumstances*) quoiqu'il arrive; *Br F* **two days in bed and you'll be as right as r.** deux jours au lit et tu seras remis; *Fig* **he doesn't have the sense to come in out of the r.** il n'a pas inventé le fil à couper le beurre; **driving/fine r.** pluie battante/fine; **freezing r.** pluie verglaçante; **heavy r.** forte *ou* grosse pluie; **light r.** pluie fine; *Geog* **r. belt** zone *f* des pluies; **r. cape** pèlerine *f*; *Am* **r. check** (*for sports event*) = billet *m* valable pour une réunion remise à cause du mauvais temps; (*for sales*) = bon *m* qui garantit le prix d'un produit soldé et qui est donné à la suite de l'épuisement des stocks avant la fin de la période des soldes; *esp Am* **or would you rather take a r. check?** (*issuing invitation*) ou est-ce que tu préfères remettre ça à plus tard?; *esp Am* **I'll take a r. check on that** (*replying to invitation*) ça sera pour une autre fois; **r. cloud** nuage *m* de pluie; **r. hat** capuche *f*; **r. hood** capuche; (*attached to anorak, jacket etc*) capuchon *m*, capuche; **r. shower** averse *f*

(b) *Fig* (*large quantity*) (*of abuse, blows etc*) pluie *f*, avalanche *f*

rain[2] **1** *v impers* pleuvoir; **it rains, it is raining** il pleut; **it is raining hard** il pleut à verse; *Br F* **it's raining cats and dogs** il tombe des cordes, il pleut comme vache qui pisse; *Prov* **it never rains but it pours** (*of misfortune*) un malheur ne vient jamais seul **2** *vi* (*of abuse, blows etc*) pleuvoir (**on sur**) **3** *vt* **to r. gifts/flowers on sb** couvrir qn de cadeaux/fleurs; **to r. blows on sb** rouer qn de coups

▶ **rain down** *vi* = **rain**[2] **2**, *vtsep* = **rain**[2] **3**

▶ **rain off** *vtsep Br Sp etc* **to be rained off** (*of match etc*) être annulé à cause du mauvais temps

▶ **rain out** *vtsep Am* = **rain off**

rainbow ['reɪnbəʊ] *n* arc-en-ciel *m*, *pl* arcs-en-ciel; **all the colours of the r.** toutes les couleurs de l'arc-en-ciel; **a dress in all the colours of the r.** une robe arc-en-ciel; *Fig* **to chase rainbows** se nourrir d'illusions; **r. coalition** coalition *f* hétéroclite; **r-coloured** aux couleurs de l'arc-en-ciel

rainbow trout *n* truite *f* arc-en-ciel

raincoat ['reɪnkəʊt] *n* imperméable *m*, *F* imper *m*

rain dance *n* danse *f* de la pluie

raindrop ['reɪndrɒp] *n* goutte *f* de pluie

rainfall ['reɪnfɔːl] *n* (*amount*) précipitations *fpl*; **average r.** précipitations moyennes, taux *m* de pluviosité; **low/high r.** précipitations faibles/importantes

rainforest ['reɪnfɒrɪst] *n* (**tropical**) **r.** forêt *f* tropicale humide

rain gauge *n* pluviomètre *m*

rainless ['reɪnlɪs] *adj* (*day etc*) sans pluie

rainmaker ['reɪnmeɪkər] *n* (*magician*) faiseur, -euse de pluie

rainmaking ['reɪnmeɪkɪŋ] *adj* (*ritual etc*) pour faire pleuvoir

rainout ['reɪnaʊt] *n Am Sp* match *m* annulé à cause du mauvais temps

rainproof[1] ['reɪnpruːf] *adj* (*coat, fabric etc*) imperméable

rainproof[2] *vt* (*fabric*) imperméabiliser

rainstorm ['reɪnstɔːm] *n* pluies *fpl* torrentielles

rainwater ['reɪnwɔːtər] *n* eau *f* de pluie

rainwear ['reɪnweər] *n* (*clothing*) vêtements *mpl* de pluie

rainy ['reɪnɪ] *adj* (*climate, weather*) pluvieux; **a r. day** un jour de pluie; **the r. season** la saison des pluies; **it has been very r. recently** il a beaucoup plu récemment; *Fig* **to put something by** *or* **keep something for a r. day** garder une poire pour la soif; *Fig* **she puts by ten pounds a week for a r. day** elle met dix livres de côté par semaine au cas où elle en aurait besoin

raise[1] [reɪz] *n* **(a)** *Am* (*pay increase*) augmentation *f* (de salaire); **to get a r.** être augmenté, avoir une augmentation **(b)** *Cards* (*poker*) relance *f*; (*bridge*) enchère *f*

raise[2] *vt* **(a)** (*lift, cause to rise*) (*one's hand, eyes, anchor*) lever; (*veil*) relever; (*weight*) lever, soulever; (*blind*) remonter; (*flag*) hisser; (*sunken ship*) renflouer; **to r. a cloud of dust** soulever un nuage de poussière; *Th* **to r. the curtain** lever le rideau; **to r. an eyebrow** *or* **one's eyebrows** (*in disapproval*) froncer les sourcils, sourciller; (*in surprise*) ouvrir des yeux ronds **he raised an eyebrow at the news** à cette nouvelle, son visage prit un air d'étonnement; **that will r. a few eyebrows** *or* **an eyebrow or two** (*cause surprise*) cela va en surprendre plus d'un; (*cause disapproval*) cela va en faire tiquer plus d'un; **eyebrows were raised yesterday when ...** (*in surprise*) il y a eu un mouvement de surprise hier quand ...; (*in disapproval*) la désapprobation s'est lue sur les visages hier quand ...; **to r. one's fist to sb** menacer qn du poing; **to r. one's glass** lever son verre (**to sb** à la santé de qn); **to r. one's glass to one's lips** porter son verre à ses lèvres; **to r. sb's hackles** hérisser qn; **to r. one's hand to sb** lever la main sur qn; **to r. one's hat to sb** soulever son chapeau pour saluer qn; *Fig* tirer son chapeau à qn; **to r. one's head** (*from lowered position*) lever la tête; (*hold erect*) dresser la tête; **to r. a patient to a sitting position** soulever un malade pour l'asseoir; **to r. sb's hopes** donner de l'espoir à qn; **don't r. your hopes too much** n'espère pas trop; *Mil, Fig* **to r. one's sights** viser plus haut; **to r. standards** (*of education, morality*) élever le niveau; (*of cleanliness, safety*) améliorer les conditions; **to r. the standard of living** améliorer le niveau de vie; **to r. sb's spirits** remonter le moral à qn; **to r. the tone** *or* **level of the conversation** élever le niveau de la conversation; **to r. the tone** *or* **level of the neighbourhood** rehausser le prestige du quartier; **to r. the rafters** (*make noise*) faire un foin d'enfer *ou* un boucan de tous les diables; **to r. the roof** (*make noise*) faire un foin d'enfer *ou* un boucan de tous les diables; (*complain*) faire une scène terrible *ou* de tous les diables

(b) (*increase in amount*) (*wages, price*) augmenter; (*temperature*) faire monter; **to r. a credit limit** déplafonner un crédit; **to r. production to a maximum** porter la production au maximum; **to r. the school-leaving age** prolonger la scolarité; **they've raised the age limit to ...** l'âge limite est passé à ...; **to r. the stakes** faire monter les enjeux; **to r. the pass mark** élever le niveau requis; *Fig* **she raised the temperature (of the room) by her condemnation of party policy** les esprits se sont échauffés lorsqu'elle a condamné la politique du parti; *Am* **to r. a cheque** falsifier le montant d'un chèque; *Cards* **I'll r. you ten** (*at poker*) plus dix; *Math* **to r. a number to the ninth power** élever un nombre à la puissance neuf

(c) (*increase in height*) **to r. (the level of) a wall** rehausser *ou* surélever un mur; **to r. the level of the ground** rehausser le niveau du sol; **to r. the ceiling on wage increases** augmenter le plafond des salaires; **she raised herself to her full height and replied ...** elle se redressa et, de toute sa hauteur, répondit ...

(d) (*increase in intensity*) **to r. sb's consciousness (of sth)** (*inform*) sensibiliser qn (à qch); (*emphasize*) faire prendre conscience à qn (de qch); **to r. one's voice** (*speak more loudly*) élever la voix; (*speak in anger*) hausser le ton; **no one raised their voice (to answer** *or* **speak)** personne ne souffla mot

(e) (*create, produce*) (*problem, matter for discussion*) soulever (**with** auprès de); (*fears, doubts, distrust*) susciter; **to r. an objection** élever *ou* soulever une objection; **to r. a question** (*make query*) poser une question; **his attitude raises certain questions** son attitude pose *ou* soulève *ou* suscite certaines questions; **his attitude raises questions about his loyalty** son attitude remet en question sa loyauté; *F* **to r. hell** *or* **a stink** (*complain*) faire une scène terrible *ou* de tous les diables (**about sth** à propos de qch); **to r. a blush/laugh** faire rougir/rire; **to r. a cheer** (*of people*) crier hourra; (*of announcement, speech etc*) soulever des hourras; **to r. a shout** (*of people*) pousser un cri; **to r. a smile** (*in oneself*) esquisser un sourire; (*in others*) provoquer *ou* faire naître un sourire; **to r. a storm of laughter/protest** déclencher *ou* soulever une tempête de rires/protestations; **to r. the alarm** donner *ou* sonner l'alarme; **to r. a loan** (*of government*) émettre *ou* lancer un emprunt; (*of individual*) faire un emprunt (**on** sur); **to r. steam** (*in boiler*) chauffer la chaudière

(f) (*collect together*) (*money*) rassembler; **to r. money for charity** mobiliser des fonds pour une œuvre de bienfaisance; **to r. an army** réunir une armée, mettre une armée sur pied; **to r. funds** (*for charity*) (*of volunteers*) collecter des fonds (**for** pour, au profit de); (*for business, government programme*) se procurer des fonds; **to r. signatures** (*for petition*) rassembler des signatures; **how much (money)**

did you r. on the car when you sold it? combien est-ce que tu t'es fait sur la vente de la voiture?; **he wanted a new motorbike but couldn't r. the money** il voulait une moto neuve mais il n'a pas pu trouver l'argent nécessaire; **to r. taxes** lever des impôts

(g) (*erect*) (*building, barn etc*) construire; (*statue*) ériger (**to** à l'effigie de)

(h) (*rear, grow*) (*children*) élever; (*cattle, poultry etc*) élever, faire l'élevage de; (*wheat, vegetables*) cultiver, faire pousser

(i) (*promote*) *Mil, Fig* **to r. sb from the ranks** promouvoir qn; *Mil* **to r. sb to the rank of lieutenant** promouvoir qn lieutenant; **to r. sb from the gutter** sortir qn du caniveau; **to r. sb to the peerage** (*give hereditary title to*) anoblir qn; (*give life title to*) conférer à qn un titre de pair

(j) (*contact*) (*by telephone*) (*person*) joindre, contacter; (*by radio*) (*ship*) entrer en contact (radio) avec; *Naut* **to r. land** apercevoir la terre

(k) (*awaken, rouse*) **to r. Cain** (*make noise*) faire un foin d'enfer *ou* un boucan de tous les diables; (*complain*) faire une scène terrible *ou* de tous les diables; **to r. the devil** (*complain*) faire une scène terrible *ou* de tous les diables; **to r. sb from his/her bed** faire lever qn, sortir qn du lit; **to r. sb from the dead** ressusciter qn; **to r. a ghost** faire apparaître un fantôme; **to r. a spirit** évoquer un esprit

(l) (*stir up*) (*nation*) soulever; (*rebellion*) provoquer

(m) (*end*) (*blocade, embargo, siege*) lever

▶ **raise up** *vtsep* lever, soulever; **she raised herself up out of her chair** elle se leva de son fauteuil

raised [reɪzd] *adj* **(a)** (*lifted*) (*arm etc*) levé; **we could hear r. voices from the next room** on entendait des gens qui parlaient fort dans la pièce d'à côté; **to say sth in a r. voice** dire qch en haussant le ton **(b)** (*elevated*) (*deck, flowerbed*) surélevé; (*embossed*) (*design, letter, motif*) en relief **(c)** *Am Culin* au levain

raiser ['reɪzər] *n* (*breeder*) (*of cattle etc*) éleveur *m*

raisin ['reɪz(ə)n] *n* raisin *m* sec; **r. bread** pain *m* aux raisins

raising ['reɪzɪŋ] *n* **(a)** (*lifting*) (*of curtain*) lever *m*; (*of sunken ship*) renflouage *m*; (*of standards*) élévation *f* **(b)** (*of prices, rents, salaries*) augmentation *f*; **r. of the school-leaving age** prolongation *f* de la scolarité **(c)** (*of army*) levée *f*; (*collecting*) (*of funds for charity*) collecte *f*; (*of taxes*) levée; **r. of money** mobilisation *f* de fonds **(d)** (*of barn, building*) construction *f*; (*of monument, statue*) érection *f* **(e)** (*of animals*) élevage *m*; (*of children*) éducation *f*; (*of crops*) culture *f* **(f)** (*of blockade, embargo, siege*) levée; **r. of the dead** résurrection *f* des morts; *Culin* **r. agent** levure *f*

Raj [rɑːdʒ] *n Br Hist* **the R.** l'empire *m* britannique en Inde

rajah ['rɑːdʒə] *n* ra(d)ja(h) *m*

rake[1] [reɪk] *n* **(a)** (*for gardener, croupier*) râteau *m* **(b)** (*for grate*) râble *m*, ringard *m*; **as thin as a r.** maigre comme un clou

rake[2] *vt* **(a)** (*collect or level with rake*) (*leaves, ground, path*) ratisser **(b)** *Mil* (*fire on with machine gun*) (*enemy forces, trenches*) mitrailler **(c)** (*search*) (*with eyes*) (*group, crowd*) détailler minutieusement; (*with searchlights*) (*sky, sea*) balayer; **to r. one's memory** fouiller dans ses souvenirs

rake[3] *n Lit* (*dissolute man*) coureur *m*, débauché *m*, libertin *m*, *Old-fashioned* roué *m*

rake[4] *n* (*slope*) (*of aircraft wings, funnel, mast etc*) (angle *m* d')inclinaison *f*; (*of stage*) pente *f*, inclinaison; **stage with a steep r.** scène fortement inclinée

rake[5] **1** *vi* (*of aircraft wings, funnel, mast etc*) être incliné; (*of stage*) être en pente *ou* incliné **2** *vt* (*funnel, mast etc*) incliner; (*stage*) construire en pente; **a steeply raked stage** une scène fortement inclinée

▶ **rake about, rake around** *vi* (*search*) fouiller (**among, in** dans)

▶ **rake in** *vtsep* **(a)** *F* (*money*) (*acquire*) amasser; **you must be raking it in!** tu dois t'en mettre plein les poches!; **that shop is raking in a fortune** ce magasin ramasse une fortune **(b)** (*in garden*) (*compost*) enfouir au râteau; (*in casino*) (*stakes*) ratisser

▶ **rake off** *vtsep* **(a)** (*remove*) (*pebbles, leaves*) enlever au râteau **(b)** *F* (*take*) empocher; **he raked off £50** il a empoché 50 livres, il s'est mis 50 livres dans la poche

▶ **rake out** *vtsep* **(a)** (*remove ashes from*) retirer *ou* enlever les cendres de **(b)** *F* (*find*) (*scarf, gloves etc*) dégoter, dénicher (**from** dans)

▶ **rake over** *vtsep* (*ground*) ratisser; *Fig* **to r. over the ashes** *or* **the past** (*revive*) remuer le passé

▶ **rake through** *vipo* (*search*) (*pockets, drawer*) fouiller dans; **the down-and-out was raking through the dustbins** le clochard fouillait dans *ou* faisait les poubelles

▶ **rake up** *vtsep* **(a)** (*collect with rake*) (*leaves*) ratisser **(b)** (*revive*) (*fire*) attiser; *Fig* **to r. up an old quarrel** raviver une ancienne querelle; **to r. up the past** remuer le passé; **to r. up sb's past** fouiller dans le passé de qn **(c)** *F* (*find with difficulty*) (*money, story etc*) dégoter, dénicher

rake-off *n* **(a)** *F* (*share of profits*) (*legal*) commission *f*; (*illegal*) ristourne *f*; **what's her r.?** (*legal*) quelle est sa part?; (*illegal*) combien est-ce qu'elle se met dans la poche? **(b)** *Am* (*deduction*) rabais *m*, réduction *f* (**on** sur)

raki [rɑː'kiː, 'rækɪ] *n* (*drink*) raki *m*

rakish ['reɪkɪʃ] *adj* **(a)** *Old-fashioned* (*dissolute*) (*behaviour, life*) débauché **(b)** (*jaunty*) (*air*) cavalier, désinvolte; **to wear one's hat at a r. angle** porter son chapeau avec désinvolture; **r. charm/smile** charme *f*/sourire *m* canaille; *Naut* **a ship built on r. lines** un navire élancé *ou* effilé

rakishly ['reɪkɪʃlɪ] *adv* d'un air désinvolte

rally[1] ['rælɪ] *n* **(a)** (*meeting*) grand rassemblement *m*; (*protest gathering*) manifestation *f* **(b)** (*improvement*) (*in health*) amélioration *f* passagère, mieux *m* momentané; *St Exch* redressement *m*, rally *m* **(c)** *Sp* (*in tennis etc*) long échange *m* **(d)** (*car race*) rallye *m*

rally[2] **1** *vt* **(a)** (*unite, win over*) (*troops, supporters*) rallier; **to r. support for a cause** s'assurer un soutien pour une cause

(b) (*recover*) (*one's strength*) reprendre; **to r. one's spirits** reprendre courage; **to r. sb's spirits** redonner courage à qn

2 *vi* **(a)** (*unite, support*) se rallier (**to, round** à); **to r. for the attack** se regrouper pour attaquer; **to r. round sb** (*help*) venir en aide à qn; **all the neighbours rallied round to help** tous les voisins sont venus apporter leur soutien; **to r. to sb's defence** accourir au secours de qn

(b) (*recover*) (*of shares*) se redresser; (*of patient*) se remettre momentanément; (*of athlete*) se reprendre, se ressaisir

(c) *Sp* (*enter car rallies*) courir *ou* participer à des rallyes; *Tennis* **they've been rallying for five minutes** l'échange dure depuis cinq minutes

rallycross ['rælɪkrɒs] *n Aut* rallycross *m*

rally driver *n* pilote *m* de rallye

rallyer ['rælɪər] *n Sp* concurrent, -ente d'un rallye

rallying ['rælɪɪŋ] *n* **(a)** (*of troops, supporters*) ralliement *m*; **r. cry/point** cri *m*/point *m* de ralliement **(b)** *Sp, Aut* **to go r.** courir *ou* participer à un rallye/des rallyes

RAM *n* **(a)** [ræm] *Comptr* (*abbr* **random access memory**) mémoire *f* vive; **R. chip** puce *f* de mémoire vive; **R. disk** mémoire à disque; **R.-resident** résident en mémoire vive **(b)** [ɑːreɪ'em] *Br* (*abbr* **Royal Academy of Music**) = Conservatoire *m* national de musique

ram[1] [ræm] *n* **(a)** (*animal*) bélier *m*; (*astrological sign*) Bélier **(b)** *Tech* (*part of pile driver*) marteau *m*; (*part of hydraulic press*) (piston *m*) plongeur *m*; **(hydraulic) r.** bélier *m* hydraulique; *Aut* **r. air** air *m* forcé; *Aut* **r. air induction** introduction *f* d'air par forçage; **r. cylinder** vérin *m* **(c)** *Hum Sl* (*sexually active man*) viril *m*, macho *m*

ram[2] *vt* (**-mm-**) **(a)** (*crash into*) (*of ship*) (*another ship, submarine*) entrer en collision avec, aborder; *Hist* (*galleon*) éperonner; (*of car*) (*tree, lorry*) heurter, percuter; **he rammed the gates with a lorry** (*knocked down*) il a défoncé le portail avec un camion; **he rammed the trolley into my ankles** il m'a heurté les chevilles avec son caddie **(b)** (*force into place*) enfoncer (**into** dans)

▶ **ram down** *vtsep* (*compact*) (*earth*) tasser; *Fig* **to r. one's hat down on one's head** enfoncer son chapeau (sur la tête); **she's always ramming religion down my throat** elle me rebat toujours les oreilles avec sa religion

▶ **ram home** *vtsep* (*emphasize*) (*the importance of something*) insister sur; **he kept ramming it home that we should ...** il n'arrêtait pas de répéter que nous devions ...; *Mil* **to r. home a charge** bourrer un canon *ou* un fusil

▶ **ram into** **1** *vtaspo* (*force*) **to r. clothes into a suitcase** bourrer une valise de vêtements; **to r. a charge into a gun** bourrer un fusil; *Fig* **the teacher rammed the dates into them** le professeur leur enfonçait *ou* leur faisait entrer les dates dans la tête; **to r. food into one's mouth** se gaver **2** *vipo* (*collide with*) emboutir, percuter; **a Jag rammed into the back of me** une Jag a embouti l'arrière de ma voiture; **they rammed into each other** ils se sont percutés

▶ **ram through** *vtsep* (*force acceptance of*) (*appointment*) imposer

Ramadan [ræmə'dɑːn] *n Rel* ramadan *m*; **during R.** pendant ramadan

ramble[1] ['ræmb(ə)l] *n* (*walk*) (*spontaneous*) balade *f*, grande promenade *f*; (*planned*) randonnée *f*; **to go on** *or* **for a r.** (*spontaneously*) faire une balade *ou* une grande promenade; (*planned*) partir en randonnée

ramble[2] *vi* **(a)** (*walk*) (*spontaneously*) se balader, faire une grande promenade (**over, through** dans); (*planned*) faire une randonnée (**over, through** dans) **(b)** (*talk in* *disconnected fashion*) parler sans suite, dire n'importe quoi (**about** de) (**c**) (*be delirious*) divaguer, *F* battre la campagne (**d**) (*meander*) (*of stream*) serpenter (**through** dans); **there was ivy rambling all over the ruins** le lierre rampait sur les ruines; **the path that rambles through the fields** le chemin sinueux qui traverse les champs

▶ **ramble on** *vi* tenir des discours sans fin, discourir; **to r. on about nothing in particular** parler pour ne rien dire; **what are you rambling on about now?** qu'est-ce que tu racontes maintenant?

rambler ['ræmblər] *n* (**a**) (*hiker*) randonneur, -euse (**b**) (*rose*) rosier *m* grimpant (**c**) *Am* (*house*) ranch *m*

rambling ['ræmblɪŋ] **1** *adj* (**a**) (*conversation, letter, speech etc*) décousu (**b**) (*path, stream etc*) sinueux; **a r. house** une maison pleine de coins et de recoins; **a r. town** une ville construite au hasard; **r. rose** rosier *m* grimpant **2** *n* (**a**) (*hiking*) randonnées *fpl*; **to go r.** partir en randonnée (**b**) **ramblings** (*delirium*) divagations *fpl*; **the ramblings of old age** les radotages *mpl* de la vieillesse

rambunctious [ræm'bʌŋkʃəs] *adj US F* (**a**) (*boisterous*) (*behaviour, child*) turbulent, chahuteur, -euse, tapageur (**b**) (*noisy*) (*meeting*) bruyant, mouvementé; (*party*) bruyant

RAMC [ɑːreɪem'siː] *n Br Mil* (*abbr* **Royal Army Medical Corps**) ≈ service *m* de santé de l'armée

ramee ['ræmɪ] *n Tex* = **ramie**

ramekin, ramequin ['ræmɪkɪn] *n Culin* ramequin *m*

ramie ['ræmɪ] *n Tex* ramie *f*

ramification [ræmɪfɪ'keɪʃən] *n* ramification *f*

ramify ['ræmɪfaɪ] **1** *vt* ramifier **2** *vi* se ramifier

ramjet ['ræmdʒet] *n Av* **r. (engine)** statoréacteur *m*

rammer ['ræmər] *n* (*for road-making*) dame *f*; (*for metal-working*) fouloir *m*, batte *f*; (*for civil engineering*) engin *m* de compactage du sol

ramp [ræmp] *n* (**a**) (*slope*) rampe *f* (**b**) *Aut* (*in garage*) pont *m* élévateur; (*connecting road*) bretelle *f* (d'accès); (*bump on road*) dos *m* d'âne; (*difference in level*) dénivellation *f*, dénivellement *m*; (*to slow traffic down*) ralentisseur *m*; *Av* **boarding r.** passerelle *f*

rampage¹ ['ræmpeɪdʒ] *n F* **to be** *or* **go on the r.** (*lose control*) se déchaîner; (*cause damage*) tout saccager; *Hum* **the boss is on the r.** le patron est complètement déchaîné; **the hooligans went on a r.** les hooligans ont tout saccagé sur leur passage

rampage² [ræm'peɪdʒ] *vi* **to r.** (**about** *or* **around**) se déchaîner; **they were rampaging through the streets** ils saccageaient tout dans les rues

rampaging [ræm'peɪdʒɪŋ] *adj* (*bulls, protestors etc*) déchaîné

rampancy ['ræmpənsɪ] *n* (*of corruption, vice*) prolifération *f*; (*of plant*) exubérance *f*

rampant ['ræmpənt] *adj* (**a**) (*corruption, poverty, vice*) qui sévit, endémique; (*plant*) exubérant, luxuriant; **to be r.** (*of corruption etc*) régner, sévir; *F* **he's a bit r. tonight** (*sexually*) il est émoustillé ce soir; **r. inflation** inflation *f* galopante (**b**) *Her* rampant; **the Lion R.** le Lion rampant

rampart ['ræmpɑːt] *n* (*fortification*); *Fig* rempart *m*

ram-raid ['ræmreɪd] *vt* **to r. a shop** dévaliser un magasin après en avoir brisé la vitrine à l'aide d'un véhicule

ramrod ['ræmrɒd] *n* (*for cleaning rifle*) écouvillon *m*; (*for loading cannon*) refouloir *m*; **to be as stiff as a r.** être raide comme un piquet; **to sit as straight as a r.** *or* **r-straight** être raide comme un piquet sur sa chaise

ramshackle ['ræmʃæk(ə)l] *adj* (*building, farm*) délabré, qui tombe en ruines; (*economy, government*) qui s'effrite *ou* s'effondre, délabré; **r. old car** vieille guimbarde *f*

ran [ræn] *see* = **ran²**

ranch¹ [rɑːntʃ] *n* ranch *m*, ferme *f* d'élevage; **cattle/mink r.** ferme d'élevage de bétail/du vison; **r. hand** employé *m* de ranch; **r. house** ranch; *Am* **r. mink** vison *m* d'élevage

ranch² **1** *vi* avoir *ou* exploiter *ou* tenir un ranch **2** *vt* (*cattle, mink*) élever, faire l'élevage de

rancher ['rɑːntʃər] *n* propriétaire *mf* de ranch; **cattle/mink r.** éleveur *mf* de bétail/visons

ranching ['rɑːntʃɪŋ] *n* (*of cattle, mink*) élevage *m*

rancid ['rænsɪd] *adj* rance; **to go r.** rancir; **to smell r.** sentir le rance

rancidity [ræn'sɪdɪtɪ], **rancidness** ['rænsɪdnɪs] *n* (*of butter, fat etc*) rancidité *f*

rancorous ['ræŋkərəs] *adj* (*attitude*) rancunier, -ière, plein de rancœur; (*remark*) amer, plein de rancœur

rancour, *US* **rancor** ['ræŋkər] *n* rancune *f*, rancœur *f*; **full of r.** (*remark etc*) amer; **the r. of her remarks/criticisms** l'amertume de ses remarques/critiques; **he is full of r.** (*permanent condition*) il est aigri; **to be full of r. against sb** avoir beaucoup de rancœur contre qn

rand [rænd] *n* (**a**) (*South African currency*) rand *m* (**b**) *Geog* **the R.** le Rand

R & B [ɑːrən'biː] *n Mus* (*abbr* **rhythm and blues**) rhythm and blues *m*

R & D [ɑːrən'diː] *n* (*abbr* **research and development**) recherche *f* et développement; **R. department** bureau *m* d'études; **R. director** directeur *m* de recherche et développement; **R. expenditure** dépenses *fpl* pour la recherche et le développement

random ['rændəm] **1** *adj* (*choice*) fait au hasard; (*sample*) prélevé au hasard; (*pattern*) irrégulier; *Math* (*error, number*) aléatoire; **I just made a r. guess** j'ai deviné tout à fait par hasard; **a r. selection of people were asked if …** on a demandé à des gens choisis au hasard si …; **r. check/sampling** contrôle *m*/échantillonnage *m* au hasard; **r. killings** tuerie *f* aveugle *ou* au hasard; *Mktg* **r. selection** sélection *f* au hasard; **r. shot** coup *m* tiré au hasard *ou* à l'aveuglette; **to be killed by a r. shot** *or* **bullet** être tué par une balle perdue; *Math* **r. variable** variable *f* aléatoire; **r. violence** violence *f* gratuite

2 *n* **at r.** au hasard; **to fire at r.** tirer au hasard *ou* à l'aveuglette

random access *n Comptr* accès *m* aléatoire *ou* sélectif; **r. file** fichier *m* à accès aléatoire; **r. memory** mémoire *f* vive

randomize ['rændəmaɪz] *vt* randomiser

randy ['rændɪ] *adj Br F* émoustillé, allumé; **to get** *or* **become r.** commencer à s'exciter; **to make sb r.** allumer qn; **to be feeling r.** être excité; **he's a r. devil** c'est un chaud lapin

ranee ['rɑːnɪ] *n* rani *f*

range¹ [reɪndʒ] *n* (**a**) (*of missile, telescope, weapon*) portée *f*; (*of car, plane*) autonomie *f*; *Mil* **out of r.** hors de portée (de tir); *Mil* **within r.** à portée de tir; **at point blank r.** à bout portant; **at a r. of 1,000 metres** à une distance de 1 000 mètres; **to fire at short/long r.** tirer à petite/grande distance *ou* à courte/longue portée; **short/medium/long-r. aircraft** court/moyen/long-courrier *m*; *Met* **short/long-r. forecast** prévisions *fpl* météorologiques à court/long terme; **to be within hearing r.** être à portée de voix; **r. of vision** champ *m* visuel; **r. finding** télémétrie *f*

(**b**) (*target practice area*) **rifle** *or* **shooting r.** *Mil* champ *m* de tir; (*at funfair*) stand *m* de tir; **rocket/torpedo r.** zone *f* d'essai de fusées/torpilles

(**c**) (*scale*) (*of prices, salaries*) échelle *f*, éventail *m*; (*of instrument, voice*) étendue *f*, registre *m*, tessiture *f*; **beyond one's r.** (*of price*) au-dessus de ses moyens; (*of note*) hors de son registre; **within one's r.** (*of price*) dans ses prix; (*of note*) dans son registre; **what is your price r.?** quel prix voulez-vous mettre?; **a house at the lower end of the r.** une maison bas de gamme; **an actor with a wide r. of expressions** un acteur qui a une gamme d'expressions très variée

(**d**) (*scope*) (*of knowledge, research*) étendue *f*; (*of inquiry, investigation*) domaine *m*; **she has a wide r. of interests** elle s'intéresse à beaucoup de choses

(**e**) (*collection, series*) (*of colours, feelings, products*) gamme *f*; (*of patterns, sizes*) choix *m*; **the shop carries a wide/limited r. of …** le magasin offre un grand choix/choix limité de …; **the coat comes in a wide r. of colours/sizes** le manteau existe dans une gamme variée de couleurs/un grand choix de tailles; **a top of the r. sports car** une voiture de sport haut de gamme; **to experience the full r. of emotions** passer par toute la gamme des émotions

(**f**) (*of hills, mountains*) chaîne *f*

(**g**) (*territory*) (*of animal, plant*) habitat *m*; *Am* (*grazing area*) prairie *f*, pâturages *mpl*; **r. cattle** bétail *m* élevé dans la prairie

(**h**) (*in surveying*) alignement *m*, direction *f*; **r. pole** *or* **rod** jalon *m*

(**i**) (*cooker*) **kitchen r.** fourneau *m* de cuisine

range² **1** *vt* (**a**) (*arrange in row*) (*troops, pupils*) faire aligner; (*tanks along border*) déployer; (*plates, books*) ranger (**along** le long de); *Fig* **to r. oneself with sb** se ranger du côté de qn; (*in political, scientific etc matters*) s'aligner sur la position de qn; *Fig* **to r. oneself against sb** s'opposer à qn; **the forces which were ranged against them** les forces alliées contre eux

(**b**) (*travel*) (*forest, sea*) parcourir, sillonner (**in search of, looking for** à la recherche de)

(**c**) (*aim*) (*weapon, telescope*) braquer (**on** sur)

(**d**) *Am* **to r. cattle** élever du bétail dans la prairie

2 *vi* (**a**) (*extend*) (*of ages, colours, marks*) aller (**from … to** de … à); (*of prices, temperatures*) varier (**from … to** entre … et); **incomes ranging from £12,000 to £15,000** *or* **between £12,000 and £15,000** revenus *mpl* de l'ordre de 12 000 à 15 000 livres; **their discussions will r. over a great many topics** leurs discussions couvriront un grand nombre de sujets

(**b**) (*travel*) (*of animals, people*) parcourir; (*of projectiles*) porter (**over a given distance** à une distance donnée); **these**

guns r. over six miles ces canons ont une portée de six mil(l)es; **they ranged over a large area** (*were found*) leur habitat était très étendu; (*roamed across*) ils parcouraient de larges étendues; *Fig* **his eyes ranged over the audience** il parcourut l'auditoire des yeux

(**c**) *Mil* (*adjust aim*) régler le tir

rangefinder ['reɪndʒfaɪndər] *n* télémètre *m*

rangeland ['reɪndʒlænd] *n Am* prairie *f*

ranger ['reɪndʒər] *n* (**a**) (*in forest, park*) garde *m* forestier (**b**) *US* (*State police officer*) policier *m*; (*soldier*) membre *m* d'un commando (**c**) *Br* **R.** (**Guide**) (guide *f*) aînée *f*

ranging ['reɪndʒɪŋ] *adj Mil* **r. fire** tir *m* de réglage; **r. pole** *or* **rod** (*surveying instrument*) jalon *m*

rangy ['reɪndʒɪ] *adj* (*thin*) élancé

rani ['rɑːnɪ] *n* rani *f*

rank¹ [ræŋk] *n* (**a**) (*position*) (*in army, navy*) grade *m*; (*in society*) rang *m* (social); *Br* **badge of r.** insigne *m* de grade; **officer of high r.** officier *m* supérieur; **to hold the r. of colonel** avoir le grade de colonel; **to reduce in r.** rétrograder; *Mil* **the ranks** les hommes *mpl* (du rang); *Mil, Fig* **to have risen from the ranks** être sorti du rang; **to reduce an NCO to the ranks** casser un gradé; **to have served in the ranks** avoir servi comme simple soldat; *Mil* **all ranks** les militaires *mpl* de tous grades; *Br Mil* **officers and other ranks** gradés et simples soldats; **the higher ranks of the civil service** les hauts fonctionnaires; **person of (high) r.** personne de haut rang; **actor/dancer of the first r.** comédien/danseur de premier ordre; *Br* **a Minister of Cabinet r.** un ministre du Cabinet; *Fig* **to pull r. (on sb)** faire jouer son grade (avec qn); *Fig* **the ranks of the homeless/unemployed** les rangs des sans-abri/chômeurs

(**b**) (*row*) (*of trees, on chessboard etc*) rangée *f*; (*of people*) rang *m*; **r. upon r.** (*of objects*) rangée après rangée; (*of people*) rang après rang; **to arrange in ranks** (*objects*) mettre en rangées; (*people*) (faire) mettre en rangs; *Mil* **close ranks!** serrez!; *Mil* **to break/close ranks** rompre/serrer les rangs; *Fig* **to break ranks** se désolidariser (**with** de, d'avec); *Fig* **to close ranks** se montrer solidaire; *Mil* **front r.** premier rang; *Br* (**taxi**) **r.** station *f* de taxis

rank² **1** *vt* (**a**) (*classify*) (*athlete, book etc*) classer (**among** parmi, au nombre de)

(**b**) *Am* (*outrank*) (*in army*) occuper un rang supérieur à; (*in office, organization etc*) être le supérieur de

(**c**) (*arrange in rows*) (*pieces of game*) mettre en rangées; (*troops*) (faire) mettre en rangs

2 *vi* (**a**) (*occupy position*) compter (**among** parmi); **to r. above sb** être le supérieur de *ou* occuper un rang supérieur à qn; **to r. below sb** occuper un rang inférieur à qn; **to r. equally** être au même niveau (**with** que); **to r. with sb** être du même niveau que qn; **in chess, a castle ranks above a bishop** aux échecs, la tour est plus forte que le fou; **this must** *or* **has to r. as the best/biggest/worst ...** ceci doit être le meilleur/plus grand/pire ...; **a car does not r. high in my order of priorities** une voiture ne vient pas en tête de mes priorités

(**b**) *Am Mil* (*be most senior*) être le plus haut en grade; *Fig* **he doesn't r.** ce n'est pas quelqu'un d'important

rank³ *adj* (**a**) *Fml* (*excessive*) (*vegetation, weeds*) envahissant, luxuriant; **to grow r.** pousser (très) rapidement (**b**) (*foul-smelling*) fétide, qui sent fort; **to be r. with sweat** sentir fort la sueur; **to smell r.** sentir fort (**c**) (*absolute*) complet, absolu; (*ignorance, stupidity, incompetence*) crasse; **he's a r. outsider** (*in competition*) c'est un outsider; **r. beginner** parfait(e) novice *mf*; **r. imposter** fieffé imposteur *m*; **r. injustice** injustice *f* flagrante

rank-and-file *n* (**a**) *Mil* (*soldiers*) simples soldats *mpl*; **ten officers and two hundred r.** dix officiers et deux cents hommes (**b**) (*ordinary members*) (*in political party, union*) base *f*; **r. feelings/opinions** sentiments/opinions des membres *ou* de la base

rank-and-filer *n* (*in army*) simple soldat *m*; (*in political party, union*) membre *m* de la base

ranker ['ræŋkər] *n Mil* (*soldier*) simple soldat *m*; (*officer*) officier *m* sorti du rang

ranking ['ræŋkɪŋ] **1** *n* (*classification*) classement *m*; **his r. is number four** il est classé quatrième **2** *adj* (**a**) *Am* (*authority, economist*) éminent; *Am Mil* **the r. officer** l'officier le plus haut en grade (**b**) **high/low r.** (*officer*) de haut grade/grade inférieur; (*diplomat, official*) de haut rang/rang inférieur; **a low r. civil servant** un petit fonctionnaire

rankle ['ræŋk(ə)l] *vi* rester sur le cœur; **it rankled with me** je ne l'ai pas digéré; **what they did still rankles with her** elle n'a toujours pas digéré ce qu'ils ont fait

rankness ['ræŋknɪs] *n* (**a**) *Fml* (*of vegetation*) exubérance *f*, luxuriance *f* (**b**) (*foul smell*) odeur *f* forte *ou* fétide

ransack ['rænsæk] *vt* (**a**) (*search*) (*room, drawer*) mettre sens dessus dessous (**b**) (*pillage*) (*store, town*) piller, mettre à sac; (*house*) (*of burglar*) dévaliser

ransom¹ ['rænsəm] *n* (*money*) rançon *f*; **to hold sb to r.** demander une rançon pour la libération de qn; *Fig* **the strikers were holding the country to r.** les grévistes exerçaient un chantage sur le pays

ransom² *vt* (*captive*) racheter

rant [rænt] *vi* déclamer avec véhémence, *F* déblatérer (**about, at** contre); **to r. and rave** fulminer, tempêter (**about, at** contre)

▶ **rant on** *vi* = rant

ranting ['ræntɪŋ] **1** *adj* (*style*) déclamatoire; (*speech*) tonitruant **2** *n* **ranting(s)** déclamation *f*; **to listen to sb's r. about sth** écouter qn s'échauffer à propos de qch; **sectarian rantings** propos *mpl* d'un sectarisme hystérique; **r. and raving, rantings and ravings** discours *m* délirant

ranunculus, *pl* **-uses, -i** [ræ'nʌŋkjʊləs, -əsɪz, -aɪ] *n Bot* renoncule *f*

rap¹ [ræp] *n* (**a**) (*slight blow*) petit coup *m* sec; **I heard a r. at the door** j'ai entendu frapper à la porte; **to give sb a r. on** *or* **over the knuckles** (*hit*), *Fig* taper sur les doigts à qn; *Fig* **the saleswoman was given a r. over the knuckles for being rude to a customer** la vendeuse s'est fait taper sur les doigts pour avoir été impolie avec un client

(**b**) *esp US Sl* (*accusation, charge*) **to beat the r.** échapper à la condamnation; **to take the r. for sth** trinquer pour qch; **you let me take the r. for you** tu m'as laissé trinquer à ta place; **r. sheet** casier *m* judiciaire

(**c**) *US F* (*conversation*) **we had a r. session last night** hier soir, on a taillé une bavette

(**d**) *Fig F* (*small amount*) **he doesn't care** *or* **give a r.** il s'en moque *ou* s'en fiche éperdument

(**e**) *Mus* **r.** (**music**) rap *m*; **r. artist** chanteur, -euse de rap

rap² (**-pp-**) **1** *vt* (*strike*) (*window, door*) frapper à; **to r. sb's knuckles** *or* **sb on** *or* **over the knuckles** (*hit*), *Fig* taper sur les doigts à qn; *Am* **to r. sb** (*criticize*) éreinter qn **2** *vi* (**a**) **to r. at/on sth** frapper sur *ou* contre qch (**b**) *US F* (*talk*) papoter, bavarder

▶ **rap out** *vtsep* (**a**) (*order, instruction*) lancer (**b**) **to r. out a message** (*by tapping*) communiquer au moyen de coups

rapacious [rə'peɪʃəs] *adj* rapace

rapaciously [rə'peɪʃəslɪ] *adv* avec rapacité

rapacity [rə'pæsɪtɪ] *n* rapacité *f*

rape¹ [reɪp] *n* (**a**) viol *m*; **to commit r.** violer; *Fig* **the r. of the tropical forests** la destruction des forêts tropicales; **r. crisis centre** centre *m* d'acceuil et d'information pour les victimes de viol; **r. victim** personne *f* violée, victime *f* d'un viol (**b**) *Arch* (*abduction*) enlèvement *m*; **the R. of the Sabine Women** l'enlèvement des Sabines

rape² *vt* (*person*) violer; *Fig* (*forest, environment, region*) détruire

rape³ *n Bot* (**summer**) **r.** colza *m*; **r.** (**seed**) **oil** huile *f* de colza

raphia ['ræfɪə] **1** *n Bot* raphia *m* **2** *adj* en raphia

rapid ['ræpɪd] *adj* (*developments, improvement, progress*) rapide; *Mil* **r. deployment force** force *f* d'intervention rapide; **r. eye movement** sommeil *m* paradoxal, phase *f* de mouvements oculaires; **r. fire** feu *m* accéléré *ou* continu; **rapid-fire** *or* **rapid-firing gun** canon *m* à tir rapide; *Fig* **a comedian with rapid-fire delivery** un comédien au débit rapide; **he was subjected to a stream of rapid-fire questions** il a été soumis à un feu roulant de questions; **r. pulse** pouls *m* rapide; **r. strides** longues enjambées *fpl*; *Fig* **we are making r. strides towards a cure for cancer** la recherche contre le cancer fait des progrès rapides; **they have had six children in r. succession** ils ont eu six enfants très rapprochés

rapidity [rə'pɪdɪtɪ] *n* rapidité *f*

rapidly ['ræpɪdlɪ] *adv* rapidement

rapids ['ræpɪdz] *npl Geog* rapides *mpl*; **to shoot the r.** descendre les rapides

rapier ['reɪpɪər] *n* rapière *f*; *Fig* **she has a r. (-like) wit** elle a un esprit mordant; **r. thrust** coup *m* d'estoc *ou* de pointe; *Fig* (*witty remark*) trait *m* d'esprit

rapist ['reɪpɪst] *n* violeur *m*, auteur *m* d'un viol/de viols

▶ **rappel down** [ræ'pel] *vi* (*in mountaineering*) descendre en rappel

rapper ['ræpər] *n Mus* chanteur, -euse de rap

rapport [ræ'pɔːr] *n* bons rapports *mpl*, affinités *fpl*; **there was an instant r. between them** ils ressentirent une sympathie immédiate; **he had a r. with his music teacher** il avait des affinités avec son professeur de musique

rapprochement [ræ'prɒʃmɒn] *n* rapprochement *m*; **to effect a r.** se rapprocher (**with sb** de qn)

rapscallion [ræp'skælɪən] *n Arch, Hum* garnement *m*

rapt [ræpt] *adj* (*attention, interest*) profond; (*look, smile*) ravi, d'extase; **a r. face** un visage attentif; **there was a r. look on her face as she listened** elle écoutait, l'air très absorbé; **to be r. in contemplation** être plongé dans ses pensées, *Litt* sabîmer dans la contemplation

raptor ['ræptər] *n Orn* rapace *m*

rapture ['ræptʃər] *n* ravissement *m*, extase *f*; **to be in raptures** être ravi *ou* enchanté (**with, over** de); **in raptures of delight** transporté de joie; **he was filled with r. at the thought/the idea** il était en extase à cette pensée/cette idée; **to go into raptures** s'extasier (**over** devant); **he goes into raptures over his new grandchild** il s'extasie *ou* il est en extase devant son dernier petit-enfant; **she went into raptures at the prospect of meeting him** elle est tombée en extase à l'idée de le rencontrer

rapturous ['ræptʃərəs] *adj* (*cries*) d'extase, de ravissement; (*applause*) frénétique; (*reception, welcome*) enthousiaste; **his face was r. with joy** il rayonnait de joie; **they were r. about their daughter's success** le succès de leur fille les rendait fous de joie

rare [reər] *adj* **(a)** (*uncommon*) rare; **very** *or* **extremely r.** très *ou* extrêmement rare, rarissime; **it is r. for him to do that** c'est rare qu'il fasse ça; *Fig* **he's a r. bird** (*strange*) il est bizarre; *F* **you're a r. bird in these parts since you got that promotion** vous vous faites rare depuis que vous avez été promu; *Ch* **r. earths** terres *fpl* rares; **r. gas** gaz *m* rare **(b)** *Culin* (*steak etc*) (*on purpose*) bleu; (*by accident*) pas assez cuit; **medium r.** à point **(c)** (*lacking oxygen*) (*air, atmosphere*) raréfié **(d)** *Old-fashioned* **we had r. fun** *or* **a r. old time** on s'est fameusement amusés; **he's a r. one for a fight** il est toujours prêt à se battre

rarebit ['ræbɪt, 'reəbɪt] *n Culin* **Welsh r.** = tranche *f* de pain grillée recouverte de fromage fondu souvent mélangé à de la moutarde et de la bière

rarefied ['reərɪfaɪd] *adj* (*thin*) (*air, gas*) raréfié; *Fig* **to live in a r. atmosphere** vivre dans un monde à part

rarefy ['reərɪfaɪ] **1** *vt* (*air, gas*) raréfier **2** *vi* (*of air, gas*) se raréfier

rarely ['reəlɪ] *adv* rarement; **r. have I** *or* **I have r. encountered anyone like him** j'ai rarement rencontré quelqu'un comme lui; **she is r. ill** elle est rarement malade, il est rare qu'elle soit malade

rareness ['reənɪs] *n* (*uncommonness*) rareté *f*

raring ['reərɪŋ] *adj* (*eager*) **r. to start** impatient de commencer; **to be r. to go** (*of person, animal*) trépigner *ou* piaffer d'impatience

rarity ['reərɪtɪ] *n* (*uncommonness*) rareté *f*; **a fine day is a r. here** une belle journée est un événement rare ici; **wild flowers are becoming (something of) a r.** les fleurs sauvages se font de plus en plus rares

rascal ['rɑːsk(ə)l] *n* **(a)** (*child*) coquin, -ine, fripon, -onne; **you little r.!** petit coquin!, petite canaille! **(b)** *Old-fashioned* (*scoundrel*) coquin *m*, vaurien *m*

rascally ['rɑːskəlɪ] *adj Old-fashioned* (*behaviour*) de coquin; (*lawyer*) retors; **r. fellow** coquin *m*, vaurien *m*; **r. trick** vilain tour *m*, tour de coquin

rase [reɪz] *vt* = **raze**

rash¹ [ræʃ] *n* **(a)** *Med* rougeur *f*, éruption *f* (cutanée); (*caused by allergy*) urticaire *f*; (*caused by chickenpox, measles, scarlet fever*) exanthème *m*, *F* boutons *mpl*; **to come out** *or* **break out in a r.** attraper des boutons; (*because of allergy*) avoir une crise d'urticaire; **strawberries bring me out in a rash** les fraises me donnent de l'urticaire; *Fig* **the very thought of him brings me out in a r.!** rien que de penser à lui ça me donne des boutons! **(b)** *Fig* (*of anonymous letters, resignations etc*) vague *f*, épidémie *f*

rash² *adj* (*person*) imprudent, téméraire; (*action, words*) imprudent, inconsidéré, irréfléchi; **don't make any r. promises!** ne faites pas de promesses en l'air!; **we decided in a r. moment to ...** nous avons décidé dans un moment de folie de ...; **that was a bit r. of you** c'était un peu risqué de ta part; *Hum* **don't do anything r., will you?** surtout, ne fais pas de folies!

rasher ['ræʃər] *n Br* tranche *f* de bacon

rashly ['ræʃlɪ] *adv* (*to behave, act, speak*) sans réfléchir, imprudemment; (*to agree, decide*) dans un moment de folie

rashness ['ræʃnɪs] *n* (*of person, action*) imprudence *f*, inconséquence *f*; **I paid for my r.** j'ai payé cher mes imprudences; **the r. of the chairman's statement** la déclaration inconsidérée du président

rasp¹ [rɑːsp] *n* **(a)** (*file*) râpe *f* **(b)** (*sound*) grincement *m*; **the r. in his voice** le ton rauque de sa voix **(c)** *Scot* (*abbr* **raspberry**) framboise *f*

rasp² **1** *vt* **(a)** (*use file on*) râper; *Fig* **the cat rasped its tongue over my face** le chat m'a léché la figure de sa langue râpeuse; **he rasped his hand over his unshaven chin** il frotta sa main sur son menton râpeux **(b)** (*say hoarsely*) **to r. (out)** dire d'une voix rauque; **to r. out an answer/a plea** répondre/supplier d'une voix rauque **2** *vi* **(a)** (*make hoarse sound*) **her breath rasped in her lungs** elle avait une respiration sifflante **(b)** (*be irritating*) **to r. on the ears** écorcher les oreilles; **the constant creaking of the door was rasping on their nerves** le grincement constant de la porte leur portait sur les nerfs

raspberry ['rɑːzb(ə)rɪ] *n* **(a)** (*fruit, flavour*) framboise *f*; **r. (bush), r. cane** framboisier *m*; **r. jam** confiture *f* de framboise; **r. tart** tarte *f* à la framboise; **r. vinegar** vinaigre *m* de framboise **(b)** *F* **to blow** *or* **give sb a r.** (*jeer*) siffler qn; **to get a r.** se faire siffler

rasping ['rɑːspɪŋ] **1** *n* **(a)** (*noise*) grincement *m* **(b)** (*shaved-off piece of metal*) copeau *m* **2** *adj* (*sound*) grinçant; **r. cough** toux *f* rauque *ou* sèche; **r. voice** voix *f* rauque

raspings ['rɑːspɪŋz] *npl Culin* (*with breadcrumbs*) chapelure *f*

Rasta ['ræstə] *n, adj* (*abbr* **Rastafarian**) rasta *mf inv*

Rastafarian [ræstə'feərɪən] *n, adj* rastafari *mf inv*

Rastafarianism [ræstə'feərɪənɪz(ə)m] *n* rastafarianisme *m*

raster ['ræstər] *n* trame *f*; **r. scan** balayage *m* de trame

rat¹ [ræt] *n* **(a)** (*animal*) rat *m*; **to be caught like a r. in a trap** être fait comme un rat; **with her hair all in rats' tails** avec ses mèches collées; *Fig* **I smell a r.** il y a quelque chose de louche; *Am F* **r. cheese** fromage *m* ordinaire; **r. poison** mort-aux-rats *f*

(b) *F Pej* (*unreliable person*) lâcheur, -euse; **you r.!** salaud!, ordure!

(c) *US F Pej* (*informer*) mouchard, -arde, indic *m*

(d) *F Pej* (*strikebreaker*) jaune *mf*, briseur, -euse de grève

(e) *Br Old-fashioned F* **rats!** (*exclamation of irritation*) zut!

rat² *vi* (-tt-) *F Pej* (*reveal information*) moucharder, cafarder

▶ **rat on** *vipo F Pej* (*person*) (*to friends, parents etc*) dénoncer; (*to police*) balancer; **to r. on a promise** revenir sur une promesse; **they ratted on our deal** ils nous ont laissé tomber dans cette affaire

ratable ['reɪtəb(ə)l] *adj* = **rateable**

ratafia [rætə'fɪə] *n* (*drink*) ratafia *m*; *Br* **r. (biscuit)** macaron *m*

ratan [ræ'tæn] *n* = **rattan**

rat-arsed ['rætɑːst] *adj Br Sl* (*drunk*) rond comme une queue de pelle

rat-a-tat(-tat)¹ ['rætətæt(tæt)] *n* (*on door*) toc toc *m*; (*on drum*) rantanplan *m*; (*of machine gun*) pétarade *f*; (*of typewriter*) tac-tac-tac *m*

rat-a-tat(-tat)² *vi* (-tt-) (*on door*) frapper; (*of machine gun*) pétarader

ratatouille [rætə'tuːiː] *n Culin* ratatouille *f*

ratbag ['rætbæg] *n Sl* (*obnoxious person*) con *m*, conne *f*; *Hum* **you r.!** petit saligaud, petite garce!

rat-catcher *n* chasseur *m* de rats

ratchet ['rætʃɪt] *n Tech* rochet *m*; **r. mechanism** (dispositif *m* d')encliquetage *m*; **r. wheel** roue *f* à rochet; **r. screwdriver** tournevis *m* à cliquet

rate¹ [reɪt] *n* **(a)** (*of inflation, tax etc*) taux *m*; **r. of adoption** (*of product*) taux d'adoption; *Mktg* **r. of churn** taux de clients passés à la concurrence; **r. of depreciation** taux d'amortissement; **r. of exchange** cours du change; **r. of growth** taux d'accroissement *ou* de croissance; **r. of increase** taux d'accroissement; *Mktg* **r. of penetration** taux de pénétration; *Mktg* **r. of renewal** taux de renouvellement; **r. of return** (*on investment*) (taux de) rendement *m*; **r. of uptake** taux de succès; **birth/crime/death r.** taux de natalité/criminalité/mortalité; **pass** *or* **success/failure r.** (*in exam etc*) pourcentage *m* de réussites/d'échecs; **at the r. of** (*amount*) à raison de; **to be paid at the r. of five pounds an hour** être payé (à raison de) cinq livres de l'heure; **to strike for higher rates of pay** faire la grève pour obtenir une augmentation de salaire; **the r. is 60p in the pound** le taux est de soixante pence par livre

(b) (*speed*) vitesse *f*; **the fearful r. of technological advance** le rythme effrayant du progrès technologique; **at the r. of ...** au rythme de ...; *F* **at a r. of knots** à toute allure; **at this rate** à ce rythme-là; (*slow speed*) à ce train-là; **at the r. things are going** du train où vont les choses; *Fig* **at any r.** en tout cas; *Av* **r. of climb** vitesse ascensionnelle; **r. of flow** (*of rivers, turbines*) débit *m*; **r. of production** (*in factory*) cadence *f ou* rythme *m* de production

(c) (*price, charge*) tarif *m*; **what are your rates?** (*for hotel room, service*) quels sont vos tarifs *ou* prix?; **to pay the full r.** payer plein tarif

(d) *Br* (*formerly*) (*tax*) (*usu pl*) **rates** impôts *mpl* locaux; **rates and taxes** impôts et contributions; **r. collector** receveur, -euse municipal(e); **r. rebate** dégrèvement *m* d'impôts locaux; **rates office** recette *f* municipale

rate[2] **1** *vt* (**a**) (*consider*) considérer (**as** comme); (*classify*) (*athlete, pianist etc*) classer (**among** parmi); (*evaluate*) (*pupil, concert, film etc*) évaluer; **I r. him among my closest friends** je le compte au nombre de *ou* le considère comme un de mes amis les plus proches; **to r. sb/sth highly** apprécier beaucoup qn/qch; **to be highly rated** être très apprécié; **how do you r. their chances of winning the contract?** à votre avis, quelles sont leurs chances de décrocher le contrat?; **I r. this restaurant very highly** je trouve ce restaurant excellent; *Br F* **I don't r. him** je ne l'apprécie pas beaucoup

(**b**) (*deserve*) mériter; **that performance should r. him third place** cette prestation devrait lui assurer la troisième place; **a battle that didn't r. a mention in the history books** une bataille qui n'a pas mérité d'apparaître dans les livres d'histoire

(**c**) *Br* (*formerly*) (*set amount of taxes on*) (*property*) établir *ou* calculer le montant des impôts locaux sur; **their house has been rated higher this year** leur maison a été classée dans la tranche supérieure cette année

2 *vi* (*be classified*) se classer, être classé (**as** comme); **in terms of efficiency, she rates higher than anyone else** en ce qui concerne l'efficacité, elle bat tout le monde; **to r. with** (*impress*) plaire à, impressionner

-rate [reɪt] *suff* **first/second -r.** de premier/second ordre

rateable ['reɪtəb(ə)l] *adj Br Admin* (*house, property*) imposable; **r. value** valeur *f* locative nette, *Spec* loyer *m* matriciel

rate-cap *vt Br Admin* (*local authority*) fixer un taux plafond pour les impôts locaux de

rate-capping ['reɪtkæpɪŋ] *n Br Admin* plafonnement *m* des impôts locaux

rated ['reɪtɪd] *adj Tech* (*load, speed, voltage*) nominal

rate-of-return analysis *n* analyse *f* du rendement

ratepayer ['reɪtpeɪər] *n Br* (*formerly*) (*local taxpayer*) contribuable *mf* (assujetti(e) aux impôts locaux)

ratfink ['rætfɪŋk] *n US Pej Sl* (*obnoxious person*) salaud *m*, ordure *f*

rather ['rɑːðər] *adv* (**a**) (*preferably*) plutôt (**than** que); **I'd r. stay** j'aimerais mieux *ou* je préférerais rester (**than** que); **I would r. that you came** je préférerais que vous veniez; **I'd r. not** je n'y tiens pas; **I'd r. you didn't do it** je préférerais que tu ne le fasses pas; **r. than leave/stay** plutôt que de partir/rester; **anything r. than that** tout sauf ça; **r. you than me!** plutôt toi que moi!; **accept? I'd r. die!** accepter? plutôt mourir!

(**b**) (*more precisely*) **or r.** ou plutôt, ou pour être plus précis

(**c**) [ⓘA4, B] (*fairly*) plutôt, assez; (*to a degree*) un peu; **she's a r.** *or* **r. a beautiful woman** c'est une femme plutôt belle; **she is r. plain** elle n'est pas très jolie; **r. a lot of people** pas mal de monde; **I r. think you know him** je crois bien *ou* il me semble que vous le connaissez; **it tastes r. like a pear** (*but I know it's not*) ça rappelle le goût de la poire; (*I'm guessing*) on dirait de la poire; **I am r. inclined to agree with you** je suis plutôt de votre avis; **I r. liked it** ça m'a assez *ou F* pas mal plu; **it's r. nice** c'est bien, *F* c'est pas mal; **r. more tired** un peu plus fatigué (**than** que)

(**d**) ['rɑː'ðɜː] *Old-fashioned* (*certainly*) (*when accepting offer*) oui alors, et comment; (*when answering question*) et comment

ratification [rætɪfɪ'keɪʃən] *n* (*by government*) ratification *f*; (*by sports authorities*) homologation *f*

ratify ['rætɪfaɪ] *vt* (*treaty*) ratifier; (*record*) homologuer; **to r. a contract** approuver un contrat

ratine [ræ'tiːn] *n Tex* ratine *f*

rating ['reɪtɪŋ] *n* (**a**) (*classification*) classement *m*; *Am Mil* **r. badge**, *Br* **badge of r.** insigne *m* de grade

(**b**) (*evaluation*) (*of employee, student etc*) appréciation *f*; (*of candidates, politicians*) cote *f* de popularité; (*for credit*) notation *f*; **r. agency** agence *f* de notation *ou* de rating; **r. scale** (*in market research*) échelle *f* de classement

(**c**) *TV* **the ratings** l'indice *m* d'écoute, le taux *m* d'audience, le taux d'écoute; **to boost the ratings** améliorer l'indice d'écoute; **to stand high in the ratings** avoir un indice d'écoute élevé; **ratings success** succès *m* d'audience; **ratings war** guerre *f* de l'audimat®, course *f* à l'audimat®

(**d**) *Br Admin* (*formerly*) (*of property*) (*setting of tax*) calcul *m* du montant des impôts locaux; (*tax*) montant *m* des impôts locaux

(**e**) *Br* (*sailor*) matelot *m*; **the ratings** les matelots et gradés

ratio, *pl* **-os** ['reɪʃɪəʊ, -əʊz] *n* (*proportion, relationship*) proportion *f*, rapport *m*; **in a r. of 25 to 1** dans une proportion *ou* un rapport de 25 pour 1; **in direct r.** directement proportionnel, en rapport direct (**to** avec), en raison directe (**to** de); **the school has a teacher-pupil r. of 1 to 10** l'école a un rapport professeur-élève de 1 pour 10

ratiocination [rætɪɒsɪ'neɪʃən] *n Fml* raisonnement *m*

ration[1] ['ræʃən], *Am* ['reɪʃən] *n* (*of bread, sugar etc*) ration *f*; **you've had your r. of TV for this evening** tu as eu ta dose de télévision pour ce soir; **rations** (*food supplies*) provisions *fpl*; **to be on short rations** avoir des rations réduites; **to put sb on short rations** réduire les rations de qn; **full rations** rations complètes; *Mil* **to draw rations** toucher sa ration; *Am Mil* **C rations** vivres *mpl*; *Br Mil* **iron rations** vivres de réserve; **r. book** *or* **card** carte *f* de rationnement

ration[2] *vt* (*bread, sugar etc*) rationner; **I was rationed to ...** ma ration était de ...; **she rations herself to one film a week** elle se limite à un film par semaine; **I'll r. you to an hour's television a day** je ne t'autoriserai à regarder la télévision qu'une heure par jour

rational ['ræʃənəl] *adj* (**a**) (*sensible*) (*behaviour, person*) raisonnable, sensé; **it seemed like the r. thing to do** il me semblait que c'était ce qu'il y avait de plus logique à faire (**b**) (*sane*) rationnel; (*lucid*) lucide; **to be quite r.** avoir toute sa tête (**c**) (*based on or using reason*) (*decision*) sensé; (*thought*) rationnel; (*animal, creature*) doué de raison; **she is not quite r. when the subject of divorce comes up** elle ne pense pas très clairement lorsqu'on parle de divorce (**d**) *Math* (*number*) rationnel

rationale [ræʃə'nɑːl] *n* (*reasoning*) raisonnement *m* (**for** de); (*written or spoken*) exposé *m* raisonné; **what's the r. for the decision?** comment peut-on expliquer cette décision?

rationalism ['ræʃənəlɪz(ə)m] *n* rationalisme *m*

rationalist ['ræʃənəlɪst] *adj, n* rationaliste *mf*

rationalistic [ræʃənə'lɪstɪk] *adj* rationaliste

rationality [ræʃə'nælɪtɪ] *n* (*of decision, thought*) rationalité *f*

rationalization [ræʃənəlaɪ'zeɪʃən] *n* (**a**) (*of action, behaviour etc*) justification *f*, rationalisation *f* (**of** de) (**b**) *Br Ind* (*of company etc*) rationalisation *f*

rationalize ['ræʃənəlaɪz] **1** *vt* (**a**) (*action, behaviour, dislike, fear etc*) justifier, rationaliser, trouver une explication logique *ou* rationnelle à (**b**) *Br Ind* (*company etc*) rationaliser

2 *vi* (**do**) **stop rationalizing!** arrête de chercher des excuses!

rationally ['ræʃənəlɪ] *adv* (**a**) (*sensibly*) raisonnablement (**b**) (*sanely*) rationnellement (**c**) (*using reason*) (*to decide, think*) rationnellement

rationing ['ræʃənɪŋ], *Am* ['reɪʃənɪŋ] *n* (*of bread, sugar etc*) rationnement *m* (**of** de); (**food**) **r.** rationnement alimentaire

ratlin(e) ['rætlɪn] *n Naut* enfléchure *f*

rat race *n Fig* jungle *f*, foire *f* d'empoigne; **to get out of the r.** sortir du système

ratrack ['rætræk] *n Ski* ratrack *m*

rat-tail *n* (*file*) (lime *f*) queue-de-rat *f*

rattan [ræ'tæn] *n Bot* rotin *m*; **r. furniture/seat** meubles *mpl*/siège *m* en rotin

rat-tat *n, vi* = **ratatat(-tat)**

ratteen [ræ'tiːn] *n Tex* = **ratine**

ratter ['rætər] *n* (*dog*) ratier *m*

rattiness ['rætɪnɪs] *n Br F* (*irritability*) irritabilité *f*

ratting ['rætɪŋ] *n* **to go r.** faire la chasse aux rats

rattle[1] ['ræt(ə)l] *n* (**a**) (*for baby*) hochet *m*; (*on pram*) boulier *m*; (*for sports fan*) crécelle *f*; (*of snake*) sonnette *f* (**b**) (*noise*) (*of bottles, chains, coins, keys*) cliquetis *m*; (*in engine*) bruit *m* (de ferraille); (*of gunfire, hailstones*) crépitement *m*; (*of door, window*) vibration *f*; (**death**) **r.** râle *m*

rattle[2] **1** *vi* (*make noise*) faire du bruit; (*of bottles*) cliqueter, s'entrechoquer; (*of chains, coins, keys*) cliqueter; (*of door, window*) vibrer; (*of engine*) faire un bruit de ferraille; (*of gunfire, hailstones*) crépiter; **the door rattled in the wind** le vent faisait vibrer la porte

2 *vt* (**a**) (*make noise with*) (*box*) secouer; (*bottles*) entrechoquer; (*chains, coins, keys*) faire du bruit avec; (*door, window*) ébranler, faire vibrer

(**b**) *F* (*make nervous*) (*person*) démonter, ébranler, faire perdre son sang froid à; **to get rattled** perdre son sang froid; **don't get rattled!** pas de panique!; **we got them rattled** on a semé la panique parmi eux; **she was badly rattled by the news** la nouvelle l'a beaucoup secouée *ou* l'a complètement démontée; **to be easily rattled** être facilement démonté

▶ **rattle along** *vi* (**a**) (*move noisily*) (*of car, train*) rouler dans un bruit de ferraille (**b**) (*move quickly*) (*in car, train*) rouler à toute allure

▶ **rattle around** *vi* **he's been rattling around in that enormous house since his wife died** il est perdu dans cette grande maison depuis la mort de sa femme

▶ **rattle away** *vi* (*talk rapidly*) jacasser

▶ **rattle down** *vi* (*of stones etc*) tomber avec fracas

▶ **rattle off** *vtsep* (*lines, recitation etc*) débiter

▶ **rattle on** *vi* (*speak at length*) ne pas arrêter de parler (**about** de)

▶ **rattle through** *vipo* (*homework, task etc*) expédier

rattlebrain [ˈræt(ə)lbreɪn] *n Old-fashioned F (foolish person)* cervelle *f* d'oiseau, tête *f* de linotte
rattlesnake [ˈræt(ə)lsneɪk], *Am* **rattler** [ˈrætlər] *n* serpent *m* à sonnette, crotale *m*
rattletrap [ˈræt(ə)ltræp] *n Old-fashioned F (car)* vieille guimbarde *f ou* bagnole *f*
rattling [ˈræt(ə)lɪŋ] **1** *n* = **rattle**[1] **(b) 2** *adj* **(a)** *(noisy)* bruyant; **r. noise** cliquetis *m* **(b)** *(fast)* rapide; **to set a r. pace** imposer un rythme très rapide; *(in race)* mener à une cadence rapide **3** *adv Old-fashioned (extremely)* **r. good** *(lunch, story etc)* excellent, fameux
rat-trap *n* **(a)** *(for animals)* piège *m* à rats, ratière *f* **(b)** *Am (rundown building)* taudis *m*
ratty [ˈrætɪ] *adj* **(a)** *Br F (irritable)* irritable, grincheux; *(annoyed)* irrité, grincheux; **to get r.** *(of adult)* prendre la mouche; *(of child)* devenir grognon **(b)** *Am F (shabby) (building, clothes)* miteux
raucous [ˈrɔːkəs] *adj* **(a)** *(hoarse)* rauque; **r. voice** voix *f* rauque *ou* éraillée **(b)** *(loud, rowdy)* **r. laughter** rires *mpl* gras; **a r. party** une soirée tapageuse *ou* bruyante; **things got a bit r. as the evening wore on** la soirée est devenue de plus en plus bruyante
raucously [ˈrɔːkəslɪ] *adv* **(a)** *(to shout etc)* d'une voix rauque **(b)** *(to celebrate)* bruyamment, de façon tapageuse
raucousness [ˈrɔːkəsnɪs] *n* **(a)** *(hoarseness)* raucité *f* **(b)** *(rowdiness)* **the r. of the party was not to his liking** il n'aimait pas le côté tapageur *ou* bruyant de la soirée
raunch(iness) [rɔːntʃ, ˈrɔːntʃɪnɪs] *n F* **(a)** *(of joke, song)* grivoiserie *f* **(b)** *(of dance, voice)* sensualité *f*
raunchy [ˈrɔːntʃɪ] *adj F* **(a)** *(joke, song) (dirty)* cochon; *(in more light-hearted way)* grivois; **that's much too r. for our viewers** c'est beaucoup trop grivois pour nos téléspectateurs **(b)** *(sexy) (dance, voice)* sexy *inv*; **there is something a little r. about her** elle a un petit quelque chose de sexy
ravage[1] [ˈrævɪdʒ] *n (damage) (caused by alcohol, disease, grief, time etc) (usu pl)* **ravages** ravages *mpl*
ravage[2] *vt (destroy) (crops, region)* ravager, dévaster; *(person)* ravager; **the invading army ravaged the land** l'armée ennemie a mis le pays à feu et à sang; **ravaged face** visage *m* ravagé
rave[1] [reɪv] *n* **(a)** *F (praise)* éloge *m* enthousiaste; *Br F* **to have a r. about sb/sth** parler avec beaucoup d'enthousiasme de qn/qch; **r. notice** *or* **review** critique *f ou* revue *f* dithyrambique **(b)** *(party)* rave *f*
rave[2] *vi* **(a)** *(be delirious)* délirer **(b)** *(talk nonsense)* divaguer, délirer (**about** à propos de); **to r. (on)** *(rage)* tempêter (**about, at** contre); **to r. at** *or* **against sb** s'emporter contre qn, être *ou* se mettre en colère contre qn **(c)** *F* **to r. about sb/sth** *(praise)* ne pas tarir d'éloges sur qn/qch, faire l'éloge de qn/qch
raven [ˈreɪv(ə)n] **1** *n (bird)* corbeau *m* **2** *adj (colour)* (noir comme du) jais, de jais; **a r.-haired beauty** une beauté aux cheveux noir corbeau *ou* de jais
ravening [ˈræv(ə)nɪŋ] *adj (hungry)* vorace; *Hum* **the r. hordes** les morfales *mpl*
ravenous [ˈræv(ə)nəs] *adj (animal)* vorace; *(person)* affamé; *(appetite)* vorace, féroce; **to be r.** avoir une faim dévorante *ou* de loup; *Fig* **to be r. for** *(fame, power)* être assoiffé *ou* avide de
ravenously [ˈræv(ə)nəslɪ] *adv (to eat)* voracement; **to be r. hungry** avoir une faim dévorante *ou* de loup
raver [ˈreɪvər] *n Br* **(a)** *F (socially active person)* fêtard, -arde, noceur, -euse; **he's a bit of a r.** il est noceur *(trendy)* il est dans le coup, il est branché **(b)** *(who goes to raves)* raver *m*
rave-up *n Br F (party)* fiesta *f*, nouba *f*; **to have a r.** faire la fiesta *ou* nouba; **the neighbours had a right old r. last night** les voisins ont fait une de ces fiestas *ou* noubas hier soir
ravine [rəˈviːn] *n* ravin *m*
raving [ˈreɪvɪŋ] **1** *adj attrib* **(a)** *(delirious)* délirant **(b)** *(angry)* furieux; **a r. lunatic** un fou furieux, une folle furieuse; **I'd have to be a r. lunatic to ...** il faudrait que je sois complètement fou pour ...; **to be r. mad** *(crazy)* être complètement fou; *F (angry)* être furax (**about** au sujet de, **with** contre); *Br F* **you are stark r. mad** *or* **bonkers** tu es complètement givré *ou* fêlé; *Fig* **she is a r. beauty** elle est d'une grande beauté; **she is no r. beauty** ce n'est pas une beauté; **to be a r. success** avoir un succès fou **2** *n* **(a)** *(delirium)* délire *m* **(b)** *(wild talk)* divagation *f*; **the ravings of a madman** les divagations d'un fou
ravioli [rævɪˈəʊlɪ] *n* [①**A13**, 7] *(pasta)* ravioli *mpl*
ravish [ˈrævɪʃ] *vt Fml* **(a)** *Lit (delight) (person)* enchanter, ravir **(b)** *(rape)* violenter, violer; *Arch (woman) (abduct)* enlever, ravir
ravishing [ˈrævɪʃɪŋ] *adj (sight, view)* magnifique, ravissant; **a r. woman, a woman of r. beauty** une femme ravissante *ou* d'une grande beauté
ravishingly [ˈrævɪʃɪŋlɪ] *adv (to play, sing)* à ravir; **r. beautiful** d'une beauté ravissante
raw[1] [rɔː] *adj* **(a)** *(uncooked) (meat, shellfish, vegetables)* cru **(b)** *(unprocessed) (data, statistics)* brut; **r. edge** *(of material)* bord *m* coupé; **r. materials** matières *fpl* premières; *Fig* **he uses his former colleagues as r. material for his plays** il s'inspire de ses anciens collègues pour ses pièces; **r. sewage** eaux *fpl* d'égout non traitées; **r. silk** soie *f* brute *ou* crue *ou* écrue *ou* grège; **r. spirits** alcool *m* pur; **r. sugar** sucre *m* brut *ou* non raffiné
(c) *(inexperienced)* inexpérimenté; **a r. recruit** un bleu; *Mil* **r. troops** troupes *fpl* non aguerries
(d) *(sore) (wound)* à vif; *(skin)* écorché; **her hands were r. with the cold** ses mains étaient bleues à cause du froid; *Fig* **the memory was still r.** le souvenir était encore cuisant *ou* douloureux; *Fig* **my nerves are r.** j'ai les nerfs à vif *ou* à fleur de peau; *Fig* **a r. deal** *(unfair treatment)* traitement *m* injuste; **to give sb a r. deal** être dur avec qn; **he's had a r. deal out of life** il n'a pas été gâté par la vie; **working mothers get a r. deal from the government** les mères qui travaillent sont très défavorisées par le gouvernement; *Fig* **to touch a r. nerve** toucher un point sensible
(e) *(unpleasant) (climate, weather)* âpre, glacial; **a r. wind** un vent âpre *ou* pénétrant; **it's a r. day** il fait glacial
(f) *Am (frank)* cru, brutal, réaliste; **the film paints a r. picture of penitentiary life** le film peint la vie carcérale de façon crue *ou* brutale *ou* réaliste
raw[2] *n* **life in the r.** la vie telle qu'elle est; **to get** *or* **touch sb on the r.** piquer *ou* toucher qn au vif; *F* **in the r.** *(naked)* nu, tout nu, *F* à poil
rawboned [ˈrɔːbəʊnd] *adj (thin and strong-looking)* mince et vigoureux
rawhide [ˈrɔːhaɪd] *n* **(a)** *(untreated leather)* cuir *m* brut *ou* vert; **r. bag/belt** sac *m*/ceinture *f* en cuir vert **(b)** *(whip)* fouet *m* à lanières
Rawlplug® [ˈrɔːlplʌg] *n* cheville *f*, tampon *m*
rawness [ˈrɔːnɪs] *n* **(a)** *(inexperience) (of recruit etc)* inexpérience *f* **(b)** *(soreness) (of skin)* écorchure *f*, éraflure *f* **(c)** *(unpleasantness) (of climate, weather)* âpreté *f*, rudesse *f*; *(of wind)* âpreté **(d)** *Am (frankness)* réalisme *m*, brutalité *f*
ray [reɪ] *n* **(a)** *(of light, sun etc)*, *Phys* rayon *m*; *Fig* **that child has brought a r. of sunshine into my life** cet enfant, c'est mon rayon de soleil; *Iron* **you're a real little r. of sunshine, aren't you!** tu as vraiment le mot pour rire, toi! **(b)** *Fig (of hope, intelligence)* lueur *f* **(c)** *(fish)* raie *f*; **electric r.** torpille *f*
rayon [ˈreɪɒn] *n Tex* rayonne *f*; **r. dress/shirt** robe *f*/chemise *f* en rayonne
raze [reɪz] *vt* **to r. (to the ground)** *(building)* raser
razor [ˈreɪzər] *n* rasoir *m*; **electric r.** rasoir électrique; **lady's r.** rasoir pour femme; **r. cut** *(hairstyle)* coupe *f* au rasoir; **r. edge** fil *m* tranchant; *(mountain ridge)* arête *f* effilée *ou* aiguë; *Fig* **to be (balanced) on a r. 's edge** *(election, match, fate)* être très incertain; **on a r. 's edge** *(in difficulty)* au bord du précipice *ou* du gouffre; **her life was on a r. 's edge for days** sa vie n'a tenu qu'à un fil pendant plusieurs jours; **r. slash** estafilade *f (laissée par un coup de rasoir)*; **she gave him a r. slash across the face** elle lui a donné un coup de rasoir au visage; **r. wire** *or Am* **ribbon** barbelés *mpl* tranchants
razorback [ˈreɪzəbæk] *n* **(a)** *(whale)* rorqual *m* **(b)** *US (wild pig)* cochon *m* sauvage
razorbill [ˈreɪzəbɪl] *n (bird)* petit pingouin *m*
razor blade *n* lame *f* de rasoir
razor clam *n Am (shellfish)* couteau *m*
razor-cut *vt (hair)* couper au rasoir
razor-sharp *adj (knife)* coupant comme un rasoir; *Fig (intelligence, mind)* vif; *(wit, reply)* acerbe
razor-shell *n Br (shellfish)* couteau *m*, solen *m*
razz [ræz] *vt Old-fashioned F (tease)* taquiner, railler, tourner en ridicule
razzamatazz [ræzəmətæz] *n* = **razzmatazz**
razzle [ˈræz(ə)l] *n Br F* **to be** *or* **go on the r.** faire la bringue *ou* la fête *ou* la nouba
razzle-dazzle *n F (flashy display)* tape-à-l'œil *m*, clinquant *m*; *Br* **to be** *or* **go on the r.** faire la bringue *ou* la fête *ou* la nouba
razzmatazz [ˈræzmətæz] *n F (flashy display)* tape-à-l'œil *m*, clinquant *m*
RC [ɑːˈsiː] *n, adj Rel (abbr* **Roman Catholic**) catholique *mf*
RCMP [ɑːsiːemˈpiː] *n Can (abbr* **Royal Canadian Mounted Police**) GRC *f*
Rd *abbr* **Road**
RDBMS [ɑːdiːbiːemˈes] *n Comptr (abbr* **relational database management system**) SGBDR *m*
re[1] [reɪ] *n Mus* ré *m*
re[2] [riː] **1** *prep (with reference to) (at top of letter)* objet *m*; *(in*

body of letter etc) en référence à, suite à **2** *n Jur* (**in**) **r. Martin v Thomas** dans l'affaire Martin contre Thomas

re- [riː-] *pref* (**a**) (*before consonant*) re-, ré-; **to rebaptize** rebaptiser; **to reheat** réchauffer (**b**) (*before vowel*) r-, ré-; **to reassure** rassurer; **to readjust** rajuster, réajuster

reach[1] [riːtʃ] *n* (**a**) (*accessibility*) atteinte *f*, portée *f*; **beyond the r. of the authorities** à l'abri des *ou* hors de la portée des autorités; **he was beyond the r. of human help** on ne pouvait plus rien faire pour lui; **a subject beyond my r.** une matière qui dépasse mon entendement; **out of r.** (*object*) hors de portée; **I'll be out of r. for a week** on ne pourra pas me contacter pendant une semaine; **keep out of the r. of children** (*instruction on medicine bottles, plastic bags etc*) ne pas laisser à la portée des enfants; **within r. of** à portée de; (*near*) à proximité de, proche de; **within arm's r.** à portée de la main; **within easy r.** (*object*) à portée de la main; (*banks, shops etc*) facilement accessible; **within everyone's r.** (*affordable*) à la portée de tous *ou* de toutes les bourses; **fifty pounds for a meal is not within my r.** je ne peux pas me permettre de mettre cinquante livres dans un repas

(**b**) (*length of arm*) extension *f*; *Boxing* allonge *f*; **he has a longer r. than any of the other contenders** il a la meilleure allonge de tous les concurrents

(**c**) (*action*) **she made a r. for the gun** elle étendit la main pour prendre le revolver

(**d**) (*area, region*) (*of river*) partie *f*; **the upper reaches of a river** le cour supérieur d'une rivière; **in the further reaches of the empire** au fin fond de l'empire

(**e**) *TV etc* (*audience size*) portée *f*

reach[2] **1** *vt* (**a**) (*arrive at*) (*conclusion, destination*) arriver à; (*goal, height*) atteindre; (*of letter, news, parcel*) parvenir à; **to r. (an) agreement** aboutir à un accord (**on** sur); **to r. a decision** prendre une décision; **to r. a ceiling** (*of imports, wages*) plafonner; **to r. the end of one's journey** arriver au bout de son voyage; **which page have you reached?** à quelle page en es-tu?; **it has reached my ears that …** j'ai entendu dire *ou* appris que …; **production has reached rock bottom** *or* **an all time low** la production est descendue à son niveau le plus bas; **unemployment is reaching the two million mark** le nombre de chômeurs atteint le seuil des deux millions

(**b**) (*gain access to*) (*beach, house*) atteindre; (*contact*) joindre, contacter; **to r. sb by telephone** joindre qn par/*ou* au téléphone; **easy/difficult to r.** (*house etc*) facile/difficile d'accès; **the town could only be reached by sea** on ne pouvait accéder à *ou* atteindre la ville que par la mer; *Fig* **nobody can r. him** (*get through to him*) on ne peut pas communiquer avec lui; **the adverts are intended to r. the over-40s** les publicités sont destinées aux *ou* sont à l'intention des plus de 40 ans; **to r. a younger/wider audience** toucher un public plus jeune/large

(**c**) (*stretch as far as*) (*one's shoulder, waist*) arriver (jusqu')à; **can you r. the ceiling?** est-ce que vous pouvez toucher le plafond?; **are the curtains long enough to r. the floor?** est-ce que les rideaux sont suffisamment longs pour descendre jusqu'au sol?

(**d**) (*hand*) **to r. sb sth** passer qch à qn

(**e**) *Am F* (*corrupt*) (*witness*) corrompre, suborner

2 *vi* (*extend*) (*of forest, property etc*) s'étendre (**to** jusqu'à); (*of noise, voice*) porter (**to** jusqu'à); **as far as the eye can r.** à perte de vue; **can you r.?** est-ce que tu peux y arriver?; **to r. for sth** *or* **to get sth** allonger *ou* étendre le bras pour prendre qch; **the policeman reached for his gun** l'agent de police mit la main sur son revolver; *Fig* **to r. for the sky** *or* **the stars** être très ambitieux, viser très haut; *Am* **r. (for the sky)!** haut les mains!; **to r. into** (*drawer, pocket*) mettre la main dans (**for** pour prendre)

▶ **reach across** *vi* allonger *ou* (é)tendre le bras (**for** pour prendre)

▶ **reach back** *vi Fig* (*of records, files etc*) remonter (**to** à)

▶ **reach down[2]** **1** *vi* (*of coat, curtains, hair etc*) descendre (**to** jusqu'à); (*of person*) allonger *ou* (é)tendre le bras (**for** pour prendre) **2** *vtsep* (*object*) (*from cupboard, shelf*) descendre; **can you r. me down that saucepan?** est-ce que tu peux me passer la casserole là-haut?; **he reached it down to her** il le lui a passé

▶ **reach out** **1** *vi* allonger *ou* (é)tendre le bras (**for** pour prendre) **2** *vtsep* **he reached out his hand for the glass** il tendit la main vers le verre

▶ **reach over** **1** *vi* = **reach across** **2** *vtsep* **to r. sb over sth** passer qch à qn; **could you r. me over the salt?** est-ce que tu peux me passer le sel?

▶ **reach up[2]** **1** *vi* (*of person*) lever le bras (**for** pour prendre); (*of snow, water*) monter (**to** jusqu'à); **her boots reached halfway up her legs** ses bottes lui montaient à mi-jambe **2** *vtsep* **to r. sb up sth** passer qch à qn

reachable [ˈriːtʃəb(ə)l] *adj* (*place, object*) accessible; (*goal, objective*) que l'on peut atteindre; **put it where it won't be r. by the kids** mets-le hors de portée des enfants

reach-me-down *n Old-fashioned Br* vieux vêtement *m*

react [rɪˈækt] **1** *vi* réagir (**against** contre; **on** sur; **to** à); **to be slow to r.** (*of chemical*) avoir une réaction lente; (*of person*) être lent à réagir; **he reacted well to the treatment** il a bien réagi au traitement; **an acid can r. with a base to form a salt** un acide et une base peuvent réagir ensemble et former un sel **2** *vt Ch* faire réagir (**sth with sth** qch avec qch)

reactance [rɪˈæktəns] *n El* réactance *f*

reactant [rɪˈæktənt] *n Ch* réactif *m*

reaction [rɪˈækʃən] *n* (**a**) (*response*) (*of chemical, person*) réaction *f*; **to show no r.** rester sans réaction; **what was her r.?** quelle a été sa réaction?, comment a-t-elle réagi?; **in r. to** en *ou* par réaction contre; *Med* **if there is any adverse r.** en cas d'effets indésirables; **the patient's adverse r.** le fait que le malade ait mal réagi (**b**) *Pol Pej* **the forces of r.** les réactionnaires *mpl*, *F* les réacs *mpl*

reactionary [rɪˈækʃən(ə)rɪ] *adj, n Pol* réactionnaire *mf*; **the reactionaries** les réactionnaires *mpl*, *F* les réacs *mpl*

reaction engine *n Av* moteur *m* à réaction, réacteur *m*

reaction motor *n Av* moteur *m* à réaction, réacteur *m*

reaction time *n* temps *m* de réaction

reaction turbine *n MecE* turbine *f* à réaction

reactivate [rɪˈæktɪveɪt] *vt* (**a**) (*start again*) (*group, club*) reconstituer, reformer (**b**) *esp Am Mil* (*return to active status*) (*ship*) remettre en service

reactive [rɪˈæktɪv] *adj Ch, Phys* réactif; *El* (*load, power*) réactif, déwatté; **r. current** courant *m* réactif; **r. marketing** mercatique *f* réactive

reactivity [rɪækˈtɪvɪtɪ] *n Ch, Phys* réactivité *f*

reactor [rɪˈæktər] *n Ch* réacteur *m*; *Nucl Phys* réacteur atomique

read[1] [riːd] *n* **to have a (bit of a) r.** faire un peu de lecture; *F* **just have a r. of this!** (*expression of astonishment, disgust*) lis-moi ça!; *Br F* **can I have a r. of your magazine?** est-ce que je peux jeter un coup d'œil à votre magazine?; *F* **this book's a good r.** ce livre est agréable à lire; **I've always enjoyed a good r.** j'ai toujours aimé avoir un bon livre à lire; **he was having a quiet r.** il lisait tranquillement; *Th* **we'll have a r. through this afternoon** nous lirons la pièce cet après-midi; *Comptr* **r. error** erreur *f* de lecture

read[2] (*pt, pp* **read** [red]) **1** *vt* (**a**) (*newspaper, book, Braille etc*), *Comptr* lire; (*writing, score*) lire, déchiffrer; **have you got anything to r.?** avez-vous de quoi lire *ou* quelque chose à lire?; **have you got enough to r.?** avez-vous assez de lecture?; **to r. sth over and over (again)** lire et relire qch; **I r. Italian** je lis *ou* je peux lire l'italien; **to r. Proust in the original** lire Proust dans le texte; **her novels have been read** [red] **and enjoyed by millions** ses romans ont été lus et appréciés par des millions de personnes; **to be widely read** [red] (*of magazine, author etc*) être très lu (**by** parmi); (*of scholar etc*) avoir beaucoup lu; **she is widely read** [red] **in history** elle a lu beaucoup de livres d'histoire; **for 'least', r. 'lease'** il faut lire "lease" au lieu de "least"; **do you r. me?** *Rad* est-ce que vous me recevez?; *Fig* est-ce que tu me comprends?; **I r. you loud and clear** *Rad* je vous reçois cinq sur cinq; *Fig* oui, oui j'ai compris; **he was reading my lips** il lisait sur mes lèvres; *Fig* **r. my lips!** (*believe me*) je te jure!; *Admin* **read** [red] **and approved** (*stamp on document*) lu et approuvé; *Fig* **to take sth as read** [red] (*evident*) considérer qch comme allant de soi; (*agreed upon*) considérer qch comme entendu; *Admin* **to take the minutes as read** [red] passer sur la lecture du procès-verbal

(**b**) (*interpret*) (*situation, sb's actions etc*) interpréter; **to r. sb's mind** *or* **thoughts** lire dans la pensée de qn; **to r. the future** lire *ou* prédire l'avenir; **she can r. him like a book** elle sait toujours ce qu'il pense; *Sp* **to r. the game well** anticiper sur les mouvements de l'adversaire; **he read** [red] **that well** (*of sportsman*) il a bien anticipé; **I read** [red] **it as 24, but it was actually 224** j'ai vu 24 mais en fait c'était 224; **to r. the temperature/a thermometer** lire la température/un thermomètre; **to r. an electricity meter** relever un compteur d'électricité; **to r. sb's palm** *or* **hand** lire les lignes de la main de qn

(**c**) (*say aloud*) (*letter, poem*) lire (à haute voix); **to r. sb sth, to r. sth to sb** lire qch à qn; **r. me that last bit again** relis-moi le dernier passage; **to r. a child a bedtime story** lire une histoire à un enfant pour qu'il s'endorme; *Rel* **to r. the lesson** lire un passage de l'Évangile; *Fig* **to r. sb a lesson** *or* **a lecture** faire la leçon à qn; **to r. a paper at a conference** présenter un exposé à une conférence; *Rad* **to r. the news** lire les informations; *TV* présenter le journal; *Jur* **to r. a will** exécuter la lecture d'un testament

(d) **to r. oneself to sleep** lire jusqu'à ce qu'on s'endorme; **he read** [red] **me to sleep** il m'a fait la lecture jusqu'à ce que je m'endorme

(e) *Br Univ* (*study*) (*French, history etc*) étudier; **to r. law/medicine** faire son droit/sa médecine

(f) (*show*) (*of measuring instrument*) indiquer; **the inscription on the monument reads ...** on peut lire sur le monument ...; **the sign on the door read** [red] **No Entry** sur l'écriteau on pouvait lire 'Défense d'entrer'

2 *vi* (a) lire; **she taught her daughter (how) to r.** elle a appris à lire à sa fille; **to r. to sb** faire la lecture à qn; **I'm very fond of reading** j'aime beaucoup lire *ou* la lecture *ou F* bouquiner; **to r. aloud** lire à haute voix; **r. quietly to yourselves** lisez en silence; **to r. about sb/sth** lire quelque chose sur qch/qn; **what are you reading about?** qu'est-ce que tu lis?; **we read** [red] **of his death in the newspaper** nous avons appris sa mort dans le journal

(b) (*interpret*) **to r. between the lines** lire entre les lignes; **she read** [red] **in the cards that I would be famous** elle a lu dans les cartes que je serais célèbre

(c) *Br Univ* **to r. for a degree** préparer un diplôme; **to r. for the Bar** faire des études de droit

(d) (*be worded*) **to r. well/badly** (*of text*) être bien/mal écrit; **his text reads like a translation** son texte sent la traduction; **the telegram reads as follows** le télégramme est libellé comme suit; **Arabic reads from right to left** l'arabe se lit de droite à gauche; **her life story reads like a fairytale** sa vie ressemble à un conte de fées

▶ **read in** *vtsep Comptr* (*data*) emmagasiner, lire et stocker en mémoire

▶ **read into** *vtaspo* **to r. sth into sth** voir qch dans qch; **don't r. too much into what she says** ne donne pas à ce qu'elle dit plus de signification que ça n'en a; **you're reading far too much into it** tu interprètes beaucoup trop

▶ **read off** *vtsep* (*names etc*) énumérer (**from** sur)

▶ **read on** *vi* (*continue to read*) **now r. on** lisez la suite; **to r. on from ...** lire à partir de ...

▶ **read out** *vtsep* (*names, list, passage etc*) lire (à haute voix); *Comptr* (*data*) sortir, extraire de la mémoire

▶ **read over** *vtsep* (*quickly*) parcourir; (*with special care*) examiner; *esp Am* (*read again*) relire

▶ **read through** *vtsep* (*skim*) parcourir; (*examine closely*) lire en détail, examiner; *Th* **to r. through a play** faire la lecture d'une pièce

▶ **read up** *vtsep* (*subject*) étudier

▶ **read up on** *vipo* = **read up**

readability [riːdəˈbɪlɪtɪ] *n* (*of book, handwriting*) lisibilité *f*

readable [ˈriːdəb(ə)l] *adj* (a) (*book, style etc*) lisible; **highly** *or* **very r.** d'une lecture très agréable (b) (*legible*) (*handwriting, disk*) lisible; **not r.** illisible

readdress [riːəˈdres] *vt* (*forward*) (*letter*) faire suivre

reader [ˈriːdər] *n* (a) (*of books, newspapers etc*) lecteur, -trice; *Am* (*company librarian*) documentaliste *mf*; **she is a great** *or* **an avid r.** c'est une grande liseuse, elle lit beaucoup; **he's not much of a r.** il n'aime pas beaucoup la lecture, il ne lit pas beaucoup; **(proof) r.** correcteur, -trice d'épreuves; **publisher's r.** lecteur, -trice dans une maison d'édition

(b) *Univ Br* = maître *m* de recherches; *US* = assistant, -ante, *Can* chargé(e) de cours

(c) (*book*) (*for teaching reading*) livre *m* de lecture; (*textbook*) livre, manuel *m*; (*anthology*) recueil *m*; **French/geography r.** livre de français/géographie; **a Melville r.** un recueil d'extraits de Melville

(d) (*machine*) lecteur *m*

readership [ˈriːdəʃɪp] *n* (a) (*of magazine, author etc*) lecteurs *mpl*; (*esp of paper*) lectorat *m*; **what is the paper's r.?** combien de personnes lisent le journal?; **r. survey** étude *f* du lectorat (b) *Br Univ* **she holds a r. in mathematics** elle est maître de recherches en mathématiques

read head *n Comptr* tête *f* de lecture

readies [ˈredɪz] *npl Br F* (*cash*) fric *m*; **£500 in r.** 500 livres en liquide; **I want the r. first** je veux le fric d'abord

readily [ˈredɪlɪ] *adv* (*willingly*) de bonne grâce, volontiers; (*easily*) facilement

readiness [ˈredɪnɪs] *n* (a) (*willingness*) empressement *m* (**to do** à faire) (b) (*agility*) (*of speech, tongue*) facilité *f* d'expression; (*of mind, wit*) vivacité *f* d'esprit (c) (*preparedness*) **to be in r.** être prêt (**for** pour); **to have everything in r.** avoir tout prêt

reading [ˈriːdɪŋ] **1** *n* (a) (*action, pastime*) lecture *f*; **r. is not his favourite activity** a lecture n'est pas son passe-temps favori; **I have a lot of r. to catch up on** j'ai beaucoup de retard à rattraper dans mes lectures; **I like a bit of light r.** j'aime bien un livre facile à lire de temps en temps; **his thesis makes (for) boring r.** sa thèse est ennuyeuse à lire; **a young woman of wide r.** une jeune femme très cultivée *ou* érudite *ou* lettrée; *Comptr* **r. to disk** lecture *f* sur disque

(b) (*saying aloud*) (*of play, poetry, will*) lecture *f*; *Parl* **first/second/third r.** (*of bill*) première/seconde/troisième lecture

(c) (*measurement*) (*of meter*) relevé *m*; (*by instrument*) indication *f*; **the fuel gauge is giving the wrong r.** la jauge d'essence n'est pas fiable; **to take a barometric/temperature r.** lire le baromètre/le thermomètre

(d) (*interpretation*) (*of facts, situation, character*) interprétation *f*; **this is one of two possible readings of the poem/novel** c'est l'une des deux lectures possibles du poème/roman

2 *adj* **to have a r. age of ten** lire comme un enfant de dix ans; **she has a r. age well in advance of her years** elle est très en avance sur son âge pour ce qui est de la lecture; **children of r. age** des enfants en âge de lire; **r. book** livre *m* de lecture; **I have a r. knowledge of Arabic** je peux lire l'arabe; **take some r. material** *or* **matter** prends de la lecture *ou* de quoi lire; **the r. public** les lecteurs *mpl*; **r. speed** (*of child, computer*) vitesse *f* de lecture

reading glasses *npl* lunettes *fpl* pour lire

reading head *n Comptr* tête *f* de lecture

reading lamp *n* (*on desk*) lampe *f* de bureau; (*by bed*) lampe de chevet

reading light *n* (*on plane, train*) liseuse *f*

reading list *n* liste *f* de livres *ou* d'ouvrages recommandés

reading room *n* (*in library*) salle *f* de lecture; (*in university*) salle d'étude

readjust [riːəˈdʒʌst] **1** *vt* (*correct*) (*prices, wages*) rajuster, réajuster; (*microscope, telescope*) remettre au point; **to r. one's clothing** se rajuster **2** *vi* (*of person*) se réadapter (**to** à)

readjustment [riːəˈdʒʌstmənt] *n* (a) (*of prices, wages*) rajustement *m*, réajustement *m*; **some r. of the telescope is necessary** il faut régler à *ou* de nouveau le télescope (b) (*of person*) réadaptation *f*

read me document *n Comptr* ouvrez-moi *m*

readmission [riːədˈmɪʃən] *n* (*to club, political party*) réintégration *f* (**to** dans); **to gain r. to a party** réintégrer un parti; **his r. to hospital was seen as a bad sign** le fait qu'il soit réadmis à l'hôpital a été interprété comme un mauvais signe

readmit [riːədˈmɪt] *vt* (*take in again*) (*person*) réintégrer (**to** dans); **he was readmitted (to hospital) last night** il a été réadmis à l'hôpital la nuit dernière

read-only *adj Comptr* **r. disk** disque *m*/disquette *f* en lecture seule; **r. file** fichier *m* en lecture seule; **r. memory** mémoire *f* morte; **r. mode** mode *m* lecture seule; **to make a file r.** mettre un fichier en lecture seule

read-out *n Comptr* affichage *m*; **r. device** unité *f* d'affichage

read-through *n* (*of script*) lecture *f* du scénario; **to give sth a quick r.** parcourir qch rapidement

readvertise [riːˈædvətaɪz] **1** *vt* (*job*) repasser une annonce pour **2** *vi* **they're readvertising** ils ont repassé l'annonce

readvertisement [riːədˈvɜːtɪsmənt] *n* deuxième annonce *f*; **this is a r.** (*notice on jobs page*) deuxième annonce d'offre d'emploi

read-write *adj Comptr* **r. head** tête *f* de lecture/écriture; **r. memory** mémoire *f* lecture-écriture; **r. protection notch** encoche *f* de protection lecture-écriture

ready[1] [ˈredɪ] **1** *adj* (a) (*prepared*) prêt (**to do** à faire, **for sth** pour qch); **to get r.** se préparer, s'apprêter (**to do** à faire, **for sth** à qch); *Old-fashioned* **to make r.** faire des préparations, se préparer (**for** pour); **to get sth r.** préparer qch; **dinner is r.** le dîner est servi, *F* à table; **I'm r. if you are, r. when you are** quand tu veux; *Sp* **r.! steady! go!** à vos marques! prêts! partez!; **to get r. for school** se préparer pour aller à l'école; **to get r. for bed** se préparer à aller se coucher; **to get a patient r. for an operation** préparer un malade pour une opération; **to get some food r.** préparer à manger; **to get a room r. for a guest** préparer une chambre pour un invité; **r. for delivery** livrable; *Com* **r. for shipping** sous palan; **r. for use** prêt à l'usage; **she's r. for anything** elle est prête à tout; **r. to go to press** bon à tirer, BAT; **are you r. to order?** (*in restaurant*) avez-vous choisi *ou* fait votre choix?; **r. to serve** (*food*) prêt à servir, tout prêt; **I'm r. to drop** (*exhausted*) je tombe de fatigue; **r. to hand** sous la main, à portée de (la) main; **r. cash** *or* **money** argent *m* liquide; **to pay in r. money** payer en espèces ou en argent liquide

(b) (*willing*) prêt, disposé (**to do** à faire); **she's always r. to help** elle est toujours prête à rendre service

(c) (*quick*) prompt, facile; **to have a r. wit** avoir l'esprit prompt *ou* d'à-propos *ou* de repartie; **to be always r. with an answer** avoir la réplique prompte; **you're always a bit too r. with advice** tu donnes toujours trop de conseils; **he's**

very r. with his fists il est prompt à se battre; **don't be too r. to condemn him** ne le condamnez pas trop rapidement, ne soyez pas trop prompt à lui jeter la pierre; **a r. source of income** une source de revenu facile; **the story found r. acceptance** l'histoire a été acceptée sans difficulté

2 *n* **(a)** *F* **the r.** (*money*) argent *m* liquide; **have you enough of the r. on you?** est-ce que tu as assez de liquide?

(b) the reporter had her notebook at the r. la journaliste avait son carnet tout prêt; **with camera at the r., she ...** son appareil photo tout prêt, elle ...; **with their guns at the r.** prêts à tirer

ready² *vt* (*the house*) préparer; **to r. oneself for action** se préparer à l'action

ready- [redɪ-] *pref* **ready-cut** précoupé

ready-made 1 *adj* (*shoes, suit*) de confection; (*curtains, excuses, phrases*) tout fait; **a r. cake** un gâteau tout fait; **r. clothes** vêtements *mpl* de confection, prêt-à-porter *m*; *Fig* **to have a r. family** avoir une famille déjà constituée **2** *n* (*garment*) (vêtement *m* de) confection *f*

ready-mix *adj* (*buns, cake etc*) fait à partir d'une préparation; (*concrete*) prémalaxé

ready reckoner *n Com* barème *m*

ready-to-wear *adj* (*shoes, suit etc*) de confection; **r. clothing** prêt-à-porter *m*

reaffirm [riːə'fɜːm] *vt* (*one's loyalty, a belief, one's intentions*) réaffirmer

reafforest [riːə'fɒrɪst] *vt* = **reforest**

reafforestation [riːəfɒrɪ'steɪʃən] *n* = **reforestation**

Reaganite ['reɪgənaɪt] *n* partisan *m* de Reagan; **R. budget/ programme** budget *m*/programme *m* reaganien

Reaganomics [reɪgə'nɒmɪks] *npl* (*usu with sing verb*) reaganisme *m*

reagent [rɪ'eɪdʒənt] *n Ch* réactif *m*

real [rɪəl] **1** *adj* **(a)** (*authentic*) (*diamond, pearl, mother*) vrai; (*gold, leather*) véritable; (*silk, flowers*) naturel; **a r. friend/ idiot** un véritable ami/idiot; **a r. disaster/shock** un véritable *ou* vrai désastre/choc; **he's made a r. effort** il a fait un véritable effort, il a fait un effort réel; **that's what I call a r. man!** ça, c'est ce que j'appelle un (vrai) homme; **the r. reason** la vraie raison (**for** pour); **she has no r. feeling for poetry** elle n'a pas le sens de la poésie; **what is his r. name?** quel est son vrai nom?; **he's a r. gentleman** c'est un vrai gentleman; *F* **it's the r. McCoy** *or* **thing** c'est du vrai de vrai; **this orange drink is not bad but it's poor stuff compared to the r. thing** cette boisson à l'orange n'est pas mauvaise, mais ça ne vaut pas le vrai jus d'orange; *F* **she swears it's the r. thing this time** (*true love*) elle jure que cette fois-ci c'est le grand amour; *F* **this is not a drill, it's the r. thing** *or* **for r.** ce n'est pas un exercice, c'est pour de vrai; *esp Am F* **is that man for r.?** il est pas vrai, ce type!; *esp Am F* **is that for r.?** c'est vrai?; *esp Am F* **get r.!** tu délires!

(b) (*actual*) (*cost, salary, world etc*), *Math, Phys* réel; *Fin* **in r. terms** en termes réels **what does that mean in r. terms?** qu'est-ce que ça signifie au bout du compte?; **in r. life** dans la réalité *ou* la vie; *Banking* **r. debit interest** intérêts *mpl* débiteurs réels; *Rel* **r. presence** présence *f* réelle; *Mktg* **r. repositioning** repositionnement *m* réel; **r. salary** salaire *m* réel; *Fin* **r. value** valeur *f* effective *ou* réelle

(c) *Sp* **r. tennis** (jeu *m* de) paume *f*; **to play r. tennis** jouer à la paume

2 *adv Am F* (*very*) vraiment, très; **a r. fine day** une très belle journée; **that's r. nice of you** c'est vraiment *ou* très gentil de votre part; **I'll see you r. soon** à très bientôt

3 *n Phil* **the r.** le réel

real ale *n Br* bière *f* anglaise brassée selon les procédés traditionnels

real estate *n Am* biens *mpl* immobiliers; **she's in r.** elle travaille dans l'immobilier

real-estate *adj Am* **r. agent** agent *m* immobilier; **r. agency** agence *f* immobilière; **r. developer** promoteur *m* immobilier

realism ['rɪəlɪz(ə)m] *n Art, Phil etc* réalisme *m*

realist ['rɪəlɪst] *adj, n Art, Phil etc* réaliste *mf*

realistic [rɪə'lɪstɪk] *adj* (*person, proposal*) réaliste; (*style*) plein de réalisme

realistically [rɪə'lɪstɪklɪ] *adv* (*to act, behave*) avec réalisme

reality [rɪ'ælɪtɪ] *n* réalité *f*; **in r.** en réalité; **to bring sb back to r.** ramener qn à la réalité; **they refuse to face the r. of their situation** ils refusent de voir la situation telle qu'elle est; **to become a r.** (*of dream, hope etc*) se réaliser, devenir réalité; **to make a dream/project (a) r.** réaliser un rêve/projet; **the realities of everyday life** les réalités de la vie quotidienne; *US TV* **r. show** reality show *m*

realizable ['rɪəlaɪzəb(ə)l] *adj* (*plan, project etc*), *Fin* réalisable; **r. securities** valeurs *fpl* réalisables

realization [rɪəlaɪ'zeɪʃən] *n* **(a)** (*of plan, project etc*), *Fin* réalisation *f* **(b)** (*awareness*) prise *f* de conscience; **there is a growing r. that ...** on commence à se rendre compte que ...; **the sudden r. that ... made her weep** elle s'est mise à pleurer quand tout d'un coup elle s'est rendu compte que ...

realize ['rɪəlaɪz] **1** *vt* **(a)** *Fin* (*asset, profit*) réaliser; **to r. a high price** (*of goods*) atteindre un prix élevé; (*of seller*) obtenir un prix élevé; **how much did they r. on the sale?** combien est-ce qu'ils ont gagné sur la vente?

(b) (*make real*) **our worst fears have been realized** nos pires craintes se sont réalisées; **our hopes were realized** nos espoirs se sont réalisés *ou* concrétisés; **he hasn't yet realized his full potential** il n'a pas encore atteint son maximum

(c) (*know, be aware of*) se rendre compte de, réaliser; **I r. that, but ...** je sais bien, mais ...

(d) (*become aware of*) se rendre compte de/que, prendre conscience de/que; **we realized that he was blind** nous nous sommes aperçus *ou* rendu compte qu'il était aveugle; **I realized it at the first glance** je m'en suis aperçu *ou* rendu compte au premier coup d'œil

2 *vi* **I'm sorry, I didn't r.** je suis désolé, je ne m'en étais pas rendu compte *ou F* je n'avais pas réalisé

really ['rɪəlɪ] **1** *adv* **(a)** (*actually*) vraiment; **things that r. exist** choses qui existent réellement; **that is r. a matter for the manager** c'est là proprement l'affaire du gérant; **is it r. true?** est-ce bien vrai? **(b)** (*intensifier*) **he r. likes you** il t'aime beaucoup; **you r. <u>must</u> go to it** il faut absolument que vous y alliez; **I r. have** *or* **ought to be going** il faut vraiment que j'y aille **(c)** (*very*) vraiment; **she's r. nice** elle est vraiment sympa **2** *int* **r.?** vraiment?; **r.!** (*indignation*) vraiment!

realm [relm] *n* **(a)** *Fml* (*kingdom*) royaume *m* **(b)** *Fig* (*of dreams, fancy etc*) monde *m*; (*of politics, science etc*) domaine *m*; **within the realms of possibility** dans le domaine du possible; **health is no longer exclusively the r. of doctors** la santé n'est plus l'apanage du médecin

real-time *adj Comptr* (*processing, system etc*) en temps réel; **r. clock** horloge *f* (en) temps réel; **r. graphics** graphiques *mpl* en temps réel; **r. management** gestion *f* en temps réel; **r. operating system** système *m* d'exploitation en temps réel

realtor ['rɪəltər] *n Am* agent *m* immobilier

realty ['rɪəltɪ] *n Jur* biens *mpl* immobiliers, (biens *mpl*) immeubles *mpl*

ream¹ [riːm] *n* (*of paper*) rame *f*; *F* **to write reams** écrire des pages et des pages; *F* **reams of statistics/information** des quantités *fpl* de statistiques/d'informations

ream² *vt* **(a)** *Tech* (*bore*) (*part*) aléser **(b)** *US* (*squeeze*) (*lemon*) presser

reamer ['riːmər] *n* **(a)** *Tech* alésoir *m* **(b)** *US* (*for lemon*) presse-citron *m inv*

reanimate [riː'ænɪmeɪt] *vt Med* r(é)animer

reap [riːp] **1** *vt* (*corn, field*) moissonner; *Prov* **he who sows the wind shall r. the whirlwind** qui sème le vent récolte la tempête; *Fig* **to r. the rewards of one's labours** recueillir le fruit de ses travaux; *Fig* **I r. no benefit from it** je n'en retire aucun avantage **2** *vi* moissonner, faire la moisson

reaper ['riːpər] *n* (*machine*) moissonneuse *f*; (*person*) moissonneur, -euse; **r. binder** moissonneuse-lieuse *f, pl* moissoneuses-lieuses; *Fig* **the (Grim) R.** la Faucheuse

reaping ['riːpɪŋ] *n* (*of corn etc*) moisson *f*; **r. hook** faucille *f*; **r. machine** moissonneuse *f*

reappear [riːə'pɪər] *vi* réapparaître

reappearance [riːə'pɪərəns] *n* réapparition *f*

reapply [riːə'plaɪ] **1** *vt* (*cream, lotion etc*) réappliquer **2** *vi* (*for grant, job, loan etc*) renouveler sa demande (**for** de)

reappoint [riːə'pɔɪnt] *vt* (*person*) renommer

reappointment [riːə'pɔɪntmənt] *n* **nobody opposed his r.** personne ne s'opposa à ce qu'il soit reconduit dans ses fonctions

reappraisal [riːə'preɪz(ə)l] *n* **(a)** *Fin* (*of property*) réévaluation *f* **(b)** (*of policy*) réexamen *m*

reappraise [riːə'preɪz] *vt* **(a)** *Fin* (*property*) réévaluer **(b)** (*policy*) réexaminer

rear¹ [rɪər] *n* **(a)** (*back part*) (*of building, car, train*) arrière *m*; **in the r.** en arrière, à l'arrière; **in the r. of the train** en queue du train; **at** *or Am* **in the r. of** (*behind*) derrière; **from the r.** par derrière; (*to recognize*) de derrière; **to bring up the r.** (*of procession*) venir en queue; (*be in last place*) être à la queue, *Pej* être la lanterne rouge; *Aut* **r. axle/door/wheel/window** essieu *m*/portière *f*/roue *f*/lunette *f* arrière *inv*; **r. drive axle** pont *m* arrière; *Br Aut* **r. lights** *or* **lamps** feux *mpl* arrière; **r. legs** (*of dog, cat etc*) pattes de derrière; (*of horse*) jambes de derrière; **r. entrance** (*of building*) entrée *f* de derrière; **r. portion** (*of train*) wagons *mpl* de queue; *Aut* **r. spoiler** aileron *m ou* spoiler *m* arrière; *Aut* **r-view** *or Am* **r-vision mirror** rétroviseur *m*, rétro *m*

(b) *(of military column)* queue *f*; **to bring up the r.** *(come at end) (of military column)* fermer la marche; **to protect one's r.** *Mil* protéger ses arrières; *Fig* assurer ses arrières

(c) *F (buttocks)* **r. (end)** derrière *m*, fesses *fpl*; **he needs a kick in the r.** il lui faut un coup de pied au derrière *ou* dans les fesses

rear² **1** *vt* **(a)** *(nurture) (child, sheep)* élever; *(plants)* cultiver **(b)** *(lift) (one's head)* relever; *Fig* **to r. its ugly head** *(of racism, violence etc)* faire son apparition **2** *vi* **to r. (up) (on its hind legs)** *(of horse)* se cabrer; **cliffs r. (up) above the shore** des falaises se dressent au-dessus du rivage

rear admiral *n Naut* contre-amiral *m*, *pl* contre-amiraux

rear-drive *adj* à traction arrière

rear-end *vt esp Am Aut* **to r. sb** *(collide with)* emboutir l'arrière de la voiture de qn

rear-engined [rɪər'endʒɪnd] *adj (car etc)* avec le moteur à l'arrière, à moteur arrière

rearguard ['rɪəgɑːd] *n Mil* arrière-garde *f*, *pl* arrière-gardes; **r. action** combat *m* d'arrière-garde; **to fight** *or* **mount a r. action** mener un combat d'arrière-garde

rearing ['rɪərɪŋ] *n* **(a)** *(of children)* éducation *f*; *(of animals)* élevage *m*; *(of plants)* culture *f* **(b) r. (up)** *(of horse)* cabrage *m*

rearm [riː'ɑːm] *vti* réarmer

rearmament [riː'ɑːməmənt] *n (of country, soldiers etc)* réarmement *m*

rearmost ['rɪəməʊst] *adj* dernier; *(carriage, compartment on train)* dernier, de queue

rear-mounted *adj (engine, gun)* monté à l'arrière

rearrange [riːə'reɪndʒ] *vt (books, furniture, flowers)* changer la disposition de; *(room, office)* aménager de façon différente; *(one's clothing)* réajuster; *(schedule)* modifier; *(appointment)* changer, reporter; **they've rearranged everything in here** tout a changé de place ici; **could we r. things?** est-ce qu'on peut s'organiser autrement?; *F* **to r. sb's face** casser la gueule à qn

rearrangement [riːə'reɪndʒmənt] *n (of books, flowers, room etc)* réarrangement *m*; *(of schedule)* modification *f*; *(of appointment)* changement *m*

rearward ['rɪəwəd] **1** *adj* **(a)** *(at back) (compartment etc)* (situé à l')arrière **(b)** *(backward) (glance, movement)* vers l'arrière **2** *adv esp Am* = **rearwards**

rearwards ['rɪəwədz] *adv esp Br (be situated)* à l'arrière; *(to glance, move)* vers l'arrière

rear-wheel drive *n Aut* propulsion *f* arrière; **car with r.** voiture *f* à traction arrière

rear-wheel steering *n Aut* roues *fpl* arrière directrices

reason¹ ['riːz(ə)n] *n* **(a)** *(cause)* raison *f* **(for** de); **there is a r. for his doing so** il y a une raison pour qu'il fasse ça; **to state one's reasons for a decision** motiver une décision; **for reasons of health** pour raisons de santé; **reasons of state** la raison d'État; *usu Iron* **for reasons best known to themselves** pour des raisons qu'eux seuls connaissent *ou* qu'ils sont les seuls à connaître; **for some** *or* **one r. or other** pour une raison ou pour une autre; **for no other r. than that I forgot** pour la simple raison que j'ai oublié; **for no particular r.** sans raison particulière; **for no r. at all** sans aucune raison; **that's no r. for refusing to help me!** ce n'est pas une raison pour refuser de m'aider!; **for that very r.** pour cette raison même; **for the very r. that he had been asked not to do it** précisément parce qu'on l'avait prié de ne pas le faire; **the r. why** la raison; **I don't know the r. why** je ne sais pas pourquoi; **the r. (why) he left** la raison pour laquelle il est parti; **the r. (why** *or* **for which) he came, his r. for coming** la raison pour laquelle il est venu; **what's the r. for it?** à quoi cela tient-il?, quelle en est la raison?; **what r. did you give for your absence?** comment as-tu expliqué ton absence?; **what r. could they give for such inhuman acts?** comment peuvent-ils justifier des actes d'une telle cruauté?; **to have every r. to believe ...** avoir tout lieu de croire ...; **I have (good) r. to believe that he's lying** j'ai de bonnes raisons de croire qu'il ment; **to have r. enough (to do sth)** avoir de bonnes raisons (de faire qch); **she complains and with (good) r.** elle se plaint et pour cause; **it's not without (good) r. that I detest him** ce n'est pas pour rien que je le déteste; **to give sb good r. for doing sth** donner de bonnes raisons à qn de faire qch; **give me one good r. why I should!** donne-moi une raison valable pour que je le fasse!; **all the more r. for going there** *or* **why I should go there** raison de plus pour y aller *ou* pour que j'y aille; *Fml* **by r. of his infirmity** en raison de son infirmité; **to be found not guilty by r. of insanity** être déclaré non-coupable pour cause de démence

(b) *(sanity, common sense)* raison *f*; **he lost his r.** il a perdu la raison; **to listen to** *or* **hear** *or* **see r.** entendre raison; **it stands to r.** il va de soi *ou* sans dire **(that ...** que ... + *ind*); **that stands to r.** ça va de soi *ou* sans dire, c'est logique; **within r.** dans des limites raisonnables

reason² **1** *vi* raisonner **(about** sur); **to r. with sb** raisonner (avec) qn; **there's no reasoning with him** il n'y a pas moyen de lui faire entendre raison, on ne peut pas raisonner avec lui; *Hum* **ours is not to r. why** il ne faut pas chercher à comprendre; **to r. from past experience** raisonner en fonction de ses expériences passées **2** *vt* **to r. that ...** estimer que ... + *ind*; **to r. sb into/out of doing sth** convaincre qn de faire/de ne pas faire qch

▶ **reason out** *vtsep (maths problem)* résoudre; *(one's differences)* résoudre en discutant; **to r. out that ...** déduire que ...

reasonable ['riːz(ə)nəb(ə)l] *adj (person, price, demand)* raisonnable; *(offer)* acceptable, raisonnable; *(effort)* acceptable; **(do) be r.** soyez *ou* tâchez d'être raisonnable; **as is only r.** ce qui est parfaitement normal; **to believe sth beyond all r. doubt** croire qch en son âme et conscience; **r. suspicions** soupçons *mpl* fondés; **r. excuse** excuse *f* valable **(for** de); **with a r. amount of luck** avec un peu de chance; **the weather/meal/film was r.** le temps/le repas/le film était passable

reasonableness ['riːz(ə)nəb(ə)lnɪs] *n (of person, offer etc)* caractère *m* raisonnable; *(of effort)* caractère acceptable; *(of suspicion)* bien-fondé *m*

reasonably ['riːz(ə)nəblɪ] *adv* **(a)** *(to behave, act)* raisonnablement, de façon raisonnable; **r. priced** d'un prix raisonnable **(b)** *(fairly, rather)* assez; **r. fit** en assez bonne forme; **if we are r. lucky** avec un peu de chance

reasoned ['riːzənd] *adj (analysis, decision etc)* raisonné

reasoning ['riːzənɪŋ] **1** *n* raisonnement *m*; **power of r.** *(ability)* capacité *f* de raisonnement; **the r. behind the decision** les raisons de cette décision; **such r. is dangerous** un tel raisonnement est dangereux **2** *adj (creature etc)* doué de raison; *(ability, process etc)* de raisonnement

reassemble [riːə'semb(ə)l] **1** *vt* **(a)** *(gather) (troops)* rassembler **(b)** *(put together) (machine)* remonter; *(frame)* rassembler **2** *vi* *(of troops)* s'assembler de nouveau; **Parliament will r. on ...** le Parlement rouvrira le ...

reassembly [riːə'semblɪ] *n (gathering together)* rassemblement *m*; *Pol* rentrée *f*; *(of machine, gun)* remontage *m*

reassert [riːə'sɜːt] *vt (conviction, belief)* réaffirmer; **her self-confidence reasserted itself** sa confiance est revenue

reassess [riːə'ses] *vt* **(a)** *(policy, situation)* reconsidérer, réexaminer **(b)** *Fin (damages)* réévaluer; **you have been reassessed** votre situation fiscale a été réexaminée

reassessment [riːə'sesmənt] *n* **(a)** *(of policy, situation)* réexamen *m* **(b)** *Fin (of damages)* réévaluation *f*

reassign [riːə'saɪn] *vt (transfer) (employee, police officer etc)* muter **(to** à); *(work, project etc)* confier **(to** à); **the work's been reassigned** le travail a été confié à quelqu'un d'autre

reassignment [riːə'saɪnmənt] *n* **(a)** *(transfer) (of employee, police officer etc)* mutation *f* **(b)** *(duties)* nouveau poste *m*, nouvelles fonctions *fpl*

reassume [riːə'sjuːm] *vt (one's duties)* reprendre

reassurance [riːə'ʃʊərəns] *n* **(a)** *(comfort)* réconfort *m*; *(guarantee)* assurance *f*; **the boss gave (them) reassurances about their jobs** le patron les a rassurés quant à leur emploi **(b)** *Br Fin* réassurance *f*

reassure [riːə'ʃʊər] *vt* **(a)** *(person)* rassurer **(about** à propos de); **to r. sb of one's esteem** assurer qn de son estime; **to feel reassured** se sentir rassuré **(about** sur) **(b)** *Br Fin* réassurer

reassuring [riːə'ʃʊərɪŋ] *adj (person, news etc)* rassurant

reassuringly [riːə'ʃʊərɪŋlɪ] *adv (to behave, act)* d'une manière rassurante

reawaken [riːə'weɪk(ə)n] **1** *vt (sleeper)* réveiller; *(interest, feeling)* ranimer, faire renaître; *(hope)* faire renaître **2** *vi (of person)* se réveiller de nouveau; *(of affection, feelings, interest)* se ranimer

reawakening [riːə'weɪk(ə)nɪŋ] *n (of person, feeling etc)* réveil *m*; *(of interest)* regain *m*; *(of idea)* renaissance *f*

rebate ['riːbeɪt] *n Com etc* **(a)** *(refund)* remboursement *m* (partiel); *(of tax)* dégrèvement *m* **(b)** *(discount on purchase)* rabais *m*, ristourne *f*

rebel¹ ['reb(ə)l] *n (opponent) (of government)* rebelle *mf*; *(armed)* rebelle, insurgé, -ée; *(in society)* rebelle, révolté, -ée; *US Hist* **the Rebels** les confédérés; **r. army/camp** armée *f*/camp *m* rebelle; **r. forces/MPs** forces *fpl*/parlementaires *mpl* rebelles; **r. leader** chef *m* des rebelles

rebel² [rɪ'bel] *vi* **(-ll-)** *(against government)* se rebeller, se soulever **(against** contre); *(against society)* se rebeller, se révolter **(against** contre); **to r. against one's fate** se révolter *ou* s'insurger contre son destin; **her stomach rebelled at the**

thought of more food elle avait l'estomac qui se soulevait rien que de penser à de la nourriture

rebellion [rɪ'beljən] *n* (*against government*) rébellion *f*, soulèvement *m* (**against** contre); (*against society*) rébellion, révolte *f* (**against** contre); **to be in r. against** être en rébellion contre; **to rise up in r.** se soulever (**against** contre)

rebellious [rɪ'beljəs] *adj* (*soldier, troops etc*) insubordonné; (*student, inhabitants*) révolté, en révolte; (*behaviour, child etc*) rebelle; **r. hair** cheveux *mpl* qui ne tiennent pas en place; **r. bit of hair** mèche *f* rebelle; **r. act** acte *m* de rébellion

rebelliously [rɪ'beljəslɪ] *adv* (*to behave, act*) d'une façon rebelle

rebelliousness [rɪ'beljəsnɪs] *n* (*of troops*) insubordination *f*; (*of students etc*) esprit *m* de rébellion

rebirth [riː'bɜːθ] *n* (*of country etc*) renaissance *f*

reboot [riː'buːt] *Comptr* **1** *vt* réamorcer **2** *vi* se réamorcer

rebore[1] ['riːbɔːr] *n Aut* réalésage *m*; **my car needs a r.** le cylindre de ma voiture a besoin d'être réalésé *ou* d'un réalésage

rebore[2] *vt Aut* réaléser

reborn [riː'bɔːn] *adj usu pred* né à nouveau; **to be r.** renaître; **hope was r.** l'espoir est revenu; **to feel r.** (*physically*) se sentir revigoré; (*spiritually*) se sentir renaître

rebound[1] ['riːbaʊnd] *n* (*of ball*) rebond *m*; **to hit a ball on the r.** frapper une balle au rebond; **he headed in the r.** il a marqué un but de la tête en prenant la balle au rebond; *Fig* **she married him on the r.** elle l'a épousé à cause d'une déception amoureuse; *Fig* **he caught her on the r.** il a commencé à la fréquenter au moment où elle sortait d'une déception amoureuse

rebound[2] [rɪ'baʊnd] *vi* (**a**) (*of ball etc*) rebondir; (*of stone*) ricocher; (*of cry, noise*) faire écho (**from** contre); *Fig* (*of joke, lie etc*) se retourner (**on** contre); **the trick he played rebounded on him** son mauvais tour s'est retourné contre lui (**b**) (*recover*) (*of person*) se ressaisir (**from** après); (*of share prices, business*) reprendre, se redresser (**from** après)

rebuff[1] [rɪ'bʌf] *n* (*of person*) rebuffade *f*; (*of suggestion etc*) refus *m*; **to meet with** *or* **suffer a r.** (*of person*) essuyer une rebuffade; (*of suggestion etc*) être repoussé

rebuff[2] *vt* (*reject*) (*advances*) repousser; (*person*) repousser, rejeter; (*offer, suggestion*) rejeter; (*allegation*) démentir; **to feel rebuffed** se sentir repoussé *ou* rejeté

rebuild [riː'bɪld] *vt* (*pt, pp* **rebuilt** [riː'bɪlt]) (*house, company*) reconstruire; (*one's life*) reconstruire, refaire; (*machine, engine*) remettre à neuf, refaire

rebuilding [riː'bɪldɪŋ] *n* (*of house, company*) reconstruction *f*; (*of machine, engine*) réfection *f*, remise *f* à neuf

rebuke[1] [rɪ'bjuːk] *n* réprimande *f*; **to administer** *or* **deliver a r. to sb** réprimander qn, faire une réprimande à qn

rebuke[2] *vt* (*person*) réprimander (**for doing sth** pour avoir fait qch)

rebus ['riːbəs] *n* rébus *m*

rebut [rɪ'bʌt] *vt* (**-tt-**) *Fml* (*accusation, hypothesis etc*) réfuter

rebuttal [rɪ'bʌt(ə)l] *n Fml* réfutation *f*

rebuy [riː'baɪ] *n Mktg* réachat *m*; **r. rate** taux *m* de réachat

rec [rek] *n F* (**a**) *Br* **r. (ground)** terrain *m* de jeux (**b**) *Am Sch* (*break*) récréation *f*, *F* récré *f*; **r. room** (*in home*) salle *f* de jeux

recalcitrance [rɪ'kælsɪtrəns] *n Fml* récalcitrance *f*

recalcitrant [rɪ'kælsɪtrənt] *adj Fml* (*horse, person*) récalcitrant; (*disease*) rebelle

recall[1] ['riːkɔːl] *n* (**a**) (*remembering*) **she has remarkable powers of r.** elle a une mémoire remarquable; **to have instant r.** avoir une excellente mémoire; **to have total r.** (être capable de) se souvenir de tous les détails de quelque chose; *Mktg* **r. test** test *m* de rappel *ou* du lendemain *ou* de mémoire (**b**) (*calling back*) (*of troops, library book, defective goods etc*) rappel *m*; (*of Parliament*) reconvocation *f*; *Mil* **to sound the r.** battre le rappel; **lost beyond r.** perdu irrévocablement; **r. slip** (*for library book*) fiche *f* de rappel

recall[2] [rɪ'kɔːl] **1** *vt* (**a**) (*remember*) se souvenir de, se rappeler; **to r. doing sth** se rappeler avoir fait qch; **to r. sth to sb** rappeler qch à qn; **legends that r. the past** légendes évocatrices du passé *ou* qui évoquent le passé; **how vividly I r. the scene!** avec quelle netteté je revois ce spectacle!

(**b**) (*call back*) (*troops, defective goods etc*) rappeler; (*library book*) demander le retour de; **the sound of the telephone recalled her to the present** la sonnerie du téléphone la ramena à la réalité

2 *vi* **as I r.** si je me rappelle bien; **as you may r.** comme vous vous en souvenez *ou* le rappelez peut-être; **as you will r.** comme vous vous en souvenez sans doute

recant [rɪ'kænt] **1** *vt* (*opinion*) rétracter, revenir sur; (*doctrinal error*) abjurer; (*doctrine*) désavouer **2** *vi* se rétracter

recantation [riːkæn'teɪʃən] *n* (*of faith, statement*) abjuration *f* (**of** de)

recap[1] ['riːkæp] *n* (**a**) *F* (*summary*) récapitulation *f*; **let's do a r.** faisons le point (**b**) *Am Aut* pneu *m* rechapé

recap[2] (**-pp-**) **1** *vt* (**a**) *F* = **recapitulate 1(a)** (**b**) *Am Aut* (*tyre*) rechaper **2** *vi F* récapituler

recapitalization [riːkæpɪtəlaɪ'zeɪʃən] *n* recapitalisation *f*

recapitalize [riː'kæpɪtəlaɪz] *vt* changer la structure financière de

recapitulate [riːkə'pɪtjʊleɪt] **1** *vt* (**a**) (*summarize*) (*discussion etc*) récapituler; **let us r. the facts** faisons le point (**b**) *Mus* (*theme*) reprendre **2** *vi* récapituler

recapitulation [riːkəpɪtjʊ'leɪʃən] *n* (**a**) (*of discussion etc*) récapitulation *f* (**b**) *Mus* reprise *f*

recapture[1] [riː'kæptʃər] *n* (*of town*) reprise *f*; (*of prisoner*) capture *f*

recapture[2] *vt* (**a**) (*take again*) (*prisoner, town*) reprendre (**b**) (*recreate*) (*era, age, atmosphere*) faire revivre, recréer; (*one's youth*) retrouver

recast [riː'kɑːst] *vt* (*pt, pp* **recast**) (**a**) (*reshape*) (*sentence, piece of writing*) remanier (**b**) *Th* (*find new cast for*) (*play*) changer la distribution de; (*find new part for*) (*actor*) donner un nouveau rôle à; **the part has been recast** le rôle a été donné à quelqu'un d'autre

recce ['rekɪ] *n F* (*exploration*) reconnaissance *f*; **to make a quick r.** faire une reconnaissance rapide (**of** de)

recede [rɪ'siːd] *vi* (**a**) (*of tide, sea*) se retirer, descendre; (*of coastline, person, thing*) s'éloigner, reculer; **the colour receded from his face** il devint livide; **as memories of the past r.** à mesure que les souvenirs du passé s'effacent (**b**) (*slope backwards*) **to have a receding chin/forehead** avoir le menton/front fuyant *ou* qui fuit; **his hair(line)** *or* **he is receding** son front se dégarnit (**c**) (*lose value*) perdre de la valeur; **the company's shares have receded five points** les actions de la société ont reculé de *ou* perdu cinq points

receipt[1] [rɪ'siːt] *n* (**a**) (*receiving*) (*of letter, parcel etc*) réception *f*; **on r. of this letter** dès réception de cette lettre; **on r. of the news** à la nouvelle (**about** de); **within one week of r.** dans un délai d'une semaine après réception; **to pay on r.** payer à (la) réception; **to acknowledge r.** accuser réception (**of** de); **we are in r. of ...** nous avons reçu ...; *Com* **r. at domicile** prise *f* à domicile; **r. of a dividend** perception *f* de dividende; **r. stamp** timbre-quittance *m*

(**b**) (*for payment*) reçu *m* (**for** de); (*in supermarket, bar*) ticket *m* de caisse; (*for letter, parcel*) récépissé *m*, accusé *m* de réception; **to give a r.** (*for meal, taxi fare etc*) donner un reçu; (*for rent*) donner une quittance

(**c**) **receipts** (*takings*) recettes *fpl*, rentrées *fpl*; **receipts and expenditure** recettes et dépenses *fpl*

receipt[2] *vt Com* acquitter, quittancer; **to r. a bill** (*in writing*) acquitter une facture; (*with stamp*) apposer le tampon 'pour acquit' sur une facture

receivable [rɪ'siːvəb(ə)l] *Com* **1** *adj* (*account, bill etc*) à recevoir **2** *n* compte *m ou* effet *m* à recevoir

receive [rɪ'siːv] **1** *vt* (**a**) (*take delivery of*) (*gift, news, letter*) recevoir; (*money etc*) recevoir, toucher; (*salary etc*) toucher; **I have received your letter** j'ai reçu votre lettre, votre lettre m'est parvenue; **received with thanks** (*on bill*) pour acquit; *Rad, TV* **to r. a broadcast** recevoir une émission; **to r. a station** capter un poste; **are you receiving me?** (*on radio*) est-ce que vous me recevez?; **to r. (the) service** (*of tennis or badminton player*) recevoir le service; *Jur* **to r. stolen goods** receler des objets volés

(**b**) (*be given*) (*greeting, blow, communion etc*) recevoir; (*refusal*) essuyer; (*criticism*) faire l'objet de; (*commission, unemployment benefit, interest*) percevoir; *Jur* **to r. thirty days** être condamné à un mois de prison; **I received the distinct impression that ...** j'ai eu la nette impression que ...; *prov* **it is better** *or* **more blessed to give than to r.** il y a plus de joie à donner qu'à recevoir; **we don't want them to r. a bad impression of us** nous ne voulons pas leur faire mauvaise impression; *St Exch* **to r. a premium** encaisser un premium

(**c**) (*welcome*) (*guests*) recevoir; **to be cordially received** (*of visitor etc*) trouver un accueil chaleureux, être bien reçu; **the proposal was well/badly received** la proposition reçut un accueil favorable/défavorable *ou* a été bien/mal reçue; **the film was well received by the critics** le film a été bien accueilli par la critique; **to r. sb into the Church** admettre qn dans l'Église; **to r. sb into one's family** admettre *ou* recevoir qn dans sa famille

2 *vi* (*of tennis or badminton player*) recevoir le service

received [rɪ'siːvd] *adj* (**a**) (*idea*) reçu; (*opinion*) admis; **the r. view is that ...** il est communément admis *ou* accepté que ..., on admet communément que ...; *Br* **r. pronunciation** = la prononciation standard du sud de l'Angleterre; **r. wisdom** sagesse *f* populaire (**b**) *Com* **r. stamp** cachet *m* d'arrivée

receiver [rɪ'siːvər] *n* **(a)** (*of stolen goods*) receleur, -euse **(b)** *Tel* récepteur *m*; **to lift** *or* **pick up the r.** décrocher; **to replace the r.** raccrocher; **r. rest** berceau *m* du récepteur **(c)** *Rad* récepteur *m*; **r. aerial** antenne *f* de réception **(d)** *Jur, Fin* **r. in bankruptcy, official r.** administrateur, -trice judiciaire, syndic *m* de faillite; **to be in the hands of the r.** être en règlement judiciaire

receivership [rɪ'siːvəʃɪp] *n Jur, Fin* liquidation *f* judiciaire; **to go into r.** se mettre en règlement judiciaire

receiving [rɪ'siːvɪŋ] **1** *n* (*of stolen goods*) recel *m* **2** *adj* **r. aerial** antenne *f* de réception; *Am* **r. blanket** petite couverture *f* légère pour bébé; *Com* **r. depot** dépôt *m* de réception; *Rad* **r. set** poste *m* récepteur; *Rad* **r. station** station *f* réceptrice; *F* **to be at** *or* **on the r. end** écoper; **to be on the r. end of sb's temper** faire les frais du mauvais caractère de qn; *F* **I've been on the r. end of customers' complaints all day** c'est moi qui me suis occupé des réclamations des clients toute la journée; *F* **it's different when you're on the r. end** c'est tout autre chose quand c'est à toi que ça arrive

recent ['riːsənt] *adj* (*development, event, past*) récent; (*acquaintance*) nouveau, *f* nouvelle; **event of r. date** événement *m* récent; **all that is quite r.** tout cela est très récent; **in r. months** au cours des derniers mois; **r. news** nouvelles *fpl* récentes *ou* fraîches; **in r. times** récemment; **the most r. edition** (*of book etc*) la dernière édition; **her most r. novel** son dernier roman

recently ['riːsəntlɪ] *adv* récemment; **as r. as yesterday** pas plus tard qu'hier; **until quite r.** jusqu'à récemment *ou* ces derniers temps; **I saw her quite r.** je l'ai vue tout dernièrement

receptacle [rɪ'septək(ə)l] *n* **(a)** (*for litter, paper, water etc*) récipient *m* **(b)** *Am El* prise *f* de courant (femelle)

reception [rɪ'sepʃən] *n* **(a)** (*welcome*) accueil *m*; **to give sb a chilly/warm r.** réserver à qn un accueil glacial/chaleureux; **what kind of r. did you get?** quel accueil est-ce qu'ils t'ont réservé?, comment est-ce qu'ils t'ont reçu?; **the play has had a favourable r.** la pièce a été accueillie favorablement *ou* bien reçue

(b) (*party*) réception *f*; (*in the evening*) réception, soirée *f*; **wedding r.** réception de mariage; **r. room** (*in hotel*) salle *f* de réception; (*in private house*) salon *m*

(c) (*in hotel*) réception *f*; (*in office, hospital*) accueil *m*; **r., the r. desk** la réception; **at** *or* **to r.** à la réception/à l'accueil; **r.** *n* chef *m* de réception

(d) *Rad, TV* réception *f*

reception centre *n* (*for refugees etc*) centre *m* d'accueil

reception class *n Br Sch* première année *f* de maternelle

reception clerk *n Am* réceptionniste *mf*

reception committee *n also Fig Hum* comité *m* d'accueil

receptionist [rɪ'sepʃənɪst] *n* réceptionniste *mf*; (*at trade fair*) hôtesse *f* d'accueil

receptive [rɪ'septɪv] *adj* (*audience, listener*) réceptif (**to an idea** à une idée); **r. to sb** compréhensif envers qn

receptiveness [rɪ'septɪvnɪs], **receptivity** [riːsep'tɪvɪtɪ] *n* (*of audience, listener*) réceptivité *f* (**to** à)

receptor [rɪ'septər] *n* **(a)** (*for antibody, drug*) récepteur *m*; **r. site** (site *m*) récepteur **(b)** (*for radio signals*) récepteur *m*

recess¹ [rɪ'ses], *Am* ['riːses] *n* **(a)** *Br* (*holidays*) (*of law courts, Parliament*) vacances *fpl*; **while Parliament is in r.** pendant les vacances parlementaires **(b)** *Am Sch* (*break*) récréation *f* **(c)** *Am Jur* (*break*) suspension *f* d'audience; **the court is now in r.** l'audience est maintenant suspendue; **we will take a ten minute r.** nous allons suspendre l'audience pendant dix minutes **(d)** (*nook*) recoin *m*; (*for bed etc*) renfoncement *m*; (*for statue*) niche *f*; **dining r.** coin *m* repas, coin salle à manger; **in the innermost recesses of the soul** dans les replis *ou* recoins les plus secrets de l'âme

recess² **1** *vt* (*place in a recess*) (*lighting, switch etc*) encastrer **2** *vi* **(a)** *Br* **Parliament will r. next week** les vacances parlementaires commenceront la semaine prochaine **(b)** *Am* (*of assembly*) suspendre la séance; (*of court*) suspendre l'audience

recession [rɪ'seʃən] *n Econ* récession *f*; **in (a) r.** en récession

recessionary [rɪ'seʃənərɪ] *adj Econ* (*conditions, policy etc*) de récession; **to have a r. effect** (*of policy etc*) entraîner une récession

recessive [rɪ'sesɪv] *adj Biol* (*gene*) récessif

recharge [riː'tʃɑːdʒ] **1** *vt* (*battery*) recharger; *Fig* **to r. one's batteries** recharger ses batteries, reprendre du poil de la bête **2** *vi* (*of battery*) se recharger

rechargeable [riː'tʃɑːdʒəb(ə)l] *adj* (*battery*) rechargeable

recherché [rə'ʃeəʃeɪ] *adj* (*film, topic*) recherché

recidivism [rɪ'sɪdɪvɪz(ə)m] *n Jur* récidivisme *m*

recidivist [rɪ'sɪdɪvɪst] *adj, n Jur* récidiviste *mf*

recidivistic [rɪsɪdɪ'vɪstɪk] *adj Jur* (*tendency etc*) à récidiver

recipe ['resɪpɪ] *n Culin; Fig* recette *f*; *Pharm* formule *f*, recette; **r. for a happy life** recette pour vivre heureux; **a r. for failure** le meilleur moyen pour échouer; **those two working together would be a r. for disaster** si ces deux-là travaillaient ensemble ce serait l'échec *ou* la catastrophe assuré(e); **r. book** livre *m* de recettes; **r. card** fiche-recette *f*, *pl* fiches-recettes, fiche-cuisine *f*, *pl* fiches-cuisines

recipient [rɪ'sɪpɪənt] *n* (*of gift, letter etc*) destinataire *mf*; (*of cheque, money*) bénéficiaire *mf*; (*of award, honour*) récipiendaire *mf*; *Med* (*of organ transplant*) receveur, -euse

reciprocal [rɪ'sɪprək(ə)l] **1** *adj* **(a)** (*agreement, friendship*) réciproque; (*concessions, trade*) mutuel, réciproque; **he dislikes me and it's r.** il ne m'aime pas et c'est réciproque *ou* je le lui rends bien; **r. marketing** mercatique *f* bilatérale; *Mktg* **r. relationships model** modèle *m* de relations réciproques **(b)** *Gram* réciproque **(c)** *Math* réciproque, inverse **2** *n Math* réciproque *f*, inverse *f*

reciprocally [rɪ'sɪprəklɪ] *adv* (*to trade*) réciproquement

reciprocate [rɪ'sɪprəkeɪt] **1** *vt* (*return*) (*compliment*) retourner; **to r. sb's kindness** payer la gentillesse de qn de retour; **he had great admiration for her but his feelings were never reciprocated** il avait beaucoup d'admiration pour elle mais ce n'était pas réciproque **2** *vi* **(a)** (*do the same*) en faire autant; (*counter-attack*) riposter **(b)** *MecE* (*of piston etc*) avoir un mouvement alternatif *ou* de va-et-vient

reciprocating [rɪ'sɪprəkeɪtɪŋ] *adj MecE* (*movement*) alternatif; (*machine*) à mouvement alternatif *ou* de va-et-vient; **r. engine** moteur *m* alternatif

reciprocation [rɪsɪprə'keɪʃən] *n* **(a)** (*of feeling*) réciprocité *f*; **I think some r. of her compliment is called for** je pense qu'il faudrait lui retourner le compliment; **these feelings met with no r.** ces sentiments n'ont pas été payés de retour; **in r. for ...** en retour de ... **(b)** *MecE* mouvement *m* alternatif, va-et-vient *m inv*

reciprocity [resɪ'prɒsɪtɪ] *n* réciprocité *f*

recirculated air [riː'sɜːkjʊleɪtɪd] *n Aut* air *m* recyclé

recital [rɪ'saɪt(ə)l] *n* **(a)** (*of poetry*) récitation *f* **(b)** *Mus* récital *m*; **to give a r.** donner un récital; **Bach r.** récital Bach **(c)** (*of events etc*) récit *m*, narration *f*; (*of complaints, details etc*) énumération *f*

recitation [resɪ'teɪʃən] *n* (*of poem etc*) récitation *f*; **to give a r.** réciter; **to give a r. from Burns** réciter du Burns

recitative [resɪtə'tiːv] *n Mus* récitatif *m*

recite [rɪ'saɪt] **1** *vt* **(a)** (*poem etc*) réciter **(b)** (*complaints, details etc*) énumérer **2** *vi* réciter; **will you r. to us?** voulez-vous nous réciter quelque chose?

reckless ['reklɪs] *adj* (*foolhardy*) (*person*) inconscient, téméraire; (*attempt, action, decision etc*) téméraire; (*driving, gambler*) imprudent; **to be a r. spender** dépenser sans compter; **to be r. with one's money** dépenser son argent inconsidérément; *Aut* **r. driver** automobiliste *mf* imprudent(e), *F* chauffard *m*

recklessly ['reklɪslɪ] *adv* (*to attempt*) témérairement; (*to drive, gamble*) imprudemment; (*to spend*) sans compter

recklessness ['reklɪsnɪs] *n* (*of attempt, person*) témérité *f*; (*of driving, gambling*) imprudence *f*

reckon ['rekən] **1** *vt* **(a)** (*consider*) (*person*) considérer (**as** comme); **to r. sb among the greatest writers** mettre qn au rang *ou* au nombre des plus grands écrivains; **he is reckoned to be one of the richest men in England** il paraît *ou* ce serait l'un des hommes les plus riches d'Angleterre

(b) (*calculate, count*) (*amount etc*) calculer, compter; **the cost has been reckoned at £100** le coût a été estimé à 100 livres

(c) *F* (*think*) penser; **I r. he's forty** je lui donne quarante ans; **I r. he'll consent** à mon avis, il consentira; **maybe we should go, what do you r.?** nous devrions peut-être y aller, qu'est-ce que tu en penses?; **the Government obviously reckons it has a good chance of winning an early election** le gouvernement a bon espoir de gagner une élection anticipée

(d) *F* (*regard favourably*) **I don't r. her chances** je ne donne pas cher de sa réussite

2 *vi* **(a)** (*calculate*) compter, calculer; **reckoning from today** à partir *ou* à compter d'aujourd'hui

(b) (*expect, plan*) compter (**to go** partir); **you should r. to be there by 6 o'clock at the latest** il faut que tu prévois d'arriver à six heures au plus tard

▶ **reckon in** *vtsep* compter

▶ **reckon on** *vipo* **to r. on sth** compter sur qch; **they had not reckoned on finding me here** ils ne comptaient pas me trouver ici

▶ **reckon up** **1** *vtsep* (*column of figures*) additionner; (*change, coins*) compter; **to r. up the cost of sth** calculer le coût de qch; **to r. up a bill** faire une facture **2** *vi* (*prepare bill*) faire la note

▶ **reckon with** *vipo* compter avec; **to have sb to r. with** avoir affaire à qn; **she's a force to be reckoned with** c'est une femme avec laquelle il faut compter **he hadn't reckoned with this response** il ne s'attendait pas à cette réaction; **you didn't r. with Superman!** c'était compter sans Superman!

▶ **reckon without** *vipo* compter sans; **he had reckoned without his rivals** il n'avait pas tenu compte de ses rivaux

reckoner ['rek(ə)nər] *n* **ready r.** barème *m*

reckoning ['rekənɪŋ] *n* (*of bill, interest etc*) calcul *m*; **by my r.** d'après mes calculs; **to be out in one's r.** s'être trompé dans ses calculs; **you're a long way out in your r.** vous êtes loin du compte; **to the best of my r.** autant je puisse en juger; *Rel* **day of r.** jour *m* du Jugement dernier; *Fig* instant *m* de vérité

reclaim¹ [rɪ'kleɪm] *vt* **(a)** (*land*) mettre en valeur; (*from undergrowth*) défricher; (*marsh*) assécher; **to r. land from the sea/the desert** conquérir du terrain sur la mer/le désert **(b)** (*lost property, suitcase etc*) récupérer; (*tax, expenses*) se faire rembourser; **to r. VAT** récupérer la TVA **(c)** *Ind* (*rubber etc*) régénérer; (*by-product*) récupérer

reclaim² ['riːkleɪm] *n* **luggage** *or* **baggage r.** (*in airport*) retrait *m* des bagages

reclamation [reklə'meɪʃən] *n* **(a)** (*of land*) mise *f* en valeur; (*from undergrowth*) défrichement *m*; (*of marsh*) assèchement *m* **(b)** (*of tax, expenses*) remboursement *m* **(c)** *Ind* (*of rubber etc*) régénération *f*; (*of by-product*) récupération *f*

reclassify [riː'klæsɪfaɪ] *vt* (*plant etc*) reclasser; (*document etc*) reclassifier

recline [rɪ'klaɪn] **1** *vt* (*one's head*) appuyer (**against** contre; **on** sur); (*seat*) incliner le dossier de **2** *vi* (*of person*) (*be lying*) être allongé *ou* étendu (**on** sur); (*lie down*) s'allonger, s'étendre; (*of head*) être appuyé (**on** sur); (*of seat*) avoir un dossier inclinable *ou* réglable

recliner [rɪ'klaɪnər] *n* (*for sunbathing*) chaise *f* longue; (*armchair*) fauteuil *m* à dossier inclinable, fauteuil relax

reclining [rɪ'klaɪnɪŋ] *adj* **to be in a r. position** (*of person*) être en position allongée *ou* couchée; (*of seat*) être incliné; **r. seat** (*in aircraft etc*) siège *m* à dossier inclinable *ou* réglable

recluse [rɪ'kluːs] *n* reclus, -use; **to live** *or* **lead the life of a r.** vivre en reclus *ou* ermite; **she has become a bit of a r.** elle est devenue assez solitaire

recognition [rekəg'nɪʃən] *n* **(a)** (*identification*) (*of person, style etc*) reconnaissance *f*; **she gave no sign of r.** elle n'a pas eu l'air de me/le/*etc* reconnaître; **to change beyond** *or* **out of all r.** devenir méconnaissable; **brand r.** (*in advertising*) identification *f* de la marque; *Mktg* **r. test** test *m* de reconnaissance

(b) (*acknowledgement*) (*of fact, government, speaker etc*) reconnaissance *f*; **to win r.** (*of artist etc*) s'imposer (**from** aux yeux de); **her work has won her international r.** son œuvre lui a permis de s'imposer sur le plan international; **to withhold r. from** (*government*) refuser de reconnaître; **in r. of his courage** en reconnaissance de son courage; **she received no r.** on ne lui accordait aucune considération

recognizable [rekəg'naɪzəb(ə)l] *adj* (*person, style etc*) reconnaissable; **he's so changed as to be no longer r.** il est devenu méconnaissable

recognizably [rekəg'naɪzəblɪ] *adv* **she is r. your daughter** on voit bien que c'est votre fille

recognizance [rɪ'kɒgnɪzəns] *n Jur* (*promise*) engagement *m*; (*money paid*) caution *f* personnelle; **to enter into recognizances** donner caution; **to enter into recognizances for sb** se porter garant *ou* caution pour qn, cautionner qn; **to be released on one's own recognizances** être remis en liberté sur engagement personnel

recognize ['rekəgnaɪz] *vt* **(a)** (*know again*) (*person, town etc*) reconnaître (**by** à); **to r. the truth when one sees it** être capable de savoir si quelque chose est vrai ou non, savoir discerner le vrai du faux; **he can certainly r. a good business opportunity** il sait repérer les bonnes affaires

(b) (*acknowledge*) (*government, fact etc*) reconnaître; *Sp* (*record*) homologuer; **to r. sb as king** reconnaître qn comme *ou* en tant que roi; **to r. defeat** accepter *ou* admettre sa défaite; **to be the first to r. a fact** être le premier à reconnaître un fait

(c) *Am* **to r. a member** (*of chairman of a meeting etc*) donner la parole à un membre; *Am* **to be recognized** (*of speaker*) avoir la parole

recognized ['rekəgnaɪzd] *adj* (*government etc*) reconnu; (*truth*) admis, accepté; (*method etc*) classique; **it is a r. fact that …** c'est un fait avéré *ou* reconnu que …; **the r. term** le terme consacré (**for** pour); *Com* **r. agent** agent *m* accrédité (**for** pour); **to be a r. authority** être une autorité reconnue (par tous) (**on** en)

recoil¹ ['riːkɔɪl] *n* (*of gun, rifle*) recul *m*; (*of spring*) détente *f*; (*of person*) mouvement *m* de recul

recoil² [rɪ'kɔɪl] *vi* (*of gun, rifle*) reculer; (*of spring*) se détendre; (*of person*) reculer (**from doing sth** à l'idée de faire qch); *Fig* (*of joke etc*) se retourner (**on** contre); **to r. (in horror/disgust)** avoir un mouvement de recul

recoilless [rɪ'kɔɪllɪs] *adj* (*rifle etc*) sans recul

recollect [rekə'lekt] **1** *vt* se rappeler, se souvenir de; **she was unable to r. what had happened** elle était incapable de se souvenir de ce qui s'était passé **2** *vi* **as far as I r.** autant que je m'en souvienne

recollection [rekə'lekʃən] *n* souvenir *m*; **my earliest recollections** mes premiers souvenirs; **her r. differs from mine** nos souvenirs ne concordent pas, ses souvenirs et les miens ne concordent pas; **I have some r. of it** j'en ai un vague souvenir; **I have no r. of it** je n'en ai *ou* je n'en garde aucun souvenir; **I have no r. of doing it** je ne me souviens pas de *ou* je ne me rappelle pas l'avoir fait; **to the best of my r.** pour autant que je me souvienne

recombinant [riː'kɒmbɪnənt] *adj Biol* **r. DNA** ADN *m* recombinant

recommend [rekə'mend] *vt* **(a)** (*praise*) (*book, restaurant, doctor*) recommander (**to** à; **for** pour); **the hotel is to be recommended for its cooking** on recommande cet hôtel pour sa cuisine; **the film has little to r. it** on ne peut pas dire grand-chose en faveur de ce film (**apart from, except** en dehors de); **the place has little to r. it apart from the weather** cet endroit n'a pas grand intérêt à part qu'il y fait beau; **the proposal has a lot to r. it** la proposition a beaucoup d'avantages *ou* d'attrait; **the hotel comes recommended** on dit beaucoup de bien de cet hôtel

(b) (*advise*) (*caution*) conseiller; **to r. sb to do sth** recommander *ou* conseiller à qn de faire qch; **I r. going** *or* **that you go via Leeds** je vous recommande *ou* conseille de passer par Leeds; **this is not to be recommended** ce n'est pas recommandé; **recommended (retail) price** prix *m* (public) conseillé

(c) *Old-fashioned* (*entrust*) **to r. sth to the care of sb** *or* **to sb's care** recommander qch aux soins de qn; **to r. one's soul to God** recommander son âme à Dieu

recommendable [rekə'mendəb(ə)l] *adj* (*book, person etc*) recommandable; **highly r.** très recommandable

recommendation [rekəmen'deɪʃən] *n* **(a)** (*advice*) recommandation *f*; **I have come on the r. of one of your customers** je viens sur la recommandation d'un de vos clients; **through personal r.** par recommandation personnelle; **one can only join the club through personal r.** on ne peut devenir membre du club qu'en étant recommandé personnellement; **my r. is that …** ce que je recommande *ou* conseille c'est que …; **to follow/ignore sb's recommendations** suivre/ne pas suivre les recommandations de qn; **the report's recommendations** les recommandations contenues dans le rapport

(b) (*commendation*) recommandation *f*; **the hotel's sole r. is its location** l'emplacement de l'hôtel est son seul intérêt

recompense¹ ['rekəmpens] *n* **(a)** (*reward*) récompense *f* (**for** de); **in r. for …** en récompense de … **(b)** *Jur* (*for damage, loss*) dédommagement *m* (**for** de, pour); **as r.** en dédommagement

recompense² *vt* **(a)** (*reward*) récompenser (**for** de) **(b)** *Jur* (*compensate*) dédommager (**for sth** de qch)

reconcilable [rekən'saɪləb(ə)l] *adj* (*ideas, opinions*) compatible, conciliable (**with** avec); **not r.** irréconciliable

reconcile ['rekənsaɪl] *vt* **(a)** (*person*) réconcilier (**with** avec); **to be reconciled with sb** se réconcilier avec qn; **to r. sb to sth** faire accepter qch à *ou* par qn; **to r. oneself** *or* **become reconciled to sth** se résigner à quelque chose **(b)** (*settle*) (*quarrel*) régler, mettre fin à; **let us r. our differences** essayons de nous entendre **(c)** (*make agree*) (*opinions, facts*) concilier; *Am Acct* (*figures, bank statement*) rapprocher; *Fin* **to r. accounts** faire cadrer *ou* accorder les comptes; **evidence which cannot be reconciled with the known facts** témoignage qui ne cadre pas avec les faits connus

reconciliation [rekənsɪlɪ'eɪʃən] *n* **(a)** (*of people*) réconciliation *f* (**between** entre; **with** avec) **(b)** (*of differences, of opinions*) conciliation *f* **(c)** (*of bank statements*) rapprochement *m*; *Acct* **r. statement** état *m* de rapprochement

recondite [rɪ'kɒndaɪt, 'rekəndaɪt] *adj Fml* (*subject, knowledge*) abscons

recondition [riːkən'dɪʃən] *vt* (*engine etc*) refaire, remettre à neuf

reconditioned [riːkən'dɪʃənd] *adj* (*engine etc*) remis en état, refait

reconditioning [riːkən'dɪʃənɪŋ] *n* (*of engine etc*) remise *f* à neuf

reconfiguration [riːkənfɪgə'reɪʃən] *n Comptr* (*of keyboard, system etc*) reconfiguration *f*

reconfigure [riːkən'fɪgər] *vt Comptr* (*keyboard, system*) reconfigurer

reconnaissance [rɪ'kɒnɪsəns] *n Mil, Fig* reconnaissance *f*; **to make a r.** faire une reconnaissance; **to be on r.** être en reconnaissance; **r. flight/mission/satellite** vol *m*/mission *f*/ satellite *m* de reconnaissance

reconnect [riːkə'nekt] *vt* (*telephone, cable etc*) rebrancher; (*pipe*) raccorder; **to r. the water supply** rétablir l'alimentation en eau; *Tel* **to r. sb** (*of operator*) rétablir la communication; (*of telephone company*) rebrancher le téléphone

reconnection [riːkə'nekʃən] *n* (*of cable, telephone etc*) rebranchement *m*; (*of pipe*) raccordement *m*; (*of water supply, telephone call*) rétablissement *m*; *Tel* **r. charge** (*for disconnected telephone*) frais *mpl* de rebranchement

reconnoitre, *US* **reconnoiter** [rekə'nɔɪtər] **1** *vt Mil, Fig* reconnaître **2** *vi* faire une reconnaissance

reconquer [riː'kɒŋkər] *vt* (*country etc*) reconquérir

reconquest [riː'kɒŋkwest] *n* (*of country etc*) reconquête *f*

reconsider [riːkən'sɪdər] **1** *vt* (*question*) reconsidérer, repenser; (*decision*) reconsidérer, réexaminer **2** *vi* reconsidérer la question; **won't you please r.?** est-ce que vous ne pourriez pas y réfléchir à nouveau?

reconsideration [riːkənsɪdə'reɪʃən] *n* (*of question*) reconsidération *f*; (*of decision*) reconsidération *f*, réexamen *m*

reconstitute [riː'kɒnstɪtjuːt] *vt* reconstituer

reconstitution [riːkɒnstɪ'tjuːʃən] *n* reconstitution *f*

reconstruct [riːkən'strʌkt] *vt* (*house etc*) reconstruire, rebâtir; (*company, corrupt computer file etc, Fig facts, crime*) reconstituer; (*one's life, a country*) reconstruire

reconstruction [riːkən'strʌkʃən] *n* (*of house, country, life etc*) reconstruction *f*; (*of file, company etc, Fig of crime*) reconstitution *f*; **economic and financial r.** restauration *f* économique et financière

reconstructive [riːkən'strʌktɪv] *adj* **r. surgery** chirurgie *f* réparatrice

reconvene [riːkən'viːn] **1** *vt* convoquer de nouveau **2** *vi* se réunir à nouveau

record¹ ['rekɔːd] **1** *n* **(a)** (*of attendance*) registre *m*; (*of proceedings*) procès-verbal *m*, *pl* procès-verbaux; (*of verdict, fact*) enregistrement *m*; **to keep a r. of sth** garder une trace de qch; **I can find no r. of it** je n'en trouve aucune mention; **to be on r.** (*of verdict, fact*) être enregistré; *Jur* **to strike sth from the r.** rayer qch du procès-verbal; **to be on r. as saying sth** avoir déclaré qch publiquement; **to go on r. as a pacifist** se déclarer pacifiste; **to put sth on r.** noter qch, consigner qch; **it is on r.** *or* **a matter of r.** c'est un fait établi **(that** que); **this is the coldest winter on r.** c'est l'hiver le plus froid que l'on ait jamais enregistré; **to say sth off the r.** dire qch en confidence; **this is strictly off the r.** ceci est strictement confidentiel, ceci doit rester entre nous; **(just) for the r.** , **to keep the r. straight** pour que les choses soient claires; **is this for the r.?** est-ce que cela est officiel?; **to put** *or* **set the r. straight** mettre les choses au clair, dissiper tout malentendu; **to leave few records** (*of ancient civilization*) laisser peu de témoignages écrits; **the Etruscans left little r. of their religious beliefs** les Étrusques n'ont laissé que peu de traces de leurs croyances

(b) (*file*) dossier *m*; *Hist, Jur* archive *f*; *Admin* registre *m*; **our records do not go back that far** nos registres *ou* nos archives ne remontent pas aussi loin; *Admin* **records management** gestion *f* des dossiers; **r. card** fiche *f*; **r. form** (*for keeping records*) bordereau *m* de saisie; **r. office** bureau *m* des archives; *Jur* greffe *m*

(c) *Comptr* (*in database*) article *m*, enregistrement *m*;

(d) (*personal history*) antécédents *mpl*; (*of criminal*) casier *m* judiciaire; (*achievements*) résultats *mpl*; **to have a good/ bad safety r.** (*of company etc*) avoir une bonne/mauvaise réputation en ce qui concerne la sécurité; *Mil, Fig* **he has a good r.** ses états de service sont bons; **his past r.** (*behaviour*) ses antécédents; (*achievements*) ses résultats antérieurs; **given your r. as a late payer** vu vos antécédents de mauvais payeur; *Jur* **to have a clean r.** avoir un casier judiciaire vierge; *Jur* **he has a r.** il a déjà été condamné, il a des condamnations antérieures; *Med* **case r.** fiche *f* de patient *ou* d'observation

(e) *Mus* (*recording*) disque *m*; **to make** *or F* **cut a r.** faire *ou* enregistrer un disque; **to play** *or* **put on a r.** mettre *ou* passer un disque; **to change a r.** changer un disque; *Fig Hum* **change the r., will you?** change de disque!; **r. buff** *or* **collector** discophile *mf*, collectionneur, -euse de disques; **r. deck** platine *f* (tourne-disque); **r. shop** magasin *m* de disques; **r. token** bon-cadeau *m* à échanger contre des disques

(f) (*best performance*) record *m*; **to set a r.** établir un record; **to hold the r.** détenir le record **(for** de); **to break** *or* **beat the r.** battre le record **(for, by** de); **to break all records** battre tous les records

2 *adj attrib* record *inv*; **in r. time** en un temps record; **unemployment is at a r. high/low** le chômage a atteint son chiffre le plus haut/bas

record² [rɪ'kɔːd] **1** *vt* **(a)** (*write down*) (*fact*) noter (par écrit), consigner, enregistrer; (*give account of*) (*events*) rapporter, relater; (*thoughts, ideas etc*) noter (par écrit), consigner, mettre sur papier; (*temperature, rainfall, hours of sunshine etc*) relever; (*of policeman*) consigner; *Jur* (*judgment*) minuter; *Parl* **to r. a vote** voter; **throughout recorded history** aussi loin que les archives remontent; *Br* **to send a letter (by) recorded delivery** envoyer une lettre en recommandé; **to r. one's opposition** indiquer par écrit son opposition; (*in speech*) faire part de son opposition

(b) (*tape*) (*song, programme*) enregistrer; **recorded** (*not live*) (*programme*) différé; **this is a recorded message** (*on telephone*) ceci est un message enregistré; **recorded highlights** extraits *mpl* pré-enregistrés; **r. button** (*on machine*) touche *f* d'enregistrement

(c) (*register*) (*earthquake, drop in sales, increase in accidents etc*) enregistrer; **the thermometer records ten degrees** le thermomètre marque dix degrés

(d) (*be evidence of*) (*battle etc*) rappeler, commémorer

2 *vi* (*of machine, performer*) enregistrer; (*of sound*) s'enregistrer; **r. /replay head** tête *f* de lecture/enregistrement

record-breaker *n* (*person*) personne qui a battu un/des record(s); (*sporting etc performance*) **it was a splendid run but I don't think it's a r.** c'était une belle prestation mais je ne pense pas que le record soit battu

record-breaking *adj* (*jump, success etc*) qui bat tous les records

record company *n* maison *f* de disques

recorder [rɪ'kɔːdər] *n* **(a)** (*machine*) (appareil *m*) enregistreur *m*; **(tape) r.** magnétophone *m*; **radio-cassette r.** radiocassette *m* **(b)** *Mus* flûte *f* à bec **(c)** *Eng Jur* = avocat, -ate nommé(e) pour remplir certaines fonctions de juge

record-holder *n* détenteur, -trice du/d'un record

recording [rɪ'kɔːdɪŋ] *n* **(a)** (*on tape etc*) enregistrement *m*; **to play a r.** passer un enregistrement; **r. artist** musicien *m* qui enregistre des disques; **r. contract** contrat *m* avec une maison de disques; **r. deck** magnétoscope *m* d'enregistrement; **r. engineer** ingénieur *m* du son; **r. head** tête *f* d'enregistrement; **r. instrument** *or* **machine** appareil *m* enregistreur; **r. session** séance *f* d'enregistrement; **r. studio** studio *m* d'enregistrement; **r. tape** ruban *m ou* bande *f* d'enregistrement **(b)** (*writing down*) relation *f* par écrit; (*giving account*) consignation *f*

record library *n* (*public*) discothèque *f*; (*personal*) collection *f* de disques

record player *n* tourne-disques *m inv*

record producer *n* producteur *m* de disques

recount [rɪ'kaʊnt] *vt* (*relate*) raconter **(to** à)

re-count¹ ['riːkaʊnt] *n* (*of people, money, votes etc*) recomptage *m*; **to do a r.** (*of money, people, votes etc*) recompter; **to call for** *or* **demand a r.** exiger un nouveau compte des voix

re-count² [riː'kaʊnt] *vt* (*money etc*) recompter; (*votes*) compter de nouveau

recoup [rɪ'kuːp] *vt* (*money, loss*) récupérer; *Jur* défalquer, faire le décompte de; **to r. one's investment** rentrer dans ses fonds

recourse [rɪ'kɔːs] *n* recours *m*; **to have r. to sth/sb** avoir recours *ou* recourir à qch/qn; **my only r. is ...** mon seul recours est ... **(to do** de faire); **she cannot remember without r. to her notes** elle ne peut pas se souvenir sans avoir recours à ses notes; **right of r.** droit *m* de recours

recover [rɪ'kʌvər] **1** *vt* **(a)** (*get back, find again*) retrouver, *Lit* recouvrer; (*one's appetite, voice*) retrouver; *Comptr* (*file, data*) récupérer; **to r. one's breath/courage** reprendre haleine/ courage; **to r. consciousness** reprendre connaissance, revenir à soi; **I am recovering my strength** mes forces me reviennent; **to r. one's money** (*lent to sb*) récupérer son argent; (*invested in project etc*) rentrer dans ses fonds; **to r. sth from sb** reprendre qch à qn; **to r. one's health** guérir, se rétablir, recouvrer la santé; **to r. oneself** *or* **one's composure** se ressaisir; **to r. one's balance** retrouver son équilibre

(b) (*obtain, collect*) (*bodies, Ind by-product*) récupérer; (*from sea*) (*body, space ship*) repêcher

2 *vi* (*of person*) (*from shock etc*) se remettre **(from** de); (*from illness*) guérir, se remettre, se rétablir **(from** de); (*in competition, race etc*) se ressaisir; (*of export market, business*) reprendre; (*of stock market, economy, country*) se redresser; (*of currency*) remonter; **to be quite recovered** (*of patient*) être tout à fait remis *ou* guéri *ou* rétabli

re-cover *vt* (*chair etc*) recouvrir

recoverable [rɪ'kʌvərəb(ə)l] *adj* (*something lost*) récupérable; (*money*) recouvrable; (*by-product, computer file etc*) récupérable; *Com* **r. packaging** emballage *m* récupérable; *Petr* **r. resources** ressources *fpl* exploitables

recovery [rɪ'kʌvərɪ] *n* **(a)** (*of something lost*) récupération *f*; (*of money*) recouvrement *m*; **beyond** *or* **past r.** irrécupérable; *Jur* **action for r. of property** (action *f* en) revendication *f*; **r. of damages** obtention *f* de dommages-intérêts

(b) (*from illness*) guérison *f*; **to be on the way** *or* **road to r.** être en voie de guérison; **the patient is making a good r.** le malade fait des progrès rapides; **she made a quick r.** elle s'est vite rétablie; **he is past** *or* **beyond r.** (*patient*) on ne peut plus rien faire pour lui, il est dans un état désespéré; **I wish you a speedy r.** je vous souhaite un prompt rétablissement

(c) (*of economy*) redressement *m*; (*of export market, business*) reprise *f*; (*of currency*) remontée *f*; **the textile industry has declined beyond r.** l'industrie textile connaît un déclin irrémédiable; **to make a r.** (*in competition, race etc*) se ressaisir

recovery room *n Med* salle *f* de réveil

recovery service *n Br Aut* service *m* de dépannage

recovery ship *n* navire *m* de récupération

recovery vehicle *n Br Aut* dépanneuse *f*

recovery vessel *n* navire *m* de récupération

re-create *vt* (*in film, play etc*) (*age, era etc*) reconstituer, recréer

recreation [rekrɪ'eɪʃən] *n* loisirs *mpl*; *Sch* (*break*) récréation *f*; **I only write poetry for r.** j'écris des poèmes uniquement pour le plaisir; *Sch* **during (the) r.** pendant la récréation; **r. centre/facilities** centre *m*/équipements *mpl* de loisirs; **r. ground** terrain *m* de jeux; **r. room** (*in hotel, hospital*) salle *f* de détente; (*in home*) salle de jeux

re-creation *n Cin, Th etc* (*of era etc*) reconstitution *f*, recréation *f*

recreational [rekrɪ'eɪʃən(ə)l] *adj* (*centre, facility etc*) de loisirs; **r. area** (*country park etc*) aire *f* réservée aux loisirs; (*playground*) terrain *m* de jeux; **r. drug** drogue *f* utilisée de façon occasionnelle; *Am* **r. vehicle** camping-car *m*, *pl* camping-cars

recriminate [rɪ'krɪmɪneɪt] *vi* récriminer

recrimination [rɪkrɪmɪ'neɪʃən] *n* récrimination *f* **(against** contre)

recriminatory [rɪ'krɪmɪnət(ə)rɪ] *adj* (*remark etc*) de récrimination

recrudescence [ri:kru:'desəns] *n Fml* recrudescence *f*

recrudescent [ri:kru:'desənt] *adj Fml* recrudescent

recruit[1] [rɪ'kru:t] *n Mil* (*in organization, company etc*) recrue *f*

recruit[2] **1** *vt* (*army*) recruter; (*employee*) embaucher **(as** pour le poste de); **to r. sb to do sth** embaucher *ou* recruter qn pour faire qch **2** *vi Mil* recruter; (*of company*) recruter, embaucher **(for** pour)

recruiting [rɪ'kru:tɪŋ] *n* (*of soldier*) recrutement *m*; (*of employee*) recrutement, embauche *f*; **r. agent/office** agent *m*/bureau *m* de recrutement; **r. officer** (*for army*) officier *m* recruteur; (*for company*) (agent) recruteur *m*; **r. sergeant** sergent *m* recruteur

recruitment [rɪ'kru:tmənt] *n* (*of soldier, new employee etc*) recrutement *m*; **r. campaign/company/scheme** campagne *f*/société *f*/programme *m* de recrutement; **r. consultant** conseil *m* en recrutement

rectal ['rekt(ə)l] *adj Med, Anat* rectal; **r. cancer** cancer *m* du rectum; **r. examination** examen *m* rectal *ou* du rectum

rectangle ['rektæŋg(ə)l] *n* rectangle *m*

rectangular [rek'tæŋgjʊlər] *adj* rectangulaire; **to be r. in shape** être rectangulaire

rectification [rektɪfɪ'keɪʃən] *n* (*of calculation, situation etc*) rectification *f*; (*of oversight*) réparation *f*; *El* redressement *m*

rectifier ['rektɪfaɪər] *n Ch* rectificateur *m*; *El* redresseur *m*

rectify ['rektɪfaɪ] *vt* (*calculation*) rectifier, corriger; (*mistake, situation, Fin entry, Ch Math*) rectifier; (*oversight*) réparer; *El* redresser

rectilineal [rektɪ'lɪnɪəl], **rectilinear** [rektɪ'lɪnɪər] *adj* rectiligne; *TV* **r. scanning** analyse *f* par lignes

rectitude ['rektɪtju:d] *n* rectitude *f*

recto ['rektəʊ] *n Typ* recto *m*

rector ['rektər] *n* **(a)** *Church of Eng* = ecclésiastique *m* préposé à l'administration d'une paroisse et titulaire du bénéfice et de la dîme; *Cathol* (*of seminary*) supérieur *m* **(b)** *Univ* recteur *m*; *Scot Sch* proviseur *m*; *Scot Univ* = personnage *m* élu par les étudiants pour les représenter

rectorial [rek'tɔ:rɪəl] *adj* (*decision, duties*) rectoral; *Scot Univ* **r. election** élection *f* d'un recteur

rectory ['rektərɪ] *n Rel* (*residence*) presbytère *m*

rectoscope ['rektəskəʊp] *n Med* rectoscope *m*

rectum, *pl* **-ums, -a** ['rektəm, -əmz, -ə] *n Anat* rectum *m*

recumbent [rɪ'kʌmbənt] *adj Lit* couché, étendu; **to be r.** être couché **(on** sur); **r. figure** (*on tomb*) gisant *m*

recuperate [rɪ'ku:pəreɪt, -'kju:-] **1** *vt* (*one's strength, money, heat*) récupérer **2** *vi* (*of person*) se remettre, se rétablir *F* récupérer, **(from** de); **he had gone to the South of France to r.** il était allé en convalescence dans le Midi; **she is still recuperating** elle est encore en convalescence

recuperation [rɪku:pə'reɪʃən, -'kju:-] *n* **(a)** (*of strength, money, heat*) récupération *f* **(b)** (*from illness*) rétablissement *m*; **powers of r.** capacités *fpl* de rétablissement

recuperative [rɪ'ku:pərətɪv, -'kju:-] *adj* (*powers*) de rétablissement

recur [rɪ'kɜ:r] *vi* **(-rr-)** (*of theme*) revenir, être répété; (*of event, Math of figures*) se reproduire; (*of illness*) réapparaître; **to r. to the mind** revenir à la mémoire; **festival that recurs every ten years** fête qui a lieu tous les dix ans

recurrence [rɪ'kʌrəns] *n* (*of illness*) réapparition *f*; (*of infectious disease*) récurrence *f*, récidive *f*; (*of theme*) répétition *f*, réapparition; (*of event*) répétition; **has there been any r. of the symptoms?** les symptômes se sont-ils manifestés à nouveau?

recurrent [rɪ'kʌrənt] *adj* (*event*) périodique, qui revient *ou* se répète périodiquement; (*fever, symptom, theme*) récurrent; (*dream, nightmare*) qui revient souvent; *Med* **r. bronchial catarrh** bronchite *f* chronique; **r. expenses** dépenses *fpl* qui reviennent périodiquement; *Math* **r. series** série *f* récurrente

recurring [rɪ'kɜ:rɪŋ] *adj* (*event*) périodique; (*theme*) qui se répète, qui réapparaît; (*dream, nightmare*) qui revient souvent; *Math* **r. decimal** fraction *f* décimale périodique; **33. 33 r.** 33, 33 à l'infini

recusant ['rekjʊzənt] *adj Rel Hist* réfractaire

recyclable [ri:'saɪkləbəl] *adj* (*container etc*) recyclable

recycle [ri:'saɪk(ə)l] *vt* (*waste, water, paper etc*) recycler; **recycled paper/glass/plastic** papier *m*/verre *m*/plastique *m* recyclé; *Fin* **to r. funds** remettre des fonds en circulation

recycling [ri:'saɪklɪŋ] *n* (*of paper etc*) recyclage *m*; (*of funds*) remise *f* en circulation; **r. facility/plant** installation *f*/usine *f* de recyclage

red [red] **1** *adj* (*comp* **redder,** *superl* **reddest) (a)** (*dress, wine, lips etc*) rouge; (*beard, hair*) roux, *f* rousse; **r. (-rimmed) eyes** yeux *mpl* rouges; **to turn** *or* **go r.** (*of person, litmus paper*) rougir, devenir rouge; (*of leaves etc*) roussir; (*of sky*) rougeoyer; **wait till the lights turn r.** attend que le feu passe au rouge; **to be r. in the face** *or* **have a r. face** (*permanent state*) être rougeaud; **to be r. (in the face) with anger/embarrassment** être rouge de colère/gêne; **was my face r.!** ce que j'étais gêné!; **there will be some r. faces on the Opposition benches** cela va causer de l'embarras dans les rangs de l'Opposition; **to be as r. as a beetroot** (*with embarrassment*) être rouge comme une tomate; **to be as r. as a lobster** (*with sunburn*) être rouge comme une écrevisse; *Fig* **to put** *or* **roll out the r. carpet for sb** recevoir quelqu'un en grande pompe, dérouler le tapis rouge pour recevoir quelqu'un; **I got the r.-carpet treatment wherever I went** on m'a reçu en grande pompe partout où je suis allé; *Am F* **it isn't worth a r. cent** ça ne vaut pas un centime; *Mil, Fig* **to be on r. alert** être en état d'alerte maximale; *Mil, Fig* **to go to** *or* **on r. alert** se mettre en état d'alerte maximale; **the mere mention of his name was like a r. rag to a bull (to him)** le simple fait d'entendre son nom le met dans une colère noire; **Little R. Riding Hood** Le Petit Chaperon Rouge

(b) (*compounds*) **r. channel** (*at airport etc*) file *f* pour les passagers qui ont des objets à déclarer à la douane; *Fin* **r. clause credit** crédit *m* "red clause"; *Am Fin* **r. herring (prospectus)** prospectus *m* préliminaire; *Old-fashioned Pej* **r. man** Peau-Rouge *m*; *Am Fin F* **r. ink** déficit *m*; *Am* **to go into r. ink** (*of person*) se mettre à découvert; (*of company*) être en déficit; *Aut* **r. light** feu *m* rouge; **to go through a r. light** brûler un feu rouge; **to get** *or* **be given the r. light** être rejeté; **r.-light district** quartier *m* des prostituées, quartier chaud; **r. meat** viande *f* rouge; **r. pepper** (*vegetable*) poivron *m* rouge

2 *n* **(a)** (*colour*) rouge *m*; **r. is my favourite colour** le rouge est ma couleur préférée; **dressed in r.** habillé de *ou* en rouge; *F* **to see r.** (*be angry*) voir rouge

(b) *Fin F* **to be in the r.** (*of company, person*) avoir un découvert, être dans le rouge; (*of account*) avoir un solde déficitaire; **to go into the r.** passer dans le rouge; **at last I'm out of the r.** enfin je ne suis plus à découvert

(c) *Pol F* rouge *mf*; **to see reds under the bed** avoir la phobie des communistes; **the reds-under-the-bed syndrome** la phobie anti-communiste

(d) (*in billiards*) bille *f* rouge; (*on roulette table*) rouge *m*

(e) (*red wine*) rouge *m*

Red Army *n* Armée *f* rouge

red-blooded *adj* (*person*) vigoureux, robuste; (*policy,* *response etc*) musclé; **the average r. male** n'importe quel homme digne de ce nom

redbreast ['redbrest] *n* (*bird*) (**robin**) **r.** rouge-gorge *m*, *pl* rouges-gorges

redbrick ['redbrɪk] *adj* (*house, building*) en brique rouge; *Br Fig* **r. universities** = universités *fpl* de province (par opposition à Oxford et Cambridge) construites à la fin du XIX siècle

redcap ['redkæp] *n* (**a**) *Br Mil F* soldat *m* de la police militaire (**b**) *Am Rail* porteur *m*

red card *n* (*in soccer*) carton *m* rouge; **to be shown the r.** (*of soccer player*) recevoir un carton rouge

Red China *n* la Chine communiste

redcoat ['redkəʊt] *n Br* (**a**) *Hist* soldat *m* anglais (du dix-huitième siècle) (**b**) (*at holiday camp*) animateur, -trice

Red Crescent *n* Croissant-Rouge *m*

Red Cross *n* Croix-Rouge *f*

redcurrant ['redkʌrənt] *n* groseille *f* (rouge); **r. bush** groseillier *m*; **r. jelly** gelée *f* de groseille(s)

redden ['red(ə)n] **1** *vt* rougir, rendre rouge **2** *vi* (*of sky*) rougeoyer; (*of leaves*) roussir; (*of person*) rougir

reddish ['redɪʃ] *adj* (*light, colour*) rougeâtre; **r. hair** cheveux qui tirent sur le roux

red dwarf *n Astron* naine *f* rouge

redecorate [riː'dekəreɪt] **1** *vt* (*flat etc*) refaire **2** *vi* refaire la peinture et les papiers

redecoration [riːdekə'reɪʃən] *n* (*of house etc*) remise *f* à neuf de la peinture et des papiers

redeem [rɪ'diːm] *vt* (**a**) (*recover*) (*pawned item*) dégager; **to r. one's good name** sauver son honneur

(**b**) (*pay off*) (*mortgaged property*) racheter, dégager; *Fig Fml* (*obligations*) s'acquitter de; **to r. a loan** racheter une dette; **to r. a mortgage** (*of mortgagor*) éteindre une hypothèque; (*of purchaser of mortgaged property*) purger une hypothèque; *Fml* **to r. one's promise (to do sth)** tenir sa promesse (de faire qch)

(**c**) (*convert*) (*bond*) obtenir le remboursement de; (*gift token*) échanger; (*coupon*) rembourser; **to r. a bond** racheter une obligation

(**d**) (*compensate for*) (*fault*) racheter, rattraper; **to r. oneself** se racheter; **it's his sole redeeming feature** c'est sa seule qualité

(**e**) *Fml* (*free*) (*slave, prisoner*) libérer, racheter; *Rel* (*of Christ*) (*mankind*) racheter

redeemable [rɪ'diːməb(ə)l] *adj Fin* (*share etc*) remboursable, rachetable; **r. coupon** (*for purchasing*) coupon *m* de remboursement; *Fig* (*manuscript*) qui peut être sauvé; **coupons are r. for cash** les coupons sont remboursables en espèces

redeemer [rɪ'diːmər] *n Rel* **the R.** le Rédempteur

redefine [riːdɪ'faɪn] *vt* redéfinir

redefinition [riːdefɪ'nɪʃən] *n* redéfinition *f*

redemption [rɪ'dem(p)ʃən] *n* (**a**) (*of item pawned*) dégagement *m* (**b**) (*of property*) rachat *m*; (*of mortgage*) (*by mortgagor*) extinction *f*; (*by purchaser*) purge *f*; (*of loan*) amortissement *m* (**c**) (*of gift token*) échange *m*; *Fin* (*of coupon*) remboursement *m*; **r. date** date *f* de remboursement (**d**) (*of fault*) rachat *m*; **to be beyond** *or* **past r.** être irrécupérable; (*of smashed car, broken toy etc*) être irréparable (**e**) (*of slave, prisoner*) rachat *m*; *Rel* rédemption *f*; *Fig* **this setback proved his r.** ce revers de fortune fut son salut

redemptive [rɪ'demtɪv] *adj esp Rel* rédempteur, -trice

red ensign *n Br Naut* pavillon *m* de la marine marchande britannique

redeploy [riːdɪ'plɔɪ] *vt Mil* (*troops etc*) redéployer; *Admin* (*employees*) réaffecter

redeployment [riːdɪ'plɔɪmənt] *n* (*of troops etc*) redéploiement *m*; (*of staff*) réaffectation *f*

redesign [riːdɪ'zaɪn] *vt* reconcevoir

redevelop [riːdɪ'veləp] *vt* (*poor district*) réaménager, revaloriser; **the docks are being redeveloped** les docks sont en cours de réaménagement

redevelopment [riːdɪ'veləpmənt] *n* (*of town, street etc*) réaménagement *m*, remise *f* en valeur; **scheduled for r.** dont le réaménagement est prévu; **r. area/costs** zone *f*/frais *mpl* de réaménagement

red-eye *n* (**a**) *Am F* whisky *m* bon marché (**b**) *Av F* **r. (flight)** = vol *m* tard dans la nuit/tôt le matin (**c**) *Phot* **to avoid the r. effect ...** pour éviter que le sujet n'apparaisse avec les yeux rouges ...

red-eyed *adj* aux yeux rouges; **to be r.** avoir les yeux rouges (**with, from** de); **she's r. from crying/staying up all night** elle a les yeux rouges d'avoir pleuré/d'avoir passé une nuit blanche

red-faced ['red'feɪst] *adj* (*naturally*) rougeaud, rubicond; (*with anger, embarrassment*) rouge, rougissant (**with** de); **a r. admission** un aveu confus

Red Flag *n* (*song*) l'Internationale *f*

red flag *n Pol* le drapeau rouge

red giant *n Astron* géante *f* rouge

Red Guards *npl* (*in China*) garde *m* rouge

red-haired *adj* aux cheveux roux; **r. man/woman** roux *m*/rousse *f*

red-handed *adj* **to be caught r.** être pris en flagrant délit *ou F* la main dans le sac

redhead ['redhed] *n* (**a**) (*person*) roux *m*, rousse *f* (**b**) *TV, Cin* (*lighting*) mandarine *f*

red-headed *adj* (**a**) (*person*) = **red-haired** (**b**) (*bird, animal*) à tête rouge

red herring *n* (*food*) hareng *m* saur; *Fig* **it was just a r.** (*false trail*) ce n'était qu'une diversion; **she's always introducing red herrings into the conversation** (*avoiding the issue*) elle détourne toujours la conversation; (*digressing*) elle fait toujours des digressions

red-hot *adj* (*food, plate etc*) brûlant; (*metal*) chauffé au rouge; *Fig* (*supporter, revolutionary etc*) ardent; (*enthusiasm*) débordant; *F* (*very good*) excellent, sensass *inv*; **to make sth r.** (*by heating*) porter qch au rouge; **Rangers are the r. favourites to win the cup** Rangers sont les grandissimes favoris de la coupe; **r. news** nouvelle *f* de dernière heure *ou* toute chaude; **r. poker** (*flower*) tritoma *m*

redial[1] [riː'daɪəl] (**-ll-**, *US* **-l-**) *Tel* **1** *vt* **to r. a number** refaire un numéro **2** *vi* refaire le numéro

redial[2] ['riːdaɪəl] *n Tel* **r. (feature)** rappel *m* du dernier numéro; **the latest model has automatic r.** le dernier modèle est muni du système de rappel du dernier numéro

Red Indian *n Offensive* Peau-Rouge *mf*, *pl* Peaux-Rouges

redirect [riːdɪ'rekt, -daɪ-] *vt* (**a**) (*letter etc*) faire suivre; (*telephone call etc*) réacheminer (**b**) (*plane etc*) dérouter (**c**) *Fig* **to r. one's energies (into sth)** réorienter son énergie (dans qch)

redirection [riːdɪ'rekʃən, -daɪ-] *n* (**a**) (*of letter etc*) réacheminement *m*, réexpédition *f* (**b**) (*of plane*) déroutement *m* (**c**) *Fig* **the situation demands the r. of some of our attention to ...** la situation exige que l'on réoriente nos efforts vers ...

rediscount [riː'dɪskaʊnt] **1** *n* réescompte *m* **2** *vt Com Am* réescompter

rediscover [riːdɪ'skʌvər] *vt* redécouvrir

redistribute [riːdɪ'strɪbjuːt] *vt* (*wealth, tasks*) redistribuer; *Pol* **to r. seats** redécouper les circonscriptions électorales

redistribution [riːdɪstrɪ'bjuːʃən] *n* (*of wealth, labour*) redistribution *f*; *Pol* **r. of seats** nouveau découpage *m* des circonscriptions

red-letter *adj* **r. day** jour *m* à marquer d'une pierre blanche; **this has been a r. day for everyone** ceci a été un jour mémorable pour tout le monde

redneck ['rednek] *n Am Pej* (*farm worker*) rustre *m*, péquenaud *m*; *Fig* réactionnaire *mf*; **r. attitude/behaviour** attitude *f*/comportement *m* réactionnaire

redness ['rednɪs] *n* (*of face, sky etc*) rouge *m*; (*of hair*) rousseur *f*

redo [riː'duː] *vt* (*pt* **redid** [riː'dɪd]; *pp* **redone** [riː'dʌn]) (*task, flat*) refaire

redolent ['redələnt] *adj Lit* (*sweet-smelling*) odoriférant, parfumé; (*strong-smelling*) qui a une odeur forte (**of** de); *Fig* (*reminiscent*) évocateur, suggestif; **r. of spring** qui exhale une odeur de printemps; **a house r. of the past** une maison qui évoque le passé

redouble [riː'dʌb(ə)l] **1** *vt* (*one's cries, entreaties*) redoubler; **to r. one's efforts** redoubler d'efforts *ou* de zèle; *Cards* **to r. spades** surcontrer pique **2** *vi* (*of noise, efforts, criticism etc*) redoubler; *Cards* surcontrer

redoubt [rɪ'daʊt] *n Mil* redoute *f*; *Fig* bastion *m*

redoubtable [rɪ'daʊtəb(ə)l] *adj* (*fearsome*) formidable; (*opponent*) redoutable

redound [rɪ'daʊnd] *vi Fml* (*of deeds*) se retourner (**upon, on** contre); **to r. to sb's credit** être à l'honneur de qn; **to r. to sb's advantage** tourner à l'avantage de qn

red-pencil *vt* (**-ll-**, *US* **-l-**) (*text*) corriger, réviser

redraft[1] ['riːdrɑːft] *n* (**a**) (*action*) (*of proposal, submission*) refonte *f* (**b**) (*resulting text*) texte *m* revu; **this is the third r.** c'est la troisième version

redraft[2] [riː'drɑːft] *vt* (*proposal, submission*) rédiger à nouveau

redress[1] [rɪ'dres] *n* (*of grievance*) réparation *f*; **to seek r.** demander réparation (**for** de); **there is no r.** il n'y a pas de recours

redress[2] *vt* (*rectify*) (*a wrong*) réparer; **to r. the balance** rétablir l'équilibre

re-dress *vt* **to r. a wound** refaire le pansement d'une blessure

Red Sea *n* mer *f* Rouge

red setter *n (dog)* setter *m* irlandais

redshank ['redʃæŋk] *n (bird)* chevalier *m* gambette

Red Shirts *npl Italian, Hist* Chemises *fpl* rouges

redskin ['redskɪn] *n Old-fashioned Pej* Peau-Rouge *mf, pl* Peaux-Rouges

red snapper *n (fish)* vivaneau *m*

Red Square *n* la Place Rouge

red squirrel *n* écureuil *m* (roux)

redstart ['redstɑːt] *n (bird)* rouge-queue *m* à front blanc, *pl* rouges-queues à front blanc

red tape *n Fig* bureaucratie *f, F* paperasserie *f*

reduce [rɪ'djuːs] **1** *vt* **(a)** *(lessen) (price)* baisser, diminuer, réduire; *(drawing, photograph)* réduire; *(tax)* baisser, alléger; *(spending)* diminuer, réduire; *(temperature)* faire baisser; *Culin (sauce)* faire réduire; **oranges have been reduced** les oranges ont baissé *ou* diminué; *Com* **reduced to £10 from £15** soldé de 15 à 10 livres; **are these shoes reduced?** est-ce que ces chaussures sont soldées *ou* en solde?; *Ind* **to r. output** ralentir la production; **to r. the risk (of sth)** réduire le risque (de qch); **to r. speed** diminuer *ou* réduire la vitesse, ralentir; **to r. stocks** déstocker des marchandises; **to r. a prison sentence** accorder *ou* consentir une remise de peine; **his prison sentence was reduced to two years** sa peine de prison a été ramenée à deux ans

(b) *(bring to a certain state)* **to r. sth to ashes/dust** réduire qch en cendres/poussière; **to r. sb to despair/silence** réduire qn au désespoir/silence; **his words reduced her to tears** ses paroles l'ont fait fondre en larmes; **to r. sb to helpless laughter** faire mourir qn de rire; **to r. sb to the ranks/the rank of …** rétrograder *ou* casser qn/descendre qn au rang de …; **to be reduced to doing sth** en être réduit à faire qch; **is this what I've been reduced to?** j'en suis donc réduit à cela?

(c) *(simplify) (problem, question)* ramener **(to** à); *(fraction, equation)* réduire; **to r. sth to a percentage** exprimer qch en pourcentage; **to r. a fraction to its lowest terms** simplifier une fraction, ramener une fraction à sa plus simple expression; **to r. two fractions to the same denominator** réduire deux fractions au même dénominateur

2 *vi (slim)* maigrir; *Culin (sauce)* se réduire

reduced [rɪ'djuːst] *adj (smaller)* réduit; **on a r. scale** à une échelle réduite; **at r. prices** au rabais, en solde; **at greatly r. prices** à prix très réduits; **at (a) r. rate** *(bus or theatre ticket etc)* à tarif réduit; **r. rate loan** prêt *m* à taux réduit; **everything r. by ten per cent** remise de dix pour cent sur tous nos articles; **r. to clear** *(sale notice)* (soldes) coup de balai; **to be/live in r. circumstances** être/vivre dans la gêne

reducer [rɪ'djuːsər] *n El* réducteur *m*; *Phot* affaiblisseur *m*

reducible [rɪ'djuːsɪb(ə)l] *adj* réductible **(to** à)

reduction [rɪ'dʌkʃən] *n* **(a)** *(of prices)* baisse *f*, diminution *f*, réduction *f*; *(of taxes)* allègement *m*; *(of costs, speed, spending)* diminution, réduction; *(of drawing, photograph, scale)* réduction; *(of temperature, voltage)* baisse; **I'll give you a r.** *(on purchase)* je vous fais un prix; **big reductions** *(sale notice)* rabais, soldes; *Jur* **r. of sentence** remise *f* de peine; *Fin* **r. in borrowings** désendettement *m*; **r. in staff** compression *f* de personnel; **r. in stocks** déstockage *m*; **r. of capital** réduction de capital; *Tech* **r. gear** (engrenage *m*) démultiplicateur *m*

(b) *(of equation)* réduction *f*

(c) *Med (of fracture)* réduction *f*

reductionism [rɪ'dʌkʃənɪz(ə)m] *n Phil* réductionnisme *m*

reductionist [rɪ'dʌkʃənɪst] *n, adj Phil* réductionniste *mf*

redundancy [rɪ'dʌndənsɪ] *n* **(a)** *Br Ind (dismissal)* licenciement *m*; **redundancies have been heavy** il y a eu beaucoup de licenciements; **the strike caused over three hundred redundancies** la grève a causé le licenciement de plus de trois cents personnes; **voluntary r.** départ *m* volontaire; **r. notice** avis *m* de licenciement; **r. payment** *or* **money** indemnité *f* de licenciement **(b)** *(of details, factory etc)* inutilité *f*; *Comptr, Ling etc* redondance *f*

redundant [rɪ'dʌndənt] *adj* **(a)** *Br (worker)* licencié; **to make sb r.** *(of employer)* licencier qn, mettre qn au chômage; *(of technology etc)* entraîner le licenciement de qn; **to be made r.** être licencié, être mis au chômage **(b)** *(details, factory etc)* superflu; *(information, knowledge)* inutile; *Comptr, Ling (file, information)* redondant; **I just feel r. round here now** j'ai l'impression de ne plus servir à rien ici

redwood ['redwʊd] *n (tree)* séquoia *m*

re-echo **1** *vt (repeat) (sound)* répercuter, renvoyer; *Fig* répéter **2** *vi (of noise, voice etc)* retentir, résonner; **the hall echoed and re-echoed to the sound of applause** la salle retentissait d'acclamations

reed [riːd] *n* **(a)** *(plant)* roseau *m*; **bed of reeds, r. bed** roselière *f*; *Fig* **broken r.** personne *f* sur laquelle on ne peut (pas) compter; **r. bunting** *(bird)* bruant *m* des roseaux; **r. warbler** *(bird)* rousserolle *f* des roseaux **(b)** *Mus (of instrument)* anche *f*; **r. pipe** tuyau *m* à anche; **r. stop** *(on organ)* jeu *m* d'anches

re-edit *vt (text)* rédiger à nouveau; *Comptr* rééditer

re-educate *vt (criminal etc, Med limb)* rééduquer

re-education *n (of criminal etc, Med of limb)* rééducation *f*

reedy ['riːdɪ] *adj* **(a)** *(covered in reeds)* plein *ou* couvert de roseaux **(b)** *(shrill) (instrument)* aigu, *f* aiguë; *(voice)* flûté, grêle

reef[1] [riːf] *n (rocks)* écueil *m*, récif *m*; *Fig* écueil; **to hit a r.** *(of ship)* faire naufrage sur un récif; *Fig* **his plans had hit a r.** ses projets s'étaient heurté à un écueil

reef[2] *n Naut (of sail)* ris *m*; **r. knot** nœud *m* plat

reef[3] *vt Naut (sail)* prendre un *ou* des ris à; **to r. the sails** prendre les ris

reefer ['riːfər] **1** *n* **(a)** *(jacket)* caban *m*, vareuse *f* **(b)** *Old-fashioned F (marijuana cigarette)* joint *m* **(c)** *Am (for transporting goods)* camion *m*/navire *m*/wagon *m* frigorifique; *(refrigerator)* chambre *f* frigorifique **2** *adj (truck etc)* réfrigéré

reek[1] [riːk] *n (bad smell)* puanteur *f*

reek[2] *vi* puer; *also Fig* **to r. of sth** puer qch; **this room reeks** ça pue ici; *Fig* **the whole affair reeks of corruption** toute cette affaire sent la corruption à plein nez

reel[1] [riːl] *n* **(a)** *Br (for film, paper, thread)* bobine *f*; *(film itself)* pellicule *f*; *(for fishing line)* moulinet *m*; *(for cable, hose etc)* dévidoir *m*; **r. to r. tape** bande *f* en bobine; **r. to r. tape recorder** magnétophone *m* à bobines; *Am F* **(right) off the r.** *(continuously)* d'une seule traite, d'affilée; *(immediately)* sans hésiter, sur-le-champ **(b)** *(dance, music)* reel *m*, quadrille *m* écossais

reel[2] *vi (sway)* chanceler; *(not walk straight)* tituber; **to go reeling down the street** descendre la rue en titubant; *Fig* **to make sb's senses r.** donner le vertige à qn; *Fig* **my head is reeling** la tête me tourne; *Fig* **I'm still reeling** *(after news)* je n'en suis toujours pas revenu; *Fig* **she was still reeling from shock at what had happened** elle était encore toute retournée par ce qui venait de se passer; **to send sb reeling** *(of punch)* envoyer valser qn; *Fig (of news, scene etc)* abasourdir qn; *Fig* **his mind** *or* **brain reeled at the thought** cette pensée lui donnait le vertige; *Fig* **the whole room was reeling** toute la salle tournoyait autour de moi/lui/*etc*

▶ **reel in** *vtsep* **to r. a fish in** remonter un poisson (avec le moulinet)

▶ **reel off** *vtsep (speech etc)* débiter

re-elect *vt (MP etc)* réélire; **she is sure to be re-elected** sa réélection est assurée; **he was re-elected (as) president** on l'a réélu président

re-election *n* réélection *f*; **to stand** *or Am* **run for r.** se représenter

reeling ['riːlɪŋ] *adj (gait)* titubant

re-embark **1** *vt (passengers)* rembarquer **2** *vi* rembarquer; *Fig* **to r. on sth** recommencer qch

re-embarkation *n* rembarquement *m*

re-emerge *vi (of person)* ressortir; *(of sun)* reparaître; **when the country re-emerges into prosperity** quand le pays connaîtra à nouveau la prospérité

re-employ *vt (former employee)* réembaucher

re-employment *n (of former employee)* réembauchage *m*

re-enact *vt* **(a)** *(enforce) (law)* remettre en vigueur **(b)** *(depict) (accident, crime, battle)* reconstituer; *(scene, mistakes)* reproduire

re-enactment *n* **(a)** *(of law)* remise *f* en vigueur **(b)** *(of accident, crime, battle)* reconstitution *f*; *(of scene, mistakes)* reproduction *f*

re-engage *vt* **(a)** *(former employee)* réembaucher **(b)** *Tech (cogwheel)* rengrener; *Aut* **to r. the clutch** rembrayer

re-engagement *n* **(a)** *(of former employee)* réembauchage *m* **(b)** *Tech (of cogwheel)* rengrènement *m*; *Aut (of clutch)* rembrayage *m*

re-enlist *vi Mil* se rengager

re-enter **1** *vi (of person, spacecraft)* rentrer; *(of musical instrument)* faire une *ou* sa rentrée; *Th* **r. Macbeth** Macbeth rentre; **to r. for an examination** se présenter de nouveau à un examen **2** *vt* **(a)** *(a room etc)* rentrer dans; **he never re-entered that house** il n'a jamais remis les pieds dans cette maison; **to r. the job market** se remettre à chercher du travail; **the spacecraft re-entered the atmosphere** le vaisseau spatial est rentré dans l'atmosphère **(b)** *(date, name)* réinscrire, inscrire de nouveau

re-entrant 1 *adj* (*angle etc*) rentrant **2** *n* angle *m* rentrant
re-entry *n* (*of person, spacecraft*) rentrée *f*; **to make its r.** (*of spacecraft*) rentrer dans l'atmosphère
re-establish *vt* (*communications, diplomatic relations etc*) rétablir
re-establishment *n* (*of communications, relations etc*) rétablissement *m*
reeve [riːv] *vt* (*pt* **rove** [rəʊv], **reeved**; *pp* **reeved, rove**) *Naut* (*rope*) passer (**through a block** dans une poulie)
re-examination *n* (**a**) (*of file, question etc*) réexamen *m* (**b**) *Jur* (*of witness*) nouvel interrogatoire *m*
re-examine *vt* (**a**) (*review*) (*file, question etc*) réexaminer (**b**) *Jur* (*witness*) interroger de nouveau
re-export[1] [riː'ekspɔːt] *n* (*of goods*) réexportation *f*
re-export[2] ['riːekspɔːt] *vt* (*goods*) réexporter
ref *n* [ref] (**a**) *Br Sp F* (*abbr* **referee**) arbitre *m* (**b**) *Com* (*abbr* **with reference to**) suite à
re-face *vt* (*building*) ravaler les façades de; (*wall*) refaire
refashion [riː'fæʃən] *vt* remodeler
refectory [rɪ'fekt(ə)rɪ] *n* réfectoire *m*; **r. table** = table longue et étroite *f* (*souvent en chêne massif, comme on en trouve dans les châteaux*)
refer [rɪ'fɜːr] *vt* (**-rr-**) (*direct*) (*matter, proposal etc*) soumettre (**to** à); **to r. a cheque to drawer** (*of bank*) retourner un chèque au tireur; **r. to drawer** (*notice on cheque*) voir le tireur; **he referred me to an article on the subject** il m'a renvoyé à un article sur la question; **to r. a matter to sb** soumettre une question à qn; **to r. a question to sb for** (**a**) **decision** soumettre une question à la décision de qn; **to r. a matter to a tribunal** soumettre une affaire à un tribunal; **the reader is referred to …** (*in book*) se reporter à …; **to r. a patient to a specialist** envoyer un malade chez un spécialiste; *Med* **she's going to r. me** elle va m'envoyer chez un spécialiste; **to r. a customer to another department** renvoyer un client à un autre service; **he just referred me back to you** il m'a renvoyé à vous; *Med* **referred pain** douleur *f* irradiée
▶ **refer to** *vipo* (**a**) (*consult*) se référer *ou* se reporter à; **to r. (back) to an expert** consulter un expert
(**b**) (*allude to*) faire allusion à; (*speak of*) parler de; **who are you referring to?** de qui parlez-vous?; **it's you I'm referring to** c'est de toi que je parle; **referred to as …** désigné sous le nom de …; **he never refers to it** il n'en parle jamais; **we won't r. to it again** nous n'en reparlons plus; *Com* **referring to …** nous référant à …; **referring to your letter** suite à votre lettre
(**c**) (*apply to*) s'appliquer à; **these measures r. to large enterprises only** ces mesures ne concernent que les grandes entreprises; **this remark refers to you** (*is aimed at*) cette remarque s'adresse à vous; (*is about*) cette remarque vous concerne
referee[1] [refə'riː] *n* (**a**) *Sp, Fig* arbitre *m* (**b**) (*for job etc*) **please give at least two referees** veuillez fournir aux moins deux références; **will you act as my r.?** voulez-vous me fournir des références?
referee[2] *vti* (*pt, pp* **refereed**) *Sp, Fig* arbitrer
reference ['ref(ə)rəns] *n* (**a**) (*to higher authority*) renvoi *m*; **without r. to the Board** sans consulter le conseil d'administration; **I'll have to make r. to my superior** il faudra que j'en réfère à mon supérieur; **terms of r.** (*of person, investigating body*) compétence *f*; (*of law*) étendue *f*; **outside the committee's terms of r.** hors de la compétence du comité
(**b**) (*consultation*) consultation *f*; (*source*) référence *f*; **for r. only** (*on library book*) consultation sur place; (*on document etc in circulation*) pour information seulement; **to keep sth for future r.** garder qch à titre d'information; **for future r., please note …** pour votre information à l'avenir, veuillez noter …
(**c**) (*allusion*) allusion *f* (**to** à); (*mention*) mention *f* (**to** de); (*connection*) rapport *m* (**to** avec); (*in book*) (*allusion*) référence *f*; (*cross-reference*) renvoi *m*; (*on map*) coordonnées *fpl*; **to make r. to a fact** faire mention d'un fait; **if any r. is made to me** si on parle de moi; **with r. to what was said …** en référence à ce qui a été dit …; **a talk on the environment with particular r. to …** un exposé sur l'environnement abordant tout particulièrement …; **with r. to my letter of the 20th March** me référant *ou* suite à ma lettre du 20 mars; **in r.** *or* **with r. to your letter** en ce qui concerne votre lettre; **with r. to what was said at the meeting** à propos de *ou* en ce qui concerne ce qui a été dit au cours de la réunion; **r. AB** (*at head of letter*) référence AB; **our/your r.** (*on letter*) notre/votre référence
(**d**) (*testimonial*) (*from bank etc*) référence *f*; (*from employer*) référence, lettre *f* de recommandation, certificat *m* de travail; **to give sb a r.** donner son avis sur qn; **to have good references** avoir de bonnes références; **he got a very bad r. from his previous employer** son ancien employeur ne l'a pas du tout recommandé; **to take up references** prendre contact avec *ou* contacter les personnes dont un candidat se recommande; **to give sb as a r.** se recommander de qn; **you may use my name as (a) r.** vous pouvez donner mon nom comme référence, vous pouvez vous recommander de moi
(**e**) *Mktg* **r. customer** client *m* de référence; **r. group** groupe *m* de référence; **r. price** prix *m* de référence; **r. sale** vente *f* de référence
(**f**) *Banking* **r. period** période *f* de référence; **r. rate** taux *m* de référence
reference book *n* livre *m* de référence
reference library *n* bibliothèque *f* d'études; (*in library*) salle *f* de références
reference number *n Com* numéro *m* de commande
reference point *n* point *m* de repère
reference room *n* (*in public library*) salle *f* de lecture; (*in university*) salle de consultation
reference work *n* ouvrage *m* de référence
referendum [refə'rendəm] *n Pol* référendum *m*, referendum *m*; **to hold a r.** organiser un référendum; **decided in a** *or* **by r.** décidé par référendum
referral [rɪ'fɜːrəl] *n* (*of case*) envoi *m*; **he/the case is a r. from Dr. Smith** c'est un patient/un cas envoyé par le Docteur Smith; **r. system** (*in hotel business*) système *m* de réservations recommandées inter-hôteliers
refill[1] ['riːfɪl] *n* (*for lighter, pen*) recharge *f*, cartouche *f*; (*for propelling pencil*) mine *f* de rechange; (*for notebook*) feuilles *fpl* de rechange; (*of drink*) autre verre *m*; **I'll have a r.** tu me remets la même chose?; **would you like a r.?** je vous ressers?; **she handed me her glass for a r.** elle m'a tendu son verre pour que je la reserve
refill[2] [riː'fɪl] *vt* (*glass etc*) remplir (à nouveau) (**with** de); (*lighter, pen etc*) recharger; (*shelves*) regarnir (**with** de)
refillable [riː'fɪləb(ə)l] *adj* (*lighter, pen*) rechargeable
refinance [riː'faɪnæns] *Fin* **1** *vt* (*loan*) refinancer **2** *vi* (*of company*) se refinancer (**on the money market** auprès du marché monétaire)
refinancing [riː'faɪnænsɪŋ] *n Fin* refinancement *m*; **to get r. from a bank** se refinancer auprès d'une banque
refine [rɪ'faɪn] *vt* (**a**) (*process, purify*) (*sugar, petroleum*) raffiner; (*metal*) affiner (**b**) (*develop*) (*technique, machine*) perfectionner
▶ **refine on, refine upon** *vipo* (*improve*) parfaire
refined [rɪ'faɪnd] *adj* (*petroleum, sugar*) raffiné; (*metal*) affiné; *Fig* (*person, taste*) raffiné, *Pej* maniéré
refinement [rɪ'faɪnmənt] *n* (**a**) (*of manners, taste, person*) raffinement *m*; **of great r.** (*person*) très raffiné; **lack of r.** vulgarité *f* (**b**) (*of technique*) perfectionnement *m*; **machine with all the latest refinements** machine dotée des derniers perfectionnements; **to make refinements to** (*machine*) perfectionner; (*plan, tactics etc*) parfaire (**c**) (*of metal etc*) = **refining**
refiner [rɪ'faɪnər] *n* (*of sugar, petroleum*) raffineur *m*; (*of metal*) affineur *m*
refinery [rɪ'faɪnərɪ] *n* (*for petroleum, sugar*) raffinerie *f*; (*for metal*) affinerie *f*
refining [rɪ'faɪnɪŋ] *n* (*of petroleum, sugar*) raffinage *m*; (*of metal*) affinage *m*
refit[1] ['riːfɪt] *n* (*of ship*) réparation *f*, remise *f* en état; (*of factory*) réaménagement *m*; **the yacht is under r.** le yacht est en cours de réparation
refit[2] [riː'fɪt] (**-tt-**) **1** *vt* (*ship*) remettre en état; (*factory*) réaménager **2** *vi* (*of ship*) être en cours de réparation; (*of factory*) être en cours de réaménagement; **while we're refitting** *Naut* pendant les réparations; *Ind* pendant le réaménagement
reflate [riː'fleɪt] **1** *vt* **to r. the economy** relancer l'économie **2** *vi* relancer l'économie
reflation [riː'fleɪʃən] *n* relance *f*
reflationary [riː'fleɪʃənərɪ] *adj* **r. measures/policy** mesures *fpl*/politique *f* de relance
reflect [rɪ'flekt] **1** *vt* (**a**) (*image*) réfléchir, refléter, renvoyer; (*light*) réfléchir, renvoyer; (*heat*) renvoyer; **to be reflected** se réfléchir (**in** sur); *TV etc* **reflected light** lumière *f* réfléchie; *Fig* **to bask** *or* **bathe in reflected glory** se parer des plumes du paon; **they basked** *or* **bathed in the reflected glory of their famous daughter** ils se glorifiaient de la célébrité de leur fille; *Fig* **her personal problems are reflected in her poor performance at school** elle a des problèmes personnels et ses résultats scolaires s'en ressentent
(**b**) (*think*) **to r. that …** penser *ou* se dire que … + *ind*
2 *vi* (*think*) réfléchir (**on** à, sur)

▶ **reflect on** *vipo* **to r. well on sb** (*of action etc*) faire honneur à qn; **to r. badly on sb** (*of action etc*) faire du tort à qn, nuire à (la réputation de) qn; **how is that going to r. on the company?** quelles en seront les conséquences *ou* répercussions pour la société?

reflecting [rɪ'flektɪŋ] *adj* (*surface etc*) réfléchissant

reflection [rɪ'flekʃən] *n* **(a)** (*image*) (*in mirror*) reflet *m*, image *f* (réfléchie); *Fig* reflet (**of** de); **to see one's r. in a mirror** voir son image dans un miroir; *Fig* **the final score was a fair r. of the Italians' superiority** le score final reflétait bien la supériorité des Italiens; **this report is not an accurate r. of the situation** ce rapport ne donne pas un aperçu exact de la situation

(b) (*action*) (*of light, sound, image*) réflexion *f*

(c) *Fig* (*on honesty, character etc*) (*negative*) blâme *m*, critique *f* (**on** de); **their conduct is a (bad) r. on all of us** leur conduite nous fait du tort à tous; **it's a good r. on the school** c'est bon pour la réputation de l'école; **it's a r. on your popularity** ça veut dire beaucoup quant à ta popularité; **it's no r. on your performance** il ne s'agit pas d'une remise en cause de votre performance, cela ne remet pas votre performance en cause

(d) (*thought*) réflexion *f* (**on** sur); **on r.** à la réflexion, en y réfléchissant, tout bien réfléchi; **to do sth without due r.** faire qch sans avoir suffisamment réfléchi; **reflections** réflexions, pensées *fpl*; **reflections on the history of ...** considérations *fpl* sur l'histoire de ...

reflective [rɪ'flektɪv] *adj* **(a)** (*thoughtful*) (*person*) réfléchi **(b)** (*surface*) réfléchissant; **r. power** pouvoir *m* réfléchissant

reflectively [rɪ'flektɪvlɪ] *adv* (*to look at*) d'un air pensif; (*to say*) d'un ton pensif

reflector [rɪ'flektər] *n* (*on bicycle, vehicle*) réflecteur *m*, cataphote® *m*, catadioptre *m*; (*on sign, of heat*) réflecteur *m*; *TV etc* **r. board** panneau *m* réflecteur

reflex¹ ['ri:fleks] *n* (*reaction*) réflexe *m*; **to have good reflexes** avoir de bons réflexes; **to test sb's reflexes** tester les réflexes de qn; **your reflexes aren't what they should be** vos réflexes sont défaillants

reflex² *adj* **(a)** réflexe; **r. action** réflexe *m* **(b)** *Math* (*angle*) rentrant; *Phot* **r. camera** (appareil *m*) reflex *m*

reflexion [rɪ'flekʃən] *n* = **reflection**

reflexive [rɪ'fleksɪv] [①**A29**, 7; **B26-27**, D] *Gram* **1** *adj* (*pronoun, verb*) réfléchi **2** *n* (*verb*) verbe *m* réfléchi; (*pronoun*) pronom *m* (personnel) réfléchi

reflexively [rɪ'fleksɪvlɪ] *adv Gram* au sens réfléchi

reflexology [ri:flek'sɒlədʒɪ] *n* (*massage*) réflexologie *f*

refloat [ri:'fləʊt] *vt* **(a)** (*ship*) renflouer, (re)mettre à flot **(b)** *Fin* (*loan*) émettre de nouveau; (*company*) renflouer, remettre à flot; *Fig* (*proposals*) présenter à nouveau

reflux ['ri:flʌks] *n* reflux *m*

reforest [ri:'fɒrɪst] *vt* (*region, land*) reboiser

reforestation [ri:fɒrɪ'steɪʃən] *n* reboisement *m*; **r. costs/programme** coûts *mpl*/programme *m* de reboisement

reform¹ [rɪ'fɔ:m] *n* (*of law, institution etc*) réforme *f*; (*of person*) retour *m* à la vertu *ou* à une conduite meilleure; (*of alcoholics, criminals, delinquents*) réinsertion *f*; **to introduce reforms** introduire *ou* apporter des réformes; **to make reforms** faire des réformes; **to be beyond r.** être irrécupérable; *Br* **r. school** (*formerly*) maison *f* de correction *ou* de redressement

reform² **1** *vt* (*improve*) (*institution, law etc*) réformer; (*system*) réformer, améliorer; (*person*) corriger, ramener à la vertu; **he's a reformed character** il s'est assagi, il a changé en bien; **a reformed alcoholic** un ancien alcoolique; **Reformed Church** Église *f* réformée **2** *vi* (*of person*) se corriger, s'amender

re-form **1** *vt* (*battalion, group etc*) reformer **2** *vi* (*of group, troops etc*) se reformer

reformat [ri:'fɔ:mæt] (**-tt-**) **1** *vt* (*text, disk*) reformater **2** *vi* reformater

reformation [refə'meɪʃən] *n* **(a)** (*of calendar, society etc*) réforme *f*; *Rel, Hist* **the R.** la Réforme **(b)** (*of person*) retour *m* à la vertu *ou* à une conduite meilleure

reformatory [rɪ'fɔ:mət(ə)rɪ] **1** *adj* (*measures etc*) réformateur, -trice **2** *n Am* centre *m* d'éducation surveillée; *Br* (*formerly*) maison *f* de correction *ou* de redressement

reformatting [ri:'fɔ:mætɪŋ] *n* (*of text, disk, page etc*) reformatage *m*

reformer [rɪ'fɔ:mər] *n* (*of religion, society*) réformateur, -trice

reformism [rɪ'fɔ:mɪz(ə)m] *n* réformisme *m*

reformist [rɪ'fɔ:mɪst] *adj, n* réformiste *mf*

refract [rɪ'frækt] *vt* (*light*) réfracter; **to be refracted** être réfracté

refracting [rɪ'fræktɪŋ] *adj* **r. angle** angle *m* de réfraction; **r. medium** milieu *m* réfringent; **r. telescope** réfracteur *m*, lunette *f* astronomique

refraction [rɪ'frækʃən] *n Phys, Opt* réfraction *f*; **double r.** biréfringence *f*

refractive [rɪ'fræktɪv] *adj Phys* réfringent; **r. index** indice *m* de réfraction

refractivity [ri:fræk'tɪvɪtɪ] *n Phys* réfringence *f*

refractor [rɪ'fræktər] *n* **(a)** *Phys* (*material*) milieu *m* réfringent; (*object*) dispositif *m* réfringent **(b)** (*telescope*) réfracteur *m*, lunette *f* astronomique

refractory¹ [rɪ'frækt(ə)rɪ] *adj Fml* (*person*) réfractaire, récalcitrant; (*animal*) récalcitrant; (*illness*) rebelle

refractory² *n* réfractaire *m*

refrain¹ [rɪ'freɪn] *n Mus, Fig* refrain *m*

refrain² *vi* se retenir, s'abstenir (**from doing** de faire); **to r. from comment** s'abstenir de tout commentaire; **he couldn't r. from smiling** il n'a pu s'empêcher de sourire; **kindly r. from smoking/talking** (*on notice*) prière de ne pas fumer/parler

refrangible [rɪ'frændʒɪb(ə)l] *adj Phys, Opt* réfrangible

re-freeze *vt* (*food*) recongeler

refresh¹ ['ri:freʃ] *n Comptr* rafraîchissement *m*, régénération *f*; **r. circuitry** circuits *mpl* de rafraîchissement; **r. rate** taux *m* de rafraîchissement, vitesse *f* de régénération

refresh² [rɪ'freʃ] *vt* (*person*) (*of bath, drink*) rafraîchir, *F* requinquer; (*of rest, amusement*) reposer, délasser; **to r. oneself** (*with food*) se restaurer; (*with drink*) se rafraîchir; (*by taking bath*) se délasser; **to awake refreshed** s'éveiller frais et dispos *ou* bien reposé; *Hum* **to r. the inner man** se désaltérer; **to r. one's memory** se rafraîchir la mémoire; *F* **let me r. your memory!** je vais vous rafraîchir la mémoire!; **can I r. your drink for you?** voulez-vous que je vous resserve?

refresher [rɪ'freʃər] *n* **r. course** cours *m* de perfectionnement

refreshing [rɪ'freʃɪŋ] *adj* (*breeze, drink*) rafraîchissant; (*sleep*) réparateur, reposant; (*bath, shower, cup of tea*) revigorant, ravigotant; **it is r.** *or* **a r. change to encounter such honesty** cela change agréablement de *ou* il est réconfortant de rencontrer une telle honnêteté; **his honesty is r.** son honnêteté est comme une bouffée d'air frais *ou* est réconfortante

refreshingly [rɪ'freʃɪŋlɪ] *adv* d'une manière qui repose *ou* fait du bien; **r. honest** d'une honnêteté réconfortante; **a r. original style** un style dont l'originalité est comme une bouffée d'air frais

refreshments [rɪ'freʃmənts] *npl* (*drinks*) rafraîchissements *mpl*; (*snacks*) collation *f*; **to order some r.** commander à manger/à boire; **refreshments will be served** une collation sera servie

refrigerant [rɪ'frɪdʒərənt] *n* (mélange *m*) réfrigérant *m*

refrigerate [rɪ'frɪdʒəreɪt] *vt* (*food etc*) réfrigérer; **r. after opening** (*notice on packet*) conserver au réfrigérateur après ouverture; **keep refrigerated** (*notice on packet*) conserver au réfrigérateur; **refrigerated meat** viande *f* frigorifiée; **refrigerated lorry** camion *m* frigorifique

refrigeration [rɪfrɪdʒə'reɪʃən] *n* (*of food etc*) réfrigération *f*; **r. industry** industrie *f* du froid

refrigerator [rɪ'frɪdʒəreɪtər] *n* (*domestic*) réfrigérateur *m*, frigidaire® *m*; (*industrial*) réfrigérateur, chambre *f* *ou* appareil *m* frigorifique; *Rail Br* **r. van**, *Am* **r. car** wagon *m* frigorifique

refuel [ri:'fjʊəl] (**-ll-**, *US* **-l-**) **1** *vt* (*ship, aircraft, racing car*) ravitailler en carburant; *Fig* **to r. speculation** alimenter les conjectures **2** *vi* (*of ship, aircraft, racing car*) se ravitailler en carburant; **to r. in flight** se ravitailler en vol

refuelling, *US* **refueling** [ri:'fjʊəlɪŋ] *n* (*of ship, aircraft, racing car*) ravitaillement *m* en carburant; **r. stop** (*of aircraft, ship*) escale *f* pour se ravitailler en carburant; (*of racing car*) arrêt *m* pour se ravitailler en carburant

refuge ['refju:dʒ] *n* (*from danger*) refuge *m*, asile *m*; (*from weather*) abri *m* (**from** contre); (*for battered women*) foyer *m*; *Br* (*island in road*) refuge; **place of r.** lieu *m* de refuge *ou* d'asile; **to seek r.** chercher refuge *ou* asile; **to take r.** (*from danger*) se réfugier (**with** chez); **to take r. from the storm** s'abriter de l'orage; *Fig* **to take r. in lying/drugs/religion** se réfugier dans le mensonge/la drogue/la religion; *Fig* **to seek r. in lying/drugs/religion** chercher refuge dans le mensonge/la drogue/la religion; **he has been accused of taking r. in evasive language** on l'a accusé de pratiquer la langue de bois; *Lit* **God is my r.** Dieu est mon refuge

refugee [refjʊ'dʒi:] *n* réfugié, -ée; **economic r.** migrant, -ante économique; **r. camp** camp *m* de réfugiés; **r. status** statut *m* de réfugié

refund¹ ['ri:fʌnd] *n* (*for ticket, tax etc*) remboursement *m*; **to obtain a r. for sth** se faire rembourser qch; **I'm due a r.** je dois être remboursé

refund² [ri:'fʌnd, rɪ-] *vt* (*money, payment etc*) rembourser; **to r. sb** rembourser qn (**sth** de qch)

refundable [rɪ'fʌndəbl] *adj* **to charge a r. deposit on sth** consigner qch
refurbish [ri:'fɜ:bɪʃ] *vt (flat, restaurant etc)* remettre à neuf
refurbishment [ri:'fɜ:bɪʃmənt] *n* remise *f* à neuf
refusal [rɪ'fju:z(ə)l] *n (of offer, invitation etc)* refus *m* (**to do** de faire); *(of cheque)* rejet *m*; **to give a flat r.** refuser (tout) net; **to meet with a r.** *(of person)* se heurter à *ou* essuyer un refus; *(of offer, invitation etc)* se heurter à un refus; **she shook her head in r.** elle a fait non de la tête; **that's his third r.** *(of show-jumper)* c'est son troisième refus; **to have first r. (on sth)** avoir la priorité (sur qch); **to give sb first r.** donner la priorité à qn; **you promised me first r. on the car** tu m'as promis que je serais le premier à qui tu proposerais (d'acheter) la voiture; *Mktg* **r. rate** taux *m* de refus
refuse[1] ['refju:s] *n (rubbish)* ordures *fpl*, détritus *m*; **household r.** ordures ménagères; **r. bag** sac *m* à ordures; **r. bin** *(in street)* poubelle *f*, boîte *f* à ordures; *(in home)* poubelle; **r. chute** vide-ordures *m inv*; **r. collection** ramassage *m ou* enlèvement *m* des ordures (ménagères); **r. collector** éboueur *m*; **r. disposal** traitement *m* des ordures; **r.-disposal unit** broyeur *m* d'ordures; **r. dump** dépôt *m* d'ordures, dépotoir *m*; **r. material** détritus
refuse[2] [rɪ'fju:z] **1** *vt (invitation, offer, Horseriding fence etc)* refuser; *(request)* rejeter, repousser; **to r. to do sth** refuser de *ou Fml* se refuser à faire qch; **I r. to believe that** je ne peux pas le croire; **to r. to comment** se refuser à tout commentaire; **to r. to fight** refuser le combat; **the car refuses to start** la voiture ne veut pas démarrer; **to r. sb sth** refuser qch à qn; **to r. sb admittance** refuser (de laisser entrer) qn; **they were refused admittance** on ne les a pas laissés entrer; **to be refused** essuyer un refus; **I don't see how we can r. them** je ne vois pas comment on peut le leur refuser; **she made me an offer I couldn't r.** elle m'a fait une proposition que je ne pouvais pas refuser; **she refused him** *(would not marry him)* elle l'a rejeté

2 *vi (of person)* refuser; *(of horse)* refuser l'obstacle
refus(e)nik [rɪ'fju:znɪk] *n Pol* refuznik *mf*
refutation [refjʊ'teɪʃən] *n (disproving)* réfutation *f*
refute [rɪ'fju:t] *vt* **(a)** *(disprove) (argument, theory etc)* réfuter; **to r. a statement** démontrer la fausseté d'une déclaration **(b)** *(deny)* **to r. an allegation** nier une allégation
regain [rɪ'geɪn] *vt* **(a)** *(get back) (person's confidence)* regagner; *(strength, money)* récupérer; *(strength, health, sight, balance, freedom)* retrouver, recouvrer; **to r. possession of sth** rentrer en *ou* reprendre possession de qch; **to r. consciousness** reprendre connaissance, revenir à soi; **to r. (lost) ground** regagner du terrain **(b)** *(reach) (a place, one's seat)* regagner
regal ['ri:g(ə)l] *adj (offer, salary, splendour etc)* royal; *(air, person)* majestueux, royal
regale [rɪ'geɪl] *vt (person)* régaler (**with** de)
regalia [rɪ'geɪlɪə] *npl (of monarch)* insignes *mpl* royaux; *(of Freemason etc)* insignes; **the mayor came first in all his r.** le maire est venu en premier avec tous les insignes de ses fonctions; *Hum* **here comes Mrs Smith in full r.** voilà Mme Smith dans ses plus beaux atours
regally ['ri:g(ə)lɪ] *adv (to entertain)* royalement; *(to behave, act)* majestueusement
regard[1] [rɪ'gɑ:d] *n* **(a)** *(admiration, respect) (for person)* respect *m*, estime *f*; *(for skill, talent etc)* respect; **to have great r. for sb** avoir beaucoup d'estime pour qn; **I have great r. for him but I don't particularly like him** j'ai beaucoup de respect pour lui mais je ne l'apprécie pas particulièrement; **to hold sb in great** *or* **high r.** tenir qn en grande *ou* haute estime; **out of r. for sb** par respect pour qn

(b) *(consideration)* égard *m*, considération *f* (**for** pour); **out of r. for** par égard pour; **without** *or* **with no r. to** sans égard pour; **without r. to race or colour** sans distinction de race ni de couleur; **to pay r. to** avoir égard à, faire attention à; **to pay no r. to** ne faire aucune attention à; **to have no r. for human life** faire peu de cas de la vie humaine

(c) *(connection)* **in this** *or* **that r.** à cet égard; **in all regards** à tous (les) égards; **with r. to** en ce qui concerne, quant à; **with r. to your letter of ...** relativement à votre lettre du ...; **having r. to** si l'on tient compte de, eu égard à

(d) *(in message etc)* **to give** *or* **send one's regards** transmettre son bon souvenir, *Fml* faire ses hommages; **(please give) my kindest** *or* **best regards to the family** (présentez) mon meilleur souvenir *ou* mes sincères amitiés à toute la famille; **kind** *or* **best regards** *(at end of letter)* meilleur souvenir, sincères amitiés, bien amicalement
regard[2] *vt* **(a)** *(admire, respect)* avoir de l'estime pour; **to r. sb highly** avoir beaucoup d'estime pour qn; **to be highly regarded** être tenu en haute estime **(b)** *(consider)* considérer (**as** comme), tenir (**as** pour) **(c)** *(concern)* regarder, concerner; **as regards ...** en ce qui concerne ..., pour ce qui est de ..., quant à ...; **she is very strict as regards discipline** elle est très sévère pour ce qui est de *ou* sur le chapitre de la discipline
regardful [rɪ'gɑ:dfʊl] *adj* **to be r. of** se soucier de
regarding [rɪ'gɑ:dɪŋ] *prep (about)* en ce qui concerne, pour ce qui est de; *F* **what's it r.?** de quoi s'agit-il?
regardless [rɪ'gɑ:dlɪs] *adv* **(a) r. of** *(consequences, danger, noise etc)* sans se soucier de; **to be r. of the danger of infection** ne pas se soucier du risque d'infection; **r. of expense** sans regarder à la dépense **(b)** *(despite everything)* quand même; **press on r.!** allez-y quand même!, continuez!
regatta [rɪ'gætə] *n* régates *fpl*
regency ['ri:dʒənsɪ] *n* régence *f*; *Br, Fr Hist* **the R.** la Régence; **R. armchair/furniture** fauteuil *m*/meubles *mpl* Régence
regenerate [rɪ'dʒenəreɪt] **1** *vt* régénérer; **to r. an industry/a political party** régénérer une industrie/un parti politique; **to r. interest in sth** raviver l'intérêt pour qch; *Fig* **to feel regenerated** se sentir régénéré **2** *vi (of industry, party etc)* se régénérer; *(of tail, organ etc)* repousser
regenerating [rɪ'dʒenəreɪtɪŋ] *adj* régénérateur, -trice
regeneration [rɪdʒenə'reɪʃən] *n* régénération *f*
regenerative [rɪ'dʒenərətɪv] *adj* régénérateur, -trice; *Med* régénératif; *Aut* **r. braking** freinage *m* à régénération
regent ['ri:dʒənt] **1** *adj Hist* régent; **prince r.** prince *m* régent **2** *n Hist, Am Sch* régent, -ente
reggae ['regeɪ] *n Mus* reggae *m*; **r. group/musicians** groupe *m*/musiciens *mpl* de reggae
regicide ['redʒɪsaɪd] *n (crime)* régicide *m*; *(person)* régicide *mf*
regime, régime [reɪ'ʒi:m] *n Pol* régime *m*; **the old r.** l'ancien régime
regimen ['redʒɪmen] *n Med* régime *m*
regiment[1] ['redʒɪmənt] *n Mil, Fig* régiment *m*; **there's enough to feed a r.** il y a de quoi nourrir un régiment
regiment[2] *vt (people)* enrégimenter, embrigader; *(education system, organization)* réglementer
regimental [redʒɪ'ment(ə)l] *Mil* **1** *adj (badge, flag etc)* régimentaire, du régiment; **r. band** fanfare *f* du régiment; **r. sergeant major** adjudant-chef *m*, *pl* adjudants-chefs **2** *npl* **regimentals** *(uniform)* uniforme *m* (militaire), tenue *f* militaire; **in full regimentals** en grande tenue d'apparat
regimentation [redʒɪmen'teɪʃən] *n Pej* discipline *f* excessive
regimented ['redzɪmentɪd] *adj* strict; **it's a very r. organization** c'est une organisation très rigide
region ['ri:dʒ(ə)n] *n (of country, body etc)* région *f*; *Fig* **in the r. of** environ; **somewhere in the r. of £500** dans les 500 livres
regional ['ri:dʒən(ə)l] *adj (accent, development, office etc)* régional; **r. correspondent** correspondant *m* de province, correspondant régional; **r. language programme** programme *m* en langue régionale; **r. paper** journal *m* régional; **r. sales manager** directeur *m* régional des ventes; **R. Tourist Board** comité *m* régional du tourisme; **r. writer** (écrivain *m*) régionaliste *mf*
regionalism ['ri:dʒənəlɪz(ə)m] *n Ling (word, expression)* régionalisme *m*
regionalization [ri:dʒən(ə)laɪ'zeɪʃən] *n* régionalisation *f*
register[1] ['redʒɪstər] *n* **(a)** *(record)* registre *m*; *Sch* cahier *m* d'appel; **to enter sth in a r.** inscrire qch sur *ou* dans un registre; **to keep a r.** tenir un registre; *Sch* **to take the r.** faire l'appel; **r. of births, marriages and deaths** registre de l'état civil; **electoral r., r. of voters** liste *f* électorale; **r. of shareholders** livre *m* des actionnaires; *Br* **r. office** bureau *m* de l'état civil **(b)** *(range) (of instrument)* registre *m*; *(of voice)* registre, tessiture *f* **(c)** *(style) (of speaking, writing)* registre *m* **(d)** *Comptr* registre *m* **(e) (cash) r.** caisse *f* enregistreuse
register[2] **1** *vt* **(a)** *(enter in records) (member, student)* inscrire; *(vehicle, ship, goods)* immatriculer; *(company)* faire enregistrer; *(birth, marriage, death)* déclarer; *(trademark)* déposer; **to r. a complaint (with sb)** se plaindre (auprès de qn); **to r. a protest** protester; **to r. a letter** recommander une lettre; **I want to send it registered** je voudrais l'envoyer en recommandé; **is the car registered in your name?** est-ce que la voiture est à votre nom?; **she is not registered at this hotel** elle n'est pas descendue à cet hôtel

(b) *(indicate, make known) (of thermometer etc) (temperature etc)* indiquer; *(of person) (astonishment, displeasure)* manifester, exprimer; **his face registered disappointment/disapproval** son visage exprimait *ou* reflétait la déception/la désapprobation; **the earthquake registered seven on the Richter scale** le séisme a atteint 7 sur l'échelle de Richter; **winds registering a hundred miles an hour** des vents atteignant 160 kilomètres/heure

(c) *(realize)* se rendre compte de, prendre la mesure de; **she hadn't registered the danger she was in** elle ne s'était pas rendue compte du danger qu'elle courait

(d) *(achieve) (progress, victory)* réaliser

2 *vi* **(a)** (*for course etc*) s'inscrire (**for** à); (*at hotel*) signer le registre; (*of voter*) se faire inscrire sur la liste électorale; **to r. with the police** se faire inscrire à la police

(b) (*of gauge, machine*) marcher, fonctionner; (*of amount, measurement*) être indiqué, apparaître; **the quake was so small it barely even registered** la secousse a été à peine perceptible

(c) *F* (*of fact, joke etc*) être compris; **he explained it to me yesterday but it didn't r.** il me l'a expliqué hier, mais je n'ai pas fait attention; **I don't think the bad news has registered (with him/her) yet** on lui a annoncé la mauvaise nouvelle mais je ne crois pas qu'il/elle ait bien réalisé; **I've been so busy his absence has barely registered** je suis tellement occupé que je me suis à peine aperçu de son absence; **I did give them the address but I don't think it registered** je leur ai bien donné l'adresse mais je ne crois pas qu'ils l'aient retenue

registered ['redʒɪstɜːd] *adj* (*member, voter*) inscrit; (*vehicle*) immatriculé; **to send sth by r. mail** envoyer qch en recommandé; **r. and insured parcel** colis *m* chargé; *Com* **r. agent** agent *m* agréé; *Fin* **r. bond** obligation *f* nominative; **r. charity** organisme *m* de bienfaisance reconnu par l'état; **r. childminder** assistante *f* maternelle agréée; **r. disabled** infirme *mf* reconnu(e); *Com* **r. name** nom *m* déposé; *Can Fin* **r. retirement savings plan** régime *m* enregistré d'épargne-retraite; **r. security** titre *m* nominatif, valeur *f* nominative; *St Exch* **r. share** action *f* nominative; **r. unemployed** inscrit au chômage; **the r. unemployed** les personnes inscrites au chômage

registered capital *n Fin* capital *m* social déclaré

registered general nurse *n Br* infirmière *f* diplômée (d'État)

registered letter *n* lettre *f* recommandée

registered nurse *n Am* infirmière *f* diplômée (d'État)

registered office *n* (*of company*) siège *m* principal *ou* social

registered stock *n Fin* effets *mpl* nominatifs

Registered Trademark *n* marque *f* déposée

registrar ['redʒɪstrɑːr] *n* **(a)** *Br* (*in registry office*) officier *m* de l'état civil; **r.'s office** bureau *m* de l'état civil; **the R. General** le Conservateur des actes de l'état civil **(b)** *Sch, Univ* secrétaire *m* général **(c) r. of companies** directeur *m* du registre des sociétés **(d)** *Br Med* chef *m* de clinique

registration [redʒɪs'treɪʃən] *n* (*of student for course etc*) inscription *f*; (*of voter*) inscription sur la liste électorale; (*of vehicle*) immatriculation *f*; (*of birth, death, marriage*) déclaration *f*; (*of trademark*) dépôt *m*; **when does r. start?** (*for university, evening classes*) quand les inscriptions commencent-elles?; **r. card** (*for foreign guests*) fiche *f* voyageur; (*for non-EC guests*) fiche de police; *Aut* **r. document** ≈ carte *f* grise; **r. fee** (*for course, exam etc*) droit *m* d'inscription; (*for letter*) taxe *f* de recommandation; **r. form** bulletin *m* d'inscription; (*in hotel*) fiche d'accueil *ou* d'arrivée *ou* d'inscription; **r. (number)** (*of car*) numéro *m* minéralogique *ou* d'immatriculation; (*of student*) (numéro) matricule *m*

registry ['redʒɪstrɪ] *n* **(a)** *Br* **r. (office)** bureau *m* de l'état civil; **to be married at a** *or* **the r. office** se marier civilement, ≈ se marier à la mairie; **r. office wedding** mariage *m* civil **(b)** *Naut* **a ship of Canadian r.** un navire immatriculé au Canada; **certificate of r.** lettre *f* de mer, certificat *m* d'inscription; (*of French ship*) acte *m* de francisation; **port of r.** port *m* d'attache

regrade [riː'greɪd] *vt* **(a)** (*nurse, employee etc*) reclasser **(b)** *Am Sch* (*homework*) renoter

regrading [riː'greɪdɪŋ] *n* (*of nurse, employee etc*) reclassement *m*; **r. dispute/strike/guidelines** conflit *m*/grève *f*/directives *fpl* concernant le reclassement

regress [rɪ'gres] *vi* régresser

regression [rɪ'greʃən] *n* régression *f*

regressive [rɪ'gresɪv] *adj* (*gene etc*) régressif

regret¹ [rɪ'gret] *n* regret *m* (**for** de); **to feel r.** éprouver du regret (**at, about** à, **about doing** d'avoir fait); **to express one's r.** exprimer ses regrets; **to have** *or* **feel a pang of r.** éprouver une pointe de regret; **to have no regrets** n'avoir aucun regret, ne rien regretter (**about** au sujet de, quant à); **my only r. is that I didn't resign earlier** je n'ai qu'un regret, c'est de ne pas avoir donné ma démission plus tôt; **(much) to my r.** à mon grand regret; **it is with deep r. that we inform you that ...** c'est à grand regret que nous vous informons que ...; **she sends (you/us) her regrets** (*is unable to come*) elle vous/nous prie de l'excuser

regret² *vt* (**-tt-**) (*be sorry for*) regretter; **to r. doing** *or* **having done sth** regretter d'avoir fait qch; **we r. any inconvenience to passengers** nous prions les voyageurs de bien vouloir nous excuser pour ce désagrément; **you'll r. this!** tu le regretteras!; **I r. to (have to) inform you that ...** j'ai le regret *ou* je regrette de (devoir) vous annoncer que ...; **then, I r. to say, she ...** puis, malheureusement, elle ...; **he bitterly regretted having spoken** il a amèrement regretté d'avoir parlé; **I r. to hear that ...** je suis désolé d'apprendre que ...; **it is to be regretted that ...** il est regrettable *ou* à regretter que ... + *sub*

regretful [rɪ'gretfʊl] *adj* (*glance, expression*) plein de regrets; (*feeling*) de regret; **to be r.** (*of person*) avoir des regrets (**about** au sujet de, quant à)

regretfully [rɪ'gretfəlɪ] *adv* (*to say*) avec regret; **r., I cannot** je regrette, je ne peux pas

regrettable [rɪ'gretəb(ə)l] *adj* (*sad*) regrettable; (*inconvenient*) fâcheux; **it is r. that ...** il est regrettable *ou* à regretter *ou* fâcheux que ... + *sub*

regrettably [rɪ'gretəblɪ] *adv* malheureusement; **r. few people were present** il est regrettable que si peu de personnes soient venues; **a joke in r. poor taste** une plaisanterie dont le mauvais goût est à déplorer; **that's r. short-sighted of him** c'est, de sa part, un manque de perspicacité regrettable

regroup [riː'gruːp] **1** *vt* regrouper **2** *vi* se regrouper, se rassembler

regrouping [riː'gruːpɪŋ] *n* regroupement *m*

regular ['regjʊlər] **1** *adj* **(a)** (*steady, even*) (*features, pulse, service etc*) régulier; (*surface*) régulier, uni; **on a r. basis** régulièrement; **to have r. bowel movements** aller régulièrement à la selle; **bran will keep you r.** le son vous fera aller régulièrement à la selle; **to be as r. as clockwork** être réglé comme du papier à musique; **to do sth as r. as clockwork** faire qch avec une régularité infaillible; **he's there every Tuesday, (as) r. as clockwork** il est là tous les mardis, il est réglé comme du papier à musique; **to keep r. hours** (*have strict timetable*) avoir un emploi du temps précis, avoir des horaires réguliers; (*go to bed and rise at reasonable time*) se lever et se coucher à heures régulières; **you should keep more r. hours** (*go to bed earlier*) vous devriez vous coucher plus tôt; **he was a man of r. habits** il avait ses habitudes

(b) (*usual*) (*doctor etc*) habituel; (*verb*) régulier; (*price, size*) normal, *Can* régulier; (*reader, listener*) fidèle; (*staff*) permanent; *Am Aut* (*gas*) ordinaire; **my r. bedtime** l'heure à laquelle je me couche habituellement; **you can stay up past your r. bedtime** tu peux te coucher plus tard que d'habitude; **a r. visitor to the house** un/une des habitué(e)s de la maison; *Journ* **r. column** chronique *f*; **r. customer** (*in bar, restaurant*) habitué, -ée; (*in shop*) fidèle client, -ente; *Mktg* chaland *m*; **r. customer rebate** ristourne *f* de fidélité; *Ind* **r. model** modèle *m* courant; **r. supplier** fournisseur *m* habituel

(c) (*professional*) (*army, soldier*) régulier

(d) *F* (*real, thorough*) (*fool, slave etc*) vrai, véritable; **a r. hero** un vrai héros; *esp Am* **a r. guy** un type réglo *ou* sympa

(e) (*normal*) (*procedure, behaviour etc*) normal

2 *n* **(a)** (*in bar, restaurant etc*) habitué, -ée

(b) *Am Aut* (*gas*) ordinaire *m*

(c) (*professional*) *Mil* régulier *m*

regularity [regjʊ'lærɪtɪ] *n* (*of features, pulse etc*) régularité *f*; **to do sth with unfailing r.** faire qch avec une régularité infaillible

regularize ['regjʊləraɪz] *vt* (*situation*) régulariser

regularly ['regjʊləlɪ] *adv* (*to attend, visit etc*) régulièrement; *Am* **the coat is r. priced at ...** le manteau coûte normalement ...

regulate ['regjʊleɪt] *vt* **(a)** (*adjust*) (*working of a machine, watch, flow of water etc*) régler; (*of valve*) contrôler **(b)** (*control*) (*people*) contrôler; **he leads a well-regulated life** il mène une vie très réglée; **rules regulating the use of additives** les réglementations qui régissent l'emploi des additifs

regulating ['regjʊleɪtɪŋ] *adj* (*knob, switch, valve*) de réglage; (*hormone, mechanism*) régulateur, -trice; **self-r.** à réglage automatique

regulation [regjʊ'leɪʃən] *n* **(a)** (*action*) (*of machine, watch etc*) réglage *m*; (*of voltage*) régulation *f*; (*of food additives etc*) réglementation *f*; (*of information*) contrôle *m*

(b) (*rule*) règlement *m*; **r. dress/speed/uniform** tenue *f*/vitesse *f*/uniforme *m* réglementaire; **black shoes are r. wear** le port de chaussures noires est réglementaire; **regulations** règlement(s); **contrary to** *or* **against (the) regulations** contraire au règlement; **in accordance with the regulations** selon le règlement; **it's not in accordance with the regulations** ce n'est pas réglementaire; **under the regulations** en vertu du règlement; **EC regulations** règlements de la CE; **safety regulations** règles *fpl* de sécurité

regulator ['regjʊleɪtər] *n* (*of temperature, speed etc*), *Banking etc* régulateur *m*; **r. valve** régulateur *m*

regulatory ['regjʊlətərɪ, regjʊ'leɪtərɪ] *adj* (*framework, provisions etc*) de contrôle; **r. body** instance *f* de contrôle, autorité *f* réglementaire; **r. framework** cadre *m* réglementaire
regulo ['regjʊləʊ] *n Br Culin* thermostat *m*
regurgitate [rɪ'gɜːdʒɪteɪt] *vt* (*food*) régurgiter; *Fig Pej* **to r. one's lecture notes** régurgiter ses cours
regurgitation [rɪgɜːdʒɪ'teɪʃən] *n* (*of food*); *Fig Pej* (*of lecture notes*) régurgitation *f*
rehab ['riːhæb] *n F* désintoxication *f*; **r. unit** centre *m* de désintoxication; **to be in r.** être en cure de désintoxication
rehabilitate [riːə'bɪlɪteɪt, riːh-] *vt* **(a)** (*criminal, drug addict, alcoholic*) réinsérer; *Med* (*stroke victim etc*) rééduquer **(b)** (*restore reputation of*) (*politician*) réhabiliter **(c)** (*restore*) (*building, area*) réhabiliter, remettre en état, rénover
rehabilitation [riːəbɪlɪ'teɪʃən, riːh-] *n* **(a)** (*of criminal, drug addict, alcoholic*) réinsertion *f*; *Med* (*of stroke victim etc*) rééducation *f*; *Med* **r. centre** centre *m* de rééducation **(b)** (*restoring of reputation*) (*of politician*) réhabilitation *f* **(c)** (*restoring*) (*of building, area*) réhabilitation *f*, remise *f* en état, rénovation *f*
rehash[1] ['riːhæʃ] *n F* (*of book, script etc*) resucée *f*; **it was a r. of her first novel** c'était une resucée de son premier roman; **it's just a r.** c'est du réchauffé
rehash[2] [riː'hæʃ] *vt F* (*rework*) (*old story etc*) remanier; (*old arguments etc*) ressasser, rabâcher
rehearsal [rɪ'hɜːs(ə)l] *n* (*of play, speech etc*) répétition *f*; **to have** *or* **hold a r.** faire une répétition; **to put a play into r.** commencer les répétitions d'une pièce; **we go into r. next week** nous commençons les répétitions la semaine prochaine; *Fig* **the naval exercises were just a r. for the real thing** les exercices navals n'étaient qu'un entraînement; *Th* **dress r.** (répétition) générale *f*; **r. room** salle *f* de répétition; **r. script** scénario *m* de répétition
rehearse [rɪ'hɜːs] **1** *vt* **(a)** (*play, part, piece of music, ballet*) répéter; (*actor, orchestra*) faire répéter; **I rehearsed what I was going to say** j'ai préparé ce que j'allais dire; **her indignation struck me as rather rehearsed** son indignation me sembla forcée; **the cast were well rehearsed** les acteurs connaissaient bien leur rôle; **she had been carefully rehearsed by her advisers** ses conseillers lui avaient soigneusement fait répété ce qu'elle devait dire **(b)** (*list*) (*complaints, arguments etc*) répéter, rabâcher **2** *vi* (*of actor, musician etc*) répéter
reheat [riː'hiːt] *vti* réchauffer
rehouse [riː'haʊz] *vt* reloger
rehousing [riː'haʊzɪŋ] *n* relogement *m*
rehydration [riːhaɪ'dreɪʃən] *n Med* réhydratation *f*
reign[1] [reɪn] *n* (*of monarch, champion etc*) règne *m*; **in** *or* **during the r. of ...** sous le règne de ...; **r. of terror** règne de la terreur; **their r. of terror/violence is at an end** la terreur/violence qu'ils faisaient régner a pris fin
reign[2] *vi* (*of monarch, champion, silence etc*) régner; **to r. supreme** (*of monarch*) régner en maître absolu; (*of champion*) être inégalé *ou* sans rival; **to r. for ten years** régner (pendant) dix ans; **silence reigned** le silence régnait; **it's the usual situation in the office: chaos reigns** c'est comme d'habitude au bureau: il y règne le plus grand chaos
▶ **reign over** *vipo* (*of monarch, silence etc*) régner sur
reigning ['reɪnɪŋ] *adj* (*monarch*) régnant; (*champion*) en titre
reimburse [riːɪm'bɜːs] *vt* (*money*) rembourser; **to r. sb (for) sth** rembourser qn de qch
reimbursement [riːɪm'bɜːsmənt] *n* (*of money, person*) remboursement *m*
reimport [riːɪm'pɔːt] *vt* réimporter
reimportation [riːɪmpɔː'teɪʃən] *n* réimportation *f*
reimpose [riːɪm'pəʊz] *vt* réimposer
rein [reɪn] *n* (*for rider, on child*) rêne *f*; (*for coachman*) guide *f*; **to pull at** *or* **on the reins** (*of horse, rider*) tirer sur les rênes; **the reins of power** les rênes du pouvoir; *Fig* **to assume** *or* **take over/hold the reins of government** prendre/tenir les rênes du gouvernement; *Fig* **to hand over the reins** (*of politician, businessman etc*) passer les rênes du pouvoir **(to** à); **to give a horse the reins** *or* **free r.** lâcher les rênes *ou* la bride à un cheval; *Fig* **to give sb a free r. (to do sth)** donner carte blanche à qn (pour faire qch); *Fig* **to give free r. to one's imagination** donner libre cours à son imagination; *Fig* **to keep a tight r. on** *or* **over sb** tenir la bride haute à qn; *Fig* **to keep a tight r. on one's spending** surveiller étroitement ses dépenses; *Fig* **to keep a tight r. on one's emotions** ne pas se laisser aller à ses émotions, maîtriser ses émotions; *Fig* **to keep a tight r. on one's imagination** ne pas se laisser emporter par son imagination
▶ **rein back 1** *vtsep* (*horse*) faire arrêter **2** *vi* (*of rider*) faire arrêter son cheval
▶ **rein in 1** *vtsep* (*horse*) serrer la bride *ou* les rênes à; *Fig* (*enthusiasm, emotions, feelings*) modérer; *Fig* **to r. sb in** (*of person in authority*) serrer la bride *ou* la vis à qn; (*of colleague, friend*) faire se modérer; **to r. in one's spending** mettre un frein à *ou* modérer ses dépenses **2** *vi* (*of rider*) ramener son cheval au pas
reincarnate[1] [riːɪn'kɑːnɪt, -eɪt] *adj* réincarné
reincarnate[2] [riː'ɪnkɑːneɪt] *vt* **to be reincarnated** se réincarner (**as** sous les traits de, sous la forme de)
reincarnation [riːɪnkɑː'neɪʃən] *n* réincarnation *f*
reindeer ['reɪndɪər] *n* renne *m*; **r. moss** *or* **lichen** cladonie *f*
reinforce [riːɪn'fɔːs] *vt* (*army, wall, fabric*) renforcer; (*foundations*) consolider; (*concrete, glass*) armer; *Fig* (*argument*) étayer (**with** avec); (*prejudices*) renforcer; (*request*) appuyer (**with** avec); **that just reinforces what I've been saying** ça ne fait que renforcer ce que j'ai dit
reinforcement [riːɪn'fɔːsmənt] *n* **(a)** (*action*) (*of army, wall, fabric*) renforcement *m*; (*of foundations*) consolidation *f*; (*of concrete, glass*) armature *f* **(b)** (*troops etc*) **reinforcements** renforts *mpl*; **to await reinforcements** attendre un renfort *ou* des renforts; **to call up reinforcements** demander des renforts
reinitialize [riːɪ'nɪʃəlaɪz] *vt Comptr* réinitialiser
reinsert [riːɪn'sɜːt] *vt* (*advert, coin, clause*) réinsérer
reinstall [riːɪn'stɔːl] *vt Comptr* réinstaller
reinstallation [riːɪnstə'leɪʃən] *n Comptr* réinstallation
reinstate [riːɪn'steɪt] *vt* (*person*) réintégrer, rétablir (dans ses fonctions); (*clause etc*) réintroduire
reinstatement [riːɪn'steɪtmənt] *n* (*of person*) réintégration *f*, rétablissement *m* (**as** en tant que, au poste de); (*of clause etc*) réintroduction *f*
reinstitute [riː'ɪnstɪtjuːt] *vt* réintroduire
reinstitution [riːɪnstɪ'tjuːʃən] *n* réintroduction *f*
reinsurance [riːɪn'ʃʊərəns, -'ʃɔːr-] *n* réassurance *f*
reinsure [riːɪn'ʃʊər, -'ʃɔːr] *vt* réassurer
reinsurer [riːɪn'ʃʊərər, -'ʃɔːr-] *n* réassureur *m*
reintegrate [riː'ɪntɪgreɪt] *vt* (*into society etc*) réinsérer
reintegration [riːɪntɪ'greɪʃən] *n* réinsertion *f*
reinterpret [riːɪn'tɜːprɪt] *vt* réinterpréter
reinterpretation [riːɪntɜːprɪ'teɪʃən] *n* réinterprétation *f*
reintroduce [riːɪntrə'djuːs] *vt* réintroduire
reintroduction [riːɪntrə'dʌkʃən] *n* réintroduction *f*
reinvest [riːɪn'vest] *vt* réinvestir
reinvestment [riːɪn'vestmənt] *n Fin* nouveau placement *m*, réinvestissement *m*
reinvigorate [riːɪn'vɪgəreɪt] *vt* (*usu passive*) revigorer
reissue[1] [riː'ɪʃuː] *n* (*of book*) réédition *f*; (*of bank note etc*) nouvelle émission *f*
reissue[2] *vt* (*book*) rééditer; (*bank note etc*) émettre de nouveau
reiterate [riː'ɪtəreɪt] *vt* (*request, promise etc*) réitérer
reiteration [riːɪtə'reɪʃən] *n* réitération *f*
reiterative [riː'ɪtərətɪv] *adj* réitératif
reject[1] ['riːdʒekt] *n Com* (*object*) article *m* de rebut, rebut *m*; *Fig* (*for job*) candidat *m* refusé *ou* qui a échoué; *F* **he's a bit of a (social) r.!** il n'est pas sortable!; *Fig* **I'm not going out with one of your rejects!** (*former boyfriend or girlfriend*) ne crois pas que je vais sortir avec un/une de tes ex!; **export rejects** marchandises *fpl* impropres à l'exportation; **r. china/***etc* (*useless*) porcelaine/*etc f* de rebut; (*imperfect*) porcelaine/*etc* de deuxième choix; **r. shop** magasin *m* d'articles de deuxième choix
reject[2] [rɪ'dʒekt] *vt* (*refuse*) (*advice, offer, proposal*) rejeter, repousser; (*doctrine*) réprouver; (*goods, manuscript, applicant*) refuser; (*suitor*) éconduire; (*of animal, parent*) (*young, child*) rejeter; **to feel rejected** se sentir rejeté; **to r. one's food** (*not want*) refuser la nourriture; *Med* (*vomit*) rendre la nourriture; *Ind* **to r. a part** mettre une pièce au rebut; *Med* **to r. a transplant** rejeter un greffon; **the machine keeps rejecting this coin** pas moyen que la machine accepte cette *ou* ma pièce
rejection [rɪ'dʒekʃən] *n* (*of offer, suggestion, transplant*) rejet *m*; (*of applicant, goods, manuscript*) refus *m*; *Med* (*of food*) (*by stomach*) régurgitation *f*; **to meet with r.** (*of applicant etc*) essuyer un refus; (*of offer, suggestion*) être rejeté; **letter of r., r. letter** lettre *f* de refus; **r. slip** note *f* refusant un manuscrit
rejig [riː'dʒɪg] *vt* **(-gg-) (a)** *F* (*rearrange*) (*text etc*) remanier **(b)** (*re-equip*) (*factory*) réaménager
rejoice [rɪ'dʒɔɪs] *vi* se réjouir (**at, over** de; **in doing** de faire); **to r. in one's freedom/independence** jouir de sa liberté/son indépendance; **we r. to hear that you are safe** nous sommes ravis d'apprendre que vous êtes sain et sauf; *Hum Iron* **he rejoiced in the name of Winterbottom** il répondait au nom délicieux de Winterbottom
rejoicing [rɪ'dʒɔɪsɪŋ] *n* **(a)** (*joy*) réjouissance *f*, allégresse *f* (**at, over** à); **there was much r. at the announcement** la nouvelle a suscité une très grande joie; **it was an occasion**

for general r. ce fut la grande liesse *ou* la liesse générale **(b)** **rejoicings** (*festivities*) réjouissances *fpl*, festivités *fpl*; **there were great rejoicings on the day of the Coronation** il y a eu de grandes réjouissances le jour du couronnement

rejoin[1] [rɪˈdʒɔɪn] *vti* (*retort*) répliquer

rejoin[2] [riːˈdʒɔɪn] **1** *vt* **(a)** (*attach*) rejoindre, réunir (**to** à) **(b)** (*return to*) (*person*) rejoindre, retrouver; *Mil* (*unit, regiment*) rallier, rejoindre; **to r. one's ship** rallier le bord; **to r. a political party** se réinscrire à un parti politique **2** *vi* (*of roads, lines etc*) se rejoindre

rejoinder [rɪˈdʒɔɪndər] *n* (*retort*) réplique *f*; **sharp r.** riposte *f*

rejuvenate [rɪˈdʒuːvɪneɪt] *vt* (*person*) rajeunir; **I feel rejuvenated after a week off** je me sens rajeuni *ou* revigoré *ou F* requinqué après une semaine de vacances; *Fig* **to r. the economy** donner un coup de fouet à l'économie

rejuvenating [rɪˈdʒuːvɪneɪtɪŋ] *adj* rajeunissant

rejuvenation [rɪdʒuːvɪˈneɪʃən] *n* rajeunissement *m*

rekey [riːˈkiː] *vt Comptr* refrapper

rekeying [riːˈkiːɪŋ] *n Comptr* refrappe *f*

rekindle [riːˈkɪnd(ə)l] **1** *vt* (*fire*) rallumer; *Fig* (*enthusiasm, hope*) ranimer, raviver; (*hatred*) ranimer, raviver, rallumer; *Fig* **a romantic dinner to r. the flame** *or* **spark** un dîner en amoureux pour ranimer la flamme **2** *vi* se rallumer

relapse[1] [rɪˈlæps] *n Med* rechute *f*; **to have** *or* **suffer a r.** avoir *ou* faire une rechute, rechuter; **his r. into alcoholism came as no surprise** le fait qu'il soit retombé dans l'alcoolisme n'a surpris personne

relapse[2] *vi Med* avoir *ou* faire une rechute, rechuter; **to r. into unconsciousness** reperdre connaissance; *Fig* **to r. into alcoholism** retomber dans l'alcoolisme

relate [rɪˈleɪt] **1** *vt* **(a)** (*narrate*) (*story etc*) raconter, *Fml* conter; (*one's adventures*) faire le récit de; **strange to r. …** chose étonnante à dire …

(b) (*connect*) (*two facts*) établir un rapport entre; **to r. sth to sth** (*link*) rattacher qch à qch

2 *vi* **(a)** (*of question etc*) se rapporter, avoir rapport, avoir trait (**to** à); **agreement relating to …** convention ayant trait à …

(b) (*of person*) **he finds it difficult to r., he can't r. (to others)** il lui est difficile de communiquer avec les autres; **I can't r. to modern music** je n'arrive pas à apprécier la musique moderne; **I don't r. to my home town any more** je ne me sens plus d'attaches avec ma ville natale

related [rɪˈleɪtɪd] *adj* **(a)** (*languages, styles*) apparenté; **the cost of the project is directly r. to …** le coût du projet est directement lié à …; **questions r. to a subject** questions relatives à un sujet; **the two events are r.** les deux événements sont liés; **closely r. species** espèces *fpl* voisines; **r. activity** activité *f* annexe; **r. ideas** idées *fpl* connexes

(b) (*people*) apparenté (**to** à); (*by blood*) parent (**to** de); (*by marriage*) parent par alliance (**to** à); **are you two r.?** êtes-vous apparentés *ou* parents *ou* de la même famille?; **we are not really r., I just call her 'auntie'** nous ne sommes pas parents *ou* de la même famille, je l'appelle juste Tatie comme ça; **we're r. by marriage** nous sommes parents par alliance; **he is closely/distantly r. to me** nous sommes proches parents/parents éloignés

-related [rɪˈleɪtɪd] *suff* **space-/industry-r.** lié à l'espace/l'industrie

relating [rɪˈleɪtɪŋ] *adj* **r. to** (*about*) relatif à, qui se rapporte à; *Admin, Jur* afférent à

relation [rɪˈleɪʃən] *n* **(a)** (*relative*) parent, -ente; **r. by marriage** parent, -ente par alliance; **what r. is he to you?** quel est son lien de parenté avec vous?; **are you any r. to …?** avez-vous un lien de parenté avec …?; **he's no r. to me** *or* **of mine** il n'est pas de ma famille; **she is my closest living r.** c'est la plus proche parente qui me reste; **I have relations in Montreal** j'ai de la famille à Montréal; **we've invited all the relations** nous avons invité toute la famille

(b) (*connection, relationship*) relation *f*, rapport *m* (**between** entre, **with** avec); **in** *or* **with r. to** relativement à, par rapport à; **to bear no r. to** n'avoir aucun rapport avec; **to bear little r. to** avoir peu de rapport avec; **relations between us are rather strained** nos relations sont plutôt tendues; **to have** *or* **enjoy friendly relations** entretenir des relations amicales *ou* des rapports amicaux (**with** avec); **how are relations between you?** comment est-ce que vous vous entendez?; **to enter into relations with sb** entrer *ou* se mettre en rapport *ou* en relations avec qn; **to break off all relations with sb** rompre toute relation *ou* cesser tout rapport avec qn; *Fml* **to have (sexual) relations** avoir des rapports sexuels (**with** avec)

(c) (*telling*) (*of adventures, story etc*) relation *f*, récit *m*

relational [rɪˈleɪʃən(ə)l] *adj Comptr* **r. database** base *f* de données relationnelle; **r. operator** opérateur *m* relationnel

relationship [rɪˈleɪʃənʃɪp] *n* **(a)** (*relations*) rapports *mpl*; (*sexual*) liaison *f*; **to have a love-hate r. with sb/sth** avoir avec qn/qch des relations *ou* des rapports dans laquel(le)s se mêlent l'amour et la haine; **she has a good r. with her mother-in-law** elle s'entend bien avec sa belle-mère; **she's been trying to get out of the r. for months** elle essaye de rompre depuis des mois; **our r. is going nowhere** notre relation ne nous mène nulle part; **patient-doctor r.** rapports patient-médecin *ou* entre le patient et le médecin; **to have a r.** (*affair*) avoir une liaison (**with** avec); **I'm already in a r.** j'ai déjà quelqu'un, je suis déjà avec quelqu'un; **he finds it difficult to have relationships with people** ça lui est difficile d'avoir des relations *ou* des rapports avec les autres; **our r. is purely professional** nos rapports *ou* relations sont purement professionnel(le)s; **what exactly is your r. with her?** quelle est la nature de *ou* quels sont vos rapports *ou* relations avec elle?

(b) (*kinship*) (*between people of same family*) lien(s) *m(pl)* de parenté; (*by marriage*) parenté *f* par alliance; (*between languages, styles etc*) parenté; **family r.** lien de parenté; **blood r.** parenté, (degré *m* de) consanguinité *f*; **what was your r. to the deceased?** quel était votre lien de parenté avec le défunt?

(c) (*connection*) (*between things*) rapport *m*, relation *f* (**between … and** entre … et); **in r. to** relativement à; *Mktg* **r. marketing** mercatique *f* relationelle

relative [ˈrelətɪv] **1** *adj* relatif; **r. to** (*compared to*) relativement à, comparé à; (*in terms of*) en fonction de, par rapport à **2** *n* **(a)** (*person*) parent, -ente; **r. by marriage** parent, -ente par alliance; **he's no r. of mine** il n'est pas de ma famille; **she is my closest living r.** c'est la plus proche parente qui me reste; **I have relatives in Montreal** j'ai de la famille à Montréal; **we've invited all the relatives** nous avons invité toute la famille **(b)** *Phil* **the r.** le relatif

relative clause *n* [①A32-33; B20-22, F] *Gram* (proposition *f*) relative *f*

relatively [ˈrelətɪvlɪ] *adv* (*fairly*) relativement, assez; **r. few people were there** il y avait assez *ou* relativement peu de gens; **r. speaking** relativement parlant

relative pronoun *n* [①A32-33; B20-22, F] *Gram* (pronom *m*) relatif *m*

relativism [ˈrelətɪvɪz(ə)m] *n Phil* relativisme *m*

relativistic [relətɪˈvɪstɪk] *adj* relativiste

relativity [reləˈtɪvɪtɪ] *n* relativité *f*; **r. theory, theory of r.** théorie *f* de la relativité

relaunch[1] [ˈriːlɔːntʃ] *n* relancement *m*

relaunch[2] [riˈlɔːntʃ] *vt Mktg* relancer

relax [rɪˈlæks] **1** *vt* **(a)** (*person*) (*of bath, meditation etc*) (*physically*) détendre, délasser, relaxer; (*mentally*) détendre, relaxer

(b) (*loosen*) (*muscles*) relâcher, décontracter, relaxer; (*discipline*) relâcher; (*policy, law*) assouplir; **to r. one's hold** *or* **grip** desserrer son étreinte; *Fig* **to r. one's grip on** relâcher son emprise sur; **to r. one's efforts** relâcher ses efforts

2 *vi* **(a)** (*of person*) (*physically*) se détendre, se délasser, se relaxer; (*mentally*) se détendre, se relaxer; **r.!** (*calm down*) du calme!; **r.!, I'm not going to hurt you** détends-toi, je ne vais pas te faire mal

(b) (*of muscles*) se relâcher, se détendre

relaxant [rɪˈlæks(ə)nt] *n* (*drug, drink etc*) relaxant *m*; *Med* **muscle r.** myorelaxant *m*, décontracturant *m*

relaxation [riːlækˈseɪʃən] *n* **(a)** (*of person*) (*physical*) détente *f*, délassement *m*, relaxation *f*; (*mental*) détente, relaxation; **fishing is his only r.** la pêche est sa seule détente; **she finds r. in reading** elle se détend en lisant; **reading is one of my favourite forms of r.** lire est une de mes façons préférées de me détendre; **r. therapy** thérapie *f* par la relaxation **(b)** (*of muscles*) décontraction *f*, relaxation *f*; (*of discipline*) relâchement *m*; (*of policy, law*) assouplissement *m*

relaxed [rɪˈlækst] *adj* (*atmosphere, person*) décontracté, détendu, *F* relax *inv*; **she takes a very r. approach** *or* **is very r. in her approach to bringing up her children** elle élève ses enfants de façon très décontractée

relaxing [rɪˈlæksɪŋ] *adj* (*climate, medication*) relaxant; **a very r. day** une vraie journée de détente; **a r. place for a holiday** un endroit tranquille pour passer des vacances

relay[1] [ˈriːleɪ] *n* **(a)** (*of people, horses*) relais *m*; (*of workers*) relève *f*; **in relays** (*to eat, work etc*) par roulement; **they worked in r. all night to put out the fire** ils se sont relayés toute la nuit pour éteindre l'incendie; **they were organized into relays** ils étaient répartis en équipes et ils se relayaient **(b)** *Sp* **r. (race)** course *f* de relais **(c)** *El, Electron, Tel* relais *m*; *Rad, TV* (*broadcasting*) retransmission *f*, radiodiffusion *f* relayée; (*broadcast*) retransmission, émission *f* retransmise;

r. station station *f ou* émetteur *m* relais, centre-répéteur *m*; **r. transmitter** réémetteur *m*

relay² [rɪ'leɪ, riː-] *vt* (*pt, pp* **relayed**) *El, Tel, Rad etc* (*telephone message, broadcast etc*) relayer; **to r. information to sb** transmettre des informations à qn

re-lay [riː'leɪ] *vt* (*carpet, tiles etc*) reposer

release¹ [rɪ'liːs] *n* **(a)** (*of hostage, prisoner*) libération *f*; (*from care, worry*) délivrance *f*, libération (**from** de); (*from obligation, responsibility*) décharge *f*, libération (**from** de); **it was a merciful r.** (*when he or she died*) ça a été une véritable délivrance; *Jur* **order of r.** (ordre *m* de) levée *f* d'écrou; *Jur* **r. on bail** mise *f* en liberté sous caution; *Br* **day r.** = jour *m* de liberté accordé aux employés d'une entreprise pour faire un stage de formation

(b) (*of bomb*) largage *m*; (*of balloons, pigeons*) lâcher *m*; (*of gas etc*) dégagement *m*; (*of steam*) échappement *m*; (*of pressure*) relâchement *m*; *Phys* (*of energy*) libération *f*; (*of spring*) détente *f*; (*of mechanism*) déclenchement *m*; (*of clutch*) débrayage *m*; *Phot* (**shutter**) **r.** (*action*) déclenchement; (*mechanism*) déclencheur *m*; *Aut* **r. lever** (*on clutch*) levier *m* de débrayage; **r.** (**lever**) (*on typewriter*) levier *ou* touche *f* de dégagement du chariot; **r. of funds** dégagement *m ou* déblocage *m* de fonds; **r. of goods** (*from warehouse*) libération de marchandises

(c) (*of book, record etc*) sortie *f*, mise *f* en vente; (*of film*) sortie; (*of document*) diffusion *f*; (*of computer software*) version *f*; (**press**) **r.** communiqué *m* de presse; **is the film on general r.?** est-ce que le film passe dans les salles?; **latest r.** (*record*) dernier disque *m*; (*film*) dernier film *m*

release² *vt* **(a)** (*liberate*) (*hostage, prisoner*) libérer; (*patient*) (*from hospital*) laisser sortir (**from** de); (*from work*) libérer; **to r. a debtor** libérer un débiteur; **to r. sb from his** *or* **her promise** délier qn de sa promesse; **to r. sb from a duty** dispenser qn d'une corvée; *Jur* **released on bail** remis en liberté sous caution

(b) (*let go*) (*balloon, carrier pigeon*) lâcher; (*bomb*) lâcher, larguer; **to r. sb's hand** lâcher la main de qn; **to r. one's hold** desserrer son étreinte, lâcher prise; **playing squash is a good way of releasing tension** le squash est un bon moyen de se détendre

(c) (*emit*) (*gas*) dégager, laisser échapper; (*fumes etc*) émettre; **to be released** (*of energy etc*) se libérer

(d) (*unblock*) (*jammed part etc*) dégager; (*spring*) détendre; (*brake*) desserrer; *Fin* (*funds*) débloquer, dégager; *Phot* (*shutter*) déclencher; **to r. the safety catch** (*on gun*) libérer le cran de sûreté; *Aut* **to r. the clutch** débrayer

(e) (*make available*) (*book, record etc*) sortir, mettre en vente; (*film*) sortir; (*news*) rendre public; (*document*) diffuser

relegate ['relɪgeɪt] *vt* (*downgrade*) reléguer (**to** à); *Fb* **to r. a team** (**to the next division**) reléguer une équipe en division inférieure; *Fig* **we relegated the old bed to the spare room** on a relégué le vieux lit dans la chambre d'amis

relegation [relɪ'geɪʃən] *n* (*of person etc*) relégation *f* (**to** à); (*of soccer club*) relégation en division inférieure; **the r. struggle** la lutte pour rester dans la division supérieure

relent [rɪ'lent] *vi* (*of person*) s'adoucir, se radoucir; (*as result of argument, persuasion*) fléchir, se laisser amadouer; (*of storm, wind, rain*) diminuer de violence, se calmer

relentless [rɪ'lentlɪs] *adj* (*person*) implacable, inflexible, intransigeant; (*hatred*) implacable; (*persecution, pain etc*) sans rémission; (*criticism*) incessant, constant; **to be r. in doing sth** mettre de l'acharnement à faire qch

relentlessly [rɪ'lentlɪslɪ] *adv* (*to beat etc*) implacablement; (*to continue, persecute etc*) sans rémission, avec acharnement; (*to argue*) continuellement, sans arrêt; (*to blow, rain*) sans interruption, continuellement

relet [riː'let] *vt* (*house etc*) relouer

relevance ['reləvəns,], **relevancy** ['reləvənsɪ] *n* **(a)** (*aptness*) (*of facts, remarks etc*) pertinence *f*; **to have** *or* **bear some r.** avoir un rapport (**to** avec); **I don't see what r. his remarks have to the situation** je ne vois pas le rapport entre ses remarques et la situation; **what r. does that have to anything?** quel rapport est-ce que ça a?

(b) (*significance*) intérêt *m*; **Latin no longer has any r. in the school curriculum** le latin ne sert plus à rien dans les programmes scolaires; **Shakespeare's plays are still full of r.** les pièces de Shakespeare sont toujours d'actualité; **whether I happen to agree or not is of no r.** (*makes no difference*) mon avis n'a aucune importance

relevant ['reləvənt] *adj* **(a)** (*apt*) (*fact, detail etc*) pertinent; **r. to** qui a un rapport avec; **to be r.** (**to sth**) avoir un rapport (avec qch); **that's not r.** ça n'a rien à voir (**to** avec); **opinions are not r.** ce n'est pas une question d'opinions; **that's hardly r.** ça n'a pas grand intérêt; **that's hardly r. to the discussion** ça n'a pas grand-chose à voir avec la discussion

(b) (*appropriate, proper*) approprié; **you should report the matter to the r. department** vous devriez en référer au service compétent; **the r. documents** les documents qui se rapportent à l'affaire; *Jur* les pièces justificatives; **to refer sb to the r. chapter of a book** renvoyer qn au chapitre correspondant; **she did not have the r. experience for the job** elle n'avait pas l'expérience requise pour le poste

(c) (*significant*) important; (*useful*) utile; **is a knowledge of Latin r. to employers?** est-ce que la connaissance du latin a encore un intérêt quelconque pour les chefs d'entreprise?; **all r. information** tous renseignements utiles; **to be highly r.** (*of experience, qualifications*) être très utile (**for** pour); **to be/remain r.** (*of book, play, idea, ideology etc*) être/rester d'actualité

reliability [rɪlaɪə'bɪlɪtɪ] *n* (*of person, firm etc*) sérieux *m*; (*of information*) sérieux, sûreté *f*; (*of source, testimony*) sûreté; (*of device, machine, car*) fiabilité *f*; **I'm not altogether sure about the r. of our witnesses** je ne suis pas vraiment sûr qu'on puisse faire confiance à nos témoins

reliable [rɪ'laɪəb(ə)l] *adj* (*firm*) sérieux; (*information*) sérieux, sûr; (*person*) fiable, sur qui on peut compter; (*source, testimony*) sûr; (*car, machine etc*) fiable; **to have sth from a r. source** *or* **on r. evidence** tenir qch de source sûre; **my memory isn't r.** je n'ai pas bonne mémoire; **the weather is not very r.** on ne peut pas se fier au temps

reliably [rɪ'laɪəblɪ] *adv* (*to operate, perform etc*) de façon fiable; **to be r. informed that ...** savoir de source sûre que ... *+ ind*

reliance [rɪ'laɪəns] *n* **(a)** (*dependence*) dépendance *f* (**on** à); **r. on alcohol** dépendance à l'alcool; **because of the country's r. on the arms industry** parce que l'économie du pays dépend de l'industrie de l'armement **(b)** (*trust*) confiance *f*; **to place r. in** *or* **on sb/sth** se fier à qn/qch

reliant [rɪ'laɪənt] *adj* **to be r. on** (*dependent on*) dépendre de (**for** pour)

relic ['relɪk] *n* **(a)** (*reminder of past, remnant*) vestige *m*; **the last surviving r. of** les derniers vestiges de; **relics of the past** vestiges du passé; *Hum* **their old r. of a car** leur vieille bagnole toute pourrie; *Lit* **relics** (*corpse*) dépouille *f* mortelle **(b)** *Rel* relique *f*

relief [rɪ'liːf] *n* **(a)** (*from pain, anxiety, poverty etc*) soulagement *m* (**from** de); **to bring r. to sb** apporter du soulagement à qn; **that's** *or* **what a r.!** quel soulagement!; **for the r. of pain** (*of pills etc*) pour soulager la douleur; **to my great r., much to my r.** à mon grand soulagement; **to feel r.** se sentir soulagé, ressentir du soulagement (**at** à; **about, over** à propos de); **his feelings of r. were short-lived** son soulagement a été de courte durée; **you can imagine my r.** *or* **the r. that I felt** tu peux imaginer mon soulagement; **to provide light** *or* **comic r.** détendre l'atmosphère, introduire une note comique; **by way of light r.** pour se détendre un peu

(b) (*help*) secours *m*, assistance *f*, aide *f*; *Am* **to be on r.** recevoir une aide sociale; **disaster/famine r.** secours *ou* assistance *ou* aide aux victimes d'un désastre/d'une famine; **tax r.** dégrèvement *m* fiscal; **r. official** responsable *mf* d'un organisme d'aide humanitaire

(c) (*replacement*) personne *f* qui assure la relève, remplaçant, -ante; **my r. didn't show up** mon remplaçant/ma remplaçante ne s'est pas présenté(e); **r. staff** (*cover staff*) personnel *m* extra; **r. train** train *m* supplémentaire; **r. troops** la relève

(d) (*liberation*) (*of city etc*) libération *f*

(e) *Art* relief *m*, modelé *m*; **printed in r.** imprimé en relief; **to stand out in r.** ressortir, se détacher (**against** sur); **to stand out in bold** *or* **sharp r.** ressortir *ou* se détacher nettement; **to bring** *or* **throw sth into r.** faire ressortir qch; *Art* **high/low r.** haut/bas-relief

(f) *Geog* relief *m* (terrestre); **an area of low r.** une zone au relief peu élevé

relief agency *n* organisme *m* d'aide humanitaire

relief driver *n* chauffeur *m* qui assure la relève

relief fund *n* caisse *f* de secours

relief map *n* (*two-dimensional*) carte *f* topographique; (*three-dimensional*) carte en relief

relief road *n Br Aut* route *f* de délestage

relief valve *n* soupape *f* de sûreté, clapet *m* de décharge

relief work *n* aide *f* humanitaire

relief worker *n* employé(e) d'un organisme humanitaire; (*after disaster*) secouriste *mf*; *Admin* suppléant, -ante

relieve [rɪ'liːv] *vt* **(a)** (*alleviate*) (*pain, anxiety, poverty*) soulager; (*boredom*) tromper; (*the situation*) remédier à; (*pressure*) réduire; **to do sth to r. the boredom** faire qch pour tromper l'ennui; **to r. oneself** (*urinate*) se soulager; **black dress relieved by** *or* **with white lace** robe noire agrémentée de dentelle blanche; **to r. the monotony we went for a walk** pour nous changer les idées nous sommes allés nous promener; *Aut, Med* **to r. congestion in** décongestionner

(**b**) (*replace*) (*person*) remplacer, relayer; *Mil, Naut* (*the guard, watch*) relever

(**c**) (*liberate*) *Mil* (*city*) libérer; (*person*) (*from obligation*) dégager, affranchir (**from** de); **to r. sb of a burden** soulager qn d'un fardeau; **to r. sb of their coat** débarrasser qn de son manteau; **to r. sb of their duties** relever qn de ses fonctions; *F Hum* **to r. sb of sth** (*steal*) soulager qn de qch

relieved [rɪ'liːvd] *adj* soulagé; **I'm very r. to hear it** je suis très soulagé de l'apprendre, c'est un grand soulagement pour moi de l'apprendre; **to feel r.** se sentir soulagé; **to be r. at the news** être soulagé en apprenant la nouvelle

religion [rɪ'lɪdʒən] *n* religion *f*; (*Catholic, Protestant*) religion, culte *m*; (*heading on form*) confession *f*; *F Pej* **to get r.** attraper le virus de la religion; **it's against my r. to work on Sundays** c'est contraire à ma religion de travailler le dimanche; *Hum* **it's against his r. to do the washing-up!** c'est contraire à sa religion de faire la vaisselle!; *Fig* **to make a r. of (doing) sth** se faire une obligation de (faire) qch; *Fig* **football is a r. with some people** le football est une religion pour certains

religiosity [rɪlɪdʒɪ'ɒsɪtɪ] *n Pej* religiosité *f*

religious [rɪ'lɪdʒəs] **1** *adj* (*person*) pieux, croyant; (*fanatic, order, service, leader, life*) religieux; (*war, book*) de religion; *Fig* (*care*) méticuleux; *Fig* **his r. attendance at every football match** sa fréquentation scrupuleuse de tous les matches de football; *Fig* **to be r. about doing sth** faire qch avec un soin méticuleux; **r. beliefs** croyances *fpl* religieuses; **r. education** *or* **instruction** instruction *f* religieuse; **r. persuasion** confession *f*; **r. programme** programme *m* à caractère religieux **2** *n inv Rel* religieux, -ieuse

religiously [rɪ'lɪdʒəslɪ] *adv* (*to behave, act*) religieusement, pieusement; *Fig* (*to attend, obey*) religieusement, scrupuleusement

religiousness [rɪ'lɪdʒəsnɪs] *n* (*of person*) piété *f*, dévotion *f*; (*of music, art*) caractère *m* religieux; *Fig* (*of attendance, obedience*) caractère *m* scrupuleux; (*in carrying out task*) extrême méticulosité *f*

reline [riː'laɪn] *vt* (*coat*) remettre une doublure à; *Aut* **to r. the brakes** changer les garnitures de freins

relinquish [rɪ'lɪŋkwɪʃ] *vt* (*give up*) (*habit, hope*) abandonner; (*plan, right, inheritance*) renoncer à; **to r. all thoughts of doing sth** abandonner toute pensée de faire qch; **to r. (one's hold on) sth** (*let go*) lâcher qch, renoncer à qch; **to r. one's hold on one's children** laisser partir ses enfants; **her mind was beginning to r. its hold on reality** elle commençait à perdre le sens de la réalité

relinquishment [rɪ'lɪŋkwɪʃmənt] *n Fml* (*of hope etc*) abandon *m* (**of** de); (*of right etc*) renonciation *f* (**of** à)

reliquary ['relɪkwərɪ] *n Rel* reliquaire *m*

relish¹ ['relɪʃ] *n* (**a**) (*liking, taste*) goût *m* (**for** pour); **to eat sth with r.** manger qch de bon appétit, savourer qch (**b**) (*pleasure*) plaisir *m*; **danger gives r. to an adventure** le danger donne du piquant à une aventure; **he used to tell the story with great r.** il se délectait à raconter cette histoire; **..., she said with great r.** ... dit-elle avec délectation (**c**) *Culin* (*pickle*) = condiments *mpl*, pickles *mpl*, *Can* achar *m*

relish² *vt* (*enjoy*) apprécier; (*dish*) goûter, savourer; *Fig* (*victory, moment*) savourer; **to r. doing sth** trouver du plaisir à *ou* aimer faire qch; **I didn't r. the prospect** cette perspective ne me disait rien; **I didn't r. the prospect/thought/idea of telling her** j'appréhendais de le lui dire; **we didn't r. the idea** l'idée ne nous souriait pas

relive [riː'lɪv] *vt* (*one's life, the past*) revivre

reload [riː'ləʊd] **1** *vt* (*ship, camera, rifle, software etc*) recharger **2** *vi* (*of ship, photographer etc*) recharger; (*of gun, software*) se recharger

relocate [riːləʊ'keɪt] **1** *vt* (*move*) (*factory, company*) réimplanter, déménager **2** *vi* (*of person, shop*) déménager; (*of company*) se réimplanter, déménager; **the firm is relocating out of Glasgow** la société se réimplante hors de Glasgow

relocation [riːləʊ'keɪʃən] *n* (*of person, shop*) déménagement *m*; (*of company*) réimplantation *f*; **r. allowance** allocation *f* de déménagement; **r. assistance** (*from employer*) contribution *f* aux frais de déménagement; **r. expenses** (*of employee*) frais *mpl* de déménagement

reluctance [rɪ'lʌktəns] *n* (*unwillingness*) réticence *f*; (*strong*) répugnance *f*; **to do sth with a show of r.** faire qch avec une réticence feinte; **to show (some) r. to do sth** se montrer peu disposé *ou* empressé à faire qch; **to do sth with r.** faire qch à regret *ou* à contrecœur

reluctant [rɪ'lʌktənt] *adj* (*consent, greeting, promise etc*) accordé à contrecœur; **to be r. to do sth** hésiter *ou* être peu disposé *ou* peu empressé à faire qch; **to feel r.** hésiter, éprouver de la répugnance (**to do** à faire); **a r. teacher** un professeur malgré lui; **I was a r. witness of their quarrel** j'étais le témoin involontaire de leur querelle

reluctantly [rɪ'lʌktəntlɪ] *adv* (*to consent, greet, promise etc*) avec répugnance, à contrecœur; **I say it r.** il m'en coûte de le dire

▶ **rely on, rely upon** [rɪ'laɪ] *vipo* (**a**) (*count on*) (*person's help, discretion*); *Iron* (*sb to be late etc*) compter sur; (*have confidence in*) (*person, judgment etc*) avoir confiance en; **I'm relying on it** j'y compte (bien); **it's a car you can r. on** c'est une voiture fiable; **he's a lawyer you can r. on** c'est un avocat sur lequel on peut compter; **we can't r. on the weather** on ne peut jamais savoir quel temps il va faire (**b**) (*be dependent on*) (*person*) dépendre de (**for sth** pour qch)

REM [ɑːriː'em] (*abbr* **rapid eye movement**) sommeil *m* paradoxal, phase *f* de mouvements oculaires

remain [rɪ'meɪn] *vi* (**a**) (*stay behind*) rester

(**b**) (*continue to be*) (*of doubts*) rester, subsister; **to r. silent** garder le silence; **to r. faithful to sb/sth** rester fidèle à qn/qch; **please r. in your seats** veuillez rester assis; **let it r. as it is** laissez-le comme cela; **one thing remains certain** une chose demeure certaine; **to r. a problem** demeurer un problème; **to r. the same** demeurer inchangé; **the crime remains unsolved** le crime n'a toujours pas été élucidé; **the fact remains that ...** il n'en est pas moins vrai que ..., toujours est-il que ...; *Old-fashioned Br* **I r., Sir, yours truly** (*at end of letter*) veuillez agréer, Monsieur, l'expression de mes sentiments distingués

(**c**) (*be left*) rester, subsister; **all that remains of ...** tout ce qui reste *ou* subsiste de ...; **much yet remains to be done** il reste encore beaucoup à faire; **it (only) remains for me to ...** il ne me reste qu'à ..., je n'ai plus qu'à ...; **it remains to be seen whether ...** reste à savoir si ...; **that remains to be seen** c'est ce que nous verrons *F* ça reste à voir

remainder¹ [rɪ'meɪndə(r)] *n* (**a**) (*of time, wine etc*) reste *m*; (*of salary, specific quantity*) restant *m*, reste; (*of amount due*) reliquat *m*; **the r. of his life** le reste *ou* le restant de sa vie; **the r.** (*remaining people*) les autres *mfpl* (**b**) *Math* reste *m*; **division with no r.** division *f* sans reste; **the r. is one** il reste un (**c**) (*book*) invendu *m* soldé

remainder² *vt* (*book*) solder

remaining [rɪ'meɪnɪŋ] *adj* (*food, money, wine etc*) qui reste, restant; **the r. travellers** le reste des voyageurs, les autres voyageurs; **our only r. hope** le seul espoir qui nous reste

remains [rɪ'meɪnz] *npl* (*of fortune, meal*) restes *mpl*; (*of old building*) ruines *fpl*, vestiges *mpl*; *Fig* **the last r. of his self-respect** les derniers vestiges de son amour-propre; (**human**) **r.** restes humains; *Old-fashioned* (**literary**) **r.** œuvres *fpl* posthumes

remake¹ ['riːmeɪk] *n* (*of film, TV series*) remake *m*, nouvelle version *f*; **to do a r. of** faire un remake de

remake² [riː'meɪk] *vt* (*pt, pp* **remade** [riː'meɪd]) (*film*) refaire, faire un remake de; (*bed*) refaire

remand¹ [rɪ'mɑːnd] *n Jur* **to be on r.** (*in custody*) être en détention préventive; (*on bail*) être en liberté provisoire (sous caution); **r. centre** *or* **home** maison *f* de détention préventive

remand² *vt Jur* **to r. (in custody)** placer en détention préventive; **to r. on bail** mettre en liberté provisoire sous caution

remark¹ [rɪ'mɑːk] *n* (**a**) (*comment*) remarque *f*, commentaire *m*; **to make** *or* **pass a r.** faire une remarque *ou* une observation *ou* un commentaire (**about** sur); **to let sth pass without r.** laisser passer qch sans commentaire; **to venture** *or* **hazard a r.** se permettre *ou* risquer une remarque *ou* une observation *ou* un commentaire; **no remarks, please!** pas de commentaires, s'il vous plaît!

(**b**) *Fml* (*notice*) attention *f*; **worthy of r.** digne d'attention; **it could not escape r. that ...** on ne pouvait pas ne pas remarquer que ..., le fait que ... ne pouvait pas passer inaperçu; **her reaction could not escape r.** sa réaction n'a pu passer inaperçue

remark² **1** *vt* (**a**) (*comment*) faire remarquer (**that ...** que ... + *ind*) (**b**) *Fml* (*note*) (*sb*) remarquer; (*sth*) remarquer, noter; **it may be remarked that ...** constatons que ... **2** *vi* **to r. on sth** (*on weather, food etc*) parler de qch; **I remarked on it to my mother** j'en ai fait la remarque à ma mère; **I remarked to her father on how well she was looking** j'ai fait remarquer à son père qu'elle avait l'air très en forme

remarkable [rɪ'mɑːkəb(ə)l] *adj* (*change, coincidence, progress etc*) remarquable (**for** par)

remarkably [rɪˈmɑːkəblɪ] *adv* (*to change, progress etc*) remarquablement, notablement; (*good, intelligent*) remarquablement; (*bad, stupid*) incroyablement

remarket [riːˈmɑːkɪt] *vt* recommercialiser

remarketing [riːˈmɑːkɪtɪŋ] *n* mercatique *f* de relance

remarriage [riːˈmærɪdʒ] *n* remariage *m*

remarry [riːˈmærɪ] **1** *vt* **(a)** (*first spouse*) se remarier avec, épouser de nouveau **(b)** (*of registrar etc*) (*divorced couple*) remarier **2** *vi* se remarier

remaster [riːˈmɑːstər] *vt* (*album*) remasteriser

rematch [ˈriːmætʃ] *n Sp* match *m* retour

remediable [rɪˈmiːdɪəb(ə)l] *adj Fml* (*situation*) remédiable; (*illness*) curable; **an easily r. fault** un défaut auquel on peut facilement remédier

remedial [rɪˈmiːdɪəl] *adj* (*treatment etc*) curatif; *Med* **r. exercises** gymnastique *f* corrective; *Sch* **r. class** classe *f* de rattrapage; **r. education** éducation *f* spécialisée; **r. teacher** enseignant, -ante chargé d'une classe de rattrapage

remedy[1] [ˈremɪdɪ] *n* (*for illness*); *Fig* remède *m* (**for** pour, contre); **it's past** *or* **beyond r.** c'est irrémédiable *ou* sans remède

remedy[2] *vt* (*situation*) remédier à; **the situation hasn't been remedied yet** on n'a pas encore remédié à la situation

remember [rɪˈmembər] **1** *vt* **(a)** [①**A43**, b, iii] (*recall*) (*sb*) se souvenir de; (*sth*) se souvenir de, se rappeler; **I r. him as being very generous** je me souviens de lui comme de quelqu'un de très généreux; **they r. me as a child** ils se souviennent de moi lorsque j'étais enfant; **she will long be remembered for her achievements** on se souviendra longtemps d'elle pour ses exploits; **he will be remembered as the man who ...** on se souviendra de lui comme de l'homme qui ...; **do you r. turning off the lights?** est-ce que tu te souviens (d')avoir éteint les lumières?; **do you r. me turning off the lights?** tu te souviens si j'ai éteint la lumiere?; **to r. that ...** se souvenir *ou* se rappeler que ... + *ind*; **the chairman, you will r., cannot vote** le président, ne l'oubliez pas, ne peut pas voter; **I can't r. his name for the moment** son nom m'échappe pour l'instant; **I'll r. his name in a minute** son nom me reviendra dans une minute; **it will be something to r. you by** ce sera un souvenir de vous; **I'll give him something to r. (me by)!** il se souviendra de moi!

(b) [①**A43**, b, iii] (*not forget*) (*lesson*) retenir, ne pas oublier; **it was a night/a holiday to r.** c'était une nuit/des vacances mémorable(s); **I'll r. to do it** je n'oublierai pas de le faire; **that's worth remembering** c'est à noter; **r.** *or* **you must r. (that) he's only ten years old** n'oubliez pas qu'il n'a que dix ans; **did you r. to turn off the lights?** est-ce que tu as pensé à éteindre les lumières?; **r. that we're going to the theatre next week** n'oublie pas que nous allons au théâtre la semaine prochaine; **r. where we are!** reprends-toi!; **I remembered myself just in time** je me suis ressaisi juste à temps

(c) (*give gift to*) ne pas oublier; **she always remembers the children at Christmas** elle n'oublie jamais les enfants à Noël; **he remembered me in his will** il ne m'a pas oublié dans son testament

(d) (*speak of*) **let us r. them in our prayers** prions pour eux; **r. me (kindly) to them** rappelez-moi à leur bon souvenir, dites-leur bien des choses de ma part; *esp Fml* **he asked to be remembered to you** il me prie de le rappeler à votre bon souvenir

(e) (*of service, monument etc*) (*the dead*) rendre hommage à

2 *vi* se souvenir, se rappeler; **as I r.** d'après mes souvenirs; **as far as I (can) r.** pour autant que je me souvienne; **if I r. rightly** si je m'en souviens bien, si j'ai bonne mémoire; **for as long as I can r.** aussi loin que remontent mes souvenirs

remembrance [rɪˈmembrəns] *n* **(a)** (*memory*) souvenir *m*; **in r. of sb/sth** en souvenir de qn/qch; **garden of r.** jardin *m* commémoratif **(b)** *Old-fashioned* (*keepsake*) souvenir *m* **(c)** *Old-fashioned* (*greeting*) **give my kind remembrances to him** rappelez-moi à son bon souvenir

Remembrance Day *or* **Sunday** *n Br, Can* (*in France*) le jour de l'Armistice; (*in Canada*) le Jour du Souvenir

remind [rɪˈmaɪnd] *vt* (*person*) rappeler à (**that ...** que ... + *ind*); **to r. sb of sth** rappeler qch à qn; **he reminds me of my brother** il me fait penser à *ou* me rappelle mon frère; **that reminds me of my childhood** cela me rappelle mon enfance; **to r. sb to do sth** faire penser à qn à faire qch; **he reminded them of their duty to ...** il leur rappela qu'il était de leur devoir de ...; **r. me about it tomorrow** rappelle-le-moi demain; **that** *or* **which reminds me!** à propos!; **I would r. you that ...** permettez-moi de vous rappeler que ...

reminder [rɪˈmaɪndər] *n* (*letter, of event*) rappel *m*; (*to jog memory*) pense-bête *m, pl* pense-bêtes; **to send/give sb a r. about sth** envoyer un rappel à qn à propos de qch; **the exhibition is a stark r. of the horrors of war** l'exposition rappelle la guerre dans toute son horreur; **such events are a r. that ...** de tels événements nous rappellent que ...; **it's a r. to myself to ...** c'est pour me rappeler de ...; *Com* **r. of account outstanding** rappel *m* de compte

reminisce [remɪˈnɪs] *vi* évoquer *ou* raconter ses souvenirs (**about** de); (*in thoughts*) évoquer le passé, repenser au passé; **to r. about the good old days** évoquer le bon vieux temps; **to r. about sb** parler de qn (en se souvenant)

reminiscence [remɪˈnɪsəns] *n* (*of past*) souvenir *m* (**about, of** de); **to write one's reminiscences** écrire ses souvenirs

reminiscent [remɪˈnɪsənt] *adj* **(a) to be in a r. mood** être enclin à *ou* d'humeur à évoquer des souvenirs **(b) r. of** (*film, music, scene etc*) qui fait penser à *ou* rappelle *ou* évoque

reminiscently [remɪˈnɪsəntlɪ] *adv* **to smile r.** sourire en pensant à qch; **to talk r. of sth** évoquer des souvenirs de qch

remiss [rɪˈmɪs] *adj* (*negligent*) négligent (**in doing** de faire); **that was very r. of her** c'était de la négligence de sa part

remission [rɪˈmɪʃən] *n* **(a)** *Jur* remise *f* de peine **(b)** *Med* rémission *f*; **to go into r.** (*of disease, patient*) entrer en phase de rémission **(c)** *Rel* rémission *f*; **to pray for the r. of sins** prier pour la rémission des péchés **(d)** (*of debt*) remise *f*; (*of duty, fee, payment*) dispense *f*; (*of tax*) dispense, exemption *f*

remit[1] [rɪˈmɪt] (**-tt-**) **1** *vt* **(a)** (*send back*) renvoyer; *Jur* (*case*) renvoyer à un autre tribunal; *Fin* **to r. a sum to sb** remettre une somme à qn **(b)** (*lessen*), *Jur* (*sentence*) remettre; *Fig Fml* (*efforts*) relâcher **(c)** (*forgive*) (*sin*) pardonner, absoudre **(d)** (*cancel*) (*debt*) remettre, faire remise de; **to r. sb's fees** dispenser qn de ses frais; **to r. sb's income tax** dispenser *ou* exempter qn de l'impôt sur le revenu **(e)** *Fml* (*postpone*) (*matter*) remettre, différer **2** *vi* **(a)** (*of debtor*) régler, payer; **please r. by cheque** veuillez régler *ou* payer par chèque **(b)** *Fml* (*abate*) (*of efforts, zeal etc*) diminuer; (*of pain, storm*) se calmer

remit[2] [ˈriːmɪt] *n* (*area of authority*) attributions *fpl*; **to exceed one's r.** aller au-delà de ses attributions; **it is outside** *or* **not part of our r.** ceci ne relève pas de nos attributions

remittance [rɪˈmɪtəns] *n Com* (*of money*) remise *f*, envoi *m* de fonds; (*money sent*) paiement *m*, règlement *m*; **return the form with your r.** renvoyez le formulaire avec votre règlement *ou* paiement; **r. advice** avis *m* de remise; **r. date** date *f* de remise

remix [ˈriːmɪks] *n Mus* (*record*) remix *m*

remnant [ˈremnənt] *n* **(a)** (*of food*) reste *m*; *Fig* (*of imperialism, former glory*) vestige *m*; *Fig* **the remnants of one's dignity/an army** ce qui subsiste *ou* reste de sa dignité/d'une armée **(b)** (*of fabric*) coupon *m*; (*of carpet*) chute *f*; **r. sale** (*of fabric*) soldes *mpl* de fins de série; **remnants** (*of fabric*) coupons, fins *fpl* de série

remodel [riːˈmɒd(ə)l] *vt* (**-ll-**, *US* **-l-**) (*bill, draft*) remanier; (*structure, Fig legislation*) modifier; **to have one's nose/chin remodelled** se faire refaire le nez/le menton

remonstrate [ˈremənstreɪt] **1** *vi* **to r. with sb** faire des remontrances à qn (**about** au sujet de); **there's no point in trying to r. with her about it** ça ne sert à rien d'en discuter avec elle; **to r. against sth** protester contre qch **2** *vt* **to r. that ...** protester en disant que ...

remorse [rɪˈmɔːs] *n* remords *m* (**for, about** de); **without r.** (*not sorry*) sans remords; (*to do sth*) sans scrupules; **to feel r.** éprouver *ou* avoir du *ou* des remords (**for having done** d'avoir fait); **a feeling/twinge of r.** un sentiment/une pointe de remords; **in a fit of r.** dans un accès de remords; **to show r.** manifester des remords

remorseful [rɪˈmɔːsfʊl] *adj* plein de remords

remorsefully [rɪˈmɔːsfəlɪ] *adv* (*to say*) d'un ton plein de remords

remorseless [rɪˈmɔːslɪs] *adj* (*person, wind*) impitoyable; (*cruelty, persecution*) incessant; *Fig* (*ambition, logic, self-interest etc*) implacable; **he was r. in the demands that he made on his employees** il ne laissait aucun répit à ses employés; **she was r. with herself** elle était très dure avec elle-même; **he was r. in his pursuit of the criminal** il n'avait de cesse qu'il n'arrête le criminel

remorselessly [rɪˈmɔːslɪslɪ] *adv* (*to hit, pursue etc*) impitoyablement; (*ambitious, logical etc*) implacablement

remorselessness [rɪˈmɔːslɪsnɪs] *n* (*of person, criticisms, attack*) acharnement *m*

remote [rɪˈməʊt] *adj* **(a)** (*far-off*) (*house, village etc*) reculé; (*ancestor*) lointain; (*cousin*) éloigné, lointain; **r. from** loin *ou* éloigné de; **in the remotest part of Asia** au fin fond de l'Asie; **in the r. future/past** dans un avenir/un passé lointain; **r. antiquity** la haute antiquité

(b) (*removed, not connected*) éloigné (**from de**); **his plays**

are r. from everyday life ses pièces sont éloignées de la vie quotidienne

(c) *Comptr* (*user*) à distance; **r. access** accès *m* à distance; **r. batch processing** télétraitement *m* par lots; **r. data entry** entrée *f* de données à distance; **r. data processing** télétraitement; **r. help** télé-assistance *f*; **r. interrogation** interrogation *f* à distance; **with a r. interrogation facility** interrogeable à distance; **r. job entry** soumission *f* de travaux à distance; **r. loading** téléchargement *m*; **r. management** télégestion *f*; **r. processing** télétraitement; **r. reading** lecture *f* à distance; **r. server software** logiciel *m* serveur télématique; **r. terminal** terminal *m* éloigné; **r. trouble-shooting** télédépannage *m*

(d) *TV etc* **r. station** téléstation *f*; **r. van** voiture *f* de reportage

(e) (*aloof*) distant, réservé; (*with mind elsewhere*) absent; **she had a rather r. look on her face** (*looked aloof*) elle avait une expression plutôt distante; (*was thinking of other things*) elle avait un air absent

(f) (*slight*) (*chance, connection, possibility, resemblance*) vague; (*prospect*) peu probable; **I haven't the remotest idea of what he meant** je n'ai pas la moindre idée de ce qu'il voulait dire; **there is a r. possibility that ...** il y a une vague possibilité que ... + *sub*; **in the r. event of a water shortage** dans l'hypothèse improbable d'une pénurie d'eau; **he hasn't the remotest chance of winning** il n'a pas la moindre chance de gagner

remote control *n* contrôle *m* à distance; (*for model aircraft, door, television etc*) télécommande *f*; (*for bomb*) commande *f* à distance; **it's all done by r.** tout est effectué par télécommande *ou* par commande à distance; *Aut* **r. locking** verrouillage *m* à distance; **r. software** logiciel *m* de prise de contrôle à distance

remote-controlled *adj* (*model aircraft, door, television etc*) télécommandé; (*bomb*) commandé à distance

remotely [rɪˈməʊtlɪ] *adv* **(a)** (*distantly*) (*situated*) loin, au loin; (*related*) de loin **(b)** (*absent-mindedly*) (*to answer etc*) d'un ton absent **(c)** (*slightly*) (*possible*) vaguement; **it's only r. connected with the subject** cela n'a qu'un faible rapport avec le sujet; **it isn't even r. connected with the subject** cela n'a même pas le moindre rapport avec le sujet; **I'm not r. interested in science fiction** la science fiction ne m'intéresse pas le moins du monde; **not r. aware** nullement conscient; **it isn't even r. possible** c'est rigoureusement impossible

remoteness [rɪˈməʊtnɪs] *n* **(a)** (*distance*) (*of house, past etc*) éloignement *m*; (*isolation*) isolement *m* **(b)** (*aloofness*) distance *f*; **her air of r.** (*aloofness*) son air distant; (*absent-mindedness*) son air absent; **the r. of her manner** son côté distant **(c)** (*of resemblance*) faible degré *m*; **the r. of her chances of success** l'improbabilité *f* de sa réussite

remote sensing *n* télédétection *f*; **r. satellite** satellite *m* de télédétection

remould¹ [ˈriːməʊld] *n Br Aut* pneu *m* rechapé

remould² [riːˈməʊld] *vt Br* **(a)** *Aut* (*tyre*) rechaper **(b)** (*clay figure, Fig image, character etc*) remodeler

remount [riːˈmaʊnt] **1** *vt* **(a)** (*get on again*) **to r. one's horse/bicycle** remonter à cheval/bicyclette, remonter sur son cheval/sa bicyclette **(b)** (*go up again*) (*stairs*) remonter **(c)** (*place on new support*) (*picture*) rentoiler; (*jewel*) remonter
2 *vi* remonter à cheval/à bicyclette

removable [rɪˈmuːvəb(ə)l] *adj* **(a)** (*component, lid, lining etc*) amovible; *Comptr* **r. disk** disque *m* amovible *ou* extractible **(b)** (*mark, spot, stain etc*) qui peut partir; **the stain's not r.** la tache est indélébile

removal [rɪˈmuːv(ə)l] *n* **(a)** (*taking away*) (*of rubbish, plate*) enlèvement *m*; (*of stain etc*) nettoyage *m*; (*of appendix, kidney, tumour etc*) ablation *f*; (*of doubt, fear*) dissipation *f*; (*of burden, worry, obstacle, threat, word*) suppression *f*; **r. of customs barriers** suppression des barrières douanières; **the r. of stains from a jacket** le détachage d'une veste; **for stain r., for the r. of stains** pour enlever les taches, pour détacher

(b) (*taking off*) (*of coat, glove etc*) enlèvement *m*; (*of tyre*) démontage *m*; (*of seal*) levée *f*; **after r. of the bandages** une fois les bandages enlevés; **after the r. of her make-up** une fois démaquillée

(c) (*dismissal*) révocation *f*, renvoi *m*; (*of civil servant, judge etc*) destitution *f*

(d) (*moving house*) déménagement *m*; **r. expenses** frais *mpl* de déménagement

removal company *n* entreprise *f* de déménagement

removal man *n* déménageur *m*

removal van *n* camion *m* de déménagement

remove¹ [rɪˈmuːv] *n* (*degree of difference*) distance *f*; **at a certain r.** à une certaine distance; **at one r.** de façon interposée; **it is but** *or* **only one r. from ...** cela est tout près de ...; **her account is several removes from the truth** son récit est assez loin de la vérité

remove² **1** *vt* **(a)** (*take away*) (*rubbish, plate*) enlever; (*stain*) enlever, faire partir (**from** de); (*source of infection*) éliminer; (*appendix, kidney, tumour*) procéder à l'ablation de, enlever; (*person*) emmener (**to** à); *Fig* (*doubt, fear*) dissiper; (*worry, obstacle, threat, word*) supprimer, éliminer; **to have a mole/wart removed** se faire enlever un grain de beauté/une verrue; **to r. sb's name from a list** rayer qn d'une liste; **she's having the plaster removed tomorrow** on lui enlève son plâtre demain; **to r. a burden from sb** soulager qn d'un fardeau; **to r. a child from school** retirer un enfant de l'école; **police removed the demonstrators** la police a fait partir les manifestants; **the judge ordered her to be removed from the court room** le juge a ordonné qu'on la fasse sortir de la salle d'audience; **he has been removed to hospital** il a été transporté à l'hôpital; **death has removed him from our midst** la mort nous l'a enlevé

(b) (*take off*) (*coat, gloves, hat*) enlever, retirer (**from sb** à qn); (*tyre*) démonter; (*seal*) lever; **to r. one's make-up** se démaquiller; **to r. the hair from one's legs** s'épiler les jambes

(c) (*dismiss*) (*executive, director*) révoquer, renvoyer; (*civil servant, magistrate*) destituer; **to r. sb from his** *or* **her position** démettre qn de ses fonctions (**as** de)

(d) (*of furniture movers*) (*furniture etc*) déménager

(e) *Euph* (*kill*) (*person*) supprimer

2 *vi Old-fashioned* (*of people, company*) déménager (**to** à)

removed [rɪˈmuːvd] *adj* (*distant*) **his feeling was not far r. from love** son sentiment n'était pas très éloigné de l'amour; **her explanation is far r. from the truth** son explication est très éloignée de la vérité; **first cousin once r.** cousin(e) issu(e) de germain

remover [rɪˈmuːvər] *n* **(a)** (*company, person*) déménageur *m*; **a company of furniture removers** une entreprise de déménagement **(b)** (*substance*) **paint r.** décapant *m*; **stain r.** détachant *m*; **hair r.** (d)épilatoire *m*; **nail varnish r.** dissolvant *m*; **make-up r.** démaquillant *m*

removing [rɪˈmuːvɪŋ] *adj* **r. cream** (*for hair*) crème *f* (d)épilatoire; (*for make-up*) crème démaquillante; (*for wrinkles*) crème antirides

remunerate [rɪˈmjuːnəreɪt] *vt Fml* (*person*) rémunérer (**for** de); (*service*) rémunérer

remuneration [rɪmjuːnəˈreɪʃən] *n Fml* (*for service etc*) rémunération *f* (**for** de)

remunerative [rɪˈmjuːnərətɪv] *adj Fml* rémunérateur, -trice

Renaissance [rɪˈneɪsəns] *n Art etc* Renaissance *f*; **R. art/literature** art *m*/littérature *f* de la Renaissance; *Fig* **he's a R. man** c'est un esprit universel

renaissance [rɪˈneɪsəns] *n* (*of industry etc*) renaissance *f*

renal [ˈriːn(ə)l] *adj Anat* (*artery, failure etc*) rénal; **r. failure** insuffisance *f* rénale

rename [riːˈneɪm] *vt* (*person, street*) rebaptiser; *Comptr* (*file*) changer le nom de, renommer

renascence [rɪˈnæsəns, -ˈneɪ-] *n Lit* (*of nationalism*) renaissance *f*; (*of interest*) regain *m*

renascent [rɪˈnæsənt, -ˈneɪ-] *adj Lit* (*interest, nationalism etc*) renaissant

renationalization [riːnæʃənəlaɪˈzeɪʃən] *n* renationalisation *f*

renationalize [riːˈnæʃənəlaɪz] *vt* renationaliser

rend [rend] *vt* (*pt, pp* **rent** [rent]) **(a)** (*pierce*) (*the silence*) déchirer; **the air was rent with her screams** l'air était déchiré par ses hurlements **(b)** *Lit* (*tear*) déchirer; **to r. sth asunder** *or* **apart** (*in two parts*) déchirer *ou* fendre qch en deux; (*in several parts*) (*car, ship etc*) déchiqueter qch; **he was rent from my arms** il fut arraché à mes bras; **a country rent by civil war** un pays déchiré par la guerre civile

render [ˈrendər] *vt* **(a)** *Fml* (*give*) (*homage, service*) rendre; (*description*) faire; (*explanation*) donner; **to r. thanks to God** rendre grâce à Dieu; *Bible* **r. unto Caesar the things which are Caesar's** rendez à César ce qui appartient à César; **to r. an account of sth** (*describe*) faire le récit de qch; *Fin* **to r. an account to sb** remettre un compte à qn; **to r. assistance to sb** prêter secours à qn; **to r. (up) a fortress** rendre une forteresse; *Lit* **to r. up one's soul** (*die*) rendre l'âme

(b) (*make, cause to be*) rendre; **the blow rendered her unconscious** le coup lui a fait perdre connaissance; **the news rendered her speechless** la nouvelle l'a laissée sans voix

(c) (*depict*) (*light*) rendre; (*perform*) (*piece of music*) interpréter

(d) (*translate*) rendre, traduire (**in, into** en)

(e) (*plaster*) (*wall etc*) plâtrer, enduire de plâtre

(f) *Culin* **to r. (down) fat** faire fondre de la graisse

rendering ['rendərɪŋ] *n* **(a)** *Fin (of account)* reddition *f* **(b)** *(of expression, features in painting)* rendu *m*; *(of music)* interprétation *f*; **his r. of what happened** sa version des faits **(c)** *(translating) (of phrase)* traduction *f* **(d)** *(of wall)* enduit *m* **(e)** *(of fat)* fonte *f*

rendezvous[1] ['rɒndɪvu:, *pl* -vu:z] *n (meeting, meeting-place)* rendez-vous *m inv* (**for** de); **to make a r. with sb** prendre rendez-vous avec qn; **to keep a r.** se rendre à un rendez-vous

rendezvous[2] *vi (pt, pp* **rendezvoused** [-vu:d]; *prp* **rendezvousing** [-vu:ɪŋ]) se réunir, se retrouver; **to r. with sb** retrouver qn

rendition [ren'dɪʃən] *n (of role etc)* interprétation *f*; *(translation) (of phrase)* traduction *f*; **to give a r. of** *(role etc)* interpréter; **they finished with a r. of the Marseillaise** ils ont terminé en chantant/jouant la Marseillaise

renegade ['renɪgeɪd] *n* **(a)** *(traitor)* renégat, -ate; **r. priest** prêtre *m* parjure **(b)** *(outlaw)* hors-la-loi *m inv*

renege, renegue [rɪ'neɪg] *vi* **(a)** manquer à *ou* revenir sur sa promesse (**on doing sth** de faire qch); **she has reneged (on her promise)** elle a manqué à sa promesse; **she has reneged (on our deal)** elle est revenue sur notre marché **(b)** *Cards* faire une fausse renonce

renegotiate [ri:nɪ'gəʊʃɪeɪt] *vt* renégocier

renegotiation [ri:nɪgəʊʃɪ'eɪʃən] *n* renégociation *f*

renew [rɪ'nju:] *vt* **(a)** *(resume) (conversation)* reprendre; **to r. one's acquaintance with sb** renouer connaissance avec qn; **to r. pressure on sb** recommencer à faire pression sur qn (**to do** pour qu'il fasse); *Mil* **to r. an attack** attaquer de nouveau; *Fig* **to r. one's attack** revenir à la charge *ou* à l'attaque (**on** concernant)

(b) *(restate) (request, promise)* renouveler

(c) *(extend) (lease, passport, bill of exchange)* renouveler; **to r. a lease** reconduire un bail; **to r. one's subscription** se réabonner, renouveler son abonnement (**to** à); **to r. a library book** faire renouveler *ou* prolonger le prêt d'un livre de bibliothèque; **to r. one's wardrobe** renouveler sa garde-robe

(d) *(revive) (hope, enthusiasm etc)* raviver

renewable [rɪ'nju:əb(ə)l] *adj (passport etc)* renouvelable; *(lease, contract)* reconductible, renouvelable; **your subscription is r. at the end of the year** *(must be renewed)* votre abonnement doit être renouvelé à la fin de l'année; *(may be renewed)* votre abonnement peut être renouvelé à la fin de l'année; **r. energy** énergie *f* renouvelable; **r. resources** ressources *fpl* renouvelables

renewal [rɪ'nju:əl] *n* **(a)** *(of acquaintance)* renouement *m*; *(of hostilities, violence, bombing)* reprise *f*; *(of enthusiasm, hopes)* regain *m*; **r. of activity** reprise *ou* regain d'activité **(b)** *(of promise, request)* renouvellement *m* **(c)** *(of lease, passport etc)* renouvellement *m*; *(of library book)* renouvellement de prêt; **r. of subscription** réabonnement *m*, renouvellement d'abonnement (**to** à); **r. clause** clause *f* de reconduction; **r. premium** prime *f* de renouvellement

renewed [rɪ'nju:d] *adj (effort, enthusiasm, vigour)* renouvelé; *(attempt, hope)* nouveau; *(activity, efforts)* redoublé; **r. bombing/outbreaks of violence** reprise *f* des bombardements/de la violence; **doctors are expressing r. concern about her condition** son état inspire de nouvelles inquiétudes aux médecins; **there is r. interest in ...** il y a un regain d'intérêt pour ...; **there has been r. military activity in the region** il y a eu un regain d'activité militaire dans la région

rennet ['renɪt] *n* présure *f*

re-nose *vt Journ (story)* réorienter

renounce [rɪ'naʊns] *vt* **(a)** *(abandon, give up) (right, title, alcohol, violence etc)* renoncer à; *Jur (nationality, inheritance)* répudier; **to r. all thought of doing sth** renoncer à toute idée de faire qch; *Lit* **to r. the world** renoncer au monde **(b)** *(disown) (treaty)* répudier, dénoncer; *(friend)* renier, désavouer; *(one's principles)* renier; **to r. one's faith** renoncer à sa foi, apostasier; **to r. Satan and all his works** renoncer à Satan, à ses pompes et à ses œuvres

renouncement [rɪ'naʊnsmənt] *n* = **renunciation**

renovate ['renəveɪt] *vt (house etc)* rénover

renovation [renə'veɪʃən] *n (of house etc)* rénovation *f*; **closed for r.** *(notice in shop window)* fermé pour cause de travaux de rénovation; **to be under r.** être en cours de rénovation; **to undergo renovations** subir des rénovations, être en rénovation; **r. project/work** projet *m*/travaux *mpl* de rénovation

renovator ['renəveɪtər] *n* rénovateur, -trice

renown [rɪ'naʊn] *n* renommée *f*, renom *m*; **woman of great** *or* **high r.** femme *f* de grand renom; **to win r.** acquérir une renommée, se faire une renommée (**as** en tant que; **for** pour)

renowned [rɪ'naʊnd] *adj (town, person)* renommé, célèbre (**for** pour; **as** comme); *(wine)* fameux; *(artist, writer)* célèbre, illustre; **Dr Hector Smith, the r. psychiatrist** le Dr Hector Smith, le célèbre psychiatre; **he is r. for being late** il est réputé pour être toujours en retard

rent[1] [rent] *n (on flat, house etc)* loyer *m*; **for r.** à louer; **how much do you pay in r.?, how much r. do you pay?** combien est-ce que tu paies de loyer?; **to live somewhere free of r.** habiter quelque part sans payer de loyer; **to be behind with the r.** être en retard pour (payer) le loyer; **Friday is r. day, it's r. day on Friday** on doit payer le loyer vendredi; *Br* **r. book** livre *m* de location; **r. collector** receveur, -euse *ou* encaisseur, -euse de loyers; **r. strike** grève *f* des loyers

rent[2] **1** *vt (flat, video, car)* louer (**from, to** à); **to r. (out) rooms** louer des chambres (**from, to** à); **she lives in a rented house** elle habite dans une maison qu'elle loue; **rented accommodation** logement *m* en location, location; **to r.** à louer *f* **2** *vi* **it rents at** *or* **for ...** cela se loue à ...

rent[3] *n (in clothing)* déchirure *f*, accroc *m*; *(in clouds)* déchirure, trouée *f*; *(in relations)* rupture *f*

rent[4] *see* **rend**

▶ **rent out** *vipo* = **rent**[2] **1**

rental ['rent(ə)l] *n* **(a)** *(hire) (of car, flat, house etc)* location *f*; **r. car/charges/company** voiture *f*/frais *mpl*/société *f* de location; **r. office** *(for car)* bureau *m* de location; **r. property** propriété *f* à louer

(b) *(money paid) (for flat, house)* loyer *m*; *(for car, equipment, television, holiday flat)* (prix *m* de) location *f*; *(for telephone)* abonnement *m*; **to pay a telephone/television r. of ...** payer ... d'abonnement pour le téléphone/de location pour la télévision; *Tel* **fixed r.** redevance *f* d'abonnement

(c) *Acct* **r. charges** charges *fpl* locatives; **r. expenses** charges *fpl* locatives; **r. income** revenus *mpl* locatifs

rent-a-mob *n F* agitateurs *mpl*

rent boy *n Br F* jeune prostitué *m*

rent-free *adj (accommodation, flat etc)* exempt de loyer; **to live somewhere r.** habiter quelque part sans payer de loyer; **a house is available r.** il y a une maison où l'on peut habiter gratuitement *ou* sans payer de loyer

renunciation [rɪnʌnsɪ'eɪʃən] *n* **(a)** *(of right, title, alcohol, violence etc)* renonciation *f* (**of** à); *Jur (of nationality, inheritance)* répudiation *f* **(b)** *(of treaty)* répudiation *f*, dénonciation *f*; *(of beliefs)* reniement *m*; *(of friend)* reniement, désaveu *m*; *(of world)* renoncement *m* (**of** à)

reoccupy [ri:'ɒkjʊpaɪ] *vt (territory)* réoccuper; *(house)* habiter à nouveau; **the house is reoccupied** la maison est réhabitée

reopen [ri:'əʊp(ə)n] **1** *vt* **(a)** *(book, frontier, investigation etc)* rouvrir; *Fig* **to r. an old wound** rouvrir une plaie **(b)** *(resume) (hostilities)* recommencer, reprendre; *(talks)* reprendre **2** *vi (of wound)* se rouvrir; *(of shop, theatre etc)* rouvrir; *(law court)* rentrer; *(of schools, talks)* reprendre; **the border has reopened** la frontière a été rouverte

reopening [ri:'əʊp(ə)nɪŋ] *n (of shop, theatre, border, investigation etc)* réouverture *f*; *(of hostilities, talks)* reprise *f*; *Fig* **this will merely lead to the r. of old wounds** ça ne fera que rouvrir d'anciennes blessures

reorder[1] [ri:'ɔ:dər] *n (to obtain more supplies)* nouvelle commande *f*; *(reminder to supplier)* commande renouvelée; **to send** *or* **put a r. in** envoyer *ou* passer une nouvelle commande (**for** de); **r. form/procedure** formulaire *m*/procédure *f* de renouvellement de commande

reorder[2] *vt (order more)* faire une nouvelle commande de; *(order again)* renouveler la commande de

reorganization [ri:ɔ:gənaɪ'zeɪʃən] *n (of company, education, files etc)* réorganisation *f*

reorganize [ri:'ɔ:gənaɪz] **1** *vt (company, filing system etc)* réorganiser **2** *vi (of company etc)* se réorganiser

Rep [rep] *US Pol* **(a)** *abbr* **Representative** **(b)** *abbr* **Republican**

rep[1] [rep] *n F (abbr* **representative***) (door to door)* représentant, -ante; *(for large company)* représentant, -ante, VRP *m* (**for** chez); **sales r.** représentant, -ante de commerce, VRP

rep[2] *vi F* travailler comme représentant, -ante (**for** chez)

rep[3] *n Br Th F (theatre)* théâtre *m*; **what's on at the local r.?** qu'est-ce qu'on joue au théâtre municipal?; **to work in r.** faire du théâtre

repackage [ri:'pækɪdʒ] *vt Mktg* reconditionner, repenser l'emballage de

repaginate [ri:'pædʒɪneɪt] *vt* remettre en pages; *(renumber)* repaginer

repaint [ri:'peɪnt] *vt* repeindre

repair[1] [rɪ'peər] *n* **(a)** *(of shoes, watch etc)* réparation *f*; *(of building, road)* réparation, réfection *f*; *(of machine)* réparation, remise *f* en état; *(of clothing)* réparation, raccommodage *m*; **to be in need of r.** avoir besoin d'être réparé; **to be in for r.** *(of car etc)* être en réparation; **to be**

(damaged) beyond r. être irréparable; **road under r.** (*road sign*) travaux; **(shoe) repairs while you wait** (*notice in shop*) cordonnerie minute; **to make repairs to sth** (*machine, car, bike*) faire des réparations sur qch; (*shoes, garment*) réparer; **to carry out repairs** effectuer des réparations; **he does all his own repairs** il fait toutes ses réparations lui-même; **to undergo repairs** *or* **be under r.** être en réparation

(b) (*condition*) **to be in good/bad r.** être en bon/mauvais état, être bien/mal entretenu; **to keep a road/car/property in (good) r.** entretenir une route/voiture/propriété

repair² *vt* (*mend*) (*shoes, watch, building, road*) réparer; (*machine*) réparer, remettre en état

repairer [rɪˈpeərə(r)] *n* (*of shoes*) cordonnier, -ière; (*of watch, machine etc*) réparateur, -trice

repair kit *n* trousse *f* à outils

repairman [rɪˈpeəmæn] *n* (*of televisions, washing machines etc*) réparateur *m*; **a computer/TV/washing machine r.** un réparateur d'ordinateurs/de télévisions/de machines à laver

repair shop *n* atelier *m* de réparations

repaper [riːˈpeɪpə(r)] *vt* (*room*) retapisser

reparation [repəˈreɪʃən] *n Fml* (*of wrong, omission*) réparation *f*; **in r. of ...** en réparation de ...; **to make r. for sth** réparer qch; **(war) reparations, r. payments** réparations *fpl*

repartee [repɑːˈtiː] *n* repartie *f*; **to be good** *or* **quick at r.** avoir la repartie facile, avoir de la repartie; **to engage in r.** faire de l'esprit

repast [rɪˈpɑːst] *n Lit* repas *m*

repatriate¹ [riːˈpætrɪeɪt] *vt* (*prisoner of war, capital etc*) rapatrier **(to** vers)

repatriate² [riːˈpætrɪət] *n* rapatrié, -ée

repatriation [riːpætrɪˈeɪʃən] *n* (*of prisoner of war, capital etc*) rapatriement *m*

repay [riːˈpeɪ, rɪ-] *vt* (*pt, pp* **repaid** [riːˈpeɪd, rɪ-]) **(a)** (*pay back*) (*money*) rendre, rembourser; (*loan, person*) rembourser **(b)** (*reward*) (*person*) récompenser **(for** de); (*give same in return for*) (*favour*) rendre; **is this how you r. me?** c'est comme ça que tu me récompenses *ou* remercies?; **to r. sb with ingratitude** payer qn d'ingratitude; **to r. a kindness** payer une gentillesse de retour; **I can never r. you for all you've done** je ne pourrai jamais vous remercier assez pour tout ce que vous avez fait; **how can I ever r. you?** pourrais- je jamais vous remercier?

repayable [riːˈpeɪəb(ə)l, rɪ-] *adj* (*loan*) remboursable

repayment [riːˈpeɪmənt, rɪ-] *n* **(a)** (*of loan, mortgage etc*) remboursement *m*; **the repayments are spread over five years** les remboursements sont échelonnés sur cinq ans **(b)** (*of kindness*) récompense *f*; **in r. of your helpfulness/support** pour te remercier de ton aide/soutien

repayment mortgage *n Br* = prêt *m* hypothécaire qu'on rembourse et qui ne produit pas de rente

repayment plan *n* calendrier *m* des paiements

repeal¹ [rɪˈpiːl] *n* (*of law*) abrogation *f*; (*of decree*) révocation *f*

repeal² *vt* (*law*) abroger; (*decree*) révoquer

repeat¹ [rɪˈpiːt] *n* (*of event, motif, attempt*) répétition *f*; *Mus* (*passage*) reprise *f*; *Mus* (*mark*) barre *f* de reprise, renvoi *m*; *Rad, TV* rediffusion *f*; **there's nothing on (television) but repeats** il n'y a que des rediffusions; **a r. of the attempt to assassinate him** une nouvelle tentative d'assassinat sur sa personne; **we get a lot of r. business** beaucoup de nos clients reviennent; **it will be a r. of last year's final** ça sera comme la finale de l'année dernière; **r. dial** recomposition *f*, renumérotation *f*; *Com* **r. order** commande *f* renouvelée; **r. purchase** achat *m* renouvelé; **r. run** (*of adverts*) passage *m* répété; **r. sale** vente *f* répétée

repeat² **1** *vt* **(a)** (*do again*) (*action, motif*) répéter; (*one's efforts, prescription, attempt*) renouveler; (*as encore*) (*song, piece of music*) bisser; *Rad, TV* (*programme*) rediffuser; *Sch* **to r. a year** redoubler; **history repeats itself** l'histoire se répète

(b) (*say again*) (*question*) répéter; (*threat, order, promise*) réitérer; **it can't be repeated too often** on ne saurait trop le répéter; *Mus* **r.** (*after a line of a song etc*) bis; **to r. oneself** se répéter; **am I repeating myself?** est-ce que je me répète?, *F* est-ce que je radote?; **I don't want to have to r. myself** je ne veux pas avoir à le répéter; **r. after me ...** répétez après moi ...

(c) (*say to others*) (*secret*) répéter; **don't r. this, but ...** ne le répète pas, mais ...

2 *vi* **(a)** (*of decimal figure*) se répéter

(b) (*of food*) donner des renvois; **it's repeating on me** ça me donne des renvois

repeat-action key *n Comptr* touche *f* de répétition

repeated [rɪˈpiːtɪd] *adj* (*action etc*) répété; (*question etc*) réitéré; (*effort*) renouvelé; **after r. failures/warnings** après des échecs/des avertissements répétés

repeatedly [rɪˈpiːtɪdlɪ] *adv* à maintes reprises

repeater [rɪˈpiːtə(r)] *n* (*rifle*) fusil *m* à répétition

repeat function *n Comptr* fonction *f* de répétition

repeating [rɪˈpiːtɪŋ] **1** *adj* **(a)** (*rifle*) à répétition **(b)** (*decimal*) périodique **2** *n* (*of word, action*) répétition *f*

repeat offender *n Jur* récidiviste *mf*

repeat performance *n Th* deuxième représentation *f*; *Fig* **I don't want a r. of the last time I left you here alone** je ne veux pas avoir la même séance que la dernière fois que je t'ai laissé seul

repeat prescription *n Med* ordonnance *f* renouvelée

repel [rɪˈpel] *vt* (**-ll-**) **(a)** (*repulse*) (*assailant*) repousser; **to r. moisture** empêcher l'infiltration de l'humidité; **like poles r. (each other)** les pôles semblables se repoussent; **a spray that repels greenfly** un aérosol qui éloigne les pucerons **(b)** (*disgust*) répugner à, dégoûter; **she was repelled by the sight** elle a été dégoûtée par ce qu'elle a vu

repellent [rɪˈpelənt] **1** *adj* (*person, sight etc*) repoussant, répugnant; **he finds her/the idea quite r.** elle/l'idée lui répugne; **r. (to water)** imperméable **2** *n* (*for insects*) insecticide *m*

-repellent [rɪˈpelənt] *suff* **moth/rust-r.** antimites/antirouille

repent [rɪˈpent] **1** *vi* se repentir **(of** de) **2** *vt* se repentir de

repentance [rɪˈpentəns] *n* repentir *m* **(for** pour); **to show r.** manifester du repentir; *Rel* venir à résipiscence, se repentir; **to show no sign of r.** ne manifester aucun signe de repentir

repentant [rɪˈpentənt] *adj* (*sinner etc*) repentant **(of** de)

repentantly [rɪˈpentəntlɪ] *adv* (*to say, look at*) d'un ton/d'un air repentant

repercussion [riːpəˈkʌʃən] *n* **(a)** (*indirect effect*) répercussion *f*; (*of scandal*) retentissement *m*; (*consequence*) contrecoup *m*; **to have repercussions** avoir des répercussions **(for, on** sur); **the repercussions are still being felt** on en ressent encore les répercussions **(b)** (*from impact, of sound*) répercussion *f*

repertoire [ˈrepətwɑː(r)] *n* (*of jokes, songs etc*), *Th* répertoire *m*; **to have a wide/limited r.** avoir un vaste répertoire/un répertoire restreint; *Th* **the two plays will be performed in r.** les deux pièces seront jouées en alternance

repertory [ˈrepət(ə)rɪ] *n Th* (*repertoire*) répertoire *m*; **to work in r.** faire du théâtre de répertoire; **what's on at the local r.?** qu'est-ce qu'on joue au théâtre municipal?; *Br* **r. company** troupe *f* à demeure; *Br* **r. theatre** théâtre *m* de répertoire

répétiteur [repetɪˈtɜː(r)] *n Th* (*of opera singer etc*) maître *m* de musique

repetition [repɪˈtɪʃən] *n* (*of word, action etc*) répétition *f*; (*of effort*) renouvellement *m*; *Mus* reprise *f*; *Sp* **it was an exact r. of last year's final** c'était exactement comme la finale de l'année dernière; **I don't want any r. of your behaviour!** que cela ne se reproduise pas!

repetitious [repɪˈtɪʃəs] *adj* (*book, speech etc*) plein de répétitions

repetitive [rɪˈpetɪtɪv] *adj* (*person*) rabâcheur; (*job*) répétitif; *Med* **r. strain** *or* **stress injury** douleur *f* due à la répétition d'un même mouvement lors d'une activité telle que taper à la machine, jouer du violon etc

rephrase [riːˈfreɪz] *vt* (*question*) formuler à nouveau, reformuler; **perhaps I should r. that ...** peut-être devrais-je m'exprimer autrement ...

repine [rɪˈpaɪn] *vi Lit* être mécontent **(at** de)

replace [rɪˈpleɪs] *vt* **(a)** (*put back*) (*object*) replacer, remettre (en place); **I replaced the book on the shelf** j'ai replacé *ou* remis le livre sur l'étagère; **r. the book when you've finished with it** remets le livre à sa place quand tu n'en auras plus besoin; *Tel* **to r. the receiver** raccrocher (le combiné) **(b)** (*substitute for*) (*person, object*) remplacer **(as** en tant que; **with** par); **to be replaced by** *or* **with** être remplacé par; **it can be replaced** (*of broken cup etc*) on peut retrouver le/la même; *Comptr* **r. all** tout remplacer

replaceable [rɪˈpleɪsəb(ə)l] *adj* (*broken cup etc*) remplaçable

replacement [rɪˈpleɪsmənt] *n* **(a)** (*putting back*) (*of object*) remise *f* en place

(b) (*substitution*) (*of person, object*) remplacement *m* **(of ... by** de ... par); **r. cost** coût *m* de remplacement; *Mktg* **r. sale** vente *f* de remplacement; **r. value** (*of stolen item*) valeur *f* de remplacement; *Com* **r. value insurance** assurance *f* "ad valorem"

(c) (*substitute*) (*for person*) remplaçant, -ante; (*for component*) pièce *f* de rechange; **we are looking for a r. for our secretary** nous cherchons quelqu'un pour remplacer notre secrétaire; **r. hip/knee joint** prothèse *f* de (la) hanche/de (la) rotule; **r. staff** personnel *m* de remplacement

replant [riːˈplɑːnt] *vt* (*shrub, garden*) replanter

replay¹ [ˈriːpleɪ] *n Sp* second match *m*, nouvelle rencontre *f*; *TV* **instant** *or* *Br* **action r.** répétition *f* immédiate d'une séquence; *TV* **(slow-motion) r.** répétition au ralenti; *TV* **to**

give *or* **show a r.** repasser une séquence; (*in slow-motion*) repasser une séquence au ralenti; *TV etc* **r. head** tête *f* de visionnement

replay² [riːˈpleɪ] *vt* **(a)** *Sp* (*match*) rejouer; *Tennis* **to r. a point** rejouer un point **(b)** (*recording*) repasser

replenish [rɪˈplenɪʃ] *vt* (*cup etc*) remplir de nouveau (**with** de); **to r. one's supplies** se réapprovisionner (**with** de); *Banking* **to r. an account** approvisionner un compte; **she kept his glass replenished** elle veillait à ce que son verre fût toujours plein; **do you need replenishing?** est-ce que je remplis ton verre?

replenishment [rɪˈplenɪʃmənt] *n* (*of cup etc*) remplissage *m*; **r. of supplies** réapprovisionnement *m*

replete [rɪˈpliːt] *adj Fml* **(a)** (*full up*) rassasié; **r. with** gorgé de **(b)** (*well-supplied*) rempli, plein (**with** de)

repletion [rɪˈpliːʃən] *n Fml* satiété *f*; **to eat to r.** manger à satiété *ou* jusqu'à être rassasié

replica [ˈreplɪkə] *n* (*of statue, painting, building*) réplique *f*; (*of document*) copie *f*; *Fig* (*of person*) portrait *m*; (*of match, dispute etc*) répétition *f*; **she is a r. of her grandmother** c'est (tout) le portrait de sa grand-mère

replicate [ˈreplɪkeɪt] *vt* (*document*) copier; (*experiment, cell, gene*) reproduire; *Comptr* (*in spreadsheet*) recopier à l'identique; **the gene can r. itself** le gène peut se reproduire

reply¹ [rɪˈplaɪ] *n* (*to letter, query etc*) réponse *f*; **I made no r.** je n'ai rien répondu; **his r. to that was …** (*in speech*) il a répondu à cela que …; **his r. to that was to march out of the room** il a réagi à cela en sortant d'un air furieux de la pièce; **what did you say in r.?** qu'est-ce que tu as répondu?; **what did you do in r.?** comment est-ce que tu as réagi?; **there was no r.** (*to telephone call*) on n'a pas répondu, ça ne répondait pas; (*to knock on door*) on n'a pas ouvert; **in r. to your letter** en réponse à votre lettre; *Com* **r. card** carte-réponse *f*, *pl* cartes-réponses; **(international) r. coupon** coupon-réponse *m* (international), *pl* coupons-réponses (internationaux); **r. paid** réponse payée; **r. slip** talon *m* à retourner

reply² *vti* répondre (**to** à); (*retort*) répliquer (**to** à); **yes, madam, he replied** oui, madame, a-t-il répondu

reply-paid *n* **r. card** carte *f* T; **r. envelope** enveloppe *f* T, enveloppe-retour *f*

repo [ˈriːpəʊ] *n F* (*abbr* **repossession**) *St Exch* réméré *m*; **r. man** = huissier *m* (chargé par une société de saisir des meubles etc non payés); *Fin* **r. rate** taux *m* des repos

report¹ [rɪˈpɔːt] *n* **(a)** (*account*), *Com* rapport *m* (**on** sur); (*of meetings*) compte rendu *m*; (*in writing*) procès-verbal *m*, *pl* procès-verbaux; (*in newspaper*) (*short*) compte rendu; (*long*) reportage *m*; (*on radio, television*) reportage; (*by eyewitness*) témoignage *m*; *Comptr* état *m*; **there was a short r. of the incident in the newspaper** l'incident a fait l'objet d'un petit article *ou* d'un entrefilet dans le journal; **to draw up** *or* **make a r. on sth** faire *ou* rédiger un rapport sur qch; (*of police officer*) dresser procès-verbal de qch; *Parl* **the bill has reached the r. stage** le projet de loi a été présenté au parlement; **r. of the board of directors** (*in annual account*) rapport de gestion; *esp Am Sch* **book r.** compte rendu de lecture; *Sch* **end-of-term r.** bulletin *m* (trimestriel); **progress r.** rapport périodique *ou* d'avancement (des travaux); *Sch* **school r.** bulletin *m* scolaire; *Mil* **sick r.** rôle *m* des malades; *Comptr* **r. form** rapport (d'édition), fiche *f* d'état; *Comptr* **r. form generator** générateur *m* d'états

(b) (*rumour*) bruit *m* (qui court), rumeur *f*

(c) (*sound*) (*of shot*) détonation *f*, coup *m* de fusil/de canon; (*of explosion*) bruit *m* d'explosion, détonation

(d) *Old-fashioned* (*reputation*) renom *m*; **man of good r.** homme *m* de bonne réputation

report² **1** *vt* **(a)** (*give account of*) rendre compte de; (*fact, incident*) rapporter; (*speech etc*) faire le compte rendu de; *Journ* faire un reportage sur; **to r. one's findings (to sb)** rendre compte des résultats de ses recherches (à qn); **little progress has been reported so far** jusqu'à présent on n'a obtenu que peu de résultats; **the president was reported by the newspapers to have …** les journaux ont rapporté *ou* raconté que le président avait …; **she is reported to be dead** elle serait morte, on dit qu'elle est morte, on la dit morte; **it is reported that …** on dit que … + *ind*; **the version reported in the press** la version parue dans la presse; **they are reported to be in France** ils seraient en France

(b) (*make known*) (*accident, theft*) signaler (**to** à); (*announce*) (*change, developments, profits, loss etc*) annoncer; *Mil* **to r. sb sick/missing** porter qn malade/absent; **to r. sb missing** (*to police*) signaler la disparition de qn; **she has been reported missing** on a signalé sa disparition; **she was reported missing five years ago** elle a été portée disparue il y a cinq ans; **nothing to r.** rien à signaler; (*on form*) néant, R.A.S.

(c) (*denounce*) **I'm going to r. you** (*to authorities*) je vais le signaler; **to r. sb to the police** dénoncer qn à la police; **to r. a pupil to the headmaster** (*of teacher*) signaler la mauvaise conduite d'un élève au directeur; **to r. a pupil for smoking** signaler le nom d'un élève surpris en train de fumer; **I'm going to r. you for smoking** je dirai au directeur que je t'ai surpris en train de fumer

2 *vi* **(a)** (*present oneself*) se présenter (**to sb** à *ou* devant qn; **to a place** à un endroit); **please r. to reception** veuillez vous présenter à la réception; **you've to r. to the headmaster** tu dois aller chez le directeur; *Mil* **to r. sick** se faire porter malade; *Mil* **to r. fit** reprendre son service (après une maladie); *Mil* **to r. to one's unit** rallier son unité; **to r. for duty** prendre son service; **you will r. for duty on Monday** vous vous présenterez à votre poste lundi; **to r. back from leave** reprendre son service après un congé

(b) (*give account*) faire un rapport (**on** sur); (*of journalist*) faire un reportage (**on** sur); **to r. (for a newspaper)** faire des reportages (pour un journal); *Parl* **to r. on a bill** rapporter un projet de loi; *TV, Rad* **reporting from Geneva is our foreign affairs correspondent …** de Genève, notre correspondant pour les affaires étrangères …; **this is Mary Smith reporting for ITN news** Mary Smith pour le journal d'ITN

▶ **report back** *vi* **(a)** (*announce return*) se présenter **(b)** (*announce findings*) rendre compte (**on sth** de qch); **to r. back to a committee** faire son rapport à un comité; **they r. back to head office once a week** ils font un rapport pour le siège une fois par semaine

▶ **report to** *vipo* **(a)** (*be accountable to*) (*person*) rendre compte à; **who do you r. to?** qui est votre supérieur?; **you'll be reporting to Mr Jones** vous travaillerez sous la direction de M. Jones; **I r. directly to the board** je n'ai pas de supérieur hiérarchique à part le conseil d'administration **(b)** (*inform of developments*) **to r. to sb** faire son rapport à qn (**on** sur), rendre compte à qn (**on** de)

reportage [repɔːˈtɑːʒ] *n Journ etc* reportage *m*

report card *n Sch* carnet *m* (de notes), bulletin *m* scolaire; **to get a good r.** avoir un bon carnet *ou* bulletin

reported [rɪˈpɔːtɪd] *adj attrib* **their last r. position was south of the river** (*given by themselves*) la dernière fois qu'ils ont donné leur position, ils étaient au sud de la rivière; (*given by third party*) ils ont été vus pour la dernière fois au sud de la rivière; **her r. lack of interest in her children** son soi-disant manque d'intérêt pour ses enfants; *Gram* **r. speech** discours *m* indirect

reportedly [rɪˈpɔːtɪdlɪ] *adv* à ce qu'on dit; **the President r. said that …** le Président aurait dit que …; **she is r. unharmed** elle serait indemne; **he is r. resident in Paris** il résiderait à Paris

reporter [rɪˈpɔːtə(r)] *n* reporter *mf*, journaliste *mf*; (*correspondent*) envoyé, -ée, reporter

reporting [rɪˈpɔːtɪŋ] *n* **(a)** (*of news*) reportage *m*; **his r. of the facts is always accurate** il rapporte toujours fidèlement les faits; **she is noted for her objective r.** elle est connue pour l'objectivité de ses reportages; **r. restrictions** restrictions *fpl* journalistiques; *esp Jur* **r. restrictions have been imposed** on a imposé des restrictions quant aux reportages **(b)** (*within company*) **r. structure** structure *f* hiérarchique **(c)** *St Exch* **r. limit** seuil *m* d'annonce obligatoire

repose¹ [rɪˈpəʊz] *n Fml or Lit* (*rest*) repos *m*; (*sleep*) sommeil *m*; **her face is beautiful in r.** son visage est très beau lorsqu'elle est détendue; **to pray for the r. of sb's soul** prier pour le repos de l'âme de qn

repose² **1** *vt* **(a)** *Fml* **to r. trust in sb** placer *ou* mettre sa confiance en qn **(b)** *Fml* (*rest*) (*one's head*) reposer **2** *vi* **(a)** (*of argument, plan*) reposer (**on** sur) **(b)** *Fml* (*rest*) reposer

reposition [riːpəˈzɪʃən] *vt* **(a)** (*move*) **she repositioned herself nearer the door** elle a changé de place pour aller se placer près de la porte **(b)** *Com* (*change market image of*) (*product, party*) repositionner

repositioning [riːpəˈzɪʃənɪŋ] *n Com* (*of product*) repositionnement *m*

repository [rɪˈpɒzɪt(ə)rɪ] *n* (*for books, furniture etc*) dépôt *m*, entrepôt *m*; *Fig Lit* (*of knowledge etc*) mine *f*

repossess [riːpəˈzes] *vt* (*for non-payment*) (*furniture, car etc*) saisir

repossession [riːpəˈzeʃən] *n* (*of furniture etc*) saisie *f*

repot [riːˈpɒt] *vt* (*plant*) rempoter

reprehend [reprɪˈhend] *vt Fml* réprimander

reprehensible [reprɪˈhensɪb(ə)l] *adj* (*behaviour, act*) répréhensible; **that was most r. of you** c'était très répréhensible de votre part

reprehensibly [reprɪˈhensɪblɪ] *adv* (*to behave, act*) de façon répréhensible

represent [reprɪ'zent] *vt* **(a)** (*depict, portray*) (*person, object*) représenter
(b) (*act as agent for*) (*person, company etc*), *Jur, Pol* représenter; **the Queen will be represented by** ... la Reine sera représentée par ...
(c) (*constitute*) représenter, constituer; **this represents a great improvement** cela constitue un grand progrès
(d) (*symbolize, embody*) (*nation, love etc*) symboliser
(e) (*typify*) représenter; **the government's policy does not r. my opinions** la politique du gouvernement n'est pas représentative de mes opinions
(f) (*describe*) (*person, object*) présenter (**to be, as** comme); **he represents himself as a model of virtue** il se présente comme *ou* il se donne pour un modèle de vertu
(g) *Fml* (*state, express*) faire remarquer, signaler (**to** à); **I will r. your grievances to management** je ferai part de vos griefs à la direction

re-present *vt* (*bill etc*) présenter à *ou* de nouveau; **to r. a cheque** représenter un chèque à l'acceptation

representation [reprɪzen'teɪʃən] *n* **(a)** *Pol* représentation *f*; **they have increased their r. to six** le nombre de leurs délégués est passé à six; **they still lacked r. in Parliament** ils n'étaient toujours pas représentés au parlement **(b)** (*in painting*) représentation *f* **(c)** (*of facts*) exposé *m* des faits; **this is a fair r. of their point of view** cela représente bien leur point de vue **(d) representations** (*complaints*) protestations *fpl*; *Fml* **to make representations** faire des démarches (**about** concernant; **to** auprès de)

representational [reprɪzen'teɪʃən(ə)l] *adj* (*art*) figuratif

representative [reprɪ'zentətɪv] **1** *n* **(a)** (*of group, company, organization etc*) représentant, -ante; (*for mail-order firm*) délégué, -ée; (**sales**) **r.** représentante, -ante, V.R.P. *m*; **to send a r. to a conference** envoyer un(e) représentant(e) *ou* se faire représenter à une conférence; **sole representatives of a firm** représentants *ou* agents exclusifs d'une maison; **last r. of an illustrious race** dernier descendant/dernière descendante d'une race illustre
(b) *US Pol* député *m*
2 *adj* **(a)** (*typical*) représentatif, typique; **a r. cross-section of the population** un échantillon représentatif de la population; *Com* **r. sample** échantillon *m* type
(b) *Pol* (*government*) représentatif

repress [rɪ'pres] *vt* **(a)** (*desire, passions, uprising*) réprimer; (*tears*) retenir **(b)** *Psy* (*unconsciously*) refouler; (*consciously*) réprimer

repressed [rɪ'prest] *adj* (*person, feelings*) refoulé; (*laughter*) étouffé; **he is very r.** il est très refoulé *ou F* coincé; **she had a very r. adolescence** elle a été refoulée à l'adolescence

repression [rɪ'preʃən] *n* **(a)** (*of desire, uprising etc*) répression *f* **(b)** *Psy* (*unconscious*) refoulement *m*; (*conscious*) répression *f*

repressive [rɪ'presɪv] *adj* (*government, law*) répressif; (*measures*) répressif, de répression

reprieve¹ [rɪ'priːv] *n Jur* (*for condemned prisoner*) (*definitive*) commutation *f* de la peine capitale; (*temporary*), *Fig* sursis *m*; *Jur* **to grant a r.** accorder une commutation de peine/un sursis; *Fig* **this is a r. for the government** cela constitue un sursis pour le gouvernement; **we've got a r.** (*for project etc*) on nous a donné un peu plus de temps

reprieve² *vt Jur* (*prisoner*) accorder une commutation de la peine capitale à; (*temporary*) accorder un sursis à; *Fig* **the shipyard has been reprieved** le chantier naval bénéficie d'un sursis

reprimand¹ ['reprɪmɑːnd] *n* (*of child*) réprimande *f*; (*of employee, accused person*) blâme *m*; **to be given a r.** (*of child*) recevoir une réprimande; (*of employee etc*) recevoir un blâme; **she was let off with a r.** elle s'en est tirée avec une réprimande/un blâme

reprimand² *vt* (*child*) réprimander (**for** pour); (*employee, accused person*) blâmer (**for** pour)

reprint¹ ['riːprɪnt] *n* (*of book*) réimpression *f*; (*of article*) nouvelle parution *f*, nouvelle publication *f*; **the book is going into its fourth r.** le livre va être réimprimé pour la quatrième fois; **separate r.** (*of article from journal*) tirage *m* à part

reprint² [riː'prɪnt] **1** *vt* (*book*) réimprimer; (*article*) faire paraître *ou* publier à nouveau; **article reprinted from The Times** article reproduit du Times **2** *vi* (*of book*) être en réimpression

reprisal [rɪ'praɪz(ə)l] *n* représailles *fpl*; **to carry out** *or* **take reprisals** exercer des représailles, user de représailles (**against** contre); **to threaten reprisals** menacer de représailles; **there have been threats of r.** il y a eu des menaces de représailles; **as a** *or* **in r. for** ... en *ou* par représailles pour ...; **r. attack/raid** attaque *f*/raid *m* de représailles

reprise [rɪ'priːz] *n Mus* reprise *f*

reproach¹ [rɪ'prəʊtʃ] *n* **(a)** (*blame*) reproche *m*; **she heaped reproaches on him** elle l'a accablé de reproches; **look of r.** regard plein de reproche; **there was a note of r. in his voice** il y avait une pointe *ou* une nuance de reproche dans sa voix; **a letter of r.** une lettre de reproches; **beyond** *or* **above r.** irréprochable **(b)** (*shame*) honte *f*; **to be a r. to** ... être la honte de...; **it is a r. to the government that** ... c'est une honte pour le gouvernement que ...; **things that have brought r. upon him** choses qui ont jeté le discrédit sur lui

reproach² *vt* reprocher (**sb for** *or* **with sth** qch à qn); **to r. oneself** s'en vouloir; **I have nothing to r. myself with** *or* **for** je n'ai rien à me reprocher; **she reproached him for not keeping his promise** elle lui a reproché de n'avoir pas tenu sa promesse

reproachful [rɪ'prəʊtʃfʊl] *adj* (*tone*) de reproche; (*look*) plein de reproche

reproachfully [rɪ'prəʊtʃfəlɪ] *adv* (*to say, look at*) d'un ton/d'un air de reproche *ou* plein de reproche

reprobate ['reprəbeɪt] *n Fml* réprouvé, -ée, *Old-fashioned Hum* vaurien, -ienne

reprocess [riː'prəʊses] *vt Ind etc* (*waste etc*) retraiter

reprocessing [riː'prəʊsesɪŋ] *n* (*of waste*) retraitement *m*; **r. plant** usine *f* de retraitement

reproduce [riːprə'djuːs] **1** *vt* (*copy*) (*painting*) reproduire; (*document*) copier **2** *vi Biol, Bot* se reproduire; (*of photocopier*) reproduire; **this print will r. well** cette estampe se prêtera bien à la reproduction

reproduction [riːprə'dʌkʃən] *n* (*of document, picture etc*), *Biol, Bot* reproduction *f*; **thousands of reproductions have been made of this picture** ce tableau a été reproduit à des milliers d'exemplaires; **r. furniture** meubles *mpl* de style

reproductive [riːprə'dʌktɪv] *adj Biol* reproducteur, -trice; **r. organs** organes *mpl* reproducteurs; **r. system** (*of animal etc*) appareil *m* reproducteur

reprogram [riː'prəʊgræm] *vt Comptr* reprogrammer; **to r. a computer to do sth** reprogrammer un ordinateur pour qu'il fasse qch

reprography [re'prɒgrəfɪ] *n* reprographie *f*

repro head ['riːprəʊ] *n* tête *f* de lecture

reproof¹ [rɪ'pruːf] *n esp Fml* réprobation *f*; (*in speech, writing*) blâme *m*; **he looked at her with r.** il l'a regardée avec réprobation; **word/look of r.** mot *m*/regard *m* de réprobation

reproof² [riː'pruːf] *vt* (*raincoat*) réimperméabiliser

reprove [rɪ'pruːv] *vt esp Fml* (*child*) réprimander, reprendre; (*person*) réprimander (**for** pour); (*action*) condamner

reproving [rɪ'pruːvɪŋ] *adj esp Fml* (*look, tone*) réprobateur, -trice

reprovingly [rɪ'pruːvɪŋlɪ] *adv* (*to say, look at*) d'un ton/d'un air réprobateur

reptile ['reptaɪl] *n* reptile *m*; **r. house** (*in zoo*) vivarium *m* pour les reptiles

reptilian [rep'tɪlɪən] **1** *adj* (*animal*) reptilien; *Pej* (*features*) de reptile **2** *n* reptile *m*

republic [rɪ'pʌblɪk] *n* république *f*

Republican [rɪ'pʌblɪkən] *adj, n US Pol* républicain, -aine

republican [rɪ'pʌblɪkən] *adj, n* républicain, -aine

republicanism [rɪ'pʌblɪkənɪz(ə)m] *n* républicanisme *m*

republication [riːpʌblɪ'keɪʃən] *n* réédition *f*

republish [riː'pʌblɪʃ] *vt* rééditer

repudiate [rɪ'pjuːdɪeɪt] *vt Fml* (*spouse, idea, treaty etc*) répudier; (*friend, opinion*) désavouer; (*offer*) repousser; (*debt, accusation*) nier; **to r. the authorship of a book** désavouer la paternité d'un livre

repudiation [rɪpjuːdɪ'eɪʃən] *n* (*of spouse, idea etc*) répudiation *f*; (*of friend, opinion*) désaveu *m*; (*of offer*) refus *m*; (*of debt, accusation*) reniement *m*

repugnance [rɪ'pʌgnəns] *n* (*abhorrence*) répugnance *f* (**for** pour); **to have a r. for sth/for doing sth** avoir de la répugnance pour qch/à faire qch

repugnant [rɪ'pʌgnənt] *adj* (*deed, person etc*) répugnant (**to** à); **to be r. to sb** répugner à qn

repulse¹ [rɪ'pʌls] *n* (*of assistance, offer etc*) refus *m*; *Mil* échec *m*; **to meet with a r.** (*of person, offer*) essuyer un refus

repulse² *vt* (*person, request, Mil assault*) repousser; *Mil* (*enemy*) repousser, refouler; **to be repulsed by sth** (*disgusted*) être révolté par qch

repulsion [rɪ'pʌlʃən] *n* **(a)** (*of person*) répulsion *f* (**for** à l'égard de); **to feel r. for sth/sb** éprouver de la répulsion à l'égard de qch/qn **(b)** *Phys* répulsion *f*

repulsive [rɪ'pʌlsɪv] *adj* **(a)** (*person, sight, smell, habit, idea etc*) repoussant, répugnant **(b)** *Phys* répulsif

repulsively [rɪ'pʌlsɪvlɪ] *adv* (*to behave, say etc*) de façon répugnante; **r. ugly** d'une laideur repoussante

repulsiveness [rɪ'pʌlsɪvnɪs] *n* **(a)** (*of person, sight, habit etc*) caractère *m* repoussant *ou* répugnant **(b)** *Phys* force *f* répulsive

repurchase¹ [riːˈpɜːtʃɪs] *n* rachat *m*; *St Exch* **r. at a profit** rachat *m* gagnant; *Mktg* **r. market** marché *m* de renouvellement; **r. period** délai *m* de réachat; **r. rate** taux *m* de réachat; **r. right** droit *m* de rachat

repurchase² *vt* racheter

reputable [ˈrepjʊtəb(ə)l] *adj* (*person, job*) honorable; (*shop, company*) de bonne réputation; (*source of information*) sûr

reputation [repjuːˈteɪʃən, repjʊ-] *n* (*of person, shop etc*) réputation *f*; **to make a r. (for oneself)** se faire une réputation; **to have a good/bad r.** avoir (une) bonne/mauvaise réputation (**as** en tant que); *Old-fashioned* **to ruin a girl's r.** entacher l'honneur d'une demoiselle; **to have a r. for frankness** avoir la réputation d'être franc; **to know sb by r.** connaître qn de réputation; **his r. had gone before him** sa réputation l'avait précédé; **to live off one's r.** vivre sur sa réputation; *Old-fashioned Pej* **he has a bit of a r.** il n'a pas très bonne réputation; **to live up to one's r.** (*of person*) se montrer à la hauteur de sa réputation; (*of book, restaurant etc*) être à la hauteur de sa réputation

repute¹ [rɪˈpjuːt] *n esp Fml* réputation *f*, renom *m*; **to know sb by r.** connaître qn de réputation; **to be held in high r.** être estimé; **of r.** (*doctor etc*) réputé, de grand renom; *Euph* **house of ill r.** maison *f* de passe

repute² *vt* (*usu passive*) **to be reputed wealthy** avoir la réputation d'être riche; **he is reputed to be a good doctor** il a la réputation d'être (un) bon médecin, il est réputé pour être bon médecin; **she is reputed to be a genius by her colleagues** c'est un véritable génie si l'on en croit ses collègues

reputed [rɪˈpjuːtɪd] *adj attrib* putatif; **his r. father** son père putatif

reputedly [rɪˈpjuːtɪdlɪ] *adv* (*supposedly*) à ce qu'on dit; **she is r. the best heart specialist** elle a la réputation d'être la meilleure cardiologue

request¹ [rɪˈkwest] *n* demande *f*, requête *f*; **r. for money** demande d'argent; **at the r. of sb, at sb's r.** à la demande de qn; **samples sent on r.** échantillons sur demande; **to make a r.** faire *ou* formuler une demande (**for** de); **to grant sb's r.** répondre à la demande de qn; **by (popular) r.** à la demande générale; *Rad* **to play a r.** passer un disque demandé par un auditeur; *Rad* **to send in a r.** envoyer une demande

request² *vt* **to r. sth from** *or* **of sb** demander qch à qn, *Fml* solliciter qch de qn; **to r. sb to do sth** demander à qn de faire qch; (*as a matter of urgency*) prier qn de faire qch; **passengers are requested not to smoke** les passagers sont priés de ne pas fumer; **as requested** (*on compliments slip etc*) conformément à votre demande

request programme, request show *n Rad* programme *m* des auditeurs, émission *f* de disques à la demande

request stop *n Br* (*for bus*) arrêt *m* facultatif

requiem [ˈrekwɪəm] *n* **r. (mass)** *Rel* messe *f* de requiem *m*, messe des morts; *Mus* requiem *m*; **to have a r. mass for sb** faire dire une messe de requiem pour qn

require [rɪˈkwaɪər] *vt* (*necessitate*) (*work, patience, care etc*) demander, exiger; (*need*) (*of person*) avoir besoin de; **to r. sth of sb** (*demand*) exiger qch de qn; **the parts don't r. any glueing** les pièces n'ont pas besoin d'être collées; **to r. sb to do sth** exiger de qn qu'il fasse qch; **you are required under the regulations to …** en vertu du règlement vous êtes tenu de …; **he had done all that was required by law** il s'était conformé à toutes les exigences de la loi; **my services are no longer required** on n'a plus besoin de mes services; *Euph* (*I've been dismissed*) j'ai été remercié; **this plant requires plenty of water** cette plante demande beaucoup d'eau; **have you everything you r.?** avez-vous tout ce qu'il vous faut *ou* tout ce dont vous avez besoin?; **I shall do whatever is required** je ferai tout ce qu'il faudra; **the qualifications required for this job** les qualités requises pour ce poste; **if required** s'il le faut, si besoin est; **when required** quand il le faut; **staff required** (*notice in shop*) on recherche du personnel

required [rɪˈkwaɪəd] *adj attrib* requis; **in the r. time** en temps voulu, dans le délai prescrit; **r. reading** ouvrages *m(pl)* à lire absolument; (*for student*) ouvrages au programme, lectures *fpl* obligatoires

requirement [rɪˈkwaɪəmənt] *n* (*need*) exigence *f*; (*condition*) condition *f* (requise); *Univ* **requirements for the course, course requirements** conditions préalables d'admission; **a qualification in Greek is no longer a r.** un diplôme de grec n'est plus nécessaire; **to meet** *or* **satisfy sb's requirements** (*wishes*) correspondre aux besoins de qn; (*demands*) satisfaire les *ou* aux exigences de qn; **to meet the government's safety requirements** répondre aux normes de sécurités mises en place par le gouvernement

requisite [ˈrekwɪzɪt] **1** *adj* (*money, papers etc*) requis (**for** pour), nécessaire (**for** à) **2** *n* **(a)** (*for travel etc*) article *m*; **toilet requisites** articles *ou* nécessaire *m* de toilette **(b)** (*condition*) condition *f* (requise); **a qualification in Greek is no longer a r.** un diplôme de grec n'est plus nécessaire

requisition¹ [rekwɪˈzɪʃən] *n* demande *f*; *Mil* réquisition *f*; *Com etc* **to put in a r. for supplies** passer une commande *f* de fournitures; **r. number** numéro *m* de référence

requisition² *vt Mil* (*supplies etc*) réquisitionner (**from** de); *Com* (*supplies*) commander, faire la demande de; *Fig* (*person*) réquisitionner (**to do** pour faire); (*person's services*) recourir à, avoir recours à

requisitioning [rekwɪˈzɪʃənɪŋ] *n Mil* **r. officer** officier *m* chargé des réquisitions

requital [rɪˈkwaɪt(ə)l] *n Fml* (*for service*) récompense *f*; (*of love*) retour *m*; **in r. of** *or* **for her services** en récompense de ses services

requite [rɪˈkwaɪt] *vt* (*service*) récompenser; **to r. sb for sth** récompenser qn de qch; **her love had never been requited** son amour n'avait jamais été payé de retour

reread [riːˈriːd] *vt* relire

reredos [ˈrɪədɒs] *n* (*in church*) retable *m*

reroute [riːˈruːt] *vt* (*plane, train etc*) dérouter (**through** via)

rerouting [riːˈruːtɪŋ] *n* (*of flight etc*) déroutement *m*; **r. of goods** déroutage *m* de marchandises

rerun¹ [ˈriːrʌn] *n* (*repeat*) (*of film*) reprise *f*; *Rad, TV* rediffusion *f*; *Fig* répétition *f*; **I wouldn't mind seeing a r. of that second goal** je voudrais bien revoir le deuxième but

rerun² [riːˈrʌn] *vt* (*film, cassette*) repasser; *Rad, TV* (*programme*) rediffuser

resale [riːˈseɪl] *n* revente *f*; **r. price maintenance** prix *m* imposé(s) (par le fabricant); **not for r.** ne peut être vendu; **r. value** valeur *f* de revente

reschedule [riːˈʃedjuːl] *vt* (*appointment, flight, departure*) modifier l'heure/la date de; *Fin* (*debt*) rééchelonner

rescheduling [riːˈʃedjuːlɪŋ] *n* (*of appointment, flight, departure*) modification *f* d'heure/de date; *Fin* (*of debt*) rééchelonnement *m*

rescind [rɪˈsɪnd] *vt* (*law*) rescinder, abroger; (*contract*) annuler, résilier

rescue¹ [ˈreskjuː] *n* (*saving*) sauvetage *m*; (*help, troops etc*) secours *mpl*; (*setting free*) délivrance *f*; **to the r.** à la rescousse; **to come/go to sb's r.** venir/aller au secours de qn; **(financial) r. package** plan *m* de sauvetage (financier)

rescue² *vt* (*from death, difficult or embarrassing situation*) sauver, secourir; (*set free*) délivrer (**from** de); **to r. sb from danger** arracher qn à un danger, sauver qn d'un danger; **to r. sb from drowning** sauver qn qui se noie; **to r. a company from bankruptcy** sauver une société de la faillite; **the rescued** (*used as pl*) les rescapés *mpl*

rescue operation *n* opération *f* de sauvetage

rescue party *n* équipe *f* de sauveteurs

rescuer [ˈreskjuːər] *n* (*from shipwreck, fire etc*) secouriste *mf*, sauveteur *m*; (*from embarrassing situation*) sauveur *m*; (*from captivity*) libérateur, -trice

rescue services *npl* services *mpl* de secours

rescue worker *n* sauveteur *m*, secouriste *mf*

research¹ [rɪˈsɜːtʃ] *n* recherche(s) *f(pl)* (**into, on** sur); **some r.** de la recherche; **a piece of r. (work)** un travail de recherche; **to do** *or* **be engaged in r.** faire des recherches (**on, into** sur); **when I finish my degree I'd like to do r.** quand j'aurai mon diplôme, j'aimerais faire de la recherche *ou* devenir chercheur; **r. establishment/laboratory/team** centre *m*/laboratoire *m*/équipe *f* de recherche; **r. budget** budget *m* consacré à la recherche; **r. finding** découverte *f* effectuée à l'occasion de recherches; **r. firm** société *f* d'études; **r. manager** chef *m* des études; **r. octane number** indice *m* d'octane recherché; **r. programme** programme *m* de recherche; **r. technique** technique *f* de recherche; **r. tool** outil *m* de recherche

research² **1** *vt* (*subject*) faire des recherches sur; (*book, thesis*) faire des recherches pour; **a well researched book** un livre bien documenté **2** *vi* faire des recherches (**on, into** sur)

research and development *n* recherche *f* et développement *m*

research assistant *n* assistant, -ante de recherche

researcher [rɪˈsɜːtʃər] *n* chercheur, -euse

research fellow *n* chercheur, -euse (*qui a reçu une bourse*)

research scientist *n* chercheur, -euse

research student *n* étudiant, -ante qui fait une thèse

research work *n* recherches *fpl*, travaux *mpl* de recherche

research worker *n* (*scientific*) chercheur, -euse; *Am* (*literary*) documentaliste *mf*

reseat [riːˈsiːt] *vt* **(a) to r. the guests** (*put in different positions*) refaire les tables; **when they were all reseated** (*had sat down again*) lorsqu'ils se sont rassis **(b)** (*pair of trousers, chair*) remettre un fond à **(c)** *Tech* (*valve*) roder

resection [riːˈsekʃən] *n Surg* résection *f*

resell [riːˈsel] *vt* (*pt, pp* **resold** [riːˈsəʊld]) revendre

reseller [riːˈselər] *n Com* revendeur *m*

resemblance [rɪˈzembləns] *n* ressemblance *f* (**to** à, avec; **between** entre); **to bear a r. to sb/sth** ressembler à qn/qch; **there is a strong family r.** il y a un air de famille très prononcé; **his testimony bears no r. to the facts** il n'y a aucune ressemblance entre son témoignage et les faits

resemble [rɪˈzemb(ə)l] *vt* ressembler à; **to r. one another** se ressembler

resent [rɪˈzent] *vt* **(a)** (*object to*) ne pas aimer du tout; **I r. your remarks** je n'aime pas du tout vos remarques; **I r. that!** je n'aime pas ça du tout! **(b)** (*feel bitter about*) éprouver de l'amertume à l'égard de; **you r. my being here** ma présence vous déplaît; **your children r. me** tes enfants m'en veulent; **he resents having to take orders from a woman** il accepte mal d'avoir une femme comme supérieur

resentful [rɪˈzentfʊl] *adj* (*remark, look*) plein de ressentiment *ou* d'amertume, amer; **to be** *or* **feel r.** éprouver de l'amertume *ou* du ressentiment (**about** à propos de, concernant)

resentfully [rɪˈzentfəlɪ] *adv* (*to behave, act*) avec ressentiment *ou* amertume; (*to speak*) d'un ton plein de ressentiment *ou* d'amertume, d'un ton rancunier; (*to look at*) avec ressentiment *ou* amertume, d'un air rancunier

resentment [rɪˈzentmənt] *n* amertume *f*, ressentiment *m* (**at** à; **over** concernant; **of** à l'égard de); **to feel r. against sb** avoir de la rancune contre qn; **there is a lot of r. about her appointment** sa nomination suscite beaucoup d'amertume

reservation [rezəˈveɪʃən] *n* **(a)** (*booking*) (*in restaurant etc*) réservation *f*; **to make a r.** réserver; **to make a r. for nine o'clock** (*in restaurant*) réserver une table pour neuf heures; **do you have a r.?** (*in restaurant, hotel*) est-ce que vous avez réservé?; (*in train*) est-ce que vous avez une réservation?; **for reservations, call ...** pour réserver appeler ...; **r. agent** agent *m* de réservation; **r. sheet** feuille *f* de réservation, bordereau *m* de réservations; **r. ticket** coupon *m* de réservation; **reservations book** agenda *m ou* livre *m* de réservation; **reservations system** système *m* de réservation

(b) (*doubt*) (*about idea, plan etc*) réserve *f*; **without r.** sans réserve; **not without** *or* **with some r.** non sans réserves; **with this r.** à cette restriction près; **to have reservations about sth** avoir des doutes à propos de qch; **to have no reservations in doing sth** n'avoir aucune hésitation à faire qch

(c) *Am* (*land*) terrain *m* réservé; **(Indian) r.** réserve *f* indienne; *Br Aut* **central r.** terre-plein *m* central, *pl* terres-pleins centraux

reservation clerk *n Am* préposé, -ée aux réservations

reservation desk *n* bureau *m* des réservations

reserve[1] [rɪˈzɜːv] *n* **(a)** (*stock*) (*of money etc*) réserve *f*; **to have great reserves of energy** avoir beaucoup d'énergie en réserve; *Pol* **he still has a r. of support in the country** il bénéficie encore d'un certain soutien parmi les électeurs; **to draw on one's reserves** (*of courage, money, skill*) puiser dans ses réserves; *Petr* **known reserves** réserves prouvées; **to keep sth in r.** garder qch en réserve (**for** pour); **in r.** en réserve; *Acct* **r. account** compte *m* de réserve; *Acct* **r. capital** capital *m* de réserve; **r. currency** monnaie *f* de réserve; *Acct* **r. funds** fonds *mpl* de réserve; **r. power/energy** réserve de puissance/énergie

(b) *Mil etc* **the reserves** (*soldiers*) la réserve *f*, les réservistes *mpl*; (*unit*) la réserve; **r. officer** officier *m* de réserve

(c) *Sp* (*substitute*) remplaçant, -ante; **to play for the reserves** jouer dans l'équipe de réserve

(d) (*for birds, game*) réserve *f*; **nature r.** réserve naturelle; *Can* **Indian r.** réserve indienne

(e) (*limitation*) **without r.** sans réserve

(f) *Br* (*at auction*) **r. (price)** prix *m* minimum; **to put a r. on sth** fixer un prix minimum à qch; **the item did not reach its r.** l'article n'a pas atteint le prix minimum fixé

(g) (*reticence*) réserve *f*; **with typical English r.** avec une réserve toute britannique

reserve[2] *vt* **(a)** (*book*) (*table, Rail seat*) réserver; *Th etc* (*seat*) louer; **reserved seat** (*on train*) place *f* réservée; (*at theatre, concert etc*) place louée **(b)** (*keep*) réserver, mettre en réserve; **to r. a seat for sb** réserver *ou* retenir une place à qn; **to r. the right to do sth** se réserver le droit de faire qch; **to r. one's strength** ménager ses forces; **all rights reserved** tous droits de reproduction réservés **(c)** (*withhold*) **to r. judgement on sth/sb** réserver son jugement sur qch/qn

reserved [rɪˈzɜːvd] *adj* (*shy*) réservé; **to be r. with sb** être réservé *ou* se tenir sur la réserve avec qn

reservedly [rɪˈzɜːvɪdlɪ] *adv* avec réserve, de manière réservée

reserve tank *n Aut, Av* réservoir *m* de secours

reservist [rɪˈzɜːvɪst] *n Mil etc* réserviste *m*

reservoir [ˈrezəvwɑːr] *n* (*for water*) réservoir *m*, bassin *m* de retenue; (*for oil*) réservoir; *Fig* **reservoirs of strength/courage** réserve *f* d'énergie/de courage

reset [riːˈset] (*pt, pp* **reset**; *prp* **resetting**) *vt* **(a)** (*watch*) remettre à l'heure; (*stopwatch, counter*) remettre à zéro; (*computer*) réinitialiser; **to r. an alarm clock** régler la sonnerie d'un réveil; *Comptr* **r. button** *or* **switch** bouton *m* de remise à zéro, bouton *m* de réinitialisation **(b)** (*precious stone etc*) remonter; *Surg* (*fracture*) réduire; (*dislocation*) remettre, remboîter **(c)** *Typ* (*text*) recomposer

resettle [riːˈset(ə)l] **1** *vt* (*refugees*) réinstaller; (*area*) repeupler **2** *vi* se réinstaller (**in** dans)

resettlement [riːˈset(ə)lmənt] *n* (*of refugees*) implantation *f*; (*of area*) repeuplement *m*

reshape [riːˈʃeɪp] *vt* (*industry etc*) réorganiser

reshuffle[1] [riːˈʃʌf(ə)l] *n* (*of Cabinet, jobs etc*) remaniement *m*

reshuffle[2] *vt* **(a)** (*staff etc*) remanier **(b)** (*cards*) battre de nouveau

reside [rɪˈzaɪd] *vi* **(a)** *Fml* (*of person*) résider (**at, in** à, dans) **(b)** *Fig* (*of power, quality*) résider (**in** dans)

residence [ˈrezɪdəns] *n* **(a)** (*stay*) séjour *m*; **to take up r. in a country** se fixer *ou* s'établir dans un pays; **whenever the Queen is in r.** quand la reine est là; **in r.** (*doctor, poet*) sur place; **place of r.** lieu *m* de résidence; **six months r.** séjour de six mois; **r. permit** permis *m* de séjour; *Am* **r. tax** taxe *f* de séjour **(b)** *Fml* (*home*) demeure *f*, maison *f*; **desirable r. for sale** belle propriété à vendre; **official r.** résidence *f* officielle **(c)** *Br Univ* **(hall of) r.** résidence *f* universitaire; **to stay in residences** vivre en résidence universitaire

residency [ˈrezɪdənsɪ] *n* **(a)** *Am Med* internat *m*; **to do one's r.** faire son internat **(b)** (*house*) (*of governor etc*) résidence *f* officielle **(c)** *Mus, Th* (*engagement*) contrat *m* (à long terme)

resident [ˈrezɪdənt] **1** *adj* résident; (*population*) fixe; *Journ* (*correspondent*) permanent; **to be r. in London** résider à Londres; **r. manager** directeur *m* qui habite sur place; *Comptr* **r. program** programme *m* résident; **r. teacher** professeur *m* à demeure, professeur résident

2 *n* **(a)** (*of country, street*) habitant, -ante; (*of hotel*) pensionnaire *mf*; (*foreigner*) résident, -ente; **to be a permanent r.** être résident permanent (**of** de); **residents' association** association *f* de riverains; **residents' parking bay** *or* **place** emplacement *m* réservé aux riverains

(b) *Am Med* interne *mf*

residential [rezɪˈdenʃəl] *adj* **(a)** (*area, neighbourhood etc*) résidentiel; **the building is reverting to r. use** l'édifice va être à nouveau utilisé comme habitation **(b)** (*course*) à temps complet; **r. seminar** séminaire *m* résidentiel **(c)** (*staff*) à demeure

residual [rɪˈzɪdjʊəl] **1** *adj* **(a)** (*unrest, resentment etc*) qui subsiste; **r. income** revenu *m* net **(b)** *Ch* résiduel **2** *n* **(a)** *Cin, TV* **residuals** (*repeat fees*) droits *mpl* de seconde diffusion **(b)** *Ch* résidu *m*

residuary [rɪˈzɪdjʊərɪ] *adj Jur* **r. legatee** légataire *mf* (à titre) universel(le)

residue [ˈrezɪdjuː] *n* **(a)** (*of army, fortune etc*) reste(s) *m(pl)*; *Jur* (*of estate*) reliquat *m* **(b)** *Ch, Ind etc* résidu *m*

residuum, *pl* **-a** [rɪˈzɪdjʊəm, -ə] *n Ch* résidu *m*

resign [rɪˈzaɪn] **1** *vi* démissionner, donner sa démission (**from** de); **he has resigned as Prime Minister** il a démissionné de son poste de Premier ministre; *Parl* **r.!, r.!** démission! démission! **2** *vt* (*position*) résigner; **to r. one's job** démissionner de son poste; **to r. sth to sb** abandonner *ou* céder qch à qn; **to r. oneself to sth/to doing sth** se résigner à qch/à faire qch

resignation [rezɪgˈneɪʃən] *n* **(a)** (*from job*) démission *f*; **to give (in)** *or* **send in** *or Fml* **tender one's r.** donner sa démission **(b)** (*attitude*) résignation *f*; **to accept one's fate with r.** accepter son sort avec résignation

resigned [rɪˈzaɪnd] *adj* résigné; **to be r. to sth** être résigné à qch; **to be r. to one's fate** s'être résigné

resignedly [rɪˈzaɪnɪdlɪ] *adv* (*to say, look at*) avec résignation, d'un ton/d'un air résigné

resilience [rɪˈzɪlɪəns] *n* (*of material, metal etc*) élasticité *f*; *Fig* (*of person*) (*physical*) résistance *f*; (*mental*) ressort *m*; (*of economy etc*) faculté *f* de reprise; **to have r.** (*of person*) avoir du ressort

resilient [rɪˈzɪlɪənt] *adj* (*material, metal*) élastique; *Fig* **to be r.** (*of person*) (*physically*) être résistant; (*mentally*) avoir du ressort; **children are more r. than adults** les enfants se remettent plus vite que les adultes; **the economy is proving remarkably r.** l'économie fait preuve d'une remarquable capacité de reprise

resin ['rezɪn] *n* résine *f*; **to tap trees for r.** gemmer des arbres
resinated ['rezɪneɪtɪd] *adj* (*wine*) résiné
resinous ['rezɪnəs] *adj* résineux
resist [rɪ'zɪst] **1** *vt* (*person, attack, corrosion, temptation etc*) résister à; (*influence, attempt*) s'opposer à, résister à; (*change*) s'opposer à, ne pas aimer; (*suggestion*) repousser; *Jur* **to r. arrest** opposer une résistance aux forces de l'ordre lors d'une arrestation; **I couldn't r. telling him** je n'ai pas pu m'empêcher *ou* me retenir de le lui dire; **I can't r. chocolates** je ne peux pas résister devant des chocolats **2** *vi* résister
resistance [rɪ'zɪstəns] *n* **(a)** (*to attack, corrosion, temptation, influence, change etc*) résistance *f* **(to** à**)**; **to put up (a)** *or* **offer r.** résister, offrir une résistance **(to** à**)**; **to make** *or* **offer no r.** n'offrir *ou* n'opposer aucune résistance; **to offer no r. to a suggestion** ne pas s'opposer à une proposition; **to meet with no r.** ne rencontrer aucune résistance; **to have no r. left** (*to illness etc*) ne plus avoir de résistance; *Fig* **to take the line of least r.** aller au plus facile, suivre la loi du moindre effort; **the (French) R.** la Résistance

(b) *El, Phys etc* résistance *f*; **r. coupling** couplage *m* par résistance; **r. thermometer** thermomètre *m* à résistance; **r. welding** soudure *f* électrique par résistance
resistance fighter *n* résistant, -ante
resistance movement *n Pol etc* résistance *f*
resistant [rɪ'zɪstənt] *adj* résistant **(to** à**)**; **to be r. to change** (*of person*) s'opposer à *ou* ne pas aimer les changements; *Med* **r. to** rebelle à
-resistant [rɪ'zɪstənt] *suff* **corrosion/heat-r.** résistant à la corrosion/la chaleur
resistor [rɪ'zɪstər] *n El* résistance *f*
resit[1] ['riːsɪt] *n Br Univ F* (*exam*) **the resits are scheduled for August** la session de rattrapage est prévue pour le mois d'août; **how many resits do you have?** combien d'examens est-ce que tu as à repasser?; **the French r. is on Monday** la deuxième session de l'examen de français est lundi
resit[2] [riː'sɪt] *vt Br* (*pt, pp* **resat** [riː'sæt]; *prp* **resitting**) (*exam, driving test*) repasser
resize [riː'saɪz] *vt Comptr* (*window*) redimensionner; **r. box** case *f* de redimensionnement
resole [riː'səʊl] *vt* ressemeler
resolute ['rezəluːt] *adj* (*person*) résolu, déterminé; (*answer, voice*) résolu, ferme; (*refusal, opposition*) ferme
resolutely ['rezəluːtlɪ] *adv* (*to say*) résolument; (*to refuse, oppose sth*) fermement
resoluteness ['rezəluːtnɪs] *n* résolution *f*, fermeté *f*
resolution [rezə'luːʃən] *n* **(a)** (*decision*) (*of individual*) résolution *f*; **to make a r. to do sth** prendre la résolution de faire qch; **have you made any New Year resolutions?** est-ce que tu as pris de bonnes résolutions pour le nouvel an?; **to keep/break a New Year r.** tenir/ne pas tenir une résolution prise à l'occasion du nouvel an

(b) (*decision*) (*of committee, meeting etc*) résolution *f*; **to put a r. to the meeting** soumettre *ou* proposer une résolution à l'assemblée; **to pass** *or* **carry** *or* **adopt a r.** adopter une résolution; **the committee passed a r. that he should be expelled** *or* **to expel him** le comité a adopté la résolution de l'expulser; **the r. was rejected** la résolution a été refusée

(c) (*firmness*) résolution *f*, fermeté *f*; **her r. was strengthened by their refusal** sa résolution s'est trouvée renforcée par leur refus; **there was a note of r. in his voice** il parla d'un ton résolu

(d) (*solving*) (*of difficulty, problem etc*) résolution *f*

(e) *Med* (*of tumour*) résolution *f*

(f) *TV, Comptr* (*of screen, image etc*) résolution *f*; **high r. screen** écran à haute résolution *ou* définition
resolve[1] [rɪ'zɒlv] *n* **(a)** (*decision*) résolution *f*; **to make a firm r. to do sth** prendre la résolution de faire qch **(b)** = **resolution (c)**
resolve[2] **1** *vt* **(a)** (*decide*) **to r. to do sth** (*of individual*) se décider *ou* se résoudre à faire qch, décider *ou* résoudre de faire qch; (*of committee*) adopter la résolution de faire qch, décider *ou* résoudre de faire qch; **the committee has resolved that ...** le comité a décidé que ...

(b) (*solve*) (*problem, difficulty*) résoudre; (*crisis, situation*) apporter une solution à

(c) *Ch* (*substance*) résoudre en ses éléments; **to r. itself** (*of substance*) se résoudre

2 *vi* **(a)** (*of person*) **to r. (up)on/against doing** décider *ou* résoudre de faire/ne pas faire

(b) *Ch* (*of chemical etc*) se résoudre **(into** en**)**

(c) *Med* (*of tumour*) se résoudre, se résorber
resolved [rɪ'zɒlvd] *adj* résolu; **to be r. to do sth** être résolu *ou* décidé à faire qch
resolving [rɪ'zɒlvɪŋ] *n* **r. power** (*of lens*) pouvoir *m* de résolution
resonance ['rez(ə)nəns] *n* (*of instrument*), *Electron* résonance *f*; (*of voice*) sonorité *f*; *Aut* **r. chamber** (*in silencer*) pot *m* de résonance; *Electron* **r. curve** courbe *f* de résonance
resonant ['rezənənt] *adj* (*sound*), *Electron* résonnant; (*voice, room*) qui résonne, sonore; **to be r. with** résonner de; **his voice was r. with emotion** sa voix vibrait d'émotion; *Electron* **r. frequency** fréquence *f* de résonance
resonate ['rezəneɪt] *vi* retentir **(with** de**)**; **his voice resonated with emotion** sa voix vibrait d'émotion
resonator ['rezəneɪtər] *n Electron etc* résonateur *m*
resort[1] [rɪ'zɔːt] *n* **(a)** (*recourse*) recours *m* **(to** à**)**; (*person resorted to*) recours, ressource *f*; **to have r. to sth** avoir recours à qch; **without r. to** sans avoir recours à, sans recourir à; **in the** *or* **as a last r.** en dernier recours *ou* ressort, en désespoir de cause; **she would be my last r.** je ne m'adresserais à elle qu'en dernier recours **(b)** **(holiday) r.** lieu *m* de vacances; **health r.** station *f* climatique *ou* thermale; **seaside r.** station balnéaire; **ski r.** station de ski; **r. hotel** hôtel *m* saisonnier *ou* touristique; **r. tax** (*hotel tax*) taxe *f* sur l'hôtellerie **(c)** (*haunt*) lieu *m* de rendez-vous **(of** pour**)**, *Pej* repaire *m* **(of** de**)**
resort[2] *vi* **to r. to** avoir recours à, recourir à; **to r. to doing sth** en venir à faire qch; **to r. to drink** se rabattre sur la boisson; **to r. to sb (for help)** avoir recours *ou* faire appel *ou* recourir à qn; **to r. to force** avoir recours à la force
resound [rɪ'zaʊnd] *vi* (*of place*) résonner, retentir **(with** de**)**; (*of voice*) résonner; *Fig* (*of event*) avoir du retentissement
resounding [rɪ'zaʊndɪŋ] *adj* (*applause, defeat, failure*) retentissant; (*laugh*) sonore; (*success, victory*) éclatant, retentissant; **her first novel was a r. success/failure** son premier roman a connu un succès/échec retentissant
resoundingly [rɪ'zaʊndɪŋlɪ] *adv* d'une manière retentissante; **to be r. successful** (*of author, play etc*) connaître un succès retentissant
resource[1] [rɪ'sɔːs, -'zɔːs] *n* **(a)** (*wealth*) **resources** ressources *fpl*; **human resources** ressources humaines; **r. market** marché *m* de ressources **(b)** (*expedient, recourse*) ressource *f*; **inner resources** ressource; **to be at the end of one's resources** être au bout de ses *ou* à bout de ressources; **he was left to his own resources** il a dû se débrouiller tout seul; *Am* **r. person** (*contact*) contact *m* **(c)** (*ingenuity*) ressource *f*; **person of great r.** personne *f* (pleine) de ressource(s)
resource[2] *vt* (*project*) financer, encadrer financièrement, humainement et matériellement
resource-based *adj* (*tourist attraction*) faisant usage de ressources naturelles ou monument déjà sur place
resourceful [rɪ'sɔːsfʊl, -'zɔːs-] *adj* (*person*) habile, ingénieux, (plein) de ressources, *F* débrouillard; (*solution etc*) habile, ingénieux; **that was very r. of you** tu as fait preuve de beaucoup de débrouillardise; **he's a r. sort of person** il a de la ressource
resourcefully [rɪ'sɔːsfəlɪ, -'zɔːs-] *adv* habilement, ingénieusement
resourcefulness [rɪ'sɔːsfʊlnɪs, -'zɔːs-] *n* (*of person, solution*) ingéniosité *f*, habileté *f*, *F* débrouillardise *f*
resourcing [rɪ'sɔːsɪŋ, -'zɔːs-] *n Br* (*of project etc*) financement *m*; **r. officer** agent *m* de financement
respect[1] [rɪ'spekt] *n* **(a)** (*admiration*) respect *m* **(for** pour**)**; **to earn** *or* **gain** *or* **win sb's r.** gagner le respect de qn; **to have great r. for sb, to hold sb in great r.** avoir beaucoup de respect pour qn; **he knows how to command r.** il sait se faire respecter; **her achievements command r.** ses réussites suscitent le respect

(b) (*consideration*) respect *m* **(for** pour**)**; **to have r. for sb** avoir du respect pour qn; **she has little r. for the truth/other people's property** elle fait peu de cas de la vérité/du bien d'autrui, elle a peu de respect pour la vérité/le bien d'autrui; **to do sth as a mark of r.** faire qch par respect; **he took his hat off as a mark of r.** il a ôté son chapeau en signe de respect; **there was a new note of r. in his voice** il y avait maintenant une note de respect dans sa voix; **he shows little r. for his parents** il ne se montre guère respectueux avec *ou* envers ses parents; **show your father a little more r.!** sois un peu plus respectueux avec *ou* envers ton père!; **out of r. for ...** par respect *ou* égard *ou* considération pour ...; **out of r. for her feelings** pour ménager sa sensibilité; **treat those plates with r.** (*they are fragile*) fais attention à ces assiettes; **treat matches with r.** (*they are dangerous*) utilisez les allumettes avec prudence; **treat mountains with r.** (*be careful*) soyez prudent en montagne; **with all due r. (to you)** sauf votre respect, sauf le respect que je vous dois, sans vouloir vous vexer *ou* offenser; **with the greatest r. to my**

colleague, I feel that ... sans vouloir critiquer ma collègue, je pense que ...; **with the greatest r., sir, I cannot agree** sans vouloir vous offenser, Monsieur, je ne suis pas d'accord

(c) respects respects *mpl*, hommages *mpl*; **(give** *or* **send) my respects to your mother** (présentez *ou* envoyez) mes hommages à votre mère; **to pay one's respects to sb** présenter ses respects *ou* ses hommages à qn; **to pay one's last respects** (*at funeral*) rendre les derniers hommages **(to** à)

(d) (*aspect*) égard *m*; **in some** *or* **certain respects** à certains égards; **in at least two respects** à au moins deux égards; **in all respects** *or* **every r.** à tous (les) égards, sous tous les rapports; **in this r.** à cet égard; **in other respects** à d'autres égards; **with r. to, in r. of** en ce qui concerne

respect[2] *vt* **(a)** (*admire*) respecter, avoir du respect pour; **he was greatly respected** il était très respecté **(for** pour); **to be universally respected** être respecté de tous **(b)** (*show consideration for*) (*person's wish, opinion etc*) respecter; **I r. myself too much to do that** je me respecte trop pour faire cela **(c)** (*comply with*) (*the law, speed limit etc*) respecter

respectability [rɪspektə'bɪlɪtɪ] *n* respectabilité *f*

respectable [rɪ'spektəb(ə)l] *adj* **(a)** (*honourable, decent*) (*family, person etc*) respectable, digne de respect; (*upbringing etc*) comme il faut; (*behaviour, clothes*) convenable, comme il faut; **he always looked so r.** il avait toujours l'air tellement comme il faut; **to be r.** (*dressed*) être présentable; **I'm not r., you answer the door** va ouvrir, je ne suis pas présentable **(b)** (*fairly good or large etc*) respectable; (*salary, mark, result*) honorable; **a r. number of people** un bon nombre de gens; **a r. sum** une somme respectable *ou* rondelette

respectably [rɪ'spektəblɪ] *adv* **(a)** de manière respectable; (*to behave, dress*) convenablement; (*brought up*) comme il faut; **to live r.** mener une existence respectable **(b)** (*rather well*) plutôt bien

respecter [rɪ'spektər] *n* **to be no r. of the law** ne pas respecter la loi; **to be no r. of persons** (*of death, taxes etc*) ne faire acception de personne; (*of person*) ne s'en laisser imposer par personne

respectful [rɪ'spektfʊl] *adj* respectueux **(to, towards** envers; **of** de); **to stand at a r. distance** se tenir à distance respectueuse

respectfully [rɪ'spektfəlɪ] *adv* (*to listen, say etc*) respectueusement, avec respect; *Old-fashioned* **(I remain) yours r.** (*at end of letter*) veuillez agréer l'expression de mes sentiments respectueux

respectfulness [rɪ'spektfəlnɪs] *n* (*of person*) respect *m*; **the r. of his answer** le respect avec lequel il a répondu

respecting [rɪ'spektɪŋ] *prep Fml* concernant, relatif à; **r. your article** à propos de votre article

respective [rɪ'spektɪv] *adj* respectif

respectively [rɪ'spektɪvlɪ] *adv* respectivement

respiration [respɪ'reɪʃən] *n* respiration *f*

respirator ['respɪreɪtər] *n Med* respirateur *m*; (*gas mask*) masque *m* à gaz; **to be on a r.** être sous respirateur

respiratory [rɪ'spɪrɪt(ə)rɪ] *adj* (*disease, organ, system*) respiratoire; **r. failure** insuffisance *f* respiratoire

respire [rɪ'spaɪər] *vti* respirer

respite ['respaɪt] *n* **(a)** (*from worry etc*) répit *m*; **to work without r.** travailler sans relâche; **the weekend was a welcome r.** le weekend a constitué un répit bienvenu **(b)** (*from obligation*) sursis *m*, délai *m*; **to get/grant a r.** obtenir/accorder un délai

resplendence [rɪ'splendəns] *n Fml* splendeur *f*, resplendissement *m*

resplendent [rɪ'splendənt] *adj Fml* resplendissant, éblouissant

resplendently [rɪ'splendəntlɪ] *adv* de manière resplendissante *ou* éblouissante; (*decorated, dressed*) somptueusement

respond [rɪ'spɒnd] *vi* **(a)** (*answer*) répondre **(to** à); *Rel* réciter *ou* chanter les répons; **he responded with a smile** il a répondu par un sourire

(b) (*react*) (*to affection, kindness etc*) répondre, être sensible **(to** à); (*to order*) répondre, réagir **(to** à); **to fail to r. to sb's advances** ne pas répondre aux avances de qn; **to r. generously to an appeal** répondre généreusement à un appel; *Fig* **to r. to pressure** céder aux pressions; *Med* **to r. to treatment** (*of patient*) réagir positivement au traitement; *Med* **she is not responding** elle ne réagit pas; **the tumour/illness is not responding to treatment** le traitement n'a pas d'effet *ou* n'agit pas sur la tumeur/la maladie; *Av, Aut* **to r. well** bien répondre; **children r. well to responsibility** les enfants aiment bien qu'on leur donne des responsabilités; *Aut, Av* **to r. to the controls** obéir aux commandes

respondent [rɪ'spɒndənt] *n* **(a)** *Jur* (*esp in divorce case*) défendeur, -eresse; (*in appeal case*) intimé, -ée **(b)** (*to questionnaire*) sondé *m*; (*in opinion poll*) personne *f* interrogée *ou* sondée, répondant *m*; **the respondents** les sondés

response [rɪ'spɒns] *n* **(a)** (*answer*) réponse *f*; *Rel* répons *m*; **he made no r.** il n'a pas répondu, il n'a pas donné de réponse; *Rel* **to make the responses at Mass** répondre la messe; **what was her r.?** (*answer*) quelle a été sa réponse?; **he smiled in r.** il a souri en guise de réponse; **in r. to your question** en réponse à votre question, pour répondre à votre question; **in r. to your letter** suite à votre lettre; **r. rate** (*to questionnaire etc*) taux *m* de réponse

(b) (*reaction*) *Med* réaction *f*; *Physiol* réponse *f*, réaction; **what was the Government's r.?** comment le gouvernement a-t-il réagi?; **the appeal met with a generous r.** les gens ont répondu généreusement à l'appel; **the decision was taken in r. to ...** la décision a été prise en réaction à ...; *Mil* **flexible r.** réponse graduée; **r. time** (*of device*) temps *m* de réponse

responsibility [rɪspɒnsɪ'bɪlɪtɪ] *n* **(a)** (*authority*) responsabilité *f*; **to have r. for sth** avoir la responsabilité de qch; **a position of r.** un poste de *ou* à responsabilité; **to have a lot of r. at an early age** avoir beaucoup de responsabilités très jeune; **to do sth on one's own r.** prendre la responsabilité de faire qch

(b) (*blame*) responsabilité *f*; **to take** *or* **accept full r. for sth** prendre *ou* accepter la responsabilité de qch; **we accept no r. for lost or stolen items** (*notice in restaurant etc*) nous déclinons toute responsabilité pour les objets perdus ou volés; **to refuse to accept any r. for the accident** décliner toute responsabilité pour *ou* quant à l'accident; **no-one has yet claimed r. for the attack** personne n'a encore revendiqué l'attaque; **the r. is mine** c'est moi qui suis responsable

(c) (*obligation*) responsabilité *f*; **sense of r.** sens *m* des responsabilités; **you have a r. to your family** vous avez la responsabilité de votre famille

(d) (*task, duty*) responsabilité *f*; **it's my r.** c'est ma responsabilité **(to do** de faire); **answering the phone is your r., not mine** c'est à toi de répondre au téléphone, pas à moi; **his new responsibilities give him no time for leisure** ses nouvelles fonctions *ou* responsabilités ne lui laissent aucune place pour ses loisirs; **bringing up children is quite a r.** élever des enfants est une grande responsabilité

responsible [rɪ'spɒnsɪb(ə)l] *adj* **(a)** (*trustworthy*) (*attitude, person*) responsable; **r. job** poste *m* à responsabilités; **no r. parent would have left the children alone** un parent responsable n'aurait pas laissé les enfants tout seuls; **try to be a bit more r. in future** essaye d'être un peu plus responsable à l'avenir; **r. tourism** (*green tourism*) tourisme *m* vert

(b) (*for accident, mistake etc*) responsable **(for** de); **to hold sb r.** tenir qn (pour) responsable **(for** de); *Jur* **to be (legally) r. for sb's actions** être solidaire des actes de qn; **he is not r. for his actions** il n'est pas responsable de ses actes

(c) (*accountable*) responsable **(for** de; **to sb** devant qn); **to be r. for sb/sth** avoir la responsabilité de qn/qch; **to make sb r. for sth** donner à qn la responsabilité de qch; **I will be r. for his safety** je me porte garant de sa sécurité; **you and she will be jointly r. for the project** vous et elle partagerez la responsabilité du projet; **she had been r. for the party's successful election campaign** c'est grâce à elle que la campagne électorale fut un succès

responsibly [rɪ'spɒnsɪblɪ] *adv* (*to behave, act*) de façon responsable

responsive [rɪ'spɒnsɪv] *adj* (*reacting*) qui réagit; (*alert*) éveillé; *Med* (*illness, rash etc*) qui réagit bien **(to** à); *Aut* (*brakes, steering etc*) qui répond bien; (*engine*) nerveux; **r. to** (*to kindness*) sensible à; (*to idea, suggestion*) réceptif à; **he is very r. to my needs** il est très attentif à mes besoins; **you're not being very r.** (*not reacting verbally*) tu ne dis rien; (*not reacting physically*) il n'y a pas de réaction de ta part, tu ne réagis pas; **people become more r. if ...** les gens sont plus réceptifs si ...; **they're not very r. tonight** (*of audience*) ils ne réagissent pas beaucoup *ou* ils sont plutôt amorphes ce soir; **most allergies are r. to this treatment** on peut guérir la plupart des allergies avec ce traitement

responsiveness [rɪ'spɒnsɪvnɪs] *n* (*of person*) (*to kindness*) sensibilité *f* **(to** à); (*to idea etc*) réceptivité *f* **(to** à); **we were pleased by their r. to the plan** la façon dont ils ont réagi au projet nous a plu

respray[1] ['riːspreɪ] *n* **the car's had a r.** la voiture a été repeinte

respray[2] [riː'spreɪ] *vt* repeindre au pistolet

rest[1] [rest] *n* **(a)** (*repose*) repos *m*; **to have** *or* **take a r.** se reposer **(from** de); **to have a good night's r.** passer une bonne nuit; **I need a r.** j'ai besoin de me reposer, j'ai besoin de repos; **my arms need a r.** j'ai besoin de me reposer les bras; **we've earned a r.** nous avons mérité un peu de repos;

to stop for a r. faire une pause; **to put** *or* **set sb's mind at r.** dissiper les craintes *ou* inquiétudes de qn, rassurer qn; **to give sb a r. from sth** permettre à qn de se reposer de qch; *F* **give it a r., will you!** (*stop doing sth, talking etc*) arrête cinq minutes, tu veux bien!; *F* **give that music a r.!** arrête un peu cette musique!; **give studying a r. for a day or two** arrête de travailler pendant un ou deux jours; **she's giving tennis a r. this year** elle a arrêté le tennis cette année; **those children give her no r.** ces enfants ne lui laissent aucun repos; **his conscience gave him no r.** sa conscience ne lui laissait pas de répit; **you must get some more r.** vous devez vous reposer davantage; **a day of r., a day's r.** un jour de repos; **the day of r.** le repos dominical; **to come to r.** (*of ball, vehicle etc*) s'arrêter, s'immobiliser; (*of bird, eyes*) se poser (**on** sur); *Am Mil* **r. and recreation** permission *f*; *Am Mil* **two days' r. and recreation** deux jours de permission; *Euph* **to be at r.** (*be dead*) reposer en paix; *Euph* **to be laid to r.** (*buried*) être enterré; *Euph* **to be** *or* **lie at r.** (*dead*) reposer en paix; *Euph* **to lay sb to r.** porter qn en terre, enterrer qn; *Fig* **to lay** *or* **put a plan to r.** (*not carry any further*) renoncer à *ou* abandonner un projet; **to lay** *or* **put allegations/doubts/suspicions to r.** dissiper des allégations/des doutes/des suspicions; **perhaps we could lay the matter to r.** (*not discuss any further*) peut-être qu'on pourrait arrêter de parler de cette affaire une bonne fois pour toutes; **the matter should be laid to r. as quickly as possible** (*resolved*) cette affaire doit être résolue au plus vite

(**b**) (*support*) support *m*; (*for billiard cue*) chevalet *m*; *Tel* (*for receiver*) étrier *m*

(**c**) *Mus* (*silence*) silence *m*

rest[2] **1** *vi* (**a**) (*relax*) se reposer, prendre du repos; **you need to r. (up)** il vous faut le repos complet; **to r. from one's work** se reposer de son travail; **to r. easy** se détendre; **to be resting** (*of actor*) = se trouver sans engagement; **she is resting comfortably** (*after operation etc*) son état est satisfaisant; **I won't r. until ...** je n'aurai de cesse que ... + *sub*; **to r. on** (*of roof etc*) reposer sur; **he was resting on his shovel** il s'appuyait sur sa pelle; **his head was resting on her shoulder** il avait la tête appuyée contre son épaule; *Fig* **to r. on one's oars** se reposer, *F* souffler; *Fig* **to r. on one's laurels** se reposer *ou* s'endormir sur ses lauriers

(**b**) (*be buried*) être enterré, reposer; **may they r. in peace!** qu'ils reposent en paix!; **r. in peace** (*inscription on gravestone*) qu'il(s)/qu'elle(s) repose(nt) en paix

(**c**) (*remain*) **there the matter rests** l'affaire en reste *ou* en est là; **I won't let it r. at that** cela ne se passera pas ainsi; **let it r.!** (*stop talking about it*) n'en parlons plus!; (*stop pursuing the matter*) ça suffit; **can't we let it r.?** (*stop talking about it*) restons-en là, je vous en prie; **r. assured** soyez certain *ou* assuré (**that** que); **a heavy responsibility rests (up)on them** une lourde responsabilité pèse sur eux; **to r. with** (*of decision, responsibility etc*) incomber à; **it rests with you to ...** il vous incombe de ...; **it doesn't r. with me to decide** ce n'est pas à moi qu'il incombe de décider

(**d**) (*be based*) **to r. on** (*of argument, fame*) reposer sur

(**e**) *Jur* **the defence/prosecution rests** = plaise au tribunal d'adopter mes conclusions

2 *vt* (**a**) (*repose*) **to r. oneself** se reposer; **to r. one's men/horses** laisser ses hommes/chevaux se reposer; **the coach wanted to r. his players** l'entraîneur voulait que son équipe se repose; **to r. one's eyes/legs** se reposer les yeux/les jambes; *Agr* **to r. a field** mettre un champ en jachère; **(God) r. his soul!** que Dieu ait son âme!, qu'il repose en paix!

(**b**) (*lean*) (*one's elbows*) appuyer (**on** sur); (*one's head*) reposer (**on** sur); (*one's hopes, confidence etc*) fonder (**on** sur)

(**c**) (*base*) (*argument, theory*) fonder (**on** sur)

(**d**) *esp Am Jur* **to r. one's case** conclure son plaidoyer; *Fig* **I r. my case** j'ai dit ce que j'avais à dire

rest[3] *n* **the r.** (*remainder*) le reste (**of** de); (*others*) les autres *mfpl*; **where's the r. (of it)?** (*of money, food etc*) où est le reste?; **the r. of the men/cups** les autres hommes/tasses; **I'm keeping the r. of it for tomorrow** je garde le reste *ou* le restant pour demain; **do you want to watch the r. of the news?** est-ce que tu veux regarder le reste des actualités?; **(as) for the r.** quant au reste, pour le reste; **and (all) the r. of it** et tout le reste; **the r. of us** nous autres, le reste (d'entre nous); **it's just another day like all the r.** c'est un jour comme un autre

rest area *n Aut Austr* aire *f* de repos

restart [riː'stɑːt] **1** *vt* (*work etc*) recommencer, reprendre; (*machine*) (re)mettre en marche; (*engine*) remettre en marche, relancer; (*computer*) réamorcer **2** *vi* (*of job etc*) recommencer, reprendre; (*of machine, engine*) se remettre en marche; (*of computer*) se réamorcer

restate [riː'steɪt] *vt* (**a**) (*repeat*) (*theory, viewpoint*) exposer de nouveau; *Mus* (*theme*) reprendre; **she restated her concern about the child's safety** elle a réitéré ses inquiétudes à propos de la sécurité de l'enfant (**b**) (*rephrase*) (*question*) reformuler, formuler de nouveau

restatement [riː'steɪtmənt] *n* (**a**) (*repetition*) (*of theory, viewpoint*) nouvel exposé *m*; **it's a point that bears r.** c'est une chose qui mérite d'être répétée (**b**) (*rephrasing*) (*of question*) nouvelle formulation *f*

restaurant ['restrɒnt] *n* restaurant *m*; *Br Rail* **r. car** wagon-restaurant *m*, *pl* wagons-restaurants; **r. chain** chaîne *f* de restaurants; **r. manager** gérant *m* de restaurant

restaurateur [restərə'tɜːr] *n* restaurateur, -trice

rest-cure *n* cure *f* de repos; *Fig* **this job is no r.** ce travail n'est pas une sinécure

rest-day *n* (*of cricketer, tennis player etc*) jour *m* de repos; (*of shift worker*) jour de congé

rested ['restɪd] *adj* reposé; **to feel r.** se sentir (bien) reposé *ou* frais et dispos

restful ['restfʊl] *adj* (*holiday, weekend, place etc*) reposant; **r. to the eyes** (*colour, lighting*) qui repose les yeux, reposant pour la vue

restfully ['restfəlɪ] *adv* (*to spend time*) paisiblement, tranquillement

rest-home *n* (**a**) (*for convalescents*) maison *f* de repos (**b**) (*for elderly*) maison *f* de retraite; **to go into/to put sb in a r.** aller en/mettre qn en maison de retraite

resting ['restɪŋ] *n* **r. place** abri *m*; **last r. place** dernière demeure *f*

restitution [restɪ'tjuːʃən] *n Fml* (*of stolen property*) restitution *f*; (*compensation*) réparation *f*; **to make r. of sth** (*give back*) restituer qch; **to make r. for sth** (*make up for*) réparer qch; (*by providing monetary compensation*) verser des dommages-intérêts pour qch; **he should make full r.** il devrait verser une compensation intégrale

restive ['restɪv] *adj* (*nervous*) (*person, crowd*) agité; (*apt to rebel*) (*person, child*) récalcitrant, indocile, rétif; (*horse*) rétif

restively ['restɪvlɪ] *adv* nerveusement

restiveness ['restɪvnɪs] *n* (*of population, because of individual's nervousness*) agitation *f*; (*because of boredom*) (*of audience*) impatience *f*; (*of child*) nature *f* turbulente; (*of horse*) nature rétive

restless ['restlɪs] *adj* (*person*) nerveux, agité; (*child*) agité, remuant; (*sea*) agité; (*wind*) incessant; **to be r. in one's sleep** *or* **a r. sleeper** avoir un *ou* le sommeil agité; **I've had** *or* **spent a r. night** j'ai passé une nuit agitée; **r. mind** esprit agité; **she's feeling a bit r.** (*in present job, situation etc*) elle a envie de voir *ou* de faire autre chose; **the audience was getting r.** l'auditoire s'impatientait

restlessly ['restlɪslɪ] *adv* (*to move*) (*of person*) avec agitation; *Lit* (*of wind*) sans cesse

restlessness ['restlɪsnɪs] *n* (*of person, sea*) agitation *f*; (*of mind*) nervosité *f*, état *m* fiévreux; (*of audience*) impatience *f*

restock [riː'stɒk] **1** *vt* (*shelves, shop*) réapprovisionner (**with** en); (*freezer*) refaire le plein de; **to r. a river (with fish)** rempoissonner une rivière **2** *vi* (*of shop*) se réapprovisionner

restoration [restə'reɪʃən] *n* (**a**) (*of monument, building, furniture etc*) restauration *f* (**b**) (*of communications, law and order*) rétablissement *m* (**c**) (*of lost property, fortune*) restitution *f*; (*of dynasty*) restauration *f*, rétablissement *m* sur le trône; *Br Hist, Fr Hist* **the R.** la Restauration; *Br* **R. comedy/literature/poetry** comédie *f*/littérature *f*/poésie *f* de (l'époque de) la Restauration

restoration fund *n* caisse *f* de restauration

restoration project *n* projet *m* de restauration

restoration work *n* travail *m* de restauration

restorative [rɪ'stɔːrətɪv, -'stɒr-] **1** *n* (*medicine*) cordial *m* **2** *adj* **the r. powers of sleep** les pouvoirs reconstituants du sommeil

restore[1] *n Comptr* **to do a r.** faire une restauration

restore[2] [rɪ'stɔːr] *vt* (**a**) (*monument, building, furniture etc*) restaurer; **to r. sth to its former glory** redonner son éclat d'antan à qch; **to be restored to its former glory** retrouver son éclat d'antan

(**b**) *Comptr* (*files*) restaurer

(**c**) (*bring back*) (*law and order, calm*) rétablir; (*peace*) rétablir, restaurer; (*confidence*) faire renaître; (*discipline, dynasty*) restaurer; **order is being restored** l'ordre est en train d'être rétabli; **to r. sb to health** rétablir la santé de qn; **to r. a company to profitability** permettre à une entreprise de redevenir bénéficiaire; **I feel quite restored** je me sens revigoré; **to r. sb to life** ramener qn à la vie; **to r. sb's strength** redonner des forces à qn; **to r. sb's sight/hearing** rendre la vue/l'ouïe à qn; **to r. the circulation** réactiver la circulation

(**d**) (*give back*) restituer, rendre (**to sb** à qn); **to r. sth to its place/former condition** remettre qch à sa place *ou* en place/ en état
restorer [rɪ'stɔːrər] *n* (**a**) (*of building, picture etc*) restaurateur, -trice (**b**) (*for hair*) régénérateur *m* capillaire
restrain [rɪ'streɪn] *vt* (*person, dog, one's curiosity*) retenir; (*passions*) refréner; (*crowd, tears*) retenir, contenir; (*anger*) contenir, refouler; **to r. oneself** se maîtriser, se contenir; **I had to r. an impulse to laugh out loud/to hit him** il a fallu que je me retienne pour ne pas rire tout haut/pour ne pas le frapper; **to r. sb from doing sth** empêcher qn de faire qch; **he had to be forcibly restrained** il a fallu le retenir de force; **to r. sb's activities** mettre un frein aux activités de qn
restrained [rɪ'streɪnd] *adj* (*feelings*) contenu; (*tone, terms*) mesuré; (*style*) sobre; (*silence*) prudent; (*response*) mitigé; **her manner was very r.** son attitude était très réservée
restraining [rɪ'streɪnɪŋ] *adj* (*influence*) modérateur; *Jur* qui retient, restrictif; **r. order** injonction *f*
restraint [rɪ'streɪnt] *n* (**a**) (*moderation*) (*of person*) modération *f*, mesure *f*; (*of style*) sobriété *f*; **to throw aside all r.** abandonner toute mesure; **to show** *or* **exercise great r.** faire preuve de beaucoup de modération; **to urge r.** demander instamment qu'on fasse preuve de modération (**in doing** en faisant)
(**b**) (*restriction*) restriction *f*; (*of powers, wages*) limitation *f*; **to put a r. on sb** contraindre qn; **to break free of all r.** se déchaîner; **to be under no r.** avoir ses coudées franches; **without r.** (*to laugh, cry, speak etc*) sans se retenir; **to impose restraints** imposer des restrictions (**on** sur); **r. of trade** restrictions commerciales; **to put sb under r.** (*mental patient*) mettre la camisole de force à qn; (*prisoner*) mettre les menottes à qn
restrict [rɪ'strɪkt] *vt* (*speed etc*) limiter, restreindre (**to** à); **to r. oneself to ...** se limiter à ..., se restreindre à ...; **he is restricted to one glass of wine a day** il n'a droit qu'à un verre de vin par jour; **fog is restricting visibility** le brouillard limite la visibilité; **membership is restricted to the over-20s** la qualité de membre est réservée aux personnes âgées de plus de 20 ans; *Banking* **to r. the supply of a currency** raréfier une monnaie
restricted [rɪ'strɪktɪd] *adj* (*sense, space, use*) restreint, limité; (*sale*) contrôlé; (*speed*) limité; **to be on a r. diet** suivre un régime sévère *ou* strict; **she feels less r. wearing trousers** elle se sent plus libre (de ses mouvements) lorsqu'elle porte un pantalon; **r. access** (*notice on factory gate etc*) accès réservé; *Comptr* **r-access system** système *m* à accès restreint; **r. area** *Aut* zone *f* à vitesse limitée; *Admin, Mil* zone interdite; *Admin* **r. document** document *m* secret; *Th* **seats with a r. view (of the stage)** des places depuis lesquelles on ne voit pas toute la scène
restriction [rɪ'strɪkʃən] *n* restriction *f*; (*of speed etc*) limitation *f*; **to place** *or* **set** *or* **impose restrictions on sth** apporter des restrictions à qch
restrictive [rɪ'strɪktɪv] *adj* (*clause, measure etc*) restrictif; *Br Ind* **r. practices** pratiques *fpl* restrictives
restring [riː'strɪŋ] *vt* (*pt, pp* **restrung** [riː'strʌŋ]) (*pearls*) enfiler de nouveau; (*violin*) remonter; (*guitar*) remplacer les cordes de; (*racket*) recorder
rest room *n Am* toilettes *fpl*
restructure [riː'strʌktʃər] *vt* (*company, industry, economy*) restructurer
restructuring [riː'strʌktʃərɪŋ] *n* restructuration *f*
rest stop *n Aut Am* aire *f* de repos; **to make a r.** faire une pause pour se détendre
restyle [riː'staɪl] *vt* (*car*) changer le style de; (*hair*) changer la coupe de
result[1] [rɪ'zʌlt] *n* (**a**) (*of action, behaviour etc*), *Math, Sp etc* résultat *m* (**of** de); **the r. is that ...** il en résulte que ...; **as a r. of ...** à la suite de ...; **without r.** sans résultat; **results** (*of exam etc*) résultats; **I tried making some jam with disastrous results** j'ai essayé de faire des confitures mais ça a été un désastre; **if they get a good r. in this match** s'ils font un bon match; **this paint gives excellent results** cette peinture donne d'excellents résultats; **to be a** *or* **the r. of sth** résulter *ou* être le résultat de qch; **as a r.** en conséquence; **to have little** *or* **no r.** avoir peu ou pas de résultats
(**b**) (*good outcome*) **to yield** *or* **show results** donner des résultats; **she knows how to get results** elle sait comment s'y prendre pour arriver à quelque chose *ou* pour avoir des résultats; *F* **we need a r.** (*obtain a successful outcome*), *Br Sp* (*win*) il faut qu'on fasse un résultat
result[2] *vi* résulter (**from** de); **it results from this that ...** il s'ensuit que ...; **consequences resulting from ...** conséquences de ...; **to r. in** (*unpleasantness, increase, decrease*) entraîner, engendrer; (*loss of life*) entraîner, provoquer; **the summit talks resulted in a treaty** le sommet a abouti à la signature d'un traité
resultant [rɪ'zʌltənt] **1** *adj attrib* qui en résulte, résultant **2** *n Math* résultante *f*
resume ['rɪzjuːm] **1** *vt* (*relations*) reprendre, renouer; (*after short break*) (*speech, negotiations, discussions, trip*) continuer, poursuivre; **to r. one's seat** reprendre sa place, se rasseoir; **to r. doing sth** se remettre à faire qch; **to r. work** se remettre au travail; **to r. one's duties** reprendre son service *ou* ses fonctions; **she resumed her maiden name** elle a repris son nom de jeune fille **2** *vi* (*of music, speaker etc*) continuer, reprendre; **we/the meeting will r. after lunch** nous reprendrons/la réunion reprendra après le déjeuner; *Cr* **play resumed at four** le match a repris à quatre heures
résumé ['reɪzjʊmeɪ, -uːmeɪ] *n* (**a**) (*summary*) résumé *m*, abrégé *m*; **to give a r. of sth** faire un résumé de qch (**b**) *Am* (*curriculum vitae*) curriculum vitae *m inv*
resumption [rɪ'zʌmpʃən] *n* (*of relationship, negotiations etc*) reprise *f*
resurface [riː'sɜːfɪs] **1** *vt* (*road*) refaire le revêtement de **2** *vi* (*of submarine*) faire surface, revenir à la surface; *esp Hum* **when did he eventually r.?** (*return*) quand est-ce qu'il a fini par refaire surface?
resurgence [rɪ'sɜːdʒəns] *n* (*of nationalism, trend, idea, ideology*) résurgence *f*, réapparition *f*; (*of disease*) réapparition; (*of company etc*) reprise *f*
resurgent [rɪ'sɜːdʒənt] *adj usu attrib* (*idea, nationalism etc*) renaissant; (*company etc*) qui connaît une reprise
resurrect [rezə'rekt] *vt* (*the dead, Fig fashion*) ressusciter; (*era*) faire revivre; (*quarrel, argument*) réveiller; (*hopes, fears*) ranimer
resurrection [rezə'rekʃən] *n* (*of the dead*); *Fig* résurrection *f*; **the R.** la résurrection du Christ; **this resulted in the r. of their old argument** cela a relancé leur querelle
resuscitate [rɪ'sʌsɪteɪt] *vt Med* (*person*) ranimer; *Fig* (*plan*) ressortir; (*ailing company*) faire repartir
resuscitation [rɪsʌsɪ'teɪʃən] *n Med* réanimation *f*, ranimation *f*; **all attempts at r. failed** toutes les tentatives de réanimation *ou* de ranimation ont échoué; *Fig* **there was a r. of interest** il y a eu un regain d'intérêt
resuscitator [rɪ'sʌsɪteɪtər] *n* (*machine*) appareil *m* de réanimation
retail[1] ['riːteɪl] *n Com* (vente *f* au) détail *m*; **to buy/sell goods r.** *or Am* **at r.** acheter/vendre des marchandises au détail; **wholesale and r. business** commerce *m* de gros et de détail; **r. bank** banque *f* de détail; **r. banking** banque de détail; **r. chain** chaîne *f* de vente au détail; **r. customer** client, -ente qui achète au détail; **r. dealer** détaillant, -ante; **r. outlet** point *m* de vente, magasin *m* de détail; **r. panel** panel *m* de détaillants; **r. price** prix *m* de détail; **r. price index** indice *m* des prix de détail; **r. sales** vente *f* au détail; **r. selling** vente au détail; **r. shipment** expédition *f* de détail; **r. trade** commerce de détail; **r. travel agent** agent *m* de voyages détaillant; **r. wholesale** demi-gros *m*
retail[2] **1** *vt* (**a**) (*goods*) vendre au détail (**b**) (*spread*) (*gossip*) colporter **2** *vi* (*of goods*) se vendre au détail (**at, for** à)
retailer ['riːteɪlər] *n* détaillant, -ante; **r. brand** marque *f* de revendeur *ou* de détaillant *ou* de distributeur; **r. margin** marge *f* du détaillant; **retailers' group** groupement *m* de détaillants
retailing ['riːteɪlɪŋ] *n* vente *f* au détail; **r. mix** marchéage *m* de distribution
retain [rɪ'teɪn] *vt* (**a**) (*keep*) (*property, control etc*) conserver, garder; (*custom, heat etc*) conserver; **to r. the right to do sth** se réserver le droit de faire qch (**b**) **to r. sb's services** s'assurer les services de qn; *Br Jur* **to r. a barrister** *or* **counsel** retenir un avocat (à l'avance); *Jur* **retaining fee** avance *f*, provision *f* (**c**) (*hold in place*) (*object*) retenir, maintenir; *Constr* **retaining wall** mur *m* de soutènement *ou* de retenue (**d**) (*remember*) garder en mémoire, mémoriser
retained [rɪ'teɪnd] *adj Acct* **r. earnings** revenu *m* non distribué; **r. profit** bénéfices *mpl* non distribués
retainer [rɪ'teɪnər] *n* (**a**) (*fee*) avance *f*, provision *f*; **to pay sb a r.** verser une avance *ou* provision à qn (**b**) *Old-fashioned* (*servant*) serviteur *m*
retake[1] ['riːteɪk] *n* (**a**) *Cin, TV* nouvelle prise *f*; **it took several retakes** il a fallu plusieurs prises (**b**) *esp Univ* (*exam*) examen *m* à repasser; (*candidate*) candidat, -ate qui repasse un examen; **how many retakes did you have to do?** combien d'examens est-ce que tu as dû repasser?; **the r. of the history exam** *or* **the history r. will be held on ...** l'examen d'histoire de la session de rattrapage aura lieu le ...
retake[2] [riː'teɪk] *vt* (*pt* **retook** [riː'tʊk]; *pp* **retaken** [riː'teɪk(ə)n]) (**a**) *Cin, TV* (*shot*) refaire, filmer à nouveau (**b**) *esp Univ* (*exam*) repasser (**c**) (*stronghold etc*) reprendre

retaliate [rɪ'tælɪeɪt] *vi* riposter, rendre la pareille; (*in speech*) riposter; *esp Mil* user de représailles (**with** par); **to r. for an attack** riposter à une attaque (**by doing** en faisant)
retaliation [rɪtælɪ'eɪʃən] *n* riposte *f*, représailles *fpl* (**against** contre); **r. for the attack** représailles contre l'attaque; **in r.** par mesure de représailles; **in r. for** en représailles de
retaliatory [rɪ'tælɪət(ə)rɪ] *adj attrib* **r. measures** *Mil* représailles *fpl*; *Econ* mesures *fpl* de rétorsion; **r. bombing** des représailles sous forme de bombardements; **to make a r. attack on a guerrilla camp** exercer des représailles contre un camp de guérilleros
retard[1] ['ri:tɑ:d] *n esp Am F Pej* (*retarded person*) demeuré, -ée
retard[2] [rɪ'tɑ:d] *vt* (*delay growth or development of*) retarder, retarder la croissance *ou* le développement de; **to be severely (mentally) retarded** être très attardé *ou* arriéré; **mentally retarded person** (personne *f*) attardé(e) *ou* arriéré(e); **the retarded** (*used as pl*) les attardés *mpl*, les arriérés *mpl*
-retardant [rɪ'tɑ:dənt] *suff* **heat/flame-r.** qui ralentit la propagation de la chaleur/des flammes
retardation [ri:tɑ:'deɪʃən] *n* (*of growth*) retard *m*; (*of mechanism*) retardement *m*; (**mental**) **r.** arriération *f* mentale
retch [retʃ] *vi* avoir des haut-le-cœur; *Fig* **to make sb r.** soulever le cœur à qn
retching ['retʃɪŋ] *n* haut-le-cœur *mpl*; **r. noises were coming from the bathroom** on entendait quelqu'un vomir dans la salle de bain
retd (*abbr* **retired**) retraité, à la retraite
retell [ri:'tel] *vt* (*pt, pp* **retold** [ri:'təʊld]) (*story*) raconter de nouveau
retelling [ri:'telɪŋ] *n* **the number of his assailants grew with each r.** chaque fois qu'il racontait l'histoire le nombre de ses attaquants augmentait
retention [rɪ'tenʃən] *n* (*of custom*) conservation *f*; (*of authority, provisions, restrictions*) maintien *m*; (*of fact, impression etc*) mémoire *f*; *Med* (*of urine etc*) rétention *f*; **to have limited powers of r.** (*memory*) avoir peu de mémoire; **to have great powers of r.** (*memory*) avoir une excellente mémoire; *Com* **r. of title** réserve *f* de propriété
retentive [rɪ'tentɪv] *adj* (*memory*) fidèle; (*person*) qui a une bonne mémoire
retentiveness [rɪ'tentɪvnɪs] *n* (*of memory*) fidélité *f*
rethink[1] ['ri:θɪŋk] *n* **to have a r.** (**about sth**) réfléchir à nouveau (à qch); **we need a complete r. of our strategy** il nous faut revoir entièrement notre stratégie; **the plan needs a complete r.** le projet doit être complètement repensé
rethink[2] [ri:'θɪŋk] *vt* (*pt, pp* **rethought** [-'θɔ:t]) (*matter, plan*) repenser, reconsidérer
reticence ['retɪsəns] *n* (*on one occasion*) réticence *f*; (*character trait*) réserve *f*; **the r. of his manner** sa réticence/réserve; **without any r.** sans réticence(s); **this r. isn't like her** elle n'est pas aussi réservée d'habitude
reticent ['retɪsənt] *adj* peu communicatif, réservé; **to be r. about sth** ne pas vouloir parler de qch, faire mystère de qch
reticently ['retɪsəntlɪ] *adv* avec réticence *ou* réserve
reticular [rɪ'tɪkjʊlər], **reticulate(d)** [rɪ'tɪkjʊlət, -leɪtɪd] *adj esp Biol* réticulé
reticulation [rɪtɪkjʊ'leɪʃən] *n esp Biol* réticulation *f*
reticule ['retɪkju:l] *n* (**a**) *Opt* réticule *m* (**b**) *Hist* (*bag*) réticule *m*
retina, *pl* **-as, -ae** ['retɪnə, -əz, -i:] *n* (*of eye*) rétine *f*
retinal ['retɪnəl] *adj* (*image etc*) rétinien; *Med* **r. detachment** décollement *m* de la rétine
retinue ['retɪnju:] *n* (*of prince etc*), *Hum* suite *f*
retire [rɪ'taɪər] **1** *vi* (**a**) (*of employee*) prendre sa retraite; **to r. from a company** prendre sa retraite d'une société; **to r. from teaching** prendre sa retraite de l'enseignement; **when I r.** quand je prendrai ma retraite; **to r. early** prendre une retraite anticipée; **to have retired** être à la retraite
(**b**) (*withdraw*) se retirer (**to** dans, à; **from** de); (*of troops*) reculer, se replier (**to** vers); (*from match, competition etc*) se retirer, abandonner; **to r. from boxing/the race** abandonner la boxe/la course; **to r. into oneself** se replier sur soi-même; *Fml* **to r. from the room** quitter la pièce; *Fml* **to r. (to bed/for the night)** (aller) se coucher
2 *vt* (**a**) (*person*) (*from work*) mettre à la retraite
(**b**) (*withdraw*), *Mil* (*troops*) retirer
retired [rɪ'taɪəd] *adj* (**a**) (*police officer, doctor etc*) retraité, à la retraite; **to be r.** être à la retraite; *Mil* **to put** *or* **place sb on the r. list** mettre qn à la retraite; **Admiral John Smith, r.** Amiral John Smith, retraité (**b**) (*secluded*) (*life*) retiré; (*place etc*) retiré, isolé
retiree [rɪtaɪə'ri:] *n US* retraité, -ée
retirement [rɪ'taɪəmənt] *n* (**a**) (*from work, army etc*) retraite *f*; **on my r.** (*when I retire*) quand je serai à la retraite; (*when I retired*) quand j'ai pris ma retraite; **to take early r.** prendre une retraite anticipée; **she's been offered early r.** on lui a proposé de prendre *ou* de faire valoir ses droits à une retraite anticipée; **to come out of r.** reprendre sa carrière; **to live in r.** (*no longer employed*) être à la retraite; (*in seclusion*) vivre retiré du monde; **compulsory r.** retraite d'office; **r. age** âge *m* de la retraite; *Br* **r. flat** appartement *m* pour retraités; **r. pension** (pension *f* de) retraite; **r. plan** système *m* de retraite; **r. present** cadeau *m* de départ en *ou* à la retraite; **r. savings fund** fonds *m* d'épargne pour la retraite, fonds d'épargne-retraite, FER *m*; **r. savings plan** plan *m* d'épargne retraite, PER *m*
(**b**) (*withdrawal*) (*of troops*) repli *m*; (*from match, competition etc*) abandon *m*
retiring [rɪ'taɪərɪŋ] *adj* (**a**) (*reserved*) réservé; **to have** *or* **be of a r. nature** avoir un *ou* être d'un naturel réservé (**b**) (*employee*) qui prend sa retraite; (*elected official*) sortant
retiring age *n* âge *m* de la retraite
retool [ri:'tu:l] **1** *vt Ind* (*factory*) rééquiper; *Am F* (*company*) réorganiser **2** *vi Ind* (*of factory*) se rééquiper; *Am F* (*of company*) se réorganiser
retort[1] [rɪ'tɔ:t] *n* (*answer*) réplique *f* (**to** à), riposte *f*; **to make a r.** lancer une réplique
retort[2] *vti* répliquer, rétorquer
retort[3] *n Ch, Ind* cornue *f*
retouch [ri:'tʌtʃ] *vt* (*photograph*) retoucher
retouching [ri:'tʌtʃɪŋ] *n* (*of photograph etc*) retouche *f*
retrace [rɪ'treɪs] *vt* (*events*) reconstituer; **to r. one's steps** revenir sur ses pas, rebrousser chemin; **to r. sb's movements** (*of police etc*) reconstituer les faits et gestes de qn
retract [rɪ'trækt] **1** *vt* (**a**) (*what one said*) rétracter; (*statement, offer etc*) revenir sur; (*opinion etc*) désavouer, rétracter (**b**) (*of animal*) (*claws*) rentrer; *Av* **to r. the undercarriage** escamoter *ou* rentrer le train d'atterrissage **2** *vi* (**a**) (*of person*) se rétracter (**b**) (*of cat's claws*) rentrer; *Av* (*of undercarriage*) s'escamoter, rentrer; (*of blade*) s'escamoter
retractable [rɪ'træktəb(ə)l] *adj Av* (*undercarriage*) rentrant, escamotable; (*handle etc*) escamotable; (*ballpoint pen*) à pointe rétractable
retraction [rɪ'trækʃən] *n* (**a**) (*of statement*) rétractation *f*; (*of opinion*) désaveu *m*, reniement *m*; **to publish a r.** (*of newspaper*) publier un désaveu (**b**) (*of claws etc*) rétraction *f*
retrain [ri:'treɪn] **1** *vt* (*employee*) recycler; *Med* (*muscle*) rééduquer **2** *vi* (*of employee*) se recycler
retraining [ri:'treɪnɪŋ] *n* (*of person*) recyclage *m*; *Med* (*of muscle*) rééducation *f*
retread[1] ['ri:tred] *n Aut* (pneu *m*) rechapé *m*
retread[2] [ri:'tred] *vt Aut* (*tyre*) rechaper
retreat[1] [rɪ'tri:t] *n* (**a**) *Mil, Fig* retraite *f*; *Mil* **to sound/beat the r.** sonner/battre la retraite; *Fig* **to beat a (hasty) r.** battre en retraite (**b**) (*of flood waters*) retrait *m*, recul *m* (**c**) *Rel* (*seclusion*) retraite *f*; **to go into** *or* **on r.** faire une retraite (**d**) (*place*) abri *m*, retraite *f*, refuge *m*; **a holiday/weekend r.** une maison paisible pour les vacances/le week-end; **a country r.** une maison paisible à la campagne
retreat[2] *vi* (**a**) *Mil* battre en retraite, reculer; (*of crowd, spectators etc*) battre en retraite, reculer (**from** de); **to r. a few hundred yards** reculer de quelques centaines de mètres; **to r. into a world of one's own** s'isoler dans son petit monde (à soi); **to r. from the public eye** se retirer du monde (**b**) (*of flood waters, glacier*) reculer
retrench [rɪ'trentʃ] **1** *vt Fin* (*expenditure*) restreindre; *Liter* (*literary work*) faire des coupures dans **2** *vi Fin* restreindre ses dépenses, faire des économies
retrenchment [rɪ'trentʃmənt] *n Fin* (*of expenditure*) réduction *f*; **policy of r.** politique *f* d'économies
retrial [ri:'traɪ(ə)l] *n Jur* nouveau procès *m*
retribution [retrɪ'bju:ʃən] *n* châtiment *m*; **in r. for sth** comme châtiment pour qch; **to exact r.** se venger; **the Day of R.** le Jugement dernier; **just r. of** *or* **for a crime** juste châtiment pour un crime
retributive [rɪ'trɪbjʊtɪv] *adj* (*measure etc*) punitif
retrievable [rɪ'tri:vəb(ə)l] *adj* (*loss, error*) réparable; *Comptr* accessible; *Fin* (*amount*) recouvrable
retrieval [rɪ'tri:v(ə)l] *n* (*recovery*) (*of lost object*) récupération *f*; (*of error, loss*) réparation *f*; (*of fortune*) rétablissement *m*, *Fin* recouvrement *m*; *Comptr* (*of data*) recherche *f*; (*of lost data*) récupération *f*; *Comptr* **r. system** système *m* de recherche; **information r. system** système de recherche documentaire; (*computer system*) système de recherche d'information; **beyond** *or* **past r.** irréparable
retrieve [rɪ'tri:v] **1** *vt* (*property*) récupérer; (*freedom*) retrouver; (*loss, error etc*) réparer; (*honour, fortune*) rétablir; (*of dog*) (*ball, game-bird etc*) rapporter; *Fin* (*assets*) recouvrer; *Comptr* (*file*) retrouver, extraire; **to r. one's losses** se refaire; **to r. the situation** sauver la situation **2** *vi Hunting* (*of dog*) rapporter

retriever [rɪ'triːvər] *n Hunting (dog)* chien *m* d'arrêt, retriever *m*
retro ['retrəʊ] *adj (fashion etc)* rétro *inv*
retro- ['retrəʊ-] *pref* rétro-
retroactive [retrəʊ'æktɪv] *adj (increase, measure etc)* rétroactif; **the increase is r. to last January** l'augmentation a un effet rétroactif à compter de janvier dernier
retroactively [retrəʊ'æktɪvlɪ] *adv (to increase, come into effect etc)* rétroactivement
retrofit ['retrəʊfɪt] *vt Av (aircraft, machine)* moderniser (**with** en y intégrant)
retroflex ['retrəʊfleks] *adj Ling* rétroflexe
retroflexion [retrəʊ'flekʃən] *n Med* rétroflexion *f*
retrograde ['retrəgreɪd] *adj (movement, step etc)* rétrograde
retrogress [retrə'gres] *vi* rétrograder
retrogression [retrə'greʃən] *n* rétrogradation *f*, rétrogression *f*; *Biol* régression *f*
retrogressive [retrə'gresɪv] *adj* rétrograde; *Biol* régressif
retrorocket ['retrəʊrɒkɪt] *n Astronaut* rétrofusée *f*
retrospect ['retrəspekt] *n* **in r.** rétrospectivement, après coup; **when I consider these events in r.** quand je pense à ces événements rétrospectivement *ou* après coup
retrospective [retrə'spektɪv] **1** *adj (review)* rétrospectif; *(measure)* à effet rétroactif **2** *n (of film director's, artist's etc work)* rétrospective *f*
retrospectively [retrə'spektɪvlɪ] *adv (to consider etc)* rétrospectivement, après coup; *(to take effect)* rétroactivement
retroussé [rə'truːseɪ] *adj (nose)* retroussé
retrovirus ['retrəʊvaɪrəs] *n Biol* rétrovirus *m*
retry [riː'traɪ] **1** *vt Jur* juger à *ou* de nouveau **2** *vi esp Comptr* réessayer
retsina [ret'siːnə] *n* retsina *m*
retune[1] ['riːtjuːn] *n Aut (of engine)* réglage *m*; **the engine needs a r.** il faut faire régler le moteur
retune[2] [riː'tjuːn] *vt Aut (engine)* régler; *Mus (instrument)* accorder
return[1] [rɪ'tɜːn] *n* **(a)** *(of person, peace, spring etc)* retour *m*; **on my r.** dès *ou* à mon retour; **on his r. to France** à son retour en France; **by r. (of post)** par retour (du courrier); **the r. to school** la rentrée (des classes); **many happy returns (of the day)!** bon anniversaire!; **r. journey** (voyage *m* de) retour; *Br Rail etc* **r. (ticket)** aller *m* (et) retour; *Br* **day r.** aller (et) retour valable pour la journée seulement; **cheap day r.** billet *m* d'aller (et) retour à tarif réduit valable pour la journée seulement; **I've lost the r. half of my ticket** j'ai perdu mon billet *ou* coupon de retour; **r. air fare** tarif *m* aérien aller-retour; **how much is the r. fare?** combien coûte l'aller (et) retour?; **r. flight/voyage** vol *m*/voyage de retour; **point of no r.** point *m* de non-retour
(b) *(of goods to supplier)* renvoi *m*; *(of stolen property)* restitution *f*; *(of overpayment)* remboursement *m*; *Tennis (of service)* renvoi (de la balle); *(library book)* livre *m* (de bibliothèque) que l'on rapporte; *(election) (of politician)* élection *f*; **r. (key)** *(on keyboard)* touche *f* (de) retour; **(carriage) r.** *(on typewriter, keyboard)* retour *m* (de chariot); *Tennis* **to make a good r. (of service)** bien renvoyer le service; **r. to office** *(of politician)* reprise *f* de fonctions; *Com* **on sale or r.** *(goods)* vendu avec possibilité de retour; **no deposit, no r.** *(on bottle)* ni retour, ni consigne; *Th* **returns may be available on the day of the performance** des places peuvent se libérer le jour de la représentation; **are there any returns?** est-ce que des places se sont libérées?; **r. address** adresse *f* de l'expéditeur; *Com* **returns** rendus *mpl*; *(of books, newspapers)* invendus *mpl*, bouillons *mpl*; *F Pol* **to announce the returns of the election** annoncer les résultats du scrutin; **early returns indicate a win for the incumbent** les premiers résultats laissent prévoir une victoire du candidat sortant
(c) *Fin (yield)* rapport *m* (**on** de); **how much r. do you get on your investment?** combien est-ce que ton investissement te rapporte?; **returns** *(profit)* bénéfices *mpl*; *Acct* **returns ledger** journal *m* des rendus; **quick returns** bénéfices réalisés rapidement; **small profits and quick returns** faibles bénéfices et ventes rapides; **to bring (in) a fair r.** rapporter un bénéfice raisonnable; **r. on capital** retour *m* sur capital; *Acct* **r. on capital employed** rendement *m* sur capital immobilisé; **r. on investment** retour sur investissement; **r. on sales** retour sur ventes
(d) *(form)* rapport *m* officiel; *(for tax)* déclaration *f*
(e) to give sth in r. donner qch en échange; *(for favour, service)* donner qch en guise de récompense *ou* de remerciement; **in r. for which ...** moyennant quoi ...; **if you will do sth in r.** si vous voulez bien faire qch en retour; **in r. for this service ...** en récompense de ce service ...; **you must expect the same treatment in r.** il faut vous attendre à la pareille; **it's a small r. for all your kindness** c'est une modeste récompense pour votre bonté; *Sp* **r. match** *or* **game** match *m* retour, revanche *f*; **I'll give you a r. match** *or* **game next week** on disputera le match retour *ou* la revanche la semaine prochaine
return[2] **1** *vi (come back)* revenir; *(go back)* retourner; *(of anxiety, fear)* revenir, reprendre; **to r. home** rentrer (chez soi); **I was returning from a journey** je rentrais de voyage; **he/spring has returned** il/le printemps est revenu *ou* est de retour; **to r. from the dead** ressusciter d'entre les morts; **her colour returned** elle a repris des couleurs; *Naut* **to r. to port** rentrer au port; **to r. to a task** reprendre une tâche; **to r. to a subject** revenir à un sujet; **to r. to one's old habits** reprendre ses vieilles habitudes; **to r. to work** reprendre le travail; *Post* **r. to sender** *(on undelivered letter)* retour à l'envoyeur
2 *vt* **(a)** *(give or send back) (book, compliment, verdict etc)* rendre; *(something stolen etc)* restituer; *(gift, ball etc)* renvoyer; *(loan)* rembourser; *(elect) (MP)* élire; **returned letter** lettre renvoyée à l'expéditeur; **returned cheque** chèque *m* retourné; **to r. a book to its place** remettre un livre à sa place; **to r. a purchase to a shop** rendre *ou* rapporter un article à un magasin; *Tennis* **to r. (the) service** renvoyer le service; *Jur* **the jury returned a verdict of guilty/not guilty** le jury a déclaré l'accusé coupable/non coupable; **to r. an animal to the wild** remettre un animal en liberté; *Mil* **to r. fire** riposter (au feu adverse); **to r. the favour** rendre la pareille; **to r. sb's greeting** rendre un salut à qn; **to r. good for evil** rendre le bien pour le mal; **to r. sb's love** aimer qn en retour; *Tel* **to r. a call** rappeler; *Pol* **to r. the result of the poll** annoncer les résultats du scrutin
(b) *Com, Fin (produce) (profit)* rapporter, dégager
(c) *Old-fashioned (answer)* répondre, répliquer
returnable [rɪ'tɜːnəb(ə)l] *adj Com (purchase, ticket etc)* qui peut être rendu; *(bottle)* consigné; **sale items are not r.** *(notice in shop)* les articles en solde ne sont ni échangés ni repris; **empties are not r.** on ne reprend pas les bouteilles, les bouteilles ne sont pas consignées; *Com* **r. packaging** emballage *m* consigné
returning [rɪ'tɜːnɪŋ] *n Br Can Pol* **r. officer** directeur, -trice du scrutin
reunification [riːjuːnɪfɪ'keɪʃən] *n (of country)* réunification *f*
reunify [riː'juːnɪfaɪ] *vt (country)* réunifier
reunion [riː'juːnɪən] *n* retrouvailles *fpl*, réunion *f*; *Am* **class r.** réunion d'anciens élèves de la même classe *ou* promotion; **to have** *or* **hold a r.** organiser une réunion *ou* des retrouvailles; **r. celebration/dinner** célébration *f*/dîner *m* de retrouvailles
reunite [riːjʊ'naɪt] **1** *vt (after quarrel) (family etc)* réconcilier; **the freed hostage was reunited with his wife** l'otage libéré a retrouvé sa femme; **the dog was reunited with its owner** le chien a retrouvé son maître; **he reunited the band for one last gig** il a reformé le groupe pour un ultime concert **2** *vi (of band)* se reformer
reupholster [riːʌp'həʊlstər] *vt Furn (chair etc)* rembourrer et recouvrir
reusable [reː'juːzəb(ə)l] *adj (paper, bottle etc)* réutilisable; *(battery)* rechargeable
reuse[1] [riː'juːs] *n (of paper, bottle etc)* réutilisation *f*
reuse[2] [riː'juːz] *vt (paper, bottle etc)* réutiliser
Rev *n Rel (abbr* **Reverend***)* révérend
rev[1] [rev] *n Aut F (abbr* **revolution***)* tour *m* (à la minute *ou* minute); **to do three thousand revs** faire trois mille tours (à la) minute; **r. counter** compte-tours *m inv*; **r. limiter** limiteur *m* de régime
rev[2] (-vv-) *Aut F* **1** *vt (engine)* emballer; **he revs the engine too hard** il fait tourner le moteur trop vite **2** *vi (of engine)* s'emballer; *(of driver)* emballer le moteur
► **rev up** *vtsep, vi* = **rev[2]**
revalidate [rɪ'vælɪdeɪt] *vt* revalider; **r. sticker** *(if travel ticket is changed)* autocollant *m* de revalidation
revaluation [riːvæljʊ'eɪʃən] *n Econ, Fin (of currency, property etc)* réévaluation *f*
revalue [riː'væljuː] *vt Econ, Fin (currency, property)* réévaluer
revamp[1] ['riːvæmp] *n F (of method, play etc)* remaniement *m*; *(of policy)* modification *f*, remaniement; *(of company)* réorganisation *f*, restructuration *f*; *(of house etc)* retapage *m*, remise *f* en état
revamp[2] [riː'væmp] *vt F (method, play etc)* remanier; *(policy)* modifier, remanier; *(company)* réorganiser, restructurer; *(house etc)* retaper, remettre en état
revanchisme [rɪ'væntʃɪz(ə)m] *n* revanchisme *m*
revanchiste [rɪ'væntʃɪst] *n, adj* revanchiste *mf*, revanchard, -e
Revd *Rel (abbr* **Reverend***)* révérend
reveal [rɪ'viːl] *vt (something hidden, secret, one's sources,*

name) révéler; (*fact*) révéler, faire connaître; (*quality etc*) laisser voir; **to r. one's identity** révéler son identité, dire *ou* donner son nom, se faire connaître; **the police do not want to r. the identity of the victim** la police ne veut pas révéler l'identité de la victime; **a medical examination revealed two cracked ribs** un examen médical a permis de découvrir deux côtes fêlées; **it was revealed that** ... on a révélé que ...

revealing [rɪ'viːlɪŋ] *adj* (*sign, comment etc*) révélateur, -trice; (*dress*) (*low-cut*) décolleté; (*skirt, dress*) (*short*) très court, qui ne cache pas grand-chose; (*blouse*) (*transparent*) transparent; **that was very r. about his intentions** cela en disait long sur ses intentions

revealingly [rɪ'viːlɪŋlɪ] *adv* (*to say*) d'un ton révélateur; **a r. low dress** une robe très décolletée

reveille [rɪ'vælɪ] *n Mil* réveil *m*; **to sound (the) r.** sonner *ou* battre le réveil

revel¹ ['rev(ə)l] *n Old-fashioned* (*often pl*) divertissement(s) *m(pl)*, réjouissances *fpl*

revel² *vi* (**-ll-**, *US* **-l-**) se réjouir, se divertir, *F* faire la noce; **to r. in sth/in doing sth** se délecter à qch/à faire qch; **to r. in one's freedom** savourer pleinement sa liberté; **enjoy it?, he positively revels in it** s'il aime ça?, tu veux dire qu'il adore ça!

revelation [revə'leɪʃən] *n* révélation *f*; **it was a r. to me** cela a été une révélation pour moi; *Bible* **(the Book of) Revelations** l'Apocalypse *f*

reveller, *US* **reveler** ['rev(ə)lər] *n* joyeux, -euse convive, *F* noceur, -euse, fêtard, -e; **there were no taxis left for the late-night revellers** il n'y avait plus de taxis pour les oiseaux de nuit

revelling ['rev(ə)lɪŋ], **revelry** ['revəlrɪ] *n* festivités *fpl*

revenge¹ [rɪ'vendʒ] *n* **(a)** vengeance *f*; **r. is sweet** la vengeance est douce; **to take** *or* **get** *or* **have (one's) r.** se venger (**for** de; **on** sur); **to want one's r.** vouloir se venger; **in r.** pour se venger (**for** de); **to do sth out of r.** faire qch par esprit de vengeance

(b) *Fig* (*esp in games*) revanche *f*; **to give sb his/her r.** laisser qn prendre sa revanche; **Liverpool got their r. for last week's defeat** Liverpool a pris la revanche de sa défaite de la semaine dernière

revenge² *vt* (*insult*) venger; **to r. oneself** *or* **be revenged** se venger (**on** sur; **for** de)

revengeful [rɪ'vendʒfʊl] *adj* (*attitude, person etc*) vindicatif; (*act*) vengeur, de vengeance

revengefully [rɪ'vendʒfʊlɪ] *adv* (*to do*) par esprit de vengeance, de façon vindicative; (*to say*) d'un ton vengeur

revenger [rɪ'vendʒər] *n* vengeur, -eresse (**of** de)

revenue ['revənjuː] *n Fin, Com* revenu *m*; (*from land, property*) revenu, rentes *fpl*; (*from sales*) recettes *fpl*; **advertising r.** recettes de publicité; **oil r.** revenu pétrolier; **the** *Br* **Inland** *or Am* **Internal R.** le fisc; **tax r.** recettes fiscales; **r. passenger mile** revenu passager-kilomètre

reverberate [rɪ'vɜːbəreɪt] *vi* (*of sound*) retentir, résonner (**off** contre); (*of light, heat*) se réverbérer (**off** contre); **the room reverberated with the children's shouts** la pièce résonnait des cris des enfants; *Fig* **the news reverberated round the world** la nouvelle a fait du bruit partout dans le monde; (*had an effect*) la nouvelle a eu des répercussions partout dans le monde

reverberation [rɪvɜːbə'reɪʃən] *n* (*of sound*) réverbération *f*; *Fig* **the announcement is still causing reverberations** la nouvelle continue à avoir des répercussions

revere [rɪ'vɪər] *vt* révérer

reverence¹ ['revərəns] *n* révérence *f*; (*for artist, doctor etc*) vénération *f*; *Rel* respect *m* religieux; **to hold sb in r.** révérer *ou* vénérer qn; *Rel* **Your** *or* **His R.** monsieur l'abbé

reverence² *vt Fml* révérer

reverend ['rev(ə)rənd] **1** *adj Rel* révérend; **the R. Father Martin** *Church of Eng* le révérend père Martin; *Cathol* l'abbé *m ou* le père Martin; **the R. Mother Superior** la révérende mère supérieure; **Right R.** (*bishop*) très révérend; **Very R.** (*dean*) très révérend; **Most R.** (*archbishop*) révérendissime

2 *n* révérend *m*; *Church of Eng* pasteur *m*; *Cathol* abbé *m*; *Cathol* **Your R.** (mon) père

reverent ['rev(ə)rənt] *adj* (*gesture, tone*) respectueux, plein de révérence, *Lit* révérencieux; **to be very r. towards sb** être très respectueux à l'égard de *ou* envers qn

reverential [revə'renʃəl] *adj* (*act*) révérenciel; (*tone, gesture etc*) révérencieux

reverently ['rev(ə)rəntlɪ] *adv* (*to treat*) avec révérence; (*to act, speak etc*) avec grand respect *ou* vénération, très respectueusement

reverie ['revərɪ] *n* rêverie *f*; **to be in a r.** être rêveur; **to be lost in r.** être perdu dans ses rêveries; **to fall into a r.** se mettre à rêver (**about** à, de)

revers [rɪ'vɪəz] *npl* (*on jacket*) revers *mpl*

reversal [rɪ'vɜːs(ə)l] *n* **(a)** (*of opinion, policy, situation*) revirement *m*; (*of roles*) renversement *m*, inversion *f*; (*of fortune*) revers *m*; **to suffer a r.** (*of person*) essuyer un revers de fortune **(b)** *Jur* (*of decision*) annulation *f* **(c)** *Phot* **r. film** pellicule *f* inversible

reverse¹ [rɪ'vɜːs] *adj* (*order, image*) inverse; **in r. order** à l'envers; *TV, Cin* **r. cut** contrechamp *m*; *Am* **r. discrimination** discrimination *f* à l'envers; *Comptr* **r. engineering** ingénierie *f* inverse; **r. side** (*of coin etc*) revers *m*; (*of fabric*) envers *m*; (*of paper*) verso *m*; *Comptr* **r. sort** (*alphabetical*) tri *m* en ordre inverse; (*of numbers*) tri *m* en ordre décroissant; *Av* **r. thrust** poussée *f* inversée; *Aut* **r. turn** virage *m* en marche arrière; *Aut* **to do** *or* **make a r. turn** faire un virage en marche arrière; *Comptr* **r. video** vidéo *f* inversée

reverse² *n* **(a)** (*opposite*) contraire *m*; **to be (quite) the r. of sth** être (tout) le contraire *ou* l'opposé de qch; **she was the r. of calm** elle était tout sauf calme; **quite the r.!** bien au contraire!; **printed in r.** imprimé à l'envers **(b)** (*back*) (*of coin*) revers *m*; (*of fabric*) envers *m*; (*of paper*) verso *m* **(c)** (*defeat*) échec *m*; (*misfortune*) revers *m*; **to suffer a r.** essuyer un revers de fortune; (*be defeated*) essuyer un échec **(d)** *Aut* (*gear*) marche *f* arrière; **in r.** en marche arrière; **to put a car into r.** mettre une voiture en marche arrière; **to do a r.** faire une marche arrière

reverse³ **1** *vt* **(a)** (*turn in opposite direction*) (*coat, picture*) retourner; *Br Tel* **to r. the charge(s)** appeler *ou* téléphoner *ou* faire un appel en PCV, *Can* faire un appel à frais virés; *Mil* **to r. arms** renverser les fusils; *Tech* **to r. steam** renverser la vapeur

(b) (*alter*) (*order, policy*) inverser, changer du tout au tout; (*situation*) renverser; (*decision*) annuler; **to r. a trend** renverser une tendance; **the roles are reversed** les rôles sont intervertis; *Aut* **to r. one's car** faire marche arrière; **to r. the car out of the garage** sortir du garage en marche arrière

2 *vi Aut* faire marche arrière; **to r. into a lamppost** rentrer dans un réverbère en faisant une marche arrière; **to r. out (of the garage)** sortir (du garage) en marche arrière

▶ **reverse out** *vtsep Typ* inverser

reverse-charge call *n Br Tel* communication *f* en PCV, *Can* appel *m* à frais virés

reverse gear *n Aut* marche *f* arrière

reversible [rɪ'vɜːsɪb(ə)l] *adj Clothing* (*fabric, jacket etc*) réversible, à double face; *Phot* (*film*) inversible; (*decree, judgment, sentence*) révocable; **the decision is not r.** la décision est irrévocable

reversing [rɪ'vɜːsɪŋ] *n Aut* marche *f* arrière; **r. beeper** *or* **bleeper** avertisseur *m* de marche arrière; **r. lights** feux *mpl* de recul

reversion [rɪ'vɜːʃən] *n* **(a)** (*to previous condition*) retour *m* (**to** à); *Biol* retour à l'état antérieur, régression *f*; *Biol* **r. to type** retour au type primitif; *Fig* **this was a not unexpected r. to type** comme on s'y attendait, le naturel a repris le dessus **(b)** *Jur* (*of property*) retour *m*, réversion *f*; **right of r.** réversion; **estate in r.** bien *m* grevé d'une réversion

reversionary [rɪ'vɜːʃənərɪ] *adj* **(a)** *Biol* (*characteristic, organ*) atavique **(b)** *Jur* (*right*) de réversion, réversible **(c)** *Fin* **r. bonus** prime *f* d'intéressement; **r. owner** nu-propriétaire *m*; **r. ownership** nue-propriété *f*

revert [rɪ'vɜːt] *vi* **(a)** (*of conversation, thoughts*) revenir (**to** à); *Biol* retourner à l'état sauvage; **to r. to type** *Biol* revenir *ou* retourner au type primitif; *Fig* laisser le naturel reprendre le dessus; **we shall r. to this matter** nous reviendrons sur cette question; **reverting to your question** pour (en) revenir à votre question; **the garden has reverted to a wilderness** le jardin est retourné à l'état sauvage; **to r. to one's maiden name** (*of divorced woman*) reprendre son nom de jeune fille **(b)** *Jur* (*of property*) revenir, retourner (**to** à)

revetment [rɪ'vetmənt] *n Constr* revêtement *m*; **r. wall** mur *m* de revêtement, épaulement *m*

review¹ [rɪ'vjuː] *n* **(a)** (*of past etc*) examen *m*; (*of policy, salary etc*) révision *f*, examen; (*of situation*) bilan *m*; **to come up for r.** (*of salary, contract etc*) devoir être réexaminé; **to be under r.** (*of policy, salary etc*) faire l'objet d'une révision, être en cours de révision; **they are keeping the question of student grants under r.** la question des allocations d'études fait l'objet de réexamens perpétuels; **to keep a question under r.** continuer d'étudier une question; **prices are subject to r.** les prix peuvent faire l'objet d'une révision; **a r. of the year** une rétrospective des événements de l'année; *TV* **r. screen** écran *m* de vision

(b) (*of book, play, film etc*) compte rendu *m*, critique *f*; **he gave it a good r.** il en a fait une bonne critique; **her last novel got very bad reviews** son dernier roman a eu de très

mauvaises critiques; **r. copy** (*of book*) exemplaire *m* fourni au critique
(**c**) (*publication*) revue *f*
(**d**) *Th* (*show*) revue *f*
(**e**) *Mil* revue *f*; **to hold a r.** passer une revue; **to pass troops in r.** passer des troupes en revue
(**f**) *Jur* (*of trial*) révision *f*

review² **1** *vt* (**a**) (*the past*) revoir, examiner; (*policy, salary*) réviser, examiner; (*facts*) passer en revue; (*situation*) faire le bilan *ou* le point de; **your progress will be reviewed every six weeks** on fera le point sur *ou* le bilan de vos progrès toutes les six semaines (**b**) (*book, film etc*) faire la critique *ou* le compte rendu de (**c**) *Mil* (*troops*) passer en revue; **to be reviewed** (*of troops*) être passé en revue (**d**) *esp Am Sch* (*revise*) (*lessons*) revoir, réviser (**e**) *Jur* (*trial*) revoir, réviser **2** *vi* (**a**) **he reviews for the Sunday Times** il rédige des critiques pour le Sunday Times (**b**) *esp Am Sch* réviser, faire des révisions

reviewer [rɪ'vju:ər] *n* (*of book, play etc*) critique *m*

revile [rɪ'vaɪl] *vt* injurier (**for** pour)

revise¹ [rɪ'vaɪz] *n Typ* épreuve *f* de révision, seconde *f*; **second** *or* **final r.** troisième épreuve, tierce *f*

revise² **1** *vt* (**a**) (*amend*) (*text*) revoir, réviser; (*proofs*) corriger, réviser; (*law, constitution*) réviser; (*decision*) revenir sur; **to r. one's opinion of sb** changer d'opinion à l'égard de qn; **to r. figures upwards/downwards** corriger des chiffres *ou* des calculs à la hausse/à la baisse (**b**) *Br* (*study*) (*lesson*) réviser, revoir, repasser **2** *vi Br* (*for exam*) réviser, faire des révisions (**for** pour)

revised [rɪ'vaɪzd] *adj* (*text*) revu, révisé; (*proof, law*) révisé; **r. edition** (*of book etc*) édition *f* revue et corrigée; **the R. Version** = la traduction de la Bible de 1884

reviser [rɪ'vaɪzər] *n* réviseur *m*; *Typ* (*of proof*) correcteur, -trice

revision [rɪ'vɪʒən] *n* révision *f*; **for r.** à revoir; *Br Sch* **to do some r.** faire des révisions

revisionism [rɪ'vɪʒənɪz(ə)m] *n Pol* révisionnisme *m*

revisionist [rɪ'vɪʒənɪst] *adj, n Pol* révisionniste *mf*

revisit [ri:'vɪzɪt] *vt* (*place*) visiter de nouveau, revisiter; (*person*) aller voir de nouveau, retourner voir; **Brideshead Revisited** Retour à Brideshead; **nuclear power revisited** (*title of article etc*) un nouveau regard *ou* une nouvelle perspective sur la question de l'énergie nucléaire

revitalize [ri:'vaɪtəlaɪz] *vt* (*person*) revigorer; (*economy*) relancer; (*industry, the arts, trade unionism etc*) donner un nouvel essor à

revival [rɪ'vaɪv(ə)l] *n* (**a**) (*of person*) réanimation *f*; **all attempts at r. failed** toutes les tentatives de réanimation ont échoué (**b**) (*of arts, industry, hope*) renaissance *f*; (*of custom, fashion*) réapparition *f*, renouveau *m*; (*of interest*) réveil *m*, renouveau; *Jur* (*of law*) remise *f* en vigueur; (*of economy*) reprise *f*; **the r. of trade** la reprise des affaires (**c**) (*of play etc*) reprise *f*; **to put on a r. of Blithe Spirit** monter une reprise de Blithe Spirit (**d**) *Rel* (*of faith*) réveil *m*, renouveau *m*; **religious r.** retour *m* à la religion; **r. meeting** = réunion *f* visant à ranimer la foi (dans une ville)

revivalism [rɪ'vaɪvəlɪz(ə)m] *n Rel* = mouvement *m* visant à ranimer la foi

revivalist [rɪ'vaɪvəlɪst] *n Rel* = personne *f* qui essaie de ranimer la foi; **r. meeting** = réunion *f* visant à ranimer la foi (dans une ville)

revive [rɪ'vaɪv] **1** *vt* (**a**) (*sb who has fainted*) ranimer; (*dying person*) réanimer; **that will r. you** voilà qui vous remontera
(**b**) (*memory, conversation*) ranimer; (*hope, interest*) raviver, faire renaître; (*custom*) faire renaître; (*fashion*) relancer; **to r. sb's spirits** remonter le moral à qn; **this role could r. his flagging career** ce rôle pourrait faire redémarrer sa carrière sur le déclin
(**c**) *Th* (*play*) remonter
2 *vi* (**a**) (*of unconscious person*) reprendre connaissance; (*of dying person*) revenir à la vie
(**b**) (*of hope, arts*) renaître; (*of custom*) revenir (à la mode), reprendre; (*of fashion*) revenir; (*of business, commerce*) reprendre; **his spirits revived** il a repris courage; **hopes have revived of finding the miners alive** l'espoir renaît de trouver les mineurs vivants

revivify [rɪ'vɪvɪfaɪ] *vt Lit* revivifier

revocable [rɪ'vəʊkəb(ə)l] *adj Jur* (*contract, law, will etc*) révocable; (*decision*) sur laquelle on peut revenir; (*order*) que l'on peut annuler; **r. letter of credit** crédit *m* documentaire révocable

revocation [revə'keɪʃən] *n* (*of will*) révocation *f*; (*of decision, order, contract*) annulation *f*; (*of law*) abrogation *f*

re-voice *vt TV etc* doubler

re-voiced *adj TV etc* doublé

revoke [rɪ'vəʊk] *vt Jur* (*will*) révoquer; (*order, contract*) annuler; (*law*) abroger; (*decision, promise*) revenir sur; (*driving licence*) retirer

revolt¹ [rɪ'vəʊlt] *n* révolte *f*; **to rise in r.** se soulever, se révolter (**against** contre); **to be in r.** être en révolte (**against** contre)

revolt² **1** *vi* (*of troops*) se révolter, se soulever, s'insurger (**against** contre) **2** *vt* (*disgust*) révolter; **to be revolted by sth** être révolté par qch

revolting [rɪ'vəʊltɪŋ] *adj* (*disgusting*) (*action*) révoltant; **it smells r.** ça a une odeur infecte; **it tastes r.** ça a un goût infâme; **that sounds r.** (*what has just been described*) ça semble répugnant

revoltingly [rɪ'vəʊltɪŋlɪ] *adv* d'une façon révoltante; **a r. bad smell** une odeur infecte

revolution [revə'lu:ʃən] *n* (**a**) *Pol, Fig* révolution *f*; *Hist* **the French/Russian R.** la Révolution française/russe; **the Industrial R.** la Révolution industrielle; **this process has brought about a r. in the industry** ce procédé a révolutionné *ou* complètement transformé l'industrie (**b**) (*of wheel*) tour *m*, révolution *f*; (*of record, turntable, propeller*) tour; (*of planet*) révolution; *Aut, MecE* **r. counter** compte-tours *m inv*; **revolutions per minute** tours à la minute

revolutionary [revə'lu:ʃən(ə)rɪ] *adj, n Pol, Fig* révolutionnaire *mf*

revolutionize [revə'lu:ʃənaɪz] *vt* (*industry*) révolutionner, transformer complètement

revolve [rɪ'vɒlv] **1** *vt* (*wheel etc*) faire tourner; *Fig* **to r. a problem in one's mind** retourner un problème dans son esprit **2** *vi* (*of wheel etc*) tourner; **to r. around sth/sb** tourner autour de qch/qn; **all my thoughts r. around you** je ne pense qu'à toi; **her life revolves around her husband** son mari est le centre de son existence; **the play revolves around ...** la pièce est centrée sur ...

revolver [rɪ'vɒlvər] *n* (*firearm*) revolver *m*

revolving [rɪ'vɒlvɪŋ] *adj* (**a**) (*planet etc*) en rotation, qui accomplit sa révolution (**b**) (*chair etc*) pivotant; (*stage*) tournant; *Banking* **r. credit** crédit *m* permanent, crédit revolving; **r. letter of credit** crédit documentaire renouvelable, crédit revolving; **r. door** tambour *m*; *Am Fig* = le va-et-vient de fonctionnaires haut-placés entre les services publics et le secteur privé; *Fin* **r. fund** fonds *m* de roulement; **r. stand** (*in store etc*) tourniquet *m*

revue [rɪ'vju:] *n Th* revue *f*

revulsion [rɪ'vʌlʃən] *n* (*disgust*) dégoût *m*, répugnance *f*; **to draw back in r.** reculer dans un mouvement de dégoût; **to be filled with r.** être rempli de dégoût; **to fill sb with r.** (*of scene, cruelty etc*) remplir qn de dégoût

reward¹ [rɪ'wɔ:d] *n* récompense *f*; **to offer a r.** offrir une récompense (**for** pour); **as a** *or* **in r. for ...** en récompense de *ou* pour ...; **to get a fair r. for** *or* **from one's labour** tirer de son travail une récompense légitime

reward² *vt* (*person*) récompenser, rémunérer (**for** de; **with** par); (*financially*) récompenser; **that's how he rewards me for my loyalty** voilà comment il me récompense de mon dévouement; **their patience was finally rewarded** ils furent finalement récompensés de leur patience

rewarding [rɪ'wɔ:dɪŋ] *adj* qui (en) vaut la peine; (*satisfying*) qui apporte des satisfactions; (*financially*) qui (en) vaut la peine financièrement, rémunérateur, -trice

rewind¹ [ri:'waɪnd] *vt* (*pt, pp* **rewound** [ri:'waʊnd]) *Cin* (*film, tape*) rembobiner; **r.** (**button**) (*on tape deck*) touche *f* 'rewind', touche pour rembobiner la bande

rewind² ['ri:waɪnd] *n Phot* (**automatic**) **r.** rembobinage *m* (automatique)

rewire [ri:'waɪər] *vt* (*house, flat*) refaire l'installation électrique de; (*plug*) recâbler

reword [ri:'wɜ:d] *vt* (*paragraph etc*) recomposer, rédiger à nouveau; **let me r. that** je vais essayer de m'exprimer autrement

rework [ri:'wɜ:k] *vt* (*idea, theme*) retravailler (sur); (*text, thesis etc*) retravailler; **to r. a letter** remanier une lettre

rewrite¹ ['ri:raɪt] *n* (*of article, filmscript etc*) nouvelle version *f*; **it needs a r.** cela demande à être réécrit; *Journ etc* **r. man** rewriter *m*; *Journ etc* **r. sub** réviseur *m*

rewrite² [ri:'raɪt] *vt* (*pt* **rewrote** [ri:'rəʊt]; *pp* **rewritten** [ri:'rɪt(ə)n]) (*letter, article*) récrire, réécrire, rédiger à nouveau; *Fig* **to r. history** réécrire l'histoire

rewriteable [ri:'raɪtəb(ə)l] *adj Comptr* réinscriptible

rewriter [ri:'raɪtər] *n Journ etc* réviseur *m*, rewriter *m*

rewriting [ri:'raɪtɪŋ] *n Journ etc* récriture *f*, rewriting *m*

Reynaud's disease ['reɪnəʊdz] *n Med* maladie *f* de Reynaud

Rgt (*abbr* **regiment**) rég

rhapsodic(al) [ræp'sɒdɪk, -ɪk(ə)l] *adj* (*description etc*) excessivement élogieux, dithyrambique; *Mus* r(h)apsodique

rhapsodize ['ræpsədaɪz] *vi* (*of person*) s'extasier (**over** sur)

rhapsody ['ræpsədɪ] *n Mus* r(h)apsodie *f*; *Fig* (*feeling*) transports *mpl*; (*in words*) dithyrambe *m*; *Fig* **to go into/be in rhapsodies** s'extasier (**over** sur); **to send sb into rhapsodies** rendre qn extatique

rhea [ˈriːə] *n* (*bird*) nandou *m*

Rhenish [ˈrenɪʃ] *adj Old-fashioned Geog* rhénan, du Rhin; **R. (wine)** vin *m* du Rhin

rheo [ˈriːəʊ], **rheostat** [ˈriːəʊstæt] *n El* rhéostat *m*

rhesus [ˈriːsəs] *n* **(a)** *Zool* **r. (monkey)** (macaque *m*) rhésus *m* **(b)** *Physiol* **r. factor** (facteur *m*) rhésus *m*; **r. positive/negative** (*blood*) rhésus positif/négatif; **I'm r. negative** je suis rhésus négatif; **r. negative mother** mère *f* rhésus négatif; **r. baby** = enfant *mf* rhésus positif souffrant d'incompatibilité avec le rhésus négatif de la mère

rhetoric [ˈretərɪk] *n* **(a)** *Pej* (*bombast*) emphase *f*, rhétorique *f*; **his speech contained nothing but r.** son discours ne consistait qu'en de belles phrases vides de sens; **it's just empty r.** ce ne sont que des mots **(b)** (*art of speaking*) rhétorique *f*

rhetorical [rɪˈtɒrɪk(ə)l] *adj* **(a)** (*style*) emphatique, ampoulé **(b)** (*term etc*) de rhétorique; **r. question** question *f* de pure forme

rhetorically [rɪˈtɒrɪklɪ] *adv* **(a)** (*to speak*) avec emphase **(b)** (*to ask*) pour la forme

rhetorician [retɒˈrɪʃən] *n* (*expert in speaking*) rhétoricien, -ienne

rheumatic [ruːˈmætɪk, rʊ-] **1** *adj Med* (*pain etc*) rhumatismal; (*person*) rhumatisant; (*finger, joint*) atteint de rhumatisme; **r. fever** rhumatisme *m* articulaire aigu; **he suffered from a r. condition** il souffrait de rhumatismes **2** *n* rhumatisant, -ante

rheumaticky [ruːˈmætɪkɪ, rʊ-] *adj F* = **rheumatic[1]**

rheumatics [ruːˈmætɪks, rʊ-], **rheumatism** [ˈruːmətɪz(ə)m, rʊ-] *n Med* rhumatisme *m*; **to have** *or* **suffer from r.** avoir des *ou* souffrir de rhumatismes

rheumatoid [ˈruːmətɔɪd, ˈrʊ-] *adj Med* rhumatoïde; **r. arthritis** polyarthrite *f* rhumatoïde

rheumatologist [ruːməˈtɒlədʒɪst, rʊ-] *n Med* rhumatologue *mf*

rheumatology [ruːməˈtɒlədʒɪ, rʊ-] *n Med* rhumatologie *f*

rheumy [ˈruːmɪ] *adj Lit* **r. eyes** yeux *mpl* chassieux

Rhineland (the) [ðəˈraɪnlənd] *n* la Rhénanie

rhinestone [ˈraɪnstəʊn] *n* faux diamant *m*; **r. earring** boucle *f* d'oreille en strass

Rhine (the) [ðəˈraɪn] *n* le Rhin; **R. wines** vins *mpl* du Rhin

rhino [ˈraɪnəʊ] *n* (*animal*) rhino(céros) *m*

rhinoceros [raɪˈnɒsərəs] *n* (*animal*) rhinocéros *m*; *Fig* **to have a hide** *or* **skin like a r.** manquer totalement de *ou* être complètement dépourvu de sensibilité

rhizome [ˈraɪzəʊm] *n Bot* rhizome *m*

Rhode Island [rəʊd-] *n* Rhode Island *m*; *Orn* **R. red** (*chicken*) Rhode-Island *f*

Rhodes[1] [rəʊdz] *n* Rhodes *f*

Rhodes[2] *n Univ* **R. scholarship** bourse *f* de Rhodes; **R. scholar** titulaire *mf* de la bourse de Rhodes

Rhodesia [rəʊˈdiːʒə, -zɪə] *n Hist* Rhodésie *f*

Rhodesian [rəʊˈdiːʒən, -zɪən] *Hist* **1** *adj* rhodésien **2** *n* Rhodésien, -ienne

rhododendron, *pl* **-ons, -a** [rəʊdəˈdendrən, -ənz, -ə] *n* rhododendron *m*; **r. bush** rhododendron

rhomb [rɒm] *n Geom* losange *m*, rhombe *m*

rhombic [ˈrɒmbɪk] *adj* rhombique

rhomboid [ˈrɒmbɔɪd] *adj, n Geom* rhomboïde *m*

rhombus, *pl* **-uses, -i** [ˈrɒmbəs, -əsɪz, -aɪ] *n Geom* = **rhomb**

Rhone (the) [ðəˈrəʊn] *n* le Rhône; **the R. valley** la vallée du Rhône

rhubarb [ˈruːbɑːb] *n Bot, Culin, Pharm* rhubarbe *f*; **r. jam** confiture *f* de rhubarbe; **r. tart/dessert** tarte *f*/dessert *m* à la rhubarbe; *Th* **r., r.** = mots *mpl* répétés par les acteurs lorsqu'ils doivent avoir l'air de parler entre eux sur scène

rhyme[1] [raɪm] *n* **(a)** (*sound*) rime *f*; **can you think of a r. for ...?** est-ce que tu peux trouver une rime pour ...?; *Fig* **without r. or reason** sans rime ni raison; **there's neither r. nor reason to it** cela ne rime à rien *ou* n'a ni rime ni raison; **r. scheme** agencement *m* des rimes **(b)** (*poem*) vers *mpl*; **children's rhymes** comptines *fpl*; **to make up a r.** faire *ou* composer des vers (**about** sur); **to speak in r.** faire des vers

rhyme[2] **1** *vi* (*of words*) rimer (**with** avec); **rhyming couplet** distique *m*; **rhyming dictionary** dictionnaire *m* de rimes **2** *vt* **to r. a word with another** faire rimer un mot avec un autre

rhymed [raɪmd] *adj* rimé

rhymester [ˈraɪmstər] *n Pej* rimailleur, -euse

rhyming slang [ˈraɪmɪŋ] *n forme f d'argot londonnienne, associée à la culture Cockney, qui substitue à un mot une expression qui rime avec lui; par ex.* stairs = apples and pears *ou* wife = trouble and strife

rhythm [ˈrɪð(ə)m] *n Mus etc* rythme *m*; (*pace*) rythme, cadence *f*; **to have a sense of r.** avoir le sens du rythme; **he's got r.** il a le sens du rythme; **to keep up a steady r.** maintenir un rythme régulier; (*of worker*) travailler à un rythme régulier; **r. of work** rythme *ou* cadence de travail

rhythm and blues *n* rhythm and blues *m*

rhythmic(al) [ˈrɪðmɪk, -ɪk(ə)l] *adj* rythmé, cadencé; (*beat*) rythmique; **to be r.** (*of person*) avoir le sens du rythme; **r. dancing** danse *f* rythmique; **r. breathing** respiration *f* cadencée

rhythmically [ˈrɪðmɪklɪ] *adv* (*to breathe, dance etc*) avec rythme, de façon rythmée *ou* cadencée

rhythm method *n* (*of birth control*) méthode *f* de la température

rhythm section *n* (*in jazz band etc*) section *f* rythmique

rib[1] [rɪb] *n* **(a)** (*of person, animal*) côte *f*; **his ribs stick out** on lui voit les côtes; **r.-tickling joke/story** une plaisanterie/histoire à mourir de rire; *Fig F* **this soup will stick to your ribs!** (*is very thick*) cette soupe vous tiendra bien au corps!; *Culin* **spare ribs** travers *m* de porc; *Culin* **r. roast** côte de bœuf **(b)** (*of aeroplane, ceiling, leaf*) nervure *f*; (*of umbrella*) baleine *f* **(c)** (*in knitting*) côte *f*; **knit two inches in r.** tricoter environ cinq centimètres (au point) de côtes

rib[2] (**-bb-**) **1** *vt F* (*person*) taquiner (**about** à propos de, au sujet de) **2** *vi Knitting* **r. for two inches** tricoter environ cinq centimètres (au point) de côtes

ribald [ˈrɪbəld, ˈraɪ-] *adj* (*joke, person, song*) grivois, paillard; (*laughter*) gras

ribaldry [ˈrɪbəldrɪ, ˈraɪ-] *n* grivoiserie *f*, paillardise *f*; **enough of this r.!** assez de paillardises!

ribbed [rɪbd] *adj* (*ceiling*) à nervures, nervuré; (*fabric*) côtelé, à côtes; *Knitting* au point de côtes; *Archit* **r. vault** voûte *f* d'ogives

ribbing [ˈrɪbɪŋ] *n* **(a)** *F* (*teasing*) taquinerie *f*; **to take a r.** se faire mettre en boîte **(b)** (*on ceiling*) nervures *fpl*; (*of fabric, knitting*) côtes *fpl*

ribbon [ˈrɪbən] *n* **(a)** (*for hair, package, typewriter*) ruban *m*; **tied with r.** attaché avec du ruban; *Horseriding* **ribbons** (*reins*) guides *fpl*; **to hang in ribbons** (*of clothes, curtains etc*) pendre en lambeaux; **to tear to ribbons** (*clothes etc*) mettre en lambeaux, déchiqueter, lacérer; *F* (*film, performance etc*) éreinter; **r. cartridge** ruban encreur; **r. cassette** cassette *f* de ruban; **r. guide** (*on printer*) guide-ruban *m*; **r. microphone** microphone *m* à ruban

(b) (*on medal*) ruban *m*; (*of order*) cordon *m*

(c) *Fig* (*of land, road etc*) bande *f* étroite, *Lit* ruban *m*; (*of smoke*) filet *m*; **r. development** concentration *f* urbaine en bordure de route

ribcage [ˈrɪbkeɪdʒ] *n Anat* cage *f* thoracique

riboflavin(e) [raɪbəʊˈfleɪvɪn] *n Ch* riboflavine *f*

ribonucleic [raɪbəʊnjuːˈkliːɪk] *adj Ch* **r. acid** acide *m* ribonucléique

rice[1] [raɪs] *n* riz *m*; **long/short grain r.** riz à grains longs/courts; **brown r.** riz complet; **to grow r.** cultiver du riz; **r. bowl** bol *m* pour le riz; *Fig* **the country was once the r. bowl of Asia** le pays a fourni autrefois tout son riz à l'Asie; **r. grower** riziculteur, -trice; **r. growing** riziculture *f*; **r.-growing** (*country, region*) rizicole

rice[2] *vt Am Culin* (*vegetables*) passer au presse-purée

rice field *n* rizière *f*

rice paddy *n* rizière *f*

rice paper *n* papier *m* de riz

rice pudding *n Culin* (*milky*) riz *m* au lait; (*solid*) gâteau *m* de riz

ricer [ˈraɪsər] *n Am Culin* presse-purée *m inv*

rice water *n* eau *f* de riz

rice wine *n* alcool *m* de riz, saké *m*

rich [rɪtʃ] **1** *adj* (*person, country, food*) riche; (*profit*) gros; (*banquet*) somptueux; (*soil*) riche, fertile; (*vegetation*) luxuriant; (*harvest, supply*) abondant; (*costume, dress*) riche, somptueux; (*furnishings*) luxueux; (*colour*) intense; (*voice*) chaud, étoffé, ample; **extremely r.** (*person*) richissime; **r. people** les riches *mpl*; **to get** *or* **grow r.** s'enrichir; **a get-r.-quick scheme** un système pour s'enrichir rapidement; **I'm richer by a hundred pounds** *or* **a hundred pounds richer** j'ai une centaine de livres de plus; **to strike it r.** faire fortune, *F* décrocher le gros lot; **r. in ...** riche *ou* abondant en ...; *Aut* **r. mixture** mélange *m* riche; *F Iron* **that's r. coming from you** venant de toi, c'est un peu fort

2 *n* **(a) riches** (*of country, seabed etc*) richesse(s) *f(pl)*

(b) the r. (*pl*) les riches *mpl*

-rich [rɪtʃ] *suff* **cotton/protein-r.** riche en coton/protéines; **iron-r.** riche *ou* à haute teneur en fer

Richard [ˈrɪtʃəd] *n* **R. the Lionheart** Richard *m* Cœur de Lion

richly [ˈrɪtʃlɪ] *adv* (*to dress*) richement, somptueusement; (*to decorate*) richement, magnifiquement; **r. deserved** bien mérité

richness [ˈrɪtʃnɪs] *n* (*of person, country, food, fuel mix, style*) richesse *f*, abondance *f*; (*of banquet*) somptuosité *f*; (*of soil*) richesse, fertilité *f*; (*of voice*) chaleur *f*, ampleur *f*; (*of colour*) intensité *f*

Richter [ˈrɪktər] *n* **R. scale** échelle *f* de Richter; **to measure five on the R. scale** (*of earthquake*) atteindre cinq sur l'échelle de Richter

rick[1] [rɪk] *n* (*of hay, straw etc*) meule *f*

rick[2] *vt* (*hay etc*) mettre en meule(s)

rick[3] *vt* (*ankle*) se tordre; **to r. one's neck** attraper un torticolis; **to r. one's back** se donner un tour de reins

rickets [ˈrɪkɪts] *npl* (ⓘA10, d) *Med* rachitisme *m*; **to have r.** être rachitique

rickety [ˈrɪkɪtɪ] *adj* **(a)** *F* (*furniture*) bancal, *pl* bancals, branlant; (*staircase*) branlant, délabré; (*bridge*) branlant; *Fig* (*explanation, alliance*) bancal, boiteux **(b)** *Med* rachitique

rickshaw [ˈrɪkʃɔː] *n* pousse-pousse *m inv*; **r. driver** conducteur *m* de pousse-pousse; **r. passenger** personne *f* se déplaçant en pousse-pousse

ricochet[1] [ˈrɪkəʃeɪ, -ʃet] *n* (*of ball, bullet etc*) ricochet *m*

ricochet[2] *vi* (**ricochetted** [ˈrɪkəʃeɪd]; **ricochetting** [ˈrɪkəʃeɪɪŋ]) (*of ball, bullet etc*) ricocher (**off** sur)

rictus, *pl* **-tus, -tusses** [ˈrɪktəs, -əsɪz] *n* rictus *m*

rid [rɪd] *vt* (*pt* **ridded, rid**; *pp* **rid**; *prp* **ridding**) (*person*) débarrasser, délivrer (**of** de); (*place*) débarrasser (**of** de); **to r. the world of poverty** délivrer le monde de la pauvreté; **to r. oneself of one's illusions** se défaire de ses illusions; **to r. sb of his enemies** délivrer qn de ses ennemis; **the kidneys r. the body of waste** les reins débarrassent le corps des déchets; **to get rid of** (*dismiss*) (*employee*) se débarrasser de, renvoyer; (*government, politician etc*) se débarrasser de; (*murder*) supprimer, éliminer; **to get rid** *or* **to r. oneself of sth** se débarrasser *ou* se défaire de qch; **I thought we were never going to get rid of them** (*guests*) j'ai cru que nous n'allions jamais arriver à nous en débarrasser *ou* à nous débarrasser d'eux; **to get rid of a cold** se débarrasser d'un rhume; **I'll get rid of it for you** je vais t'en débarrasser; **I've got rid of my car** je me suis débarrassé de ma voiture; **we can't get rid of the house** nous n'arrivons pas à vendre la maison; *Cards* **to get rid of a card** se défausser d'une carte; **to be well rid of sth/sb** être bien débarrassé de qch/qn; **you're well rid of him!** tu en es bien débarrassé!

riddance [ˈrɪd(ə)ns] *n* **good r.!** bon débarras!; *F* **good r. to bad rubbish!** bon débarras, on ne perd pas grand-chose!

ridden [ˈrɪd(ə)n] **1** *pp see* **ride**[2] **2** *adj* **to be r. with** *or* **by guilt** être bourrelé de remords *ou* accablé par le remords

-ridden [ˈrɪd(ə)n] *suff* **debt-r.** criblé *ou* accablé de dettes; **disease-r.** rongé par la maladie; **guilt-r.** bourrelé de remords, accablé par le remords

riddle[1] [ˈrɪd(ə)l] *n* (*puzzle*) devinette *f*; *Fig* (*person, event*) énigme *f*; **to speak** *or* **talk in riddles** parler par énigmes; **to ask sb a r.** poser une devinette à qn

riddle[2] *n Gardening* (*for earth, gravel etc*) crible *m*

riddle[3] *vt* **(a)** (*gravel*) cribler **(b) to r. sb with bullets** cribler qn de balles; **riddled with** (*holes*) criblé de; (*spelling mistakes*) cousu de; (*corruption*) en proie à; (*cancer*) rongé par

ride[1] [raɪd] *n* **(a)** (*journey*) (*on bicycle, motorbike, car*) tour *m*, promenade *f*; (*in taxi*) course *f*; (*on horse*) promenade; (*in train*) voyage *m*; (*on merry-go-round*) tour (de manège); (*in boat, helicopter, plane*) tour; **to go for a r. in a car** *or* **a car r.** aller se promener *ou* aller faire un tour en voiture; **we went for a r. in my car** nous sommes allés faire un tour dans ma voiture; **to go for** *or* **take a r.** (*on bicycle, motorbike*) aller se promener *ou* aller faire un tour à bicyclette/à moto; (*on horse*) faire une promenade à cheval; **to have a r. on** (*bicycle*) monter sur; (*horse*) monter à; **to give a child a r. on one's back** porter un enfant sur son dos; **the car gives a very smooth r.** la voiture a de bonnes qualités routières; *Fig* **he did not have an easy r.** (*at interview, press conference etc*) on ne l'a pas épargné; *Fig* **to give sb a rough r.** en faire baver *ou* voir à qn; **we're in for a bumpy r.** (*in plane, car etc*) ça va secouer; *Fig* nous sommes bien partis pour en baver; *Fig* **to be** *or* **come along for the r.** venir juste pour voir; **he has three rides today** (*of jockey*) il a trois montes aujourd'hui; **to take sb for a r.** emmener qn faire une promenade (**on a horse** à cheval; **in one's car** en voiture); *Fig F* (*cheat*) faire marcher qn, mener qn en bateau; *Am Fig F* (*in order to kill*) emmener qn en voiture pour lui faire la peau; *Fig F* **he's been taken for a r.** (*cheated*) il s'est fait avoir; *Aut* **r. absorbency** absorption *f* des inégalités de la route

(b) (*distance*) trajet *m*; *Br* **it's a 70p r. on the bus** il y en a pour 70p en autobus; **it's only a short r. away by car** il n'y en a pas pour longtemps en voiture; **it's a quarter of an hour's r. on a bicycle** il y en a pour un quart d'heure à bicyclette

(c) *Am Aut* (*lift*) **can I give you a r.?** est-ce que je peux vous emmener *ou* conduire quelque part?; **could you give me a r. into town?** est-ce que tu peux m'emmener *ou* me conduire en ville?; **does everyone have a r. to the church?** est-ce que tout le monde a un véhicule pour aller à l'église?; **do you have a r. to the airport?** est-ce que quelqu'un vous emmène *ou* conduit à l'aéroport?

(d) (*path in forest*) allée *f* cavalière

(e) (*attraction at funfair*) attraction *f*

(f) (*passenger in taxi*) client, -e

(g) *Vulg Sl* (*sexually*) **a good r.** un bon coup

ride[2] (*pt* **rode** [rəʊd]; *pp* **ridden** [ˈrɪd(ə)n]) **1** *vi* **(a)** (*on horse*) faire du cheval, monter à cheval; (*on bicycle*) faire de la bicyclette; (*on motorbike*) faire de la moto; **he was riding when I saw him** il était à cheval/bicyclette/moto quand je l'ai vu; **can you r.?** (*on horse*) est-ce que vous savez monter à cheval?; **she doesn't r. much** (*on horse*) elle ne monte pas souvent à cheval; **I'm going riding this morning** (*on horse*) je vais faire du cheval ce matin; **he rides well** (*on horse*) il monte bien (à cheval), il est bon cavalier; **he rode into town on his horse/bicycle** il est allé en ville à cheval/bicyclette; **to r. to hounds** faire de la chasse à courre; **to r. on an elephant** aller à dos d'éléphant; **it's the first time I've ridden in a Porsche** c'est la première fois que je roule en *ou* que je monte dans une Porsche; **to r. on sb's knee** (*of child*) être à califourchon sur le genou de qn; **to r. to a place** aller *ou* se rendre à un endroit (**on horseback** à cheval; **on a bicycle** à bicyclette); **to r. to work on the bus** aller *ou* se rendre en bus à son travail; **he prefers to r. at the back of the bus** il préfère s'asseoir au fond du bus; **I don't mind riding in the back** *or Am* **in back** je veux bien m'asseoir à l'arrière; *Fig* **to be riding for a fall** courir à sa perte; **to be riding high** connaître une période de succès; **to r. up/down** (*in lift*) monter/descendre; **he's riding in the 3. 30** (*taking part in horserace*) il dispute la course de 3h30

(b) *Fig* **to let sth r.** laisser courir qch

(c) *Aut* **this car rides very smoothly** cette voiture a de bonnes qualités routières

(d) (*of ship*) **to r. at anchor** être au mouillage

2 *vt* **(a) she rode her horse across the fields** elle a fait traverser le champ à son cheval; **she rode her horse at the fence** elle a dirigé son cheval sur la barrière; **he's a very easy horse to r.** c'est un cheval très facile à monter; **to r. an ass/elephant** être monté à dos d'âne/d'éléphant; *Horseracing* **Comet ridden by Martin** Comet monté par Martin; **to r. a good/bad race** (*of horse*) bien/mal courir; (*of jockey*) bien/mal monter; **witches r. broomsticks** les sorcières chevauchent des balais *ou* des manches à balai; **to know how to r. a bike** savoir faire du vélo *ou* de la bicyclette; **can I r. your bike?** est-ce que je peux monter sur ta bicyclette?; **to r. 50 kilometres** aller *ou* faire 50 kilomètres (à cheval *ou* en voiture *etc*); **to r. the waves** *Naut* (*of ship*) voguer sur les flots; *Sp* (*of surfer*) chevaucher les vagues; *Naut* **to r. the storm** soutenir le choc de la tempête; *Fig* attendre que l'orage passe; *Boxing* **to r. a punch** (*of boxer*) encaisser un coup; *Am* **to r. sb up/down** (*in elevator*) faire monter/descendre qn; **to r. sb down** (*on horse*) (*trample*) piétiner qn; **to r. a horse into the ground** monter un cheval jusqu'à l'épuisement

(b) *Am* (*travel in*) (*bus, train*) prendre (**to** jusqu'à)

(c) *esp Am F* (*harass*) **to r. sb** être (toujours) sur le dos de qn; **stop riding me!** fiche-moi la paix!

▶ **ride on** *vipo Fig* (*depend on*) **there's a lot riding on this election** l'enjeu de cette élection est important; **what's riding on it?** quelle conséquence est-ce que ça peut avoir?

▶ **ride out 1** *vtsep* **to r. out the storm** *Naut* étaler la tempête; *Fig* surmonter la crise; *Fig* **to r. out a problem/crisis** survivre à un problème/une crise; *Am* **to r. sb out of town** faire quitter la ville à qn **2** *vi* **we rode out to meet them** nous sommes partis à leur rencontre en vélo/à cheval

▶ **ride up** *vi* (*of skirt etc*) remonter

rider [ˈraɪdər] *n* **(a)** (*on horse*) cavalier, -ière; (*on racehorse*) jockey *m*; (*in circus*) écuyer, -ère; (*on bicycle*) cycliste *mf*; (*on motorcycle*) motocycliste *mf*; **to be a good r.** (*on horse*) bien monter à cheval, être bon cavalier; (*on motorcycle*) bien savoir faire de la moto; *Sp* être un bon/une bonne motocycliste

(b) (*to bill*) clause *f* additionnelle (**to** à); (*to document*) annexe *f* (**to** à); (*to contract*) avenant *m* (**to** à); **to add a r. (recommending) that …** ajouter une clause recommandant que …

riderless [ˈraɪdələs] *adj* (*horse*) sans cavalier

ridership [ˈraɪdəʃɪp] *n Am* nombre *m* total d'utilisateurs des transports en commun

ridesharing [ˈraɪdʃeərɪŋ] *n Am* = partage *m* d'un véhicule pour se rendre sur son lieu de travail

ridge¹ [rɪdʒ] *n* **(a)** (*of roof, mountain*) arête *f*, crête *f*; **r. roof** toit *m* en dos d'âne; **r. tile** (tuile *f*) faîtière *f* **(b)** (*chain of hills, mountains*) chaîne *f*; *Met* **r. of high pressure** dorsale *f* barométrique **(c)** (*on surface*) strie *f*; (*on sand*) ride *f*; (*in ploughed field*) crête *f* de labour

ridge² *vt* **(a)** (*roof*) enfaîter **(b)** (*surface*) strier, sillonner; (*sand*) rider, strier

ridged [rɪdʒd] *adj* (*surface*) strié, ridé

ridgepole [ˈrɪdʒpəʊl] *n* (*of roof*) panne *f* faîtière; (*of tent*) mât *m* de faîte

ridgetree [ˈrɪdʒtriː] *n* (*of roof*) panne *f* faîtière

ridgeway [ˈrɪdʒweɪ] *n Br* route *f* des crêtes

ridicule¹ [ˈrɪdɪkjuːl] *n* ridicule *m*; **to hold sb/sth up to r.** tourner qn/qch en ridicule *ou* en dérision; **to lay oneself open to r.** s'exposer au ridicule; **object of r.** objet *m* de risée

ridicule² *vt* ridiculiser, tourner en ridicule (**for** à cause de)

ridiculous [rɪˈdɪkjʊləs] **1** *adj* (*behaviour, person etc*) ridicule; **to make sb/sth look r.** rendre qn/qch ridicule, ridiculiser qn/qch; **to make oneself look r.** se rendre ridicule, se ridiculiser; **it's r. that ...** il est ridicule que ... + *sub*; **to pay a r. price for sth** (*pay little*) payer qch un prix ridicule *ou* dérisoire; (*pay a lot*) payer qch beaucoup trop cher; *F* **don't be r.** ne sois pas ridicule **2** *n* **the r.** le ridicule *m*; **to verge on the r.** friser le ridicule; **from the sublime to the r.** du sublime au ridicule

ridiculously [rɪˈdɪkjʊləslɪ] *adv* (*to act, dress etc*) d'une façon ridicule, ridiculement; (*easy, expensive, low etc*) ridiculement; **r. rich** immensément riche

ridiculousness [rɪˈdɪkjʊləsnɪs] *n* (*of appearance, behaviour, situation etc*) ridicule *m*

riding [ˈraɪdɪŋ] *n* **(a)** (*of horse*) équitation *f*; (*skill*) monte *f*; **r. is her favourite hobby** l'équitation est son passe-temps favori; **r. cap** bombe *f*; **r. boots/breeches/costume** bottes *fpl*/culotte *f*/tenue *f* de cheval; **r. crop** *or* **whip** cravache *f*; **r. habit** amazone *f*; **r. instructor** professeur *m* d'équitation, maître *m* de manège; **r. kit** tenue de cheval; **r. lesson** leçon *f* d'équitation; **r. school** école *f* d'équitation, manège *m*; **r. techniques** techniques *fpl* de l'équitation

(b) *Aut* **smooth r.** suspension *f* douce

(c) (*district, region*) *Can Pol* circonscription *f* électorale; *Br Hist* **the East/West/North R.** la division est/ouest/nord du comté d'Yorkshire

rife [raɪf] *adj* (*widespread*) répandu; **to be r.** (*of corruption, crime, disease etc*) régner, sévir; (*of rumours*) aller bon train; **the city was r. with disease** la ville était en proie à la maladie, la maladie régnait dans la ville; **the city was r. with rumour** les rumeurs allaient bon train dans la ville; **the police force is r. with corruption** la corruption règne dans la police

riff [rɪf] *n Mus* riff *m*

riffle¹ [ˈrɪf(ə)l] *n Am* (*ripple*) rides *fpl* sur l'eau, ondulations *fpl* de l'eau; (*shoal*) banc *m*

riffle² *vt* (*cards*) battre; (*pages*) feuilleter

▶ **riffle through** *vipo* feuilleter

riffraff [ˈrɪfræf] *n Pej* racaille *f*; **he's just r.** c'est un vaurien

rifle¹ [ˈraɪf(ə)l] *vt* (*flat, office etc*) mettre sens dessus dessous; (*person's pockets, filing cabinet, drawer*) fouiller; (*tomb*) violer

rifle² *n* fusil *m*; (*for hunting*) fusil (de chasse); **r. club** société *f* de tir; *Mil* **R. Corps** corps *m* des fusiliers *ou* des chasseurs à pied; *TV, Rad* **r. mike** micro *m* canon; **r. practice** (exercice *m* de) tir *m* au fusil; **r. shot** coup *m* de fusil; **within r. shot** à portée de fusil

rifleman, *pl* **-men** [ˈraɪf(ə)lmən] *n Mil* fusilier *m*, fantassin *m*

rifling [ˈraɪflɪŋ] *n* (*on gun barrel*) (*grooves*) rayures *fpl*

rift [rɪft] *n* (*in earth, rock etc*) fissure *f*, crevasse *f*; (*in clouds etc*) éclaircie *f*; *Fig* (*in relationship*) rupture *f*; *Pol* (*in party*) scission *f*; *Fig* **to heal the r. between two people** réconcilier deux personnes; **to heal the r. in a party** réconcilier les adversaires au sein d'un parti; *Geol* **r. valley** rift *m*

rig¹ [rɪg] *n* **(a)** (*of ship*) gréement *m* **(b)** (**oil**) **r.** derrick *m*; (*at sea*) plate-forme *f* pétrolière **(c)** *Am* (*truck*) semi-remorque *m*, *pl* semi-remorques **(d)** *F* (*outfit*) = **rigout**

rig² *vt* **(-gg-)** **(a)** *Naut* (*ship*) gréer **(b)** *F* (*manipulate dishonestly*) (*election etc*) truquer; **to r. the market** *Com* manipuler le marché; *St Exch* manipuler la Bourse; **to r. prices** fixer illégalement les prix; **to r. a game** truquer un jeu

▶ **rig out** *vtsep* (*dress*) (*person*) attifer, accoutrer (**as** en); **to r. oneself out** s'accoutrer (**in** dans, avec)

▶ **rig up** *vtsep* (*aerial, shelter*) monter, installer; *F* **to r. something up** faire une installation de fortune

rigamarole [ˈrɪgəmərəʊl] *n F* = **rigmarole**

rigger [ˈrɪgər] *n* **(a)** (*of ship*) gréeur *m*; **square r.** (*ship*) navire *m* gréé en carré **(b)** (*of plane*) monteur-régleur *m*, *pl* monteurs-régleurs

rigging [ˈrɪgɪŋ] *n* **(a)** (*on ship*) gréement *m*; (*of ship*) gréage *m* **(b)** *F* (*of election*) truquage *m*; (*of market*) hausse *f ou* baisse *f* factice; (*of prices*) fixation *f* illégale

right¹ [raɪt] **1** *adj* **(a)** (*correct, accurate*) (*answer etc*) bon, *f* bonne, exact, juste; (*word*) exact, juste; **that can't be r.** ça ne peut pas être ça, ça ne peut pas être juste; **have you got the r. amount?** avez-vous le compte exact?; **is this the r. house?** est-ce la bonne maison?, est-ce bien la maison?; **what's the r. time?** quelle heure est-il (exactement)?, quelle est l'heure juste *ou* exacte?; **my watch is r.** ma montre est à l'heure; **to be r.** (*of person*) avoir raison (**to do** de faire); **you're quite r.!** vous avez bien raison!; **to be r. about sth** avoir raison à propos de qch; **you were r. about him being a crook** vous aviez raison de dire que c'est une canaille; **you were quite r. to call the police** vous avez bien fait d'appeler la police; **it doesn't look r.** (*of answer, dress etc*) ça ne va pas; **the r. side of the material** l'endroit *m* du tissu; **r. side** *or* **way up** à l'endroit; **we're on the r. road** nous sommes sur le bon chemin *ou* la bonne route; *Fig* **to be on the r. lines** être dans la bonne direction; **that's r.!** parfaitement!, c'est ça!; **r. (you are)!** entendu!, d'accord!; *F* **r.?** d'accord?; *Am* **r. on!** *Br, Austr* **too r.!** exactement!, bien parlé!; **he's on the r. side of forty** il n'a pas encore quarante ans; **to get on the r. side of sb** s'insinuer dans les bonnes grâces de qn; **to keep on the r. side of the law** respecter la loi

(b) (*morally good*) bien; (*fair*) juste; **it's not r. to steal** ce n'est pas bien de voler; **it's not r. that ...** ce n'est pas juste que ... + *sub*; **I can't accept the money – it wouldn't look r.** je ne peux pas accepter l'argent, ça ferait mauvais effet; **it's only r.** ce n'est que justice; **I thought it r. to attend** j'ai jugé bon *ou* à propos d'y aller; **to do the r. thing** se conduire honnêtement *ou* honorablement; *Old-fashioned Br* **I hope he's going to do the r. thing by you** (*marry you*) j'espère qu'il va agir honorablement à ton égard (et demander ta main)

(c) (*most appropriate*) **the r. thing to do** la meilleure chose à faire; **in the r. place** à la bonne place; **to be in the r. place at the r. time** être là où il faut quand il le faut; **the r. man/woman in the r. place** l'homme/la femme qu'il faut pour la tâche; **you came at the r. time** vous êtes venu au bon moment; **now is not the r. time to mention it** ce n'est pas le moment d'en parler; **to wait for the r. moment** attendre le bon moment *ou* le moment opportun; **to know the r. people** avoir des relations, connaître les gens qu'il faut

(d) (*mentally, physically well*) **to be in one's r. mind** avoir toute sa raison, être en possession de toutes ses facultés; **no one in their r. mind would do such a thing** aucune personne sensée ne ferait une chose pareille; *F* **he's not quite r. in the head** il n'a pas toute sa tête; **I'm not feeling quite r.** je ne me sens pas très bien, *F* je ne me sens pas dans mon assiette; *F* **as r. as** *Br* **rain** *or Am* **a trivet** en parfaite santé

(e) (*as intensifier*) *Br F* (*idiot, swindle etc*) vrai; **I felt a r. fool** je me suis senti vraiment stupide; **he's all r.** c'est un brave type; *Sl* **she's a bit of all r.!** voilà une jolie pépée!

(f) (*righthand*) droit; **on the r. side** à *ou* sur la droite; *Comptr* **r. arrow key** touche *f* flèche vers la droite; **r. bank** (*of river*) rive *f* droite; **r. hand** main *f* droite; **on my r. hand** sur *ou* à ma droite; **he's my r. hand** c'est mon bras droit; **r. justification** justification *f* à droite; **r. justified** justifié à droite; *TV, Cin* **r. pan** panoramique *m* horizontal GD

2 *n* **(a)** (*morality*) droit *m*, bien *m*; **r. and wrong** le bien et le mal; **to know r. from wrong** faire la différence entre le bien et le mal; **to teach sb r. from wrong** apprendre à qn la différence entre le bien et le mal; **to be in the r.** avoir raison; **by rights** en toute justice

(b) (*entitlement*) droit *m* (**to** à; **to do** de faire); **by what r.?** de quel droit?, à quel titre?; **what r. have you to do that?** de quel droit faites-vous cela?; **to exercise a r.** exercer un droit; **r. to know** droit de savoir; **r. to vote** droit de vote; *Jur* **r. of abode** (*of refugee etc*) droit de séjour; **r. of reply** droit de réponse *ou* de rectification; **r. of way** *Jur* servitude *f ou* droit de passage; *Aut* priorité *f*; **there is no r. of way across this land** il n'y a pas de droit de passage sur cette terre; **to have r. of way** (*on road*) avoir (la) priorité; **to hold the film/translation rights to a book** détenir les droits d'adaptation cinématographique/de traduction d'un livre; **all rights reserved** tous droits réservés; **it belongs to him by r.** cela lui appartient de droit; **to possess sth in one's own r.** avoir qch en propre; **she is famous in her own r.** c'est elle-même une célébrité; **the rights of man** les droits de l'homme; **human/animal rights** les droits de l'homme/l'animal;

women's rights les droits de la femme; **to be within one's rights** être dans son droit (**in doing** en faisant); **to know one's rights** connaître ses droits; *St Exch* **rights issue** émission *f* de nouvelles actions à taux préférentiel, émission de droits

(**c**) (*order*) **to put** *or* **set sth to rights** arranger qch, mettre qch en ordre; **I'll soon have this kitchen set to rights** j'aurai vite fait de remettre de l'ordre dans la cuisine; **to put** *or* **set the world to rights** refaire le monde; **to put** *or* **set things to rights** remettre de l'ordre

(**d**) (*right-hand side*) droite *f*, côté *m* droit; **on the r.** à droite; **on your r.** sur *ou* à votre droite; **to drive on the r.** rouler *ou* conduire à droite; **to keep to the r.** tenir sa droite

(**e**) *Boxing etc* (*blow*) droit *m*; **with a r. to the jaw** d'un droit à la mâchoire

(**f**) *Pol* **the r.** la droite; **a government of the r.** un gouvernement de droite; **to be to** *or* **on the r.** être à droite; **to be to the r. of sb** (*more right-wing than*) être plus à droite que qn

3 *adv* (**a**) (*straight*) (tout) droit; **he went r. at him** il est allé droit vers lui; **to put a mistake r.** corriger *ou* rectifier une erreur; **to put things r.** arranger les choses; **to put one's watch r.** mettre sa montre à l'heure; **to put sb r.** (*give directions*) aider qn; (*open eyes*) détromper qn, désabuser qn (**about** au sujet de); **drink this, it'll soon put you r.** bois ça, ça te remettra d'aplomb; **to do sth r. away** *or* **off** (*immediately*) faire qch sur-le-champ *ou* immédiatement; (*at the first attempt*) faire qch du premier coup; **I'll be r. back** je reviens tout de suite; **r. now** (*immediately*) tout de suite; (*at the moment*) en ce moment; **he was here r. now** il était là il y a une minute

(**b**) (*completely*) **r. to the end of the peninsula** jusqu'au bout de la presqu'île; **a wall r. round the house** un mur tout autour de la maison; **he turned r. round** il a fait un tour complet; **r. at the top** tout en haut; *Fig* **you have to go r. to the top if you want to get anything done** il faut aller tout en haut de la hiérarchie pour arriver à quelque chose; **r. at the back** tout au fond; **to go r. through sth** traverser qch de part en part; **somebody had cut r. through the cable** quelqu'un avait sectionné le câble; **she walked r. up to me** elle se dirigea tout droit vers moi; **the water came r. up to her shoulders** l'eau lui arrivait jusqu'aux épaules; **r. up until the last moment** jusqu'à la dernière minute; **the dress came r. down to her ankles** la robe lui arrivait jusqu'aux chevilles; **r. reverend/honourable** très révérend/honorable

(**c**) (*exactly*) exactement; **r. in the middle** au beau *ou* en plein milieu; **r. in the middle of the harvest** en pleine moisson; **r. behind** juste derrière; **the wind was r. behind us** nous avions le vent en plein dans le dos; **to be r. behind sb** (*in support*) soutenir qn à fond; **he parked r. in front of the gate** il s'est garé en plein devant le portail; **I'll be waiting r. here** j'attends ici, je ne bouge pas; **it was r. here on the table** il était là sur la table

(**d**) (*correctly*) (*to answer*) correctement; (*to guess*) juste; **if I remember r.** si je me souviens bien; **did I hear r.?** est-ce que j'ai bien entendu?; **you did r. to wait** vous avez bien fait d'attendre; **to act r.** bien agir

(**e**) (*well*) bien; **nothing goes r. with me** rien ne me réussit; **I'm sure it'll all come r. for you** je suis sûr que tout s'arrangera pour vous; **I got your letter all r.** j'ai bien reçu votre lettre; **to see sb r.** (*financially*) veiller à ce que qn ne soit pas à court d'argent; **r. enough, she could have been more tactful** (*I agree with you*) c'est vrai elle aurait pu être plus délicate; **it was a mistake r. enough** c'était bien une erreur; **he's to blame r. enough** c'est bien de sa faute (à lui)

(**f**) (*to the right-hand side*) (*to look, turn*) à droite; *F* **r., left and centre** (*everywhere*) de tous les côtés; *F* **he owes money r., left and centre** il doit de l'argent à droite et à gauche; *F* **he cheated us r., left and centre** il nous a eus sur tous les tableaux

(**g**) *Br Dial F* (*very*) très; **I was r. glad to hear it** j'étais très heureux de l'apprendre

right[2] *vt* (**a**) (*put upright*) (*boat, car etc*) redresser; **to r. itself** (*of boat*) se redresser (**b**) (*correct*) (*a wrong*) réparer; (*mistake*) corriger, rectifier; **to r. itself** (*of situation*) s'arranger; (*of problem*) se résoudre

right angle *n* angle *m* droit; **at right angles to ...** à angle droit avec ...

right-angled *adj* à angle droit; (*triangle etc*) rectangle

righteous ['raɪtʃəs] **1** *adj* (*person*) droit, vertueux; *Bible* juste; (*anger, indignation*) juste, justifié; *Pej* **r. tone of voice** ton *m* satisfait **2** *npl* **the r.** les bons *mpl*, les justes *mpl*

righteously ['raɪtʃəslɪ] *adv* (*to live, behave*) vertueusement; (*to deny, protest*) de manière offensée; *Pej* (*to say*) d'un ton satisfait; **he became r. indignant** il s'indigna

righteousness ['raɪtʃəsnɪs] *n* (*of person*) droiture *f*, vertu *f*; *Bible* **those who hunger and thirst after r.** ceux qui ont soif de justice

rightful ['raɪtfʊl] *adj* (*heir, king, claim, owner*) légitime; (*inheritance*) auquel on a droit; **to have one's r. share** avoir sa juste part; **she insisted on being given her r. share** elle insista pour qu'on lui donne la part à laquelle elle avait droit

rightfully ['raɪtfəlɪ] *adv* légitimement; (*inherited*) à juste titre; **it is r. mine** cela m'appartient légitimement

right-hand *adj* (*glove etc*) de la main droite; (*bend, drawer etc*) de droite; **to have r. drive** (*of car*) avoir la conduite à droite, avoir le volant à droite; **on the r. side** sur le côté droit; *Fig* **r. man/woman** bras *m* droit

right-handed 1 *adj* (*person*) droitier; (*tool, scissors etc*) pour droitiers; (*screw*) vis *f* dont le pas est à droite; **r. blow** coup *m* du droit, droit *m* **2** *adv* (*to play, hit etc*) de la main droite

right-hander ['raɪt'hændər] *n* (**a**) (*person*) droitier, -ière (**b**) (*blow*) coup *m* du droit, droit *m*

righting ['raɪtɪŋ] *n* (*of boat, wrong*) redressement *m*

rightist ['raɪtɪst] **1** *n* (*person*) homme *m*/femme *f* de droite **2** *adj* (*ideas, politics etc*) de droite

rightly ['raɪtlɪ] *adv* (*correctly*) (*to act, judge, guess*) bien; (*to choose*) avec raison; (*justifiably*) (*to believe, be annoyed, concerned*) à juste titre, avec raison; **r. or wrongly** à tort ou à raison; **I can't r. say** je ne saurais dire au juste; **I don't r. know** je ne sais pas exactement *ou* au juste; **and r. so** et à juste titre, et avec raison

right-minded *adj* sensé

rightness ['raɪtnɪs] *n* (*of decision, cause*) légitimité *f*; (*of answer*) justesse *f*, exactitude *f*

righto [raɪ'təʊ] *int Br F* OK!, d'accord!

right of recourse *n* droit *m* de recours

right-on *adj F* politiquement correct

right-thinking *adj* sensé

right-to-lifer *n Am* personne *f* qui est contre l'avortement

right triangle *n Am* triangle *m* rectangle

right whale *n Zool* baleine *f* franche

right wing *n Mil, Sp* aile *f* droite; *Pol* droite *f*

right-wing *adj Pol* (*attitude, government, policy etc*) de droite; **he is very r.** il est très à droite

right-winger *n Pol* personne *f* de droite

righty-ho [raɪtɪ'həʊ] *int Br F* OK!, d'accord!

rigid ['rɪdʒɪd] *adj* (*metal, plastic etc*) rigide; *Fig* (*discipline, principles, rules etc*) rigide, strict, inflexible; (*etiquette*) rigide; **she's very r. in her ideas** elle a des idées très rigides *ou* inflexibles; **r. with fear** pétrifié; *Br F* **to be bored r.** s'ennuyer ferme; *Br F* **it shook me r.** (*shocked me*) ça m'a fichu un sacré coup

rigidity [rɪ'dʒɪdɪtɪ] *n* (*of metal, plastic*) rigidité *f*, raideur *f*; *Fig* (*of discipline, principles, rules etc*) rigidité, inflexibilité *f*; (*of etiquette*) rigidité

rigidly ['rɪdʒɪdlɪ] *adv* rigidement; (*censored, controlled*) sévèrement, strictement; **r. opposed to ...** rigoureusement opposé à ...

rigmarole ['rɪgmərəʊl] *n F* (**a**) (*process*) procédure *f* compliquée; **to go through a whole r.** faire tout un tas de démarches (**b**) (*speech*) galimatias *m*

rigor ['rɪgər] *n* (**a**) *US* = **rigour** (**b**) *Med* **r. mortis** ['mɔːtɪs] rigidité *f* cadavérique

rigorous ['rɪgərəs] *adj* (*discipline, training, climate, analysis etc*) rigoureux

rigorously ['rɪgərəslɪ] *adv* rigoureusement

rigorousness ['rɪgərəsnɪs] *n* rigueur *f*

rigour, *US* **rigor** ['rɪgər] *n* rigueur *f*; **the r. of the law** la sévérité de la loi; **the rigours of prison life/the Scottish climate** les rigueurs de la vie en prison/du climat écossais

rigout ['rɪgaʊt] *n F* (*outfit*) tenue *f*, *Pej* accoutrement *m*; **to be in full r.** être en grande tenue

rile [raɪl] *vt F* (*person*) agacer, exaspérer; **to r. sb (up) about sth** faire (en)rager qn à propos de qch; **don't get riled!** ne t'énerve pas!

Riley ['raɪlɪ] *n F* **to lead** *or* **live the life of R.** mener la grande vie

rill [rɪl] *n Lit* ruisselet *m*, petit ruisseau *m*

rim[1] [rɪm] *n* (*of cup, glass, crater etc*) bord *m*; (*of wheel*) jante *f*; (*of dirt, soap etc*) dépôt *m*, trace *f*; **spectacle rims** monture *f* de lunettes; **countries on the Pacific R.** pays *mpl* de la ceinture pacifique; **Pacific R. economy** économie *f* des pays de la ceinture pacifique; *TV, Cin* **r. light** éclairage *m* rasant

rim[2] *vt* (**-mm-**) (*wheel*) janter; (*of hills etc*) (*valley*) border; **nails rimmed with dirt** des ongles ourlés de crasse

rime[1] [raɪm] *n Lit* (*frost*) givre *m*, gelée *f* blanche

rime[2] *n, vti Arch* = **rhyme**

rimless ['rɪmlɪs] *adj* (*spectacles*) sans monture

-rimmed ['rɪmd] *suff* **horn/steel-r.** (*spectacles*) avec une monture en écaille/en acier

rimming ['rɪmɪŋ] *n TV, Cin* éclairage *m* frisant

rind [raɪnd] *n* (*of melon, lemon etc*) écorce *f*, zeste *m*; (*of cheese*) croûte *f*; (*of bacon*) couenne *f*; **a piece of orange/lemon r.** un zeste *ou* un morceau d'écorce de citron/d'orange

ring¹ [rɪŋ] *n* **(a)** (*band*) (*for finger*) anneau *m*; (*with stone, for marking birds*) bague *f*; (*for keys*) porte-clés *m inv*; (*for napkin*) rond *m* de serviette; *Gym* **the rings** les anneaux *mpl*; *Mus* **The R. (Cycle** *or* **of the Nibelung)** La Tétralogie; *MecE* **retaining r.** plaquette *f* de fixation; **r. spanner** clé *f* à œil; *Comptr* **r. structure** structure *f* en anneau

(b) (*circle*) (*of people, chairs etc*) cercle *m*; (*in water, of smoke*) rond *m*; (*burner on stove*) feu *m*, brûleur *m*; (*around planet*) anneau *m*; (*around sun, moon*) halo *m*; (*of tree*) anneau *ou* cercle annuel; (*stain*) marque *f*, trace *f*; **the cup will leave a r.** la tasse va faire une marque; **sitting in a r.** assis en cercle *ou* en rond; *Geol* **R. of Fire** ceinture *f* de feu; **to have rings round one's eyes** avoir des cernes sous les yeux *ou* les yeux cernés; **they formed a r. round her** ils ont formé un cercle autour d'elle; **to draw** *or* **put a r. round sth** entourer qch d'un cercle; *Fig* **to make** *or* **run rings round sb** (*at chess, tennis etc*) complètement dominer qn; (*in quiz game, general knowledge test etc*) être bien meilleur que qn; **(swimming) r.** bouée *f*

(c) (*enclosure*) (*at circus*) arène *f*, piste *f*; (*for boxing, wrestling*) ring *m*; (*for bullfight*) arène; (*for showjumping*) enceinte *f*; **the r.** (*boxing as sport*) la boxe *f*; *Boxing* **to retire from the r.** abandonner la boxe; *St Exch* **the R.** le Parquet; *Fig* **to throw** *or* **toss one's hat into the r.** faire connaître son intention de participer

(d) (*organization*) (*of people*) groupe *m*, cercle *m*; (*gang*) bande *f*; *Com* cartel *m*; (*of spies, drug traffickers*) réseau *m*

ring² *vt* **(a)** (*bird*) baguer **(b)** (*of police, troops etc*) (*building etc*) encercler; (*item on list etc*) entourer d'un trait de crayon; **to r. sb/sth round** *or* **about** *or* **in** (*surround*) encercler *ou* entourer qn/qch (**with** de)

ring³ *n* **(a)** (*sound*) (*of bells, telephone*) sonnerie *f*; (*of small bell, coins*) tintement *m*; (*of voice*) timbre *m*; **there was a r. at the door** on a sonné; **a r. of bells** (*set of bells*) un carillon; *Tel* **I hung up on the sixth r.** j'ai raccroché à la sixième sonnerie; *Fig* **the name has a familiar r. to it** ce nom me dit quelque chose; **the r. of truth** l'accent *m* de la vérité; *Fig* **it has a hollow r.** cela sonne creux **(b)** *Br Tel F* (*communication*) coup *m* de fil; **to give sb a r.** passer un coup de fil à qn

ring⁴ (*pt* **rang** [ræŋ]; *pp* **rung** [rʌŋ]) **1** *vi* **(a)** (*of bell, telephone, person*) sonner; (*of small bell*) tinter; (*of alarm*) retentir; **this will cause the alarm to r.** cela déclenchera l'alarme; **to r. at the door** sonner à la porte; **the bell is ringing for dinner** on sonne pour le dîner; **to r. for sb** sonner qn; **to r. for some coffee** (*by pushing bell*) sonner pour demander du café; (*by telephoning*) téléphoner pour demander du café; **to r. for room service** sonner pour appeler le service en chambre

(b) *esp Br Tel* téléphoner; **to r. round** passer une série de coups de fil

(c) (*resonate*) (*of street etc*) résonner, retentir (**with** de); (*of ears*) bourdonner; **her words still r. in my ears** ses paroles résonnent encore à mes oreilles

(d) *Fig* **to r. true** être convaincant; **to r. false** sonner faux; *Fig* **his answer did not r. true** sa réponse sonnait faux

2 *vt* **(a)** (*bell*) (faire) sonner; (*alarm*) déclencher; **to r. the doorbell** sonner à la porte; *Fig* **does that r. a bell?** est-ce que cela vous rappelle *ou* vous dit quelque chose?; *Fig* **the name rings a bell** ce nom me dit quelque chose; *Fig* **to r. the changes** introduire des changements

(b) *esp Br Tel* téléphoner à, appeler, passer un coup de fil à

▶ **ring back** *esp Br Tel* **1** *vi* rappeler **2** *vtsep* (*person*) rappeler

▶ **ring down** *vtsep Th* **to r. down the curtain** sonner pour faire baisser le rideau; *Fig* **to r. down the curtain on sth** marquer la fin de qch

▶ **ring in 1** *vi esp Br Tel* **to r. in sick** appeler pour dire qu'on est malade; **the boss wants her to r. in every hour** le patron veut qu'elle appelle toutes les heures **2** *vtsep* **to r. in the New Year** marquer la nouvelle année par une volée de cloches

▶ **ring off** *vi esp Br Tel* raccrocher

▶ **ring out 1** *vi* (*of bell, telephone*) sonner; (*of voice, shot*) retentir **2** *vtsep* **to r. out the Old Year** marquer la fin de l'année en sonnant les cloches

▶ **ring up** *esp Br* **1** *vi Tel* téléphoner **2** *vtsep* **(a)** *Tel* (*person*) téléphoner à, appeler, passer un coup de fil à **(b)** *Th* **to r. up the curtain** sonner pour faire lever le rideau; *Fig* **to r. up the curtain on sth** marquer le début de qch **(c) to r. an amount up** (*on cash register*) enregistrer une somme; **to r. up a profit** réaliser un bénéfice

ring binder *n* classeur *m* à anneaux

ringed [rɪŋd] *adj* **(a)** (*wearing ring*) (*bird*) bagué **(b)** (*with marking*) (*plover etc*) à collier

ringer ['rɪŋər] *n* **(a)** (*of bell*) sonneur, -euse, carillonneur, -euse **(b)** *Am Horseracing* cheval *m* substitué à un autre **(c)** *F* **to be a dead r. for sb** être le sosie de qn **(d)** *Sl* (*stolen car with altered plates*) voiture *f* maquillée

ring finger *n* annulaire *m*

ringing ['rɪŋɪŋ] **1** *adj* (*bell*) qui tinte *ou* sonne; (*voice, laughter etc*) sonore, retentissant; **I still have a r. sound in my ears** j'ai encore les oreilles qui sifflent; **in r. tones** d'une voix vibrante **2** *n* (*of large bell, telephone*) sonnerie *f*; (*of small bell*) tintement *m*; (*in ears*) bourdonnement *m*; *Br Tel* **r. tone** tonalité *f* de sonnerie

ringleader ['rɪŋli:dər] *n Pej* (*of gang*) chef *m* de bande; (*of rebellion, in mischief etc*) meneur, -euse

ringlet ['rɪŋlɪt] *n* (*curl*) anglaise *f*, boucle *f* (de cheveux); **to wear one's hair in ringlets** porter les cheveux en boucles, porter des anglaises

ringmaster ['rɪŋmɑ:stər] *n* (*of circus*) = Monsieur Loyal

ring-necked ['rɪŋnekt] *adj* (*bird, snake*) à collier; **r. dove** pigeon *m* ramier, palombe *f*

ring-pull *n* bague *f* (d'ouverture); **r. can** boîte *f* qui s'ouvre à l'aide d'une bague (d'ouverture)

ring road *n Br* périphérique *m*

ringside ['rɪŋsaɪd] *n* premier rang *m*; **at the r.** au premier rang; **to have a r. seat** (*at circus, boxing match*) avoir une place au premier rang; *Fig* être aux premières loges; **to have a r. view of sth** être bien placé pour voir qch

ring-tailed *adj* à queue zébrée

ringworm ['rɪŋwɜ:m] *n Med* teigne *f*

rink [rɪŋk] *n* (*for ice-skating*) patinoire *f*; (*for roller-skating*) piste *f*

rinkydink [rɪŋkɪ'dɪŋk] *adj US F* (*poor quality*) à la gomme

rinse¹ [rɪns] *n* **(a)** (*of bottle, hands etc*) rinçage *m*; **to give sth a r.** rincer qch; **r. cycle** (*in washing machine*) cycle *m* de rinçage, rinçage *m* **(b)** (*hair colouring*) rinçage *m* (colorant); **to have a r.** se faire faire un rinçage (colorant)

rinse² *vt* **(a)** (*washing, cup etc*) rincer; **to r. soap out of a sponge/clothes** rincer une éponge/des vêtements pour enlever le savon; **to r. one's hands** se passer les mains à l'eau; (*remove soap*) se rincer les mains; **to r. one's mouth** se rincer la bouche **(b)** (*with hair colouring*) **to r. one's hair** se faire un rinçage (colorant); **to r. sb's hair** faire un rinçage (colorant) à qn

▶ **rinse down** *vtsep* (*meal, pill*) **can I have some water to r. the pill down with?** puis-je avoir de l'eau pour avaler mon cachet?; **a little glass of something to r. it down?** un petit verre de quelque chose pour le faire passer?

▶ **rinse out² 1** *vtsep* (*cup, bucket etc*) rincer; **to r. out the dirt/soap** rincer pour enlever la saleté/le savon; *Fig* **go and r. your mouth out!** va te laver la bouche! **2** *vi* (*of stain, dye*) partir à l'eau

riot¹ ['raɪət] *n* (*uprising*) émeute *f*; *Fig* **there will be a r.** (*when people find out*) ça va faire scandale; *Fig* **a r. of colour** une explosion de couleurs; **to run r.** (*of person*) se déchaîner; (*of plants, inflation*) devenir incontrôlable; **my imagination was running r.** j'ai commencé à imaginer toutes sortes de choses; *F* **he's/it's a r.** (*amusing*) il est/c'est tordant

riot² *vi* **(-t-)** faire une émeute; (*of football supporters, demonstrators*) (*to fight*) se battre; (*to destroy things*) se livrer à de violentes manifestations; (*of prisoners*) se mutiner

Riot Act *n* loi *f* britannique anti-émeutes; *Fig* **to read sb the riot act** réprimander qn sévèrement, *F* engueuler qn

rioter ['raɪətər] *n* émeutier, -ière; (*football fans, demonstrators*) vandale *m*, casseur *m*; (*prisoners*) mutin *m*

riot gear *n* matériel *m* anti-émeute

rioting ['raɪətɪŋ] **1** *adj* **r. football hooligans** des hooligans qui cassent tout sur leur passage; **r. mob** bande *f* d'émeutiers; (*of football fans*) bande des vandales *ou* des casseurs **2** *n* émeutes *fpl*; (*fighting*) bagarres *fpl*; **r. broke out when …** des *ou* les bagarres ont éclaté quand …

riotous ['raɪətəs] *adj* **(a)** (*crowd etc*) violent; *Jur* **to charge sb with r. behaviour** accuser qn d'avoir eu un comportement séditieux; **r. living** vie *f* déréglée **(b)** *F* (*amusing*) (*party, occasion*) très gai et très bruyant; (*laughter*) exubérant; **we had a r. time** on a bien rigolé; **a r. success** un franc succès, un succès retentissant

riotously ['raɪətəslɪ] *adv* violemment; *F* **to be r. funny** être à se tordre de rire; **a r. funny film** un film extrêmement drôle

riot police *n* la police anti-émeute

RIP [ɑ:raɪ'pi:] (*abbr* **Rest In Peace**) Repose en paix

rip¹ [rɪp] *n* (*in fabric*) déchirure *f*; **there's a r. in your jacket** il y a une déchirure à ta veste

rip² (-pp-) **1** *vt* (*fabric etc*) déchirer; **to r. to pieces** *or* **shreds** (*garment*) déchirer en lambeaux; (*letter*) déchirer en mille morceaux; *Fig* (*play, film, director etc*) éreinter; (*argument*) mettre en pièces; **it's ripped to pieces** *or* **shreds** (*garment, carpet*) il est en lambeaux

2 *vi* **(a)** (*of fabric etc*) se déchirer

(b) *F* **to r. along** aller *ou* avancer à toute vitesse *ou* à fond de train; **the explosion ripped through the building** le choc de l'explosion s'est propagé dans tout le bâtiment; **let her** *or* **it r.!** (*of car, motorboat etc*) mets les gaz!, fonce!

(c) *F* (*be angry*) **to let r.** laisser éclater sa colère (**about** au sujet de); **to let r. (with) a stream of abuse** lancer une bordée d'injures; **to let r. at sb** s'en prendre à qn (**about** au sujet de); **to let r. against the government** s'en prendre *ou* s'attaquer au gouvernement (**for** au sujet de); **she really let r.** (*spoke her mind, let hair down etc*) elle s'est déchaînée

▶ **rip apart 1** *vtsep* déchirer; *Fig* éreinter, mettre en pièces **2** *vi* se déchirer

▶ **rip away** *vtsep* arracher

▶ **rip into** *vipo F* (*person*) attaquer violemment

▶ **rip off** *vtsep* **(a)** (*by tearing, remove quickly*) arracher; (*one's jacket*) enlever en toute hâte; **they ripped off their clothes** ils se sont déshabillés en toute hâte **(b)** *F* (*steal*) piquer; *F* **to r. sb off** (*cheat*) arnaquer qn; *F* **you were ripped off** tu t'es fait arnaquer

▶ **rip open 1** *vtsep* (*person*) éventrer; (*cheek*) déchirer; (*garment*) (*open quickly*) ouvrir d'un mouvement; **the bayonet ripped open his stomach** la baïonnette l'a éventré; **to r. open a letter** décacheter une lettre en la déchirant; **to r. open a package** ouvrir un paquet en le déchirant; **jeans ripped open at the knee** un jean déchiré au genou **2** *vi* se déchirer

▶ **rip out** *vtsep* (*remove*) (*fireplace, light fittings etc*) enlever; (*page from book*) arracher

▶ **rip up** *vtsep* **(a)** (*tear*) (*letter*) déchirer **(b)** (*remove*) (*floorboards*) arracher; (*pavement*) creuser

riparian [raɪˈpeərɪən] *adj, n Fml* riverain, -aine; (*wildlife*) des rivières

ripcord [ˈrɪpkɔːd] *n* (*on parachute*) corde *f* d'ouverture, cordelette *f* de déclenchement; (*on hot-air balloon*) corde de déchirure

ripe [raɪp] *adj* (*fruit, grain*) mûr; (*cheese*) bien fait, bien à point; (*vulgar*) grossier; **to live to a r. old age** vivre vieux, vivre jusqu'à un âge avancé; *Hum* **the r. old age of sixteen** l'âge avancé de seize ans; **the time is r. for speaking the truth** le temps est venu de dire la vérité; **the time is not yet r.** le temps n'est pas encore venu; **r. for change/revolution** mûr *ou* prêt pour le changement/la révolution; **the company is r. for takeover** la société est prête pour être rachetée; **a site r. for development** un site bon à exploiter; **to smell r.** (*of fruit*) avoir un parfum de fruit mûr; *Pej* (*of person*) sentir mauvais

ripen [ˈraɪp(ə)n] **1** *vt* (*fruit, grain*) (faire) mûrir; (*cheese*) affiner **2** *vi* (*of fruit, Fig of plan etc*) mûrir; (*of cheese*) se faire; *Fig* **to r. into manhood** atteindre l'âge d'homme

ripeness [ˈraɪpnɪs] *n* (*of fruit, grain etc*) maturité *f*; *Fig* (*of comments, language*) grossièreté *f*

ripening [ˈraɪp(ə)nɪŋ] **1** *adj* **(a)** *Lit* (*sun*) qui fait mûrir **(b)** (*fruit, grain*) mûrissant, qui mûrit; (*cheese*) qui se fait **2** *n* (*of fruit, grain*) maturation *f*, mûrissage *m*, mûrissement *m*; (*of cheese*) affinage *m*

rip-off *n F* **it's a r.!** (*too expensive*) c'est du vol!; (*not money's worth*) c'est de l'arnaque!; **r. prices** des prix astronomiques; **r. merchant** arnaqueur, -euse

riposte¹ [rɪˈpɒst] *n Fencing* riposte *f*; **to make a r.** riposter

riposte² *vi* (*in argument etc*), *Fencing* riposter

ripper [ˈrɪpər] *n* (*killer*) éventreur *m*

ripping [ˈrɪpɪŋ] *adj Old-fashioned Br F* épatant, formidable; **a r. yarn** une histoire épatante

ripple¹ [ˈrɪp(ə)l] *n* **(a)** (*wave*) (*on water*) ride *f*; (*in corn, hair*) ondoiement *m*, ondulation *f*; *Fig* **a r. of excitement ran through the crowd** un frémissement d'excitation a parcouru la foule; *TV, Cin* **r. dissolve** fondu *m* par ondulation; *Fig* **r. effect** (*of action, investment etc*) effet *m* multiplicateur **(b)** (*noise*) (*of stream*) murmure *m*, gazouillement *m*; (*of conversation, voices*) murmure(s); (*of laughter, applause*) vague *f* **(c)** (*ice-cream*) **raspberry/strawberry r.** = glace *f* vanille panachée à la framboise/fraise

ripple² **1** *vi* **(a)** (*form ripples*) (*of water*) se rider; (*of corn, hair*) onduler, ondoyer; (*of muscles*) saillir **(b)** (*make sound*) (*of stream*) murmurer, gazouiller; **laughter/applause rippled through the audience** des vagues de rires/d'applaudissements ont traversé le public **2** *vt* (*of wind*) (*water, sand*) rider; **he rippled his muscles** il a fait saillir ses muscles

rip-roaring *adj F* (*party*) tumultueux; **a r. success** un succès retentissant

ripsaw [ˈrɪpsɔː] *n* scie *f* à refendre

riptide [ˈrɪptaɪd] *n* courant *m* de retour

RISC [rɪsk] *n Comptr* (*abbr* **reduced instruction set chip/computer**) RISC

rise¹ [raɪz] *n* **(a)** (*appearance*) (*of sun, moon*) lever *m*; *Fig* **to give r. to sth** donner lieu à qch

(b) (*ascent*) (*of theatre curtain*) lever *m*; (*of leader, party*) ascension *f*; (*to power*) accession *f*; (*in rank*) avancement *m*, promotion *f*; (*of industry, technology*) essor *m*; (*in ground*) éminence *f*; **her r. to fame came overnight** elle est devenue célèbre du jour au lendemain; *F* **to take** *or* **get a r. out of sb** (*tease*) faire enrager qn

(c) (*increase*) (*in pressure etc*) hausse *f* (**in** de); (*in level of river*) crue *f*; (*of temperature*) augmentation *f*, élévation *f*; (*of tide*) montée *f*; (*of price*) hausse, augmentation; *Br* **(pay) r.** augmentation (de salaire); *Br* **to get a r.** (*in salary*) être augmenté; **the r. and fall** (*of empire, politician etc*) la grandeur et la décadence; **the book charts his r. and fall** le livre retrace son ascension et sa chute; **the r. and fall of the tide** le flux et le reflux; **food prices are on the r.** le prix des denrées est en hausse; **a big r. in house prices is on the way** une hausse *ou* augmentation importante des prix de l'immobilier se prépare

rise² *vi* (*pt* **rose** [rəʊz]; *pp* **risen** [ˈrɪz(ə)n]) **(a)** (*get up*) *Fml* (*from bed, chair*) se lever; (*from knees, after fall*) se relever; (*from the dead*) ressusciter; (*of Parliament, court*) (*at end of day*) lever *ou* clore la séance; (*at end of session*) entrer en vacances; (*on entry of judge*) se lever; **all r.!** (*in courtroom*) levez-vous s'il vous plaît!; **to r. from the table** se lever de table; **to r. on its hind legs** (*of horse*) se cabrer; **to r. early/late** (*from bed*) se lever tôt/tard; *F* **r. and shine!** debout!; **Christ is risen** le Christ est ressuscité

(b) (*appear, emerge*) (*of sun, star, moon*) se lever; **a picture rose in my mind** une image s'est présentée à mon esprit; **a feeling of panic rose in me** un sentiment de panique s'est emparé de moi; **to r. from the ashes of sth** renaître des cendres de qch; **new buildings are rising all the time** on n'arrête pas de construire

(c) (*ascend*) (*of theatre curtain*) se lever; (*of road, ground, sap etc*) monter; (*of smoke, balloon*) monter, s'élever (**from** de); *Fig* (*in society*) s'élever; *Th* **the curtain rose at 7. 30** le lever de rideau a eu lieu à 19h30; **to r. off the ground** (*of plane*) quitter le sol, décoller; **to r. in the saddle** faire du trot enlevé; **to r. to the surface** (*of fish; Fig of anger*) faire surface; (*of doubts, conflict*) se faire jour; **to r. to the bait** mordre à l'hameçon; **a murmur rose from the crowd** une rumeur s'est élevée parmi la foule; **the boat rose and fell on the water** le bateau se balançait sur l'eau; **trees rising a hundred feet above the plain** arbres qui s'élèvent à trente mètres au-dessus de la plaine; **his voice rose above the noise of the crowd** sa voix s'élevait au-dessus du bruit de la foule; **this book never rises above the level of potboiler** ce livre n'est que de la littérature alimentaire; *Fig* **to r. above events/one's difficulties** ne pas se laisser abattre par les événements/ses problèmes; **she seems to r. above that kind of petty jealousy** elle semble être au-dessus de ce genre de jalousie mesquine; **try to r. above it** tâche de rester au-dessus de la mêlée; **to r. to the occasion/challenge/task** se montrer à la hauteur de la situation/du défi/de la tâche; **to r. to fame** devenir célèbre; **to r. to power** accéder au pouvoir; **to r. in the world** faire son chemin; **he rose from nothing** il est parti de rien; **to r. to the rank of colonel** monter jusqu'au grade de colonel; **to r. through the ranks** monter les échelons un à un; **to r. in sb's esteem** monter dans l'estime de qn

(d) (*increase in amount, intensity*) (*of temperature*) monter, augmenter; (*of wind*) se lever; (*of voice*) s'élever; (*of hope*) grandir; (*of tide, pressure, river, water level*) monter; (*of dough*) lever; (*of prices*) monter, augmenter; **prices are rising** les prix montent *ou* sont à la *ou* en hausse; **everything has risen in price** tout a augmenté, tous les prix ont augmenté; **the river has risen by two metres** la rivière est montée de deux mètres; **the wind has risen to gale force** le vent se mit à souffler en tempête; **my spirits rose at the sight of the mountains** j'ai repris courage à la vue des montagnes; **her colour rose** ses joues s'empourprèrent

(e) (*become erect*) (*of hair*) se hérisser; **the dog's hackles rose** le chien s'est hérissé de colère; **the hair on the back of her neck rose** ses poils se sont hérissés

(f) (*revolt*) se soulever, se révolter (**against** contre); **to r. in arms** prendre les armes; **to r. in protest against sth** se soulever *ou* se révolter contre qch

(g) (*originate*) (*of river*) prendre sa source (**at** à; **in** dans); (*of difficulty, quarrel*) provenir, naître (**from** de)

▸ **rise up** *vi (revolt)* = **rise**²
riser ['raɪzər] *n* **(a)** **early r.** lève-tôt *mf inv*; **late r.** lève-tard *mf inv* **(b)** *(on staircase)* contremarche *f* **(c)** *(pipe)* tuyau *m* de montée
rise time *n Comptr* temps *m* de montée
risibility [rɪzɪ'bɪlɪtɪ] *n Lit (of situation etc)* caractère *m* risible *ou* ridicule; *(of offer)* caractère dérisoire
risible ['rɪzɪb(ə)l] *adj Lit (idea, plan etc)* risible, ridicule; *(offer)* dérisoire
rising ['raɪzɪŋ] **1** *adj* **(a)** *(sun)* levant
(b) *(road, artist, politician etc)* qui monte; **the r. generation** la nouvelle *ou* la jeune génération; **r. ground** élévation *f* du terrain, éminence *f*; **r. trot** trot *m* enlevé
(c) *(pressure, temperature)* en hausse; *(tide)* montant; *(stock market)* orienté à la hausse; **r. prices** la hausse des prix
2 *n* **(a)** *(of Parliament)* levée *f*, clôture *f*; **I don't like early r.** je n'aime pas me lever tôt
(b) *(of sun, moon)* lever *m*; *(of star)* lever, ascension *f*
(c) *(of theatre curtain)* lever *m*; *(of sap)* montée *f*
(d) *(of river)* montée *f*
(e) *(revolt)* insurrection *f*, révolte *f*, soulèvement *m*
3 *prep* **he's r. sixty** il va sur (ses) soixante ans
rising damp *n Constr* humidité *f* par capillarité
rising star *n* étoile *f* montante; *Mktg* produit *m* d'avenir
risk¹ [rɪsk] *n (danger)* risque *m* **(of doing** de faire); *(in insurance)* risque; **at r.** *(life, person, child)* en danger; *Med (person, population)* à risque; *(job)* menacé; **to place** *or* **put sth at r.** risquer qch; **to place** *or* **put sb at r.** faire courir un danger à qn; **is there any r. of that happening?** est-ce qu'il y a un risque que cela se produise?; **there's no r. of that happening** pas de danger que ça se passe, ça ne risque pas d'arriver; **to be full of risks** comporter beaucoup de risques; **to run risks** courir des risques; **to run the r. of losing everything** courir le risque *ou* risquer de tout perdre; **to take risks** prendre des risques; **I'm not taking any risks** je ne veux prendre aucun risque, je ne veux rien risquer; **I'll take that r.** j'en prends le risque; **with no r. of infection** sans risque d'infection; **at the r. of his life** au péril de sa vie; **at the r. of sounding conceited** au risque de paraître prétentieux; **at considerable r. to herself** en courant (elle-même) un risque considérable; **at one's own r.** à ses risques et périls; **it's too much of a r.** c'est un trop grand risque; *Jur* **risks and perils at sea** fortune *f* de mer; **the investment is a good/bad r.** c'est un bon/mauvais investissement; **he is a good/bad r.** *(for insurance purposes)* on peut l'assurer sans crainte/il serait trop risqué de l'assurer; *Fig* **he is a bad** *or* **not a good r.** *(as potential husband, employee etc)* ce n'est pas quelqu'un en qui on peut avoir confiance; **to be a fire/health/security r.** constituer un risque d'incendie/pour la santé/pour la sécurité; **r. analysis** analyse *f* des risques; *Acct* **r. asset ratio** coefficient *m* de solvabilité; **r. factor** facteur *m* de risque; **r. management** gestion *f* des risques; **r. management tool** instrument *m* de maîtrise du risque; **r. monitoring** suivi *m ou* surveillance *f* des risques; *St Exch* **r-reward ratio** ratio *m* risque-rentabilité; **r. spreading** répartition *f* des risques
risk² *vt* **(a)** *(endanger) (life, reputation etc)* risquer; **to r. one's neck** *or* **skin** risquer sa peau **(b)** *(take the chance of) (defeat, failure)* courir le risque de; **I'll r. it** je vais risquer le coup; **to r. sb's anger** s'exposer à la colère de qn; **she won't r. leaving** elle ne se risquera pas à partir; **to r. breaking one's leg** risquer de *ou* courir le risque de se casser une jambe
risk capital *n esp Br Fin* capital *m* à risque
riskiness ['rɪskɪnɪs] *n (of venture etc)* risques *mpl*
risk-taker *n* preneur *m* de risque
risky ['rɪskɪ] *adj (job, venture etc)* risqué
risotto [rɪ'zɒtəʊ] *n Culin* risotto *m*
risqué ['rɪskeɪ, 'riː-] *adj (story etc)* osé
rissole ['rɪsəʊl] *n Culin* croquette *f*
rite [raɪt] *n Rel* rite *m*; *Rel* **the last rites** les derniers sacrements *mpl*; **r. of passage** rite de passage; *Mus* **The R. of Spring** le Sacre du printemps
ritual ['rɪtjʊəl] **1** *adj (dance, killing)* rituel; *Fig* **there was r. condemnation of him in the press** la presse l'a condamné pour la forme **2** *n Rel, Fig* rituel *m*; *Fig* **to make a r. of sth** (se) faire un rituel de qch; **it's become a bit of a r.** c'est devenu comme un rituel; **he went through his nightly r. of locking the doors** il a verrouillé les portes selon son rituel de tous les soirs
ritualism ['rɪtjʊəlɪz(ə)m] *n Pej* ritualisme *m*
ritualist ['rɪtjʊəlɪst] *adj, n Pej* ritualiste *mf*
ritualistic [rɪtjʊə'lɪstɪk] *adj Pej* ritualiste
ritually ['rɪtjʊəlɪ] *adv (killed)* rituellement, selon les rites
ritz [rɪts] *n Am F* tape-à-l'œil *m inv*; **to put on the r.** se mettre sur son trente et un, *Pej* faire du tape-à-l'œil
ritzy ['rɪtsɪ] *adj F (glamorous) (party, occasion etc)* chic
rival¹ ['raɪv(ə)l] **1** *adj (company, faction etc)* rival; *(forces, claim etc)* opposé **2** *n* rival, -ale, concurrent, -ente; **to be rivals for sth** être en compétition pour qch; **to be rivals in business/love** être rivaux en affaires/amour; **to be without** *or* **have no r.** ne pas avoir d'égal, être inégalé
rival² **(-ll-,** *US* **-l-)** *vt* **(a)** *(compete with)* rivaliser avec **(in** de) **(b)** *(equal)* égaler **(for, in** en); **it rivals anything to be seen in Paris** ça vaut largement tout ce que l'on peut voir à Paris; **New York cannot r. London for historic interest** New York ne vaut pas Londres du point de vue de l'intérêt historique; **her rudeness is rivalled only by her dishonesty** chez elle, l'impolitesse n'a d'égale que la malhonnêteté; **elegance/effrontery that could scarcely be rivalled** élégance/effronterie sans égale
rivalry ['raɪvəlrɪ] *n* rivalité *f* **(between** entre); **the party is torn by personal rivalries** le parti est divisé par des rivalités d'ordre personnel; **in r. with sb** en concurrence *ou* rivalité avec qn **(for** pour)
riven ['rɪv(ə)n]) *adj pred Lit* **a country r. by war** un pays déchiré par la guerre
river ['rɪvər] *n (small)* rivière *f*; *(flowing into sea)* fleuve *m*; *Fig (of lava)* coulée *f*; *(of blood)* flot *m*; *F* **to sell sb down the r.** trahir qn, vendre qn; *US F* **he's up (the) r.** *(in prison)* il est en taule; *Br* **the R. Thames,** *US* **the Thames R.** la Tamise; **r. bank** rive *f*; **r. port/traffic** port *m*/trafic *m* fluvial; **r. safety** sécurité *f* de la navigation fluviale; **r. users** usagers *mpl* des rivières
river basin *n* bassin *m* du fleuve
riverbed ['rɪvəbed] *n* lit *m* de la rivière
river blindness *n* onchocercose *f*
river mouth *n* embouchure *f* de la rivière/du fleuve
river police *n* police *f* fluviale
riverside ['rɪvəsaɪd] *n* bord *m* de l'eau, rive *f*; **to walk along the r.** marcher le long de la rive; **r. house/pub** maison *f*/pub *m* au bord de l'eau; **r. properties** propriétés *fpl* riveraines
rivet¹ ['rɪvɪt] *n* rivet *m*; **r. head/hole** tête *f*/trou *m* de rivet; **r. gun** pistolet *m* à river
rivet² *vt Tech* river, riveter; *Fig (eyes)* fixer **(on** sur); *Fig* **all eyes were riveted on her** tout le monde avait les yeux rivés sur elle; *Fig* **to be riveted to the spot** être rivé *ou* cloué sur place; **I was riveted to the television** j'étais cloué devant la télévision; **to be absolutely riveted** être absolument fasciné **(by** par); *Tech* **riveted joint** rivure *f*
riveter ['rɪvɪtər] *n (person)* riveur, -euse; *(machine)* riveteuse *f*, riveuse *f*
riveting ['rɪvɪtɪŋ] **1** *n* rivetage *m*; **r. machine** riv(et)euse *f* **2** *adj Fig (story etc)* fascinant
Riviera (the) [ðərɪvɪ'eərə] *n* **the (French) R.** la Côte d'Azur
rivulet ['rɪvjʊlɪt] *n* ruisselet *m*; *Fig (of sweat etc)* filet *m*
Riyadh [rɪ'jæd] *n* R(i)yad, Riad
riyal [rɪ'jæl] *n (coin)* rial *m*
RN [ɑː'ren] *abbr* **(a)** *Br Mil* **Royal Navy** **(b)** *Am Med* **registered nurse**
RNA [ɑːre'neɪ] *n (abbr* **ribonucleic acid)** ARN *m*
RNLI [ɑːrene'laɪ] *n Br (abbr* **Royal National Lifeboat Institution)** = société *f* nationale de sauvetage en mer
roach [rəʊtʃ] *n* **(a)** *(fish)* gardon *m* **(b)** *Am F (cockroach)* cafard *m*, blatte *f*; **r. motel** piège *m* à cafards; **r. powder** poudre *f* pour tuer les cafards **(c)** *Sl (of marijuana cigarette)* filtre *m* de joint; **r. clip** pince *f* pour joint
road [rəʊd] *n* **(a)** route *f* **(to** de); *(small and narrow)* chemin *m*; *(in town)* rue *f*; *(roadway)* chaussée *f*; *Fig (path)* voie *f*, chemin **(to** de); **the London/Paris r.** la route de Londres/Paris; **the r. into town** la route qui mène en ville; **across** *or* **over the r.** *(building etc)* en face; **the woman from across the r.** la dame d'en face; **by r.** par la route; **to send sth by r.** envoyer qch par route; *F* **get out of the r.!** ne gène *ou* bloque pas le passage!; *Fig* **it was getting in the r. of solving the problem** cela empêchait de résoudre le problème; *F* **sorry, am I in your r.?** pardon, je vous bloque le passage?; **to be off the r.** *(of car)* être en panne; *(of driver)* ne pas pouvoir conduire; *(banned)* s'être fait retirer son permis de conduire; **to step into the r.** descendre du trottoir; **the r. is up** la route est en travaux; *esp Am* **to burn up the r.** *(of driver)* brûler de la gomme; **down/up the r.** *(to live, work)* un peu plus loin dans cette rue; **I ran down the r.** j'ai dévalé la rue, j'ai descendu la rue en courant; *Fig* **no-one can see what is down the r.** personne ne peut savoir ce que l'avenir réserve; **a few years down the r.** dans quelques années; **yes, when I'm seventy, but that's a long way down the r. (yet)** oui, quand j'aurai soixante-dix ans, mais ce n'est pas pour tout de suite; *F* **one for the r.** un petit verre avant de partir; *Prov* **all roads lead to Rome** tous les chemins mènent à Rome; **the r. to hell is paved with good intentions** l'enfer

est pavé de bonnes intentions; **approach r.** route d'accès; **the price on the r.** (*of car*) le prix clé en main; **after three hours on the r.** après trois heures de route; **to be on the r.** (*travelling*) être en route *ou* chemin *ou* voyage; (*of salesman, theatre company, pop group etc*) être en tournée; (*work as salesman*) être représentant; **that car shouldn't be on the r.** cette voiture ne devrait pas rouler; *Fig* **to be on the r. to recovery/success** être sur le chemin de la guérison/du succès; **to be on the right r.** *Aut* être sur la bonne route; *Fig* être sur la bonne voie; *Fig* **we'd like to go a little further down this r.** nous aimerions aller un peu plus loin dans ce sens *ou* cette direction; *Fig* **we don't want to go down the r. of military intervention** nous ne voulons pas nous engager dans la voie d'une intervention armée; **somewhere along the r.** en chemin; *Fig* **to come to the end of the r.** (*of relationship etc*) toucher à sa fin; *Fig F* **let's get this show on the r.** allez, c'est parti, on y va!; *F* **let's hit the r.!** en route!; **hit the r.!** fiche le camp!; **r. accidents/user** accidents *mpl*/usager *m* de la route; *Am Sl* **r. apple** (*dung*) crottin *m*; **r. conditions** état *m* des routes; **r. feel** (*of car*) sensation *f* au volant; **r. haulage** camionnage *m*, transports *mpl* routiers; **r. haulage company** entreprise *f* de transports routiers; **r. haulage forwarding agent** groupeur *m* routier; **r. haulier** transporteur *m* routier, affréteur *m* routier; **r. junction** carrefour *m*; **r. marking** marquage *m* au sol; *Br* **r. metal** empierrement *m*; **r. noise** (*when driving*) bruit *m* de roulement; **r. safety** sécurité *f* routière; **he's got no r. sense** il n'a pas conscience des dangers de la circulation; *Mktg* **r. show** tournée *f* de présentation; **r. sign** panneau *m* (routier *ou* de signalisation); *Br* **r. system/transport** réseau *m*/transports *mpl* routier(s); **r. train** train *ou* convoi *m* routier; **r. transport** transports *mpl* routiers; **r. transport company** entreprise *f* de transport routier; **r. tyre noise** bruit *m* de roulement; *Aut* **r. wheel** roue *f*; **r. works** *or* **repairs** travaux *mpl* de voirie

(b) *Naut* **road(s)** rade *f*

(c) *US Rail* chemin *m* de fer

roadbed ['rəʊdbed] *n* (*for road*) empierrement *m*; *Rail* terre-plein *m*

roadblock ['rəʊdblɒk] *n* barrage *m* routier

roadbuilding ['rəʊdbɪldɪŋ] *n* construction *f* de routes; **r. programme** programme *m* pour construire des routes

road company *n Am Th* troupe *f* itinérante

road-fund *adj Br* **r. licence** ≈ vignette *f*; **r. tax** taxe *f* routière

road hog *n F* chauffard *m*

roadholding ['rəʊdhəʊldɪŋ] *n* (*of car*) **r. (ability)** tenue *f* de route *ou* de cap

roadhouse ['rəʊdhaʊs] *n* **(a)** *Old-fashioned* hôtellerie *f* en bord de route **(b)** *Am* café *m*/restaurant *m* pour les automobilistes/camionneurs

roadie ['rəʊdɪ] *n F* roadie *m*

road manager *n* (*of pop group etc*) organisateur *m* de tournées

road map *n* carte *f* routière

road movie *n* road movie *m*

road race *n Cycling* course *f* cycliste sur route

road racer *n* (*bicycle*) bicyclette *f* de compétition; (*cyclist*) routier *m*

road rage *n* = forte agressivité *f* engendrée par la conduite des autres automobilistes

roadroller ['rəʊdrəʊlər] *n* rouleau *m* compresseur

roadshow ['reʊdʃəʊ] *n* tournée *f*, spectacle *m* itinérant

roadside ['rəʊdsaɪd] *n* bord *m* de (la) route; **r. inn/cafe/hotel** auberge *f*/café *m*/hôtel *m* situé(e) au bord de la route; **r. advertising** affichage *m* routier; *Aut* **r. assistance** assistance *f* technique aux véhicules, assistance dépannage; **r. camera** caméra *f* en bord de route; **r. repairs** (*by driver*) réparations *fpl* de fortune; (*by mechanic*) dépannage *m*

roadstead ['rəʊdsted] *n Naut* rade *f*

roadster ['rəʊdstər] *n Old-fashioned Aut* torpédo *m*

roadsweeper ['reʊdswiːpər] *n* balayeur, -euse; (*vehicle*) balayeuse *f*

road tax *n Aut* taxe *f* différentielle sur les véhicules à moteur; *Br* **have you paid your r.?** ≈ est-ce que tu as acheté ta vignette?; *Br* **r. disc** ≈ vignette *f*

road test *n* test *m* de roulage

road-test *vt* (*car*) essayer sur route; *Fig* tester

road testing *n* essai *m* routier

Road Traffic Act *n* loi *f* de la circulation routière

roadway ['rəʊdweɪ] *n* chaussée *f*

roadwork ['rəʊdwɜːk] *n* (*by boxer, athlete etc*) entraînement *m* consistant à courir le long de la route; **to do r.** courir le long de la route

roadworthiness ['rəʊdwɜːðɪnɪs] *n* (*of vehicle*) état *m* de marche

roadworthy ['rəʊdwɜːðɪ] *adj* (*vehicle*) en état de marche *ou* de rouler

roam [rəʊm] **1** *vi* errer; **to r. about the streets** (*of child etc*) traîner dans les rues; **to r. about the world** courir le monde **2** *vt* (*the streets*) parcourir; (*the seas*) sillonner; (*the world*) courir

roamer ['rəʊmər] *n* vagabond, -onde; **to be (something** *or* **a bit of) a r.** aimer rouler sa bosse

roaming ['rəʊmɪŋ] **1** *adj* errant, vagabond **2** *n* vagabondage *m*, errance *f*

roan [rəʊn] **1** *adj* (*horse, cow*) rouan **2** *n* (*horse*) (cheval *m*) rouan *m*; (*cow*) vache *f* rouanne

roar[1] [rɔːr] *n* (*of person*) hurlement *m*; (*of anger*) vocifération *f*; (*of lion, wind, engine*) rugissement *m*; (*of thunder*) grondement *m*; (*of sea*) mugissement *m*; (*of crowd, spectators etc*) clameurs *fpl*; (*of furnace*) ronflement *m*; (*of applause*) tonnerre *m*; (*of traffic*) vrombissement *m*; **to give a r.** (*of person*) hurler; (*of lion*) rugir; **the crowd gave a r. of approval** la foule a poussé un hurlement d'approbation; **roars of laughter** grands éclats *mpl* de rire

roar[2] **1** *vi* (*of person*) hurler; (*in anger*) vociférer; (*of crowd*) hurler; (*of lion, wind, engine*) rugir; (*of thunder*) gronder; (*of sea*) mugir; (*of furnace*) ronfler; **to r. with laughter** hurler de rire **2** *vt* (*order*) hurler, vociférer; **to r. one's approval** manifester son approbation par des hurlements

▶ **roar by** *vi* (*of car etc*) passer dans un bruit de tonnerre

▶ **roar on** *vtsep* **they roared their team on** (*encouraged*) ils ont crié de toutes leurs forces pour encourager leur équipe

▶ **roar out** *vtsep* = **roar**[2]

▶ **roar past** *vi* = **roar by**

roaring[1] ['rɔːrɪŋ] **1** *adj* (*person*) hurlant; (*lion, wind, engine*) rugissant; (*thunder*) grondant; **a r. fire** une belle flambée; *Geog* **the R. Forties** les quarantièmes *mpl* rugissants; **the R. Twenties** les années folles; *F* **to be r. drunk** être complètement bourré *ou* rond; **to do a r. trade** faire un gros commerce, vendre beaucoup **(in** de); **r. success** succès fou **2** *n* = **roar**[1]

roast[1] [rəʊst] **1** *n* **(a)** *Culin* rôti *m*; **a pork r., a r. of pork** un rôti de porc; **pot r.** rôti à la cocotte **(b)** *Am F* (*of celebrity etc*) = soirée ou émission en l'honneur d'une vedette, et au cours de laquelle cette dernière fait l'objet de taquineries et de flatteries **2** *adj Culin* (*pork, chestnuts etc*) rôti; **r. beef** rôti *m* de bœuf, rosbif *m*; **r. potatoes** pommes de terre *fpl* rôties au four

roast[2] **1** *vt* **(a)** (*meat*) (faire) rôtir; (*chestnuts*) rôtir; (*almonds*) (faire) griller; (*coffee*) torréfier, griller; **to r. oneself in front of the fire** se (faire) rôtir *ou* se (faire) griller devant le feu **(b)** *F* (*criticize*) (*book, film etc*) éreinter **(c)** *Am F* (*tease*) (*person*) railler, mettre en boîte **2** *vi* (*of meat etc*) rôtir; (*of coffee*) se torréfier; *F* **I was roasting in the sun** je grillais au soleil

roaster ['rəʊstər] *n* **(a)** *Br Culin* (*chicken*) volaille *f* à rôtir; (*pan*) (*with lid*) cocotte *f* **(b)** (*for coffee*) brûloir *m*, torréfacteur *m*

roasting ['rəʊstɪŋ] **1** *adj F* **r. (-hot)** brûlant; **it's r. in here** il fait une chaleur à crever ici; **we're r. here** on cuit ici **2** *n* **(a)** (*of meat*) rôtissage *m*; (*of coffee*) torréfaction *f*; **r. chef** rôtisseur *m*; **r. jack** tournebroche *m*; **r. pan** plat *m* à rôtir **(b)** *F* (*reprimand*) semonce *f*; **to give sb a r.** (*reprimand*) passer un savon à qn; (*criticize*) éreinter qn

rob [rɒb] *vt* **(-bb-)** (*person*) voler; (*bank, house*) dévaliser; **to r. sb of sth** voler qch à qn; (*deprive*) priver qn de qch; *Fig* **the illness robbed him of his health for years to come** la maladie lui a rendu la santé fragile pour de longues années; **the illness had robbed him of his good looks** la maladie lui avait fait perdre sa beauté; **to r. the till** voler la caisse; *Prov* **to r. Peter to pay Paul** déshabiller Pierre pour habiller Paul; *Sp* **he was robbed of victory** il a été privé de sa victoire; *esp Fb F* **we were robbed!** nous aurions dû gagner!

robber ['rɒbər] *n* voleur, -euse

robbery ['rɒbərɪ] *n* vol *m*; **armed r.** vol à main armée; **highway r.** vol de grand chemin, brigandage *m*; *Fig* **it's highway** *or* **daylight r.!** c'est du vol (organisé)!; *Fig* **it's nothing short of r.!** c'est du vol!

robe[1] [rəʊb] *n* **(a)** (*of priest, judge etc*) robe *f*; **magistrate in his robes** magistrat *m* en robe **(b)** (*dressing gown*) (*heavy*) robe *f* de chambre; (*light, for women*) peignoir *m*; (*bathrobe*) sortie *f* de bain, peignoir (de bain) **(c)** *Am* (*blanket*) couverture *f*

robe[2] **1** *vt* (*judge, priest*) revêtir d'une robe **2** *vi* (*of judge etc*) revêtir sa robe

robin ['rɒbɪn] *n* **r. (-redbreast)** (*bird*) rouge-gorge *m*, *pl* rouges-gorges; *US* **r. 's-egg blue** (*colour*) bleu vert *inv*

robing ['rəʊbɪŋ] *n* **r. room** (*for judge etc*) vestiaire *m*

Robin Hood *n* Robin des Bois *m*

robot ['rəʊbɒt] *n* robot *m*; *Fig* robot, automate *m*

robotics [rəʊ'bɒtɪks] *n* [①A10, C] (*usu with sing verb*) robotique *f*; **r. research/expert** recherche *f*/expert *m* dans le domaine de la robotique
robotize ['rəʊbətaɪz] *vt esp Am* (*assembly line*) robotiser
robust [rəʊ'bʌst] *adj* (*person, faith, appetite*) robuste, solide; (*machine, suitcase etc*) solide; (*coffee, wine*) corsé; (*defence, speech, statement*) vigoureux, musclé
robustness [rəʊ'bʌstnɪs] *n* (*of person*) robustesse *f*; (*of machine, suitcase, appetite, faith*) solidité *f*, robustesse; (*of coffee, wine*) goût *m* corsé; (*of defence, speech etc*) vigueur *f*
roc [rɒk] *n Myth* (*bird*) rock *m*
rock¹ [rɒk] *n* **(a)** (*substance*) roche *f*; **cut in(to) the r.** creusé dans le roc; **a layer of r.** une couche rocheuse
(b) (*at seaside, boulder, rock face*) rocher *m*; *Am* (*stone*) pierre *f*; *Fig* roc *m*; *Geog F* **the R.** (*Gibraltar*) le Rocher de Gibraltar; *Fig* **she was an absolute r. during the crisis** elle nous a été d'un grand secours pendant cette épreuve; **you're a r.!** tu es formidable!; *Naut* **to run onto the rocks** s'échouer sur des rochers; *Fig* **on the rocks** (*marriage, relationship*) en pleine débâcle; (*company*) en faillite; (*whisky*) avec des glaçons, *Can* sur glace; **fall of rocks** chute *f* de pierres, éboulis *m* rocheux; **to be as solid as a r.** être solide comme le roc; *Am Prov* **to be between a r. and a hard place** être confronté à un choix impossible; *Fig* **to reach** *or* **hit r. bottom** (*of prices*) être au plus bas; (*of person, morale*) toucher le fond; *Am F* **r. hound** (*professional*) géologue *mf*; (*amateur*) collectionneur, -euse de pierres; **r. lobster** langouste *f*; **r. painting** peinture *f* rupestre; *Fig* **r. solid** (*support, morale etc*) solide comme le roc
(c) *esp Am Sl* (*diamond*) diamant *m*
(d) *Br* (*sweet*) sucre *m* d'orge; **a stick of r.** un sucre d'orge
(e) *Sl* **rocks** (*testicles*) couilles *fpl*; **to get one's rocks off** (*have sex*) baiser
rock² *n* **(a)** (*rocking motion*) **to give the cradle a r.** balancer un peu le berceau **(b)** *Mus* rock *m*; **r. and roll, r. 'n' roll** rock-and-roll *m*; **r. concert/group/singer** concert *m*/groupe *m*/ chanteur, -euse de rock
rock³ **1** *vt* (*baby*) bercer; (*boat, cradle*) balancer; (*violently*) (*building; Fig person*) secouer, ébranler; **to r. a baby to sleep** bercer un enfant pour qu'il s'endorme; *Fig* **to r. the boat** faire des vagues; *Fig* **don't r. the boat** ne fais pas d'histoires; *Fig* **the Government has been rocked by the latest sex scandal** le gouvernement a été secoué par la dernière histoire de mœurs **2** *vi* **(a)** (*sway*) se balancer; (*of building, ground*) trembler; **to r. (backwards and forwards) in one's chair** se balancer sur sa chaise; **to r. with laughter** être secoué par le fou rire **(b)** (*dance*) danser le rock
rock-and-roll facility *n TV, Cin* (*for dubbing*) dispositif *m* de marche avant-arrière synchronisé
rock-bottom *adj* (*prices*) les plus bas, très bas
rock-bound *adj* (*bay etc*) encerclé de rochers
rock bun *n Culin* rocher *m*
rock cake *n Culin* rocher *m*
rock-climb *vi* faire de la varappe
rock climber *n* varappeur, -euse
rock climbing *n* varappe *f*; **to go r.** faire de la varappe
rock crystal *n Miner* cristal *m* de roche
rocker ['rɒkər] *n* **(a)** (*on cradle, rocking chair etc*) bascule *f*; *F* **to be off one's r.** être timbré *ou* givré; **to go off one's r.** devenir givré **(b)** *Aut, MecE* culbuteur *m*; **r. arm** culbuteur; **r. arms** culbuteurs *mpl*, culbuterie *f* **(c)** *Am F* (*rocking chair*) fauteuil *m* à bascule, rocking-chair *m*, *pl* rocking-chairs, *Can* berceuse *f* **(d)** *Mus* (*person*) rocker *m* **(e)** *Br Hist* (*as opposed to mod*) rocker *m*
rockery ['rɒkərɪ] *n* (*in garden*) rocaille *f*
rocket¹ ['rɒkɪt] *n* (*firework, missile*) fusée *f*; **to fire** *or* **launch a r.** lancer une fusée; *Fig* **to give sb a r.** engueuler qn (**about** au sujet de); *Fig* **he's just had a r. from the boss** il vient de se faire engueuler par le patron; **r. attack** attaque *f* à la roquette; **r. base** base *f* de lancement de fusées; **r. fuel** propergol *m*; *Fig* (*strong drink*) dynamite *f*; **r. launcher** lance-fusées *m inv*, lance-roquettes *m inv*
rocket² *vi* (*of prices*) monter en flèche; **to r. to fame** devenir célèbre très rapidement; **to r. away/past** (*of car etc*) filer/ passer à toute allure
rocket³ [rɒ'ket] *n* (*plant*) roquette *f*
rocketry ['rɒkɪtrɪ] *n* (*science*) étude *f ou* technologie *f ou* technique *f* des fusées; (*weaponry*) arsenal *m* de fusées
rock face *n* paroi *f* rocheuse
rockfall ['rɒkfɔːl] *n* éboulement *m*; **beware of rockfalls** chute de pierres
rock garden *n* rocaille *f*
rock-hard *adj* (*soil etc*) dur comme (de) la pierre
Rockies (the) [ðə'rɒkɪz] *npl* les (Montagnes) Rocheuses *fpl*
rocking ['rɒkɪŋ] **1** *adj* (*movement*) oscillant; (*building*) branlant; **a r. movement** des oscillations **2** *n* (*of baby*) bercement *m*; (*of boat, cradle*) balancement *m*; (*of chair*) balancement, oscillation *f*
rocking chair *n* fauteuil *m* à bascule, rocking-chair *m*, *pl* rocking-chairs, *Can* berceuse *f*
rocking horse *n* cheval *m* à bascule
rock melon *n Am* cantaloup *m*
Rock of Ages *n Rel* Jésus-Christ *m*
Rock of Gibraltar *n Geog* Rocher *m* de Gibraltar
rock plant *n* plante *f* rupestre
rock pool *n* (*at seaside*) flaque *f ou* mare *f* dans les rochers
rock salmon *n Br* roussette *f*
rock salt *n* sel *m* gemme
rockslide ['rɒkslaɪd] *n* (*action*) éboulement *m* de rochers; (*result*) éboulis *m*
rocky ['rɒkɪ] *adj* **(a)** (*path*) rocailleux; (*soil*) rocailleux, pierreux; (*shoreline, terrain*) rocheux; **r. outcrop** affleurement *m* rocheux **(b)** *Fig* (*unstable*) difficile; (*marriage, relationship*) instable, branlant; **his business is in a r. condition** ses affaires vont mal; **I feel a bit r.** (*unwell*) je ne suis pas dans mon assiette; **it's been a r. year for the oil industry** ça a été une année difficile pour l'industrie pétrolière; **to have a r. road ahead** avoir des problèmes en perspective; **to go through a r. patch** traverser une période difficile
Rocky Mountains *npl* Montagnes *fpl* Rocheuses
rococo [rə'kəʊkəʊ] *adj, n Art etc* rococo *m*
rod [rɒd] *n* **(a)** (*stick*) (*wooden*) baguette *f*; (*metal*) tige *f*; (*of curtain*) tringle *f*; (*for fishing*) canne *f* à pêche; *Old-fashioned* (*for administering punishment*) verge *f*; **to fish with r. and line** pêcher à la ligne; **r. fishing** pêche *f* à la ligne; **fuel r.** barreau *m* de combustible; *Fig* **to make a r. for one's own back** se préparer des ennuis; *Prov* **spare the r. and spoil the child** qui aime bien châtie bien; *Fig* **a r. to beat oneself with** des verges pour se faire battre; **that would be giving them a r. to beat us with** ce serait leur donner des bâtons pour nous faire battre; **to rule sb with a r. of iron** gouverner qn avec une main de fer
(b) (*symbol of office*) verge *f*
(c) *Old-fashioned* (*measure*) perche *f* (= approx 5m)
(d) *Am Sl* (*gun*) flingue *m*, pétard *m*
(e) *Sl* (*penis*) bite *f*
rode *see* **ride²**
rodent ['rəʊdənt] *n* rongeur *m*; **r. characteristics/habitat** caractéristiques *fpl*/habitat *m* des rongeurs; *Br* **r. operative** employé, -ée chargé(e) de la dératisation
rodent-like *adj* qui fait penser à un rongeur
rodeo ['rəʊdɪəʊ, rəʊ'deɪəʊ] *n* rodéo *m*; **r. rider** cavalier *m* pratiquant le rodéo
rodomontade [rɒdəmɒn'teɪd, -'tɑːd] *n Lit* rodomontade *f*
roe¹ [rəʊ] *n* **r. (deer)** chevreuil *m*
roe² *n* (*of fish*) œufs *mpl* (de poisson); **soft r.** laite *f*, laitance *f*
roebuck ['rəʊbʌk] *n* chevreuil *m* (mâle)
roentgen ['rɜːntgən] *n* Röntgen *m*, Roentgen *m*; **r. equivalent man** = unité *f* employée pour évaluer l'effet biologique d'un rayonnement radioactif; **measurements are given in r. equivalent man** les mesures sont données en Röntgen Equivalent Man
rogation [rəʊ'geɪʃən] *n Rel* rogations *fpl*; **R. Week** la semaine des Rogations; **R. Sunday** le dimanche avant l'Ascension
Roger ['rɒdʒər] *int* **R.!** (*in radio message*) bien reçu!
roger ['rɒdʒər] *vt Br Sl* baiser
rogue [rəʊg] *n* (*dishonest*) filou *m*, crapule *f*; (*mischievous*) coquin, -ine, fripon, -onne; (*maverick*) franc-tireur, *pl* francs-tireurs; **rogues' gallery** collection *f* de portraits de criminels; *Fig Hum* bande *f* de personnes à la mine patibulaire; **r. (elephant/buffalo)** (éléphant *m*/buffle *m*) solitaire *m*; **r. gene** gène *m* aberrant; **r. policeman** policier *m* corrompu
roguery ['rəʊgərɪ] *n* (*dishonesty*) crapulerie *f*, malhonnêteté *f*; (*mischievousness*) côté *m* farceur; (*of child*) espièglerie *f*
roguish ['rəʊgɪʃ] *adj* (*smile, look etc*) espiègle, coquin, fripon
roguishly ['rəʊgɪʃlɪ] *adv* (*to smile, wink*) avec espièglerie, d'un air coquin *ou* fripon
roguishness ['rəʊgɪʃnɪs] *n* = **roguery**
ROI [ɑːrəʊ'aɪ] *n* (*abbr* **return on investment**) retour *m* sur investissement
roisterer ['rɔɪstərər] *n Lit* fêtard, -arde
role, rôle [rəʊl] *n Th, Fig* rôle *m*; *Fig* **to play an important/a leading r.** jouer un rôle important/prépondérant; *Psy* **r. model** modèle *m*, exemple *m*; **children need a r. model** les enfants ont besoin de quelqu'un à qui s'identifier
role-play, rôle-play **1** *vt* jouer **2** *n* = **role-playing**
role-playing, rôle-playing *n* (*for training purposes, at school*) jeu *m* de rôle; (*in psychotherapy*) psychodrame *m*

rolf [rɒlf] *vi Am Sl* vomir
roll[1] [rəʊl] *n* **(a)** (*of paper*) rouleau *m*; (*of fat, flesh*) bourrelet *m*; *esp Am* (*of paper money*) liasse *f*; **a r. of film** une pellicule (photo); **r. film** pellicule *f* en bobine
(b) (*bread*) petit pain *m*; *Br* **jam r.** (gâteau *m*) roulé *m* à la confiture; **spring r.** rouleau *m* de printemps; **ham/cheese r.** ≈ sandwich *m* au jambon/fromage
(c) (*noise*) (*of drum, thunder*) roulement *m*
(d) (*movement*) (*of ball, dice etc*) roulement *m*; (*of ship, vehicle*) roulis *m*; (*of sea*) houle *f*; (*of aircraft*) (vol *m* en) tonneau *m*; (*in canoe*) esquimautage *m*; **to walk with a r.** se balancer *ou* se dandiner en marchant; **to have a r. on the ground** (*of horse etc*) se rouler par terre; **to do a r.** (*in high jump*) sauter en rouleau; *Fig F* **to have a r. in the hay** faire des galipettes dans le foin; *F* **to be on a r.** (*of gambler, football team*) avoir la chance de son côté; *Fig* (*have good momentum going*) être bien parti; **western r.** (*high jump*) rouleau *m* costal; *Aut* **r. cage** cage *f* de roulement
(e) (*list*) liste *f*; *Mil Br* **r. of honour,** *US* **honor r.** liste *f* de ceux qui sont morts pour la patrie; *Jur* **to strike sb off** *or* **from the rolls** rayer qn du tableau; **to call the r.** faire l'appel
roll[2] **1** *vt* **(a)** (*cigarette, paper, carpet etc*) rouler; (*marble, ball, car*) faire rouler; **to r. sth along the ground** faire rouler qch sur le sol; **to r. string into a ball** rouler de la ficelle en pelote; **to r. one's own** (*cigarettes*) rouler ses cigarettes; **to r. a snowball** faire une boule de neige; *Cin F* **r. 'em!** ça tourne!; **to r. one's eyes** rouler les yeux; **to r. one's r's** rouler les r; *Culin* **loin of mutton boned and rolled** carré de mouton roulé; **to r. an umbrella** plier un parapluie; **to r. itself into a ball** (*of animal*) se mettre en boule; **he is a chauffeur and gardener rolled into one** il est à la fois chauffeur et jardinier; **this room is a bedroom and study rolled into one** cette pièce sert à la fois de chambre et de bureau
(b) (*flatten*) (*lawn*) rouler, passer au rouleau; (*road*) cylindrer; (*metal*) laminer; (*gold*) planer
(c) *Am F* **to r. a drunk** (*rob*) dévaliser un ivrogne
2 *vi* **(a)** (*of ball, ship etc*) rouler; (*of aircraft*) faire un tonneau *ou* des tonneaux; **to r. on the ground/in the grass** (*of person, animal*) se rouler par terre/dans l'herbe; **the car rolled to a stop** la voiture s'est progressivement arrêtée; *Fig* **heads will r.** il va y avoir des têtes qui vont tomber; *Fig* **someone's head will r. for this** quelqu'un va payer pour cela; *F* **to be rolling in money** *or* **it** rouler sur l'or; *F* **to r. with laughter** se tordre (de rire), se tenir les côtes; *F* **he/the film had them rolling in the aisles** il/ce film les faisait se tordre de rire; *Fig F* **to get sth rolling** (*started*) mettre qch en route; (*conversation, discussion*) lancer qch; *Fig* **to get the ball rolling** mettre les choses en train; **to r. with the punches** (*of boxer*) encaisser les coups de l'adversaire; *Fig* encaisser
(b) (*of thunder*) gronder; **to hear the drums rolling** entendre le roulement des tambours
(c) (*of hills, prairie*) onduler; **the hills rolled away into the distance** il y avait des collines à perte de vue
(d) (*of camera, machine etc*) tourner; *TV, Cin* **r.!** moteur!; **the cameras were rolling** les caméras tournaient; *Cin* **the credits started to r.** le générique commença à défiler; **it's too late, the presses are rolling** c'est trop tard, c'est déjà sous presse; **to get the presses rolling** mettre les rotatives en route
▶ **roll about 1** *vi* (*of marble, ball etc*) rouler çà et là; (*of person, animal*) se rouler; (*of ship*) rouler; **to r. about on the floor** *or* **ground** (*of person*) se rouler par terre; (*of object*) rouler par terre; **to r. about in pain/laughing** se tordre de douleur/de rire **2** *vtsep* **to r. sth about** faire rouler qch
▶ **roll along** *vi* **(a)** (*of ball, car etc*) rouler **(b)** *F* (*arrive*) arriver, se pointer
▶ **roll around 1** *vi* = **roll about 1**, = **roll round 2** *vtsep* = **roll about 2**
▶ **roll away 1** *vi* (*of marble, ball etc*) rouler au loin; (*of clouds*) s'éloigner; (*of mist*) se retirer **2** *vtsep* **to r. sth away** rouler qch
▶ **roll back 1** *vi* (*of car*) reculer, rouler en arrière; **her eyes rolled back in her head** ses yeux se révulsèrent **2** *vtsep Mil* **to r. back the enemy** faire reculer l'ennemi; **to r. back a carpet** rouler un tapis (pour faire de la place); **to r. back reforms** faire marche arrière; **to r. back the frontiers of science/the state** faire reculer les frontières de la science/de l'état; **to r. back the years** revivre le passé; *Am Com* **to r. back prices** baisser les prix
▶ **roll by** *vi* (*of car*) passer (en roulant); (*of time*) s'écouler
▶ **roll down 1** *vi* (*of tears*) couler; **to r. down a hill** (*of car, children*) débouler une pente; **the tears rolled down his cheeks** les larmes coulaient le long de ses joues; **2** *vtsep* **to r. sth down** descendre qch (en le faisant rouler); **to r. down a blind/car window** baisser un store/la vitre d'une voiture; **she rolled down the car window** elle a baissé la vitre; **to r. down one's sleeves** se retourner les manches
▶ **roll in 1** *vi* **(a)** (*of waves*) déferler; (*of mist, clouds, train*) arriver; *F* (*of orders, spectators etc*) affluer; *F* (*of person*) rappliquer, s'amener; *F* **she rolled in to work three hours late** elle s'est amenée au travail avec trois heures de retard **(b)** (*at hockey*) remettre la balle en jeu **2** *vtsep* **to r. sth in** faire entrer qch en le faisant rouler; **to r. the ball in** (*in hockey*) remettre la balle en jeu
▶ **roll off** *vi* tomber (en roulant); **to r. off the shelf/the table** rouler de l'étagère/de la table; **sweat was rolling off his back** la sueur lui coulait dans le dos; **cars are rolling off the production line** les voitures sortent de la chaîne de production
▶ **roll on 1** *vi* (*of time*) s'écouler; *F* **r. on tonight/the holidays!** vivement ce soir/les vacances! **2** *vtsep* **to r. one's stockings/a condom on** mettre ses bas/un préservatif; **to r. paint on** étendre de la peinture au rouleau
▶ **roll out 1** *vi* (*of ball etc*) rouler (à l'extérieur); **to r. out of bed** (*of person*) se sortir du lit; *F* **we rolled out of the pub at midnight** nous sommes sortis du pub à minuit; **the train rolled out of the station** le train quitta la gare **2** *vtsep* **to r. sth out** (*through door etc*) faire sortir qch en le faisant rouler; **to r. a carpet out** dérouler un tapis; **to r. out any bumps** (*in lawn*) faire disparaître des inégalités au rouleau; **to r. out the dough** étendre la pâte au rouleau
▶ **roll over 1** *vi* (*of person*) (*once*) se retourner; (*many times*) se rouler; (*of car etc*) (*once*) capoter; (*several times*) faire des tonneaux; **to r. over on the ground** rouler sur le sol; **to r. over (and over) on the bed/the ground** se rouler sur le lit/par terre; **the car rolled over and over and then fell into the ravine** la voiture a déboulé dans le ravin; *Fig* **he'll soon r. over** (*give in*) il se ravisera bientôt **2** *vtsep* **(a)** (*person, stone*) retourner **(b)** *Fin* (*renew*) renouveler (*extend*) prolonger
▶ **roll round** *vi* (*of season etc*) arriver
▶ **roll up 1** *vi* (*of blind*) remonter; *F* (*arrive*) (*of guests*) rappliquer, se pointer, s'amener; (*of customers, spectators*) rappliquer en foule; **to r. up into a ball** (*of animal*) se mettre *ou* se rouler en boule; **r. up!, r. up!** venez nombreux! **2** *vtsep* (*map etc*) rouler; (*trousers*) relever, retrousser; (*blind, car window*) remonter; **to r. sth up in sth** (*for protection*) envelopper qch (**in** de); **to r. up one's sleeves** retrousser ses manches; **to r. oneself up in a blanket** s'enrouler dans une couverture
rollaway [ˈrəʊləweɪ] *esp Am* **1** *n* (*bed*) lit *m* pliant sur roulettes **2** *adj* **r. bed/table** lit *m*/table *f* pliant(e) sur roulettes
rollback [ˈrəʊlbæk] *n Am* (*of prices, inflation*) baisse *f*, réduction *f*
rollbar [ˈrəʊlbɑːr] *n* (*on vehicle*) arceau *m* de sécurité
roll call *n* appel; **to have a r., to take the r.** faire l'appel
rolled [rəʊld] *adj* **(a)** (*paper etc*) en rouleau, roulé; **r. in a blanket** roulé dans une couverture **(b)** (*lawn*) passé au rouleau, roulé; (*metal etc*) laminé; (*umbrella*) plié; **r. gold** plaqué or; **r.-gold watch** montre en plaqué or; **r. oats** flocons *mpl* d'avoine
rolled-up *adj* (*sleeves, trousers*) retroussé, relevé; (*paper etc*) enroulé; (*carpet*) roulé
roller [ˈrəʊlər] *n* **(a)** (*for paint, garden etc*) rouleau *m*; (*for metal*) laminoir *m*; *Comptr* (*in printer*) rouleau; (*in mouse*) galet *m*; (*for hair*) rouleau, bigoudi *m*; **to put rollers in (one's hair), to put one's hair in rollers** se mettre des rouleaux *ou* des bigoudis; **my hair's in rollers** j'ai des rouleaux *ou* des bigoudis sur la tête; **road r.** rouleau compresseur; **r. bandage** bandage *m* enroulé; *TV* **r. caption** déroulant *m*; **r. map** carte *f* sur rouleau; *TV* **r. prompter** prompteur *m* déroulant
(b) (*on chair etc*) roulette *f*; **r. bearing** roulement *m* à rouleaux; **r. conveyor** transporteur *m* à rouleaux
(c) (*wave*) rouleau *m*
(d) *Am F* **high r.** (*gambler*) gros parieur *m*
roller blind *n* store *m* sur rouleau
roller coaster *n* (*at funfair*) montagnes *fpl* russes; **the r. fortunes of a company/a party** les hauts et les bas que connaît une société/un parti
roller-coaster *vi esp Am* (*of road*) faire des montagnes russes; (*of economy*) connaître des hauts et des bas prononcés
roller skate *n* patin *m* à roulettes
roller-skate *vi* faire du patin à roulettes
roller-skating *n* patin *m* à roulettes; **r. rink/clothes** piste *f*/vêtements *mpl* de patin à roulettes; **to go r.** aller faire du patin à roulettes

▶ **rollick about** ['rɒlɪk] *vi* faire la fête

rollicking ['rɒlɪkɪŋ] **1** *adv* **to get r. drunk** se saoûler; **it's a r. good read!** (*of book*) c'est un livre excellent!; **to have a r. good time** bien se marrer **2** *adj* **r. laughter** rires *mpl* bruyants **3** *n Br F* **to give sb a (right) r.** (*tell off*) engueuler qn

rolling ['rəʊlɪŋ] **1** *adj* **(a)** (*ball etc*) roulant, qui roule; (*mist*) qui avance; (*boat*) qui roule, qui a du roulis; *Fig* (*subject to review*) (*programme*) réexaminé à intervalles réguliers; *F* **to be r. drunk** être ivre mort; *Prov* **a r. stone gathers no moss** pierre qui roule n'amasse pas mousse; *Fig* **he's a r. stone** il ne reste jamais très longtemps au même endroit; *Fig* **r. strikes** grèves tournantes

(b) (*thunder*) qui gronde

(c) (*hills, prairie, ground*) ondulant, onduleux; (*gait*) chaloupé; (*sea*) gros, houleux; **to have a r. gait** avoir une démarche chaloupée; **r. countryside** paysage ondulant *ou* ondulé

2 *n* **(a)** (*of ship, vehicle*) roulis *m*; *Aut* **r. resistance** résistance *f* au roulement

(b) (*of road, lawn*) cylindrage *m*; (*of metal*) laminage *m*

rolling mill *n* laminoir *m*

rolling pin *n Culin* rouleau *m* (à pâtisserie)

rolling stock *n Rail* matériel *m* roulant

rollmop ['rəʊlmɒp] *n Culin* rollmops *m*

rollneck ['rəʊlnek] **1** *adj* (*sweater*) à col roulé **2** *n* (*sweater*) (pull *m* à) col *m* roulé

roll-on *n* **(a) r. (deodorant)** déodorant *m* à bille **(b)** *Old-fashioned* (*corset*) gaine *f* (élastique)

roll-on/roll-off *adj* (*ferry, traffic etc*) de type roll on-roll off, roulier; (*port*) à roulage direct; (*cargo*) à manutention horizontale *ou* de type roll on-roll off

rollout marketing ['rəʊlaʊt] *n* mercatique *f* expansionniste

roll-top *n* **r. (desk)** bureau *m* à cylindre

roll-up, roll-your-own *n Br F* (*cigarette*) cigarette *f* roulée

roly-poly ['rəʊlɪ'pəʊlɪ] **1** *n* **(a)** *F* (*plump person*) **he's a bit of a r.** il est plutôt grassouillet **(b)** *Br Culin* **r. (pudding)** gâteau *m* roulé à la confiture **2** *adj F* (*person*) boulot, grassouillet

ROM [rɒm] *n Comptr* (*abbr* **read only memory**) mémoire *f* morte, (mémoire) ROM *f*

romaine [rəʊ'meɪn] *n Am* **r. (lettuce)** (laitue *f*) romaine *f*

Roman ['rəʊmən] **1** *adj* (*law, numeral etc*) romain; **R. candle** (*firework*) chandelle *f* romaine; *Rel* **R. Catholic** catholique; **R. Catholicism** catholicisme *m*; **R. nose** nez *m* busqué *ou* aquilin; **the Holy R. Empire** le Saint Empire romain (germanique) **2** *n* Romain, -aine; *Bible* **Epistle to the Romans** Épître *f* aux Romains

roman ['rəʊmən] *n, adj Typ* romain *m*; **in r.** (*word, abbreviation*) en romain

Romance [rə'mæns, 'rəʊ-] *n Ling* le roman; **R. languages/words** langues *fpl*/mots *mpl* roman(e)s; **student of R. languages** romaniste *mf*

romance¹ [rə'mæns, 'rəʊ-] *n* **(a)** (*book*) histoire *f ou* roman *m* d'amour; (*film*) histoire d'amour; *Liter, Hist* roman de chevalerie *ou* d'aventures; **the age of r.** l'époque des chevaliers **(b)** (*between people*) idylle *f*; (*affair*) aventure *f* (amoureuse); (*love*) amour *m*; **a holiday r.** un amour *ou* une idylle de vacances; **r. is in the air** il y a de l'amour dans l'air **(c)** (*charm*) (*of place, situation*) poésie *f* **(d)** *Mus* romance *f*

romance² **1** *vi Old-fashioned* exagérer, inventer à plaisir **2** *vt esp Am* (*person*) faire la cour à

romancing [rə'mænsɪŋ, 'rəʊ-] *n* (*exaggeration*) exagération *f*, invention *f*

Romanesque [rəʊmə'nesk] *adj Archit* roman

Romania [rə'meɪnɪə] *n* Roumanie *f*

Romanian [rə'meɪnɪən] **1** *adj* roumain **2** *n* **(a)** Roumain, -aine **(b)** *Ling* roumain *m*

romanize ['rəʊmənaɪz] *vt Typ* (*text*) transcrire en caractères romains

Romans(c)h [rəʊ'mænʃ] *adj, n Ling* romanche *m*

romantic [rə'mæntɪk, rəʊ-] **1** *adj* **(a)** (*love, landscape, spot etc*) romantique; *Pej* (*impractical*) (*scheme, notion*) romanesque; **he's very r.** il est très romantique; **a r. dinner for two** un dîner romantique *ou* en tête à tête; **r. young woman** jeune fille sentimentale *ou* romantique; **to play the r. lead** (*in film, play*) être le jeune premier/la jeune première; **r. adventure** aventure *f* romanesque; **r. novelist** auteur *m* de romans d'amour; **r. play/comedy** pièce *f*/comédie *f* romantique **(b)** *Art, Liter, Mus* romantique **2** *n* (*person*) romantique *mf*

romantically [rə'mæntɪklɪ, rəʊ-] *adv* (*to behave*) de façon romantique; **to be r. involved with sb** avoir des relations amoureuses avec qn

romanticism [rə'mæntɪsɪz(ə)m, rəʊ-] *n* **(a)** *Art, Liter, Mus* romantisme *m* **(b)** (*of person*) idées *fpl* romanesques

romanticist [rə'mæntɪsɪst, rəʊ-] *n* romantique *mf*

romanticize [rə'mæntɪsaɪz, rəʊ-] **1** *vt* (*idea, incident etc*) romancer; **to r. war** glorifier la guerre **2** *vi* donner dans le romanesque

Romany ['rəʊmənɪ] **1** *adj* (*custom, life, language etc*) tzigane **2** *n* **(a)** tzigane *mf* **(b)** *Ling* tzigane *m*

Rome [rəʊm] *n* **(a)** Rome *m ou f*; *Prov* **R. was not built in a day** = Paris ne s'est pas fait en un jour; *Prov* **when in R., (do as the Romans do)** il faut adopter les usages de l'endroit où l'on se trouve **(b)** *Rel* **(the Church of) R.** l'Église *f* de Rome; **to go over to R.** passer au catholicisme

Romeo ['rəʊmɪəʊ] *n* Roméo *m*; *Hum* **he's a bit of a R.** c'est un Roméo

romp¹ [rɒmp] *n* **to have a r. with a child** chahuter avec un enfant; **the book is a r. through two centuries of French history** le livre nous promène à travers deux siècles d'histoire de France; **the film/play is an enjoyable r.** ce film/cette pièce constitue un divertissement agréable; **sex romps** ébats *mpl* amoureux

romp² *vi* **to r. (about** *or* **around)** (*of child, animal etc*) s'ébattre (bruyamment), gambader; **to r. away with a race** gagner une course haut la main; **to r. home** (*of candidate, horse, runner*) arriver dans un fauteuil; **to r. through an examination** passer un examen sans effort *ou F* les doigts dans le nez; **to r. through one's work** faire son travail sans effort; **the book romps through two centuries of French history** ce livre traverse deux siècles d'histoire de France

romper ['rɒmpər] *n* **r. suit, rompers** (*for baby*) barboteuse *f*

rondo ['rɒndəʊ] *n Mus* rondeau *m*

roneo®¹ ['rəʊnɪəʊ] *n* document *m/etc* ronéotypé *ou* ronéoté

roneo®² *vt* (*document*) ronéotyper, ronéoter

roo [ru:] *n Austr F* kangourou *m*; **r. bar** = arceau *m* de sécurité

rood [ru:d] *n* **(a)** *Rel* crucifix *m*; **r. arch** arche *f* du jubé; **r. loft** (galerie *f* du) jubé *m*; **r. screen** jubé **(b)** *Arch* (*measurement*) rood *m*, quart *m* d'arpent

roof¹ [ru:f] *n* (*of building, vehicle*) toit *m*; (*of tunnel, cave, mine*) plafond *m*; **to be without** *or* **not have a r. over one's head** se trouver sans logement; **at least you have a r. over your head** au moins, tu as un endroit pour vivre; **to live under one** *or* **the same r.** habiter sous le même toit *ou* dans le même bâtiment; **shops and sports facilities under one** *or* **the same r.** des boutiques et des aménagements sportifs dans un même endroit; **not under <u>my</u> r.** pas chez moi; *F* **to go through** *or* **hit the r.** (*get angry*) sortir de ses gonds; *F* **to go through the r.** (*of inflation, prices*) connaître une flambée; *Lit* **the r. of heaven** la voûte des cieux; **the r. of the mouth** la voûte du palais; *Fig* **the r. of the world** le toit du monde; **r. light** lucarne *f*; (*in vehicle*) plafonnier *m*; *Aut* **r. pillar** montant *m* de toit; **r. timbering** *or* **timbers** combles *mpl*

roof² *vt Constr* (*house etc*) couvrir (**with** de); **to r. sth in** *or* **over** recouvrir qch d'un toit; **a house roofed with slate/thatch** une maison à toit d'ardoises/de chaume

-roofed [-ru:ft] *suff* **slate-r.** à toit d'ardoises

roofer ['ru:fər] *n Constr* (*of building etc*) couvreur *m*

roof garden *n* jardin *m* aménagé sur le toit

roofing ['ru:fɪŋ] *n* (*operation*) pose *f* de la toiture; (*material*) toiture *f*; **r. material/tiles/felt** matériaux *mpl*/tuiles *fpl*/feutre *m* de couverture

roofless ['ru:flɪs] *adj* (*building*) sans toit, à ciel ouvert

roof rack *n* (*on car*) galerie *f*

rooftop ['ru:ftɒp] *n* toit *m*; *Fig* **to shout** *or* **proclaim sth from the rooftops** crier qch sur les toits

rooftree ['ru:ftri:] *n* poutre *f* de faîte, faîtage *m*

rook¹ [rʊk] *n* **(a)** (*bird*) freux *m* **(b)** (*in chess*) tour *f*

rook² *vt Old-fashioned F* (*cheat*) (*person*) rouler (**out of** de)

rookery ['rʊkərɪ] *n* (*of rooks, seals*) colonie *f*; (*of penguins*) rookerie *f*

rookie ['rʊkɪ] *n Am F* (*in army*) recrue *f*, bleu *m*; (*in sport*) novice *mf*; (*addition to a team*) nouveau membre *m*; *Am* **r. cop** flic *m* débutant, bleu

room¹ [ru:m] *n* **(a)** (*in house etc*) pièce *f*; (*in hotel*) chambre *f*; (*bedroom*) chambre; (*large, public*) salle *f*; **one's rooms** ses appartements *mpl*; **to live in rooms** vivre dans un meublé; **(furnished) rooms to let** chambres (meublées) à louer; **r. and board** chambre et pension; **double/single r.** chambre pour deux personnes/une personne; **r. with twin beds** chambre à deux lits; **r. 22 wants some coffee** (*in hotel*) du café pour la chambre 22; *Euph F* **the smallest r. in the house** (*toilet*) le petit coin; *Am* **men's r., ladies r.** toilettes *fpl*; **the r. fell silent** le silence s'est fait dans la pièce *ou* dans la salle; **the whole r. burst out laughing** toute la salle a éclaté de rire; **serve at r. temperature** (*of wine*) servir chambré; **to keep sth at r. temperature** garder qch à la température ambiante *ou* de la pièce; **r. attendant** (*in hotel*) femme *f* de chambre; **r. availability chart** planning *m* de disponibilité des chambres; **r. card** fiche *f* de la chambre; **r. change** (*in *hotel*) délogement *m*; **r. clerk** réceptionniste *mf*; **r. divider** cloison *f*, écran *m*; **r. key** clé *f* de la chambre; **your r. key** la clé de votre chambre; **r. night** (*in hotel*) nuitée *f*; **r. number** numéro *m* de chambre; **r. occupancy** (*in hotels*) occupation *f* des chambres, taux *m* d'occupation; **r. rack** (*in hotel*) room-rack *m*, tableau *m* (de l'état) des chambres; **r. rack card** (*in hotel*) fiche client, fiche d'occupation; **r. sale** vente *f* de chambre; **r. service manager** responsable *mf* du service à l'étage

(**b**) (*space*) place *f* (**for** pour); (**some**) **r.** de la place; **there's no r. to breathe in here** on étouffe ici; **to give sb r. to move** donner à qn plus d'espace *ou* de place pour bouger; **to take up a lot of r.** prendre beaucoup de place; **there's no r. to move in his flat** on n'a pas la place de bouger dans son appartement; *F* **there isn't (enough) r. to swing a cat in here** c'est vraiment exigu ici; **to have r. for manoeuvre** avoir une marge de manœuvre; **there is r. for negotiation** il existe une marge de négociation; **to make r. for sb** faire de la *ou* une place à qn; *Fig* laisser le champ libre à qn; **to make r. for sth** faire de la place pour qch; **to leave (sb) some r. (for sth)** laisser de la place (à qn) (pour qch); **is there r. for one more?** (*person*) est-ce qu'il y a encore de la place pour une personne?; **r. for one more inside!** (*on bus*) il y a encore de la place pour une personne; *Fig* **there's r. for doubt** le doute est permis; **there is no r. for doubt** aucun doute n'est possible; **there is r. for improvement** cela laisse à désirer, on peut/il peut/vous pouvez/*etc* faire mieux; **there's no r. for slackers in this company** les fainéants n'ont pas leur place dans cette société

room² *vi Old-fashioned* vivre en meublé; *Am* **to r. with sb** partager un logement avec qn; **to r. together** vivre ensemble dans le même logement

-roomed [ru:md] *suff* **two/three-r.** (*house etc*) de deux/trois pièces

roomer ['ru:mər] *n Am* locataire *mf* en meublé

roomette [ru:'met] *n Am Rail* compartiment *m* avec couchette

roomful ['ru:mfʊl] *n* (*of people, objects etc*) salle *f* pleine; (*of soldiers*) chambrée *f*; **a r. of students** une salle pleine d'étudiants

roominess ['ru:mɪnɪs] *n* (*of house etc*) dimensions *fpl* spacieuses *ou* généreuses; (*of clothing*) coupe *f* confortable *ou* ample; (*of car*) dimensions spacieuses

rooming ['ru:mɪŋ] *n Am* **r. house** maison *f* de rapport

roommate ['ru:mmeɪt] *n Br* (*sharing room*) camarade *mf* de chambre; *Am* (*sharing apartment or house*) = personne *f* avec qui l'on partage un appartement ou une maison

room service *n* (*in hotel*) service *m* dans les chambres; **to provide r.** servir dans les chambres; **to call r.** appeler le service en chambre *ou* le garçon d'étage

roomy ['ru:mɪ] *adj* (*house*) spacieux, où l'on a de la place; (*clothes*) ample; (*car*) spacieux; (*suitcase*) grand

roost¹ [ru:st] *n* perchoir *m*; (*for domestic fowl*) juchoir *m*; *Fig* (*for person*) logement *m*, gîte *m*; **to go to r.** se percher: *Fig* **to come home to r.** (*of crime, mistake etc*) se retourner contre son auteur; *Fig* **your chickens have come home to r.** ça s'est retourné contre toi, ça a fait boomerang

roost² *vi* se percher

rooster ['ru:stər] *n* coq *m*

root¹ [ru:t] *n* (**a**) (*of plant, tooth*), *Math, Ling* racine *f*; **to pull up a plant by the roots** déraciner une plante; **to pull sb's hair out by the roots** arracher les cheveux de qn; **to touch up one's roots** (*of person with dyed hair*) refaire ses racines; **to take r.** (*of plant*); *Fig* prendre racine *ou* pied; *Fig* **to destroy sth r. and branch** extirper qch; **a r. and branch reform** une réforme complète; *Am* **r. cellar** = cave *f* où l'on stocke les légumes à racine comestible; *Comptr* **r. (directory)** racine, répertoire *m* principal

(**b**) (*cause*) (*of problem etc*) cause *f*, origine *f*; **to have its roots in sth** (*of crisis etc*) avoir ses origines dans qch; *Prov* **money is the r. of all evil** l'argent est la source de tous les maux; **to get to the r. of things** aller au fond des choses; **to strike at the r. of the problem** aller à la source du problème; **r. cause** cause première

(**c**) (*ethnic, class, cultural origins*) *Fig* **my roots are in Canada** mes racines sont au Canada; **I don't have any roots** je n'ai pas de racines; *Fig* **to put down roots** s'intégrer; **to get back to one's roots** retrouver ses racines

root² **1** *vt* (*cuttings*) enraciner (**in** dans); *Fig* **rooted to the spot** *or* **ground** cloué *ou* figé sur place; **her behaviour is rooted in her political convictions** son comportement trouve ses origines dans ses convictions politiques **2** *vi* (*of cuttings*) s'enraciner, prendre racine

root³ **1** *vi* (*of pig*) fouiller avec le groin **2** *vt* (*of pig*) (*earth*) fouiller

▶ **root about, root around** *vi* fouiller; **to r. about** *or* **around for one's keys/a pen** fouiller pour trouver ses clés/un stylo; **to r. around in a drawer** fouiller dans un tiroir

▶ **root for** *vipo esp Am F* (*cheer, support*) encourager; **to r. for a candidate** appuyer un candidat; **we'll be rooting for you** nous sommes de votre côté

▶ **root out** *vtsep* (**a**) (*remove*) (*plant*) déraciner; *Fig* **to r. out abuse** supprimer *ou* extirper des abus (**b**) *F* (*find*) trouver, dénicher; **see if you can r. him out of the pub** essayez de le faire décoller du pub

▶ **root through** *vipo* fouiller dans

▶ **root up** *vtsep* (*plant*) déraciner; (*carrots, potatoes*) arracher

root beer *n Am* = boisson *f* gazeuse (faite avec les racines de certaines plantes)

root canal *n* (*of tooth*) canal *m* de la racine; **to have r. treatment** subir un traitement endodontique

root crops *npl Agr* (cultures *fpl* de) racines *fpl* alimentaires

rooted ['ru:tɪd] *adj* (*plant*) enraciné; (*cutting*) qui a des racines; *Fig* (*prejudice*) enraciné; **deeply r.** bien ancré *ou* enraciné (**in** dans)

rooting ['ru:tɪŋ] *n* enracinement *m*; **r. compost** compost *m* spécial pour boutures

rooting out *n* (*of abuse etc*) extirpation *f*, éradication *f*

rootless ['ru:tlɪs] *adj* (*plant, person*) sans racines

rootstock ['ru:tstɒk] *n* (*of plant*) souche *f*

root vegetable *n* légume *m* à racine comestible

rope¹ [rəʊp] *n* corde *f*; *Naut* cordage *m*; (*of pearls*) sautoir *m*; *Boxing etc* **the ropes** les cordes; **to be on the ropes** (*of boxer*) se retrouver dans les cordes; *Fig* (*of company, economy etc*) battre de l'aile; **to be on the ropes financially** être sur la corde raide; **to have sb on the ropes** *Boxing* mettre qn dans les cordes; *Fig* acculer qn, mettre qn dans une position difficile; *Br F* **it's money for old r.** c'est grassement payé pour pas grand-chose; **wire r.** câble *m* métallique; **a piece of r.** une corde; **bell r.** (*in house*) cordon *m* de sonnette; (*in belltower*) corde de cloche; **to put on the r.** (*of climbers*) s'encorder; (**climbers on the**) **r.** (alpinistes *mpl* en) cordée *f*; *F* **to know the ropes** connaître les ficelles; *F* **to learn the ropes** apprendre les ficelles; *F* **to show** *or* **teach sb the ropes** mettre qn au courant, former qn; **the r.** (*death by hanging*) la pendaison; **to bring back the r.** remettre la pendaison en vigueur; *Fig* **to give sb enough r. (to hang himself/herself)** donner à qn la corde pour se pendre; *Fig* **to give sb lots** *or* **plenty of r.** donner du mou à qn

rope² *vt* (**a**) (*person, object*) lier (avec une corde) (**to** à); **to r. climbers (together)** encorder des alpinistes; **climbers roped together** (alpinistes *mpl* en) cordée *f* (**b**) *Am* (*animal*) prendre au lasso

▶ **rope in** *vtsep F* **to r. sb in** (*to help etc*) recruter qn (**to do** pour faire); **don't let yourself get roped in** ne te laisse pas embringuer là-dedans

▶ **rope off** *vtsep* séparer (par une corde); **part of the field has been roped off** une partie du champ a été fermée par des cordes

▶ **rope up** **1** *vi* (*of climbers*) s'encorder **2** *vtsep* attacher avec de la corde

rope ladder *n* échelle *f* de corde

rope maker *n* cordier *m*

rope-soled ['rəʊpsəʊld] *adj* (*sandals etc*) à semelles de corde

rop(e)y ['rəʊpɪ] *adj Br F* (*unreliable*) (*translation etc*) minable; (*ill*) (*person*) patraque; **to feel a bit r.** se sentir patraque, ne pas être dans son assiette

ro-ro ['rəʊrəʊ] *adj* = **roll-on/roll-off**

Rorschach ['rɔ:ʃɑ:k] *n Psy* **R. test** test *m* de Rorschach

rosary ['rəʊzərɪ] *n Rel* rosaire *m*, chapelet *m*; **to say the** *or* **one's r.** dire *ou* réciter son rosaire *ou* son chapelet

rose¹ [rəʊz] **1** *n* (**a**) (*flower*) rose *f*; (*on hat etc*) rosette *f*; (*on watering can*) pomme *f*; (**ceiling**) **r.** rosace *f*; **r. (bush)** rosier *m*; *Fig* **life is not a bed of roses, life is not all roses** tout n'est pas rose dans la vie; *Fig* **her life wasn't a bed of roses** tout n'était pas rose dans sa vie; *Prov* **there is no r. without a thorn** il n'y a pas de rose sans épine; *Fig* **to come up always smelling of roses** s'en sortir toujours très bien; *Fig* **to come up roses** marcher parfaitement; *Fig* **to put the roses back in sb's cheeks** (*of holiday, sea air etc*) redonner des couleurs à qn; *Hist* **the Wars of the Roses** la guerre des Deux-Roses; **r. petal** pétale *m* de rose

(**b**) (*colour*) rose *m*; **r. brick/paint** brique *f*/peinture *f* rose; **r. pink** rose; **r. red** vermillon *m*

2 *adj* (*colour*) rose

rose² *pt see* **rise²**

rosé ['rəʊzeɪ] *n* (vin *m*) rosé *m*

roseate ['rəʊzɪeɪt] *adj Lit* rose

rosebay ['rəʊzbeɪ] *n Bot* laurier-rose *m*, *pl* lauriers-roses

rose bed *n* parterre *m* de rosiers

rosebud ['rəʊzbʌd] *n* bouton *m* de rose; **r. mouth** bouche *f* en cerise

rose-coloured *adj* rose, rosé; **to see things** *or* **the world through r. glasses** *or* **spectacles** voir tout en rose, voir la vie en rose

rose-cut *adj* (*diamond etc*) (taillé) en rose

rose garden *n* roseraie *f*

rose grower *n* rosiériste *mf*

rosehip ['rəʊzhɪp] *n* églantine *f*; **r. jelly** gelée *f* d'églantine; **r. syrup** sirop *m* d'églantine

rosemary ['rəʊzmərɪ] *n Bot, Culin* romarin *m*; **r. bush** buisson *m* de romarin

rose-pink *adj* (*dress etc*) (couleur de) rose

rose quartz *n* pseudo-rubis *m inv*, rubis *m* de Bohême

rose-red *adj* (*complexion etc*) vermeil

rose-tinted ['rəʊztɪntɪd] *adj* rose, rosé; **to see things** *or* **the world through r. glasses** *or* **spectacles** voir tout en rose, voir la vie en rose

rosetree ['rəʊztriː] *n* rosier *m* sur tige

rosette [rəʊ'zet] *n* **(a)** (*badge*) rosette *f*; *Sp etc* (*prize*) cocarde *f* **(b)** *Archit* (*carving*) rosette *f*; (*window*) rosace *f*

rose-water *n* eau *f* de rose; **r. perfume** parfum *m* à l'eau de rose

rose window *n Archit* rosace *f*, rose *f*

rosewood ['rəʊzwʊd] *n* bois *m* de rose; **r. desk/table** bureau *m*/table *f* en bois de rose

rosie ['rəʊzɪ] *n Br Sl* **r. (lee)** (*tea*) thé *m*

rosin¹ ['rɒzɪn] *n* colophane *f*

rosin² *vt Mus* (*bow*) traiter à la colophane

rosiness ['rəʊzɪnɪs] *n* couleur *f* rose, rose *m*; **the r. of her cheeks** le rose de ses joues

ROSPA ['rɒspə] *n Br* (*abbr* **Royal Society for the Prevention of Accidents**) ≈ société *f* pour la prévention des accidents

roster¹ ['rɒstər] *n Mil etc* **(duty) r.** liste *f* (de service)

roster² *vt esp Am* (*person*) mettre sur une liste (de service)

rostrum, *pl* **-a, -ums** ['rɒstrəm, -ə, -əmz] *n* (*for speaker*) estrade *f*, tribune *f*; (*for prizewinner*) podium *m*; (*for conductor*) estrade; *TV* **r. camera** caméra *f* banc-titre, caméra d'animation; *TV* **r. cameraman** opérateur *m* banc-titre

rosy ['rəʊzɪ] *adj* (*pink*) rose, rosé; *Fig* (*future*) prometteur, tout rose; **r. cheeks** joues roses *ou* vermeilles; **her r. complexion** son teint de rose; *Fig* **to paint everything in r. colours** peindre tout sous un jour favorable *ou* en rose; *Fig* **to paint a r. picture of sth** dépeindre qch sous un jour optimiste; *Fig* **a r. prospect** une perspective attrayante; *Fig* **to take a r. view of things** voir les choses sous un jour optimiste *ou* la vie en rose

ROT [ɑːrəʊ'tiː] *n* (*abbr* **recording off transmission**) enregistrement *m* à conserver

rot¹ [rɒt] *n* **(a)** (*in plant, wood etc*) pourriture *f*; (*of food*) putréfaction *f*; *Fig* **the r. has set in** (*among employees, players etc*) les choses ont commencé à aller mal; *Fig* **to stop the r.** empêcher les choses de se dégrader, remonter la pente; *Fig* **we have stopped the r.** on remonte la pente **(b)** *F esp Old-fashioned* (*nonsense*) bêtises *fpl*, inepties *fpl*; **to talk (utter** *or* **absolute) r.** dire des bêtises *ou* des inepties *ou* des imbécillités; **(what) r.!** n'importe quoi!

rot² **(-tt-) 1** *vi* (*of leaves, wood, material etc*) pourrir; (*of food*) se décomposer, se putréfier; (*of manure*) se décomposer; *Fig* **they let him r. in prison** ils l'ont laissé croupir en prison **2** *vt* (faire) pourrir, décomposer; **oil rots rubber** l'huile désagrège le caoutchouc; **sugar rots your teeth** le sucre gâte les dents *ou* donne des caries

▶ **rot away** *vi, vtsep* = **rot²**

▶ **rot down** *vi* (*of compost material*) se décomposer

rota ['rəʊtə] *n esp Br* liste *f* de service; **we have a r. for the housework** nous faisons le ménage (chacun) à tour de rôle; **according to a r.** (chacun) à tour de rôle

Rotarian [rəʊ'teərɪən] *n, adj* rotarien *m*

Rotary ['rəʊtərɪ] *n* **R. Club** Rotary Club *m*

rotary ['rəʊtərɪ] **1** *adj* (*movement, pump, engine*) rotatif; (*switch*) tournant; *Typ* **r. printing press** (machine *f*) rotative *f*, *F* roto *f*; **r. clothesline** *or* **clothes dryer** séchoir *m* parapluie **2** *n Am Aut* (*roundabout*) sens *m* giratoire

rotate [rəʊ'teɪt] **1** *vi* **(a)** (*of earth etc*) tourner; (*on pivot*) pivoter **(b)** (*in job*) remplir des fonctions à tour de rôle; **the presidency rotates every two years among members** les membres assument la présidence à tour de rôle tous les deux ans **2** *vt* **(a)** (*knob, dial*) (faire) tourner; (*on pivot*) faire pivoter **(b)** (*duties*) remplir à tour de rôle; (*housework*) faire à tour de rôle; *Agr* (*crops*) alterner

rotating [rəʊ'teɪtɪŋ] **1** *adj* (*which can move*) tournant, rotatif; (*which is moving*) en rotation; **2** *n* rotation *f*; (*of crops*) alternance *f*

rotation [rəʊ'teɪʃən] *n* **(a)** (*of planet*) rotation *f*; (*of machine*) rotation, tour *m*; **rotations per minute** tours-minute *mpl* **(b)** (*in job*) roulement *m*; **by** *or* **in r.** par roulement, à tour de rôle; *Agr* **r. of crops** alternance *f* des cultures, assolement *m*

rotator [rəʊ'teɪtər] *n* (*device*) appareil *m* rotateur

rotatory [rəʊ'teɪtərɪ] *adj* rotatoire

rote [rəʊt] *n* **r. learning** apprentissage *m* par cœur; **to learn sth by r.** apprendre qch par cœur

rotgut ['rɒtgʌt] *n Br F Pej* (*wine, spirits*) tord-boyaux *m inv*

rotisserie [rəʊ'tiːsərɪ, -'tɪs-] *n* (*spit*) rôtissoire *f*

rotogravure ['rəʊtəʊgrə'vjʊər] *n* rotogravure *f*

rotor ['rəʊtər] *n* (*of turbine, helicopter*) rotor *m*; **r. arm** (*of engine*) rotor de distributeur; **r. blade** pale *f* de rotor

Rotovator® ['rəʊtəveɪtər] *n Br* motoculteur *m*

rotten ['rɒt(ə)n] *adj* **(a)** (*leaves, wood, egg, fruit etc*) pourri; **to smell r.** sentir le pourri; **to go r.** pourrir; *Br Hist* **r. borough** bourg *m* pourri

(b) *F* (*bad, of poor quality*) (*book, film etc*) nul, pourri; (*actor, golfer etc*) nul; (*job, day etc*) sale; **to feel r.** (*ill*) être mal fichu; **I feel r. about this but ...** (*sorry*) ça me rend malade mais ...; **I felt r. about it** (*sorry*) j'en étais malade; **to look r.** avoir l'air mal fichu; **he played a r. game** il a joué affreusement mal, il a été lamentable; **what r. luck!** quelle guigne!; **to have r. luck** avoir la guigne; **r. weather** temps pourri, temps de chien; **the weather was r.** il a fait un temps de chien; **it's been a r. summer** (*with bad weather*) ça a été un été pourri; **she's been having a r. time of it lately** elle vient de traverser une sale période

(c) *F* (*unpleasant*) **a r. trick** un sale tour, un tour vache *ou* de cochon; **you r. bastard!** espèce de pourriture!; **what a r. bastard he is** quelle pourriture; **don't be r.!** ne sois pas vache!; **that was a r. thing to do** c'était un sale tour; **she's r. to the core** elle est pourrie jusqu'à la moelle

rottenly ['rɒt(ə)nlɪ] *adv* (*to behave*) affreusement mal, de façon abominable *ou* épouvantable

rottenness ['rɒt(ə)nnɪs] *n* **(a)** (*of leaves, wood, fruit etc*) pourriture *f* **(b)** *F* (*of performance etc*) caractère *m* lamentable, nullité *f*

rotter ['rɒtər] *n Old-fashioned Br F* sale type *m*, propre *m* à rien

rotting ['rɒtɪŋ] *adj* qui pourrit, en putréfaction

rotund [rəʊ'tʌnd] *adj* (*large and round*) rond; (*plump*) rond, rondelet; (*speech, style*) grandiloquent; **his r. figure** ses formes arrondies

rotunda [rəʊ'tʌndə] *n Archit* rotonde *f*

rotundity [rəʊ'tʌndɪtɪ] *n* (*of person*) rotondité *f*, embonpoint *m*; (*of speech, style*) grandiloquence *f*

rouble, *US* **ruble** ['ruːb(ə)l] *n* (*currency*) rouble *m*

roué ['ruːeɪ] *n Old-fashioned* roué *m*, débauché *m*

rouge¹ [ruːʒ] *n* (*make-up*) rouge *m* (à joues)

rouge² *vt* **to r. (one's cheeks)** se mettre du rouge aux joues, se farder

rough¹ [rʌf] **1** *adj* **(a)** (*uneven, not smooth*) (*material*) rude, rugueux; (*surface*) rugueux; (*skin*) rêche; (*road*) défoncé; (*terrain etc*) accidenté; (*ground*) inégal, raboteux; (*uncultivated*) (*land, pasture*) en friche; *F* **to give sb the r. edge of one's tongue** parler brutalement à qn

(b) (*unrefined, unpolished*) (*manners*) grossier, fruste; (*speech*) bourru, rude; (*style*) fruste; **in a** *or* **its r. state** à l'état brut; **to knock the r. edges off sb/sth** dégrossir qn/qch; **r. book** brouillard *m*; *TV, Cin* **r. cut** premier montage *m*; **r. diamond** brave homme *m*/femme *f* sous des dehors de rustre; **r. draft** brouillon *m*; *TV, Cin* **r. edit** montage bout à bout; *TV, Cin* **r. focus** première mise *f* au point; **r. layout** (*of page etc*) prémaquette *f*, esquisse *f*, squelette *f*; **r. paper** papier *m* brouillon; **r. sketch** ébauche *f*, esquisse; *Sch* **r. work** brouillon

(c) *F* (*ill, not working properly*) **to feel/look r.** se sentir/avoir l'air patraque; **the engine sounds a bit r.** le moteur ne semble pas tourner très rond

(d) (*violent*) (*person, behaviour, treatment*) brutal; (*wind*) violent; **to suffer r. treatment** (*people*) être maltraité; (*objects*) souffrir; **to be r. with sb** brutaliser qn, rudoyer qn; **she's terribly r. with the children** elle est très brutale avec les enfants; **you were too r.** tu as été trop brutal; **don't be so r. with her** sois moins brutal avec elle; **to come in for some r. treatment** se faire maltraiter; **this is a r. neighbourhood** c'est un quartier dur; *F* **r. customer** violent *m*; **a r. crossing** (*on ferry etc*) une traversée agitée; **r. sea(s)** mer *f* grosse *ou* houleuse; **due to r. handling** parce qu'on l'a malmené; *F Fig* **r. stuff** brutalités *fpl*; *Sl* **r. trade** (*in homosexual relationship*) partenaire *m* homosexuel prolo

(e) (*harsh, hard*) (*voice, wine*) rude, âpre; *F* **to give sb/sth a r. time** *or* **ride** être vache avec qn/esquinter qch; **don't give**

me a r. time ne me rends pas la vie difficile; *F* **he's had a r. time of it** il en a bavé, il a bouffé de la vache enragée; *F* **he's had a r. deal** ça a été très dur pour lui; **he received some r. handling from the press** la presse l'a présenté de façon défavorable; **to make it** *or* **things r. for sb** rendre la vie difficile à qn; *F* **it was r. on her** c'était dur pour elle; **it's r. on the skin** c'est mauvais pour la peau; **divorce is r. on children** le divorce est dur pour les enfants; **you were too r. on them** tu as été trop sévère avec eux; **it's r. having to work on Saturdays** c'est dur de devoir travailler le samedi; **they've had a lot of r. luck recently** ils n'ont pas eu beaucoup de chance dernièrement; **r. justice** justice *f* sommaire; **r. work** gros travaux *mpl*

(f) (*approximate*) (*calculation, estimate etc*) approximatif; **r. guess** approximation *f*; **at a r. guess** *or* **estimate** approximativement; **as a r. guide, one metre equals three feet** un mètre équivaut approximativement à trois pieds; **could you give me a r. idea of how long it will take?** pourriez-vous me donner une idée approximative du temps que ça va prendre?, pourriez-vous me dire en gros combien de temps cela va prendre?; **I have a r. idea of what it's about** j'ai une petite idée de ce dont il s'agit

2 *adv* rudement, grossièrement; **to play r.** jouer brutalement; (*in business, relationship*) ne pas faire de cadeaux; *F* **to sleep r.** coucher à la dure; *F* **to live r.** vivre à la dure

3 *n* **(a)** (*ground*) terrain *m* accidenté; *Golf* **to be in the r.** être dans l'herbe longue; *Fig* **to take the r. with the smooth** prendre le bon avec le mauvais

(b) *F* (*hooligan*) voyou *m*

(c) *F* (*in sexual sense*) **she likes a bit of r.** elle aime s'envoyer un prolo de temps en temps

(d) (*of drawing etc*) ébauche *f*; (*sketch of layout etc*) crayonné *m*; **to do sth in r.** faire qch au brouillon

rough² *vt F* **to r. it** vivre à la dure; **we'll just have to r. it** il faudra qu'on fasse avec les moyens du bord

▶ **rough out** *vtsep* (*drawing etc*) ébaucher; (*plan, project, play, novel*) ébaucher, concevoir dans ses grandes lignes

▶ **rough up** *vtsep* **(a)** (*person's hair*) ébouriffer **(b)** *F* **to r. sb up** tabasser qn

roughage ['rʌfɪdʒ] *n* (*in food*) fibres *fpl* (alimentaires)

rough-and-ready *adj* (*meal*) vite préparé; (*accommodation, construction*) sommaire; (*person*) rustre; (*conditions, solution*) grossier

rough-and-tumble *n* bousculade *f*, mêlée *f*; **the children were having a bit of a r.** les enfants chahutaient; *Fig* **the r. of politics** la jungle de la politique; *Fig* **the r. world of publishing** la jungle de l'édition

roughcast¹ ['rʌfkɑːst] *n Constr* crépi *m*; **r. surface/wall** surface *f*/mur *m* crépi(e)

roughcast² *vt* (*pt, pp* **roughcast**) *Constr* (*wall etc*) crépir

roughen ['rʌf(ə)n] **1** *vt* (*surface*) rendre rugueux **2** *vi* **(a)** (*of surface*) devenir rugueux **(b)** (*of sea*) grossir, devenir houleux

rough-hewn [rʌf'hjuːn] *adj* (*lumber, statue etc*) dégrossi

roughhouse ['rʌfhaʊs] *n F* **there was a bit of a r. in the pub last night** il y a eu de la bagarre au pub hier soir

roughly ['rʌflɪ] *adv* **(a)** (*crudely*) (*to build*) grossièrement; **r. made table** table de conception grossière; **to sketch sth r.** faire un croquis sommaire de qch **(b)** (*harshly*) (*to behave, answer*) rudement **(c)** (*violently*) brutalement; **to treat sb r.** maltraiter *ou* malmener *ou* rudoyer qn **(d)** (*approximately*) **r. (speaking)** approximativement, en gros, grosso modo; **to estimate sth r.** estimer qch approximativement; **they live in r. the same area** ils habitent approximativement dans le même quartier

roughneck ['rʌfnek] *n* **(a)** *Am F* (*hooligan*) voyou *m* **(b)** (*on oil rig*) = personne *f* travaillant sur une plate-forme pétrolière

roughness ['rʌfnɪs] *n* **(a)** (*of surface*) caractère *m* rugueux; (*of skin*) caractère rêche; (*of ground*) inégalité *f*; (*of road*) mauvais état *m* **(b)** (*of sea*) agitation *f*; (*of wind*) violence *f* **(c)** (*of voice*) âpreté *f*, rudesse *f*

roughrider ['rʌfraɪdə(r)] *n* dresseur *m* de chevaux

roughshod ['rʌfʃɒd] *adj* **to ride r. over** (*person*) traiter cavalièrement, fouler aux pieds; (*objections*) fouler aux pieds

rough-spoken *adj* au langage grossier

roulette [ruː'let] *n* (*game*) roulette *f*; **to play r.** jouer à la roulette; **r. table** table *f* de roulette; **r. wheel** roulette

Roumania [ruː'meɪnɪə, rʊ-] *n* = **Romania**

Roumanian [ruː'meɪnɪən, rʊ-] *n, adj* = **Romanian**

round¹ [raʊnd] **1** *adj* **(a)** (*in shape*) rond, circulaire; (*cheeks, stomach, earth*) rond; **to become r.** s'arrondir; **to have r. shoulders** avoir le dos rond; **r. brackets** parenthèses *fpl*; *Mus* **a good r. top C** un mi du haut parfait; **r. dance** ronde *f*; **r. hand(writing)** écriture *f* ronde

(b) (*number*) rond; **in r. figures** en chiffres ronds; **a r. dozen** une douzaine exactement; **r. sum** compte *m* rond

2 *n* **(a)** (*shape*) (*of bread*) tranche *f*; *Art* **sculpture in the r.** ronde-bosse *f*; **theatre in the r.** théâtre *m* en rond; *Culin* **r. of beef** gîte *m* à la noix; **a r. of sandwiches** = un sandwich

(b) (*stage of match, tournament, election etc*) manche *f*, tour *m*; *Boxing* round *m*; (*of golf*) partie *f*; **to play a r. of golf** faire une partie de golf; **he only went three rounds** (*of boxer*) il n'a fait que trois rounds; **in the first r., in r. 1** (*of boxing match*) au cours du premier round; **to have a r. of cards** faire une partie de cartes; *Horseriding* **clear r.** sans-faute *m inv*; **to have** *or* **get a clear r.** faire un sans-faute; **to be/get through to the next r.** se qualifier/s'être qualifié pour la manche suivante

(c) (*series*) (*of talks, visits*) série *f*; (*of drinks*) tournée *f*; **to stand a r. of drinks** payer une tournée (générale); **whose r. is it?** qui paye cette tournée?; **it's my r.** c'est moi qui paye cette tournée, c'est ma tournée

(d) (*route*) **rounds** (*of milkman etc*) tournée *f*; (*of doctor*) visites *fpl*; (*of policeman*) ronde *f*; **delivery r.** livraisons *fpl*, tournée; *Fig* **the daily r.** la routine de tous les jours; **the daily r. of cooking and cleaning** les travaux quotidiens de cuisine et de ménage; **one continual r. of pleasure** une succession perpétuelle de plaisirs; **to go** *or* **do the rounds** (*of story, rumour etc*) circuler; (*of virus, cold etc*) circuler, se propager; **the story went** *or* **did the rounds (of the village)** l'histoire a fait le tour (du village); **to be on** *or* **make** *or* **do one's rounds** (*of doctor*) faire ses visites; (*of policeman*) faire sa ronde; (*of milkman etc*) faire sa tournée; **to do a hospital r.** faire sa visite à l'hôpital, visiter ses malades; **to do a paper r.** distribuer un/le journal *ou* des/les journaux; **to do** *or* **go the rounds of the travel agencies/***etc* faire le tour des agences de voyages/*etc*

(e) *Mil* (*bullet*) balle *f*; (*cartridge*) cartouche *f*; *Mil* **r. of ten shots** salve *f* de dix coups; **to fire a r.** tirer un coup; *Fig* **r. of applause** applaudissements *mpl*; **let's have a big r. of applause for her** on l'applaudit bien fort!

(f) *Mus* canon *m*

round² **1** *adv* autour; **garden with a wall right** *or* **all r.** jardin avec un mur tout autour; **taking it all r., taken all r.** (*on the whole*) dans l'ensemble, en général; **all r., it was a good result** dans l'ensemble, c'était un bon résultat; **the villages/people r. about** les villages/gens des alentours; **r. here** par ici; **all (the) year r.** (pendant) toute l'année; **the long way r.** le chemin le plus long; **to have one's hat/jumper on the wrong way r.** avoir son chapeau/son pull à l'envers; **to do sth the wrong way r.** (*in the wrong order*) faire qch à l'envers; **it's the other way r.** (*quite the opposite*) c'est (tout) le contraire; **try the key the other way r.** essaie la clef dans l'autre sens; **to go r. (to sb's)** passer (chez qn); **to order the car r.** demander qu'on amène la voiture; **to ask sb r.** inviter qn (chez soi); **he brought his friend r. (with him)** il a amené son ami (avec lui); **he'll be r.** il passera

2 *prep* **(a)** (*position*) autour de; **sitting r. the table** assis autour de la table; **he's 95 cm r. the chest** il fait 95 cm de tour de poitrine; **shells were exploding r. (about) him** des obus éclataient autour de lui; *Br* **he's r. the pub** il est au pub; *Br* **he's r. his brother's** il est chez son frère

(b) (*motion*) autour de; **to look r. the room** parcourir une pièce du regard; **to travel r. the world** parcourir le monde; **she walked r. the town centre** elle s'est promenée dans le centre-ville; **to go r. (and r.) sth** (*in circle*) tourner autour de qch; **to go r. an obstacle** contourner un obstacle; **to go r. the corner** (*of person*) tourner le coin; (*of vehicle*) prendre le virage; **the grocer r. the corner** l'épicier du coin; **if you are r. this way next week** si vous passez par ici la semaine prochaine

(c) (*approximately*) **r. about** environ; **r. (about) midday** vers midi; **she's r. about forty** elle a la quarantaine

round³ *vt* **(a)** (*shape*) (*object*), *Ling* (*vowel*) arrondir **(b)** *Naut* (*headland*) doubler, franchir; (*island*) contourner; **to r. a corner** (*of car*) prendre un virage; (*of person*) tourner un coin

▶ **round down** *vtsep* (*figure etc*) arrondir (**to** à) (*à un chiffre inférieur*)

▶ **round off** *vtsep* **(a)** (*sentence etc*) conclure; (*negotiations etc*) conclure, achever; **to r. off one's speech** achever son discours; **to r. things off …** pour finir …; **we rounded the meal off with a bottle of brandy** nous avons fini le repas avec une bouteille de cognac **(b)** (*figures*) arrondir

▶ **round on** *vipo* s'en prendre à; **she rounded on him for no reason** elle lui est tombée dessus sans aucune raison

▶ **round up** *vtsep* **(a)** (*gather*) (*cattle*) rassembler; (*local criminals*) faire une rafle de; **r. up the usual suspects** rassemblez les suspects habituels; **to r. everyone up for a**

meeting rassembler tout le monde pour une réunion **(b)** (*number etc*) arrondir **(to** à) (*à un chiffre supérieur*); **to r. an amount up** arrondir une somme **(to** à)

roundabout ['raʊndəbaʊt] **1** *n Br* **(a)** (*at fairground, in playground*) manège *m*; *F* **what you gain on the swings you lose on the roundabouts** ce que tu gagnes d'un côté, tu le perds de l'autre **(b)** *Aut* rond-point *m, pl* ronds-points; *Spec* sens *m* giratoire **2** *adj* (*method, statement, approach, route etc*) détourné, indirect; **to take a r. way** faire un détour; **to hear of sth in a r. way** apprendre qch indirectement; **to lead up to a question in a r. way** aborder une question de biais

rounded ['raʊndɪd] *adj* arrondi; (*breasts*) plein

roundel ['raʊnd(ə)l] *n* (*on wood, stone*) œil-de-bœuf *m, pl* œils-de-bœuf; (*on aircraft*) cocarde *f*

rounders ['raʊndəz] *npl Br Sp* = jeu *m* similaire au baseball

round-eyed *adj* aux yeux ronds; **to listen in r. amazement** écouter les yeux ronds

Roundhead ['raʊndhed] *n Br Hist* Tête *f* ronde; **R. army/victory** armée *f*/victoire *f* des Têtes rondes

roundhouse ['raʊndhaʊs] *n Rail* rotonde *f*

roundly ['raʊndlɪ] *adv* (*to praise, criticize etc*) franchement, carrément; **r. beaten** battu à plate(s) couture(s)

roundness ['raʊndnɪs] *n* rondeur *f*

round robin *n* **(a)** = pétition *f* dont les signatures sont disposées en cercle (*afin de ne pas révéler qui a signé le premier*) **(b)** *US Sp* poule *f*

round-shouldered [raʊnd'ʃəʊldəd] *adj* (*person*) voûté; **to be r.** être voûté, avoir le dos voûté

roundsman, *pl* **-men** ['raʊndzmən] *n Br Com* livreur *m*

Round Table *n* Table *f* ronde

round table *n Pol, Ind etc* table *f* ronde; **r. conference** table ronde

round-the-clock 1 *adj* (*activity etc*) de jour et de nuit; **police are keeping a r. vigil on them** la police les surveille de jour comme de nuit **2** *adv* (*to work, study*) vingt-quatre heures sur vingt-quatre; **open r.** ouvert vingt-quatre heures sur vingt-quatre

round trip *n* (*there and back*) voyage *m* d'aller-retour, aller (et) retour *m*; **r. flight** vol *m* aller-retour; **r. passenger** passager *m* aller-retour

round-trip *adj Am* (*ticket etc*) aller (et) retour

roundup ['raʊndʌp] *n* (*of cattle*) rassemblement *m*; (*of criminals*) rafle *f*; **here is a r. of the news** voici un résumé des informations *ou* des actualités

roundworm ['raʊndwɜːm] *n* ascaride *m*

rouse [raʊz] *vt* **(a)** (*awaken*) (*person*) (*from sleep*) (r)éveiller; (*make more active*) secouer, *F* remuer; **to r. sb from a daydream** tirer qn de sa rêverie; **I was suddenly roused by a loud cry** soudain, un cri m'a fait sortir de ma torpeur; **to r. oneself** se secouer; **to r. oneself to do sth** s'efforcer de faire qch; **to r. sb to action** pousser qn à agir; **to r. sb from his apathy** faire sortir qn de son apathie; **to r. the camp** donner l'alerte au camp **(b)** (*cause*) (*indignation etc*) soulever; (*admiration*) susciter; *Lit* **to r. the passions** éveiller les passions; **to r. sb to anger** susciter la colère de qn

roused [raʊzd] *adj* (*angry*) en colère

rousing ['raʊzɪŋ] *adj* (*speech*) stimulant; (*welcome*) enthousiaste; (*music*) qui fait vibrer les cœurs; **r. cheers** applaudissements frénétiques

roustabout ['raʊstəbaʊt] *n F Am* débardeur *m*; *Austr* homme *m* à tout faire, manœuvre *m*

rout¹ [raʊt] *n Mil* déroute *f*; **to put troops to r.** mettre des troupes en déroute; *Fig* **the election was a r. for the government** l'élection a été une débâcle pour le gouvernement

rout² *vt Mil, Fig* mettre en déroute

▶ **rout out** *vtsep* **(a)** (*get rid of*) évincer **(from, of** de) **(b)** (*find*) (*information*) dénicher

route¹ [ruːt], *Am* [ruːt, raʊt] *n* **(a)** (*of traveller*) itinéraire *m*; (*of plane, ship*) route *f*, voie *f*; (*of parade*) parcours *m*; (*on mountain*) course *f*; *Am* (*of mailman etc*) tournée *f*; *Fig* (*to failure, success etc*) voie **(to** de); **to be en r.** être en route **(for a town** pour une ville); *Fig* **he's en r. for success** il est sur la voie du succès; **to map out a r.** établir un itinéraire; **sea r.** route maritime; **bus r.** (*service*) ligne *f* d'autobus; (*direction taken*) itinéraire *ou* parcours d'un autobus; **are you on a bus r.?** est-ce qu'un autobus passe près de chez vous?; **all routes** (*road sign*) toutes directions; *Comptr* **r. finder software** logiciel *m* cartographique de recherche d'itinéraires; **r. map** carte *f* routière; *Mil* **r. march** marche *f* d'entraînement (au pas de route)

(b) *Am* (*highway*) route *f* nationale; **R. 66** la (route) nationale 66

route² *vt* (*parcel etc*) router, acheminer **(through, via** par); (*bus, train, flight etc*) faire passer **(via** par; **through** par, à travers); **the flight was routed via Turkey** notre itinéraire passait par la Turquie

routine [ruː'tiːn] **1** *n* **(a)** (*habit*) routine *f*; **to establish a working r.** organiser son travail, s'organiser; **to do sth as a matter of r.** faire qch de façon systématique; **the daily r.** le train-train quotidien

(b) *Th* (*of dancer*) enchaînement *m* (de pas de danse); (*of comic*) numéro *m*; **to go through one's r.** (*of dancer*) faire son enchaînement; (*of comic*) faire son numéro; **to practise one's r.** répéter son enchaînement/son numéro; *Fig F* **don't give me that r.** arrête ton numéro

(c) *Comptr* sous-programme *m*

2 *adj* **(a)** (*normal*) de routine; (*procedures*) d'usage; **it's just r.** (*said by official*) c'est une simple formalité; **r. enquiries** (*of police*) constatations *fpl* d'usage; **it's just a r. enquiry** c'est simplement pour les constatations d'usage; **r. examination** examen *m* de routine; **it was a r. flight** c'était un vol sans histoire

(b) (*boring, uninspired*) (*work, tasks*) routinier; **r. performance** représentation qui n'a rien de particulier

routinely [ruː'tiːnlɪ] *adv* (*systematically*) (*to check, proceed etc*) systématiquement

routing ['ruːtɪŋ] *n* (*action*) routage *m*; (*route*) itinéraire *m*; *TV etc* **r. switcher** grille *f* de régie

rove [rəʊv] **1** *vi* (*of person*) rôder, vagabonder; **his eyes roved from one to the other** son regard allait de l'un à l'autre **2** *vt* (*the countryside, country*) parcourir; (*the seas*) (*of pirate etc*) écumer

rover ['rəʊvər] *n* vagabond, -onde; (*scout*) routier *m*

roving ['rəʊvɪŋ] **1** *adj* vagabond; (*ambassador*) itinérant; **to have a r. commission** avoir une grande liberté de manœuvre; *F* **he has a r. eye** c'est un dragueur; *Journ* **r. reporter** reporter *m* qui va sur le terrain; (*on larger scale*) grand reporter **2** *n* vagabondage *m*; **r. life** vie *f* de nomade

row¹ [rəʊ] *n* (*of chairs, knitting*) rang *m*; (*of trees*) rangée *f*; (*of houses*) ligne *f*, rangée; (*in street names*) rue *f*; (*of people*) (*one beside the other*) rang, rangée; (*one behind the other*) file; (*of cars*) (*one beside the other*) rangée; (*one behind the other*) file; *Comptr* (*in spreadsheet*) ligne; **in a r.** en rang *ou* ligne; **to put things in a r.** mettre des objets en rang, aligner des objets; **two Sundays in a r.** deux dimanches de suite *ou* d'affilée; **in rows** par rangs; **in two rows** sur deux rangs; **in the front/third r.** (*seat etc*) au premier/troisième rang; **r. of figures** ligne de chiffres; **r. of medals** rangée *ou F* brochette *f* de décorations; *Am* **r. house** maison *f* (*qui fait partie d'une rangée de maisons attenantes*); **r. houses** rangée de maisons attenantes

row² *n* (*in boat*) promenade *f* en canot; **to go for a r.** canoter

row³ 1 *vi* (*in boat*) ramer; *Sp* faire de l'aviron; **to r. hard** ramer de toutes ses forces, *Spec* faire force de rames **2** *vt* (*boat*) faire aller à la rame; (*person*) transporter en canot

row⁴ [raʊ] *n* **(a)** (*noise*) chahut *m*, tapage *m*, vacarme *m*; **I can't concentrate with all this r. going on** je ne peux pas me concentrer avec tout ce chahut *ou* tapage *ou* vacarme; **make less r.!** faites moins de chahut *ou* de tapage *ou* de vacarme!; **to make** *or* **kick up a r.** (*be noisy*) faire du chahut *ou* tapage *ou* du vacarme; (*protest*) faire toute une histoire **(about** au sujet de)

(b) (*quarrel*) dispute *f*, querelle *f*, *F* scène *f*; **family r.** querelle de famille; **to have a r.** se disputer, se quereller **(with** avec); *F* **to get into a r. with sb** (*into quarrel*) se disputer avec qn; *F* **I got into a r. with the bus driver** je me suis disputé avec le chauffeur du bus; *Scot* **the boss gave me a r. for being late** le patron m'a enguirlandé parce que j'étais en retard; **the r. in Parliament over defence policy** la controverse au Parlement au sujet de la politique de défense

row⁵ *vi* (*quarrel*) se disputer, se quereller **(with** avec; **about** à propos de)

rowan ['raʊən, 'rəʊ-] *n* (*tree*) sorbier *m* (domestique), cormier *m*; (*berry*) sorbe *f*, corme *f*

rowboat ['rəʊbəʊt] *n Am* bateau *m* à rames

rowdiness ['raʊdɪnɪs] *n* tapage *m*, chahut *m*

rowdy ['raʊdɪ] **1** *adj* tapageur, -euse, chahuteur, -euse; **to be r.** chahuter **2** *n* (*person*) voyou *m*

rowdyism ['raʊdɪɪz(ə)m] *n* tapage *m*, chahut *m*

rowel ['raʊəl] *n* (*on spur*) molette *f*

rower ['rəʊər] *n* (*of boat*) rameur, -euse

rowing¹ ['rəʊɪŋ] *n* (*in boat*) canotage *m*; *Sp* aviron *m*; *Br* **r. boat** bateau *m* à rames; *Sp* **r. club** club *m* d'aviron; *Gym* **r. machine** rameur *m*

rowing² ['raʊɪŋ] *n* (*quarrelling*) disputes *fpl*, querelles *fpl*

rowlock ['rɒlək] *n Br* tolet *m*

royal ['rɔɪəl] **1** *adj* **(a)** (*visit, family etc*) royal; *Fig* (*splendid*) royal, princier; **His/Her R. Highness** Son Altesse Royale; **Their R. Highnesses** Leurs Altesses Royales; **Your R.**

Highness Votre Altesse Royale; **the r. we** le 'nous' de majesté; *Parl* **r. assent** assentiment *m* du souverain (*nécessaire pour faire passer une loi*); **r. blue** bleu *m inv* roi *ou* (de) France; **r. charter** acte *m* du souverain; *Cards* **r. flush** quinte *f* royale; *Culin* **r. icing** = glaçage *m* fait à partir de blancs d'œufs; **r. jelly** gelée *f* royale; **r. warrant** brevet *m* de fournisseur du souverain

(**b**) (*in names of organizations etc*) **R. Automobile Club** = Touring Club *m* de France; **R. Academy of Dramatic Art** = Conservatoire *m* national d'art dramatique; **R. Academy of Music** = Conservatoire *m* national de musique; **R. Air Force** Armée *f* de l'air britannique; **R. Army Medical Corps** corps *m* médical de l'armée britannique; **R. Canadian Air Force** Armée de l'air canadienne; **R. Canadian Mounted Police** Gendarmerie *f* royale du Canada; *Br* **R. Commission** = commission *f* nommée par le monarque sur recommandation du premier ministre; *Br Mil* **R. Engineers** = section *f* du génie civil de l'armée britannique; **R. Mail** la poste britannique; **R. Marines** les Marines de l'armée britannique; **R. National Lifeboat Institution** = société *f* nationale de sauvetage en mer; **R. Navy** Marine *f* nationale britannique; **R. School of Music** École *f* royale de musique; **R. Society for the Protection of Birds** = ligue *f* pour la protection des oiseaux; **R. Society for the Prevention of Cruelty to Animals** = Société *f* protectrice des animaux; **R. Ulster Constabulary** Police *f* royale de l'Ulster

2 *n F* membre *m* de la famille royale; **the Royals** la famille royale

royalism ['rɔɪəlɪz(ə)m] *n* royalisme *m*

royalist ['rɔɪəlɪst] *adj, n* royaliste *mf*

royally ['rɔɪəlɪ] *adv* (*to entertain, welcome etc*) royalement

royalty ['rɔɪəltɪ] *n* (**a**) (*rank, position*) royauté *f*; **hotel patronized by r.** hôtel fréquenté par les membres de la famille royale; **is he r.?** est-ce qu'il fait partie de la famille royale?; **we were treated like r.** nous avons été traités comme des princes (**b**) *Com* (*for invention etc*) redevance *f*; **royalties** (*for author, singer, musician*) droits *mpl* d'auteur; *Petr* royalties *fpl*; **to do sth on a r. basis** être rémunéré en droits d'auteur

rozzer ['rɒzər] *n Old-fashioned Br Sl* (*policeman*) flic *m*

RP [ɑː'piː] *n* (*abbr* **received pronunciation**) = prononciation *f* de l'anglais considérée comme la norme

RPI [ɑːpiː'aɪ] *n* (*abbr* **retail price index**) indice *m* des prix de détail

rpm [ɑːpiː'em] *n Aut etc* (*abbr* **revolutions per minute**) tours/minute *mpl*

R & R [ɑːrən'dɑːr] *n US Mil* (*abbr* **rest and recreation**) permission *f*

RRP [ɑːrɑː'piː] *n Br* (*abbr* **recommended retail price**) prix *m* public conseillé

RSC [ɑːres'siː] *n Br Th abbr* **Royal Shakespeare Company**

RSI [ɑːre'saɪ] *n Med abbr* **repetitive strain** *or* **stress injury**

RSM [ɑːre'sem] *n* (**a**) *Br Mil* (*abbr* **regimental sergeant-major**) adjudant-chef *m* (**b**) *Br abbr* **Royal School of Music**

RSPB [ɑːrespiː'biː] *n Br abbr* **Royal Society for the Protection of Birds**

RSPCA [ɑːrespiːsiː'eɪ] *n Br* (*abbr* **Royal Society for the Prevention of Cruelty to Animals**) ≈ SPA *f*

RSPCC [ɑːrespiːsiː'siː] *n Br* (*abbr* **Royal Society for the Prevention of Cruelty to Children**) ≈ fondation *f* pour l'enfance

RSVP [ɑːresviː'piː] (*abbr* **répondez s'il vous plaît**) (*on invitation*) RSVP

RT [ɑː'tiː] (*abbr* **return ticket**) AR *m*

Rt Hon *Br Pol* (*abbr* **Right Honourable**) très honorable

RTW [ɑːtiː'dʌb(ə)ljuː] (*abbr* **round the world**) tour du monde

rub[1] [rʌb] *n* frottement *m*; (*massage*) friction *f*; **to give sth a r.** frotter qch; (*massage*) frictionner qch; (*to dry it*) donner un coup de torchon à qch; (*to polish it*) astiquer qch; *Fig* **there's the r.!** c'est là toute la difficulté!, *F* c'est là le hic!

rub[2] (**-bb-**) **1** *vt* frotter; (*massage*) frictionner; (*polish*) astiquer; **to r. one's eyes/chin** se frotter les yeux/le menton; **to r. one's leg with liniment** se frictionner la jambe avec un onguent; **to r. itself against sth** (*of cat etc*) se frotter contre qch; **to r. one's hands (together) (in** *or* **with satisfaction)** se frotter les mains (de satisfaction); **to r. sb's hands** frictionner les mains à qn; **to r. sth dry** sécher qch en le frottant; **to r. sth through a sieve** passer qch au tamis; *Fig* **to r. shoulders with** côtoyer, coudoyer; *Fig* **I don't have two pennies to r. together** je n'ai pas un sou; *F* **he hasn't got two brain cells to r. together** il n'a pas deux sous de jugeote

2 *vi* (*of straps, shoes etc*) frotter; (*of person, animal*) se frotter (**against** contre); **these shoes r.** ces chaussures me font mal

▶ **rub against 1** *vipo* frotter (contre) **2** se frotter contre

▶ **rub along** *vi F* (**a**) (*manage*) se débrouiller (**b**) (*get on*) **we r. along (together) very well** nous nous entendons très bien

▶ **rub away** *vtsep* = **rub off**

▶ **rub down** *vtsep* (**a**) (*prepare for decorating*) (*wall*) regratter; (*paintwork*) poncer (**b**) (*dry etc*) **to r. a horse down** bouchonner un cheval; **to r. sb down** frictionner qn; **to r. oneself down** (*dry oneself*) se frictionner

▶ **rub in** *vtsep* (*lotion, polish etc*) **r. the ointment in** faites bien pénétrer la pommade; **put some polish on the cloth and r. it in** mettez un peu de cirage sur le chiffon et frottez bien; **to r. a hole in sth** faire un trou dans qch à force de frotter; *Fig* **there's no need to r. it in!** ce n'est pas la peine d'insister; *Fig F* **to r. sb's nose in it** mettre le nez de qn dans son caca; *Fig* **to r. salt in(to) the wound** remuer le couteau dans la plaie

▶ **rub into** *vtaspo* **r. the ointment into the skin** faites bien pénétrer la pommade dans la peau; *Culin* **to r. the butter into the flour** ajouter le beurre à la farine en malaxant le mélange

▶ **rub off 1** *vtsep* enlever en frottant **2** *vi* **this paint rubs off easily** cette peinture s'enlève facilement; *Fig* **to r. off on sb** (*of manners, enthusiasm etc*) déteindre sur qn; *Fig* **some of it is bound to r. off** il y aura forcément des influences

▶ **rub out** *vtsep* (*word etc*) effacer, gommer; *Sl* **to r. sb out** (*murder*) descendre *ou* but(t)er qn

▶ **rub up 1** *vtas* **to r. oneself up against sb/sth** se frotter contre qn/qch; *Fig* **to r. sb up the wrong way** prendre qn à rebrousse-poil **2** *vi* **to r. up against sb/sth** se frotter contre qn/qch

rubber[1] ['rʌbər] *n* (**a**) *Br* (*eraser*) gomme *f*; (*for blackboards*) chiffon *m*

(**b**) (*substance*) caoutchouc *m*; *Fig* **my legs feel like r.** j'ai les jambes en coton; **r. ball/gloves** balle *f*/gants *mpl* en caoutchouc; **r. boots** bottes *fpl* en caoutchouc; *F* **r. cheque** chèque *m* en bois; *Am Pol F* **the r. chicken circuit** = série *f* de visites dans de petites villes au cours d'une campagne électorale; **r. overshoes,** *Am* **rubbers** caoutchoucs *mpl*; **r. ring** bouée *f* gonflable; *Aut* **r. sleeve** manchon *m* en caoutchouc; **r. stamp** tampon *m*; *F* **r. stamp parliament** parlement *m* qui ne fait qu'entériner les lois

(**c**) *Sl* (*condom*) préservatif *m*, capote *f*; **r. goods** préservatifs

rubber[2] *n Cards* rob(re) *m*; **to play a r.** faire un robre

rubber band *n* élastique *m*

rubber dinghy *n* bateau *m* pneumatique

rubberize ['rʌbəraɪz] *vt* (*fabric*) caoutchouter

rubberneck[1] ['rʌbənek] *n Am F* (**a**) (*at scene of accident etc*) badaud, -aude, curieux, -ieuse (**b**) (*tourist*) touriste *mf*

rubberneck[2] *vi Am F* (**a**) (*at scene of accident etc*) faire le badaud (**b**) (*of tourist*) faire le touriste

rubber plant *n* caoutchouc *m*

rubber plantation *n* plantation *f* d'hévéas

rubber planter *n* planteur, -euse d'hévéas

rubber-stamp *vt* (*document etc*) apposer un cachet sur, estampiller; *Fig* (*decision*) approuver sans discussion

rubber tree *n* arbre *m* à gomme

rubbery ['rʌbərɪ] *adj* caoutchouteux

rubbing ['rʌbɪŋ] *n* frottement *m*, frottage *m*; *Med etc* friction *f*; *Art* (*of brass etc*) frottis *m*; *Art* **to take a r. of an inscription** faire un frottis d'une inscription; *Am* **r. alcohol** alcool *m* à 90 (degrés); **r. down** = **rubdown**

rubbish[1] ['rʌbɪʃ] *n* (**a**) *Br* (*refuse*) détritus *mpl*; (*household products*) ordures *fpl*; **r. collection** ramassage *m* des ordures

(**b**) (*junk*) *F* saleté(s) *f(pl)*; **the house was full of r.** (*trashy items*) la maison était pleine de petites cochonneries; **shall I keep this stuff? – no, it's just r.** je garde ces trucs? – non, c'est bon à jeter; **it's amazing how much r. one accumulates** c'est incroyable toutes les cochonneries qu'on peut accumuler

(**c**) *Fig* (*nonsense*) bêtises *fpl*; **to talk r.** dire des bêtises; **(what) r.!, what a load of (old) r.!** quelles foutaises!; **her latest book is a load of r.** son dernier livre est vraiment nul; **the play is absolute r.** la pièce est nulle

rubbish[2] *vt F* (*book, plan etc*) éreinter, descendre en flammes

rubbish bin *n* boîte *f* à ordures, poubelle *f*

rubbish chute *n* vide-ordures *m inv*

rubbish dump *n* dépotoir *m*, décharge *f* publique

rubbish heap *n* dépotoir *m*, décharge *f* publique; *Fig* **to throw sb/sth on the rubbish heap** se débarrasser de qn/qch

rubbishy ['rʌbɪʃɪ] *adj Br* (*worthless*) sans valeur; (*poor quality*) de mauvaise qualité; (*book, play*) nul

rubble ['rʌb(ə)l] *n* décombres *mpl*; **to reduce a town to r.** réduire une ville à des décombres; **from the r. of his marriage** des ruines de son mariage

rubdown ['rʌbdaʊn] *n* (*of person*) friction *f*; (*of horse*) bouchonnement *m*, bouchonnage *m*; (*of wood, paintwork*) frottement *m*; **to give sb a good r.** bien frictionner qn

rube [ru:b] *n Am F* paysan *m*, péquenaud *m*

Rube Goldberg ['ru:b'gəʊldbɜ:g] *adj Am* (*device*) de bric et de broc; (*plan etc*) tarabiscoté

rubella [ru:'belə] *n Med* rubéole *f*; **r. injection/vaccine** piqûre *f*/vaccin *m* contre la rubéole

Rubicon ['ru:bɪkən] *n* Rubicon *m*; *Fig* **to cross the R.** franchir le Rubicon

rubicund ['ru:bɪkənd] *adj Lit* rubicond, rougeaud

ruble ['ru:b(ə)l] *n US* = **rouble**

rubric ['ru:brɪk] *n* rubrique *f*

ruby ['ru:bɪ] **1** *n* (*gem*) rubis *m*; **r. earrings/necklace** boucles *fpl* d'oreille/collier *m* en rubis **2** *adj* **r. (red)** rouge rubis *inv*; **r. lips** lèvres *fpl* vermeilles; **r. port** porto *m* rouge; **r. wedding** noces *fpl* de vermeil

RUC [ɑ:ju:'si:] *n Br* (*abbr* **Royal Ulster Constabulary**) = Police *f* royale de l'Ulster

ruche[1] [ru:ʃ] *n* (*on sleeves etc*) ruché *m*

ruche[2] *vt* (*sleeve etc*) garnir d'un ruché

ruck[1] [rʌk] *n* **(a)** (*in rugby*) mêlée *f* ouverte; *Fig* **the (common) r.** le commun; **to rise above the r.** se distinguer de la masse **(b)** *F* (*fight*) bagarre *f*

ruck[2] *vi* (*in rugby*) former une mêlée ouverte

ruck[3] *n* (*in cloth*) faux pli *m*

ruck[4] **1** *vt* (*sheet*) froisser **2** *vi* (*of sheet*) se froisser

rucksack ['rʌksæk] *n Br* sac *m* à dos

ruckus ['rʌkəs] *n esp Am F* (*argument, controversy*) bagarre *f*; (*noise*) chahut *m*, vacarme *m*; **to make a r.** faire du chahut *ou* du vacarme; (*complain noisily*) faire un scandale; **to cause a r.** (*of news etc*) faire du foin

ruction ['rʌkʃən] *n F* dispute *f*; **there'll be ructions** il va y avoir du grabuge *ou* de la casse

rudder ['rʌdər] *n* (*on boat*) gouvernail *m*; (*on plane*) gouverne *f*; *Av* **rudders** empennage *m*

rudderless ['rʌdəlɪs] *adj* (*ship*) sans gouvernail; *Fig* (*country etc*) qui va à la dérive

ruddiness ['rʌdɪnɪs] *n* (*of complexion*) teint *m* coloré

ruddy ['rʌdɪ] **1** *adj* **(a)** (*complexion*) rougeaud, haut en couleur; (*sky*) rougeâtre; **r. glow** (*of fire*) lueur *f* rouge **(b)** *Br Sl* fichu; **you r. fool!** espèce d'imbécile!; *Br Sl* **r. hell!** nom de dieu! **2** *adv Br Sl* **it's r. cold** il fait rudement froid; **r. fast/slow** bigrement rapide/lent

rude [ru:d] *adj* **(a)** (*impolite*) impoli, mal élevé (**to** envers) **(b)** (*indecent*) (*word, joke etc*) indécent, obscène; **he made a r. gesture** il a fait un geste obscène **(c)** *Lit* (*primitive*) (*tool*) grossier, rudimentaire; (*drawing*) primitif **(d)** *Fig* (*violent*) (*shock, surprise etc*) violent; *Fig* **to receive a r. awakening** recevoir un choc; *Fig* **it was a bit of a r. awakening** le réveil a été brutal **(e)** (*vigorous*) **to be in r. health** jouir d'une santé robuste

rudely ['ru:dlɪ] *adv* **(a)** (*impolitely*) (*to speak, interrupt*) impoliment, grossièrement **(b)** *Lit* (*primitively*) (*made, drawn*) primitivement, grossièrement **(c)** *Fig* (*violently*) violemment; **to be r. awakened** être réveillé brusquement; *Fig* sortir brusquement de sa torpeur; **they were r. awakened to the difficulties which such an operation entails** ils se rendirent soudain compte des difficultés qu'une telle opération implique

rudeness ['ru:dnɪs] *n* **(a)** (*impoliteness*) impolitesse *f*, grossièreté *f* **(b)** (*indecency*) (*of joke, story*) obscénité *f* **(c)** *Lit* (*primitiveness*) (*of tool*) caractère *m* rudimentaire *ou* grossier

rudiment ['ru:dɪmənt] *n Anat* rudiment *m*; **rudiments** (*of grammar etc*) rudiments, notions *fpl* élémentaires

rudimentary [ru:dɪ'ment(ə)rɪ] *adj* (*tail, knowledge etc*) rudimentaire; (*equipment, tool etc*) (*primitive*) rudimentaire; (*essential*) de base; **to have a r. grasp of sth** comprendre les rudiments de qch; **I speak r. Chinese** j'ai des rudiments de chinois

rue[1] [ru:] *vt Fml* (*action*) regretter amèrement; **to r. the day when …** regretter le jour où …; **you'll r. the day** (*that you did this*) tu vas le regretter

rue[2] *n Bot, Culin* rue *f*

rueful ['ru:fʊl] *adj* (*glance, smile*) désabusé

ruefully ['ru:fʊlɪ] *adv* (*to laugh, say*) d'un air désabusé

ruefulness ['ru:fʊlnɪs] *n* (*of glance, smile*) caractère *m* désabusé

ruff[1] [rʌf] *n* (*on costume*) collerette *f*; *Hist* fraise *f*; (*on bird, animal*) collier *m*, cravate *f*

ruff[2] *vt Cards* couper (avec un atout)

ruffian ['rʌfɪən] *n* brute *f*; **young ruffians** petits voyous *mpl*

ruffle[1] ['rʌf(ə)l] *n* **(a)** *Clothing* (*at wrist*) manchette *f* (en dentelle); (*at throat*) jabot *m* plissé **(b)** (*of bird*) collier *m*, cravate *f*

ruffle[2] *vt* (*of wind*) (*surface of water*) troubler, rider; (*grass*) agiter; (*sb's hair*) ébouriffer; **to r. its feathers** (*of bird*) hérisser ses plumes; **to r. sb's feelings** *or* **sb's feathers** froisser qn; **to r. sb's composure** faire perdre contenance à qn

ruffled ['rʌfəld] *adj* **(a)** (*hair, feathers etc*) ébouriffé; (*clothes, sheets*) en désordre; *Fig* **to smooth sb's r. feathers** apaiser qn **(b)** *Fig* **to be r.** (*disconcerted*) être déconcerté; (*annoyed, irritated*) être irrité; **to get r.** perdre contenance; (*get annoyed*) s'irriter

rug [rʌg] *n* **(a)** (*blanket*) couverture *f*; **travelling r.** couverture de voyage, plaid *m* **(b)** (*carpet*) (petit) tapis *m*, carpette *f*; *Fig* **to pull the r. (out) from under sb's feet** couper l'herbe sous le pied à qn **(c)** *F* (*toupee*) postiche *m*

rugby ['rʌgbɪ] *n* **r. (football)** rugby *m*; **r. ball/ground** ballon *m*/terrain *m* de rugby; **r. league** rugby *ou* jeu *m* à treize; **r. player** rugbyman *m*, joueur *m* de rugby; **r. tackle** plaquage *m*; **r. union** rugby à quinze

rugged ['rʌgɪd] *adj* **(a)** (*ground, country*) accidenté; (*rock, hill*) découpé; **r. features** traits *mpl* rudes *ou* irréguliers; **a man with r. good looks** un homme à la beauté brute **(b)** (*equipment, vehicle etc*) robuste **(c)** (*manners*) bourru, rude; **r. independence** indépendance *f* farouche; **r. individualist** individualiste *mf* farouche *ou* forcené(e); **r. life** vie *f* rude *ou* dure

ruggedness ['rʌgɪdnɪs] *n* **(a)** (*of ground, country*) aspect *m* accidenté; (*of rock*) aspect découpé; **the r. of his features** ses traits taillés au couteau **(b)** (*of vehicle etc*) robustesse *f*

rugger ['rʌgər] *n Br F* rugby *m*; *Pej* **r. bugger** supporter *m* de rugby

ruin[1] ['ru:ɪn] *n* (*of building etc*); *Fig* ruine *f*; **the castle is a r.** le château est en ruine(s); **to fall into/lie in ruin(s)** tomber/être en ruine(s); **to be in ruins** (*of building, economy*) être en ruine(s); (*of career*) être fini; (*of hopes*) être anéanti; **the r. of my career/hopes** la fin de ma carrière/mes espoirs; **to go to r.** (*of building, economy, country*) tomber en ruine(s); (*of person*) sombrer; **he's on the road to r.** il va *ou* court à la ruine *ou* à sa perte; **to be the r. of sb** être la perte de qn; **it will be the r. of him** ça le perdra; **gambling has led to his r.** le jeu l'a perdu *ou* l'a mené à sa perte; **r. is staring us in the face** la ruine nous pend au nez

ruin[2] *vt* (*harvest, dress*) abîmer; (*person*) ruiner; (*person's life, future, holiday, day*) gâcher; **to r. one's eyesight** s'user la vue *ou* les yeux; **to r. one's health** se ruiner la santé; **being a miner had ruined his lungs** il s'était esquinté les poumons à la mine; **ruined castle** château *m* en ruine(s); **the meal's ruined** le repas est gâché *ou F* fichu; **to r. sb's plans** faire échouer les projets de qn; **he ruined my chances of playing in the World Cup** il a rendu impossible ma participation à la Coupe du monde **we're ruined** (*financially*) nous sommes ruinés; **tourists are ruining the town** les touristes massacrent la ville; **the small villages along the coast have been ruined by mass tourism** les petits villages de la côte ont perdu tout leur charme à cause du tourisme de masse; **they're ruining that child** ils pourrissent cet enfant

ruination [ru:ɪ'neɪʃən] *n* ruine *f*, perte *f*; **to be the r. of sb** être la perte de qn

ruinous ['ru:ɪnəs] *adj* (*expense etc*) ruineux; **in a r. condition** (*of building, economy*) en ruine; **tobacco and alcohol are r. to the health** le tabac et l'alcool ruinent la santé

ruinously ['ru:ɪnəslɪ] *adv* **r. expensive** ruineux

rule[1] [ru:l] *n* **(a)** (*principle*) règle *f*; (*regulation*) règlement *m*; (*custom*) coutume *f*; **according to the rules** (*of game etc*) d'après la règle; (*regulation*) d'après le règlement; **it's a r. that …** c'est un fait établi que…, il est évident que…; **I'm sorry, but that's the r.** *or* **those are the rules** je suis désolé mais c'est le règlement; **to lay** *or* **set sth down as a r.** poser qch comme règle générale; **as a (general) r.** en règle générale; **the exception proves the r.** l'exception confirme la règle; **snow is the r. rather than the exception in winter** en hiver, normalement, il neige; **to make it a r. to do sth** se faire un principe de faire qch; **we must make it a r. that everyone contributes equally** nous devons poser comme principe que chacun contribue à part égale; **rules and regulations** la réglementation; **there are too many rules and regulations** la réglementation est trop lourde; *Ind* **work(ing) to r.** grève *f* du zèle; **to work to r.** faire la grève du zèle; **to play according to** *or* **to observe the rules (of the game)** jouer selon les règles (du jeu); **it's against the rules** c'est contre les règles; **to bend** *or* **stretch the rules** contourner *ou* oublier le règlement; **rules of conduct** règles de conduite; **the r. of the road** (*for cars*) le code de la route; (*for ships*) les règles de route; *Math* **r. of three** règle de trois; **as a r. of thumb, allow one pound of meat for four people** en règle générale, compter une livre de viande pour quatre personnes; **ground r.** règle de base; **Queensberry rules** (*in boxing*) règles du marquis de Queensberry

(b) (*authority*) autorité *f*; *Pol* gouvernement *m*; **under British r.** sous l'autorité britannique; **the r. of law** l'autorité de la loi; **majority r., the r. of the majority** règle *f* majoritaire
(c) (*for measuring*) règle *f*; **pocket r.** règle *ou* mètre *m* de poche; **folding r.** mètre pliant
(d) (*of religious order*) règle *f*

rule² *vt* **1** (a) (*country, people*) gouverner; (*one's passions, emotions*) maîtriser, dominer; **to r. a nation** régner sur une nation; **to r. sb** (*dominate*) dominer qn; **don't let him r. your life** ne le laisse pas mener ta vie; **don't let your heart r. your head** ne laisse pas tes émotions l'emporter sur la raison; *Lit* **to r. the waves** tenir la mer, être maître *ou* maîtresse des mers; *Fig* **to r. the roost** régner, faire la loi
(b) (*decide*) décider (**that ...** que ... + *ind*); **the chairperson ruled her** *or* **her remark out of order** le président a déclaré que sa remarque n'était pas valable
(c) (*paper*) rayer; **ruled paper** papier *m* rayé *ou* réglé
2 *vi* (a) (*of monarch*) régner (**over** sur); **Arsenal r. OK!** (*in graffiti*) vive Arsenal!
(b) (*of judge*) statuer (**on sth** sur qch); **to r. in favour of/against sb** (*of judge, umpire etc*) décider en faveur de/contre qn

▶ **rule off** *vtsep* faire *ou* tracer un trait; **she ruled off a 2cm margin** elle a tracé une marge de 2cm

▶ **rule out** *vtsep* **to r. sth out** exclure qch; **a possibility that can't be ruled out** une possibilité que l'on ne saurait exclure *ou* écarter *ou* éliminer; **the police have ruled out murder** la police exclut la possibilité d'un meurtre; **the presence of hostages ruled out an attack** la présence d'otages rendait toute attaque impossible

rule book *n* (*of club etc*) règlement *m*; **to throw away the r.** faire fi des règles *fpl*

rule-governed ['ruːlgʌvənd] *adj* qui suit des règles

ruler ['ruːlər] *n* (a) (*of country*) dirigeant, -ante; (*sovereign*) souverain, -aine (**of, over** de) (b) (*for measuring*) règle *f*; *Comptr* **r. line** règle

ruling ['ruːlɪŋ] **1** *adj* (*passion*) dominant; (*concern, consideration*) premier; *Pol* (*party*) au pouvoir; (*class*) dirigeant **2** *n* (*of judge, umpire etc*) décision *f*; **to give** *or* **hand down a r. in favour of sb** décider en faveur de qn

rum¹ [rʌm] *n* rhum *m*

rum² *adj* (*comp* **rummer**, *superl* **rummest**) *Old-fashioned Br F* (*story etc*) drôle, bizarre; **a r. character** un drôle de type *ou* de numéro; **it was a bit of a r. do** c'était un peu louche

Rumania [ruː'meɪnɪə, rʊ-] *n* = **Romania**

Rumanian [ruː'meɪnɪən, rʊ-] = **Romanian**

rumba ['rʌmbə] *n* (*dance, music*) rumba *f*; **to do the r.** faire la rumba; **to play a r.** jouer une rumba; **r. tune/step** air *m*/pas *m* de rumba

rumble¹ ['rʌmb(ə)l] *n* (a) (*of thunder, gunfire*) grondement *m*; (*of voices*) bruit *m* confus; (*of cart*) roulement *m*; *Aut* ronflement *m*; (*of stomach*) gargouillement *m*; **my stomach gave a r.** mon estomac a gargouillé; **rumbles of discontent in the hall** des murmures de protestation dans la salle; **this caused rumbles of discontent in the press/party** cela a soulevé des vagues dans la presse/au sein du parti; **r. strip** (*on road*) bande *f* d'avertissement sonore (b) *Am Sl* (*gang-fight*) échauffourée *f*

rumble² **1** *vi* (a) (*of thunder, gunfire etc*) gronder; (*of stomach*) gargouiller; **a cart rumbled along the street** une charrette qui passait remplit la rue de son fracas (b) *Am Sl* (*fight*) (*of street gang*) prendre part à une échauffourée **2** *vt Br F* (*see through*) (*scheme, plot etc*) deviner, découvrir; (*person*) deviner le jeu de; **we've been rumbled** on a deviné notre jeu

▶ **rumble on** *vi* (*drone on*) (*of person*) ne pas cesser de parler (**about** de); (*carry on*) (*of dispute*) traîner

rumbling ['rʌmblɪŋ] **1** *n* (a) (*of thunder*) grondement *m*; (*of tanks, underground train*) roulement *m*; (*of stomach*) gargouillements *mpl*, borborygmes *mpl* (b) *Fig* (*of discontent etc*) grognement *m*; **there have been rumblings about the proposal** la proposition a été accueillie avec des grognements **2** *adj* **a r. noise** un grondement

rumbustious [rʌm'bʌstjəs] *adj F* (*person, behaviour*) exubérant; (*child*) exubérant, turbulent; *Th* (*farce*) joyeux

ruminant ['ruːmɪnənt] *adj, n Zool* ruminant *m*

ruminate ['ruːmɪneɪt] *vi* (a) *Fml* (*of person*) ruminer; **to r. over** *or* **about** *or* **on sth** retourner qch dans sa tête (b) (*of animal*) ruminer

rumination [ruːmɪ'neɪʃən] *n* (a) *Fml* (*of person*) rumination *f* (b) (*of animal*) rumination *f*

ruminative ['ruːmɪnətɪv] *adj Fml* (*look, voice*) plein de questionnement

ruminatively ['ruːmɪnətɪvlɪ] *adv Fml* (*to say*) d'un ton méditatif; (*to gaze*) d'un air méditatif

rummage ['rʌmɪdʒ] *n* (*search*) **to have a r. (around/about)** fouiller, fourrager (**in** dans); **I had a quick r. in my/his suitcase** j'ai rapidement fouillé ma/sa valise; *Am* **r. sale** vente *f* de charité *ou* de bienfaisance

▶ **rummage about, rummage around** *vi* fouiller, fourrager (**among** dans); **what are you rummaging around here for?** qu'est-ce que tu farfouilles?

▶ **rummage in, rummage through** *vipo* (*pockets, drawer etc*) fouiller dans, fourrager dans

rummy ['rʌmɪ] *n Cards* rami *m*; **to play r.** jouer au rami

rumour¹, *US* **rumor** ['ruːmər] *n* rumeur *f*, bruit *m* (qui court); **r. has it** *or* **there's a r. going round that ...** le bruit court que ..., on raconte que ...; **rumours have been circulating** des rumeurs ont circulé (**that** selon lesquelles; **about** au sujet de); **so r. has it** c'est ce qu'on dit; **to hear a r. that ...** entendre dire que ...; **there are rumours of a takeover** on parle de *ou* d'un rachat; **have you heard any rumours about what's going to happen?** est-ce que vous avez entendu parler de ce qui va se passer?; **it's only a r.** ce n'est qu'une rumeur *ou* qu'un bruit qui court *ou* qu'un on-dit; **r. monger** colporteur, -euse de rumeurs

rumour², *US* **rumor** *vt* (*always passive*) **it is rumoured that ...** le bruit court que ...; **he is rumoured to be ...** le bruit court *ou* on dit qu'il est...; **he was rumoured to be in hiding** le bruit courait qu'il se cachait; **so it was rumoured** c'est ce qu'on a dit

rumoured, *US* **rumored** ['ruːməd] *adj* **the r. takeover of the company/cancellation of the project** la rumeur selon laquelle l'entreprise serait rachetée/le projet serait annulé; **the table was sold for a r. £2m** selon la rumeur, la table aurait été vendue 2 millions de livres

rump [rʌmp] *n* (a) (*of animal*) croupe *f*; (*of bird*) croupion *m*; *F* (*of person*) postérieur *m*; **r. steak** romsteck *m* (b) *F* (*of army, political party etc*) restant *m*; **the r. Yugoslavia** ce qui reste de la Yougoslavie; *Br Hist* **R. Parliament** Parlement *m* croupion

rumple ['rʌmp(ə)l] *vt* (*dress etc*) chiffonner, friper, froisser; (*sheets*) froisser; (*person's hair*) ébouriffer

rumpled ['rʌmpəld] *adj* (*dress etc*) chiffonné, fripé, froissé; (*sheets*) froissé; (*hair*) ébouriffé; **to look r.** (*of person*) avoir l'air ébouriffé

rumpus ['rʌmpəs] *n F* (*noise*) chahut *m*, vacarme *m*; (*argument, protest*) bagarre *f*; **to kick up** *or* **make** *or* **raise** *or* **cause a r.** (*be noisy*) faire un chahut à tout casser; (*protest*) faire du raffut (**about** au sujet de); **there's been a bit of a r. about her appointment** il y a eu toute une histoire à propos de sa nomination; *Am* **r. room** salle *f* de jeux

rumpy-pumpy [rʌmpɪ'pʌmpɪ] *n Hum F* (*sex*) partie *f* de jambes en l'air

run¹ [rʌn] *n* (a) (*on foot*) course *f*; **he took a short r. and cleared the gate** après un court élan il a franchi la barrière; **at a r.** en courant; **to break into a r.** se mettre à courir; **to go for a r.** (*jog*) aller courir; **to take the dog for a r.** aller faire courir le chien; **we've got them on the r.** nous les avons mis en déroute; **to be on the r.** (*from police*) être en fuite *ou F* en cavale; (*of soldiers, rebels etc*) être en fuite *ou* en déroute; (*be busy*) courir; *F* **to make a r. for it** (*escape*) se tirer; (*to get out of rain, catch train etc*) se grouiller; *F* **to have a (good) r. for one's money** en avoir pour son argent; *F* **to give sb a (good) r. for their money** en donner pour son argent à qn; *Fig* en faire voir (de toutes les couleurs) à qn; **she's making a r. for the Presidency** (*bid*) elle se lance dans la course des présidentielles; **to make ten runs** (*in cricket match*) marquer dix points; *F* **to have the runs** (*diarrhoea*) avoir la courante
(b) (*for pleasure*) (*in car etc*) balade *f*; **to go for a r.** (*in the car*) aller se balader en voiture; **he gave me a r. home** il m'a raccompagné en voiture
(c) (*journey*) trajet *m*; **our town is a two-hour r. (by train/by car) from London** notre ville est à deux heures (de train/de voiture) de Londres; **he used to do the London (to) Glasgow r.** (*of pilot, bus or train driver*) il faisait la ligne Londres Glasgow
(d) (*of book*) tirage *m*; (*of product*) série *f*
(e) (*sequence, series*) série *f*, suite *f*; **the recent r. of events** la récente série d'événements; **a r. of bad luck** une série *ou* suite de malheurs; **we had a r. of good luck last week** la semaine dernière la chance nous a souri; *Cards* **r. of three** suite de trois cartes; **the r. of the cards was against me** la suite de cartes n'était pas en ma faveur; **in the long r.** en fin de compte; **in the short r.** à court terme; **to have a long r.** (*of fashion, person in power*) tenir longtemps; (*of play*) tenir longtemps l'affiche; *Th* **after its record r. in London** après être resté à l'affiche à Londres pendant un temps record; *Th* **during its six-month r.** pendant les six

mois où elle a tenu l'affiche; *Th* **it will soon finish its r.** cela ne sera bientôt plus à l'affiche

(f) (*rush*) (*on Stock Exchange*) ruée *f*; **a r. on the banks** un retrait massif des dépôts bancaires; **r. on the red** (*in roulette etc*) série *f* à la rouge; **a r. on the dollar** une ruée sur le dollar; **there's been a big r. on tickets** les gens se sont rués sur les billets

(g) (*type*) **the ordinary r. of mankind** le commun des mortels; **in the ordinary r. of things** en temps normal; **out of the common r.** hors du commun

(h) (*freedom*) **to give sb the r. of one's house** mettre sa maison à la disposition de qn; **to have the r. of the house** être libre d'aller partout dans la maison; **the children were allowed the r. of the fields behind the house** les enfants ont eu le droit d'aller jouer dans les champs derrière la maison

(i) (*in stocking*) maille *f* qui file, échelle *f*

(j) (*for skier*) piste *f*

(k) (*of salmon*) remontée *f*

(l) (*enclosure*) **(chicken) r.** enclos *m* des poulets

(m) *Mus* roulade *f*

run² (*pt* **ran** [ræn]; *pp* **run**; *prp* **running**) **1** *vi* **(a)** courir (**towards** à, vers); **to come running towards sb** accourir vers qn; **to r. up/down the street** monter/descendre la rue en courant; **r. up to your grandmother's** cours chez ta grand-mère; **I'll just r. across** *or* **round** *or* **over to the shop** je fais un saut à l'épicerie; **r. along!** allez-vous-en!; **the tram runs on special tracks** le tramway roule sur des rails spéciaux; **to r. to fetch** *or* **get help** courir chercher de l'aide; **she ran for the police** elle a couru chercher la police; **don't come running to me for help** ne viens pas me chercher quand tu auras besoin d'aide; *Fig* **she went running to the press with the story** elle a couru répéter l'histoire à la presse; *Fig* **he's running scared** il a la frousse

(b) (*flee*) fuir, s'enfuir, se sauver; **r. for it!** sauve qui peut!; **to r. for one's life** s'enfuir pour sauver sa peau

(c) (*compete in race*) (*of athlete, horse*) courir; **to r. for Parliament** se présenter à la députation; **to r. for office** se porter candidat; **to r. for President** *or* **the Presidency** se porter candidat *ou* se présenter aux élections présidentielles

(d) (*flow*) couler; **the river runs into a lake** la rivière débouche *ou* se jette dans un lac; **the floor was running with water** le sol ruisselait; **the streets were running with blood** le sang coulait dans les rues; **my nose is running** j'ai le nez qui coule; **the tears were running down her cheeks** les larmes coulaient le long de son visage; **the ice cream is beginning to r.** la glace commence à fondre; **the water had run cold** l'eau qui coulait était froide; **the water for my bath had just started to r. cold** j'ai eu juste assez d'eau chaude pour mon bain *Fig* **my blood ran cold** mon sang se glaça

(e) (*of ship*) **to r. before the wind** courir vent arrière; **to r. aground** (*of ship*) échouer; *Fig* (*of project etc*) capoter

(f) (*go*) **I must r. (along)** il faut que je file; **the lease has only a year to r.** il ne reste qu'un an de bail, le bail expire dans un an; *Th* **the play has been running for a year** la pièce est à l'affiche depuis un an; **the film is currently running in Hull** le film est actuellement sur les écrans à Hull; **the conversation ran something like this** voilà en gros ce qui s'est dit; **few buses are running because of the strike** à cause de la grève, il y a peu de bus qui circulent; **this train is not running today** ce train ne circule pas aujourd'hui; **the buses stop running at midnight** après minuit il n'y a plus de bus; **trains running to Paris** trains à destination de Paris; **trains running between London and Manchester** trains qui circulent entre Londres et Manchester; **to be running late** (*of person, bus, train etc*) avoir du retard; **the train is running approximately twenty minutes late** le train aura environ vingt minutes de retard; **our programmes are running ten minutes late** il y a un retard de dix minutes dans nos programmes; **it runs in the family** c'est de famille

(g) (*operate*) (*of machine*) fonctionner, marcher; **the hotel runs like clockwork** l'hôtel marche sans problème; **the engine's running** le moteur marche *ou* tourne *ou* est en marche; **the engine is running smoothly** le moteur tourne rond; **the car runs on unleaded petrol** la voiture roule à l'essence sans plomb; *Comptr* **the software runs on this machine** le logiciel peut être utilisé sur cette machine; *El* **this machine runs off the mains** cet appareil se branche sur (le) secteur

(h) (*pass*) (*of road, railway etc*) passer; **the line runs from ... to ...** la ligne va de ... jusqu'à ...; **the road runs alongside the river** la route suit *ou* longe la rivière; **to r. north and south** être orienté nord-sud; **the road runs quite close to the village** la route passe tout près du village; **the tunnel runs right through the Alps** le tunnel traverse les Alpes; **a tunnel running beneath the Channel** un tunnel qui passe sous la Manche; **to r. to seed** (*of plant*) monter en graine; **to r. to fat** (*of person*) prendre de l'embonpoint

(i) **to r. high** (*of sea*) être grosse *ou* houleuse; **feelings** *or* **tempers are running high** les esprits sont échauffés; **his funds are running low** ses fonds baissent; **our stores are running low** nos provisions s'épuisent *ou* tirent à leur fin; **the river had run dry** la rivière s'est asséchée

(j) (*of colour in fabric*) déteindre; (*of ink*) couler; **colour that runs in the wash** couleur qui déteint au lavage

(k) (*of stocking*) filer, se démailler

(l) (*of salmon*) remonter les rivières

2 *vt* **(a)** **to r. a race** courir *ou* disputer une course; **to r. a kilometre** courir un kilomètre; **to r. an errand** faire une course; **to r. the blockade** forcer le blocus; **things must r. their course** il faut que les choses suivent leur cours; **to allow things to r. their course** laisser faire les choses; **the illness/crisis/recession had run its course** la maladie/crise/récession était terminée; **to r. a fox to earth** chasser un renard jusqu'à son terrier; **to r. sb hard** *or* **close** talonner qn; *F* **I'm run off my feet** je suis débordé

(b) (*drive*) **to r. the car into the garage** rentrer la voiture dans le garage; **to r. one's car into a wall/tree** mettre la voiture dans un mur/arbre; **to r. sb (in)to town/back home** conduire qn en ville/reconduire qn chez lui

(c) (*smuggle*) (*drugs, arms*) faire la contrebande de

(d) (*operate*) (*machine*) faire fonctionner, faire marcher; **I can't afford to r. a car** je n'ai pas les moyens d'entretenir une voiture; **the house is too expensive to r.** la maison coûte trop cher à entretenir; **this computer runs most software** on peut utiliser la plupart des logiciels sur cet ordinateur; *Comptr* **to r. a programme** exécuter *ou* faire tourner un programme; **to r. trains between Glasgow and Inverness** assurer un service de trains entre Glasgow et Inverness; **they are running an extra train** ils ont mis un train supplémentaire; *Av* **to r. the engines** (*for checking*) faire le point fixe; **to r. tests** effectuer des essais

(e) (*manage*) (*business, theatre*) diriger; (*shop, hotel*) tenir; (*farm*) exploiter; (*newspaper, magazine*) rédiger; **stop trying to r. my life for me!** cesse de vouloir diriger ma vie!

(f) (*enter in competition*) (*horse*) faire courir; *Pol* **to r. a candidate** présenter un candidat

(g) (*pass*) faire passer; **to r. the vacuum cleaner over the carpet** passer l'aspirateur sur la moquette; **to r. pipes through a wall** faire passer des tuyaux à travers un mur; **to r. one's fingers over sth** promener ses doigts sur qch; *Mus* **to r. one's fingers over the keys** passer les doigts sur les touches; **she ran her eye over the page** ses yeux parcoururent la page; **he ran his eye over the room** il parcourut la pièce du regard; **to r. a comb/brush through one's hair** se donner un coup de peigne/de brosse; **he ran his hand through his hair** il a passé sa main dans ses cheveux

(h) (*make flow*) (*water etc*) faire couler (**into sth** dans qch); **to r. a bath** faire couler un bain

(i) (*have, carry*) **to r. a (high) temperature** faire de la température, avoir de la fièvre; **to r. a deficit** avoir un déficit; **to r. a story/an article** (*of newspaper etc*) publier un article

▶ **run about 1** *vi* courir çà et là (**in** dans); **I've been running about all day** (*been busy*) j'ai couru toute la journée **2** *vipo* (*shops*) courir; **there were people running about the streets in their pyjamas** il y avait des gens en pyjama qui couraient dans les rues; **to r. about the streets** (*of children*) courir les rues

▶ **run across** *vipo* (*person*) rencontrer par hasard; (*information, book, photo album etc*) tomber sur

▶ **run after** *vipo* (*chase, also sexually*) courir après; **to r. after sb** (*chase*) courir après qn; (*coddle*) dorloter qn; *Fig* **to r. after men/women** courir les garçon/filles; **she spends half her life running after her kids** elle passe son temps à être derrière les enfants; **he's got all these assistants running after him the whole time** il a tout un tas d'assistants qui passent sans arrêt derrière ce qu'il fait

▶ **run around** *vi, vipo* = **run about**; **he was sure his wife was running around** il était sûr que sa femme le trompait

▶ **run around with** *vipo F* (*be friendly with*) fréquenter; (*have affair with*) sortir avec

▶ **run away** *vi* (*of person*) s'enfuir, se sauver; (*from home etc*) (*of child, teenager etc*) faire une fugue; (*of horse*) s'emballer; **they have run away to get married** ils se sont enfuis pour se marier; **to r. away from home** faire une fugue; *Fig* **to r. away from the facts** se refuser à l'évidence; **to r. away from one's responsibilities** fuir ses responsabilités; **to r. away with sb** partir avec qn; **to r. away with sth** emporter qch, partir avec qch; **the favourite ran away with the race** le favori a gagné la course haut la main; **don't r. away with the idea that I'm rich** ne va pas t'imaginer que je suis riche; **his imagination runs away with him** il a une imagination galopante; **she lets her enthusiasm r. away with her** elle se laisse emporter par son enthousiasme

▶ **run back 1** *vi* (*of person*) revenir en courant; *F* **to come running back** (*of errant husband etc*) revenir **2** *vtsep* (*take back by car*) ramener

▶ **run by** *vi, vtsep* = **run past**

▶ **run down 1** *vi* **(a)** (*of person*) descendre en courant

(b) (*of clockwork, clock*) s'arrêter (faute d'être remonté); (*of battery*) se décharger

2 *vtsep* **(a)** (*in car etc*) renverser; **to r. sb down in one's car** renverser qn avec sa voiture; **she was almost run down by a bus** elle a failli se faire renverser par un bus **(b)** (*find*) (*person, object*) découvrir, dénicher

(c) (*criticize*) dénigrer; **he's always running himself down** il se diminue tout le temps

(d) (*reduce*) (*number of employees*) diminuer; (*stocks*) laisser s'épuiser; (*production*) réduire progressivement; (*industry, factory*) fermer progressivement; **you've run the battery down** vous avez déchargé la pile; (*of car*) vous avez vidé *ou* déchargé la batterie, vous avez mis la batterie à plat

▶ **run in 1** *vi* entrer en courant **2** *vtsep* **(a)** *F* (*arrest*) arrêter; **to be** *or* **get run in** se faire pincer **(for** pour) **(b)** *Aut* (*engine*) roder; *Br* **running in** (*notice on car*) en rodage

▶ **run into** *vipo* (*in vehicle*) (*tree, car*) rentrer dans, entrer en collision avec; (*on foot*) (*person*) foncer dans; **you should be more careful, you nearly ran into me!** tu devrais faire attention, tu as failli me rentrer dedans!; *Fig* (*meet*) rencontrer par hasard; **to r. into debt** faire des dettes, s'endetter; **to r. into difficulties** rencontrer des difficultés; **takings r. into five figures** la recette atteint les cinq chiffres; **the cost will r. into millions** le coût va s'élever à des millions

▶ **run off 1** *vi* **(a)** fuir, s'enfuir, se sauver; **to r. off with the cash** partir en emportant l'argent; **to r. off with sb** (*elope with*) s'enfuir avec qn **(b)** (*of liquid*) s'écouler; *Am Sl* **to r. off at the mouth** parler sans arrêt **2** *vtsep* **(a)** (*make copies of*) copier, reproduire; *Typ* **machine that runs off ten copies a minute** machine qui imprime dix feuilles par minute **(b)** (*write quickly*) (*article*) pondre **(c)** (*liquid*) faire écouler **(d)** (*lose by running*) **you'll soon r. off those few extra pounds** vous n'aurez pas de mal à perdre ces quelques kilos en trop si vous courez régulièrement

▶ **run on 1** *vi* **(a)** (*keep running*) (*of person*) continuer à courir **(b)** (*of verse*) enjamber; *Typ* (*of words*) se rejoindre, être liés; (*of text*) suivre sans alinéa; *Typ* **r. on** (*instruction*) alinéa *m* à supprimer; **how much longer is this going to r. on for?** (*of meeting, film etc*) ça va durer encore combien de temps?; *F* **he <u>does</u> r. on, doesn't he!** (*talks a lot*) quand il est parti celui-là, il ne s'arrête plus; **he can r. on for hours if you let him** si tu le laisses faire il peut tenir le crachoir pendant des heures **2** *vtsep Typ* **to r. on the text** faire suivre le texte sans alinéa

▶ **run out 1** *vi* **(a)** (*from house etc*) sortir en courant; *Fig* **to r. out on sb** abandonner qn

(b) (*of lease*) expirer; (*money, supplies etc*) s'épuiser; **time is running out** il ne reste plus beaucoup de temps

2 *vtsep* **(a)** *Cr* (*batsman*) mettre hors jeu pendant sa course

(b) to r. sb out of town faire quitter la ville à qn

▶ **run out of** *vipo* (*money, food, cigarettes, wine, ideas etc*) ne plus avoir de; **to r. out of provisions** épuiser ses provisions; **we are running out of sugar** nous allons nous trouver à court de sucre; **we're/you're running out of time** il nous/vous reste peu de temps; **I've run out of cigarettes** je n'ai plus de cigarettes; **I'm running out of patience** ma patience est à bout, je perds patience **(with** avec)

▶ **run over 1** *vipo* **(a)** (*document*) parcourir; *Th* **to r. over one's lines** revoir son texte **(b)** (*exceed*) **to r. over the allotted time** excéder le temps imparti **2** *vtsep* (*person*) (*in car*) renverser; **he's been run over** (*injured*) il s'est fait renverser; (*killed*) il s'est fait écraser; **the car ran over his legs** la voiture lui est passé sur les jambes **3** *vi* **(a)** (*of vessel or contents, bath, cup etc*) déborder; **to r. over with energy/enthusiasm** déborder d'énergie/d'enthousiasme **(b)** (*continue for too long*) (*of speech, TV programme etc*) déborder

▶ **run past 1** *vi* (*of person*) **to r. past sb/sth** passer devant qn/qch en courant **2** *vtaspo F* **can I r. something past you?** puis-je vous demander vos impressions?; **to r. an idea/proposal past sb** demander à qn ce qu'il pense d'une idée/proposition; **r. that one past me again** dis-moi ça encore une fois

▶ **run through 1** *vi* (*of person*) traverser *ou* passer en courant

2 *vipo* **(a)** (*go over, rehearse etc*) (*text etc*) revoir; **let's just r. through the procedure one more time** reprenons une dernière fois la marche à suivre; *Th* **to r. through one's part** répéter son rôle; **I'll r. through your speech with you** je vous ferai répéter votre discours

(b) (*pass through*) **a murmur ran through the crowd** un murmure a parcouru la foule; **that song keeps running through my head** j'ai cette chanson dans la tête; **money runs through his fingers like water** l'argent lui brûle les doigts

(c) (*use up*) (*money etc*) dépenser; (*case of wine, coffee*) consommer; **he runs through a dozen shirts a week** il lui faut une douzaine de chemises par semaine

3 *vtsep* (*stab*) transpercer **(with a sword** d'une épée)

▶ **run to** *vipo* (*of amount, number*) monter à, s'élever à; **I don't think our budget will r. to that** je ne crois pas que notre budget nous permette cela; **today's newspaper runs to 32 pages** le journal d'aujourd'hui a 32 pages; **I can't** *or* **my money won't r. to a car** je ne peux pas me permettre financièrement d'avoir une voiture

▶ **run up 1** *vi* (*to the flat etc above*) monter en courant; **to r. up to sb** courir vers qn; **people came running up** (*to me etc*) des gens sont arrivés en courant **2** *vipo* **to r. up the stairs** monter l'escalier en courant **3** *vtsep* **(a)** (*overdraft*) laisser grossir; (*debts*) laisser accumuler; **he ran up a huge phone bill** (*his own*) il s'est ruiné en téléphone; (*sb else's*) il m'a/nous a/les a/*etc* ruiné(s) en téléphone **(b)** (*raise*) (*flag*) hisser **(c)** (*sew quickly*) (*dress etc*) confectionner à la hâte

▶ **run up against** *vipo* (*difficulties*) se heurter à

runabout ['rʌnəbaʊt] *n Aut* petite voiture *f*

runaround ['rʌnəraʊnd] *n F* **to give sb the r.** (*give contradictory instructions etc*) faire tourner qn en bourrique; (*by telling lies etc*) faire marcher qn

runaway ['rʌnəweɪ] **1** *n* (*person*) fuyard, -arde, fugitif, -ive; (*child, teenager*) fugueur, -euse; (*horse*) cheval *m* emballé *ou* échappé **2** *adj* **(a)** (*prisoner, slave*) en fuite, *F* en cavale; (*child, teenager*) fugueur, -euse; (*horse*) emballé, échappé; **r. lorry/train** camion *m*/train *m* fou **(b)** (*victory*) remporté haut la main; **the play has been a r. success** la pièce a connu un immense succès **(c)** (*inflation*) galopant

rundown ['rʌndaʊn] *n* **(a)** (*summary*) résumé *m* détaillé; **give me a r. on what's been happening** racontez-moi en détail ce qui s'est passé; *TV, Cin* **r. sheet** feuille *f* d'ordre de passage à l'antenne **(b)** (*reduction*) (*of staff, production*) diminution *f*, réduction *f*

run-down *adj* **(a)** (*battery*) à plat **(b)** (*building*) délabré; (*person*) fatigué

rune [ruːn] *n* rune *f*

run-flat *adj* (*tyre*) anti-crevaison

rung [rʌŋ] *n* (*on ladder*) échelon *m*, barreau *m*; (*on chair*) barreau, bâton *m*; *Fig* **on the bottom** *or* **lowest r. of the ladder** (*in organization etc*) tout en bas de l'échelle

runic ['ruːnɪk] *adj* (*letters, verse*) runique

run-in *n F* (*quarrel*) prise *f* de bec; **to have a r. with the law** avoir des démêlés avec la justice **(about** au sujet de)

runnel ['rʌn(ə)l] *n Lit* ruisseau *m*; (*in street*) caniveau *m*

runner ['rʌnər] *n* **(a)** (*in race*) coureur, -euse; *Horseracing* partant *m*; **she's a very fast r.** elle court très vite **(b)** (*messenger*) messager *m*, courrier *m*; (*for film crew*) stagiaire *mf*, grouillot *m*; *esp US* **bank r.** garçon *m* de recette **(c)** (*of guns, drugs etc*) contrebandier *m* **(d)** (*on plant*) stolon *m*; (*on strawberry*) marcotte *f* **(e)** (*on sleigh*) patin *m*; (*on skate*) lame *f* de patin; (*on drawer*) coulisseau *m*; *Aut* (*for seats*) glissière *f* **(f)** (*carpet*) chemin *m* **(g)** (*for desk*) rallonge *f* **(h)** *F* **to do a r.** prendre la tangente

runner bean *n* haricot *m* d'Espagne, haricot à rames

runner-up *n* (*in race, competition etc*) second, -onde **(to** après); **fifteen runners-up will also receive prizes** les quinze suivants recevront également des prix; *Mktg* **r. firm** entreprise *f* "dauphin"

running[1] ['rʌnɪŋ] **1** *adj* (*pattern etc*) continu; (*battle, feud etc*) incessant; **they have a r. battle about housework** ils se bagarrent continuellement à propos des travaux ménagers; **to give a r. commentary** *Sp* faire un commentaire simultané **(on, about** de); **r. expenses** dépenses *fpl* courantes; *Mil* **r. fire** feu *m* roulant; **r. hand** écriture *f* cursive; **r. repairs** petites réparations *fpl*; **r. sore** plaie *f* qui suppure; *Sewing* **r. stitch** point *m* devant, point droit; *Journ* **r. story** actualité *f* en pleine évolution; **r. total** total *m* provisoire; (*in elections*) estimations *fpl*; **to keep a r. total of sth** calculer qch au fur et à mesure; **r. water** (*in house etc*) eau *f* courante; (*stream etc*) eau qui coule; **to rinse sth in r. water** rincer qch à l'eau courante

2 *n* **(a)** (*on foot*) course *f* à pied; **to make the r.** (*in race*); *Fig* mener la course; *Fig* **to make all the r.** (*in relationship*) toujours prendre les devants; **to be in the r.** avoir des chances; **she's in the r. for the nomination** elle a des chances d'être nommée; **to be out of the r.** n'avoir aucune chance

(b) *(working, operation) (of machine)* marche *f*, fonctionnement *m*; *(of train)* marche, circulation *f*; **r. in** *(of engine)* rodage *m*; **we apologize for the late r. of this train** nous vous prions d'excuser le retard de ce train; **in r. order** en bon état (de marche); **r. costs** frais *mpl* d'entretien; *Naut* **r. lights** feux *mpl* de position

(c) *(management) (of hotel, restaurant etc)* direction *f*; *(of railway)* exploitation *f*

(d) *(smuggling) (of arms, drugs)* introduction *f* en contrebande

(e) *(of water)* écoulement *m*, ruissellement *m*

(f) *Comptr (of program)* exécution *f*

(g) *TV etc* **r. order** ordre *m* de passage; *TV, Cin* **r. speed** *(of tape, film)* vitesse *f* de déroulement *ou* de défilement

running[2] *adv* de suite; **three years r.** trois ans de suite; **we talked for two hours r.** nous avons parlé pendant deux heures d'affilée *ou* de suite

running board *n Aut* marchepied *m*

running down *n* **(a)** *(criticism) (of person, play etc)* dénigrement *m* **(b)** *(reduction) (of staff)* réduction *f*, diminution *f*; *(of industry, factory)* réduction *ou* diminution de la production

running head *n Typ* titre *m* courant

running jump *n Sp* saut *m* avec élan; *F* **go (and) take a r.!** va te faire voir (ailleurs)!, va te faire cuire un œuf!

running mate *n Pol* candidat *m* à la vice-présidence

running-on *n (of engine)* auto-allumage *m*

running shoe *n* chaussure *f* de course

running title *n Typ* titre *m* courant

running track *n* piste *f*

runny [ˈrʌnɪ] *adj (mixture)* liquide, *Pej* trop liquide; *(nose)* qui coule

run-off *n* **(a)** *Sp* **r. (race)** finale *f*; *Pol* **r. (election)** élection *f* pour départager deux candidats **(b)** *(water) (from field etc)* eaux *fpl* de ruissellement **(c)** *Am (for desk)* rallonge *f*

run-of-the-mill *adj (film, play etc)* ordinaire, sans rien de particulier

run-on *n Typ* texte *m* continu sans alinéa

run-out *n* **(a)** *Ski* zone *f* d'arrivée **(b)** *(of film, tape)* amorce *f* de fin de bobine

run-proof, run-resist *adj (stocking etc)* indémaillable

runt [rʌnt] *n (of litter)* le plus faible *(d'une portée)*; *Pej (of man)* avorton *m*

run-through *n (of text etc)* lecture *f*; *Th* répétition *f*; *Th* **to have a r.** répéter

runtime system [ˈrʌntaɪm] *n Comptr* système *m* en phase d'exécution

run-up *n* **(a)** *Sp (of high-jumper, pole-vaulter, bowler)* élan *m*; *Av* **the pilot was making his r. to the target** le pilote fonçait sur l'objectif **(b)** *(period)* période *f* préparatoire; **in the r. to the exams/election** dans la période qui précède/a précédé/*etc* les examens/les élections

runway [ˈrʌnweɪ] *n Av* piste *f*; **r. lights** feux *mpl* de la piste d'atterrissage

rupee [ruːˈpiː] *n (currency)* roupie *f*

rupture[1] [ˈrʌptʃər] *n (in negotiations, marriage, of container, pipeline etc)* rupture *f*; *Med (of artery)* éclatement *m*, rupture; *Med (hernia)* hernie *f*

rupture[2] **1** *vt (relations)* rompre; *(container, pipeline etc)* percer, faire éclater; *Med (blood vessel, appendix etc)* se rompre; *(spleen)* se faire éclater; **to r. oneself** se faire une hernie **2** *vi (of container, pipeline etc)* éclater, se rompre; *(of blood vessel, appendix)* se rompre; *(of spleen)* éclater

ruptured [ˈrʌptʃəd] *adj (relations, container, pipeline)* rompu; *Med (organ)* hernié; *(blood vessel, appendix)* rompu; *(spleen)* éclaté

rural [ˈrʊər(ə)l] *adj (life, custom etc)* rural

ruse [ruːz] *n* ruse *f*, stratagème *m*, subterfuge *m*

rush[1] [rʌʃ] *n* **(a)** *(plant)* jonc *m*; **r. bed** jonchaie *f* **(b)** *(material)* jonc *m*, paille *f*; **made from rushes** fait de joncs; **r. mat** natte *f* de jonc; **r. matting** tapis *m* de jonc

rush[2] *n* **(a)** *(dash)* course *f* précipitée, ruée *f*; **to make a r. at sb** s'élancer *ou* se jeter *ou* se précipiter sur qn; **to make a r. for the exit/the phones** se précipiter vers la sortie/les téléphones; **to get lost in the r.** se perdre dans la bousculade; **let's leave before the r. starts** partons avant la bousculade; **there was a r. for the papers** on s'arrachait les journaux

(b) *(hurry)* hâte *f*, empressement *m*; **in a r.** en (toute) hâte; **there's no r. (for it)** ce n'est pas pressé; **life is too much of a r. in London** à Londres, la vie va trop vite; **to be in a (bit of a) r.** être (un peu) pressé; **in the r. to finish the article, he forgot to check the spelling** dans sa hâte de terminer l'article, il a oublié de vérifier l'orthographe; **we left in such a r. that …** nous sommes partis avec une telle précipitation que …; **what's all the r. for?** qu'est-ce qui presse tant?; **there's a bit of a r. on** il y a quelque chose d'assez pressé; **a r. job** *(urgent)* un travail urgent; *(hurried)* un travail bâclé; **to have a r. job on** avoir un travail urgent à faire; **r. order** commande *f* urgente

(c) *(surge)* **a r. of cold air** une bouffée d'air froid; **a r. of water** une arrivée soudaine d'eau; *Fig* **a r. of blood to the head** un coup de sang; **we had a r. (of customers) in the afternoon** les clients sont arrivés en masse l'après-midi

(d) *(demand)* ruée *f* **(on** sur)

(e) *Cin* **rushes** épreuves *fpl*, production *f* journalière, rushes *mpl*; **to see the rushes** voir les épreuves

rush[3] **1** *vi (move fast)* se précipiter, se ruer **(at** sur; **towards** vers); *(hurry)* se dépêcher **(to do** de faire); *(of blood)* affluer **(to** à); *(of vehicle)* foncer; **I must r.** il faut que je me dépêche; **there's no point in rushing** ça ne sert à rien de se dépêcher *ou* de se précipiter; **he came rushing down the stairs** il a dégringolé l'escalier; **a stream that rushes down the mountain side** un ruisseau qui dévale le flanc de la montagne; *Prov* **fools r. in (where angels fear to tread)** = agir sans réfléchir peut avoir des conséquences fâcheuses; **to r. to conclusions** conclure trop hâtivement; **the blood rushed to his cheeks/head** le sang lui est monté au visage/à la tête; **to r. upstairs** monter l'escalier à toute vitesse *ou* à la hâte; **to r. forward** se précipiter (en avant)

2 *vt* **(a)** *(hurry) (task)* faire trop vite; **they had obviously rushed the work** à l'évidence, ils avaient travaillé trop vite; *Pej* **a rushed job** un travail fait à la hâte *ou F* à la va-vite; **a horse that rushes its fences** un cheval qui se précipite sur les obstacles avec trop d'impétuosité; *Fig* **don't r. your fences!** réfléchissez donc!

(b) *(hurry) (person)* bousculer; **don't r. me** laissez-moi le temps de souffler, ne me bousculez pas; **I won't be rushed** je ne veux pas qu'on me bouscule; **let's not r. things** ne nous précipitons pas; **to be rushed off one's feet** courir à droite et à gauche; **I've been rushed off my feet all day** j'ai passé ma journée à courir à droite et à gauche

(c) *(transport quickly)* transporter d'urgence; **he was rushed to hospital** on l'a transporté d'urgence à l'hôpital; **please r. me your latest catalogue** *(notice on advertising material)* envoyez-moi d'urgence votre dernier catalogue

(d) *(attack) (position)* prendre d'assaut; **to rush sb** attaquer qn; **the audience rushed the platform** le public a envahi l'estrade

(e) *Br F (charge a lot)* **how much did they r. you for that?** combien est-ce qu'ils t'ont fait cracher pour ça?

▶ **rush about, rush around** *vi* courir çà et là

▶ **rush away** **1** *vi* partir précipitamment; **do you have to r. away?** est-ce qu'il faut vraiment que vous partiez aussi vite? **2** *vtsep (person)* emmener d'urgence

▶ **rush back** *vi* revenir en toute hâte *ou F* revenir en vitesse

▶ **rush into** **1** *vipo* **to r. into a room** entrer précipitamment *ou* faire irruption dans une pièce; *Fig* **to r. into things** agir sans réfléchir; **to r. into marriage/divorce** se marier/divorcer trop vite **2** *vtsep* **to r. sb into sth** forcer qn à faire qch trop vite; **to be rushed into doing sth** être obligé *ou* contraint à faire qch précipitamment; **to be rushed into a decision/answer** être contraint à *ou* obligé de prendre une décision/donner une réponse à la hâte; **don't let yourself be rushed into anything** ne te sens pas obligé de faire quoi que ce soit à la hâte

▶ **rush off** *vi, vtsep* = **rush away**

▶ **rush out** **1** *vi* sortir précipitamment **(of** de) **2** *vtsep (product)* sortir à la hâte; *(troops)* envoyer d'urgence

▶ **rush through** **1** *vipo* **the wind was rushing through the tunnel** le vent s'engouffrait dans le tunnel; **to r. through one's work** faire son travail à la hâte *ou F* en vitesse **2** *vtsep* **to r. a bill through (the House)** faire passer un projet de loi à la hâte; **to r. an order/application through** traiter une commande/une demande en urgence

▶ **rush up** **1** *vi (go upstairs etc)* monter à toute vitesse; **to r. up to sb** *(to say hello etc)* se précipiter sur qn **2** *vtsep Mil* **to r. up reinforcements** amener *ou* envoyer des renforts en toute hâte

rushfull [ˈrʌʃfʊl] *n Journ* premier reportage *m*

rush hour *n* heures *fpl* d'affluence *ou* de pointe; **r. traffic** circulation *f* aux heures de pointe *ou* d'affluence

rushing [ˈrʌʃɪŋ] *adj (wind, river)* déchaîné, *Lit* impétueux

rusk [rʌsk] *n* ≈ biscotte *f*; *(for baby)* gros biscuit *m*

russet [ˈrʌsɪt] **1** *n* **(a)** *(colour)* brun *m* roux **(b)** *(apple)* reinette *f* grise **2** *adj (colour)* brun roux *inv*

Russia [ˈrʌʃə] *n* Russie *f*

Russian [ˈrʌʃən] **1** *adj* russe; (*history*) de la Russie; (*teacher, lesson, dictionary*) de russe; **R. language student** étudiant, -ante de russe; **R. roulette** roulette *f* russe; **R. salad** salade *f* russe; **R. service** (*from silver salver onto plate*) service *m* à la russe **2** *n* **(a)** (*person*) Russe *mf* **(b)** *Ling* russe *m*
Russianization [rʌʃənaɪˈzeɪʃən] *n* (*of population, republic etc*) russification *f*
Russianize [ˈrʌʃənaɪz] *vt* russifier
Russify [ˈrʌsɪfaɪ] *vt* = **Russianize**
Russky [ˈrʌskɪ] *n F* ruskof *m*
Russophile [ˈrʌsəʊfaɪl] *adj, n* russophile *mf*
rust[1] [rʌst] **1** *n* (*on metal, wheat etc*) rouille *f*; *Br F* **r. bucket, r. heap** (*car*) bagnole *f* toute rouillée; **r. inhibitor, r. preventer** antirouille *m inv* **2** *adj* **r. (coloured), r. red** rouille *inv*
rust[2] **1** *vi* (*of metal*) se rouiller **2** *vt* (*metal, wheat etc*) rouiller; **badly rusted** très rouillé
▶ **rust away** *vi* (*of metal etc*) être rongé *ou* mangé par la rouille
▶ **rust through** *vi* être rongé *ou* mangé par la rouille
rustic [ˈrʌstɪk] **1** *adj* (*bench, charm etc*) rustique **2** *n* paysan, -anne, campagnard, -arde, *Pej* rustaud, -aude
rusticate [ˈrʌstɪkeɪt] *vt Br Univ Fml* (*student*) renvoyer temporairement
rustication [rʌstɪˈkeɪʃən] *n Br Univ Fml* (*of student*) renvoi *m* temporaire
rusticity [rʌˈstɪsɪtɪ] *n* rusticité *f*
rustiness [ˈrʌstɪnɪs] *n* (*of metal*) rouillure *f*, rouille *f*; **because of the r. of my French** parce que mon français est un peu rouillé
rustle[1] [ˈrʌs(ə)l] *n* (*of leaves*) bruissement *m*, frémissement *m*; (*of silk, dress*) frou-frou *m*; (*of paper*) froissement *m*
rustle[2] **1** *vi* (*of leaves*) bruire, frémir; (*of silk, dress*) faire frou-frou, froufrouter; (*of paper*) froisser; **to hear papers rustling** entendre des froissements de papier **2** *vt* (*leaves*) faire bruire, faire frémir; (*silk, dress*) faire froufrouter; (*paper*) froisser
rustle[3] *vt* (*cattle etc*) voler
▶ **rustle up** *vtsep F* (*meal, snack*) (se débrouiller pour) faire; **she can always r. up a good meal** elle se débrouille toujours pour servir un bon repas; **to r. up some coffee** faire du café; **to r. up support** rassembler des partisans
rustler [ˈrʌslər] *n* (*of cattle*) voleur, -euse (de bétail); (*of horses*) voleur, -euse (de chevaux)
rustling [ˈrʌslɪŋ] *n* **(a)** = **rustle**[1] **(b)** (*of cattle*) vol *m*
rustproof[1] [ˈrʌstpruːf] *adj* (*paint, treatment etc*) antirouille *inv*; (*metal*) résistant à la rouille, inoxydable
rustproof[2] *vt* (*metal*) protéger contre la rouille
rustproofing [ˈrʌstpruːfɪŋ] *n* (*substance*) produit *m* antirouille; (*process*) application *f* d'un produit antirouille (**of** sur)
rust-resistant *adj* (*metal*) résistant à la rouille
rusty [ˈrʌstɪ] *adj* **(a)** (*iron etc*) rouillé; **to get r.** se rouiller; *Fig* **my French is getting r.** mon français est un peu rouillé; **my playing is very/a bit r.** je suis très/un peu rouillé; **the pianist sounded/the batsman looked a bit r.** le pianiste était/le batteur semblait un peu rouillé **(b)** (*colour*) rouille *inv*; **a r. red** un marron rouille
rut[1] [rʌt] *n* (*groove*) ornière *f*; *Fig* **to get into a r.** s'encroûter; *Fig* **to be (stuck) in a r.** être prisonnier d'une routine; *Fig* **to get out of the r.** sortir de l'ornière
rut[2] *vt* **(-tt-)** (*path*) sillonner d'ornières; **deeply rutted** (*path etc*) coupé par les ornières
rut[3] *n* (*of stag etc*) rut *m*
rut[4] *vi* **(-tt-)** (*of stag etc*) être en rut
rutabaga [ruːtəˈbeɪgə] *n Am* rutabaga *m*
ruthless [ˈruːθlɪs] *adj* (*person*) impitoyable, sans pitié; (*act*) brutal; (*determination, schedule, pace*) impitoyable; **to be r. in enforcing the law** être impitoyable dans l'application de la loi; **he was r. in shortening the text** il n'a pas fait de sentiments quand il s'est agi d'abréger le texte; **I'm going to have to be r.** il faut que j'y aille carrément
ruthlessly [ˈruːθlɪslɪ] *adv* (*to act, say*) impitoyablement
ruthlessness [ˈruːθlɪsnɪs] *n* (*of person, act*) nature *f* impitoyable
rutted [ˈrʌtɪd] *adj* (*road etc*) plein d'ornières
rutting [ˈrʌtɪŋ] *n* (*of stag etc*) rut *m*; **r. season** saison *f* du rut
RV [ɑːˈviː] *n* **(a)** *Am Aut* (*abbr* **recreational vehicle**) camping-car *m*, *pl* camping-cars **(b)** (*abbr* **Revised Version**) traduction *f* de la Bible de 1884
Rwanda [rʊˈændə] *n* Rwanda *m*, Ruanda *m*
Rwandan [rʊˈændən] **1** *n* Rwandais, -aise, Ruandais, -aise **2** *adj* rwandais, ruandais
rye [raɪ] *n* **(a)** (*plant*) seigle *m*; **r. bread** pain *m* de seigle **(b)** *Am* **r. (whiskey)** whisky *m* de seigle
rye-grass *n* ivraie *f* vivace

S

S, s [es] **(a)** *(letter)* S, s *m*; **two S's** *or* **Ss** deux S **(b) S(-shaped) hook** crochet *m* en S; *Aut* **S bend** virage *m* en S **(c) S** *(abbr* **south)** S; *(abbr* **small)** *(on clothes label)* S **(d)** *Br Hist (abbr* **shilling(s))** shilling(s) *m(pl)*

's [s, z] **(a)** *(shortened form of* **is, has, us)** **it's raining** il pleut; **he's found a knife** il a trouvé un couteau; **let's go!** partons! **(b)** [①A15-16,D] *(genitive case)* **the pupil's books** les livres de l'élève; **the pupils' books** les livres des élèves; **in an hour's time** dans une heure **(c)** *(forming pl)* **the Thomas's** les Thomas, la famille Thomas; **a series of o's** une série d'o

SA [es'eɪ] *n* **(a)** *(abbr* **Salvation Army)** Armée *f* du Salut **(b)** *(abbr* **South Africa)** Afrique *f* du Sud

Saar [sɑːr] *n* **the S.** la Sarre

Sabbath ['sæbəθ] *n* **(a)** *Rel* **S. (day)** *(Jewish)* (jour *m* du) sabbat *m*; *(Christian)* dimanche *m*; **S. day observance** observance *f* du sabbat/dimanche; **to keep/break the S.** observer/violer le sabbat/dimanche **(b) witches' S.** sabbat *m* (de sorcières)

sabbatical [sə'bætɪk(ə)l] **1** *n Univ* année *f*/trimestre *m* sabbatique, congé *m* sabbatique *(accordé(e) à un professeur etc pour faire des recherches etc)*; **to be on s.** *(of teacher etc)* être en année/en cours de trimestre sabbatique **2** *adj Univ* **s. year/term** année *f*/trimestre *m* sabbatique *(accordé(e) à un professeur etc pour faire des recherches etc)*

sable¹ ['seɪb(ə)l] *n* **(a)** *(animal)* zibeline *f* **(b) s. (fur)** zibeline *f*; **s. coat** manteau de zibeline

sable² **1** *n Arch, Lit (colour)* sable *m* **2** *adj Lit* noir; *Her* sable

sabot ['sæbəʊ] *n (clog)* sabot *m*

sabotage¹ ['sæbətɑːʒ] *n* sabotage *m*

sabotage² *vt (project, bridge etc)* saboter

saboteur [sæbə'tɜːr] *n* saboteur, -euse

sabre, *US* **saber** ['seɪbər] *n (sword)* sabre *m*; **s. cut** *(blow)* coup *m* de sabre; *(scar)* balafre *f*; *Fig* **s. rattling** *(words, talk)* propos *mpl* agressifs; *(action)* actes *mpl* agressifs

sac [sæk] *n Biol* sac *m*; **yolk s.** membrane *f* vitelline; **ink s.** *(of squid, sepia etc)* poche *f* d'encre

saccharin ['sækərɪn] *n Ch etc* saccharine *f*

saccharine ['sækəriːn] *adj Ch* saccharin; *Fig, Pej (smile etc)* mielleux; *(story, film etc)* édulcoré

sacerdotal [sæsə'dəʊt(ə)l] *adj* sacerdotal

sachet ['sæʃeɪ] *n* sachet *m*

sack¹ [sæk] *n* **(a)** *(bag)* (grand) sac *m*; **s. of coal/flour** sac de charbon/farine; *F* **to hit the s.** se pieuter; **s. race** course *f* en sac **(b)** *F* **to give sb the s.** virer qn, mettre qn à la porte; **to get the s.** être viré, être mis à la porte

sack² *vt* **(a)** *F (dismiss from job)* virer, mettre à la porte **(b)** *(put in sacks) (coal etc)* ensacher, mettre en sac

sack³ *n Mil etc (plundering)* sac *m*, pillage *m*

sack⁴ *vt (plunder) (town etc)* mettre à sac

sack⁵ *n Arch (wine)* = vin *m* blanc sec d'Espagne

sackcloth ['sækklɒθ] *n* **(a)** *Tex* toile *f* à sacs, grosse toile **(b)** *Bible etc* **s. and ashes** le sac et la cendre; *Fig* **he wasn't exactly wearing s. and ashes** il n'avait pas tellement l'air désolé *ou* contrit; **I'm not going to go around in s. and ashes just because I forgot our anniversary** je ne vais quand même pas porter le deuil parce que j'ai oublié notre anniversaire de mariage

sackful ['sækfʊl] *n (of flour etc)* plein sac *m*

sacking¹ ['sækɪŋ] *n* **(a)** *F (dismissal from job) (of employee)* renvoi *m* **(b)** = **sackcloth (a)**

sacking² *n (plundering) (of town etc)* sac *m*, mise *f* à sac

sackload ['sækləʊd] *n* = **sackful**

sacrament ['sækrəmənt] *n Rel* sacrement *m*; **to take** *or* **receive the sacraments** communier; **the (Most) Holy S., the Blessed S.** le saint Sacrement

sacramental [sækrə'mentəl] **1** *adj* sacramentel **2** *npl Rel* **the sacramentals** les sacramentaux *mpl*

sacred ['seɪkrɪd] *adj* **(a)** *(held in awe) (place etc)* sacré; **s. to the memory of ...** à la mémoire de ... **(b)** *Rel* sacré; *(music)* sacré, religieux; **s. books** livres d'Église, livres saints; **s. place** lieu saint; **s. cow** *Rel* vache sacrée; *Fig (institution)* institution intouchable; *(idea)* idée sacrée *ou* sacro-sainte; **the S. Heart** le Sacré-Cœur **(c)** *(serious) (promise)* sacré, inviolable; *(duty)* sacré; **nothing was s. to him** il ne respectait rien; **is nothing s. any more?** on ne respecte vraiment plus rien!

sacredness ['seɪkrɪdnɪs] *n* **(a)** *(of place etc)* caractère *m* sacré **(b)** *(of oath)* caractère *m* sacré, inviolabilité *f*; *(of duty)* caractère sacré

sacrifice¹ ['sækrɪfaɪs] *n* **(a)** *(act of sacrificing)* sacrifice *m* **(of** de); **to make great sacrifices** faire de grands sacrifices; **to make the supreme s.** faire le sacrifice suprême; **he succeeded at the s. of his health** il a réussi au prix de sa santé *ou* en sacrifiant sa santé; **it was a real s.** *(selling sth)* on y a perdu énormément **(b)** *(person, animal)* victime *f* sacrifiée; **to offer (up) sth/sb as a s.** offrir qch/qn en sacrifice **(to** à)

sacrifice² **1** *vt* sacrifier; **to s. oneself** se sacrifier **(for** pour); **to s. one's career/independence** sacrifier sa carrière/son indépendance; *Fig* **the Prime Minister sacrificed one of his Ministers to appease the press** le Premier Ministre a sacrifié un de ses ministres pour calmer la presse **2** *vi* **to s. to idols** sacrifier aux idoles

sacrificial [sækrɪ'fɪʃəl] *adj (rites, dagger, lamb)* du/de sacrifice; *Fig* **s. lamb** *or* **victim** victime *f* à sacrifier

sacrilege ['sækrɪlɪdʒ] *n Rel, Fig* sacrilège *m*

sacrilegious [sækrɪ'lɪdʒəs] *adj* sacrilège

sacristan ['sækrɪstən] *n Rel* sacristain *m*

sacristy ['sækrɪstɪ] *n Rel* sacristie *f*

sacrosanct ['sækrəʊsæŋkt] *adj usu Iron* sacro-saint, *pl* sacro-saint(e)s

sacrum ['seɪkrəm, 'sæk-] *n Anat* sacrum *m*

SAD [eseɪ'diː] *n (abbr* **Seasonal Affective Disorder)** dépression *f* saisonnière

sad [sæd] *adj (comp* **sadder,** *superl* **saddest) (a)** triste; **a s. old bicycle** une pauvre vieille bicyclette; **a s.-looking lettuce** une salade toute flétrie; **to become s.** s'attrister; **to look s.** avoir l'air triste; **to make sb s.** attrister qn, affliger qn; **we were very s. to hear of our friend's death** nous avons été désolés d'apprendre la mort de notre ami; **to be s. at heart** avoir le cœur gros *ou* serré

(b) *(depressing) (news, place, memories etc)* triste; **that's very s. news** c'est bien triste; **a s. reflection** *or* **comment on our society** cela en dit long sur notre société; **it's s. that no one seems to care about the elderly** il est triste que personne ne semble se soucier des personnes âgées; **he came to a s. end** il a eu une triste fin; **s. to say** malheureusement

(c) *F (pathetic) (person)* minable; **to be a s. case** être minable

sadden ['sæd(ə)n] *vt (person)* attrister, affliger

saddle¹ ['sæd(ə)l] *n* **(a)** *(on horse, bicycle)* selle *f*; **hunting s.** selle anglaise; **in the s.** en selle, monté; *Fig* **to be in the s.** *(in control)* tenir les rênes (du pouvoir); **to rise in the s.** faire du trot enlevé **(b)** *Culin (of mutton, venison)* selle *f* **(c)** *Geol (of mountain)* col *m*

saddle² *vt* **(a)** *(horse)* seller **(b)** *F* **to s. sb with sth** mettre qch sur les bras de qn, charger *ou* encombrer qn de qch; **I've been saddled with this project** on m'a mis ce projet sur les bras; **she's saddled with five children** elle a cinq enfants sur les bras; **saddled with debts** grevé de dettes

▶ **saddle up** **1** *vi (of rider)* seller **2** *vtsep (horse)* seller

saddleback ['sæd(ə)lbæk] *n* **(a)** *Archit* toit *m* en bâtière **(b)** *(of hill)* ensellement *m* **(c)** *(pig)* cochon *m* noir avec une ceinture blanche

saddlebag ['sæd(ə)lbæg] *n Horseriding, Cycling etc* sacoche *f* de selle

saddlecloth ['sæd(ə)lklɒθ] *n* couverture *f ou* tapis *m* de selle

saddle horse *n* cheval *m* de selle, monture *f*

saddler ['sædlər] *n* sellier *m*

saddle room *n* sellerie *f*

saddlery ['sædlərɪ] *n (trade, articles)* sellerie *f*, bourrellerie *f*

saddle soap *n* = savon *m* spécial pour nettoyer le cuir

saddle sore *n* plaie *f* provoquée par le port de la selle; **to have a s.** *(of horse)* avoir le dos meurtri à cause de la selle; *(of rider)* avoir mal aux fesses (d'avoir été en selle)

saddle-sore *adj* **to be s.** *Horseriding* avoir mal aux fesses (d'avoir été en selle); *Cycling* avoir mal aux fesses (d'avoir fait du vélo)
saddling ['sædlɪŋ] *n* (*of horse*) sellage *m*
Sadducee ['sædjʊsiː] *n* Saducéen, -éenne
sadism ['seɪdɪz(ə)m] *n* sadisme *m*
sadist ['seɪdɪst] *n* sadique *mf*
sadistic [sə'dɪstɪk] *adj* sadique
sadistically [sə'dɪstɪklɪ] *adv* sadiquement, avec sadisme
sadly ['sædlɪ] *adv* **(a)** (*in an unhappy way*) (*to reply, smile*) tristement, d'un air triste **(b)** (*deplorably*) malheureusement; **s., this is so** c'est, hélas *ou* malheureusement, le cas **(c)** (*greatly*) vraiment; **you're s. mistaken** tu te trompes lourdement; **he is s. missed** il nous/leur manque beaucoup; **compassion is s. lacking in our society** la compassion fait tristement défaut dans notre société
sadness ['sædnɪs] *n* tristesse *f*, mélancolie *f*
sadomasochism [seɪdəʊ'mæsəkɪz(ə)m] *n* sadomasochisme *m*
sadomasochist [seɪdəʊ'mæsəkɪst] *n* sadomasochiste *mf*
sadomasochistic [seɪdəʊmæsə'kɪstɪk] *adj* sadomasochiste
s. a. e. [eseɪ'iː] *n Com etc* (*abbr* **stamped addressed envelope**) enveloppe *f* timbrée avec son adresse
safari [sə'fɑːrɪ] *n* safari *m*; **on s.** en safari; **to go on s.** faire un safari, aller en safari; **s. holiday** safari; **s. jacket** saharienne *f*; **s. park** réserve *f* d'animaux sauvages; **s. suit** ensemble *m* avec saharienne
safe¹ [seɪf] *n* **(a)** (*strongbox*) coffre-fort *m*, *pl* coffres-forts; *Banking* **night** *or* **deposit s.** coffre *m* de nuit **(b)** **(meat) s.** garde-manger *m inv*
safe² **1** *adj* **(a)** (*not in danger*) en sécurité; **s. from sth** à l'abri de qch; **to be s. from recognition** ne pas risquer d'être reconnu; **at last we are s.** enfin nous voilà en sécurité *ou* saufs *ou* hors de danger; **I'm glad to hear you're s.** je suis content d'apprendre qu'il ne t'est rien arrivé; **your daughter's not s. with him** votre fille court un risque en le fréquentant; **to come home s.** rentrer sain et sauf; **s. and sound** sain et sauf

(b) (*not dangerous*) (*street, town*) sûr; (*chemical, water etc*) sans danger; (*building, bridge etc*) solide; **she assured me the water was perfectly s. for drinking** elle m'a assuré qu'on pouvait boire l'eau sans danger; **not s.** dangereux; **is it s. to leave him alone?** est-ce qu'il n'y a pas de danger à le laisser seul?; **is the meat/water s. (to eat/drink)?** est-ce qu'on peut manger la viande/boire l'eau sans risque?; **to make a bomb s.** désamorcer une bombe; **it's as s. as houses** (*not dangerous*) cela ne présente aucun risque; **s. beach for children** plage où les enfants peuvent se baigner en (toute) sécurité; **at a s. distance** à distance respectueuse; *Med* **s. dose** dose *f* inoffensive; **s. driver** conducteur, -trice prudent(e); **s. load** (*for lorry*) charge *f* admissible; (*for lift*) charge maximum; *El* charge de sécurité; **s. sex** rapports *mpl* sexuels protégés; **to practise s. sex** se protéger (*contre les maladies sexuellement transmissibles*); **a s. sex campaign** une campagne visant à promouvoir l'utilisation du préservatif

(c) (*not entailing risk*) (*conversation, novel etc*) sûr; **it's a s. guess that ...** on ne prend pas beaucoup de risques en disant que ...; **it is s. to say that ...** on peut dire à coup sûr que ...; **(in order) to be on the s. side** pour plus de sûreté, pour être plus sûr; **it's as s. as houses** *or Br* **as the Bank of England** (*of investment*) c'est de l'or en barres; *Prov* **better s. than sorry** deux précautions valent mieux qu'une; **it's a pretty s. assumption** *or* **bet that ...** il y a fort à parier que ...; **s. investment** placement sûr *ou* de tout repos; **to wish sb a s. journey** souhaiter bon voyage à qn; **to have a s. journey** faire bon voyage

(d) (*secure*) (*place etc*) sûr; **in s. keeping** en lieu sûr, en sûreté; **to give sth to sb for s. keeping** confier qch à qn; **it's in his s. keeping** c'est sous sa garde; **in s. hands** entre (de) bonnes mains; **he's a s. pair of hands** (*of goalkeeper*) il a les mains très sûres; (*of manager, minister etc*) il est très fiable; **to put sb/sth in a s. place** mettre qn/qch en lieu sûr; *Fin* **s. custody** garde *f* en dépôt de titres; **s. retreat** asile assuré *ou* sûr; *Br Parl* **s. seat** siège *m* assuré

2 *adv* **to play (it) s.** ne rien risquer
safe-blower *n* perceur *m* de coffres-forts à l'explosif
safe-breaker *n* perceur *m* de coffres-forts
safe-conduct *n* sauf-conduit *m*, *pl* sauf-conduits
safe-cracker *n* = **safe-breaker**
safe deposit *n* dépôt *m* en coffre-fort; **s. (box)** coffre *m* bancaire
safeguard¹ ['seɪfgɑːd] *n* garantie *f* (**against** contre); **s. clause** clause *f* de sauvegarde
safeguard² **1** *vt* (*sb's interests, rights*) sauvegarder, protéger **2** *vi* **to s. against sth** se protéger contre qch
safe house *n* (*for spies, terrorists*) cachette *f* sûre
safekeeping [seɪf'kiːpɪŋ] *n* **in s.** en lieu sûr, en sûreté; **to give sth to sb for s.** confier qch à qn; **it's in his s.** c'est sous sa garde
safely ['seɪflɪ] *adv* **(a)** (*to work, play, use a tool etc*) en toute sécurité; (*to drive, ride*) sans danger; **to arrive s.** (*of person*) bien arriver; (*after dangerous journey*) arriver sain et sauf; (*of parcel etc*) arriver sans dommage; (*of ship etc*) arriver à bon port; **to land s.** atterrir sans problème; **to put sth s. away** mettre qch en lieu sûr *ou* en sûreté; **the bomb has been s. defused** la bombe a été désamorcée et ne présente plus aucun danger; **the kids are s. tucked up in bed** les enfants sont bien sagement au lit

(b) (*with certainty*) avec certitude; **I can s. say that ...** je puis dire avec certitude *ou* à coup sûr que ...; **you can s. expect her to remember** vous pouvez être sûr qu'elle s'en souviendra
safeness ['seɪfnɪs] *n* **(a)** **a feeling of s.** un sentiment de sécurité *ou* de sûreté **(b)** (*of bridge*) solidité *f*; (*of nuclear power, electrical appliances*) sûreté *f* **(c)** (*certainty*) (*of deal, investment, choice etc*) sûreté *f*; (*cautiousness*) (*of style, writing*) assurance *f*
safety ['seɪftɪ] *n* (*of person*) sécurité *f*; (*of thing*) sûreté *f*; **to seek s. in flight** chercher son salut dans la fuite; **to guarantee sb's s.** (*of police etc*) assurer la protection de qn; *prov* **there's s. in numbers** plus on est nombreux, moins on court de risques; **for s. 's sake** pour plus de sûreté; **in a place of s.** en lieu sûr; **road s.** sécurité routière; *Aut* **s. cage** habitacle *m* de sécurité; *Aut* **s. cell** cellule *f* de sécurité; **she's very s. conscious** elle se préoccupe beaucoup de la sécurité; **s. device** dispositif *m* de sécurité; **s. drill** exercice *m* d'évacuation; **s. feature** (*device*) dispositif de sécurité; (*characteristic*) caractéristique *f* pour assurer la sécurité; **s. features** (*on car*) aménagements *mpl ou* dispositifs *mpl* de sécurité; *Aut etc* **s. glass** verre *m* de sécurité; *Min* **s. lamp** lampe *f* de sûreté; **s. margin** marge *f* de sécurité; **s. matches** allumettes *fpl*; **s. measures** consignes *fpl* de sécurité; **s. mechanism** mécanisme *m* de sécurité; **s. net** filet *m*; *Fig* mesure *f* de sûreté; **s. regulations** réglementation *f* sur la sécurité; **s. standards** normes *fpl* de sécurité; *Com* **s. stock** stock *m* de sécurité; **s. valve** *Tech* soupape *f* de sûreté; *Fig* soupape
safety belt *n* ceinture *f* de sécurité
safety catch *n* (*on gun*) cran *m* de sûreté; (*on bonnet*) crochet *m* de sécurité; (*on door*) cran d'arrêt
safety chain *n* (*on door*) chaîne *f* de sûreté; (*of bracelet etc*) chaînette *f* de sûreté
safety deposit box *n* coffre(-fort) *m*
safety first *n* mesures *fpl* de prévention des accidents; **do they teach you any s.?** est-ce qu'ils vous apprennent la prévention?; **to take a s. approach** avoir une approche très prudente; **s.!** la sécurité d'abord!
safety lock *n* verrouillage *m* de sécurité
safety pin *n* épingle *f* de nourrice *ou* de sûreté
saffron ['sæfrən] **1** *n* **(a)** *Culin, Pharm* safran *m*; **s. (crocus)** (*plant*) safran; **wild** *or* **meadow s.** safran des prés **(b)** (*colour*) safran *m*; **s. yellow** jaune safran *inv* **2** *adj* safran *inv*
sag¹ [sæg] *n* **(a)** (*of roof etc*) affaissement *m*, fléchissement *m*; (*in line, rope etc*) flèche *f*, ventre *m* **(b)** (*drop*) (*in prices, support etc*) baisse *f*
sag² *vi* **(-gg-)** (*of platform, roof etc*) s'affaisser, fléchir; (*of cheek, breast etc*) pendre; (*of cable, rope*) (*state*) être détendu, pendre; (*action*) se détendre; (*of curtain*) pendre au milieu; (*of prices, support etc*) baisser, fléchir; **the gate was sagging on its hinges** le portail était branlant; **he's beginning to s. a little** il faiblit un peu
saga ['sɑːgə] *n Liter* saga *f*; *F* **the continuing s. of our washing machine** le feuilleton de notre machine à laver
sagacious [sə'geɪʃəs] *adj Fml* (*person, mind, remark etc*) sagace, avisé; (*action*) plein de sagesse
sagaciously [sə'geɪʃəslɪ] *adv Fml* avec sagacité
sagacity [sə'gæsɪtɪ] *n Fml* (*of person, remark*) sagacité *f*, perspicacité *f*
sage¹ [seɪdʒ] *Lit* **1** *adj* (*person, conduct etc*) sage, prudent **2** *n* (*wise man*) philosophe *m*, sage *m*
sage² *n Bot, Culin* sauge *f*; **s. green** (*colour*) vert *m* cendré *inv*; **s. tea** tisane *f* de sauge
sagely ['seɪdʒlɪ] *adv Lit* sagement, prudemment
sagging ['sægɪŋ] *adj* (*roof etc*) affaissé; (*gate etc*) penché d'un côté; (*breast, cheek etc*) pendant; (*line etc*) courbe; (*rope*) lâche; (*prices, market, support etc*) en baisse; (*enthusiasm, demand*) fléchissant, faiblissant
Sagittarius [sædʒɪ'teərɪəs] *n Astron* le Sagittaire; **I am S.** je suis Sagittaire *ou* du Sagittaire
sago ['seɪgəʊ] *n Culin* sagou *m*; **s. palm** (*tree*) sagoutier *m*; **s. pudding** dessert de sagou au lait

Sahara [sə'hɑːrə] *n* **the S. (Desert)** le Sahara
sahib ['sɑːɪb] *n* sahib *m*
said *see* **say**[2]
sail[1] [seɪl] *n* **(a)** (*on boat*) voile *f*; **square s.** voile carrée; **to hoist/lower a s.** hisser/amener une voile; **to make s.** (*set sail*) prendre la mer; (*spread sails*) hisser les voiles; **under s.** (*of ship*) sous voile(s), à la voile; **under full s.** toutes voiles dehors; **to set s.** prendre la mer; **to set s. for ...** partir pour ...; **s. ho!** voilier en vue!; **a fleet of twenty s.** une flotte de vingt voiles *ou* de vingt voiliers **(b)** (*journey*) traversée *f*; **it will be a three hours' s.** la traversée durera trois heures; **to go for a s.** faire de la voile **(c)** (*of windmill*) aile *f*, volant *m*, toile *f*
sail[2] **1** *vi* **(a)** (*of sailing ship*) faire voile; (*of any ship*) naviguer, faire route; *Sp* **do you s.?** est-ce que vous faites de la voile?; *Fig* **to s. (a bit) close to the wind** prendre des risques
(b) (*start voyage*) prendre la mer; **we s. at noon** nous partons à midi
(c) (*travel by sea*) voyager par mer; **to s. over the seas** parcourir les mers; **they sailed around the Mediterranean** ils ont fait le tour de la Méditerranée; **to s. round a cape** contourner un promontoire
(d) (*of glider*) planer; **there were clouds sailing by** des nuages voguaient dans le ciel; **the ball/stone sailed through the air** le ballon/caillou vola; **his toupet went sailing out of the open window** son postiche s'est envolé par la fenêtre ouverte
(e) to s. into a room entrer majestueusement dans une pièce; *F* **to s. through an examination** réussir un examen sans problèmes *ou F* les doigts dans le nez
2 *vt* (*sailing boat*) manœuvrer; (*ship*) piloter, commander; **to s. a toy boat on a pond** faire naviguer un petit bateau sur un bassin; **to s. the seas** parcourir les mers
sailboard[1] ['seɪlbɔːd] *n Sp* planche *f* à voile
sailboard[2] *vi Sp* faire de la planche à voile *ou* du véliplanche
sailboarder ['seɪlbɔːdər] *n Sp* (véli)planchiste *mf*
sailboarding ['seɪlbɔːdɪŋ] *n Sp* planche *f* à voile, véliplanchisme *m*
sailboat ['seɪlbəʊt] *n Am* voilier *m*, bateau *m* à voile
sailcloth ['seɪlklɒθ] *n Tex* (*for sails*) toile *f* à voile(s); (*for clothes*) toile
sailing ['seɪlɪŋ] *n* **(a)** (*activity*) (*in sailing ship, sailing boat*) navigation *f* à voile; (*in any ship*) navigation; *Sp* voile *f*; **to go s.** faire de la voile; *Fig* **it's (all) plain s.** cela va tout seul; **s. before the wind** allure *f* du vent arrière; **s. orders** ordre *m* d'appareiller, instructions *fpl* pour l'appareillage **(b)** (*departure*) départ *m*, appareillage *m*; **the 12 o'clock s.** le bateau de midi; **s. card** liste *f* des navires en partance; **s. schedule** horaires *mpl* de départ
sailing boat *n Br* voilier *m*, bateau *m* à voile
sailing ship *n* voilier *m*, navire *m* à voiles
sailmaker ['seɪlmeɪkər] *n* voilier *m*
sailor ['seɪlər] *n* marin *m*; **to be a good s.** avoir le pied marin; **to be a bad s.** être sujet au mal de mer; **s. hat** (*for women*) canotier *m*; (*for boys*) chapeau *m* de marin; **s. suit** costume *m* marin (*d'enfant*)
sainfoin ['sænfɔɪn] *n* (*plant*) sainfoin *m*
saint [seɪnt] *n* **(a)** saint *m*, sainte *f*; **s. 's day** fête *f* de saint, fête patronale; **All Saints' (Day)** la Toussaint; *Fig* **I'm no s.** je ne suis pas un saint; *F* **to try the patience of a s.** lasser la patience d'un saint **(b)** (*usu* [sənt]) **S. Bernard** (*dog*) saint-bernard *m inv*; **S. David's Day** la Saint-David; **S. George** Saint Georges; **S. Helena** (*island*) Sainte-Hélène *f*; **S. John the Baptist** Saint Jean-Baptiste; **the S. Lawrence (River)** le (fleuve) Saint-Laurent; **S. Peter's** (la cathédrale *ou* l'église) Saint-Pierre **(c) the Communion of Saints** la Communion des Saints
sainted ['seɪntɪd] *adj Old-fashioned F* **my s. aunt!** mes aïeux!
sainthood ['seɪnthʊd] *n* sainteté *f*
saintliness ['seɪntlɪnɪs] *n* sainteté *f*
saintly ['seɪntlɪ] *adj* (*life, action etc*) de saint; *Iron* **to put on a s. air** prendre un air de petit saint
sake[1] [seɪk] *n* **(a) to do sth for the s. of sb** *or* **for sb's s.** faire qch pour qn *ou* par égard pour qn; **I forgive you for her s.** je vous pardonne par égard pour elle; **do it for the s. of your family** faites-le pour (l'amour de) votre famille; **they stayed together for the s. of the children** *or* **for the children's s.** ils sont restés ensemble à cause des enfants; **for all our sakes, tell no one** ne le dis à personne dans notre intérêt à tous; **do it for my s.** (*do it to please me*) faites-le pour me faire plaisir; **for God's s., for goodness' s., for heaven's s. , for Pete's s., for pity's s.** pour l'amour de Dieu *ou* du ciel; **all for the s. of a few pence!** tout ça pour quelques malheureux pence!; **for the s. of peace** dans l'intérêt de la paix; **for old times' s.** en souvenir du passé; **for economy's s.** par économie; **art for art's s.** l'art pour l'art; **this is talking for talking's s.** *or* **for the s. of talking** c'est parler pour parler; **let's say, for the s. of argument** *or* **for argument's s. ...** admettons que ...; **you're just saying that for the s. of an argument** *or* **of arguing!** tu dis cela uniquement par provocation
(b) *US F* **sakes alive!, sakes!** grand Dieu!, par exemple!
sake[2] ['sɑːkɪ] *n* (*drink*) saké *m*
sal [sæl] *n* **s. ammoniac** sel *m* ammoniac; **s. volatile** (solution *f* de) sels volatils anglais
salaam[1] [sə'lɑːm] *n F* salutation *f* (chez les musulmans)
salaam[2] **1** *vt* saluer **2** *vi* saluer
salacious [sə'leɪʃəs] *adj* (*story, person*) salace
salaciousness [sə'leɪʃəsnɪs] *n* (*of story, person*) salacité *f*
salad ['sæləd] *n* salade *f*; **cheese/ham s.** salade au fromage/jambon; **green s.** salade (verte); **fruit s.** macédoine *f ou* salade de fruits; **s. bar** (*in restaurant*) buffet *m* de salades; **s. bowl** saladier *m*; *Fig* **s. days** années *f* de jeunesse *ou* d'inexpérience; **s. oil** huile *f* de table
salad cream *n* = sauce *f* de salade (en bouteille)
salad dressing *n* vinaigrette *f*
salamander ['sæləmændər] *n* salamandre *f*
salami [sə'lɑːmɪ] *n* salami *m*
salaried ['sælərɪd] *adj Ind, Com* **(a)** (*personnel*) salarié; **s. employee** salarié, -ée; **s. staff** salariés **(b)** (*employment*) rémunéré
salary ['sælərɪ] *n* salaire *m*; (*of civil servant*) traitement *m*; **s. plus commission** salaire fixe plus commission; **s. earner** salarié, -ée; **s. level** niveau *m* de rémunération *ou* de salaires; **s. scale** barème *m ou* grille *f ou* échelle *f* des salaires
salaryman, *pl* **-men** ['sælərɪmæn -men] *n* employé de bureau japonais
sale [seɪl] *n* **(a)** (*act, event*) vente *f*; **sales** (*turnover*) chiffre *m* d'affaires; **sales and marketing** vente-marketing *f*; **sales and marketing department** service *m* vente-marketing; **house for s.** maison à vendre; **business for s.** fonds à céder; **to put sth up for s.** mettre qch en vente; **article for which there is no s.** article qui ne se vend pas; **on s.** *Br* (*available to buy*) en vente; *Am* (*at reduced price*) en solde; *Com* **s. at arrival/departure** vente à l'arrivée/au départ; **s. by private agreement** vente à l'amiable; **s. of stock** écoulement *m* de stocks; **s. or return basis** vente avec faculté de retour; **bill of s.** acte *m* de vente; **s. by auction, auction s.** vente aux enchères; *Jur* **compulsory s.** adjudication *f* forcée; **sales acumen** astuce *f* du vendeur; **s. agreement** compromis *m* de vente; **sales analysis** analyse *f* des ventes; **sales area** (*in store*) surface *f* de vente; (*district*) région *f* desservie; **sales audit** audit *m* de vente; **sales campaign** campagne *f* de vente; **sales commission** commission *f* de vente; **sales contract** contrat *m* de vente; **sales counter** comptoir *m* de vente; **sales drive** campagne *f* de vente; **sales figures** chiffre *m* de vente; **sales floor** surface *f* de vente; **sales force** force *ou* équipe *f* de vente; **sales forecast** prévision *f* des ventes; **sales goal** objectif *m* de vente; **sales incentive holiday** voyage *m* d'encouragement pour les bons vendeurs; **sales invoice** facture *f* de vente; *Acct* **sales ledger** grand livre *m* des ventes, journal *m* des ventes; **sales letter** lettre *f* de vente; **sales licence** licence *f* de vente; **sales literature** littérature *f* commerciale; **sales meeting** réunion *f* de représentants; **sales monopoly** monopole *m* de vente; **sales network** réseau *m* de vente; **sales objective** objectif *m* de vente; **sales outlet** point *m* de vente; **sales pitch** arguments *mpl* de vente; (*verbal*) boniment *m*, argumentation *f*; **s. price** prix *m* de vente; **sales promoter** promoteur *m* de ventes; **sales promotion** promotion *f* des ventes, animation *f* des ventes; **sales quota** quota *m* de ventes; **sales rally** rallye *m* de stimulation; **sales target** objectif *m* de vente; **sales tax** taxe *f* sur le chiffre d'affaires, TCA *f*; **sales team** équipe *f* de vente; **sales technician** agent *m* technico-commercial; **sales technique** technique *f* de vente; **sales tool** instrument *m* de vente; **sales volume** volume *m* des ventes; *Mktg* **sales wave** vague *f* de vente
(b) *Com* **(clearance) s.** *or* **sales** soldes *mpl*; **in the s.,** *Am* **on a.** (*article*) en solde; **I got it in a s.** je l'ai acheté en solde; **I got it in the sale(s)** je l'ai acheté pendant les soldes; **s. price** prix *m* soldé
saleability [seɪlə'bɪlɪtɪ] *n Com* facilité *f* d'écoulement
saleable ['seɪləb(ə)l] *adj* (*goods etc*) vendable
sale of work *n* vente *f* de charité
saleroom ['seɪlruːm] *n* salle *f* de(s) vente(s)
sales agent *n* agent *m* commercial
sales and marketing director *n* directeur *m* des ventes et du marketing
sales assistant *n Br Com* vendeur, -euse

salesclerk ['seɪlzklɜ:k] *n Am* vendeur, -euse *f*
sales consultant *n* conseiller *m* commercial
sales department *n* service *m* commercial, service des ventes
sales director *n* directeur *m* des ventes
sales engineer *n* ingénieur *m* technico-commercial, ingénieur commercial, ingénieur des ventes
salesgirl ['seɪlzgɜ:l] *n* vendeuse *f*
salesman, *pl* **-men** ['seɪlzmən] *n* vendeur *m*; (*sales rep*) représentant *m* (de commerce)
sales manager *n* directeur *m* commercial, chef *m ou* responsable *mf* des ventes
salesmanship ['seɪlzmənʃɪp] *n* technique *f* de vente
salesperson, *pl* **-people** ['seɪlzpɜ:sən, -pi:p(ə)l] *n* **(a)** (*for company*) représentant, -ante (de commerce) **(b)** (*in shop*) vendeur, -euse
sales representative *or F* **rep** *n* représentant *m ou* agent *m* commercial
saleswoman, *pl* **-women** ['seɪlzwʊmən, -wɪmɪn] *n* **(a)** (*for company*) représentante *f* (de commerce) **(b)** (*in shop*) vendeuse *f*
Salic ['seɪlɪk] *adj Hist* **S. law** loi *f* salique
salient ['seɪlɪənt] **1** *adj* **(a)** (*angle etc*) saillant **(b)** (*characteristic*) saillant, frappant; **the s. points of an argument** les points forts d'une argumentation **2** *n* (*in trench warfare etc*) saillant *m*
saline ['seɪlaɪn] **1** *adj* (*spring, water*) salin, salé; *Med* **s. drip** goutte-à-goutte *m inv* de solution saline; **s. solution** solution *f* saline **2** *n Med* (*salt solution*) sérum *m* physiologique
salinity [sə'lɪnɪtɪ] *n* salinité *f*
saliva [sə'laɪvə] *n* salive *f*
salivary [sə'laɪvərɪ] *adj* (*glands etc*) salivaire
salivate ['sælɪveɪt] *vi also Fig* saliver
salivation [sælɪ'veɪʃən] *n* salivation *f*
sallow[1] ['sæləʊ] *n* (*willow*) saule *m*
sallow[2] *adj* (*complexion*) jaunâtre
sallowness ['sæləʊnɪs] *n* (*of complexion*) ton *m* jaunâtre
Sally ['sælɪ] *n Br F* **the S. Army** l'Armée *f* du Salut
sally ['sælɪ] *n* **(a)** *Mil* sortie *f*; (*excursion*) excursion *f*, sortie; **his first s. into travel writing** sa première tentative de récit de voyage **(b)** *Old-fashioned* **s. (of wit)** boutade *f*, trait *m* d'esprit
▶ **sally forth, sally out** *vi* **(a)** (*go out*) sortir; *Hum* (*go for walk*) partir en promenade **(b)** *Mil* faire une sortie **(c)** *Lit* (*go out*) sortir; **young students who are now about to s. forth into the world** de jeunes étudiants sur le point de se lancer dans le monde
salmon ['sæmən] **1** *n* **(a)** (*usu inv in pl*) (*fish*) saumon *m*; **s. steak** darne *f* de saumon; **young s.** tacon *m*, saumoneau *m*; **s. ladder** *or* **leap** *or* **pass** échelle *f* à saumon(s); **s. trout** truite *f* saumonée **(b)** (*colour*) **s. (pink)** (rose *m*) saumon *m inv* **2** *adj* (*colour*) **s. (pink)** (rose) saumon *inv*
salmonella [sælmə'nelə] *n* salmonelle *f*; **to have s. (poisoning)** avoir une salmonellose
salon ['sælɒn] *n* **(a)** (*of fashion designer, hairdresser etc*) salon *m*; *Art* **the S.** le Salon; **(beauty) s.** institut *m ou* salon de beauté; **hairdressing s.** salon de coiffure **(b)** *Liter* salon *m* **(c)** (*drawing room*) salon *m*
saloon [sə'lu:n] *n* **(a)** *Am* (*bar*) saloon *m*, bar *m*; **billiard s.** salle *f* de billard; *Am* **s. keeper** patron, -onne de saloon *ou* de bar; *Br* **s. bar** = bar plutôt élégant **(b)** *Naut* (*of steamship*) salon *m*; (*on yacht*) cabine *f* **(c)** *Br Aut* **s. (car)** berline *f*; **two-door s.** coach *m*; **four-door s.** berline
salopettes [sælə'pets] *npl Ski* (*garment*) combinaison *f*
salsa ['sælsə] *n* **(a)** (*chilli sauce*) = sauce *f* piquante à base de tomates, d'oignons et de piment **(b)** *Mus* salsa *f*
salsify ['sælsɪfɪ] *n* (*plant*) salsifis *m*
SALT [sɔ:lt] *n Mil* (*abbr* **Strategic Arms Limitation Talks**) négociations *fpl* SALT; **S. agreements** accords *mpl* SALT
salt[1] [sɔ:lt] **1** *n* **(a)** (*on roads*), *Culin, Ch* sel *m*; **kitchen s.** gros sel; **rock s.** sel gemme; **sea s.** sel marin, sel de mer; **table s.** sel de table; **(bath) salts** sels de bain; *Old-fashioned* **(liver) salts** sels; **to take a story with a pinch** *or* **grain of s.** ne pas prendre une histoire au pied de la lettre; **he's not worth his s.** il ne vaut rien; **any athlete worth his/her s.** n'importe quel(le) athlète digne de ce nom, n'importe quel athlète qui se respecte; *Old-fashioned* **to sit (at table) above/below the s.** être assis au haut bout/au bas bout de la table; *Fig* **to rub s. in sb's wounds** remuer le couteau dans la plaie; *Fig* **the s. of the earth** le sel de la terre; **s. spoon** cuiller *f* à sel; *Hist* **s. tax** gabelle *f*
(b) (*interest*) **to add s. to sth** mettre un peu de sel à qch, mettre du piment à qch
(c) *Naut F* **old s.** vieux loup *m* de mer
2 *adj* **(a)** (*food*) **too s.** trop salé; **s. cod** morue *f* salée
(b) (*rocks, ground*) salifère

salt[2] *vt* **(a)** (*food*) saler **(b)** = **salt down**
▶ **salt away** *vtsep* (*save*) (*money etc*) économiser, mettre en lieu sûr
▶ **salt down** *vtsep* (*preserve with salt*) (*meat, fish etc*) saler
salt beef *n* bœuf *m* salé
saltbox ['sɔ:ltbɒks] *n* boîte *f* à sel; *US* (*house*) = maison *f* à toit penchant (*avec deux étages à l'avant et un étage à l'arrière*)
saltcellar ['sɔ:ltselər] *n* (*for salt*) salière *f*
salted ['sɔ:ltɪd] *adj* (*butter, herring etc*) salé
salt flats *npl* marais *m* salant
salt-free *adj* (*diet etc*) sans sel
saltine ['sɔ:lti:n] *n Am Culin* biscuit *m* salé
saltiness ['sɔ:ltɪnɪs] *n* (*of water etc*) salinité *f*; (*of food etc*) salure *f*
salting ['sɔ:ltɪŋ] *n* (*of meat etc*) (*for preserving*) salaison *f*; (*for flavouring*) salage *m*
salt lake *n* lac *m* salé
salt lick *n* (*stone*) pierre *f* salée; (*ground*) terre *f* salée
salt marsh *n* marais *m* salant
saltmill ['sɔ:ltmɪl] *n* moulin *m* à sel
salt mine *n* mine *f* de sel
salt pan *n* marais *m* salant, salin *m*
saltpetre, *US* **saltpeter** [sɒlt'pi:tər] *n* salpêtre *m*
saltwater ['sɔ:ltwɔ:tər] *adj, attrib* **s. fish** poisson *m* de mer
salt water *n* eau *f* salée
saltworks ['sɔ:ltwɜ:ks] *n* (*for sea salt*) salin *m*; (*for rock salt*) saline *f*; (*salt refinery*) raffinerie *f* de sel
saltwort ['sɔ:ltwɜ:t] *n Bot* **(a)** soude *f*; **prickly s.** kali *m* **(b)** (*salicornia*) salicorne *f*
salty ['sɔ:ltɪ] *adj* **(a)** (*taste, sauce, water etc*) salé **(b)** *F* (*anecdote, book*) piquant; (*licentious*) salé, corsé
salubrious [sə'lu:brɪəs] *n Fml* salubre, sain; *Fig* **one of his less than s. friends** un de ses amis pas très fréquentables
salubriousness [sə'lu:brɪəsnɪs] *n Fml* salubrité *f*
saluki [sə'lu:kɪ] *n* (*dog*) sloughi *m*
salutary ['sæljʊt(ə)rɪ] *adj* salutaire; **to have a s. effect on sb** faire du bien à qn
salutation [sæljʊ'teɪʃən] *n Fml* salutation *f*; (*in letter*) titre *m* de civilité; **in s.** en guise de salut
salute[1] [sə'lu:t] *n Mil, Naut etc* (*gesture*) salut *m*; **to return sb's s.** rendre son salut à qn; **to take the s.** (*at march past*) passer les troupes en revue; **to fire a s.** tirer une salve; **to fire a ten-gun s.** saluer de dix coups
salute[2] **1** *vt* (*person*) saluer; *Lit* **to s. sb's achievements** saluer les exploits de qn; **I s. you** je te tire mon chapeau **2** *vi Mil, Naut* saluer, faire le salut militaire
salvage[1] ['sælvɪdʒ] *n* **(a)** (*salvaging*) (*of ship etc*) sauvetage *m*; (*of waste material*) récupération *f* **(b)** (*objects salvaged*) objets *mpl* sauvés (*après une catastrophe*) **(c)** (*money*) indemnité *f ou* prime *f* de sauvetage; (*paid to salvage tug*) indemnité de remorquage
salvage[2] *vt* (*ship etc*) sauver; (*items from fire etc*) sauver, récupérer; (*car etc*) récupérer; *F* (*dish, essay etc*) rattraper; **to s. something from the ruins of one's career** sauver quelque chose de la faillite qu'a été sa carrière; **salvaged goods** matériel récupéré
salvage company *n* compagnie *f* spécialisée dans le remorquage et le renflouage de navires
salvage tug *n* remorqueur *m* (*pour les sauvetages*)
salvage vessel *n* navire *m* de relevage
salvation [sæl'veɪʃən] *n* salut *m*; **to work out one's own s.** travailler à son (propre) salut; **you've been my s.** vous m'avez sauvé; **beyond s.** irrécupérable
Salvation Army *n* Armée *f* du Salut
salvationist [sæl'veɪʃənɪst] *n* salutiste *mf*
salve[1] [sælv, sɑ:v] *n Pharm* baume *m*, onguent *m*; *Fig* baume
salve[2] [sælv] *vt Fml* adoucir, apaiser; (*conscience*) soulager
salver ['sælvər] *n* (*tray*) plateau *m* (*en argent etc*)
salvia ['sælvɪə] *n* (*plant*) sauge *f* (*ornementale*)
salvo ['sælvəʊ] *n Mil, Naut, Fig* salve *f*; **to fire a s.** tirer une salve; **s. of applause** salve d'applaudissements
SAM [sæm] *n Mil* (*abbr* **surface-to-air missile**) missile *m* sol-air
Samaritan [sə'mærɪt(ə)n] **1** *adj* samaritain **2** *n* Samaritain, -aine; *Bible* **the Good S.** le bon Samaritain; **to be a good S.** se conduire en bon Samaritain; **the Samaritans** (*telephone service*) ≈ SOS *m* Amitié
samba[1] ['sæmbə] *n* (*dance*) samba *f*
samba[2] *vi* danser la samba
sambo ['sæmbəʊ] *n Offensive, Sl* bougnoul *m*
same [seɪm] **1** *adj* même; **at the s. time that …** au moment même où …; **he's the s. age as me** il est du même âge que moi; **in the s. way** de la même façon; **we are going the s. way** nous allons dans la même direction; **do you still feel the s. way?** est-ce que vos sentiments sont toujours les

mêmes?; **she's still the s. (old) Sarah** c'est toujours notre bonne vieille Sarah; **one and the s. thing** une seule et même chose; **the very s. thing** tout à fait *ou* exactement la même chose; **the** *or* **that very s. day** le jour même; **the very s. situation** la même situation exactement; **it is always/it is no longer the s. thing** c'est toujours/ce n'est plus la même chose; **it all amounts** *or* **comes to the s. thing** tout cela revient au même; *F* **it's the s. difference** c'est bonnet blanc et blanc bonnet; **at the s. time** en même temps; (*at once*) à la fois, du même coup; **that s. man is now a millionaire** ce même homme est maintenant millionnaire

2 *pron* **the s.** le même, la même, *pl* les mêmes; *Fml* (*that one*) celui-là même, celle-là même, *pl* ceux-là mêmes, celles-là mêmes; **it's the s. everywhere** c'est la même chose *ou* c'est pareil *ou Fml* il en est de même partout; **it's all the s., it's just the s.** c'est exactement la même chose; *F* c'est tout comme; **if it's all the s. to you** si cela ne vous fait rien, si ça vous est égal; **it's much the s.** c'est à peu près la même chose; **low-alcohol lager just isn't the s.** la bière à faible teneur en alcool, ça n'est tout simplement pareil *ou* pas la même chose; **the house isn't the s. without her** la maison n'est pas pareille sans elle; **he had an accident and he's never been the s. since** il a eu un accident et il n'est plus le même depuis; *F* **(the) s. again?** (*whisky etc*) encore un?; *F* **(the) s. again!** remettez ça!; *F* **s. here!** et moi aussi!, et moi de même!; **a Happy New Year to you! – (the) s. to you!** je vous souhaite une bonne année! – vous de même!; *F* **(the) s. to you, you bastard!** toi pareil, espèce de salaud!; **I would have done the s.** j'aurais fait la même chose *ou* de même, j'aurais agi de la même façon

3 *adv* **the s.** de la même façon; **to think/feel/act the s.** penser/sentir/agir de même; **they taste all the s.** ils ont tous le même goût; **all these houses look the s. to me** je trouve que ces maisons se ressemblent toutes; **all her songs sound the s.** toutes ses chansons se ressemblent; **all the s.** (*nevertheless*) quand même, tout de même; **when I am away things go on just the s.** quand je suis absent tout continue à marcher comme d'habitude

same-day delivery *n Com* livraison *f* le jour même

same-day value *n Banking* valeur *f* jour

sameness ['seɪmnɪs] *n* **(a)** (*being identical*) identité *f*, similitude *f* **(b)** (*monotony*) monotonie *f*

samey ['seɪmɪ] *adj F* monotone

samosa [sə'məʊsə] *n* samosa *m*

samovar ['sæməvɑːr] *n* samovar *m*

sampan ['sæmpæn] *n* (*boat*) sampan(g) *m*

sample¹ ['sɑːmp(ə)l] *n Com etc* (*of cloth etc*) échantillon *m*; (*of ore, blood, urine*) prélèvement *m*; **a s. of one's work** un échantillon de son travail; *Com* **up to s.** pareil *ou* conforme à l'échantillon; *Com* **not up to s.** non conforme à l'échantillon; **to take a s.** faire un prélèvement; **to take a blood s.** faire une prise de sang; **s. book/card** catalogue *m*/carte *f* d'échantillons; **that's a pretty fair s. of his bad temper** c'est un aperçu de son mauvais caractère; *Mktg* **s. survey** enquête *f* par sondage

sample² *vt* (*wine, dish*) goûter à, déguster; (*experience*) essayer

sampler ['sɑːmplər] *n Sewing* = modèle *m* de broderie

sampling ['sɑːmplɪŋ] *n* prélèvement *m ou* prise *f* d'échantillons, échantillonnage *m*; (*of food, wine etc*) dégustation *f*; **s. error** erreur *f* d'échantillonnage; *Com, Ind* **random s.** prélèvement d'échantillons au hasard

samurai ['sæmʊraɪ] *n inv* samouraï *m*

sanatorium, *pl* **-iums, -ia** [sænə'tɔːrɪəm, -ɪəmz, -ɪə] *n* sanatorium *m*

sanctification [sæŋ(k)tɪfɪ'keɪʃən] *n* sanctification *f*

sanctified ['sæŋ(k)tɪfaɪd] *adj* (*person*) sanctifié; (*thing*) consacré

sanctify ['sæŋ(k)tɪfaɪ] *vt* **(a)** (*person, thing*) sanctifier; (*day, land etc*) consacrer **(b) sanctified by time** consacré par le temps

sanctimonious [sæŋ(k)tɪ'məʊnɪəs] *adj* d'une piété suffisante; (*air*) de petit saint; **don't be so s.** ne sois pas si moralisateur

sanctimoniously [sæŋ(k)tɪ'məʊnɪəslɪ] *adv* d'un air de petit saint

sanction¹ ['sæŋ(k)ʃən] *n* **(a)** *Jur* **(punitive) s.** sanction *f* (pénale); *Pol* **to impose (economic) sanctions on a country** prendre des sanctions économiques contre un pays; **accused of sanctions busting** accusé de ne pas respecter des sanctions (*contre un pays, une organisation etc*) **(b)** *Fml* (*consent*) sanction *f*, autorisation *f*; **without their s.** sans leur consentement

sanction² *vt* **(a)** *Jur* (*ratify*) (*law etc*) ratifier **(b)** (*authorize*) sanctionner, autoriser; **sanctioned by usage** consacré par l'usage

sanctity ['sæŋ(k)tɪtɪ] *n* **(a)** *Rel* (*of person, life etc*) sainteté *f* **(b)** (*of land, oath etc*) caractère *m* sacré; (*of private life etc*) inviolabilité *f*

sanctuary ['sæŋ(k)tj(ʊ)ərɪ] *n* **(a)** *Rel* (*place*) sanctuaire *m* **(b)** (*refuge*) sanctuaire *m*, refuge *m*; **to take s.** trouver asile **(c)** (*for birds*) refuge *m*; **wild life s.** réserve *f* zoologique

sanctum ['sæŋ(k)təm] *n Rel, Fig* (*room etc*) sanctuaire *m*

Sanctus ['sæŋ(k)təs] *n Rel, Mus* sanctus *m*

sand¹ [sænd] *n* sable *m*; **the coast offers mile after mile of shining sands** la côte vous offre des kilomètres de sable doré; *Constr, Fig* **to build on s.** bâtir sur le sable; **on the sand(s)** (*on the beach*) sur la plage; (*on sandbank*) sur un banc de sable; *prov* **the sands of time are running out for us** nous n'aurons bientôt plus le temps, le temps qui nous est imparti sera bientôt écoulé

sand² *vt* **(a)** (*with sandpaper*) (*make smoother*) poncer; (*remove paint, varnish from*) décaper au papier de verre **(b)** (*cover with sand*) (*pathway etc*) sabler; (*floor*) répandre du sable sur

▶ **sand down** *vtsep* = **sand² (a)**

sandal ['sænd(ə)l] *n* sandale *f*

sandalwood ['sænd(ə)lwʊd] *n* (bois *m* de) santal *m*

sandbag¹ ['sændbæg] *n Mil etc* sac *m* de sable

sandbag² *vt* **(-gg-) (a)** *Mil* (*building*) protéger avec des sacs de sable **(b)** (*hit*) assommer (*d'un coup de gourdin sur la nuque*)

sandbank ['sændbæŋk] *n* banc *m* de sable

sand bar *n* ensablement *m* (*à l'embouchure d'un fleuve*)

sandblast ['sændblɑːst] *vt* décaper au jet de sable, sabler

sandblasting ['sændblɑːstɪŋ] *n* (*of surface*) décapage *m ou* décapement *m* au (jet de) sable

sandboy ['sændbɔɪ] *n* **as happy as a s.** gai comme un pinson, heureux comme un poisson dans l'eau

sand castle *n* château *m* de sable

sand dune *n* dune *f*

sand eel *n* lançon *m*

sander ['sændər] *n* (*tool*) ponceuse *f*

sand flea *n* puce *f* pénétrante, chique *f*; (*crustacean*) puce de mer

sandglass ['sændglɑːs] *n* sablier *m*

sand hopper *n* (*crustacean*) puce *f* de mer

Sandhurst ['sændhɜːst] *n Br Mil* = Saint-Cyr

sanding ['sændɪŋ] *n* **(a)** (*with sandpaper*) (*smoothing*) ponçage *m*; (*removal of paint, varnish*) décapage *m* au papier de verre; **s. disc** disque *m* en papier de verre **(b)** (*spreading of sand*) sablage *m*

sanding down *n* = **sanding (a)**

sandman ['sændmæn] *n Fig* marchand *m* de sable

sand martin *n* (*bird*) hirondelle *f* de rivage

sandpaper¹ ['sændpeɪpər] *n* papier *m* de verre

sandpaper² *vt* frotter *ou* poncer au papier de verre

sandpiper ['sændpaɪpər] *n* (*bird*) bécasseau *m*

sandpit ['sændpɪt] *n* sablière *f*, sablonnière *f*, carrière *f* de sable; (*for children*) bac *m* à sable

sandshoes ['sændʃuːz] *npl Br* rythmiques *fpl*

sandstone ['sændstəʊn] *n* grès *m*; **s. buildings** bâtiments en grès

sandstorm ['sændstɔːm] *n* tempête *f* de sable

sand trap *n Am Golf* bunker *m*

sandwich¹ ['sændwɪtʃ] *n* sandwich *m*, *pl* sandwichs, sandwiches; **ham/cheese s.** sandwich au jambon/fromage; **open s.** canapé *m*; *US* **hero** *or* **submarine s.** gros sandwich coupé dans une baguette; *Culin* **s. (cake)** génoise *f* fourrée; **s. filling** garniture *f*; **s. loaf** pain *m* de mie

sandwich² *vt* intercaler **(between** entre), *F* coincer **(between** entre); **to be sandwiched between two people** être coincé entre *ou F* pris en sandwich entre deux personnes

sandwich bar *n* sandwicherie *f*

sandwich board *n* panneau *m* (*que porte l'homme-sandwich*)

sandwich course *n Sch* cours *m* comprenant des stages

Sandwich Islands *n* îles *fpl* Sandwich

sandwich man *n* homme-sandwich *m*, *pl* hommes-sandwiches

sandy ['sændɪ] *adj* **(a)** (*earth etc*) sableux, sablonneux; (*path*) sablonneux, de sable; **s. beach** plage de sable; **are the beaches s.?** est-ce que ce sont des plages de sable?; *Naut* **s. bottom** fond de sable; **my hair is all s.** (*full of sand*) mes cheveux sont pleins de sable **(b)** (*in colour*) (*hair etc*) roux pâle *inv*, blond roux *inv*

sane [seɪn] *adj* (*person*) sain d'esprit; (*views, speech etc*) raisonnable, sensé; **to be s.** (*of person*) avoir toute sa raison

sanely ['seɪnlɪ] *adv* raisonnablement; **he spoke quite s.** il a dit des choses très sensées

sang *see* sing
sang-froid [sɒŋ'frwɑː] *n* sang-froid *m*
sanguinary ['sæŋgwɪnərɪ] *adj Lit* (*battle*) sanglant; (*tyrant*) sanguinaire
sanguine ['sæŋgwɪn] *adj Lit* **(a)** (*complexion etc*) d'un rouge sanguin, rubicond **(b)** (*temperament*) sanguin; (*person, disposition etc*) confiant, optimiste (**about** quant à); **to be of a s. disposition** être porté à l'optimisme
sanguinely ['sæŋgwɪnlɪ] *adv* avec confiance, avec optimisme
sanitarium [sænɪ'teərɪəm] *n Am* = **sanatorium**
sanitary ['sænɪt(ə)rɪ] *adj* hygiénique, sanitaire; **s. disposal bag** sachet *m* pour garniture périodique; **s. engineer** technicien *m* en équipement sanitaire; **s. inspector** inspecteur, -trice de la salubrité publique; **s. towel,** *Am* **s. napkin** *or* **pad** serviette *f* hygiénique; **s. ware** équipement *m* de salle de bain
sanitation [sænɪ'teɪʃən] *n* (*system*) système *m* sanitaire; **the s. here is appalling** les conditions sanitaires ici sont affreuses; **there's no s. in the camps** il n'y a pas d'installations sanitaires dans les camps
sanitize ['sænɪtaɪz] *vt esp Am* (*clean*) aseptiser; (*sterilize*) stériliser; *Fig* (*document, novel etc*) expurger; **sanitized label** (*on toilet*) bandelette *f* de propreté pour WC
sanity ['sænɪtɪ] *n* **(a)** (*of person*) santé *f* mentale; **there are doubts about his s.** on se demande s'il est sain d'esprit **(b)** (*of plan, policy etc*) bon sens *m*
sanserif [sæn'serɪf] *Typ* **1** *n* sanserif **2** *adj* sanserif, sans empattement, sans patte
Sanskrit ['sænskrɪt] *adj, n Ling* sanscrit *m*, sanskrit *m*
Santa (Claus) ['sæntə(klɔːz)] *n* le Père Noël
sap[1] [sæp] *n* **(a)** (*of plant*) sève *f*; **the s. is rising** la sève monte; *Fig* **to feel the s. rising** être tout ragaillardi **(b)** *F* (*gullible person*) niguedouille *f*; (*idiot*) andouille *f*
sap[2] *n Mil etc* (*trench*) sape *f*
sap[3] *n Am* (*cosh*) gourdin *m*
sap[4] *vt* **(-pp-)** *Mil, Fig* saper, miner; **the fever has sapped (him of) his strength** la fièvre l'a miné
saphead ['sæphed] *n Am F* andouille *f*
sapless ['sæplɪs] *adj* (*plant, wood*) sans sève, desséché
sapling ['sæplɪŋ] *n* (*young tree*) jeune arbre *m*
sapper ['sæpər] *n Mil* sapeur *m*; (*in charge of laying mines*) mineur *m*; *F* **the sappers** le génie
sapphic ['sæfɪk] *adj* (*in prosody*) saphique; *Lit* (*lesbian*) saphique; *Old-fashioned* **s. vice** saphisme *m*
sapphire ['sæfaɪər] **1** *n* **(a)** (*precious stone*) saphir *m* **(b)** (*colour*) (couleur *f* de) saphir *m* **2** *adj* (*in colour*) (couleur de) saphir *inv*
sappiness ['sæpɪnɪs] *n* (*of tree etc*) abondance *f* de sève, teneur *f* en sève
sappy ['sæpɪ] *adj* **(a)** (*tree etc*) plein de sève; (*timber*) vert **(b)** *Old-fashioned F* (*stupid*) bête, stupide
saraband ['særəbænd] *n* (*dance, music*) sarabande *f*
Saracen ['særəs(ə)n] *Hist* **1** *adj* sarrasin **2** *n* Sarrasin, -ine
sarcasm ['sɑːkæz(ə)m] *n* (*characteristic, remark*) sarcasme *m*; **his constant s.** ses sarcasmes continuels
sarcastic [sɑː'kæstɪk] *adj* sarcastique; **s. remark** sarcasme *m*, remarque *f* sarcastique
sarcastically [sɑː'kæstɪklɪ] *adv* d'une manière sarcastique
sarcoma [sɑː'kəʊmə] *n Med* sarcome *m*
sarcophagus, *pl* **-phagi** [sɑː'kɒfəgəs, -fədʒaɪ] *n* sarcophage *m*
sardine [sɑː'diːn] *n* (*fish*) sardine *f*; **the passengers were packed in like sardines** les passagers étaient serrés comme des sardines; **s. boat** sardinier *m*
Sardinia [sɑː'dɪnɪə] *n* Sardaigne *f*
Sardinian [sɑː'dɪnɪən] **1** *adj* sarde **2** *n* **(a)** Sarde *mf* **(b)** *Ling* sarde *m*
sardonic [sɑː'dɒnɪk] *adj* (*expression, laugh*) sardonique
sardonically [sɑː'dɒnɪklɪ] *adv* d'une manière sardonique, sardoniquement
sarge [sɑːdʒ] *n Mil F* sergent *m*
sari ['sɑːrɪ] *n* (*garment*) sari *m*
Sark [sɑːk] *n* (île *f* de) Sercq
sarky ['sɑːkɪ] *adj F* sarcastique
sarnie ['sɑːnɪ] *n Br F* casse-croûte *m inv*
sarong [sə'rɒŋ] *n* (*garment*) sarong *m*
sarsaparilla [sɑːsəpə'rɪlə] *n* (*plant*) salsepareille *f*; (*drink*) boisson *f* à la salsepareille
sartorial [sɑː'tɔːrɪəl] *adj Fml* (*matters, taste*) vestimentaire; (*trade*) de tailleur; **s. elegance** élégance *f* vestimentaire; *F* **he is a s. disaster area** il n'a aucun sens de l'élégance vestimentaire
SAS [eseɪ'es] *n Br Mil* (*abbr* **special air service**) ≈ GIGN *m*
sash[1] [sæʃ] *n* (*on dress*) large ceinture *f* à nœud bouffant; (*worn by officer*) écharpe *f*
sash[2] *n Constr* (*of window*) châssis *m* mobile; **s. window** fenêtre *f* à guillotine
sashay ['sæʃeɪ] *vi Am F* **he sashayed across to the bar** (*walked affectedly*) il s'est approché du bar avec une nonchalance affectée; **I'll just s. down to Joe's place** (*go*) je vais juste faire un tour chez Joe
sashcord ['sæʃkɔːd] *n* corde *f* de fenêtre
sashimi ['sæʃɪmɪ] *n* sashimi *m*
Sask *abbr* **Saskatchewan**
sasquatch ['sæskwætʃ] *n* = géant *m* des légendes du Nord-Ouest des États-Unis et du Sud-Ouest du Canada
sass [sæs] *vt US F* (*be insolent to*) répondre à
Sassenach ['sæsənæk] *Scot Hum or Pej* **1** *n* Anglais, -aise **2** *adj* anglais
sassy ['sæsɪ] *adj US F* effronté, insolent
sat *see* **sit**
Satan ['seɪt(ə)n] *n* Satan *m*
satanic [sə'tænɪk] *adj* satanique, diabolique
satanically [sə'tænɪklɪ] *adv* sataniquement, diaboliquement
satanism ['seɪtənɪz(ə)m] *n* satanisme *m*
satanist ['seɪtənɪst] *n* sataniste *mf*
satchel ['sætʃəl] *n* sacoche *f*; *Sch* cartable *m*
sate [seɪt] *vt* **(a)** *Fml* (*hunger*) rassasier, assouvir; (*desire etc*) assouvir; (*person*) rassasier **(b)** = **satiate**
sateen [sə'tiːn] *n Tex* satinette *f*, satin *m* de coton
satellite ['sætəlaɪt] *n* **(a)** (*natural, manmade*) satellite *m*; **artificial s.** satellite artificiel; **manned/unmanned s.** satellite habité/non habité; **(tele)communications s.** satellite de télécommunications; **meteorological** *or* **weather s.** satellite météorologique; **to watch sth on s. (TV)** regarder qch sur (une chaîne de télévision) satellite; **s. antenna** antenne *f* satellite; **s. communication system** système *m* de communication par satellite; *TV* **s. dish** antenne *f* parabolique; **s. link** liaison *f* par satellite; **s. picture** *Phot* photo *f* satellite; *Met* animation *f* satellite; **s. station** station *f* satellite; *TV* **s. television** télévision *f* par satellite; **s. transmission** transmission *f* par satellite; **s. transponder** transpondeur *m* satellite; **s. up-link** liaison *f* par satellite
(b) s. (state) (état *m*) satellite *m*; **s. (town)** ville *f* satellite
satiate ['seɪʃɪeɪt] *vt Fml* rassasier (**with** de)
satiated ['seɪʃɪeɪtɪd] *adj Fml* (*with food*) rassasié; (*with pleasure*) comblé
satiation [seɪʃɪ'eɪʃən] *n Fml* **(a)** (*process*) assouvissement *m* **(b)** (*state*) satiété *f*; **to reach (a point of) s.** (*when eating, drinking*) être rassasié; **to eat until one has reached (a point of) s.** manger à satiété
satiety [sə'taɪɪtɪ] *n* = **satiation (b)**
satin ['sætɪn] *n Tex* satin *m*; **s. finish** (*of paper etc*) apprêt *m* satiné; **s. flower** stellaire *f*; **s. paper** papier *m* satiné
satinette [sætɪ'net] *n Tex* satinette *f*
satire ['sætaɪər] *n* satire *f*; **a s. on sth** une satire de qch
satirical [sə'tɪrɪk(ə)l] *adj* satirique
satirically [sə'tɪrɪklɪ] *adv* satiriquement
satirist ['sætɪrɪst] *n* (*writer*) satiriste *mf*; (*comedian*) chansonnier *m*, comédien, -ienne satirique
satirize ['sætɪraɪz] *vt* faire la satire de; (*in literature*) satiriser
satisfaction [sætɪs'fækʃən] *n* **(a)** (*pleasure*) satisfaction *f*, contentement *m* (**at, with** de); **to have the s. of doing sth** avoir la satisfaction de faire qch; **it gives me great s. to know that ...** je suis très satisfait d'apprendre que ...; **to one's complete s.** à sa satisfaction totale; **s. or your money back** remboursement garanti; *Com* **s. guaranteed** satisfaction garantie **(b)** (*act*) (*of creditor*) désintéressement *m*; (*of condition*) accomplissement *m*; (*of hunger, desire*) assouvissement *m*; **to demand s.** (*in duel*) demander réparation
satisfactorily [sætɪs'fækt(ə)rɪlɪ] *adv* de manière *ou* de façon satisfaisante
satisfactory [sætɪs'fækt(ə)rɪ] *adj* satisfaisant; (*pupil*) qui donne satisfaction; **the result is not very s.** le résultat n'est pas très satisfaisant *ou* laisse à désirer; **to bring negotiations to a s. conclusion** mener à bien des négociations; *Med* **the patient is s.** *or* **in a s. condition** l'état du malade est satisfaisant
satisfied ['sætɪsfaɪd] *adj* (*customer etc*) content, satisfait (**with** de); *Iron* **not s. with that she then broke the other chair** comme ça ne lui suffisait pas, elle a cassé l'autre chaise
satisfy ['sætɪsfaɪ] *vt* **(a)** (*make happy*) satisfaire, contenter; *Sch* **to s. the examiners** (*of examinee*) être reçu à l'examen; **(in order) to s. your curiosity** pour satisfaire votre curiosité **(b)** (*convince*) convaincre, assurer; **I am satisfied that he was telling the truth** je suis convaincu *ou* persuadé *ou* sûr qu'il disait la vérité **(c)** (*creditors*) désintéresser; (*condition*) remplir; *Math* (*equation*) satisfaire à; (*sb's honour*) faire réparation à, satisfaire à; **to s. demand** satisfaire à la demande
satsuma [sæt'suːmə] *n* satsuma *f*
saturate ['sætʃəreɪt] *vt* **(a)** (*soak*) imprégner, saturer (**with** de)

(**b**) *Ch, Phys* (*solution*) saturer; *Com* **to s. the market** saturer le marché

saturated ['sætʃəreɪtɪd] *adj* (**a**) (*ground, clothing etc*) détrempé, saturé d'eau; **to become s. with sth** s'imprégner de qch; *Fig* être saturé de qch; *Com* **the market is s.** le marché est saturé (**b**) *Ch, Phys* (*solution, compound etc*) saturé, intense; **s. fat** graisse *f* saturée (**c**) (*colour*) saturé, intense

saturation [sætʃə'reɪʃən] *n* imprégnation *f*, saturation *f*; *Ch, Phys* saturation; **the media's s. coverage of the affair** la couverture médiatique outrancière de l'affaire; *Mil* **s. bombing** bombardement *m* en masse; **s. point** point *m* de saturation; **the market has reached s. point** le marché est saturé, le marché est arrivé à saturation

Saturday ['sætədɪ] *n* samedi *m* [①A75-6, B-C; B58-9, B-C] **he's coming on S.** il vient samedi; **he comes on Saturdays** il vient le samedi; **he comes every S.** il vient tous les samedis

Saturn ['sætɜːn] *n Astron* Saturne *f*; *Myth* Saturne *m*

saturnalia [sætə'neɪlɪə] *n* saturnales *fpl*

saturnine ['sætənaɪn] *adj Lit* (*gloomy*) taciturne, sombre

saturnism ['sætənɪz(ə)m] *n Med* saturnisme *m*

satyr ['sætər] *n Myth etc* satyre *m*

sauce [sɔːs] *n* (**a**) *Culin* sauce *f*; **tomato s.** sauce tomate; **white s.** sauce blanche *ou* béchamel; **caper s.** sauce aux câpres; *Prov* **what's s. for the goose is s. for the gander** ce qui est bon pour l'un l'est aussi pour l'autre; **s. boat** saucière *f* (**b**) *Old-fashioned, F* (*impudence*) culot *m*, toupet *m*

saucepan ['sɔːspən] *n* casserole *f*; **double s.** bain-marie *m*, *pl* bains-marie; **s. lid** couvercle *m* de casserole

saucer ['sɔːsər] *n* soucoupe *f*; **flying s.** soucoupe volante; *F* **eyes like saucers** yeux comme des soucoupes

saucily ['sɔːsɪlɪ] *adv F* (*in risqué manner*) d'un air coquin

sauciness ['sɔːsɪnɪs] *n F* (**a**) (*impertinence*) impertinence *f* (**b**) (*risqué quality*) (*of joke, nightdress etc*) côté *m* coquin

saucy ['sɔːsɪ] *adj F* (**a**) (*impertinent*) impertinent, effronté (**b**) (*risqué*) (*person, joke, nightdress etc*) coquin; *Old-fashioned* **s. little hat** petit chapeau coquet

Saudi ['saʊdɪ] **1** *adj* saoudien **2** *n F* (**a**) (*person*) Saoudien, -ienne (**b**) (*country*) Arabie *f* séoudite *ou* saoudite

Saudi Arabia *n* Arabie *f* saoudite

Saudi Arabian 1 *n* Saoudien, -ienne **2** *adj* saoudien

sauerkraut ['saʊəkraʊt] *n* choucroute *f*

sauna ['sɔːnə] *n* sauna *m*

saunter[1] ['sɔːntər] *n* balade *f*; **to go for a s. in the park** aller se balader dans le parc; **at a s.** (*to arrive*) tranquillement

saunter[2] *vi* **to s. (along)** se balader; **to s. along** *or* **down the street** descendre la rue en flânant; **to s. up to sb** s'approcher de qn tranquillement; **she sauntered in, half an hour late** elle est arrivée tranquillement, une demi-heure en retard; **she sauntered past as if nothing had happened** elle est passée d'un pas tranquille comme s'il ne s'était rien passé

saurian ['sɔːrɪən] *adj, n* (*reptile*) saurien *m*

sausage ['sɒsɪdʒ] *n Culin* (*fresh*) saucisse *f*; (*preserved, hard, dry*) saucisson *m*; *Br Fig, F* **not a s.** que dalle; **I was left without a s.** il ne me restait que dalle; *F, Hum* **you silly old s. you!** que tu es bête *ou* nigaud!; *F* **s. dog** saucisse *f* à pattes, teckel *m*; *Br* **s. roll** ≈ friand *m*; **s. skin** boyau *m*

sausagemeat ['sɒsɪdʒmiːt] *n* chair *f* à saucisse

sauté[1] ['səʊteɪ] **1** *adj* sauté; **s. potatoes** pommes de terre sautées **2** *n* sauté *m*

sauté[2] *vt* (faire) sauter

sautéed ['səʊteɪd] *adj* sauté

savage[1] ['sævɪdʒ] **1** *adj* (**a**) (*fierce*) (*animal, criticism*) féroce; (*blow*) brutal, féroce; (*person*) enragé; **to make a s. attack on sb** attaquer sauvagement qn (**b**) (*primitive*) (*people, custom etc*) sauvage, barbare **2** *n* sauvage *mf*

savage[2] *vt* (**a**) (*attack physically*) (*of animal*) attaquer sauvagement (**b**) (*criticize*) (*person, play*) éreinter; (*proposal, plan*) critiquer violemment

savagely ['sævɪdʒlɪ] *adv* (*to beat, attack*) sauvagement, férocement; (*to criticize*) violemment

savageness ['sævɪdʒnɪs], **savagery** ['sævɪdʒ(ə)rɪ] *n* (*fierceness*) (*of animal, blow, attack, criticism*) férocité *f*

savanna(h) [sə'vænə] *n* savane *f*

save[1] [seɪv] *n Fb* arrêt *m*; **to make a s.** arrêter la balle

save[2] **1** *vt* (**a**) (*rescue*) (*person, animal*) sauver; **to s. sb's life** sauver la vie à *ou* de qn; *Fig* **she can't run to s. her life** elle est incapable de courir; *Fig* **to s. one's (own) neck** *or* **skin** sauver sa peau; **the doctors could not s. him** les médecins n'ont pas pu le sauver; **to s. sb from falling** empêcher qn de tomber; **this saved us from financial disaster** ça nous a sauvé d'une catastrophe financière; *Fb etc* **to s. a goal** arrêter le ballon; *Sp* **to s. the game** sauver le match; **to s. the situation** sauver la situation; *Rel* **to s. one's soul** sauver son âme; **to s. sth from a fire** récupérer qch des décombres d'un incendie; **God s. the King/the Queen!** vive le Roi/la Reine!

(**b**) (*keep for future*) (*old jars, old wrapping paper etc*) garder, mettre de côté; (*money*) économiser, épargner, mettre de côté; (*collect*) (*stamps, cigarette coupons, petrol vouchers etc*) collectionner; **I'm saving this one for later** je garde celui-ci pour plus tard; **to s. oneself for sth** se réserver pour qch; **s. a dance for me** réservez-moi une danse

(**c**) (*not waste*) (*money, work etc*) économiser; (*expenditure, effort*) éviter; (*space*) gagner; **to s. time** gagner du temps, économiser du temps; **I am saving my strength** je me ménage, je ménage mes forces; **I might as well have saved my breath** j'aurais mieux fait d'économiser ma salive; **I saved £10 by buying it there** j'ai économisé dix livres en l'achetant là; **s. pounds on washing machines** faites des économies sur l'achat d'une machine à laver

(**d**) (*spare*) **to s. sb sth** éviter *ou* épargner qch à qn; **this has saved him a great deal of expense/trouble** cela lui a évité *ou* épargné beaucoup de dépense/peine; **this will s. us having to do it again** ça nous évitera de devoir le refaire; **to s. sb the trouble of doing sth** éviter *ou* épargner à qn la peine de faire qch; **to s. sb from sth** épargner qch à qn; **to s. sb from doing sth** épargner à qn la peine de faire qch

(**e**) *Comptr* sauvegarder; **to s. sth to disk** sauvegarder qch sur une disquette; **s. command** commande *f* de sauvegarde; **s. as command** article *m* 'enregistrer sous'

2 *vi* (*save money*) économiser, épargner; **I've never been able to s.** je n'ai jamais pu économiser *ou* épargner; **they are saving for their holiday/a new car** ils économisent pour leurs vacances/pour acheter une voiture neuve; **s. on heating costs by insulating your house** économisez sur vos frais de chauffage en isolant votre maison

save[3] *Arch, Lit* **1** *prep* sauf, excepté, à l'exception de **2** *conj* **s. that ...** sauf que ..., excepté que ...

▶ **save up 1** *vi* (*save money*) économiser, faire des économies **(for** pour**)**; **we're saving up to go to Canada/buy a fridge** nous économisons pour aller au Canada/pour acheter un réfrigérateur **2** *vtsep* (*keep for future*) (*money etc*) économiser, mettre de côté; (*collect*) (*stamps, petrol vouchers etc*) collectionner

save-as-you-earn *adj Br Fin* **s. scheme** = plan *m* d'épargne à contributions mensuelles produisant des intérêts exonérés d'impôts

saveloy ['sævəlɔɪ] *n Culin* cervelas *m*

saver ['seɪvər] *n* (*person who saves money*) épargnant, -ante

saving[1] ['seɪvɪŋ] **1** *adj* (*redeeming*) **her/its s. grace** ce qui la/le rachète

2 *n* (**a**) (*rescue*) (*of lives etc*) sauvetage *m*; (*of person, souls*) salut *m*; **this was the s. of him** cela a été son salut

(**b**) (*act of saving money*) économie *f*, épargne *f*; **savings** économies; *Econ* dépôts *mpl* d'épargne; **to live on one's savings** vivre de ses économies; **to make savings** faire des économies; *US* **savings and loan association** caisse *f* d'épargne-logement; **(National) Savings Bank** ≈ Caisse *f* (Nationale) d'Épargne; **(national) savings certificate** ≈ bon *m* d'Épargne; **savings club** club *m* d'épargne; **savings plan** plan *m* d'épargne; *Fin* **savings scheme** plan *m* d'épargne

(**c**) *Comptr* sauvegarde *f*

saving[2] *Arch, Lit* **1** *conj* = **save[3]** 2 **2** *prep* sauf; **s. your presence** sauf votre respect

savings account *n* compte *m* d'épargne

saviour, *US* **savior** ['seɪvjər] *n* sauveur *m*; *Rel* **Our S.** Notre Sauveur

savory ['seɪvərɪ] *n Bot, Culin* sarriette *f*

savour[1], *US* **savor** ['seɪvər] *n* saveur *f*, goût *m*

savour[2], *US* **savor 1** *vt* (*success, moment etc*) savourer **2** *vi* (*of thing*) **to s. of sth** sentir qch; **the whole affair savours of corruption** tout cela sent la corruption

savoury, *US* **savory** ['seɪvərɪ] **1** *adj* (**a**) (*appetizing*) (*taste, dish*) savoureux, appétissant; **he looked even less s. than the other tramps** il avait l'air encore plus repoussant que les autres clochards; **he doesn't have a very s. reputation** il a une sale réputation (**b**) *Culin* (*not sweet*) (*dish*) salé; **s. omelette** omelette salée **2** *n Culin* (*hors d'œuvre*) hors d'œuvre *m inv* (*chaud ou froid*); (*course*) entremets *m* salé

Savoy [sə'vɔɪ] *n* (**a**) *Geog* Savoie *f* (**b**) **s. (cabbage)** chou *m* frisé de Milan, *pl* choux

savvy[1] ['sævɪ] *n Sl* (*common sense*) jugeote *f*

savvy[2] *vt Sl* piger; **s.?** tu piges?

saw[1] [sɔː] *n* (*tool*) scie *f*; **metal s.** scie à métaux; **circular s.** scie circulaire; **s. blade** lame *f* de scie; **s. cut** trait *m* de scie; **s. tooth** dent *f* de scie

saw² *vt* (*pt* **sawed** [sɔːd] ; *pp* **sawn** [sɔːn], **sawed**) scier

saw³ *n Lit* (*saying*) adage *m*, dicton *m*

saw⁴ *see* **see¹**

▶ **saw off** *vtsep* couper *ou* enlever à la scie

▶ **saw up** *vtsep* (*wood*) débiter

sawbones ['sɔːbəʊnz] *n Old-fashioned F* chirurgien *m*

sawbuck ['sɔːbʌk] *n Am* **(a)** = **sawhorse** **(b)** *F* (*ten-dollar bill*) billet *m* de dix dollars

sawdust ['sɔːdʌst] *n* sciure *f* (de bois)

sawfish ['sɔːfɪʃ] *n* poisson-scie *m*, *pl* poissons-scies

sawhorse ['sɔːhɔːs] *n Carp* chevalet *m* de sciage, chèvre *f*

sawing ['sɔːɪŋ] *n* (*of wood*) sciage *m*

sawing up *n* (*of wood*) débitage *m*

sawmill ['sɔːmɪl] *n* scierie *f*

sawn-off ['sɔːnɒf] *adj* **s. shotgun** carabine *f* à canon scié

sawyer ['sɔːjər] *n* scieur *m* (de long)

sax [sæks] *n Mus F* saxo *m*; **s. player** saxophoniste *mf*

saxifrage ['sæksɪfreɪdʒ] *n* (*plant*) saxifrage *f*

Saxon ['sæks(ə)n] **1** *adj* saxon **2** *n* **(a)** Saxon, -onne **(b)** *Ling* saxon *m*

Saxony ['sæksənɪ] *n* Saxe *f*

saxophone ['sæksəfəʊn] *n Mus* saxophone *m*

saxophonist [sæk'sɒfənɪst] *n Mus* saxophoniste *mf*

say¹ [seɪ] *n* **to have one's s.** dire ce qu'on a à dire; **to have a s. in a discussion** avoir son mot à dire dans un débat; **let me have my s.** laissez-moi parler; **I have no s. in the matter** je n'ai pas voix au chapitre

say² (*pt, pp* **said** [sed]; *3rd sing pr* **says** [sez]) **1** *vt* **(a)** [①A73,viii] (*utter*) dire; **to s. sth to sb** dire qch à qn; **to s. sth again** répéter qch, redire qch; **to s. hello/goodbye (to sb)** dire bonjour/au revoir (à qn); **s. hello to her from me** dis-lui bonjour de ma part; **to s. goodbye to one's chances of winning** dire adieu à ses chances de gagner; **to s. yes/no to an offer** accepter/refuser une offre; *F* **I wouldn't s. no to a glass of beer** je boirais bien *ou* volontiers un verre de bière; **to s. a word** dire un mot; **you have only to s. the word** vous n'avez qu'un mot à dire; **I didn't s. a word** je n'ai pas dit un mot; **it's for him/not for him to s.** c'est/ce n'est pas à lui de décider; *Tel* **who shall I s. is calling?** c'est de la part de qui?; **why he did it I can't** *or* **couldn't s.** (*I have no idea*) je ne sais pas pourquoi il l'a fait; **I can't s.** (*I'm not allowed to tell you*) je ne peux pas le dire; **there's no saying what might happen if …** on ne sait pas ce qui pourrait se passer si …; **it goes without saying that …** il va de soi *ou* cela va sans dire que …; **what did you s.?** (*repeat what you said*) pardon?, qu'avez-vous dit?; **whatever he may s.** quoi qu'il en dise; **what do you s. to a drink?** ça te dit de prendre un verre?; **good morning, she said** bonjour, dit-elle; **he said that you were here** il a dit que vous étiez ici; **as I said in my letter** comme je l'ai dit dans ma lettre; **the Bible says** *or* **it says in the Bible that …** comme il est écrit dans la Bible …; **it says in the newspaper that …** on dit dans le journal que …; **the church clock says ten** le cadran de l'église marque dix heures; **what does your watch s.?** quelle heure est-il à ta montre?; **the sign said ten more kilometres** la pancarte indiquait qu'il restait dix kilomètres; **let it be said** soit dit en passant; **you don't mean to s. he's 86** vous n'allez pas me dire qu'il a 86 ans; **one might as well s. …** autant dire …; **I must s. that …** j'avoue que …, je dois dire que …; **it has to** *or* **must be said** il faut le dire; **that is to s.** c'est-à-dire; **have you said anything about it to him?** est-ce que vous lui en avez parlé?; **the less said the better** moins nous parlerons, mieux cela vaudra; **to s. nothing of …** et je ne parle pas de …; **getting there will be difficult enough to s. nothing of getting home again** se rendre là-bas va déjà être assez difficile alors je ne parle pas de revenir ici; **he has very little to s. for himself** il est peu communicatif; **what have you got to s. for yourself?** eh bien, expliquez-vous!; **there's a lot to be said for it** c'est une bonne idée; **there is little/much to be said for beginning now** on n'a pas/on a intérêt à commencer dès maintenant; **you're honest, I'll s. that for you** je dirais en votre faveur que vous êtes honnête; **the way you dress says something about you as a person** la manière dont les gens s'habillent est révélatrice de leur personnalité; **his response says a lot about …** sa réponse en dit long sur …; **don't s. you've forgotten already!** ne (me) dis pas que tu as déjà oublié!; *F* **you don't s. (so)!** pas possible!, ça alors!; **you can s. that again!, you said it!** vous l'avez dit!, comme vous dites!; **need I s. more?** est-il besoin d'en dire davantage?; **they s. that …, it is said that …** on dit que …, on prétend que …; **I've heard it said that …** j'ai entendu dire que …; **he is said to be rich, they s. he is rich** on le dit riche, on dit qu'il est riche; **what do you s., Amanda, should we go?** qu'en penses-tu Amanda, on y va?; **what do you s. to that?** qu'en dites-vous *ou* pensez-vous?; **is he stupid? – I wouldn't s. that** est-ce qu'il est bête? – je n'irais pas jusque-là; **on the whole I should s. not** dans l'ensemble, je ne crois pas *ou* je crois que non; **it is difficult to s. (when/where/which)** il est difficile de dire (quand/où/quel); **didn't I s. so!** je vous l'avais bien dit!; **I should s. so!** et comment donc!; **what did I s.?** (*I was right*) qu'est-ce que j'avais dit?; **let us** *or* **shall we** *or* **shall I s.** disons; **if I had, s., £100,000 to spend** si j'avais, mettons *ou* disons, 100 000 livres à dépenser; **other countries such as Germany, s. or France** d'autres pays comme par exemple l'Allemagne ou la France; **she didn't accept their offer – I should s. not!** elle n'a pas accepté leur offre – il ne manquerait plus que ça!

(b) (*recite*) (*prayer etc*) dire; **to s. one's prayers** dire *ou* faire ses prières; **to s. mass** dire la messe

2 *vi* **I'm not saying** je ne dis rien; *F* **says you!** que tu dis!; **I mean to s.!** tout de même!, quand même!; **as they s., as people s.** comme on dit; **as one might s.** comme qui dirait; *F* **s., I've got an idea** dites donc, j'ai une idée; *Old-fashioned Br* **I s.!**, *Am* **s.!** (*exclamatory*) dites donc!; *Old-fashioned Br* **I s.!** (*expressing surprise*) pas possible!, fichtre!; **I'll s.!** et comment donc!

SAYE [eseɪwaɪ'iː] *n Br Fin* (*abbr* **save-as-you-earn**) = plan *m* d'épargne à contributions mensuelles produisant des intérêts exonérés d'impôts

saying ['seɪɪŋ] *n* proverbe *m*, dicton *m*; **as the s. goes** (*according to the proverb*) comme dit le proverbe

say-so *n F* (*permission*) permission *f*; **I can't do it without her s.** je ne peux pas le faire sans sa permission; **on sb's s.** avec la permission de qn

SC [es'siː] (*abbr* **South Carolina**) Caroline *f* du Sud

scab¹ [skæb] *n* **(a)** (*on wound*) croûte *f* **(b)** *Vet* (*disease*) gale *f* **(c)** *Ind Sl* (*person*) jaune *m*, briseur, -euse de grève; **s. labour** des briseurs de grève; **s. miner** mineur qui ne fait pas grève

scab² *vi* **(-bb-)** **(a)** (*of wound*) former une croûte **(b)** *Ind Sl* (*replace strikers*) remplacer les grévistes; (*betray workmates*) trahir ses camarades

▶ **scab over** *vi* = **scab² (a)**

scabbard ['skæbəd] *n* (*for sword*) fourreau *m*; (*for dagger*) gaine *f*

scabby ['skæbɪ] *adj* **(a)** *Vet* (*sheep etc*) galeux **(b)** (*sore etc*) croûteux, scabieux **(c)** *F* (*contemptible*) (*behaviour etc*) dégoûtant **(d)** *F* (*grotty*) (*coat, room etc*) pouilleux, -euse

scabies ['skeɪbiːz] *n Med* gale *f*

scabious ['skeɪbɪəs] *n* (*plant*) scabieuse *f*

scabrous ['skeɪbrəs] *adj* **(a)** (*surface etc*) rugueux, raboteux **(b)** (*topic, tale etc*) scabreux, risqué

scads [skædz] *npl Am F* des tas (**of** de)

scaffold ['skæf(ə)ld] *n* **(a)** (*for execution*) échafaud *m*; **to go to the s.** monter à *ou* sur l'échafaud **(b)** *Constr* échafaudage *m*

scaffolding ['skæfəldɪŋ] *n* échafaudage *m*

scalable font ['skeɪləb(ə)l] *n Typ* police *f* de taille variable

scalawag ['skæləwæg] *n esp Am F* = **scallywag**

scald¹ [skɔːld] *n* (*on hand etc*) brûlure *f*

scald² *vt* **(a)** (*burn*) (*hand etc*) ébouillanter; **to s. oneself** s'ébouillanter **(b)** *Culin* (*fruit, vegetables*) échauder, ébouillanter; (*milk etc*) faire chauffer sans bouillir; (*pot, container*) échauder, ébouillanter

scalding ['skɔːldɪŋ] **1** *adj* **s. (hot)** (*liquid*) brûlant; **a s. hot day** une journée torride; *Lit* **s. tears** larmes brûlantes **2** *n* (*burning*) brûlure *f*; **the boiling water caused s. on her arms and face** elle s'est ébouillanté les bras et le visage

scale¹ [skeɪl] *n* **(a)** (*on fish, reptile etc*) écaille *f*; *Med* (*on skin*) squame *f* **(b)** *Metal* **scale(s)** écailles *fpl* de fer **(c)** (*incrustation*) (*in pipes, kettle etc*) tartre *m*, incrustation *f*; (*on teeth*) tartre; **boiler s.** tartre; **s. remover** détartrant *m*

scale² **1** *vt* (*fish*) écailler; (*teeth*) détartrer; (*boiler, pipe*) désincruster, détartrer **2** *vi* (*of skin*) (se) desquamer; (*of paint etc*) s'écailler

scale³ *n* [①A10,e] (*for weighing*) balance *f*; (*for letters*) pèse-lettres *m inv*; (*in bathroom etc*) pèse-personne *m*, *pl* pèse-personnes; (*for baby*) pèse-bébé *m*, *pl* pèse-bébés; **pair of scales** balance *f* à plateaux; **to tip the scales at 100 kilos** peser 100 kilos; *Fig* **to tip the scales** faire pencher la balance; **s. (pan)** plateau *m* (de balance); (*deep*) bassin *m*; **platform scales** bascule *f*; **letter scales** pèse-lettres; **bathroom scales** pèse-personne; **baby scales** pèse-bébé

scale⁴ *vt* (*climb*) (*wall etc*) escalader; (*mountain, cliff*) escalader, faire l'ascension de

scale⁵ *n* **(a)** (*grading system*) échelle *f*; (*of thermometer*) échelle (graduée), graduations *fpl*; (*of prices etc*) **sliding s.** (*of salaries, prices*) échelle mobile; **sliding s. tariff** tarif dégressif; **at the top of the (social) s.** en haut *ou* au sommet de l'échelle (sociale); **to judge sth on a s. of one to ten** noter qch sur dix

(b) (*size*) (*of map, drawing etc*) échelle *f*; **small/large-s. map** carte à petite/à grande échelle; **to draw sth to s.** dessiner qch à l'échelle; **to be in/out of s.** être/ne pas être à l'échelle; **on a national s.** à l'échelle nationale; **the s. of a problem/crisis/disaster/project** l'ampleur *ou* l'importance d'un problème/d'une crise/d'un sinistre/d'un projet

(c) *Mus* gamme *f*; **major/minor s.** gamme majeure/mineure; **to practise one's scales** faire des gammes

scale[6] *vt Typ* (*font*) ajuster la taille de

▶ **scale down** *vtsep* **(a)** (*draw to smaller scale*) réduire l'échelle de; *Typ* (*font*) réduire (la taille de) **(b)** (*prices, demands etc*) réduire; (*expectations*) calmer; **to s. down production** ralentir la production

▶ **scale up** *vtsep* (*prices, demands etc*) augmenter; *Typ* (*font*) agrandir

scale model *n* maquette *f*, modèle *m* réduit

scales [skeɪlz] *npl see* **scale**[3]

scaling[1] ['skeɪlɪŋ] *n* **(a)** (*removal of incrustation*) (*of teeth*) détartrage *m*; (*of boiler, pipes*) détartrage, désincrustation *f* **(b)** (*deposit inside pipe, boiler, kettle etc*) tartre *m*, calcaire *m*; (*process of incrustation*) formation *f* du tartre, entartrage *m*

scaling[2] *n* **(a)** (*climbing*) escalade *f* **(b)** (*grading*) (*of prices, salaries etc*) graduation *f*; *Typ* (*of font*) ajustement *m* de la taille

scaling down *n* réduction *f*, diminution *f*; (*proportionately*) réduction proportionnelle

scaling up *n* augmentation *f*

scallion ['skæljən] *n Bot* échalote *f*

scallop[1] ['skɒləp, 'skæl-] *n* **(a)** (*mollusc*) **s. (shell)** peigne *m*, coquille *f* Saint-Jacques; *Culin* coquille Saint-Jacques; *Culin* (*of veal etc*) escalope *f* **(b)** *Sewing etc* feston *m*

scallop[2] *vt* **(a)** *Culin* (*fish etc*) faire cuire en coquille(s) **(b)** *Sewing* festonner; **scalloped handkerchief** mouchoir festonné

scallywag ['skælɪwæg] *n* **(a)** *F* chenapan *m*; **little s.** (*child*) petit(e) coquin, -ine **(b)** *US Hist* = partisan *m* des Républicains après la guerre de Sécession

scalp[1] [skælp] *n Anat* cuir *m* chevelu; (*war trophy*) scalp *m*

scalp[2] *vt* **(a)** (*in war*) scalper; *Hum* (*of hairdresser*) ratiboiser **(b)** *F* (*tickets*) revendre au noir

scalpel ['skælp(ə)l] *n Surg* scalpel *m*

scalper ['skælpər] *n* **(a)** *St Exch Sl* spéculateur *m* sur variation minimale **(b)** *esp Am F* (*ticket tout*) = revendeur *m* de billets au marché noir

scaly ['skeɪlɪ] *adj* (*fish*) écailleux; (*skin*) squameux

scam [skæm] *n F* arnaque *f*

scamp [skæmp] *n* fripouille *f*; *F* **little s.** (*child*) petit(e) coquin, -ine

scamper[1] ['skæmpər] *n* (*playful run*) course *f* folâtre *ou* allègre; (*quick run*) course rapide

scamper[2] *vi* (*run playfully*) gambader; **it scampered up the tree** il a grimpé à l'arbre en un clin d'œil; **they all scampered across the bridge** ils ont traversé le pont à toute vitesse; *Fig* **the programme scampered through the 18th century in ten minutes** l'émission a survolé le XVIIIème siècle en dix minutes

▶ **scamper away, scamper off** *vi* (*of mice*) filer; (*of animals*) détaler; (*of person*) décamper

scampi ['skæmpɪ] *n Culin* scampi *m*

scan[1] [skæn] *n* **(a)** (*look*) regard *m* appuyé; **after a quick s. around the room they left** ils examinèrent rapidement la pièce et s'en allèrent **(b)** *Electron, Rad etc* balayage *m*; *Comptr* lecture *f* au scanneur **(c)** *Med* examen *m* au scanne(u)r; (*in pregnancy*) échographie *f*; **to have a s.** se faire faire un examen au scanner; (*in pregnancy*) se faire faire une échographie

scan[2] **(-nn-) 1** *vt* **(a)** (*in prosody*) (*verse*) scander **(b)** (*examine closely*) scruter, examiner minutieusement; (*the horizon*) scruter **(c)** (*glance at, over*) jeter un coup d'œil sur; (*book etc*) feuilleter, parcourir **(d)** *Electron, Rad etc* (*image, soundtrack*) balayer; *Med* examiner au scanne(u)r; (*in pregnancy*) faire une échographie à; *Comptr* (*text, graphics*) passer *ou* lire au scanne(u)r, scanner; **scanned input** entrée *f* (à partir du) scanne(u)r **2** *vi* (*in prosody*) **this line doesn't s.** ce vers est faux

▶ **scan in** *vtsep Comptr* (*graphics*) insérer par scanne(u)r, capturer au scanne(u)r

scandal ['skænd(ə)l] *n* **(a)** (*outrage*) scandale *m*; **it's a s.** c'est un scandale; **to create** *or* **cause a s.** causer un scandale **(b)** (*gossip*) médisance *f*; *F, Pej or Hum* **s. sheet** journal *m* à scandale

scandalize ['skændəlaɪz] *vt* scandaliser, choquer

scandalmonger ['skænd(ə)lmʌŋgər] *n* colporteur, -euse d'histoires scandaleuses

scandalmongering ['skænd(ə)lmʌŋgərɪŋ] **1** *n* **it's just s.** c'est fait exprès pour faire du scandale; **to put a stop to this s.** mettre un terme à tous ces racontars **2** *adj* (*journalist etc*) qui cherche le scandale

scandalous ['skændələs] *adj* (*conduct, event, prices etc*) scandaleux

scandalously ['skændələslɪ] *adv* scandaleusement

Scandinavia [skændɪ'neɪvɪə] *n* Scandinavie *f*

Scandinavian [skændɪ'neɪvɪən] **1** *adj* scandinave **2** *n* Scandinave *mf*

scanner ['skænər] *n Med, Comptr* scanne(u)r *m*; **radar s.** explorateur *m ou* balayeur *m* radar; (*radar aerial*) antenne *f* (de) radar; *Aut* (*to break alarm codes*) scanner *m*

scanning ['skænɪŋ] *n* **(a)** (*in prosody*) (*of verse*) scansion *f* **(b)** (*close examination*) examen *m* minutieux; *Electron, Rad etc* (*of image, soundtrack*) balayage *m*; *Comptr* passage *m* au scanne(u)r, scannérisation *f*; **radar s.** exploration *ou* balayage radar

scansion ['skænʃən] *n* (*in prosody*) scansion *f*

scant [skænt] *adj attrib* insuffisant, peu abondant; **they paid s. regard to what he said** ils ont à peine fait attention à ce qu'il disait

scantily ['skæntɪlɪ] *adv* peu abondamment; (*insufficiently*) insuffisamment; **s. dressed** *or* **clad** très peu vêtu; **she came to the party rather s. clad** elle est venue à la soirée dans une tenue des plus légères

scantiness ['skæntɪnɪs] *n* (*of supplies etc*) insuffisance *f*; (*of vegetation*) rareté *f*, pauvreté *f*

scanty ['skæntɪ] *adj* (*supply etc*) peu abondant; (*insufficient*) insuffisant, à peine suffisant; **a s. meal** un maigre repas; **a s. little dress** une robe qui ne cache pas grand-chose

scapegoat ['skeɪpgəʊt] *n* (*who takes the blame*) bouc *m* émissaire; (*on whom frustrations are taken out*) souffre-douleur *m inv*

scapegrace ['skeɪpgreɪs] *n Old-fashioned* (*good-for-nothing*) vaurien, -ienne, bon *m*/bonne *f* à rien

scapula, *pl* **-ae** ['skæpjʊlə, -iː] *n Anat* omoplate *f*

scapular ['skæpjʊlər] *adj Anat etc* scapulaire

scar[1] [skɑːr] *n* (*mark of wound*) cicatrice *f*; (*on face, caused by knife etc*) balafre *f*; **s. tissue** tissu *m* cicatriciel; **the scars that the old mine workings have left on the hills** les cicatrices laissées sur les collines par les anciennes mines; **he carried the (mental) scars for the rest of his life** il est resté marqué à vie

scar[2] **(-rr-) 1** *vt* (*leg, face etc*) marquer d'une cicatrice; (*face*) (*with knife etc*) balafrer; **to be scarred** porter *ou* avoir des cicatrices; *Fig* **to be scarred for life** (*by experience etc*) être marqué à vie; **war-scarred** (*of country etc*) dévasté par la guerre **2** *vi* (*of wound*) faire une cicatrice

scar[3] *n* (*in mountain range etc*) rocher *m* escarpé

▶ **scar over** *vi* cicatriser

scarab ['skærəb] *n* (*precious stone*), *Ent* scarabée *m*

scarce ['skeəs] **1** *adj* (*animal, water, edition, substance, news etc*) rare; (*commodities*) rare, peu abondant; *F* **to make oneself s.** s'éclipser, s'esquiver **2** *adv Arch, Lit* = **scarcely**

scarcely ['skeəslɪ] *adv* [①A72,a,iv] à peine, *Fml* guère; **I have s. any left** il ne m'en reste presque plus, *Fml* il ne m'en reste guère; **she could s. speak** c'est à peine si elle pouvait parler, elle pouvait à peine parler; **s. ever** presque jamais; **he had s. come in** *or* **s. had he come in when the telephone rang** à peine était-il rentré que le téléphone sonna; **she was s. 21 years old** elle avait à peine 21 ans; **it is s. likely that …** il est peu vraisemblable que …; **they would s. destroy their own home, would they?** ils n'iraient pas jusqu'à détruire leur propre maison!

scarcity ['skeəsɪtɪ], **scarceness** ['skeəsnɪs] *n* (*rarity*) rareté *f*; (*lack*) manque *m*, disette *f*; **to have s. value** être précieux parce que rare; **because of their s. value** parce qu'ils sont rares

scare[1] [skeər] *n* panique *f*; *F* **you gave me an awful s.** vous m'avez fait une drôle de peur; **a bomb s.** une alerte à la bombe; **a s. over poisoned food** une panique à propos de nourriture empoisonnée

scare[2] **1** *vt* (*alarm*) effrayer, alarmer; (*frighten*) faire peur à, effrayer; **they scared him into leaving** (*intentionally*) ils lui ont fait peur jusqu'à ce qu'il parte; (*unintentionally*) ils lui ont fait peur au point qu'il est parti; **the high costs scared them off the idea** les coûts élevés leur en ont fait abandonner l'idée; *F* **to s. the pants off sb** faire une peur bleue à qn **2** *vi* s'effrayer, s'alarmer; **I don't s. easily** je ne m'effraie pas facilement *ou* pour rien

▶ **scare away, scare off** *vtsep* (*frighten*) (*person*) faire fuir; (*birds, deer etc*) effaroucher; (*discourage, put off*) faire fuir, effrayer

scarecrow ['skeəkrəʊ] *n Agr, Fig* épouvantail *m*; **to be dressed like a s.** être habillé à faire peur

scared [skeəd] *adj* (*look*) apeuré, effrayé; **to be s. of sb/sth** avoir peur de qn/qch; **I'm not s. of you** tu ne me fais pas peur, je n'ai pas peur de toi; **he's s. of his own shadow** il a peur de son ombre; **to be s. to death** *or* **out of one's wits**; *F* **to be s. stiff** avoir une peur bleue **(of** de)

scaredy-cat ['skeədɪkæt] *n F* (*in children's language*) froussard, -arde

scaremonger ['skeəmʌŋgər] *n* alarmiste *mf*

scaremongering ['skeəmʌŋgərɪŋ] *n* alarmisme *m*

scarf, *pl* **scarfs, scarves** [skɑ:f(s), skɑ:vz] *n* écharpe *f*; (*of silk*) foulard *m*; **football s.** écharpe aux couleurs d'une équipe de football

scarface ['skɑ:feɪs] *n* balafré, -ée

scarification [skærɪfɪ'keɪʃən] *n Agr, Med* scarification *f*

scarify[2] ['skærɪfaɪ] *vt* **(a)** (*skin, ground*) scarifier **(b)** *F* = **scare**[2] **1**

scarily ['skeərɪlɪ] *adv* à faire peur; **we came s. close to being killed** on est passé à deux doigts de la mort

scarlatina [skɑ:lə'ti:nə] *n Med* scarlatine *f*

scarlet ['skɑ:lɪt] **1** *adj* écarlate; **to blush** *or* **go** *or* **turn s.** devenir cramoisi *ou* écarlate; *Cathol* **s. hat** chapeau *m* de cardinal; *Old-fashioned, Hum* **s. woman** poule *f* **2** *n* écarlate *m*

scarlet fever *n Med* scarlatine *f*

scarlet pimpernel *n* (*plant*) mouron *m* rouge

scarlet runner *n* haricot *m* d'Espagne

scarp [skɑ:p] *n* **(a)** *Geog* (*of hill*) escarpement *m* **(b)** *Mil* (*in fortifications*) escarpe *f*

scarper ['skɑ:pər] *vi Br F* se tirer, déguerpir

scary ['skeərɪ] *adj F* (*frightening*) effrayant, qui fait peur; **it's s. here** ça fiche la frousse içi

scat [skæt] *int F* filez!, fichez le camp!

scathing ['skeɪðɪŋ] *adj* (*remark, sarcasm etc*) acerbe, mordant, cinglant; **she was s. about security arrangements** elle a fait des remarques acerbes au sujet des mesures de sécurité

scathingly ['skeɪðɪŋlɪ] *adv* d'une manière acerbe; (*to remark*) d'un ton cinglant *ou* acerbe

scatological [skætə'lɒdʒɪk(ə)l] *adj* (*joke etc*) scatologique

scatology [skə'tɒlədʒɪ] *n* scatologie *f*

scatter[1] ['skætər] *n* (*of shot etc*) éparpillement *m*, dispersion *f*, écartement *m*; **s. cushion** petit coussin *m* décoratif; **s. rug** petit tapis *m*; (*by bed*) descente *f* de lit

scatter[2] **1** *vt* (*army etc*) disperser; (*clouds etc*) dissiper; (*birds*) faire envoler; (*leaves, papers etc*) éparpiller; (*sow*) (*corn, seed*) semer à la volée; *Phys* (*of surface*) (*light*) diffuser **2** *vi* (*of crowd etc*) se disperser; (*of birds etc*) s'égailler; (*of army*) se débander; (*of clouds etc*) se dissiper; (*of shot*) s'éparpiller

scatterbrain ['skætəbreɪn] *n F* étourdi, -ie, tête *f* de linotte

scatterbrained ['skætəbreɪnd] *adj F* étourdi, écervelé

scattered ['skætəd] *adj* dispersé, éparpillé, épars; **s. showers** averses éparses; **s. light** lumière diffuse; **s. over the floor** éparpillé sur le sol; **houses s. here and there on the plain** des maisons çà et là dans la plaine

scattering ['skætərɪŋ] *n* (*small number*) petit nombre *m*; (*small quantity*) petite quantité *f*; **there was a s. of snow on the mountains** il y avait de la neige çà et là sur les montagnes; **he only has a s. of followers** il n'a qu'un petit nombre de disciples

scattiness ['skætɪnɪs] *n Br F* (*absent-mindedness*) étourderie *f*; (*craziness*) loufoquerie *f*

scatty ['skætɪ] *adj Br F* (*absent-minded*) étourdi, écervelé; (*crazy*) barjo, barge

scavenge ['skævɪndʒ] **1** *vi* (*hunt*) fouiller; **to s. in the dustbins** fouiller *ou* faire les poubelles; **to s. for information/news** être à l'affût des informations/nouvelles **2** *vt* récupérer; (*in engine*) (*burnt gas*) balayer, refouler

scavenger ['skævɪndʒər] *n* **(a)** (*person, animal*) fouilleur, -euse d'ordures; (*animal living off dead prey*) animal *m* nécrophage; **he's a real s.** (*gets things from other people's rubbish*) c'est le roi de la récupération **(b)** *Arch* (*street cleaner*) éboueur *m*

scenario [sɪ'nɑ:rɪəʊ] *n Cin, Th, Fig* scénario *m*

scene [si:n] *n* **(a)** *Th, Cin* (*place of action*) scène *f*; *Fig* (*of event*) théâtre *m*, lieu *m*; *Th* **s. change, change of s.** changement *m* de décor *ou* de scène; *Fig* **a change of s. would do him good** un changement d'air *ou* de décor lui ferait du bien; *Th* **the s. is set in London** l'action se passe à Londres; **to set the s.** planter le décor; *Fig* **her success set the s. for more women to enter music** son succès a permis à un plus grand nombre de femmes d'avoir une carrière musicale; **the political/sporting s.** la scène politique/sportive; **the modern poetry s. in Paris** la poésie moderne à Paris; **this athlete is a newcomer to the international s.** cet athlète est nouveau sur la scène sportive internationale; **to arrive** *or* **come on the s.** faire son apparition; (*of police*) arriver sur les lieux (du crime/de l'accident/*etc*); **to be first on the s.** être le premier sur les lieux; **the s. of the crime/accident** les lieux du crime/de l'accident; *F* **it's not my s.** ce n'est pas mon genre; *F* **to make the s.** devenir célèbre

(b) *Th* (*subdivision of play*) scène *f*; **s. two** scène deux

(c) *Th* (*scenery*) décor *m*; **scenes painted by ...** décors par ...; *also Fig* **behind the scenes** dans la *ou* les coulisse(s)

(d) *Fig* (*episode*) scène *f*, spectacle *m*; **it was a touching s.** c'était une scène émouvante *ou* un spectacle émouvant; **I can just picture the s.** je vois d'ici la scène

(e) (*sight*) vue *f*; **the s. from the window** la vue de la fenêtre; **a s. of devastation** un spectacle de désolation

(f) *F* (*fuss*) **now don't make a s.!** ne fais pas une scène!

scene dock *n TV, Th* magasin *m* de décors

scene painter *n* décorateur *m* de théâtre

scenery ['si:nərɪ] *n* **(a)** *Th* décor(s) *m(pl)*; *Fig F* **you need a change of s.** vous avez besoin de changer d'air *ou* de décor **(b)** (*countryside*) paysage *m*; (*view*) vue *f*

scene-set *n TV etc* mise *f* en place

sceneshifter ['si:nʃɪftər] *n Th* machiniste *mf*

scenic ['si:nɪk] *adj* **(a)** (*countryside*) pittoresque; (*route etc*) panoramique; **s. route** (*for tourists*) route *f* touristique, itinéraire *m* panoramique; **an area of great s. beauty** une région qui offre de très beaux panoramas; **s. railway** (*for tourists*) petit train *m* touristique **(b)** *Th* scénique; **s. cloth** rideau *m* de fond scénique; **s. designer** décorateur *m*, décoratrice *f*; *TV etc* **s. treatment** scénographie *f*; *TV etc* **s. workshop** atelier *m* de décors

scent[1] [sent] *n* **(a)** (*smell*) parfum *m*; (*of flowers*) odeur *f*, *Lit* senteur *f* **(b)** (*liquid*) parfum *m* **(c)** (*in hunting*) fumet *m*, vent *m*; **s. gland** *or* **organ** glande *f* à sécrétion odoriférante; **to pick up the s.** (*of hounds*) trouver la piste; **to be on the s.** être sur la piste(of de); **to lose** *or* **be thrown off the s.** perdre la trace *ou* la piste; **to throw the police off the s.** mettre la police en déroute, semer la police **(d)** (*sense of smell*) (*of dog*) odorat *m*, flair *m*

scent[2] *vt* **(a)** (*of hounds etc*) **to s. game** flairer *ou* sentir le gibier; *Fig* **to s. dishonesty/***etc* flairer la malhonnêteté/*etc*; **keen-scented dog** chien au nez *ou* à l'odorat fin **(b)** (*of flower etc*) (*the air*) parfumer, embaumer; **to s. sth with sth** (*with perfume etc*) parfumer *ou* imprégner qch de qch

scented ['sentɪd] *adj* (*soap etc*) parfumé

scentless ['sentlɪs] *adj* (*flower*) inodore, sans odeur

sceptic, *US* **skeptic** ['skeptɪk] *n* sceptique *mf*

sceptical, *US* **skeptical** ['skeptɪk(ə)l] *adj* sceptique

sceptically, *US* **skeptically** ['skeptɪklɪ] *adv* sceptiquement, avec incrédulité

scepticism, *US* **skepticism** ['skeptɪsɪz(ə)m] *n* scepticisme *m*

sceptre, *US* **scepter** ['septər] *n* sceptre *m*

schedule[1] ['ʃedju:l, *US* 'skedju:l] *n* **(a)** (*plan*) programme *m*; (*for work*) plan *m* (de travail), planning *m*; *Rail etc* (*timetable*) horaire *m*; **to be behind/ahead of s.** être en retard/en avance sur les prévisions; **we're on s. (for March)** nous sommes dans les délais (pour mars); **everything went off according to s.** tout a marché comme prévu; **I work to a very tight s.** mon emploi du temps est très chargé; **on s.** (*train, bus etc*) à l'heure

(b) *Com* (*list*) (*of items*) nomenclature *f*; (*of machines*) inventaire *m*; (*of prices*) barème *m*; *Admin* (*of taxes*) cédule *f*

(c) *Jur* (*to law, articles of association etc*) annexe *f*

schedule[2] *vt* **(a)** (*make plan for*) programmer, inscrire au programme, faire le programme de; (*put in timetable*) (*train etc*) inscrire à l'horaire; **the mayor is scheduled to make a speech** le maire doit prononcer un discours; **it's scheduled for three o'clock** c'est prévu pour quinze heures **(b)** *Br* (*class*) **to s. as an ancient monument** classer (comme) monument historique **(c)** *Com* (*list*) (*item*) inscrire sur une liste **(d)** *Jur* (*add as appendix*) ajouter en annexe

scheduled ['ʃedju:ld, *US* 'skedju:ld] *adj* **(a)** (*flight, services etc*) régulier; **to arrive at the s. time** arriver à l'heure prévue *ou* annoncée *ou* indiquée; *TV* **a change to our s. programme** un changement dans notre grille des programmes **(b)** *Fin* **S. Territories** zone *f* sterling

scheduler ['ʃedju:lər, *US* 'skedju:lər] *n Comptr* (*package*) logiciel *m* de planification (de projets)

scheduling ['ʃedju:lɪŋ, *US* 'skedju:lɪŋ] *n* ordonnancement *m*; *TV* programmation *f*; *TV etc* **s. director** directeur *m* des programmes

schema, *pl* **-ata** ['ski:mə, -ətə] *n Fml* schéma *m*

schematic [skɪ'mætɪk] *adj* schématique

scheme[1] [ski:m] *n* **(a)** (*arrangement*) arrangement *m*, combinaison *f*; (*system*) système *m*; **colour s.** combinaison de(s) couleurs; **I like the colour s. on this carpet** j'aime le mélange de couleurs de ce tapis; **where does mankind fit into the s. of things?** quelle est la place de l'humanité dans l'univers?; **where does it come in your s. of things?** quelle place cela a-t-il dans votre conception des choses?

(**b**) (*plan*) plan *m*, projet *m*

(**c**) *Pej* (*intrigue*) intrigue *f*, *F* magouille *f*; **the best laid schemes** les combinaisons *ou F* les combines les mieux étudiées

(**d**) *esp Br* **pension s.** caisse *f* de retraite; **(housing) s.** cité *f*

scheme² **1** *vi* intriguer, *F* magouiller **2** *vt* (*plot*) machiner, combiner; **to s. sb's downfall** comploter pour renverser qn

schemer ['ski:mər] *n Pej* intrigant, -ante

scheming ['ski:mɪŋ] **1** *adj* intrigant **2** *n* intrigues *fpl*, machinations *fpl*

scherzo ['skeətsəʊ] *n Mus* scherzo *m*

schism ['s(k)ɪz(ə)m] *n* schisme *m*

schismatic [s(k)ɪz'mætɪk] *adj, n* schismatique *mf*

schist [ʃɪst] *n Miner* schiste *m*; **mica s.** micaschiste *m*

schizo ['skɪtsəʊ] *adj, n F* schizo(phrène) *mf*

schizoid ['skɪtsɔɪd] *adj, n Psy* schizoïde *mf*

schizophrenia [skɪtsəʊ'fri:nɪə] *n Psy* schizophrénie *f*

schizophrenic [skɪtzəʊ'frenɪk] *adj, n* schizophrène *mf*, schizophrénique *mf*

schlep(p) [ʃlep] *esp Am F* **1** *vt* (*carry, drag*) trimballer, transbahuter **2** *vi* faire un tour, traîner

schlock [ʃlɒk] *n Am F* camelote *f*, saloperies *fpl*; **s. film** navet *m*

schlong [ʃlɒŋ] *n Am Sl* (*penis*) zob *m*

schmal(t)z [ʃmɔ:lts] *n F* sensiblerie *f*

schmaltzy ['ʃmɔ:ltsɪ] *adj F* (*film, novel, music etc*) à l'eau de rose, à la guimauve

schmooze [ʃmu:z] *vi F* (*chat people up at social gathering*) faire des mondanités

schmuck [ʃmʌk] *n Am Sl* (*fool*) con *m*, conne *f*

schnapps [ʃnæps] *n* schnaps *m*

schnitzel ['ʃnɪts(ə)l] *n* côtelette *f* de veau

schnozzle ['ʃnɒz(ə)l] *n Sl* (*nose*) naze *m*

scholar ['skɒlər] *n* (**a**) (*learned person*) savant, -ante, érudit, -ite; **I'm not much of a s.** je ne suis pas très savant; **Latin s.** latiniste *mf* (**b**) *Sch, Univ* (*winner of scholarship*) boursier, -ière (**c**) *Arch* (*pupil*) élève *mf*, écolier, -ière

scholarly ['skɒləlɪ] *adj* savant, érudit

scholarship ['skɒləʃɪp] *n* (**a**) (*learning*) savoir *m*, érudition *f* (**b**) *Sch, Univ* (*sum of money*) bourse *f* (d'études)

scholastic [skə'læstɪk] **1** *adj* (*philosophy, theology*) scolastique; *Sch Fml* (*work, success etc*) scolaire **2** *n Phil, Rel* scolastique *m*

school¹ [sku:l] *n* (**a**) [①**A6**,d,i] (*for children*) école *f*; *Admin* établissement *m* scolaire; (*from 11 to 15*) collège *m*; (*from 15 to 18*) lycée *m*; **to go to s.** aller en classe *ou* à l'école/au collège/au lycée; **which s. do you go to?** à quelle école/à quel collège/à quel lycée est-ce que tu vas?; **I went to** *or* **was at s. with her** je suis allé à l'école/au collège/au lycée avec elle; **I'm still at s.** je vais encore à l'école; **at s.** à l'école *ou* en classe/au collège/au lycée; **there is no s. tomorrow** il n'y a pas d'école *ou* il n'y a pas classe demain; **when does s. start?** (*primary*) à quelle heure est-ce que la classe commence?; (*secondary*) à quelle heure est-ce que les cours commencent?; **nursery s.** (école *f*) maternelle; *Br* **primary** *or Am* **elementary s.** école primaire, *Admin* établissement d'enseignement primaire; *Br* **comprehensive s.** établissement d'enseignement secondaire polyvalent; **grammar s.** *Br* ≈ lycée, *Am* ≈ école primaire; **high s.** (*from 11 to 15*) collège *m*; (*from 15 to 18*) lycée *m*; **independent** *or* **private s.** école *ou* collège libre; **public s.** *Br* école privée, *Am* école publique; **state s.** école publique *ou* d'Etat, établissement public; *Br Hist* **approved s.** centre *m* d'éducation surveillée; **Sunday s.** catéchisme *m*; **the whole s. knew it** toute l'école le savait; **the upper/lower s.** (*the pupils*) les grandes/petites classes; **(of) s. age** (d')âge scolaire; **s. attendance** (*going to school*) scolarisation *f*; (*not being absent*) présence *f* à l'école; **s. book** livre *m* de classe, livre scolaire; **s. buildings** bâtiments *mpl* scolaires; **the s. buildings** les bâtiments de l'école; **s. day** journée *f* de classe; **s. friend** camarade *mf ou F* copain, copine de classe *ou* d'école, **s. hours** heures *fpl* de cours; **s. magazine** journal *m* de l'école; **schools broadcasting** émissions *fpl* scolaires; **schools programmes** programmes *mpl* éducatifs; **schools radio** radio *f* scolaire; **s. report** livret *m* scolaire, bulletin *m* (scolaire); **s. trip** voyage *m* scolaire; **s. uniform** uniforme *m* scolaire

(**b**) [①**A6**,d,i] (*part of university*) département *m*, institut *m*; *Am* (*college, university*) faculté *f*, université *f*; *Am* **to be at s.** être à l'université; **s. of art, art s.** école *f* des beaux-arts; **s. of dancing** académie *f ou* école de danse; **fencing s.** académie *ou* salle *f* d'escrime; *Br* **driving s., s. of motoring** auto-école *f*, *pl* auto-écoles; **summer s.** cours *m* de vacances, université d'été

(**c**) *Art, Phil etc* (*group*) école *f*; (*following a master*) disciples *mpl*; **the Flemish s.** l'école flamande; **the Platonic s.** l'école de Platon; **s. of thought** école (de pensée); *F* **to be brought up in the s. of hard knocks** être élevé à la dure; **she is one of the old s.** elle est de la vieille école

school² *vt* (**a**) (*educate*) (*person*) instruire, faire l'éducation de (**b**) (*train*) (*child, sb's mind*) former; (*horse*) dresser; **to s. oneself** se discipliner

school³ *n* (*of fish*) banc *m*; (*of porpoises*) bande *f*

school board *n* conseil *m* d'établissement

schoolboy ['sku:lbɔɪ] *n* écolier *m*; (*11 to 15*) collégien *m*; (*15 to 18*) lycéen *m*; **s. slang** argot *m* scolaire

schoolchild, *pl* **-children** ['sku:ltʃaɪld, -tʃɪldrən] *n* écolier, -ière

schooldays ['sku:ldeɪz] *n* (*period of life*) vie *f* scolaire; **in my s.** quand j'étais à l'école

schoolfellow ['sku:lfeləʊ] *n Old-fashioned* camarade *mf* de classe *ou* d'école

schoolgirl ['sku:lgɜ:l] *n* écolière *f*; (*11 to 15*) collégienne *f*; (*15 to 18*) lycéenne *f*

schoolhouse ['sku:lhaʊs] *n* (**a**) (*school building*) école *f* (**b**) (*head's residence*) maison *f* du directeur/de la directrice (*faisant corps avec l'école*)

schooling ['sku:lɪŋ] *n* (**a**) (*education*) instruction *f*, éducation *f*; (*sending up to school*) scolarisation *f*; **he paid for his nephew's s.** il a subvenu aux frais d'études de son neveu; **compulsory s.** scolarisation obligatoire (**b**) (*of horse*) dressage *m*

schoolkid ['sku:lkɪd] *n F* écolier, -ière

school leaver *n* élève *mf* en âge de quitter l'école

school-leaving age *n* âge *m* de fin de scolarité

schoolma'am, schoolmarm ['sku:lmɑ:m] *n Old-fashioned F* institutrice *f*; *still current in Fig* **she's a real s.** elle est tellement pédante

schoolmaster ['sku:lmɑ:stər] *n Old-fashioned* (*in primary school*) instituteur *m*, maître *m* (d'école); (*in secondary school*) professeur *m*

schoolmate ['sku:lmeɪt] *n* camarade *mf* de classe

schoolmistress ['sku:lmɪstrɪs] *n Old-fashioned* (*in primary school*) institutrice *f*, maîtresse *f* (d'école); (*in secondary school*) professeur *m*

schoolroom ['sku:lru:m] *n* salle *f* de classe

schoolteacher ['sku:lti:tʃər] *n* (*in primary school*) instituteur, -trice, maître *m*/maîtresse *f* (d'école); (*in secondary school*) professeur *m*

schoolteaching ['sku:lti:tʃɪŋ] *n* enseignement *m*

school year *n* année *f* scolaire

schooner¹ ['sku:nər] *n Naut* schooner *m*, goélette *f*

schooner² *n* (*sherry glass*) grand verre *m* à xérès; *Am* (*beer glass*) grand verre à bière

sciatic [saɪ'ætɪk] *adj Anat* (*nerve*) sciatique

sciatica [saɪ'ætɪkə] *n Med* sciatique *f*

science ['saɪəns] *n* science *f*; **pure/applied s.** science pure/sciences appliquées; **natural s.** sciences naturelles; **social s.** sciences sociales; **s. teacher** professeur *m* de sciences; **s. park** parc *m* scientifique

science fiction *n* science-fiction *f*, anticipation *f*

scientific [saɪən'tɪfɪk] *adj* scientifique; **let's be s. about this** faisons preuve d'esprit scientifique; **s. research** recherche *f* scientifique

scientifically [saɪən'tɪfɪklɪ] *adv* scientifiquement

scientist ['saɪəntɪst] *n* scientifique *mf*, homme *m* de science

scientistic [saɪən'tɪstɪk] *adj Pej* prétendument scientifique

sci-fi ['saɪfaɪ] *F* **1** *n* science-fiction *f* **2** *adj* de science-fiction

Scilly ['sɪlɪ] *n* **the S. Isles, the Scillies** les Sorlingues *fpl*

scimitar ['sɪmɪtər] *n* cimeterre *m*

scintillate ['sɪntɪleɪt] *vi* scintiller; **scintillating with wit** pétillant d'esprit

scintillating ['sɪntɪleɪtɪŋ] *adj* (*wit, conversation etc*) étincelant, pétillant; (*book, match etc*) brillant; *Iron* **it wasn't exactly s.** ce n'était pas particulièrement brillant

scintillation [sɪntɪ'leɪʃən] *n* (*of wit etc*) éclat *m*

scion ['saɪən] *n* (**a**) (*of plant*) scion *m*, greffon *m* (**b**) *Lit* (*of noble family etc*) (*descendant*) descendant *m*, rejeton *m*

scissor *vt* (dé)couper avec des ciseaux

scissor bill *n* (*bird*) bec-en-ciseaux *m*, *pl* becs-en-ciseaux

scissors ['sɪzəz] *n* [①**A10**,e] **(pair of) s.** ciseaux *mpl*; **s.** (*in wrestling*), *Gym etc* ciseaux; (*in high jump*) saut *m* en ciseaux; *Swimming* **s. kick** ciseaux; *Fig* **a s.-and-paste job** (*of book etc*) du réchauffé

sclerosis, *pl* **-oses** [sklɪə'rəʊsɪs, -əʊsi:z] *n Med* sclérose *f*

scoff¹ [skɒf] *n* (*mocking*) **we had a good s. at his expense** nous nous sommes bien moqués de lui

scoff² *vi* (*mock*) se moquer; **to s. at** (*sb*) railler, se moquer de; (*sth*) se moquer de; **don't s.** ne te moque pas!; **to s. at danger** faire fi du danger

scoff³ *n esp Br F* (*food*) boustifaille *f*, bouffe *f*

scoff⁴ *vt esp Br F* (*eat*) bouffer

scoffing ['skɒfɪŋ] **1** *adj* (*mocking*) moqueur, railleur **2** *n* moquerie(s) *f(pl)*, raillerie(s) *f(pl)*

scold¹ [skəʊld] *n Old-fashioned* (*woman*) mégère *f*

scold² **1** *vi* gronder, criailler **2** *vt* gronder, réprimander; **to s. sb for doing sth** gronder qn d'avoir fait qch; **she scolded him for being late** elle l'a grondé à cause de son retard

scolding ['skəʊldɪŋ] **1** *adj* (*tone*) de réprimande **2** *n* (*reprimand*) gronderie(s) *f(pl)*, réprimande *f*, semonce *f*; **to give sb a good s.** sermonner qn; *F* remonter les bretelles à qn; **constant s.** des réprimandes continuelles

scoliosis [skɒlɪ'əʊsɪs] *n Med* scoliose *f*

scollop ['skɒləp] *n, vt* = **scallop**

sconce [skɒns] *n* **(a)** (*with handle*) bougeoir *m* **(b)** (*on wall*) applique *f*

scone [skɒn, skəʊn] *n Culin* = sorte *f* de petit pain sucré que l'on consomme beurré au thé de 5 heures

scoop¹ [sku:p] *n* **(a)** (*device*) (*for flour, rice etc*) pelle *f*; (*for ice cream*) cuiller *f* à glace, portionneuse *f*; (*for mashed potato*) cuiller à faire des boules de purée; *Naut* (*bailer*) épuisette *f*, écope *f*; (*of dredger*) godet *m*; *Fishing* **s. net** drague *f* **(b)** (*portion*) cuillerée *f*; **a s. of ice-cream/mashed potato/***etc* une boule de glace/purée/*etc* **(c)** *Journ F* scoop *m*, primeur *f*, exclusivité *f*; **to make a s.** faire un scoop **(d)** *Clothing* **s. neck** décolleté *m* arrondi

scoop² *vt* **(a)** (*shovel*) (*water from a boat*) écoper; (*earth*) enlever; **to s. sth into sth** évider qch dans qch; **to s. ice cream into a cone** mettre de la glace dans un cornet **(b)** *Journ* **to s. a story** avoir un scoop; **to s. the other papers** publier avant les autres journaux

▶ **scoop out** *vtsep* (*wood, tomato etc*) évider; **to s. the water out of a boat** écoper un bateau

▶ **scoop up** *vtsep* (*sand, coal, flour etc*) (*with hands*) prendre à pleines mains; (*with scoop*) (*sand, mud etc*) ramasser; (*water*) puiser; (*ice cream, mashed potato*) faire des boules de; **she scooped up the last of her soup** elle finit son assiette d'un coup de cuillère; **he scooped up the book from the floor** il ramassa le livre qui était par terre; **the helicopter scooped him up** l'hélicoptère le repêcha; **she scooped the baby up (in her arms)** elle a saisi le bébé (dans ses bras)

scoot [sku:t] *vi F* **to s. (off** *or* **away)** filer, déguerpir; **he came scooting up to me** il se précipita sur moi; **it's time to s.!** allez, on se casse!

scooter ['sku:tər] *n* (*for child*) trottinette *f*, patinette *f*; **(motor) s.** scooter *m*

scope [skəʊp] *n* (*of action, law etc*) portée *f*, étendue *f*; (*of science etc*) domaine *m*; (*of undertaking*) envergure *f*; (*for sb's movements etc*) espace *m*, place *f*; **s. of cover** (*in insurance*) objet *m* de garantie; **the guidelines leave a lot of s. for interpretation** les instructions laissent une grande place à l'interprétation; **it's beyond** *or* **outside my s.** cela n'est pas de mon ressort, cela n'est pas de *ou* ne rentre pas dans ma compétence; **it is beyond the s. of my comprehension how ...** je ne comprends absolument pas comment ...; **to have no/a lot of s. for manoeuvre** n'avoir aucune/avoir une grande marge de manœuvre; **it's outside the s. of this enquiry** cela n'entre pas dans les limites de cette enquête; **to give full** *or* **free s. to sb** laisser le champ libre à qn; **to give full** *or* **free s. to one's imagination** laisser libre cours à son imagination; **there's little s. for people with your qualifications** il y a peu de possibilités pour des gens avec des qualifications telles que les vôtres

scorch¹ [skɔ:tʃ] *n* **s. (mark)** trace *f* de brûlure

scorch² **1** *vt* (*of fire etc*) (*clothes etc*) (légèrement) brûler; (*of sun*) (*grass etc*) brûler, dessécher; *Culin* (*meat etc*) laisser brûler; *Mil* **scorched earth policy** tactique *f ou* politique *f* de la terre brûlée **2** *vi* (*of material etc*) brûler

scorch³ *vi Br F* (*move quickly*) **he scorched after her** il courut après elle; **to s. down the road** (*of person, car*) descendre la rue à toute vitesse; **she scorched past the other competitors** elle a dépassé les autres concurrents à toute vitesse; **she went scorching past us in her new car** elle passa devant nous comme une fusée dans sa nouvelle voiture

▶ **scorch along** *vi Br F* (*of car, runner*) passer à toute allure

scorcher ['skɔ:tʃər] *n F* (*hot day*) journée *f* torride

scorching ['skɔ:tʃɪŋ] **1** *adj* (*sun*) brûlant, ardent; (*wind*) brûlant; (*heat, day*) torride **2** *adv* **s. hot** (*water, drink, saucepan etc*) brûlant; (*day*) torride; *F* **it's s. hot here** il fait une chaleur à crever ici

score¹ [skɔ:r] *n* **(a)** *Sp etc* score *m*, marque *f*; (*in quiz*) score; **after 20 minutes there was still no s.** après 20 minutes le score était toujours zéro à zéro; **what's the s.?** quel est le score *ou* la marque?; **to keep the s.** marquer *ou* compter les points; *Cards* tenir la marque; **what was your s.?** combien tu as fait *ou* marqué?; *Fig, F* **to know the s.** savoir ce qu'il en est

(b) (*line made by cutting*) rayure *f*, rainure *f*; (*deeper*) entaille *f*; (*on rock etc*) strie *f*

(c) old s. *or* **scores** (*dispute*) vieille(s) rancœur(s) *f(pl)*; **to have an old s. to settle with sb** avoir un vieux compte à régler avec qn; **to pay off** *or* **settle old scores** régler de vieux comptes

(d) (*reason, grounds*) critère *m*; **on what s. was her application rejected?** sur quels critères sa candidature a-t-elle été rejetée?; **don't worry on that s.** n'ayez aucune crainte sur ce point *ou* à ce sujet

(e) *Mus* partition *f*; **full s.** partition d'orchestre

(f) [ⓘ**A12**,1,h,i; **B56**,A,d; **B56**,C,3] (*pl* **score**) (*twenty*) **a s.** vingt, une vingtaine; *Arch* **three or four s. people** entre soixante et quatre-vingt personnes; *F* **you can find them by the s.** on les trouve à la pelle; *F* **scores** (*a large number*) un grand nombre; *F* **scores of people** une foule de gens

score² **1** *vt* **(a)** *Sp* (*goal, try, points*) marquer; **to s. a hit** (*with song*) faire un tube; *Fig* (*of idea etc*) faire un tabac; (*of person*) faire des ravages; *Fig* **to s. a success** remporter un succès; *Fig F* **to s. points off sb** river son clou à qn

(b) (*cut line in*) (*cylinder, ground, paper, wood etc*) rayer; (*leather etc*) inciser; (*rock etc*) strier; **she scored her name on the bench** elle grava son nom sur le banc; **s. the meat/fish with a sharp knife** faites des petites entailles dans la viande/le poisson avec un couteau bien aiguisé; **mountainside scored by torrents** flanc de montagne creusé *ou* raviné par les torrents; **water had scored grooves into the rock** l'eau avait creusé des rainures dans le rocher

(c) *Mus* **scored for piano, violin and flute** pour piano, violon et flûte

(d) *Sl* **to s. drugs** acheter de la drogue *ou F* de la dope

2 *vi* **(a)** *Sp* (*of football player, team*) marquer; (*in rugby*) marquer un essai; (*in basketball*) marquer un panier

(b) (*keep the score*) compter *ou* marquer les points

(c) *Fig* **that's where he scores** (*that's where he has the advantage*) c'est là qu'il est le plus fort; **this is where the new Renault really scores** c'est là que la nouvelle Renault est vraiment super; **he scores on looks but not much else** il est mignon mais ça s'arrête là

(d) (*with knife, scissors*) découper; **s. along the dotted line** découper le long des pointillés

(e) *Sl* (*have sex*) (*of man*) se faire une nénette; (*of woman*) se faire un mec

(f) *Sl* (*buy drugs*) acheter de la drogue *ou F* de la dope

▶ **score off** **1** *vipo F* (*win point in argument etc*) **to s. off sb** river son clou à qn **2** *vtsep* (*delete*) rayer; **s. his name off the list** rayez son nom de la liste

▶ **score out** *vtsep* (*delete*) rayer

scoreboard ['skɔ:bɔ:d] *n* tableau *m* d'affichage

scorecard ['skɔ:kɑ:d] *n Sp* carte *f ou* fiche *f* de score; *Golf* carte *f* du parcours; (*at shooting range*) carton *m*

scorer ['skɔ:rər] *n Sp* **(a)** (*person who keeps score*) personne qui marque les points **(b)** *Fb etc* (*person who scores goal, point etc*) buteur *m*; **the team's top (goal) s.** le meilleur buteur de l'équipe

scoring ['skɔ:rɪŋ] *n* **(a)** *Sp* **to open the s.** ouvrir la marque; **there was no s. until ...** aucun point *ou Fb etc* but n'avait été marqué jusqu'à ce que ... **(b)** (*grooves etc*) (*on surface*) rayure *f*; (*on rock*) stries *fpl*, striation *f*; (*on cylinder etc*) rayures **(c)** *Mus* (*of piece of music*) orchestration *f*, arrangement *m*

scorn¹ [skɔ:n] *n* dédain *m*, mépris *m*; **to pour s. on sth** rejeter qch avec mépris

scorn² *vt* **(a)** dédaigner, mépriser; **she scorned their help** elle a dédaigné leur aide **(b) to s. to do sth** dédaigner de faire qch

scornful ['skɔ:nfʊl] *adj* (*person, smile etc*) dédaigneux, méprisant; **to be s. of sb/sth** dédaigner *ou* mépriser qn/qch, traiter qn/qch avec mépris *ou* dédain

scornfully ['skɔ:nfəlɪ] *adv* dédaigneusement, avec mépris

Scorpio ['skɔ:pɪəʊ] *n Astron* Scorpion *m*; **I'm a S.** je suis (du) Scorpion

scorpion ['skɔ:pɪən] *n* (*animal*) scorpion *m*

Scot [skɒt] *n* [ⓘ**A21**,d,ii] Écossais, -aise

Scotch [skɒtʃ] [ⓘ**A21**,d,ii] **1** *adj* (*not used in Scotland*) écossais; **S. broth** potage *m*; *Br Culin* **S. egg** = œuf *m* enrobé de chair à saucisse et pané; **S. mist** bruine *f*, crachin *m*; *F* **what do think that is then?, S. mist?** si tu allais à la mer, tu n'y trouverais pas d'eau; **S. pine** *or* **fir** pin *m* d'Écosse; *esp Am* **S. tape**® Scotch *m*; **S. terrier** scottish-terrier *m*, *pl* scottish-terriers; **S. whisky** whisky *m* écossais **2** *n* **(a)** (*whisky*) scotch *m* **(b)** (*not used in Scotland*) **the S.** *npl* les Écossais *mpl*

scotch [skɒtʃ] *vt* (*project etc*) mettre fin à, faire échouer; (*rumour*) mettre fin à, mettre un terme à
Scotchman, *pl* **-men** ['skɒtʃmən] *n* [①A21,d,ii] (*not used in Scotland*) Écossais *m*
Scotchwoman, *pl* **-women** ['skɒtʃwʊmən, -wɪmɪn] *n* [①A21,d,ii] (*not used in Scotland*) Écossaise *f*
scot-free ['skɒt'friː] *adj F* **to get off s.** (*unpunished*) s'en tirer à bon compte
Scotland ['skɒtlənd] *n* Écosse *f*; **S. Yard** Scotland Yard *m*
Scots [skɒts] [①A21,d,ii] **1** *adj* écossais; **the S. Guards** la Garde écossaise; **S. pine** *or* **fir** pin *m* d'Écosse **2** *n Ling* écossais *m*
Scotsman, *pl* **-men** ['skɒtsmən] *n* [①A21,d,ii] Écossais *m*
Scotswoman, *pl* **-women** ['skɒtswʊmən, -wɪmɪn] *n* [①A21,d,ii] Écossaise *f*
Scott [skɒt] *int Old-fashioned* **Great S.!** Grand Dieu!
Scotticism ['skɒtɪsɪz(ə)m] *n* expression *f* écossaise
Scottie ['skɒtɪ] *n F* scottish-terrier *m*, *pl* scottish-terriers
Scottish ['skɒtɪʃ] *adj* [①A21,d,ii] écossais; **S. terrier** scottish-terrier *m*, *pl* scottish-terriers
scoundrel ['skaʊndr(ə)l] *n* scélérat *m*, vaurien *m*; *F* (*child, puppy etc*) chenapan *m*
scour¹ ['skaʊər] *vt* (*saucepan etc*) récurer; (*floor etc*) frotter; (*in metalwork*) (*metal surface*) décaper; **the stream had scoured a channel in the hillside** le cours d'eau avait creusé un passage dans la colline
scour² *n* **to give a saucepan/the bath a good s.** bien récurer une casserole/la baignoire
scour³ **1** *vi* = **scour about** **2** *vt* (*search*) (*countryside*) parcourir, battre; (*woods, house*) fouiller; **to s. the country for sb** battre la campagne à la recherche de qn
▶ **scour about** *vi* (*search widely*) battre la campagne
scourer ['skaʊərər] *n* (**pan** *or* **pot**) **s.** (*metal*) tampon *m* à récurer; (*sponge*) éponge *f* à récurer
scourge¹ [skɜːdʒ] *n* (**a**) (*affliction*) fléau *m* (**b**) *Arch, Lit* (*whip*) fouet *m*; *Rel* (*for self-flagellation*) discipline *f*; *Fig* **he was the s. of ...** il était la terreur de ...
scourge² *vt* (**a**) *Arch, Lit* (*whip*) fouetter, flageller; *Rel* **to s. oneself** se donner la discipline (**b**) *Lit* (*afflict*) (*of war, famine, drought*) dévaster; (*of corruption*) accabler
scouring ['skaʊərɪŋ] *n* (*scrubbing*) récurage *m*, frottage *m*; (*in metalwork*) décapage *m*; **s. pad** (*metal*) tampon *m* à récurer; (*sponge*) éponge *f* à récurer; **s. powder** poudre *f* à récurer
Scouse [skaʊs] *Br F* **1** *adj* de Liverpool **2** *n Ling* dialecte *m* de Liverpool
Scouser ['skaʊsər] *n F* personne *f* originaire de Liverpool
scout¹ [skaʊt] *n* (**a**) (*person*), *Mil* éclaireur *m*; *Old-fashioned Br Aut* dépanneur *m* (*employé par les organismes d'assistance automobile*); (**boy**) **s.** (*Catholic*) scout *m*; (*non-Catholic*) éclaireur *m*; *Am* (**Girl**) **S.** guide *f*, éclaireuse *f*; *Cin, Sp etc* (**talent**) **s.** dénicheur, -euse de talents; *Am F* **a good s.** (*fellow*) un bon gars; **s. camp** camp *m* de scouts (**b**) (*aircraft*) avion *m* de reconnaissance
scout² *vi Mil etc* aller en reconnaissance; *Cin, Sp etc* **to s. for talent** être à la recherche de futurs talents
scout³ *n F* (*search*) **to have a s. around for sth** chercher qch; **I had a good s. around** j'ai bien cherché
scout⁴ *n Univ* (*servant*) garçon *m* de service (*spécialement à Oxford*)
▶ **scout about, scout around** *vi* (*search*) chercher (**for sth** qch)
scouting ['skaʊtɪŋ] *n* scoutisme *m*; **the S. Movement** le mouvement scout
scoutmaster ['skaʊtmɑːstər] *n* chef *m* de troupe
scow [skaʊ] *n Naut* chaland *m*
scowl¹ [skaʊl] *n* air *m* renfrogné; **to look at sb with a s.** regarder qn d'un air renfrogné
scowl² *vi* se renfrogner; **to s. at sb** menacer qn du regard, regarder qn d'un air menaçant
scowling ['skaʊlɪŋ] *adj* renfrogné
Scrabble® ['skræb(ə)l] *n* scrabble®
scrabble ['skræb(ə)l] *vi* **to s.** (**about** *or* **around**) (*scrape*) gratter; (*grope*) tâtonner; **I was scrabbling about in the dark trying to find my key** je tâtonnais dans le noir pour trouver ma clef; **beggars were scrabbling about in the dirt for coins** des mendiants grattaient dans la saleté pour trouver des pièces; **to s. about for work** chercher du travail désespérément
scrag¹ [skræg] *n* **the s. of the neck** la nuque; *Culin* **s.** (**end**) **of mutton** collet *m* de mouton
scrag² *vt* (**-gg-**) *Old-fashioned F* (*tease, rag*) tourmenter
scraggy ['skrægɪ] *adj* (*person etc*) maigre, maigrichon, maigrelet; (*piece of meat*) maigrichon, maigrelet
scram [skræm] *vi* (**-mm-**) *F* filer, ficher le camp; **s.!** file!, fiche le camp!
scramble¹ ['skræmb(ə)l] *n* (**a**) (*rush, struggle*) bousculade *f*; *Hist* **the s. for Africa** la lutte des puissances coloniales pour se répartir l'Afrique; **a s. for jobs** une bataille pour l'emploi; **a s. for profits** une course effrénée aux profits; **there was a s. for the door** il y a eu une ruée vers la porte (**b**) (*climb*) ascension *f* difficile (**c**) *Av F* (*takeoff*) décollage *m* d'urgence (**d**) *Br Sp* (**motorcycle**) **s.** motocross *m inv*
scramble² **1** *vi* (**a**) **to s. for sth** (*struggle*) se battre *ou* se bousculer pour avoir qch
(**b**) (*move, often with difficulty*) **to s. up/down/in/out** monter/descendre/entrer/sortir péniblement; **we scrambled over the rocks** nous avons grimpé par-dessus les rochers; **to s. up a hill** grimper une colline à quatre pattes
(**c**) (*move with speed*) **to s. up a ladder/tree** monter à une échelle/un arbre à toute vitesse; **he scrambled into his trousers** il a enfilé son pantalon à toute vitesse
(**d**) *Av F* (*take off*) décoller d'urgence
(**e**) *Sp* faire du motocross
2 *vt* (**a**) *Culin* (*eggs*) brouiller; **scrambled eggs** œufs *mpl* brouillés
(**b**) *Tel, Electron etc* (*message*) brouiller; **scrambled** (*encoded*) brouillé, codé, crypté
(**c**) *Av F* (*aircraft*) faire décoller d'urgence
scrambler ['skræmblər] *n* (**a**) *Tel etc* (*device*) brouilleur *m* (**b**) *Br Sp* (*on motorbike*) motard *m* de motocross
scrambling ['skræmblɪŋ] *n* (**a**) *Tel, Electron etc* (*of message*) brouillage *m* (**b**) *Br Sp* (**motorcycle**) **s.** motocross *m*
scrap¹ [skræp] *n* (**a**) (*piece*) (*of paper*) morceau *m*, bout *m*; (*of land etc*) parcelle *f*; (*of ribbon, information, evidence*) bout; (*of bread etc*) petit morceau; (*for scrapbook*) image *f*; (*cutting from newspaper*) coupure *f*; **to fight over the scraps** se disputer les restes; **to tear sth into scraps** déchirer qch en morceaux; **scraps** (*of food*) restes *mpl*; (*of cloth*) bouts; **not a s. of evidence** pas la moindre preuve; **there isn't a s. of truth in what she says** il n'y a pas une parcelle de vérité dans ce qu'elle dit; **to catch scraps of a conversation** saisir des bouts *ou* des bribes de conversation
(**b**) **s. iron, s. metal** ferraille *f*; **s. paper** (papier *m*) brouillon *m*; **to sell sth for s.** vendre qch à la casse
scrap² *vt* (**-pp-**) (**a**) (*discard*) (*part etc*) mettre au rebut; (*machine*) mettre hors service; (*nuclear missiles etc*) abandonner la construction de; (*project*) laisser tomber, abandonner (**b**) (*send for scrap*) (*car, lorry etc*) mettre à la ferraille *ou* à la casse
scrap³ *n F* (*fight*) bagarre *f*; (*quarrel*) dispute *f*; **to have a s.** (*fight*) se bagarrer; (*quarrel*) se disputer; **to get into a s.** (*fight*) se bagarrer; (*quarrel*) se disputer (**with sb** avec qn)
scrap⁴ *vi* (**-pp-**) *F* (*fight*) se bagarrer; (*quarrel*) se disputer
scrapbook ['skræpbʊk] *n* album *m* (*de découpages*)
scrap dealer *n* marchand *m* de ferraille
scrape¹ [skreɪp] *n* (**a**) (*action with scraper*) coup *m* de grattoir *ou* de racloir; (*wound on skin*) éraflure *f*; (*thin layer*) (*of butter etc*) mince couche *f*; (*sound*) (*of violin etc*) grincement *m*; **to give sth a s. with one's nail** gratter qch avec son ongle; **she had given the car a nasty s. on the side** elle avait fait une belle éraflure sur le côté de la voiture (**b**) *F* (*difficulty*) embarras *m*; **to get into a s.** se mettre dans l'embarras *ou F* le pétrin; **to get out of a s.** se tirer d'affaire *ou* d'embarras
scrape² **1** *vt* (**a**) (*scratch*) (*skin, polished surface etc*) érafler; **to s. one's shins** s'érafler les tibias; **to s. the bottom** (*of ship*) sillonner *ou* talonner le fond
(**b**) (*clean*) (*dirt, burnt part*) racler (**off** de); (*paint, wallpaper, surface*) gratter (**off** de); (*wall*) ravaler; *Culin* (*carrots etc*) gratter; (*in tanning*) (*skin*) racler, dépiler; **to s. one's shoes** racler *ou* décrotter ses chaussures; **to s. one's plate clean** racler son assiette; *Naut* **to s. a ship's bottom** nettoyer la carène d'un navire; *Fig* **to s. the (bottom of the) barrel** (*with money*) racler les fonds de tiroir; (*be reduced to extremes*) être tombé bien bas
(**c**) **with her hair scraped back** les cheveux tirés
(**d**) (*achieve laboriously*) **to s. a living** gagner tout juste sa vie *ou F* sa croûte; **to s. a win** arracher une victoire; **to s. a pass** (*in exam*) réussir de justesse
2 *vi* (**a**) (*scratch*) gratter; (*make sound*) (*of wheel, pen, violin etc*) grincer; **branches that s. against the shutters** branches qui frottent contre les volets
(**b**) **to s.** *or* **s. away** (**on the fiddle**) gratter du violon
(**c**) *F* (*succeed with difficulty*) **to s. home** (*win game, race*) gagner de justesse; **to s. into college** réussir de justesse à rentrer à l'université
▶ **scrape along** *vi* (*just manage financially etc*) vivoter, s'en tirer péniblement
▶ **scrape by** *vi* (**a**) = **scrape along** (**b**) (*just succeed*) (*in an exam*) réussir de justesse
▶ **scrape in** *vi* (*just succeed*) (*in entering university etc*)

entrer de justesse; (*in winning election*) gagner de justesse; *Sp* (*in qualifying*) se qualifier de justesse
▶ **scrape off** *vtsep* (*remove*) (*paint etc*) racler, gratter
▶ **scrape out** *vtsep* (*saucepan*) récurer; (*pipes*) nettoyer
▶ **scrape through 1** *vi* = **scrape by (b) 2** *vipo* **to s. through an examination** être reçu de justesse à un examen; **the Bill only just scraped through its first reading** le projet de loi a été adopté de justesse en première lecture
▶ **scrape together** *vtsep* (*save with difficulty*) (*sum of money*) rassembler
▶ **scrape up** *vtsep* **(a)** = **scrape together (b)** *Hum* **he scraped himself up off the floor** il a fini par se relever; **we had to s. him up off the ground** il a fallu le ramasser à la petite cuillère

scraper ['skreɪpər] *n* racloir *m*, grattoir *m*; *Aut etc* (**ice**) **s.** raclette *f*, grattoir (*pour pare-brise*); **door** *or* **shoe s.** décrottoir *m*, grattoir

scrapheap ['skræphiːp] *n* tas *m* de ferraille; **to throw sth on the s.** mettre qch à la ferraille *ou* au rebut; *Fig* **to throw sb on the s.** laisser tomber qn comme une vieille savate; **he ended up on the s.** (*through redundancy etc*) on l'a mis au rebut; **to consign ideas/projects to the s.** mettre des idées/projets au rebut; **lots of companies are on the s.** beaucoup d'entreprises sont hors de combat

scrapie ['skreɪpɪ] *n Vet* scrapie *f*

scraping ['skreɪpɪŋ] *n* **(a)** (*sound*) (*of pen, saw, violin etc*) grincement *m*; (*scratching*) grattement *m*; *Fig* **bowing and s.** salamalecs *mpl* **(b)** (*thin layer*) (*of butter etc*) mince couche *f*

scrapman, *pl* **-men** ['skræpmən] *n* ferrailleur *m*, casseur *m*

scrap merchant *n* marchand *m* de ferraille

scrapple ['skræp(ə)l] *n Am Culin* = (genre de) friand *m* fait de farine de maïs et de morceaux de porc que l'on fait frire à la poêle

scrappy ['skræpɪ] *adj* (*collection etc*) hétérogène, hétéroclite; (*speech, film, novel*) décousu; (*work, performance*) inégal; *Sp* **a s. second half** une seconde mi-temps inégale; **s. knowledge** connaissances fragmentaires

scratch¹ [skrætʃ] *n* **(a)** (*mark, cut*) égratignure *f*, éraflure *f*; (*made by claw*) griffure *f*; (*on polished surface, record etc*) rayure *f*; **it's nothing, just a s.** ce n'est rien, juste une égratignure; **he came out of it without a s.** il s'en est sorti indemne, il s'en est sorti sans la moindre égratignure; *Am* **s. paper** brouillon *m*

(b) (*blow*) (*with fingernail*) coup *m* d'ongle; (*with claw*) coup de griffe

(c) (*repeated action*) (*of pen*) grincement *m*; **could you give my back a s.?** tu peux me gratter le dos?; **to give one's head a s.** se gratter la tête

(d) *Fig F* **to start from s.** partir de rien; (*restart*) repartir à zéro; **to build a house from s.** construire une maison de bout en bout; **to write a dictionary from s.** écrire un dictionnaire totalement nouveau; **she built the business up from s.** elle a monté l'affaire à partir de rien; **to come up to s.** être à la hauteur, faire le poids; **to bring sb up to s.** mettre qn à niveau; (*prepare for exam*) préparer qn; **to bring sth up to s.** mettre qch à niveau; **he's not up to s.** il ne fait pas le poids, il n'est pas à la hauteur; **the work was not up to s.** le travail n'était pas à la hauteur; *Golf* **s. player** (*in tournament*) joueur, -euse classé(e) zéro

scratch² 1 *vt* **(a)** (*of cat, person etc*) griffer; (*of thorn etc*) (*skin*) égratigner, érafler; (*glass, record etc*) rayer; **he was badly scratched** il était tout écorché; **to s. oneself** s'égratigner, s'érafler; (*with nails*) se griffer; **to s. one's name on a bench** graver son nom sur un banc; *Fig* **she quickly scratched a few notes on her pad** elle griffonna rapidement quelques notes sur son calepin; **to s. a hole** creuser un trou avec les griffes; *Fig* **to s. the surface (of the problem)** ne faire qu'effleurer le problème; *Fig* **s. any patriot and you will invariably find a bigot** si l'on gratte un peu, on trouve un fanatique derrière chaque patriote

(b) (*rub*) (*metal, itchy skin*) gratter; **to s. one's head** se gratter la tête; *Fig* **you s. my back and I'll s. yours** rends-ma service et je te renverrai l'ascenseur

(c) (*of bird, animal*) (*ground*) gratter

(d) (*delete*) **to s. sb off** *or* **from a list** rayer *ou* biffer qn d'une liste; **to s. sb from a team** exclure qn d'une équipe; *Horseracing* **to s. a horse** déclarer forfait pour un cheval; (*of stewards*) scratcher un cheval

2 *vi* **(a)** (*of person, animal*) (*to relieve itch*) se gratter; (*of bird, animal*) (*in the ground*) gratter; (*of thorns, branches etc*) piquer; (*of wool, new clothes*) gratter; **don't s.!** (*yourself*) arrête de te gratter!; (*stop scratching me*) arrête de me griffer!; **a cat that scratches** un chat qui griffe; **to s. at the door** gratter à la porte

(b) (*of pen etc*) grincer, gratter

(c) *Sp* (*of entrant*) déclarer forfait

scratch³ *adj* (*meal etc*) improvisé, sommaire; *Sp* **s. team** équipe *f* improvisée
▶ **scratch about, scratch around** *vi* **to s. about** *or* **around for sth** essayer de dénicher qch
▶ **scratch out** *vtsep* **(a)** (*remove by scratching*) **to s. sb's eyes out** arracher les yeux à qn **(b)** (*delete*) (*word*) rayer, biffer, raturer; (*with penknife*) gratter, effacer
▶ **scratch together** *vtsep* = **scrape together**

scratching ['skrætʃɪŋ] *n* **(a)** (*with fingernail*) coups *mpl* d'ongle; (*damaging*) (*action*) rayage *m*; (*on surface*) rayures *fpl* **(b)** (*to relieve itch*) grattement *m* **(c)** (*sound*) grattement *m*; (*of pen nib*) grincement *m*; (*of record*) craquement(s) *m(pl)*

scratchpad ['skrætʃpæd] *n Am Comptr* bloc-notes *m*, *pl* blocs-notes; **s. memory** mémoire *f* bloc-notes

scratchy ['skrætʃɪ] *adj* **(a)** (*drawing*) peu assuré; **s. writing** pattes *fpl* de mouche **(b)** (*pen etc*) (*messy*) qui gratte; (*noisy*) qui grince (*sur le papier*); (*material etc*) (*coarse*) rugueux, grossier; (*that irritates skin*) qui gratte (la peau); (*record*) qui craque

scrawl¹ [skrɔːl] *n Pej* (*writing*) griffonnage *m*, gribouillage *m*; **this s. is supposed to be your answer?** est-ce que c'est votre réponse, ces gribouillages-là?

scrawl² *Pej* **1** *vt* (*letter etc*) griffonner, gribouiller **2** *vi* écrire comme un chat

scrawny ['skrɔːnɪ] *adj* (*neck*) maigre, décharné; (*piece of meat*) maigrichon

scream¹ [skriːm] *n* **(a)** (*cry*) cri *m* perçant *ou* aigu, hurlement *m*; **a s. of pain** un cri *ou* un hurlement de douleur; **screams of laughter** de grands éclats de rire **(b)** *F* (*amusing thing, person*) **it was a s.** c'était à se tordre (de rire); **he's a s.** il est tordant

scream² 1 *vi* (*once*) pousser un cri perçant *ou* aigu, hurler; (*repeatedly*) pousser des cris aigus, hurler; (*of rabbit, hare*) couiner; (*of jet, missile*) faire un bruit perçant; **jets screamed overhead** des jets sont passés au-dessus de nos têtes dans un bruit assourdissant; **to s. with pain** crier *ou* hurler de douleur; **to s. with laughter** rire à gorge déployée *ou* aux éclats; **everyone's screaming about high prices** tout le monde pousse les hauts cris à propos des prix élevés; **the poster screams at you** l'affiche vous saute à la figure

2 *vt* **to s. abuse** hurler des injures; **to s. oneself hoarse** crier à en avoir la voix rauque; **the headlines screamed "guilty"** le mot "coupable" s'étalait en grosses lettres sur les premières pages des journaux

screaming ['skriːmɪŋ] **1** *adj* (*person*) criard; (*headlines*) tape-à-l'œil *inv*; (*missile, jet*) qui fait un bruit perçant **2** *n* (*of terror etc*) cris *mpl*, hurlements *mpl*; (*of birds etc*) cris perçants

screamingly ['skriːmɪŋlɪ] *adv F* **s. funny** tordant, à se tordre (de rire)

scree [skriː] *n Geol* éboulis *m*

screech¹ [skriːtʃ] *n* (*cry*) cri *m* perçant *ou* aigu; (*of tyres, brakes etc*) crissement *m*; **a s. of laughter** un éclat de rire perçant

screech² 1 *vi* (*of person, parrot etc*) pousser des cris perçants *ou* aigus; (*of tyres*) crisser; **the car screeched to a halt** la voiture s'est arrêtée dans un crissement de pneus; **she does tend to s. on the high notes** elle a tendance à hurler les notes aiguës **2** *vt* (*orders, insults*) hurler

screeching ['skriːtʃɪŋ] **1** *adj* (*laugh*) perçant, aigu; (*tyres*) qui crissent **2** *n* (*cries*) cris *mpl* perçants *ou* aigus; (*of tyres*) crissement *m*

screech owl *n* effraie *f*

screed [skriːd] *n usu Pej* (*long book*) pavé *m*; (*long article*) article *m* à rallonge; **to write screeds** en écrire des tartines; **she wrote me a s.** (*long letter*) elle m'a écrit une lettre qui fait des kilomètres

screen¹ [skriːn] *n* **(a)** (*in front of fire*) écran *m*; (*against draught*) paravent *m*; (*partition*) cloison *f*; (*wrought iron etc*) grille *f*; **choir s.** (*in church*) grille de chœur; **rood s.** jubé *m*; **s. of trees** rideau *m* d'arbres; **to act as a s. for a criminal** couvrir un criminel; **the shop was just a s. for her criminal activities** le magasin n'était qu'une couverture pour ses activités criminelles; **protective/safety s.** écran de protection/de sécurité; **fire s.** écran ignifuge

(b) *Cin, TV etc* écran *m*; **the s.** (*cinema*) l'écran; **television s.** écran de télévision; **the big s.** (*cinema*) le grand écran; **the small s.** (*television*) le petit écran; **a picture/a face appeared on the s.** une image/un visage est apparu(e) sur l'écran; **s. adaptation** adaptation *f* à l'écran; **s. image** image *f* à l'écran

(c) *Comptr* écran *m*; **on s.** sur (l')écran; **to bring up the next s.** amener l'écran suivant; **this takes you back/**

forwards a s. *or* **s. by s.** ceci vous fait avancer/reculer écran par écran; **s. controller** contrôleur *m* d'écran; **s. display** affichage *m*; **s. down command** commande *f* écran vers le bas, commande écran suivant; **s. dump** impression *f* écran; **s. font** fonte *f* écran; **s. generation** génération *f* d'écrans; **s. line** ligne-écran *f*; **s. memory** mémoire *f* écran; **s-oriented** orienté écran; **s. painting** modification *f* du papier peint; **s. refresh** rafraîchissement *m ou* régénération *f* de l'écran; **s. saver** économiseur *m* d'écran; **s. up command** commande *f* écran vers le haut, commande écran précédent

(**d**) *El, Electron* écran *m*; **fluorescent s.** écran fluorescent

(**e**) *Constr, Min* (*sieve*) crible *m*, tamis *m*, sas *m*; *Am* (*ventilation grill in door*) grille *f* de ventilation

screen² *vt* (**a**) (*conceal*) (*sth*) masquer, dissimuler, cacher; (*behind a screen*) cacher derrière un écran *ou* un paravent; (*protect*) abriter, protéger; (*from harmful influences etc*) mettre à l'abri (**from** de); **to s. sth from view** cacher *ou* masquer *ou* dérober qch aux regards *ou* à la vue

(**b**) *Cin* (*film*) projeter, passer; (*show on television*) passer à l'écran

(**c**) (*personnel*) trier, sélectionner; (*job applicants*) examiner; (*immigrants etc*) filtrer; (*news etc*) filtrer, passer au crible; *Med* (*person*) faire passer un test de dépistage à; **s. sb for security** contrôler qn pour des raisons de sécurité

(**d**) (*sieve etc*) (*gravel, coal, ore, grain etc*) cribler, passer au crible

▶ **screen off** *vtsep* (*part of room*) séparer par un paravent/une cloison/un rideau/*etc*; **their house is screened off (from ours) by a row of trees** nous ne pouvons voir leur maison de la nôtre à cause de la rangée d'arbres qui les sépare; **the nurses screened off the dying man** les infirmières ont tiré les rideaux/ont mis des paravents autour du lit du mourant

▶ **screen out** *vtsep* éliminer, écarter

screen actor *n Cin* acteur *m* de cinéma

screen actress *n Cin* actrice *f* de cinéma

screening ['skri:nɪŋ] *n* (**a**) *Cin* (*of film*) projection *f*, passage *m* à l'écran; (*on television*) passage à l'écran; **when the film had its first s.** quand le film est passé pour la première fois à l'écran; *TV, Cin* **s. room** salle *f* de projection

(**b**) (*of personnel*) triage *m*, sélection *f*; (*of immigrants, news etc*) filtrage *m*; (*of job applicants*) examen *m* sélectif; *Med* (*of contagious patients*) dépistage *m*; **s. for a disease** dépistage d'une maladie; *Med* **to have a s.** se faire faire un test de dépistage

(**c**) (*sieving*) (*of gravel, coal etc*) criblage *m*; (*of grain*) sassement *m*

screenplay ['skri:npleɪ] *n Cin* scénario *m*

screen rights *npl Cin* droits *mpl* d'adaptation à l'écran

screen test *n Cin* bout *m* d'essai

screen wash *n Aut* lave-glace *m*

screenwriter ['skri:nraɪtər] *n Cin* scénariste *mf*

screen writing *n TV, Cin* écriture *f* de scénarios

screw¹ [skru:] *n* (**a**) (*for fixing*) vis *f*; *HydE* **Archimedes'** *or* **Archimedean s.** vis d'Archimède; *F* **to have a s. loose** avoir une case de vide *ou* une araignée au plafond; *F* **to put the screws on sb, to tighten the s. on sb** mettre la pression sur qn; **s. cap** *or* **top** (*of bottle*) bouchon *m* à vis; (*of jar*) couvercle *m* à vis; **s. thread** pas *m ou* filet *m* de vis

(**b**) *Av, Naut* **s. (propeller)** hélice *f*; **twin-s.** hélice double

(**c**) (*turn of screw*) tour *m* de vis; (*turn of screwdriver*) coup *m* de tournevis; **give it another s.** serrez-le encore un peu

(**d**) *Old-fashioned* (*twist*) (*of tobacco*) papillote *f*; (*of paper*) tortillon *m*

(**e**) *Billiards* effet *m*; **to put (a** *or* **some) s. on the ball** donner de l'effet à la balle

(**f**) *Br Sl* (*prison officer*) maton, -onne

(**g**) *Vulg* (*sexual intercourse*) baise *f*; **what she needs is a good s.** c'est une mal-baisée; **to have a good s.** baiser un bon coup; **she's a good s.** c'est un bon coup

(**h**) *Old-fashioned Br F* (*salary*) salaire *m*, paye *f*

screw² **1** *vt* (**a**) (*fix*) visser; **to s. sth (on) to sth** visser qch à *ou* sur qch; **screwed together** vissés l'un(e) à l'autre; **to s. one's head round to see sth** se tordre le cou pour voir qch; **to s. one's face into a smile** *or* **grin** se forcer à sourire, faire une grimace plutôt qu'un sourire

(**b**) *F* (*cheat*) (*sb*) avoir, rouler; **we've been screwed!** on s'est fait avoir!; **to s. money from** *or* **out of sb** extorquer de l'argent à qn; **they're out to s. you for every penny you've got** ils essayent de vous extorquer tout l'argent que vous avez

(**c**) *Billiards* (*ball*) donner de l'effet à

(**d**) *Vulg* (*have sexual intercourse with*) s'envoyer, sauter, baiser; *Fig* **s. you!** va te faire foutre!; **s. him!** qu'il aille se faire foutre!

2 *vi* (**a**) (*of tap etc*) tourner; **the knobs s. into the drawer** les boutons se vissent sur le tiroir

(**b**) *Billiards* (*of ball*) rebondir de travers, dévier

(**c**) *Vulg* (*have sexual intercourse*) baiser, s'envoyer en l'air

▶ **screw around** *vi* (**a**) *F* (*mess around*) glander (**b**) *Vulg* (*be promiscuous*) baiser *ou* coucher avec tout le monde

▶ **screw back** *vi Billiards* (*of player*) faire de l'effet rétrograde, faire un rétro; (*of ball*) revenir en arrière

▶ **screw down** *vtsep* (*secure*) fixer *ou* tenir avec une/des vis

▶ **screw off** **1** *vtsep* (*lid*) dévisser **2** *vi* se dévisser

▶ **screw on** **1** *vtsep* (*attach*) visser; *F* **he's got his head screwed on, his head's screwed on the right way** il a la tête solide *ou* la tête sur les épaules **2** *vi* se visser

▶ **screw up** **1** *vtsep* (**a**) (*tighten by screwing*) visser; (*nut*) serrer; **to s. sth up tight** visser qch à bloc; **to s. up a piece of paper** froisser une feuille de papier; **to s. up one's eyes** plisser les yeux; **to s. up one's face** grimacer; **to s. up one's courage** prendre son courage à deux mains

(**b**) *Sl* (*spoil*) (*job*) bousiller, foutre en l'air; **this has screwed up my plans** ça m'a foutu mes plans en l'air; **he screwed up the interview** il a complètement merdé à l'entretien

(**c**) *Sl* (*make neurotic*) **to s. sb up** foutre qn en l'air; **her parents' divorce has really screwed her up** le divorce de ses parents l'a vraiment foutue en l'air

2 *vi* (**a**) (*of lid, nut etc*) se visser

(**b**) **her face screwed up in distaste** *or* **disgust** elle fit une grimace de dégoût

(**c**) *Sl* (*make a mess of sth*) merder

screwball ['skru:bɔ:l] *adj, n esp Am F* dingue *mf*

screwdriver ['skru:draɪvər] *n* (**a**) (*tool*) tournevis *m*; **crossheaded s.** tournevis cruciforme; **s. blade/handle** lame *f*/poignée *f* de tournevis (**b**) (*cocktail*) vodka-orange *f, pl* vodkas-orange

screwed [skru:d] *adj Br F* (*drunk*) bourré, rond

screw-on *adj* (*earrings*) à vis; *Phot* (*lens*) détachable, mobile

screwy ['skru:ɪ] *adj F* dingue, loufoque

scribble¹ ['skrɪb(ə)l] *n* (**a**) (*act of scribbling*) griffonnage *m*, gribouillage *m* (**b**) (*bad handwriting*) écriture *f* illisible, pattes *fpl* de mouche; **that's not drawing, it's just (a) s.** ce n'est pas du dessin, c'est du gribouillage

scribble² **1** *vt* (*a few words, notes*) griffonner, gribouiller **2** *vi* gribouiller; (*write quickly, in notebook etc*) griffonner; **don't s. on the walls** ne gribouille pas sur les murs; **I used to s. a bit** j'écrivais un peu, quoi, autrefois

▶ **scribble down** *vtsep* (*write*) = **scribble² 1**

scribbler ['skrɪblər] *n* (**a**) (*person who scribbles*) griffonneur, -euse, gribouilleur, -euse (**b**) *F* (*inferior writer*) écrivailleur, -euse

scribbling ['skrɪblɪŋ] *n* (*bad handwriting*) griffonnage *m*, gribouillage *m*; *F* **scribblings** (*inferior writings*) écrits *mpl* de deuxième zone; **s. paper** (papier *m*) brouillon *m*; **s. pad** bloc-notes *m inv*

scribe [skraɪb] *n Hist* (*person*) scribe *m*

scrimmage¹ ['skrɪmɪdʒ] *n* (**a**) (*struggle*) mêlée *f*, bagarre *f*, bousculade *f* (**b**) *US Fb* mêlée *f*

scrimmage² **1** *vi* se bousculer **2** *vt US Fb* (*ball*) mettre en mêlée

scrimp [skrɪmp] *vi* **to s. (and save)** faire des économies de bouts de chandelle

scrip [skrɪp] *n Fin* (*shares*) valeurs *fpl*, titres *mpl*, actions *fpl*; **s. (certificate)** certificat *m* d'actions provisoire; **s. issue** titres attribués à un actionnaire (*au lieu de dividende etc*), émission *f* d'actions gratuites

script¹ [skrɪpt] *n* (**a**) (*manuscript*) manuscrit *m*; *Sch* (*in exam*) copie *f*; *Th* texte *m*; *Cin* scénario *m*, script *m*; **to read from a s.** (*of newsreader, politician etc*) lire ses notes; *also Fig* **that's not in the s.** ce n'est pas prévu au programme; *Cin, TV* **s. editor** scénariste *mf* (de réécriture); **s. girl** scripte *f* (**b**) (*as opposed to print*) écriture *f* script; **Gothic s.** écriture gothique; *Typ* **s. (type)** cursive *f*

script² *vt* écrire le script pour

scripted ['skrɪptɪd] *adj* (*remark etc*) préparé à l'avance

scriptural ['skrɪptʃər(ə)l] *adj Rel* scripturaire

scripture ['skrɪptʃər] *n* (**a**) **(Holy) S., the Scriptures** l'Écriture *f* sainte, les (saintes) Écritures; *Sch* **s. lesson** cours *m* d'histoire sainte (**b**) *Sch* instruction *f* religieuse

scriptwriter ['skrɪptraɪtər] *n Cin etc* scénariste *mf*

scriptwriting ['skrɪptraɪtɪŋ] *n* écriture *f* de scénarios

scrofula ['skrɒfjʊlə] *n Med* scrofule *f*

scrofulous ['skrɒfjʊləs] *adj* (**a**) *Med* scrofuleux (**b**) (*corrupt*) dépravé

scroll¹ [skrəʊl] *n* (**a**) (*roll of paper, parchment*) rouleau *m*; **the Dead Sea Scrolls** les manuscrits *mpl* de la mer Morte (**b**) (*decoration*), *Archit etc* spirale *f*; (*of Ionic capital*) volute *f*; (*in writing*) enjolivement *m*, arabesque *f*; (*in engraving etc*) cartouche *m* (*encadrant un titre*); (*of violin*) crosse *f* (**c**)

Comptr défilement *m*; **s. bar** barre *f ou* bande *f* de défilement; **s. box** ascenseur *m*, cage *f* d'ascenseur; **s. lock (key)** touche *f* d'arrêt de défilement

scroll² *Comptr* **1** *vi* défiler **2** *vt* faire défiler

▶ **scroll down** *Comptr* **1** *vi* (*of operator*) faire défiler de haut en bas; (*of text*) défiler de haut en bas **2** *vipo* **to s. down a page** passer à la page suivante

▶ **scroll through** *vipo Comptr* (*text*) parcourir

▶ **scroll up** *Comptr* **1** *vi* (*of operator*) faire défiler de bas en haut; (*of text*) défiler de bas en haut **2** *vipo* **to s. up a page** passer à la page précédente

scrolling ['skrəʊlɪŋ] *n Comptr* défilement *m*

Scrooge [skru:dʒ] *n F* grippe-sou *m*

scrotal ['skrəʊtəl] *adj Anat* scrotal

scrotum ['skrəʊtəm] *n Anat* scrotum *m*

scrounge [skraʊndʒ] *F* **1** *vt* (*meal, cigarette*) se faire offrir; **to s. money** taper les gens; **to s. sth from** *or* **off sb** se faire offrir qch par qn; **to s. money from sb** taper qn; **can I s. a cigarette off you?** tu m'offres une cigarette?; **could I s. a lift from someone?** est-ce que quelqu'un peut m'emmener?; **she managed to s. together the money** elle a réussi à trouver l'argent en tapant les gens

2 *vi* **to s. round for sth** essayer de se faire offir *ou* payer qch; **to s. off sb** vivre aux crochets de qn, profiter de qn

3 *n* **he's on the s.** il cherche quelqu'un à taper; **he's always on the s.** c'est un tapeur

scrounger ['skraʊndʒər] *n F* tapeur, -euse; (*living off state etc*) profiteur, -euse; (*getting invitations to meals*) pique-assiette *mf inv*

scrub¹ [skrʌb] *n* (*bushes*) broussailles *fpl*; (*land*) brousse *f*; (*in Mediterranean country*) garrigue *f*

scrub² *n* **(a)** (*with brush*) **give your hands a good s.** frottez-vous bien les mains; **to give the table a good s.** frotter la table (à la brosse); *US* **s. brush** brosse *f* dure **(b)** *Am* **s. team** équipe *f* de deuxième ordre

scrub³ *vt* (**-bb-**) **(a)** (*clean*) (*pot*) récurer; (*floor*) frotter (avec une brosse *ou* à la brosse); *Naut* (*deck etc*) briquer; **to s. one's hands** bien se laver *ou* se frotter les mains **(b)** *F* (*cancel*) annuler; (*tape*) effacer; **she's been scrubbed from the team** on l'a virée de l'équipe

▶ **scrub down** *vtsep* (*walls etc*) lessiver; **go and s. yourself down** va te décrasser

▶ **scrub off** **1** *vtsep* enlever, frotter (pour faire partir) **2** *vi* s'enlever

▶ **scrub out** *vtsep* (*stain, mud, dirt etc*) faire partir; (*pots*) récurer

▶ **scrub up** *vi Med* (*wash*) (*of surgeon*) se brosser les mains (*avant d'opérer*)

scrubber ['skrʌbər] *n* **(a)** (*implement*) **(pan) s.** tampon *m* à récurer **(b)** *Br F* (*promiscuous woman*) pute *f*, putain *f*, marie-couche-toi-là *f inv*

scrubbing ['skrʌbɪŋ] *n* **(a)** (*cleaning*) (*of pot*) récurage *m*; (*with brush*) nettoyage *m* avec une brosse dure; *Br* **s. brush** brosse *f* dure *ou* de chiendent **(b)** = **scrub² (a)**

scrubland ['skrʌblænd] *n* brousse *f*

scruff [skrʌf] *n* **(a)** (*part of neck*) nuque *f*; (*skin*) peau *f* du cou; **to take sb by the s. of the neck** saisir qn par la peau du cou **(b)** *F* (*scruffy person*) **he's a real s.!** il est vraiment peu soigné!, il fait vraiment négligé!; **a s. like you** quelqu'un d'aussi peu soigné que toi

scruffily ['skrʌfɪlɪ] *adv* **s. dressed** débraillé, *F* dépenaillé

scruffiness ['skrʌfɪnɪs] *n* (*in dress, appearance*) négligence *f*; (*of district*) état *m* de délabrement

scruffy ['skrʌfɪ] *adj* (*person*) (*badly dressed*) peu soigné, débraillé, *F* dépenaillé; (*clothes etc*) sale, en piteux état; (*hotel*) minable; (*district*) délabré; **this jacket's getting a bit s.** cette veste commence à s'user; **a s. old van** un vieux camion tout pourri *ou* déglingué

scrum [skrʌm] *n Rugby* mêlée *f*; *F* (*pushing, shoving*) mêlée, bousculade *f*; **s. cap** protège-oreilles *m inv*; **s. half** demi *m* de mêlée

scrummage ['skrʌmɪdʒ] *n* = **scrum**

scrump [skrʌmp] *vi Br F* chiper des fruits (*dans un verger etc*)

scrumptious ['skrʌm(p)ʃəs] *adj F* épatant, fameux

scrumpy ['skrʌmpɪ] *n Br* cidre *m* fermier

scrunch¹ [skrʌntʃ] *n* (*of boots on snow etc*) crissement *m*

scrunch² **1** *vt* (*with teeth*) croquer avec les dents; **to s. a cigarette into the ground** écrabouiller une cigarette sur le sol; **to s. a piece of paper into a ball** faire une boule avec une feuille de papier **2** *vi* (*make scrunching sound*) craquer; (*of snow*) crisser

▶ **scrunch up** *vtsep* (*paper*) écraser; **to s. one's face up in disgust** faire une grimace de dégoût

scrunchy ['skrʌntʃɪ] *adj* (*cereal etc*) qui craque sous la dent

scruple¹ ['skru:p(ə)l] *n* scrupule *m*; **to have scruples about sth** avoir des scrupules à propos de qch; **to have scruples about doing sth** avoir des scrupules à faire qch; **he has no scruples about lying to them** il n'a aucun scrupule à leur mentir

scruple² *vi Fml* **not to s. to do sth** ne pas avoir de scrupules à faire qch

scrupulous ['skru:pjʊləs] *adj* **(a)** (*person, conscience etc*) scrupuleux; **the newspaper was s. about checking its sources** le journal vérifiait très soigneusement ses sources **(b)** (*care, work*) scrupuleux, minutieux

scrupulously ['skru:pjʊləslɪ] *adv* **(a)** (*with moral correctness*) scrupuleusement **(b)** (*carefully*) scrupuleusement, minutieusement; **s. clean** d'une propreté rigoureuse

scrupulousness ['skru:pjʊləsnɪs] *n* (*quality*) esprit *m* scrupuleux; **his s. in noting down all his expenses** les scrupules qu'il avait à relever toutes les dépenses

scrutineer [skru:tɪ'nɪər] *n* (*of votes*) scrutateur, -trice

scrutinize ['skru:tɪnaɪz] *vt* scruter, sonder; (*examine in depth*) examiner soigneusement; (*votes*) vérifier

scrutiny ['skru:tɪnɪ] *n* (*examination*) examen *m* minutieux *ou* attentif; **to come under s.** faire l'objet d'un examen

SCSI ['skʌzɪ] *n Comptr* (*abbr* **small computer systems interface**) SCSI *f*; **SCSI card** carte *f* SCSI

scuba ['sku:bə] *n* scaphandre *m* autonome; **s. diver** plongeur, -euse autonome; **s. diving** plongée *f* sous-marine autonome

scud [skʌd] *vi* (**-dd-**) filer comme le vent; **the clouds were scudding across the sky** les nuages filaient à travers le ciel

scuff¹ [skʌf] **1** *vt* frotter, racler (*avec les pieds*); (*leather, shoes etc*) érafler **2** *vi* marcher en traînant les pieds; **to s. through the autumn leaves** marcher dans les feuilles mortes

scuff² *n* **s. (mark)** éraflure *f*; (*on floor*) rayure *f*

▶ **scuff up** *vtsep* (*raise into the air*) (*snow, dust*) soulever (*en traînant les pieds*)

scuffed [skʌft] *adj* (*shoe*) éraflé; (*floor*) rayé

scuffing ['skʌfɪŋ] *n* (*on piston*) rayures *fpl* (d'usure)

scuffle¹ ['skʌf(ə)l] *n* échauffourée *f*, bagarre *f*

scuffle² *vi* se battre, se bagarrer

scull¹ [skʌl] *n* (*oar*) (*one of a pair*) aviron *m* de couple; (*used at stern*) godille *f*; (*boat*) scull *m*

scull² **1** *vi* (*row in pair*) ramer *ou* nager en couple; (*at stern*) godiller **2** *vt* (*row in pair*) faire avancer en couple; (*at stern*) faire avancer à la godille

scullery ['skʌlərɪ] *n Br* arrière-cuisine *f*, *pl* arrière-cuisines; **s. maid** fille *f* de cuisine

sculling ['skʌlɪŋ] *n* (*rowing*) (*in pair*) nage *f* à couple; (*at stern*) nage à la godille

sculpt [skʌlpt] *Art* **1** *vt* (*statue*) sculpter **2** *vi* faire de la sculpture

sculptor ['skʌlptər] *n Art* sculpteur *m*

sculptress ['skʌlptrɪs] *n Art* femme *f* sculpteur, sculptrice *f*

sculptural ['skʌlptʃər(ə)l] *adj* (*art*) sculptural

sculpture¹ ['skʌlptʃər] *n* (*art or object*) sculpture *f*

sculpture² **1** *vt* (*carve*) (*statue, stone etc*) sculpter; **she has finely sculptured features** elle a le visage très fin **2** *vi* faire de la sculpture

scum [skʌm] *n* **(a)** (*film of dirt*) pellicule *f* de crasse; (*froth*) écume *f*, mousse *f*; **to take the s. off sth** (*off boiled food*) écumer qch, enlever l'écume de qch; (*off bath etc*) enlever la crasse de qch **(b)** *Pej* (*people*) **the s. of society** le rebut de la société; **the s. of the earth** la lie de la société; **he's/they're s.** c'est une ordure/ce sont des ordures

scunner ['skʌnər] *n Scot* dégoût *m*; **to take a s. to sth/sb** prendre qch/qn en dégoût

scupper¹ ['skʌpər] *n Naut* dalot *m*

scupper² *vt F* (*ship, project etc*) couler, saborder; **we're scuppered!** on est fichus!

scurf [skɜ:f] *n* (*on head*) pellicules *fpl*; (*on skin*) désquamation *f*

scurfy ['skɜ:fɪ] *adj* (*head etc*) pelliculeux; (*skin*) squameux

scurrility [skə'rɪlɪtɪ] *n* (*of language, person*) grossièreté *f*; (*of attack*) ignominie *f*

scurrilous ['skʌrɪləs] *adj* (*language etc*) grossier, injurieux; (*person*) grossier; (*attack*) ignoble

scurrilously ['skʌrɪləslɪ] *adv* (*coarsely*) grossièrement; (*insultingly*) injurieusement

scurrilousness ['skʌrɪləsnɪs] *n* = **scurrility**

scurry¹ ['skʌrɪ] *n* (*dash*) course *f* précipitée, débandade *f*

scurry² *vi* (*dash*) aller à pas précipités, *F* filer

▶ **scurry away, scurry off** *vi* (*of mice*) filer; (*of people*) décamper; (*of animals*) détaler

scurvy ['skɜ:vɪ] *n Med* scorbut *m*; **to get s.** attraper le scorbut

scutcheon ['skʌtʃən] *n Her* écu *m*, écusson *m*

scuttle¹ ['skʌt(ə)l] *n* (*container*) **(coal) s.** seau *m* à charbon

scuttle² *n Naut* (*hatch*) écoutille *f*; *Am* (*in ceiling*) trappe *f*

scuttle³ *vt Naut* (*ship*) saborder

scuttle⁴ *vi* (*run*) courir à pas précipités

▶ **scuttle away, scuttle off** *vi* (*of crab, insect etc*) déguerpir; (*of person*) décamper
scuttling ['skʌtlɪŋ] *n* (*of ship*) sabordage *m*
Scylla ['sɪlə] *n Lit* **to be between S. and Charybdis** être tiraillé entre deux maux
scythe¹ [saɪð] *n Agr* faux *f*
scythe² *vt* (*corn etc*) faucher
▶ **scythe through** *vipo* (*with a weapon*) faucher; **her stick scythed through the air** son bâton fendit l'air
SDI [esdi:'aɪ] *n Mil* (*abbr* **strategic defence initiative**) initiative *f* de défense stratégique
SDLP [esdi:el'pi:] *n* (*abbr* **Social Democratic and Labour Party**) = parti *m* politique d'Irlande du Nord
SDP [esdi:'pi:] *n* (*abbr* **Social Democratic Party**) Parti *m* Social Démocrate
SE (*abbr* **south east**) SE
sea [si:] *n* **(a)** mer *f*; **at the bottom of the s.** au fond de la mer; **by the s.** au bord de la mer; **by s.** par (voie de) mer; **beyond** *or* **over the sea(s)** au delà des mers; **to go to s.** (*become sailor*) devenir marin; (*set sail*) (*of person, ship*) prendre la mer; **to put (out) to s.** (*of ship*) prendre la mer *ou* le large; **the open s., the high seas** le large, la haute mer; **on the high seas, out at s.** en haute mer, en pleine mer, au grand large; *Fig* **to be all at s.** (*perplexed*) être complètement perdu; **heavy** *or* **strong s.** grosse mer, mer grosse *ou* houleuse; **there's a heavy s.** il y a de la mer; *Naut* **to run before the s.** avoir la mer de l'arrière; **s. air** air marin *ou* de la mer; **s. breeze** brise *f* de mer *ou* du large; *F* **old s. dog** vieux loup *m* de mer; **s. lane** couloir *m* maritime; **to find** *or* **get one's s. legs** s'habituer à la mer; **he hasn't found his s. legs** il n'a pas encore le pied marin; **s. monster** monstre *m* marin; **s. power** puissance *f* navale; **s. salt** sel *m* de mer; **S. Scout** scout *m* marin; **s. travel** voyages *mpl* en mer; **room with a s. view** chambre avec vue sur la mer; **s. voyage** voyage en mer
(b) *Fig* (*of faces*) mer *f*; (*of blood*) bain *m*; *Lit* (*of troubles*) multitude *f*
sea anemone *n* anémone *f* de mer, actinie *f*
sea bass *n* bar *m*, loup *m*
sea bathing *n* baignade *f* en mer
sea battle *n* bataille *f* navale
seabed ['si:bed] *n* fond *m* de la mer
seabird ['si:bɜ:d] *n* oiseau *m* de mer
seaboard ['si:bɔ:d] *n* (*coastline*) littoral *m*; (*coastal region*) bord *m* de la mer, région *f* côtière
seaboots ['si:bu:ts] *npl* bottes *fpl* de marin *ou* de mer
seaborne ['si:bɔ:n] *adj* (*trade*) maritime; (*goods*) transporté par mer
sea calf *n* veau *m* marin, phoque *m*
sea captain *n* capitaine *m* de marine marchande
sea change *n Fig* bouleversement *m*; **it caused a s. in British politics** cela a provoqué un raz-de-marée sur la scène politique britannique
sea chest *n Naut* coffre *m* de marin *ou* de bord
sea coast *n* côte *f*
sea cow *n* vache *f* marine
sea crossing *n* traversée *f*
sea cucumber *n* concombre *m* de mer, holothurie *f*
sea eagle *n* aigle *m* de mer
sea elephant *n* éléphant *m* de mer
seafarer ['si:feərər] *n* (*sailor*) marin *m*
seafaring ['si:feərɪŋ] *adj* **s. man** (*sailor*) marin *m*; **a s. people** un peuple de navigateurs
sea fight *n* combat *m* naval
sea fish *n* poisson *m* de mer
sea fishery *n* pêche *f* maritime
sea fishing *n* pêche *f* maritime
sea floor *n* fond *m* de la mer
sea fog *n* brouillard *m* marin
seafood ['si:fu:d] *n* (*no pl*) fruits *mpl* de mer; **s. restaurant** restaurant *m* de fruits de mer
sea freight *n* fret *m* maritime; **s. services** messageries *fpl* maritimes
seafront ['si:frʌnt] *n* (*area facing sea*) bord *m* de (la) mer; (*promenade*) esplanade *f*, front *m* de mer; **house on the s.** maison sur le front de mer
sea god *n Myth* dieu *m* marin *ou* de la mer
seagoing ['si:gəʊɪŋ] *adj* (*ship*) de mer; (*nation*) de navigateurs
sea-green *n, adj* bleu-vert *m inv*
seagull ['si:gʌl] *n* (*bird*) mouette *f*, goéland *m*
seahorse ['si:hɔ:s] *n* hippocampe *m*
seal¹ [si:l] *n* **(a)** (*animal*) phoque *m*; **elephant s.** éléphant *m* de mer; **grey s.** phoque gris; **fur s.** otarie *f* à fourrure; **s. cull** abattage *m* de phoques **(b)** (*skin*) (peau *f* de) phoque *m*
seal² *vi* (*hunt seals*) chasser le phoque; **to go sealing** aller à la chasse au phoque
seal³ *n* **(a)** (*on deed etc*) sceau *m*; (*on letter, bottle of wine etc*) cachet *m*; (*on door etc*) scellés *mpl*; *Com* (*on goods for export*) plomb *m*; *Jur* **given under my hand and s.** signé et scellé par moi; **under the s. of silence/secrecy** sous le sceau du silence/du secret; **to give one's s. of approval to sth** donner son approbation à qch; **to set one's s. to sth** (*to mark with one's seal*) mettre son sceau sur qch; (*to authorize*) autoriser qch, confirmer qch; (*to give approval to*) donner son approbation à qch; **to set the s. on sth** (*on alliance, friendship*) sceller; (*on fate, defeat*) décider de; **this event set the s. on their fate** cet événement allait décider de leur sort; **under s.** sous scellés; *Rel* **under the s. of confession** dans le secret de la confession; *Jur* **official s.** (*affixed to property etc*) scellé *m*
(b) (*instrument*) sceau *m*; *Admin* **the Great S.** le grand sceau (*employé pour les actes publics*)
(c) *Tech* (*device for making airtight*) joint *m* d'étanchéité; (*airtight join*) joint étanche; **in order to get a good s.** pour obtenir une bonne étanchéité
seal⁴ *vt* **(a)** (*put seal on*) (*deed etc*) sceller; (*letter, bottle*) cacheter; (*at customs*) (*goods*) (faire) plomber; *Jur* (*door etc*) apposer les scellés sur; **to s. sb's fate** (*of event etc*) décider du sort de qn; **his fate is sealed** son sort est décidé
(b) (*close*) (*letter etc*) cacheter; (*block*) (*mineshaft, pipe*) obturer, boucher; (*jar*) fermer hermétiquement; (*box*) sceller; (*make airtight*) rendre étanche, étancher; (*of joint etc*) assurer l'étanchéité de; *Culin* (*meat*) saisir; **sealed with a kiss** (*of letter*) fermé avec un baiser; **the frontier has been sealed** la frontière est fermée; **my lips are sealed** (*I am not allowed to say*) il m'est défendu de parler; (*I shall not say*) je ne dirai pas un mot
▶ **seal in** *vtsep* (*contain*) enfermer; **fry the meat at a high temperature to s. in the flavour** faites revenir la viande à feu vif afin de lui conserver toute sa saveur
▶ **seal off** *vtsep* (*isolate*) isoler; **the area was sealed off by the police** le quartier a été bouclé par la police
▶ **seal up** *vtsep* = **seal⁴ (b)**
sealant ['si:lənt] *n* produit *m* d'étanchéité
sealed [si:ld] *adj* (*envelope*) cacheté; (*train*) plombé; (*box, door*) scellé; **in a s. jar** dans un bocal fermé hermétiquement; *Aut* **s. beam unit** bloc *m* optique; *Com* **s. bid** soumission *f* cachetée; *Com* **s.-bid pricing** fixation *f* d'un prix de soumission; *Aut* **s. cooling system** circuit *m* de refroidissement pressurisé; **s. envelope** pli *m* cacheté; *Mil, Naut* **s. orders** ordres *mpl* cachetés
sealer ['si:lər] *n* **(a)** (*ship*) bateau *m* pour la chasse aux phoques **(b)** (*seal hunter*) chasseur *m* de phoques
sea level *n* niveau *m* (moyen) de la mer; **500 metres above/below s.** 500 mètres au-dessus/au-dessous du niveau de la mer
sealing¹ ['si:lɪŋ] *n* (*seal hunting*) chasse *f* au phoque
sealing² *n* **(a)** (*putting on seal*) (*on deed etc*) scellage *m*; (*of letter etc*) cachetage *m*; (*at customs*) (*of goods*) plombage *m*; **s. wax** cire *f* à cacheter **(b)** (*closing*) (*of letter*) cachetage *m*; (*of pipe etc*) obturation *f*; **s. compound** lut *m*, mastic *m*; *Aut* (*for radiator*) anti-fuite *m inv*
sea lion *n* otarie *f*
sea loch *n Scot* bras *m* de mer
Sea Lord *n Br* lord *m* de l'Amirauté
sealskin ['si:lskɪn] *n* (peau *f* de) phoque *m*; **s. coat** manteau *m* en (peau de) phoque
seam¹ [si:m] *n* **(a)** *Sewing* couture *f*; (*in metal pipe, between boards etc*) joint *m*; (*weld*) soudure *f*; **flat s.** couture rabattue *ou* plate; **French s.** couture double *ou* anglaise; **a ship's seams** les coutures d'un navire; *Fig* **bursting at the seams** (*of room, building etc*) plein à craquer; **to be coming apart at the seams** (*of garment*) craquer de partout; *Fig* (*of economy, system etc*) aller à vau-l'eau **(b)** (*wrinkle*) (*on face etc*) ride *f* **(c)** *Min etc* (*of coal etc*) veine *f*
seam² *vt* **(a)** *Sewing* (*garment*) faire une couture à **(b) face seamed with scars** visage couvert de cicatrices
seaman, *pl* **-men** ['si:mən] *n* marin *m*; (*ordinary sailor*) matelot *m*, marin; *Br* **ordinary s.** matelot de troisième classe *ou* de pont; *Br* **able(-bodied) s.** matelot de deuxième classe; *Br* **leading s.** matelot (breveté) de première classe, quartier-maître *m*, *pl* quartier(s)-maîtres
seamanship ['si:mənʃɪp] *n* qualités *fpl* de navigateur; **thanks to his s.** grâce à ses qualités de navigateur
seam bowler *n Cr* = lanceur *m* qui se sert des joints de la balle pour lui donner de l'effet
sea mile *n* mille *m* marin *ou* nautique
sea mist *n* brume *f* marine
seamless ['si:mlɪs] *adj* **(a)** (*stocking*) sans couture; (*in metalworking*) (*tube etc*) sans soudure **(b)** *Fig* (*changeover, whole*) continu; **a s. transition** un passage très progressif

seamlessly ['si:mlɪslɪ] *adv Fig* très progressivement
seamstress ['semstrɪs] *n* couturière *f*
seamy ['si:mɪ] *adj* sordide; **one of the city's seamier districts** l'un des quartiers les plus sordides de la ville; **the s. side of life/politics** le côté sordide de l'existence/la politique
seance ['seɪɒns] *n* (*of spiritualists*) séance *f* de spiritisme
sea otter *n* loutre *f* marine *ou* de mer
seaplane ['si:pleɪn] *n Av* hydravion *m*
seaport ['si:pɔ:t] *n* port *m* maritime *ou* de mer
sear[1] [sɪər] *adj Lit* (*withered*) flétri, desséché
sear[2] *vt* **(a)** (*to burn*) brûler; (*a wound*) cautériser; *Fig* **the image would forever be seared on his memory** l'image resterait à tout jamais gravé dans sa mémoire **(b)** *Culin* (*meat etc*) saisir **(c)** *Fig Lit* (*harden*) (*conscience etc*) endurcir; (*heart*) durcir, dessécher
search[1] [sɜ:tʃ] *n* recherche(s) *f(pl)*; (*in a drawer etc*) fouille *f*; *Jur* perquisition *f*; (*at customs*) visite *f*; **to have a s. for sth** chercher qch; **her s. for her son/the truth** la recherche de son fils/la vérité; **in s. of sth** à la recherche de qch; **to be in s. of sth** être en quête de qch, être à la recherche de qch; *Comptr* **to do a s. for sth** rechercher qch; *Comptr* **s. and replace** recherche *f* et remplacement *m*; *Comptr* **s. and replace command** commande *f* de recherche et remplacement; *Comptr* **s. and replace function** fonction *f* recherche et remplacement; *Comptr* **s. command** commande *f* de recherche; *Comptr* **s. direction** direction *f* de la recherche; **to make a s.** faire des recherches; **right of s.** droit *m* de visite; (*at sea*) droit de recherche
search[2] **1** *vt* (*place, house, drawer, box, suspect, sb's pockets, one's memory*) fouiller; (*face*) scruter; (*at customs*) (*ship, sb's bags*) visiter; *Comptr* (*file, directory*) rechercher dans; *Comptr* **to s. and replace sth** rechercher et remplacer qch; *Jur* **to s. a house** faire une perquisition *ou* une visite domiciliaire; *Jur* **to s. the scene of a crime** fouiller le lieu d'un crime; *F* **s. me!** je n'ai pas la moindre idée! **2** *vi* faire des recherches; *Comptr* effectuer une recherche; **to s. after the truth** rechercher la vérité; **to s. for sb/sth** (re)chercher qn/qch
▶ **search out** *vtsep* chercher
▶ **search through** *vipo* fouiller
searcher ['sɜ:tʃər] *n* (*member of search party*) sauveteur *m*; **he was a s. after truth** c'était un homme qui recherchait la vérité
searching ['sɜ:tʃɪŋ] **1** *adj* (*examination*) minutieux; (*look*) scrutateur; **s. questions** questions de fond **2** *n* (*of suspect, house, ship etc*) fouille *f*; (*at customs*) visite *f*; *Jur* perquisition *f*
searchlight ['sɜ:tʃlaɪt] *n* projecteur *m*; (*beam*) faisceau *m* d'un/du projecteur; **to turn a s. on sth** braquer un projecteur sur qch
search party *n* expédition *f* de secours
search warrant *n Jur* mandat *m ou* ordre *m* de perquisition
searing ['sɪərɪŋ] *adj* (*pain*) fulgurant; (*criticism, indictment etc*) virulent
seascape ['si:skeɪp] *n* **(a)** (*view*) vue *f* sur la mer **(b)** (*picture*) marine *f*
sea serpent *n* serpent *m* de mer
sea shanty *n Mus* chanson *f* de marin
seashell ['si:ʃel] *n* coquille *f* de mer, coquillage *m*
seashore ['si:ʃɔ:r] *n* bord *m* de (la) mer; (*beach*) plage *f*
seasick ['si:sɪk] *adj* **to be s.** avoir le mal de mer; **to be a little/very s.** avoir un léger/fort mal de mer
seasickness ['si:sɪknɪs] *n* mal *m* de mer, *Spec* naupathie *f*; **s. tablets** cachets contre le mal de mer
seaside ['si:saɪd] *n* bord *m* de (la) mer; **at the s.** au bord de la mer; **s. resort** station *f* balnéaire; **a s. village/boarding house** un village/une pension au bord le mer
sea snake *n* serpent *m* de mer
season[1] ['si:z(ə)n] *n* [①**A6-7**,d,v; **A75**,B,1,c; **B4**,A,3,c; **B58**,B,1,c] **(a)** (*period of year*) saison *f*; **the four seasons** les quatre saisons; **the rainy s.** la saison des pluies; **hunting s.** saison de la chasse; **close/open s.** (*in hunting*) chasse fermée/ouverte; *Fishing* pêche *f* fermée/ouverte; **the tourist s.** la saison touristique; **S.'s Greetings** meilleurs vœux de fin d'année

(b) (*for fruit, vegetables etc*) saison *f*; **oysters are in/out of season** c'est/ce n'est pas la saison des huîtres; **strawberries are in s.** c'est la saison des fraises; **in s.** (*of animal*) en rut; (*of female*) en chaleur; *Com* **the high s.** la haute saison; *Com* **the slack s.** , **the off s.** la morte-saison

(c) *F* (*season ticket*) abonnement *m*

(d) *Th* saison *f*; *TV, Cin* cycle *m*; **a s. of French films** un cycle de films français

(e) *Sp* saison *f*; **the football/cricket/***etc* **s.** la saison de football/cricket/*etc*
season[2] **1** *vt* (*dish*) assaisonner; (*wood*) dessécher; (*barrel*) aviner; (*wine*) mûrir **2** *vi* (*of wood*) se sécher; (*of wine etc*) mûrir, se faire
seasonable ['si:zənəb(ə)l] *adj* **(a) s. weather** un temps de saison **(b)** *Lit* (*help, advice*) opportun, à propos
seasonal ['si:zən(ə)l] *adj* (*changes etc*) des saisons; (*trade, occupation*) saisonnier, -ière; **s. adjustment** ajustement *m* saisonnier; **s. affective disorder** dépression *f* saisonnière; **s. employment** emploi *m* saisonnier; **s. fluctuation** fluctuation *f* saisonnière; **s. worker** (ouvrier *m*) saisonnier *m*, (ouvrière *f*) saisonnière *f*
seasonally ['si:zən(ə)lɪ] *adv* selon la saison; **s. adjusted unemployment figures** chiffres *mpl* du chômage en données corrigées des variations saisonnières
seasoned ['si:zənd] *adj* **(a)** *Culin* (*dish*) assaisonné; **highly s. dish** plat *m* relevé *ou* épicé **(b)** (*wood, cigar etc*) sec, *f* sèche; (*wine*) mûr, fait **(c)** *Fig* (*soldier*) aguerri; **s. traveller** voyageur, -euse expérimenté(e); **a s. political campaigner** un militant politique chevronné
seasoning ['si:zənɪŋ] *n* **(a)** (*act*) *Culin* (*of dish*) assaisonnement *m*; (*of wood*) séchage *m*; (*of wine*) maturation *f*; (*of troops*) aguerrissement *m* **(b)** *Culin* (*condiment*) assaisonnement *m*, condiment *m*
season ticket *n Rail, Th, Fb* abonnement *m*; **s. holder** abonné, -ée
seat[1] [si:t] *n* **(a)** (*chair*) (*in Parliament, on bus, train etc*) siège *m*; (*in theatre*) place *f*; (*of toilet*) lunette *f*, siège; (*bench*) (*in park etc*) banc *m*; *Aut* **car s.** siège de voiture; *Av* **ejection** *or* **ejector s.** siège éjectable; *Aut, Th etc* **flap** *or* **folding s.** strapontin *m*; *F* **to be in the hot s.** être sur la sellette; **to book a s.** (*on train, in theatre*) réserver une place; **s. number** numéro *m* de place (assise); **s. pitch** espacement *m* des sièges

(b) (*somewhere to sit*) place *f*; **there were no seats left** il n'y avait plus de places; **to take a s.** s'asseoir; **to keep one's s.** rester assis; **keep a s. for me** gardez-moi une place; *Pol* **to have a s. in the House** avoir un siège à l'Assemblée; **to have a s. on the Council** être conseiller (municipal); **to have a s. on the board** avoir un siège au conseil d'administration

(c) (*part*) (*of chair*) siège *m*, fond *m*; *F* (*of person*) derrière *m*, fesses *fpl*; (*of trousers*) fond

(d) (*centre*) (*of government*) siège *m*; (*of disease*) foyer *m*; *Med* (*of pain etc*) siège; **a s. of learning** haut lieu *m* du savoir; **the s. of the emotions** le siège des émotions; **country s.** château *m*

(e) *Horseriding* (*way of sitting*) assiette *f*; **to have a good s.** avoir une bonne assiette

(f) *Tech* (*of valve*) siège *m*
seat[2] *vt* **(a)** (*cause to sit*) (*child etc*) (faire) asseoir; (*guests*) (*decide where to place*) placer; (*show to seat*) faire asseoir; **you will be seated in five minutes, madam** votre table sera prête dans cinq minutes, madame; **to remain seated** rester assis; *Fml* **please be seated** veuillez vous asseoir, je vous prie de vous asseoir **(b)** (*accommodate*) **bus which seats thirty** autobus à trente places (assises); **this table seats twelve** on tient à douze à cette table; **the hall seats two hundred** deux cents personnes peuvent tenir dans la salle **(c)** *Tech* (*valve*) assurer *ou* ajuster l'assise de
seatback [si:tbæk] *n* dossier *m*
seat belt *n Aut, Av* ceinture *f* de sécurité
-seater ['si:tər] *suff* **a two/single/***etc***-s.** *Aut* une voiture à deux places/une place/*etc*; *Av* un avion biplace *ou* à deux places/à une place/*etc*
seating ['si:tɪŋ] *n* (*allocation of seats*) allocation *f* des sièges *ou* des places; (*positioning*) placement *m*; (*seats*) (*in hall etc*) sièges *mpl*; *Tech* (*of valve*) siège; **there is more s. upstairs** il y a encore des places en haut; **s. arrangements** (*at dinner*) plan *m* de table; **s. capacity** nombre *m* de places (assises); (*of stadium etc*) capacité *f* d'accueil; **s. plan** (*at dinner*) plan de table/tables
SEATO ['si:təʊ] *n Mil* (*abbr* **Southeast Asia Treaty Organization**) OTASE *f* (Organisation *f* du Traité de l'Asie du Sud-Est)
seat-of-the-pants *adj F* **the project has been a bit of a s. operation** le projet a été mené au pif
sea trout *n* truite *f* saumonée
sea urchin *n* oursin *m*
sea wall *n* digue *f*
seaward ['si:wəd] **1** *adv* (*also* **seawards**) vers la mer, du côté du large **2** *adj* **s. breeze** brise du large **3** *n* **to s.** du côté du large, vers le large
seawater ['si:wɔ:tər] *n* eau *f* de mer; **s. therapy** thalassothérapie *f*
seaway ['si:weɪ] *n Naut* route *f*; **the St. Lawrence S.** la voie maritime du Saint-Laurent

seaweed ['si:wi:d] *n* algue *f*
seaworthiness ['si:wɜ:ðɪnɪs] *n* (état *m* de) navigabilité *f*
seaworthy ['si:wɜ:ðɪ] *adj* (*of ship*) en (bon) état de navigabilité
sebaceous [sɪ'beɪʃəs] *adj* (*gland, cyst*) sébacé
sebum ['si:bəm] *n Physiol* sébum *m*
sec [sek] *n F* = **second¹ (a)**; **half a s.!, just a s.!** une seconde!, deux secondes!
secant ['si:kənt] *Math* **1** *adj* sécant **2** *n* sécante *f*
secateurs [sekə'tɜ:z] *npl Br* sécateur *m*
secede [sɪ'si:d] *vi* faire sécession; (*from party*) se séparer, faire scission (**from** de)
secession [sɪ'seʃən] *n* sécession *f*; (*from party*) scission *f*; *US Hist* **the War of S.** la Guerre de Sécession
secessionist [sɪ'seʃənɪst] *adj, n* scissionniste *mf*; *US Hist* sécessionniste *mf*
seclude [sɪ'klu:d] *vt* tenir retiré *ou* éloigné *ou* écarté (**from** de)
secluded [sɪ'klu:dɪd] *adj* (*place*) écarté, retiré; **s. life** vie retirée *ou* de reclus; **to live a s. life** vivre une vie retirée *ou* de reclus
seclusion [sɪ'klu:ʒən] *n* solitude *f*; (*of village, farm*) isolement *m*; **in s.** retiré du monde; **to live in s.** vivre dans la solitude, vivre en reclus
second¹ ['sekənd] *n* **(a)** (*of time*) seconde *f*; **in a split s.** en une fraction de seconde; **for a s.** pendant une seconde; **wait a s.!** attendez une seconde *ou* un instant!; **I won't be a s.** je reviens tout de suite, j'en ai pour deux secondes; **s. hand** (*on clock, watch*) trotteuse *f* **(b)** *Math, Astron* seconde *f*
second² **1** *adj* **(a)** second, deuxième; **the s. of March** le deux mars; **twenty-/thirty-s.** vingt-/trente-deuxième; **Charles the S.** Charles Deux *ou* II; **our roads are s. to none** nos routes sont les meilleures du monde; **to be s. in line for the throne** être deuxième prétendant au trône; **I'm s. in line for promotion** je suis deuxième sur la liste des gens à promouvoir; **to be s. in command** commander en second; **to marry a s. time** *or* **for the s. time** se marier pour la deuxième *ou* seconde fois; **Spain's s. city** la deuxième ville d'Espagne; **the s. largest city in the world/in Portugal** la deuxième ville du monde/du Portugal; **to take a s. helping** (*at meal*) se resservir; **he's the s. oldest player in the team** après le doyen de l'équipe c'est lui le plus vieux; **she knew she would never be more than s. best** (*in person's affection*) elle savait qu'elle ne serait jamais plus qu'un second choix; (*of athlete*) elle savait qu'elle serait toujours deuxième; **we're not happy with s. best** nous ne nous contenterons pas d'un pis-aller; **in a fight with him you'll come off s. best** si tu t'affrontes à lui, tu n'en sortiras pas vainqueur; **s. ballot** deuxième tour *m*; **s. chance** deuxième chance; **s. childhood** deuxième enfance; *Rel* **the S. Coming** le second avènement; **s. cousin** cousin, -ine issu(e) de germain; **s. floor** *Br* deuxième étage *m*; *Am* premier étage; **to live on the s. floor** *Br* habiter au deuxième (étage); *Am* habiter au premier étage; *Sch* **s. form** ≈ (classe *f* de) cinquième *f*; *Aut* **s. gear** seconde *f*; **to take a s. holiday** reprendre des vacances; **s. home** résidence *f* secondaire; **my s. home** (*country*) mon deuxième pays; (*family*) ma deuxième famille; **s. language** seconde *ou* deuxième langue *f*; *Journ* **s. lead** (*second most important newspaper story*) gros titre *m* de deuxième ordre; **s. nature** seconde nature *f*; **it has become s. nature to her** elle le fait presque par instinct; **s. opinion** deuxième avis *m*; **in the s. place** deuxièmement, en second lieu; **to take s. place** passer second; **s. rate** médiocre, inférieur; (*artist etc*) de second ordre; *Parl* **s. reading** deuxième lecture *f*; **on s.** *Br* **thoughts** *or Am* **thought** tout bien réfléchi; **to have s. thoughts** avoir des hésitations (**about sth** au sujet de qch); **are you having s. thoughts?** est-ce que vous hésitez?; **I've had s. thoughts** j'ai bien réfléchi, j'ai changé d'avis; *Mus* **s. violin** second *ou* deuxième violon *m*; **to get one's s. wind** (*in race etc*) trouver un second souffle; *Fig* (*after feeling tired*) trouver un second souffle, se remettre

(b) (*another*) **a s. Camus/Churchill** un nouveau Camus/Churchill

2 *n* **(a)** (*in order*) second *m*, seconde *f*, deuxième *mf*; *Sp etc* **to come in a good s.** arriver second en très bonne position derrière le vainqueur; *Mil etc* **s. in command** commandant *m* en second; *Br Univ* **to get a s.** être reçu à la licence avec mention assez bien; *Br Univ* **upper/lower s.** (*degree*) mention *f* bien/assez bien; *Aut* **to start in s.** démarrer en seconde; *F* **anyone for seconds?** (*at meal*) qui veut se resservir?; *F* qui veut du rabiot *ou* du rab?

(b) *Mus* **major/minor s.** seconde *f* majeure/mineure

(c) *Com* **seconds** articles *mpl* de deuxième choix, produits *mpl* de second choix

(d) (*in duel*) témoin *m*; *Boxing* soigneur *m*

second³ *vt* **(a)** (*support*) (*person*) seconder; (*in debate etc*) (*motion*) appuyer **(b)** [sɪ'kɒnd] *Br Mil etc* (*detach*) (*officer*) mettre en disponibilité *ou* hors cadre (*pour fonctions spéciales etc*); **to be seconded** être mis hors cadre, être détaché (**to** à; **from** de)
secondary ['sekənd(ə)rɪ] *adj* secondaire; (*evidence*) indirect; (*rôle etc*) peu important, accessoire; **s. meaning of a word** sens dérivé d'un mot; **of s. importance** d'importance secondaire; *Br formerly* **s. modern** = collège *m* offrant un enseignement semi-professionnel; *Med* **s. cancer** métastase *f*; **s. education** enseignement *m* secondaire *ou* du second degré; *Med* **s. infection** surinfection *f*; **s. road** route *f* secondaire *ou* départementale; **s. sector** secteur *m* secondaire
secondary school *n* école *f* secondaire; *Admin* établissement *m* d'enseignement secondaire
second chamber *n Parl* deuxième chambre *f*
second class **1** *n Rail* deuxième classe *f* **2** *adv* **to travel s.** voyager en seconde (classe)
second-class *adj* (*ticket, carriage*) de seconde (classe); **s. citizen** citoyen, -enne de deuxième *ou* seconde classe; *Br Univ* **s. degree** = licence *f* avec mention assez bien; **s. mail** courrier *m* (à tarif) non urgent
second-degree *adj Med* **s. burns** brûlures *fpl* au deuxième degré
seconder ['sekəndər] *n* personne *f* qui soutient une proposition; **I need a s.** il me faut quelqu'un qui soutienne ma proposition
second-generation *adj* (*immigrant etc*) de la deuxième génération
second-guess *vt* **to s. sb** anticiper ce que qn va dire/faire
second-hand **1** *adv* (*to buy*) d'occasion; **to hear news s.** recevoir des nouvelles de seconde main *ou* d'un tiers **2** *adj* (*car, book, furniture etc*) d'occasion; (*news etc*) de seconde main; **s. bookshop** librairie *f* d'occasion; **s. clothes shop** boutique *f* de vêtements d'occasion; **s. dealer** (*in clothes*) fripier, -ière; (*in books*) bouquiniste *mf*; **the s. market** le marché de l'occasion
secondly ['sekəndlɪ] *adv* deuxièmement, en second lieu
secondment [sɪ'kɒndmənt] *n Br Mil etc* détachement *m* (**to** à; **from** de); **to be on s. to another department** être détaché auprès d'un autre service
second name *n* nom *m* de famille
second person *n Gram* deuxième personne *f*
second-row forward *n Rugby* avant *m* de deuxième ligne
second sight *n* clairvoyance *f*, seconde vue *f*
secrecy ['si:krɪsɪ] *n* secret *m*; **in s.** en secret; **why all the s.?** pourquoi tous ces secrets?; **there's no s. about it** ça n'a rien de secret; **business conducted in complete s.** affaires menées dans le plus grand secret; **to swear sb to s.** faire jurer le silence à qn
secret ['si:krɪt] **1** *adj* secret, -ète; (*place*) secret, caché; **to keep sth s.** tenir *ou* garder qch secret, cacher qch, taire qch; **he'd kept it s. from me for years** il me l'avait caché pendant des années; **desk with a s. compartment** bureau à secret; **s. meeting/assembly** réunion/assemblée secrète; **s. admirer** admirateur *m* secret, admiratrice *f* secrète; **s. ballot** vote *m* au scrutin secret; **s. door** porte cachée *ou* dérobée; *Mil, Fig* **s. weapon** arme *f* secrète

2 *n* secret *m*; **in s.** en secret; **can you keep a s.?** est-ce que tu peux garder un secret?; **it can be our little s.** ça sera notre petit secret à nous; **I make no s. of it** je n'en fais pas mystère, je ne le cache pas; **to let sb into the s.** mettre qn dans le secret; **the s. is not to press too hard** l'astuce consiste à ne pas appuyer trop fort; **it's no s.** ce n'est pas un secret; **an open s.** un secret de Polichinelle
secret agent *n* agent *m* secret
secretarial [sekrə'teərɪəl] *adj* (*work*) de secrétariat; **s. college/course** école *f*/cours *m* de secrétariat; **s. post** poste *m* de secrétaire; **s. service** service *m* de secrétariat; **s. staff** personnel *m* de secrétariat
secretariat [sekrə'teərɪət] *n* secrétariat *m*
secretary ['sekrət(ə)rɪ] *n* **(a)** secrétaire *mf*; **private s.** secrétaire particulier, -ière; *Br* **company s.** secrétaire *m* général; **(1st/2nd/3rd) s.** (*to ambassador*) ≈ secrétaire d'ambassade **(b) s. (bird)** serpentaire *m*, secrétaire *m*
secretary-general *n* secrétaire *m* général
Secretary of State *n Br* ministre *m*; *US* ≈ Ministre des Affaires étrangères
secrete¹ [sɪ'kri:t] *vt* (*of gland etc*) sécréter
secrete² *vt* (*hide*) cacher
secretion [sɪ'kri:ʃən] *n Physiol* sécrétion *f*
secretive ['si:krɪtɪv] *adj* (*person*) secret, -ète; (*in negative sense*) cachottier; (*behaviour*) fermé; **why are you being so s. about it?** pourquoi fais-tu tant de cachotteries là-dessus?
secretively ['si:krɪtɪvlɪ] *adv* avec dissimulation
secretiveness ['si:krɪtɪvnɪs] *n* caractère *m* secret; (*on particular occasion*) cachotterie *f*
secretly ['si:krɪtlɪ] *adv* en secret; (*to think etc*) secrètement

secret police *n* police *f* secrète
Secret Service *n* = Deuxième Bureau *m*
sect [sekt] *n* secte *f*
sectarian [sek'teərɪən] **1** *adj* (*attitude, cult*) sectaire; **s. killing** assassinat *m* sectaire; **s. quarrels** querelles *fpl* partisanes **2** *n* sectaire *mf*
sectarianism [sek'teərɪənɪz(ə)m] *n* sectarisme *m*; (*attitude*) esprit *m* sectaire
section¹ ['sekʃən] *n* **(a)** (*part*) section *f*, portion *f*; (*of structure, company*) division *f*, partie *f*; (*of tube, railway etc*) tronçon *m*; *Com* (*of store*) rayon *m*; (*in shop*) secteur *m*; *US Rail* (*of sleeping car*) compartiment *m*; (*component, prefabricated part*) élément *m*; (*of document, text etc*) partie; (*of law etc*) article *m*; *Mus* (*in orchestra*) section; *Mil* (*fighting unit*) (*of infantry section*) groupe de combat; (*of fusiliers, grenadiers*) équipe *f*; *Am* (*area*) lotissement *m*; *Av* **nose s.** partie avant, nez *m*; **tail section** partie arrière, queue *f*; **the bookcase comes in sections** la bibliothèque est démontable; *Journ* **sports/travel/financial/TV s.** rubrique *f* sport/voyage/finances/télé; **all sections of the population** toutes les couches de la population, toutes les catégories sociales; **s. manager** chef *m* de section
(b) (*cut*) *Geom* section *f*; *Archit, Constr etc* coupe *f*, profil *m*, section; (*in metalwork*), *Constr* profilé *m*; (*thin slice*) tranche *f*, lamelle *f*; **microscopic s.** mince lame *f*, plaque *f* (*pour examen au microscope*); **conic/plane s.** section conique/plane; **horizontal s.** coupe *ou* section horizontale
section² *vt* **(a)** (*cut*) sectionner **(b)** (*send to mental hospital*) faire interner
sectional ['sekʃən(ə)l] *adj* **(a)** (*interests*) particulier; (*rivalries*) interne **(b)** (*drawing etc*) en coupe, en profil; (*area*) de section **(c) s. furniture** mobilier *m* modulaire
sectionalism ['sekʃənəlɪz(ə)m] *n US* régionalisme *m*, esprit *m* de clocher
sector ['sektər] *n* **(a)** *Geom, Astron, Mil, Comptr* secteur *m*; *Admin* **public/private s.** secteur public/privé; **public s. spending** dépenses *fpl* publiques **(b)** *Geom* (*instrument*) compas *m* de proportion
secular ['sekjʊlər] *adj Rel* (*history, art etc*) laïque, séculier; (*music*) profane; **s. priest** (prêtre *m*) séculier *m*
secularism ['sekjʊlərɪz(ə)m] *n* **(a)** laïcisme *m* **(b)** *Phil* laïcité *f*
secularization [sekjʊləraɪ'zeɪʃən] *n* (*of church property etc*) sécularisation *f*; (*of school*) laïcisation *f*
secularize ['sekjʊləraɪz] *vt* (*property, priest*) séculariser; (*school*) laïciser
secure¹ [sɪ'kjʊər] *adj* **(a)** (*free from anxiety*) (*person*) tranquille, en paix; *Psy* sûr de soi; (*future, nomination*) assuré; **you make me feel s.** tu me donnes confiance; **to feel s. of victory** être assuré *ou* certain de la victoire; *Fml* **s. in the knowledge that ...** sachant avec certitude que ...
(b) (*safe*) (*valuables*) en sûreté; (*investment, place*) sûr; **s. communications** communications inviolables; **s. from attack** à l'abri d'une attaque; **the prisoner is s.** le prisonnier est en lieu sûr
(c) (*door, plank, foundations, lock etc*) solide; (*foothold, grasp*) ferme, sûr; **that rope doesn't look very s.** cette corde n'a pas l'air très solide; **to make the boat s.** bien amarrer le bateau
secure² *vt* **(a)** (*keep out of danger*) mettre en sûreté; (*prisoner*) mettre en lieu sûr; **to s. a pass** (*in mountains*) garder un défilé
(b) (*immobilize*) (*sth which is loose*) bien fixer; (*flapping shutter etc*) attacher, fixer; (*cargo*) arrimer; **doors and windows should be properly secured** les portes et les fenêtres doivent être bien fermées
(c) *Jur, Com* (*borrower*) garantir; **to s. a debt by mortgage** hypothéquer une créance; *Fin* **to s. a loan** garantir un emprunt, nantir un prêt; *Fin* **to s. by warrant** warranter
(d) (*obtain*) obtenir; (*objective*) atteindre; **to s. sth for sb** (*future, victory, holiday etc*) assurer qch pour qn; **he secured his future with the company by ...** il a assuré son avenir dans l'entreprise en ...
secured [sɪ'kjʊəd] *adj Jur* (*loan*) garanti; *Fin* **s. bond** obligation *f* cautionnée
securely [sɪ'kjʊəlɪ] *adv* **(a)** (*safely*) en sécurité; **to be s. protected** être parfaitement protégé; **he is s. behind bars** il est hors d'état de nuire **(b)** (*firmly*) solidement; **s. tightened** bien serré; **make sure your seatbelt is s. fastened** assurez-vous que vous avez bien attaché votre ceinture de sécurité
securitization [sɪkjʊərɪtaɪ'zeɪʃən] *n St Exch* titrisation *f*
securitize [sɪ'kjʊərɪtaɪz] *vt St Exch* titriser
security [sɪ'kjʊərɪtɪ] *n* **(a)** (*of lock, person etc*) sécurité *f*, sûreté *f*; **to live in s.** vivre en sécurité; **s. of tenure** (*in job*) sécurité de l'emploi; (*as tenant*) jouissance *f* d'une location; **(job) s.** sécurité de l'emploi
(b) (*at military base, during state visit etc*) sécurité *f*; **s. alert** alerte *f* au danger; **s. blanket** (*for child*) objet *m* transitionnel; **a s. blanket** *or* **cordon has been thrown around the airport** un déploiement de forces de l'ordre a été organisé autour de l'aéroport; *Admin, Mil etc* **s. clearance** habilitation *f*; (*document*) laissez-passer *m*; **s. code** code *m* confidentiel; **the (United Nations) S. Council** le Conseil de sécurité (des Nations Unies); **s. deposit** dépôt *m* de garantie; **s. device** dispositif *m* de sûreté; *Comptr* **s. level** niveau *m* de sécurité; **s. measures** mesures *fpl* de sécurité; *Comptr* **s. password** mot *m* de passe sécuritaire; **s. personnel** gardiens *mpl*; **he's/it's a s. risk** il/cela constitue un danger *ou* un risque pour la sécurité; **(maximum) s. wing** quartier *m* de haute sécurité
(c) (*safeguard*) sécurité *f*; **there's a further s. against theft** il y a un dispositif de sécurité antivol supplémentaire
(d) *Com, Jur* (*financial guarantee*) garantie *f*; (*for payment of debt*) caution *f*, cautionnement *m*; (*collateral*) nantissement *m*; (*person*) garant, -ante; **s. for a debt** (*money etc*) garantie d'une créance; **to stand s. for sb** se porter garant *ou* caution pour qn; **to give sth as (a) s.** donner qch en cautionnement; **to lend money on s. /without s.** prêter de l'argent sur nantissement/sur gage à découvert
(e) *St Exch* **securities** titres *mpl*, papiers *mpl* valeurs, valeurs *fpl* (mobilières); **government securities** fonds *mpl* d'État; **the securities market** le marché des valeurs, le marché *m* des titres; *US* **Securities and Exchange Commission** = Commission *f* des opérations de Bourse; **securities house** société *f* de bourse; **securities lodged as collateral** titres déposés en nantissement; **securities issued** valeurs *fpl* émises
(f) (social) s. sécurité *f* sociale; **to live on s.** vivre des allocations
security-coded *adj* (*radio*) codé, à code de sécurité; *Aut* **s. immobilizer** antidémarrage *m* codé
security firm *n* société *f* de gardiennage
security forces *npl* forces *fpl* de sécurité
security guard *n* vigile *m*; (*for premises*) garde *m*; (*carrying money*) convoyeur *m* de fonds
security officer *n* vigile *m*, agent *m* de sécurité
security patrol *n* patrouille *f* de sûreté *ou* de protection
sedan [sɪ'dæn] *n* **(a)** *Am Aut* voiture *f* de tourisme; **four-door s.** berline *f* **(b)** *Hist* **s. chair** chaise *f* à porteurs
sedate¹ [sɪ'deɪt] *adj* (*person*) posé, pondéré, réfléchi; (*lifestyle*) calme; (*deportment*) composé, calme
sedate² *vt Med* donner un sédatif à
sedately [sɪ'deɪtlɪ] *adv* posément
sedation [sɪ'deɪʃən] *n Med* sédation *f*; **to be under s.** être sous sédatifs *ou* sous calmants
sedative ['sedətɪv] *adj, n Med* sédatif *m*, calmant *m*
sedentary ['sedəntrɪ] *adj* (*posture*) assis; (*job etc*) sédentaire; **s. life** vie sédentaire
sedge [sedʒ] *n* (*plant*) joncs *mpl*, roseaux *mpl*; **s. warbler** (*bird*) phragmite *m* des joncs
sediment ['sedɪmənt] *n* sédiment *m*; (*in bottle*) dépôt *m*; (*in wine*) lie *f*; *Ch* résidu *m*
sedimentary [sedɪ'ment(ə)rɪ] *adj Geol* (*layer, rock*) sédimentaire
sedimentation [sedɪmen'teɪʃən] *n* sédimentation *f*
sedition [sɪ'dɪʃən] *n* sédition *f*
seditious [sɪ'dɪʃəs] *adj* séditieux
seduce [sɪ'djuːs] *vt* séduire; **they seduced him away from the company with ...** ils ont réussi à le convaincre de quitter l'entreprise en lui faisant miroiter ...; **to s. sb into doing sth** convaincre qn de faire qch
seducer [sɪ'djuːsər] *n* séducteur, -trice
seduction [sɪ'dʌkʃən] *n* **(a)** (*sexual*) séduction *f* **(b)** (*attractiveness*) (*usu pl*) attrait *m*, charme *m*; **the seductions of such a lifestyle** les attraits *ou* charmes d'un tel style de vie
seductive [sɪ'dʌktɪv] *adj* (*look, charm*) séducteur; (*music, argument, speech*) charmeur; (*smile*) aguichant; **s. offer** offre *f* séduisante *ou* attrayante *ou* alléchante
seductively [sɪ'dʌktɪvlɪ] *adv* avec séduction; **s. attractive** très attirant
seductiveness [sɪ'dʌktɪvnɪs] *n* (*of offer etc*) caractère *m* séduisant *ou* attrayant *ou* alléchant; (*of woman*) séduction *f*, charme *m*; (*of style*) charme
sedulous ['sedjʊləs] *adj Fml* assidu, scrupuleux
sedulously ['sedjʊləslɪ] *adv Fml* scrupuleusement
see¹ [siː] [①**A40**,C,1,a; **B33**,2,b,i] (*pt* **saw** [sɔː]; *pp* **seen** [siːn]) **1** *vt* **(a)** (*with eyes*) voir; **I saw it with my own eyes** je l'ai vu de mes propres yeux, je l'ai de mes yeux vu; **the cathedral can be seen from a long way off** on voit la cathédrale de très loin; **to s. the sights of the town** visiter les monuments de

la ville; **there's nothing to s.** il n'y a rien à voir; **I can't s. anything** je ne vois rien; **the moment I saw him** dès que je l'ai aperçu *ou* vu; **did you s. that programme last night?** tu as vu cette émission hier soir?; **now s. what you've done!** regarde ce que tu as fait!; **s. page 50** voir page 50; **s. above** se reporter plus haut; **s. (on) the back** voir au verso; **I'm not fit to be seen** je ne suis pas présentable; **to s. things** (*hallucinate*) avoir des hallucinations *ou* des visions; **it has to be seen to be believed** il faut le voir pour le croire; **the squalor in which they live has to be seen to be believed** ils vivent dans une misère, il faut le voir pour le croire; **to s. sb do** *or* **doing sth** voir qn faire qch; **I saw him fall** je l'ai vu tomber; **to s. sb coming** voir venir qn; *Fig* **they saw you coming a mile off** ils t'ont vu arriver de loin; **to s. one's way** voir où l'on va; **I can't s. a way out of this problem** je ne vois pas d'issue à ce problème; **could you s. your way to lending me your car?** est-ce que par hasard, tu pourrais me prêter ta voiture?; **to s. the back of sb** se débarrasser de qn; **to s. sense** *or* **reason** entendre raison; **I'll s. him in hell first!** qu'il aille au diable!, qu'il aille se faire pendre!; **he has seen a great deal of the world** (*he has travelled a great deal*) il a beaucoup voyagé; (*he has a great deal of experience*) il a une vaste expérience; **the city hasn't seen such crowds in decades** la ville n'a pas connu une foule pareille depuis des dizaines d'années; **the country saw many changes** le pays a connu de grands changements; *Mil* **the first time he saw action** quand il a reçu le baptême du feu; *Mil* **he saw action in the desert** il a combattu dans le désert

(b) (*understand*) comprendre, saisir; (*the error of one's ways etc*) reconnaître; **I don't s. how/why/where ...** je ne vois pas comment/pourquoi/où ...; **I don't s. the need** *or* **necessity for ...** je ne vois pas l'intérêt de ...; **they cannot s. the truth** la vérité leur échappe; **I can't s. the difference** je ne vois pas la différence; **I don't s. the point** je ne vois pas l'intérêt; **he can't s. a joke** il ne comprend pas la plaisanterie; **I s. what you mean** je vois ce que vous voulez dire; **I don't s. that at all!** (*I don't agree*) je ne suis pas du tout d'accord!

(c) (*observe*) **to s. oneself in one's children** se reconnaître dans ses enfants; **I don't know what you s. in her** je ne vois pas ce que tu lui trouves; **it remains to be seen whether ...** (il) reste à savoir si ...; **whether this is true remains to be seen** (il) reste à savoir si ceci est vrai; **I can't s. any sense** *or* **the sense in continuing this discussion** je ne vois pas l'intérêt de continuer cette discussion; **I s.** *or* **saw in the paper that ...** j'ai vu dans le journal que ...; **he never lived to s. the project finished** il est mort avant que le projet ne soit achevé; **I s. (that) you're a sports fan** je vois que vous êtes un fan de sport

(d) (*perceive sth in a certain way*) voir, percevoir; **I s. things differently now** aujourd'hui je vois les choses autrement; **this is how I s. it** voici comme je perçois la chose

(e) (*envisage*) voir; **what do you s. happening next?** d'après vous, qu'est-ce qui va se passer ensuite?; **how do you s. the situation in a year's time?** comment pensez-vous que la situation aura évolué dans un an?; **I don't s. myself still doing this in a year's time** je ne me vois *ou* m'imagine pas faire encore cela dans un an; **how do you s. things developing?** comment est-ce que vous envisagez l'avenir?; **I can't s. them accepting this** je ne peux pas croire qu'ils vont accepter cela; **they say this will be more efficient but I don't s. it** ils disent que cela sera plus efficace, mais je n'y crois pas; **I don't s. any chance of that** à mon avis c'est peu probable; **I can't s. you as a boxer** je ne te vois pas en boxeur; **I can't s. myself doing this** je ne me vois *ou* m'imagine pas en train de faire cela

(f) (*examine*) examiner; **let me s. that letter again** repassez-moi cette lettre (pour que je la relise)

(g) (*investigate, enquire, discover*) **I'll s. what I can do** je vais voir ce que je peux faire; **let's s. what happens if ...** voyons ce qu'il se passe si ...

(h) (*make sure*) **to s. (to it) that everything is in order** s'assurer que tout est en ordre; **I shall s. (to it) that he comes** je me charge de le faire venir; **s. (to it) that you don't miss the train!** faites attention de ne pas manquer le train!; *F* **he'll s. you (all) right** il s'occupera de toi

(i) (*meet*) (*person*) voir; (*visitor*) recevoir; (*doctor, solicitor etc*) consulter, voir; **he sees a great deal of the Longs** il fréquente *ou* voit beaucoup les Long; **we don't s. much of each other** nous ne nous voyons pas souvent; **when shall I s. you again?** quand est-ce que je vais vous revoir?; **are you seeing another woman?** est-ce que tu as *ou* vois une autre femme?; **s. you soon!, (I'll) be seeing you!** à bientôt!; **(I'll) s. you Thursday!** à jeudi!; *F* **s. you!** salut!, à plus [aplys]!; **to go to** *or* **and s. sb** aller voir qn; **I can't s. him today** (*visitor*) je ne peux pas le recevoir aujourd'hui

(j) (*speak to*) **I want to s. the manager** je veux voir le directeur; **can I s. you for a minute in my office?** je peux vous voir un instant dans mon bureau?; **I'd like to s. you on business** je voudrais vous parler affaires

(k) (*escort, accompany*) **to s. sb home** reconduire qn *ou* accompagner qn jusque chez lui/elle; **I saw him to the station** je l'ai accompagné jusqu'à la gare; **I'll s. you to the door** je vous accompagne jusqu'à la porte

(l) (*at cards*) **I'll s. you** je demande à voir; **I'll s. your hundred** je vous suis à cent

2 *vi* **(a)** voir; **she can't s. very well** (*her sight is poor*) elle ne voit pas très bien, sa vue n'est pas très bonne; (*on specific occasions*) elle ne voit pas très bien; **cats can s. in the dark** les chats voient clair la nuit; **as far as the eye can s.** à perte de vue; *Old-fashioned F* **s. here!** (*annoyance*) dites donc!, voyons!

(b) (*understand*) voir; **as far as I can s.** autant que je puisse en juger; **I s.** je vois, je comprends; **ah, I s.!** ah, je vois!; **do you s.?**; *F* **s.?** tu vois?; **you s., I never liked them** voyez-vous, je ne les ai jamais aimés

(c) (*observe*) voir; **s. for yourself** voyez par vous-même; **seeing is believing** on ne peut nier ce qu'on voit de ses propres yeux; **we shall s.** nous verrons (bien); **we'll soon s.** on le saura vite; **we'll soon s. if ...** on saura vite si ...; **I'll be a good musician one day, you'll s.** je serai un bon musicien un jour, vous verrez; **s.! I told you he wouldn't let us down** tu vois! je t'avais dit qu'il ne nous laisserait pas tomber

(d) (*examine*) voir; **can I s.?** je peux voir?; **let me s.!, let's s.!** fais voir!; **have you got a free room? – let me s.** est-ce que vous avez une chambre libre? – voyons (voir); **it was, let me s., in 1938** c'était, voyons (voir), en 1938

(e) (*consider*) voir; **can we go to the beach, Mummy? – we'll** *or* **I'll s.** est-ce qu'on peut aller à la plage, maman? – je verrai *ou* on verra

(f) (*find out*) (aller) voir

see[2] *n Rel* (*of bishop*) siège *m* épiscopal, évêché *m*; (*of archbishop*) archevêché *m*; **the Holy S.** le Saint-Siège

▶ **see about** *vipo* **(a)** (*attend to*) s'occuper de; **I'll have to s. about that old door** il faudra que je m'occupe de cette vieille porte **(b)** (*consider*) voir; **I'll s. about it** je verrai ça; *Iron* **we'll (soon) s. about that!** c'est ce qu'on va voir!

▶ **see across** *vtas* (*escort to other side of*) **to s. sb across the road** aider qn à traverser la rue

▶ **see in 1** *vi* (*look in*) voir à l'intérieur; **the curtains were drawn, so we couldn't s. in** les rideaux étaient tirés, nous ne pouvions rien voir à l'intérieur **2** *vtsep* (*escort in*) (*person*) faire entrer; **to s. the new year in** faire le réveillon du nouvel an

▶ **see into** *vipo* (*interior of room, building etc*) voir; **to s. into the future** voir l'avenir; **to s. into sb's heart** lire dans le cœur de qn

▶ **see off** *vtsep* **(a) to s. sb off at the station** accompagner qn (jusqu')à la gare; **we'll come to s. you off** nous viendrons vous dire au revoir **(b) to s. sb off (the premises)** (*escort*) accompagner qn jusqu'à la sortie; (*make sure they go*) s'assurer du départ de qn **(c)** (*in fight etc*) **she saw off two bigger girls** elle a battu deux filles plus grandes qu'elle; **the dogs saw them off** les chiens les ont fait fuir

▶ **see out** *vtsep* **(a)** (*escort to door*) accompagner jusqu'à la porte; **I'll s. myself out** je connais le chemin, ce n'est pas la peine de me raccompagner **(b)** (*stay until end of*) voir la fin de; (*undertaking*) mener à bonne fin; **I'll s. another year out here then go home** je vais passer une autre année ici puis je rentrerai; **I don't think these boots will s. the winter out** je ne crois pas que ces bottes feront l'hiver; **he isn't expected to s. out the week** il y a peu de chances qu'il survive jusqu'à la fin de la semaine; **he'll s. us all out!** (*will survive us*) il nous enterrera tous!

▶ **see over, see round** *vipo* (*tour*) (*house etc*) visiter, voir

▶ **see through 1** *vipo* (*not be deceived by*) (*person*) deviner les intentions de; **I saw through him** j'ai deviné ses intentions, je l'ai percé à jour; **I saw through their little game** j'ai vite compris leur petit jeu

2 *vtas* **(a)** (*stay until end of*) **to s. a show/film through** assister à un spectacle/regarder un film jusqu'au bout; **to s. a matter through** mener une affaire à bonne fin *ou* jusqu'au bout; **I'll s. it through** je tiendrai jusqu'au bout

(b) (*help to cope*) aider; **£20 should s. me through (to Monday)** 20 livres devraient me suffire (jusqu'à lundi); **friends and relatives are seeing her through this bad time** ses amis et sa famille l'aident à traverser cette période difficile; **200 gallons should s. us through the winter** 200 gallons devraient nous suffire pour l'hiver

▶ **see to** *vipo* (*deal with*) s'occuper de; **I'll have to get it seen to** il faut que je m'en occupe; **I'll s. to it** je vais m'en occuper, je m'en charge; **I'll s. to it that you're not disturbed** je ferai en sorte que vous ne soyez pas dérangé

▶ **see up** *vtsep (accompany)* **to s. sb up** faire monter qn

seed[1] [siːd] *n* **(a)** graine *f*; *(of apple, pear, grapes etc)* pépin *m*; **mustard s.** graine de moutarde; **s. vessel** péricarpe *m*; **seed(s)** *(in gardening, agriculture)* semence(s) *fpl*, graine(s); **to go** *or* **run to s.** *(of plant)* monter en graine; *(of land)* tomber en friche; *(of person)* se laisser aller; *Fig* **the seeds of discord** les germes *mpl* de la discorde; **to sow (the) seeds of discord/doubt** semer la discorde/le doute; **s. pearls** semence de perles; **s. potatoes** pommes *fpl* de terre de semence

(b) *Arch, Lit* = **semen**

(c) *Bible, Lit (descendants)* descendance *f*, lignée *f*; **the s. of Abraham** la descendance d'Abraham

(d) *Tennis* tête *f* de série

seed[2] **1** *vi (of plant)* monter en graine; *(of cereals)* venir à graine **2** *vt* **(a)** *(sow with seeds) (field etc)* semer; *Met* **to s. clouds** provoquer la pluie **(b)** *(remove seeds from) (melons, grapes etc)* épépiner **(c)** *Tennis* **to s. the players** classer les joueurs; **seeded players** têtes *fpl* de série; **she was seeded tenth** elle était classée dixième

seed bed *n* (couche *f* de) semis *m*, germoir *m*

seed box *n* boîte *f* à semis

seedcake ['siːdkeɪk] *n Culin* gâteau *m* parfumé au carvi

seed capital *n* capital *m* initial *ou* de départ

seed corn *n* grain *m* de semence; *Fig* embryon *m*

seediness ['siːdɪnɪs] *n* **(a)** *(of clothes)* état *m* miteux; *(of building)* état minable; **the s. of the area surprised him** il fut surpris de voir à quel point l'endroit était minable **(b)** *F (feeling of being unwell)* indisposition *f*

seedless ['siːdlɪs] *adj (grapes etc)* sans pépins

seedling ['siːdlɪŋ] *n (plant grown from seed)* (jeune) plant *m*; **seedlings** semis *m*

seed merchant *n* grainetier, -ière

seed money *n* mise *f* de fonds

seedsman, *pl* **-men** ['siːdzmən] *n* grainetier *m*

seed tray *n* terrine *f* à semis

seedy ['siːdɪ] *adj* **(a)** *(shabby) (person)* miteux; *(hotel etc)* minable, miteux **(b)** *F (unwell)* mal fichu, patraque; **to feel s.** se sentir patraque, être mal fichu, ne pas être dans son assiette **(c)** *(full of seeds)* plein de pépins

seeing ['siːɪŋ] **1** *adj Am* **s. eye dog** chien *m* d'aveugle **2** *conj* **s. (that** *or F* **as how) ...** vu que ... + *ind*, étant donné que ... + *ind*; **s. as how it's all so simple, why don't you do it yourself?** pourquoi ne le fais-tu pas toi-même puisque c'est si simple? **3** *n* **s. is believing** voir c'est croire

seek [siːk] *(pt, pp* **sought** [sɔːt]) **1** *vt* **(a)** *(look for) (sth lost, job etc)* chercher; *(sb's friendship, promotion etc)* rechercher; *(sb)* chercher; **to be actively seeking employment** être en recherche effective d'emploi; **to s. one's fortune** chercher fortune; **to s. shelter** chercher un abri; **they sought shelter under a tree** ils se sont réfugiés sous un arbre

(b) *(request)* **to s. sth from** *or* **of sb** demander qch à qn; **to s. sb's help** rechercher *ou* demander l'aide de qn; **to s. advice** demander conseil

(c) to s. to do sth essayer *ou* tenter de faire qch; **she sought in vain to convince them of her innocence** elle tenta en vain de les convaincre de son innocence

2 *vi* **s.!** *(to dog)* cherche!; *Prov* **s. and you** *or Arch* **ye shall find** quand on cherche on trouve

▶ **seek after** *vipo (look for) (truth)* chercher; **to be much sought after** être très recherché *ou* demandé

▶ **seek out** *vtsep (find) (person)* trouver

seeker ['siːkər] *n* chercheur, -euse; **a s. after truth** un chercheur/une chercheuse de vérité; **pleasure seekers** gens *mpl* en quête de plaisirs

seek time *n Comptr* temps *m* d'accès

seem [siːm] **1** *vi* sembler, paraître, avoir l'air; **to s. tired** paraître *ou* sembler *ou* avoir l'air fatigué; **how did she s. to you?** comment l'as-tu trouvée?; **do whatever seems best (to you)** fais au mieux; **how does it s. to you?** qu'en pensez-vous?; **it seems like a dream** on croit rêver; **it all seems a long time ago now** ça me paraît loin maintenant; **it doesn't s. right, them getting away with it** ça ne semble pas juste qu'ils s'en tirent à bon compte; **she seems to be** *or* **she seems (like) a nice person** elle a l'air bien; **I s. to have heard his name somewhere** il me semble avoir entendu son nom quelque part; **I seemed to be floating on a cloud** j'avais l'impression de flotter sur un nuage; **I s. to have dropped your vase** je crois (bien) que j'ai laissé tomber votre vase; **I can't s. to get it right** je n'y arrive pas; **she seemed to be trying to say something** elle semblait essayer de dire quelque chose

2 *v impers* **it seems (that) ..., it would s. that ...** il paraît que ... + *ind*, il semble que ... + *ind or sub*; **it seemed best to ...** il semblait préférable de ...; **it seems like only yesterday** c'est comme si c'était hier; **it seems likely that this will happen soon** cela risque d'arriver bientôt; **it seems to me that ...** il me semble que ...; **it seemed to me (that) I was dreaming** il me semblait *ou* j'avais l'impression que je rêvais; **it seemed as though** *or* **as if ...** il semblait que ... + *sub*, on aurait dit que ...+ *ind*; **it seems so, it would s. so** à ce qu'il paraît; **it seems not, it wouldn't s. so** il paraît que non; **it seems to be raining** on dirait qu'il pleut; **there doesn't s. to be any butter left** j'ai l'impression qu'il n'y a plus de beurre

seeming ['siːmɪŋ] *adj* apparent

seemingly ['siːmɪŋlɪ] *adv* apparemment

seemliness ['siːmlɪnɪs] *n Fml* bienséance *f*

seemly ['siːmlɪ] *adj Fml* convenable, bienséant

seen [siːn] **1** *pp see* **see[1]** **2** *adj attrib Sch* **a s. translation** une traduction préparée

seep [siːp] *vi* suinter; *(into sth)* s'infiltrer; **the water was seeping into the earth** l'eau s'infiltrait dans la terre; **information was seeping out** des renseignements filtraient

seepage ['siːpɪdʒ] *n* **(a)** *(act)* suintement *m*; *Fig (of workers)* fuite *f* **(b)** *(lost liquid)* fuite *f*, déperdition *f*

seer [sɪər] *n Lit* prophète *m*, prophétesse *f*

seersucker ['sɪəsʌkər] *n Tex* coton *m* gaufré

seesaw[1] ['siːsɔː] **1** *n* bascule *f*, tapecul *m* **2** *adj (movement)* de bascule, de va-et-vient; *Fin* **s. effect** effet *m* balançoire

seesaw[2] *vi* **(a)** *(play on a seesaw)* jouer à la bascule, faire du tapecul **(b)** *(of machine part etc)* basculer; *Fig (oscillate)* osciller

seethe [siːð] *vi (of liquid)* bouillonner; *(of crowd etc)* s'agiter; **the street is seething with people** la rue grouille de monde; **to be seething (with anger)** bouillir de colère; **he's absolutely seething** il est fou de rage; **the country was seething with discontent** le mécontentement agitait tout le pays

seething ['siːðɪŋ] *adj (liquid)* bouillonnant; **a s. mass of worms** une masse grouillante de vers

see-through *adj* transparent

segment[1] ['segmənt] *n (of sphere, circle, worm)* segment *m*; *(of orange)* quartier *m*; *(of population, public opinion)* partie *f*; **s. of a line** segment *m* linéaire

segment[2] [seg'ment] **1** *vt* couper en segments, segmenter **2** *vi (of worm)* se segmenter

segmentation [segmən'teɪʃən] *n Biol, Mktg* segmentation *f*

segregate ['segrɪgeɪt] *vt (sth)* isoler, mettre à part; *(sb)* séparer **(from** de); *(races)* soumettre à la ségrégation

segregation [segrɪ'geɪʃən] *n* séparation *f*, isolement *m*; *Pol* ségrégation *f*; **policy of s.** ségrégationnisme *m*

segregationist [segrɪ'geɪʃənɪst] *adj, n Pol* ségrégationniste *mf*

segue ['segweɪ] *n TV etc* transition *f* musicale

sei [seɪ] *adj* **s. whale** rorqual *m* boréal

seismic ['saɪzmɪk] *adj* sismique; *Fig (shock waves, changes)* gigantesque

seismograph ['saɪzməgrɑːf] *n* sismographe *m*

seismologist [saɪz'mɒlədʒɪst] *n* sismologue *mf*

seismology [saɪz'mɒlədʒɪ] *n* sismologie *f*

seize [siːz] *vt* **(a)** *(grab)* saisir; **to s. hold of sb/sth** saisir *ou* empoigner qn/qch; **to s. hold of an idea** se jeter sur une idée; **to s. sb by the throat** saisir qn à la gorge; **to s. the opportunity of doing sth** sauter sur *ou* saisir l'occasion de faire qch; **to be seized with fright/panic/doubt** être saisi de peur/panique/doute **(b)** *(take for oneself)* s'emparer de; *(fortress)* prendre; *(enemy ship)* capturer; *Jur (drugs, stolen goods etc)* saisir; *(person)* arrêter **(c)** *(understand) (meaning, implication etc)* saisir; **to s. the meaning of sth** prendre *ou* saisir le sens de qch

▶ **seize on** *vipo (grasp) (idea)* saisir; **to s. on a pretext for leaving** saisir *ou* sauter sur un prétexte pour partir

▶ **seize up** *vi MecE etc (become stuck) (of part, machine etc)* (se) gripper, coincer; *(of engine)* caler; **my knee's seized up** *(completely)* mon genou est coincé; *(partially)* mon genou est ankylosé

▶ **seize upon** *vipo* = **seize on**

seizing ['siːzɪŋ] *n Mil (of fortress)* prise *f*; *(of enemy ship)* capture *f*; *Jur (of property, goods)* saisie *f*

seizure ['siːʒər] *n* **(a)** *(of fortress)* prise *f*; *(of enemy ship)* capture *f*; *Jur (of property, goods)* saisie *f* **(b)** *Med* crise *f*, attaque *f*; **(apoplectic) s.** attaque d'apoplexie; *F* **he just about had a s. when he found out!** il a failli faire une crise quand il a su!

seldom ['seldəm] *adv* [①A72,a,iv] rarement; **he is s. seen** on le voit rarement; **such things are s. seen now** de telles choses se font rares de nos jours; **s. have I heard such nonsense** j'ai rarement entendu des bêtises pareilles

select¹ [sɪ'lekt] *adj* (*exclusive*) de (premier) choix, d'élite; (*club*) très fermé, select; (*audience*) choisi
select² *vt* choisir, sélectionner; *Comptr, Sp* sélectionner; **to s. from ...** choisir parmi ...; **s. 'enter'** tapez 'entrée'; **to s. an option** activer une option
selectable [sɪ'lektəb(ə)l] *adj Comptr* qui peut être sélectionné
select committee *n Br Parl* commission *f* d'enquête
selected [sɪ'lektɪd] *adj* choisi; *Com* de choix; *Liter* **s. passages** morceaux *mpl* choisis
selection [sɪ'lekʃən] *n* **(a)** (*act of choosing*) choix *m*, sélection *f*; (*for team*) sélection; **to make a s.** faire un choix; *Biol* **natural s.** sélection naturelle; *Mktg* **s. method** méthode *f* de sélection; **s. procedure** procédure *f* de sélection; (*for staff*) démarche *f* de sélection **(b)** (*range*) choix *m*; **a wide s.** un grand choix; **a narrow s.** un choix limité; **a good s. of wines** un bon choix de vins; **they don't have a very good s.** ils n'ont pas beaucoup de choix **(c)** (*thing(s) chosen*) **selections from Byron** morceaux *mpl* choisis de Byron; *Horseracing* **our selections** nos pronostics
selection box *n* **(a)** (*of chocolates*) assortiment *m* de chocolats **(b)** *Comptr* rectangle *m* de sélection
selective [sɪ'lektɪv] *adj* sélectif; **to be s.** (*of person*) savoir choisir, choisir avec discernement; **he's very s. about what he eats** il est très difficile sur la nourriture; **you should be more s. about your friends** tu devrais mieux choisir tes amis; **to be s. in the application of a law** appliquer la loi en fonction de ses intérêts; **s. breeding** élevage *m* à base de sélection
selective entry *n Sch* sélection *f* sur concours/après examen du dossier
selectively [sɪ'lektɪvlɪ] *adv* de manière sélective
selectivity [sɪlek'tɪvɪtɪ] *n* sélectivité *f*
selectman, *pl* -men [sɪ'lektmən] *n US* (*in New England*) = conseiller *m* municipal
selector [sɪ'lektər] *n* **(a)** *Sp* sélectionneur, -euse **(b)** *Tel, Aut* sélecteur *m*; *Aut* **s. lever** (*in automatic gearbox*) levier *m* de sélection
selenium [sɪ'li:nɪəm] *n* sélénium *m*
self, *pl* **selves** [self, selvz] **1** *n* **(a) that wasn't his real s.** il n'était pas lui-même; **he's quite his old** *or* **former s. again** (*he has recovered*) il est complètement rétabli; (*his character has returned to normal*) il est tout à fait comme auparavant; **she is a shadow of her former s.** elle n'est plus que l'ombre d'elle-même; **she was her usual cheerful/ tactless s.** comme à son habitude, elle était gaie/blessante; **preoccupation with s.** préoccupation *f* de sa propre personne; *Old-fashioned* **your good selves** vous-mêmes, vous
(b) *Psy* **the s.** (*personality*) la personnalité; (*ego*) le moi; **two selves in one body** deux personnalités dans une seule personne; **the notion of the s.** la notion du moi
(c) (*flower*) fleur *f* de couleur uniforme
2 *pron* (*on cheque*) **pay s.** payez à moi-même
self- [self] *pref* **(a)** (*of and by oneself*) auto-; **s.-analysis** autoanalyse *f* **(b)** (*in oneself*) de soi-même; **s.-belief** confiance *f* en soi **(c)** (*automatic*) automatique; **s.-closing** à fermeture automatique
self-abasement *n* rabaissement *m* de soi-même
self-abnegation *n* = **self-denial**
self-absorbed [-əb'zɔ:bd] *adj* égocentrique
self-abuse *n Old-fashioned* masturbation *f*
self-acting *adj* automatique
self-addressed ['selfə'drest] *adj* **s. envelope** enveloppe *f* à son propre nom
self-adhesive *adj* autocollant; **s. label** étiquette *f* autocollante
self-adjusting *adj* à autoréglage, à réglage automatique; **s. tappet** poussoir *m* auto-régleur
self-advertisement *n* publicité *f* qu'on se fait à soi-même; **to indulge in s.** aimer se faire de la publicité
self-advocacy *n esp Am Admin* (*of mentally handicapped person*) affirmation *f* de soi
self-aggrandizement *n* autoglorification *f*
self-analysis *n* autoanalyse *f*
self-apparent *adj* évident
self-appointed *adj* **a s. critic of the régime** une personne qui s'érige en critique du régime; **a s. spokesperson** un porte-parole qui s'est lui-même désigné; **s. moral guardians** des moralisateurs qui s'érigent en censeurs
self-appraisal *n* auto-évaluation *f*; **s. scheme** système *m* d'auto-évaluation
self-assembly 1 *adj* (*furniture etc*) à monter soi-même **2** *n* **flat-packed for s.** en pièces détachées à monter soi-même
self-assertive *adj* décidé; **be more s.** vous devriez vous affirmer davantage
self-assertiveness *n* affirmation *f* de soi
self-assessment *n* auto-évaluation *f*
self-assurance *n* assurance *f*
self-assured *adj* sûr de soi, plein d'assurance
self-aware *adj* conscient de soi-même
self-awareness *n* conscience *f* de soi
self-belief *n* confiance *f* en soi; **to have s.** croire en soi-même
self-betterment *n* (*material*) amélioration *f* de sa condition; (*spiritual*) progrès *mpl* spirituels
self-catering 1 *adj* (*holiday*) en appartement meublé; (*flat*) meublé avec cuisine équipée; **s. accommodation** meublé *m* de tourisme; **s. apartment** meublé *m*, location *f* de vacances, appartement *m* en location; **s. holiday** vacances *fpl* en location; **to be on a s. holiday** être en location **2** *adv* **to go s.** louer un meublé pour ses vacances
self-censorship *n* autocensure *f*; **to practise s.** s'autocensurer
self-centred, *US* **-centered** [self'sentəd] *adj* égocentrique
self-certification *n* = système *m* dans lequel les employés n'ont pas besoin de certificat médical pour justifier d'une absence
self-check routine *n Comptr* routine *f* d'autotest
self-cleaning *adj* (*oven*) autonettoyant
self-coloured, *US* **-colored** *adj* uni
self-composed *adj* posé, calme
self-composure *n* calme *m*
self-concept *n* (*self-image*) image *f* de soi
self-confessed ['selfkən'fest] *adj* **as a s. pervert, I ...** tout perverti que je suis, je ...; **he is a s. workaholic** de son propre aveu, c'est un bourreau de travail
self-confidence *n* confiance *f* en soi, assurance *f*
self-confident *adj* sûr de soi, plein d'assurance
self-congratulation *n* autosatisfaction *f*
self-congratulatory *adj* (*person*) qui fait de l'autosatisfaction; (*remarks, tone*) d'autosatisfaction, dénotant l'autosatisfaction
self-conscious *adj* **(a)** (*person*) embarrassé, gêné, contraint; **he's very s. about his large nose** il est très complexé par son gros nez **(b)** (*affected*) (*writing style etc*) affecté **(c)** *Phil* conscient, qui a conscience de soi
self-consciously *adv* avec gêne *ou* embarras
self-consciousness *n* **(a)** (*embarrassment*) contrainte *f*, embarras *m*, gêne *f* **(b)** (*affectedness*) (*of writing style etc*) affectation *f* **(c)** *Phil* conscience *f* de soi
self-contained ['selfkən'teɪnd] *adj* **(a)** (*person*) réservé; (*uncommunicative*) peu communicatif; (*independent*) indépendant **(b)** (*apartment*) indépendant, avec entrée particulière
self-contempt *n* mépris *m* de soi-même; **to be full of s.** se mépriser
self-contradictory *adj* contradictoire
self-control *n* maîtrise *f* de soi; **to exercise s.** faire un effort sur soi-même; **to have no s.** ne pas savoir se maîtriser; **to lose one's s.** perdre tout empire sur soi-même, ne plus se maîtriser *ou* se contrôler; **to regain one's s.** se ressaisir
self-controlled *adj* **to be s.** (*of person*) avoir du sang-froid
self-correcting ['selfkə'rektɪŋ] *adj* à correction automatique, autocorrecteur, -trice
self-critical *adj* **to be s.** être critique à l'égard de soi-même; **you're too s.** tu es trop sévère avec toi-même
self-criticism *n* autocritique *f*
self-deception *n* aveuglement *m*; **it's pure s. on his part** il se fait des illusions
self-defeating ['selfdɪ'fi:tɪŋ] *adj* **that would be s.** cela irait à l'encontre du but recherché
self-defence, *US* **-defense** *n Jur* légitime défense *f*; **to kill sb in s.** tuer qn en (état de) légitime défense; **a course in s.** un cours d'autodéfense *ou* de self-défense
self-delusion *n* illusion *f*; **it is nothing but s. on her part** elle se fait des illusions
self-denial *n* abnégation *f*
self-denying ['selfdɪ'naɪɪŋ] *adj* qui fait preuve d'abnégation; **a s. life** une vie de sacrifice
self-deprecation ['selfdeprɪ'keɪʃən] *n* dénigrement *m* de soi-même
self-deprecatory *adj* (*person*) qui se dénigre; (*remarks*) critique envers soi-même
self-destruct *vi* s'autodétruire
self-destruction *n* autodestruction *f*
self-destructive *adj* (*behaviour, character*) suicidaire
self-determination *n Pol* autodétermination *f*
self-discipline *n* autodiscipline *f*
self-doubt *n* manque *m* de confiance en soi
self-drive *adj* (*car*) sans chauffeur
self-educated *adj* autodidacte
self-effacing ['selfɪ'feɪsɪŋ] *adj* qui aime à s'effacer
self-employed 1 *adj* qui travaille à son (propre) compte, indépendant **2** *npl* **the s.** les travailleurs *mpl* indépendants

self-employment *n* travail *m* à son propre compte, travail en indépendant
self-esteem *n* estime *f ou* respect *m* de soi, amour-propre *m*; **to suffer from low s.** avoir peu d'estime de soi
self-evident *adj* évident en soi, qui saute aux yeux
self-evidently *adv* à l'évidence
self-examination *n* (*of conscience*) examen *m* de conscience; (*of breast*) autopalpation *f*
self-explanatory *adj* qui s'explique de soi-même
self-expression *n* libre expression *f*
self-fertilization *n Biol* autofécondation *f*
self-fertilizing ['self'fɜːtɪlaɪzɪŋ] *adj Biol* autofécondant
self-financing **1** *adj* (*entreprise*) qui s'autofinance **2** *n* autofinancement *m*
self-fulfilling *adj* **s. prophecy** = prédiction *f* qui se réalise dès qu'on en parle
self-fulfilment *n* accomplissement *m* de soi
self-governing *adj* autonome
self-government *n* autonomie *f*
self-hatred *n* haine *f* de soi
self-help *n* efforts *mpl* personnels; **s. group** = groupe *m* visant à aider les gens à atteindre un but grâce à des efforts personnels
self-hypnosis *n* autohypnose *f*
self-ignition *n Aut* auto-allumage *m*
self-image *n* image *f* qu'on a de soi-même, image de soi
self-importance *n* suffisance *f*, présomption *f*
self-important *adj* suffisant, présomptueux
self-imposed ['selfɪm'pəʊzd] *adj* (*task etc*) dont on a pris de soi-même la responsabilité; (*exile*) volontaire
self-improvement *n* amélioration *f* personnelle; (*material*) amélioration de sa condition
self-induction *n El* self-induction *f*, auto-induction *f*; **s. coil** bobine *f* de self-induction; *F* self *f*
self-indulgence *n* sybaritisme *m*, habitude *f* de ne rien se refuser; **a typical example of the author's stylistic s.** un exemple typique de la complaisance stylistique de l'auteur envers lui-même
self-indulgent *adj* sybarite, qui ne se refuse rien; (*writer, artist etc*) complaisant envers soi-même; (*novel, film etc*) complaisant
self-inflicted ['selfɪn'flɪktɪd] *adj* (*damage etc*) que l'on s'inflige à soi-même; **s. wound** mutilation *f* volontaire
self-interest *n* intérêt *m* (personnel); **to act from** *or* **out of s.** agir dans un but intéressé
self-interested *adj* intéressé
selfish ['selfɪʃ] *adj* égoïste
selfishly ['selfɪʃlɪ] *adv* égoïstement; **to act s.** agir en égoïste
selfishness ['selfɪʃnɪs] *n* égoïsme *m*
self-justification *n* justification *f* (de ses propres actes); **his attempts at s.** ses tentatives pour se justifier
self-knowledge *n* connaissance *f* de soi
selfless ['selflɪs] *adj* désintéressé, altruiste
selflessness ['selflɪsnɪs] *n* désintéressement *m*, altruisme *m*
self-loading *adj* (*gun*) automatique
self-loathing *n* dégoût *m* de soi-même
self-locking *adj* (*door etc*) à verrouillage *ou* fermeture automatique; *MecE* à blocage automatique, auto-bloqueur; (*nut*) indesserrable
self-love *n* narcissisme *m*
self-made *adj* **s. man** self-made-man *m*
self-mockery *n* moquerie *f* à l'égard de soi-même
self-mocking *adj* (*tone, remarks*) empreint d'ironie à l'égard de soi-même
self-motivated *adj* capable de prendre des initiatives
self-motivation *n* motivation *f*
self-obsessed ['selfəb'sest] *adj* obsédé par soi-même
self-opinionated *adj* entêté; **he's very s.** il veut toujours avoir raison
self-op studio *n* (*in broadcasting*) studio *m* de reportage
self-parking *adj Aut* (*wipers*) à retour automatique
self-perpetuating ['selfpə'petjʊeɪtɪŋ] *adj* qui se reproduit indéfiniment
self-pity *n* attendrissement *m* sur soi-même; **full of s.** attendri sur soi-même; **to wallow in s.** s'apitoyer sur son sort
self-pitying *adj* qui s'apitoie sur son sort
self-pollination *n Bot* autopollinisation *f*
self-portrait *n* autoportrait *m*
self-possessed ['selfpə'zest] *adj* maître de soi, qui a beaucoup de sang-froid
self-possession *n* sang-froid *m*, maîtrise *f* de soi
self-praise *n* éloge *m* de soi-même; **I'm not saying that in s.** ce n'est pas laudatif à mon égard
self-preservation *n* **(instinct for) s.** instinct *m* de conservation
self-proclaimed ['selfprə'kleɪmd] *adj* autoproclamé
self-propelled, -propelling [selfprə'peld, -'pelɪŋ] *adj* (*vehicle*) automoteur, -trice, autopropulsé
self-publicist *n* **he is an accomplished s.** il sait soigner sa publicité
self-raising, *Am* **-rising** *adj* (*flour*) contenant de la levure chimique
self-regard *n* = **self-esteem**
self-regulating *adj MecE* autorégulateur, -trice, à autoréglage; (*economy*) qui se régule d'elle-même
self-regulation *n* autorégulation *f*
self-reliance *n* indépendance *f*
self-reliant *adj* indépendant
self-repairing bumper [selfrɪ'peərɪŋ] *n Aut* pare-chocs *m* auto-réparable
self-replicate *vi* s'autoreproduire
self-replicating ['selfreplɪkeɪtɪŋ] *adj* autoreproducteur, -trice
self-replication ['selfreplɪ'keɪʃən] *n* autoreproduction *f*
self-respect *n* respect *m* de soi, amour-propre *m*; **have you no s.?** tu n'as pas d'amour-propre?; **to lose all s.** perdre toute dignité
self-respecting *adj* qui se respecte; **no s. journalist/doctor** aucun journaliste/médecin qui se respecte
self-restraint *n* retenue *f*; **to exercise s.** se contenir, se retenir
self-righteous *adj* pharisaïque; **stop being so s.!** cesse d'être aussi content de toi!
self-righteousness *n* pharisaïsme *m*, satisfaction *f* de soi
self-righting *adj* (*lifeboat etc*) à redressement automatique
self-rule *n Pol* autonomie *f*
self-sacrifice *n* abnégation *f*
selfsame ['selfseɪm] *adj* identique, absolument le même
self-satisfaction *n* contentement *m* de soi, fatuité *f*, suffisance *f*
self-satisfied *adj* (*person*) content de soi, suffisant; (*look*) suffisant; **to look s.** avoir l'air content de soi-même
self-sealing *adj* (*envelope*) autocollant
self-seeking ['self'siːkɪŋ] *adj* (*person*) égoïste
self-service *n Com* libre-service *m*; **s. petrol station** station *f* libre-service; **s. restaurant** self *m* (service)
self-serving *adj* égoïste, intéressé
self-starter *n* **(a)** *Old-fashioned Aut* démarreur *m* (automatique) **(b)** (*person*) personne *f* très motivée et capable d'initiatives
self-styled ['selfstaɪld] *adj* soi-disant *inv*, prétendu
self-sufficiency *n* indépendance *f*; *Econ* **national s.** autarcie *f*
self-sufficient *adj* (*independent*) indépendant, autosuffisant; **the country is s. in foodstuffs** le pays pourvoit à ses propres besoins en denrées alimentaires
self-supporting *adj* indépendant; (*person*) qui pourvoit à ses besoins; (*business*) qui couvre ses frais; *Archit* (*vault*) autoportant
self-tapping *adj* **s. screw** vis *f* autotaraudeuse
self-taught *adj* **(a)** (*person*) autodidacte **(b)** (*skills*) que l'on a acquis tout seul
self-test[1] *Comptr n* autotest *m*; **the printer does a s.** l'imprimante procède à une vérification de ses fonctions; **s. button** bouton *m* d'autotest; **s. program** programme *m* d'autotest
self-test[2] *vi* s'autotester
self-willed ['self'wɪld] *adj* obstiné, volontaire
self-winding ['self'waɪndɪŋ] *adj* (*watch*) à remontage automatique
sell[1] [sel] *n* **(a)** **hard s.** vente par des méthodes agressives; **soft s.** vente par des méthodes de suggestion *ou* de persuasion **(b)** *Old-fashioned F* (*trick*) attrape-nigaud *m*, *pl* attrape-nigauds
sell[2] (*pt, pp* **sold** [səʊld]) **1** *vt* **(a)** vendre; (*goods*) vendre, placer; **to s. sb sth, to s. sth to sb** vendre qch à qn; **he sold it to me for £10** il me l'a vendu (pour) 10 livres; **to s. sth for cash** vendre qch au comptant; **to s. sth on credit** vendre qch à crédit; **to s. sth privately** vendre qch de gré à gré; **a shop that sells clothes/furniture** un magasin de vêtements/meubles; **the album/book sold nearly a million copies** l'album/le livre s'est vendu à près d'un million d'exemplaires; **the Guardian sells roughly 400,000 copies a day** le Guardian tourne à environ 400 000 exemplaires par jour; **to s. sb into slavery/prostitution** vendre qn comme esclave/prostituée; **to s. sth at a loss** vendre qch à perte; **to sell sth at a profit** faire un bénéfice en vendant qch; *Lit* **to s. one's life dearly** vendre chèrement sa vie; **to s. one's soul** vendre son âme

(b) (*cause to be sold*) faire vendre; **scandal sells newspapers** ce sont les scandales qui font vendre les journaux; **you need at least one major star to s. the film** il faut au moins une star pour que le film fasse recette

(c) **to s. oneself** (*in interview etc*) se faire valoir; *F* se vendre; **to s. oneself short** ne pas se montrer à sa juste valeur; **you have to s. yourself more to the electorate** il faudrait vous vendre mieux auprès des électeurs; **to s. an idea to the electorate** faire passer une idée auprès des électeurs; **to s. a party to the electorate** vendre les idées d'un parti auprès des électeurs; **they had difficulty selling the changes to the workforce** ils ont eu des difficultés à faire accepter les changements aux ouvriers; *F* **I couldn't s. my father the idea** je n'ai pas pu faire accepter l'idée à mon père; *F* **to be sold on an idea** être emballé par une idée

(d) (*betray*) (*secret, one's country etc*) vendre; **to s. oneself** se vendre; **to s. sb down the river** (*betray*) trahir qn

2 *vi* (a) (*of product etc*) se vendre; **to s. well/badly** se vendre bien/mal; **to s. like hot cakes** se vendre comme des petits pains; **shares in the company are selling at 109 pence** les actions de cette compagnie s'échangent à 109 pence

(b) (*work in sales*) être dans la vente; **to be good at selling** être (un) bon vendeur; **I'm not selling** (*my car etc*) je ne vends pas

▶ **sell forward** *vtas, vi Fin* vendre à terme

▶ **sell off** *vtsep* (*dispose of at low price*) (*of shop*) solder; (*stock, goods*) liquider; (*of person*) vendre; **to s. off goods** écouler des marchandises

▶ **sell out 1** *vtsep* (a) **the concert is sold out** il n'y a plus de billets pour le concert; **the tickets are sold out** tous les billets ont été vendus; **the edition is sold out** l'édition est épuisée; **I'm sold out** j'ai tout vendu; **the supermarket was sold out of butter** le supermarché était à court de beurre

(b) *St Exch* (*portfolio of shares*) réaliser

(c) (*betray*) (*person, principles etc*) vendre, trahir

2 *vi* (a) (*sell all stocks*) **to s. out (of sth)** se trouver à court (de qch); **have you got any bread? – no, I'm afraid we've sold out** est-ce que vous avez du pain? – non, nous n'en avons plus

(b) (*sell business*) liquider; (*sell shares*) retirer sa participation d'une/de la société; **to sell out to sb** vendre sa participation à qn

(c) (*betray cause*) trahir sa cause

▶ **sell up 1** *vtsep* **to s. up a business/property** vendre (complètement) une affaire/propriété **2** *vi* (*sell property*) vendre ses effets; (*sell business*) vendre son fonds; **he sold up and went to Canada** il a tout vendu et est parti au Canada

sell-by-date *n Com* date *f* limite de vente; *Fig F* **to be past one's s.** avoir fait son temps

seller ['selər] *n* (a) (*person*) vendeur, -euse; (*stockist*) marchand, -ande (**of** de); *Fin* (*of stocks*) réalisateur *m*; **s. 's market** marché *m* à la hausse (b) **good/bad s.** (*item*) article *m* qui se vend bien/mal

selling ['selɪŋ] *n* (*of goods etc*) vente *f*, écoulement *m*; **buying and s.** la vente et l'achat; **the job doesn't involve much s.** le travail ne fait pas intervenir beaucoup de vente; **s. price** prix *m* de vente; **s. points** points *mpl* forts; **s. rate** (*of currency*) taux *m* de vente

selling off, selling out *n* (*of stock*) liquidation *f*; *Fin* (*of shares etc*) (re)vente *f*, réalisation *f*

sell order *n St Exch* injonction *f* à la vente

Sellotape® ['seləteɪp] *n* ruban *m* adhésif, scotch® *m*

sellotape ['seləteɪp] *vt* **to s. sth to sth** scotcher qch à qch

sellout ['selaʊt] *n* (a) **this play's a s.** on joue à guichets fermés; **this line has been a s.** cet article s'est vendu à merveille (et il ne nous en reste plus) (b) (*act of betrayal*) trahison *f*

selvage, selvedge ['selvɪdʒ] *n* (*of fabric*) lisière *f*

semantic [sɪ'mæntɪk] *adj Ling* sémantique; **a purely s. distinction** une distinction purement sémantique

semantically [sɪ'mæntɪklɪ] *adv* sémantiquement, du point de vue sémantique

semantics [sɪ'mæntɪks] *npl* [①A10,c] *Ling* (*usu with sing verb*) sémantique *f*; *Fig* **that's just s.** ce ne sont que des discours

semaphore¹ ['seməfɔːr] *n* sémaphore *m*; *Rail etc* **s. signal** signal *m* à bras

semaphore² *vt* (*message*) transmettre par sémaphore

semblance ['sembləns] *n* (*appearance*) apparence *f*, semblant *m*; **to re-establish a** *or* **some s. of order** rétablir un semblant d'ordre; **a (mere) s. of friendship** un semblant d'amitié

semen ['siːmen] *n Physiol* sperme *m*

semester [sɪ'mestər] *n Am* semestre *m*

semi ['semɪ] *n Br F* maison *f* jumelée

semi- ['semɪ] *pref* semi-, demi-

semiautomatic ['semɪɔːtə'mætɪk] **1** *adj* semi-automatique **2** *n* arme *f* semi-automatique

semibreve ['semɪbriːv] *n Br Mus* ronde *f*

semicircle ['semɪsɜːk(ə)l] *n* demi-cercle *m*, *pl* demi-cercles

semicircular ['semɪ'sɜːkjʊlər] *adj* demi-circulaire, semi-circulaire

semicolon ['semɪ'kəʊlən] *n* point-virgule *m*, *pl* points-virgules

semiconductor ['semɪkən'dʌktər] *n El* semi-conducteur *m*

semiconscious ['semɪ'kɒnʃəs] *adj* à demi conscient

semiconsciousness ['semɪ'kɒnʃəsnɪs] *n* demi-inconscience *f*

semidarkness ['semɪ'dɑːknɪs] *n* demi-jour *m*, pénombre *f*

semidetached ['semɪdɪ'tætʃt] **1** *adj* (*house*) jumelé, jumeau, *f* jumelle; *Fig* **a s. member of the Government** = un membre du gouvernement en qui le Premier ministre ne peut pas totalement avoir confiance **2** *n* maison *f* jumelée

semi-documentary *n* film *m* semi-documentaire

semifinal ['semɪ'faɪn(ə)l] *n Sp* demi-finale *f*, *pl* demi-finales; **to reach the semifinals** atteindre les demi-finales

semifinalist ['semɪ'faɪnəlɪst] *n Sp* demi-finaliste *mf*

semi-finished goods *npl* produits *mpl* semi-finis

semi-graphics *n* [①A10,c] *Comptr* semi-graphisme *m*

semi-invalid *n* **he's a s.** il ne peut presque plus se déplacer

semiliterate ['semɪ'lɪtərɪt] *adj* quasi illettré

semi-manufactured product [-mænjʊ'fæktʃəd] *n* demi-produit *m*

seminal ['semɪnəl] *adj* (a) *Physiol, Bot* séminal; **s. fluid** sperme *m*, liquide *m* séminal (b) (*event, work*) fructueux

seminar ['semɪnɑːr] *n Univ* séminaire *m*

seminarist ['semɪnərɪst] *n Cathol* séminariste *m*

seminary ['semɪnərɪ] *n Cathol* séminaire *m*

semi-obscurity *n* (*darkness*) pénombre *f*; *Fig* quasi-obscurité *f*

semi-official *adj* semi-officiel

semiology [semɪɒlədʒɪ] *n* sém(é)iologie *f*

semiotic [semɪ'ɒtɪk] *adj* sémiotique

semiotics [semɪ'ɒtɪks] *npl* [①A10,c] (*usu with sing verb*) sémiotique *f*

semi-precious *adj* semi-précieux, fin

semiquaver ['semɪkweɪvər] *n Br Mus* double croche *f*

semi-retired *adj* **he is s.** il est en retraite partielle

semi-retirement *n* retraite *f* partielle

semi-skilled *adj* (*worker*) spécialisé

semi-skimmed ['semɪ'skɪmd] *adj* **s. milk** lait *m* demi-écrémé

Semite ['semaɪt] *n* Sémite *mf*

Semitic [sɪ'mɪtɪk] *adj* sémitique

semitone ['semɪtəʊn] *n Br Mus* demi-ton *m*

semitropical ['semɪ'trɒpɪkəl] *adj* = **subtropical**

semivowel ['semɪ'vaʊəl] *n* semi-voyelle *f*, *pl* semi-voyelles

semolina [semə'liːnə] *n* semoule *f*

SEN [esiː'en] *n Br Med* (*abbr* **State Enrolled Nurse**) infirmier, -ière diplômé(e) d'État

Sen (a) (*abbr* **senator**) sénateur (b) (*abbr* **senior**) aîné, père

senate ['senɪt] *n* (a) *Pol* Sénat *m*; **s. house** Sénat (b) *Univ* conseil *m* d'université

senator ['senətər] *n Pol* sénateur *m*

senatorial [senə'tɔːrɪəl] *adj* sénatorial

send [send] *vt* (*pt, pp* **sent** [sent]) (a) (*dispatch*) (*sth*) envoyer; (*in business letters, administration etc*) faire parvenir; (*by post*) (*letter etc*) envoyer, expédier; (*money*) remettre; (*person*) envoyer; **to s. word to sb** envoyer un mot à qn, faire savoir qch à qn; **to s. one's love to sb** envoyer *ou* faire ses amitiés à qn; **to s. clothes to the laundry** donner du linge à blanchir; **to s. a child to school** envoyer un enfant à l'école; **to s. sb to prison** envoyer qn en prison; **to s. sb on an errand** envoyer qn faire une course; **to s. sb for sth** envoyer qn chercher qch; *Comptr* **s. to the printer** envoyer à *ou* vers *ou* sur l'imprimante

(b) (*cause to move, change etc*) **force that sends sth in a certain direction** force qui fait marcher *ou* qui pousse qch dans une certaine direction; **it sends a current down the wire** il fait passer un courant dans le fil; **it sent a shiver down my spine** cela m'a fait un frisson dans le dos; **the blow sent him sprawling** le coup l'a renversé; **that sent him into fits of laughter** cela l'a fait éclater de rire; **you'll s. me mad** vous allez me rendre fou; **the rain sent us scurrying for shelter** nous avons couru nous abriter dès que la pluie a commencé; **to s. sb into a panic/a fit of depression/a rage** paniquer/déprimer/enrager qn; **to s. sb's profits tumbling** faire chuter les bénéfices de qn; *F* **to s. sb packing, to s. sb about his/her business** envoyer promener qn

(c) *Lit* (*grant*) (*sth*) accorder, envoyer; **s. him/her victorious** que Dieu lui donne *ou* lui accorde la victoire; **what fortune sends us** ce que la fortune nous envoie

(d) *Old-fashioned, F* (*thrill*) **it sends me** ça me transporte

▶ **send along** *vtsep* envoyer; **s. him along!** (*send him to see me*) envoyez-le-moi; (*tell him to see me*) dites-lui de venir me voir

▶ **send away 1** *vtsep* (a) (*send to another place*) envoyer; **to be sent away to school** être envoyé à l'école (b) (*dismiss*) renvoyer, congédier **2** *vi* (*write to obtain something*) écrire

▶ **send away for** *vipo* (*write to obtain*) demander par courrier; **s. away for your free copy now** demandez maintenant votre exemplaire gratuit

▶ **send back** *vtsep* (*return*) (*sb, sth*) renvoyer; (*food in restaurant*) renvoyer à la cuisine

▶ **send down** *vtsep* **(a)** (*send to lower place*) faire descendre **(b)** (*cause to fall*) (*prices, temperature etc*) faire descendre **(c)** *Br Univ* (*expel*) renvoyer, expulser **(d)** *Br F* (*send to prison*) envoyer en prison, coffrer

▶ **send for** *vipo* **(a)** (*summon*) (*sb, sth*) envoyer chercher; **we sent for a couple of pizzas** nous nous sommes fait livrer deux pizzas; **we sent for the doctor** nous avons appelé le médecin, nous avons envoyé chercher le médecin **(b)** = **send away for**

▶ **send in 1** *vtsep* (*send to a place*) (*invoice, bill*) soumettre; (*request etc*) remettre; (*dinner*) (faire) servir; **he has sent in his bill (to us/them)** il nous/leur a envoyé sa note; **many viewers sent in comments on the programme** de nombreux spectateurs ont envoyé leurs commentaires sur l'émission; **s. Mrs Jones in** faites entrer Mme Jones; **to s. the army in** envoyer l'armée **2** *vi* (*write to obtain sth*) faire une demande écrite (**for sth** de qch)

▶ **send off 1** *vtsep* (*by post*) envoyer, expédier; *Fb etc* (*player*) renvoyer *ou* expulser du terrain **2** *vi* = **send away 2**

▶ **send on** *vtsep* (*forward*) (*letter*) faire suivre; (*order*) transmettre; (*luggage*) expédier à l'avance; *Fb etc* (*player*) envoyer sur le terrain

▶ **send on ahead** *vtas* (*luggage etc*) envoyer à l'avance; (*person*) envoyer en reconnaissance

▶ **send out 1** *vtsep* **(a)** (*person*) envoyer dehors; (*pupil*) mettre à la porte; **to s. sb out for more food/wine** envoyer qn chercher de la nourriture/du vin **(b)** (*leaflets*) lancer, expédier; (*invitations*) envoyer **(c)** (*signals, heat etc*) émettre; **the chimney/engine sent out billows of smoke** la cheminée/le moteur crachait des tourbillons de fumée **2** *vi* (*for food, wine*) envoyer chercher

▶ **send up** *vtsep* **(a)** (*send to higher place*) (*sb, sth*) faire monter; (*rocket*) lancer **(b)** (*prices, temperature etc*) faire monter *ou F* grimper **(c)** *Br F* (*parody*) se moquer de, parodier; (*play, part*) faire une parodie de; **he sent her up as an eccentric duchess** il l'avait caricaturée sous les traits d'une duchesse excentrique **(d)** *Am F* (*send to prison*) envoyer en taule, coffrer

sender ['sendər] *n* (*of letter, fax, goods*) expéditeur, -trice; (*of radio message*) transmetteur *m*

sending ['sendɪŋ] *n* envoi *m*; **s. by rail** expédition *f* par chemin de fer; **s. depot** dépôt *m* d'expédition

send-off *n F* **we went to the station to give her a good s.** nous sommes allés à la gare pour marquer son départ; **to give sb a good s.** (*funeral*) faire à qn de belles funérailles; **to give sb a big s.** venir nombreux pour dire au revoir à qn

send-up *n Br F* satire *f*, parodie *f*; **is this a s.?** est-ce qu'on se moque de moi?

Senegal [senɪ'gɔːl] *n* Sénégal *m*

Senegalese [senɪgə'liːz] **1** *adj* sénégalais **2** *n* Sénégalais, -aise

senescence [sɪ'nesəns] *n Med* sénescence *f*

senile ['siːnaɪl] *adj* sénile; **s. dementia** démence *f* sénile

senility [sɪ'nɪlɪtɪ] *n* sénilité *f*

senior ['siːnjər] **1** *adj* (*in age*) aîné; (*in rank, position etc*) plus haut placé; (*longer-serving*) plus ancien; *Mil etc* (*officer*) supérieur; **Bernard Long s.** Bernard Long père; **he's two years s. to me** il est mon aîné de deux ans; **s. in rank** de grade supérieur; **the s. boys/girls of a school** les garçons/filles des grandes classes; **s. executive** cadre *m* supérieur; **(the) s. management** la direction; *Sch* **s. master/mistress** professeur *m* principal; **the s. officer** l'officier *m* commandant; **I'll report you to your s. officer** je vais vous signaler à votre supérieur; **s. official** haut fonctionnaire *m*; **s. partner** associé *m* principal; **s. reporter** grand reporter *m*; *Br* **the S. Service** la marine

2 *n* **(a)** (*in age*) aîné, -ée; **she is his s. by three years, she is three years his s.** elle est son aînée de trois ans; **to be sb's s.** (*in age*) être l'aîné de qn; (*in rank*) être d'un rang plus élevé que qn; **the seniors** (*pupils*) les grand(e)s

(b) *US Sch* étudiant, -ante de quatrième (et dernière) année

senior citizen *n* personne *f* âgée

seniority [siːnɪ'ɒrɪtɪ] *n* **(a)** (*in age*) priorité *f* d'âge, supériorité *f* d'âge; **he was chairman by virtue of s.** il était président en raison de son âge **(b)** (*in rank*) ancienneté *f* (de grade); **to be promoted by s.** avancer (de grade) *ou* être promu à l'ancienneté; **to have s. over sb** avoir plus d'ancienneté que qn

senna ['senə] *n Bot* séné *m*; *Pharm* **s. pods** follicules *mpl* de séné

sensation [sen'seɪʃən] *n* **(a)** (*power of feeling*) sensibilité *f*; (*feeling*) (*of well-being, discomfort, heat, cold etc*) sensation *f*; **I had the s. of falling** j'avais la sensation de tomber **(b)** (*excitement*) **to create** *or* **make** *or* **cause a s.** (*of event etc*) faire sensation; **the film was the s. of the year** le film a été l'événement de l'année; **s.-hungry readers** des lecteurs avides de sensationnel

sensational [sen'seɪʃən(ə)l] *adj* **(a)** (*film, novel, press etc*) à sensation **(b)** *F* (*excellent*) sensationnel, fantastique

sensationalism [sen'seɪʃənəlɪz(ə)m] *n* **(a)** recherche *f* du sensationnel **(b)** *Phil* sensualisme *m*, sensationnisme *m*

sensationalist [sen'seɪʃənəlɪst] **1** *n* (*with news*) colporteur *m* de nouvelles à sensation; (*who overdramatizes*) personne *f* ayant tendance à dramatiser **2** *adj* (*article, style, journalism*) à sensation; **to be s.** (*of tabloids, reporting*) faire du sensationnel

sensationalize [sen'seɪʃənəlaɪz] *vt* (*event etc*) faire du sensationnel sur; **it's been so sensationalized that ...** on a fait tant de battage là-dessus que ...

sensationally [sen'seɪʃ(ə)nəlɪ] *adv* **(a) the murder was treated s. in the tabloids** les tabloïdes ont fait du meurtre une histoire à sensations **(b)** *F* (*successful, good*) d'une manière sensationnelle *ou* fantastique; **they did s. well in the first round** ils ont été fantastiques dans les premières épreuves

sense[1] [sens] *n* **(a)** (*faculty*) sens *m*; **the five senses** les cinq sens; **to have a keen s. of smell/hearing** avoir l'odorat fin/l'ouïe fine; **she seemed to have a sixth s.** elle semblait posséder un sixième sens; **to be in possession of all one's senses** jouir de toutes ses facultés; **pleasures of the senses** plaisirs sensuels *ou* des sens; **s. impression** sensation *f*; **s. organs** organes *mpl* des sens

(b) have you taken leave of your senses? avez-vous perdu l'esprit *ou* la raison?; **to come to one's senses** (*be sensible again*) revenir à la raison; (*regain consciousness*) revenir à soi; **to bring sb to his senses** ramener qn à la raison

(c) (*feeling*) sensation *f*, sens *m*; (*awareness*) sentiment *m*, conscience *f*; **she has a s. for what is likely to sell** elle a du flair pour deviner ce qui va se vendre; **a s. of achievement** un sentiment d'accomplissement; **to have a s. of belonging** avoir le sentiment d'être intégré; **s. of colour/beauty** sens des couleurs/de la beauté; **s. of injustice** sentiment d'injustice; **a s. of pleasure/warmth** une sensation de plaisir/chaleur; **to lose all s. of reality/time** perdre la notion de la réalité/du temps

(d) (*rationality*) bon sens *m*; **common s.** sens *m* commun; **good s.** bon sens; **to talk s.** parler raison; **there's no s. in that, that doesn't make s.** cela n'a pas de sens, cela ne rime à rien; **it would make more s. if ...** cela serait plus intelligent si ...; **there's a lot of s. in what she says** ce qu'elle dit est très sensé; **it doesn't make s. to do that** cela n'a pas de sens de faire une chose pareille; **it makes good political/business s. to ...** il est bon sur le plan politique/commercial de ...; **it makes more s. to do this first** c'est plus logique de commencer par cela; **that makes good s.** c'est logique, c'est une bonne idée; **where's the s. in that?** à quoi ça sert?; **there's no s. in doing that** ça ne sert à rien; **to have the (good) s. to do sth** avoir l'intelligence *ou* le bon sens de faire qch; **to have more s. than to do sth** avoir assez de bon sens pour ne pas faire qch

(e) (*meaning*) (*of word etc*) sens *m*, signification *f*; **these words don't make s.** ces mots n'ont pas de sens *ou* sont incompréhensibles; **now the sentence makes more s.** maintenant la phrase a plus de sens; **does this sentence make s.?** cette phrase veut-elle dire quelque chose?; **you're not making s.** vous êtes illogique; **make s.!** sois logique!; **I can't make s. of it** je n'arrive pas à le comprendre; **in the literal/figurative s.** au sens propre/figuré; **in every s. of the word, in more senses than one** dans tous les sens du terme; **in a s.** d'une certaine façon, dans un (certain) sens; **in the s. that ...** en ce sens que ..., au sens où ...; **in the normal s. (of the word)** à proprement parler; **in no s., not in any s.** en aucun cas; **this is not in any real s. a change of policy** ça ne représente pas du tout un changement de politique; **in a very real s.** véritablement

sense[2] *vt* **(a)** (*know intuitively*) sentir; (*have premonition*) pressentir; **I sensed no difference in his mood from last time** je n'ai décelé chez lui aucun changement d'humeur par rapport à la dernière fois; **I sensed that she was hiding something** j'avais le pressentiment qu'elle cachait quelque chose **(b)** *Phil* percevoir par le sens **(c)** *Electron etc* détecter

senseless ['senslɪs] *adj* **(a)** (*unconscious*) sans connaissance, inanimé; **to fall s.** tomber sans connaissance; **to knock/beat sb s.** assommer qn **(b)** (*pointless*) (*action*) insensé, stupide, absurde; **a s. killing** un meurtre gratuit; **a s. remark** une remarque stupide; **what a s. waste (of human life)** (*one person*) voilà une vie humaine absurdement gâchée; (*more than one person*) **que de vies humaines gâchées**

senselessly ['senslɪslɪ] *adv* absurdement

senselessness ['senslɪsnɪs] *n* (*stupidity*) absurdité *f*

sensibility [sensɪ'bɪlɪtɪ] *n* **(a)** (*of person*) sensibilité *f*, émotivité *f*; **I do not want to offend anyone's sensibilities** je ne veux pas heurter la susceptibilité de qui que ce soit **(b)** (*of organ etc*) sensibilité *f*

sensible ['sensɪb(ə)l] *adj* **(a)** (*rational*) (*person, decision*) sensé, raisonnable; **it would be more s. to ...** il serait plus raisonnable de ...; **be s.** soyez raisonnable; **s. choice** choix judicieux; **s. clothes** vêtements commodes *ou* pratiques; **s. person** personne sensée *ou* pleine de bon sens; **s. shoes** chaussures confortables et pratiques **(b)** *Arch, Lit* (*aware*) conscient **(of** de); **to be s. of the fact that ...** être sensible au *ou* apprécier le fait que ... **(c)** *Fml* (*perceptible*) (*quantity, difference etc*) sensible, appréciable

sensibly ['sensɪblɪ] *adv* **(a)** (*rationally*) (*to behave, discuss*) raisonnablement; (*to decide, divide*) judicieusement; **to be s. dressed** porter des vêtements pratiques **(b)** (*perceptibly*) sensiblement, perceptiblement

sensitive ['sensɪtɪv] *adj* **(a)** (*person, skin*) sensible; (*portrayal, interpretation*) plein de sensibilité; **he's very s. about his accent** il est très susceptible sur son accent; **to be s. to noise** être sensible au bruit; **to be s. to the cold** (*of person*) être frileux, -euse **(b)** *Fin* (*market*) sensible; *Phot* (*plate*) impressionnable, sensible à la lumière; (*paper*) sensible, sensibilisé; *Phot etc* **s. layer** couche *f* sensible; **s. to sth** sensible à qch **(c)** (*question, issue etc*) délicat, sensible; (*document, information*) confidentiel

sensitively ['sensɪtɪvlɪ] *adv* sensiblement, d'une manière sensible; (*to write etc*) avec sensibilité

sensitiveness ['sensɪtɪvnɪs], **sensitivity** [sensɪ'tɪvɪtɪ] *n* (*of person, skin, machine, instrument etc*) sensibilité *f*; *Phot* impressionnabilité *f*, rapidité *f*; (*of question etc*) caractère *m* délicat; (*of document, information etc*) caractère confidentiel

sensitization [sensɪtaɪ'zeɪʃən] *n Med, Phot* sensibilisation *f*

sensitize ['sensɪtaɪz] *vt* sensibiliser; *Phot* **sensitized paper** papier *m* sensible *ou* sensibilisé

sensitizer ['sensɪtaɪzər] *n Phot* sensibilisateur *m*

sensor ['sensər] *n Electron* détecteur *m*, capteur *m*

sensory ['sensərɪ] *adj* (*nerve etc*) sensoriel; **s. organs** organes *mpl* des sens

sensual ['sensjʊəl] *adj* **(a)** sensuel; (*instinct*) animal; **s. pleasures** plaisirs *mpl* des sens **(b)** (*person, art*) sensuel, voluptueux

sensualism ['sensjʊəlɪz(ə)m] *n* **(a)** sensualité *f* **(b)** *Phil* sensualisme *m*

sensualist ['sensjʊəlɪst] *n* **(a)** sensualiste *mf*, voluptueux, -euse **(b)** *Phil* sensualiste *mf*

sensuality [sensjʊ'ælɪtɪ] *n* sensualité *f*

sensuous ['sensjʊəs] *adj* (*pleasure, life, charm etc*) sensuel, voluptueux

sensuously ['sensjʊəslɪ] *adv* voluptueusement, avec volupté

sensuousness ['sensjʊəsnɪs] *n* volupté *f*

sent *see* **send**

sentence[1] ['sentəns] *n* **(a)** [①**A72-3**; **B59-61**] *Gram* phrase *f*; *Mktg* **s. completion** phrases à compléter **(b)** *Jur* (*conviction*) condamnation *f*, sentence *f*; (*period in prison*) peine *f*; **life s.** condamnation à perpétuité; **s. of death, death s.** condamnation à mort, arrêt *m* de mort; **under s. of death** condamné à mort; **to pass (a) s.** prononcer une condamnation *ou* une sentence; **while he was serving his s.** pendant qu'il purgeait sa peine

sentence[2] *vt Jur* condamner; **to s. sb to a month's imprisonment/to death** condamner qn à un mois de prison/ à mort

sententious [sen'tenʃəs] *adj Fml* (*person, speech etc*) sentencieux

sententiousness [sen'tenʃəsnɪs] *n Fml* (*of person*) caractère *m* sentencieux; (*of writing etc*) ton *m* sentencieux

sentient ['sentɪənt] *adj Fml* sensible

sentiment ['sentɪmənt] *n* **(a)** (*opinion*) sentiment *m*, opinion *f*, avis *m*; **these are my sentiments** voilà mon sentiment *ou* mon opinion; **my sentiments exactly** je partage entièrement votre avis; **noble sentiments** sentiments nobles **(b)** (*sentimentality*) sentimentalité *f*; (*mawkish*) sensiblerie *f* **(c)** *Arch, Lit* (*emotion*) sentimentalité *f*

sentimental [sentɪ'ment(ə)l] *adj* sentimental; **s. value** valeur *f* sentimentale; **don't be so s.!** ne sois pas si sentimental!

sentimentalism [sentɪ'mentəlɪz(ə)m] *n* sentimentalisme *m*; (*mawkishness*) sensiblerie *f*

sentimentalist [sentɪ'mentəlɪst] *n* personne *f* sentimentale; **he's/she's a s.** c'est un sentimental/une sentimentale

sentimentality [sentɪmen'tælɪtɪ] *n* sentimentalité *f*; (*mawkishness*) sensiblerie *f*

sentimentalize [sentɪ'mentəlaɪz] **1** *vi* faire du sentiment **2** *vt* (*novel, work, situation etc*) romancer

sentimentally [sentɪ'ment(ə)lɪ] *adv* sentimentalement; (*mawkishly*) avec sensiblerie

sentinel ['sentɪn(ə)l] *n Mil* factionnaire *m*, sentinelle *f*; *Fig* **the s. of democracy** le garant *ou* gardien de la démocratie; **to stand s. over sth** être de garde à qch; *Fig* protéger qch

sentry ['sentrɪ] *n Mil* factionnaire *m*, sentinelle *f*; **to be on** *or* **to do s. duty, to stand s.** être en sentinelle *ou* de faction; **to relieve a s.** relever une sentinelle; **s. box** guérite *f*

sepal ['sep(ə)l] *n Bot* sépale *m*

separable ['sep(ə)rəb(ə)l] *adj* séparable

separate[1] ['sep(ə)rət] *n* (*print*) tiré *m* à part

separate[2] **1** *adj* (*parts, box, booklet etc*) séparé, détaché **(from** de); (*distinct*) distinct; (*independent*) indépendant; (*times, days*) différent; **the two issues are quite s.** les deux problèmes sont distincts; **to keep sth s. (from sth else)** séparer qch (de qch d'autre); **to sleep in s. rooms/beds** (*of married couple*) faire chambre/lit à part; **use a s. piece of paper** utilisez une feuille séparée; **it's now become a s. company** c'est maintenant une société indépendante; **they went their/we went our s. ways** ils sont partis chacun de leur côté/nous sommes partis chacun de notre côté **2** *npl Com* **separates** coordonnés *mpl*

separate[3] ['sepəreɪt] **1** *vt* séparer **(from** de); (*milk*) écrémer; (*members of a family etc*) désunir; (*sb from his family etc*) détacher; **to s. eggs** séparer les blancs des jaunes; **s. two eggs** prenez deux oeufs, séparez les blancs des jaunes; **murder cases can be separated under four headings** on distingue quatre types de meurtres; **to s. two boxers** séparer deux boxeurs; **he is separated (from his wife)** il est séparé (de sa femme); **the Channel separates England from France** la Manche sépare la France et l'Angleterre; **the gulf that separates him from his colleagues** l'abîme entre lui et ses collègues, l'abîme qui le sépare de ses collègues; **what separates their language from other African languages is ...** ce qui distingue leur langue des autres langues africaines c'est ...; **to s. the men from the boys** faire un tri

2 *vi* (*of group of people, man and wife*) se séparer; **when we separated for the night** quand nous nous sommes quittés pour la nuit; **to s. from sb** se séparer de qn, rompre avec qn

▶ **separate off** *vtsep* séparer

▶ **separate out 1** *vi* se séparer **2** *vtsep* séparer **(from** de)

separately ['sep(ə)rətlɪ] *adv* séparément; **are you paying s.?** (*in shop, restaurant etc*) est-ce que vous payez séparément?; **not to be sold s.** (*on multiple pack, promotional item etc*) ne peut être vendu séparément; **wash s.** (*on garment label etc*) laver séparément; **keep this s.** gardez ceci à part

separation [sepə'reɪʃən] *n* séparation *f* **(from sb** d'avec qn); (*of milk*) écrémage *m*; **(judicial) s.** séparation (judiciaire); **s. of powers** séparation des pouvoirs; *Mil* **s. allowance** = allocation *f* faite à la femme d'un soldat; *Psy* **s. anxiety** peur *f* de l'abandon

separatism ['sepərətɪz(ə)m] *n* séparatisme *m*

separatist ['sepərətɪst] *adj, n* séparatiste *mf*

separator ['sepəreɪtər] *n Tech, Comptr* séparateur *m*

sepia ['si:pɪə] *n Art* sépia *f*; **s. (drawing)** (dessin *m* à la) sépia

sepoy ['si:pɔɪ] *n Mil* cipaye *m*

sepsis ['sepsɪs] *n Med* septicité *f*

September [sep'tembər] *n* [①**A75-6**,**B-C**; **B58-9**,**B-C**] septembre *m* **in S.** au mois de septembre, en septembre; **(on) the first/the seventh of S.** le premier/le sept septembre

septet [sep'tet] *n Mus* septuor *m*

septic ['septɪk] *adj Med* septique; **to become** *or* **go s.** s'infecter; **I have a s. finger** j'ai un doigt infecté; **s. poisoning** septicémie *f*; **s. tank** fosse *f* septique

septicaemia, *US* **septicemia** [septɪ'si:mɪə] *n Med* septicémie *f*

septuagenarian [septjʊədʒɪ'neərɪən] *n, adj* septuagénaire *mf*

Septuagesima [septjʊə'dʒesɪmə] *n Rel* **S. (Sunday)** (le dimanche de) la Septuagésime

Septuagint ['septjʊədʒɪnt] *n* version *f* (de la Bible) des Septante, Septante *f*

septum, *pl* **-a** [septəm, -ə] *n Anat* septum *m*; *Bot* cloison *f*

sepulchral [sɪ'pʌlkrəl] *adj Lit* sépulcral

sepulchre, *US* **sepulcher** ['sepəlkər] *n* sépulcre *m*; **the Holy S.** le Saint Sépulcre

sequel ['si:kwəl] *n* (*to novel etc*) suite *f*; **as a s. to these events** comme suite à ces événements; **action that had an unfortunate s.** acte qui a entraîné des suites malheureuses

sequence ['si:kwəns] *n* **(a)** (*order*) ordre *m*; (*in time*) ordre,

succession *f*; **what's the s. of events going to be?** quelle est le programme?; **in some sort of s.** dans un ordre quelconque; **in s.** l'un après l'autre; **out of s.** (*one item*) mal rangé; (*set of pictures, items*) dans le désordre; **the films were deliberately shown out of s.** les films ont été présentés dans le désordre exprès; **logical s.** enchaînement *m* logique
(b) (*series*) (*of events, disasters etc*) suite *f*, série *f*
(c) *Cards, Mus, Cin, Comptr* séquence *f*; *Comptr* **s. check(ing)** contrôle *m* de séquence; *Mus* **a chord s.** une suite d'accords; *Gram* **s. of tenses** concordance *f* des temps

sequencer ['siːkwənsər] *n Comptr* coordonnateur *m*, séquenceur *m*

sequencing ['siːkwənsɪŋ] *n Comptr* mise *f* en séquence

sequential [sɪ'kwenʃəl] *adj* séquentiel; (*teaching, history etc*) continu; *Comptr* **s. file** fichier *m* séquentiel; *Comptr* **s. processing** traitement *m* séquentiel

sequentially [sɪ'kwenʃəlɪ] *adv* séquentiellement

sequester [sɪ'kwestər] *vt* **(a)** *Fml* (*confiscate*) confisquer; *Jur* (*property of debtor*) séquestrer, mettre sous séquestre **(b)** *Lit* **to s. oneself (from the world)** se retirer (du monde); **to lead a sequestered life** vivre une vie de reclus; **a sequestered corner of the property** un coin isolé de la propriété

sequestrate [sɪ'kwestreɪt] *vt* confisquer; *Jur* (*property of debtor*) séquestrer, mettre sous séquestre

sequestration [siːkwe'streɪʃən] *n* confiscation *f*; *Jur* séquestration *f*, mise *f* sous séquestre

sequin ['siːkwɪn] *n* (*on dress etc*) paillette *f*

sequined ['siːkwɪnd] *adj* à paillettes

sequoia [sɪ'kwɔɪə] *n* (*tree*) séquoia *m*

seraglio [se'rɑːlɪəʊ] *n* sérail *m*, -ails

seraph, *pl* **seraphs, seraphim** ['serəf, -əfs, -əfɪm] *n* séraphin *m*

seraphic [sɪ'ræfɪk] *adj* séraphique

Serb [sɜːb] **1** *adj* serbe **2** *n* Serbe *mf*

Serbia ['sɜːbɪə] *n* Serbie *f*

Serbian ['sɜːbɪən] **1** *adj* serbe **2** *n* **(a)** Serbe *mf* **(b)** *Ling* serbe *m*

Serbo-Croat [sɜːbəʊ'krəʊæt], **Serbo-Croatian** [sɜːbəʊkrəʊ'eɪʃən] **1** *adj* serbo-croate **2** *n* **(a)** Serbo-croate *mf* **(b)** *Ling* serbo-croate *m*

sere [sɪər] *adj Lit* (*vegetation*) desséché; (*lake*) asséché

serenade[1] [serə'neɪd] *n* sérénade *f*

serenade[2] *vt* donner une sérénade à

serendipitous [serən'dɪpɪtəs] *adj Lit* génial et fortuit

serendipity [serən'dɪpɪtɪ] *n Lit* don *m* de faire des trouvailles

serene [sɪ'riːn] *adj* **(a)** (*sky, sea, person*) serein, calme, tranquille; (*sky*) clair; **her face wore a s. look** son visage exprimait le calme *ou* la sérénité **(b)** (*in title*) sérénissime; **His S. Highness** son Altesse sérénissime

serenely [sɪ'riːnlɪ] *adv* calmement, avec sérénité

serenity [sɪ'renɪtɪ] *n* sérénité *f*, calme *m*

serf [sɜːf] *n* serf *m*, serve *f*

serfdom ['sɜːfdəm] *n* servage *m*

serge [sɜːdʒ] *n Tex* serge *f*; **cotton s.** sergé *m*; **s. suit** costume en sergé

sergeant ['sɑːdʒənt] *n* (*in infantry, air force*) sergent *m*; (*in artillery, armoured corps, cavalry*) maréchal *m* des logis; **(police) s.** brigadier *m*; **quartermaster s., staff s.** (*in infantry, air force*) sergent fourrier *ou* comptable; (*in artillery, armoured corps, cavalry*) maréchal des logis fourrier *ou* comptable; *Jur* **s. at arms** huissier *m*

sergeant-major *n Mil* adjudant *m*; **regimental s.** adjudant-chef *m*, *pl* adjudants-chefs

serial ['sɪərɪəl] **1** *adj* **(a)** *Mus* (*belonging to series*) sériel
(b) (*arranged in series*) en série; (*forming series*) formant série
(c) *Comptr* (*printer*) série *inv*; **s. interface** interface *f* série; **s. to parallel convertor** convertisseur *m* série-parallèle; **s. cable** câble *m* série; **s. data** données *fpl* série; **s. input** entrée *f* série; **s. output** sortie *f* série; **s. port** port *m* série; **s. printer port** port *m* d'imprimante série
2 *n* (*story published in parts*) (*in magazine*) feuilleton *m*, roman-feuilleton *m*, *pl* romans-feuilletons; *Rad* feuilleton (radiophonique); *TV* feuilleton (télévisé); **it was first published in s. form** cela a d'abord été publié sous forme de feuilleton; **s. drama** feuilleton; **s. writer** feuilletoniste *mf*

serialization [sɪərɪəlaɪ'zeɪʃen] *n* mise *f* en feuilleton, publication *f* en feuilleton; (*TV, Rad*) adaptation *f* en feuilleton; **s. rights** droits *mpl* de reproduction en feuilleton

serialize ['sɪərɪəlaɪz] *vt* (*novel etc*) publier en feuilleton, adapter en feuilleton; *TV, Rad* diffuser en feuilleton; **serialized in six parts** (*novel etc*) publié en six épisodes; *TV, Rad* diffusé en six parties; **it's being serialized in the Observer** ça sort en feuilleton dans l'Observer

serial killer *n* meurtrier *m* en série

serially ['sɪərɪəlɪ] *adv* **(a)** en *ou* par série **(b)** *Journ* en feuilleton

serial number *n Ind* numéro *m* de série; (*of engine*) numéro matricule

serial rights *npl* droits *mpl* de reproduction en feuilleton

seriatim [sɪərɪ'eɪtɪm] *adv Fml* point par point

sericulture ['serɪkʌltʃər] *n* sériciculture *f*

series ['sɪəriːz] *n* **(a)** série *f*; (*of colours*) échelle *f*, gamme *f*; (*of books*), *TV, Rad* série; **a s. of terrorist attacks** une série d'attaques terroristes; **in s.** en série, en succession; *TV* **s. producer** producteur *m* de série télévisée **(b)** *El* **connection in s., s. connection** montage *m* en série; *El* **s. winding** enroulement *m* en série

series-connected *adj Comptr* connecté en série

series-wound motor *n* moteur *m* à enroulements série

serif ['serɪf] *n Typ* serif *m*

seriocomic [sɪərɪəʊ'kɒmɪk] *adj* moitié sérieux moitié comique

serious ['sɪərɪəs] *adj* **(a)** (*grave, critical*) sérieux, grave; **things are becoming s.** cela devient sérieux; **s. crime squad** police *f* criminelle; **s. injury** blessure grave; **s. mistake** grosse faute
(b) (*in earnest, thoughtful*) (*person, decision, newspaper etc*) sérieux; **she's not really a s. novelist** (*not considered a real novelist*) ce n'est pas un écrivain majeur; **to be s. about sth** parler sérieusement à propos de qch; **is he s. about emigrating?** est-ce qu'il envisage sérieusement d'émigrer?; **I have never seen him so s. about a girl** je ne l'ai jamais vu aussi sérieux avec une fille; **I'm s.** je ne plaisante pas; **are you s.?** tu parles sérieusement?; **surely you're not s.?** vous n'êtes pas sérieux?, vous plaisantez?; **I was being s. when I said ...** je ne plaisantais pas quand j'ai dit ...; **I have never given the subject s. thought** je n'y ai jamais pensé sérieusement; *F* **an evening of s. drinking** une soirée bien arrosée; *F* **s. money** beaucoup de fric; **the s. press** la presse sérieuse

seriously ['sɪərɪəslɪ] *adv* **(a)** (*gravely, critically*) sérieusement, gravement; **s. ill** gravement malade; **s. wounded** grièvement blessé; *Mil* **the s. wounded** les grands blessés; **the project is s. late** le projet est vraiment en retard; **he got it s. wrong** il s'est complètement trompé
(b) (*in earnest*) (*to talk*) sérieusement; **to take sth s.** prendre qch au sérieux; **to take oneself s.** se prendre au sérieux; **she takes everything far too s.** elle prend tout bien trop au sérieux; **if we are to be taken s. as a world class football team** pour qu'on nous prenne au sérieux en tant qu'équipe de football de niveau international; **you can't s. expect them to believe that** vous ne pouvez pas penser sérieusement qu'ils vont croire ça; **but s., what will you do?** plaisanterie à part, qu'allez-vous faire?

serious-minded *adj* (*person*) réfléchi, sérieux; **s. people** les gens sérieux

seriousness ['sɪərɪəsnɪs] *n* **(a)** (*gravity*) (*of situation, illness etc*) gravité *f* **(b)** (*of tone, personality etc*) sérieux *m*; **in all s.** sérieusement

serjeant ['sɑːdʒənt] *n* **S. at Arms** *Parl* commandant *m* militaire du Parlement; *Hist* (*attendant*) huissier *m* d'armes

sermon ['sɜːmən] *n* **(a)** *Rel* sermon *m*; (*in Protestant church*) prêche *m*; **to deliver a s.** faire un sermon; **collection of sermons** sermonnaire *m*; *Bible* **the S. on the Mount** le Sermon sur la Montagne **(b)** *Fig* sermon *m*; **to give sb a s.** sermonner qn; **the editor does tend to go in for sermons** le rédacteur en chef a tendance à faire des sermons

sermonize ['sɜːmənaɪz] *vi Pej* sermonner, prêcher

sermonizing ['sɜːmənaɪzɪŋ] *n Pej* prêchi-prêcha *m inv*

seroconversion [sɪərəʊkən'vɜːʃən] *n Med* séroconversion *f*

serous ['sɪərəs] *adj Anat etc* (*fluid etc*) séreux; *Anat* **s. membrane** séreuse *f*

serpent ['sɜːpənt] *n* serpent *m*

serpentine ['sɜːpəntaɪn] *adj Lit* serpentin; (*path*) sinueux, tortueux

SERPS [sɜːps] *n Br* (*abbr* **State Earnings-Related Pension Scheme**) = pension *f* de retraite versée par l'État et calculée en fonction des salaires

serrated [se'reɪtɪd] *adj* en dents de scie; **s. edge** denture *f*; **knife with a s. edge, s. knife** couteau-scie *m*

serration [se'reɪʃən] *n* denture *f*

serried ['serɪd] *adj Lit* serré; **in s. ranks** en rangs serrés

serum, *pl* **-ums, -a** ['sɪərəm, -rəms, -rə] *n Physiol* sérum *m*; **blood s.** sérum sanguin

servant ['sɜːvənt] *n* **(a)** (*of God, the community etc*) serviteur *m*, servante *f*; **public servants** employés *mpl* d'un service public, employés de la fonction publique; *Arch Fml* **your most humble and obedient s.** votre très humble serviteur **(b)** (*in household*) domestique *mf*; (*female*) bonne *f*; (*in 19th century and before*) (*male*) serviteur *m*; (*female*) servante *f*; **the servants** les domestiques; (*19th century and before*) les serviteurs; **a large staff of servants** une nombreuse domesticité; **servants' quarters** appartement des domestiques

serve[1] [sɜːv] *n Tennis* service *m*; **(it's) your s.!** à vous de servir!

serve[2] **1** *vt* **(a)** *(master, cause etc)* servir; **to s. God/one's country** servir Dieu/sa patrie; **to have served one's country well** avoir bien servi sa patrie, *Lit* bien mériter de la patrie; **he has served the company faithfully** il a rendu de grands services à la société; **to s. one's own interests** servir ses propres intérêts; *Old-fashioned* **he served me very badly** *(treated)* il a très mal agi envers moi

(b) *(of thing)* être utile à; **to s. the purpose** faire l'affaire; **that old computer does not really s. my purpose** ce vieil ordinateur ne convient pas à mes besoins; **tool that serves several purposes** outil qui sert à plusieurs usages; **this dictionary should s. the purposes of most users** ce dictionnaire devrait rendre service à la majorité des utilisateurs; **it has served its purpose and has been discarded** il a bien servi et on s'en est débarrassé; **I think this one's served its purpose** *(is useless)* je crois qu'il a fait son temps, celui-ci; **if my memory serves me right** si j'ai bonne mémoire

(c) *(complete)* *(prison sentence)* purger; *(apprenticeship)* faire; **to s. one's sentence** *or* **one's time** purger sa peine; **he served a sentence of five years' imprisonment** il a fait cinq ans de prison; **to have served ten years** *(in army)* avoir dix ans de service; *(in prison)* avoir fait dix ans de prison; *Pol* **to s. a term of office** exercer un mandat (présidentiel/de député/*etc*)

(d) *(of bus, rail service, TV station etc)* *(region, population etc)* desservir

(e) *(in shop)* **to s. a customer** servir un client; **are you being served?** est-ce qu'on s'occupe de vous?; **I'm being served, thank you** on s'occupe de moi, merci; **we don't s. (alcohol to) people under eighteen** *(in bar)* nous ne servons pas d'alcool aux moins de dix-huit ans

(f) *(at table etc)* **to s. sb with soup/vegetables** servir du potage/des légumes à qn; **to s. a dish** servir un plat; **dinner is served, madam** Madame est servie; **s. chilled** servir très frais; *Rel* **to s. mass** servir la messe; **serves four** *(on packet, in recipe)* pour quatre personnes; **beef served in a mushroom sauce** bœuf servi avec une sauce aux champignons

(g) *Tennis* **to s. the ball** servir; **he served the ball into ...** il a envoyé la balle de service dans ...; **to s. an ace** faire un ace

(h) *Jur* **to s. a writ/a summons on sb, to s. sb with a writ/a summons** délivrer *ou* signifier *ou* notifier une assignation/une citation à qn

(i) it serves you right! c'est bien fait pour toi!, tu n'as que ce que tu mérites!; **it serves him right for not listening to me** il ne m'a pas écouté, c'est bien fait pour lui; **it would have served you right** tu l'aurais bien mérité

(j) *(of male animal)* *(female)* couvrir

2 *vi* **(a)** *(carry out duty etc)* **to s. in the army** servir dans l'armée; **to s. in the war with sb** faire la guerre avec qn; **she served under three presidents** elle a servi sous trois présidents; **to s. in a government** servir dans un gouvernement

(b) *(meet requirements)* *(of tool, plan etc)* **the boxes s. as tables** les boîtes tiennent lieu de tables; **to s. as a pretext/as an example** servir de prétexte/d'exemple; **it serves to remind us how vulnerable we all are** il est bon de nous rappeler à quel point nous sommes vulnérables; **events in Bosnia s. to demonstrate just how fragile peace is** les événements de Bosnie démontrent à quel point la paix est fragile

(c) *(in shop)* être vendeur, -euse

(d) to s. (at table) servir à table

(e) *Rel* **to s. (at mass)** servir la messe

(f) *Tennis* servir

▶ **serve out** *vtsep* **(a)** *(food)* servir **(b)** *(prison sentence)* purger; *(term of office)* finir, aller jusqu'au bout de; **before she had served out her term of office** avant la fin de son mandat; **to s. out one's time** *(in post etc)* aller jusqu'au bout de son mandat; *Mil* finir son temps de service; *Pej* **the Chairman was just serving out his time** le Président se contentait d'attendre la retraite

▶ **serve up 1** *vtsep* *(dinner etc)* servir; *Fig* *(programme, excuse etc)* sortir, pondre; *(performance)* servir **2** *vi* servir

server ['sɜːvər] *n* **(a)** *(at table)* serveur, -euse **(b)** *Tennis* serveur, -euse **(c)** *Rel (at mass)* servant *m* d'autel **(d)** *(tray)* plateau *m* (de service) **(e)** *(utensil)* **(set of) salad/fish servers** service *m* à salade/à poisson **(f)** *Comptr* **(file) s.** serveur *m*; **s. administrator** administrateur *m* de serveur; **s. engine** processeur-serveur *m*

service[1] ['sɜːvɪs] *n* **(a)** service *m*; **in the s. of God/of one's country** au service de Dieu/de son pays; **to die in the King's/Queen's s.** mourir au service du roi/de la reine; **I am (entirely) at your s.** je suis à votre (entière) disposition; **to do sb a s.** rendre (un) service à qn; **to be of some s.** se rendre utile; **to be of s. to sb** être utile à qn; **can I be of any s. to you?** puis-je vous être utile *ou* vous aider en aucune manière?; **to bring** *or* **put into s.** *(piece of machinery, vehicle etc)* mettre en service; **this pen has given me good s.** ce stylo m'a bien servi; **to offer one's services** offrir ses services; **his services to education** les services qu'il a rendus à l'enseignement; **services rendered** services rendus; *Econ* **goods and services** biens *mpl* et services; *Comptr* **s. bureau** société *f* de traitement à façon; *Av* **s. ceiling** *(of aircraft)* plafond *m* pratique; *Journ* **s. column** rubrique *f* services

(b) *Old-fashioned* **to be in/go into s.** *(of servant)* être/devenir domestique; **to go into s. with sb** entrer au service de qn

(c) *(with army, firm etc)* service *m*; *Com* **promotion according to length of s.** avancement à l'ancienneté; *Com* **to give many years of loyal s. to a company** faire de nombreuses années de bons et loyaux services dans une société; *Mil* **fit/unfit for s.** apte/inapte au service; *Mil* **to see s.** faire la guerre; *Naut* **s. afloat/ashore** service à bord/à terre; **military** *or Br Hist* **national s.** service militaire *ou* national; **when I was doing my military s.** quand j'étais au régiment; **active s.** service actif; **the civil s.** l'administration *f*, la fonction publique; **to be in the civil s.** être fonctionnaire; **the Foreign** *or* **Diplomatic S.** le service diplomatique, la diplomatie; *F* la carrière; **the Secret S.** = le Deuxième Bureau

(d) *(in shop, restaurant etc)* service *m*; **the s. there is good/slow** *(in restaurant)* le service y est de qualité/lent; **s. is included** le service est compris; **s. not included** service non-compris; **24-hour s.** *(open 24 hours)* ouvert 24 heures sur 24; *(service carried out within 24 hours)* travail effectué dans les 24 heures; **s. accommodation** hébergement *m* avec restauration; **s. bell** *(in hotel)* sonnette *f* (pour appeler un employé de l'hôtel); *Br* **s. flat** résidence *f* hôtelière

(e) *(system)* *(rail, air, postal etc)* service *m*; *(for water, gas, electricity)* distribution *f*; **bus s.** service d'autobus/de cars; **we have a good bus/train s.** notre ville est bien desservie par les autobus/par le chemin de fer; **goods** *or* **freight s.** service de marchandises; **passenger s.** service de voyageurs; **public services** services publics; **postal/telephone services** services postaux/téléphoniques; **social/medical services** services sociaux/médicaux; **it provides a s. to the community** cela offre un service aux gens; *TV, Rad* **s. area** zone *f* de desserte, région *f* desservie; **s. sector** secteur *m* tertiaire, tertiaire *m*

(f) *Mil* **the s.** *(army)* l'armée *f*; *(navy)* la marine; *(air force)* l'armée de l'air; **s. personnel** personnel *m* militaire; **s. rifle** fusil *m* réglementaire *ou* de l'armée; **s. vehicle** véhicule *m* militaire *ou* de l'armée; **Joint Services Staff College** ≈ École *f* d'État-major interarmes

(g) *(maintenance)* entretien *m*; *Aut* révision *f*; *Mil (of gun)* service *m*; **my car needs a complete s.** ma voiture a besoin d'une révision complète; **after-sales s.** service après vente; *Aut* **s. area** *or Am* **centre** locaux *mpl* de service; **s. contract** contrat *m* d'entretien; *Aut* **s. history** historique *m* d'entretien; **s. manual** *or* **handbook** manuel *m* d'entretien; **s. road** route *f* réservée aux véhicules de livraison

(h) *Rel* office *m*, culte *m*; **to attend s.** assister à l'office *ou* au culte; **the marriage s.** la cérémonie du mariage

(i) *Jur (of deed, writ)* délivrance *f*, signification *f*

(j) *(crockery)* service *m*; **tea/dinner s.** service à thé/de table

(k) *Tennis* service *m*

service[2] *vt* **(a)** *(do maintenance work to)* entretenir; *(car)* faire la révision de; *(domestic appliance)* assurer l'entretien de **(b)** *(in breeding)* *(of bull, stallion)* *(female)* couvrir **(c)** *(provide services to)* pourvoir aux besoins de; *Fin (loan, debt)* rembourser

serviceable ['sɜːvɪsəb(ə)l] *adj (in functioning state)* en état de fonctionner; *(useable)* utilisable; *(useful)* pratique

service agreement *n* contrat *m* de service

service area *n* aire *f* de services *(au bord d'une autoroute)*; **service areas** *(in hotel)* locaux *mpl* de service

service bay *n Aut (in garage)* zone *f* de travail

service bus *n Austr, New Zealand* autocar *m*

service car *n Austr, New Zealand* autocar *m*

service center *n Am Ant* aire *f* de services *(au bord d'une autoroute)*

service charge *n* service *m*; **there's a ten per cent s.** il y a dix pour cent de service; **rent plus s.** loyer plus les charges

service company *n* entreprise *f* prestataire de services

service court *n Tennis* rectangle *m* de service

serviced ['sɜːvɪst] *adj* (*apartment etc*) avec service d'entretien; **s. accommodation** résidence *f* hôtelière; **s. apartment** appartement *m* dans une résidence hôtelière
service engineer *n* (*for electrical, gas appliance etc*) ingénieur *m* chargé de l'entretien, technicien *m* de maintenance
service fault *n* faute *f* de service
service hatch *n* passe-plats *m inv*
service industry *n Econ* branche *f* du tertiaire
service life *n* durée *f* de vie
service lift *n Br* ascenseur *m* de service
service line *n Tennis* ligne *f* de service
serviceman, *pl* **-men** ['sɜːvɪsmən] *n* militaire *m*; *Br Hist* **national s.** appelé *m*
service provider *or* **supplier** *n* prestataire *m* de service(s)
services ['sɜːvɪsɪs] *npl* **(a)** (*on motorway*) services *mpl*; (*place*) aire *f* de services; **s. 10 km** (*on sign*) aire de services, 10 km **(b) the (armed) services** les forces *fpl* armées
service station *n Aut* station-service *f*, *pl* stations-service
servicewoman, *pl* **-women** ['sɜːvɪswʊmən, -wɪmɪn] *n* femme *f* soldat; *F* soldate *f*
servicing ['sɜːvɪsɪŋ] *n* entretien *m*; **s. manual** manuel *m* d'entretien
serviette [sɜːvɪ'et] *n Br* serviette *f* de table
servile ['sɜːvaɪl] *adj* (*person, behaviour*) servile
servility [sɜː'vɪlɪtɪ] *n* servilité *f*
serving ['sɜːvɪŋ] **1** *adj* (*soldier*) au service; **the longest-s. official** la personnalité officielle ayant le plus d'ancienneté **2** *n* (*portion*) (*of food*) portion *f*; **s. dish** plat *m*, assiette *f* de service
serving hatch *n* passe-plats *m inv*
servitude ['sɜːvɪtjuːd] *n* (*slavery*) servitude *f*, esclavage *m*; **to be sold into s.** être vendu comme esclave; *Jur* **penal s. for life** (*imprisonment*) travaux forcés à perpétuité
servo ['sɜːvəʊ] **1** *n F* = **servomechanism 2** *adj Aut* **s. brake** servofrein *m*
servo-assistance *n* servo-assistance *f*
servocontrol [sɜːvəʊkən'trəʊl] *n* servocommande *f*
servomechanism [sɜːvəʊ'mekənɪz(ə)m] *n* servomécanisme *m*
servomotor [sɜːvəʊ'məʊtər] *n* servomoteur *m*
servo-unit *n* servo-commande *m*
sesame ['sesəmɪ] *n* **(a)** (*plant*) sésame *m*; **s. oil** huile *f* de sésame; **s. seeds** graines *fpl* de sésame **(b) open s.** (*magic formula*) sésame, ouvre-toi!
session ['seʃən] *n* **(a)** (*period of activity*) séance *f*; **morning/evening s.** (*at swimming pool etc*) séance du matin/soir; **skiing tuition at £10 per 3-hour s.** cours de ski à 10 livres par séance de 3 heures; **training s.** séance d'entraînement; **we had a long s. on the phone** nous sommes restés très longtemps au téléphone; **I've just had a long s. with the lawyers** je viens d'avoir un long entretien avec les avocats; *F* **she has a complaining s. every morning** régulièrement, tous les matins, il faut qu'elle se plaigne
(b) (*meeting*) session *f*; *Parl* **the autumn s.** la session d'automne; **the House is now in s.** la Chambre siège actuellement
(c) *US, Scot Sch, Univ* (*term*) trimestre *m* (scolaire/universitaire); (*year*) année *f* (scolaire/universitaire)
session artist *n Mus* artiste *mf* de studio
session musician *n Mus* musicien, -ienne de studio
set[1] [set] *n* **(a)** (*group*) (*of keys, boxes, chess pieces etc*) jeu *m*; (*of problems, rules, symptoms, pans etc*) série *f*; (*of glasses, china*) service *m*; (*of tyres, wheels*) train *m*; (*of turbines*) batterie *f*; (*of stamps, butterflies etc*) (*collection*) collection *f*; (*series*) série; (*of sb's works*) œuvres *fpl* complètes; (*of lingerie*) parure *f*; *Comptr* (*of characters, instructions*) jeu, ensemble *m*; *Math* ensemble; **s. of bills of exchange** jeu de lettres de change; **s. of data** ensemble de données; **s. of teeth** denture *f*, dentition *f*; (*artificial*) dentier *m*; **s. of golf clubs** jeu de crosses; **s. of bells** sonnerie *f* (*d'église etc*); *Old-fashioned* **toilet s., dressing-table s.** garniture *f* de toilette; **construction s.** jeu de construction; **a s. of cooking utensils** une batterie de cuisine; **a s. of sheets** une parure de lit; **a s. of screwdrivers** une série de tourne-vis; **a s. of tests** une batterie de tests; **to collect the (whole) s.** rassembler toute la collection, faire la collection; **chairs, the s. of six, £200** chaises, 200 livres les six; *Math* **s. theory** théorie *f* des ensembles
(b) (*of people*) groupe *m*; *Pej* **literary/political s.** coterie *f* littéraire/politique; **he got in with the literary/political s.** il s'est mêlé au groupe de ceux qui s'intéressaient à la littérature/politique; **the smart s.** les élégants; **I'm not one of their s.** je ne suis pas de leur monde
(c) *Br Sch* **top/bottom s.** classe *f* des forts/des plus faibles
(d) (*position*) (*of public opinion*) tendances *fpl*; **his anxiety was betrayed in the s. of his shoulders** la position de ses épaules trahissait son anxiété; **I could tell she was angry by the s. of her jaw** je voyais sa colère à ses machoires serrées
(e) (*in hairdressing*) mise *f* en plis
(f) (*apparatus*) **(radio) s.** poste *m* de radio; **(television) s.** téléviseur *m*, poste de télévision
(g) *Constr* **(paving) s.** pavé *m* d'échantillon
(h) *Th* (*scenery*) décor *m*; *TV, Cin* plateau *m* (de tournage); **on s.** *Th* sur scène; *TV, Cin* sur le plateau; **rehearsal on the s.** *Th* répétition *f* sur scène; *Cin* répétition sur le plateau; **s. dressing** agencement *m* des éléments du décor
(i) *Mus etc* (*performance*) set *m*; **the band played two sets** le groupe a joué deux sets
(j) (*tool*) **nail s.** chasse-clou(s) *m inv*; **saw s.** tourne-à-gauche *m inv*
(k) *Tennis* manche *f*, set *m*
(l) (*of badger*) terrier *m*
set[2] (*pt, pp* **set**; *prp* **setting**) **1** *vt* **(a)** (*place*) (*sth on or against sth, sth before sb*) mettre, poser; **to s. one's glass on the table** poser son verre sur la table; **to s. sth before sb** présenter qch à qn; **to s. a dish in front of sb** servir un plat à qn; **to s. a stake in the ground** enfoncer *ou* planter un pieu dans la terre; **to s. one's hand/seal to a document** apposer sa signature/son sceau à un acte; **to s. sb on his feet again** remettre qn sur pied; **her eyes are set too close together** elle a les yeux trop rapprochés; **the house is set in the heart of the woods** la maison est située au milieu des bois; **to s. a match to sth** mettre le feu à qch; **to s. a value on sth** décider de la valeur de qch; **to s. a proposal before the board** présenter un projet au conseil d'administration; **to s. one's heart on sth** avoir qch à cœur, vouloir absolument qch; **to s. the table** mettre le couvert *ou* la table; **to s. the table for two** mettre deux couverts; **to s. a trap (for sb)** tendre un piège (à qn)
(b) (*story, film*) situer; **where is the story/film set?** où est-ce que l'histoire/le film se passe?; *Th* **to s. a scene** monter un décor; **the second act is set in a street** le second acte se passe dans une rue
(c) (*adjust*) (*mechanism, watch etc*) régler; **to s. one's watch by the town clock** régler sa montre sur l'horloge de la ville; **to s. the alarm clock for** *or* **at five o'clock** mettre le réveil à cinq heures; **to s. the milometer to zero** ramener *ou* remettre le compteur à zéro; **to s. one's hat straight** remettre son chapeau droit; **to have one's hair set** se faire faire une mise en plis
(d) (*mount*) (*stone*) monter, sertir; **set with diamonds** orné *ou* incrusté de diamants; **(with) all sails set** toutes voiles dehors
(e) (*prepare*) (*trap, also Fig*) dresser, tendre
(f) (*fix*) (*date, day*) fixer, arrêter; **to s. a date for a meeting** fixer une date de réunion; **to s. a price** fixer *ou* établir un prix; **to s. the rate of sth** tarifer qch; **to s. limits to sth** fixer des limites à qch; **to s. prices high/low** fixer les prix hauts/bas; **to s. an age limit at ...** fixer une limite d'âge à ...; **to s. oneself a target** se fixer un but; **to s. a fashion/trend** lancer une mode/tendance; **to s. a record** établir un record; **to s. oneself a task** s'imposer une tâche; **to s. sb a problem** poser un problème à qn; *Sch* **to s. an essay** donner un sujet de dissertation; *Sch* **to s. a book** mettre un livre au programme; **to s. an exam(ination) paper** choisir les questions d'une épreuve écrite; **to s. the page margins** marger la page
(g) (*cause to start*) **to s. sb to do sth** faire faire qch à qn; **to s. a man to work** mettre un homme au travail; **that set me thinking** cela m'a fait réfléchir *ou* m'a donné à réfléchir; **to s. the dog barking** faire aboyer le chien; **to s. people talking** (*provoke comment*) faire parler les gens; **to s. sth going** mettre qch en train; **to s. a mechanism going** mettre un mécanisme en marche; **to s. sb free** libérer qn, rendre sa liberté à qn
(h) *Mus* **to s. a melody half a tone higher/lower** chanter/jouer un air un demi-ton plus haut/bas; **to s. words to music** mettre des paroles en musique
(i) *Surg* (*bone, limb*) remettre; (*fracture*) réduire
(j) *Typ* composer; **to s. type** composer; **to s. a page** composer une page
(k) (*of plant*) (*fruit*) donner, porter
2 *vi* **(a)** (*of sun, moon*) se coucher; **we saw the sun setting** nous avons vu le coucher du soleil
(b) (*become firm*) (*of jelly*) prendre; (*of broken bone*) se recoller; (*of cement*) prendre, durcir; **her features had set in an expression of determination** ses traits s'étaient durcis en une expression de très forte détermination; *Fig* **public opinion was beginning to s. against the proposal** l'opinion publique commençait à se durcir contre la proposition
(c) (*in hunting*) (*of dog*) tomber en arrêt

set[3] *adj* **(a)** (*face*) immobile, aux traits rigides; (*look*) fixe; (*smile*) figé; **(hard) s.** ferme, figé; (*cement*) bien pris

(b) (*prepared*) **to be (all) s. to do sth** être prêt à faire qch; **to be all s.** (*ready to begin*) être prêt à commencer; *Sp* **(get) s.!** en position, attention!; *Journ* **sterling s. to fall** la livre sterling sur le point de chuter

(c) (*determined*) **to be (dead) s. on sth** être résolu *ou* déterminé à qch; **to be (dead) s. on doing sth** être résolu *ou* déterminé à faire qch; **to be dead s. against sb/sth** être résolument contre qn/qch

(d) (*fixed*) (*ideas, opinions etc*) arrêté; (*time, price*) fixé; (*way*) prédéterminé; **he has a s. way of doing it** il a sa méthode pour le faire; **to be s. in one's ways** avoir ses habitudes, être coincé dans ses habitudes; **at s. hours** à heures fixes; **with no s. purpose** sans but précis; *Sch* **s. books** ouvrages *mpl* au programme; **one of our s. books is 'Oliver Twist'** un des ouvrages au programme est 'Oliver Twist'; **s. dinner** (menu *m* de) table *f* d'hôte; (*at fixed price*) menu à prix fixe; **s. forms of behaviour** comportements fixés par l'usage; **s. form of prayer** prière liturgique; **s. price** prix *m* fixe; **s. speech** discours *m* composé à l'avance *ou* préparé; *Sch* **s. subject** matière *f* obligatoire; **s. task** tâche *f* assignée; **to give sb a s. task to do** assigner à qn une tâche bien précise

▶ **set about** *vipo* **(a)** (*start*) **to s. about a piece of work** se mettre à *ou* entreprendre un travail; **to s. about doing sth** se mettre à faire qch; **I don't know how to s. about it** je ne sais pas comment m'y prendre **(b)** (*attack*) **to s. about sb** attaquer qn

▶ **set against** *vtaspo* **(a)** (*cause to oppose*) **to s. sb against sb** dresser qn contre qn; *F* monter (la tête à) qn contre qn; **it had set members of the family one against the other** cela avait dressé les membres de la famille les uns contre les autres; **something's set him against the idea** quelque chose lui en a fait détester l'idée; **to s. oneself** *or* **one's face against sth** s'opposer résolument à qch

(b) (*weigh against*) **to s. sth against sth** contre-balancer qch par qch; **to s. the benefits against the costs** évaluer les bénéfices par rapport aux coûts

(c) *Fin* (*offset*) **to s. expenses against taxes** déduire les dépenses des impôts

(d) (*compare*) **to set sth against sth** comparer qch à qch; **we must s. the government's promises against its achievements** nous devons examiner les promesses du gouvernement à la lumière de ses actions

▶ **set apart** *vtsep* **(a)** (*distinguish*) distinguer **(from** de); **what sets them apart from other companies is …** ce qui les distingue des autres sociétés c'est … **(b)** (*isolate*) (*person*) isoler; **they set themselves apart** ils faisaient bande à part

▶ **set aside** *vtsep* **(a)** (*abandon temporarily*) (*job, task*) mettre de côté; **could you s. aside what you're working on for a while?** pouvez-vous laisser ce que vous êtes en train de faire un moment?

(b) (*not consider*) ne pas prendre en ligne de compte, laisser de côté; **setting that aspect aside** sans prendre cet aspect en ligne de compte, si on laisse de côté cet aspect; **to s. aside one's personal feelings** mettre de côté tout sentiment personnel

(c) (*save*) (*money*) mettre de côté *ou* en réserve; (*hours, weekend etc*) réserver; **to s. aside some money every week** mettre de l'argent de côté chaque semaine

(d) *Jur* (*judgement, verdict etc*) casser, infirmer; (*claim*) rejeter; (*will*) annuler

▶ **set back** *vtsep* **(a)** *Constr etc* **house set back (from the road)** maison en retrait (de la route) **(b)** (*delay*) retarder le progrès de; **the news may s. him** *or* **his recovery back** la nouvelle risque de retarder sa guérison; **this decision will s. the economy back ten years** cette décision va faire revenir l'économie dix ans en arrière **(c)** *F* (*cost*) **it set me back £5,000** ça m'a coûté 5 000 livres; **that new car must have set her back a bit** cette nouvelle voiture a dû lui coûter un fric fou

▶ **set by** *vtsep* = **set aside (c)**

▶ **set down** *vtsep* **(a)** (*put down*) poser, déposer; **the train stops to s. down passengers only** ce train ne prend pas de voyageurs **(b) to s. sth down in writing** coucher qch par écrit; **condition set down in the contract** condition énoncée dans le contrat; **permissible levels of pollution are set down in the regulations** les taux de pollution tolérés sont fixés dans les réglementations

▶ **set forth 1** *vi Arch, Lit* (*leave*) se mettre en route, partir **2** *vtsep* (*present*) (*case etc*) présenter, mettre en avant; **the document sets forth a detailed description of …** le document présente une description détaillée de …

▶ **set in 1** *vi* (*take hold*) (*of gangrene, fog, winter, cynicism*) s'installer; **night was setting in** la nuit tombait; **the rain had set in** la pluie ne s'arrêtait plus **2** *vtsep Sewing* (*sleeve*) monter

▶ **set off 1** *vtsep* **(a)** (*ignite*) (*rocket*) faire partir; (*bomb*) faire exploser

(b) (*cause*) (*explosion, alarm, argument, chain of events*) déclencher

(c) (*cause to do sth*) **this answer set them off (laughing)** cette réponse a déclenché les rires; **one look at his face set me off again** en le voyant, mon fou rire a repris de plus belle; **if you say anything it'll only s. him off (crying) again** si tu dis quoi que ce soit, il va se remettre à pleurer; **the smallest amount of pollen will s. her off** la moindre dose de pollen lui déclenche une réaction allergique; **don't mention Maradona or you'll s. him off again** surtout ne prononce pas le nom de Maradona sinon il va recommencer; **someone mentioned the war and of course that set Uncle Arthur off** quelqu'un mentionna le mot guerre, et évidemment, oncle Arthur embraya aussitôt sur le sujet

(d) (*enhance*) mettre en relief *ou* en valeur; (*colour, person's best points*) faire ressortir, faire valoir, rehausser; **those curtains really s. the room off** ces rideaux mettent vraiment la pièce en valeur

(e) *Fin* (*debt*) compenser; **to s. off a gain against a loss** compenser une perte par un gain; **can I s. these expenses off against my tax liability?** est-ce que je peux déduire ces frais de mes impôts?

(f) *Comptr* (*num lock, insert, etc*) désactiver

2 *vi* (*depart*) se mettre en route, partir; **to s. off on a journey** partir; **to s. off again** se remettre en route; **to s. off running** partir en courant

▶ **set on 1** *vipo* (*attack*) attaquer **2** *vtsep Comptr* (*num lock, insert etc*) activer **3** *vtaspo* **(a)** (*cause to follow*) **to s. the police on the tracks of a thief** mettre la police aux trousses d'un voleur; **to s. sb (off) on the wrong track** mettre qn sur une fausse piste; **to s. sb on his way** mettre qn sur les rails **(b)** (*cause to attack*) **to s. a dog on sb** lâcher un chien sur qn

▶ **set out 1** *vtsep* (*arrange*) disposer; (*goods*) étaler; (*one's ideas*) exposer; **his work is well set out** son travail est bien présenté

2 *vi* **(a)** (*depart on journey*) se mettre en route, partir; **just as he was setting out** au moment de son départ; **to s. out for school** partir pour l'école; **to s. out again** repartir; **to s. out in pursuit/in search of sb** se mettre à la poursuite/à la recherche de qn

(b) (*start job etc*) **I didn't realize when I set out how difficult it would be** je n'avais pas réalisé combien ce serait difficile lorsque j'ai commencé; **I didn't s. out with any preconceptions** au départ, je n'avais aucune idée préconçue

(c) (*intend*) **I didn't s. out to attack the government** je n'avais aucune intention d'attaquer le gouvernment; **they deliberately set out to cause trouble** ils avaient l'intention de créer des problèmes; **his theory sets out to prove that …** sa théorie a pour objet de prouver que …

▶ **set to 1** *vi* **(a)** (*start working*) se mettre au travail *ou* à l'œuvre **(b)** *F* (*of two people*) (*start arguing*) avoir une prise de bec; (*start fighting*) en venir aux mains **2** *vipo* (*start doing*) **to s. to work** se mettre au travail *ou* à l'œuvre

▶ **set up 1** *vtsep* **(a)** (*erect*) (*mast*) dresser; (*statue*) ériger; (*computer system, stereo system, model train set*) installer; (*machine, tent, tripod etc*) monter; (*barrier*) élever; **to s. sth up again** (*because it has fallen*) relever qch; *Fig* **to s. up a barrier between people** mettre une barrière entre les gens

(b) (*arrange*) (*dinner, meeting, appointment*) organiser; (*system, link*) établir; **I've set things up (so that …)** j'ai organisé les choses (de telle manière que …); **will you s. things up for the meeting?** veux-tu t'occuper d'organiser la réunion?

(c) (*establish*) (*committee, tribunal*) instituer, constituer; (*business*) créer, fonder; (*programme*) monter; (*distinction, connection*) établir; **to s. up an account** ouvrir un compte; **to s. up house** *or* **home** s'installer dans une maison; **to s. sb up in business** aider qn à monter une affaire; **to s. oneself up as a lawyer** monter un cabinet d'avocat

(d) *Med etc* (*cause*) (*infection, irritation*) provoquer, causer

(e) *F* (*fabricate evidence against sb*) (*usu passive*) **I've been set up** on m'a monté le coup, on m'a bien eu

(f) (*invigorate*) (*person*) revivifier; **a fortnight in the country will s. you up** une quinzaine à la campagne va vous remettre d'aplomb

(g) *Typ* (*text*) composer

2 *vi* **(a)** (*establish oneself*) **to s. up in business** se mettre à son compte; **to s. up as a chemist** s'établir pharmacien(ne);

he has set up for himself il s'est établi à son compte; **to s. up overseas** s'implanter à l'étranger
(**b**) (*claim to be*) **to s. up as a critic** se poser en critique
▶ **set upon** *vipo* attaquer; **to be set upon by sb** être attaqué par qn
set-aside *n EC* gel *m* des terres
setback ['setbæk] *n* (**a**) (*reversal, stroke of bad luck*) mésaventure *f*; *Fin, St Exch* tassement *m*, repli *m*; *Med* rechute *f*; **they encountered a number of setbacks** ils ont eu de nombreux déboires; **to suffer a s.** (*of patient*) rechuter; **the dollar suffered a s. today** le dollar a connu un repli aujourd'hui; **to suffer a s. in one's plans** voir ses plans compromis; **this will prove a s. in his career** cela va compromettre sa carrière (**b**) *Archit* décrochement *m*
set designer *n Th* décorateur, -trice de théâtre; *Cin* décorateur, -trice de cinéma; *TV* décorateur, -trice pour la télévision
set expression *n* (*in language*) expression *f* figée
set-in *adj Sewing* **s. sleeve** manche *f* rapportée
set menu *n* menu *m* fixe
setmeter ['setmi:tər] *n TV etc* audimètre *m*
set phrase *n* (*in language*) expression *f* figée
set piece *n* (**a**) *Culin* pièce *f* montée; (*fireworks*) pièce montée, pièce d'artifice; *Sp* tactique *f*; **s. speech** cheval *m* de bataille (**b**) *TV, Cin* élément *m* de décor
set point *n Tennis* balle *f* de set
set-square *n* équerre *f* (à dessin)
sett [set] *n* (**a**) *Constr* (**paving**) **s.** pavé *m* d'échantillon (**b**) (*of badger*) terrier *m*
settee [se'ti:] *n* canapé *m*; **bed s.** canapé-lit *m*, *pl* canapés-lits
setter ['setər] *n* (**a**) (*person*) (*of diamonds etc*) sertisseur *m*; *Typ* (**type**) **s.** compositeur, -trice (**b**) (*dog*) setter *m*; **Irish s.** setter irlandais
setting ['setɪŋ] **1** *adj* (**a**) (*sun, star*) couchant
(**b**) **slow-/quick-s. cement** ciment *m* à prise lente/rapide
2 *n* (**a**) (*act of adjusting*) réglage *m*
(**b**) (*act of mounting*) (*of specimen, jewel*) montage *m*; (*result*) monture *f*
(**c**) *Typ* composition *f*; **s. width** largeur *f* de composition
(**d**) (*act of fixing, arranging*) (*of date etc*) désignation *f*; **s. up of an account** ouverture *f* d'un compte; **s. up of a business** création *f ou* fondation *f* d'une entreprise
(**e**) (*of sun etc*) coucher *m*
(**f**) *Surg* (*of broken bone*) recollement *m*; (*of fracture*) réduction *f*
(**g**) (*hardening*) (*of cement*) affermissement *m*, prise *f*; **s. lotion** lotion *f* pour mise en plis
(**h**) (*location*) (*of story, festival etc*) cadre *m*; *Th* mise *f* en scène; **a novel in an 18th century s.** un roman dans un décor 18ème siècle
(**i**) (*arrangement*) **s. for violin** arrangement *m* pour violon; (**place**) **s.** (*at table*) couvert *m*; **the s. to music of ...** la mise en musique de ...
(**j**) (*on washing machine, iron etc*) réglage *m*; **try a higher s.** (*of oven, iron, microwave etc*) augmentez la température; **what s. was it on?** sur quoi était-elle réglée?
(**k**) *Comptr* (*of tabs etc*) (*action*) pose *f*; (*position*) positionnement *m*; **printer settings** paramètres *mpl* de l'imprimante
settle[1] ['set(ə)l] *n* (*seat*) = banquette *f* en bois avec un dossier
settle[2] **1** *vt* (**a**) (*make stable*) (*put carefully in place*) mettre bien en place; (*person, population etc*) (*country*) coloniser, peupler; (*one's affairs*) régler, mettre de l'ordre dans; **to s. one's feet in the stirrups** bien installer ses pieds dans les étriers; **she had settled herself in an armchair** elle s'était installée dans un fauteuil; **to s. an invalid for the night** installer un malade pour la nuit; **to s. the children for the night** mettre les enfants au lit
(**b**) (*calm*) (*person, nerves etc*) apaiser, calmer; **give me something to s. my stomach** donnez-moi quelque chose pour l'estomac; **to s. sb's doubts** dissiper les doutes de qn
(**c**) (*fix*) (*day, venue etc*) fixer, déterminer; **it's as good as settled** c'est comme si c'était fait; **everything is settled, it's settled** l'affaire est conclue; **that's settled then** c'est entendu *ou* convenu
(**d**) (*resolve*) (*question*) résoudre, décider; (*quarrel, dispute, account*) régler; (*debt*) payer; **to s. a matter** régler une question; **to s. accounts** *or* **old scores** *or* **an old score with sb** régler des comptes avec qn; **to s. one's differences (with sb)** se mettre d'accord (avec qn); **questions not yet settled** questions en suspens; **that settles it!** voilà qui est réglé!; **s. it among yourselves** arrangez cela entre vous; **to s. a matter out of court** régler une question à l'amiable; **to s. one's bills** payer ses factures; *F* **that settled him** *or* **his hash** (*that put a stop to him*) ça lui a réglé son compte; (*that put a stop to his boasting*) ça lui a rabattu le caquet
(**e**) (*bestow*) **to s. an annuity on sb** constituer une rente à qn; **to s. all one's property on one's wife** mettre tous ses biens au nom de sa femme
2 *vi* (**a**) (*of person, people*) s'établir, se fixer (**in a place** dans un lieu); (*of bird, insect etc*) se poser; **to s. in an armchair** s'installer dans un fauteuil; **she had settled in a corner** elle s'était installée dans un coin; **they settled along the Ohio** ils se sont installés au bord de l'Ohio; **she lived here a few years, but didn't s.** elle a vécu ici quelques années, mais ne s'est pas installée définitivement; (*never felt at home*) elle a vécu ici quelques années, mais ne s'est jamais habituée; **the snow is settling** la neige tient; **to s. to work/to do sth** se mettre sérieusement au travail/à faire qch; **he can't s. to anything** il n'arrive pas à se concentrer sur quoi que ce soit; **I couldn't s.** (*in bed*) je n'arrivais pas à m'endormir; *Fig* **a look of despair/contentment had settled on his face** le désespoir/la satisfaction se lisait sur son visage
(**b**) (*of liquid, beer*) reposer; (*of sediment*) se déposer; (*of dust*) retomber; **to let s.** (*dregs etc*) laisser déposer; (*wine*) laisser se rasseoir; (*solution*) laisser reposer; **allow the mixture to s.** laissez reposer le mélange
(**c**) (*of ground, pillar etc*) prendre son assiette, s'asseoir; (*of foundation etc*) s'affaisser; **let your food s. before you go swimming** attendez d'avoir digéré avant d'aller nager
(**d**) (*of excitement*) s'apaiser, se calmer; **the weather is settling** le temps se calme
(**e**) *Jur* **to s.** (**out of court**) régler l'affaire (à l'amiable)
▶ **settle down 1** *vi* (**a**) (*make oneself comfortable*) s'installer; **they settled down by the fire/to watch TV** ils s'installèrent près de la cheminée/pour regarder la télévision; **to s. down to sleep** s'apprêter à dormir; **it took the children some time to s. down to sleep** les enfants ont mis du temps à se décider à dormir; **to s. down with a book** s'installer avec un livre
(**b**) (*give serious attention to sth*) **to s. down to work** se mettre sérieusement au travail; **to s. down to a job** s'attaquer *ou* se mettre à une tâche
(**c**) (*adopt regular life*) se ranger, s'assagir; (*of situation*) s'arranger, redevenir normal; (*of excitement*) se calmer; **it's time you settled down and got married** il est temps que tu te ranges et que tu te maries; **he's not someone you could imagine settling down with** ce n'est pas le genre de personne avec qui on peut imaginer se marier; **s. down, children!** calmez-vous, les enfants!, du calme, les enfants!; **he's beginning to s. down at school** il commence à s'habituer à l'école; **things are settling down** (*becoming more definite*) les choses commencent à prendre tournure; (*calming down*) les choses sont en train de se calmer; **as soon as the market settles down** aussitôt que le marché se sera stabilisé
2 *vtsep* (**a**) (*make comfortable*) **to s. the baby down for the night** installer le bébé pour la nuit
(**b**) (*make calm*) **to s. a class down** calmer une classe
▶ **settle for** *vipo* (*accept*) accepter; **I settled for £100** j'ai accepté 100 livres; **I insist on the best quality, I never s. for (anything) less** j'exige ce qu'il y a de mieux, je n'accepte jamais rien en dessous; **we haven't got any brandy, will you s. for Scotch?** nous n'avons pas de cognac, est-ce qu'un whisky fera l'affaire?
▶ **settle in 1** *vi* (*become established*) s'installer, s'établir; **to s. in in a new school** s'habituer à une nouvelle école; **to s. in at a job** s'habituer à un emploi; **to s. in at a company** s'intégrer à une société **2** *vtsep* (*help become established*) (*new employee, person in new home*) aider à s'installer
▶ **settle on** *vipo* (*decide on*) décider de; **have you settled on a name for the baby/a date for the wedding?** avez-vous décidé d'un prénom pour le bébé/d'une date pour le mariage?; **they couldn't s. on a price** ils n'ont pas réussi à se mettre d'accord sur un prix
▶ **settle up** *vi* (**a**) (*pay bill*) payer (**b**) (*pay debt*) s'acquitter; **I'll s. up with you tomorrow** je vous réglerai demain
▶ **settle with** *vipo* **to s. with sb** (*pay debt*) régler ses comptes avec qn
settled ['set(ə)ld] *adj* (**a**) (*stable, calm*) (*life*) stable; (*idea, habit*) fixe, enraciné; (*intention*) bien arrêté; (*person, character*) rassis, réfléchi; (*bearing etc*) tranquille, calme; **s. weather** temps stable; **I am a man of s. habits** je suis un homme d'habitudes; **she is s. in her job** elle est habituée à son emploi (**b**) (*established in home*) (*person*) installé, établi; **to get s.** s'installer (**c**) (*colonized*) colonisé
settlement ['set(ə)lmənt] *n* (**a**) (*action*) (*of people in a country*) établissement *m*, installation *f*; (*of country*) colonisation *f*
(**b**) (*of ground*) tassement *m*, affaissement *m*
(**c**) (*of matter*) règlement *m*; (*of difference*) arrangement *m*; (*of question*) résolution *f*, décision *f*; (*of treaty etc*)

conclusion *f*; *Com* (*of account*) règlement, paiement *m*; *St Exch* liquidation *f*; *Com* **in (full) s.** pour solde de tout compte; *St Exch* **s. day** jour *m* de (la) liquidation *ou* du règlement; *Fin* **s. discount** remise *f* pour règlement rapide; *Fin* **s. period** délai *m* de règlement, terme *m* de liquidation; *St Exch* **s. price** cours *m* de compensation *ou* de règlement; *Fin* **s. value** valeur *f* transactionnelle

(d) (*agreement*) accord *m*; **they have reached a s.** ils sont arrivés à un accord; *Jur* **s. of an annuity** constitution *f* de rente (**on** en faveur de); **marriage s.** contrat *m* de mariage

(e) (*colony*) colonie *f*; **penal s.** colonie pénitentiaire

(f) *US* (*small community*) village *m*

settler ['setlər] *n* (*colonist*) colon *m*

settling ['setlɪŋ] *n* **(a)** = **settlement** (*a*) **(b)** (*of liquid*) clarification *f* **(c)** (*of ground*) affaissement *m* **(d)** = **settlement (c)**

set-to *n F* (*fight*) bagarre *f*; (*argument*) prise *f* de bec

setup ['setʌp] *n F* **(a)** (*organization*) fonctionnement *m*; **it's an odd s.** (*company*) c'est une drôle de boîte; (*marriage, relationship*) c'est un drôle de ménage; (*collection of people*) c'est une drôle d'équipe; **you've got a nice s. here** vous êtes bien installé ici **(b)** *esp Am* (*something rigged*) machination *f*, coup *m* monté

seven ['sev(ə)n] *adj, n* sept *m*; **two sevens are fourteen** deux fois sept (font) quatorze; *Cards* **the s. of hearts** le sept de cœur; **the s. deadly sins** les sept péchés capitaux; **s.-league boots** bottes *fpl* de sept lieues; *Lit* **to sail the s. seas** parcourir les océans; *F* **the s.-year itch** le cap difficile des sept ans de mariage; *F* **to have the s.-year itch** arriver au cap difficile des sept ans de mariage

seven-bit character *n Comptr* caractère *m* à sept bits

seven-bit data *n Comptr* données *fpl* à sept bits

sevenfold ['sev(ə)nfəʊld] **1** *adj* septuple **2** *adv* sept fois autant; **to increase s.** septupler

seventeen [sev(ə)n'tiːn] *adj, n* dix-sept *m*; **she's s.** elle a dix-sept ans

seventeenth [sev(ə)n'tiːnθ] **1** *adj* dix-septième **2** *n* **(a)** (*of month*) dix-sept *m*; **(on) the s. of May** le dix-sept mai **(b)** (*person, thing*) dix-septième *mf* **(c)** (*fraction*) dix-septième *m*

seventh ['sev(ə)nθ] **1** *adj* septième; **to be in s. heaven** être aux anges *ou* au septième ciel; **Edward the S.** Édouard Sept; *Rel* **S.-day Adventist** adventiste *mf* du septième jour **2** *n* **(a)** (*of month*) sept *m*; **(on) the s. (of May)** le sept (mai) **(b)** (*person, thing*) septième *mf*; **you're the s. this morning to ask me that** tu es la septième personne qui me demande *ou* à me demander ça ce matin **(c)** (*fraction*) septième *m* **(d)** *Mus* (*interval*) septième *f*

seventieth ['sev(ə)ntɪɪθ] **1** *adj* soixante-dixième, *Belg Swiss* septantième **2** *n* **(a)** (*person, thing*) soixante-dixième *mf* **(b)** (*fraction*) soixante-dixième *m*

seventy ['sev(ə)ntɪ] *adj, n* soixante-dix *m*, *Belg Swiss* septante *mf*; **s.-one** soixante et onze; **s.-five** soixante-quinze; **s.-nine** soixante-dix-neuf; **to be in one's seventies** être septuagénaire

sever ['sevər] **1** *vt* (*cut off*) (*arm, finger, leg*) sectionner (**at** au niveau de); (*friendship, link, relationship*) rompre; (*communications*) interrompre; **to s. one's connections with sb** couper les liens avec qn; **to s. sth from sth** séparer qch de qch; **a severed head** une tête coupée **2** *vi* (*of rope etc*) (se) rompre

several ['sev(ə)r(ə)l] **1** *adj* **(a)** [ⓘB14,B,1,a] (*a number of*) plusieurs; **I've been there s. times** j'y suis allé plusieurs fois; **he and s. others** lui et plusieurs autres **(b)** *Lit* (*respective*) respectif; **they have their s. reasons for wanting ...** ils avaient chacun leurs raisons de vouloir ...; **they went their s. ways** ils s'en allèrent, chacun de son côté; **we've decided to go our s. ways** nous avons décidé de suivre chacun notre chemin **2** *pron* plusieurs *mfpl*; **s. of us/of them/***etc* plusieurs d'entre nous/d'entre eux/*etc*; **s. of our party heard it** plusieurs membres de notre groupe l'ont entendu

severally ['sevrəlɪ] *adv Fml* séparément, individuellement

severance ['sevərəns] *n* séparation *f* (**from** de); (*of relations etc*) rupture *f*; *Ind* **s. pay** compensation *f* pour perte d'emploi

severe [sɪ'vɪər] *adj* **(a)** (*person, measures*) sévère, strict (**with** envers); **a s. reprimand** une verte réprimande **(b)** (*winter, weather*) rigoureux, rude; (*illness, wound*) grave; **a s. blow** un coup dur; **to suffer s. hardship** connaître de grosses difficultés; **s. loss** grosse *ou* forte perte; **s. pain** douleur violente *ou* vive; **she was in s. pain** elle a énormément souffert **(c)** (*style etc*) sévère, austère

severely [sɪ'vɪəlɪ] *adv* **(a)** (*punished, dealt with etc*) sévèrement, avec sévérité **(b)** (*wounded*) grièvement; (*ill*) gravement; **her patience was s. tried by his behaviour** sa patience a été durement éprouvée par son comportement **(c)** (*to frown, dress etc*) sévèrement, de façon austère

severity [sɪ'verɪtɪ] *n* **(a)** (*of person, punishment, criticism*) sévérité *f*; (*of conditions*) dureté *f* **(b)** (*of weather, climate etc*) rigueur *f*, rudesse *f*; (*of illness, loss, injury*) gravité *f*; (*of pain*) violence *f* **(c)** (*of style*) sévérité *f*, austérité *f*

Seville [sə'vɪl] *n* Séville *f*; **S. orange** orange *f* amère

sew [səʊ] (*pt* **sewed** [səʊd]; *pp* **sewn** [səʊn], *occ* **sewed**) **1** *vi* coudre **2** *vt* coudre; **hand/machine sewn** cousu (à la) main/à la machine

▶ **sew on** *vtsep* (*button*) (*put on*) coudre; (*put back on*) recoudre

▶ **sew up** *vtsep* **(a)** (*close by sewing*), *Surg* (*wound, cut etc*) recoudre **(b)** *F* **it's all sewn up** tout est arrangé; **we've got it all sewn up** l'affaire est dans le sac; **to have the elections/the match sewn up** avoir gagné les élections/le match d'avance

sewage ['suːɪdʒ] *n* eau(x) *f(pl)* d'égout(s); **s. disposal** évacuation *f* des eaux usées; **s. farm** *or* **works** champs *mpl* d'épandage; **s. system** système *m* du tout-à-l'égout

sewer[1] ['səʊər] *n* (*person who sews*) couseur, -euse; **to be a good/bad s.** être bon/mauvais couturier

sewer[2] ['suːər] *n* (*pipe*) égout *m*; **main s.** égout collecteur; *Fig* **s. of vice** cloaque *m* de vice; **he's got a mind like a s.** il a l'esprit mal placé; (*he interprets everything sordidly*) c'est un véritable obsédé sexuel

sewerage ['suːərɪdʒ] *n* **(a)** (*system of sewers*) système *m* d'égouts **(b)** = **sewage**

sewer rat *n* rat *m* d'égout

sewing ['səʊɪŋ] *n* **(a)** (*activity*) couture *f*; **s. basket** boîte *f* à couture; **s. cotton** *or* **thread** fil *m* à coudre; **s. kit** nécessaire *m* de couture; **s. machine** machine *f* à coudre; **s. needle** aiguille *f* à coudre **(b)** (*work*) ouvrage *m* (à l'aiguille); **the s. on this shirt is terrible** cette chemise est très mal cousue

sewn *see* **sew**

sex[1] [seks] *n* sexe *m*; **he's got s. on the brain** il a l'esprit dans la culotte; **to have s. with sb** (*on ongoing basis*) avoir des rapports sexuels avec qn; (*on one occasion*) coucher avec qn; **how many times have you had s. with him?** combien de fois est-ce que vous avez eu des rapports avec lui?; **but no s., right?** en tout bien tout honneur; **a novel full of s.** un roman plein de passages érotiques; **the fair(er)** *or* **weaker s.** le beau sexe; **the s. act** l'acte sexuel; **s. aid** gadget *m* érotique; **s. appeal** attrait *m* sexuel, sex-appeal *m*; **to have a s. change** (*operation*) changer de sexe; **s. change operation** opération *f* de changement de sexe; *Biol* **s. determination** détermination *f* du sexe; **to have a low/high s. drive** avoir un appétit sexuel faible/élevé; **s. industry** industrie *f* du sexe; **s. life** vie *f* sexuelle; *Hum* **how's your s. life?** et ta vie amoureuse, comment ça va?; *F* **s. mad** qui ne pense qu'au sexe; **to be s. mad** ne penser qu'au sexe; **s. maniac** obsédé, -ée sexuel(le); **s. object** objet *m* sexuel; **s. organs** organes *mpl* sexuels; **s. shop** sex-shop *m*; **s.-starved** en manque (de sexe); **s. therapist** sexologue *mf*; **s. toy** gadget *m* érotique; **s. tourism** tourisme *m* sexuel; *Psy* **the s. urge** le désir sexuel

sex[2] *vt* (*person, animal*) déterminer le sexe de

sexagenarian [seksədʒɪ'neərɪən] *adj, n* sexagénaire *mf*

sex crime *n* crime *m* sexuel

sex discrimination *n* discrimination *f* sexiste

sexed [sekst] *adj* **(a)** *Biol* sexué **(b)** *Psy* **highly s.** qui a une forte libido

sex education *n* éducation *f* sexuelle

sex fiend *n esp Journ* maniaque *mf* sexuel(le)

sex industry *n* industrie *f* du sexe

sexiness ['seksɪnɪs] *n* caractère *m* sexy; **the s. of her appearance** son air sexy; **they are all agreed on his s.** ils sont tous d'accord pour dire qu'il est sexy; **the s. of the way she walks** sa démarche sexy

sexism ['seksɪz(ə)m] *n* sexisme *m*

sexist ['seksɪst] **1** *adj* sexiste **2** *n* sexiste *mf*

sex kitten *n F* nana *f* très sexy

sexless ['sekslɪs] *adj* **(a)** *Biol* (*neuter*) asexué **(b)** (*person*) asexué; (*marriage etc*) où il n'y a pas/plus de relations sexuelles

sex offender *n* délinquant *m* sexuel, délinquante *f* sexuelle

sexologist [sek'sɒlədʒɪst] *n* sexologue *mf*

sexology [sek'sɒlədʒɪ] *n* sexologie *f*

sexploitation [seksplɔɪ'teɪʃən] *n F* exploitation *f* commerciale de la sexualité

sexploits ['seksplɔɪts] *npl F, Hum* aventures *fpl* sexuelles

sexpot ['sekspɒt] *n F* femme *f*/homme *m* très sexy

sex scandal *n* scandale *m* sexuel

sex symbol *n* symbole *m* sexuel

sextant ['sekstənt] *n Geom, Naut* sextant *m*

sextet [seks'tet] *n Mus* sextuor *m*; (*jazz band*) sextet *m*

sexton ['sekst(ə)n] *n Rel* sacristain *m* et sonneur *m* de cloches (et fossoyeur *m*)

sextuple ['sekstjʊp(ə)l] *adj, n* sextuple *m*

sextuplet ['sekstjʊplɪt] *n* **(a)** (*child*) sextuplé, -ée **(b)** *Mus* sextolet *m*

sexual [ˈseksjʊəl] *adj* sexuel; **s. attraction** attirance *f* sexuelle; **s. discrimination** discrimination *f* sexiste, sexisme *m*; **s. harassment** harcèlement *m* sexuel; **s. intercourse** rapports *mpl* sexuels; **the s. organs** les organes *mpl* sexuels; **s. reproduction** reproduction *f* sexuelle
sexuality [seksjʊˈælɪtɪ] *n* sexualité *f*
sexually [ˈseksjʊəlɪ] *adv* sexuellement; **to be s. active** avoir des rapports sexuels; **to be s. attracted to sb** éprouver une attirance sexuelle pour qn; **s. transmitted disease** maladie *f* sexuellement transmissible
sexy [ˈseksɪ] *adj F* (*person, clothes*) sexy; (*book, film*) érotique; *Mktg* (*product*) branché; *Fig* **skiing has become very s.** le ski est devenu très chic; **hi there s.!** (*man*) salut, beau gosse!; (*woman*) salut, ma beauté!
sez [sez] *int Sl* **s. you!** (*that's what you think*) tu parles!; (*you're not telling the truth*) et ta sœur!
SF [esˈef] *n* (*abbr* **Science Fiction**) S.F. *f*, anticipation *f*
SFA [eseˈeɪ] *n Sp* (*abbr* **Scottish Football Association**) Fédération *f* écossaise de football
Sgt *Mil* (*abbr* **Sergeant**) Sgt
sh [ʃ] *int* chut!
shabbily [ˈʃæbɪlɪ] *adv* **(a)** (*furnished, dressed etc*) pauvrement **(b)** (*to treat, behave*) mesquinement
shabbiness [ˈʃæbɪnɪs] *n* **(a)** (*of clothing etc*) aspect *m* râpé *ou* usé; (*of furniture etc*) piètre état *m*; (*of person*) apparence *f* pauvre *ou* miteuse **(b)** (*of conduct etc*) mesquinerie *f*, petitesse *f*
shabby [ˈʃæbɪ] *adj* **(a)** (*clothing etc*) râpé, usé; (*furniture, room, house etc*) pauvre, minable; **to become s.** (*of material*) s'élimer; **to look s.** (*of person*) avoir l'air minable *ou* miteux; **s. genteel** pauvre mais digne **(b)** (*conduct*) mesquin, petit; **a s. excuse** un prétexte mesquin; **s. trick** mesquinerie *f*
shack [ʃæk] *n* (*hut*) cabane *f*, hutte *f*; *Pej* (*house*) baraquement *m*; *F Hum* **nice little s. you have here** c'est une belle petite baraque que vous avez
▶ **shack up** *vi Sl* (*cohabit*) **to s. up (together)** se mettre à la colle; **to s. up with sb** (*start to live with*) se mettre à la colle avec qn; **are they still shacking up together?** est-ce qu'ils vivent toujours ensemble?
shackle [ˈʃæk(ə)l] *vt* (*prisoner*) enchaîner, mettre les fers à; *Fig* **shackled by convention** entravé par les conventions
shackles [ˈʃæk(ə)lz] *npl* (*on prisoner etc*) fers *mpl*; *Fig* **the s. of convention** le carcan des conventions sociales; **to throw off the s. of convention** rejeter le carcan des conventions sociales
shacktown [ˈʃæktaʊn] *n Am F* bidonville *m*
shade¹ [ʃeɪd] *n* **(a)** (*darkness*), *Art* ombre *f*; **in the s. of a tree** à l'ombre d'un arbre; **a tree provided some s.** un arbre donnait de l'ombre; **temperature in the s.** température à l'ombre; *Fig* **to put sb in the s.** éclipser qn, faire de l'ombre à qn; *Myth Lit* **the Shades** (*the underworld*) les Enfers *mpl*

(b) (*nuance*) (*of colour, opinion*) nuance *f*; **different shades of blue** différentes nuances de bleu; *Comptr* **shades of grey** niveaux *mpl ou* tons *mpl* de gris; **a s. longer** un tantinet plus long; **a s. too big** un tantinet trop grand; **he is a s. better** il va un tout petit peu mieux; **a s. (too) sweet** un petit peu (trop) sucré; **a s. of irony** une nuance d'ironie; **just a s.** un petit peu

(c) *Lit* (*ghost*) ombre *f*, fantôme *m*; *Fig* **shades of 1968** ça rappelle 1968

(d) (*device*) **(eye) s.** visière *f*; **(lamp) s.** abat-jour *m inv*; *Am* **(window) s.** store *m* (de fenêtre); *F* **shades** (*sunglasses*) lunettes *fpl* de soleil
shade² **1** *vt* **(a)** (*put in darkness*) ombrager, donner de l'ombre à; (*of hat*) (*face*) obscurcir; **to s. sth from the sun** protéger qch du soleil; **to s. one's eyes with one's hand** s'abriter les yeux de la main; **to s. a light** voiler *ou* masquer une lumière **(b)** *Art* (*drawing*) ombrer, mettre des ombres à **2** *vi* **blue that shades into green** bleu qui se fond en vert; **these categories s. into one another** ces catégories se confondent
▶ **shade away, shade off** **1** *vtsep* (*change by degrees*) (*colours*) dégrader **2** *vi* **red shading off into pink** du rouge qui se fond en rose
shadeband [ˈʃeɪdbænd] *n Aut* bande *f* pare-soleil
shaded [ˈʃeɪdɪd] *adj* **(a)** (*path etc*) ombragé; (*lamp etc*) à abat-jour **(b)** *Art* (*drawing*) ombré; (*area on diagram, map*) hachuré
shadeless [ˈʃeɪdlɪs] *adj* sans ombre
shadiness [ˈʃeɪdɪnɪs] *n* **(a)** (*of path etc*) ombre *f*, ombrage *m* **(b)** *F* (*suspiciousness*) (*of affair etc*) aspect *m* louche; (*of person*) réputation *f* suspecte
shading [ˈʃeɪdɪŋ] *n* **(a)** *Art* (*on drawing*) ombres *fpl*; (*on map etc*) hachures *fpl* **(b) subtle shadings of meaning** (*nuances*) nuances *fpl* de sens subtiles
shadow¹ [ˈʃædəʊ] **1** *n* **(a)** ombre *f*; (*dark area*) obscurité *f*; (*on picture, photograph*) noir *m*; **in the s.** (*in the shade*) à *ou* dans l'ombre; (*in dark place*) dans l'obscurité; **to cast a s.** jeter une ombre; *Fig* **this cast a s. over the festivities** cela a jeté une ombre sur la fête; *Fig* **coming events cast their shadows** les événements à venir se font pressentir; *Fig* **to catch at shadows, to run after a s.** se bercer d'illusions; **town nestling in the s. of a mountain** ville nichée à l'ombre d'une montagne; **a figure (standing) in the shadows** une silhouette (se tenant) dans l'ombre; *Fig* **to be afraid of one's own s.** avoir peur de son ombre; **not the s. of a doubt** pas l'ombre d'un doute; **to be a (mere) s. of one's/its former self** (*of person, country*) n'être que l'ombre de soi-même; **the s. of death/war** l'ombre de la mort/guerre; **under the s. of a terrible accusation** sous le coup d'une accusation terrible; *Med* **a s. on the right lung** un voile au poumon droit; **to have (dark) shadows round** *or* **under one's eyes** avoir les yeux cernés; **eye s.** (*make-up*) ombre à paupières

(b) (*person*) (*constant companion*) compagnon *m*/ compagne *f* inséparable; (*person following someone*) = personne *f* qui prend qn en filature; **the dog was her s.** le chien la suivait comme son ombre; **to put a s. on sb** faire suivre qn

2 *adj Br Pol* fantôme; **s. cabinet** cabinet *m* fantôme; **the S. Home Secretary** le Ministre de l'Intérieur du cabinet fantôme
shadow² *vt* **(a)** (*cast shadows over*) ombrager **(b)** (*follow*) (*person*) filer, pister, prendre en filature
shadow boxing *n* shadow-boxing *m*, boxe *f* dans le vide; *Fig* attaque *f* rituelle *ou* de pure forme
shadowing [ˈʃædəʊɪŋ] *n* (*of suspect etc*) filature *f*
shadow printing *n Comptr* impression *f* ombrée
shadow puppet *n* ombre *f* chinoise
shadowy [ˈʃædəʊɪ] *adj* **(a)** (*path etc*) ombragé, ombreux **(b)** (*vague*) (*project*) indécis, vague; **a s. form** une silhouette vague
shady [ˈʃeɪdɪ] *adj* **(a)** (*tree etc*) qui donne de l'ombre; (*place, lane etc*) ombragé **(b)** *F* (*suspicious*) (*person, transaction, business etc*) louche; (*financier, affair*) véreux; **the s. side of politics** les dessous *mpl* de la politique
shaft¹ [ʃɑːft] *n* **(a)** (*of spear etc*) hampe *f*, bois *m*; (*of golf club, tool*) manche *m* **(b)** *esp Lit* (*arrow*) flèche *f*, trait *m*; *Fig* **shafts of wit** des traits d'esprit **(c)** (*beam*) (*of light*) rayon *m*; (*of lightning*) éclair *m* **(d)** (*of column*) fût *m*; (*of feather*) tige *f* **(e)** *MecE* arbre *m*; (*stationary*) axe *m*; **driving s.** arbre moteur; **transmission s.** arbre de transmission; **propeller s.** arbre porte-hélice, arbre d'hélice; *Aut* **s. pin** fusée *f* **(f)** (*on horse-drawn vehicle*) brancard *m*
shaft² *n* **(a)** *Min* puits *m*; **air** *or* **ventilation s.** puits d'aérage, conduit *m* d'air; **to sink a s.** creuser *ou Tech* foncer un puits **(b)** *Br* **lift** *or Am* **elevator s.** cage *f* (d'ascenseur)
shaft³ *vt Sl* **(a)** (*have sexual intercourse with*) tringler **(b)** *Fig* (*cheat*) entuber; **to get shafted** se faire entuber
shag¹ [ʃæg] *n* **(a)** (*of carpet*) long poil *m*; **s. pile (carpet)** moquette *f* très moelleuse **(b)** (*tobacco*) tabac *m* fort (*coupé fin*)
shag² *n* (*bird*) cormoran *m* huppé
shag³ *n Br Vulg* (*sex act*) **to have a s.** tirer un coup
shag⁴ *vti Br Vulg* (*have sexual intercourse* (*with*)) baiser
▶ **shag out** *vtsep Br Sl* (*exhaust*) crever; **I'm shagged out** je suis crevé
shagged [ʃægd] *adj Br Sl* (*exhausted*) crevé, claqué
shagger [ˈʃægər] *n Br Vulg* baiseur *m*
shaggy [ˈʃægɪ] *adj* (*hairy*) poilu; (*pony etc*) à longs poils; (*hair*) hirsute, ébouriffé; (*beard*) hirsute, touffu; (*eyebrows*) en broussailles; (*carpet*) poilu, à long poil; **s. dog story** = histoire *f* farfelue
shah [ʃɑː] *n* s(c)hah *m* (d'Iran)
shake¹ [ʃeɪk] *n* **(a)** (*act of shaking*) secousse *f*; (*trembling*) (*of hand, voice etc*) tremblement *m*; *US* (*earthquake*) tremblement de terre; **to give sth a good s.** bien secouer *ou* agiter qch; **to give oneself a s.** se secouer; **a s. of the head** un hochement de tête; *F* **to be all of a s.** trembler de tous ses membres; *F* **to have the shakes** (*to be trembling*) (*with fear*) avoir les chocottes; (*with illness, from alcohol*) avoir la tremblote; **with a s. in his voice** d'une voix tremblotante; *Fig* **in two shakes (of a lamb's tail)** en un rien de temps; *F* en moins de deux

(b) *Culin* **milk s.** milk-shake *m*

(c) *F* **to be no great shakes** ne pas casser des briques, ne pas casser trois pattes à un canard; *F* **he is no great shakes as a writer/at German** comme écrivain/en allemand, il ne casse pas des briques
shake² (*pt* **shook** [ʃʊk]; *pp* **shaken** [ˈʃeɪk(ə)n]) **1** *vt* **(a)** secouer; (*liquid, bottle etc*) agiter; (*building etc*) ébranler, secouer;

Fig (*opinion, sb's faith*) ébranler; **s. well (before using)** (*on carton etc*) bien agiter avant l'emploi; **to s. one's head** (*in disbelief etc*) secouer *ou* hocher la tête; (*to indicate 'no'*) faire non de la tête; **to s. one's fist at sb** menacer qn du poing; **to s. hands with sb** serrer la main à *ou* de qn; **to s. sb's hand, to s. sb by the hand** donner une poignée de main à qn; **the French s. hands more often** les Français se serrent la main plus souvent; **they shook hands on it** ils ont topé; **to s. oneself free (from sth)** se dégager (de qch) d'une secousse; *Fig* se dégager (de qch); **to s. sb out of his/her complacency/apathy** faire sortir qn de sa suffisance/son apathie; **to s. the snow from one's head** secouer sa tête pour se débarrasser de la neige; **that has shaken my faith in him** cela a ébranlé la confiance que j'avais en lui; **event that shook the country** événement qui a bouleversé le pays; **she was badly shaken by the accident** elle a été terriblement bouleversée par l'accident; **to feel shaken after a fall** se ressentir d'une chute; *F* **that'll s. him!** ça va le choquer

(b) *Austr Sl* (*rob*) voler

2 *vi* **(a)** trembler; (*of voice*) trembloter, chevroter; **her hand was shaking** sa main tremblait; **the whole building shook** (*after explosion etc*) tout le bâtiment a tremblé; **the door shakes whenever a bus passes** à chaque fois qu'un bus passe, ça fait trembler la porte; **the ground shook** le sol a tremblé; **to s. with fright/rage** trembler *ou* frémir de crainte/colère; **in a voice shaking with emotion** d'une voix émue *ou* tremblotante; *F* **to s. in one's shoes** trembler *ou* grelotter de peur; *F* trembler dans ses baskets

(b) *F* **to s. on it** (*shake hands*) toper

▶ **shake down 1** *vtsep* **(a)** (*cause to fall*) **to s. down apples/***etc* faire tomber des pommes/*etc* en secouant l'arbre **(b)** *Am F* (*extort money from*) **to s. sb down for ten dollars** faire cracher dix dollars à qn **(c)** *Am F* (*search*) (*person, apartment etc*) fouiller **2** *vi* **(a)** (*fall*) (*of fruits etc*) tomber **(b)** (*settle down*) (*get used to routine, job*) s'habituer; *F* **to s. down (for the night)** se mettre au pieu, se pieuter

▶ **shake off** *vtsep* **(a)** (*remove by shaking*) **to s. the dust off sth** secouer la poussière de qch **(b)** (*get rid of*) (*illness, cold, depression etc*) se débarrasser de **(c)** *F* (*escape from*) (*person*) se débarrasser de; (*other runner*) semer; **I can't s. him off** il ne me lâche pas d'une semelle; **she's always phoning me up, I can't s. her off** elle me téléphone sans cesse, je n'arrive pas à m'en débarrasser

▶ **shake out** *vtsep* **(a)** (*remove dust from*) (*rug, tablecloth etc*) secouer; (*empty*) (*bag*) vider en le secouant **(b)** (*remove by shaking*) (*dirt, sand etc*) faire sortir en secouant; **he picked up his shoes and shook the sand out** il a ramassé ses chaussures et en a secoué le sable **(c)** (*unfurl*) (*sail, flag*) déferler

▶ **shake up** *vtsep* **(a)** (*mix by shaking*) (*liquid, container etc*) secouer; **don't s. the lemonade up** ne secoue pas la limonade **(b)** (*plump up*) (*pillow etc*) secouer **(c)** (*upset*) (*person*) secouer; **she looked pretty shaken up** elle a l'air assez secouée; **he was badly shaken up after the accident** l'accident lui a fait un coup **(d)** (*arouse from indifference etc*) secouer; **he needs shaking up** il a besoin qu'on le secoue

shakedown ['ʃeɪkdaʊn] *n* **(a)** *Am F* (*extortion*) chantage *m*, extorsion *f* **(b)** *Am F* (*search*) fouille *f* **(c)** *F* (*improvised bed*) lit *m* de fortune

Shaker ['ʃeɪkər] *n Rel* = membre *m* d'une secte protestante du XVIIIème siècle, aujourd'hui presque disparue, qui prêchait le célibat

shaker ['ʃeɪkər] *n* **sugar s.** saupoudreuse *f* (*pour le sucre*); **salad s.** panier *m* à salade; **cocktail s.** shaker *m*

Shakespearian, Shakespearean [ʃeɪks'pɪərɪən] *adj* shakespearien

shake-up *n F* (*of staff*) remaniement *m*

shakily ['ʃeɪkɪlɪ] *adv* (*to walk*) à pas chancelants; (*to write*) d'une main tremblante; (*to speak*) d'une voix chevrotante

shakiness ['ʃeɪkɪnɪs] *n* (*of building, chair etc*) manque *m* de stabilité *ou* de solidité; (*of person, health, knowledge*) faiblesse *f*; (*of hand*) tremblement *m*; (*of voice*) chevrotement *m*; (*of position*) précarité *f*

shaking ['ʃeɪkɪŋ] *n Med* tremblement *m*

shako ['ʃækəʊ] *n Mil* (*headgear*) s(c)hako *m*

shaky ['ʃeɪkɪ] *adj* (*furniture etc*) branlant, peu solide; (*health*) faible, chancelant; (*position*) précaire; (*hand*) tremblant, vacillant; (*writing*) tremblé; (*voice*) mal assuré; (*knowledge*) pas très sûr; **to be s. on one's legs** *or F* **one's pins** ne pas tenir sur ses jambes *ou F* quilles; **I feel very s.** (*I am trembling*) je suis tout tremblant; (*I feel unsteady on my feet*) je ne me sens pas bien solide sur mes jambes; (*I feel rather unwell*) je suis patraque *ou* tout chose; **his English is s.** il est faible en anglais

shale [ʃeɪl] *n* schiste *m* argileux *ou* ardoisier, argile *f* schisteuse; **s. oil** huile *f* de schiste

shall [①A56-7,b; B36,K,1,a] (*stressed* [ʃæl], *unstressed* [ʃəl]) *modal aux v* (*pr* **shall**; *pt, cond* **should** *stressed* [ʃʊd], *unstressed* [ʃəd]; *Arch* **shouldst** [ʃʊdst]; *no other parts*; **shall not** *and* **should not** *are often contracted into* **shan't** [ʃɑːnt], **shouldn't** ['ʃʊd(ə)nt]) **(a)** (*with full meaning, denotes duty or command*) *Fml* **he s. do it if I order it** il sera obligé de le faire si je le lui ordonne; **he s. not do it** je lui interdis de le faire; **he says he won't do it – he s.!** il dit qu'il ne le fera pas – je l'ordonne!; **you shall do it!** vous le ferez, je le veux!; *Jur* **ships s. carry three lights** les navires sont tenus de porter trois feux

(b) (*making suggestion, asking permission*) **s. I open the window?** voulez-vous que j'ouvre la fenêtre?; **I'll make some coffee, s. I?** je vais faire du café, d'accord?; **let's go in, s. we?** rentrons, voulez-vous?

(c) [①A51,a,i: A72,a,iii] (*future*) **you shan't have any!** tu n'en auras pas!; **you s. pay for this!** vous me le payerez!; **tomorrow I s. go and he will arrive** demain, moi je partirai et lui il arrivera; **will you be there? – I s.** y serez-vous? – oui (, j'y serai); **will you be there? – no, I s. not** *or* **I shan't** y serez-vous? – non(, je n'y serai pas); **I s. explain the situation to you and you will listen** je vais vous expliquer la situation et vous allez m'écouter; **as we s. see** comme nous le verrons, comme nous allons le voir

shallot [ʃə'lɒt] *n* échalote *f*

shallow ['ʃæləʊ] *adj* **(a)** (*water, dish etc*) peu profond; (*soil*) superficiel; **s.-rooted** (*tree*) à enracinement superficiel; **s. breathing** respiration *f* faible; **the s. end** (*of swimming pool*) le petit bain **(b)** *Fig* (*superficial*) (*person, mind etc*) superficiel; (*friendship*) de surface

shallowness ['ʃæləʊnɪs] *n* **(a)** (*of water, dish etc*) peu *m* de profondeur **(b)** *Fig* (*of person, mind*) caractère *m* superficiel, superficialité *f*

shallows ['ʃæləʊz] *npl* (*in sea etc*) bas-fond *m*, *pl* bas-fonds, haut-fond *m*, *pl* hauts-fonds

shalt [ʃælt] *2nd pers sing modal aux v Arch, Bible* **thou s. not kill** tu ne tueras point

shaly ['ʃeɪlɪ] *adj* schisteux

sham¹ [ʃæm] **1** *adj* faux, truqué; (*illness etc*) simulé, feint; (*piety*) apparent; **s. peace** paix *f* de pacotille **2** *n* feinte *f*, trompe-l'œil *m inv*; *F* chiqué *m*; **it was nothing but a s.** c'était du chiqué; **that's all s.** *F* tout ça, c'est de la frime; **he's a s.** c'est un imposteur; **you big s., you're not sad at all!** espèce de comédien, tu n'es pas triste du tout!; **the elections were a s.** les élections n'étaient qu'une imposture

sham² (-mm-) **1** *vt* feindre, simuler; **to s. sickness** faire semblant d'être malade **2** *vi* **he's only shamming** c'est une comédie qu'il nous joue, il fait semblant

shaman ['ʃæmən] *n* chaman *m*

shamanism [ʃæmə'nɪz(ə)m] *n* chamanisme *m*

shamanistic [ʃæmə'nɪstɪk] *adj* relatif au chamanisme

shamateur ['ʃæmətɜːr] *n Sp F* = athlète/*etc* prétendument amateur mais qui, en réalité, perçoit de l'argent

shamble ['ʃæmb(ə)l] *vi* **to s. (along)** aller à pas traînants; **to s. up to sb** approcher qn d'un pas traînant

shambles ['ʃæmb(ə)lz] *npl* (*usu with sing verb*) (*disorder*) désordre *m*, fouillis *m*; (*department, company, accounts*) foutoir *m*; (*reception*) désastre *m*; **what a s.!** quelle pagaille!; **it's a bloody s.!** quel foutoir!; **the match was a s.** le match était totalement nul; **the cupboard was in a s.** le placard était rangé n'importe comment

shambolic [ʃæm'bɒlɪk] *adj F* bordélique

shame¹ [ʃeɪm] *n* **(a)** (*disgrace, guilt etc*) honte *f*; **hooligans are the s. of our country** les hooligans sont la honte de notre pays; **to bring s. on one's family/country** faire honte à sa famille/son pays; *also Fig* **to put sb to s.** faire honte à qn; **to my s.** à ma grande honte; **s. (up)on you!** quelle honte!; **for s.!** vous n'avez pas honte!; **he hid his face in s.** il s'est caché la face de honte; **to blush for** *or* **with s.** rougir de honte; **without s.** effronté, éhonté; **she is utterly without s.** elle n'a aucune pudeur; **to be past all s., to be lost to all s.** avoir perdu toute honte; **to have no s.** (*no scruples*) n'avoir aucune honte; **have you no s.?** tu n'as pas honte?; **six cakes, have you no s.?** six gâteaux! faut pas te gêner!

(b) (*pity*) dommage *m*; **it would be a s. to …** il serait dommage de …; **it's a s. you can't come** c'est dommage que vous ne puissiez pas venir; **what a s.!** quel dommage!; *Parl* **s.!** = cri *m* des députés anglais à la Chambre des communes pour manifester leur désapprobation ou leur indignation

shame² *vt* (*cause to feel ashamed*) faire honte à; (*bring shame on*) couvrir de honte; **to be shamed into doing sth** faire qch par amour-propre; **they tried to s. her into donating more** ils ont essayé de lui faire honte pour qu'elle donne davantage

shamefaced [ˈʃeɪmfeɪst] *adj* (*ashamed*) (à l'air) honteux; (*embarrassed*) embarrassé, décontenancé

shamefacedly [ʃeɪmˈfeɪsɪdlɪ] *adv* d'un air honteux; (*with embarrassment*) d'un air embarrassé

shameful [ˈʃeɪmfʊl] *adj* honteux, scandaleux

shamefully [ˈʃeɪmfəlɪ] *adv* honteusement, scandaleusement; **s. ignorant** honteusement ignorant

shamefulness [ˈʃeɪmfʊlnɪs] *n* honte *f*, infamie *f*

shameless [ˈʃeɪmlɪs] *adj* **(a)** (*without shame*) (*person, conduct*) éhonté, effronté; **he was quite s. about it all** il ne montrait aucun scrupule; *usu Hum* **a s. (little) hussy** une diablesse **(b)** (*immodest*) (*person*) sans pudeur, dévergondé; (*conduct*) impudique

shamelessly [ˈʃeɪmlɪslɪ] *adv* **(a)** (*without shame*) effrontément **(b)** (*immodestly*) (*to carry on, have affair etc*) avec impudeur

shamelessness [ˈʃeɪmlɪsnɪs] *n* **(a)** (*lack of shame*) effronterie *f* **(b)** (*sexual immodesty*) impudeur *f*; (*of conduct*) impudicité *f*

shaming [ˈʃeɪmɪŋ] *adj* humiliant

shammy [ˈʃæmɪ] *n* **s. (leather)** peau *f* de chamois

shampoo¹ [ʃæmˈpuː] *n* shampo(o)ing *m*; **liquid/dry s.** shampo(o)ing liquide/sec; **carpet s.** shampo(o)ing pour moquette; **to give sb a s.** faire un shampo(o)ing à qn; **s. and set** shampo(o)ing et mise en plis

shampoo² *vt* **to s. one's hair** se faire un shampo(o)ing; **to s. sb** *or* **sb's hair** faire un shampo(o)ing à qn; **to s. a carpet** shampouiner une moquette

shamrock [ˈʃæmrɒk] *n* (*plant*) trèfle *m*; **the land of the s.** = l'Irlande *f*

shamus [ˈʃeɪməs] *n Am F* (détective *m*) privé *m*

shandy [ˈʃændɪ], *US* **shandygaff** [ˈʃændɪgæf] *n* panaché *m*; **a lager s.** un panaché à la bière blonde

Shanghai [ʃæŋˈhaɪ] *n* Shanghai *m*, Changhai *m*

shanghai [ʃæŋˈhaɪ] *vt F Naut* **to s. sb** embarquer qn de force sur un navire à court d'équipage; *Fig* **to s. sb into doing sth** (*force*) forcer qn à faire qch

Shangri-La [ʃæŋgrɪˈlɑː] *n* paradis *m* terrestre

shank [ʃæŋk] *n* **(a)** *Culin* (*of beef*) jarret *m*; (*of horse's leg*) canon *m*; *F* **to go** *or* **ride on Shanks' pony** y aller à pinces **(b)** (*of key, rivet*) tige *f*; *Typ* (*of letter*) corps *m*, tige; *Naut* (*of anchor*) verge *f*

shan't *see* **shall**

shantung [ʃænˈtʌŋ] *n Tex* shant(o)ung *m*

shanty¹ [ˈʃæntɪ] *n* (*hut*) bicoque *f*, cabane *f*; **s. town** bidonville *m*

shanty² *n Naut* **(sea) s.** chanson *f* de marin

SHAPE [ʃeɪp] *n Mil* (*abbr* **Supreme Headquarters Allied Powers, Europe**) quartier *m* général des forces alliées de l'OTAN en Europe

shape¹ [ʃeɪp] *n* **(a)** (*form*) forme *f*; **what s. is it?** de quelle forme est-ce?; **they were the same s.** ils étaient de la même forme, ils avaient la même forme; **a cake in the s. of a …** un gâteau en forme de …; **oblong/triangular in s.** de forme oblongue/triangulaire; **spherical in s.**, **of spherical s.** de forme sphérique; **trees of all shapes** des arbres de toutes les formes; **my hat was knocked out of s.** mon chapeau a été déformé; **to get out of s., to lose (its) s.** se déformer; **to mould sth into s.** donner forme à qch; *Journ etc F* **to knock an article into s.** mettre un article au point; *F* **to knock** *or* **lick a team into s.** faire quelque chose d'une équipe; **to give s. to a plan** donner corps à un projet; **to take s.** prendre forme *ou* tournure; **this is the s. of things to come** c'est ça l'avenir, *esp Pej* voilà ce qui nous attend; **progress, in the s. of motorways/supermarkets** le progrès que représentent les autoroutes/les supermarchés; **wealth in the s. of a large house** la richesse symbolisée par la possession d'une grande maison; **no communication in any s. or form** aucune communication de quelque forme que ce soit; **something in the s. of …** une espèce *ou* une sorte de …; **help arrived in the s. of …** l'aide est arrivée sous la forme de …

(b) (*condition*) **to keep in/get back into s.** (*physically*) garder/retrouver la forme; **to be in good/poor s.** (*of person etc*) être en bonne/petite forme; *F* **she was in pretty bad s.** (*very ill, badly injured*) elle était mal en point *ou* dans un sale état; **what sort of s. is he in?** (*after accident, ordeal*) dans quel état est-il?; **he's in no s. to be doing this kind of work!** il n'est pas en état de faire ce genre de travail!

(c) (*figure, human figure*) forme *f*; **two shapes loomed up in the darkness** deux formes surgirent dans l'obscurité

shape² **1** *vt* (*clay etc*) façonner, modeler; (*block of stone etc*) tailler; *Fig* (*plan*) former; **to s. sth out of sth** façonner qch avec qch; **to s. the clay into an urn** donner à l'argile la forme d'une urne; **to s. sb's character** façonner le caractère de qn; **to s. the destiny of man** diriger *ou* régler la destinée de l'homme; **to s. the course of public opinion** manipuler l'opinion publique; **the war shaped her perception of the army** la guerre a influencé sa perception de l'armée **2** *vi* = **shape up (a)**

▸ **shape up** *vi* **(a)** (*turn out*) **to s. up well** promettre; (*of affair*) prendre bonne tournure; **let's see how he shapes up in his new job** voyons comment il va s'en tirer dans son nouvel emploi; **the new player is shaping up well** le nouveau joueur promet beaucoup; *esp Am F* **s. up or ship out!** secouez-vous sinon c'est la porte! **(b)** (*prepare to tackle*) **to s. up to a problem/situation** s'attaquer à un problème/faire face à une situation

shaped [ʃeɪpt] *adj* **(a)** façonné, taillé; (*in metalwork*) (*piece*) profilé, embouti **(b)** **well/badly s.** bien/mal formé; **an awkwardly s. room** une pièce de forme bizarre; **s. like an egg** en forme d'œuf

-shaped [ʃeɪpt] *suff* **egg/heart/***etc***-s.** en forme d'œuf/de cœur/*etc*

shapeless [ˈʃeɪplɪs] *adj* informe

shapelessness [ˈʃeɪplɪsnɪs] *n* manque *m* de forme

shapeliness [ˈʃeɪplɪnɪs] *n* (*of woman*) beauté *f* de forme, belles proportions *fpl*; (*of legs*) galbe *m*

shapely [ˈʃeɪplɪ] *adj* bien fait; **a s. leg** une jambe bien galbée; **to be s.** (*of woman*) être bien faite *ou F* bien roulée

shaper [ˈʃeɪpər] *n* (*who creates projects etc*) personne *f* qui lance des projets

shaping [ˈʃeɪpɪŋ] *n* (*of block of stone etc*) façonnement *m*, façonnage *m*; **the s. of his character** le développement *ou* la formation de son caractère; **the s. of a policy** la conception d'une politique

shard [ʃɑːd] *n* (*of pottery*) tesson *m*

share¹ [ʃeər] *n Agr* (*of plough*) soc *m* (de charrue)

share² *n* **(a)** (*part*) part *f*; **in equal shares** en parts égales; **to have a s. in sth** participer à qch; **to have a s. in the profits** participer aux bénéfices; **you had a s. in this** (*you are partly responsible*) vous y êtes pour quelque chose; (*you contributed*) votre participation a été importante; **I had no s. in this decision** je n'ai aucune responsabilité dans cette décision; **to come in for a s. of the blame** être reconnu responsable; **to take a s. of the profits** prendre sa part des bénéfices; **to take a s. of the blame** reconnaître sa part de responsabilité; **the lion's s.** la part du lion; *Mktg* **s. point** point *m* de part de marché; **s. in profits** (*participation*) participation *f* aux bénéfices; (*amount*) tantième *m*; **to give sb a s. of the profits** donner à qn une part des bénéfices; *F* **to go shares** partager (**with** avec); *F* **I went half shares with him** (*in buying sth*) on l'a acheté à deux; **(fair) s.** part équitable; **I'm entitled to a fair s. of the profits** j'ai droit à ma part des bénéfices; **I've had my s. of worries** j'ai eu mon lot de soucis; **she's had more than her (fair) s. of problems** elle a eu largement son lot de problèmes; *F* **we've had more than our fair s. of rain and then some** question pluie, nous avons été servis; *Jur* **legal s.** (*of inheritance*) réserve *f* légale; **to pay one's s.** payer sa (quote-)part; **to do one's s., to take** *or* **bear one's s. of the burden** participer; **he doesn't do his s.** il ne fait pas sa part; **to have a s. in an undertaking** avoir un intérêt *ou* être intéressé dans une entreprise

(b) *Fin* action *f*, titre *m*; **to hold** *or* **have shares** détenir des actions, être actionnaire; **to have shares in a company** détenir des actions dans une société; **to own 51% of the shares** détenir 51% du capital; **s. account** compte-titres *m*; **s. capital** capital *m* social; **s. dealing** opérations *fpl* de Bourse, négoce *m* de titres; **s. index** indice *m* boursier; **s. issue** émission *f* d'actions; **s. market** marché *m* des valeurs mobilières; **s. owner** détenteur *m* d'actions; **s. ownership** actionnariat *m*; **s. price index** indice *m* des cours d'actions

share³ **1** *vt* partager; **to s. sth with sb** partager qch avec qn; **to s. a bathroom** (*of tenants*) partager une salle de bain; **a shared bathroom** une salle de bain commune; **to s. sb's opinion** partager l'avis de qn; **to s. one's ideas/impressions with sb** partager des idées/impressions avec qn; *Iron* **thank you very much for sharing that with me** c'est vachement intéressant ce que tu dis!; **he shares all his secrets with me** il me fait part de tous ses secrets; **they s. an interest in music** ils partagent le même intérêt pour la musique

2 *vi* partager; **to s. and s. alike** partager équitablement; **to s. in sth** (*in blame, praise etc*) partager qch; **to s. in the profits** participer aux *ou* avoir part aux bénéfices; **to s. in sb's grief/happiness** partager la douleur/le bonheur de qn

▸ **share out** *vtsep* (*loot etc*) partager, distribuer, répartir; (*work*) répartir, distribuer

share certificate *n* certificat *m* d'action(s) *ou* de titre(s)

sharecropper [ˈʃeəkrɒpər] *n Agr* métayer, -ère

sharecropping [ˈʃeəkrɒpɪŋ] *n Agr* métayage *m*

shareholder [ˈʃeəhəʊldər] *n Fin* actionnaire *mf*; **the shareholders** l'actionnariat *m*, les actionnaires; **minority/**

majority s. actionnaire minoritaire/majoritaire; **small s.** petit porteur *m*; **shareholders' funds** capitaux *mpl* propres, haut *m* de bilan; **shareholders' meeting** réunion *f ou* assemblée *f* des actionnaires

shareholding [ˈʃeəhəʊldɪŋ] *n Fin* (*shares*) participation *f*; (*share ownership*) actionnariat *m*

share option *n* possibilité *f* d'acheter des actions

share-out *n* partage *m*, répartition *f*

shareware [ˈʃeəweər] *n Comptr* shareware *m*, logiciel *m* en libre essai, logiciel contributif; **s. programs** sharewares *mpl*

sharing [ˈʃeərɪŋ] *n* **(a)** (*of loot, property etc*) distribution *f*, partage *m* **(b)** (*participation*) participation *f*, partage *m*; **profit s.** participation aux bénéfices

shark [ʃɑːk] *n* **(a)** (*fish*) requin *m* **(b)** *F* (*ruthless person*) requin *m* **(c)** *Am F* (*talented person*) as *m*; **to be a s. at math** être calé en maths, être une bête en maths

sharkskin [ˈʃɑːkskɪn] *n* peau *f* de requin

sharp [ʃɑːp] **1** *adj* **(a)** (*knife, edge*) tranchant, affilé; (*spear, tooth, point*) aigu, pointu

(b) (*features etc*) anguleux, tiré; (*peak etc*) pointu; (*angle*) saillant, aigu; (*curve*) prononcé; (*ascent, descent*) raide; (*roof*) pointu, en pointe; (*turning*) brusque; (*outline, focus, Phot image*) net, *f* nette; *Fig* **to be at the s. end** être en première ligne; **s. rise/drop in prices** forte *ou* nette hausse/baisse des prix; **s. contrast** contraste marqué *ou* net; **this accident brings into s. relief the need for extra precautions** cet accident démontre à quel point il est nécessaire de prendre des précautions supplémentaires

(c) (*sight*) perçant; (*hearing*) fin; (*cunning, shrewd*) rusé, malin; (*unscrupulous*) peu scrupuleux; **to have a s. mind** avoir l'esprit vif; **he's as s. as a needle** (*quick to understand*) il a l'esprit vif; (*cunning*) il est malin comme un singe; **s. practice(s)** procédés indélicats *ou* peu honnêtes

(d) (*wind*) vif, perçant; (*cold*) pénétrant, piquant; **it's a bit s. this morning** il fait frisquet ce matin; **a s. frost** une forte gelée; **s. pain** douleur aiguë

(e) (*fast*) rapide; (*trot*) vif

(f) (*harsh*) (*voice, words*) cinglant; (*person*) brusque; **to make a s. retort** (*to reply in a sharp tone*) répondre d'une voix cassante; (*to make a cutting reply*) répondre de façon cinglante; **a s. reproof** une verte réprimande; **in a s. tone** d'un ton brusque; **a s. tongue** une langue acérée *ou* caustique

(g) (*taste*) âpre, piquant; (*sauce*) piquant; (*apple etc*) acide; (*wine*) vert

(h) (*sound*) perçant, aigu

(i) *Mus* (*note*) dièse; **you're s.** (*to singer*) vous chantez trop aigu; (*to violinist*) vous jouez trop aigu; **a semitone s.** un demi-ton trop haut

(j) *F* (*in dress*) classe *inv*; **to be a s. dresser** s'habiller classe

2 *n Mus* dièse *m*; **double s.** double dièse *m*

3 *adv* **(a) s. pointed pencil** crayon taillé fin; **s. edged** (*knife etc*) tranchant, affilé

(b) (*to turn*) brusquement, court; **turn s. right** prenez à angle droit; **the road turns s. right** la route fait un virage serré à droite

(c) (*punctually*) **at four o'clock s.** à quatre heures sonnantes *ou* précises *ou F* tapantes

(d) *F* **look s.!** dépêchez-vous!, remuez-vous!

(e) *Mus* (*to sing, play*) trop aigu

sharpen [ˈʃɑːp(ə)n] **1** *vt* **(a)** (*knife, tool etc*) affiler, aiguiser; (*stick etc*) tailler en pointe, aiguiser; (*pencil*) tailler; (*angle*) rendre plus saillant; (*feature, contrast*) accentuer; **to s. its claws** (*of cat etc*) faire ses griffes

(b) to s. sb's wits éveiller l'esprit de qn, *F* dégourdir qn

(c) (*pain, animosity*) aviver; (*passion, desire*) exciter; (*of walk etc*) (*appetite*) aiguiser, ouvrir

(d) to s. one's voice prendre un ton plus acerbe *ou* âpre

(e) *Culin* (*sauce*) donner du piquant à

(f) *Mus* (*note*) diéser

2 *vi* **(a)** (*of faculties etc*) s'aiguiser

(b) (*of tone*) devenir plus acerbe *ou* âpre

(c) (*of sound*) devenir plus perçant *ou* aigu

sharpener [ˈʃɑːp(ə)nər] *n* (*device*) aiguisoir *m*; **(knife) s.** aiguisoir *m* (pour couteaux); **(pencil) s.** taille-crayon *m*, *pl* taille-crayon(s)

sharpening [ˈʃɑːp(ə)nɪŋ] *n* (*of tool etc*) affilage *m*, aiguisage *m*

sharper [ˈʃɑːpər] *n* escroc *m*; *Cards* tricheur, -euse

sharp-eyed *adj* (*good at finding things*) à qui rien n'échappe; (*keen-sighted*) à la vue perçante

sharply [ˈʃɑːplɪ] *adv* **(a) s. pointed** très pointu **(b) this contrasts s. with** ... ceci contraste nettement avec ...; **s. in focus** très net; **to bring sth s. home, to bring sth s. into focus** faire apparaître de façon évidente **(c)** (*to drop, descend, brake*) brusquement; (*to turn*) brusquement, court; **he looked up s. when I mentioned her name** il a brusquement levé les yeux lorsque j'ai mentionné son nom **(d)** (*to reprimand*) sévèrement; (*to reply*) d'un ton brusque; **he looked s. at her** (*angrily, warning etc*) il l'a regardée sévèrement; (*trying to understand*) il l'a regardée d'un œil pénétrant

sharpness [ˈʃɑːpnɪs] *n* **(a)** (*of knife edge etc*) tranchant *m*; (*of contours, photograph*) netteté *f*; (*of contrast*) caractère *m* marqué; **s. of focus** (*of photo*) netteté *f*; (*of analysis etc*) précision *f*; *Aut etc* **s. of the turn** raideur *f* du virage

(b) (*of mind, hearing*) finesse *f*; (*of child*) intelligence *f*; **s. of sight** acuité *f* visuelle

(c) (*of pain*) violence *f*; **there's a s. in the air** il fait frisquet

(d) (*of tone, reprimand*) sévérité *f*, âpreté *f*; (*of tone*) brusquerie *f*; (*of character, voice*) aspérité *f*

(e) (*taste*) (*of sauce*) piquant *m*; (*of apple etc*) acidité *f*

(f) (*of sound*) acuité *f*, qualité *f* perçante

sharpshooter [ˈʃɑːpʃuːtər] *n Mil* tireur *m* d'élite

sharp-sighted *adj* (*keen-sighted*) à la vue perçante; (*observant*) observateur, -trice

sharp-tongued [ʃɑːpˈtʌŋd] *adj* caustique

sharp-witted *adj* vif, *f* vive

shatter [ˈʃætər] **1** *vt* **(a)** (*smash*) fracasser, briser en éclats; (*bone*) briser en plusieurs morceaux **(b)** (*hopes*) briser, renverser; (*silence*) rompre **(c)** (*health, nerves*) détraquer; *F* **I was absolutely shattered!** (*stunned*) j'ai été scié!; (*exhausted*) j'étais complètement crevé! **2** *vi* se briser (en éclats), se fracasser; **the windscreen shattered** le pare-brise a volé en éclats

shattering [ˈʃætərɪŋ] *adj* (*blow*) écrasant; **s. news** des nouvelles renversantes

shatterproof [ˈʃætəpruːf] *adj* (*glass, windscreen*) feuilleté

shave¹ [ʃeɪv] *n* rasage *m*; **to have a s.** se raser; (*be shaved*) se faire raser; **this razor gives you a really close s.** avec ce rasoir vous pouvez vraiment vous raser de près; *F* **that was a close s.!** vous l'avez/il l'a/*etc* échappé belle!, il était moins une!

shave² **1** *vt* **(a)** (*face, legs etc*) raser; (*remove hair from face of*) (*person*) faire la barbe à; **to s. sb's head** raser la tête à qn; **to s. one's legs** se raser les jambes **(b)** (*wood*) planer; (*corner*) rogner; **to s. prices** rogner les prix **(c)** (*brush against*) effleurer **2** *vi* se raser; **to start shaving** (*of boy*) commencer à se raser

shave³ *n* (*tool*) plane *f*, racloir *m*

▶ **shave off** *vtsep* **to s. off one's moustache** se raser la moustache; **to s. off a piece of cheese/sausage** couper une mince tranche de fromage/saucisson; **you'll need to s. a bit more off the drawer** il faut raboter un peu plus le tiroir; **this has shaved a few points off the government's lead in the polls** cela a légèrement rogné l'avance du gouvernement dans les sondages

shaven [ˈʃeɪv(ə)n] *adj* (*monk*) tonsuré; (*head, chin*) rasé; **clean s.** (*man*) sans barbe ni moustache; (*face*) glabre

shaver [ˈʃeɪvər] *n* **(a) (electric) s.** rasoir *m* électrique; **s. socket** prise *f* pour rasoir électrique **(b)** *Old-fashioned F* **(young) s.** (*lad*) gosse *m*, gamin *m*

Shavian [ˈʃeɪvɪən] **1** *n* admirateur, -trice de George Bernard Shaw **2** *adj* (*of Shaw*) de George Bernard Shaw; (*like Shaw*) à la George Bernard Shaw

shaving [ˈʃeɪvɪŋ] *n* **(a) s. brush** blaireau *m*; **s. cream** crème *f* à raser; **s. foam** mousse *f* à raser; **s. mirror** miroir *m* à raser; **s. soap** savon *m* à barbe; **s. stick** bâton *m* de savon à barbe **(b)** (*small piece shaved off*) (*of wood, metal*) copeau *m*

shawl [ʃɔːl] *n* châle *m*

she [ʃiː] **1** *pers pron* [①A26-7,a-c] **(a)** elle; (*of ship*) il; **s. was running** elle courait; **what's s. doing?** qu'est-ce qu'elle fait?; **here s. comes!** la voici (qui vient)!; **s. sails at ten o'clock** (*of ship*) il part à dix heures; **she's had it, this old car** elle est bonne pour la casse, cette vieille voiture **(b)** (*stressed*) elle; **s. and I** elle et moi; **<u>she</u> knows nothing about it** elle n'en sait rien, elle; *esp Lit* **s. of whom you speak** celle dont vous parlez **2** *n F* femelle; **it's a s.** (*of newborn child*) c'est une petite fille; (*of animal*) c'est une femelle

she- [ʃiː] *pref* **s.-ass** ânesse *f*; **s.-bear** ours *m* femelle, ourse *f*; **s.-cat** chatte *f*; **s.-devil** diablesse *f*

sheaf, *pl* **-ves** [ʃiːf, -vz] *n* (*of corn etc*) gerbe *f*; (*of papers*) liasse *f*; **I had a whole s. of letters this morning** j'ai reçu toute une pile de lettres ce matin

shear [ʃɪər] (*pt* **sheared**; *pp* **shorn** [ʃɔːn], **sheared**) **1** *vt* **(a)** (*sheep etc*) tondre; *Fig* **to be shorn of sth** être dépouillé *ou* privé de qch **(b)** (*cut*) (*branch etc*) couper; **to s. through sth** trancher qch **(c)** *Phys etc* cisailler **2** *vi* (*of material*) se fendre

▶ **shear off** *vi* se détacher

shearer [ˈʃɪərər] *n* **(a)** (*person*) (*of sheep*) tondeur, -euse **(b)** (*machine*) (*for sheep*) tondeuse *f*

shearing [ˈʃɪərɪŋ] *n* **(a)** (*of sheep*) tonte *f*; **s. time** tonte *f* **(b)** **shearings** (*of wool*) tontes *fpl*
shears [ʃɪəz] *n* [ⓘA10,e] **(pair of) s.** (*large scissors*) cisaille(s) *f*; (*for sheep, at hairdresser*) tondeuse *f*; **(garden) s.** sécateur *m*; *Sewing etc* **pinking s.** ciseaux *mpl* à denteler
sheath [ʃi:θ] *n* (*pl* [ʃi:ðz, ʃi:θs]) (*protective sleeve*) manchon *m* protecteur; (*for sword, umbrella etc*) fourreau *m*; (*for scissors*) étui *m*; (*for knife, electric cable*) gaine *f*; *Anat* (*of organ*) enveloppe *f*; (*of muscle*) gaine; *Bot* gaine; **(contraceptive) s.** préservatif *m*; **s. dress** (*garment*) fourreau; **s. knife** couteau *m* à gaine
sheathe [ʃi:ð] *vt* **(a)** (*sword etc*) (re)mettre au fourreau, rengainer; (*knife etc*) engainer; **sheathed in** gainé de **(b)** *El* (*cable*) gainer
sheathing [ˈʃi:ðɪŋ] *n El* (*sheath*) (*of cable*) gaine *f*
sheave [ʃi:v] *vt* (*corn etc*) mettre en gerbes
Sheba [ˈʃi:bə] *n* **the Queen of S.** la reine de Saba
shebang [ʃɪˈbæŋ] *n Sl* **the whole s.** tout le bazar
shebeen [ʃɪˈbi:n] *n Dial Irish* débit *m* de boissons clandestin
shed¹ [ʃed] *n* (*larger*) hangar *m*; (*smaller*) remise *f*; **lean-to s.** appentis *m*; **(garden) s.** cabane *f* de jardin; *Rail* **(engine) s.** remise de locomotives; **tool s.** cabane à outils; **bicycle s.** (*small*) remise à vélo; (*big*) hangar à vélo; **cattle s.** étable *f*
shed² (*pt, pp* **shed**; *prp* **shedding**) **1** *vt* **(a)** (*drop, get rid of*) (*leaves, teeth, skin, horns etc*) perdre; (*of lorry etc*) (*load*) renverser; **snakes s. their skin** les serpents muent; **its feathers s. water** l'eau lui glisse sur les plumes; **to s. its leaves** (*of plant*) s'effeuiller; **to s. jobs** supprimer des emplois; **to s. labour** licencier de la main-d'œuvre; *El* **to s. the load** délester; **he shed 20 pounds in a month** il a perdu œ kilos en un mois; **to s. one's clothes** se dépouiller de ses vêtements
(b) (*spill*) (*tears, blood*) répandre, verser; (*light*) diffuser; **before more blood is shed** avant que davantage de sang ne soit versé; *Fig* **to s. light on sth** faire *ou* jeter la lumière sur qch
2 *vi* (*of cat*) perdre ses poils
she'd [ʃi:d] **(a) = she had**, *see* **have² (b) = she would**, *see* **will³**
shedding [ˈʃedɪŋ] *n* **(a)** (*of leaves, teeth etc*) perte *f*, chute *f*; *El* **load s.** délestage *m* **(b)** (*of blood*) effusion *f*
sheen [ʃi:n] *n* reflet *m*; **hair with a golden s.** cheveux aux reflets d'or; *Fig* **to take the s. off sb's reputation/image** ternir la réputation/l'image de qn
sheep [ʃi:p] *n* (*inv in pl*) mouton *m*; *Fig* **the black s. (of the family/***etc***)** la brebis galeuse; *Fig* **lost** *or* **stray s.** brebis perdue *ou* égarée; **they follow one another like s.** ce sont des moutons de Panurge; *Fig* **to separate the s. from the goats** *or* **the s. and the goats** séparer les brebis d'avec les boucs; **to make s.'s eyes at sb** faire les yeux doux à qn
sheep-dip *n* **(a)** (*place*) enclos *m* (*avec bain désinfectant*) **(b)** (*disinfectant*) bain *m* désinfectant (*pour les moutons*)
sheepdog [ˈʃi:pdɒg] *n* (chien *m* de) berger *m*; **Old English s.** berger *m* anglais sans queue; **s. trial** concours *m* de chiens de berger
sheep farmer *n* éleveur *m* de moutons
sheep farming *n* élevage *m* de moutons
sheepfold [ˈʃi:pfəʊld] *n* parc *m* à moutons
sheepish [ˈʃi:pɪʃ] *adj* (*embarrassed*) penaud; **to look s.** rester penaud
sheepishly [ˈʃi:pɪʃlɪ] *adv* d'un air penaud
sheepishness [ˈʃi:pɪʃnɪs] *n* (*embarrassment*) air *m* penaud
sheep pen *n* parc *m* à moutons
sheep shearer *n* (*person*) tondeur, -euse (*de moutons*); (*machine*) tondeuse *f* mécanique
sheep shearing *n* tonte *f*
sheepskin [ˈʃi:pskɪn] *n* **(a)** (*skin*) peau *f* de mouton; **s. (jacket)** veste *f* en mouton **(b)** *esp US* (*diploma*) diplôme *m*
sheer¹ *vi Naut* embarder, faire une embardée
sheer² **1** *adj* **(a)** (*pure*) pur, véritable; **this accident was caused by s. carelessness** c'est la négligence et elle seule qui est à l'origine de l'accident; **that's s. carelessness!** c'est de la négligence pure et simple!; **it's s. madness** *or* **lunacy** *or* **folly** c'est de la folie pure (et simple), c'est de la pure folie; **with a look of s. disbelief** avec un air d'incrédulité absolue; **a s. waste of time** une pure perte de temps; **out of s. malice** par pure méchanceté; **it was s. stupidity** c'était franchement stupide; **in s. desperation she wrote to him** en désespoir de cause elle lui écrivit; **by s. chance** tout à fait par hasard; **by s. necessity** par pure nécessité
(b) (*perpendicular*) (*cliff, path etc*) perpendiculaire, à pic, abrupt, escarpé
(c) *Tex* fin, transparent; **s. silk stockings** bas *mpl* de soie extra-fins
2 *adv* **(a)** (*completely*) (*crazy*) complètement; **this goes s. against everything I've ever been taught** ceci va complètement à l'encontre de tout ce qu'on m'a toujours appris; **the tree was torn s. out by the roots** l'arbre a été littéralement déraciné
(b) (*to drop etc*) perpendiculairement, à pic, à plomb
▶ **sheer away** *vi* (*move away*) (*of vehicle, boat*) faire une embardée; *F* **to s. away from a subject** éviter un sujet
sheet¹ [ʃi:t] *n* **(a)** (*on bed*) drap *m*; **fitted s.** drap-housse *m*; *F* **to get between the sheets** se mettre au lit; *F* se pieuter; *F* **what's he like between the sheets?** comment est-il au lit?
(b) (*of paper*) feuille *f*, feuillet *m*; **loose s., fly s.** feuille volante; *Com* **order s.** bulletin *m* de commande; *Ind* **time** *or* **work** *or* **job s.** feuille de présence
(c) (*of glass*) feuille *f*; (*of metal*) feuille, tôle *f*, plaque *f*; *Culin* **baking s.** plaque à pâtisserie; **s. glass** verre *m* à vitres; **s. metal** tôle; **s. mill** laminoir *m* à tôles, tôlerie *f*
(d) (*of water, foam*) nappe *f*; (*of flame*) rideau *m*; (*of ice*) couche *f*; **the rain was coming down in sheets** la pluie tombait à verse; **s. lightning** éclairs *mpl* diffus, éclairs en nappe(s)
sheet² *n Naut* (*rope*) écoute *f*; **s. bend** nœud *m* d'écoute; *Old-fashioned F* **to be three sheets in the wind** (*drunk*) avoir du vent dans les voiles
▶ **sheet down** *vi* (*of rain*) tomber à verse; **it was sheeting down** il pleuvait à verse
sheet-fed *adj Comptr* à alimentation feuille par feuille; **s. printer** imprimante *f* feuille à feuille
sheetfeed [ˈʃi:tfi:d] *n Comptr* alimentation *f* feuille par feuille, feuille à feuille *m*; (*device*) dispositif *m* d'alimentation papier
sheet feeder *n Comptr* dispositif *m* d'alimentation
sheeting [ˈʃi:tɪŋ] *n* (*fabric*) toile *f* pour draps; **(plastic) s.** bâche(s) *f(pl)* (en plastique)
sheet music *n* partition *f*; **they sell s.** ils vendent des partitions
sheik(h) [ʃeɪk, ʃi:k] *n* cheik *m*, scheik *m*
sheik(h)dom [ˈʃeɪkdəm, ˈʃi:k-] *n* territoire *m* d'un/du sheik
sheila [ˈʃi:lə] *n Austr Sl* (*girl*) nana *f*
shekel [ˈʃek(ə)l] *n* **(a)** *Hist* (*coin, weight*) sicle *m* **(b)** *F* **shekels** (*money*) fric *m*, flouse *m*
shelf, *pl* **shelves** [ʃelf, ʃelvz] *n* **(a)** (*in shelving unit*) tablette *f*; (*in cupboard*) planche *f*, rayon *m*; (*in bookcase*) rayon; (*of sideboard*) étagère *f*; (*in oven*) plateau *m*; **(set of) shelves** étagère; **these machines can be bought off the s.** ces machines sont disponibles en stock; **to stay on the shelves** (*of goods*) (*not get sold*) ne pas se vendre; (*not sell well*) être difficile à vendre; *F* **to be on the s.** (*abandoned*) être laissé pour compte; (*of unmarried woman*) être en passe de devenir vieille fille; *Aut* **(window) s.** plage *f* arrière; (*at front*) vide-poche *m*; *Mktg* **s. facing** frontal *m* de rayonnage, frontale *f*; **s. space** rayonnage *m*
(b) (*of cliff, rock face*) rebord *m*, saillie *f*; (*in oceanography*), *Geog* terrasse *f*, plate-forme *f*, *pl* plates-formes; (*of rock, sand*) banc *m*; **continental s.** plate-forme continentale
shelf filler *n* (*person in supermarket*) réassortisseur, -euse;
shelf life *n* (*of goods*) durée *f* de conservation sur les rayons avant la vente; **the s. is six months** la durée de conservation avant vente est de six mois; *Fig* **to have a short s.** (*of ideas, pop groups etc*) avoir une durée de vie courte
shelf stacker *n* (*person in supermarket*) réassortisseur, -euse
shell¹ [ʃel] *n* **(a)** (*of mollusc, snail, egg, nut*) coquille *f*; (*of lobster, turtle*) carapace *f*; (*of oyster, mussel, turtle*) écaille *f*; (*of pea etc*) cosse *f*; (*of chrysalis*) enveloppe *f*; **shells** (*on beach etc*) coquillages *mpl*; *Fig* **to come out of/retire into one's s.** sortir de/rentrer dans sa coquille; **I'm just an empty s.** je me sens tout vide; **s. pink** (*colour*) rose *m* pâle **(b)** *Naut* (*of ship etc*) carcasse *f*, squelette *m*, coque; *Constr* (*of building*) charpente *f*; (*damaged*) carcasse; **the burnt-out s. of a car/house** la carcasse brûlée d'une voiture/maison **(c)** (*bomb*) obus *m*
shell² **1** *vt* **(a)** (*nuts etc*) écaler, décortiquer; (*peas*) écosser; (*oysters, mussels*) écailler; (*prawns*) éplucher **(b)** *Mil* bombarder **2** *vi* **nuts that s. easily** noix faciles à décortiquer; **peas that s. easily** pois faciles à écosser
▶ **shell out** *F* **1** *vtsep* cracher, casquer; **I was shelling out £100 a week on petrol** je casquais 100 livres d'essence par semaine **2** *vi* casquer, banquer
she'll [ʃi:l] **= she will**, *see* **will³**
shellac¹ [ʃeˈlæk] *n* gomme-laque *f*; *Ch* shellac *m*
shellac² *vt* **(shellacked) (a)** traiter à la gomme-laque **(b)** *US Sp Sl* (*defeat*) battre à plate(s) couture(s)
shellacking [ʃəˈlækɪŋ] *n US Sp Sl* **to get a s.** se faire battre à plate(s) couture(s)
shelled [ʃeld] *adj* (*nuts etc*) écalé; (*peas*) écossé
shellfire [ˈʃelfaɪər] *n* tir *m* d'obus; **to be under s.** subir des tirs d'obus; **we came under heavy s.** nous avons subi un pilonnage intensif

shellfish [ˈʃelfɪʃ] *n* **(a)** *(mollusc)* mollusque *m* (comestible), coquillage *m*; *(crustacean)* crustacé *m* **(b)** *(collectively)* mollusques *mpl* et crustacés *mpl*; *Culin* fruits *mpl* de mer
shelling [ˈʃelɪŋ] *n Mil* bombardement *m*
shell program *n Comptr* logiciel *m* shell
shell-shaped *adj* en forme de coquillage, conchoïde
shell shock *n* psychose *f* traumatique, syndrome *m* commotionnel
shellshocked [ˈʃelʃɒkt] *adj Med, Mil* commotionné; *Fig* **to feel s.** être en état de choc
shell suit [ˈʃelsjuːt] *n* survêtement *m*
shelter¹ [ˈʃeltər] **(a)** *(place)* refuge *m*; *(from rain, bombs, at bus stop etc)* abri *m*; *(bus stop)* abribus *m*; *(for the homeless etc)* asile *m*, refuge; *(for guards)* abrivent *m*; *Mil* **air raid s.** abri contre les attaques aériennes, abri de défense passive **(b)** *(protection)* **under s.** à l'abri, à couvert; **to take s. under/from sth** s'abriter *ou* se mettre à l'abri sous/de qch; **to seek s. under a tree** chercher à s'abriter sous un arbre; **to find s.** trouver un abri; *(of refugee etc)* trouver asile *ou* refuge; **to give s. to sb** abriter qn; *(give asylum etc)* offrir un asile *ou* un refuge à qn
shelter² **1** *vt* abriter; *(lost person etc)* donner asile à, recueillir; **to s. sb/sth from the rain** abriter qn/qch de la pluie **2** *vi* s'abriter, se mettre à l'abri *ou* à couvert **(from** de); **to s. under a tree** s'abriter sous un arbre; **to s. from the wind** s'abriter du vent; **to s. from the rain** s'abriter de la pluie
sheltered [ˈʃeltəd] *adj* abrité, protégé **(against, from** de); **s. housing** foyers *mpl* *(pour personnes handicapées, personnes âgées, femmes battues etc)*; **to have had** *or* **led a s. life** avoir eu une vie protégée, à l'écart des réalités de l'existence; **you've led a s. life!** tu n'as rien vu!; **s. workshop** atelier *m* pour les handicapés qui ont besoin de travailler dans des conditions particulières
shelve [ʃelv] **1** *vt* **(a)** *(fit with shelves)* *(cupboard etc)* munir *ou* garnir de rayons **(b)** *(put on shelves)* *(books etc)* mettre sur les rayons **(c)** *(postpone)* *(question etc)* ajourner; *(project)* mettre en veilleuse; **the project has been shelved for 6 months** le projet a été mis de côté pendant 6 mois **2** *vi* *(slope downwards)* **the land shelves down to the sea** le terrain descend en pente douce jusqu'à la mer
shelving [ˈʃelvɪŋ] *n* **(a)** *(no pl)* *(shelves)* rayons *mpl*, rayonnage *m*; **adjustable s.** rayons amovibles **(b)** *(postponing)* *(of question etc)* ajournement *m*
shemozzle [ʃɪˈmɒz(ə)l] *n US F (fight)* bagarre *f*
shenanigans [ʃɪˈnænɪgənz] *npl F* manigances *fpl*; **he's having s. with my wife** il a une aventure avec ma femme
shepherd¹ [ˈʃepəd] *n* berger *m*, *Lit* pâtre *m*; *Rel* **the Good S.** le bon Pasteur; *Bible* **the Lord is my S.** l'Éternel est mon berger; **German s. (dog)** berger allemand; **s. dog** chien *m* de berger; **s.'s pie** hachis *m* parmentier; *Bot* **s.'s purse** capselle *f*, bourse-à-pasteur *f*, *pl* bourses-à-pasteur
shepherd² *vt* *(sheep)* garder; *Fig (of priest) (his flock)* guider; *(tourists etc)* conduire, piloter; **we were shepherded into the next room** nous avons été conduits dans la pièce suivante
shepherdess [ʃepəˈdes] *n* bergère *f*
sherbet [ˈʃɜːbət] *n* **(a) s. (powder)** limonade *f* en poudre *(pour préparer une boisson gazeuse)* **(b)** *Am (water ice)* sorbet *m*
sheriff [ˈʃerɪf] *n* **(a)** *Br Admin* shérif *m* *(représentant de la Couronne dans un comté)* **(b)** *Scot Jur* juge *m* de première instance **(c)** *US* chef *m* de la police *(d'un comté)*, shérif *m*; **deputy s.** = citoyen *m* assermenté faisant fonction d'agent de police
sherry [ˈʃerɪ] *n* vin *m* de Xérès, xérès *m*; **s. glass** = verre *m* à madère
she's [ʃiːz] **(a) = she is,** *see* **be (b) = she has,** *see* **have²**
Shetland [ˈʃetlənd] *n* **(a) the S. Islands, the Shetlands** les îles *fpl* Shetland; **S. pony** poney *m* shetlandais *ou* de Shetland **(b)** *Tex* shetland *m*
shew [ʃəʊ] *(pt* **shewed** [ʃəʊd]; *pp* **shewn** [ʃəʊn]) *Arch, Lit* = **show²**
Shia [ˈʃiːə] *n* **(a)** *(religion)* chiisme *m* **(b)** *(person)* chiite *mf*
shibboleth [ˈʃɪbəleθ] *n Bible* schibboleth *m*; *Fig (of party etc)* mot *m* d'ordre; **outworn shibboleths** *(doctrines)* doctrines vieux-jeu *ou* désuètes
shield¹ [ʃiːld] *n* **(a)** *(worn on arm)* bouclier m; *Her* écu *m*, écusson *m*; **he used his body as a s. to protect the president** il a fait un bouclier de son corps pour protéger le président; *Fig* **a s. against sth** une protection contre qch; **s. bearer** écuyer *m*
(b) *(around nuclear reactor)* bouclier *m*; *(on cable)* blindage *m*; *Astron* **heat s.** bouclier thermique; *Aut* **sun s.** pare-soleil *m inv*
(c) *(in spray painting)* masque *m*, cache *m*
(d) *(police badge)* plaque *f* de policier
(e) *Sp (trophy)* plaque *f*
shield² *vt* **(a)** protéger **(from, against** contre); **to s. sb from criticism** protéger qn des critiques; **to s. sb from punishment** soustraire qn à une punition; **to s. sb from danger** protéger qn contre le danger; **to s. sb with one's (own) body** faire un bouclier de son corps à qn; **to s. one's eyes** se protéger les yeux **(b)** *(in spray painting)* *(surfaces)* masquer **(c)** *El, Rad* blinder; **shielded cable** câble *m* blindé
shift¹ [ʃɪft] *n* **(a)** *(of position etc)* changement *m*; *(of tide, current)* renverse *f*; *(of wind)* saute *f*; **s. in meaning** glissement *m* de sens; **there has been a s. in public opinion** il y a eu un glissement de l'opinion publique; **a s. to the right/left** un glissement à droite/gauche; *Aut* **(gear) s.** levier *m* de vitesses; *Ling* **consonant/vowel s.** mutation *f* consonantique/vocalique; *Astron* **red s.** décalage *m* vers le rouge
(b) *Ind etc* *(work period)* poste *m*; *(group of workers)* équipe *f*, brigade *f* *(d'ouvriers)*; **day/night s.** *(period)* poste de jour/nuit; *(workers)* équipe de jour/nuit; **to work in shifts** travailler par équipes, se relayer; **to work eight-hour shifts** travailler par poste(s) de huit heures, faire les trois-huit; **we each did three-hour shifts** nous nous sommes relayés toutes les trois heures
(c) *(dress)* robe *f* fourreau; *Arch (undergarment)* chemise *f* *(de femme)*
(d) *Old-fashioned* **to make s.** s'arranger
shift² **1** *vt* **(a)** *(move)* changer de place; *(with difficulty)* bouger, déplacer; **could you s. your car?** pouvez-vous déplacer votre voiture?; **the drawer's stuck, I can't s. it** le tiroir est coincé, je ne peux le faire bouger; **they've shifted offices again** ils ont déménagé de nouveau; **he keeps getting shifted to a different job** on n'arrête pas de le muter; **he's shifted his position** *(in negotiations)* il a changé de position; **once she's decided on something it's impossible to s. her** une fois qu'elle a pris une décision, il est impossible de lui faire changer d'avis; **to s. a stain** *(of washing powder etc)* enlever une tache; **to s. the blame onto sb** rejeter la responsabilité sur qn; *Th* **to s. the scenery** changer le décor; *Aut* **to s. the gears** changer de vitesse
(b) *F (sell)* vendre; **we've been shifting these at 50 a day** *(selling them)* on en vend 50 par jour; **I've got to s. this work by 4. 00** *(finish)* il faut que j'aie terminé ce travail avant 4 heures
2 *vi* **(a)** *(move)* *(of person, object)* bouger, se déplacer; *(change places)* changer de place; *Naut (of cargo)* se désarrimer, se déplacer; **it won't s.** *(of object etc)* ça ne veut pas bouger!; **this stain won't s.** cette tache ne veut pas partir; *Th* **the scene shifts** la scène change; **the wind has shifted (round)** le vent a tourné *ou* viré; **could you s.?** *(out of the way)* pouvez-vous dégager?; **could you possibly s. a little?** pourriez-vous vous déplacer un peu?; **the building is shifting** l'immeuble bouge; **he wouldn't s.** *(in negotiations etc)* il est resté ferme sur ses positions; **he shifted nervously from foot to foot** il oscillait d'un pied sur l'autre avec nervosité
(b) *F (move quickly)* se magner (le train); **I didn't know she could s. so fast** je ne savais pas qu'elle pouvait se magner à ce point-là; **this car can really s.!** cette voiture est un vrai bolide!; **that's really shifting** ça, c'est de la vitesse
(c) *F* **to s. for oneself** *(manage)* se débrouiller; **she can** *or* **knows how to s. for herself** elle est débrouillarde
▶ **shift about, shift around** **1** *vtsep* *(object)* changer de place; **we've shifted the office around** nous avons changé la disposition du bureau; **he's always being shifted around** *(in job)* il est tout le temps muté; *(in location in office etc)* on le change tout le temps de place; *(from town to town etc)* on le fait tout le temps déménager **2** *vi* **(a)** *(fidget)* bouger **(b)** *(move around)* changer de place; *(change jobs)* changer d'emploi
▶ **shift along** *vi* *(move on seat etc)* se décaler; **s. along a bit** pousse-toi
▶ **shift over** *vi* **s. over!** pousse-toi!
▶ **shift up** *vi* **(a) = shift along (b)** *Am Aut* passer à la vitesse supérieure
shift-click *Comptr* **1** *n* majuscule-clic **2** *vi* faire un majuscule-clic
shift-drag *n Comptr* majuscule-glisser *m*
shiftily [ˈʃɪftɪlɪ] *adv* sournoisement
shiftiness [ˈʃɪftɪnɪs] *n* sournoiserie *f*, fausseté *f*
shifting [ˈʃɪftɪŋ] **1** *adj* qui se déplace; *(relationship, scene etc)* changeant; *(wind etc)* inégal; *Fig* **the s. sands of public opinion** l'opinion publique toujours versatile **2** *n* *(moving)* *(of sth by sb)* déplacement *m*; *(movement)* *(of sth)* mouvement *m*, déplacement; *(of cargo)* désarrimage *m*; *(change)* *(of position, direction etc)* changement *m*; *Th* **scene s.** changement de décors; *Aut* **(gear) s.** changement de vitesse

shift key *n* (*on typewriter, computer*) touche *f* des majuscules
shiftless [ˈʃɪftlɪs] *adj* **(a)** (*lazy*) paresseux **(b)** (*lacking resourcefulness*) peu débrouillard, qui manque d'initiative *ou* de ressource
shiftlessness [ˈʃɪftlɪsnɪs] *n* **(a)** (*laziness*) paresse *f* **(b)** (*lack of resourcefulness*) manque *m* de ressource *ou* d'initiative
shift lock *n Comptr* (*facility*) dispositif *m* de blocage; (*key*) touche *f* de blocage *ou* fixe-majuscules
shiftwork [ˈʃɪftwɜːk] *n Ind* travail *m* par équipes *ou* par roulement
shiftworker [ˈʃɪftwɜːkər] *n Ind* ouvrier, -ière qui fait les trois-huit
shifty [ˈʃɪftɪ] *adj* (*person*) louche; (*look*) sournois; (*behaviour*) ambigu, -uë; **s. eyes** regard *m* fuyant; **there is something s. about him** il y a quelque chose de louche chez lui
Shiism [ˈʃiːɪz(ə)m] *n* chiisme *m*
Shiite [ˈʃiːaɪt] **1** *n* chiite *mf* **2** *adj* chiite
shillelagh [ʃɪˈleɪlə] *n* gourdin *m* irlandais
shilling [ˈʃɪlɪŋ] *n* shilling *m*; *Fig* **to cut sb off without a s.** déshériter qn; *Hist* **to take the king's/queen's s.** = s'engager dans l'armée
shillyshally [ˈʃɪlɪʃælɪ] *vi F* hésiter, tergiverser
shillyshallying [ˈʃɪlɪʃælɪɪŋ] *n F* hésitation *f*, tergiversation *f*
shimmer¹ [ˈʃɪmər] *n* lueur *f*; (*of sea, silk etc*) miroitement *m*; (*in heat*) reflets *mpl*; (*of TV picture*) scintillement *m*; **a s. of light** une lueur; **the s. of the moon on the lake** les reflets de la lune sur le lac
shimmer² *vi* (*of sea*) miroiter; (*of silk*) chatoyer
shimmering [ˈʃɪmərɪŋ] *adj* (*sea*) miroitant; (*silk*) chatoyant
shimmy¹ [ˈʃɪmɪ] *n* **(a)** *US Aut* (*movement of front wheels*) flottement *m* des roues avant **(b)** (*dance*) shimmy *m*
shimmy² *vi* **(a)** *Aut* (*of wheels*) osciller **(b)** (*dance*) danser le shimmy
shin [ʃɪn] *n* tibia *m*; *Culin* jarret *m* (de bœuf), gîte *m* de devant; **to kick sb in the shins** donner un coup de pied dans les tibias à qn; *Sp* **s. guard** *or* **pad** jambière *f*
▶ **shin up (-nn-) 1** *vipo* (*climb*) **to s. up a tree** grimper à un arbre **2** *vi* (*climb*) grimper
shinbone [ˈʃɪnbəʊn] *n Anat* tibia *m*
shindig [ˈʃɪndɪg] *n F* **(a)** (*party*) fête *f* **(b)** = **shindy (a)**
shindy [ˈʃɪndɪ] *n F* **(a)** (*din*) raffut *m*, ramdam *m*; **to kick up a s.** (*make a din*) faire du raffut *ou* du ramdam; **to kick up a s. about sth** (*protest loudly*) faire du raffut pour protester contre qch **(b)** *US* = **shindig (a)**
shine¹ [ʃaɪn] *n* **(a)** (*brightness*) éclat *m*; (*on shoes etc*) brillant *m*; (*on textiles etc*) luisant *m*; **to take the s. off sth** délustrer qch, ternir qch; *Fig* ternir qch, entacher qch **(b)** (*action*) **to give one's shoes a s.** cirer ses chaussures; **to give the brass a s.** astiquer les cuivres **(c)** *F* **to take a s. to sb** s'enticher de qn
shine² (*pt, pp* **shone** [ʃɒn]) **1** *vi* (*of sun etc*) briller; (*of polished article*) (re)luire; *Fig* (*excel*) briller; **the moon/the sun is shining** il y a un clair de lune/il fait soleil; **the sun was shining straight into my eyes** j'avais le soleil dans les yeux; **the light from the torch shone on a piece of paper** la lumière de la lampe de poche éclaira un morceau de papier; **her face was shining with joy** son visage rayonnait de joie; **her eyes shone with enthusiasm** ses yeux brillaient d'enthousiasme; *Fig* **to s. at Maths/Latin** être brillant en maths/latin; *Fig* **he doesn't s. in company** il ne brille pas en société
2 *vt* **(a) to s. a light on sth** (*illuminate*) éclairer qch (*avec une lampe etc*); (*direct at*) braquer une lampe sur qch
(b) (*pt, pp* **shined** [ʃaɪnd]) (*polish*) (*shoes etc*) polir, cirer; (*brass*) astiquer
shiner [ˈʃaɪnər] *n F* (*black eye*) œil *m* poché, *F* œil au beurre noir
shingle¹ [ˈʃɪŋg(ə)l] *n* **(a)** *Constr* (*wooden tile*) bardeau *m*, aisseau *m* **(b)** *Am* (*sign*) (*of doctor, lawyer etc*) plaque *f* (*de cuivre*); **to put one's s. up** (*to open business*) s'installer **(c)** (*hairstyle*) coupe *f* à la garçonne
shingle² *vt* **(a)** *Constr* (*roof*) couvrir de bardeaux **(b) to s. sb** *or* **sb's hair** couper les cheveux de qn à la garçonne
shingle³ *n* (*no pl*) (*on beach*) galets *mpl*; **s. beach** plage *f* de galets
shingles [ˈʃɪŋg(ə)lz] *n* (①**A10**,d) *Med* zona *m*
shingly [ˈʃɪŋglɪ] *adj* (*covered in pebbles*) couvert de galets; (*beach*) de galets
shininess [ˈʃaɪnɪnɪs] *n* éclat *m*, brillance *f*; (*due to wear*) lustrage *m*
shining [ˈʃaɪnɪŋ] *adj* brillant, (re)luisant; (*face*) rayonnant; **a s. example** un exemple éclatant *ou* insigne (**of sth** de qch)
▶ **shinny up** [ˈʃɪnɪ] *vipo, vi Am F* = **shin up**
Shintoism [ˈʃɪntəʊɪz(ə)m] *n* shintoïsme *m*, shintô *m*
shiny [ˈʃaɪnɪ] *adj* brillant, luisant; **clothes made s. by long wear** vêtements lustrés par l'usage
ship¹ [ʃɪp] *n* **(a)** navire *m*; (*smaller*) bateau *m*; (*esp warship*) bâtiment *m*; **to go by s.** aller en bateau; **to send sth by s.** envoyer qch par bateau; **is there a doctor/swimming pool on the s.?** y a-t-il un docteur/une piscine à bord?; **sailing s.** voilier *m*, navire à voiles; **passenger s.** paquebot *m*; **merchant s.** navire marchand, cargo *m*; **container s.** navire porte-conteneurs; **depot** *or* **supply s.** ravitailleur *m*; **training s.** navire-école *m*, *pl* navires-écoles; *Fig* **the s. of State** le char de l'État; **the s. of the desert** (*camel*) le chameau; *Fig* **when my s. comes home** *or* **in** dès que j'aurai fait fortune; *Fig* **to be like ships that pass in the night** (*of lovers*) être des amants de passage; **s.'s biscuit** biscuit *m* de mer; **s.'s boat** embarcation *f* de bord; **s.'s boy** mousse *m*; **s.'s carpenter** charpentier *m* de bord; **s.'s chandler** shipchandler *m*, fournisseur *m* de navires; **the s.'s company** l'équipage *m*; **s.'s manifest** manifeste *m*
(b) (*spaceship*) vaisseau *m*; *F* (*aeroplane*) avion *m*
ship² (-pp-) 1 *vt* **(a)** *Com* (*to send by sea, rail etc*) envoyer, expédier **(b)** (*to take on board*) (*cargo etc*) embarquer; **to s. water** (*of ship*) embarquer de l'eau; **to s. oars** rentrer *ou* border les avirons **2** *vi* **(a)** (*of passenger*) s'embarquer; (*of sailor*) armer sur un navire **(b)** (*be delivered*) sortir des usines
▶ **ship off** *vtsep F* (*send*) (*thing, person*) expédier; **his mother shipped him off to boarding school** sa mère l'a expédié dans un pensionnat
▶ **ship out 1** *vtsep* (*send*) (*goods*) expédier; (*troops etc*) envoyer **2** *vi esp Am F* (*leave*) mettre les voiles; *see* = **shape up**
shipboard [ˈʃɪpbɔːd] *adj attrib* à bord d'un/du navire
ship-broker *n* courtier *m* maritime
shipbuilder [ˈʃɪpbɪldər] *n* constructeur *m* de navires
shipbuilding [ˈʃɪpbɪldɪŋ] *n* construction *f* navale; **a s. firm** une entreprise de construction navale; **the s. industry** l'industrie *f* de la construction navale
shipload [ˈʃɪpləʊd] *n* chargement *m*, cargaison *f*; *Fig* **by the s., in shiploads** en masse
shipmate [ˈʃɪpmeɪt] *n* compagnon *m ou* camarade *m* de bord
shipment [ˈʃɪpmənt] *n* (*sending*) expédition *f*, envoi *m*; (*goods sent*) envoi; **the containers awaiting s.** les conteneurs prêts pour l'expédition; **three shipments of …** trois cargaisons *ou* chargements de …
shipowner [ˈʃɪpəʊnər] *n* armateur *m*, propriétaire *m* de navire, fréteur *m*
shipped bill [ʃɪpt] *n Com* connaissement *m* embarqué
shipped weight *n Com* poids *m* embarqué
shipper [ˈʃɪpər] *n* expéditeur *m*
shipping [ˈʃɪpɪŋ] *n* (*ships*) navires *mpl* (*d'un pays, d'un port etc*); (*sending*) expédition *f*, envoi *m*; **dangerous to** *or* **for s.** dangereux pour la navigation; **s. address** adresse *f* de livraison; **s. agent** agent *m* maritime, commissionnaire *mf* de transport; **s. bill** connaissement *m*; **s. company** compagnie *f* de navigation; **s. conference** conférence *f* maritime; **s. costs** frais *mpl* d'expédition; (*by ship*) frais *mpl* d'embarquement; **s. (department)** service *m* expédition, expéditions; **s. documents** documents *mpl* d'expédition, documents maritimes; **s. exchange** bourse *f* de fret; **s. instructions** instructions *fpl* pour l'expédition; **s. instructions form** formulaire *m* présentant les instructions pour l'expédition; **s. intelligence** nouvelles *fpl* maritimes; **s. lanes** routes *fpl* de navigation; **s. line** ligne *f ou* compagnie maritime; **s. marks** marques *fpl* d'expédition; **s. note** permis *m* d'embarquement; **s. office** agence *f* maritime; **s. routes** routes *fpl* de navigation
shipshape [ˈʃɪpʃeɪp] *adj* (très) bien rangé; (*documents etc*) en bon ordre; **everything's s.** tout est à sa place; **to get a room s.** ranger une pièce, mettre de l'ordre dans une pièce; *Old-fashioned* **s. and Bristol fashion!** impeccable!
shipwreck¹ [ˈʃɪprek] *n* naufrage *m*; **to suffer s.** (*of ship*) faire naufrage; *Fig* **the s. of one's hopes** le naufrage de ses espoirs
shipwreck² *vt* (*usu in passive*) **to be shipwrecked** faire naufrage
shipwrecked [ˈʃɪprekt] *adj* naufragé
shipwright [ˈʃɪpraɪt] *n* constructeur *m* de navires; (*on board ship*) charpentier *m* du bord
shipyard [ˈʃɪpjɑːd] *n* chantier *m* naval, chantier de constructions navales; **s. worker** ouvrier *m* de chantier naval
shire [ʃaɪər] *n* comté *m*; **s. horse** = cheval *m* anglais de gros trait
Shires [ʃaɪəz] *npl* = comtés *mpl* ruraux du centre de l'Angleterre
shirk [ʃɜːk] **1** *vt* (*obligation etc*) manquer à, se soustraire à; (*task*) renâcler à; (*a duty*) esquiver; (*one's duty*) négliger; **to s. doing sth** se défiler (pour ne pas faire qch); **to s. the**

question esquiver *ou* éluder la question **2** *vi* (*avoid work*) tirer au flanc; **stop shirking!** arrête de tirer au flanc *ou* de te défiler devant le travail!

shirker [ˈʃɜːkər] *n F* tire-au-flanc *m*; **she's no s.** elle n'a rien d'un tire-au-flanc

shirr [ʃɜːr] *vt Sewing* bouillonner

shirring [ˈʃɜːrɪŋ] *n Sewing* bouillonné *m*

shirt [ʃɜːt] *n* chemise *f*; (*with short sleeves*) chemisette *f*; *Sp* maillot *m*; **sports** *or* **casual s.** chemise sport; *F* **he's a stuffed s.** il est guindé; **to change one's s., to put on a clean s.** changer de chemise; *F* **to put one's s. on a horse** parier sa chemise sur un cheval; *F* **he'd have the s. off your back** il te mangerait la laine sur le dos; *F* **he'd give you the s. off his back** il donnerait sa chemise; *F* **to lose one's s.** (*lose everything*) y laisser sa chemise; *Am* (*lose one's temper*) s'emporter, prendre la mouche; *F* **keep your s. on!** ne vous emballez pas!, calmez-vous!; *Hist* **Red/Black/Brown Shirts** Chemises rouges/noires/brunes; **s. collar** col *m* de chemise; **s. cuff** poignet *m* de chemise; **s. front** plastron *m ou* devant *m* de chemise

shirting [ˈʃɜːtɪŋ] *n* shirting *m*

shirtlifter [ˈʃɜːtlɪftər] *n Offensive Sl* tante *f*, homosexuel *m*

shirtmaker [ˈʃɜːtmeɪkər] *n* chemisier, -ière

shirtsleeve [ˈʃɜːtsliːv] *n* manche *f* de chemise; **to be in one's shirtsleeves** être en bras *ou* en manches de chemise

shirt-tail *n* pan *m* de chemise

shirtwaister, *Am* **shirtwaist** [ˈʃɜːtweɪst(ər)] *n* (*dress*) robe *f* chemisier

shirty [ˈʃɜːtɪ] *adj Br F* irritable; **to get s.** se fâcher

shit[1] [ʃɪt] **1** *n* **(a)** *Vulg* (*excrement, Fig rubbish*) merde *f*; (*nonsense*) conneries *fpl*; **to have a s.** chier; **to have the shits** (*to have diarrhoea*) avoir la chiasse; (*to be frightened*) faire dans son froc; **bird/dog s.** merde d'oiseau/de chien; *Fig* **the s. will really hit the fan** il y en aura pour tout le monde, il y aura de la merde pour tout le monde; **tough s.!** pas de bol!; **this is a s. book** c'est un livre de merde; **he doesn't give a s.** il s'en fout, *Vulg* il n'en a rien à branler; **to beat the s. out of sb** démolir qn; **to scare the s. out of sb** foutre une trouille bleue à qn; **to bore the s. out of sb** faire crever qn d'ennui; **I'm not taking any more of his s.** je ne le laisserai plus m'emmerder; **to be in the s.** être dans la merde; **to be up s. creek (without a paddle)** être dans la merde jusqu'au cou; **s. stirrer** fouille-merde *mf, pl* fouille-merdes; *Am* **no s.!** arrête tes conneries!
(b) *Vulg* (*person*) salaud *m*, salope *f*
(c) *Sl* (*heroin*) came *f*; (*marijuana*) shit *m*
2 *int* merde!

shit[2] (*pt, pp* **shat** [ʃæt], **shitted** [ˈʃɪtɪd]) *Vulg* **1** *vi* chier; **they'll s. on us from a great height** ils vont bien se foutre de nous **2** *vt* chier; **I was shitting myself** je chiais dans mon froc; **he'll s. a brick** il chiera dans son froc

shite [ʃaɪt] *n, vti Vulg* = **shit**

shit(e)house [ˈʃɪthaʊs, ˈʃaɪt-] *n Vulg* (*toilet*) chiottes *m ou fpl*, gogues *mpl*

shitface [ˈʃɪtfeɪs] *n Vulg* gueule *f* de con

shit-hot *adj Sl* vachement bien

shitless [ˈʃɪtlɪs] *adj Sl* **to be scared s.** chier dans son froc; **to be bored s.** s'emmerder profondément

shit-scared *adj* **to be/look s.** avoir/avoir l'air d'avoir une trouille bleue

shitty [ˈʃɪtɪ] *adj Sl* (*nappies, trousers*) plein de merde; (*weather, job*) merdique, de merde; **I feel s.** je me sens vasouillard; (*feel guilty etc*) je me trouve dégueulasse; **that was a s. thing to say/do to someone** c'était dégueulasse de dire/faire ça à quelqu'un; **he was really s. to her** il a été vraiment dégueulasse avec elle; **to get the s. end of the stick** se récolter la merde

shiver[1] [ˈʃɪvər] *n* (*from cold, fear*) frisson *m*; **it sent cold shivers down my back** cela m'a fait froid dans le dos; **to feel a s.** avoir un frisson; *F* **to have the shivers** avoir la tremblote; *F* **it gives me the shivers to think of it** ça me donne des frissons quand j'y pense

shiver[2] *vi* **(a)** frissonner, trembler (**with cold/fear** de froid/peur); **to s. like a leaf** *or* **a jelly** trembler comme une feuille **(b)** (*of sail*) faseyer, ralinguer

shiver[3] *n* (*fragment*) éclat *m*, fragment *m*; **to break sth into shivers** casser qch en mille morceaux

shiver[4] **1** *vt* (*break*) casser en morceaux; *Arch, Hum* **s. me timbers!** tonnerre de Dieu! **2** *vi* (*break*) se casser en morceaux

shivering [ˈʃɪvərɪŋ] **1** *adj* frissonnant; (*with cold*) grelottant **2** *n* frissonnement *m*; **to have a s. fit** être pris de frissons

shivery [ˈʃɪvərɪ] *adj* = **shivering 1**; **to feel s.** avoir des frissons; (*feverish*) se sentir fiévreux; **it gives you a s. feeling** cela donne le frisson

shoal[1] [ʃəʊl] *n* (*shallow*) haut-fond *m, pl* hauts-fonds; (*sandbank*) banc *m* de sable

shoal[2] *n* (*of fish*) banc *m*; *F* (*of people*) foule *f*, multitude *f*; (*of letters, applications etc*) grande quantité *f*, tas *m*

shock[1] [ʃɒk] *n* **s. of hair** tignasse *f*

shock[2] *n* **(a)** (*impact*) choc *m*; (*of collision etc*) impact *m*; (*jolt*), *Geol* secousse *f*; **to stand the s.** résister au choc; **slight (earthquake) shocks were felt** on a senti de petites secousses; **s. wave** onde *f* de choc; *Fig* **the news sent s. waves through the financial world** la nouvelle a provoqué des ondes de choc dans le monde de la finance
(b) (*emotional blow*) coup *m*; (*caused by bad news etc*) *Med* choc *m*; **it was a s. to find out I'd got no money left/I'd won** ça m'a fait un choc de découvrir que je n'avais plus d'argent/que j'avais gagné; **the news of his death came as a terrible s. to all of us** la nouvelle de sa mort nous a tous énormément choqués; **the s. killed him, he died of the s.** le choc l'a tué; **be prepared for a s.** prépare-toi à un choc; *Med* **post-operative s.** choc post-opératoire; **to be in s.** être en état de choc; **to go into s.** entrer en état de choc; **in a state of s.** en état de choc; *F Hum* **s. horror story** histoire *f* abominable; *F Hum* **s. horror!** l'horreur!
(c) (electric) s. décharge *f*; **to get a(n electric) s.** recevoir une décharge; *Fig* **s. treatment** traitement *m* de choc; **electric s. treatment** traitement *m* par électrochocs

shock[3] *vt* (*person*) (*scandalize*) choquer; **to s. the eye/ear** choquer la vue/l'oreille; **a book that shocked the public** un livre qui a fait scandale; **easily shocked** qui se choque facilement; **to be shocked at** *or* **by sth** (*scandalized*) être choqué de *ou* scandalisé par qch; **she wanted to s. them into action** elle voulait les choquer pour les faire réagir; **to s. sb out of doing sth** dissuader qn de faire qch en lui faisant peur; **I was shocked to hear that …** j'ai été choqué d'apprendre que …; **millions were shocked by pictures of the famine** des millions de personnes ont été choquées *ou* bouleversées par les images de la famine

shockable [ˈʃɒkəb(ə)l] *adj* **he's easily/not easily s.** il se choque facilement/ne se choque pas facilement

shock absorbent *adj* antichoc

shock absorber *n Aut etc* amortisseur *m*

shocked [ʃɒkt] *adj* (*person, voice etc*) (*scandalized*) choqué; (*stunned*) atterré; **there was a s. silence when …** il y eut un silence atterré lorsque …

shocker [ˈʃɒkər] *n F* **(a)** (*shocking news*) **that was a real s.** ça a été un rude coup **(b)** (*bad mistake*) faute *f* énorme; (*in behaviour*) grosse bourde *f* **(c)** (*novel*) roman *m* à sensations; (*film*) film *m* à sensations **(d)** (*person*) **he really is a s.!** il est vraiment impossible!

shocking [ˈʃɒkɪŋ] **1** *adj* (*sight etc*) (*scandalizing*) choquant; (*revolting*) abominable, affreux; (*news*) atterrant, bouleversant; (*weather*) abominable, exécrable; (*pain*) atroce; **to be in a s. state** être dans un état lamentable; **s. behaviour** (*scandalizing*) comportement scandaleux; (*unworthy*) conduite indigne; **how s.!** quelle horreur!; **the s. truth about conditions in our prisons** la terrible vérité sur les conditions de vie dans nos prisons; **their s. ignorance** leur scandaleuse ignorance; **s. pink** rose criard **2** *adv F* **he carried on something s.!** il nous a fait une scène abominable!

shockingly [ˈʃɒkɪŋlɪ] *adv* (*to behave*) scandaleusement; (*to treat*) abominablement; *F* (*extremely*) (*expensive etc*) affreusement; **they did s. in the exam** leurs résultats à l'examen ont été lamentables; **s. deprived** dans une misère atroce; **s. immoral** d'une immoralité scandaleuse; **a s. low-cut dress** une robe outrageusement décolletée; **in s. bad taste** du dernier mauvais goût

shockproof [ˈʃɒkpruːf] *adj* **(a)** (*scientific instrument etc*) antichoc **(b)** *F* (*person*) qui ne se choque pas facilement

shock tactics *npl* tactique *f ou* action *f* de choc

shock therapy *n* électrochocs *mpl*

shock troops *npl* troupes *fpl* d'assaut *ou* de choc

shod *see* **shoe**[2]

shoddily [ˈʃɒdɪlɪ] *adv* **s. made** mal fait; **to treat sb s.** traiter qn peu honorablement; **to behave s. (towards sb)** se conduire mesquinement (envers qn)

shoddiness [ˈʃɒdɪnɪs] *n* (*of material, workmanship*) mauvaise qualité *f*; **the s. of their treatment of him** leur mesquinerie envers lui

shoddy[1] [ˈʃɒdɪ] *n Tex* (*cloth*) drap *m* de laine d'effilochage, laine *f ou* tissu *m* de récupération

shoddy[2] *adj* (*goods etc*) de camelote, de pacotille; (*conduct*) mesquin; (*workmanship*) médiocre; **s. goods** camelote *f*

shoe[1] [ʃuː] *n* **(a)** (*for foot*) chaussure *f*, soulier *m*; **a pair of shoes** une paire de chaussures; **lace-up shoes** richelieus *m*; **high-heeled shoes** chaussures à talons hauts; **to put on/take off one's shoes** se chausser/se déchausser, mettre/

enlever ses chaussures; **to shake** *or* **quake in one's shoes** être dans ses petits souliers; *Fig* **to step into sb's shoes** prendre la place de qn, succéder à qn; *Fig* **I wouldn't like to be in his shoes** je ne voudrais pas être à sa place; **put yourself in my shoes** mets-toi à ma place; *Fig* **to be waiting for dead men's shoes** attendre la mort de qn (*pour le remplacer*); **s. leather** cuir *m* pour chaussures; *Fig* **you might as well save your s. leather** c'est inutile que vous y alliez; **I've worn out a lot of s. leather** j'ai marché des kilomètres; **s. rack** porte-chaussures *m inv*

(b) (*horseshoe*) fer *m* à cheval; **to cast** *or* **throw a s.** (*of horse*) perdre un fer, se déferrer

(c) *Aut* (*of brake*) mâchoire *m*; *Aut* **s. expander** écarteur *m* de mâchoire

(d) (*of sledge etc*) patin *m*

shoe[2] *vt* (*pt, pp* **shod** [ʃɒd]; *prp* **shoeing**) **(a)** (*provide with shoes*) chausser; **to be well shod** être bien chaussé **(b)** (*pt, pp also* **shoed**) (*horse*) ferrer

shoeblack [ˈʃuːblæk] *n* cireur *m*

shoebrush [ˈʃuːbrʌʃ] *n* brosse *f* à chaussures

shoe cream *n* cirage *m* en crème

shoehorn[1] [ˈʃuːhɔːn] *n* chausse-pied *m*, *pl* chausse-pieds

shoehorn[2] *vt Fig* **we can s. a few more in** on peut en faire tenir encore quelques-uns

shoeing [ˈʃuːɪŋ] *n* (*of horse*) ferrage *m*, ferrure *f*

shoelace [ˈʃuːleɪs] *n* lacet *m* (de chaussure); *Fig* **he's not fit to tie your shoelaces** il n'est pas digne de cirer vos chaussures

shoemaker [ˈʃuːmeɪkər] *n* (*who makes shoes*) fabricant *m* de chaussures; (*who makes and sells shoes*) chausseur *m*; (*shoe repairer*) cordonnier *m*; *Prov* **let the s. stick to his last** cordonnier, mêlez-vous de votre pantoufle!

shoemender [ˈʃuːmendər] *n* cordonnier *m*

shoe polish *n* cirage *m*

shoe-polishing machine *n* machine *f* à cirer les chaussures

shoe repairs *npl* cordonnerie *f*

shoeshine [ˈʃuːʃaɪn] *n US* **(a)** (*action*) cirage *m* de chaussures **(b)** (*person*) cireur *m* de chaussures; **s. boy** petit cireur de chaussures

shoeshop [ˈʃuːʃɒp] *n* magasin *m* de chaussures

shoestring [ˈʃuːstrɪŋ] *n* lacet *m* de chaussure; *Fig F* **on a s.** à peu de frais; *F* **they're doing it on a s.** ils tirent sur la corde; *F* **a film made on a s. (budget)** un film réalisé à peu de frais

shoe tree *n* embauchoir *m*

shone *see* **shine**[2]

shoo [ʃuː] *int* (*to animal, children*) allez!, ouste!

▸ **shoo away, shoo off** *vtsep* (*scare away*) (*chickens etc*) chasser

shoo-in *n Am* **to be a s. for President/the Championship** être le vainqueur assuré pour les éléctions présidentielles/les championnats

shook *see* **shake**[2]

shoot[1] [ʃuːt] *n* **(a)** *Bot* (*plant*) pousse *f*; (*on a plant*) rejet *m*, scion *m*; (*of vine*) sarment *m*, pampre *m*; **young** *or* **tender s.** tendrille *f*, tendron *m* **(b)** *Cin, TV* tournage *m*; **he has a s. all afternoon** il a une prise de vue tout l'après-midi **(c)** = **chute** **(d)** (*shooting contest*) concours *m* de tir; *esp Br* (*hunting party*) partie *f* de chasse; (*land*) chasse *f* gardée **(e)** *F* **the whole (bang) s.** (*everything*) tout le bazar **(f)** *F Euph* **oh s.!** miel!

shoot[2] (*pt, pp* **shot** [ʃɒt]) **1** *vi* **(a)** (*move rapidly*) se précipiter; (*of star*) filer; **he shot into the room** il est entré dans la pièce en éclair *ou* en trombe; **to s. forward** foncer *ou* s'élancer à toute allure; **to s. ahead** prendre la tête; **he's always shooting across to New York** il va sans arrêt à New York; **the cat shot out of his arms** le chat bondit de ses bras

(b) (*of pain*) élancer; **I've got pains shooting through my shoulder** j'ai des élancements dans l'épaule

(c) (*of tree, bud etc*) pousser, bourgeonner; (*of plant*) germer

(d) (*fire gun*) tirer; (*hunt*) chasser; **don't s.!** ne tirez pas!; **to s. straight** bien viser; **to s. at sb/sth** tirer *ou* faire feu sur qn/qch; **to be shot at** se faire tirer dessus; *Fig* **to s. from the hip** parler sans réfléchir

(e) *Cin* tourner; *Phot* (*take photo*) prendre la/une photo

(f) *Fb, Hockey* shooter

(g) *Am F* **s.!** (*say what you want to*) allez-y!

2 *vt* **(a)** (*pass rapidly*) (*rapids*) franchir; *Aut* **to s. the (traffic) lights** griller *ou* brûler le feu rouge

(b) (*move rapidly*) (*bolt*) pousser; *Fishing* (*net*) jeter; *Fig* **he had shot his bolt** il avait brûlé ses dernières cartouches; **we were shot out of the car** nous avons été éjectés de la voiture; *Am F* **to s. the breeze** (*chat*) bavarder; (*exaggerate*) en rajouter; *F* **to s. a line** (*boast*) faire du baratin; **he's just shooting a line** ce qu'il raconte, c'est du baratin

(c) (*unleash*) (*arrow*) décocher; (*projectile*) lancer; (*bullet*) tirer; *Fb* **he shot the ball into the net** il a envoyé le ballon dans le filet; **to s. a glance at sb** lancer *ou* décocher un regard à qn; **the chimney shot a shower of sparks into the air** la cheminée envoya un jet d'étincelles dans l'air; *F* **to s. heroin** se shooter à l'héroïne; *Sl* **to s. one's load** *or* **wad** (*ejaculate*) décharger

(d) (*person*) (*hit with bullet*) atteindre d'un coup de feu; (*kill*) tuer d'un coup de feu; (*wound*) blesser d'un coup de feu; (*spy*) abattre; (*partridge, woodsnipe etc*) tirer; (*hunt*) (*game*) chasser; **I've been shot** j'ai reçu une balle; **a man was shot (and killed) yesterday** un homme a été tué par balle hier; **everybody remembers the day Kennedy was shot** tout le monde se souvient du jour où Kennedy a été assassiné; **to be shot in the arm** être atteint au bras; **the robbers tried to s. their way out** les voleurs tentèrent de se sauver en tirant des coups de feu; **to s. sb dead** tuer qn par balle; **to s. sb through the head** tirer une balle dans la tête de qn; **she was shot through the heart** elle a été tuée d'une balle en plein cœur; **to s. oneself in the foot** se tirer dans le pied; *Fig* (*spoil one's chances*) se faire du tort à soi-même; **to s. holes in sb's argument/case** démonter les arguments/la théorie de qn; **to s. sb/sth to pieces** mettre qn/qch en pièces; *Mil* **to be (court-martialled and) shot** être passé par les armes, être fusillé; *Fig F* **I'll be shot** je suis foutu; *Fig F* **you'll get me shot** tu vas me faire avoir des ennuis

(e) *Cin* (*film*) tourner; (*scene, actor*) filmer; *Phot* photographier; *TV, Cin* **to s. sound** effectuer une prise de son

(f) **to s. dice** lancer les dés; **to s. pool** faire une partie de billard; *Fb* **to s. the ball into the net** envoyer le ballon dans les filets; **to s. a goal/a basket** marquer un but; *Golf* **to s. a 64** faire le parcours en 64 coups

▸ **shoot back** **1** *vi* **(a)** (*fire back*) riposter **(b)** (*into its shell, into office*) disparaître **2** *vtsep* (*return quickly*) envoyer; **the candidate shot back his answers** le candidat répondait du tac au tac

▸ **shoot down** *vtsep* **(a)** (*cause to fall by gunfire etc*) (*person*) abattre (par balle); (*plane*) abattre, descendre **(b)** (*show to be wrong or unacceptable*) (*person, argument, proposal etc*) descendre; **she was shot down in flames when ...** elle a été descendue en flammes lorsque ...

▸ **shoot off** **1** *vi* **(a)** (*leave quickly*) partir comme une flèche; **I've got to s. off now** il faut que je me sauve **(b)** *Sl* (*ejaculate*) décharger **2** *vtsep* **(a)** (*remove by bullet or shell*) emporter par une balle/par un obus; **he had a foot shot off** il a eu un pied fauché par un obus **(b)** (*fire*) **she shot off a few rounds into the darkness** elle a tiré dans le noir; **he shot off an entire magazine** il a vidé son chargeur; *Fig* **to s. off a letter/memo to sb** envoyer une lettre/un mémo à qn; *Sl* **to s. one's mouth off** (*be indiscreet*) ouvrir sa grande gueule (**about sth** à propos de qch)

▸ **shoot out** **1** *vi* (*emerge quickly*) (*of water, flames*) jaillir; **to s. out of a side street** déboucher brusquement d'une rue latérale **2** *vtsep* **(a)** (*extend quickly*) (*sparks etc*) lancer; **the snake shot out its tongue** le serpent a dardé sa langue **(b)** (*extinguish, destroy etc with gunshots*) (*light, window*) tirer dans; **his right eye had been shot out** il avait perdu l'œil droit dans une fusillade **(c)** *F* **to s. it out** régler ses comptes à coups de feu

▸ **shoot up** **1** *vtsep* **they shot the bar up** ils ont mitraillé le bar; **he was badly shot up in the war** il a été sérieusement blessé à la guerre; **he's been shot up** il a reçu des balles (dans la peau) **2** *vi* **(a)** (*of plants, children*) pousser; (*of rocket*) s'élever; (*of prices*) monter en flèche; (*of fountain etc*) jaillir; **he's really shot up!** (*he's grown*) qu'est-ce qu'il a poussé!; **new tower blocks are shooting up all over the city** de nouvelles tours poussent dans toute la ville **(b)** *Sl* (*with drugs*) se shooter

shooter [ˈʃuːtər] *n Sl* (*gun*) flingue *m*, feu *m*

shooting [ˈʃuːtɪŋ] **1** *adj* **s. pains** douleurs *fpl* lancinantes

2 *n* **(a)** (*gunfire*) coups *mpl* de feu; (*killing*) fusillade *f*; (*of spies, revolutionaries etc*) mise *f* à mort; (*hunting*) chasse *f*; **there was no s.** (*in robbery etc*) aucun coup de feu n'a été tiré; **there was a s.** il y a eu une fusillade; **anyone who witnessed the s. is asked to contact the police** tout témoin de la fusillade est prié de prendre contact avec la police; **pigeon s.** tir *m* aux pigeons; **s. gallery** (stand *m* de) tir; **the s. season** la saison de la chasse

(b) *Cin* (*of film*) tournage *m*; **s. starts next week on her new film** le tournage de son nouveau film commence la semaine prochaine; **s. angle** angle *m* de prise de vue; **s. plan** plan *m* de travail; **s. script** découpage *m* (technique)

shooting brake *n Br Aut* break *m*

shooting match *n* concours *m* de tir; *Fig F* **the whole s.** (*things*) tout le bazar; (*people*) le ban et l'arrière-ban

shooting party *n* partie *f* de chasse

shooting range *n* champ *m* de tir
shooting star *n* étoile *f* filante
shooting stick *n* canne-siège *f, pl* cannes-sièges
shoot-out *n F* échange *m* de coups de feu, fusillade *f*; **they settled it with a s.** ils ont réglé leurs comptes à coups de feu
shop[1] [ʃɒp] *n* **(a)** *Com* (*building*) magasin *m*; (*small*) boutique *f*; **I'm just going down to the shops** je sors faire des courses; **the ones you buy in shops** ceux que l'on achète en magasin; **you can't get these in the shops** on ne les trouve pas en magasin; **the new book should reach the shops in July** le nouveau livre devrait être en vente en juillet; **grocer's s.** épicerie *f*; **baker's s.** boulangerie *f*; **shoe s.** magasin de chaussures; **duty-free s.** boutique hors taxes; **mobile s.** boutique ambulante; *Old-fashioned* **s.!** il y a quelqu'un?; **to set up s.** (*to open a shop*) ouvrir un magasin; (*to set up as shopkeeper*) s'établir comme commerçant, -ante; **to set up s. as a hairdresser** ouvrir un salon de coiffure; **to set up s. on one's own** se mettre à son compte; **to keep (a) s.** tenir un magasin; **to mind the s.** garder le magasin; *Fig* assurer la permanence; *also Fig* **to shut up s.** fermer boutique; (*at the end of the day*) fermer le magasin; *Fig F* **you've come to the wrong s.** vous vous trompez de porte; *F* **he was staggering about all over the s.** il titubait fortement; **they're all over the s. on defence policy** leur politique de défense n'est absolument pas cohérente; **my notes are all over the s.** c'est la pagaille dans mes notes; **the defence was all over the s.** c'était la pagaille dans la défense; **s. front** devanture *f* de magasin; **s. window** vitrine *f*; (*display*) étalage *m*; **in the s. window** dans la *ou* en vitrine; *Mktg* **s.'s own brand** marque *f* de magasin *ou* de détail(lant)
(b) *F* (*act of shopping*) courses *fpl*, shopping *m*; **I do my big s. on a Friday** je fais mes grosses courses le vendredi
(c) *Ind etc* (*workshop*) atelier *m*; **assembly s.** atelier de montage; **pattern s.** atelier de modelage; **repair s.** atelier de réparations; **carpenter's s.** atelier de menuiserie; **closed s.** = entreprise *f* qui n'admet que du personnel appartenant à un certain syndicat; **the s. floor** l'atelier; (*workforce*) les ouvriers *mpl*
(d) *F* **to talk s.** parler boutique
shop[2] **(-pp-) 1** *vi* **to s., to go shopping** (aller) faire ses courses; (*for food*) aller aux provisions; (*at market*) aller faire son marché; **to go shopping for clothes** aller acheter des vêtements, *Can* magasiner **2** *vt Br Sl* (*betray*) (*person*) dénoncer
▶ **shop around** *vi* comparer les prix
shop assistant *n* vendeur, -euse (de magasin), employé, -ée de magasin
shopfitter [ˈʃɒpfɪtər] *n* installateur *m ou* agenceur *m* de magasins
shop foreman *n* chef *m* d'atelier
shopgirl [ˈʃɒpgɜːl] *n Old-fashioned* vendeuse *f*, employée *f* de magasin
shop-in-shop *n Com* boutiquage *m*, magasin *m* à l'intérieur d'une grande surface
shopkeeper [ˈʃɒpkiːpər] *n* commerçant, -ante
shoplifter [ˈʃɒplɪftər] *n* voleur, -euse à l'étalage
shoplifting [ˈʃɒplɪftɪŋ] *n* vol *m* à l'étalage
shopman, *pl* **-men** [ˈʃɒpmən] *n US* mécanicien *m* (*dans un atelier de réparations*)
shopper [ˈʃɒpər] *n* **(a)** (*person*) **streets crowded with shoppers** des rues pleines de gens qui font leurs courses; **for the convenience of shoppers** (*sign in shop*) pour mieux servir nos clients **(b)** *F* (*bag*) sac *m* à provisions
shopping [ˈʃɒpɪŋ] *n* courses *fpl*; **to do one's/the s.** faire ses/les courses; (*for food*) aller aux provisions; (*at market*) faire son marché; **I hate s.** (*for food etc*) je déteste faire les courses; (*for clothes, wandering round shops*) je déteste faire du shopping; **to do one's Christmas s.** faire ses achats de Noël; **I had a lot of heavy s.** j'étais lourdement chargé d'achats; **I haven't got much s. to do** je n'ai pas beaucoup de courses à faire; **s. bag/basket** sac *m*/panier *m* à provisions; **Saturday is my main s. day** le samedi est le jour où je fais mes grosses courses; **only three s. days to Christmas** il ne reste plus que trois jours pour faire les courses avant Noël; **s. street** rue *f* commerçante; **my weekly s. trip** mes courses hebdomadaires; **for my next s. trip** la prochaine fois que j'irai faire les courses
shopping arcade *n* galerie *f* marchande
shopping centre *n* (*district*) magasins *mpl*; (*complex of shops*) centre *m* commercial
shopping channel *n TV* chaîne *f* de télé-achat
shopping list *n* liste *f* de commissions; *Fig* liste de revendications
shopping mall *n* centre *m* commercial
shopping plaza *n* centre *m* commercial
shopping precinct *n* centre *m* commercial
shopping trolley *n* caddie *m*®
shopsoiled [ˈʃɒpsɔɪld] *adj Br* (*article*) défraîchi; (*display goods*) qui a fait l'étalage
shop steward *n* porte-parole *m inv* des ouvriers, délégué *m* syndical
shoptalk [ˈʃɒptɔːk] *n F* **no s., OK?** on ne parle pas métier *ou* affaires *ou F* boutique, d'accord?
shopwalker [ˈʃɒpwɔːkər] *n Br* chef *m* de rayon
shopworn [ˈʃɒpwɔːn] *adj Am* = **shopsoiled**
shore[1] [ʃɔːr] *n* (*coast*) côte *f*; (*shoreline*) rivage *m*; (*of sea, lake, river*) bord *m*; **on the s.** sur le rivage; (*on beach*) sur la plage; (*by sea*) au bord de la mer; *Naut* **on s.** à terre; **to go on s.** se rendre à terre; (*disembark*) débarquer; *Lit* **distant shores** de lointains rivages; **she rarely visits our shores** elle visite rarement nos contrées; **to keep rabies from our shores** empêcher la rage d'atteindre nos côtes
shore[2] *n Constr etc* étai *m*, étançon *m*
shore[3] *vt* = **shore up**
▶ **shore up** *vtsep* (*support*) (*house, wall*) étayer, étançonner; *Fig* (*government*) étayer, consolider
shore excursion *n* excursion *f* (lors d'une escale)
shore leave *n Naut* permission *f* à terre
shoreline [ˈʃɔːlaɪn] *n* rivage *m*; (*by sea*) côte *f*
shoreward(s) [ˈʃɔːwəd(z)] *adv* vers la terre
shorn[1] [ʃɔːn] *adj* **(a)** (*head*) rasé **(b)** (*sheep*) tondu
shorn[2] *see* **shear**
short[1] [ʃɔːt] **1** *adj* **(a)** (*physically*) court; (*person*) petit, de petite taille; **to be s. in the arm/leg** avoir les bras courts/les jambes courtes; (*of garment*) être court au niveau des bras/des jambes; **(at) a s. distance from the station** à peu de distance de la gare; **to have s. hair** avoir les cheveux courts; **to go by the shortest road, to go the shortest way** aller par le chemin le plus court; **a s. history of France** un précis d'histoire de France; **s. back and sides** (*haircut*) coupe *f* dégagée autour des oreilles; *Horseracing etc* **s. odds** *or* **price** faible cote *f*; **at s. range** à courte portée; **s. trousers** culottes *fpl* courtes
(b) (*in time*) court, bref; **to take quick s. breaths** respirer à petits coups rapides; **the days are getting shorter** les jours raccourcissent; **s. and sweet** court mais bon; **that was s. and sweet!** c'était court mais c'était bien!; **in s.** (*to sum up*) bref, en résumé, en somme; **Bill is s. for William** Bill est le diminutif de William; **the s. answer is 'no'** en deux mots, la réponse est non; **a s. drink** un petit verre; **we've just got time for a s. game** nous avons juste le temps de faire une petite partie; **at s. intervals** à intervalles rapprochés; **to have a s. memory** avoir la mémoire courte; **s. order cook** = cuisinier *m* qui prépare les plats au fur et à mesure des commandes; **s. syllable** syllabe *f* brève; **to have a s. temper** s'emporter facilement; **for a s. time** pour un petit moment; **a s. time ago** il y a peu de temps; *Ind* **to be on s. time** être en chômage partiel; *Ling* **s. vowel** voyelle *f* brève; **to make s. work of sth** (*problem, difficulty*) résoudre qch en un clin d'œil; **he made s. work of his meal** il a avalé son repas en une minute; **you sure made s. work of that!** tu n'y es pas allé par quatre chemins!; **he made s. work of his opponent** il s'est débarrassé de son adversaire en un rien de temps
(c) (*abrupt*) **to be s. with sb** être cassant avec qn; **he was very s. with me** il a été très brusque avec moi
(d) (*insufficient, lacking*) (*weight, measure etc*) insuffisant; **to give sb s. measure** donner à qn moins que la quantité que l'on fait payer; **money is very s.** *or* **is in very s. supply** on est à court d'argent; **water is in s. supply** l'eau se fait rare; **it is two francs s.** il manque deux francs; **I am twenty francs s.** il me manque vingt francs; **50 s. of the thousand** mille moins 50; **to be s. of sth** (*of person*) être à court de qch, manquer de qch; **I'm a bit s. of cash** je suis un peu à court d'argent; **the country is s. of engineers** le pays manque d'ingénieurs; *F Hum* **he's a few sandwiches s. of a picnic** il a une case vide; **he's a bit s. on common sense** il manque un peu de bon sens; *Fin* **s. payment** moins-perçu *m*
(e) (*less than*) **little** *or* **not far s. of it** peu s'en faut; **he is not far s. of thirty** il frise la trentaine; **it is little s. of folly** c'est de la folie (pure); **it was nothing s. of a masterpiece** ce n'était rien moins qu'un chef-d'œuvre; **nothing s. of violence would compel him** il n'y a que la violence qui l'y obligerait
(f) *St Exch* court, en position courte; *Fin* **s. bills, bills at s. date** billets *mpl ou* traites *fpl* à courte échéance; **s. position** position *f* vendeur; **s. sale** vente *f* à découvert
2 *n* **(a)** *Cin* (*short film*) court métrage *m*, court *m*
(b) (*drink*) alcool *m* fort
(c) *El F* (*short circuit*) court-circuit *m*, *pl* courts-circuits

(d) *(in prosody) (syllable)* brève *f*; *Ling (vowel)* voyelle *f* brève

3 *adv* **(a) hair cut s.** cheveux coupés court

(b) to stop s. s'arrêter (tout) net; *F* s'arrêter pile; **to stop s. of doing sth** se retenir de faire qch; **it just stops s. of being criminal** c'est à la limite de la criminalité; **she stopped s. of actually calling him a liar** pour un peu, elle le traitait de menteur; **to cut sb s.** couper la parole à qn; *F* **to be caught s.** *(need to relieve oneself)* être pris d'un besoin pressant; *(not have enough money)* être à court d'argent

(c) to go s. se priver; **to go s. of sth** se priver de qch; **we're running s. of ...** *(supplies etc)* on est presqu'à court de ...; **we are running s. of provisions, our provisions are running s.** nos vivres vont bientôt s'épuiser; **to fall s.** *(of arrow, bomb etc)* ne pas arriver jusqu'à la cible; **to fall s. of sb's expectations** décevoir qn; **to fall s. of one's duty** manquer à son devoir; **it falls far s. of what we need** c'est loin de suffire à nos besoins; **s. of a miracle we are ruined** à moins d'un miracle, nous sommes perdus; **there's not much we can do s. of selling the house** il n'y a pas grand-chose à faire à part vendre la maison

(d) *Fig* **to sell sb s.** *(betray)* trahir qn; *(trick)* rouler qn; **to sell oneself s.** ne pas se montrer à sa juste valeur

(e) *St Exch* **to buy s.** acheter à court terme; **to sell s.** vendre à découvert

short[2] *vti El F* = **short-circuit[2]**

shortage [ˈʃɔːtɪdʒ] *n (of money, food etc)* manque *m*, pénurie *f*; **the paper s.** la crise du papier; **we have constant staff shortages** nous manquons constamment de personnel; **there is no s. of applicants** on ne manque pas de candidats

short-arse *n Br Sl* nabot *m*; **he/she is a little s.** il/elle est un peu court(e) sur pattes, *Pej* il/elle a le cul un peu bas

shortbread, shortcake [ˈʃɔːtbred, -keɪk] *n Culin* = sablé *m*

short break *n (holiday)* mini-séjour *m*

short-change *vt (intentionally)* voler *(en rendant la monnaie)*; *(accidentally)* ne pas rendre assez de monnaie à; *Fig (cheat)* posséder

short-circuit[1] *n El* court-circuit *m*, *pl* courts-circuits

short-circuit[2] **1** *vt El; Fig* court-circuiter **2** *vi El* se mettre en court-circuit

shortcode [ˈʃɔːtkəʊd] *n Telecom* code *m* abrégé; **s. dialling** numérotation *f* abrégée

shortcoming [ˈʃɔːtkʌmɪŋ] *n (flaw) (usu pl)* **shortcomings** défauts *mpl*, imperfections *fpl*

shortcrust [ˈʃɔːtkrʌst] *adj Culin* **s. pastry** pâte *f* brisée

shortcut [ˈʃɔːtˈkʌt] *n* raccourci *m*; *Fig* **don't try to take shortcuts** n'essayez pas d'aller trop vite; **there are no shortcuts** on ne peut pas aller plus vite que la musique; **useful shortcuts** des trucs; *Comptr* **s. key** touche *f* de raccourci

short-dated *adj Fin (bill)* à courte échéance; *(paper)* court

shorten [ˈʃɔːt(ə)n] **1** *vt (skirt etc)* raccourcir; *(text, task)* abréger; *(stay)* écourter; **Albert is often shortened to Bert** on utilise souvent le diminutif Bert à la place d'Albert; *Culin* **to s. pastry** travailler la pâte avec une matière grasse **2** *vi (of days etc)* raccourcir

shortening [ˈʃɔːtnɪŋ] *n* **(a)** *(of days)* raccourcissement *m* **(b)** *(of text)* raccourcissement *m*, abrégement *m* **(c)** *Culin* matière *f* grasse

shortfall [ˈʃɔːtfɔːl] *n* manque *m*; *(financial)* déficit *m*

short-focus lens *n Phot* objectif *m* à courte focale

shorthaired [ˈʃɔːtheəd] *adj (person)* aux cheveux courts; *(animal)* à poil ras

shorthand [ˈʃɔːthænd] *n (writing system)* sténo(graphie) *f*; **to take a speech down in s.** sténographier un discours, prendre un discours en sténo; **s. typing** sténodactylographie *f*; **s. typist** sténodactylo(graphe) *mf*; **s. writer** *or* **reporter** sténographe *mf*; **s. writing** écriture *f* sténographique; *Fig* **this is s. for ...** c'est l'abréviation de ..., en bref, ça signifie ...

shorthanded [ʃɔːtˈhændɪd] *adj* **to be s.** manquer de personnel

short-haul *adj (flight, route)* court-courrier; **s. aircraft** (avion *m)* court-courrier *m*

shorthorn [ˈʃɔːthɔːn] *n* shorthorn *m*

shortish [ˈʃɔːtɪʃ] *adj* assez *ou* plutôt court; *(person)* courtaud

short-legged *adj* aux jambes courtes

shortlist[1] [ˈʃɔːtlɪst] *vt Br* sélectionner, retenir la candidature de; **to s. a candidate** retenir une candidature *(en vue d'une sélection ultérieure)*; **you've been shortlisted** on a retenu votre candidature

shortlist[2] *n* liste *f* des candidats retenus

short-lived *adj (joy, triumph etc)* bref, éphémère, de courte durée

shortly [ˈʃɔːtlɪ] *adv* **(a)** *(soon)* bientôt, prochainement; *(in a couple of minutes)* sous peu; **s. after(wards)** *(soon afterwards)* peu (de temps) après; **President Smith who was s. to be** *or* **would s. be re-elected** le président Smith qui allait bientôt être réélu **(b)** *(abruptly) (to answer etc)* brusquement, sèchement

shortness [ˈʃɔːtnɪs] *n* **(a)** *(physical) (of arm, skirt)* peu *m* de longueur; *(of person)* petite taille *f* **(b)** *(in time) (of life)* brièveté *f*, courte durée *f*; **s. of memory** manque *m* de mémoire **(c)** *(abruptness)* brusquerie *f* **(d)** *(lack) (of supplies etc)* manque *m*, insuffisance *f*

short pastry *n Culin* pâte *f* brisée

short-range *adj Mil* à courte portée; *(forecast)* à court terme

shorts [ʃɔːts] *npl* [ⓘA10,e] *(short trousers)* short *m*; *Am (underwear)* caleçon *m*; **a pair of s.** un short

shortsheet [ˈʃɔːtʃiːt] *vt US (bed)* mettre en portefeuille

shortsighted [ʃɔːtˈsaɪtɪd] *adj* **(a)** *Opt* myope **(b)** *Fig (approach etc)* imprévoyant; **that was very s. of you/him** ça n'était pas faire preuve de beaucoup de prévoyance

shortsightedness [ʃɔːtˈsaɪtɪdnɪs] *n* **(a)** *Opt* myopie *f* **(b)** *Fig (of approach etc)* imprévoyance *f*

short-staffed [ʃɔːtˈstɑːft] *adj* à court de personnel; **to be s.** manquer de personnel

short-stay car park *n* parking *m* courte durée

short story *n* nouvelle *f*

short-tempered *adj* vif, d'un caractère emporté

short-term *adj (prisoner)* qui purge une peine de prison de courte durée; *(contract)* de courte durée; *(solution, memory)*, *Fin* à court terme; **s. borrowings** emprunts *mpl* à court terme; **s. loan** emprunt à court terme

short-termism [ʃɔːtˈtɜːmɪz(ə)m] *n* politique *f* du court terme

short-time *adj* **s. worker/working** chômeur *m*/chômage *m* partiel

short wave *n* ondes *fpl* courtes

short-winded *adj* au souffle court; **to be s.** manquer de souffle

shorty [ˈʃɔːtɪ] *n F* petit *m*, petite *f*; **come on, s.!** allez, le petit!

shot[1] [ʃɒt] *n* **(a)** *(act of firing, sound)* coup *m* (de feu); **pistol s.** coup de pistolet; **warning s.** coup d'avertissement; *Naut* coup de semonce; **to fire a s.** tirer un coup de feu; **without firing a s.** sans tirer un (seul) coup de feu; **parting s.** *(remark)* remarque *f ou* réplique *f* qu'on lance en partant, dernière remarque; **he's a good s.** c'est un bon tireur; *F* **a big s.** un type important, un grand manitou, *Sl* une grosse légume; **a s. across the bows** un tir d'avertissement; *Fig* un avertissement; **to fire a s. across the bows** tirer un coup en guise d'avertissement; *Fig* donner un avertissement

(b) *(inv in pl) (projectiles) (from shotgun)* plomb *m*; **bird s.** cendrée *f*; *Fig* **like a s.** *(to leave)* comme une flèche; *(to accept)* d'emblée, sans hésitation; *Metal* **lead s.** grenaille *f* de plomb

(c) *Sp (of shot putter)* poids *m*; **to put the s.** lancer le poids

(d) *Sp (in tennis, golf etc)* coup *m*; *(in football, hockey)* shoot *m*; **good s.!** bien joué!; *Tennis etc* **drop s.** amortie *f*; **passing s.** passing-shot *m*; **to make a long s.** *(aim from a distance)* viser de loin; *Fig (guess wildly)* deviner au hasard; *(take a risk)* prendre un (gros) risque; **not by a long s.** il s'en faut de beaucoup; *Fig* **to take a s. in the dark** *(make a wild guess)* donner une réponse complètement au hasard; *F* y aller au pifomètre; **I'm going to take a s. in the dark and say 1,000** je vais donner un chiffre au hasard, disons 1 000; *Fig* **to call the shots** prendre les décisions; *Fig* **<u>they</u> call the shots** c'est eux qui décident

(e) *Phot* photo *f*; *Cin* plan *m*, prise *f* de vue; **you can get a good s. of the castle from here** d'ici vous prendrez bien le château; **high angle s.** plongée *f*; *TV, Cin* **s. list** liste *f* des prises (de vue)

(f) *F (injection)* une piqûre *f*; *F (drink) (of brandy etc)* petit verre *m*; **a s. in the arm** *(injection)* une piqûre au bras; *Fig (stimulation)* un coup de fouet; **to give sb a s.** faire une piqûre à qn

(g) *Fig (attempt)* **I'll have a s. at it/at doing it** je vais essayer *ou* tenter le coup; **I had a s. at learning Swahili** j'ai essayé d'apprendre le swahili; **it's worth having a s. at** ça vaut le coup; **her second s. at the presidency** sa deuxième tentative pour obtenir la présidence; **she made** *or* **had a good s. at it** elle a fait tout ce qu'elle pouvait; *esp Am F* **give it your best s.** fais de ton mieux

(h) *F (turn)* tour *m*; **it's your s.** *(in game)* à vous de jouer; **to have a s. of sth** essayer qch; **it's my s. next** c'est mon tour; **you've had two shots already** tu as déjà essayé deux fois

shot[2] *adj* **(a) to get s. of sb/sth** se débarrasser de qn/qch; **to be s. of sb/sth** être débarrassé de qn/qch **(b) s. silk** soie *f* changeante

shotgun [ˈʃɒtgʌn] *n* fusil *m* de chasse; *TV, Cin* **s. mike** micro *m* canon; *F* **s. wedding** mariage *m* forcé

shot put *n Sp* poids *m*, lancer *m* du poids

shot putter *n Sp* lanceur, -euse de poids

should [ʃʊd] *modal aux v* [①A56-7,b] (a) (*duty or command*) **you s. do it at once** vous devriez le faire tout de suite; **you s. have come earlier** vous auriez dû arriver plus tôt; **you/he/** *etc* **s. not have gone** il ne fallait pas y aller; **a present?, oh you shouldn't have!** un cadeau?, vous n'auriez pas dû!; **it was an accident that s. have been foreseen** c'était un accident à prévoir; **you s. have seen her!** il fallait la voir!, si vous l'aviez vue!; **you shouldn't laugh at him** vous avez tort de vous moquer de lui; **I shouldn't do that if I were you** je ne ferais pas ça si j'étais toi; **I don't remember – well you s.** je ne m'en souviens pas – eh bien tu devrais

(b) (*expression of opinion*) **she s. have arrived by this time** elle devrait être arrivée à l'heure qu'il est; **that s. suit you!** voilà qui fera sans doute votre affaire!; **this weather s. be ideal for anglers** ce temps devrait être idéal pour les pêcheurs; **what s. I have said?** qu'est-ce que j'aurais dû dire?; *Iron* **I s. worry!** (*I don't worry about it*) ce n'est pas mon affaire!; *Iron* **you s. worry about getting fat!** tu ne risques pas de grossir!; *Iron* **you s. complain!** tu n'as aucune raison de te plaindre!

(c) (*exclamatory, in rhetorical questions*) **why s. you suspect me?** pourquoi me soupçonner?; **how s. I not be happy?** comment ne serais-je pas heureux?; **who s. I meet but Martin!** (et) voilà que je rencontre Martin!

(d) [①A52,b] (*in subordinate clauses*) **he ordered that they s. be released** il ordonna qu'on les relâchât; **she insisted that he s. wear his hair short** elle a exigé qu'il porte les cheveux courts; **I didn't want to, but he told me I s.** je ne voulais pas, mais il m'a dit que je devais le faire

(e) [①A51,13] (*in conditional clauses*) **if he s. come** *or Fml* **s. he come, let me know** s'il vient, faites-le-moi savoir; **s. the occasion arise, s. it (so) happen** le cas échéant; **in case she s. not be there** au cas où elle ne serait pas là

(f) **my holiday was over, the next day I s. be far away** mes vacances étaient finies, le lendemain je serais bien loin

(g) [①A51,13] (*in the main clause of conditional sentences*) **we s. come if we were invited** nous viendrions si on nous invitait; **had you written to me I s. have answered you** si vous m'aviez écrit, je vous aurais répondu

(h) (*in softened affirmation*) **I s. like a drink** je prendrais bien quelque chose; **I s. have thought that you would have known better** j'aurais pensé que vous auriez été plus avisé; **I shouldn't be surprised (if…)** cela ne me surprendrait pas (que … + *pr sub*)

shoulder¹ [ˈʃəʊldər] *n* (*of person*), *Culin* épaule *f*; (*of hill etc*) épaulement *m*; (*of mountain*) contrefort *m*; **round shoulders** dos *m* rond *ou* voûté; **he's got broad shoulders** il est large d'épaules; *Fig* il a bon dos; **too tight across the shoulders** (*of coat etc*) trop étroit de carrure; **off-the-s. dress** robe *f* dégageant les épaules; **slung across** *or* **over the s.** (*bag, rifle etc*) en bandoulière; **to look over one's s.** vérifier si on est suivi; **to tell sb sth straight from the s.** dire qch carrément *ou* brutalement à qn; **to have a good head on one's shoulders** avoir la tête sur les épaules; **to rub shoulders with millionaires/film stars** côtoyer des millionnaires/stars du cinéma; **to lay the blame on sb's shoulders** rejeter la faute sur qn; *F* mettre la faute sur le dos de qn; *Fig* **to put one's s. to the wheel** se mettre à l'œuvre avec énergie; **to stand head and shoulders above the rest** (*be far taller*) dépasser les autres d'une tête; *Fig* (*be far better*) surpasser tous les autres; **s. high** à la hauteur des épaules; **to carry sb s. high** porter qn en triomphe; **s. to s.** (*side by side*) côte à côte, épaule contre épaule; **hard s.** (*on road*) bas-côté *m*; **soft s.** (*on road*) accotement non stabilisé; **s. belt** baudrier *m*; **s. braid** fourragère *f*; **s. harness** *Av* bretelles *fpl*; *TV, Cin* harnais *m* caméra; **s. knot** aiguillette *f*; *TV, Cin* **s. pod** crosse d'épaule *f*

shoulder² *vt* (a) (*push*) pousser avec l'épaule; **to s. one's way through the crowd** se frayer un passage à travers la foule à coups d'épaule; **to s. sb out of the way** *or* **aside** écarter *ou* repousser qn d'un coup d'épaule; **she shouldered the door open** elle ouvrit la porte d'un coup d'épaule (b) (*put on shoulder*) (*object*) mettre sur l'épaule; **to s. one's gun** mettre son fusil sur l'épaule; *Fig* **to s. the responsibility** endosser la responsabilité; *Mil* **to s. arms** se mettre au port d'armes; **s. arms!** portez armes!

shoulder bag *n* sac *m* en *ou* à bandoulière

shoulder blade *n* omoplate *f*; (*of horse etc*) paleron *m*

shoulder loop *n US Mil etc* patte *f* d'épaule, épaulette *f*

shoulder pad *n* épaulette *f*; *US Fb* protège-épaule *m*, *pl* protège-épaules

shoulder rate *n* (*in tourism*) tarif *m* moyenne saison

shoulder season *n* (*in tourism*) moyenne saison *f*

shoulder strap *n* (*of bag etc*) bretelle *f*, bandoulière *f*; (*on dress, dungarees*) épaulette *f*, bretelle; (*on underwear*) bretelle; *Mil etc* patte *f* d'épaule, épaulette

shout¹ [ʃaʊt] *n* (*of joy, pain etc*) cri *m*; **shouts of laughter** éclats *mpl* de rire; **there was a s. of 'no more taxes!'** on cria 'plus d'impôts!'; *Br F* **it's my s.** (*my turn to buy the drinks*) c'est ma tournée

shout² 1 *vi* crier, pousser un cri/des cris; **there's no need to s.** inutile de crier; **to s. at sb** crier contre qn, *F* crier après qn; **don't s. at me** baisse le ton!, *F* ne me crie pas après!; **to s. for sb** appeler qn de toutes ses forces; **to s. for help** crier *ou* appeler au secours; **to s. to sb to do sth** crier à qn de faire qch; *Fig* **it's nothing to s. about** (*to boast about*) il n'y a pas de quoi se vanter; *Fig* **to have something to s. about** avoir quelque raison de se réjouir **2** *vt* crier; (*insults etc*) vociférer; **to s. oneself hoarse** s'enrouer à force de crier; **look out!, he shouted** attention!, cria-t-il

▶ **shout down** *vtsep* (*person*) huer, conspuer; (*proposal*) conspuer; **the speaker was shouted down** l'orateur n'a pas réussi à se faire entendre

▶ **shout out** 1 *vi* **I shouted out in pain** je hurlais de douleur **2** *vtsep* crier

shouting [ˈʃaʊtɪŋ] *n* cris *mpl*; (*uproar*) clameur *f*; **there was a lot of s.** on criait beaucoup; *Fig* **it's all over bar the s.** c'est dans le sac, c'est du tout cuit

shove¹ [ʃʌv] *n* poussée *f*; (*with shoulder etc*) coup *m*; **to give sth/sb a s.** pousser qch/qn, donner une poussée à qch/à qn; *Fig* **he's lazy, he just needs a little s.** il est paresseux, il a juste besoin qu'on le pousse un peu

shove² 1 *vt* (*person, object*) pousser; **to s. sb/sth along** *or* **forward** pousser qn/qch en avant, faire avancer qn/qch; **to s. sth into a drawer** fourrer qch dans un tiroir **2** *vi* pousser; **stop shoving!** arrêtez de pousser!; **she shoved past me** elle m'a bousculé en passant

▶ **shove around** *vtsep* (a) (*push*) bousculer (b) *F* (*bully*) malmener; **I don't like being shoved around** je n'aime pas passer pour quantité négligeable

▶ **shove aside, shove away** *vtsep* (*push away*) (*person, object*) écarter d'une poussée

▶ **shove off** 1 *vi F* (*leave*) décamper; **s. off!** fiche le camp! **2** *vtsep* (*launch*) (*boat*) pousser au large

▶ **shove over** *vi F* (*move over*) se pousser

shove-halfpenny, -ha'penny [ˈʃʌvheɪpnɪ] *n Br* = (jeu *m* du) galet *m*

shovel¹ [ˈʃʌv(ə)l] *n* pelle *f*; *Constr etc* **power/steam s.** pelle mécanique/à vapeur

shovel² *vt* (**-ll-**) (*coal etc*) pelleter, prendre *ou* jeter à la pelle; *F* **to s. food into one's mouth** s'empiffrer

▶ **shovel away** *vtsep* (*snow etc*) déblayer

▶ **shovel up** *vtsep* (*grain etc*) ramasser *ou* entasser à la pelle

shoveler [ˈʃʌvələr] *n* (*duck*) souchet *m*

shovelful [ˈʃʌvəlfʊl] *n* (*of sand etc*) pelletée *f*

show¹ [ʃəʊ] *n* (a) (*exhibition*) exposition *f*; (*agricultural etc*) concours *m*, comice *m*; (*of animals*) foire *f*; **to be on s.** être exposé; **motor/air s.** salon *m* de l'automobile/de l'aviation; **fashion s.** présentation *f* de collections; **dog s.** exposition canine; **s. animal** animal *m* de concours; *TV etc* **s. copy** copie *f* antenne *ou* exploitation; **s. format** format *m* de présentation; *TV* **s. print** copie antenne *ou* exploitation; **s. window** vitrine *f* (*de magasin*); (*display*) étalage *m*

(b) (*play etc*) spectacle *m*; (*on television, radio*) émission *f*; **to go to a s.** aller au spectacle; *Th* **to stop the s.** (*be a success*) faire un tabac; **the s. must go on** *Th* le spectacle continue; *Fig* il faut continuer (*malgré le décès de qn etc*); *Th* **to steal the s.** (r)emporter la vedette; *Fig* **let's get this s. on the road** allez, c'est parti, on y va!; *Fig* **to run the s.** être à la tête de *ou* diriger l'affaire; *Fig* **to make a s. of oneself** se donner en spectacle; **film s.** séance *f* de cinéma; *Rad, TV* **talk** *or* **chat s.** talk-show *m*; **one-man s.** solo *m*; **travelling s.** (*at a fair*) spectacle forain; *Th F* **s. stopper** acteur, -trice/chanteur, -euse/numéro *m/etc* qui fait un tabac

(c) (*act of showing*) (*appearance*) apparence *f*; (*pretence*) semblant *m*, simulacre *m*; (*ostentation*) parade *f*, ostentation *f*; **to vote by s. of hands** voter à mains levées; **it's all a s.** (*not genuine*) ce n'est qu'une façade; **to do sth for s.** (*to impress*) faire qch pour la forme; (*show off skills etc*) épater pour la galerie; **to be fond of s.** aimer l'éclat *ou* la parade; **s. of generosity** affectation *f* de générosité; **s. of strength** démonstration *f* de force; **to make a s. of resistance** faire semblant *ou* mine de résister; **to make a s. of being angry** faire semblant *ou* faire mine d'être fâché; **to make a great s. of friendship** faire de grandes démonstrations d'amitié; **to make a s. of learning** étaler sa culture

(d) **to put up a good s.** (*of athlete, competitor etc*) bien se défendre; **the party put up a good s.** le parti s'est bien débrouillé; *Old-fashioned F* **good s.!** très bien!, bravo!; *F* **it**

was a poor *or* **bad s.** c'était plutôt manqué; **it's a pretty poor s.** c'est vraiment lamentable

show² (*pt* **showed** [ʃəʊd]; *pp* **shown** [ʃəʊn]) **1** *vt* (**a**) (*display*) (*thing, quality etc*) montrer; (*allow to be seen*) faire voir, laisser voir; (*passport*) présenter; (*gratitude etc*) témoigner; (*one's feelings*) manifester, laisser voir, laisser paraître; (*courage, enthusiasm*) montrer, faire montre de; **to s. sth to sb, to s. sb sth** montrer *ou* faire voir qch à qn; **to s. sb how to do sth** montrer à qn comment faire qch; **to s. one's wares** étaler ses marchandises; **to s. one's cards** *or* **one's hand** *Cards* découvrir son jeu; *Fig* (*make one's intentions known*) jouer cartes sur table; **the picture shows three figures** le tableau représente trois personnes; **to have sth to s. for one's money** en avoir pour son argent; **to s. one's legs** montrer ses jambes; *F* **that dress shows everything she's got** cette robe ne cache pas grand-chose; **he won't s. his face here again** il ne se montrera plus ici; **a colour that doesn't s. the dirt** une couleur qui n'est pas salissante; **to s. oneself** se montrer, se faire voir; (*at a reception etc*) faire acte de présence; **to s. itself** se montrer; (*of emotion, tendency*) se manifester; **to s. a profit** faire ressortir un bénéfice, dégager des profits; **to s. a loss** accuser *ou* faire ressortir une perte; **to s. great improvement** faire apparaître une grande amélioration; **to s. a taste for sth** témoigner d'un goût pour qch; **his face showed his delight** la joie se voyait sur son visage; **she showed no sign of having heard anything** (*didn't reveal she had*) elle n'a pas montré qu'elle avait entendu; (*didn't seem to have*) elle n'a pas montré si elle avait entendu; **to s. one's age** faire bien son âge; **to s. oneself (to be) a coward** se montrer lâche; **she showed herself to be a hard worker** elle s'est révélée *ou* avérée dure à la tâche; **he showed me no mercy** il n'a fait preuve d'aucune pitié envers moi; **to s. willing** faire preuve de bonne volonté

(**b**) (*indicate*) indiquer; **a diagram shows how the system works** un diagramme indique le fonctionnement du système; **place shown on a map** lieu indiqué sur une carte; **to s. the time/the temperature** (*of watch, thermometer etc*) indiquer l'heure/la température

(**c**) (*prove, demonstrate*) prouver, démontrer; **these remarks show how worried the government is** ces remarques témoignent de l'inquiétude du gouvernement; **a mere glance will s. that …** il suffit d'un coup d'œil pour se rendre compte que …; **which only** *or* **all goes to s. that …** ce qui prouve que …; **it just shows you how lucky we are** ça vous montre la chance que nous avons; *F* **I'll s. you!** je vous apprendrai!; *Jur* **to s. cause or reason** (*set out one's reasons*) exposer ses raisons; (*offer valid reasons*) offrir des raisons valables

(**d**) (*film*) passer, projeter; (*TV programme*) diffuser; *TV* **this programme will be shown tomorrow** cette émission passera (à l'écran) demain

(**e**) (*escort, lead*) **to s. sb the way** indiquer *ou* montrer le chemin à qn; **to s. sb to his/her room** conduire qn à sa chambre; **to s. sb round the town** faire visiter *ou* faire voir la ville à qn; **we were shown over the house** on nous a fait visiter la maison; **to s. sb into a room** introduire *ou* faire entrer qn dans une pièce

2 *vi* (**a**) (*be or become visible*) se montrer, paraître, se voir; (*of buds*) sortir; **your slip's showing** votre jupon dépasse; **she lets her feelings s. too much** elle laisse trop voir ses sentiments; **it shows in your face** cela se voit *ou* se lit sur votre visage; **she's used to getting what she wants – it shows!** elle a l'habitude d'obtenir ce qu'elle veut – ça se voit!; **it doesn't s.** ça ne se voit pas, on ne dirait pas; **ah well, it just** *or* **all goes to s.!** eh oui, c'est la vie!

(**b**) *F* (*arrive*) se pointer; **he didn't s.** il n'est pas venu

▶ **show in** *vtsep* (*escort inside*) faire entrer

▶ **show off 1** *vtsep* (*flaunt*) faire montre *ou* étalage de; (*show to advantage*) faire valoir, mettre en valeur; **they like to s. off their culture** ils aiment bien faire étalage de leur culture; **he likes to s. off his muscles/knowledge** il aime bien exhiber ses muscles/connaissances; **she was showing off her new car** elle exhibait sa nouvelle voiture; **she came in to s. off her new baby** elle est venue faire admirer son nouveau-né; **coat that shows off the figure well** manteau qui marque *ou* dessine bien la taille; **wearing white shows off a tan** porter du blanc met le bronzage en valeur

2 *vi* (*try to impress*) se donner des airs; *F* faire de l'épate; (*with clothes, possessions etc*) parader, se pavaner; **to s. off in front of sb** chercher à épater qn; **stop showing off!** arrête de faire l'important *ou* de te donner des airs!; **you don't have to drive that fast, you're just showing off** ce n'est pas la peine de conduire aussi vite, tu cherches juste à nous épater

▶ **show out** *vtsep* (*escort out*) reconduire, accompagner jusqu'à la porte; **it's okay, I'll s. myself out** inutile de vous déranger, je saurai retrouver le chemin (tout seul)

▶ **show through** *vi* se voir au travers; **her knickers showed through under her dress** on voyait ses sous-vêtements au travers de sa robe

▶ **show up 1** *vtsep* (**a**) (*reveal*) (*impostor etc*) démasquer, dénoncer; (*flaw etc*) révéler; **he's been shown up** il est grillé

(**b**) (*shame*) faire honte à, embarrasser; (*deliberately humiliate*) humilier, vexer; **you're always showing me up in front of other people!** (*embarrassing me*) tu me mets toujours dans l'embarras devant les gens!

(**c**) (*escort upstairs*) accompagner en haut

2 *vi* (**a**) (*be evident*) (*against a background*) se dessiner, se détacher, ressortir; **the dirt really shows up on a white carpet** la saleté ressort vraiment sur une moquette blanche

(**b**) *F* (*arrive*) venir; **to fail to s. up** ne pas se présenter; **they'll s. up at twelve** ils s'amèneront à midi; **you're the boss, you really ought to s. up** tu es le patron, tu devrais vraiment y aller *ou* te montrer

show apartment *n* appartement *m* témoin

showbiz [ˈʃəʊbɪz] *n F* industrie *f ou* monde *m* du spectacle, showbiz *m*; **s. personality** personnalité *f* du showbiz *ou* du monde du spectacle

showboat [ˈʃəʊbəʊt] *n US* bateau-théâtre *m*, *pl* bateaux-théâtres

show business *n* industrie *f ou* monde *m* du spectacle; **that's s.!** c'est ça, la vie d'artiste!

showcase [ˈʃəʊkeɪs] *n Com* vitrine *f*; *Fig* **the exhibition will be a s. for Italy's best furniture designers** l'exposition sera la vitrine de tous les meilleurs créateurs de mobilier d'Italie

showdown [ˈʃəʊdaʊn] *n F* (*confrontation*) confrontation *f*

shower¹ [ˈʃaʊər] *n* (**a**) (*of rain*) averse *f*; (*of blows, stones*) volée *f*; (*of sparks*) gerbe *f*; (*of insults*) avalanche *f*; **heavy s.** (*of rain*) ondée *f*, grosse averse

(**b**) (*for washing*) (*act, device*) douche *f*; **to have** *or* **take a s.** prendre une douche, se doucher; **he was in the s. for half an hour** il est resté une demi-heure sous la douche; *Old-fashioned* **s. bath** bain-douche *m*, *pl* bains-douches; **s. head** pommeau *m* de la douche; **s. room** salle *f* de douches *ou* d'eau

(**c**) *Astron* **meteor s.** essaim *m* de météores

(**d**) *Am F* (*party*) réception *f* où chacun apporte un cadeau

(**e**) *Br F Pej* (*group*) **what a s.!** quelle bande *ou* quel tas de crétins!

shower² **1** *vt* verser; (*water*) faire gicler (**onto** sur); **to s. blows on sb** faire pleuvoir des coups sur qn; **to s. gifts/honours on sb** combler qn de cadeaux/d'honneurs; **I've been showered with invitations** je suis submergé d'invitations; **to s. compliments on sb** inonder qn de compliments **2** *vi* (*take a shower*) prendre une douche, se doucher

▶ **shower down** *vi* (*of rocks*) tomber; *Fig* (*of compliments, insults*) pleuvoir; **rocks showered down on us** des pierres s'abattirent sur nous

shower cabinet *n* cabine *f* de douche

shower cap *n* bonnet *m* de douche

shower curtain *n* rideau *m* de douche

shower gel *n* gel *m* de douche

showerproof [ˈʃaʊəpruːf] *adj Tex* imperméable

shower unit *n* bloc-douche *m*, *pl* blocs-douches

showery [ˈʃaʊərɪ] *adj* (*weather*) pluvieux; **it's s. (weather)** le temps est à l'averse

show girl *n* girl *f*

showground [ˈʃəʊgraʊnd] *n* (*fairground*) champ *m* de foire; (*for equestrian event etc*) terrain *m* de concours hippique/*etc*

show house *n* maison *f* témoin

showily [ˈʃəʊɪlɪ] *adv* **s. dressed** habillé de façon voyante

showiness [ˈʃəʊɪnɪs] *n* faste *m*, ostentation *f*; (*of jewellery*) clinquant *m*; (*of dress, decoration*) luxe *m* criard *ou* tapageur

showing [ˈʃəʊɪŋ] *n* (**a**) (*exhibition*) exposition *f* (**b**) (*of film*) projection *f*; *TV, Cin* présentation *f*; **the first s. will be at …** la première projection aura lieu à … (**c**) (*performance*) performance *f*; **a poor s. by our team** une déplorable performance de la part de notre équipe; **on this s. we don't stand a chance in the championship** vu cette performance, on n'a pas une chance de gagner le championnat (**d**) *esp Fml* **on your own s.** (*admission*) comme vous le dites vous-même

showing off *n* vantardise *f*

show jumper *n* (*horse*) sauteur *m*

show jumping *n* jumping *m*, concours *mpl* de sauts d'obstacles

showman, *pl* -men [ˈʃəʊmən] *n* (*at fair*) forain *m*; *Fig* **he's a real s.** il a le sens du spectacle

showmanship ['ʃəʊmənʃɪp] *n* (*of person*) sens *m* du spectacle; **the s. of his act** son numéro spectaculaire; *Fig Pej* **it's just s.** c'est du cinéma
shown *see* **show**[2]
show-off *n F* (*person*) m'as-tu-vu *mf inv*, *F* frimeur, -euse; **John's a terrible s.** John est un sacré prétentieux; **don't be a s.** (*with clothes, possessions, skills*) arrête de faire de l'épate *ou F* de frimer
showpiece ['ʃəʊpi:s] *n* (*in exhibition etc*) œuvre *f*; *Fig* **the locals regarded the new theatre as something of a s.** les gens du quartier considéraient le nouveau théâtre comme leur joyau
showplace ['ʃəʊpleɪs] *n* (*scenic place*) endroit *m* pittoresque
showring ['ʃəʊrɪŋ] *n* (*at auction*) (*for horses, cattle etc*) arène de vente; (*at equestrian event*) arène de concours hippique
showroom ['ʃəʊru:m] *n* (*for purchasing*) magasin *m*; (*display only*) salle *f ou* salon *m* d'exposition; (*for cars etc*) salle d'exposition, show-room *m*; **electricity s.** magasin d'électroménager (*où l'on peut aussi payer ses factures d'électricité*); **in s. condition** à l'état neuf
show trial *n* procès-spectacle *m*
showy ['ʃəʊɪ] *adj* (*appearance, dress*) voyant, *Pej* tapageur, tape-à-l'œil *inv*; (*jewellery*) clinquant; (*decoration, wallpaper*) criard, tape-à-l'œil; **he's a bit s. in the way he dresses** la façon dont il s'habille est un peu voyante; **he's a bit s. in the way he acts** il se fait un peu trop remarquer
shrapnel ['ʃræpn(ə)l] *n Mil* (*fragments*) éclats *mpl* d'obus; **s. wound** blessure *f* provoquée par des éclats d'obus
shred[1] [ʃred] *n* (*of fabric, paper etc*) lambeau *m*; (*of meat etc*) morceau *m*; **to tear sth (in)to shreds** (*into small pieces*) déchiqueter qch; (*into strips*) mettre qch en lambeaux; **to tear sb's reputation to shreds** démolir la réputation de qn; **to tear sb to shreds** démolir qn; **to tear sb's argument/a play to shreds** démolir l'argument de qn/une pièce; **his reputation was in shreds** sa réputation était ruinée; **his argument was in shreds** son argument était réduit à néant; **her dress was all in shreds** sa robe était tout en lambeaux; **there isn't a s. of evidence** il n'y a pas la moindre preuve; **anyone with a s. of decency would have refused** n'importe qui ayant un minimum de décence aurait refusé; **not a s. of truth** pas un grain de vérité; **without a s. of clothing on** nu comme un ver
shred[2] *vt* (**-dd-**) (*sth*) déchirer en lambeaux; (*confidential documents*) déchiqueter, broyer; *Culin* (*grate*) couper en lamelles
shredder ['ʃredər] *n* (*device*) (*for confidential documents*) déchiqueteuse *f*, broyeuse *f*
shredding ['ʃredɪŋ] *n* (*of fabric, confidential documents*) déchiquetage *m*, broyage *m*; **s. machine** déchiqueteuse *f*, broyeuse *f*
shrew [ʃru:] *n* (**a**) *Zool* (*animal*) musaraigne *f* (**b**) *Pej* (*woman*) mégère *f*
shrewd [ʃru:d] *adj* (*person etc*) sagace; (*businessman*) astucieux; **he's a s. man** c'est une fine mouche; **s. answer** réponse *f* adroite; **that was a s. move** c'était bien joué; **I've got a s. idea that …** je suis porté à croire que …; **to make a s. guess** deviner juste; **I could make a pretty s. guess** ce n'est pas difficile à deviner
shrewdly ['ʃru:dlɪ] *adv* astucieusement
shrewdness ['ʃru:dnɪs] *n* sagacité *f*, finesse *f*
shrewish ['ʃru:ɪʃ] *adj Pej* (*woman*) acariâtre
shriek[1] [ʃri:k] *n* (*of person, animal*) cri *m* aigu *ou* perçant; **shrieks of joy** cris joyeux; **shrieks of laughter** grands éclats *mpl* de rire; **to give a s.** pousser un cri perçant
shriek[2] **1** *vi* (*of person*) pousser un cri aigu *ou* perçant; (*of wind*) hurler; **to s. with laughter/pain** hurler de rire/douleur **2** *vt* **to s. (out) a warning** pousser un cri d'avertissement
shrieking ['ʃri:kɪŋ] *n* cris *mpl* aigus *ou* perçants
shrift [ʃrɪft] *n F* **to give sb short s.** expédier qn, envoyer promener qn; **I got short s. from him** il m'a envoyé promener, *Iron* il m'a bien reçu
shrike [ʃraɪk] *n* (*bird*) pie-grièche *f*, *pl* pies-grièches
shrill[1] [ʃrɪl] *adj* (*voice, sound etc*) aigu, *f* aiguë, perçant; (*complaint etc*) véhément; **in a s. voice** d'une voix perçante; **a s. whistle** (*sound*) un coup de sifflet strident
shrill[2] *vi Lit* pousser un son aigu *ou* strident; **a whistle shrilled** un coup de sifflet déchira l'air
shrillness ['ʃrɪlnɪs] *n* (*of sound*) acuité *f*, stridence *f*
shrilly ['ʃrɪlɪ] *adv* (*to say*) d'un ton aigu; (*to protest*) de façon virulente
shrimp[1] [ʃrɪmp] *n* (*crustacean*) crevette *f* (grise); *F Pej* (*short person*) nabot, -ote; **s. boat** crevettier *m*; **s. net** haveneau *m*
shrimp[2] *vi* **to go shrimping, to s.** pêcher la crevette, aller à la pêche à la crevette
shrine [ʃraɪn] *n* (**a**) (*saint's tomb*) tombeau *m* de saint(e) (**b**) (*reliquary*) châsse *f*, reliquaire *m* (**c**) (*place of pilgrimage*) lieu *m* de pèlerinage
shrink[1] [ʃrɪŋk] *n F* (*psychiatrist*) psy *mf*
shrink[2] (*pt* **shrank** [ʃræŋk]; *pp* **shrunk** [ʃrʌŋk], *as adj* **shrunken** ['ʃrʌŋk(ə)n]) **1** *vi* (**a**) (*become smaller*) (se) rétrécir, rapetisser; (*of income, budget*) diminuer; (*of material etc*) rétrécir; (*of person*) (*out of shyness etc*) se faire tout petit; **tropical rainforests are shrinking in size** la surface des forêts tropicales humides est en train de diminuer; **he is beginning to s. (with age)** il commence à se tasser; **to s. in the wash** rétrécir au lavage; *Fig* **to s. into oneself** rentrer en soi-même
(**b**) (*move away*) reculer; **to s. from sth** reculer devant *ou* se dérober à qch; **to s. in horror** reculer d'horreur; **to s. from doing sth** reculer *ou* répugner à faire qch
2 *vt* (*fabric*) (*deliberately*) faire rétrécir; **I've shrunk my pullover** (*accidentally*) mon pull a rétréci; **fully shrunk material** tissu irrétrécissable
▶ **shrink back** *vi* (*move away*) avoir un mouvement de recul; **to s. back in horror** reculer d'horreur
shrinkage ['ʃrɪŋkɪdʒ] *n* (**a**) (*of wood*) retrait *m*; *Tex etc* rétrécissement *m* (**b**) *Com* (*through pilferage*) coulage *m*
shrinking ['ʃrɪŋkɪŋ] *n* (**a**) (*act of becoming smaller*) = **shrinkage** (*a*) (**b**) (*act of moving back*) **s. from sth** recul *m* devant qch; **she's no s. violet** elle n'est pas timide; **stop acting like a s. violet** arrête de faire ton/ta timide
shrink-wrap *vt* emballer sous film plastique
shrink-wrapped *adj* sous film plastique
shrink-wrapping *n* (**a**) (*process*) emballage *m* sous film plastique (**b**) (*material*) film *m* plastique
shrive [ʃraɪv] *vt* (*pt* **shrove** [ʃrəʊv]; *pp* **shriven** ['ʃrɪv(ə)n]) *Arch* (*a penitent*) confesser, absoudre
shrivel ['ʃrɪv(ə)l] (**-ll-**, *US* **-l-**) **1** *vt* (*skin*) rider; (*apple*) rider, ratatiner; (*of sun*) (*plants*) dessécher **2** *vi* (*of plant, apple*) se rider, se ratatiner
▶ **shrivel up 1** *vi* (*of plant, skin*) se ratatiner; *Fig* **I shrivelled up with embarrassment** je serais rentré dans un trou de souris tellement j'étais gêné **2** *vtsep* (*apple, skin*) ratatiner; (*plants, leaves*) complètement dessécher
shrivelled ['ʃrɪv(ə)ld] *adj* ratatiné
shroud[1] [ʃraʊd] *n* (*for dead body*) linceul *m*, suaire *m*; *Fig* **in a s. of mystery** enveloppé de mystère; *Lit* **under a s. of darkness** sous les voiles de la nuit
shroud[2] *n* (**a**) *Naut* hauban *m* (**b**) **s. (lines)** (*of parachute*) suspentes *fpl*
shroud[3] *vt* (*body*) ensevelir; *Fig* (*sth*) envelopper, voiler (**in** de); **shrouded in mist/mystery** enveloppé de brume/mystère; **shrouded in gloom** (*meeting, person*) plongé dans la tristesse
Shrove [ʃrəʊv] *adj* **S. Tuesday** Mardi *m* gras
Shrovetide ['ʃrəʊvtaɪd] *n Rel* les jours *mpl* gras
shrub [ʃrʌb] *n* (*plant*) arbrisseau *m*, arbuste *m*
shrubbery ['ʃrʌbərɪ] *n* massif *m* d'arbustes; **the ball disappeared into the s.** la balle disparut dans les massifs (d'arbustes)
shrug[1] [ʃrʌg] *n* **s. (of the shoulders)** haussement *m* d'épaules; **with a s. (of his shoulders)** en haussant les épaules; **he gave a s. of contempt** il haussa les épaules en signe de mépris
shrug[2] (**-gg-**) **1** *vt* **to s. one's shoulders** hausser les épaules **2** *vi* hausser les épaules
▶ **shrug off** *vtsep* (*treat as unimportant*) (*problem, other people's feelings etc*) ignorer; (*danger*) dédaigner, mépriser
shrunken ['ʃrʌŋk(ə)n] *adj Tex* rétréci; (*features etc*) ratatiné; **s. with age** (*person*) tassé par l'âge; **s. heads** (*in anthropology*) têtes *fpl* réduites
shuck[1] [ʃʌk] *Am* **1** *n* (*of peas, beans*) cosse *f*, gousse *f*; (*of sweet corn*) spathe *f*; (*of nut*) écale *f*; (*of oyster, clam*) coquille *f* **2** *int F* **shucks!** mince (alors)!, flûte (alors)!
shuck[2] *vt Am* (**a**) (*peas, beans*) écosser; (*sweet corn*) éplucher; (*nuts*) écaler; (*oysters, clams*) écailler; *F* (*garment*) ôter (**b**) = **shuck off**
▶ **shuck off** *vtsep Am* (*rid oneself of*) (*bad habit*) se défaire de
shudder[1] ['ʃʌdər] *n* (*of person*) frisson *m*, frémissement *m*; (*of engine*) vibration *f*; *F* **it gives me the shudders** j'en ai des frissons
shudder[2] *vi* frissonner (**with** de); (*of machine, vehicle, ship etc*) vibrer; **I s. to think of it** *or* **at the thought of it** j'ai des frissons rien que d'y penser; **I s. to think what went into this soup** je frémis à l'idée de ce qu'il peut y avoir dans cette soupe; **I s. to think** je n'ose y penser; **the bus shuddered to a halt** le bus s'immobilisa en vibrant
shuffle[1] ['ʃʌf(ə)l] *n* (**a**) (*in walking*) traînement *m* de pieds, pas *m* traînant; (*in dancing*) frottement *m* de pieds; **soft shoe s.** = danse *f* de music-hall (*exécutée en chaussons*) (**b**)

Cards mélange *m*; **to give the cards a s.** battre *ou* mélanger les cartes

shuffle² **1** *vt* (*mix*) (*papers etc*) brasser; *Cards* battre, mélanger; **to s. one's feet** (*in walking*) traîner les pieds; **he stood there shuffling his feet** il était là debout dansant d'un pied sur l'autre **2** *vi* **(a)** (*drag one's feet*) traîner les pieds; **she shuffled into the room** elle entra dans la pièce en traînant les pieds; **the children were shuffling in their seats** les enfants s'agitaient sur leur chaise **(b)** *Cards* mélanger

▶ **shuffle along** *vi* (*walk dragging one's feet*) avancer en traînant les pieds

▶ **shuffle off** **1** *vi* (*walk away dragging one's feet*) s'en aller en traînant les pieds; **the badger shuffled off into the bushes** le blaireau disparut dans les buissons en trottinant **2** *vtsep* (*set aside*) (*responsibility*) rejeter (**onto sb** sur qn); **to s. a job off onto sb** refiler un boulot à qn; *Hum* **to s. off this mortal coil** mourir

shuffleboard ['ʃʌf(ə)lbɔːd] *n* (jeu *m* de) palet *m*

shuffling ['ʃʌflɪŋ] *adj* (*gait*) traînant

shufti, shufty ['ʃʊftɪ] *n Br F* coup *m* d'œil; **have a s. at this** jettes-y un coup d'œil; **can I have a s.?** je peux jeter un coup d'œil?

shun¹ [ʃʌn] *int Mil etc F* (*attention!*) garde-à-vous!

shun² *vt* (**-nn-**) (*sb, sth*) fuir, éviter; (*publicity*) fuir; **to s. society** fuir le monde; **to s. everybody** éviter tout le monde

shunt¹ [ʃʌnt] *n El* shunt *m*, dérivation *f*

shunt² **1** *vt* **(a)** *Rail* (*train, carriages*) manœuvrer; **to s. a train onto a siding** aiguiller un train sur une voie de garage; *F* **we were shunted into another room** on nous a parqués dans une autre pièce; *F* **the responsibility was shunted back and forth between departments** la responsabilité a été renvoyée de service en service

(b) *El* (*circuit etc*) shunter, dériver; (*condenser*) monter en dérivation

(c) *F* (*to push*) pousser; **he just shunted me out of his way** il m'a poussé hors de son chemin; **s. that box of files over here, will you?** passe-moi ce carton de dossiers, tu veux!

2 *vi F* **I spent the day shunting back and forth between the two offices** j'ai passé ma journée à faire la navette entre les deux bureaux

shunter ['ʃʌntər] *n Rail* (*train*) locomotive *f* de manœvre

shunting ['ʃʌntɪŋ] *n* **(a)** *Rail* manœuvre *f*; **s. engine** locomotive *f ou* machine *f* de manœuvre; **s. operations** manœuvres *fpl* de triage; **s. yard** gare *f* de triage **(b)** *El* dérivation *f*, shuntage *m*

shush¹ [ʃʌʃ] *int* chut!

shush² *vt* (*sb*) faire taire

shut¹ [ʃʌt] *adj* fermé; **to find the door s.** trouver la porte fermée, trouver porte close; *F* **to keep one's mouth s.** avoir la bouche cousue; **keep your mouth s.!** ferme-la!; **they always keep the door s.** ils gardent toujours la porte fermée; **keep the door s.!** ferme la porte!

shut² (*pt, pp* **shut**; *prp* **shutting**) **1** *vt* (*door, shop, box, book etc*) fermer; **to s. the door on sb** *or* **in sb's face** fermer la porte au nez de qn; **to s. one's eyes** fermer les yeux; **to s. one's ears to sth** refuser d'entendre qch; **to s. one's mind to the possibility that ...** se refuser à l'éventualité que ...; **s. your mind to it!** ne pense pas à ça!; **to s. one's finger in the door** se pincer le doigt dans la porte; *F* **to s. sb's mouth (for him)** faire taire qn; *Sl* **s. your mouth** *or* **face!** la ferme!, ta gueule!

2 *vi* (*of door, lid etc*) (se) fermer; (*of shop, museum etc*) fermer; **the door won't s.** la porte ne ferme pas; **the door shut to** la porte s'est fermée (toute seule)

▶ **shut away** *vtsep* s'enfermer; **to s. oneself away** s'enfermer; **to s. oneself away from the world** s'isoler du monde; **these objects have been shut away for centuries** ces objets sont restés enfermés pendant des siècles

▶ **shut down** **1** *vtsep* (*factory, airport etc*) fermer; (*production*) arrêter; *Tech* (*steam, power*) couper; *Av* (*engine*) couper, arrêter; *Comptr* (*system*) arrêter **2** *vi* (*of factory etc*) (*through lack of work*) fermer temporairement; (*for holiday*) fermer; (*permanently*) fermer ses portes; (*of TV station etc for the night*) arrêter ses programmes; *Comptr* (*of system*) s'arrêter

▶ **shut in** *vtsep* (*confine*) (*sb, sth*) enfermer; **to s. oneself in** s'enfermer; **to feel shut in** avoir un sentiment d'étouffement; **we're shut in by hills** nous sommes entourés de collines

▶ **shut off** *vtsep* **(a)** (*stop*) (*electricity, water*) couper; *Aut* (*engine*) couper, arrêter; **to s. off funds** couper des crédits **(b)** (*block*) (*road*) couper; (*pipe, exit*) boucher **(c)** (*isolate*) isoler (**from** de); **she shut herself off from other people** elle s'isolait du reste des gens; **to be shut off from society** être exclu du monde; **you shouldn't s. yourself off so** tu ne devrais pas t'isoler comme ça

▶ **shut out** *vtsep* **(a)** (*exclude*) (*person*) exclure; (*air, light, competition*) bloquer; (*memory etc*) chasser; **the trees s. out the view** les arbres bouchent la vue; **to s. sb out from** *or* **of sth** exclure qn de qch; **I've shut her out of my life** je l'ai rayée de ma vie **(b)** (*keep outside*) **to s. sb out (of doors)** fermer la porte à qn; **I've shut myself out (of my house)** je me suis enfermé dehors; **he's taken the keys and has shut me out** il a pris les clefs et du coup je suis enfermé dehors **(c)** *Am Sp* (*prevent from scoring*) empêcher de marquer

▶ **shut up** **1** *vtsep* **(a)** (*confine*) (*sb, sth*) enfermer; **to s. oneself up** s'enfermer chez soi; **to s. sb up (in prison)** emprisonner qn

(b) (*close*) (*room*) fermer; **to s. up shop** (*close shop at end of day*) fermer le magasin; (*close shop permanently*) fermer boutique; (*of theatre etc*) fermer ses portes

(c) (*close completely*) (*west wing etc*) condamner; (*opening etc*) obstruer, boucher; **to s. up a house** (*when going away*) boucler une maison

(d) *F* (*make quiet*) (*person*) faire taire; (*using threats or violence*) réduire au silence; **s. those kids up!** faites taire ces gamins!; **that ought to s. him up** (*stop him boasting*) ça devrait lui rabattre son caquet; (*stop him complaining*) ça devrait le calmer

2 *vi F* se taire; **s. up!** tais-toi!; (*aggressive*) *Sl* la ferme!, ta gueule!; **he never knows when to s. up** il ne sait pas se taire *ou* la fermer quand il faut; **to s. up about sth** la fermer à propos de qch

shutdown ['ʃʌtdaʊn] *n* (*of factory*) (*temporary*) fermeture *f* temporaire; (*permanent*) fermeture; (*of machine, computer*) mise *f* hors tension, arrêt *m*

shut-eye *n F* roupillon *m*; **to have** *or* **get a bit of s.** roupiller, coincer la bulle

shut-in **1** *adj* **to have a s. feeling** (*in room etc*) se sentir enfermé; (*in relationship*) se sentir prisonnier, -ière **2** *n Am* invalide *mf* confiné chez lui/elle

shut-off *n* (*of funds*) coupure *f*; **s. (device)** dispositif *m* d'arrêt automatique

shut-out *n* **(a)** *Ind* lock-out *m inv* **(b)** *Cards* **s. bid** ouverture *f* préventive **(c)** *Am Sp* (*win*) éclatante victoire *f*

shutter ['ʃʌtər] *n* **(a)** (*on window*) volet *m*; **(slatted) shutters** persiennes *fpl*; **(folding) shutters** volets pliants; **to open/close the shutters** ouvrir/fermer les volets; **to put up the shutters** (*of shop*) fermer la/les devanture(s), mettre les volets; *Fig* (*close shop permanently*) fermer boutique **(b)** *Phot* obturateur *m*; **to release the s.** actionner l'obturateur; **s. release** déclencheur *m* (d'obturateur); **s. speed** vitesse *f* d'obturation

shuttered ['ʃʌtəd] *adj* (*window*) (*with shutters*) à volets; (*with shutters closed*) à volets fermés; **the house has s. windows** la maison a des volets

shuttering ['ʃʌtərɪŋ] *n* (*for concrete*) coffrage *m*

shutting ['ʃʌtɪŋ] *n* (*act of closing*) (*of door, box, factory*) fermeture *f*

shutting down *n* = **shutdown**

shuttle¹ ['ʃʌt(ə)l] *n* **(a)** *Tex, Sewing etc* navette *f* **(b)** (*train, bus, plane etc*) navette *f*; **s. service** service *m* de navettes, navette; *Astronaut* **space s.** navette spatiale; **to engage in s. diplomacy** faire la navette entre deux parties lors de négociations **(c)** = **shuttlecock**

shuttle² **1** *vi* faire la navette (**between** entre) **2** *vt* **to s. sb back and forth** *or* **to and fro** (*of shuttle bus etc*) véhiculer qn d'un endroit à un autre; *Pej* (*from office to office etc*) envoyer qn à droite et à gauche; *F* balader qn; **to s. back and forth** (*tape*) faire avancer et reculer rapidement pour repérer un point précis; **to s. a document to and fro** transbahuter un document d'un endroit à un autre

shuttlecock ['ʃʌt(ə)lkɒk] *n Sp* volant *m*

shy¹ *n* **(a)** (*throw*) (*of stone etc*) jet *m*, lancement *m*; **to take a s. at sth with a stone** tirer sur qch avec un caillou; **5p a s.** (*at fairs*) 5 pence le coup **(b)** *Old-fashioned F* (*attempt*) (*to achieve sth*) essai *m*, tentative *f*; **to have a s. at doing sth** s'essayer à faire qch

shy² *adj* (*comp* **shyer**, *superl* **shyest**) **(a)** (*person, child*) timide; (*bird*) sauvage, farouche; **to make sb s.** intimider qn; **to be s. of people** être gêné *ou* mal à l'aise en société; **to be s. of doing sth** hésiter à faire qch; **he fought s. of admitting his interest** il a fait tout ce qu'il a pu pour ne pas avoir à admettre qu'il était intéressé **(b)** *esp Am* **to be s. of** (*lack*) (*sth*) manquer de; **we're still 500 dollars s.** il nous manque encore 500 dollars

shy³ *vi* (*pt, pp* **shied**; *prp* **shying**) (*of horse*) s'effaroucher; **to s. at sth** (*of horse*) s'effaroucher devant qch; *Fig* (*of person*) renâcler devant qch

shy[4] (*pt, pp* **shied**; *prp* **shying**) *vt* (*throw*) (*stone etc*) lancer, jeter (**at sb** à qn)
▶ **shy away** *vi* (*retreat in fear, nervousness*) **to s. away from sth/doing sth** éviter qch/de faire qch; **to s. away from an idea** se méfier d'une idée; **he has shied away from driving since the accident** il évite de conduire depuis l'accident
Shylock ['ʃaɪlɒk] *n F Pej* usurier *m*
shyly ['ʃaɪlɪ] *adv* (*to smile, suggest, look on etc*) timidement; (*to blush*) de timidité
shyness ['ʃaɪnɪs] *n* (*of person, child*) timidité *f*; (*of animal*) caractère *m* farouche; **to lose one's s.** s'enhardir
shyster ['ʃaɪstər] *n esp Am Pej F* (*lawyer*) avocassier *m*; (*businessman*) escroc *m*
SI [e'saɪ] *n Tech* (*abbr* **Système International**) SI *m*; **SI units** unités *fpl* de SI
si [si:] *n Mus* si *m*
Siam [saɪ'æm] *n Hist* Siam *m*
Siamese [saɪə'mi:z] **1** *adj Hist* siamois; **S. cat** (chat *m*) siamois *m*; **S. twins** (*brothers*) frères *mpl* siamois; (*sisters*) sœurs *fpl* siamoises **2** *n* **(a)** *Hist* (*person*) Siamois, -oise **(b)** *Ling, Hist* siamois *m* **(c)** (*cat*) siamois *m*
siamesed [saɪə'mi:zd] *adj Aut* (*joined together*) siamois
Siberia [saɪ'bɪərɪə] *n* Sibérie *f*
Siberian [saɪ'bɪərɪən] **1** *adj* sibérien **2** *n* Sibérien, -ienne
sibilance ['sɪbɪləns] *n TV, Rad* sifflante *f*
sibilant ['sɪbɪlənt] **1** *adj* sifflant **2** *n Ling* sifflante *f*
sibling ['sɪblɪŋ] *n* (*brother*) frère *m*; (*sister*) sœur *f*; **s. rivalry** rivalité *f* entre enfants de la même famille
sibyl ['sɪbɪl] *n* sibylle *f*
sibylline ['sɪbɪlaɪn] *adj* (*book etc*) sibyllin
sic [sɪk] *adv* sic, ainsi
siccative ['sɪkətɪv] *adj, n* siccatif *m*
Sicilian [sɪ'sɪlɪən] **1** *adj* sicilien **2** *n* Sicilien, -ienne
Sicily ['sɪsɪlɪ] *n* Sicile *f*
sick [sɪk] **1** *adj* **(a)** (*ill*) malade; (*humour*) noir; (*joke*) macabre; **to be s.** (*ill*) être malade; **to report s.** se faire porter malade; **to be s. in the head** (*mad*) être malade de la tête; *Fig* **you have to be pretty s. to desecrate somebody's grave** il faut être vraiment malade pour profaner la tombe de quelqu'un; *Fig* **to have a s. mind** avoir l'esprit malade; **s. bed** lit *m* de malade; *Mil* **to go on s. parade** demander à voir un médecin; **s. list** liste *f* des malades; **s. note** mot *m* d'excuse (expliquant qu'on est malade), certificat *m* médical
(b) to be s. (*vomit*) rendre; **to feel s.** avoir mal au cœur; **to make oneself s.** (*on purpose*) se faire vomir; (*by eating too much chocolate etc*) se rendre malade; **he was as s. as a cat** *or* **a dog** il a été malade comme un chien; *Fig* il en a fait une maladie; **to be s. to one's stomach** avoir mal au cœur; *Fig* en être malade, en faire une maladie; *Fig* **it makes me s.** cela m'écœure; *Fig* **you make me s.!** tu m'écœures!; *Fig* **he was very s. at** *or* **about failing his exam** son échec à l'examen l'a complètement bouleversé; **I'm s. about having to cancel my holiday** je suis malade de devoir annuler mes vacances; *Fig* **she looked pretty s. when she didn't get the prize** elle avait l'air plutôt écœurée quand elle n'a pas reçu le prix; *Fig* **to be s. with jealousy** être malade de jalousie; *Lit* **to be s. at heart** être navré; **s. feeling** malaise *m*; **s. headache** migraine *f*
(c) to be s. of sth être las de qch; **to grow s. of sth** se dégoûter de qch; **I'm s. of spaghetti every night/your constant complaining** j'en ai assez de manger des spaghetti tous les soirs/que vous vous plaigniez sans cesse; **I'm s. and tired** *or* **I'm s. to death of it** j'en ai assez, j'en ai marre
2 *n* **(a) the s.** (*pl*) les malades *mpl*
(b) *Br F* (*vomit*) vomi *m*
▶ **sick up** *vtsep Br F* (*vomit*) vomir, rendre
sick bay *n* infirmerie *f*; *Naut* poste *m* des malades
sick benefit *n* prestations *fpl* en cas de maladie
sick building syndrome *n* = syndrome *m* comprenant des maux de tête *etc* qu'on retrouve chez des personnes résidant ou travaillant dans des bâtiments équipés de la climatisation, *Can* syndrome des bâtiments malsains
sicken ['sɪk(ə)n] **1** *vi* (*become ill*) tomber malade; (*of plants*) languir, dépérir; **to be sickening for an illness/for something** couver une maladie/quelque chose; *Fig, Lit* **to s. of sth** se lasser *ou* se dégoûter de qch **2** *vt* (*make nauseous*) donner mal au cœur à, donner envie de vomir à; *Fig* (*disgust*) dégoûter, donner la nausée à; *Fig* **his business methods s. me** ses procédés en affaires me révoltent *ou* me rendent malade
sickening ['sɪknɪŋ] *adj* (*disgusting*) écœ)urant, dégoûtant; (*smell*) nauséabond; (*sight*) révoltant; *F* **how perfectly s.!** (*annoying*) c'est vraiment écœurant!; *F* **she's so good at maths – I know, it's s.** elle est tellement bonne en maths – je sais, c'est écœurant; **there was a s. crunch as the boats collided** il y a eu un craquement sinistre lorsque les bateaux sont entrés en collision
sickeningly ['sɪknɪŋlɪ] *adv* (de façon) à vous soulever le cœur *ou* à vous écœurer
sickle ['sɪk(ə)l] *n* faucille *f*; *Med* **s. cell anaemia** drépanocytose *f*
sick leave *n* congé *m* de maladie
sickliness ['sɪklɪnɪs] *n* **(a)** (*of person*) état *m* maladif; (*of complexion*) pâleur *f* **(b)** (*of cake*) goût *m* écœurant
sickly ['sɪklɪ] *adj* **(a)** (*person*) maladif, souffreteux; (*plant*) étiolé, rabougri; (*colour, light*) faible, pâle; (*complexion*) pâle; (*pallor*) maladif; (*sun*) blafard; (*smile*) pâle **(b)** *Old-fashioned* (*climate*) malsain, insalubre **(c)** (*taste*) écœurant; *Fig* (*sentiment*) qui écœure, qui dégoûte; (*story, tune*) plein de sensiblerie, à la guimauve; **s. sweet** douceâtre
sickness ['sɪknɪs] *n* (*illness*) maladie *f*; (*nausea*) mal *m* de cœur; **you agreed to stay with him in s. and in health** vous aviez accepté de rester avec lui qu'il soit malade ou en bonne santé; **(bouts of) s.** (*nausea*) nausée(s) *f(pl)*; **sleeping s.** maladie du sommeil; **altitude** *or* **mountain s.** mal des montagnes; **morning s.** nausées matinales
sickness benefit *n Br Admin* (*payments*) indemnité *f* journalière,
sick pay *n* indemnité *f* journalière (*payé par l'employeur en cas de longue maladie*)
sickroom ['sɪkru:m] *n* chambre *f* de malade; (*in school etc*) infirmerie *f*
side[1] [saɪd] *n* **(a)** (*of person, animal*) côté *m*, flanc *m*; **to be lying on one's s.** être couché sur le côté; **right/left s.** côté droit/gauche; **by sb's s.** à côté de qn; **by** *or* **at my s.** à côté de moi, à mes côtés; **they were standing s. by s.** ils se tenaient l'un à côté de l'autre; *Fig* **they worked s. by s. with their former enemies** ils ont travaillé en étroite collaboration avec leurs anciens ennemis; *F* **to split** *or* **burst one's sides (laughing)** se tenir les côtes (de rire), se tordre (de rire); **s. of bacon** flèche *f* de lard; **s. of beef** demi-carcasse *f* de bœuf
(b) (*part*) (*of house, box, triangle etc*) côté *m*; (*of mountain*) flanc *m*, versant *m*; (*of ditch, vase*) paroi *f*; (*of ship*) bord *m*, côté; *Math* (*of equation*) membre *m*; **to put two boxes s. by s.** mettre deux boîtes l'une à côté de l'autre
(c) (*surface*) côté *m*; (*of record*) face *f*; **the right/wrong s. of a fabric** l'endroit *m*/l'envers *m* d'un tissu; **the under/upper s. of sth** le dessous/le dessus de qch; **printed on one s. only** imprimé d'un seul côté; **on the other s. of the paper** (*when looking at the front*) au verso; (*when looking at the back*) au recto; **buttered s. up** (*of slice of bread*) le côté beurré vers le haut; *Fig* **the other s. of the picture** le revers de la médaille; **the right/wrong s. (of sth)** le bon/mauvais côté (de qch); *Com* **this s. up** haut!; **on this s. (of)** de ce côté(-ci) (de); **on that s. (of)** de ce côté-là (de); **on the other s. (of sth)** de l'autre côté (de qch); **with a dog on either s.** flanqué de deux chiens; **on both sides** des deux côtés, de part et d'autre; **on all sides, on every s.** de tous les côtés; (*everywhere*) partout; **on the left/right hand s.** à (main) gauche/droite; **on the south s.** du côté sud; **the tower leans on** *or* **to one s.** la tour penche d'un côté; **to put sth on** *or* **to one s.** mettre qch de côté; **to take sb on** *or* **to one s.** prendre qn à part *ou* en particulier; **to stand on** *or* **to one s.** se tenir à l'écart *ou* à part; **from all sides, from every s.** de tous (les) côtés, de toutes parts; **from s. to s.** d'un côté à l'autre; *Fig* **to get on the right s. of sb** gagner les faveurs de qn; **to be on the right s. of sb** être dans les petits papiers de qn; *Fig* **to get on the wrong s. of sb** prendre qn à rebrousse-poil; **to be on the right s. of the law** avoir la loi pour soi; **to be on the wrong s. of the law** aller contre la loi; **to be on the right s. of forty** avoir moins de quarante ans; **to be on the wrong s. of forty** avoir quarante ans bien sonnés; **it costs the wrong s. of £1,000** ça coûte plus de 1 000 livres; **it's a bit on the expensive/long/hot s.** c'est plutôt cher/long/chaud
(d) (*aspect*) (*of situation, argument etc*) aspect *m*, côté *m*; (*of personality*) côté; **I could see the funny s. of the situation** je voyais le côté drôle de la situation; **I can't see the funny s. of that** je ne vois pas ce qu'il y a de drôle là-dedans; **his good s.** ses bons côtés; **to have a jealous/thoughtful s.** avoir un côté jaloux/méditatif; **there are many sides to her character** elle a bien des facettes à son caractère; **I had never seen that s. of him before** je n'avais jamais vu cet aspect de sa personnalité; **the good/bad s. of the business** le bon/mauvais côté de l'affaire; **to look on the bright s. (of things)** voir les choses du bon côté, prendre les choses du bon côté; **he always looks on the gloomy s. of things** il voit tout en noir; **to hear/look at both sides of the question** (*consider both aspects*) considérer les deux aspects de la question; (*consider arguments for and against*)

envisager le pour et le contre; **you haven't heard my s. of the story!** vous n'avez pas entendu ma version de l'histoire!

(e) (*in dispute*) côté *m*; *Sp* équipe *f*, camp *m*; **the two sides to the dispute will meet on Monday** les deux partis se recontreront lundi; **to be on the right/wrong s.** être du bon/mauvais côté; **to take sides** choisir son camp, prendre parti; **to refuse to take sides** refuser de prendre parti; **to take sides with sb, to take the s. of sb** se ranger avec *ou* du côté de qn; **he's on our s.** il est avec nous *ou* de notre côté; **whose s. are you on?** de quel côté êtes-vous?; **to change sides** changer de camp, virer de bord; *Pol etc* faire volte-face; **they fought on our s.** ils se sont battus à nos côtés; **they were on the other s.** (*in war etc*) ils étaient de l'autre côté; **time is on our s.** le temps travaille pour nous; *Fb* **a club/national s.** une équipe locale/nationale; **to pick sides** faire les équipes; **to let the s. down** trahir *ou* décevoir ses amis/*etc*

(f) (*lineage*) côté *m*; **on his mother's s.** du côté maternel *ou* de sa mère

(g) *Old-fashioned Br F* (*affectation*) **to put on s.** se donner des airs; **there's no s. to her at all** c'est quelqu'un de très simple

(h) *Fig* **he does a bit of gardening on the s.** il a un petit boulot: il fait du jardinage; *F* **to make something** *or* **a bit on the s.** se faire des extras; *F* **profits on the s.** de la gratte; *F* **to have a bit on the s.** (*have lover*) (*of man*) avoir une petite amie *ou* une maîtresse; (*of woman*) avoir un petit ami *ou* un amant; **he has his bit on the s. every Tuesday** il a son cinq à sept tous les mardis

(i) *Billiards* **to put s. on a ball** donner de l'effet à une balle

(j) (*in compounds*) **s. aisle** (*in church, cathedral*) bas-côté *m*; *Th etc* passage *m* latéral *ou* de côté; *Am* **s. chair** chaise *f* (*de salle à manger etc*); **s. chapel** (*in church, cathedral*) chapelle *f* latérale; **it is served with a s. dish of potatoes** nous le servons avec des pommes de terre en accompagnement; **s. door** porte *f* latérale; *Fig* **to enter a profession by the s. door** entrer dans une profession par la petite porte; **s. entry** *or* **entrance** entrée *f* sur le côté; **s. face** profil *m*; **with a s. glance at her** en la regardant de côté *ou* du coin de l'œil, en lui jetant un regard en coin; **s. issue** question *f* d'importance *ou* d'intérêt secondaire; **the s. issues of a question** les à-côtés *mpl* d'une question; **s. panel** (*of vehicle*) ridelle *f*; **s. pocket** poche *f* laterale *ou* de côté; **s. rail** (*of ship*) rambarde *f*; (*of bridge*) garde-fou *m*; **s. table** petite table *f*, desserte *f*; **s. view** vue *f* de côté; **s. wall** (*of tyre*) flanc *m*; **s. window** (*of car*) vitre *f* latérale

side² *vi* **to s. with sb** (*support*) prendre le parti de qn; **to s. against sb** prendre parti contre qn

sideboard ['saɪdbɔːd] *n* **(a)** (*piece of furniture*) buffet *m* **(b)** *Br* **sideboards** (*whiskers*) favoris *mpl*

sideburns ['saɪdbɜːnz] *npl* (*whiskers*) favoris *mpl*

sidecar ['saɪdkɑːr] *n* **(a)** (*of motor bike*) side-car *m*, *pl* side-cars **(b)** *esp Am* (*cocktail*) = cocktail *m* composé de cointreau, de cognac et de jus de citron

-sided [-'saɪdɪd] *suff* **a four-s. figure** une figure à quatre côtés; **a many-s. debate** (*with many facets*) un débat qui touche à bien des problèmes; (*with many participants*) un débat auquel on confronte des opinions très diverses; **three-s. contract** contrat à trois parties *ou* tripartite

side drum *n Mus* tambour *m*

side effect *n* (*of medication etc*) effet *m ou* réaction *f* secondaire

side-impact bar *n Aut* renfort *m* anti-impact latéral

sidekick ['saɪdkɪk] *n F* acolyte *mf*; *Hum* **can I bring along a couple of sidekicks?** est-ce que je peux emmener quelques copains?

sidelight ['saɪdlaɪt] *n* **(a)** *Phot etc* lumière *f* de côté; *Fig* **to throw a s. on a subject** donner un aperçu sur un sujet **(b)** *Constr* (*window*) fenêtre *f* latérale **(c) sidelights** *Br Aut* feux *mpl* de position; *Naut* feux de côté

sideline¹ ['saɪdlaɪn] *n* **(a)** *Fb etc* ligne *f* de touche; *Fig* **to be on the sidelines** (*excluded*) rester sur la touche; **I prefer to stay on the sidelines** je préfère ne pas m'en mêler; **all his life he has stayed on the sidelines** toute sa vie, il est resté à l'écart; **to watch from the sidelines** *Sp* regarder de la ligne de touche; *Fig* être là en spectateur **(b)** (*secondary job*) petit boulot *m*; **it's just a s.** (*which earns money*) c'est un petit à-côté; **we sell guide books as a s.** en plus de nos activités principales, nous vendons des guides

sideline² *vt Am Sp* (*usu passive*) **to be sidelined** être mis sur *ou* rester sur la touche *Fig* **to be feeling sidelined** avoir l'impression d'avoir été laissé sur la touche

sidelong ['saɪdlɒŋ] **1** *adv* (*to fall*) à l'oblique, obliquement, de côté; (*to look at sb*) de côté, du coin de l'œil **2** *adj* (*glance*) oblique, de côté; **to give sb a s. glance** regarder qn de côté *ou* du coin de l'œil

sidereal [saɪ'dɪərɪəl] *adj Astron* sidéral

side road *n* chemin *m* latéral; (*minor road*) route *f* secondaire

side-saddle **1** *n* selle *f* de dame *ou* de femme **2** *adv* **to ride s.** monter en amazone

side salad *n* salade *f*

sideshow ['saɪdʃəʊ] *n* (*at fair*) (*stall*) stand *m* de foire; (*show*) spectacle *m* de foire; *Fig* (*secondary matter*) affaire *f* d'importance secondaire

sideslip¹ ['saɪdslɪp] *n* **(a)** *Aut, Cycling, Ski* dérapage *m* **(b)** *Av* glissade *f* (sur l'aile), glissement *m* latéral

sideslip² *vi* **(a)** *Aut, Cycling, Ski* déraper **(b)** *Av* glisser sur l'aile

sidesman, *pl* **-men** ['saɪdzmən] *n Br Rel* = marguillier *m* adjoint

sidesplitting ['saɪdsplɪtɪŋ] *adj F* (*joke*) tordant

sidesplittingly ['saɪdsplɪtɪŋlɪ] *adv F* **s. funny** drôle à se tordre de rire

sidestep ['saɪdstep] **1** *vi* faire un pas de côté; *Boxing etc* esquiver **2** *vt* (*tackle*) éviter; (*player*) passer; *Fig* (*question*) éviter

side street *n* rue *f* latérale *ou* transversale; (*small street*) petite rue

sidestroke ['saɪdstrəʊk] *n Swimming* nage *f* indienne

sideswipe¹ ['saɪdswaɪp] *n* (*blow*) coup *m* sur le côté; **to take a s. at sb** frapper qn sur le côté; *Fig* faire une remarque désagréable sur qn en passant; *Fig* **that was a s. at the Prime Minister** c'était une allusion malveillante à propos du Premier Ministre

sideswipe² *vt Am* (*car etc*) donner un coup dans *ou* cogner le côté de

sidetrack¹ ['saɪdtræk] *Am Rail* voie *f* secondaire

sidetrack² *vt Fig* (*divert from aim*) distraire; (*divert from subject*) faire dévier **(from** de); **they tried to s. him onto something else** ils ont essayé de le faire dévier sur un autre sujet; **he's easily sidetracked** il se laisse facilement distraire; **to be** *or* **get sidetracked** (*be diverted from one's aim*) se détourner de son but; (*digress*) s'écarter de son sujet

sidewalk ['saɪdwɔːk] *n Am* trottoir *m*; **s. café** terrasse *f* de café

sideways ['saɪdweɪz] **1** *adv* latéralement; (*to look*) en biais; (*to turn sth*) en travers, de biais; **to lean/fall s.** se pencher/se tomber sur le côté; **to slide s.** (*of door etc*) coulisser latéralement; **to walk s.** marcher en crabe; **to put sth s. on to sth** mettre qch à angle droit avec qch **2** *adj* de côté; **s. motion** mouvement *m* latéral

side whiskers *npl* favoris *mpl*

sidewinder ['saɪdwaɪndər] *n* **(a)** (*snake*) serpent *m* à sonnettes cornu **(b)** *US* (*blow*) coup *m* sur le côté

siding ['saɪdɪŋ] *n Rail* voie *f* de garage; *Br* (*secondary line*) embranchement *m*; (*of factory*) voie de raccordement; **goods s.** voie de chargement

sidle ['saɪd(ə)l] *vi* **to s. up to sb** se glisser auprès de qn; **to s. out of the room** se glisser hors de la salle; **to s. along** s'avancer de côté *ou F* de guingois

SIDS [sɪdz] *n Med* (*abbr* **sudden infant death syndrome)** mort *f* subite du nourrisson

siege [siːdʒ] *n Mil, Fig* siège *m*; **to lay s. to a town** assiéger une ville; **to raise the s.** lever le siège; **to declare a state of s.** déclarer l'état de siège; **to be under s.** être assiégé; **they have a s. mentality** ils se sentent persécutés; *Mil Hist* **s. gun** pièce *f* de siège

Siena [sɪ'enə] *n* Sienne *f*

sienna [sɪ'enə] **1** *n* (*earth*) terre *f* de Sienne; **raw/burnt s.** terre de Sienne naturelle/brûlée **2** *adj* (*colour*) **s. (brown)** terre de Sienne *inv*

sierra [sɪ'eərə] *n Geog* sierra *f*

siesta [sɪ'estə] *n* sieste *f*; **to take a s.** faire la sieste

sieve¹ [sɪv] *n* (*with coarse mesh*) crible *m*; (*with fine mesh*) tamis *m*; (*for powders and liquids*) sas *m*; (*for liquids*) passoire *f*; **to pass sth through a s.** passer qch au tamis/au crible; *F* **he's got a memory like a s.** il a la tête comme une passoire; **this bucket leaks like a s.** ce seau est une vraie passoire

sieve² *vt* = **sift 1 (a)**

sift [sɪft] **1** *vt* **(a)** (*flour*) tamiser, passer au tamis; (*sand etc*) cribler, passer au crible; **to s. sugar over a cake** saupoudrer un gâteau de sucre **(b)** *Fig* (*examine*) (*evidence*) examiner minutieusement, passer au crible; **to s. the facts** passer les faits au crible **2** *vi* (*of dust etc*) filtrer **(through** à travers); **the sand sifted through his fingers** le sable lui coulait entre les doigts

▶ **sift out** *vtsep* (*remove by sifting*) (*impurities*) ôter en tamisant; *Fig* (*unsuitable candidates etc*) éliminer

▶ **sift through** *vipo* (*facts, evidence*) parcourir

sifter ['sɪftər] *n* **(a)** (*sieve*) tamis *m*, crible *m* **(b)** (*for sugar*) saupoudroir *m*

sifting ['sɪftɪŋ] *n* tamisage *m*, criblage *m*; *Fig* (*examination*) (*of evidence etc*) examen *m* minutieux

sigh¹ [saɪ] *n* soupir *m*; **heavy/deep/long(-drawn) s.** gros/profond/long soupir; **he breathed** *or* **heaved a s. of relief** il a poussé un soupir de soulagement; **with a s.** en soupirant, avec un soupir

sigh² *vi* soupirer, pousser un soupir; *Lit* (*of wind*) gémir; **to s. with relief** pousser un soupir de soulagement; *Old-fashioned* **to s. for sth/sb** soupirer pour *ou* après qch/qn

sighing ['saɪɪŋ] *n* soupirs *mpl*; *Lit* (*of wind*) plainte *f*

sight¹ [saɪt] *n* **(a)** (*faculty*) vue *f*; **to have good/bad s.** avoir une bonne/mauvaise vue; **to have long s.** avoir la vue longue, être presbyte; **short s.** myopie *f*; **to lose one's s.** perdre la vue

(b) (*act of seeing*) **to catch s.** *or* **get a s. of sb/sth** apercevoir *ou* entrevoir qn/qch; **to lose s. of sb/sth** perdre qn/qch de vue; **to lose s. of the fact that …** perdre de vue (le fait) que …; **I can't bear the s. of him, I hate the very s. of him** je ne peux pas le sentir *ou* le voir; **I can't stand the s. of blood** je ne supporte pas la vue du sang; **to shoot sb at** *or* **on s.** faire feu *ou* tirer sur qn à vue; *Mus* **to play at s.** déchiffrer; *Com, Fin* **bill payable at s.** effet payable à vue; *Com* **we need to have s. of it first** il faut le voir d'abord; **to buy goods s. unseen** acheter des marchandises sans les avoir vues; **at first s.** à première vue, au premier abord; **at first s. everything seemed normal** à première vue, tout semblait normal; **to fall in love at first s.** avoir le coup de foudre (**with** pour); **it was (a case of) love at first s.** ce fut le coup de foudre; **to know sb by s.** connaître qn de vue; **to find favour in sb's s.** trouver grâce aux yeux de qn; *Fin* **s. bill** effet *m* à vue; *Tech* **s. check** contrôle *m* à vue, contrôle visuel; *Fin* **s. deposit** dépôt *m* à vue; *Fin* **s. draft** traite *f* à vue; *Fin* **s. letter of credit** crédit *m* utilisable à vue; *Med* **to have a s. test** faire vérifier sa vue

(c) (*range of vision*) **to come into s.** (ap)paraître; **to be within s.** être à portée de vue, être en vue; **to be (with)in s. of land** avoir la terre en vue; **it sank within s. of land** il a coulé près des côtes; **land in s.!** terre!; **keep him in s.** ne le perdez pas de vue; **out of s.** caché aux regards; *Old-fashioned Sl* (*excellent*) sensas; **to vanish out of s.** disparaître; **to put sth out of s.** faire disparaître qch, cacher qch; **keep it out of s. of the kids** fais attention à ce que les gamins ne le voient pas; **to keep out of s.** se cacher, se dérober; **out of my s.!** hors de ma vue!, hors d'ici!; *Prov* **out of s. out of mind** loin des yeux, loin du cœur

(d) (*aiming device*) (*of firearm*) viseur *m*; **front s.** guidon *m*; **back s.** cran *m* de mire; (*circular*) œilleton *m*; (*of sextant*) lumière *f*; **angle of s.** angle *m* de visée *ou* de site, site *m*; **line of s.** (*of optical instrument*) ligne *f* de visée; (*of firearm*) ligne de mire *ou* de tir; **to take a s. on sth** viser qch, mirer qch; *Mil* **telescopic s.** hausse *f* téléscopique, hausse à lunette; **to adjust sights** prendre *ou* régler la hausse; **to have sb/sth in one's sights** avoir qn/qch en ligne de mire; *Fig* avoir qn/qch en vue; *Fig* **to have** *or* **set one's sights on sth/sb** avoir des vues sur qch/qn; **to set one's sights on becoming rich** avoir la ferme intention de devenir riche; *Fig* **to lower one's sights** viser moins haut

(e) (*spectacle*) spectacle *m*; **sad s.** spectacle navrant; **it's a s. to see** cela vaut la peine d'être vu; **it was a s. for sore eyes** cela faisait plaisir à voir; **you're a s. for sore eyes!** c'est un plaisir de te voir!; **what a s. you are!, you do look a s.!** (*wet, dirty*) te voilà dans un drôle d'état!; (*ridiculous*) de quoi tu as l'air comme ça!; **the sights** (*scenic places*) les sites *mpl* pittoresques; (*of a city etc*) les monuments *mpl*, les curiosités *fpl*; **we're going to see the sights** nous allons visiter la ville/la région/*etc*

(f) *Fig F* **not by a long s.** loin de là; *F* **a damn s. longer/harder/more expensive** vachement plus long/difficile/cher

(g) *Aut* **s. glass** hublot *m* de contrôle; **s. (hole)** (*for inspection purposes*) regard *m*

sight² *vt* **(a)** (*see*) (*person, object, land*) apercevoir; (*star, planet etc*) observer; **a golden eagle has been sighted here twice** on a aperçu un aigle royal ici à deux reprises **(b) to s. a gun** (*aim*) viser; (*adjust sights of*) régler la lunette d'un fusil

sighted ['saɪtɪd] **1** *adj* qui voit **2** *npl* **the s.** les voyants *mpl*

sighting ['saɪtɪŋ] *n* **several sightings of teal have been reported** on a vu des sarcelles à plusieurs reprises; **this is the first s. this year** c'est première fois qu'on le/la/les voit cette année

sightless ['saɪtlɪs] *adj* aveugle; *Fig* (*eyes*) éteint

sightlessness ['saɪtlɪsnɪs] *n* cécité *f*

sightly ['saɪtlɪ] *adj* **not very s.** pas très beau à voir

sight-read *vti Mus* déchiffrer

sight-reading *n Mus* déchiffrage *m*

sightsee ['saɪtsiː] *vi* visiter des monuments

sightseeing ['saɪtsiːɪŋ] *n* **I don't really enjoy s.** je n'aime pas tellement faire le touriste; **we spent the day s.** nous avons passé la journée à visiter le pays/les monuments; **to go s.** visiter la ville/la région/*etc*; **s. tour** visite *f* guidée; **a s. tour of Paris** un tour de Paris

sightseer ['saɪtsiːər] *n* touriste *mf*

sign¹ [saɪn] *n* **(a)** (*gesture*) signe *m*; **to make a s. /signs to sb** faire (un) signe/des signes à qn; **s. of the cross** signe de la croix; **to make the s. of the cross** se signer; **s. of recognition** signe de reconnaissance; *Telecom* **call s.** indicatif *m* d'appel

(b) (*indication*) indice *m*, indication *f*; **a sure s.** un signe qui ne trompe pas; **it's a sure s. that …** à n'en pas douter, c'est le signe que …; **it's a good/bad s.** c'est bon/mauvais signe; **s. of the times** signe des temps; **as a s. of …** en signe de …; **no s. of …** (*no trace of*) nulle *ou* aucune trace de …; **there is no s. of an end to the recession** il n'y a aucun élément qui indiquerait la fin de la récession; **he gave no s. of having heard anything** il n'a manifesté en aucune façon avoir entendu quoi que ce soit; **to show no s. of life** ne donner aucun signe de vie, ne pas donner signe de vie; **there was no s. of her** elle n'y était pas; **is there any s. of him yet?** il ne serait pas arrivé, par hasard?; **is there any s. of the missing child?** est-ce qu'il y a une trace de l'enfant disparu?; **there is little s. of progress in the negotiations** les négociations ne semblent pas avancer; **if there's the slightest s. of unrest** s'il y a le moindre signe d'agitation; **all the signs are that …** tout porte à croire que …; **the room showed signs of having been recently occupied** il était clair que la pièce avait récemment été occupée

(c) (*of pub, inn etc*) enseigne *f*; (*notice*) panneau *m*; **(shop) s.** enseigne, écriteau *m*; **a 'for sale' s.** un écriteau 'à vendre'; **neon s.** enseigne *ou* réclame *f* au néon; **(road) s.** panneau de signalisation (routière); **road signs** (*collectively*) signalisation *f* routière; **follow the signs for Manchester** suivre les panneaux indiquant Manchester; **traffic s.** panneau de signalisation (routière)

(d) (*symbol*) symbole *m*; **plus/minus s.** signe *m* plus/moins; **s. of the zodiac** signe du zodiaque; **lucky s.** signe de chance

sign² **1** *vt* **(a)** (*one's name, a document, cheque etc*) signer; (*bill of exchange*) accepter; (*contract*) signer, passer; *Fin* **to s. a bill** viser un effet; **to s. a deal** passer un marché; **the letter was signed by the president** la lettre portait la signature du président *ou* était signée de la main du président; *Jur* **signed, sealed and delivered in the presence of …** fait et signé en présence de …

(b) (*say in sign language*) **to s. sth** dire qch dans le langage des sourds-muets

(c) *Old-fashioned* (*indicate by gesture*) **to s. assent** faire signe que oui; **to s. sb to do sth** faire signe à qn de faire qch

(d) *Fb etc* (*player*) embaucher, engager; **he was signed to United for £1,000,000** il a été embauché par United pour 1 000 000 livres, il a signé un contrat de 1 000 000 livres avec United

2 *vi* **(a)** (*write signature*) signer; **to s. by proxy, to s. per pro** signer par procuration; **s. here** signez là; *Fb etc* **he signed for United** il a signé avec United

(b) (*know sign language*) connaître le langage des sourds-muets; (*use sign language*) communiquer dans le langage des sourds-muets

(c) (*indicate by gesture*) **to s. to sb to do sth** faire signe à qn de faire qch

▶ **sign away** *vtsep* (*concede by signing*) (*right etc*) signer la cession de; **to s. sth away to sb** céder qch par écrit à qn; **you're signing your life away** c'est comme si tu signais ton arrêt de mort; **to s. one's freedom away** renoncer à sa liberté (*en signant un contrat etc*)

▶ **sign for** *vipo* (*acknowledge receipt of*) (*delivery, registered letter etc*) signer pour accuser réception de, émarger

▶ **sign in** **1** *vi* (*sign when entering*) (*of employee*) pointer; (*of hotel guest*) signer à l'entrée; **all visitors must s. in** tous les visiteurs doivent signer en entrant **2** *vtsep* (*gain entrance for*) signer pour faire entrer; **I'm a member, so I can s. you in** je suis membre, donc je peux vous faire entrer

▶ **sign off** *vi* **(a)** *Rad, TV* terminer l'émission (*en jouant l'indicatif*) **(b)** (*close letter*) finir une lettre; **I'll s. off now and go to bed** je vais finir cette lettre maintenant et aller au lit

▶ **sign on** **1** *vtsep Mil* (*person*) engager; (*hire*) (*worker*) embaucher **2** *vi* **(a)** (*of worker*) être engagé, se faire embaucher; (*of soldier*) s'engager **(b)** *Br F* (*register for unemployment benefit*) s'inscrire au chômage; **Tuesday is my day for signing on** je pointe le mardi **(c)** *Comptr* ouvrir une session

▶ **sign out** **1** *vi* (*sign when leaving*) (*of employee*) pointer; (*of hotel guest*) signer à la sortie; **visitors must s. out** les visiteurs doivent signer en sortant **2** *vtsep* (*indicate* *departure of)* **could you s. me out?** est-ce que vous pouvez noter que je suis parti?

▶ **sign over** *vtsep* **to s. sth over to sb** céder qch à qn (par écrit)

▶ **sign up 1** *vi* **(a)** *(register)* s'inscrire **(for a course/***etc* à un cours/*etc*) **(b)** *(enlist)* *(of soldier)* s'engager **2** *vtsep Sp, Th etc* *(player, actor etc)* *(hire)* donner un contrat à, engager; **can I s. you up as a driver?** est-ce que je peux vous inscrire comme chauffeur?

signal[1] ['sɪgn(ə)l] *n* **(a)** signal *m*, -aux; *Fig* signe *m*; **warning s.** signal avertisseur *ou* d'avertissement; **alarm s.** signal d'alarme *ou* d'alerte; **all clear s.** signal de fin d'alerte; **time s.** signal horaire; *Sp etc* **starting s.** signal de *ou* du départ; *Tel* **call** *or US* **line s.** indicatif *m* d'appel; *Am* **busy s.** signal de ligne occupée; **to give/send/receive a s.** faire/envoyer/ recevoir un signal; **when I give the s.** quand je donne/ donnerai le signal; *Fig* **he's putting out a lot of confusing signals** son attitude n'est pas claire; *Fig* **we don't want to send the wrong signals** nous ne voulons pas induire les gens en erreur (par notre comportement); **you're sending all the wrong signals if you want her to realize you're attracted to her** si tu veux qu'elle comprenne que tu es attiré par elle, il faut que ton attitude le montre; **his statement sent all the right signals** sa déclaration a clairement laissé voir ses intentions; **the demonstration is a clear s. to the government to change its policy** la manifestation signifie clairement que le gouvernement doit changer de politique; **traffic signals** feux *mpl* de circulation; **light s.** signal lumineux; *Mil* **arm** *or* **hand s.** signal à bras; **semaphore s.** signal sémaphorique; *Naut* signal à bras; **flag s.** *Mil* signal par fanion(s); *Naut* signal à pavillon; *Rail* signal par drapeau; **Morse signals** signaux Morse; **stop s.** signal d'arrêt immédiat; *Naut* **s. book** livre *m* des signaux; *Rail* **s. box** poste *m* d'aiguillage; **s. communications** télécommunications *fpl*, transmissions *fpl*; **s. flag** *Mil* fanion *m* de signalisation; *Naut* pavillon *m* pour signaux; **s. flare** *(rocket)* fusée *f* éclairante; *(stationary)* feu *m* de Bengale; **s. lamp** *(for making signals)* lampe *f ou* projecteur *m* de signalisation; *(serving as a signal)* (lampe) témoin *m*; **s. light** *Naut* fanal *m*, -aux; *Mil* voyant *m* (lumineux); *Br Mil* **Signals** transmissions; *Br Mil* **Signals officer** officier *m* des transmissions; *Am* **s. red** vermillon *m* chinois; **s. rocket** fusée de signalisation

(b) *Electron, Rad etc* **input/output s.** signal *m* d'entrée/de sortie

signal[2] (-ll-, *US* -l-) **1** *vi* faire un signal/des signaux **(to** à); **I signalled to him (to stop)** je lui ai fait signe (de s'arrêter); **she signalled for the bill** elle a fait signe qu'on lui apporte l'addition; *Aut etc* **to s. before stopping** *(with hand)* prévenir *ou* avertir avant de s'arrêter; *Aut* **he didn't s. before he turned** *(with light)* il n'a pas mis son clignotant avant de tourner; *(with hand)* il n'a pas fait signe avant de tourner

2 *vt* *(order)* transmettre; *(train, ship)* faire signe à; *Aut* **to s. that one is turning** *(with hand)* signaler un changement de direction; *(with light)* mettre son clignotant avant de tourner; **the train was signalled to stop** le train a reçu le signal de s'arrêter; **this signals the start of the rainy season** cela indique le début *ou* c'est le signe du début de la saison des pluies; **her resignation signalled the beginning of the end** sa démission a marqué le début de la fin; **he signalled the car on** il a fait signe à la voiture d'avancer

signal[3] *adj attrib Lit* *(success)* éclatant, remarquable; *(failure)* notoire; *(service)* insigne; *(importance)* capital; **a s. lack of sth** un manque flagrant de qch

signalize ['sɪgnəlaɪz] *vt* *(victory, success)* marquer

signaller ['sɪgnələr] *n* signaleur *m*

signalling, *US* **signaling** ['sɪgnəlɪŋ] *n* **(a)** *(act)* signalisation *f*; *(sending signals)* transmission *f* de signaux; **s. flag** *Mil* fanion *m* de signalisation; *Naut* pavillon *m* pour signaux; *Rail* drapeau *m* **(b)** *(signals)* signaux *mpl*

signally ['sɪgnəlɪ] *adv Lit* remarquablement, d'une façon éclatante; **... which he had s. failed to do ...** ce qu'il avait totalement manqué de faire; **the performance was s. lacking in enthusiasm** l'interprétation manquait singulièrement d'enthousiasme

signalman, *pl* **-men** ['sɪgnəlmən] *n* signaleur *m*; *(using semaphore)* sémaphoriste *m*; *Rail* bloqueur *m*

signatory ['sɪgnət(ə)rɪ] **1** *n* signataire *mf* **(to a treaty** d'un traité) **2** *adj* *(nation)* signataire

signature ['sɪgnətʃər] *n* **(a)** signature *f*; *Admin* visa *m*; **to put one's s. to a letter** apposer sa signature au bas d'une lettre; **his s. was on the letter** la lettre portait sa signature; *Com etc* **for s.** pour signature; **s. book** parapheur *m*; **s. by proxy** signature par procuration; **s. stamp** griffe *f* **(b)** *Typ* *(mark)* signature *f*; *(pages)* cahier *m* d'imprimerie **(c)** *Mus* **(key) s.** armature *f*

signature tune *n Rad, TV* *(of programme)* indicatif *m*

signboard ['saɪnbɔːd] *n* *(of pub, shop etc)* enseigne *f*

signet ['sɪgnɪt] *n* **s. ring** chevalière *f*; *Hist* *(for sealing)* anneau *m* sigillaire

significance [sɪg'nɪfɪkəns] *n* **(a)** *(importance)* importance *f*, portée *f*; **event of no/of great s.** événement sans importance/de la plus haute importance **(b)** *(meaning)* *(of word, gesture etc)* signification *f*; **what is the s. of this ceremony?** que signifie cette cérémonie?; **she gave him a look of deep s.** elle lui glissa un regard très significatif

significant [sɪg'nɪfɪkənt] *adj* **(a)** *(event, difference, improvement etc)* important, significatif; *(amount of money)* important; **do you think this is s.?** pensez-vous que cela a de l'importance?; **what's s. about it is that ...** ce qu'il y a d'important là-dedans c'est que ...; *US F* **s. other** = conjoint *mf*, partenaire *mf* **(b)** *(word, gesture)* significatif; *(look)* lourd de sens

significantly [sɪg'nɪfɪkəntlɪ] *adv* **(a)** *(appreciably)* *(to differ)* sensiblement; **s. cheaper** sensiblement moins cher; **it's not s. different** ça ne fait pas une grosse différence; **there have been s. fewer problems** on a eu nettement moins de problèmes **(b)** *(in a meaningful way)* *(to look at etc)* d'une manière significative; **she paused s. at this point** à ce moment-là, elle s'est interrompue et son silence était lourd de sens; **s., no one mentioned it** personne n'a mentionné ce point, ce qui, en soi, était très significatif

signification [sɪgnɪfɪ'keɪʃən] *n Fml* *(of word, event)* signification *f*, sens *m*

significative [sɪg'nɪfɪkətɪv] *adj* révélateur **(of** de)

signify ['sɪgnɪfaɪ] **1** *vt* **(a)** *(indicate)* signifier, indiquer; **a broad forehead signifies intelligence** un front large est (un) signe d'intelligence **(b)** *(mean)* signifier, vouloir dire; *(make known)* *(one's intentions etc)* signifier, faire connaître **2** *vi* importer; **it doesn't s.** cela n'a aucune importance, peu importe

signing ['saɪnɪŋ] *n* **(a)** *(of document etc)* signature *f*; *(of deed)* passation *f*; *Com* *(of bill)* acceptation *f*; **s. for the post** émargement *m* du courrier; **a manager with s. authority** un fondé de pouvoir **(b)** *(sign language)* langage *m* des sourds-muets; **her s. is excellent** elle connaît très bien le langage des sourds-muets **(c)** *Fb etc* transfert *m*

signing-in *n* *(of employees)* pointage *m*

sign language *n* mimique *f*; *(of the deaf)* langage *m* des sourds-muets; **to speak in s.** parler par gestes; **to use s.** *(to deaf person, foreigner etc)* s'exprimer par gestes

sign-off *n TV* annonce *f* de la fin des émissions

sign painter *n* *(of lettering)* peintre *m* en lettres; *(of pub signs etc)* peintre d'enseignes

signpost[1] ['saɪnpəʊst] *n* poteau *m* indicateur; *Fig* jalon *m*, point *m* de repère

signpost[2] *vt* *(road etc)* signaliser, marquer de poteaux indicateurs; *Fig* *(thesis, meaning, differences etc)* signaler; **well/badly signposted road** route qui est bien/mal signalisée; **signposted footpath** sentier *m* balisé

signposting ['saɪnpəʊstɪŋ] *n* signalisation *f* des routes; *Fig* **despite obvious s. from the author, some readers failed to spot that ...** bien que l'auteur ait placé des indices très clairs ici et là, certains lecteurs n'ont pas vu que ...

sign writer *n* *(of lettering)* peintre *m* en lettres; *(of pub signs etc)* peintre d'enseignes

Sikh [siːk] *adj, n Rel* sikh, -e

silage ['saɪlɪdʒ] *n Agr* fourrage *m* ensilé

silence[1] ['saɪləns] *n* silence *m*; **s.!** silence!; *(notice in library etc)* défense de parler; **there was a sudden s.** soudain, il y a eu un silence; **to break the s.** rompre le silence; **a shot broke the s.** un coup de feu déchira le silence; **to reduce sb to s.** réduire qn au silence, faire taire qn; **there's been complete s. from head office** le siège est resté totalement silencieux; **a deafening s.** un silence éloquent; **to suffer in s.** souffrir en silence; **to buy sb's s.** acheter le silence de qn; **to write to sb after five years' s.** écrire à qn après un silence de cinq ans; **to pass over sth in s.** passer qch sous silence; **the s. of the night** le silence de la nuit; *Prov* **s. is golden** le silence est d'or

silence[2] *vt* *(person)* réduire au silence, faire taire; *(the opposition)* réduire au silence; *(pupils etc)* imposer le silence à; *(one's conscience, criticism)* faire taire; *(complaints)* étouffer; *Mil* *(enemy fire)* faire cesser, faire taire; *(muffle)* *(noise)* amortir, étouffer; **that really silenced him!** *(made speechless)* ça l'a laissé sans voix!

silencer ['saɪlənsər] *n* **(a)** *Br Aut* *(on exhaust)* silencieux *m* **(b)** *(on gun)* silencieux *m*

silent ['saɪlənt] *adj* **(a)** *(person, place etc)* silencieux; *(taciturn)* silencieux, taciturne, peu loquace; **to fall s.** devenir silencieux; **he's trying to come across as the strong, s. type** il veut qu'on le prenne pour un mec viril; *Hum* **he's the**

strong, **s. type** c'est un viril; **to keep s.** observer le silence; (*not reveal information*) garder le silence, se taire (**about** sur); **to remain s.** rester muet; **be s.!** taisez-vous!; **they stood a minute in s. memory of ...** ils ont observé une minute de silence à la mémoire de ...; **to give sb the s. treatment** ne pas adresser la parole à qn; **s. as the grave** muet comme une tombe; **the document is s. on this point** le document ne dit rien sur ce point; **s. actor/actress** acteur/actrice de film(s) muet(s); **s. camera** caméra *f* muette; **s. film** *or* **movie** film *m* muet; **stars of the s. screen** vedettes du cinéma muet; **the s. majority** la majorité silencieuse; *Rel* **s. order** ordre *m* silencieux; *Com* **s. partner** commanditaire *m*, bailleur *m* de fonds; **s. protest** manifestation *f* silencieuse
(**b**) *Ling* (*letter*) muet; **the k is s.** le k ne se prononce pas, le k est muet

silently ['saɪləntlɪ] *adv* (*to walk, move, do sth*) sans faire de bruit, silencieusement; (*to nod, sit*) en silence; (*to change sth*) discrètement

silex ['saɪleks] *n Miner* silex *m*

silhouette[1] [sɪlu:'et] *n* silhouette *f*; **in s.** en silhouette; *TV, Cin* **s. lighting** éclairage *m* en contre-jour

silhouette[2] *vt* silhouetter, projeter en silhouette; **to be silhouetted against a light background** se détacher (en silhouette) sur un fond clair; **a tree silhouetted against the sky** un arbre qui se détachait *ou* qui se découpait sur le ciel

silica ['sɪlɪkə] *n Ch* silice *f*; **s. gel dessicant crystals** cristaux *mpl* dessicatifs de silica-gel

silicate ['sɪlɪkət] *n Ch* silicate *m*

siliceous [sɪ'lɪʃəs] *adj Ch* siliceux

silicon ['sɪlɪkən] *n Ch* silicium *m*; **s. chip** puce *f ou* pastille *f* de silicium; **s. technology** technologie *f* du silicium; **S. Valley** Silicon Valley *f*; **s. wafer** tranche *f* de silicium

silicone ['sɪlɪkəʊn] *n Ch* silicone *f*; **s. implant** implant *m* en silicone; **s. rubber** caoutchouc *m* silicone

silicosis [sɪlɪ'kəʊsɪs] *n Med* silicose *f*

silk [sɪlk] *n* (**a**) (*fabric, fibre*) soie *f*; **raw s.** soie grège *ou* écrue; **artificial s.** rayonne *f*; **a black s. dress** une robe de soie noire; **s. fabric(s), silk(s)** soierie *f*; **s. finish** similisage *m*; **s. screen printing** sérigraphie *f*; **s. stockings** bas de *ou* en soie; **s. yarn** fil de soie (**b**) *Horseracing* **silks** (*of jockey*) casaque *f* (**c**) *Br Jur F* (*King's, Queen's Counsel*) conseiller *m* du roi/de la reine; (*collectively*) conseillers du roi/de la reine; **to take s.** être nommé conseiller du roi/de la reine

silken ['sɪlk(ə)n] *adj Lit* (**a**) *Tex* de soie; *Fig* (*curls*) soyeux, de soie (**b**) (*voice, words*) doux, *Pej* doucereux, mielleux

silkiness ['sɪlkɪnɪs] *n* (**a**) (*of fabric*) nature *f* soyeuse (**b**) (*of voice, words*) moelleux *m*, *Pej* mielleux *m*

silkworm ['sɪlkwɜ:m] *n* ver *m* à soie; **s. breeder** sériciculteur *m*, magnanier, -ière; **s. breeding** sériciculture *f*, magnanerie *f*; **s. moth** bombyx *m* (du mûrier); **s. nursery** *or* **farm** magnanerie

silky ['sɪlkɪ] *adj* soyeux; **s. voice** voix moelleuse, *Pej* voix mielleuse; **s. soft hair** cheveux doux comme de la soie

sill [sɪl] *n Constr etc* (*of door*) seuil *m*; (*of window*) rebord *m*, appui *m*; (*of frame*) sole *f*, semelle *f*; *Aut* bas *m* de marche

sillabub ['sɪləbʌb] *n Culin* = entremets *m* sucré semblable au sabayon

silliness ['sɪlɪnɪs] *n* sottise *f*, bêtise *f*; **that's enough s. for one morning** assez de bêtises pour ce matin

silly ['sɪlɪ] **1** *adj* (*person*) sot, *f* sotte, stupide; (*question, answer*) stupide; **don't be so s.!** ne sois pas si bête!; **I'll pay – don't be s.** je vais payer – il n'en est pas question!; **(you) s. fool** *or* **ass!** imbécile!, espèce d'idiot!; **it would make me look s.** j'aurais l'air bête *ou* ridicule; **that was a s. thing to do!** ça *ou* ce n'était pas très intelligent!; **to say something s.** dire une bêtise; **but that's s., she was here half an hour ago** mais c'est ridicule, elle était ici il y a une demi-heure; **there was a new manager every week, it was** *or* **things were getting s.** il y avait un nouveau gérant chaque semaine, ça en devenait ridicule; **it was s. of me to ask** c'était idiot de ma part de demander ça; **he's forgotten his umbrella, (the) s. man** il a oublié son parapluie, cet idiot; *Journ F* **the s. season** = la période creuse des mois d'été; **to laugh oneself s.** mourir de rire; **to worry sb s.** rendre qn malade d'inquiétude; **she's been worrying herself s.** elle est morte d'inquiétude; **she'll worry herself s.** elle se rendra malade d'inquiétude (**about** à cause de); **to knock sb s.** étourdir *ou* assommer qn
2 *n F* idiot, -ote; **don't be such a s.!** que tu es bête!

sillybilly ['sɪlɪbɪlɪ] *n F* (*to child*) gros bêta *m*; **don't be such a s.!** ne sois pas si bête!; **oh, I am a s.!** oh, que je suis bête!

silo ['saɪləʊ] *n Agr, Mil* silo *m*

silt[1] [sɪlt] *n* boue *f*; (*in waterway*) dépôt *m*, vase *f*, limon *m*

silt[2] *vt* = **silt up 2**

► **silt up 1** *vi* (*of harbour etc*) s'envaser **2** *vtsep* (*fill with silt*) (*port, canal*) envaser

silting up *n* (*of port, canal etc*) envasement *m*

silver[1] ['sɪlvər] **1** *n* (**a**) (*metal*) argent *m*; **is that spoon s.?** est-ce que cette cuiller est en argent?; *Prov* **he was born with a s. spoon in his mouth** il est né coiffé; *Prov* **every cloud has a s. lining** à quelque chose malheur est bon; **to look for the s. lining** regarder le bon côté des choses; **s. gilt** vermeil *m*, argent recouvert d'or; **s. grey** gris argenté *inv*; **s. paper** papier *m* d'étain, papier argenté *ou* d'argent; **s. plate** (*layer of silver*) plaqué *m* argent; (*silver-plated objects*) argenterie *f*; **s. plating** argenture *f*; **stars of the s. screen** stars du grand écran; **s. service** (*in restaurant*) service *m* de grande classe; **s. service waiter/waitress** serveur *m*/serveuse *f* pour service au guéridon; **s. tongued** (*voice etc*) argentin; **s. wedding** noces *fpl* d'argent
(**b**) *Br* (*coins*) pièces *fpl* en argent; **a pound in s.** une livre en argent, une livre en pièces *ou* en monnaie d'argent
(**c**) (*silverware*) argenterie *f*
(**d**) *Sp etc* **s. (medal)** médaille *f* d'argent; **to get a s. in the shot put** remporter une médaille d'argent au lancer du poids
2 *adj* (**a**) (*made of silver*) en argent
(**b**) **s. (-coloured)** argent *inv*

silver[2] *vt* (*mirror*) étamer; (*cutlery etc*) argenter; *Lit* (*waves etc*) argenter

silver birch *n* bouleau *m* blanc

silver bromide *n* bromure *m* d'argent

silverfish ['sɪlvəfɪʃ] *n* (**a**) (*fish*) argentine *f* (**b**) (*insect*) lépisme *m*, petit poisson *m* d'argent

silver fox *n* renard *m* argenté

silver-haired *adj* aux cheveux argentés

silver-plate *vt* argenter

silver-plated *adj* argenté

silverside ['sɪlvəsaɪd] *n Br Culin* gîte *m* à la noix

silversmith ['sɪlvəsmɪθ] *n* orfèvre *m*

silverware ['sɪlvəweər] *n* argenterie *f*

silverwork ['sɪlvəwɜ:k] *n* orfèvrerie *f*

silvery ['sɪlvərɪ] *adj Lit* (*cloud, water*) argenté; (*scales etc*) d'argent; (*laugh*) argentin

simian ['sɪmɪən] **1** *adj Zool* simien; *Fig* (*gait, appearance etc*) simiesque **2** *n Zool* simien *m*

similar ['sɪmɪlər] *adj* semblable (**to** à), pareil (**to** à), similaire; *Math* (*triangles*) semblable; **your case is s. to mine** votre cas est semblable au mien; **they are s. in appearance** d'apparence, ils sont semblables; **the two women are s.** les deux femmes se ressemblent; **there was a s. mistake on page 1** il y avait une erreur semblable page 1; **something s. happened to me** il m'est arrivé quelque chose de semblable

similarity [sɪmɪ'lærɪtɪ] *n* ressemblance *f*; *Math* (*of triangles*) similitude *f*; **there the s. ends** c'est là que s'arrête la comparaison

similarly ['sɪmɪləlɪ] *adv* pareillement; **they were s. dressed** ils/elles étaient habillé(e)s de la même façon; **s., ...** de même ...

simile ['sɪmɪlɪ] *n* comparaison *f*

similitude [sɪ'mɪlɪtju:d] *n Fml* (*resemblance*) ressemblance *f*, similitude *f*; (*comparison*) comparaison *f*

SIMM [sɪm] *n Comptr* (*abbr* **single in-line memory module**) SIMM *m*

simmer[1] ['sɪmər] *n Culin* **to keep sth at a s.** *or* **on the s.** (faire) mijoter qch, faire cuire qch à petit feu *ou* à feu doux

simmer[2] **1** *vi* (**a**) *Culin etc* (*of liquid*) frémir; (*of food in pot*) mijoter, cuire à petit feu *ou* à feu doux (**b**) *Fig* (*of revolt, discontent etc*) fermenter; **he was simmering with rage** il bouillonnait de rage **2** *vt Culin* (*stew etc*) mijoter, mitonner

► **simmer down** *vi* (*of person*) se calmer

simnel ['sɪmn(ə)l] *n Br* **s. (cake)** gâteau *m* de Pâques *ou* de la mi-carême

simon crane ['saɪmən] *n TV, Cin* grue *f* hydraulique

simony ['saɪmənɪ] *n Rel* simonie *f*

simper[1] ['sɪmpər] *n* minauderies *fpl*; **..., he said with a s.** ..., dit-il en minaudant; **the s. she puts on when ...** la façon dont elle minaude quand ...

simper[2] *vi* minauder, mignarder; (*smile affectedly*) sourire avec affectation; **I could hear him simpering down the phone to her** je l'entendais lui dire des minauderies au téléphone

simpering ['sɪmpərɪŋ] **1** *adj* mignard, affecté **2** *n* minauderie *f*; **I've had enough of her s.** j'en ai assez de ses minauderies

simple ['sɪmp(ə)l] *adj* (*method etc*) simple, élémentaire; (*character*) simple, naturel; (*naive*) simple, naïf, crédule; **he's a bit s.** il est un peu simplet; **for the s. reason that ...** pour la simple raison que ...; **I'm not so s. as to believe that** je n'ai pas la naïveté de croire cela; **to become simpler** se simplifier; **the simplest thing to do is to ...** le plus simple est de ...; **a meal that is s. to prepare** un repas qui est simple à préparer; **he won't understand, keep it s.** il ne va

rien comprendre, reste simple; **let's keep it s.** restons simples; **it's as s. as that** c'est aussi simple que ça; **in s. terms** avec des mots simples; **reduced to its simplest terms** réduit à sa plus simple expression; **to have s. tastes** avoir des goûts simples; **that's the s. truth** c'est la vérité pure et simple; *St Exch* **s. position** position *f* élémentaire; *Gram* **s. sentence** proposition *f* indépendante
simple fracture *n* fracture *f* simple
simple-hearted [sɪmp(ə)l'hɑːtɪd] *adj* simple, ingénu, candide
simple interest *n Com* intérêts *mpl* simples
simple-minded *adj* simple (d'esprit), simplet, -ète; (*naive*) naïf, candide
simple-mindedness [sɪmp(ə)l'maɪndɪdnɪs] *n* simplicité *f*; (*naiveness*) naïveté *f*, candeur *f*
simpleness ['sɪmp(ə)lnɪs] *n* = **simplicity**
simple-rank order *n Mktg* classement *m* simple
simpleton ['sɪmp(ə)ltən] *n* nigaud, -aude, niais, -aise
simplex ['sɪmpleks] *n Ling* (*of word*) forme *f* de base
simplicity [sɪm'plɪsɪtɪ] *n* **(a)** (*candour*) (*of child etc*) candeur *f*, simplicité *f*; (*foolishness*) bêtise *f*, sottise *f* **(b)** (*of problem, dress etc*) simplicité *f*; **it's s. itself** c'est simple comme bonjour
simplification [sɪmplɪfɪ'keɪʃən] *n* simplification *f*
simplify ['sɪmplɪfaɪ] *vt* simplifier
simplistic [sɪm'plɪstɪk] *adj* simpliste; **am I being too s.?** est-ce que je simplifie trop?
simply ['sɪmplɪ] *adv* **(a)** (*in simple manner*) (*to speak, act*) simplement; (*dressed*) avec simplicité **(b)** (*absolutely*) absolument; **it's s. impossible** c'est tout bonnement impossible; **I s. won't do it** je refuse absolument de le faire; **I was s. amazed by it** j'en étais tout à fait abasourdi **(c)** (*just*) tout simplement; **purely and s.** purement et simplement; **it's s. a matter** *or* **question of time** c'est une simple question de temps, c'est tout simplement une question de temps
simulacrum, *pl* **-a** [sɪmjʊ'leɪkrəm, -ə] *n Fml* simulacre *m*
simulate ['sɪmjʊleɪt] *vt* **(a)** (*imitate*) (*illness etc*) simuler, feindre; (*enthusiasm etc*) affecter; **simulated leather** similicuir *m*; **simulated fur** fausse fourrure *f*; **simulated marble** marbre *m* artificiel; (*painted*) faux marbre **(b)** *Tech* simuler; **simulated test marketing** marché-test *m* simulé
simulation [sɪmjʊ'leɪʃən] *n* simulation *f*
simulator ['sɪmjʊleɪtər] *n Tech* (*device*) simulateur *m*; **flight s.** simulateur de vol
simultaneity [sɪməltə'neɪɪtɪ] *n* simultanéité *f*
simultaneous [sɪməl'teɪnɪəs] *adj* simultané; **s. with …** qui a lieu en même temps que …; **s. broadcast** émission diffusée simultanément, retransmission *f* simultanée; *Math* **s. equation** identités *fpl* remarquables; **s. interpreting** interprétation *f* simultanée
simultaneously [sɪməl'teɪnɪəslɪ] *adv* simultanément; **s. with** en même temps que
sin[1] [sɪn] *n* péché *m*; *F* (*against taste etc*) offense *f*; **sins of omission/commission** péchés par omission/action; **original s.** péché originel; **the seven deadly sins** les sept péchés capitaux; **the forgiveness of sins** le pardon des offenses; *Old-fashioned Hum* **to live in s.** vivre dans le péché; *F Hum* **for my sins, I was appointed …** pour mes péchés, j'ai été nommé …; *F* **if it's not a s. to ask …** s'il est permis de poser la question …; *F* **it would be a s. to stay indoors on a day like this** c'est un crime de rester à l'intérieur par une si belle journée; *Sp F* **s. bin** prison *f*
sin[2] *vi* (**-nn-**) pécher, commettre un péché/des péchés; **to s. against** (*the proprieties*) pécher contre, blesser; (*a rule etc*) manquer à; **more sinned against than sinning** plus à plaindre qu'à blâmer
Sinai ['saɪnaɪ] *n* Sinaï *m*; **the S. Peninsula** la presqu'île de Sinaï; **Mount S.** le mont Sinaï
since [sɪns] **1** *adv* **(a)** depuis; **I've not seen him s.** je ne l'ai pas revu depuis; **he's been in perfect health ever s.** depuis (lors), sa santé est parfaite

(b) (*ago*) **she had long s. given up hope of promotion** elle avait, depuis longtemps, abandonné tout espoir de promotion; **long s.** (*for a long time*) depuis longtemps; (*a long time ago*) il y a longtemps; **not long s.** il n'y a pas très longtemps; *Old-fashioned* **many years s.** il y a bien des années

2 *prep* [①B29,9] depuis; **s. his death** depuis sa mort; **s. early June** dès les premiers jours de juin; **I've been here (ever) s. lunch** je suis là depuis le déjeuner; **she has lived here s. 1984** elle vit ici depuis 1984; **she had lived there s. 1933** elle vivait là depuis 1933; **I haven't seen her s. Christmas** je ne l'ai pas vue depuis Noël; **s. then, s. that time** depuis ce temps-là, depuis lors; **s. when?** depuis quand?; *F* **s. when do you come into a room without knocking?** depuis quand est-ce qu'on entre sans frapper?; **s. seeing you** depuis que je vous ai vu

3 *conj* **(a)** [①B29,9] (*in time*) depuis que; **s. I've been here** depuis que je suis ici; **it's a long time s. I saw her** il y a longtemps que je ne l'ai vue, ça fait longtemps que je ne l'ai pas vue; **(ever) s. I have lived in London** depuis que j'habite (à) Londres; **s. he had been there** depuis qu'il était là

(b) (*because*) puisque; **I'll do it s. it's you that's asking** je le ferai puisque c'est vous qui me le demandez
sincere [sɪn'sɪər] *adj* sincère; **he is completely s.** il est de bonne foi
sincerely [sɪn'sɪəlɪ] *adv* sincèrement; **it is my s. held conviction that …** je suis sincèrement convaincu que …; **yours s.,** *esp Am* **s. yours** (*letter ending*) veuillez agréer, Monsieur/*etc*, l'expression de mes sentiments distingués *ou* les meilleurs
sincerity [sɪn'serɪtɪ] *n* (*of person*) sincérité *f*, bonne foi *f*; (*of emotion*) sincérité; **in all s.** de la meilleure foi du monde, en toute sincérité
sine [saɪn] *n Math* (*of angle*) sinus *m*
sinecure ['saɪnɪkjʊər] *n* sinécure *f*
sine die [siːneɪ'diːeɪ, 'saɪnɪ'daɪɪ] *adv Jur* sine die
sine qua non ['siːneɪkwɑː'nəʊn] *n* condition *f* sine qua non
sinew ['sɪnjuː] *n Anat* tendon *m*
sinewy ['sɪnjuːɪ] *adj* **(a)** (*meat*) tendineux **(b)** (*arm etc*) musclé, nerveux
sinful ['sɪnfʊl] *adj* (*pleasure, deed*) coupable; (*waste*) scandaleux; **it is s. to …** c'est un crime *ou Old-fashioned* un péché de …; **I am a s. wretch** je suis un misérable pécheur; **s. city** ville de perdition; **s. life** vie de péchés; **s. person** pécheur *m*, pécheresse *f*; **s. world** monde de pécheurs
sinfully ['sɪnfʊlɪ] *adv* (*to act*) d'une façon coupable; **it is s. wasteful to …** c'est un gaspillage honteux de …
sinfulness ['sɪnfʊlnɪs] *n* (*of behaviour, act*) caractère *m* scandaleux; **his/her s.** son état de pécheur/pécheresse; **a life of s.** une vie de péché
sing [sɪŋ] (*pt* **sang** [sæŋ]; *pp* **sung** [sʌŋ]) **1** *vi* **(a)** (*of person, bird*) chanter; **I can't s.** je ne sais pas chanter **(b)** (*of the wind etc*) siffler; (*of the ears*) tinter, bourdonner; **the kettle is singing** la bouilloire chante *ou* siffle **(c)** *Sl* (*inform*) moucharder, balancer **2** *vt* (*song*) chanter; **s. me a song** chante-moi une chanson; **Sinatra sings the Beatles** Sinatra chante les Beatles; *Fig* **to s. another** *or* **a different tune** changer de ton; **to s. sb to sleep** chanter quelque chose pour endormir qn; **to s. sb's praises** chanter les louanges de qn
▶ **sing along** *vi* **s. along if you like** chantez avec moi/nous/*etc* si vous voulez
▶ **sing of** *vipo Lit* chanter
▶ **sing out 1** *vi* (*sing loudly*) chanter (plus) fort; *F* **s. out if you need me** (*call*) appelle-moi si vous avez/tu as besoin de moi **2** *vtsep* (*note*) chanter clairement
▶ **sing up** *vi* (*sing louder*) chanter plus fort
singable ['sɪŋəb(ə)l] *adj* chantable
Singapore [sɪŋə'pɔːr] *n* Singapour *m*
Singaporean [sɪŋə'pɔːrɪən] **1** *adj* singapourien, -ienne **2** *n* Singapourien, -ienne
singe[1] [sɪndʒ] *n* **s. (mark)** légère brûlure *f*
singe[2] *vt* (*accidentally*) brûler légèrement; (*clothes, hair*) roussir; (*deliberately*) (*poultry, hair*) flamber
singer ['sɪŋər] *n* chanteur, -euse; **s. songwriter** auteur-compositeur-interprète *mf*
Singhalese [sɪŋgə'liːz] *adj, n* = **Sinhalese**
singing ['sɪŋɪŋ] **1** *adj* (*bird*) qui chante; **to have a fine s. voice** chanter admirablement **2** *n* (*of person, bird*) chant *m*; **his s. is awful** il chante atrocement; **s. lesson** leçon *f* de chant
singing telegram *n* télégramme *m* chanté
single[1] ['sɪŋg(ə)l] *n* **(a)** (*record*) 45 tours *m*; (*cd or cassette*) single *m*; (*ticket*) aller *m* simple; (*banknote*) (*one pound*) billet *m* d'une livre; (*one dollar*) billet d'un dollar; *Phot* **s. camera** monocaméra *f* **(b)** (*unmarried person*) célibataire *mf*; **a package holiday for singles** des vacances organisées pour célibataires **(c)** *Tennis etc* **singles** simple *m*; **men's/women's singles** simple messieurs/dames
single[2] *adj* **(a)** (*just one*) seul; **one s. case of …** un cas unique de …; **every s. day** tous les jours; **to do sth in a s. movement** faire qch d'un seul geste; **not a s. one** pas un seul, pas un; **I haven't seen a s. soul** je n'ai pas vu âme qui vive; **in a s. sum** en une fois; **don't say a s. word** ne dites pas un (seul) mot; **s. market** marché *m* unique; **s. price** prix *m* unique; *Typ* **s. quotes** guillemets *mpl* en accent simple, guillemets simples; *Comptr* **s. sheet feed** alimentation *f* feuille à feuille; *Typ* **s. spacing** interlignage *m* simple; *Comptr* **s. user licence** licence *f* individuelle d'utilisation; *Comptr* **s. user system** système *m* un seul utilisateur; **s. yellow line** (*on road*) ≈ ligne *f* jaune discontinue

(b) (*for one person, not double etc*) (*bed*) à une place, pour une personne; (*room*) à un lit, pour une personne; *Naut* (*cabin*) individuel, -elle; **in s. rank** sur un rang; **s. combat** combat *m* singulier; *Bot* **s. flower** fleur *f* simple; **s. occupancy** (*of hotel room*) occupation *f* par une seule personne; **s. (room) supplement** supplément *m* chambre individuelle; **s. seater** (*car*) monoplace *f*; (*plane*) monoplace *m*

(**c**) (*not married*) célibataire, non-marié(e); **a s. man/woman** un/une célibataire; **he remained s.** il est resté célibataire; **s. parent** parent *m* isolé

▶ **single out** *vtsep* (*choose from many*) isoler, choisir; **she was singled out for praise** elle a fait l'objet de félicitations particulières; **why s. him out (for blame)?** pourquoi le blâmer en particulier?

single-breasted [sɪŋg(ə)l'brestɪd] *adj* **s. jacket** veston *m* droit

single-column *adj Typ* à une colonne

single-cylinder *adj Aut etc* **s. engine** moteur *m* monocylindrique

single-decker [sɪŋg(ə)l'dekər] *n Br* autobus *m* sans impériale

single-density *adj Comptr* (*disk*) à simple densité

single-drive *adj* (*computer*) à un seul lecteur de disquettes

single-engined [sɪŋg(ə)l'endʒɪnd] *adj* **s. aircraft** (avion *m*) monomoteur *m*

Single European Market *n* Marché *m* unique européen

single-handed [sɪŋg(ə)l'hændɪd] **1** *adv* **I did it s.** je l'ai fait tout seul; **to sail s.** naviguer seul **2** *adj* **thanks to his s. efforts** grâce aux efforts qu'il a fourni, seul

single-handedly [sɪŋg(ə)l'hændɪdlɪ] *adv* seul, tout seul

single-lane *adj* (*traffic*) à voie unique

single-lens *adj Phot* **s. camera** appareil-photo *m* monoculaire; **s. reflex** (*camera*) reflex *m* monoculaire

single-line *adj Aut* **s. traffic only** circulation *f* à une (seule) voie

single-minded *adj* (*in pursuit of a goal*) (*person*) constant; (*determination, pursuit of power*) farouche; (*convictions*) absolu; (*determined*) (*attitude, deeds*) résolu; **he was s. in his pursuit of power** sa soif de pouvoir était sans bornes

single-mindedly [sɪŋg(ə)l'maɪndɪdlɪ] *adv* résolument

single-mindedness [sɪŋg(ə)l'maɪndɪdnɪs] *n* (*constancy*) constance *f*; (*determination*) résolution *f*

singleness ['sɪŋg(ə)lnɪs] *n* **with s. of purpose** avec un seul but en vue; **his s. of purpose** sa détermination

single-parent family *n* famille *f* monoparentale

single-phase *adj El* **s. current** courant *m* uniphasé *ou* monophasé

singles bar *n* bar *m* pour célibataires

single-sex *adj* **s. school** école *f* non-mixte

single-sided *adj Comptr* (*disk*) à une seule face

single-spaced [sɪŋg(ə)l'speɪst] *adj Typ* à interligne simple

single-spoke *adj* (*steering wheel*) monobranche

singlet ['sɪŋglɪt] *n Br* maillot *m* de corps; (*of cotton, flannel*) gilet *m*; *Sp* maillot

singleton ['sɪŋg(ə)ltən] *n Cards, Math* singleton *m*

single-track *adj* **s. railway** chemin *m* de fer à voie unique; **s. road** route *f* à une seule voie

singly ['sɪŋglɪ] *adv* (*one by one*) séparément, un à un; *Com* **articles sold s.** articles qui se vendent séparément *ou* à la pièce; **people entered s. or in pairs** les gens sont entrés seuls ou par deux

singsong ['sɪŋsɒŋ] **1** *adj* (*tone*) chantant; **in a s. voice** d'un ton chantant **2** *n F* (*singing session*) concert *m* improvisé; **to have a s.** pousser la chansonnette

singular ['sɪŋgjʊlər] **1** *adj* (**a**) *Gram* (*number*) singulier, -ière (**b**) (*remarkable*) rare, remarquable; (*strange*) singulier, bizarre **2** *n* [①A14-15,C] *Gram* singulier *m*; **in the s.** au singulier

singularity [sɪŋgjʊ'lærɪtɪ] *n* (*remarkableness*) particularité *f*; (*strangeness*) bizarrerie *f*

singularize ['sɪŋgjʊləraɪz] *vt* singulariser

singularly ['sɪŋgjʊləlɪ] *adv* (*remarkably*) singulièrement, remarquablement; **I was s. unimpressed** cela ne m'a vraiment pas impressionné

Sinhalese [sɪn(h)ə'li:z] **1** *adj* cing(h)alais **2** *n* (**a**) (*person*) Cing(h)alais, -aise (**b**) *Ling* cing(h)alais *m*

sinister ['sɪnɪstər] *adj* (**a**) (*event, smile, atmosphere, appearance*) sinistre; (*air*) menaçant (**b**) *Her* senestre, sénestre

sink¹ [sɪŋk] *n* (**a**) (*basin*) (*in kitchen*) évier *m*; **to pour sth down the s.** jeter qch dans l'évier; *Fig, Lit* **s. of iniquity** lieu *m* de perdition *ou* de tous les vices; **s. unit** bloc-évier *m*, *pl* blocs-éviers (**b**) *Geol etc* bétoire *f*

sink² (*pt* **sank** [sæŋk]; *pp* **sunk** [sʌŋk]; *Arch & as adj* **sunken** ['sʌŋkən]) **1** *vi* (**a**) (*in water*) disparaître dans l'eau; (*of ship*) sombrer, couler; **to s. like a stone** (*of person*) couler à pic; *Fig* **here goes! s. or swim!** allons-y! il faut risquer le tout pour le tout!; **to s. into the mud/the snow** s'enfoncer dans la boue/la neige; **to s. into quicksand** s'enliser dans des sables mouvants

(**b**) **to s. into one's memory** (*of facts etc*) se graver dans la mémoire; **to s. into oblivion** tomber dans l'oubli; **to s. into poverty/a life of crime/depression** s'enfoncer dans la pauvreté/le crime/la dépression; **to s. into a deep sleep** s'endormir profondément; **to s. into a coma** sombrer dans le coma; **sunk in thought** plongé dans ses pensées

(**c**) (*subside*) **to s. (down)** (*of ground*) s'affaisser; (*of wall, building etc*) s'affaisser, se tasser; **to s. (down) into an armchair** (*of person*) se laisser tomber *ou* s'effondrer dans un fauteuil; **to s. to the ground** (se laisser) tomber à terre; **her heart sank at the news** à cette nouvelle son cœur s'est serré; **his spirits sank** il perdit tout courage; **the sun is sinking** le soleil baisse

(**d**) (*decrease*) (*of prices etc*) baisser; **the pound has sunk** la livre a chuté *ou* baissé; **they've sunk to the bottom of the league table** ils sont tombés tout en bas du classement; **the patient is sinking fast** le malade baisse *ou* décline rapidement; **her voice sank to a whisper** sa voix s'est réduite à un murmure; **he has sunk in my estimation** il a baissé *ou* diminué dans mon estime; **how could anyone s. so low?** comment peut-on tomber aussi bas?

2 *vt* (**a**) (*ship*) couler, faire sombrer, envoyer au fond; *F* **we're sunk** nous sommes fichus

(**b**) (*well*) creuser, forer; (*stake etc*) enfoncer; **stone sunk into the wall** pierre encastrée dans le mur; **to s. one's teeth into sth** enfoncer ses dents dans qch; **they sank their differences** ils ont fait abstraction de leurs différences

(**c**) *F* (*to drink*) s'envoyer; **to s. a pint** s'envoyer une pinte de bière

(**d**) *Fin* (*debt*) amortir

(**e**) **to s. money in a project** (*invest*) investir des capitaux dans un projet

(**f**) **to s. the ball** *Billiards* mettre la bille dans la blouse; *Golf* envoyer la balle dans le trou

▶ **sink in** *vi* (**a**) (*be absorbed*) (*of liquid*) pénétrer (**b**) (*be understood*) **her remark didn't s. in until later** ce n'est que plus tard que j'ai/il a/*etc* compris le sens de sa remarque; **the lesson hasn't sunk in** la leçon n'a pas été retenue; **it was beginning to s. in that things had changed** je commençais/il commençait/*etc* à comprendre que les choses avaient changé

sinker ['sɪŋkər] *n* (*of fishing rod*) plomb *m*

sinking ['sɪŋkɪŋ] **1** *adj* (*ground*) qui s'enfonce, qui s'affaisse; (*wall etc*) qui se tasse; (*ship*) qui fait naufrage; **with a s. heart** avec un serrement de cœur; **I'm getting that s. feeling that something has happened** j'ai le pressentiment qu'il s'est passé quelque chose; **I get that s. feeling every time I think about what happened** à chaque fois que je pense à ce qui s'est passé, j'ai l'estomac qui se serre

2 *n* (**a**) (*of ship*) engloutissement *m*; (*intentional, in war etc*) torpillage *m*

(**b**) (*subsiding*) (*of ground etc*) affaissement *m*; (*of building etc*) tassement *m*

(**c**) (*of well*) creusage *m*, forage *m*

(**d**) *Fin* (*of debt*) amortissement *m*; **s. fund** fonds *m* *ou* caisse *f* d'amortissement

sinless ['sɪnlɪs] *adj* sans péché; (*pure*) innocent, pur

sinner ['sɪnər] *n* pécheur *m*, pécheresse *f*

sinning ['sɪnɪŋ] *n* péché *m*

Sinologist [saɪ'nɒlədʒɪst, sɪ-] *n* sinologue *mf*

Sinology [saɪ'nɒlədʒɪ, sɪ-] *n* sinologie *f*

sinuosity [sɪnjʊ'ɒsɪtɪ] *n* sinuosité *f*

sinuous ['sɪnjʊəs] *adj* (**a**) (*movement, river etc*) sinueux, tortueux (**b**) (*supple*) (*person*) souple, agile

sinus ['saɪnəs] *n Anat* sinus *m*; **I've got a bit of s. trouble** j'ai un problème de sinus

sinusitis [saɪnə'saɪtɪs] *n Med* sinusite *f*

Sioux [su:] **1** *adj* sioux *inv* **2** *n inv* (**a**) Sioux *mf* (**b**) *Ling* sioux *m*

sip¹ [sɪp] *n* petite gorgée *f*; **to drink sth in sips** siroter qch, boire qch à petits coups; **have a s. and see if you like it** goûte pour voir si tu aimes

sip² (**-pp-**) **1** *vt* (*tea, wine etc*) boire à petites gorgées *ou* à petits coups, siroter **2** *vi* **to s. at sth** boire qch à petites gorgées

siphon¹ ['saɪf(ə)n] *n* siphon *m*

siphon² *vt* (*liquid*) siphonner

▶ **siphon off** *vtsep* (**a**) (*liquid*) siphonner (**b**) *Fin* (*money, supplies etc*) détourner; (*staff*) prendre; **they siphoned off all the profits** ils ont détourné *ou F* pompé tous les bénéfices

sir [sɜ:r, sər] *n* (**a**) (*as form of address to a superior, esp Am to an equal*) monsieur *m*; **yes, s.** oui, monsieur; *Mil etc* (*to superior officer*) oui, mon capitaine/mon colonel/*etc*; *Naut* oui, commandant/amiral/*etc*; **dinner is served, s.** monsieur est servi; **Dear S.** (*in letter*) Monsieur; (*less formal*) Cher Monsieur; **Dear Sirs** Messieurs; *Sch F* **s. told me** le maître me l'a dit **(b)** (*title*) sir (= *titre d'un baronet et d'un knight; ne s'emploie jamais sans le prénom, ainsi Sir Walter Scott, Sir Walter*)

sire[1] ['saɪər] *n* **(a)** (*in breeding*) père *m*; (*stallion*) étalon *m* **(b)** *Arch, Lit* (*father*) père *m*; *Arch* (*address to sovereign*) sire *m*

sire[2] *vt* (*of stallion, man*) engendrer

siren ['saɪərən] *n* **(a)** *Myth, Fig* sirène *f*; **s. song** chant de sirène **(b)** *Ind, Naut etc* (*of factory, ship*) sirène *f*

sirloin ['sɜːlɔɪn] *n Culin* aloyau *m* (*de bœuf*); **s. steak** steak *m* d'aloyau

sirocco [sɪ'rɒkəʊ] *n Met* siroc(c)o *m*

sirup ['sɪrəp] *n Am* = **syrup**

sis [sɪs] *n F* (*sister*) sœurette *f*; *F* frangine *f*

sisal ['saɪs(ə)l] *n* (*plant, fibre*) sisal *m*

sissy ['sɪsɪ] *Pej* **1** *n* (*cowardly child etc*) poule *f* mouillée; (*effeminate man, boy*) garçon *m* efféminé; **that's a game for sissies!** c'est un jeu de filles! **2** *adj* (*cowardly*) lâche, peureux; (*effeminate*) efféminé; **s. game** jeu de filles; **he thinks it's s. to …** il pense que ça fait efféminé de …

sister ['sɪstər] *n* **(a)** (*in family*) sœur *f*; **sisters unite!** (*to female workers, feminists*) sœurs, unissez-vous!; **s. company** société-sœur *f*; **s. nations** nations *fpl* sœurs; **s. ship** sister-ship *m* **(b)** *Rel* religieuse *f*, (bonne) sœur *f*; **S. of Mercy** sœur de la Charité; **come in, S.** entrez, ma sœur **(c)** (*nurse*) infirmière-chef *f*; **thank you, s.** merci madame/ mademoiselle

sisterhood ['sɪstəhʊd] *n* **(a)** *Rel* communauté *f* religieuse (*de sœurs*) **(b)** (*solidarity*) solidarité *f* féminine; **the s.** (*women*) la communauté des femmes

sister-in-law, *pl* **sisters-in-law** *n* belle-sœur *f*, *pl* belles-sœurs

sisterly ['sɪstəlɪ] *adj* de sœur; **in a s. fashion** en sœur

Sistine ['sɪstiːn, -taɪn] *adj* **the S. chapel** la chapelle Sixtine

Sisyphus ['sɪsɪfəs] *n* Sisyphe *m*

sit (*pt, pp* **sat** [sæt]; *prp* **sitting**) **1** *vi* **(a)** (*of person*) s'asseoir; **to be sitting** (*in armchair, on ground etc*) être assis; **s.!** (*to dog*) assis!; **we usually s. in the living room** nous sommes d'ordinaire dans le salon; **where would you like me to s.?, where shall I s.?** où est-ce que je me mets?; **she was sitting reading** elle était assise à lire *ou* en train de lire; **I'm fed up with sitting at home** j'en ai assez de rester enfermé à la maison; **don't just s. there, say something!** mais enfin, dis quelque chose!; **don't just s. there, do something!** eh bien, allez, remue-toi!; **to s. at (the) table** (*take one's seat*) s'asseoir *ou* se mettre à (la) table, s'attabler; **they were sitting at (the) table** ils étaient à table, ils étaient attablés; **we were sitting at lunch/dinner** nous étions en train de déjeuner/dîner; **he sits for hours over his books** il passe des heures penché sur ses livres; *F* **to s. tight** (*not move*) ne pas bouger de sa place; (*not give in*) ne pas céder

(b) to s. in Parliament = être député

(c) (*of assemblies*) siéger, être en séance; **the court is sitting** la séance est ouverte

(d) *F* (*of object*) **the diskette was sitting on the radiator** la disquette était *ou* se trouvait sur le radiateur; **I found it sitting on the fridge** je l'ai trouvé sur le frigo; **the car was sitting in the drive** la voiture était stationnée dans l'allée

(e) (*of bird*) être perché; **to s. (on eggs)** (*of hen*) couver (*des œufs*)

(f) (*of responsibility*) **to s. heavy on sb** peser sur qn

(g) to s. well/badly (*of jacket etc*) tomber bien/mal; **the jacket sits well/badly on him** la veste lui va bien/ne lui va pas

2 *vt* **(a) to s. a child on the table** asseoir un enfant sur la table

(b) *Br Sch etc* (*exam*) passer

▶ **sit about, sit around** *vi* (*hang around*) traîner; (*do nothing*) ne rien faire

▶ **sit back** *vi* **(a)** (*lean back*) **to s. back in one's chair** s'appuyer sur le dossier de sa chaise/son fauteuil **(b)** *F* (*relax*) se relaxer; **to s. back and let the others do the work** (*not intervene*) regarder les autres travailler; **the authorities just sat back and did nothing** les autorités n'ont pas daigné faire quoi que ce soit; **we can't just s. back and do nothing** nous ne pouvons pas rester comme ça sans rien faire

▶ **sit down 1** *vi* s'asseoir; **to be sitting down** être assis; **please s. down** asseyez-vous, *Fml* veuillez vous asseoir; **to s. down again** se rasseoir; (*at table*) se remettre à (la) table; **to s. down at (the) table** se mettre à table, s'attabler; **to s. down to a meal** se mettre à table pour un repas; **to s. down to a game of bridge** s'installer pour faire une partie de bridge; **I think we should s. down and talk about it** je crois qu'il faut qu'on en discute *ou* en parle **2** *vtas* (*child etc*) asseoir; *F* **s. yourself down!** asseyez-vous donc!

▶ **sit for** *vipo* **(a)** *Br* (*be candidate in*) (*exam*) passer **(b)** (*pose for*) **to s. for one's portrait** se faire faire son portrait

▶ **sit in** *vi* **(a)** (*at meeting etc*) assister sans participer; **do you mind if I s. in for a while?** cela vous ennuie-t-il si je reste à écouter un moment? **(b) to s. in for sb** (*replace*) remplacer qn **(c)** (*occupy building, office etc*) faire grève avec occupation des locaux

▶ **sit in on** *vipo* (*attend as observer*) **to s. in on a rehearsal/a meeting** assister à une répétition/une réunion (sans y participer)

▶ **sit on** *vipo F* **(a)** (*not deal with*) (*proposal, suggestion etc*) ne pas s'occuper de; (*deliberately*) faire traîner; **they sat on it for two months** ils ne s'en sont pas occupés pendant deux mois **(b)** (*repress*) rembarrer

▶ **sit out 1** *vi* (*sit down outside*) s'asseoir dehors; (*be seated outside*) être assis dehors **2** *vtsep* **(a)** (*not participate in*) (*game etc*) ne pas prendre part à; **I'll s. this one out** (*dance*) je ne veux pas danser celle-ci; **I'll s. out this round** (*of card game etc*) je passe mon tour **(b)** (*wait until end of*) (*conference etc*) rester (patiemment) jusqu'à la fin de; **he sat out the war in Switzerland** il est resté en Suisse en attendant la fin de la guerre

▶ **sit through** *vipo* (*wait until end of*) rester pendant toute la durée de; **he sat through the whole play** il est resté jusqu'à la fin de la pièce; **to s. through dinner** rester à table jusqu'à la fin du repas; **we had to s. through two hours of Wagner** nous avons dû nous payer deux heures de Wagner

▶ **sit up 1** *vi* (*straighten one's back*) se tenir droit (*sur sa chaise, son lit etc*), se redresser; (*from lying position*) se dresser *ou* se mettre sur son séant; **s. up straight!** tiens-toi droit!; *Fig* **to make sb s. up** étonner qn, épater qn; *Fig* **her competitors are beginning to s. up and take notice** ses concurrents commencent à prendre conscience de son existence; **to s. up (and beg)** (*of dog*) faire le beau; **to s. up (late)** veiller; **to s. up for sb** (*wait up for*) (rester debout à) attendre qn, veiller en attendant le retour de qn; **to s. up with a sick man** garder *ou* veiller un malade; **to s. up to (the) table** (*sit closer*) approcher sa chaise de la table; (*come to table*) venir à table

2 *vtsep* **to s. sb up** soulever qn pour l'asseoir; **to s. sb up against a wall** adosser qn contre un mur

sitar ['sɪtɑːr, sɪ'tɑːr] *n* sitar *f*

sitcom ['sɪtkɒm] *n TV, Rad* sitcom *m*

sit-down 1 *n* (*act*) **come and have a s.** venez vous asseoir **2** *adj* **s. meal** repas *m* servi à table; *Ind* **s. strike** grève *f* sur le tas

site[1] [saɪt] *n* **(a)** (*position*) (*of building etc*) emplacement *m*, situation *f*; (*archaeological etc*) site *m*; *Med* (*of pain etc*) siège *m*; **the s. of a battle/a historic meeting** le site d'une bataille/d'une réunion historique; **(camp) s.** (terrain *m* de) camping *m* **(b)** **(building) s.** chantier *m* (de construction); **on s.** sur place; **to be on s.** être à pied d'œuvre; **s. manager** chef *m* de chantier

site[2] *vt* (*building, stadium*) placer; (*factory*) implanter; **to be sited** être situé

sit-in *n inv* sit-in *m*; (*strike*) occupation *f* des locaux

siting ['saɪtɪŋ] *n* emplacement *m*

sitter ['sɪtər] *n* **(a)** *Art* modèle *m* **(b)** *F* (*child minder*) gardien, -ienne d'enfants **(c)** (*hen*) couveuse *f* **(d)** *Sp F* **to miss a s.** rater un but/une balle/*etc* facile; **you gave him a s.** tu lui as fait une excellente passe

sitting ['sɪtɪŋ] **1** *adj* (*seated*) assis; (*hare*) au gîte; *Fig* **to be a s. duck** (*easy target for criticism etc*) être une cible facile; *Art* **a s. figure** une figure assise; **a s. hen** une poule en train de couver; *Parl* **our s. member** le député qui nous représente actuellement

2 *n* (*for portrait etc*) pose *f*; (*of committee, court etc*) séance *f*; **s. and standing room** places assises et places debout; **to paint a portrait in three sittings** faire un portrait en trois séances; **first/second s.** (*for meals*) premier/ deuxième service; **to serve 500 people in** *or* **at one s.** servir 500 personnes à la fois; **to write two chapters at one s.** écrire deux chapitres d'un trait *ou* d'un (seul) jet

sitting room *n* (*in house*) salon *m*, salle *f* de séjour

sitting tenant *n* locataire *mf* dans les lieux

situate ['sɪtjʊeɪt] *vt* (*house etc*) situer; **from where we were situated …** d'où nous nous trouvions …; **pleasantly situated house** maison bien située; **awkwardly situated** (*person*) dans une situation *ou* une position embarrassante; **he's well situated to know what's going on** il est bien placé pour savoir ce qui se passe

situation [sɪtjʊ'eɪʃən] *n* **(a)** (*of building, town*) situation *f*, emplacement *m* **(b)** (*political etc*) situation *f*; **to explain the s.** exposer la situation; **to find oneself in an unfortunate s.** se trouver dans une situation déplorable; *F* **what's** *or* **how's**

the coffee s.? combien nous reste-t-il de café?; *F* **we're in a staff shortage s.** nous n'avons pas assez de personnel; **what to do in an emergency s.** que faire en cas d'urgence **(c)** *Old-fashioned* (*employment*) emploi *m*, position *f*; **to look for/find a s.** chercher/trouver un emploi; **situations vacant/wanted** (*in advertisements*) offres *fpl*/demandes *fpl* d'emploi

situation comedy *n TV, Rad* sitcom *m*

sit-upon *n Old-fashioned F* derrière *m*, postérieur *m*

six [sɪks] **1** *adj, n* six *m*; **number s.** (le) numéro six; **twenty-s.** vingt-six; **s. fours** *or* **four sixes are twenty-four** six fois quatre *ou* quatre fois six font vingt-quatre; **s. and a half** six et demi; **at s. (o'clock)** à six heures; **at s. thirty** à six heures et demie; **to be s. (years old)** avoir six ans; **double s.** (*at dominoes etc*) double-six *m*, *pl* doubles-six; *Cards* **the s. of hearts** le six de cœur; *F* **it's s. of one and half a dozen of the other** c'est blanc bonnet et bonnet blanc, c'est kif-kif; **we're all** *or* **everything's at sixes and sevens** tout est sens dessus dessous; *F* **to be s. feet under** être six pieds sous terre; **a s-cylinder car** une six cylindres; **the S. Counties** = l'Irlande *f* du Nord; *Hist* **the S. Day War** la guerre des six jours; **s-seater (car)** voiture à six places

2 *n Cr* six points (*marqués par le batteur*); **he scored five sixes** il a marqué cinq fois six points; *F* **to knock for s.** (*person*) (*knock down*) étendre; (*flabbergast*) abasourdir; (*enemy etc*) battre à plate(s) couture(s), écraser; (*project etc*) ficher en l'air; **that's knocked everything for s.** ça a tout fiché en l'air

sixfold ['sɪksfəʊld] **1** *adj* sextuple **2** *adv* au sextuple; **to increase s.** sextupler

six-foot *adj* (*beam*) de six pieds; **a s. bodyguard** un garde du corps très baraqué

six-footer *n* homme *m*/femme *f* mesurant six pieds, *F* armoire *f* à glace; **he's obviously going to be a s.** on voit bien qu'il va atteindre les deux mètres

six-pack *n Com* (*of bottles, cans*) pack *m* de six

sixpence ['sɪkspəns] *n* **(a)** (*sum*) six pence **(b)** *formerly* (*coin*) pièce *f* de six pence

sixpenny ['sɪkspənɪ] *adj Old-fashioned* (*sweet etc*) qui coûte six pence; (*stamp*) de six pence; **s. piece** pièce *f* de six pence

sixpennyworth [sɪks'penɪwəθ] *n Old-fashioned* **to buy s. of chocolate** acheter pour six pence de chocolat

six-shooter *n* six-coup *m*

six-sided *adj* qui a six côtés, hexagonal

sixteen [sɪks'tiːn] *adj, n* seize *m*; **she is s.** elle a seize ans

sixteenth [sɪks'tiːnθ] **1** *adj* seizième; **Louis the S.** Louis XVI; **(on) the s. (of August)** le seize (août); *esp Am Mus* **s. note** double croche *f* **2** *n* **(a)** (*person, thing*) seizième *mf* **(b)** (*fraction*) seizième *m*

sixth [sɪksθ] **1** *adj* **(a)** sixième; **Henry the S.** Henri VI; **(on) the s. (of December)** le six (décembre); **s. sense** sixième sens *m* **(b)** *Eng Sch* **the s. form** ≈ les classes *fpl* de première et de terminale; **s. form college** lycée *m* de préparation aux examens O levels et A levels; **s. former** = élève de première ou de terminale **2** *n* **(a)** (*person, thing*) sixième *mf* **(b)** (*fraction*) sixième *m* **(c)** *Mus* sixte *f*

sixthly ['sɪksθlɪ] *adv* sixièmement

sixtieth ['sɪkstɪɪθ] *adj, n* soixantième *mf*

sixty ['sɪkstɪ] *adj, n* soixante *m*; **s. one** soixante et un; **s.-third** soixante-troisième; **about** *or* **some s. books** une soixantaine de livres; **she's in her sixties** elle a la soixantaine, elle a plus de soixante ans; **in the Sixties** dans les années soixante

sixty-four *adj, n* soixante-quatre *m*; *F* **the s. (thousand) dollar question** la question cruciale

sizable ['saɪzəb(ə)l] *adj* = **sizeable**

size¹ [saɪz] *n* **(a)** (*of building, room*) grandeur *f*; (*of town, country, island*) superficie *f*; (*of carpet, machine, car*) dimensions *fpl*, taille *f*; (*of apple, cake, print*) grosseur *f*, taille; (*of problem, undertaking*) importance *f*, ampleur *f*; *Comptr* (*of file etc*) taille; **of equal** *or* **the same s., of a s.** de (la) même grandeur/taille/*etc*; **I was surprised by the s. of the bill** j'ai été étonné par le montant de la note; **bicycles/people come in all shapes and sizes** il y a des bicyclettes/des gens de toutes les formes et de toutes les tailles; **books arranged according to s.** livres disposés par ordre de taille; **it's the s. of an egg** c'est gros comme un œuf; **to grow/decrease in s.** augmenter/diminuer de taille; **actual** *or* **full s.** grandeur nature; **a town of that s.** une ville de cette importance; *F* **that's about the s. of it** c'est un peu ça; **to cut a piece to s.** tailler une pièce à la dimension *ou* à la cote; *F* **to cut sb down to s.** rabattre le caquet à qn, remettre qn à sa place; *Comptr* **s. box** case *f* de dimensionnement, case de contrôle de taille

(b) (*of person*) taille *f*; *Com* (*of clothes*) taille; (*of shirt*) encolure *f*; (*of shoes, gloves, hat*) pointure *f*; (*of book, paper*) format *m*; **a boy half/twice his s.** un garçon deux fois moins/plus grand que lui; **a s. larger/smaller** (*shoes*) une pointure au-dessus/en-dessous; (*dresses etc*) une taille au-dessus/en-dessous; **what s. do you take?, what's your s.?, what s. are you?** (*in shoes*) quelle pointure chaussez-vous?; (*in dresses, shirts etc*) quelle est votre taille?; **s. ten shoes** ≈ chaussures *fpl* de pointure 44; **I've nothing in your s.** je n'ai rien à votre taille/à votre pointure; **to try sth for s.** essayer qch (*pour voir si la taille va*); *F* **try this one for s.** prends ça

size² *vt* (*classify according to size*) (*objects*) classer par grosseur *ou* par dimension; (*adjust size of*) adapter les dimensions de

size³ *n Tech* apprêt *m*; (*glue*) colle *f*, encollage *m*

size⁴ *vt Tech* (*wallpaper*) apprêter, encoller

▶ **size up** *vtsep* **to s. sb up** évaluer qn, jauger qn; **they soon sized him up** ils ont eu vite fait de le jauger

sizeable ['saɪzəb(ə)l] *adj* assez grand, plutôt grand; (*difference*) assez important; (*fine, sum*) assez élevé

sized [saɪzd] *adj* **fair s.** (*quite large*) assez grand; **medium s.** de grandeur *ou* de taille moyenne; **large/small s.** de grande/petite taille; (*book, paper etc*) de grand/petit format

sizing ['saɪzɪŋ] *n Tech* **(a)** (*process*) apprêtage *m*; (*of wallpaper*) collage *m*, encollage *m* **(b)** (*substance*) colle *f*; (*in painting*) apprêt *m*

sizzle¹ ['sɪz(ə)l] *n* (*of something frying*) grésillement *m*

sizzle² *vi* (*of frying pan, sausages etc*) grésiller

sizzler ['sɪz(ə)lər] *n F* journée *f* de canicule; **it was a real s. (of a day)** on se serait cru dans un four, on crevait de châleur

sizzling ['sɪzlɪŋ] **1** *adj* (*heat, temperature*) torride; (*food*) grésillant **2** *adv* **s. hot** (*food*) tout grésillant; *F* (*day*) torride **3** *n* grésillement *m*

skate¹ [skeɪt] *n* (*fish*) raie *f*

skate² *n* **(ice/roller) s.** patin *m* (à glace/à roulettes); *Fig F* **to get one's skates on** se dépêcher

skate³ *vi* (*on ice*) patiner, faire du patin; (*on roller skates*) faire du patin à roulettes; **he skated across the lake** il a traversé le lac en patins à glace; *Fig F* **to s. round sth** tourner autour du pot

▶ **skate over** *vipo* **(a)** (*skate across surface of*) parcourir en patin **(b)** (*discuss superficially*) (*subject*) ne faire qu'effleurer; (*difficulties*) passer rapidement sur

skateboard¹ ['skeɪtbɔːd] *n Sp* planche *f* à roulettes; *F* skate-board *m*, *pl* skate-boards, skate *m*, *Can* rouli-roulant® *m*, *pl* rouli-roulants

skateboard² *vi Sp* faire de la planche à roulettes *ou F* du skate *ou Can* du rouli-roulant

skateboarder ['skeɪtbɔːdər] *n Sp* personne *f* pratiquant le skate(-board); **a champion s.** un champion du skate-board

skateboarding ['skeɪtbɔːdɪŋ] *n* skate(-board) *m*; **to go s.** aller faire du skate-board

skater ['skeɪtər] *n* patineur, -euse

skating ['skeɪtɪŋ] *n* (*on ice*) patinage *m*; (*on roller skates*) patin *m* à roulettes; **s. rink** patinoire *f*; (*for roller skating*) piste *f*

skean dhu ['skiːən'duː] *n Scot* = dague *f* décorative que l'on porte dans la chaussette

skedaddle [skɪ'dæd(ə)l] *vi F* (*run off*) déguerpir, prendre ses jambes à son cou

skeet [skiːt] *n Sp* **s. (shooting)** (genre de) ball-trap *m*

skein [skeɪn, skiːn] *n* **(a)** (*of silk, wool*) écheveau *m* **(b)** (*of wild geese*) vol *m*

skeletal ['skelɪt(ə)l] *adj* squelettique; *Fig* (*presentation etc*) sommaire

skeleton ['skelɪt(ə)n] *n* **(a)** (*of human being, animal etc*) squelette *m*; *Fig* **s. in the cupboard** *or Am* **in the closet** secret *m* honteux (de la famille); **to have a s. in the cupboard** *or Am* **in the closet** avoir un squelette dans le placard; **s. at the feast** rabat-joie *m inv*, trouble-fête *m inv*; **he's a living s.** c'est un vrai squelette **(b)** *Fig* (*of building etc*) charpente *f*, squelette *m*; (*of novel, essay*) canevas *m*, esquisse *f*; **s. staff/crew** personnel *m*/équipage *m* réduit

skeleton key *n* passe-partout *m*; (*thief's*) fausse clef *f*, rossignol *m*

skeptic, skeptical *etc US* = **sceptic, sceptical** *etc*

sketch¹ [sketʃ] *n* **(a)** *Art, Liter* croquis *m*, esquisse *f*; **character s.** portrait *m* littéraire; **to make a s. of sth** faire le croquis de qch; **preliminary s.** premier jet *m*; **(parliamentary) s. writer** = journaliste *mf* spécialiste de l'actualité parlementaire qu'il/qu'elle présente de façon humoristique; **s. pad** bloc *m* à croquis; **s. map** plan *m* sommaire **(b)** *Fig* (*of project*) exposé *m*, ébauche *f*; **she drew a brief s. of the situation** elle a fait un bref résumé de la situation **(c)** *Th, TV* sketch *m*, saynète *f*

sketch² *vt* **(a)** *Art* (*landscape, building etc*) esquisser, croquer; (*person, thing*) faire un *ou* le croquis de **(b)** = **sketch out**

▶ **sketch in** *vtsep* (*draw roughly*) dessiner sommairement, esquisser; *Fig* (*details*) esquisser

▶ **sketch out** *vtsep* (*draw up outline of*) (*novel*) faire le canevas *ou* l'ébauche de; (*provide outline of*) (*project etc*) esquisser, ébaucher

sketchbook ['sketʃbʊk] *n* cahier *m* de croquis

sketchily ['sketʃɪlɪ] *adv* sans les détails, *Pej* d'une manière incomplète *ou* vague; (*to remember*) vaguement

sketching ['sketʃɪŋ] *n* **to do some s.** faire des croquis; **to go s.** aller faire des croquis; **s. block** *or* **pad** bloc *m* à croquis

sketchy ['sketʃɪ] *adj* (*work*) qui manque de fini; (*drawing*) qui manque de détails; (*knowledge*) superficiel, sommaire; (*ideas*) plutôt vague; **I'm a bit s. on this** mes connaissances sont un peu sommaires

skew[1] [skju:] *n* **on the s.** de *ou* en biais, en oblique

skew[2] **1** *adj* en biais, oblique **2** *adv* de *ou* en biais

skew[3] **1** *vi* (*of truck etc*) biaiser, obliquer **2** *vt* (*distort*) (*results*) biaiser

skewbald ['skju:bɔ:ld] *adj* (*horse*) pie *inv*

skewer[1] ['skju:ər] *n Culin* brochette *f*; (*large, for whole pig etc*) broche *f*

skewer[2] *vt Culin* (*pieces of meat, vegetables etc*) mettre sur une brochette; (*whole pig etc*) embrocher; **his hand had been skewered to the table** il s'est fait embrocher la main à la table

skew-whiff ['skju:'wɪf] *adj Br F* de travers; *F* de traviole

ski,[1] *pl* **skis** [ski:, -i:z] *n* ski *m*; **s. binding** fixation(s) *f(pl)*; **s. boots** chaussures *fpl* de ski; *Aut* **s. box** coffre *m* porte-skis; *Aut* **s. carrier** porte-skis *m*; **s. centre** station *f* de ski; **s. club** club *m* de ski; *Aut* **s. flap** trappe *f* à skis; **s. instructor** moniteur, -trice de ski; **s. jump** saut *m* à ski; (*structure*) tremplin *m*; **s. jumper** sauteur *m*; **s. jumping** saut à ski(s); **s. lift** remonte-pente *m*, *pl* remonte-pentes, téléski *m*; **s. pants** fuseau *m*; **s. pass** carte *f ou* forfait *m* de remonte-pente; *Aut* **s. rack** porte-skis; **s. resort** station de ski; **s. run** *or* **slope** piste *f* de ski; **s. stick, s. pole** bâton *m* de ski; **s. suit** combinaison *f* de ski; **s. tow** remonte-pente; **s. wax** fart *m*

ski[2] *vi* (*pt, pp* **skied**) skier, faire du ski; (*move*) aller à *ou* en skis; **he skis well** il skie bien; **to learn to s.** apprendre à skier *ou* à faire du ski; **to s. down the slope** descendre la piste à *ou* en skis; **we skied back** nous sommes rentrés à *ou* en skis

skid[1] [skɪd] *n* **(a)** *Aut* (*action*) dérapage *m*; **to go into a s.** déraper, faire un dérapage; **to correct a s.** redresser **(b)** (*device*), *Com* palette *f* sur patins; *Av* (*for landing etc*) patin *m*; *Fig F* **to put the skids under sb** (*hurry*) faire se magner qn; (*bring about ruin of*) glisser des peaux de bananes à qn; *Fig F* **to be on the skids** (*of economy, company, marriage etc*) battre de l'aile; **he's on the skids** il va mal finir

skid[2] **(-dd-) 1** *vi* (*of car, tyre etc*) déraper; (*of wheel*) patiner; **his glasses went skidding across the table** ses lunettes ont glissé jusqu'à l'autre bout de la table **2** *vt* (*car*) faire faire un dérapage à

skidlid ['skɪdlɪd] *n Aut Sl* casque *m* de moto

skidmark ['skɪdmɑ:k] *n* (*on road*) trace *f* de dérapage; *Fig F Hum* (*on underpants, nappy etc*) trace

skidpan ['skɪdpæn] *n Aut* terrain *m* de dérapages

skid row *n Am F* quartier *m* pauvre; **he's heading for s. row** il va finir clochard; **after two years on s. row** après deux années dans la rue

skier ['ski:ər] *n* skieur, -euse

skiff [skɪf] *n* esquif *m*, yole *f*; (*in rowing*) skiff *m*

skiffle ['skɪf(ə)l] *n Mus* skiffle *m*; **s. group** skiffle-group *m inv*

ski-flying *n Ski* vol *m* à ski

skiing ['ski:ɪŋ] *n* ski *m*; **to go s.** faire du ski; **we went on a s. holiday** nous sommes allés aux sports d'hiver; **s. centre** station *f* de sports d'hiver; **s. instructor** moniteur, -trice de ski; **s. resort** station de ski

skilful, *US* **skillful** ['skɪlfʊl] *adj* adroit, habile; **to be s. at** *or* **in (doing) sth** être habile à (faire) qch; **to be s. with one's hands** être habile *ou* adroit de ses mains

skilfully, *US* **skillfully** ['skɪlfʊlɪ] *adv* habilement, adroitement

skilfulness, *US* **skillfulness** ['skɪlfʊlnɪs] *n* habileté *f*, adresse *f*

skill [skɪl] *n* **(a)** (*ability*) habileté *f*, adresse *f*; (*manual*) dextérité *f*; (*as translator, negotiator, footballer, driver*) talent *m*; (*on basis of learning*) connaissances *fpl*; **technical s.** connaissance *f* technique; **s. in doing sth** talent *ou* habileté pour faire qch; **lack of s.** manque de don; **a game involving no s.** un sport/un jeu n'exigeant aucune aptitude particulière; **repairing pianos requires great s.** réparer les pianos demande une grande compétence; **language skills** connaissances en langues; **I don't have the necessary skills** je n'ai pas les connaissances nécessaires; **an archaeologist requires many skills** un archéologue doit posséder de nombreuses aptitudes; **they have very different skills** ils ont des aptitudes très différentes; *Iron* **it's one of my special skills** je sais si bien le faire

(b) (*trade*) métier *m*; (*learned technique*) technique *f*; **learn new skills** apprenez de nouvelles techniques

skilled [skɪld] *adj* habile; (*work*) de spécialiste; **to be s. in doing sth** être habile à faire qch; **highly s. staff** personnel très qualifié; **s. labour** main-d'œuvre *f* qualifiée; **s. manual worker** ouvrier *m* spécialisé, OS *m*; **s. worker** ouvrier, -ière qualifié(e)

skillet ['skɪlɪt] *n Am* poêle *f* (à frire)

skillful, skillfully *etc US* = **skilful, skilfully** *etc*

skim[1] [skɪm] *n* **just give it a quick s.** (*read through quickly*) jetez-y un coup d'œil rapide

skim[2] **(-mm-) 1** *vt* **(a)** (*stock, gravy etc*) écumer; (*milk*) écrémer; *Mktg* écrémer; **skim(med) milk** lait *m* écrémé **(b)** (*pass lightly over*) (*surface*) effleurer, raser; **to s. stones on water** faire des ricochets; *Fig* **the book just skims the surface (of the problem)** le livre se contente de survoler le problème **2** *vi* **to s. along** *or* **over the ground** (*fly just above*) voler au ras du sol; (*move on surface*) raser le sol; **to s. over the water** (*fly just above*) voler à fleur d'eau; (*move on surface*) raser l'eau; *Fig* **the author skims over the real problem** l'auteur survole les vrais problèmes

▶ **skim off** *vtsep* (*remove by skimming*) (*cream, fat etc*) enlever, prélever; *Fig* **to s. the cream off sth** prendre la meilleure partie de qch; **the accounts department skims off the best recruits** la comptabilité récupère les meilleures recrues

▶ **skim through** *vipo* (*read superficially*) (*novel, document etc*) lire en diagonale

skimmer ['skɪmər] *n* (*for milk*) écrémeuse *f*

skimp [skɪmp] **1** *vt* (*food, fabric of dress*) lésiner sur; *F* (*one's work*) bâcler **2** *vi* lésiner sur tout; (*live parsimoniously*) vivre chichement; **they skimped on the cost of the new road** ils lésinaient sur le coût de la nouvelle route

skimpily ['skɪmpɪlɪ] *adv* (*furnished etc*) parcimonieusement; **s. made** (*dress*) étriqué; **s. dressed** légèrement vêtu

skimpiness ['skɪmpɪnɪs] *n* insuffisance *f*; (*of garment*) aspect *m* étriqué

skimpy ['skɪmpɪ] *adj* insuffisant; **s. meal** maigre repas; **s. skirt** jupe étriquée; **to be s. with sth** (*be mean*) lésiner sur qch

skin[1] [skɪn] *n* **(a)** peau *f*; *Fig* **to have a thin/thick s.** être/ne pas être susceptible; **to cast** *or* **throw its s.** (*of snake etc*) muer; **I always wear cotton next to my s.** je porte toujours du coton sur la peau; **to strip to the s.** se mettre tout nu; **she was soaked to the s.** elle était trempée jusqu'aux os; *F* **she's nothing but** *or* **she's all s. and bone** elle n'a que la peau et les os; **I nearly jumped out of my s.** cela m'a fait sursauter; **to escape by the s. of one's teeth** s'échapper de justesse; **to save one's (own) s.** sauver sa peau; (*escape criticism, scandal etc*) se tirer d'affaire; *F* **to get under sb's s.** (*annoy*) ennuyer qn; (*get on sb's nerves*) taper sur les nerfs de qn; *F* **I've got her under my s.** je l'ai dans la peau; *F* **it's no s. off my nose** ça n'a aucune conséquence pour moi; **s. cancer** cancer *m* de la peau; **s. complaint** maladie *f* de peau; **s. deep** (*emotions*) à fleur de peau; (*wound*) superficiel; **beauty is only s. deep** la beauté n'est pas tout; **s. disease** maladie de peau; *F* **s. flick** film *m* porno; *F* **s. game** escroquerie *f*, filouterie *f*; *F* **s. mag(azine)** magazine *m* porno

(b) (*of dead animal*) peau *f*

(c) (*of fruit, sausage*) peau *f*; (*of onion*) pelure *f*; *Culin* **potatoes (cooked) in their skins** pommes *fpl* de terre en robe de chambre *ou* en robe des champs

(d) *Naut* (*of canoe*) bordé *m* extérieur; (*of ship*) bordé extérieur, enveloppe *f*, coque *f*; *Av* (*of fuselage*) revêtement *m*

(e) (*on milk, sauce, custard etc*) peau *f*, pellicule *f*

(f) *Sl* (*skinhead*) skin *mf*

(g) *Sl* (*for roll-up*) papier *m* à cigarette

skin[2] *vt* **(-nn-)** (*rabbit, cat etc*) écorcher, dépouiller; (*tomato etc*) peler, éplucher; **to s. one's knees** s'écorcher les genoux; *Prov* **there's more than one way to s. a cat** il y a plus d'une façon d'arriver à ses fins; *F* **to s. sb alive** écorcher qn, estamper qn

skin care *n* soins *mpl* de la peau

skin cream *n* crème *f* de beauté

skin diver *n* plongeur, -euse, sous-marin(e) autonome

skin diving *n* plongée *f* sous-marine autonome

skinflint ['skɪnflɪnt] *n F* pingre *mf*, grippe-sou *m*, *pl* grippe-sous

skinful ['skɪnfʊl] *n F* **he's had a s.** (*of alcohol*) il a pris une (bonne) cuite

skin graft *n Med* greffe *f* de peau

skinhead ['skɪnhed] *n* skinhead *mf*; **s. gang** bande de skinheads

skinless [ˈskɪnlɪs] *adj* (*sausage etc*) sans peau
skinned [skɪnd] *adj* (*rabbit*) à qui on a enlevé la peau; **to keep one's eyes s.** ouvrir l'œil; **keep your eyes s.** ouvre l'œil (et le bon); **to keep one's eyes s. for sb/sth** guetter qn/qch; **I'll keep my eyes s. for one** j'en guette un
-skinned [-skɪnd] *suff* **dark/fair-s.** à la peau mate/claire
skinniness [ˈskɪnɪnɪs] *n* maigreur *f*; (*no negative overtones*) minceur *f*
skinny [ˈskɪnɪ] *adj* maigre; (*without negative overtones*) mince; (*sweater, pullover etc*) collant
skinny-dip¹ *n Am F* baignade *f* tout nu *ou* à poil
skinny-dip² *vi Am F* nager *ou* se baigner tout nu *ou* à poil
skinny-malinky [skɪnɪməˈlɪŋkɪ] *n F* asperge *f*
skint [skɪnt] *adj Br F* **to be s.** être sans le sou, être fauché
skin test *n* cuti-réaction *f*, *pl* cuti-réactions
skintight [ˈskɪntaɪt] *adj* (*garment*) collant, moulant
skip¹ [skɪp] *n* (*jump*) (petit) saut *m*, gambade *f*; *Am* **s. rope** corde *f* à sauter
skip² *n F* (*skipper*) cap'taine *m*
skip³ (**-pp-**) **1** *vi* (**a**) (*of lambs, children*) sautiller, gambader; (*with rope*) sauter à la corde; **they came skipping out of school** ils sont sortis de l'école en gambadant; **to s. from one subject to another** sauter d'un sujet à un autre; **to read without skipping** lire sans rien sauter
(**b**) *F* **I skipped across to Paris** j'ai fait un saut à Paris; **he's just skipped out to the shops** il vient d'aller faire des courses; **if you s. through the work too fast ...** si vous travaillez à la va-vite ...
(**c**) *F* (*leave without paying*) filer à l'anglaise
2 *vt* (**a**) (*meal, year at school, stage in process*) sauter; (*in planning trip etc*) (*not go to*) ne pas aller à; (*word, line etc*) (*intentionally*) omettre; (*accidentally*) sauter (par-dessus), passer; *Comptr* (*command*) sauter; *Sch* **to s. a class** (*play truant*) sécher un cours; (*move up*) sauter une classe; **my heart skipped a beat** mon cœur a fait un bond; *F* **to s. bail** se dérober à la justice (*alors qu'on jouit de la liberté provisoire*); *F* **they've skipped the country** ils ont quitté le pays; *F* **s. it!** (*that's enough*) ça suffit!; (*forget it*) passons!, laisse courir!
(**b**) *Am* **to s. rope** sauter à la corde
skip⁴ *n Constr, Min etc* benne *f*
▶ **skip off** *vi Br F* (*leave*) filer, décamper
▶ **skip over** *vipo* (*omit*) (*word, line etc*) (*intentionally*) omettre; (*accidentally*) sauter (par-dessus), passer
skipper¹ [ˈskɪpər] *n* (**a**) *Naut* capitaine *m*, patron *m*; *Av* commandant *m* de bord; *Sp, F* capitaine, chef *m* (**b**) *F* (*who leaves without paying bill*) client *m* qui part sans payer *ou* qui file à l'anglaise
skipper² *vt F* (*ship*) être le commandant de; (*plane*) être le commandant à bord de; (*sports team*) être le chef de
skipping [ˈskɪpɪŋ] *n* (*with rope*) saut *m* à la corde; *Br* **s. rope** corde *f* à sauter
skirl [skɜːl], *Scot* [skɪrl] *n Scot* (*of bagpipes*) son *m* aigu
skirmish¹ [ˈskɜːmɪʃ] *n Mil* escarmouche *f*, échauffourée *f*; *Fig* altercation *f*
skirmish² *vi Mil* se livrer à une guerre d'escarmouches; **they are still skirmishing in the hills** il y a encore des escarmouches dans les collines; *Fig* **they've been skirmishing for months** il y a des accrochages depuis des mois entre eux
skirmisher [ˈskɜːmɪʃər] *n Mil* tirailleur *m*
skirt¹ [skɜːt] *n* (**a**) (*garment*) jupe *f*; (*of overcoat, uniform etc*) pan *m*, basque *f*; *Offensive, Sl* (**bit of**) **s.** gonzesse *f*, pépé *f*; *Culin* **s. of beef** = flanchet *m* de bœuf (**b**) (**saddle**) **s.** petit quartier *m* (de la selle) (**c**) (*of hovercraft*) jupe *f* (**d**) (*in engine*) (*of piston*) jupe *f*; *Aut* **s. clearance** jeu *m* à la jupe
skirt² *vt* (*village, hill, problem*) contourner; (*of person*) (*wall*) longer, serrer; **the path skirts the wood** le sentier côtoie *ou* contourne le bois
▶ **skirt around** *vipo* = **skirt²**
skirting [ˈskɜːtɪŋ] *n Br Constr* **s. (board)** plinthe *f*
skit [skɪt] *n Liter, Mus, Th* pièce *f* satirique, satire *f*; **a s. on the current crisis** une satire sur la crise actuelle
skitter [ˈskɪtər] *vi* (*move quickly*) **to s. away** *or* **off** (*of spider etc*) s'enfuir; **the pencil skittered across the floor** le crayon glissa sur le sol
skittish [ˈskɪtɪʃ] *adj* (**a**) (*horse*) ombrageux (**b**) (*person*) (*playful*) espiègle; (*frivolous*) frivole
skittishly [ˈskɪtɪʃlɪ] *adv* (*playfully*) avec espièglerie; (*frivolously*) frivolement
skittishness [ˈskɪtɪʃnɪs] *n* (**a**) (*of horse*) caractère *m* ombrageux (**b**) (*of person*) (*playfulness*) espièglerie *f*; (*frivolousness*) frivolité *f*
skittle [ˈskɪt(ə)l] *n* **s. (pin)** quille *f*; **(game of) skittles** (jeu *m* de) quilles *fpl*; **to play skittles** jouer aux quilles; **s. alley** (terrain *m* de) jeu de quilles
skive [skaɪv] *vi Br F* tirer au flanc
▶ **skive off** *vi Br F* (*leave work etc*) s'esquiver
skiver [ˈskaɪvər] *n Br F* tire-au-flanc *m inv*
skiving [ˈskaɪvɪŋ] *n Br F* manque *m* de travail; **there's too much s. round here** on tire trop au flanc ici
skivvy¹ [ˈskɪvɪ] *n Br Pej* bonniche *f*, bonne *f* à tout faire; *Fig* **I'm not your s.!** je ne suis pas ta bonne!
skivvy² *vi Br* faire la bonne (à tout faire); *Fig* **I'm not skivvying for you** je ne suis pas ta bonne
skua [ˈskjuːə] *n* (*bird*) stercoraire *m*
skulduggery [skʌlˈdʌgərɪ] *n F* magouille *f*; **political/financial s.** magouille politique/financière
skulk [skʌlk] *vi* (**a**) (*hide*) se cacher (**b**) (*move furtively*) rôder; **to s. in/out** entrer/sortir furtivement
skull [skʌl] *n* crâne *m*; **s. and crossbones** tête *f* de mort et tibias; **he's got a thick s.** il a la tête dure; *F* **can't you get that into your thick s.?** est-ce que tu ne peux pas te rentrer ça dans le crâne?; *F* **I was bored out of my s.** je crevais d'ennui; *Sl* **to be out of one's s.** (*drunk*) être bourré; **to get out of one's s.** se bourrer la gueule
skullcap [ˈskʌlkæp] *n* (*of priest etc*) calotte *f*
skunk [skʌŋk] *n* (*animal*) mouffette *f*; (*fur*) scons(e) *m*, skons *m*, skun(k)s *m*; *F, Pej* (*person*) mufle *m*, salaud *m*
sky¹ [skaɪ] *n* ciel *m*, *pl* cieux, (*in Art*) ciels; **under the open s.** (*to picnic, wander*) au grand air; **to sleep under the open s.** dormir à la belle étoile; *Fig* **the s.'s the limit** il n'y a pas de limite; **to praise sb to the skies** porter qn aux nues; *Prov* **red s. at night, shepherd's delight** rouge le soir, l'espoir; *Prov* **red s. in the morning, shepherd's warning** ≈ araignée du matin, chagrin; **the bridge was blown s. high** le pont a volé en éclats; **his project was blown s. high** son projet a été anéanti; **prices are s. high** les prix sont astronomiques; **s. blue** bleu *m* ciel, bleu azur; *TV etc* **s. cloth** rideau *m* de fond
sky² *vt* (*pt, pp* **skied**) *Cr, Tennis etc* (*ball*) envoyer en chandelle
sky-blue *adj* bleu ciel *inv*, bleu azur *inv*
skydiver [ˈskaɪdaɪvər] *n Av, Sp* parachutiste *mf* qui pratique la chute libre
skydiving [ˈskaɪdaɪvɪŋ] *n Av, Sp* parachutisme *m* en chute libre
Skye [skaɪ] *n* (l'île *f* de) Skye *f*; **S. terrier** skye-terrier *m*, *pl* skye-terriers
skyjack [ˈskaɪdʒæk] *vt F* (*plane*) détourner
skyjacker [ˈskaɪdʒækər] *n F* pirate *m* de l'air
skyjacking [ˈskaɪdʒækɪŋ] *n F* piraterie *f* aérienne
skylark¹ [ˈskaɪlɑːk] *n* (*bird*) alouette *f* des champs
skylark² *vi F* (*play about*) rigoler, batifoler
skylarking [ˈskaɪlɑːkɪŋ] *n F* rigolade *f*
skylight [ˈskaɪlaɪt] *n* (*in roof, ceiling*) jour *m*; (*in attic*) (lucarne *f*) faîtière *f*; (*hinged*) (châssis *m ou* fenêtre *f ou* lucarne à) tabatière *f*
skyline [ˈskaɪlaɪn] *n* (*horizon*) (ligne *f* d')horizon *m*; (*of city*) silhouette *f*; **it radically alters the s.** ça change radicalement le profil de la ville
skypilot [ˈskaɪpaɪlət] *n Old-fashioned Mil Sl* (*padre*) aumônier *m* militaire
skyrocket¹ [ˈskaɪrɒkɪt] *n* fusée *f*
skyrocket² *vi F* (*of prices etc*) monter en flèche
skyscape [ˈskaɪskeɪp] *n Art* paysage *m* céleste
skyscraper [ˈskaɪskreɪpər] *n* gratte-ciel *m*, *pl* gratte-ciel(s)
skyward(s) [ˈskaɪwəd(z)] *adv* (*to fly*) dans le ciel; (*to look*) vers le ciel
skyway [ˈskaɪweɪ] *n Am* (**a**) *Av* couloir *m* aérien (**b**) (*flyover*) saut-de-mouton *m*; (*raised road*) route *f* surélevée
sky(-)writing *n* publicité *f* aérienne
S&L [esəˈnel] *n Am* (*abbr* **savings and loan association**) société *f* immobilière
slab [slæb] *n* (**a**) (*of stone, marble etc*) plaque *f*, dalle *f*; (*of timber*) plaque; (*in mortuary*) table *f*; (**paving**) **s.** dalle; **butcher's s.** étal *m* de boucher (**b**) (*of cake*) (grosse) tranche *f*; (*of chocolate*) plaque *f*, tablette *f*; (*of meat*) pavé *m*
slack¹ [slæk] *n* (**a**) (*in cable, belt*) mou *m*; *MecE* jeu *m* (nuisible); **to take up the s. in a cable** mettre un câble au raide; *Fig* **to take up the s.** relancer le marché (**b**) *Naut* (*sea*) mer *f* étale (**c**) (*trousers*) **slacks** pantalon *m*
slack² *adj* (**a**) (*rope etc*) mou, *f* molle, lâche; (*screw*) desserré; (*handshake, grip*) mou; **to be** *or* **hang s.** (*of rope*) avoir du mou; *Fig* **to have a s. rein on sth** diriger qch sans fermeté *ou* mollement
(**b**) (*careless*) (*person, attitude, work*) négligent; (*lazy*) *F* flemmard; (*analysis*) flou; **things are getting far too s. around here** il y a beaucoup trop de relâchement ici; **to get** *or* **become s.** (*of person*) se laisser aller, se relâcher; **to be s. in** *or* **about doing sth** être négligent en faisant qch; **security at the base is very s.** les mesures de sécurité à la base militaire ne sont pas du tout strictes

(c) (*not busy*) (*market, economy*) peu actif; (*business*) stagnant; **business is s.** les affaires ne marchent pas fort; **we're s. this afternoon** (*in business etc*) nous ne sommes pas très occupés cet après-midi; **when things are a bit slacker** quand les choses se calmeront; **s. periods** moments de creux, périodes calmes; **the s. season** la morte-saison, la saison creuse; **s. time** période d'accalmie

slack³ *vi F* (*of person*) (*become negligent*) se laisser aller; (*in one's work, efforts*) se relâcher; **dear me, I must be slacking!** mon Dieu, je vieillis!

slack⁴ *n* (*coal*) menu charbon *m*, poussier *m*

▶ **slack off 1** *vi* (*diminish*) (*of pressure, demand, rain etc*) se calmer **2** *vtsep MecE* (*diminish*) (*pressure*) relâcher

slacken ['slæk(ə)n] **1** *vt* (*pace, efforts*) ralentir; (*rope*) détendre, relâcher, donner du mou à; (*sail*) donner du mou à; **to s. speed** diminuer la vitesse, ralentir (la marche); **to s. the reins** lâcher la bride *ou* les rênes **2** *vi* (*of person*) se relâcher, devenir négligent; (*of rope*) prendre du mou; (*of speed*) ralentir; (*of storm*) se calmer; (*of energy, enthusiasm*) retomber; **business is slackening** les affaires stagnent

▶ **slacken off** *vi, vtsep* = **slack off**

slackening ['slæk(ə)nɪŋ] *n* (*of zeal*) ralentissement *m*, diminution *f*; (*of strength, speed*) diminution; (*of rope, efforts*) relâchement *m*; **s. of speed** ralentissement

slacker ['slækər] *n F* paresseux, -euse, *F* flemmard, -arde

slackly ['slæklɪ] *adv* **(a)** (*to hang*) mollement **(b)** (*carelessly*) négligemment

slackness ['slæknɪs] *n* **(a)** (*negligence*) négligence *f*; (*laziness*) paresse *f*, *F* flemme *f*; (*laxity*) mollesse *f*; (*of discipline*) laxisme *m* **(b)** (*of muscles etc*) relâchement *m*; (*of rope*) mou *m* **(c)** *Com* (*of business*) stagnation *f*

slag¹ [slæg] *n* **(a)** *Metal* (*of metal*) scorie(s) *f(pl)*; (*of blast furnace*) crasse *f*, laitier(s) *m(pl)*; *Min* déchets *mpl* miniers; *Geol* **volcanic s.** scories volcaniques; **s. heap** *Metal* crassier *m*; *Min* terril *m* **(b)** *Pej Sl* (*woman*) salope *f*

slag² *vt Br Sl* débiner

▶ **slag off** *vtsep Br Sl* (*denigrate*) se moquer de; (*behind sb's back*) dénigrer

slagging ['slægɪŋ] *n Br Sl* **to give sb a s.** débiner qn

slain [sleɪn] **1** *adj Lit* mort **2** *npl Lit* **the s.** les morts *mpl* **3** *pp see* **slay**

slake [sleɪk] *vt* **(a)** *Lit* **to s. one's thirst** étancher *ou* apaiser sa soif, se désaltérer **(b)** *Ch* (*lime*) éteindre; **slaked lime** chaux *f* éteinte

slalom ['slɑːləm] *n Ski* slalom *m*

slam¹ [slæm] *n* (*of door etc*) claquement *m*; **he shut the door after him with a s.** il claqua la porte derrière lui

slam² (-mm-) **1** *vt* **(a)** (*door*) (faire) claquer; **to s. the door in sb's face** claquer la porte au nez de qn; **she slammed the book (down) on the table** elle a flanqué le livre sur la table; **he slammed the phone down** il raccrocha d'un geste furieux; *Fb* **he slammed the ball into the back of the net** il a logé le ballon au fond des filets; **she slammed her fist into his face** elle lui a flanqué son poing dans la figure; **he slammed the money down on the counter** il jeta rageusement l'argent sur le comptoir

(b) *F* (*criticize severely*) critiquer; (*person*) éreinter; **he was slammed in the press** il a été éreinté par la presse

2 *vi* (*of door etc*) claquer; **to s. out of the house** sortir de la maison en claquant la porte

slam³ *n Cards* (*at bridge*) chelem *m*, schelem *m*; *Cards, Sp* **grand s.** grand chelem; **to make a s.** faire (le) chelem

▶ **slam on** *vtsep F* **to s. on the brakes** freiner à fond

slammer ['slæmər] *n Sl* (*prison*) taule *f*

slander¹ ['slɑːndər] *n* calomnie *f*; *Jur* diffamation *f* verbale

slander² *vt* calomnier; *Jur* diffamer

slanderer ['slɑːndərər] *n* détracteur, -trice; *Jur* diffamateur, -trice

slanderous ['slɑːndərəs] *adj* (*words, article*) calomnieux; *Jur* diffamatoire

slanderously ['slɑːndərəslɪ] *adv* calomnieusement; *Jur* de façon diffamatoire

slang¹ [slæŋ] *n* (*in general, of specific group*) argot *m*; **s. words** mots d'argot, mots argotiques; **prisoners'/schoolboy s.** argot des prisonniers/écoliers; **s. phrase** *or* **expression** expression argotique

slang² *vt F* (*person*) (*abuse*) injurier; (*reprimand*) engueuler

slangily ['slæŋɪlɪ] *adv* (*to express oneself*) en argot

slanging match ['slæŋɪŋ] *n F* prise *f* de bec, engueulade *f*; **they were having a s.** ils se sont engueulés

slangy ['slæŋɪ] *adj* (*style, language, term*) argotique

slant¹ [slɑːnt] *n* **(a)** (*oblique angle*) biais *m*, biseau *m*; **on the** *or* **at a s.** de biais, obliquement **(b)** (*emphasis*) perspective *f*; **to put a different s. on things** apporter une perspective différente sur les choses; **to put a left-/right-wing s. on events** interpréter les événements dans une perspective de gauche/de droite; **these historians put a different s. on events** ces historiens ont envisagé les événements sous un angle différent; **report with a s. to it** reportage tendancieux

slant² **1** *vi* (*slope*) être en pente, être incliné; (*of handwriting*) pencher (**to** à) **2** *vt* **(a)** (*angle*) incliner **(b)** *Fig* (*bias*) fausser; **the article was slanted** l'article était orienté; **slanted news** informations tendancieuses *ou* faussées

slant-eyed *adj* aux yeux bridés; **to be s.** avoir les yeux bridés

slanting ['slɑːntɪŋ] *adj* (*roof*) en pente, incliné; (*writing*) couché, penché

slantwise, slantways ['slɑːntwaɪz, -weɪz] *adv* en *ou* de biais

slap¹ [slæp] **1** *n* (*with hand*) claque *f*, tape *f*; (*of waves*) clapotis *m*; **s. in the face** gifle *f*; *Fig* (*rebuff*) gifle, affront *m*, soufflet *m*; **s. on the back** tape dans le dos; *Fig* félicitations *fpl*; **to get a s. on the back for one's efforts** être félicité pour les efforts que l'on a fournis; *Br Hum, F* **they were having a bit of s. and tickle on the sofa** ils se faisaient un câlin sur le divan **2** *adv F* **s. (bang) in the middle** en plein milieu; **the car went s. bang into the wall** la voiture est rentrée dans le mur de plein fouet; **they ran s. bang into each other** ils se sont rentrés en plein dedans

slap² *vt* (-pp- [slæpt]) **(a)** (*person*) (*with open hand*) donner une claque *ou* une tape à; **to s. sb's face, to s. sb in the face** gifler qn; **to s. sb on the back** donner une tape sur le dos à qn; *Fig* (*congratulate*) féliciter qn **(b)** (*put brusquely*) **she slapped the money on the table** elle a jeté *ou* flanqué l'argent sur la table

▶ **slap around** *vtas* battre, *F* cogner

▶ **slap down** *vtsep* **(a)** (*put down brusquely*) jeter; *F* flanquer, balancer **(b)** *F* (*repress*) (*person*) rembarrer; (*put in his place*) remettre à sa place; (*suggestion*) rejeter

▶ **slap on** *vtsep* **he slapped on some aftershave** il s'est aspergé de lotion après-rasage; *F* **they slapped on another £50** ils ont augmenté le prix de 50 livres; **the paint had been just slapped on** la peinture avait été appliquée n'importe comment

slapdash ['slæpdæʃ] **1** *adj* sans soin(s); (*work*) à la six-quatre-deux; (*person*) expéditif; **to do sth in a s. manner** faire qch à la va-vite *ou* à la six-quatre-deux; **s. worker** saboteur, -euse **2** *adv* sans soin(s), à la va-vite, à la six-quatre-deux

slap-happy *adj F* (*careless*) insouciant; **this work's a bit s.** ce travail a été fait à la va-vite

slaphead ['slæp(h)ed] *n Sl* (*bald person*) crâne *m* d'œuf

slapping ['slæpɪŋ] *n* (*blows*) claques *fpl*, gifles *fpl*

slapstick ['slæpstɪk] *n Th* **s. (comedy)** comédie *f* bouffonne, farce *f*

slap-up *adj Br F* **s. meal** festin *m*, repas *m* somptueux

slash¹ [slæʃ] *n* **(a)** (*cut*) entaille *f*; (*on the face*) estafilade *f*, balafre *f* **(b)** *Sewing* (*in sleeve*) crevé *m* **(c)** *Typ* barre *f* oblique **(d)** *Br Sl* **to have a s.** (*urinate*) pisser un coup

slash² **1** *vt* (*cut*) (*flesh*) taillader; (*face*) balafrer; (*rope etc*) couper *ou* trancher net; *Fig* (*shorten*) (*text etc*) couper radicalement; (*criticize*) (*novel etc*) éreinter; *F* casser; (*reduce*) (*prices, interest rates*) casser; (*unemployment, spending*) réduire de façon radicale; **he slashed the sack open** il a fendu le sac d'un coup de couteau; **prices slashed** prix sacrifiés; *Sewing* **slashed sleeve** manche *f* à crevés

2 *vi* **to s. at sb with a knife** donner des coups de couteau à qn; **to s. about with a knife** donner des coups de couteau dans tous les sens; **they slashed through the undergrowth** ils se sont taillés un chemin dans les sous-bois

slashing ['slæʃɪŋ] *adj* (*criticism*) mordant, cinglant

slat [slæt] *n* (*of shutter etc*) lame *f*, lamelle *f*, planchette *f*; (*of bed*) traverse *f*

slate¹ [sleɪt] *n* **(a)** *Geol* ardoise *f*; *Constr* (feuille *f* d')ardoise; **s. blue** bleu ardoise *m inv*; **s.-colour(ed)** ardoisé; **s. grey** (gris *m*) ardoise *inv*; **a s. grey colour** une couleur d'ardoise; **s. quarry** ardoisière *f*; **s. roof** toit *m* d'ardoises; **s. worker** *or* **quarryman** ardoisier *m*

(b) **(writing) s.** ardoise *f*; *Br F* **put it on my s.** (*as debt*) mettez-le moi sur mon ardoise; *Fig* **to wipe the s. clean** faire table rase (du passé); **I have a clean s.** (*have no debts*) je n'ai pas de dettes; (*have committed no offence*) mon casier judiciaire est vierge; **to start again with a clean s.** repartir sur de nouvelles bases; **s. pencil** crayon *m* d'ardoise

(c) *TV etc* clap *m*

slate² *vt* **(a)** *Constr* (*roof*) couvrir d'ardoises *ou* en ardoise; **slated roof** toit d'ardoises **(b)** *Am Pol* (*candidate*) inscrire sur la liste; **to be slated to do sth** être susceptible de faire qch; **he was slated for promotion but …** il aurait dû être promu mais …

slate³ *vt Br F* (*criticize severely*) (*person, book, decision, government*) critiquer, éreinter, *F* casser

slater ['sleɪtər] *n* **(a)** (*person*) couvreur *m* (en ardoises) **(b)** *Dial* (*woodlouse*) cloporte *m*

slating ['sleɪtɪŋ] *n Br F* (**a**) (*reprimand*) savon *m*; **he got a s. from the PM** il s'est fait passer un savon par le Premier Ministre (**b**) (*severe criticism*) critique *f* acerbe; **the play got a s. in the press** la pièce a été éreintée *ou F* cassée par la presse
slatted ['slætɪd] *adj* (*shutters etc*) à lames, à planchettes
slattern ['slætən] *n* femme *f* mal soignée, souillon *f*
slatternly ['slætənlɪ] *adj* (*woman*) mal soigné; (*habit, dress*) négligé
slaty ['sleɪtɪ] *adj Geol* ardoisier; (*colour*) ardoisé
slaughter[1] ['slɔːtər] *n* (**a**) (*of cattle, sheep etc*) abattage *m* (**b**) (*of people*) tuerie *f*, carnage *m*, massacre *m*; **the senseless s. of innocent civilians** le massacre insensé de civils innocents
slaughter[2] *vt* (**a**) (*cattle, sheep*) abattre (**b**) (*kill*) (*people*) tuer, massacrer; *F* (*defeat heavily*) (*opponent*) battre à plate(s) couture(s), massacrer
slaughterer ['slɔːtərər] *n* (**a**) (*of cattle, sheep*) abatteur *m*, tueur *m* (**b**) (*of people*) tueur, -euse
slaughterhouse ['slɔːtəhaʊs] *n* abattoir *m*
slaughtering ['slɔːtərɪŋ] *n* (**a**) (*of cattle, sheep*) abattage *m* (**b**) (*of people*) tuerie *f*, carnage *m*, massacre *m*
Slav [slɑːv] **1** *adj* slave **2** *n* Slave *mf*
slave[1] [sleɪv] *n* esclave *mf*; **to be sb's s.** être l'esclave de qn; **to be the s. of** *or* **a s. to one's passion** être esclave de sa passion; **to be a s. to duty** ne connaître que son devoir; **to be a s. to convention** être esclave des conventions; **to be a s. to one's work** être esclave de son travail; **s. camera** caméra *f* asservie *ou* esclave; *Aut* **s. cylinder** récepteur *m*; **s. driver** garde *m* d'esclaves; *Fig F* garde-chiourme *m, pl* garde(s)-chiourme(s); **s. labour** travail *m* d'esclave; *Fig* esclavage *m*
slave[2] *vi* travailler comme un nègre (**over** à); **to s. over a hot stove** trimer à ses fourneaux
▶ **slave away** *vi* (*work hard*) trimer (**over, at** sur)
slaver[1] ['sleɪvər] *n* (**a**) (*ship*) (bâtiment *m*) négrier *m* (**b**) (*person*) marchand *m* d'esclaves; (*of blacks*) négrier *m*; **white s.** personne *f* pratiquant la traite des blanches
slaver[2] ['slævər] *n* (*saliva*) bave *f*, salive *f*
slaver[3] *vi* (*dribble*) baver (**over** sur)
slavery ['sleɪvərɪ] *n* esclavage *m*; **to sell sb into s.** vendre qn comme esclave; **to reduce to s.** (*person*) réduire en esclavage; (*a people*) asservir; **white s.** traite *f* des blanches; **this work is sheer s.** ce travail est un véritable esclavage
slave trade *n* traite *f* des noirs, commerce *m ou* traffic *m* des esclaves; **white s.** traite des blanches
slave trader *n* marchand *m* d'esclaves
Slavic ['slɑːvɪk] *adj, n* slave *m*
slavish ['sleɪvɪʃ] *adj* (*submission*) d'esclave; (*imitation*) servile
slavishly ['sleɪvɪʃlɪ] *adv* (*to imitate*) servilement
slavishness ['sleɪvɪʃnɪs] *n* servilité *f*
Slavonic [slə'vɒnɪk] **1** *adj* slave; **student of S. languages** slavisant, -ante **2** *n Ling* slave *m*; **Church S., Old S.** slavon *m*
slaw [slɔː] *n esp Am Culin* salade *f* de chou cru
slay [sleɪ] *vt* (*pt* **slew** [sluː]; *pp* **slain** [sleɪn]) *Lit* tuer; *esp US Journ* assassiner; **the slain** (*npl*) les morts *mpl*; *F* **this one will really s. you** (*of joke etc*) celle-là va vous faire mourir de rire
slayer ['sleɪər] *n Lit* (*killer*) tueur, -euse; *esp US Journ* (*murderer*) assassin *m* (**of** de)
slaying ['sleɪɪŋ] *n Lit* (*killing*) (*of dragon*) destruction *f*; (*of person*) meurtre *m*; *esp US Journ* (*murder*) assassinat *m*, meurtre *m*
sleaze [sliːz] *n F* corruption *f*; (*gossip in newspapers, on TV*) ragots *mpl* sordides; (*dirt, immorality*) perversité *f*; *esp Am* **s. ball** fumier *m*, ordure *f*; **the s. factor will affect his chances in the election** tous les ragots sordides qui ont circulé à son sujet risquent de compromettre son succès aux élections; **the s. factor in politics** la corruption de la vie politique
sleaziness ['sliːzɪnɪs] *n F* (*of place etc*) sordide *m*
sleazo ['sliːzəʊ] *n F* personne *f* louche; **he's a s.** c'est un type louche
sleazy ['sliːzɪ] *adj F* sordide, glauque
sled [sled] *n, vi Am* = **sledge**[1,2]
sledge[1] [sledʒ] *n* (*means of transport*) traîneau *m*; (*toy*) luge *f*
sledge[2] *vi* (*travel*) aller en traîneau; (*play*) faire de la luge; **to go sledging** se promener en traîneau, faire une promenade en traîneau; (*of children*) aller faire de la luge
sledge[3] *n* = **sledgehammer**
sledgehammer ['sledʒhæmər] *n* (*tool*) masse *f*; **to have (all) the subtlety of a s.** manquer totalement de subtilité; *F* **s. arguments** arguments massue(s); **a s. blow** (*punch*) un coup de massue; *Fig* (*to industry etc*) un coup fatal; **to use a s. to crack a walnut** employer les grands moyens (pour régler un problème mineur)
sleek[1] [sliːk] *adj* (**a**) (*smooth*) (*hair, fur etc*) lisse et brillant; (*person*) (*well-groomed*) trop pomponné; **s. horse** cheval d'un beau poil; **a s. black limousine** une limousine d'un noir brillant; **the car's s. lines** la ligne aérodynamique de la voiture (**b**) (*unctuous*) (*manner*) mielleux, onctueux
sleek[2] *vt* (*hair, horse's coat*) lisser
▶ **sleek down** *vtsep* **to s. down one's hair** se lisser les cheveux; (*with oil*) se brillantiner les cheveux
sleekly ['sliːklɪ] *adv* (**a**) **to glisten s.** luire (**b**) (*unctuously*) (*to talk, act*) mielleusement, onctueusement
sleekness ['sliːknɪs] *n* (**a**) (*of skin, satin*) luisant *m* (**b**) (*of manners*) onctuosité *f*
sleep[1] [sliːp] *n* sommeil *m*; *F* (*substance in eye*) chassie *f*; **short s.** somme *m*; **deep** *or* **sound s.** sommeil profond; **beauty s.** sommeil avant minuit (*considéré comme le plus réparateur*); **to go to** *or* **drop off to s.** s'endormir, s'assoupir; **to go to** *or* **drop off to s. again** se rendormir; **to send sb to s.** endormir qn; *Med* **to put sb to s.** endormir qn; *Vet* **to put an animal to s.** piquer un animal; **to read oneself to s.** lire pour s'endormir; **to rouse sb from his/her s.** réveiller qn, arracher qn au sommeil; **to have a good (night's) s.** bien dormir; **I need my s.** j'ai besoin de beaucoup de sommeil; **to get two hours' s.** dormir deux heures; **I didn't get a wink of s. all night** je n'ai pas fermé l'œil de la nuit; (*stayed up working etc*) j'ai passé une nuit blanche; **a night without s.** une nuit blanche; **to rub the s. out of one's eyes** se frotter les yeux pour se réveiller; **I won't lose any s. over it** cela ne m'empêchera pas de dormir; **in my s.** (*to cry, talk, call out*) en dormant; **to walk in one's s.** être somnambule; **my foot's gone to s.** j'ai des fourmis dans le pied, j'ai le pied engourdi
sleep[2] (*pt, pp* **slept** [slept]) **1** *vi* (**a**) (*not be awake*) dormir; **to s. like a log** dormir à poings fermés, dormir comme une souche *ou* comme un loir; **to s. soundly** dormir profondément; **to s. the night through** dormir toute la nuit; **to s. through a noise** ne pas être réveillé par un bruit; **I slept right through the alarm** je n'ai pas entendu le réveil; **I haven't slept a wink all night** je n'ai pas fermé l'œil de (toute) la nuit; **to s. (for) six hours** dormir six heures; **to try to s.** chercher le sommeil; **he can't s. for thinking about it** il n'en dort pas; **to s. late** faire la grasse matinée; **I'll s. on it** la nuit porte conseil; **s. on it** la nuit porte conseil

(**b**) (*spend a night*) coucher; **to s. rough** coucher sur la dure; **to s. on the floor/in a bed** coucher par terre/dans un lit; **the bed had not been slept in** le lit n'avait pas été défait

2 *vt* (**a**) **a house that sleeps ten people** une maison où l'on peut coucher à dix; **this room sleeps four** on peut coucher à quatre dans cette chambre

(**b**) *Lit* **to s. the sleep of the just** dormir du sommeil du juste
▶ **sleep around** *vi F* (*be promiscuous*) coucher avec n'importe qui
▶ **sleep away** *vtsep* **to s. the day/the hours away** passer la journée/les heures à dormir *ou* en dormant
▶ **sleep in** *vi* (**a**) (*have a lie-in*) faire la grasse matinée; (*wake up too late*) ne pas se réveiller à l'heure (**b**) (*of servant*) coucher à la maison
▶ **sleep off** *vtsep F* (*remove by sleeping*) (*headache*) faire passer en dormant; **to s. off one's hangover, to s. it off** cuver son vin/sa bière/*etc*
▶ **sleep out** *vi* (*not sleep at home*) découcher; (*in open air*) coucher à la belle (étoile); (*of servant*) coucher à domicile, venir en journée
▶ **sleep together** *vi* coucher ensemble
▶ **sleep with** *vipo* **to s. with sb** coucher avec qn
sleeper ['sliːpər] *n* (**a**) (*person*) dormeur, -euse; **a late s.** un couche-tard; **to be a light/heavy s.** avoir le sommeil léger/profond; **to be a good s.** (*of baby*) bien dormir; **s. night** (*in hotels*) nuitée *f* (**b**) *Br Rail* (*on track*) traverse *f* (**c**) *Rail* (*carriage*) wagon-lit *m, pl* wagons-lits; (*train*) train-couchette *m* (**d**) *Am* (*pajamas*) **sleeper(s)** pyjama *m* d'enfant (**e**) (*spy*) espion *m* en sommeil (**f**) (*earring*) dormeuse *f*
sleepily ['sliːpɪlɪ] *adv* d'un air endormi; **a village nestled s. in the hills** un village blotti tranquillement contre les collines
sleepiness ['sliːpɪnɪs] *n* (**a**) (*desire to sleep*) envie *f* de dormir, somnolence *f* (**b**) (*of town*) calme *m*, *Pej* apathie *f*
sleeping ['sliːpɪŋ] **1** *adj* dormant, endormi; *Prov* **let s. dogs lie** ne réveillez pas le chat qui dort; *Com* **s. partner** commanditaire *m*; (*who supplies capital*) bailleur *m* de fonds

2 *n* sommeil *m*; **the house has s. accommodation for ten** c'est une maison où dix personnes peuvent dormir; **there's no s. accommodation here** il n'y a rien pour dormir; **this is the s. accommodation here** c'est ici qu'on dort; **what are the s. arrangements?** et pour dormir, comment on fait?; **she was a bit vague about the s. arrangements** elle est restée

vague concernant les lits; **s. quarters** chambre(s) *f(pl)*, dortoir(s) *m(pl)*; *Mil* chambrée *f*; *Med* **s. sickness** maladie *f* du sommeil
sleeping bag *n* sac *m* de couchage
sleeping car, sleeping carriage *n Rail* wagon-lit *m*, *pl* wagons-lits
sleeping draught *n* sirop *m* somnifère
sleeping pill *n* somnifère *m*
sleeping policeman *n F* ralentisseur *m*
sleeping tablet *n* somnifère *m*
sleepless ['sli:plɪs] *adj* sans sommeil; (*night*) d'insomnie; **to have a s. night** ne pas fermer l'œil de la nuit, passer une nuit blanche; *Lit* **s. vigilance** vigilance sans faille
sleeplessly ['sli:plɪslɪ] *adv* sans dormir
sleeplessness ['sli:plɪsnɪs] *n* insomnie *f*
sleepwalk ['sli:pwɔ:k] *vi* (*be a sleepwalker*) être somnambule; **he's sleepwalking** il marche en dormant; **I was sleepwalking last night** j'ai eu une crise de somnambulisme la nuit dernière; *Fig* **we are sleepwalking into disaster** nous allons tout droit à la catastrophe sans nous en rendre compte
sleepwalker ['sli:pwɔ:kər] *n* somnambule *mf*
sleepwalking ['sli:pwɔ:kɪŋ] *n* somnambulisme *m*
sleepy ['sli:pɪ] *adj* **(a)** somnolent; **to be** *or* **feel s.** avoir envie de dormir, avoir sommeil; **to make sb (feel) s.** endormir qn; **s. look** air endormi **(b) s. little town** petite ville endormie
sleepyhead ['sli:pɪhed] *n F* endormi, -ie; **wake up, s.!** debout, paresseux/paresseuse!
sleet[1] [sli:t] *n* **(a)** (*icy rain*) pluie *f* mêlée de neige **(b)** *Am* (*ice*) verglas *m*
sleet[2] *v impers* **it's sleeting** il tombe de la neige fondue
sleeve [sli:v] *n* **(a)** (*of garment*) manche *f*; **short s.** manche courte; **s. hole** (*in dress etc*) emmanchure *f*; *Fig F* **he's got something up his s.** il a une idée derrière la tête; **he's got a surprise up his s.** il nous/leur/*etc* réserve une surprise; **to have more than one trick up one's s.** avoir plus d'un tour dans son sac; **s. board** (*for ironing sleeves*) jeannette *f* **(b)** *MecE* chemise *f*, fourreau *m*, gaine *f* (souple); (*tubular casing*) douille *f* **(c)** (*of record*) pochette *f*; **s. notes** annotations *fpl* sur la pochette
sleeved [sli:vd] *adj* (*garment*) à manches
-sleeved [-sli:vd] *suff* **long/short-s.** à manches longues/courtes
sleeveless ['sli:vlɪs] *adj* (*dress, pullover etc*) sans manches
sleigh [sleɪ] *n* traîneau *m*; **s. bell** grelot *m*, clochette *f* (*sur un traîneau*); **s. ride** promenade *f* en traîneau
sleight [slaɪt] *n* (*conjuring trick*) tour *m* de passe-passe; **it's done by s. of hand** c'est de la prestidigitation; **by s. of hand** par un tour de passe-passe
slender ['slendər] *adj* **(a)** mince; (*figure*) svelte, fluet; **s. waist** taille fine **(b)** (*hope*) ténu; (*income*) modique, maigre, modeste; **the slenderest of margins** une marge des plus étroites; **there is a very s. chance that ...** il y a une chance très faible que ...; **s. means** de maigres ressources; **of s. means** qui a de petits moyens
slenderize ['slendəraɪz] *vt Am* amincir
slenderly ['slendəlɪ] *adv* **s. built** à la taille fine
slenderness ['slendənɪs] *n* **(a)** minceur *f*; (*of person, waist*) sveltesse *f* **(b)** (*of fortune*) modicité *f*; (*of resources*) maigreur *f*
slept *see* **sleep[2]**
sleuth[1] ['slu:θ] *n F usu Hum* limier *m*, détective *m*; **a good bit of s. work** un travail de fin limier
sleuth[2] *vi F* faire le détective
sleuthhound ['slu:θhaʊnd] *n* (*dog*) limier *m*; *F* (*detective*) limier, détective *m*
slew[1] [slu:] *n* (*turn*) virage *m*; *Aut* (*180 degree turn*) tête-à-queue *m inv*
slew[2] **1** *vt* faire pivoter **2** *vi* pivoter; (*of car*) (*turn right round*) faire un tête-à-queue; **the car slewed off the track** la voiture a dérapé hors de la piste
slew[3] *n F* (*large number*) tas *m*
slew[4] *see* **slay**
▶ **slew around, slew round 1** *vtsep* (*rotate*) faire pivoter; **she slewed the car round** elle a fait pivoter la voiture; (*180 degree turn*) elle a fait un tête-à-queue **2** *vi* (*rotate*) pivoter; (*of car*) (*through 180 degrees*) faire un tête-à-queue
slice[1] [slaɪs] *n* **(a)** (*of bread, cake, meat etc*) tranche *f*; (*of pizza*) part *f*; (*of apple*) quartier *m*; **(round) s.** (*of lemon, sausage etc*) rondelle *f*; **s. of bread and butter** tartine *f* beurrée; **apple s.** tartelette *f* aux pommes; **to take a large s. of the credit for sth** s'attribuer une large part du mérite de qch; **a. s. of the profits** une part des bénéfices; **a s. of life** une tranche de vie **(b)** (*utensil*) **fish s.** truelle *f* (à poisson); **cake s.** pelle *f* à tarte **(c)** *Sp* coup *m* qui fait dévier la balle à droite; *Tennis* balle coupée
slice[2] **1** *vt* **(a)** couper *ou* découper en tranches; **to s. thinly** (*meat*) couper en tranches fines; (*onions etc*) émincer; **to s. sth in two** *or* **in half** couper qch en deux; *Am* **no matter how thin you s. it it's still baloney** par quelque bout que tu le prennes, c'est un bobard **(b)** (*ball*) *Tennis* couper; *Golf, Rugby* faire dévier à droite **2** *vi* **this meat slices easily** cette viande est facile à couper
▶ **slice into** *vipo* (*cut easily*) couper facilement; **the knife sliced into the flesh** le couteau a pénétré dans la chair
▶ **slice off** *vtsep* (*remove by slicing*) (*piece*) trancher, couper, détacher; **to s. off the tip of one's finger** se trancher le bout du doigt
▶ **slice through** *vipo* (*cut easily*) couper sans effort; **the knife sliced through the rope** le couteau a tranché la corde; *Fig* **the river slices through the city** la rivière coupe la ville en deux; **to s. through the enemy lines** transpercer les lignes adverses; **he sliced through the red tape** il a éliminé toute la paperasserie d'un seul coup
▶ **slice up** *vtsep* (*cut into slices*) couper *ou* découper en tranches
sliced [slaɪst] *adj* (*bread, ham etc*) en tranches; *F* **he thinks it's the best thing since s. bread** il pense que c'est ce qu'on a fait de mieux depuis l'invention du fil à couper le beurre
slicer ['slaɪsər] *n Culin* (*device*) couteau *m* à découper; (*electric*) couteau électrique; **(bacon) s.** coupe-jambon *m inv*
slick[1] [slɪk] *adj F* (*skilful, deft*) habile, adroit; (*catch, change-over*) adroit; (*movie*) bien fait, *Pej* malin, -igne; **s. talker** beau parleur *m*
slick[2] *n* **(oil) s.** nappe *f* de pétrole; (*on beach and sea*) marée *f* noire
▶ **slick back** *vtsep* (*comb back with oil etc*) **to s. back one's hair** se lisser les cheveux en arrière
▶ **slick down** *vtsep* (*comb down with oil etc*) **to s. one's hair down** se lisser les cheveux
▶ **slick up** *vi F* (*make oneself attractive*) se faire beau
slicker ['slɪkər] *n Am* **(a)** (*raincoat*) imperméable *m*; (*oilskin*) ciré *m* **(b)** (*person*) **(city) s.** homme *m* de finance habile, *Pej* requin *m*
slickly ['slɪklɪ] *adv usu Pej* (*skilfully*) habilement; (*cunningly*) habilement, adroitement
slickness ['slɪknɪs] *n usu Pej* (*skill, deftness*) habileté *f*, adresse *f*; (*cunning*) ruse *f*
slide[1] [slaɪd] *n* **(a)** (*action*) glissade *f*, glissement *m*; (*of land*) glissement de terrain; **to have a s.** (*of person*) faire une glissade; **the alarming s. of the economy** le dérapage alarmant de l'économie; **a s. in prices/popularity** une chute des prix/de la popularité; **a mud s.** une coulée de boue; **a rock s.** un éboulement

(b) (*place*) (*on snow or ice*) glissoire *f*; (*in playground*) toboggan *m*; *Av* **(escape) s.** toboggan d'évacuation

(c) *Mus* (*ornament*) coulé *m*; (*in violin playing etc*) glissade *f*; (*part of trombone etc*) coulisse *f*; **s. guitar** slide guitar *f*

(d) *Tech* (*sliding part*) pièce *f* qui glisse *ou* qui coulisse; (*of slide rule*) coulisseau *m*, réglette *f*; (*in rowing*) glissière *f*

(e) (*of microscope*) **(object) s.** (plaque *f ou* lame *f*) porte-objet *m*, *pl* porte-objet(s); (*what is on the slide*) préparation *f*

(f) *Phot* **(colour) s.** diapositive *f* (en couleur); *F* diapo *f* (en couleur); **lecture illustrated with slides** conférence *f* avec projections

(g) *Br* **(hair) s.** barrette *f*
slide[2] (*pt, pp* **slid** [slɪd]) **1** *vi* **(a)** (*slip*) (*of mechanism between runners etc*) coulisser; (*of person*) glisser; **to s. (on ice)** (*of person*) glisser (sur la glace), faire une glissade/des glissades; **she slid on the floor** elle a glissé sur le parquet; **the dish slid off the table/onto the floor** le plat a glissé de la table/sur le sol; *Fig* **to let things** *or* **everything s.** laisser tout aller à la dérive; (*lose interest in everything*) se désintéresser de tout; **the country was sliding into anarchy** le pays glissait vers l'anarchie; **prices/profits had begun to s.** les prix/profits avaient commencé à chuter

(b) (*move quietly*) (*into room, behind curtain etc*) se glisser; **the snake slid through the grass** le serpent s'est glissé entre les herbes; **the pilot slid into the cockpit** le pilote s'est glissé dans le cockpit; **to s. over a delicate subject** glisser sur un sujet délicat

2 *vt* (faire) glisser; **to s. sth into one's pocket** glisser qch dans sa poche
▶ **slide down 1** *vi* (*go down by sliding*) descendre en glissant; (*of prices*) chuter **2** *vipo* (*go down by sliding*) descendre en glissant; **to s. down a rope** se laisser couler *ou* glisser le long d'une corde; **to s. down the banisters** glisser le long de la rampe; **it's sliding down the charts** il perd des places au hit-parade
▶ **slide off 1** *vi* **(a)** (*be removed by sliding*) **the lid slides off** pour enlever le couvercle, il faut le faire glisser *ou* coulisser;

it keeps sliding off ça n'arrête pas de glisser **(b)** *F* *(sneak away)* filer en douce **2** *vtsep* *(lid etc)* faire glisser

▶ **slide out 1** *vi* **(a)** *(come out by sliding)* sortir en glissant **(b)** *F* *(sneak outside)* se glisser dehors **2** *vtsep* *(drawers, battery)* enlever en faisant glisser

▶ **slide out of** *vipo* *(evade)* se sortir de; **to s. out of doing the housework** échapper aux tâches ménagères; **I'd like to see him s. out of that one** j'aimerais bien voir comment il va se tirer d'affaire

slide fastener *n esp Am* fermeture *f* éclair *ou* à glissière

slide matte *n TV etc* cache *m* latéral

slide projector *n* projecteur *m* pour diapositives

slide show *n* présentation *f* de diapositives

sliding ['slaɪdɪŋ] *adj* glissant; *(panel)* coulissant, mobile; *(roof)* ouvrant; **s. door** porte *f* coulissante; *MecE* **s. parts** organes *mpl* mobiles; *Econ* **s. scale** *(of prices etc)* échelle *f* mobile; **s. seat** *(in rowing boat)* banc *m* à coulisses *ou* à glissières; *Aut* siège *m* réglable *ou* mobile; **s. sunroof** toit *m* ouvrant coulissant

slight¹ [slaɪt] *adj* **(a)** *(small)* *(pain, mistake etc)* léger, petit; *(intelligence, difference etc)* faible; *(damage)* peu important; *(wound)* sans gravité; **a s. accident** un petit incident; **a s. improvement** un léger mieux; *St Exch* **s. rise** hausse *f* de faible amplitude; **not the slightest danger/interest/***etc* pas le moindre danger/intérêt/*etc*; **to take offence at the slightest thing** se vexer pour un rien; **I haven't the slightest (idea)** je n'en ai pas la moindre idée; **not in the slightest** pas du tout, pas le moins du monde; **they weren't (in) the slightest bit interested, they weren't interested in the slightest** ils n'étaient pas le moins du monde intéressés; **there's a s. chance of some sunshine tomorrow** il y a une petite chance qu'il fasse beau demain

(b) *(thin)* ténu; *(person)* menu; *(figure)* frêle

slight² *n* *(affront)* affront *m*

slight³ *vt* *(person)* *(affront)* faire un affront à; *(treat without consideration)* traiter sans considération, manquer d'égards pour *ou* à; **to feel slighted** se sentir vexé *ou* froissé

slighting ['slaɪtɪŋ] *adj* *(tone)* de mépris, de dédain; *(remark)* plein de mépris

slightingly ['slaɪtɪŋlɪ] *adv* avec dédain, dédaigneusement

slightly ['slaɪtlɪ] **(a)** *(to a small degree)* légèrement, un peu; **s. better** un (petit) peu mieux; **I know him s.** je le connais un peu **(b) s. built** menu

slightness ['slaɪtnɪs] *n* **(a)** *(small extent)* *(of mistake etc)* légèreté *f*; *(of difference)* petitesse *f*; *(of damage)* insignifiance *f* **(b)** *(thinness)* **the s. of her arms** ses bras menus; **her s.** son corps menu

Slim [slɪm] *n* *(Aids)* maladie *f* de la maigreur

slim¹ [slɪm] *adj* *(comp* **slimmer,** *superl* **slimmest)** *(person)* svelte; *(fingers etc)* fuselé, menu; *(book etc)* mince; *(chance, hope etc)* petit; **tall and s.** élancé; **his first s. volume** son premier petit opuscule

slim² **(-mm-) 1** *vt* amincir **2** *vi* maigrir; **to be slimming** être au régime, suivre un régime amaigrissant; **dress that is slimming** robe qui mincit

▶ **slim down 1** *vtsep* *(reduce)* *(labour force)* réduire; **the company is slimming down its electronics operation** la société réduit ses activités dans le domaine de l'électronique **2** *vi* **(a)** *(lose weight)* maigrir **(b)** *(become smaller in size)* *(of company, army etc)* diminuer de taille

slime [slaɪm] *n* **(a)** *(mud)* vase *f*; **the primeval s.** la boue préhistorique **(b)** *(on fish etc)* humeur *f* visqueuse; *(of slug)* bave *f*; **what's this horrible s.?** qu'est-ce que c'est ce truc dégueulasse? **(c)** *F* *(person)* ordure *f*

slimeball ['slaɪmbɔːl] *n F* *(person)* mec *m* répugnant

sliminess ['slaɪmɪnɪs] *n* **(a)** état *m* vaseux; *(of fish etc)* viscosité *f* **(b)** *F* *(servility)* servilité *f*, obséquiosité *f*

slimly ['slɪmlɪ] *adv* **s. built** svelte

slimmer ['slɪmər] *n* personne *f* qui suit un régime amaigrissant; **ideal for slimmers** l'idéal pour maigrir

slimming ['slɪmɪŋ] *n* amincissement *m*; **s. can be bad for you** les régimes peuvent vous faire du mal; **s. club** centre *m* d'amaigrissement; **s. course** cure *f* d'amaigrissement; **s. diet** régime *m* amaigrissant; **s. pill** pilule *f* amaigrissante

slimness ['slɪmnɪs] *n* *(of person)* minceur *f*, sveltesse *f*; *(of book etc)* minceur

slimy ['slaɪmɪ] *adj* **(a)** *(consistency)* vaseux; *(mud)* gras; *(paste etc)* visqueux, gluant; **the frog felt all s.** la grenouille était toute visqueuse **(b)** *(tracks of slug)* visqueux; *(covered in slime)* couvert de vase; *(fish)* couvert d'une sécrétion visqueuse; *(slug etc)* couvert de bave; **it was a horrible s. mess** c'était parfaitement dégueulasse **(c)** *F* *(person)* servile, obséquieux; **he's a real s. creep** c'est un vrai lèche-bottes

sling¹ [slɪŋ] *n* **(a)** *Med* écharpe *f*; *(of rifle etc)* bretelle *f*; *(for hoisting)*, *Naut etc* élingue *f*; *(for hoisting people)* agui *m*; **to have one's arm in a s.** avoir le bras en écharpe **(b)** *(weapon)* fronde *f*

sling² *vt* *(pt, pp* **slung** [slʌŋ]) **(a)** *(hang)* suspendre; **to s. sth over one's shoulder** jeter qch sur l'épaule; **to s. sth across one's chest** mettre qch en bandoulière; *F* **to s. one's hook** mettre les bouts **(b)** *(throw)* lancer, jeter; **s. that paper over, will you?** lance-moi le journal, s'il te plaît; **they were slinging insults at each other** ils se lançaient des insultes

▶ **sling off** *vtsep F* **to s. sb off a course** virer qn d'un cours

▶ **sling out** *vtsep F* **(a)** *(dismiss)* *(person)* flanquer dehors; **he was slung out of the army** il s'est fait jeter de l'armée **(b)** *(throw away)* jeter, balancer

▶ **sling up** *vtsep* *(hoist)* hisser *(avec une grue)*

slingback ['slɪŋbæk] **1** *n* chaussure *f* à talon ouvert, sandale *f* **2** *adj* *(shoe)* à talon ouvert

slingshot ['slɪŋʃɒt] *n esp Am* fronde *f*

slink [slɪŋk] *vi* *(pt, pp* **slunk** [slʌŋk]) **to s. off** *or* **away** partir en catimini, s'éclipser; **to s. in/out** entrer/sortir furtivement; **she was slinking about in a velvet dress** elle ondulait dans sa robe en velours

slinkily ['slɪŋkɪlɪ] *adv F* *(to move)* avec des ondulations; **s. cut dress** robe qui suit bien les courbes du corps; **she sidled s. up to him** elle s'est dirigée vers lui en roulant des hanches

slinking ['slɪŋkɪŋ] *adj* furtif

slinky ['slɪŋkɪ] *adj F* *(figure)* svelte, mince; *(clothing)* collant, ajusté; *(walk)* ondulant

slip¹ [slɪp] *n* **(a)** *(fall)* **he had a s. on the ice** il a fait une chute sur la glace; **he had a nasty s.** il est mal tombé, il a fait une mauvaise chute

(b) *(error)* faute *f* d'inattention *ou* d'étourderie; *(in speaking)* lapsus *m*; **to make a s.** faire une erreur; *(in speaking)* faire un lapsus; **s. of the pen** petite erreur *f* d'orthographe; **she made a s. of the tongue** sa langue a fourché; **it was a s., I meant to say ...** ma langue a fourché, je voulais dire ...; *Prov* **there's many a s. twixt cup and lip** il y a loin de la coupe aux lèvres

(c) to give sb the s. fausser compagnie à qn; **s. stitch** *Knitting* maille *f* glissée; *Sewing* point *m* perdu

(d) *Geol* *(of land)* glissement *m*; *(of rocks)* éboulement *m*

(e) *(by thing)* glissement *m*; *(in share values etc)* chute *f*; *(in standards)* baisse *f*; *Aut* *(of clutch)* patinage *m*

(f) *(garment)* combinaison *f* *(de femme)*; **half** *or* **waist s.** jupon *m*; **your slip's showing** votre jupon dépasse; **(pillow) s.** taie *f* d'oreiller

(g) *(of ferry)* cale *f* de chargement; **the ship is still on the slips** le navire est toujours sur cale(s) *ou* en construction

(h) *Th* **the slips** les coulisses *fpl*

(i) *Cr* *(player)* chasseur *m* posté à droite du garde-guichet; **the slips** *(position)* la station à droite du garde-guichet

(j) *(in pottery)* *(for decoration)* engobe *m*

slip² **(-pp-) 1** *vi* **(a)** *(slide)* glisser; *(of knot)* couler, courir; *(of earth etc)* s'ébouler; *(of prices)* chuter; *MecE etc* *(of clutch, belt etc)* patiner, glisser; *TV* **the picture keeps slipping** l'image descend; **his foot slipped** son pied a glissé; **I slipped on a banana skin** j'ai glissé sur une peau de banane; **to s. from sb's hands** *or* **grasp** *(of vase, book etc)* glisser des mains *ou* des doigts de qn; **to s. through sb's fingers** filer entre les doigts de qn; **to s. into bad habits** prendre de mauvaises habitudes; **an error that has slipped into the text** une faute qui s'est glissée dans le texte; **the patient slipped into a coma** le malade est tombé dans le coma; **money just slips through his fingers** l'argent lui file entre les doigts; **they let the terrorists s. through their fingers** ils ont laissé filer les terroristes; **he let his guard s.** il a baissé sa garde; **don't let your concentration s.** ne relâche pas ta concentration; **the record has slipped to number 22** le disque est descendu en 22ème position; **the quality is slipping** la qualité baisse

(b) *(move quickly, smoothly etc)* **to s. into bed** se glisser *ou* se couler dans son lit; **to s. into one's dressing gown** passer *ou F* enfiler sa robe de chambre; **she slipped into the next room** elle s'est glissée dans la pièce voisine; **just s. round** *or* **over to the post office** fais un saut jusqu'au bureau de poste

(c) *(make mistake)* faire une (faute d')étourderie; **you're slipping** *(performing below one's usual standard)* tu baisses!; **he slipped and said 'twenty' by mistake** sa langue a fourché et il a dit 'vingt' par erreur

(d) to let s. *(opportunity, word, secret)* laisser échapper; **she let s. a few swear words** elle a laissé échapper quelques jurons; **to let (it) s. that ...** laisser échapper que ...

2 *vt* **(a)** *Aut* **to s. the clutch** laisser patiner l'embrayage; **to s. its chain** *or* **leash** *or* **lead** *(of animal)* se détacher; **the dog has slipped its collar** le chien s'est dégagé de son collier; **his name has slipped my mind** son nom m'échappe; **to s. sb's attention** échapper à qn

(b) *(put)* *(sth into sb's hand, a letter into the post box)* glisser; **he slipped it into his pocket** il l'a glissé dans sa poche; **to s. sth into the conversation** glisser qch dans la conversation; **to s. the bolt (home)** pousser le verrou à fond; **I slipped my arm round her waist** j'ai glissé mon bras autour de sa taille; *F* **to s. something** *or* **one over on sb** rouler qn

(c) *Naut* **to s. a cable** larguer *ou* filer une amarre par le bout; **to s. one's moorings** filer le corps-mort

(d) *Knitting* *(stitch)* glisser

(e) *Med* **to s. a disc** se faire une hernie discale

slip³ *n* **(a)** *(piece)* *(of paper)* bout *m*; *(coupon)* bon *m*; *(docket)* fiche *f*; *(of land etc)* bande *f* étroite; **pay s.** bulletin *m* de paie; **sales s.** récépissé *m*; *Journ* **s. page** page *f* volante; *Journ* **s. sheet** encart *m* **(b)** *Old-fashioned F* **s. of a girl** jeune fille fluette; *(young)* fillette *f* **(c)** *(in horticulture)* bouture *f*; *(for grafting)* scion *m*

▶ **slip away** *vi* *(of person)* *(get away)* filer; *(leave work early)* s'éclipser; *(of lead in elections etc)* s'effriter; **the patient was slipping away** le malade s'éteignait doucement; **control of the party was slipping away from her** elle perdait peu à peu son emprise sur le parti; **my life seemed to be slipping away from me** ma vie m'échappait; **you're slipping away from me** *(in relationship)* tu t'éloignes de moi

▶ **slip back 1** *vi* **(a)** *(return)* revenir **(into** dans) **(b)** *(get worse)* *(of work)* se dégrader **2** *vtsep* *(put back)* remettre

▶ **slip by 1** *vi* **(a)** *(of time, years etc)* passer; *(fast)* fuir **(b)** *(pass unnoticed)* *(of person)* passer sans se faire remarquer **2** *vipo* **to s. by sb** *(of errors, escapee)* échapper à qn

▶ **slip down 1** *vi* *(slide down)* descendre en glissant; *(of socks)* descendre; **this whisky slips down very nicely** ce whisky descend tout seul **2** *vipo* **to s. down a pole** glisser le long d'un poteau; **they've slipped down the league** ils sont descendus au classement

▶ **slip in 1** *vi* *(enter quickly, inconspicuously)* entrer sans se faire remarquer; *(enter room, house quickly, inconspicuously)* se glisser dans une pièce/une maison/*etc*; **a few mistakes slipped in** *(in text)* quelques erreurs se sont glissées dans le texte **2** *vt* *(insert inconspicuously)* glisser; **she slipped in several references to ...** elle a placé plusieurs allusions à ...

▶ **slip off 1** *vtsep* *(jacket, shoes)* enlever **2** *vi* *(of person)* s'éclipser

▶ **slip on** *vtsep* *(put on quickly)* *(garment)* passer, *F* enfiler

▶ **slip out** *vi* **(a)** *(escape)* s'échapper; **the soap slipped out of my hands** le savon m'a glissé des mains; **to let sth s. out** laisser échapper qch; **the secret has slipped out** le secret a transpiré; **it slipped out that ...** le bruit s'est répandu selon lequel ... **(b)** *(leave quickly, inconspicuously)* *(to avoid sb/sth)* filer (à l'anglaise); **I'm just slipping out for a few minutes** je m'éclipse quelques minutes, je reviens dans une minute; **could you s. out and buy me some chocolate?** tu pourrais faire un saut à l'épicerie/*etc* pour m'acheter du chocolat?

▶ **slip past 1** *vi* passer **2** *vipo* **to s. past sb/sth** se glisser devant qn/qch **3** *vtaspo F* **to s. one past sb** rouler qn

▶ **slip through** *vi* *(of errors etc)* échapper à l'attention; **too many mistakes are slipping through** il y a trop d'erreurs qui nous/leur/*etc* échappent

▶ **slip up** *vi* *(make mistake)* se tromper; *(socially etc)* faire une gaffe, gaffer

slipcase ['slɪpkeɪs] *n* *(for books)* étui *m*

slipcover ['slɪpkʌvər] *n esp Am* **(a)** *(for furniture)* housse *f* **(b)** *(book cover)* jaquette *f*

slipknot ['slɪpnɒt] *n* nœud *m* coulant

slip-on 1 *n F* **(a) slip-ons** *(shoes)* mocassins *mpl* **(b)** *Am* *(sweater)* pull-over *m*, *pl* pull-overs, pull *m* **2** *adj* **s. shoes** mocassins *mpl*

slipover ['slɪpəʊvər] *n* débardeur *m*

slippage ['slɪpɪdʒ] *n* *(in production)* retard *m*; **there's too much s.** *(loss of time)* on perd de plus en plus de temps; **s. in prices** dérapage *m* des prix

slipped disc [slɪpt] *n Med* hernie *f* discale

slipper ['slɪpər] *n* **(a)** *(footwear)* *(backless)* mule *f*; *(with back)* chausson *m*, pantoufle *f* **(b)** *MecE* *(of brake)* patin *m*

slipper baths *npl Old-fashioned* bains *mpl* publics

slipperiness ['slɪpərɪnɪs] *n* **(a)** *(of surface)* nature *f* glissante **(b)** *(of person)* caractère *m* rusé

slippery ['slɪpərɪ] *adj* **(a)** *(pavement, fish etc)* glissant; *(difficult)* *(subject, concept)* délicat; **it's s. (underfoot)** ça glisse; *Fig* **to be on s. ground** être sur un terrain glissant; *Fig* **it's a s. slope** nous sommes/il est/*etc* sur une pente glissante; **this was the start of the s. slope that led to (his) alcoholism** ce fut le début de la déchéance qui l'a mené à l'alcoolisme **(b)** *(devious)* *(person)* retors; **he's as s. as an eel** il glisse comme une *ou* est aussi insaisissable qu'une anguille

slippy ['slɪpɪ] *adj F* **(a)** *(slippery)* glissant **(b)** *Old-fashioned Br F* *(quick)* **you'll have to be pretty s. about it** il va falloir que tu fasses ficelle; **look s.!** grouille-toi!

slip road *n Br Aut* bretelle *f*

slipshod ['slɪpʃɒd] *adj* *(negligent)* *(person, attitude)* négligent; *(work)* négligé, bâclé; **book written in a s. manner** livre écrit sans soin

slipstream¹ ['slɪpstriːm] *n* *(of car, boat etc)* sillage *m*, remous *mpl*; *Av* souffle *m ou* vent *m* de l'hélice; *Fig* **to be dragged along in sb's s.** se laisser entraîner par qn

slipstream² *vt* *(car)* se mettre dans le sillage de

slip-up *n F* gaffe *f*; **there's been a s.** il y a eu une gaffe de faite; **to make a s.** faire une gaffe

slipway ['slɪpweɪ] *n Naut* *(for building, repairing)* cale *f ou* chantier *m* de construction; *(for launching)* slip *m*

slit¹ [slɪt] *n* fente *f*; *(between curtains etc)* entrebâillement *m*; *(for shooting through)* meurtrière *f*; **s.-eyed** aux yeux bridés; **to be s.-eyed** avoir les yeux bridés; **s. pocket** *(in outer garment)* fente *f* verticale donnant accès aux vêtements de dessous; *(false pocket)* fausse poche *f*; *Mil* **s. trench** tranchée *f*

slit² *vt* *(pt, pp* **slit**; *prp* **slitting)** *(make slit in)* fendre; *(envelope)* ouvrir; *Surg* *(flesh)* inciser; **the knife had slit his leg open** le couteau lui avait ouvert la cuisse; **the blow slit his cheek** le coup lui a déchiré la joue; **to s. sb's throat** couper la gorge à qn; **to s. open a sack** éventrer un sac; **slit skirt** jupe fendue

slither¹ ['slɪðər] *n* glissement *m*

slither² *vi* glisser; *(of snake, worm)* ramper; **the dog was slithering about on the ice** le chien dérapait sur la glace; **to s. down a hill** déraper dans une pente

sliver ['slɪvər] *n* *(thin slice)* petite tranche *f*; *(of wood)* éclat *m*

Sloane (Ranger) [sləʊn('reɪndʒər)] *n Br F* jeune fille *f* BCBG

Sloaney ['sləʊnɪ] *adj Br F* BCBG

slob [slɒb] *n F* *(untidy, rude)* rustaud *m*; *(lazy)* flemmard, -arde; **big fat s.** gros lard *m*

slobber¹ ['slɒbər] *n* *(saliva)* bave *f*, salive *f*

slobber² *vi* *(salivate)* baver; **stop slobbering on me** arrête de me baver dessus

▶ **slobber over** *vipo* *(of dog, baby)* *(person, shoulder)* baver; *(kiss etc)* *(person)* faire des bises baveuses à; **he doesn't like them slobbering all over him** il n'aime pas qu'ils lui bavent dessus

sloe [sləʊ] *n* **(a)** *(fruit)* prunelle *f*; **s. gin** = (alcool *m* de) prunelle **(b) s. (bush** *or* **tree)** prunellier *m*

slog¹ [slɒg] *n F* **(a)** *(blow)* coup *m* (violent); **to give the ball a real s.** frapper dans la balle un bon coup **(b)** *(hard work)* boulot *m* pénible; **it was a bit of a s.** on en a bavé; **a hard s.** *(great effort, reading book)* un gros effort; *(walk, ride)* un trajet pénible; **it's a long s. to the top** *(of hill, in organization)* on en bave pour arriver en haut

slog² **(-gg-)** *F* **1** *vt* *(hit)* *(person, object)* cogner, battre; *Cr* *(ball)* frapper fort sur; **he slogged his way through the text** il a déchiffré le texte avec grande difficulté **2** *vi* *(work hard)* turbiner, trimer; **they slogged for miles** *(walking)* ils marchèrent à grand-peine pendant des kilomètres

▶ **slog along** *vi F* *(keep walking)* marcher d'un pas lourd *ou* péniblement

▶ **slog away** *vi F* *(keep working, trying)* trimer

▶ **slog away at** *vipo F* **(a)** *(work hard at)* travailler avec acharnement à **(b)** *(keep hitting)* continuer à frapper

▶ **slog on** *vi F* **(a)** = **slog along (b)** *(keep working)* continuer à trimer; **I think I'll s. on a little longer** je pense que je vais continuer à bosser encore un peu

slogan ['sləʊgən] *n Pol, Com* slogan *m*; **election/advertising s.** slogan électoral/publicitaire

slogger ['slɒgər] *n F* **(a)** *Boxing, Cr* cogneur *m* **(b)** *(hard worker)* bûcheur, -euse

sloop [sluːp] *n Naut* sloop *m*

slop¹ [slɒp] *n* **(a) slops** *(pig food)* soupe *f* à cochons; *Pej* *(food)* brouet *m*; *(spilt drinks)* *(on table etc)* boissons *fpl* renversées; **s. basin** = récipient *m* utilisé pour vider les fonds de tasses; **s. pail** seau *m* hygiénique **(b)** *F* *(sentimentality)* bêtises *fpl* à l'eau de rose

slop² **(-pp-) 1** *vt* *(spill)* *(liquid)* renverser **(over the table** sur la table) **2** *vi* *(of liquids)* déborder

▶ **slop about, slop around** *vi* **(a)** *F* *(walk in water, mud etc)* patauger, barboter **(b)** *(of liquid)* clapoter **(c)** *Fig F* **he just slops around the house all day** il passe toute la journée à traîner *ou F* à glandouiller chez lui

▶ **slop out** *vi* *(in prison)* vider les seaux hygiéniques

▶ **slop over** *vi* = **slop² 2**

slope¹ [sləʊp] *n* **(a)** *(incline)* pente *f*, inclinaison *f*; *(in road, railway)* rampe *f*; **steep/gentle s.** pente raide/douce; *Mil* **with rifle at the s.** l'arme sur l'épaule **(b)** *(hill)* pente *f*; *(of* *mountain)* versant *m*; *Ski* piste *f*; **on the slopes of the Himalayas** sur les pentes de l'Himalaya; **on the northern s.** sur le versant nord; **halfway down/up the s.** à mi-pente

slope² **1** *vi* (*of ground etc*) être en pente; (*not be straight*) (*of picture etc*) pencher; **to s. forward** *or* **to the right/backward** *or* **to the left** (*of writing*) pencher à droite/à gauche; **the garden slopes down to the river** le jardin descend (en pente) vers la rivière; **the ground slopes up to the house** le terrain monte en pente vers la maison **2** *vt* incliner; *Mil* **to s. arms** mettre l'arme sur l'épaule; **s. arms!** arme sur l'épaule!

▶ **slope away, slope off** *vi F* (*leave furtively*) décamper, filer

sloping ['sləʊpɪŋ] *adj* (*roof*) en pente; **s. shoulders** épaules tombantes; **s. (hand)writing** écriture couchée *ou* penchée

sloppily ['slɒpɪlɪ] *adv* **(a)** (*carelessly*) sans soin **(b)** *F* (*sentimentally*) avec sensiblerie

sloppiness ['slɒpɪnɪs] *n* **(a)** (*carelessness*) (*in work*) manque *m* de soin, négligence *f*; (*of style*) négligence **(b)** *F* (*sentimentality*) sentimentalité *f* excessive

slopping out ['slɒpɪŋ] *n* (*in prison*) vidange *f* des seaux hygiéniques

sloppy ['slɒpɪ] *adj* **(a)** (*careless*) (*work, person*) négligé; (*worker*) négligent; (*organization, approach*) nul, *f* nulle; (*language, spelling*) relâché **(b)** *F* (*sentimental*) (*novel*) guimauve; (*person*) fleur bleue; **s. sentimentality** sensiblerie *f*

sloppy joe *n F Br* (*sweater*) pull-over *m* très ample; *Am* (*hamburger*) steak *m* haché servi en sandwich

slosh [slɒʃ] **1** *vi* (*of liquid*) (*move around*) clapoter **2** *vt* **(a)** (*spill*) (*water etc*) renverser **(b)** *F* (*apply liberally*) (*paint on wall etc*) flanquer **(c)** *Br Sl* (*hit*) (*person*) flanquer un coup à, tabasser

▶ **slosh about, slosh around** *vi* **(a)** *F* (*walk in water, mud etc*) patauger, barboter **(b)** (*of liquid*) clapoter

sloshed [slɒʃt] *adj Br Sl* (*drunk*) bourré, rond

slot¹ [slɒt] *n* **(a)** (*groove*) (*in vending machine, head of screw etc*) fente *f*; *Comptr* emplacement *m*; **to put a coin in the s.** (*of vending machine etc*) introduire une pièce de monnaie dans la fente; *Comptr* **expansion s.** emplacement pour carte d'extension

(b) (*in broadcasting schedule, waiting list etc*) créneau *m* horaire; (*for aircraft in flight control*) créneau; **we've missed our s.** nous avons raté notre créneau; **there's a s. for somebody with editorial skills** il y a un créneau pour quelqu'un ayant une formation de rédacteur; **to fill a s.** boucher un trou; *Rad, TV* **prime time s.** heure *f* de grande écoute

slot² (-tt-) **1** *vt* **to s. sth into sth** insérer *ou* mettre qch dans qch; **to s. sb into a job** caser qn dans un travail; **where can we s. him in?** comment est-ce qu'on peut l'intégrer? **2** *vi* s'introduire, se glisser (**into sth** dans qch); **it slots well into our programme** cela s'insère bien dans notre programme; **she slotted into the department well** elle s'est bien intégrée au service

▶ **slot in 1** *vtsep* (*fit in*) (*patient, customer etc*) prendre; **to s. a book in a space on a shelf** glisser un livre dans un espace sur une étagère **2** *vi* (*fit in*) **the book will s. in here** le livre rentrera là-dedans

▶ **slot together 1** *vtsep* (*pieces*) encastrer l'un dans l'autre/les uns dans les autres **2** *vi* s'encastrer l'un dans l'autre/les uns dans les autres

sloth [sləʊθ] *n* **(a)** (*laziness*) paresse *f* **(b)** (*animal*) paresseux *m*; **s. bear** ours *m* jongleur; **s. monkey** loris *m* lent

slothful ['sləʊθfʊl] *adj* paresseux, -euse

slothfully ['sləʊθfəlɪ] *adv* paresseusement

slothfulness ['sləʊθfʊlnɪs] *n* paresse *f*

slot-in card *n Comptr* carte *f* enfichable

slot machine *n* (*vending machine*) distributeur *m* (automatique); (*gambling machine*) machine *f ou* appareil *m* à sous

slot meter *n* compteur *m* à pièces

slouch¹ [slaʊtʃ] *n* **(a)** (*way of walking*) démarche *f* mollasse; (*deportment*) allure *f* avachie *ou* molle; **s. of the shoulders** épaules tombantes; **s. hat** (grand) chapeau mou *ou* rabattu **(b)** *F* **he's no s.** il n'est pas empoté

slouch² *vi* (*hold oneself badly*) être avachi; (*walk badly*) avoir une démarche mollasse; **don't s.!** tenez-vous droit!

▶ **slouch about, slouch around** *vi* (*in town*) traîner; (*at home, in front of television*) traînasser

slough¹ [slaʊ] *n* (*bog*) bourbier *m*, fondrière *f*; *Lit* **to be in a s. of despair/gloom** sombrer dans le désespoir/la tristesse

slough² [slʌf] *n* (*of reptile, insect*) mue *f*; **to cast its s.** muer

slough³ **1** *vi* (*of reptile etc*) muer **2** *vt* **to s. its skin** (*of reptile, insect*) muer; *Lit* **to s. a bad habit** se débarrasser d'une mauvaise habitude

▶ **slough away** *vi* = **slough off 2**

▶ **slough off 1** *vtsep* = **slough³** *2* **2** *vi* (*become detached*) (*of scab etc*) se détacher, tomber

Slovak ['sləʊvæk] **1** *adj* slovaque **2** *n* **(a)** (*person*) Slovaque *mf* **(b)** *Ling* slovaque *m*

Slovakia [sləʊ'vækɪə] *n* Slovaquie *f*

Slovakian [sləʊ'vækɪən] *adj, n* = **Slovak**

sloven ['slʌv(ə)n] *n* **(a)** (*untidy person*) mal soigné, -ée; (*woman*) souillon *f* **(b)** *Old-fashioned* (*careless worker*) saboteur, -euse

Slovene ['sləʊviːn] *adj, n* = **Slovenian**

Slovenia [sləʊ'viːnɪə] *n* Slovénie *f*

Slovenian [sləʊ'viːnɪən] **1** *adj* slovène **2** *n* **(a)** (*person*) Slovène *mf* **(b)** *Ling* slovène *m*

slovenliness ['slʌv(ə)nlɪnɪs] *n* (*of work, appearance*) négligence *f*

slovenly ['slʌv(ə)nlɪ] *adj* **(a)** (*untidy*) (*person*) mal soigné; (*dress*) débraillé **(b)** (*negligent*) (*person*) négligent; (*work*) négligé, bousillé; (*style*) débraillé; **done in a s. way** fait sans soin

slow¹ [sləʊ] **1** *adj* **(a)** (*not fast*) lent; (*boring*) (*film, show etc*) ennuyeux; (*stupid*) (*person*) simple; **I'm being a bit s. this morning** je suis un peu lent ce matin; **to be s. over doing sth** mettre longtemps à faire qch; **business is s.** les affaires languissent *ou* ne vont pas fort; **to be s. to do sth** (*of person*) être lent à faire qch; **s. to act** *or* **to take action** lent à agir; **progress has been s.** les progrès ont été lents; **this method is s. but sure** cette méthode est lente mais sûre; **he wasn't s. to respond** *or* **in responding** il n'a pas été long à répondre; **he's been s. to get it done** il a mis du temps à le faire; **sorry I was s. getting back to you** désolé d'avoir mis du temps à vous rappeler; **you're very s. today** tu es très lent aujourd'hui; *F* **to be as s. as treacle** *or Am* **molasses (in winter)** être lent comme un escargot *ou* une tortue; **to be s. off the mark** (*in race*) démarrer en douceur; (*to start sth*) prendre son temps pour faire qch; (*to understand*) être lent à la détente; **a s. child** un enfant attardé; **to cook sth in a s. oven** faire cuire qch à four doux; *US Sl* **to do a s. burn** avoir la moutarde qui vous monte au nez; **it's s. work** ça ne va pas vite; **she's a s. worker** elle travaille lentement

(b) (*clock, watch*) en retard; **my watch is five minutes s.** ma montre retarde de cinq minutes

2 *adv* lentement; **to go s.** aller lentement; (*as industrial action*) faire la grève perlée; **to run s.** (*of engine*) tourner au ralenti; (*of clock*) retarder; **s.!** (*on road sign*) ralentir!; *Naut* **s. ahead/astern!** en avant/en arrière doucement!; **s. moving** (*traffic*) au ralenti; (*queue, crowd, river, film, etc*) lent; **s. spoken** qui parle lentement; **s. burning** à combustion lente; (*in explosives*) (*powder*) lent

slow² *vti* = **slow down, slow up**

▶ **slow down, slow up 1** *vi* (*go more slowly*) ralentir; *Aut* (*of engine*) prendre le ralenti; **to s. down** *or* **up (to a stop)** s'arrêter; *Fig* **s. down a bit** doucement!; **as he got older he slowed down** à mesure qu'il prenait de l'âge il a ralenti son rythme **2** *vtsep* ralentir; **I'll only s. you down** je vais vous retarder

slowcoach ['sləʊkəʊtʃ] *n Br F* lambin, -ine, traînard, -arde

slow-cook *vt* mijoter, faire cuire à feu doux

slowdown ['sləʊdaʊn] *n* (*slowing*) (*in business etc*) ralentissement *m*; *Am* (*industrial action*) travail *m* au ralenti

slowing ['sləʊɪŋ] *n* **s. (down** *or* **up)** ralentissement *m*

slow lane *n Aut* voie *f* lente

slowly ['sləʊlɪ] *adv* lentement; **the time/morning has gone very s.** le temps/la matinée a passé très lentement; **to run s.** (*engine*) tourner au ralenti; **he's s. realizing that ...** il se rend compte peu à peu que ...; **s. but surely** lentement mais sûrement; **to cook sth s.** faire cuire qch à feu doux

slow motion *n Cin etc* **(in) s.** (au) ralenti *m*

slow-motion replay *n* ralenti *m*

slowness ['sləʊnɪs] *n* (*lack of speed*) lenteur *f*; (*of mind*) lourdeur *f*, lenteur; (*of film, show etc*) lenteur; (*of clock etc*) retard *m*

slowpoke ['sləʊpəʊk] *n Am F* lambin, -ine, traînard, -arde

slow-release *adj Med* (*medicine*) retard *inv*

slow running *n MecE* ralenti *m*

slow-running jet *n Aut* gicleur *m* de ralenti

slow train *n Rail* (train *m*) omnibus *m*

slow-worm *n* orvet *m*, serpent *m* de verre

SLR [esel'ɑːr] *n Phot* (*abbr* **single-lens reflex**) reflex *m* monoculaire

sludge [slʌdʒ] *n* (*mud*) vase *f*, fange *f*; *Ind* boue *f*; (*in engine*) cambouis *m*; **sewage s.** vidanges *fpl*

sludgy ['slʌdʒɪ] *adj* (*muddy*) vaseux; *Ind* boueux

slug¹ [slʌg] *n Zool* limace *f*; **s. pellet** pastille *f* anti-limace

slug² *n* **(a)** (*bullet*) balle *f*, plomb *m* **(b)** *F* (*of brandy etc*) goutte *f*, coup *m*

slug[3] *n Am F* (*blow*) coup *m* violent

slug[4] *vt esp Am F* (*hit*) (*person, ball*) frapper; **he slugged me with a piece of wood** il m'a frappé avec un bâton

▶ **slug out** *vtsep F, also Fig* **to s. it out** (*of two people*) se rentrer dedans; **he slugged it out with him** il s'est battu avec lui

slugfest ['slʌgfest] *n Am Boxing F* combat *m*

sluggard ['slʌgəd] *adj, n Lit* paresseux, -euse, fainéant, -ante

sluggish ['slʌgɪʃ] *adj* (*person, day*) (*lazy*) paresseux, *F* flemmard; (*not energetic*) léthargique; (*mind*) lent, engourdi; (*response, attempt, engine*) mou, *f* molle; (*river, pulse etc*) lent, paresseux; (*market*) stagnant; (*sales*) médiocre; (*organization, bureaucracy*) lourd; **the economy is s.** l'économie est au ralenti; **at a s. pace** au ralenti

sluggishly ['slʌgɪʃlɪ] *adv* **(a)** (*lazily*) paresseusement **(b)** (*slowly*) lentement

sluggishness ['slʌgɪʃnɪs] *n* **(a)** (*of person*) paresse *f*, *F* flemme *f*; (*of mind*) lenteur *f* **(b)** (*of river etc*) lenteur *f*; *Aut* (*of engine*) mollesse *f*; (*of organization, bureaucracy*) lourdeur *f*

sluice[1] [slu:s] *n* **(a)** (*structure*) écluse *f* **(b)** = **sluicegate (c)** (*action*) *F* **to give sth a s. down** laver qch à grande eau

sluice[2] *vt* (*wash*) laver à grande eau

▶ **sluice down** *vtsep* (*wash down*) laver à grande eau; **to s. oneself down with cold water** s'asperger d'eau fraîche

▶ **sluice out 1** *vtsep* **(a)** *HydE* (*release*) (*water from reservoir*) laisser échapper (par les vannes) **(b)** (*rinse*) (*cup, pot etc*) rinser **2** *vi* (*of water etc*) (*flow out in great quantity*) couler à flots

sluicegate ['slu:sgeɪt] *n* porte *f* d'écluse, vanne *f*

sluiceway ['slu:sweɪ] *n* canal *m*, -aux à vannes

slum[1] [slʌm] *n* (*district*) bas quartier *m*, quartier pauvre; (*house*) taudis *m*; **s. clearance** suppression *f* des taudis; **s. landlord** propriétaire *mf* d'un taudis

slum[2] *vt* **(-mm-)** *F* **to s. it** zoner; *Fig Hum* **I'm slumming it tonight** j'ai décidé de zoner ce soir

slumber[1] ['slʌmbər] *n Lit* sommeil *m*; **her s. was** *or* **her slumbers were interrupted by …** son sommeil a été interrompu par …; *Fig* **the country had finally awoken from its slumbers** le pays était enfin sorti de sa torpeur; *Fig Lit* **he awoke from his intellectual slumbers** il est sorti de ses hibernations intellectuelles; **s. wear** vêtements *mpl* de nuit

slumber[2] *vi* sommeiller, dormir (paisiblement)

slumber party *n Am* = soirée *f* en pyjama entre fillettes, où les invitées restent dormir chez leur hôte

slummy ['slʌmɪ] *adj* sordide; **the s. area of town** les bas quartiers

slump[1] [slʌmp] *n Econ* (*of prices etc*) effondrement *m*; **s. in prices** dégringolade *f* des prix; **the s. in oil prices** l'effondrement des prix du pétrole; **there's been a s. in the pound** la livre a chuté; *Econ* **the s.** la crise *ou* dépression économique

slump[2] *vi* **(a)** (*of person*) s'effondrer, s'affaisser (**into a chair** dans un fauteuil); **the editor was slumped unconscious over his desk** le rédacteur était effondré sans connaissance sur son bureau **(b)** *Econ* (*of prices, pound*) (*fall suddenly*) s'effondrer, *F* dégringoler; (*of economy, demand*) chuter

slung *see* **sling[2]**

slunk *see* **slink**

slur[1] [slɜ:r] *n* **(a)** (*insult*) insulte *f*; (*on reputation*) tache *f*; **a racial s.** une réfléxion raciste; **to cast a s. on sb's reputation** porter atteinte à *ou* ternir la réputation de qn **(b)** *Mus* (*sign*) liaison *f*; (*passage*) coulé *m* **(c)** (*in speech*) mauvaise articulation *f*; **in a drunken s.** de la voix traînante d'un ivrogne; **to speak with a s.** mal articuler; (*as result of stroke etc*) parler d'une voix traînante

slur[2] **(-rr-) 1** *vt* **(a)** (*words*) mal articuler; **his speech was slurred** il articulait mal; (*because of stroke etc*) il parlait d'une voix traînante **(b)** *Mus* (*two notes*) lier; (*passage*) couler; **slurred notes** notes liées coulant **2** *vi* (*speak indistinctly*) mal articuler ses mots, manger la moitié de ses mots

▶ **slur over** *vipo* (*not deal with fully*) **to s. over a fact** passer *ou* glisser sur un fait

slurp [slɜ:p] **1** *vt* (*soup etc*) faire du bruit en mangeant; (*tea*) faire du bruit en buvant **2** *vi* (*eating*) faire du bruit en mangeant; (*drinking*) faire du bruit en buvant

▶ **slurp up** *vtsep* (*soup*) avaler en faisant du bruit

slush [slʌʃ] *n* **(a)** (*snow*) neige *f* fondue **(b)** *F* (*sentimentality*) sensiblerie *f*

slush fund *n Pol F* caisse *f* noire

slush money *n F* dessous-de-table *mpl*

slushy ['slʌʃɪ] *adj* **(a)** (*from snow*) détrempé par la neige **(b)** *F* (*novel, film etc*) guimauve; (*person*) fleur bleue

slut [slʌt] *n* **(a)** (*dirty woman*) souillon *f* **(b)** (*promiscuous woman*) salope *f*, *Vulg* pute *f*

sluttish ['slʌtɪʃ] *adj* **(a)** (*dirty*) sale; **to lead a s. existence** vivre salement **(b)** (*promiscuous*) (*behaviour etc*) de pute; **s. woman** salope *f*

sluttishness ['slʌtɪʃnɪs] *n* **(a)** (*dirtiness*) saleté *f* **(b)** (*promiscuity*) conduite *f* immorale

sly [slaɪ] **1** *adj* (*comp* **slyer**, *superl* **slyest**) **(a)** (*cunning*) rusé; **he's a s. dog** c'est un fin matois **(b)** (*dishonest*) sournois **(c)** (*mischievous*) malin, *f* -igne, espiègle; **s. grin** sourire espiègle **2** *n* **on the s.** à la dérobée, en cachette

slyboots ['slaɪbu:ts] *n F* petit malin *m*, petite maligne *f*

slyly ['slaɪlɪ] *adv* **(a)** (*cunningly*) avec ruse **(b)** (*dishonestly*) sournoisement **(c)** (*mischievously*) d'une manière espiègle, avec espièglerie

slyness ['slaɪnɪs] *n* **(a)** (*cunning*) ruse *f* **(b)** (*dishonesty*) sournoiserie *f* **(c)** (*mischievousness*) espièglerie *f*

smack[1] [smæk] **1** *n* **(a)** (*blow*) claque *f*; **s. in the face** gifle *f*; *Fig F* **s. (in the eye)** affront *m*, rebuffade *f*; **to give a child a s. on the bottom** donner une fessée à un enfant **(b)** (*sound*) claquement *m*; **with a s. of his lips** avec un claquement de langue; **the s. of the waves** le fouettement des vagues **(c)** *F* (*loud kiss*) gros baiser *m* retentissant, grosse bise *f* **2** *adv* **to go s.** (*make sound*) faire clac; *F* **to bump s. into a tree** rentrer en plein dans un arbre; **to bump s. into a lamppost** se prendre un lampadaire; **s. in the middle** en plein milieu, au beau milieu; **he caught him s. on the chin** il l'a frappé en plein sur le menton

smack[2] *vt* (*hit*) frapper, taper (*avec le plat de la main*); (*person*) donner une claque à; **to s. sb's face** donner une gifle à qn, gifler qn; **to s. a child's bottom** donner une fessée à un enfant

smack[3] *n Naut* (**fishing**) **s.** bateau *m* de pêche

smack[4] *n Sl* (*heroin*) héro *f*

smack[5] *n* (*slight taste*) (*of garlic etc*) léger goût *m*

▶ **smack of** *vipo* (*have slight taste of*) avoir un léger goût de; *Fig* **to s. of heresy** sentir l'hérésie *ou* le brûlé *ou* le fagot

smacker ['smækər] *n* **(a)** *F* (*big kiss*) grosse bise *f*, gros baiser *m* **(b)** *Sl* (*pound*) livre *f*; (*dollar*) dollar *m*

smacking ['smækɪŋ] *n* (*spanking*) fessée *f*; **to give sb a s.** donner une fessée à qn

small [smɔ:l] **1** *adj* **(a)** (*not large*) petit; (*dose etc*) petit, faible; **to make sth smaller** rapetisser qch; **to make oneself s.** se faire tout petit; **s. arms** armes *fpl* portatives; *Com* **s. business** petite entreprise *f*, PME *f*; **s. businessman** patron *m* de PME; *Typ* **s. capitals**, *F* **s. caps** petites capitales *fpl*; **s. child** (*young*) enfant en bas âge, petit enfant; (*small in size*) enfant de petite taille; **a s. coffee** une petite tasse (de café); **a s. white coffee please!** un petit crème, s'il vous plaît!; **s. details** de menus détails; **the smallest details** les moindres détails; **of s. dimensions** de petites dimensions; **he's a s. eater** il a un petit appétit; *Aut* **s. end** (*of connecting rod*) pied *m*; **a s. hotel** un hôtel modeste; **the s. hours** les petites heures du jour; **s. investor** petit porteur *m*; *Typ* **s. letters** minuscules *fpl*; **in s. numbers** en petit nombre; **the smallest number of people possible** le moins de gens possible; **the s. print** (*in contract etc*) les petits caractères; **s. screen** petit écran *m*; **s. shopkeeper** petit commerçant *m*; **s. T-shirt** T-shirt de petite taille; *Typ* **s. type** petits corps *mpl*; **s. voice** voix fluette, petite voix; **s. income** revenu modique *ou* modeste

(b) (*not important*) peu important; *Br F* **to be s. beer** (*of sb, sth*) être insignifiant; **this was s. beer** c'était de la petite bière; **of no s. consequence** très important, qui porte à conséquence; **she took no s. pride in …** elle n'était pas peu fière de …; **it makes not the smallest difference** ça ne fait pas la moindre différence; **it was no s. surprise to me** cela m'a beaucoup surpris; **it's s. wonder that …** ce n'est guère étonnant que … + *sub*; **s. change** petite monnaie *f*; **s. fry** menu fretin *m*; **a s. matter** une bagatelle; **I do some acting, in a s. way** je fais un peu de théâtre; **he's a farmer in a s. way** il tient une petite exploitation agricole; **in her own s. way she had …** dans la limite de ses moyens, elle avait …

(c) (*petty*) mesquin; **I felt very s.** (*ashamed*) je n'étais pas fier; (*humiliated*) je me suis senti très humilié; **to make sb look** *or* **feel s.** humilier qn, rabaisser qn; **s. mind** esprit mesquin

2 *n* **(a)** **s. of the back** creux *m ou* chute *f* des reins

(b) *F* **smalls** lingerie *f*, sous-vêtements *mpl*; **to wash one's smalls** faire sa petite lessive

(c) (*small size*) (*in T-shirt etc*) petite taille *f*

3 *adv* **(a)** (*to chop etc*) menu, fin

(b) (*to write*) petit; **to think s.** voir petit

small ads *npl Journ F* petites annonces *f*

smallholder ['smɔ:lhəʊldər] *n Agr* petit cultivateur *m*

smallholding ['smɔ:lhəʊldɪŋ] *n Agr* petite ferme *f*

small intestine *n Anat* intestin *m* grêle

smallish ['smɔ:lɪʃ] *adj* assez *ou* plutôt petit

small-minded *adj* à l'esprit mesquin *ou* étroit
smallness ['smɔːlnɪs] *n* **(a)** (*of income*) petitesse *f*, modicité *f*; (*of sum*) faible montant *m* **(b)** (*pettiness*) **the s. of his mind** sa mesquinerie
smallpox ['smɔːlpɒks] *n Med* petite vérole *f*, variole *f*; **a s. case** un cas de variole
small-scale *adj* **(a)** (*model*) réduit; (*map*) à petite échelle **(b)** (*business*) peu important, de peu d'importance **(c)** *Comptr* **s. integration** intégration *f* à petite échelle
small talk *n* banalités *fpl*; (*at drinks party etc*) conversation *f* mondaine; **I'm no good at s.** j'ai horreur d'avoir à échanger des banalités; **to make s. with sb** faire la conversation à qn
small-time *adj F* insignifiant, médiocre; **s. crook** petit escroc *m*
small-town *adj F* provincial, de province; **a s. attitude** une mentalité provinciale
▶ **smarm down** [smɑːm] *vtsep* **to s. down one's hair** se brillantiner les cheveux
▶ **smarm up to** *vipo F Pej* lécher les bottes à
smarminess ['smɑːmɪnɪs] *n F Pej* caractère *m* doucereux; **his s. gets on my nerves** ses flagorneries me tapent sur les nerfs
smarmy ['smɑːmɪ] *adj F Pej* doucereux, flagorneur; **a s. git** un lèche-bottes *inv*
smart¹ [smɑːt] *n* (*pain*) douleur *f* cuisante
smart² *vi* **(a)** (*of wound, graze etc*) brûler; **my eyes are smarting** les yeux me brûlent **(b)** (*of person*) souffrir; **to s. under an insult** souffrir sous le coup d'une insulte
smart³ **1** *adj* **(a)** (*clever*) habile, intelligent; (*shrewd*) malin, *f* -igne, rusé; (*quick-thinking*) à l'esprit vif; (*resourceful*) qui a des idées, *F* dégourdi, débrouillard; *Comptr* intelligent; **it isn't s. to break the law** ce n'est pas malin de ne pas respecter la loi; **to be too s. for sb** être trop intelligent pour qn; **trying to be s., eh?** tu essaies de faire le malin, hein?; **don't try to be s. with me** n'essaie pas de faire le malin avec moi; **that wasn't very s., was it?** ce n'était pas très malin, tu ne trouves pas?; **s. lad wanted** on recherche un jeune garçon intelligent; **s. businesswoman** femme d'affaires habile; **s. answer** réponse habile; *F* **s. aleck** *or* **Alec** petit malin *m*; **s. bomb/missile** bombe *f* intelligente/engin *m* intelligent; **the s. money is on JJ for chairman** les gens au parfum prédisent JJ comme PDG; **a s. move** une sage décision; *F* **he's a s. one** c'est un malin
(b) (*dress, person, building etc*) (*elegant*) élégant, chic *inv*; (*attractive*) coquet, pimpant; **to make oneself s.** se faire beau/belle; (*for interview etc*) bien s'habiller; **you do look s.** comme tu es beau/belle!; **the s. set** la haute; **to be a s. dresser** bien s'habiller
(c) (*quick*) vif, rapide; (*prompt*) prompt; **s. pace** allure vive; **that's s. work** vous avez vite fait; **a s. box on the ear** une bonne gifle; **s. reprimand** réprimande assez sèche
2 *adv* **look s. (about it)!** dépêchez-vous!, remuez-vous!
smartarse, *Am* **smartass** ['smɑːtɑːs, -æs] *F* **1** *n* petit malin *m*, petite maligne *f*; **don't be such a s.!** arrête de faire le malin! **2** *adj* (*answer*) malin, *f* -igne
smart card *n* carte *f* à puce *ou* à mémoire; **s. reader** lecteur *m* de cartes à puce *ou* de cartes à mémoire
smarten ['smɑːt(ə)n] *vt* **to s. (the appearance of) sth** arranger qch; **to s. one's pace** accélérer, activer
▶ **smarten up** **1** *vtsep* **(a)** (*make more elegant*) (*sth*) donner du chic à; (*make more presentable*) arranger; **to s. oneself up** se faire beau **(b)** *F* (*improve*) **you'd better s. up your ideas** *or* **your act!** tu ferais bien de te reprendre; (*to lazy person*) tu ferais bien de te secouer **2** *vi* **(a)** (*make oneself elegant*) se faire beau **(b)** *F* (*improve performance*) se reprendre
smarting ['smɑːtɪŋ] **1** *adj* (*pain, eyes*) brûlant **2** *n* douleur *f* cuisante
smartish ['smɑːtɪʃ] *adv Br F* vite fait, en vitesse; **you'd better get ready pretty s.** tu ferais mieux de te préparer vite fait
smartness ['smɑːtnɪs] *n* **(a)** (*cleverness*) habileté *f*, intelligence *f*; (*shrewdness*) ruse *f*; (*quickness of thought*) vivacité *f* (d'esprit); (*resourcefulness*) débrouillardise *f* **(b)** (*elegance*) élégance *f*, chic *m* **(c)** (*speed*) rapidité *f*
smarty-pants ['smɑːtɪpænts] *n F* petit malin *m*, petite maligne *f*
smash¹ [smæʃ] **1** *n* **(a)** (*heavy blow*) coup *m* violent; (*loud noise*) fracas *m*; *Tennis* smash *m* **(b)** (*collision*) collision *f*; (*accident*) accident *m*; (*pile-up*) télescopage *m* **(c)** (*failure*) (*in business*) débâcle *f*; (*bankruptcy*) faillite *f* **(d)** **s. (hit)** gros succès *m* **2** *adv* **to go s.** (*of firm, bank*) faire faillite
smash² **1** *vt* **(a)** **to s. sth on** *or* **against sth** heurter *ou* lancer qch contre qch avec violence; **to s. sth open** ouvrir qch d'un coup violent; **she smashed him over the head with a chair** elle lui a cassé une chaise sur la tête; **she smashed her fist into his face** elle lui a fichu son poing dans la figure; **he smashed the ball into the back of the net** d'un tir terrible, il a envoyé le ballon au fond des filets; *Tennis* **to s. the ball** faire un smash, smasher
(b) **to s. sth (to pieces)** briser qch (en mille morceaux); (*shatter*) fracasser qch; **to s. the door open** enfoncer la porte
(c) (*destroy*) (*sb, sth*) anéantir; (*army etc*) écraser; *Sp* (*record*) pulvériser; **to s. a drugs ring** démanteler un réseau de trafiquants de drogue
2 *vi* **(a)** (*strike*) se heurter violemment **(into sth** contre qch); **the car smashed into the wall** la voiture est allée s'écraser contre le mur
(b) **to s. (in pieces)** éclater (en mille morceaux)
(c) (*of firm etc*) faire faillite
▶ **smash down** *vtsep* (*door etc*) défoncer
▶ **smash in** *vtsep* **(a)** (*break open*) (*door etc*) enfoncer, défoncer; (*safe*) forcer **(b)** *F* **to s. sb's face in** casser la figure *ou F* la gueule à qn; **I'll s. your face in** je te casse la gueule
▶ **smash open** *vtsep* **(a)** = **smash in** (*a*) **(b)** (*box etc*) ouvrir en cassant d'un coup de marteau/*etc*; **he smashed his head open on a rock** il s'est ouvert la tête en heurtant un rocher
▶ **smash up** *vtsep* (*sth*) briser en morceaux; (*car etc*) démolir; **they smashed the place up in revenge** ils ont tout démoli pour se venger
smash-and-grab *adj* **s. raid** rafle *f* (*après bris de devanture*)
smashed [smæʃt] *adj Sl* (*drunk*) bourré, rond; (*on drugs*) camé; **to get s.** (*drunk*) se bourrer; (*on drugs*) se camer
smasher ['smæʃər] *n* **what a s.!** (*attractive person*) il/elle est vachement bien!; **that's a s.!** (*car etc*) il/elle est génial(e)!
smashing ['smæʃɪŋ] *adj* **(a)** (*blow*) violent **(b)** *esp Br F* (*excellent*) super, génial; **we had a s. time** c'était vachement bien
smash-up *n Aut, Rail etc F* (*collision*) télescopage *m*
smattering ['smæt(ə)rɪŋ] *n* (*of French, maths etc*) connaissances *fpl* sommaires; **to have a s. of English** savoir un peu d'anglais; **to have a s. of chemistry** avoir quelques notions de chimie
smear¹ [smɪər] *n* **(a)** (*stain*) tache *f*, souillure *f*; (*defamation*) diffamation *f*; (*spoken*) calomnie *f*; **they resorted to s. tactics** ils eurent recours à la diffamation/la calomnie **(b)** (*for microscope*) (*vaginal etc*) frottis *m*
smear² **1** *vt* **(a)** (*stain*) barbouiller, salir (**with** avec); (*non-pejorative sense, cover*) enduire (**with** de); **their faces were smeared with coaldust** ils avaient le visage tout barbouillé de charbon; **to s. sth with grease, to s. grease on sth** étaler de la graisse sur qch; **the walls were smeared with blood** les murs étaient tout maculés de sang; **to s. oneself with grease, to s. grease on oneself** s'enduire de graisse
(b) (*page of writing etc*) maculer, barbouiller; **don't s. the paint!** ne salis pas la peinture; **the colours had been smeared into one another** les couleurs s'étaient mélangées; **to get smeared** (*of outline*) s'estomper; **the rain has smeared the address** la pluie a en partie effacé l'adresse
(c) (*defame*) diffamer; (*verbally*) calomnier; (*person's reputation*) salir
2 *vi* (*of paint etc*) couler; (*of ink*) baver
smear campaign *n* campagne *f* de calomnies
smear test *n Med* frottis *m* vaginal
smeary ['smɪərɪ] *adj* (*stained*) taché, barbouillé; (*with blurred outlines*) aux contours estompés; (*windows etc*) sale
smell¹ [smel] *n* **(a)** **(sense of) s.** odorat *m*; (*of animals*) flair *m*; **to have a keen sense of s.** avoir l'odorat très développé; (*of dog etc*) avoir beaucoup de flair
(b) (*odour*) (*of flowers*) odeur *f*, parfum *m*, senteur *f*; **(bad) s.** mauvaise odeur; **there's a bad s.** ça sent mauvais; **what's that s.?** quelle est cette odeur?; **stale s.** (*of beer etc*) relent *m*; **it has no s.** ça n'a pas d'odeur; **(pleasant) s. of cooking** bonne odeur de cuisine; **the s. was unbearable** l'odeur était intolérable; **to take a s. at sth** sentir qch, renifler qch; *Fig* **a s. of death** une odeur de mort; *Fig* **I don't like the s. of this at all** ça ne me plaît pas du tout, c'est louche
smell² (*pt, pp* **smelt** [smelt], *occ* **smelled**) **1** *vt* (*inhale smell of*) (*sth*) sentir; (*flowers*) respirer l'odeur de; (*of dog*) (*sth*) flairer, renifler; (*perceive smell of*) (*sth*) sentir l'odeur de; (*odour*) sentir; *Fig* (*danger etc*) sentir, flairer; **I can s. something burning** je sens quelque chose qui brûle; **I can s. gas** je sens le gaz; **I can s. cooking/chocolate** je sens une odeur de cuisine/chocolat; *Fig* **I s. a rat** il y a quelque chose de louche
2 *vi* **(a)** (*of flower etc*) sentir; **to s. good/bad/strong(ly)** sentir bon/mauvais/fort; **to s. of violets** sentir la violette; **it smells like lemon** ça sent le citron, on dirait du citron; **to s. of gas** sentir le gaz; **these flowers don't s.** ces fleurs n'ont pas d'odeur, ces fleurs ne sentent rien

(b) *(have bad smell)* sentir (mauvais); **it smells (awful)!** ça pue!; **his breath smells** il a mauvaise haleine

(c) *(have sense of smell)* **he can't s.** il n'a pas d'odorat

▶ **smell out** *vtsep* (a) *(discover by smelling) (of dog)* flairer; *Fig (of person) (secret)* découvrir (b) **his cigarettes are smelling the office out** ses cigarettes empestent *ou* empuantissent le bureau

smelliness ['smelɪnɪs] *n* mauvaise odeur *f*, puanteur *f*

smelling ['smelɪŋ] *adj* **sweet s.** qui sent bon; **s. salts** sels *mpl*

smelly ['smelɪ] *adj* (a) malodorant, puant; **it's s. in here** ça sent mauvais ici; **to be s.** sentir mauvais; **he's got s. feet** il pue des pieds; **am I still s.?** je sens encore (mauvais)? (b) *F (objectionable, unpleasant)* dégueulasse

smelt[1] [smelt] *n (fish)* éperlan *m*

smelt[2] *vt (ore)* fondre; *(metal)* extraire par fusion

smelter ['smeltər] *n* haut-fourneau *m*

smelting ['smeltɪŋ] *n (of ore)* fonte *f*, fusion *f*; *(of metal)* extraction *f* par fusion; **s. works** fonderie *f*

smidgen ['smɪdʒən] *n F* **a s. of sth** un tout petit peu de qch

smile[1] [smaɪl] *n* sourire *m*; **with a s.** en souriant, avec un sourire; **with a s. on his lips** le sourire aux lèvres; **to give sb a s.** adresser un sourire à qn, sourire à qn; **she was all smiles** elle était toute souriante *ou* tout sourire; *(pretence)* elle était tout sucre tout miel; **that'll take** *or* **wipe the s. off his face!** cela va lui faire passer l'envie de sourire!

smile[2] **1** *vi* sourire; **to s. at sb** sourire à qn, adresser un sourire à qn; **fortune smiles on him** la fortune lui sourit; **to keep smiling,** *Lit* **to s. in the face of adversity** garder le sourire; **he always comes up smiling** il garde toujours le sourire; *Phot* **s.!** souriez!; **she smiled back (at him)** elle lui rendit son sourire **2** *vt* **to s. a bitter smile** sourire amèrement, avoir un sourire amer; **to s. a welcome to sb** accueillir qn avec *ou* par un sourire; **to s. one's gratitude** exprimer sa gratitude par un sourire

smiling ['smaɪlɪŋ] *adj* souriant; **s. faces** visages souriants

smilingly ['smaɪlɪŋlɪ] *adv* en souriant, avec un sourire

smirch[1] [smɜːtʃ] *n* tache *f*, salissure *f*, souillure *f*

smirch[2] *vt* salir, souiller

smirk[1] [smɜːk] *n (affected smile)* sourire *m* affecté; *(mocking)* petit sourire supérieur; *(gloating)* petit sourire narquois

smirk[2] *vi (affectedly)* sourire d'un air affecté; *(mockingly)* sourire d'un air supérieur; *(gloatingly)* sourire d'un air narquois

smite [smaɪt] *vt* (*pt* **smote** [sməʊt]; *pp* **smitten** ['smɪt(ə)n]) (a) *Arch, Lit (strike) (the enemy)* frapper, battre (b) **to be smitten with blindness** être frappé de cécité; **to be smitten with remorse** être pris de remords; **to be smitten with a desire to do sth** être pris d'un *ou* du désir de faire qch; *F* **to be smitten with a girl** être amoureux fou d'une jeune fille; **he's totally smitten** il est sous le charme

▶ **smite down** *vtsep Arch, Lit* abattre

smith [smɪθ] *n* forgeron *m*; *(who shoes horses)* maréchal-ferrant *m*, *pl* maréchaux-ferrants

smithereens [smɪðə'riːnz] *npl* **the ship was blown to s.** l'explosion a réduit le navire en miettes; **he was blown to s. in the explosion** il a été déchiqueté dans l'explosion; **to smash sth to s.** briser qch en mille morceaux

smithy ['smɪðɪ] *n* forge *f*; *(for shoeing horses)* (atelier *m* de) maréchalerie *f*

smitten *see* **smite**

smock[1] [smɒk] *n (garment)* blouse *f*, sarrau *m*

smock[2] *vt Sewing (dress etc)* orner de smocks

smocking ['smɒkɪŋ] *n* smocks *mpl*

smog [smɒg] *n* smog *m*

smoke[1] [sməʊk] *n* (a) *(substance)* fumée *f*; **tobacco s.** fumée de tabac; *Fig F* **to go up in s.** *(of building, papers etc)* partir en fumée; *F* **he had s. coming out of his ears** *(was angry)* ses yeux lançaient des éclairs; *Prov* **(there's) no s. without fire** il n'y a pas de fumée sans feu; **s. signals** signaux *mpl* de fumée

(b) *(act of smoking)* **let's have a s.** si on fumait (une cigarette/une pipe/un cigare)?; **I always have a s. at about 10** je me fume toujours ma petite cigarette aux alentours de dix heures

(c) *F (cigarette)* cigarette *f*; *(cigar)* cigare *f*

(d) *(marijuana)* joint *m*

(e) *Br Sl* **the (Big) S.** Londres *m*

smoke[2] **1** *vi* (a) *(smoke tobacco)* fumer; **do you s.?** (est-ce que) vous fumez?; **do you mind if I s.?** est-ce que ça vous dérange si je fume?; *F* **to s. like a chimney** *(of person)* fumer comme un pompier *ou* un sapeur (b) *(emit smoke, vapour)* fumer; *(of lamp)* fumer; **the horses' flanks were smoking** les chevaux étaient tout fumants **2** *vt* (a) *(tobacco)* fumer; **to s. a pipe/cigarettes** fumer la pipe/des cigarettes; **to s. twenty a day** fumer vingt cigarettes par jour (b) *Culin (ham, meat, fish)* fumer

▶ **smoke out** *vtsep* (a) *(flush out with smoke) (insects)* enfumer pour les chasser; *Fig* faire sortir; *(bandits, snipers)* débusquer (b) *(fill with smoke)* enfumer (c) **my pipe is smoked out** j'ai fini ma pipe

smoke bomb *n* bombe *f* fumigène

smoked [sməʊkt] *adj Culin (ham, fish)* fumé; **s. glass** verre *m* fumé

smoke detector *n* détecteur *m* de fumée

smoke-filled ['sməʊkfɪld] *adj* plein de fumée, enfumé

smokeless ['sməʊklɪs] *adj (fuel)* sans fumée; **s. zone** zone *f* où il est interdit de brûler du charbon afin de limiter la pollution atmosphérique

smoker ['sməʊkər] *n* (a) *(of tobacco)* fumeur, -euse; **cigarette/pipe s.** fumeur de cigarettes/pipe; **heavy s.** gros fumeur; **s.'s cough** toux *f* de fumeur (b) *Rail etc F (compartment)* compartiment *m* fumeurs

smoke screen *n Mil* rideau *m ou* écran *m* de fumée; *Fig (comments, action etc)* tentative *f* de dissimulation

smokestack ['sməʊkstæk] *n (of train, factory etc)* cheminée *f*; *esp Am* **s. industries** industries *fpl* lourdes

smoking ['sməʊkɪŋ] **1** *adj* fumant, qui fume **2** *n* (a) *(of tobacco) (habit)* tabagisme *m*; **the effects of s. on the foetus** les effets du tabagisme sur le fœtus; **s. can damage your health** fumer nuit à votre santé; **no s. (allowed)** défense de fumer; **s. area** zone *f* fumeurs; **s. carriage** voiture *f* fumeurs; *Rail* **s. compartment** compartiment *m* fumeurs; **s. jacket** veste *f* d'intérieur; **s. room** fumoir *m*; **s. seat** place *f* fumeur (b) *Culin (of ham etc)* fumage *m*

smoky ['sməʊkɪ] *adj* (a) *(atmosphere, room, town)* enfumé (b) *(ceiling etc)* noirci par la fumée; **s. grey** gris *m* fumée *inv*; **s. blue** gris bleu *inv*; *Geol* **s. quartz** quartz *m* fumé (c) *(fire, lamp)* qui fume (d) *(taste)* de fumée

smolder, smoldering *US* = **smoulder, smouldering**

smooch [smuːtʃ] *F* **1** *vi* (a) *(kiss)* se bécoter; *(cuddle)* se peloter (b) *(dance)* danser un slow **2** *n* **to have a s.** *(kiss)* se bécoter; *(cuddle)* se peloter; *(dance)* danser un slow

smoochy ['smuːtʃɪ] *adj F (music)* doux et romantique

smooth[1] [smuːð] *adj* (a) *(surface, paper)* lisse; *(skin)* doux, *f* douce; *(road etc)* uni, égal; *(forehead)* sans rides; *(mixture, sauce etc)* onctueux, -euse; **to make s.** *(jagged edges)* lisser; *(hair)* défriser; *(road, surface)* aplanir; **the steps were worn s.** les marches étaient devenues lisses; *Br F* **as s. as a baby's bottom** *(skin, face etc)* doux comme une peau de bébé; **as s. as a millpond** *(sea)* d'un calme plat; **s. chin** *(without a beard)* menton glabre; *(close-shaven)* menton rasé de près; **a s. shave** un rasage parfait

(b) *(gentle)* doux, *f* douce; *(trip, flight etc) (comfortable)* confortable; *(without problems)* sans anicroches; *(wine)* moelleux; *(style)* coulant; *(person)* doucereux, mielleux; **the conference got off to a s. start** la conférence a commencé très bien; **to ensure a s. passage for a bill** s'assurer qu'un projet de loi sera adopté sans difficulté; **to make things s. for sb** faciliter les choses pour qn; **he's a s. operator** il sait s'y prendre; *TV etc* **s. cut** montage *m* régulier; **s. ride** conduite aisée; *Fig* **the bill had a s. ride** le projet de loi est passé sans problème; **s. running** *(of machine)* fonctionnement doux *ou* régulier; *(of project)* déroulement sans anicroches; **the s. running of the department** le bon fonctionnement du service; **s. talker** beau parleur *m*; **to have a s. tongue** être doucereux; *F* **s. type** *or* **character** personne mielleuse

smooth[2] *n* **to give one's hair a s. (down)** lisser ses cheveux, se lisser les cheveux; **to give sth a s. down with sandpaper** égaliser qch avec du papier de verre; **you have to take the rough with the s.** il faut prendre le bon avec le moins bon

smooth[3] *vt (feathers, hair etc)* lisser; *(plank)* aplanir; *(ground)* égaliser; *(garment)* défroisser; **to s. one's brow** dérider son front; **to s. the way for sb/sth** faciliter les choses pour qn/qch

▶ **smooth away** *vtsep (problems, fears etc)* faire oublier

▶ **smooth back** *vtsep* **to s. back one's hair** mettre ses cheveux en arrière

▶ **smooth down** *vtsep (make smooth) (feathers, hair etc)* lisser; *(wood)* égaliser

▶ **smooth off** *vtsep (make smooth) (angle)* adoucir

▶ **smooth out** *vtsep* (a) *(map, sheets)* défroisser; *(remove by smoothing) (crease)* faire disparaître (b) = **smooth over**

▶ **smooth over** *vtsep (make easier)* **to s. over difficulties** aplanir des difficultés; **to s. things over** arrondir les angles

smoothbore ['smuːðbɔːr] *adj* à canon lisse

smoothie ['smuːðɪ] *n F* baratineur, -euse

smoothly ['smuːðlɪ] *adv (to work, function)* sans heurts, sans problèmes; *(of car, engine etc)* en douceur; **to run s.** *(of car)* rouler en douceur; *(of meeting, project)* se dérouler sans heurts; **everything's going s.** tout va bien, *F* tout marche comme sur des roulettes, tout baigne; **the journey went s.** le voyage s'est déroulé sans problèmes; **the interview went quite s. until I ...** l'entretien s'est bien passé jusqu'à ce que je ...

smoothness ['smu:ðnɪs] *n* **(a)** (*of surface*) égalité *f*; (*of skin, fur*) douceur *f*, satiné *m*; (*of sea*) calme *m* **(b)** (*of operation of machine*) douceur *f*, régularité *f*; (*of machine, administration etc*) bon fonctionnement *m*; (*of style*) fluidité *f* **(c)** (*suavity*) (*of person*) air *m* doucereux

smooth-running *adj* (*machine etc*) qui marche bien; (*project*) qui se déroule sans heurts

smooth-spoken *adj* doucereux, mielleux

smooth-talk *vt* **to s. sb** prendre qn par les sentiments, *F* embobiner qn; **to s. sb into doing sth** embobiner qn pour qu'il fasse qch; **let's see if he can s. his way out of this one** voyons si cette fois-ci il réussit à s'en sortir à force de baratin

smooth-talking *adj* doucereux, mielleux

smooth-tongued ['smu:ð'tʌŋd] *adj* doucereux, mielleux

smoothy ['smu:ðɪ] *n F* = **smoothie**

smote *see* **smite**

smother ['smʌðər] **1** *vt* **(a)** (*stifle*) (*person*) étouffer, suffoquer; (*fire*) étouffer; (*sound*) éteindre, étouffer; (*cry*) étouffer, retenir; (*oath, groan, yawn*) réprimer; *Fig* (*person, criticism, call for inquiry, scandal*) étouffer; (*one's feelings*) cacher; **to s. sb with kisses** étouffer qn de baisers **(b)** (*cover*) couvrir; **strawberries smothered in** *or* **with cream** fraises recouvertes de crème; **to be smothered in furs** être emmitouflé dans des fourrures **2** *vi* suffoquer, étouffer

smothered ['smʌðəd] *adj* (*cry*) sourd, étouffé; (*sound*) étouffé

smother-love *n F* amour *m* étouffant d'une mère

smoulder, *US* **smolder** ['sməʊldər] *vi* (*of coal etc*) brûler lentement *ou* sans flamme; (*of fire, rebellion etc*) couver (sous la cendre); **to s. with anger/passion** se consumer de colère/passion

smouldering, *US* **smoldering** ['sməʊldərɪŋ] *adj* (*coal etc*) qui brûle sans flamme; (*fire, dissent, passion, jealousy etc*) qui couve (sous la cendre)

smudge¹ [smʌdʒ] *n* tache *f*, salissure *f*; (*slip with pen*) bavure *f* de stylo; **you've got a s. on your nose** tu as une tache sur le nez; **the house was just a white s. in the distance** la maison n'était qu'une tache blanche dans le lointain

smudge² **1** *vt* (*ink*) étaler; (*drawing, paint*) salir; (*eye makeup*) faire couler; **don't kiss me or you'll s. my lipstick** ne m'embrasse pas sinon mon rouge à lèvres va s'en aller **2** *vi* (*of ink, writing*) s'étaler; (*of paint*) couler

smudgy ['smʌdʒɪ] *adj* (*face etc*) sali; (*text*) taché; (*handwriting, drawing*) sale; **the heat had made her make-up s.** la chaleur avait fait couler son maquillage

smug [smʌg] *adj* (*tone, look*) suffisant, satisfait de soi-même; **he has a s. look** il a un air suffisant, il a l'air content de lui; **stop looking so s.** arrête de te croire supérieur; **he was s. about his success** sa réussite le rendait plein de suffisance

smuggle ['smʌg(ə)l] **1** *vt* (*arms, drugs etc*) faire de la contrebande de; (*when coming through customs*) faire passer en fraude; **to s. sth into/out of the country** (faire) entrer/sortir qch en contrebande; **to s. sb into/out of a country** faire entrer qn clandestinement dans un pays/sortir qn clandestinement d'un pays; **they are being smuggled into France by boat** on les fait entrer clandestinement en France par bateau; **to s. sth into a room** apporter qch subrepticement dans une pièce **2** *vi* (*of arms or drugs smuggler*) faire de la contrebande; (*when coming through customs*) frauder

▶ **smuggle in** *vtsep* (*into country*) (*arms, drugs etc*) introduire en contrebande; (*when coming trhough customs*) faire passer en fraude; (*into prison etc*) introduire illégalement

▶ **smuggle out** *vtsep* (*from country*) (*arms, drugs etc*) faire sortir en contrebande; (*when coming through customs*) faire sortir en fraude; (*from prison etc*) faire sortir illégalement

smuggler ['smʌglər] *n* (*of drugs, arms etc*) contrebandier, -ière; (*when coming through customs*) fraudeur, -euse

smuggling ['smʌglɪŋ] *n* (*of drugs, arms etc*) contrebande *f*; (*when coming through customs*) fraude *f*; **drug s.** trafic *m* de stupéfiants; **s. operation** opération *f* de contrebande

smugly ['smʌglɪ] *adv* (*to look at*) d'un air suffisant; (*to say*) d'un ton suffisant; **he's so s. self-righteous** il est tellement suffisant

smugness ['smʌgnɪs] *n* suffisance *f*

smut [smʌt] *n* **(a)** (*soot*) parcelle *f* de suie; (*soot mark*) tache *f* de suie (**on the face** au *ou* sur le visage) **(b)** (*obscenity*) cochonneries *fpl*, grivoiseries *fpl*; **to talk s.** dire des cochonneries; **that book's/film's just s.** il n'y a que des cochonneries dans ce livre/film **(c)** *Agr* (*on grain crops*) charbon *m*

smuttiness ['smʌtɪnɪs] *n* (*lewdness*) (*of remark etc*) grivoiserie *f*, grossièreté *f*

smutty ['smʌtɪ] *adj* **(a)** (*remark, conversation etc*) grossier, grivois **(b)** (*dirty*) noirci, noir, sali (*de suie*)

snack¹ [snæk] *n* casse-croûte *m inv*, collation *f*; **if you eat too many snacks between meals ...** si vous grignotez (trop) entre les repas ...; **to have a s.** casser la croûte, manger un morceau sur le pouce; **s. bar** snack(-bar) *m*

snack² *vi* manger entre les repas; **I've been snacking on chocolates all day** aujourd'hui je me suis nourri de chocolat

snaffle¹ ['snæf(ə)l] *n Horseriding* **s. (bit)** mors *m* brisé; **s. (bridle)** bridon *m*

snaffle² *vt Br F* (*take, steal*) piquer

▶ **snaffle up** *vtsep Br F* (*bargains, cakes etc*) rafler

snafu [snæ'fu:] *Am Sl* **1** *adj* en (grand) désordre, chaotique **2** *n* grosse gaffe *f*

snag¹ [snæg] *n* **(a)** (*protrusion*) (*of tree*) aspérité *f* **(b)** *Fig* (*problem*) accroc *m*; *Fig* **to strike a** *or* **hit a** *or* **come across a s.** se heurter à un obstacle *ou* à une anicroche; **that's the s.!** voilà le hic!; **the s. is that it's too expensive** le hic c'est que c'est trop cher **(c)** (*tear*) (*in garment*) accroc *m*

snag² **(-gg-)** **1** *vt* (*dress etc*) faire un accroc à; (*stocking etc*) accrocher **2** *vi* (*of clothes*) s'accrocher

snail [sneɪl] *n* escargot *m*; **at a s.'s pace** à pas d'escargot; *Aut* **s. cam** came *f* en colimaçon

snail mail *n F* = terme humoristique désignant les services postaux par opposition aux messageries électroniques

snake¹ [sneɪk] *n* **(a)** (*reptile*) serpent *m*; *Fig* (*person*) faux jeton *m*; **common s., grass s.** couleuvre *f* à collier; *Fig* **a s. in the grass** un faux jeton; *US F* **snakes alive!** grand Dieu! **(b)** *Fin* serpent *m* monétaire

snake² *vi* (*of road etc*) serpenter

snakebite ['sneɪkbaɪt] *n* morsure *f* de serpent

snake charmer *n* charmeur *m* de serpents

snakes and ladders *npl* (*game*) = le jeu de l'oie

snakeskin ['sneɪkskɪn] *n* peau *f* de serpent

snap¹ [snæp] **1** *n* **(a)** (*action*) (*of teeth*) coup *m* de dents; **to have a s. at sth** (*of dog etc*) essayer de happer qch; **with a s. of the fingers** claquant ses doigts; **s. fastener** bouton-pression *m*, *pl* boutons-pression; **s. lock** serrure *f* à ressort

(b) (*sound*) (*of teeth, whip etc*) coup *m* sec, claquement *m*; (*of sth breaking*) crac *m*; **I heard a s.** j'ai entendu un crac

(c) (*cold weather*) **cold s.** courte période *f* de temps froid, coup *m* de froid

(d) *Culin* **ginger s.** biscuit *m* sec au gingembre

(e) *Phot F* instantané *m*; **holiday snaps** photos *fpl* de vacances

(f) *Cards* = (jeu *m* de) bataille *f*

2 *adj* instantané, imprévu; **s. decision** décision *f* immédiate; **to call a s. election** décider du jour au lendemain de faire des élections; **s. vote** vote *m* de surprise

3 *adv* **to go s.** (*make sound*) faire clac; (*break cleanly*) (se) casser net; **s. went my stick!** et crac! ma canne se cassa!

4 *int* **(a)** *Cards* **s.!** bataille!

(b) *F* (*in identical situation*) **I'm going to Paris – s.!** je vais à Paris – ça par exemple! moi aussi!; **do you like my new tie? – yes, but look, s.!** tu aimes ma nouvelle cravate? – oui, mais regarde, j'ai la même!

snap² **(-pp-)** **1** *vi* **(a)** (*of dog etc*) **to s. at sb/sth** essayer de mordre qn/qch

(b) (*of teeth, whip etc*) claquer, faire un bruit sec; **to s. (shut)** (*of fastener, door etc*) se fermer avec un bruit sec; **he snapped to attention** il se mit au garde-à-vous en un quart de seconde

(c) (*of stick, rope etc*) **to s. (in two)** (*break cleanly*) (se) casser net; (*break with sound*) se rompre avec un bruit sec

(d) (*speak abruptly*) parler sèchement; **to s. at sb** s'adresser à qn d'un ton sec *ou* cassant; **there's no need to s.** ce n'est pas la peine de me parler sur ce ton

(e) *Phot* **tourists snapping away with their cameras** des touristes qui n'arrêtent pas de prendre des photos

2 *vt* **(a)** (*whip etc*) faire claquer; **to s. one's fingers** (faire) claquer ses doigts; **to s. one's fingers at sb** narguer qn, faire la nique à qn

(b) (*break*) (*stick etc*) casser, rompre; **to s. sth in two** casser qch en deux

(c) *Phot F* (*take photo of*) prendre; (*facial expression etc*) saisir; **she snapped him eating a cake** elle l'a pris en photo en train de manger un gâteau

(d) (*say sharply*) **to s. an order at sb** lancer un ordre à qn d'un ton sec; **mind your own business!, he snapped (at me)** occupe-toi de ce qui te regarde, dit-il d'un ton cassant

▶ **snap back** *vi* (*of trigger etc*) revenir brusquement

▶ **snap off** **1** *vtsep* (*break off*) (*with hands etc*) arracher; (*with teeth*) enlever d'un coup de dents; (*accidentally*) (*end of* *stick etc)* casser; *Fig F* **to s. sb's head off** rembarrer qn vivement **2** *vi (break off)* se casser

▸ **snap out 1** *vtsep (say sharply) (order)* donner d'un ton sec **2** *vi F (return to normal mood)* **s. out of it!** fais pas la tête *ou* la gueule; **I'm sure she'll s. out of it soon** je suis sûr qu'elle va finir par se dérider

▸ **snap to 1** *vi (close with snap) (of lid, door etc)* se (re)fermer avec un bruit sec **2** *vtas* (re)fermer (avec un bruit sec)

▸ **snap up** *vtsep* **(a)** *(seize in jaws)* saisir, happer **(b)** *(buy, take quickly etc)* rafler; **to s. up a bargain** sauter sur *ou* saisir une occasion; **the tickets are being snapped up like hot cakes** les billets s'arrachent comme des petits pains

snapdragon ['snæpdræg(ə)n] *n (flower)* muflier *m*, gueule-de-loup *f*, *pl* gueules-de-loup

snappily ['snæpılı] *adv (to reply)* d'un ton hargneux

snappish ['snæpıʃ] *adj (person, dog)* hargneux

snappishly ['snæpıʃlı] *adv (to reply)* d'un ton hargneux

snappishness ['snæpıʃnıs] *n* hargne *f*

snappy ['snæpı] *adj* **(a)** *(person, tone, reply, dog)* hargneux **(b)** *(style, prose etc)* vif, *f* vive, plein d'allant; *(organization)* dynamique; *(slogan, campaign)* plein de punch; *F* **make it s.!** grouille-toi!, magne-toi!; **he's a s. dresser** il s'habille chic *ou F* classe

snapshot ['snæpʃɒt] *n Phot, Fig F* instantané *m*; *Comptr (of screen)* instantané *m*, impression *f* immédiate

snare[1] [sneər] *n (in hunting)* lacet *m*, collet *m*; *Fig* piège *m*; **to lay** *or* **set a s.** *(for animal)* poser un collet; *(for opponent)* tendre un piège; **to be caught in a s.** *(of animal)* être pris au lacet; *Fig (of person)* être pris au piège

snare[2] *vt (bird)* prendre au filet; *(rabbit)* prendre au collet *ou* au lacet; *Fig (person)* prendre au piège

snare drum *n Mus* caisse *f* claire

snarl[1] [snɑːl] *n (sound) (of dog, person)* grondement *m*, grognement *m*; *(of tiger)* feulement *m*

snarl[2] *vi (show teeth)* montrer les dents; *(make sound) (of person, dog)* grogner, gronder; *(of tiger)* feuler; **to s. at sb** *(of person, dog)* grogner *ou* gronder contre qn; **go away!, he snarled** va-t-en, gronda-t-il

snarl[3] *n (entanglement) (of ropes, wires etc)* enchevêtrement *m*; *(of traffic)* embouteillage *m*

snarl[4] **1** *vi (become entangled)* s'emmêler, s'enchevêtrer **2** *vt (entangle)* emmêler, enchevêtrer

▸ **snarl up 1** *vtsep* **to s. up the traffic** provoquer des embouteillages; **to s. up a system** paralyser un système; **the traffic gets snarled up at the traffic lights** la circulation bouchonne aux feux; **I got snarled up on the ringroad** je suis resté coincé dans un bouchon sur le périphérique **2** *vi (of traffic)* bouchonner; *(of system, country etc)* être paralysé

snarling ['snɑːlıŋ] **1** *adj* grondant, grognant **2** *n (sound)* grondement *m*, grognement *m*

snarl-up *n (of traffic)* embouteillage *m*, bouchon *m*; *(in system etc)* paralysie *f*; **there's a s. in the switchboard** le standard est saturé

snatch[1] [snætʃ] *n* **(a)** *(grab)* mouvement *m* vif *(pour saisir qch)*; *F (kidnapping)* kidnapping *m*, enlèvement *m*; *F (robbery)* vol *m*; *Sp (in weightlifting)* arraché *m*; **to make a s. at** *or* **for sth** chercher à saisir qch; **to carry out a wages/jewellery s.** *(theft)* voler la paye/des bijoux; **s. squad** = groupe *m* de policiers ou de soldats formé pour arrêter les meneurs etc dans les manifestations

(b) *(short period)* courte période *f*; *(small piece)* fragment *m*; **s. of sleep** petit somme *m*; **in** *or* **by snatches** *(to sleep)* par intervalles; *(to work)* de façon intermittente, à bâtons rompus; **to overhear snatches of conversation** surprendre des bouts *ou* des bribes de conversation; **I could hear a s. of music** quelques notes de musique me parvenaient

(c) *esp US Sl (female pubic area)* chatte *f*

snatch[2] **1** *vt (object)* saisir, empoigner; *(kidnap) (baby)* kidnapper; *(steal) (money, handbag)* voler; *Sp (in weightlifting) (weight)* arracher; **to s. sth from sb** arracher qch à qn; **to s. sth out of sb's hands** arracher qch des mains de qn; **to s. an opportunity** saisir une occasion; **to s. something to eat** manger sur le pouce; **to s. a bit of sleep** faire un petit somme; **I snatched three hours' sleep** j'ai fait un petit somme de trois heures **2** *vi* saisir brusquement *ou* arracher les objets; **don't s.!** on n'arrache pas les choses des mains des gens!

▸ **snatch at** *vipo (try to grab)* tâcher de saisir; **to s. at an opportunity** saisir une occasion (au vol)

▸ **snatch away** *vtsep (grab)* arracher, enlever **(from** de); **he snatched away the book I was reading** il m'a arraché des mains le livre que je lisais; **he snatched it away from me/George** il me l'a arraché des mains/il l'a arraché des mains de George

▸ **snatch up** *vtsep (pick up quickly)* ramasser vivement; **she snatched up the baby** elle s'est emparée vivement du bébé

snazzy ['snæzı] *adj F (shirt, tie, car)* classe *inv*; **he's a s. dresser** il s'habille classe

sneak[1] [sniːk] *n* **(a)** *Sch F (telltale)* cafard, -arde, mouchard, -arde; **s. thief** chipeur, -euse, chapardeur, -euse **(b) s. preview** *(of exhibition, film etc)* avant-première *f*; **to have a s. preview of sth** *(of exhibition, film etc)* voir qch en avant-première; *(of book, product etc)* avoir la primeur de qch; **I've had a s. preview of his novel** j'ai lu quelques passages de son roman avant sa parution

sneak[2] **1** *vi* **(a)** *(tell tales)* moucharder, cafarder

(b) *(move furtively)* **to s. past the guard** passer devant la garde sans se faire voir; **to s. into the cinema without paying** entrer au cinéma sans payer

2 *vt (remove surreptitiously) (from desk, room etc)* subtiliser; *(deliver surreptitiously) (cigarettes, whisky etc)* donner en cachette; *(letter)* glisser; **to s. a glance at sb** glisser un œil vers qn; **they sneaked him past the guards** ils le firent passer sans que les gardes le voient; **someone must have sneaked it into my suitcase** quelqu'un a dû le glisser dans ma valise; **she sneaked her boyfriend into her bedroom** elle fit subrepticement entrer son petit ami dans sa chambre

▸ **sneak about, sneak around** *vi (move furtively)* rôder

▸ **sneak away** *vi* = **sneak off**

▸ **sneak in 1** *vi (enter furtively)* entrer sans se faire repérer; **to s. in without paying** entrer sans payer **2** *vtsep (bring in furtively) (object)* introduire furtivement *ou* subrepticement; **I'll s. you in after dark** je te ferai entrer discrètement à la nuit tombée

▸ **sneak off** *vi (leave furtively)* filer; **he sneaked off and joined another team** il a filé en douce et a rejoint une autre équipe

▸ **sneak on** *vipo esp Br F (tell tales on)* moucharder

▸ **sneak out 1** *vi (leave furtively)* filer; **to s. out of a room** sortir d'une pièce sans se faire voir **2** *vtsep (take out furtively) (object)* emporter subrepticement; *(person)* faire sortir subrepticement

sneakers ['sniːkəz] *npl esp Am* tennis *mpl*

sneaking ['sniːkıŋ] *adj* **I have a s. respect for him** j'avoue que j'ai un certain respect pour lui; **to have a s. feeling** *or* **suspicion that ...** avoir comme une vague impression que ...

sneaky ['sniːkı] *adj* sournois

sneer[1] [snıər] *n (smile)* sourire *m* de mépris; *(laugh)* ricanement *m*; *(remark)* sarcasme *m*

sneer[2] **1** *vi (smile)* sourire d'un air moqueur; *(laugh)* ricaner; **to s. at sb** se moquer de qn; *(address scornful remarks to)* lancer des sarcasmes à qn **2** *vt* **'you couldn't do that,' he sneered** 'tu n'en serais pas capable', a-t-il lancé en ricanant

sneerer ['snıərər] *n* moqueur, -euse, ricaneur, -euse

sneering ['snıərıŋ] **1** *adj (face, look)* ricaneur; *(remark, laughter)* sarcastique **2** *n (laughing)* ricanement *m*; *(remarks)* sarcasmes *mpl*

sneeringly ['snıərıŋlı] *adv (contemptuously)* avec mépris; *(sarcastically)* d'un air sarcastique; *(laughing scornfully)* en ricanant

sneeze[1] [sniːz] *n* éternuement *m*

sneeze[2] *vi* éternuer; **she sneezed all over her plate** elle a éternué sur son assiette

▸ **sneeze at** *vipo F* **that's not to be sneezed at** il ne faut pas cracher dessus

sneezing ['sniːzıŋ] *n* éternuement *m*; **his s. irritates me** ses éternuements m'agacent; **s. fit** crise *f* d'éternuements; **s. powder** poudre *f* à éternuer

snick[1] [snık] *n (notch)* entaille *f*, encoche *f*

snick[2] *vt* **(a)** *(wood etc)* entailler, faire une entaille dans; *(fabric)* faire une fente dans **(b)** *Cr (ball)* couper légèrement

snicker ['snıkər] *n, vi* = **snigger**

snide [snaıd] *adj F (scornful)* méprisant; *(sarcastic)* sarcastique; **she was very s. about it** elle s'est montrée très méprisante/très sarcastique à ce sujet

sniff[1] [snıf] *n* reniflement *m*; **to take a s. at sth** renifler qch; **with a s. of disgust** avec un reniflement de dégoût; **I caught a s. of his aftershave** j'ai senti son after-shave; **there's still a s. of gas** ça sent toujours le gaz; **to have a little s.** *(smell)* renifler un petit coup; *F (have a slight cold)* avoir un léger rhume

sniff[2] **1** *vi* renifler; **he sniffed with disdain** il a reniflé avec dédain **2** *vt* **(a)** *(investigate by smelling)* flairer, renifler; *(detect) (good meal, danger etc)* flairer; **the dog sniffed my hand** le chien m'a flairé la main **(b)** *(inhale) (snuff etc)* humer, renifler; *(cocaine, glue)* sniffer

▸ **sniff at** *vipo* **(a)** *F (disdain)* **the offer is not to be sniffed at** il ne faut pas cracher sur une proposition comme celle-ci **(b)** *(smell)* flairer, renifler; **the dog sniffed at my hand** le chien m'a flairé la main

▶ **sniff out** *vtsep* (*discover by smelling*) (*of dog*) (*person, object*) détecter, flairer; *Fig* (*scandal etc*) déterrer
sniffer dog ['snɪfər] *n* chien *m* renifleur
sniffle[1] ['snɪf(ə)l] *n* (*slight cold*) petit rhume *m* (de cerveau); **to have a s.** *or* **the sniffles** avoir un petit rhume
sniffle[2] *vi* **(a)** (*sniff repeatedly*) renifler **(b)** (*cry*) pleurnicher
sniffy ['snɪfɪ] *adj F* **(a)** (*disdainful*) dédaigneux; **to be s. about sth** (*take exception to sth*) voir qch d'un mauvais œil; (*regard with contempt*) considérer qch avec mépris **(b)** (*bad-smelling*) **it's a bit s. in here** ça pue un peu ici **(c)** (*with cold*) **I'm still a bit s.** je renifle encore
snifter ['snɪftər] *n* **(a)** *Old-fashioned F* (*drink*) goutte *f*, petit verre *m* **(b)** *Am* (*glass*) verre *m* à cognac
snigger[1] ['snɪgər] *n* (*stifled laughter*) ricanement *m*; (*at dirty story etc*) petit rire *m* grivois
snigger[2] *vi* (*stifle laughter*) ricaner (**at** à propos de)
sniggering ['snɪgərɪŋ] *n* (*stifled laughter*) ricanement *m*; **her s. irritates me** ses ricanements m'agacent
snip[1] [snɪp] *n* **(a)** (*cut*) petite entaille *f*; (*act of cutting with scissors*) coup *m* de ciseaux **(b)** (*piece cut off*) (*of paper, fabric*) morceau *m* coupé, bout *m* **(c)** *Br F* (*bargain*) affaire *f* (avantageuse), occasion *f*; **to get a s.** faire une affaire; **at £25 it's a s.** à 25 livres c'est une affaire
snip[2] *vt* **(-pp-)** couper; **s. s.** clac clac
▶ **snip off** *vtsep* couper
snipe[1] [snaɪp] *n inv* (*bird*) bécassine *f*
snipe[2] *vi Mil* tirer; *Fig* (*criticize*) critiquer; **to s. at sb** *Mil* tirer sur qn (*d'une position embusquée*); *Fig* critiquer qn sournoisement; **to s. at the enemy** canarder l'ennemi; **to be sniped at** se faire canarder
sniper ['snaɪpər] *n Mil* tireur *m* embusqué; **to be killed by a s.'s bullet** être tué par un tireur embusqué; **s. fire** tir *m* d'embuscade
sniping ['snaɪpɪŋ] **1** *n Mil* tir *m* d'embuscade; *Fig* critique *f* sournoise (**at sb** de qn) **2** *adj* (*criticism, remarks etc*) sournois
snippet ['snɪpɪt] *n* (*small piece*) bout *m*, morceau *m* (coupé); (*of book etc*) court extrait *m*; (*of conversation*) bribes *fpl*
snitch[1] [snɪtʃ] *n Sl* **(a)** (*informer*) balance *f* **(b)** (*nose*) pif *m*
snitch[2] *Sl* **1** *vi* (*inform*) moucharder; **to s. on sb** balancer qn **2** *vt* (*steal*) chaparder
snivel[1] ['snɪv(ə)l] *n* (*whine*) pleurnichement *m*; **to say sth with a s.** dire qch en pleurnichant
snivel[2] *vi* **(-ll-**, *US* **-l-)** (*whine*) pleurnicher
sniveller, *US* **sniveler** ['snɪv(ə)lər] *n* pleurnicheur, -euse
snivelling, *US* **sniveling** ['snɪv(ə)lɪŋ] **1** *adj* (*person*) (*whining*) pleurnicheur, -euse; **you s. little idiot!** espèce de pleurnicheur! **2** *n* (*whining*) pleurnicherie *f*
snob [snɒb] *n* snob *mf*; **she's a bit of a s.** c'est une snobinarde; **a music s.** un snob en matière de musique
snobbery ['snɒbərɪ] *n* snobisme *m*; **inverted s.** snobisme à rebours; **intellectual s.** snobisme intellectuel
snobbish ['snɒbɪʃ] *adj* snob *inv*
snobbishness ['snɒbɪʃnɪs] *n* snobisme *m*
snog[1] [snɒg] *n Br F* **to have a s.** se bécoter
snog[2] *Br F* **1** *vi* (*of couple*) se bécoter **2** *vt* embrasser
snogging ['snɒgɪŋ] *n Br F* bécotage *m*
snood [snu:d] *n* (*hairnet*) résille *f*
snook [snu:k] *n F* **to cock a s. at sb** (*make gesture at*) faire un pied de nez à qn; *Fig* (*defy*) faire la nique à qn
snooker[1] ['snu:kər] *n* (*game*) billard *m* snooker; (*shot*) snooker *m*
snooker[2] *vt* **to s. sb** (*in game*) empêcher qn de frapper la boule directement; *Fig F* mettre qn dans une impasse; *Fig F* **now I've snookered myself** je suis coincé maintenant; **to be snookered** (*in game*) se trouver dans l'impossibilité de frapper la boule directement; *Fig* être coinçé, être dans une impasse
snoop[1] [snu:p] *n F* **(a)** = **snooper (b) I'll have a s. around** je vais jeter un petit coup d'œil
snoop[2] *vi F* fourrer son nez partout, fouiner; **he was snooping behind the lab** il fouinait derrière le labo
▶ **snoop around** *vi F* fourrer son nez partout; **to s. around in sb's papers/desk** fouiller dans les papiers/le bureau de qn
▶ **snoop on** *vipo F* (*spy on*) (*person*) espionner
snooper ['snu:pər] *n F* **(a)** (*official investigator*) fouine *f* **(b) he's a terrible s.** il fourre son nez partout
snooty ['snu:tɪ] *adj F* arrogant, hautain
snooze[1] [snu:z] *n F* petit somme *m*; **to have a s.** faire un petit somme; **s. button** (*on alarm*) bouton *m* de rappel
snooze[2] *vi F* sommeiller, faire un petit somme; (*be not quite asleep*) somnoler
snore[1] [snɔ:r] *n* ronflement *m*
snore[2] *vi* ronfler
snorer ['snɔ:rər] *n* ronfleur, -euse
snoring ['snɔ:rɪŋ] *n* ronflement *m*; **the sound of his s.** le bruit de ses ronflements; **his s. could be heard halfway down the corridor** on l'entendait ronfler du milieu du couloir
snorkel[1] ['snɔ:k(ə)l] *n Swimming* tuba *m*; (*of submarine*) schnorchel *m*, schnorkel *m*
snorkel[2] *vi* **to s., to go snorkelling** faire de la plongée avec un tuba
snort[1] [snɔ:t] *n* **(a)** (*exhalation*) reniflement *m*; (*of horse etc*) ébrouement *m* **(b)** (*expressing impatience, disgust*) grognement *m* d'impatience/de dégoût; (*of anger*) grommellement *m*; **s. of laughter** court éclat *m* de rire; **she gave a s. of disbelief** elle a reniflé *ou* pouffé en signe d'incrédulité **(c)** *Sl* (*of drink*) petit coup *m*; (*of cocaine*) prise *f*; **he had a quick s. of whisky** il s'est jeté un petit whisky derrière la cravate
snort[2] **1** *vi* (*exhale*) renifler bruyamment; (*of horse*) s'ébrouer; **to s. with laughter** pouffer de rire; **to s. in disbelief** pouffer en signe d'incrédulité; **to s. with anger** s'étrangler de colère; *Fig F* **to s. at sth** dédaigner qch **2** *vt* **(a)** (*answer*) grogner; **that's preposterous!, she snorted** c'est absurde!, a-t-elle jeté **(b)** *Sl* (*cocaine*) sniffer
snorter ['snɔ:tər] *n Sl* **(a)** *Br* (*strong letter*) lettre *f* carabinée; **that's a real s.** (**of a problem**) ça va nous/vous/*etc* donner du fil à retordre **(b)** (*short drink*) (*of alcohol*) goutte *f*, petit verre *m*
snot [snɒt] *n F* (*from nose*) morve *f*; **a bit of s.** de la morve; **s. rag** tire-jus *m inv*
snotty ['snɒtɪ] *adj F* **(a)** (*handkerchief*) sale, dégoûtant; (*nose*) couvert de morve; **s.(-nosed)** cradingue, crade; **some s.(-nosed) little brat** un petit morveux **(b)** (*arrogant*) arrogant; **one of those incredibly s. officials** un de ces officiels qui pètent plus haut que leur cul
snout ['snaʊt] *n* **(a)** (*of animal*) museau *m*; (*of pig, hedgehog*) groin *m*; (*of boar*) boutoir *m*; (*of gun*) bout *m* (du canon); *F* (*nose*) naze *m*, tarin *m*, pif *m* **(b)** *Br Prison Sl* (*tobacco*) tabac *m* **(c)** *Br Sl* (*police informer*) indic *m*
snow[1] [snəʊ] *n* **(a)** neige *f*; **eternal s.** neiges éternelles; **the s. line** la limite des neiges (éternelles); **to be s. blind** souffrir de cécité des neiges; **s. goggles** lunettes *fpl* de ski; **s.** *Br* **tyres** *or Am* **tires** pneus *mpl* neige **(b)** *TV, Rad* neige *f* **(c)** *Sl* (*cocaine*) neige *f*
snow[2] *v impers* neiger; **it's snowing** il neige
▶ **snow in** *vtsep* (*usu passive*) **to be snowed in** être bloqué par la neige
▶ **snow off** *vtsep* (*usu passive*) **the match was snowed off** le match a été annulé à cause de la neige
▶ **snow under** *vtsep* (*usu passive*) **snowed under with work** débordé de travail
▶ **snow up** *vtsep* (*usu passive*) **to be snowed up** être bloqué par la neige
snowball[1] ['snəʊbɔ:l] *n* **(a)** boule *f* de neige; *F* **he hasn't a s. 's chance (in hell)** il n'a pas l'ombre d'une chance; **s. fight** bataille *f* de boules de neige; **s. selling** vente *f* à la boule de neige **(b) s. (tree** *or* **bush)** boule-de-neige *f*, *pl* boules-de-neige, obier *m* **(c)** (*drink*) snowball *m*
snowball[2] *vi* **(a)** (*of story, debts etc*) faire boule de neige **(b)** (*fight with snowballs*) se battre à coups de boules de neige
snow bank *n Can* banc *m* de neige
snow blindness *n* cécité *f* des neiges
snowboot ['snəʊbu:t] *n* après-ski *m*, *pl* après-skis
snowbound ['snəʊbaʊnd] *adj* (*person, airport*) bloqué par la neige
snowcapped ['snəʊkæpt] *adj* couronné de neige
snow chain *n* chaîne *f* à neige
snowdrift ['snəʊdrɪft] *n* congère *f*
snowdrop ['snəʊdrɒp] *n* (*flower*) perce-neige *m inv*
snowfall ['snəʊfɔ:l] *n* chute *f* de neige
snow fence *n* (*on road*) paraneige *m*
snowfield ['snəʊfi:ld] *n* champ *m* de neige
snowflake ['snəʊfleɪk] *n* flocon *m* de neige
snow goose *n* oie *f* des neiges
snow leopard *n* léopard *m* des neiges, once *f*
snowman, *pl* **-men** ['snəʊmæn, -men] *n* bonhomme *m* de neige; **they built** *or* **made a s.** ils ont fait un bonhomme de neige; **the abominable s.** l'abominable homme des neiges
snowmobile ['snəʊməʊbi:l] *n Am* (*open*) motoneige *m*; (*enclosed*) autoneige *f*
snowplough, *US* **-plow** ['snəʊplaʊ] *n Rail, Ski etc* chasse-neige *m inv*
snowshoe ['snəʊʃu:] *n* raquette *f* (*pour la neige*)
snowstorm ['snəʊstɔ:m] *n* tempête *f* de neige
snowsuit ['snəʊsu:t] *n* combinaison *f* de ski
snow(-)white **1** *adj also Fig* blanc comme la neige **2** *n* **S. (and the seven dwarfs)** Blanche-Neige *f* (et les sept nains)
snowy ['snəʊɪ] *adj* neigeux; (*day etc*) de neige; (*field etc*)

enneigé; (*season*) des neiges; **s. (white) hair** cheveux blancs (comme la neige)

SNP [esen'piː] *n Pol* (*abbr* **Scottish National Party**) parti *m* nationaliste écossais

snub¹ [snʌb] *n* (*refusal*) rebuffade *f*; (*insult*) affront *m*; **to meet with a s.** être rejeté d'une rebuffade

snub² *vt* (**-bb-**) (*person*) faire un affront à; **I said hello but he just snubbed me** je lui ai dit bonjour mais il m'a ignoré *ou* m'a snobé

snub³ *adj* (*nose*) (plat et) retroussé

snub-nosed ['snʌbnəʊzd] *adj* au nez retroussé; **s. revolver** revolver au canon court

snuff¹ [snʌf] *n* tabac *m* à priser; **to take s.** priser; **a pinch of s.** une prise; **s. (coloured)** (couleur) tabac *inv*

snuff² *vt* **(a)** (*extinguish*) (*candle*) moucher; (*hope, enthusiasm etc*) éteindre **(b)** *Br Sl* **to s. it** (*die*) clamecer, clamser, passer l'arme à gauche **(c)** (*sniff*) (*air*) humer

▶ **snuff out** *vtsep* (*life*) mettre un terme à; (*opposition*) étouffer; *F* (*person*) éliminer

snuffbox ['snʌfbɒks] *n* tabatière *f*

snuffer ['snʌfər] *n* (*for candle*) mouchette *f*

snuffle¹ ['snʌf(ə)l] *n* **(a)** (*sniff*) reniflement *m*; *F* **snuffles** (*cold*) rhume *m* **(b)** (*nasal tone*) voix *f* nasillarde

snuffle² *vi* **(a)** (*sniff*) renifler; (*have a cold*) avoir un rhume **(b)** (*speak in nasal tone*) nasiller, parler en nasillant

snuff movie *n* = film *m* qui contient les images d'une mort en direct

snug [snʌg] **1** *adj* (*house etc*) confortable, où l'on est bien; (*person*) (*sheltered*) bien à l'abri; (*warm*) bien au chaud; (*bed*) douillet; (*jacket*) bien chaud; **to make oneself s.** se mettre à son aise; **to lie s. in bed** être bien au chaud dans son lit; *F* **as s. as a bug in a rug** tranquille comme Baptiste; **it's a s. fit** (*of machine part etc*) ça s'emboîte parfaitement; (*of clothing*) c'est bien ajusté; **it's a bit of a s. fit, it's a bit too s.** (*too tight*) (*of clothing*) c'est un peu trop serré **2** *n Br* petite arrière-salle *f* (*dans un pub*)

snuggery ['snʌgərɪ] *n* petite pièce *f* intime (et confortable); *Br* (*in pub*) petite arrière-salle *f*

snuggle ['snʌg(ə)l] **1** *vi* **to s. under the covers** se pelotonner sous les couvertures; **village snuggling in the valley** village niché dans la vallée **2** *vt* **to s. a child close to one** serrer un enfant dans ses bras

▶ **snuggle down** *vi* (*make oneself comfortable*) **to s. down in bed** se blottir (bien au chaud) dans son lit

▶ **snuggle up** *vi* (*come close*) se pelotonner, se blottir (**to sb** contre qn); **to s. up with a good book** s'installer bien confortablement avec un bon livre

snugly ['snʌglɪ] *adv* confortablement; (*warmly*) bien au chaud; **s. wrapped** (*in blanket etc*) douillettement enveloppé; **garment that fits s.** vêtement bien ajusté; **this piece should fit s. into …** cette pièce devrait s'emboîter parfaitement *ou* exactement dans …

So. **(a)** (*abbr* **South**) S. **(b)** (*abbr* **Southern**) S.

so [səʊ] **1** *adv* **(a)** [①A5] (*to such an extent*) si, tellement; **it's so easy** c'est si *ou* tellement facile; **I was so disappointed** j'étais tellement déçu; **we're so pleased you could come** nous sommes tellement *ou* si contents que vous ayez pu venir; **she isn't so very old** elle n'est pas tellement *ou* si vieille; **the young and the not so young** les jeunes et les moins jeunes; **I'm not so sure of that** je n'en suis pas si sûr; **so serious a wound** une blessure aussi grave; **what's so important about this case?** qu'est-ce que cette affaire a de si important?; **he's not so clever as she is** il n'est pas aussi intelligent qu'elle; **she wouldn't be so stupid as to do that** elle ne serait pas bête au point de faire cela, elle ne serait pas assez bête pour faire cela; **would you be so kind as to …?** voudriez-vous avoir la gentillesse de …?; **I was so hungry I could have eaten it all** j'avais si faim que j'aurais pu tout manger; **he's so rich that he doesn't know what he's worth** il est riche au point d'ignorer le montant de sa fortune; **I loved her so (much)** je l'aimais tant; **we enjoyed ourselves so much** nous nous sommes tellement amusés; **it's not so much that I dislike them, more that I don't <u>like</u> them** ce n'est pas tant qu'ils me déplaisent, ça serait plutôt qu'ils ne me plaisent pas; **you do exaggerate so!** tu exagères tellement!

(b) [①A28,i] (*in this way*) ainsi, de cette façon, de cette manière; **stand just so** tenez-vous ainsi *ou* comme ça; **while he was so occupied …** pendant qu'il était ainsi occupé …; **as X is to Y, so Y is to Z** X est à Y ce que Y est à Z; **she so arranged things that …** elle a fait en sorte que … + *sub*; **I have been so informed** c'est ce que l'on m'a dit; **so I believe** c'est ce que je crois; **it so happened that I was there** le hasard a voulu que je fusse là, il s'est trouvé que j'étais là; **and so on, and so forth** et ainsi de suite; **so to speak** *or* **say** pour ainsi dire; **has the train gone? – I think so** est-ce que le train est parti? – je crois *ou* je pense que oui; **he's clever – do you think so?** il est intelligent – vous trouvez?; **I suppose so, I expect so** je (le) suppose; **I hope so** je l'espère bien, j'espère bien; **I'm afraid so** j'en ai bien peur, je le crains; **I didn't say so** moi, je n'ai pas dit cela; **is she really ill? – so it seems** elle est donc vraiment malade? – à ce qu'il paraît; **so I told him** c'est ce que je lui ai dit; **there is a train at six or so I was told** il y a un train à six heures, ou du moins c'est ce qu'on m'a dit; **I'm not very organized – so I see!** je ne suis pas très organisé – c'est ce que je vois!; **I told you so!** je vous l'avais bien dit!; **so much so that …** à tel point que …, tellement que …; **(much) more so** (bien) plus encore; **that's so** c'est bien vrai; **is that so?** vraiment?; **that being so** (*as this is the case*) puisqu'il en est ainsi; (*should this prove the case*) dans ces conditions; **so be it!** soit!, qu'il en soit ainsi!; **if so** s'il en est ainsi; **why so?** pourquoi cela?; **how so?** comment cela?; **perhaps so** cela se peut; **quite so** parfaitement, absolument; **a hundred pounds or so** une centaine de livres; **a week or so** une huitaine de jours; **a little girl <u>so</u> high** une petite fille grande comme ça; **she's right and so are you** elle a raison et vous aussi; **and so am I/are we** et moi/et nous aussi; **he thinks he can do it – so he can** il pense qu'il peut le faire – en effet il le peut; **you're late! – so I am!** vous êtes en retard! – c'est vrai!; **it was Mr Smith – so it was!** c'était Monsieur Smith – en effet!; *F* **they aren't French – they are so!** ils ne sont pas français – si!

(c) [①A69,b,vii; B55,B] (*purpose*) **so that, so as to** afin que + *sub*, pour que + *sub*, afin de + *inf*, pour + *inf*; **she stood up so as to** *or* **so that she could see better** elle s'est levée afin de *ou* pour mieux voir; **she sat down so that I could see better** elle s'est assise afin que *ou* pour que je puisse mieux voir; **we hurried so as not to be late, we hurried so that we shouldn't be late** nous nous sommes dépêchés pour ne pas être *ou* afin de ne pas être en retard

(d) [①A69,b,viii; B55,B] (*consequence*) **so that** de sorte que; **the flight was cancelled so that we had to stay at home** le vol a été annulé de sorte que *ou* si bien que nous avons dû rester à la maison; **the crates had fallen over so that we couldn't get past** comme les caisses étaient tombées, nous n'avons pas pu passer

(e) *F* **so so** (*not too bad*) comme ci comme ça; **the cooking is only so so** la cuisine n'est pas terrible

2 *conj* **(a)** (*therefore*) donc, c'est pourquoi; **she has a bad temper, so be careful** elle a mauvais caractère, donc faites attention; **he wasn't there, so I came back again** il n'était pas là, donc je suis revenu; **so what?** et alors?; **it's very expensive – so? what am I supposed to do about it?** c'est très cher – et alors? que voulez-vous que j'y fasse?; **so, we're a bit late, what difference does that make?** et alors, nous sommes un peu en retard, quelle différence cela fait-il?

(b) so there you are! vous voilà donc!; **so that's what it is!** ah! c'est comme ça!; **so you're not coming?** vous ne venez donc pas?; **so, what do we do?** eh bien, qu'est-ce qu'on fait?

soak¹ [səʊk] *n* **(a) give them a good s.** mets-les bien à tremper; **to have a good s. (in the bath)** prendre un bon bain **(b)** *F* (*drunkard*) poivrot, -ote

soak² **1** *vt* **(a)** (*of liquid, person*) tremper (**in sth** dans qch); (*beans etc*) faire tremper; **the rain soaked me to the skin** la pluie m'a trempé jusqu'aux os; **soaked with blood/sweat** plein de sang/trempé de transpiration; **I got soaked** je me suis tout trempé; (*by rain*) je me suis fait tremper **(b)** *F* (*customer*) écorcher; **to s. the rich** faire payer les riches **2** *vi* baigner, tremper (**in sth** dans qch); (*of liquid*) s'infiltrer, s'imbiber (**into sth** dans qch); **to leave a saucepan to s.** laisser une casserole tremper

▶ **soak in** **1** *vi* (*of liquid*) pénétrer, être absorbé; *Fig* **has it soaked in yet?** est-ce qu'il a/est-ce que tu as/*etc* pigé? **2** *vtsep* (*absorb*) **to s. in water** s'imprégner d'eau, absorber l'eau; **she went to the main square to s. in the atmosphere** elle est allée sur la place principale pour s'imprégner de son atmosphère

▶ **soak through** *vi* **(a)** (*seep through to other side*) s'infiltrer à travers **(b)** (*be absorbed*) pénétrer, s'infiltrer

▶ **soak up** *vtsep* (*liquid*) absorber, boire; **to s. up water** s'imprégner d'eau, absorber de l'eau; *Fig* **to s. up the sun** se rôtir au soleil; **to s. up the atmosphere** s'imprégner de l'atmosphère

soaked [səʊkt] *adj* trempé; (*ground*) détrempé; **s. to the skin, s. through** trempé jusqu'aux os

soaking ['səʊkɪŋ] **1** *n* trempage *m*; **give the beans a good s.** faites tremper les haricots pendant plusieurs heures; **give the clothes a good s.** mettez le linge à tremper pendant un bon moment; **to get a s.** se faire tremper **2** *adj* (*wet*) trempé;

you're absolutely s.! vous êtes tout trempé! 3 *adv* **s. wet** trempé; **to get s. wet** se tremper; (*in rain*) se faire tremper
so-and-so *n F* **(a)** (*unspecified person*) Untel *m*, Unetelle *f*; **Mr. S.** Monsieur Untel; **Mrs. S.** Madame Unetelle **(b)** *Pej* (*unpleasant person*) type *m*; **a crafty s.** une fine mouche, un malin; **you old s.!** (*reproving*) espèce de vilain!; **the old s.!** (*angry*) le salaud!; (*admiring, surprised*) le bougre!; **you greedy old s.** espèce de gourmand!; **don't cry, you silly old s.!** faut pas pleurer, espèce d'idiot!
soap[1] [səʊp] *n* savon *m*; **a bar** *or* **cake of s.** un morceau de savon; (*small*) une savonnette; *US Sl* **no s.!** rien à faire; **shaving s.** savon à barbe; *F* **soft s.** (*flattery*) flatterie *f*; **to wash sth with s.** savonner qch; **s. bubble** bulle *f* de savon; *TV* **s. (opera)** feuilleton *m*; **s. powder** lessive *f* en poudre
soap[2] *vt* (*clothes etc*) savonner
▶ **soap down** *vtsep* savonner
soapbox ['səʊpbɒks] *n* (*for soap*) caisse *f* à savon; (*child's cart*) voiture *f* pour enfant; **s. orator** personne *f* qui harangue les foules; *Fig* **to get up on a s.** faire un discours improvisé, haranguer les foules
soapdish ['səʊpdɪʃ] *n* porte-savon *m*, *pl* porte-savons
soapflakes ['səʊpfleɪks] *npl* savon *m* en paillettes
soapiness ['səʊpɪnɪs] *n* (*of sth*) caractère *m* savonneux
soapstone ['səʊpstəʊn] *n* stéatite *f*
soapsuds ['səʊpsʌdz] *npl* (*lather*) mousse *f* de savon; (*water*) eau *f* savonneuse
soapy ['səʊpɪ] *adj* **(a)** (*water*) savonneux; (*body*) couvert de savon; (*taste*) de savon; **this beer tastes s.** cette bière a un goût de savon **(b)** *F* (*flattering*) (*person, voice*) doucereux, onctueux
soar [sɔːr] *vi esp Lit* (*fly up*) prendre son essor, s'élever; (*glide*) planer; (*of spirits*) remonter en flèche; **rents have soared** les loyers ont augmenté de façon vertigineuse
soaring ['sɔːrɪŋ] **1** *adj* (*bird, arrow*) qui monte *ou* s'élève dans les airs; (*steeple*) élancé; (*price, popularity etc*) qui monte en flèche; **the s. flight of the eagle** le vol majestueux de l'aigle **2** *n* (*rising*) (*of bird*) essor *m*; (*of prices*) hausse *f*
sob[1] [sɒb] *n* sanglot *m*; *Am* **s. sister** journaliste *f* qui fait le courrier du cœur; *F* **s. story** histoire *f* à faire pleurer dans les chaumières; *F* **to tell sb a s. story** raconter une histoire pour apitoyer qn; *F* **s. stuff** sensiblerie *f*, *F* mélo *m*
sob[2] (-bb-) **1** *vi* sangloter **2** *vt* (*say*) dire en sanglotant; **she sobbed herself to sleep** elle s'est endormie en sanglotant
▶ **sob out** *vtsep* **(a)** (*say*) dire en sanglotant **(b)** **to s. one's heart out** pleurer à chaudes larmes
s. o. b. [esəʊ'biː] *n esp Am Sl* (*abbr* **son of a bitch**) fils *m* de pute, salaud *m*
sobbing ['sɒbɪŋ] **1** *adj* **in a s. voice** d'une voix brisée par les sanglots **2** *n* sanglots *mpl*
sober[1] ['səʊbər] *adj* **(a)** (*not drunk*) sobre; **as s. as a judge** sobre comme un chameau; (*serious*) sérieux comme un pape; **when he's s. (again)** quand il sera dessoûlé **(b)** (*moderate*) sobre, modéré; (*calm*) calme, posé; (*face*) grave; (*colours, dress*) sobre; **s. opinion** opinion réfléchie; **the s. truth** la simple vérité
sober[2] *vt* dessoûler; **this news sobered him** cette nouvelle l'a dégrisé
▶ **sober down 1** *vi* (*become calmer*) s'assagir **2** *vtsep* dégriser
▶ **sober up 1** *vi* (*become less drunk*) se dégriser; **s. up!** reprends-toi! **2** *vtsep* dessoûler; (*of news etc*) dégriser
sobering ['səʊbərɪŋ] *adj* qui dégrise; **it's had a s. effect on him** ça l'a dégrisé; **it's a s. thought** ça vous fait réfléchir
sober-minded *adj* (*serious*) sérieux, réfléchi
soberness ['səʊbənɪs] *n* **(a)** (*not drinking*) sobriété *f* **(b)** (*of style, dress, character*) sobriété *f*; (*seriousness*) sérieux *m*
sobersides ['səʊbəsaɪdz] *n Old-fashioned F* (*solemn person*) bonnet *m* de nuit
sobriety [səʊ'braɪətɪ] *n also Fig* sobriété *f*
Soc (a) *abbr* **society (b)** *abbr* **Socialist**
so-called [səʊ'kɔːld] *adj* **(a)** (*so named*) appelé ainsi, ainsi nommé; **the s. temperate zone** la zone dite tempérée **(b)** (*supposed*) **a s. doctor** un soi-disant *ou* un prétendu docteur; **s. progress** de prétendus progrès
soccer ['sɒkər] *n* football *m*; *F* foot *m*; **s. match** match *m* de football *ou F* de foot; **s. player** footballeur, -euse; **s. boots** chaussures *fpl* de foot; **s. pitch** terrain *m* de football
sociability [səʊʃə'bɪlɪtɪ] *n* sociabilité *f*
sociable ['səʊʃəb(ə)l] *adj* sociable; **I had a drink with them to be s.** j'ai pris un verre avec eux pour me montrer sociable; **to become more s.** (*of person*) (*become less shy*) s'apprivoiser; (*become more friendly*) devenir plus sociable; **I'm not feeling very s. at the moment** je n'ai pas envie de voir du monde en ce moment; **I'm not in a s. mood** je ne suis pas d'humeur à voir du monde
sociably ['səʊʃəblɪ] *adv* sociablement; **she's not very s. inclined** elle n'est pas très mondaine
social ['səʊʃəl] **1** *adj* **(a)** social; **to have a busy s. life** (*see a lot of people*) voir beaucoup de monde; (*go out a lot*) sortir beaucoup; **work is getting in the way of my s. life** j'ai trop de travail pour pouvoir sortir; **since he's been married he's had to give up his s. life** depuis son mariage, il ne voit presque plus personne; **to be sb's s. equal** être l'égal de qn sur le plan social; **s. benefits system** système *m* de prévoyance; **s. class** classe *f* sociale; *Old-fashioned Euph* **s. disease** maladie *f* vénérienne; **s. drinker** personne *f* qui ne boit de l'alcool que dans les soirées; **s. drinking** consommation *f* d'alcool lors de réunions amicales; **s. engineering** mesures *fpl* prises pour influencer les structures sociales; **s. evening** (*party*) soirée *f*; (*gathering*) réunion *f*; **s. group** catégorie *f* socio-professionnelle, CSP *f*; **the s. ladder** l'échelle *f* sociale; **s. marketing** mercatique *f* sociale; **the s. order** l'ordre *m* social; **s. outcast** marginal, -ale; **to take sth into s. ownership** nationaliser qch; **s. position** rang *m* dans la société; **s. reformer** réformateur, -trice de la société; **to be on** *or* **get s. security** percevoir des allocations; **s. security contributions** cotisations *fpl* de sécurité sociale; **s. security provisions** prévoyance *f* sociale
(b) *Zool* social; **man is a s. animal** l'homme est un animal grégaire
2 *n* (*party*) soirée *f*
social climber *n* arriviste *mf*
social climbing *n* arrivisme *m*
social democrat *n Pol* social-démocrate *mf*, *pl* sociaux-démocrates
social fund *n Br Admin* fonds *m* de solidarité
socialism ['səʊʃəlɪz(ə)m] *n* socialisme *m*
socialist ['səʊʃəlɪst] *adj, n* socialiste *mf*
socialite ['səʊʃəlaɪt] *n* membre *m* de la haute société, homme *m*/femme *f* du monde
socialize ['səʊʃəlaɪz] **1** *vi* **to s. with sb** fréquenter qn; (*chat*) bavarder avec qn; **he won't s.** il n'accepte jamais une invitation; **they do a lot of socializing** ils voient beaucoup de gens **2** *vt Econ* (*property*) nationaliser; *US* **socialized medicine** médecine *f* d'État
socially ['səʊʃəlɪ] *adv* socialement; **to be s. active** (*go out a lot*) sortir beaucoup; (*see a lot of people*) voir beaucoup de monde; **we don't do much s.** nous sortons peu, nous fréquentons peu de gens; **I saw her s. for a while, but nothing beyond that** je l'ai vaguement fréquentée pendant un temps, mais rien de plus; **I don't know him s. at all, just at work** en dehors du travail, je ne le connais pas du tout; **s. mobile** mobile sur le plan social
social sciences *npl* sciences *fpl* humaines
social services *npl* services *mpl* sociaux *ou* d'assistance sociale
social work *n* œuvres *fpl* sociales; (*professional*) travail *m* de l'assistant social; **s. department** assistance *f* sociale
social worker *n* assistant, -ante social(e)
society [sə'saɪətɪ] *n* **(a)** (*community, companionship*) société *f*; **he's a danger** *or* **menace to s.** c'est un danger pour la société; **to avoid the s. of one's colleagues** éviter la compagnie de ses collègues; **this word isn't used in polite s.** on n'utilise pas ce mot chez les gens bien élevés; **(high) s.** le beau monde, la haute société; *Journ* **s. news** *or* **column** *or* **pages** mondanités *fpl*; **consumer s.** société de consommation; **s. people** gens *mpl* du monde; **a s. wedding** un mariage dans le grand monde
(b) (*body*) société *f*; (*association*) association *f*; **charitable s.** œuvre *f* de bienfaisance *ou* de charité; *Br* **National S. for the Prevention of Cruelty to Children** organisation *f* de protection de l'enfance; *Rel* **the S. of Friends** la Société des Amis, les Quakers *mpl*; **the S. of Jesus** les Jésuites *mpl*
sociocultural [səʊsɪəʊ'kʌltʃər(ə)l] *adj* socioculturel
socioeconomic [səʊsɪəʊiːkə'nɒmɪk] *adj* socio-économique; **s. grouping** classification *f* socio-économique
sociolinguistic [səʊsɪəʊlɪŋ'gwɪstɪk] *adj* sociolinguistique
sociolinguistics [səʊsɪəʊlɪŋ'gwɪstɪks] *n* [ⓘA10,c] sociolinguistique *f*
sociological [səʊsɪəʊ'lɒdʒɪk(ə)l] *adj* sociologique
sociologist [səʊsɪ'ɒlədʒɪst] *n* sociologue *mf*
sociology [səʊsɪ'ɒlədʒɪ] *n* sociologie *f*
sociometry [səʊsɪ'ɒmɪtrɪ] *n* sociométrie *f*
sociopath ['səʊsɪəpæθ] *n* inadapté, -ée
socioprofessional [səʊsɪəʊprə'feʃən(ə)l] *adj* socioprofessionnel; **s. group** catégorie *f* socioprofessionnelle, CSP *f*
sock[1] [sɒk] *n* (*Am pl also* **sox**) (*garment*) chaussette *f*; **(ankle) socks** socquettes *fpl*; *Br Fig F* **to pull one's socks up** se secouer; *Br F* **put a s. in it, will you!** ferme-la!
sock[2] *n F* (*blow*) gnon *m*, beigne *f*; (*in the eye*) cocard *m*; **to give sb a s. on the jaw** flanquer une beigne à qn

sock³ *vt F* (*hit*) (*person*) flanquer une beigne à; **s. it to me!** (*show me what you can do*) montre-moi ce que tu sais faire
socket ['sɒkɪt] *n Anat* (*of eye*) orbite *f*; (*of tooth*) alvéole *f*; (*of bone*) cavité *f* articulaire, glène *f*; (*of pipe*) (*in plumbing*) emboîtement *m*, manchon *m*; *esp Br* (*for electric plug*) prise *f* (de courant); (*of lightbulb*) douille *f*; (*tool*) douille, embout *m*; **ball and s. joint** *Anat* énarthrose *f*; *Tech* articulation *f*; **microphone s.** prise microphone; **s. set** jeu *m* d'embouts
Socrates ['sɒkrəti:z] *n* Socrate *m*
Socratic [sɒ'krætɪk] *adj* socratique
sod¹ [sɒd] *n* (*piece of turf*) motte *f* de gazon; **to cut** *or* **turn the first s.** donner le premier coup de bêche; **under the s.** (*buried*) enterré
sod² *n esp Br Sl* (*obnoxious person or thing*) **he's a real s.** c'est un vrai salaud; **you silly s.** espèce d'imbécile!; **you stupid s.!** andouille!; **poor s.!** pauvre bougre!; **he's a rude s.** quel ours!; **the kid's being an absolute little s.!** ce gosse est une vraie peste!; **this problem/screw is a real s.!** ce putain de problème/cette putain de vis!; **odds and sods** petits bouts *mpl*, bribes *fpl* et morceaux *mpl*
sod³ *vt esp Br Sl* (*to damn*) **s. you!** va te faire foutre!; **s. them!** ils peuvent toujours aller se faire voir!; **s. the party, I'm tired** la soirée, je m'en fous, je suis fatigué; **s. it!** merde, alors!
▶ **sod off** *vi esp Br Sl* (*go away*) foutre le camp; **s. off!** fous-moi le camp!; **I told him to s. off** je lui ai dit d'aller se faire voir
soda ['səʊdə] *n Ch etc* soude *f*; **caustic s.** soude caustique; **washing s.** carbonate *m* de soude; **bicarbonate of s., baking s.** bicarbonate *m* de soude; **s. bread** = pain *m* levé au bicarbonate de soude; *Am* **s. cracker** biscuit *m* au bicarbonate de soude; *Am* **s. fountain** cafétéria *f*; **s. (water)** eau *f* de Seltz, soda *m*
sod-all *esp Br Sl* **1** *n* (*nothing*) que dalle; **that's got s. to do with it!** ça n'a foutrement rien à voir avec ça; **they do s. all day** ils n'en fichent pas une rame de la journée **2** *adj attrib* **I have s. money** je n'ai pas un putain de rond; **they've got s. hope of winning** ils n'ont pas une putain de chance de gagner
sodden ['sɒd(ə)n] *adj* (*field*) (dé)trempé; (*clothes etc*) trempé; **s. with drink** imbibé d'alcool
sodding ['sɒdɪŋ] *adj esp Br Sl* (*as intensifier*) **this s. weather/government/car** ce putain de temps/de gouvernement/cette putain de voiture; **you s. bastard!** enculé!
sodium ['səʊdɪəm] *n Ch* sodium *m*; **s. chloride** chlorure *m* de sodium
Sodom ['sɒdəm] *n* Sodome *f*
sodomite ['sɒdəmaɪt] *n* sodomite *m*
sodomize ['sɒdəmaɪz] *vt* sodomiser
sodomy ['sɒdəmɪ] *n* sodomie *f*
Sod's law [sɒdz] *n* loi *f* de l'emmerdement maximum
sofa ['səʊfə] *n* canapé *m*; **s. bed** canapé-lit *m*, *pl* canapés-lits
soft [sɒft] **1** *adj* **(a)** (*substance, ground, cheese etc*) mou, *f* molle; (*pillow, carpet, fabric, toilet paper etc*) doux, *f* douce, moelleux; (*rock, pencil etc*) tendre; (*hat*) mou; (*leather*) souple; **a nice s. bed** un lit moelleux; **this bed is too s.** ce lit est trop mou; **as s. as silk** doux comme de la soie; **s. to the touch** doux au toucher; **to become** *or* **get s.** s'amollir; **s. skin** peau douce *ou* veloutée; **s. mouth** (*of horse*) bouche tendre *ou* sensible; **s. shoe shuffle** = danse *f* de music-hall (*exécutée en chaussons*)

(b) (*gentle*) (*voice, music, rain, wind etc*) doux, *f* douce; (*shade, blue etc*) tendre; *Ling* **s. consonant** consonne *f* douce; *Av, Astronaut* **s. landing** atterrissage *m* en douceur; **s. light** lumière *f* douce *ou* atténuée *ou* tamisée; **s. lighting** éclairage *m* doux *ou* atténué; **s. outline** contour *m* flou; **s. step** pas feutré *ou* de loup; **s. water** eau *f* douce *ou* non calcaire; **s. words** mots doux *ou* tendres

(c) (*person*) (*not strict*) coulant; (*easy*) (*job, life etc*) tranquille; *F* **to be s. on sb** (*fond of*) être amoureux *ou* entiché de qn; (*lenient towards*) être coulant avec qn; **you mustn't be so s. with** *or* **on them** il faut les traiter plus sévèrement; **to have a s. spot for sb** avoir un faible pour qn; *F* **to be a s. touch** (*of person*) (*easy to get money from*) être facile à taper; (*easy to take advantage of*) être bonne poire; **to have a s. heart** avoir le cœur tendre; **s. option** solution *f* de facilité

(d) *F* (*stupid*) stupide, bête; **don't be s.!** ne sois pas bête!; **he's gone s. in the head!** il a perdu la boule!

(e) *Comptr, Typ* **s. hyphen** tiret *m* conditionnel; **s. page break** changement *m* conditionnel de page; **s. reset** simple réinitialisation *f*; **s. return** retour *m* de chariot conditionnel, changement *m* de ligne facultatif; **s. space** espace-ressort *m*

2 *adv F* **don't talk s.!** ne dis pas de bêtises!
softback ['sɒftbæk] *n* (livre *m* de) poche *m*; **s. version** version *f* poche
softball ['sɒftbɔ:l] *n Am Sp* = variante *f* du baseball qui se joue avec une balle plus grande et plus molle
soft-boiled *adj* (*egg*) mollet
soft copy *n Comptr* visualisation *f* sur écran
soft-core *adj* **s. pornography** pornographie *f* peu explicite, *F* soft *m*
soft-cover *n esp Am* (livre *m* de) poche *m*
soft currency *n Fin* devise *f* faible
soft drinks *npl* boissons *fpl* non alcoolisées
soft drugs *npl* drogues *fpl* douces
soften ['sɒf(ə)n] **1** *vt* (*wax etc*) ramollir; (*skin*) adoucir; (*leather*) assouplir; (*person*) (*physically*) ramollir; (*emotionally*) attendrir; (*colour*) adoucir, atténuer; (*voice, personality, water etc*) adoucir; (*light, contrast etc*) atténuer; (*one's tone*) radoucir; (*person's anger*) calmer, atténuer; **troops softened by idleness** troupes amollies par l'oisiveté; **the government has softened its stance in its talks with the unions** le gouvernement a adouci sa position lors des négociations avec les syndicats; *Fig* **to s. the blow** faire passer le choc/amortir le choc

2 *vi* (*of wax etc*) se ramollir; (*of skin etc*) s'adoucir; (*of meat*) s'attendrir; (*of person*) se radoucir; (*of anger*) se calmer; **the union's stance has softened** le syndicat a adouci sa position
▶ **soften up 1** *vtsep* **(a)** (*make softer*) adoucir **(b)** *Mil etc* (*prisoner, suspect etc*) réduire la résistance de **(c)** (*hard-hearted person*) amadouer **2** *vi* = **soften 2**
softener ['sɒf(ə)nər] *n* **water s.** adoucisseur *m* d'eau; **fabric s.** adoucissant *m*
softening ['sɒf(ə)nɪŋ] *n* (*of wax etc*) ramollissement *m*; (*of leather*) assouplissement *m*; (*of character, attitudes, water*) adoucissement *m*; (*of light, contrast, outlines*) atténuation *f*; *Hum* **he has suffered from a s. of the brain** son cerveau s'est ramolli; **there has been a s. of attitudes** il y a eu un adoucissement *ou* un fléchissement des attitudes
soft-faced hammer ['sɒftfeɪst] *n* maillet *m*
soft focus *n Phot* flou *m* artistique, point *m* diffus; *Fig* **to see things in s.** avoir une vision idéaliste du monde
soft-focus *adj Phot* **s. lens** objectif *m* pour créer des effets de flou
soft fruit *n* baies *fpl* (*comestibles*)
soft furnishings *npl Br Com* tissus *mpl* d'ameublement; (*carpets and curtains*) tapis *mpl* et rideaux
softheaded [sɒft'hedɪd] *adj F* bête, niais
softhearted *adj* au cœur tendre, sensible; **he's too s.** il a trop de cœur
softie ['sɒftɪ] *n F* = **softy**
soft loan *n Fin* prêt *m* offrant des conditions avantageuses
softly ['sɒftlɪ] *adv* (*to talk, whisper, tap etc*) doucement; (*to walk*) sans bruit; (*tenderly*) tendrement; (*to land*) en douceur; **the room is s. lit** l'éclairage de la pièce est doux; **the prisoners are treated too s.** les prisonniers ne sont pas traités assez sévèrement
softly-softly *adj* (*approach etc*) doux, *f* douce
softness ['sɒftnɪs] *n* **(a)** (*of skin, fabric, climate etc*) douceur *f* **(b)** (*of character*) mollesse *f*; (*of outlines*) flou *m* **(c)** *F* (*foolishness*) niaiserie *f*
soft(-)pedal 1 *vi* **(a)** *Mus* mettre la pédale douce **(b)** *F* (*not emphasize strongly*) y aller doucement, ne pas trop insister **2** *vt Fig* atténuer, amoindrir
soft porn *n* pornographie *f* peu explicite, *F* soft *m*; **s. film** film *m* érotique; **s. magazines** presse *f* de charme
soft-sectored ['sɒftsektəd] *adj Comptr* (*disk*) formaté par programme, à secteurs logiciels
soft sectoring ['sektərɪŋ] *n Comptr* formatage *m* logiciel
soft sell *n Com* vente *f* par des méthodes de suggestion ou de persuasion
soft shoulder *n Aut* accotement *m* non stabilisé
soft-soap *vt F* flatter, passer la pommade à
soft-spoken *adj* **to be very s.** avoir la voix très douce
soft tissue *n Anat* parties *fpl* charnues
soft-top *n Aut* décapotable *f*
soft verge *n Aut* accotement *m* non stabilisé
software ['sɒftweər] *n Comptr* logiciel *m*, software *m*; **all the s. written for …** tous les logiciels réalisés pour …; **a piece of s. that …** un logiciel qui …; **s.-controlled** contrôlé par logiciel; **s. company** fabricant *m ou* éditeur *m* de logiciels; **s. error** erreur *f* de logiciel; **s. house** éditeur *m* de logiciel; **s. package** logiciel; **s. problem** problème *m* de logiciel; **s. tool** outil *m* logiciel; **s. writer** concepteur *m* de logiciel
software-compatible *adj* compatible du point de vue logiciel
softwood ['sɒftwʊd] *n Carp etc* bois *m* tendre
softy ['sɒftɪ] *n F* (*gentle person*) cœur *m* sensible; (*coward*) couard, -arde; **to be a terrible s.** (*sentimental*) être

sentimental à l'excès; **you know I'm a big s.** (*can't say no*) tu sais que je suis trop gentil

SOGAT ['səʊgæt] *n Br abbr* **Society of Graphical and Allied Trades**

soggy ['sɒgɪ] *adj* (*ground*) détrempé, imbibé; (*clothes, carpet, shoes, bread*) trempé; (*cake*) imbibé

soh [səʊ] *n Mus* sol *m inv*

soil[1] [sɔɪl] *n* **(a)** (*earth*) terre *f*; **to cultivate the s.** cultiver la terre; **alluvial s.** terrain *m* d'alluvion(s); *Lit* **one's native s.** sa terre natale **(b)** *Old-fashioned* **night s.** (*excrement*) excréments *mpl* humains

soil[2] **1** *vt* (*clothes, sheet, underwear*) souiller, salir; **they had soiled the carpet with mud** ils avaient maculé la moquette de boue; *Fig* **to s. one's hands** se salir les mains; *Fig* **to s. sb's reputation** salir la réputation de qn **2** *vi* **fabric that soils easily** tissu salissant *ou* qui se salit facilement

soiled [sɔɪld] *adj* souillé, sali; *Fig* (*reputation*) entaché; **s. linen** linge *m* sale; **if it's s. the shop won't exchange it** si c'est sale la boutique ne fera pas l'échange; **some slightly s. items at reduced prices** des articles légèrement salis à prix réduits

soirée ['swɑːreɪ] *n* soirée *f*

soixante-neuf [swæsɑːnt'nɜːf] *n* soixante-neuf *m*

sojourn[1] ['sɒdʒɜːn] *n Lit* séjour *m*

sojourn[2] *vi Lit* séjourner

sol [sɒl] *n Mus* sol *m inv*

solace[1] ['sɒləs] *n Lit* consolation *f*, soulagement *m*; **to find s. in sth** trouver une consolation dans qch

solace[2] *vt Lit* (*person*) consoler; **I solaced myself with this thought** cette pensée m'a consolé

sola of exchange ['səʊlə] *n Fin* seule *f* de change

solar ['səʊlər] *adj* (*system, energy etc*) solaire; **s. battery** pile *f* solaire; **s. cell** pile solaire; **s. panel** panneau *m* solaire; *Anat* **s. plexus** plexus *m* solaire; **s.-powered** à énergie solaire

solarium, *pl* **-ia** [səʊ'leərɪəm, -ɪə] *n* solarium *m*

sold *see* **sell**[2]

solder[1] ['sɒldər, 'səʊldər] *n* soudure *f*

solder[2] *vt* souder

soldering ['sɒldərɪŋ, 'səʊldərɪŋ] *n* soudure *f*; **s. iron** fer *m* à souder

soldier[1] ['səʊldʒər] *n* soldat *m*, militaire *m*; **private s.** simple soldat, (soldat de) deuxième classe *m*; **when I grow up I want to be a s.** quand je serai grand je serai soldat; **an old s.** un ancien soldat, un vétéran; **s. of fortune** soldat de fortune; **tin s.** soldat de plomb; **s. ant** (fourmi *f*) soldat

soldier[2] *vi* (*be a soldier*) faire le métier de soldat

▶ **soldier on** *vi Br* (*persevere*) persévérer; **we soldiered on through the blizzard** nous avons progressé à grand peine dans le blizzard; **I'll s. on with this for another half hour** je vais encore m'escrimer là-dessus pendant une demi-heure

soldiering ['səʊldʒərɪŋ] *n* la carrière militaire *ou* des armes; **he was tired of s.** il en avait assez du métier de soldat; **to go s.** se faire soldat

soldierlike, soldierly ['səʊldʒəlaɪk, -lɪ] *adj* de soldat

soldiery ['səʊldʒərɪ] *n* (*no pl*) *Old-fashioned* (*soldiers*) soldats *mpl*, militaires *mpl*

sole[1] [səʊl] *n* (*of foot*) plante *f*; (*of shoe*) semelle *f*

sole[2] *vt* (*shoe*) (*fit with sole*) mettre une semelle à; (*resole*) ressemeler

sole[3] *n* (*fish*) sole *f*; **Dover s.** (vraie) sole

sole[4] *adj* seul, unique; (*legatee*) universel; **his s. reason** son unique raison; **s. agency** représentation *f* exclusive; **s. agency contract** contrat *m* de représentation exclusive; *Com* **s. agent** représentant *m ou* agent *m* exclusif; **s. contract** contrat *m* exclusif; **s. right** droit *m* exclusif; **s. trader** entreprise *f* unipersonnelle

solecism ['sɒlɪsɪz(ə)m] *n Ling* solécisme *m*; *Fml* (*social error*) bévue *f*

solely ['səʊllɪ] *adv* seulement, uniquement; **I went there s. to see it** j'y suis allé dans le seul but de le voir

solemn ['sɒləm] *adj* **(a)** (*oath etc*) solennel; (*duty*) sacré; (*question*) grave; *Jur* **s. agreement** contrat *m* solennel; **s. warning** avertissement *m* formel **(b)** (*person*) grave, sérieux; (*tone, atmosphere*) solennel; **to look s.** avoir l'air solennel

solemness ['sɒləmnɪs] *n* = **solemnity (a)**

solemnity [sə'lemnɪtɪ] *n* **(a)** (*of occasion, ceremony*) solennité *f*; (*of expression, attitude*) gravité *f*, sérieux *m*; **with all s.** en toute solennité **(b)** *Lit* **the solemnities** (*religious festival*) les fêtes *fpl* solennelles, les solennités *fpl*

solemnization [sɒləmnaɪ'zeɪʃən] *n* (*of marriage*) célébration *f*

solemnize ['sɒləmnaɪz] *vt* (*religious festival*) solenniser, célébrer; (*marriage*) célébrer

solemnly ['sɒləmlɪ] *adv* **(a)** (*to promise etc*) solennellement **(b)** (*seriously*) gravement; (*to speak*) avec solennité

solenoid ['sɒlənɔɪd] *n El* solénoïde *m*; **s. switch** contacteur *m* à solénoïde

solfa ['sɒlfɑː] *n Mus* **tonic s.** solfège *m*

solicit [sə'lɪsɪt] **1** *vt* **(a)** solliciter (**from sb** de qn); (*votes*) solliciter, briguer **(b)** (*of prostitute*) (*customers*) racoler **2** *vi* (*of prostitute*) racoler

solicitation [səlɪsɪ'teɪʃən] *n* sollicitation *f*

soliciting [sə'lɪsɪtɪŋ] *n Jur* (*of prostitute*) racolage *m*

solicitor [sə'lɪsɪtər] *n* **(a)** *Br Jur* = homme *m* de loi qui remplit à la fois les fonctions d'avocat et de notaire; (*for property, wills etc*) notaire *m*; (*in court cases etc*) avocat *m*; **S. General** conseiller *m* juridique de la Couronne **(b)** (*seeking trade etc*) solliciteur, -euse

solicitous [sə'lɪsɪtəs] *adj Lit* (*eager*) soucieux, désireux (**of sth** de qch); (*concerned*) préoccupé; (*caring*) plein de sollicitude; **s. attention to detail** soin méticuleux des détails

solicitously [sə'lɪsɪtəslɪ] *adv* avec sollicitude

solicitousness [sə'lɪsɪtəsnɪs], **solicitude** [sə'lɪsɪtjuːd] *n* sollicitude *f*, préoccupation *f*

solid ['sɒlɪd] **1** *adj* (*brick, stone, Fig business*) solide; (*mass, line*) compact; (*gold, silver*) massif; (*tyre*) plein; (*wall*) plein, sans ouvertures; (*in a single piece*) en une seule pièce, d'un seul tenant; *Fig* **a s. wall of demonstrators** un mur compact de manifestants; **frozen s.** (*water, pond*) gelé jusqu'au fond; *Fig* **there is s. support for the proposal** il y a une majorité de gens en faveur de la proposition; *Pol etc* **the union was s. behind him** le syndicat était tout entier derrière lui; **the town was s. for Labour** la ville a massivement voté Travailliste; **the workers were s. behind the strike** les employés étaient tous pour la grève; **s. food** nourriture *f* solide; **to become s.** (*of fluid*) se solidifier; **s. as a rock** (*ice, mud*) dur comme de la pierre; *Fig* solide comme le roc; **to build on s. foundations** bâtir sur des fondations solides; *Fig* construire sur des bases solides; **on s. ground** sur un terrain ferme; **man of s. build** homme bien charpenté; **s. common sense** solide bon sens; **to have s. reasons for believing sth** avoir de bonnes raisons de croire qch; **a good s. meal** un repas consistant; **some good s. research** des recherches bien concrètes; *Geom* **s. angle** angle *m* solide; **to sleep/work for nine s. hours** dormir/travailler neuf heures d'affilée; **three days' s. rain** trois jours de pluie continue; **s. vote** vote *m* massif

2 *n* solide *m*; **solids** (*food*) aliments *mpl* solides; **is the baby on solids yet?** le bébé mange-t-il déjà des aliments solides?

3 *adv* **to sleep/work for nine hours s.** dormir/travailler neuf heures d'affilée

solidarity [sɒlɪ'dærɪtɪ] *n* solidarité *f*; **to show s. with sb** faire preuve de solidarité envers qn; **S.** (*in Poland*) Solidarité *f*

solid fuel *n* combustible *m* solide

solidification [səlɪdɪfɪ'keɪʃən] *n* solidification *f*; (*of oil*) congélation *f*

solidify [sə'lɪdɪfaɪ] **1** *vt* **(a)** solidifier; (*oil*) congeler **(b)** *Fig* (*union, fact*) consolider **2** *vi* **(a)** se solidifier; (*of oil*) se congeler **(b)** *Fig* (*of opinions etc*) se consolider

solidity [sə'lɪdɪtɪ] *n* solidité *f*

solidly ['sɒlɪdlɪ] *adv* **(a)** solidement; (*without interruption*) sans interruption, sans s'arrêter; **s. held** tenu fermement *ou* solidement; **s. built man** homme bien charpenté **(b)** (*to vote*) massivement; **we're s. behind you** nous vous soutenons à fond

solid-state *adj* (*physics*) des solides; (*electronics, circuit, device*) à semi-conducteurs; **s. electronics** semi-conducteurs *mpl*

soliloquize [sə'lɪləkwaɪz] *vi* faire un monologue, soliloquer

soliloquy [sə'lɪləkwɪ] *n* soliloque *m*, monologue *m*

solitaire [sɒlɪ'teər] *n* **(a)** (*game with pegs etc*) solitaire *m*; *Am Cards* (jeu *m* de) patience *f*, réussite *f* **(b) s. (diamond)** solitaire *m*

solitary ['sɒlɪt(ə)rɪ] **1** *adj* solitaire; (*on one's, its own*) seul, solitaire; (*isolated*) isolé; **not a s. one** pas un seul; **s. confinement** (*in prison*) régime *m* (d'isolement) cellulaire; **to be kept in s. confinement** être détenu en régime (d'isolement) cellulaire **2** *n F* régime *m* (d'isolement) cellulaire; **he got three months' s.** il a pris trois mois de cachot

solitude ['sɒlɪtjuːd] *n* solitude *f*; **to live in s.** vivre dans la solitude

solo ['səʊləʊ] **1** *n* **(a)** *Mus* solo *m*; **violin s.** solo de violon; **s. album** album *m* solo **(b)** *Cards* **s. (whist)** whist *m* de Gand **2** *adv* **to fly s.** voler seul; *Mus* **to play s.** jouer en solo; **to go s.** *Cards* jouer seul; (*of business partner, member of rock group etc*) faire une carrière en solo **3** *adj* **s. flight** vol *m* en solo; **s. guitar** guitare *f* solo

soloist ['səʊləʊɪst] *n Mus* soliste *mf*

Solomon Islands ['sɒləmən'aɪləndz] *npl* îles *fpl* Salomon

solstice ['sɒlstɪs] *n* solstice *m*; **the winter/summer s.** le solstice d'hiver/d'été

solubility [sɒljʊ'bɪlɪtɪ] *n* (*of a salt etc*) solubilité *f*
soluble ['sɒljʊb(ə)l] *adj* **(a)** soluble (**in water** dans l'eau) **(b)** (*problem*) soluble
solution [sə'luːʃən] *n* **(a)** (*act of solving*) (*of difficulty, equation*) résolution *f*, solution *f* **(b)** (*answer*) (*to problem*) solution *f*; **there is no real s. to this** il n'y a aucune solution dans ce cas **(c)** (*fluid*) solution *f*; **salt in s.** sel *m* en solution
solvable ['sɒlvəb(ə)l] *adj* (*problem*) soluble
solve [sɒlv] *vt* (*problem, equation, riddle*) résoudre; (*mystery*) éclaircir
solvency ['sɒlvənsɪ] *n Com, Jur* solvabilité *f*
solvent ['sɒlvənt] **1** *adj* **(a)** *Com, Jur* solvable **(b)** (*liquid*) dissolvant, solvant **2** *n* dissolvant *m*, solvant *m*
solvent abuse *n* utilisation *f* de solvants hallucinogènes
solvent abuser [ə'bjuːzər] *n* toxicomane *mf* utilisant des solvants hallucinogènes
Som *abbr* **Somerset**
Somali [sə'mɑːlɪ] **1** *adj* somali, somalien **2** *n* **(a)** Somali, -ie; **the S.** (*pl*) les Somalis *mpl* **(b)** *Ling* somali *m*
Somalia [sə'mɑːlɪə] *n* Somalie *f*
Somaliland [sə'mɑːlɪlænd] *n Hist* Somalie *f*
somatic [sə'mætɪk] *adj Biol* somatique
sombre, *US* **somber** ['sɒmbər] *adj* (*colour etc*) sombre; (*person, look*) sombre, (*mood*) maussade; **to be in a s. mood** être d'humeur maussade
sombrely, *US* **somberly** ['sɒmbəlɪ] *adv* (*to look at sb etc*) d'un air sombre; **s. dressed** habillé de couleurs sombres
sombrero [sɒm'breərəʊ] *n* sombrero *m*
some [sʌm] [①**A34-35**,a; **B14-15**,B] **1** *adj* **(a)** (*not specified*) **s. (sort of an) excuse** une excuse quelconque; **he'll come s. day** il arrivera un de ces jours; **s. days she is better** certains jours elle va mieux; **s. books are difficult to read** certains livres sont difficiles à lire, il y a des livres qui sont difficiles à lire; **s. people say ...** certaines personnes disent ..., il y en a qui disent ...; **s. fool left the door open** un imbécile a laissé la porte ouverte; **s. bureaucrat decided the road would be here** un bureaucrate quelconque a décidé que la route passerait ici; **s. book or other** un livre quelconque

(b) [①**B4-5**,B] (*certain quantity, number*) de; **to drink s. water** boire de l'eau; **I ate s. fruit** j'ai mangé des fruits; **s. strange people appeared** d'étranges personnes *ou* des personnes étranges ont fait leur apparition; **s. people** des personnes; (*a few*) quelques personnes; **s. people think ...** il y a des gens qui pensent ...; **I felt s. uneasiness** je ressentais quelque inquiétude; **that would be s. help** cela faciliterait un peu les choses; **in s. measure, to s. degree** jusqu'à un certain point, dans une certaine mesure; **s. distance away** à quelque distance, à une certaine distance; **s. days ago** il y a quelques jours; **for s. time** pendant quelque temps *ou* un certain temps; **he has been waiting for s. time** il attend depuis quelque temps *ou* depuis un certain temps; **it will be s. time** *or* **s. little while before it's finished** ça va prendre un certain temps *ou* un moment avant que ça soit fini; **at s. length** assez longuement

(c) *F* (*intensive*) **(that was) s. storm!** quelle tempête!; **she's s. girl!** c'est une fille formidable!; **that was s. meal!** ce que nous avons bien mangé!, *F* ce qu'on s'est mis!; **s. people!** il y a des gens, vraiment!; **s. father you are!** quel père tu fais!

(d) *Iron* **s. hope!** quelle illusion!

2 *pron* **(a)** (*people*) certain(e)s, quelques-uns, quelques-unes; **s. or all of them** tous ou seulement certains d'entre eux; **s. believe that ...** certains croient que ..., il y en a qui croient que ...; **they went off, s. one way, s. another** ils se sont dispersés, les uns d'un côté, les autres de l'autre *ou Lit* qui d'un côté, qui de l'autre; **s. of my friends** certains de mes amis

(b) (*things, quantity*) (*referring to countable nouns*) quelques-uns, quelques-unes; (*referring to uncountable nouns*) un peu; **s. of the guests had already left** quelques invités étaient déjà partis; **s. of the money has been recovered** on a retrouvé une partie de l'argent; **I have s.** j'en ai; **give me s.** donnez-m'en; **I've s. more** (*I have some left*) j'en ai encore; (*I have some others*) j'en ai d'autres; **s. of the time** une partie du temps; **Norway has s. of the most beautiful scenery in the world** les paysages de la Norvège sont parmi les plus beaux du monde; **at least there's <u>some</u> left** (*not nothing*) il en reste quand même un peu

3 *adv* **(a)** (*approximately*) environ, quelque *inv*; **s. thirty pounds** une trentaine de livres, quelque trente livres; **s. fifteen minutes** un bon quart d'heure; **s. few minutes ago** il y a quelques minutes

(b) *Am F* (*intensive*) **to go it s.** y aller en plein; **it annoyed him s.** ça l'a plutôt énervé

somebody ['sʌmbədɪ] **1** *pron* [①**A34**,a; **B15**,2] (*some person*) quelqu'un; **s. told me so** quelqu'un *ou* on me l'a dit; **s. I know told me** quelqu'un que je connais me l'a dit; **he's not s. you can trust** ce n'est pas quelqu'un en qui on peut avoir confiance; **s. is knocking** on frappe; **s. is missing** il manque quelqu'un; **s. (or other) has told him** quelqu'un lui a dit; **is this s.'s wallet?** est-ce que ce portefeuille est à quelqu'un?; **s. important** quelqu'un d'important; **we need s. a bit taller/who speaks Russian** il nous faut quelqu'un d'un peu plus grand/qui parle russe; *F* **Mr S. (or other)** quelqu'un; **there was a Mr S. (or other) to see you** il y a M. Machin (Truc) qui voulait te voir; **s. else** quelqu'un d'autre; **he went and s. else came along** il est parti et un autre est venu

2 *pron, n* (*pl* **somebodies** ['sʌmbədɪz]) (*important person*) **he's (a) s.** c'est un personnage, ce n'est pas le premier venu; **she thinks she's s.** elle se croit quelqu'un, elle ne se prend pas pour n'importe qui; **I want to be s.** je veux être quelqu'un

someday ['sʌmdeɪ] *adv* un jour
somehow ['sʌmhaʊ] *adv* **(a)** (*in some way or other*) d'une façon ou d'une autre, d'une manière ou d'une autre; **we'll manage it s. (or other)** nous y parviendrons tant bien que mal; **s. we got there on time** nous nous sommes débrouillés pour arriver à l'heure **(b)** (*for some reason or other*) **I never liked her s.** pour une raison ou pour une autre elle ne m'a jamais été sympathique; **s. (or other) it's different** il y a pourtant une différence; **s. it doesn't seem right** je ne sais pas pourquoi mais j'ai l'impression que c'est faux
someone ['sʌmwʌn] *pron* = **somebody 1**
someplace ['sʌmpleɪs] *adv Am* = **somewhere**
somersault[1] ['sʌməsɔːlt] *n* (*on ground or accidental*) culbute *f*; (*in air*) saut *m* périlleux; **to turn** *or* **do a s.** (*on ground or accidentally*) faire la culbute; (*in air*) faire un saut périlleux; (*of car*) faire un tonneau
somersault[2] *vi* (*of person*) (*on ground or accidentally*) faire la/des culbute(s); (*in air*) faire un/des saut(s) périlleux; (*of car*) faire un/des tonneau(x); **the car somersaulted twice** la voiture a fait deux tonneaux; **he's good at somersaulting** il est doué pour les culbutes/les sauts périlleux
something ['sʌmθɪŋ] [①**A34-35**,a; **B15**,2] **1** *n, pron* **(a)** quelque chose *m*; **I've brought you a little s.** je vous ai apporté un petit quelque chose *ou* une bricole; **say s.** dites quelque chose; **s. or other** une chose ou une autre; **s. or other was bothering her** quelque chose l'ennuyait; **Anne s. (or other)** Anne je ne sais plus quoi; **there's s. about him I don't like** il y a en lui quelque chose qui me déplaît; **s. tells me she'll come** quelque chose me dit qu'elle viendra; **s. has happened** il est arrivé quelque chose; **was it s. I said?** est-ce que j'ai dit quelque chose (qu'il ne fallait pas)?; **s. to drink/eat/read** quelque chose à boire/manger/lire; **to ask for s. to drink** demander (quelque chose) à boire; **can I get you s.?** est-ce que je peux vous offrir quelque chose (à manger/à boire)?; **let's have s. to eat** mangeons quelque chose; **it must have been s. he ate that made him ill** ça doit être quelque chose qu'il a mangé qui l'a rendu malade; **s. to live for** une raison de vivre; **to have s. to cry/be annoyed about** avoir une bonne raison de pleurer/se fâcher; **to have s. to hang on to** avoir quelque chose à quoi se raccrocher; **s. new** quelque chose de nouveau *ou* de neuf; **I've s. else to do** j'ai autre chose à faire; **he's s. in a bank** il travaille dans une banque; **in the year eleven hundred and s.** en l'an onze cent et quelque chose; **she's eighty s.** elle a quatre-vingts ans et quelques, *F* elle a quatre-vingts ans et des poussières; **a certain (indefinable) s.** un je-ne-sais-quoi; **he has seen s. of the world** (*is mature, experienced*) il connaît la vie; (*has travelled*) il a pas mal voyagé; **her plan has s. in it, there's s. in her plan** son projet mérite considération; **there's s. in what you say** il y a de la vérité dans ce que vous dites; **she has s. to do with it** elle y est pour quelque chose; **it's s. to do with the way he speaks** ça a un rapport avec la façon dont il parle; **well, that's s.** c'est déjà quelque chose!; **that was quite s.!** c'était vraiment quelque chose!; **she's an accountant or s.** elle est comptable ou quelque chose comme ça; **is it broken or s.?** c'est cassé ou quoi?; **she's off work with a cold or s.** elle n'est pas venue travailler à cause d'un rhume, je crois; **he bought it from a man in a bar or s.** je crois qu'il l'a acheté à un type dans un bar

(b) there's s. of an improvement il y a une certaine amélioration; **she's s. of a miser** elle est un peu *ou* quelque peu avare

2 *adv* **(a) it looks s. like a guinea pig** ça ressemble à un cochon d'Inde; **s. like 500** 500 environ, quelque chose comme 500; **is this s. like him?** est-ce que ça lui ressemble un peu?; **s. like that** quelque chose comme ça

(b) *F* (*intensifying*) **he treated me s. shocking** il m'a traité d'une façon abominable; **he fancies her s. rotten** il en est amoureux comme pas possible

sometime ['sʌmtaɪm] **1** *adv* (*often written as two words*) **s. (or other)** un jour ou l'autre; **you'll have to make your mind up s.** tôt ou tard, il faudra que tu prennes une décision; **the last time I saw him was s. in August** la dernière fois que je l'ai vu, c'était en août; **we'll talk about it s. before/after Christmas** on en reparlera à un moment ou à un autre avant/après Noël; **I'll do it s.** je vais le faire; **I hope to go there s.** j'espère y aller un jour; **s. before 7 o'clock** avant 7 heures; **s. last year** au cours de l'année dernière; **s. in August** pendant le mois d'août; **s. before last Tuesday** avant mardi dernier; **s. between 1927 and 1931** entre 1927-1931; **s. soon** bientôt; *F* **see you s.!** à bientôt!
2 *adj attrib Lit* **Mr Martin, my s. tutor** M. Martin, autrefois mon professeur

sometimes ['sʌmtaɪmz] *adv* quelquefois, parfois; **s. one, s. the other** tantôt l'un, tantôt l'autre

somewhat ['sʌmwɒt] **1** *adv* un peu, quelque peu; **it's s. difficult** c'est assez difficile **2** *n* **he was s. of a coward** il était assez poltron; **this was s. of a relief** ce fut, en quelque sorte, un soulagement

somewhere ['sʌmweər] *adv* **(a)** (*in or to some place*) quelque part; **it's s. in the Bible** cela se trouve quelque part dans la Bible; **s. near us** pas bien loin de nous; **s. along the way** sur le chemin, quelque part en chemin; **now we're getting s.!** voilà un premier résultat!, enfin nous avançons!; **I need s. quiet to work** j'ai besoin d'un endroit calme pour travailler; **s. in the world** quelque part (dans le monde); **s. in France** quelque part en France; **s. else** ailleurs, autre part; **s. or other** je ne sais où; **he lives s. near Oxford** il habite dans les environs d'Oxford
(b) (*approximately*) **he is s. around fifty** il a à peu près cinquante ans; **it costs s. in the region of £500** cela coûte environ 500 livres; **there were s. around 50 kilobytes left** il restait environ 50 kilo-octets

sommelier ['sɒməljeɪ] *n* sommelier *m*

somnambulism [sɒm'næmbjʊlɪz(ə)m] *n* somnambulisme *m*

somnambulist [sɒm'næmbjʊlɪst] *n* somnambule *mf*

somniferous [sɒm'nɪfərəs] *adj* somnifère, soporifique; *Fig* soporifique

somnolence ['sɒmnələns] *n Fml* somnolence *f*

somnolent ['sɒmnələnt] *adj Fml* somnolent

son [sʌn] *n* fils *m*; *Am* **s. of a bitch** (*obnoxious person*) fils de pute, salaud *m*; *Am F* **s. of a gun** coquin *m*; **the S. of God** le fils de Dieu; **the S. of Man** le fils de l'homme; *Fig* **a s. of the people** un fils du peuple; **OK, s.?** (*lad*) OK, mon petit gars?

sonar ['səʊnɑːr] *n Naut* sonar *m*

sonata [sə'nɑːtə] *n Mus* sonate *f*

sonatina [sɒnə'tiːnə] *n Mus* sonatine *f*

sonde [sɒnd] *n Met etc* sonde *f*

son et lumière [sɒneɪ'luːmjeər] *n* spectacle *m* son et lumière, son et lumière *m*

song [sɒŋ] *n* **(a)** chanson *f*, *Lit* chant *m*; *Rel* cantique *m*; **marching s.** chanson de route; **give us a s.** chantez-nous quelque chose; *F* **to buy sth for a s.** acheter qch pour rien *ou* pour une bouchée de pain; *F* **it went for a s.** cela s'est vendu pour une bouchée de pain; *F* **he made a great s. and dance about it** il en a fait tout un plat; *Lit* **s. of victory** chant de victoire; **s. of praise** *Lit* louanges *fpl*; *Rel* cantique *m*; *Lit* **with a s. in one's heart** la joie au cœur, le cœur léger; *Bible* **the S. of Songs, the S. of Solomon** le Cantique des Cantiques; **s. book** recueil *m* de chansons, chansonnier *m*; **a festival of French s.** un festival de la chanson française *F* **to be on s.** (*of engine*) tourner rond; (*of team*) être en bonne forme
(b) (*singing*) chant *m*; **to burst** *or* **break into s.** se mettre à chanter; **the s. of the birds** le chant *ou* le ramage des oiseaux

songbird ['sɒŋbɜːd] *n* oiseau *m* chanteur

songster ['sɒŋstər] *n* **(a)** (*singer*) chanteur *m* **(b)** (*poet*) poète *m*, chantre *m* **(c)** = **songbird**

songstress ['sɒŋstrɪs] *n* (*singer*) chanteuse *f*

songwriter ['sɒŋraɪtər] *n Mus* (*writes the music*) compositeur, -trice (de chansons); (*writes the words*) parolier *m*; (*writes both*) auteur-compositeur *m*

sonic ['sɒnɪk] *adj Phys* acoustique, audible; *Av* (*speed*) sonique; **s. boom** bang *m*

son-in-law *n* gendre *m*, beau-fils *m*, *pl* beaux-fils

sonnet ['sɒnɪt] *n* (*in poetry*) sonnet *m*

sonny ['sʌnɪ] *n F* mon petit gars *m*, fiston *m*; **look here, s. Jim** *or* **boy** attention, mon petit gars

sonority [sə'nɒrɪtɪ] *n* sonorité *f*

sonorous ['sɒnərəs] *adj* sonore; **s. voice** voix sonore *ou* timbrée

sonorously ['sɒnərəslɪ] *adv* (*to speak*) d'une voix sonore; **the organ boomed s.** l'orgue résonnait

sonorousness ['sɒnərəsnɪs] *n* sonorité *f*

soon [suːn] *adv* [ⓘA23,3,a,ii] **(a)** (*within a short time*) bientôt; **how s. can you get here?** combien de temps vous faut-il pour y aller?; **s. after** peu après; **s. after four** (un) peu après quatre heures; **it will s. be three years since ...** voici bientôt trois ans que ..., cela fera bientôt trois ans que ...; **he'll be here very s.** il sera ici sous peu, il sera ici très bientôt; **must you leave so s.?** vous faut-il partir si tôt?; **too s.** trop tôt, avant l'heure; **an hour too s.** (*to arrive etc*) avec une heure d'avance; **they were s. making friends** ils se sont bien vite fait des amis; **it ended all too s.** cela a fini bien trop tôt; **none too s.** juste à temps
(b) [ⓘB29-30,11] **as s. as** aussitôt que, dès que; **I'll see him as s. as he comes** je le verrai aussitôt *ou* dès qu'il arrivera; **as s. as I arrived in London** dès mon arrivée à Londres; **as s. as he saw them** dès qu'il les a vus; **as s. as possible** le plus tôt possible, aussitôt que possible, dès que possible
(c) sooner (*earlier*) plus tôt; **we would have got there sooner, if ...** nous serions arrivés plus tôt, si ...; **the sooner you begin the sooner you will have finished** plus tôt vous commencerez plus vite vous aurez fini; **the problem should be dealt with sooner rather than later** il faut faire face au problème le plus tôt possible; **the sooner the better** le plus tôt sera le mieux; **sooner or later** tôt ou tard; **no sooner said than done** (aus)sitôt dit, (aus)sitôt fait; **no sooner had he finished than he was arrested** à peine eut-il fini qu'il fut arrêté
(d) (*preference*) **I would just as s. stay** j'aime autant rester; **I would die sooner than give in** je mourrais plutôt que de céder; **I would sooner die** j'aimerais mieux mourir; **someone will have to do it – sooner you than me!** quelqu'un devra le faire – il vaudrait mieux que ce soit vous, plutôt que moi
(e) soonest (*to do sth*) aussitôt que possible; **it will be next week at the soonest** ce sera la semaine prochaine au plus tôt; *Prov* **least said soonest mended** moins on en dit, mieux ça vaut

soot [sʊt] *n* suie *f*

sooth [suːθ] *n Arch* **in s.** en vérité

soothe [suːð] *vt* (*pain, burn etc*) calmer, apaiser; (*the mind*) tranquilliser; (*person*) apaiser; **to s. sb's anger** apaiser la colère de qn

▸ **soothe down** *vtsep* (*make less angry, worried*) (*person*) calmer

soothing ['suːðɪŋ] *adj* calmant, apaisant; *Med* lénitif; **in a s. voice** d'une voix apaisante

soothingly ['suːðɪŋlɪ] *adv* (*to say*) d'un ton apaisant

soothsayer ['suːθseɪər] *n Arch* devin *m*, devineresse *f*

soothsaying ['suːθseɪɪŋ] *n Arch* divination *f*

sooty ['sʊtɪ] *adj* **(a)** (*covered in soot*) couvert de suie; (*black*) noir de suie **(b)** (*deposit*) de suie; (*ressembling soot*) fuligineux

sop¹ [sɒp] *n* **(a)** (*bread*) morceau *m* de pain trempé **(b)** *Lit* (*concession*) concession *f*; **as a s. to his conscience** pour soulager sa conscience; **he just said that as a s. to her feelings** il a dit ça seulement pour lui plaire *ou* (*if she is angry etc*) pour l'amadouer; **a concession that was not much more than a s. to the unions** une concession qui n'avait pour but que d'amadouer les syndicats

sop² *vt* (**-pp-**) (*bread*) (faire) tremper

▸ **sop up** *vtsep* (*mop up*) (*liquid*) éponger; **the paper towel sopped up the water** l'essuie-tout a absorbé toute l'eau

sophism ['sɒfɪz(ə)m] *n* sophisme *m*

sophist ['sɒfɪst] *n* sophiste *mf*

sophistical [sə'fɪstɪk(ə)l] *adj* sophistique, captieux

sophisticate [sə'fɪstɪkɪt] *n* personne *f* sophistiquée

sophisticated [sə'fɪstɪkeɪtɪd] *adj* (*person*) sophistiqué; (*in matters of food, wine, conversation, tastes etc*) raffiné; (*style*) recherché, sophistiqué; (*plan*) subtil; (*machinery*) (très) perfectionné; (*technology*) sophistiqué; **for the s. look this winter ...** si vous voulez être élégante cet hiver ...; **our more s. readers** nos lecteurs les plus cultivés; **teenagers think it's very s. to ...** les adolescents pensent que ça fait très bien de ...

sophistication [səfɪstɪ'keɪʃən] *n* (*of person*) (*appearance*) raffinement *m*, sophistication *f*; (*tastes*) goûts *mpl* raffinés; (*of style, dress*) recherche *f*; (*of machinery*) (degré *m* de) perfectionnement *m*

sophistry ['sɒfɪstrɪ] *n* **(a)** (*reasoning*) sophistique *f*; **to indulge in s.** se laisser aller à la sophistique **(b)** (*example*) sophisme *m*

Sophocles ['sɒfəkliːz] *n* Sophocle *m*

sophomore ['sɒfəmɔːr] *n Am Univ* étudiant, -ante de seconde année; **I'm a s.** je suis en deuxième année (de fac)

soporific [sɒpə'rɪfɪk] **1** *adj* somnifère, soporifique **2** *n* somnifère *m*

soppiness ['sɒpɪnɪs] *n Br F* (*sentimentality*) sentimentalisme *m*, sensiblerie *f*

sopping ['sɒpɪŋ] *adj* trempé; **s. wet** tout trempé; (*person*) trempé jusqu'aux os

soppy ['sɒpɪ] *adj Br F* **(a)** (*sentimental*) (*person*) gnangnan *inv*; (*sentiment*) fadasse; (*story, film etc*) à l'eau de rose **(b)** (*silly*) stupide, bête; **don't be s.!** ne sois pas si bête!

soprano, *pl* **-os, -i** [sə'prɑːnəʊ, -əʊz, -iː] *n Mus* (*singer*) soprano *mf, pl* soprani, sopranos; **s. voice** voix *f* de soprano

sorb [sɔːb] *n* **(a) s. (apple)** (*fruit*) sorbe *f* **(b) s. (tree)** sorbier *m*

sorbet ['sɔːbeɪ] *n Culin* (*water ice*) sorbet *m*

sorbitol ['sɔːbɪtɒl] *n* sorbitol *m*

sorcerer ['sɔːs(ə)rər] *n* sorcier *m*

sorceress ['sɔːs(ə)rɪs] *n* sorcière *f*

sorcery ['sɔːs(ə)rɪ] *n* sorcellerie *f*

sordid ['sɔːdɪd] *adj* sordide; (*place etc*) sale, crasseux; (*business, motives*) bas, vil

sordidly ['sɔːdɪdlɪ] *adv* sordidement

sordidness ['sɔːdɪdnɪs] *n* sordidité *f*; (*of place etc*) saleté *f*; (*of business, motives*) bassesse *f*

sore[1] [sɔːr] *adj* **(a)** (*painful*) douloureux, endolori; (*eyes, throat, gums*) irrité; **s. to the touch** douloureux au toucher; **s. throat** mal *m* de gorge; **I've (got) a s. throat** j'ai mal à la gorge, j'ai la gorge irritée; **to have a s. finger** avoir mal au doigt; **it's still s.** ça fait toujours mal; *Fig* **it's a s. point** *or* **subject with him** il est très sensible sur ce point

(b) *esp Am F* (*annoyed*) embêté (**about** au sujet de); (*upset*) chagriné (**about** par); **Mom's s. because I forgot her birthday** Maman a de la peine parce que j'ai oublié son anniversaire

(c) *Am F* (*angry*) en rogne; **to be** *or* **get s.** se ficher en rogne

(d) *Lit* **to be in s. need of sth** avoir grandement besoin de qch; **s. trial** cruelle épreuve

sore[2] *n Med* plaie *f*; *Fig* **to (re)open an old s.** raviver une plaie ancienne; **(running) s.** ulcère *m*

sorehead ['sɔːhed] *n esp Am F* ronchon, -onne

sorely ['sɔːlɪ] *adv* **(a)** *Lit* **s. wounded** gravement *ou* grièvement blessé **(b)** (*greatly*) gravement, grandement; **s. distressed** dans une grande *ou* profonde détresse; **s. needed** dont on a grandement besoin; **s. tempted** fortement tenté; **s. tried** cruellement éprouvé

soreness ['sɔːnɪs] *n Med* douleur *f*

sorghum ['sɔːgəm] *n* (*plant*) sorg(h)o *m*

sorrel[1] ['sɒrəl] *n* (*plant*) oseille *f*

sorrel[2] **1** *adj* (*horse*) alezan **2** *n* (*colour, horse*) alezan *m*

sorrow[1] ['sɒrəʊ] *n* douleur *f*, chagrin *m*; **to my s.** à mon (grand) regret; **more in s. than in anger** avec plus de tristesse que de colère; *Bible* **the Man of Sorrows** l'Homme *m* de douleur

sorrow[2] *vi esp Lit* s'affliger, être affligé (**over** *or* **at** *or* **about sth** de qch); **to s. for** *or* **after sb/sth** pleurer qn/qch

sorrowful ['sɒrəfʊl] *adj* (*person*) triste, affligé, chagriné; (*news, situation*) triste, attristant; **s. look** regard attristé *ou* désolé

sorrowfully ['sɒrəfəlɪ] *adv* tristement

sorrowing ['sɒrəʊɪŋ] *adj* affligé

sorry ['sɒrɪ] *adj* **(a)** (*regretful*) fâché, chagriné, désolé (**about sth** de qch); **she's s. she did it** *or* **for having done it** elle regrette de l'avoir fait; **to be s. not to have done sth** regretter *ou* avoir du regret de ne pas avoir fait qch; **I'm only s. we couldn't have stayed longer** je regrette que nous n'ayons pas pu rester plus longtemps; *F* **you'll be s.!** il vous en cuira, vous vous en repentirez; **you'll be s. you ever came here!** vous allez regretter d'être venu ici!; **I'll make him s.** je le lui ferai regretter; **I'll make him s. (that) he ever came here** je lui ferai regretter d'être venu ici; **I'm s. I ever let him in the house** je regrette de l'avoir laissé entrer dans la maison; **I'm (very) s. to hear that …** je regrette (infiniment) que …, je suis désolé d'apprendre que …; **you won't be s. you bought a …** vous ne regretterez pas d'avoir acheté un …; **I'm s. to say that …** je regrette d'avoir à vous dire que …; **I'm so s. to keep you waiting** excusez-moi de vous faire attendre; **(I'm) s.!** pardon!, excusez-moi!; **s.?** (*what?*) pardon?; **s., did you really mean what you said earlier?** à propos, parliez-vous sérieusement tout à l'heure?; **I'm s., but that's crap!** je suis désolé, mais c'est de la merde!; **so s.!** vraiment désolé; **s., I can't help** désolé, je ne peux rien pour vous; **to feel s. for sb** (*take pity on*) avoir pitié de qn; (*feel sympathy for*) plaindre qn; **I'm s. for him** (*I feel pity for him*) il me fait pitié; (*I sympathize with him*) je le plains; **to look s. for oneself** faire grise mine; **he's just feeling s. for himself** il s'apitoie sur son sort; **once you've stopped feeling s. for yourself** une fois que tu auras fini de te plaindre; **I'm just feeling a bit s. for myself** je suis un peu déprimé; **I don't usually feel this s. for myself** d'habitude, je ne me laisse pas aller comme ça; **to say one is s. (for sth)** demander pardon (pour qch); **say s. to the lady** (*to child*) demande pardon à la dame

(b) (*pitiful*) misérable, piteux; **to be in a s. plight** être dans une mauvaise passe; **to be in a s. state** être dans un piteux état; **to cut a s. figure** faire piètre figure; **it was/they were a s. sight** c'était/ils offraient un spectacle navrant; **the whole s. tale** toute cette malheureuse affaire

sort[1] [sɔːt] *n* **(a)** [①A13,3,a] (*kind*) sorte *f*, genre *m*, espèce *f*; **all sorts of people** des gens de toutes sortes; **it takes all sorts (to make a world)** il faut de tout (pour faire un monde); **what s. of tree is it?** quelle sorte d'arbre est-ce?; **what s. of day did you have?** comment s'est passée ta journée?; **what s. of a man is he?** quelle sorte d'homme est-ce?; **she's not the s. to give in easily** elle n'est pas du genre à abandonner facilement; **I know your s.!** je connais les gens comme toi!; *F* **she's a good s.** c'est une fille sympa; **we don't want your s. here** nous ne voulons pas de gens comme vous ici; **this** *or F* **these s. of people** les gens de cette espèce, ces gens-là; **you get all sorts at these parties** on rencontre toutes sortes de gens dans ces soirées; **I've heard all sorts of things about him** j'en ai entendu de toutes les couleurs sur son compte; **I can't stand that s. of thing** je ne peux pas souffrir ce genre de chose; **something of the s.** *or* **of that s.** quelque chose de pareil *ou* de semblable *ou* dans ce genre-là; **nothing of the s.** (*not in the least*) pas du tout!; **he's a liar – he's nothing of the s.!** c'est un menteur – pas du tout!; **I've a s. of feeling that …** j'ai comme l'impression que …; **the trees formed a s. of arch** les arbres formaient comme une arche; **that's my s. of holiday** voilà des vacances comme je les aime; *Pej* **coffee of a s.** du soi-disant café; **a peace of sorts** une paix, si l'on peut dire; **he is some s. of writer** il est écrivain mais je ne sais pas quel genre de livres il écrit; *Pej* **a writer of sorts** un écrivaillon; **to make some s. of (a) reply** répondre d'une façon quelconque *ou* tant bien que mal; **to be out of sorts** (*a little unwell*) être mal fichu, ne pas être dans son assiette; (*in a bad mood*) être de mauvaise humeur

(b) *F* (*used adverbially*) **s. of** (*a bit*) plutôt, un peu; (*in a way*) d'une certaine façon; **it's s. of heavy** c'est un peu lourd, c'est plutôt lourd; **I s. of feel that …** j'ai dans l'idée que …, j'ai comme l'impression que …; **I s. of expected it** je m'en doutais un peu; **it's getting s. of late** il se fait tard, quoi; **did he say sorry? – s. of** il s'est excusé? – en quelque sorte; **he s. of apologized** d'une certaine façon, il s'est excusé

(c) *Old-fashioned* (*manner*) **in this s.** de cette manière *ou* façon; **in some s.** en quelque sorte, d'une certaine manière

(d) (*order*), *Comptr* tri *m*; **to have a quick s. through the mail** faire un tri rapide du courrier, trier rapidement le courrier; **to do a s.** trier; *Comptr* **s. routine** routine *f* de tri

sort[2] **1** *vt* (*make selection from*) (*sth*) faire le tri de; (*put together*) assortir; (*papers etc*) classer; *Comptr* trier; **to s. the letters** (*in post office*) trier les lettres; **to s. things into categories** classer des choses par catégories; **s. these documents into piles** triez ces documents et faites-en des piles; **it's the kind of drink that sorts the men from the boys** c'est une boisson d'hommes; **situations like this s. the men from the boys** des situations comme celle-ci vous permettent de voir qui est un homme

2 *vi Comptr* trier; (*of file, data*) se trier; **s. on this field to a new file** trier à partir de ce champ et sauvegarder les données réordonnées dans un nouveau fichier

▶ **sort out** *vtsep* **(a)** (*eliminate by sorting*) trier, sélectionner; **to s. out the foreign stamps from the British ones** séparer les timbres étrangers des timbres britanniques

(b) (*organize*) (*papers, desk etc*) mettre de l'ordre dans; **it's time she sorted herself out** il est temps qu'elle se reprenne; **give me a few minutes to get (myself) sorted out** *or* **to s. myself out** (*on arrival in office, at home etc*) donnez-moi quelques minutes pour souffler; (*arrange papers for meeting etc*) donnez-moi quelques minutes pour m'organiser; **to s. out who's sleeping where** décider qui dort où; **to s. out a room/some clothes for sb** (*allocate*) préparer une chambre/des vêtements pour qn; **I'll go and s. the tickets out** (*make arrangements for, obtain*) je vais m'occuper des billets; **I've sorted out the tickets** j'ai tout arrangé en ce qui concerne les billets

(c) (*establish, clarify*) **we never sorted out what really happened** nous n'avons jamais compris ce qui s'était vraiment passé; **let's s. out how much we owe you** voyons combien nous vous devons; **to s. out the details** mettre au clair les détails; **you've got to s. out your priorities** il faut que tu définisses ce qui prime pour toi

(d) *F* (*deal with*) (*problem*) régler; (*difficult person*) régler son compte à; **everything's sorted out now** tout est arrangé *ou* réglé maintenant; **two aspirins ought to s. out that headache** deux aspirines devraient avoir raison de ce mal de tête

▶ **sort through** *vipo* (*search among*) (*old clothes, papers etc*) faire un *ou* le tri dans; **to s. through the mail** dépouiller le courrier

sorta ['sɔːtə] *F* = **sort of**

sort code *n Banking* numéro *m* d'agence

sorter ['sɔːtər] *n* **(a)** (*person*) trieur, -euse; (*who classifies*) classeur, -euse **(b)** (*device*) machine *f* trieuse; (**letter**) **s.** trieur *m* de lettres

sortie ['sɔːtiː] *n Mil, Av etc* sortie *f*; **I make the occasional s. to the shops** de temps en temps, je vais faire un tour dans les magasins

sorting ['sɔːtɪŋ] *n* triage *m*, tri *m*; (*classifying*) classement *m*; *Comptr* tri; *Comptr* **s. algorithm** algorithme *m* de tri; **s. office** (*in post office*) bureau *m ou* centre *m* de tri

SOS [esəʊ'es] *n* SOS *m*; **to send (out) an S.** envoyer un SOS; *Fig* **relief organizations are sending out an S. for food and clothing** les organisations d'aide demandent d'urgence de la nourriture et des vêtements; **S. call** appel *m* de détresse

sot [sɒt] *n* ivrogne *m*

sottish ['sɒtɪʃ] *adj* (*person*) abruti par l'alcool; (*behaviour*) d'ivrogne

sotto voce [sɒtəʊ'vəʊtʃɪ] *adv* (*to speak*) tout bas

soufflé ['suːfleɪ] *n Culin* soufflé *m*; **cheese/spinach s.** soufflé au fromage/aux épinards; **s. dish** moule *m* à soufflé

sough[1] [saʊ] *n Lit* (*of wind*) murmure *m*

sough[2] *vi Lit* (*of wind*) murmurer

sought *see* **seek**

sought-after *adj* (*job, car etc*) recherché; **much s.** très recherché

soul [səʊl] *n* **(a)** (*spirit*) âme *f*; **to throw oneself body and s. into sth** se donner corps et âme à qch; *Old-fashioned* **upon my s.!** sur mon âme!; **he's the s. of discretion** il est la discrétion même; **departed souls** les âmes des trépassés *ou* des disparus; **to pray for sb's s.** prier pour l'âme de qn; **to sell one's s.** vendre son âme; *Fig* **this music's/drama's got no s.** cette musique/ce théâtre n'a pas d'âme; **God rest her s.!** que Dieu ait son âme!; **All Souls' Day** la Fête des Morts

(b) (*person*) âme *f*; **population of two thousand souls** population de deux mille âmes; **without meeting a (living) s.** sans rencontrer âme qui vive; **there wasn't a s. in the street** il n'y avait pas un chat dans la rue; **I promise I won't tell a s.** je promets que je ne le dirai à personne; **he's a good s.** c'est une bonne âme; **she's a happy s.** elle a un tempérament heureux *ou* optimiste; **poor s.!** le/la pauvre!; **poor little s.!** pauvre petit(e)!

(c) s. (music) soul *f*, soul music *f*; *esp US* **s. brother/sister** frère *m*/sœur *f*; **s. food** = nourriture *f* traditionnelle des Noirs américains; **s. singer** chanteur, -euse de soul

soul-destroying ['səʊldɪstrɔɪɪŋ] *adj* (*job etc*) abrutissant, d'une monotonie mortelle

soulful ['səʊlfʊl] *adj* (*with deep feeling*) tendre; (*music*) qui touche l'âme

soulfully ['səʊlfəlɪ] *adv* (*to sing*) tendrement; *Pej* (*sentimentally*) avec sensiblerie

soulless ['səʊllɪs] *adj* **(a)** (*person*) sans âme **(b)** (*job*) abrutissant

soullessly ['səʊllɪslɪ] *adv* sans émotion; **the house had been s. renovated** on a rénové la maison sans aucune sensibilité

soullessness ['səʊllɪsnɪs] *n* (*of person*) manque *m* de sensibilité; (*of building*) côté *m* inhumain; **the s. of my surroundings** le décor inhumain qui est le mien

soulmate ['səʊlmeɪt] *n* âme *f* sœur

soul-searching *n* examen *m* de conscience; **after a lot of s.** après un profond examen de conscience

soul-stirring *adj* émouvant

sound[1] [saʊnd] *n Phys, Mus etc* son *m*; (*of door, car engine, wind etc*) bruit *m*; **the device recognizes the s. of your voice** l'appareil reconnaît le son de votre voix; **the s. of one's own voice** le son de sa (propre) voix; **he likes (listening to) the s. of his own voice** il aime s'écouter parler; **there was not a s. to be heard** on n'entendait pas le moindre bruit; **no s. escaped his lips** pas un son ne sortait de ses lèvres; **not a s. could be heard** le silence était total; **the s. of a dog barking/a door closing** le bruit d'un chien qui aboie/d'une porte qui se ferme; **every violin has its own s.** chaque violon a sa propre sonorité; **within (the) s. of ...** à portée du son de ...; *TV etc* **to turn up/turn down the s.** augmenter/diminuer le volume; **I don't like the s. of it** cela ne me dit rien qui vaille; **he's angry by the s. of it** on dirait bien qu'il est fâché; *F* **today's sounds** (*music*) les sons d'aujourd'hui; **it has a 60's s. to it** ça ressemble à la musique des années 60; **s. archives** phonothèque *f*, archives *fpl* sonores; **s. balance engineer** ingénieur *m* du son; **s. detector** (*of missile*) détecteur *m* par le son; **s. generator** générateur *m* de son; **s. hole** (*of violin*) ouïe *f*, esse *f*; (*of guitar*) ouïe; **s. level** niveau *m* sonore; **s. logo** logo *m* sonore; **s. mixer** table *f ou* console *f* de mixage; **s. recording** enregistrement *m* du son, enregistrement sonore; **s. reel** bande *f* son; **s. studio** auditorium *m ou* studio *m* d'enregistrement

sound[2] **1** *vi* **(a)** (*make sound*) sonner, résonner; (*resound*) retentir; **the trumpet sounded** la trompette retentît *ou* sonna

(b) (*seem*) paraître, sembler, avoir l'air; **name that sounds French** nom qui sonne français; **she sounds French** elle a l'air d'être française; **the translation still sounds a bit French** la traduction sonne toujours un peu français; **that sounds like trouble!** voilà les ennuis!; **he sounds like my kind of guy** c'est le genre de type avec qui je m'entendrais; **you s. like the kind of person we're looking for** je crois que vous êtes la personne qu'il nous faut; **it still sounds a bit wrong** (*of words, music*) ça sonne encore un peu faux; **that sounds odd!** cela paraît bizarre!; **what about an omelette? – that sounds good!** que dirais-tu d'une omelette? – bonne idée!; **'attractive four-bedroomed house', how does that s.?** 'belle maison avec quatre chambres à coucher', qu'est-ce que tu en penses?; **their suggestion sounds interesting** leur suggestion semble intéressante; **how does that s. to you?** (*referring to suggestion*) qu'est-ce que tu en dis?; **she sounded interested/happy** elle semblait intéressée/heureuse; **the noise sounded a long way off** le bruit semblait venir de loin; **it sounds like Mozart** on dirait du Mozart; **he doesn't s. like a man to ...** d'après ce que vous dites il ne serait pas homme à ...

2 *vt* **(a)** (*trumpet, retreat*) sonner; (*the alert, the alarm*) donner; *Aut* **to s. one's horn** klaxonner; *Lit* **to s. sb's praises** chanter les louanges de qn

(b) (*pronounce*) (*letter*) prononcer; **the h is not sounded** l'h ne se prononce pas *ou* est muet

(c) *Med* (*person, person's chest*) ausculter; **he sounded my chest** il m'a ausculté

sound[3] *n Med* (*probe*) sonde *f*

sound[4] **1** *vt* **(a)** *Naut, Med* sonder **(b) to s. public opinion** sonder l'opinion publique **2** *vi* (*of whale*) plonger au fond

sound[5] *n* (*channel*) détroit *m*, bras *m* de mer

sound[6] **1** *adj* **(a)** (*lungs, foundations*) sain; (*wood*) sans tare; (*bridge, engine*) (*in good condition*) en bon état; (*not damaged*) non endommagé; **s. in body and mind** sain de corps et d'esprit; **of s. mind** sain d'esprit; *F* **to be s. in wind and limb** (*of person*) avoir bon pied bon œil; **I'm as s. as a bell** je suis en parfaite santé

(b) (*argument, knowledge, basis*) solide; (*reason, reasoning*) valable; (*policy etc*) sage; (*investment*) sûr, solide, fiable; (*goalkeeper, manager, musician, lawyer etc*) bon, fiable; **ecologically s. legislation** législation juste du point de vue écologique; **s. doctrine** doctrine saine; *Rel* (*orthodox*) doctrine orthodoxe; **a s. piece of advice** un bon conseil; **s. financial position** situation financière saine; **s. business** entreprise saine *ou* solide; **he's pretty s. on his grammar** il a de bonnes bases en grammaire; **it makes good s. sense** c'est tout à fait raisonnable

(c) a s. sleep un sommeil profond; **I'm a s. sleeper** je dors bien; **to give sb a s. thrashing** administrer une bonne correction à qn

2 *adv* **to be s. asleep** être profondément endormi, dormir à poings fermés

▶ **sound off** *vi F* (*express opinions forcefully, complain*) **to s. off about sth** faire de grands laïus sur qch; **to s. off at sb** engueuler qn; **she's always sounding off about rude shop assistants** elle est toujours en train de se plaindre des vendeuses peu aimables

▶ **sound out** *vtsep* (*ascertain opinion, allegiance of*) (*person*) sonder

sound barrier *n Av* mur *m* du son

soundbite ['saʊndbaɪt] *n* petite phrase *f*

sound board *n* (*of piano*) table *f* d'harmonie; (*of organ*) tamis *m*; (*of pulpit*) abat-voix *m inv*

sound box *n* (*of string instrument*) caisse *f* de résonance; (*of record player*) diaphragme *m*

sound check *n* soundcheck *m*

sound effects *npl* effets *mpl* sonores, bruitage *m*; **s. man** bruiteur *m*

sound engineer *n* ingénieur *m* du son,

sounder ['saʊndər] *n Naut* sondeur *m*

sounding[1] ['saʊndɪŋ] *n Mil* **the s. of the retreat** le signal de la retraite

sounding[2] *n* **(a)** *Naut* (*act*) sondage *m*; **echo s.** sondage par ultra-sons **(b)** *Naut* **soundings** (*measurements*) sondages *mpl*; (*bottom*) fonds *mpl*; **to take soundings** sonder, prendre le fond; *Fig* sonder

sounding board *n* (*of pulpit etc*) abat-voix *m inv*; (*of piano*) table *f* d'harmonie; (*of organ*) tamis *m*; *Fig* **to use sb as a s.** tester ses idées sur qn

sounding lead [led] *n* (plomb *m* de) sonde *f*
sounding line *n* (ligne *f* de) sonde *f*
soundless ['saʊndlɪs] *adj* muet, silencieux
soundlessly ['saʊndlɪslɪ] *adv* silencieusement, sans bruit
soundly ['saʊndlɪ] *adv* **(a)** (*solidly*) solidement **(b)** (*to reason*) sainement; (*wisely*) judicieusement; **to invest s.** investir dans des valeurs sûres; **he argued s.** son argumentation était solide **(c)** (*to sleep*) profondément; **to thrash sb s.** (*with stick etc*) administrer une bonne correction à qn; *Sp* **we were s. beaten** nous avons été battus à plate(s) couture(s)
soundness ['saʊndnɪs] *n* **(a)** (*of merchandise, mind etc*) bon état *m*; (*of company*) solidité *f*; (*solvency*) solvabilité *f* **(b)** (*of argument, reasoning, decision etc*) validité *f*; (*of judgment*) justesse *f*; (*of advice, policy*) sagesse *f*; (*of doctrine*) orthodoxie *f*
soundproof[1] ['saʊndpruːf] *adj* (*room etc*) insonorisé; (*material*) insonore; **s. hood** capot *m* antibruit
soundproof[2] *vt* (*room etc*) insonoriser
soundproofing ['saʊndpruːfɪŋ] *n* (*material*) matériau *m* isolant *ou* insonore; (*act*) insonorisation *f*
sound system *n* système *m* audio
soundtrack ['saʊndtræk] *n Cin* bande *f ou* piste *f* sonore; **s. (album)** (*record etc*) bande originale
sound wave *n Phys* onde *f* sonore
soup [suːp] *n* soupe *f*; (*thin*) potage *m*; **onion/fish s.** soupe à l'oignon/de poisson; *Fig F* **to be in the s.** être dans le pétrin; *Fig F* **to land sb in the s.** mettre qn dans le pétrin; **s. ladle** louche *f*; **s. plate** assiette *f* creuse; **s. spoon** cuillère *f* à soupe; **s. tureen** soupière *f*
▶ **soup up** *vtsep F* (*car, engine*) gonfler
soupçon ['suːpsɒn] *n* (*of garlic, sarcasm*) soupçon *m*, pointe *f*
souped-up ['suːptʌp] *adj F* gonflé; **a s. job** (*car, motorcycle*) une bagnole/une moto au moteur gonflé
soup kitchen *n* soupe *f* populaire
sour[1] ['saʊər] *adj* **(a)** (*fruit etc*) aigre, acide; (*milk, cream, bread etc*) aigre; (*wine*) suret, verjuté; (*soil*) acide; **to turn s.** (*of food*) (s')aigrir, surir; *Fig* (*of situation, relationship*) tourner à l'aigre; *F* tourner au vinaigre; **to turn sth s.** (faire) aigrir qch; **to smell s.** sentir l'aigre; *Fig* **the plan went s. on him** (*went wrong*) le projet a mal tourné pour lui; *Fig* **s. grapes** rancœur *f*; **it was just s. grapes that made her say that** elle a simplement dit ça par rancœur **(b)** (*person*) revêche, aigre; **he's s. about being left out** il est amer parce qu'on l'a laissé à l'écart
sour[2] **1** *vi* surir, (s')aigrir; **her temper has soured** son caractère s'est aigri **2** *vt* (*milk, character etc*) aigrir; *Culin* **soured cream** crème *f* aigre; **soured by disappointment** (*person*) aigri par une déception; **these events have soured their relationship** ces événements ont aigri leur relation
source [sɔːs] **1** *n* (*of river, misfortune, light etc*) source *f*; (*of heat, infection etc*) foyer *m*; **the Rhone has its s. in the Alps** le Rhône prend sa source dans les Alpes; **a good s. of vitamin C** une bonne source de vitamine C; **this book is a good s. of information about ...** ce livre est une bonne source d'informations sur ...; **I have it from a good s.** je le sais *ou* tiens de source sûre; **a historian's/reporter's sources** les sources d'un historien/reporter
2 *adj attrib* **s. disk** disque *m* source; (*floppy*) disquette *f* source; *Comptr* **s. document** document *m* de base, document source; **s. drive** unité *f* source *ou* d'origine; **s. file** fichier *m* source; **s. language** (*in translation, interpreting*) langue *f* de départ; *Comptr* langage *m* source; **s. materials** (*of book*) sources *fpl*; *Comptr* **s. program** programme *m* source; **s. text** texte *m* de départ
sour cream *n Culin* crème *f* aigre
sour-dough *n* **s. loaf** pain *m* au levain
sourface ['saʊəfeɪs] *n F* = **sourpuss**
sourfaced ['saʊəfeɪst] *adj* (*person*) au visage rébarbatif; (*look*) revêche; (*reply*) aigre
sourly ['saʊəlɪ] *adv* (*to answer*) aigrement; (*to look at sb*) d'un air revêche
sourness ['saʊənɪs] *n* **(a)** (*of fruit etc*) aigreur *f*, acidité *f*; (*of milk*) aigreur **(b)** (*of person*) aigreur *f*
sourpuss ['saʊəpʊs] *n F* grincheux, -euse; (*kill-joy*) rabat-joie *m inv*
sousaphone ['suːsəfəʊn] *n Mus* sousaphone *m*
sous chef ['suːʃef] *n* second *m*, assistant *m* du chef de cuisine
souse[1] [saʊs] *n Culin* saumure *f*, marinade *f*
souse[2] *vt* plonger, immerger (**in** dans); *Culin* (*herring*) faire mariner; **to s. sth with water** arroser qch d'eau
soused [saʊst] *adj* **(a)** *Culin* mariné; **s. herrings** harengs *mpl* marinés **(b)** *Sl* (*drunk*) bourré, pété; **to get s.** se soûler
south [saʊθ] **1** *n* sud *m*, midi *m*; **the s.** (*region of a country*) le sud, le midi; **house facing the s.** maison (exposée) au sud *ou* au midi; **to the s. (of sth)** au sud (de qch); **the S. of France** le sud *ou* le midi (de la France); *US* **the S.** les États *mpl* du sud (des États-Unis)
2 *adv* au sud; (*to travel*) vers le sud; **s. of a place** (*to be situated*) au sud d'un endroit; **to face s.** (*of building etc*) être orienté au sud; **s. by east** sud-quart-sud-est; **s. by west** sud-quart-sud-ouest; **to go s.** (*to southern part of country*) aller dans le sud
3 *adj* sud *inv*; (*wind*) du sud; (*wall, window*) orienté au sud; **s. side** côté *m* sud; **on the s. side** du côté sud; **the s. coast** la côte sud
South Africa *n* Afrique *f* du Sud
South African **1** *adj* sud-africain **2** *n* Sud-africain, -aine
South America *n* Amérique *f* du Sud
South American **1** *adj* sud-américain, de l'Amérique du Sud **2** *n* Sud-Américain, -aine
southbound ['saʊθbaʊnd] *adj* (*train etc*) allant vers le sud
southeast [saʊθ'iːst] **1** *n* sud-est *m*; *Naut* suet *m inv* **2** *adv* au sud-est; (*to travel*) vers le sud-est; **s. by east** sud-est-quart-est; **s. by south** sud-est-quart-sud **3** *adj* du sud-est; **the S. Asian Treaty Organization** l'Organisation *f* du Traité de l'Asie du Sud-Est
southeasterly [saʊθ'iːstəlɪ] **1** *adj* (*wind etc*) du sud-est; **to travel in a s. direction** voyager en direction du sud-est **2** *adv* vers le sud-est
southeastern [saʊθ'iːstən] *adj* (du) sud-est
southerly ['sʌðəlɪ] **1** *adj* (*wind*) du sud; (*current*) qui se dirige vers le sud; **to travel in a s. direction** voyager vers le sud; **s. point** point situé au sud *ou* vers le sud; **the most s. point of the United States** le point situé le plus au sud des États-Unis; **s. aspect** (*of house*) exposition *f* au midi *ou* au sud; *Naut* **to steer a s. course** faire route vers le sud; (*change course*) mettre le cap au sud **2** *adv* vers le sud
southern ['sʌðən] *adj* **(a)** (*cooking, people*) (du) sud, du midi; (*climate*) (du) sud, du midi, méridional; (*country, temperament*) méridional; (*region of the world*) austral; **s. Italy** l'Italie du sud; **the countries of s. Europe** les pays de l'Europe méridionale; **the s. hemisphere** l'hémisphère *m* sud *ou* austral; *Astron* **the S. Cross** la Croix du Sud; **s. lights** aurore *f* australe **(b)** *US Hist* (*army etc*) sudiste
southerner ['sʌðənər] *n* **(a)** habitant, -ante du sud, méridional, -ale **(b)** *US Hist* sudiste *mf*
south-facing *adj* (*window, building etc*) orienté vers le sud
South Korea *n* Corée *f* du sud
South Pacific *n* Pacifique *m* sud
southpaw ['saʊθpɔː] *n Boxing etc* gaucher, -ère
South Pole *n* pôle *m* sud
South Sea Islands *npl* Océanie *f*
South Seas *npl* mers *fpl* du Sud
south-south-east, *Naut* **sou'sou'east** [saʊ(θ)saʊ(θ)'iːst] **1** *adj, n* sud-sud-est *m* **2** *adv* au sud-sud-est; (*to travel*) vers le sud-sud-est
south-south-west, *Naut* **sou'sou'west** [saʊ(θ)saʊ(θ)'west] **1** *adj, n* sud-sud-ouest *m*; *Naut* susuroît *m* **2** *adv* au sud-sud-ouest; (*to travel*) vers le sud-sud-ouest
South Vietnam *n Hist* Sud Vietnam *m*
southward ['saʊθwəd] **1** *adj* au *ou* du sud **2** *adv* vers le sud; **s. bound** allant vers le sud
southwards ['saʊθwədz] *adv* vers le sud
southwest, *Naut* **sou'west** [saʊ(θ)'west] **1** *n* sud-ouest *m*; *Naut* suroît *m* **2** *adv* au sud-ouest; (*to travel*) vers le sud-ouest; **s. by west** sud-ouest-quart-ouest; **s. by south** sud-ouest-quart-sud **3** *adj* du sud-ouest; **s. wind** vent (du) sud-ouest
southwesterly, *Naut* **sou'westerly** [saʊ(θ)'westəlɪ] **1** *adj* (*wind etc*) du sud-ouest; **to travel in a s. direction** voyager vers le sud-ouest **2** *adv* vers le sud-ouest
southwestern [saʊθ'westən] *adj* (*region*) sud-ouest; **to travel in a s. direction** voyager vers le sud-ouest
South Yemen *n* Yémen *m* du Sud
souvenir [suːvə'nɪər] *n* souvenir *m*; **s. shop** boutique *f* de souvenirs
sou'wester [saʊ'westər] *n* **(a)** *Naut* (*wind*) (vent *m* du) sud-ouest *m* **(b)** (*hat*) suroît *m*
sovereign ['sɒvrɪn] **1** *adj* souverain, suprême; **the s. good** le bien souverain; **s. rights** droits *mpl* de souveraineté **2** *n* **(a)** (*monarch*) souverain, -aine, monarque *m* **(b)** *Br Hist* (*coin*) = souverain *m* (*pièce d'or de la valeur d'une livre*)
sovereignty ['sɒvrəntɪ] *n* souveraineté *f*
Soviet ['səʊvɪət] **1** *n* **(a)** (*council*) soviet *m*; **Supreme S.** Soviet suprême **(b) the Soviets** (*people*) les Soviétiques *mpl* **2** *adj* soviétique; **the Union of S. Socialist Republics** l'Union *f* des Républiques socialistes soviétiques
sovietization [səʊvɪətaɪ'zeɪʃən] *n* soviétisation *f*
Soviet Union *n* Union *f* soviétique
sow[1] [səʊ] (*pt* **sowed** [səʊd]; *pp* **sown** [səʊn], **sowed**) **1** *vt*

(*seeds, field*) semer; **to s. a field with wheat** ensemencer un champ de blé; *Fig* **to s. (the seeds of) discord/doubt** semer la discorde/le doute **2** *vi* semer

sow² [saʊ] *n* (*female pig*) truie *f*; (*wild*) laie *f*

sower ['səʊər] *n* (*person*) semeur, -euse; (*device*) semoir *m*

sowing ['səʊɪŋ] *n* (*task*) ensemencement *m*; **s. time** *or* **season** (saison *f* des) semailles

sox [sɒks] *npl Am* = **socks,** *see* **sock¹**

soya ['sɔɪə] *n Br* **s. bean** graine *f* de soya *ou* de soja, pois *m* chinois; **s. flour/oil** farine *f*/huile *f* de soja; **s. sauce** sauce *f* de *ou* au soja

soybean ['sɔɪbiːn] *n Am* graine *f* de soja

soy sauce [sɔɪ] *n* sauce *f* au *ou* de soja

sozzled ['sɒz(ə)ld] *adj Sl* (*drunk*) pété, bourré; **to get s.** se soûler

spa [spɑː] *n* (*spring*) source *f* thermale; (*in sports centre, health farm etc*) jacuzzi® *m*; **s. (town)** station *f* thermale; **s. bath** bain *m* bouillonnant; **s. hotel** hôtel *m* médicalisé; **s. resort** station hydrominérale

space¹ [speɪs] *n* **(a)** espace *m*; (*room*) place *f*; **he sat staring into s.** il était assis le regard perdu dans le vide; **open spaces** (*green*) espaces verts; (*not built on*) étendues *fpl* non bâties; **wide open spaces** grands espaces; **living s.** espace vital; **in a confined s.** dans un espace restreint; *Com* **to sell s. (in a newspaper)** vendre de l'espace (dans un journal); **to take up a lot of s.** prendre *ou* occuper beaucoup de place; **there's no s. left** il n'y a plus de place; **this cupboard is a great s. saver** avec ce placard on gagne beaucoup de place

(b) *Astronaut* espace *m*; **the conquest of s.** la conquête de l'espace; **outer s.** espace extra-atmosphérique; **s. blanket** couverture *f* de survie; **s. mission** mission *f* spatiale; **s. shot** lancement *m* d'engin dans l'espace; **s. suit** scaphandre *m ou* combinaison *f* de cosmonaute

(c) (*free area, place*) espace *m* libre; (*interval*) espacement *m*, intervalle *m*; (*on form etc*) blanc *m*, espace; **a s. in the timetable** un créneau dans l'emploi du temps; **a (parking) s.** une place de parking

(d) (*between lines of writing etc*) interligne *m*; *Typ* espace *m* blanc; **blank s.** (*between letters*) intervalle *m* entre les lettres

(e) (*period*) espace *m*, intervalle *m*; **in the s. of a year** dans *ou* en l'espace d'un an; **after a short s. of time** après un court intervalle

space² *vt* (*trees, words, visits*) espacer; (*troops, payments*) échelonner; **evenly spaced** régulièrement espacés; **the posts are spaced ten feet apart** les poteaux sont plantés à dix pieds d'intervalle

▶ **space out** *vtsep* **(a)** (*arrange at intervals*) = **space² (b)** *Sl* **to be spaced out** (*under influence of drugs*) être parti *ou* fait

space age *n* ère *f* de l'exploration spatiale

space-age *adj* (*technology etc*) de l'an 2000

spacebar ['speɪsbɑːr] *n Typ* barre *f* d'espacement

spacecraft ['speɪskrɑːft] *n* véhicule *m ou* vaisseau *m* spatial, astronef *m*

space flight *n* vol *m ou* voyage *m* spatial

space heater *n esp Am* chauffage *m* d'appoint

space invaders® *npl* envahisseurs *mpl* venus de l'espace

spacelab ['speɪslæb] *n* laboratoire *m* spatial

spaceman, *pl* **-men** ['speɪsmæn, -men] *n* astronaute *m*

space probe *n* (*rocket*) sonde *f* spatiale

spacer ['speɪsər] *n MecE* pièce *f* d'écartement

space rocket *n* fusée *f* spatiale *ou* interplanétaire

space rule *n Typ* filet *m* maigre

space-saving *adj* qui permet de gagner de la place; (*furniture etc*) compact; **if you're looking for some s. ideas** si vous cherchez des idées pour gagner de la place

spaceship ['speɪsʃɪp] *n* véhicule *m ou* vaisseau *m* spatial, astronef *m*

space shuttle *n* navette *f* spatiale

space station *n* station *f* spatiale

space-time *n Phys* espace-temps *m*

space travel *n* voyages *mpl* dans l'espace; (*science*) astronautique *f*

spacewalk ['speɪswɔːk] *n Astronaut* marche *f* dans l'espace

spacewoman, *pl* **-women** ['speɪswʊmən, -wɪmɪn] *n* astronaute *f*

spacing ['speɪsɪŋ] *n* (*of trees etc*) espacement *m*, écartement *m*; *Typ* (*of letters, lines*) espacement; **in single/double s.** (*with typewriter*) à simple/double interligne

spacious ['speɪʃəs] *adj* (*kitchen, house, car boot*) spacieux, vaste; (*clothes*) ample

spaciousness ['speɪʃəsnɪs] *n* (*of kitchen, house, car boot*) dimensions *fpl* spacieuses

spade¹ [speɪd] *n* (*tool*) bêche *f*; (*child's*) pelle *f*; *Prov* **to call a s. a s.** appeler les choses par leur nom, appeler un chat un chat

spade² *vt* (*earth etc*) bêcher

spade³ *n* **(a)** *Cards* pique *m*; **ace of spades** as *m* de pique; **to play a s., to play spades** jouer pique **(b)** *Offensive Sl* (*negro*) nègre *m*, négresse *f*

spadeful ['speɪdfʊl] *n* pelletée *f*

spadework ['speɪdwɜːk] *n* (*with spade*) travaux *mpl* à la bêche; *Fig* travaux préliminaires

spaghetti [spə'getɪ] *n* [ⒾA13,7] *Culin* spaghetti *mpl*; *El F* (*cables, wires*) souplisseau *m*; *Br F* **s. junction** échangeur *m* sur plusieurs niveaux; **it's like s. junction around here!** tous ces échangeurs, c'est compliqué!; *Cin* **s. western** western *m* spaghetti

Spain [speɪn] *n* Espagne *f*

span¹ [spæn] *n* **(a)** (*of hand*) empan *m*; **wing s.** (*of bird, aircraft*) envergure *f* **(b)** (*between two points of support*) portée *f*; (*of arch*) largeur *f*; (*of bridge*) travée *f*; **single s. bridge** pont *m* à travée unique **(c)** (*duration, period of time*) durée *f*; **the party's twenty-year s. in power is coming to an end** les vingt années de pouvoir du parti arrivent à leur fin **(d)** (*extent*) (*of knowledge, interests, activity etc*) étendue *f*

span² *vt* **(-nn-) (a)** (*of bridge etc*) (*river etc*) enjamber; **once the river had been spanned** une fois qu'on a eu construit un pont pour traverser la rivière **(b)** (*include*) couvrir; **her knowledge spans a wide range of subjects** ses connaissances couvrent une grande variété de sujets; **his life spans nearly the whole century** sa vie embrasse presque tout le siècle; *Mus* **to s. an octave** couvrir une octave

span³ *n* (*pair*) (*of horses, oxen*) paire *f*, couple *m*

spangle¹ ['spæŋg(ə)l] *n Tex etc* paillette *f*; (*large*) paillon *m*

spangle² *vt* pailleter (**with** de); **spangled with silver** pailleté d'argent

Spaniard ['spænɪəd] *n* [ⒾA20,d] Espagnol, -ole

spaniel ['spænjəl] *n* épagneul *m*; **cocker/springer s.** épagneul cocker/springer

Spanish ['spænɪʃ] [ⒾA20,d] **1** *adj* espagnol; **S. fly** mouche *f* d'Espagne, cantharide *f*; *Mus* **S. guitar** guitare *f* espagnole; **S. omelette** omelette *f* à l'espagnole; **S. onion** oignon *m* d'Espagne **2** *n* **(a)** *Ling* espagnol *m*; **S. teacher** professeur d'espagnol **(b) the S.** (*pl*) les Espagnols *mpl*

Spanish-American *adj* hispano-américain; *Hist* **the S. war** la guerre hispano-américaine

Spanish Inquisition *n Hist, Fig* Inquisition *f* espagnole

spank¹ [spæŋk] *n* fessée *f*

spank² *vt* (*child*) fesser, donner une fessée à

▶ **spank along** *vi* (*go fast*) aller bon train

spanking ['spæŋkɪŋ] **1** *n* fessée *f*; **to give a child a s.** donner une fessée à un enfant **2** *adj Old-fashioned F* **(a)** (*excellent*) épatant **(b) to go at a s. pace** aller bon train **3** *adv Old-fashioned F* **s. new** flambant neuf; **a s. good time was had** on s'est diablement bien amusé

spanner ['spænər] *n Br* clef *f*; **adjustable s.** clef à molette; **box s.** clef à douille *ou* à tire-fonds; *Fig* **to throw a s. in the works** mettre des bâtons dans les roues à qn; **that's really thrown a s. in the works!** cela nous/leur/*etc* a vraiment mis des bâtons dans les roues; **so that's the s. in the works** alors, c'est ça le hic

spar¹ [spɑːr] *n Naut* espar *m*; *Av* **wing s.** longeron *m* d'aile

spar² *n Miner* spath *m*

spar³ *vi* **(-rr-) to s. with sb** *Boxing* s'entraîner avec qn; *Fig* (*argue*) jouter avec qn

spare¹ ['speər] **1** *adj* **(a)** (*surplus*) (*copy, trousers*) en plus; (*free*) disponible; **have you got a s. plastic bag?** est-ce que tu as un sac en plastique qui ne te sert pas?; **with the s. cash they bought a table** avec l'argent qui leur restait ils ont acheté une table; **that left a few hours s.** ça a laissé quelques heures libres; **is this bed s.?** est-ce que ce lit est libre?; **we have a s. bed** (*can put you/him up for the night*) nous avons un lit qui ne sert pas; *F* **is this cake going s.?** si vous ne savez pas quoi faire de ce gâteau je le prends; *F* **if you have any tickets going s.** si vous avez des tickets en trop; *F* **if you hear of any flats going s.** si vous entendez parler d'appartements qui se libèrent; **s. parts** pièces *fpl* de rechange, pièces détachées; **s. room** chambre *f* d'ami(s); **s. time** temps *m* libre; **in my s. time** à mes heures perdues; **I don't get much s. time** je n'ai pas beaucoup de temps libre; **s. tyre** *or Am* **tire** pneu *m* de rechange; *Br F* (*around waist*) bourrelet *m* de graisse, pneu; *Aut* **s. wheel** roue *f* de secours

(b) (*frugal*) (*meal etc*) frugal; (*style, room*) dépouillé

(c) (*thin*) (*person*) sec, *f* sèche; **he was tall and s.** il était grand et mince

(d) *Br F* (*mad*) **to drive sb s.** rendre qn dingue; **he'll go s. if he finds out** il va être fou s'il apprend ça

2 *n* (*spare part*) pièce *f* de rechange, pièce détachée; (*tyre*)

pneu *m* de rechange; **I've lost my pencil, have you got a s.?** j'ai perdu mon crayon, en as-tu un à me prêter?

spare[2] *vt* **(a)** (*in negative constructions*) (*be grudging of*) **to s. no expense** ne pas regarder à la dépense; **to s. no pains** se donner beaucoup de mal; **to s. no effort** ne pas ménager ses efforts

(b) (*go without*) se passer de; **can you s. that much money?** pouvez-vous vous en passer?; **can you s. the time?** avez-vous le temps?; **we can't s. him** il nous est indispensable, nous ne pouvons pas nous passer de lui; **to have nothing to s.** n'avoir que le strict nécessaire, ne rien avoir de superflu; **to have enough and to s. (of sth)** avoir plus qu'il n'en faut (de qch); **there is room to s.** la place ne manque pas; **I cannot s. the time to finish it** je n'ai pas le temps de le finir; **to have no time to s.** ne pas avoir le temps; **to have no time to s. for sb/sth** ne pas avoir de temps à consacrer à qn/qch; **when I have time to s.** quand j'ai des loisirs, quand j'ai du temps libre; **whenever I have a minute to s.** dès que j'ai une minute; **I have a minute to s., so send her in** j'ai une minute à lui consacrer, faites-la donc entrer; **to catch a train with five minutes to s.** prendre un train avec cinq minutes de battement; **we caught the plane with absolutely no time to s.** nous avons attrapé l'avion vraiment de justesse; **we'll have at least half an hour to s.** nous aurons au minimum une demi-heure de battement; **to s. sb some sugar/ten pounds** donner à qn du sucre/dix livres; **are you sure you can s. it?** tu es sûr que ça ne te dérange pas?; *Iron* tu es sûr que ça ne va pas te manquer?; **can you s. a couple of people this afternoon?** est-ce que vous pourriez vous passer de quelques personnes cet après-midi?; **can you s. me a few moments?** pouvez-vous m'accorder quelques minutes?; **to s. a thought for sb** penser à qn

(c) (*show mercy towards*) (*person, horse*) ménager; (*person condemned to die*) faire grâce à; **to s. sb's life** épargner la vie de qn; **s. me!** (*do not kill me*) de grâce!, épargnez-moi!; *Fig* (*don't expose me to that etc*) par pitié, pas ça!; **if she is spared** (*lives*) si elle vit; **death spares no one** la mort n'épargne personne; **the flood spared nothing** l'inondation n'a rien épargné; **to s. sb's feelings** ménager qn, épargner qn; **tell me, don't s. my feelings** dis-moi, n'essaye pas de me ménager; **the report spared no one** le rapport ne ménageait personne; **s. my blushes!** ne me faites pas rougir!; **he doesn't s. himself** il ne se ménage pas; **to s. sb the trouble of doing sth** éviter à qn la peine de faire qch; **you could have spared yourself/us the trouble** vous auriez pu vous/nous éviter cette peine; **s. me the details!** (*don't tell me*) épargne-moi les détails!; **I'll s. you the rest** je vous fais grâce du reste

sparing ['speərɪŋ] *adj* (*economical*) économe; **to be s. with the butter** ménager le beurre; **she is very s. with her money** elle fait très attention à son argent; **he is s. with his praises** il est avare de louanges

sparingly ['speərɪŋlɪ] *adv* (*to eat*) sobrement; (*moderately*) modérément, avec modération; **to use sth s.** utiliser qch avec modération; **apply the cream s. to the affected area** appliquer la crème en couche fine sur la région touchée

spark[1] [spɑːk] *n* **(a)** (*glowing particle*) étincelle *f*; (*from fire*) flammèche *f*; **the s. of life** l'étincelle de la vie; *Fig* **sparks flew** ça a fait des étincelles; **he hasn't a s. of imagination** il manque totalement d'imagination; **he hasn't a s. of generosity in him** il n'est pas généreux pour deux sous; **a bright s.** (*intelligent person*) une tête; *F Iron* **you're a bright s.** tu es un rapide, toi!; **who's the bright s. who ...?** qui est le petit malin qui ...?

(b) *El etc* étincelle *f*; *Aut* **s. advance** correcteur *m* d'avance; **s. gap** *El* distance *f* explosive *ou* d'éclatement; (*in engine*) éclateur *m*, pont *m* d'allumage; **spark(ing) plug** bougie *f* (d'allumage); **s. plug spanner** clé *f* à bougies

(c) *Naut, Av Old-fashioned F* **sparks** (*radio operator*) radio *m*; (*electrician*) électricien *m*

spark[2] *vi* jeter des étincelles; (*of dynamo etc*) cracher; **to s. across the terminals** (*of current*) jaillir entre les bornes

▶ **spark off** *vtsep* (*initiate*) (*revolution, reaction etc*) déclencher, provoquer; (*idea etc*) donner naissance à; **this remark sparked off a discussion about ...** cette remarque a déclenché *ou* donné lieu à une discussion au sujet de ...

sparkle[1] ['spɑːk(ə)l] *n* **(a)** (*spot of light*) étincelle *f*; (*lasting only short time*) brève lueur *f* **(b)** (*act, state of sparkling*) scintillement *m*; (*of eyes*) éclat *m*, pétillement *m*; (*of diamond*) feux *mpl*; **wine that has lost its s.** vin qui ne pétille plus; *Fig* **if the s. has gone out of your marriage ...** si la magie a disparu de votre mariage ...; **he's got no s. about him** il est plutôt terne; **he's lost his s.** il a perdu sa joie de vivre

sparkle[2] *vi* (*of jewel, tinsel, metal, snow etc*) étinceler, scintiller; (*of surface of lake*) miroiter; (*of wine*) pétiller, mousser; **her eyes sparkled (with joy)** ses yeux pétillaient (de joie); **sparkling with wit** (*book*) plein d'esprit

sparkler ['spɑːklər] *n* **(a)** (*firework*) cierge *m* magique **(b)** *F* (*diamond*) diam *m*

sparkling ['spɑːklɪŋ] **1** *adj* étincelant, brillant; (*conversation*) brillant; (*wine*) mousseux, pétillant; (*lemonade*) gazeux; **he was a s. conversationalist** sa conversation était des plus brillantes **2** *adv* **s. clean** étincelant de propreté, d'une propreté étincelante

sparring ['spɑːrɪŋ] *n Boxing* entraînement *m*; (*arguing*) échanges *mpl* verbaux; **it was just a little good-natured s.** (*verbal*) ce n'était qu'une petite bagarre amicale; *Boxing* **s. match** match *m* d'entraînement; *Fig* **I could hear them having a s. match in the corridor** je les entendais se disputer dans le couloir; **s. partner** *Boxing* partenaire *m* d'entraînement, sparring-partner *m*; *Fig* adversaire *m*

sparrow ['spærəʊ] *n* (*bird*) moineau *m*; **hedge s.** fauvette *f* d'hiver

sparrowhawk ['spærəʊhɔːk] *n* (*bird*) épervier *m*

sparse [spɑːs] *adj* (*trees, population*) clairsemé, épars; **s. hair** cheveux rares *ou* clairsemés

sparsely ['spɑːslɪ] *adv* peu abondamment; **s. covered with trees** aux arbres clairsemés; **s. furnished** à peine meublé; **s. populated** peu peuplé

sparseness ['spɑːsnɪs] *n* (*of population*) faible densité *f*; (*of vegetation*) manque *m*

Sparta ['spɑːtə] *n* Sparte *f*

Spartan ['spɑːtən] **1** *adj Hist, Fig* spartiate; *Fig* **to lead a s. life** vivre en spartiate, mener une vie de spartiate **2** *n Hist* Spartiate *mf*; *Fig* spartiate

spasm ['spæz(ə)m] *n Med* spasme *m*; *Fig* (*of coughing, jealousy*) accès *m*; *Med* **to go into spasms** avoir des spasmes; **to work in spasms** travailler par à-coups; **after a sudden s. of feverish activity** après un accès soudain d'activité fébrile

spasmodic [spæz'mɒdɪk] *adj Med* spasmodique; *Fig* (*irregular*) irrégulier; (*intermittent*) intermittent; **s. work** travail fait par à-coups

spasmodically [spæz'mɒdɪklɪ] *adv Med* spasmodiquement; *Fig* (*irregularly*) irrégulièrement; (*intermittently*) de façon intermittente; (*to work*) par à-coups

spastic ['spæstɪk] **1** *adj Med* spastique; (*paralysis etc*) spasmodique; *Offensive Sl* (*performance, attempt etc*) minable, nul **2** *n Med* handicapé, -ée moteur

spat[1] [spæt] *n* (*of oysters etc*) naissain *m*

spat[2] *n* (*item of clothing*) demi-guêtre *f*, *pl* demi-guêtres

spat[3] *n Am F* (*quarrel*) querelle *f*

spat[4] *vi* (-tt-) *Am F* (*quarrel*) se quereller

spat[5] *see* **spit**[4]

spate [speɪt] *n* (*of river*) crue *f*; *Fig* (*of letters etc*) avalanche *f*; (*of abuse*) torrent *m*; **river in (full) s.** rivière en crue; *Fig* **to be in full s.** être en plein dans son sujet; **a s. of burglaries** une série de cambriolages; **there's been a sudden s. of orders** il y a eu une soudaine avalanche *ou* un soudain déluge de commandes

spatial ['speɪʃəl] *adj Math, Phys etc* spatial; **s. awareness** conscience *f* de l'espace

spatiotemporal [speɪʃɪəʊ'tempərəl] *adj* spatio-temporel

spatter[1] ['spætər] *n* (*of liquid*) éclaboussure *f*; *Ind* (*of solder*) projection *f*; *esp Am F* **s. movie** = film *m* d'horreur où le sang gicle

spatter[2] **1** *vt* éclabousser (**with** de); **the wall was spattered with grease** le mur était couvert d'éclaboussures *ou* tout éclaboussé de graisse **2** *vi* (*of liquid*) jaillir, gicler; **the rain spattering down on the pavement** la pluie qui rebondit sur le trottoir

-spattered [-spætəd] *suff* **blood/mud/oil-s.** couvert d'éclaboussures de sang/de boue/d'huile

spatula ['spætjʊlə] *n Pharm, Surg, Culin etc* spatule *f*

spavin ['spævɪn] *n Vet* éparvin *m*

spawn[1] [spɔːn] *n* **(a)** (*of frog, fish etc*) frai *m*, œufs *mpl*; *Lit, Pej* (*offspring*) progéniture *f* **(b)** **(mushroom) s.** blancs *mpl* de champignon, mycélium *m*

spawn[2] **1** *vi* (*of fish etc*) frayer; *F* (*of people*) se multiplier **2** *vt* (*of fish, frog etc*) (*eggs*) déposer; *Fig, F* engendrer, donner naissance à; **the organization/movement spawned various offshoots** l'organisation/le mouvement a donné naissance à plusieurs ramifications

spawning ['spɔːnɪŋ] *n Zool* frai *m*; **s. ground** frayère *f*; **s. season** frai

spay [speɪ] *vt Vet* châtrer

speak [spiːk] (*pt* **spoke** [spəʊk]; *pp* **spoken** ['spəʊk(ə)n]) **1** *vi* **(a)** (*talk*) (*of person*) parler; **can he s.?** est-ce qu'il parle?, est-ce qu'il sait parler?; **without speaking** sans parler, sans rien dire; **to s. to sb** parler à qn (**about sth** de qch); **he spoke slowly/hesitatingly/too quickly** il s'est exprimé *ou* il a parlé lentement/avec hésitation/trop rapidement; **she hasn't spoken to me since** elle ne m'a pas adressé la parole depuis; **I can't give you a rise, you'll have to s. to the boss** je ne peux pas vous donner une augmentation, il va falloir que vous vous adressiez au patron; **they're not speaking (to each other)** ils ne s'adressent pas *ou* plus la parole; **I hate it when Mum and Dad aren't speaking** j'ai horreur des fois où Papa et Maman refusent de se parler; **isn't it about time you two started speaking again?** est-ce que vous ne devriez pas faire la paix?; **I'll s. to him about it** je lui en toucherai un mot, je lui en parlerai; **I know her/him to s. to** on se dit bonjour; **roughly speaking** approximativement; **legally/morally speaking** légalement/moralement parlant; **so to s.** pour ainsi dire; *Tel* **who's speaking?** qui est à l'appareil?; (*before transferring call*) c'est de la part de qui?; **Mr Thomas? – yes, speaking** M. Thomas? – lui-même

(**b**) (*give a speech*) faire un discours; **he spoke on the subject of ...** il a parlé *ou* traité de ...; **to have the right to s.** avoir le droit de se faire entendre, avoir droit à la parole

2 *vt* (**a**) (*a word, the truth*) dire; **she has never spoken a word to me** elle ne m'a jamais adressé la parole, elle ne m'a jamais dit un mot; **he didn't s. a word about it** il n'en a pas soufflé mot; **to s. one's mind** dire ce qu'on pense; **to s. one's lines** (*in play*) dire son rôle

(**b**) (*language*) parler; **do you s. French?** parlez-vous français?; **English is spoken everywhere** l'anglais est parlé partout; **English spoken** (*on sign*) on parle anglais; *also Fig* **to s. the same language** parler le même langage

(**c**) *Lit* (*show*) (*feeling, emotion*) indiquer, témoigner de; **eyes that s. affection** yeux qui témoignent de l'amitié

▶ **speak against** *vipo* (*motion, bill, proposal*) se prononcer contre; **she spoke passionately against the practice** elle a condamné cette pratique avec virulence

▶ **speak for** *vipo* (**a**) (*person*) (*speak on behalf of*) parler pour; (*speak in support of*) plaider pour; **I'm sure I s. for everyone when I say ...** je suis sûr que j'exprime la pensée générale lorsque je dis ...; **speaking for myself** pour ma part, en ce qui me concerne; **I'll tell him when to leave, I can s. for myself!** c'est moi qui lui dirai de partir, je suis parfaitement capable de le faire moi-même!; **he is old enough to s. for himself** (*ask for something*) il est assez grand pour le demander tout seul; (*say something*) il est assez grand pour le dire lui-même; *F usu Hum* **s. for yourself!** parle pour toi!; **the facts s. for themselves** ces faits se passent de commentaires *ou* parlent d'eux-mêmes; **it doesn't s. very well for her chances of winning** ça ne laisse présager rien de bon quant à ses chances de victoire

(**b**) **to be spoken for** (*to be reserved*) être réservé; (*of man, woman*) (*at dance etc*) être accompagné; (*have girlfriend, boyfriend*) avoir un(e) petit(e) ami(e); (*have wife, husband*) être marié

▶ **speak of** *vipo* (**a**) (*talk about*) parler de; **speaking of ...** à propos de ..., en parlant de ...; **it's nothing to s. of** ce n'est rien, n'en parlons plus; **there's nothing on television/in the town or nothing to s. of, anyway** il n'y a rien de spécial à la télévision/en ville; **to s. well/highly of sb/sth** dire du bien/beaucoup de bien de qn/qch; **he is well spoken of** il a une bonne réputation, on dit du bien de lui; **to s. ill of sb** dire du mal de qn, médire de qn (**b**) (*indicate*) être significatif de; **this speaks of large-scale corruption** c'est le signe d'une corruption à grande échelle

▶ **speak out** *vi* (**a**) (*speak with courage*) oser parler, oser prendre la parole; **to s. out against injustice** oser dénoncer l'injustice (**b**) (*speak loudly*) parler (plus) fort

▶ **speak up** *vi* (**a**) (*speak louder*) parler plus fort *ou* plus haut (**b**) (*take active part in discussion etc*) prendre la parole, participer à la discussion; **she speaks up in class/meetings** elle prend la parole en classe/lors de réunions (**c**) = **speak out** (**a**)

▶ **speak up for** *vipo* (*person*) parler en faveur de; **why don't you s. up for yourself?** pourquoi est-ce que tu ne te défends pas?; **you've got to learn to s. up for yourself** il faut que tu apprennes à défendre tes intérêts

speakeasy ['spi:ki:zɪ] *n US* débit *m ou* bar *m* clandestin

speaker ['spi:kər] *n* (**a**) (*in dialogue*) interlocuteur, -trice; **as a s. of Italian** *or* **an Italian s. myself ...** moi qui parle italien ...; **there are very few surviving speakers of the language** il reste très peu de personnes qui parlent cette langue; **there were three speakers on the tape** il y avait trois personnes (qui parlaient) sur la bande; **I'm a plain s.** j'appelle les choses par leur nom, je dis ce que je pense, je dis les choses comme elles sont

(**b**) (*at meeting, in discussion programme*) intervenant, -ante; (*at conference*) conférencier, -ière; (*political, orator*) orateur *m*; *US TV* (*announcer*) speaker *m*, speakerine *f*; **we have three speakers this evening** nous avons trois intervenants ce soir; **the next s. will be ...** la parole est maintenant à ...; **to be a good s.** s'exprimer très bien

(**c**) *Parl* **the S.** *Br, Can* = le Président (des Communes); *US* = le Président du Congrès; **Mr/Madam S.** Monsieur/Madame le Président

(**d**) (*loudspeaker*) haut-parleur *m*, *pl* haut-parleurs, enceinte *f*

speaking ['spi:kɪŋ] **1** *adj* (*doll, robot etc*) parlant **2** *n* **plain s.** franchise *f*, franc-parler *m*; **public s.** art *m* oratoire; **unaccustomed as I am to public s.** bien que je n'aie pas l'habitude de parler en public; **s. a foreign language is easier than writing it** parler une langue étrangère, c'est plus facile que de l'écrire; **he finds s. very difficult** il a du mal à parler; **we're no longer on s. terms** on ne s'adresse plus la parole; **s. tube** tube *m* acoustique; *Naut, Aut etc* porte-voix *m inv*; *Av* aviophone *m*

-speaking [-'spi:kɪŋ] *suff* **Chinese/Russian-s.** (*as mother tongue*) de langue maternelle chinoise/russe; (*as learnt language*) qui parle chinois/russe; **slow-s.** qui s'exprime lentement; **plain-s.** qui appelle les choses par leur nom

speaking clock *n Br Telecom* horloge *f* parlante

speaking part *n* (*in play*) rôle *m* parlant

spear[1] [spɪər] *n* (**a**) *Mil* lance *f*; (*in hunting*) épieu *m*; (*for throwing*) javelot *m*; **to be a s.-carrier** *Th* être figurant; *Fig* avoir un rôle mineur (**b**) *Fishing* harpon *m*

spear[2] *vt* (**a**) (*pierce*) (*person*) transpercer *ou* (*kill*) tuer d'un coup de lance; (*olive, piece of food etc*) piquer (*avec une fourchette etc*) (**b**) *Fishing* (*fish*) harponner

spear[3] *n* (*of grass*) brin *m*; **spears of asparagus, asparagus spears** pointes *fpl* d'asperges

spear fishing *n* pêche *f ou* chasse *f* (sous-marine) au harpon

spear gun *n* fusil *m* à harpon

spearhead[1] ['spɪəhed] *n* (*of spear*) fer *m* de lance; *Mil* (*of attack*) pointe *f*; *Fig* (*of organization etc*) fer de lance

spearhead[2] *vt Mil* **they spearheaded the crossing of the river** ils ont forcé les premiers le passage du fleuve; *Fig* **to s. a movement** être le fer de lance d'un mouvement

spearmint ['spɪəmɪnt] *n* (*plant, flavour*) menthe *f* verte; (*chewing gum*) chewing-gum *m* à la menthe verte

spec [spek] *n F* **we've got it on s. for a week** on l'a à l'essai pour une semaine; **to buy sth on s.** acheter qch à tout hasard

special ['speʃəl] **1** *adj* spécial, particulier (**to** à); (*friend*) intime; **nothing s.** rien de particulier; **the food was OK but nothing s.** la nourriture était assez bonne mais elle n'avait rien d'exceptionnel; **are you doing anything s. for your birthday?** tu fais quelque chose de spécial pour ton anniversaire?; **what's so s. about the 19th November?** qu'est-ce que le 19 novembre a de si spécial?; **to pay s. attention (to sth)** faire particulièrement attention (à qch); **for someone s.** (*on card*) pour quelqu'un qui m'est cher; **s. case** cas *m* particulier; **s. characteristic** particularité *f*; **s. clause** clause *f* particulière; *Journ* **our s. correspondent** notre envoyé spécial; **s. delivery** envoi *m* en exprès; **to mail sth s. delivery** envoyer qch en exprès; **s. diet** régime *m* spécial; *Fin* **s. drawing rights** droits *mpl* de tirage spéciaux; **s. edition** édition *f* spéciale, hors *m* série; **s. feature** particularité *f*; **s. indications** (*on ticket*) indications *fpl* spéciales; *Journ etc* **s. issue** numéro *m* spécial; *Br* **s. licence** = dispense *f* de bans; *Br* **they were married by s. licence** ils se sont mariés avec dispense de bans; **for s. occasions** pour les jours de fête, pour les occasions spéciales; **s. offer** offre *f* spéciale; **s. pleading** plaidoyer *m* partial; **s. powers** pouvoirs *mpl* d'exception; *Com* **s. price** prix *m* spécial; **s. rate** tarif *m* préférentiel *ou* spécial; *Br* **s. school** = école *f* pour les enfants handicapés; **to get s. treatment** bénéficier d'un traitement de faveur

2 *n* (*train*) train *m* spécial; **s. (edition)** *Journ* édition *f* spéciale; (*programme*) émission *f* spéciale; **today's s.** (*in restaurant*) plat *m* du jour

special agent *n* (*spy etc*) agent *m* secret

Special Air Service *n Br* = **SAS**

Special Branch *n Br* (*police*) service *m* de renseignements

special constable *n* auxiliaire *m* de police

special effects *npl Cin, TV etc* trucages *mpl*, effets *mpl* spéciaux; **s. engineer** truquiste *m*; **s. generator** générateur *m* d'effets spéciaux, truqueur *m*

specialist ['speʃəlɪst] *n* spécialiste *mf*; **to become a s. in electronics** *or* **an electronics s.** se spécialiser dans l'électronique; *Med* **heart/lung/cancer s.** cardiologue *mf*/pneumologue *mf*/cancérologue *mf*; **what are your s.**

subjects? dans quels sujets vous spécialisez-vous?; **it requires s. skills** ça demande les compétences d'un spécialiste; **it's s. work** c'est un travail de spécialiste; **if you don't have the s. knowledge** si vous n'avez pas les connaissances d'un spécialiste; **s. bookshop** librairie *f* spécialisée; *TV etc* **s. channel** chaîne *f* spécialisée; **s. dictionary** dictionnaire *m* spécialisé; **s. press** presse *f* d'information spécialisée, presse spécialisée

speciality [speʃɪ'ælɪtɪ] *n* **(a)** (*of store, restaurant, region etc*) spécialité *f*; (*area of study*) (*of student*) matière *f* principale; (*of researcher*) sujet *m* de recherches; **his s. is Vietnamese art** il se spécialise dans l'art du Vietnam; *also Iron* **that's my s.** c'est ma spécialité, je suis spécialiste; **skiing holidays our s.** (*in advertisement*) les sports d'hiver sont notre spécialité; **s. goods** produits *mpl* de spécialité, produits spécialisés; **s. restaurant** restaurant *m* de spécialités; **s. shop** magasin *m* spécialisé **(b)** *Jur* = **specialty (a)**

specialization [speʃəlaɪ'zeɪʃən] *n* spécialisation *f* (**in** dans)

specialize ['speʃəlaɪz] *vi* (*of shop, researcher etc*) se spécialiser (**in** dans); *Iron* **she specializes in that sort of blunder** elle est spécialiste de ce genre de gaffes

specialized ['speʃəlaɪzd] *adj* (*work, subject*) spécialisé

specially ['speʃəlɪ] *adv* (*in particular*) spécialement, particulièrement; **I'm s. interested in antique furniture** je m'intéresse plus particulièrement *ou* surtout aux antiquités; **I went there s. to see them** j'y suis allé dans le seul but de les voir, j'y suis allé exprès pour les voir; **I waited up s.** je suis resté debout exprès; **s. designed to ...** spécialement conçu pour ...; **I s. asked you not to ...** je t'avais bien demandé de ne pas ...; **it's not s. good** ce n'est pas particulièrement bon; **s. at night** surtout le soir; **they had a cake s. made** ils ont fait faire un gâteau spécialement

specialty ['speʃəltɪ] *n Am* = **speciality (a)**

specie ['spiːʃiː] *n* (*no pl*) *Fin* espèces *fpl* (monnayées)

species ['spiːʃiːz] *n inv* **(a)** *Biol* espèce *f*; **the human s.** l'espèce humaine; **the origin of s.** l'origine *f* des espèces **(b)** (*type*) espèce *f*, sorte *f*

specific [spɪ'sɪfɪk] **1** *adj* (*particular*) spécifique; (*clear*) (*statement, example, rule, aim*) précis; (*command*) explicite; **or, to be s., ...** ou, pour être précis, ...; **in this s. case** dans ce cas précis *ou* particulier; **to be s.** (*of person*) être explicite; **she was pretty s. about her intentions** elle a été très précise quant à ses intentions; **could you be a bit more s.?** pourriez-vous être plus précis?, pourriez-vous préciser? **2** *n Med* spécifique *m* (**for** contre); *US Ind* **specifics** (*precise description*) description *f* précise; (*characteristics*) caractéristiques *fpl*; *F* **to get down to specifics** en venir aux faits précis

specifically [spɪ'sɪfɪk(ə)lɪ] *adv* spécifiquement; (*precisely*) précisément; **your name was mentioned s.** votre nom a été bien précisément mentionné; **you must state quite s. what the requirements are** vous devez bien spécifier les conditions requises; **I s. told you not to ...** je t'ai dit très précisément de ne pas ...; **I s. asked for a small portion** j'ai bien demandé une petite portion; **we were s. forbidden to ...** il nous était expressément défendu de ...; **it is s. designed for use in ...** c'est (tout) spécialement conçu pour une utilisation dans ...; **a book which is s. written for people who ...** un livre écrit tout particulièrement pour les gens qui ...

specification [spesɪfɪ'keɪʃən] *n* **(a)** (*act*) (*of details etc*) spécification *f* **(b)** (*description*) (*of car*) caractéristiques *fpl*; (*of work to be done*) prescriptions *fpl*; *Constr, Ind* **specifications** (*of contract*) cahier *m* des charges; *Mktg* **s. buying** achats *mpl* spécifiés **(c)** (*condition, stipulation*) spécification *f*; **there's no s. about the number of times you can enter** on ne précise pas combien de fois il vous est permis d'entrer; **their only s. was that the press should not be told** la seule condition qu'ils avaient posée était que la presse ne devait pas être informée

specific gravity *n Phys* densité *f*

specificity [spesɪ'fɪsɪtɪ] *n* spécificité *f*

specify ['spesɪfaɪ] *vt* (*conditions etc*) spécifier, préciser; **I specified blue** j'ai spécifié la couleur bleue; **specified load** charge prévue *ou* prescrite; **unless otherwise specified** sauf indication contraire

specimen ['spesɪmɪn] *n* spécimen *m*; (*sample*) spécimen, échantillon *m*; **the finest specimens in his collection** les plus belles pièces de sa collection; **that's a magnificent s.** (*butterfly etc*) c'est un très beau spécimen; **a s. of sb's handwriting** un échantillon *ou* exemple de l'écriture de qn; *Med* **to take a s. of sb's blood, to take a blood s. from sb** faire une prise de sang à qn; *F* **a s.** (*of urine*) un prélèvement d'urine; *F* **an odd s.** (*person*) un drôle de type; *F* **you're a pretty pathetic s., aren't you!** tu es vraiment lamentable!; **s. copy** spécimen; **s. page** page *f* spécimen, page type; **s. signature** spécimen de signature

specious ['spiːʃəs] *adj* (*appearance*) spécieux, trompeur; (*argument etc*) captieux, spécieux

speciousness ['spiːʃəsnɪs] *n* (*of argument, promises*) caractère *m* spécieux

speck [spek] *n* **(a)** (*mark*) petite tache *f*; (*of colour, ink*) point *m*; (*on fruit*) tavelure *f*; *Med* **specks (in front of the eyes)** = une mouche (*devant les yeux*) **(b)** (*small piece*) (*of dust*) grain *m*, atome *m*; **the ship was only a s. on the horizon** le navire n'était qu'un point à l'horizon

speckle[1] ['spek(ə)l] *n* petite tache *f*; (*of colour*) point *m*; (*on animal, egg*) moucheture *f*, tacheture *f*

speckle[2] *vt* tacheter, moucheter

speckled ['spek(ə)ld] *adj* tacheté, moucheté; (*plumage*) grivelé; (*hen*) tacheté; **bird s. with white** oiseau tacheté de blanc

specs [speks] *npl F* **(a)** (*spectacles*) carreaux *mpl* **(b)** *Ind* (*specifications*) spécifications *fpl*

spectacle ['spektək(ə)l] *n* **(a)** (*show, sight*) spectacle *m*; **to make a s. of oneself** se donner en spectacle **(b)** [①A10,e] **(pair of) spectacles** (paire *f* de) lunettes *fpl*; **to put on one's spectacles** mettre *ou* chausser ses lunettes; **s. case** étui *m* à lunettes

spectacled ['spektək(ə)ld] *adj* à lunettes

spectacular [spek'tækjʊlər] **1** *adj* spectaculaire **2** *n Th, Cin* superproduction *f*; **an ice-skating s.** une revue de patinage artistique

spectacularly [spek'tækjʊləlɪ] *adv* (*to improve, collapse etc*) de façon spectaculaire

spectate [spek'teɪt] *vi esp Sp* **to s. at** (*match etc*) assister à; **I prefer to s.** je préfère être spectateur/spectatrice

spectator [spek'teɪtər] *n* spectateur, -trice; **the spectators** les spectateurs; **we don't want any spectators** nous ne voulons pas qu'on nous regarde; **s. sport** sport *m* que l'on se contente de regarder en spectateur; **it makes an excellent TV s. sport** c'est un sport très télévisuel

specter ['spektər] *n Am* = **spectre**

spectral ['spektr(ə)l] *adj* **(a)** *Phys, Ch* spectral; **s. colours** couleurs *fpl* spectrales **(b)** (*ghostly*) spectral

spectre ['spektər] *n* spectre *m*, fantôme *m*; *Fig* **the s. of war/famine** (*threat*) le spectre de la guerre/famine

spectrogram ['spektrəʊgræm] *n* spectrogramme *m*

spectrograph ['spektrəʊgræf] *n* spectrographe *m*

spectrometer [spek'trɒmɪtər] *n* spectromètre *m*

spectroscope ['spektrəskəʊp] *n* spectroscope *m*

spectroscopy [spek'trɒskəpɪ] *n* spectroscopie *f*

spectrum, *pl* **-tra** ['spektrəm, -trə] *n* **(a)** *Phys etc* spectre *m*; **the colours of the s.** les couleurs spectrales *ou* du spectre; **s. analysis** analyse *f* spectrale **(b)** (*of opinions*) éventail *m*; **a wide s. of opinions** un large éventail d'opinions; **the whole s. of political opinion** tout l'éventail des opinions politiques; **across the political s.** dans l'ensemble des tendances politiques

speculate ['spekjʊleɪt] *vi* **(a)** **to s. on** *or* **about sth** (*wonder*) spéculer *ou* méditer sur qch; (*conjecture*) faire des conjectures sur qch **(b)** *Fin* spéculer; **to s. on the Stock Exchange** spéculer en Bourse

speculating ['spekjʊleɪtɪŋ] *n Fin* spéculation *f*

speculation [spekjʊ'leɪʃən] *n* **(a)** (*wondering*) spéculation *f*, méditation *f*; (*conjecture*) conjecture *f* (**on, about** sur); **it was pure s. on his part** c'était (une) pure conjecture de sa part **(b)** *Fin* spéculation *f*; **to buy sth on s.** acheter qch à titre de spéculation

speculative ['spekjʊlətɪv] *adj also Fin* spéculatif, -ive; **these are merely s. assumptions** ce sont là de pures hypothèses *ou* de pures conjectures; *St Exch* **s. security** valeur *f* de spéculation, valeur spéculative

speculatively ['spekjʊlətɪvlɪ] *adv* (*to suggest, argue*) à titre d'hypothèse; (*to invest*) spéculativement

speculator ['spekjʊleɪtər] *n* spéculateur, -trice; *St Exch* joueur, -euse en Bourse; spéculateur, -trice

speculum, *pl* **-ums, -a** ['spekjʊləm, -əmz, -ə] *n Med* spéculum *m*

speech [spiːtʃ] *n* **(a)** (*faculty*) la parole; **to lose the power of s.** perdre la parole; **her s. was slow and deliberate** elle parlait lentement en pesant ses mots; **to be slow of s.** parler lentement; **to be abrupt in one's s.** parler d'une manière brusque; *Comptr* **s. chip** puce *f* de traitement de la parole; **s. defect** trouble *m* d'élocution; **s. impediment** défaut *m* d'élocution; *Comptr* **s. recognition** reconnaissance *f* de la parole, reconnaissance vocale

(b) (*language*) (*of a people*) langue *f*; (*of a region etc*) parler *m*; **things which people say in everyday s.** des choses que les gens disent dans la langue de tous les jours

(**c**) (*address*) discours *m*, allocution *f*; **to give** *or* **make a s.** faire *ou* prononcer un discours *ou* une allocution; **s.!, s.!** un discours!, un discours!; *Br Sch* **s. day** = distribution *f* des prix; **s. making** (*speeches*) discours *mpl*
(**d**) [①A61,21; A73,viii] *Gram* **part of s.** partie *f* du discours; **direct/indirect s.** discours *m ou* style *m* direct/indirect; **figure of s.** figure *f* de rhétorique

speech community *n Ling* communauté *f* de langue

speechify ['spi:tʃɪfaɪ] *vi Pej* discourir, pérorer

speechifying ['spi:tʃɪfaɪɪŋ] *n Pej* beaux discours *mpl*, laïus *m*

speechless ['spi:tʃlɪs] *adj* (**a**) (*struck dumb*) interdit, interloqué, muet; **to be s. with anger/fear/rage** être muet de colère/peur/rage; **emotion left him s.** l'émotion l'a laissé muet; **I was s.** (*with anger, surprise etc*) j'étais sans voix; **I'm s.!** je ne sais pas quoi dire! (**b**) (*for physiological reasons*) incapable de parler

speechlessly ['spi:tʃlɪslɪ] *adv* sans voix

speech therapist *n* orthophoniste *mf*

speech therapy *n* orthophonie *f*

speechwriter ['spi:tʃraɪtər] *n* rédacteur, -trice de discours

speed[1] [spi:d] *n* (**a**) vitesse *f*, rapidité *f*; (*of engine, machine*) vitesse, régime *m*; *Phot* (*of film*) vitesse; (*of lens*) rapidité; **the s. of light/sound** la vitesse de la lumière/du son; *Lit* **to make all s.** faire diligence, se hâter; **with all possible s.** aussi rapidement *ou* aussi vite que possible; **the s. with which she learnt/the building was completed** la vitesse à laquelle elle a appris/le bâtiment a été terminé; *Aut etc* **at s.** (*to travel*) à grande vitesse; **at top** *or* **full s.** à toute vitesse; (*of runners*) à toutes jambes; **to drive at top s.** rouler à toute vitesse *ou* à toute allure; *Naut* **full s. ahead/astern!** en avant/en arrière toute!; **car with a maximum s. of 150 km an hour** voiture qui plafonne à 150 km à l'heure; **cruising s.** vitesse *ou* régime de croisière; *Av* **take-off s.** vitesse de décollage; **to gather/lose s.** prendre/perdre de la vitesse; **to reduce s.** ralentir; **to pick up s.** (*of train, car*) prendre de la vitesse; *Aut* **s. sensor** capteur *m* de vitesse
(**b**) (*gear*) vitesse *f*; **five-s. gearbox** boîte *f* à cinq vitesses
(**c**) *Arch* **to wish sb good s.** souhaiter bonne chance à qn
(**d**) *F* (*amphetamine*) amphétamine *f*, *F* amphé *f*

speed[2] **1** *vi* (**a**) (*pt, pp* **sped** [sped] *or* **speeded**) (*hasten*) se hâter, se presser; (*go fast*) aller vite; *Aut etc* (*go fast*) faire de la vitesse; **the car was speeding towards us** la voiture arrivait sur nous à toute vitesse; **we are speeding towards a crisis** nous allons à grands pas vers une crise
(**b**) (*pt, pp* **speeded**) *Aut* (*exceed speed limit*) faire un excès de vitesse; **I was caught speeding** j'ai eu une contravention pour excès de vitesse
(**c**) *F* **to be speeding** (*be under effect of amphetamines*) être sous amphés
2 *vt* (*pt, pp* **sped** *or* **speeded**) *Arch, Lit* **to s. sb on his/her way** (*wish a good journey*) souhaiter bon voyage à qn; *esp Hum* (*encourage to leave*) encourager *ou* presser qn à partir plus vite; *Arch* **God s. (you)!** bon voyage!

▶ **speed along 1** *vi* (*in car, on bike*) rouler vite; *F* foncer; (*on foot*) marcher *ou* courir vite; **the work is speeding along** le travail avance à bonne allure **2** *vtsep* (*work*) faire avancer *ou* progresser en vitesse

▶ **speed back 1** *vi* (*of person, driver*) rentrer à toute vitesse; **she sped back to Edinburgh** elle est retournée à Édimbourg à toute vitesse **2** *vtsep* (*person*) ramener à toute vitesse

▶ **speed off 1** *vi* (*on foot, in car*) partir à toute allure **2** *vtsep* **they sped him off to hospital** ils l'ont transporté à l'hôpital à toute vitesse

▶ **speed up 1** *vi* (*of driver, runner etc*) accélérer; (*of work, pace*) s'accélérer; (*work faster*) travailler plus rapidement **2** *vtsep* (*staff, project*) activer; (*job*) activer, accélérer; **to s. things up** accélérer *ou* activer les choses

speedboat ['spi:dbəʊt] *n* vedette *f*; (*with outboard motor*) hors-bord *m inv*

speed bump *n* ralentisseur *m*

speed cop *n F* motard *m*

speedily ['spi:dɪlɪ] *adv* rapidement

speediness ['spi:dɪnɪs] *n* rapidité *f*

speeding ['spi:dɪŋ] *n Aut* (*exceeding speed limit*) excès *m* de vitesse; **s. fine** contravention *f* pour excès de vitesse; **s. laws** réglementation *f* de la vitesse

speeding up *n* accélération *f*

speed limit *n* limitation *f* de vitesse; **to exceed the s.** faire un excès de vitesse; **exceeding the s.** excès *m* de vitesse

speed merchant *n F* fou *m* du volant

speedo ['spi:dəʊ] *n F* = **speedometer**

speedometer [spi:'dɒmɪtər] *n Aut etc* compteur *m* (de vitesse)

speedster ['spi:dstər] *n* (*car*) bolide *m*; (*driver*) fou *m* du volant, *Pej* chauffard *m*

speed trap *n* contrôle *m* de vitesse-surprise

speed-up *n* accélération *f*

speedway ['spi:dweɪ] *n* (**a**) *Sp* (*motorcycle racing*) speedway *m*; (*track*) circuit *m* de speedway; *Am* (*for cars*) circuit automobile; **s. rider** pilote *m* de speedway (**b**) *Am* (*fast road*) = autoroute *f*

speedwell ['spi:dwel] *n* (*plant*) véronique *f*

speedwriting ['spi:draɪtɪŋ] *n* écriture *f* abrégée

speedy ['spi:dɪ] *adj* (*person, work, response etc*) rapide, prompt; (*car*) rapide; **s. revenge** prompte vengeance

speleologist [spi:lɪ'ɒlədʒɪst] *n* spéléologue *mf*

speleology [spi:lɪ'ɒlədʒɪ] *n* spéléologie *f*

spell[1] [spel] *n* (*magic words*) formule *f* magique, charme *m*; (*enchanted state*) sort *m*, maléfice *m*, charme; **to cast a (magic) s. over sb, to put a (magic) s. on sb** jeter un sort à qn, ensorceler qn; **to break the s.** rompre le charme; **under a s.** sous un charme, ensorcelé

spell[2] (*pt, pp* **spelt, spelled** [spelt, speld]) **1** *vt* (**a**) (*out loud*) épeler; (*in writing*) orthographier; **how is it spelt?, how do you s. it?** comment ça s'épelle *ou* s'écrit?; **how do you s. 'Mississippi'?** comment écrit-on 'Mississippi'?; **can you s. that for me?** (*on telephone etc*) pouvez-vous me l'épeler?; **it's spelt** *or* **you s. it with an 'o'** ça s'écrit avec un 'o'
(**b**) **what do these letters s.?** quel mot forment ces lettres?
(**c**) (*signify*) signifier; **to s. disaster** être un désastre; **this spells disaster** on est perdu; **it would s. disaster** cela serait un désastre
2 *vi* orthographier *ou* écrire correctement; **he can't s.** il est nul en orthographe; **she can't s. very well** elle n'est pas très bonne en orthographe

spell[3] *n* (**a**) (*period*) période *f*; *Austr* (*rest period*) repos *m*; **to rest for a (short) s.** se reposer pendant quelque temps; **a long s. of cold weather** une longue période de froid; **during the cold s.** pendant le coup de froid; **we're in for a s. of wet weather** le temps se met à la pluie; **to suffer from dizzy spells** être sujet à des vertiges; **it's his second s. in prison** c'est son deuxième séjour en prison; **the end of the party's long s. in power is in sight** le parti est en train de vivre ses derniers moments au pouvoir
(**b**) (*turn*) (*of duty*) tour *m*; **to do a s. of duty** faire un tour de service; **to take spells at the pumps** se relayer aux pompes; **do you want to take a s. at the wheel?** tu veux me relayer au volant?

spell[4] *vt* (**a**) *Am F* (*relieve*) (*person*) relayer, relever (*dans son travail*) (**b**) *Austr* (*allow to rest*) (*horse*) laisser reposer

▶ **spell out** *vtsep* (*address, name etc*) (*pronounce individual letters of*) épeler; (*have difficulty in reading*) déchiffrer péniblement; *Fig* (*explain explicitly*) expliquer bien clairement; **... even though I spelled my name out for him** ... bien que je lui aie épelé mon nom; *Fig* **do I have to s. it out for you?** faut-il que je te fasse un dessin?; *Fig* **I'll s. it out for you** je vais te le dire clairement

spellbinder ['spelbaɪndər] *n* (*speaker*) orateur, -trice captivant(e)

spellbinding ['spelbaɪndɪŋ] *adj* envoûtant

spellbound ['spelbaʊnd] *adj* (*fascinated*) envoûté, fasciné; **to hold sb s.** envoûter qn, fasciner qn

spell-check *n Comptr* correction *f* orthographique; **to do** *or* **run a s. on a document** effectuer une correction orthographique sur un document

spell-checker *n Comptr* correcteur *m* orthographique *ou* d'orthographe

speller ['spelər] *n* (**a**) (*person*) **to be a good/a bad s.** être fort/faible en orthographe (**b**) (*book*) alphabet *m*

spelling ['spelɪŋ] *n* [①A74] orthographe *f* **his s. is atrocious** son orthographe est déplorable; **s. mistake** faute *f* d'orthographe; **s. test** test *m* d'orthographe

spend[1] [spend] *n esp Com* dépenses *fpl*

spend[2] (*pt, pp* **spent** [spent]) **1** *vt* (**a**) (*money*) dépenser; **to s. one's money on cigarettes** dépenser son argent en cigarettes; **her father has spent a great deal on her education** son père a dépensé beaucoup pour ses études; **to s. money on sb** dépenser son argent pour qn; **she spends money like water** l'argent lui fond *ou* glisse entre les mains; *Br F* **to s. a penny** (*urinate*) faire pipi
(**b**) (*pass*) (*time*) passer; **to s. the night** passer la nuit; **to s. Sunday in the country** passer le dimanche à la campagne; **haven't you got any better ways of spending your time?** c'est tout ce que tu trouves à faire pour t'occuper?; **could you please s. a little time talking to her about it?** pourrais-tu prendre un peu de temps pour lui en parler?; **how do you s. your weekends?** qu'est-ce que tu fais le week-end?
(**c**) (*expend*) (*time, energy*) consacrer; **to s. time on (doing) sth** consacrer *ou* employer du temps à (faire) qch; **to s. a lot of effort on a job** se donner beaucoup de mal pour un travail; **if you spent a bit more care on ...** si tu apportais *ou* mettais un peu plus de soin à ...

(d) (*usu passive*) (*use up*) (*one's strength, ammunition*) épuiser; **her strength/energy was all but spent** elle n'avait presque plus de forces/d'énergie

2 *vi* dépenser

spendable ['spendəb(ə)l] *adj* **s. income** revenu *m* dépensable

spender ['spendər] *n* **to be a big s.** être très dépensier; **they are the biggest arms s.** ce sont eux qui dépensent le plus en armement

spending ['spendɪŋ] *n* dépense *f*; **public s.** dépenses *fpl* publiques; **s. money** argent *m* disponible pour les loisirs; (*pocket money*) argent de poche; **s. power** pouvoir *m* d'achat; **s. spree** vague *f* de dépenses; **to go on a s. spree** faire des folies

spendthrift ['spendθrɪft] *n* dépensier, -ière; **s. habits** habitudes *fpl* dépensières

spent[1] [spent] *adj* (a) (*tired*) épuisé (b) (*used up*) épuisé; **s. bullet** balle *f* morte; **s. match** allumette *f* usagée

spent[2] *see* **spend**[2]

sperm[1] [spɜːm] *n Physiol* sperme *m*; **s. bank** banque *f* de sperme; **s. donor** donneur *m* de sperme

sperm[2] *n* **s. whale** cachalot *m*; **s. oil** huile *f* de spermaceti

spermaceti [spɜːmə'setɪ] *n* spermaceti *m*, blanc *m* de baleine

spermatozoon, *pl* **-oa** [spɜːmətəʊ'zəʊɒn, -əʊə] *n* spermatozoïde *m*

spermicidal [spɜːmɪ'saɪd(ə)l] *adj* spermicide

spermicide ['spɜːmɪsaɪd] *n* spermicide *m*

spew[1] [spjuː] *vti* (*vomit*) vomir, *Sl* dégueuler; *Sl* **it makes you want to s.!** ça fait gerber!

spew[2] *n F* (*vomit*) vomi *m*, *Sl* dégueulis *m*

▶ **spew forth, spew out** 1 *vi* (*of lava, flames etc*) jaillir, fuser (**from, of** de); *Fig* (*of propaganda, lies, etc*) fuser 2 *vtsep* (*lava, Fig propaganda*) déverser

▶ **spew up** *vi, vtsep* (*vomit*) vomir, *Sl* dégueuler

sphagnum, *pl* **-a** ['sfægnəm, -ə] *n* **s. (moss)** sphaigne *f*

sphere [sfɪər] *n* (a) *Astron, Geom* sphère *f*; **the celestial s.** la sphère céleste (b) (*field*) domaine *m*, sphère *f*; (*social circle*) milieu *m*, sphère; **to extend one's s. of activity** étendre sa sphère d'activité; **that is not within my s.** cela n'est pas de mon domaine *ou* de mon ressort; **in the political s.** sur le plan politique; **in political/academic spheres** dans les milieux politiques/universitaires; **s. of influence** sphère *ou* zone *f* d'influence

spherical ['sferɪk(ə)l] *adj* sphérique

spheroid ['sfɪərɔɪd] *n* sphéroïde *m*

sphincter ['sfɪŋktər] *n* sphincter *m*

sphinx, *pl* **sphinxes** [sfɪŋks, 'sfɪŋksɪz] *n Myth* sphinx *m*

sphinx-like *adj* de sphinx; (*smile*) énigmatique

spice[1] [spaɪs] *n* (a) *Culin* épice *f*; **mixed spice(s)** épices mélangées; **s. rack** étagère *f ou* présentoir *m* à épices (b) *Fig* sel *m*, piquant *m*; **to give s. to a story** pimenter un récit; **the s. of life** le sel *ou* le piquant de la vie; **the s. of adventure** le piment de l'aventure

spice[2] *vt* (a) (*cake, drink etc*) épicer (b) *Fig* (*story etc*) pimenter, relever

spiciness ['spaɪsɪnɪs] *n* (a) (*of food*) caractère *m* épicé (b) *Fig* (*of story*) piquant *m*, sel *m*

spick [spɪk] 1 *adj* **s. and span** reluisant de propreté, propre comme un sou neuf; (*person*) tiré à quatre épingles 2 *n Am Offensive, Sl* (*Spanish-American*) latino *mf*

spicy ['spaɪsɪ] *adj* (a) *Culin* (*spiced*) épicé; (*taste*) relevé (b) *Fig* (*story, conversation etc*) piquant, croustillant; (*risqué*) salé, épicé, poivré; **to tell s. stories** en dire de vertes

spider ['spaɪdər] *n* (a) araignée *f*; **s.'s web,** *Am* **s. web** toile *f* d'araignée (b) *Br* (*for luggage*) fixe-bagages *m inv* (c) *F* (*wheelbrace*) clé *f* en croix

spider crab *n* araignée *f* de mer

spiderman, *pl* **-men** ['spaɪdəmæn, -men] *n Br* ouvrier *m* qui travaille au sommet des édifices

spider monkey *n* atèle *m*, singe-araignée *m*, *pl* singes-araignées

spidery ['spaɪdərɪ] *adj* (*resembling a spider*) qui ressemble à une araignée; **s. handwriting** pattes *fpl* de mouches

spiel [ʃpiːl, spiːl] *n F* baratin *m*, speech *m*; (*of salesman*) boniment *m*; **he gave me some s. about having been held up at the airport** il m'a servi tout un baratin comme quoi il avait été bloqué à l'aéroport

▶ **spiel off** *vtsep Am F* (*recite*) débiter

spiffing ['spɪfɪŋ] *adj Old-fashioned Br F* épatant

spigot ['spɪgət] *n* (a) (*stopper*) (*of barrel*) fausset *m* (b) *US* (*faucet for water etc*) robinet *m* (c) (*handle of tap*) clef *f* (de robinet)

spike[1] [spaɪk] *n* (a) (*of railing, helmet*) pointe *f*; (*of barbed wire etc*) piquant *m*; **impaled on the spikes of the railings** empalé sur la grille; **s. heel** (*on woman's shoes*) talon *m* aiguille; **s. (nail)** clou *m* à large tête *ou* à tête de diamant; **s. file** pique-notes *m inv*; *Sp* **spikes** (*running shoes*) chaussures *fpl* à pointes (b) *Bot* épi *m*; **s. lavender** lavande *f* aspic *m* (c) *El* pointe *f ou* crête *f* de tension (d) *Journ* pique *f*; **on the s.** rejeté

spike[2] *vt* (a) (*fit with spikes*) armer de pointes; **spiked gate** grille *f* à pointes *ou* garnie de pointes; *Sp* **spiked shoes** chaussures *fpl* à pointes (b) (*thwart*) (*affair*) faire avorter; (*plan*) contrecarrer, entraver; *Fig* **to s. sb's guns** priver qn de ses moyens d'action, mettre qn hors d'action (c) (*add alcohol to*) (*drink*) corser (d) *Journ* (*story, article*) rejeter, *F* balancer

spiked [spaɪkt] *adj Journ* rejeté

spikenard ['spaɪknɑːd] *n Lit* (*ointment*) nard *m* (indien)

spiky ['spaɪkɪ] *adj* (a) (*with sharp points*) piquant; **s. hair** (*short*) cheveux *mpl* en brosse; (*of punk etc*) cheveux hérissés (b) *F* (*touchy, irritable*) susceptible, chatouilleux, -euse

spill[1] [spɪl] *n* (*fall*) **to have** *or* **take a s.** culbuter; (*from bicycle, horse*) tomber, faire une chute, *F* ramasser *ou* se prendre une pelle

spill[2] (*pt, pp* **spilt, spilled** [spɪlt, spɪld]) 1 *vt* (*liquid, salt*) renverser; (*blood*) verser; **without spilling a drop** sans laisser tomber une goutte; *Fig* **to s. the beans** vendre la mèche 2 *vi* (*of liquid*) se répandre, couler; **some wine had spilled on the carpet** du vin s'était répandu sur le tapis

spill[3] *n* (*for lighting fire etc*) allume-feu *m inv*

▶ **spill out** 1 *vi* (*of liquid etc*) déborder; *Fig* (*of words*) sortir; **the crowd started spilling out of the stadium** la foule commença à se déverser hors du stade 2 *vtsep* (*liquid*) renverser; *Fig* (*story*) répandre

▶ **spill over** *vi* (*of liquid*) déborder, se déverser; *Fig* (*of scandal, conflict*) se répandre (**into** dans); **the population has spilled over into the surrounding areas** la population s'est déversée sur les zones avoisinantes; **the conflict could s. over into neighbouring countries** le conflit risquerait de s'étendre aux pays voisins

spillage ['spɪlɪdʒ] *n* (*action*) déversement *m* accidentel; (*liquid*) liquide *m* déversé; **there's been a diesel s. on the M25** un chargement de gasoil s'est renversé sur la M25

spill light *n TV etc* lumière *f* parasite, mouche *f*

spillover ['spɪləʊvər] *n* (*excess population*) surpopulation *f*

spillway ['spɪlweɪ] *n HydE* déversoir *m*

spin[1] [spɪn] *n* (a) (*turning movement*) tournoiement *m*; (*of ball etc*) (mouvement *m* de) rotation *f*; (*of washing machine*) essorage *m*; *Av* vrille *f*; **to give sth a s.** (*in spin dryer*) essorer qch; **give the washing a quick s.** donne un petit coup d'essorage au linge; *Sp* **to put s. on a ball** donner de l'effet à une balle; **there was a lot of s. on that ball** il y avait beaucoup d'effet dans cette balle; **to go into a s.** *Aut* faire un tête-à-queue; *Fig* perdre la tête; *Fig* **the news sent him into a s.** la nouvelle l'a complètement paniqué; *Av* **flat s.** vrille à plat, tonneau *m*; *Fig F* **to be in a flat s.** ne pas savoir où donner de la tête; *Cr* **s. bowler** lanceur *m* qui donne de l'effet à la balle

(b) *F* (*short journey*) (*in car etc*) tour *m*, promenade *f*; **to go for a s.** aller faire un tour

(c) *Austr F* (*luck*) coup *m* de chance; (*bad luck*) malchance *f*

spin[2] (*pt, pp* **spun** [spʌn]; *prp* **spinning**) 1 *vt* (a) (*wool, cotton etc*) filer; **to s. its web** (*of spider*) tisser sa toile; **to s. a top** lancer une toupie; **to s. a coin** jouer à pile ou face (b) = **spin-dry** 2 *vi* (a) (*of top etc*) tourner; (*of suspended object*) tournoyer; (*of compass*) être affolé, s'affoler; **my head's spinning** la tête me tourne; **the room's spinning** (*because I'm dizzy, drunk etc*) la pièce tourne (autour de moi); **the blow sent him spinning** le coup l'a envoyé rouler (b) (*of wheel*) patiner (*sur place*); *Fishing* pêcher à la cuillère; **to s. for fish** pêcher, lancer

▶ **spin out** *vtsep* (*prolong*) (*speech*) délayer; (*discussion*) faire durer, prolonger; (*affair, story*) faire traîner en longueur; **to s. out one's money** économiser; **to s. out one's drink** faire durer sa boisson

▶ **spin round** 1 *vi* (*turn*) (*of car*) faire un tête-à-queue; (*of person*) pivoter, virevolter; (*turn around sharply*) se retourner vivement, faire volte-face; **she spun round in her chair** elle pivota sur sa chaise; **to s. round and round** tournoyer, tourbillonner 2 *vtsep* (*turn fast*) (*wheel, person etc*) faire tourner; (*several times*) (*person*) faire tournoyer

spina bifida [spaɪnə'bɪfɪdə] *n* spina-bifida *m*

spinach ['spɪnɪtʃ] *n* (*plant*) épinard *m*; *Culin* épinards *mpl*

spinal ['spaɪn(ə)l] *adj* spinal, vertébral; **s. column** colonne *f* vertébrale, *Spec* rachis *m*; **s. cord** moelle *f* épinière; **s. curvature** déviation *f* de la colonne vertébrale; **s. injury** lésion *f* de la colonne vertébrale

spindle ['spɪnd(ə)l] *n* (a) *Tex* fuseau *m*; **s.-shaped** fusiforme, fuselé (b) *MecE etc* arbre *m*, axe *m*, mandrin *m*; (*of potter's wheel etc*) pivot *m*; (*of axle, shaft*) fusée *f*

spindleshanks ['spɪnd(ə)lʃæŋks] *n Old-fashioned F* (*person*) grand échalas *m*
spindly ['spɪndlɪ] *adj* (*person*) maigrelet; (*legs*) grêle; (*furniture etc*) peu solide, peu robuste
spin doctor *n Pol* porte-parole *mf* d'un parti dont le rôle est de présenter la politique de son parti à la presse d'une manière favorable
spindrift ['spɪndrɪft] *n* embrun(s) *m*(*pl*), poudrin *m*
spin-dry *vt* (*clothes*) (faire) essorer
spin-dryer *n* essoreuse *f* (centrifuge)
spin-drying *n* essorage *m*
spine [spaɪn] *n* **(a)** *Anat* épine *f* dorsale, colonne *f* vertébrale, *Spec* rachis *m*; **s. chiller** (*story*) histoire *f* à vous glacer le sang; (*novel, film*) roman *m*/film *m* d'épouvante **(b)** *Geog* arête *f* **(c)** (*of book*) dos *m* **(d)** (*spike*) (*of plant, fish, hedgehog etc*) piquant *m*, épine *f*
spineless ['spaɪnlɪs] *adj* **(a)** (*person*) (*lacking character*) mou, *f* molle, sans caractère; (*lacking courage*) poltron, lâche **(b)** (*without spines*) (*plant, fish etc*) sans épines, sans piquants
spinet [spɪ'net] *n Mus* épinette *f*
spinnaker ['spɪnəkər] *n Naut* spinnaker *m*, spi *m*
spinner ['spɪnər] *n* **(a)** *Tex* fileur, -euse; *Fig* **s. of tales** *or* **yarns** conteur, -euse **(b)** *Fishing* cuillère *f* **(c)** *Cr* (*bowler*) lanceur *m* qui donne de l'effet à la balle; (*ball*) balle *f* avec de l'effet
spinneret ['spɪnəret] *n* (*of spider etc*) filière *f*
spinney ['spɪnɪ] *n Br* petit bois *m*, bosquet *m*
spinning ['spɪnɪŋ] **1** *adj* tournant, tournoyant; **my s. head** ma tête qui tourne/tournait **2** *n* **(a)** *Tex* (*of wool, cotton etc*) filage *m*; *Ind* filature *f* **(b)** **s. motion** *or* **movement** mouvement *m* rotatif *ou* de rotation
spinning factory *n Ind* filature *f*
spinning jenny *n Tex, Hist* métier *m* à filer
spinning mill *n Ind* filature *f*
spinning top *n* toupie *f*
spinning wheel *n* rouet *m*
spin-off *n* (*advantage*) retombée *f*, avantage *m ou* bénéfice *m* supplémentaire; (*by-product*) sous-produit *m*, *pl* sous-produits, (produit *m*) dérivé *m*; **the film is a s. from a TV series** le film est tiré d'une série télévisée; **a s. of the Olympics was meant to be the creation of permanent jobs** on estimait qu'une des retombées des Jeux Olympiques serait la création d'emplois permanents
spinster ['spɪnstər] *n* célibataire *f*, femme *f*/fille *f* non mariée, *Pej* vieille fille
spinsterhood ['spɪnstəhʊd] *n* état *m* de vieille fille
spiny ['spaɪnɪ] *adj Biol, Zool* épineux; (*covered in spines*) épineux, couvert d'épines *ou* de piquants
spiny anteater *n* échidné *m*
spiny lobster *n* langouste *f*
spiracle ['spaɪərək(ə)l] *n* (*of whale etc*) évent *m*; (*of insect*) stigmate *m*
spiral¹ ['spaɪər(ə)l] **1** *n* spirale *f*; (*single curve*) spire *f*, tour *m*; **in a s.** en spirale; *Av* **s. (climb/dive)** montée *f*/descente *f* en spirale *ou* en vrille; **wage-price** *or* **inflationary s.** course *f ou* spirale des prix et des salaires **2** *adj* spiral, en spirale; **s. binding** reliure *f* en spirale; **s. staircase** escalier *m* en spirale *ou* en colimaçon *ou* en hélice *ou* à vis
spiral² *vi* (**-ll-**, *US* **-l-**) (*form a spiral*) former une spirale; (*turn*) tourner en spirale; (*rise*) (*of steam, smoke*) s'élever en spirale; **spiralling prices** dérapage *m* des prix
▶ **spiral down** *vi* (*of plane*) descendre en spirale *ou* en vrille; (*of steps*) descendre en spirale *ou* en colimaçon
▶ **spiral up** *vi* (*of rocket etc*) s'élever *ou* monter en spirale; (*of smoke*) s'élever en spirale; (*of steps*) monter en spirale *ou* en colimaçon; (*of prices*) monter en vrille
spirally ['spaɪərəlɪ] *adv* en spirale
spire ['spaɪər] *n Archit* (*of church*) aiguille *f*, flèche *f*
spirit¹ ['spɪrɪt] *n* **(a)** (*soul*) esprit *m*, âme *f*; **I'll be with you in s.** je serai avec vous en pensée; *Bible* **the poor in s.** les pauvres d'esprit; *Rel, prov* **the s. is willing but the flesh is weak** l'esprit est prompt, mais la chair est faible

(b) (*incorporeal being*) esprit *m*; **the (Holy) S.** le Saint-Esprit, l'Esprit saint; **evil s.** esprit malin, mauvais génie *m*; **to raise a s.** évoquer un esprit; **to believe in spirits** croire aux esprits *ou* aux revenants; **s. writing** = écrits *mpl* dictés au médium par les esprits

(c) (*person*) esprit *m*; **the leading s.** (*in undertaking*) l'âme *f*, le chef; (*of revolt*) le meneur, la meneuse

(d) (*mood, attitude*) esprit *m*, disposition *f*; **the s. of the age** l'esprit du siècle; **the s. of liberty** l'esprit de liberté; **that was not the s. of the agreement** ce n'était pas l'esprit de cet accord; **to have the party s.** avoir envie de s'amuser; **to enter into the s. of sth** entrer dans l'esprit de qch; **to enter into the s. of the thing** entrer de bon cœur dans la partie; **to take sth in the right/wrong s.** prendre qch bien/mal; **he took it in the s. in which it was intended** il l'a pris comme il fallait; *F* **that's the s.!** à la bonne heure!

(e) (*courage*) caractère *m*, courage *m*; (*ardour*) ardeur *f*, entrain *m*; **man of unbending s.** homme au caractère inflexible; **woman of s.** (*having strong character*) femme de caractère; (*brave*) femme courageuse; **to show s.** montrer du caractère *ou* du courage; **to have s.** avoir de l'allant; **the pianist played with more s. than skill** le pianiste jouait avec plus d'ardeur que de talent; **his s. was broken** quelque chose s'était brisé en lui; **to be in good spirits** (*cheerful*) être gai; (*in a good mood*) être de bonne humeur; **to be in high spirits** être en train *ou* en verve; **to be in low spirits** (*depressed*) être abattu; (*feel sad*) se sentir tout triste; **to keep up one's spirits** ne pas perdre courage; **to raise** *or* **revive sb's spirits** remonter le moral à qn; **their spirits rose** ils reprirent courage; **with s.** (*to say sth, react*) énergiquement; **... she replied with s.** ... répondit-elle avec beaucoup de verve

(f) spirits (*drinks*) spiritueux *mpl*; **wines and spirits** vins *mpl* et spiritueux; **methylated spirits** alcool *m* dénaturé *ou* à brûler; **surgical s.** = alcool à 90°; *Th etc* **s. gum** gomme *f* arabique (*pour coller de faux cheveux etc*); **s. lamp/stove** lampe *f*/réchaud *m* à alcool
spirit² *vt* **they spirited him out of the back door** ils l'ont fait sortir discrètement par la porte de derrière; **to s. weapons into a building** introduire des armes dans un bâtiment; **the film spirits us back to 18th century France** le film nous transporte dans la France du 18ème siècle
▶ **spirit away, spirit off** *vtsep* (*remove secretly, quickly*) (*person*) faire disparaître *ou* enlever comme par enchantement; (*object*) subtiliser, escamoter
spirited ['spɪrɪtɪd] *adj* **(a)** (*person*) (*lively*) vif, animé; (*passionate*) plein de fougue *ou* de verve; (*intrepid*) intrépide; (*horse*) fougueux **(b)** (*style, reply etc*) plein de verve; **s. attack** attaque pleine de fougue; **s. discussion** discussion vive *ou* animée; *Mus* **to give a s. performance** jouer avec brio *ou* avec verve
spiritless ['spɪrɪtlɪs] *adj* **(a)** (*style*) sans vie; (*conversation etc*) qui manque d'entrain **(b)** (*person*) (*lacking courage, character*) sans courage, sans caractère; (*cowardly*) lâche; (*lacking vigour, passion*) sans vigueur, sans ardeur; (*weak*) mou, *f* molle
spirit level *n Carp etc* niveau *m* à bulle d'air *ou* à alcool
spiritual ['spɪrɪtjʊəl] **1** *adj Rel* spirituel; (*not material, physical*) spirituel, immatériel; **s. father** père *m* spirituel; **France/Cambridge is my s. home** la France est ma terre spirituelle/Cambridge, c'est la ville où je me sens chez moi; **his s. home is probably 18th century Holland** c'est probablement dans la Hollande du 18ème siècle qu'il se sentirait le plus à l'aise; **s. life** vie spirituelle **2** *n Mus* **(negro) s.** negro-spiritual *m*, *pl* negro-spirituals
spiritualism ['spɪrɪtjʊəlɪz(ə)m] *n* **(a)** (*belief in spirits*) spiritisme *m* **(b)** *Phil* spiritualisme *m*
spiritualist ['spɪrɪtjʊəlɪst] *n, adj* **(a)** (*believing in spirits*) spirite *mf* **(b)** *Phil* spiritualiste *mf*
spirituality [spɪrɪtjʊ'ælɪtɪ] *n* (*of soul, person*) spiritualité *f*
spiritually ['spɪrɪtjʊəlɪ] *adv* spirituellement
spirituous ['spɪrɪtjʊəs] *adj Fml* spiritueux, alcoolique; **s. liquor** alcool *m* fort, spiritueux *m*
spirt [spɜːt] *n, vti* = **spurt**
spit¹ [spɪt] *n* **(a)** *Culin* broche *f* **(b)** *Geog* **s. (of land)** pointe *f* (de terre), langue *f* (de terre)
spit² *vt* (**-tt-**) *Culin* (*put on a spit*) (*meat etc*) embrocher, mettre à la broche
spit³ *n* **(a)** (*saliva*) salive *f*; (*act of spitting*) crachement *m*; **he wiped the s. from his face** il essuya le crachat de son visage; **a gob of s.** un crachat; *F* **he's the s. of his father** c'est son père tout craché; *F* **s. and polish** astiquage *m*, fourbissage *m*; **a s. and sawdust bar** un bar tout simple **(b)** (*of rain*) crachin *m*
spit⁴ (*pt, pp* **spat** [spæt]; *prp* **spitting**) **1** *vi* (*of person, cat, pen*) cracher; (*of fire*) crépiter; (*of hot fat*) grésiller; **to s. in sb's face, to s. at sb** cracher au visage à qn; **I wouldn't trust him further than I could s.** je n'ai pas la moindre confiance en lui; **it's spitting (with rain)** il crachine, il fait du crachin **2** *vt* (*saliva, blood, insults*) cracher
spit⁵ *n* (*depth of spade*) profondeur *f* de fer de bêche; **to dig the ground two spits deep** labourer la terre à deux fers de bêche
▶ **spit back** *vi* (*of engine*) avoir des retours de flamme (au carburateur)
▶ **spit out** *vtsep* (*expel from mouth*) cracher; (*sth bad*) recracher; **you're fired!, he spat out** vous êtes viré!, lança-t-il; *F* **s. it out!** (*say what you want to*) accouche!, vide ton sac!
▶ **spit up** *vtsep* (*blood*) cracher

spite [spaɪt] *n* **(a)** *(malice)* rancune *f*; *(ill will)* malveillance *f*; *(pique)* dépit *m*; **from** *or* **out of s.** *(out of maliciousness)* par pure malice *ou* méchanceté; **he broke her toy out of pure** *or* **sheer s.** il a cassé son jouet par pure méchanceté envers elle; **she went to a different university out of s.** *(to annoy sb)* elle est allée dans une autre université pour ennuyer son monde **(b) in s. of ...** en dépit de ..., malgré ...; **in s. of everything** malgré tout; **in s. of the fact that I had warned her, in s. of my having warned her** en dépit du fait que je l'avais prévenue, bien que je l'aie prévenue

spite[2] *vt (person)* vexer, contrarier; **he does it to s. me** il le fait pour me tracasser *ou* m'ennuyer

spiteful ['spaɪtfʊl] *adj* méchant, malveillant; *(because of a grudge)* rancunier, vindicatif; **s. remark** observation méchante; **s. tongue** langue *f* de vipère

spitefully ['spaɪtfəlɪ] *adv* par malveillance, méchamment, par dépit *ou* rancune; **'that's a stupid idea', he said s.** 'c'est une idée stupide', dit-il méchamment

spitefulness ['spaɪtfʊlnɪs] *n* méchanceté *f*, malveillance *f*; *(because of grudge)* rancœur *f*

spitfire ['spɪtfaɪər] *n (person)* furie *f*

spitroast ['spɪtrəʊst] *vt Culin* cuire à la broche; **s. lamb** agneau à la broche

spitting ['spɪtɪŋ] *n* crachement *m*; **no s.** *(on sign)* défense de cracher; *F* **within s. distance of the front door** à deux pas de la porte d'entrée; *F* **he's the s. image of his father** c'est son père tout craché

spittle ['spɪt(ə)l] *n (saliva)* salive *f*; *(of animal)* bave *f*; **she was covered in s.** elle était couverte de crachats

spittoon [spɪ'tuːn] *n* crachoir *m*

spitz [spɪts] *n (dog)* loulou *m*

spiv [spɪv] *n Br F* filou *m*; *(on black market)* profiteur *m ou* trafiquant *m* du marché noir

spivvy ['spɪvɪ] *adj Br F (appearance, clothes)* tape-à-l'œil *inv*, tapageur; **do I look a bit s. in this?** n'ai-je pas l'air un peu filou avec ça?

splash[1] [splæʃ] **1** *n* **(a)** *(action) (of water, molten metal)* éclaboussement *m*; *(of waves)* clapotement *m*, clapotis *m*; **to fall into the water with a s.** tomber dans l'eau en faisant floc *ou* flac; *Fig F* **to make a (big) s.** faire sensation; **s. back** *(for sink etc)* panneau *m* protecteur; *Journ* **s. headline** manchette *f*; *Journ* **s. story** sujet *m* à sensation **(b)** *(mark, amount) (of mud, ink etc)* éclaboussure *f*; *(of colour, light)* tache *f*; *F* **a whisky and s.** un whisky soda; **just a s., please** *(of water etc)* très peu *ou* juste un soupçon, s'il vous plaît **2** *int* floc!, flac!, ploc!

splash[2] **1** *vt* éclabousser **(with water** d'eau); **to s. water at one another** se jeter de l'eau; *Journ* **a photo was splashed across the front page** une photo s'étalait en première page; **to s. one's way across a river** traverser une rivière en pataugeant; **to s. oneself** *(with water etc)* s'éclabousser; *(with paint etc)* se tacher; **to s. oneself/one's face with water** s'asperger/s'asperger la figure d'eau; **he really splashes the aftershave on** il s'asperge de lotion après-rasage **2** *vi (of liquid)* faire des éclaboussures; *(of waves)* clapoter; *(of tap)* cracher; *(of person, animal)* barboter, patauger

▶ **splash about, splash around 1** *vtsep (spread by splashing) (water)* faire jaillir, faire gicler; *F* **to s. one's money about** claquer son argent **2** *vi (of person, animal)* barboter, patauger

▶ **splash down** *vi Astronaut (land in sea)* amerrir

▶ **splash out** *Br F* **1** *vi (spend more money than usual)* claquer des ronds; **I've splashed out on a new hat** je me suis offert un nouveau chapeau; **you <u>have</u> been splashing out, haven't you!** tu as fait des frais *ou* des folies, dis-moi! **2** *vtsep* **we splashed out £500 on a new ...** nous avons dépensé *ou F* claqué 500 livres dans un nouveau ...

▶ **splash up 1** *vi (be thrown up) (of liquid, mud etc)* gicler **2** *vtsep (liquid, mud etc)* faire gicler

splashdown ['splæʃdaʊn] *n (of spacecraft)* amerrissage *m*

splat [splæt] *int* splof; **the fruit landed s. on the ground** le fruit tomba sur le sol avec un splof

splatter[1] ['splætər] *n* éclaboussure *f*

splatter[2] **1** *vt* **to s. sb with mud, to s. mud over sb** éclabousser qn de boue; **blood was splattered everywhere** tout était éclaboussé de sang **2** *vi (of liquid)* jaillir, gicler; **the tomato splattered against the wall** la tomate a giclé sur le mur

splay[1] [spleɪ] *vt (one's fingers)* écarter; *Archit etc* **to s. the sides of a window** ébraser *ou* évaser une fenêtre; **to walk with splayed feet** marcher en canard; **splayed opening** ouverture ébrasée *ou* évasée

splay[2] *adj (knees etc)* tourné en dehors

▶ **splay out 1** *vtsep (spread) (one's fingers)* écarter **2** *vi Archit etc* s'évaser

splayfooted [spleɪ'fʊtɪd] *adj (person)* **to be s.** marcher en canard

spleen [spliːn] *n* **(a)** *Anat* rate *f* **(b)** *Fml (anger)* bile *f*; **in a fit of s. ...** dans un accès de mauvaise humeur ...; **to vent one's s. on sb** décharger sa mauvaise humeur sur qn **(c)** *Arch, Lit (melancholy)* spleen *m*

splendid ['splendɪd] *adj (gown, occasion, view)* splendide, superbe, magnifique; *(meal)* magnifique; *(opportunity)* splendide; **we had a s. time** c'était formidable; **a policy of s. isolation** une politique isolationniste; *Fig* **he sat in s. isolation** il était assis, superbe dans sa solitude; **that's s., thanks very much!** c'est formidable, merci beaucoup!

splendidly ['splendɪdlɪ] *adv* splendidement, magnifiquement; **s. dressed** superbement vêtu; **they got along s.** ils s'entendirent magnifiquement bien

splendiferous [splen'dɪfərəs] *adj F usu Hum* magnifique, rutilant

splendour, *US* **splendor** ['splendər] *n* splendeur *f*, magnificence *f*; **the mountains in all their s.** les montagnes dans toute leur splendeur

splice[1] [splaɪs] *n (in rope, cable etc)* épissure *f*; *Carp* enture *f*; *Cin (in film)* (point *m* de) collage *m*; *(in magnetic tape)* raccord *m*

splice[2] *vt Naut etc (rope, cable)* épisser; *Carp (two pieces of wood)* enter; *Cin (film)* coller; *(magnetic tape)* raccorder, faire un raccord à; *Old-fashioned F* **to s. the mainbrace** boire un coup; *F* **to get spliced** *(marry)* se caser

splicing ['splaɪsɪŋ] *n Naut (of rope, cable)* épissage *m*; *Carp (of two pieces of wood)* enture *f*; *(of film, magnetic tape)* collage *m*

spliff [splɪf] *n Sl* joint *m*, cigarette *f* de marijuana

splint[1] [splɪnt] *n Med* attelle *f*, éclisse *f*; **to put a limb in splints** éclisser un membre

splint[2] *vt Med (broken limb)* éclisser

splinter[1] ['splɪntər] *n (of wood, glass, shrapnel)* éclat *m*; *(in finger etc)* écharde *f*; *Surg (of fractured bone)* esquille *f*; **I've got a s. in my finger** j'ai une écharde dans le doigt

splinter[2] **1** *vt (sth)* briser en mille morceaux; *(violently)* faire voler en éclats; *(oar, mast)* craquer **2** *vi (shatter)* éclater; *(violently)* voler en éclats; *(of oar, mast etc)* craquer, éclater; *(of bone)* se briser; *Fig (of political party)* éclater

splinter group *n Pol* groupe *m* séparatiste

splinterproof ['splɪntəpruːf] *adj (glass)* se brisant sans éclats

split[1] [splɪt] *n* **(a)** *(in floorboard etc)* fente *f*; *(small)* fissure *f*; *(in rock etc)* crevasse *f*; *(in dress, robe etc)* déchirure *f*; *(in skin)* gerçure *f*

(b) *(division) (in group)* division *f*, scission *f*; *(in personality)* dédoublement *m*; *(of screen)* éclatement *m*; **a three/four-way s. (in the voting)** division en trois/quatre (de l'électorat); **there was a s. in the party over ...** il y avait une division *ou* une scission dans le parti à propos de ...; **to heal the s.** effacer les divisions

(c) *(share in profits, loot etc)* part *f*; **they suggested a fifty-fifty s. of the profits** ils ont proposé de partager les bénéfices fifty-fifty

(d) banana s. banana *f* split

(e) *Gym* **to do the splits** faire le grand écart

(f) *(in meaning of word etc)* distinction *f*

split[2] *(pt, pp* **split**; *prp* **splitting) 1** *vt* **(a)** *(wood etc)* fendre; *(slate)* (re)fendre; *(rock etc)* cliver; *(tear)* déchirer; **to s. one's head (on sth)** s'ouvrir la tête (sur qch); *F* **to s. one's sides laughing** *or* **with laughter** se tenir les côtes; *Fig* **to s. hairs** ergoter, couper les cheveux en quatre

(b) *(divide) (amount of money, people into groups etc)* diviser **(into equal shares** en parts égales); **to s. sth in two** *or* **in half** *or* **down the middle** couper qch en deux; *Nucl Phys* **to s. the atom** fissionner l'atome; **to s. a company** scinder une société; *Pol* **to s. the party** provoquer une scission dans le parti; **this split the party three ways** ceci a divisé *ou* scindé le parti en trois; **to s. the vote** disperser les voix; **the Labour Party paid the price of a split vote** le parti travailliste a fait les frais de la division; **to s. one's vote,** *esp US* **to s. the ticket** partager ses votes entre plusieurs candidats; **to s. shares** fractionner des actions; **to s. a bottle** *(share)* partager une bouteille; **to s. the difference** partager la différence; *F* **can you s. a fiver for me?** pouvez-vous me faire la monnaie de cinq livres?

2 *vi* **(a)** *(of wood etc)* se fendre; *(of rock)* se cliver; *(of skin etc)* se gercer; *(of dress etc)* se déchirer; *(of seam in dress etc)* craquer; *Fig (of political party etc)* se scinder; *F* **my head's splitting** j'ai un mal de tête fou

(b) *Sl (leave)* mettre les bouts

split[3] *adj* **s. ends** *(in hair)* fourches *fpl*; **I tend to get s. ends**

j'ai des cheveux qui ont tendance à fourcher; [①A41,vii] *Gram* **s. infinitive** infinitif *m* éclaté (*lorsqu'un mot s'intercale entre 'to' et le verbe*); **s. peas** pois *mpl* cassés; *Psy* **he has a s. personality** il souffre d'un dédoublement de personnalité; *MecE* **s. pin** goupille *f* (fendue); *Comptr* **s. screen** écran *m* divisé, multi-écran *m*; **to work a s. shift** avoir une journée de travail discontinue

▶ **split away** *vi* = **split off 1**

▶ **split off 1** *vi* (*become detached*) se séparer, se détacher (*par clivage*); *Fig* (*leave group*) se séparer **2** *vtsep* (*break off*) détacher (*par clivage*)

▶ **split on** *vipo Br Sl* (*inform on*) (*person*) dénoncer; (*accomplice, friend*) donner

▶ **split open 1** *vi* (*burst open*) se fendre, s'ouvrir **2** *vtsep* (*break open*) ouvrir; **to s. one's head open** s'ouvrir la tête

▶ **split up 1** *vtsep* **(a)** (*divide*) (*money, work, loot*) répartir, partager; (*couple, people fighting*) séparer; (*organization, party*) diviser, scinder; (*break up into several parts*) (*party etc*) fragmenter; **we split the work up amongst ourselves** nous nous sommes réparti le travail; **I don't want to s. you and Joyce up** je ne veux pas te séparer de Joyce; **the police tried to s. the crowd up** la police a essayé de disperser la foule

(b) (*break down, analyse*) (*meaning of a word*) analyser, décomposer; **it should be split up into paragraphs** il faudrait le décomposer *ou* diviser en paragraphes; *Ch* **to s. up a compound into its elements** dédoubler un composé en ses éléments

2 *vi* (*divide*) **the compound had split up into its elements** le composé s'était divisé en ses éléments; **the party split up (into three groups)** le parti s'est divisé (en trois groupes); **Paul and Anne have split up** Paul et Anne se sont séparés *ou* ont rompu; **the rock group split up in 1992** le groupe de rock s'est séparé en 1992

split-level *adj Archit* (*building, room etc*) à deux niveaux; **s. grill** grill *m* à deux étages

split second *n* quart *m* de seconde

split-second *adj* **with s. timing** avec un minutage réglé au dixième de seconde; **trapeze work requires s. timing** le trapèze requiert une synchronisation réglée au dixième de seconde

splitter (box) ['splɪtər] *n Aut* doubleur *m* de gamme

splitting ['splɪtɪŋ] **1** *adj F* **to have a s. headache** avoir un mal de tête fou **2** *n* **(a)** *Nucl Phys* **s. of the atom** fission *f* de l'atome **(b)** = **splitting up**

splitting up *n* **(a)** (*act of breaking up*) fragmentation *f*; (*of sth*) division *f*, fractionnement *m* **(b)** (*division*) (*of piece of land etc*) division *f*; (*of two people etc*) séparation *f*; (*of political party etc*) scission *f*

split-up *n* (*in political party*) division *f*, scission *f*; (*of couple*) séparation *f*, rupture *f*; (*of friends*) séparation

split-view mirror *n Aut* rétroviseur *m* à double miroir

splodge¹ [splɒdʒ] *n F* (*stain*) (*of colour, ink*) pâté *m*; (*piece*) (*of ice-cream, ketchup etc*) plâtrée *f*

splodge² *vt F* (*stain*) tacher, barbouiller (**with** de); **he splodged a great lump of cream on top** il balança une grosse cuillerée de chantilly par-dessus

splotch¹ [splɒtʃ] *n F* (*of colour, ink*) tache *f*

splotch² *vt F* tacher, barbouiller (**with** de)

splurge¹ [splɜːdʒ] *n F* **(a)** (*ostentation*) esbroufe *f*, épate *f* **(b)** (*extravagant spending*) folles dépenses *fpl*; **I have a bit of a s. from time to time** je m'autorise quelques folies de temps en temps; **let's have a s. and give the biggest party ever** et si on claquait du fric et qu'on organisait la plus grande fête qu'on ait jamais vue

splurge² *vi F* = **splurge out**

▶ **splurge out** *vi F* (*spend extravagantly*) faire des dépenses extravagantes; **to s. out on sth** faire des folies pour qch

splutter¹ ['splʌtər] *n* **(a)** (*speech*) bredouillement *m* **(b)** (*of engine*) bafouillage *m*; **the engine gave a s. and died** le moteur a toussé puis est mort

splutter² **1** *vt* (*excuse, threat*) bredouiller **2** *vi* (*of person*) (*because of surprise, emotion*) bafouiller; (*because of anger*) s'étrangler; (*of engine*) bafouiller; **the engine finally spluttered into life** finalement, le moteur a toussé puis a démarré

▶ **splutter out 1** *vtsep* = **splutter²** *1* **2** *vi* (*of fire, firework etc*) s'éteindre avec un crépitement

spoil¹ [spɔɪl] *n* (*usu pl*) butin *m*; *Fig* **to claim one's share of the spoil(s)** demander sa part du gâteau; **one of the spoils of war** une prise de guerre

spoil² (*pt, pp* **spoiled, spoilt** [spɔɪld, spɔɪlt]) **1** *vt* **(a)** (*ruin*) (*evening, holiday, view*) gâcher; (*goods, decorations etc*) abîmer; **her hat was spoilt by the rain** son chapeau a été abîmé par la pluie; **the picnic was spoilt by the rain** le pique-nique a été gâché par la pluie; **to get spoilt** *or* **spoiled** (*of object*) s'abîmer; **to s. sb's fun** gâter *ou* gâcher le plaisir de qn; **it spoils (the beauty of) the view** ça gâche la vue; **to s. sb's appetite** couper l'appétit *ou* la faim à qn; **to s. the market** gâter le marché; **to s. the surprise** tout gâcher (*en dévoilant une surprise*); **don't s. the surprise for me** ne me gâche pas tout; **to s. the ending of a film/book (for sb)** gâcher un film/livre (à qn) en lui révélant la fin; **spoiled goods** marchandises *fpl* avariées; *Pol* **spoilt paper** bulletin *m* nul

(b) (*indulge*) (*person*) gâter; **a spoilt child** un enfant gâté; **we're spoilt here, not many cities have 20 theatres** nous sommes gâtés ici, peu de villes comptent 20 théâtres; **to be spoilt for choice** avoir l'embarras du choix

2 *vi* **(a)** (*of fruit, fish etc*) s'abîmer

(b) to be spoiling for a fight avoir envie de se battre; *F* chercher la bagarre

spoilage ['spɔɪlɪdʒ] *n Typ* déchets *mpl* de tirage

spoiler ['spɔɪlər] *n Av* déporteur *m*; *Aut* béquet *m*, becquet *m*, spoiler *m*; *Pol etc* (*candidate*) = candidat *m* qui se présente dans le but pur et simple de compromettre les chances d'un autre candidat; *Journ* = tactique *f* utilisée pour s'approprier le scoop d'un journal rival

spoilsport ['spɔɪlspɔːt] *n F* trouble-fête *mf inv*, rabat-joie *mf inv*; **don't be a s.!** ne joue pas les trouble-fête *ou* les rabat-joie!

spoke¹ [spəʊk] *n* **(a)** (*of wheel*) rayon *m*; **s. wheel** roue *f* à rayons **(b)** (*airport*) aéroport *m* d'apport **(c)** *Br Fig* **to put a s. in sb's wheel** mettre des bâtons dans les roues à qn

spoke² *see* **speak**

spoken ['spəʊk(ə)n] **1** *pp see* **speak 2** *adj* **s. language** langue *f* parlée; **the s. word** la parole; **my s. French is quite good** en français, je suis assez bon à l'oral

spoken-voice *adj* (*record*) parlé

spokeshave ['spəʊkʃeɪv] *n Carp* (*tool*) vastringue *f*

spokesman, *pl* **-men** ['spəʊksmən] *n* (*of party etc*) porte-parole *m inv*; **to act as s. for sb** être le porte-parole de qn; (*on one occasion*) prendre la parole au nom de qn

spokesperson ['spəʊkspɜːsən] *n* porte-parole *m inv*

spokeswoman, *pl* **-women** ['spəʊkswʊmən, -wɪmɪn] *n* (*femme f*) porte-parole *f inv*

spoliation [spəʊlɪ'eɪʃən] *n Fml* (*despoiling*) spoliation *f*

spondaic [spɒn'deɪɪk] *adj* (*in prosody*) spondaïque

spondee ['spɒndiː] *n* (*in prosody*) spondée *m*

spondulicks, spondulix [spɒn'djuːlɪks] *npl F* fric *m*

sponge¹ [spʌndʒ] *n* **(a)** (*for washing etc*), *Zool* éponge *f*; **to throw in the s.** *Boxing* jeter l'éponge; *Fig* s'avouer vaincu, abandonner la partie; **to have a s. bath** se laver avec une éponge; *Tex* **s. cloth** tissu *m* éponge; **s. fisher** pêcheur, -euse d'éponges **(b)** (*action*) coup *m* d'éponge; **to give sth a s.** passer l'éponge sur *ou* donner un coup d'éponge à qch **(c) s. (cake)** gâteau *m* mousseline, gâteau de savoie; **s. biscuit** = madeleine *f*

sponge² **1** *vt* **(a)** éponger, passer l'éponge sur **(b)** *F* (*cadge*) (*meal etc*) écornifler, grappiller; **to s. sth off** *or* **from sb** chiper *ou* taper qch à qn **2** *vi F* (*be parasite*) faire le parasite

▶ **sponge down** *vtsep* (*wash*) (*person*) doucher avec une éponge; (*horse*) éponger; (*car*) nettoyer à l'éponge

▶ **sponge off 1** *vtsep* (*stain*) enlever à l'éponge **2** *vipo F* (*parents, friends etc*) vivre aux crochets *ou* aux dépens de; **they're just sponging off the state!** ce ne sont que des parasites de l'État!

▶ **sponge on** *vipo F* = **sponge off 2**

▶ **sponge out** *vtsep* (*blood etc*) enlever à l'éponge; (*wound*) nettoyer à l'éponge

▶ **sponge up** *vtsep* (*liquid*) éponger

sponge bag *n* trousse *f* de toilette *ou* de voyage

sponger ['spʌndʒər] *n F* parasite *m*

sponginess ['spʌndʒɪnɪs] *n* spongiosité *f*; (*of cake, pastry*) moelleux *m*; (*of road surface*) caractère *m* mou; (*of soles*) souplesse *f*

spongy ['spʌndʒɪ] *adj* spongieux; (*cake, pastry*) moelleux; (*road surface*) mou, *f* molle; (*soles*) souple

sponsor¹ ['spɒnsər] *n* (*for athlete, team, festival, programme, giving money*) sponsor *m*; (*introducing new member to club, for student*) parrain *m*; (*at baptism*) parrain, marraine *f*; *Jur* garant *m*, répondant *m*, caution *f* (**for sb** de qn); **to stand s. to a child** (*at baptism*) tenir un enfant sur les fonts (baptismaux)

sponsor² *vt* **(a)** (*athlete, team, charity walker, festival etc*) sponsoriser; (*student*) parrainer; *Rad, TV* (*programme*) sponsoriser, parrainer; **sponsored walk** marche *f* sponsorisée (pour aider une œuvre de charité) **(b)** *Jur* (*act as guarantor for*) être le garant de, répondre de, se porter caution pour **(c)** *Rel* (*act as godparent to*) parrainer

sponsoring ['spɒnsərɪŋ] *n Mktg* parrainage *m*, mécénat *m*
sponsorship ['spɒnsəʃɪp] *n* **(a)** (*of athlete, team, festival etc, Rad, TV of programme*) parrainage *m*, sponsorat *m*; (*of student*) parrainage; *Mktg* **under the s. of** sous le patronage de; *Sp etc* **s. deal** contrat *m* de parrainage **(b)** *Jur* garantie *f*, caution *f* **(c)** *Rel* (*by godparent*) parrainage *m*
spontaneity [spɒntə'niːɪtɪ, -'neɪ-] *n* spontanéité *f*
spontaneous [spɒn'teɪnɪəs] *adj* (*person, gesture*) spontané; (*act, confession*) volontaire; **s. combustion** combustion *f* spontanée
spontaneously [spɒn'teɪnɪəslɪ] *adv* spontanément; **she s. offered to help** elle a spontanément proposé son aide
spoof[1] [spuːf] *n F* **(a)** (*play, film etc*) satire *f* (**on** de); **s. thriller** satire de film à sensations **(b)** (*trick*) blague *f*; **they erected some s. factories to fool the enemy** ils ont installé des usines factices pour tromper l'ennemi; **he sent round a s. memo about redundancies** il a fait passer une fausse circulaire *ou F* une circulaire bidon parlant de licenciements
spoof[2] *vt F* (*parody, satirize*) parodier, caricaturer
spook [spuːk] *n F* **(a)** (*ghost*) fantôme *m* **(b)** *Am* (*spy*) espion, -ionne
spooky ['spuːkɪ] *adj F* (*story etc*) qui fait peur; (*place*) sinistre; (*strange*) dingue; **it's s. here at night** c'est sinistre ici le soir; **he's a s. sort of person** il est du genre sinistre
spool[1] [spuːl] *n* **(a)** *Tex* bobine *f*, can(n)ette *f*; (*of sewing machine*) can(n)ette; **s. of thread** bobine de coton (à coudre) **(b)** *Fishing* tambour *m* (de moulinet) **(c)** *El* (corps *m* de) bobine *f*; *Phot, Cin* bobine (de film); **take-up s.** bobine enrouleuse; (**ribbon**) **s.** (*for typewriter*) bobine du ruban
spool[2] *vt Tex* bobiner; *Comptr* spouler, mettre en (file d')attente
spooler ['spuːlər] *n Comptr* (*for printing*) spouleur *m*, pilote *m* de mise en file d'attente
spoon[1] [spuːn] *n* **(a)** (*utensil*) cuillère *f*, cuiller *f*; **serving s.** cuillère de service *ou* à service **(b)** *Golf* bois *m* numéro 3, spoon *m*; *Fishing* **s. (bait), trolling s.** cuillère *f*
spoon[2] **1** *vt* **(a)** (*liquid*) prendre *ou* verser à l'aide d'une cuillère; **to s. syrup/gravy onto sth** verser un sirop/une sauce sur qch à l'aide d'une cuillère; **he spooned soup into his mouth** il enfournait de grandes cuillerées de soupe **(b)** *Fishing* pêcher à la cuillère **2** *vi Old-fashioned F* (*of couple*) se faire des mamours
▶ **spoon out** *vtsep* (*serve*) (*sauce etc*) servir (avec une cuillère)
▶ **spoon up** *vtsep* (*eat*) manger à la cuillère
spoonbill ['spuːnbɪl] *n* (*bird*) spatule *f* (blanche)
spoonerism ['spuːnərɪz(ə)m] *n* contrepèterie *f*
spoon-feed *vt* (*pt, pp* **-fed** [-fed]) nourrir à la cuillère; *Fig* (*student etc*) mâcher le travail à
spoonful ['spuːnfʊl] *n* cuillerée *f*
spoor [spʊər] *n* (*in hunting*) foulées *fpl*, piste *f*
sporadic [spə'rædɪk] *adj* sporadique; (*showers*) épars, isolé; (*work, Mil firing*) intermittent
sporadically [spə'rædɪk(ə)lɪ] *adv* sporadiquement; (*to fire, work*) par intervalles, à intermittence
spore [spɔːr] *n Biol* spore *f*
sporran ['spɒrən] *n Scot* = aumônière *f* en cuir parfois agrémentée de fourrure, portée sur le devant du kilt
sport[1] [spɔːt] *n* **(a)** sport *m*; **aquatic/winter sports** sports nautiques/d'hiver; **sports commentator** commentateur *m* sportif; **sports editor** rédacteur *m* en chef sportif; **sports facilities** installations *fpl* sportives; **sports** *or US* **s. jacket** *or* **coat** veste *f* sport; *Journ* **sports page** rubrique *f* sportive, page *f* des sports; **sports paper** journal *m* sportif; **sports press** presse *f* sportive; **sports programme** émission *f* sportive; *TV etc* **sports results** résultats *mpl* sportifs; **sports shop** magasin *m* de sport

(b) *F* **a (good** *or* **real) s.** (*good loser*) un beau joueur, une belle joueuse; (*generous, fair, lively person*) une personne sympa; **you're a real s.** tu es vraiment sympa; **a bad s.** (*bad loser*) un mauvais perdant, une mauvaise perdante; **come on, be a s.!** allez, sois sympa!; *esp Austr* **hello, (old) s.!** salut, mon vieux!

(c) *Old-fashioned* (*amusement*) jeu *m*, divertissement *m*, amusement *m*; **in s.** pour rire, par plaisanterie; **to make s. of sth** s'amuser *ou* se moquer de qch; **to have good s.** (*in hunting*) faire bonne chasse; (*in fishing*) faire bonne pêche *ou* bonne prise

(d) *Bot, Biol* variété *f* anormale, type *m* anormal
sport[2] **1** *vt* (*wear*) (*red waistcoat, carnation etc*) arborer **2** *vi* **(a)** *Old-fashioned* (*amuse oneself*) se divertir, s'amuser **(b)** *Biol, Bot* (*of plants, animals*) produire une variété anormale
sporting ['spɔːtɪŋ] *adj* **(a)** (*to do with sport*) sportif, -ive; **s. event** manifestation *f* sportive; **s. man/woman** (*horseracing enthusiast*) turfiste *mf* **(b)** (*fair, reasonable*) **it's very s. of him** c'est très chic de sa part; **you've got a s. chance** tu as tes chances; **to give sb a s. chance** donner sa chance à qn; **I'll make you a s. offer** je vais vous faire une offre honnête; **in a s. spirit** avec un esprit sportif, sportivement **(c)** *Old-fashioned* (*fond of hunting or fishing*) amateur de chasse/de pêche
sportingly ['spɔːtɪŋlɪ] *adv* sportivement
sportive ['spɔːtɪv] *adj Old-fashioned* (*joking*) badin; (*playful*) folâtre
sports car *n* voiture *f* de sport
sportscast ['spɔːtskɑːst] *n Am Rad, TV* émission *f* sportive
sportscaster ['spɔːtskɑːstər] *n Am Rad, TV* journaliste *m* sportif, journaliste *f* sportive
sports centre *n* complexe *m ou* centre *m* sportif
sports club *n* club *m* de sport
sports day *n Sch* = journée *f* de compétition sportive au sein d'un établissement scolaire
sports ground *n* terrain *m* de sport *ou* de jeux
sportsman, *pl* **-men** ['spɔːtsmən] *n* **(a)** (*player*) sportif *m*; (*hunter*) chasseur *m*; (*angler*) pêcheur *m* **(b) he's a real s.** (*fair-minded person*) il a l'esprit sportif; (*good loser*) il est beau joueur
sportsmanlike ['spɔːtsmənlaɪk] *adj* sportif, -ive; **in a s. way** sportivement
sportsmanship ['spɔːtsmənʃɪp] *n* **(a)** (*skill*) habileté *f ou* qualités *fpl* de sportif **(b)** (*fair-mindedness*) esprit *m* sportif, sportivité *f*
sportsperson ['spɔːtspɜːsən] *n* (*player*) sportif *m*, sportive *f*
sports saloon *n* berline *f* sport
sportswear ['spɔːtsweər] *n* vêtements *mpl* de sport
sportswoman, *pl* **-women** ['spɔːtswʊmən, -wɪmɪn] *n* **(a)** (*player*) sportive *f* **(b) she's a real s.** (*fair-minded person*) elle a l'esprit sportif; (*good loser*) elle est belle joueuse
sporty ['spɔːtɪ] *adj F* **(a)** (*fond of sport*) sportif, -ive **(b)** (*jacket etc*) gai; (*car*) sportif, -ive; **it's a bit too s.** c'est un peu trop sport
spot[1] [spɒt] *n* **(a)** (*place*) endroit *m*, lieu *m*; **a remote s.** un endroit écarté *ou* isolé; **beauty s.** site *m* touristique; *Aut* **a black s.** (*on road*) un point noir; **an unemployment black s.** une zone particulièrement touchée par le chômage; **X marks the s.** (*of crime etc*) la croix indique le lieu; **the police are on the s.** la police est sur les lieux; **to have sb on the s.** (*reporter, representative, agent etc*) avoir qn sur place; **our reporter on the s., Mary Smith** notre correspondante sur place, Mary Smith; *F* **to put sb on the s.** (*put in difficult position*) mettre qn dans une situation difficile; (*force to answer difficult question*) embarrasser qn par des questions; **to be fined on the s.** recevoir une amende sur-le-champ; **to do sth on the s.** (*straightaway*) faire qch sur place *ou* sur-le-champ; **to be killed on the s.** être tué sur le coup, être tué net; *F* **her performance failed to hit the high spots** sa représentation n'a pas été brillante; *F* **to be in a (tight) s.** (*in predicament*) être dans le pétrin; *F* **to get into a bit of a s.** se ficher dans le pétrin; **night s.** boîte *f* de nuit; **weak s.** point faible; **to find sb's weak s.** trouver le défaut dans la cuirasse de qn, trouver le point faible de qn; **blind s.** *Anat* point aveugle; *Aut* angle *m* aveugle; *F* **that's your blind s.** c'est là où vous refusez de voir clair

(b) (*stain*) tache *f*, macule *f*; (*on fruit etc*) tavelure *f*

(c) (*pimple*) bouton *m*; **to come out in spots** se couvrir de boutons; **it makes me come out in spots** ça me donne des boutons

(d) (*dot*) (*of colour*) (*on shirt, tie etc*) pois *m*; (*on playing card, domino*) point *m*; *Billiards* mouche *f*; **blue tie with red spots** cravate bleue à pois rouges; **a leopard's spots** la tacheture *ou* la moucheture d'un léopard; *F* **to knock spots off sb** (*beat*) battre qn à plate(s) couture(s); **she knocks spots off him** (*is much better than*) il ne lui arrive pas à la cheville; **the new Peugeot knocks spots off the ...** face à la nouvelle Peugeot, le ... ne fait pas le poids; *Med* **a s. on the lung** un voile au poumon

(e) *Br F* (*small amount*) (*of rain, wine*) goutte *f*; **a s. of whisky** une larme de whisky; **what about a s. of lunch?** si nous déjeunions?; **to do a s. of work** faire un peu de travail; **a s. of bother** *or* **trouble** un petit ennui; **to get into a s. of bother** s'attirer des ennuis

(f) (*spotlight*), *Th* projecteur *m*; (*in home, on exhibition stand*) spot *m*

(g) *TV, Rad* (*time reserved for adverts, specific commentator*) créneau *m*
spot[2] **(-tt-) 1** *vt* **(a)** (*mark with spots*) tacher, moucheter; (*stain, mark*) tacher, souiller; *Billiards* (*ball*) mettre sur la mouche

(b) (*notice*) (*person, object*) repérer, apercevoir; *Horseracing etc* (*winner*) prédire, repérer; *Mil* (*enemy* *positions etc*) repérer, observer; (*trains etc*) repérer; (*talent*) dénicher; **to s. sb doing sth** apercevoir qn en train de faire qch; **I spotted her in the crowd** je l'ai repérée au milieu de la foule; **to s. a mistake** détecter une erreur; **to s. an opportunity** repérer une occasion; **well spotted!** (*when noticing mistake*) bien vu!; (*when finding sb in crowd*) quel œil!; **I'd never have spotted it** je ne l'aurais jamais remarqué; **she was last spotted in the pub** la dernière fois qu'on l'a vue elle était au pub; **I spotted him as a potential troublemaker** j'ai très vite repéré qu'il était un agitateur

2 *vi* **it's spotting (with rain)** il pleuviote

spot buying *n Fin* achat *m* au comptant

spot cash *n Com* (argent *m*) comptant *m*

spot check *n* (*without notice*) contrôle *m* surprise; (*random check*) contrôle par sondage(s)

spot-check *vt* (*randomly*) contrôler par sondage(s); (*at random intervals*) contrôler à intervalles irréguliers; (*without notice*) faire des contrôles surprises de; **athletes are regularly spot-checked for anabolic steroids** on effectue souvent des contrôles surprises sur les athlètes pour détecter les anabolisants

spot deal *n* = **spot transaction**

spot height *n Geog* altitude *f*

spotless ['spɒtlɪs] *adj* (*shirt, reputation*) sans tache, immaculé; (*house, kitchen*) impeccable

spotlessly ['spɒtlɪslɪ] *adv* **s. clean** impeccable; **s. white** d'une blancheur immaculée *ou* parfaite

spotlessness ['spɒtlɪsnɪs] *n* propreté *f*

spotlight[1] ['spɒtlaɪt] *n Th, Cin* (*beam*) lumière *f* de projecteur; (*device*) spot *m*, projecteur *m* (à faisceau concentré); (*in home, on exhibition stand etc*) spot *m*; *Aut* projecteur auxiliaire orientable; **to hold the s.** *Th* occuper le centre de la scène (*dans la lumière du projecteur*); *Fig* avoir *ou* tenir la vedette; *Fig* **she has always been in** *or* **has never been out of the s.** elle n'a pas cessé de tenir la vedette *ou* d'être sur la sellette

spotlight[2] *vt* (*person, object*), *Th* diriger les projecteurs sur; *Fig* mettre en vedette

spotlighting ['spɒtlaɪtɪŋ] *n* (*in home*), *Th, Cin* éclairage *m* à effet

spot market *n St Exch* marché *m* au comptant

spot news *n* brève *f*

spot-on *adj F* exact, au point; **that's s.** c'est exact; **his answer was s.** sa réponse était parfaitement exacte *ou* correcte; **the missiles were s.** les missiles ont atterri en plein dans le mille

spot price *n Fin* cours *m* spot

spot rate *n Fin* cours *m* à vue, cours spot

spotter ['spɒtə(r)] *n Mil, Av* observateur *m*; **s. plane** avion *m* d'observation; **train s.** = personne *f* qui regarde passer des trains (*pour repérer les différents modèles*); **talent s.** dénicheur, -euse de talent

spotting ['spɒtɪŋ] *n* **train/plane s.** repérage *m* de trains/d'avions

spot trading *n Fin* négociations *fpl* au comptant

spot transaction *n St Exch* opération *f ou* transaction *f* au comptant

spotty ['spɒtɪ] **1** *adj* **(a)** (*marked with spots*) moucheté, tacheté; (*covered with stains*) plein de taches **(b)** (*pimply*) (*face, person*) couvert de boutons, boutonneux; **a s. adolescent** un adolescent boutonneux **2** *n F* **hi there, s.!** salut, le boutonneux/la boutonneuse!

spot-weld[1] *vt* souder par points

spot-weld[2] *n* soudure *f* par points

spot-welding *n* soudure *f* par points

spouse [spaʊz] *n Admin, Jur* conjoint, -ointe; *Arch, Lit* époux *m*, épouse *f*

spout[1] [spaʊt] *n* **(a)** (*of teapot, kettle etc*) bec *m*; (*of watering can*) canon *m*, goulot *m*; **s. (hole)** (*of whale*) évent *m*; *Constr* **rainwater s.** (*of gutter*) tuyau *m* de décharge, gargouille *f*, chantepleure *f*; *Sl* **to be up the s.** (*of plans, finances, economy*) être fichu *ou* foutu; (*of woman*) (*be pregnant*) être en cloque; *Sl* **to put sth up the s.** (*plans, finances, economy etc*) faire capoter qch **(b)** (*jet of liquid*) jet *m*; **a s. of water shot up** un jet d'eau partit

spout[2] **1** *vi* **(a)** (*of liquid*) jaillir, rejaillir; (*more forcefully*) gicler; (*of whale*) lancer un jet d'eau/d'air, souffler **(b)** *Fig F* (*of person*) parler à jet continu, dégoiser; **what's he spouting on about now?** qu'est-ce qu'il est en train de débiter maintenant? **2** *vt* **(a)** (*of person*) (*water etc*) faire jaillir, lancer; **the pipe spouted water everywhere** de l'eau jaillissait du tuyau **(b)** *Fig F* (*speech, nonsense*) dégoiser *ou* débiter à jet continu

▶ **spout out 1** *vi* (*of water, lava etc*) jaillir, sortir en giclant; **the liquid was spouting out of the barrel** le liquide sortait du tonneau en giclant, le liquide jaillissait du tonneau **2** *vtsep* **(a)** (*lava*) cracher; **the pipe spouted out water** de l'eau jaillissait du tuyau **(b)** *Fig F* (*utter*) (*statistics etc*) débiter

sprain[1] [spreɪn] *n Med* entorse *f*; (*less serious*) foulure *f*

sprain[2] *vt* (*ankle, wrist*) se fouler; (*more seriously*) se faire une entorse à; **sprained ankle** foulure *f* à la cheville; (*more serious*) entorse *f* à la cheville

sprang *see* **spring[2]**

sprat [spræt] *n* (*fish*) sprat *m*, harenguet *m*

sprawl[1] [sprɔːl] *n* **(a)** (*position*) position *f* affalée **(b)** (*of houses etc*) étendue *f*; **an urban s.** une agglomération

sprawl[2] *vi* **(a)** (*of person*) s'affaler, s'étaler; **he was lying sprawled (out) on the sofa** il était affalé sur le divan; **to send sb sprawling** faire tomber qn de tout son long; **to go sprawling** s'étaler par terre **(b)** (*of town etc*) s'étendre de tous les côtés; (*of plant*) s'étendre, se déployer

sprawling ['sprɔːlɪŋ] *adj* **(a)** (*person*) affalé **(b)** (*suburbs, plants*) tentaculaire; **s. handwriting** écriture *f* irrégulière et étalée

spray[1] [spreɪ] *n* (*of plant*) brin *m*, ramille *f*; **s. of flowers** branche *f* de fleurs, rameau *m* fleuri; *Archit, Sewing etc* chute *f* de fleurs; **s. of diamonds** aigrette *f* de diamants

spray[2] *n* **(a)** (*liquid*) (*of seawater*) embrun *m*, poudrin *m*; (*water in particles*) poussière *f* d'eau, eau *f* vaporisée; (*of perfume, fuel etc*) jet *m* atomisé *ou* pulvérisé; (*for hair*) spray *m* coiffant, laque *f*

(b) (*act of spraying*) coup *m* de vaporisateur; (*of perfume, paint etc*) jet *m*; **to give sth a s.** (*fields, roses etc*) pulvériser qch; (*walls etc*) peindre qch au pistolet; (*hair*) mettre du spray *ou* de la laque sur qch

(c) (*device*) (*for hair spray, paint etc*) bombe *f*; (*for hair, non-gas operated*) atomiseur *m*, vaporisateur *m*; **deodorant s.** désodorisant *m* atomiseur; **perfume s.** atomiseur à parfum; **fly s.** atomiseur *ou* bombe insecticide; **s. can** atomiseur, bombe; *Ind* **s. drying** (*of milk etc*) séchage *m* par atomisation; **s. nozzle** gicleur *m*

spray[3] **1** *vt* **(a)** (*perfume, hair conditioner, deodorant*) atomiser, vaporiser; (*paint, chemicals*) pulvériser; **he sprayed water all over me** il m'a aspergé d'eau; **to s. a solution up one's nostrils** se vaporiser un liquide dans le nez; *Ind* **to s. dry** sécher par atomisation; **slogan sprayed on a wall** slogan écrit à la bombe sur un mur; **this liquid is sprayed on the oil slick** ce liquide est pulvérisé sur le pétrole; **three layers of paint are sprayed onto the metal** on passe trois couches de peinture au pistolet sur le métal; **she sprays her hair in position** elle se coiffe en se mettant du spray

(b) (*cover with spray*) asperger, arroser; (*plants etc*) bassiner; (*tree*) passer au vaporisateur; (*with paint-sprayer*) peindre au pistolet; **to s. the crops/the fields** pulvériser les récoltes/champs; **to s. sth with machine-gun fire** mitrailler qch

2 *vi* **water sprayed up in our faces** de l'eau éclaboussait nos visages

sprayer ['spreɪə(r)] *n* **(a)** vaporisateur *m*, pulvérisateur *m*; (*for paint*) pistolet *m* **(b)** (*vehicle, plane*) arroseuse *f*

spray gun *n* (*for paint etc*) pistolet *m*, pulvérisateur *m*

spray paint *n* peinture *f* au pistolet

spread[1] [spred] *n* **(a)** (*of land etc*) étendue *f*; (*of wings, sails etc*) envergure *f*; *Com* (*between two rates*) différence *f*; (*in interest rates*) différentiel *m* de taux d'intérêt; *St Exch* écart *m*; *Am* (*ranch*) ranch *m*; *St Exch* **s. of investments** diversification *f* des placements; **we have a good s. of products** (*range*) nous avons un bel éventail *ou* une belle gamme de produits

(b) (*expansion*) (*of education*) diffusion *f*; (*of doctrine, disease*) propagation *f*; (*of ideas*) expansion *f*, dissémination *f*

(c) *F* (*big meal*) festin *m*, repas *m* somptueux; **cold s.** repas froid

(d) *Journ etc* double page *f*

(e) *Culin* pâte *f* à tartiner; **cheese s.** fromage *m* à tartiner; **chocolate s.** chocolat *m* à tartiner

spread[2] (*pt, pp* **spread**) **1** *vt* **(a)** (*one's arms etc*) étendre; (*net*) tendre; (*sails*) déployer; (*one's fingers*) écarter; **a bird with its wings spread** un oiseau aux ailes déployées; **to s. one's wings** (*of bird*), *Fig* déployer ses ailes

(b) (*distribute*) (*sand, straw*) répandre; (*manure, fertilizer*) épandre; (*terror*) semer; (*news*) répandre, rapporter; (*lies etc*) colporter; (*disease*) propager; **to s. sb's fame (abroad)** faire connaître la réputation de qn; *Fig* **he's in danger of spreading himself too thin** il risque de faire trop de choses à la fois; **the payments are spread over several months** les paiements sont échelonnés *ou* étalés *ou* répartis sur plusieurs mois; **if we can s. the work over three months** si nous pouvons répartir le travail sur trois mois; **could you s. the word?** voulez-vous passer le mot?

(c) (*apply*) **to s. butter on a slice of bread** étendre *ou* étaler du beurre sur une tranche de pain, tartiner une tranche de pain de beurre; **to s. ointment on a burn** appliquer *ou* mettre de la pommade sur une brûlure; **to s. the paint evenly** étendre *ou* étaler la peinture en couches égales

(d) to s. a surface with sth recouvrir *ou* enduire une surface de qch; *Old-fashioned Am* **to s. the table** dresser *ou* mettre la table, mettre le couvert

2 *vi* **(a)** (*stretch*) (*of forest, city, suburbs*) s'étendre, s'étaler; (*of desert*) s'étendre

(b) (*of rumour, news, ideas etc*) se répandre, se propager; (*of disease, fire, theory, epidemic etc*) se propager, s'étendre (**to** à, jusqu'à); (*of smell, smoke, sound*) se répandre (**throughout** dans); (*of fame*) s'étendre (**throughout** dans); (*of cancer*) se généraliser; (*of evil*) s'étendre, se généraliser; (*of group of people*) se disperser; **the fire is spreading** l'incendie gagne; **her ideas are spreading** ses idées font tache d'huile

(c) (*of butter, paste, cheese etc*) **it spreads easily** c'est facile à tartiner

▶ **spread about, spread around** *vtsep* **(a)** (*rumour, disease etc*) répandre; **have you been spreading it around that I …?** est-ce que tu as été raconter partout que je …? **(b)** *Euph* **he spreads himself about a bit** (*is promiscuous*) il couche à droite et à gauche

▶ **spread out 1** *vtsep* **(a)** (*open out*) (*map etc*) déployer, étaler; **the plain lay spread out in front of us** la plaine s'étalait *ou* se déployait devant nous; **a bird with its wings spread out** un oiseau aux ailes déployées; **to s. oneself out** (*on sofa etc*) s'étendre, s'allonger; **he spread his papers out on the desk** il étala ses papiers sur le bureau

(b) (*space out in time*) (*deliveries, payments*) échelonner; **to s. out over several financial years** étaler sur plusieurs exercices

2 *vi* (*of person*) (*on sofa etc*) s'étendre, s'allonger; (*of troops, rescue party etc*) se disperser; **give yourself room to s. out** (*doing craft work etc*) accordez-vous de l'espace pour vous étaler

spread eagle *n Her* aigle *f* éployée; (*in skating*) grand aigle *m*

spread-eagled [-'iːg(ə)ld] *adj* étalé de tout son long

spreader ['spredər] *n* **(a)** (*person*) (*of idea*) propagateur, -trice; (*of news*) rapporteur, -euse; (*of rumour*) colporteur, -euse, propagateur, -trice **(b)** *Agr, Constr* épandeur *m*, épandeuse *f*; (*for putty, plaster etc*) spatule *f*

spreading ['spredɪŋ] **1** *adj* **under a s. chestnut tree** sous un châtaignier bien déployé **2** *n* (*act of spreading*) (*of lies*) colportage *m*; (*of disease, doctrine, rumours*) propagation *f*; (*of ideas*) dissémination *f*; (*of paint etc*) étendage *m*

spreadsheet ['spredʃiːt] *n Comptr* feuille *f* de calcul; (*software*) tableur *m*

spree [spriː] *n* nouba *f*; **to have a s., to go (out) on a s.** faire la nouba; **to go on a shopping** *or* **spending s.** aller claquer son argent dans les magasins; **a s. of looting** des saccages

sprig [sprɪg] *n* brin *m*

sprightliness ['spraɪtlɪnɪs] *n* vivacité *f*

sprightly ['spraɪtlɪ] *adj* (*person, tune*) vif; (*old person*) alerte, fringant; **her s. commentary on current events** ses commentaires pétillants sur l'actualité; **he's very s. for 80** il est très fringant pour ses 80 ans

spring¹ [sprɪŋ] *n* **(a)** (*of water*) source *f*; *Fig Lit* (*of custom etc*) source, origine *f*; **hot** *or* **thermal s.** source thermale; **hot** *or* **thermal springs** eaux thermales; **mineral s.** source d'eau minérale; **s. water** eau *f* de source

(b) [①A6-7,d,v] (*season*) printemps *m*; **in (the) s.** au printemps; **a lovely s. evening** une belle soirée de printemps; **to have s. fever** être amoureux, *Can* avoir la fièvre du printemps; **s. flowers** fleurs printanières; **s. tide** grande marée *f*, marée de vive eau; **s. vegetables** primeurs *mpl*

(c) (*leap*) saut *m*, bond *m*

(d) (*elasticity*) élasticité *f*; **the s. of a bow** la force *ou* la souplesse d'un arc; **with a s. in his step** d'un pas léger; **the s. had gone out of her step** sa démarche avait perdu de sa souplesse; *Carp* **there's too much s. in this type of wood** ce type de bois est trop souple

(e) (*device*) ressort *m*; **(watch) s.** ressort (de montre); **springs, s. suspension** (*of car etc*) suspension *f* à ressort(s); **s. lock** serrure *f* à pompe

spring² (*pt* **sprang** [spræŋ]; *pp* **sprung** [sprʌŋ]) **1** *vi* **(a)** (*jump*) bondir, sauter; **to s. to one's feet** se lever vivement *ou* d'un bond; **to s. into action** (*of person*) passer à l'action; **he sprang into life when I mentioned the subject** il a semblé revivre quand j'ai mentionné le sujet; **the engine sprang to life** le moteur partit d'un coup; **to s. to sb's defence** (*in words*) prendre vivement la défense de qn; (*in case of assault etc*) se précipiter pour porter secours à qn; **the lid sprang open** le couvercle a sauté; **the door sprang open** la porte s'est ouverte d'un coup; **the lever springs out** le levier sort tout d'un coup; **to s. into public view** être propulsé sur la scène publique; **he sprang to fame overnight** il est devenu célèbre du jour au lendemain; **they sprang to attention** d'un bond, ils se mirent au garde-à-vous; **one thing that immediately springs to mind is …** une chose qui vient immédiatement à l'esprit est …; *Lit* **a tear sprang to her eye** une larme surgit dans ses yeux; *Lit* **an oath sprang to his lips** un juron lui est monté aux lèvres

(b) (*to originate, come into being*) **to s. from** venir de, provenir de; **hope springs eternal** l'espérance reste toujours vivace; **to s. into existence** surgir, apparaître soudain; *F* **where did you s. from?** d'où sortez-vous?

(c) (*warp*) (*of wood*) gauchir, se déformer, se déjeter

2 *vt* **(a) to s. a leak** faire une voie d'eau

(b) (*partridge etc*) (faire) lever

(c) (*trap*) faire jouer; (*mine*) faire sauter

(d) (*car*) munir de ressorts; **sprung carriage** voiture suspendue

(e) *F* (*help to escape from prison*) faire échapper de prison

▶ **spring back** *vi* (*move back suddenly*) (*of object*) se redresser, repartir en arrière; **the branch sprang back** la branche s'est redressée; **she sprang back in horror** elle recula d'un bond, horrifiée

▶ **spring forward** *vi* (*rush forward*) s'élancer *ou* se précipiter en avant

▶ **spring on** *vtaspo* (*confront with*) **to s. a question on sb** (*unexpectedly*) poser à qn une question inattendue; (*point-blank*) poser une question à brûle-pourpoint à qn; **to s. a surprise on sb** faire une surprise à qn; **I wish you wouldn't s. things on me like that** (*without warning*) j'aimerais bien que tu arrêtes de me prendre par surprise; **sorry to have to s. this on you** désolé de vous demander ça à la dernière minute

▶ **spring up** *vi* **(a)** (*jump to one's feet*) se lever vivement *ou* d'un bond **(b)** (*appear suddenly*) **a breeze sprang up** une brise s'est levée; **an intimacy sprang up between them** l'intimité naquit entre eux; **a doubt sprang up in his mind** un doute a germé dans son esprit; **the company sprang up almost overnight** la société s'est montée quasiment du jour au lendemain; **to (begin to) s. up** (*of plant etc*) (commencer à) pousser; **McDonalds are springing up all over the place** les McDonalds poussent partout comme des champignons

spring balance *n* peson *m*

springboard ['sprɪŋbɔːd] *n Gym, Swimming, Fig* tremplin *m*

springbok ['sprɪŋbɒk] *n* (*antelope*) springbok *m*

spring chicken *n Culin* poussin *m*; *F* **she's no s.** elle n'est plus toute jeune

spring-clean¹ *n* nettoyage *m* de printemps; **to give a house a s.** faire le nettoyage de printemps dans une maison

spring-clean² **1** *vt* (*house*) nettoyer à fond **2** *vi* faire le nettoyage de printemps, *Can* faire le grand ménage

spring-cleaning *n* grand nettoyage *m* de printemps

springe [sprɪndʒ] *n* (*snare*) lacet *m*, collet *m*

springer ['sprɪŋər] *n* **s. (spaniel)** épagneul *m* springer

springiness ['sprɪŋɪnɪs] *n* effet *m* de ressort; (*of hair*) gonflant *m*; (*of mattress*) élasticité *f*; (*of turf, ground*) souplesse *f*

springing ['sprɪŋɪŋ] *n* (*of car, bed*) suspension *f*

springless ['sprɪŋlɪs] *adj Tech* sans ressort(s)

springlike ['sprɪŋlaɪk] *adj* (*weather etc*) de printemps; (*dress*) printanier

spring-loaded *adj* à ressort

spring mattress *n* matelas *m* à ressorts

spring onion *n* ciboule *f*

spring roll *n Culin* rouleau *m* de printemps

springtide ['sprɪŋtaɪd] *n Lit* = **springtime 1**

springtime ['sprɪŋtaɪm] **1** *n* printemps *m*; **in s.** au printemps **2** *adj attrib* (*weather, feeling*) printanier

springy ['sprɪŋɪ] *adj* élastique, qui fait ressort; (*brake pedal*) flexible; (*carpet*) moelleux; (*wood*) élastique; (*hair*) qui ont du volume; **with a s. step** (*to walk*) d'un pas léger

sprinkle¹ ['sprɪŋk(ə)l] *n* (*of salt, sugar, nutmeg etc*) pincée *f*; **a s. of rain** quelques gouttes *fpl* de pluie

sprinkle² *vt* (*cake, pie etc*) (*with sugar, salt etc*) saupoudrer (**with sth** de qch); (*with liquid*) arroser légèrement (**with sth** de qch); **to s. the floor with sand** répandre du sable par terre; **he should s. a few well-known names in the text** il devrait introduire quelques noms fameux par-ci par-là dans le texte; **a house or two was sprinkled here and there on the hillside** quelques maisons étaient éparpillées sur la colline

sprinkler ['sprɪŋklər] *n* **(a)** (*for lawns etc*) arroseur *m*; (**rotary**) **s.** arroseur (rotatif); (**fire**) **s.** (*extinguisher*) extincteur *m* (automatique) d'incendie; **s. head** (*of shower*) pommeau *m*; (*of watering can*) pomme *f*; **s. system** (*in ceiling*) noyage *m* en pluie **(b)** *Rel* goupillon *m*, aspersoir *m* **(c)** (*for sugar*) saupoudreuse *f*

sprinkling ['sprɪŋklɪŋ] *n* **(a)** (*action*) (*with sugar etc*) saupoudrage *m*; (*with water*) arrosage *m* léger; *Rel* **s. of holy water** aspergès *m*, aspersion *f*; *US* **s. can** arrosoir *m* **(b)** (*quantity*) (*of nutmeg, sugar etc*) pincée *f*; **a s. of gravel** une légère couche de gravier; **a s. of knowledge** quelques connaissances; **with a liberal s. of literary references** avec moult références littéraires données ici et là; **with a larger than usual s. of mistakes** avec ça et là encore plus de fautes que d'habitude; **a s. of new faces in the congregation** quelques nouvelles têtes ici et là dans la congrégation; **there was now a s. of grey among the auburn hair** il y avait maintenant quelques fils d'argent dans la chevelure auburn

sprint^1 [sprɪnt] *n Sp* sprint *m*; (*acceleration, spurt*) pointe *f* de vitesse; *Sp, Fig F* **to put on a s.** (*run*) piquer un sprint; **you'll need to put on a bit of a s. if you're going to finish that translation in time** il va falloir que tu passes la seconde si tu veux finir cette traduction à temps; **there was a s. finish** il y a eu un sprint à l'arrivée; **he has a good s. finish** il est très rapide dans les sprints de fins de courses

sprint^2 *vi Sp* sprinter; **I was good at sprinting** j'étais bon dans les courses de vitesse; **to s. past sb** sprinter pour dépasser qn; **the little boy sprinted off** le petit garçon s'élança à toutes jambes; **he sprinted upstairs** il est monté en courant; **he sprinted after her** il a couru derrière elle à toute vitesse; **I had to s. for the bus** j'ai dû courir *ou F* piquer un sprint pour attraper le bus

sprinter ['sprɪntər] *n Sp* sprinter *m*

sprite [spraɪt] *n* lutin *m*, esprit *m* (follet), farfadet *m*

sprocket ['sprɒkɪt] *n MecE* **(a)** (*tooth*) dent *f* (de pignon) **(b)** **s. (wheel)** pignon *m* de chaîne

sprog [sprɒg] *n Sl* (*child*) môme *mf*, gosse *mf*

sprout^1 [spraʊt] *n Bot* **(a)** (*shoot*) pousse *f* **(b)** (**Brussels**) **sprouts** choux *mpl* de Bruxelles

sprout^2 **1** *vi* **(a)** (*of plant*) pousser; (*of branch, shrub*) bourgeonner; (*of seed*) germer **(b)** = **sprout up 2** *vt* **(a)** **to s. horns** (*of animal*) pousser des cornes; *F* **to s. a moustache** se laisser pousser la moustache **(b)** (*seeds*) faire germer

▶ **sprout up** *vi* (*of plants, F of child*) pousser; *Fig* (*of new buildings, towns etc*) pousser comme un champignon/des champignons; (*of new community, sect*) surgir, naître

spruce^1 [spru:s] *adj* (*person*) (très) soigné, tiré à quatre épingles; (*house, room*) (très) soigné, bien entretenu

spruce^2 *n* (*tree*) **s. (fir)** (sapin *m*) épicéa *m*; **Norway s.** sapin de Norvège

▶ **spruce up** *vtsep* (*make neat*) (*house, room*) donner de l'éclat à; **to s. oneself up** se faire beau/belle; **all spruced up** sur son trente et un

spruceness ['spru:snɪs] *n* (*of person*) mise *f* soignée; (*of house, room etc*) propreté *f*

sprung^1 [sprʌŋ] *adj* (*mattress etc*) à ressorts

sprung^2 *see* **spring**^{2}

spry [spraɪ] *adj* (*comp* **spryer,** *superl* **spryest**) vif, actif, plein d'allant

spud [spʌd] *n* **(a)** *F* (*potato*) patate *f*; *Mil Sl* **s. bashing** corvée *f* de patates, (corvée de) pluches *fpl* **(b)** (*weeding hoe*) sarcloir *m*

spume [spju:m] *n Arch, Lit* (*of sea*) écume *f*

spun^1 [spʌn] *adj Tex* câblé; **s. silk** soie *f* filée; **s. sugar** sucre *m* filé; *US* (*candy floss*) barbe *f* à papa

spun^2 *see* **spin**^{2}

spunk [spʌŋk] *n* **(a)** *Old-fashioned F* (*courage*) cran *m*; **to have plenty of s.** avoir du cran **(b)** *Br Vulg* (*semen*) foutre *m*

spunky ['spʌŋkɪ] *adj Old-fashioned F* (*brave*) courageux, qui a du cran

spur^1 [spɜ:r] *n* **(a)** (*for riding*) éperon *m*; *Fig* **to win one's spurs** faire ses preuves **(b)** *Fig* (*stimulus*) stimulant *m*; **this hope was the s. that drove her on** cet espoir fut l'aiguillon qui la fit aller de l'avant; **to do sth on the s. of the moment** faire qch sous l'impulsion du moment *ou* sur un coup de tête; **it was a s.-of-the-moment decision** j'ai pris/il a pris/*etc* cette décision sur un coup de tête **(c)** (*of cock*) ergot *m*; (*of fighting cock*) éperon *m* **(d)** *Geog* éperon *m*, contrefort *m*; (*of railway line*) épi *m*; (*to motorway*) bretelle *f* d'accès, voie *f* d'accélération **(e)** *Bot* éperon *m*

spur^2 *vt* (**-rr-**) (*horse*) éperonner, talonner; *Fig* **to s. sb into action** pousser qn à agir; **booted and spurred** botté et éperonné

▶ **spur on** *vtsep* **(a)** (*horse*) éperonner, talonner **(b)** *Fig* (*motivate*) aiguillonner, stimuler; **spurred on by a desire to** … stimulé *ou* aiguillonné par un désir de …; **this spurred us on to redouble our efforts** ceci nous a stimulés et fait redoubler d'efforts

spurge [spɜ:dʒ] *n* (*plant*) euphorbe *f*, épurge *f*

spurious ['spjʊərɪəs] *adj* (*false*) faux, *f* fausse; (*argument, objection*) non valable; (*distinction, reasoning*) douteux; (*writings*) apocryphe; (*edition*) de contrefaçon

spuriously ['spjʊərɪəslɪ] *adv* faussement

spuriousness ['spjʊərɪəsnɪs] *n* fausseté *f* (**of** de); (*of distinction*) non-validité *f*; (*of text*) caractère *m* apocryphe

spurn [spɜ:n] *vt* (*offer*) rejeter avec mépris; (*person, person's advances*) repousser avec mépris; **she's feeling spurned** (*by lover, boyfriend*) elle se sent rejetée

spurt^1 [spɜ:t] *n* **(a)** (*of liquid*) jaillissement *m*, jet *m*, giclée *f* **(b)** (*sudden effort*) effort *m* soudain; (*burst of energy*) poussée *f* d'énergie; *Sp* (*of speed*) effort de vitesse; *Cycling F* emballage *m*; **a s. of anger/jealousy** un bref moment de colère/jalousie; **a s. of energy** une poussée d'énergie; **to put on a s.** (*when running*) démarrer; *Cycling F* emballer; (*in work etc*) donner un coup de collier; **there's been a sudden s. of activity** il y a eu un regain d'activité; **she tends to work in spurts** elle a tendance à travailler par à-coups; *Sp* **final s.** pointe *f* finale, rush *m*

spurt^2 **1** *vi* **(a)** (*of liquid*) jaillir, gicler **(b)** *Sp* produire son effort; **she spurted past the other competitors** elle a produit son effort et a dépassé les autres concurrents; **he spurted into the lead** *Sp* il a produit son effort et s'est placé en tête de la course; *Fig* il est soudain venu se placer en tête **2** *vt* (*of person*) (*liquid*) faire jaillir, faire gicler; (*of fountain pen*) gicler; **the pipe spurted water everywhere** de l'eau jaillissait du tuyau; **the pen spurted ink onto the carpet** l'encre jaillit du stylo et tacha la moquette

▶ **spurt out 1** *vi* = **spurt**^{2} **1 (a) 2** *vtsep* = **spurt**^{2} **2**

sputnik ['spʊtnɪk] *n Astronaut* spoutnik *m*

sputter ['spʌtər] **1** *vt* (*say while spitting saliva*) dire en lançant des postillons **2** *vi* (*mumble*) bredouiller; (*talk while spitting saliva*) lancer des postillons en parlant; *Aut* (*of engine*) tousser; (*of pen*) fuir irrégulièrement; (*of kindling wood*) pétiller; (*of meat on grill, candle*) grésiller; (*of flame*) grésiller, crépiter; **the engine sputtered into life** le moteur toussa avant de démarrer

▶ **sputter out** *vi* (*stop burning*) **the candle sputtered out** la bougie s'est éteinte en grésillant

sputum, *pl* **-a** ['spju:təm, -ə] *n Med* crachat *m*

spy^1, *pl* **spies** [spaɪ, spaɪz] *n Pol, Ind* espion, -ionne; (*for police, prison warden etc*) *F* mouchard, -arde; **s. master** chef *m* de réseau; **s. network** *or* **ring** réseau *m* d'espionnage; *Av* **s. plane** avion-espion *m*, *pl* avions-espions; **s. satellite** satellite-espion *m*, *pl* satellites-espions; **another s. scandal would ruin us** la découverte d'un autre espion et le scandale qui en résulterait équivaudrait à notre perte

spy^2 **1** *vi* espionner; **to s. on sb** épier *ou* espionner qn; **I had the feeling I was being spied on all the time** j'avais l'impression qu'on m'épiait tout le temps **2** *vt* (*notice*) apercevoir, voir

▶ **spy out** *vtsep* **to s. out the land** explorer le terrain

spyglass ['spaɪglɑ:s] *n Old-fashioned* lunette *f* d'approche, longue-vue *f*, *pl* longues-vues

spyhole ['spaɪhəʊl] *n* (*in wall, floor*) trou *m*; (*in door*) judas *m*

spying ['spaɪɪŋ] *n* espionnage *m*

Sq (*abbr* **Square**) place, square

sq (*abbr* **square**) carré

sq. ft. (*abbr* **square foot/feet**) pied(s) carré(s)

SQL [eskju:'el] *n Comptr abbr* **structured query language**

SQL engine *n Comptr* processeur *m* SQL

Sqn. Ldr. *Br Mil, Av abbr* **Squadron Leader**

squab [skwɒb] *n* **(a)** (*young pigeon*) pigeonneau *m* sans plumes **(b)** *Br Aut* coussin *m*

squabble^1 ['skwɒb(ə)l] *n* querelle *f*, chamaillerie *f*

squabble^2 *vi* se quereller, se chamailler (**with** avec)

squabbler ['skwɒblər] *n* querelleur, -euse, chamailleur, -euse

squabbling ['skwɒblɪŋ] *n* querelles *fpl*, chamailleries *fpl*

squad [skwɒd] *n* **(a)** (*of workmen etc*) brigade *f*, équipe *f*; *Sp* équipe; **rescue s.** équipe de secours; **s. car** voiture *f* de police **(b)** *Mil* escouade *f*; **firing s.** peloton *m* d'exécution

squaddie ['skwɒdɪ] *n Br F* (*private soldier*) bidasse *m*

squadron ['skwɒdrən] *n* **(a)** *Mil, Av* escadron *m*; **fighter/bomber s.** escadron de chasse/bombardiers; *Br* **s. leader** (*rank*) = commandant *m* **(b)** *Naut* escadre *f*

squalid ['skwɒlɪd] *adj* (*dirty*) sale; (*sordid*) sordide

squalidly ['skwɒlɪdlɪ] *adv* de façon sordide

squalidness ['skwɒlɪdnɪs] *n* = **squalor**
squall¹ [skwɔ:l] *n* (*cry*) cri *m* rauque *ou* discordant
squall² *vi* (*cry*) crier; *F* brailler
squall³ *n* (*gust*) bourrasque *f*, rafale *f*; *Naut* grain *m*
squalling ['skwɔ:lɪŋ] **1** *adj* criard; *F* braillard **2** *n* criaillerie *f*
squally ['skwɔ:lɪ] *adj* (*weather*) à rafales; *Naut* à grains; **it's s. today** il y des bourrasques *ou Naut* des grains aujourd'hui
squalor ['skwɒlər] *n* (*dirtiness*) saleté *f*; (*poverty*) misère *f*; **to die in s.** mourir dans la misère
squander ['skwɒndər] *vt* (*money, time, Fig talents*) gaspiller; (*fortune*) dissiper, dilapider, *F* claquer; *Fig* (*natural resources*) dilapider
squandering ['skwɒndərɪŋ] *n* (*of money, time*) gaspillage *m*; (*of fortune*) dissipation *f*
square¹ [skweər] **1** *n* **(a)** (*shape*) (*of chocolate etc*), *Geom* carré *m*; (*on chessboard etc*) case *f*; (*on map*) carreau-module *m*, *pl* carreaux-modules; **to divide a map into squares** quadriller une carte; **to fold sth into a s.** plier qch en carré; *Fig* **to be back at s. one** être revenu à son point de départ; *Fig* **let's start again from s. one** repartons du point de départ; (*in relationship*) repartons à zéro; **(silk) s.** carré *ou* foulard *m* (de soie)
(b) *Math* (*of number*) carré *m*; **magic s.** carré magique
(c) (*of town, village*) place *f*; (*with garden*) square *m*; *Mil* terrain *m* de manœuvre(s)
(d) (*for drawing, measuring angles*) équerre *f*; **set s.** équerre à dessin; **to cut sth on the s.** couper qch à angles droits; **out of s.** qui n'est pas d'équerre
(e) *F* **he's a s.** (*old-fashioned*) il est vieux jeu
2 *adj* **(a)** [①B56,C,4] (*figure, shoulders, neckline, Naut sail, Math metre, centimetre etc*) carré; **nine metres s.** de neuf mètres sur neuf, de neuf mètres au carré; **nine s. metres** neuf mètres carrés; **a s. mile** = 2,5 kilomètres carrés; **the S. Mile** = la City (*de Londres*); *Fig* **to be a s. peg in a round hole** ne pas être à sa place; *F* **s. eyes** (*person*) téléphage *m*; **s. measure** mesure *f* de surface *ou* de superficie; **s. pin socket** prise *f* mâle à fiche carrée; *Naut* **s. rigger** navire *m* gréé en carré; **s.-headed** à tête carrée
(b) (*right-angled*) *Typ* **s. brackets** crochets *mpl*; **s. corner** coin *m* à angle droit; *Electron etc* **s. wave** onde *f* carrée *ou* rectangulaire
(c) *Fig* (*refusal, denial*) net, catégorique; (*meal*) copieux; **what he needs is a good s. meal** tout ce dont il a besoin, c'est d'un vrai repas; **to get things s.** (*arrange*) arranger les choses; (*put in order*) mettre tout en ordre; **to make an account s.** régler un compte; **to be s. with sb** être quitte envers qn; **they are (all) s.** (*in competition*) ils sont à égalité; (*debts to each other have been paid*) ils sont quittes; **to get s. with sb** (*get even*) régler son compte à qn; (*settle bills etc*) être quitte envers qn; **to get things s. with sb** (*arrange matters*) arranger les choses avec qn; **a s. deal** une affaire honnête; **he always gives you a s. deal** il est toujours loyal en affaires
(d) *Old-fashioned F* vieux jeu *inv*, *F* ringard; **you're so s.** qu'est-ce que tu peux être vieux jeu *ou F* ringard
3 *adv* **(a)** (*at right angles*) à angles droits; *Tech* d'équerre **(to, with** avec); **set s. upon its base** d'aplomb sur sa base; **he hit him (fair and) s. on the jaw** il l'a frappé en plein sur le menton
(b) (*to act*) honnêtement; **fair and s.** loyalement, carrément
square² **1** *vt* **(a)** (*block of marble, wood*) carrer, équarrir
(b) (*account*) régler; **to s. accounts with sb** (*pay money owed*) régler (ses comptes avec) qn; (*get revenge*) régler son compte à qn; **to s. matters** arranger les choses; **to s. one's practice with one's principles** accorder ses actions avec ses principes; **how do you s. it with your conscience?** comment arrangez-vous cela avec votre conscience?; **it's OK, I'll s. it with him** ça va, j'arrangerai ça avec lui
(c) [①C56,C,4,F] (*bribe*) acheter, soudoyer, *F* graisser la patte à
(d) *Geom, Fig* **to s. the circle** faire la quadrature du cercle; **it's like squaring the circle** c'est la quadrature du cercle
(e) *Math* (*number, expression*) élever *ou* mettre au carré; **four squared** quatre au carré
(f) (*divide into squares*) (*sheet of paper*) quadriller; **squared paper** papier quadrillé *ou* à carreaux
(g) *Sp* **to s. the match** (*of team, player*) égaliser; **that goal squares the match** avec ce but, ils ont égalisé
2 *vi* **(a) the end and the side should s. with each other** le bout et le côté doivent se raccorder
(b) (*coincide*) s'accorder (**with** avec); **the theory does not s. with the facts** la théorie ne correspond pas aux faits
▶ **square away** *vtsep Am* (*tidy*) (*books*) ranger; (*room*) arranger
▶ **square off** **1** *vtsep* **(a)** (*divide into squares*) (*sheet of paper*) quadriller **(b)** *Carp etc* (*make square*) (*end of a plank*) mettre d'équerre, équarrir **2** *vi esp Am* (*assume fighting position*) se mettre en position de combat
▶ **square up** **1** *vi* **(a)** (*settle debts*) régler ses dettes *ou* comptes; **can we s. up later?** pouvons-nous nous arranger *ou* faire nos comptes plus tard?; **to s. up with sb** (*pay money owed*) régler (ses comptes avec) qn; *Fig* (*get even with*) se venger de qn, régler son compte à qn **(b)** (*face with determination*) **to s. up to the difficulties/to sb** faire face aux difficultés/à qn **(c)** (*assume fighting position*) se mettre en position de combat **2** *vtsep Carp etc* (*make square*) (*end of plank*) mettre d'équerre, équarrir
square-bashing *n Br Mil Sl* = exercice *m*
square-built *adj* (*person*) aux épaules carrées; (*short and sturdy*) trapu; (*building*) carré
square dance *n* danse *f* à quatre
squarely ['skweəlɪ] *adv* **(a)** (*directly*) carrément; **s. built** bâti en carré; (*person*) aux épaules carrées; **look me s. in the eyes** regarde-moi bien dans les yeux; **stand it s. on its base** placez-le bien en équilibre sur son socle **(b)** (*honestly*) carrément, honnêtement; (*to act*) loyalement
squareness ['skweənɪs] *n* **(a)** (*shape*) forme *f* carrée **(b)** *Old-fashioned F* (*of person, views*) conservatisme *m*
square number *n Math* carré *m*
square root *n* racine *f* carrée
square ruler *n* carrelet *m*, règle *f* quadrangulaire
square-shouldered ['skweə'ʃəʊldəd] *adj* aux épaules carrées
square-toed *adj* (*shoes*) à bout carré
squaring ['skweərɪŋ] *n* **(a)** (*of account*) règlement *m* **(b) the s. of the circle** la quadrature du cercle
squash¹ [skwɒʃ] *n* **(a)** (*crush*) **there was a dreadful s. at the doors** la foule s'écrasait aux portes; **it was a s., but everyone got in the car** nous étions serrés comme des sardines mais tout le monde a tenu dans la voiture; *Old-fashioned* **s. hat** chapeau *m* mou **(b)** (*crowd*) cohue *f* **(c)** *Br* **orange/lemon s.** (*concentrate, drink*) sirop *m* d'orange/de citron **(d)** *Sp* **s.**, *Fml* **s. rackets** (*game*) squash *m*; **s. court** court *m* de squash
squash² **1** *vt* écraser, aplatir; *Fig* (*revolt etc*) écraser, étouffer; *Fig* (*person*) remettre à sa place, rembarrer; *Fig* **she looked rather squashed** (*humiliated*) elle avait l'air plutôt dépité **2** *vi* (*become squashed*) s'écraser, s'aplatir; **to s. into a room/car** se serrer dans une pièce/voiture
squash³ *n Am* (*vegetable*) courge *f*
▶ **squash up** **1** *vi* (*sit, stand together closely*) se serrer **2** *vtsep* écraser
squashy ['skwɒʃɪ] *adj* (*fruit*) trop mûr; (*easily squashed*) qui s'écrase facilement; (*ground*) bourbeux, détrempé
squat¹ [skwɒt] *n* **(a)** (*posture*) posture *f* accroupie **(b)** (*place*) squat *m*
squat² **(-tt-)** **1** *vi* **(a)** (*crouch down*) s'accroupir; (*of animal*) se tapir; **she was squatting by the fire** elle était accroupie au coin du feu **(b)** (*occupy house illegally*) squatter; **to s. on a piece of land** occuper un terrain illégalement **2** *vt* (*occupy illegally*) (*house*) squatter
squat³ *adj* (*person*) ramassé, trapu; (*object, building etc*) écrasé; (*arc*) surbaissé
squatter ['skwɒtər] *n* squatter *m*
squaw [skwɔ:] *n* squaw *f*
squawk¹ [skwɔ:k] *n* **(a)** (*of bird, F of person*) cri *m* rauque; **a s. of protest** un tollé; **to give a s. of outrage** pousser un cri d'indignation **(b)** *F* (*complaint*) rouspétance *f*
squawk² *vi* **(a)** (*of bird*) pousser des cris rauques; *F* (*of person, baby*) brailler; **to s. with rage/in protest** pousser des cris de rage/en signe de protestation **(b)** *F* (*complain*) rouspéter **(c)** *Sl* (*inform*) moucharder
squeak¹ [skwi:k] *n* **(a)** (*noise*) (*of animal, person*) couinement *m*, cri *m* aigu; (*of unoiled door, wheel etc*) grincement *m*; **to let out a s.** pousser un couinement; *F* **I don't want to hear another s. out of you** je ne veux pas entendre le moindre murmure **(b)** *F* **that was a near** *or* **narrow s.** nous l'avons/il l'a/*etc* échappé belle!
squeak² **1** *vi* (*of animal*) couiner; (*of person*) pousser des cris aigus, couiner; (*of machine part etc*) grincer; (*of shoes*) crisser **2** *vt* crier d'une petite voix aiguë
squeaking ['skwi:kɪŋ] *n* (*of animal*) couinements *mpl*; (*of door etc*) grincement *m*
squeaky ['skwi:kɪ] *adj* (*shoes*) qui crissent; **s. voice** petite voix aiguë; **s. hinges** gonds grinçants
squeaky-clean *adj F* (*person*) blanc/*f* blanche comme neige; (*image, reputation*) sans tache
squeal¹ [skwi:l] *n* cri *m* aigu; (*of animal*) cri perçant; (*of brakes*) grincement *m*; (*of tyres*) crissement *m*

squeal² **1** *vi* **(a)** (*scream*) pousser des cris aigus, couiner; (*of tyres*) crisser; (*of brakes*) grincer; **to s. like a stuck pig** crier comme un porc qu'on égorge **(b)** *F* (*complain*) protester, jeter les hauts cris **(c)** *Sl* (*inform*) moucharder; **to s. on sb** dénoncer qn **2** *vt* crier d'une voix aiguë *ou* perçante

squealer ['skwi:lər] *n Sl* (*informer*) mouchard, -arde

squealing ['skwi:lɪŋ] *n* cris *mpl* aigus; (*of tyres*) crissement *m*; (*of brakes*) grincement *m*

squeamish ['skwi:mɪʃ] **1** *adj* sensible; *F* chochotte; **to feel s.** avoir des nausées, avoir mal au cœur; **it makes me feel s.** ça me donne mal au cœur; **I'm s. about seeing blood** je ne supporte pas la vue du sang; **don't be so s.!** ne fais pas le dégoûté!, *F* ne fais pas ta chochotte! **2** *npl* **the s.** les petites natures *fpl*; **this programme/film is not for the s.** cette émission/ce film est réservé à ceux qui ont l'estomac bien accroché

squeamishness ['skwi:mɪʃnɪs] *n* sensibilité *f*

squeegee ['skwi:dʒi:] *n* **(a)** (*mop*) balai *m* en caoutchouc; (*for window cleaning*) racloir *m* (*avec bordure de caoutchouc*) **(b)** *Phot etc* raclette *f*; **roller s.** rouleau *m* en caoutchouc

squeeze¹ [skwi:z] *n* compression *f*; (*of hand*) serrement *m*; (*hug*) étreinte *f*; **a. s. of lemon** quelques gouttes *fpl* de citron; **to give sth a s.** (*toothpaste*) serrer qch; (*cloth*) essorer qch; (*lemon*) presser qch; **to give sb's hand a s.** serrer la main à qn; **to give sb a s.** serrer qn dans ses bras; **credit s.** restriction *f* de crédit; *F* **to put the s. on sb** mettre la pression sur qn; **to put the s. on prices/wages** bloquer les prix/salaires; **it'll be a s. but I think we should all fit in** on sera serrés mais je crois que tout le monde tiendra; **it was a tight s.** (*but we fitted in*) on tenait tout juste; **it's something of a s. getting into these jeans** quelle gymnastique pour enfiler ce jean

squeeze² **1** *vt* **(a)** (*sponge, lemon*) presser; (*hug*) (*person*) embrasser, étreindre; (*wring*) (*cloth*) essorer; **to s. sb's hand** serrer la main à qn; **to s. the life out of sb** (*of bear, person*) étouffer qn; **to s. liquid out of sth** faire sortir un liquide de qch; **to s. the water out of a sponge** essorer une éponge; **to s. the juice out of a lemon** extraire le jus d'un citron; **to s. sth into a box** faire entrer qch de force dans une boîte; **he squeezed his way under the fence** il s'est glissé *ou* faufilé sous le grillage; **to s. prices/wages** bloquer les prix/salaires; **I think we can just s. you in** (*find time for in schedule etc*) je crois qu'on pourra vous trouver un petit moment; (*in class, car etc*) je crois qu'on pourra vous trouver une petite place; **to s. money out of sb** extorquer de l'argent à qn

(b) *Fig* (*put pressure on*) pressurer; **we'll have to s. him a bit harder** il va falloir qu'on augmente encore la pression sur lui; **to s. the working class/rich** pressurer les classes ouvrières/les riches; **the British car industry has been squeezed by foreign competition** l'industrie automobile britannique subit la pression de la concurrence étrangère

2 *vi* **to s. into a crowded train** entrer de force dans un train bondé; **to find a little parking space to s. into** trouver une petite place de parking où se faufiler; **any room for one more to s. in?** y a-t-il encore une toute petite place?; **we squeezed under the fence** nous nous sommes glissés *ou* faufilés sous le grillage

▶ **squeeze out** *vtsep* (*juice etc*) extraire; **to s. out a tear** y aller de sa (petite) larme; *F* **they're trying to s. me out** (*off company board etc*) ils essaient de se débarrasser de moi

▶ **squeeze through** **1** *vi* se faufiler, se glisser **2** *vipo* **to s. through a narrow window** se glisser par une fenêtre étroite

▶ **squeeze up** *vi* (*sit, stand together closely*) **to s. up (together)** se serrer (les uns contre les autres); **s. up a bit so Jane can sit down** serrez-vous un peu pour que Jane puisse s'asseoir

squeezebox ['skwi:zbɒks] *n F* accordéon *m*, concertina *m*

squeezer ['skwi:zər] *n* presse *f*; **lemon s.** presse-citrons *m inv*

squelch¹ [skweltʃ] *n* (*of mud*) bruit *m* de succion; (*of wet shoes etc*) gargouillement *m*, gargouillis *m*

squelch² *vi* **to s. through the mud** patauger dans la boue; **they squelched across the muddy farmyard** ils ont traversé la cour de la ferme en pataugeant; **the water squelched in his shoes** l'eau gargouillait dans ses chaussures

squib [skwɪb] *n* **(a)** (*firework*) pétard *m*, serpenteau *m*; *Fig* **to be a damp s.** faire l'effet d'un pétard mouillé **(b)** (*satire*) satire *f*, brocard *m*

squid [skwɪd] *n* calmar *m*, calamar *m*

squiffy ['skwɪfɪ] *adj Old-fashioned Br F* un peu ivre, gris, éméché

squiggle ['skwɪg(ə)l] *n* (*mark, line*) trait *m ou* ligne *f* en paraphe; (*writing*) gribouillis *m*

squiggly ['skwɪglɪ] *adj* tortueux, -euse, sinueux, -euse

squint¹ [skwɪnt] *n* **(a)** (*eye defect*) strabisme *m*; **he has a slight s.** il louche légèrement **(b)** (*sideways glance*) regard *m* de côté *ou* de travers; **I had a s. at his paper** j'ai jeté un coup d'œil oblique sur son journal; *F* **let's have a s. at it!** faites voir!

squint² *vi* **(a)** (*have eye defect*) loucher **(b)** (*look through half-closed eyes*) plisser les yeux; **they're all squinting because of the sun** ils font tous la grimace à cause du soleil **(c)** (*look sideways*) **to s. at sth/sb** regarder qch/qn de côté *ou* de travers *ou* furtivement

squint³ *adj* **(a)** **s. eyes** yeux *mpl* louches **(b)** *F* (*crooked*) de travers, *F* de traviole

squint-eyed *adj* au regard louche

squinting ['skwɪntɪŋ] *n* strabisme *m*

squire¹ ['skwaɪər] *n* **(a)** *Br* (*local landowner*) châtelain *m* **(b)** *Hist* (*attendant to knight*) écuyer *m* **(c)** *Br F* **evening, s.** 'soir, patron

squire² *vt* (*lady*) servir de cavalier à, escorter

squirearchy ['skwaɪərɑ:kɪ] *n* classe *f* des châtelains

squirm¹ [skwɜ:m] *n* (*of pain etc*) tortillement *m*

squirm² **1** *vi* (*of worm etc*) se tordre, se tortiller; (*with embarrassment*) être très mal à l'aise; **he was squirming with embarrassment** il se tordait d'embarras; **to s. with delight** se tortiller de joie; **to s. out of a situation** se sortir d'une situation; **to s. out of one's commitments** se défiler de ses obligations; **his over-politeness makes me s.** sa politesse excessive me met extrêmement mal à l'aise; **his prose makes me s.** sa prose me donne des boutons; **the sight of all that blood made me s.** tout ce sang m'a donné la nausée

2 *vt* **to s. one's way out of a situation** se sortir d'une situation; **to s. one's way out of one's commitments** se défiler de ses obligations

squirrel ['skwɪr(ə)l] *n* **(a)** (*animal*) écureuil *m* **(b)** *Com* **s. (fur)** petit-gris *m*

▶ **squirrel away** *vtsep* mettre de côté

squirt¹ [skwɜ:t] *n* **(a)** (*of liquid*) jet *m*, giclée *f*; **to add a s. of soda** ajouter une giclée d'eau de Seltz; **to give sb a s. with a water pistol** arroser qn avec un pistolet à eau **(b)** *F* (*insignificant person*) morveux, -euse, péteux, -euse

squirt² **1** *vt* (*liquid etc*) faire gicler; **to s. soda water into a glass** mettre une giclée d'eau de Seltz dans un verre; **he squirted a little deodorant under each arm** il se vaporisa du déodorant sur chaque aisselle **2** *vi* (*of liquid etc*) gicler, jaillir; **water was squirting out everywhere** l'eau giclait de partout

squish¹ [skwɪʃ] *n F* (*sound*) bruit *m* d'écrabouillement; **the s. of mud underfoot** le gargouillement de la boue sous les pieds

squish² *F* **1** *vt* (*squash*) écraser **2** *vi* **the mud squished beneath his feet** la boue gargouillait sous ses pieds

squishy ['skwɪʃɪ] *adj F* (*ground*) détrempé; (*fruit etc*) mou, *f* molle; **the ground's s. underfoot** le sol gargouille sous les pas

Sr (*abbr* **Senior**) Sr

SRAM ['esræm] *n Comptr* (*abbr* **static random access memory**) mémoire *f* vive statique

Sri Lanka [sri:'læŋkə] *n* Sri Lanka *m*

Sri Lankan [sri:'læŋkən] **1** *adj* srilankais **2** *n* Sri Lankais, -aise

SRN [esɑ:r'en] *n Br Med abbr* **State Registered Nurse**

SS [es'es] *n Naut* (*abbr* **steamship**) **the SS Normandie** = le Normandie SS

St **(a)** (*abbr* **Street**) = rue **(b)** (*abbr* **Saint**) S(t), *f* Ste

st (*abbr* **stone**) = 6,35 kg

stab¹ [stæb] *n* **(a)** (*with dagger*) coup *m* de poignard; (*with knife*) coup de couteau; *Fig* **s. in the back** coup de Jarnac, attaque *f* déloyale; **s. of pain** élancement *m*; **a s. of remorse/envy** une pointe de remords/de jalousie; **s. wound** (*with dagger*) coup(s) de poignard; (*with knife*) coup(s) de couteau; **he had severe s. wounds in the chest** il était dans un état grave, ayant reçu des coups de couteau dans la poitrine **(b)** *F* (*attempt*) **to have a s. at sth** essayer de faire qch; **I'll have a s.** je vais essayer

stab² (**-bb-**) **1** *vt* (*person*) (*with dagger*) poignarder; (*with knife*) donner un coup/des coups de couteau à; **to s. sb with a fork/pair of scissors** donner un coup/des coups de fourchette/ciseaux à qn; **to s. sb to death** tuer qn à coups de couteau, poignarder qn; **to s. sb in the back** poignarder qn dans le dos; *Fig* tirer dans le dos de qn; **he's been stabbed** il a été poignardé; **he stabbed his knife into the tabletop** il planta son couteau dans la table; **she stabbed a piece of sausage with her fork** elle piqua un morceau de saucisse avec sa fourchette

2 *vi* **to s. at sb** (*with knife*) porter un coup de couteau à qn; (*with dagger*) porter un coup de poignard à qn; **he stabbed at the map with his finger** il a indiqué un point sur la carte avec son doigt; **to s. at sb with one's finger** menacer qn du doigt

stabbing ['stæbɪŋ] **1** *adj* **s. pain** élancement *m*, douleur *f* lancinante **2** *n* (*act*) (*with dagger*) coups *mpl* de poignard; (*with knife*) coups de couteau; (*murder*) meurtre *m* à coups de couteau; (*attack*) coup(s) de couteau; **there was a s. in the pub last night** quelqu'un s'est fait poignarder au pub hier soir; **to die in a s.** mourir poignardé; **the number of stabbings has increased** le nombre d'attaques à l'arme blanche est en hausse

stability [stə'bɪlɪtɪ] *n* (*of building*) stabilité *f*, solidité *f*; (*economic, of aircraft, chemical compound etc*) stabilité; **mental s.** équilibre *m* mental

stabilization [steɪbɪlaɪ'zeɪʃən] *n* (*of economy, aircraft*), *Phys, El* stabilisation

stabilize ['steɪbɪlaɪz] **1** *vt* (*economy, ship, exchange rate*) stabiliser **2** *vi* se stabiliser

stabilizer ['steɪbɪlaɪzər] *n* **(a)** *Naut* stabilisateur *m*; *Av* stabilisateur, empennage *m*; *Aut* **s. bar** barre *f* stabilisatrice **(b)** (*in foodstuffs, explosives etc*) stabilisant *m*

stabilizing ['steɪbɪlaɪzɪŋ] *adj* stabilisateur, -trice; **to have** *or* **exert a s. effect on prices** exercer une action stabilisatrice sur les prix; **her new job had a s. effect on her** son nouvel emploi a eu un effet stabilisateur *ou* équilibrant sur elle

stabilizing agent *n* (*in foodstuffs etc*) agent *m* stabilisant

stable[1] ['steɪb(ə)l] *n* **(a)** (*building*) écurie *f*; *Fig* **to lock the s. door after the horse has bolted** fermer la cage quand les oiseaux se sont envolés **(b)** (*horses*) chevaux *mpl* (*d'une certaine écurie*); *Horseracing, Aut etc* écurie *f*; *Fig* (*of boxers, film-stars*) équipe *f*; (*of publications, newspapers*) empire *m*; **racing s.** écurie de courses; **s. companion** *or* **mate** (*horse*) cheval *m* de la même écurie; *Fig* (*person*) (*in sport, film*) membre *m* de la même équipe; **they are political s. mates** ils partagent les mêmes idées politiques

stable[2] *vt* (*horse*) loger dans une écurie; **we can s. three horses** nous avons de la place pour trois chevaux

stable[3] *adj* **(a)** (*steady*) (*marriage, job, surface, economy, political situation*), *Ch, Phys* stable; (*ground, stairs, stepladders*) solide; **s. currency** monnaie stable; **the government is becoming more s.** le gouvernement se stabilise; **to be in a s. condition** (*of patient*) être dans un état stationnaire; **s. state** état stable, état de stabilité **(b)** (*well-balanced*) (*person*) équilibré; **he's perfectly s.** il est parfaitement équilibré; **he's not s.** il n'est pas équilibré, il est instable

stableboy ['steɪblbɔɪ] *n* garçon *m* d'écurie

stablelad ['steɪbllæd] *n* lad *m*

stabling ['steɪblɪŋ] *n* **(a)** (*of horses*) logement *m* dans une écurie **(b)** (*space in stables*) **we have plenty of s.** nous ne manquons pas de place aux écuries

staccato [stə'kɑːtəʊ] **1** *adj* (*note*) staccato; (*style, dialogue of play*) haché; (*voice*) saccadé **2** *adv Mus* staccato **3** *n Mus* staccato *m*; **she replied in a rapid s.** elle répondit d'un ton rapide et saccadé

stack[1] [stæk] *n* **(a)** (*of hay etc*) meule *f*; (*of wood, coal, plates etc*) pile *f*, tas *m*; (*of weapons*) faisceau *m*; **stacks** (*in library*) rayonnages *mpl*; **s. room** (*in library*) réserve *f*

(b) *F* **stacks of ...** (*a lot of*) des tas de ..., beaucoup de ...; **I've stacks of work to do** j'ai plein de boulot; **I've got stacks of things to read** j'ai une tonne de choses à lire; **we've got stacks of time** on a largement le temps; **to make stacks of money** ramasser l'argent à la pelle; **stacks** *or* **a s. of letters/complaints** des tonnes de courrier/plaintes

(c) (*of chimney*) souche *f*, corps *m*; (*of locomotive etc*) cheminée *f*

(d) *Geog* (*rock formation*) haut rocher *m* (*au large d'une côte*)

(e) *Av* (*aircraft waiting to land*) = avions *mpl* dans le ciel en attente d'un créneau d'atterrissage

(f) *Comptr* pile *f*; **s. pointer** pointeur *m* de pile

stack[2] *vt* **(a)** (*put in stacks*) (*hay*) mettre en meule(s); (*wood, coal, plates etc*) empiler, entasser; (*weapons*) mettre en faisceaux; **the odds were stacked against them** tout était contre eux; *Sl* **a woman stacked the way she is** une femme roulée comme elle **(b)** *Am* **to s. the cards** tricher aux cartes; **the jury was stacked against him** le jury avait un parti pris contre lui **(c)** *Av* (*aircraft waiting to land*) mettre en attente d'atterrissage **(d)** (*fill*) (*shelf, room*) bourrer

▶ **stack up** *vtsep* (*objects, books etc*) empiler

stacker ['stækər] *n* (*on printer*) dispositif *m* d'alimentation feuille à feuille; (*for output*) récepteur *m* (de sortie d'imprimante)

stacking chairs ['stækɪŋ] *npl* chaises *fpl* superposables

stadium, *pl* **-iums, -ia** ['steɪdɪəm, -ɪəmz, -ɪə] *n Sp etc* stade *m*

staff[1] [stɑːf] *n* **(a)** (*stick*) bâton *m*; (*of banner, lance*) hampe *f*; (*of bishop*) crosse *f*; *Naut* (*of flag*) mât *m*; (*in surveying*) mire *f*; *US* **at half s.** (*of flag*) en berne; *Lit* **the s. of life** (*bread*) le pain

(b) [①A11,g,iii] (*personnel, employees*) personnel *m*; **when he joined the s.** quand il est entré dans le personnel; **how many people are there on the s.?** combien de personnes y a-t-il en tout?; **domestic s.** domestiques *mfpl*; *Journ* **editorial s.** rédaction *f*; **teaching s.** personnel enseignant; **nursing s.** infirmiers *mpl*, infirmières *fpl*; **office s.** personnel de bureau; **sales-support s.** personnel de soutien commercial; **senior** *or* **managerial s.** cadres *mpl* supérieurs; **s. association** syndicat *m* du personnel; *Journ* **s. correspondent** envoyé *m* de la rédaction, correspondant *m* permanent; **s. cutback** réduction *f* de personnel; **s. management** direction *f* du personnel; **s. nurse** = infirmière diplômée; **s.-student ratio** rapport *m* entre le nombre de professeurs et le nombre d'étudiants; **s. reshuffle** remaniement *m* du personnel; **s. turnover** roulement *m* du personnel

(c) *Mil* (*officers*) état-major *m*, *pl* état-majors; **general s.** état-major général; **chief of s.** chef *m* d'état-major; **joint chiefs of s.** état-major interarmées; **S. College** = École *f* supérieure de guerre; **s. officer** officier *m* d'état-major

(d) *Mus* (*pl* **staves** [steɪvz]) portée *f*

staff[2] *vt* (*office etc*) pourvoir en personnel; **the office is almost entirely staffed by women** le personnel du bureau est presque entièrement composé de femmes; **the office is only staffed between the hours of 2 and 4** il y a quelqu'un au bureau de 2h à 4h seulement

staffer ['stɑːfər] *n F* membre *m* du personnel; *Journ* journaliste *mf* permanent(e)

staffing ['stɑːfɪŋ] *n* (*finding staff*) recrutement *m* de personnel; **s. arrangements** organisation *f* du personnel; **s. level** niveau *m* d'effectif; **s. problems** problèmes *mpl* de personnel

staff nurse *n Med* = infirmière *f* diplômée

staff room *n Sch* salle *f* des professeurs

Staffs *abbr* **Staffordshire**

stag [stæg] *n* **(a)** (*animal*) cerf *m* **(b)** *Br St Exch F* (*premium hunter*) loup *m*

stag beetle *n Ent* lucane *m*, cerf-volant *m*, *pl* cerfs-volants

stage[1] [steɪdʒ] *n* **(a)** *Th* (*place*) scène *f*; *TV, Cin* plateau *m*; **the s.** (*theatre*) le théâtre; **to go on the s.** (*take up acting*) devenir acteur/actrice; **front of the s.** avant-scène *f*; **to come on (the) s.** entrer en scène; **to set the s.** monter les décors; *Fig* préparer le terrain; *Fig* **now the s. was set for ...** maintenant tout était prêt pour ...; **s. directions** indications *fpl* scéniques; **s. door** entrée *f* des artistes; **s. effects** effets *mpl* scéniques; **s. left/right** côté cour/jardin; **s. lighting** éclairage *m* de plateau

(b) (*platform*) estrade *f*; (*for workmen*) échafaudage *m*; (*of microscope*) platine *f*

(c) (*phase*) stade *m*, étape *f*; **to be at a particular s.** (*in one's development etc*) en être à un certain stade; **to go through a particular s.** (*in one's development etc*) traverser un certain stade; **at this s.** à ce point, à ce moment; **in the larval s.** à l'état de larve, au stade larvaire; **to do sth in (successive) stages** faire qch par étapes (successives); **at what s. in its development?** à quel moment *ou* stade de son développement?; **at this s. in the project** à ce stade du projet; **at a later s. in his life** à un stade plus avancé de sa vie; **to pay in easy stages** payer en petits versements; **to do sth one s. at a time** faire qch étape par étape; **s. of production** phase *f* de production

(d) (*part of journey*) étape *f*; *Hist* (*for stagecoach etc*) relais *m*; **s. by s.** d'étape en étape; **we did the journey in easy stages** nous avons fait le voyage en petites étapes; *Br* **fare s.** = (changement *m* de) section *f* (*de l'itinéraire d'un autobus*)

(e) s. (coach) diligence *f*

(f) *Astronaut* (*of rocket*) étage *m*

stage[2] *vt* **(a)** *Th etc* mettre en scène; (*play*) monter, porter à la scène; (*demonstration etc*) organiser, faire; (*coup*) monter; **to s. a comeback** faire un come-back; **the whole incident had been staged** l'incident avait été monté de toutes pièces **(b)** (*phase*) **staged payments** paiements *mpl* échelonnés; **carefully staged reduction of nuclear weapons** réduction soigneusement étagée des armes nucléaires

stagecraft ['steɪdʒkrɑːft] *n Th* technique *f* de la scène

stage fright *n* trac *m*

stagehand ['steɪdʒhænd] *n Th* machiniste *mf*; *TV* machiniste de plateau

stage-manage *vt Th* mettre en scène; *Fig Pej* (*demonstration etc*) organiser depuis les coulisses

stage manager *n* régisseur *m*, chef *m* de plateau

stage name *n* nom *m* de théâtre

stager ['steɪdʒər] *n* **old s.** vieux routier *m*

stage school *n* école *f* avec enseignement du théâtre
stage-struck *adj* épris *ou* féru de théâtre
stage whisper *n* aparté *m*
stagey ['steɪdʒɪ] *adj Pej* = **stagy**
stagflation [stæg'fleɪʃən] *n Econ* stagflation *f*
stagger¹ ['stægər] *n* **(a)** pas *m* chancelant **(b)** *Vet* **staggers** vertigo *m*
stagger² **1** *vi* chanceler, tituber; **she staggered beneath the weight** elle chancela sous le poids; **to s. along** marcher en chancelant *ou* en titubant; **to s. to one's feet** se relever en chancelant **2** *vt* **(a)** (*overwhelm*) (*person*) stupéfier; **to be staggered** tomber à la renverse; **I'm staggered!** je n'arrive pas à le croire! **(b)** (*hours of work, holidays etc*) échelonner
staggered ['stægəd] *adj* **s. junction** carrefour *m* décalé; **s. payments** paiements *mpl* échelonnés
staggering ['stægərɪŋ] **1** *adj* (*news*) renversant, atterrant; (*price*) incroyable; **s. blow** coup *m* de massue; **s. increase in prices** hausse vertigineuse des prix; **it cost a s. £4,000** ça a coûté la somme incroyable de 4000 livres **2** *n* (*of hours of work, holidays*) échelonnement *m*
staghorn ['stæghɔːn] *n* bois *mpl* de cerf
staghunt(ing) ['stæghʌnt(ɪŋ)] *n* chasse *f* au cerf
staging ['steɪdʒɪŋ] *n* **(a)** *Th* (*of play*) mise *f* à la scène; **s. area** décor *m* **(b)** (*set, scenery*) scénographie *f* **(c) s. post** *Hist* (*for coaches*) relais *m* (de diligences); *Av* escale *f* aérienne; *Fig* étape *f*
stagnant ['stægnənt] *adj* (*water*) stagnant; (*trade, business*) en stagnation, dans le marasme
stagnate [stæg'neɪt] *vi* (*of water, trade, business, Fig of person*) stagner
stagnation [stæg'neɪʃən] *n* (*of water*) stagnation *f*; (*of trade*) stagnation, marasme *m*
stag night *or* **party** *n* (*before wedding*) enterrement *m* de la vie de garçon; (*otherwise*) soirée *f* entre hommes; **to have a s.** (*before wedding*) enterrer sa vie de garçon
stagy ['steɪdʒɪ] *adj Pej* théâtral
staid [steɪd] *adj* sérieux, -euse
staidness ['steɪdnɪs] *n* sérieux *m*
stain¹ [steɪn] *n* **(a)** (*mark*) tache *f*; **to remove a s.** enlever une tache **(from** de); *Fig* **without a s. on his character** sans atteinte à sa réputation; **to leave a s. on sb's reputation** entacher la réputation de qn; **a grease/blood s.** une tache de graisse/sang; **s. remover** détachant *m* **(b)** (*dye*) colorant *m*; **(wood) s.** teinture *f* (pour bois)
stain² **1** *vt* **(a)** (*mark*) tacher **(with** de); *Fig* (*person's reputation*) entacher, souiller, ternir; **hands stained with blood** mains tachées *ou* souillées de sang; *Fig* **hands stained with the blood of innocent people** mains tachées du sang d'innocents **(b)** (*dye*) (*wood*) teindre, teinter; (*glass*) peindre **2** *vi* **material that stains easily** tissu qui se tache facilement
stained glass [steɪnd] *n* (*material*) verre *m* coloré; (*windows*) vitraux *mpl*
stained-glass window *n* vitrail *m*, -aux
staining ['steɪnɪŋ] *n* (*of wood*) teinture *f*
stainless ['steɪnlɪs] *adj* (*reputation*) sans tache
stainless steel *n* acier *m* inoxydable; *F* inox *m*; **s. knives** des couteaux en acier inoxydable *ou F* en inox
stair ['steər] *n* [①A10,f] **(a) stair(s)** (*flight of stairs*) escalier *m*; **she took the stairs** elle prit l'escalier; **I met him on the stairs** je l'ai rencontré dans l'escalier; **back stairs** escalier de service; **s. carpet** tapis *m* d'escalier **(b)** (*step*) marche *f*, degré *m*
staircase ['steəkeɪs] *n* (*stairs*) escalier *m*; (*structure*) cage *f* d'escalier; **secret s.** escalier dérobé
stairway ['steəweɪ] *n* = **staircase**
stairwell ['steəwel] *n* cage *f* d'escalier
stake¹ [steɪk] *n* **(a)** (*piece of wood, metal*) pieu *m*; (*for marking land*) jalon *m*, fiche *f*; (*for tethering animal*) piquet *m*; (*in horticulture*) tuteur *m*; (*for vine*) échalas *m*; (*in surveying*) jalon; *F* **to pull up stakes** (*leave*) partir; (*leave one's home*) déménager; **s. boat** bateau *m* de ligne de départ
(b) (*for execution*) **to die** *or* **be burned at the s.** mourir sur le bûcher; **she went to the s. for her beliefs** on l'a brûlée pour ses croyances; *Fig* **but I'm not going to go to the s. for it** mais je n'ai aucune intention de mourir pour ça
(c) (*in gambling*), *Fig* mise *f*, enjeu *m*; **the stakes are down** les jeux sont faits; **to play for high stakes** jouer gros jeu; **our honour is at s.** il y va de notre honneur, notre honneur est en jeu; **there's a lot at s.** de lourds intérêts sont en jeu; **to have large sums at s. in an enterprise** avoir de fortes sommes engagées dans une entreprise; **to have a s. in sth** avoir des intérêts dans qch; *Horseracing* **stakes** (*prize*) prix *m*
stake² *vt* **(a)** (*mark out*) (*piece of land etc*) jalonner, piqueter; (*in surveying*) (*line, road etc*) jalonner; **to s. a claim** *Min* jalonner une concession; *Fig* faire valoir ses droits
(b) (*support with stakes*) (*object*) soutenir avec des pieux; (*vine etc*) échalasser; (*tomatoes*) tuteurer
(c) (*in gambling*) (*amount of money*) mettre en jeu, jouer; *Fig* (*reputation, job etc*) risquer; **to s. twenty francs** miser *ou* jouer vingt francs; **to s. everything** *or* **one's all** jouer son va-tout, mettre tout en jeu; **I'd s. my life on it** j'en mettrais ma tête à couper
(d) *Am F* (*person*) (*provide with money*) financer; (*provide needs of*) subvenir aux besoins de
▶ **stake off** *vtsep* = **stake²** **(a)**
▶ **stake out** *vtsep* **(a)** = **stake²** (*a*) **(b)** (*keep under observation*) (*building etc*) surveiller
stakeholder ['steɪkhəʊldər] *n* personne *f* participant à une affaire, partie *f* prenante
stakeout ['steɪkaʊt] *n* surveillance *f*; **to be on s.** faire le guet; **he was caught in a s.** la police faisait le guet et on l'a arrêté
staking ['steɪkɪŋ] *n* **(a)** (*marking off*) (*of piece of land etc*) jalonnement *m*, piquetage *m* **(b)** (*support*) (*of vine*) échalassage *m*; (*of tomatoes*) tuteurage *m*
stalactite ['stæləktaɪt], *Am also* [stə'læktaɪt] *n Geol* stalactite *f*
stalagmite ['stæləgmaɪt], *Am also* [stə'lægmaɪt] *n Geol* stalagmite *f*
stale¹ [steɪl] *adj* **(a)** (*not fresh*) qui n'est pas frais/*f* fraîche; (*bread, cake*) rassis; (*air*) vicié; **s. breath** mauvaise haleine *f*; **s. smell** odeur *f* de renfermé; (*of beer, perfume etc*) relent *m*
(b) *Fig* (*old*) (*excuse, cliché, argument etc*) vieux, *f* vieille; *Com* **s. bill** connaissement *m* périmé; **s. joke** plaisanterie éculée; **s. news** nouvelle plus très fraîche; **it soon becomes s. and boring** on s'en lasse rapidement et ça devient ennuyeux
(c) (*person*) qui a perdu sa fraîcheur; **to go s.** (*of athlete etc*) se surentraîner; (*of actor, musician etc*) perdre son inspiration; **I'm s.** (*of athlete, executive*) je suis vidé; (*of actor, writer, musician*) je n'ai plus d'inspiration; **I'm feeling a bit s.** j'ai un peu perdu de ma fraîcheur; *F* **it's gone s. on me** ça ne m'intéresse plus, j'ai perdu mon enthousiasme; **her marriage had gone s.** son mariage avait perdu de sa passion
(d) *Fin* (*market*) lourd, plat
stale² *vi* (*of news etc*) perdre de son intérêt; **pleasure that never stales** plaisir toujours nouveau
stalemate¹ ['steɪlmeɪt] *n Chess* pat *m*; *Fig* **negotiations have reached a s.** les négociations sont dans l'impasse; *Fig* **it's s. between them** ils sont dans une impasse; *Fig* **it's s.** c'est l'impasse
stalemate² *vt Chess* **Black is stalemated** les Noirs sont pat; *Fig* **this has stalemated the talks** cela a mis les négociations dans l'impasse; *Mktg* **stalemated industry** industrie *f* dans l'impasse
staleness ['steɪlnɪs] *n* **(a)** (*of bread*) état *m* rassis; (*of beer etc*) évent *m*; (*stale smell*) odeur *f* de renfermé; (*of beer, perfume etc*) relent *m* **(b)** (*of news*) manque *m* de fraîcheur
Stalinism ['stɑːlɪnɪz(ə)m] *n* stalinisme *m*
Stalinist ['stɑːlɪnɪst] *adj, n* stalinien, -ienne
stalk¹ [stɔːk] *n* (*way of walking*) (*imposing*) démarche *f* majestueuse; (*disdainful*) démarche hautaine
stalk² **1** *vi* (*walk haughtily*) marcher *ou* s'avancer l'air hautain; **to s. out of a room** sortir d'une pièce l'air hautain **2** *vt* **(a)** (*of animal*) (*prey*) être sur les traces de; (*of hunter*) (*game*) traquer; (*deer*) chasser à l'approche; *Fig* (*person*) suivre furtivement; (*of private detective*) filer; (*of murderer*) traquer **(b)** (*prowl about in*) (*corridor, street*) rôder dans
stalk³ *n* **(a)** (*of plant*) tige *f*; (*of fruit*) queue *f*; (*of wheat, corn*) chaume *m*; (*of bunch of grapes*) rafle *f*, râpe *f*; (*of cabbage*) trognon *m*; *Zool* pédoncule *m*, pédicule *m*; **s.-eyed** aux yeux pédonculés; **her eyes came out/were (out) on stalks** les yeux lui sont sortis/sortaient de la tête **(b)** (*of wineglass*) pied *m* **(c)** *Aut* (*for controls*) tige *f*, manette *f*
stalker ['stɔːkər] *n* (*hunter*) chasseur *m* à l'approche
stalking ['stɔːkɪŋ] *n* (*in hunting*) chasse *f* à l'approche; **s. horse** (*in hunting*) cheval *m* d'abri; *Fig* (*pretext*) prétexte *m*; *Pol* **we'll use him as a s. horse** on va s'en servir comme d'un candidat bidon
stall¹ [stɔːl] *n* **(a)** (*in stable*) stalle *f*; (*in byre*) case *f*
(b) (*for selling etc*) étalage *m* (en plein vent), éventaire *m*; (*at exhibition etc*) stand *m*; **(market) s.** place *f ou* emplacement *m* (au marché); **newspaper s.** kiosque *m* à journaux; **I bought it at a fruit s.** je l'ai acheté chez le petit marchand de fruits; *also Fig* **to set out one's s.** déballer sa marchandise
(c) choir s. stalle *f*; *Th* **(orchestra) stalls** fauteuils *mpl* d'orchestre; **a seat in the stalls** un fauteuil d'orchestre
(d) *Med* (*for finger*) doigtier *m*

(**e**) (*act of stalling*) *Aut* (*of engine*) calage *m*; **I thought his story was just a s. to gain time** j'ai pensé qu'il ne cherchait qu'à gagner du temps avec son histoire

(**f**) *Horseracing* **(starting) stalls** stalle *f* (de départ)

stall[2] **1** *vt* (**a**) *Aut* (*engine*) caler (**b**) (*put in stalls*) (*cattle*) mettre à l'étable (**c**) (*hold off*) **try and s. them for half an hour** essaie de les retenir une demi-heure; **I think he's deliberately stalling us** je crois qu'il nous fait attendre délibérément; **they tried to s. us with some nonsense** ils ont tenté de nous retarder avec des bêtises **2** *vi* (**a**) (*of engine*) caler; *Av, Fig* (*of campaign*) être en perte de vitesse (**b**) **to s. (for time)** chercher à gagner du temps; **stop stalling!** arrête de tergiverser!; **we'll have to s. on this for another week or so** il faudra que nous gagnions environ une semaine de plus pour ça

stall-feed *vt* (*pt, pp* **stall-fed** [-fed]) (*cattle*) engraisser à l'étable

stallholder ['stɔːlhəʊldər] *n* étalagiste *mf*, marchand, -ande en plein vent; **I've agreed to be a s. at the fête** j'ai accepté de tenir un stand à la fête

stalling ['stɔːlɪŋ] *n Aut* **to prevent s.** pour empêcher que le moteur ne cale

stallion ['stæljən] *n* étalon *m*

stalwart ['stɔːlwət] **1** *adj* (*strong*) robuste, vigoureux; (*brave*) vaillant; *Fig* (*defender*) résolu; (*supporter*) fidèle; (*refusal*) inébranlable; **they put up a s. defence** ils se sont défendus d'arrache-pied **2** *n Pol* **a party s.** un pilier du parti

stamen ['steɪmən] *n Bot* étamine *f*

stamina ['stæmɪnə] *n* résistance *f*

stammer[1] ['stæmər] *n* (*permanent*) bégaiement *m*; (*out of nervousness etc*) bégaiement, balbutiement *m*; **man with a s.** homme qui bégaie, bègue *m*

stammer[2] **1** *vi* (*normally*) bégayer; (*out of nervousness etc*) bégayer, balbutier **2** *vt* = **stammer out**

▶ **stammer out** *vtsep* (*excuse etc*) bégayer, balbutier

stammerer ['stæmərər] *n* bègue *mf*

stammering ['stæmərɪŋ] *n* bégaiement *m*; (*through nervousness etc*) bégaiement, balbutiement *m*

stamp[1] [stæmp] *n* (**a**) **(postage) s.** timbre(-poste) *m*, *pl* timbres(-poste); *Br* **(National Insurance) s.** = mois *m* de cotisation à l'assurance chômage; *Jur* **s. duty** droit *m* de timbre, timbre *m* fiscal; **s. hinge** charnière *f*; **s. machine** distributeur *m* automatique de timbres-poste

(**b**) (*device for marking*) tampon *m*; (*esp for metal*) estampe *f*, étampe *f*; (*esp for gold etc*) poinçon *m*; **signature s.** griffe *f*; **date s.** (timbre *m*) dateur *m*; **rubber s.** tampon *ou* timbre de caoutchouc; **s. pad** tampon (encreur)

(**c**) (*mark*) marque *f* (apposée); *Ind* estampille *f ou* marque de contrôle; *Fig* **it needs his s. of approval** il faut son approbation; **to bear the s. of genius** porter l'empreinte du génie; **to leave one's s. on sth** marquer qch de son empreinte; **there are few politicians of her s.** (*calibre*) il y a peu de politiciens de sa trempe, *Pej* il y a peu de politiciens de son espèce

(**d**) (*in metalwork*) étampeuse *f*, estampeuse *f*

(**e**) (*of foot*) battement *m* de pied (*d'impatience, de colère*); **with a s. of the foot** en frappant du pied; **ceaseless s. of feet** (*as expression of impatience, enthusiasm*) piétinement *m* perpétuel; **the ceaseless s. of feet past my window** le bruit continuel des pas devant ma fenêtre

stamp[2] **1** *vt* (**a**) **to s. one's foot** taper du pied; **he stamped the toy to pieces** il a écrabouillé le jouet à coups de talon; **he stamped the snow/mud off his boots** il tapait du pied pour faire tomber la neige/boue; **he stamped the earth down** il a tassé la terre avec le pied

(**b**) (*imprint mark on*) (*object*) imprimer sur; (*gold, silver*) poinçonner; (*coins etc*) frapper, estamper; (*leather*) frapper, estamper, gaufrer; **each article is stamped with the manufacturer's mark** chaque article porte la marque du fabricant; **a design is stamped on the butter** un dessin est imprimé dans le beurre; *Fig* **he was determined to s. his mark on the party** il était déterminé à marquer le parti de son empreinte

(**c**) (*mark with ink*) (*document*) timbrer, estampiller; (*passport*) viser; (*letter*) timbrer, affranchir; (*goods*) estampiller; *Fin* **to s. a bill** viser un effet; **they s. the details on your cheque** ils tamponnent les détails sur votre chèque; **a machine that stamps the date on ...** une machine qui marque *ou* tamponne la date sur ...

(**d**) (*put postage stamp on*) (*letter, parcel*) timbrer, affranchir

(**e**) (*in metalwork*) (*metal objects*) étamper, estamper

(**f**) *Fig* **to s. sb/sth (as) ...** donner à qn/qch le caractère de ...; **this stamped him (as) a rebel** à partir de là, on lui a collé l'étiquette de rebelle

2 *vi* **to s. upstairs/outside** monter l'escalier/sortir d'un pas bruyant

▶ **stamp about, stamp around** *vi* (*stamp feet*) trépigner, piétiner; (*for warmth*) battre la semelle

▶ **stamp on 1** *vipo* (**a**) (*step on*) (*cockroach, worm*) écraser (avec le talon) (**b**) *Fig* (*repress*) (*person*) écraser, bafouer; (*suggestions*) fouler aux pieds **2** *vtsep* (*date etc*) tamponner, marquer

▶ **stamp out** *vtsep* (**a**) (*eradicate*) (*rebellion*) écraser; (*abuse, resistance, independence etc*) éradiquer; (*epidemic, inflation*) enrayer (**b**) (*extinguish by stamping*) (*fire*) éteindre en piétinant (**c**) (*in metalwork*) (*sheet metal*) découper à la presse *ou* à l'emporte-pièce

stamp album *n* album *m* de timbres-poste

stamp collector *n* philatéliste *mf*

stamped [stæmpt] *adj* (**a**) (*with seal*) estampillé (**b**) **s. addressed envelope** enveloppe *f* timbrée

stampede[1] [stæm'piːd] *n* (*rush, flight*) (*of troops, horses etc*) fuite *f* précipitée, débandade *f*; **several people were injured in the s.** plusieurs personnes ont été blessées dans la panique; **there was a s. for the door** tout le monde s'est précipité vers la porte

stampede[2] **1** *vi* (*rush*) se ruer, se précipiter **(for, towards** vers, sur); (*flee*) fuir en désordre *ou* à la débandade; (*of cattle etc*) partir à la débandade **2** *vt* (*cattle, people*) semer la panique parmi; **to s. a nation into war** précipiter un peuple dans la guerre; **to s. sb into doing sth** presser qn à faire qch, bousculer qn pour qu'il fasse qch; **I don't want to s. you into (making) a decision** je ne veux pas te presser *ou* te bousculer dans ta décision

stamping ['stæmpɪŋ] *n* (**a**) (*with feet*) piétinement *m*, trépignement *m*; *F* **this was one of my old s. grounds** j'y allais tout le temps (**b**) (*in metalwork*) estampage *m*, étampage *m*; (*item*) pièce *f* estampée; **s. press** estampeuse *f* (**c**) (*of letters, parcels*) affranchissement *m*, timbrage *m*

stamping out *n* (*of rebellion etc*) écrasement *m*; (*of abuse etc*) enraiement *m*; (*of disease*) éradication *f*

stance [stæns] *n* (*posture*) position *f*; *Fig* position, attitude *f*; *Golf, Cr etc* (*of player*) posture *f*; **she took up her usual s. at the window** elle s'est mise à la fenêtre comme à son habitude; **the government's s. on this** la position *ou* l'attitude du gouvernement là-dessus

stanch [stɑːntʃ] *vt* = **staunch**[2]

stanchion ['stɑːnʃən] *n* étançon *m*, étai *m*

stand[1] [stænd] *n* (**a**) (*position*) position *f* (**on** concernant); **to take up a s. near the door** se poster *ou* prendre position près de la porte; **to take a s.** prendre position et s'y tenir; **to take a firm s.** ne pas transiger; **you should take a firmer s. with them** tu devrais adopter une attitude plus ferme envers eux; **to make a s. against an abuse** s'opposer résolument à un abus; **to make a s. (against the enemy)** (*of troops*) faire face (à l'ennemi)

(**b**) *Th* représentation *f*; (*by band*) concert *m*

(**c**) (*for taxis*) station *f*

(**d**) (*support*) (*of lamp etc*) support *m*, pied *m*; (*for motorbike etc*) béquille *f*; **(revolving) s.** (*for books, postcards etc*) tourniquet *m*; *TV etc* **s. lamp** lumière *f* sur pied; *TV etc* **s. microphone** microphone *m* sur pied

(**e**) (*stall*) (*in open air*) étalage *m*, étal *m*; (*at exhibition etc*) stand *m*

(**f**) (*at sports ground, for watching procession*) tribune *f*; **the stands** les tribunes

(**g**) *Agr* (*crop*) récolte *f* sur pied; (*of trees*) peuplement *m*

(**h**) *Jur* (*witness box*) barre *f* des témoins; **to take the s.** venir à la barre

stand[2] (*pt, pp* **stood** [stʊd]) **1** *vi* (**a**) (*have upright position*) être debout, se tenir debout; (*maintain upright position*) rester debout; (*assume upright position*) se lever; **she stood with her back to me** elle se tenait debout en me tournant le dos; **to be/keep standing** être/rester debout; **I was too weak to s.** j'étais trop faible pour me tenir debout; **I could hardly s.** je pouvais à peine me tenir debout; *Fig* **to s. on one's own two feet** se débrouiller tout seul; *F* **he hasn't/you haven't/***etc* **a leg to s. on** ça ne tient pas; **I've lost everything but what I s. up in** j'ai tout perdu sauf ce que j'ai sur le dos; **to s. six feet high** (*of object*) avoir six pieds de haut, mesurer six pieds; (*of person*) mesurer six pieds; **the house is still standing** la maison tient toujours debout; **not a stone (of the building) was left standing** le bâtiment avait été complètement détruit; *Sch* **s.!** levez-vous!; *Mil* **to s. to attention** se mettre au garde-à-vous

(**b**) (*be situated, be*) se trouver, être; **a chapel stands at the top of the hill** une chapelle se dresse au sommet de la colline; **a car was standing at the door** il y avait une voiture à la porte; **the monument stands as a memorial to his life's**

work le monument a été érigé pour célébrer l'œuvre de sa vie; **I found the door standing open** j'ai trouvé la porte ouverte; **nothing stands between you and success** rien ne s'oppose à votre succès; **a man stood in the doorway** un homme se tenait à la porte; **I'll s. at** *or* **by the window** je me mettrai à la fenêtre; **I didn't know where to s.** je ne savais où me mettre; **I stood and looked at him, I stood looking at him** je suis resté à le regarder; **I was standing a few feet away from him** je me tenais à quelques pas de lui; **to s. talking/watching** rester à parler/regarder; **don't just s. there! do something!** ne reste pas là les bras ballants! fais quelque chose!; **don't s. in the passage!** ne reste pas là, tu gênes le passage!; **if you insist on leaving school at 16 I won't s. in your way** si tu veux vraiment arrêter tes études à 16 ans, je ne m'y opposerai pas; **to leave sb standing (there)** laisser qn planté (là); *Sp etc* **to be left standing** être laissé sur place; **to leave the competition standing** *Sp* griller la concurrence; *Fig* laisser les autres très loin derrière; **s. and deliver!** la bourse ou la vie!; **we're standing right behind you** nous sommes avec vous; **with the union standing behind him** avec le soutien du syndicat

(c) (*maintain position*) **to s. fast** *or* **firm** (*not retreat*) tenir, tenir bon; **to s. still** se tenir immobile; **time seemed to s. still** le temps semblait s'être arrêté; **we s. or fall together** nous sommes solidaires (les uns des autres); **I shall s. or fall by the issue** mon sort dépend du résultat; **to s. alone** faire face *ou* tenir tête seul; **to s. on ceremony** faire des manières; **she's standing on her dignity** elle exige le respect qui lui est dû; **she doesn't s. on her dignity at these occasions** elle ne fait pas la fière dans de telles circonstances

(d) (*remain valid*) tenir, se maintenir; **the passage must s.** le passage doit rester comme il est *ou* sans modification; **the bet stands** le pari tient; **the objection stands** cette objection est toujours valable; **what you said last week, does that still s.?** et ce que tu as dit la semaine dernière, ça tient toujours?

(e) (*be in certain state*) être, se trouver; **to s. convicted of ...** avoir été déclaré coupable de ..., être convaincu de ...; **to s. in need of ...** avoir besoin de ...; **you s. in danger of getting killed** vous risquez de vous faire tuer; **to s. to lose £5,000** risquer de perdre 5 000 livres; **to s. to win a lot of money** avoir des chances de gagner beaucoup d'argent; **no-one stands to gain from a quarrel like this** personne n'a rien à gagner d'une telle querelle; **to s. as security for a debt** assurer une créance; **to s. guarantor** *or* **surety for sb** se porter garant envers qn, cautionner qn; **to s. (as candidate) for Parliament** se présenter *ou* se porter candidat à la députation; **the thermometer stood at 30°** le thermomètre marquait 30°; **the debt now stands at $3.5 billion** la dette s'élève à présent à $3,5 milliards; **the balance stands at £50** le reliquat de compte est de cinquante livres; **the amount standing to your credit** votre solde créditeur; **how do we s.?** (*in work etc*) où en sommes-nous?; (*financially*) où en sont nos comptes?; **as matters s., as it stands** au point où en sont les choses, dans l'état actuel des choses; **to know how things s.** être au fait de la situation; **I don't know where I s.** j'ignore quelle est ma situation *ou* ma position; **how do you s. with him?** quelle est votre position vis-à-vis de lui?; **you never know how** *or* **where you s. with her** on ne sait jamais sur quel pied danser avec elle; **I s. corrected** je reconnais mon erreur

(f) (*remain motionless*) **to allow a liquid to s.** laisser reposer *ou* laisser déposer un liquide

2 *vt* **(a)** (*place upright*) mettre, poser, placer; **to s. sth on the table** mettre *ou* poser qch sur la table; **to s. sth against the wall** dresser qch contre le mur; **to s. sth upright** mettre qch debout

(b) to s. one's ground tenir bon *ou* ferme; **s. your ground!** (*don't retreat*) ne reculez pas d'une semelle!; (*don't give up opposition*) tenez ferme!, ne lâchez pas prise!

(c) (*endure*) supporter, soutenir, subir; **to s. the cold** supporter le froid; **to s. a shock** résister à *ou* supporter un choc; **his argument does not s. investigation** son argument ne tient pas; **to s. comparison with sb/sth** soutenir la comparaison avec qn/qch; **he can't s. her** il ne peut pas la souffrir *ou* la sentir; **I won't s. such behaviour** je ne supporterai pas une pareille conduite; **I can't s. it any longer** (*heat, cold, discomfort etc*) je ne tiens plus; (*emotional tension, cruelty etc*) je n'en peux plus

(d) *F* (*pay for*) payer, offrir; **to s. sb a drink** payer à boire à qn; **to s. sb a dinner** payer un dîner à qn; **I'll s. you** c'est moi qui paie

(e) to s. a chance (of doing sth) avoir de bonnes chances (de faire qch); **if this initiative is to s. a chance ...** si vous voulez que cette initiative ait la moindre chance de succès ...

▶ **stand about, stand around** *vi* (*be standing, doing nothing*) se tenir là; **there were a lot of people standing around talking** il y avait beaucoup de monde qui se tenait là à parler; **I can't afford to pay people to s. around all day doing nothing** je n'ai pas les moyens de payer les gens à ne rien faire

▶ **stand aside** *vi* **(a)** (*be standing apart*) se tenir à l'écart **(b)** (*move aside*) s'écarter; **to s. aside to let sb pass** s'effacer pour laisser passer qn; *Fig* **to s. aside in favour of sb** se désister en faveur de qn

▶ **stand away** *vi* (*move away*) s'éloigner **(from** de)

▶ **stand back** *vi* **(a)** (*of person*) (*move away*) (se) reculer; (*keep in background*) se tenir en arrière; **s. well back please!** reculez(-vous) bien, s'il vous plaît **(b)** (*of building etc*) être situé en retrait; **a house standing back from the road** une maison située en retrait (de la route)

▶ **stand by 1** *vi* **(a)** (*be ready*) se tenir prêt; *Naut* se tenir paré; *Mil* **the troops are standing by** les troupes sont en état d'alerte; *Naut* **s. by!** paré!, attention!

(b) (*wait*) attendre, patienter; **viewers were told to s. by for further developments** on demanda aux téléspectateurs de patienter et d'attendre la suite des événements

(c) (*not get involved*) se tenir là (*sans intervenir*); **people just stood by and watched him being beaten up** les gens restèrent là à le regarder se faire cogner

2 *vipo* **(a)** (*stand next, near to*) (*of person*) se tenir près de *ou* à côté de

(b) (*person*) (*support, defend*) soutenir, défendre; (*take side of*) se ranger du côté de; **she stood by her friend throughout the trial** elle a soutenu son amie tout au long du procès

(c) (*keep, honour*) (*promise*) rester fidèle à; **I s. by what I said** je m'en tiens à ce que j'ai dit

▶ **stand down** *vi* (*retire*) (*from team, position etc*) se retirer; (*of candidate*) retirer sa candidature **(in favour of** en faveur de); *Mil* quitter son service; *Jur* (*of witness*) quitter la barre

▶ **stand for** *vipo* **(a)** *esp Br* (*present oneself as candidate for*) se présenter à; **to s. for parliament** se présenter au parlement; **to s. for the chairmanship** se présenter à la présidence; **to s. for election** se présenter aux élections; **half the committee are standing for re-election** la moitié des membres du comité se représente

(b) (*mean, represent*) (*sth*) signifier, vouloir dire; **'tsp' stands for 'teaspoonful'** 'tsp' signifie 'teaspoonful'; **the letters AA s. for 'Alcoholics Anonymous'** les lettres AA veulent dire 'Alcooliques Anonymes'; **our party stands for freedom and democracy** notre parti est celui de la liberté et de la démocratie

(c) (*tolerate*) (*sth*) supporter, tolérer; **I won't s. for it** je ne supporterai pas cela

▶ **stand in** *vi* (*act as replacement*) assurer le remplacement

▶ **stand in for** *vipo* (*act as replacement for*) (*person*) remplacer; *Cin* (*actor*) doubler; **a little party with fruit juice standing in for champagne** une petite fête où le jus de fruit tient lieu de champagne

▶ **stand off 1** *vi* (*remain at a distance*) se tenir éloigné *ou* à l'écart **2** *vipo Naut* **to s. off the coast** être au large

▶ **stand out** *vi* **(a)** (*be noticeable*) (*of objects*) ressortir; *Pej* détonner; (*protrude*) faire saillie; **to s. out in sharp relief** ressortir, se détacher; *Fig* se distinguer; **to s. out against sth** faire contraste avec qch; **mountains that s. out against the horizon** montagnes qui se dessinent à *ou* sur l'horizon; **the qualities that s. out in his work** les qualités marquantes de son œuvre; **she stands out in a crowd** on la remarque dans la foule; *Fig* **characteristics that make him s. out in the crowd** traits qui le caractérisent; *F* **that stands out a mile!** (*is very obvious*) ça se voit comme le nez au milieu de la figure!; **it really stands out that he's not a local** ça se voit *ou* se remarque vraiment qu'il n'est pas d'ici

(b) (*adopt firm position*) résister **(against** à), tenir bon *ou* ferme **(against** contre)

▶ **stand out for** *vipo* (*sth*) insister sur

▶ **stand over 1** *vi* (*be postponed*) rester en suspens; **to let a question s. over, to allow a question to s. over** remettre une question à plus tard, laisser une question en suspens **2** *vipo* **to s. over sb** (*lean over*) se pencher sur qn; (*watch*) surveiller qn de près; **if I don't s. over him, he does nothing** si je ne suis pas toujours sur son dos, il ne fait rien

▶ **stand to 1** *vi Mil etc* être prêt, être en état d'alerte; **s. to!** aux armes! **2** *vtas Mil etc* mettre en état d'alerte

▶ **stand together** *vi* être *ou* rester solidaire

▶ **stand up 1** *vi* **(a)** (*rise to one's feet*) se lever, se mettre debout; (*to be standing up*) se tenir debout; **this lamp won't s. up straight** cette lampe ne tient pas droite; **s. up!** levez-vous!, debout!; **we must s. up and be counted!** il ne faut pas nous laisser faire! **(b)** *(be valid)* se tenir, être valide; **there isn't enough evidence for the charge to s. up in court** il n'y a pas suffisamment de preuves pour que l'accusation tienne au tribunal **2** *vtsep* **(a)** *F (fail to meet)* poser un lapin à **(b)** *(put in upright position) (object)* mettre debout; **to s. a child up (again)** (re)mettre un enfant sur ses pieds

▶ **stand up for** *vipo (defend) (person)* soutenir, défendre; **only Chris stood up for her** seul Chris l'a soutenue *ou* s'est mis de son côté; **s. up for what you believe in** défendez ce en quoi vous croyez

▶ **stand up to** *vipo (resist, oppose) (sb)* tenir tête à; *(endure) (of object)* résister à; **it won't s. up to that sort of treatment** ça ne résistera pas à ce genre de traitement; **it doesn't s. up to close analysis** ça ne résiste pas à une analyse poussée

stand-alone *n Comptr* poste *m* autonome, monoposte *m*; **s. computer** ordinateur *m* autonome; **s. workstation** station *f* de travail autonome

standard¹ ['stændəd] *n* **(a)** *(flag etc)* bannière *f*; *Mil* étendard *m*; *Naut* pavillon *m*; *Mil, Fig* **s. bearer** porte-drapeau *m*, *pl* porte-drapeaux

(b) *(accepted length, quantity etc)* étalon *m*, référence *f*; **to use sth as a s.** prendre qch comme référence; *Fin* **gold/silver s.** étalon (d')or/d'argent; *Rail* **s. gauge** voie *f* normale; **s. model** *(of car)* voiture *f* de série; *(of machine)* modèle *m* standard *ou* de série

(c) *(set requirement)* norme *f*; **to meet government standards** être conforme aux normes établies par le gouvernement; **to make a product comply with standards** adapter un produit aux normes; **standards and practices** normes et usages; **standards catalogue** catalogue *m* de normes; **standards committee** organisme *m* de normalisation; **standards conversion** *(in broadcasting)* transcodage *m*; **standards converter** *(in broadcasting)* transcodeur *m*

(d) *(level, quality)* niveau *m*; **to have high/low standards** *(of person)* être exigeant/ne pas être exigeant; *(of school)* exiger un bon niveau/ne pas exiger un bon niveau; **they have no standards** ils ne sont pas exigeants du tout; **s. of living** niveau de vie; **everyone has his own standards** chacun voit midi à sa porte; **to raise the standards of behaviour** améliorer la discipline; **a high s. of playing/academic achievement** un niveau de jeu/de réussite académique élevé; **he sets very high standards for his students** il exige de ses étudiants un niveau très élevé; **not to come up to s.** ne pas atteindre le niveau exigé; **my cooking isn't up to your s.** ma cuisine n'est pas à la hauteur de la vôtre

(e) *(in horticulture)* **s. rose (tree)** rosier *m* sur tige

standard² *adj* **(a)** *(length, width etc)* standard *inv*, normalisé; **s. measure** mesure *f* étalon; **s. thickness** *(of iron etc)* épaisseur *f* type *ou* courante; **s. weight** poids *m* normal; **British s. time** heure *f* légale anglaise

(b) *(usual) (criticism, problem, behaviour, approach)* classique; *(price)* normal; **headrests are s.** *or* **are fitted as s.** les appuis-têtes sont montés en série; **s. authors** auteurs *mpl* classiques; **s. edition** *(of an author)* édition *f* courante; **s. English** l'anglais *m* standard; **s. spelling/pronunciation** orthographe *f*/prononciation *f* correcte; **a s. French dictionary** un dictionnaire général de la langue française; **one of his s. jokes** une de ses plaisanteries habituelles; **to come in s. sizes** *(of clothes)* exister dans les tailles standards; **the cooking is fairly s.** la cuisine n'a rien de sensationnel; **s. practice** pratique *f* courante; **that's s.** c'est normal; **s. class** deuxième classe *f*; **s. closure** *(for letter)* formule *f* de politesse pour terminer une lettre; **s. cost** coût *m* standard *ou* préétabli; **s. deviation** *(in statistics)* écart *m* type; **s. document** document *m* type; **s. opening** *(for letter)* formule de politesse pour commencer une lettre; **s. rate** taux *m* normal; **s. service** service *m* standard; **s. shipping note** permis *m* d'embarquement standard, avis *m* d'expédition standard

standardization [stændədaɪ'zeɪʃən] *n* standardisation *f*; *(of weights etc)* étalonnage *m*, étalonnement *m*; *(of methods etc)* uniformisation *f*

standardize ['stændədaɪz] **1** *vt* normaliser, standardiser; *(weights etc)* étalonner; *(methods, conditions)* uniformiser **2** *vi* **to s. on sth** adopter qch comme standard

standard lamp *n* lampadaire *m*

stand-by **1** *n* **(a)** *(substitute person)* **to act as a s.** remplacer qn

(b) *(sth held in reserve)* réserve *f*; **to have a sum in reserve as a s.** avoir une somme en réserve en cas de besoin; **a fruitcake can be a useful s. for unexpected guests** il est toujours bon d'avoir un cake en réserve pour les invités surprises; *Rail* **s. engine** locomotive *f* de réserve

(c) *Mil etc (state of readiness)* (état *m* d')alerte *f*; **to be on s.** *(of troops, firemen etc)* être en état d'alerte; **s. mode** *(of printer etc)* veille *f*; **in s. mode** en veille

(d) *Av etc* **s. (passenger)** passager *m* (en) standby; **s. (ticket)** standby *m*; **to be on s.** être en standby

2 *adv* **to fly s.** voler en standby

standee [stæn'di:] *n esp Am (in bus)* voyageur, -euse debout; *Th* spectateur, -trice debout

stand-in **1** *n (person)* remplaçant, -ante; *(actor)* doublure *f* **2** *adj* remplaçant; **a s. teacher/speaker/***etc* un remplaçant

standing ['stændɪŋ] **1** *adj* **(a)** *(in upright position)* debout; **s. crops** récoltes *fpl* sur pied; *Sp* **s. jump** saut *m* sans élan; **s. ovation** ovation *f* debout; **s. passengers** voyageurs *mpl* debout; *Sp* **s. start** départ *m* debout; **s. stone** *(monument)* menhir *m*; **s. water** eau *f* stagnante *ou* dormante

(b) *(permanent) (price)* fixe; *Mil* **s. army** armée *f* de métier; *Acct* **s. charges** charges *fpl* locatives; **s. committee** commission *f* permanente; *Com* **s. expenses** frais *mpl* généraux; **I have a s. invitation** je peux aller chez lui/elle/eux quand je veux; **you have a s. invitation** tu peux venir chez moi/nous quand tu veux; **s. joke** grosse plaisanterie *f*; **he's become a s. joke** il est devenu un objet de risée; **s. rule** règle *f* fixe

2 *n* **(a)** *(upright position)* station *f* debout; **no s.!** *(in bus etc)* défense de voyager debout; *Rail, Th etc* **s. room** place(s) *f(pl)* debout; **s. (room) only** il ne reste que des places debout

(b) **of long s.** *(friends)* de longue date; **friend of twenty years' s.** ami de vingt ans

(c) *(position) (of country, firm)* rang *m*, position *f*; *(of party, person)* popularité *f*; **financial s.** situation *f* financière; **social s.** position sociale

standing order *n Banking* virement *m* automatique, ordre *m* de prélèvement permanent; *Com* **to place a s. for sth** passer une commande permanente de qch

standing orders *npl Parl* règlement(s) *m(pl)* *(d'une assemblée etc)*

stand-off *n (between opponents)* impasse *f*

stand-off (half) *n Rugby* demi *m* d'ouverture

stand-offish [stænd'ɒfɪʃ] *adj (person)* peu accessible, distant, réservé; **to be s.** se mettre *ou* se tenir sur son quant-à-soi

stand-offishness [stænd'ɒfɪʃnɪs] *n* raideur *f*, réserve *f*

standpipe ['stændpaɪp] *n (in street)* colonne *f* d'alimentation

standpoint ['stændpɔɪnt] *n* point *m* de vue; **from the s. of ...** du point de vue de ...; **from a late 20th-century s.** dans une perspective de fin de XXe siècle

standstill ['stændstɪl] *n* arrêt *m*, immobilisation *f*; **traffic has come to a s.** la circulation est immobilisée; **to bring to a s.** arrêter; *(railways, production etc)* paralyser; **many factories are at a s.** beaucoup d'usines chôment; **the railways are at a s.** les chemins de fer sont paralysés

stand-up **1** *adj* **(a)** *(collar)* droit, montant **(b)** *(meal)* pris debout **(c)** *Boxing* **s. fight** combat *m* en règle; **they just about had a s. fight!** ils ont failli se battre!; **to have a s. argument** avoir une dispute en règle **(d)** **s. comedian** *or* **comic** comique *mf* (de scène); **s. comedy** spectacle *m* comique **2** *n (comedy)* spectacle *m* comique; **to do s.** faire des spectacles comiques

stank *see* **stink²**

Stanley knife® ['stænlɪ] *n* cutter *m*

stannic ['stænɪk] *adj Ch* stannique

stanza, *pl* **-as** ['stænzə, -əz] *n (in poetry)* strophe *f*

staphylococcus, *pl* **-cocci** [stæfɪləʊ'kɒkəs, -'kɒksaɪ] *n* staphylocoque *m*

staple¹ ['steɪp(ə)l] *n (for papers)* agrafe *f*; *(for cable etc)* crampon *m*; **wire s.** (clou *m*) cavalier *m*; **s. gun** agrafeuse *f*; **s. remover** arrache-agrafes *m inv*

staple² *vt (piece of paper, cheque etc)* agrafer (**to** à); *Constr etc* fixer avec un crampon, agrafer; **to s. two pieces of paper together** agrafer deux morceaux de papier

staple³ *n (basic foodstuff)* aliment *m* de base; **staples** *(goods)* biens *mpl* de première nécessité; **sex scandals are a s. of the tabloid press** la presse à sensation se nourrit des scandales sexuels; **such accusations are a s. of the annual conference** ces accusations reviennent régulièrement à chaque conférence annuelle; *Econ* **s. (commodity)** produit *m* de première nécessité; **s. convenience goods** produits de première nécessité; **s. crop** culture *f* de base; **s. diet** alimentation *f* de base; *Fig* pain *m* quotidien; **to grow up on a s. diet of television and violence** grandir nourri de télévision et de violence

stapler ['steɪplər] *n (device)* agrafeuse *f*

stapling ['steɪplɪŋ] *n (of papers)* fixation *f* à l'aide d'agrafes, agrafage *m*; *(of cables etc)* fixation à l'aide de crochets *ou* crampons; **s. machine** agrafeuse *f*

star¹ [stɑːr] *n* **(a)** *Astron* étoile *f*; **shooting s.** étoile filante; **the**

morning s. l'étoile du matin; **the pole s.** l'étoile polaire, la polaire; **he was born under a lucky s.** il est né sous une bonne étoile; *Fig* **to reach for the stars** essayer d'atteindre les sommets; *Fig F* **to see stars** voir les étoiles en plein midi, voir trente-six chandelles; **the stars and stripes** (*American flag*) la bannière étoilée

(b) (*insignia*) (*of order*) plaque *f*; *Mil* (*on shoulder of uniform*) étoile *f*; **S. of David** étoile de David; **three s. brandy** cognac *m* trois étoiles; **three s. hotel** hôtel *m* trois étoiles; **s. rating** (*of hotel*) classement *m* par étoiles

(c) (*shape*) (*on horse's forehead*) étoile *f*; *Typ* astérisque *m*; *Comptr* **in a s. configuration** connecté en étoile; *Comptr* **s. structure** structure *f* en étoile

(d) *Cin etc* (*person*) étoile *f*, vedette *f*, star *f*; *Mktg* vedette, star; **film** *or* **movie s.** étoile *ou* star *ou* vedette du cinéma; **rock s.** star du rock; **to get s. billing** tenir le haut de l'affiche; **s. mentality** mentalité *f* de star; **s. part** rôle *m* de vedette; *Sp* **s. player** joueur, -euse vedette; **s. presenter** animateur, -trice vedette; **s. turn** numéro *m* de premier ordre; *F* (*of performance, conference, evening*) clou *m*

star² (**-rr-**) **1** *vt* **(a)** (*mark with asterisk*) (*word etc*) marquer d'un astérisque

(b) *Cin, Th, TV etc* (*of film, play etc*) (*actor*) mettre en scène dans le rôle principal, avoir pour vedette; **the film/play stars Katherine Hepburn (as** *or* **in the role of)** le film/la pièce met en scène Katherine Hepburn dans le rôle principal (de); **'The Last Metro' starring Catherine Deneuve and Gérard Depardieu** 'le Dernier Métro' avec Catherine Deneuve et Gérard Depardieu dans les rôles principaux

2 *vi Cin, Th, TV etc* (*of actor, actress*) être en vedette; **he starred as a gangster** il avait un rôle de gangster; **to have a starring role** avoir un des premiers rôles

starboard ['stɑːbəd] *n Naut* tribord *m*; **on the s. side, to s.** à tribord; **on the s. bow** par tribord devant; **hard a-s.!** tribord toute!

starch¹ [stɑːtʃ] *n* (*for collar, tablecloth etc*) amidon *m*, empois *m*; *Culin* (*from potatoes*) fécule *f*; (*from rice, corn, wheat etc*) amidon

starch² *vt* (*collar, tablecloth etc*) empeser, amidonner

starched [stɑːtʃt] *adj* empesé, amidonné

starchy ['stɑːtʃɪ] *adj* **(a)** *Ch* amylacé; **s. foods** féculents *mpl* **(b)** *F* (*person, manner*) guindé

star-crossed *adj* **s. lovers** amants *mpl* maudits

stardom ['stɑːdəm] *n Cin, Th etc* (*state*) célébrité *f*, vedettariat *m*; **to rise to s.** devenir une vedette, atteindre la célébrité; **dreams of s.** rêves *mpl* de célébrité

stardust ['stɑːdʌst] *n* **(a)** *Astron* amas *m* stellaire **(b)** (*magic dust*) poudre *f* magique; **to have s. in one's eyes** être plein d'illusions

stare¹ [steər] *n* regard *m* fixe; **glassy/stony s.** regard terne/dur; **vacant s.** regard vague; **to have a long s. at sb/sth** fixer longuement qn/qch

stare² **1** *vi* regarder fixement; (*with astonishment*) ouvrir de grands yeux; **to s. into the distance** regarder au loin; **don't s.!** ne regarde pas comme ça; **it's rude to s.** ce n'est pas poli de dévisager les gens; **to s. at sb/sth** (*look at hard*) regarder qn/qch fixement, fixer qn/qch; (*begin to look at*) porter son regard sur qn/qch; (*be stupefied by*) regarder qn/qch d'un air hébété; **to s. at sb** (*look at insolently*) regarder qn effrontément, dévisager qn; **what are you staring at?** que regardez-vous comme ça?

2 *vt* **to s. sb in the face** dévisager qn; **it's staring you in the face** (*it's obvious*) ça vous saute aux yeux; **the answer was staring me in the face all the time** la réponse était sous mon nez depuis le début

▶ **stare out** *vtsep* **to s. sb out** fixer qn jusqu'à ce qu'il/elle détourne les yeux

starfish ['stɑːfɪʃ] *n* étoile *f* de mer, astérie *f*

stargaze ['stɑːgeɪz] *vi* **(a)** *F* (*look at stars*) regarder les étoiles **(b)** (*daydream*) rêvasser, bayer aux corneilles

stargazer ['stɑːgeɪzər] *n* **(a)** (*astrologist*) astrologue *mf*; *F* (*astronomer*) passionné, -ée d'astronomie **(b)** (*daydreamer*) rêveur, -euse, rêvasseur, -euse

stargazing ['stɑːgeɪzɪŋ] *n* **(a)** (*astrology*) astrologie *f*; *F* (*looking at stars*) étude *f* des étoiles **(b)** (*daydreaming*) rêvasserie(s) *f(pl)*

staring ['steərɪŋ] *adj* **s. eyes** yeux *mpl* fixes

stark [stɑːk] **1** *adj* (*contrast*) absolu, fort; (*light*) cru; (*furnishing, black and white*) austère, sobre; (*truth, facts*) brut; (*landscape*) nu; **this stands in s. contrast to …** ceci se démarque nettement de …; **s. realism** (*of novel, painting*) réalisme *m* brut; **a very s. flat** un appartement très nu *ou* sobre; **the s. simplicity of …** la sobre *ou* l'austère simplicité de …; **the s. desolation of the region** l'absolue désolation de la région; **s. madness** folie *f* pure; **the s. towns of the North** les mornes villes du Nord

2 *adv* **s. naked** tout nu; **s. staring mad** complètement fou

starkers ['stɑːkəz] *adj, adv Br F* tout nu, *f* toute nue

starkness ['stɑːknɪs] *n* (*of furnishing etc*) austérité *f*, sobriété *f*; (*of landscape*) nudité *f*; **the s. of the contrast between …** le contraste violent entre …

starless ['stɑːlɪs] *adj* sans étoiles

starlet ['stɑːlɪt] *n Cin etc* starlette *f*, starlet *f*

starlight ['stɑːlaɪt] *n* lumière *f* des étoiles; **in the** *or* **by s.** à la lumière des étoiles; **s. night** nuit *f* étoilée

starling ['stɑːlɪŋ] *n* (*bird*) étourneau *m*

starlit ['stɑːlɪt] *adj* (*sky*) étoilé; **s. night** nuit *f* étoilée

star-of-Bethlehem *n* (*plant*) ornithogale *m* (à ombelle), *F* dame *f* d'onze heures

starred [stɑːd] *adj Typ* (*asterisked*) marqué d'un astérisque

starry ['stɑːrɪ] *adj* (*sky*) étoilé, (par)semé d'étoiles; **s. night** nuit *f* étoilée

starry-eyed *adj* (*person*) naïf, *f* naïve; **the children stood s. in front of the Christmas tree** les enfants étaient debout devant le sapin de Noël, émerveillés; **a s. scheme** un projet utopique; **she was all s. about him until …** elle était tout émerveillée par lui jusqu'à ce que …

starshell ['stɑːʃel] *n Mil* obus *m* éclairant *ou* à étoiles

star-spangled ['stɑːspæŋg(ə)ld] *adj* étoilé; **the S. Banner** (*flag*) la bannière étoilée; (*national anthem*) l'hymne *m* national des États-Unis

start¹ [stɑːt] *n* **(a)** (*beginning*) commencement *m*, début *m*; (*of journey, race*) départ *m*; *Aut* démarrage *m*; *Av* envol *m*; **for a s.** pour commencer; **at the s.** au début; **at the very s.** au tout début; **from the s.** dès le début; **there were problems from the s.** il y a eu des problèmes dès le début; **I never liked him, right from the s.** il m'a toujours déplu, dès le début; **from s. to finish** du début (jusqu')à la fin; **£5 isn't much, but it's a s.** 5 livres ce n'est pas grand-chose, mais c'est un début; **I've cleaned the kitchen – well, it's a s.** j'ai nettoyé la cuisine – eh bien, c'est déjà ça; **she had a good s. in life** elle a bien débuté dans la vie; **to make a s.** (*begin work*) commencer; (*begin journey*) se mettre en route; **to make a s. on sth** commencer qch; **to make a fresh s. in one's life** refaire sa vie; **to make a good s.** bien commencer; **to make a fresh s.** recommencer; *Sp* **false s.** faux départ; **to give sb a s.** (*in business etc*) lancer qn; *Sp* laisser qn partir le premier, donner un peu d'avance à qn; **to give sb a 60 metre(s) s.** donner à qn 60 mètres d'avance; **to have a s. on sb** être en avance sur qn

(b) (*starting place*) départ *m*; **the runners lined up at the s.** les coureurs se rangèrent sur la ligne de départ

(c) (*sudden movement*) (*with fear, surprise*) tressaillement *m*, sursaut *m*, soubresaut *m*; **to wake with a s.** se réveiller en sursaut; **he gave a s.** il a tressailli, il a sursauté; **to give sb a s.** faire sursauter qn; **you gave me such a s.!** tu m'as fait peur!

start² **1** *vi* **(a)** (*begin*) commencer; (*in career*) débuter; **to s. again** recommencer; **the story starts with a murder** l'histoire commence par un meurtre; **well, to s. at the beginning …** bon, commençons par le commencement …; **you'd better s. by telling me your name** vous devriez commencer par me dire votre nom; **let's s. with the cost** commençons par le coût; **to s. the way one means to go on** donner la mesure dès le début; **starting Monday** à partir de lundi; **she had started as a doctor** elle avait débuté *ou* commencé en tant que médecin; **to s. in business** se mettre *ou* se lancer dans les affaires; **to s. with** (*in the first place*) au début; **there were only six members to s. with** il n'y avait que six membres au début; **to s. on a job** commencer *ou* entamer un travail

(b) *Br F* (*begin crying*) se mettre à pleurer; (*begin fighting*) se mettre à se battre; **now don't <u>you</u> s.!** tu ne vas pas t'y mettre aussi!

(c) (*move suddenly*) (*with surprise, fear etc*) sursauter, tressaillir, tressauter; **he started at the sound of my voice** il a tressailli au son de ma voix; **she started with surprise** surprise, elle sursauta; **to s. out of one's sleep** se réveiller en sursaut

(d) (*begin journey*) partir, se mettre en route; **to s. again** repartir, se remettre en route; **to s. on a journey** commencer un voyage; **we s. tomorrow** nous partons demain

(e) (*begin to move*) (*of car*) démarrer; (*of train*) partir, s'ébranler; (*of engine*) partir, démarrer; **the engine won't s.** le moteur refuse de partir *ou* de démarrer

2 *vt* **(a)** (*work, campaign etc*) commencer; (*conversation, talks etc*) entamer; (*a fashion, rumour etc*) lancer; **to s. a job** démarrer un travail; **to s. a meeting** débuter une séance; **to s. legal proceedings** engager une action en justice; **to s. a fire** provoquer un incendie; **you started it** c'est toi qui as commencé; **to s. doing sth, to s. to do sth** commencer *ou* se mettre à faire qch; **to s. crying again** se remettre à pleurer; **it's just started raining** il se met à pleuvoir; **now you've started something!** en voilà une affaire!; **if you s. him on this subject he will never stop** si vous le lancez sur ce sujet il ne tarira pas; **we started him in the sales department** nous l'avons fait débuter au service des ventes; **to get started** (*of person*) (*on task*) commencer, s'y mettre; (*on journey*) partir, se mettre en route; (*in career etc*) débuter, démarrer; **to help sb get started in life** aider qn à démarrer dans la vie; **when does he s. school?** quand est-ce qu'il commence l'école?

(b) *Sp* (*runners etc*) donner le signal du départ à; (*in hunting*) (*stag, hare*) lever; *Horseriding* **to s. a horse at a gallop** faire partir un cheval au galop

(c) (*set up*) (*company, newspaper*) lancer; (*business*) fonder; **to s. sb in business** lancer qn dans les affaires

(d) (*cause to function*) (*machine*) mettre en marche, lancer; (*car*) démarrer; (*engine*) mettre en marche; (*computer, pump*) amorcer

▶ **start in on** *vipo esp Am* (*attack*) s'attaquer à

▶ **start off 1** *vi* **(a)** (*begin journey*) = **start² 1** (*d*) **(b)** (*begin*) commencer; **you s. off** (*in discussion etc*) commencez; **she started off by talking about …** elle commença en parlant de …

2 *vtsep* **(a)** (*begin*) commencer; **s. your talk off with a reference to …** commencez votre discours en mentionnant …; **he lent us a couple of thousand pounds to s. us off** (*in business etc*) il nous a prêté quelques milliers de livres pour nous aider à démarrer; **here are three specimens to s. you off** (*with your collection*) voici trois spécimens pour commencer; **the pianist played a few bars to s. them off** (*in singing etc*) le pianiste a joué quelques mesures d'introduction; **what started the whole thing off?** comment tout a-t-il commencé?

(b) to s. sb off (on a subject) lancer qn sur un sujet; **don't s. him off on that!** (*get him talking about it*) ne le lance pas sur ce sujet!; **the baby's crying again, what started him off this time?** le bébé s'est remis à pleurer, qu'est-ce qu'il a cette fois?; **dad's finally calmed down, don't you s. him off again** papa s'est enfin calmé, ne va pas l'énerver

▶ **start on** *vipo* (*begin quarrelling with, shouting at etc*) s'en prendre à

▶ **start out** *vi* (*begin*) commencer, débuter; (*begin journey*) se mettre en route (**for** pour); **she started out as a postwoman/driving a van** elle a commencé *ou* débuté comme factrice/conductrice de camion; **he started out to write a novel** au départ il voulait écrire un roman

▶ **start over** *vi Am* (*start again*) recommencer

▶ **start up 1** *vi* **(a)** (*start functioning*) (*of engine*) démarrer, se mettre en marche **(b)** (*in business*) s'installer; **to s. up in business** monter sa propre affaire; **he decided to s. up by himself** il a décidé de se mettre à son compte **2** *vtsep* **(a)** (*cause to function*) (*engine, car*) mettre en marche, démarrer; (*machine*) mettre en marche **(b)** (*company, newspaper*) lancer; (*business*) fonder; (*restaurant, school*) ouvrir

start bit *n Comptr* bit *m* de départ

start code *n Comptr* code *m* de départ

starter ['stɑːtər] *n* **(a)** *Sp* (*competitor*) partant *m*; **to be an early s.** (*start work early*) commencer son travail de bonne heure; **to be a slow s.** être lent à démarrer; *Br* **s. flat** = appartement *m* convenant à ceux qui achètent pour la première fois

(b) *Sp etc* (*official*) starter *m*; **to be under s.'s orders** attendre le signal du starter

(c) (*device*) *Aut* démarreur *m*; *MecE* dispositif *m* de mise en marche; *El* (rhéostat *m*) démarreur, rhéostat de démarrage; **s. solenoid** électrovalve *f* de starter

(d) *esp Br Culin* entrée *f*, hors-d'œuvre *m inv*; **would you like a s.?** désirez-vous une entrée?; *F* **for starters** (*as a first course*) en entrée; *Fig* (*for a start*) pour commencer, (tout) d'abord

starter motor *n* démarreur *m*

starting ['stɑːtɪŋ] *n* **(a)** (*beginning*) commencement *m*, début *m*; (*causing to start*) (*of war, fight etc*) instigation *f*; **s. point** *or* **place** point *m* de départ; *Horseracing* **s. price** dernière cote *f* avant le départ; **s. salary** salaire *m* de départ; (*of civil servants*) traitement *m* initial, traitement de départ; **s. signal** signal *m* de *ou* du départ **(b)** (*of business etc*) mise *f* en route *ou* en train **(c)** (*of engine etc*) mise *f* en marche, démarrage *m*; (*of machine*) lancement *m*

starting block *n* starting-block *m*, *pl* starting-blocks

starting handle *n Br Aut* manivelle *f*

starting line *n Sp* ligne *f* de départ

starting motor *n MecE* moteur *m* de démarrage

starting pistol *n Sp* pistolet *m* de starter

starting post *n* (poteau *m* de) départ *m*

starting up *n* = **starting (b)**, **(c)**

startle ['stɑːt(ə)l] *vt* (*alarm*) effrayer, alarmer; (*cause to jump*) faire sursauter; **she was startled to see him so pale** sa pâleur l'alarma

startled ['stɑːt(ə)ld] *adj* effrayé; **to give a s. cry** crier d'effroi

startling ['stɑːtlɪŋ] *adj* (*noise etc*) effrayant; (*news, event etc*) renversant; **s. resemblance** ressemblance saisissante

start-up *n* **(a)** (*of machine*) démarrage *m* **(b)** (*of new business*) ouverture *f*, lancement *m*; **there have been 500 start-ups this year** il y a eu 500 créations d'entreprises cette année; **s. capital** capital *m* initial, capital de départ; **s. costs** (*of company*) frais *mpl* d'établissement

starvation [stɑː'veɪʃən] *n* privation *f ou* manque *m* de nourriture, inanition *f*; **millions are threatened with s. if …** des millions de gens vont peut-être mourir de faim si …; **to die of s.** mourir de faim; **prisoners were kept on a s. diet** les prisonniers étaient presque entièrement privés de nourriture; **a s. diet of rice and a few vegetables** une alimentation très pauvre à base de riz et de quelques légumes; **I'm on a s. diet** (*to slim*) je suis un régime draconien; **s. wages** des salaires de misère

starve [stɑːv] **1** *vi* (*lack food*) manquer de nourriture; (*endure hunger*) souffrir de la faim; **to s. (to death)** mourir de faim; *F* **I'm starving** (*hungry*) je meurs *ou* je crève de faim **2** *vt* (*deprive of food*) (*person*) priver de nourriture; **to s. sb (to death)** faire mourir qn de faim; **they were prepared to s. themselves to death rather than give in** ils étaient prêts à se laisser mourir de faim plutôt que de capituler; **to s. a city into surrender** affamer une ville pour l'amener à se rendre; *Fig* **to s. sb/sth of sth** priver qn/qch de qch

▶ **starve out** *vtsep Mil etc* (*town, garrison*) affamer (*pour le/la/etc faire sortir*)

starved [stɑːvd] *adj* affamé; **she looks half s.** elle a l'air famélique; **s. of affection** privé d'affection; **I'm feeling s. of affection** je suis en manque d'affection; *F* **I'm s.** (*hungry*) je crève de faim

starving ['stɑːvɪŋ] *adj* affamé; **the s. millions** tous ceux qui souffrent de la faim

Star Wars *npl Mil* guerre *f* des étoiles

stash¹ [stæʃ] *n F* **(a)** (*of arms*) cache *f*; (*of biscuits etc*) réserve *f* (secrète); **a s. of drugs was discovered** de la drogue a été découverte; **I hid my s.** (*of drugs*) j'ai caché ma part de drogue **(b)** (*place*) planque *f*

stash² *vt F* (*object*) (*hide*) cacher, planquer; (*put*) ficher

▶ **stash away** *vtsep* = **stash²**

stasis ['steɪsɪs] *n* stase *f*

state¹ [steɪt] *n* **(a)** (*condition*) état *m*, condition *f*; (*situation*) situation *f*; **to be in a good s. of repair** être en bon état; *Iron* **here's a nice** *or* **a pretty s. of affairs** nous voilà bien!, c'est du joli *ou* du propre!; **a body in a s. of rest/motion** un corps au repos/en mouvement; **to declare a s. of war/emergency** déclarer l'état de guerre/d'urgence; **s. of consciousness** état de conscience; **s. of health** état de santé; **what's the current s. of play?** où en sont-ils?; **what's the current s. of play on our project?** où en est notre projet?; **I am not in a fit s. to travel** je ne suis pas en état de voyager; **he was in a s. of panic** il a été pris de panique; **she was in a s. of terror** elle était terrifiée; **the married s.** le mariage; **the single s.** le célibat; **in a solid/liquid s.** à l'état solide/liquide; **nitrogen is more easily transportable in its liquid s.** l'azote est plus facilement transportable à l'état liquide; **s. of mind** état d'esprit; **to be in a terrible s.** (*emotionally*) être dans tous ses états; (*of room, papers etc*) être dans un état désastreux; **this represents the s. of the art in …** c'est la pointe de la technologie en matière de …

(b) (*rank*) rang *m*; (*ceremony*) pompe *f*, apparat *m*; **she lived in a style befitting her s.** elle avait un train de vie digne de son rang; **to live in s.** mener grand train; **to travel in s.** voyager en grand apparat; **to dine in s.** dîner en grande pompe; **to lie in s.** (*of body*) être exposé; **lying in s.** (*of body*) exposition *f*; **he was in his robes of s.** il était en costume d'apparat; **s. apartments** salons *mpl* d'apparat; **s. ball** grand bal *m* officiel; **s. carriage, s. coach** voiture *f* d'apparat; **s. funeral** funérailles *fpl* nationales; **the S. Opening of Parliament** = l'ouverture *f* officielle du Parlement britannique en présence du souverain

(c) *Pol* (*country, nation*) état *m*; **the S.** l'État; **Church and S.** l'Église et l'État; **Secretary of S.** *Br* secrétaire *m* d'État, *US* = Ministre *m* des Affaires étrangères; **s.-aided industry** industrie *f* subventionnée par l'État; **affairs of S.** affaires *fpl* d'État; **s. documents** documents *mpl* officiels; **the s. education system** l'enseignement *m* public; **s.-owned industry** industrie du secteur public; **s. intervention**

intervention *f* de l'État; **s. monopoly** monopole *m* de l'état; **s.-run** public; *Fr Hist* **the States General** les États généraux

(d) (*administrative region in some countries*) état *m*; **the United States of America,** *F* **the States** les États-Unis (d'Amérique)

state² *vt* **(a)** (*declare*) déclarer; (*conditions, demands, reasons, objections*) énoncer; (*claim etc*) exposer, formuler; *Math, Fig* (*problem*) poser, énoncer; **this condition was expressly stated** cette condition était clairement énoncée; **the receipt should s. the source of payment** le reçu doit stipuler l'origine du paiement; **please s. below ...** veuillez noter en bas ...; **I have stated my opinion** j'ai donné mon opinion; **they stated their opposition to that measure** ils ont clairement fait savoir leur opposition à cette mesure; **I can s. with certainty that ...** je peux affirmer avec certitude que ...; *Jur* **to s. the case** faire l'exposé des faits; **please s. your name and address (and qualifications)** veuillez décliner vos nom et adresse (et qualités)

(b) (*fix*) (*time, date*) **at the stated times** aux heures indiquées; **on the stated dates** aux jours indiqués; **at stated intervals** à intervalles fixes

state capitalism *n* capitalisme *m* d'État

state church *n* église *f* d'État

state control *n* étatisme *m*; **to bring an industry under s.** étatiser une industrie

statecraft ['steɪtkrɑːft] *n* savoir *m* d'un homme d'État

State Department *n US* = Ministère *m* des Affaires étrangères

State Enrolled Nurse *n Br Med* = infirmier, -ière diplômé(e) d'État

Statehouse ['steɪthaʊs] *n US* = bâtiment *m* où siège le corps législatif d'un État

stateless ['steɪtlɪs] *adj* apatride; **s. person** apatride *mf*

statelessness ['steɪtlɪsnɪs] *n* apatridie *f*

stateliness ['steɪtlɪnɪs] *n* **(a)** (*grandeur*) majesté *f*, grandeur *f* **(b)** (*dignity*) dignité *f*

stately ['steɪtlɪ] *adj* **(a)** (*imposing*) majestueux, imposant; **the s. homes of England** les châteaux *mpl* de l'Angleterre **(b)** (*dignified*) plein de dignité; (*noble*) noble, élevé; **s. bearing** allure pleine de majesté

statement ['steɪtmənt] *n* **(a)** déclaration *f*; (*of facts*) exposé *m*, énoncé *m*; (*official, to Press, House of Commons*) communiqué *m*; *Jur* (*made by witness etc*) déposition *f*; **she made the following s. ...** elle a déclaré que ...; **I have no further statement(s) to make** je n'ai plus rien à ajouter; *Fig* **the film is making a s.** il y a un message dans ce film; *Fig* **someone who wears jeans to a wedding reception is making a s.** quelqu'un qui va à un mariage en jeans veut faire comprendre quelque chose; **a s. appeared in the press to the effect that ...** il fut affirmé dans la presse que ...; **a bare s. of the facts** un simple énoncé des faits; *Jur* **to take sb's s.** prendre la déposition de qn; **to volunteer a s.** faire une déposition de son propre gré; **to call him a thief is nothing more than a s. of fact** le traiter de voleur, c'est une constatation

(b) (*received from bank, credit card company*) **s. (of account)** relevé *m* de compte; **monthly s.** fin *f* de mois; **s. of affairs** (*in bankruptcy*) bilan *m* de liquidation

state-of-play report *n* état *m* de situation

state-of-the-art *adj* (*technology, design etc*) de pointe, très avancé; **it's very s.** c'est le nec plus ultra, c'est très moderne

state police *n US* police *f* d'État

State Registered Nurse *n Br Med* infirmier, -ière diplômé(e)

stateroom ['steɪtruːm] *n* **(a)** *Naut* cabine *f*; *Am Rail Old-fashioned* (compartiment *m* de) wagon-lit *m* **(b)** *esp Br* (*in palace etc*) chambre *f* d'apparat, grand appartement *m*

state school *n* école *f* publique, établissement *m* public

state sector *n* secteur *m* public

stateside ['steɪtsaɪd] **1** *adv* aux États-Unis **2** *adj* des États-Unis, américain

statesman, *pl* **-men** ['steɪtsmən] *n* homme *m* d'État

statesmanlike ['steɪtsmənlaɪk] *adj* (*attitude etc*) d'homme d'État; *Fig* stratégique

statesmanship ['steɪtsmənʃɪp] *n* art *m* de gouverner; **a decision which shows considerable s.** une décision qui prouve des qualités d'homme d'État

state system *n* (*education*) **the s.** le public

state trooper *n US* policier *m* (*qui dépend d'un État*)

State university *n US* = université *f* subventionnée et contrôlée par un État

state visit *n* visite *f* officielle

statewide ['steɪtwaɪd] *adj, adv* partout dans un/l'État

static ['stætɪk] **1** *n* électricité *f* statique; (*on telephone line*) parasites *mpl* **2** *adj* **(a)** (*electricity*) statique **(b)** (*not moving*) statique; (*unchangeable*) immuable; *Pej* (*relationship etc*) qui stagne; **the situation remains s.** la situation reste inchangée; **s. lap belt** ceinture *f* ventrale statique; *Comptr* **s. RAM, s. random access memory** mémoire *f* vive statique; *TV, Cin* **s. shot** plan *m* fixe

statics ['stætɪks] *npl* [①A10,c] *Phys* (*usu with sing verb*) statique *f*

station¹ ['steɪʃən] *n* **(a)** **(railway) s.** gare *f*; **underground** *or Am* **subway s.** station *f* de métro; **bus** *or Br* **coach s.** gare routière; *Rail* **passenger/goods s.** gare de voyageurs/de marchandises; **s. hotel** hôtel *m* de la gare

(b) (*place*) position *f*, place *f*; (*post*) poste *m*; **to take up one's s.** (*take one's place*) prendre sa place; (*go to one's post*) se rendre à son poste; *Rel* **the stations of the Cross** le chemin de la Croix; *Mil etc* **action stations** postes de combat; *Mil, Fig* **action stations!** à vos postes!; **naval s.** station *f* navale; (*port*) port *m* de guerre; **military s.** poste militaire; (*garrison*) garnison *f*; *Naut* **lifeboat s.** station de sauvetage; *Met* **weather s.** station météo(rologique); **police s., s.** commissariat *m* (de police), poste (de police); **fire s.** poste *ou* caserne *f* de pompiers; **power s.** centrale *f* électrique; **atomic power s.** centrale atomique; *Aut* **filling s., petrol s.,** *Am* **gas s.** poste d'essence, station-service *f*, *pl* stations-service; **s. waiter** chef *m* de rang

(c) **(radio/television) s.** station *f* (de radio)/chaîne *f* (de télévision); *TV, Rad* **s. ident** *or* **identification** indicatif *m* de chaîne; *TV* **s. manager** directeur *m* de station; **s. presetting** *Rad* programmation *f* des stations; *TV* programmation des chaînes

(d) *Austr, NZ* (*farm*) = ferme *f* (et ses dépendances); **sheep s.** élevage *m* de moutons

(e) (*social condition*) position *f*, condition *f*; (*rank*) rang *m*; **s. in life** situation *f* sociale; *Old-fashioned* **to marry below** *or* **beneath one's s.** faire une mésalliance, se mésallier

station² *vt* (*person in a place*) placer, mettre; (*soldier*) désigner son poste à; (*troops*) poster; **to be stationed at ...** *Mil* être stationné *ou* être en garnison à ...; *Naut* être en station à ...; **he stationed himself behind a door** il s'est posté derrière une porte

stationary ['steɪʃən(ə)rɪ] *adj* **(a)** (*not moving*) immobile; (*car*) (*parked*) en stationnement; (*not moving*) à l'arrêt; **to remain s.** rester immobile; *Mil* **s. target** cible *f* fixe **(b)** (*fixed*) fixe; (*permanent*) à demeure

stationer ['steɪʃənər] *n* papetier *m*; **s.'s (shop)** papeterie *f*

stationery ['steɪʃən(ə)rɪ] *n* papeterie *f*; (*writing paper*) papier *m* à lettres; **office/school s.** fournitures *fpl* de bureau/scolaires; **hotel s.** papier à lettres fourni par un/l'hôtel; **headed s.** papier à en-tête; *Br Admin* **the S. Office** le Service des fournitures et des publications de l'Administration

station manager *n Am Aut, Rail* chef *m* de gare

station master *n Rail* chef *m* de gare

station wagon *n* break *m*

statism ['steɪtɪz(ə)m] *n* étatisme *m*

statist ['steɪtɪst] *adj* étatiste

statistic [stə'tɪstɪk] *n* (*statistical item*) élément *m* d'un/du tableau statistique; **statistics** statistiques *fpl*; **a worrying s.** un chiffre inquiétant; **to become just another s.** (*unimportant person*) n'être plus qu'un numéro; **he became just another s.** (*was killed*) il est juste venu s'ajouter aux statistiques (des morts); **vital statistics** statistiques démographiques; *F* (*of woman*) mensurations *fpl*

statistical [stə'tɪstɪk(ə)l] *adj* statistique; **s. data** données *fpl* statistiques; **s. tables** statistiques *fpl*

statistically [stə'tɪstɪk(ə)lɪ] *adv* statistiquement

statistician [stætɪs'tɪʃən] *n* statisticien, -ienne

statistics [stə'tɪstɪks] *npl* [①A10,c] (*usu with sing verb*) (*science*) statistique *f*

stator ['steɪtər] *n MecE, El* (*of turbine*) stator *m*

statuary ['stætjʊərɪ] **1** *adj* (*art, marble etc*) statuaire **2** *n* **(a)** (*art*) statuaire *f*, art *m* statuaire **(b)** (*statues*) statues *fpl*

statue ['stætjuː] *n* statue *f*; **don't stand there like a s.!** ne reste pas là comme une souche!

statuesque [stætjʊ'esk] *adj* sculptural

statuette [stætjʊ'et] *n* statuette *f*

stature ['stætjər] *n* stature *f*, taille *f*; **to be short of s.** être de petite taille; **it will increase her s.** (*of author etc*) sa réputation y gagnera; **he grew in s. as he ...** (*in reputation*) il acquit une certaine réputation à mesure qu'il ...; **a writer of some international s.** un écrivain ayant une certaine renommée internationale; **a politician of his s.** un homme politique de son envergure

status ['steɪtəs] *n* (*position*) statut *m*; (*marital*) situation *f* de famille; (*prestige, standing*) prestige *m*, standing *m*; **(personal) s.** statut (personnel); *Admin* **civil s.** état *m* civil; **social s.** rang *m* social; **with no official s.** sans titre officiel;

he's only interested in the job because of the s. that attaches to it cet emploi ne l'intéresse qu'en raison du prestige qui y est attaché; *Comptr* **s. box** zone *f* d'état; *Comptr* **s. printout** (*of printer*) impression *f* des paramètres de l'imprimante; **s. report** état du projet, état de situation
status-conscious *adj* attaché à son standing
status enquiry *n* (*about creditworthiness*) prise *f* de renseignements sur la solvabilité; **s. department** service *m* des renseignements commerciaux
status line *n Comptr* ligne *f* d'état *ou* de statut
status quo ['steɪtəs'kwəʊ] *n* statu quo *m inv*; **to maintain the s.** maintenir le statu quo
status symbol *n* marque *f* de prestige *ou* de standing
statute ['stætjuːt] *n Jur* loi *f*, ordonnance *f*; *Br Pol* (*act*) acte *m* du Parlement; **s. of limitations** = période *f* précisée par la loi au bout de laquelle il y a prescription; **the s. of limitations in this country is ten years** dans ce pays, il y a prescription de dix ans; **statutes** (*of company*) statuts *mpl*, règlements *mpl*; **s. book** code *m* (des lois); **to put sth in the s. book** faire passer qch en loi; (*of trade union etc*) faire passer qch dans le règlement; **s. law** droit *m* écrit
statutory ['stætjʊt(ə)rɪ] *adj* **(a)** (*established by law*) établi par la loi; (*by regulations*) réglementaire; (*offence*) prévu par la loi; **s. duty** devoir *m* défini par la loi; **s. holiday** jour *m* férié, fête *f* légale; **there is no s. obligation to …** il n'y a aucune obligation légale de …; **s. sick pay** indemnités *fpl* de maladie prévues par la loi; *US Jur* **s. rape** détournement *m* de mineur; **s. regulations** règlements *mpl* statutaires; **s. reserve** réserve *f* statutaire; **s. rights** droits *mpl* statutaires **(b)** (*according to law*) statutaire, conforme aux statuts
staunch¹ [stɔːntʃ] *adj* (*person*) sûr, dévoué; (*supporter*) dévoué, loyal; **a s. Catholic** un(e) catholique à tout crin; **a s. socialist** un(e) socialiste convaincu(e)
staunch² [stɔːntʃ] *vt* (*blood*) étancher; **to s. a wound** étancher le sang d'une blessure
staunchly ['stɔːntʃlɪ] *adv* avec fermeté; (*with resolve*) avec résolution; **s. Catholic/republican area** région résolument catholique/républicaine
staunchness ['stɔːntʃnɪs] *n* (*of person*) fermeté *f*; (*loyalty*) dévouement *m*
stave¹ [steɪv] *n* **(a)** (*wooden stick*) bâton *m*; **staves** (*of barrel*) douves *fpl* **(b)** (*in prosody*) (*of poem*) stance *f*, strophe *f* **(c)** *Mus* portée *f*
▶ **stave in** *vtsep* (*pt, pp* **staved, stove** [stəʊv]) (*break*) (*barrel, ship's sides*) défoncer, enfoncer
▶ **stave off** *vtsep* (*keep away*) (*problem etc*) détourner, écarter; (*danger*) prévenir, parer à; (*disaster*) conjurer; **to s. off a cold** éviter un rhume; **to s. off hunger** tromper la faim
stay¹ [steɪ] *n* **(a)** (*in a town etc*) séjour *m*; (*at friend's house*) visite *f*; **fortnight's s.** séjour de quinze jours **(b)** *Jur, Fig* **s. of execution** sursis *m*; *Jur* **s. of proceedings** suspension *f* d'instances
stay² **1** *vi* **(a)** (*not move, remain*) rester; **s. there!** tenez-vous là!; **s. where you are!** restez où vous êtes!; *F* **to s. put** ne pas bouger; (*refuse to move*) refuser de bouger; *F* **I'll s. put, I'm staying put** j'y suis, j'y reste; **to s. still** rester tranquille; **to s. at home** rester à la maison *ou* chez soi; **to s. in bed** rester au lit; (*when ill*) garder le lit; **to s. to** *or* **for dinner** rester (à *ou* pour) dîner; **computers are here to s.** les ordinateurs sont entrés dans les mœurs; **this word is here to s.** ce mot est entré dans la langue; **these changes are here to s.** ces changements sont passés dans les mœurs; **the weather stayed fine/wet all week** le temps est resté au beau/à la pluie toute la semaine; **it stays dark until after eight in winter** il fait nuit jusqu'à plus de huit heures en hiver; **if the weather stays like this** si le temps se maintient; **it won't s. in position** impossible de le/la faire tenir en place

(b) (*reside*) (*for short time*) séjourner; **I stayed 5 years in the States** j'ai passé *ou* habité cinq années aux États-Unis; **where are you staying?** où loges-tu?; **he has come to s.** (*for a visit*) il est venu passer quelques jours chez nous; (*for good*) il est venu habiter chez nous; **to s. at a hotel** être à l'hôtel; **I'm staying at a hotel** je suis descendu à l'hôtel; **to s. with sb** loger chez qn; (*for holiday*) passer quelque temps chez qn; **we're staying with relations** nous sommes chez des parents

(c) *Sp* (*endure*) **a horse that can s.** un cheval qui a du fond; **to s. with sth** s'atteler à qch; **it won't be finished unless you s. with it** ce ne sera jamais fini à moins que tu ne t'y tiennes

(d) *Arch* (*stop*) s'arrêter; (*still used in*) **s.!** (*to dog*) pas bouger!

(e) *Scot* (*live*) habiter, demeurer

2 *vt* **(a)** *esp Lit* (*stop*) (*person's progress*) arrêter; (*epidemic*) enrayer; **to s. sb's arm** *or* **hand** retenir le bras de qn; **to s. one's hand** se retenir

(b) *Jur etc* remettre; (*decision etc*) ajourner; **to s. judgement** surseoir à un/au jugement

(c) (*endure*) **she can s. five kilometres** elle peut tenir cinq kilomètres; **to s. the course** tenir le rythme; *Sp* **will he s. the distance?** tiendra-t-il la distance?

stay³ *n* **(a)** (*support*) soutien *m*; *Constr, MecE etc* étai *m*, étançon *m*; *Naut* (*for mast*) étai *m*; (*for bonnet*) béquille *f* **(b)** **stays** (*corset*) corset *m*
▶ **stay away** *vi* (*not approach*) ne pas s'approcher (**from** de); (*not attend*) ne pas assister (**from** à); **to s. away from school** ne pas aller à l'école; **to s. away from danger** se tenir à l'écart du danger; **you can play outside but s. away from the road** tu peux jouer dehors mais ne va pas sur la route
▶ **stay behind** *vi* rester en arrière; (*after school, work*) rester plus tard
▶ **stay down** *vi* **(a)** *Sch* (*repeat year*) redoubler **(b)** (*of hair, lid etc*) tenir en place; **I've tried to eat but nothing will s. down** j'ai essayé de manger mais je ne garde rien **(c)** (*under water*) **the turtle/diver can s. down for …** la tortue/le plongeur peut rester sous l'eau pendant …
▶ **stay in** *vi* **(a)** (*not go out*) ne pas sortir; (*stay in house*) rester à la maison **(b)** (*of screw, fitting etc*) rester en place
▶ **stay off** **1** *vi* **(a)** (*not go to work, school*) rester à la maison **(b)** (*hold off*) (*of bad weather*) ne pas arriver; **we're hoping the rain will s. off a little longer** nous espérons que la pluie attendra encore un peu **2** *vipo* **(a)** (*keep away from*) (*main roads, private property etc*) éviter, ne pas passer par; (*alcohol, drugs, sweets etc*) ne pas prendre, éviter; **s. off the whisky!** pas de whisky! **(b)** (*not attend*) (*school, work etc*) ne pas aller à
▶ **stay on** *vi* **(a)** (*remain longer*) rester plus longtemps **(b)** (*remain in place*) (*of hat, wig etc*) tenir *ou* rester en place; (*of sticker etc*) tenir
▶ **stay out** *vi* **(a)** (*stay outside*) rester dehors; (*not come home*) ne pas rentrer; **to s. out all night** découcher; **to s. out late** rentrer tard; **to s. out until all hours of the night** rester dehors jusque très tard dans la nuit **(b)** *Ind* (*continue strike*) poursuivre *ou* continuer la grève **(c)** (*not interfere*) **to s. out of sth** ne pas se mêler de qch; **s. out of this!** ne t'en mêle pas!
▶ **stay over** *vi* prolonger son séjour, rester plus longtemps; **you can s. over if you like** (*spend the night*) tu peux dormir ici si tu veux
▶ **stay up** *vi* **(a)** (*not go to bed*) ne pas se coucher, veiller; **to s. up late** se coucher *ou* veiller tard; **we stayed up all night talking** nous sommes restés à parler toute la nuit; **my parents always s. up until I get home** mes parents attendent toujours jusqu'à ce que je sois rentré pour aller se coucher; **don't s. up for me** ne m'attends pas pour aller dormir

(b) (*remain in place*) (*of picture, shelf, tent, trousers*) tenir; **the decorations stayed up until February** les décorations sont restées en place jusqu'en février

(c) *Br* (*at university*) **he used to s. up over the vacations** il restait (travailler) à l'université pendant les vacances

stay-at-home *adj, n* casanier, -ière
stayer ['steɪər] *n* **(a)** *Sp* (*runner*) coureur *m* de fond; (*cyclist*) stayer *m*; (*horse*) stayer, cheval *m* qui a du fond **(b)** (*person who perseveres*) personne *f* persévérante; **she's a real s.** elle va jusqu'au bout de ce qu'elle entreprend; **gifted but not a s.** doué mais manque de suivi *ou* de persévérance
staying ['steɪɪŋ] *n* **s. power** résistance *f*, endurance *f*; **to have good s. power** (*of horse*) avoir du fond
stay-over *n* (*re-used hotel room*) chambre *f* en recouche, recouche *f*
stays list *n* (*at hotel*) liste *f* des clients en recouche
STD [estiː'diː] *n* **(a)** *Br Telecom* (*abbr* **subscriber trunk dialling**) **S. code** indicatif *m* régional **(b)** *Med* (*abbr* **sexually transmitted disease**) MST *f*
stead [sted] *n* **(a)** **to stand sb in good s.** être fort utile à qn **(b)** *esp Lit* **in sb's s.** à la place *ou* au lieu de qn
steadfast ['stedfɑːst] **1** *adj* ferme, stable; **s. in love/in adversity** constant en amour/dans l'adversité; **they were s. in their refusal to compromise** ils se sont montrés très déterminés dans leur refus du compromis **2** *adv* (*to hold, stand*) sans fléchir
steadfastly ['stedfɑːstlɪ] *adv* (*to refuse*) fermement; (*to love, serve etc*) avec constance; **she has s. refused to identify her sources** elle a toujours refusé de désigner ses sources
steadfastness ['stedfɑːstnɪs] *n* (*determination*) fermeté *f*; (*constancy*) constance *f*
steadicam operator ['stedɪkæm] *n TV, Cin* opérateur *m* steadicam

steadily ['stedɪlɪ] *adv* **(a)** *(solidly)* fermement **(b)** *(at regular rate)* régulièrement; *(without stopping)* sans arrêt; *(without jolting)* sans à-coups; *(constantly)* continuellement; *(to work)* assidûment; **to walk s.** *(not stagger)* bien tenir sur ses jambes; **s. increasing output** rendement augmentant de façon régulière; **his health grows s. worse** sa santé empire régulièrement; **to work s. at sth** travailler assidûment à qch; **they were s. gaining on us** inexorablement, ils nous rattrapaient **(c)** *(calmly)* d'une manière posée; **she looked at him s.** elle l'a fixé du regard, elle l'a regardé fixement

steadiness ['stedɪnɪs] *n* **(a)** *(of table, hand etc)* fermeté *f*; **s. of hand** sûreté *f* des gestes; **s. of hand is vital for surgeons** il est vital que les chirurgiens aient la main sûre **(b)** *(regularity)* *(of movement, action)* régularité *f*; *(perseverance)* assiduité *f*, persévérance *f*; *(stability)* stabilité *f*; **s. of purpose** constance *f* (avec laquelle l'on poursuit ses objectifs); *St Exch* **s. of prices** bonne tenue *f* des prix **(c)** *(calm)* *(of person)* calme *m*; *(non-volatility)* régularité *f*

steady¹ ['stedɪ] **1** *adj* **(a)** *(stable, solid)* *(table, ladder etc)* stable; **to make a bookshelf s.** rendre une étagère stable; **to hold sth s.** bien tenir qch; **to keep s.** ne pas bouger; **to be s. on one's feet** *or* **legs** être d'aplomb sur ses jambes; **to have a s. hand** avoir la main sûre; **with a s. hand** d'une main sûre *ou* ferme

(b) *(regular)* *(rate, increase, growth)* continu, soutenu; *(income)* fixe, régulier; *(pulse)* égal; *Com* *(market)* soutenu; *(person)* *(in work, lifestyle etc)* régulier; **s. breeze** brise *f* étale; *Com* **s. demand for ...** demande suivie pour ...; *Sp* **to play a s. game** avoir un jeu régulier; **beneath her s. gaze** sous son regard soutenu; **s. increase** augmentation *f* régulière; **s. pace** allure *f* régulière; **to drive at a s. 90** rouler constamment à 90; **s. prices** prix *mpl* stables; **s. progress** progrès *mpl* constants; **s. rain** pluie *f* persistante; **s. worker** travailleur *m* régulier *(concernant la productivité)*; **to be s. in one's affections** être constant dans ses affections; **he hasn't been in s. work for years** il n'a pas (eu) de travail stable depuis des années

(c) *(calm)* posé; **s. horse** cheval *m* calme; **in a s. voice** d'une voix posée

(d) he has a s. girlfriend il a la même copine depuis longtemps; **I don't have a s. boyfriend** je n'ai pas vraiment de petit ami

2 *adv F* **they are going s. now** ça devient sérieux entre eux deux; **they've been going s. for two years now** ça fait deux ans qu'ils sortent ensemble

3 *int* **s.!** *(don't move)* ne bougez pas!; *(watch out you don't fall)* attention (de ne pas tomber)!; *F* **s. (on)!** *(gently)* doucement!

4 *n F* *(boyfriend, girlfriend)* **my s.** mon petit ami, ma petite amie

steady² **1** *vt* raffermir, affermir; **to s. one's hand** s'assurer que sa main ne tremble pas; **to s. oneself** retrouver son équilibre; **to s. oneself against sth** s'appuyer contre qch; **to s. one's nerves** calmer ses nerfs; **marriage has steadied him** le mariage lui a donné un certain équilibre **2** *vi* *(of boat etc)* retrouver son équilibre; **prices are steadying** les prix se raffermissent

▶ **steady down** *vi* *(become a calmer person)* se calmer

steak [steɪk] *n Culin* *(beef)* bifteck *m*, steak *m*; *(cut from the ribs)* entrecôte *f*; *(of meat, fish)* tranche *f*; *(of salmon)* darne *f*; **fillet s.** *(beef)* tournedos *m*; **s. and chips** steak frites; **s. and kidney pie/pudding** tourte *f*/pudding *m* à la viande et aux rognons de bœuf; **s. knife** couteau *m* à viande; **s. tartare** steak tartare

steakhouse ['steɪkhaʊs] *n* grill *m*

steal¹ [sti:l] *n esp Am F* *(bargain)* affaire *f*; **at $35 it's a s.!** à 35 dollars, c'est une affaire!

steal² *(pt* **stole** [stəʊl]; *pp* **stolen** ['stəʊl(ə)n]) **1** *vt* *(property, person's idea, husband)* voler (**from sb** à qn); **I've had my purse stolen** on m'a volé mon porte-monnaie; **to s. money from the till** *(of employee)* prendre de l'argent *ou* se servir dans la caisse; **to s. sb's heart** prendre le cœur de qn; **to s. a kiss** voler un baiser; **to s. a few hours from one's studies** laisser ses études de côté pendant quelques heures; **to s. a glance at sb** jeter un coup d'œil furtif à qn; **to s. a march on sb** devancer qn; *Th* **to s. the show** ravir la vedette; **to s. sb's thunder** couper l'herbe sous le pied de qn

2 *vi* **(a)** voler (**from sb** qn); *Bible* **thou shalt not s.** tu ne voleras point; **to be caught stealing** être pris en train de voler

(b) *(move quietly)* **to s. away/in/out** s'en aller/entrer/sortir sans bruit; **she stole into the room** elle s'est faufilée *ou* glissée dans la pièce; **to s. up on sb** se glisser vers qn; *Fig* *(of old age etc)* prendre qn par surprise

stealing ['sti:lɪŋ] *n* vol *m*; **s. is wrong** c'est mal de voler

stealth [stelθ] *n* ruse *f*; **by s.** par la ruse; *(furtively)* à la dérobée, furtivement; **to do good by s.** faire le bien en restant dans l'ombre; *Mil* **s. bomber** avion *m* furtif

stealthily ['stelθɪlɪ] *adv* furtivement, à la dérobée

stealthiness ['stelθɪnɪs] *n* *(of action etc)* caractère *m* furtif; *(of person)* manières *fpl* furtives; **his s. in defaming his rivals** la ruse avec laquelle il parvenait à diffamer ses rivaux

stealthy ['stelθɪ] *adj* furtif; *(look)* dérobé, à la dérobée; **with a s. step** à pas furtifs *ou* feutrés *ou* de loup

steam¹ [sti:m] *n* vapeur *f* (d'eau); *(condensation)* buée *f*; *MecE etc* **to get up** *or* **to raise s.** mettre la chaudière sous pression; **to get up s.** *(of person)* rassembler toutes ses forces *ou* toute son énergie; **at full s.** à toute vapeur; *Naut* **full s. ahead!** en avant toute!; **to run out of s.** *(of engine etc)* ne plus être sous pression; *F* *(of project, campaign etc)* s'essouffler; *F* *(of person)* manquer de souffle; *F* **I'm running out of s.** je commence à peiner; *Fig* **to let off s.** se défouler; **to proceed under its own s.** *(of damaged ship etc)* parvenir à naviguer sans être remorqué; *Fig* **I'll get there under my own s.** j'irai par mes propres moyens; **s. cooking** cuisson *f* à la vapeur; **s. power** vapeur; **s. room** chambre *f* de vapeur; *Constr etc* **s. shovel** pelleteuse *f*

steam² **1** *vt* passer à la vapeur, étuver; *Culin* *(vegetables etc)* cuire à la vapeur *ou* à l'étuvée; **to s. open an envelope** décacheter une lettre à la vapeur

2 *vi* **(a)** *(give off steam)* fumer; **horses steaming with sweat** chevaux fumants (de sueur)

(b) *(cook in steam)* *(of vegetables etc)* cuire à la vapeur

(c) to s. ahead *(of ship, locomotive)* avancer (à la vapeur); *Fig* *(make rapid progress)* avancer à toute vapeur; **the train steamed out of the station** le train quitta la gare dans un nuage de fumée; **the ferry steamed into port** le ferry entra dans le port; *Fig F* **he came steaming into the room** *(fast)* il est entré dans la pièce à toute pompe; *(angry)* il est entré dans la pièce en fulminant

▶ **steam off** **1** *vtsep* *(stamp)* décoller à la vapeur **2** *vi* *(of ship)* s'éloigner (en fumant)

▶ **steam up** **1** *vi* *(become covered in condensation)* *(of window, windscreen, glasses etc)* s'embuer **2** *vtsep* *(usu passive)* **to get all steamed up** *(of windows, glasses etc)* se couvrir de buée, s'embuer; *Fig F* *(lose one's composure)* s'énerver

steam bath *n* bain *m* de vapeur

steamboat ['sti:mbəʊt] *n* (bateau *m* à) vapeur *m*

steamed [sti:md] *adj* *(vegetables etc)* à la vapeur

steam engine *n MecE* machine *f* à vapeur; *Rail* locomotive *f* à vapeur

steamer ['sti:mər] *n* **(a)** *(ship)* (bateau *m* à) vapeur *m* **(b)** *Culin* *(saucepan)* cuiseur *m* à vapeur; *(insert for saucepan)* panier *m* de cuisson à la vapeur

steaming ['sti:mɪŋ] **1** *adj* **(a)** fumant **(b)** *Fig F* *(angry)* fumant de colère; *(drunk)* bourré, pété **2** *adv* **s. hot** bien chaud; *F* **s. drunk** bourré, pété **3** *n* **(a)** *Culin* cuisson *f* à la vapeur *ou* à l'étuvée **(b)** *Sl* *(street robbery by gangs)* = vol *m* de sacs à main pratiqué en bande

steam iron *n* fer *m* à vapeur

steam radio *n Hum* radio *f*; **in the days of s.** aux débuts de la radio

steamroller¹ ['sti:mrəʊlər] *n Constr* rouleau *m* compresseur; *Fig* force *f* écrasante

steamroller² *vt Constr* *(road)* passer au rouleau compresseur; *Fig* *(the opposition etc)* écraser; **to s. a bill through Parliament** imposer un projet de loi au Parlement; **he steamrollered his plans through the committee** il a imposé ses projets au comité

steamship ['sti:mʃɪp] *n* bateau *m* à vapeur

steamy ['sti:mɪ] *adj* *(full of steam)* plein de vapeur; *(covered in steam)* couvert de buée; *Fig F* *(novel, movie, scene)* torride

steed [sti:d] *n Lit* coursier *m*, destrier *m*

steel¹ [sti:l] *n* **(a)** *(metal)* acier *m*; **rolled s.** acier laminé; **a grip/a will of s.** une poigne/une volonté de fer; **nerves of s.** nerfs *mpl* d'acier; **s. knife/ladder** couteau *m*/échelle *f* en acier; **s. plate** plaque *f* d'acier **(b)** *Arch, Lit* *(sword)* fer *m*, épée *f*; *(blade)* lame *f* **(c)** *(for sharpening knives)* affiloir *m*, fusil *m*

steel² *vt* **to s. oneself** *or* **one's heart to do sth** s'armer de courage pour faire qch; **to s. oneself against sth** se blinder contre qch

steel band *n* ruban *m* d'acier; *Mus* steel band *f*

steelclad ['sti:lklæd] *adj* couvert *ou* revêtu d'acier; *(knight)* bardé de fer

steel industry *n* sidérurgie *f*

steel mill *n* aciérie *f*

steel-plated *adj* cuirassé

steel wool *n* paille *f* de fer

steelwork ['sti:lwɜ:k] *n* **(a)** *Tech* tôleries *fpl*; **constructional s.** profilés *mpl* pour constructions **(b)** (*usu with sing verb*) **steelworks** (*factory*) aciérie *f*

steelworker ['sti:lwɜ:kər] *n* ouvrier *m* de l'industrie sidérurgique

steely ['sti:lɪ] *adj* **(a)** (*of steel*) d'acier **(b)** (*hard*) dur; (*gaze etc*) d'acier; (*determination*) inflexible; **s. blue** (bleu) acier

steelyard ['sti:ljɑ:d, 'stɪljəd] *n* (balance *f*) romaine *f*

steep¹ [sti:p] *adj* **(a)** (*path, hill, street*) escarpé, raide; (*slope*) raide; (*cliff*) à pic; **s. climb** (*hill*) pente *f* raide; **the plane went into a s. climb/dive** l'avion monta à la verticale/ descendit en piqué; **s. gradient** forte pente, pente raide *ou* rapide; **s. rise in prices** hausse *f* considérable des prix **(b)** *F* (*excessive*) (*price etc*) excessif; **that's pretty s.!** (*of price*) c'est un peu raide!; **that's a bit s.!** (*unreasonable*) c'est un peu fort!

steep² **1** *vt* (*clothes, food*) faire tremper; (*hides*) tremper; **terrace steeped in sunshine** terrasse baignée de soleil; **steeped in prejudice** imbibé de préjugés; **steeped in history** imprégné d'histoire; **to s. oneself in the atmosphere of the Middle Ages** se tremper *ou* se plonger dans l'atmosphère du Moyen Age **2** *vi* tremper; *Culin* mariner

steepen ['sti:p(ə)n] *vi* (*of slope etc*) devenir plus raide; (*of prices*) augmenter

steeple ['sti:p(ə)l] *n* (*bell tower*) clocher *m*; (*spire*) flèche *f* (de clocher)

steeplechase ['sti:p(ə)ltʃeɪs] *n Sp, Horseracing* steeple-chase *m, pl* steeple-chases, steeple *m*

steeplechaser ['sti:p(ə)ltʃeɪsər] *n* (*rider*) cavalier *m* qui monte en steeple-chases; (*horse, athlete*) steeple-chaser *m*

steeplechasing ['sti:p(ə)ltʃeɪsɪŋ] *n Sp, Horseracing* steeple-chases *mpl*

steeplejack ['sti:p(ə)ldʒæk] *n* réparateur *m* de clochers et de cheminées d'usines

steeply ['sti:plɪ] *adv* (*to drop*) en pente raide, à pic; (*to climb*) à pic; **road that climbs s.** route à forte pente; **to rise s.** (*of path*) monter à pic; *Fig* (*of prices*) monter en flèche

steepness ['sti:pnɪs] *n* (*of slope*) escarpement *m*

steer¹ [stɪər] **1** *vt* (*car*) conduire, diriger; (*ship*) gouverner; (*yacht*) barrer; (*person*) diriger (**towards** vers); **to s. sb out of trouble** sortir qn du pétrin; **to s. a northerly course, to s. north** faire route vers le nord; (*turn north*) mettre le cap sur le nord; *Fig* **to s. a middle course** trouver un compromis; **to s. the conversation away from a subject** détourner la conversation; **to s. the conversation round to another subject** aiguiller la conversation sur un autre sujet; **to s. a country out of a crisis** faire sortir un pays de la crise

2 *vi* (*of person*) conduire; (*of ship*) gouverner; **to s. for sth** se diriger vers qch; **to s. clear of sth/sb** éviter qch/qn

steer² *n* (*bull*) bœuf *m*

steerage ['stɪərɪdʒ] *n Old-fashioned Naut* (*third-class accommodation*) entrepont *m*; **to travel s.** voyager dans l'entrepont

steerageway ['stɪərɪdʒweɪ] *n Naut* vitesse *f* nécessaire pour gouverner

steering ['stɪərɪŋ] *n* (*act*) (*of car*) direction *f*; (*mechanism*) (*of car*) timonerie *f*, (boîte *f* de) direction; (*of ship*) appareil *m* à gouverner; (*of plane*) direction; *Aut* **s. arm** bras *m* de direction; *Aut* **s. box** boîtier *m* de direction; *Aut* **s. geometry** géométrie *f* du train avant; *Aut* **s. play** jeu *m* à la direction; *Aut* **s. rod** bielle *f* de direction

steering column *n Aut* colonne *f* de direction; **s. lock** antivol *m* de direction

steering committee *n Pol etc* comité *m* d'organisation

steering lock *n Aut* angle *m* de braquage; (*anti-theft*) antivol *m* de direction

steering wheel *n Aut* volant *m*; *Naut* roue *f* du gouvernail

steersman, *pl* **-men** ['stɪəzmən] *n Naut* homme *m* de barre, timonier *m*

stellar ['stelər] *adj* stellaire

stem¹ [stem] *n* **(a)** *Bot* (*of plant*) tige *f*, *Spec* pédoncule *m*; (*of leaf*) queue *f*, *Spec* pétiole *m* **(b)** (*of glass*) pied *m*; (*of tobacco pipe*) tuyau *m*; (*of valve*) tige *f*; *Mus* (*of note*) queue *f*; **s. glass** verre *m* à pied **(c)** *Ling* (*of word*) radical *m* **(d)** (*of ship*) étrave *f*; **from s. to stern** de l'avant à l'arrière; *Fig* **the party is split from s. to stern on this issue** le parti est totalement divisé sur cette question

stem² *vi* **(-mm-) to s. from sth** (*of problems, errors, theories etc*) provenir de qch; (*of models, versions, designs etc*) être issu de qch; **much harm stemmed from this** il en est résulté beaucoup de mal

stem³ **1** *vt* (*hold back*) (*flow of liquid etc*) arrêter, contenir; *Fig* **to s. an epidemic** enrayer une épidémie; *Fig* **to s. the tide of ...** arrêter le flot de ...; *Fig* **to s. the rise in unemployment/ crime** enrayer la montée du chômage/de la criminalité; *Fig* **to s. the advance of fascism/an army** bloquer l'avancée du fascisme/d'une armée **2** *vi Ski* faire un stem

stem⁴ *n Ski* (virage *m* en) stem *m*; **s. Christie/parallel** stem christie/parallèle

stemmed [stemd] *adj* (*glass*) à pied

stemware ['stemweər] *n Am* (*glasses*) verres *mpl*

stench [stentʃ] *n* odeur *f* nauséabonde, puanteur *f*; *Fig* **the s. of corruption** l'odeur nauséabonde de la corruption

stencil¹ ['stens(ə)l] *n* **(a)** (*device*) pochoir *m*; **coloured by s.** colorié au pochoir; **s. plate** pochoir **(b)** (*work*) peinture *f* au pochoir **(c)** (*typewritten copy etc*) stencil *m*; **s. paper** papier *m* stencil

stencil² **(-ll-,** *US* **-l-) 1** *vt* (*leaf, flower etc*) peindre au pochoir; *Ind, Com* (*packing case*) marquer; (*letter etc*) polycopier, tirer au stencil **2** *vi* peindre au pochoir

sten gun [sten] *n* mitraillette *f*

stenographer, *US* **stenographist** [stə'nɒgrəfər, -fɪst] *n* sténographe *mf*; *F* sténo *mf*

stenography [stə'nɒgrəfɪ] *n* sténographie *f*

stenotyper ['stenətaɪpər] *n* sténotype *m*

stenotypist ['stenətaɪpɪst] *n* sténotypiste *mf*

stenotypy ['stenətaɪpɪ] *n* sténotypie *f*

stentorian [sten'tɔ:rɪən] *adj* (*voice*) de stentor

step¹ [step] *n* **(a)** (*movement, sound*) pas *m*; **with quick steps** d'un pas rapide; **to take a s.** faire un pas (**back** en arrière; **forward** en avant); **one s. forward, two steps back** un pas en avant et deux pas en arrière; *esp Lit* **to turn one's steps towards a place** diriger ses pas *ou* se diriger vers un lieu; **a child's first steps** les premiers pas d'un enfant; **at every s.** à chaque pas; **s. by s.** pas à pas; (*little by little*) petit à petit, graduellement, progressivement; **within a few steps of the house** à quelques pas de la maison; **it's quite a s.** (*quite a long way*) ce n'est pas tout près; (*quite a big change*) c'est une décision importante; **that's a great s. forward** c'est déjà un grand pas de fait, c'est déjà un grand progrès; **a s. in the right direction** un pas dans la bonne voie; **you'll have to watch your s.** il va falloir que tu fasses attention où tu mets les pieds; *Fig* fais attention à ce que tu fais; *Fig* **they fought us every s. of the way** ils nous ont combattu sans répit *ou* sur chaque point; *Fig* **we're behind you every s. of the way** nous sommes avec vous sur toute la ligne

(b) (*in walking, dancing*) pas *m*; **marching s.** pas ordinaire; **to be in s.** marcher au pas, être au pas; **to fall into s.** se mettre au pas; **to keep (in) s.** rester au pas; **to break s.** rompre le pas; *Fig* **to be out of s. with sb** être à contre-courant de qn; *Fig* **supply has got out of s. with demand** l'offre ne correspond plus à la demande

(c) (*action, measure*) démarche *f*, mesure *f*; **to take the necessary steps** faire *ou* entreprendre les démarches nécessaires; **to take steps to do sth** prendre des mesures pour faire qch; **the first s. will be to ...** la première chose à faire, ce sera de ...

(d) (*of staircase*) marche *f*, degré *m*; (*of ladder*) échelon *m*; (*of stepladders*) marche; **flight of steps** escalier *m*, volée *f* de marches; (*outside building*) perron *m*; **mind the s.** attention à la marche; **to go up a s.** (*be promoted*) monter en grade; **it's a s. up from the old house** c'est un peu mieux que la vieille maison; **this new job is a s. up for me** ce nouveau travail va me permettre de progresser dans ma carrière; **to cut steps** (*in mountaineering*) tailler

(e) (*stage*) étape *f*; **it is a simple two-s. procedure** c'est une procédure simple en deux étapes; **the next s. is to ...** l'étape suivante consiste à ...

(f) (*ladder*) **(pair of) steps** escabeau *m*, échelle *f* double; *Av* **steps** passerelle *f*

step² *vi* (**stepped** [stept]) (*take a step, steps*) faire un pas/des pas; (*walk*) marcher, aller; **to s. on sb's foot** marcher sur le pied de qn; **s. this way** venez par ici; **s. inside for a moment** entrez pour un moment; **he stepped carefully over the cat** il enjamba soigneusement le chat; **to s. off a ladder** descendre d'une échelle; *F Hum* **he stepped under a bus** il est passé sous un bus

▶ **step aside** *vi* s'écarter; **to s. aside to let sb pass** s'écarter pour laisser passer qn; **it's time the chairman stepped aside** il est temps que le président se retire et laisse la place à quelqu'un d'autre

▶ **step back** *vi* faire un pas en arrière; *Fig* **if we could s. back into the last century** si nous pouvions revenir au siècle passé; **sometimes it helps to s. back and look at things** il est parfois bon de prendre du recul

▶ **step down** **1** *vtsep* (*decrease*), *El* (*current*) dévolter; *MecE* **to s. down the gear** démultiplier la transmission **2** *vi* **(a)** (*resign*) démissionner; **he stepped down in favour of the other candidate** (*withdrew*) il s'est retiré en faveur de l'autre candidat **(b)** (*descend*) descendre (**from** de)

▸ **step forward** *vi* faire un pas en avant; *Fig* (*of volunteer etc*) se désigner, se porter volontaire

▸ **step in** *vi* entrer (**to** dans); (*intervene*) intervenir, s'interposer

▸ **step on** *vipo* (*tread on*) (*sth*) marcher sur; *F* **to s. on the gas, to s. on it** *Aut* appuyer sur l'accélérateur *ou F* sur le champignon; (*hurry*) se dépêcher, *F* se grouiller; **to s. on the brakes** donner un coup de frein brusque

▸ **step out** *vi* (**a**) (*go outside house etc*) sortir (**b**) (*walk faster*) allonger *ou* forcer le pas; **to s. out briskly** marcher rapidement (**c**) *Old-fashioned* **to be stepping out with sb** (*courting*) sortir avec qn

▸ **step up 1** *vi* **to s. up to sb/sth** s'approcher de qn/qch; **s. up!, s. up!, come and see ...** approchez! approchez! venez voir ...; **he stepped up onto the platform** il est monté sur le podium **2** *vtsep* (*increase, intensify*) accroître, augmenter

stepbrother ['stepbrʌðər] *n* demi-frère *m*, *pl* demi-frères (= *fils du beau-père ou de la belle-mère*)

stepchild, *pl* **-children** ['steptʃaɪld, -tʃɪldrən] *n* beau-fils *m*, belle-fille *f*, *pl* beaux-fils, belles-filles

stepdaughter ['stepdɔːtər] *n* belle-fille *f*, *pl* belles-filles

stepfather ['stepfɑːðər] *n* beau-père *m*, *pl* beaux-pères

stepladder ['steplædər] *n* escabeau *m*

stepless transmission ['steplɪs] *n Aut* transmission *f* à variateur continue

stepmother ['stepmʌðər] *n* belle-mère *f*, *pl* belles-mères

steppe [step] *n Geog* steppe *f*

stepper ['stepər] *n El* **s. motor** moteur *m* pas-à-pas

stepping stone ['stepɪŋ] *n* pierre *f* (pour passer une rivière/*etc* à gué); *Fig* tremplin *m*

stepping up *n* (*of production etc*) augmentation *f*; (*of campaign etc*) intensification *f*

stepsister ['stepsɪstər] *n* demi-sœur *f*, *pl* demi-sœurs (= *fille du beau-père ou de la belle-mère*)

stepson ['stepsʌn] *n* beau-fils *m*, *pl* beaux-fils

stereo[1], *pl* **-os** ['sterɪəʊ, -əʊz, 'stɪə-] **1** *n* (**a**) (*equipment*) chaîne *f* stéréo (**b**) (*sound*) stéréo *f*; **to listen to sth in s.** écouter qch en stéréo; **s. signal** signal *m* stéréo; **s. transmitter** émetteur *m* stéréo (**c**) *Typ* = **stereotype**[1] (*b*) **2** *adj* (*equipment*) stéréo *inv*; (*recording, broadcast*) en stéréo

stereophonic [sterɪə'fɒnɪk, stɪə-] *adj* stéréophonique

stereoscope ['sterɪəskəʊp, 'stɪər-] *n Opt* stéréoscope *m*

stereoscopic [sterɪəʊ'skɒpɪk, stɪə-] *adj* stéréoscopique; **s. film** film *m* en 3D *ou* en relief

stereotype[1] ['sterɪətaɪp, 'stɪə-] *n* (**a**) *Fig* stéréotype *m* (**b**) *Typ* cliché *m*

stereotype[2] *vt* (**a**) *Fig* stéréotyper (**b**) *Typ* stéréotyper, clicher

stereotyped ['sterɪətaɪpt, 'stɪə-] *adj Typ, Fig* stéréotypé; **the s. idea of a farmer** le stéréotype de l'agriculteur

stereotypical [sterɪə'tɪpɪkəl, stɪə-] *adj* stéréotypé; **the s. image of ...** le stéréotype de ...

stereotyping ['sterɪətaɪpɪŋ, 'stɪə-] *n* fabrication *f* de stéréotypes; **the s. of women** les stéréotypes que l'on colle aux femmes

sterile ['steraɪl] *adj* stérile

sterility [ste'rɪlɪtɪ] *n* stérilité *f*

sterilization [sterɪlaɪ'zeɪʃən] *n* stérilisation *f*

sterilize ['sterɪlaɪz] *vt* stériliser; **sterilized milk** lait *m* stérilisé

sterilizer ['sterɪlaɪzər] *n* (*device*) stérilisateur *m*

sterilizing ['sterɪlaɪzɪŋ] *n* stérilisation *f*

sterling ['stɜːlɪŋ] **1** *adj* (*silver*) de bon aloi, fin; *Fig* vrai, solide; **a s. fighter** un combattant inlassable; **s. qualities** qualités solides; **pound s.** livre *f* sterling; **the s. area** la zone sterling **2** *n* (*currency*) (livre *f*) sterling *m*; **to pay in s.** payer en livres sterling

stern[1] [stɜːn] *adj* sévère; **we are made of sterner stuff** nous, nous sommes d'une autre trempe

stern[2] *n Naut* arrière *m*

sternly ['stɜːnlɪ] *adv* sévèrement

sternness ['stɜːnnɪs] *n* sévérité *f*

sternum, *pl* **-a, -ums** ['stɜːnəm, -ə, -əmz] *n Anat* sternum *m*

steroid ['stɪərɔɪd, 'ste-] *n Bio, Ch* stéroïde *m*

stertorous ['stɜːtərəs] *adj Med, Lit* stertoreux, ronflant

stet[1] [stet] *n Typ* bon *m*

stet[2] *vt* (**-tt-**) *Typ* (*word on proofs*) maintenir

stethoscope ['steθəskəʊp] *n Med* stéthoscope *m*

stetson ['stets(ə)n] *n* chapeau *m* mou à larges bords

stevedore ['stiːv(ə)dɔːr] *n* docker *m*, arrimeur *m*

stew[1] [stjuː] *n* (**a**) *Culin* ragoût *m*; **Irish s.** ragoût de mouton à l'irlandaise; *F* **to be in a s.** (*of person*) être dans tous ses états (**b**) *Arch* (*brothel*) bordel *m*

stew[2] **1** *vt Culin* (*meat etc*) faire cuire en ragoût; **to s. apples** faire une compote de pommes **2** *vi Culin* (*of meat*) mijoter; *F* **to let sb s. in his/her own juice** laisser qn cuire dans son jus, laisser mariner qn

steward ['stjuəd] *n* (**a**) (*of estate*) régisseur *m*, intendant *m*; *Naut* (*manager of provisions*) distributeur *m*, commis *m ou* agent *m* aux vivres; *Naut, Av* (*attendant*) steward *m*; *Naut* **s.'s mate** cambusier *m* (**b**) (*at sporting event*) commissaire *m*; (*at demonstration etc*) membre *m* du service d'ordre; (*at dance*) organisateur, -trice; *Horseracing* **a s.'s inquiry** une enquête des commissaires; *Ind* **shop s.** délégué *m* d'atelier *ou* d'usine *ou* du personnel

stewardess [stjuə'des] *n Naut* hôtesse *f*; *Av* **air s.** hôtesse de l'air

stewardship ['stjuədʃɪp] *n* économat *m*, intendance *f*; *Fig* **under his s. the situation improved markedly** quand il était responsable, les choses s'étaient nettement améliorées

stewed [stjuːd] *adj Culin* **s. beef** ragoût *m* de bœuf, bœuf *m* (à la) mode; **s. fruit** compote *f* de fruits; **this tea is s.** ce thé a trop infusé

stewing ['stjuːɪŋ] *n* **s. beef** bœuf *m* pour ragoût; **s. pears** poires *fpl* à cuire; **s. pan** = **stewpan**

stewpan ['stjuːpæn] *n* (grande) casserole *f*

stewpot ['stjuːpɒt] *n* cocotte *f*, fait-tout *m inv*

St. Ex. *Fin* (*abbr* **Stock Exchange**) Bourse *f*

stick[1] [stɪk] *n* (**a**) (*piece of wood*) bâton *m*; (*small piece of wood*) morceau *m* de bois; *Fig* **the big s.** la manière forte, (la politique de) la force; *Fig* **you're giving him a s. to beat you with** vous lui donnez des verges pour vous faire fouetter *ou* le bâton pour vous faire battre; (**walking**) **s.** canne *f*; **to gather sticks** ramasser du bois sec *ou* du petit bois; **cocktail** *or* **cherry s.** bâtonnet *m* (*pour cerise de cocktail*); (**swizzle**) **s.** (*for cocktails etc*) agitateur *m*; **not a s. was left standing** tout était rasé; **my few sticks of furniture** mes quelques meubles; *Prov* **sticks and stones may break my bones (but words will never hurt me)** les chiens aboient, la caravane passe; **s. figure** bonhomme *m* dessiné *ou* composé de bâtonnets; *TV* **s. mike** micro *m* tenu à la main; *F* **he lives out in the sticks** il habite un trou perdu, il vit dans la brousse; *Sl* **to be up the s.** (*pregnant*) être en cloque

(**b**) *Old-fashioned F* (*person*) **he's/she's a funny old s.** c'est un drôle de personnage; **he's/she's a good old s.** c'est un type/une fille bien; **a dry old s.** un pince-sans-rire; *Old-fashioned* **Jeremy, old s.!** Jeremy, vieille branche!

(**c**) (*of barley sugar, chewing gum, glue etc*) bâton *m*; (*of deodorant*) applicateur *m*; (*of dynamite*) bâtonnet *m*

(**d**) *Culin* **s. of celery** branche *f* de céleri; **s. of rhubarb** tige *f* de rhubarbe

(**e**) *Mil, Av* **s. of bombs** chapelet *m* de bombes

(**f**) *F* **to take a lot of s.** (*to be criticized*) se faire taper sur les doigts; (*to be mocked*) se faire mettre en boîte; *F* **to give sb s. (for sth)** (*criticize*) taper sur les doigts de qn (à cause de qch); (*laugh at*) se payer la tête de qn (à cause de qch); *F* **to give it some s.** (*exert oneself*) s'y mettre

stick[2] (*pt, pp* **stuck** [stʌk]) **1** *vt* (**a**) (*insert*) piquer, enfoncer (**sth into sth** qch dans qch), planter, fixer (**sth on a spike** qch sur une pointe); **to s. a pin into sth** enfoncer une épingle dans qch; **she stuck the spade into the ground** elle a planté la bêche dans le sol; **to s. pigs** chasser le sanglier à l'épieu

(**b**) *F* (*put*) mettre; **to s. one's hat on one's head** mettre *ou* planter son chapeau sur sa tête; **s. it in your pocket** fourrez-le dans votre poche; **s. it in the corner** collez ça dans le coin; **s. it on the table** mettez ça sur la table

(**c**) (*attach with glue, sticky tape*) coller; **to s. sth on(to) sth** coller qch à *ou* sur qch; **their trunk was stuck all over with labels** leur malle était couverte d'étiquettes

(**d**) *Br F* (*endure*) supporter, endurer; **to s. it** tenir le coup, tenir bon; **I can't s. it any longer** je n'en peux plus; **I can't s. him** je ne peux pas le sentir

(**e**) (*in horticulture*) (*peas etc*) ramer; (*plants*) mettre des tuteurs à

(**f**) **to be stuck** (*unable to move*) être coincé; (*in mud etc*) être embourbé; (*mentally, in a problem etc*) être bloqué *ou* en panne; **to get stuck in a bog** s'embourber dans un marécage; **he got his head stuck** sa tête est restée coincée; **I got stuck on the last question** j'ai séché sur la dernière question; **there's something stuck in the pipe** il y a quelque chose de coincé dans le tuyau; **here I am stuck in hospital for six weeks** me voilà cloué à l'hôpital pour six semaines; **I was stuck at Heathrow for six hours** j'ai été bloqué six heures à Heathrow; **to be stuck in a job** être coincé dans un emploi; **the book's finished but I'm stuck for a title** le livre est fini mais je ne trouve pas de titre; **stuck for money** à court d'argent; *F* **I'm stuck with it/him** (*can't get rid of*) je ne peux pas m'en débarrasser; *F* **we're stuck with it** (*decision etc*) il faut s'y résigner

(**g**) *F* **you can s. your job** ton boulot tu peux te le mettre où je pense

2 *vi* (**a**) **sewing left with a needle sticking in it** ouvrage laissé avec une aiguille piquée dedans; **the point was sticking through the lining** la pointe avait percé la doublure; **don't leave the spade sticking in the ground** ne laisse pas la pelle plantée dans le sol

(**b**) (*adhere*) (se) coller, s'attacher, tenir (**to** à); *Culin* (*of rice etc*) attacher; **the stamp won't s.** le timbre ne colle pas; **the name stuck** ce nom leur/lui/*etc* est resté

(**c**) (*of key, drawer, mechanism*) (se) coincer; (*in sand, bog etc*) s'enfoncer; *Aut* (*of valve, cut-out*) rester collé; *Fig* **the words stuck in his throat** les mots lui restèrent dans la gorge; **it sticks in my throat** (*of situation, sb's arrogance etc*) c'est dur à digérer; **to s. fast** (*of boat*) s'enliser; **the lift has stuck** l'ascenseur est coincé

▶ **stick around** *vi F* (*wait*) attendre; (*stay*) rester

▶ **stick at** *vipo* (**a**) (*persevere with*) s'acharner à (faire); **s. at it!** persévérez! (**b**) (*stop in face of*) **to s. at nothing** ne reculer devant rien

▶ **stick by** *vipo* (**a**) (*remain loyal to*) **to s. by a friend** ne pas abandonner un ami (**b**) (*continue to affirm*) maintenir; **I s. by what I said** je maintiens ce que j'ai dit

▶ **stick down** *vtsep* (**a**) *F* (*put down*) **s. it down anywhere** mettez-le *ou* collez-le n'importe où; **to s. sth down in a notebook** inscrire qch sur un carnet (**b**) (*with glue*) (*envelope*) coller

▶ **stick in 1** *vtsep* (**a**) (*with glue*) coller (**b**) *F* (*put in*) mettre, *F* coller; (*knife etc*) enfoncer (**c**) *F* **to get stuck in** (*start working*) s'y mettre; (*start eating*) se mettre à manger; **to get stuck into sth** (*work etc*) se mettre à qch; (*food*) se mettre à manger qch; **let's get stuck in!** allons, on s'y met! **2** *vi* (**a**) (*of knife etc*) s'enfoncer; **she threw the knife at the wall and it stuck in** elle a lancé le couteau contre le mur et il s'y est planté (**b**) *F* (*persevere*) **just s. in there!** tenez bon!

▶ **stick on 1** *vtsep* (*stamp etc*) coller, fixer; *Sl* **to s. one on sb** (*hit*) coller *ou* ficher un marron à qn; *F* **to be stuck on sb** être fou de qn; *F* **he is stuck on the idea** il s'enthousiasme pour cette idée **2** *vi* (*adhere*) adhérer; (*to stay stuck on*) rester collé

▶ **stick out 1** *vtsep* (**a**) (*cause to protrude*) faire dépasser, sortir; **to s. out one's tongue** tirer la langue; **to s. out one's hand** tendre la main; **to s. out one's chest** bomber la poitrine; **he stuck his head out (of the window)** il sortit la tête (par la fenêtre); *F* **to s. one's neck out (for sb)** prendre des risques (pour qn)

(**b**) *F* **to s. it out** (*persevere*) persévérer

2 *vi* (**a**) (*protrude*) faire saillie, ressortir; **to s. out (beyond sth)** dépasser (de qch); **his ears s. out** il a les oreilles décollées; **her teeth s. out** elle a les dents qui avancent

(**b**) *F* (*be noticeable*) se voir, se remarquer; **the way she dresses makes her s. out** la manière dont elle s'habille fait qu'elle ne passe pas inaperçue; **it sticks out a mile** c'est clair comme le jour; **it sticks out like a sore thumb** ça détonne, ça jure

▶ **stick out for** *vipo F* (*insist on*) **to s. out for sth** s'obstiner à demander qch

▶ **stick to** *vipo* (**a**) (*like glue*) coller à; **the rice had stuck to the pan** le riz avait collé *ou* attaché à la casserole; **her shirt stuck to her back** elle avait la chemise collée au dos; **the name stuck to him** ce nom lui est resté; **to s. to sb like a limpet** *or* **like a leech** *or* **like glue** se cramponner *ou* s'accrocher à qn, coller qn

(**b**) (*remain true to*) **to s. to one's promise** tenir sa promesse; **s. to it!** (*don't give in*) persévérez!; *F* **to s. to one's guns** ne pas en démordre; **to s. to an opinion** maintenir une opinion, ne pas démordre d'une opinion

(**c**) (*restrict oneself to*) **to s. to (the) facts** s'en tenir aux faits; **to s. to the point** ne pas s'écarter de la question; **to s. to the text** serrer le texte de près

(**d**) (*continue to affirm*) **I s. to what I said** je maintiens ce que j'ai dit; **she's sticking to her version of what happened** elle maintient sa version des faits; **that's my story and I'm sticking to it** c'est ma version et je m'y tiens

(**e**) (*keep*) **s. to what you've got!** contente-toi de ce que tu as!

(**f**) (*not leave*) **to s. to one's post** rester à son poste; **he sticks to his room** il ne sort pas de sa chambre

▶ **stick together 1** *vi* (**a**) (*with glue etc*) être collé (**b**) (*of friends etc*) **it's amazing they've stuck together** c'est incroyable qu'ils soient restés ensemble; **they always s. together** ils sont inséparables; (*show solidarity*) ils sont toujours solidaires **2** *vtsep* coller (ensemble)

▶ **stick up 1** *vtsep* (**a**) *F* (*erect*) (*fence*) ériger; (*signpost*) mettre, planter (**b**) *Sl* (*raise*) **s. 'em up!** haut les mains! (**c**) *F* (*attach to wall etc*) (*notice, poster etc*) afficher (**d**) *F* **to s. up a bank** attaquer une banque à main armée **2** *vi* (*point upwards*) se dresser; **his hair's sticking up** il est ébouriffé; **an overturned table with its legs sticking up in the air** une table à l'envers avec les pieds en l'air

▶ **stick up for** *vipo* (*defend*) prendre la défense de, soutenir; **to s. up for one's rights** défendre ses droits; **she can s. up for herself** elle peut se défendre toute seule

▶ **stick with** *vipo* (**a**) (*remain loyal to*) rester fidèle à (**b**) (*stay near*) rester avec; **the other runners couldn't s. with him** les autres coureurs ne pouvaient pas le suivre (**c**) (*persevere with*) (*English, tennis etc*) continuer; **to s. with doing sth** continuer à faire qch; **I'm sticking with my old car for now** je garde ma vieille voiture pour le moment

sticker ['stɪkər] *n* (**a**) (*label*) étiquette *f* gommée; *US F* (*poster*) affiche *f*; *US F* (*election poster*) affiche électorale (**b**) *F* (*determined person*) personne *f* persévérante; **she's a s.** elle ne manque pas de persévérance

stickiness ['stɪkɪnɪs] *n* (*of substance, hands etc*) moiteur *f*; (*of product*) nature *f* gluante *ou* collante

sticking ['stɪkɪŋ] *adj Br* **s. plaster** pansement *m* adhésif, sparadrap *m*; **s. point** point *m* de désaccord

stick insect *n Ent* phasme *m*

stick-in-the-mud *F* **1** *n* **he's an old s.** (*killjoy*) c'est un rabat-joie; (*fogey*) c'est un vieux réac **2** *adj* (*attitude, person etc*) (*killjoy*) rabat-joie; (*fogey*) réac

stickleback ['stɪklbæk] *n* (*fish*) épinoche *f*

stickler ['stɪklər] *n* **to be a s. for discipline** être à cheval sur la discipline

stick-on *adj* (*label*) adhésif; **s. soles** semelles *fpl* autocollantes

stick-up *n F* attaque *f* à main armée, braquage *m*; **this is a s.!** ceci est un hold-up!

sticky ['stɪkɪ] *adj* (**a**) (*substance, hands*) poisseux, gluant; (*paper etc*) collant, adhésif; (*climate*) moite; *F* **s. bun** petit pain *m* sucré; **to have s. fingers** avoir les doigts poisseux; *F* (*be a thief*) être voleur; *Comptr* **s. key** touche *f* à auto-maintien; **s. label** étiquette *f* autocollante, étiquette gommée; **s. tape** ruban *m* adhésif; **s. weather** temps *m* lourd; *Br Fig F* **to be on a s. wicket** être dans une situation difficile (**b**) *F* (*awkward*) (*problem, situation*) difficile; **is he being s. about it?** est-ce qu'il fait des histoires (à ce sujet)?; **he will come to a s. end** il finira mal

stiff[1] [stɪf] **1** *adj* (**a**) (*rigid, hard*) raide, rigide, dur; (*brush*) dur; (*person, manner*) raide, guindé; (*stubborn*) inflexible, obstiné; *Fin* (*market, commodity*) ferme; **s. joint** articulation *f* ankylosée; **to grow s.** (*of joint*) s'ankyloser; **to be quite s.** (*with sitting still*) être engourdi; (*after exercise*) être tout courbaturé; (*through lack of exercise*) être raide, manquer de souplesse; **he is very s.** (*formal*) il est d'un abord difficile; *F* **exams scare me s.** j'ai une peur bleue des examens; **I was bored s.** je m'ennuyais à mourir; **I was frozen s.** j'étais frigorifié; **a s. smile** un sourire forcé; **book bound in s. covers** livre relié en carton; **s. neck** torticolis *m*; **to offer s. resistance** (*of person*) résister opiniâtrement, tenir bon; (*of thing*) tenir bon; **s. style** style *m* guindé *ou* empesé

(**b**) (*door-handle, hinge etc*) qui fonctionne mal; (*paste, batter*) ferme; (*soil, clay*) dur; **the handle is s.** la poignée est dure; *Naut* **s. breeze** forte brise *f*

(**c**) (*exam*) difficile; **I sent them a s. letter** je leur ai envoyé une lettre bien sentie; **s. price** prix *m* élevé; **s. sentence** peine *f* sévère; **you need a s. drink** tu as besoin d'un remontant; **a s. whisky** un whisky bien tassé; **that's a bit s.!** (*going too far*) c'est un peu fort!

2 *n* (**a**) *Sl* (*corpse*) macchabée *m*

(**b**) *Am F* (*ordinary working man*) prolo *m*

stiff[2] *vt Sl* (*kill*) buter

stiffen ['stɪf(ə)n] **1** *vt* (**a**) (*wall, beam, plate etc*) renforcer; (*with starch*) (*collar etc*) empeser; **age has stiffened his joints** l'âge lui a raidi les articulations; **this action stiffened their resolve** cette action a raffermi leur résolution (**b**) (*paste*) rendre ferme, donner de la consistance à; (*drink*) corser (**c**) **to s. the entrance exams** rendre les examens d'entrée plus difficiles **2** *vi* (**a**) (*become rigid*) (se) raidir, devenir raide; (*of person*) se raidir; **opposition is stiffening** l'opposition se durcit (**b**) (*of paste etc*) devenir ferme, prendre de la consistance; *Naut* (*of wind*) fraîchir

stiffener ['stɪf(ə)nər] *n* (**a**) (*in shoe*) contrefort *m*; (*in collar*) baleine *f* (de col) (**b**) *F* (*drink*) remontant *m*

stiffening ['stɪf(ə)nɪŋ] *n* (**a**) (*action*) raidissement *m*, renforcement *m*; (*of resistance*) durcissement *m*; **s. of the joints** ankylose *f* (**b**) (*for cloth*) amidon *m*

stiffly ['stɪflɪ] *adv* (*to bow*) avec raideur; (*to answer, greet etc*) avec froideur; (*to resist*) obstinément

stiff-necked ['stɪfnekt] *adj* (*stubborn*) obstiné, entêté

stiffness ['stɪfnɪs] *n* (**a**) (*of limbs, beam etc*) raideur *f*, rigidité *f*; (*of spring etc*) dureté *f*; *Fin* (*of market*) fermeté *f*; **s. of the legs** (*after exercise*) courbatures *fpl* dans les jambes;

(through lack of exercise) raideur, manque *m* de souplesse; *(after sitting)* engourdissement *m* des jambes; **s. of manner** raideur, air *m* guindé **(b)** *(of paste)* fermeté *f*, consistance *f*; *(of soil)* dureté *f*, fermeté **(c)** *(of price)* montant *m* élevé; *(of exam)* difficulté *f*

stiffy ['stɪfɪ] *n Sl* **to have a s.** *(erection)* triquer, avoir la trique

stifle ['staɪf(ə)l] **1** *vt (person)* étouffer, suffoquer; *(shouts, cries, yawn, laugh)* étouffer; *(rebellion)* réprimer; *(cry)* retenir **2** *vi* suffoquer, étouffer

stifled ['staɪf(ə)ld] *adj (cry etc)* étouffé; **with a s. voice** d'une voix éteinte

stifling ['staɪflɪŋ] *adj* étouffant, suffocant; *(sensation)* d'étouffement; **it's s. here!** on étouffe ici!

stigma, *pl* **-as, -ata** ['stɪgmə, -əz, 'stɪgmətə, stɪg'mɑːtə] *n* **(a)** *(pl usu* **stigmas)** *(social disgrace)* honte *f*; **there is no longer any s. in being a single mother** il n'y a plus de honte à être mère célibataire **(b) stigmata** *(of saint)* stigmates *mpl* **(c)** *(pl* **stigmata)** *Biol (of insect etc)* stigmate *m* **(d)** *(pl* **stigmas)** *Bot (of pistil)* stigmate *m*

stigmatic [stɪg'mætɪk] *n Rel* stigmatisé, -e

stigmatize ['stɪgmətaɪz] *vt* stigmatiser; **stigmatized as a coward** marqué comme lâche; **stigmatized as illegitimate** entaché de bâtardise

stile¹ [staɪl] *n* **(a)** *(in fence, hedge etc)* échalier *m* **(b)** *(turnstile)* tourniquet *m*

stile² *n Constr (of door etc)* montant *m*

stiletto, *pl* **-os, -oes** [stɪ'letəʊ, -əʊz] *n* **(a)** *(dagger)* stylet *m* **(b) s. heels, stilettos** talons *mpl* aiguille **(c)** *Sewing etc* poinçon *m*

still¹ [stɪl] **1** *adj (motionless)* immobile; *(calm)* calme; *(silent)* silencieux; *(wine)* non mousseux; *(orange juice, mineral water)* non gazeux; *TV, Cin* **s. frame** image *f* fixe; **s. water** eau *f* dormante; *Prov* **s. waters run deep** il faut se méfier de l'eau qui dort **2** *adv* **to keep s.** ne pas bouger, se tenir *ou* rester tranquille; **sit s.!** restez *ou* tenez-vous tranquille!; **to stand s.** *(not move)* ne pas bouger, se tenir immobile; *(of science etc)* ne pas faire de progrès; **her heart stood s.** son cœur cessa de battre **3** *n* **(a) in the s. of the night** dans le calme de la nuit **(b)** *Cin* photo *f (tirée du film)*

still² *vt (person)* tranquilliser, calmer, apaiser; **to s. sb's fears** calmer les craintes de qn

still³ **1** *adv* **(a)** *(up to now)* encore; **he is s. here** il est encore *ou* toujours ici; **he's s. not here** il n'est toujours pas là; **it's stuck – s.?** c'est coincé – encore?; **I s. have 500 francs** il me reste 500 francs, j'ai encore 500 francs; **I have s. to thank you** il me reste à vous remercier; **it s. remains to be seen** ça reste à voir; **I s. can't see what was wrong with my suggestion** je ne vois toujours pas en quoi ma suggestion était mauvaise; **in spite of his faults, I love him s.** malgré ses défauts je l'aime toujours

(b) *(even)* encore; **s. more/less** encore plus/moins; **s. more worrying ...** plus inquiétant encore ...; **if you can reduce the price s. further** si vous pouvez réduire encore le prix

(c) *(nonetheless, all the same)* pourtant; **he's s. the boss** c'est pourtant lui le patron; **but that s. doesn't justify ...** mais cela ne justifie pourtant pas ...; **OK, but I s. think we ought to do it** d'accord, mais je pense qu'on devrait quand même le faire; **it s. won't make me change my mind** je ne vais pas changer d'avis pour autant; **but s., if she did accept, wouldn't it be marvellous!** peut-être, mais si elle acceptait ce serait formidable!

2 *conj* cependant, pourtant, néanmoins, toutefois; **s. the fact remains that ...** toujours est-il que ..., il n'en reste pas moins vrai que ...; **s., what else could I have done?** qu'aurais-je pu faire d'autre, enfin?

still⁴ *n (for distilling)* alambic *m*

stillbirth ['stɪlbɜːθ] *n* enfant *m* mort-né; **the number of stillbirths** la mortinatalité

stillborn ['stɪlbɔːn] *adj* mort-né, -ée, *pl* mort-nés, -ées; *Fig (project etc)* avorté, mort-né

still life *n (pl* **still lifes)** *Art* nature *f* morte

stillness ['stɪlnɪs] *n* tranquillité *f*; *(of person)* calme *m*, repos *m*; *(of place, atmosphere)* tranquillité, paix *f*

stilt [stɪlt] *n* **(a)** *(for walking)* échasse *f*; **to walk on stilts** marcher sur des échasses **(b)** *Constr* pilotis *m*

stilted ['stɪltɪd] *adj (style, manner etc)* guindé, raide

Stilton ['stɪlt(ə)n] *n* fromage *m* de Stilton, stilton *m*

stimulant ['stɪmjʊlənt] **1** *n (tea, coffee etc)* excitant *m*; *Med* stimulant *m*; *(for heart)* tonicardiaque *m* **2** *adj attrib* **it has a s. effect** ça a un effet stimulant

stimulate ['stɪmjʊleɪt] *vt* **(a)** *(person, enthusiasm)* stimuler; *(mind, appetite etc)* aiguiser; *Ind (production)* encourager, activer **(b)** *Med (liver etc)* stimuler

stimulating ['stɪmjʊleɪtɪŋ] *adj (competition, work)* stimulant; *(music)* entraînant; *(book)* stimulant, qui donne à penser; **it's s. to work with talented people** c'est stimulant de travailler avec des gens qui ont du talent

stimulation [stɪmjʊ'leɪʃən] *n* stimulation *f*; **to need s.** avoir besoin d'être stimulé; **s. marketing** mercatique *f* de stimulation *ou* de stim

stimulative ['stɪmjʊlətɪv] **1** *adj* stimulant **2** *n* stimulant *m*

stimulus, *pl* **-i** ['stɪmjʊləs, -aɪ] *n* **(a)** *(incentive)* encouragement *m*; **to give a s. to trade** donner un coup de fouet au commerce; *Mktg* **s. response** réponse *f* stimulée **(b)** *Physiol* stimulus *m*; **to apply a s. to a muscle** exciter un muscle

sting¹ [stɪŋ] *n* **(a)** *(of bee)* dard *m*, aiguillon *m*; *(of scorpion)* aiguillon; *(of nettle)* poil *m* piquant **(b)** *(injury) (from wasp etc)* piqûre *f*; *Fig (of joke)* pointe *f*; *(of wound)* douleur *f* cuisante; *(of attack)* vigueur *f*, mordant *m*; **with the s. of the wind in our faces** le visage fouetté par le vent; **joke with a s. in it** plaisanterie qui comporte une pointe; **to have a s. in the tail** *(of story etc)* avoir une fin inattendue; *Lit* **the s. of remorse** l'aiguillon du remords; *Fig* **to take the s. out of sth** affaiblir qch **(c)** *esp US Sl (con trick)* arnaque *f*; *(by police)* coup *m* monté

sting² *(pt, pp* **stung** [stʌŋ]) **1** *vt* **(a)** *(of bees, nettles etc)* piquer; **a bee stung her finger** *or* **stung her on the finger** une abeille lui a piqué le doigt; **that reply stung her (to the quick)** cette réponse l'a piquée (au vif); **smoke that stings the eyes** fumée qui picote les yeux; **this stung him into action** cela l'a incité à agir

(b) *F (cheat)* **to s. sb for £50** rouler qn en lui faisant payer 50 livres, dépouiller qn de 50 livres; **to be stung** essuyer le coup de fusil; **could I s. you for a tenner?** *(borrow)* est-ce que je peux te taper dix livres?

2 *vi (of parts of the body)* cuire; *(of cut, graze)* picoter, brûler; *(of bees, nettles etc)* piquer; **my eyes were stinging** les yeux me brûlaient; **this is going to s. a bit** ça va faire un peu mal; **that stung!** *(of remark etc)* c'est blessant!

stingily ['stɪndʒɪlɪ] *adv* mesquinement, chichement

stinginess ['stɪndʒɪnɪs] *n (of person)* pingrerie *f*; *(of portion etc)* insuffisance *f*

stinging ['stɪŋɪŋ] *adj (pain etc)* cuisant; *(blow, answer)* cinglant; **s. nettle** ortie *f* brûlante; **s. remark** remarque *f* blessante

stingray ['stɪŋreɪ] *n (fish)* pastenague *f*

stingy ['stɪndʒɪ] *adj (person)* chiche, pingre; **a s. portion** une mini-portion; **to be s. with one's money** être avare (avec son argent); **to be s. with the cream** lésiner sur la crème

stink¹ [stɪŋk] *n* **(a)** *(smell)* puanteur *f* **(b)** *F (trouble)* grabuge *m*; **to raise** *or* **kick up a s.** faire un esclandre *ou* du grabuge; **there'll be a s.!** il va y avoir du grabuge

stink² *vi (pt* **stank** [stæŋk], **stunk** [stʌŋk]; *pp* **stunk)** *(of place, person etc)* puer, empester; **it stinks in here** ça pue ici; **to s. of garlic** puer *ou* empester l'ail; *F* **to s. of money** puer le fric; *F* **this film/book stinks!** ce film/livre est nul!; **the whole business stinks of corruption** tout ça sent la corruption à plein nez

▶ **stink out** *vtsep (fill with bad smell) (room etc)* empester

stinkbomb ['stɪŋkbɒm] *n* boule *f* puante

stinker ['stɪŋkər] *n F* **(a)** *(difficult problem, question etc)* casse-tête *m*, *pl* casse-tête(s); *(unpleasant letter)* lettre *f* carabinée; **the algebra paper was a s.** on a eu une composition d'algèbre carabinée; **I had a s. of a cold** j'avais un rhume carabiné **(b)** *(person)* individu *m* méprisable, salaud *m*

stinkhorn ['stɪŋkhɔːn] *n Bot* phallus *m* impudique

stinking ['stɪŋkɪŋ] **1** *adj* puant; *Sl (disgusting)* dégueulasse; **a s. cold** un gros rhume **2** *adv F* **to be s. rich** puer le fric

stinkpot ['stɪŋkpɒt] *n Old-fashioned, F (unpleasant person)* salaud *m*; **what a s.!** *(smelly)* qu'est-ce qu'il pue!

stint¹ [stɪnt] *n* **(a)** *(period)* temps *m*, période *f*; *(amount of work)* besogne *f* assignée; **to do one's daily s.** accomplir sa tâche quotidienne; **if you do a regular s. (with the weights/your clarinet)** si tu travailles régulièrement (tes haltères/ta clarinette); **do you want a s. at the wheel?** est-ce que tu veux prendre un peu le volant?; **I did the last s.** c'est moi qui ai pris le dernier tour; **after a long s. at the keyboard** après être resté longtemps au clavier; **she had a two-year s. in the army** elle a fait deux ans dans l'armée **(b)** *(restriction)* restriction *f*; **without s.** sans limite; *(to spend money)* sans compter

stint² *vt (money, effort)* épargner; **don't s. the cream/whisky** ne lésine pas sur la crème/le whisky; **to s. oneself** se sacrifier; **to s. sb of sth** priver qn de qch, refuser qch à qn; **to give without stinting** donner sans compter; **he doesn't s. his praise** il n'est pas avare de compliments

▶ **stint on** *vipo* lésiner sur

stipend ['staɪpend] *n* traitement *m*, appointements *mpl* (*d'un ecclésiastique, d'un magistrat*)

stipendiary [staɪ'pendjərɪ] **1** *adj* qui reçoit des appointements fixes; *Br* **s. magistrate** juge *m* d'un tribunal d'instance (*à Londres et dans les grandes villes*) **2** *n Br* = **stipendiary magistrate**

stipple ['stɪp(ə)l] *Art* **1** *vt* (*drawing*) faire en pointillé **2** *vi* pointiller

stipulate ['stɪpjʊleɪt] *vt* (*date, condition etc*) stipuler; **to s. (in writing) that ...** stipuler (par écrit) que ...; **within the period stipulated** dans le délai prescrit; **to s. the terms of a contract** fixer les conditions d'un contrat

stipulation [stɪpjʊ'leɪʃən] *n* condition *f*; *Jur* stipulation *f*; **the only s. I make is that ...** la seule condition que je pose c'est que ...; **on the s. that ...** à condition que ...

stir[1] [stɜːr] *n* (**a**) (*act of stirring liquid etc*) **to give sth a s.** remuer *ou* tourner qch (**b**) (*agitation*) agitation *f*, émoi *m*; **there was a great s.** il y eut un grand remue-ménage; **to make** *or* **cause a s.** faire du bruit, faire sensation; **the news caused a s. in the town** la nouvelle a mis la ville en émoi

stir[2] (**-rr-**) **1** *vt* (*set in motion*) (*leaves, water*) remuer, faire bouger; (*tea etc*) remuer, tourner; (*move emotionally*) (*person*) émouvoir, remuer; (*emotions*) agiter; (*curiosity, interest*) éveiller; *Culin* (*sauce, cream etc*) tourner; (*mixture*) agiter; (*fire*) activer, attiser; **not a breath stirs the leaves** pas un souffle ne remue *ou* ne fait trembler les feuilles; **to s. sb to pity** provoquer la compassion de qn; **events that s. the soul** événements qui remuent l'âme; **these words stirred her to action** ces mots l'ont fait agir; *F* **s. yourself** *or* **your stumps!** remue-toi!; *Br F* **to s. it** (*make trouble*) fomenter la discorde

2 *vi* (**a**) (*move*) bouger, remuer; **don't s. from here** ne bougez pas d'ici; **he did not s. out of the house** il n'est pas sorti de la maison; **he is not stirring yet** (*is still in bed*) il n'est pas encore levé; **to s. in one's sleep** remuer dans son sommeil; **the audience were stirring in their seats** les spectateurs s'agitaient dans leur fauteuil

(**b**) *Br F* (*set people against each other*) semer la zizanie

stir[3] *n Sl* (*prison*) taule *f*; **in s.** en taule

▶ **stir up** *vtsep* (**a**) (*salad etc*) remuer; (*of wind*) remuer, faire bouger; (*fire*) ranimer, activer (**b**) (*rebellion, dissent*) fomenter (**c**) (*workers, crowd etc*) inciter à la révolte; **to s. up hatred** attiser les haines; **to s. up trouble** fomenter la discorde; **to s. things up** faire bouger les choses

stir-crazy *adj esp Am Sl* fou, *f* folle, détraqué (*à cause d'une longue période de détention*)

stir-fry[1] *n* sauté *m*

stir-fry[2] *vt Culin* faire sauter *ou* frire rapidement; **stir-fried vegetables** légumes *mpl* sautés

stirrer ['stɜːrər] *n* (**a**) *Br F* (*person who provokes trouble*) personne *f* qui sème la zizanie (**b**) *Ch, Phot* (*device*) agitateur *m*

stirring ['stɜːrɪŋ] **1** *adj* (*moving*) émouvant; **s. times** une époque passionnante; **it's s. stuff** c'est passionnant **2** *n* (**a**) *Br F* (*troublemaking*) **s. is her speciality** semer la zizanie, c'est sa spécialité (**b**) **stirrings** (*beginnings*) frémissement *m*; **the first stirrings of passion** les premiers frémissements de la passion; **the first stirrings of revolt/resistance** les premiers signes de la révolte/de la résistance

stirrup ['stɪrəp] *n* (**a**) *Horseriding* étrier *m*; **to put one's feet in the stirrups** chausser les étriers; **s. cup** coup *m* de l'étrier; **s. leather** *or* **strap** étrivière *f*; **s. pump** pompe *f* portative (**b**) *Med* **stirrups** étriers *mpl*

stitch[1] [stɪtʃ] *n* (**a**) *Sewing* point *m*; (*in knitting, crochet*) maille *f*; *Surg* (point de) suture *f*; (**machine**) **s.** piqûre *f* (à la machine); **to put a few stitches in a garment** faire un point à un vêtement; *F* **he hasn't got a dry s. on him** il est trempé jusqu'aux os; *F* **without a s. on** nu comme un ver; **to drop a s.** (*in knitting, crochet*) sauter une maille; **dropped s.** (*in knitting, crochet*) maille coulée; **to make a s.** (*in knitting, crochet*) faire une maille; **to put stitches in a wound** faire une suture à *ou* suturer une plaie, recoudre une plaie; **she had to have ten stitches** ils ont dû lui faire dix points de suture; **when are you having the stitches out?** quand allez-vous vous faire retirer vos points de suture?; *Prov* **a s. in time saves nine** un point à temps en épargne cent, un point fait à temps en vaut mille

(**b**) (*pain*) **s. (in the side)** point *m* de côté; **I've got a s.** j'ai un point de côté

(**c**) *F* **we were in stitches** (*laughing*) on se tordait de rire; **his story/the film had us in stitches** son histoire était tordante/le film était tordant *ou* à se tordre de rire; **he had us in stitches** il nous a fait (nous) tordre de rire

stitch[2] *vt* (**a**) (*clothing*) coudre; (*leather*) piquer; **to (machine) s.** piquer (à la machine); **to s. sth onto sth** coudre qch sur qch (**b**) *Surg* (*wound*) suturer (**c**) (*in bookbinding*) (*book*) brocher

▶ **stitch down** *vtsep* coudre; (*repair*) recoudre

▶ **stitch up** *vtsep* (**a**) (*repair by sewing*) (*bag etc*) recoudre (**b**) (*of surgeon*) (*person, wound*) recoudre; **we'll soon have you stitched up** on va vous faire quelques points de suture et ce sera fini (**c**) *Sl* (*falsely incriminate*) faire porter le chapeau à; **I've been stitched up** on m'a fait porter le chapeau

stitching ['stɪtʃɪŋ] *n* (**a**) (*act*), *Sewing* couture *f*; (*in leather*) piqûre *f*; (*ornamental*) broderie *f*; *Surg* suture *f*; (*in bookbinding*) brochage *m*, brochure *f* (**b**) *Sewing* (*stitches*) points *mpl*, piqûres *fpl*; **the stitching's coming undone** les piqûres se sont défaites

stoat [stəʊt] *n* hermine *f*

stochastic [stɒ'kæstɪk] *adj* stochastique

stock[1] [stɒk] *n* (**a**) (*supply*) provision *f*, approvisionnement *m*, stock *m*; (*in forestry*) peuplement *m*; *Ind* stock; **s. of plays** répertoire *m*; **to lay in a s. of food** faire provision de vivres, s'approvisionner en vivres; *Com* **s. (in trade)** marchandises *fpl* (en magasin), stock; *Fig* **double entendre was her s. in trade** l'ambiguïté, c'était sa spécialité; **old s.** fonds *mpl* de boutique; **surplus s.** surplus *mpl*; **s. in hand** marchandises *fpl ou* existence *f* en magasin, stock; **stocks are low** il y a peu de marchandises en stock; **while stocks last** jusqu'à épuisement des stocks; **to take s.** *Com* faire *ou* dresser l'inventaire; *Fig* faire le bilan; *Fig* **to take s. of sb** évaluer qn; (*by looking at*) toiser qn; **to take s. of the situation** faire le bilan de la situation, faire le point de la situation; **in s.** en magasin, en stock; **to be out of s.** (*of goods*) manquer en magasin; (*of book*) être épuisé; **we're out of s.** nous sommes en rupture de stock; *Rail* **locomotive s.** effectif *m ou* dotation *f* en locomotives; *Cin* (**film**) **s.** film *m* vierge, films *ou* bandes *fpl* vierges; **s. availability** disponibilité *f* en stock; **s. book** livre *m* des inventaires; **s. issued docket** bon *m* de sortie; **s. keeping** tenue *f* des stocks; **s. level** niveau *m* de stock; **s. outage** rupture *f* de stock; **s. received docket** bon d'entrée; **s. replacement** renouvellement *m* des stocks; **s. sheet** fiche *f* de stock; **s. shrinkage** coulage *m* de stock; **s. turnaround** *or* **turnover** rotation *f* des stocks

(**b**) (*livestock*) bétail *m*; **grazing s.** bétail, animaux *mpl* sur pied; **fat s.** bétail de boucherie

(**c**) *Fin* fonds *mpl*, valeurs *fpl*, actions *fpl*; **government s.** fonds d'État, fonds *ou* effets *mpl* publics, rentes *fpl* (sur l'État); *Fig* **her s. is going up/down** ses actions sont en hausse/en baisse; **stocks and shares** valeurs mobilières, valeurs de bourse, titres *mpl*; **s. index** indice *m* boursier

(**d**) (*of tree*) (*trunk*) tronc *m*; (*stump*) bloc *m*; (*in horticulture*) sujet *m*, ente *f*, porte-greffe *m*; *Fig* (*lineage*) souche *f*; **he's of German s.** il est d'origine allemande

(**e**) (*of rifle*) fût *m*, bois *m*, monture *f*; (*of whip*) manche *m*; (*of plough*) macheron *m*; *Naut* (*of anchor*) jas *m*

(**f**) *Naut* **stocks** cales *fpl*; **to be on the stocks** être sur cales, être en construction; *Fig* (*of new novel etc*) être en chantier

(**g**) **stocks** (*for punishment*) pilori *m*

(**h**) *Ind* (*raw materials*) matières *fpl* premières

(**i**) *Culin* **beef/chicken/vegetable s.** bouillon *m* de bœuf/poulet/légumes

(**j**) (*plant*) matthiole *f*, giroflée *f* des jardins

(**k**) (*neckwear*) col-cravate *m* (*d'équitation*), *pl* cols-cravates; (*of English clergy*) plastron *m* en soie noire

stock[2] *adj* (*conventional*) habituel; **he has three s. speeches** il a, en tout et pour tout, trois discours qu'il ressort périodiquement; **s. answer** réponse *f* classique; *Th* **s. company** troupe *f* à demeure (*dans une ville*); **s. phrase** expression *f* toute faite, expression consacrée; *Th* **s. play** *or* **piece** pièce *f* de *ou* du répertoire; *TV* **s. shot** image *f ou* document *m* d'archives

stock[3] *vt* (**a**) (*supply*) (*shop*) approvisionner (**with** de, en); (*farm*) monter en bétail; (*house*) approvisionner (**with** de); (*pond*) empoissonner; (*forest*) peupler (**with** de); **this shop is well stocked** ce magasin est bien approvisionné; **to have a well-stocked cellar** avoir une cave bien remplie (**b**) (*have, keep in stock*) (*goods*) avoir *ou* tenir *ou* garder en magasin *ou* en dépôt, stocker; **I don't s. this article** je ne vends pas cet article; **we s. all leading makes of furniture** nous faisons toutes les grandes marques de meubles

▶ **stock up 1** *vi* (*build up a stock*) faire des provisions *ou* des réserves; **to s. up with sth** bien s'approvisionner en *ou* de qch **2** *vtsep* (*larder, cellar*) approvisionner

stockade[1] [stɒ'keɪd] *n* (**a**) (*fort*) palissade *f*, palanque *f* (**b**) *US Mil* (*prison*) bloc *m*; **to be in the s.** être au bloc

stockade[2] *vt* palissader, palanquer

stock breeder *n* éleveur *m*

stock breeding *n* élevage *m*

stockbroker [ˈstɒkbrəʊkər] *n* agent *m* de change; *Br F* **s. belt** banlieue *f* aisée
stock-car *n Sp* stock-car *m*; **s. racing** course *f* de stock-cars
stock check *n* contrôle *m* des stocks
stock control *n Com* gestion *f* des stocks; **s. system** système *m* de contrôle de stocks
stock cube *n* bouillon-cube *m*, *pl* bouillons-cubes, bouillon *m* en cube
Stock Exchange *n* Bourse *f* (*de Londres*)
stock exchange *n* bourse *f* des valeurs
stock farm *n* élevage *m*
stock farmer *n* éleveur *m*
stock farming *n* élevage *m*
stockfish [ˈstɒkfɪʃ] *n* stockfisch *m*, merluche *f*
stockholder [ˈstɒkhəʊldər] *n Fin* actionnaire *mf*, porteur *m ou* détenteur *m* de titres
stockily [ˈstɒkɪlɪ] *adv* **s. built** trapu
stockiness [ˈstɒkɪnɪs] *n* stature *f* trapue
stockinet(te) [stɒkɪˈnet] *n Tex* **wool/cotton s.** jersey *m* de laine/coton
stocking [ˈstɒkɪŋ] *n* (*garment*) bas *m*; *Old-fashioned* (*knee-length sock*) chaussette *f*; *Med* **elastic** *or* **support s.** bas à varices; **body s.** combinaison *f* (une pièce); **s. filler** petit cadeau *m* de Noël; **s. mask** = bas utilisé comme masque par les bandits; *Knitting* **s. stitch** (point *m* de) jersey *m*
stockist [ˈstɒkɪst] *n Com* revendeur *m*; (*agent*) stockiste *m*
stock keeper *n Com* magasinier *m*
stockless purchase plan [ˈstɒklɪs] *n Com* plan *m* d'achat sans stock
stock list *n St Exch* cours *mpl* de la Bourse; *Com* inventaire *m*, inventaire des stocks
stockman, *pl* **-men** [ˈstɒkmən] *n* **(a)** (*man who works with livestock*) gardien *m* de bestiaux; (*owner*) bouvier *m* **(b)** *Am* (*warehouseman*) magasinier *m*
stock market 1 *n Com* marché *m* des titres *ou* des valeurs, marché boursier **2** *adj* boursier; **s. crash** krach *m* boursier; **s. gamble** spéculation *f* boursière; **s. value** valeur *f* en Bourse
stockpile¹ [ˈstɒkpaɪl] *n* (*of sugar, ammunition etc*) stocks *mpl* de réserve *ou* de sécurité; **nuclear s.** réserve(s) *f*(*pl*) d'armements nucléaires
stockpile² *vt* (*goods*) stocker; (*arms*) entasser, accumuler
stockpiling [ˈstɒkpaɪlɪŋ] *n* stockage *m*, constitution *f* de réserves; (*of nuclear weapons*) accumulation *f*
stockpot [ˈstɒkpɒt] *n Culin* marmite *f*
stock rider *n Austr* cowboy *m*
stockroom [ˈstɒkruːm] *n* magasin *m*, réserve *f*, resserre *f*
stock-still *adv* **to stand s.** rester (complètement) immobile; **he suddenly stood s.** soudain, il s'immobilisa
stock take *n* inventaire *m* des stocks
stocktaking [ˈstɒkteɪkɪŋ] *n Com, Ind* (établissement *m ou* levée *f* d')inventaire *m*, inventaire des stocks; **s. is in February** on fait l'inventaire en février
stocky [ˈstɒkɪ] *adj* trapu; (*horse*) ragot
stockyard [ˈstɒkjɑːd] *n* parc *m* à bétail *ou* à bestiaux
stodge [stɒdʒ] *n F* (*food*) aliment *m* bourratif, étouffe-chrétien *m*; **the s. we get in the canteen** les trucs bourratifs qu'on nous sert à la cantine
stodgy [ˈstɒdʒɪ] *adj* **(a)** (*meal, food*) bourratif **(b)** (*book*) indigeste; (*style*) lourd; (*person*) ennuyeux à force de sérieux, assommant
stogie [ˈstəʊgɪ] *n Am* cigare *m* bon marché, *pl* cigares bon marché
stoic [ˈstəʊɪk] *adj, n* stoïque *mf*; *Antiq* **S.** stoïcien, -ienne
stoical [ˈstəʊɪk(ə)l] *adj* stoïque
stoically [ˈstəʊɪklɪ] *adv* stoïquement
stoicism [ˈstəʊɪsɪz(ə)m] *n* stoïcisme *m*
stoke [stəʊk] *vt* (*fire*) entretenir; (*furnace*) alimenter, entretenir le feu de; (*steam engine*) chauffer le foyer de; *Fig F* **the way he stokes his food in** la façon dont il engouffre sa nourriture
▶ **stoke up 1** *vtsep* = **stoke 2** *vi* **(a)** *Naut* pousser les feux; *Rail* alimenter le feu **(b)** *F* (*eat heavily*) bouffer (comme quatre), bâfrer
▶ **stoke up on** *vipo F* (*eat a lot of*) se bourrer de
stoker [ˈstəʊkər] *n Rail* chauffeur *m*; *Naut* mécanicien *m*; (*of blast furnace*) chargeur *m*
STOL [stɒl] *n Mil, Av* (*abbr* **short takeoff and landing**) **(a)** (*system*) décollage *m* et atterrissage *m* courts **(b)** (*aircraft*) ADAC *m*
stole¹ [stəʊl] *n* **(a)** *Rel* étole *f* **(b)** (*garment*) étole *f* (*de vison etc*)
stole² *see* **steal²**
stolen¹ [ˈstəʊlən] *adj* (*car, property etc*) volé; **s. goods** objets volés; **he was charged with receiving s. goods** on l'a inculpé de recel (de marchandises volées)
stolen² *see* **steal²**
stolid [ˈstɒlɪd] *adj* flegmatique, impassible; **his s. exterior concealed ...** sous des dehors impassibles, il cachait ...
stolidity [stɒˈlɪdɪtɪ] *n* flegme *m*
stolidly [ˈstɒlɪdlɪ] *adv* flegmatiquement
stolidness [ˈstɒlɪdnɪs] *n* flegme *m*
stoma, *pl* **-ata** [ˈstəʊmə, -ətə] *n* stomate *m*
stomach¹ [ˈstʌmək] *n* (*organ*) estomac *m*; (*front of abdomen*) ventre *m*; **pain in the s.** mal *m* d'estomac; **upset s., s. upset** troubles *mpl* de la digestion; *Pharm* **to be taken on an empty s.** à prendre à jeun; **to drink on an empty s.** boire lorsqu'on a l'estomac vide, boire à jeun; **to turn sb's s.** soulever le cœur à qn, écœurer qn; **to have a cast iron s.** avoir un estomac à toute épreuve *ou* d'autruche; **an army marches on its s.** une armée ne se bat pas le ventre vide; **first s.** (*of ruminants*) panse *f*; **to have a large s.** (*be fat*) avoir un gros ventre; **s. ache** douleurs *fpl* d'estomac, *F* mal *m* de ventre; **to have s. ache** avoir mal au ventre; **s. pump** pompe *f* stomacale; *Fig* **to have no s. for sth** (*not feel like*) ne pas se sentir d'humeur à qch; *Fig* **he had no s. for a fight** il n'avait pas le cœur à se battre
stomach² *vt* (*support*) (*sth*) supporter, endurer; (*person*) supporter; **I can't s. it any longer** j'en ai plein le dos, j'en ai ras le bol; **I can't s. oysters** je ne peux pas avaler les huîtres
stomp [stɒmp] *vi* frapper du pied; **to s. out of the room** quitter la pièce en martelant des pieds; **I wish you wouldn't s. around like that** j'aimerais que tu arrêtes de marteler des pieds comme ça; **he was stomping up and down** il arpentait la pièce d'un pas lourd; **she stomped off** elle est partie en tapant des pieds
stone¹ [stəʊn] *n* **(a)** (*piece of rock*) pierre *f*; (*pebble*) caillou *m*, -oux; *Constr* mœllon *m*, pierre de taille; (*gravestone*) pierre tombale; **not to leave a s. standing** tout raser *ou* démolir; **to throw stones at sb** lancer des pierres sur *ou* à qn; *Fig* **who's going to cast the first s. (at him)?** qui lui jettera la (première) pierre?; *Fig* **to leave no s. unturned** mettre tout en œuvre, remuer ciel et terre (**to do sth** pour accomplir qch); **a s. 's throw from here** à deux pas d'ici
(b) (*precious stone*) pierre *f*; **precious stones** (*in raw state*) pierres précieuses; (*cut*) pierreries *fpl*, pierres précieuses
(c) (*material*) pierre *f* (*à bâtir*); **the S. Age** l'âge de (la) pierre; **s. axe** hache *f* de pierre; **s. coloured** beige; **s. cutter** (*person who cuts blocks*) tailleur *m ou* équarrisseur *m* de pierres; **s. floor** sol *m* dallé; **s. jug** cruche *f* de grès; **s. saw** scie *f* à pierre *ou* de carrier
(d) *Med* calcul *m*
(e) (*of fruit*) noyau *m*
(f) *Br* (*unit of weight*) = 6,348kg
stone² *vt* **(a)** (*fruit*) dénoyauter **(b)** (*person*) attaquer *ou* assaillir à coups de pierres, lapider; (*as punishment*) lapider; (*car etc*) lancer des pierres contre; **to s. sb to death** lapider qn (*jusqu'à ce que mort s'ensuive*); *Br Sl* **s. the crows!, s. me!** ça alors!
stone-blind *adj* complètement aveugle
stonechat [ˈstəʊntʃæt] *n* (*bird*) traquet *m* pâtre
stone-cold 1 *adj* froid comme le marbre; **the tea is s.** ce thé est complètement froid *ou* glacé **2** *adv* **s. sober** complètement sobre
stonecrop [ˈstəʊnkrɒp] *n* (*plant*) orpin *m*
stoned [stəʊnd] *adj* **(a)** *Sl* **to be s.** (*on drugs*) être pété *ou* défoncé; (*drunk*) être bourré **(b)** (*fruit*) dénoyauté
stone-dead 1 *adj* raide mort **2** *adv* raide mort; **the blow killed him s.** le coup l'a tué instantanément; *Fig* **to kill a proposal s.** sonner le glas d'une proposition; **the teacher killed French s. for her** le professeur l'a complètement dégoûtée du français
stone-deaf *adj* complètement sourd, sourd comme un pot
stoneground [ˈstəʊngraʊnd] *adj* (*flour*) à l'ancienne
stonemason [ˈstəʊnmeɪs(ə)n] *n* maçon *m*
stone sub *n Journ* correcteur *m* de mise en page
stonewall [stəʊnˈwɔːl] *vi* **(a)** *Sp* pratiquer un jeu défensif pour tenir jusqu'à la fin **(b)** *Parl, Fig* faire de l'obstruction
stonewalling [stəʊnˈwɔːlɪŋ] *n* **(a)** *Sp* jeu *m* défensif **(b)** *Parl, Fig* obstructionnisme *m*
stoneware [ˈstəʊnweər] *n* poterie *f* de grès
stonewashed [ˈstəʊnwɒʃt] *adj* (*jeans etc*) délavé
stonework [ˈstəʊnwɜːk] *n* maçonnerie *f*
stonily [ˈstəʊnɪlɪ] *adv* froidement; (*to look at sb*) d'un air glacial; (*to reply*) d'un ton glacial
stoniness [ˈstəʊnɪnɪs] *n* **(a)** (*of soil*) nature *f* pierreuse **(b)** (*of heart*) dureté *f*; (*of look*) froideur *f*
stoning [ˈstəʊnɪŋ] *n* (*of person*) lapidation *f*
stony [ˈstəʊnɪ] *adj* **(a)** (*full of, covered in stones*) pierreux, rocailleux **(b)** (*hard like stone*) dur comme la pierre **(c)** (*lacking in emotion*) dur; (*reception*) froid; (*look, stare,*

silence) glacial, -ials *ou* -iaux; **s. heart** cœur *m* de glace *ou* de marbre **(d)** *Br F* **s. broke** sans le sou, dans la dèche; **I'm s. broke** je n'ai pas un sou, je suis fauché (comme les blés)

stony-hearted [stəʊnɪ'hɑːtɪd] *adj* au cœur de pierre; **to be** *or* **remain s.** être *ou* rester de glace *ou* marbre; **he's s.** il a un cœur de pierre

stood *see* **stand**[2]

stooge[1] [stuːdʒ] *n* **(a)** *Th* faire-valoir *m inv* (*d'un comique*) **(b)** *Fig, F* (*person who is manipulated*) larbin *m*

stooge[2] *vi Th* **to s. for a comedian** servir de faire-valoir à un comique

stook[1] [stuːk] *n Agr* tas *m* de gerbes, moyette *f*

stook[2] *vt Agr* mettre en moyettes

stool [stuːl] *n* **(a)** (*seat*) tabouret *m*; (*with steps*) escabeau *m*; **folding s.** pliant *m*; **piano s.** tabouret de piano; *Fig* **to fall between two stools** être assis entre deux chaises; **prayer s.** prie-Dieu *m inv* **(b)** *Med* **stools** selles *fpl*, fèces *fpl* **(c)** (*in horticulture*), *Agr* pied *m* mère, plante *f* mère

stool pigeon *n F* (*informer*) indicateur, -trice, *F* indic *mf*, balance *f*

stoop[1] [stuːp] *n* (*posture*) dos *m* rond, épaules *fpl* voûtées; **to have a s.** avoir le dos rond *ou* les épaules voûtées; **to walk with a s.** marcher les épaules voûtées, marcher voûté

stoop[2] **1** *vi* (*bend down*) se pencher, se baisser; (*have bent back*) avoir le dos rond, être voûté; *Fig* (*abase oneself*) s'abaisser, s'avilir (**to do sth** à *ou* jusqu'à faire qch); (*deign*) daigner (**to do sth** faire qch); *Lit* **to s. to conquer** s'abaisser pour triompher; **she stooped to pick up the pin** elle s'est baissée pour ramasser l'épingle; **he was beginning to s.** il commençait à se voûter; *Fig* **he would s. to anything** c'est un homme prêt à toutes les bassesses; *Fig* **I never thought they'd s. so low as to ...** je ne pensais pas qu'ils s'abaisseraient jusqu'à ... **2** *vt* (*head*) pencher, incliner; (*back*) courber, arrondir

stoop[3] *n Am* (*porch*) porche *m* (*avec perron*); (*platform*) terrasse *f* surélevée (*devant une maison*)

stooping ['stuːpɪŋ] *adj* penché (en avant); (*permanently*) voûté

stop[1] [stɒp] *n* **(a)** (*halt*) arrêt *m*; (*pause*) arrêt, halte *f*, pause *f*; *Av* (*in flight*) escale *f*; **to put a s. to sth** arrêter *ou* faire cesser qch, mettre fin à qch; **ten minutes' s.** dix minutes d'arrêt; **to come to a s.** s'arrêter; (*of car*) stopper; **to make a s.** faire (une) halte; (*for short period*) faire une pause; **we made four stops along the way** nous nous sommes arrêtés *ou* nous avons fait halte quatre fois en chemin; **the bus/train makes a s. at ...** le bus/le train s'arrête à ...; **to bring sth to a s.** arrêter qch; **let's have a s. for lunch** faisons une pause pour le déjeuner; **we travelled without a s.** nous avons voyagé sans escale; **we had a s. at the castle on the way back** nous nous sommes arrêtés au château sur le chemin du retour; **(bus) s.** arrêt (d'autobus); **request s.** arrêt facultatif; *Aut* **s. sign** stop *m*; *Am* **s. street** = rue *f* non prioritaire

(b) (*full stop*) point *m*; (*in telegram*) stop *m*

(c) *Mus* (*on organ*) jeu *m*, registre *m*; **to pull out a s.** tirer un registre; *Fig F* **to pull out all the stops** faire un effort surhumain (**to do sth** pour faire qch)

(d) *Carp, MecE etc* dispositif *m* de blocage, arrêt *m*, taquet *m*, butée *f*; (*for door*) heurtoir *m*; *MecE* (*for end of travel*) butoir *m*

(e) *Opt, Phot* (*of lens*) diaphragme *m*; *Phot* **s. bath** bain *m* d'arrêt

(f) *Ling* occlusive *f*

stop[2] **(-pp-) 1** *vt* **(a)** (*halt*) arrêter; (*traffic*) arrêter, interrompre; (*clock*) arrêter; (*machine*) arrêter, stopper; *Boxing* (*blow*) parer; (*fight*) interrompre; (*abuse, evil practice, rumours*) mettre fin à, faire cesser; (*strike*) briser, enrayer; **s. thief!** au voleur!; **to s. an opponent** *Fb* arrêter un adversaire; *Boxing* mettre un adversaire K.O.; **this bullet will s. a man at 200 metres** cette balle arrêtera un homme à 200 mètres; *Mil Sl* **to s. a bullet** prendre une balle; **the curtains s. the light** les rideaux cachent la lumière; **to s. sb's doing sth** *or* **sb (from) doing sth** empêcher qn de faire qch; **I couldn't s. myself** je n'ai pas pu m'en empêcher; **to s. sth being done** empêcher que qch (ne) se fasse; **nothing will s. her** rien ne l'arrêtera; **what's stopping you?** qu'est-ce qui vous retient?, qu'est-ce qui vous en empêche?; **to s. the bleeding** arrêter l'hémorragie; **dumping nuclear waste should be stopped** il faut qu'on arrête de jeter n'importe où les déchets nucléaires; **it ought to be stopped** (*put an end to*) il faut que cela cesse

(b) (*cease*) (*efforts, visits, work*) cesser; *Com* **to s. payment** cesser les paiements; **to s. doing sth** arrêter *ou* cesser de faire qch; **to s. smoking/drinking** s'arrêter *ou* cesser de fumer/boire; **he never stops talking** il n'arrête pas de parler, il parle sans cesse; **s. that noise!** arrête ce bruit!; **s. it!** (*to naughty child*) ça suffit!, assez!; (*you're hurting me*) arrête!; **it has stopped raining** il a cessé de pleuvoir, la pluie a cessé

(c) (*block*) (*hole*) boucher, fermer; (*pipe*) obstruer, obturer; *Br* (*tooth*) plomber; **to s. one's ears** se boucher les oreilles; **to s. a gap** (*around door etc*) boucher un espace; *Fig* combler une lacune; *Com* **to s. (payment of) a cheque** faire opposition à un chèque; **to s. sb's wages** retenir le salaire de qn; **to s. so much out of sb's wages** faire une retenue de tant sur le salaire de qn; **to s. sb's pension** supprimer la pension de qn; *Mil* **all leave is stopped** toutes les troupes sont consignées, toutes les permissions sont suspendues

(d) (*in horticulture*) (*plant*) pincer

(e) *Mus* **to s. a string** presser une corde; **to s. a flute** boucher les trous d'une flûte

2 *vi* **(a)** (*halt*) s'arrêter; (*of ship, car*) s'arrêter, stopper; **to s. short** *or* **dead** s'arrêter net *ou F* pile; **to s. and talk to sb** s'arrêter pour parler à qn; **to do a hundred kilometres without stopping** faire cent kilomètres sans s'arrêter *ou* sans arrêt *ou* (tout) d'une traite; **we stopped in Caen** nous nous sommes arrêtés à Caen; **to go through a station without stopping** passer dans une gare sans s'y arrêter; *Naut* **to s. at a port** faire escale à *ou* dans un port

(b) (*cease*) (*of rain, pain, headache, person doing sth*) s'arrêter, cesser; **my watch has stopped** ma montre s'est arrêtée; **to work fifteen hours without stopping** travailler pendant quinze heures d'affilée *ou* de suite; **to s. for lunch** faire une pause pour déjeuner; **he never stops** (*working, talking etc*) il ne s'arrête jamais; **she stopped in the middle of a sentence** elle s'arrêta au milieu d'une phrase; **he never stops to think** il ne prend jamais le temps de réfléchir; **she doesn't know when to s.** elle ne sait pas s'arrêter; **she did not s. at that** elle ne s'en tint pas là; **he'll s. at nothing** rien ne l'arrêtera; **s. a moment!** arrêtez un instant!; **the matter will not s. there** l'affaire n'en demeurera pas là; **the rain has stopped** la pluie a cessé

(c) (*stay*) rester; **to s. at home** rester à la maison; **she's stopping with us for a few days** elle est venue passer quelques jours chez nous; **we decided to s. at a hotel** nous avons décidé de descendre à l'hôtel; **we stopped at a hotel for two weeks** nous avons passé deux semaines à l'hôtel

▶ **stop away** *vi* (*not come*) ne pas venir; (*not go*) ne pas y aller

▶ **stop by** *vi* (*visit briefly*) faire une petite visite; **s. by any time** tu peux passer quand tu veux; **I'll s. by at the post office on my way home** je passerai à la poste en rentrant à la maison; **we'll s. by and see you next week** nous passerons te voir la semaine prochaine

▶ **stop down** *vi Phot* réduire l'ouverture

▶ **stop in** *vi* **(a)** (*visit*) **to s. in to see sb** passer voir qn **(b)** *Br* (*stay at home*) rester chez soi

▶ **stop off** *vi* (*stay briefly*) faire (une) halte; **they're stopping off at Bali for a couple of days on their way home** ils font étape à Bali pour quelques jours en rentrant

▶ **stop out** *vi Br* (*not come home*) **to s. out all night** découcher, ne pas rentrer de toute la nuit; **to s. out (till) late** rentrer tard

▶ **stop over** *vi* (*stay briefly*) faire escale, faire halte; **we stopped over at Manchester on the flight to Toronto** nous avons fait escale à Manchester en route pour Toronto

▶ **stop up 1** *vtsep* (*block*) (*hole*) boucher; (*pipe*) obstruer, obturer **2** *vi* **(a)** *Br* (*not go to bed*) **to s. up late** veiller tard; **to s. up all night** veiller toute la nuit **(b)** *Phot* augmenter l'ouverture

stop-(and-)go *adj* **s. policy** alternance *f* de coups de frein et d'accélérations, stop-and-go *m inv*

stop bit *n Comptr* bit *m* d'arrêt

stopcock ['stɒpkɒk] *n* robinet *m* d'arrêt

stop code *n Comptr* code *m* d'arrêt

stopgap ['stɒpgæp] *n* bouche-trou *m*, *pl* bouche-trous; **s. measure** pis-aller *m inv*

stoplight ['stɒplaɪt] *n* **(a)** (*in street*) feu *m* rouge **(b)** (*on car*) stop *m*

stop-limit order *n St Exch* ordre *m* stop à cour limité

stop-list *n Banking* (*for lost cheques*) liste *f* de chèques volés ou perdus

stop(-)off *n* escale *f*

stopover ['stɒpəʊvər] *n* (*break in journey*) escale *f*; *Rail* (*option of breaking journey*) faculté *f* d'arrêt; **s. ticket** billet *m* avec (faculté d')arrêt

stoppage ['stɒpɪdʒ] *n* **(a)** (*of traffic*) arrêt *m*, interruption *f*; *Mil etc* (*of pay, leave*) suspension *f*; (*of work*) arrêt, interruption; (*by discontented employees*) débrayage *m*; (*longer*) grève *f* **(b)** (*obstruction*) (*of pipe*) obstruction *f*, engorgement *m*; *Med* occlusion *f* **(c)** (*of salary*) retenue *f*

stopper[1] ['stɒpər] *n* (*of bottle etc*) bouchon *m*; (*of pipe*) obturateur *m*

stopper² *vt* (*carafe, flask etc*) boucher
stopping ['stɒpɪŋ] **1** *adj Rail* **s. train** train *m* omnibus **2** *n* **(a) s. place** (point *m* d')arrêt *m*, halte *f* **(b)** (*act of ending*) cessation *f*; (*of service*) suppression *f*; **s. of payment** suspension *f* de paiement **(c)** *Br* (*in tooth*) plombage *m*
stop-press *adj, n Br Journ* **s. (news)** informations *fpl* de dernière heure
stopwatch ['stɒpwɒtʃ] *n* chronomètre *m*; **they used a s. to time them** ils les ont chronométrés
storage ['stɔːrɪdʒ] *n* **(a)** (*act of storing*), *Com, El* emmagasinage *m*, emmagasinement *m*; (*of heat*) accumulation *f*; *Comptr* stockage *m*; **to put sth into s.** mettre qch en dépôt; *Comptr* **s. capacity** capacité *f* de stockage; *El* **s. cell** élément *m* d'accumulateur; *Com* **s. costs** frais *mpl* d'entreposage; *Comptr* **s. device** dispositif *m* de stockage; **(night) s. heater** radiateur *m* à accumulation (*qui fonctionne pendant la nuit*); *Comptr* **s. medium** support *m* de stockage; **s. tank** (*for petrol, water*) réservoir *m* d'emmagasinage *ou* de stockage; (*for water*) citerne *f*; *Aut* **s. tray** vide-poche *m*; **s. unit** (*furniture*) meuble *m ou* élément de rangement
(b) (*available space*) (*in store, for storing*) espace *m* disponible; (*of business*) entrepôts *mpl*, magasins *mpl*; **the kitchen has plenty of s. space** la cuisine a beaucoup d'espace de rangement; **there is additional s. for luggage in the rack above your head** vous pouvez également déposer vos bagages dans les casiers au-dessus de vos têtes
(c) (*cost*) frais *mpl* d'entrepôt, magasinage *m*
store¹ [stɔːr] *n* **(a)** (*supply*) provision *f*, approvisionnement *m*; **to have a good s. of wine** avoir une bonne cave; **a s. of jokes** un stock d'histoires drôles; **his vast s. of knowledge** ses vastes connaissances, sa culture impressionnante; **to lay in a s. of sth** faire une provision de qch, s'approvisionner en qch; **to lay in stores** s'approvisionner; **to hold** *or* **keep sth in s.** tenir *ou* garder qch en réserve; **what the future holds in s. for us** ce que l'avenir nous réserve; **I have a surprise in s. for her** je lui ménage *ou* réserve une surprise; **to set great/little s. by sth** faire grand/peu de cas de qch
(b) stores (*supplies*) provisions *fpl*, approvisionnement *m*; (*food and drink*) provisions, vivres *mpl*
(c) *Com, Ind* (*warehouse etc*) entrepôt *m*, magasin *m*; (*for furniture*) garde-meuble *m*, *pl* garde-meubles; *Mil, Naut* (*in barracks*) magasin
(d) *esp Am* (*shop*) magasin *m*; **general s.** épicerie *f*; *not Am* **the village s.** l'épicerie du village; **toy/book s.** magasin de jouets/librairie *f*; *not Am* **(department** *or* **big) s.** grand magasin; *Mktg* **s. audit** contrôle *m* des points de vente; *Mktg* **s. brand** marque *f* de magasin; **s. manager** chef *m* de magasin
(e) *Comptr* mémoire *f*
store² **1** *vt* **(a)** (*put in a store*) (*hay, corn*) emmagasiner; (*beetroot etc*) mettre en silo; (*take into store*) (*furniture*) prendre en dépôt; (*put in store*) (*furniture*) mettre en dépôt; **squirrels s. food for the winter** les écureuils font des provisions pour l'hiver
(b) (*accumulate*) amasser, accumuler; (*put in reserve*) mettre en réserve; (*electricity, heat*) emmagasiner; **s. in a cool place** conserver au frais
(c) *Comptr* stocker
(d) (*supply*) approvisionner **(with** en); **he stored the larder with enough tinned goods to last the winter** il a rempli le placard avec assez de boîtes de conserve pour passer l'hiver
2 *vi* **goods that don't s. well** marchandises qui ne se conservent *ou* ne se gardent pas bien
▶ **store away** *vtsep* (*put away for future*) emmagasiner; *Fig* **he's storing it all away** il enregistre tout
▶ **store up** *vtsep* = **store² 1 (b)**; **to s. up problems for oneself** se garantir des problèmes pour l'avenir; **feelings of resentment that have been stored up over the years** des sentiments d'amertume qui se sont accumulés au fil des ans
store-bought *adj* qu'on trouve dans le commerce
store detective *n* vigile *m*
storefront ['stɔːfrʌnt] *n Am* devanture *f* de magasin
storehouse ['stɔːhaʊs] *n* magasin *m*, entrepôt *m*, dépôt *m*; *Fig* **a s. of information** une mine de renseignements
storekeeper ['stɔːkiːpər] *n* magasinier *m*; (*in hospital*) dépensier, -ière; *Am* (*shopkeeper*) commerçant, -ante
storeroom ['stɔːruːm] *n* (*for food*) office *m*; (*for old furniture etc*) débarras *m*; (*in school, offices etc*) réserve *f*; *Ind* halle *f* de dépôt; *Naut* soute *f* aux vivres *ou* à provisions, magasin *m*, cambuse *f*
store(s)man, *pl* **-men** ['stɔː(z)mən] *n* manutentionnaire *m*, magasinier *m*
storey, *US* **story** ['stɔːrɪ] *n* (*of building*) étage *m*; *Br* **on the third s.**, *Am* **on the fourth s.** au troisième étage; **single** *or* **one s. house** maison sans étage *ou* de plain-pied
-storeyed, *US* **-storied** ['stɔːrɪd] *suff* **two-s. house** maison à un étage; **one-s.** *or* **single-s. house** maison sans étage *ou* de plain-pied
storing ['stɔːrɪŋ] *n Com* magasinage *m*
stork [stɔːk] *n* (*bird*) cigogne *f*
storm¹ [stɔːm] *n* **(a)** *Met* orage *m*; (*wind*) tempête *f*; **rain s.** tempête de pluie; **there's a s. coming** le temps est à l'orage; *Fig* **a s. in a teacup** une tempête dans un verre d'eau; *Fig* **political s.** ouragan *m ou* tourmente *f* politique; *Fig* **to bring a s. about one's ears** déclencher un tollé général; *Fig* **to cause a s.** faire l'effet d'une bombe; **s. damage** dommages *mpl ou* dégâts *mpl* causés par l'orage *ou* la tempête
(b) (*of insults*) bordée *f*; (*of applause, protest*) tempête *f*; **to raise a s. of laughter** déchaîner l'hilarité générale
(c) *Mil* assaut *m*; **to take a stronghold by s.** prendre d'assaut une place forte; *Fig* **to take the audience by s.** soulever l'auditoire; **the play took Broadway by s.** la pièce a connu un succès foudroyant à Broadway; *Fig* **to take sb by s.** (*emotionally*) bouleverser qn
storm² **1** *vi* (*of person*) tempêter, pester; **to s. at sb** s'emporter contre qn; **to s. into/out of the room** entrer dans/quitter la pièce comme un ouragan; **she was storming about the place like a madwoman** elle se démenait dans la pièce comme une folle; **she went storming into the lead** elle est venue prendre la tête comme un ouragan **2** *vt* **(a)** *Mil* (*attack*) donner l'assaut à; (*capture*) prendre d'assaut, emporter d'assaut, enlever **(b)** (*say angrily*) fulminer
stormbound ['stɔːmbaʊnd] *adj* bloqué par une tempête
storm cloud *n* nuée *f* d'orage; *Fig* nuage *m* à l'horizon *ou* menaçant
storm cone *n* cône *m* de tempête
storm door *n* (élément *m* extérieur de la) double-porte *f*
storm drain *n* égout *m* pluvial
storming ['stɔːmɪŋ] *n Mil* prise *f* d'assaut **(of** de); **the s. of the Bastille** la prise de la Bastille
storm lantern *n* lampe-tempête *f*, *pl* lampes-tempêtes
storm sewer *n* égout *m* pluvial
storm troops *npl* troupes *fpl* d'assaut; *German Hist* sections *fpl* d'assaut
storm warning *n* avis *m* de tempête
stormy ['stɔːmɪ] *adj* (*weather, sky*) orageux; (*sea*) démonté; **the weather is s.** le temps est orageux *ou* à l'orage; *Fig* **s. discussion** discussion *f* orageuse; **s. life** vie *f* tumultueuse; **s. meeting** réunion *f* houleuse; **s. marriage** mariage *m* orageux; **s. petrel** (*bird*) pétrel *m*
story¹ ['stɔːrɪ] *n* **(a)** (*tale, account*) histoire *f*; **to tell a s.** raconter *ou* conter une histoire; **there is a s. that ...** on raconte que ...; **as the s. goes** à ce que l'on raconte; *Fig* **that is quite another s.** ça, c'est une autre histoire; *F* **it's the (same) old s.** *or* **the old, old s.** c'est toujours la même histoire; *F* **it's the s. of my life** c'est le genre de chose qui m'arrive tout le temps; **it's a long s.** c'est toute une histoire, c'est une longue histoire; **these bruises tell their own s.** ces meurtrissures en disent long; **each photo tells its** *or* **a s.** toutes les photos racontent une histoire; **she can tell a good s.** elle en connaît de bonnes; **so, to cut a long s. short ...** bref, pour résumer ...; *Mktg* **s. completion** histoire *f ou* scénario *m* à compléter
(b) short s. nouvelle *f*, conte *m*; **short s. writer** nouvelliste *mf*
(c) (*plot*) (*of novel, play etc*) intrigue *f*
(d) *Journ F* affaire *f*, information *f*; **who have we got on the s.?** qui est sur l'affaire?; **they decided to publish the s.** ils ont décidé de publier l'information
(e) *F* (*lie*) histoire *f*, conte *m*; **to tell stories** raconter des histoires
story² *n Am* (*of building*) = **storey**
storyboard ['stɔːrɪbɔːd] *n* story-board *m*, *pl* story-boards, scénarimage *m*, scénario-maquette *m*
storybook ['stɔːrɪbʊk] *n* livre *m* de contes, livre d'histoires; **it looks like a s. castle** cela ressemble à un château de conte de fées; **it had a s. ending** ça s'est terminé comme un conte de fées
storyline ['stɔːrɪlaɪn] *n* intrigue *f*; **it was quite hard to follow the s.** j'ai/il a/*etc* eu du mal à suivre le fil de l'histoire
storyteller ['stɔːrɪtelər] *n* **(a)** conteur, -euse; **to be a good/bad s.** être bon/mauvais conteur **(b)** *F* (*esp said to children*) (*liar*) menteur, -euse; **you big s.!** gros menteur!, grosse menteuse!
storytelling ['stɔːrɪtelɪŋ] *n* **(a)** art *m* de conter; **to be good at s.** avoir l'art de raconter des histoires **(b)** *F* (*telling lies*) mensonges *mpl*
stoup [stuːp] *n Rel* bénitier *m*
stout¹ [staʊt] *adj* **(a)** (*fat*) corpulent, fort; **to grow s.** prendre de l'embonpoint **(b)** (*solid*) (*door, shoes, beam*) solide; (*cloth*) renforcé **(c)** (*strong*) (*shoulders, legs, arms etc*) fort,

vigoureux; (*brave*) brave, vaillant; (*resolute*) ferme, résolu; *Old-fashioned* **s. fellow** (*brave*) homme vaillant *ou* courageux; (*sturdy*) costaud *m*; **s. heart** cœur *m* vaillant; **to put up a s. resistance** se défendre vaillamment

stout² *n* (*beer*) stout *m*, bière *f* brune forte

stouthearted [staʊt'hɑːtɪd] *adj Lit* courageux, intrépide

stoutly ['staʊtlɪ] *adv* **(a)** (*vigorously*) fortement, vigoureusement; (*to deny sth*) catégoriquement; **she s. maintained that ...** elle affirmait énergiquement que ... **(b)** (*sturdily*) (*built*) solidement

stoutness ['staʊtnɪs] *n* **(a)** (*fatness*) embonpoint *m* **(b)** (*solidity*) solidité *f* **(c)** (*vigorousness*) (*of resistance etc*) fermeté *f*, vigueur *f*

stove [stəʊv] *n* **(a)** (*cooker*) cuisinière *f*; (*oven*) fourneau *m*; (*small, portable*) réchaud *m*; **electric/gas s.** cuisinière électrique/à gaz; **oil s.** poêle *m* à pétrole; (*heater*) calorifère *m* à mazout **(b)** *Ch, Ind* étuve *f*, four *m*

stovepipe ['stəʊvpaɪp] *n* **(a)** tuyau *m* de poêle **(b) s. hat** chapeau *m* tuyau de poêle

stow [stəʊ] *vt* **(a)** (*put away*) ranger, mettre; *Sl* **s. it!** (*shut up*) la ferme!; (*that's enough*) ça suffit! **(b)** *Naut* (*cargo*) arrimer; (*anchor, ship's boats*) saisir **(c) to s. sth full of sth** remplir qch de qch

▶ **stow away 1** *vtsep* = **stow (a)**; *F* **to s. away a huge meal** s'envoyer un repas énorme; *F* **he can certainly s. it away** il a un bon coup de fourchette **2** *vi* (*hide*) s'embarquer clandestinement

stowage ['stəʊɪdʒ] *n Naut* (*of goods*) arrimage *m*; (*space*) espace *m* utile; (*cost*) frais *mpl* d'arrimage; *Aut* **s. bin** vide-poche *m*, bac *m* de rangement

stowaway ['stəʊəweɪ] *n Naut, Av* passager *m ou* voyageur *m* clandestin

strabismus [stræ'bɪzməs] *n Med* strabisme *m*

straddle¹ ['stræd(ə)l] *vt* **(a)** (*be on both sides of*) (*horse*) enfourcher; (*chair*) se mettre à califourchon sur; (*wall*) se mettre à califourchon *ou* à cheval sur; **their empire straddled the Mediterranean** leur empire couvrait la Méditerranée; **to s. a river** (*of bridge*) enjamber une rivière; **the village straddles the border** le village est à cheval sur la frontière; **her life straddled two centuries** sa vie est à cheval sur deux siècles; **a company that straddles two continents** une entreprise qui a des intérêts dans deux continents

(b) *Am Pol etc* (*question*) refuser de se compromettre sur; **to s. the fence** ne pas prendre parti, ne pas s'engager

straddle² *n* **(a)** *Sp* (*in high jump*) rouleau *m* ventral **(b)** *St Exch* stellage *m*

strafe [streɪf] *vt Mil* mitrailler en rase-mottes

straggle ['stræg(ə)l] *vi* **(a)** (*walk in disorderly fashion*) marcher sans ordre; (*not keep up*) rester en arrière, traîner; **other climbers straggled behind and got lost** d'autres grimpeurs sont restés à la traîne et se sont perdus; **his hair straggled over his jacket collar** les mèches de sa nuque pendouillaient sur le col de son veston **(b)** (*of plants*) pousser en désordre; **the roses are straggling everywhere** les roses poussent dans tous les sens

straggler ['stræglər] *n* (*person*) traînard, -arde; *Naut* (*ship, sailor*) retardataire *m*, lanterne *f* rouge

straggling ['stræglɪŋ] *adj* **a few s. houses** quelques maisons *fpl* éparpillées; **s. hairs** mèches *fpl* rebelles

straggly ['stræglɪ] *adj* (*branches, hair*) épars; (*beard*) rare; **a s. line of refugees** une file étirée de réfugiés

straight [streɪt] **1** *adj* **(a)** (*not curved*) (*back, leg, line etc*) droit; (*trajectory*) rectiligne; (*movement*) en ligne droite; *Tennis* **to win in three s. sets** gagner en trois sets; *Am* **she got s. As in the exam** (*all As*) elle n'a obtenu que des mentions très bien à l'examen; **he always gets s. As** il a toujours vingt sur vingt; *Fig* **to play with** *or* **keep a s. bat** se conduire honorablement; **to have a s. back** avoir le dos bien droit, se tenir bien droit; **s. edge** (*tool*) règle *f* (à araser); *Cards* **s. flush** quinte *f* flush; **s. hair** cheveux *mpl* raides; **s. line** (ligne *f*) droite *f*; *Boxing* **s. right/left** direct *m* du droit/gauche; *Horseracing, Fin* **s. tip** tuyau *m* sûr *ou* de source sûre

(b) (*honest*) honnête, loyal; (*frank*) franc, *f* franche; (*answer*) sans équivoque, franc; **s. as a die** d'une droiture absolue; **to be s. with sb** agir loyalement avec qn *ou* envers qn; **be s. with me, is he ...?** sois franc avec moi, est-il ...?; **I want a s. answer!** je veux une réponse franche; **to play a s. game** jouer franc jeu; **s. talking** conversation très franche; **it's time for some s. talking** il est temps que nous ayons une conversation très franche

(c) (*serious, conventional*) **to keep a s. face** garder son sérieux; **I couldn't keep a s. face** je n'ai pas pu m'empêcher de rire

(d) *F* (*heterosexual*) hétéro(sexuel)

(e) *Pol* **s. fight** campagne *f* électorale à deux candidats

(f) (*neat*) pur; **s. whisky** whisky *m* sec; **to drink one's whisky s.** boire son whisky sec

(g) (*aligned*) droit; **your tie isn't s.** votre cravate n'est pas droite *ou* est de travers; **your skirt isn't s.** ta jupe est de travers; **to put a picture s.** redresser un tableau; **to put the room s.** remettre de l'ordre dans la pièce; *Fig* **to put things** *or* **matters s.** arranger les choses; (*sort problem out*) débrouiller l'affaire; **to put sb s.** révéler son erreur à qn; **you ought to put her s. about what he's (really) like** tu devrais lui dire la personne qu'il est vraiment; **let's try to get things s.** essayons d'y voir clair; **let's get this s., he left at two o'clock?** mettons les choses au clair, il est parti à deux heures?; *F* **get this s.!** comprends-moi bien!; *F* **I need five hundred pounds to get me s.** il me faut cinq cents livres pour me remettre d'aplomb *ou* me refaire

2 *n* **(a) to be out of (the) s.** n'être pas d'aplomb, être de travers; **to cut a material on the s.** couper une étoffe de droit fil; **the s. and narrow** le droit chemin; **to keep on** *or* **stick to the s. and narrow** rester dans le droit chemin

(b) *Sp* **the s.** (*on race track*) la ligne droite; **the back s.** la ligne opposée *ou* d'en face; **the home s.** la (dernière) ligne droite; *Fig* **we're on the home s. now** nous sommes dans la dernière ligne droite

(c) *Sl* (*heterosexual*) hétéro *mf*

3 *adv* **(a)** (*in straight line*) droit; **to fly s. as an arrow** voler droit comme une flèche; **to shoot s.** tirer juste; **to go s.** aller droit; (*of criminal*) vivre honnêtement; (*of drug addict*) se désintoxiquer; **keep** *or* **go s. on** continuez tout droit; **to read a book s. through** (*from beginning to end*) lire un livre d'un bout à l'autre; (*without stopping*) lire un livre d'une traite

(b) (*without delay*) directement; **it comes s. from Paris** ça vient directement *ou* tout droit de Paris; **I'll be s. back** je reviens directement; **to come/go** *or* **get s. to the point** aller/venir droit au fait; **to get s. on with one's work** se mettre directement au travail; **to walk s. in** entrer sans frapper; **s. away** immédiatement, aussitôt, tout de suite; *F* **s. off** sur-le-champ, tout de suite; *F* **I can't tell you s. off** je ne peux pas vous le dire tout de suite

(c) (*directly*) directement; **to drink s. from the bottle** boire à (même) la bouteille; **it is s. across the road** c'est juste en face; **s. above sth** juste au-dessus de qch; **to look sb s. in the face** regarder qn bien en face; **he looked s. through me** il m'a regardé sans me voir; **we drove s. through Nantes** nous avons traversé Nantes sans nous arrêter; *F* **to let sb have it s.** dire son fait à qn; **I told him s. (out) what I thought of it** je lui ai dit carrément *ou* tout net ce que j'en pensais; **to come s. out with sth** dire qch tout net; **to tell** *or* **give sb sth s. from the shoulder** dire qch carrément à qn; *Th* **to play a part s.** jouer un rôle de façon classique

(d) (*honestly*) honnêtement; **to deal s. with people** être loyal en affaires; **to play s.** jouer franc jeu; *Br Sl* **s. up!** sans blague!

(e) (*clearly*) **I can't see s.** je ne vois pas clair; **I can't think s.** mon cerveau refuse de fonctionner

straight actor *n Th* comédien *m* dramatique

straightaway ['streɪtəweɪ] **1** *adv* immédiatement, tout de suite **2** *adj Am* en ligne droite

straight-edged *adj* (*knife*) à tranchant droit

straighten ['streɪt(ə)n] **1** *vt* (*make straight*) rendre droit; (*nail, rod etc*) redresser; (*bar*) défausser; (*put in order*) ranger, mettre en ordre; **to s. one's back** se redresser; **to s. one's hair** se recoiffer; (*take curls out*) se défriser les cheveux; **to s. one's tie** arranger sa cravate; **to s. one's affairs** mettre de l'ordre dans ses affaires **2** *vi* (*of person*) se redresser; (*of thing, road etc*) devenir droit

▶ **straighten out 1** *vtsep* **(a)** (*make straight*) redresser; (*bar*) défausser; **he straightened out the crumpled bedclothes** il a remis les draps en place **(b)** (*put right*) (*one's affairs*) arranger, mettre en ordre; **I will try to s. things out** je vais essayer d'arranger les choses **2** *vi* (*become straight*) (*of river, road etc*) redevenir droit

▶ **straighten up 1** *vtsep* **(a)** (*put straight*) (*picture etc*) redresser **(b)** (*put in order*) (*room etc*) mettre de l'ordre dans **2** *vi* (*straighten one's back*) se redresser

straight-faced ['streɪt'feɪst] *adj* impassible; **to give a s. answer** répondre sans perdre son sérieux

straightforward [streɪt'fɔːwəd] *adj* **(a)** (*person, conduct*) franc, *f* franche; **to give a s. answer to a question** répondre sans détours à une question; **to be quite s. about it** y aller franc jeu **(b)** (*simple*) simple; **it's a very s. cooker to use** c'est une cuisinière très simple à utiliser **(c)** (*clear*) manifeste; **a case of s. racism** un exemple de racisme manifeste

straightforwardly [streɪt'fɔːwədlɪ] *adv* **(a)** (*to act*) avec droiture, loyalement; (*to speak*) franchement, d'une manière franche, sans détours **(b)** (*simply*) facilement; **it can be assembled s. enough** le montage est assez facile; **you then quite s. remove the lid** puis vous ôtez le couvercle tout simplement *ou* très facilement **(c)** (*clearly*) manifestement; **to be s. wrong** (*of person*) avoir manifestement tort

straightforwardness [streɪt'fɔːwədnɪs] *n* (*of person*) franchise *f*; (*of matter, question*) simplicité *f*

straightline depreciation ['streɪtlaɪn] *n Acct* amortissement *m* linéaire

straight man *n Th* (*comedian's*) faire-valoir *m inv*

straightness ['streɪtnɪs] *n* **(a)** (*of line*) rectitude *f* **(b)** (*of conduct*) droiture *f*, rectitude *f*

straight part *n Th* rôle *m* sérieux

straight ticket *n US Pol* liste *f* non panachée

strain¹ [streɪn] *n* **(a)** (*tension*) tension *f*; *Phys* (*ratio*) rapport *m* de la déformation, allongement *m* unitaire; **the s. on the rope was too great** la corde était soumise à une trop grande tension; **to relieve the s. on** *or* **take the s. off a beam** soulager une poutre; *MecE* **breaking s.** force *f ou* contrainte *f* à la rupture, effort *m* de rupture; **to take the s.** (*of beam*) (*be subjected to*) être soumis à la tension; (*to support*) supporter la tension; (*of person*) supporter la tension nerveuse; **it would be** *or* **put too great a s. on my finances** ce serait trop lourd pour ma bourse; **the long hours put a s. on her marriage** ses horaires impossibles ont occasionné des tensions dans son mariage; **the s. of modern life** la tension de la vie moderne; **the s. of business life** la fatigue propre au monde des affaires; **all this driving's getting a bit of a s.** tous ces déplacements en voiture commencent à me fatiguer; **I find it a s.** je trouve cela fatigant; **the s. was beginning to tell (on them/***etc***)** la tension devenait visible; **mental s.** surmenage *m* (intellectuel); **eye s.** fatigue *f* des yeux

(b) *Med* entorse *f*; (*less serious*) foulure *f*; **s. in the back** tour *m* de reins

strain² **1** *vt* **(a)** (*cable*) tendre, surtendre; **to s. one's ears** tendre l'oreille; **to s. one's eyes** (*overuse*) se fatiguer *ou* s'abîmer les yeux *ou* la vue **(doing sth** à faire qch); (*make effort*) s'efforcer **(to see sth** pour voir qch); **to s. one's voice** (*overuse*) se fatiguer la voix; (*make effort*) forcer sa voix; **to s. every nerve to do sth** mettre toute sa force à faire qch; **to s. relations** tendre les rapports **(between** entre); **to s. one's resources** grever ses ressources jusqu'à la limite

(b) *MecE* (*part*) déformer; **I've strained my wrist/ankle** je me suis foulé le poignet/la cheville; (*more seriously*) je me suis fait une entorse au poignet/à la cheville; **to s. one's back** se faire mal au dos; **to s. one's heart** se fatiguer le cœur; **to s. a muscle** se froisser un muscle; **to s. oneself** (*overexert oneself*) se surmener, s'éreinter **(doing sth** à faire qch); *Iron* **he doesn't (exactly) s. himself** on ne peut pas dire qu'il se foule (la rate); *Iron* **don't s. yourself, will you!** surtout ne te foule pas!

(c) (*liquid*) filtrer, passer; (*stock*) tamiser, passer; (*vegetables*) faire égoutter

2 *vi* **(a)** (*make great effort*) peiner; **to s. at a door** essayer d'ouvrir une porte; **to s. at a rope/at the oars** tirer sur une corde/sur les rames; **the author doesn't s. after effect** l'auteur ne cherche pas à faire de l'effet; **to s. at the leash** (*of dog*) tirer sur la laisse; *Fig* (*be restless*) ne pas tenir en place; (*be rebellious*) se rebeller

(b) (*of beam*) fatiguer, travailler; (*of rope*) être trop tendu

(c) *MecE* (*of piece of metal*) gauchir, se fausser

(d) *Lit* **to s. at sth** (*be unwilling*) se faire un scrupule de qch; **to s. at doing sth** avoir des scrupules à faire qch

(e) (*of liquid*) filtrer **(through** à travers)

strain³ *n* **(a)** *Biol* (*of virus*) souche *f*; (*of grain, plant*) variété *f*; (*of animal*) race *f*, lignée *f* **(b) a s. of weakness** un fond de faiblesse; **he said much more in the same s.** il s'est étendu longuement dans ce sens; **other stories/films in the same s.** d'autres histoires/films dans la même veine **(c)** *esp Lit* **strains** (*sounds, music*) accents *mpl*; **sweet strains** doux accords *mpl*

strained [streɪnd] *adj* **(a)** (*rope, conversation, atmosphere etc*) tendu; **s. nerves** nerfs *mpl* tendus; **s. relations** rapports *mpl* tendus **(b)** *Med* **s. ankle** cheville *f* foulée **(c)** (*forced*) (*laughter*) forcé, contraint; (*language, interpretation*) forcé, exagéré **(d)** (*liquid*) filtré; (*stock*) tamisé; (*vegetables*) égoutté

strainer ['streɪnər] *n Culin* passoire *f*; **tea s.** passe-thé *m inv*, passette *f* à thé; **milk s.** passoire

strait [streɪt] *n* **(a)** détroit *m*; **the Straits of Gibraltar** le détroit de Gibraltar; **the Straits of Dover** le Pas de Calais **(b) to be in dire** *or* **desperate straits** être dans une situation désespérée; (*financially*) avoir de gros problèmes financiers

straitened ['streɪtənd] *adj* **in s. circumstances** dans une situation (financière) difficile

straitjacket¹ ['streɪtdʒækɪt] *n* camisole *f* de force; *Fig* carcan *m*; *Fig* **a financial s.** un carcan financier

straitjacket² *vt Fig* gêner, entraver; **to be straitjacketed by a lack of investment/by censorship** être bloqué par le manque d'investissement/par la censure

straitlaced ['streɪt'leɪst] *adj* collet monté *inv*

strand¹ [strænd] *n Lit* (*shore*) rive *f*, grève *f*

strand² *vt* (*ship*) échouer; **tourists stranded by the air controllers' strike** touristes bloqués à cause de la grève des aiguilleurs du ciel

strand³ *n* **(a)** (*piece*) (*of rope*) brin *m*, toron *m*; *Sewing* (*of cotton*) brin; (*of cloth*) fil *m*; (*of hair*) mèche *f* **(b)** *Fig* (*of plot*) fil *m*; **to unravel the strands of a complicated affair** démêler les fils d'une affaire compliquée

stranded ['strændɪd] *adj* **(a)** (*ship*) échoué; **s. whale** baleine échouée (sur la plage) **(b)** (*person*) **to leave sb s.** laisser qn en rade; **to be s.** rester en rade; **s. tourists** touristes bloqués

strange [streɪndʒ] *adj* **(a)** (*unusual*) étrange, bizarre; **they didn't write – (that's) s.** ils n'ont pas écrit – (c'est) bizarre; **s. beasts** bêtes *fpl* fantastiques; **she wears the strangest clothes** elle porte les vêtements les plus bizarres; **she's a s. girl** c'est une fille bizarre; **it's a s. thing** c'est (une chose) étrange; **s. to say, I've never met him** bien que cela paraisse bizarre, je ne l'ai jamais rencontré; **it's s. that you haven't heard of it** c'est bizarre que tu n'en aies pas entendu parler; **it was s. to see her in a dress** ça faisait bizarre *ou* drôle de la voir en robe; **s. how some faces stick in your mind** c'est bizarre *ou* drôle comme certains visages restent gravés dans la mémoire; **they've got a s. way of saying thank you** ils ont une drôle de façon de dire merci; **it felt s. to be back in Scotland again** cela m'a fait bizarre de revenir en Écosse

(b) (*unfamiliar*) **s. faces** des visages *mpl* nouveaux *ou* inconnus; **a s. place/house** un endroit/une maison qu'on ne connaît pas; **I can't work with s. tools** je ne peux pas travailler avec des outils qui ne sont pas les miens; **don't talk to s. men** ne parle pas aux étrangers

(c) *Arch* (*foreign*) étranger; **in a s. land** dans un pays étranger

strangely ['streɪndʒlɪ] *adv* bizarrement; **it all seemed s. familiar** tout avait un étrange goût de déjà-vu; **he's behaving very s.** il se conduit de manière très étrange; **s. enough, he felt nothing** ce qui est bizarre c'est qu'il n'a rien senti

strangeness ['streɪndʒnɪs] *n* **(a)** (*unusual quality*) bizarrerie *f* **(b)** (*unfamiliarity*) (*of surroundings etc*) étrangeté *f*

stranger ['streɪndʒər] *n* (*from somewhere else*) étranger, -ère; (*someone not known*) inconnu, -ue; **don't talk to strangers** ne parle pas aux inconnus; **I'm a s. here** je ne suis pas d'ici; **they're strangers (to us)** nous ne les connaissons pas; **you're quite a s. these days!** vous vous faites rare; *F* **hello, s.!** salut toi! on ne te voit plus!; (*to unknown person*) bonjour, l'étranger; **to become a s. to sb** devenir étranger à qn; **they had become complete strangers to one another** ils étaient devenus des étrangers l'un pour l'autre; **to become a s. to sth** perdre l'habitude de qch; **he's a s. /no s. to fear** il ne connaît pas/il connaît bien la peur; **she's no s. to controversy/success** elle a l'habitude de la polémique/du succès; **I spy strangers!** (*in House of Commons*) je demande le huis clos!

strangle ['stræŋg(ə)l] *vt* (*person*). *Fig* étrangler; (*laugh*) étouffer

strangled ['stræŋg(ə)ld] *adj* (*person*) étranglé; (*voice, laughter*) étouffé

stranglehold ['stræŋg(ə)lhəʊld] *n* **(a)** (*in wrestling*) étranglement *m* **(b)** *Fig* **to have a s. on sb** tenir qn à la gorge; **to have a s. on sth** avoir la mainmise sur qch; **economic s.** mainmise économique; **to break the s. on a country's economy** mettre fin à la mainmise sur l'économie d'un pays

strangler ['stræŋglər] *n* (*person*) étrangleur, -euse

strangling ['stræŋglɪŋ] *n* étranglement *m*

strangulate ['stræŋgjʊleɪt] *vt* **(a)** *Med* (*intestine*) étrangler; **strangulated hernia** hernie *f* étranglée **(b) = strangle**

strangulation [stræŋgjʊ'leɪʃən] *n* strangulation *f*; *Fig* **economic s.** asphyxie *f* économique

strap¹ [stræp] *n* (*of leather, canvas*) sangle *f*, lanière *f*, courroie *f*; (*on bra etc*) bretelle *f*; (*on shoe*) lanière, patte; (*for watch*) bracelet *m*; (*on underground train, bus*) poignée *f*; **watch s.** bracelet de montre; **(trouser) s.** (*under foot*) sous-pied *m*, *pl* sous-pieds; **to give sb the s.** (*punishment*) fouetter qn (avec une sangle)

strap² *vt* (-pp- [stræpt]) **(a)** (*attach*) (*object*) attacher avec une sangle, sangler; (*trunk*) boucler; **to s. sth to sth** sangler qch à qch **(b)** (*punish*) **to s. a child** frapper un enfant avec une sangle **(c)** *Med* (*broken limb etc*) bander

▶ **strap down** *vtsep* (*containers etc*) arrimer; (*prisoner, patient*) attacher

▶ **strap in** *vtsep* (*passenger*) attacher; **to s. oneself in** s'attacher, attacher sa ceinture

▶ **strap up** *vtsep* **(a)** (*suitcase*) sangler **(b)** *Med* = **strap²(c)**

straphang ['stræphæŋ] *vi* voyager debout (*en se tenant à la courroie ou à la poignée*)

straphanger ['stræphæŋər] *n* (*in underground etc*) voyageur, -euse debout; **after 15 years of being a s.** (*commuting*) après être allé au travail pendant quinze ans en métro

strapless ['stræplɪs] *adj* (*dress, bra etc*) sans bretelles; **s. top** bustier *m*

strap-line *n Journ* surtitre *m*

strapped [stræpt] *adj F* **to be s. (for cash)** être à court d'argent, être fauché

strapping ['stræpɪŋ] *adj* solide, robuste; **s. fellow** grand gaillard; **tall s. girl** fille grande et costaude

strata ['strɑːtə] *npl see* **stratum**

stratagem ['strætədʒəm] *n* stratagème *m*

strategic [strə'tiːdʒɪk] *adj* stratégique; **s. business area** domaine *m* d'activité stratégique; **s. business plan** plan *m* stratégique d'entreprise; **s. business unit** unité *f* d'activité stratégique; **s. management** gestion *f* stratégique; **s. marketing** mercatique *f* stratégique; **s. planning** planification *f* stratégique

strategically [strə'tiːdʒɪk(ə)lɪ] *adv* stratégiquement; **s. placed** placé à un endroit/aux endroits stratégique(s)

strategist ['strætədʒɪst] *n* stratège *m*

strategy ['strætɪdʒɪ] *n* stratégie *f*

stratification [strætɪfɪ'keɪʃən] *n* stratification *f*

stratified ['strætɪfaɪd] *adj* (*formation, society*) stratifié

stratify ['strætɪfaɪ] **1** *vt* stratifier **2** *vi* se stratifier

stratosphere ['strætəsfɪər] *n* stratosphère *f*

stratum, *pl* **-a** ['strɑːtəm, -ə] *n* [①A13,5] *Geol* strate *f*, couche *f*; *Fig* couche; **the various strata of society** les différentes couches sociales

straw [strɔː] *n* **(a)** paille *f*; **it's not worth a s.** cela ne vaut pas un clou *ou* un pet de lapin; *Fig* **to clutch** *or* **grasp at straws** se raccrocher à de faux espoirs; *Prov* **a drowning man will clutch at a s.** = quand on se noie on est prêt à se raccrocher à n'importe quoi; *Fig* **straws in the wind** un signe, un indice; *Prov* **it's the last s. that breaks the camel's back** c'est la goutte d'eau qui fait déborder le vase; **it's the last s.!** ça c'est le comble *ou* le bouquet!; **s. hat** chapeau *m* de paille; *Fig* **man of s.**, *Am* **s. man** homme de paille; **s. mat** paillasson *m*; **s. mattress** paillasse *f*

(b) (*for drinking*) paille *f*; **to drink lemonade through a s.** boire de la limonade avec une paille

(c) (*colour*) (jaune *m*) paille *f*

strawberry ['strɔːb(ə)rɪ] *n* **(a)** (*fruit, flavour*) fraise *f*; **s. (plant)** fraisier *m*; **wild s.**, *Am* **field s.** fraise des bois; **s. bed** planche *f ou* plant *m* de fraisiers; **s. field** fraiseraie *f*; **s. ice cream** glace *f* à la fraise; **s. jam** confiture *f* de fraises **(b) s. (colour)** fraise *inv*; **s. mark** (*on skin*) fraise *f*

strawberry blonde **1** *adj* blond vénitien *inv* **2** *n* femme *f*/fille *f* aux cheveux blond vénitien

straw-coloured *adj* jaune paille *inv*

straw poll *n* sondage *m* d'opinion

stray¹ [streɪ] **1** *n* **(a)** (*animal*) animal *m* égaré; (*dog*) chien *m* errant; *Jur* animal sans maître **(b) waifs and strays** (*children*) enfants *mpl* abandonnés **(c)** *Rad* **strays** parasites *mpl*, friture *f* **2** *adj* **(a)** (*animal*) égaré, perdu; *Jur* sans maître **(b)** *Fig* (*example, specimen*) isolé; **s. bullet** balle *f* perdue; **here are a few s. thoughts on the project** voilà quelques idées en vrac concernant le projet; **any s. thoughts you might have ...** si vous avez des idées ...

stray² *vi* (*of person, animal*) s'égarer, errer; (*of sheep*) s'écarter du troupeau; **the plane had strayed off course** l'avion s'était écarté de sa route; **the sheep will s. onto the road** les moutons vont se sauver sur la route; *Fig* **to s. from the right path** s'écarter du droit chemin; **to let one's thoughts s.** laisser vagabonder *ou* vaguer ses pensées; **to s. from the point** s'écarter du sujet

streak¹ [striːk] *n* **(a)** (*stripe*) raie *f*, rayure *f*; (*of mist, vapour, dirt*) traînée *f*; (*of light*) rai *m*, trait *m*; **a s. of sunlight** un rayon de soleil; **the first streaks of dawn** les premières lueurs de l'aube; **like a s. of lightning** comme un éclair; **streaks of grey hair** mèches *fpl* de cheveux gris; **I've had a s. of luck** je tiens le filon; **winning/losing s.** (*in sport*) suite *f* de victoires/défaites; **to be on a winning s., to hit a winning s.** être en veine; **there's a s. of Irish blood in her** elle a un peu de sang irlandais

(b) *Fig* (*tendency*) tendance *f*; **to have a jealous/mean/cruel s.** être d'une nature jalouse/avare/cruelle; **there was a s. of cowardice in him** il avait un côté lâche

(c) *F* (*act of running naked*) **to do a s.** = courir nu (en public)

streak² **1** *vt* rayer, strier (**with** de); **fur streaked with black** pelage rayé de noir; **streaked with tears** strié de larmes; **her face was streaked with dirt/blood** elle avait des traces de saleté/sang sur le visage; **wall streaked with damp** mur plein de traces d'humidité; **white marble streaked with red** marbre blanc veiné de rouge; **his hair was streaked with silver** ses cheveux étaient parsemés de fils d'argent; **to have one's hair streaked** se faire faire des mèches

2 *vi* **(a)** (*run, move etc fast*) **to s. along/past** aller/passer comme un éclair; **to s. off** partir à toute allure; **the Ferrari streaked past him** la Ferrari le dépassa en trombe; **the rocket streaked up into the sky** la fusée partit comme un éclair dans le ciel

(b) *F* (*run naked*) courir nu (en public)

streaker ['striːkər] *n F* = personne *f* qui court nu(e) (en public)

streaking ['striːkɪŋ] *n* (*streaks*) raies *fpl*, rayures *fpl*, bandes *fpl*; (*in hairdressing*) effet *m* de mèches

streaky ['striːkɪ] *adj* **(a)** (*paint*) irrégulier; (*pattern*) strié; (*mirror, plates etc*) couvert de traces; (*cloud*) effiloché; **her make-up had gone s.** son maquillage avait dégouliné **(b) s. bacon** bacon *m* entrelardé

stream¹ [striːm] *n* **(a)** (*brook*) ruisseau *m*; **mountain s.** torrent *m*

(b) (*flow*) (*of light, blood, water*) flot(s) *m(pl)*, jet *m*; (*of lava*) coulée *f*; (*of tears, words, congratulations, insults*) flot *m*, torrent *m*; (*of people, cars*) flot; **in one continuous s.** à jet continu; **a s. of water shot out of the tap** l'eau jaillit à flot du robinet; *Liter* **s. of consciousness** monologue *m* intérieur; **s. feed** (*on photocopier*) alimentation *f* automatique

(c) (*current*) courant *m*; **with the s.** dans le sens du courant, au fil de l'eau; **against the s.** contre le courant, à contre-courant; *Fig* **to go with the s.** suivre le mouvement; *Fig* **to go against the s.** aller à contre-courant; **the main s. of public opinion** le courant de l'opinion publique

(d) to come on s. (*of oil*) commencer à couler; (*of new power station etc*) entrer en production; **to go off s.** (*of oil*) cesser de couler; (*of power station etc*) cesser de produire

(e) *Br Sch* groupe *m* de niveau

stream² **1** *vi* **(a)** (*of liquid*) couler à flots, ruisseler; **people were streaming over the bridge** un flot continu de gens traversait le pont; **people streamed out of the stadium** des flots de gens sortaient du stade; **the sunlight streams in(to the room)** le soleil entre à flots (dans la chambre) **(b)** (*of surface*) ruisseler (**with** de); **his eyes were streaming** (*he was crying*) il était ruisselant de larmes; (*his eyes were watering*) il avait les yeux qui pleuraient **(c)** (*of hair, garment, banner*) flotter (au vent) **2** *vt* **(a) to s. blood** ruisseler de sang **(b)** *Br Sch* **to s. pupils** répartir les élèves selon leur niveau d'aptitude

streamer ['striːmər] *n* **(a)** (*flag*) banderole *f*; **(paper) streamers** serpentins *mpl* (de carnaval) **(b)** *Journ* (*headline*) titre *m* flamboyant, bandeau *m*, cinq colonnes *fpl* à la Une **(c)** *Comptr* streamer *m*, dévideur *m*

streaming ['striːmɪŋ] **1** *adj* (*liquid*) qui coule; *F* **to have a s. cold** avoir un gros rhume **2** *n Br Sch* répartition *f* par niveaux

streamline ['striːmlaɪn] *vt* **(a)** (*car etc*) caréner **(b)** *Fig* (*method, economy*) rationaliser; (*department, company, army etc*) dégraisser

streamlined ['striːmlaɪnd] *adj* **(a)** *Aut, Av* caréné; (*fuselage*) aérodynamique; (*ship*) hydrodynamique **(b)** *Fig* (*system, economy*) rationalisé; (*department, organization, army etc*) dégraissé

streamlining ['striːmlaɪnɪŋ] *n* **(a)** (*of bodywork*) carénage *m*, profilage *m* **(b)** *Fig* (*of system, economy*) rationalisation *f*; (*of department, organization, army etc*) dégraissage *m*

street [striːt] *n* rue *f*; **back s.** petite rue écartée; *Pej* rue pauvre; (*dangerous*) rue mal fréquentée; **the High S.** la Grand-rue; **to turn** *or* **throw sb (out) into the s.** jeter qn à la rue; **to walk the streets** courir les rues, battre le pavé; (*of prostitute*) faire le trottoir; **on the s.** dans la rue; **to be on the street(s)** (*of prostitute*) faire le trottoir; (*of homeless people*) être à la rue; **the whole s. heard the row** toute la rue a entendu la dispute; **the man in the s.** Monsieur Tout-le-Monde, l'homme de la rue; *F* **she's streets ahead of the rest of the class** elle est largement en tête de la classe; *Fig* **that's right up my s.** c'est tout à fait mon rayon; *Old-fashioned* **s. Arab** gamin *m* des rues; **s. furniture** mobilier *m* urbain; **s. life** (*activity*) animation *f* (des rues); **s. photographer** photographe *mf* de la rue, photostoppeur, -euse; **s. theatre** théâtre *m* de rue; **s. urchin** gamin, -ine des rues; **s. value** (*of drugs*) prix *m* à la revente

streetcar ['striːtkɑːr] *n Am* tramway *m*

street cred *n* image *f* de marque; **to have a lot of s.** être très branché; **it gives him a lot of s.** ça lui donne une bonne image de marque; **they're gaining s.** leur image de marque s'améliore; **this won't do much for my s.** ça va craindre pour mon image de marque

street guide *n* indicateur *m* des rues

street lamp *n* réverbère *m*

street level *n* rez-de-chaussée *m inv*; **below s.** au sous-sol

street light *n* réverbère *m*

street lighting *n* éclairage *m* urbain *ou* des rues

street map *n* plan *m*

street market *n* marché *m* en plein air; *St Exch* marché après Bourse

street musician *n* musicien, -ienne des rues

street party *n* = fête *f* de rue organisée en célébration d'un événement national

street plan *n* plan *m*

street sweeper *n* (*person*) balayeur, -euse; (*machine*) balayeuse *f*

street trader *n* marchand *m* ambulant, marchande *f* ambulante

streetwalker ['stri:twɔ:kər] *n* racoleuse *f*

streetwise ['stri:twaɪz] *adj* averti, malin

strength [streŋθ] *n* (**a**) (*of person, acid, player, team*) force *f*; *Ch* (*of solution*) titre *m*; *El* (*of current*) intensité *f*; (*of beam, rope*) solidité *f*; (*of emotion*) force, intensité; **solution at full s., full-s. solution** solution *f* concentrée; **s. of character** force de caractère; **s. of purpose** détermination *f*; **s. of will** résolution *f*, volonté *f*; **by sheer (physical) s.** uniquement grâce à la force physique; **to recover** *or* **regain one's s.** reprendre des forces; **you must keep up your s.** il faut garder vos forces; **she doesn't know her own s.** elle ne connaît pas sa force; **to build up one's s. again** reprendre des forces; **to lose s.** s'affaiblir; *Fig* **to do sth on the s. of what one has been told** faire qch en se fiant à *ou* en s'appuyant sur ce qu'on vous a dit; **convicted on the s. of eye-witness evidence** condamné sur la foi des déclarations des témoins oculaires; **he got a good job on the s. of his qualifications** il a obtenu un bon emploi grâce à ses diplômes; **s. of a friendship** solidité d'une amitié; **s. of materials** résistance *f* des matériaux; **to go from s. to s.** (*of person's health*) aller de mieux en mieux; (*of project etc*) avancer à pas de géant; (*of company, new writer etc*) connaître une réussite de plus en plus remarquable; **we went from s. to s.** (*in business or political relationship*) nous avons progressé à pas de géant; (*in personal relationship*) nous nous entendions de mieux en mieux; *Mktg* **strengths and weaknesses** forces et faiblesses *fpl*

(**b**) (*numbers*) **to be present in great s.** être présents en grand nombre; **they were there in full s.** ils y étaient au grand complet

(**c**) *Mil* (*of army*), *Fig* effectif(s) *m(pl)*; **wartime/peacetime s.** effectif de guerre/de paix; **to be under s.** avoir un effectif insuffisant; **to bring a battalion/department up to s.** compléter l'effectif d'un bataillon/service; **there are 30 of us when we're at full s.** nous sommes 30 quand nous sommes au complet

strengthen ['streŋθ(ə)n] **1** *vt* (*wall, house, position, friendship*) consolider; (*beam, material, law, pound sterling*) renforcer; (*person, body*) fortifier; (*sb's authority*) (r)affermir; *Ch* (*solution*) augmenter la concentration de; *Typ* (*colour*) charger; **it would s. my hand** *or* **position** cela renforcerait ma position; **this merely strengthened their resolve** ça n'a fait que renforcer leur détermination **2** *vi* (*of resolve, position etc*) se renforcer, s'affermir; (*of sterling etc*) se raffermir; (*of patient, industry, country etc*) prendre *ou* reprendre des forces

strengthening ['streŋθ(ə)nɪŋ] **1** *adj* (*tonic*) fortifiant **2** *n* (*of material*) renforcement *m*; (*of wall, building*) consolidation *f*; (*of sb's authority*) (r)affermissement *m*; **there was a s. of opposition** l'opposition s'est renforcée; **there was a slight s. of the pound on foreign markets** il y a eu un léger renforcement de la livre sur les marchés étrangers

strenuous ['strenjʊəs] *adj* (*work, match, day at the office*) fatigant; (*campaigner*) zélé; (*effort, opposition*) acharné; (*denial*) formel, énergique; **to make s. efforts to get sth done** faire des efforts acharnés pour accomplir qch; **a s. advocate of sth** un défenseur passionné de qch; **a s. opponent of sth** un adversaire acharné de qch; **s. life** vie *f* harassante

strenuously ['strenjʊəslɪ] *adv* vigoureusement; (*to work, oppose*) avec acharnement; (*to deny*) formellement, énergiquement

strenuousness ['strenjʊəsnɪs] *n* (*of work*) dureté *f* (*de l'effort physique exigé*); (*of opposition*) acharnement *m*

strep throat [strep] *n US* **to have a s.** avoir mal à la gorge

streptococcal [streptəʊ'kɒk(ə)l] *adj Med* streptococcique

streptococcus, *pl* **-cocci** [streptəʊ'kɒkəs, -'kɒk(s)aɪ] *n Med* streptocoque *m*

streptomycin [streptəʊ'maɪsɪn] *n Med* streptomycine *f*

stress¹ [stres] *n* (**a**) (*mental*) stress *m*, tension *f*; **to be under a lot of s.** être en proie au stress, être très tendu; **how does he react under s.?** comment réagit-il sous le stress *ou* sous la pression?; **I work better under s.** je travaille mieux sous la pression; **this puts our relationship under s.** ça crée des tensions dans nos relations; **how to cope with s.** comment vivre avec le stress; **some people thrive on s.** certaines personnes travaillent mieux sous la pression; **a major s. factor** un important facteur de stress *ou* de tension; **the stresses and strains of modern life** les tensions et les pressions de la vie moderne

(**b**) *MecE etc* (*tension*) tension *f*, travail *m*; *MecE* (*in components*) sollicitation *f*; **to be in s.** (*of beam*) travailler; **s. limit** limite *f* de travail *ou* de fatigue

(**c**) (*emphasis*) insistance *f*; *Ling* accent *m* tonique; (*in prosody*) accentuation *f*; **to put s. on sth** insister sur qch; **to lay s. on** (*fact*) insister sur, faire ressortir; (*word*) insister sur; (*syllable*) accentuer, appuyer sur; **the s. falls on the last syllable** l'accent tonique tombe sur la dernière syllabe; **there was too much s. on memorization of facts** on demandait d'apprendre trop de faits par cœur

stress² *vt* (**a**) (*emphasize*) insister sur; (*fact*) faire ressortir; (*word*) souligner, insister sur; **she stressed that no decision had been taken** elle a insisté sur *ou* souligné le fait qu'aucune décision n'avait été prise (**b**) *Ling* (*syllable*) accentuer, appuyer sur; **stressed syllable** syllabe *f* accentuée (**c**) *MecE* (*beam*) charger, fatiguer, faire travailler; **to be stressed** (*of beam*) travailler

stressed [strest] *adj MecE* sollicité; (*beam etc*) sous tension; (*person*) stressé, sous tension, tendu; (*syllable*) accentué; **to let oneself get s.** se laisser gagner par le stress

stressed-out *adj* (complètement) stressé

stressful ['stresfʊl] *adj* (*situation, job*) stressant

stress mark *n* accent *m*

stress-related *adj* dû au stress; **s. illnesses** maladies *fpl* dues au stress

stretch¹ [stretʃ] *n* (**a**) (*act of stretching*) **with a yawn and a s.** en bâillant et en s'étirant; **to have a s.** s'étirer; **at full s.** au maximum de ses capacités; **by no s. of the imagination could it be called a democracy** même avec beaucoup d'imagination *ou* même en faisant un gros effort d'imagination, on ne pourrait pas dire qu'il s'agit d'une démocratie; **it's not ready yet, not by a long s.** ce n'est pas encore prêt, et il s'en faut de beaucoup; *Mus* **s. of the fingers** (*at the piano*) écart *m* des doigts

(**b**) (*elasticity*) élasticité *f*; **with two-way s.** (*of elastic fabric*) extensible dans les deux sens; **s. fabric** tissu *m* extensible

(**c**) (*of country, water*) étendue *f*; (*of land*) bande *f*; (*of road*) section *f*; (*of time, silence etc*) période *f*; **for a long s. of time** (pendant) longtemps, pendant une longue période de temps; **at a s., at one s.** (tout) d'un trait, d'affilée; **she's been working for hours at a s.** voilà des heures qu'elle travaille sans désemparer; *F* **to do a five-year s.** (*in prison*) faire cinq ans de prison

stretch² **1** *vt* (**a**) (*extend*) (*elastic, belt, cable, spring*) tendre; (*shoes, gloves*) détendre, élargir; (*sb's patience*) éprouver, exercer; (*meaning of a word*) forcer; (*arm*) allonger; (*hand*) tendre, avancer; (*leg*) étirer; **to s. oneself** s'étirer; **to s. one's neck to see sth** tendre le cou pour voir qch; **to s. one's legs** (*take short walk etc*) se dégourdir les jambes; **to s. its wings** (*of bird*) déployer ses ailes; *Fig* **to s. one's wings** voler de ses propres ailes; **he stretched his arm through the broken window** il allongea le bras à travers le carreau cassé; **to s. the truth** exagérer; **to s. a point** faire une exception (**for sb** en faveur de qn); *F* **that's stretching it a bit!** vous y allez/il y va/*etc* un peu fort!; *Art* **to s. the canvas on the frame** tendre la toile sur le châssis; **to s. a rope across a room** tendre une corde à travers une pièce; **to s. an awning over the deck** établir une tente sur le pont

(**b**) (*put demands on*) demander un effort maximum à; (*resources*) grever jusqu'à la limite; **to be fully stretched** (*of person*) être à son rendement maximum; (*of resources, services*) être sollicité à fond; **she needs a job that will s. her** elle a besoin d'un travail qui la pousse à donner le maximum

(**c**) (*make last*) (*income, supplies etc*) tirer au maximum sur; **we should be able to s. the food until the weekend** nous devrions pouvoir faire durer les provisions jusqu'au week-end; **our money could be stretched to last until**

Christmas nous pourrions faire durer notre argent jusqu'à Noël

2 *vi* **(a)** (*become longer*) s'allonger; (*of person, rope*) s'étirer; (*of elastic*) se détendre; (*of gloves etc*) se détendre, s'élargir; **the rope stretched across the ravine** le corde allait d'un côté à l'autre du ravin; **it's rude to s.!** (*with arm*) il est impoli d'allonger le bras comme ça!; **she stretched across the table** elle allongea le bras *ou* tout le corps en travers de la table; **he stretched down under the table to pick up ...** il allongea le bras *ou* le corps sous la table pour ramasser ...; **I have to s. up to reach the top shelf** il faut que je m'étire pour atteindre l'étagère du haut

(b) (*of terrain, road etc*) s'étendre; **the road stretches away into the distance** la route s'étire dans le lointain

(c) my resources won't s. to that mes moyens (pécuniaires) ne vont pas jusque-là; **the dish will s. to six helpings** on pourra faire six portions; **there is enough material here to s. to two books** il y a assez de matière pour en faire deux livres

▶ **stretch out 1** *vi* **(a)** (*extend limbs*) s'étirer; (*of horse when racing*) aller ventre à terre **(b)** (*extend*) (*of road, valley etc*) s'étendre; **a barren future stretched out ahead of her** un avenir sombre se profilait devant elle **2** *vtsep* (*extend*) (*arm*) allonger; (*hand*) tendre, avancer; **to lie stretched out on the ground** être étendu par terre; **we could s. the meat out till Sunday** nous pourrions faire durer la viande jusqu'à dimanche

stretcher ['stretʃər] *n* **(a)** (*for casualty*) brancard *m*, civière *f*; **he was carried** *or* **taken off on a s.** on l'a emmené sur une civière *ou* un brancard; **he's a s. case** *Med* il faut l'emporter sur une civière; *Fig F* (*having been beaten up etc*) il est bon pour l'hôpital **(b)** *Art* **(canvas) s.** châssis *m*

▶ **stretcher off** *vtsep* (*remove on stretcher*) emmener sur une civière

stretcher bearer *n* brancardier *m*, ambulancier *m*

stretcher party *n* détachement *m ou* équipe *f* de brancardiers

stretching ['stretʃɪŋ] *n* **s. of the rules** entorse *f* au règlement

stretch mark *n Obst* vergeture *f*

stretchy ['stretʃɪ] *adj* élastique, extensible

strew [struː] *vt* (*pp* **strewed** [struːd] *or* **strewn** [struːn]) **to s. sth over the floor** (*on purpose*) jeter *ou* répandre qch sur le plancher, (re)couvrir le plancher de qch; (*accidentally*) répandre qch sur le plancher; **the ground was strewn with rushes** une jonchée de roseaux recouvrait le sol, le sol était jonché de roseaux; **the bomb exploded, strewing the crowd with pieces of broken glass** la bombe explosa, couvrant la foule de débris de verre; **his clothes were strewn everywhere in the house** ses vêtements étaient éparpillés partout dans la maison; **toys were strewn over** *or* **around** *or* **on the floor** des jouets jonchaient le plancher; **references to classical literature are strewn throughout his work** son œuvre est émaillée de références à la littérature classique

strewth [struːθ] *int Br Sl* ça alors!

striated [straɪ'eɪtɪd] *adj* strié

stricken[1] ['strɪk(ə)n] *adj esp Lit* (*person, voice, look*) affligé; **he looked s.** il avait l'air affligé; **s. with grief** accablé de douleur; **s. with guilt** accablé par les remords; **s. by** *or* **with polio** atteint de polio; **s. by** *or* **with blindness** frappé de cécité; **the s. city** la ville sinistrée; **the s. vessel** le vaisseau en détresse *ou* naufragé; **the s. animal hid in the bushes** l'animal blessé se cacha dans les fourrés

stricken[2] *see* **strike[2]**

strict [strɪkt] *adj* **(a)** (*teacher, boss, parent etc*) strict, sévère; **to be s. with sb** être sévère *ou* strict avec *ou* envers qn

(b) (*ruling, etiquette*) strict, péremptoire; (*discipline, regime*) sévère, strict; (*fast*) strict, austère; **s. deadline** délai *m* de rigueur; **s. morals** morale *f* rigide, mœurs *fpl* sévères; **s. Muslim** musulman de stricte obédience; **she gave s. orders not to be woken** elle a donné l'ordre formel *ou* strict qu'on ne la réveille pas

(c) (*exact*) exact, strict; **the s. minimum** le strict minimum; **in the s. sense of the word** au sens strict du mot; **to observe s. neutrality** observer la neutralité la plus stricte; **in strictest confidence** à titre tout à fait *ou* strictement confidentiel

strictly ['strɪktlɪ] *adv* **(a)** (*sternly*) strictement, sévèrement; (*treated, brought up*) avec rigueur **(b)** (*totally*) strictement; **s. confidential** strictement confidentiel; **smoking (is) s. prohibited** il est strictement *ou* formellement interdit de fumer; **it is s. forbidden** c'est strictement défendu, c'est formellement interdit **(c)** (*exactly*) exactement, rigoureusement; **s. (speaking)** à proprement parler; **this rule was s. observed** cette règle a été rigoureusement *ou* strictement observée

strictness ['strɪktnɪs] *n* **(a)** (*of discipline*) sévérité *f* **(b)** (*of rules*) rigueur *f*; **their s. in applying the rules** la rigueur avec laquelle ils appliquaient le règlement **(c)** (*of interpretation*) exactitude *f*

stricture ['strɪktʃər] *n Fml* **(a)** (*usu pl*) **strictures** (*criticism*) critiques *fpl*; **to pass strictures (up)on sb/sth** diriger ses critiques contre qn/qch **(b)** (*restriction*) restriction *f*, limitation *f* **(c)** *Med* (*of ureter*) rétrécissement *m*; (*of intestine*) étranglement *m*

stride[1] [straɪd] *n* **(a)** (grand) pas *m*, enjambée *f*; (*when running*) foulée *f*; **to shorten/lengthen one's s.** ralentir/allonger le pas; *Fig* **to make great strides** faire de grands progrès *ou* des progrès rapides; *Fig* **to take sth in one's s.** *or US* **in s.** (*do easily*) faire qch sans le moindre effort; (*not be disconcerted by*) ne pas se laisser troubler par qch; **she left him after 6 months, but he took it all in his s.** après six mois, elle l'a quitté brusquement, mais il ne s'est pas laissé troubler pour autant; **these things happen, you just have to learn to take them in your s.** ce sont des choses qui arrivent, il faut savoir les accepter; **eventually you come to take it all in your s.** on finit par s'y faire; **to get into** *or F* **to hit one's s.** (*in walking*) prendre son allure normale; *Sp* (*of runner*) trouver son rythme; (*in working*) prendre la cadence; *Fig* **to put sb off his/her s.** faire perdre la cadence à qn

(b) *esp Austr F* **strides** (*trousers*) fute *m*, futal *m*

stride[2] (*pt* **strode** [strəʊd]; *pp* **stridden** ['strɪd(ə)n]) **1** *vi* marcher à grands pas *ou* à grandes enjambées; **she strode into the room** elle est entrée dans la pièce à grandes enjambées; **to s. along/away** avancer/s'éloigner à grands pas; **science is striding further ahead each year** chaque année, la science avance *ou* progresse à pas de géant; **she just strode straight up to him and said ...** elle se dirigea droit vers lui et dit ...; **Bonaparte strode impatiently up and down the room** Bonaparte arpentait impatiemment la pièce; **to s. over sth** enjamber qch

2 *vt Lit* **he strode the deck/the streets** il arpentait le pont/les rues

stridency ['straɪdənsɪ] *n* stridence *f*; (*of protests*) véhémence *f*

strident ['straɪdənt] *adj* strident; (*colour*) criard; (*protest*) véhément

stridently ['straɪdəntlɪ] *adv* (*to talk*) d'une voix stridente; (*to laugh, shout*) de façon stridente; (*to protest*) avec véhémence

strife [straɪf] *n* contestation *f*; **domestic s.** querelles *fpl* de ménage; **political/sectarian s.** des luttes *fpl* politiques/sectaires; **after years of industrial s.** après des années de conflits sociaux

strike[1] [straɪk] *n* **(a)** *Ind* grève *f*; **teachers'/miners' s.** grève des professeurs/mineurs; **postal s.** grève des postiers; **power s.** = grève des employés de l'EDF; **an unofficial s.** = grève qui n'est pas soutenue par les syndicats; **lightning s.** grève surprise; **sit-down s.** grève sur le tas; **sympathy s.** grève de solidarité; **to be on s.** être en grève, faire grève; **to go on** *or* **come out on s.** se mettre en grève; **to bring people out on s.** amener des gens à faire grève; **to go on hunger s.** (*of prisoner*) faire la grève de la faim; **there have been calls for s. action** on a appelé à la grève; **the dispute could easily lead to s. action** le conflit pouvait très facilement amener une grève; **s. notice** préavis *m* de grève

(b) *Min* (*of ore, oil*) rencontre *f*; (*of bed*) découverte *f*; **there has been a major oil s.** il y a eu une découverte d'un important gisement de pétrole; *Fig F* **lucky s.** coup *m* de veine

(c) (*blow*) coup *m*; (*of clock*) sonnerie *f*; *Mil* raid *m* (**on** sur); *Fishing* (*by angler*) ferrage *m*; (*by fish*) mordage *m*; (*in baseball*) balle *f* manquée (*par le batteur*); (*in tenpin bowling*) honneur *m* double; *Mil* **first s. weapon** arme *f* de première frappe; *Mil, Av* **air s.** raid, intervention *f* aérienne; **s. aircraft** avion(s) *m(pl)* d'assaut

strike[2] (*pt* **struck** [strʌk]; *pp* **struck,** *Arch, Lit* **stricken** ['strɪk(ə)n]) **1** *vt* **(a)** (*hit*) (*person, piano key*) frapper; **to s. sb in the face** frapper qn à la figure; **to be struck by a stone** être frappé par une pierre; **to s. sb a blow** porter *ou* assener un coup à qn; **they got what they wanted without striking a blow** ils ont obtenu ce qu'ils voulaient sans coup férir; **to be struck by a huge wave** essuyer un coup de mer; **ready to s. a blow for freedom of speech** prêt à se battre pour défendre la liberté de parole; **who struck the first blow?** qui a frappé le premier?; *Fig* **in his speech he struck a blow for freedom/those who ...** par son discours, il a fait avancer la cause de liberté/de ceux qui ...; *Fig* **to s. a blow at sth** taper sur qch; *Mus* **to s. a chord** plaquer un accord; *Fig* **that strikes a chord (with me)** je me retrouve là-dedans; *Fig* **that strikes a familiar note** cela fait l'effet du déjà vu/du déjà entendu, ça me rappelle des choses; **to s. the right/wrong**

note sonner juste/faux; **the clock strikes the hour and half hour** l'horloge sonne l'heure et la demi-heure; **the clock struck the hour** l'horloge sonna l'heure juste; **as the clock struck 10** lorsque l'horloge sonna dix heures

(**b**) (*collide with*) frapper contre, heurter; **his head struck the pavement** sa tête a heurté le trottoir; **to s. (the) bottom** (*of ship*) toucher (le fond), talonner; **struck by lightning** (*house*) frappé par la foudre; (*tree, person*) foudroyé; **lightning had struck the house** la foudre était tombée sur la maison; **to s. a mine** (*of ship*) heurter une mine; **to s. a pedestrian** (*of car*) heurter un piéton; **a sound struck my ear** un bruit attira mon attention

(**c**) **to s. terror into sb** frapper qn de terreur; **it struck fear into their hearts** ils furent glacés d'effroi; **to s. sb with surprise** frapper qn d'étonnement; **struck with panic/terror** pris de panique/terrorisé; **to be struck dumb/blind** être frappé de mutisme/cécité; **he was struck dead by a heart attack** il a été emporté par une crise cardiaque; **the bullet hit her in the head, striking her dead** la balle l'a frappée en pleine tête, la tuant sur le coup; *Lit* **he struck his opponent dead** il a tué son adversaire d'un coup

(**d**) (*match*) allumer, frotter; (*sparks*) faire jaillir; *Old-fashioned Br Sl* **s. a light!** nom de Dieu!

(**e**) (*impress*) impressionner; (*the eye, imagination*) frapper; **how does she s. you?** quelle impression vous fait-elle?; **he strikes me as (being) sincere** il me paraît sincère; **the place struck her as familiar** l'endroit lui a paru familier; **that is how it struck me** voilà l'effet que cela m'a fait; **did it never s. you that you weren't wanted there?** ne vous est-il jamais venu à l'esprit que vous étiez de trop?; **what struck me was his brazen impudence** ce qui m'a frappé, c'est son impudence sans nom; **the thought struck me that ...** l'idée m'est venue *ou* il m'est venu à l'idée que ...; **it strikes me that we'd do better to say no** j'ai la nette impression que nous ferions mieux de dire non

(**f**) (*discover*) (*path*) tomber sur, découvrir; (*gold*) découvrir; **to s. oil** atteindre une nappe de pétrole, rencontrer *ou* toucher le pétrole; *Fig* trouver un filon; *F* **she has struck it rich** elle a fait fortune

(**g**) (*lower*) (*tent*) démonter; *Naut* (*sail*) amener, caler; *Th* **to s. the set** démonter le décor; **to s. camp** lever le camp; **to s. one's flag** *or* **one's colours** *Naut* amener *ou* rentrer son pavillon, mettre pavillon bas; *Fig* (*surrender*) se rendre

(**h**) **to s. an attitude** poser

(**i**) **to s. a bargain** faire *ou* conclure un marché; **to s. a balance between X and Y** trouver un équilibre entre X et Y; **to s. an agreement/deal (with sb)** conclure un accord/un marché (avec qn)

(**j**) (*delete*) enlever; **that remark must be struck** *or US* **stricken from the record** cette remarque doit être retirée du procès-verbal

(**k**) (*of plant*) **to s. root** prendre racine

(**l**) (*coin, medal*) frapper

2 *vi* (**a**) (*attack*) (*of enemy*) attaquer; (*of assassin, burglar etc*) frapper; (*of disaster, earthquake etc*) survenir; (*with dagger, club etc*) frapper; (*of serpent*) foncer; *Fig* **to s. at sth** menacer qch; **these reforms s. deep at the heart of our traditional way of life** ces réformes mettent en péril notre mode de vie traditionnel; **to s. home** faire mouche; *Prov* **s. while the iron is hot** il faut battre le fer tant qu'il est chaud; **the terrorists struck twice** les terroristes ont frappé deux fois; **where the missile struck** là où le missile a frappé

(**b**) (*of clock*) sonner

(**c**) *Ind* se mettre en grève; **to s. for better conditions** se mettre en grève pour de meilleures conditions de travail; **striking workers** ouvriers en grève

(**d**) (*travel, head*) prendre (*une certaine direction*); **to s. across country** prendre à travers champs; **they then struck west** ils sont ensuite partis vers l'ouest

(**e**) (*of cutting*) prendre (racine)

▶ **strike back 1** *vtsep* (*hit with return blow*) **to s. sb back** rendre son coup à qn; **if anyone strikes me I s. him back** si quelqu'un me frappe, je rends le coup **2** *vi* (*hit return blow*) rendre le coup; *Fig* (*retaliate*) effectuer des représailles; **to s. back at the enemy** répliquer à l'ennemi, contre-attaquer; **the government struck back at its critics** le gouvernement a répondu à ceux qui le critiquaient

▶ **strike down** *vtsep* (*knock down*) renverser; (*kill*) abattre; *Fig* **struck down by disease** terrassé par la maladie

▶ **strike off 1** *vtsep* (**a**) (*remove by hitting*) enlever d'un coup; (*sb's head*) trancher (**b**) (*delete*) **to s. off a name from a list, to s. a name off a list** biffer *ou* rayer un nom d'une liste; **to be struck off** (*of doctor, solicitor*) être radié (**c**) *Com* (*deduct*) **to s. off £5** faire une réduction de *ou* déduire cinq livres (**d**) *Typ* (*number of copies*) tirer **2** *vi* (*travel, head*) **to s. off to the left** (*of person*) prendre à gauche; (*of road*) tourner à gauche; **we left the path and struck off into the depths of the forest** nous avons quitté le sentier et nous nous sommes enfoncés dans la forêt

▶ **strike on** *vipo* (*discover*) tomber sur

▶ **strike out 1** *vtsep* (*delete*) (*word*) rayer, biffer, barrer; **s. out whichever does not apply** rayer la mention inutile

2 *vi* (**a**) (*hit out*) **to s. out at sb** allonger *ou* porter un coup à qn; *Fig* (*criticize, attack*) attaquer qn; **to s. out right and left** frapper à droite et à gauche

(**b**) (*travel, head*) **I struck out for the shore** (*swimming*) j'ai commencé à nager *ou* (*rowing*) j'ai commencé à ramer dans la direction du rivage; *Fig* **to s. out in a new direction** (*in life, thinking etc*) prendre une direction nouvelle

(**c**) (*become independent*) **to s. out for oneself, to s. out on one's own** voler de ses propres ailes

(**d**) *Baseball* sortir (du jeu)

▶ **strike up 1** *vtsep* (*song*) entonner; (*piece of music*) commencer de *ou* à jouer; **to s. up a friendship with sb** se lier d'amitié avec qn, se prendre d'amitié pour qn; **to s. up an acquaintance with sb** lier connaissance avec qn; **to s. up a conversation with sb** entrer en conversation avec qn; **they immediately struck up a conversation** ils sont immédiatement entrés en conversation **2** *vi* **on his arrival the band struck up** à son arrivée, la fanfare attaqua un morceau

strike ballot *n* = vote *m* avant que les syndicats ne décident d'une grève

strikebound ['straɪkbaʊnd] *adj* paralysé par une/la grève; (*commuters*) coincé par une/la grève

strikebreaker ['straɪkbreɪkər] *n Ind* briseur, -euse de grève

strike force *n Mil* (**a**) (*capacity*) force *f* de frappe (**b**) (*unit*) détachement *m ou* brigade *f* d'intervention; (*larger*) force *f* d'intervention

strike fund *n* = caisse *f* de prévoyance permettant d'aider les grévistes

strike-out mode *n Comptr* mode *m* barré

strike pay *n* allocation *f* de grève

strike price *n Fin* **s. price** (*for share*) prix *m* d'exercice

striker ['straɪkər] *n* (**a**) *Ind* gréviste *mf* (**b**) *Sp, Fb* buteur *m*; *Cr* = batteur *m* qui reçoit; *Baseball* batteur (**c**) (*device*) frappeur *m*; (*of clock*) marteau *m*; (*of firearm*) percuteur *m*; *Aut* **s. plate** gâche *f* de porte

strike-thru mode *n Comptr* mode *m* barré

striking ['straɪkɪŋ] **1** *adj* (**a**) (*sight, similarity, difference, appearance*) frappant, saisissant; (*feature*) saillant; (*situation*) dramatique; **he was a s. figure** c'était un personnage impressionnant; **of s. beauty** d'une beauté frappante

(**b**) **s. clock** pendule *f* à sonnerie

(**c**) (*workers*) en grève

2 *n* (**a**) (*of coins*) frappe *f*

(**b**) **within s. distance** à quelques kilomètres; **we were within s. distance of the summit** nous étions tout près du sommet; **we haven't finished, but we're within s. distance** nous n'avons pas encore fini, mais on en est tout près; **s. surface** (*for match*) frottoir *m*

(**c**) (*of clock*) sonnerie *f*; **s. mechanism** sonnerie

strikingly ['straɪkɪŋlɪ] *adv* d'une manière frappante *ou* saisissante; **s. beautiful** d'une beauté frappante

striking off *n* (*of name*) suppression *f*; (*of lawyer, doctor*) radiation *f*

Strine [straɪn] *n Hum F* anglais *m* australien

string¹ [strɪŋ] *n* (**a**) (*cord*) ficelle *f*; (*piece of string*) bout *m* de ficelle; (*of puppet*) fil *m*; **ball of s.** pelote *f* de ficelle; *Fig* **to have sb on a s.** mener qn par le bout du nez; *Fig* **to keep sb on a s.** (*in uncertainty*) laisser qn dans l'incertitude; (*keep control over*) tenir qn en laisse; *Fig* **(with) no strings (attached)** sans conditions, sans condition aucune; **with strings attached** avec des conditions; *Fig* **to pull the strings** tirer les ficelles; *Fig* **to pull strings** faire jouer ses relations *ou F* le piston; **s. bag** filet *m* (à provisions); *Br* **s. vest** maillot *m* de corps à grosses mailles

(**b**) (*of violin, piano, bow*) corde *f*; *Tennis* **strings** (*of racket*) cordes, cordage *m*; **the strings of a violin** la monture d'un violon; **guitar/violin s.** corde de guitare/de violon; **the strings** (*in orchestra*) (*instruments, players*) les cordes; **a s. of horses** un groupe de chevaux; **our first s.** (*athlete, horse etc*) le meilleur; **our second s.** (*athletes, horse*) nos athlètes/notre cheval numéro deux; *Fig* **to have more than one s. to one's bow** avoir plus d'une corde à son arc

(**c**) (*of onions, islands*) chapelet *m*; (*of medals*) brochette *f*; (*of vehicles*) file *f*; (*of barges*) train *m*; (*of words, shops, defeats*) série *f*; **s. of beads** collier *m*; *Rel* chapelet; **s. of pearls** collier de perles; **a whole s. of children/names** toute une kyrielle d'enfants/de noms

(d) *Comptr* suite *f*, chaîne *f*; **s. of characters** suite de caractères; **s. variable** variable *f* de chaîne

string² *vt* (*pp, pt* **strung** [strʌŋ]) (a) (*fit with strings*) (*tennis racket*) corder; (*violin*) mettre les cordes à, monter; (*bow*) bander; **to be highly strung** (*of person, horse etc*) être nerveux; (*likely to suffer for emotional reasons*) être émotif (b) (*pearls*) enfiler; **to s. fairy lamps across a garden** accrocher des guirlandes de lampions dans un jardin; *Fig* **to s. sentences together** enfiler des phrases; **he can't s. two sentences together** il est incapable d'aligner trois mots (c) *Culin* **to s. beans** ôter les fils des haricots

▶ **string along** *vtsep F* (*deceitfully encourage*) duper, tromper; **they're just stringing you along** ils se moquent de toi; **let's s. them along a bit longer** et si on les faisait marcher encore un peu

▶ **string along with** *vipo F* (*accompany*) accompagner, faire route avec

▶ **string out 1** *vi* (*form long line*) s'espacer; *Sp* **the field strung out behind** le peloton des coureurs s'effilochait **2** *vtsep* (a) (*in time*) **to s. sth out** faire durer qch; **the TV series was strung out over six weeks** le feuilleton (de) télé a traîné pendant six semaines (b) (*in space*) **the troops were strung out over two hundred kilometres** les troupes s'échelonnaient sur 200 kilomètres; **you're all too strung out, get closer together** vous êtes trop clairsemés, rapprochez-vous les uns des autres

▶ **string up** *vtsep F* (*hang*) pendre haut et court

string band *n* orchestre *m* à cordes

string bass *n* contrebasse *f*

string bean *n* haricot *m* vert

stringboard [ˈstrɪŋbɔːd] *n Constr* limon *m* (d'escalier)

stringed [strɪŋd] *adj Mus* (*instrument*) à cordes

stringency [ˈstrɪndʒənsɪ] *n* (*of rules*) rigueur *f*, sévérité *f*; *Fin* (*of market*) resserrement *m*

stringent [ˈstrɪndʒənt] *adj* (*rule*) rigoureux, -euse, strict; (*savings*) rigoureux; *Fin* (*market*) tendu, serré

stringently [ˈstrɪndʒəntlɪ] *adv* rigoureusement, strictement

stringer [ˈstrɪŋər] *n* (*journalist*) reporter *m* local, stringer *m*, stringman *m*

stringing [ˈstrɪŋɪŋ] *n* (*act*) (*of violin*) montage *m*; (*of racket*) cordage *m*; (*of bow*) bandage *m*

string orchestra *n* orchestre *m* à cordes

stringpiece [ˈstrɪŋpiːs] *n Constr* longrine *f*

string-puller [ˈstrɪŋpʊlər] *n F* **he could be a useful s.** il peut nous/leur/*etc* être utile s'il fait jouer ses relations

string quartet *n* quatuor *m* à cordes

stringy [ˈstrɪŋɪ] *adj* (a) (*vegetables*) fibreux, -euse, filandreux, -euse; **s. meat** viande *f* filandreuse (b) (*person*) élancé

strip¹ [strɪp] *n* (a) (*of cloth, paper*) bande *f*; (*of metal*) lame *f*, lamelle *f*; (*of ground*) bande, langue *f*; **narrow s.** bandelette *f*; *Fig* **to tear sb off a s.** donner *ou* passer un savon à qn, laver la tête à qn; *Med* **dressing s.** bande à pansement; *Av* **(landing) s.** piste *f* (d'atterrissage); **s. cartoon, comic s.** bande *f* dessinée, BD *f* (b) *Sp* (*clothes*) (*of football team*) tenue *f*

strip² *n* **to do a s.** (*undress*) se déshabiller, se dévêtir; (*for show*) faire un strip-tease; **s. club** boîte *f* de strip-tease; *Cards* **s. poker** strip-poker *m*; **s. show** (spectacle *m* de) strip-tease *m*

strip³ **(-pp-) 1** *vt* (a) (*undress*) déshabiller, dévêtir; **to s. sb to the skin, to s. sb naked** mettre qn à poil; **stripped to the waist** nu jusqu'à la ceinture, torse nu

(b) (*deprive*) **to s. sb of sth** dépouiller *ou* déposséder qn de qch; **to s. sb of his/her clothes** dépouiller qn de ses vêtements; **trees stripped of their leaves** arbres dépouillés de leurs feuilles; **stripped of all his worldly goods** dépouillé de tous ses biens; **to be stripped of one's title/rank/office** être dépouillé de son titre/rang/poste

(c) (*bed*) défaire; *El* (*cable*) dénuder; *Phot* (*plate*) pelliculer; **to s. a tree** (*of leaves*) effeuiller un arbre; (*of bark*) écorcer un arbre; (*of branches*) ébrancher un arbre; (*of fruit*) (*of person*) cueillir les fruits sur un arbre; (*of bird*) manger tous les fruits d'un arbre; **to s. a wall** (*remove wallpaper*) arracher le papier d'un mur; (*remove paint*) enlever *ou* gratter la peinture d'un mur; **thieves have stripped the house** les cambrioleurs ont complètement vidé la maison; *Mil F* **to s. an NCO** dégrader un sous-officier; **to s. an engine/a gun** démonter un moteur/un fusil; *Aut* **stripped chassis** châssis *m* nu

(d) (*remove*) **to s. sth from sth** enlever *ou* ôter qch de qch **2** *vi* (*undress*) se déshabiller, se dévêtir; **to s. to the waist** se mettre nu jusqu'à la ceinture

▶ **strip down 1** *vtsep* (*dismantle*) (*engine, gun*) démonter; (*remove non-essential parts from*) (*bike etc*) enlever les parties non essentielles de; *Fig* **to s. a theory down to (its) essentials** simplifier une théorie pour n'en garder que l'essentiel **2** *vi* (*undress*) se déshabiller; **to s. down to one's underwear** se mettre en sous-vêtements

▶ **strip off 1** *vi* (a) (*undress*) se déshabiller, *F* se dépoiler (b) (*of wallpaper etc*) se décoller, s'enlever **2** *vtsep* (*remove*) (*paint*) gratter; (*wallpaper*) décoller; **to s. the paint off a wall** enlever *ou* gratter la peinture d'un mur

stripe¹ [straɪp] *n* (a) (*on cloth*) rayure *f*, raie *f*; (*on animal's coat*) rayure, zébrure *f*; *Mil* galon *m*; (*magnetic*) piste *f*; **black with a red s.** noir à raie rouge; **to mark sth with stripes** rayer *ou* zébrer qch; *Mil* **long service s.** chevron *m*; *Mil* **to get/lose a s.** être promu/dégradé (b) *Am* **a man of that s.** un homme de ce genre

striped [straɪpt] *adj* (*socks, material etc*) à raies, à rayures; (*animal's coat*) rayé, zébré; **red and blue s. jacket** veston rayé rouge et bleu

strip light *n* (*in the home*) néon *m*; *TV, Cin* rampe *f* au néon fluorescente, rame *f* de cyclorama, éclairage *m* du cyclo

strip lighting *n* éclairage *m* au néon *ou* fluorescent

stripling [ˈstrɪplɪŋ] *n* tout jeune homme *m*

strip mining *n esp Am Min* exploitation *f* à ciel ouvert

strippagram [ˈstrɪpəgræm] *n* = message *m* d'adieu/ d'anniversaire délivré par une jeune fille ou un jeune homme qui fait un strip-tease

stripped-down [strɪptˈdaʊn] *adj* **s. version** version *f* simplifiée

stripper [ˈstrɪpər] *n* (a) (*striptease artist*) strip-teaseuse *f*; **(male) s.** strip-teaseur *m* (b) **(paint) s.** décapant *m*; **wallpaper s.** produit *m* pour décoller le papier peint

strip-search¹ *n* fouille *f* d'une personne dévêtue; **to undergo a s.** devoir se déshabiller afin d'être fouillé

strip-search² *vt* **to s. sb** faire déshabiller qn pour le/la fouiller

striptease [ˈstrɪptiːz] *n* (spectacle *m* de) strip-tease *m*; **to do a s.** faire un strip-tease; **s. artist** strip-teaseur *m*, strip-teaseuse *f*

stripy [ˈstraɪpɪ] *adj* = **striped (a)**

strive [straɪv] *vi* (*pt* **strove** [strəʊv]; *pp* **striven** [ˈstrɪv(ə)n]) **to s. to do sth** s'efforcer de faire qch, faire des efforts pour faire qch; **to s. for** *or* **after sth** essayer d'obtenir qch; **to s. after effect** chercher à faire de l'effet; **s. as we might** malgré tous nos efforts; **to s. against sb** lutter contre qn

strobe [strəʊb] *n Phys etc* stroboscope *m*; **s. lighting** éclairage *m* stroboscopique

stroboscope [ˈstrəʊbəskəʊp] *n* stroboscope *m*

strode *see* **stride²**

stroke¹ [strəʊk] *n* (a) (*blow*) coup *m*; **to receive twenty strokes** (*with whip, cane etc*) recevoir vingt coups; *Fig* **at a s.** d'un coup; **to abolish a practice at a s.** abolir un usage d'un seul coup; **s. of lightning** coup de foudre

(b) (*movement*) (*of wing, oar*) coup *m*; *MecE* (*of piston etc*) mouvement *m*, course *f*; *Cr, Tennis etc* coup; *Swimming* (*style*) nage *f*; (*arm movement*) mouvement des bras; (*in breast stroke*) brasse *f*; **she was only a few strokes from the bank** elle était à quelques mètres seulement de la rive; **to lengthen the s.** (*in rowing*) allonger la nage; **to keep s.** (*in rowing*) nager ensemble, garder la cadence; *Fig* **to be off one's s.** n'être pas au mieux de sa forme; *Fig* **to put sb off his/her s.** déconcerter qn; **not to do a s. of work** ne rien faire; **s. of (good) luck** coup de chance, aubaine *f*; **s. of wit/ of genius** trait *m* d'esprit/de génie; **bold s.** coup hardi; *Golf* **s. play** concours *m* par coups

(c) (*of clock*) coup *m*; **on the s. of nine** sur le coup de neuf heures, à neuf heures sonnantes *ou* tapantes; **to arrive on the s.** arriver à l'heure juste

(d) *Med* attaque *f*; **to have a s.** avoir une attaque

(e) (*mark*) trait *m*; *Typ* barre *f* oblique; (*of pencil, brush*) coup *m* de crayon/de pinceau; (*of pen*) trait de plume; **at the s. of a pen** d'un coup de crayon; **with a few bold strokes of the brush** de trois coups de pinceau; *Fig* **to put the finishing strokes to one's work** apporter les dernières touches *ou* mettre la dernière main à son travail

(f) (*oarsman*) chef *m* de nage; **to row s.** donner la nage, être chef de nage; **s. oar** (*oar*) aviron *m* du chef de nage; (*person*) chef de nage

stroke² (*in rowing*) **1** *vt* (*boat*) être chef de nage de **2** *vi* être chef de nage, donner la nage

stroke³ *n* (a) (*caress*) caresse *f*; **to give sb/sth a s.** caresser qn/qch (b) *esp Am* (*remark*) **(positive) s.** encouragement *m*; **to give sb a s.** encourager qn

stroke⁴ *vt* (*caress*) (*fur, sb's hair*) caresser; **to s. one's chin** se caresser le menton; **to s. one's hair down** *or* **into place** lisser ses cheveux; **s. the ointment evenly over the ...** passer la pommade en couche régulière sur le ...; **he just stroked the ball into the net** il fit glisser le ballon dans les buts

-stroke [-strəʊk] *suff* **two/four-s. engine** moteur *m* à deux/à quatre temps

stroll[1] [strəʊl] *n* tour *m*, *F* balade *f*; **to take** *or* **go for a s.** aller faire un tour

stroll[2] *vi* flâner, *F* se balader; **to s. around town** flâner en ville; **she strolled in an hour late and didn't even say sorry** elle est arrivée tranquillement avec une heure de retard et ne s'est même pas excusée; **he strolled across to me** il s'avança tranquillement vers moi

stroller ['strəʊlər] *n* **(a)** (*person*) flâneur, -euse, promeneur, -euse **(b)** *Am* (*pushchair*) poussette *f* (d'enfant)

strolling ['strəʊlɪŋ] *adj Th* **s. player** comédien *m* ambulant, comédienne *f* ambulante; **s. players** troupe *f* ambulante

strong [strɒŋ] **1** *adj* (*comp* **stronger** ['strɒŋgər]; *superl* **strongest** ['strɒŋgɪst]) **(a)** (*physically powerful*) (*person, horse etc*) fort; **he's not very s.** (*not muscular*) il n'est pas très fort; (*not healthy*) il n'est pas très robuste; **to be s. in the arm** avoir beaucoup de force dans le bras; **she's as s. as a horse** *or* **an ox** elle est forte comme un cheval *ou* un bœuf; **to be getting stronger** (*after illness*) reprendre ses forces; **his eyesight is not as s. as it was** sa vue a baissé, sa vue n'est pas aussi bonne qu'elle était

(b) (*belief, will, currency, feelings, food, tastes, drink*) fort; (*wind, voice, light*) fort, puissant; (*character*) fort, ferme; (*nerves, constitution*) solide; (*country*) puissant; (*colour*) vif; (*protest, plea*) puissant, énergique; *Com* (*market*) ferme; *El* (*current*) fort, intense; (*supporter*) ardent, vigoureux; **there's s. evidence that he committed suicide/the economy is recovering** tout porte à croire qu'il s'est suicidé/qu'il va y avoir une reprise de l'économie; **she's a s. character** elle a une forte personnalité; **he's a s. candidate for the post** il a le profil idéal pour le poste; **this is a s. possibility** il y a de fortes chances; **to have s. reasons for doing sth** avoir de bonnes raisons de faire qch; **if you have s. feelings about it** si cela vous tient très à cœur; **he comes from a s. Catholic family** il vient d'une famille très catholique; **the religion which is strongest in Scandinavia** la religion qui prédomine en Scandinavie; **the pound is getting stronger** la livre sterling se raffermit; **to be in a s. position** (*politically, financially, militarily*) être dans une position de force; **s. conviction** ferme conviction *f*; **you've got to be s. and say 'no'** il faut être ferme et dire 'non'; **be s.** (*be brave*) sois courageux *ou* fort; **company two hundred s.** compagnie forte de deux cents personnes; **the wind is growing stronger** le vent forcit; **to give s. support to sb/a measure** appuyer fortement qn/une mesure; **to be s. on sth** (*good at*) être fort en qch; *Mus* **s. beat** temps *m* fort; **a s. chance** une forte chance; **a s. accent** un fort accent; **s. verb** verbe *m* fort; **s. syllable** syllabe *f* accentuée; **s. likeness** grande *ou* forte ressemblance *f*; **s. measures** mesures *fpl* draconiennes; *Fig* **I found the book rather s. meat** j'ai trouvé ce livre plutôt salé; **s. point** point fort; **politeness is not her s. point** la politesse n'est pas son fort; **to have a s. smell** sentir fort; *Ch* **s. solution** solution forte *ou* concentrée; *Cards* **s. suit** (couleur) longue *f*; *Fig* **languages are not my s. suit** les langues ne sont pas mon fort; **s. wind** grand vent

(c) (*resistant*) (*rope, cloth, shoes*) solide, résistant

(d) s. language (*forceful*) langage *m* énergique *ou* vigoureux; (*swearwords*) grossièretés *fpl*; **to write in s. terms to sb** écrire une lettre énergique à qn; **to put sth in the strongest possible terms** exprimer qch dans des termes les plus énergiques possible

2 *npl* **the s.** les forts *mpl*, les puissants *mpl*

3 *adv F* **to be still going s.** (*be in good condition etc*) (*of athlete*) avoir encore un bon rythme; (*of old person, party, company etc*) se porter toujours bien; **how's grandfather? – still going s.** comment va le grand-père? – toujours solide; **you're pitching it a bit s.** vous y allez un peu fort

strong-arm[1] *adj* **to use s. methods** *or* **tactics** utiliser la manière forte; **by s. methods** à la méthode forte

strong-arm[2] *vt Am F* rouer de coups

strong-box *n* coffre-fort *m*, *pl* coffres-forts

stronghold ['strɒŋhəʊld] *n* (*fortress*) forteresse *f*; *Fig* bastion *m*; **s. of trade unionism** bastion du syndicalisme

strongly ['strɒŋlɪ] *adv* **(a)** (*solidly*) solidement **(b)** (*forcefully*) (*to believe*) fortement; (*to support, oppose, endorse*) vigoureusement, énergiquement; **the sun shone s.** le soleil brillait fort; **he argued s. in favour of/against …** il s'est montré très partisan de/opposé à …; **to be s. in favour of sth** être fortement en faveur *ou* chaud partisan de qch; **s. worded letter** lettre dans laquelle on ne mâche pas ses mots; **I don't feel s. about it** je n'y attache pas une grande importance; **I feel very s. that they should be punished** je suis convaincu qu'ils devraient être punis

strongman ['strɒŋmæn] *n* **(a)** (*powerful man*) homme *m* à poigne **(b)** (*in circus*) Monsieur Muscle *m*; **could you do your s. act with this coffee jar?** viens nous faire admirer ta force, on a besoin d'ouvrir un pot de café

strong-minded *adj* **to be s.** (*of person*) avoir de la volonté; **s. person** forte tête *f*

strong-mindedness [strɒŋ'maɪndɪdnɪs] *n* force *f* de caractère

strongroom ['strɒŋruːm] *n* chambre *f* forte

strong-willed [strɒŋ'wɪld] *adj* = **strong-minded**

strontium ['strɒntɪəm] *n Ch* strontium *m*

strop[1] [strɒp] *n* **(razor) s.** cuir *m* (à repasser *ou* à rasoir), affiloir *m*

strop[2] *vt* (-pp-) (*razor*) affiler *ou* repasser sur le cuir

strophe ['strəʊfɪ] *n* (*in poetry*) strophe *f*

stroppiness ['strɒpɪnɪs] *n Br F* (*insolence*) insolence *f*; (*awkwardness*) mauvais caractère *m*; (*aggressiveness*) agressivité *f*

stroppy ['strɒpɪ] *adj Br F* (*insolent*) insolent; (*not cooperative*) contrariant; (*aggressive*) agressif, hargneux; **she got a bit s. when I asked her if …** elle est montée sur ses grands chevaux quand je lui ai demandé si …; **don't get s. with me!** ce n'est pas la peine de monter sur tes grands chevaux

strove *see* **strive**

struck *see* **strike**[2]

structural ['strʌktʃər(ə)l] *adj* **(a)** *Phil, Geol etc* structural; (*relating to structure*) structurel; **s. linguistics** linguistique *f* structurale **(b)** *Constr* de construction; **s. damage** dégâts *mpl* de structure; **s. engineer** (ingénieur *m*) constructeur *m*; **s. fault** défaut *m* de construction; **s. iron/steel** fer *m*/acier *m* de construction

structuralism ['strʌktʃər(ə)lɪz(ə)m] *n Psy, Ling* structuralisme *m*

structurally ['strʌktʃər(ə)lɪ] *adv* **(a)** (*to think, analyse*) structurellement; **s., the novel is …** du point de vue de la structure, le roman est … **(b) the building is sound s.** la structure du bâtiment est saine

structure[1] ['strʌktʃər] *n* **(a)** (*of building, society, language etc*) structure *f* **(b)** (*building, monument*) construction *f*, édifice *m*, bâtiment *m*; **the social s.** l'édifice social; *Mil etc* **command s.** structure *f* de commandement; *Econ* **price s.** structure des prix

structure[2] *vt* (*organization*) structurer; (*novel etc*) structurer, architecturer

structured ['strʌktʃəd] *adj* structuré; **highly s.** très structuré; **s. interview** entretien *m* structuré *ou* centré; *Comptr* **s. query language** langage *m* d'interrogation structuré; **s. questionnaire** questionnaire *m* structuré

struggle[1] ['strʌg(ə)l] *n* lutte *f* (**for** pour; **against** contre); **fierce/desperate s.** lutte acharnée/désespérée; **he gave in without a s.** il n'a opposé aucune résistance; **the class s.** la lutte des classes; **s. for freedom** lutte pour la liberté; **life is a s.** la vie est un combat; **the s. for life/for existence** la lutte pour la vie/pour l'existence; **it's a s. getting the kids to wash properly** il faut se battre pour que les enfants se lavent correctement; **it'll be a s. but I think we'll make it** ce sera difficile *ou* dur, mais je crois que nous y arriverons; **I finished the book but it was a real s.** j'ai terminé le livre mais ça a été très dur; **I had a s. getting him to change his mind** j'ai eu du mal à le faire changer d'avis; **he's not worried about the s. that many people have just to make ends meet** il se fiche que des tas de gens doivent se battre pour arriver à joindre les deux bouts

struggle[2] *vi* lutter (**with** avec; **against** contre; **for** pour); (*move violently*) se débattre, se démener; **to s. to do sth** avoir du mal à faire qch; **she struggled to control her temper** elle a eu du mal à ne pas s'emporter; **the child struggled and kicked** l'enfant se débattait des pieds et des mains; **she was struggling with her umbrella** elle se débattait avec son parapluie; **he struggled to his feet** il s'est levé avec difficulté; **to s. along** (*walking etc*) marcher *ou* avancer péniblement; **we are struggling along** (*in life, with work etc*) nous nous débrouillons tant bien que mal; **he struggled through the hole in the wall** avec difficulté il réussit à passer par le trou du mur; **the more he struggled the deeper he sank in the mud** plus il se débattait plus il s'enfonçait dans la boue; **let's s. on for another month/couple of kilometres or so** essayons de tenir encore un mois/kilomètre ou deux; **the climbers struggled back to camp** les grimpeurs sont rentrés au camp tant bien que mal; **we struggled through** nous avons surmonté tous les obstacles; **to be struggling (badly)** (*in one's job, university course etc*) avoir du mal; **the team is struggling** (*in match, to retain position in league etc*) l'équipe a des difficultés; **to s. against circumstances** lutter contre les événements; **to s. with death** lutter contre la mort; **to s. with one's conscience/homework** être aux prises avec sa conscience/

ses devoirs; **we have to s. to make ends meet** nous avons du mal à joindre les deux bouts; **many companies are struggling** (*financially*) beaucoup d'entreprises ont du mal *ou* sont en difficulté; **I had to s. to make myself understood** j'ai eu de la peine *ou* du mal à me faire comprendre; **he was obviously struggling for** *or* **to find the right word** il avait visiblement de la peine à trouver le mot juste

struggling ['strʌglɪŋ] *adj* (*artist etc*) qui vit péniblement; (*masses*) laborieux; **when I was a s. young actor** quand je débutais comme acteur

strum¹ [strʌm] *n* **the s. of a guitar** le son d'une guitare

strum² (**-mm-**) **1** *vt* (*guitar*) pincer les cordes de; **to s. (out) a tune** (*on guitar*) jouer un air **2** *vi* (*on a guitar*) pincer les cordes

strumming ['strʌmɪŋ] *n* **a gentle s. from the guitar** les doux accords de la guitare; *Pej* **his s. gets on my nerves** les raclements de sa guitare me tapent sur les nerfs

strumpet ['strʌmpɪt] *n Arch, Lit* prostituée *f*

strung *see* **string²**

strung-out *adj esp Am Sl* (*on heroin*) en manque

strung-up *adj* (*person*) tendu

strut¹ [strʌt] *n Constr* (*support*) étai *m*; (*crosspiece*) traverse *f*; (*in roofing*) jambe *f* de force; (*of roof truss*) contrefiche *f*; *Av* pilier *m*, mât *m*

strut² *n* (*walk*) démarche *f* affectée

strut³ **1** *vi* (**-tt-**) se pavaner; (*after victory, compliment etc*) se rengorger; **to s. in/out** entrer/sortir en se pavanant **2** *vt esp Am F* **to s. one's stuff** frimer

▶ **strut about, strut around** *vi* (*parade oneself*) se pavaner; (*walk around self-importantly*) parader

struth [stru:θ] *int Br Sl* ça alors!

strychnine ['strɪkni:n] *n* strychnine *f*

stub¹ [stʌb] *n* **(a)** (*of pencil*) bout *m*; (*of cigarette, cigar*) mégot *m*; (*of dog's tail*) bout de queue; **s. axle** fusée *f* de direction **(b)** (*of cheque*) talon *m*, souche *f*

stub² *vt* (**-bb-**) **to s. one's toe (on** *or* **against sth)** se heurter *ou* se cogner le pied contre qch, buter contre qch

▶ **stub out** *vtsep* (*cigarette*) écraser

stubble ['stʌb(ə)l] *n* **(a)** *Agr* chaume *m*, éteule *f*; **to clear a field of s.** chaumer un champ; **to burn the s.** brûler les chaumes; **s. field** chaume **(b)** (*on face*) barbe *f* piquante (*de plusieurs jours*)

stubbly ['stʌblɪ] *adj* **(a)** *Agr* (*field*) couvert de chaume *ou* d'éteule **(b) s. beard** barbe *f* piquante (*de plusieurs jours*); **s. chin** menton *m* qui pique

stubborn ['stʌbən] *adj* **(a)** (*person*) entêté, têtu, obstiné; (*determination, resistance*) farouche; **their s. refusal to surrender** leur refus obstiné de se rendre; **as s. as a mule** têtu comme un mulet *ou* une mule **(b)** (*stain, infection*) rebelle

stubbornly ['stʌbənlɪ] *adv* obstinément, avec entêtement; **she s. refused to give up hope** elle a refusé obstinément d'abandonner espoir

stubbornness ['stʌbənnɪs] *n* (*of person*) entêtement *m*, obstination *f*, opiniâtreté *f*; (*of determination, resistance*) inflexibilité *f*

stubby ['stʌbɪ] *adj* (*person*) trapu; **s. fingers** doigts *mpl* boudinés

stucco¹ ['stʌkəʊ] *n* stuc *m*; **s. work** stucage *m*

stucco² *vt* (*pt, pp* **stuccoed**; *prp* **stuccoing**) stuquer; **stuccoed decorations** des décorations en stuc

stuck *see* **stick²**

stuck-up *adj F Pej* snob; (*conceited*) prétentieux

stud¹ [stʌd] *n* **(a)** (*nail*) clou *m* à grosse tête; (*as ornament*) clou doré; (*of pedestrian crossing*) clou; **studs** (*on football boots*) crampons *mpl* **(b)** (*of dress shirt*) bouton *m* (double); **(collar) s.** bouton de col **(c)** *Tech* (*short pin*) goujon *m*, tourillon *m*; **s. (bolt)** goujon **(d)** *Constr* poteau *m*, montant *m*; **s. wall** mur *m* de séparation **(e) s. (earring)** boucle *f* (d'oreille)

stud² *vt* (**-dd-**) **(a)** (*fit with studs*) garnir de clous, clouter; **studded door** porte garnie de clous *ou* cloutée; **studded tyre** pneu *m* clouté; *Fig* **studded with stars** (*sky*) parsemé d'étoiles; **her dress was studded with jewels** sa robe était constellée de pierreries **(b)** *Constr* (*partition*) établir la charpente de

stud³ *n* **(a) to be at s.** (*of horse*) être à la monte; (*of dog*) faire des saillies; **to put a horse to s.** utiliser un cheval comme étalon **(b)** (*stallion*) étalon *m*; *Fig Sl* (*man*) mec *m* bien monté; **he's a real s.** c'est un vrai tombeur **(c)** *Cards* **s. (poker)** poker *m*

studbook ['stʌdbʊk] *n* stud-book *m*

student ['stju:dənt] *n* **(a)** *Univ* étudiant, -ante; *Sch* élève *mf*; **law/medical/arts s.** étudiant en droit/en médecine/en lettres; **the s. body** les étudiants *mpl*; *US* **s. driver** apprenti(e) conducteur, -trice; **s. flat/house** appartement *m*/maison *f* d'étudiants; **s. life** vie *f* d'étudiant; **s. rate** (*for travel etc*) tarif *m* étudiant; **s. radio** radio *f* universitaire; **s. riots** émeutes *fpl* étudiantes; **students' union** syndicat *m* étudiant **(b)** (*observer etc*) (*of human nature etc*) observateur, -trice **(of** de); **students of Middle East politics will know that ...** ceux qui étudient la politique du Moyen-Orient savent que ...

student grant *n* bourse *f*

student nurse *n* élève *f* infirmière

student teacher *n* professeur *m* en cours de formation

stud farm *n* haras *m*

stud fastener *n* pression *f*

studhorse ['stʌdhɔ:s] *n* étalon *m*

studied ['stʌdɪd] *adj* (*style, attitude, posture*) étudié, recherché; (*move, act*) prémédité, calculé; (*negligence*) voulu; **s. elegance** élégance *f* recherchée

studio ['stju:dɪəʊ] *n* (*of artist, photographer*) atelier *m*, studio *m*; **(film/television) s.** studio de cinéma/de télévision; **recording s.** studio d'enregistrement; *Rad* auditorium *m*; *TV* **s. audience** public *m* (*présent lors d'un enregistrement*); **s. bed** canapé-lit *m*, *pl* canapés-lits; **s. (broadcast) camera** caméra *f* en studio; *Am* **s. apartment,** *Br* **s. flat** studio; **s. control console** pupitre *m* de régie; **s. couch** divan *m*; **s. manager** directeur *m* de studio; **s. monitor** écran *m* de contrôle studio; **s. rehearsal** répétition *f* en studio; **s. supervisor** chef *m* de studio; **s. talkback** interphone *m* de studio

studious ['stju:dɪəs] *adj* **(a)** (*person, atmosphere*) studieux; **person of s. habits** personne studieuse **(b)** (*careful*) **with s. attention** avec une attention soutenue; **because of his s. avoidance of the topic** parce qu'il évitait soigneusement le sujet

studiously ['stju:dɪəslɪ] *adv* **(a)** (*listen to teacher*) studieusement **(b)** (*carefully*) attentivement; **she s. avoided me** elle s'ingéniait à m'éviter; **he was s. polite** il était d'une politesse étudiée

studiousness ['stju:dɪəsnɪs] *n* **(a)** (*eagerness to study*) amour *m* de l'étude **(b)** (*carefulness*) empressement *m*, zèle *m* **(in doing sth** à faire qch)

stud mare *n* (jument *f*) poulinière *f*

study¹ ['stʌdɪ] *n* **(a)** (*investigation*) étude *f* **(of** de); (*report*) étude, rapport *m*; **to make a s. of sth** étudier qch; **I've made a special s. of ...** je me suis spécialisé dans ...; *Scol, Univ* **studies** études; **Department of Classical Studies** Section des lettres classiques; **s. tour** voyage *m* d'étude **(b)** (*room*) cabinet *m* de travail, bureau *m*; *Sch* salle *f* d'étude **(c)** *Old-fashioned* **brown s.** (*reverie*) rêverie *f*; **to be (lost) in a brown s.** être plongé *ou* absorbé dans ses réflexions *ou* dans de vagues rêveries **(d)** *Art, Mus* étude *f*; *F* **her face was a s.!** il fallait voir sa tête!

study² **1** *vt* (*language, music, part*) étudier; (*terrain, stars*) observer; *Scol, Univ* (*French, law*) faire des études de; (*plans*) examiner, étudier; (*question*) mettre à l'étude; **she studied history at Yale** elle a étudié l'histoire à Yale; **he studied her face for signs of emotion** il examina son visage pour y détecter des signes d'émotion

2 *vi* étudier; **you ought to s. harder** tu devrais étudier davantage; **he's studying** il étudie; (*he's at college etc*) il fait ses études; **she's studying to be a doctor** elle fait des études de médecine; **to s. for an examination** se préparer pour un examen, préparer un examen; **he studied under Professor ...** il a étudié avec le Professeur ..., il a été l'élève du Professeur ...

study group *n* groupe *m* d'étude

study period *n* heure *f* de permanence *ou* d'étude

study trip *n* voyage *m* d'études

stuff¹ [stʌf] *n* **(a)** (*substance*) matière(s) *f(pl)*, substance *f*, *F* truc *m*; **here's some s. to put on that burn** voilà de quoi soigner cette brûlure; **there's some sticky s. in the saucepan** il y a quelque chose qui colle dans la casserole; **he is of the s. that heroes are made of** il est du bois dont on fait les héros; *F* **she writes good s.** elle écrit de bons trucs; *F* **there was some s. about unions on the news** ils ont dit un truc sur les syndicats aux informations; **dangerous s., acid** c'est dangereux, l'acide; *F* **this wine is good s.** ce vin, c'est du bon; **I don't like that s. you gave me** je n'aime pas ce que vous m'avez donné là

(b) (*objects*) truc *m*; (*possessions*) affaires *fpl*

(c) (*more vaguely*) **come on, do your s.!** allons, montre-nous ce que tu sais faire!; **he knows his s.** il s'y connaît; **that's the s.!** voilà ce qu'il faut!; **good s.!** (*well done etc*) bien!; **old s.** vieilleries *fpl*; **silly s.** sottises *fpl*, balivernes *fpl*; *Old-fashioned* **s. and nonsense!** ça, c'est de la bêtise!

(d) *Tex* **(woollen) s.** étoffe *f* de laine

(e) *Sl* (*drug*) came *f*

stuff² *vt* (**a**) (*fill*) bourrer (**with** de); (*chair, cushion*) rembourrer (**with** de); *Culin* (*chicken etc*) farcir; (*zoological specimen*) empailler, naturaliser; *Vulg* (*have sex with*) se faire; **her pockets are stuffed with sweets** elle a des bonbons plein les poches; *F* **to s. oneself, to s. one's face** s'empiffrer; **his head was stuffed with romantic ideas** il avait la tête bourrée *ou* farcie d'idées romanesques; *Br Vulg* **get stuffed!** va te faire foutre!; *Br Vulg* **he can get stuffed** il peut aller se faire foutre

(**b**) (*shove*) **to s. sth into sth** fourrer qch dans qch; **to s. one's fingers in one's ears** se boucher les oreilles (avec les doigts); *Br Vulg* **you can s. it** (**up your arse**)! tu peux te le mettre où je pense!; *Br Vulg* **s. your job!** ton boulot, tu peux te le mettre où je pense; *Br Vulg* **s. this, I'm going home!** et puis merde, je rentre!

▶ **stuff up** *vtsep* (*hole etc*) boucher; **I'm all stuffed up with a cold** j'ai le nez complètement bouché avec ce rhume; **I'm** *or* **my nose is stuffed up** j'ai le nez bouché

stuffed [stʌft] *adj* (*olives, tomatoes etc*) farci; (*owl, fox, rabbit etc*) empaillé; *F* **s. shirt** individu *m* suffisant

stuffing ['stʌfɪŋ] *n* (*filling for meat, poultry etc*) farce *f*; (*for upholstery*) bourre *f*, rembourrage *m*; **horsehair s.** matelassure *f* de crin; *F* **to knock the s. out of sb** (*defeat heavily*) mettre la pâtée à qn; (*of blow, attacker, illness*) mettre qn K.O.

stuffy ['stʌfɪ] *adj* (**a**) (*room etc*) mal ventilé, mal aéré; **to smell s.** sentir le renfermé; **it's a bit s. in here** on manque d'air ici (**b**) (*standoffish*) collet monté; (*over-conventional*) vieux jeu *inv*; **don't be so s.** (*don't be offended*) il n'y a pas de quoi te scandaliser (**c**) **to feel s.** (*have blocked nose*) avoir le nez bouché

stultify ['stʌltɪfaɪ] *vt* (*make stupid*) (*of work*) abrutir, assommer

stultifying ['stʌltɪfaɪɪŋ] *adj* (*work*) abrutissant

stumble¹ ['stʌmb(ə)l] *n* (*when walking*) trébuchement *m*; (*of horse*) faux pas *m*

stumble² *vi* (**a**) (*when walking*) trébucher; (*of horse*) faire un faux pas, broncher; **to s. off** partir en trébuchant; **she stumbled over my briefcase** elle a trébuché sur ma serviette (**b**) **to s. when one speaks** (*hesitate*) hésiter en parlant; (*confuse words etc*) s'embrouiller en parlant; **she stumbled through her speech** elle s'est embrouillée tout au long de son discours

▶ **stumble across** *vipo* (*find*) tomber sur par hasard

▶ **stumble along** *vi* avancer en trébuchant

▶ **stumble (up)on** *vipo* = **stumble across**

stumbling ['stʌmblɪŋ] **1** *adj* (*speech*) hésitant; **she took her first s. steps** elle a fait ses premiers pas **2** *n* **s. block** pierre *f* d'achoppement

stump¹ [stʌmp] *n* (**a**) (*of tree*) souche *f*, chicot *m*; (*of tooth*) reste *m* d'une dent cassée; *F* chicot; (*of arm, leg*) moignon *m*; (*of pencil*) bout *m*; (*of cigar*) bout, *F* mégot *m*; (*of tail, column, mast*) tronçon *m*; (*of cabbage*) trognon *m* (**b**) *F* **stumps** (*legs*) pattes *fpl*, quilles *fpl*; **stir your stumps!** remuez-vous!, grouillez-vous! (**c**) *Pol F* **to be on the s.** faire campagne; **s. orator** *or* **speaker** orateur *m* (**d**) *Cr* piquet *m*; **to draw stumps** enlever les piquets, cesser le match

stump² **1** *vt* (**a**) (*baffle*) coller; **to be stumped for an answer** ne savoir que répondre, sécher; **it stumped me** ça m'a désarçonné; **this one has got me stumped** alors là, je sèche (**b**) *Cr* mettre hors jeu (*un batteur qui est sorti de son camp*) (**c**) *esp Am Pol F* **she stumped the country from one end to the other** elle a parcouru le pays d'un bout à l'autre pour sa campagne électorale **2** *vi esp Am Pol F* faire campagne

▶ **stump along** *vi* (*walk heavily*) marcher *ou* avancer d'un pas lourd; (*limping*) marcher *ou* avancer, en clopinant

▶ **stump off** *vi* (*annoyed*) partir d'un pas lourd

▶ **stump up** *Br F* **1** *vtsep* (*pay*) cracher **2** *vi* casquer

stumpy ['stʌmpɪ] *adj* (*person, thing*) trapu; (*figure*) ramassé; **s. pencil** petit bout *m* de crayon

stun [stʌn] *vt* (**-nn-**) (**a**) (*make unconscious*) étourdir, assommer (**b**) *Fig* (*shock*) abasourdir; **the news stunned us** cette nouvelle nous a fait l'effet d'un coup de massue *ou* nous ont abasourdis; **we were stunned to hear of your accident** nous avons été consternés d'apprendre que vous aviez eu un accident; **to be stunned** être stupéfait; **stunned with surprise** stupéfié, frappé de stupeur

stung *see* **sting²**

stun grenade *n* grenade *f* incapacitante

stun gun *n* (*in science fiction*) pistolet *m* paralysant; (*for animals*) fusil *m* hypodermique

stunner ['stʌnər] *n F* (**a**) **he's/she's a s.** il/elle est vachement beau/belle, il/elle est canon (**b**) (*excellent thing*) chose *f* extraordinaire, *F* truc *m* super

stunning ['stʌnɪŋ] *adj* (**a**) (*blow*) étourdissant, abrutissant; (*misfortune*) accablant, bouleversant (**b**) (*shocking*) renversant; (*amazing, excellent*) formidable, épatant; **she's really s.** (*beautiful*) elle est éblouissante; **his/her s. good looks** sa beauté éblouissante

stunningly ['stʌnɪŋlɪ] *adv* **s. beautiful** d'une beauté éblouissante; **s. dressed** magnifiquement vêtu

stunt¹ [stʌnt] *vt* (*person, thing*) arrêter dans sa croissance; (*growth*) ralentir très fortement; **the economy had been stunted by the lack of investment** l'économie avait été freinée dans son développement par la faiblesse de l'investissement

stunt² *n* (**a**) (*skilful act*) tour *m* de force; *Cin* cascade *f*; **to do one's own stunts** (*of actor, actress*) ne pas se faire doubler dans les scènes dangereuses; *Av* **to perform stunts** faire des acrobaties (**b**) (*sth done to gain attention, for publicity*) coup *m* de pub; *usu Pej* **to pull a s.** faire un coup de pub

stunted ['stʌntɪd] *adj* (*tree, person*) rabougri; (*intellect, development*) atrophié; **to become s.** (*of tree, person*) se rabougrir

stunt flying *n Av* vol *m* acrobatique

stunt man *n Cin* cascadeur *m*

stunt pilot *n Av* pilote *m* de voltige

stunt woman *n Cin* cascadeuse *f*

stupefaction [stju:pɪ'fækʃən] *n* stupeur *f*, stupéfaction *f*

stupefy ['stju:pɪfaɪ] *vt* (**a**) (*astound*) abasourdir, stupéfier; **I'm absolutely stupefied** (**by what has happened**) je n'en reviens pas, j'en suis stupéfait (**b**) (*make insensitive*) abrutir; *Med* stupéfier, engourdir

stupefying ['stju:pɪfaɪɪŋ] *adj* stupéfiant

stupendous [stju:'pendəs] *adj* prodigieux, *F* formidable

stupendously [stju:'pendəslɪ] *adv* prodigieusement

stupid ['stju:pɪd] **1** *adj* stupide, sot, *f* sotte, bête; **I did a s. thing** j'ai fait une bêtise; **don't be s.!** ne faites pas l'idiot!; **how s. of me!** que je suis bête!; **I'm not s., you know!** je ne suis pas idiot quand même!; **what a s. place to put it!** c'est idiot de l'avoir mis là!; **a s. record/film** un disque/film idiot; **I don't want your s. book!** je ne veux pas de ton livre idiot!; *F* **to drink oneself s.** s'abrutir d'alcool **2** *n F* (*term of address*) **of course not, s.!** bien sûr que non, gros bêta/grosse bêtasse!

stupidity [stju:'pɪdɪtɪ] *n* stupidité *f*; (*action, remark*) bêtise *f*

stupidly ['stju:pɪdlɪ] *adv* stupidement, bêtement; **rather s., I agreed** bêtement, j'ai accepté

stupor ['stju:pər] *n* stupeur *f*; **in a drunken s.** abruti par la boisson

sturdily ['stɜ:dɪlɪ] *adv* (**a**) (*constructed*) fortement; **s. built** solide (**b**) (*to refuse, defend etc*) résolument

sturdiness ['stɜ:dɪnɪs] *n* (**a**) (*of person, plant etc*) vigueur *f*, robustesse *f*; (*of table, piece of equipment*) solidité *f* (**b**) (*of resolve, opposition*) résolution *f*, fermeté *f*

sturdy ['stɜ:dɪ] *adj* (**a**) (*person*) vigoureux, robuste; (*table, furniture*) solide; **a s. fellow** un gaillard robuste (**b**) (*opposition, resistance*) résolu, ferme

sturgeon ['stɜ:dʒ(ə)n] *n* (*fish*) esturgeon *m*

stutter¹ ['stʌtər] *n* bégaiement *m*; **he has a s.** il est bègue, il bégaie

stutter² **1** *vi* bégayer; **the engine stuttered into life** le motteur toussa avant de démarrer **2** *vt* bégayer

stutterer ['stʌtərər] *n* bègue *mf*

stuttering ['stʌtərɪŋ] **1** *adj* bègue; **s. machine-gun fire** le crépitement des mitrailleuses **2** *n* bégaiement *m*

sty¹, *pl* **sties** [staɪ, staɪz] *n Agr, Fig* porcherie *f*

sty², stye [staɪ] *n Med* orgelet *m*

Stygian ['stɪdʒɪən] *adj Lit* d'une noirceur impénétrable; **S. gloom** ténèbres *fpl* impénétrables

style¹ [staɪl] *n* (**a**) (*manner*) style *m*, manière *f*; (*of car etc*) type *m*, modèle *f*; (*of clothes*) mode *f*; (*of hair*) coiffure *f*; **s. of living** style *ou* train *m* de vie; **Gothic/Byzantine s.** style gothique/byzantin; **building in the classical s.** bâtiment *m* de style classique; **that's not my s.** ce n'est pas mon genre *ou* style; **that's the s.!** c'est cela!, bravo!; **you've got to admire his s.!** on ne peut qu'admirer la façon dont il s'y prend!; **something in that s.** quelque chose de ce genre *ou* style; **in the latest s.** à la (dernière) mode, *F* dernier cri; *Comptr* **s. bar** barre *f* de style; **s. sheet** feuille *f* de style

(**b**) (*in writing, speaking*) style *m*; (*way of writing*) manière *f* d'écrire; **written in a humorous s.** écrit dans un style humoristique; **written in the s. of a 1940s thriller** écrit dans le style du roman policier des années 1940; **this writer lacks s.** (*good style*) cet écrivain manque de style

(**c**) (*distinction, sophistication*) chic *m*, classe *f*; **she has s.** elle a de l'allure *ou* de la classe; **to live in (grand** *or* **great) s.** mener grand train, vivre sur un grand pied; **they arrived in s.** ils ont fait leur entrée en grande pompe; **let's do things in s.** faisons bien les choses; **let's travel in s.** voyageons en grand style

(**d**) (*of calendar*) **old/new s.** vieux/nouveau style *m*
(**e**) (*tool in engraving*) burin *m*; *Bot* style *m*

style[2] *vt* (**a**) (*design*) créer; **dress styled by X** robe créée par X; **hair styled by X** coiffé(e) par X (**b**) (*designate*) (*sb*) dénommer; (*sth*) appeler; **to s. oneself doctor** se faire appeler docteur

styling ['staɪlɪŋ] *n* façon *f*; (*of car*) ligne *f*; **hair s.** coiffure *f*; **s. mousse/gel** mousse *f* coiffante/gel *m* coiffant

stylish ['staɪlɪʃ] *adj* qui a de la classe; (*clothes*) élégant, chic *inv*; (*camerawork, design*) artistique; **a s. writer** un écrivain qui a du style

stylishly ['staɪlɪʃlɪ] *adv* élégamment, avec chic, avec classe

stylishness ['staɪlɪʃnɪs] *n* élégance *f*, chic *m*, classe *f*; (*of prose*) élégance

stylist ['staɪlɪst] *n* styliste *mf*; **hair s.** coiffeur, -euse (d'art); (*shop sign*) = coiffure *f* (d'art)

stylistic [staɪ'lɪstɪk] *adj* stylistique, du *ou* de style

stylistically [staɪ'lɪstɪk(ə)lɪ] *adv* du point de vue de la stylistique

stylistics [staɪ'lɪstɪks] *npl* [①**A10**,c] (*usu with sing verb*) stylistique *f*

stylization [staɪlaɪ'zeɪʃən] *n* stylisation *f*

stylize ['staɪlaɪz] *vt Art* styliser; **stylized flowers** fleurs stylisées

stylus, *pl* **-i, -uses** ['staɪləs, -aɪ, -əsɪz] *n* (*in engraving etc*) style *m*; (*on record player*) pointe *f* de lecture; (*made of sapphire*) saphir *m*; (*made of diamond*) diamant *m*

stymie ['staɪmɪ] *vt F* **this question stymied me** cette question m'a coincé; **to be stymied** être dans une impasse

styptic ['stɪptɪk] *Med* **1** *adj* styptique, astringent; **s. pencil** pierre *f* d'alun **2** *n* styptique *m*, astringent *m*

suasion ['sweɪʒ(ə)n] *n Arch, Lit* persuasion *f*; **to subject sb to moral s.** agir sur la conscience de qn

suave [swɑːv] *adj* affable, courtois, *Lit* urbain, *Pej* doucereux, mielleux

suavely ['swɑːvlɪ] *adv* avec affabilité, affablement, *Pej* de façon doucereuse, doucereusement

suaveness ['swɑːvnɪs], **suavity** ['swɑːvɪtɪ] *n* affabilité *f*, courtoisie *f*, *Lit* urbanité *f*, *Pej* manières *fpl* doucereuses, airs *mpl* mielleux

sub[1] [sʌb] *n F* (**a**) (*subscription*) (*to club, union etc*) cotisation *f*; **to pay one's subs** payer sa cotisation (**b**) *Sp* (*substitute*) remplaçant *m* (**c**) *Naut* (*submarine*) sous-marin *m* (**d**) *Journ* (*subeditor*) secrétaire *mf* de rédaction

sub[2] (**-bb-**) *F* **1** *vi* (**a**) (*substitute*) **to s. for sb** remplacer qn (**b**) *Journ* (*subedit*) mettre un article au point, travailler comme secrétaire de rédaction **2** *vt Journ* (*article*) mettre au point, corriger

sub-account *n Acct* sous-compte *m*

subagent [sʌb'eɪdʒənt] *n* sous-agent *m*

subalpine [sʌb'ælpaɪn] *adj* subalpin

subaltern ['sʌbəltən] *n Mil* (officier *m*) subalterne *m*

subaqua [sʌb'ækwə] *adj* **s. diving** plongée *f* sous-marine; **s. club** club *m* de plongée sous-marine

subatomic [sʌbə'tɒmɪk] *adj* subatomique

subbed [sʌbd] *adj Journ* corrigé

subclass ['sʌbklɑːs] *n* sous-classe *f*

subclause ['sʌbklɔːz] *n esp Jur* (*of contract*) paragraphe *m*

subcommittee ['sʌbkəmɪtɪ] *n* sous-comité *m*; (*in larger organizations*) sous-commission *f*

subconscious [sʌb'kɒnʃəs] *adj, n Psy* subconscient *m*

subconsciously [sʌb'kɒnʃəslɪ] *adv* subconsciemment

subcontinent [sʌb'kɒntɪnənt] *n* sous-continent *m*; **the Indian s.** le sous-continent indien

subcontract[1] [sʌb'kɒntrækt] *n* (contrat *m* de) sous-traitance *f*

subcontract[2] [sʌbkən'trækt] *vt* (*work, order*) sous-traiter; **to s. a job (out) to sb** sous-traiter un travail avec qn

subcontracting ['sʌbkəntræktɪŋ] *n* sous-traitance *f*; **the s. firm** le sous-traitant

subcontractor ['sʌbkəntræktər] *n* sous-traitant *m*

subculture ['sʌbkʌltʃər] *n* (**a**) (*in sociology*) groupe *m ou* phénomène *m* culturel secondaire; **youth s.** phénomène *m* culturel propre à la jeunesse (**b**) (*in bacteriology*) repiquage *m*, culture *f* secondaire

subcutaneous [sʌbkjʊ'teɪnɪəs] *adj* sous-cutané

subdeacon [sʌb'diːkən] *n Rel* sous-diacre *m*

subdirectory ['sʌbdɪrektərɪ] *n Comptr* sous-répertoire *m*

subdivide [sʌbdɪ'vaɪd] **1** *vt* subdiviser, sous-diviser **2** *vi* se subdiviser

subdivision [sʌbdɪ'vɪʒən] *n* subdivision *f*

subdominant [sʌb'dɒmɪnənt] *n Mus* sous-dominante *f*

subdue [səb'djuː] *vt* (**a**) (*tribe, enemy etc*) subjuguer, soumettre, assujettir; (*fire*) maîtriser; (*angry impulse*) dompter, réprimer; (*emotions*) maîtriser, dominer (**b**) (*light, heat, voice*) adoucir; (*light, pain*) atténuer

subdued [səb'djuːd] *adj* (*person*) (*quieter than usual*) inhabituellement calme; (*sad*) triste; (*heat, sound*) adouci; **s. colours** couleurs *fpl* sobres; **s. conversation** conversation *f* à voix basse; **s. light** demi-jour *m*, lumière *f* tamisée; **it's a very s. tone for him** c'est un ton très modéré qui ne lui ressemble pas; **in a s. tone** *or* **voice** à voix basse, à mi-voix

subedit [sʌb'edɪt] *Journ* **1** *vi* mettre au point un article, travailler comme secrétaire de rédaction **2** *vt* (*article*) mettre au point

subediting [sʌb'edɪtɪŋ] *n* mise *f* au point, correction *f*

subeditor [sʌb'edɪtər] *n Journ* secrétaire *mf* de rédaction; (*in publishing*) rédacteur, -trice; *Journ* **assistant s.** secrétaire *mf* adjoint(e)

subfamily ['sʌbfæmɪlɪ] *n Biol* sous-famille *f*

subfolder ['sʌbfəʊldər] *n Comptr* sous-dossier *m*

sub-frame *n Aut* faux-châssis *m*, sous-châssis *m*

subfusc [sʌb'fʌsk] *adj* (*clothing*) sombre

subgenus, *pl* **-genera** ['sʌbdʒiːnəs, -dʒenərə] *n Biol* sous-genre *m*

subgroup ['sʌbgruːp] *n* sous-groupe *m*

subhead, subheading ['sʌbhed(ɪŋ)] *n* sous-titre *m*

subhuman [sʌb'hjuːmən] **1** *adj* sous-humain; (*intelligence, behaviour*) inférieur à celui/celle des humains **2** *n* sous-homme *m*

subject[1] ['sʌbdʒɪkt] *n* (**a**) (*of conversation, book, fugue*) sujet *m*; (*of legal case*) objet *m*; *Sch, Univ* matière *f*; **this will be the s. of my next lecture** ma prochaine conférence portera sur ce sujet; **to wander from the s.** s'écarter du sujet, faire une digression; **while we are on the s.** à ce propos, pendant que nous sommes sur ce sujet; **on the s. of** à propos de; **to change the s.** parler d'autre chose, changer de sujet; **to change the s., has anyone seen Andy?** pour changer de sujet, est-ce que quelqu'un a vu Andy?; **don't try to change the s.!** n'essaie pas de changer de sujet *ou* de détourner la conversation; *Sch, Univ* **science subjects** matières *fpl* scientifiques; **s. matter** (*of letter*) contenu *m*; (*of book*) sujet; (*of contract*) objet
(**b**) *Biol, Med etc* sujet *m*; **to be the s. of an experiment** servir de sujet d'expérience
(**c**) [①**A72-3**,a; **B17**,D,1] *Gram* (*of verb*) sujet *m*
(**d**) *Art, Phot* sujet *m*
(**e**) (*of monarch*) sujet, -ette; **British s.** sujet britannique

subject[2] *adj* (**a**) (*state, country*) assujetti, soumis; **s. to military laws** justiciable des tribunaux militaires
(**b**) (*liable*) **s. to** (*rheumatism, hayfever etc*) sujet à; **to be s. to violent changes of mood/fits of jealousy** avoir tendance à avoir des sautes d'humeur/des crises de jalousie; **prices s. to 5% discount** prix bénéficiant d'une remise de 5%; **s. to stamp duty** soumis au timbre; **all trains will be s. to delay** des retards sont à prévoir sur toutes les lignes; **we're all s. to taxation** nous sommes tous assujettis à l'impôt; **an area that is s. to avalanches** une zone d'avalanches; **I'm very s. to colds** j'attrape des rhumes facilement; **s. to variation** variable
(**c**) (*conditional*) **s. to ...** sous réserve de ...; **s. to payment** moyennant paiement; **s. to your consent** sous réserve de votre consentement; **it's all s. to her approval** tout dépend de *ou* est subordonné à son approbation

subject[3] [səb'dʒekt] *vt* (**a**) (*subjugate*) (*people, nation*) soumettre, assujettir, subjuguer (**b**) (*force to undergo*) soumettre, exposer (**sb/sth to sth** qn/qch à qch); **to s. sb to torture** mettre qn à la torture, torturer qn; **to s. sb/sth to an examination** faire subir un examen à qn/qch, soumettre qn/qch à un examen; **to be subjected to much criticism** être en butte à de nombreuses critiques; **metal subjected to great heat** métal exposé à une forte chaleur; **to s. oneself to sth** se soumettre à qch; **to s. sth to tax** soumettre qch à l'impôt

subjection [səb'dʒekʃən] *n* soumission *f*, assujettissement *m* (**to** à); **in a state of s.** dans la sujétion

subjective [səb'dʒektɪv] *adj* subjectif

subjectively [səb'dʒektɪvlɪ] *adv* subjectivement

subjectivism [səb'dʒektɪvɪz(ə)m] *n* subjectivisme *m*

subjectivity [sʌbdʒek'tɪvɪtɪ] *n* subjectivité *f*

subjoin [sʌb'dʒɔɪn] *vt* (*list*) ajouter, adjoindre

sub judice ['sʌb'dʒuːdɪsɪ] *adj Jur* **the case is s.** l'affaire n'est pas encore jugée

subjugate ['sʌbdʒʊgeɪt] *vt* (*people, nation*) assujettir, subjuguer

subjugation [sʌbdʒʊ'geɪʃən] *n* assujettissement *m*, subjugation *f*

subjunctive [səb'dʒʌŋktɪv] [①**A51-2**,14; **B30-31**,G] *Gram* **1** *adj* subjonctif **2** *n* subjonctif *m*; **in the s. (mood)** au (mode) subjonctif

sublease[1] ['sʌbliːs] *n* (**a**) (*document, type of contract*) sous-bail *m*, *pl* sous-baux; (*of farm*) sous-ferme *f* (**b**) (*act*) sous-location *f*

sublease[2] [sʌb'liːs] *vt* (*apartment*) sous-louer; (*land*) sous-affermer

sub-lessee *n* sous-locataire *mf*
sub-lessor *n* sous-bailleur, -bailleresse
sublet [sʌb'let] *vt (pt, pp* **-let**; *prp* **-letting**) *(apartment)* sous-louer; *(land)* sous-affermer
sub-letting *n* sous-location *f*
sub-lieutenant *n Naut* enseigne *m* (de vaisseau) de première classe
sublimate[1] ['sʌblɪmeɪt] *n Ch* sublimé *m*
sublimate[2] *vt* **(a)** *(feeling, instinct)* sublimer **(b)** *Ch (solid)* sublimer
sublimation [sʌblɪ'meɪʃən] *n* sublimation *f*
sublime[1] [sə'blaɪm] **1** *adj (thought, poet, F little dress etc)* sublime; **s. indifference** suprême indifférence **2** *n* **the s.** le sublime; **to go from the s. to the ridiculous** *or Br Sl* **the gorblimey** passer du sublime au ridicule
sublime[2] **1** *vt Ch (solid)* sublimer **2** *vi Ch (of solid)* se sublimer
sublimely [sə'blaɪmlɪ] *adv* **(a) s. beautiful** d'une beauté sublime **(b)** *(indifferent)* suprêmement; **he remained s. unaware of what was going on** il n'a jamais rien su de ce qui se passait
subliminal [sʌb'lɪmɪn(ə)l] *adj Psy* subliminal, subliminaire; **s. advertising** publicité *f* subliminale; **s. message** message *m* subliminal
sublimity [sʌb'lɪmɪtɪ] *n* sublimité *f*
sub-machine-gun *n* mitraillette *f*
submarine [sʌbmə'ri:n] **1** *adj (cable, volcano)* sous-marin **2** *n* **(a)** *Naut* sous-marin *m*; **midget** *or* **pocket s.** sous-marin de poche **(b)** *Am (sandwich)* gros sandwich *m*
submariner [sʌb'mærɪnər] *n* sous-marinier *m*
sub-market *n* sous-marché *m*
submediant [sʌb'mi:dɪənt] *n Mus* sous-dominante *f*
submenu ['sʌbmenju:] *n Comptr* sous-menu *m*
submerge [səb'mɜ:dʒ] **1** *vt* **(a)** *(put in liquid)* immerger **(in** dans) **(b)** *(cover) (field etc)* submerger, inonder; **submerged in details** perdu dans les détails **2** *vi* plonger; *(of submarine)* effectuer sa plongée
submerged [səb'mɜ:dʒd] *adj (field etc)* submergé, inondé; *(submarine)* en plongée; *(reef)* sous-marin; *Fig* **s. in work** submergé de travail, qui croule sous le travail
submergence [səb'mɜ:dʒəns] *n* submersion *f*
submersible [səb'mɜ:sɪb(ə)l] *Naut* **1** *adj* submersible **2** *n* (bateau *m*) submersible *m*, sous-marin *m*
submersion [səb'mɜ:ʃən] *n* submersion *f*
submission [səb'mɪʃən] *n* **(a)** *(to person's will, authority)* soumission *f*; *(to defeat)* résignation *f*; *(in wrestling)* abandon *m*; **to starve/beat sb into s.** réduire qn par la famine/violence **(b)** *(of matter to arbitration)* soumission *f*; *(of proof of identity)* présentation *f* **(c)** *Jur* plaidoirie *f*; **in my s. ...** selon ma thèse ...; **it's my s. that ...** j'ai la conviction que ...
submissive [səb'mɪsɪv] *adj (tone, look)* soumis; *(person)* docile; **to be sexually s.** être soumis sur le plan sexuel
submissively [səb'mɪsɪvlɪ] *adv* avec soumission, docilement
submissiveness [səb'mɪsɪvnɪs] *n* soumission *f*, docilité *f*
submit [səb'mɪt] **(-tt-) 1** *vi (to sb, sb's will, superior power)* se soumettre; *(to necessity)* se plier; *(to discipline)* s'astreindre; *(to misfortune)* se résigner; *(in wrestling)* abandonner; **to s. to authority** se soumettre à l'autorité

2 *vt* soumettre; **to s. sth for sb's approval/for sb's inspection** soumettre *ou* présenter qch à l'approbation/à l'inspection de qn; **to s. proof of identity** présenter des pièces d'identité; **to s. that ...** représenter *ou* alléguer que ...; *Jur* **I s. that there is no case against my client** je plaide le non-lieu; **I s. that you are not in fact ...** j'affirme que vous n'êtes pas en fait ...; **the author submits that ...** l'auteur affirme que ...
subnormal [sʌb'nɔ:məl] *adj (person, behaviour)* arriéré; *(temperature)* au-dessous de la normale; **educationally s.** arriéré
suborder ['sʌbɔ:dər] *n Biol* sous-ordre *m*
subordinate[1] [sə'bɔ:dɪnət] **1** *adj (rank)* inférieur, subalterne; *(role)* accessoire; **s. to** subordonné à; *Gram* **s. clause** proposition *f* subordonnée **2** *n* subordonné, -ée
subordinate[2] [sə'bɔ:dɪneɪt] *vt* subordonner **(to** à); **everything is subordinated to religion** tout est subordonné à la religion
subordination [səbɔ:dɪ'neɪʃən] *n* subordination *f* **(to** à)
suborn [sə'bɔ:n] *vt Jur (witness)* suborner
suborning [sə'bɔ:nɪŋ] *n Jur* subornation *f*
subplot ['sʌbplɒt] *n Liter, Th* intrigue *f* secondaire
subpoena[1] [sə'pi:nə] *n Jur (of witness)* citation *f*, assignation *f*
subpoena[2] *vt (pt, pp* **subpoenaed)** *Jur* **to s. sb (to appear)** assigner qn à comparaître, citer qn; **to s. sb as witness** citer qn à comparaître; **to s. a witness** assigner un témoin à comparaître; **he has been subpoenaed** il a été cité à comparaître
sub-postmaster *n Br* receveur *m* d'un bureau de poste *(dans un village)*
sub-postmistress *n Br* receveuse *f* d'un bureau de poste *(dans un village)*
sub-post office *n Br* petit bureau *m* de poste
sub-prefect *n Fr Admin* sous-préfet *m*
subprogram ['sʌbprəʊgræm] *n Comptr* sous-programme *m*
subroutine ['sʌbru:ti:n] *n Comptr* sous-programme *m*
subscribe [səb'skraɪb] **1** *vi* **(a)** *(contribute, give money)* souscrire **(to** à); **to s. to a newspaper** *(become a subscriber)* s'abonner à un journal; *(be a subscriber)* être abonné à un journal; *Com* **to s. to a service** s'abonner à un service; *Fin* **to s. to a loan** souscrire un prêt; **to s. to a share issue** souscrire à une émission d'actions

(b) to s. to an opinion souscrire à une opinion; **I don't s. to that theory** je ne souscris pas à cette théorie; **I cannot s. to that** je ne suis pas d'accord avec cela

2 *vt* **(a)** *(money)* verser; **to s. ten pounds** verser dix livres; *Fin* **to s. shares** souscrire des actions; **subscribed capital** capital *m* souscrit, souscription *f*

(b) *Fml (one's name)* souscrire; **to s. one's name to a document** apposer sa signature à un document
subscriber [səb'skraɪbər] *n* **(a)** *(to newspaper)* abonné, -ée; **telephone s.** abonné du *ou* au téléphone **(b)** *(to charity)* souscripteur *m* **(c)** *Fml (of document)* signataire *mf*, souscripteur *m*; **the s.** le soussigné, la soussignée
subscriber trunk dialling *n* (téléphone *m*) automatique *m*
subscript ['sʌbskrɪpt] *n Typ* indice *m*; **s. 3** 3 en indice
subscription [sʌb'skrɪpʃən] *n* **(a)** *(to newspaper)* abonnement *m*; **to take out a s. to a paper** s'abonner à un journal, prendre un abonnement à un journal; **s. to a club** cotisation *f* à un club; **s. TV** télévision *f* par abonnement

(b) s. to a charity souscription *f* à une œuvre de bienfaisance; **to get up a s.** se cotiser; **monument erected by public s.** monument élevé par souscription publique; *Fin* **s. to a loan** souscription à un emprunt; **s. list** liste *f* de souscription *ou* des souscripteurs

(c) *(to an opinion)* adhésion *f* **(to** à); *(to an act, a decision etc)* approbation *f* **(to** de)
subscription fee *n* frais *mpl* d'inscription; *(for share purchase)* droit *m* de souscription
subsection ['sʌbsekʃən] *n* subdivision *f*; *(in text)* paragraphe *m*
subsequent ['sʌbsɪkwənt] *adj* suivant, ultérieur, *Fml, Jur* subséquent; **at a s. meeting** au cours d'une séance ultérieure; **any s. corrections** toutes corrections ultérieures; **the investigation and all the s. recriminations** l'enquête et toutes les plaintes qui s'en sont suivies; **s. events proved us right** la suite des événements a prouvé *ou* les événements ultérieurs ont prouvé que nous avions raison; **s. to this** à la suite de ceci, par la suite
subsequently ['sʌbsɪkwəntlɪ] *adv* plus tard, par la suite; **s. to sth** postérieurement à qch
subservience [səb'sɜ:vɪəns] *n* soumission *f*, servilité *f*; *(to fashion)* assujettissement *m*
subservient [səb'sɜ:vɪənt] *adj* **(a)** *(servile)* obséquieux, servile; **s. to sb** soumis à qn **(b)** *(subordinate)* subordonné; **to make sth s. to sth** subordonner qch à qch
subset ['sʌbset] *n Math* sous-ensemble *m*
subside [səb'saɪd] *vi* **(a)** *(of ground, building)* s'affaisser, se tasser; *F* **to s. into an armchair** s'affaler dans un fauteuil **(b)** *(of water)* baisser, diminuer; *(of blister, bump)* dégonfler; **the flood is subsiding** la crue diminue **(c)** *(of storm, excitement, fever)* s'apaiser, se calmer
subsidence ['sʌbsɪdəns, səb'saɪdəns] *n* **(a)** *(of building, road)* affaissement *m*; *(of land, foundations)* tassement *m* **(b)** *(of river)* décrue *f*, baisse *f*; *Med (of tumour)* délitescence *f*; *(of fever)* apaisement *m* **(c)** *Geol* subsidence *f*
subsidiarity [səbsɪdɪ'ærɪtɪ] *n* subsidiarité *f*
subsidiary [səb'sɪdɪərɪ] **1** *adj* subsidiaire, auxiliaire; *Com* **s. account** sous-compte *m*; *Fin* **s. company** filiale *f* **2** *n Fin (company)* filiale *f*
subsidize ['sʌbsɪdaɪz] *vt (project, industry, person)* subventionner; **to be subsidized by the State** *or* **the government** recevoir une subvention de *ou* être subventionné par l'État; **why should I carry on subsidizing you?** je ne vois pas pourquoi je continuerais à te donner de l'argent!; **subsidized industry** industrie *f* subventionnée
subsidy ['sʌbsɪdɪ] *n* subvention *f*; **export/building s.** prime *f* *ou* subvention à l'exportation/à la construction
subsist [səb'sɪst] *vi (stay alive)* tirer sa subsistance, vivre **(on** de); *(remain in existence)* subsister; **custom that still subsists** coutume qui existe *ou* subsiste encore (de nos jours)
subsistence [səb'sɪstəns] *n* subsistance *f*; **means of s.** moyens

m de subsistance; **s. (allowance)** frais *mpl* de subsistance; **to live at s. level** avoir tout juste de quoi vivre; **a bare s. wage** un salaire à peine suffisant pour vivre; **s. economy** économie *f* de subsistance; **s. farming** autoconsommation *f*

subsoil ['sʌbsɔɪl] *n* sous-sol *m*

subsonic [sʌb'sɒnɪk] *adj Av* subsonique

subspecies ['sʌbspiːʃiːz] *n Biol* sous-espèce *f*

substance ['sʌbstəns] *n* **(a)** (*matter*) substance *f*, matière *f*; *Rel* (*spiritual, bodily*) substance **(b)** (*essential element*) (*of article, argument*) fond *m*, substance *f*, essentiel *m*; **I agree in s.** je suis d'accord sur le fond **(c)** (*strength, solidity*) solidité *f*; **the candidate was long on image but short on s.** le candidat faisait bonne impression mais manquait d'épaisseur; **book of s.** livre solide; **his argument has little s.** son argument n'a rien de solide; **he's a man of s.** (*financially*) il a du bien; (*intellectually etc*) c'est un homme d'envergure

substandard [sʌb'stændəd] *adj* de qualité inférieure; **it's s. English/French** ce n'est pas du bon anglais/français

substantial [səb'stænʃəl] *adj* **(a)** (*significant*) (*point, progress, reduction*) important; (*progress, difference*) grand; (*reason, evidence*) valable; **s. proof** preuve *f* concluante *ou* valable; **a s. number of …** un nombre important de … **(b)** (*meal*) substantiel, copieux; (*structure, book*) solide; (*cloth*) résistant **(c)** (*company*) solide, bien assis; (*sum of money*) gros; (*profit, loss*) important

substantially [səb'stænʃəlɪ] *adv* **(a)** (*considerably*) considérablement; **it's now s. improved** cela s'est maintenant considérablement amélioré; **this contributed s. to our success** cela a largement contribué à notre succès **(b)** (*for the most part*) **they are s. the same** dans l'ensemble *ou* pour l'essentiel ils sont pareils; **the text is s. unaltered** le texte est dans l'ensemble *ou* pour l'essentiel resté inchangé **(c)** (*solidly*) (*built*) solidement

substantiate [səb'stænʃɪeɪt] *vt* (*statement*) prouver, justifier; (*corroborate*) corroborer; (*claim, accusation etc*) prouver *ou* établir le bien-fondé de

substantiation [səbstænʃɪ'eɪʃən] *n* (*of statement*) justification *f*; (*corroboration*) confirmation *f*; (*of accusation, charge*) preuves *fpl*

substantival [sʌbstən'taɪv(ə)l] *adj Gram* substantivé

substantive ['sʌbstəntɪv] **1** *adj* **(a)** (*measures, issue*) important; *Jur* **s. law** droit *m* positif **(b)** *Gram* substantif **2** *n Gram* substantif *m*

substantively ['sʌbstəntɪvlɪ] *adv* **(a)** *Gram* substantivement **(b)** (*considerably*) considérablement

substation ['sʌbsteɪʃən] *n El etc* sous-station *f*

substitute[1] ['sʌbstɪtjuːt] *n* **(a)** (*foodstuff, drug*) succédané *m*; **as a s. for …** comme succédané de …; **coffee s.** ersatz *m* de café; **there's no s. for parental love** rien ne remplace l'amour parental; **low-alcohol lager is a poor s. for the real thing** la bière à faible teneur en alcool n'a rien de comparable avec la vraie bière; *Mktg* **s. product** produit *m* de substitution **(b)** (*person*) remplaçant, -ante, suppléant, -ante; *Sp* remplaçant; *Jur, Rel* substitut *m*; **as a s. for …** en remplacement de …, pour remplacer …; **to act as a s. for sb/sth** remplacer qn/qch, se substituer à qn/à qch

substitute[2] **1** *vt* substituer; *Sp* remplacer; **to s. margarine for butter** remplacer le beurre par la margarine **2** *vi* **to s. for sb** remplacer *ou* suppléer qn

substitution [sʌbstɪ'tjuːʃən] *n* substitution *f*, remplacement *m*; *Sp* remplacement; *Sp* **to make a s.** faire un remplacement

substitution(al) market [sʌbstɪtjuːʃən((ə)l)] *n Mktg* marché *m* de substitution, marché environnant

substratum, *pl* **-a, -ums** [sʌb'strɑːtəm, -ə, -əmz] *n* couche *f* inférieure; *Geol, Phil* substrat *m*

substring ['sʌbstrɪŋ] *n Comptr* sous-chaîne *f*

substructure ['sʌbstrʌktʃər] *n* (*of building*) fondement *m*; (*of road*) infrastructure *f*

subsume [sʌb'sjuːm] *vt* subsumer; **to s. X under Y** incorporer X à Y

subsystem ['sʌbsɪstəm] *n* sous-système *m*

subtenancy ['sʌbtenənsɪ] *n* sous-location *f*

subtenant ['sʌbtenənt] *n* sous-locataire *mf*

subtend [səb'tend] *vt* sous-tendre

subterfuge ['sʌbtəfjuːdʒ] *n* subterfuge *m*; **to resort to s.** user de subterfuge; **this was a s. to …** c'était un subterfuge pour …

subterranean [sʌbtə'reɪnɪən] *adj* souterrain

subtitle[1] ['sʌbtaɪt(ə)l] *n Cin, TV, Typ* sous-titre *m*; **film with English subtitles** film sous-titré en anglais

subtitle[2] *vt Cin, TV etc* sous-titrer

subtitled ['sʌbtaɪt(ə)ld] *adj Cin, TV* (*film, programme*) sous-titré

subtitling ['sʌbtaɪtlɪŋ] *n Cin, TV* sous-titrage *m*

subtle ['sʌt(ə)l] *adj* (*person, mind, reasoning, perfume, charm*) subtil; (*cunning*) rusé, astucieux; **s. distinction** distinction *f* ténue *ou* subtile; **you are being too s.** vous finassez; **s. irony** fine ironie *f*; **s. remark** observation *f* subtile

subtlety ['sʌt(ə)ltɪ] *n* **(a)** (*of distinction, mind, reasoning*) subtilité *f*; (*of policy*) subtilité, raffinement *m*, finesse *f* **(b)** (*subtle thing*) subtilité *f*

subtly ['sʌt(ə)lɪ] *adv* subtilement, avec finesse; (*to argue etc*) avec subtilité; **s. different** légèrement différent

subtonic [sʌb'tɒnɪk] *n Mus* note *f* sensible, sensible *f*

subtotal ['sʌbtəʊt(ə)l] *n* sous-total *m*, total *m* partiel

subtract [səb'trækt] *vt* soustraire, retrancher **(from** de)

subtraction [səb'trækʃən] *n* [①A71,7; B56,C,4] soustraction *f* **(from** de)

subtropical [sʌb'trɒpɪk(ə)l] *adj* subtropical

subtype ['sʌbtaɪp] *n* sous-type *m*

suburb ['sʌbɜːb] *n* banlieue *f*; (*nearer city*) faubourg *m*; **the suburbs** la banlieue; **in the suburbs** en banlieue; **in the suburbs of Paris** dans la banlieue de Paris; **garden s.** cité-jardin *f*, *pl* cités-jardins

suburban [sə'bɜːbən] *adj* suburbain; (*house, station, train*) de banlieue; *Pej* (*narrow-minded*) (*person*) à l'esprit étroit; (*life*) étriqué; **even the city centre's s.** même le centre-ville sent la banlieue

suburbanite [sə'bɜːbənaɪt] *n* banlieusard, -arde

suburbia [sə'bɜːbɪə] *n* la banlieue

subvention [səb'venʃən] *n* subvention *f*

subversion [səb'vɜːʃən] *n Pol etc* subversion *f*

subversive [səb'vɜːsɪv] **1** *adj* subversif **(of** de) **2** *n* individu *m* subversif; **a group of subversives** un groupe subversif

subvert [səb'vɜːt] *vt* renverser, subvertir

subway ['sʌbweɪ] *n* **(a)** *Br* (*walkway under road etc*) passage *m* souterrain, souterrain *m* **(b)** *esp Am Rail* métro *m*

sub-zero *adj* au-dessous de zéro; **s. temperatures** températures *fpl* en-dessous de zéro

succeed [sək'siːd] **1** *vi* **(a)** (*be successful*) réussir; **hard workers always s.** les grands travailleurs arrivent *ou* réussissent toujours; **how to s. in business** comment réussir dans les affaires; **young man who will s.** jeune homme qui ira loin; **to s. in doing sth** réussir *ou* arriver à faire qch; **she always succeeds** tout lui réussit; **I/the plan only succeeded in making things worse** je n'ai/le projet n'a réussi qu'à aggraver la situation; **to s. in one's attempt to …** réussir à …; *prov* **if at first you don't s., try and try again** pour réussir il faut persévérer; *Prov* **nothing succeeds like success** la réussite appelle la réussite

(b) to s. to the throne *or* **the Crown** succéder à la couronne; **to s. to an office/estate** hériter d'une fonction/d'une propriété; *Jur* **right to s.** droits *mpl* de succession

2 *vt* (*person, thing*) succéder à; **George III was succeeded by George IV** George IV succéda à *ou* fut le successeur de George III

succeeding [sək'siːdɪŋ] *adj* **(a)** (*following*) suivant; (*in future*) futur, à venir **(b)** (*successive*) successif; **with each s. year** d'année en année

success [sək'ses] *n* succès *m*, réussite *f*; **we wish you s.** bonne chance!; **to meet with** *or* **to achieve s.** avoir *ou* remporter du succès; **the film was a great s. in Italy** le film a eu énormément de succès en Italie; **without s.** sans succès, en vain; **to score a s.** remporter un succès; **to be a s.** (*go well, work out well etc*) réussir, être réussi, être un succès; (*be popular*) (*of film, book etc*) être un succès; (*of party, cake*) être une réussite, être réussi; **the cake was a big s.** (*everyone liked it*) le gâteau a eu beaucoup de succès; **to be a s. with sb** (*be popular etc*) avoir un *ou* du succès auprès de qn; **it was a huge** *or* **great s.** cela a eu un succès fou; **the company has been one of the few successes of recent years** l'entreprise fait partie des quelques exemples de réussite de ces dernières années; **the film has been his biggest s. to date** ce film a été son plus grand succès à ce jour; **to make a s. of sth** réussir qch; **he made a big s. of it** il a très bien réussi; **a second attempt met with no better s.** une seconde tentative n'a pas eu plus de succès; **s. fee** prime *f* de rendement; **s. rate** (*of operation, treatment etc*) taux *m* de succès; **s. story** histoire *f* d'une réussite

successful [sək'sesfʊl] *adj* (*project*) couronné de succès; (*outcome*) heureux; (*play*) qui a du succès; **to be s. in doing sth** réussir à faire qch; (*after an effort*) arriver *ou* parvenir à faire qch; **were you s.?** avez-vous réussi?; *F* est-ce que ça a marché?; **he is s. in everything** tout lui réussit, il réussit dans tout ce qu'il entreprend; **a s. businesswoman** une femme d'affaires qui a réussi; **to be s. at the polls** sortir victorieux du scrutin; **s. candidates** *Pol* candidats *mpl* élus; *Sch* candidats reçus; **to bring an operation to a s. conclusion** mener à bien une opération; **a s. evocation of a bygone age** une évocation fort réussie d'une époque révolue; *Com* **s. tenderer** adjudicataire *mf*

successfully [sək'sesfəlɪ] *adv* avec succès; **when we've s. completed this stage of the operation** quand nous aurons mené à bien cette partie de l'opération

succession [sək'seʃən] *n* **(a)** *(series) (of victories, visitors etc)* succession *f*, série *f*, suite *f*; **an endless s. of ...** une suite ininterrompue de ...; **in s.** successivement; **for two years in s.** pendant deux années consécutives *ou* de suite; **in close s.** se succédant de près; **in rapid s.** coup sur coup; **a rapid s. of governments** une succession rapide de gouvernements; **a long s. of kings** une longue suite de rois

(b) *(to throne), Jur* succession *f*; *(descendants)* lignée *f*; **he was third in s. to the throne** c'était le troisième dans l'ordre de succession au trône; **to settle the s.** régler la succession; **at the time of his s. to the throne** au moment de son avènement; **law of s.** droit *m* des successions; **right of s.** droits de succession

successive [sək'sesɪv] *adj* successif; **on five s. Sundays** cinq dimanches consécutifs *ou* de suite; **s. generations** les générations *fpl* successives

successively [sək'sesɪvlɪ] *adv* successivement

successor [sək'sesər] *n* successeur *m* **(to** à); **the s. to the throne** l'héritier *m* du trône; **my first car and its successors** ma première voiture et celles qui lui ont succédé *ou* qui sont venues ensuite

succinct [sʌk'sɪŋ(k)t] *adj (account, writer)* succinct

succinctly [sʌk'sɪŋ(k)tlɪ] *adv* succinctement

succinctness [sʌk'sɪŋ(k)tnɪs] *n* concision *f*

succour[1], *US* **succor** ['sʌkər] *n Lit* secours *m*, aide *f*; **to give s.** porter secours *ou* assistance

succour[2], *US* **succor** *vt Lit* venir en aide à, venir à l'aide de; *(the poor)* secourir

succulence ['sʌkjʊləns] *n* succulence *f*

succulent ['sʌkjʊlənt] **1** *adj* **(a)** *(food)* succulent **(b)** *Bot* **s. leaf** feuille *f* charnue **2** *n Bot* plante *f* grasse

succumb [sə'kʌm] *vi* succomber **(to** à), céder **(to** à); **to s. to one's injuries** succomber à *ou* mourir de ses blessures; **we have all succumbed to her charm** son charme nous a tous conquis, nous avons tous succombé à son charme; **I eventually succumbed** j'ai fini par céder

such [sʌtʃ] **1** *adj* **(a)** *(of that kind)* tel, pareil; **beasts of prey s. as the lion or the tiger** des bêtes fauves telles que le lion ou le tigre; **s. a man** un tel homme; **on s. an occasion** en semblable occasion, en une telle occasion, en une occasion pareille; **why do you ask s. a question?** pourquoi demander une chose pareille?, pourquoi poser une question pareille?; **did you ever see s. a thing!** a-t-on jamais vu pareille chose!; **you wouldn't have s. a thing as a corkscrew, would you?** vous n'auriez pas un tire-bouchon, par hasard?; **s. is not my intention** ce n'est pas là mon intention; **if s. were the case** s'il en était ainsi, si tel était le cas; **the village boasts a bus, s. as it is** le village a un autobus, si l'on peut dire; **s. books as these are always useful** les livres de ce genre sont toujours utiles; **in s. cases** en pareils cas; **in s. weather** par un temps pareil; **how can you tell s. lies?** comment pouvez-vous mentir de la sorte?, comment pouvez-vous dire des mensonges pareils?; **she has s. ideas!** elle a de ces idées!; **s. courage** tant de courage, un tel courage; **some s. plan was in my mind** j'avais dans l'esprit un projet de ce genre; **there is no s. thing** cela n'existe pas; **if there were no s. thing as money** si l'argent n'existait pas; **I said no s. thing** je n'ai rien dit de semblable *ou* de pareil; **no s. thing!** pas du tout!; *Jur* **persons guilty of s. offences** personnes coupables des délits susmentionnés

(b) on s. (and s.) a day in s. (and s.) a place tel jour en tel endroit; **your letter of s. and s. a date** votre lettre du tant; **s. a one** un tel, une telle

(c) she arranges things in s. a way that she is free on Saturdays elle s'arrange de manière à être libre le samedi; **his kindness was s. as to make us feel ashamed** sa bonté était telle que nous en étions confus; *Fml* **to take s. steps as shall be considered necessary** prendre toutes les mesures qui paraîtront nécessaires; *Fml* **until s. time as is convenient to me** jusqu'à ce que cela me convienne

2 *adv* [①A5] **s. large houses** de si grandes maisons; **I had never heard s. good music** je n'avais jamais entendu d'aussi bonne musique; **he's not s. a good player as you** ce n'est pas un aussi bon joueur que vous; **s. a clever woman** une femme si intelligente; **it was s. a long time ago** il y a si longtemps de cela; **he is s. a liar** il est tellement menteur, c'est un tel menteur; **s. an enjoyable day** une journée si *ou* tellement agréable; **we had s. a good time** on s'est tellement *ou* si bien amusé(s), on s'est tant amusé(s); **don't be in s. a hurry** ne soyez pas si pressé; **you gave me s. a fright!** vous m'avez fait une (telle) peur!

3 *pron* **(a) he enjoys cakes, ices and s.** il mange avec plaisir des gâteaux, des glaces et autres choses de ce genre

(b) that's not for s. as you cela n'est pas pour quelqu'un comme toi; **s. as have the money can afford it** ceux qui ont de l'argent peuvent se l'offrir; **I haven't many, but I will send you s. as I have** je n'en ai pas beaucoup, mais je vous enverrai ce que j'ai; **s. is life!** c'est la vie!

(c) she was a very brave woman and well known as s. c'était une femme très courageuse, et elle était bien connue en tant que telle; **history as s. is too often neglected** l'histoire en tant que telle est trop souvent négligée; **the text as s. is fine but ...** le texte en soi est bien mais ...; **I wasn't scared as s.** je n'avais pas vraiment peur

suchlike ['sʌtʃlaɪk] *F* **1** *adj* semblable, pareil **2** *pron* **beggars, tramps and s.** mendiants, vagabonds et autres gens de la sorte; **concerts, theatres and s.** concerts, théâtres, et autres choses de ce genre

suck[1] [sʌk] *n* **(a) to give sth a s.** sucer qch; **to have** *or* **take a s. at a sweet** sucer un bonbon **(b) to give a child s.** donner à téter *ou* la tétée à un enfant

suck[2] **1** *vt* sucer; *(mother's milk)* téter; *(drink, sweets)* sucer, suçoter; *(handkerchief)* mordiller; *(pipe)* tirer sur; *(not smoking)* sucer; *Tech (liquid, air)* aspirer; **to s. sth through a straw** aspirer qch avec une paille; **to s. one's fingers** se sucer les doigts; **to s. one's thumb** sucer son pouce; **to s. poison out of a wound** extraire le poison d'une blessure en la suçant; *Fig* **to s. sb dry** sucer qn jusqu'à la moelle; **the dust is sucked into the bag** la poussière est aspirée dans le sac; *Fig* **to get sucked into a conspiracy** être entraîné dans une conspiration

2 *vi* **(a)** *(with mouth)* sucer; *(of baby, animal)* téter (le lait); *(of pump)* aspirer; **to s. at a sweet** sucer *ou* suçoter un bonbon; **to s. on one's pipe** tirer sur sa pipe; *(not smoking)* sucer sa pipe; **to s. on a straw** tirer sur *ou* aspirer avec une paille

(b) *esp US Sl (be very bad, unpleasant etc)* être merdique; **this city sucks** cette ville est merdique

▶ **suck down** *vtsep (of whirlpool etc)* engloutir, entraîner vers le fond

▶ **suck in** *vtsep (with mouth)* sucer; *(draw in by vacuum)* aspirer; *(of air pump)* aspirer; *(in vortex)* engloutir; *(cheeks)* creuser; *(knowledge)* absorber; **to get sucked in** *(to conspiracy, plot etc)* se laisser entraîner **(to** dans)

▶ **suck off** *vtsep Vulg (sexually)* sucer, faire une pipe à

▶ **suck out** *vtsep (with mouth) (juice)* sucer; **to s. out the poison from a wound** aspirer *ou* sucer le poison d'une blessure

▶ **suck up** *vtsep Tech (liquid, air)* sucer, aspirer, pomper; **these gases get sucked up into the upper atmosphere** ces gaz sont aspirés dans les couches supérieures de l'atmosphère

▶ **suck up to** *vipo F Pej (ingratiate oneself with)* faire de la lèche à, lécher les bottes *ou Sl* le cul à

sucker[1] ['sʌkər] *n* **(a)** *F (gullible person)* niais *m*, nigaud *m*; **to be a s. for a pretty/handsome face** ne pas savoir résister à un joli visage **(b)** *(of octopus etc)* suçoir *m*; *(of bloodsucker, on machine)* ventouse *f* **(c)** *(of plant)* rejeton *m*, rejet *m*; *(of tree)* drageon *m*, surgeon *m*; **to throw out suckers** *(of tree)* drageonner, surgeonner

sucker[2] **1** *vt esp Am F (dupe)* pigeonner; **he suckered them out of a million dollars** il les a eus d'un million de dollars **2** *vi (of tree)* drageonner

sucking ['sʌkɪŋ] **1** *adj* **s. pig** cochon *m* de lait **2** *n (of baby)* succion *f*; *(of pump)* aspiration *f*

suckle ['sʌk(ə)l] **1** *vt (child, young)* allaiter; *(baby)* donner le sein *ou* donner à téter à **2** *vi (of baby, animal)* téter

suckling ['sʌklɪŋ] *n* **(a)** *(act)* allaitement *m* **(b)** *Arch (child)* nourrisson, -onne, enfant *mf* au sein; *(animal)* jeune animal *m* qui tète encore; *(still used in)* **s. pig** cochon *m* de lait

sucrose ['su:krəʊs] *n Ch* saccharose *m*

suction ['sʌkʃən] *n* succion *f*; *(of water in pump)* aspiration *f*; *(of air)* aspiration, appel *m*; **to adhere by s.** faire ventouse; *Aut etc* **s. cup** *or* **pad** ventouse *f*; **s. pump** pompe *f* aspirante; **s. stroke** temps *m* de l'aspiration

Sudan (the) [ðəsu:'dæn] *n* le Soudan

Sudanese [su:də'ni:z] **1** *adj* soudanais, soudanien **2** *n* Soudanais, -aise, Soudanien, -ienne

sudden ['sʌd(ə)n] *adj* **(a)** soudain, subit; *(movement, bend)* brusque; **this is rather s.** c'est plutôt inattendu; **it was a very s. decision** j'ai/il a/*etc* pris cette décision très vite; **it's all so s.** tout est arrivé si vite; **their marriage was rather s.** leur mariage s'est fait assez soudainement *ou* brusquement; **s. death** mort *f* soudaine *ou* subite; *Fb* **s. death play-off** épreuve *f* des penalties; **s. infant death syndrome** mort subite du nourrisson; **s. rise** hausse *f* subite; **s. shower** averse *f* subite **(b) all of a s.** soudain, tout à coup, tout d'un coup

suddenly ['sʌd(ə)nlɪ] *adv* soudain, tout à coup, tout d'un coup; (*to move*) brusquement; **she died s.** elle est morte subitement; **it happened so s.** c'est arrivé si vite; **then s. he was gone** et puis soudain, il avait disparu; **she very s. changed her mind** elle a changé d'avis très soudainement

suddenness ['sʌd(ə)nnɪs] *n* soudaineté *f*; (*of movement*) brusquerie *f*

suds [sʌdz] *npl* **(soap) s.** (*foam*) mousse *f* de savon; (*soapy water*) eau *f* savonneuse

sue [su:] **1** *vt Jur* **to s. sb (at law)** intenter un procès à qn, poursuivre qn en justice; **to s. sb for damages** poursuivre qn en dommages-intérêts; **to s. sb for libel** poursuivre qn pour diffamation **2** *vi* **(a)** *Jur* **to s. for a separation** plaider en séparation; **to s. for libel** attaquer en diffamation; **to s. for a divorce** entamer une procédure de divorce; **if you print that story I'll s.** si vous publiez cette histoire, je vous fais un procès **(b) to s. for peace** demander la paix

suede [sweɪd] *n* (*for shoes*) daim *m*; (*for gloves, jacket etc*) (peau *f* de) suède *m*; **s. gloves** gants de suède; **s. shoes** chaussures en daim; *Sl* **s. head** crâne *m* rasé

suet ['su:ɪt] *n Culin* graisse *f* de rognon; **s. dumpling** boulette *f* de graisse de bœuf; **s. pudding** pudding *m* fait avec de la farine et de la graisse de bœuf

Suez ['su:ɪz, 'sʊɪz] *n* Suez; **the S. Canal** le canal de Suez; **the S. crisis** la crise de Suez

suffer ['sʌfər] **1** *vt* (*undergo*) (*loss, indignity, consequence*) subir; (*pain*) endurer; (*sorrow*) subir, éprouver; (*tolerate, endure*) supporter, tolérer; **to s. defeat** essuyer *ou* subir une défaite; **to s. hunger** souffrir de la faim; **she doesn't s. fools gladly** elle ne peut pas supporter *ou* souffrir les imbéciles

2 *vi* (*of person, business, marriage, relations, health etc*) souffrir; (*of economy*) être perturbé; (*of profits*) subir une perte; **to s. from rheumatism** souffrir de rhumatismes; **to s. for one's misdeeds** supporter les conséquences de ses méfaits; **you'll s. for it** il vous en cuira, vous allez le payer; **I'll make (sure) you s. for this!** tu me le paieras!; **to be made to s. for what others have done** payer pour les actions d'autrui; **to s. from neglect** pâtir d'un manque de soins; **the country suffers from labour troubles** le pays est en proie à l'agitation ouvrière; **his good name has suffered** sa réputation a souffert; **she started drinking and her work suffered** elle a commencé à boire et son travail en a pâti; **the vines have suffered from the frost** les vignes ont souffert de la gelée

sufferance ['sʌf(ə)rəns] *n* tolérance *f* **(of** de**)**; **children are admitted on s.** l'entrée des enfants est tolérée; **I get the feeling I'm just here on s.** j'ai l'impression de n'être ici que parce qu'on m'y tolère

sufferer ['sʌf(ə)rər] *n* **to be a s. from ill health** avoir une mauvaise santé; **sufferers from asthma/arthritis, asthma/arthritis sufferers** personnes sujettes à l'asthme/l'arthrite

suffering ['sʌf(ə)rɪŋ] **1** *adj* souffrant, qui souffre **2** *n* souffrance *f*; **the depression caused great s.** la dépression a causé de grandes souffrances; **cheerful in spite of his s.** gai malgré ses souffrances

suffice [sə'faɪs] *Fml* **1** *vi* suffire; **that will s. for me** cela me suffira **2** *vt* (*person*) suffire à, être suffisant pour; **s. (it) to say that I got nothing out of it** il suffit de dire que je n'en ai rien obtenu

sufficiency [sə'fɪʃənsɪ] *n Fml* quantité *f* suffisante, *Arch* suffisance *f*; **to have a s. of sth** avoir assez de qch; **to have no more than a bare s.** avoir tout juste assez; (*of food, money*) avoir tout juste de quoi manger/vivre

sufficient [sə'fɪʃənt] **1** *adj* (*reason, explanation*) suffisant; **s. care/attention** suffisamment de *ou* assez de soins/d'attention; **lack of s. food/funds** insuffisance *f* de nourriture/de moyens; **this is s. to feed them** cela suffit pour les nourrir; **a hundred francs will be s. (for me)** cent francs (me) suffiront; **one light will be s.** une lampe suffira; **this work is not s.** ce travail n'est pas suffisant; **an apology is no longer s.** une excuse ne suffit plus; **it was s. to give her the address and she would find her way there** il suffisait de lui donner l'adresse et elle trouvait son chemin; **this news was s. to make him worry** cette nouvelle suffit à l'inquiéter; **they didn't have s. warning** on ne les a pas prévenus suffisamment à l'avance; **is that s. time for you?** cela vous donne-t-il suffisamment de temps?; **let me know in s. time so that I can ...** prévenez-moi suffisamment à l'avance pour que je puisse ...; **with s. supplies** avec des réserves suffisantes, avec suffisamment de réserves; **there was nowhere near s. heating in the building** l'immeuble était loin d'être suffisamment chauffé

2 *n* assez; **have you had s. (to eat)?** avez-vous assez mangé?; **they don't have s. to live on** ils n'ont pas assez pour vivre

sufficiently [sə'fɪʃəntlɪ] *adv* suffisamment, assez; **to be s. tactful to ...** avoir suffisamment de tact pour ...

suffix[1] ['sʌfɪks] *n Gram, Comptr* suffixe *m*

suffix[2] ['sʌfɪks, sʌ'fɪks] *vt Gram, Comptr* suffixer

suffocate ['sʌfəkeɪt] **1** *vt* (*kill*) étouffer; (*of smell*) suffoquer; *Fig* **all initiative was suffocated** la moindre initiative était étouffée; *Fig* **the secret police suffocated any dissent** la police secrète étouffa toutes les dissensions **2** *vi* étouffer, suffoquer **(with rage** de colère**)**; **they were suffocating for lack of oxygen** ils étouffaient à cause du manque d'oxygène; **the stowaways suffocated (to death)** les passagers clandestins périrent étouffés

suffocating ['sʌfəkeɪtɪŋ] *adj* suffocant, étouffant; **it's s. (in) here** on étouffe ici

suffocation [sʌfə'keɪʃən] *n* suffocation *f*, étouffement *m*; **to die of s.** mourir étouffé *ou* par asphyxie

suffragan ['sʌfrəgən] *adj, n Rel* **bishop s., s. (bishop)** (évêque *m*) suffragant *m*

suffrage ['sʌfrɪdʒ] *n Pol* (*right to vote*) droit *m* de vote; **universal s.** suffrage *m* universel; **women's s.** droit de vote pour les femmes

suffragette [sʌfrə'dʒet] *n Pol, Hist* suffragette *f*

suffuse [sə'fju:z] *vt esp Lit* se répandre sur; **a blush suffused her cheeks** ses joues s'empourprèrent; **eyes suffused with tears** yeux baignés de larmes; **suffused with light** inondé de lumière

sugar[1] ['ʃʊgər] *n* **(a)** sucre *m*; **granulated s.** sucre cristallisé; **lump s.** sucre en morceaux; **lump** *or* **cube of s.** morceau *m* *ou* carré *m* de sucre; **caster s.** sucre semoule; (*finer*) sucre en poudre; **icing s.** sucre glace; **brown s.** cassonade *f*; **help yourself to s.** prenez donc du sucre; **milk, no s., please** avec du lait, sans sucre, s'il vous plaît; **he takes two spoonfuls of s.** *ou* **two sugars** il prend deux sucres; **s. basin** *or* **bowl** sucrier *m*; **s. mouse** souris *f* en sucre; **s. pea** mange-tout *m* *inv*; **s. refinery** raffinerie *f* (de sucre), sucrerie *f*; **s. shaker** saupoudreuse *f* (pour le sucre); **(pair of) s. tongs** pince *f* à sucre

(b) milk s. sucre *m* de lait, lactose *f*; *Physiol* **blood s.** glucose *m* sanguin; **blood s. level** taux *m* de sucre dans le sang

(c) *F* (*term of address*) (mon) trésor *m*

(d) *Euph* **oh s.!** oh mercredi!

sugar[2] *vt* (*coffee etc*) sucrer; (*pill*) dragéifier, recouvrir de sucre; **sugared almond** dragée *f*; *Fig* **to s. the pill** dorer la pilule

sugar almond *n* dragée *f*

sugar beet *n* betterave *f* à sucre

sugar cane *n* canne *f* à sucre

sugar-coat *vt* recouvrir de sucre; *Fig* (*unpleasant measure*) faire passer

sugar-coated *adj* recouvert de sucre; (*almond*) lissé; **s. pill** pilule *f* dragéifiée

sugar daddy *n F* **she's found herself a s.** elle s'est trouvé un homme d'âge mûr qui l'aide financièrement, *Pej* elle s'est trouvé un vieux friqué; *F* **I've no intention of being your s.** je n'ai pas l'intention de t'entretenir

sugar-free *adj* sans sucre

sugarloaf ['ʃʊgələʊf] *n* pain *m* de sucre; **s. mountain** montagne *f* en pain de sucre

sugar maple *n* érable *m* à sucre

sugarplum ['ʃʊgəplʌm] *n* bonbon *m*; **yes, my s.** oui, mon petit chou

sugary ['ʃʊgərɪ] *adj* **(a)** (*containing sugar*) sucré; (*sprinkled with sugar*) saupoudré de sucre; **to go s.** (*of jam*) se cristalliser; **s. taste** goût *m* sucré **(b)** (*smile, tone*) mielleux, sucré; (*tone*) doucereux

suggest [sə'dʒest] *vt* **(a)** (*propose*) (*sth*) suggérer, proposer **(to sb** à qn**)**; *Jur* **I s. that ...** n'est-il pas vrai que ...?; **she suggested going for a walk** elle a suggéré *ou* proposé de faire une promenade; **what do you s. I do?** que suggérez-vous que je fasse?; **I shall do as you s.** je ferai comme vous le suggérez; **a solution suggested itself to me** une solution m'est venue à l'esprit; **or was it a conspiracy, as some have suggested?** ou s'agissait-il d'une conspiration comme on l'avait suggéré auparavant?; *Com* **suggested retail price** prix *m* conseillé

(b) (*inspire, recommend*) (*idea*) inspirer, faire naître; **common sense would s. we give up** le bon sens nous dirait *ou* conseillerait d'abandonner

(c) (*insinuate, imply*) insinuer; **are you suggesting that I am lying?** est-ce que vous insinuez que je mens?; **which suggests that it was an accident** ce qui semblerait indiquer qu'il s'agissait d'un accident; **are eggs as scarce as the price would s.?** les œufs sont-ils aussi rares que le prix le laisse supposer?; **the marks in the sand s. a person of**

about ... les traces sur le sable indiquent la présence d'une personne d'environ ...

(**d**) (*evoke*) évoquer; **what do these abstract forms s. to you?** que vous suggèrent *ou* évoquent ces formes abstraites?

suggestible [sə'dʒestɪb(ə)l] *adj* (**a**) *Psy* suggestible (**b**) (*easily influenced*) influençable

suggestion [sə'dʒestʃən] *n* (**a**) [①A57-8,c-d] (*proposal*) suggestion *f*, proposition *f*; **to be open to suggestions** être prêt à accueillir des suggestions; **at her s. I stayed at home** suivant son conseil, je suis resté chez moi; **to make a s.** faire une suggestion *ou* proposition; **practical s.** conseil *m* pratique; **suggestions for improvement** propositions en vue d'une amélioration; **to be full of suggestions** être fécond en idées *ou* en conseils; **it was only a s.** ce n'était qu'une suggestion; **suggestions box** boîte *f* à idées

(**b**) *Jur* **my s. is that you were not there at the time** n'est-il pas vrai que vous étiez absent à ce moment-là?

(**c**) *Psy etc* suggestion *f*; **hypnotic s.** suggestion hypnotique; **adverts work by s.** les publicités fonctionnent à la suggestion

(**d**) (*insinuation*) indication *f*; **there is no s. that he might be guilty** rien/personne ne suggère *ou* dit qu'il est coupable

(**e**) (*hint*) **to speak with just a s. of a foreign accent** parler avec une pointe d'accent étranger; **s. of regret** nuance *f ou* pointe *f* de regret

suggestive [sə'dʒestɪv] *adj* (**a**) (*reminiscent, thought-provoking*) suggestif; **s. of sth** évocateur de qch (**b**) (*indecent, erotic*) (*lyrics, dance etc*) suggestif; **s. joke** plaisanterie *f* grivoise

suggestively [sə'dʒestɪvlɪ] *adv* d'une façon suggestive

suggestiveness [sə'dʒestɪvnɪs] *n* (*of picture etc*) caractère *m* suggestif

suicidal [su:ɪ'saɪd(ə)l] *adj* suicidaire; **it would be s. (to do it)** ce serait du suicide *ou* ce serait suicidaire (d'agir de la sorte); *Fig* **as far as your career is concerned it would be s.** sur le plan professionnel, ça serait du suicide; **s. tendencies** tendances *fpl* au suicide *ou* suicidaires; **to be feeling s.** se sentir suicidaire, avoir des idées de suicide; **an absolutely s. bit of driving** une conduite complètement suicidaire

suicide ['su:ɪsaɪd] *n* (**a**) (*act*) suicide *m*; **to commit s.** se suicider; **attempted s., s. attempt** tentative *f* de suicide; *Fig* **to commit political/economic/financial s.** se suicider politiquement/économiquement/financièrement; *Fig* **it would be s. to go there** ce serait du suicide d'y aller; **mass s.** suicide collectif; *Mil* **s. mission** mission *f* suicide; **s. note** lettre *f* (*laissée par un suicidé*); **s. pact** = accord *m* de suicide collectif passé entre deux personnes ou plus; **s. squad** équipe *f* (en mission) suicide

(**b**) (*person*) suicidé, -ée; **there was an attempted s. in the next bed** il y avait quelqu'un qui avait tenté de se suicider dans le lit d'à côté

suit[1] [s(j)u:t] *n* (**a**) (*clothing*) ensemble *m*; (*man's*) complet *m*, costume *m*; (*woman's*) tailleur *m*; **two-piece/three-piece s.** complet deux/trois pièces; **s. of armour** armure *f* complète; *Av, Astronaut* **flying** *or* **flight s.** combinaison *f* de vol; **pressure s.** combinaison pressurisée; **space s.** combinaison de cosmonaute

(**b**) *Cards* couleur *f*; *Fig* **politeness is not his strong** *or* **long s.** la politesse n'est pas son fort; **to follow s.** fournir à la couleur (demandée); *Fig* en faire autant, faire de même

(**c**) *Jur* **s. (at law)** (*lawsuit*) procès *m* (civil); (*act of suing*) poursuites *fpl* judiciaires; **to bring a s. against sb** intenter un procès à qn, poursuivre qn en justice; **criminal s.** action *f ou* procès criminel(le); **to be a party in a s.** être en cause

(**d**) *Old-fashioned, Lit* (*request*) prière *f*, demande *f*; **to press one's s. with a girl** (*when courting*) faire une cour assidue à une jeune fille

suit[2] **1** *vt* (**a**) (*of clothes, colours etc*) aller à; (*of arrangement, time, job etc*) convenir à; **to be suited to** *or* **for sth** être fait pour qch; **blue suits you** le bleu te va bien; **this climate/this food does not s. me** ce climat/cette nourriture ne me convient pas; **this hat suits you** ce chapeau vous va (bien); **clothes not suited to the climate** vêtements ne convenant pas au climat; **the premises are not suited for display purposes** les locaux ne se prêtent pas à la présentation des marchandises; **he is not suited to be a doctor** il n'est pas fait pour être médecin; **they are suited to** *or* **s. each other** ils sont faits l'un pour l'autre; **a small job in the country would s. me very well** un petit emploi en province m'irait *ou* me conviendrait très bien; **she found a house that suited her** elle a trouvé une maison à son gré; **marriage suits you** le mariage vous réussit; **that suits me best** c'est ce qui m'arrange le mieux; **that suits me (just) fine** *or F* **down to the ground** ça me va à merveille, ça me convient parfaitement; **I shall do it when it suits me** je le ferai quand cela me conviendra; **you can't just come and go when(ever) it suits you** tu ne peux pas aller et venir à ta guise; **(would) two o'clock s. you?** est-ce que deux heures vous conviendrait?; **s. yourself** faites comme vous voudrez; **we have something to s. every taste/pocket** nous en avons pour tous les goûts/toutes les bourses

(**b**) *Am* (*dress in suit*) vêtir d'un costume; **his followers were suited in black** ses disciples étaient vêtus d'un costume noir

(**c**) (*adapt*) adapter (**sth to sth** qch à qch); *esp Fml* **to s. the action to the word** joindre les gestes à la parole

2 *vi* **that date does not s.** cette date ne convient pas; **would tomorrow s.?** demain conviendrait-il?

suitability [s(j)u:tə'bɪlɪtɪ] *n* (*of date, arrangement, character*) convenance *f*; (*of comment, translation*) à-propos *m*; (*of decision, action etc*) bien-fondé *m*; (*of a person for a job*) capacité *f*; **they doubted his s. as a husband for her** ils n'étaient pas sûrs qu'il était le mari qu'il lui fallait; **we've got doubts about the s. of this film/book for young children** nous ne sommes pas sûrs que ce film/livre convienne aux jeunes enfants; **s. of a candidate for a post** aptitude *f* d'un candidat pour un poste

suitable ['s(j)u:təb(ə)l] *adj* (*subject, work*) convenable, qui convient; (*candidate*) valable; (*date, title, clothes, example*) adéquat; **we have found nothing s.** nous n'avons rien trouvé qui convienne; **wherever you think s.** où bon vous semblera; **the most s. date** la date qui conviendra le mieux; **is tomorrow s.?** demain te convient-il?; **s. expression** expression *f* pertinente *ou* appropriée; **s. marriage** union *f* bien assortie; **I've nothing s. to wear** je n'ai rien de convenable à me mettre; **with a s. note of sarcasm** avec une touche de sarcasme appropriée; **s. to** *or* **for sth** bon *ou* propre *ou* approprié à qch; **he's not s. for our Christine** ce n'est pas l'homme qu'il faut à notre Christine; **is it a book s. for children?** est-ce un livre pour les enfants?, est-ce que ce livre convient aux enfants?; **s. for children of seven years and under** pour les enfants de sept ans ou moins; **to make sth s. for sth** adapter qch à qch

suitably ['s(j)u:təblɪ] *adv* convenablement; (*to say*) à propos; **s. impressed/embarrassed** très impressionné/gêné; **s. matched** bien assortis; *Iron* **I hope you're s. impressed!** j'espère que tu es content maintenant!

suitcase ['s(j)u:tkeɪs] *n* valise *f*; **I'm still living out of a s.** je ne suis pas encore installé; **I've been travelling around, living out of a s.** j'ai voyagé un peu partout sans jamais vraiment m'installer

suite [swi:t] *n* (**a**) **s. (of rooms)** suite *f*, appartement *m* (**b**) (*furniture*) **(three piece) s.** canapé *m* avec deux fauteuils assortis, salon *m* trois pièces; **bathroom s.** (meubles *mpl* de) salle *f* de bains; **bedroom s.** (meubles de) chambre *f* à coucher (**c**) *Mus* suite *f*; **orchestral s.** suite d'orchestre (**d**) (*of prince*) suite *f*

suiting ['s(j)u:tɪŋ] *n Com* (*cloth*) tissu *m* de confection; **men's suitings** tissus pour complets

suitor ['s(j)u:tər] *n* (**a**) *Arch, Hum* soupirant *m* (**b**) *Jur* plaideur, -euse

sulfa, sulfate *etc US* = **sulpha, sulphate** *etc*

sulk[1] [sʌlk] *n* bouderie *f*; **to be in a s.** bouder; **to have (a fit of) the sulks** bouder, faire la tête

sulk[2] *vi* bouder, faire la tête

sulkily ['sʌlkɪlɪ] *adv* (*to reply*) d'un ton boudeur; (*look at sb*) d'un air boudeur; **he retreated s. to his room** il partit dans sa chambre en boudant

sulkiness ['sʌlkɪnɪs] *n* bouderie *f*

sulking ['sʌlkɪŋ] *n* bouderie *f*

sulky ['sʌlkɪ] *adj* boudeur; **to be s.** bouder; **to look s.** avoir un air boudeur, faire la tête; (*of model*) prendre un air boudeur

sullen ['sʌlən] *adj* (*person*) maussade, renfrogné, morose; (*silence*) obstiné, buté; *Lit* (*sky, clouds*) maussade

sullenly ['sʌlənlɪ] *adv* d'un air maussade *ou* renfrogné; (*to obey*) de mauvaise grâce

sullenness ['sʌlənnɪs] *n* maussaderie *f*, air *m* renfrogné

sullied ['sʌlɪd] *adj* souillé, terni

sully ['sʌlɪ] *vt* (**a**) *Lit* (*make dirty*) souiller, ternir (**b**) *Fig* (*reputation*) entacher, salir; **to s. one's hands** se salir les mains

sulpha, *US* **sulfa** ['sʌlfə] *n* **s. drug** sulfamide *f*

sulphate, *US* **sulf-** ['sʌlfeɪt] *n* sulfate *m*; **copper s.** sulfate de cuivre

sulphide, *US* **sulf-** ['sʌlfaɪd] *n* sulfure *m*; **hydrogen s.** sulfure d'hydrogène, hydrogène *m* sulfuré

sulphonamide, *US* **sulf-** [sʌl'fɒnəmaɪd] *n* sulfamide *m*

sulphur, *US* **sulf-** ['sʌlfər] *n* soufre *m*; **s. dioxide** anhydride *m* sulfureux; **s. mine** soufrière *f*; *Geol* **s. spring** source *f* sulfureuse

sulphureous, *US* **sulf-** [sʌl'fjʊərɪəs] *adj* sulfureux; (*coloured*) couleur de soufre *inv*, soufré

sulphuric, *US* **sulf-** [sʌl'fjʊərɪk] *adj* (*acid*) sulfurique
sulphurous, *US* **sulf-** ['sʌlfərəs, -fjʊər-] *adj* **(a)** = **sulphureous** **(b)** *Ch* (*acid*) sulfureux
sultan ['sʌltən] *n* sultan *m*
sultana [sʌl'tɑːnə] *n* **(a)** *Culin* (*fruit*) raisin *m* de Smyrne **(b)** (*female sultan*) sultane *f*
sultanate ['sʌltəneɪt] *n* sultanat *m*
sultriness ['sʌltrɪnɪs] *n* **(a)** (*of climate etc*) chaleur *f* étouffante; (*of atmosphere*) lourdeur *f*; **the s. of the weather** le temps lourd **(b)** *Fig* (*sensuality*) sensualité *f*, volupté *f*
sultry ['sʌltrɪ] *adj* **(a)** (*heat*) étouffant, suffocant; (*weather*) lourd, orageux; **it is s.** il fait très lourd **(b)** (*voice, look*) sensuel, voluptueux
sum[1] [sʌm] *n* **(a)** (*amount*) (*of money etc*) somme *f*; (*total*) somme, total *m*; (*of account*) montant *m*; **in s.** en somme, somme toute; **a nice little s.** une jolie petite somme, une somme rondelette; **the s. of sb's efforts** la somme des efforts de qn; **the whole is greater than the s. of its parts** l'ensemble est encore meilleur que la somme des éléments qui le compose; *Acct* **s. payable** somme à payer; **s. total** somme totale; *Fig* (*of sb's efforts etc*) totalité *f*; **is that the s. total of what you've done today?** c'est tout ce que vous avez fait aujourd'hui?
(b) *Math* (*problem*) problème *m*, exercice *m* (d'arithmétique); *Sch* **sums** (*arithmetic*) calcul *m*; **to do a s. in one's head** faire un calcul de tête; **to do sums** faire du calcul *ou* de l'arithmétique
sum[2] *vt* (**-mm-**) (*numbers*) additionner; *Math* (*series*) sommer
▶ **sum up 1** *vtsep* **(a)** (*summarize*) résumer, faire un résumé de; **to s. up what one has said before** se résumer, résumer les faits; *Jur* **to s. up the case** *or* **the evidence** (*of judge*) résumer les débats; **to s. up a situation in a word** résumer une situation en un mot **(b)** (*assess quickly*) **to s. up the situation at a glance** évaluer la situation d'un coup d'œil; **to s. sb up** juger *ou* évaluer qn **(c)** (*add*) (*numbers*) faire la somme de, totaliser **2** *vi* (*summarize*) résumer; **to s. up I will say that ...** en résumé je dirai que ...; **in summing up the judge said ...** dans son résumé, le juge a dit ...
sumac(h) ['s(j)uːmæk, 'ʃuː-] *n* (*plant*) sumac *m*
summarily ['sʌmərɪlɪ] *adv* sommairement
summarize ['sʌməraɪz] *vt* (*book etc*) résumer sommairement; (*debate etc*) récapituler
summary ['sʌmərɪ] **1** *adj* (*brief*) sommaire; **s. account** (*providing summary*) résumé *m*; *Jur* référé *m*; *Acct* **s. balance sheet** bilan *m* condensé; **s. dismissal** renvoi *m* sommaire; **he was dealt rather s. justice** on lui a rendu une justice plutôt sommaire; *Jur* **s. offences** délits *mpl* qui peuvent être jugés en procédure sommaire; **s. proceedings** affaire *f* sommaire; **s. report** rapport *m* récapitulatif
2 *n* sommaire *m*, résumé *m*, aperçu *m*; (*of book*) argument *m*; (*of commercial operations*) récapitulation *f*, relevé *m*; *TV, Rad* **s. of the news, news s.** rappel *m* des titres
summation [sʌ'meɪʃən] *n* **(a)** (*addition*) sommation *f*, addition *f* **(b)** (*total*) somme *f*, total *m* **(c)** (*summary*) résumé *m*; **the exhibition was a s. of his life's work** l'exposition résumait parfaitement son œuvre **(d)** *Am Jur* résumé *m* des débats (*par le juge*)
summer[1] ['sʌmər] *n* [①A6-7,d,v] été *m*; **in s.** en été; **in the s.** pendant l'été; **in the s. of 1945** pendant l'été 1945; **a s.('s) day** un jour d'été; **winter and s. alike, I live in the country** été comme hiver j'habite la campagne; **next s.** l'été prochain; **Indian s.** été de la Saint-Martin, été indien; *Lit* **many summers ago** il y a bien longtemps; *Lit* **a girl of 12 summers** une fille de 12 printemps; **s. break** petites vacances *fpl* d'été; **s. clothes** habits *mpl* ou vêtements *mpl* d'été; **the s. holidays** les vacances *ou* congés *mpl* d'été; *Scol* les grandes vacances; **s. season** saison *f* d'été, période *f* estivale; **s. visitor** estivant, -ante
summer[2] **1** *vi* (*by the sea etc*) passer l'été; (*of cattle*) estiver **2** *vt* (*cattle*) estiver
summerhouse ['sʌməhaʊs] *n* (*in garden*) pavillon *m*
summer resort *n* station *f* estivale
summer school *n* cours *mpl ou* université *f* d'été
summertime ['sʌmətaɪm] *n* (*season*) (saison *f* d')été *m*
summer time *n Admin* (*by clock*) heure *f* d'été, *Can* heure avancée
summery ['sʌmərɪ] *adj* d'été, estival; **you look very s. in that** ça *te donne un petit avi estival*
summing-up [sʌmɪŋ'ʌp] *n Jur* résumé *m* des débats (*par le juge*); **in her s. up the judge said ...** dans son résumé (des débats) le juge a dit ...
summit ['sʌmɪt] *n* **(a)** (*of mountain*) sommet *m*, cime *f*; *Fig* **the s. of greatness** le faîte *ou* sommet des grandeurs; **to be at the s. of one's power/fame** être au sommet *ou* à l'apogée du pouvoir/de sa gloire **(b)** *Pol* sommet *m*; **s. conference** conférence *f* au sommet; **talks will be held at s. level** des négociations auront lieu au sommet
summiteer [sʌmɪ'tɪər] *n Pol* participant, -ante à un sommet
summon ['sʌmən] *vt* **(a)** (*call*) (*servant, help, police, doctor*) appeler, faire venir; (*assembly, person to meeting, employee*) convoquer; *Jur* citer à comparaître; **business summoned him back to London** les affaires l'ont rappelé à Londres; **to s. a defendant/a witness to appear** citer *ou* assigner un défendeur/un témoin; **s. the next witness!** faites entrer le témoin suivant **(b)** = **summon up**
▶ **summon up** *vtsep* **(a)** (*courage, help, support etc*) faire appel à; **to s. up all one's strength** rassembler toutes ses forces; **summoning up all her courage ...** prenant son courage à deux mains ...; (*more serious*) rassemblant tout son courage ... **(b)** (*memory*) faire resurgir; (*spirits*) invoquer
summons[1], *pl* **-ses** ['sʌmənz, -zɪz] *n* **(a)** (*order to attend etc*) convocation *f* **(b)** *Jur* citation *f* (à comparaître), assignation *f* (à comparaître); **to issue a s.** lancer une assignation; **to serve a s. on sb** citer qn à comparaître; **to take out a s. against sb** faire assigner qn
summons[2] *vt Jur* citer à comparaître, assigner, appeler en justice
sump [sʌmp] *n* **(a)** (**oil**) **s.** carter *m* à huile; **to drain the s.** faire la vidange; **s. guard** protection *f* de carter; **s. pan** carter d'huile **(b)** *Min etc* puisard *m* **(c)** (*cesspool*) fosse *f* d'aisance
sumptuous ['sʌm(p)tjʊəs] *adj* somptueux
sumptuously ['sʌm(p)tjʊəslɪ] *adv* somptueusement
sumptuousness ['sʌm(p)tjʊəsnɪs] *n* somptuosité *f*
sun[1] [sʌn] *n* soleil *m*; **the s. is shining** il fait (du) soleil, le soleil brille; **the s. rises/sets** le soleil se lève/se couche; **rising/setting s.** soleil levant/couchant; **against the s.** face au soleil; **to have the s. in one's eyes** avoir le soleil dans les yeux; **let's get out of the s.** mettons-nous à l'abri du soleil; **too much s. can be harmful** de trop longues expositions au soleil peuvent être dangereuses; **to take the s.** prendre le soleil; **to catch the s.** (*of person*) (*get suntanned*) bronzer; (*get sunburnt*) prendre des coups de soleil; (*of garden etc*) voir le soleil, **to get a touch of the s.** prendre *ou* attraper un coup de soleil; **every species/subject under the s.** toutes les espèces existantes/tous les sujets possibles; **there's nothing new under the s.** (il n'y a) rien de nouveau sous le soleil; **to try everything under the s.** essayer tout ce qu'il est possible d'imaginer; **to call sb every name** *or* **everything under the s.** traiter qn de tous les noms; **nothing under the s. was going to stop her now** rien ni personne n'allait l'arrêter maintenant; *Fig* **to have a place in the s.** avoir une place au soleil; *Sl* **she thinks the s. shines out of his arse** elle n'a rien vu d'aussi beau que lui; **s. awning** store *m*; *Naut* **s. deck** pont-promenade *m*, *pl* ponts-promenades; *Aut* **s. gear** planétaire *m*; **s. helmet** casque *m* (colonial); **s. oil/lotion** huile *f*/lotion *f* solaire; *Aut* **s. shield** pare-soleil *m inv*; **s. terrace** terrasse *f*; *Aut* **s. visor** pare-soleil; *Aut* **s. wheel** roue *f* solaire
sun[2] *vt* (**-nn-**) exposer au soleil; **to s. oneself** prendre le soleil, *F* faire le lézard
sunbaked ['sʌnbeɪkt] *adj* (*earth*) brûlé par le soleil
sunbathe ['sʌnbeɪð] *vi* prendre un bain de soleil, se faire bronzer
sunbather ['sʌnbeɪðər] *n* personne *f* qui prend un bain/des bains de soleil; **suddenly the park was full of sunbathers** soudain le parc s'est rempli de gens venus prendre un bain de soleil
sunbathing ['sʌnbeɪðɪŋ] *n* bains *mpl* de soleil
sunbeam ['sʌnbiːm] *n* rayon *m* de soleil
sunbed ['sʌnbed] *n* (*for tanning*) lit *m* à ultraviolets; (*in garden etc*) (fauteuil *m*) relax *m*
sunblind ['sʌnblaɪnd] *n* store *m*
sunblock ['sʌnblɒk] *n* écran *m* total
sunburn ['sʌnbɜːn] *n* coup *m* de soleil; **suffering from s.** souffrant de coups de soleil
sunburnt, sunburned ['sʌnbɜːnt, -bɜːnd] *adj* brûlé par le soleil; **to get s.** attraper *ou* prendre un coup de soleil
sunburst ['sʌnbɜːst] *n Met* éclaircie *f*; (*brooch*) broche *f* (en forme de) soleil
sundae ['sʌndeɪ] *n Culin* = glace *f* aux fruits recouverte d'un coulis, de noix, de crème Chantilly *etc*
Sunday ['sʌndɪ] *n* [①A75-6,B-C; B58-9,B-C] dimanche *m* **I expect him on S.** *or* **this (coming) S.** je l'attends dimanche; **he comes on Sundays** il vient le dimanche; **she comes every S.** elle vient tous les dimanches; **in one's S. clothes** *or* **one's S. best** dans ses habits du dimanche; **to put on one's S. best** s'habiller en dimanche, s'endimancher; *Br* **S. lunch** déjeuner *m* du dimanche; **S. paper** journal *m* du dimanche; *F* **the Sundays** (*newspapers*) les journaux du dimanche
Sunday school *n Rel* catéchisme *m*; **S. teacher** catéchiste *mf*, personne *f* qui fait le catéchisme

sunder ['sʌndər] *Lit* **1** *vt* détruire **2** *vi* (*of ship's hull*) se rompre; (*of bridge, empire*) s'écrouler

sundial ['sʌndaɪəl] *n* cadran *m* solaire, gnomon *m*

sundown ['sʌndaʊn] *n* coucher *m* du soleil; **at s.** au coucher du soleil

sundowner ['sʌndaʊnər] *n F* (**a**) *Br* (*drink*) = boisson *f* alcoolisée prise le soir (**b**) *Austr* (*tramp*) clochard *m*

sun-drenched ['sʌndren(t)ʃt] *adj* (*beach etc*) baigné *ou* arrosé de soleil

sun-dried ['sʌndraɪd] *adj* séché au soleil

sundry ['sʌndrɪ] **1** *adj* divers; **on s. occasions** à diverses reprises; **s. expenses** frais *mpl* divers, dépenses *fpl* diverses **2** *n* (**a**) **all and s.** tout le monde; **this is not for all and s. to hear** je ne veux pas que tout le monde entende ça (**b**) **sundries** (*items*) articles *mpl* divers; (*costs*) frais *mpl* divers

sunfish ['sʌnfɪʃ] *n* môle *f*, poisson-lune *m*, *pl* poissons-lunes

sunflower ['sʌnflaʊər] *n* (*plant*) tournesol *m*, soleil *m*, hélianthe *m*; **s. seeds** graines *fpl* de tournesol; **s. (seed) oil** huile *f* de tournesol

sung *see* **sing**

sunglasses ['sʌnglɑːsɪz] *npl* lunettes *fpl* de soleil

sun-god *n* dieu *m* soleil

sungun ['sʌngʌn] *n TV, Cin* sun-gun *m*, éclairage *m* sur batterie

sunhat ['sʌnhæt] *n* chapeau *m* de soleil

sunk *see* **sink**[2]

sunken[1] ['sʌŋk(ə)n] *adj* (*rock*) immergé; (*wreck*) englouti; (*cheeks*) creux; (*garden etc*) encaissé, en contrebas; **s. eyes** yeux *mpl* creux *ou* enfoncés; **s. chest** poitrine *f* creuse

sunken[2] *see* **sink**[2]

Sun King *n* Roi *m* Soleil

sun lamp *n* lampe *f* à bronzer

sunless ['sʌnlɪs] *adj* sans soleil

sunlight ['sʌnlaɪt] *n* (lumière *f* du) soleil *m*; **in the s.** au soleil, en plein soleil; **to keep out of the s.** éviter la lumière du soleil; **keep it out of the s.** protégez-le du soleil, évitez-lui le soleil

sunlit ['sʌnlɪt] *adj* éclairé par le soleil; (*full of sunlight*) ensoleillé

sun lounge *n* solarium *m*

sunniness ['sʌnɪnɪs] *n* (*of place*) ensoleillement *m*; *Fig* **the s. of her disposition** ses bonnes dispositions

sunny ['sʌnɪ] *adj* (**a**) (*day, place*) ensoleillé; (*building*) éclairé par le soleil; (*side*) exposé au soleil; **it's s.** il fait (du) soleil; *esp Am* **s. side up** (*fried egg*) sur le plat (**b**) *Fig* (*face*) radieux, rayonnant; (*person*) joyeux; **to have a s. disposition** être d'une nature joyeuse; *Fig* **to look on the s. side of things** voir le bon côté des choses; *F* **to be on the s. side of 40** ne pas avoir encore atteint la quarantaine

sun parlor *n* solarium *m*

sun porch *n* solarium *m*

sunray ['sʌnreɪ] *n* rayon *m* de soleil, rayon solaire; **s. lamp** (*for tanning*) lampe *f* à bronzer; *Med* lampe à ultraviolets; *Med* **s. treatment** héliothérapie *f*

sunrise ['sʌnraɪz] *n* lever *m* du soleil; **at s.** au soleil levant, au lever du soleil; *F* **s. industry** industrie *f* de l'avenir *ou* du futur

sunroof ['sʌnruːf] *n Aut* toit *m* ouvrant; (*of hotel etc*) toiture-terrasse *f*, solarium *m*

sunset ['sʌnset] *n* coucher *m* du soleil; **at s.** au soleil couchant, au coucher du soleil

sunshade ['sʌnʃeɪd] *n* (*parasol*) ombrelle *f*; (*for table etc*) parasol *m*; (*in car*) pare-soleil *m inv*

sunshine ['sʌnʃaɪn] *n* (**a**) (*light*) (clarté *f ou* lumière *f* du) soleil *m*; **in the s.** au soleil; **in the bright** *or* **brilliant s.** en plein soleil; **they need more s.** il leur faut davantage de soleil; **period of s.** période d'ensoleillement; *Aut* **s. roof** toit *m* ouvrant; **the S. State** = la Floride (**b**) *F* **hello s.!** (*to girl, woman*) bonjour ma jolie!; (*to boy, man*) salut mon vieux!; *F Iron* **where d'you think you're going, s.?** eh, tu vas où comme ça, mon coco?

sun-soaked *adj* (*beach etc*) baigné de soleil

sunspot ['sʌnspɒt] *n* (**a**) (*on the sun*) tache *f* solaire, tache du soleil (**b**) (*holiday resort etc*) (*for summer holiday*) station *f* estivale; **it's our favourite winter s.** c'est là que nous préférons aller prendre du soleil pendant nos vacances d'hiver

sunstroke ['sʌnstrəʊk] *n Med* insolation *f*; **to get s.** attraper une insolation

suntan ['sʌntæn] *n* bronzage *m*, hâle *m*; **to get a s.** (se faire) bronzer; **she's got a tremendous s.** elle a un bronzage magnifique; **s. lotion/oil** lotion *f*/huile *f* solaire

suntanned ['sʌntænd] *adj* bronzé, hâlé

suntrap ['sʌntræp] *n* coin *m* très ensoleillé

sun-up *n Am* lever *m* du soleil; **at s.** au lever du soleil

sun-worship *n Rel* culte *m* du soleil

sun-worshipper *n Rel* adorateur, -trice du soleil; *Fig* (*on beach etc*) amateur, -trice de soleil

sup[1] [sʌp] *n esp Scot, North Eng* petite gorgée *f*; **to take a s. of soup** prendre une goutte de bouillon

sup[2] (**-pp-** [sʌpt]) **1** *vt esp Scot, North Eng* boire à petites gorgées **2** *vi Old-fashioned* (*have supper*) souper (**off, on** de)

▶ **sup up** *esp Scot, North Eng* **1** *vtsep* (*drink up*) finir **2** *vi* finir son verre

super ['suːpər] **1** *adj F* (*excellent*) super *inv*, formidable, génial **2** *n* (**a**) *Am F* (*in apartment block*) concierge *mf*, gardien *m* (d'immeuble) (**b**) *F* = **supervisor** (**c**) *Aut* (*petrol*) super *m*

superable ['suːpərəb(ə)l] *adj* surmontable

superabundance [suːpərə'bʌndəns] *n* surabondance *f* (**of** de)

superabundant [suːpərə'bʌndənt] *adj* surabondant

superabundantly [suːpərə'bʌndəntlɪ] *adv* surabondamment

superannuate [suːpər'ænjʊeɪt] *vt* (*person*) mettre à la retraite; *Fig* (*thing*) mettre au rancart, remiser

superannuated [suːpər'ænjʊeɪtɪd] *adj* (*person*) (mis) en *ou* à la retraite, retraité; (*ideas*) suranné; (*system, equipment*) démodé

superannuation [suːpərænjʊ'eɪʃən] *n* retraite *f*; **s. fund** caisse *f* des retraites

superb [suː'pɜːb] *adj* (*athlete, performance, food, accommodation, novel, singing*) excellent; (*animal, view, weather, film, picture etc*) superbe

superbly [suː'pɜːblɪ] *adv* superbement

supercargo ['suːpəkɑːgəʊ] *n Naut* subrécargue *m*

supercharge ['suːpətʃɑːdʒ] *vt Aut, Av etc* (*engine*) suralimenter, surcomprimer; **supercharged engine** moteur *m* suralimenté *ou* surcomprimé *ou* à compresseur

supercharger ['suːpətʃɑːdʒər] *n Aut, Av etc* compresseur *m*, surpresseur *m*

supercilious [suːpə'sɪlɪəs] *adj* hautain, dédaigneux

superciliously [suːpə'sɪlɪəslɪ] *adv* avec hauteur, dédaigneusement

superciliousness [suːpə'sɪlɪəsnɪs] *n* hauteur *f*

superconductor [suːpəkən'dʌktər] *n Phys, El* supraconducteur *m*

supercooling ['suːpə'kuːlɪŋ] *n* sous-refroidissement *m*

supercritical [suːpə'krɪtɪk(ə)l] *adj Nucl Phys* supercritique, surcritique

super-duper ['suːpə'duːpər] *adj F* super, superchouette

superego ['suːpəriːgəʊ] *n Psy* surmoi *m*

superelevation [suːperelɪ'veɪʃən] *n* (*of road*) dévers *m*

supererogation [suːpererə'geɪʃən] *n Fml* surérogation *f*

superficial [suːpə'fɪʃəl] *adj* (**a**) superficiel; **he has a s. charm** il a un charme superficiel; **to have a s. knowledge of sth** avoir des connaissances superficielles de qch; **s. learning** vernis *m* de connaissances (**b**) *Med* **s. wound** blessure *f* superficielle

superficiality [suːpəfɪʃɪ'ælɪtɪ] *n* superficialité *f*

superficially [suːpə'fɪʃəlɪ] *adv* superficiellement

superfine ['suːpəfaɪn] *adj* (**a**) *Com etc* surfin, superfin (**b**) (*mind etc*) raffiné

superfluity [suːpə'fluːɪtɪ] *n* superfluité *f*; **s. of good things** surabondance *f* de biens; **s. of words** surabondance de paroles

superfluous [suː'pɜːflʊəs] *adj* superflu, *Lit* superfétatoire; **it would be s. to mention …** il serait superflu de mentionner …; *F* **I'm starting to feel a bit s.** je commence à me sentir un peu de trop ici; **s. weight** excédent *m* de poids

superfluously [suː'pɜːflʊəslɪ] *adv* d'une manière superflue

superfluousness [suː'pɜːflʊəsnɪs] *n* superfluité *f*

Superglue®[1] ['suːpəgluː] *n* super-glu® *f*

superglue[2] *vt* coller à la super-glu®

supergrass ['suːpəgrɑːs] *n Br Sl* indic *m* (*très précieux pour la police*)

superhighway ['suːpəhaɪweɪ] *n Am Comptr* autoroute *f*

superhuman [suːpə'hjuːmən] *adj* surhumain

superimpose [suːpərɪm'pəʊz] *vt* superposer, surimposer; *Phot, Cin* faire une surimpression de, surimprimer; *Fig* **a Western culture superimposed on an indigenous one** une culture occidentale venue se superposer à une culture indigène

superimposition [suːpərɪmpə'zɪʃən] *n* superposition *f*, *Phot, Cin* surimpression *f*

superintend [suːpərɪn'tend] *vt* diriger, surveiller; **to s. the election** présider au scrutin

superintendence [suːpərɪn'tendəns] *n* direction *f*, surveillance *f*

superintendent [suːpərɪn'tendənt] *n* (**a**) (*director*) directeur, -trice; (*of works etc*) surveillant, -ante, chef *m*; *US F* **sidewalk s.** passant, -ante qui regarde les travaux de construction (**b**) (*police officer*) commissaire *m* (de police) (**c**) *Am* (*of apartment block*) concierge *mf*, gardien *m* (d'immeuble)

superior [suː'pɪərɪər] **1** *adj* (**a**) (*position, officer, quality*) supérieur (**to** à); *Geog* **Lake S.** le lac Supérieur; **to be s. in numbers to the enemy** être supérieur en nombre à l'ennemi, avoir la supériorité du nombre sur l'ennemi; **they were overcome by s. numbers** ils ont succombé sous le nombre, ils ont été vaincus par le nombre; **she felt s. to her colleagues** elle se sentait supérieure à ses collègues; *Typ* **s. letter** lettre *f* supérieure; *Typ* **s. number** chiffre *m* supérieur

(b) (*arrogant*) (*person*) orgueilleux; (*air*) de supériorité; **with a s. smile** avec un sourire condescendant

2 *n* supérieur, -eure; **he is your s.** il est votre supérieur; **to be sb's s. in courage** être plus courageux que qn; **Father S.** père *m* supérieur; **Mother S.** mère *f* supérieure

superiority [suːpɪərɪˈɒrɪtɪ] *n* supériorité *f*; **s. in men and materials** supériorité en hommes et en matériel; *Mil, Av* **air s.** supériorité aérienne; **s. complex** complexe *m* de supériorité

superlative [suːˈpɜːlətɪv] **1** *adj* **(a)** (*excellent*) excellent **(b)** *Gram* superlatif **2** *n* [①A18-19,4; A22,c; B10-11,E; B12-13,F] *Gram* superlatif *m*; **in the s.** au superlatif; *Fig* **to speak in superlatives** s'exprimer par superlatifs

superlatively [suːˈpɜːlətɪvlɪ] *adv* extrêmement, au plus haut degré; **s. fit** dans une forme excellente

superman, *pl* **-men** [ˈsuːpəmæn, -men] *n* surhomme *m*, *Hum F* superman *m*

supermarket [ˈsuːpəmɑːkɪt] *n* supermarché *m*; **s. prices** prix *mpl* dans les supermarchés

supermarketing [ˈsuːpəmɑːkɪtɪŋ] *n* supermercatique *f*

supermini [ˈsuːpəmɪnɪ] *n Aut* citadine *f*

supermodel [ˈsuːpəmɒd(ə)l] *n* supermodel *m*

supernatural [suːpəˈnætʃərəl] **1** *adj* surnaturel **2** *n* surnaturel *m*

supernaturally [suːpəˈnætʃərəlɪ] *adv* de manière surnaturelle

supernova [suːpəˈnəʊvə] *n Astron* supernova *f*, *pl* supernovæ

supernumerary [suːpəˈnjuːm(ə)rərɪ] **1** *adj* surnuméraire; (*staff*) en surnombre **2** *n* surnuméraire *m*; *Th, Cin* figurant, -ante

superphosphate [suːpəˈfɒsfeɪt] *n* superphosphate *m*

superpose [suːpəˈpəʊz] *vt* superposer (**upon, on** à); (*planks etc*) étager

superpower [ˈsuːpəpaʊər] *n Pol* superpuissance *f*; **s. talks** négociations *fpl* entre les superpuissances

superscript [ˈsuːpəskrɪpt] *Typ* **1** *adj* (*number*) en exposant; **s. 3** 3 en exposant **2** *n* (*number*) exposant *m*

superscription [suːpəˈskrɪpʃən] *n* (*on coin*) inscription *f*

supersede [suːpəˈsiːd] *vt* (*sb, sth*) remplacer; (*sb*) prendre la place de, supplanter; **this catalogue supersedes previous issues** ce catalogue annule les précédents; **method now superseded** méthode périmée; **the RWQ20 has long been superseded by smaller models** la RWQ20 a depuis longtemps été supplantée par des modèles plus petits

supersensitive [suːpəˈsensɪtɪv] *adj* hypersensible

supersonic [suːpəˈsɒnɪk] *adj* (*plane, speed*) supersonique; **s. boom** *or* **bang** bang *m*

superstar [ˈsuːpəstɑːr] *n Cin, Sp* superstar *f*

superstition [suːpəˈstɪʃən] *n* superstition *f*

superstitious [suːpəˈstɪʃəs] *adj* superstitieux

superstitiously [suːpəˈstɪʃəslɪ] *adv* superstitieusement

superstore [ˈsuːpəstɔːr] *n* hypermarché *m*

superstructure [ˈsuːpəstrʌktʃər] *n* superstructure *f*

supertanker [ˈsuːpətæŋkər] *n Naut* superpétrolier *m*, supertanker *m*

supertax [ˈsuːpətæks] *n* surimposition *f*, surtaxe *f*

supertonic [suːpəˈtɒnɪk] *n Mus* sus-tonique *f*

superuser [ˈsuːpəjuːzər] *n Comptr* gros utilisateur *m*

supervene [suːpəˈviːn] *vi esp Fml* survenir; **if no complications s.** s'il ne survient pas de complications

supervention [suːpəˈvenʃən] *n Fml* survenue *f*

super-VGA *n Comptr* Super-VGA *m*

supervise [ˈsuːpəvaɪz] *vt* **(a)** (*keep watch on*) (*children, prisoners*) surveiller **(b)** (*department, thesis*) diriger

supervision [suːpəˈvɪʒən] *n* **(a)** (*keeping watch on*) surveillance *f*; **children are under the s. of trained instructors at all times** les enfants se trouvent toujours sous la surveillance de moniteurs diplômés **(b)** (*control*) (*of department, thesis*) direction *f*

supervisor [ˈsuːpəvaɪzər] *n* **(a)** (*person who keeps watch over sb/sth*) surveillant, -ante **(b)** (*manager*) directeur, -trice **(c)** *Univ* (*for PhD etc*) directeur *m* de thèse(s)

supervisory [suːpəˈvaɪz(ə)rɪ] *adj* (*committee etc*) de surveillance; **s. board** conseil *m* de surveillance; **a s. function** une fonction de surveillance; **a s. role** un rôle de surveillant

superwoman, *pl* **-women** [ˈsuːpəwʊmən, -wɪmɪn] *n Hum F* superwoman *f*

supine[1] [ˈsuːpaɪn] *adj* **(a)** (*lying on back*) couché *ou* étendu sur le dos **(b)** (*inactive*) mou, *f* molle, indolent

supine[2] *n Gram* supin *m*

supper [ˈsʌpər] *n* [①A6,d,iii] (*early evening meal*) dîner *m*; (*snack before going to bed*) souper *m*; **to have s.** dîner; (*before bed*) souper; *Fig* **you'll have to sing for your s.** c'est un prêté pour un rendu, c'est donnant, donnant; **the Last S.** la Cène, le dernier repas (du Seigneur); *Rel* **the Lord's S.** la communion, la cène, l'eucharistie *f*

suppertime [ˈsʌpətaɪm] *n* l'heure *f* du dîner; (*before bed*) l'heure du souper; **(it's) s.!** à table!

supplant [səˈplɑːnt] *vt* (*person*) supplanter, prendre la place de, évincer

supple [ˈsʌp(ə)l] *adj* (*limb, object, material*) souple, flexible; (*person*) souple; **to become s.** s'assouplir; **s.-limbed** aux membres souples

supplement[1] [ˈsʌplɪmənt] *n* (*of newspaper, for travel, of angle*) supplément *m*

supplement[2] [ˈsʌplɪment] *vt* (*book*) ajouter un supplément à; **to s. one's income by writing articles** augmenter ses revenus en écrivant des articles

supplementary [sʌplɪˈment(ə)rɪ] *adj* supplémentaire (**to** de); *Math* **s. angle** angle *m* supplémentaire; *Br formerly* **s. benefit** = allocation *f* versée par l'État à ceux qui ont les plus faibles revenus; **s. cover** garanties *fpl* complémentaires; **s. income** revenus *mpl* annexes

suppleness [ˈsʌp(ə)lnɪs] *n* souplesse *f*

suppliant [ˈsʌplɪənt] **1** *adj* (*attitude, gesture*) suppliant, de supplication **2** *n* suppliant, -ante

supplicant [ˈsʌplɪkənt] *n* suppliant, -ante

supplicate [ˈsʌplɪkeɪt] *Fml, Lit* **1** *vt* (*person*) supplier (**to do sth** de faire qch); (*sb's protection*) solliciter humblement **2** *vi* supplier

supplicating [ˈsʌplɪkeɪtɪŋ] *adj* suppliant, de supplication

supplication [sʌplɪˈkeɪʃən] *n* **(a)** (*act*) supplication *f* **(b)** (*request*) supplique *f*

supplier [səˈplaɪər] *n Com* fournisseur, -euse; **s. code** code *m* fournisseur; *Acct* **s. credit** crédit-fournisseur *m*, avoir-fournisseur *m*

supply[1] [səˈplaɪ] *n* **(a)** (*act of supplying*) approvisionnement *m*, fourniture *f*; **electricity s.** alimentation *f* en électricité; *Econ* **s. and demand** l'offre *f* et la demande; **s.-side economics** théorie *f* économique de l'offre; *Mil* **s. lines** lignes *fpl* de ravitaillement; **s. pipe** (*for fuel*) conduite *f* d'arrivée du combustible; **s. price** prix *m* d'offre; *Naut* **s. ship** ravitailleur *m*

(b) (*stock*) provision *f*; **to get (in) a fresh s. of sth** se réapprovisionner en qch; **money/information is in short s.** on manque d'argent/d'informations; **supplies** (*for office, photography*) fournitures *fpl*; **supplies of money** fonds *mpl*, ressources *fpl*; **food supplies** vivres *mpl*; **to cut off** *or* **stop the enemy's supplies** couper l'ennemi de ses approvisionnements; **supplies and services** fournitures et services *mpl*

(c) *Sch* **s. teacher** suppléant, -ante, remplaçant, -ante; **to do s. teaching** faire des remplacements

supply[2] **1** *vt* **(a)** fournir, approvisionner (**sb with sth** qn en qch); (*market*) alimenter; (*goods*) fournir, procurer; (*information*) fournir; (*services*) assurer; (*water, gas etc*) amener; **to s. oneself with sth** s'approvisionner en qch; **the tradesmen who s. us** nos fournisseurs; *El* **to s. a factory with current** alimenter une usine en courant; **the arteries that s. the brain** les artères qui amènent le sang au cerveau; **to s. proof** fournir des preuves

(b) (*omission*) réparer; (*need*) répondre à; **to s. sb's needs** pourvoir *ou* subvenir aux besoins de qn

2 *vi* **to s. for sb** (*of teacher etc*) assurer l'intérim *ou* la suppléance de qn

support[1] [səˈpɔːt] *n* **(a)** (*act of supporting*) appui *m*, soutien *m*; (*of arch, vault*) soutènement *m*; **moral s.** appui *ou* soutien moral; **to give s. to a proposal** appuyer une proposition; **this discovery lends s. to those who have argued …** cette découverte va dans le sens de ceux qui soutiennent que …; **the rebels have little s.** les rebelles bénéficient d'un soutien limité; **there is widespread s. for the government/these policies** le gouvernement/ces politiques bénéficie(nt) d'un très large soutien; **can I expect your s.?** est-ce que je peux compter sur votre soutien?; **to produce documents in s. of an allegation** produire des pièces à l'appui d'une allégation *ou* pour appuyer une allégation; *Jur* fournir les pièces au soutien; **to argue in s. of a measure** défendre une mesure; **in s. of this theory** à l'appui de cette théorie; *Mil* **air s.** appui *ou* soutien aérien; **with (financial) s. from the council** avec l'appui (financier) du conseil; **insufficient air for the s. of life** air en quantité insuffisante pour permettre la vie; **their son was their only means of s.** leur fils était leur seul soutien; **to be without means of s.** être sans ressources; *Mil* **s. unit** unité *f* de soutien

(b) (*person, thing supporting*) soutien *m*; (*of arch, vault*) appui *m*, support *m*, soutien; (*in horticulture*) tuteur *m*; **she is the s. of the family** c'est elle qui fait vivre la famille; *Sp*

(athletic) s. suspensoir *m*; *US* **price supports** subventions *fpl*; **s. market** marché *m* support *ou* d'appui; **s. services** services *mpl* de soutien *ou* généraux; **s. staff** personnel *m* de soutien *ou* des services généraux; **s. stockings** bas *mpl* à varices

support² *vt* **(a)** (*hold up*) (*vault, arch*) supporter, soutenir; *MecE* (*load*) supporter, résister à; (*prices*) soutenir; **I supported him with my arm** je lui ai donné le bras; **he supported himself on a stick/my arm** il s'appuyait sur un bâton/mon bras

(b) (*encourage, aid*) (*person, claims*) appuyer; (*theory*) soutenir; (*government, project*) apporter son soutien à; (*charitable event*) sponsoriser; (*charitable organization*) faire une donation à; *Sp* (*team*) supporter; *Mil* (*troops*) soutenir; (*of new discoveries etc*) (*theory*) renforcer; **proof that supports a case** preuves à l'appui d'une cause; **his theory is supported by facts** sa théorie est corroborée par les faits; *Parl* **to s. the motion** soutenir la motion; **to be supported by sb** (*in a proposal*) être soutenu par qn; **environmentalists s. the bill** les écologistes soutiennent le projet de loi; **the mayor, supported by the clergy** le maire, avec le soutien du clergé; **his parents supported him in his attempt to become an actor** ses parents l'ont soutenu lorsqu'il a essayé de devenir acteur

(c) (*help to exist*) (*life*) entretenir; (*person*) soutenir financièrement, pourvoir aux besoins de; **to have a wife and three children to s.** avoir une femme et trois enfants à charge; **it was impossible to s. his family on his meagre salary** il lui était impossible de subvenir aux besoins de sa famille avec son maigre salaire; **hospital supported by voluntary contributions** hôpital financé par les souscriptions volontaires; **to s. oneself** se suffire (à soi-même), gagner sa vie

(d) *Comptr* permettre l'utilisation de, supporter; **this package, which is supported by all ABC workstations ...** ce progiciel, qui peut être utilisé sur tous les postes de travail ABC ...

supportable [sə'pɔːtəb(ə)l] *adj* **(a)** (*bearable*) supportable, tolérable **(b)** (*theory etc*) soutenable

supporter [sə'pɔːtər] *n* **(a)** (*person*) (*of opinion*) défenseur *m*, tenant *m*; (*of party*) partisan *m*, sympathisant *m*; (*of politician*) partisan, -ane; *Sp* (*of team*) supporter *m*; **supporters' club** club *m* des supporters **(b)** (*device*) soutien *m*, support *m*

supporting [sə'pɔːtɪŋ] *adj Cin* (*film, programme*) supplémentaire; *Th, Mus* **s. act** première partie *f*; **in the days when the Beatles were one of the s. acts** quand les Beatles se produisaient en première partie; *Th* **the s. cast** les seconds *ou* deuxièmes rôles *mpl*; **there is an excellent s. cast** les seconds rôles sont excellents; *Th, Cin* **s. role** *or* **part** second rôle; **s. wall** mur *m* d'appui *ou* de soutènement

supportive [sə'pɔːtɪv] *adj* (*parent, friend, ally etc*) qui soutient; **to be s.** prêter son appui; **she's been very s.** elle l'a/nous a/*etc* bien soutenu(s); **she's usually so s.** d'habitude, elle fait tout ce qu'elle peut pour les/nous/*etc* aider; **I was trying to be as s. as I could** je faisais de mon mieux pour les/*etc* aider; **you could be more s.!** vous pourriez me/nous/*etc* soutenir un peu plus!; **to be s. of sb's efforts** soutenir qn dans ses efforts

supportiveness [sə'pɔːtɪvnɪs] *n* soutien *m*, appui *m*

suppose [sə'pəʊz] *vt* **(a)** [①**A46**,9,a,iii] (*assume*) supposer; (*imagine*) imaginer; (*think*) croire, penser; **you mustn't s. that ...** il ne faut pas vous imaginer que ...; **what makes you s. that I trust you?** qu'est-ce qui vous fait croire que j'ai confiance en vous?; **I don't s. he'll do it** je ne crois pas qu'il le fera; **will you go? – I s. so** irez-vous? – probablement; **please can I stay up late? – oh, I s. so** s'il te plaît est-ce que je peux veiller tard? – bon, si tu veux; **I don't think he'll come – no, I s. not** *or* **I don't s. so** je ne crois pas qu'il viendra – non, sans doute *ou* probablement pas; **I don't s. you remember me** vous ne vous souvenez sans doute pas de moi; **I s. you can't remember <u>that</u> either!** tu ne te souviens probablement pas de ça non plus!; **supposing** *or* **(let us) s. (that) you're right** supposons *ou* en supposant *ou* mettons que vous ayez raison; **s.** *or* **supposing you were ill** supposez que vous soyez malade; **s. we <u>do</u> stay another year, what then?** suppose qu'en effet, nous restions une année de plus, et après?; **supposing** *or* **s. he came back** si, par supposition, il revenait, supposons qu'il revienne; **s. I was talking to him, what of it?** et si j'étais en train de lui parler, qu'est-ce que ça peut faire?; **yes, but s. I were to die** oui, mais si je venais à mourir; *F* **s. we change the subject** et si nous changions de sujet; **just supposing it <u>did</u> happen** supposons que ça se produise; **the plan supposes we can keep inflation under 1.5%** le projet part du principe que nous arriverons à maintenir l'inflation au-dessous de 1,5%; **that supposes rather more enthusiasm than I think will be forthcoming** cela suppose un enthousiasme qui ne viendra pas, à mon avis

(b) to be supposed to do sth être censé faire qch; **she's supposed to be in London** (*they say she is, she should be*) elle est censée être à Londres; **the film's supposed to be very good** à ce qu'il paraît, c'est un très bon film; **it's supposed to have been discovered by ...** on dit que cela a été découvert par ...; **there is supposed to be a well in the garden** on dit qu'il y a un puits dans le jardin; **I'm not supposed to do it** je ne suis pas censé le faire; **you're not supposed to know that** (*so keep quiet about it*) vous n'êtes pas censé le savoir; (*so I won't tell you*) je n'ai pas à vous le dire; **you're not supposed to park here** vous n'avez pas le droit de vous garer ici; **don't ask me! – <u>you're</u> supposed to be in charge!** ne me demande pas ça! – je croyais pourtant bien que c'était toi le responsable!; **you're supposed to be my friend!** je vous croyais mon ami!; **could you lend me the key? – well, I'm not supposed to, but ...** pourriez-vous me prêter la clef? – eh bien, je ne devrais pas, mais ...; **the computer's not supposed to make a noise like that** l'ordinateur ne devrait pas faire un tel bruit; **how am I supposed to work in conditions like these!** comment veut-on que je travaille dans de telles conditions!; **how is anybody supposed to make sense of that!** comment est-on censé s'y retrouver?

supposed [sə'pəʊzd] *adj attrib* (*presumed, alleged*) présumé

supposedly [sə'pəʊzɪdlɪ] *adv* soi-disant

supposition [sʌpə'zɪʃən] *n* [①**A56**,a,v] supposition *f*, hypothèse *f*; **unfounded s.** supposition gratuite; **on the s. that ...** à supposé que ...+ *sub*, dans l'hypothèse où ... + *cond*; **on the s. that she had caught the train** dans l'hypothèse où elle aurait pris le train

suppositious [sʌpə'zɪʃəs] *adj Fml* supposé

supposititious [səpɒzɪ'tɪʃəs] *adj Fml* (*false*) faux, *f* fausse

suppository [sə'pɒzɪtrɪ] *n Pharm* suppositoire *m*

suppress [sə'pres] *vt* **(a)** (*uprising*) réprimer, étouffer; (*newspaper, association*) supprimer; (*malpractice*) faire disparaître **(b)** (*scandal*) étouffer; (*sob*) étouffer, ravaler; (*feelings, emotions*) réprimer, refouler; (*emotion*) dominer; **to s. one's feelings** se contenir, faire taire ses sentiments; **to s. a cough** réprimer son envie de tousser **(c)** (*hide*) cacher, dissimuler; (*keep silent about*) passer sous silence; (*fact*) ne pas révéler; *Jur* faire disparaître; (*name*) taire, ne pas donner **(d)** *Rad, El* déparasiter

suppressed [sə'prest] *adj* (*feeling etc*) étouffé, réprimé; **s. anger** colère *f* refoulée; **s. excitement** agitation *f* contenue

suppression [sə'preʃən] *n* **(a)** (*of uprising, malpractice*) répression *f*; (*of book, newspaper*) interdiction *f* **(b)** (*of emotions*) refoulement *m*; *Med* (*of sweat, urine*) suppression *f*; **the minister demanded the s. of the story** le ministre a exigé que l'on étouffe l'affaire **(c)** (*of truth, fact, evidence*) dissimulation *f*; **she could not tolerate this s. of the truth** elle ne pouvait tolérer que l'on dissimule la vérité de cette manière **(d)** *Rad* antiparasitage *m*

suppressor [sə'presər] *n* **(a)** (*person*) **the s. of the uprising** celui qui dirige/dirigeait/*etc* la répression **(b)** *Rad* (*device*) (dispositif *m ou* appareil *m*) antiparasite *m*; **s. grid** grille *f* de freinage

suppurate ['sʌpjʊreɪt] *vi* (*of wound, sore*) suppurer

suppurating ['sʌpjʊreɪtɪŋ] *adj Med* purulent, suppurant

suppuration [sʌpjʊ'reɪʃən] *n* suppuration *f*

supranational [suːprə'næʃən(ə)l] *adj* supranational

suprarenal gland [suːprə'riːn(ə)l] *n Anat* glande *f* surrénale

supremacist [sʊ'preməsɪst] *n* = personne *f* croyant en la supériorité d'un groupe, racial ou autre

supremacy [sʊ'preməsɪ] *n* suprématie *f*; **white s.** la suprématie de la race blanche

supreme [sʊ'priːm] *adj* suprême; **to reign s.** (*of monarch*) régner en souverain absolu; *Fig* (*of champion etc*) régner; **to make the s. sacrifice** (*die*) se sacrifier; *Rel* **the S. Being** l'Être *m* suprême; **S. Commander** commandant *m* en chef; *US Jur* **S. Court** Cour *f* suprême

supremely [sʊ'priːmlɪ] *adv* suprêmement; **we are s. happy** nous jouissons d'un bonheur suprême, nous sommes suprêmement heureux

supremo, *pl* **-s** [sʊ'priːməʊ, -məʊz] *n Br* grand chef *m*, *F* big boss *m*

Supt *abbr* **superintendent**

surcharge¹ ['sɜːtʃɑːdʒ] *n* (*additional charge*) supplément *m*; (*as penalty*) majoration *f* d'impôt; **s. on a letter** surtaxe *f* d'une lettre; **there's a s. for late bookings** il y a un supplément à payer pour les réservations de dernière minute

surcharge[2] *vt* (*letter etc*) surtaxer; **if motorists were surcharged for …** si on surtaxait les automobilistes pour …

surd [sɜːd] *n* **(a)** *Math* quantité *f* irrationnelle **(b)** *Ling* (*consonant*) sourde *f*

sure [ʃʊər] **1** *adj* (*convinced, definite*) sûr, certain; (*judgement, shot*) sûr; (*remedy, cure*) infaillible; (*profit, success*) sûr, assuré; **to be s. of** *or* **about sth** être sûr *ou* certain de qch; **I'm s. of it** j'en suis sûr *ou* certain; **I'm not so s. of** *or* **about that** je n'en suis pas bien sûr *ou* certain; (*implying permission won't be given*) ça, ça m'étonnerait; **I can't be s., but I think it was two o'clock** je n'en suis pas tout à fait sûr, mais je pense qu'il était deux heures; **I'm s. you're mistaken** je suis sûr que vous vous trompez; **are you quite s. he hasn't left yet?** êtes-vous bien sûr qu'il n'est pas encore parti?; **I'm s. you must be** *or* **you're very tired** je suis sûr que vous êtes très fatigué; **to be s. of oneself** être sûr de soi; **I don't know, I'm s.** ma foi, je ne sais pas; **we're all very grateful, I'm s., but …** nous vous/leur/*etc* en sommes certainement très reconnaissants, mais …; **to make s. of sth** s'assurer de qch; **make s. (that) the door is shut** assurez-vous que la porte est fermée, verifiez que la porte est fermée; **I'll just go and make s.** je vais vérifier; **to make s. of a seat** s'assurer une place; **don't be too** *or* **so s.!** vous êtes bien sûr de vous!; **what makes you so s.?** comment pouvez-vous en être si sûr?; **with a s. hand** d'une main assurée; **there is only one s. way of doing it** il n'y a qu'un moyen sûr de le faire; *Iron* **that's a s. way of failing the interview** c'est un moyen sûr d'échouer à l'entretien; **it's a s. thing** c'est une certitude *ou* une chose certaine; *esp Am F* **s. thing!** bien sûr!, pour sûr!; **I don't know for s.** je n'en suis pas bien sûr; **tomorrow for s.** demain sans faute; **she won't come, that's for s.** elle ne viendra pas, c'est certain; **it's s. to be fine** il fera sûrement beau; **he's s. to come** il viendra sûrement *ou* à coup sûr; **be s. to come early** ne manquez pas d'arriver de bonne heure; **be s. and ask him what time he's coming!** assure-toi de l'heure à laquelle il arrivera; **be s. not to lose it, be s. that you don't lose it** prenez garde de ne pas le perdre

2 *adv* **(a)** *esp Am F* (*really*) vraiment; **it s. is cold** il fait vraiment froid; **it s. was difficult** c'était vraiment *ou* bien difficile; **you s. do know your history!** vous vous y connaissez vraiment *ou F* drôlement bien en histoire!

(b) as s. as fate, as s. as eggs are *or F* **is eggs** aussi vrai qu'il fait jour, aussi sûr que deux et deux font quatre; **s. enough he was there** il était bien là; **she'll come s. enough** elle viendra, tu peux compter là-dessus; **no, it's whisky s. enough** non, c'est bien du whisky; *F* **for s.!**, *esp Am* **s.!** mais oui!, bien sûr!

surefooted [ʃʊəˈfʊtɪd] *adj* au pied sûr; **to be s.** avoir le pied sûr; *Fig* **the Prime Minister gave a s. performance in the debate** le Premier ministre a très bien intervenu lors du débat

surely [ˈʃʊəlɪ] *adv* **(a)** (*in a sure manner*) **slowly but s.** lentement mais sûrement **(b)** (*certainly*) assurément, sans doute; **he will s. come** il viendra sûrement; **s. you don't believe that!** vous ne croyez quand même pas cela!; **s. you're not going to leave us?** vous n'allez quand même pas nous quitter?; *esp Am* **will you help me? – s.!** voulez-vous m'aider? – bien sûr!; **it's all gone – s. not?** il n'y en a plus – c'est pas vrai!

sureness [ˈʃʊənɪs] *n* (*of hand, judgement etc*) sûreté *f*; (*of remedy*) efficacité *f*; (*certainty*) certitude *f*; **the s. of his aim** la précision de son tir

surety [ˈʃʊərətɪ] *n Jur* (*person*) caution *f*, garant, -ante; *Com* donneur *m* d'aval; **to stand s. for sb** se porter caution pour qn, se rendre *ou* se porter garant de qn; **s. for a debt** garant d'une dette; **s. for a loan** sûreté *f* en garantie d'un crédit; **in his own s. of £5000** sous (sa propre) caution de cinq mille livres

surf[1] [sɜːf] *n* ressac *m*

surf[2] **1** *vi Sp* faire du surf **2** *vt* **to s. the Internet** naviguer dans *ou* surfer sur l'Internet

surface[1] [ˈsɜːfɪs] *n* **(a)** (*exterior, face*) surface *f*; **the earth's s.** la surface de la terre; **to rise to the s. of the water** remonter *ou* revenir à la surface de l'eau; **to rise** *or* **come to the s.** (*of submarine*) revenir en surface *ou* à la surface; **to break s.** faire surface; **smooth/even s.** surface lisse/unie; **his politeness is only on the s.** sa politesse est toute de surface; **on the s. she is very calm** en surface, elle est très calme; **meaning that lies below the s.** signification *f* cachée; **we're still very much on the s. of the problem** nous n'avons pas encore attaqué le fond du problème; **to send a letter by s. mail** envoyer une lettre par voie de terre/de mer; **s. transport** transport *m* terrestre et/ou maritime; **by s. transport** par voie de terre et/ou de mer; **s. water** eau *f* superficielle, eaux de surface; *Min* **s. work** travail *m* au jour; *Min* **s. worker** ouvrier *m* du jour

(b) (*area*) aire *f*, étendue *f*, superficie *f*; *Geom* **s. of revolution** surface *f* de révolution *ou* de rotation; **working s.** plan *m* de travail; (*in office*) surface utile; *Av* **lifting s.** surface portante *ou* de sustentation

(c) *Constr* (*of road*) revêtement *m*; **temporary s.** chaussée *f* provisoire

surface[2] **1** *vt* (*treat surface of*) apprêter la surface de; (*in papermaking*) calandrer; *Constr* (*road*) revêtir (**with** de); **they surfaced the back yard with concrete** ils ont recouvert la surface de la cour d'une couche de béton **2** *vi* **(a)** (*of submarine, whale etc*) faire surface; (*return to surface*) revenir en surface, remonter à la surface **(b)** *F* (*of person*) (*reappear, regain consciousness*) refaire surface

surface grammar *n Ling* grammaire *f* de surface

surface-mounted *adj Comptr* (*chips*) monté en surface

surface noise *n* (*on recording*) bruit *m* de surface

surface speed *n* (*of submarine*) vitesse *f* en surface

surface structure *n Ling* structure *f* de surface

surface tension *n Phys* tension *f* superficielle *ou* de surface

surface-to-air *adj Mil* **s. missile** missile *m* sol-air

surface-to-surface *adj Mil* **s. missile** missile *m* sol-sol

surfacing [ˈsɜːfɪsɪŋ] *n Constr* (*of/on road etc*) revêtement *m*

surfboard [ˈsɜːfbɔːd] *n Sp* planche *f* de surf, surf *m*

surfboarder, surfboarding [ˈsɜːfbɔːdər, -ɪŋ] = **surfer, surfing**

surfeit[1] [ˈsɜːfɪt] *n* (*excess*) surabondance *f*; **to have a s. of oysters/of music** être rassasié d'huîtres/de musique

surfeit[2] *vt* gorger, rassasier (**with** de); **to s. oneself with sth** se gorger de qch jusqu'à s'en dégoûter; **surfeited with pleasure** blasé *ou* écœuré par les plaisirs

surfer [ˈsɜːfər] *n* surfeur, -euse; **(Internet) s.** internaute *mf*, navigateur, -trice *ou* surfeur, -euse de l'Internet

surfing [ˈsɜːfɪŋ] *n* surf *m*

surfrider, surfriding [ˈsɜːfraɪdər, -ɪŋ] = **surfer, surfing**

surge[1] [sɜːdʒ] *n* (*of sea*) houle *f*; *El* (*of electricity*) surtension *f*; *Fig* (*of activity*) poussée *f*; (*of enthusiasm*) accès *m*; *Fig* **the s. of the crowd** les remous *mpl* de la foule; **a s. of anger** un flot *ou* une vague de colère; **there has been a s. of public interest in …** il y a eu un mouvement *ou* une poussée de l'intérêt public pour …; **she felt a s. of fury** elle sentit la fureur monter en elle; **these seasonal surges in production/sales** ces poussées saisonnières de la production/des ventes

surge[2] *vi* (*of sea*) être houleux; (*of waters*) se soulever; *El* (*of power*) être en surtension; *Fig* **the crowd surged along the street/onto the pitch** la foule s'est répandue en flots dans la rue/sur le terrain; **the crowd surged back** la foule a reflué

▶ **surge up** *vi* (*well up*) monter d'un seul coup; **anger surged up within her** un flot de colère est monté en elle; **a figure surged up out of the darkness** une silhouette surgit de l'ombre

surgeon [ˈsɜːdʒ(ə)n] *n* chirurgien *m*; *US Admin* **S. General** ministre *m* de la santé

surgery [ˈsɜːdʒərɪ] *n* **(a)** (*technique etc*) chirurgie *f*; (*operation*) intervention *f* chirurgicale; **major/minor s.** grande/petite chirurgie; **he'll need s.** il faudra l'opérer; **heart s.** chirurgie du cœur; **he's had heart s.** il a eu une opération du cœur; **the s. was successful** l'opération a réussi; **a clever piece of s.** une opération habile **(b)** *Br* (*place*) (*of doctor*) cabinet *m* (de consultation); (*of dentist*) cabinet; **s. (hours)** heures *fpl* de consultation **(c)** *Br Pol* (*of MP etc*) consultation *f* publique; **town councillors hold weekly surgeries** les conseillers municipaux tiennent des consultations hebdomadaires

surgical [ˈsɜːdʒɪk(ə)l] *adj* chirurgical; **s. boot** chaussure *f* orthopédique; **s. collar** minerve *f*; **s. instruments** instruments *mpl* de chirurgie; **s. spirit** alcool *m* à 90°; *Fig* **with s. precision** avec une précision mathématique

surging [ˈsɜːdʒɪŋ] *adj* **a s. sea** une mer houleuse; **a s. mass of people** un flot pressé de gens

surliness [ˈsɜːlɪnɪs] *n* (*mood*) humeur *f* maussade; (*of expression*) air *m* bourru; (*of remark*) ton *m* bourru

surly [ˈsɜːlɪ] *adj* (*person*) maussade, revêche; (*tone, look, remark*) bourru

surmise[1] [ˈsɜːmaɪz] *n* conjecture *f*

surmise[2] [sɜːˈmaɪz] *vt* conjecturer; **as you may well have surmised** comme vous l'avez peut-être deviné, comme vous le soupçonnez peut-être

surmount [sɜːˈmaʊnt] *vt* **(a)** (*be on top of*) surmonter; **column surmounted by a cross** colonne surmontée d'une croix **(b)** (*overcome*) (*obstacle, difficulty*) surmonter; (*emotion*) maîtriser

surmountable [sɜːˈmaʊntəb(ə)l] *adj* surmontable

surname [ˈsɜːneɪm] *n* [①B8,10] nom *m* de famille; **s. and Christian** *or* **first names** nom et prénoms *mpl*

surpass [sɜːˈpɑːs] *vt* **(a)** (*be superior to*) (*person*) surpasser;

(*rivals*) devancer; **to s. sb in kindness** renchérir sur la bonté de qn; **he has surpassed himself** il s'est surpassé; *Iron* **you've surpassed yourself this time** vous vous êtes surpassé cette fois (**b**) (*exceed*) dépasser, excéder; **the result surpassed my hopes** le résultat a dépassé mes espérances; **this surpasses all previous records** ceci surpasse tous les records précédents

surpassing [sɜːˈpɑːsɪŋ] *adj* sans égal, sans pareil; **of s. beauty** d'une beauté incomparable *ou* sans pareille

surplice [ˈsɜːplɪs] *n Rel* surplis *m*

surplus [ˈsɜːpləs] **1** *n* surplus *m*, excédent *m*; **to have a s. of sth** avoir qch en excès; **EC grain surpluses** excédents de céréales de la CE; **government s.** surplus *mpl* du gouvernement **2** *adj* (*items*) en trop, en surplus, excédentaire; **s. food/wine/oil** excédent *m* alimentaire/de vin/d'huile; **s. to requirements** en trop; **s. population/ products** population *f*/produits *mpl* excédentaire(s); *Com* **s. stock** surplus *mpl*

surprise¹ [səˈpraɪz] **1** *n* surprise *f*; **to take sb by s.** surprendre qn, prendre qn au dépourvu; **to give sb a s.** faire une surprise à qn; **it was a s. to see her there** ce fut une surprise de la voir là; **what a s. to see you here!** je ne m'attendais pas à vous rencontrer ici; **what a pleasant s.!** quelle bonne surprise!; **the party was meant to be a s.** la fête était censée être une surprise; **to spoil the s.** gâcher la surprise; **it was no s. to learn that he had a criminal record** il n'y avait rien d'étonnant à ce qu'il ait un casier judiciaire; **he's in for a bit of a s.!** s'il savait ce qu'on lui prépare!; **s., s.!, it's us!** surprise!, c'est nous!; **to my great s., much to my s.** à ma grande surprise, à mon grand étonnement; **imagine my s. when …** imaginez comme j'ai été surpris quand …, imaginez quelle a été ma surprise *ou* quel a été mon étonnement quand …

2 *adj* surprise; **the President's s. announcement** l'annonce surprise du président; **s. party** surprise-partie *f*, *pl* surprises-parties; **s. visit** visite *f* à l'improviste, visite(-) surprise; **to pay sb a s. visit** aller chez qn sans le prévenir

surprise² *vt* (**a**) (*astonish*) surprendre, étonner; **nothing surprises him** rien ne l'étonne; **you could s. yourself** tu pourrais t'étonner toi-même; **to be surprised at sth** être surpris *ou* étonné de qch; **I am surprised to see you** *or* **at seeing you** je m'étonne de vous voir, je suis surpris de vous voir; **I should be surprised if he came back** cela m'étonnerait qu'il revienne; **there can't be many people who don't have a phone – you'd be surprised** il ne doit pas y avoir beaucoup de gens qui n'ont pas le téléphone – ne crois pas ça; **I wouldn't** *or* **shouldn't be surprised if they knew already** cela ne me surprendrait pas qu'ils le sachent déjà; **it doesn't s. me in the least** ça ne m'étonne pas du tout; **I was agreeably surprised** j'ai été agréablement surpris; **I'm surprised at you!** tu m'étonnes!

(**b**) (*catch unawares*) surprendre; **to s. sb in the act** surprendre qn en flagrant délit, prendre qn sur le fait

surprised [səˈpraɪzd] *adj* (*look*) étonné, surpris; (*expression*) de surprise; **don't look so s.** ne prends pas un air aussi étonné

surprising [səˈpraɪzɪŋ] *adj* surprenant, étonnant; **well, it's not s., is it?** ça n'a vraiment rien de surprenant; **it wouldn't be s. if he was in the plot** ça n'aurait rien de surprenant s'il était du complot; **that's s. coming from him** (venant) de sa part, c'est surprenant

surprisingly [səˈpraɪzɪŋlɪ] *adv* étonnamment; **I found him s. young** je lui ai trouvé l'air étonnamment jeune; **s. enough, he agreed** cela peut paraître surprenant, mais il a accepté; **not s., she changed her mind** comme on pouvait s'y attendre *ou* évidemment, elle a changé d'avis

surreal [səˈrɪəl] **1** *adj* surréaliste **2** *n* surréalisme *m*

surrealism [səˈrɪəlɪz(ə)m] *n* surréalisme *m*

surrealist [səˈrɪəlɪst] *adj, n* surréaliste *mf*

surrealistic [sərɪəˈlɪstɪk] *adj* surréaliste

surrealistically [sərɪəˈlɪstɪk(ə)lɪ] *adv* d'une manière *ou* dans un style surréaliste

surrender¹ [səˈrendər] *n* (**a**) (*act of surrendering*) (*of army, fortress*) reddition *f*; **no s.!** nous ne nous rendrons pas! (**b**) *Jur* (*of possessions, rights*) abandon *m*, cession *f*; (*of right to property*) restitution *f*; (*of rights, authority*) abdication *f*; **to make a s. of principle** transiger avec ses principes (**c**) (*in insurance*) (*of policy*) rachat *m*; **s. value** valeur *f* de rachat

surrender² **1** *vi* se rendre; *Mil* faire (sa) soumission, rendre les armes; **to s. to the police** se constituer prisonnier, se livrer à la police; *Fig* **all right! I s.!** ça va! je me rends!; **to s. to temptation** céder à la tentation

2 *vt* (**a**) (*fortress*) rendre, livrer

(**b**) (*right, possessions*) abandonner, céder; (*right*) abdiquer; **she was instructed to s. her children to the care of the social services** on l'a obligé à laisser la garde de ses enfants à l'autorité des services sociaux; **to s. all hope of sth** abandonner *ou* renoncer à tout espoir de qch; **to s. an advantage** laisser un avantage; **to s. control of sth** abandonner la direction de qch

(**c**) (*in insurance*) (*policy*) racheter

surreptitious [sʌrəpˈtɪʃəs] *adj* subreptice, clandestin

surreptitiously [sʌrəpˈtɪʃəslɪ] *adv* subrepticement, clandestinement

surreptitiousness [sʌrəpˈtɪʃəsnɪs] *n* caractère *m* subreptice

surrogacy [ˈsʌrəgəsɪ] *n* maternité *f* de substitution

surrogate [ˈsʌrəgɪt] *n* (*person*) suppléant, -ante, substitut *m*; *Rel, Jur* subrogé, -ée; (*thing*) succédané *m* (**for** *or* **of sth** de qch); **s. mother** mère *f* porteuse; **s. motherhood** maternité *f* de substitution

surround¹ [səˈraʊnd] *n* encadrement *m*, bordure *f*

surround² *vt* entourer; *Mil* (*enemy*) entourer, cerner; (*town*) investir; **the crowd surrounded the car** la foule a assiégé la voiture; **surrounded by** *or* **with dangers** cerné de dangers; **he likes to be surrounded by …** il aime être entouré de …; **give up!, you're surrounded!** rendez-vous!, vous êtes cernés!; **the decision has been surrounded by controversy** la décision n'a pas cessé d'être controversée

surrounding [səˈraʊndɪŋ] *adj* entourant, environnant; **the s. country** le pays alentour *ou* environnant

surroundings [səˈraʊndɪŋz] *npl* (**a**) (*environment*) environnement *m*, milieu *m*; **in its natural s.** dans son milieu naturel; **to be in familiar s.** être en pays de connaissance (**b**) (*surrounding area*) (*of city etc*) environs *mpl*, alentours *mpl*

surtax¹ [ˈsɜːtæks] *n Admin* surtaxe *f*; (*on income*) = surtaxe progressive sur le revenu

surtax² *vt* surtaxer

surveillance [sɜːˈveɪləns] *n* surveillance *f*, contrôle *m*; **to keep sb under s.** surveiller qn; **to be under s.** être sous surveillance

survey¹ [ˈsɜːveɪ] *n* (**a**) (*study*) (*of subject, situation*) étude *f*; (*of opinions, voting intentions*) sondage *m*; (*for market research*) enquête *f*; **s. research** recherche *f* par sondage (**b**) (*inspection*) inspection *f*, visite *f*; *Br* (*of house, flat*) expertise *f* (**c**) (*in surveying*) (*action*) levé *m*; **aerial s.** levé aérophotogrammétrique; **to make a s. of an estate** relever un domaine; **quantity s.** métrage *m*, métré *m*, toisé *m*

survey² [sɜːˈveɪ] *vt* (**a**) (*look at*) (*countryside etc*) regarder, scruter; (*question*) étudier, mettre à l'étude (**b**) (*in market research*) (*population*) enquêter; **to s. the scale of the damage** contempler l'ampleur du désastre; **to s. the situation** examiner la situation (**c**) (*inspect*) (*ship, building*) inspecter, faire l'expertise de l'état de; *Br* **to have a house surveyed** faire expertiser une maison (**d**) (*in surveying*) (*city, property*) relever, lever le(s) plan(s) de; (*coast*) hydrographier, faire l'hydrographie de

surveying [sɜːˈveɪɪŋ] *n* (**a**) *Constr* expertise *f*; (*for mapmaking*) topographie *f*; **quantity s.** métrage *m*, métré *m*, toisé *m*; **s. instruments** instruments *mpl* topographiques (**b**) (*inspection*) inspection *f*, visite *f*

surveyor [səˈveɪər] *n* (*of land*) géomètre *mf* expert; **naval s.** (ingénieur *m*) hydrographe *m*; **s.'s table** planchette *f*; *Admin* **land s. and valuer, district s.** cadastreur *m*; (**quantity**) **s.** métreur *m* vérificateur; *Naut* **marine s.** visiteur *m* *ou* inspecteur *m* de navires; *Br* (**property**) **s.** (architecte *mf*) expert *m*

survivable [səˈvaɪvəb(ə)l] *adj* **a s. attack** une attaque à laquelle on peut survivre; **the conditions were not s.** il était impossible de survivre dans de telles conditions

survival [səˈvaɪv(ə)l] *n* (**a**) (*continued existence*) (*of tradition*) survivance *f*; (*of injured person etc*) survie *f*; **her s. as party leader** sa survie en tant que tête du parti; **it's a question of s.** c'est une question de survie; *Biol, Fig* **the s. of the fittest** la survie du plus apte (**b**) (*remaining part*) (*of ancient custom*) vestige *m*; **a s. of times past** un vestige du passé

survival bag *n* sac *m* de couchage de survie

survivalism [səˈvaɪvəlɪz(ə)m] *n* = préparation *f* à une catastrophe nucléaire ou autre

survivalist [səˈvaɪv(ə)lɪst] *n* = personne *f* qui se prépare à une catastrophe nucléaire ou autre

survival kit *n* équipement *m* de survie

survive [səˈvaɪv] **1** *vi* survivre; (*of custom*) survivre, subsister; **enough to s. on** de quoi survivre; **those who survived** les survivants *mpl*; **those toys wouldn't s. two minutes with our kids** ces jouets ne survivraient pas plus de deux minutes avec nos gamins; *F* **it's not serious, you'll s.** ce n'est pas grave, tu t'en remettras; *F* **it'll be awful, I don't know how I'll s.!** ça va être horrible, je ne sais pas comment je vais m'en sortir!; *F* **how's things? – I'm surviving** comment ça va? – pas trop mal

2 *vt* (*of person*) survivre à; (*of house, clothes*) supporter;

he will s. us all il nous enterrera tous; **he is survived by a family of four** il laisse derrière lui une famille de quatre personnes; **to s. an injury** survivre à une blessure; **to s. an illness** réchapper d'une maladie; **I couldn't s. another meeting with him** je ne supporterais pas une autre réunion avec lui; **to s. a recession** (*of company*) survivre à une récession

surviving [sə'vaɪvɪŋ] *adj* (*person*) survivant; (*remains, copy*) qui reste; **the only s. member of ...** le seul survivant de ...; **there is one s. sister** une des sœurs est encore en vie, il y a une sœur encore en vie

survivor [sə'vaɪvər] *n* survivant, -ante; **he is the sole s. of his family** il est le seul qui reste de sa famille; **the survivors of the disaster** les rescapés *mpl*; **earthquake/flood s.** rescapé, -ée d'un tremblement de terre/d'une inondation; **she's a s.** (*in politics, business etc*) c'est une battante; *Pej* c'est une miraculée

susceptibility [səseptɪ'bɪlɪtɪ] *n* **(a)** (*liability to be affected*) susceptibilité *f*; **s. to a disease** prédisposition *f* à une maladie; **s. to pain** sensibilité *f* à la douleur **(b)** *Fml* (*sensitivity*) sensibilité *f*, susceptibilité *f*; **to avoid wounding any susceptibilities** éviter de blesser la susceptibilité de qui que ce soit

susceptible [sə'septɪb(ə)l] *adj* (*liable to be affected*) sensible (**to** à); (*touchy*) susceptible, qui se froisse facilement; **s. to media influences** sensible à l'influence des médias; **s. to a disease** prédisposé à une maladie; **this will make you less s. to colds** ceci vous rendra plus résistant au rhume; **s. to cold** frileux; *Fml* **s. of proof** qui peut être prouvé, démontrable

suspect[1] ['sʌspekt] **1** *adj* suspect **2** *n* **(a)** suspect, -ecte **(b)** *Mktg* client *m* potentiel, suspect *m*; **s. pool** clients potentiels

suspect[2] [sə'spekt] *vt* **(a)** (*person*) (*of crime etc*) soupçonner; **to s. sb of sth/of having done sth** soupçonner qn de qch/d'avoir fait qch

(b) (*have intuition of*) (*reason, truth*) soupçonner; (*danger*) flairer, subodorer; **he suspects nothing** il ne se doute de rien; **does your husband s. anything?** est-ce que ton mari se doute de quelque chose?; **I never suspected it for a moment** je n'avais pas le moindre soupçon, je ne m'en suis jamais douté

(c) (*doubt*) (*authenticity of a work etc*) avoir des doutes sur; **to s. sb's motives** mettre en doute les raisons de qn

(d) (*consider likely*) croire, penser; **I suspected as much** je m'en doutais; **I s. that what she really means is ...** je pense que ce qu'elle veut vraiment dire, c'est ...; **I s. you're right** je crois bien que tu as raison

suspected [sə'spektɪd] *adj* **a s. person** un(e) suspect(e); *Med* **a s. case of typhoid** un cas présumé de typhoïde; **he has a s. fracture** on craint qu'il (n')ait une fracture

suspend [sə'spend] *vt* **(a)** (*hang*) suspendre, pendre; **to s. sth from the ceiling** suspendre *ou* pendre qch au plafond **(b)** (*stop*) (*bus service, work*) suspendre; *Jur* **to s. judgment** surseoir au jugement; *Jur* **to s. proceedings** suspendre les poursuites; *Com* **to s. payment** suspendre ses paiements **(c)** (*exclude temporarily*) (*officer, footballer etc*) suspendre; (*jockey*) mettre à pied; (*newspaper*) suspendre; **to s. sb from his/her office** suspendre qn de ses fonctions; **to s. a pupil (from school)** renvoyer un élève (provisoirement); **suspended on full pay** *Admin* suspendu sans suppression de traitement; *Mil* suspendu sans suppression de solde

suspended [sə'spendɪd] *adj* suspendu; (*particles*) en suspension; *Jur* en suspens, suspendu; **she was given a s. prison sentence of six months** elle a été condamnée à six mois de prison avec sursis; **to be in a state of s. animation** (*of person, animal*), *Fig Hum* être en hibernation; **the scheme is in a state of s. animation** le projet est en suspens

suspender [sə'spendər] *n* **(a)** *Br* (*for stocking*) jarretelle *f*; (*for sock*) fixe-chaussette *m*, *pl* fixe-chaussettes; **s. belt** porte-jarretelles *m inv* **(b)** *Am* **(pair of) suspenders** (*braces*) (paire *f* de) bretelles *fpl*

suspense [sə'spens] *n* **(a)** (*uncertainty*) suspense *m*, incertitude *f*; *Liter, Cin etc* suspense; **to keep** *or* **hold sb in s.** tenir *ou* garder qn en haleine; **the s. is killing me** ce suspense me rend fou; *Iron* quel suspense! **(b)** *Jur* **the question remains in s.** la question reste posée *ou* en suspens; *Fin* **s. account** compte *m* d'ordre

suspension [sə'spenʃən] *n* **(a)** (*of car etc*) suspension *f*; *Aut* **s. bush** bague *f* de suspension; *Aut* **s. geometry** géométrie *f* de la suspension **(b)** (*of hostilities, supplies etc*) suspension *f*; *Jur* (*of judgement*) surséance *f*; *Com* **s. of payments** suspension de paiements **(c)** (*of official, officer etc*) suspension *f*; (*of jockey*) mise à pied **(d)** *Ch* **(substance in) s.** (substance *f* en) suspension *f*

suspension bridge *n* pont *m* suspendu

suspension cable *n* câble *m* porteur

suspension chain *n MecE* chaîne *f* de suspension

suspension file *n* hamac *m*, dossier *m* suspendu

suspension points *npl Typ, Gram* points *mpl* de suspension

suspensory [sə'spensərɪ] *adj Anat* (*ligament*) suspenseur; *Med* **s. bandage** suspensoir *m*

suspicion [sə'spɪʃən] *n* **(a)** (*belief of guilt*) soupçon *m*; *Jur* suspicion *f*; **not the shadow** *or* **ghost of a s.** pas l'ombre d'un soupçon; **to be under s.** être soupçonné; **to have (one's) suspicions about sb** avoir des doutes sur qn, soupçonner qn; **to arouse s.** éveiller *ou* faire naître les soupçons; **to arouse** *or* **awaken sb's suspicions** éveiller les soupçons de qn; **above s.** au-dessus de tout soupçon; **praise free from any s. of flattery** louanges aucunement suspectes de flatterie; **to be right in one's suspicions** soupçonner juste; *Jur* **to arrest/detain sb on s.** arrêter/détenir qn préventivement; **on s. of arson** sous la présomption d'incendie volontaire; **detention on s.** détention *f* préventive; **I had my suspicions about it** je m'en doutais, j'avais mes soupçons là-dessus; **I had no s. of it** je n'avais pas le moindre soupçon

(b) (*characteristic, quality*) défiance *f*, suspicion *f*; **to look at sb with s.** regarder qn avec défiance; **the s. in her eyes/voice** la défiance dans ses yeux/sa voix

(c) (*hint*) petite dose *f*, soupçon *m* (**of** de); (*of irony, malice*) pointe *f*

suspicious [sə'spɪʃəs] *adj* **(a)** (*arousing suspicions*) suspect, louche; **it looks s.** cela me paraît louche *ou* suspect; **a s. character** un individu louche *ou* suspect; **he died in s. circumstances** il est mort dans des circonstances suspectes **(b)** (*having suspicions*) méfiant, soupçonneux; **she has a very s. mind** elle est très soupçonneuse *ou* méfiante; **to be** *or* **feel s. about** *or* **of sb/sth** avoir des soupçons à l'endroit *ou* à l'égard de qn/sur qch; **her behaviour made me s.** sa conduite a éveillé mes soupçons

suspiciously [sə'spɪʃəslɪ] *adv* **(a)** (*to act*) d'une manière suspecte *ou* louche; **he was s. eager to leave** l'empressement qu'il avait de partir était suspect; **it sounded s. as though she had lost it** on aurait dit qu'elle l'avait perdu; **it looks s. like the one I lost** il ressemble étrangement à celui que j'ai perdu; **two texts that are s. similar** deux textes qui sont étrangement similaires; **it looks s. like measles (to me)** cela m'a tout l'air d'une rougeole **(b)** (*to watch, ask*) d'un air méfiant, avec méfiance; (*to think*) avec méfiance

suspiciousness [sə'spɪʃəsnɪs] *n* **(a)** (*causing suspicion*) (*of behaviour, parcel etc*) caractère *m* suspect *ou* louche **(b)** (*feeling suspicion*) (*of person, in voice etc*) caractère *m* soupçonneux, méfiance *f*

suss [sʌs] *vt Br F* = **suss out**

▶ **suss out** *vtsep Br F* (*work out*) (*person*) classer; (*system, technique*) piger; **I finally sussed out what she was doing** j'ai fini par piger ce qu'elle faisait; **to have sth sussed out** avoir pigé qch; **I've got him sussed out** j'ai pigé quel genre de type c'est

sussed [sʌst] *adj Sl* **to be s.** (*well-informed*) être au jus

sustain [sə'steɪn] *vt* **(a)** (*support*) (*person, weight, growth, pace, level*) soutenir, supporter; **enough oxygen to s. life** suffisamment d'oxygène pour que la vie soit possible; **to s. the body** sustenter le corps; **evidence to s. an assertion** témoignages pour appuyer une affirmation; *Mus* **to s. a note** tenir *ou* prolonger une note **(b)** (*suffer, receive*) (*loss*) éprouver, essuyer, subir; (*attack*) soutenir; **to s. an injury** recevoir une blessure, être blessé **(c)** *Jur* **to s. an objection** (*of court*) admettre une objection; **objection sustained** objection admise

sustainable [sə'steɪnəb(ə)l] *adj* **(a)** (*rate, lifestyle*) que l'on peut maintenir **(b)** *Ecol* (*forest*) viable; **s. growth** croissance *f* durable

sustained [sə'steɪnd] *adj* soutenu; **s. applause** applaudissements *mpl* prolongés; *Mil* **s. fire** feu *m* soutenu *ou* nourri; *Mus* **s. note** tenue *f*

sustaining [sə'steɪnɪŋ] *adj* (*food, meal*) nourrissant; **the s. power of faith** le soutien que constitue la foi

sustenance ['sʌstənəns] *n* **(a)** (*act*) subsistance *f*; **necessary for the s. of our bodies** nécessaire à notre subsistance; **means of s.** moyens *mpl* de subsistance **(b)** (*food*) aliments *mpl*, nourriture *f*

suttee [sʌ'ti:] *n Hindu Rel* (*practice*) satî *m*; (*widow*) satî *f*

suture[1] ['su:tʃər] *n* **(a)** *Anat, Bot* suture *f* **(b)** *Surg* (*action*) suture *f*; (*stitch*) point *m* de suture; (*thread*) fil *m* pour sutures

suture[2] *vt Surg* (*wound*) suturer

suzerain ['su:zəreɪn] *n* suzerain, -aine

suzerainty ['su:zərəntɪ] *n* suzeraineté *f*

svelte [svelt] *adj* svelte

Svengali [svenˈgælɪ] *n* manipulateur, -trice

SVGA [esviːdʒiːˈeɪ] *n Comptr* (*abbr* **super video graphics array**) SVGA *m*; **S. monitor** moniteur *m* SVGA

swab¹ [swɒb] *n* **(a)** (*floorcloth*) serpillière *f*; *Naut* vadrouille *f*; *Mil* écouvillon *m* **(b)** *Med* (*material*) tampon *m*; (*specimen*) prélèvement *m*; (*smear*) frottis *m*; **s. of cotton wool** tampon d'ouate; **to take a s. of sb's throat** faire un prélèvement dans la gorge de qn

swab² *vt* (**-bb-**) **(a)** (*clean with floorcloth*) nettoyer, essuyer; **to s. the decks** laver le pont **(b)** = **swab down (c)** = **swab out**

▶ **swab down** *vtsep* (*clean*) (*courtyard*) laver à grande eau; *Naut* (*deck*) laver

▶ **swab out** *vtsep* (*clean out*), *Mil* (*firearm*) écouvillonner; *Med* (*wound*) nettoyer avec un tampon

swaddle [ˈswɒd(ə)l] *vt* emmailloter (**with, in** de)

swaddling [ˈswɒdlɪŋ] *n Arch* **s. clothes** maillots *mpl*, langes *mpl*

swag [swæg] *n F* (*of thief*) butin *m*; *Austr* (*of tramp*) baluchon *m*

swagger¹ [ˈswægər] *n* (*in walk*) démarche *f* balancée et crâneuse; (*carefree manner*) air *m* cavalier *ou* désinvolte; **to walk with a s.** se pavaner; *Mil* **s. stick** *or* **cane** badine *f*

swagger² *vi* **(a)** (*strut*) **when he walks, he swaggers** il marche en se pavanant; **to s. (about)** se pavaner; **to s. in/out** entrer/sortir en se pavanant **(b)** (*boast*) fanfaronner, faire le faraud; **to s. about sth** se vanter de qch

swaggering [ˈswægərɪŋ] **1** *adj* (*air*) crâneur **2** *n* = **swagger¹**; (*boasting*) fanfaronnades *fpl*, rodomontades *fpl*

swagman, *pl* **-men** [ˈswægmæn, -mən] *n Austr F* chemineau *m* (*qui porte son baluchon*)

Swahili [swɑːˈhiːlɪ] **1** *adj* souahéli, swahéli, swahili **2** *n* **(a)** (*pl* **Swahili(s)**) Souahéli, -ie, Swahéli, -ie, Swahili, -ie, *pl* -i(s) **(b)** *Ling* souahéli *m*, swahéli *m*, swahili *m*

swain [sweɪn] *n* **(a)** *Lit, Arch* (*rustic*) jeune berger *m* **(b)** *Old-fashioned, Hum* (*suitor*) soupirant *m*

SWALK [swɔːlk] (*abbr* **sealed with a loving kiss**) (*written on envelope*) = scellée d'un tendre baiser

swallow¹ [ˈswɒləʊ] *n* (*act of swallowing*) déglutition *f*; (*mouthful*) (*of water*) gorgée *f*; **at one s.** d'un seul coup *ou* trait

swallow² *n* (*bird*) hirondelle *f*; *Prov* **one s. doesn't make a summer** une hirondelle ne fait pas le printemps; *Br Swimming* **s. dive** saut *m* de l'ange

swallow³ **1** *vt* **(a)** (*food, drink*) avaler; (*oyster*) gober; **to s. sth whole** avaler qch tout rond; **to s. one's words** (*speak indistinctly*) avaler ses mots **(b)** (*believe*) (*story*) gober, avaler; **to s. the bait** (*of person*) se laisser prendre à l'appât; **I told her a lie and she swallowed it** je lui ai raconté un mensonge et elle l'a gobé *ou* avalé; **her story is hard to s.** son histoire est difficile à avaler **(c)** (*accept without protest*) (*insult*) avaler; (*one's anger, pride*) ravaler **2** *vi* avaler; **to s. hard** (*when nervous, afraid*) avaler sa salive

▶ **swallow down** *vtsep* (*drink, pill*) avaler

▶ **swallow up** *vtsep* (*engulf*) engloutir, engouffrer; *Fig* **they were soon swallowed up by** *or* **in the mist** ils ont vite été engloutis par le brouillard; **the small country/company was swallowed up** le petit pays/la petite société a été englouti(e)

swallow-dive *vi Br Swimming* faire le saut de l'ange

swallowtail [ˈswɒləʊteɪl] *n* **(a)** (*forked tail*) queue *f* fourchue **(b)** *Old-fashioned F* (*coat*) queue-de-morue *f*, *pl* queues-de-morue **(c) s. (butterfly)** machaon *m*, grand porte-queue *m*

swallow-tailed *adj* **(a)** (*bird*) à queue fourchue **(b) s. coat** = **swallowtail (b)**

swamp¹ [swɒmp] *n* marais *m*, marécage *m*; *Am* **s. fever** malaria *f*

swamp² *vt* (*flood*) inonder; (*field*) submerger; (*boat*) remplir d'eau; *F* **to be swamped with sth** (*work, orders, requests*) être submergé *ou* débordé de qch; (*letters, offers of help*) être submergé de qch

swampy [ˈswɒmpɪ] *adj* (*terrain*) marécageux

swan¹ [swɒn] *n* cygne *m*; **mute s.** cygne commun *ou* muet; **black s.** cygne noir; *Am Swimming* **s. dive** saut *m* de l'ange; *Fig* **s. song** chant *m* du cygne

swan² *vi* (**-nn-**) *F* **to s. around** se balader, musarder; **he just sort of swans around the office all day** il ne fait que musarder dans le bureau toute la journée; **she came swanning in at a quarter to ten** elle est arrivée les mains dans les poches à dix heures moins le quart; **where's he swanning off to now?** où est-ce qu'il va encore traîner?; **don't think you can come swanning back just when you feel like it** ne crois pas que tu peux revenir les mains dans les poches quand tu en as envie; **a swanning sort of job** un boulot plutôt tranquille *ou F* peinard

swank¹ [swæŋk] *F* **1** *n* **(a)** (*ostentation*) épate *f*; **I've had enough of all this s.** j'en ai assez de toute cette esbroufe **(b)** (*ostentatious person*) frimeur, -euse; (*boastful person*) crâneur, -euse **2** *adj esp Am* = **swanky**

swank² *vi F* se donner des airs, faire de l'épate

swanky [ˈswæŋkɪ] *adj F* (*person*) prétentieux, poseur; (*restaurant, dinner, hotel*) hyperchic; (*car*) tapageur

swan-necked [ˈswɒnnekt] *adj* (*person*) au cou de cygne

swannery [ˈswɒnərɪ] *n* réserve *f* de cygnes

swansdown [ˈswɒnzdaʊn] *n Tex* (*cotton fabric*) molleton *m*

swap¹ [swɒp] *n* (*exchange*) troc *m*, échange *m*; (*object, article*) objet *m ou* article *m* à échanger/qu'on a échangé; *St Exch* swap *m*, échange *m* financier; **to do a s.** faire un troc *ou* un échange; **it wasn't a very good s.** ce n'était pas un échange très équitable; **it's a good s.** c'est un échange avantageux; **she took my old car as a s. for this one** elle a pris ma vieille voiture en échange de celle-ci; **swaps** (*in stamp collecting etc*) doubles *mpl*

swap² (**-pp-**) **1** *vt* **(a) to s. sth for sth** échanger *ou* troquer qch contre *ou* pour qch; **I'll s. you mine for yours** je t'échange le mien contre le tien; *F* **(I'll) s. you!** je te l'échange!; **to s. places with sb** changer de place avec qn; **to s. insults/ideas** échanger des insultes/idées; **to s. stories** échanger ses impressions **(b)** *St Exch* swaper **2** *vi* faire du troc; **shall we s.?** si nous faisions un échange?

SWAPO [ˈswɑːpəʊ] *n Pol* (*abbr* **South-West Africa People's Organization**) SWAPO *f*

sward [swɔːd] *n Lit* gazon *m*, pelouse *f*

swarm¹ [swɔːm] *n* (*of bees, people, children*) essaim *m*; (*of locusts*) vol *m*; (*of gnats, people*) nuée *f*; (*of small boats*) fourmillement *m*; **there were swarms of tourists** il y avait des nuées de touristes

swarm² **1** *vi* **(a)** (*of bees*) essaimer; (*of people*) accourir en masse, se presser (**round** autour de; **in** dans); **the crowd swarmed over the pitch** la foule a fait irruption sur *ou* a envahi le terrain **(b)** (*of place*) fourmiller, grouiller (**with** de) **2** *vt* = **swarm up**

▶ **swarm up** *vipo* (*climb*) (*tree, mast*) grimper à; **they all swarmed up the side of the ship** ils grimpèrent comme un seul homme sur les flancs du navire

swarming *n* (*in beekeeping*) essaimage *m*

swarthiness [ˈswɔːðɪnɪs] *n* teint *m* basané *ou* bistré

swarthy [ˈswɔːðɪ] *adj* (*complexion*) basané, bistré, *Pej* noiraud

swash¹ [swɒʃ] *n* (*of waves*) clapotis *m*

swash² *vi* (*of water*) clapoter

swashbuckler [ˈswɒʃbʌklər] *n* bravache *m*

swashbuckling [ˈswɒʃbʌklɪŋ] **1** *adj* fanfaron; **s. film** (*with musketeers*) film *m* de cape et d'épée; (*with pirates*) film de corsaires; **s. tale** fanfaronnade *f*; **s. hero** héros *m* superbe **2** *n* fanfaronnades *fpl*, rodomontades *fpl*

swashplate [ˈswɒʃpleɪt] *n Aut* plateau *m* oscillant

swastika [ˈswɒstɪkə] *n* svastika *m*, croix *f* gammée

swat¹ [swɒt] *n* (*blow*) tape *f*; **to take a s. at** (*person, dog etc*) donner une tape à; (*insect*) donner un coup de tapette à; **fly s.** (*swatter*) tapette *f* tue-mouches

swat² *vt* (**-tt-**) taper; (*insect*) écraser

swath [swɔːθ] *n Agr* = **swathe¹**

swathe¹ [sweɪð] *n Agr* andain *m*; *Fig* **the cannons had cut great swathes through the troops** les canons avaient décimé les troupes

swathe² *vt* emmailloter, envelopper; **head swathed in bandages** tête enveloppée de bandages; **swathed in mist** baigné de brume

sway¹ [sweɪ] *n* **(a)** (*movement*) balancement *m*, oscillation *f*, mouvement *m* de va-et-vient; *Rail* (*of trucks*) mouvement de lacet **(b)** (*control, power*) empire *m*, domination *f*; **under her s.** sous son empire, sous son influence; **to have** *or* **hold s. over a people/country** avoir *ou* tenir un peuple/pays sous sa domination; **emotions that no longer hold any s. over me** des émotions qui n'ont plus aucun empire *ou* aucune emprise sur moi

sway² **1** *vi* se balancer, osciller; (*of drunkard*) vaciller; (*remain undecided*) rester indécis, hésiter; **to s. in the wind** (*of trees*) se balancer dans le vent; **he swayed back up to the bar** il revint au bar en vacillant; **public opinion is prone to s. this way and that** l'opinion publique oscille souvent d'un côté et de l'autre

2 *vt* **(a)** (*trees*) faire osciller, faire se balancer; **she sways her hips when she walks** elle balance *ou* roule les hanches en marchant

(b) (*influence*) **considerations that s. our opinions** considérations qui influencent nos opinions; **to s. sb from his/her course** détourner qn de ses projets; **to refuse to be swayed** refuser de se laisser influencer; **what can we say or do to s. you?** que pouvons-nous dire ou faire pour vous convaincre *ou* (*make you change your mind*) vous faire changer d'avis?; **what finally swayed them was …** ce qui les a finalement décidés a été …; **it was close but one thing swayed it** (*in vote etc*) la lutte était serrée mais une chose a fait pencher la balance

swaying ['sweɪɪŋ] **1** *adj* qui se balance de-ci de-là, qui oscille; **s. motion** balancement *m*, mouvement *m* de va-et-vient **2** *n* balancement *m*, oscillation *f*, mouvement *m* de va-et-vient; (*of boat, car*) roulis *m*

Swazi ['swɑːzɪ] **1** *adj* souazi **2** *n* **(a)** Souazi, -ie **(b)** *Ling* le dialecte souazi

Swaziland ['swɑːzɪlænd] *n* Souaziland *m*

swear [sweər] (*pt* **swore** [swɔːr]; *pp* **sworn** [swɔːn]) **1** *vt* **(a)** jurer; (*on oath*) déclarer sous la foi du serment; **to s. an oath** faire un serment, jurer; **to s. sth on the Bible** jurer qch sur la Bible; **to s. to do sth** jurer de faire qch; **I could have sworn I heard a shout** j'aurais juré avoir entendu un cri; **it wasn't me, I s. (it)!** ce n'était pas moi, je le jure!; **to s. allegiance to sb/sth** prêter serment d'allégeance à qn/qch; **to s. revenge** jurer *ou* faire serment de se venger; **to s. sb to secrecy** faire jurer le secret à qn

(b) (*utter swearwords*) **bloody idiot!, she swore** espèce d'abruti!, proféra-t-elle

2 *vi* **(a)** (*use swearwords*) jurer, proférer *ou* lâcher un juron/des jurons; **to s. at sb** injurier qn; **to s. like a trooper** jurer comme un charretier

(b) (*give one's word*) jurer

▸ **swear by** *vipo* **(a)** (*invoke*) jurer par; **to s. by one's honour** jurer sur l'honneur; **to s. by all that one holds sacred** jurer sur tout ce qu'on a de plus sacré **(b)** (*have confidence in*) se fier à; **she swears by him/those vitamin tablets** elle ne jure que par lui/par ces vitamines; **it's marvellous stuff, we all s. by it** c'est merveilleux, nous ne jurons plus que par ça!

▸ **swear in** *vtsep* (*jury, witness*) faire prêter serment à

▸ **swear off** *vipo* (*alcohol etc*) jurer de renoncer à

▸ **swear to** *vipo* (*on oath*) attester *ou* certifier sous serment; **I s. to it** je l'atteste; **I would s. to it** j'en jurerais, *F* j'en mettrais ma main au feu, *F* j'en mettrais ma tête à couper; **I couldn't** *or* **wouldn't s. to it** je n'en mettrais pas ma main au feu, je n'en mettrais pas ma tête à couper

swearing ['sweərɪŋ] *n* (*use of swearwords*) jurons *mpl*, gros mots *mpl*; **there's too much s. on television** il y a trop de grossièretés à la télévision

swearing in *n* **after the s. of the jury** après que le jury eut prêté serment

swearword ['sweəwɜːd] *n* gros mot *m*, juron *m*

sweat[1] [swet] *n* **(a)** sueur *f*, transpiration *f*; **covered in s.** (*of people, clothes*) couvert *ou* trempé de sueur; **by the s. of one's brow** à la sueur de son front; **the s. was pouring off him** il dégoulinait de sueur; **to be in a s., to be all of a s.** suer, être en nage; *Fig* (*to be excited*) être tout excité; *Fig* **to be in a s. about sth** avoir des sueurs froides à cause de qch; *Fig* **to work oneself (up) into a s.** se faire du mauvais sang **(about sth** au sujet de qch); **to break into a s.** se mettre à transpirer; **to be in a cold s.** avoir des sueurs froides; *F* **it was a real s. getting this piano up the stairs** monter le piano par l'escalier, c'était vraiment tuant; *F* **no s.** pas de problème; *Old-fashioned Mil* **old s.** vieux troupier

(b) (*on wall etc*) suintement *m*

sweat[2] **1** *vi* suer, transpirer; (*of walls*) suinter; (*of cheese*) suer; *Fig F* (*work hard*) peiner; *F* (*worry*) se faire de la bile, se faire un sang d'encre; **to s. profusely** suer à grosses gouttes; **Johnny was sweating over his lessons** Johnny potassait ses leçons; **I've been sweating over this piece of work for the last three hours** ça fait trois heures que je m'escrime à faire ce travail **2** *vt* (*person, horse*) faire suer; (*workers*) exploiter; *Culin* (*onions*) faire revenir *ou* blondir; *Am Fig F* (*suspect*) cuisiner; *F* **to s. blood** suer sang et eau; *F* **to s. buckets** être en nage

▸ **sweat off** *vtsep* (*lose by exercise*) (*weight*) perdre en faisant de l'exercice; (*in sauna*) perdre en transpirant

▸ **sweat out** *vtsep* **(a)** (*cure*) (*cold*) chasser *ou* guérir en transpirant **(b)** *F* **to s. it out** (*endure*) prendre son mal en patience, tenir jusqu'au bout **(c)** *Sl* **to s. one's guts out** s'échiner

sweatband ['swetbænd] *n* (*of hat*) cuir *m* intérieur; *Sp* bandeau *m* en éponge

sweat duct *n Anat* conduit *m* sudorifère

sweated ['swetɪd] *adj* **s. labour** (*work*) travail *m* exténuant et mal rétribué, travail d'esclave; (*people*) main-d'œuvre *f* exploitée; **s. goods** articles *mpl* produits par des ouvriers exploités

sweater ['swetər] *n* (*garment*) pullover *m*, pull *m*

sweat gland *n Anat* glande *f* sudoripare

sweatiness ['swetɪnɪs] *n* (*of body etc*) moiteur *f*

sweating ['swetɪŋ] **1** *adj* (*person*) en sueur; (*hand, body*) moite; (*wall*) suintant **2** *n* transpiration *f*; *Med* sudation *f*; (*of wall*) suintement *m*; **s. room** (*in Turkish bath*) étuve *f*, salle *f* de sudation

sweatshirt ['swetʃɜːt] *n Sp* sweat-shirt *m*, *pl* sweat-shirts, sweat *m*

sweatshop ['swetʃɒp] *n* atelier *m* où les ouvriers sont exploités; *Fig Hum* **it's a real s. here** c'est le bagne ici

sweaty ['swetɪ] *adj* (*person*) en sueur; (*hands, palms*) moite; (*work*) qui fait transpirer; (*shirt etc*) imprégné de sueur *ou* de transpiration; (*smell*) de sueur, de transpiration; **to get s.** (*of person*) suer, transpirer; **s. afternoon** après-midi d'une chaleur humide; **s. socks** chaussettes puantes (de sueur)

Swede [swiːd] *n* [①A20,d] (*person*) Suédois, -oise

swede [swiːd] *n* (*plant*) rutabaga *m*

Sweden ['swiːd(ə)n] *n* Suède *f*

Swedish ['swiːdɪʃ] [①A20,d] **1** *adj* suédois **2** *n Ling* suédois *m*

sweep[1] [swiːp] *n* **(a)** (*single stroke of broom, paintbrush, scythe*) coup *m* de balai/de pinceau/de faux; (*cleaning*) balayage *m*; **at one s.** d'un seul coup; **to give a room a good s. (out)** balayer une chambre à fond; **this room could do with a s.** cette chambre a bien besoin d'un coup de balai; *Fig* **to make a clean s.** (*replace staff etc*) faire table rase; (*in gambling*) rafler le tout; **the thieves made a clean s.** les voleurs ont tout enlevé *ou* raflé

(b) (*movement*) (*with arm*) mouvement *m* circulaire; *Mil, Av* balayage *m*; **with a wide s. of the arm** d'un geste large; **s. of the eye** regard *m* circulaire; **s. hand** (*on clock, watch*) trotteuse *f* centrale

(c) (*area covered*) *Mil* (*of gun*) portée *f*; (*of lighthouse*) balayage *m*, portée; (*of wings*) envergure *f*; (*of knowledge*) étendue *f*

(d) *Rad, Electron* **scan(ning) s.** balayage *m*

(e) (*rapid flow*) (*of river*) course *f ou* flot *m* rapide

(f) (*curve*) courbe *f*, courbure *f*; (*of river*) boucle *f*; *Archit* (*of arch*) courbure; **to make a wide s. to take a bend** prendre du champ pour effectuer un virage; **s. of a car's lines** galbe *f* d'une voiture; **a fine s. of grass/of country** une belle étendue de gazon/de pays

(g) (chimney) s. (*person*) ramoneur *m*

(h) *F* (*sweepstake*) sweepstake *m*

sweep[2] (*pt, pp* **swept** [swept]) **1** *vt* (*room, streets, dust etc*) balayer; (*chimney*) ramoner; *Naut* (*channel*) (*for mines*) draguer; **her dress sweeps the ground** sa robe balaie le sol; **a storm swept the town** un orage ravagea la ville; **the deck was swept by a huge wave** une grosse vague balaya le pont; **to s. the horizon with a telescope** parcourir *ou* balayer l'horizon avec un télescope; **to s. the seas** parcourir les mers; **to s. the board** (*in gambling*) rafler le tout; *Fig* avoir un succès fou; **the latest craze to s. the country** la dernière tocade à envahir le pays; **the most outlandish rumours swept the besieged city** les rumeurs les plus folles parcouraient la ville assiégée; *Fig* **to s. a matter under the carpet** enterrer une question; **a wave swept him overboard** une lame l'a entraîné par-dessus bord; **she was swept to power on a wave of nationalism** elle a été propulsée au pouvoir par une vague de nationalisme; **the victorious army swept all before it** l'armée victorieuse a tout balayé sur son passage

2 *vi* **(a)** (*with broom*) balayer

(b) (*move rapidly*) avancer avec un mouvement rapide et uni; **she swept into/out of the room** elle est entrée dans/sortie de la salle d'un air majestueux; **to s. round the corner** (*of car*) tourner le coin de la rue en décrivant un large virage; **the plague swept over Europe** la peste a ravagé toute l'Europe; **the beam swept across the sea** le faisceau lumineux balaya la mer; **the rolling prairies s. away into the distance** les prairies ondoyantes se perdent dans le lointain; **the road sweeps round the lake** la route décrit une courbe autour du lac

(c) *Naut* **to s. for mines** draguer des mines

▸ **sweep along 1** *vi* (*move rapidly*) avancer rapidement **2** *vtsep* (*carry forward*) (*of current etc*) entraîner, emporter; **we were swept along by a tide of nationalism** nous avons été balayés par une vague nationaliste

▸ **sweep aside** *vtsep* (*move aside*) écarter d'un geste large; **to s. aside opposition** écarter l'opposition; **they were swept aside by the crowd** ils ont été repoussés par la foule

▸ **sweep away** *vtsep* (*snow, clouds*) balayer; (*malpractice, abuse*) supprimer; **the bridge was swept away by the torrent** le pont a été emporté par le torrent

▸ **sweep by** *vi* (*move past rapidly*) (*of car*) passer à toute vitesse; (*of person*) (*majestically*) passer majestueusement; (*disdainfully*) passer dédaigneusement

▸ **sweep down 1** *vtsep* **the current sweeps the logs down with it** le courant emporte *ou* entraîne le bois **2** *vi* **(a)**

(attack) **the enemy swept down upon us** l'ennemi s'abattit *ou* fonça sur nous **(b)** *(curve downwards)* **hills sweeping down to the sea** des collines qui descendent vers la mer

▶ **sweep in** *vi (approach, enter rapidly)* **the wind sweeps in** le vent s'engouffre; **she swept in** elle a fait son entrée d'un air majestueux

▶ **sweep off** *vtsep (remove forcefully)* enlever *ou* emporter avec violence; **he swept her off to Paris for the weekend** il l'a emmenée en week-end à Paris; **to be swept off one's feet by sb** être emballé par qn; **to s. sb off his/her feet** enthousiasmer qn; *(in love affair)* faire perdre la tête à qn

▶ **sweep on** *vi (advance rapidly) (of flood)* avancer régulièrement; *(continue)* continuer d'avancer (irrésistiblement)

▶ **sweep out 1** *vtsep (clean) (room)* balayer (à fond) **2** *vi (leave majestically)* **she swept out (of the room)** elle est sortie (de la pièce) d'un air majestueux

▶ **sweep past** *vi* = **sweep by**

▶ **sweep up 1** *vtsep (collect by sweeping) (dust, leaves etc)* balayer, ramasser; *(sweep into a pile)* ramasser en tas; **with her hair swept up into a chignon** avec ses cheveux relevés en chignon; **she swept up her two babies and ...** en toute hâte, elle prit ses deux bébés dans ses bras et ... **2** *vi* **(a)** *(clean up)* balayer **(b)** *(arrive)* **the car swept up to the door** la voiture a roulé majestueusement jusqu'à la porte

sweepback ['swi:pbæk] *n Av* (angle *m* de) flèche *f*

sweeper ['swi:pər] *n* **(a)** *(person)* balayeur, -euse; *Fb* arrière *m* volant **(b)** *(machine) (for industrial use)* balayeuse *f*; *(for domestic use)* balai *m* (mécanique)

sweeping ['swi:pɪŋ] **1** *adj (gesture)* large; *(movement)* circulaire; **s. changes** changements *mpl* radicaux; **s. generalization** *or* **statement** généralisation *f* hâtive; *Art* **s. line** ligne *f* allongée *ou* élancée; **low s. lines** *(of car)* lignes basses et allongées; **s. plain** vaste plaine *f*; **s. reform** réforme *f* radicale **2** *n* **sweepings** *(refuse)* balayures *fpl*, ordures *fpl*; *Fig (of a country, society)* rebut *m*

sweepingly ['swi:pɪŋlɪ] *adv (too generally) (to describe things, criticize etc)* de façon trop générale *ou* hâtive

sweeping up *n* balayage *m*, ramassage *m*

sweepstake ['swi:psteɪk] *n Horseracing* sweepstake *m*

sweet [swi:t] **1** *adj* **(a)** *(in taste)* doux, *f* douce; *(cream, cake, fruit)* sucré; **as s. as honey** doux comme le miel; **to taste s.** avoir une saveur douce; *Culin* **s. and sour sauce** sauce aigre-douce; **to have a s. tooth** aimer les sucreries

(b) *(of flower)* **to smell s.** avoir une odeur agréable, sentir bon; *(of rose)* embaumer; *Fig* **the s. smell of success** la douceur du succès; *Fig* **it hardly smells very s.** ça ne sent pas très bon

(c) s. breath haleine *f* fraîche

(d) *(sound)* doux, *f* douce, mélodieux; *(flattery)* doux à l'oreille

(e) *(pleasant)* agréable; *(smile)* doux, *f* douce; **revenge is s.** douce est la vengeance; *F* **to keep sb s.** s'assurer les bonnes grâces de qn; **a s. old lady** une vieille dame charmante; **that's very s. of you** c'est bien gentil à vous; **a s. little dress** une gentille petite robe, une petite robe exquise; **a s. girl** une gentille petite fille; **what a s. kitten!** quel petit chat adorable!; **that puppy's ever so s.!** qu'il est mignon, ce chiot!; **to say** *or* **whisper s. nothings to sb** *or* **in sb's ear** conter fleurette à qn, dire des mots doux à l'oreille de qn; *F* **s. talk** flatterie *f*, boniment *m*; **s. temper** caractère *m* doux *ou* aimable

(f) *Old-fashioned F* **to be s. on sb** avoir un béguin pour qn

(g) *(intensifier)* **she'll do it in her own s. time** elle le fera quand elle le jugera bon; **it's only going to be of benefit to his own s. self** c'est à sa petite pomme qu'ira tout le bénéfice; **he'll go his own s. way** il fera ce qui lui plaira; *F* **you bet your s. life I am!** je pense bien!; *Sl* **s. bugger-all** que dalle

(h) *(engine)* doux, *f* douce; **s. running** *(of machine)* fonctionnement régulier

2 *n esp Br (piece of confectionery)* bonbon *m*; *(dessert)* dessert *m*; **sweets** *(confectionery)* sucreries *fpl*, confiseries *fpl*, friandises *fpl*; **s. shop** confiserie *f*; **my s.!** mon chéri!, ma chérie!; **be a s.!** sois un amour!

sweetbread ['swi:tbred] *n Culin* **veal/lamb s.** ris *m* de veau/d'agneau

sweet cherry *n Bot* merisier *m*

sweetcorn ['swi:tkɔ:n] *n Culin* maïs *m* doux

sweeten ['swi:t(ə)n] *vt (food, drink)* sucrer; *(air)* désodoriser; *(breath)* purifier; *(task)* adoucir, rendre plus agréable; **to s. the pill** dorer la pilule; **to s. sb's temper** adoucir qn; **to s. sb** *(bribe etc)* graisser la patte à qn

sweetener ['swi:t(ə)nər] *n* **(a)** *Culin* édulcorant *m*; **artificial s.** édulcorant de synthèse **(b)** *F (bribe)* pot-de-vin *m*; **to give sb a s.** graisser la patte à qn, verser un pot-de-vin à qn

sweetening ['swi:t(ə)nɪŋ] *n (substance)* édulcorant *m*; **what s. did you use?** avec quoi l'avez-vous sucré?

sweetheart ['swi:thɑ:t] *n* amoureux, -euse; **(my) s.!** mon amour!, mon cœur!; **they have been sweethearts since childhood** ils s'aiment depuis leur enfance; **a childhood s.** un amour d'enfance; *Ind* **s. agreement** = accord *m* officieux

sweetie ['swi:tɪ] *n F* **(a)** *Br (confectionery)* bonbon *m* **(b) s. (pie)** *(term of endearment)* mon mignon, ma mignonne; **he's such a s.** il est croquignolet; **be a s. and ...** sois mignon tu veux et ...

sweetish ['swi:tɪʃ] *adj* sucré; *(unpleasantly)* douceâtre

sweetly ['swi:tlɪ] *adv* **(a)** *(to sing)* mélodieusement; **the engine's running s.** le moteur tourne bien; **he kicked the ball s. into the corner of the net** il a mis la balle dans le coin du filet comme à l'entraînement **(b)** *(pleasantly)* agréablement, gentiment; **to smile s.** sourire gentiment

sweetmeat ['swi:tmi:t] *n Old-fashioned, Lit (sweet)* bonbon *m*; **sweetmeats** sucreries *fpl*, douceurs *fpl*

sweetness ['swi:tnɪs] *n* **(a)** *(of honey, victory, revenge etc)* douceur *f*; **I prefer the s. of this beer** je préfère cette bière parce qu'elle est plus douce **(b)** *(of person, gesture etc)* gentillesse *f*, charme *m*; **she's s. itself when you are there** c'est la douceur personnifiée quand tu es là; **now that he's got what he wanted he's all s. and light** maintenant qu'il a eu ce qu'il voulait il est tout miel

sweet pea *n Bot* pois *m* de senteur

sweet potato *n* patate *f* douce

sweet-scented, sweet-smelling *adj (flower, plant)* odorant, odoriférant; *(room)* parfumé

sweet-talk[1] *n F* baratin *m*

sweet-talk[2] *vt F* baratiner; **to s. sb into doing sth** baratiner qn pour lui faire faire qch; **you can't s. your way around me this time** cette fois, tu ne m'auras pas par la flatterie *ou* ce n'est pas la peine de me baratiner

sweet-tempered *adj* doux, *f* douce, agréable

sweet violet *n Bot* violette *f* odorante

sweet william ['wɪljəm] *n Bot* œillet *m* de(s) poète(s)

swell[1] [swel] **1** *n* **(a)** *Naut* houle *f* **(b)** *(of sound)* augmentation *f*; *Lit* **the majestic s. of the organ** les accents *mpl* majestueux de l'orgue **(c)** *Mus (of organ) (device)* soufflet *m*; **s. box** boîte *f* expressive **(d)** *Old-fashioned F (well-dressed man)* élégant *m* **2** *adj Am F (excellent)* épatant; *Iron* **that's just s.!** ça, c'est la meilleure!; **a s. guy** un chic type

swell[2] *(pt* **swelled**; *pp* **swollen** ['swəʊl(ə)n], *occ* **swelled) 1** *vt* (r)enfler, gonfler; *Mus (note)* enfler; **the river was swollen by the rain** la pluie avait grossi la rivière; **eyes swollen with tears** yeux gonflés de larmes; **all this has helped to s. the ranks of the unemployed** tout cela est venu grossir le nombre de chômeurs; **to s. the number(s)** grossir les effectifs

2 *vi* enfler; *(of part of the body)* se tuméfier; *(of wood)* gonfler; *(of number, crowd)* augmenter, grossir; *(of sea)* se soulever; *(of music)* s'enfler; **her arm is swelling** son bras enfle; **his heart swelled with pride** son cœur se gonflait d'orgueil; **the problem had swollen to massive proportions** le problème avait pris des proportions énormes

▶ **swell out** *vi (be swollen)* être bombé; *(expand)* bomber; **the sails s. out** les voiles se gonflent

▶ **swell up** *vi (of injured part of body etc)* enfler; *esp Lit* **all swollen up with pride** tout bouffi d'orgueil

swellheaded [swel'hedɪd] *adj F* vaniteux, suffisant

swelling ['swelɪŋ] **1** *adj* qui s'enfle *ou* se gonfle; *(sail)* gonflé; *(numbers)* croissant **2** *n* **(a)** *(of number)* augmentation *f*; *(of column)* renflement *m* **(b)** *Med (of face)* tuméfaction *f*, gonflement *m*, enflure *f*; *(on forehead)* bosse *f*, enflure; *(growth)* tumescence *f*, tumeur *f*

swelter ['sweltər] *vi* étouffer *ou* être accablé de chaleur

sweltering ['sweltərɪŋ] *adj (heat)* étouffant, accablant; **s. (hot) day** journée *f* étouffante *ou* d'une chaleur accablante; **it's s. in here** on étouffe ici

swept *see* **sweep**[2]

sweptwing ['sweptwɪŋ] *adj Av (aircraft)* à ailes en flèche

swerve[1] [swɜ:v] *n* écart *m*, déviation *f*; *Aut* embardée *f*; *Sp* **to put a** *or* **some s. on the ball** faire dévier une balle

swerve[2] **1** *vi (of pedestrian, cyclist, footballer)* faire un écart; *(of horse)* se dérober; *(of car)* faire un écart *ou* une embardée; *(of ball)* décrire une courbe; *Fig (from truth etc)* s'écarter; **the cyclist was swerving in and out of the traffic** le cycliste zigzaguait entre les voitures; **to s. to avoid sb/sth** *(of car, driver)* faire une embardée pour éviter qn/qch; *Fig* **she never swerves from her duty** elle ne s'écarte jamais de son devoir **2** *vt (ball)* dévier; **to s. the car** faire un écart avec la voiture

swift [swɪft] **1** *adj* rapide; *(reaction etc)* prompt; **as s. as an arrow** vif *ou* rapide comme l'éclair; *Lit* **s. of foot** rapide à la course; *Lit* **s. to anger** toujours prêt à s'emporter, irascible **2** *n* (*bird*) martinet *m*

swift-flowing *adj* (*river*) au cours rapide

swift-footed *adj* rapide à la course

swiftly ['swɪftlɪ] *adv* (*to run etc*) vite, rapidement; (*to react etc*) promptement

swiftness ['swɪftnɪs] *n* (*speed*) rapidité *f*, vitesse *f*; (*of reply etc*) promptitude *f*

SWIFT transfer *n Fin* virement *m* SWIFT

swig¹ [swɪg] *n F* lampée *f*; **to take a s. at the bottle** boire un coup à la bouteille; **he took a s. of whisky** il a bu une lampée *ou* gorgée de whisky; **fancy a s.?** (*passing bottle etc*) un petit coup?

swig² *vt* (-gg-) *F* (*beer, lemonade etc*) boire à grands traits *ou* à grands coups

▶ **swig down** *vtsep F* (*beer etc*) boire *ou* descendre d'un seul trait

swill¹ [swɪl] *n* **(a)** (*for pigs*) pâtée *f*; *Fig Pej* **this horrible s.** (*food, drink*) cette saloperie **(b)** *esp Br* (*act of rinsing*) lavage *m* à grande eau; **to give sth a s. (out)** laver *ou* rincer qch à grande eau

swill² *vt* **(a)** *F* (*drink*) boire avidement **(b)** *esp Br* = **swill out**

▶ **swill out** *vtsep esp Br* (*rinse*) laver à grande eau; **to s. out a basin** rincer une cuvette à grande eau

swim¹ [swɪm] *n* **(a)** (*for leisure*) baignade *f*; (*for exercise*) nage *f*; **to have** *or* **take a s.** se baigner; **to go for a s.** (*for leisure*) aller se baigner; (*for exercise*) aller nager; **coming for a s.?** tu viens te baigner?; **did you enjoy your s.?** (*for leisure*) tu t'es bien baigné?; (*for exercise*) tu as bien nagé?; **it was a long s. to the shore** il a fallu nager longtemps pour atteindre le rivage; **I have a big breakfast after my morning s.** le matin je prends un gros petit-déjeuner après avoir nagé; **that's a long s.!** à la nage cela fait loin!; **s. bladder** (*of fish*) vessie *f* natatoire **(b)** *Fig F* **to be in the s. (of things)** être dans le coup

swim² (*pt* **swam** [swæm]; *pp* **swum** [swʌm]; *prp* **swimming**) **1** *vi* (*of person, animal*) nager; (*of fat, scum*) (*float*) surnager, flotter; *Fig* (*of eyes, vision*) se brouiller; **to s. like a fish** nager comme un poisson; **to s. to the shore** gagner le rivage à la nage; **to s. over** *or* **across a river** traverser une rivière à la nage; **they swam under the net** ils sont passés sous le filet (en nageant); **let's s. back** rentrons (à la nage)!; *Fig* **to s. with the tide** suivre le courant; *Sp* **to s. for one's country** faire partie de l'équipe nationale de natation; **to go swimming** (*for leisure*) aller se baigner; (*for exercise*) aller nager; **the meat was swimming in gravy** la viande nageait dans la sauce; **eyes swimming with tears** yeux noyés *ou* baignés de larmes; **to make sb's head s.** faire tourner la tête à qn; **my head is swimming** la tête me tourne, j'ai la tête qui tourne; **everything swam before my eyes** tout semblait tourner autour de moi

2 *vt* (*river*) traverser *ou* passer à la nage; **to s. the Channel** traverser la Manche à la nage; **to s. four lengths** nager *ou* faire quatre longueurs; **to s. the breast stroke** nager la brasse; **she swam one stroke and ...** elle fit une brasse et ...; **to s. a race** faire une course de natation (**with sb** contre qn)

swimmer ['swɪmər] *n* (*person*) nageur, -euse

swimming ['swɪmɪŋ] *n* nage *f*; *esp Sp* natation *f*; *Br* **s. costume** maillot *m* de bain; **s. instructor** maître *m* nageur; **s. lesson** leçon *f* de natation; **s. match** concours *m* de natation; **s. pool** piscine *f*; **s. trunks** slip *m* de bain

swimmingly ['swɪmɪŋlɪ] *adv F* au mieux, à merveille; **everything is going s.** tout va comme sur des roulettes

swimsuit ['swɪms(j)uːt] *n* maillot *m* de bain

swimwear ['swɪmweər] *n* maillots *mpl* de bain

swindle¹ ['swɪnd(ə)l] *n* escroquerie *f*, filouterie *f*; **it's a s.** c'est une escroquerie

swindle² *vt* escroquer, filouter, *F* rouler; **to s. sb out of sth** escroquer qch à qn; **I'm afraid you've been swindled** j'ai bien peur que tu ne te sois fait rouler

swindler ['swɪndlər] *n* escroc *m*, filou *m*

swine [swaɪn] *n* (*inv in pl*) **(a)** *Sl* (*man*) salaud *m*; (*woman*) garce *f*; **this is a s. to deal with!** c'est une belle saloperie!; **(dirty** *or* **filthy) s.!** sale cochon *m*! **(b)** *Arch, Dial* (*pig*) cochon *m*, porc *m*, *Arch, Lit* pourceau *m*; *Vet* **s. fever** peste *f* porcine

swineherd ['swaɪnhɜːd] *n Old-fashioned, Lit* porcher *m*, gardeur *m* de cochons

swing¹ [swɪŋ] *n* **(a)** (*movement*) (*of pendulum*) oscillation *f*, balancement *m*, va-et-vient *m*; (*of crank*) tour *m*; *Boxing, Golf* swing *m*; *Fig* **the s. of the pendulum** le mouvement de balancier; **to give a child a s.** (*on swing*) pousser un enfant (sur une balançoire); *F* **to take a s. at sb** balancer un coup de poing à qn; *Golf* **he took a huge s. at the ball** il prit un grand élan pour frapper la balle; **s. of a door** ouverture *f* d'une porte; **to be in full s.** (*of party etc*) battre son plein; (*of organization*) être en pleine activité; **when the season is in full s.** quand la saison bat son plein; **he has dramatic swings in mood** il a des sautes d'humeur incroyables; *Fig* **sudden s. of** *or* **in public opinion** revirement *m* inattendu de l'opinion publique; *Pol* **s. to the left** glissement *m* à gauche *ou* vers la gauche; *Econ* **seasonal swings** variations *fpl* saisonnières; **s. glass** *or* **mirror** miroir *m* à bascule; (*full length*) psyché *f*

(b) (*rhythmic movement*) mouvement *m* rythmé; **to walk with a s.** marcher d'un pas rythmé *ou* d'un pas cadencé; **song that goes with a s.** chanson très rythmée; *F* **everything went with a s.** (*of party*) tout a baigné; *F* **to get into the s. of things** se mettre au courant *ou* dans le bain; *Mus* **s. (music)** swing *m*

(c) (*in playground, hanging from tree etc*) balançoire *f*; *Fig, F* **what you gain on the swings, you lose on the roundabouts, it's swings and roundabouts** ce qu'on gagne d'un côté on le perd de l'autre; *F* **it's a swings and roundabouts situation** c'est une situation où l'on n'a rien à perdre ni à gagner; **s. boat** balançoire *f* (en forme de bateau)

swing² (*pt, pp* **swung** [swʌŋ]) **1** *vi* (*on child's swing*) se balancer; (*change direction*) changer de direction; *Mus* swinguer; *Old-fashioned F* (*be up to date*) être dans le vent; (*be going well*) (*of party*) battre son plein; **to s. (to and fro)** se balancer; (*of bell*) se balancer; (*of pendulum*) osciller; **shop sign that swings (to and fro) in the wind** enseigne de magasin qui ballotte au vent; *F* **to s. for a crime** être pendu pour un crime; **to s. (on** *or* **round an axis)** tourner *ou* pivoter sur un axe; **the door swings on its hinges** la porte tourne sur ses gonds; **to s. open** (*of door*) s'ouvrir; **to s. to** (*of door*) se refermer; **to s. (at anchor)** (*of ship*) éviter (sur l'ancre); *Mil* **the whole line swung to the left** toute la ligne fit une conversion vers la gauche; **to s. along** (*walk*) marcher d'un pas balancé; **to s. into the saddle** sauter à cheval *ou* en selle; **to s. from branch to branch** se balancer d'une branche à une autre; **to s. into action** passer à l'action

2 *vt* (*to and fro*) (faire) balancer; (*pendulum*) faire osciller; (*turn*) faire tourner; *Av* (*propeller*) lancer; (*hammock*) suspendre, pendre, accrocher; *Mus* (*tune etc*) interpréter en swing; **to s. one's arms** balancer les bras; **to s. one's hips (in walking)** balancer les hanches; *Boxing* **to s. a blow** balancer un coup; **to s. oneself into the saddle** sauter à cheval *ou* en selle; **to s. a child** faire balancer un enfant; *Cr* **to s. the ball** faire dévier la balle en l'air; **to s. the voting in favour of sb** faire pencher la balance en faveur de qn; *F* **to s. a deal** (*bring it off*) mener une affaire à bien; *F* **if we get their support I think we can s. it** si on arrive à obtenir leur soutien, je crois qu'on est bon; *F* **to s. it so that ...** (*arrange things*) arranger les choses de manière (à ce) que ...

▶ **swing at** *vipo* (*aim blow at*) **to s. at sb** balancer un coup de poing à qn; **he swung wildly at the ball** il prit un grand élan pour frapper la balle

▶ **swing back** *vi* (*of door*) se rabattre; (*of pendulum, branch*) revenir; **public opinion swung back** il y eut un revirement d'opinion

▶ **swing out** *vi* (*of car, driver*) faire un écart; (*from side road*) déboucher

▶ **swing round 1** *vi* (*turn around*) (*of person*) se retourner vivement; (*of public opinion, person etc*) faire volte-face; (*of car*) virer (brusquement), faire un brusque virage; **the car swung right round** la voiture a fait un tête-à-queue; **this part swings round on this pivot** cette pièce tourne autour de ce pivot; *Fig* **to s. round behind the party leadership** se rallier à la direction du parti **2** *vtsep* (*turn round suddenly*) (*car*) faire faire un brusque virage à; (*dancer*) faire tourner; *Fig* **to s. sb round** convaincre qn; **to s. a car right round** faire faire un tête-à-queue à une auto

swing bridge *n* pont *m* tournant *ou* pivotant

swing door *n* porte *f* battante

swingeing ['swɪndʒɪŋ] *adj* (*increase, reduction etc*) énorme; (*attack, criticism*) violent; **s. blow** coup *m* bien envoyé; **s. cuts** compressions *fpl* budgétaires démesurées; **s. damages** forts dommages-intérêts *mpl*; **s. majority** majorité *f* écrasante

swinger ['swɪŋər] *n* **(a)** *Old-fashioned F* (*lively, trendy person*) **to be a s.** être dans le vent **(b)** (*partner-swapper*) échangiste *mf*

swinging ['swɪŋɪŋ] **1** *adj* (*to and fro*) balançant; (*mirror*) à bascule; *Old-fashioned F* (*person*) dans le vent; **with s. arms** les bras ballants; **s. blow** coup *m* balancé; **s. door** porte *f* battante; **s. London** le Londres branché des années soixante; **the s. Sixties** les folles années *fpl* soixante; *Old-fashioned* **s. party** réception *f* endiablée; **s. stride** allure *f* rythmée *ou* cadencée *ou* dégagée; **s. tune** air *m* qui swingue

2 *n* (*to and fro*) balancement *m*; (*of pendulum*) oscillation *f*; **s. motion** balancement

swingometer [swɪŋ'ɒmɪtər] *n* tableau *m* des estimations (*des résultats des élections*)

swing shift *n Am Ind* (*workers*) équipe *f* assurant la relève (*surtout celle de mi-journée*); (*period*) journée *f* de travail mi-jour mi-nuit

swing-wing *adj* (*aircraft*) à géométrie variable

swinish ['swaɪnɪʃ] *adj F* (*behaviour*) dégueulasse; **that s. brother of yours** ton dégueulasse de frère

swipe[1] [swaɪp] *n F* (*with fist or stick*) coup *m* de poing/de bâton; *Cr, Golf* coup à toute volée; **I gave myself a s. round the head with it** je me suis donné un coup sur la tête avec; **to take a s. at sb** (*aim blow at*) balancer un coup (de poing) à qn; *Fig* (*in satire etc*) taper sur qn

swipe[2] **1** *vi* **to s. at the ball** (*hit it*) frapper la balle de toutes ses forces; **he swiped at the ball but missed** il a voulu frapper la balle de toutes ses forces mais il a frappé dans le vide **2** *vt F* **(a)** (*hit*) (*person*) (*with fist or stick*) donner un coup de poing/de bâton à; *Cr, Golf* (*ball*) frapper de toutes ses forces; **I managed to s. myself in the eye** j'ai réussi à me donner un coup dans l'œil **(b)** (*steal*) (*sth, sb's girlfriend*) chiper **(c)** (*pass through credit card reader*) passer au pressographe

swirl[1] [swɜːl] *n* (*of water*) remous *m*; (*of gases*) tourbillonnement *m*; (*of cream etc*) spirale *f*; **a s. of dust** un tourbillon de poussière; **a s. of skirts** un tournoiement de jupes

swirl[2] **1** *vi* tournoyer, tourbillonner **2** *vt* faire tournoyer

swirling ['swɜːlɪŋ] *adj* tourbillonnant, tournoyant

swish[1] [swɪʃ] *n* **(a)** (*sound*) (*of water*) bruissement *m*; (*of dress*) froufrou *m*; (*of curtains being drawn*) frôlement *m*; (*of whip*) sifflement *m*; (*of scythe, tyres*) crissement *m* **(b)** (*blow with whip*) coup *m* de fouet; **the cow flicked away the flies with a s. of its tail** la vache chassait les mouches avec sa queue

swish[2] **1** *vi* (*of water*) bruire; (*of silk*) froufrouter; (*of whip*) siffler **2** *vt* (*stick, cane*) faire siffler; **to s. its tail** (*of animal*) battre l'air de sa queue

swish[3] *adj esp Br F* (*elegant*) (*person*) élégant, chic; (*flat, car*) super

Swiss [swɪs] **1** *adj* suisse; **the S. government** le gouvernement helvétique; **S. cheese** emmenthal *m*; **S. cheese (plant)** caoutchouc *m*; **S. French** suisse romand; **S. German** suisse alémanique; **S. roll** roulé *m* **2** *n* (*inv in pl*) Suisse *m*, Suissesse *f*

switch[1] [swɪtʃ] *n* **(a)** interrupteur *m*; *F* bouton *m*; (*more than 2 positions*) commutateur *m*; **two-way s.** va-et-vient *m*; **s. gear** appareillage *m* de commutation *ou* de distribution

(b) (*change*) (*in policy, opinion*) revirement *m*; (*of resources, emphasis*) changement *m*; **to make a s.** effectuer un changement; **to make the s. from gas to electricity** passer du gaz à l'électricité

(c) *Am Rail* (*point*) aiguille *f*; (*siding*) voie *f* de raccordement *ou* de garage

(d) (*stick*) baguette *f*, badine *f*; (*for caning pupil*) canne *f*; **(riding) s.** petite cravache *f*

(e) *Comptr* (*in DOS*) paramètre *m*

switch[2] **1** *vt* **(a)** *El* (*current*) commuter

(b) (*change*) (*places etc*) changer de; (*lever*) changer la position de; (*exchange*) échanger; **to s. the conversation (to something else)** détourner la conversation; **to s. the conversation to money** faire passer la conversation sur le sujet de l'argent; **why do you always have to s. the conversation to ...?** pourquoi faut-il toujours que tu en reviennes à des questions de ...?; **can I s. it for another one?** puis-je l'échanger contre un autre?; **he's been switched to another department** il a été muté dans un autre service

(c) *Am Rail* (*train*) aiguiller; **to s. a train onto a branch line** aiguiller un train sur un embranchement

(d) (*hit with stick*) donner un coup de baguette à; **to s. its tail** (*of cow*) battre l'air de sa queue

2 *vi* (*change*) **to s. (from gas) to electricity** passer (du gaz) à l'électricité; **I see no reason to s. to another brand** je ne vois vraiment pas pourquoi je changerais de marque; **they switched to another topic when I arrived** ils ont changé de conversation quand je suis arrivé; **she later switched to teaching** par la suite, elle s'est réorientée vers l'enseignement

▶ **switch back** *vi* (*revert to*) **to s. back (from electricity) to gas** repasser (de l'électricité) au gaz; **we switched back to gas** nous sommes revenus au gaz; **to s. back to BBC2** remettre sur BBC2

▶ **switch off 1** *vtsep* (*radio, light, heating etc*) couper, éteindre; (*printer etc*) éteindre; **it switches itself off** ça s'éteint automatiquement; **they switched off the power** ils ont coupé le courant; **s. the light off when you go out!** éteignez la lampe *ou* n'oubliez pas d'éteindre quand vous sortirez!; *Aut* **to s. off the ignition** *or* **the engine** couper le moteur **2** *vi* (*of person*) (*turn off lights etc*) éteindre; (*of appliance etc*) s'éteindre; **where does it s. off?** où est l'interrupteur?, où est-ce que cela s'éteint?; *F* **to s. off (completely)** (*stop listening*) décrocher

▶ **switch on 1** *vtsep* (*radio, TV, heating etc*) mettre (en marche); (*light, current*) mettre; (*electricity, printer*) allumer; *Aut* **to s. on the ignition** *or* **the engine** mettre le contact; **to s. on the charm** faire du charme; **to be switched on** (*of person*) *F* (*be up to date*) être bien au courant de ce qui se passe; *Sl* (*be under influence of drugs*) être défoncé; *F* **they switched me on to new ideas** ils m'ont initié aux idées nouvelles **2** *vi* (*of heating, light, computer, TV*) s'allumer; **most people s. on after eight o'clock** la plupart des gens regardent la télévision/écoutent la radio après vingt heures

▶ **switch over** *vi* **(a)** *Rad, TV* **to s. over (to another station/channel)** changer de station/chaîne; **let's s. over to Channel 4** et si on mettait la 4? **(b) to s. over to modern languages** (*of student*) réorienter ses études vers les langues vivantes; **we switched over to gas** nous sommes passés au gaz

▶ **switch round 1** *vtsep* (*exchange one for the other*) échanger; **someone's switched these photos round** quelqu'un a échangé ces photos; **why don't we s. the desks round?** et si on changeait les bureaux de place? **2** *vi* (*change places*) changer de place; (*in job*) (*alternate*) tourner

switchback ['swɪtʃbæk] *n* (*road*) route *f* en lacets; (*railway*) voie *f* ferrée en lacets; (*bend*) virage *m* en lacet; *Br* (*at fair*) montagnes *fpl* russes

switchblade ['swɪtʃbleɪd] *n Am* couteau *m* à cran d'arrêt

switchboard ['swɪtʃbɔːd] *n* **(a)** *Tel* central *m* (téléphonique); (*in office*) standard *m*; **s. line** ligne *f* principale; **s. operator** standardiste *mf* **(b)** *El* tableau *m* (commutateur *ou* de distribution)

switched line [swɪtʃt] *n* (*in datacomms*) ligne *f* commutée

switched network *n Comptr* réseau *m* commuté

switcher ['swɪtʃər] *n TV* console *f* vidéo, pupitre *m* de mélange vidéo

switchman, *pl* **-men** ['swɪtʃmən] *n Am Rail* aiguilleur *m*

Switzerland ['swɪtsələnd] *n* Suisse *f*; **German(-speaking) S.** la Suisse alémanique; **French(-speaking) S.** la Suisse romande; **Italian(-speaking) S.** la Suisse italienne

swivel[1] ['swɪv(ə)l] *n* (*device*) pivot *m*; **s. arm** bras *m* pivotant; **s. base** socle *m* pivotant; **s. chair** *or* **seat** siège *m* tournant, chaise *f* pivotante; **s. joint** (joint *m* à) rotule *f*; **s. pin** pivot *m* de fusée

swivel[2] **(-ll-,** *US* **-l-) 1** *vi* pivoter, tourner **2** *vt* faire pivoter

▶ **swivel round 1** *vi* (*turn*) pivoter, tourner; **to s. round on one's heels** pivoter sur ses talons **2** *vtsep* faire pivoter

swivelling, *US* **swiveling** *adj* (*screen, arm etc*) pivotant, mobile

swiz(z) [swɪz] *n Br Sl* (*sth unfair*) **it's a s.!, what a s.!** c'est pas juste!

swizzle ['swɪz(ə)l] *n* **(a)** *Am F* (*cocktail*) cocktail *m*; **s. stick** agitateur *m* **(b)** *Br Sl* = **swiz(z)**

swollen ['swəʊl(ə)n] *adj* enflé, gonflé; (*face*) bouffi; (*stomach*) ballonné; **his arm was very s.** il avait le bras très enflé; **s. glands** ganglions *mpl*; **the river is s.** la rivière est en crue; *Fig F* **to suffer from** *or* **to have a s. head** avoir la grosse tête

swollen-headed *adj F* vaniteux, qui a la grosse tête

swoon[1] [swuːn] *n Old-fashioned* évanouissement *m*, défaillance *f*; **to fall** *or* **go into a s.** s'évanouir, se pâmer

swoon[2] *vi Old-fashioned* **(a)** (*faint*) s'évanouir **(b)** (*in rapture*) se pâmer

swoop[1] [swuːp] *n* (*of plane*) descente *f* en piqué (**upon** sur); (*of falcon on its prey*) descente; **police s.** (*on nightclub etc*) descente de police; **cocaine found in drugs s.** de la cocaïne découverte à la suite d'une descente de police; *F* **at one (fell) s.** d'un seul coup

swoop[2] *vi* **the hawk swooped down on its prey** (*dived*) le faucon a plongé sur sa proie; (*caught it*) le faucon a fondu sur sa proie; **the gunship swooped down over the village** l'hélicoptère de combat est descendu en piqué sur le village; **the swallows were swooping and whirling** les hirondelles tourbillonnaient; **the police swooped on the nightclub** la police a fait une descente dans la boîte de nuit

swoosh[1] [swuːʃ] *n* (*of water*) bruissement *m*; (*of wind*) sifflement *m*

swoosh[2] **1** *vi* **the water swooshes round the toilet then ...** l'eau tourbillone dans la cuvette des toilettes puis ...; **the waves swooshed over the deck** les vagues déferlaient sur le pont; **you could hear the liquid swooshing around in the tank** on entendait le liquide clapoter dans le réservoir; **the rocket/whip swooshes through the air** la fusée/le fouet siffle dans l'air

2 *vt* **he swooshed it down the loo** il l'a fait disparaître dans les toilettes; **she then swooshed it out with clean water** (*rinsed*) elle l'a ensuite rincé à grande eau; **s. the detergent all over the stain** répandre le détergent généreusement sur la tache
swop[2] [swɒp] *n, vti* = **swap**
sword [sɔːd] *n* épée *f*, *Arch, Lit* glaive *m*; *Mil, Naut* sabre *m*; **to draw one's s.** tirer son épée, dégainer; **to cross swords with sb** croiser l'épée *ou* le fer avec qn; *Fig* (*argue*) se disputer avec qn; (*in debate*) se mesurer avec qn; **to put the inhabitants to the s.** passer les habitants au fil de l'épée; *Prov* **those that live by the s. shall die by the s.** ceux qui ont vécu par le fer *ou* par l'épée périront par le fer *ou* par l'épée; *Lit* **the S. of Justice** le glaive de la Justice; **the S. of Damocles** l'épée de Damoclès; **s. arm** bras *m* droit; **s. cut** (*blow*) coup *m* de sabre; (*wound*) blessure *f* faite avec le sabre; (*on face*) balafre *f*; **s. dance** danse *f* du sabre
swordbearer ['sɔːdbeərər] *n* (*esp municipal*) officier *m* qui porte le glaive
swordbelt ['sɔːdbelt] *n* ceinturon *m*
swordfight ['sɔːdfaɪt] *n* combat *m* à l'épée
swordfish ['sɔːdfɪʃ] *n* espadon *m*
swordplay ['sɔːdpleɪ] *n* (*technique*) escrime *f* à l'épée; **the very realistic s. in the fight scenes** le réalisme des scènes de combat à l'épée; **verbal s.** joute *f* oratoire
swordsman, *pl* **-men** ['sɔːdzmən] *n* épéiste *m*, tireur *m* d'épée; **good** *or* **fine s.** fine lame *f*, bonne épée *f*
swordsmanship ['sɔːdsmənʃɪp] *n* habileté *f* à l'épée, talents *mpl* d'escrimeur
swordstick ['sɔːdstɪk] *n* canne *f* à épée, canne-épée *f*, *pl* cannes-épées
sword-swallower ['sɔːdswɒləʊər] *n* avaleur *m* de sabres
swore *see* **swear**
sworn[1] [swɔːn] *adj attrib* (*declaration*) sous serment; (*witness*) qui a prêté serment; **s. enemies** ennemis *mpl* jurés
sworn[2] *see* **swear**
SWOT [swɒt] *n Mktg* (*abbr* **strengths, weaknesses, opportunities, threats**) forces, faiblesses, opportunités et menaces *fpl*; **S. analysis** analyse *f* des forces, faiblesses, opportunités et menaces
swot[1] [swɒt] *n Br Sch F* (*person*) bûcheur, -euse, bosseur, -euse, *Pej* bachoteur, -euse
swot[2] *vi* (**-tt-**) *Br Sch F* bûcher, bosser, *Pej* bachoter
▶ **swot up** *Br Sch F* **1** *vtsep* (*maths etc*) potasser, bûcher **2** *vi* = **swot**[2]
▶ **swot up on** *vipo Br Sch F* (*maths etc*) potasser, bûcher
swotting ['swɒtɪŋ] *n Br Sch F, Pej* bachotage *m*; **I'd better do some s.** je ferais mieux de bûcher
swum *see* **swim**[2]
swung *see* **swing**[2]
swung dash *n Typ* tilde *m*
sybarite ['sɪbəraɪt] *adj, n* sybarite *mf*
sybaritic [sɪbə'rɪtɪk] *adj* sybaritique, sybarite
sycamore ['sɪkəmɔːr] *n* (*maple*) sycomore *m*, faux platane *m*; *Am* (*plane tree*) platane
sycophancy ['sɪkəfənsɪ] *n Fml* flagornerie *f*
sycophant ['sɪkəfənt] *n Fml* flagorneur, -euse
sycophantic [sɪkə'fæntɪk] *adj Fml* flagorneur
syllabic [sɪ'læbɪk] *adj* syllabique
syllabification [sɪlæbɪfɪ'keɪʃən] *n* syllabation *f*
syllabify [sɪ'læbɪfaɪ] *vt* (*word*) découper en syllabes
syllable ['sɪləb(ə)l] *n* syllabe *f*; **short s.** (*in prosody*) brève *f*; **long s.** (*in prosody*) longue *f*; *Fig* **to explain sth in words of one s.** expliquer qch en termes très simples
syllabub ['sɪləbʌb] *n Culin* = sabayon *m*
syllabus, *pl* **-i, -uses** ['sɪləbəs, -aɪ, -əsɪz] *n Sch, Univ* (*of course*) programme *m*; **on the s.** au programme; **to take a subject off the s.** enlever une matière du programme; **s. design** conception *f* de programme
syllogism ['sɪlədʒɪz(ə)m] *n* (*in logic*) syllogisme *m*
syllogistic [sɪlə'dʒɪstɪk] *adj* (*in logic*) syllogistique
sylph [sɪlf] *n* (**a**) *Myth* sylphe *m*, sylphide *f* (**b**) *Lit* (*slim woman*) sylphide *f*; *F* **she's no s.** elle n'a rien d'une sylphide
sylph-like *adj* (*waist etc*) de sylphide; (*woman*) à la taille de sylphide
sylvan ['sɪlvən] *adj Lit* sylvestre
symbiosis, *pl* **-ses** [sɪmb(a)ɪ'əʊsɪs, -iːz] *n Biol, Fig* symbiose *f*
symbiotic [sɪmb(a)ɪ'ɒtɪk] *adj Biol, Fig* symbiotique
symbol[1] ['sɪmb(ə)l] *n* symbole *m* (**of, for** de); *Am* **road symbols** pictogrammes routiers
symbol[2] *vt Am* = **symbolize**
symbolic [sɪm'bɒlɪk] *adj* symbolique; **s. logic** logique *f* symbolique
symbolically [sɪm'bɒlɪklɪ] *adv* symboliquement
symbolism ['sɪmbəlɪz(ə)m] *n* symbolisme *m*
symbolist ['sɪmbəlɪst] *adj, n* symboliste *mf*
symbolization [sɪmbəlaɪ'zeɪʃən] *n* symbolisation *f*
symbolize ['sɪmbəlaɪz] *vt* symboliser
symmetrical [sɪ'metrɪk(ə)l] *adj* symétrique
symmetrically [sɪ'metrɪklɪ] *adv* symétriquement
symmetry ['sɪmɪtrɪ] *n* symétrie *f*
sympathetic [sɪmpə'θetɪk] *adj* (**a**) (*kind, understanding*) (*person*) compréhensif, -ive; (*stronger*) compatissant; (*letter*) de sympathie, qui marque la sympathie; (*look, smile*) de sympathie; **he's always very s.** il est toujours prêt à vous écouter; **I didn't find him very s.** (**about it**) je ne l'ai pas trouvé très compréhensif; **you could try to be more s.** (**towards her**) tu pourrais essayer de te montrer plus compréhensif (envers elle); **to be s. to a proposal** être bien disposé à l'égard d'une proposition; **s. audience** auditoire *m* bien disposé; **her novel got a very s. reception** son roman a été très bien accueilli

(**b**) (*pain*) sympathique; *Phys* (*vibration*) due à la résonance; *Mus* **s. string** corde *f* qui vibre par résonance
sympathetically [sɪmpə'θetɪklɪ] *adv* (**a**) (*showing understanding*) avec bienveillance; (*showing pity*) avec compassion; **the new play was s. received** la nouvelle pièce a été bien accueillie (**b**) *Med* par sympathie; *Phys* (*to vibrate*) par résonance
sympathize ['sɪmpəθaɪz] *vi* (**a**) (*show sympathy*) compatir; (*have understanding*) comprendre; **I s. because I used to have similar problems** je compatis car j'ai connu des problèmes du même genre; **I s. with your point of view but ...** je comprends votre point de vue mais ...; **I do s.** (*feel pity etc*) je compatis; (*feel understanding*) je (vous) comprends très bien (**b**) (*agree*) **those who s. with Professor Smith in his view that ...** ceux qui s'associent au Professeur Smith pour dire que ...; **to s. with a cause** *etc* avoir des sympathies pour une cause *etc*
sympathizer ['sɪmpəθaɪzər] *n* (**a**) (*person in agreement*) sympathisant, -ante (**with a cause** d'une cause); **a rebel/an IRA s.** un sympathisant des rebelles/de l'IRA (**b**) (*person who shows sympathy, understanding*) **to be a s. in sb's grief** compatir au chagrin de qn; **we have received many letters from sympathizers** nous avons reçu de nombreuses lettres de personnes qui voulaient nous témoigner leur sympathie
sympathy ['sɪmpəθɪ] *n* (**a**) (*compassion*) compassion *f*; **to have s. for sb** éprouver de la compassion pour qn; **to show s. to sb** faire preuve de compassion envers qn; **you have my deepest s.** *Fml* (*on bereavement etc*) je vous présente toutes mes condoléances; *Hum* (*on your new girlfriend etc*) je te souhaite bien du plaisir; **a letter of s.** une lettre de condoléances; **we'd all like to express our s. on this tragic loss** nous aimerions tous vous exprimer nos condoléances à la suite de cette perte tragique; **our sympathies are with the families of the dead** nous compatissons avec les familles des victimes; **I don't need s., I need help** ce n'est pas de compassion dont j'ai besoin, c'est d'une aide; **if you do catch a cold don't expect any s. from me!** si tu attrapes un rhume, ne compte pas sur moi pour te plaindre

(**b**) (*understanding, support etc*) sympathie *f* (**for sb** pour qn); **to feel s. for sb** éprouver de la sympathie pour qn; **popular sympathies are on his side** il a l'opinion pour lui; **to view a proposal with s.** regarder une proposition d'un bon œil; **to be in s. with sb's ideas** partager les idées de qn; **my s. is** *or* **my sympathies are with the opposition** ma sympathie va à l'opposition; **she was accused of having communist/federalist sympathies** on l'accusait d'avoir des sympathies pour les communistes/les fédéralistes; **to strike** *or* **come out** (**on strike**) **in s.** se mettre en grève de solidarité (**with** avec); **prices went up in s.** les prix sont montés par contrecoup; *Phys* **string that vibrates in s.** corde qui vibre par résonance; *Physiol* **the temperature of the other hand falls in s.** la température de l'autre main tombe par réaction; *Ind* **s. strike** grève *f* de solidarité
symphonic [sɪm'fɒnɪk] *adj Mus* symphonique
symphony ['sɪmfənɪ] *n Mus* (**a**) (*composition*), *Fig* symphonie *f*; **s. concert** concert *m* symphonique; **s. orchestra** orchestre *m* symphonique (**b**) *Am* (*orchestra*) orchestre *m* symphonique
symposium, *pl* **-ia, -iums** [sɪm'pəʊzɪəm, -ɪə, -ɪəmz] *n* symposium *m*; (*collection*) recueil *m* d'articles (*de spécialistes*)
symptom ['sɪm(p)təm] *n Med, Fig* symptôme *m*; **to show all the symptoms of ...** présenter tous les symptômes de ...
symptomatic [sɪm(p)tə'mætɪk] *adj* symptomatique (**of** de)
synagogue ['sɪnəgɒg] *n* synagogue *f*
synapse ['sɪnæps] *n* synapse *f*
sync [sɪŋk] *n* (*abbr* **synchronization**) **in s.** (*of film etc*) synchronisé; **out of s.** (*of film etc*) mal synchronisé; **the engine is a bit out of s.** le moteur ne tourne pas très rond; **to be in s. with the times** être en harmonie avec son temps;

to be out of s. with the times être déphasé; **he's somehow out of s. with the others** (*not in tune, not thinking the same way etc*) il est un peu décalé *ou* déphasé par rapport aux autres; **her ideas are out of s. with ...** ses idées sont en décalage par rapport à ...; **the translation is out of s.** il y a un décalage dans cette traduction

synchromarketing [sɪŋkrəʊ'mærkətɪŋ] *n* synchromercatique *f*

synchromesh ['sɪŋkrəʊmeʃ] *n Aut* synchronisation *f*, synchronisateur *m*, synchro *m*; **s. on all gears** boîte de vitesses avec rapports synchronisés; **s. gearbox** boîte *f* de vitesses synchronisée

synchronic [sɪŋ'krɒnɪk] *adj* (*synchronous*) synchrone; *Ling* (*descriptive*) synchronique

synchronism ['sɪŋkrənɪz(ə)m] *n* synchronisme *m*

synchronization [sɪŋkrənaɪ'zeɪʃən] *n* synchronisation *f*

synchronize ['sɪŋkrənaɪz] **1** *vt* (*watches, actions, movements, events*) synchroniser (**sth with sth** qch avec qch); *El* (*generators*) coupler en phase **2** *vi* (*of events*) arriver *ou* avoir lieu simultanément; **we'll try to s. with you** nous essaierons de nous synchroniser avec vous

synchronized ['sɪŋkrənaɪzd] *adj* synchronisé; *El* **s. generators** générateurs *mpl* synchronisés *ou* en phase; **s. sound** son *m* synchrone; *Sp* **s. swimming** natation *f* synchronisée

synchronizer ['sɪŋkrənaɪzər] *n El, Comptr* synchronisateur *m*

synchronizing generator ['sɪŋkrənaɪzɪŋ] *n TV etc* générateur *m* de synchro

synchronous ['sɪŋkrənəs] *adj* synchrone (**with** de)

syncline ['sɪŋklaɪn] *n Geol* synclinal *m*

syncopate ['sɪŋkəpeɪt] *vt* syncoper; **syncopated music** musique *f* syncopée; **syncopated rhythm** rythme *m* syncopé

syncopation [sɪŋkə'peɪʃən] *n Mus* syncope *f*

syncope ['sɪŋkəpɪ] *n Med, Gram* syncope *f*

syncretic [sɪŋ'kretɪk] *adj* syncrétique

syncretism ['sɪŋkrətɪz(ə)m] *n* syncrétisme *m*

syndic ['sɪndɪk] *n* syndic *m*

syndicalism ['sɪndɪkəlɪz(ə)m] *n* syndicalisme *m*

syndicalist ['sɪndɪkəlɪst] *n, adj* syndicaliste *mf*

syndicate[1] ['sɪndɪkət] *n* (**a**) *Com, Fin* syndicat *m*; *US* (*criminal organization*) association *f* de malfaiteurs; *Am* (*news agency*) agence *f* de presse; *US* (*chain of newspapers*) chaîne *f* de journaux; **member of a s., s. member** syndicaliste *mf* (**b**) (*board of syndics*) conseil *m* de syndics

syndicate[2] ['sɪndɪkeɪt] *vt Journ* (*article*) publier simultanément dans plusieurs journaux; *Fin* **syndicated loan** prêt *m* en participation

syndication [sɪndɪ'keɪʃən] *n Journ* (*of article*) publication *f* simultanée dans plusieurs journaux; **s. agency** agence *f* de presse

syndrome ['sɪndrəʊm] *n Med, Fig* syndrome *m*

synectics [sɪ'nektɪks] *n* [①A10,c] synectique *f*

synergism ['sɪnədʒɪz(ə)m] *n* synergisme *m*

synergy ['sɪnədʒɪ] *n* synergie *f*

synod ['sɪnəd] *n* (**a**) *Rel* synode *m*; **the General S.** le conseil d'administration de l'Église anglicane (**b**) (*council*) assemblée *f*, convention *f*

synonym ['sɪnənɪm] *n* synonyme *m*

synonymous [sɪ'nɒnɪməs] *adj* synonyme (**with** de); **their name is s. with quality** leur nom est synonyme de qualité

synonymously [sɪ'nɒnɪməslɪ] *adv* (*to use a word*) comme synonyme (**with** de); **these two words can be used s.** ces deux mots peuvent être employés comme synonymes

synonymy [sɪ'nɒnɪmɪ] *n* synonymie *f*

synopsis, *pl* **-pses** [sɪ'nɒpsɪs, -psi:z] *n* résumé *m*; (*of science, film*) synopsis *m*

synoptic [sɪ'nɒptɪk] *adj* synoptique

synovia [sɪ'nəʊvɪə, saɪ-] *n Physiol, Anat* synovie *f*

synovial [sɪ'nəʊvɪəl] *adj Med* **s. fluid** liquide *m* synovial; **s. membrane** membrane *f* synoviale

syntactic(al) [sɪn'tæktɪk, -ɪk(ə)l] *adj Gram, Comptr* syntaxique, syntactique

syntax ['sɪntæks] *n Gram, Comptr* syntaxe *f*; *Comptr* **s. error** erreur *f* de syntaxe

synthesis, *pl* **-es** ['sɪnθɪsɪs, -i:z] *n* synthèse *f*

synthesize ['sɪnθəsaɪz] *vt* (*elements*) synthétiser; (*product*) faire la synthèse de

synthesizer ['sɪnθəsaɪzər] *n* synthétiseur *m*

synthetic [sɪn'θetɪk] **1** *adj* (*product, fibre etc*) synthétique; *F* **s. smile** sourire artificiel *ou* factice **2** *n* [①A10,c] **synthetics** matières *fpl* synthétiques

synthetically [sɪn'θetɪklɪ] *adv* synthétiquement

syph [sɪf] *n F* = **syphilis**

syphilis ['sɪfɪlɪs] *n Med* syphilis *f*

syphilitic [sɪfɪ'lɪtɪk] *adj, n Med* syphilitique *mf*

syphon ['saɪf(ə)n] *n, vt* = **siphon**

Syria ['sɪrɪə] *n* Syrie *f*

Syrian ['sɪrɪən] **1** *adj* syrien **2** *n* Syrien, -ienne

syringe[1] ['sɪrɪndʒ, sɪ'rɪndʒ] *n* seringue *f*

syringe[2] *vt* (*wound etc*) seringuer; **to s. (out) the ears** laver les oreilles avec une seringue

syrup ['sɪrəp] *n* (**a**) (*sweet liquid*) sirop *m*; **rosehip/maple s.** sirop d'hibiscus/d'érable; *Pharm* **cough s.** sirop pectoral, sirop pour *ou* contre la toux (**b**) (*Br* **golden**) **s.** mélasse *f* raffinée (**c**) (*sentimentality*) douceur *f* affectée

syrupy ['sɪrəpɪ] *adj* sirupeux; *Fig* (*tone*) mielleux, doucereux; **s. music/prose** musique/prose à l'eau de rose

system ['sɪstəm] *n* (**a**) (*structure, organization*) système *m*; **the feudal s.** le régime féodal; **the s.** (*established order*) l'ordre *m* établi, le système; **you can't beat the s.** on ne peut rien contre le système; *Astron* **the solar s.** le système solaire; *Anat* **nervous/muscular s.** système nerveux/musculaire; **the digestive s.** l'appareil *m* digestif; **bad for the s.** mauvais pour l'organisme; **it's a bit of a shock to the s.** ça fait un choc; *F* **to get sth out of one's s.** se libérer de qch; *F* **to get sb out of one's s.** (*after romance*) se sortir qn de la tête

(**b**) (*network*) (*railway, telephone etc*) réseau *m*; **road/river s.** réseau routier/fluvial; **s. of pulleys** système *m* de poulies; **central heating s.** installation *f* de chauffage central

(**c**) *Comptr* **the XYZ is an excellent s.** le XYZ est un excellent ordinateur; **operating s.** système *m* d'exploitation; **to return to s.** retourner *ou* revenir au système; **s. bus** bus *m* système; **s. crash** panne *f* du système; **s. file** fichier *m* système; **s. folder** dossier *m* système; **s. manufacturer** fabricant *m* d'ordinateurs; **s. privilege** privilège *m* d'accès au système; **s. program** programme *m* système

(**d**) *Comptr* **systems** analyse *f* fonctionnelle

(**e**) (*method*) système *m*; (*methodicalness*) méthode *f*; **to lack s.** manquer de méthode *ou* d'organisation

systematic [sɪstə'mætɪk] *adj* systématique, méthodique; **the s. destruction of the forest** la destruction systématique de la forêt; **she's very s.** elle a de l'ordre *ou* de la méthode

systematically [sɪstə'mætɪklɪ] *adv* systématiquement, avec méthode; (*to destroy etc*) systématiquement

system(at)ization [sɪstəm(ət)aɪ'zeɪʃən] *n* systématisation *f*

system(at)ize ['sɪstəm(ət)aɪz] *vt* systématiser

systemic [sɪs'ti:mɪk] *adj* (*insecticide*), *Ling* systémique

system prompt *n Comptr* invite *f* du système, message *m* d'attente du système

systems analysis *n Comptr* analyse *f* fonctionnelle

systems analyst *n Comptr* analyste-programmeur *m*

systems board *n Comptr* carte *f* système

systems buying *n Mktg* achat *m* de système

systems contracting *n Mktg* contrats *mpl* de système

system(s) disk *n Comptr* disquette *f* système

system software *n Comptr* logiciel *m* d'exploitation, logiciel système

systole ['sɪstəlɪ] *n Med* systole *f*

T

T, t [tiː] *n* (*letter*) T, t *m*; **to cross one's t's** barrer ses t; **to a T** à la perfection; **she has the accent off to a T** (*of actress etc*) elle maîtrise l'accent à perfection, elle maîtrise parfaitement l'accent; **that's you to a T** c'est tout à fait toi; **my job suits me to a T** mon travail me convient à merveille

TA [tiː'eɪ] *n* **(a)** *Br Mil* (*abbr* **Territorial Army**) armée *f* territoriale **(b)** *Am Univ* (*abbr* **teaching assistant**) = étudiant, -ante de deuxième cycle qui assure quelques heures de cours en échange d'une bourse d'étude

ta [tɑː] *n, int Br F* merci *m*

TAB [tæb] *n Med* (*abbr* **typhoid-paratyphoid A and B**) (vaccin *m*) TAB *m*; **he has had a T. injection** on lui a fait le TAB

tab[1] [tæb] *n* **(a)** (*on garment*) (*maker's name tab*) griffe *f*; (*owner's name tab*) étiquette *f*; (*on boot*) tirant *m*; (*on file*) onglet *m*; (*for file, removable*) cavalier *m*; (*on can*) languette *f*; (*on lace*) ferret *m*; *Fig* **to keep tabs on sb/sth** avoir qn/qch à l'œil, ne pas perdre qn/qch de vue; **to keep tabs on expenses** contrôler les dépenses; **to keep tabs on sb's movements** surveiller les moindres mouvements de qn

(b) (*loop*) (*for hanging*) attache *f*, patte *f*

(c) *esp Am* (*bill*) (*in restaurant*) addition *f*; (*in hotel*) note *f*; *F* **to pick up the t.** (*for meal, accommodation*) régler l'addition *ou* la note; (*for government programme, research etc*) payer; (*for damage done by others*) casquer, raquer

(d) (*on typewriter, word processor etc*) (*position*) colonne *f*; (*in text, figures*), *Comptr* tabulation *f*; **t. (key)** tabulateur *m*, touche *f* de tabulation; **to set tabs** régler *ou* positionner les tabulateurs **(at** à); **t. points** points *mpl* de tabulation; **t. setting** (*act*) pose *f* de tabulations; (*result*) tabulations *fpl*; **t. stop** taquet *m* de tabulation

tab[2] *vt* (*text*) poser des tabulations dans; (*figures*) disposer en colonne(s)

tabard ['tæbəd] *n* (*garment*) tabar(d) *m*

Tabasco® [tə'bæskəʊ] *n* Tabasco® *m*

tabbing ['tæbɪŋ] *n Comptr* (*act*) pose *f* de tabulations; (*result*) tabulations *fpl*

tabbouleh ['tæbʊleɪ] *n* taboulé *m*

tabby ['tæbɪ] *n* **t. (cat)** chat *m* tigré *ou* moucheté

tabernacle ['tæbənæk(ə)l] *n Rel* **(a)** (*receptacle*) tabernacle *m* **(b)** (*place of worship*) temple *m*

table[1] ['teɪb(ə)l] *n* **(a)** (*piece of furniture*) table *f*; (*small and round*) guéridon *m*; **card** *or* **gaming t.** table de jeu; **changing/ironing t.** table à langer/repasser; **nest of tables** table gigogne; **to set** *or Br* **lay the t.** mettre *ou* dresser la table *ou* le couvert; **to sit down to (the) t.** se mettre à table; **to be at (the) t.** être attablé *ou* à table; **to be (sitting) at the breakfast/dinner t.** être à table pour le petit déjeuner/(le) dîner; **to leave the t.** se lever *ou* sortir de table, quitter la table; **he has awful t. manners** il se tient très mal à table; **mind your t. manners!** tiens-toi bien à table!; *F* **to drink sb under the t.** mieux tenir l'alcool que qn; **he drank us under the t.** il était encore debout alors que nous roulions sous la table; **I could drink you under the t. any day!** je te parie que je peux boire plus que toi!; **two drinks and I'm under the t.** deux verres et je suis complètement paf!; *Parl* **to lay a bill on the t.** *Br, Can* (*submit*) déposer un projet de loi; *US* (*suspend*) ajourner la discussion d'un projet de loi; *Fig* **to give sb money under the t.** donner un dessous de table *ou* un pot-de-vin à qn; *Fig* **to get back to the negotiating t.** reprendre les pourparlers; *Fig* **management has nothing new to put on the t.** la direction n'a rien de nouveau à proposer; *Fig* **the offer is still on the t.** la proposition tient toujours; *Fig* **to turn the tables on sb** retourner la situation, renverser les rôles; *Fig* **the tables have been turned** les rôles sont renversés; **high** *or F* **top t.** (*at banquet etc*) table d'honneur; *Rel* **the Lord's T., the communion t.** la sainte table; *Geog* **T. Bay/Mountain** la baie/montagne de la Table; **t. knife/linen/wine** couteau *m*/linge *m*/vin *m* de table; **t. centre** décor *m* de table; **t. lamp** petite lampe *f*; **t. leg/top** pied *m*/dessus *m* de table; **t. mat** set *m* de table; **t. napkin** serviette *f* de table; **t. runner** chemin *m* de table; **t. tent** (*cards on tables in restaurants*) carte *f* de menu suggéré

(b) (*group of diners*) table *f*, tablée *f*; **she kept the entire t. amused** elle a distrait tout le monde à table; *Am* **to wait (on) t.** travailler comme serveur/serveuse; *Am* **I'm not going to wait t. all my life** je ne vais pas être serveur/serveuse toute ma vie; **t. service** service *m* à table; **t. talk** menus propos *mpl*, propos légers

(c) (*food*) table *f*; **she keeps a good t.** on mange bien chez elle; **the restaurant has a hot and cold t.** le restaurant propose des plats chauds et des plats froids

(d) (*list*) (*of facts, figures etc*) table *f*, tableau *m*; (*of fares*) liste *f*; **t. of contents** table des matières; *Math* **twelve times t.** table de (multiplication par) douze; *Sp* **(league) t.** classement *m*; **where is the team in the (league) t.?** quel est le classement de l'équipe?; *Ch* **periodic t.** (*of the elements*) tableau de la classification périodique; *Naut* **tide t.** annuaire *m ou* indicateur *m* des marées; *Comptr* **t. look-up** consultation *f* de table

(e) *Geog* (*plateau*) plateau *m*

(f) (*slab*) (*of stone etc*) plaque *f*, tablette *f*; *Rel* **the Tables of the Law** les Tables *fpl* de la Loi

(g) *Mus* (*sounding board*) table *f* d'harmonie

table[2] *vt* **(a)** *Br, Can Parl* (*submit*) (*proposal, resolution*) présenter; (*bill*) déposer; (*amendment*) proposer; **to t. a motion of confidence** poser la question de confiance **(b)** *US* (*suspend*) (*proposal, resolution, bill etc*) ajourner la discussion de; (*enquiry*) ajourner

tableau, *pl* **-eaux** *or* **-eaus** ['tæbləʊ, -əʊz] *n Th* tableau *m*; **t. vivant** tableau vivant

tablecloth ['teɪb(ə)lklɒθ] *n* nappe *f*

table d'hôte [tɑːbl'dəʊt] *n* menu *m*; **t. dinner** dîner *m* à prix fixe

table-hop *vi Am* = aller de table en table dans un restaurant ou une réception, pour montrer qu'on a des relations

tableland ['teɪb(ə)llænd] *n Geog* plateau *m*

table-rapping ['teɪb(ə)lræpɪŋ] *n* (*in spiritualism*) coups *mpl* frappés sur un guéridon

table salt *n* sel *m* de table

tablespoon ['teɪb(ə)lspuːn] *n* **(a)** (*utensil*) cuiller *f ou* cuillère *f* à soupe **(b)** (*quantity*) cuillerée *f* à soupe **(of** de), = 18 ml

tablespoonful ['teɪb(ə)lspuːnfʊl] *n* cuillerée *f* à soupe **(of** de)

tablet ['tæblɪt] *n* **(a)** (*pill*) (*for swallowing*) comprimé *m*, cachet *m*; (*for sucking*) pastille *f* **(b)** (*slab*) (*of clay, slate etc*) tablette *f*; (*inscribed stone*) plaque *f* commémorative **(c)** (*bar*) (*of soap*) pain *m* **(d)** *Scot* (*sweet*) fondant *m* au caramel

table tennis *n* tennis *m* de table, ping-pong *m*; **table-tennis player** joueur, -euse de ping-pong, pongiste *m*; **table-tennis ball/bat** balle *f*/raquette *f* de ping-pong

tableware ['teɪb(ə)lweər] *n* vaisselle *f*

table wine *n* vin *m* de table

tabloid ['tæblɔɪd] **1** *n* (*format*) tabloïd *m*; **the tabloids** les tabloïds; *Pej* (*popular press*) la presse populaire à scandales *ou* à sensations **2** *adj* **t., in t. form** (*news etc*) en condensé *ou* raccourci; **the t. press** la presse petit format; *Pej* (*popular press*) la presse populaire à scandales *ou* à sensations; **t. format** format *m* tabloïd

tabloidese [tæblɔɪ'diːz] *n* style *m* tabloïde

taboo, tabu[1] [tə'buː] *Rel, Fig* **1** *n* tabou *m*, *pl* -ous; **there is a t. on the subject/place** le sujet/l'endroit est tabou **2** *adj* (*subject, place etc*) tabou (*often inv in pl*); **to declare sth t.** déclarer qch tabou; **these subjects are t.** ces sujets sont tabou(s)

taboo, tabu[2] *vt Rel, Fig* (*sth*) interdire, déclarer tabou; (*sb*) déclarer tabou

tabular ['tæbjʊlər] *adj* (*information, statistics*) tabulaire, disposé en table(s) *ou* tableau(x); **in t. form** (*information, statistics etc*) sous forme de table(s) *ou* tableau(x); **t. ledger** grand livre *m* (à colonnes)

tabulate ['tæbjʊleɪt] *vt* (*arrange in table*) (*figures, facts*) présenter sous forme de table(s) *ou* de tableau(x); (*on word processor etc*) (*figures etc*) mettre en colonnes; **to t. data** classer des données

tabulation [tæbjʊ'leɪʃən] *n* (*of figures etc*) présentation *f* sous forme de table(s) *ou* tableau(x); (*on typewriter*) mise *f* en colonnes

tabulator ['tæbjʊleɪtər] *n* **(a)** (*on typewriter, word processor etc*) tabulateur *m* **(b)** (*machine*) tabulatrice *f*

tacheometer [tækɪ'ɒmɪtər] *n* tachéomètre *m*

tachistoscope [tə'kɪstəskəʊp] *n* tachistoscope *m*

tachograph ['tækəʊgræf] *n Aut* tachygraphe *m*

tachometer [tæ'kɒmɪtər] *n Aut* tachymètre *m*, compte-tours *m*

tachycardia [tækɪ'kɑːdɪə] *n Med* tachycardie *f*

tachycardiac [tækɪ'kɑːdɪæk] *adj Med* tachycardique

tachymeter [tæ'kɪmɪtər] *n* tachéomètre *m*

tacit ['tæsɪt] *adj* (*admission, consent*) tacite

tacitly ['tæsɪtlɪ] *adv* (*to admit, consent*) tacitement

taciturn ['tæsɪtɜːn] *adj* taciturne

taciturnity [tæsɪ'tɜːnɪtɪ] *n* taciturnité *f*

Tacitus ['tæsɪtəs] *n Hist* Tacite *m*

tack[1] [tæk] *n* **(a)** (*fastener*) (*for carpet*) clou *m*; (*for upholstery*) broquette *f*, semence *f*; (*for poster, notice etc*) punaise *f*; *F* **to get down to brass tacks** en venir aux faits

(b) *Sewing* (*stitch*) point *m* de bâti; **to take out the tacks** retirer le bâti

(c) (*course*), *Naut* bord *m*, bordée *f*; *Fig* voie *f*; *Naut* **to make a t.** faire *ou* courir *ou* tirer un bord *ou* une bordée; **to be/run/sail on the starboard/port t.** être/courir/faire route tribord amures/bâbord amures; *Fig* **to be on the right t.** être sur la bonne voie; *Fig* **to be on the wrong t.** être sur la mauvaise voie, faire fausse route; *Fig* **let's try another t.** essayons une autre tactique, changeons de tactique; *Fig* **to go off on a fresh t.** (*in career*) changer de voie; (*in conversation*) passer à un autre sujet

tack[2] **1** *vt* **(a)** (*fasten*) **to t. (down)** clouer; (*poster*) punaiser **(to à)**; *Fig* **to t. sth on** (*add*) rajouter qch **(to à)** **(b)** *Sewing* **to t. (down/in/on/together)** bâtir, faufiler; **to t. up a hem** faire le bâti d'un ourlet, faufiler un ourlet **2** *vi* (*of ship*) louvoyer, faire *ou* courir *ou* tirer un bord *ou* une bordée; **to t. to port** virer (de bord) sur bâbord

tack[3] *n Horseriding* (*harness*) sellerie *f*; **t. room** sellerie

tack[4] *n Naut* (*ship's biscuits*) biscuits *mpl* de marin

tackiness ['tækɪnɪs] *n* **(a)** (*stickiness*) (*of paint, varnish*) adhésivité *f*; (*of glue*) viscosité *f* **(b)** *F* (*shabbiness*) (*of shop, neighbourhood etc*) apparence *f* minable; (*vulgarity*) (*of remark, joke etc*) goût *m* douteux; (*of clothes, jewellery*) aspect *m* bon marché; (*of person*) vulgarité *f*

tacking ['tækɪŋ] *n* **(a)** (*of carpet*) clouage *m* **(b)** *Sewing* bâti *m*, faufilage *m*; **to take out the t.** retirer le bâti **(from** de); **t. stitch** point *m* de bâti; **t. thread** fil *m* à bâtir, faufil *m* **(c)** (*of ship*) **t. (about)** louvoiement *m*

tackle ['tæk(ə)l] *n* **(a)** (*equipment*) (*for hobby, sport*) attirail *m*, matériel *m*, équipement *m*; *Naut etc* (*for lifting*) appareil *m* de levage; **under ship's t.** sous palan; **fishing t.** articles *mpl* de pêche **(b)** *Fb, Hockey* tacle *m*; *Rugby* plaquage *m*, placage *m*

tackle[2] *vt* **(a)** (*deal with*) (*problem, task*) s'attaquer à; (*pudding etc*) attaquer; (*subject*) aborder; *Sch* (*homework*) se mettre à; **to t. a thief** attraper un voleur; **I don't know how to t. it** je ne sais pas comment m'y prendre **(b)** (*speak to*) **to t. sb (about sth)** parler à qn (de qch), dire deux mots à qn (au sujet de qch) **(c)** *Fb, Hockey* tacler; *Rugby* plaquer

tackler ['tæklər] *n Fb, Hockey* tacleur *m*; *Rugby* plaqueur *m*

tackling ['tæklɪŋ] *n Fb, Hockey* tacle *m*; *Rugby* plaquage *m*, placage *m*; **you need to work on your t.** il faut que vous amélioriez vos tacles/vos plaquages

tacky ['tækɪ] *adj* **(a)** (*sticky*) (*paint, varnish*) collant, qui n'est pas sec/*f* sèche; (*glue*) qui commence à prendre; (*surface*) collant, poisseux **(b)** *F* (*shop, neighbourhood etc*) minable, moche; (*vulgar*) (*remark, joke etc*) d'un goût douteux; (*clothes, jewellery*) minable, à deux sous; (*person*) vulgaire; **a t. colour-scheme** une association de couleurs hideuse; **what a t. way to treat someone** quelle façon minable de traiter quelqu'un

taco ['tɑːkəʊ] *n Culin* crêpe *f* de maïs

tact [tækt] *n* (*of person*) tact *m*; (*in difficult situation*) délicatesse *f*; **a matter requiring t.** un problème qu'il faut aborder avec tact; **to show a lack of/great t.** faire preuve de peu/beaucoup de tact

tactful ['tæktfʊl] *adj* (*person*) plein de tact, diplomate; (*in difficult situation*) délicat; (*answer, remark*) plein de tact, diplomatique; (*question, reference*) délicat; **to be t.** (*of person*) avoir du tact; **that wasn't very t. of him** il a manqué de tact, ce n'était pas très délicat de sa part; **she was her usual t. self** elle a fait preuve de son tact habituel; **the t. thing would have been to say nothing** il aurait mieux valu ne rien dire; **that wasn't very t.** quel manque de tact, ce n'était pas très délicat

tactfully ['tæktfəlɪ] *adv* (*to behave, act*) avec tact *ou* délicatesse *ou* diplomatie; **I t. refrained from asking him** par tact *ou* délicatesse, je me suis retenu de lui poser la question

tactfulness ['tæktfʊlnɪs] *n* = **tact**

tactic ['tæktɪk] *n Mil, Fig* tactique *f*, manœuvre *f*; **tactics** la tactique; **to use delaying tactics** utiliser une tactique pour gagner du temps

tactical ['tæktɪk(ə)l] *adj Mil, Fig* **(a)** (*move, weapon etc*) tactique; **t. mistake** erreur *f* (de) tactique; **t. voter** = personne *f* qui fait un vote utile; **t. voting** vote *m* utile; **t. withdrawal** retrait *m* stratégique **(b)** (*person, conduct*) adroit

tactically ['tæktɪklɪ] *adv* (*to behave, act*) adroitement; **t. (speaking)** *Mil* du point de vue de la tactique; *Fig* du point de vue tactique

tactician [tæk'tɪʃən] *n Mil, Fig* tacticien, -ienne

tactile ['tæktaɪl] *adj* (*organ, reflex etc*) tactile

tactless ['tæktlɪs] *adj* (*person*) qui manque de tact; (*answer, remark*) dépourvu de tact, qui manque de tact; (*question, reference*) indélicat; **that was a bit t. of you** tu as fait preuve d'un certain manque de tact, ce n'était pas très délicat de ta part

tactlessly ['tæktlɪslɪ] *adv* (*to behave, act*) sans tact *ou* délicatesse; **she asked him, rather t., about his first wife** avec un manque de tact évident, elle lui a posé des questions sur sa première femme

tad [tæd] *n F* **(a) a t.** (*of milk, sugar etc*) un peu; (*somewhat*) quelque peu **(b)** (*child*) gosse *mf*

Tadjik ['tɑːdʒɪk, tɑː'dʒiːk] *n* = **Tadzhik**

tadpole ['tædpəʊl] *n* têtard *m*

Tadzhik ['tɑːdʒɪk, tɑː'dʒiːk] *n* Tadjik *mf*; **T. Soviet Socialist Republic** République *f* socialiste soviétique du Tadjikistan

Tadzhiki [tɑː'dʒɪkiː, -'dʒiːkiː] **1** *n Ling* tadjik *m* **2** *adj* tadjik

Tadzhikistan [tɑːdʒɪkɪ'stɑːn] *n* Tadjikistan *m*

taffeta ['tæfɪtə] *n* (*fabric*) taffetas *m*; **t. dress/skirt** robe/jupe en *ou* de taffetas

taffrail ['tæfreɪl] *n Naut* (*structure*) couronnement *m*; (*rail*) lisse *f* de couronnement

Taffy ['tæfɪ] *n F esp Pej* (*Welshman*) Gallois *m*; **hey, T.!** hé, toi le Gallois!

taffy ['tæfɪ] *n* **(a)** *Am* (*sweet*) caramel *m* (dur), *Can* tire *f* **(b)** *Am Sl* (*flattery*) flagornerie *f*

tag[1] [tæg] *n* **(a)** (*for identification*) (*on garment*) marque *f*; (*label*) étiquette *f*; (*on animal*) agrafe *f*; (*on file*) onglet *m*; *Comptr* (*label*) marque *f*; (*of data*) préfixe *m*; (*of program*) étiquette

(b) (*end piece*) (*on cord, shoelace*) ferret *m*; (*of material etc*) bout *m*; *esp Am* **t. end** (*of day, speech, procession etc*) fin *f*; (*of conversation*) bribes *fpl*; (*of supplies, sale goods etc*) restes *mpl*; [①**A46**,8,b; **B61**,3] *Gram* **t. (question)** tag *m*

(c) (*epithet, nickname*) surnom *m*

(d) (*quotation*) citation *f*; (*trite saying*) lieu *m* commun, cliché *m*

(e) *Am* (*paper etc flag*) insigne *m*, cocarde *f*

(f) (*game*) jeu *m* de chat; (*with sanctuary*) jeu de chat perché; **to play** *or* **have a game of t.** jouer à chat; (*with sanctuary*) jouer à chat perché

tag[2] **(-gg-)** **1** *vt* **(a)** (*clothing*) marquer; (*merchandise, software*) étiqueter; (*cattle*) mettre une agrafe à; (*file*) mettre un onglet à; *Comptr* (*data*) marquer **(b)** (*term*) (*person*) qualifier, traiter **(as** de); (*nickname*) surnommer **(c)** *Am* (*for traffic offence*) (*vehicle*) coller une contravention *ou F* un papillon sur; (*person*) mettre une contravention à **(d)** (*in game of tag*) toucher; *Baseball* **to t. sb (out)** mettre un coureur hors jeu **(e)** *esp Am F* (*follow*) (*person*) suivre; (*of police etc*) filer **2** *vi* **to t. after sb** suivre qn

▶ **tag along** *vi* (*follow*) suivre; **mind if I t. along?** est-ce que je peux venir avec vous?; **to t. along behind** (*lagging*) traîner derrière

▶ **tag on 1** *vi* **to t. on to sb** coller (aux talons de) qn **2** *vtsep* **to t. sth on** (*add*) rajouter **(to à)**

Tagalog [tə'gɑːlɒg] *n* **(a)** (*person*) Tagal *m*, Tagalog *m* **(b)** *Ling* tagal *m*, tagalog *m*

tagboard ['tægbɔːd] *n Am* carton *m*

tag day *n Am* jour *m* de quête

tagliatelle [tæljə'telɪ] *n Culin* tagliatelles *fpl*

tag line *n* (*in play*) mot *m* de la fin; (*in poem*) dernier vers *m*; (*of entertainer etc*) slogan *m*; *Journ* chute *f*

tag question *n* [①**A46**,8,b; **B61**,3] *Gram* tag *m*

Tahiti [tə'hiːtɪ] *n* Tahiti *m*; **in T.** à Tahiti

Tahitian [tə'hiːʃən] **1** *adj* tahitien **2** *n* Tahitien, -ienne

tai chi ['taɪtʃiː] *n* tai-chi *m*, tai-chi-chuan *m*

taiga ['taɪgɑː] *n Geog* taïga *f*

tail[1] [teɪl] *n* **(a)** (*of animal, bird, fish, reptile*) queue *f*; **to spread its t.** (*of peacock*) faire la roue; **with his t. between his legs** (*of dog*), *Fig* la queue entre les jambes; *Fig* **to turn t.**

prendre ses jambes à son cou, montrer les talons; *Fig* **to keep one's t. up** ne pas se laisser abattre; *Fig* **the t.'s wagging the dog** c'est le monde à l'envers; **the t. of the hostages is wagging the dog of foreign policy** le problème des otages décide de la politique étrangère; **t. feather** (penne *f*) rectrice *f*

(b) (*of shirt*) pan *m*; (*of coat*) basque *f*, pan; **tails, t. coat** habit *m*, queue-de-pie *f*; **to see sb out of the t. of one's eye** voir qn du coin de l'œil

(c) (*of comet, kite, plane*) queue *f*; (*of car, ski*) arrière *m*; (*of coin*) pile *f*, revers *m*; **story with a sting in the t.** histoire qui se termine sur une pointe de méchanceté; *Aut F* **to sit on sb's t.** coller qn; **tails!** pile!; **t. end** (*of material*) bout *m*; (*of procession*) queue; (*of storm*) fin *f*, queue; (*of conversation, film etc*) fin, toutes dernières minutes *fpl*; *Av* **t. assembly** dérive *f*; *TV* **t. slate** clap *m* de fin; *Av* **t. unit** empennage *m*

(d) *F* (*someone following*) personne *f* en filature; **to put a t. on sb** filer qn; **we've got a t.** quelqu'un nous file, nous sommes suivis; **to be on sb's t.** suivre qn de près; (*of detective*) filer qn

(e) *F* (*buttocks*) derrière *m*

(f) *Am Vulg* (*woman in sexual terms*) **she's a great piece of t.** elle est très baisable; **he's looking for some t.** il cherche une fille à baiser, il cherche à tirer un coup

tail² **1** *vt* **(a)** *F* (*follow*) filer, prendre en filature **(b)** (*lamb etc*) couper la queue à **2** *vi* **to t. after sb** suivre qn de près; (*of several persons one behind another*) suivre qn à la queue leu leu

▶ **tail away** *vi* (*of attendance, clientele etc*) diminuer, décroître; (*of voice*) s'affaiblir; (*of book etc*) se terminer en queue de poisson; (*of competitors in race etc*) s'espacer, s'égrener; (*of column on the march*) s'allonger; (*of interest, enthusiasm, support*) diminuer

▶ **tail back** *vi* (*of traffic*) bouchonner; **the traffic tailed back all the way to ...** les voitures étaient pare-chocs contre pare-chocs jusqu'à ...

▶ **tail off** *vi* = **tail away**

tailback ['teɪlbæk] *n Aut* (*queue*) bouchon *m*, embouteillage *m*, point *m* noir

tailboard ['teɪlbɔːd] *n* (*on lorry*) porte *f* à rabattement arrière; (*on car*) hayon *m* (arrière)

-tailed [teɪld] *suff* **short/long-t.** à queue courte/longue

tailgate¹ ['teɪlgeɪt] *n* = **tailboard**

tailgate² *Aut F* **1** *vt* **to t. sb** coller qn **2** *vi* **don't t.!** ne roulez pas trop près!

tailhopping ['teɪlhɒpɪŋ] *n Ski* ruade *f*

tailings ['teɪlɪŋz] *npl* (*from mining*) déchets *mpl*

taillamp ['teɪllæmp] *n Am Aut* feu *m* arrière

taillight ['teɪllaɪt] *n Am Aut* feu *m* arrière

tailor¹ ['teɪlər] *n* (*for men*) tailleur *m*; (*for women*) couturière *f*; **t.'s chalk** craie *f* de tailleur; **t.'s dummy** mannequin *m*; *Fig Pej* **he looks like a t.'s dummy** il est tout endimanché

tailor² *vt* (*suit*) faire, façonner; *Fig* (*speech*) adapter (**to, to suit** à); **(woman's) tailored suit** tailleur *m*; **the tailored look is back** la mode des tailleurs ajustés est de retour; **a tailored shirt** une chemise cintrée; **a tailored skirt** une jupe de tailleur

tailoring ['teɪlərɪŋ] *n* **(a)** (*profession*) métier *m* de tailleur **(b)** (*work*) ouvrage *m* de tailleur

tailor-made *adj* (*suit etc*) fait sur mesure; **t. for** (*specially designed*) conçu pour; (*suited*) fait pour; **it's t. for me** c'est du sur mesure, c'est juste ce qu'il me faut; **the part's t. for her** ce rôle lui va à merveille

tailpiece ['teɪlpiːs] *n* (*to document, speech etc*) appendice *m*; (*to letter*) post-scriptum *m inv*; *Mus* (*on stringed instrument*) cordier *m*; *Typ* cul-de-lampe *m*, *pl* culs-de-lampe

tailpipe ['teɪlpaɪp] *n Aut* tuyau *m* d'échappement

tailplane ['teɪlpleɪn] *n Av* stabilisateur *m*

tailrace ['teɪlreɪs] *n* (*for mill*) bief *m* d'aval

tailshaft ['teɪlʃɒːft] *n Aut* arbre *m* de sortie

tailskid ['teɪlskɪd] *n Av* béquille *f* de queue

tailspin ['teɪlspɪn] *n Av* (descente *f* en) vrille *f*; **to go into a t.** vriller; *Fig* (*panic*) s'affoler, paniquer (**about** de); (*of economy, interest rates*) s'effondrer; **the news sent her into a t.** la nouvelle l'a affolée *ou* paniquée

tailwind ['teɪlwɪnd] *n Av* vent *m* arrière

taint¹ [teɪnt] *n* (*of food*) corruption *f*, décomposition *f*; (*of air, water*) contamination *f*, pollution *f*; (*of reputation, corruption*) souillure *f*; *Fig* (*of madness*) tare *f*; **the t. of sin** la tache *ou* souillure du péché; **book with no t. of bias** livre sans trace de préjugés

taint² *vt* (*contaminate*) (*food*) gâter; (*air, water*) contaminer, polluer; (*minds, morals*) infecter, vicier, corrompre; (*reputation*) souiller, entacher

tainted ['teɪntɪd] *adj* (*air, water*) contaminé, pollué; (*food*) gâté; (*meat*) avarié; *Fig* (*reputation*) souillé, entaché; (*money*) sale

Taiwan [taɪ'wɑːn] *n* Taïwan

Taiwanese [taɪwə'niːz] **1** *adj* taïwanais **2** *n* Taïwanais, -aise

Tajik ['tɑːdʒɪk, tɑː'dʒiːk] *n* = **Tadzhik**

take¹ [teɪk] *n* **(a)** (*recording*) (*of film, scene*) prise *f* de vue(s); (*of record*) enregistrement *m*; *TV, Cin* **t. sheet** liste *f* des prises; **we'll do that t. again** on va refaire cette prise/cet enregistrement **(b)** (*catch*) (*of fish, game*) prise *f* **(c)** (*money*) (*of restaurant, shop*) recette *f*; **our t. is up this week** nos recettes sont en hausse cette semaine; *F* **to be on the t.** toucher des pots-de-vin

take² (*pt* **took** [tʊk]; *pp* **taken** ['teɪk(ə)n]) **1** *vt* **(a)** (*grasp*) (*knife, somebody's hand*) prendre; **to t. sth again** reprendre qch; **to t. sth in one's hand** prendre qch dans la main; **you're taking your life in your hands doing that** c'est ta vie que tu risques en faisant cela; **to t. sb's arm** (*lean on etc*) prendre le bras de qn; **to t. sb by the arm, to t. sb's arm** (*to prevent escape*) attraper qn par le bras; **to t. sb in one's arms** prendre qn dans ses bras; **to t. (hold of) sb** saisir *ou* empoigner qn; **to t. (hold of) sth** se saisir *ou* s'emparer de qch; **to t. sb by the throat/collar** prendre qn à la gorge/au collet; **to t. the opportunity to do** *or* **of doing sth** profiter de l'occasion pour faire qch; **t. your partners** (*at dance*) invitez vos partenaires

(b) (*remove*) (*book, pen etc*) prendre; **to t. sth (away) from sb** enlever *ou* prendre qch à qn; (*steal*) prendre *ou* voler qch à qn; **to t. one number from another** soustraire *ou* ôter un chiffre d'un autre; **to t. sth from the table/out of a drawer** prendre qch sur la table/dans un tiroir; **to t. sth from one's pocket** prendre qch dans sa poche; **to t. a saucepan off the heat** ôter *ou* retirer une casserole du feu; **to t. sth out of sb's hands** prendre qch des mains de qn; *Fig* **to t. the food out of sb's mouth** retirer le pain de la bouche de qn; **to t. sth off the market** retirer qch du marché

(c) (*hold*) (*of container, building etc*) contenir, avoir une capacité de; **this bus takes fifty passengers** c'est un car de cinquante places

(d) (*tolerate*) (*heat, criticism, insolence, pressure*) supporter; **she can't t. a joke** elle ne comprend pas la plaisanterie; **I can't t. any more** je n'en peux plus; **I can't t. any more of him** je ne peux plus le supporter; **I can't t. much more of this** je commence à en avoir assez, je ne vais pas supporter cela bien longtemps; **he can't t. his drink** il ne supporte pas l'alcool; *esp Am* **I'm not taking any!** je ne marche pas!; **he can t. it** il sait encaisser

(e) (*lead*) (*person*) amener (**to** à); (*away*) emmener; (*in car*) conduire (**to** à); (*of road*) (*person*) mener (**to** à); **to t. the dog for a walk** aller promener le chien; **to t. oneself to bed** aller se coucher; *Hum* **I can't t. you anywhere** tu n'es pas sortable; **to t. sb home** (*on foot, by car etc*) raccompagner *ou* ramener qn; (*to meet parents*) amener qn chez ses parents *ou* à la maison; **he's taking me (out) to dinner/the theatre** il m'emmène au restaurant/au théâtre; **to t. sb (along) with one** emmener qn avec soi; **to t. sb round a museum** faire visiter un musée à qn; **she took me round the exhibition** elle m'a fait faire le tour de l'exposition; **to t. sb round a house** faire visiter une maison à qn; **to t. sb across the road** faire traverser la rue à qn; **her job takes her all over the world** son travail l'amène à voyager dans le monde entier; **the scandal has taken her to the top of the best-seller list** le scandale l'a propulsée en haut de la liste des best-sellers; **whatever took him there?** qu'allait-il faire là-bas?; **to t. sb to court** intenter un procès contre qn

(f) (*carry*) (*flowers, sweets etc*) apporter (**to** à); (*one's coat*) prendre; **will this train t. me to Cambridge?** est-ce que ce train va à *ou* passe par Cambridge?; **to t. sb to hospital** transporter qn à l'hôpital; **to t. sth along** *or* **over** *or* **round** apporter qch (**to sb** à qn); **to t. sth with one** emporter qch; **t. some food with you** emportez des provisions; **to t. sth down(stairs)** descendre qch; *F* **you can't t. it with you** (*money when you die*) tu ne l'emporteras pas avec toi dans la tombe; **to t. a problem/matter to sb** soumettre un problème/une affaire à qn

(g) (*go by*) (*bus, shortcut, road*) prendre; **t. the turning on the left** prenez à gauche

(h) (*require*) (*of journey, work etc*) (*time*) prendre; (*of engine, machine*) (*diesel, paraffin etc*) consommer; **it takes an army/courage** il faut une armée/du courage (**to do** pour faire); **it takes one to know one** il faut en être un/une pour savoir ce que c'est; **it took four of us to carry him** il a fallu s'y mettre *ou* nous avons dû nous y mettre à quatre pour le porter; **that will t. some explaining** voilà qui va demander des explications; **the work took some doing** le travail a été difficile; **it will t. him two hours** il en aura pour deux heures; **it took us longer than I expected** cela nous a pris plus de temps que je ne pensais; **how long does it t. to get there?** combien de temps faut-il pour y aller?; **how long**

does it t.? (*for journey, job to be done etc*) combien de temps est-ce que cela prend?; **I took an hour to do it** *or* **over it** j'ai mis une heure à *ou* cela m'a pris une heure pour le faire; **it takes a clever man to do that** bien malin *ou* habile qui peut le faire; **she's got what it takes to be a leader** elle a l'étoffe d'un chef; **she's got what it takes** (*for job etc*) elle a les qualités requises; **he doesn't have what it takes to be a politician** il n'a pas l'étoffe d'un politicien; *Gram* **verb that takes a preposition** verbe qui réclame *ou* nécessite une préposition; **noun that takes an 's' in the plural** nom qui prend un 's' au pluriel

(i) (*adopt*) (*precautions, measures*) prendre; **to t. legal advice** consulter un avocat; **to t. legal proceedings** entamer *ou* engager des poursuites judiciaires; **to t. the veil** prendre le voile; **to t. holy orders** entrer dans les ordres; **to t. a dislike to sb** prendre qn en aversion *ou* en grippe; **to t. a decision about sth** prendre une décision concernant qch; **to t. the view that …** penser *ou* estimer *ou* considérer que …

(j) (*occupy*) (*flat, house*) louer; (*seat*) prendre; **all the seats are taken** toutes les places sont prises; **please t. a seat** asseyez-vous, *Fml* veuillez vous asseoir, **t. your seats!** prenez vos places!

(k) (*consume*) (*tablet, sugar etc*) prendre; **to t. something to drink** prendre quelque chose à boire; **how do you t. your coffee?** qu'est-ce que tu prends dans ton café?; **to t. drugs** (*of addicts etc*) se droguer; (*in hospital etc*) prendre des médicaments; **to be taken twice a day** à prendre deux fois par jour; **not to be taken internally** à usage externe; **are you taking anything for that cold?** est-ce que tu soigne ce rhume?, est-ce que tu prends quelque chose pour ce rhume?

(l) (*do, perform*) (*walk, trip*) faire; (*holiday*) prendre; **t. a look at this!** regarde-moi ça!; **t. your pick** faites votre choix; **to t. a bath** (*wash*) prendre un bain; *Am F* (*lose money*) perdre gros; *Fb* **to t. a penalty** tirer un penalty; **to t. a print from a negative** tirer une épreuve d'un négatif; **to t. a photograph of sb/sth** prendre qn/qch en photo; **to have one's photograph taken** se faire photographier *ou* prendre en photo; **to t. a good photo(graph)** (*be photogenic*) être photogénique; *Rel* **to t. a service** célébrer un office; *Sch* **he takes them for English** il leur enseigne l'anglais; **to t. the part of Hamlet** jouer (le rôle d')Hamlet

(m) (*record*) (*temperature, letter, notes, name and address*) prendre

(n) (*capture*) (*power, town*) s'emparer de; (*prize*) gagner, remporter; **to t. a woman** (*sexually*) prendre une femme; **t. him alive!** attrapez-le vivant!; **to t. sb prisoner** faire qn prisonnier; **to t. sb by surprise** prendre qn par surprise, surprendre qn; *Chess etc* **to t. a piece** prendre une pièce; *Cards* **to t. a trick** faire une levée

(o) (*experience, feel*) **to t. fright** prendre peur; **to be taken ill** tomber malade

(p) (*assume*) **to t. sb/sth for sb/sth** prendre qn/qch pour qn/qch; **I took you for an Englishman** je vous croyais anglais; **what do you t. me for?** pour qui tu me prends?; **to t. the news as** *or* **to be true** tenir la nouvelle pour vraie; **how old do you t. her to be?** quel âge est-ce que tu lui donnes?; **I t. it that you agree** je présume que vous êtes d'accord; **she took your silence to mean refusal** elle a interprété votre silence comme *ou* a pris votre silence pour un refus

(q) (*pass successfully*) (*bend*) prendre; (*obstacle*) sauter

(r) (*consider*) (*case*) prendre; **t. (for example) the pensioners** prenez (par exemple) les *ou* le cas des retraités; **taking one thing with another** l'un dans l'autre

(s) (*accept, receive*) (*client, guest*) prendre; (*cheque*) accepter; *F* **t. it or leave it!** c'est à prendre ou à laisser; *F* **t. five!** cinq minutes de pause!, reposez-vous cinq minutes!; **to t. sth well/badly** bien/mal prendre qch; **he took the news better than I thought he would** il a pris la nouvelle mieux que je ne l'aurais cru; **to t. sb/sth the wrong way** (*misunderstand*) mal comprendre qn/qch; **don't t. this the wrong way, but …** (*be offended*) ne le prends pas mal, mais …; **I wonder how she'll t. it** je me demande quelle tête elle fera *ou* comment elle va le prendre; **I'll t. it here** (*phone call*) je le prends ici; **I took a phone call for her yesterday** j'ai pris un coup de fil pour elle hier; *Old-fashioned* **to t. a wife** prendre femme; **do you t. this man to be your lawful wedded husband?** (*in wedding ceremony*) consentez-vous à prendre M. Lapoire pour époux?; **to t. a chance** *or* **risk** *or* **gamble** risquer le coup; *Com etc* **to t. so much a week** faire (une recette de) tant par semaine; **what** *or* **how much will you t. for it?** combien en voulez-vous?; **does this machine t. pound coins?** cette machine accepte-t-elle les pièces d'une livre?; **to t. the hook** *or* **bait** (*of fish*) mordre à l'hameçon; *Fig* tomber dans le panneau; **to t. a beating** (*be punched*) recevoir une rossée; (*be defeated*) essuyer une défaite; **to t. a bet** tenir un pari; **to t. all responsibility** assumer toute la responsabilité; **we must t. things as we find them** *or* **as they come** il faut prendre les choses comme elles sont *ou* comme elles viennent; **t. it from me!** croyez-moi!; **to t. sb seriously** prendre qn au sérieux; **nylon does not t. dyes well** le nylon ne prend pas bien la teinture; **to t. heavy loads** (*of crane, engine etc*) supporter de lourdes charges; **it won't t. your weight** ça ne supportera pas ton poids

(t) (*newspaper, magazine etc*) **what paper do you t.?** (*buy at shop*) quel journal achetez-vous?; (*subscribe to*) à quel journal êtes-vous abonné?

(u) *Scol* (*sit*) (*exam*) passer, se présenter à; (*study*) (*subject*) faire; (*course*) suivre; **I didn't t. Latin at school** je n'ai pas fait de latin au lycée; **she took her degree last year** elle a obtenu son diplôme l'an dernier

(v) (*copy, quote*) (*passage from author*) emprunter (**from** à); (*quotation, figures*) (*from book, report etc*) tirer (**from** de); **the title is taken from the Bible** le titre vient de la Bible; **the word is taken from (the) Latin** ce mot vient du latin

(w) (*use*) (*eggs, flour etc*) prendre; **t. the scissors to it** vas-y avec les ciseaux; **t. a hammer to it** prends un marteau; **I'll have to t. bleach to this stain** il faudra que je nettoie cette tache à l'eau de javel; **his father took a stick to him** son père lui a donné des coups de bâton

2 *vi* (*be successful*) (*of fire, graft, plant cutting, vaccine, dye etc*) prendre

▶ **take aback** *vtas* (*surprise*) décontenancer, interloquer (**with** par)

▶ **take after** *vipo* (*be like*) (*one's father etc*) (*in looks*) ressembler à; (*in personality*) tenir de

▶ **take apart** *vtsep* (*dismantle*) (*machine etc*) démonter; *Fig* (*criticize*) (*project etc*) démolir; *Fig* **to t. sb apart** (*in fight*) démolir qn; (*scold*) passer un savon à qn

▶ **take away 1** *vtsep* **(a)** (*remove*) (*from person*) (*licence*) retirer (**from sb** à qn); (*furniture*) confisquer; (*from place*) (*person, thing*) enlever (**from** de); *Math* (*number*) soustraire, ôter (**from** de); **they took his books and files away from him** ils lui ont confisqué ses livres et ses dossiers; **to t. a child away from school** retirer un enfant de l'école; **it takes away the fun** ça gâche tout

(b) (*lead*) (*person*) emmener; (*carry*) (*thing*) emporter; (*wounded person*) transporter; **what takes you away so soon?** qu'est-ce qui vous fait partir de si bonne heure?; **his work took him away from his family for long periods** son travail le tenait éloigné de sa famille pendant de longues périodes; *Br* **sandwiches to t. away** sandwich(e)s *mpl* à emporter; **not to be taken away** (*on book in library*) exclu du prêt

2 *vi* **to t. away from the pleasure/value of sth** diminuer le plaisir/la valeur de qch; **I don't want to t. away from his achievements in the past, but …** je ne veux pas minimiser ses performances passées mais …

▶ **take back** *vtsep* **(a)** (*lead*) (*person*) reconduire, ramener, raccompagner; **they took him back to hospital/his family** ils l'ont reconduit à l'hôpital/dans sa famille **(b)** (*return*) (*book etc*) rapporter (**to** à); **that takes me back to my childhood** cela me rappelle mon enfance; **it takes you back a bit, doesn't it?** ça ne nous rajeunit pas tout ça, hein? **(c)** (*accept*) (*former employee, unsold goods*) reprendre; **she's a fool to t. him back** (*husband etc*) elle est idiote d'accepter qu'il revienne **(d)** (*withdraw*) (*what one said*) retirer; (*one's word*) retirer, reprendre; (*gift*) reprendre; **I t. it (all) back** je retire tout ce que j'ai dit

▶ **take down** *vtsep* **(a)** (*remove*) (*poster etc*) enlever; (*plate etc*) (*from cupboard, shelf etc*) descendre; (*coat, picture etc*) (*from hook*) décrocher **(b)** (*lower*) (*one's trousers, one's pants*) baisser **(c)** (*destroy*) (*wall etc*) démolir; *F* **to t. sb down a peg or two** remettre qn à sa place, rabattre son caquet à qn **(d)** (*dismantle*) (*scaffolding, circus tent*) démonter **(e)** (*record*) (*name, address, instructions etc*) noter; (*notes*) prendre; **they took down everything she said** ils ont noté tout ce qu'elle disait; **to t. down a letter in shorthand** prendre une lettre en sténo

▶ **take in** *vtsep* **(a)** (*lead*) (*person*) faire entrer; (*carry*) (*washing, harvest etc*) rentrer

(b) (*admit, receive*) (*orphan*) recueillir; (*lodge*) (*person*) héberger, loger, recevoir; (*lodgers*) prendre; **to t. in sewing/washing** faire la couture/la lessive à domicile

(c) (*reduce*) (*skirt, sleeve*) reprendre; *Naut* **to t. in sail** prendre un ris; **to t. in the slack** (*on rope*) reprendre du mou

(d) (*cover*) (*several countries etc*) comprendre, englober; (*questions, possibilities*) embrasser; **the tour takes in all the important towns** l'excursion passe par toutes les villes importantes

(e) (*understand*) (*intellectually*) comprendre, se rendre compte de; (*emotionally*) (*bad news*) réaliser, bien comprendre; **it took me a while to t. in the full implications of this news** il m'a fallu un certain temps pour mesurer entièrement la portée de cette nouvelle; **he took in the situation at a glance** en un clin d'œil il a compris ce qu'il se passait; **to t. it all** *or* **everything in** (*listen*) être tout oreilles

(**f**) (*deceive*) tromper, rouler (**with** avec); **to be taken in** se faire avoir; **I've been taken in** on m'a eu, je me suis fait rouler; **to allow oneself to be taken in** se laisser avoir *ou* duper *ou* tromper; **to be taken in by appearances** se laisser tromper par les apparences

(**g**) *Am* (*see, visit*) (*museum*) visiter; **to t. in the sights** visiter la ville; **to t. in a movie/show** aller au cinéma/théâtre

▶ **take off 1** *vtsep* (**a**) (*remove*) (*glasses, hat, make-up, lid*) enlever; (*clothing*) enlever, retirer, ôter; (*leg*) amputer; **t. your feet off the table!** retire *ou* enlève tes pieds de la table!; **to t. sb's attention off sth** détourner l'attention de qn; **he never took his eyes off us** il ne nous quittait pas des yeux; **to t. a couple of pounds off** (*off price*) baisser le prix *ou* faire un rabais de quelques livres; (*by dieting etc*) perdre quelques kilos; **to t. sb off a list** rayer qn d'une liste; **to t. sth off sb's hands** débarrasser qn de qch; **I'll t. the baby off your hands for a few hours** je vais garder le bébé pendant quelques heures, ça te libérera; **to t. sth off the market** retirer qch du marché; **t. your hands off me!** bas les pattes!; **to t. a load off sb's mind** ôter un poids à qn *ou* de la poitrine de qn; **to t. years off sb** (*of clothes, diet etc*) rajeunir qn; **to t. the passengers off** (*from ship*) (*by boat*) débarquer les passagers; **the injured man was taken off the ship by helicopter** le blessé a été évacué du bateau par hélicoptère

(**b**) (*lead*) (*person*) emmener (**to** à, chez, en); **to t. oneself off** s'en aller, *F* décamper

(**c**) (*cancel*) (*train, bus etc*) supprimer; (*show, programme*) annuler

(**d**) (*mimic*) imiter

(**e**) **to t. some time off** prendre un congé; **to t. three days off** prendre trois jours de congé; **I'm going to t. the day off tomorrow** demain je prends ma journée

2 *vi* (**a**) (*leave*) (*of plane*) décoller (**for** pour); (*of athlete*) prendre son appel (**from** de); (*of person*) partir (**for** pour); (*hurriedly*) s'en aller, *F* décamper, filer; **she's taken off for two weeks in the Caribbean** elle est partie passer deux semaines aux Caraïbes

(**b**) *F* (*succeed*) (*of company etc*) prendre un grand essor, être en plein essor; (*of film, book etc*) faire un tabac; **the craze never took off in France** cette mode n'a jamais pris en France

▶ **take on 1** *vtsep* (**a**) (*accept*) (*task*) entreprendre; (*responsibility*) assumer; **to t. sb on** (*accept challenge of*) se battre contre qn; **to t. sb on at tennis** défier qn au tennis; **to t. it on oneself to do sth** prendre sur soi de faire qch; **to t. on passengers** (*of train etc*) prendre *ou* embarquer des voyageurs

(**b**) (*hire*) (*worker*) engager, embaucher

(**c**) (*acquire*) (*colour, appearance*) prendre (**of** de); **the word takes on another meaning** le mot prend une autre signification

(**d**) (*escort*) (*person*) **in the end, he took me on to the station** en fin de compte, il m'a emmené jusqu'à la gare

2 *vi Old-fashioned Br F* (*be upset*) s'en faire; **she does t. on so** elle s'en fait pour un rien

▶ **take out** *vtsep* (**a**) (*remove*) sortir (**of** de); (*tooth*) arracher; (*stain*) ôter, enlever; *Fig F* **it really takes it out of you!** (*is tiring*) c'est vraiment épuisant!; *Fig F* **to t. it out on sb/sth** passer sa colère sur qn/qch; *Fig* **to t. sb out of himself/herself** changer les idées de qn

(**b**) (*carry*) (*chairs, washing etc*) sortir; *Am* **sandwiches to t. out** sandwich(e)s *mpl* à emporter

(**c**) (*dog*) promener, sortir; **to t. sb out to the theatre/a restaurant** emmener qn au théâtre/restaurant; **why don't you t. me out more often?** pourquoi est-ce qu'on ne sort pas plus souvent tous les deux?; **he's taking me out to dinner tonight** il m'invite au restaurant ce soir; **he's been taking her out for a couple of months** il sort avec elle depuis quelques mois

(**d**) (*obtain*) (*permit, licence*) prendre, obtenir; (*insurance policy, subscription*) souscrire à; **to t. out insurance** contracter une assurance

(**e**) *esp Am* (*destroy*) détruire; (*kill*) éliminer

▶ **take over 1** *vtsep* (**a**) (*become responsible for*) (*restaurant, company etc*) prendre la direction de; **to t. over sb's job** remplacer qn; **he took over the family business** il a repris l'entreprise familiale (**b**) (*buy out*) (*company*) racheter (**c**) (*overrun*) (*country*) envahir; **she takes the place over** (*of bossy person etc*) elle joue les despotes (**d**) **to t. over the lead** (*in race, polls*) prendre la tête **2** *vi* (**a**) *Mil, Pol* (*assume power*) prendre le pouvoir; (*succeed*) prendre la succession (**from** de); (*of new manager etc*) prendre la direction (**b**) (*relieve*) prendre la relève ce (**from** de)

▶ **take to** *vipo* (**a**) (*go to*) **to t. to the road** prendre la route; **to t. to one's heels** *or* **to flight** prendre ses jambes à son cou; **to t. to one's bed** prendre le lit, s'aliter; **to t. to the hills** se réfugier dans les collines; **to t. to the boats** monter dans les canots de sauvetage

(**b**) (*adopt*) (*bad habits*) prendre; **he's taken to going for early-morning runs** il a pris l'habitude d'aller courir tous les matins tôt; **to t. to drink** *or* **drinking** se mettre à boire *ou* à la boisson

(**c**) (*like*) (*person*) éprouver de la sympathie pour; **they took to each other instantly** ils se sont tout de suite plu; **I didn't t. to him/it** il/ça ne m'a pas plu; **to t. to a game** prendre goût à un jeu

▶ **take up 1** *vtsep* (**a**) (*lead*) (*person*) faire monter; **there's a lift to t. you up** vous pouvez monter en ascenseur; **the lift took us up to the 25th floor** l'ascenseur nous a amenés au 25e étage

(**b**) (*carry*) (*suitcase, shopping etc*) monter

(**c**) (*lift*) (*carpet*) enlever, déclouer; (*paving stones, railway tracks*) enlever; (*street*) dépaver, défoncer; *Rail* (*passengers*) prendre; **to t. up a book from the table** prendre un livre sur la table

(**d**) (*shorten*) (*skirt*) raccourcir; **to t. up the slack** (*in cable*) retendre le câble

(**e**) (*accept*) (*challenge*) relever; (*offer*) accepter; (*suggestion*) retenir; *St Exch* (*shares*) souscrire à; **to t. up a bet** tenir un pari; **to t. sb up on an offer** accepter l'offre de qn; **can I t. you up on your offer?** est-ce que ton offre tient toujours?; **I'll t. you up on that one day** je te prendrai au mot un de ces jours

(**f**) (*discuss*) (*subject, problem etc*) parler de, discuter (de); **I'd like to t. you up on what you said about ...** si vous le permettez, j'aimerais revenir sur ce que vous avez dit à propos de ...; **I'll have to t. you up on that** je ne suis pas du tout d'accord là-dessus

(**g**) (*absorb*) (*water*) absorber

(**h**) (*adopt*) (*idea etc*) adopter; **to t. up an attitude on sth** prendre *ou* adopter une attitude à l'égard de qch

(**i**) (*begin*) (*career*) embrasser; (*hobby, studies*) se mettre à; (*continue*) (*task, book etc*) reprendre, se remettre à; **to t. up one's duties** entrer en fonctions; **to t. up (the thread of) the conversation** reprendre le fil de la conversation

(**j**) (*occupy*) (*space, time*) occuper, prendre; (*attention*) absorber, occuper; **he is entirely taken up with his business** il est complètement absorbé par ses affaires

2 *vi* **to t. up with sb** se lier avec qn

takeaway ['teɪkəweɪ] *Br* **1** *adj* (*meal, sandwich etc*) à emporter **2** *n* (**a**) (*café, restaurant*) café *m*/restaurant *m* qui fait des plats à emporter (**b**) (*sandwich*) sandwich *m* à emporter; (*dish, meal*) plat *m* à emporter; **a Chinese t.** un plat chinois à emporter

take-home *adj* **t. pay** salaire *m* net

taken ['teɪkən] *adj* (**a**) (*seat, table*) occupé, pris (**b**) (*impressed*) impressionné (**with** par); **he was very much t. with the idea** l'idée l'enchantait; **I was not t. with her** elle ne m'a pas fait bonne impression

takeoff ['teɪkɒf] *n* (**a**) (*mimicry*) imitation *f*; **to do a t. of sb** imiter qn (**b**) (*departure*) (*of plane*) décollage *m*; (*of high-jumper, long-jumper etc*) appel *m*; **t. slot** (*for plane*) créneau *m* horaire de décollage (**c**) (*success*) (*of country, industry etc*) essor *m*

takeout ['teɪkaʊt] *adj, n Am* = **takeaway**

takeover ['teɪkəʊvər] *n* (**a**) (*of company*) prise *f* de contrôle, rachat *m*; **t. bid** OPA *f*, offre *f* publique d'achat; **to be the subject of a t. bid** être l'objet d'une OPA; **t. fever** opeamania *f*; **ripe for t.** opéable (**b**) *Pol* prise *f* de pouvoir

taker ['teɪkər] *n* (*of lease*) preneur *m*; (*at auction etc*) acheteur *m*, preneur; **any takers?** (*to go to cinema etc*) est-ce qu'il y a des amateurs?; **I put it up for sale but there were no takers** je l'ai mis en vente mais il n'y a pas eu d'amateurs

take-up *n* (**a**) (*of benefits*) réclamation *f*; **the level of t. has been low** peu de gens ont profité de l'offre; **there has been a 10% t. of the grants** 10% des subventions ont été attribuées (**b**) *Tech* **t. spool/reel** bobine *f* réceptrice/enrouleuse; **t. point** (*of clutch*) point *m* de prise

taking ['teɪkɪŋ] **1** *adj Old-fashioned* (*person*) attirant, séduisant; (*smile, manners*) engageant **2** *n* (**a**) (*of city etc*) prise *f*; **the money/job is his for the t.** il n'a qu'à accepter l'argent/le poste (**b**) *Com* **takings** recette *f* (**c**) *Old-fashioned* **to be in a t.** être agité

talc [tælk] *n* (*toiletry, mineral*) talc *m*
talcum ['tælkəm] *n* **t. (powder)** talc *m*
tale [teɪl] *n* **(a)** (*story*) conte *m*; (*legend*) légende *f*; **thereby hangs a t.** il y a toute une histoire là-dessous; **his drawn face told the t. of his sufferings** ses traits tirés en disaient long sur ses souffrances; **she lived to tell the t.** elle a survécu **(b)** (*lie*) histoire *f*; **to tell tales** raconter des histoires **(c)** (*account, report*) récit *m*; **to tell tales** (*sneak*) rapporter, cafarder; *Fig* **to tell tales out of school** (*be indiscreet*) être indiscret, trop parler
talebearer ['teɪlbeərər] *n* (*sneak*) rapporteur, -euse, cafard *m*
talent ['tælənt] *n* **(a)** (*ability*) talent *m*, don *m*; **to have a t. for sth** être doué en *ou* pour qch, avoir du talent pour qch; **to have a t. for annoying everyone/getting into trouble** avoir le don d'agacer tout le monde/de s'attirer des ennuis; **he has no t. for business** il n'a pas le don des affaires; **a woman of** *or* **with t.** une femme talentueuse *ou* de talent
(b) (*person with ability*) talent *m*; *TV Sl* (*actors, presenters etc*) artistes *mpl*
(c) *Br F* (*people of the opposite sex*) (*women*) belles nanas *fpl*, belles minettes *fpl*; (*men*) beaux mecs *mpl*; **what's the local t. like?** comment sont les nénettes/les mecs par ici?; **where does the t. hang out?** où est-ce qu'on trouve de belles nanas/de beaux mecs?
(d) *Hist* (*coin*) talent *m*
talented ['tæləntɪd] *adj* talentueux, de talent; (*performance*) plein de talent
talent scout, talent spotter *n* dénicheur, -euse de talent(s), imprésario *m*; *Sp* recruteur *m*
taletelling ['teɪltelɪŋ] *n* rapportage *m*, cafardage *m*
talisman, *pl* **-mans** ['tælɪzmən] *n* talisman *m*
talk¹ [tɔːk] *n* **(a)** (*conversation*) entretien *m*, conversation *f*; **to have a t. with sb** (*chat*) parler *ou* s'entretenir avec qn; **we had an interesting t.** nous avons eu une conversation intéressante; **it's time you and I had a little t.** il est temps que nous ayons une petite conversation; **it's time we had a t. about your behaviour** il est temps que nous discutions *ou* parlions de votre conduite; **that was just sales t.** tout ça ce n'était que des boniments
(b) (*discussion*) **there is some t. of his returning** il est question qu'il revienne; **there has been t. of it** on en a parlé, il en a été question; *Pol etc* **talks** dialogue *m*, pourparlers *mpl*; **to start talks** engager le dialogue, entrer en pourparlers; **peace talks** négociations *fpl ou* pourparlers de la paix
(c) (*rumour*) **there is some t. of his returning** le bruit court qu'il va revenir; **it's the t. of the town** on ne parle que de cela; **she's the t. of the town** elle défraie la chronique; **their behaviour is causing a lot of t.** leur conduite fait jaser; **it's just t.** ce ne sont que des racontars
(d) (*words, speech*) langue *f*, langage *m*; **baby t.** babil *m* enfantin; **double t.** (*unclear*) propos *mpl* ambigus; (*false*) propos insincères; **small t.** banalités *fpl*, conversation *f* banale, propos sans importance; **to make** *or* **indulge** *or* **engage in small t.** parler de choses et d'autres, parler à bâtons rompus; **I'm no good at small t.** je ne suis pas doué pour faire la conversation
(e) (*bravado*) **to be all t.** (*of person*) être fort en gueule; **he's all t. and no action** il parle beaucoup, mais il ne fait pas grand-chose
(f) (*lecture*) exposé *m* (**on** sur); **to give a t. on** *or* **about sth** faire un exposé sur qch
talk² **1** *vi* **(a)** (*converse*) parler; (*chat*) bavarder (**of, about** de; **with** avec); **to t. to** *or* **with sb** parler à *ou* avec qn, s'entretenir avec qn; **to t. to oneself** parler tout seul; **she didn't t. to me the whole evening** elle ne m'a pas dit un mot de la soirée; **who do you think you are talking to!** à qui croyez-vous donc parler?; **to t. of** *or* **about doing sth** parler de faire qch; **to t. and t.** parler sans arrêt; **don't all t. at once** ne parlez pas tous en même temps; *Iron, Hum* surtout, ne parlez pas tous en même temps; **you're the only one I can t. to** tu es le seul auquel je puisse parler *ou* me confier; **that's no way to t.!** il ne faut pas dire des choses pareilles!; (*referring to bad language*) en voilà un langage!; **he likes to hear himself t.** il s'écoute parler; **to t. through one's hat** dire *ou* débiter des sottises; *F* **now you're/we're talking!** voilà qui est mieux!; *F* **<u>you</u> can** *or* **can't t.!** tu peux (bien) parler, toi!; **to make a prisoner t.** faire parler un prisonnier; **his accomplices are afraid he'll t.** ses complices ont peur qu'il ne parle; *F* **he talks big** il fanfaronne; **money talks** avec de l'argent on peut tout faire; **what are you talking about?** (*asking question*) de quoi parlez-vous?; (*expressing disbelief*) qu'est-ce que vous racontez?; **I don't know what you're talking about** (*in answer to accusation*) je ne sais pas ce que vous voulez dire; **she knows what she is talking about** elle sait de quoi elle parle, elle s'y connaît; **t. about luck/laugh** tu parles d'une chance/d'un fou rire
(b) (*about problem, in reprimanding way*) **to t. to sb** dire un mot *ou* deux mots à qn, parler à qn; **<u>I'll</u> t. to him!** je vais lui dire deux mots!, je vais lui en toucher deux mots!
(c) (*gossip*) cancaner, jaser; **people will t.** on va jaser; **you know how people t.** tu sais comme les gens sont cancaniers *ou* comme les langues vont bon train; **we don't want people to t.** il ne faut pas faire jaser; **this will give them something to t. about** voilà quelque chose qui va les faire jaser; **the whole town was talking about it** toute la ville en parlait; **to get oneself talked about** faire parler de soi
(d) (*speak*) parler; **to learn to t.** apprendre à parler; **can he t.?** (*of bird*) est-ce qu'il parle?; **is the baby talking yet?** est-ce que le bébé parle?
(e) (*lecture*) **to t. on the radio** faire un discours *ou* parler à la radio
(f) how much are we talking about? il faut compter combien?, çe va chercher dans les combien?; **we're talking about at least £10,000** il faut compter au moins 10 000 livres, ça va chercher au moins dans les 10 000 livres
2 *vt* (*speak*) (*French etc*) parler; **to t. nonsense** dire des bêtises; **to t. politics** parler politique; **to t. (common) sense** tenir des propos raisonnables; **do t. sense!** sois sérieux!; **to t. (some) sense into sb** faire entendre raison à qn; **to t. oneself hoarse** s'enrouer à force de parler; **to t. oneself into a job** (*by trying to impress*) obtenir un emploi grâce à son baratin; **you've just talked yourself into a job** (*by saying that*) ce que vous avez dit là m'a convaincu et vous avez le poste; **to t. oneself out of trouble** se tirer d'affaire grâce à son baratin; **t. yourself out of that one!** vas-y, essaie de t'en sortir cette fois-ci!; **she can t. her way out of anything** avec son bagou elle arrive toujours à se tirer d'affaire; **to t. sb into/out of doing sth** persuader/dissuader qn de faire qch; **to t. sb into a better frame of mind** remonter le moral à qn en lui parlant; **to t. sb out of a bad mood** rendre à qn sa bonne humeur en lui parlant
▶ **talk away 1** *vtsep* **to t. the night away** passer la nuit à parler; **to t. a child's fears away** rassurer un enfant en lui parlant **2** *vi* ne pas s'arrêter de parler
▶ **talk back** *vi* (*answer cheekily*) répondre avec insolence (**to** à), répliquer; **don't t. back to me!** je te défends de me répondre
▶ **talk down 1** *vi* **to t. down to sb** parler avec condescendance *ou* comme à un inférieur à qn **2** *vtsep* **(a)** (*silence*) réduire au silence en parlant **(b)** (*plane, pilot*) donner des instructions d'atterrissage à; **the priest talked the man down from the parapet** le prêtre a persuadé l'homme de descendre du parapet
▶ **talk out** *vtsep* **to t. things out** discuter la chose à fond; *Parl* **to t. a bill out** prolonger les débats de façon qu'un projet de loi ne puisse être voté avant la clôture
▶ **talk over** *vtsep* (*question*) discuter (de), débattre; **let's t. it over** discutons-en
▶ **talk round 1** *vtas* (*sb*) persuader, faire changer d'avis à; **I talked them round to my way of thinking** je les ai amenés à partager mon avis **2** *vipo* **to t. round the problem** *or* **issue** tourner autour du pot
▶ **talk up 1** *vtsep* (*film, book etc*) vanter; **to t. up sb's chances** surestimer les chances de qn; **the Chancellor is trying to t. up the economy** le Chancelier s'est montré optimiste pour tenter de redynamiser l'économie **2** *vi Am* (*speak openly, without hesitation*) parler franchement
talkathon ['tɔːkəθɒn] *n Am* (*in Congress, on television etc*) débat-marathon *m*
talkative ['tɔːkətɪv] *adj* (*person*) (*chatty*) causant, loquace; (*chatterbox*) bavard; **he's very t.** il est très bavard, *F* il a la langue bien pendue, il n'a pas sa langue dans sa poche
talkativeness ['tɔːkətɪvnɪs] *n* (*of person*) loquacité *f*
talkback ['tɔːkbæk] *n* interphone *m*
talker ['tɔːkər] *n* (*conversationalist*) **to be a good t.** avoir de la conversation; **to be a brilliant t.** briller dans la conversation; **my father was never much of a t.** mon père n'a jamais été très bavard
talkie ['tɔːkɪ] *n Old-fashioned Cin F* film *m* parlant *ou* parlé
talking ['tɔːkɪŋ] **1** *adj* parlant; **t. doll** poupée *f* qui parle; *Cin* **t. film** film *m* parlant *ou* parlé; *TV* **t. head** plan *m* de dialogue; **t. shop** lieu *m* de palabres; **the United Nations is accused of being a t. shop** on accuse les Nations Unies de ne faire que de la parlotte **2** *n* **(a)** (*discussion, conversation*) **that's enough t.** assez parlé; **to do all the t.** (*in conversation*) faire la conversation à soi tout seul; **let me do the t.** laisse-moi parler **(b)** (*chatter*) bavardage *m*; **no t., please!** pas de bavardage!
talking book *n* (*for the blind*) livre *m* enregistré
talking point *n* sujet *m* de conversation

talking-to *n F* (*scolding*) réprimande *f*, semonce *f*; **to give sb a t.** passer un savon à qn (**about** sur; **for** pour); **he needs a good t.** il a besoin d'un bon savon
talk show *n Rad, TV* talk-show *m, pl* talk-shows
talky ['tɔːkɪ] *adj Am* (*book, film etc*) saturé de dialogues
tall [tɔːl] **1** *adj* (*person*) grand; (*building etc*) grand, haut, élevé; **how t. are you?** combien mesurez-vous?; **she's taller than I am** elle est plus grande que moi; **he was taller by a head** *or* **stood a (whole) head taller than me** il me dépassait d'une tête; **she's growing taller** elle grandit; **he has grown t.** (qu'est-ce qu')il a grandi; **how t. is that mast?** quelle est la hauteur de ce mât?; **tree five metres t.** arbre de cinq mètres de hauteur; **I'd love a t. glass of something cold** je boirais volontiers un grand verre de quelque chose de bien frais; *Fig* **a t.** *Br* **story** *or Am* **tale** une histoire invraisemblable *ou* à dormir debout; *Fig* **that's a t. order** voilà qui va être difficile *ou* compliqué
2 *adv Fig* **to walk** *or* **stand t.** marcher la tête haute
tallboy ['tɔːlbɔɪ] *n Br* grande commode *f*
tallness ['tɔːlnɪs] *n* (*of person*) taille *f*; (*of building etc*) hauteur *f*
tallow ['tæləʊ] *n* (*fat*) suif *m*; **t. candle** chandelle *f*
tally¹ ['tælɪ] *n* **(a)** (*record*) (*of merchandise*) pointage *m*; **to keep a t. of goods/names** pointer des marchandises/des noms **(b)** (*calculation*) compte *m*; **to keep (a) t. of one's score** noter son score; **to keep (a) t. of one's spending** tenir le compte de ses dépenses; **who's keeping t.?** qui fait les comptes *ou Sp* compte les points?
tally² **1** *vt* (*goods*) pointer **2** *vi* (*of figure, report etc*) correspondre (**with** à), concorder (**with** avec); **these accounts do not t.** ces comptes ne correspondent *ou* ne concordent pas
tally-ho *int, n* (*in hunting*) taïaut *m*, tayaut *m*
Talmud ['tælmʊd] *n Rel* Talmud *m*
Talmudic [tæl'mʊdɪk] *adj* (*scholar etc*) talmudique
Talmudist ['tælmʊdɪst] *n* Talmudiste *m*
talon ['tælən] *n* (*of bird*) serre *f*, griffe *f*; *Fig* (*of person*) griffe
tamable ['teɪməb(ə)l] *adj* = **tameable**
tamarind ['tæmərɪnd] *n* (*fruit*) tamarin *m*; **t. (tree)** tamarinier *m*
tamarisk ['tæmərɪsk] *n* (*plant*) tamaris *m*
tambour ['tæmbʊər] *n* **(a)** *Sewing* **t. (frame)** tambour *m* à broder; **t. lace** dentelle *f* (brodée) sur tulle **(b)** *Archit, Mus* tambour *m*
tambourine [tæmbə'riːn] *n Mus* tambourin *m*
tame¹ [teɪm] *adj* **(a)** (*animal*) (*unafraid*) familier; (*domesticated*) apprivoisé; *Am* (*plant, land*) cultivé; **the squirrels are very t.** les écureuils sont très familiers *ou* ne sont pas farouches; **to grow** *or* **become t.** (*of animal*) s'apprivoiser **(b)** (*person*) soumis, docile; (*story, speech, film, show etc*) fade, banal; **the story's ending was rather t.** l'histoire se terminait sur une note plutôt banale; *Hum* **we have a t. builder who does that sort of thing** on a un ouvrier très serviable qui fait ce genre de choses; **we've our own t. Spaniard here** on a un Espagnol de service ici
tame² *vt* (*animal*) apprivoiser; (*lion*) dompter; *Am* (*plant, wilderness*) cultiver; (*person, passion*) dominer; **to t. the elements** dominer les éléments
tameable ['teɪməb(ə)l] *adj* (*animal*) qu'on peut apprivoiser; (*lion etc*) domptable
tamely ['teɪmlɪ] *adv* (*to submit*) sans résistance, docilement; **the story ends very t.** l'histoire se termine de façon très banale; **a t. worded letter of complaint** une lettre de réclamation timide
tamer ['teɪmər] *n* (*of lions etc*) dompteur, -euse
Tamil ['tæmɪl] **1** *adj* tamoul, tamil (*no f*) **2** *n* **(a)** (*person*) Tamoul, -oule, Tamil *m* **(b)** *Ling* tamoul *m*, tamil *m*
taming ['teɪmɪŋ] *n* (*of animal*) apprivoisement *m*; (*of lion, Fig of person*) domptage *m*; **the T. of the Shrew** la Mégère Apprivoisée
tammy ['tæmɪ] *n F* (*cap*) béret *m* écossais
tam-o'-shanter [tæmə'ʃæntər] *n* béret *m* écossais
tamp [tæmp] *vt Constr* (*earth*) damer; (*pipe, tobacco*) bourrer
▶ **tamp down** *vtsep* = **tamp**
tampax® ['tæmpæks] *n* tampon *m*
▶ **tamper with** ['tæmpər] *vipo* (*interfere with*) (*mechanism etc*) toucher à, *F* trifouiller; (*lock*) essayer d'ouvrir; (*rules*) truquer; (*register*) falsifier; (*accounts, document*) truquer, tripatouiller; **to t. with sb's mail** ouvrir le courrier de qn; *Horseracing* **to t. with a horse** doper un cheval; **to t. with a witness** suborner un témoin
tampon ['tæmpɒn] *n Surg* (*of cotton wool, gauze*) tampon *m*; (*to absorb menstrual flow*) tampon (périodique)
tan¹ [tæn] **1** *n* **(a)** (*on skin*) bronzage *m*, hâle *m*; **to get a (good) t.** bronzer; **to have a t.** être bronzé *ou* hâlé; **to lose one's t.** perdre son bronzage **(b)** (*colour*) marron *m* clair **2** *adj* (*colour, shoes*) marron clair *inv*; **t. gloves** des gants *mpl* en cuir marron clair
tan² (**-nn-**) **1** *vt* (*leather*) tanner; (*of sun*) (*skin*) hâler, donner un hâle à; *F* **to t. sb** *or* **sb's hide** tanner le cuir à qn **2** *vi* (*of complexion*) se hâler, bronzer; **I t. easily** je bronze facilement
tandem ['tændəm] *n* (*bicycle*) tandem *m*; **to do sth in t.** faire qch ensemble; **the party and the unions must work in t.** le parti et les syndicats doivent travailler ensemble; **in t.** (*of horses, turbines etc*) en tandem
tang [tæŋ] *n* **(a)** (*flavour*) saveur *f* piquante, piquant *m*; **a t. of irony** une pointe d'ironie; **the t. of the morning air** l'air *m* vif du matin **(b)** (*of knife*) soie *f*; (*of file*) queue *f*
tangent ['tændʒənt] *n Geom* tangente *f*; **at a t. to a curve** tangentiellement à une courbe; *Fig* **to go off at a t.** changer de sujet
tangential [tæn'dʒenʃəl] *adj Geom etc* tangentiel; *Fig* secondaire; **that is t. to the main issue** étant donné le sujet, ceci est secondaire
tangerine [tændʒə'riːn, 'tænd-] **1** *n* mandarine *f* **2** *adj* (*colour*) mandarine *inv*
tangibility [tæn(d)ʒɪ'bɪlɪtɪ] *n* tangibilité *f*
tangible ['tæn(d)ʒɪb(ə)l] *adj* **(a)** (*palpable*) tangible, palpable; **t. assets** *Jur* biens *mpl* corporels; *Acct* actif *m* corporel; *Acct* **t. fixed assets** immobilisations *fpl* corporelles **(b)** (*real*) réel; **t. difference** différence *f* sensible
tangibly ['tæn(d)ʒɪblɪ] *adv* **(a)** (*palpably*) tangiblement **(b)** (*really*) sensiblement
Tangier(s) [tæn'dʒɪər, -'dʒɪəz] *n* Tanger *m*
tanginess ['tæŋɪnɪs] *n* saveur *f* piquante, piquant *m*
tangle¹ ['tæŋg(ə)l] *n* (*bundle, confusion*) (*of undergrowth*) fouillis *m*; (*of branches, hair, threads, barbed wire, roads*) enchevêtrement *m*; **to be (all) in a t.** (*of string etc*) être (tout) embrouillé; (*of wool, hair*) être (tout) emmêlé; *Fig* (*of person*) ne savoir plus où on en est; **his finances are in such a t.** ses comptes sont tellement embrouillés; **her private life is in a terrible t.** sa vie privée est un véritable sac de nœuds; **to get into a t.** (*of string, business*) s'embrouiller; (*of wool, hair*) s'enchevêtrer; (*making speech, explaining sth*) s'embrouiller, s'emmêler; **to get into an emotional t.** se mettre dans une situation compliquée sur le plan affectif
tangle² **1** *vt* = **tangle up** **2** *vi* (*of string etc*) s'embrouiller, s'emmêler, s'enchevêtrer
▶ **tangle up** *vtsep* **(a)** (*make confused*) (*threads, hair*) embrouiller, (em)mêler; (*question*) embrouiller; **to get tangled up** (*of threads, wires etc*) s'emmêler; **to get tangled up in sth** (*in rope, net*) (*of animal, person*) être enchevêtré dans qch; **she had got tangled up in some barbed wire** elle était prise dans des barbelés **(b)** (*involve*) **he got himself tangled up in the Smith case** il s'est retrouvé impliqué dans l'affaire Smith; **they got tangled up in something dishonest** ils ont été mêlés à une affaire malhonnête
▶ **tangle with** *vipo F* (*quarrel, fight with*) s'en prendre à; **I wouldn't t. with him if I was you** à ta place je ne me frotterais pas à lui; **to t. with the law** avoir des démêlés avec la justice
tangled ['tæŋg(ə)ld] *adj* (*hair, love life etc*) embrouillé, emmêlé
tango¹ ['tæŋgəʊ] *n* (*dance*) tango *m*
tango² *vi* danser le tango; *Fig* **it takes two to t.** (*sexual*) il faut être deux pour ces choses-là; (*share responsibility*) tu as ta/il a sa/*etc* part de responsabilité
tangy ['tæŋɪ] *adj* (*flavour*) qui a un goût piquant; **the t. sea air** l'air *m* vif de la mer
tank [tæŋk] *n* **(a)** (*container*) (*for water, petrol etc*) réservoir *m*; **water t.** réservoir à eau *ou* d'eau; *Naut* caisse *f* à eau; *Rail* caisse à eau, soute *f* (à eau); (*alongside track*) château *m* d'eau; **storage t.** réservoir de stockage; **a full t. (of fuel)** un plein (réservoir de carburant); *Aut, Av* **fuel** *or Br* **petrol** *or Am* **gas(oline) t.** réservoir de carburant; *Am* **t. truck** camion-citerne *m, pl* camions-citernes; *Rail* **t. wagon** *or Am* **car** wagon-citerne *m, pl* wagons-citernes
(b) *Ind etc* (*for processing etc*) cuve *f*, bac *m*; *Pol* **think t.** comité *m ou* groupe *m* d'experts; **(air/buoyancy) t.** caisson *m* (à air/de flottabilité)
(c) *Mil* char *m*; **the tanks** les blindés *mpl*; **t. warfare** guerre *f* combattue à l'aide de chars
▶ **tank along** *vi F* (*go fast*) (*of driver, car etc*) foncer
▶ **tank up** *Br* **1** *vi Aut* (*fill fuel tank*) faire le plein d'essence **2** *vtsep* (*usu passive*) *Sl* **to get tanked up** (*drunk*) se prendre une biture; **to be tanked up** être bourré *ou* bituré
tankard ['tæŋkəd] *n* chope *f*; *Arch* **a t. of ale** un pot de bière
tank commander *n* commandant *m* de char
tanker ['tæŋkər] *n Naut* navire-citerne *m, pl* navires-citernes; *Rail* wagon-citerne *m, pl* wagons-citernes; *Naut* **oil t.** (navire *m*) pétrolier *m*; **t. (aircraft)** avion-citerne *m, pl* avions-citernes; (*for refuelling*) avion *m* de ravitaillement; **t. lorry** *or Am* **truck** camion-citerne *m, pl* camions-citernes
tank regiment *n* régiment *m* de chars

tank top *n* (*garment*) débardeur *m* en laine
tank trap *n* fossé *m* antichar
tanned [tænd] *adj* (*leather*) tanné; (*face, complexion*) hâlé, bronzé; (*deeply, naturally*) basané
tanner[1] ['tænər] *n* (*person*) tanneur *m*
tanner[2] *n Br Hist Sl* (*coin*) (pièce *f* de) six pence *mpl*
tannery ['tænərı] *n* tannerie *f*
tannic ['tænık] *adj* (*acid*) tannique
tannin ['tænın] *n* tan(n)in *m*
tanning ['tænıŋ] *n* **(a)** (*act of tanning hides*) tannage *m*; **t. (trade)** tannerie *f* **(b)** *F* (*beating*) raclée *f*; **to give sb a good t.** flanquer une bonne raclée à qn
tannoy® ['tænɔı] *n* système *m* de haut-parleurs; **an announcement came over the t.** il y a eu une annonce au haut-parleur
tansy ['tænzı] *n* (*plant*) tanaisie *f*
tantalize ['tæntəlaız] *vt* tourmenter, mettre au supplice
tantalizing ['tæntəlaızıŋ] *adj* terriblement alléchant; **it's t.** c'est un vrai supplice de Tantale
tantalizingly ['tæntəlaızıŋlı] *adv* **the cool water was t. near** cette eau fraîche à proximité était un véritable supplice; **we came t. close to solving it** c'était exaspérant *ou* rageant de voir à quel point nous étions près de la solution
tantamount ['tæntəmaʊnt] *adj* équivalent (**to** à); **to be t. to sth** équivaloir à qch; **that's t. to saying I'm a liar** cela revient à dire que je mens
tantrum ['tæntrəm] *n* (*of child*) caprice *m*; (*of adult*) colère *f*; **to throw a t.** (*of child*) faire un caprice; (*of adult*) piquer une colère
Tanzania [tænzə'nıə] *n* Tanzanie *f*
Tanzanian [tænzə'nıən] **1** *adj* tanzanien **2** *n* Tanzanien, -ienne
Taoism ['taʊız(ə)m] *n* taoïsme *m*
Taoist ['taʊıst] *n* taoïste *mf*
tap[1] [tæp] *n* **(a)** *Br* (*for water*) robinet *m*; (*plug*) bonde *f*; **to turn on/turn off the t.** ouvrir/fermer le robinet; *Fig* **to turn on the t.** (*cry*) pleurer; *Fig* **to turn off the t.** fermer le robinet; **on t.** (*of beer etc*) à la pression; *Fig* **to be on t.** (*of person, thing*) être (toujours) disponible; **they've got cheap labour on t.** ils ont de la main-d'œuvre pas chère à volonté; **t. water** eau *f* du robinet **(b)** *esp Am El* prise *f* (intermédiaire) **(c)** (*action*) (*into pipe*) branchement *m*; (*of telephone communication*) écoute *f*; *Telecom* **who authorized the t.?** qui a autorisé la mise sur écoute?
tap[2] *vt* **(-pp-)** **(a)** (*barrel*) percer, mettre en perce; (*tree*) inciser, entailler; (*pine tree*) gemmer; (*wine*) tirer; (*natural resources etc*) exploiter; (*water course*) capter; (*gas or water pipe*) faire un branchement sur; **we must t. all the resources we have** nous devons puiser dans toutes nos ressources; **to t. a telephone conversation** écouter une communication téléphonique à l'aide d'une table d'écoutes; **the phones are tapped** les téléphones sont sur écoute; *F* **to t. sb for fifty francs** taper qn de cinquante francs **(b)** *MecE* (*nut, screw*) tarauder, fileter
tap[3] *n* **(a)** (*light blow, sound*) petit coup *m*; (*with hand*) tape *f*; **t. at the door** coup léger *ou* discret à la porte; **there was a t. on the window** on frappa à la fenêtre; **a t. on the shoulder** une tape sur l'épaule **(b)** *Mil* **to play taps** sonner l'extinction des feux
tap[4] **(-pp-)** **1** *vt* (*strike lightly*) (*surface*) taper légèrement, tapoter; (*hit gently*) (*person*) donner un petit coup à; **she tapped me on the shoulder** (*to attract attention*) elle m'a tapé sur l'épaule **2** *vi* **(a)** **to t. at** *or* **on the door** frapper doucement à la porte **(b)** **to t. (dance)** faire des claquettes
▶ **tap out** *vtsep* **(a)** **to t. out the rhythm** marquer le rythme; **to t. out the rhythm on the table** taper le rythme sur la table; **to t. out a message** (*in morse code*) émettre un message; **to t. out a message on the central heating pipes** transmettre un message en tapant sur les tuyaux du chauffage central **(b)** **to t. out one's pipe** débourrer sa pipe
tap dance *n* numéro *m* de claquettes
tap dancer *n* danseur, -euse de claquettes
tap dancing *n* claquettes *fpl*; **to do t.** faire des claquettes
tape[1] [teıp] *n* **(a)** (*ribbon*) (*of cotton*) ruban *m*; (*of cloth, paper*) bande *f*; *Sp* bande d'arrivée; **masking t.** ruban-cache *m*; (**(self-)adhesive** *or F* **sticky**) **t.** ruban adhésif, scotch® *m*; *Pharm* **adhesive t.** sparadrap *m*; *El* **insulating t.** ruban isolant, chatterton *m*; **t. (measure)** mètre *m* (ruban); (*dressmaker's*) centimètre *m*; *Sp* **to breast the t.** franchir la ligne d'arrivée *ou* arriver le premier; *Horseracing* **the tapes** (*at start*) les rubans
(b) (*in recording*) (*length of tape*) bande; (*cassette*) cassette *f* (audio); **magnetic** *or* **recording t.** bande magnétique; **(video) t.** cassette vidéo; **pre-recorded t.** bande enregistrée; **a techno t.** une cassette de techno; **to get** *or* **put sth on t.** enregistrer qch; **I've got it on t.** je l'ai en cassette
tape[2] *vt* **(a)** (*parcel*) scotcher; (*electric wire*) guiper; **to t. sth to sth** scotcher qch à qch **(b)** *Fig* **I've got him taped** je sais comment il est *ou* ce qu'il vaut **(c)** (*record*) enregistrer; **she was taped talking to them** elle a été enregistrée en train de leur parler; **taped music** musique *f* enregistrée
▶ **tape up** *vtsep* (*parcel, broken object*) scotcher
tape backup *n Comptr* sauvegarde *f* sur bande; **t. system** système *m* de sauvegarde sur bande; **t. unit** unité *f* de sauvegarde sur bande
tape deck *n* platine *f* cassette(s), *pl* platines cassettes
tape drive *n* lecteur *m* de bandes
tape library *n* collection *f* de cassettes
taper[1] ['teıpər] *n* **(a)** (*candle*) bougie *f* filée; *Rel* cierge *m* **(b)** (*to light candle, fire etc*) allume-feu *m inv*
taper[2] *n Archit, Constr etc* (*shape*) conicité *f*, cône *m*
taper[3] **1** *vt* tailler en pointe *ou* en cône; (*hair*) effiler; *Archit* (*column*) fuseler, diminuer **2** *vi* s'effiler; **column that tapers upwards** colonne *f* taillée en pointe; **her hair tapers in to the neck** ses cheveux sont effilés sur son cou; **it tapers to a point** c'est taillé en pointe
▶ **taper off** **1** *vi* (*of line, long thin object*) s'amincir, se rétrécir; (*get smaller gradually*) (*of production, numbers etc*) diminuer, se réduire **2** *vtsep* (*long thin object*) effiler; (*production etc*) réduire, diminuer
tape reader *n Comptr* lecteur *m* de bande
tape-record *vt* enregistrer
tape recorder *n* magnétophone *m*
tape recording *n* enregistrement *m*
tapered ['teıpəd] *adj* (*hair*) effilé; (*column, candle*) en fuseau; **t. trousers** fuseau *m*
tapering ['teıpərıŋ] **1** *adj* en pointe; (*finger*) effilé, fuselé; *Archit* (*column*) en fuseau; *Fin* **t. rate** tarif *m* dégressif **2** *n* (*in hairdressing*) effilage *m*
tape streamer *n Comptr* streamer *m*, dévideur *m* (de bande)
tapestry ['tæpıstrı] *n* tapisserie *f*; **t. maker** *or* **weaver** tapissier, -ière
tape unit *n Comptr* unité *f* de bande
tapeworm ['teıpwɜːm] *n* ténia *m*, ver *m* solitaire
taping ['teıpıŋ] *n* (*recording*) enregistrement *m*
tapioca [tæpı'əʊkə] *n* tapioca *m*
tapir ['teıpər] *n* (*often inv in pl*) (*animal*) tapir *m*
tappet ['tæpıt] *n MecE* poussoir *m*; **t. clearance** jeu *m* aux culbuteurs
tapping[1] ['tæpıŋ] *n Telecom* **(telephone) t.** écoutes *fpl* (de communications téléphoniques)
tapping[2] *n* (*knocking*) petits coups *mpl*; (*with hand*) tapotement *m*
taproom ['tæpruːm] *n* bar *m*
taproot ['tæpruːt] *n Bot* racine *f* pivotante, pivot *m*
tar[1] [tɑːr] *n* **(a)** (*for roads, in cigarettes*) goudron *m*; *Fig F* **to spoil the ship for a ha'porth of t.** tout gâcher pour des économies de bouts de chandelle; **t. paper** papier *m* goudronné **(b)** *Old-fashioned Naut F* **(Jack) t.** (*sailor*) loup *m* de mer
tar[2] *vt* **(-rr-)** (*road, wood*) goudronner; (*pavement*) bitumer; *Naut* (*boat*) goudronner, brayer; **to t. and feather sb** rouler qn dans le goudron et les plumes; *Fig* **we're all tarred with the same brush** on nous a tous mis dans le même panier *ou* sac
taradiddle ['tærədıd(ə)l] *n F* (*lie*) bobard *m*
tarantella [tærən'telə] *n* (*dance*), *Mus* tarentelle *f*
tarantula [tə'ræntjʊlə] *n* (*spider*) tarentule *f*
tardily ['tɑːdılı] *adv Fml* **(a)** (*late*) tardivement; (*too late*) en retard **(b)** (*slowly*) lentement
tardiness ['tɑːdınıs] *n Fml* **(a)** (*lateness*) retard *m* **(b)** (*slowness*) lenteur *f* (**in doing sth** à faire qch)
tardy ['tɑːdı] *adj Fml* **(a)** (*late*) (*payment, reaction*) tardif **(b)** (*slow*) lent; (*unhurried*) peu empressé
tare[1] [teər] *n Bible* **tares** (*weeds*) ivraie *f*
tare[2] *n Com* tare *f*; (*of lorry*) poids *m* net; (*of vehicle*) poids à vide
tare[3] *vt Com* (*goods*) tarer; (*vehicle*) peser à vide
target[1] ['tɑːgıt] **1** *n Mil, Fig* cible *f*, objectif *m*; (*person*) cible; **moving t.** objectif mobile *ou* mouvant; **to land on t.** (*of bomb etc*) atteindre son objectif; **sitting t.** cible facile; *Fig* **to be an easy t.** être une cible facile; *Fig* **we're on t. (to meet the deadline)** nous sommes dans les temps (pour ce qui est du respect des échéances); **the project is/we're behind t.** le projet a/nous avons pris du retard; **to set oneself a t.** se fixer un but *ou* un objectif
2 *adj attrib* **t. area** zone *f* visée; **t. cost** coût *m* ciblé; *Comptr* **t. disk** disque *m*/disquette *f* de destination, disque/disquette cible; *Comptr* **t. drive** unité *f* de destination; *Comptr* **t. file** fichier *m* de destination; **t. population** population-cible *f*; **t. pricing** fixation *f* du prix en fonction de l'objectif; **t. readership** lectorat *m* cible; *Com* **t.-return pricing** fixation du prix en fonction du taux de rentabilité souhaité; **t. sales figure** chiffre *m* de ventes ciblé

target² *vt* **(a)** *Mil, Fig (aim at) (place, building etc)* viser, prendre pour cible; *Com (market)* cibler; **they targeted the magazine at 18-to-25-year-olds** le magazine a été conçu pour des lecteurs appartenant à la tranche 18-25 ans; **services should be better targeted** il faudrait qu'on cible mieux les services **(b)** *(direct) (missiles, advertising campaign)* diriger

target audience *n Rad, TV* public *m* cible *ou* visé

target date *n Com etc (for delivery etc)* date *f* ciblée *ou* visée

targeted ['tɑːgɪtɪd] *adj* visé, ciblé

target figure *n* objectif *m*

target group *n* groupe *m* cible

target language *n* langue *f* d'arrivée, langue cible

target market *n* marché *m* cible

target practice *n* exercices *mpl* de tir

target setting *n* arrêt *m* des objectifs

targetting ['tɑːgɪtɪŋ] *n* **(a)** *(setting targets)* détermination *f* d'objectifs; **because of unrealistic t.** en raison d'objectifs non réalistes **(b)** *Mktg* ciblage *m* **(c)** *(of funds, resources etc)* **we need better t. of resources** il nous faut mieux cibler les ressources

tariff ['tærɪf] **1** *n* **(a)** *(at customs)* tarif *m*; **reduced t.** tarif réduit; **full t.** plein tarif; **t. barrier** *or* **wall** barrière *f* douanière *ou* tarifaire **(b)** *(price list)* tarif *m*, tableau *m* des prix **2** *adj* tarifaire

tarmac®¹ ['tɑːmæk] *n* **(a)** *Constr* macadam *m*, goudron *m* **(b)** *Av (runway)* piste *f*

tarmac² *vt (pt, pp* **tarmacked***) (road etc)* goudronner, macadamiser

tarmacadam [tɑːmə'kædəm] *n* = **tarmac¹ (a)**

tarn [tɑːn] *n (in mountains)* petit lac *m* de montagne

tarnish¹ ['tɑːnɪʃ] *n* ternissure *f*

tarnish² **1** *vt (surface of metal, person's reputation)* ternir **2** *vi (of metal etc)* se ternir

tarnishing ['tɑːnɪʃɪŋ] *n (of metal)* ternissure *f*

tarot ['tærəʊ] *n Cards* tarot *m*; **t. cards** tarots

tarp [tɑːp] *n Am F* = **tarpaulin**

tarpaulin [tɑː'pɔːlɪn] *n (fabric)* toile *f* goudronnée; *(sheet)* bâche *f*, prélart *m*

tarragon ['tærəgən] *n (plant), Culin* estragon *m*; **t. vinegar** vinaigre *m* à l'estragon

tarry¹ ['tɑːrɪ] *adj* **(a)** *(made of tar)* goudronneux, bitumineux **(b)** *(covered, stained with tar)* couvert de goudron

tarry² ['tærɪ] *vi Lit* **(a)** *(stay)* rester, demeurer **(at** *or* **in a place** dans un endroit) **(b)** *(delay)* s'attarder **(over sth** sur qch)

tarsus, *pl* **-i** ['tɑːsəs, -aɪ] *n Anat* tarse *m*

tart¹ [tɑːt] *n* **(a)** *esp Br Culin* tarte *f*; *(small)* tartelette *f* **(b)** *F (prostitute)* putain *f*, poule *f*; *Pej (promiscuous woman)* pute *f*; *(woman)* pépée *f*, *Pej* grognasse *f*; *Pej* **the silly t.** cette andouille

tart² *adj (in taste)* au goût âpre, aigrelet; *(tone)* acerbe, aigre

▶ **tart up** *vtsep F usu Pej (room, car etc)* retaper; **to t. oneself up** se faire beau; **this car's just a tarted up version of the …** cette voiture n'est qu'une version améliorée du …

tartan ['tɑːt(ə)n] *n Tex (cloth or pattern)* tartan *m*, écossais *m*; **t. shirt** chemise *f* écossaise

Tartar ['tɑːtər] **1** *adj* tatar **2** *n* **(a)** Tatar, *f* Tatare **(b)** *Fig Pej (man)* homme *m* intraitable; *(woman)* mégère *f*

tartar ['tɑːtər] *n (on teeth), Ch* tartre *m*

tartaric [tɑː'tærɪk] *adj Ch (acid etc)* tartrique

tartly ['tɑːtlɪ] *adv (to say)* d'un ton acerbe

tartness ['tɑːtnɪs] *n (of fruit, wine, tone)* aigreur *f*

tarty ['tɑːtɪ] *adj Sl Pej (clothes etc)* vulgaire; **to look t.** avoir l'air d'une pute

task [tɑːsk] *n* **(a)** travail *m*, -aux, tâche *f*; **these are your tasks** voici votre travail; **their t. is to …** leur travail *ou* tâche consiste à …; **the unpleasant t. of informing the parents** la tâche désagréable d'informer les parents; **it's an endless t.** c'est un travail sans fin; **to set sb a t.** imposer une tâche à qn **(b) to take sb to t. for (doing) sth** prendre qn à partie *ou* réprimander qn pour (avoir fait) qch

taskforce ['tɑːskfɔːs] *n Mil* corps *m* expéditionnaire; *Fig (to investigate)* commission *f*; *(to do special job)* groupe *m* de travail

taskmaster, taskmistress ['tɑːskmɑːstər, -mɪstrɪs] *n* **he is a hard t.** il est terriblement exigeant; *(stronger)* c'est un véritable tyran

Tasmania [tæz'meɪnɪə] *n* Tasmanie *f*

Tasmanian [tæz'meɪnɪən] **1** *adj* tasmanien **2** *n* Tasmanien, -ienne

TASS [tæs] *n (abbr* **telegraphic news agency of the Soviet Union)** TASS *f*

tassel ['tæs(ə)l] *n* **(a)** *(on furniture, clothing etc)* gland *m* **(b)** *Bot (on corn)* barbe *f*

tasselled ['tæs(ə)ld] *adj* à glands, orné de glands

taste¹ [teɪst] *n* **(a)** *(flavour)* goût *m*, saveur *f*; **it has a burnt t.** cela a un goût de brûlé; **this drink has no t.** cette boisson n'a pas de goût *ou* est insipide; *Fig* **the whole business left a nasty t. in my mouth** toute cette histoire m'a franchement dégoûté *ou* m'a laissé un méchant arrière-goût

(b) *(sense of)* **t.** goût *m*

(c) *(small amount)* **a t. of cheese** *etc* un petit peu de fromage *etc*; **a t. of wine** *etc* une petite gorgée de vin *etc*; **have a t. of this claret** goûtez-moi ce bordeaux; *Fig* **to give sb a t. of the whip** faire tâter du fouet à qn; **this was my first t. of freedom** c'était la première fois que je goûtais à la liberté; **she's already had a t. of prison** elle a déjà tâté de la prison; **is this a t. of things to come?** est-ce là un avant-goût de ce qui nous attend?; **to give sb a t. of their own medicine** rendre à qn la monnaie de sa pièce

(d) *(liking)* goût *m* **(for** pour); **to have a t. for** *(music etc)* aimer, avoir le goût de; **to have expensive tastes** avoir des goûts de luxe; **to acquire** *or* **develop a t. for sth** prendre goût à qch; **to find sth to one's t.** trouver qch à son goût; *Culin* **add sugar to t.** on ajoute du sucre à volonté; **it's a matter of t.** c'est une question de goût; *prov* **everyone to his t.** des goûts et des couleurs on ne discute pas, chacun ses goûts

(e) *(judgement)* goût *m*; **she has excellent t. in dress** elle s'habille avec (beaucoup de) goût; **to be in perfect t.** être d'un goût parfait; **in bad t.** de mauvais goût; **it would be bad t. to wear that to a funeral** il serait de mauvais goût de porter cela à un enterrement

taste² **1** *vt* **(a)** *(distinguish taste of)* sentir, percevoir la saveur de; **I can't t. anything when I have a cold** les aliments n'ont plus aucun goût quand je suis enrhumé; **can't you t. the cinnamon?** tu ne sens pas la cannelle?; **I can t. something like cloves in it** ça sent un peu le clou de girofle

(b) *(sample quality of) (dish)* goûter; *(wines, teas etc)* déguster

(c) *(get a little taste of)* goûter de *ou* à; *(liquid)* boire une petite gorgée de; *Fig (whip, prison etc)* tâter de; **I haven't even tasted it** je n'y ai pas même goûté; **he had not tasted food for three days** il n'avait pas mangé depuis trois jours; **to t. happiness/success** goûter au bonheur/à la réussite

2 *vi* **the cake tasted of lemon** le gâteau avait un goût de citron; **it tastes like spinach** ça a un goût d'épinard; **to t. good/bad** être bon/mauvais, avoir un bon/mauvais goût; **it tastes fine to me** moi je trouve ça bon; **it tastes salty** c'est salé; **it tastes funny** ça a un drôle de goût; **it doesn't t. of anything to me** moi, je trouve que ça ne sent rien; *esp Lit* **to t. of despair/defeat** connaître le désespoir/la défaite

taste bud *n* papille *f* gustative

tasteful ['teɪstfʊl] *adj (remark, action)* de bon goût; *(decoration)* fait avec goût

tastefully ['teɪstfəlɪ] *adv* avec goût

tastefulness ['teɪstfʊlnɪs] *n* bon goût *m*

tasteless ['teɪstlɪs] *adj* **(a)** *(food etc)* sans goût, fade, insipide; **the poison is t. and odourless** le poison est inodore et sans saveur **(b)** *(clothes, remarks etc)* de mauvais goût

tastelessly ['teɪstlɪslɪ] *adv (to dress, furnish etc)* sans goût

tastelessness ['teɪstlɪsnɪs] *n* **(a)** *(of food)* insipidité *f*, fadeur *f* **(b)** *(of person, clothes, remark etc)* manque *m* de goût

taster ['teɪstər] *n* **(a)** *(person) (of wines, teas etc)* dégustateur, -trice **(b)** *(foretaste)* **this is just a t. (of what's to come)** ceci n'est qu'un avant-goût (de ce qui va suivre)

tastiness ['teɪstɪnɪs] *n* saveur *f ou* goût *m* agréable

tasting ['teɪstɪŋ] *n (of wines)* dégustation *f*

tasty ['teɪstɪ] *adj* **(a)** *(dish, meal)* savoureux; **it's not very t.** ça n'a pas beaucoup de goût; **a t. morsel** un mets succulent **(b)** *Br F (good-looking)* bien foutu; **she's a t. piece** c'est un beau morceau

tat¹ [tæt] *n see* **tit²**

tat² *n F (junk)* camelote *f*

ta-ta [tæ'tɑː] *int Br F* au revoir!

Tatar ['tɑːtər] **1** *adj* tatar; **T. Republic** République *f* de Tatarie **2** *n* Tatar *m*, Tatare *f*

Tatary ['tɑːtərɪ] *n* Tatarie *f*

tater ['teɪtər] *n Br Sl (potato)* patate *f*

tatter ['tætər] *n* lambeau *m*, loque *f*; **in tatters** en lambeaux, en loques; *Fig (reputation, confidence)* anéanti; **to tear sb's reputation to tatters** ruiner la réputation de qn

tattered ['tætəd] *adj (clothes)* en loques, en lambeaux; *(person)* déguenillé, loqueteux

tattie ['tætɪ] *n esp Scot F (potato)* patate *f*

tattle¹ ['tæt(ə)l] *n (gossip, rumour)* commérages *mpl*, potins *mpl*

tattle² *vi (gossip)* commérer, cancaner

tattler ['tætlər] *n (gossip, rumour-monger)* commère *f*, cancanier, -ière

tattoo[1] [tə'tuː] *n Mil* (**a**) (*drum signal*) retraite *f* (du soir); **to beat** *or* **sound the t.** battre *ou* sonner la retraite (**b**) (*parade*) parade *f* militaire
tattoo[2] *n* (*design*) tatouage *m*; **a t. of an anchor, an anchor t.** un tatouage représentant une ancre; **t. artist** tatoueur *m*
tattoo[3] *vt* tatouer
tattooing [tə'tuːɪŋ] *n* tatouage *m*
tattooist [tə'tuːɪst] *n* tatoueur *m*
tatty ['tætɪ] *adj F* (*in poor condition*) miteux; (*of poor quality*) minable
taught *see* **teach[2]**
taunt[1] [tɔːnt] *n* (*words*) sarcasme *m*, raillerie *f*
taunt[2] *vt* accabler de sarcasmes; **to t. sb into action** pousser qn à agir en usant de sarcasmes; **to t. sb with sth** railler qn à propos de qch
taunting ['tɔːntɪŋ] *adj* sarcastique, railleur
tauntingly ['tɔːntɪŋlɪ] *adv* d'un ton sarcastique *ou* railleur
Taurus ['tɔːrəs] *n Astron* le Taureau; **I'm (a) T.** je suis Taureau
taut [tɔːt] *adj* (*rope*) tendu; (*muscle*) tendu, contracté; (*prose, style, sentence*) dépouillé; **she looked t.** elle avait l'air tendu; **t. situation** situation *f* tendue
tauten ['tɔːt(ə)n] **1** *vt* (*cable etc*) tendre **2** *vi* se tendre
tautness ['tɔːtnɪs] *n* (*of cable etc*) raideur *f*; (*of muscles*) tension *f*; (*of piece of prose*) caractère *m* dépouillé
tautological [tɔːtə'lɒdʒɪk(ə)l] *adj* tautologique
tautology [tɔː'tɒlədʒɪ] *n* tautologie *f*
tavern ['tæv(ə)n] *n* (*in proper names*), *Lit* taverne *f*, cabaret *m*
tawdriness ['tɔːdrɪnɪs] *n* (*of piece of jewellery*) clinquant *m*, faux éclat *m*; (*of decor*) clinquant; **there was a t. about everything in the hotel** tout dans l'hôtel était d'un luxe tapageur
tawdry ['tɔːdrɪ] *adj* (**a**) (*clothing, ornament*) tape-à-l'œil, tapageur; (*decor*) clinquant; **t. jewellery** clinquant *m*, toc *m*; **a t. hotel** un hôtel à la décoration tape-à-l'œil (**b**) (*conduct, motive etc*) lâche
tawny ['tɔːnɪ] *adj* fauve; **t. eagle** aigle *m* ravisseur; **t. owl** chouette *f* hulotte; **t. port** porto *m* qui a jauni dans le fût
tax[1] [tæks] *n* (**a**) *Admin* impôt *m*, taxe *f*; **you pay out a small fortune in t.** on paye une petite fortune en impôts; **before t.** hors taxe, HT; (*income*) avant impôt; **direct/indirect t.** impôt direct/indirect; **income t.** impôt sur le revenu; **capital gains t.** impôt sur les plus-values; *Br* **value added t.**, *US* **processing t.** taxe à la valeur ajoutée; **to levy a t. on sth** frapper qch d'un droit; **t. allowance** déduction *f* fiscale, abattement *m* fiscal; **t. assessment** avis *m* d'imposition, fixation *f* de l'impôt; **t. benefit** avantage *m* fiscal; **t. burden** charge *f ou*; pression *f* fiscale, poids *m* de la fiscalité; **t. code** barème *m* fiscal; **t. clearance** quitus *m* fiscal; **t. consultant** conseiller *m* fiscal, fiscaliste *mf*; **t. credit** avoir *m* fiscal; **t. cut** baisse *f ou* réduction *f* des impôts; **t. domicile** foyer *m ou* domicile *m* fiscal; **t. exempt** exempt d'impôts; **t. exemption** exonération *f ou* exemption *f* d'impôts, exonération fiscale; **t. expert** expert *m* fiscal; **t. impact** incidence *f* fiscale; **t. incentive** incitation *f* fiscale; **t. law** droit *m* fiscal; **t. loophole** échappatoire *f* fiscale; **t. paid** *adj* net d'impôt; **t. point** date *f* de facturation; **t. provision** disposition *f* fiscale; **t. reduction** abattement *m* fiscal; **t. refund** remise *f* fiscale; (*on goods*) détaxe *f*; **t. relief** dégrèvement *m* (fiscal); **t. revenue** recettes *fpl* fiscales; **t. shelter** manœuvre *f* pour diminuer les impôts à payer; **t. specialist** fiscaliste *mf*; **t. stamp** timbre *m* fiscal; **t. system** système *m* fiscal, fiscalité *f*, régime *m* d'imposition; **t. tolerance** tolérance *f* fiscale
(**b**) (*strain*) charge *f*
tax[2] *vt* (**a**) *Admin* (*person*) imposer, frapper d'un impôt; (*luxury items etc*) taxer; **to t. income** imposer le revenu; **to be heavily taxed** être lourdement imposé; **small businesses are being taxed out of existence** accablées d'impôts, les petites entreprises disparaissent; **we're being taxed out of existence** on nous accable d'impôts; *Br Aut* **taxed** avec vignette
(**b**) (*put under strain*) mettre à l'épreuve; **to t. sb's intellect/imagination** éprouver l'intelligence/l'imagination de qn; **to t. sb's patience to the limit** abuser sérieusement de la patience de qn
(**c**) *esp Lit* (*accuse*) **to t. sb with sth** taxer qn de qch; **to t. sb with doing sth** accuser qn d'avoir fait qch
taxable ['tæksəbl] *adj* (**a**) (*income, land etc*) imposable, taxable; **to make sth t.** imposer qch; **t. income** revenu *m* imposable, assiette *f* d'impôt; **t. profit** bénéfice *m* imposable; **t. transaction** opération *f* imposable (**b**) *Jur* **costs t. to sb** frais *mpl* à la charge de qn
taxation [tæk'seɪʃən] *n* (*imposing taxes*) imposition *f*; (*taxes*) charges *fpl* fiscales (*tax revenue*) impôts *mpl*, taxes *fpl*
tax authorities *npl* administration *f* fiscale
tax avoidance *n* évasion *f* fiscale
tax bracket *n* tranche *f* d'imposition
tax centre *n* centre *m* des impôts, CDI *m*
tax collection *n* recouvrement *m* d'impôts, perception *f* d'impôts
tax collector *n* percepteur *m* (d'impôt), receveur *m* des impôts
tax-deductible *adj* déductible des impôts
tax deduction *n* prélèvement *m* fiscal; **t. at source** perception *f* à la source
tax disc *n Br* (*on vehicle*) vignette *f*
tax evasion *n* fraude *f ou* évasion *f* fiscale
tax exile *n* = personne *f* vivant à l'étranger pour fuir le fisc
tax-free *adj* exempt d'impôts
tax-free shop *n* boutique *f* hors taxes
tax-free shopping *n* shopping *m* hors taxes
tax haven *n* paradis *m* fiscal
taxi[1] ['tæksɪ] *n* taxi *m*; **to go by t.** aller en taxi; **t. driver** chauffeur *m* de taxi; **t. fare** prix *m* de la course; **t. fares** tarif *m* des taxis; **t. rank** *or esp Am* **stand** station *f* de taxis
taxi[2] *vi* (*pt, pp* **taxied**; *prp* **taxying**) (*of aircraft*) rouler; **the plane taxied back to the terminal** l'avion regagna le terminal
taxicab ['tæksɪkæb] *n* taxi *m*
taxidermist ['tæksɪdɜːmɪst] *n* taxidermiste *mf*
taxidermy ['tæksɪdɜːmɪ] *n* taxidermie *f*
taximeter ['tæksɪmiːtər] *n* taximètre *m*, compteur *m* (de taxi)
taxing ['tæksɪŋ] *adj* (*job, course*) ardu; **these long hours are very t.** ces longues journées sont complètement éreintantes
tax inspector *n* inspecteur *m* des impôts
taxiplane ['tæksɪpleɪn] *n* avion-taxi *m*, *pl* avions-taxis
tax man *n* fisc *m*
tax office *n* (bureau *m* de) perception *f*
taxonomic [tæksə'nɒmɪk] *adj* taxonomique
taxonomy [tæk'sɒnəmɪ] *n* taxonomie *f*
taxpayer ['tækspeɪər] *n* contribuable *mf*
tax rebate *n* abattement *m ou* dégrèvement *m* fiscal
tax return *n* (*form*) déclaration *f* d'impôt, feuille *f* d'impôts; **to make one's t.** faire sa déclaration d'impôt
tax year *n* année *f* d'imposition, exercice *m* fiscal
TB [tiː'biː] *n Med* (*abbr* **tuberculosis**) BCG *m*
T-bar *n Ski* téléski *m*, tire-fesses *m inv*
T-bone *n Culin* **T. steak** steak *m* d'aloyau
tbs, tbsp *Culin* (*abbr* **tablespoonful**) cuillerée *f* à soupe
T-card *n* fiche *f* en T
TCP® [tiːsiː'piː] *n* (*antiseptic*) ≈ Merchryl® *m*
TD [tiː'diː] *n Irish Pol abbr* = membre *m* de la chambre basse du Parlement irlandais
tea [tiː] *n* (**a**) (*leaves, drink*) thé *m*; (*herbal infusion*) tisane *f*, infusion *f*; **camomile** *etc* **t.** infusion de camomille *etc*; **to drink t.** boire *ou* prendre du thé; **a cup of t.** une tasse de thé; **t. and coffee making facilities** nécessaire *m* pour préparer le thé et le café; **China t.** thé de Chine; **black/green t.** thé noir/vert; **t. blend** mélange *m* des thés
(**b**) [①A6,d,iii] *esp Br* (*meal*) (**afternoon**) **t.** thé *m*, = goûter *m*; **high t.** repas *m* du soir; *Scot* **t.** (*dinner*) dîner *m*; **to ask sb to t.** inviter qn à (venir) prendre le thé; **to give a t. party** inviter des gens pour le thé; (*for children*) organiser un goûter; **t. service** *or* **set** service *m* à thé; **t. table** table *f* à thé
(**c**) (*plant*) thé *m*
tea bag *n* sachet *m* de thé
tea boy *n* larbin *m*
tea break *n* = pause-café *f*, *pl* pauses-café
tea caddy *n* boîte *f* à thé
teacake ['tiːkeɪk] *n Br Culin* (genre *m* de) petit pain *m*
teach[1] [tiːtʃ] *n F* (*teacher*) prof *mf*
teach[2] (*pt, pp* **taught** [tɔːt]) **1** *vt* (*subject*) enseigner; **to t. sb sth, to t. sth to sb** enseigner *ou* apprendre qch à qn; **to t. sb (how) to do sth** apprendre à qn à faire qch; **to t. oneself sth** apprendre qch tout seul; **your Japanese is very good, who taught you?** tu parles très bien japonais, qui t'a appris?; **I taught myself** j'ai appris tout seul; **who taught you to drive!** où as-tu appris à conduire!; **can you t. me the butterfly stroke?** est-ce que tu peux m'apprendre la nage papillon?; **he teaches the young pupils** il fait la classe *ou* l'école aux petits; **she teaches the piano** elle est professeur de piano; **he teaches French** il enseigne le français, il est professeur de français; *Am* **to t. school** enseigner; (*as profession*) être dans l'enseignement; **the way history is taught** la manière dont on enseigne l'histoire; *Prov* **you can't t. your grandmother to suck eggs** ce n'est pas au vieux singe qu'on apprend à faire la grimace; *F* **to t. sb a lesson** donner une leçon à qn; *F* **that'll t. him!** ça lui apprendra!; *F* **to t. sb a thing or two** dégourdir qn; *F* **I'll t. you to speak to me like that!** je vous apprendrai à me parler comme ça!

2 *vi* enseigner; (*as profession*) être dans l'enseignement; **she has taught abroad** elle a enseigné à l'étranger; **when you've been teaching for 25 years ...** quand tu as passé 25 ans dans l'enseignement ...

teachable ['ti:tʃəb(ə)l] *adj* **(a)** (*person*) qui apprend facilement **(b)** (*subject*) enseignable; **it's not t.** c'est impossible à enseigner; **it's not easily t.** cela n'est pas facile à enseigner

teacher ['ti:tʃər] *n* (*at primary school*) instituteur, -trice, maître *m*/maîtresse *f* d'école; (*at secondary school*) professeur *m*, enseignant, -ante; **history/French/maths t.** professeur d'histoire/de français/de maths; **to become a t.** devenir professeur; **t.'s pet** chouchou *mf* du professeur; **t.-pupil ratio** taux *m* d'encadrement des élèves

teacher training *n* formation *f* pédagogique; **to do one's t.** suivre une formation pédagogique; **to get one's t. certificate** obtenir son certificat d'aptitude pédagogique; **t. college** école *f* normale

tea chest *n* caisse *f* à thé

teach-in *n* séminaire *m*

teaching ['ti:tʃɪŋ] *n* **(a)** (*profession, action*) enseignement *m*; **a low/high standard of maths/language t.** un niveau élevé/bas dans l'enseignement des maths/des langues; **to go into t.** entrer dans l'enseignement; **t. aids** matériel *m ou* équipement *m* pédagogique; *Med* **t. hospital** = centre *m* hospitalier universitaire, CHU *m*; **t. method** méthode *f* d'enseignement; **t. practice** stage *m* pratique d'enseignement; **the t. profession** (*teachers*) le corps enseignant; **the t. staff** (*of primary school*) les instituteurs *mpl*; (*of secondary school*) les professeurs *mpl*
(b) (*classes*) cours *mpl*; **most of the t. is done in the morning** la plupart des cours ont lieu le matin
(c) (*doctrine*) doctrine *f*; **teachings** préceptes *mpl*

tea cloth *n* torchon *m*

tea cosy *n* couvre-théière *m*, *pl* couvre-théières

teacup ['ti:kʌp] *n* tasse *f* à thé

teacupful ['ti:kʌpfʊl] *n* (*measure*) tasse *f* (**of** de)

teak [ti:k] *n* (*wood, tree*) teck *m*, tek *m*

teal [ti:l] *n* (*pl usu* **teal**) (*duck*) sarcelle *f*

tea lady *n* = employée *f* qui sert le thé dans une entreprise

tea leaf *n* feuille *f* de thé; *Br Sl* (*thief*) voleur, -euse; (**used**) **tea leaves** marc *m* de thé; **to read the tea leaves** lire dans le marc de thé

team[1] [ti:m] *n* [ⓘA11,g,i] (*of players, workers etc*) équipe *f*; (*of horses, oxen*) attelage *m*; **football t.** équipe de football; **member of a t., t. member** membre *m* d'une équipe; *Sp* équipier *m*; **he's one of the t.** il fait partie de l'équipe; **a t. effort** un travail d'équipe; **t. games** jeux *mpl* d'équipe; **he's not much of a t. player** (*at football*), *Fig* il n'a pas l'esprit d'équipe; **t. spirit** l'esprit *m* d'équipe; **t. sports** sports *mpl* d'équipe

team[2] *vti* = **team up**

▶ **team up 1** *vi* s'associer (**with sb** avec qn); **the two companies have teamed up to work on this project** les deux entreprises se sont associées pour travailler sur ce projet **2** *vtsep* associer, mettre en collaboration (**with** avec)

team-mate *n Sp* coéquipier *m*

teamster ['ti:mstər] *n* **(a)** (*of mules etc*) conducteur *m* (*d'attelage*), charretier *m* **(b)** *US* (*trucker*) camionneur *m*, routier *m*

teamwork ['ti:mwɜ:k] *n* (*combined effort*) travail *m* d'équipe; (*ability to work together*) collaboration *f*; *Sp* jeu *m* d'équipe; **success due to t.** réussite due à un travail d'équipe

tea plant *n* arbre *m* à thé, théier *m*

tea plantation *n* plantation *f* de thé

tea planter *n* planteur *m* de thé

teapot ['ti:pɒt] *n* théière *f*

tear[1] [tɪər] *n* (*from eye*) larme *f*; **in tears** en larmes; **on the verge of tears** au bord des larmes; **to burst into tears** fondre en larmes, éclater en sanglots; **to bring tears to sb's eyes** faire venir des larmes aux yeux de qn; **to shed bitter tears/tears of joy** verser des larmes amères/de joie; **crocodile tears** larmes de crocodile

tear[2] [teər] *n* (*rip*) déchirure *f*; (*in garment*) accroc *m*

tear[3] (*pt* **tore** [tɔ:r]; *pp* **torn** [tɔ:n]) **1** *vt* (*dress, letter etc*) déchirer; **to t. a muscle** (*of person*) se déchirer un muscle; **torn tendon** tendon *m* déchiré; **to t. a hole in sth** faire un trou *ou* un accroc à qch; **to t. sth in two** *or* **in half** déchirer qch en deux; **to t. sth open** ouvrir qch en le déchirant; **to t. sth to pieces** (*document, bank note etc*) déchirer qch en mille morceaux; *Fig* (*film, argument etc*) mettre qch en pièces; **the fox was torn to pieces by the hounds** le renard a été déchiqueté *ou* mis en pièces par la meute; *Fig* **to t. sb to pieces** mettre qn en pièces, écharper qn; *Fig* **they'll t. you to pieces** ils vont vous mettre en pièces, vous allez vous faire écharper; *Fig* **to t. sb's character to shreds** *or* **pieces** démolir qn; **country torn by civil war** pays déchiré par la guerre civile; **torn between two feelings** tiraillé entre deux émotions; *Fig* **that's torn it** il ne manquait plus que ça; *Fig* **to t. one's hair** s'arracher les cheveux
2 *vi* **(a)** (*of material, muscle etc*) se déchirer
(b) to t. at sth déchirer qch

▶ **tear about, tear around 1** *vi* (*rush around*) courir partout; **I've been tearing around on my bike all day** j'ai pédalé comme un fou toute la journée; **he's always tearing around** il est toujours à se démener; **he tears about from auction to auction** il est toujours à courir d'une vente aux enchères à une autre **2** *vipo* **he spends most of his time tearing around the country** il passe la plus grande partie de son temps à sillonner le pays; **to t. around the shops** faire des courses en vitesse; **to t. around a museum** parcourir un musée à toute vitesse

▶ **tear along 1** *vi* (*go fast*) aller à toute vitesse, *F* foncer; **to t. along at top speed** aller à toute vitesse; **to t. along at 100 mph** foncer à 100 à l'heure **2** *vipo* (*go fast on*) **he was tearing along the road** (*in vehicle, on bike*) il dévalait la rue; (*on foot*) il descendait la rue à toute vitesse

▶ **tear away 1** *vtsep* (*remove by tearing*) arracher (**from** de) **2** *vtas* **to t. oneself away from** (*leave reluctantly*) (*television, book etc*) s'arracher de; **I couldn't t. myself away from the place** je n'arrivais pas à me décider à partir **3** *vi* (*leave at high speed*) partir à toute vitesse; (*of car*) démarrer en trombe

▶ **tear down** *vtsep* (*take down forcefully*) (*poster etc*) arracher (**from** de); (*wall, building etc*) démolir; (*statue*) renverser

▶ **tear into** *vipo* **(a)** (*attack physically*) attaquer, assaillir; **the lion's teeth tore into the antelope's flesh** le lion lacéra la chair de l'antilope de *ou* avec ses crocs **(b)** (*attack verbally*) incendier, passer un savon à

▶ **tear off 1** *vtsep* (*detach by tearing*) arracher (**from** de); **he had had one of his arms torn off by a machine** il avait eu le bras arraché par une machine; *F* **to t. sb off a strip, to t. a strip off sb** donner *ou* passer un savon à qn **2** *vi* = **tear away 3**

▶ **tear out 1** *vtsep* (*remove by tearing*) arracher (**from** de); **to t. a page out of a book** arracher une page d'un livre; *Fig* **he was tearing his hair out** il s'arrachait les cheveux **2** *vi* (*leave at high speed*) partir en trombe; **she tore out of the house after them** elle sortit en trombe de la maison derrière eux

▶ **tear up 1** *vtsep* **(a)** (*tear into small pieces*) (*letter etc*) déchirer; (*ground, fields etc*) (*of tanks, car wheels etc*) labourer; (*deliberately*) (*of JCB*) défoncer; (*contract*) déchirer; *Fig* oublier **(b)** (*pull up*) (*plant, tree*) déraciner; (*railings, telegraph pole*) arracher **2** *vipo* (*go up fast*) **to t. up the stairs** monter l'escalier quatre à quatre

tearaway ['teərəweɪ] *n Br* casse-cou *m inv*

teardrop ['tɪədrɒp] *n* larme *f*

tear duct *n Anat* canal *m* lacrymal

tearful ['tɪəfʊl] *adj* (*person*) en pleurs; (*farewell*) déchirant; **in a t. voice** avec des larmes dans la voix; **she gets all t.** les larmes lui montent aux yeux

tearfully ['tɪəfəlɪ] *adv* (*crying*) en pleurant; (*on verge of tears*) les larmes aux yeux

tear gas *n* gaz *m* lacrymogène; **t. bomb** bombe *f* lacrymogène

tearing ['teərɪŋ] *n* (*of fabric etc*) déchirement *m*; **a t. sound** un bruit de déchirure; *F* **to be in a t. hurry** être terriblement pressé

tearjerker ['tɪədʒɜ:kər] *n F* (*film, book*) mélo *m*

tearless ['tɪəlɪs] *adj* **t. grief** chagrin *m* sans larmes

tear-off ['teərɒf] *adj* (*label etc*) perforé; (*reply slip etc*) détachable; **t. calendar** calendrier *m* éphéméride

tearoom ['ti:ru:m] *n* salon *m* de thé

tea rose *n* rose *f* thé

tearstained ['tɪəsteɪnd] *adj* (*face*) (*dirty*) barbouillé de larmes; (*in tears*) baigné de larmes

tease[1] [ti:z] *n* **(a)** (*person*) taquin, -ine; **he's a t.** il est taquin **(b)** (*sexual*) (*woman*) allumeuse *f*; **don't be a t.** arrête de m'allumer

tease[2] **1** *vt* **(a)** (*person*) taquiner; (*dog etc*) embêter; (*maliciously*) tourmenter; **to t. sb about sth** taquiner qn à propos de qch **(b)** (*sexually*) allumer **(c)** *Tex* (*comb out*) (*fabric etc*) effiler, effilocher; (*wool*) démêler **(d) he teased the wire through the slot** avec beaucoup de minutie, il a réussi à mettre le fil dans la fente; **he teased the engine into life** il a réussi à démarrer la voiture à force de la bichonner **2** *vi* **don't worry, he's just teasing** ne t'inquiète pas, il fait ça pour rire

▶ **tease out** *vtsep* **(a)** *Fig* **she carefully teases out the important facts** elle prend soin de dégager les faits importants; **to t. information out of sb** faire donner des informations à qn **(b)** *Tex* = **tease**[2] **1(c)**

teasel ['ti:z(ə)l] *n* **(a)** (*plant*) cardère *f* **(b)** *Tex* carde *f*
teaser ['ti:zər] *n* **(a)** = **tease**[1] **(b)** *F* (*problem*) question *f* difficile, colle *f*; (*advert*) teaser *f*
teashop ['ti:ʃɒp] *n* salon *m* de thé
teasing ['ti:zɪŋ] **1** *adj* (*tone etc*) taquin **2** *n* (*provoking*) taquinerie *f*
teasingly ['ti:zɪŋlɪ] *adv* (*in a teasing tone*) sur le ton de la taquinerie; (*in order to tease*) pour taquiner
teaspoon ['ti:spu:n] *n* cuillère *f ou* cuiller *f* à café
teaspoonful ['ti:spu:nfʊl] *n* cuillerée *f* à café
tea strainer *n* passe-thé *m inv*, passoire *f ou* passette *f* à thé
teat [ti:t] *n* (*of woman*) mamelon *m*, bout *m* de sein, téton *m*; (*of cow etc*) trayon *m*; (*of feeding bottle*) tétine *f*
teatime ['ti:taɪm] *n* l'heure *f* du thé
tea towel *n* torchon *m*
tea urn *n* = grande bouilloire *f* servant à faire le thé pour les collectivités
teazel, teazle ['ti:z(ə)l] *n* = **teasel**
tech [tek] *n Br F* (*abbr* **technical college**) = lycée *m* technique
technical ['teknɪk(ə)l] *adj* (*term, dictionary, problem etc*) technique; **don't get t.** n'emploie pas de termes trop techniques; (*difficulty*) d'ordre technique; **t. director** *or* **manager** directeur *m* technique; **t. hitch** incident *m* technique; *Boxing* **t. knockout** victoire *f* sur un adversaire qui ne peut pas continuer; *Jur* **t. offence** quasi-délit *m*, *pl* quasi-délits; **t. specifications** spécifications *fpl* techniques; **t. standard** norme *f* technique
technical college *n Br* = lycée *m* technique
technical drawing *n* dessin *m* industriel
technicality [teknɪ'kælɪtɪ] *n* **(a)** (*of term*) technicité *f* **(b)** (*detail*) détail *m* technique; (*technical term*) terme *m* technique; *Jur* **she was acquitted on a t.** elle a été acquittée sur un point de droit
technically ['teknɪklɪ] *adv* **(a)** techniquement; (*to express oneself*) en termes techniques; **t., it shouldn't be able to fly** d'un point de vue technique, il ne devrait pas pouvoir voler **(b)** (*strictly, in reality*) en réalité; **t. (speaking), you're not allowed to do that** théoriquement tu n'as pas le droit de faire ça
technician [tek'nɪʃən] *n* technicien, -ienne
Technicolor® ['teknɪkʌlər] *adj, n Cin* Technicolor *m*
technique [tek'ni:k] *n* technique *f*; **his t. is poor** il manque de technique
technocracy [tek'nɒkrəsɪ] *n* technocratie *f*
technocrat ['teknəkræt] *n* technocrate *mf*
technological [teknə'lɒdʒɪk(ə)l] *adj* technologique
technologist [tek'nɒlədʒɪst] *n* technologue *mf*, technologiste *mf*
technology [tek'nɒlədʒɪ] *n* technologie *f*; **the lastest t.** la technologie de pointe *ou* la plus avancée; **t. transfer** transfert *m* de technologie
technophobia [teknəʊ'fəʊbɪə] *n* technophobie *f*
techy ['tetʃɪ] *adj* = **tetchy**
tectonic [tek'tɒnɪk] *adj* tectonique
tectonics [tek'tɒnɪks] *npl* [①**A10,c**] tectonique *f*
Ted [ted] *n Br F* (*teddy boy*) ≈ blouson *m* noir
tedder ['tedər] *n Agr* (*machine*) faneuse *f*
teddy ['tedɪ] *n* **(a)** *Br F* **t. boy** ≈ blouson *m* noir **(b)** **t. (bear)** (*toy*) ours *m* en peluche
tedious ['ti:dɪəs] *adj* (*job, speech etc*) ennuyeux, fastidieux; (*person, film*) ennuyeux; **how t. for you!** comme c'est ennuyeux!; **as he explained in t. detail** comme il l'a expliqué en de fastidieux détails
tediously ['ti:dɪəslɪ] *adv* d'une manière ennuyeuse, fastidieuse
tediousness, tedium ['ti:dɪəsnɪs, -dɪəm] *n* (*of job, existence, film*) manque *m* d'intérêt
tee[1] [ti:] *n Golf* (*support for ball*) tee *m*; (*piece of ground*) tertre *m ou* point *m* de départ
tee[2] *vt Golf* (*ball*) mettre sur un tee
▶ **tee off** *vi Golf* jouer le départ
▶ **tee up 1** *vi Golf* placer la balle sur le tee **2** *vtsep Golf* **to t. up the ball** placer la balle sur le tee; *Fig* **to t. up a deal** préparer le terrain pour obtenir un contrat; **to t. up a job for sb** apporter un travail à qn sur un plateau
teem [ti:m] *vi* **(a)** grouiller, fourmiller (**with** de); (*with ideas*) regorger (**with** en) **(b) the rain was teeming down** la pluie tombait à verse; **it's teeming with rain** il tombe des cordes
teeming ['ti:mɪŋ] *adj* **(a)** grouillant **(b) in the t. rain** sous la pluie battante
teen [ti:n] *adj F* = **teenage**; **t. idol** idole *f* des jeunes
teenage ['ti:neɪdʒ] *adj* (*boy, girl etc*) adolescent, jeune; (*problems*) de l'adolescence; (*party, novels*) d'adolescents; **in her t. years** quand elle était adolescente; **t. magazine** magazine *m* pour adolescents
teenager ['ti:neɪdʒər] *n* adolescent, -ente
teens [ti:nz] *npl* **one's t.** l'adolescence *f*; **to be in one's t.** être adolescent(e); **to be hardly out of one's t.** avoir juste vingt ans
teeny-bopper ['ti:nɪbɒpər] *n F* petite minette *f*
teeny(-weeny) ['ti:nɪ('wi:nɪ)], **teensy(-weensy)** ['ti:nzɪ('wi:nzɪ)] *adj F* minuscule, tout petit; **just a t. drop, please** juste une toute petite goutte, s'il vous plaît
teeshirt ['ti:ʃɜ:t] *n* tee-shirt *m*, T-shirt *m*
teeter[1] ['ti:tər] *n esp Am* (*seesaw*) jeu *m* de bascule, tapecul *m*
teeter[2] *vi* (*be unsteady*) chanceler; *Fig* **to t. on the brink of ruin/war** être à deux doigts de la ruine/d'un conflit armé
teethe [ti:ð] *vi* (*usu in progressive tenses*) faire ses (premières) dents, percer ses dents
teething ['ti:ðɪŋ] *n* dentition *f*, poussée *f* dentaire; **t. ring** anneau *m* de dentition; *Fig* **t. troubles** difficultés *fpl* initiales
teetotal [ti:'təʊt(ə)l] *adj* qui ne boit jamais d'alcool
teetotalism [ti:'təʊtəlɪz(ə)m] *n* abstention *f* de toute boisson alcoolisée; **after two weeks of enforced t.** après une quinzaine de jours au régime sec
teetotaller, *US* **teetotaler** [ti:'təʊt(ə)lər] *n* personne *f* qui ne boit jamais d'alcool
TEFL ['tef(ə)l] *n* (*abbr* **Teaching of English as a Foreign Language**) enseignement *m* de l'anglais langue étrangère; **T. course** formation *f* en anglais langue étrangère
tegument ['tegjʊmənt] *n* tégument *m*
tel (*abbr* **telephone**) tél.
telebanking ['telɪbænkɪŋ] *n* monétique *f*; (*home banking*) banque *f* à domicile
telecast[1] ['telɪkɑ:st] *n TV* émission *f* de télévision
telecast[2] *vt* (*pt, pp* **telecast**) téléviser
telecine ['telɪsɪnɪ] *n* télé-cinéma *m*
telecomms ['telɪkɒmz] *npl* télécommunications *fpl*
telecommunications [telɪkəmju:nɪ'keɪʃənz] *n* télécommunications *fpl*; **t. engineer** technicien *m* des télécommunications; **t. industry** industrie *f* des télécommunications; **t. link** liaison *f* de télécommunications; **t. satellite/network** satellite *m*/réseau *m* de télécommunications
telecommute ['teləkəmju:t] *vi* faire du télétravail, télétravailler
telecommuter ['teləkəmju:tər] *n* télétravailleur, -euse
telecommuting ['teləkəmju:tɪŋ] *n* télétravail *m*
teleconference ['telɪkɒnf(ə)rəns] *n* téléconférence *f*
teleconferencing ['telɪkɒnf(ə)rənsɪŋ] *n* téléconférences *fpl*
telefilm ['telɪfɪlm] *n* téléfilm *m*, film *m* télévisé
telegenic [telɪ'dʒenɪk] *adj* télégénique
telegram ['telɪgræm] *n* télégramme *m*; **greetings t.** télégramme de félicitations; **t. form** formule *f* de télégramme
telegraph[1] ['telɪgrɑ:f] *n* télégraphe *m*; *F* **bush t.** téléphone *m* arabe; **t. pole/wire** poteau *m*/fil *m* télégraphique
telegraph[2] **1** *vt* (*news*) télégraphier; (*person*) télégraphier à; *Sp* **to t. a punch/pass/***etc* téléphoner un coup/une passe/*etc* **2** *vi* télégraphier
telegrapher [tɪ'legrəfər] *n US* télégraphiste *mf*
telegraphese [telɪgrə'fi:z] *n* langage *m ou* style *m* télégraphique
telegraphic [telɪ'græfɪk] *adj* télégraphique; **t. money order** mandat *m* télégraphique; **t. payment** paiement *m* télégraphique
telegraphist [tɪ'legrəfɪst] *n* télégraphiste *mf*
telegraphy [tɪ'legrəfɪ] *n* télégraphie *f*
telejector ['telɪdʒektər] *n TV* projecteur *m* de télévision
telekinesis [telɪkɪ'ni:sɪs] *n* télékinésie *f*
telemarket ['telɪma:kɪt] *n* télémarché *m*
telemarketing ['telɪmɑ:kɪtɪŋ] *n* télémercatique *f*
telematics [telɪ'mætɪks] *n* [①**A10,c**] télématique *f*
Telemessage® ['telɪmesɪdʒ] *n Br* télégramme *m*
telemeter ['telɪmi:tər] *n* (*in surveying*) appareil *m* de télémesure; *Mil etc* télémètre *m*
teleological [telɪə'lɒdʒɪk(ə)l] *adj Phil* téléologique
teleology [telɪ'ɒlədʒɪ] *n Phil* téléologie *f*
telepathic [telɪ'pæθɪk] *adj* télépathique; (*person*) télépathe; **you must be t.!** tu dois avoir des dons de télépathie!; **tell me, I'm not t.!** dis-le moi, je ne suis pas médium!
telepathically [telɪ'pæθɪklɪ] *adv* (*to communicate*) par télépathie
telepathy [tɪ'lepəθɪ] *n* télépathie *f*
telepayment ['telɪpeɪmənt] *n* télépaiement *m*
telephone[1] ['telɪfəʊn] *n* [①**A71,5**] téléphone *m*; **to be on the t.** (*be subscriber*) avoir le téléphone, être abonné au téléphone; (*be speaking on it*) être au téléphone; **to speak to sb on the t.** avoir qn au téléphone; **come on, get off the t.!** allez, raccroche!; **you're wanted on the t.** on vous demande au téléphone; **to have a good t. manner** savoir bien parler au téléphone; *Mil* **field t.** téléphone de campagne; **public t.** téléphone public; **t. booking** réservation *f* par téléphone;

Am **t. booth** cabine *f* téléphonique; **t. code area** circonscription *f* téléphonique; **t. conversation** entretien *m* téléphonique; **t. help desk** assistance *f* téléphonique; **t. interview** entretien *m* téléphonique *ou* par téléphone; **t. interviewing** enquête *f* téléphonique, sondage *m* par téléphone; **t. jack** fiche *f* téléphonique; *Br* **t. kiosk** cabine *f* téléphonique; **t. line/network** ligne *f*/réseau *m* téléphonique; **t. link** liaison *f* téléphonique; **t. marketing** mercaphonie *f*, mercatique *f* téléphonique, téléaction *f*; **t. memo** fiche *f* téléphonique; **t. message** message *m* téléphoné *ou* téléphonique; **t. message pad** bloc *m* télémémo; **t. prospecting** télédémarchage *m*, démarchage *m* à distance; **t. reservation** réservation *f* par téléphone *ou* téléphonique; **t. services** services *mpl* téléphoniques; **t. subscriber** abonné *m* au téléphone; **t. survey** enquête *f* téléphonique

telephone[2] **1** *vi* téléphoner **(to** à**)**; **to t. for a taxi** appeler un taxi (par téléphone) **2** *vt* (*message*) téléphoner; (*person*) téléphoner à; **to t. a warning** envoyer un avertissement par téléphone; **to t. a bomb-warning to the police** prévenir la police par téléphone d'une alerte à la bombe

telephone book *n* annuaire *m* (du téléphone), annuaire téléphonique, bottin *m*

telephone box *n* cabine *f* téléphonique

telephone call *n* appel *m* téléphonique

telephone directory *n* annuaire *m* (du téléphone), annuaire téléphonique, bottin *m*

telephone exchange *n* central *m* téléphonique

telephone number *n* [①A71,5] numéro *m* de téléphone

telephone operator *n* téléphoniste *mf*, standardiste *mf*

telephone sales *npl* ventes *fpl* par téléphone, téléventes *fpl*

telephone salesman *n* télévendeur *m*, télé-acteur *m*

telephone saleswoman *n* télévendeuse *f*, télé-actrice *f*

telephone selling *n* vente *f* par téléphone, télévente *f*

telephone switchboard *n* standard *m* téléphonique

telephonic [telɪ'fɒnɪk] *adj* téléphonique

telephonist [tɪ'lefənɪst] *n Br* téléphoniste *mf*

telephony [tɪ'lefənɪ] *n* téléphonie *f*

telephotography [telɪfə'tɒgrəfɪ] *n* téléphotographie *f*

telephoto lens [telɪ'fəʊtəʊ] *n* téléobjectif *m*

teleprinter ['telɪprɪntər] *n* téléimprimeur *m*

Teleprompter® ['telɪprɒm(p)tər] *n TV* téléprompteur *m*, télésouffleur *m*

telesales *n* télévente(s) *f(pl)*, phoning *m*; **t. person** télévendeur *m*, télévendeuse *f*, télé-acteur *m*, télé-actrice *f*

telescope[1] ['telɪskəʊp] *n* **(reflecting) t.** télescope *m* (à réflexion *ou* à miroir); **(refracting) t.** lunette *f* (d'approche), longue-vue *f*, *pl* longues-vues; *Astron* réfracteur *m*; **radio t.** radiotélescope *m*

telescope[2] **1** *vt* (*train etc*) télescoper; *Fig* (*condense*) condenser **(into** en**)** **2** *vi* (*of train etc*) se télescoper; **parts made to t.** pièces qui s'emboîtent

telescopic [telɪs'kɒpɪk] *adj* **(a)** télescopique; (*visible with telescope*) visible au télescope; *Phot* **t. lens** téléobjectif *m*; **t. sight** (*of rifle*) lunette *f* **(b)** (*expanding*) télescopique; (*gangway etc*) coulissant; **t. damper** amortisseur *m* télescopique; **t. tripod** trépied *m* télescopique; **t. umbrella** parapluie *m* télescopique

teleselling ['telɪselɪŋ] *n* télévente *f*

teleshopping ['telɪʃɒpɪŋ] *n* télé-achat *m*

teletext ['telɪtekst] *n TV* télétexte *m*

telethon ['telɪθɒn] *n TV* téléthon *m*

teletype® ['telɪtaɪp] *n* télétype *m*

teletyper ['telɪtaɪpər] *n* télétype *m*

teletypewriter [telɪ'taɪpraɪtər] *n US* = **teleprinter**

televiewer ['telɪvjʊər] *n* téléspectateur, -trice

televise ['telɪvaɪz] *vt* téléviser

television [telɪ'vɪʒən] *n* télévision *f*; (*set*) téléviseur *m*, (poste *m* de) télévision; **closed-circuit t.** télévision à *ou* en circuit fermé; **colour t.** télévision (en) couleur; **colour t. (set)** téléviseur couleur; **pay t.** télévision payante; **what's on t.?** qu'est-ce qu'il y a à la télévision?; **I saw it on t.** je l'ai vu à la télévision; **have you been on t.?** êtes-vous passé à la télévision?; **to watch t.** regarder la télévision; **from a t. point of view** d'un point de vue télévisuel; **it makes/doesn't make good t.** ça a/n'a pas un bon impact télévisuel; **t. advertising** publicité *f* télévisée; **t. archives** archives *fpl* télévisuelles; **t. audience** (*reached by advertising*) audience *f* de téléspectateurs; **t. broadcaster** télédiffuseur *m*; **t. broadcasting network** réseau *m* de télédistribution; **t. campaign** campagne *f* télévisée; **t. commentary** téléreportage *m*; **t. commercial** publicité *f* télévisée; **t. drama** drame *m* télévisé; **t. interview** interview *f* télévisée *ou* à la télévision; **t. journalist** journaliste *mf* de télévision; **t. news** journal *m* télévisé, JT *m*, actualités *fpl* télévisées; **t. network** réseau télévisuel; **t. on demand** télévision à la demande; **t. play** pièce *f* de théâtre pour la télévision; **t. receiver** récepteur *m* de télévision; **t. rights** droits *mpl* de télédiffusion; **t. room** salle *f* de télévision; **t. sponsoring** parrainage-télévision *m*; **t. viewer** téléspectateur *m*, téléspectatrice *f*; **t. viewing panel** panel *m* de téléspectateurs

television camera *n* caméra *f* de télévision; **it's my first time in front of the television cameras** c'est la première fois que je suis devant les caméras

television channel *n* chaîne *f* de télévision

television guide *n* journal *m* de télévision

television licence *n* (*fee*) redevance *f* télé(visuelle)

television personality *n* vedette *f* de la télévision

television programme *n* émission *f* de télévision, programme *m* télévisé

television screen *n* écran *m* de télévision

television show *n* spectacle *m* télévisé

television studio *n* studio *m* de télévision

television tie-in *n* partenariat *m* avec la télévision

televisual [telɪ'vɪʒʊəl] *adj* télévisuel

teleworking ['telɪwɜːkɪŋ] *n* télétravail *m*

telewriting ['telɪraɪtɪŋ] *n* téléécriture *f*

telex ['teleks] *n* télex *m*; **to send sth by t.** télexer qch; **t. operator** télexiste *mf*; **t. transfer** virement *m* par télex

telex[2] *vt* (*message*) télexer; **I'll t. you** je vous enverrai un télex

tell [tel] (*pt, pp* **told** [təʊld]) **1** *vt* **(a)** (*say*) dire; (*story etc*) raconter; **to t. the truth** dire la vérité; **to t. a lie** dire un mensonge; **to t. sb sth** dire qch à qn; **I know — Dennis told me** je sais — Dennis me l'a dit; **she doesn't t. me anything** elle ne me dit *ou* raconte rien; **to t. sb a joke** raconter une blague à qn; **to t. sb a lie** dire *ou* raconter un mensonge à qn; **can you t. me the way to the station?** pouvez-vous m'indiquer le chemin de la gare?; **I can't t. you how pleased I am** je ne saurais vous dire combien je suis content; **we are told that ...** on nous informe *ou* dit que ...; **I told you no!** je t'ai dit non!; **it's just as I told you** c'est exactement ce que je t'avais dit; **I told you so!, didn't I t. you!, what did I t. you!** je te l'avais bien dit!; **you're telling me!** à qui le dis-tu?, tu l'as dit!; **are you telling me (that) you spent £50 on that?** tu ne vas pas me dire que tu as payé 50 livres pour ça?; **t. me another!** à d'autres!; *esp US F* **t. him goodbye (for me)!** dis-lui au revoir de ma part!; **I'll t. you what happened** je vais vous raconter ce qui est arrivé; *F* **(I) t. you what!** (*solving problem, making suggestion*) bon!; **t. me something about yourself** parlez-moi un peu de vous(-même); **to hear t. of ...** entendre parler de ...; **to hear t. that ...** entendre dire que ...; **that would be telling!** ça c'est mon secret!; *F* **to t. teacher** rapporter, cafarder; **to t. the time** (*of clock*) donner l'heure; **to t. sb the time** (*of person*) dire l'heure qu'il est *ou* donner l'heure à qn; **to t. sb about sb** parler de qn à qn; **she wrote to t. me of her father's death** elle m'a écrit pour m'annoncer la mort de son père; **t. me what you know about it** dites-moi ce que vous en savez; **let me t. you ...** permets-moi de te dire ...; **it's not so easy, let me t. you!** ce n'est pas si facile, je t'assure *ou* je te le dis!; **what does this t. us about his character?** qu'est-ce que cela nous apprend sur son caractère?; **this example tells us nothing about the meaning of the word** cet exemple ne nous renseigne absolument pas sur le sens du mot

(b) (*discern*) **it's difficult to t. the difference between them** c'est difficile de les différencier; **to t. good from bad** *or* **right from wrong** discerner le bien du mal; **you can hardly t. him from his brother** c'est à peine si on peut le distinguer de son frère; **in the dark it was hard to t. friend from foe** dans l'obscurité il était difficile de distinguer ses amis de ses ennemis; **one can t. him by his voice** on le reconnaît à sa voix; **she can't t. the time** elle ne sait pas lire l'heure; **one** *or* **you can t. (that) she's lived abroad** on voit qu'elle a vécu à l'étranger; **I can t. it from the look in your eyes** ça se lit dans tes yeux; **I could t. they were lying** je voyais bien qu'ils mentaient; **we couldn't t. if he was angry or not** nous n'arrivions pas à savoir s'il était en colère ou non; **nobody can t. what the future has in store for us** on ne peut pas savoir ce que l'avenir nous réserve; **there's no telling what he might do!** je ne sais pas comment il va réagir!

(c) (*order etc*) **to t. sb to do sth** dire à qn de faire qch; **you can't t. me what to do!** tu n'as pas à me dire ce que je dois faire!; **t. him to come** dis-lui de venir; **do as you are told!** fais ce qu'on te dit; **she'll do as she's told!** elle fera ce qu'on lui dira (de faire)!

(d) (*count*) (*votes*) compter; *Rel* **to t. one's beads** égrener son chapelet; **all told** au total; **I made £100 out of it all told** en tout j'ai gagné 100 livres; **I had quite a good holiday all told** en fin de compte *ou* tout compte fait j'ai passé de bonnes vacances

2 *vi* **(a)** *(say)* **please don't t.** ne dis rien, s'il te plaît; **time will t.** qui vivra verra; **more than words can t.** plus qu'on ne saurait dire

(b) *(discern)* **it's difficult** *or* **hard to t.** c'est difficile à dire; **it's too early to t.** il est trop tôt pour se prononcer; **who can t.?, there's no telling!** qui sait?; **you never can t.** on ne sait jamais; **it's a male – how can you t.?** c'est un mâle – comment le sais-tu?

(c) *(have effect)* *(of drug etc)* produire son effet; *(of sleepless nights etc)* se faire sentir; **breeding will t.** bon sang ne saurait mentir; **it will t. against you** cela vous nuira

▶ **tell apart** *vtas (distinguish)* **I can't t. them apart** je n'arrive pas à les distinguer l'un de l'autre *ou* à les différencier

▶ **tell of** *vipo* **(a)** *(of story, poem etc)* raconter l'histoire de **(b)** *(indicate, reveal)* **faces which t. of ...** des visages dans lesquels se lit ...; **rings under her eyes told of sleepless nights** on voyait à ses yeux cernés qu'elle avait passé des nuits blanches

▶ **tell off 1** *vtas F (scold)* gronder (**about sth** à propos de qch); **he told them off in no uncertain terms** il leur a dit leurs quatre vérités **2** *vtsep Mil etc (assign) (sb for duty)* désigner

▶ **tell on** *vipo* **(a)** *(affect badly)* **the heat is telling on him** il commence à souffrir de la chaleur; **his age is beginning to t. on him** il commence à accuser son âge; **the effects of the embargo were beginning to t. on the country's economy** les effets de l'embargo commençaient à se faire sentir sur l'économie du pays **(b)** *F (inform on)* dénoncer; **I'll t. on you!** je le dirai!

teller ['telər] *n* **(a)** *(of story etc)* conteur, -euse **(b)** *(in bank etc)* guichetier, -ière; *Parl (of votes)* scrutateur *m*

telling ['telıŋ] **1** *adj* **(a) t. blow** coup *m* bien asséné *ou* qui porte; **what he said had a t. effect** ce qu'il a dit a porté; **a t. criticism/remark** une critique/remarque bien sentie; **a t. speech** un discours percutant **(b)** *(revealing)* révélateur, -trice; **her remarks were very t.** ses remarques étaient très révélatrices **2** *n* **the t. of tales plays an important part in their culture** les contes oraux jouent un rôle important dans leur culture; **it loses nothing in the t.** ça ne perd rien à être raconté

telling off *n F* réprimande *f*; **to give sb a t.** gronder qn

telltale ['telteıl] *n (person)* rapporteur, -euse, cafard, -arde; **a t. sign** un signe révélateur; **a t. odour** une odeur qui ne trompe pas

tellurium [te'lʊərıəm] *n Ch* tellure *m*

telly ['telı] *n esp Br F* télé *f*; **on the t.** à la télé; **t. addict** accro *mf* de la télé

temerity [tı'merıtı] *n* témérité *f*, audace *f*; **she had the t. to accuse me!** elle a eu l'audace de m'accuser!

temp¹ [temp] *n F* intérimaire *mf*; *(temporary secretary)* secrétaire *mf* intérimaire; **to do t. work** faire de l'intérim; *(as secretary)* être secrétaire intérimaire

temp² *vi F* faire de l'intérim; *(as secretary)* être secrétaire intérimaire

temp³ *(abbr* **temperature)** température

temper¹ ['tempər] *n* **(a)** *(anger)* colère *f*; *(bad mood)* mauvaise humeur *f*; **in an outburst of t.** dans un mouvement de colère; **to be in a t.** être en colère; **to be in a good/bad t.** être de bonne/mauvaise humeur; **to send sb into a t.** mettre qn en colère; *F* **t.(, t.)!** du calme!, on se calme!; **to keep one's t.** rester calme, garder son calme; **to lose one's t.** se mettre en colère, s'emporter; **to fly into a t.** piquer une colère **(b)** *(character)* caractère *m*, tempérament *m*; **fiery/even t.** caractère fougueux/égal; **she's got (quite) a t.** elle a un sacré caractère; **to have a quick t.** s'emporter facilement **(c)** *Metal (of steel)* coefficient *m* de dureté, trempe *f*

temper² *vt* **(a)** *Tech (steel, blade)* donner la trempe à; *(metal)* recuire, adoucir **(b)** *(moderate)* *(action etc)* modérer, adoucir; *(one's grief etc)* maîtriser; *(one's enthusiasm etc)* tempérer, modérer; **to t. justice with mercy** faire preuve de clémence **(c)** *(piano)* accorder par tempérament

tempera ['tempərə] *n Art* **to paint in t.** peindre a tempera; **t. painting** peinture *f* à la tempera

temperament ['temp(ə)rəmənt] *n (character)* caractère *m*, tempérament *m*; **an outburst** *or* **show of t.** un coup de colère

temperamental [temp(ə)rə'ment(ə)l] *adj* **(a)** *(difference etc)* du tempérament; **he has a t. aversion to conflict/hard work** fondamentalement il déteste les conflits/le travail **(b)** *(person)* capricieux, fantasque; *(machine)* capricieux; **his knee has been a bit t. since his accident** son genou lui joue des tours depuis son accident

temperamentally [temp(ə)rə'ment(ə)lı] *adv (by nature)* de nature; **t. different** d'un tempérament différent; **they were t. unsuited** *(of couple)* leurs caractères étaient incompatibles; **she's t. unsuited to this sort of work** elle n'est pas de nature à *ou* elle n'a pas le caractère pour faire ce genre de travail

temperance ['temp(ə)rəns] *n* **(a)** *(moderation)* *(in taking pleasure, eating, drinking etc)* tempérance *f*, modération *f*, retenue *f* **(b)** *(abstinence from alcohol)* tempérance *f*, sobriété *f*; **t. hotel** = hôtel *m* où l'on ne sert pas d'alcool; **t. society/movement** ligue *f*/mouvement *m* antialcoolique

temperate ['temp(ə)rət] *adj* **(a)** *(climate, zone etc)* tempéré **(b)** *(language etc)* modéré, mesuré

temperature ['temp(ə)rətʃər] *n* température *f*; **fall in t., t. drop** chute *f* de température; **room t.** température ambiante; **at room t.** *(of wine)* chambré; **the t. was in the thirties** il faisait plus de trente degrés; *Med* **to take sb's t.** prendre la température de qn; **to have a raised t., to have** *or* **to run a t.** avoir de la température *ou* de la fièvre; **he's got a t. of forty** il a quarante de fièvre; *Fig* **to judge the t. of a meeting** prendre la température d'une réunion; **to raise/lower the t.** faire monter/faire baisser la température; **t. chart** feuille *f* de température; **t. gauge** jauge *f* de température; **t. sensor** capteur *m* de température

tempered ['tempəd] *adj (steel)* trempé, recuit; **t. safety glass** verre *m* de sécurité trempé

-tempered [-tempəd] *suff* **to be good/bad-t.** *(habitually)* avoir un bon/mauvais caractère; *(on one occasion)* être de bonne/mauvaise humeur; **to be quick-t.** s'emporter facilement

tempest ['tempıst] *n Lit* tempête *f*, tourmente *f*

tempestuous [tem'pestjʊəs] *adj* **(a)** *(weather, wind etc)* de tempête **(b)** *(meeting etc)* orageux, tempétueux; *(person, mood, relationship etc)* turbulent, agité

tempestuously [tem'pestjʊəslı] *adv* **(a)** *Lit* **the winds blew t. outside** un vent tempétueux soufflait au dehors **(b)** *(violently)* *(to argue etc)* violemment

tempestuousness [tem'pestjʊəsnıs] *n* **(a)** *(of weather)* violence *f* **(b)** *(of meeting)* caractère *m* orageux; *(of crowd)* turbulence *f*, agitation *f*

temping ['tempıŋ] *n* intérim *m*

Templar ['templər] *n Hist* **(Knight) T.** Templier *m*, chevalier *m* du Temple

template ['templıt] *n* **(a)** *(in metalworking)*, *Carp etc* gabarit *m*, calibre *m*, patron *m* **(b)** *Comptr (for keyboard)* réglette *f*

temple¹ ['temp(ə)l] *n Rel* temple *m*

temple² *n Anat* tempe *f*

tempo, *pl* **-i** ['tempəʊ, -i:] *n Mus* tempo *m*; *Fig* **strikes that upset the t. of production** grèves qui perturbent le rythme de la production

temporal¹ ['tempər(ə)l] *adj* **(a)** *(power etc)* temporel **(b)** *Gram* temporel

temporal² *adj Anat (bone etc)* temporal

temporarily ['temp(ə)rərılı, tempə'reərılı] *adv* temporairement; *(for the present time)* momentanément, temporairement; **we were t. delayed** nous avons été retardés quelques minutes

temporary ['temp(ə)rərı] *adj* *(office, entrance etc)* temporaire; *(hearing loss etc)* momentané, passager; *(work, employee)* intérimaire; **the improvement is only t.** l'amélioration n'est que passagère *ou* momentanée; **on a t. basis** temporairement; *(to work)* par intérim; **to exercise t. command** commander par intérim; **this will at least give you t. relief** cela vous soulagera pendant un moment; **t. appointment** poste *m* temporaire; *Admin* emploi *m* amovible; **t. contract** *(for employment)* contrat *m* de mission d'intérim, contrat temporaire; **t. file** fichier *m* temporaire; *Jur* **t. injunction** injonction *f* temporaire; **t. job** emploi temporaire; **t. manager** directeur *m* intérimaire; **t. replacement** suppléance *f*; **t. surface** *(of road)* revêtement *m* provisoire; **t. work** intérim *m*; **t. worker** intérimaire *mf*

temporize ['tempəraız] *vi Fml (seek to gain time)* temporiser, chercher à gagner du temps

tempt [tem(p)t] *vt* tenter; **to t. sb to do sth** inciter qn à faire qch; **to let oneself be tempted** se laisser tenter, céder à la tentation; **I'm tempted to try** je suis tenté *ou* j'ai envie d'essayer; **the fine weather tempted us to go out** le beau temps nous a donné envie de sortir; **to t. providence/fate** tenter la providence/le sort; **don't t. me!** ne me tente pas!

temptation [tem(p)'teıʃən] *n* tentation *f*; **to throw** *or* **put t. in sb's way** exposer qn à la tentation; **to give in** *or* **yield to t.** succomber *ou* céder à la tentation; *Bible* **lead us not into t.** ne nous soumets pas à la tentation; **there's a great t. to say that ...** on est très tenté de dire que ...

tempter ['tem(p)tər] *n* tentateur *m*

tempting ['tem(p)tıŋ] *adj* tentant, alléchant; *(meal)* appétissant

temptingly ['tem(p)tıŋlı] *adv* d'une manière tentante; **the grapes glistened t. in their bowl** les grappes dans le plat étaient brillantes et appétissantes; **the cool water beckoned t.** l'eau fraîche donnait envie de se baigner

temptress ['tem(p)trɪs] *n Lit, Hum* tentatrice *f*
ten [ten] *num adj, n* dix *m*; **number t.** le numéro dix; **some** *or* **about t. years ago** il y a une dizaine d'années; **three tens are thirty** trois fois dix font trente; **tens of thousands** des dizaines de milliers; **the T. Commandments** les dix commandements *mpl*; *Rugby* **t. metre line** ligne *f* des dix mètres; **they're t. a penny** il y en a à la pelle; **t. to one he'll mention it** je vous parie qu'il en parlera; **the top t.** (*in record charts*) palmarès *m* des dix meilleurs *ou* des dix meilleures ventes
tenable ['tenəb(ə)l] *adj* **(a)** (*position, fortress etc*) tenable; (*theory*) soutenable; *Mktg* **t. firm** entreprise *f* défendable **(b) appointment t. for three years** poste auquel on est nommé pour trois ans
tenacious [te'neɪʃəs] *adj* tenace; **t. memory** excellente mémoire *f*
tenaciously [te'neɪʃəslɪ] *adv* avec ténacité; (*stubbornly*) obstinément
tenacity, tenaciousness [te'næsɪtɪ, te'neɪʃəsnɪs] *n* ténacité *f*; (*of memory*) sûreté *f*
tenancy ['tenənsɪ] *n* location *f*; **expiration of t.** expiration *f* de bail, échéance *f* de location; **during my t.** pendant la période de ma location
tenant[1] ['tenənt] *n* locataire *mf*; **t. in possession, sitting t.** occupant, -ante; **t. farmer** métayer *m*
tenant[2] *vt* (*house etc*) occuper comme locataire; **only half the farms were still tenanted** il n'y avait de locataires que dans la moitié des fermes
tenantry ['tenəntrɪ] *n, no pl* (*tenants*) métayers *mpl*
tench [tenʃ] *n* (*fish*) tanche *f*
tend[1] [tend] *vt* (*sick person etc*) soigner; (*machine etc*) surveiller; (*sheep etc*) garder; (*garden, fire*) entretenir
tend[2] *vi* **(a) doctrine that tends towards socialism** doctrine socialisante, doctrine qui penche vers le socialisme; **blue tending to green** bleu tirant sur le vert; **her tastes t. towards the exotic** elle a une attirance pour les choses exotiques; **I t. to(wards) the view that ...** j'ai tendance à penser que ...

(b) to t. to do sth avoir tendance à faire qch; **to t. to skid** (*of car*) déraper facilement; **she tends to exaggerate** elle a tendance à exagérer; **we t. to think of man as being separate from nature** nous avons tendance à considérer que l'homme ne fait pas partie de la nature; **some people like that kind of film, but I t. not to** il y a des gens qui aiment ce genre de film, moi (je n'aime) pas trop
▶ **tend to** *vipo* (*look after*) s'occuper de
tendency ['tendənsɪ] *n* tendance *f* **(to** à); **t. to drink** penchant *m* pour la boisson; **he has artistic tendencies** il a des dons artistiques; **to have a t. to (do) sth** avoir (une) tendance à (faire) qch; **a growing t.** une tendance de plus en plus marquée
tendentious [ten'denʃəs] *adj* tendancieux
tendentiously [ten'denʃəslɪ] *adv* tendancieusement
tendentiousness [ten'denʃəsnɪs] *n* caractère *m* tendancieux
tender[1] ['tendər] *n Naut* (*boat*) navire *m* annexe; (*for supplies*) ravitailleur *m*; *Rail* tender *m*
tender[2] *adj* **(a)** (*meat*) tendre; **to make meat t.** attendrir la viande

(b) (*sensitive*) tendre, sensible; **t. conscience** conscience *f* délicate *ou* susceptible; **t. to the touch** sensible *ou* douloureux au toucher; **t. heart** cœur *m* tendre *ou* sensible; **to touch sb on a t. spot** toucher qn à un endroit sensible; *Fig* toucher le point sensible chez qn

(c) (*plant etc*) délicat, fragile; *esp Lit, Hum* **a child of t. years** un(e) petit(e) enfant

(d) (*affectionate*) (*person, sentiment etc*) tendre, affectueux; **they bade each other a t. farewell** ils se sont tendrement dit au revoir; **t. look** regard doux *ou* tendre; *Iron* **I leave him to your t. mercies** je l'abandonne à vos soins
tender[3] *n Com* soumission *f*, offre *f*; **to invite tenders for a job, to put a job out to t.** mettre un travail en adjudication; **to make** *or* **put in a t. for sth** soumissionner *ou* faire une soumission pour qch; **a call for t.** un appel d'offres; **by t.** par voie d'adjudication; **t. documents** documents *mpl* d'appel d'offres; **t. form** formule *f* de soumission; **t. insurance** assurance *f* offre; **t. price** prix *m* d'offre; *Jur, Com* **legal t.** cours *m* légal, monnaie *f* libératoire; **to be legal t.** (*of money*) avoir cours, avoir force libératoire
tender[4] **1** *vt* (*one's services, money etc*) offrir; **to t. one's resignation** présenter sa démission; **to t. one's apologies** faire *ou* présenter ses excuses; *Jur* **to t. money in discharge of debt** faire une offre réelle; **please t. exact fare** veuillez avoir la monnaie exacte **2** *vi Com* **to t. for sth** soumissionner (pour) qch, faire une soumission pour qch; **to t. for a contract** soumissionner à une adjudication
tenderer ['tendərər] *n Com* soumissionnaire *mf*; **successful t.** adjudicataire *mf*
tenderfoot, *pl* **-foots, -feet** ['tendəfʊt(s), -fiːt] *n esp Am* (*in wild place*) nouveau venu *m*
tenderhearted [tendə'hɑːtɪd] *adj* au cœur tendre *ou* sensible; **to be too t.** avoir trop de cœur
tenderheartedness [tendə'hɑːtɪdnɪs] *n* compassion *f*, sensibilité *f*
tenderize ['tendəraɪz] *vt Culin* (*meat*) attendrir
tenderizer ['tendəraɪzər] *n Culin* attendrisseur *m*
tenderloin ['tendəlɔɪn] *n Culin* (*of beef etc*) filet *m*
tenderly ['tendəlɪ] *adv* **(a)** (*to touch, hold sth*) doucement, délicatement **(b)** (*to look at, feel*) tendrement, avec tendresse
tenderness ['tendənɪs] *n* **(a)** (*of meat*) tendreté *f* **(b)** (*of plant*) délicatesse *f*, fragilité *f*; (*of conscience*) délicatesse **(c)** (*affection*) tendresse *f*, affection *f* **(for** pour)
tendon ['tendən] *n Anat* tendon *m*
tendril ['tendrɪl] *n Bot* vrille *f*, cirre *m*
tenement ['tenɪmənt] *n* **t. (building)** immeuble *m* d'habitation, *Pej* vieil immeuble d'habitation en mauvais état; **t. flat** appartement *m*, *Pej* appartement dans un vieil immeuble
tenet ['tenɪt, 'tiː-] *n* (*dogma*) doctrine *f*, dogme *m*; (*belief*) croyance *f*
tenfold ['tenfəʊld] **1** *adj* décuple **2** *adv* au décuple; **to increase t.** décupler
ten-gallon *adj* **t. hat** = chapeau *m* de cowboy haut et à larges bords
Tenn *abbr* **Tennessee**
tenner ['tenər] *n F Br* (*ten-pound note*) billet *m* de dix livres; *US* (*ten-dollar bill*) billet de dix dollars; **it cost a t.** ça a coûté dix livres/dollars
tennis ['tenɪs] *n Sp* **(lawn) t.** tennis *m*; **to play t.** jouer au tennis; **table t.** tennis de table; **deck t.** deck-tennis *m*; **(real** *or* **royal** *or US* **court) t.** (jeu *m* de) paume *f*; **t. ball** balle *f* de tennis; **t. club** club *m* de tennis; **t. court** court *m* de tennis; (*in real tennis*) jeu de paume; *Med* **t. elbow** tennis elbow *m*; **t. player** joueur, -euse de tennis; **t. racquet** *or* **racket** raquette *f* de tennis; **t. shoes** chaussures *fpl* de tennis, tennis *fpl ou mpl*
tenon ['tenən] *n Carp* tenon *m*; **t. saw** tenonneuse *f*
tenor ['tenər] *n* **(a)** *Mus* (*voice, singer*) ténor *m*; **t. clef** clé *f* d'ut quatrième ligne; **t. sax(ophone)** saxo(phone) *m* ténor; **t. voice** voix *f* de ténor **(b)** (*general sense*) (*of letter etc*) contenu *m*, sens *m* général
tenpence ['tenpəns, -pens] *n Br* (pièce *f* de) dix pence *mpl*
tenpenny ['tenpənɪ] *adj Br* de *ou* à dix pence; **t. stamp** timbre *m* de dix pence
tenpin ['tenpɪn] *n* quille *f*; *Br* **t. bowling,** *Am* **tenpins** jeu *m* de quilles; (*in bowling alley*) bowling *m*
tense[1] [tens] *n* [①A39,7; B28-30,F] *Gram* temps *m*; **verb in the present/the future t.** verbe au (temps) présent/futur
tense[2] *adj* **(a)** (*nerves, situation, silence, moment etc*) tendu; (*muscle*) contracté, noué; **t. voice** voix *f* étranglée (par l'émotion); **to be t.** (*of person*) être tendu **(b)** (*cord etc*) tendu, raide
tense[3] **1** *vt* tendre; **he tensed himself as the door opened** il se raidit au moment où la porte s'ouvrit **2** *vi* se raidir
▶ **tense up** *vtsep, vi* = **tense**[3]
tensely ['tenslɪ] *adv* **he waited t. for the judge's decision** l'air tendu, il attendait la décision du juge; **we watched t. as he approached the door** le regard tendu, nous le regardâmes s'approcher de la porte; **she spoke t.** on sentait la tension dans sa voix
tenseness ['tensnɪs] *n* **(a)** (*of nerves, situation etc*) tension *f* **(b)** (*of muscles etc*) contraction *f*
tensile ['tensaɪl] *adj* (*stretchable*) extensible, élastique; (*metal*) ductile; **t. load** charge *f* de traction; **t. strength** limite *f* d'élasticité; **t. stress** contrainte *f* de tension *ou* de traction
tension ['tenʃən] *n* **(a)** (*of mind, nerves, Pol in region etc*) tension *f*; **t. headache** maux *mpl* de tête nerveux **(b)** (*of cord, muscular etc*) tension *f*; *Phys* (*of fluid*) tension, force *f* élastique; *El* tension, voltage *m*; **to keep a cable under t.** garder un câble sous tension **(c)** *MecE* (*stress*) (force *f* de) traction *f*; (*of spring*) tension *f*; **to be in t.** être en traction
tent [tent] *n* tente *f*; **bell t.** tente conique; **oxygen t.** tente à oxygène; **to pitch/strike tents** monter/démonter les tentes; **t. peg** piquet *m* de tente; **t. pole** mât *m* de tente
tentacle ['tentək(ə)l] *n Biol, Fig* tentacule *m*
tentative ['tentətɪv] *adj* d'essai; (*hesitant*) hésitant; (*conclusion*) provisoire; **to make a t. move towards peace** faire un petit pas vers la paix; **t. offer** offre *f* préliminaire *ou* d'essai; **it was just a t. suggestion** ce n'était qu'une suggestion
tentatively ['tentətɪvlɪ] *adv* à titre d'essai; (*hesitantly*) avec hésitation; (*to conclude*) provisoirement

tenterhooks ['tentəhʊks] *n* **to be on t.** être au supplice *ou* sur le gril *ou* sur des charbons ardents; **to keep sb on t.** faire languir qn, mettre qn sur des charbons ardents
tenth [tenθ] **1** *adj* dixième **2** *n* **(a)** (*of month*) dix *m*; **(on) the t. (of May)** le dix (mai) **(b)** (*person, thing*) dixième *mf* **(c)** (*fraction*) dixième *m* **(d)** *Mus* (intervalle *m* de) dixième *f*
tenting ['tentɪŋ] *n* toile *f* de tente
tenuous ['tenjʊəs] *adj* (*argument, link etc*) ténu, faible
tenuously ['tenjʊəslɪ] *adv* de façon ténue
tenuousness ['tenjʊəsnɪs] *n* (*of argument, link etc*) fragilité *f*
tenure ['tenjər] *n* **(a)** *Hist, Jur* (*of property*) tenure *f*; **system of land t.** régime *m* foncier **(b)** *Jur* (*period*) (*of office, property etc*) (période *f* de) jouissance *f ou* (d')occupation *f*; (*permanency of employment*) titularisation *f*; **during his t. of office** pendant qu'il exerçait ses fonctions
tepee ['ti:pi:] *n* tipi *m*, wigwam *m*
tepid ['tepɪd] *adj* (*water etc*) tiède; (*feeling, welcome etc*) tiède, mitigé
tepidly ['tepɪdlɪ] *adv* mollement, de façon mitigée
tepidness ['tepɪdnɪs] *n* tiédeur *f*
tercentenary [tɜ:sen'ti:nərɪ], **tercentennial** [tɜ:sen'tenɪəl] *adj, n* tricentenaire *m*
tercet ['tɜ:sɪt] *n* (*in prosody*) tercet *m*
term [tɜ:m] *n* **(a)** (*word, expression*) terme *m*; **technical/scientific t.** terme *ou* expression *f* technique/scientifique; **he spoke of him in the most flattering terms** il a parlé de lui en des termes les plus flatteurs; **I told her in no uncertain terms** je le lui ai dit carrément *ou* sans mâcher mes mots; **in terms of difficulty I'd say it was in the medium range** si on considère le degré de difficulté, je dirais c'était moyennement difficile; **in terms of salary/pollution** du point de vue du salaire/de la pollution; **in terms of time, I think we're talking about twelve weeks** question temps, je pense qu'il faut compter douze semaines; **in layman's terms** pour parler clairement; **in financial terms** financièrement parlant, en matière de finance; **I was thinking more in terms of a family car/something under £50** je voyais plus une voiture du genre voiture familiale/quelque chose de moins de 50 livres; **in personal/political terms it was a disaster** d'un point de vue personnel/politique ça a été une catastrophe
(b) (*relations*) **to be on good/bad terms with sb** être en bons/mauvais termes avec qn; **to be on friendly terms with sb** être en bons termes avec qn; **we remained on friendly terms** nos relations sont restées amicales; **to be on the best of terms with sb** être au mieux avec qn, être dans les meilleurs termes avec qn; **we're not on those kind of terms** nous ne nous connaissons pas aussi bien; **to come to terms with sth** accepter qch, se faire à qch
(c) (*in logic*), *Math* terme *m*; **to express one quantity in terms of another** exprimer une quantité en fonction d'une autre
(d) *Com etc* **terms** (*conditions*) conditions *fpl*; (*of contract*) clauses *fpl*, termes *mpl*; **terms and conditions of a contract** conditions d'un contrat; **on these terms I accept** à ces conditions j'accepte; **make** *or* **name your own terms** fixez vos conditions; **under the terms and conditions of the contract** selon les termes du contrat; **to dictate terms** imposer ses conditions; **to come to** *or* **make terms** s'arranger (**with sb** avec qn); **terms of credit** conditions de crédit; **terms of exchange** termes d'échange; **terms of reference** (*of commission etc*) attributions *fpl*, mandat *m*; **terms of payment** conditions *ou* termes de paiement; **terms of trade** termes de l'échange; **weekly terms** (*in hotel etc*) pension *f* par semaine; **on easy terms** avec facilités de paiement; **not on any terms** à aucun prix
(e) (*period*) terme *m*, période *f*, durée *f*; *Sch, Univ* trimestre *m*; (*of court*) session *f*; **to serve a t. of five years (in prison)** faire cinq ans de prison; **during her t. of** *or* **in office** (*of president, mayor etc*) pendant son mandat; *Com* **long-/short-t. transaction** opération *f* à long/court terme; **a long-t. policy** une politique à longue échéance; **in the long t.** à la longue; **in the short t.** à court terme; *Sch, Univ* **in t. time, during t.** pendant le trimestre; *Sch, Univ* **half t. (holiday)** congé *m* de mi-trimestre
(f) (*limit*) terme *m*, fin *f*; *Com* (*of bill of exchange*) (terme d')échéance *f*; **to have reached (full) t.** (*of pregnancy*) être à terme; **to set** *or* **put a t. to sth** mettre fin *ou* un terme à qch; *Fin* **t. deposit** dépôt *m* à terme; *Fin* **t. draft** traite *f* à terme; *Fin* **t. insurance cover** couverture *f* à terme; *Fin* **t. loan** crédit *m* à terme
term² *vt* designer, appeler; **that is what I would t. a stupid answer** voilà ce que j'appelle une réponse idiote
termagant ['tɜ:məgənt] *n Lit* mégère *f*, virago *f*
terminal ['tɜ:mɪn(ə)l] **1** *adj* (*phase, stage*) terminal; (*illness*) incurable; *Med* **I'm afraid it's t.** je crains que vous ne soyez/qu'il ne soit/*etc* condamné; **t. station** terminus *m*; **t. bonus** (*in insurance*) = bonus *m* versé au titulaire d'une assurance-vie, au terme de celle-ci; *Med* **t. case** malade *mf* en phase terminale; *F* **t. boredom** ennui *m* mortel **2** *n* **(a)** *El* (*of battery*) pôle *m*; **t. voltage** tension *f* aux bornes **(b)** (*rail, bus*) terminus *m*, gare *f* terminus; (*maritime*) gare maritime; (*for containers*) terminal *m*; *Av* **(air) t.** aérogare *f*; **t. building** (*at airport*) aérogare *f* **(c)** *Comptr* (poste *m*) terminal *m*; **t. emulation** émulation *f* de terminal
terminally ['tɜ:mɪn(ə)lɪ] *adv Med* **to be t. ill** être en phase terminale; **the t. ill** (*npl*) les malades *mpl* incurables *ou* condamnés
terminate ['tɜ:mɪneɪt] **1** *vt* (*employment, project, commitment*) mettre un terme à, mettre fin à; (*contract etc*) résilier; **the project was terminated in 1987** on a mis fin au projet en 1987; **to t. a pregnancy** (*of doctor*) interrompre une grossesse, pratiquer une IVG; (*of woman*) avoir une IVG; **to have one's pregnancy terminated** avoir une IVG **2** *vi* (*of word etc*) se terminer, finir (**in** en, par); (*of line etc*) se terminer, aboutir (**in, at** à); (*of train*) avoir son terminus (**at** à); **this train terminates here** terminus du train!
termination [tɜ:mɪ'neɪʃən] *n* **(a)** (*of trial etc*) fin *f*, conclusion *f*; (*of relations, dealings etc*) cessation *f*; *Jur* (*of obligation etc*) résolution *f*, résiliation *f*; **t. of pregnancy** interruption *f* (volontaire) de grossesse, IVG *f*; **t. clause** clause *f* de résiliation **(b)** *Gram* terminaison *f*, désinence *f*
terminator ['tɜ:mɪneɪtər] *n Comptr* terminateur *m*
terminological [tɜ:mɪnə'lɒdʒɪk(ə)l] *adj* terminologique
terminologist [tɜ:mɪ'nɒlədʒɪst] *n* terminologue *mf*
terminology [tɜ:mɪ'nɒlədʒɪ] *n* terminologie *f*
terminus, *pl* **-i, -uses** ['tɜ:mɪnəs, -aɪ, -əsɪz] *n Rail etc* (gare *f*) terminus *m*; **t. hotel** (*at train station*) hôtel *m* de gare
termite ['tɜ:maɪt] *n* (*insect*) termite *m*
term paper *n US* dissertation *f* trimestrielle
tern [tɜ:n] *n* (*bird*) sterne *f*; **arctic t.** sterne arctique
ternary ['tɜ:nərɪ] *adj Ch, Math etc* ternaire
terrace¹ ['terɪs] *n* **(a)** *Constr, Geol, Agr* terrasse *f*; *Fb etc* **the terraces** les gradins *mpl* **(b)** *Br* **t. (of houses)** rangée *f* de maisons attenantes
terrace² *vt* (*garden etc*) disposer en terrasse(s); (*hillside etc*) terrasser
terraced ['terɪst] *adj* **(a)** (*garden*) en terrasse; **t. hillsides** collines cultivées en terrasses **(b)** *Br* **t. house** = maison *f* située dans une rangée d'habitations attenantes; **t. houses** (*row*) rangée *f* de maisons attenantes
terracotta [terə'kɒtə] *n* terre *f* cuite; (*colour*) ocre *m* foncé
terra firma ['terə'fɜ:mə] *n* la terre ferme, *F* le plancher des vaches; **to be back on t. again** être de retour sur le plancher des vaches; *Fig* (*in known area etc*) se retrouver en terrain connu
terrain [tə'reɪn] *n Mil, Geog* terrain *m*
terrapin ['terəpɪn] *n* (*reptile*) tortue *f* d'eau douce
terrarium, *pl* **-ia, -iums** [te'reərɪəm, -ɪə, -ɪəmz] *n* terrarium *m*
terrestrial [tɪ'restrɪəl] **1** *adj* (*globe, plant, life, TV programmes etc*) terrestre; **t. broadcasting** diffusion *f* terrestre *ou* hertzienne **2** *n* (*inhabitant of the Earth*) terrien, -ienne
terrible ['terɪb(ə)l] *adj* terrible; (*accident, crime, shock*) affreux, épouvantable; (*film, teacher etc*) nul; (*coffee, food etc*) infecte; (*injury*) très grave; **what a t. thing to say** c'est horrible de dire ça; **I'm t. at maths** je suis nul en math; **he's a t. talker** (*talks a lot*) c'est un sacré bavard; **going without a meal isn't so t.** ce n'est pas si terrible de sauter un repas
terribly ['terɪblɪ] *adv* **(a)** (*badly*) terriblement; (*to behave*) de manière atroce; **the economy has performed t.** les résultats économiques sont désastreux; **t. injured** très gravement blessé **(b)** *F* (*very*) très; **t. busy** très *ou* terriblement occupé; **t. worried** terriblement *ou* affreusement inquiet; **that's t. kind of you** vous êtes vraiment trop aimable; **he's t. keen to meet you** il a vraiment envie de te rencontrer; **not t. interesting** pas très intéressant; **are you interested? – not t.** ça vous intéresse? – pas vraiment
terrier ['terɪər] *n* (*dog*) (chien *m*) terrier *m*; *Fig* **he's a real t.** il n'abandonne jamais; **bull t.** bull-terrier *m*, *pl* bull-terriers
terrific [tə'rɪfɪk] *adj F* (*excellent*) génial; (*enormous*) énorme; **we had a t. time** c'était génial; **t.!** génial!; **a t. noise** un bruit énorme; **a t. pace** une allure vertigineuse
terrifically [tə'rɪfɪklɪ] *adv F* (*very*) très; **it was t. hot** il faisait terriblement chaud
terrified ['terɪfaɪd] *adj* (*look, person*) terrifié; **to be t. of sb** avoir une peur bleue de qn; **they're t. of losing their jobs** ils tremblent à l'idée de perdre leur emploi; **to be t. (that)** être terrifié *ou* mort de peur (à l'idée que + *sub*)
terrify ['terɪfaɪ] *vt* terrifier, faire très peur à; **this remark terrified me** cette remarque m'a terrifié; **it terrifies me what he'll do next** je suis terrifié à la pensée de ce qu'il pourrait faire

terrifying ['terɪfaɪɪŋ] *adj* terrifiant, terrible, épouvantable
terrifyingly ['terɪfaɪɪŋlɪ] *adv* (*difficult, dangerous*) épouvantablement; (*to scream*) d'une manière terrifiante; **to come t. close to death** passer à deux doigts de la mort, frôler la mort
terrine [te'riːn] *n* terrine *f*
territorial [terɪ'tɔːrɪəl] **1** *adj* **(a)** (*possessions, tax, claim etc*) territorial **(b) a t. animal** un animal qui a tendance à protéger son territoire; **gorillas are very t. creatures** les gorilles mettent toujours beaucoup d'acharnement à défendre leur territoire; **the sales director is highly t.** le directeur des ventes est prêt à tout pour défendre son territoire; **they're very t. about their part of the office** ils veulent que personne ne s'immisce dans leur partie du bureau **2** *n Br Mil* **T.** territorial *m*
Territorial Army *n Br* force *f* armée constituée de réservistes volontaires
territoriality [terɪtɔːrɪ'ælɪtɪ] *n* territorialité *f*
territorial waters *npl* eaux *fpl* territoriales
territory ['terɪt(ə)rɪ] *n* (*of state, animal*) territoire *m*; *Fig* **I'm afraid this isn't my t.** désolé, ce n'est pas mon domaine; *Fig* **this will be familiar t. for his readers** le lecteur se retrouvera en terrain familier
terror ['terər] *n* **(a)** (*fear*) terreur *f*, effroi *m*, épouvante *f*; **a look of t.** un regard épouvanté; **to be in (a state of) t.** être terrorisé; **to be in t. of one's life** craindre pour sa vie; **to go in t. of sb** avoir une peur bleue de qn; *F* **to have a holy t. of sth** craindre qch comme la peste; **a reign of t.** un régime de terreur; *Fr Hist* **the T.** la Terreur; **t. campaign, campaign of t.** campagne *f* de terreur

(b) (*person*) **he was the t. of the countryside** c'était la terreur du pays; *F* **she's a little** *or* **a holy t.** c'est un petit diable; *F* **he's a t. for being late** il est épouvantable avec sa manie d'être toujours en retard; *F* **he's a t. for the whisky/chocolate biscuits** c'est un fou de whisky/de petits gâteaux au chocolat
terrorism ['terərɪz(ə)m] *n* terrorisme *m*
terrorist ['terərɪst] **1** *n* terroriste *mf* **2** *adj* terroriste; **t. attack** attentat *m* (terroriste); **t. bombing** attentat à la bombe
terrorize ['terəraɪz] *vt* terroriser
terror-stricken, terror-struck *adj* (*expression, look*) de terreur; **to be t.** être saisi de terreur
terry ['terɪ] *adj, n Tex* **t. (towelling)** tissu *m* éponge; **t. towel** serviette *f* éponge
terse [tɜːs] *adj* abrupt, brusque
tersely ['tɜːslɪ] *adv* abruptement, brusquement
terseness ['tɜːsnɪs] *n* (*of reply etc*) brusquerie *f*; (*of style*) caractère *m* abrupt
tertiary ['tɜːʃɪərɪ] *adj, n* tertiaire *m*; **t. education** enseignement *m* du troisième cycle; **t. sector** secteur *m* tertiaire
Terylene® ['terɪliːn] *n Br Tex* tergal® *m*; **T. skirt** jupe en tergal
TESL ['tes(ə)l] *n* (*abbr* **Teaching English as a Second Language**) enseignement *m* de l'anglais deuxième langue
TESOL ['tesɒl] *n* (*abbr* **Teaching English to Speakers of Other Languages**) enseignement *m* de l'anglais langue étrangère
TESSA ['tesə] *n Br* (*abbr* **tax exempt special savings account**) plan *m* d'épargne exonéré d'impôts
test¹ [test] *n* **(a)** (*trial, check etc*) épreuve *f*; (*scientific*) test *m*; **to put sth to the t.** mettre qch à l'épreuve *ou* à l'essai, éprouver qch; **to undergo a t.** subir une épreuve; **to pass** *or* **stand the t.** soutenir *ou* supporter l'épreuve; **method that has stood the t. of time** méthode *f* éprouvée; **it was a t. of our friendship** ça a mis notre amitié à l'épreuve; **endurance t.** épreuve d'endurance; *Aut etc* **road t.** essai *m* sur route; *Nucl Phys* **nuclear t.** essai nucléaire; *Aut* **t. centre** (*for repairs*) centre *m* d'essai; *Mktg* **t. city** ville-test *f*, *pl* villes-tests; *Mktg* **t. site** site-témoin *m*, *pl* sites-témoins

(b) *Sch, Med etc* (*examination*) examen *m*; **eye/blood t.** examen des yeux/du sang; *Sch* **French/Maths t.** examen *ou* interrogation *f* de français/math; *Med etc* **blood t.** prise *f* de sang; *Aut* **driving t.** permis *m* de conduire; **hearing t.** examen de l'ouïe; *Cin etc* **screen t.** bout *m* d'essai; **t. certificate** certificat *m* d'essai; *Br Sch* **t. paper** (*questions*) sujets *mpl* d'examen; (*answers*) copie *f* d'examen; *Mus* **t. piece** morceau *m* imposé

(c) *Cr, Rugby* **t. (match)** match *m* international
test² **1** *vt* (*try out*) (*car, computer system, method etc*) essayer, tester; (*weights and measures etc*) contrôler, vérifier; (*sb's sight*) examiner; (*procedure*) expérimenter; (*beam etc*) sonder; (*water etc*) analyser; **to t. sb's hearing** faire passer des tests auditifs à qn; **to t. sb's blood** faire une analyse de sang à qn; **to t. sb's fitness** tester l'endurance de qn; **to t. sb's knowledge** tester les connaissances de qn; *Sch* **to t. a class in algebra** faire faire un examen d'algèbre à une classe; *Med* **to t. sb for AIDS** faire subir le test de dépistage du SIDA à qn; **to t. an athlete for steroids** faire subir des tests à un athlète pour détecter l'usage de stéroïdes; **to t. a drug on sb/animals** expérimenter un médicament sur qn/des animaux

2 *vi* (*of scientist etc*) expérimenter; **to t. for AIDS/TB** procéder à un test de dépistage du SIDA/de la tuberculose; **she tested positive for AIDS** son test de dépistage du SIDA s'est révélé positif; *Sp* **he tested positive for banned substances** son contrôle antidopage s'est révélé positif; **to t. for alkaloids** faire la réaction des alcaloïdes; **one, two, testing** (*in soundcheck*) un, deux, essai
▶ **test out** *vtsep* (*person, idea etc*) mettre à l'épreuve; **to t. out a scheme** essayer un projet; **to t. out an idea on sb** tester une idée sur qn
testament ['testəmənt] *n* **(a)** (*will*) testament *m*; **to make one's (last will and) t.** tester, faire son testament **(b)** (*tribute*) preuve *f*, témoignage *m*; **the victory was a t. to her bravery** cette victoire a été le témoignage de son courage **(c)** *Bible* **the Old/the New T.** l'Ancien/le Nouveau Testament *m*
testamentary [testə'ment(ə)rɪ] *adj* testamentaire
test area *n* zone-test *f*, *pl* zones-tests
testate ['testeɪt] *adj Jur* **to die t.** mourir en laissant un testament valable
testator, *f* **testatrix,** *pl* **-trices, -trixes** [tes'teɪtər, -'teɪtrɪks, -trɪsiːz, -trɪksɪz] *n* testateur, -trice
test ban *n* interdiction *f* des essais nucléaires; **t. treaty** traité *m* de prohibition des essais nucléaires
test-bed *n* banc *m* d'essai
test bench *n* banc *m* d'essai
test card *n TV* mire *f* (de réglage)
test case *n Jur* affaire *f* qui fait jurisprudence
test chart *n TV* mire *f* (de réglage)
test drive *n Aut* course *f* d'essai; (*on road*) essai *m* sur route; **to take a car for a t.** essayer une voiture
test-drive *vt Aut* essayer
tester¹ ['testər] *n* **(a)** (*person*) contrôleur, -euse; (*device*) appareil *m* de contrôle **(b)** (*sample*) (*of cosmetic*) échantillon *m*
tester² *n* (*canopy over bed*) baldaquin *m*, ciel *m*
test flight *n Av* vol *m* d'essai
test-fly *vt* **to t. a plane** faire le vol d'essai d'un avion
testicle ['testɪk(ə)l] *n* testicule *m*
testify ['testɪfaɪ] **1** *vi Jur* témoigner; **to t. in sb's favour/against sb** témoigner en faveur de qn/contre qn; **to t. to a fact** (*of things*) témoigner d'un fait; (*of person*) attester *ou* affirmer un fait, témoigner d'un fait **2** *vt* **(a)** (*one's regret, faith etc*) témoigner **(b)** *Jur* déclarer, affirmer sous serment
testily ['testɪlɪ] *adv* d'un ton irrité
testimonial [testɪ'məʊnɪəl] *n* **(a)** (*character reference*) (*given by company, director*) références *fpl*; (*letter of recommendation*) lettre *f* de recommandation **(b)** (*tribute*) témoignage *m* d'estime; *Fb* **t. (match)** jubilé *m*; **t. advertising** témoignage
testimony ['testɪmənɪ] *n* (*of senses etc*) témoignage *m*; *Jur* attestation *f*; (*of witness*) déposition *f*; **to bear t. to sth** témoigner de qch, rendre témoignage de qch; **in t. whereof** en foi de quoi
testing ['testɪŋ] **1** *adj* (*problem, time, experience etc*) difficile **2** *n* (*of machine, bridge etc*) essai *m*, épreuve *f*; (*of drug, cosmetic*) expérimentation *f*; **animal t.** expérimentation animale *ou* sur les animaux; **t. laboratory** laboratoire *m* d'essai de produits
testis, *pl* **testes** ['testɪs, 'testiːz] *n* testicule *m*
test market *n* marché-test *m*, *pl* marchés-tests, marché *m* témoin
test-market *vt* tester sur le marché
testosterone [tes'tɒstərəʊn] *n* testostérone *f*
test pattern *n TV* mire *f*
test pilot *n Av* pilote *m* d'essai
test run *n Aut* course *f* d'essai; *Comptr* essai *m* de programme, passage *m* d'essai
test track *n Aut* piste *f* d'essai
test tube *n* éprouvette *f*, tube *m* à essai
test-tube baby *n* bébé-éprouvette *m*, *pl* bébés-éprouvette
testy ['testɪ] *adj* irritable
tetanus ['tetənəs] *n Med* tétanos *m*; **t. injection** piqûre *f* antitétanique
tetchily ['tetʃɪlɪ] *adv* d'un ton irrité
tetchiness ['tetʃɪnɪs] *n* irritation *f*
tetchy ['tetʃɪ] *adj* irritable
tête-à-tête ['teɪtɑː'teɪt] **1** *adv* tête-à-tête **2** *n* (*pl* **tête-à-têtes**) tête-à-tête *m inv*
tether¹ ['teðər] *n* (*for tying horse etc*) longe *f*, attache *f*; *Fig* **to be at the end of one's t.** être à bout, *F* être au bout du rouleau
tether² *vt* (*horse etc*) attacher

tetrachloride [tetrə'klɔːraɪd] *n* tétrachlorure *m*
tetragon ['tetrəgən] *n* quadrilatère *m*
tetragonal [te'trægən(ə)l] *adj* quadrilatère
tetrahedron [tetrə'hiːdrən, -'hed-] *n* tétraèdre *m*
tetrameter [te'træmɪtər] *n* (*in poetry*) tétramètre *m*
Teutonic [tjuː'tɒnɪk] *adj* teuton, teutonique; *Hist* **the T. Order (of Knights)** l'ordre *m* Teutonique
Tex *abbr* **Texas**
Texan ['teks(ə)n] **1** *adj* texan **2** *n* Texan, -ane
text [tekst] *n* (*of manuscript, author, in computing*) texte *m*; (*passage from Bible*) citation *f* tirée de l'Écriture sainte; *Sch* **set texts** textes imposés; **t. area** zone *f* de texte; **t. block** bloc *m* de texte; **t. buffer** mémoire *f* tampon de texte; *Comptr* **t. editor** éditeur *m* de texte; **t. input** entrée *f ou* introduction *f* de texte; **t. layout** disposition *f* de texte; **t. mode** mode *m* texte; **t. processing** traitement *m* de texte; **t. processing capabilities** potentiel *m* de traitement de texte; **t. processor** (unité *f* de) traitement de texte
textbook ['tekstbʊk] *n Sch etc* manuel *m*; **physics/algebra t.** manuel *ou* livre *m* de physique/d'algèbre; **t. definition** définition *f* classique; *Fig* **a t. example** un exemple parfait *ou* typique (**of** de); **this was a t. example of how not to impress your boss** c'était l'exemple parfait de ce qu'il ne faut pas faire devant son patron; **a t. landing** (*of plane*) un atterrissage parfait
text editing *n* édition *f* de texte, mise *f* en forme de texte; **t. feature** fonction *f* d'éditeur de texte, fonction d'édition
text file *n Comptr* fichier *m* texte
textile ['tekstaɪl] **1** *adj* textile **2** *n* (*fabric*) tissu *m*; (*raw material*) textile *m*; **the t. industries** l'industrie *f* textile
text processor *n* texteur *m*, logiciel *m* de traitement de texte
text-size *adj* (*newspaper*) plein format
textual ['tekstjʊəl] *adj* textuel; **t. error** erreur *f* de texte
textually ['tekstjʊəlɪ] *adv* textuellement
texture ['tekstʃər] *n* (*of fabric*) tissage *m*; (*of skin, wood etc*) texture *f*, grain *m*; *Fig* (*of prose*) texture *f*; *Tex* **close/loose t.** tissage serré/lâche; **it'll improve the t. of your life** ça améliorera la qualité de votre vie
TFT [tiːef'tiː] *n* (*abbr* **thin film transistor**) transistor *m* en couche mince
TGWU [tiːdʒiːdʌbljuː'juː] *n Br* (*abbr* **Transport and General Workers' Union**) = syndicat *m* des transports et des travailleurs confédérés
Thai [taɪ] **1** *adj* thaïlandais; *Ling* thaï **2** *n* **(a)** Thaïlandais, -aise **(b)** *Ling* thaï *m*
Thailand ['taɪlænd] *n* Thaïlande *f*
thalassotherapy [θæləsəʊ'θerəpɪ] *n* thalassothérapie *f*
thalidomide [θə'lɪdəmaɪd] *n* thalidomide *f*; **t. baby** bébé *m* victime de la thalidomide
Thames [temz] *n* **the T.** la Tamise; *Fig* **he'll never set the T. on fire** il n'a pas inventé l'eau chaude
than [ðæn, *unstressed* ð(ə)n] *conj* (*in comparison of inequality*) que; (*with numbers*) de; **I have more/less t. you** j'en ai plus/moins que vous; **more t. twenty** plus de vingt; **more t. once** plus d'une fois; **he's taller t. me** *or* **t. I am** *or Fml* **t. I** il est plus grand que moi; **I know her better t. you** je la connais mieux que toi; **I feel better t. ever** je me sens mieux que jamais; **she would do anything rather t. let him suffer** elle ferait n'importe quoi plutôt que de le laisser souffrir; **no sooner had we entered t. the music began** nous étions à peine entrés que la musique a commencé; **any person other t. himself** tout autre que lui; **it was none other t. her old friend** ce n'était nul autre que son vieil ami
thane [θeɪn] *n Eng, Scot Hist* ≈ baron *m*
thank [θæŋk] *vt* remercier; (*God*) rendre grâce(s) à; **to t. sb for sth** remercier qn de *ou* pour qch; **to t. sb for doing sth.** remercier qn d'avoir fait qch; **t. God!, t. heaven(s)!, t. goodness!** Dieu merci!; **t. you** merci, je te/vous remercie; **will you have some tea? – no, t. you** veux-tu du thé? – non merci *ou* non je te remercie; **yes, t. you** oui, s'il te plaît; **are you comfortable? – yes, t. you** tu es bien installé? – oui, je te remercie *ou* merci; **t. you very much** merci beaucoup, merci bien; **t. you for coming** merci d'être venu; *F Iron* **t. you for nothing!** je te remercie!; *Iron* **I'll t. you to mind your own business!** je te prie de t'occuper de ce qui te regarde!; **you can t. your lucky stars you're not dead** tu peux remercier ta bonne étoile de ne pas être mort; **to have sb to t. for sth** devoir qch à qn; *Iron* **you have only yourself to t. for it** c'est à toi seul qu'il faut t'en prendre; **the curtains are torn — we've got the cat to t. for that** les rideaux sont déchirés — c'est le chat qui a fait ce beau travail
thankful ['θæŋkfʊl] *adj* reconnaissant; **to be t. to sb for sth** être reconnaissant à qn de qch, *esp Fml* savoir gré à qn de qch; **to be t. that ...** être bien content que ...; **at least that's something to be t. for** voilà au moins quelque chose de positif; **you should be t. you weren't charged extra** vous pouvez vous estimer heureux *ou* vous devriez être content qu'on ne vous ait pas fait payer de supplément
thankfully ['θæŋkfəlɪ] *adv* **(a)** (*gratefully*) avec reconnaissance, avec gratitude **(b)** (*fortunately*) heureusement; **t. no one was hurt** heureusement *ou* Dieu merci, personne n'a été blessé
thankfulness ['θæŋkfʊlnɪs] *n* reconnaissance *f*, gratitude *f*
thankless ['θæŋklɪs] *adj* (*task etc*) ingrat
thanks [θæŋks] **1** *npl* [①**A10**,f] remerciements *mpl*; **give him my t.** remerciez-le de ma part; **to give t. to sb for sth** remercier qn de *ou* pour qch; **to offer** *or* **give t. to God** rendre grâce à Dieu; **to propose a vote of t. to sb** voter des remerciements à qn; **t. be to God!** (rendons) grâce à Dieu!; **that's all the t. I get!** voilà comment on me remercie!

2 *int F* **t.!** merci!; **t. very much!, t. a lot!** merci beaucoup!, merci bien!; **many t. for ...** mille mercis pour ...; **t. for your letter** merci pour *ou* de ta lettre; **t. for coming** merci d'être venu; **no t.** non merci; *F Iron* **t. for nothing!** je te remercie!

3 *prep* **t. to him/to his help** grâce à lui/à son aide; **no t. to you/them** on ne peut pas dire que ce soit grâce à toi/eux
thanksgiving [θæŋks'gɪvɪŋ] *n* action *f* de grâce(s); **T. Day** *US* = fête *f* célébrée le 4e jeudi de novembre; *Can* le jour de l'action de grâces (*fête célébrée le 2e lundi d'octobre*)
thank you *n* remerciement *m*; **t. note** mot *m* de remerciement; **t. letter** lettre *f* de remerciement; **a big t. from all of us** un grand merci de nous tous; **say t.** dis merci
that[1] [ðæt] [①**A30**,9; **B13-14**,6,A] **1** *dem pron* (*pl* **those** [ðəʊz]) **(a)** cela, ça, ce; **give me t.** donnez-moi ça; **what's t.?** qu'est-ce (que c'est) que cela *ou* ça?; **who's t.?** qui est-ce?; **t.'s Mr Thomas** c'est M. Thomas; **is t. you, Anne?** est-ce toi *ou* c'est toi Anne?; **those are my things** ce sont mes affaires; **those are my orders** voilà mes ordres; **is t. all the luggage you're taking?** c'est tout ce que tu emportes comme bagages?; **t.'s where he lives** c'est là qu'il habite; **after/before t.** après/avant cela; **t. was two years ago** il y a deux ans de cela, c'était il y a deux ans; **with t. she took out her handkerchief** là-dessus, elle a sorti son mouchoir; **what do you mean by t.?** qu'entendez-vous par là?; **t. is** *or* **t.'s to say** c'est-à-dire; **so <u>that's</u> settled** bon, ça c'est réglé *ou* voilà qui est réglé; **it was a bad meal and an expensive one at t.** non seulement le repas n'était pas bon mais en plus il était cher; **t.'s right!, t.'s it!** c'est cela!, ça y est!; **t.'s all** c'est tout, voilà tout; **t.'s strange!** voilà qui est curieux!; *F* **good stuff, t.!** ah c'est bon ça!; **and t.'s t.!, so t.'s t.!** et puis voilà!, voilà tout!; **t. will do** ça suffit, c'est bon; **t.'s enough of t.!** en voilà assez!

(b) (*opposed to* **this, these**) celui-là, *f* celle-là, *pl* ceux-là, *f* celles-là; **this is new and t.'s old** celui-ci est neuf et celui-là est vieux

(c) (*indefinite, as antecedent to a relative*) celui, *f* celle, *pl* ceux, *f* celles; **what's t. (that) you're holding?** qu'est-ce que tu as dans la main?; **all those that I saw** tous ceux que j'ai vus; **one of those who were present** (l')un de ceux qui étaient présents; **I'm not one of those who ...** je ne suis pas du genre à *ou* de ceux qui ...; **all those present at the wedding** tous ceux qui ont assisté au mariage

2 *dem adj* (*pl* **those**) ce; (*before vowel or h mute*) cet, *f* cette, *pl* ces; (*for emphasis and in opposition to* **this, these**) ce ... -là, cet ... -là, cette ... -là, *pl* ces ... -là; **t. book** ce livre(-là); **those books** ces livres(-là); **compare t. edition with these two** comparez cette édition-là avec ces deux-ci; **t. one** celui-là, celle-là; **at t. time** à ce moment-là, à cette époque; **in those days** en ce temps-là, à cette époque; **everybody is agreed on t. point** tout le monde est d'accord là-dessus; **t. fool of a gardener** cet imbécile de jardinier; *Dial* **t. there table** cette table-là; *Dial* **how's t. there son of yours?** et ton fils, comment il va?; **well, how's t. leg of yours?** eh bien, et cette jambe *ou* comment va votre jambe?; **it's t. wife of his who's to blame** c'est la faute de sa femme; **all those flowers that you have there** toutes ces fleurs que vous avez là; **what about t.** *or* **those five pounds you owe me?** et ces cinq livres que tu me dois?

3 *dem adv* **(a)** (*with adj or adv of quantity*) **t. high** aussi haut que ça; **it was about t. big** c'était grand comme ça; **can you swim t. far?** tu peux nager aussi loin?; **I don't go there t. often** (*not much*) je n'y vais pas très souvent; **I don't go there <u>that</u> often** je n'y vais pas aussi souvent que ça; **I don't have t. much confidence in him to believe all he says** je n'ai pas assez confiance en lui pour croire tout ce qu'il raconte

(b) (*so*) tellement, si; **is she t. tall?** est-elle si grande (que ça)?; **he's t. stupid he ...** il est tellement stupide qu'il ...
that[2] [ðæt, *unstressed* ðət] [①**A32**,a-d; **B20**,F,1-3] *rel pron sing, pl* (*sometimes omitted*) **(a)** (*for subject*) qui; (*for object*) que; **the letter t. came yesterday** la lettre qui est arrivée hier; **the**

letter t. I sent you la lettre que je vous ai envoyée; **you're the only person t. can help me** vous êtes la seule personne qui puisse m'aider; **miser t. he was, he would not pay** avare comme il était, il n'a pas voulu payer

(b) (*governed by prep which always follows* **that**) lequel, *f* laquelle, *pl* lesquels, *f* lesquelles; **the envelope t. I put it in** l'enveloppe dans laquelle je l'ai mis; **the woman t. we're talking about** la femme dont nous parlons; **the person t. I gave it to** la personne à laquelle *ou* à qui je l'ai donné; **not t. I know of** pas que je sache, pas à ma connaissance

(c) (*after expression of time*) où, que; **the time t. I saw him** la fois *ou* le jour où je l'ai vu; **during the years t. she had spent in prison** pendant les années qu'elle avait passées en prison

that[3] [ðæt, *unstressed* ðət] *conj* [①**A68-69**,2,a] **(a)** (*introducing subordinate clause; often omitted*) que; **she said t. she would come** elle a dit qu'elle viendrait; **I'll see to it t. everything is ready** je veillerai à ce que tout soit prêt; **he's so ill t. he can't work** il est tellement malade qu'il est incapable de travailler; **to wish/hope t.** souhaiter/espérer que + *sub or ind*; **I wish t. it had never happened** je voudrais que cela ne soit jamais arrivé; **I hope t. you'll come** j'espère que vous viendrez

(b) so t., in order t. (afin) que, pour que + *sub*; (*same subject in both clauses*) afin de + *inf*, pour + *inf*; **they kept quiet so t. he could sleep** ils n'ont pas fait de bruit pour que *ou* afin qu'il puisse dormir; **come nearer so t. I can see you** approchez, que je vous voie; **put it there so t. it won't be forgotten** mettez-le là pour qu'on ne l'oublie pas; **I sold it so t. I would have the money** je l'ai vendu afin d'avoir *ou* pour avoir l'argent

(c) *esp Lit* (*exclamatory*) **t. he should behave like this!** dire qu'il se conduit comme cela!; **oh t. it were possible!** oh, si c'était possible!

thatch[1] [θætʃ] *n* (*roof*) chaume *m*; *F* (*hair*) crinière *f*; **under this great t. of hair** sous cette épaisse crinière, sous cette masse de cheveux

thatch[2] *vt* (*roof*) couvrir de *ou* en chaume; **thatched cottage** chaumière *f*; **thatched roof** toit *m* de chaume

thatcher [ˈθætʃər] *n* couvreur *m* en chaume

Thatcherism [ˈθætʃərɪz(ə)m] *n* thatcherisme *m*

Thatcherite [ˈθætʃəraɪt] *adj, n* thatcherien, -ienne

thaw[1] [θɔː] *n Met* dégel *m*, fonte *f* des neiges; **the t. is setting in** c'est le dégel; *Fig* **a t. in relations** un dégel *ou* une détente des relations

thaw[2] **1** *vt* (*snow etc*) dégeler; (*frozen food*) décongeler **2** *vi* (*of snow, ice*) fondre; (*of frozen food etc*) se décongeler; (*of lake etc*) dégeler; *Fig* (*of person*) (*relax*) se dégeler; **it's thawing** il dégèle

► **thaw out 1** *vi* (*of frozen food etc*) se décongeler; (*of lake etc*) dégeler; (*of person*) (*become warm*) se réchauffer; **come in and t. out** entrez et réchauffez-vous **2** *vtsep* (*frozen food*) décongeler

thawing [ˈθɔːɪŋ] *n* (*of river etc*) dégel *m*; (*of snow*) fonte *f*; (*of frozen food*) décongélation *f*; **a t. in relations** un dégel *ou* une détente des relations

the[1] [ðiː; *unstressed before consonant* ðə; *unstressed before vowel* ðɪ] *def art* **(a)** [①**A6-8; B3-4**,A] le, *f* la, (*before vowel or h mute*) l', *pl* les; **at/to the ...** au ..., à la ..., *pl* aux ...; **of/from the ...** du ..., de la ..., *pl* des ...; **t. father and (t.) mother** le père et la mère; **I spoke to t. driver** j'ai parlé au conducteur; **t. roof of t. house** le toit de la maison; **t. arrival of t. guests** l'arrivée des invités; **at** *or* **on t. corner** au coin; **on t. other side** de l'autre côté; **on t. Monday he fell ill** le lundi il est tombé malade; **I'll see him in t. summer** je le verrai cet été; **in t. summer of 1946** pendant l'été 1946, en été 1946; **in t. year 1314** en l'an 1314; **t. Greeks** les Grecs; **t. Martins** (*family*) les Martin; **Edward t. Seventh** Édouard Sept; **t. England of today** l'Angleterre d'aujourd'hui; **he's t. best-looking man I know** c'est le plus bel homme que je connaisse; *F* **well, how's t. throat then?** eh bien, et cette gorge?; *F* **t. wife** (*my/your wife*) ma/ta femme; **Mrs Long, t. managing director of the firm** Mme. Long, PDG de l'entreprise; **t. impudence/cheek of it!** quelle audace/quel culot!; **the concept of t. beautiful/good** le concept du beau/bon; **words borrowed from t. French** mots empruntés au français; **t. poor** les pauvres; **Catherine t. Great** Catherine la Grande; **she's got t. measles/flu** elle a la rougeole/grippe; **t. golden eagle lives in mountainous regions** l'aigle royal vit dans les régions montagneuses; **who invented t. wheel?** qui a inventé la roue?; **to be paid by t. hour** être payé à l'heure; **eight apples to t. kilo** huit pommes au kilo; **thirty miles to t. gallon** = dix litres aux cent kilomètres; **to play t. trumpet/drums** jouer de la trompette/de la batterie; **I was absent at t. time** j'étais absent à cette époque *ou* à ce moment-là; **do leave t. child alone!** mais laissez-le donc, cet enfant!; **she's giving up her job – t. woman's mad!** elle quitte son emploi – c'est une folle!

(b) (*stressed*) [ðiː] **her father is Professor Smith, <u>the</u> Professor Smith** son père est le professeur Smith, le fameux *ou* le célèbre professeur Smith; **Maurice's is <u>the</u> shop for furniture** pour les meubles, la maison Maurice est la meilleure qui soit

the[2] *adv* **I am all t. more/t. less surprised that ...** j'en suis d'autant plus/d'autant moins surpris que ...; **he ran all t. faster** il a couru d'autant plus vite; **t. longer the wait t. bigger the disappointment** plus on attend plus on est déçu; **t. sooner t. better** le plus tôt sera le mieux; **t. less said about it t. better** moins on en parlera mieux cela vaudra; **t. more he drinks t. thirstier he gets** plus il boit, plus il a soif

theatre, *US* **theater** [ˈθɪətər] *n* **(a)** (*building, drama*) théâtre *m*; **open air t.** théâtre en plein air; **to go to the t.** aller au théâtre *ou* au spectacle; **the English t.** le théâtre anglais **(b)** **(lecture) t.** amphithéâtre *m*; *Br Med* **(operating) t.** salle *f* d'opération; **in t.** en salle d'op **(c)** (*area*) **the t. of war** le théâtre de la guerre; **t. (nuclear) weapon** arme *f* de théâtre

theatre bill *n* affiche *f* de théâtre

theatre company *n* compagnie *f* théâtrale

theatre critic *n* critique *mf* théâtral(e) *ou* de théâtre

theatre(-)goer, *US* **theater-** *n* amateur, -trice de théâtre

theatre(-)going, *US* **theater- 1** *adj* **the t. public** ceux qui vont au théâtre **2** *n* fréquentation *f* des théâtres

theatre sister *n Med* infirmière *f* au bloc opératoire

theatre workshop *n* atelier *m* de théâtre

theatrical [θɪˈætrɪk(ə)l] *adj* **(a)** *Th* théâtral; **t. company** compagnie *f* théâtrale **(b)** *Fig* (*attitude etc*) théâtral

theatrically [θɪˈætrɪklɪ] *adv* **(a)** *Th* théâtralement **(b)** *Fig* théâtralement, avec affectation

theatricals [θɪˈætrɪkəlz] *npl* **(amateur) t.** théâtre *m* d'amateurs; *Fig* **we don't need all the t.!** épargnez-nous toute cette mise en scène *ou* toute cette comédie!

thee [ðiː] *pers pron objective case, Arch, Dial, Lit* **(a)** (*unstressed*) te; (*before a vowel or h mute*) t'; **we beseech t.** nous te supplions; **sit t. down** assieds-toi **(b)** (*stressed*) toi; **he thinks of t.** il pense à toi

theft [θeft] *n* vol *m*; **t. cover** garantie *f* vol; *Aut* **t. deterrent faceplate** cache-radio *m*; **t. insurance** assurance *f* vol; **t. risk** risque *m* de vol

theftproof [ˈθeftpruːf] *adj* (*vehicle etc*) muni d'un dispositif antivol; (*lock etc*) antivol, de sécurité

their [ðeər] [①**A30**,8; **A42**,3; **B19-20**,E,1] *poss adj* **(a)** leur, *f* leur, *pl* leurs; **t. neighbour(s)** leur(s) voisin(s); **t. father and mother** leur père et leur mère, leurs père et mère; **t. eyes are blue** ils ont les yeux bleus; **they have a car of t. own** ils ont leur propre voiture; **they've lost t. hats** ils ont perdu leur chapeau; **T. Majesties** Leurs Majestés **(b)** [①**A27-8**,g] *F* (*after indef pron or to replace his/her*) son, *f* sa, *pl* ses; **someone's left t. umbrella** quelqu'un a laissé son parapluie; **each candidate should bring t. ...** chaque candidat doit amener son ...

theirs [ðeəz] *poss pron* [①**A30**,8; **B20**,E,2] **(a)** le leur, la leur, *pl* les leurs; **this house is t.** cette maison est la leur *ou* est à eux/elles *ou* leur appartient; **a friend of t.** un ami à eux/elles, un de leurs amis; **that damn dog of t.!** leur sacré chien!; **I'm interested in them and (in) t.** (*their family*) je m'intéresse à eux et aux leurs; *Fml* **t. is not to reason why** il ne leur revient pas d'en questionner la raison **(b)** [①**A27-8**,g] *F* (*indef or to replace his/hers*) le sien, la sienne

theism [ˈθiːɪz(ə)m] *n Rel* théisme *m*

theist [ˈθiːɪst] *n* théiste *mf*

theistic [θiːˈɪstɪk] *adj Rel* théiste

them [ðem, ðəm] **1** *pers pron pl objective case* [①**A26**; **A42**,3; **B17**,2] **(a)** (*unstressed*) (*direct*) les *mf*; (*indirect*) leur *mf*; (*after prepositions*) eux, *f* elles; **I like t.** je les aime bien; **have you seen t.?** les avez-vous vu(e)s?; **give t. some** donnez-leur-en; **speak to t.** parlez-leur; **look at t.** regardez-les; **they took the keys away with t.** ils ont emporté les clefs avec eux

(b) (*stressed*) eux, *f* elles; **I'm thinking of t.** c'est à eux/elles que je pense; **it's t.!** c'est eux/elles!, ce sont eux/elles!, les voilà!; **we're not as rich as t.** nous ne sommes pas aussi riches qu'eux

(c) (*other prep combinations*) **every one of t. was killed** ils ont tous été tués; **there were three of t.** (*of people*) ils/elles étaient trois; (*of objects*) il y en avait trois; **it was nice/good of them to come** c'est gentil de leur part d'être venus/c'est bien qu'ils soient venus; **give me half of t.** donnez-m'en la moitié; **several/many/most of t.** plusieurs/beaucoup/la plupart d'entre eux; **neither of t.** ni l'un ni l'autre; **none of t.** aucun d'entre eux

(d) [①A27-8,g] *F (as indef pron)* **when anyone comes she says to t. …** quand quelqu'un vient elle lui dit …
2 *adj Dial (those)* ces

thematic [θiː'mætɪk] *adj Mus etc* thématique

theme [θiːm] *n* (a) *(of speech etc)* sujet *m*, thème *m*; **t. advertising** publicité *f* thématique; **t. evening** soirée *f* à thème; **t. restaurant** restaurant *m* à thème; **t. weekend** week-end *m* à thème (b) *Sch, Am (essay)* dissertation *f* (c) *Art, Lit, Mus etc* thème *m*, motif *m*; *Mus* **t. with variations** thème et variations *fpl*

themed [θiːmd] *adj* thématique; *TV* **t. channel** chaîne *f* thématique; **t. evening** soirée *f* thématique

theme music *n Rad, TV (of programme)* générique *m*; *Cin (in film)* thème *m* principal de la musique d'un/du film

theme park *n* parc *m* à thème

theme song, theme tune *n* = **theme music**

themselves [ðəm'selvz, *stressed* ðem-] *pers pron pl* [①A29] (a) *(emphatic)* eux-mêmes, *f* elles-mêmes; **they did it t.** ils l'ont fait eux-mêmes; **they t. are resigned to it** eux-mêmes s'y sont résignés; **they were standing in a corner by t.** ils étaient tout seuls dans un coin; **they were whispering among t.** ils chuchotaient entre eux; **the houses t. were quite elegant, but …** les maisons elles-mêmes étaient assez belles, mais … (b) *(reflexive)* [①B26,D] se; **they've hurt t.** ils se sont fait mal; **they don't see t. living here forever** ils ne se voient pas vivre ici toute leur vie (c) [①A27-8,g] *F (indef use)* **if anybody hurts t.** si quelqu'un se fait mal

then [ðen] **1** *adv* (a) *(at that time)* alors, en ce temps-là, à cette époque; **what were you doing t.?** que faisiez-vous alors?; **the t. existing system** le système qui existait à cette époque *ou* en ce temps-là; **in the conditions t. prevailing, in the t. prevailing conditions** dans les conditions d'alors *ou* de l'époque; **t. and there** séance tenante, sur-le-champ
(b) *(after, next)* puis, ensuite, alors; *(in space)* puis; **we'll have soup first (and) t. some fish** on prendra d'abord du potage (et) ensuite du poisson; **what t.?** et puis (quoi)?, et (puis) après?; **on the left the church, t. a few old houses** à gauche l'église, puis quelques vieilles maisons
(c) *(in addition)* d'ailleurs, et aussi, et puis; **and t. there are the children to be considered** et puis *ou* et aussi il faut penser aux enfants
(d) **but t.** mais; **she lost her temper, but t. that's hardly surprising** elle s'est énervée, mais à vrai dire ce n'est pas étonnant; **it's beautiful material, but t. it is expensive** c'est du beau tissu, mais c'est vrai qu'il coûte cher
(e) **before t.** avant cela; **will you have finished by t.?** est-ce que vous aurez fini d'ici là?; **by t. it will be too late** à ce moment-là il sera trop tard; **between now and t.** d'ici là; **(every) now and t.** de temps en temps, de temps à autre; **(ever) since t., from t. on** dès lors, depuis ce temps-là; **until t.** *(referring to past time)* jusqu'alors; *(until future time)* jusque-là
(f) *(in that case)* donc, alors; **if you want to go, t. go!** si tu veux y aller, (eh bien) vas-y!; **well t., you're coming?** alors tu viens?; **right t. …** bon …, bien …; **(but) t. you should have told him so** en ce cas vous auriez dû le lui dire; **you knew all the time t.?, t. you knew all the time?** donc tu le savais depuis le début?
2 *adj (in front of noun)* **the t. Foreign Secretary** le Ministre des Affaires Étrangères d'alors *ou* de l'époque; **his t. wife** son épouse d'alors

thence [ðens] *adv Fml, Lit* (a) *(from there)* de là; **we went to Paris and (from) t. to Rome** nous sommes allés à Paris et de là à Rome (b) *(from that time)* = **thenceforth** (c) *(as a result of that)* pour cette raison, par conséquent

thenceforth, thenceforward ['ðens'fɔːθ, -'fɔːwəd] *adv Fml, Lit* **(from) t.** dès lors

theocracy [θiː'ɒkrəsɪ] *n* théocratie *f*

theocratic [θiːə'krætɪk] *adj* théocratique

theodolite [θiː'ɒdəlaɪt] *n (in surveying)* théodolite *m*

theologian [θiːə'ləʊdʒ(ɪ)ən] *n* théologien *m*

theological [θiːə'lɒdʒɪk(ə)l] *adj* théologique; **t. college** séminaire *m*

theologically [θiːə'lɒdʒɪklɪ] *adv* théologiquement; *(from a theological point of view)* d'un point de vue théologique

theology [θiː'ɒlədʒɪ] *n* théologie *f*

theorem ['θɪərəm] *n Math, Phys etc* théorème *m*

theoretical [θiːə'retɪk(ə)l] *adj (reasoning etc)* théorique; *(doctrine)* théorétique; **it's only t.** ce n'est que de la théorie

theoretically [θiːə'retɪklɪ] *adv* théoriquement, du point de vue théorique; **t., individuals can travel where they like** théoriquement *ou* en théorie, les individus peuvent voyager où ils le désirent

theoretician [θiːərɪ'tɪʃən] *n* théoricien, -ienne

theorist ['θiːərɪst] *n* théoricien, -ienne

theorize ['θiːəraɪz] *vi* théoriser

theorizing ['θiːəraɪzɪŋ] *n* théorisation *f*

theory ['θiːərɪ] *n* théorie *f*; **in t.** en théorie; **I have a t. about that** j'ai mon idée là-dessus

theosophical [θiːə'sɒfɪk(ə)l] *adj* théosophique

theosophist [θiː'ɒsəfɪst] *n* théosophe *mf*

theosophy [θiː'ɒsəfɪ] *n* théosophie *f*

therapeutic [θerə'pjuːtɪk] *adj Med, Fig* thérapeutique

therapeutically [θerə'pjuːtɪklɪ] *adv* thérapeutiquement; *(from therapeutic point of view)* d'un point de vue thérapeutique

therapeutics [θerə'pjuːtɪks] *npl* [①A10,c] *Med* thérapeutique *f*

therapist ['θerəpɪst] *n* (a) *(psychological)* psychothérapeute *mf* (b) *(in general)* thérapeute *mf*

therapy ['θerəpɪ] *n Med* (a) *(psychological)* psychothérapie *f* (b) *(in general)* thérapie *f*; **speech t.** orthophonie *f*

there [ðeər, *unstressed* ðər] **1** *adv* (a) [①A23,3,b] *(in that place)* là; **the keys aren't t.** les clefs ne sont pas là *ou* n'y sont pas; **put it t.** mets-le là; *(extending hand)* serre-moi la main; **she's still t.** elle est encore là, elle y est toujours; **does he work t.?** c'est là qu'il travaille?; **we're t.!** nous voilà arrivés!; **who's t.?** qui est là?; *F* **to be all t.** *(alert, shrewd)* être malin; *(in full possession of one's faculties)* avoir toute sa raison *ou* toute sa tête; *F* **she's not all t.** elle a un (petit) grain, elle est un peu marteau; **I'm going t.** j'y vais; **t. and back** aller et retour; **t. and then** séance tenante, sur-le-champ; *Fig* **I've been t.** je suis passé par là, j'ai connu ça; *F* **to be t. for sb** être là auprès de qn; **give me that book t.** donnez-moi ce livre-là; **that man t.** cet homme-là; **your friend t.** votre ami; **hey! you t.!** hé, vous là-bas!; **move along t., please!** circulez, s'il vous plaît; **t. they are!** les voilà!; **t. she comes!** la voilà (qui arrive)!; **we go to Paris and from t. to Rome** nous allons à Paris et de là à Rome; **somewhere round t.** *or* **near t.** quelque part par là; **put it over t.** mettez-le là-bas *ou* par là; **down t.** en bas; **up t.** là-haut; **in t.** là-dedans; **under t.** là-dessous; **t.'s a dear!** tu seras gentil!; **t. you are!** *(here's what you asked for)* (et) voilà!; **just press the button and t. you are!** *(it's done)* vous n'avez qu'à appuyer sur le bouton et ça y est!
(b) **t. is/are** il y a; **t. was/were** il y avait, il était; **t. will be** il y aura; **t. was once a king** il était *ou* il y avait une fois un roi; **t. was singing and dancing** on a chanté et dansé; **will t. be food?** est-ce qu'il y aura à manger?; **t.'s a page missing** il manque une page; **t. is only one** il n'y en a qu'un; **t.'s one slice left** il reste une tranche; **t. are** *or F* **t.'s two slices left** il reste deux tranches; **t.'s nothing we can do to help them** on ne peut rien faire pour les aider; **t.'s no need to shout** c'est inutile de crier; **t. isn't any** il n'y en a pas; **t.'s someone at the door** il y a quelqu'un à la porte; **t. comes a time when …** il arrive un moment où …; **t.'s the bell ringing** voilà la cloche qui sonne
(c) *(in that matter)* quant à cela, dans ce domaine, sur ce sujet; **t. 's** *or* **t. lies the difficulty** voilà le problème, le problème est là; *F* **t. you have me!, you've got me t.!** ça, ça me dépasse
(d) *(at this point)* là; **we'll have to stop t. for today** nous nous arrêterons là pour aujourd'hui
2 *int* voilà!; **t. now, that's done!** là! voilà qui est fait!; **t. now, that wasn't too painful, was it?** alors, ça n'a pas été trop douloureux, hein?; **t. (you are), I told you so** là! je te l'avais bien dit!; **t.!, t.! (now) don't worry!** allons, allons, ne t'inquiète pas!; **I'll do as I like, so t.!** je ferai comme il me plaira, et puis c'est tout!

thereabouts ['ðeərə'baʊts] *adv* (a) *(with place) (nearby)* près de là; *(in that area)* dans le voisinage; **in Brighton or t.** à Brighton ou quelque part par là (b) *(with number, quantity, distance etc) (approximately)* à peu près, environ; **the parcel weighs two kilos or t.** le colis pèse environ deux kilos

thereafter [ðeər'ɑːftər] *adv Fml, Lit* après (cela), par la suite

thereby [ðeə'baɪ *when at the end of clause*; 'ðeəbaɪ *when preceding verb*] *adv Fml* ainsi, de cette façon; *prov* **t. hangs a tale!** c'est toute une histoire!

therefore ['ðeəfɔːr] *adv* donc, aussi; **I think, t. I am** je pense, donc je suis; **I should t. be grateful if you would …** je vous serais donc reconnaissant *ou* aussi vous serais-je reconnaissant de bien vouloir …; **they had t. decided to …** ils avaient donc décidé de …; **you are his friend and t. mine** vous êtes son ami et donc vous êtes aussi le mien

therefrom [ðeə'frɒm] *adv Lit, Fml* de là; **it follows t. that …** cela signifie donc que …

therein [ðeər'ɪn] *adv Lit, Fml* (a) *(in that matter)* en cela; **t. you are mistaken** en cela vous vous trompez (b) *(in that place)* (là-)dedans; **and all the furniture t.** *(in house)* et tous les meubles qu'elle contient

thereof [ðeər'ɒv] *adv Lit, Fml* de cela, en; **in lieu t.** au lieu de

cela; **he drank t.** il y but; **the building and the owner t.** l'immeuble et le propriétaire de celui-ci
there's [ðeəz] = **there is, there has**
thereto [ðeə'tuː] *adv Lit, Fml* à cela, y; **the house and the garden pertaining t.** la maison et le jardin qui va avec celle-ci
thereupon ['ðeərə'pɒn] *adv Fml* **(a)** (*at which point*) sur ce, sur quoi, là-dessus; **t. he left** sur quoi il est parti **(b)** *Lit* **there is much to be said t.** il y aurait beaucoup à dire là-dessus *ou* à ce sujet
therewith [ðeə'wɪð, -'wɪθ] *adv Fml, Lit* **(a)** (*with that*) avec cela **(b)** = **thereupon (a)**
therm [θɜːm] *n Br Phys etc* thermie *f*
thermal[1] ['θɜːm(ə)l] *adj* **(a)** thermal; *Comptr* **t. paper** papier *m* thermique *ou* thermosensible; *Comptr* **t. printer** imprimante *f* thermique *ou* thermoélectrique; **t. springs** eaux *fpl ou* sources *fpl* thermales; *Comptr* **t. transfer** transfert *m* thermique; **t. underwear** sous-vêtements *mpl* en thermolactyl® **(b)** *Phys* thermal, thermique, calorifique; **t. energy** énergie *f* thermique *ou* calorifique; *Nucl Phys* **t. reactor** pile *f ou* réacteur *m* à neutrons thermiques; **t. unit** unité *f* thermique
thermal[2] *n* **(a)** *Met, Av* thermique *m*, ascendance *f* thermique **(b)** *F* **thermals** (*underwear*) (sous-vêtements *mpl* en) thermolactyl® *m*
thermic ['θɜːmɪk] *adj Phys etc* thermique, calorifique
thermionic [θɜːmɪ'ɒnɪk] *adj Electron* thermoélectronique, thermionique
thermistor [θɜː'mɪstər] *n* thermistor *m*
thermocouple ['θɜːməʊkʌp(ə)l] *n El* couple *m* thermoélectrique, thermocouple *m*
thermodynamic [θɜːməʊdaɪ'næmɪk] *adj* thermodynamique
thermoelectric [θɜːməʊɪ'lektrɪk] *adj* thermoélectrique
thermometer [θə'mɒmɪtər] *n* thermomètre *m*
thermonuclear [θɜːməʊ'njuːklɪər] *adj Nucl Phys, Mil* thermonucléaire
thermopile ['θɜːməʊpaɪl] *n El* pile *f* thermoélectrique
thermoplastic [θɜːməʊ'plæstɪk] *adj, n* thermoplastique *m*
Thermos® ['θɜːməs] *n* **T. (flask)** (bouteille *f*) thermos *m or f inv*
thermostat ['θɜːməstæt] *n* thermostat *m*, calorstat *m*
thermostatic [θɜːmə'stætɪk] *adj* thermostatique; **t. control** réglage *m* (de la température) par thermostat; **t. switch** thermocontact *m*
thermostatically [θɜːmə'stætɪklɪ] *adv* **t. controlled** réglé par thermostat
thesaurus, *pl* **-i** [θɪ'sɔːrəs, -aɪ] *n* dictionnaire *m* de synonymes
these *see* **this**
thesis, *pl* **theses** ['θiːsɪs, -iːz] *n* (*in logic*), *Univ etc* thèse *f*; **to uphold/defend a t.** soutenir/défendre une thèse; **PhD** *or* **doctoral t.** thèse de doctorat
Thespian ['θespɪən] *Lit, Hum* **1** *adj* tragique, dramatique **2** *n* acteur, -trice (de théâtre)
they [ðeɪ] **1** *pers pron pl* [①**A26**; **B17**,1] (*unstressed*) ils, *f* elles; (*stressed*) eux, *f* elles; (*with dem force*) ceux, *f* celles; **t. are dancing** ils/elles dansent; **here t. come** les voici (qui arrivent); **t. alone can ...** eux seuls/elles seules peuvent ...; **we are as rich as t. are** nous sommes aussi riches qu'eux/qu'elles; *Lit* **t. who believe** ceux/celles qui croient

2 *indef pron* [①**A27**,e; **B15**,2,c] **(a)** (*people*) on; **t. say that ...** on dit que ...

(b) [①**A27-28**,g] *F* (*after indef pron or to replace he/she*) **nobody ever admits they're wrong** on ne veut jamais reconnaître qu'on a tort; **each candidate must be told that t. should ...** chaque candidat doit être informé qu'il doit ...
they'd [ðeɪd] = **(a) they had,** *see* **have**[2] **(b) they would,** *see* **will**[3]
they'll [ðeɪl] = **they will,** *see* **will**[3]
they're [ðeər] = **they are,** *see* **be**
they've[2] [ðeɪv] = **they have,** *see* **have**[3]
thiamine ['θaɪəm(a)ɪn] *n Bio, Ch* thiamine *f*
thick [θɪk] **1** *adj* **(a)** (*walls, material etc*) épais, *f* épaisse; (*book, thread etc*) gros, *f* grosse; (*lips*) épais, gros; **wall one metre t.** mur d'un mètre d'épaisseur; *F* **to give sb a t. ear** arranger le portrait de qn; **the t. end of a stick** le gros bout d'un bâton; *Fig* **to have a t. skin** avoir la peau dure; *F* **can't you get it into your t. skull** *or* **head that ...?** tu ne peux pas faire entrer dans ta petite tête que ...?

(b) (*dense*) (*forest, undergrowth*) épais, *f* épaisse, touffu; (*carpet*) épais; (*hair*) abondant, épais; (*voice*) (*from alcohol*) aviné; (*from sleep*) ensommeillé; (*from concussion, lust*) étouffé; **t. eyebrows** sourcils *mpl* touffus *ou* épais; **the leaves were/snow was t. on the ground** il y avait une belle épaisseur de feuilles/neige sur le sol; *Fig* **Conservative voters aren't very t. on the ground in these parts** ici les gens qui votent conservateur ne sont pas légion

(c) (*liquid*) épais, *f* épaisse, visqueux; (*mist*) dense, épais; (*darkness*) profond; **t. mud** boue *f* grasse; **the air was t. with smoke** l'air était plein de fumée

(d) *F* **to be very t. with sb** être très copain avec qn; *prov* **they're as t. as thieves** ils s'entendent comme larrons en foire

(e) *F* (*excessive*) **that's a bit t.!** ça c'est un peu raide *ou* un peu fort!

(f) *F* (*stupid*) abruti, bouché; **to be as t. as two short planks** *or* **a brick** être bête comme ses pieds

2 *n* **in the t. of the forest** au beau milieu de la forêt; **in the t. of (the) battle** au cœur de la bataille; **when you are in the t. of it** *or* **of things** dans le feu de l'action; **we soon found ourselves in the t. of things** nous nous sommes vite retrouvés au cœur de l'action; **in the t. of the fight** au (plus) fort *ou* au vif de la mêlée; **to go through t. and thin for sb** faire n'importe quoi pour qn; **to follow sb** *or* **stick to sb through t. and thin** soutenir qn *ou* se rallier à qn quoiqu'il arrive

3 *adv* **(a)** (*in a thick layer*) en couche épaisse; **snow lay t. on the ground** une neige épaisse *ou* une épaisse couche de neige couvrait le sol; **to cut the bread t.** couper le pain en tranches épaisses; *F* **to lay it on a bit t.** exagérer

(b) his blows fell t. and fast il frappait à coups redoublés, les coups pleuvaient dru; **insults were flying t. and fast** les insultes pleuvaient dru; **letters were coming in t. and fast** les lettres pleuvaient *ou* affluaient
thicken ['θɪk(ə)n] **1** *vt* (*wall etc*) épaissir; (*sauce*) épaissir, lier **2** *vi* (*of tree trunk, figure, air etc*) (s')épaissir; (*of sauce*) épaissir; *esp Hum* **the plot thickens ...** l'intrigue se corse ...
thickener, thickening ['θɪk(ə)nər, 'θɪk(ə)nɪŋ] *n* épaississant *m*; **thickening agent** agent *m* épaississant
thicket ['θɪkɪt] *n* fourré *m*
thickhead ['θɪkhed] *n F* abruti, -ie
thickheaded [θɪk'hedɪd] *adj F* (*stupid*) bête, bouché
thickie ['θɪkɪ] *n Br F* idiot, -ote; **so that a t. like me can understand** de sorte qu'un lourdaud *ou* idiot comme moi puisse comprendre; **he's a complete t.** ce n'est pas une flèche; **I was a t. at maths** j'étais nul en maths
thick-lipped *adj* lippu
thickly ['θɪklɪ] *adv* **(a)** (*in thick layer(s)*) en couche(s) épaisse(s); (*cut sth*) en tranches épaisses; **to spread butter t.** étaler généreusement du beurre **(b)** (*densely*) dru; **the snow fell t.** la neige tombait dru; **t. wooded** très boisé **(c) to speak t.** (*with suppressed rage, lust*) parler d'une voix étouffée; (*when drunk*) avoir la voix avinée
thickness ['θɪknɪs] *n* **(a)** (*of wall etc*) épaisseur *f*; (*of lips etc*) grosseur *f*; **roll the pastry out to a t. of 1/8 of an inch** étalez la pâte jusqu'à ce qu'elle fasse environ 3 mm d'épaisseur **(b)** (*of forest etc*) épaisseur *f*; (*of hair, beard etc*) abondance *f* **(c)** (*of liquid*) consistance *f*; (*of fog*) épaisseur *f*; (*of voice*) étouffement *m* **(d)** (*layer*) (*of paper etc*) couche *f*
thicko ['θɪkəʊ] *n Br F* = **thickie**
thickset ['θɪk'set] *adj* (*person*) trapu
thick-skinned *adj* (*animal, fruit*) à la peau épaisse; *Fig* (*person*) qui a la peau dure
thick-sliced *adj* (*bread*) coupé en tranches épaisses
thief, *pl* **thieves** [θiːf, θiːvz] *n* voleur, -euse; **horse t.** voleur *m* de chevaux; **stop t.!** au voleur!; *F* **thieves' kitchen** repaire *m* de voleurs; *Prov* **set a t. to catch a t.** à fripon, fripon et demi *prov* **once a t. always a t.** qui a volé volera
thieve [θiːv] **1** *vi* voler, commettre des vols **2** *vt* voler
thieving ['θiːvɪŋ] **1** *adj* voleur, -euse; **keep your t. hands off!** bas les pattes! **2** *n* vol *m*
thigh [θaɪ] *n* cuisse *f*; **t. boots** cuissardes *fpl*
thighbone ['θaɪbəʊn] *n Anat* fémur *m*
thigh-length *adj* (*dress, coat*) qui descend jusqu'à mi-cuisse; **t. boots** cuissardes *fpl*
thimble ['θɪmb(ə)l] *n Sewing* dé *m* (à coudre); **hunt the t.** (*game*) = cache-tampon *m inv*
thimbleful ['θɪmb(ə)lfʊl] *n* (*of brandy etc*) doigt *m*
thimble printer *n Comptr* imprimante *f* à tulipe
thin[1] [θɪn] (*comp* **thinner,** *superl* **thinnest**) **1** *adj* **(a)** (*paper etc*) mince, fin; (*thread etc*) ténu, fin; (*material*) fin, mince, léger; (*person*) maigre, mince; (*air*) raréfié; **to grow** *or* **become thinner** (*of person*) maigrir; **to get** *or* **become thinner** (*of air*) se raréfier; **as t. as a rake** maigre comme un clou, sec comme un coup de trique; *Fig* **this was only the t. end of the wedge** à partir de là, ce fut l'escalade; *Typ* **t. stroke** délié *m*; **t. film transistor** transistor *m* en couche mince

(b) (*sparse*) (*hair etc*) clairsemé, rare; (*population, audience*) clairsemé; **attendance has been rather t. recently** le taux de présence est très bas en ce moment; **his hair was getting t.** ses cheveux s'éclaircissaient; **t. on the ground** peu nombreux; **t. beard** barbe peu fournie (**c**) (*liquid*) clair, peu consistant; (*blood*) appauvri; **t. soup** potage *m* clair; **t. voice** voix *f* fluette *ou* grêle

(**d**) *Fig* **my patience is wearing t.** ma patience a des limites!; **my patience was wearing t.** je commençais à perdre patience; **his excuse was rather t.** son excuse était un peu légère; **to have a t. time (of it)** (*not enjoy oneself*) s'ennuyer, s'embêter; (*go through hard times*) manger de la vache enragée

2 *adv* **to spread sth t.** étaler qch en couche fine *ou* mince; **they cut the cheese as t. as possible** ils ont coupé le fromage aussi fin que possible

3 *n see* **thick 2**

thin[2] (**-nn-**) **1** *vt* (*paint*) diluer, délayer; (*sauce*) allonger, éclaircir **2** *vi* (*of trees, crowd, hair etc*) s'éclaircir; (*of liquid*) devenir clair; **his hair is thinning** il perd ses cheveux

▶ **thin down** *vtsep* (*dilute*) (*paint*) diluer, délayer; (*sauce*) allonger, éclaircir

▶ **thin out 1** *vi* (*become less dense*) (*of hair*) s'éclaircir; **he's thinning out on top** il se dégarnit sur le dessus du crâne **2** *vtsep* (*make less dense*) (*plants*) éclaircir; (*hair*) éclaircir, désépaissir

thine [ðaɪn] *Arch, Lit* **1** *poss pron* le tien, *f* la tienne, *pl* les tiens, *f* les tiennes; **for thee and t.** pour toi et les tiens; **what is mine is t.** ce qui est à moi est à toi **2** *poss adj* (*used instead of* **thy** *before a noun or adj beginning with a vowel or h mute*) ton, *f* ta, *pl* tes

thing [θɪŋ] *n* (**a**) chose *f*, *F* truc *m*; **a t. of beauty** une belle chose; **the things of this world** les choses de ce monde; **chocolate, sweets, and things (like that)** le chocolat, les bonbons, et autres choses de ce style; *F* **what's that t.?** qu'est-ce que c'est que ce machin-là?; *F* **where's that scraper t.?** où est le machin pour gratter?; **my things** (*clothes etc*) mes vêtements *mpl*; (*belongings*) mes affaires *fpl*; **winter things** (*clothes*) vêtements d'hiver; **bring along your swimming things** apportez vos affaires de bain; **to pack (up) one's things** faire ses valises; **I didn't bring a lot of things** (*on holiday*) je n'ai pas pris beaucoup d'affaires

(**b**) *F* (*person*) (*with adj expressing pity, contempt etc*) être *m*, créature *f*; **poor t.!** le/la pauvre!; **you silly t.!** sot/sotte que tu es!; **poor little things!** pauvres petits!; **she's a dear old t.** c'est une petite vieille bien sympathique

(**c**) (*action, remark, fact etc*) chose *f*; **that was a silly t. to do** ça, ce n'est pas très malin de ta/sa/*etc* part; **what a silly/nasty t. to say!** c'est vraiment stupide/méchant de dire ça *ou* une chose pareille; **the things you say!** les choses que tu peux dire parfois!; **how could you do such a t.?** comment avez-vous pu faire une chose pareille?; **how could you say such a t.!** comment avez-vous pu dire une chose pareille!; **did you ever hear of such a t.?** on n'a pas idée d'une chose pareille!; **you take things too seriously** vous prenez les choses trop au sérieux; **she gets things done** avec elle, le travail avance bien; **to think things over** réfléchir; **it's just one of those things** ce sont des choses qui arrivent; **it's a t. you need to give careful consideration to** c'est une chose à laquelle tu dois porter une grande attention; **to talk of one t. and another** parler de choses et d'autres; **it's been one t. after the other** (*problems*) on a eu des problèmes en cascade *ou* une cascade de problèmes; **what with one t. and another we haven't had time** on a été pris par plein de choses et on n'a pas eu le temps; **that's the very t.** c'est juste ce qu'il faut; **the t. is this** voici ce dont il s'agit; **the t. is, I haven't got any money** le problème, c'est que je n'ai pas d'argent; **the only t. left is to ...** il ne reste plus qu'à ...; **the important t. is that ...** l'important c'est que ...; **the t. to remember is that ...** ce dont il faut se souvenir est que ...; **that's quite another t.** ça, c'est tout autre chose; **neither one t. nor another** ni l'un(e) ni l'autre; **and another t.** en plus; *F* **he's on to a good t.** il est sur un bon filon *ou* un bon coup; **I don't know a t. about algebra** je n'y connais absolument rien en algèbre; **it doesn't mean a t. to me** (*I don't understand it at all*) je n'y comprends (absolument) rien; (*it isn't at all familiar to me*) ça ne me dit absolument rien; (*it doesn't concern me at all*) ça ne me concerne pas; **there isn't a t. we can do about it** il n'y a absolument rien que nous puissions y faire; **to know a t. or two** (*to know a few tricks etc*) avoir plus d'un tour dans son sac; (*to be well informed*) en savoir long; *F* **she's got a t. about French** (*loves it*) le français, c'est son truc; (*hates it*) le français, ce n'est pas son truc; *F* **he's got a t. about that, it's a t. with him** c'est son idée fixe; *F* **do your (own) t.!** fais comme il te plaira!; **things are going badly** ça va mal; **as things are** les choses étant comme elles sont; *F* **how are things?, how's things?** comment ça va?

(**d**) **the latest t. in shoes** la dernière mode en matière de chaussures; **it's the (very) latest t.** c'est tout ce qu'il y a de plus moderne; **he looks quite the t.** il est vraiment très chic; **the t. (to do)** (*etiquette*) l'usage *m*; **it's not the done t.** cela ne se fait pas

(**e**) *F* (*penis*) machin *m*

thingummy, thingamy, thingumajig, thingumabob, thingy ['θɪŋəmɪ, -dʒɪg, -bɒb, 'θɪŋɪ] *n F* (*object*) truc *m*, machin *m*, bidule *m*; (*person*) machin *m*, machine *f*, trucmuche *mf*

think[1] [θɪŋk] *n* **to have a t.** réfléchir; **what do you say? – I'll have a t. about it** qu'en dis-tu? – je vais réfléchir; *F* **you've got another t. coming!** tu peux toujours courir!

think[2] (*pt, pp* **thought** [θɔːt]) **1** *vi* penser, réfléchir; **to t. aloud** penser tout haut; **to t. (long and) hard** bien réfléchir, *F* se creuser la tête; *F* **to t. big** être ambitieux; **I did it without thinking** je l'ai fait sans réfléchir *ou* sans y penser; **I'm sorry, I wasn't thinking** désolé, je l'ai fait/dit sans réfléchir; **I was so pressed for time that I wasn't even thinking** (*during exam*) j'étais tellement pris par le temps que j'écrivais n'importe quoi; **you just don't t., do you!** (*are inconsiderate, careless etc*) jamais tu ne réfléchis, hein!; **t. before you speak** réfléchissez avant de parler; **just t. a minute!** réfléchissez un peu!; **give me time to t.** laissez-moi une minute que je réfléchisse; **you t. too much** tu réfléchis trop; **to t. again** se raviser; **you can (just) t. again!** tu peux toujours courir!; **it makes you t.** ça vous fait réfléchir; **I'd t. twice about that, if I were you** j'y réfléchirais à deux fois si j'étais toi; **to t. on one's feet** savoir prendre des décisions rapidement

2 *vt* (**a**) (*imagine, suppose*) **what are you thinking?** à quoi pensez-vous?; **I know what you're thinking** je sais ce que vous pensez *ou* ce que vous vous dites, je sais à quoi vous pensez; **I was just thinking 'I wonder where he is' when ...** j'étais justement en train de me dire 'je me demande où il est' lorsque ...; **I (really) can't t. why/what/where ...** je me demande bien pourquoi/ce que/où ...; **I can't t. what you mean** je n'arrive pas à comprendre *ou* voir ce que vous voulez dire; **what will people t.?** que vont penser les gens?; **he thinks he knows everything** il s'imagine tout savoir; **one would have thought that ...** c'était à croire que ...; **anyone would t. she was asleep** on dirait qu'elle dort; **who'd have thought it!** qui l'eût cru?!; **just t.!** songez donc!; **to t. that he's only twenty!** et dire qu'il n'a que vingt ans!; **and to t. it used to cost just ...!** quand je pense qu'avant ça ne coûtait que ...; **t. what we could do with all that money!** pense *ou* songe à tout ce que nous pourrions faire avec tout cet argent; **I have been thinking that ...** l'idée m'est venue que ...; *esp Lit* **I only thought to help you** ma seule pensée était de vous aider; **did you t. to bring any money?** avez-vous pensé *ou* songé à apporter de l'argent?; **to t. evil/kind thoughts** avoir de sombres/douces pensées

(**b**) [①**A46,9,a,iii**] (*believe, have as opinion*) **do you t. you could do it? – I t. I could** pensez-vous que cela vous serait possible? – je pense que oui; **it's better to get it over with, don't you t.?** il vaut mieux en finir, ne croyez-vous pas?; **I thought I heard her** j'ai cru l'entendre; **I thought it was all over** je croyais que tout était fini; **everyone asked him what he thought** chacun lui a demandé son avis; **what do <u>you</u> t., Jenny?** et toi, qu'en penses-tu, Jenny?; **well what do you t.? does it suit me?** alors, qu'est-ce que tu en penses, ça me va?; **I t. she's pretty/nice** je la trouve jolie/sympa; **everyone thought he was mad** on le tenait pour fou; **I rather t. it's going to rain** j'ai dans l'idée qu'il va pleuvoir; **it is thought that ...** on suppose que ... + *ind*; **I t. so** je pense que oui; **I don't t. so, I t. not** je pense que non; **that's what I t. (too)** c'est (aussi) mon impression; **so I thought, I thought so, I thought as much** c'est bien ce que je pensais; **I (should) hardly t. so** c'est peu probable; **I should t. so!** je crois bien!; **do you t. they'll agree? – I should t. so** croyez-vous qu'ils accepteront? – je pense que oui; **he's going to apologize – I should t. so (too)!** il va s'excuser – j'espère bien!; **he apologized – I should t. so (too)!** il s'est excusé – ce n'est pas trop tôt!; **I shouldn't t. so** je ne crois pas; *F* **that's what you t.!** c'est ce que tu crois!, tu te fais des idées!

(**c**) (*judge*) juger, considérer, croire; **if you t. it necessary to ...** si vous jugez nécessaire de ...; **I hardly t. it likely that ...** il me semble peu probable que ... + *sub*; **to t. fit** *or* **t. it proper to ...** juger bon *ou* convenable de ...; **you thought her (to be) a fool** vous l'avez prise pour une sotte; **they were thought to be rich** on les disait *ou* supposait riches; (*they passed for rich*) ils passaient pour (être) riches

(**d**) (*expect*) **I little thought I would see him again** je ne m'attendais guère à le revoir

(**e**) *F* **designers are thinking pink** le rose, c'est la couleur in chez les stylistes; **the company is thinking expansion** le maître mot dans la société, c'est expansion

▶ **think about** *vipo* (**a**) penser à; **what are you thinking about?** à quoi penses-tu?; **do you still t. about her?** pensez-vous encore à elle?; **he can't sleep for thinking about it** il perd le sommeil à force d'y penser, *F* il n'en dort plus; **that's worth thinking about** cela mérite réflexion; **quite cheap when you t. about it** plutôt bon marché quand on y pense

(**b**) (*consider*) (*proposal etc*) réfléchir à; **what do you say? – I'll t. about it** qu'en dites-vous? – j'y songerai *ou* réfléchirai; **that will give them something to t. about** voilà qui va leur donner matière à réflexion; **to t. about doing sth** envisager de *ou* songer à faire qch

(**c**) (*take into account*) penser à; **I've got my family/future to t. about** il faut que je pense à ma famille/mon avenir

(**d**) (*have opinion about*) penser de; **what do you t. about him?** que pensez-vous de lui?; **what do you t. about it?** qu'en pensez-vous?

▶ **think back** *vi* repenser; **to t. back on past events** repenser à des événements passés; **when I t. back** quand j'y repense; **t. back to what you were doing in 1975** songez à *ou* rappelez-vous ce que vous faisiez en 1975; **thinking back, I suppose I never really liked him** réflexion faite, je crois que je ne l'ai jamais vraiment aimé

▶ **think of** *vipo* (**a**) (*be attentive to*) penser à, songer à; **to t. of others** penser aux autres; **I've got the children/the children's education to t. of** il faut que je songe aux enfants/à l'éducation des enfants; **I can't t. of everything!** je ne peux pas penser à tout!

(**b**) (*reflect on*) penser à; **we're thinking of you** nous pensons à toi; **I was thinking of how much times have changed** je songeais combien les temps ont changé; **when I t. of what might have happened!** quand je pense à ce qui aurait pu arriver!; **it's rather silly, when you (come to) t. of it** c'est plutôt bête, quand on y pense; **come to t. of it, I did see her that night** maintenant que j'y pense, je l'ai vue cette nuit-là; **what am I thinking of?** où ai-je la tête?; **what were you thinking of, letting the child out on his own?** où avais-tu la tête, pour laisser cet enfant sortir seul?; **we wouldn't t. of letting our daughter travel alone** il ne nous viendrait pas à l'esprit de laisser notre fille voyager seule; **I couldn't t. of it!** c'est impossible!

(**c**) (*recall, bring to mind*) (*name etc*) se rappeler (de); **I can't t. of their number at the moment** je n'arrive pas à me rappeler leur numéro là maintenant; **I can't t. of the right word** le mot juste m'échappe

(**d**) (*imagine*) imaginer, se figurer; **just t. of it, a holiday in the Caribbean!** imagine, des vacances aux Caraïbes!; **and it weighs two tons, (just) t. of that!** et figure-toi que ça pèse deux tonnes!

(**e**) (*have opinion about*) penser de; **what do you t. of him?** que penses-tu de lui?; **what do you t. of it?** qu'en pensez-vous?; **what do you t. of this picture?** que dites-vous de ce tableau?; **I don't t. much of the idea/her taste** je ne trouve pas que cette idée soit très bonne/qu'elle ait très bon goût; **to t. a lot of** *or* **highly of sb** avoir une haute opinion de qn; **to t. a great deal of oneself, to t. too much of oneself** avoir une haute idée de soi-même *ou* de sa personne; **to t. too much of sth** attacher trop d'importance à qch; **I told her what I thought of her** je lui ai dit son fait; **to t. well/badly of sb** avoir une bonne/mauvaise opinion de qn; **he is well thought of** il est bien vu *ou* considéré

(**f**) **to t. of doing sth** envisager de *ou* songer à faire qch; **what were you thinking of giving her?** que pensais-tu lui donner?

(**g**) (*have idea of*) imaginer, penser à, avoir l'idée de; (*solution*) imaginer; **the longest word I could t. of** le mot le plus long auquel je puisse penser; **I've thought of a way of persuading her** j'ai pensé à *ou* imaginé un moyen de la persuader; **try every method you can t. of** essayez toutes les méthodes que vous puissiez imaginer; **who thought of coming to this restaurant?** qui a eu l'idée de venir dans ce restaurant?; **why didn't you phone? – I didn't t. of it** pourquoi n'avez-vous pas téléphoné? – je n'y ai pas pensé; **who thought of the idea?** qui a eu cette idée?; **what a clever idea!, now why didn't I t. of that?** quelle idée géniale!, pourquoi n'y ai-je pas pensé *ou* songé?; **t. of a number** pensez à un chiffre; **I thought of him as being tall** je le voyais grand

▶ **think out** *vtsep* (*plan, solution*) imaginer; **he likes to t. things out for himself** il aime juger des choses par lui-même; **see if you can t. something out** essaie d'imaginer *ou* de trouver une solution; **well thought out plan** projet bien étudié; **carefully thought out answer** réponse bien pesée

▶ **think over** *vtsep* (*question etc*) réfléchir à; **I'll t. it over** j'y réfléchirai; **t. it over (carefully)** réfléchissez-y *ou* songez-y bien; **on thinking it over** réflexion faite, à la réflexion

▶ **think through** *vtas* (*plan etc*) bien considérer; **I thought it through all night** j'y ai réfléchi toute la nuit; **the scheme has not been properly thought through** le plan n'a pas été considéré suffisamment en détail

▶ **think up** *vtsep* (*project, method*) imaginer; **who thought that idea up?** qui a eu cette idée?

thinkable ['θɪŋkəb(ə)l] *adj* concevable, imaginable; **is it t. that ...?** peut-on imaginer que ... + *sub*?; **it is scarcely** *or* **barely t. that ...** il est difficilement concevable *ou* imaginable que ... + *sub*

thinker ['θɪŋkər] *n* penseur, -euse

thinking ['θɪŋkɪŋ] **1** *adj* pensant, qui pense; **the paper for t. people** le journal pour les gens qui réfléchissent; **the t. man's pin-up** la pin-up des intellectuels; **any t. person would agree that ...** n'importe qui réfléchissant un tant soit peu serait d'accord pour dire que ...

2 *n* (**a**) (*process of thought*) pensée(s) *f(pl)*, réflexion(s) *f(pl)*; **to do some t.** réfléchir un peu; **he did some hard t.** il a sérieusement réfléchi; **we'd better do a bit of quick t.** nous ferions bien de réfléchir en vitesse; **to put on one's t. cap** cogiter; **good t.!** bien vu!

(**b**) (*opinion*) opinion *f*, avis *m*; **to my (way of) t.** à mon avis; **I hope to bring you round to my way of t.** j'espère vous amener à mon opinion *ou* à mon point du vue; **she influenced the t. of a generation** elle a influencé la façon de penser de toute une génération

thinking distance *n Aut* temps *m* de réaction

think-tank *n* comité *m ou* groupe *m* d'experts

thin-lipped *adj* aux lèvres minces; **he was rather t.** (*displeased*) il avait les lèvres plutôt pincées

thinly ['θɪnlɪ] *adv* (*in thin layers*) en couche(s) mince(s); (*in thin slices*) en tranches fines; **t. sown wheat** blé *m* clairsemé; **t. populated** peu peuplé; **t. clad** (*lightly*) légèrement vêtu; (*inadequately*) vêtu insuffisamment; **a t. veiled allusion** une allusion à peine voilée

thinner ['θɪnər] *n* (*for paint etc*) diluant *m*

thinness ['θɪnnɪs] *n* (**a**) (*of sheet of paper etc*) minceur *f*; (*of material etc*) légèreté *f*; (*of person*) minceur; (*excessive*) maigreur *f* (**b**) (*of liquid*) fluidité *f*; (*of air*) raréfaction *f*

thinning ['θɪnɪŋ] *adj* **his t. hair** ses cheveux qui commencent à se clairsemer

thinning agent *n* diluant *m*

thin-skinned *adj Fig* (*person*) susceptible, trop sensible

thin-sliced *adj* (*bread*) coupé en tranches fines, finement coupé

third [θɜːd] **1** *num adj, n* (*day, floor etc*) troisième *mf*; **Edward the T.** Édouard III; **(on) the t. (of May)** le trois (mai); **every t. day** tous les trois jours; **the t. age** le troisième âge; *F* **t. degree** interrogatoire *m* serré; **to give sb the t. degree** faire subir un interrogatoire serré à qn; (*treat roughly*) cuisiner qn; *Hist* **the T. Estate** le Tiers État; **t. gear** troisième vitesse *f*; (*gearwheel*) pignon *m* de troisième

2 *n* (**a**) (*fraction*) tiers *m*; **to lose a t./two thirds of one's money** perdre le tiers/les deux tiers de son argent; **one t. full** plein au tiers

(**b**) *Mus* tierce *f*

(**c**) *Br Univ* **to get a t. (class honours degree) in history** obtenir la mention 'passable' en histoire

(**d**) *Aut* **to go into t.** passer en troisième

third-degree burn *n Med* brûlure *f* du troisième degré

thirdly ['θɜːdlɪ] *adv* troisièmement, en troisième lieu

third party *n Jur* (*person*) tiers *m*, tierce personne *f*; **t. cover** assurance *f* aux tiers; **t. fire and theft insurance** assurance au tiers vol et incendie; **t. holder** tiers détenteur *m*; **t. owner** tiers possesseur *m*

third person *n Gram* troisième personne *f*; **to act through a t.** (*in negotiation etc*) passer par une tierce personne

third rate *adj* médiocre, de troisième ordre

Third Reich *n Hist* Troisième Reich *m*

Third World *n* tiers-monde *m*

thirst[1] [θɜːst] *n* soif *f*; *Fig esp Lit* **the t. for** *or* **after knowledge** la soif de connaissances; **to satisfy one's t. for adventure** satisfaire sa soif d'aventures

thirst[2] *vi Arch, Lit* être altéré *ou* avide (**for** de); *Lit* **to t. for blood/revenge** être altéré de sang/de vengeance

thirstily ['θɜːstɪlɪ] *adv* avidement

thirsty ['θɜːstɪ] *adj* (*person*) qui a soif; (*stronger*) assoiffé; (*earth etc*) desséché; *F* (*car*) qui consomme énormément; **to be** *or* **feel t.** avoir soif; **I'm t.** j'ai soif; **to make sb t.** donner soif à qn; *F* **all this talking is t. work** de parler autant, cela donne soif *ou* cela vous sèche le gosier; *Fig Lit* **t. for blood/for riches** assoiffé *ou* altéré *ou* avide de sang/de richesses

thirteen [θɜː'tiːn] *num adj, n* treize *m*; **she's t. (years old)** elle a treize ans; **at t. hundred hours** à treize heures

thirteenth [θɜː'tiːnθ] **1** *num adj, n* treizième *mf*; **(on) the t. (of May)** le treize (mai); **Friday the t.** vendredi treize **2** *n* (*fraction*) treizième *m*

thirtieth ['θɜːtɪɪθ] *num adj, n* trentième *mf*; **(on) the t. (of June)** le trente (juin)

thirty [ˈθɜːtɪ] *num adj, n* trente *m*; **t.-three** trente-trois; **t.-first** trente et unième; **t.-second** trente-deuxième; **(on) the t.-first (of May)** le trente et un (mai); **about t. guests** une trentaine d'invités; **to be t. (years old)** avoir trente ans; **the thirties** les années trente; **he leaves at two-t.** il part à deux heures trente

this [ðɪs] [①A30,9; B13-4,6,A] **1** *dem pron* (*pl* **these** [ðiːz]) **(a)** ceci, ce; **what's t.?, what are these?** qu'est-ce que c'est (que ceci *ou F* que ça)?; **who's t.?** qui est-ce?; *Tel* **who is t.?** qui est à l'appareil?; **you'll be sorry for t.** vous le regretterez; **at t.** sur ce, là-dessus; **it ought to have happened before t.** cela aurait dû être fait depuis longtemps; **after t.** après cela, ensuite; **t. is curious** c'est curieux, voilà qui est curieux; **t. is what she told me** voici ce qu'elle m'a dit; **t. is Mr. Ford** je vous présente M. Ford; **these are my children** voici mes enfants; **t. is where she lives** c'est ici qu'elle habite; **these are things we cannot do without** ce sont des choses dont on ne peut se passer; **listen to t.** écoutez bien ceci; **eat/drink some of t.** mangez-/buvez-en un peu; **what's t. (that) I hear?** qu'est-ce que j'apprends?; **do it like t.** fais comme ceci; **what's all t.?** (*these objects*) qu'est-ce que c'est que tout ça?; (*what's happening?*) qu'est-ce qu'il y a?, qu'est-ce qui se passe?

(b) (*opposed to* **that**) **will you have t. or that?** voulez-vous ceci ou cela?; *F* **they were talking about t. and that** ils parlaient de choses et d'autres

(c) (*referring to sth already mentioned*) celui-ci, *f* celle-ci, *pl* ceux-ci, *f* celles-ci; **I prefer these to those** je préfère ceux-ci à ceux-là

2 *dem adj* (*pl* **these**) ce, (*before vowel or h mute*) cet, *f* cette, *pl* ces; (*for emphasis and in opposition to* **that, those**) ce ... -ci, cet ... -ci, cette ... -ci, *pl* ces ... -ci; **t. book** ce livre(-ci); **these books** ces livres(-ci); **t. morning** ce matin; **t. afternoon** cet(te) après-midi; **t. week** cette semaine; **one of these days** un de ces jours; **(in) these days, in t. day and age** de nos jours; **by t. time** à l'heure qu'il est; **to run t. way and that** courir de-ci de-là; **he will tell you that in t. or that case you should ...** il vous dira qu'en tel ou tel cas il faut ...; **for t. reason ...** voilà pourquoi ..., pour cette raison ...; *F* **t. here house** cette maison(-ci); *F* **I've known him these three years** je le connais depuis trois ans

3 *dem adv* aussi ... que ceci; **t. high, as high as t.** aussi haut que ceci *ou* que cela *ou* que ça; **t. far** jusqu'ici, jusque-là; **can you eat t. much?** pourras-tu manger tout cela?; **t. much is certain ...** ceci au moins est sûr ...

thistle [ˈθɪs(ə)l] *n* chardon *m*

thistledown [ˈθɪs(ə)ldaʊn] *n* duvet *m* de chardon

thither [ˈðɪðər] *adv Arch, Lit* là; *Lit* **to run hither and t.** courir çà et là

tho' [ðəʊ] *conj, adv F, Lit* = **though**

thole, tholepin [ˈθəʊl(pɪn)] *n Naut* tolet *m*

thong [θɒŋ] *n* lanière *f* de cuir; (*of whip*) lanière; *Am, Austr* **a pair of thongs** (*sandals*) des tongs *fpl*

thoracic [θɔːˈræsɪk] *adj* thoracique

thorax, *pl* **thoraces** [ˈθɔːræks, θɔːˈreɪsiːz] *n* thorax *m*

thorn [θɔːn] *n* **(a)** *Bot* épine *f*; *Fig* **to be a t. in sb's flesh** *or* **side** être un sujet continuel d'irritation pour qn **(b)** (*tree*) épine *f*

thornback [ˈθɔːnbæk] *n* (*fish*) raie *f* bouclée

thornbush [ˈθɔːnbʊʃ] *n* (arbrisseau *m*) épineux *m*

thornless [ˈθɔːnlɪs] *adj* sans épines

thorny [ˈθɔːnɪ] *adj* épineux; *Fig* **t. question** question *f* épineuse

thorough [ˈθʌrə] *adj* (*search etc*) minutieux; (*knowledge*) approfondi; (*understanding*) profond; (*job*) consciencieux; **to be t. in one's work** travailler consciencieusement; **to give a room a t. cleaning** nettoyer une pièce à fond; **it needs a t. revision** il/elle a besoin d'une révision en profondeur; **a t. scoundrel** un fieffé coquin; **to make a t. nuisance of oneself** se rendre complètement insupportable

thoroughbred [ˈθʌrəbred] **1** *adj* (*cheval*) pur-sang *inv*; (*dog etc*) de race **2** *n* (*horse*) pur-sang *m inv*; (*animal*) animal *m*, -aux de race; **she's a real t.** (*person*) elle a de la classe

thoroughfare [ˈθʌrəfeər] *n* voie *f* de communication; **busy t.** (*street*) rue *f* très passante; (*road*) importante voie de communication; **one of the main thoroughfares of the town** une des rues principales *ou* une des artères de la ville; **no t.** (*on sign*) (*no through road*) rue barrée; (*no access*) passage interdit (au public)

thoroughgoing [ˈθʌrəgəʊɪŋ] *adj* (*search, inspection etc*) minutieux; (*knowledge, revision etc*) approfondi; (*changes*) profond; (*reform*) en profondeur; **such a t. rogue as him** un fieffé coquin de cette espèce

thoroughly [ˈθʌrəlɪ] *adv* (*to know language etc*) parfaitement; (*to know sth, to clean sth*) à fond; (*stupid*) complètement; **to be t. bored** s'ennuyer mortellement; **t. honest** d'une honnêteté à toute épreuve; **t. untrustworthy** totalement indigne de confiance

thoroughness [ˈθʌrənɪs] *n* (*of work*) minutie *f*; **the t. of his knowledge** ses connaissances très complètes

those *see* **that[1]**

thou[1] [ðaʊ] *pers pron Arch, Bible* (*unstressed*) tu; (*stressed*) toi; **t. seest** tu vois; **t. art** tu es; **hearest t.?** entends-tu?; **t. and I** toi et moi

thou[2] [θaʊ] *n F* (*abbr* **thousand**) mille *m inv*

though [ðəʊ] **1** *conj* **(a)** (*in spite of the fact that*) quoique, bien que + *sub*; **t. she is poor she is generous** quoiqu'elle soit pauvre, elle est généreuse; **I respect him t. I don't like him** je le respecte, bien qu'il ne me soit pas sympathique; **t. I am a father** tout père que je suis; **t. not handsome, he was attractive** sans être beau, il avait du charme; **I think I did quite well, t. I say so** *or* **it myself** je ne m'en suis pas mal sorti, si je peux me permettre de le dire

(b) this statement, terrible t. it be cette déclaration, pour terrible qu'elle soit; **strange t. it may seem** si étrange que cela puisse sembler; **even t. you'll laugh at me** même si vous vous moquez de moi

(c) as t. comme si; **it looks as t. she's gone** il semble qu'elle soit partie; **as t. nothing had happened** comme si de rien n'était

2 *adv* cependant, pourtant; **it's not what I want t.** mais ce n'est pas ce que je veux; **I didn't mean it t.** mais je ne disais pas ça sérieusement; **he had promised to go, he didn't t.** il avait promis d'y aller, cependant, il n'en a rien fait; **did she t.!** elle a dit/fait cela?

thought[1] [θɔːt] *n* **(a)** (*thinking*) pensée *f*; **contemporary t.** la pensée contemporaine; **capable of t.** capable de penser

(b) (*idea*) pensée *f*, idée *f*; **he hasn't a t. in his head** il n'a pas une idée dans la tête; **happy t.** heureuse idée; **what a nice/kind t.!** quelle agréable/douce pensée!; **dark** *or* **gloomy thoughts** de sombres pensées; **that's** *or* **there's a t.** (*good idea*) ça, c'est une idée; (*that's true*) ça, c'est vrai; **now there's a t., why don't we ...?** j'ai une idée, et si nous ...?; (*sb else's thought*) ça c'est une bonne idée, et si nous ...?; **it's quite a t.!** (*pleasant*) le rêve!; (*unpleasant*) quelle horreur!; **to read sb's thoughts** lire dans les pensées de qn; **t. reader** liseur, -euse de pensées; **the mere t. of it** rien que d'y penser; **have you ever given it a single t.?** y avez-vous jamais pensé?; **I didn't give it another t.** je n'y ai pas repensé; **what are your thoughts on the matter?** quelle est votre opinion sur ce sujet?; **to collect one's thoughts** rassembler ses idées; **her thoughts were elsewhere** son esprit était ailleurs

(c) (*reflection*) réflexion *f*, considération *f*; (*meditation*) pensées *fpl*, rêverie *f*, méditation *f*; **after much t.** après mûre réflexion; **to give a great deal of t. to sth** réfléchir beaucoup à qch; **on second thoughts** réflexion faite, à la réflexion; **to be deep** *or* **lost in t.** être perdu *ou* absorbé dans ses pensées, être plongé dans ses réflexions

(d) (*intention*) intention *f*, dessein *m*; **I had no t. of offending you** je n'avais pas l'intention de vous offenser; **you must give up all thought(s) of seeing him** il faut renoncer à le voir, il ne faut plus penser à le voir; **his one t. is to get money** il ne pense qu'à l'argent

(e) *Old-fashioned F* **a t. too sweet** un rien trop sucré

thought[2] *pt, pp see* **think[2]**

thoughtful [ˈθɔːtfʊl] *adj* **(a)** (*pensive*) (*person, expression*) pensif, méditatif; **to look t.** avoir l'air pensif

(b) (*considerate*) (*person*) attentionné; **he was t. enough to warn me** il a eu la prévenance de m'avertir; **it was very t. of her to ...** c'était très attentionné de sa part de ...; **that wasn't very t.** ce n'était pas très gentil de sa/ta/*etc* part; **how t. (of you)!** comme c'est gentil (de ta part)!; **it was a very t. gesture (on his part)** c'était une belle preuve d'attention (de sa part); *Fml* **he was always t. of others' needs** il a toujours été très attentif aux besoins des autres

(c) (*to which thought has been given*) (*analysis, book*) profond; **he gave me his usual t. advice** comme d'habitude, il m'a aidé avec ses sages conseils

thoughtfully [ˈθɔːtfəlɪ] *adv* **(a)** (*pensively*) pensivement, d'un air pensif *ou* méditatif **(b)** (*considerately*) avec prévenance

thoughtfulness [ˈθɔːtfʊlnɪs] *n* **(a)** (*pensiveness*) méditation *f* **(b)** (*consideration*) prévenance *f*

thoughtless [ˈθɔːtlɪs] *adj* **(a)** (*ill-considered*) irréfléchi, étourdi; **t. action** acte *m* inconsidéré **(b)** (*inconsiderate*) **t. of others** qui manque d'égards *ou* de prévenance pour les autres; **that was t. of me** j'ai fait ça sans réfléchir; **it was very t. of you not to have phoned** ce n'était pas très gentil de ta part de ne pas téléphoner

thoughtlessly [ˈθɔːtlɪslɪ] *adv* **(a)** (*without thinking*) étourdiment, sans réfléchir **(b)** (*inconsiderately*) **to treat sb**

t. manquer d'égards envers qn; **he very t. left it locked** il l'a laissé fermé sans se soucier des autres le moins du monde; **they t. took the whole lot** sans aucun égard, ils ont pris le tout

thoughtlessness ['θɔːtlɪsnɪs] *n* (**a**) (*lack of forethought*) irréflexion *f*, étourderie *f* (**b**) (*lack of consideration*) manque *m* d'égards *ou* de prévenance

thought-out *adj* **well/poorly t. plan** projet bien/mal conçu; **carefully t. answer** réponse bien pesée; **this needs a carefully t. answer** il va falloir bien réfléchir avant de répondre

thought-provoking *adj* qui invite à la réflexion, qui donne à *ou* fait réfléchir

thousand ['θaʊz(ə)nd] [①A12,1,h,i; B56,A,c-d] **1** *num adj* mille *inv*; **a t. years** mille ans; **the year 4000 B.C.** l'an quatre mille av. J-C. ; *Jur, Admin* **the year one t. nine hundred and thirty** l'an mil neuf cent trente; *Culin* **T. Island dressing** mayonnaise *f* au ketchup et aux cornichons; **about a t. men** un millier d'hommes; **three hundred t. people** trois cent mille personnes; *F* **I've got a t. and one things to ask you/to do** j'ai mille choses à vous demander/faire; **no, no, a t. times no!** non, non, et cent fois non!

2 *n* mille *m inv*; **a t.** mille; **a. t. and one** mille un; **how many people were there? – about a t.** combien de gens étaient là? – un millier; **thousands of people** des milliers de gens; **in thousands** par milliers; **in hundreds of thousands** par centaines de mille; **she's one in a t.** c'est la femme entre mille

thousandfold ['θaʊz(ə)n(d)fəʊld] **1** *adj* multiplié par mille **2** *adv* mille fois autant

thousandth ['θaʊz(ə)n(t)θ] *num adj, n* millième *mf*

thraldom ['θrɔːldəm] *n Lit* esclavage *m*, assujetissement *m*, servitude *f*

thrall [θrɔːl] *n Lit* **kept in t.** maintenu en esclavage *m*

thrash [θræʃ] **1** *vt* (*beat*) (*sb, animal*) battre, rosser, rouer de coups; (*defeat heavily in game etc*) battre à plate(s) couture(s); **to t. sb soundly** donner une bonne raclée à qn; **to t. the water** donner des coups dans l'eau; **to t. one's arms and legs in the air** se débattre des mains et des pieds **2** *vi* (*of water*) battre, clapoter (**against** contre); **a sea of thrashing limbs** un océan de bras et de jambes qui se débattaient; **the doctor was trying to avoid his thrashing limbs** le docteur essayait d'éviter ses coups de pieds et ses coups de poings

▶ **thrash about, thrash around 1** *vtsep* **to t. one's arms and legs about** se débattre des mains et des pieds **2** *vi* (*move furiously*) (*of person*) se débattre (des mains et des pieds); (*of fish*) remuer, se débattre; **the fish thrashed about in the net** le poisson se débattait dans le filet

▶ **thrash out** *vtsep* (**a**) (*discuss thoroughly*) discuter à fond; **to t. it out with sb** en débattre avec qn (**b**) (*reach*) (*solution, truth etc*) arriver à

thrashing ['θræʃɪŋ] *n* (*beating*) volée *f* (de coups), *F* raclée *f*; *Sp etc* défaite *f*; **to give sb a t.** donner une raclée à qn; **they were given a t. at the elections** ils ont pris une raclée aux élections; **to give one's opponent a t.** battre son adversaire à plate(s) couture(s)

thread[1] [θred] *n* (**a**) (*of cotton, nylon, silk etc*) fil *m*; (**length of**) **t.** (*of cotton, silk etc*) brin *m*, bout *m*; **gold t.** fil d'or; **button t.** fil à boutons; *Fig* **his life hung by a t.** sa vie ne tenait qu'à un fil; **to lose the t. of the conversation** perdre le fil de la conversation; **to gather up the threads of a story** retrouver le fil d'une histoire (**b**) *Tech* (*of screw, bolt etc*) filet *m*, filetage *m* (**c**) *esp Am F* **threads** (*clothes*) fringues *fpl*

thread[2] **1** *vt* (**a**) (*needle, beads*) enfiler (**through sth** dans qch); **to t. one's way between the cars** se faufiler entre les voitures (**b**) *Tech* (*screw etc*) fileter; (*pipe, nut etc*) tarauder **2** *vi* (**a**) **we threaded through the crowd** nous nous sommes faufilés à travers la foule (**b**) **to t. into sth** (*of screw etc*) se visser dans qch; **the tape threads through these holes** la bande passe par ces trous

threadbare ['θredbeər] *adj* (*clothes etc*) râpé, élimé, usé jusqu'à la corde; *Fig* (*subject, argument, joke etc*) rebattu

thread mark *n* (*in banknote*) filigrane *m*

threadworm ['θredwɜːm] *n* oxyure *m*

threat [θret] *n* menace *f*; **to make threats** faire des menaces; **to utter a t.** proférer une menace; **to make idle threats** lancer des menaces en l'air; **it was no idle t.** ce n'était pas une menace en l'air; **there is a t. of rain** il y a un risque de pluie; **to see sb/sth as a t.** considérer qn/qch comme une menace; **is that a t. or a promise?** est-ce qu'il faut que je m'en/qu'il s'en/*etc* réjouisse ou pas; **if we exist under the t. of nuclear war** si nous vivons sous la menace d'une guerre nucléaire

threaten ['θret(ə)n] **1** *vt* (*sb*) menacer; *Jur* (*sb*) intimider; **to t. sb with sth** menacer qn de qch; (**to be**) **threatened with sth** (être) menacé de qch; **a species threatened with extinction** une espèce en voie de disparition; **the threatened strike didn't come off** cette menace de grève n'a pas abouti; **the sky threatened rain** la pluie menaçait, le ciel était menaçant; **to t. to do sth** menacer de faire qch; **this situation threatens to become dangerous** cette situation menace de devenir dangereuse **2** *vi* **a storm is threatening** l'orage menace

threatening ['θret(ə)nɪŋ] *adj* (*tone, appearance*) menaçant; (*letter*) de menaces; *Jur* d'intimidation; **the weather looks t.** le temps est menaçant; **t. language** menaces *fpl* (verbales)

threateningly ['θret(ə)nɪŋlɪ] *adv* de manière menaçante

three [θriː] *num adj, n* trois *m*; **every t. months** tous les trois mois; **twenty-t.** vingt-trois; **t. and a half** trois et demi; **to be t. (years old)** avoir trois ans; **he leaves at t. thirty** *or* **at half past t.** il part à trois heures trente *ou* à trois heures et demie; **to come in t. by t.** *or* **in threes** entrer (trois) par trois; *Pol* **the Big T.** les Trois *mpl* Grands *mpl*; **t.-engine(d) aircraft** trimoteur *m*; *Th* **t. act play** pièce *f* en trois actes; **t.-pointed** à trois pointes; **t. seater** triplace *m*; **t. sided** *or* **t. party conversations** conversations *fpl* tripartites; **t. star hotel/brandy** hôtel *m*/cognac *m* trois-étoiles; **t.-stranded rope** corde *f* à trois cordons

three-colour(ed), *US* **three-color(ed)** *adj* tricolore; *Phot* trichrome; **t.-colour process** trichromie *f*

three-cornered *adj* triangulaire; **a t. discussion** un débat à trois; **t. hat** tricorne *m*

three-course *adj* (*meal*) à trois plats

three-D 1 *adj F* = **three-dimensional 2** *n* **in t.** en trois dimensions

three-dimensional *adj* tridimensionnel

threefold ['θriːfəʊld] **1** *adj* triple; **a t. increase in the membership figures** une augmentation au triple du nombre d'adhérents **2** *adv* trois fois autant; **to increase t.** tripler

three-four *adj Mus* **t. time** mesure *f* à trois temps

three-handed *adj Cards etc* **t. game** partie *f* à trois

three-legged *adj* (*stool etc*) à trois pieds; **t. race** (*game*) = course *f* dont les participants sont attachés deux à deux par une jambe

three-line whip *n Br Pol* = obligation *f* absolue faite aux députés de prendre part à un vote et de suivre les recommandations de leur parti

threepence ['θrep(ə)ns] *n Br* trois pence *mpl*

threepenny ['θrep(ə)nɪ] *adj Br* coûtant trois pence, à *ou* de trois pence; *Hist* **t. bit** pièce *f* de trois pence

three-piece *adj* en trois pièces; *Mus* **t. band** trio *m*; **t. suit** (*clothes*) (costume *m*) trois-pièces *m inv*; **t. suite** (*furniture*) salon *m* trois pièces

three-pin *adj* **t. plug** prise *f* à trois fiches

three-ply *adj* (*wool etc*) à trois fils; (*rope*) à trois brins; (*tissues, toilet paper*) à trois épaisseurs

three-point *adj Av* **t. landing** atterrissage *m* trois points; *Aut* **t. seatbelt** ceinture *f* trois points; *Aut* **t. turn** demi-tour *m* en trois manœuvres

three-quarter 1 *adj* **t. face portrait** portrait *m* de trois-quarts; **t. length coat** trois-quarts *m inv*; *Aut* **t. vision** visibilité *f* de trois-quart **2** *n Rugby* **t.** (**back**) trois-quarts *m*; **the t. line** la ligne des trois-quarts

three-ring *adj Am* **t. circus** = cirque *m* contenant trois arènes et montrant plusieurs numéros à la fois; *Fig* cirque, chantier *m*

threescore ['θriːskɔːr] *adj Arch, Lit* soixante; **t. (years) and ten** soixante-dix ans

threesome ['θriːsəm] *n* (*three people*) groupe *m* de trois personnes; *Golf* partie *f* à trois; **do you want to make up a t.?** (*in games*) veux-tu faire le troisième?; (*going out etc*) veux-tu te joindre à nous (deux)?; **we went as a t.** nous y sommes allés à trois

three-speed *adj* à trois vitesses; **t. gearbox** boîte *f* trois vitesses

three-storey(ed), *US* **-story, -storied** *adj* (*house*) à trois étages

three-way *adj* (*division etc*) en trois; (*discussion etc*) à trois; *Br Pol* **t. marginal** = circonscription *f* où trois candidats ont d'égales chances de succès; *Aut* **t. catalytic convertor** catalyseur *m* à trois voies

three-wheeled vehicle *n* trois-roues *m*

three-wheeler *n Aut* (petite) voiture *f* à trois roues; (*tricycle*) tricycle *m*

threnody ['θrenədɪ] *n Lit* thrène *m*, chant *m* funèbre

thresh [θreʃ] *vt* (*wheat*) battre; *Fig* **to t. the water** (*of ship's screw, of whale's tail etc*) battre l'eau

thresher ['θreʃər] *n* (*person*) batteur, -euse en grange; (*machine*) batteuse *f*

threshing [ˈθreʃɪŋ] *n* (*of wheat*) battage *m*; **t. floor** aire *f* de battage; **t. machine** batteuse *f*
threshold [ˈθreʃəʊld] *n* **(a)** (*of door etc*) seuil *m*, pas *m* de la porte; **on the t.** sur le seuil; *Fig* **on the t. of a great discovery** au seuil d'une grande découverte; **to cross the t.** franchir le seuil; *Fig* **to be on the t. of life** être au seuil de la vie **(b)** *Phys etc* (*of fission, reaction*) seuil *m*; **to have a low boredom t.** être prédisposé à l'ennui, s'ennuyer facilement; **to have a low/high pain t.** mal tolérer/bien tolérer la douleur; *Physiol* **t. of audibility** *or* **of hearing** seuil d'audibilité
threw *see* **throw**[2]
thrice [θraɪs] *adv Lit* trois fois
thrift [θrɪft] *n* économie *f*, épargne *f*; **t. shop** = magasin *m* spécialisé dans la vente d'articles d'occasion
thriftily [ˈθrɪftɪlɪ] *adv* avec économie; (*live*) frugalement
thriftiness [ˈθrɪftɪnɪs] *n* économie *f*, épargne *f*
thriftless [ˈθrɪftlɪs] *adj* (*spendthrift*) dépensier; (*improvident*) imprévoyant
thriftlessness [ˈθrɪftlɪsnɪs] *n* gaspillage *m*; (*improvidence*) imprévoyance *f*
thrifty [ˈθrɪftɪ] *adj* économe, épargnant
thrill[1] [θrɪl] *n* (*exciting feeling*) (vive) émotion *f*; (*trembling*) frisson *m*, tressaillement *m*; **t. of pleasure** frisson de plaisir; **the t. of riding a motorbike** le frisson que donne la moto; **to get a t. out of sth** se donner des sensations fortes avec qch; **it gave me quite a t.** ça m'a fait quelque chose; **all the thrills of the big wheel** tous les frissons que procure la grande roue; **all the thrills and spills of the circus** toutes les joies et tous les frissons que procure le cirque; *F* **go on, give us a t., let's see you dance!** allez, montre-nous ce que tu sais faire, danse!
thrill[2] **1** *vt* (*of experience, thought, prospect*) exalter; (*of sb's touch*) faire frémir *ou* frissonner, donner des frissons à; (*of conjuror etc*) (*audience, children*) faire vibrer; **a novel/film that will t. you** un roman/film qui vous fera frémir; **he was absolutely thrilled with his present** son cadeau le transportait de joie *ou* le ravissait; **she's thrilled with her new car** elle est ravie de sa nouvelle voiture; **I'm thrilled for you** je suis très heureux pour vous; **to be thrilled at the sight of sth** être fou de joie à la vue de qch; *F* **to be thrilled to bits** être fou de joie; **we were absolutely thrilled** (*F* **to bits**) **to hear your news/to have won the holiday** nous avons été ravis *ou* hyper-contents d'avoir de vos nouvelles/ d'avoir gagné les vacances
2 *vi esp Lit* tressaillir, frissonner (de joie)
thriller [ˈθrɪlə*r*] *n* (*play, film, novel*) pièce *f*/film *m*/roman *m* à suspense, thriller *m*
thrilling [ˈθrɪlɪŋ] *adj* passionnant; (*sight*) saisissant; *Sp* **t. finish** arrivée *f* palpitante; *Iron* **how t. for you!** c'est passionnant, ce qui t'arrive!
thrive [θraɪv] *vi* (*pt, pp* **thrived** [θraɪvd]; *Arch, US pt* **throve** [θrəʊv]; *pp* **thriven** [ˈθrɪvn]) (*grow well*) (*of child, plant*) (bien) se développer; (*of adult*) bien se porter; (*of business etc*) bien marcher, bien aller; (*prosper*) (*of person*) prospérer; (*develop potential*) s'épanouir; **children who t. on milk** enfants à qui le lait profite bien; **plant that thrives in all soils** plante qui s'accommode de tous les sols; **to t. on danger** se nourrir du danger; **to t. on other people's misfortunes** s'engraisser de la misère d'autrui; **some people t. on stress** certaines personnes s'épanouissent dans le stress; **do I like it? I t. on it!** si j'aime ça? mais, j'adore!
thriving [ˈθraɪvɪŋ] *adj* (*physically*) (*plant*) vigoureux; (*person*) vigoureux, bien portant; (*prosperous*) (*person, business*) prospère, florissant
thro' [θruː] *prep F* = **through**
throat [θrəʊt] *n Anat* gorge *f*; (*gullet*) gorge, gosier *m*; **the back of the t.** le fond de la gorge, l'arrière-gorge *f*, *pl* arrière-gorges; **to cut sb's t.** couper la gorge à qn; *Fig* **he's cutting his own t.** il travaille à sa propre ruine; *Fig, Com* **they're cutting each other's throats** ils se font une concurrence désastreuse; **to grab sb by the t.** attraper *ou* saisir qn à la gorge; **to have a sore t.** avoir mal à la gorge; **to clear one's t.** s'éclaircir la voix *ou* la gorge, se racler la gorge; *Fig F* **she's always ramming** *or* **shoving** *or* **forcing it down my t.** elle m'en rebat toujours les oreilles; *F* **there's no need to jump down my t.!** inutile de me sauter dessus!; *F* **they're always at each other's throats** ils se battent continuellement; *F* **if you pour enough wine down his t. ...** si tu lui verses assez de vin ...; **t. microphone** laryngophone *m*; *Med* **t. spray** insufflateur *m*
throatiness [ˈθrəʊtɪnɪs] *n* (*of voice*) qualité *f* gutturale
throaty [ˈθrəʊtɪ] *adj* (*voice, laugh*) guttural
throb[1] [θrɒb] *n* (*of pulse, heart etc*) pulsation *f*; (*of engine*) vrombissement *m*; **the t. of the tom-toms** les vibrations *fpl* des tam-tams; **she felt a sudden t. of pain in her arm** soudain, elle ressentit un élancement dans le bras
throb[2] *vi* (**-bb-**) (*of heart, pulse etc*) battre fort; (*of engine*) vrombir; (*of tom-toms*) vibrer; **a city throbbing with activity** une ville palpitante d'activité; **my finger is throbbing** j'ai des élancements dans le doigt, *F* mon doigt me lance; **my head is throbbing** j'ai une douleur lancinante dans la tête
throbbing [ˈθrɒbɪŋ] **1** *adj* (*heart, pulse etc*) qui bat fort; (*engine*) vrombissant; (*pain*) lancinant; **the t. rhythm of the drums** les tambours qui battent fort *ou* qui vibrent **2** *n* (*of heart, pulse etc*) battement *m* (fort), pulsations *fpl*; (*of engine*) vrombissement *m*; (*of wound, infection etc*) élancements *mpl*
throes [θrəʊz] *npl* **the t. of death** *or* **death t.** les affres *fpl* de la mort; *Fig* **the death t. of the old regime** l'agonie *f* de l'ancien régime; **the company is in its death t.** l'entreprise est à l'agonie; **a country in the t. of revolution** un pays en proie à la révolution *ou* dans la tourmente de la révolution; *F* **we're in the t. of moving house** nous sommes en plein déménagement; *F* **don't disturb him while he's in the t. of writing** ne le dérange pas en pleine inspiration; **in the t. of a divorce** dans la tourmente d'un divorce
thrombosis, *pl* **thromboses** [θrɒmˈbəʊsɪs, -iːz] *n Med* thrombose *f*; **coronary t.** infarctus *m* du myocarde
throne [θrəʊn] *n* trône *m*; *F* (*lavatory*) trône; **to come to** *or* **ascend** *or Lit* **mount the t.** monter sur le trône; **the heir to the t.** l'héritier *m* au trône; **the power behind the t.** (*of king etc*), *Fig* l'Éminence *f* grise
throneroom [ˈθrəʊnruːm] *n* salle *f* du trône; *F Hum* **in the t.** (*on the toilet*) sur le trône
throng[1] [θrɒŋ] *n* foule *f*; **a t. of angels** une multitude d'anges
throng[2] **1** *vi* affluer; (*gather*) s'assembler en foule; **to t. to Paris/the main cities/the square** affluer à Paris/dans les grandes villes/sur la place; **to t. round sb** se presser autour de qn; **they thronged into the square** ils arrivèrent en foule sur la place **2** *vt* emplir; **the room was thronged with people** la pièce était bondée
thronging [ˈθrɒŋɪŋ] *adj* **a t. mass** une foule grouillante
throttle[1] [ˈθrɒt(ə)l] *n Aut etc* étrangleur *m*, obturateur *m*, papillon *m* (des gaz); (*on motorbike*) poignée *f* d'accélération; (*in plane*) commande *f* des gaz; *MecE* (*in steam engine*) régulateur *m*, prise *f* de vapeur; *Aut* **to open/ to close the t.** ouvrir/fermer les gaz; **t. (control** *or* **lever)** (*on motorbike, speedboat, plane*) manette *f* des gaz; **at full t.** à pleins gaz; **t. cable** câble *m* d'accélération
throttle[2] *vt* (*strangle*), *Fig* étrangler
▶ **throttle back, throttle down 1** *vi* (*slow engine*) mettre le moteur au ralenti; (*cut, close off fuel*) couper *ou* fermer les gaz; **the pilot/rider gradually throttled back** le pilote/ motard coupa les gaz progressivement **2** *vtsep* (*engine*) mettre au ralenti
through [θruː] **1** *prep* **(a)** (*place*) à travers; **t. a hedge** au travers d'une haie; **to go t. sb's garden** passer par le jardin de qn; **I was wandering t. the garden/trees** j'errais dans le jardin/parmi les arbres; **to go t. a tunnel** passer dans un tunnel; **the nail/arrow went t. the wood/wall** le clou/la flèche traversa le bois/le mur; **the path goes** *or* **leads t. the forest** le sentier traverse la forêt; **I'm on my way t. Paris** je traverse Paris; **let's have dinner when I'm on my way t. Paris** on pourrait dîner ensemble pendant mon passage à Paris; **to look t. the window/a telescope/a hole** regarder par la fenêtre/dans un télescope/par un trou; **she came in t. the window** elle est entrée par la fenêtre; **to go t. someone's pockets** fouiller les poches de qn; *Aut* **to go t. a red light** brûler un feu (rouge); *F* **he's been t. it** *or* **t. a lot** il en a bavé, il en a vu de dures; **to speak t. one's nose** parler du nez; **she got t. her exam** elle a été reçue à son examen; *F* **to put sb t. it** rendre la vie dure à qn; **I'm halfway t. this book** j'ai lu la moitié de ce livre
(b) (*time*) **all t. his life** durant *ou* pendant toute sa vie; **t. the ages** à travers les âges; *esp Am* **Monday t. Friday** de lundi à vendredi, du lundi au vendredi
(c) (*by means of*) **t. sb** par qn, par l'entremise *ou* l'intermédiaire de qn; **t. sth** par le *ou* au moyen de qch; (*as a result of*) en conséquence de qch, par suite de qch, à cause de qch; **to send sth t. the post** envoyer qch par la poste; **t. ignorance** par ignorance; **absent t. illness** absent par suite *ou* pour cause de maladie; **to act t. fear** agir sous le coup de la peur; **it's (all) t. me that he missed his train** c'est à cause de moi qu'il a manqué son train; **t. failing to lock the door ...** pour n'avoir pas fermé la porte à clé ...
(d) *esp Am* **to be t. doing sth** avoir fini de faire qch; **are you t. telling me what to do?** tu as fini de me dire ce que j'ai à faire?
2 *adv* **(a)** (*place*) à travers; **the water poured t.** l'eau

coulait à travers; **the nail has come t.** le clou est passé à travers; **to let sb t.** laisser passer qn; **her trousers are t. at the knees** son pantalon est déchiré aux genoux; **he's t. in the living-room** il est de l'autre côté, dans le salon; **will you be t. tomorrow?** (*are you coming here?*) est-ce que tu viens demain?; **England are t. to the semi-final** l'Angleterre s'est qualifiée pour *ou* jouera la demi-finale; *Sp* **France are not t.** la France n'est pas qualifiée; **to be soaked t.** (*of person*) être trempé jusqu'aux os; (*of jacket etc*) être complètement trempé

(**b**) (*from one end to the other*) d'un bout à l'autre; (*to the end*) jusqu'au bout, jusqu'à la fin; **to read a book (right) t.** lire un livre d'un bout à l'autre; **to see** *or* **carry sth t.** mener qch à bien; **I slept all night t.** j'ai dormi d'une traite cette nuit; **we'll stay t. until Friday** nous resterons jusqu'à vendredi; **I was aware all t. that ...** j'étais conscient tout du long de ce que ...; **we must go t. with it** il faut aller jusqu'au bout; **to be t. with sth** (*to have finished sth*) avoir fini qch; (*with scissors etc*) avoir fini avec qch; (*to have had enough of*) avoir (eu) assez de qch; **are you t. with your work?** avez-vous fini votre travail?; **I'm t. with you** j'en ai fini avec toi; **we're t.** c'est fini entre nous; *esp Am* **to be t.** (*to have stopped talking etc*) avoir terminé *ou* fini; *F* (*to be done for*) être fichu

(**c**) **to book t. to Paris** prendre un billet direct pour Paris; *Tel* **to get t. to sb** obtenir la communication avec qn; *F* **I can't get t. to him** (*make him understand*) je n'arrive pas à lui faire comprendre quoi que ce soit; *Tel* **I'll put you t. to the secretary** je vous passe la/le secrétaire; *Tel* **you're t.** vous avez la communication, vous êtes en ligne

(**d**) **to be good/bad t. and t.** (*of person*) être bon/mauvais de bout en bout *ou* de part en part; **to know sb t. and t.** connaître qn comme si on l'avait fait; **to know a district t. and t.** connaître un quartier comme sa poche

3 *adj* (*train, road, ticket*) direct; *Com* **t. bill** connaissement *m* direct; **t. carriage** transport *m* direct; **t. fare** tarif *m* direct; **t. freight** marchandises *fpl* en transit; **t. passenger** (*on same vehicle to final destination*) passager *m* 'direct'; **t. passenger to Paris** voyageur, -euse direct(e) pour Paris; **no t. road** (*on sign*) voie *f* sans issue; **t. train** train *m* direct; **t. traffic** transit *m*; **closed to t. traffic** (*on sign*) interdit aux non-résidents, riverains autorisés

throughout [θruːˈaʊt] **1** *prep* **t. the country** dans tout le pays; **t. the world** à travers le monde; **t. the year** pendant toute l'année; **t. her life** durant *ou* pendant toute sa vie **2** *adv* (*place*) partout; (*time*) tout le temps; **the coat is lined t.** le manteau est entièrement doublé; **they remained loyal t.** ils sont restés loyaux du début à la fin

throughput [ˈθruːpʊt] *n* débit *m*

through-the-wall automated teller machine *n* guichet *m* automatique

throughway [ˈθruːweɪ] *n Am* autoroute *f*

throve *see* **thrive**

throw[1] [θrəʊ] *n* (**a**) (*action*) jet *m*, lancement *m*; *Sp* (*of javelin, discus etc*) lancer *m*; (*in wrestling*) (*of opponent*) mise *f* à terre; **his longest t. so far** son meilleur jet jusqu'à présent; **3 throws for 50p** (*at fair etc*) 3 essais pour 50 pence; **it's your t.** (*of javelin, dice etc*) à toi de lancer; **a t. of the dice** un coup de dés (**b**) (*of crankshaft*) maneton *m*, bras *m* de manivelle (**c**) *Am* (*cover*) couvre-lit *m*, *pl* couvre-lits; (*scarf*) écharpe *f*

throw[2] (*pt* **threw** [θruː]; *pp* **thrown** [θrəʊn]) **1** *vt* (**a**) (*ball etc*) lancer, jeter; *Sp* (*discus, javelin etc*) lancer; **to t. sth at sb/sth** lancer *ou* jeter qch à qn/qch; **to t. sth in sb's face** jeter qch à la figure de qn; *Fig* **don't t. that in my face** ne me faites pas de reproches à ce sujet; **to t. sb a kiss** envoyer un baiser à qn; **to t. the dice** jeter les dés; **to t. a five/a six** (*at dice*) avoir un cinq/six; **to t. a glance at sb** jeter un coup d'œil à *ou* sur qn; **to t. oneself forwards/backwards** se jeter en avant/arrière; **to t. oneself into sth** (*into river etc*) se jeter dans qch; *Fig* (*into undertaking*) se lancer à corps perdu dans qch; **to t. oneself on sb's mercy** s'en remettre à la merci de qn; *Fig* **she threw herself at him** (*in relationship*) elle s'est jetée à sa tête; **to t. temptation in sb's way** exposer qn à la tentation; **to t. the blame on sb** rejeter la faute sur qn; **to t. a sheet over sth** couvrir qch d'un drap; **to t. a shawl over one's shoulders** jeter un châle sur ses épaules; **to t. sb into prison** jeter *ou* mettre qn en prison; **to t. sb to the lions** jeter qn aux lions; **to t. into confusion** (*government, court, assembly*) semer la confusion au sein de; **to t. a switch** appuyer sur un interrupteur; **to t. open the door** ouvrir la porte toute grande; **to t. open one's house to sb** ouvrir sa maison à qn; **to t. sb out of work** mettre qn au chômage

(**b**) (*image, shadow*) projeter (**on** sur); *Fig* **to t. light on the matter** éclairer la question

(**c**) *F* **to t. a fit** piquer une crise; **to t. a party** organiser une soirée

(**d**) (*opponent*) renverser; **to t. its rider** (*of horse*) désarçonner son cavalier; **to be thrown** (*of rider*) vider les arçons, être désarçonné

(**e**) **to t. its skin** (*of reptile*) muer

(**f**) (*of animals*) **to t. a litter** mettre bas

(**g**) *Cer* (*pot*) tourner, façonner au tour

(**h**) *F* (*disconcert*) déconcerter; **his question threw me for a moment** pendant un moment, je n'ai su que répondre (à sa question); **I was completely thrown** j'étais complètement déconcerté

(**i**) *Sp F* (*deliberately lose*) (*match, race etc*) perdre délibérément

2 *vi* **she can t. a hundred metres** elle est capable de lancer à cent mètres; **I can't t. straight** je n'arrive pas à lancer droit

▶ **throw about, throw around** *vtsep* jeter çà et là; (*scatter*) éparpiller, disséminer; **to t. a ball around** jouer à la balle; **to t. one's money about** *or* **around** gaspiller son argent; **to t. one's arms about** *or* **around** faire de grands gestes; **to t. oneself about** se démener; **to be thrown about** (*in vehicle etc*) être ballotté; **to like to t. one's weight around** aimer faire sentir sa force

▶ **throw aside** *vtsep* (*throw to one side*) jeter sur le côté; *Fig* (*discard*) (*career, everything one's worked for etc*) renoncer à; (*person*) rejeter, écarter; (*prejudices, fears, hatred etc*) se débarrasser de

▶ **throw away** *vtsep* (**a**) (*discard*) jeter (**b**) (*waste*) gaspiller; **to t. away a chance** laisser passer une occasion; **to t. away one's life** (*waste*) gâcher sa vie; (*sacrifice for nothing*) se sacrifier inutilement; **don't t. yourself away on a waster like him** ne gâche pas ta vie pour un bon à rien pareil; **you're just throwing money away buying that stuff** tu gaspilles vraiment ton argent en achetant ce truc; **to t. away a line** (*of actor*) énoncer une phrase avec une indifférence calculée

▶ **throw back** *vtsep* (**a**) (*return by throwing*) (*fish into water etc*) rejeter; (*ball etc*) renvoyer, relancer; *Fig* **to t. sth back in sb's face** jeter qch à la figure de qn (**b**) (*reflect*) (*of mirror*) (*image etc*) refléter, réfléchir; (*light, heat*) réverbérer (**c**) (*open forcefully*) (*shutters etc*) repousser (**d**) **to t. one's head back** rejeter la tête en arrière (**e**) *Fig* **to be thrown back upon sb/sth** être forcé de se rabattre sur qn/qch

▶ **throw down** *vtsep* (*throw from height*) jeter (*du haut de qch*); (*throw to the ground*) jeter à *ou* par terre; (*cast aside quickly*) jeter; *Cards* abattre; **to t. oneself down** se jeter sur le sol; **to t. down one's arms** jeter ses armes; *Fig* (*surrender*) se rendre; *F* **it's throwing it down!** (*raining*) qu'est-ce qui tombe!

▶ **throw in** *vtsep* (**a**) (*throw into a place*) jeter dedans; *Fb* **to t. in the ball** remettre la balle en jeu; **to t. in one's hand** *or* **one's cards** (*leave game*) abandonner *ou* quitter la partie; *Fig* (*admit defeat*) s'avouer vaincu; **to t. in the towel** *Boxing* jeter l'éponge; *Fig* (*admit defeat*) s'avouer vaincu, jeter l'éponge (**b**) (*add*) ajouter; (*give as extra*) donner en plus; **if you buy that table I'll t. in the bookcase** si vous achetez cette table, je vous donne la bibliothèque en supplément (**c**) (*remark, word*) placer (**d**) **to t. in one's lot with sb** partager le sort de qn

▶ **throw off** *vtsep* (**a**) (*remove hastily*) (*one's clothes*) enlever *ou* ôter très rapidement; (*mask*) enlever d'un coup (**b**) (*get rid of*) (*cold etc*) guérir de; (*pursuer etc*) se débarrasser de; (*oppressive regime*) se libérer de; (*old image*) secouer, se débarrasser de (**c**) (*write hastily*) (*poem etc*) composer au pied levé (**d**) **to t. sb off his bicycle** faire tomber qn de sa bicyclette; **to t. off its rider** (*of horse*) désarçonner son cavalier (**e**) (*put off*) **to t. the dogs/the police off the scent** semer les chiens/la police

▶ **throw on** *vtsep* (*put on hastily*) (*clothes*) mettre *ou* passer à la hâte; (*wood on fire*) jeter

▶ **throw out** *vtsep* (**a**) (*eject*) jeter dehors; (*person*) (*from job, pub, nightclub*) mettre à la porte; (*from school, private club, political party*) exclure

(**b**) (*discard*) jeter *ou* mettre au rebut; (*reject*) (*bill etc*) rejeter, repousser; **the takeover will t. a lot of people out of work** le rachat va mettre beaucoup de monde au chômage

(**c**) (*give out*) (*rays etc*) jeter, émettre; (*heat etc*) répandre; **to t. out roots** donner des racines

(**d**) **to t. out one's chest** bomber la poitrine

(**e**) (*challenge etc*) lancer; **to t. out a suggestion** émettre une proposition (*sans insister*)

(**f**) (*disconcert*) (*speaker etc*) troubler, déconcerter; **to t. sb out in his calculations** tromper les calculs de qn

(**g**) *Cr* (*batsman*) mettre hors jeu en lançant la balle sur le guichet

▶ **throw over** *vtsep* (*friend etc*) abandonner; (*lover etc*) *F* lâcher, plaquer; **to t. sb over for sb else** laisser tomber qn pour qn d'autre

▶ **throw together** *vtsep* **(a)** *F* (*make hurriedly*) (*meal*) préparer en vitesse **(b)** (*gather together hurriedly*) assembler à la hâte; **a few paintings/facts thrown together** quelques tableaux/faits assemblés à la hâte; **the film looks as if it's been thrown together** le film semble bâclé; **chance had thrown us together** le hasard nous avait réunis

▶ **throw up 1** *vtsep* **(a)** (*throw upwards*) jeter en l'air; (*raise high*) (*hands etc*) lever haut, mettre haut; **to t. up one's hands in despair** lever les mains en l'air de désespoir
(b) *F* (*vomit*) vomir, rendre
(c) (*build hurriedly*) (*house etc*) construire à toute vitesse
(d) (*abandon*) (*project etc*) renoncer à, abandonner; **to t. up one's job** quitter son emploi; **to feel like throwing everything up** avoir envie de tout plaquer
(e) (*reveal*) révéler, indiquer; **recent events have thrown up anomalies in the law** les derniers événements ont révélé des anomalies dans la loi; **the discussion threw up some new ideas** la discussion a amené de nouvelles idées
2 *vi F* (*vomit*) vomir, rendre

throwaway¹ ['θrəʊəweɪ] *adj* **(a)** (*disposable*) (*nappy, lighter*) à jeter, jetable **(b) it was just a t. line** *or* **remark** il/elle/*etc* a dit ça comme ça

throwaway² *n esp Am F* (*leaflet*) prospectus *m*

throwback ['θrəʊbæk] *n* **(a)** *Biol* régression *f*; **he's a t. to his great-grandfather** il a hérité (des caractéristiques) de son arrière-grand-père **(b)** *Fig* retour *m* (en arrière); **it's a t. to the 16th century** c'est un retour au 16ème siècle

thrower ['θrəʊər] *n* (*of javelin, ball etc*) lanceur, -euse; **discus t.** discobole *m*

throw-in *n Fb, Rugby* remise *f* en jeu, touche *f*

throwing ['θrəʊɪŋ] *n* (*of projectile etc*) jet *m*, lancement *m*; *Sp* (*of discus etc*) lancer *m*

throw-outs *npl Com* rebuts *mpl*

thru [θru:] *prep, adv, adj US F* = **through**

thrum [θrʌm] *vi* **(a)** (*drum*) (*with fingers*) tambouriner **(b)** (*vibrate*) vrombir

thrush¹ [θrʌʃ] *n* (*bird*) grive *f*

thrush² *n Med* muguet *m*

thrust¹ [θrʌst] *n* **(a)** (*push*) poussée *f*; *Fencing* coup *m* d'estoc; *Fig Mil, Com etc* poussée; **a bayonet t.** un coup de baïonnette; **with a single t. of his knife** d'un seul coup de couteau; *Fencing* **t. and parry** la botte et la parade; **the cut and t. of political debate** le jeu d'attaques et de ripostes des débats politiques **(b)** (*of argument*) **the general** *or* **main t. of an argument** l'idée générale d'une argumentation; **the argument has two main thrusts** l'argumentation a deux aspects principaux **(c)** *MecE* poussée *f*, butée *f*; **t. washer** rondelle *f* de butée

thrust² (*pt, pp* **thrust**) **1** *vt* pousser (avec force); **to t. sth into sth** enfoncer *ou* fourrer qch dans qch; **to t. one's hands into one's pockets** fourrer *ou* plonger les mains dans ses poches; **to be thrust into a position of responsibility** être parachuté à un poste à responsabilités; **to t. oneself** *or* **one's way through the crowd** se frayer un chemin à travers la foule **2** *vi* **to t. at sb** (*with end of stick etc*) porter un coup à qn; *Fencing* porter un coup d'estoc à qn

▶ **thrust aside, thrust away** *vtsep* (*reject*) repousser *ou* écarter d'un geste brusque; *Lit* **to t. temptation aside** repousser *ou* écarter la tentation

▶ **thrust forward** *vtsep* (*push forward*) pousser en avant; *Fig* **to t. oneself forward** se mettre en avant

▶ **thrust on, thrust upon** *vtaspo* (*force on*) **to. t. sth on sb** forcer qn à accepter qch; **to t. an opinion on sb** imposer son opinion à qn; **the responsibility was thrust upon me** on m'en a imposé la responsabilité; **and some have greatness thrust upon them** et à certains la grandeur *ou* la noblesse s'impose; **to t. oneself (up)on sb** s'imposer à qn *ou* chez qn

▶ **thrust out** *vtsep* (*one's arm, leg*) allonger brusquement; (*chest*) bomber; **he thrust his head out of the car window** il passa brusquement la tête par la vitre de la voiture

thruster ['θrʌstər] *n Astronaut* (*rocket engine*) propulseur *m*

thrustful ['θrʌstfʊl] *adj* = **thrusting**

thrusting ['θrʌstɪŋ] *adj* (*dynamic*) entreprenant, dynamique

thruway ['θru:weɪ] *n Am* autoroute *f*

thud¹ [θʌd] *n* bruit *m* sourd

thud² *vi* (**-dd-**) tomber avec un bruit sourd; **his feet went thudding along the corridor** ses pas résonnaient sourdement dans le couloir; **my heart was thudding against my ribs** mon cœur cognait sourdement dans ma poitrine; **the missile thudded into its target** le missile frappa sa cible avec un bruit sourd

thug [θʌg] *n* brute *f*

thumb¹ [θʌm] *n* pouce *m*; *F* **he's all thumbs** il est maladroit; *Fig* **to be under sb's t.** être sous la domination de qn; **she's got him right under her t.** elle le mène à la baguette; *F* **to stick out like a sore t.** choquer la vue; *F* **thumbs up!** bravo!; *F* **to give the thumbs up/down to a proposal** accepter/rejeter une proposition

thumb² 1 *vt* **(a) to t. a book** feuilleter *ou* parcourir un livre; **well thumbed book** livre qui a beaucoup servi **(b) to t. one's nose at sb** faire un pied de nez à qn **(c)** *F* **to t. a lift** *or* **ride** faire de l'auto-stop *ou* du stop; **I thumbed a lift with a Dutch motorist** un conducteur hollandais m'a pris en stop
2 *vi* **to t. through a book** feuilleter *ou* parcourir un livre

thumb index *n* onglets *mpl*

thumb-indexed ['θʌm'ɪndekst] *adj* (*edition etc*) à onglets

thumbmark ['θʌmmɑ:k] *n* marque *f* de pouce

thumbnail ['θʌmneɪl] *n* ongle *m* du pouce; *Fig* **t. sketch** description *f* concise

thumbprint ['θʌmprɪnt] *n* empreinte *f* de pouce

thumbscrew ['θʌmskru:] *n Tech* vis *f* à oreilles; (*for torture*) = instrument *m* de torture utilisé pour écraser les pouces des prisonniers

thumbstall ['θʌmstɔ:l] *n Med* doigtier *m* pour pouce

thumbtack ['θʌmtæk] *n Am* punaise *f*

thump¹ [θʌmp] *n* **(a)** (*sound*) bruit *m* sourd; **with a loud t.** avec un gros bruit sourd **(b)** (*blow with fist*) coup *m* de poing; **he's given himself a t. on the head** il s'est donné un coup sur la tête

thump² 1 *vt* (*person*) cogner; (*repeatedly*) bourrer de coups; (*table*) cogner sur; **don't t. it down like that, be careful!** (*put down heavily*) ne le cogne pas comme ça en le posant, fais attention!; **he thumped his fist on the table** il cogna du poing sur la table **2** *vi* (*on table etc*) cogner; **my heart was thumping** mon cœur battait la chamade; **the upstairs neighbours were thumping about** les voisins d'en haut martelaient le sol; **stop thumping about!** vous voulez bien cesser ce boucan!

▶ **thump out** *vtsep* (*play heavily*) **to t. out a tune** (*on piano*) marteler un air

thumping ['θʌmpɪŋ] *adj F* **a t. great ...** un/une énorme ...; **a t. headache** un mal de tête de tous les diables; **a t. big lie** un gros mensonge

thunder¹ ['θʌndər] *n* tonnerre *m*; **clap of t.** coup *m* de tonnerre; **peal** *or* **roll of t.** roulement *m ou* grondement *m ou* coup de tonnerre; **there's t. in the air** le temps est à l'orage; **voice like t.** voix *f* tonnante *ou* tonitruante; **with a face like t.** le visage fulminant de colère; *Fig* **to steal sb's t.** couper ses effets à qn; *Old-fashioned* **what in t. do you think you're doing?** tonnerre de Dieu! mais qu'est-ce qui te prend?

thunder² 1 *vi* **(a)** *Met* tonner; (*of guns, waves*) faire un bruit de tonnerre; **it's thundering** il tonne; **it's thundering and lightening** il y a du tonnerre et des éclairs
(b) (*move noisily*) **the avalanche thundered down** l'avalanche dévala dans un bruit de tonnerre; **the train thundered past** le train passa dans un bruit de tonnerre; **lorries thundered through the village** des camions traversèrent le village dans un bruit de tonnerre
(c) (*of speaker*) tonitruer, tonner; **to t. against sb/sth** tonitruer contre qn/qch; **he thundered about the need for greater vigilance** il tonnait *ou* tonitruant sur la nécessité d'une plus grande vigilance
2 *vt* (*order*) ordonner d'une voix tonitruante; **get out!, he thundered** dehors!, tonitrua-t-il *ou* dit-il d'une voix tonitruante

thunderbolt ['θʌndəbəʊlt] *n* coup *m* de foudre; *Fig* (*astounding event etc*) coup *m* d'éclat; (*piece of news*) nouvelle *f* foudroyante; **the news came like a t.** cette nouvelle m'a/l'a/*etc* stupéfait

thunderclap ['θʌndəklæp] *n* coup *m* de tonnerre

thundercloud ['θʌndəklaʊd] *n* nuage *m* orageux

thundering ['θʌnd(ə)rɪŋ] *adj* (*sound etc*) tonnant, tonitruant; **t. applause** tonnerre *m* d'applaudissements; **to be in a t. rage** être dans une colère bleue; *Old-fashioned F* **what a t. nuisance!** que c'est embêtant!; *Old-fashioned F* **what a t. (great) lie!** quel mensonge énorme!

thunderous ['θʌnd(ə)rəs] *adj* (*voice etc*) tonnant, tonitruant; **t. applause** tonnerre *m* d'applaudissements, applaudissements *mpl* à tout rompre

thunderstorm ['θʌndəstɔ:m] *n* orage *m*

thunderstruck ['θʌndəstrʌk] *adj* abasourdi; **I was t. by the news** cette nouvelle m'a stupéfait *ou* stupéfié

thundery ['θʌndərɪ] *adj* (*sky*) orageux; (*weather*) orageux, d'orage; **the weather's t.** le temps est orageux *ou* à l'orage; **t. shower** averse *f* accompagnée de tonnerre

thurible ['θjʊərɪb(ə)l] *n Rel* encensoir *m*

Thursday ['θɜ:zdɪ] *n* [①**A75-6**,B-C; **B58-9**,B-C] jeudi *m*; **Maundy T.**

jeudi saint; **he's coming on T.** il viendra jeudi; **every T. morning** tous les jeudis matins
thus [ðʌs] *adv* **(a)** *esp Lit* (*in this way*) ainsi, de cette façon, de cette manière; **t. prepared** ainsi préparé, préparé de cette façon **(b)** (*therefore*) ainsi, donc; **t., when he arrived** donc, lorsqu'il est arrivé **(c) t. far** (*as far as this*) jusqu'ici; (*as far as that*) jusque-là; **t. much** autant que cela (et pas davantage)
thwack¹ [θwæk] *n* (*blow*) coup *m*; (*with hand*) claque *f*, *F* taloche *f*; (*noise*) claquement *m*; **with a t.** avec un coup sec; **I gave myself a t. on the shin** je me suis donné un coup dans le tibia
thwack² *vt* (*hit hard*) (*ball, head*) frapper; (*slap*) gifler; **I thwacked my head on the beam** je me suis cogné la tête contre la poutre
thwart¹ [θwɔːt, *Naut* θɔːt] *n* (*in rowing boat*) banc *m* de nage
thwart² *vt* (*person*) contrarier; (*plot, scheme*) déjouer; **to be thwarted** (*of person*) essuyer un échec
thy [ðaɪ] *poss adj* (*before a vowel* **thine**) *Arch, Lit* ton, *f* ta, *pl* tes
thyme [taɪm] *n Bot, Culin* thym *m*; **wild t.** serpolet *m*
thymus [ˈθaɪməs] *n Anat* thymus *m*, glande thymique *f*
thyristor [θaɪˈrɪstər] *n* thyristor *m*
thyroid [ˈθaɪrɔɪd] *adj, n* thyroïde *f*
thyself [ðaɪˈself] *pers pron Arch, Lit* toi(-même); (*reflexive*) te
ti [tiː] *n Mus* si *m*
tiara [tɪˈɑːrə] *n* **(a)** diadème *m* **(b)** *Rel* tiare *f*
Tiberius [taɪˈbɪərɪəs] *n* Tibère *m*
Tiber (the) [ðəˈtaɪbər] *n* le Tibre
Tibet [tɪˈbet] *n* Tibet *m*
Tibetan [tɪˈbet(ə)n] **1** *adj* tibétain **2** *n* **(a)** Tibétain, -aine **(b)** *Ling* tibétain *m*
tibia [ˈtɪbɪə] *n Anat* tibia *m*
tic [tɪk] *n Med* tic *m*; **a nervous t.** un tic nerveux
tich [tɪtʃ] *n Br F* **a (little) t.** (*person*) un (petit) bout de chou
tichy [ˈtɪtʃɪ] *adj Br F* minuscule
tick¹ [tɪk] *n* **(a)** (*sound*) (*of clock*) tic-tac *m* **(b)** *Br F* (*moment*) instant *m*; **just a t.!, half a t.!** un instant!, une seconde!; **it'll only take me a couple of ticks** je vais faire ça en deux secondes **(c)** (*mark*) marque *f*, coche *f*; **to put a t. against a name** cocher un nom **(d)** *St Exch* **t. size** échelon *m* de cotation
tick² **1** *vi* **to t.** (*of clock*) faire tic-tac, tictaquer; **the minutes are ticking by** les minutes passent; *F* **I'd like to know what makes him t.** je voudrais bien savoir ce qui le motive **2** *vt* = **tick off (a)**
tick³ *n* (*parasite*) (*on cattle etc*) tique *f*
tick⁴ *n Br F* (*credit*) crédit *m*; **to buy** *or* **get sth on t.** acheter qch à crédit
tick⁵ *n* (*mattress cover*) enveloppe *f*, housse *f* (*à matelas*)
▶ **tick away** *vi* **time is ticking away** le temps passe
▶ **tick off** *vtsep* **(a)** (*mark with tick*) (*article on list etc*) pointer; (*name*) cocher **(b)** *Br F* (*reprimand*) attraper, enguirlander; **to get ticked off** se faire rembarrer **(c)** *Am F* (*irritate*) **to t. sb off** embêter qn; **he's really ticked off** il est drôlement en rogne
▶ **tick over** *vi* (*of engine*) tourner au ralenti; **the engine is ticking over nicely** le moteur tourne bien; **my business is just ticking over** les affaires vont doucement; **business is ticking over nicely** les affaires tournent bien; **it keeps my brain ticking over** ça fait travailler ma cervelle
ticker [ˈtɪkər] *n* **(a)** *Sl* (*watch*) montre *f*; (*clock*) pendule *f*; (*heart*) palpitant *m* **(b)** *St Exch* téléimprimeur *m*, téléscripteur *m*; **t. tape** bande *f* de téléimprimeur; **to be given a t. tape welcome** être accueilli sous une pluie de serpentins
ticket¹ [ˈtɪkɪt] *n* **(a)** (*railway, air, theatre, lottery etc*) billet *m*; (*underground, bus, for cloakroom etc*) ticket *m*; *Th etc* **complimentary t.** billet de faveur; *Rail etc* **single t.** billet simple, (billet d')aller *m*; **return t.** billet d'aller-retour, aller-retour *m inv*; **left-luggage t., cloakroom t.** bulletin *m ou* ticket de consigne; **platform t.** ticket de quai; **season t.** carte *f* d'abonnement; **season-t. holder** abonné, -ée; *Aut F* **(parking) t.** P.V. *m inv*, papillon *m*; **to get a (parking) t.** attraper un P.V.; **t. holders only** (*on sign*) réservé aux personnes munies de billets
(b) *Com* **(price) t.** étiquette *f*; **this doesn't have a t. on it** il n'y a pas de prix sur cet article
(c) *esp Am Pol* (*list of candidates*) liste *f* des candidats; *F* **the Democratic t.** (*policies*) le programme du parti démocrate
(d) *Naut F* **to get one's (master's) t.** passer (son brevet de) capitaine
(e) *F* **it was just the t.!** voilà juste ce qu'il me fallait
ticket² *vt* **(ticketed)** (*goods*) étiqueter
ticket agency *n* agence *f* spécialisée dans la vente de billets de théâtre (*qui vend des billets pour les spectacles les plus populaires*)
ticket barrier *n* portillon *m* automatique
ticket collector *n* contrôleur, -euse
ticket desk *n* guichet *m*
ticketing [ˈtɪkɪtɪŋ] *n* (*issuing of tickets*) billetterie *f*
ticket inspector *n* contrôleur, -euse
ticket machine *n* billetterie *f* automatique, distributeur *m* automatique de billets
ticket office *n Rail* billetterie *f*
ticket punch *n* (*of ticket inspector*) poinçon *m*; (*for use by passenger*) composteur *m*
ticket tout *n* revendeur *m* de billets
ticket window *n* guichet *m*
ticking¹ [ˈtɪkɪŋ] *n* (*of clock*) tic-tac *m*
ticking² *n Tex* toile *f ou* coutil *m* à matelas
ticking off *n Br F* (*reprimand*) engueulade *f*, savon *m*; **to get a t.** (se) prendre un savon; **to give sb a t.** passer un savon à qn
tickle¹ [ˈtɪk(ə)l] *n* chatouillement *m*; **he gave her a t.** il lui a fait des chatouilles; **to have a t. in one's throat** avoir un chatouillement dans la gorge
tickle² **1** *vt* **(a)** (*sb*) chatouiller; *F* (*amuse*) amuser; **to t. the palate** (*of food, wine*) chatouiller le palais; *F* **to t. sb's fancy** amuser qn; *F* **to be tickled to death** *or* **tickled pink at** *or* **by sth** (*be amused*) s'amuser beaucoup de qch; (*be delighted*) être enchanté *ou* ravi de qch **(b)** *Fishing* (*trout*) pêcher à la main **(c)** *Hum* **to t. the ivories** pianoter, tapoter **2** *vi* **hey, that tickles!** eh, ça chatouille!; **you're tickling!** tu me chatouilles!
tickler [ˈtɪklər] *n esp Br F* (*problem*) os *m*; (*delicate subject*) sujet *m* délicat
tickling [ˈtɪklɪŋ] **1** *adj* qui chatouille **2** *n* chatouillement *m*
ticklish [ˈtɪklɪʃ] *adj* **(a)** (*person*) chatouilleux, -euse **(b)** (*touchy*) chatouilleux; (*subject, task etc*) délicat; **to be in a t. situation** se trouver dans une situation délicate
tickly [ˈtɪklɪ] *adj* (*blanket, pullover*) qui grattouille; (*cough*) irritant, d'irritation; **a t. throat** une irritation dans la gorge
ticktack [ˈtɪktæk] *n Br Horseracing* = signaux *mpl* utilisés entre les bookmakers; **t. man** aide *m* de bookmaker (qui fait des signaux à bras)
tick-tack-toe *n Am* morpion *m*, jeu *m* des petites croix
tidal [ˈtaɪd(ə)l] *adj* **(a)** de la marée; (*energy etc*) marémoteur, -trice **(b)** (*river etc*) à marée; **t. harbour** port *m* à *ou* de marée
tidal basin *n* bassin *m* à flot
tidal wave *n* raz de marée *m inv*; (*on river*) barre *f* de flot; *Fig* (*of enthusiasm etc*) vague *f*
tidbit [ˈtɪdbɪt] *n US* = **titbit**
tiddler [ˈtɪdlər] *n Br F* (*small fish*) petit poisson *m*; (*minnow*) épinoche *f*; (*child*) bambin *m*, mioche *mf*
tiddl(e)y [ˈtɪdlɪ] *adj Br F* (*small*) minuscule
tiddlywinks [ˈtɪdlɪwɪŋks] *n* jeu *m* de puce
tide [taɪd] *n* **(a)** marée *f*; **ebb t.** marée descendante, jusant *m*; **high/low t.** marée haute/basse; **neap t.** marée de morte-eau; **spring t.** grande marée, marée de vive eau; *Naut* **to go out with the t.** partir à la marée; **rise/fall of the t.** montée *f*/ baisse *f* de l'eau; *also Fig* **against the t.** à contre-courant; *Fig* **the rising t. of discontent** la vague croissante du mécontentement; *Fig* **the t. of events** le cours des événements; *Fig* **when the t. of the battle turned** quand le cours de la bataille changea; *Fig* **the t. has turned** le vent a tourné; **t. gate** porte *f* à flot; **t. race** raz *m* de marée; **t. table** annuaire *m ou* indicateur *m* des marées
(b) *Arch* (*season*) temps *m*, saison *f*
▶ **tide over** *vtas* aider à surmonter une difficulté, *F* dépanner; **can you lend me five pounds to t. me over till Monday?** pourrais-tu me prêter cinq livres pour me dépanner jusqu'à lundi?
tidemark [ˈtaɪdmɑːk] *n* **(a)** (*mark left by tide*) laisse *f* de haute mer **(b)** *Br F* (*line of dirt*) (*in bath etc*) ligne *f* de crasse
tidewater [ˈtaɪdwɔːtər] *n* eau *f* de marée; *US* (*coastal land*) côte *f*
tideway [ˈtaɪdweɪ] *n* lit *m* de la marée
tidily [ˈtaɪdɪlɪ] *adv* avec ordre; (*dressed etc*) avec soin, soigneusement; **he puts everything away t. in a drawer at night** il range tout bien en ordre *ou* soigneusement dans un tiroir le soir
tidiness [ˈtaɪdɪnɪs] *n* (*of room, files etc*) ordre *m*; (*of person*) goût *m* de l'ordre; (*in appearance, dress, of handwriting*) soin *m*
tidings [ˈtaɪdɪŋz] *npl Lit* nouvelle(s) *f(pl)*
tidy¹ [ˈtaɪdɪ] *adj* **(a)** (*desk, room*) bien rangé, en ordre; (*handwriting*) net, soigné; (*hair*) soigné; **to have a t. mind** être méthodique, avoir l'esprit clair; **a clean and t. room**

une pièce propre et nette; **he's very t.** (*in habits*) il est très ordonné; (*in appearance*) il est très soigné **(b)** *F* (*considerable*) assez considérable; (*profit*) joli petit; **a t. sum** une somme rondelette

tidy[2] *n* vide-poches *m inv*; **sink t.** coin *m* d'évier

tidy[3] *vt* (*room*) ranger, mettre de l'ordre dans; **to t. one's hair** s'arranger les cheveux

▶ **tidy away** *vtsep* (*put away*) (*books etc*) ranger

▶ **tidy up 1** *vi* (*clear things away*) ranger **2** *vtsep* (*room*) ranger, mettre de l'ordre dans; (*file, essay*) faire le ménage dans; **to t. things up** ranger; **to t. oneself up** faire un bout de toilette

tidy-out *n* nettoyage *m* par le vide

tidy-up *n* **to give a room a t.** ranger une pièce

tie[1] [taɪ] *n* **(a)** (*link*) lien *m*; **he has no ties to the place** il n'y a rien qui l'attache à cet endroit; **family ties** liens de famille; **ties of friendship** liens d'amitié **(b)** (*of rope, straw, wicker etc*) lien *m*; (*for plastic bag*) cordon *m* **(c)** (*neck tie*) cravate *f*; **bow t.** nœud *m* papillon; **black t.** (*on invitation*) = smoking *m*; **old school t.** = cravate portée par les anciens élèves d'une école; **it's the old school t.** (*that's why he got the job etc*) ce sont les vieilles relations *ou* amitiés d'école **(d)** *Constr etc* crampon *m*; *Am Rail* traverse *f* **(e)** *Mus* liaison *f* **(f)** *Sp* (*match, race*) match *m*/course *f* à égalité; **(cup) t.** (*match*) = match de coupe

tie[2] (*pt, pp* **tied**, *prp* **tying**) **1** *vt* **(a)** (*piece of string, neck tie etc*) nouer; (*knot*) faire; (*shoelace, hood strings*) attacher, nouer; (*dog to kennel etc*) attacher; (*sb to post*) attacher, ligoter; **to t. sth to sth** attacher qch à qch; **to t. two things together** lier deux choses entre elles, attacher deux choses l'une à l'autre; *also Fig* **to t. sb's hands** lier les mains à qn; **to be tied hand and foot** être ligoté; **to have one's hands tied (behind one's back)** avoir les mains liées (derrière le dos); *Fig* **to have one's hands tied** avoir les mains liées, être pieds et poings liés

(b) (*restrict*) **he was tied to his desk** il est resté rivé à son bureau; **the children kept her tied to the house** elle était clouée chez elle à cause des enfants; **she felt tied by her sense of duty** elle se sentait contrainte par son sens du devoir

(c) (*link*) **to be tied to** avoir un lien avec

(d) *Mus* (*two notes*) lier

2 *vi Sp etc* être *ou* arriver à égalité (**with** avec); (*of candidates*) obtenir un nombre égal de suffrages; *Sch* **to t. for first place** être premier ex æquo (**with** avec)

▶ **tie back** *vtsep* (*hair, curtains*) attacher (en arrière)

▶ **tie down** *vtsep* **(a)** (*prevent from moving by tying*) **to t. sb down** immobiliser qn en l'attachant; **to t. sth down** assujettir qch **(b)** (*restrict to certain conditions*) assujettir à certaines conditions; **children t. you down** les enfants représentent une contrainte; **this ticket doesn't t. you down to specific dates** ce billet vous laisse libre de changer vos dates de départ; **to t. sb down to facts** obliger qn à ne pas s'écarter des faits; **tied down to one's job** accaparé par son travail

▶ **tie in 1** *vi* (*correspond*) (*of facts, story*) concorder, cadrer, *F* coller (**with** avec); **the two versions don't t. in** les deux versions ne concordent *ou F* ne collent pas **2** *vt* **to t. sth in with sth** faire concorder *ou F* coller qch avec qch; **this sequence has to be tied in with the rest of the film** il faut qu'on intègre cette séquence au reste du film

▶ **tie on** *vt* (*attach by tying*) (*label etc*) attacher avec une ficelle

▶ **tie up 1** *vtsep* **(a)** (*tie together*) (*parcel etc*) attacher, ficeler; (*hair*) nouer, attacher; (*top of bag*) lier, ficeler; (*injured arm etc*) bander, panser; **her hair was tied up with a ribbon** ses cheveux étaient attachés par un ruban; **there were various strands of the plot to t. up in the last episode** il y avait, dans l'histoire, beaucoup de péripéties qui demandaient une conclusion au dernier épisode

(b) (*prevent from moving*) (*animal*) attacher; (*person*) ligoter; (*boat*) amarrer

(c) (*prevent from being spent*) (*capital*) immobiliser; **my capital is tied up in stocks and shares** mon capital est immobilisé sous forme d'actions *ou* en actions

(d) *F* **to be tied up** (*busy*) être très occupé, avoir beaucoup à faire; **he's going to be tied up all afternoon** il va être pris tout l'après-midi; **to get oneself tied up** s'embrouiller; *Am* **the traffic was all tied up** il y avait un embouteillage

(e) to be tied up with sth (*be connected*) être lié à qch; **it's tied up with the increase in the bank rate** c'est lié à l'augmentation des taux d'intérêt; **our firm is tied up with theirs** notre maison a des accords avec la leur; **he's much too tied up with his work** son travail l'accapare vraiment

2 *vi* **(a)** (*of boat*) jeter l'ancre

(b) (*connect, make sense*) avoir des rapports

▶ **tie up with** *vipo* (*fit in with*) concorder *ou* cadrer *ou* coller avec

tie beam *n Constr* longrine *f*

tie-break, tie-breaker *n Tennis* tie-break *m, pl* tie-breaks; (*in TV game etc*) question *f* visant à départager les candidats, question subsidiaire

tie clip *n* fixe-cravate *m, pl* fixe-cravates

tied [taɪd] *adj* **(a)** *Br* **t. cottage** *or* **house** = logement *m* de fonction; **t. house** (*pub*) = débit *m* de boissons astreint par bail à vendre la bière d'une certaine brasserie **(b)** *Mus* **t. notes** notes *fpl* liées

tied up *adj* (*capital*) immobilisé

tie-dye *vt* = teindre qch en le nouant pour que la couleur soit irrégulière

tie-in *n* rapport *m*, association *f*; (*film from book*) film *m* tiré d'un livre; (*book from film, TV series*) livre *m* tiré d'un film/d'un feuilleton; **we've got a film t.** nous avons vendu les droits pour le cinéma; *Mktg* **t. promotion** promotion *f* collective

tie-on *adj* **t. label** étiquette *f* à œillets

tiepin ['taɪpɪn] *n* épingle *f* de cravate

tier [tɪər] *n* étage *m*; (*of seats etc*) rangée *f*; **tiers of an amphitheatre** gradins *mpl* d'un amphithéâtre; **two-t. postal system** courrier *m* à deux vitesses; **to arrange sth in tiers** disposer qch par étages, étager qch; **to rise in tiers** s'étager

tiered ['tɪəd] *adj* **t. seating** sièges *mpl* disposés en gradins; **three-t. cake** pièce montée *f* à trois étages; **three-t. stand** (*for cakes etc*) étagère *f* à trois tablettes

tie-rod *n Aut* barre *f* d'accouplement

Tierra del Fuego [tɪ'eərədel'fweɪgəʊ] *n* la Terre de Feu

tie-tack mike *n* micro *m* cravate

tie-up *n* **(a)** *Am Aut* (*traffic jam*) embouteillage *m*; *Am* (*of work*) suspension *f* forcée **(b)** (*connection*) (*between two things*) rapport *m*

TIF [tiːaɪ'ef] (*abbr* **transport international ferroviaire**) TIF *m*

tiff [tɪf] *n* petite querelle *f* (*souvent entre amoureux*)

tiffin ['tɪfɪn] *n* (*Anglo-Indian*) déjeuner *m*

tig [tɪg] *n* (*game*) (jeu *m* de) chat *m*

tiger ['taɪgər] *n* (*animal*), *Fig* tigre *m*; *Fig* **we've got a t. by the tail** on va se faire bouffer

tiger lily *n* lis *m* tigré

tiger moth *n* écaille *f*

tiger's-eye [taɪgəz'aɪ] *n* (*stone*) œil *m* de tigre

tight [taɪt] **1** *adj* **(a)** (*clothes*) serré; (*skintight*) collant, moulant; (*mortise etc*) bien ajusté; (*knot, screw*) serré; (*cord etc*) raide, tendu; **to draw a cord t.** serrer un cordon; **to keep a t. hold over sb** tenir la bride haute à qn; **too t.** (*clothes*) étriqué, trop serré, trop juste; **t. shoes** chaussures *fpl* trop petites *ou* trop étroites; **it's a bit t.** (*of clothes*) c'est un peu juste; **the key's a bit t. in the lock** la clé ne tourne pas bien dans la serrure, la serrure est dure; **to have a t. feeling across the chest** avoir une barre sur la poitrine; **it's going to be t. but we should just make it** ça va être juste, mais nous devrions y arriver; **there was just room to park, but it was a t. squeeze** il y avait tout juste la place pour se garer; *F* **to be in a t. corner** *or* **a t. spot** être dans une mauvaise passe, *F* être dans le pétrin; **to run a t. ship** bien mener sa barque; **t. rules** règles *fpl* (très) strictes

(b) (*money*) rare; *Sp* (*race*) serré, chaudement disputé; (*schedule*) chargé; **it should be a t. finish** (*in race*) l'arrivée devrait être serrée; *F* **money's a bit t. at the moment** je suis/nous sommes/*etc* un peu à court (d'argent) en ce moment

(c) (*mean with money*) pingre, radin; **she's a bit t. with money** elle est un peu pingre

(d) *F* (*drunk*) soûl, *F* pété; **to get t.** prendre une cuite

(e) (*joint*) hermétique

(f) (*turn, corner*) serré; *Aut* (*lock*) faible, petit

2 *adv* **(a)** (*firmly*) fortement; **to hold sth t.** serrer fort qch; **to hold sb t.** (*child, lover etc*) serrer qn fort (contre soi); (*person attempting to escape*) bien tenir qn; **hold t.!** tenez bon!, tenez ferme!; **to screw a nut up t.** serrer un écrou à fond *ou* à bloc; **to squeeze sth t.** serrer qch étroitement *ou* fort; **to sit t.** ne pas bouger

(b) (*to seal, shut*) hermétiquement; (*properly*) bien; **shut t., t. shut** (*door, eyes*) bien fermé

tight-arsed ['taɪtɑːst], *US* **tight-assed** ['taɪtæst] *adj Sl* coincé

tighten ['taɪt(ə)n] **1** *vt* (*screw, knot etc*) serrer, resserrer; (*nut*) bloquer; (*spring*) bander, tendre; (*blockade, restrictions*) renforcer; **to t. one's grip on sth** resserrer son emprise sur qch; **to t. one's belt** serrer sa ceinture; *Fig* se serrer la ceinture **2** *vi* (*of knot etc*) se (res)serrer; (*of spring, cable etc*) se tendre; **her lips tightened** elle serra les lèvres

▶ **tighten up 1** *vtsep* **(a)** (*screw etc*) resserrer; (*shoelaces*) refaire **(b)** (*blockade, restrictions, regulations*) renforcer;

the company has tightened up (its) security la société a renforcé ses mesures de sécurité **2** *vi* (*in discipline, security etc*) devenir plus ferme *ou* strict; **to t. up on sth** renforcer qch

tightening ['taɪt(ə)nɪŋ] *n* (*of blockade etc*) renforcement *m*; *Fin* (*of credit etc*) resserrement *m*

tightfisted [taɪt'fɪstɪd] *adj F* radin; **to be t.** être près de ses sous

tight-fitting *adj* (*dress, trousers*) moulant; (*suit, joint etc*) bien ajusté; (*door, lid*) qui ferme bien

tightknit ['taɪt'nɪt] *adj* (*community*) uni, dont les membres sont étroitement liés

tight-lipped *adj* les lèvres serrées; *Fig* **to be t.** ne rien dire (**about sth** au sujet de qch); **they kept a t. silence** ils ont gardé le silence, *F* ils sont restés bouche cousue; **you're being very t. about this** tu es très peu loquace là-dessus

tightly ['taɪtlɪ] *adv* **(a)** (*firmly*) fermement; **to hold on t. to sth** se cramponner à qch; **to squeeze sth t.** serrer qch étroitement *ou* fort; **to fit t.** être bien ajusté; **to fit too t.** être (trop) serré *ou* (trop) juste; **we were t. packed** *F* nous étions serrés comme des sardines; **don't screw it on too t.** ne le serre pas trop fort **(b)** (*to seal, close*) hermétiquement; (*properly*) bien; **eyes t. shut** yeux *mpl* bien fermés

tightness ['taɪtnɪs] *n* **(a)** *Med* (*of chest*) oppression *f*; (*of link, clothing*) étroitesse *f*; (*of embrace*) force *f* **(b)** (*of joint*) étanchéité *f* **(c)** (*of regulations, security*) rigueur *f*

tightrope ['taɪtrəʊp] *n* corde *f* raide; **to walk a t.** marcher sur une corde raide; *Fig* être sur une corde raide; **t. walker** funambule *mf*; *Fig* **political t. walking** acrobatie *f* politique; **we're walking a diplomatic t.** au point de vue diplomatique nous sommes sur une véritable corde raide

tights [taɪts] *npl* [ⓘ**A10**,e] (*garment*) collant *m*

tightwad ['taɪtwɒd] *n Am F* avare *m*, radin, -ine

tigress ['taɪgrɪs] *nf* (*animal, Fig fierce woman*) tigresse *f*

Tigris (the) [ðə'taɪgrɪs] *n* le Tigre

tike [taɪk] *n F* = **tyke**

'til [tɪl] *prep, conj Lit* = **until**

tilde ['tɪldə] *n Gram* tilde *m*

tile[1] [taɪl] *n* (*of roof etc*) tuile *f*; (*on ground, floor*) carreau *m*; *F* **to spend a night on the tiles** faire la bringue toute la nuit; **(floor) t.** carreau de pavage *ou* de revêtement de sol; **(wall) t.** carreau de revêtement mural; **t. kiln** tuilerie *f*; **t. works** tuilerie

tile[2] *vt* (*roof*) couvrir de tuiles; (*floor*) carreler

tiled [taɪld] *adj* (*roof*) de *ou* en tuiles; (*floor*) carrelé, en carrelage; (*wall*) carrelé, revêtu de carrelage

tiling ['taɪlɪŋ] *n* **(a)** (*activity*) (*on roof*) pose *f* des tuiles; (*on floor*) carrelage *m*, pose des carreaux **(b)** (*covering*) (*of roof*) (couverture *f* en) tuiles *fpl*; (*of floor*) carrelage *m*

till[1] [tɪl] *vt Agr* (*field etc*) labourer, cultiver

till[2] *n Com* tiroir-caisse *m*, *pl* tiroirs-caisses; **pay at the t.** payez à la caisse; *Fig F* **to be caught with one's hand in the t.** être surpris la main dans le sac; **t. money** encaisse *f*

till[3] **1** *prep* jusqu'à; **t. tomorrow** jusqu'à demain; **t. now** jusqu'ici, jusqu'à maintenant; **t. then** jusque-là, jusqu'alors; **from morning t. night** du matin (jusqu')au soir; **(goodbye) t. Thursday!** à jeudi!; **wait t. after the holidays** attendez jusqu'après les vacances; **not t. Monday** pas avant lundi; **he won't come t. after dinner** il ne viendra qu'après le dîner; **I'd never heard of it t. now** c'est la première fois que j'en entends parler

2 *conj* jusqu'à ce que + *sub*; **we won't go t. all the doors are shut** nous ne partirons pas tant que toutes les portes ne seront pas fermées; **I have to wait t. all the doors are shut** je dois attendre jusqu'à ce que toutes les portes soient fermées; **t. I met you ...** avant de te rencontrer ...; **to laugh t. one cries** rire aux larmes; **I'm not going t. I get my money** je ne sortirai d'ici que lorsque j'aurai mon argent

tillage ['tɪlɪdʒ] *n* **(a)** *Agr* (*activity*) labour *m*, labourage *m*, culture *f* **(b)** (*land*) terres *fpl* en labour

tiller[1] ['tɪlər] *n Naut* barre *f* franche (de direction); **who was at the t.?** qui était à la barre?

tiller[2] *n* (*ploughman*) laboureur *m*; *Lit* **a t. of the soil** un homme de la terre

tilt[1] [tɪlt] *n* **(a)** (*angle*) inclinaison *f*, pente *f*; (*in dancing*) tilt *m*; **to give sth a t.** incliner qch; *Aut* **t. adjustment steering wheel** volant *m* réglable en inclinaison; **t. and slide sunroof** toit *m* ouvrant entrebâillant et coulissant; **t. cab** (*on truck*) cabine *f* basculante **(b)** *Hist* (*lance blow*) coup *m* de lance; *Fig* **to have a t. at sb** lancer une pointe à qn; **(at) full t.** à toute vitesse, *F* à fond de train; **to run full t. into sth** donner en plein contre qch, rentrer en plein dans qch

tilt[2] **1** *vi* **(a)** (*incline*) (*state*) pencher; (*act*) incliner, pencher; *Fig* pencher (**towards** pour); **to t. backwards/forwards** incliner *ou* pencher vers l'arrière/vers l'avant **(b)** *Hist* (*joust*) jouter (**at** contre); **to t. at windmills** se battre contre des moulins à vent; *Fig* **to t. at sb** (*in debate etc*) lancer une pointe à qn **2** *vt* (*barrel, one's chair etc*) pencher, incliner; **to t. one's hat over one's eyes** rabattre son chapeau sur les yeux; **to t. one's chair back** se balancer sur sa chaise

▶ **tilt over** *vi* (*fall*) se renverser

tilted ['tɪltɪd] *adj* incliné, penché

tilth [tɪlθ] *n Agr* **(a)** (*ploughing*) labour *m* **(b)** (*soil turned up*) couche *f* arable; (*tilled land*) cultures *fpl*

tilting ['tɪltɪŋ] **1** *adj* **(a)** (*at an angle*) incliné, penché **(b)** (*able to be tilted*) inclinable **2** *n Hist* (*jousting*) joute *f*

timber[1] ['tɪmbər] **1** *n* **(a)** (*wood*) bois *m*; **building t.** bois de construction *ou* de charpente; **standing t.** bois sur pied, arbres *mpl*; **to fell t.** abattre *ou* couper des arbres; **to put an area under t.** boiser une région; **t. line** limite *f* des arbres; **t. raft** train *m* de bois *ou* de flottage **(b)** (*beam*) poutre *f*, madrier *m*; (*of ship*) membre *m* **2** *int* **t.!** attention à l'arbre (qui tombe)!

timber[2] *vt* (*mine shaft, tunnel etc*) boiser, cuveler

timbered ['tɪmbəd] *adj* **(a)** (*house etc*) en bois; **half t.** à *ou* en colombage **(b)** (*land*) boisé

timber hitch *n Naut* nœud *m* de bois *ou* d'anguille

timbering ['tɪmbərɪŋ] *n* **(a)** (*of region*) boisage *m*, boisement *m* **(b)** (*of mine shaft*) boisage *m*, cuvelage *m* **(c)** *Constr* (*wooden frame*) armature *f*; **half t.** colombage *m*

timber merchant *n* marchand *m* de bois

timber trade *n* commerce *m* du bois

timberwork ['tɪmbəwɜːk] *n* **(a)** (*activity*) charpenterie *f* **(b)** (*framework*) charpente *f*

timber yard *n* chantier *m* de bois (de charpente)

timbre ['tæmbr] *n* (*of voice*) timbre *m*

Timbuktu [tɪmbʌk'tuː] *n* Tombouctou *m*

time[1] [taɪm] *n* **(a)** temps *m*; **in (the course of) t.** avec le temps, à la longue; **it's just a matter of t.** ce n'est qu'une question de temps; **a race against t.** une course contre la montre; *Prov* **t. is money** le temps c'est de l'argent; **t. will tell** *or* **show** qui vivra verra; **my t. is my own** je suis libre de mon temps; **when I have the t.** quand j'aurai le temps; **to have t. on one's hands** avoir du temps libre; **now that the children have grown up I have t. on my hands** maintenant que les enfants sont grands, j'ai du temps à moi; **to have no t. to do sth** ne pas avoir le temps de faire qch; **I've no t. for him** il m'embête; **I've got no t. for people like that!** les gens comme ça me cassent les pieds; **to gain t.** gagner du temps; **to play for t.** chercher à gagner du temps; **you've got plenty of t.** vous avez tout votre temps; **there's no t. to lose** il n'y a pas de temps à perdre; **to make up for lost t.** rattraper le temps perdu; **to lose no t. doing sth** s'empresser *ou* se hâter de faire qch; **to waste t.** perdre du temps; **to make t. to do sth** trouver le temps de faire qch; **I can always make t. for you** pour vous, je suis toujours là; *Am Sl* **to make t. with sb** (*chat up*) draguer qn; (*have sex with*) se faire qn, s'envoyer qn; **it takes t.** cela prend du temps; **t.'s up!** c'est l'heure!; *Br* **t., gentlemen, please!** (*in pub*) on ferme!; *Fb etc* **to play extra t.** jouer les prolongations *fpl*; *Fb etc* **two minutes into extra t.** deux minutes de prolongations; *F* **to do t.** (*go to prison*) faire de la taule; **convict nearing the end of his t.** prisonnier qui a bientôt fait *ou* fini son temps; **if I had my t. over again** si j'avais à recommencer (ma vie); **she's seen a few things in her t.** elle a vu pas mal de choses dans sa vie

(b) (*period*) **in a short t.** (*quickly*) en peu de temps; (*soon*) sous peu; **in three weeks' t.** dans trois semaines; **in a month's t.** dans un mois; **in no t. (at all), in next to no t.** en un rien de temps, en moins de rien; **within the required t.** dans le délai prescrit; **to take a long t. over sth** mettre longtemps à faire qch; **to take t. over sth/to do sth properly** prendre le temps qu'il faut pour qch/pour faire qch; **take your t.!** prenez (tout) votre temps!; **you took your t.!** tu as pris ton temps!, tu en as mis un (de ces) temps!; **what a (long) t. he is taking!** il n'en finit pas!, il prend son temps!; **to take the t. and trouble to check the facts** ne ménager ni son temps ni sa peine pour vérifier les faits; **she took the t. to explain it to us** elle a pris le temps de nous l'expliquer; **we haven't seen him for a long t.** voilà longtemps que nous ne l'avons (pas) vu; **for some t. past** depuis quelque temps; **for some t. (to come)** pendant quelque temps; **a short t. after, after a short t.** peu (de temps) après; **after a t.** après quelque temps, au bout d'un certain temps; **after a long t.** longtemps après; **all this t.** pendant tout ce temps; **she does it all the t.** elle le fait toujours *ou* tout le temps; **you knew all the t., didn't you?** tu le savais pourtant, n'est-ce pas? *Cin* **running t.** (*of film*) durée *f* de projection; *Sp* **1 minute 34 seconds is her best/a good t.** 1 minute 34 secondes, c'est son meilleur temps/c'est un bon temps

(c) (*age*) époque *f*; **sign of the times** signe *m* des temps; **in times past, in former times** autrefois, jadis, dans le temps; **the good old times** le bon vieux temps; **in happier times** en un *ou* des temps plus heureux; **in times to come** à l'avenir; **in our times** *or* **these times** de nos jours; **to be ahead of** *or* **in advance of one's t.** être en avance sur son temps; **it was a very popular car in its t.** c'était une voiture très populaire à l'époque (où elle est sortie); **she was probably a good singer in her t.** en son temps, c'était sûrement une bonne chanteuse; **that was before my t.** c'était avant que je sois né; **very advanced for its t.** très en avance sur son temps *ou* sur l'époque; **to move with the times** *F* être à la page; **to be behind the times** retarder *ou* être en retard sur son siècle, *F* ne pas être à la page; **times are bad** les temps sont difficiles *ou* durs; **hard times** des temps difficiles; **to have fallen on hard times** connaître des temps difficiles

(d) (*moment*) moment *m*; **I didn't know it at the t.** (*at that moment*) je n'en savais rien à ce moment-là; (*at that period*) je n'en savais rien à cette époque; **at that t.** en ce temps-là; **at the present t.** à l'heure qu'il est, actuellement, à présent; **at one t. it was different** autrefois *ou* dans le temps, ce n'était pas comme ça *ou* c'était différent; **at no t.** jamais, à aucun moment; **at no t. did I say that …** je n'ai jamais dit que …, à aucun moment je n'ai dit que …; **at times** parfois, quelquefois, par moments; **at all times** toujours; **(at) any t. (you like)** n'importe quand, quand vous voudrez; **if at any t. …** si à l'occasion …; **some t. or other** un jour ou l'autre; **some t. next month** dans le courant du mois prochain; **this t. next year** l'an prochain à pareille époque *ou* à la même date; **by the t. (that) I got there** lorsque je suis arrivé; **from t. to t.** de temps en temps, de temps à autre; **from that t. (onwards)** dès lors, à partir de ce moment-là; **at the proper t.** en temps utile; **we shall see when the t. comes** nous verrons (cela) quand le moment sera venu; **now is the t./our t./your t. to …** c'est le (bon) moment pour …; **to choose one's t.** choisir son heure *ou* le moment; **this is no t.** *or* **this is not the t. to …** ce n'est pas le moment de …; **in due t. and place** en temps et lieu; **all in good t.** chaque chose en son temps; **in her own good t.** à son heure; **t. of (the) year** époque *f* de l'année; **at my/her/their/***etc* **t. of life** à mon/son/leur/*etc* âge; **it was holiday t.** c'était l'époque des vacances; **before one's/its t.** prématurément; **his t. had not yet come** son heure n'était pas encore venue; **to be nearing her t.** (*of pregnant woman*) approcher de son terme; **the t. for talking is past** ce n'est plus le moment de parler

(e) [①A75,A; B58,A] (*time of day etc*) heure *f*; **Greenwich mean t.** heure de Greenwich; **standard t.** heure du fuseau; **(standard) t. belt** *or* **t. zone** fuseau *m* horaire; *Br* **summer t.**, *Am* **daylight saving t.** heure d'été, *Can* heure avancée; **what's the t.?** quelle heure est-il?; **do you have the t.?** vous avez l'heure?; **what t. do you make it?** quelle heure avez-vous?; **to look at the t.** regarder l'heure; (*look at one's watch*) regarder sa montre; **watch that keeps (good) t./that loses t./that gains t.** montre qui est toujours à l'heure/qui retarde/qui avance; **what are you doing here at this t. of day/night?** qu'est-ce que tu fais ici à cette heure-ci?; **at any t. of the day or night** à n'importe quelle heure du jour ou de la nuit; **to pass the t. of day with sb** parler de la pluie et du beau temps avec qn; **this t. tomorrow** demain à la même heure; **at the t. of delivery** au moment de la livraison; **at a given t.** à un moment donné *ou* déterminé; **dinner t.** heure du dîner; **(dead) on t.** à l'heure (pile); **to run on t.** (*of trains etc*) être à l'heure; **to be ahead of/behind t.** être en avance/en retard; **I was just in t. to see it** je suis arrivé juste à temps pour le voir; **to start in good t.** s'y prendre (bien) à temps; (*on journey*) se mettre en route de bonne heure; **it is t. we left** il est temps de partir; **it's t. he understood** il est temps qu'il comprenne; *F* **it's high t.!, and about t. too!** ce n'est pas *ou* c'est pas trop tôt!; **t. signal** signal *m* horaire

(f) *Ind etc* **to put in t.** faire des heures; **to be paid by t.** être payé à l'heure; **to work** *or* **to be on short t.** être en chômage partiel; **to be on t. and a half/double t.** être payé une fois et demie/deux fois le taux horaire; **t. and motion study** étude *f* des temps et mouvements; **t. and motion expert** spécialiste *mf* des temps et mouvements; **t. off in lieu** repos *m* compensateur

(g) **to have a good t. (of it)** bien s'amuser; (*lead a pleasant life*) mener une vie agréable; *F* **to have a high old t.** faire la noce; **to have the t. of one's life** s'amuser comme un fou; **to have a bad** *or* **hard** *or* **rough t. (of it)** (*long period*) manger de la vache enragée, en voir de dures; (*shorter period*) passer un mauvais quart d'heure; **to have an easy t. of it** se la couler douce; **to give sb a hard** *or* **rough** *or* **tough t.** en faire voir de dures à qn, en faire voir de toutes les couleurs à qn

(h) (*occasion*) fois *f*; **five times** cinq fois; **this is the third t.** c'est la troisième fois; **next t.** la prochaine fois; **another t.** une autre fois; **the first t. I saw her** la première fois que je l'ai vue; **to do sth several times over** faire qch plusieurs fois *ou* à plusieurs reprises; **four times running** quatre fois de suite, à quatre reprises; **t. and t. again, t. after t.** à maintes reprises, maintes et maintes fois; **he succeeds every t.** il réussit à chaque coup; **every t. that …** chaque fois que …; **to do two things at a t.** faire deux choses à la fois; **to run upstairs four at a t.** monter l'escalier quatre à quatre; **for weeks at a t.** des semaines durant *ou* d'affilée; **it costs me £6 a t. to have my hair cut** une coupe de cheveux me coûte six livres; **at the same t. we must not forget that …** en même temps, nous ne devons pas oublier que …; **at the same t. will you also check the names of …** par la même occasion, vous vérifierez aussi les noms de …; **to do two things at the same t.** faire deux choses à la fois *ou* en même temps; *Prov* **you can't be in two places at the same t.** on ne peut être à la fois au four et au moulin

(i) (*in multiplication*) **four times two is eight** quatre fois deux font huit; **three times as big as the other** trois fois plus grand que l'autre; **six times as much** six fois autant

(j) *Mus* mesure *f*; **t. (value)** (*of note*) valeur *f*; **double/triple t.** mesure à deux/trois temps; **in strict t.** en mesure; **to keep t., to be in t.** être en mesure; **to get out of t.** perdre la mesure; **t. signature** fraction *f* indiquant la mesure; *Gym etc* **in quick t.** au pas accéléré

time² *vt* **(a)** (*set time of*) fixer l'heure de; *Phot* (*exposure*) calculer; **the meeting has been timed for 6 o'clock** l'heure de la réunion a été fixée à 6 heures; **to t. one's arrival to coincide with one's friend's** s'arranger pour arriver en même temps que son ami; **to t. a blow/a remark** choisir le moment de *ou* pour porter un coup/placer un mot; **well timed** (*remark etc*) opportun, à propos; **badly timed** (*remark etc*) inopportun, mal à propos

(b) (*measure time of*) *Sp etc* (*person, race*) chronométrer; (*runner*) prendre le temps de; *Mil etc* (*operation etc*) minuter; **to t. a journey** calculer la durée d'un voyage; **to t. how long it takes sb to do sth** mesurer le temps que qn met à faire qch; **t. yourself doing it** mesure le temps que tu mets à le faire

(c) *Aut etc* (*ignition etc*) caler; **to t. the valves** caler la distribution

time and date signal *n* signal *m* horodateur

time and date stamp *n* horodateur *m*

time and date stamping *n* horodatage *m*

time and motion studies *npl* organisation *f* scientifique du travail, OST *f*

time bill *n Fin* traite *f* à date fixe

time bomb *n* bombe *f* à retardement; *Fig* **you're sitting on a t.** vous êtes sur une poudrière

time card *n* fiche *f* de pointage

time clause *n Gram* proposition *f* temporelle

time clock *n* (*in factory etc*) pendule *f* de pointage, horloge *f* pointeuse *ou* contrôleuse, pointeuse *f*

time-consuming *adj* (*job etc*) qui prend beaucoup de temps

time difference *n* décalage *m* horaire

time exposure *n Phot* temps *m* de pose

time-honoured ['taɪmɒnəd] *adj* (*custom etc*) consacré (par l'usage), vénérable, séculaire

timekeeper ['taɪmkiːpər] *n* **(a)** (*official*) *Ind* contrôleur *m* (de présence); *Sp* chronométreur *m* **(b)** **to be a good t.** (*of person, watch*) être toujours à l'heure; **to be a poor t.** (*of person*) être toujours en retard; (*of watch*) (*be slow*) retarder; (*be fast*) avancer

timekeeping ['taɪmkiːpɪŋ] *n* **(a)** *Ind* (*regulation*) contrôle *m ou* pointage *m* de présence; *Sp etc* (*calculation of time*) chronométrage *m* **(b)** **good t.** (*punctuality*) (*of person*) ponctualité *f*; (*of watch*) exactitude *f*; **her t. was poor** elle ne respectait pas les horaires

time-lapse *adj* **t. photography** accéléré *m*

timeless ['taɪmlɪs] *adj* (*scene, appeal, novel etc*) intemporel; *Phil* atemporel; (*eternal*) éternel

timeliness ['taɪmlɪnɪs] *adj* (*of remark etc*) opportunité *f*, à-propos *m*

timely ['taɪmlɪ] *adj* opportun, à propos; **I made a t. escape** je me suis échappé juste à temps

time machine *n* machine *f* à remonter le temps

time-out *n esp Am* **(a)** *Sp* temps *m* mort; **to take t.** faire un temps mort **(b)** **to take t.** (*pause*) faire une pause; **I'm taking t. from my job** j'ai pris un congé; **I think you need t. from looking after the kids** je pense que tu as besoin de t'éloigner des gosses pendant quelque temps

timepiece ['taɪmpiːs] *n* (*clock*) pendule *f*; (*watch*) montre *f*

time pricing *n Mktg* fixation *f* des prix en fonction du moment

timer ['taɪmər] *n* **(a)** (*person*) chronométreur *m* **(b)** (*device*) *Aut etc* commutateur *m* d'allumage, temporisation *f*; (*on electric appliance etc*) minuterie *f*; *Culin* compte-minutes *m inv*; **egg t.** sablier *m*

time release *n* (*for accommodation*) location *f* après désistement

time(-)saving 1 *adj* (*device, method*) qui permet de gagner du temps **2** *n* gain *m ou* économie *f* de temps

timescale ['taɪmskeɪl] *n* période *f* (de temps); **the overall t.** la durée totale; **what sort of t. were you thinking of?** (*for completing the job, being absent from work etc*) de combien de temps allez-vous avoir besoin?; **the t. of a novel** la période sur laquelle s'échelonne un roman

time-sensitive *adj* qui requiert un minutage très précis

time-served ['taɪmsɜːvd] *adj* (*toolmaker etc*) qui a fait son apprentissage

timeserver ['taɪmsɜːvər] *n Pej* **(a)** (*opportunist*) opportuniste *mf* **(b)** (*lazy worker*) employé, -ée qui fait de la présence

timeserving ['taɪmsɜːvɪŋ] *n Pej* **(a)** (*opportunism*) opportunisme *m* **(b)** (*laziness*) paresse *f*

time-share 1 *adj* (*flat, house*) en multi-propriété **2** *n* appartement *m*/maison *f* en multi-propriété

time-sharing system *n* système *m* à temps partagé

time sheet *n* feuille *f* de présence; (*weekly*) semainier *m*

time slot *n* créneau *m ou* tranche *f* horaire

timespan ['taɪmspæn] *n* intervalle *m* de temps

time switch *n El* minuterie *f*

timetable[1] ['taɪmteɪb(ə)l] *n* **(a)** (*of departures etc*) horaire *m*; *Rail* horaire *m*, indicateur *m* **(b)** *Sch* emploi *m* du temps; *Ind* plan *m* de mise en exécution; (*for negotiations, meetings etc*) calendrier *m*; **to work to a t.** travailler selon un emploi du temps

timetable[2] **1** *vt* établir un emploi du temps/un calendrier/un horaire pour; **it's been timetabled for 9 o'clock** cela a été prévu pour 21 heures; **to t. sth to coincide with sth else** prévoir qch pour que cela coïncide avec qch d'autre **2** *vi* établir un emploi du temps/un calendrier/un horaire

time travel *n* voyage *m* dans le temps

time trial *n Sp* épreuve *f* contre la montre

time unit *n Tel* unité *f*

time value *n St Exch* valeur *f* temporelle

time warp *n* (*in science fiction*) faille *f* spatio-temporelle; **it's like going into a t.** c'est comme être transporté dans le passé/le futur

time-wasting *n* perte *f* de temps; *Sp* **the referee clamped down hard on t.** l'arbitre a sévèrement pénalisé ceux qui jouaient la montre

timework ['taɪmwɜːk] *n* travail *m* à l'heure; **to be on t.** travailler à *ou* être payé à l'heure

timeworn ['taɪmwɔːn] *adj* (*worn*) usé (par le temps)

timid ['tɪmɪd] *adj* timide, peureux

timidity [tɪ'mɪdɪtɪ] *n* timidité *f*

timidly ['tɪmɪdlɪ] *adv* timidement

timing ['taɪmɪŋ] *n* **(a)** *Sp etc* (*of movement*) rythme *m*; **good/bad t.** (*of remark*) à-propos *m*/manque *m* d'à-propos; (*of action*) opportunité *f*/inopportunité *f*; **good t., we've just started dinner!** tu arrives juste à temps, nous venons à peine de commencer à dîner!; **the actors' t. was awful** la synchronisation entre les acteurs était terrible; **a comedian with a perfect sense of t.** un comédien qui contrôle parfaitement le rythme de son débit; **he has no sense of t.** (*of what is suitable*) il n'a aucun sens de l'à-propos; **we must get the t. right between us** il faut que nous nous synchronisions; **how's that for t.!, we've finished one day before the deadline** quel minutage!, nous avons terminé un jour avant la date limite; **they're still discussing the t. of the election** ils sont encore en train de discuter de la date *ou F* du timing des élections; **the t. of the election to coincide with ...** la date des élections choisie pour coïncider avec ...; **the t. of the election is crucial** il ne faudra pas se tromper quand nous choisirons/ils choisiront/ *etc* la date des élections; **the t. of the announcement was criticized** on a critiqué le manque d'à-propos de cette annonce

(b) *Phot* (*of exposure*) calcul *m*

(c) (*measuring of time*), *Sp etc* chronométrage *m*; *Mil etc* (*of opération*) minutage *m*

(d) *Aut etc* distribution *f*; (*of ignition*) réglage *m*; (*of valve*) calage *m*; *Aut* **t. case** carter *m* de distribution; *Aut* **t. gear** pignon *m* de distribution

timorous ['tɪmərəs] *adj* timoré, timide

timorously ['tɪmərəslɪ] *adv* timidement

timpani ['tɪmpənɪ] *npl Mus* timbales *fpl*

timpanist ['tɪmpənɪst] *n Mus* timbalier *m*

tin[1] [tɪn] *n* **(a)** (*metal*) étain *m*; **t.-bearing** stannifère; **t. mine** mine *f* d'étain **(b) t. (plate)** fer-blanc *m*; *F* **he's just a little t. god** ce n'est qu'un petit tyran *m* d'opérette; *Mil etc F* **t. hat** casque *m*; **t. mug** timbale *f*; *Old-fashioned F* **t. pan alley** = le monde de la musique populaire; **t. roof** toit *m* en tôle; **t. soldier** soldat *m* de plomb; **t. whistle** flûte *f* en métal **(c)** (*mould*) (*for cake*) moule *m*; (*for tart*) tourtière *f* **(d)** *esp Br* **t. (can)** boîte *f* en fer-blanc; (*containing food*) boîte de conserves; **t. of sardines** boîte de sardines

tin[2] *vt* (-nn-) *esp Br* (*put in cans*) (*sardines etc*) mettre en boîtes

tincture[1] ['tɪŋ(k)tjər] *n* **(a)** (*of iodine etc*) teinture *f* **(b)** (*colour*) teinte *f*, nuance *f*

tincture[2] *vt* teindre, colorer

tinder ['tɪndər] *n* amadou *m*

tinderbox ['tɪndəbɒks] *n* briquet *m* (à silex); *Fig* **the country is a t.** le pays est une poudrière

tine [taɪn] *n* (*of fork*) dent *f*, fourchon *m*; (*of antler*) andouiller *m*

tinfoil ['tɪnfɔɪl] *n* papier *m* (d')étain, papier (d')aluminium, *F* papier alu

ting[1] [tɪŋ] *n* (*of bell*) tintement *m*

ting[2] **1** *vi* tinter **2** *vt* faire tinter

ting-a-ling *n, adv* drelin drelin *m*; (*electrical*) dring dring *m*

tinge[1] [tɪn(d)ʒ] *n* nuance *f*, soupçon *m*; **a t. of irony** une pointe *ou* une note d'ironie

tinge[2] *vt* teinter, colorer; **sky tinged with pink** ciel teinté de rose; **words tinged with malice** paroles teintées de malice; **memories tinged with sadness** souvenirs empreints de tristesse

tingle[1] ['tɪŋg(ə)l] *n* (*feeling*) (*of skin*) picotement *m*, fourmillement *m*; **a t. of fear ran up her spine** un frisson de peur lui remonta le long du dos; **a t. of excitement ran up her spine** un frisson d'enthousiasme la parcourut; **she felt a t. of anticipation** elle tressaillit de plaisir à cette idée

tingle[2] *vi* (*prickle*) picoter; **my hand tingles** j'ai des picotements dans la main; **to t. with impatience** vibrer d'impatience; **her legs tingled with cold** le froid lui donnait des picotements dans les jambes; **breeze that makes the blood t.** brise qui fouette le sang; **champagne that makes your mouth t.** champagne qui vous chatouille la bouche

tingling ['tɪŋglɪŋ] **1** *adj* (*prickling*) **t. sensation** picotement *m* **2** *n* = **tingle**[1]

tingly ['tɪŋglɪ] *adj* **t. sensation** picotement *m*; **my arm has gone all t.** j'ai des picotements dans tout le bras, tout mon bras me picote; **the sauna made me (feel) t. all over** le sauna m'a ravigoté

tininess ['taɪnɪnɪs] *n* petitesse *f* (extrême)

tinker[1] ['tɪŋkər] *n esp Pej* (*who repairs pots and pans*) rétameur *m* ambulant; (*gypsy*) bohémien *m*; *Br F* **you little t.!** espèce de petit coquin!; *F* **he doesn't give a t.'s cuss** il s'en moque *ou* s'en fiche comme de sa première chemise *ou* comme de l'an quarante

tinker[2] *vi* bricoler (**with** avec); **to t. with a text** trafiquer un texte; **to t. with the radio** passer du temps à rafistoler le poste de radio; **someone's been tinkering with the water heater** quelqu'un a trafiqué *ou* tripoté le chauffe-eau

tinkle[1] ['tɪŋk(ə)l] *n* (*of bells, glasses*) tintement *m*; *Br F* **I'll give you a t.** (*telephone*) je vous passerai un coup de fil

tinkle[2] **1** *vi* tinter; **to t. on the piano** pianoter **2** *vt* (*small bell*) faire tinter; *F usu Hum* **to t. the ivories** (*play the piano*) pianoter

tinkling ['tɪŋklɪŋ] *n* (*of bells, glasses*) tintement *m*

tinned [tɪnd] *adj Br* (*meat etc*) en boîte; **t. foods** conserves *fpl*; **to eat t. fruit** manger des fruits en conserve

tinnitus [tɪn'aɪtəs] *n Med* acouphène *m*

tinny ['tɪnɪ] *adj* (*sound*) grêle; (*loudspeaker, radio*) qui rend un son grêle; **to sound t.** rendre un son métallique *ou* grêle, faire un bruit de casserole; *Pej* **a t. car** une voiture pas robuste pour un sou; **food with a t. taste** aliment *m* qui a un goût d'étain *ou* de boîte de conserve

tin-opener *n esp Br* ouvre-boîte(s) *m*, *pl* ouvre-boîtes

tinpot ['tɪnpɒt] *adj F* de rien du tout; **a t. dictator** un dictateur en carton-pâte

tinsel ['tɪns(ə)l] **1** *n* (*Christmas decoration*) guirlandes *fpl* de Noël; *Fig Pej* clinquant *m*; **T. Town** = Hollywood *f* **2** *adj Fig Pej* clinquant

tinsmith ['tɪnsmɪθ] *n* (*maker of tin objects*) ferblantier *m*

tint[1] [tɪnt] *n* (*shade*) teinte *f*, nuance *f*; (*in hairdressing*) colorant *m*, couleur *f*; **red with a blue t.** teinte rouge avec une nuance de bleu; **warm tints** tons *mpl* chauds; **half t.** demi-teinte *f*, *pl* demi-teintes

tint[2] *vt* (*colour*) teinter, colorer; *Opt* **tinted glasses** verres *mpl* teintés; **to have one's hair tinted** se faire un rinçage; **tinted**

windows vitres *fpl* teintées; *Aut* **tinted shadeband** pignon *m* de distribution

tintack ['tɪntæk] *n* broquette *f*, clou *m* de tapisserie

tinting ['tɪntɪŋ] *n* coloration *f*

tintinnabulation [tɪntɪnæbjʊ'leɪʃən] *n* tintinnabulement *m*

tiny ['taɪnɪ] *adj* minuscule; **a t. bit** un tout petit peu; **a t. little house** une toute petite maison; **in a t. voice** d'une toute petite voix

tip¹ [tɪp] *n* (*end*) bout *m*, extrémité *f*; (*pointed*) pointe *f*; (*of walking stick etc*) bout ferré, embout *m*; *Billiards* (*of cue*) procédé *m*; (*of cigarette*) bout *m* (filtre); **steel t.** (*of shoe*) fer *m*; **on the tips of one's toes** sur la pointe des pieds; **to be a politician/musician to the tips of one's fingers** être politicien/musicien jusqu'au bout des doigts; **to have sth on the t. of one's tongue** avoir qch sur le bout de la langue; **from t. to toe** de la tête aux pieds; *Fig* **that's just the t. of the iceberg** (et) ce n'est que la partie émergée de l'iceberg; *Culin* **asparagus tips** pointes *fpl* d'asperge

tip² *vt* (-pp-) (*put tip on*) (*walking stick etc*) embouter; (*shoe*) mettre un bout à; **arrow tipped with poison** flèche à bout empoisonné

tip³ *n* (a) (*payment*) pourboire *m*; **to give sb a t.** donner un pourboire à qn (b) *Horseracing, St Exch etc* (*advice*) tuyau *m*; **to give sb a t.** renseigner *ou F* tuyauter qn; **to take a t. from sb** suivre le conseil de qn; **if you take my t. ...** si vous m'en croyez ...; **a book full of useful tips on how to save energy** un livre plein de tuyaux utiles *ou* plein de bons trucs pour économiser l'énergie

tip⁴ (-pp-) **1** *vt* (a) (*give money to*) donner un pourboire à (b) *Horseracing, St Exch etc* donner comme favori; **to t. a certain horse to win** pronostiquer qu'un certain cheval sera le gagnant; **she's widely tipped for the job** on estime qu'elle a toutes ses chances pour le poste, on la donne comme favorite pour le poste; **he is strongly tipped to become Home Secretary** il est pressenti pour le poste de ministre de l'Intérieur **2** *vi* (*of customer*) **she tips well** elle donne toujours de bons pourboires

tip⁵ *n* (a) (*for rubbish*) dépotoir *m*; *F* **this room's a t.!** cette pièce est un vrai dépotoir! (b) *Constr etc* chantier *m* de versage

tip⁶ *vt* (a) (*pour*) (*stones, earth, rubbish*) déverser; **to t. sth into sth** verser qch dans qch; **to t. sth on the ground** déverser qch par terre; **no tipping** (*on sign*) dépôt d'ordures interdit, décharge interdite (b) (*cause to lean*) faire pencher, faire incliner; **to t. one's hat over one's eyes** rabattre son chapeau sur ses yeux; **to t. one's hat to sb** tirer son chapeau à qn

▶ **tip off** *vtsep* (*police, journalist*) informer, *F* tuyauter; **to be tipped off about sth** avoir des renseignements sur qch, *F* être tuyauté sur qch

▶ **tip out** *vtsep* déverser, décharger; **to t. sth out on the ground** déverser qch par terre

▶ **tip over 1** *vtsep* (*overturn*) renverser; (*boat*) chavirer **2** *vi* (*overturn*) se renverser, basculer; (*of boat etc*) chavirer

▶ **tip up 1** *vtsep* (*tilt upwards*) (*seat*) soulever; (*cart*) faire basculer **2** *vi* (*tilt upwards*) (*of seat etc*) se soulever, basculer

tip-off *n* renseignement *m*, *F* tuyau *m*; (*warning*) avertissement *m*; **to give sb a t.** renseigner *ou F* tuyauter qn; **the police received a t.** la police a été informée

tipped [tɪpt] *adj* **t. cigarettes** cigarettes *fpl* à bout filtre; **t. or plain?** filtre ou sans filtre?

-tipped [tɪpt] *suff* **gold/silver-t.** à bout doré/d'argent

tipper ['tɪpər] *n* (a) **t. (truck** *or Br* **lorry)** camion *m* à benne (b) **to be a generous t.** (*in restaurant etc*) donner des pourboires généreux

tippet ['tɪpɪt] *n* (*fur*) pèlerine *f*, collet *m*

Tippex® ['tɪpeks] *n* correcteur *m* liquide, *F* blanco *m*, tippex® *m*

▶ **Tippex**® **out** *vtsep* effacer avec un correcteur liquide

tipping ['tɪpɪŋ] **1** *adj* (*wagon etc*) basculant, à bascule **2** *n* (*giving money*) distribution *f* de pourboires; (*system*) (système *m* des) pourboires *mpl*; **is t. normal?** est-ce qu'il est normal de donner des pourboires?

tipple¹ ['tɪp(ə)l] *n F* (*drink*) **time for a quick t.?** on a le temps de prendre un petit verre?; **what's your t.?** qu'est-ce que vous prenez habituellement?; **gin was my t.** je buvais du gin à l'époque

tipple² *vi F* picoler

tipple³ *n Am Min* (*apparatus*) basculeur *m* de wagons; (*place*) décharge *f*

tippler ['tɪplər] *n F* picoleur, -euse

tippy-toe ['tɪpɪtəʊ] *n, adv, vi Am* = **tiptoe**

tipsily ['tɪpsɪlɪ] *adv* (*to say*) d'une voix qui accuse l'ivresse; (*to walk*) en titubant

tipsiness ['tɪpsɪnɪs] *n* (légère) ivresse *f*

tipstaff, *pl* **-staffs** ['tɪpstɑːf, -stɑːfs] *n Br Jur* huissier *m*

tipster ['tɪpstər] *n Horseracing etc* pronostiqueur *m*

tipsy ['tɪpsɪ] *adj* gris, *F* pompette; **slightly t.** un peu éméché; **to get t.** se griser, s'enivrer

tiptoe¹ ['tɪptəʊ] **1** *n* **on t.** sur la pointe des pieds **2** *adv* sur la pointe des pieds

tiptoe² *vi* marcher sur la pointe des pieds; **to t. in/out** entrer/sortir sur la pointe des pieds

tiptop ['tɪptɒp] *adj* excellent; (*hotel etc*) de premier ordre; **I feel t.** je me sens en pleine forme

tip-up *adj* (*barrow etc*) à bascule; **t. seat** strapontin *m*

TIR [tiːaɪ'ɑːr] (*abbr* **transport international de marchandises per route**) TIR *m*

tirade [taɪ'reɪd] *n* diatribe *f* (**against** contre); **t. of invective** bordée *f* d'injures

tire¹ ['taɪər] **1** *vt* fatiguer; (*to weary*) lasser; **to t. oneself doing sth** se fatiguer à faire qch **2** *vi* se fatiguer; (*to weary*) se lasser (**of sb/sth** de qn/qch); **he never tires of telling me** il ne se lasse pas de me le dire; **they tired of his complaining** *or* **complaints** ils se sont fatigués *ou* lassés de ses plaintes

▶ **tire out** *vtsep* (*exhaust*) épuiser *ou* briser de fatigue; **to t. oneself out** se fatiguer; **she was tired out** elle n'en pouvait plus (de fatigue)

tire² *n US* = **tyre**

tired ['taɪəd] *adj* fatigué; (*weary*) las, *f* lasse; **to get t.** se fatiguer; *Hum* **it makes me t. just watching them/thinking about it** ça me fatigue rien que de les voir/d'y penser; *F Hum* **t. and emotional** (*drunk*) dans les vignes du Seigneur; **to be t. of sth** être las de qch, en avoir assez de qch; **to grow** *or* **get t. of sb/sth** se lasser *ou* se fatiguer de qn/qch; **my eyes get t. very easily** mes yeux se fatiguent très facilement; **to grow** *or* **get t. of doing sth** se lasser de faire qch; *F* **I'm t. of you** j'en ai assez de vous; **t. of arguing, he consented** de guerre lasse, il a donné son consentement; *F* **t. old carpet** vieux tapis *m* usé; **t. phrase** expression *f* usée; **in a t. voice** d'une voix lasse *ou* fatiguée

tiredly ['taɪədlɪ] *adv* avec lassitude

tiredness ['taɪədnɪs] *n* fatigue *f*; *Med* asthénie *f*

tireless ['taɪəlɪs] *adj* (*worker, campaigner etc*) infatigable; (*efforts*) inlassable

tirelessly ['taɪəlɪslɪ] *adv* infatigablement, inlassablement

tiresome ['taɪəsəm] *adj* (*boring*) assommant, ennuyeux; (*irritating, annoying*) fatigant, exaspérant; **how t.!** que c'est ennuyeux *ou* assommant!

tiring ['taɪərɪŋ] *adj* (*work, speech, person etc*) fatigant

tiro, *pl* **-o(e)s** ['taɪrəʊ, -əʊz] *n* = **tyro**

'tis [tɪz] = **it is**, *see* **be**

tissue ['tɪsjuː] *n* (*cloth*), *Biol* tissu *m*; (*paper handkerchief*) mouchoir *m* en papier; **t. (paper)** papier *m* de soie; *Fig* **t. of lies** tissu de mensonges

tiswas ['tɪzwɒz] *n F* = **tizzy**

tit¹ [tɪt] *n* (*bird*) mésange *f*; **blue t.** mésange bleue; **coal t.** mésange noire; **great t.** (mésange) charbonnière *f*

tit² *n* **t. for tat** un prêté pour un rendu; **to give sb t. for tat** rendre la pareille à qn; (*verbally*) répondre du tac au tac

tit³ *n Sl* (a) (*breast*) nichon *m*, téton *m*, néné *m*; **to get on sb's tits** (*annoy, irritate*) porter sur le système à qn (b) (*idiot*) imbécile *mf*; **I felt a right t.** je me suis senti vraiment bête, j'ai eu l'impression d'être un parfait imbécile

Titan ['taɪt(ə)n] *n Myth* Titan *m*; *Fig* **t.** titan *m*

titanic [taɪ'tænɪk] *adj* titanesque

titanium [taɪ'teɪnɪəm] *n Ch* titane *m*

titbit ['tɪtbɪt] *n* (*food*) morceau *m* de choix; (*sweet*) friandise *f*; (*of gossip*) potin *m*

titch, titchy [tɪtʃ, 'tɪtʃɪ] *Br F* = **tich, tichy**

titfer ['tɪtfər] *n Old-fashioned Br Sl* (*hat*) galurin *m*, bitos *m*

tit-for-tat *adj* (*killing, expulsions etc*) fait en représailles *ou* en riposte

tithe [taɪð] *n* dîme *f*; **t. barn** grange *f* de la dîme *ou* aux dîmes

Titian ['tɪʃɪən] **1** *n* (*the painter*) le Titien **2** *adj* (*hair*) acajou *inv*

titillate ['tɪtɪleɪt] **1** *vt* (*readers, viewers*) émoustiller; (*senses*) émoustiller, titiller; (*palate*) chatouiller **2** *vi* (*of film, book etc*) titiller les sens

titillating ['tɪtɪleɪtɪŋ] *adj* titillant, émoustillant

titillation [tɪtɪ'leɪʃən] *n* titillation *f*

titivate ['tɪtɪveɪt] *vt Old-fashioned* (*sb*) faire beau, pomponner; (*sth*) pomponner, bichonner; **to t. oneself** se faire beau, se pomponner

title¹ ['taɪtl] *n* (a) (*of book, chapter*) titre *m*; (*of article, act*) titre, intitulé *m*; **the story that gives the collection its t.** l'histoire qui donne son titre à la collection; **the t. is taken from ...** le titre est tiré de ...; **to publish fifty titles a year** publier cinquante titres par an

(b) (*of person*) titre *m*; **to give sb a t.** donner un titre à qn, titrer qn; **to have a t.** (*of nobility*) avoir un titre de noblesse, être titré

(c) *Sp* titre *m*; **to hold the t.** détenir le titre (de champion); *Boxing* **t./non t. fight** combat *m* comptant/ne comptant pas pour le titre

(d) *Jur* **t. to property** titre *m* de propriété; **t. (deed)** titre (constitutif) de propriété, acte *m* de propriété; **t. holder** propriétaire *mf*

(e) *Cin, TV* **titles** (*credits*) générique *m*

title² *vt* (*book etc*) intituler

title bar *n Comptr* barre *f* de titre

titled ['taɪtld] *adj* (*person*) titré; **to be t.** avoir un titre (de noblesse)

titleholder ['taɪtlhəʊldər] *n Sp* tenant, -ante du titre

title music *n* musique *f* de générique

title page *n Typ* (page *f* de) titre *m*; (*with embellishments*) frontispice *m*

title piece *n* (*of anthology*) conte *m*/morceau *m* qui donne son titre au recueil

title rôle *n Th* rôle *m* qui donne son titre à la pièce

title track *n Mus* (*of album*) morceau *m* qui donne son titre à l'album

titmouse ['tɪtmaʊs] *n* (*bird*) mésange *f*

titrate ['taɪtreɪt] *vt Ch, Ind* (*solution*) titrer

titter¹ ['tɪtər] *n* (*suppressed laughter*) rire *m* étouffé; (*nervous laughter*) petit rire nerveux *ou* bête

titter² *vi* (*in suppressed way*) avoir un petit rire étouffé; (*laugh nervously*) rire nerveusement *ou* bêtement

tittering ['tɪtərɪŋ] *n* petits rires *mpl*

tittie ['tɪtɪ] *n Sl* = **titty**

tittle ['tɪt(ə)l] *n* = **jot¹**

tittle-tattle¹ *n* (*gossip*) potins *mpl*, *F* cancans *mpl*

tittle-tattle² *vi* (*gossip*) *F* cancaner

titty ['tɪtɪ] *n Sl* (*breast*) nichon *m*; *Fig* **that's tough t., that's his tough t.** (c'est) tant pis pour lui

titular ['tɪtjʊlər] *adj* titulaire; (*function, office etc*) nominal; **t. possessions** terres *fpl* attachées à un titre

tizzy ['tɪzɪ] *n F* **to be in a t.** ne (pas) savoir où donner de la tête; **to get into a t.** se mettre dans tous ses états

T-junction *n* bifurcation *f* en T

TNT [tiːen'tiː] *n* (*abbr* **trinitrotoluene**) TNT *m*

to [tuː, *unstressed* tə] **1** *prep* **(a)** à; **to go to church/to school** aller à l'église/à l'école; **what school do you go to?** à quelle école allez-vous?, *F* tu vas où à l'école?, tu es dans quelle école?; **I'm off to bed** je vais au lit *ou* me coucher; **I'm off to Paris** je pars pour Paris; **he went to France/to Japan** il est allé en France/au Japon; **she returned home to her family** elle est rentrée auprès de sa famille; **I am going to the grocer's** je vais chez l'épicier; **from town to town** de ville en ville; **flights to the Continent** vols à destination de l'Europe; **the road to London** la route de Londres; **a journey to Paris** un voyage à Paris; **the shortest way to the station** le plus court chemin pour aller à la gare

(b) (*towards*) vers, à; **to the east** vers l'est; **to the trains** (*on sign*) accès aux quais; **to the right** à droite; **to the left** à gauche; **the rooms to the back** les chambres de derrière

(c) (*next to*) **elbow to elbow** coude à coude; **I told him so to his face** je le lui ai dit en face; **to clasp sb to one's heart** serrer qn sur son cœur; **to fall to the ground** tomber à *ou* par terre

(d) (*of time*) **from morning to night** du matin au soir; **from day to day** de jour en jour; **the day to day running of the school** l'administration de tous les jours de l'école; **ten minutes to six** six heures moins dix; **it's ten to** il est moins dix

(e) (*until*) jusqu'à; **to this day** jusqu'à ce jour; **to count up to ten** compter jusqu'à dix; **moved to tears** ému (jusqu')aux larmes; **fight to the death** bataille *ou* combat à mort; **to a high degree** à un haut degré; **generous to a fault** généreux à l'excès; **accurate to a millimetre** exact au millimètre près; **a year to the day** un an jour pour jour; **to cut sth down to a minimum** réduire qch au minimum

(f) (*purpose*) **to this end** à cet effet, dans ce but

(g) (*result*) **to my despair** à mon grand désespoir; **to everyone's surprise** à la surprise de tous; **to put to flight** mettre en fuite; **to pull to pieces** mettre en pièces

(h) what tune is it sung to? sur quel air cela se chante-t-il?

(i) (*of*) **heir to sb/to an estate** héritier de qn/d'une propriété; **ambassador to the King of Sweden** ambassadeur auprès du roi de Suède; **apprentice to a joiner** apprenti chez un menuisier; **the key to the door** la clef de la porte; **the answer to a question** la réponse à une question

(j) (*in comparisons*) **superior to** supérieur à; **compared to this** comparé à *ou* en comparaison de celui-ci; **that's nothing to what I have seen** cela n'est rien à côté de ce que j'ai vu

(k) (*expressing a proportion*) **three is to six as six is to twelve** trois est à six ce que six est à douze; **six votes to four** six voix contre quatre; **three goals to nil** trois buts à zéro; **to bet ten to one** parier dix contre un

(l) to all appearances selon les apparences; **not to my taste** pas à mon goût; **to the best of my recollection** (pour) autant que je m'en souvienne

(m) to drink to sb boire à la santé de qn

(n) (*concerning*) **what did she say to my suggestion?** qu'est-ce qu'elle a dit de ma proposition?; **is that all there is to it?** c'est tout?; **there's nothing to it** (*it's easy*) c'est simple comme bonjour; **there's nothing** *or* **there isn't a lot to these cameras** ils ne sont pas bien compliqués, ces appareils-photos

(o) (*used to form the dative*) à; **to give sth to sb** donner qch à qn; **he gave it to her** il le lui a donné; **who did you give it to?** à qui l'avez-vous donné?; **to speak to sb** parler à qn; *Fml* **to whom?** à qui?; **what's it to you?** qu'est-ce que ça peut te faire?; **to keep sth to oneself** garder qch pour soi; **he has been a father to me** il a été un père pour moi; **known to the ancients** connu des anciens

2 [①**A40-41**,b] (*with the infinitive*) **(a)** (*purpose, result*) pour; **he came to help me** il est venu (pour) m'aider; **we must eat (in order) to live** il faut manger pour vivre; **so to speak** pour ainsi dire; **born to rule** né pour régner; **happy to do it** heureux de le faire; **ready to listen** prêt à écouter; **old enough to go to school** en âge d'aller à l'école; **built to house 10 people** construit pour loger 10 personnes; **too hot to drink** trop chaud pour qu'on puisse le boire; **to hear her speak, you'd think she owned the place!** à l'entendre, on dirait que c'est elle le propriétaire des lieux!; **he left the house never to return to it again** il quitta la maison pour ne plus y revenir

(b) [①**A53**,c,iii] **I have a letter to write** j'ai une lettre à écrire; **I have a lot to do** j'ai beaucoup à faire; **there was not a sound to be heard** on n'entendait pas le moindre bruit; **he isn't one to forget his friends** il n'est pas homme à oublier ses amis; **there's a tendency to forget that** on a tendance à l'oublier; **I have no desire to do that** je n'ai aucun désir de le faire

(c) to lie is shameful, it is shameful to lie il est honteux de mentir; **to be or not to be** être ou ne pas être; **it is better to do nothing** il vaut mieux ne rien faire; **he learned to do it** il a appris à le faire; **I refuse to do it** je refuse de le faire

(d) (*inf in finite clause*) **I want him to know** je veux qu'il sache; **it seemed to grow** il/elle semblait grandir

(e) (*in headline*) **a hundred employees to go** cent employés vont être mis au chômage; **Clinton to meet Major** entretiens entre Mr Clinton et Mr Major

(f) (*with ellipsis of verb*) **you ought to** vous devriez le faire; **I want to** j'ai envie de le faire; (*I would like to*) je voudrais bien; **take it, it would be absurd not to** prenez-le, ce serait absurde de ne pas le faire *ou* de manquer l'occasion; **we shall have to** il le faudra bien, nous serons bien obligés

3 *adv* (*stressed*) **(a) to pull the door to** fermer la porte; **to turn to** *or* **set to with a will** se mettre résolument à l'ouvrage; **to come to** (*to one's senses*) reprendre connaissance

(b) to go to and fro aller et venir; (*of shuttle bus etc*) faire la navette

toad [təʊd] *n* **(a)** (*animal*) crapaud *m*; *F Pej, Hum* (*person*) crapule *f*; **you lying t.!** espèce de salaud de menteur! **(b)** *Br Culin* **t. in the hole** = saucisses *fpl* cuites au four dans de la pâte à crêpes

toadstool ['təʊdstuːl] *n* champignon *m* vénéneux

toady¹ ['təʊdɪ] *n* lèche-bottes *mf inv*

toady² *vi* **to t. to sb** lécher les bottes à qn

to-and-fro *adj* **t. movement** mouvement *m* de va-et-vient

toast¹ [təʊst] *n* **(a)** (*toasted bread*) pain grillé *m*, toast *m*; **piece** *or* **slice** *or* **round of t.** toast, tartine *f* grillée, rôtie *f*; **as warm as t.** bien chaud **(b)** (*tribute*) toast *m*; **to give** *or* **propose a t.** porter un toast; **to drink a t. to sb** boire à la santé de qn; **the t. was the future** on a porté un toast à l'avenir; **to be the t. of the town** être la célébrité de la ville

toast² **1** *vt* **(a)** (*bread*) griller, faire griller; *F* **to t. one's feet (in front of the fire)** se rôtir les pieds (devant le feu); **toasted cheese** toast *m* au fromage; **toasted sandwich** sandwich *m* grillé **(b) to t. sb** porter un toast à (la santé de) qn, boire à la santé de qn **2** *vi* (*of bread*) griller; **it toasts well** ça fait du bon pain grillé

toaster ['təʊstər] *n* grille-pain *m inv*; **sandwich t.** grill *m* (électrique)

toastie, toasty ['təʊstɪ] *n F* sandwich *m* grillé

toasting fork [ˈtəʊstɪŋ] *n* fourchette *f* à rôties
toast master *n* = maître *m* de cérémonies, animateur *m* (de réception)
toast rack *n* porte-toasts *m inv*, porte-rôties *m inv*
tobacco, *pl* **-os** [təˈbækəʊ, -əʊz] *n* **(a)** tabac *m*; **chewing t.** tabac à chiquer *ou* mâcher; **t.-coloured** tabac *inv*; **t. smoke** fumée *f* de tabac; **t. pouch** blague *f* à tabac; **t. tin** boîte *f* à tabac, tabatière *f* **(b) t. (plant)** tabac *m*
tobacconist [təˈbækənɪst] *n Br* (*person*) buraliste *mf*; **t.'s (shop)** (bureau *m ou* débit *m* de) tabac *m*
toboggan¹ [təˈbɒgən] *n* (*for children*), *Sp* luge *f*; **t. run** piste *f* de luge
toboggan² *vi* (*of child*), *Sp* faire de la luge; **to t. down a slope** descendre une pente en luge
tobogganing [təˈbɒgənɪŋ] *n* luge *f*; **to go t.** faire de la luge
toby jug [ˈtəʊbɪ] = pot *m* à bière décoratif (*en forme de gros bonhomme à tricorne*)
tocsin [ˈtɒksɪn] *n* tocsin *m*
tod [tɒd] *n Br Sl* **on my/his/***etc* **t.** tout seul
today [təˈdeɪ] **1** *adv* aujourd'hui; **it's a week ago t.** ça fait une semaine aujourd'hui; **t. week** aujourd'hui en huit; *F* **he's the kind who'll be here t. and gone tomorrow** (*in job, relationship etc*) c'est le genre de type qui ne peut pas se fixer; **a here t. and gone tomorrow fashion** une mode qui ne durera pas

2 *n* aujourd'hui *m*; **t.'s the day ...!** c'est aujourd'hui que ...!; **t.'s paper** le journal d'aujourd'hui *ou* du jour; **t.'s date is ...** aujourd'hui, nous sommes le ...; **t.'s date/price** la date/le prix du jour; **t.'s special** plat *m* du jour; **the young people of t.** les jeunes d'aujourd'hui
toddle¹ [ˈtɒd(ə)l] *n F* (*short walk*) petite promenade *f*, balade *f*; **I'm going for a t.** je vais faire un tour, je vais me balader
toddle² *vi* **(a)** (*of young child*) marcher à petits pas chancelants; **she's just started toddling** elle commence à peine à marcher **(b)** *F* (*of adult*) trottiner; **I'd better be toddling (along)** (*leaving*) il faut que j'y aille; **I'm just going to t. into town** je vais juste faire un tour en ville
▶ **toddle off** *vi F* (*leave*) partir, lever le camp
toddler [ˈtɒdlər] *n* enfant *mf* qui commence à marcher
toddy [ˈtɒdɪ] *n* grog *m*
to-do *n F* remue-ménage *m inv*; **what a t.!** quelle histoire!; **there was a great t. about it** l'affaire a fait grand bruit
toe¹ [təʊ] *n* **(a)** *Anat* orteil *m*, doigt *m* de pied; **big/little t.** gros/petit orteil; **on the tips of one's toes** sur la pointe des pieds; **to tread** *or* **stand on sb's toes** marcher sur les pieds de qn; *Fig* **I hope I'm not treading on any toes** j'espère que je n'empiète sur les plates-bandes de personne; *Fig* **to be on one's toes** être en alerte, être vigilant; *Fig* **to keep people on their toes** faire en sorte que les gens restent vigilants **(b)** (*of shoe etc*) bout *m*, pointe *f*
toe² *vt* **(a)** *Fb* (*ball*) frapper de la pointe du pied **(b)** *Sp* **to t. the line** *or* **the mark** s'aligner; *Fig* **to t. the line** obéir, s'exécuter; *Fig* **to t. the party line** s'aligner sur la position officielle du parti
toecap [ˈtəʊkæp] *n* bout *m* rapporté
-toed [-təʊd] *suff* **two/three/***etc***-t.** à deux/trois/*etc* orteils; **square/pointed/***etc***-t.** (*shoes*) à bouts carrés/pointus/*etc*
toehold [ˈtəʊhəʊld] *n* (*in climbing*) prise *f* de pied; *Fig* **to gain a t. in the market** mettre un pied sur le marché; **to maintain a t. on reality** garder un lien, si ténu soit-il, avec la réalité
toe-in *n Aut* pincement *m* des roues avant
toenail [ˈtəʊneɪl] *n* ongle *m* d'orteil
toe-out *n Aut* ouverture *f*, pincement *m* négatif
toepiece [ˈtəʊpiːs] *n* (*on ski*) butée *f*
toerag [ˈtəʊræg] *n Br Sl* merdeux, -euse
toff [tɒf] *n Old-fashioned Br F* aristo *mf*; **the toffs** le gratin
toffee [ˈtɒfɪ] *n* caramel *m* au beurre; *F* **he can't sing for t.** il ne sait pas chanter pour deux sous; **t. apple** pomme *f* d'amour
toffee-nosed [ˈtɒfɪnəʊzd] *adj esp Br F* snob, snobinard
tofu [ˈtɒfuː] *n* tofu *m*
▶ **tog up, tog out** [tɒg] *vtsep F* (*dress smartly*) fringuer; **to t. oneself up** bien se fringuer, se mettre sur son trente et un; **to be (all) togged up** (*dressed up*) être sur son trente et un; (*for tennis, football etc*) être en tenue
toga [ˈtəʊgə] *n* (*garment*) toge *f*
together [təˈgeðər] **1** *adv* ensemble; **to go** *or* **belong t.** aller ensemble; **we stand or fall t.** nous sommes tous solidaires; **t. with** (*as well as*) ainsi que; (*at the same time as*) en même temps que; **t. with the French, the Swedes objected** les Suédois émirent une objection, de même que les Français; **to gather** *or* **collect** *or* **bring t.** réunir, rassembler; **to gather t.** (*come together*) se réunir, se rassembler; **to add t.** additionner; **to act t.** agir de concert; **to be t. again** (*of couple, partners*) être de nouveau ensemble; **to get t. again** (*of couple, partners*) se remettre ensemble; **the family will all be t. at Christmas** la famille sera réunie à Noël; **all t.** (*everybody gathered*) tous ensemble; (*at the same time*) tous à la fois; **all t. now!** (*sing*) tous en chœur maintenant!; **all t. now! — push!** tous ensemble maintenant! — poussez!; **all t. it cost us £480** l'ensemble nous a coûté 480 livres; **for hours t.** des heures durant, pendant des heures et des heures; *F* **she's really got it t.** (*in life*) elle sait ce qu'elle fait; (*in job etc*) elle domine son sujet; **I never thought he would get it t.** je n'aurais jamais pensé qu'il y arriverait

2 *adj esp Am F* (*person*) équilibré; **the band weren't very t.** (*didn't play in unison*) le groupe ne jouait pas vraiment ensemble
togetherness [təˈgeðənɪs] *n* (*unity*) unité *f*, harmonie *f*; **the earlier feeling of t. had gone out of their relationship** le sentiment de former un couple uni qu'ils avaient éprouvé auparavant avait disparu; **the feeling of t. generated by a family Christmas** ce sentiment de chaleureuse communion que l'on ressent lors des Noëls passés en famille; **we all had a feeling of t. at the party conference** nous avons tous éprouvé un sentiment de cohésion lors du congrès du parti
toggle¹ [ˈtɒg(ə)l] *n* **(a)** (*on duffel coat etc*) olive *f*, barrette *f* **(b)** *El* **t. switch** interrupteur *m* à bascule, basculeur *m*; *Comptr* **t. key** touche *f* à deux positions *ou* à bascule
toggle² *vi Comptr* alterner (**between** entre); **to t. sth on/off** sélectionner/désélectionner qch
Togo [ˈtəʊgəʊ] *n* Togo *m*
Togolese [təʊgəˈliːz] **1** *adj* togolais **2** *n* Togolais, -aise
togs [tɒgz] *npl F* (*clothes*) fringues *fpl*, frusques *fpl*
toil¹ [tɔɪl] *n Fml, Lit* dur labeur *m*, peine *f*; **a life of t. and trouble** une vie de douleur et de peine; *Hum* **the t. and tribulation of bringing up children** les affres dans lesquelles nous jette l'éducation des enfants
toil² **1** *vi* (*work hard*) travailler dur (**at** à), peiner (**at** sur); **to be toiling** (*having difficulty in race, finishing meal etc*) peiner; **I'm toiling to finish this drink as it is** j'ai déjà assez de mal à finir ce verre; **to t. up a hill** gravir péniblement une colline; **to t. on** (*continue work*) continuer péniblement son travail; (*continue journey*) continuer péniblement sa route

2 *vt* **he toiled his way through a mass of papers** il a dû laborieusement lire tout un tas de documents
toiler [ˈtɔɪlər] *n* travailleur, -euse
toilet [ˈtɔɪlɪt] *n* **(a)** (*lavatory*) (*device*) cabinets *mpl*; (*room*) cabinet de toilette; **toilets** toilettes *fpl*; **to go to the t.** aller aux cabinets; **he's still in** *or* **on the t.** il est encore aux toilettes; **to throw sth down the t.** jeter qch dans les toilettes **(b)** *Old-fashioned* (*washing and dressing*) toilette *f*; **to make** *or* **perform one's t.** faire sa toilette; (*still used in*) **t. case** nécessaire *m ou* trousse *f* de toilette; **t. table** (table *f* de) toilette, coiffeuse *f*
toilet block *n* bloc *m* sanitaire
toilet paper *n* papier *m* hygiénique
toiletries [ˈtɔɪlɪtrɪz] *npl* articles *mpl* de toilette
toilet roll *n* rouleau *m* de papier hygiénique
toilet seat *n* siège *m* des toilettes
toilet soap *n* savon *m* de toilette
toilet tissue *n* papier *m* hygiénique
toilet training *n* apprentissage *m* de la propreté
toilet water *n* eau *f* de toilette
toils [tɔɪlz] *npl Lit, Fig* (*net*) filets *mpl*
toilsome [ˈtɔɪlsəm] *adj Lit* pénible
toing and froing [tuːɪŋənˈfrəʊɪŋ] *n* va-et-vient *m*
Tokay [təˈkaɪ] *n* (*wine*) tokai *m*, tokaï *m*, tokay *m*
token [ˈtəʊk(ə)n] *n* **(a)** (*indication*) (*of identity, respect etc*) marque *f*, témoignage *m*; **in t.** *or* **as a t. of sincerity** en signe *ou* en témoignage de bonne foi; **by the same t.** (*therefore*) donc; (*equally*) pareillement; **a t. black person/t. woman** un noir/une femme qui est là pour la forme; *Mil etc* **a t. force** une force symbolique; **t. payment/strike** paiement *m*/grève *f* symbolique *ou* d'avertissement

(b) (*disc etc*) (*for vending machine etc*) jeton *m*; **gift t.** bon *m* d'achat; **book t.** chèque-livre *m*, *pl* chèques-livres; **record t.** chèque-disque *m*, *pl* chèques-disques

(c) *Old-fashioned* (*symbol*) signe *m*; **love t.** gage *m* d'amour
tokenism [ˈtəʊkənɪz(ə)m] *n* = pratique *f* qui consiste à nommer une ou deux personnes des minorités (femme, noir etc) pour donner l'impression d'une libéralisation; **the appointment of a woman to the board was nothing but t.** ils ont nommé une femme au conseil d'administration uniquement pour la forme
token ring network *n Comptr* réseau *m* en anneau à jeton
Tokyo [ˈtəʊkɪəʊ] *n* Tokyo
told *see* **tell**
Toledo [tɒˈleɪdəʊ] *n* Tolède
tolerable [ˈtɒlərəb(ə)l] *adj* **(a)** (*pain etc*) tolérable, supportable

(b) *(acceptable)* passable; *(quite good)* assez bon; **we're in t. health** nous nous portons assez bien
tolerably ['tɒlərəblɪ] *adv* passablement; **I'm t. well** je me porte assez bien; **it was t. well done** c'était assez bien fait
tolerance ['tɒlərəns] *n* **(a)** *(religious etc)* tolérance *f*; **to show great t.** faire preuve de beaucoup de tolérance *ou* d'une grande indulgence **(b)** *(for drug, alcohol)* tolérance *f* **(of, for** à); **increasing t.** *(to drug)* accoutumance *f* **(c)** *MecE etc* tolérance *f*, écart *m* admissible
tolerant ['tɒlərənt] *adj* **(a)** tolérant; *(parent etc)* tolérant, indulgent **(b)** *Med* **t. of a drug** *(patient)* qui tolère une drogue
tolerantly ['tɒlərəntlɪ] *adv* avec tolérance; **to be t. disposed toward sb/sth** se montrer tolérant envers qn/qch
tolerate ['tɒləreɪt] *vt* **(a)** *(pain, contradiction etc)* tolérer, supporter; *(person, behaviour)* supporter; **I will not t. this behaviour** je ne supporterai pas une telle conduite **(b)** *Med (drug)* tolérer
toleration [tɒlə'reɪʃən] *n* tolérance *f*
toll¹ [təʊl] *n* **(a)** *(charge)* péage *m*, droit *m* de passage; *Fig* **to take its t.** *(of disease etc)* faire beaucoup de victimes; *(have severe effect)* laisser des traces **(of sb** sur qn); **accident that takes a heavy t. of human life** accident qui cause beaucoup de morts; **the years had taken their t.** *or* **a heavy t. on her health** sa santé s'était affaiblie avec le temps **(b)** *Am* **to call t. free** appeler gratuitement
toll² *n* *(of bell)* tintement *m*, son *m* (de cloche); *(for death)* glas *m*
toll³ **1** *vt* *(bell)* sonner; **the church clock tolled midday** l'horloge de l'église a sonné midi; **to t. sb's death** sonner le glas pour la mort de qn **2** *vi* *(of bell)* tinter, sonner; *(for death)* sonner le glas; **to t. for the dead** sonner pour les morts
toll bar *n* barrière *f* (de péage)
toll booth *n* poste *f* de péage
toll bridge *n* pont *m* à péage, pont payant
toll call *n Am Tel* communication *f* interurbaine
toll-free number *n Am* numéro *m* vert
toll gate *n* barrière *f* (de péage)
toll house *n* péage *m*
tolling ['təʊlɪŋ] *n* *(of bell)* tintement *m*; *(for death)* glas *m*
toll road *n* route *f* à péage
tollway ['təʊlweɪ] *n Am* autoroute *f* à péage
Tom [tɒm] *n* **(a)** Thomas, Tom; *F* **any T., Dick or Harry** n'importe qui, le premier venu; **T. Thumb** le Petit Poucet **(b) t. (cat)** matou *m*
tomahawk ['tɒməhɔːk] *n* hache *f* de guerre, tomahawk *m*
tomato, *pl* **-oes** [tə'mɑːtəʊ, -əʊz, *Am* tə'meɪtəʊ] *n* tomate *f*; **t. juice** jus *m* de tomate; **t. ketchup** ketchup *m*; **t. purée** concentré *m* de tomates; **t. sauce** *(for pasta etc)* sauce *f* tomate; *(ketchup)* ketchup
tomb [tuːm] *n* tombe *f*, tombeau *m*
tombac ['tɒmbæk] *n Metal* tombac *m*
tombola [tɒm'bəʊlə] *n Br* tombola *f*
tomboy ['tɒmbɔɪ] *n* garçon *m* manqué
tomboyish ['tɒmbɔɪɪʃ] *adj* *(behaviour etc)* de garçon manqué
tombstone ['tuːmstəʊn] *n* pierre *f* tombale
tome [təʊm] *n* *(volume)* tome *m*; *(large book)* gros livre *m*; *F (book)* bouquin *m*
tomfool [tɒm'fuːl] *adj F* idiot; **t. scheme** projet *m* insensé
tomfoolery [tɒm'fuːlərɪ] *n F* âneries *fpl*, bêtises *fpl*
tommy ['tɒmɪ] *n Br* *(soldier)* simple soldat *m* (de l'armée britannique), *F* troufion *m*; *Mil* **T. gun** mitraillette *f*
tommyrot ['tɒmɪrɒt] *n Old-fashioned F* bêtises *fpl*, inepties *fpl*; **that's all t.** tout ça, c'est de la blague
tomography [tə'mɒgrəfɪ] *n Med* tomographie *f*
tomorrow [tə'mɒrəʊ] **1** *adv* demain; **t. morning** demain matin; **t. night** demain soir; **t. week** demain en huit

2 *n* demain *m*; **the day after t.** après-demain; **t.'s breakfast** le petit déjeuner de demain; **who knows what t. holds?** qui sait ce que demain nous réserve?; **t. never comes** c'est maintenant ou jamais; **t. is another day** ça ira mieux demain; *Prov* **never put off till t. what you can do today** il ne faut pas remettre au lendemain ce qu'on peut faire le jour même; *F* **she was eating like there was no t.** elle mangeait comme si son dernier jour était arrivé; *Fig* **what will the world be like t.?** à quoi ressemblera le monde demain?; **the cities of t., t.'s cities** les villes de demain
tomtit ['tɒmtɪt] *n* *(bird)* mésange *f* bleue
tom-tom ['tɒmtɒm] *n* tam-tam *m*, *pl* tam-tams
ton [tʌn] *n* **(a)** *(weight)* tonne *f*; *Br* **(long) t.** tonne longue (= 1 016 kg); *US* **(short** *or* **net) t.** tonne courte (= 907 kg); **metric t.** tonne (métrique) (= 1 000 kg); *F* **this suitcase weighs a t.** cette valise est rudement lourde *ou* pèse une tonne **(b)** *F* **tons of ...** *(lots of)* des tonnes de ...; **we've tons of time** nous avons tout notre temps; **there's tons of it** il y en a des tas **(c)** *esp Br Sl (100 mph)* vitesse *f* de cent milles à l'heure; *(score of 100)* cent *m*; *(£100)* cent livres *fpl*; **to do a t.** *(of vehicle, driver etc)* faire du cent milles à l'heure
tonal ['təʊn(ə)l] *adj* tonal
tonality [təʊ'nælɪtɪ] *n* tonalité *f*
tone¹ [təʊn] *n* **(a)** *(sound)* son *m*; *(quality)* sonorité *f*; *(of voice, musical instrument)* timbre *m*; *Tel* **ringing t.** tonalité *f* d'appel; **record your message after the t.** laissez votre message après le bip sonore

(b) *(sound of voice)* ton *m*, timbre *m*; **I knew by the t. of his voice** j'ai compris au ton *ou* timbre de sa voix; **in an impatient t.** avec impatience; **in an angry t. of voice** sur le ton de la colère; **I don't like your t. (of voice), don't take that t. with me** je vous prierai de ne pas me parler sur ce ton; **in a low t.** à voix basse; **to give a serious t. to a discussion** donner un ton sérieux à une discussion; **it was the t. of the letter I didn't like** c'est le ton de cette lettre qui ne m'a pas plu

(c) *(in acoustics)*, *Mus* ton *m*; **whole t.** ton entier; **quarter t.** quart *m* de ton

(d) *Art etc (of colour)* ton *m*, nuance *f*; *Phot (of print)* ton; **warm tones** tons chauds; *Art* **half t.** similigravure *f*, *F* simili *f*

(e) *Ling* ton *m*, accent *m* tonique, accent de hauteur; **t. language** langue *f* à ton

(f) *Med (of muscles etc)* tonicité *f*, tonus *m*
tone² *vt* *(picture)* adoucir les tons de; *Phot (print)* virer; **toned paper** papier *m* teinté, papier crémé
▶ **tone down** *vtsep* **(a)** *(make less bright)* *(colour etc)* adoucir, atténuer **(b)** *(moderate)* *(remarks etc)* modérer, adoucir; **the editor had to t. down the article** le rédacteur a dû atténuer les termes de l'article
▶ **tone in** *vi* *(of colour etc)* s'harmoniser **(with** avec)
▶ **tone up** **1** *vtsep* *(make stronger)* *(muscles)* tonifier **2** *vi* *(become stronger)* *(of muscles)* se tonifier
▶ **tone with** *vipo* *(match, nearly match)* *(of colour, wallpaper etc)* s'harmoniser avec
tone arm *n* *(of record player)* bras *m* de lecture
tone control *n* *(on radio etc)* touche *f* de tonalité
tone-deaf *adj* incapable de reconnaître les notes; *(not appreciating music)* qui n'a aucun sens musical
tone-deafness *n* incapacité *f* à reconnaître les notes; *(lack of musical appreciation)* manque *m* de sens musical
toneless ['təʊnlɪs] *adj* *(voice)* blanc, *f* blanche, atone
tonelessly ['təʊnlɪslɪ] *adv* *(to say)* d'une voix blanche *ou* atone
tone poem *n Mus* poème *m* symphonique
toner ['təʊnər] *n* **(a)** *(cosmetic)* astringent *m*, lotion *f* astringente **(b)** *(for photocopier, laser)* toner *m*; **t. cartridge** *or* **cassette** cartouche *f* de toner; **t. low warning** signal *m* de baisse du toner
Tonga ['tɒŋgə] *n* Tonga *fpl*
Tongan ['tɒŋgən] **1** *adj* tongan **2** *n* **(a)** Tonguien, -ienne **(b)** *Ling* tongan *m*
tongs [tɒŋz] *npl* [ⓘA10,e] **(pair of) t.** pince(s) *f(pl)*; *(in glassmaking)* moraillles *fpl*; **fire t.** pincettes *fpl*; *Culin* **sugar t.** pince à sucre
tongue¹ [tʌŋ] *n* **(a)** *Anat, Culin* langue *f*; **to stick one's t. out** tirer la langue **(at sb** à qn); **the dog's t. was hanging out** le chien tirait la langue; **his t. was hanging out** *(from thirst)* il crevait de soif; *(in expectation)* il en bavait d'envie; **to have a ready** *or* **glib t.** avoir la langue déliée *ou* bien pendue; **hold your t.!** taisez-vous!; **to find one's t.** retrouver la parole *ou* sa langue; **have you lost your t.?** tu as perdu ta langue?; *Fig* **with one's t. in one's cheek** en plaisantant; **she was being t. in cheek** elle plaisantait; **it's hard to get your t. round these words** ces mots sont difficiles à prononcer

(b) *esp Lit (language)* langue *f*, idiome *m*; **the German t.** la langue allemande; *esp Bible* **the gift of tongues** le don des langues

(c) *(of land, flame)* langue *f*; *(of shoe)* patte *f*, languette *f*; *(of bell)* battant *m*; *Mus (of oboe)* anche *f*; *Carp* languette
tongue² *vt Mus* **to t. a passage** *(on wind instrument)* détacher les notes d'un passage avec la langue
tongue-and-groove *Carp* **1** *n* *(joint, edge)* assemblage *m* à languette; *(wood)* lattes *fpl* à languette **2** *vt* *(boards, slats)* pratiquer des languettes et des rainures sur
tongue-in-cheek *adj* *(remark, article)* fait pour plaisanter, ironique
tongue-lash *vt* tancer vertement
tongue-lashing *n* **to give sb a t.** tancer qn vertement
tongue-tied *adj* *(with shyness etc)* muet, -ette; *(with surprise etc)* interdit; **it's not like her to be t.** ça ne lui ressemble pas de rester sans rien dire
tongue twister *n* mot *m*/phrase *f* difficile à prononcer

tonguing [ˈtʌŋɪŋ] *n Mus* (*on wind instrument*) coup *m* de langue

tonic [ˈtɒnɪk] **1** *adj* **(a)** *Med etc* tonique, fortifiant **(b)** *Gram* (*accent*) tonique; *Mus* (*note*) tonique **2** *n* **(a)** *Med* tonique *m*, remontant *m*, fortifiant *m*; *Fig* **to be a t. for sb** (*of news etc*) réconforter *ou* remonter qn; **he's a t.** il vous remonte le moral, il est stimulant **(b) t. (water)** tonique *m*; **gin and t.** gin-tonic *m*, *pl* gin-tonics **(c)** *Mus* tonique *f*; **t. solfa** solfège *m*

tonicity [təʊˈnɪsɪtɪ] *n* (*of muscles etc*) tonicité *f*

tonight [təˈnaɪt] **1** *adv* (*evening*) ce soir; (*night*) cette nuit **2** *n* (*evening*) ce soir; (*night*) cette nuit; **t.'s main news** et voici les titres du journal *ou* de l'actualité

toning [ˈtəʊnɪŋ] *n Phot* (*of prints*) virage *m*

toning down *n* (*of colour, remarks*) atténuation *f*, adoucissement *m*

tonnage [ˈtʌnɪdʒ] *n Naut* tonnage *m*; **register(ed) t.** tonnage net; **t. certificate** certificat *m* de jaugeage

tonne [tʌn] *n* tonne *f* (métrique)

tonneau cover [ˈtɒnəʊ] *n Aut* bâche *f*

tonsil [ˈtɒns(ə)l] *n Anat* amygdale *f*; **to have one's tonsils out** se faire opérer des amygdales

tonsillectomy [tɒnsɪˈlektəmɪ] *n* amygdalectomie *f*

tonsillitis [tɒnsɪˈlaɪtɪs] *n Med* angine *f*, *Spéc* amygdalite *f*; **to have t.** avoir une angine *ou Spéc* amygdalite

tonsure[1] [ˈtɒnʃər] *n* tonsure *f*

tonsure[2] *vt* (*monk*) tonsurer

tontine [tɒnˈtiːn] *n* (*in insurance*) tontine *f*

ton-up *adj Old-fashioned Br F* **t. boys** = fous *mpl* de moto

tonus [ˈtəʊnəs] *n Med* tonicité *f*, tonus *m*

too [tuː] *adv* **(a)** [①A5,B] (*excessively*) trop; **it's t. difficult** c'est trop difficile; **t. difficult a job** un travail trop difficile; **t. many people** trop de gens; **t. far** trop loin; **to work t. much** *or* **t. hard** travailler trop, trop travailler; **50p t. much** 50p de trop; **this job's t. much for me** ce travail est au-dessus de mes forces; **I've listened to him t. long** je l'ai trop écouté; **I know her all** *or* **only t. well** je ne la connais que trop; **you're t. kind** vous êtes très *ou* trop gentil; **he's not t. well today** il ne va pas très bien aujourd'hui; *F* **t. right!** et comment!, vous l'avez dit!

(b) (*also*) aussi, également; **you're coming t.** vous venez aussi; **she t. is a painter** elle aussi est peintre

(c) (*moreover*) en *ou* de plus; **30° in the shade and in September t.** 30° à l'ombre et en septembre en plus

toodle-oo, toodle-pip [ˈtuːdlˈuː, -ˈpɪp] *int Old-fashioned Br F* (*goodbye*) salut!

took *see* **take**[2]

tool[1] [tuːl] *n* **(a)** (*implement*) outil *m*; **(set of) tools** outillage *m*; **garden** *or* **gardening tools** outils de jardinage; **power t.** outil à moteur; **t. holder** porte-outil *m*; **t. rack** râtelier *m* à outils; **t. set** jeu *m* d'outils; **you have to learn the tools of your trade** on ne peut pratiquer un métier sans apprentissage **(b)** *Fig* (*means, instrument*) instrument *m*; **to use sb as a t.** utiliser qn; **he was a mere t. in their hands** il n'était qu'un instrument entre leurs mains **(c)** *Sl* (*penis*) bite *f*

tool[2] *vt* **(a)** (*leather, binding*) ciseler; *MecE* (*wrought iron*) usiner, travailler; **tooled leather** cuir *m* repoussé **(b)** = **tool up 1 (a)**

▶ **tool up 1** *vtsep* **(a)** (*equip with tools*) (*factory etc*) outiller **(b)** *Sl* **to be tooled up** (*carry weapons*) être armé **2** *vi* (*become equipped with tools*) s'outiller

tool bag *n* sac *m* à outils; *Cycling* sacoche *f*

tool bar *n Comptr* barre *f* d'outils

toolbox [ˈtuːlbɒks] *n* boîte *f ou* coffre *m* à outils; *Comptr* boîte à outils

tooling [ˈtuːlɪŋ] *n* (*of leather, binding*) ciselage *m*; *MecE* usinage *m*

tool kit *n* trousse *f* à outils

tool-maker *n* fabricant *m* d'outils, outilleur *m*

tool shed *n* reserre *f*, remise *f*

toot[1] [tuːt] *n Naut* coup *m* de sirène; *Aut* coup de klaxon; *Aut* **to give sb a t.** donner un coup de klaxon à qn, klaxonner qn

toot[2] **1** *vt* **to t. a horn/a trumpet** sonner du cor/de la trompette; *Aut* **to t. the horn** klaxonner; *Aut F* **to toot sb** klaxonner qn **2** *vi* (*of person*) sonner du cor; (*of instrument*) sonner; *Aut* (*of driver*) klaxonner

tooth[1], *pl* **teeth** [tuːθ, tiːθ] *n* **(a)** dent *f*; **(set of) teeth** denture *f*, dentition *f*; **first** *or* **milk teeth** dents de lait; **buck teeth** dents proéminentes; **(set of) false teeth** dentier *m*, *F* râtelier *m*; **to have a fine set of teeth** avoir de belles dents; **to cut one's teeth** faire *ou* percer ses dents; *Fig* **to cut one's teeth on sth** se faire les dents sur qch; **to have a t. out** se faire arracher une dent; **to kick sb in the teeth** donner un coup de pied à qn dans les dents; *Fig* traiter qn avec mépris; *Fig* **to fling sth in sb's teeth** reprocher qch à qn; **in the teeth of all opposition** malgré *ou* en dépit de toute opposition; **to show** *or* **bare one's teeth** montrer les dents; **armed to the teeth** armé jusqu'aux dents; **to give a law teeth** renforcer une loi; **to fight t. and nail** se battre bec et ongles; **a meal/book you can get your teeth into** un repas/livre consistant; *F* **a job you can get your teeth into** un boulot dans lequel on peut s'en donner à cœur joie; **I want to get my teeth into the problem** je veux m'attaquer à ce problème; **to grit one's teeth** serrer les dents; *F* **I'm fed up to the back teeth with it** j'en ai plein le dos de ce truc-là; *F* **she's a bit long in the t.** elle n'est plus toute jeune; *F* **I'm getting a bit long in the t. for that** je commence à me faire un peu trop vieux pour ça; **t. glass** *or* **mug** verre *m* à dents; **t. powder** poudre *f* dentifrice

(b) (*of saw, comb, cog*) dent *f*; **teeth** (*of wheel*) denture *f*

toothache [ˈtuːθeɪk] *n* mal *m ou* rage *f* de dents; **to have t.** avoir mal aux dents

toothbrush [ˈtuːθbrʌʃ] *n* brosse *f* à dents

tooth decay *n* carie *f* dentaire

toothed [tuːθt] *adj* **(a)** (*animal*) denté; (*leaf etc*) dentelé **(b)** *MecE etc* **t. belt** courroie *f* crantée; **t. wheel** roue *f* dentée

tooth fairy *n* = la petite souris

toothless [ˈtuːθlɪs] *adj* sans dents, édenté; *Fig* (*law etc*) qu'on n'a pas les moyens de faire respecter; **the committee has been criticized for being t.** on a reproché son impuissance à la commission

toothpaste [ˈtuːθpeɪst] *n* pâte *f* dentifrice, dentifrice *m*

toothpick [ˈtuːθpɪk] *n* cure-dent(s) *m*, *pl* cure-dents

toothsome [ˈtuːθsəm] *adj* (*tasty*) savoureux

toothy [ˈtuːθɪ] *adj* aux dents *fpl* saillantes, *Pej* aux dents de cheval; **to give a big t. grin** sourire à pleines dents; **t. pegs** (*in children's language*) dents

tooting [ˈtuːtɪŋ] *n Aut* coups *mpl* de klaxon

tootle[1] [ˈtuːt(ə)l] *vi Aut* (*toot*) corner, klaxonner

tootle[2] *vi Br F* (*go*) (*in car*) rouler tranquillement; (*on foot*) se balader

▶ **tootle along** *vi Br F* (*go*) aller tout tranquillement; **well, I'll t. along now** bon, je vais me mettre en route

toots [tʊts] *n F* **are you ready, t.?** (*to woman*) tu es prête, poupée?; (*to toddler*) tu es prêt(e), doudou?

tootsy [ˈtʊtsɪ] *n F* (*in children's language*) (*foot*) peton *m*; (*toe*) doigt *m* de pied

top[1] [tɒp] *n* **(spinning** *or* **peg) t.** (*toy*) toupie *f*

top[2] **1** *n* **(a)** (*highest point*) (*of tree, mountain*) haut *m*, sommet *m*, cime *f*, faîte *m*; (*of tower, head*) sommet; (*of page, map*) haut; (*end*) (*of table*) bout *m*; **he always sat at the t. of the table** à table, c'était toujours lui qui présidait; **to make it to the t.** (*in profession, sport, music etc*) se faire une place parmi les grands; **at the t. of the stairs** en haut de l'escalier; **at the t. of the street** au bout de la rue; **at the t. of the tree** en haut de l'arbre; *Fig* au sommet de sa profession; **it went right to the t.** (*of complaint, request etc*) cela est remonté jusqu'au sommet *Sch* **to be (at) the t. of the class** être le premier/la première de la classe; **to be (at) the t. of the bill** (*of actor, singer etc*) être en haut de l'affiche; **from t. to bottom** de haut en bas; (*to search a flat etc*) de fond en comble; **from t. to toe** de la tête aux pieds; **to shout/sing at the t. of one's voice** crier/chanter à tue-tête; **to be on** *or* **at the t. of one's form** être *ou* se sentir en pleine forme; *Irish F* **(the) t. of the morning (to you)** bien le bonjour!; *Mil* **to go over the t.** (sortir des tranchées pour) aller à l'assaut; *F* **over the t.** (*overdone*) excessif; **I find her a bit over the t.** je trouve qu'elle exagère un peu; **turnip/carrot tops** fanes *fpl* de navets/de carottes

(b) (*surface*) (*of table etc*) surface *f*, dessus *m*; (*of bus*) impériale *f*; **t. of the milk** crème *f* du lait

(c) (*part*) (*of shoe*) dessus *m*; (*of box, pan etc*) couvercle *m*; (*of bottle etc*) bouchon *m*, capsule *f*; (*of pen etc*) capuchon *m*; (*of dress*) haut *m*, corsage *m*; (*separate garment*) haut; *F* **to blow one's t.** sortir de ses gonds; **t. boots** bottes *fpl* à revers

(d) on t. of (*on*) sur; **on t. (of the pile)** sur le dessus (de la pile); **to put sth on t. of sth** mettre qch sur qch; **to put sth right on the t. of sth** mettre qch tout en haut de qch; **just put it on t.** mets-le sur le dessus; **a cake with a cherry on t.** un gâteau avec une cerise dessus; **to be on t.** (*be in control*) avoir le dessus; **to be on t. of the situation** maîtriser la situation; **you mustn't let things get on t. of you** il ne faut pas te laisser dépasser par les événements; **to come out on t.** prendre le dessus; **it's just one thing on t. of another** ça n'arrête jamais; **on t. of it all** et pour comble (de malheur), et en plus de tout cela; **to be** *or* **to feel on t. of the world** être *ou* se sentir en pleine forme

(e) *F* **the tops** la crème, le gratin; **he's (the) tops!** c'est un as!; *F* **he's tops with me** pour moi, c'est le meilleur

(f) the Big T. (*in circus*) le chapiteau

(**g**) *Aut* (*gear*) quatrième *f*/cinquième *f*, *Spéc* prise *f* directe; **in t.** au rapport supérieur

2 *adj* (**a**) (*highest*) du dessus, du haut, d'en haut; (*floor, stair*) dernier; *F* **the t. brass** (*in army*) les officiers *mpl* supérieurs; (*in company etc*) les gros bonnets *mpl*; **the t. people** (*prominent people*) les gens *mpl* en vue; (*in an organization*) les gros bonnets *mpl*; **all the t. people in New York eat there** c'est un restaurant où se retrouve toute l'élite new-yorkaise; **t. coat** (*of paint*) dernière couche *f*; *F* **to pay t. dollar for sth** dépenser beaucoup d'argent pour qch; **to be/to feel on t. form** être/se sentir en pleine forme; *Aut* **t. gear** quatrième/cinquième vitesse *f*, prise *f* directe, vitesse supérieure; **t. security** sécurité *f* maximum; **he was given t. security** il a bénéficié du maximum de sécurité; **t. shelf** étagère *f* du dessus *ou* du haut; **t. speed** vitesse *f* maximum, vitesse de pointe; **to travel at t. speed** (*of plane, train etc*) aller à sa vitesse maximale; **car with a t. speed of 150 kph** voiture avec un plafond de 150 km/h; **t. table** (*at banquet, in college etc*) table *f* d'honneur

(**b**) (*best, major*) premier; **she got the t. mark** *or* **came t. in history** elle a eu la meilleure note en histoire; **the country's t. ten companies** les dix premières sociétés du pays; **one of the world's t. ten players** un des dix meilleurs joueurs mondiaux; **t. pupil** premier, -ière de la classe

top[3] *vt* (**-pp-**) (**a**) (*remove top of*) (*tree, plant*) écimer; (*tree*) étêter; **to t. and tail carrots** retirer les fanes et couper les bouts des carottes

(**b**) (*provide top for*) surmonter, couronner, coiffer (**with** de); *Culin* (*dessert etc*) garnir (**with** de); *Fig* **and to t. it all** et pour comble (de malheur), et en plus de tout cela

(**c**) (*exceed*) excéder, surpasser; **the takings have topped a thousand pounds** les recettes dépassent mille livres; **to t. sb by a head** dépasser qn d'une tête

(**d**) (*reach top of*) (*hill etc*) atteindre le sommet de

(**e**) (*be at top of*) **to t. a list/a class** être à la tête d'une liste/de la classe; **topping the bill tonight we have ...** le clou de cette soirée est ...; **to t. the charts** (*of record, singer*) être à la première place *ou* en tête des hit-parades

(**f**) *Golf* (*ball*) calotter

(**g**) *Sl* **to get topped** (*be killed*) se faire buter; **to t. oneself** (*commit suicide*) se foutre en l'air

▶ **top off** *vtsep* (*complete*) (*evening*) couronner; **topped off with a cherry** garni d'une cerise

▶ **top out** *Br Constr* **1** *vtsep* (*building*) célébrer l'achèvement de la construction de **2** *vi* célébrer l'achèvement de la construction d'un immeuble

▶ **top up 1** *vtsep* (*add more to*) (*glass etc*) remplir; **to t. up one's life assurance premium** augmenter les versements de son assurance-vie; *F* **let me t. you up** vous en reprendrez bien un peu?; *Aut* **to t. up the battery/the oil/the tank/***etc* ajouter de l'eau/de l'huile/de l'essence/*etc*; **the government tops up the rest** (*pays the balance*) le gouvernement met l'argent qui manque *ou* rajoute la différence **2** *vi Aut* (*with oil*) ajouter de l'huile; (*with petrol*) faire le plein

topaz ['təʊpæz] *n* (*gem*) topaze *f*

top-bracket *adj* de première catégorie

topcoat ['tɒpkəʊt] *n* pardessus *m*, manteau *m*

top copy *n* copie *f* originale

top dog *n Fig F* chef *m*; **to be t.** (*have the advantage*) avoir le dessus

top-down *adj* (*management*) contrôlé par le haut; *Mktg* **t. forecasting** prévisions *fpl* hiérarchisées

top-drawer *adj* (**a**) *Old-fashioned F* (*upper class*) de la haute (**b**) = **top-flight**

top-dress *vt Agr* fumer en surface

tope [təʊp] *vi Old-fashioned F* boire, picoler

topee ['təʊpɪ] *n* casque *m* colonial

toper ['təʊpər] *n Old-fashioned F* picoleur, -euse

top-flight *adj* de premier ordre, excellent

top hat *n* chapeau *m* haut de forme

top-heavy *adj* trop lourd du haut; *Naut* (*ship*) trop chargé dans les hauts; *Fig* (*organization*) dont les dirigeants sont trop nombreux

top-hole *adj Old-fashioned Br F* épatant, au poil

topi ['təʊpɪ] *n* = **topee**

topic ['tɒpɪk] *n* (*of text, discussion*) matière *f*; (*of conversation*) sujet *m*, thème *m*

topical ['tɒpɪk(ə)l] *adj* (**a**) (*question*) d'actualité; **matters of t. interest** des questions d'actualité; **it's very t.** c'est tout à fait d'actualité; **a few t. references in the text** quelques références à l'actualité dans le texte (**b**) (*index*) (organisé) par matières

topicality [tɒpɪ'kælɪtɪ] *n* actualité *f*

topically ['tɒpɪklɪ] *adv* (*to write etc*) sur des thèmes d'actualité

topknot ['tɒpnɒt] *n* (*of bird*) huppe *f*; (*hair*) petit chignon *m*

topless ['tɒplɪs] *adj* (*dancer*) aux seins nus; **to go t.** (*women*) faire du monokini; **t. beach** plage *f* seins nus; **t. bathing is permitted on some beaches only** le bronzage en monokini n'est permis que sur certaines plages

top-level *adj* (*talks etc*) au plus haut niveau

top-loader *n* (*washing machine*) machine *f* à laver à chargement par le haut

topmast ['tɒpməst] *n Naut* mât *m* de hune

topmost ['tɒpməʊst] *adj* le plus haut, le plus élevé

topnotch ['tɒpnɒtʃ] *adj Old-fashioned F* de premier ordre

top of the range *n* article *m*/modèle *m* haut de gamme

top-of-the-range *adj* haut de gamme

topographer [tə'pɒgrəfər] *n* topographe *m*

topographic(al) [tɒpə'græfɪk(əl)] *adj* topographique

topographically [tɒpə'græfɪklɪ] *adv* topographiquement

topography [tɒ'pɒgrəfɪ] *n* topographie *f*

topologic(al) [tɒpə'lɒdʒɪk(əl)] *adj* topologique

topology [tə'pɒlədʒɪ] *n* topologie *f*

-topped [-tɒpt] *suff Lit* **cloud-t. peaks** sommets couronnés de nuages; **ivory-t. walking stick** canne à pommeau d'ivoire

topper ['tɒpər] *n F* (*top hat*) haut *m* de forme

topping ['tɒpɪŋ] **1** *adj Old-fashioned Br F* excellent, formidable **2** *n Culin* (*for dessert, pizza etc*) garniture *f*; **ice-cream with raspberry t.** glace recouverte d'un coulis de framboises

topple ['tɒp(ə)l] **1** *vi* (*fall*) tomber; *Fig* (*of government etc*) tomber; (*of share prices*) chuter; **he toppled into the pool/over the edge of the cliff** il a culbuté dans la piscine/par-dessus la falaise **2** *vt* faire tomber; (*building etc*) faire s'écrouler; (*government etc*) renverser

▶ **topple down, topple over** *vi, vtsep* = **topple**

top-rank(ing) *adj* haut placé; **t. civil servant** haut fonctionnaire *m*

topsail ['tɒps(ə)l] *n Naut* hunier *m*

top-secret *adj* (*information etc*) top secret, -ète

top-security *adj* **t. prison/wing** prison *f*/aile *f* *ou* quartier *m* de haute surveillance

topside ['tɒpsaɪd] *n* (**a**) *Culin* (*of beef*) tende *f* de tranche (**b**) *Naut* **topsides** (*of ship*) accastillage *m*

topsoil ['tɒpsɔɪl] *n Agr* couche *f* arable

topsy-turvy [tɒpsɪ'tɜːvɪ] **1** *adj* sens dessus dessous; **everything's t.** (*of organization etc*) c'est la confusion totale **2** *adv* **the whole world's turned t.** c'est le monde à l'envers

top ten *or* **twenty** *n* (*hit records*) hit-parade *m*; **in the t.** au hit-parade

top-up *n Aut* (remplissage *m* d')appoint *m*; **let me give you a t.** (*when serving drinks*) vous en reprendrez bien un peu?; **t. loan/finance** prêt *m*/fonds *m* complémentaire

toque [təʊk] *n* (*hat*) toque *f*

tor [tɔːr] *n* (*hill*) pic *m*, butte *f* rocheuse

torch [tɔːtʃ] *n* (**a**) (*flame*) torche *f*, flambeau *m*; *Fig* **the t. of liberty** le flambeau de la liberté; *Fig* **to carry a t. for sb** avoir un faible pour qn; **to put sth to the t.** mettre le feu à qch (**b**) (*for welding*) chalumeau *m* (**c**) *Br* (**electric**) **t.** lampe *f* (électrique) (de poche), torche *f* électrique

torchbearer ['tɔːtʃbeərər] *n* porte-flambeau *m inv*

torchlight ['tɔːtʃlaɪt] *n* lumière *f* de torche(s) *ou* de flambeau(x); (*of electric torch*) lumière d'une/de la torche (électrique); **by t.** à la lumière des torches *ou* des flambeaux/d'une torche électrique; **t. procession** retraite *f* aux flambeaux

torch song *n* chanson *f* d'amour

tore *see* **tear**[3]

toreador ['tɒrɪədɔːr] *n* toréador *m*, torero *m*

torment[1] ['tɔːment] *n esp Lit* tourment *m*, supplice *m*; **the torments of jealousy** les tourments de la jalousie; **he suffered torments** il souffrait le martyre; **to be in t.** être au supplice

torment[2] [tɔː'ment] *vt* (*cause suffering to*) (*sb*) tourmenter, (*stronger*) torturer; (*pester*) (*sb, animal etc*) harceler; **tormented with remorse** tourmenté par les remords, en proie aux remords; **tormented soul** âme *f* tourmentée

tormentor [tɔː'mentər] *n* bourreau *m*

torn *see* **tear**[3]

tornado, *pl* **-oes** [tɔː'neɪdəʊ, -əʊz] *n* tornade *f*

torpedo[1] *pl* **-oes** [tɔː'piːdəʊ, -əʊz] *n* (**a**) *Naut etc* torpille *f*; **t. boat** vedette *f* lance-torpilles; **t. tube** (tube *m*) lance-torpilles *m inv* (**b**) **t. (fish)** (poisson *m*) torpille *f*

torpedo[2] *vt* (*ship, Fig peace*) torpiller

torpid ['tɔːpɪd] *adj* engourdi, torpide; **t. state** (*of animal*) engourdissement *m*

torpor ['tɔːpər], **torpidity** [tɔː'pɪdɪtɪ] *n* torpeur *f*, engourdissement *m*

torque [tɔːk] *n MecE, Phys etc* moment *m* de torsion *ou* de rotation; *Aut* couple *m*, torque *m*; **starting t.** couple de *ou* au démarrage; **t. converter** convertisseur *m* de couple; **t. plate**

plateau *m* absorbeur de couple; **t. wrench** clé *f* dynamométrique

torrent ['tɒrənt] *n* torrent *m*; **it's raining in torrents** il pleut à torrents *ou* à verse; **t. of abuse/of tears** torrent *ou* déluge *m* d'injures/de larmes

torrential [tɒ'renʃəl] *adj* torrentiel; **t. rain** pluie *f* diluvienne *ou* torrentielle

torrid ['tɒrɪd] *adj* (*heat, region, love affair*) torride

torsion ['tɔːʃən] *n* torsion *f*; *Aut etc* **t. bar** barre *f* de torsion

torso, *pl* **-os** ['tɔːsəʊ, -əʊz] *n Anat, Art* torse *m*

tort [tɔːt] *n Jur* acte *m* dommageable, préjudice *m*, délit *m* civil

tortoise ['tɔːtəs] *n* tortue *f* (terrestre)

tortoiseshell ['tɔːtəsʃel] *n* écaille *f* (de tortue); **t. cat** chat *m* écaille de tortue; **t. comb** peigne *m* en écaille

tortuous ['tɔːtjʊəs] *adj* (*path, means*) tortueux; **to have a t. mind** avoir l'esprit tordu

tortuously ['tɔːtjʊəslɪ] *adv* tortueusement

tortuousness ['tɔːtjʊəsnɪs] *n* (*of path, thinking etc*) caractère *m* tortueux

torture[1] ['tɔːtʃər] *n* **(a)** torture *f*; **instruments of t.** instruments *mpl* de torture; **t. chamber** chambre *f* de torture; **t. victim** victime *f* de torture **(b)** *Fig* (*physical, mental pain*) torture *f*, supplice *m*; **wearing these shoes is t.** c'est un vrai supplice de porter ces chaussures

torture[2] *vt* (*sb*) torturer; *Fig* (*by making sb wait etc*) mettre au supplice; *Fig* (*text etc*) torturer; **tortured by remorse** torturé *ou* tenaillé par le remords

torturer ['tɔːtʃərər] *n* tortionnaire *m*; *Hist* bourreau *m*

Tory ['tɔːrɪ] *adj, n Br Pol* tory *m*

Toryism ['tɔːrɪɪz(ə)m] *n Br Pol* torysme *m*

tosh [tɒʃ] *n Old-fashioned Br F* bêtises *fpl*, blague(s) *f(pl)*

toss[1] [tɒs] *n* **(a)** (*of ball etc*) lancer *m*, lancement *m*; **it was decided by the t. of a coin** on a décidé cela (en tirant) à pile ou face; **to win/lose the t.** gagner/perdre à pile ou face; **to argue the t.** discuter inutilement *ou* pour rien **(b) t. of the head** brusque mouvement *m* de tête **(c)** (*fall*) **to take a t.** (*from horse etc*) faire une chute **(d)** *Br Sl* **he doesn't give a toss (what happens** *etc*) il n'en a rien à fiche (de ce qui arrivera *etc*)

toss[2] **(-ss-) 1** *vt* (*ball etc*) lancer, jeter en l'air; (*of bull*) (*sb*) projeter en l'air; (*of sea etc*) secouer, ballotter; **to t. sth to sb** jeter qch à qn; **to t. sb in a blanket** faire sauter qn en l'air sur une couverture; **to t. the salad** remuer *ou* tourner *ou F* fatiguer la salade; **to t. a pancake** faire sauter une crêpe; **to t. a coin** jouer à pile ou face; **who's going to pay? – I'll t. you for it** qui va payer? – décidons-le à pile ou face; **to t. one's head** relever la tête avec dédain

2 *vi* **(a) to t. for sth** jouer qch à pile ou face

(b) to t. and turn in bed se tourner et se retourner dans son lit

(c) (*of waves*) s'agiter; **to t. on the waves** être ballotté par les flots; **to pitch and t.** (*of ship*) tanguer

▶ **toss about, toss around** *vtas* (*ball*) lancer, taper dans; *Fig F* (*idea*) étudier; **the ship, tossed about by the waves, ...** le bateau, agité *ou* secoué *ou* ballotté par les vagues, ...; **let's t. the idea around for a while** creusons un peu pour voir

▶ **toss across** *vtsep* envoyer; **t. the newpaper across, will you?** envoie-moi le journal, s'il te plaît

▶ **toss away** *vtsep* (*get rid of*) jeter

▶ **toss back** *vtsep* (*ball, Fig report, proposal etc*) renvoyer; (*one's hair*) rejeter en arrière

▶ **toss off 1** *vtsep* **(a)** (*drink quickly*) (*drink*) avaler d'un trait **(b)** (*complete quickly*) (*task, essay, article*) expédier **(c)** *Br Vulg* (*masturbate*) branler **2** *vi Br Vulg* (*masturbate*) se branler

▶ **toss out** *vtsep* jeter; *F* (*rubbish*) balancer; **to t. sb out of a club** (*physically, cancel membership*) mettre qn à la porte *ou F* jeter qn d'un club

▶ **toss over** *vtsep* = **toss across**

▶ **toss up 1** *vtsep* (*throw up*) lancer, envoyer; **t. that brush up, will you** lance-moi *ou* envoie-moi la brosse, s'il te plaît; **to t. sth up into the air** lancer *ou* envoyer qch en l'air **2** *vi* (*with coin*) tirer à pile ou face; **let's t. up for it** jouons-le *ou* décidons-le à pile ou face

tosser ['tɒsər] *n Br Sl* branleur *m*

tossing ['tɒsɪŋ] *n* (*of boat etc*) ballottement *m*

toss-up *n* **(a)** (*with coin*) coup *m* de pile ou face; **in the event of a tie the winner will be decided by a t.** en cas d'égalité, on tirera à pile ou face pour désigner le gagnant **(b)** *F* **in the end it was a t. between Majorca and Rhodes** finalement, nous avons dû choisir entre Majorque et Rhodes; **it's a t. which is best** il est impossible de dire quel est le meilleur; **I don't know, it's a t.** je ne sais pas, c'est kif-kif

tot [tɒt] *n* **(a)** (*child*) (*tiny*) **t.** tout(e) petit(e) enfant *mf*; **books for tiny tots** livres pour les tout-petits **(b)** (*small quantity*) (*of whisky etc*) (petite) goutte *f*

▶ **tot up 1** *vtsep* (*add*) additionner; (*total*) faire le total de; **she has totted up 2,500 hours flying time** elle totalise 2 500 heures de vol **2** *vi* (*of expenses etc*) s'élever (**to** à)

total[1] ['təʊt(ə)l] **1** *adj* total, global; **t. amount** somme *f* totale *ou* globale, montant *m* total; **t. eclipse** éclipse *f* totale; **t. failure** échec *m* complet; **they were in t. ignorance of it** ils l'ignoraient complètement; **the t. population** la population totale; **t. war** guerre *f* totale; *Com* **t. annual expenses** consommations *fpl* de l'exercice; **t. asset value** valeur *f* de bilan; **t. constructive loss** perte *f* totale; **t. fixed cost** coût *m* fixe total; **t. guarantee** garantie *f* totale; **t. insured value** valeur totale assurée; **t. loss** perte totale; **t. loss settlement** règlement *m* en perte totale; **t. payable** total *m* à payer; **t. quality control** contrôle *m* de la qualité totale; **t. quality management** gestion *f* de la qualité totale; **t. receipts** total des recettes; **t. sales** ventes *fpl* totales, chiffre *m* d'affaires global; **t. unit cost** coût complet unitaire

2 *n* total *m*; (*sum of money*) montant *m*; **grand t.** total global; **there are a t. of thirteen inspectors in the whole country** au total, il y a treize inspecteurs dans tout le pays; **sum t.** somme *f* totale; **the t. amounts to £100** la somme *ou* le montant s'élève à 100 livres; **a t. of 102 hours/people** un total de 102 heures/personnes; **in t.** au total

total[2] (*pt, pp* **totalled,** *Am* **totaled**) *vt* **(a)** (*add up*) (*expenditure*) additionner, totaliser **(b)** (*amount to*) se chiffrer à; **to t. £100** s'élever à *ou* se monter à 100 livres **(c)** *US F* (*write off*) (*car*) bousiller, déglinguer, fusiller

totalitarian [təʊtælɪ'teərɪən] *adj Pol* totalitaire

totalitarianism [təʊtælɪ'teərɪənɪz(ə)m] *n Pol* totalitarisme *m*

totality [təʊ'tælɪtɪ] *n* totalité *f*

totalizator ['təʊtəlaɪzeɪtər] *n Horseracing* (*for bets*) totalisateur *m*, totaliseur *m*

totalize ['təʊtəlaɪz] *vt* additionner, totaliser

totalling ['təʊtəlɪŋ] *n* chiffrage *m*

totally ['təʊtəlɪ] *adv* totalement

tote[1] [təʊt] *n Horseracing F* = **totalizator**

tote[2] *vt esp Am* (*goods etc*) transporter; (*bag, gun*) porter; **t. bag** (sac *m*) fourre-tout *m inv*

totem ['təʊtəm] *n* totem *m*; **t. pole** mât *m* totémique

totemic [təʊ'temik] *adj* totémique

totemism ['təʊtəmɪz(ə)m] *n* totémisme *m*

t'other, tother ['tʌðər] *adj, pron Dial, F* = **the other**

totter ['tɒtər] *vi* **(a)** (*of person*) chanceler, tituber; **to t. in/out** entrer/sortir d'un pas mal assuré *ou* chancelant **(b)** (*of building, government*) chanceler

tottering ['tɒtərɪŋ] *adj* (*person*) chancelant, titubant; (*building, regime*) chancelant; **t. steps** pas *mpl* chancelants *ou* mal assurés

tottery ['tɒtərɪ] *adj* chancelant

toucan ['tuːkæn] *n* (*bird*) toucan *m*

touch[1] [tʌtʃ] *n* **(a)** (*act of touching*) toucher *m*, contact *m*; **I felt a t. on my arm** j'ai senti qu'on me touchait le bras; **the engine starts at the first t. of the starter** le moteur démarre du premier coup

(b) (*sense*) toucher *m*; **hard/soft to the t.** dur/mou au toucher

(c) (*feel*) contact *m*; **the cold t. of marble** le contact froid du marbre

(d) (*light blow*) léger coup *m*; (*with paintbrush*) touche *f*; (*with pencil*) coup de crayon; **t. of** *or* **with a stick** léger coup de baguette; **to give one's horse a t. of the spurs** toucher son cheval de l'éperon; **to add a few touches to a picture** faire quelques retouches à un tableau; **to put the finishing touch(es)** *or* **to add the final t. to sth** mettre la dernière main à qch; **sculptor with a bold/light t.** sculpteur au ciseau hardi/délicat; **to have a light t.** (*on piano*) avoir un toucher délicat; (*in cooking*) avoir des doigts de fée; (*in writing*) avoir un style raffiné; **delicate t. (with** *or* **of the brush)** coup de pinceau délicat; *Fig* **there were some nice touches in the film** il y avait quelques notes bien vues dans le film; **he's lost his t.** il a perdu la main; **this house needs a woman's t.** il faut qu'une femme s'occupe de cette maison

(e) (*hint*) nuance *f*, soupçon *m*; **t. of garlic** pointe *f ou* soupçon d'ail; **a t. of bitterness** une nuance d'amertume; **there's a t. of colour in her cheeks** ses joues ont pris un peu de couleur; **the first touches of autumn** les premières teintes de l'automne; **a t. of originality** une note d'originalité; **to have a t. of flu** être un peu grippé

(f) (*communication*) contact *m*; **to be in t. with sb** être *ou* se tenir en contact avec qn, être en rapport avec qn; **they're still in t.** ils ont maintenu le contact *ou* sont toujours en contact; **to get in t. with sb** joindre *ou* contacter qn, prendre contact *ou* se mettre en contact avec qn; **to get in t. with the police** prendre contact avec la police; **I'll be in t.** je vous ferai signe; **to put sb in t. with sb** mettre qn en relations *ou* en rapport avec qn; **to keep** *or* **stay in t. with sb** rester en contact avec qn; **keep in t.!** on reste en contact!; **to keep sb in t. with sth** tenir qn au courant de qch; **to be out of t. with foreign affairs** ne plus être au courant des affaires étrangères; **to be out of t.** *or* **to have lost t. with sb** ne plus être en contact avec qn; **to lose t. with reality** perdre le contact avec la réalité; **the President has lost t. with the electorate** le Président a perdu le contact avec son électorat

(**g**) *Sp* touche *f*; **kick into t.** envoi *m* en touche; *Fig F* **to kick a proposal into t.** mettre une proposition au placard; **the ball has gone into t.** le ballon est sorti en touche

(**h**) *Sl* (*financially*) **to make a t.** taper quelqu'un; **easy** *or* **soft t.** (*person*) pigeon *m*; **I'm no easy** *or* **soft t.** il n'y a pas écrit "pigeon" sur mon front

touch[2] **1** *vt* (**a**) (*be in contact with*) toucher; (*finger, handle*) toucher à; *Fencing* (*one's opponent*) toucher; **to t. sth with one's finger** toucher qch du doigt; **to t. sb on the shoulder** toucher qn à l'épaule; **to t. sb on the arm** toucher le bras à qn; **I never touched him!** (*didn't hit*) je ne l'ai même pas touché; **he touched his hat to me** il m'a salué en touchant son chapeau; **t. wood!** je touche/touchons du bois!; *F* **I wouldn't t. it with a bargepole** *or Am* **a ten foot pole** je ne voudrais pas y toucher, même avec des pincettes; *F* **I wouldn't t. him with a bargepole** *or Am* **a ten foot pole** je ne veux rien avoir à faire avec lui; **nobody will t. him these days** personne ne veut plus rien avoir à faire avec lui; **stolen, are they, sorry, can't t. them** elles sont volées, hein, désolé, je ne veux rien avoir à faire avec ça; **to t. (the) bottom** (*of ship*) toucher le fond; **he touched the bell** (*pushed button*) il a appuyé sur (le bouton de) la sonnette; **the curtains t. the floor** les rideaux descendent jusqu'au plancher; **the law can't t. her** la loi ne peut rien contre elle; **I never t. wine** je ne bois jamais de vin; **you haven't touched your meat!** tu n'as pas touché à ta viande!; **stains that other detergents won't t.** des taches contre lesquelles les autres détergents ne peuvent rien; **you haven't really touched the problem of … in your essay** vous n'avez pas vraiment abordé le problème de … dans votre essai; **if it's against the law, we won't t. it** si c'est illégal, nous ne nous en mêlerons pas

(**b**) (*rival*) **when it comes to reliability, no other car can t. it** pour ce qui est de la fiabilité, aucune voiture ne peut l'égaler; **there's no one to t. him in comedy** il est sans égal dans les comédies; **there's only one other company that can t. them** il n'y a qu'une autre entreprise qui puisse rivaliser avec eux *ou* qui soit à leur niveau

(**c**) (*produce an effect on*) (*sth*) avoir un effet sur; **this quiet corner of the country was scarcely touched by the war** ce petit coin du pays n'a presque pas été touché par la guerre; **to t. sb on a raw** *or* **tender spot** toucher qn à un endroit sensible; **flowers touched by the frost** fleurs atteintes par la gelée

(**d**) (*move*) (*sb*) toucher, émouvoir; **to be touched by sb's kindness** être touché de *ou* par la bonté de qn

(**e**) *esp Fml* (*concern*) (*sb*) toucher, regarder; **the question touches you closely** la question vous touche de près

(**f**) *F* **to t. sb for a fiver** taper qn de cinq livres

2 *vi* (*of people, things*) se toucher; **don't t.!** n'y touchez pas!; **please do not t.** (*on notice*) prière de ne pas toucher; **the two ships touched** les deux navires ont touché; *Naut* **to t. at a port** faire escale à un port

▶ **touch down 1** *vi* (**a**) *Rugby* marquer un essai; *Am Fb* faire un touché-en-but, toucher dans les buts (**b**) *Astronaut, Av* (*land*) atterrir; (*in mid-journey*) faire escale **2** *vtsep* (*ball*) *Rugby* plaquer au sol; *Am Fb* toucher dans les buts

▶ **touch off** *vtsep* (*detonate*) (*canon etc*) décharger; (*mine*) faire partir, faire exploser; (*revolt, quarrel*) déclencher

▶ **touch on** *vipo* (*make brief reference to*) (*subject*) aborder; **her speech didn't even t. on this problem** elle n'a même pas abordé *ou* effleuré ce problème dans son discours

▶ **touch up** *vtsep* (**a**) (*add paint etc to*) (*painting*) faire des retouches à; (*colours of sth*) aviver, rafraîchir; (*story*) enjoliver; (*piece of work*) retaper; **to t. up (the paint on) a window frame** *etc* donner un coup de pinceau à un châssis de fenêtre *etc*; **to t. up one's make-up** rafraîchir son maquillage; **to t. up a photograph** retoucher une photo (**b**) *Br Sl* (*touch sexually*) toucher, peloter

▶ **touch upon** *vipo* = **touch on**

touch-and-go *adj* (*affair*) très risqué, hasardeux; **it's t. whether we'll have time** il n'est pas du tout sûr que nous ayons *ou* aurons le temps; **it's t. whether he'll live** il a une chance sur deux de s'en sortir; **right up to the minute they signed it was t.** jusqu'au moment où ils ont signé, rien n'était sûr

touchdown ['tʌtʃdaʊn] *n* (**a**) *Rugby* essai *m*; *Am Fb* touché-en-but *m, pl* touchés en-but, touché-à-terre *m, pl* touchés-à-terre (**b**) *Astronaut, Av* atterrissage *m*

touché ['tu:ʃeɪ] *int* touché!

touched [tʌtʃt] *adj* (**a**) (*moved*) touché, ému (**b**) *F* **t. (in the head)** toqué, timbré

touchiness ['tʌtʃɪnɪs] *n* susceptibilité *f*

touching ['tʌtʃɪŋ] **1** *adj* (*moving*) touchant, émouvant **2** *n* **t. is not allowed, no t.!** il est défendu de toucher **3** *prep Fml* concernant

touchingly ['tʌtʃɪŋlɪ] *adv* d'une manière touchante *ou* émouvante

touch-judge *n Rugby* juge *m* de touche

touchline ['tʌtʃlaɪn] *n Fb etc* ligne *f* de touche

touch screen *n* écran *m* tactile; **t. computer** ordinateur *m* à écran tactile

touch-sensitive *adj Comptr* (*screen etc*) tactile; (*key, switch*) à effleurement

touchstone ['tʌtʃstəʊn] *n* pierre *f* de touche

touch-type *vi* taper au toucher

touch-typing *n* dactylographie *f* au toucher

touchwood ['tʌtʃwʊd] *n* amadou *m*

touchy ['tʌtʃɪ] *adj* (*person*) susceptible (**about** sur); (*subject*) délicat; **to be t.** (*of person*) se froisser *ou* s'offusquer facilement; **she's very t. on that point** elle est très susceptible *ou* chatouilleuse là-dessus

tough [tʌf] **1** *adj* (**a**) (*meat etc*) dur, coriace; (*material, metal*) dur, résistant

(**b**) (*resistant, strong*) (*person*) fort, solide; **you have to be t. to …** il faut être solide *ou* résistant *ou F* costaud pour …; **to become t.** s'endurcir; *F* **a t. guy** un dur (à cuire); **as t. as old boots** coriace; (*steak*) dur comme de la semelle

(**c**) (*mentally*) fort; (*stubborn*) opiniâtre; (*strict*) dur, sévère; **she's a t. customer** (*not easy to deal with*) elle n'est pas commode; (*mentally resistant*) c'est une dure (à cuire); **is he t. enough to be sales director?** a-t-il la force de caractère nécessaire à un directeur des ventes?; **we'll have to get t. with them** il faudra que nous nous montrions plus durs avec eux; *prov* **when the going gets t., the t. get going** c'est dans les moments difficiles que les vrais hommes entrent en action

(**d**) (*difficult*) (*question, job, climb*) dur, ardu; *Hum* **it's t. at the top** (*in job etc*) c'est dur au sommet; **it was a t. job** c'était une rude besogne; **to give sb a t. time** faire passer un mauvais quart d'heure à qn; **they had a t. time when their parents died** ils en ont connu de dures quand leurs parents sont morts

(**e**) *F* (*unfortunate*) dur; **that's t. on the rest of them** c'est dur pour ceux qui restent; **it's t. for him, great for us** c'est dur pour lui, mais génial pour nous; **well, isn't that just t.!** quel dommage!; **t. luck!** pas de chance!; **that's your t. luck!** ce n'est pas de chance pour toi!, c'est tant pis pour toi

2 *n* voyou *m*

3 *adv* (*to talk, act*) comme un dur

▶ **tough out** *vtas F* **to t. it out** (*face up to sth*) faire front; (*endure sth*) tenir le coup

toughen ['tʌf(ə)n] **1** *vt* durcir; (*sb*) endurcir; **toughened glass** verre *m* trempé **2** *vi* durcir; (*of person*) s'endurcir

▶ **toughen up** *vti* = **toughen**

toughie ['tʌfɪ] *n F* (**a**) (*person*) dur *m* (**b**) (*question, problem*) casse-tête *f inv*; **question 5 was a real t.** la question 5 était une horreur; **this tooth's a real t.** (*won't come out*) cette dent est horriblement difficile à enlever

toughly ['tʌflɪ] *adv* (**a**) (*to fight*) vigoureusement (**b**) (*to argue, refuse*) avec opiniâtreté; **a t. worded reply** une réponse très dure

toughness ['tʌfnɪs] *n* (**a**) (*of wood etc*) dureté *f*, résistance *f* (**b**) (*of person*) (*physical strength*) force *f*, solidité *f*; (*resistance to fatigue*) résistance *f*; (*mentally*) force de caractère; (*inflexibility*) ténacité *f*, opiniâtreté *f* (**c**) (*of task*) difficulté *f*

toupee ['tu:peɪ] *n* postiche *m*

tour[1] [tʊər] *n* (**a**) (*journey to different places*) voyage *m*; (*excursion*) excursion *f*; **conducted** *or* **guided t.** voyage organisé; (*of museum, city, factory etc*) visite *f* (guidée); **to go on a t. of the Highlands** partir en voyage dans les Highlands; **to go on a bus t. of Paris** faire une visite guidée de Paris en bus; **the PM was taken on a t. of the factory/hospital** le Premier Ministre a fait la visite de l'usine/l'hôpital; **would you like a t. of the garden?** voulez-vous que je vous fasse visiter le jardin?; **would you like a t. of the new offices?** aimeriez-vous visiter nos nouveaux bureaux?; **package t.,** *Am* **all-expense t.** voyage à forfait *ou* à prix forfaitaire; **cycle** *or* **cycling t.** excursion *ou* randonnée *f* à bicyclette; **walking t.** excursion *ou* randonnée à pied

(b) **t. of inspection** tournée *f* d'inspection; *Mil etc* **t. of duty** service *m*; *Mil* **to do a t. of duty** servir

(c) (*by orchestra, theatre company etc*) tournée *f*; **during their European t.** *or* **t. of Europe** pendant leur tournée européenne *ou* en Europe; **concert t.** tournée de concerts; **to go on t.** partir en tournée; **to take a play on t.** jouer une pièce en tournée

tour² 1 *vt* (a) (*country*) voyager dans; (*hospital, factory etc*) visiter (b) *Mus, Th* **to t. the provinces** (*of orchestra, company*) faire une tournée en province; (*of play*) passer en province 2 *vi* (a) **we're just touring around** nous ne faisons que visiter la région; **we decided to t. through the Loire Valley** nous avons décidé de visiter la Vallée de la Loire (b) (*of orchestra, theatre company etc*) **we spend most of the year touring** nous passons la plus grande partie de l'année en tournée; **we go touring every summer** nous partons en tournée tous les étés

tour brochure *n* brochure *f ou* catalogue *m* de voyages

tour conductor, tour director *n Am* (*courier*) accompagnateur, -trice

tourer ['tʊərər] *n* (*car*) voiture *f* de tourisme; (*cycle*) vélo *m* de randonnée

tour group *n* groupe *m* (de touristes)

tour guide *n* (*person*) accompagnateur, -trice

touring ['tʊərɪŋ] 1 *n* **to do some t.** faire un circuit 2 *adj* **t. bike** *or* **cycle** vélo *m* de randonnée; **t. car** voiture *f* de tourisme; **t. caravan** caravane *f* de tourisme; *Th* **t. company** troupe *f* en tournée; **we had a t. holiday in the North of Italy** pour nos vacances nous avons visité le Nord de l'Italie; **t. site** (*caravan site*) terrain *m* de caravaning

tourism ['tʊərɪz(ə)m] *n* tourisme *m*

tourism-generated ['tʊərɪz(ə)mdʒenəreɪtɪd] *adj* généré par le tourisme

tourist ['tʊərɪst] *n* touriste *mf*; **t. agency** agence *f ou* bureau *m* de tourisme; **t. area** zone *f* touristique; **t. attraction** attrait *m ou* attraction *f ou* site *m* touristique; **t. centre** centre *m ou* ville *f* touristique; *Av etc* **t. class** classe *f* touriste; **t. enclave** enclave *f* touristique; **t. restaurant/pub** restaurant *m*/pub *m* pour touristes; **t. season** saison *f* touristique; **the t. trade** le tourisme; **t. traffic** trafic *m* touristique; **t. trail** sentier *m* touristique; *F* **t. trap** attrape-touristes *m inv*

tourist board *n* comité *m* du tourisme

tourist destination *n* destination *f* touristique

tourist guide *n* (*book*) guide *m* touristique; (*person*) guide *mf* (touristique)

touristic [tʊə'rɪstɪk] *adj* touristique

tourist industry *n* industrie *f* touristique

tourist information centre *n* syndicat *m* d'initiative, office *m* du tourisme

tourist night *n* nuitée *f*

tourist route *n* itinéraire *m* touristique

touristy ['tʊərɪstɪ] *adj F Pej* (trop) touristique

tour leader, tour manager *n Am* accompagnateur, -trice

tournament ['tʊənəmənt] *n Sp, Hist* tournoi *m*

tourniquet ['tʊənɪkeɪ] *n Med* garrot *m*

tour operator *n* tour opérateur *m*, voyagiste *m*

tour package *n* forfait *m* voyage

tousle ['taʊz(ə)l] *vt* (*sb's hair*) ébouriffer; **tousled hair** cheveux *mpl* ébouriffés

tout¹ [taʊt] *n* (a) (*for hotels*) rabatteur, -euse; (*for shows etc*) racoleur *m*; (*of tickets*) revendeur, -euse de billets (au marché noir) (b) (**racing**) **t.** (*who sells tips*) vendeur, -euse de tuyaux; **according to the touts** d'après les gens qui s'y connaissent

tout² 1 *vi* **to t. for custom** racoler des clients 2 *vt* (*one's services*) offrir; **she had touted her article around all the newspapers** elle avait fait le tour de tous les journaux pour essayer de placer son article; **to t. a product (around)** faire l'article d'un produit; **to t. one's wares** vendre sa marchandise

tow¹ [təʊ] *n* (*act of towing*) **to give sb/sth a t.** remorquer qn/qch; **to take a car in t.** prendre une voiture en remorque; **to be taken in t.** se mettre en remorque; **to be on** *or* **in t.** être en remorque; (*of boat*) être à la traîne; *F* **he always has his family in t.** il trimbale toujours toute sa famille avec lui; *F* **with six assistants in t.** avec six assistants dans son sillage; *Aut* **t. ball** rotule *f* d'attelage; **t. hook** croc *m* de remorque; **t. rope** câble *m* de remorquage; **t. weight** poids *m* remorqué

tow² *vt* (*boat, car*) remorquer; (*barge*) (*from towpath*) haler

tow³ *n* (*fibres*) étoupe *f* (blanche), filasse *f*

▶ **tow away** *vtsep* remorquer, prendre en remorque; (*of police*) emmener à la fourrière; **you'll get towed away** tu vas te retrouver à la fourrière

towage ['təʊɪdʒ] *n* (a) (*act*) remorquage *m* (b) (*charge*) (frais *mpl* de) remorquage *m*

toward [tə'wɔːd, twɔːd] *prep esp Am* = **towards**

towards [tə'wɔːdz, twɔːdz] *prep* (a) (*of direction*) vers; **t. the town** vers la ville, du côté de la ville; **he came t. me** il est venu vers moi; **it's out t. Versailles** c'est du côté de Versailles

(b) (*of time*) vers; **t. evening** vers le soir; **t. the end of his life** vers *ou* sur la fin de sa vie

(c) (*directed at*) (*of feelings, behaviour, attitude*) envers, à l'égard de; **her feelings t. me** ses sentiments envers *ou* pour moi, ses sentiments à mon égard; **they behaved strangely t. us** ils se sont conduits d'une manière étrange envers nous *ou* à notre égard

(d) (*contributing to*) pour; **to save t. the children's education** économiser pour *ou* en vue de l'éducation des enfants; **to contribute (something) t. the cost of ...** participer à l'achat de ...; **would you like to give something t. it?** voulez-vous donner quelque chose?, voulez-vous participer?

towbar ['təʊbɑːr] *n Aut* timon *m* de remorque; (*of glider*) barre *f* de remorquage

towel¹ ['taʊəl] *n* serviette *f* (de toilette); **hand t.** essuie-main(s) *m, pl* essuie-mains; *Fig* **to throw in the t.** jeter l'éponge; **roller t.** essuie-main(s) (*pour rouleau*), serviette sans fin; **tea t.**, *Am* **dish t.** torchon *m* (à vaisselle); **sanitary t.** serviette hygiénique *ou* périodique

towel² *vt* (-ll-, *US* -l-) essuyer *ou* frotter avec une serviette; **to t. oneself (dry)** (*after bath etc*) s'essuyer

towelhead ['taʊəlhed] *n Offensive Sl* (*Arab*) bougnoule *mf*

towelling, *US* **toweling** ['taʊəlɪŋ] *n* (*fabric*) tissu-éponge *m*; **t. robe** peignoir *m* en tissu-éponge

towel rail *n* porte-serviettes *m inv*

tower¹ ['taʊər] *n* (a) *Archit, Constr* tour *f*; **the T. of Babel** la tour de Babel; **the T. of London** la Tour de Londres; **she's a t. of strength** c'est quelqu'un sur qui on peut compter en cas de problème, c'est quelqu'un de solide; **he is a t. of strength in the defence line** (*in football*) c'est le pilier de la défense; **church t.** clocher *m*; **clock t.** tour de l'horloge; *HydE* **water t.** château *m* d'eau; *Av* **control t.** tour de contrôle (b) *Comptr* boîtier *m* vertical, tour *f* (c) (*for camera*) échafaudage *m* pour caméra

tower² *vi* (*climb very high into air*) monter très haut

▶ **tower above, tower over** *vipo* (*be much higher than*) dominer, dépasser de beaucoup, être beaucoup plus grand que; (*in ability*) être bien meilleur que

tower block *n Br* tour *f*

towering ['taʊərɪŋ] *adj* (*building, cliff etc*) très haut, très grand; (*person*) très grand; (*ambitions*) sans bornes; **a t. great figure of a man** un géant; **in a t. rage** au paroxysme de la colère

tower system *n Comptr* système *m* à boîtier vertical, système *m* à tour

towheaded ['təʊhedɪd] *adj* aux cheveux (blond) filasse

towing rod ['təʊɪŋ] *n* barre *f* de remorquage

towing rope *n* câble *m* de remorquage

towing weight *n* charge *f* remorquable

towline ['təʊlaɪn] *n* (câble *m* de) remorque *f*

town [taʊn] *n* (a) ville *f*; **fortified t.** place *f* forte; **the whole t. is talking about it** toute la ville en parle; **to go out on the t.** faire la bombe *ou* la noce; **t. clerk** secrétaire *mf* de mairie, secrétaire de municipalité; **t. house** (*house in town*) maison *f* de ville; (*town residence*) résidence *f* en ville; **t. house hotel** grande maison *f* en ville aménagée en hôtel; **t. life** vie *f* urbaine

(b) (*without article*) **to go into t.** aller *ou* se rendre à la *ou* en ville; **she's in t. shopping** elle est en train de faire ses courses en ville; **he's out of t.** il est à la campagne *ou* en voyage; **the best pizzas in t.** les meilleures pizzas de la ville; **man about t.** mondain *m*; *Fig F* **to go to t.** (*make great effort*) se mettre en quatre; *Fig F* **they really went to t.** (*on redecoration, doing a job etc*) ils ont vraiment mis le paquet; (*preparing a party etc*) ils ont vraiment fait les choses en grand; *Fig F* **I really went to t. on the third question** je me suis vraiment foulé pour la troisième question; *Fig F* **no need to go to t. on it** ce n'est pas la peine de trop se fatiguer; **to live in T.** (*in London*) habiter Londres

town and gown *n Univ* les habitants *mpl* de la ville et les étudiants *mpl*

town centre *n* centre *m* de la ville, centre(-)ville *m*

town council *n* conseil *m* municipal

townee, townie ['taʊnɪ] *n F* habitant, -ante de la ville

town hall *n* hôtel *m* de ville, mairie *f*

town planner *n* urbaniste *mf*

town planning *n* urbanisme *m*

townsfolk ['taʊnzfəʊk] *npl* habitants *mpl ou* gens *mpl* de la ville/des villes, citadins *mpl*

township [ˈtaʊnʃɪp] *n* **(a)** (*small town*) commune *f*, bourg *m* **(b)** *Admin Am* municipalité *f*, *Can* canton *m*; *US* (*in New England*) commune *f* **(c)** (*in S Africa*) banlieue *f* noire
townsman, *pl* **-men** [ˈtaʊnzmən] *n* habitant *m* de la ville, citadin *m*
townspeople [ˈtaʊnzpiːp(ə)l] *npl* habitants *mpl ou* gens *mpl* de la ville/des villes, citadins *mpl*
townswoman, *pl* **-women** [ˈtaʊnzwʊmən, -wɪmɪn] *n* habitante *f* de la ville, citadine *f*
towpath [ˈtəʊpɑːθ] *n* chemin *m* de halage
towrope [ˈtəʊrəʊp] *n* (câble *m* de) remorque *f*
tow-start[1] *n* **to give sb a t.** démarrer qn en remorque
tow-start[2] *vt* démarrer en remorque
tow truck *n Am* dépanneuse *f*
toxaemia, *Am* **toxemia** [tɒkˈsiːmɪə] *n Med* toxémie *f*
toxic [ˈtɒksɪk] *adj* (*substance, waste etc*) toxique; *Med* **t. shock syndrome** syndrome *m* de choc septique
toxicologic(al) [tɒksɪkəˈlɒdʒɪk, -ɪk(ə)l] *adj Med* toxicologique
toxicologist [tɒksɪˈkɒlədʒɪst] *n Med* toxicologue *mf*
toxicology [tɒksɪˈkɒlədʒɪ] *n Med* toxicologie *f*
toxin [ˈtɒksɪn] *n Bio, Ch* toxine *f*
toy [tɔɪ] *n* jouet *m*; **he's like a child with a new t.** il est comme un enfant avec un nouveau jouet; **t. dog** (*animal*) chien *m* de manchon, bichon *m*; **t. poodle** (*animal*) caniche *m* nain; **t. soldier** soldat *m* de plastique/de plomb; **t. trumpet** trompette *f* d'enfant
▶ **toy with** *vipo* (*play with*) jouer avec; **to t. with one's food** jouer avec sa nourriture; **to t. with an idea** caresser une idée; **to t. with sb** s'amuser avec qn; **to t. with sb's affections** jouer avec le cœur de qn
toy boy *n F* jeune amant *m* (*d'une femme plus âgée*); **she's got herself a t.** elle s'est déniché un petit jeune *ou* un jeune amant
toy shop *n* magasin *m* de jouets
tpi *Comptr* (*abbr* **tracks per inch**) pistes *fpl* par pouce
trace[1] [treɪs] *n* **(a)** (*vestige*) trace *f*, vestige *m*; **they could find no t. of him** ils n'ont retrouvé aucune trace de lui; **there's not a t. of it** (*there's nothing left of it*) il n'en reste pas trace; **there's not a t. of your wallet anywhere in the house** ton portefeuille n'est nulle part dans la maison; **he has disappeared without t.** il a disparu sans laisser de trace; **the last remaining traces of an ancient civilization** les derniers vestiges d'une civilisation ancienne
(b) (*small amount*) trace *f*, quantité *f* infime; (*of irony, sarcasm*) soupçon *m*; **traces of cyanide/poison** des traces de cyanure/poison; **he said with a t. of amusement** dit-il, l'air légèrement amusé; **there was the t. of a smile on her face** il y avait l'ombre d'un sourire sur son visage; *Ch* **t. element** oligo-élément *m*, *pl* oligo-éléments
trace[2] *vt* **(a)** (*outline*) (*plan, scheme etc*) exposer **(b)** (*draw*) (*plan, diagram*) tracer, faire le tracé de; (*copy*) (*drawing*) calquer; **to t. sth in the sand/dirt with a stick** dessiner qch dans le sable/la poussière avec un bâton **(c)** (*follow tracks of*) (*person, animal*) suivre la trace *ou* la piste de; (*locate*) (*lost property*) recouvrer; (*influence etc*) retracer, retrouver; **they traced him as far as Paris** *or* **to Paris** on a suivi sa piste jusqu'à Paris; **to t. the evil to its source** remonter à la source du mal
▶ **trace back** *vtsep* (*uncover origins of*) **to t. sth back to its source** remonter jusqu'à l'origine de qch; **to t. one's family back to William the Conqueror** faire remonter son arbre généalogique jusqu'à Guillaume le Conquérant
▶ **trace out** *vtsep* = **trace[2] (a)**
trace[3] *n* (*part of harness*) trait *m*; **in the traces** attelé; *Fig* **to kick over the traces** (*of person*) (*rebel*) ruer dans les brancards; (*break free*) s'émanciper
tracer [ˈtreɪsər] *n Mil etc* **t. bullet** (balle) traçante *f*; **t. shell** traçant *m*
tracery [ˈtreɪsərɪ] *n* **(a)** *Archit* (*of rose window*) réseau *m*, remplage *m* **(b)** (*of leaf etc*) nervures *fpl*
trachea, *pl* **-eae** [trəˈkiːə, -iːiː] *n Anat* trachée *f*
tracheal [trəˈkiːəl] *adj Anat* trachéal
tracheostomy [trækɪˈɒstəmɪ] *n Surg* trachéotomie *f*
tracheotomy [trækɪˈɒtəmɪ] *n Surg* trachéotomie *f*
trachoma [trəˈkəʊmə] *n Med* trachome *m*
tracing [ˈtreɪsɪŋ] *n* (*copy*) calque *m*; **t. paper** papier-calque *m*
track[1] [træk] *n* **(a)** (*marks left*) (*of animal*) trace(s) *f(pl)*, piste *f*, foulées *fpl*; (*of person*) trace(s), piste; (*of wheel*) sillon *m*; **to follow in sb's tracks** suivre la voie tracée par qn; **to be on sb's t.** être sur la piste de qn; **to throw sb off the t.** dépister qn, *F* semer qn; *Fig F* **to be off the t.** divaguer; **to be on the right t.** être sur la (bonne) voie; *Fig* **to be on the wrong t.** (*in search, guess etc*) se fourvoyer, être sur la mauvaise piste; **to keep t. of sb/sth** suivre les progrès de qn/qch; **I've lost t. of her** je l'ai perdue de vue; **I've lost t. of all the times I've** … je ne compte plus les fois où j'ai …; *F* **to make tracks** (*leave*) partir, filer; **to stop in one's tracks** s'arrêter net; **to stop sb in his/her tracks** arrêter qn net
(b) (*path*) piste *f*, chemin *m*, sentier *m*; *Rail* voie *f* (ferrée); (*for running*) piste; **cycle t.** piste cyclable; *Sp* **(running) t.** piste; **the train left the t.** le train a déraillé; *Sp* **t. and field events** épreuves *fpl* d'athlétisme; *Rail* **single-t./double-t. line** ligne *f* à une voie/à deux voies
(c) (*in recording process, on disk*) piste *f*; (*song*) (*on record, CD etc*) morceau *m*; **sound t.** piste sonore; *Comptr* **tracks per inch** pistes par pouce
(d) (*of tracked vehicle*) chenille *f*; **t./half-t. vehicle** véhicule *m* chenillé/semi-chenillé
(e) (*distance between wheels*) écartement *m* des roues, voie *f*
track[2] **1** *vt* (*animal, thief etc*) suivre à la piste, pister; (*fugitive*) traquer; (*missile*) suivre la trajectoire de **2** *vi* (*of gear wheels etc*) être en alignement; (*of camera*) faire un travelling; **the band of rain that is tracking across the country** le front de pluie qui se déplace à travers le pays
▶ **track down** *vtsep* (*discover*) (*criminal, prey etc*) dépister; (*information*) découvrir; (*missing object*) retrouver; **they tracked her down to her hide-out** ils ont remonté sa trace *ou* sa piste jusqu'à sa cachette
track arm *n Aut* bras *m* de direction
trackball [ˈtrækbɔːl] *n Comptr* boule *f* de commande, trackball *m ou f*
tracked [trækt] *adj* (*vehicle*) chenillé
tracker [ˈtrækər] *n* **(a)** (*of game*) traqueur *m*; **t. dog** chien *m* policier **(b)** *TV* machiniste *m* de travelling
track event *n Sp* épreuve *f* sur piste
tracking [ˈtrækɪŋ] *n Cin* **t. shot** travelling *m* en poursuite; *Astronaut etc* **t. station** station *f* de dépistage; **t. systems** systèmes *mpl* de repérage et poursuite
tracking down *n* (*of criminal, cause etc*) dépistage *m*
tracklayer [ˈtrækleɪər] *n Rail* (*person*) poseur *m* de voie
tracklaying [ˈtrækleɪɪŋ] *n Rail* **t. vehicle** véhicule *m* à chenilles
trackless [ˈtræklɪs] *adj* **(a)** (*place*) sans chemins, sans sentiers **(b)** *Am* **t. trolley** trolleybus *m*
track racing *n Sp* courses *fpl* de *ou* sur piste
track record *n* (*record time*) (*of racehorse, car*) record *m* de la piste; *Fig* (*of person, company*) antécédents *mpl*; **he doesn't have a very good t. for punctuality** il n'est pas réputé pour sa ponctualité; **in view of his t. of getting home late every Friday night** … vu l'habitude qu'il a de rentrer tard tous les vendredis soirs …; **a company with a good/poor t. in winning export orders** une entreprise avec un bon/mauvais palmarès sur le plan des commandes à l'exportation; **no wonder the insurance is high with your t.!** pas étonnant que l'assurance soit chère avec ton palmarès!; **given the government's t. in the field of cutting benefits** vu les antécédents du gouvernement en matière de réduction des prestations sociales
track rod *n Aut* biellette *f* de direction, barre *f* d'accouplement, bielle *f* de connexion
track shoes *npl Sp* chaussures *fpl* de course
tracksuit [ˈtræks(j)uːt] *n Sp* survêtement *m*
tract[1] [trækt] *n* **(a)** (*of land*) étendue *f* **(b)** *Anat* (*respiratory, digestive*) appareil *m*
tract[2] *n* (*pamphlet*) brochure *f*, tract *m*
tractable [ˈtræktəb(ə)l] *adj* (*person, character*) docile; (*material*) facile à ouvrer; **a t. problem** un problème que l'on peut résoudre
traction [ˈtrækʃən] *n* **(a)** *Tech* traction *f*, tirage *m*; **t. cable** câble *m* tracteur; *Aut* **t. control** contrôle *m* de traction; **t. engine** locomobile *f*; **t. wheels** (*of engine etc*) roues *fpl* motrices **(b)** *Med* traction *f*; **in t.** en traction
tractive [ˈtræktɪv] *adj* tractif; (*force*) de traction
tractor [ˈtræktər] *n* **(a)** (*vehicle*) tracteur *m*; (*of lorry*) tracteur routier; **t.-drawn** tracté; **t. driver** conducteur, -trice de tracteur; **(b)** *Comptr* **t. feed** (*device*) dispositif *m* d'alimentation par entraînement; (*facility*) alimentation *f* par entraînement; **t. holes** (*on tractor wheel*) trous *mpl* à ergots; **t. pin** (*in tractor wheel*) ergot *m* de tracteur; **t. wheel** (*on printer etc*) roue *f* d'entraînement
trad [træd] *n Br Mus F* jazz *m* traditionnel
tradable [ˈtreɪdəb(ə)l] *adj* négociable
trade[1] [treɪd] *n* **(a)** (*commerce*) commerce *m*, affaires *fpl*, négoce *m*, échanges *mpl* commerciaux; *Am* (*commercial transaction*) transaction *f* (commerciale); (*swap*) échange *m*; **to do a t.** faire un échange; **(illicit) t.** trafic *m*; **to be in t.** être dans le commerce; **wholesale/retail t.** commerce de gros/de détail; **balance of t.** balance *f* commerciale; **the tea t.** le commerce du thé; **the t. in animal skins** le commerce des

peaux; **it's good for t.** cela fait marcher le commerce; **we don't get much t. nowadays** les affaires ne marchent pas très bien ces temps-ci; **she's doing a roaring t.** elle fait des affaires en or; **t. agreement** accord *m* commercial; **t. ban** interdiction *f* de commerce; **t. bloc** union *f* douanière; **t. centre** place *f* commerciale; **t. exhibition** exposition *f* commerciale; **t. mission** mission *f* commerciale; **t. policy** politique *f* commerciale; *St Exch* **t. price** prix *m* de négociation; **t. register** Registre *m* du Commerce; **t. route** route *f* commerciale; **t. tribunal** tribunal *m* de commerce; **he's t.** (*not old money*) c'est un nouveau-riche

(**b**) (*profession*) métier *m*; (*as a body*) (corps *m* de) métier; **to be in the t.** être du métier; **to follow** *or* **carry on a t.** exercer un métier; **to learn a t.** apprendre un métier; **he's a plumber by t.** il est plombier de son état *ou* métier; **everyone to his t.** chacun son métier; **it's what we in the t. call a ...** c'est ce que, dans le métier, on appelle un ...; **the building t.** le bâtiment; **the publishing t.** l'édition *f*; **the printing t.** l'imprimerie *f*; **t. advertising** publicité *f* auprès des intermédiaires; **t. allowance** remise *f* entre professionnels; **t. body** syndicat *m* professionnel; **t. journal** journal *m* professionnel, revue *f* professionnelle; *Br Aut* **t. plate** plaque *f* d'immatriculation provisoire; **t. press** presse *f* spécialisée, presse professionnelle; **t. promotion** promotion *f* auprès des intermédiaires; **t. publication** revue *f* spécialisée *ou* professionnelle; **t. references** références *fpl* commerciales

trade² **1** *vi* (**a**) faire du commerce, commercer, faire le commerce *ou* le négoce (**in sth** de qch; **with sb** avec qn); **the company trades under the name of ...** l'entreprise opère sous le nom de ...; **he trades from a small stall in the market** il tient un petit étal au marché (**b**) *Am* (*to shop*) se ravitailler (**at, with** chez) (**c**) *St Exch* (*of shares*) s'échanger (**at** à) **2** *vt* (**a**) **to t. sth for sth** échanger *ou* troquer qch contre qch; **to t. places with sb** changer de place avec qn; **to t. insults/blows** échanger des insultes/coups (**b**) *St Exch* négocier

▶ **trade down** *vi* (**a**) *St Exch* acheter des valeurs basses (**b**) (*of car, home owner etc*) changer pour un modèle/un appartement/*etc* moins cher

▶ **trade in** *vtsep* (*give in part exchange*) (*car etc*) donner en reprise

▶ **trade off** *vtsep* **they have traded off quality against speed** ils ont fait primer la rapidité sur la qualité; **you can't ask me to t. off reputation against profit** vous ne pouvez pas me demander de choisir entre ma réputation et un profit; **you have to t. one thing off against another** il faut faire des choix

▶ **trade on** *vipo* (*exploit*) (*sb's ignorance*) exploiter, tirer profit de

▶ **trade up** *vi* (**a**) *St Exch* acheter des valeurs hautes (**b**) (*of car, home owner etc*) changer pour un modèle/un appartement/*etc* plus cher

tradeable ['treɪdəb(ə)l] *adj St Exch* négociable

trade association *n* association *f* professionnelle, groupement *m* professionnel, corps *m* de métier

trade barriers *npl* barrières *fpl* douanières

trade cycle *n* cycle *m* économique

trade debtor *n Acct* compte *m ou* créance *f* client

Trade Descriptions Act *n Br* ≈ loi *f* sur la publicité mensongère

trade directory *n* annuaire *m* de commerce

trade discount *n* remise *f* commerciale, escompte *m* commercial *ou* professionnel

traded option ['treɪdɪd] *n St Exch* option *f* négociable

trade embargo *n* embargo *m* commercial

trade fair *n* foire *f ou* exposition *f* commerciale, salon *m* professionnel

trade gap *n* déficit *m*

trade-in *n* objet *m* donné en reprise; **will you take my old car as a t.?** est-ce que vous reprendrez ma vieille voiture?; **what's its t. value?** quelle est sa valeur de reprise?; **t. allowance** valeur *f* de reprise; **t. facility** facilité *f* de reprise

trademark ['treɪdmɑːk] *n* marque *f* (de fabrique), marque de commerce; *Fig* **these close-up shots are her t.** ces gros-plans sont sa marque *ou* sa signature; **t. registration** dépôt *m* de marque

trade name *n* (*of product*) appellation *f* commerciale; (*of firm*) raison *f* commerciale

trade-off *n* (**a**) (*compromise*) compromis *m*; **you're going to have a t. between speed and quality** si l'on va plus vite, ce sera au détriment de la qualité; **we do not believe there is a t. between ... and ...** nous ne croyons pas qu'il y ait incompatibilité entre ... et ... (**b**) *esp Am* (*exchange*) échange *m*

trader ['treɪdər] *n* (**a**) (*person*) négociant, -ante, commerçant, -ante, marchand, -ande; *St Exch* opérateur *m*, spéculateur *m* (**b**) (*ship*) navire *m* marchand

trades [treɪdz] *npl* (*winds*) (vents *mpl*) alizés *mpl*

trade secret *n* secret *m* de fabrication

trade show *n* salon *m* professionnel, foire *f* commerciale

tradesman, *pl* **-men** ['treɪdzmən] *n* marchand *m*, fournisseur *m*; **tradesmen's entrance** entrée *f* des fournisseurs

trade union *n* syndicat *m* (ouvrier); **she's very active in the t.** c'est une syndicaliste militante; **t. council** conseil *m* syndical; **t. member** syndiqué *m*

trade unionism *n* syndicalisme *m* (ouvrier)

trade unionist *n* (ouvrier, -ière) syndiqué(e)

trade wind *n* (vent *m*) alizé *m*

trading ['treɪdɪŋ] *n* commerce *m*, négoce *m*; **France is our most important t. partner** la France est notre principal partenaire commercial; *Acct* **t. and profit and loss account** compte *m* de résultat; *St Exch* **t. day** jour *m* de Bourse; *Br Com, Ind* **t. estate** zone *f* industrielle; **t. hours** *Fin* heures *fpl* d'ouverture; *St Exch* horaires *fpl* des criées; *St Exch* **t. instrument** outil *m* de spéculation; **t. loss** perte *f*; *St Exch* **t. member** intermédiaire *m* négociateur; *St Exch* **t. month** mois *m* d'échéance; *St Exch* **t. order** ordre *m* de négociation; **t. partners** partenaires *mpl* commerciaux; **t. results** résultats *mpl* de l'exercice; *St Exch* **t. session** séance *f* boursière; **t. stamp** timbre-prime *m*, *pl* timbres-prime(s)

trading account *n Acct* compte *m* d'exploitation générale

trading company *n* société *f* commerciale

trading floor *n St Exch* parquet *m*, corbeille *f*

trading licence *n* carte *f* de commerce

trading post *n Hist* comptoir *m*, établissement *m* (*aux Indes, au Canada etc*)

trading year *n* année *m* d'exploitations, exercice *m* (financier)

tradition [trəˈdɪʃən] *n* tradition *f*; **t. has it that ...** selon la tradition ...; **it has become a t.** c'est passé dans la tradition; **the t. is to ...** la tradition veut que l'on ... + *sub*

traditional [trəˈdɪʃənəl] *adj* traditionnel

traditionalism [trəˈdɪʃənəlɪz(ə)m] *n* traditionalisme *m*

traditionalist [trəˈdɪʃənəlɪst] *adj, n* traditionaliste *mf*

traditionally [trəˈdɪʃənəlɪ] *adv* traditionnellement

traduce [trəˈdjuːs] *vt Fml, Lit* calomnier, diffamer

traffic ['træfɪk] *n* (**a**) circulation *f*, trafic *m*; **heavy t.** circulation intense; **ocean t.** navigation *f* au long cours; **road t.** circulation routière; **rail(way) t.** trafic ferroviaire; **through t.** circulation directe; **southbound t. should avoid ...** les conducteurs se dirigeant vers le sud ont intérêt à éviter ...; **t. news** sécurité *f* routière; **t. pollution** pollution *f* automobile; *Rad* **t. programme** informations *fpl* routières; **t. regulations** règlements *mpl* sur la circulation; **t. sign** panneau *m* de signalisation (routière), signal *m* routier

(**b**) (*movement of people*) passage *m*; (*on telephone network*) volume *m* de communications

(**c**) *Pej* (*trade*) trafic *m*

traffic² *vti* (*pt, pp* **trafficked** ['træfɪkt]) *Pej* trafiquer (**in** de); *Fig* **reporters who t. in human misery** journalistes qui exploitent la misère humaine

trafficator ['træfɪkeɪtər] *n Old-fashioned Br Aut* flèche *f* de direction

traffic builder *n Mktg* article *m* d'appel

traffic calming *n* ralentissement *m* de la circulation

traffic circle *n Am* sens *m* giratoire

traffic cone *n* cône *m* de signalisation (pour la circulation routière)

traffic control *n* régulation *f* de la circulation

traffic cop *n F* flic *m*

traffic island *n* refuge *m*

traffic jam *n* embouteillage *m*, encombrement *m*, bouchon *m*

trafficker ['træfɪkər] *n Pej* trafiquant, -ante (**in** de, en); **drug t.** trafiquant de drogue

traffic lights *npl, US* **traffic light** *n* feux *mpl* (tricolores), feux de signalisation (routière); **at the next t.** au(x) prochain(s) feu(x)

traffic offence *n* infraction *f* au code de la route

traffic patrol *n* patrouille *f* de la circulation (routière)

traffic police *n* (*in town*) police *f* de la route

traffic policeman *n* (*in town*) agent *m* de la circulation

traffic signals *npl* = **traffic lights**

traffic warden *n Br* contractuel, -elle

tragedian [trəˈdʒiːdɪən] *n* (*dramatist*) auteur *m* tragique; (*actor*) tragédien *m*

tragedienne [trədʒiːdɪˈen] *n* (*actress*) tragédienne *f*

tragedy ['trædʒɪdɪ] *n* (*accident, disaster*), *Th* tragédie *f*; **to make a t. out of sth** prendre qch au tragique; **the t. of his death** sa mort tragique; **it will be a t. if ...** ce serait une tragédie *ou* un drame si …; **the real t. was that …** ce qu'il y avait de vraiment tragique, c'était que …

tragic ['trædʒɪk] *adj* tragique; **t. actor/actress** tragédien *m*/tragédienne *f*; *F* **to put on a t. act** jouer la comédie pour se faire plaindre; **the t. side of the story is that …** ce que cette histoire a de tragique c'est que …; *Iron* **how t. for you!** c'est bête ce qui t'arrive!; **t. dad in rescue bid** (*newspaper headline*) un père tente un sauvetage désespéré

tragically ['trædʒɪklɪ] *adv* tragiquement; **he died at a t. early age** c'est tragique qu'il soit mort si jeune

tragicomedy [trædʒɪ'kɒmɪdɪ] *n* tragi-comédie *f*, *pl* tragi-comédies

tragicomic(al) [trædʒɪ'kɒmɪk, -ɪk(ə)l] *adj* tragi-comique

trail[1] [treɪl] *n* **(a)** (*of blood*) traînée *f*; (*of smoke*) panache *m*; (*of meteor*) queue *f*; *Mil* (*of gun carriage*) flèche *f*, crosse *f*; **a t. of broken promises** une série de promesses non tenues

(b) (*marks left*) (*of animal, person*) piste *f*, trace *f*; (*of snail*) trace; **to pick up the t.** (*of hounds*) retrouver la trace; **false t.** fausse piste; **to be on the t. of sb** être sur la piste de qn; **the criminals left with the police hot on their t.** les criminels sont partis avec la police sur leurs talons; **the t. was cold by then** la piste était déjà froide; **to leave a t. of destruction** tout détruire sur son passage

(c) (*path*) sentier *m* (battu); (*in forest, cross-country skiing*) piste *f*

trail[2] **1** *vt* **(a)** (*pull*) (*sth*) traîner après soi; (*of car etc*) (*caravan etc*) remorquer; *Fig* **to t. one's coat** se montrer délibérément provocateur **(b)** (*track*) (*animal, criminal*) traquer, pister, suivre à la piste; (*of crook*) (*victim*) suivre, filer **(c)** *Cin, TV* annoncer **2** *vi* **(a)** (*drag*) traîner; **your skirt is trailing (on the ground)** votre jupe traîne (par terre) **(b)** (*move slowly*) avancer lentement **(c)** (*of plant*) grimper, ramper **(d) to be trailing** (*be last*) être à la traîne; **our team is trailing at the bottom of the league** notre équipe se traîne en fin de classement

▶ **trail away** *vi* **his voice trailed away in embarrassment** il se tut, gêné; **her voice trailed away in the distance** sa voix se perdit dans le lointain

▶ **trail behind** *vi* **(a)** (*linger*) traîner derrière (les autres), être à la traîne; *Fig* (*of team etc*) être en retard sur les autres **(b)** (*be towed*) se faire remorquer, être en remorque; **with a boat trailing behind** avec un bateau en remorque

▶ **trail off** *vi* (*of voice*) diminuer jusqu'à s'éteindre; **her voice trails off** sa voix diminue jusqu'à devenir inaudible; **his voice trailed off in mid-sentence** il s'interrompit au milieu de sa phrase

trail bike *n* moto *f* de cross

trailblazer ['treɪlbleɪzər] *n* pionnier, -ière

trailblazing ['treɪlbleɪzɪŋ] *adj* (*work*) de pionnier; (*discovery*) qui ouvre la voie

trailer ['treɪlər] *n* **(a)** *Aut etc* (*behind vehicle*) remorque *f*; *Am* (*towed*) caravane *f*; (*mobile home*) camping-car *m*; *Aut* **t. hitch** fourche *f* d'attelage; **t. park** terrain *m* aménagé pour les caravanes/camping-cars **(b)** *Cin, TV* bande-annonce *f*, *pl* bandes-annonces (**for** de)

trailing ['treɪlɪŋ] *adj* **(a)** (*skirt etc*) traînant **(b)** (*plant*) grimpant, rampant **(c)** *Aut* **t. arm** bras *m* tiré; *Aut* **t. brake shoe** segment *m* de frein secondaire; *Aut* **t. shoe** segment *m* secondaire; *Av* **t. edge** (*of wing*) bord *m* de fuite **(d)** *Comptr* **t. spaces** espaces *fpl* à droite; **t. zeroes** zéros *mpl* à droite **(e)** *Mktg* **t. firm** entreprise *f* à la traîne

trail mix *n* (*dried fruit & nuts*) fruits *mpl* secs

trail net *n Fishing* traîne *m*, chalut *m*, traîneau *m*

train[1] [treɪn] *n* **(a)** *Rail* train *m*; (*underground*) rame *f*; **passenger/goods t.** train de voyageurs/de marchandises; **express train** train express; **slow** *or* **stopping t.** train omnibus; **relief t.** train supplémentaire; **the 5 o'clock t.** le train de 5 heures; **the Cardiff t., the t. to Cardiff** le train de Cardiff; **she wasn't on the t.** elle n'était pas dans le train; **by t.** (*to travel*) par *ou* en chemin de fer, en train; **to the trains** (*on sign*) accès aux quais; **t. journey** voyage *m* en *ou* par chemin de fer, voyage en train

(b) (*of carriages, barges*) train *m*, convoi *m*; (*of events, circumstances*) succession *f*, série *f*, enchaînement *m*; *Min* traînée *f* (de poudre); **t. of thought** enchaînement d'idées; **to set** *or* **put sth in t.** mettre qch en route

(c) *Tech* (*system of gears*) système *m* d'engrenages

(d) (*retinue*) (*of prince etc*) suite *f*, cortège *m*, équipage *m*; *Mil* équipage, train *m*; **the evils that follow in the t. of war** les maux que la guerre engendre

(e) (*of dress*) traîne *f*, queue *f*; (*of peacock*) queue

train[2] **1** *vt* **(a)** (*person*) former, instruire; (*animal*) dresser; (*character, mind*) former; (*ear*) exercer; *Sp* (*runner, racehorse etc*) entraîner; **he was trained at the Academy of Dramatic Art** il sort de l'Académie des Arts Dramatiques; **to t. sb for sth/to do sth** exercer qn à qch/à faire qch; **to t. sb in the use of a machine/weapon** apprendre à qn à se servir d'une machine/d'une arme; **to t. oneself to do sth** s'exercer à faire qch

(b) (*in horticulture*) (*fruit tree, vine*) palisser, mettre en espalier

(c) (*direct*) (*telescope, spotlight etc*) braquer, diriger (**on** sur); *Mil* (*gun*) pointer; *Naut* (*gun*) orienter, diriger

2 *vi* s'exercer; *Mil* faire l'exercice; *Sp* s'entraîner; **to t. for sth** s'exercer *ou* se préparer à qch; **to t. as a typist** suivre des cours de dactylographie; **she trained as a typist** elle est dactylographe de formation; **to t. as a ballet dancer** suivre une formation de danseur de ballet

▶ **train up** *vtsep* (*employees*) donner une formation complémentaire à

train bearer *n* demoiselle *f*/garçon *m* d'honneur

trained [treɪnd] *adj* (*person, worker etc*) formé; (*chien etc*) dressé; (*eye*) exercé; *Sp* entraîné; **highly/poorly t.** très bien/peu entraîné; **t. nurse** infirmière *f* diplômée; *Hum* **her husband is very well t.** (*does as he's told*) son mari est très bien dressé

trainee [treɪ'niː] *n* stagiaire *mf*; **t. manager, management t.** stagiaire de direction

trainer ['treɪnər] *n* **(a)** (*person*) (*of animals*) dresseur *m*; *Sp, Horseracing* (*of athletes, football team, racehorses*) entraîneur *m*; (*for job*) formateur *m*; *US Mil* pointeur *m* **(b)** *Av* **t.** (**aircraft**) avion-école *f*, *pl* avions-écoles **(c) trainers** (*shoes*) chaussures *fpl* de sport

training ['treɪnɪŋ] *n* **(a)** (*of person*) formation *f*; *Sp* entraînement *m*; (*of animal*) dressage *m*; **physical t.** éducation *f* physique; **vocational t.** formation professionnelle; **I'm a historian by t.** je suis historien de formation; *Fig* **it's good t. for when you're a parent** ça vous prépare pour quand vous aurez des enfants; *Mil* **military t.** instruction *f* militaire; *Sp* **to go into t.** s'entraîner; **to be in t.** (*being trained*) être à l'entraînement; (*fit*) être bien entraîné; **to be out of t.** ne plus être en forme; **t. contract** contrat *m* d'apprentissage; **t. period** stage *m*, stage de formation; **t. programme** programme *m* de formation; **t. scheme** plan *m* de formation; **t. session** entraînement *m*

(b) (*in horticulture*) (*of plant, fruit tree*) palissage *m*; *Mil* (*of gun*) orientation *f*

training base *n Mil* base *f* école

training centre *n* centre *m* de formation

training college *n* école *f* (de formation) professionnelle

training course *n* stage *m* (de formation professionnelle)

training manual *n* manuel *m* d'utilisation

training ship *n* navire-école *m*, *pl* navires-écoles

trainload ['treɪnləʊd] *n* **t. of coal** train *m* chargé de houille; **t. of tourists** plein train de touristes; **they were arriving by the t.** ils arrivaient par trains entiers

train-spotter *n* = personne *f* dont le passe-temps est de repérer les numéros des trains; *Fig Sl* **he's a bit of a t., is Derek** il est vraiment rasoir, ce Derek

trainspotting ['treɪnspɒtɪŋ] *n* = activité *f* consistant à repérer et répertorier les numéros des trains

train station *n* gare *f* de chemin de fer

traipse [treɪps] *vi F* **to t. through the streets** battre le pavé; **to t. around** traîner ça et là; **to t. around the shops** traîner dans les magasins; **we had to t. all the way back to …** il a fallu qu'on se retape tout le trajet jusqu'à …

trait [treɪt] *n* (*of character etc*) trait *m*

traitor ['treɪtər] *n* traître *m* (**to** à); **to turn t.** passer à l'ennemi, se vendre (à l'ennemi)

traitorous ['treɪt(ə)rəs] *adj* traître, *f* traîtresse, fourbe, perfide

traitorously ['treɪt(ə)rəslɪ] *adv* traîtreusement

traitress ['treɪtrɪs] *n Old-fashioned* traîtresse *f*

trajectory [trə'dʒekt(ə)rɪ] *n* trajectoire *f*; *Fig* (*of company*) itinéraire *m*

TRAM [træm] *n* (*abbr* **transputer module**) module *m* de transputer

tram [træm] *n Br* (*vehicle*) tramway *m*; **to go by t.** aller en tramway; **t. driver** conducteur *m* de tramway

tramcar ['træmkɑːr] *n Old-fashioned Br* tramway *m*

tramline ['træmlaɪn] *n* **(a)** (*route*) ligne *f* de tramways **(b) tramlines** (*track*) voie *f* de tramway; *Tennis* couloir *m*

trammel[1] ['træm(ə)l] *n Lit* **the trammels of routine** *etc* les entraves *fpl* de la routine *etc*

trammel[2] *vt* (**-ll-**, *US* **-l-**) *Lit* entraver, empêtrer; **trammelled by prejudices** entravé par les préjugés

tramp[1] [træmp] *n* **(a)** (*vagabond*) chemineau *m*, vagabond, -onde, clochard, -arde **(b)** *Naut* **t. steamer** tramp *m* **(c)** (*sound*) bruit *m* de pas marqués; **I heard the (heavy) t. of the guard** j'ai entendu le pas lourd du gardien **(d)** (*walk*) promenade *f* à pied **(e)** *esp Am F, Pej* (*loose woman*) traînée *f*

tramp² **1** *vi* **(a)** (*walk heavily*) marcher lourdement; **to t. on sth** piétiner *ou* écraser qch; **I wish you'd stop tramping on my foot!** j'aimerais bien que tu arrêtes de m'écraser le pied **(b)** (*travel on foot*) se promener *ou* voyager à pied; **to t. wearily along** suivre péniblement son chemin **2** *vt* **to t. the streets** battre le pavé; **to t. the country** parcourir le pays à pied

tramp³ *n Aut* (*of wheels*) rebondissement *m*, martèlement *m*

trample ['træmp(ə)l] **1** *vi* **to t. on sth/sb** piétiner *ou* écraser qch/qn; **to t. on sb's feelings** fouler aux pieds les susceptibilités de qn **2** *vt* (*ground*) piétiner; **to t. sb/sth underfoot** piétiner qn/qch, fouler qn/qch aux pieds; *Fig* fouler qn/qch aux pieds; **to t. down the grass** fouler l'herbe; **the child was trampled to death (by the crowd)** l'enfant est mort piétiné (par la foule)

trampoline¹ ['træmpəli:n] *n Gym etc* trampoline *m*

trampoline² *vi* faire du trampoline

tramway ['træmweɪ] *n* rails *mpl* de tramway; (*system*) réseau *m* de tramway

trance [trɑ:ns] *n Med* (*catalepsy*) catalepsie *f*; **(hypnotic) t.** transe *f*, hypnose *f*; **to send** *or* **put sb into a t.** hypnotiser qn, mettre qn en transe; **to go into a t. (state)** (*in spiritualism etc*) se mettre en transe; **he's been wandering around in a t. ever since ...** il erre en transe *ou* dans un état de transe depuis que ...

tranny ['trænɪ] *n* **(a)** *esp Br F* (*transistor radio*) transistor *m* **(b)** (*transparency*) diapositive *f*

tranquil ['træŋkwɪl] *adj* tranquille, serein, calme

tranquillity, *US also* **tranquility** [træŋ'kwɪlɪtɪ] *n* tranquillité *f*, calme *m*, sérénité *f*

tranquillize, *US* **tranquilize** ['træŋkwɪlaɪz] *vt* (*sb, state of mind etc*) tranquilliser, calmer, apaiser; (*animal*) anesthésier

tranquillizer, *US* **tranquilizer** ['træŋkwɪlaɪzər] *n Med etc* tranquillisant *m*, calmant *m*; **to be on tranquillizers** être sous calmants

transact [træn'zækt] *vt* **to t. business with sb** faire des affaires avec qn; **the business was successfully transacted** la transaction *ou* l'affaire a été conclue à notre/sa/*etc* satisfaction

transaction [træn'zækʃən] *n* **(a)** (*act of transacting*) **open for the t. of business from ...** ouvert au commerce à partir de ... **(b)** (*instance of transacting*) opération *f* (commerciale); *St Exch, Fin* transaction *f*; **cash t.** opération *ou* marché *m* au comptant; **business transactions** affaires *fpl*, commerce *m* **(c) transactions** (*of learned society*) mémoires *mpl*, procès verbaux *mpl*, comptes *mpl* rendus des séances

transalpine [trænz'ælpaɪn] *adj* transalpin

transatlantic [trænzət'læntɪk] *adj* transatlantique; **t. carrier** transporteur *m* transatlantique

transaxle ['trænzaeks(ə)l] *n Aut* boîte-pont *f*, *pl* boîtes-ponts

transceiver [træn'si:vər] *n Rad* émetteur-récepteur *m*, *pl* émetteurs-récepteurs

transcend [træn'send] *vt* **(a)** (*go beyond*) transcender, aller au delà de **(b)** (*be superior to*) surpasser

transcendence, transcendency [træn'sendəns(ɪ)] *n Fml* transcendance *f*

transcendent [træn'sendənt] *adj* transcendant

transcendental [trænsen'dent(ə)l] *adj Phil* transcendental

transcendentalism [trænsen'dentəlɪz(ə)m] *n Phil* transcendentalisme *m*

transcoder [trænz'kəʊdər] *n* transcodeur *m*

transcontinental [trænzkɒntɪ'nent(ə)l] *adj* transcontinental, -aux

transcribe [træns'kraɪb] *vt* **(a)** (*write out*) copier, transcrire; (*shorthand*) traduire; *Acct* **to t. entries** transcrire des écritures **(b)** *Mus* (*piece of music for another instrument*) transcrire

transcript ['trænskrɪpt] *n* transcription *f*, copie *f*; (*of shorthand notes*) traduction *f*; *Am Scol, Univ* livret *m* scolaire

transcription [træns'krɪpʃən] *n* **(a)** (*written copy*) = **transcript** **(b)** *Mus* transcription *f*

transducer [trænz'dju:sər] *n* transducteur *m*

transect [træn'sekt] *vt* couper transversalement

transept ['trænsept] *n* (*of church*) transept *m*; **(arm of the) t.** croisillon *m*

transfer¹ ['trænsfɜ:r] *n* **(a)** (*act*) (*of person, object, department etc*) transfert *m*; (*of employee etc*) mutation *f*; *Jur* (*of right etc*) transfert, transmission *f*; (*of property*) translation *f*, mutation; **t. of title** cession *f* de titre; *Fin* (*of shares*) transfert; (*disposal*) (*of assets, shares etc*) cession; *Com* **t. advice** avis *m* de virement; *Banking etc* (*of money from one account to another*) transfert, virement *m*; **t. of capital** transfert de capitaux; **t. of power** passation *f* des pouvoirs; **t. cheque** chèque *m* de virement; **t. of funds** virement de fonds, transfert de fonds; *Fin* **t. order** ordre *m* de virement; **t. parameter** (*in datacomms*) paramètre *m* de transfert; **t. bus** (*for tourists*) navette *f* de transfert; **t. to main airport** pré-acheminement *m*; **t. from main airport** post-acheminement *m*; **t. transport** transport *m* d'acheminement; *Av* **t. passengers** voyageurs *mpl* en transit; *Comptr* **t. speed** vitesse *f* de transfert; *Br* **(capital) t. tax** droits *mpl* de succession; (*between living persons*) droit de mutation; *Can* **t. (ticket)** correspondance *f*; *Sp* **the new striker has asked for a t.** le nouveau buteur a demandé son transfert

(b) (*document*) *St Exch* (feuille *f* de) transfert *m*; *Jur* **(deed of) t.** acte *m* de cession

(c) *Cer, Sewing etc* (*design*) décalque *m*

(d) *Aut* **t. (gear)box** boîte *f* de transfert

transfer² [træns'fɜ:r] **(-rr-)** **1** *vt* **(a)** (*sth, sb, from one place to another*) transférer; (*employee, soldier etc*) muter; *Jur* (*rights etc*) transmettre; (*privilege etc*) céder; (*attention*) déplacer (**to** sur); *Banking etc* (*sum of money*) virer; (*dispose of*) (*assets, shares etc*) céder; **to t. one's affections to another person** transférer son affection sur quelqu'un d'autre; **let's t. this desk into the blue room** mettons ce bureau dans la pièce bleue; **to t. a call** transférer un appel; *Br Tel* **transfer(red) charge call** communication *f* en PCV **(b)** *Typ, Sewing etc* (*drawing*) calquer, décalquer

2 *vi* **(a) to t. to a different department** (*of person*) être transféré dans un autre service; **to t. from one course to another** changer de cours; *Fb* **to t. to a different team** obtenir son transfert dans une autre équipe

(b) (*to change trains etc*) changer; **to t. to a different plane** *etc* changer d'avion *etc*; **we then t. back to the train at ...** puis on reprend le train à ...

transferable [træns'fɜ:rəb(ə)l] *adj* transmissible; *Jur* (*right, property*) cessible, communicable, transférable; **non t.** (*on ticket etc*) non cessible; *Fin* **t. by endorsement** transmissible par endossement; **t. credit** crédit *m* transférable; **t. document** document *m* transmissible; **t. letter of credit** crédit transférable

transfer desk *n Av* (*at airport*) guichet *m* de transit

transferee [trænsfə'ri:] *n* cessionnaire *mf*

transference ['trænsfərəns] *n* transfert *m*; **(thought) t.** transmission *f* de pensée

transfer fee *n Fb etc* (*of player*) prix *m* de transfert

transfer lounge *n Av* (*at airport*) salle *f* de transit

transfiguration [trænsfɪgjʊ'reɪʃən] *n* transfiguration *f*

transfigure [træns'fɪgər] *vt* transfigurer; **her face was transfigured with happiness** la joie avait transfiguré son visage

transfix [træns'fɪks] *vt* **(a)** (*with lance etc*) transpercer **(b)** *Fig* rendre immobile; **transfixed with fear** pétrifié *ou* cloué par la peur; **they were transfixed by the sight/her singing** (*impressed*) ils étaient hypnotisés par le spectacle/son chant

transform [træns'fɔ:m] *vt* transformer (**into** en), métamorphoser; *El* (*current*) transformer

transformation [trænsfə'meɪʃən] *n* transformation *f* (**into** en); (*of person*) métamorphose *f* (**into** en)

transformational [trænsfə'meɪʃ(ə)nl] *adj Ling* transformationnel

transformer [træns'fɔ:mər] *n El* transformateur *m*; **t. station** station *f* transformatrice

transfuse [træns'fju:z] *vt Med* (*blood*) transfuser; *Fig Lit* **in a voice transfused with emotion** d'une voix emplie d'émotion

transfusion [træns'fju:ʒ(ə)n] *n Med* **(blood) t.** transfusion *f* de sang, transfusion sanguine; **to give sb a t.** faire une transfusion à qn

transgress [trænz'gres] *Fml* **1** *vt* (*law etc*) transgresser, enfreindre **2** *vi* enfreindre la loi; (*sin*) pécher

transgression [trænz'greʃən] *n Fml* (*of law etc*) transgression *f*, infraction *f* (**of** à); (*sin*) péché *m*

transgressor [trænz'gresər] *n Fml* (*of law etc*) transgresseur *m*; (*sinner*) pécheur *m*, pécheresse *f*

tranship [træn'ʃɪp] **1** *vt* (*passengers, goods*) transborder **2** *vi* changer de bateau

transhipment [træn'ʃɪpmənt] *n* transbordement *m* **t. bill of lading** connaissement *m* de transbordement

transience ['trænzɪəns] *n* (*of phenomenon etc*) nature *f* passagère *ou* transitoire

transient ['trænzɪənt] **1** *adj* transitoire; (*happiness etc*) passager, -ère; (*beauty etc*) éphémère; *Am* **t. visitor** client, -ente de passage **2** *n Am* client, -ente de passage

transire [træn'saɪər] *n Com* passavant *m*, laissez-passer *m inv*

transistor [træn'zɪstər] *n Electron* transistor *m*; **t. (set** *or* **radio)** transistor, poste *m* à transistors

transistorize [træn'zɪstəraɪz] *vt* transistoriser

transit ['trænsɪt] *n* **(a)** (*of goods*) transit *m*; **goods in t.** marchandises *fpl* en transit; **goods lost in t.** marchandises perdues en cours de route; *Com* **t. bill** passavant *m*; *Com* **t. declaration** déclaration *f* de transit **(b)** (*of people*) (*through country etc*) voyage *m*; **t. hotel** hôtel *m* de passage *ou* de transit; **t. passenger** passager *m* en transit; **t. camp** camp *m* provisoire; **t. lounge** salle *f* de transit **(c)** *Astron* (*of planet over face of sun, heavenly body through meridian*) passage *m*; **t. circle** cercle *m* méridien

transit duty *n* droit *m* de transit

transition [træn'zɪʃ(ə)n] *n* transition *f*; **t. from day to night/from fear to hope** passage *m* du jour à la nuit/de la crainte à l'espoir; *Ch* **t. element** élément *m* de transition; **t. period** période *f* de transition, période transitoire

transitional [træn'zɪʃən(ə)l] *adj* transitionnel, de transition; *Archit, Art* **t. style** style *m* de transition

transitive ['trænzɪtɪv] *Gram* **1** *adj* transitif **2** *n* (*verb*) transitif *m*; **in the t.** à la forme transitive, transitivement

transitively ['trænsɪtɪvlɪ] *adv Gram* transitivement

transitory ['trænsɪt(ə)rɪ] *adj* transitoire, passager, -ère; (*happiness, desire etc*) passager; (*glory etc*) de courte durée

transit visa *n* visa *m* de transit

translatable [træns'leɪtəb(ə)l] *adj* traduisible

translate [træns'leɪt] **1** *vt* **(a)** (*book etc*) traduire (**from** de; **into** en); **to t. words into action(s)** *or* **deeds** passer des paroles à l'acte; *F* **can you t. that (into plain English), please?** tu peux traduire (en langage de tous les jours), s'il te plaît; **we can now t. these figures into a graph** nous pouvons maintenant traduire ces chiffres en un graphe; **to t. a novel into film terms** adapter un roman à l'écran

(b) *Rel* (*bishop*) transférer (**to** à); *Bible* **Enoch was translated (to heaven)** Énoch fut enlevé au ciel

2 *vi* (*of person*) faire de la traduction; (*of writing*) se traduire; **this expression translates literally as ...** la traduction littérale de cette expression est ...; **it doesn't really t. into film** cela se laisse difficilement adapter à l'écran; **how does that t. into economic reality?** comment est-ce que ça se traduit sur le plan économique?

translation [træns'leɪʃən] *n* **(a)** (*of book etc*) traduction *f*; *Sch* (*Latin, Russian etc*) version *f*; (*of novel into film etc*) adaptation *f*; **a lot of the beauty is lost in t.** le texte perd beaucoup de sa beauté à la traduction; **a t. problem** un problème de traduction; **simultaneous t.** traduction simultanée **(b)** *Rel* (*of bishop*) translation *f*; *Bible* (*to heaven*) enlèvement *m* (au ciel)

translation agency *n* bureau *m ou* agence *f* de traduction

translation company *n* cabinet *m ou* société de traduction

translation table *n Comptr* table *f* de traduction

translator [træns'leɪtər] *n* traducteur, -trice

transliterate [trænz'lɪtəreɪt] *vt* (*in different or phonetic characters*) translit(t)érer, transcrire

transliteration [trænzlɪtə'reɪʃən] *n* (*in different or phonetic characters*) translit(t)ération *f*, transcription *f*

translucence [trænz'lu:səns] *n* translucidité *f*

translucent [trænz'lu:sənt] *adj* translucide

transmigrate [trænzmaɪ'greɪt] *vi* (*of people*) migrer; (*of soul*) transmigrer

transmigration [trænzmaɪ'greɪʃən] *n* (*of people*) migration *f*; (*of soul*) transmigration *f*

transmissible [trænz'mɪsɪb(ə)l] *adj* transmissible

transmission [trænz'mɪʃən] *n* **(a)** *Rad, TV, Phys* (*action*) transmission *f* **(b)** (*programme*) *TV* programme *m* télévisé; *Rad* programme radiodiffusé **(c)** *Aut* transmission *f*; **t. brake** frein *m* sur transmission; **t. shaft** arbre *m* de transmission; **t. speed** vitesse *f* de transmission

transmit [trænz'mɪt] *vt* **(-tt-)** (*disease, radio waves*) transmettre; *Rad, TV* (*programme*) diffuser; *MecE* **to t. a motion to sth** communiquer un mouvement à qch

transmitter [trænz'mɪtər] *n Telecom etc* transmetteur *m*; *Rad, TV* (poste *m*) émetteur *m*, poste d'émission; *Telecom, Rad* **t. receiver** émetteur-récepteur *m*, *pl* émetteurs-récepteurs; *TV, Rad* **t. van** car *m* de transmission

transmogrify [trænz'mɒgrɪfaɪ] *vt Hum* transformer, métamorphoser (**into** en)

transmutation [trænzmju:'teɪʃən] *n Fml* transmutation *f* (**into** en)

transmute [trænz'mju:t] *vt* transformer, changer (**into** en); (*in alchemy*) transmuer

transom ['trænsəm] *n* **(a)** *Archit* (*of window, door*) traverse *f*, linteau *m* **(b)** *Am* (*window over door*) imposte *f*

transparency [træns'pærənsɪ, -'peər-] *n* **(a)** (*quality*) transparence *f*; (*of water, excuse etc*) limpidité *f* **(b)** (*picture*) *Phot* diapositive *f*; (*for overhead projector*) transparent *m*; *Phot* **colour t.** diapositive en couleur

transparent [træns'pærənt, -'peər-] *adj* **(a)** (*glass etc*) transparent; (*eau, quartz etc*) limpide **(b)** (*obvious*) évident, clair, transparent

transparently [træns'pærəntlɪ, -'peər-] *adv* (*obviously*) de toute évidence; **that's t. obvious** c'est clair comme de l'eau de roche

transpiration [trænspɪ'reɪʃən] *n* transpiration *f*

transpire [træns'paɪər] **1** *vi* **(a)** (*turn out*) **it transpired that ...** il s'est avéré que ... **(b)** (*happen*) arriver, se passer **(c)** *Physiol, Bot* transpirer **2** *vt* (*of body, plant etc*) (*fluid*) exsuder; (*smell*) exhaler

transplant[1] ['trænsplɑ:nt, 'trɑ:-] *n* **(a)** *Surg* (*act of transplanting*) (*of organ*) transplantation *f*, greffe *f*; (*of skin*) greffe; (*transplanted organ etc*) transplant *m*, greffon *m*; **heart/kidney/liver t.** greffe du cœur/rein/foie **(b)** (*in horticulture*) plant *m* repiqué

transplant[2] [træns'plɑ:nt, trɑ:-] *vt* **(a)** *Surg* (*organ*) transplanter, greffer **(b)** (*population etc*) transplanter, transporter **(c)** (*in horticulture*) (*trees etc*) transplanter; (*plants*) repiquer

transplantation [trænsplɑ:n'teɪʃən, -trɑ:-] *n* transplantation *f*

transponder [trænz'pɒndər] *n* transpondeur *m*

transport[1] ['trænspɔ:t] *n* **(a)** (*of goods, passengers, troops etc*) transport *m*; **public t.** transports en commun; **road/rail t.** transport routier/ferroviaire; **t. allowance** prime *f* de transport; **t. costs** frais *mpl* de transport; **t. cover** garantie *f* transport; **t. document** titre *m ou* document *m* de transport; **t. museum** musée *m* des transports

(b) [①A26-27,c] (*means of transport*) moyen *m* de transport; *Naut* **(troop) t.** (bâtiment *m* de) transport *m*; *Av* **t. (aircraft** *or* **plane)** (avion *m* de) transport; (*for cargo*) avion cargo; *F* **have you got t.?** (*car*) est-ce que vous avez un moyen de transport?

(c) *Lit* (*emotion*) **t. of joy** transports *mpl* de joie; **to go into a t. of joy** être transporté de joie

transport[2] [træns'pɔ:t] *vt* **(a)** (*passengers, goods*) transporter; **to t. under armed guard** convoyer **(b)** (*usu passive*) *Lit* **to be transported with joy** être transporté de joie

transportable [træns'pɔ:təb(ə)l] *adj* transportable

transportation [trænspɔ:'teɪʃən] *n* **(a)** transport *m*; (*means of transport*) moyen *m* de transport; **t. advertising** affichage *m* transport; **t. agreement** contrat *m* de transport; **t. company** société *f* de transport; *Am* **t. desk** (*in hotel*) bureau *m* de voyages; **t. insurance** assurance *f* transport **(b)** *Jur, Hist* (*to colonies*) transportation *f*

transport café *n Br* routier *m*

transport company *n* entreprise *f ou* compagnie *f* de transport

transporter [træns'pɔ:tər] *n* (*vehicle*) transporteur *m*, transporteuse *f*; (*person*) entrepreneur *m* de transports; **car t.** (*lorry*) camion *m* pour transport d'automobiles; *Rail* wagon *m* transporteur de voitures

transport police *n Br* = service *m* d'ordre des chemins de fer

transpose [træns'pəuz] *vt* **(a)** (*words, terms of equation etc*) transposer **(b)** *Mus* transposer

transposition [trænspə'zɪʃən] *n* (*of letters etc*), *Mus* transposition *f*

transputer [træns'pju:tər] *n Comptr* transputeur *m*

transsexual [træn(z)'seksjuəl] *adj, n* transsexuel, -elle

transship [træn(z)'ʃɪp] = **tranship**

transshipment [træn(z)'ʃɪpmənt] = transhipment

Trans-Siberian [træn(z)saɪ'bɪərɪən] *adj* **T. Railway** chemin *m* de fer transsibérien, Transsibérien *m*

transubstantiation [trænsəbstænʃɪ'eɪʃən] *n Rel* transsubstantiation *f*

Transvaal ['trɑ:nzvɑ:l] *n* **the T.** le Transvaal; **a T. farmer** un fermier transvaalien

transversal [trænz'vɜ:s(ə)l] **1** *adj* transversal **2** *n Geom* transversale *f*

transversally [trænz'vɜ:səlɪ] *adv* transversalement

transverse ['trænzvɜ:s] *adj* (*section, muscle*) transversal; *Anat* (*colon*) transverse; *Constr* **t. beam** traverse *f*; **t. engine** moteur *m* transversal; *Geom* **t. line** transversale *f*

transversely ['trænzvɜ:slɪ] *adv* (*mounted*) transversalement, en travers

transvestism [trænz'vestɪz(ə)m] *n* tra(ns)vestisme *m*

transvestite [trænz'vestaɪt] *n* travesti, -ie

trap[1] [træp] *n* **(a)** (*in hunting etc*) piège *m*; (*pit*) trappe *f*; *Fig* piège, ruse *f*, attrape *f*; **to set a t.** (*for animal, Fig for person*) dresser *ou* tendre un piège (**for** à); **to catch an animal in a t.** prendre une bête au piège; **she's fallen into her own t.** elle est prise à son propre piège; **he fell into the t.** il s'y laissa prendre, il tomba dans le piège; **to walk** *or* **fall straight into the t.** tomber en plein dans le piège; *Mil* **tank t.** (obstacle *m*) antichar *m*; **radar** *or* **speed t.** zone *f* de contrôle de vitesse

(b) t. (door) trappe *f*

(c) *Sl* (*mouth*) gueule *f*; **shut your t.!** ta gueule!, la ferme!; **you would have to go and open your big t.!** il a fallu que tu ouvres ta grande gueule!

(d) *Sp* (*for clay pigeons*) (projecteur *m*) ball-trap *m*, *pl*

ball-traps; (*for live pigeons*) boîte *f* de lancement; (*in dog racing*) box *m* (de départ)
(**e**) *Tech* (*for water, oil etc*) collecteur *m*; (*in plumbing*), *Constr* siphon *m*
(**f**) (*horse-drawn vehicle*) cabriolet *m*
(**g**) *esp Am Mus* **traps** instruments *mpl* à percussion

trap[2] **(-pp-) 1** *vt* (**a**) (*animal, person*) prendre au piège, piéger; **to t. sb into saying sth** faire dire qch à qn en usant de ruse; **to t. sb into making a false move** piéger qn pour qu'il fasse un faux pas; **she trapped him into marriage** elle l'a obligé à se marier avec elle en usant de ruse; **to t. one's finger in the door** se coincer le doigt dans la porte; **I was trapped in the lift for two hours** je suis resté coincé dans l'ascenseur pendant deux heures; **the climbers were trapped by an avalanche** les alpinistes ont été bloqués par une avalanche; **trapped by the flames** cerné par les flammes; **to feel trapped** (*in a relationship*) se sentir prisonnier *ou F* coincé
(**b**) (*in pipe*) (*gas etc*) arrêter
(**c**) *Sp* (*stop*) (*ball*) bloquer
2 *vi* (*set traps*) tendre des pièges, *Can* trapper

trapeze [trəˈpiːz] *n* trapèze *m*; **t. artist** trapéziste *mf*, voltigeur, -euse

trapezium [trəˈpiːzɪəm] *n Geom* trapèze *m*

trapezoid [ˈtræpɪzɔɪd] *n Geom* trapézoïde *m*

trapper [ˈtræpər] *n* (*hunter*) trappeur *m*

trappings [ˈtræpɪŋz] *npl* (**a**) (*of power, success etc*) signes *mpl* extérieurs, apparat *m*; **the t. of authority** les signes extérieurs de l'autorité (**b**) (*for horses*) harnachement *m*, caparaçon *m*

Trappist [ˈtræpɪst] *adj, n Rel* trappiste *m*

trapshooting [ˈtræpʃuːtɪŋ] *n Sp* ball-trap *m*

trash [træʃ] *n* (*worthless objects*) camelote *f*; *Am* (*refuse*) détritus *mpl*, déchets *mpl*, ordures *fpl*; (*people*) vermine *f*, racaille *f*; (*nonsense*) sottise *f*; (*literature*) littérature *f* de bas étage; **the food was t.** la nourriture était très mauvaise; **she's t.** elle ne vaut rien; **those people are t.** c'est de la racaille, ces gens-là; **to talk a lot of t.** dire des tas d'imbécilités

trash can *n Am* poubelle *f*, boîte *f* à ordures

trash icon *n Am Comptr* icône *f* de la corbeille

trashy [ˈtræʃɪ] *adj* (*goods etc*) de pacotille; (*literature*) de bas étage

trauma, *pl* **-as, -ata** [ˈtrɔːmə, -əz, -ətə] *n Med, Psy* trauma *m*; *Med* traumatisme *m*

traumatic [trɔːˈmætɪk] *adj Med* traumatique; *Fig* (*experience, journey, exam*) traumatisant

traumatism [ˈtrɔːmətɪz(ə)m] *n Med* traumatisme *m*

traumatize [ˈtrɔːmətaɪz] *vt Med, Fig* traumatiser

travail [ˈtræveɪl] *n* (**a**) *Lit* (*labour, hard work*) dur labeur *m* (**b**) *Arch, Lit* (*childbirth pains*) douleurs *fpl* de l'enfantement, travail *m*

travel[1] [ˈtræv(ə)l] *n* (**a**) voyages *mpl*; **t. was slower in those days** on voyageait plus lentement à cette époque; **what do you spend on t. (to and from work)?** à combien vous reviennent vos déplacements (pour aller et revenir du travail)?; **when are you next off on your travels?** quand repartez-vous en voyage?; **I met him on my** *or* **in the course of my travels** j'ai fait sa connaissance au cours d'un de mes voyages; **t. allowance** indemnité *f* de déplacement; **t. bag** sac *m* de voyage; **t. book** (*account*) récit *m* de voyage; (*guide*) guide *m* de voyage; **t. directory** guide *m* de voyages; **t. documents** documents *mpl* de voyage; *Am* **t. group charter** achat *m* de bloc-sièges; **t. medical insurance** assurance *f* médicale de voyage; **t. trade** industrie *f* du voyage
(**b**) *MecE etc* (*of piston*) course *f*

travel[2] **(-ll-,** *US* **-l-) 1** *vi* (**a**) (*journey*) voyager; (*journey around*) faire des voyages; (*of news*) circuler, se répandre; **he has travelled a great deal** *or* **widely** il a beaucoup voyagé; **to t. round the world** faire le tour du monde; **to t. all over the world** voyager partout dans le monde, courir le monde; **to t. through a country** (*visit all parts of*) parcourir un pays; (*on way to another destination*) traverser un pays; **light travels faster than sound** la lumière va *ou* se propage plus vite que le son; **news travels fast round here** les nouvelles vont vite par ici; **the train was travelling at 150 km an hour** le train roulait à 150 km à l'heure; **that's travelling!** (*is fast*) ça c'est de la vitesse!; **we were really travelling** nous allions très vite; **this wine won't t.** ce vin voyage mal
(**b**) *Com* **to t. (for a firm)** voyager (pour une maison), représenter une maison; **to t. on business** voyager pour affaires; **to t. in wine** être représentant en vins
(**c**) *MecE* (*of part*) se mouvoir, se déplacer; (*of electric current*) se déplacer
2 *vt* (*country*) parcourir; **to t. the length and breadth of the country** parcourir le pays de long en large; **I t. this road every day** je prends cette route tous les jours

travel agency *n* agence *f* de voyages

travel agent *n* agent *m* de voyages; **t.'s voucher** bon *m* d'agence *ou* d'échange, voucher *m*

travelator [ˈtrævəleɪtər] *n* trottoir *m ou* tapis *m* roulant

travel bureau *n* agence *f* de voyage

travel company, travel firm *n* voyagiste *mf*

travel expenses *npl* frais *mpl* de déplacement

travel guide *n* guide *m* touristique

travel insurance *n* assurance *f* (de) voyage

travelled, *US* **traveled** [ˈtrævəld] *adj* **much** *or* **well t.** (*person*) qui a beaucoup voyagé; **much t.** (*road*) très fréquenté

traveller, *US* **traveler** [ˈtræv(ə)lər] *n* voyageur, -euse; (*salesperson*) représentant, -ante; *Br* (*living in caravan etc*) nomade *mf*; **I'm not a good t.** je supporte mal les voyages; **frequent t.** personne *f* qui est souvent en voyage

traveller's cheque, *US* **traveler's check** *n* chèque *m* de voyage

travelling, *US* **traveling** [ˈtræv(ə)lɪŋ] **1** *adj* (*circus*) ambulant, forain; (*preacher*) itinérant; *MecE* (*walkway etc*) roulant; (*crane*) mobile; **t. show** (*at a fair*) spectacle *m* forain **2** *n* voyages *mpl*; **to do a lot of t.** beaucoup voyager; **there isn't a lot of t. in this job** on ne voyage pas beaucoup dans ce travail; *Cin* **t. platform** travelling *m*; **t. scholarship** bourse *f* de voyage; *Cin* **t. shot** prise *f* de vue en travelling, plan *m* travelling

travelling clock *n* réveil *m* de voyage

travelling companion *n* compagnon *m* de voyage

travelling expenses *npl* (*cost of journey*) frais *mpl* de voyage *ou* de route; *Com etc* frais de déplacement

travelling people *npl* nomades *mfpl*

travelling salesman *n* voyageur *m* de commerce

travel literature *n* documentation *f* touristique

travelogue, *US* **travelog** [ˈtrævəlɒg] *n* (*film*) documentaire *m* de voyage

travel programme *n* (*travelogue*) programme *m* de voyage

travel rug *n* couverture *f* de voyage

travel-sick *adj* **she always gets t.** elle est toujours malade en voyage

travel-sickness *n* mal *m* des transports; **t. pill** cachet *m* contre le mal des transports

travel-size *adj* (*shampoo etc*) de voyage

travelstained [ˈtræv(ə)lsteɪnd] *adj* sali par le voyage

travel-weary *adj* fatigué par le(s) voyage(s)

travel writer *n* auteur *m* de récit(s) de voyage(s)

traverse[1] [ˈtrævəs] *n* (**a**) *MecE, Constr etc* (*of chassis, frame etc*) traverse *f*, entretoise *f* (**b**) *Geom* (ligne *f*) transversale *f*; (*in surveying*) cheminement *m* (**c**) (*in mountaineering, skiing*) (*across face of escarpment*) traverse *f*, vire *f*

traverse[2] **1** *vt Lit* (*region, bridge, sea*) traverser **2** *vi* (*in mountaineering, skiing*) traverser, prendre une traverse; (*of horse*) se traverser

travesty[1] [ˈtrævəstɪ] *n* (*of play etc*) travestissement *m*; **a t. of the truth** un travestissement de la vérité; **it was a t. of justice** c'était une parodie de justice

travesty[2] *vt* (*story, figure etc*) parodier, travestir

trawl[1] [trɔːl] *n* (**a**) *Fishing* **t. (line)** palangre *f*; **t. (net)** chalut *m*, traille *f* (**b**) *Fig* (*search*) ratissage *m*

trawl[2] **1** *vi Fishing* pêcher au chalut *ou* à la traille; *Fig* **to t. for business** aller à la pêche au client **2** *vt* (*net*) traîner; (*fish*) prendre à la traille *ou* au chalut; *Fig* **she trawled the small-ads for bargains** elle épluchait les petites annonces à la recherche de bonnes affaires; *Fig* **he trawled the singles bars** il écumait les bars pour célibataires

trawler [ˈtrɔːlər] *n* (**a**) (*ship*) chalutier *m* (**b**) (*man*) pêcheur *m* au chalut, chalutier *m*

trawlerman, *pl* **-men** [ˈtrɔːləmən] *n* = **trawler (b)**

trawling [ˈtrɔːlɪŋ] *n Fishing* pêche *f* au chalut, chalutage *m*

tray [treɪ] *n* (**a**) (*for carrying*) plateau *m*; (*of trunk etc*) casier *m*, châssis *m*; (*in office etc*) corbeille *f* (à correspondance); (*of printer*) bac *m*; (*for selling ice-cream etc*) éventaire *m*; **tea t.** plateau à thé; **to bring/take sth in on a t.** apporter/prendre qch sur un plateau; **a t. of sandwiches** un plateau de sandwiches; **in-t.** (*in office etc*) corbeille de la correspondance reçue; **out-t.** (*in office etc*) corbeille du courrier à expédier/des documents à classer (**b**) *Phot etc* cuvette *f*

traycloth [ˈtreɪklɒθ] *n* napperon *m* (*de plateau*)

treacherous [ˈtretʃərəs] *adj* (*person, character*) traître, *f* traîtresse, déloyal; (*action*) déloyal; (*roads, mountains, ice*) traître

treacherously [ˈtretʃərəslɪ] *adv* (*act*) en traître, traîtreusement, perfidement; **we drove in t. bad conditions** nous avons conduit dans des conditions terriblement mauvaises; **it can get t. icy up there** il y a parfois un verglas traître par là-haut

treachery [ˈtretʃərɪ] *n* trahison *f*, perfidie *f*; **act of t.** trahison, perfidie

treacle ['triːk(ə)l] *n* mélasse *f*; **t. tart** tarte *f* à la mélasse
treacly ['triːklɪ] *adj also Fig* sirupeux
tread¹ [tred] *n* **(a)** (*footstep*) pas *m*; (*sound*) bruit *m* de pas; **I heard his familiar t. on the path** j'ai entendu son pas familier sur le chemin; **heavy t.** pas lourd; *esp Lit* **to walk with measured t.** marcher à pas mesurés
(b) (*of shoe*) semelle *f*; (*of stepladder etc*) échelon *m*; *Rail* (*of track*) surface *f ou* table *f* de roulement
(c) *Aut* (*of tyre*) (*outer layer*) bande *f* de roulement, chape *f*; (*pattern*) sculpture *f*; *Aut* **t. depth safety indicator, t. wear indicator** indicateur *m* d'usure; *Aut* **t. plate** repose-pied *m*, *pl* repose-pieds; **there isn't much t. left** (*on tyre*) le pneu est presque lisse; **the t. marks of a heavy vehicle on the sand** les empreintes *fpl* de pneus d'un véhicule lourd sur le sable
tread² (*pt* **trod** [trɒd]; *pp* **trodden** ['trɒd(ə)n]) **1** *vi* marcher; **to t. in/on sth** marcher dans/sur qch; **watch where you t.** regarde ou tu mets les pieds; *Fig* **we shall have to t. carefully** *or* **warily** il va falloir marcher sur des œufs *ou* faire très attention
2 *vt* **(a)** (*ground*) marcher sur; **to think that he has trodden this very soil!** quand je pense qu'il a foulé ce sol; **to t. sth underfoot** écraser qch du pied, fouler qch aux pieds; *Fig* **to t. sb underfoot** écraser qn; **don't t. it into the carpet!** ne marche pas dessus, ça va s'incruster dans la moquette!; **to t. mud/dirt into the carpet** mettre de la boue/de la terre sur le tapis (avec ses chaussures); **well-trodden path** chemin *m* battu; (*much used*) chemin (très) fréquenté; *Old-fashioned* **to t. a path** suivre un chemin; *Fig* **he trod the same path as his father before him** il a suivi la même voie que son père; **to t. grapes** fouler la vendange; **to t. water** *Swimming* flotter en remuant les jambes; *Fig* faire du surplace
(b) *Orn* (*of male bird*) (*female bird*) couvrir, côcher
▶ **tread down** *vtas* (*grass etc*) piétiner
treading ['tredɪŋ] *n* (*of grapes*) foulage *m*
treadle ['tred(ə)l] *n* (*of sewing machine etc*) pédale *f*; **t. machine** machine *f* à pédale
treadmill ['tredmɪl] *n Hist* (*in prisons*) moulin *m* de discipline; *Fig* (*routine*) besogne *f* (quotidienne) ingrate; **the same old t.** le train-train quotidien
treason ['triːz(ə)n] *n* trahison *f*; **high t.** haute trahison
treasonable ['triːz(ə)nəb(ə)l] *adj* (*remarks etc*) traître, *f* traîtresse, perfide; (*act*) de trahison
treasure¹ ['treʒər] *n* **(a)** trésor *m*; **art treasures** trésors *ou* richesses *fpl* artistiques; **t. hunt** chasse *f* au(x) trésor(s) **(b)** *Fig F* (*person*) trésor *m*; **my home help's a real t.** ma femme de ménage est une perle
treasure² *vt* (*person*) (*prize*) estimer; (*have affection for*) chérir; (*object, freedom*) tenir beaucoup à; (*advice*) faire beaucoup de cas de; (*memory*) chérir; **to t. sth in one's memory** garder précieusement le souvenir de qch
treasure-house *n Old-fashioned* trésor *m*
treasurer ['treʒərər] *n* trésorier, -ière
treasure-trove *n Jur* trésor *m* (qu'on a découvert); *Fig* **the museum is a real t.** le musée est une véritable caverne d'Ali-Baba; *Fig* **the book was a t. of anecdotes** le livre était une mine d'anecdotes
treasury ['treʒərɪ] *n* (*funds*) trésor *m* (public); (*place*) trésorerie *f*; (*of cathedral etc*) trésor; **the T.** (*government department*) = le ministère *m* de l'Économie et des Finances; *Fin* **t. bonds** *or* **bills** bons *mpl* du Trésor; *Com, Fin* **T. Department** Direction *f* du Trésor; *Fin* **t. swap** échange *m* cambiste
treat¹ [triːt] *n* (*pleasure*) plaisir *m*; **these chocolates are a real t.** ces chocolats sont un véritable délice *ou* un vrai régal; **to give sb a t.** gâter qn; **to give oneself a t.** faire un petit extra, se faire plaisir; **it's my t.** (*I'm paying*) c'est moi qui paie; **it would be a great t. to go to the theatre** ce serait un véritable plaisir d'aller au théâtre; **it's a t. seeing you look so well!** c'est un plaisir de te voir aussi en forme!; **to have a t. in store for sb** avoir une surprise pour qn; **if you haven't seen the film yet you've got a t. in store** si tu vas voir le film tu vas (l')adorer; *F* **to go down a t.** être très apprécié; **that whisky went down a t.!** ce whisky m'a fait du bien!; **it worked a t.** (*of plan*) ça a marché comme sur des roulettes; (*of machine, system*) ça a marché à merveille
treat² **1** *vt* **(a)** (*behave towards, use*) traiter; **to t. sb well** bien traiter qn; **to t. sb badly** mal traiter qn, ne pas bien traiter qn; **to t. sb/an animal roughly** malmener *ou* maltraiter qn/un animal; **my father still treats me like a child** mon père me traite encore comme un enfant; **he doesn't t. things seriously** il ne prend pas les choses au sérieux; **to t. sth as a joke** prendre qch comme une plaisanterie; **you t. this place like a hotel!** ce n'est pas un hôtel ici!
(b) (*metal, paper etc*) traiter; *Med* (*patient, illness*) traiter; **to t. sb for rheumatism** soigner qn qui souffre de rhumatismes; **she was treated in hospital** elle a reçu des soins à l'hôpital; **to t. wood with creosote** traiter le bois à la créosote
(c) *Liter, Mus etc* (*subject, theme*) traiter; **to t. a subject thoroughly/superficially** traiter un sujet à fond/de manière superficielle
(d) **to t. sb to sth** offrir qch à qn; **to t. oneself to sth** s'offrir qch; **to t. sb to the theatre** inviter qn au théâtre; **I'll t. you to an ice-cream** je t'offre une glace; **to t. oneself to oysters** s'offrir des huîtres; **I'll t. you** (*pay for you*) je t'invite; *Iron* **he treated us to a fair old display of petulance** nous avons eu droit à une belle démonstration de mauvaise humeur
2 *vi Fml* (*negotiate*) **to t. with sb** traiter *ou* négocier avec qn; **to t. with the enemy** pactiser avec l'ennemi
▶ **treat of** *vipo Fml* (*deal with*) traiter de
treatise ['triːtɪz] *n* traité *m* (**on** de)
treatment ['triːtmənt] *n* **(a)** (*of person*) traitement *m*; **to give special/preferential t. to sb** réserver un traitement spécial/un traitement de faveur à qn; **to receive good/bad t.** être bien/mal traité; *F* **to give sb the (full) t.** (*beat up*) rosser qn **(b)** (*of metal, paper etc*), *Med* traitement *m* **(c)** *Liter, Mus etc* (*of subject, theme*) traitement *m*, façon *f* de traiter; **the subject is given fuller t. elsewhere** le sujet est traité à fond ailleurs
treaty ['triːtɪ] *n* **(a)** (*international*) (*peace, trade*) traité *m* **(b)** (*between individuals*) accord *m*; (*contract*) contrat *m*; **to sell sth by private t.** vendre qch de gré à gré *ou* à l'amiable
treble¹ ['treb(ə)l] **1** *adj* (*triple*) triple; *Mus* **t. clef** clef *f* de sol; **t. voice** (voix *f* de) soprano *m* (*masculin*) **2** *adv* trois fois plus; **t. the number** le triple; **t. the amount** trois fois plus **3** *n* **(a)** *Mus* (*person, voice*) soprano *m* **(b)** *Electron* aigus *mpl*; **we could do with a bit more t.** il faudrait un peu plus d'aigus; **t. control** touche *f* de tonalité aiguë
treble² **1** *vt* (*value, number*) tripler **2** *vi* tripler
treble seat *n Aut* trois places *f*
trebly ['treblɪ] *adv* trois fois plus
tree¹ [triː] *n* **(a)** [①B5,1,a,ii] arbre *m*; **fruit t.** arbre fruitier; **timber t.** arbre de haute futaie; *Fig* **to be at the top of the t.** être au sommet; *Fig* **to get to the top of the t.** arriver au sommet de sa profession; *Fig F* **to be up a (gum) t.** être dans une impasse *ou* dans le pétrin; *esp Am F* **to be out of one's t.** (*be crazy*) débloquer; *F* **money doesn't grow on trees!** l'argent ne pousse pas sur les arbres; *F* **good trainers don't grow on trees** les bons entraîneurs ne courent pas les rues; *Bible* **the t. of life** l'arbre de vie; *Geog* **the t. line** la limite des arbres; **above/below the t. line** au-dessus/en-dessous de la limite des arbres; **t. trunk** tronc *m* d'arbre
(b) **family t.** arbre *m* généalogique
(c) *Hist* **gallows t.** gibet *m*, potence *f*
(d) **(shoe) t.** embauchoir *m* (pour chaussures)
tree² *vt* (*chase up a tree*) (*animal, prey*) obliger à se réfugier sur un arbre
tree creeper *n* (*bird*) grimpereau *m* des bois
tree diagram *n* organigramme *m*
tree fern *n* fougère *f* arborescente
tree frog *n* rainette *f* verte
treehouse ['triːhaʊs] *n* cabane *f* construite dans un arbre
treeless ['triːlɪs] *adj* sans arbres
tree pipit *n* (*bird*) pipit *m* des arbres
tree structure *n Comptr* arborescence *f*, structure *f* arborescente
tree surgeon *n* arboriculteur, -trice (qui s'occupe de la régénération des arbres)
treetop ['triːtɒp] *n* cime *f* d'un/de l'arbre; *Av* **to skim the treetops** voler en rase-mottes
trefoil ['triːfɔɪl, 'tref-] *n Bot, Her etc* trèfle *m*
trek¹ [trek] *n* (*hike*) marche *f*; **a long t.** (*especially on foot*) un trajet long et pénible; **it's quite a t. to the shops** ça fait une trotte pour aller jusqu'aux boutiques; **it's a long t. back up from the beach** le chemin est long et pénible pour remonter de la plage; *South African Hist* **the Great T.** le Grand Trek
trek² *vi* **(-kk-)** *vi* (*make long journey*) faire un trajet long et pénible (*à pied*); (*as holiday activity*) faire du trekking; *F* **to t. to the shops** aller jusqu'aux boutiques à pied; *F* **and I had to t. all the way back to the shops** et il a fallu que je me retape tout le trajet à pied jusqu'aux boutiques; **he trekked all over the country** il a sillonné le pays
trekking ['trekɪŋ] *n* (*as holiday activity*) randonnée *f*, trekking *m*; **a t. holiday in Nepal** des vacances *fpl* de trekking au Népal
trellis¹ ['trelɪs] *n* treillis *m*, treillage *m*; **t. window** fenêtre *f* treillissée
trellis² *vt* **(a)** (*window etc*) treillisser, treillager **(b)** (*vine*) échalasser

trelliswork ['trelɪswɜːk] *n* treillis *m*, treillage *m*

tremble¹ ['tremb(ə)l] *n* tremblement *m*; **to be all of a t.** être tout tremblant

tremble² *vi* (*vibrate*) trembler; (*shiver*) trembler, frissonner; (*with emotion*) frémir; (*of voice*) trembler; **to t. like a leaf** trembler comme une feuille; **to t. with fear** trembler de peur; **where are they? – I t. to think!** où sont-ils? –je n'ose y penser!

trembling ['tremblɪŋ] **1** *adj* tremblant **2** *n* tremblement *m*; (*of leaf*) frémissement *m*; **in fear and t.** tout tremblant

tremendous [trɪ'mendəs] *adj* **(a)** (*enormous*) immense, énorme; **there was a t. crowd** il y avait un monde fou; **a t. difference** une énorme différence; **a. t. lot of sth** une quantité énorme de qch **(b)** *F* (*excellent*) formidable; **thanks, that's t.** merci, c'est formidable

tremendously [trɪ'mendəslɪ] *adv* (*enormously*) extrêmement; **it was t. successful** ce fut un grand succès

tremolo ['treməlәʊ] *n Mus* trémolo *m*

tremor ['tremər] *n* **(a)** (*of emotion*) tremblement *m*, frémissement *m*; (*of fear*) frisson *m*; *Med* tremblement, trémulation *f* **(b)** (*of windows etc*) tremblement *m*; **earth t.** secousse *f* sismique

tremulous ['tremjʊləs] *adj* tremblotant, frémissant; (*smile*) timide, craintif; **to be t. with fear/emotion/joy** frémir de peur/émotion/joie; **t. voice** voix *f* tremblante *ou* chevrotante

tremulously ['tremjʊləslɪ] *adv* en tremblant, en tremblotant; (*timidly*) timidement

trench¹ [tren(t)ʃ] *n* **(a)** *Agr* tranchée *f*, fossé *m*; (*for draining*) rigole *f*; **water** *or* **irrigation t.** fossé d'irrigation; **t. plough** rigoleuse *f* **(b)** *Mil* tranchée *f*; **communication t.** boyau *m*, -aux; **t. warfare** guerre *f* de tranchées

trench² **1** *vt* (*ground*) creuser un fossé *ou* une tranchée dans **2** *vi* creuser des fossés *ou* des tranchées

trenchant ['tren(t)ʃənt] *adj* (*style, tone*) tranchant, net, incisif; (*reply, epigram*) mordant, caustique

trencher ['tren(t)ʃər] *n Hist* tranchoir *m*, tailloir *m*

trencherman, *pl* **-men** ['tren(t)ʃəmən] *n Old-fashioned* **good** *or* **stout t.** gros mangeur *m*

trench coat *n* trench-coat *m*, *pl* trench-coats

trend¹ [trend] *n* (*of public opinion etc*) tendance *f*; (*fashion*) mode *f*; (*of watercourse etc*) direction *f*; **upward/downward t.** tendance à la hausse/la baisse; **to set** *or* **start a t.** lancer une mode; **a t. towards ...** une tendance vers ...; **current trends** tendances actuelles; **if present trends continue** si les tendances actuelles se poursuivent; *Mktg* **t. analysis** analyse *f* des tendances

trend² *vi* se diriger, s'orienter (**to, towards** vers)

trendiness ['trendɪnɪs] *n Br F* côté *m* branché *ou* à la mode; **the t. of his haircut/views** sa coupe/ses idées à la mode; **the t. of the decor** le décor branché

trendsetter ['trendsetər] *n* lanceur, -euse de modes *ou* de nouvelles tendances

trendsetting ['trendsetɪŋ] *adj* (*innovation, design etc*) qui lance une mode

trendy ['trendɪ] *Br F* **1** *adj* (*clothes, person, views etc*) branché **2** *n Pej* (*person*) personne *f* branchée

trepan¹ [trɪ'pæn] *n Surg, Min* trépan *m*

trepan² *vt* (-nn-) *Surg* trépaner

trepanning [trɪ'pænɪŋ] *n Surg* trépanation *f*

trepidation [trepɪ'deɪʃən] *n* (*anxiety*) agitation *f* nerveuse; **he stood there in t. before the headmaster** il se tenait tout tremblant devant le directeur de l'école; **he opened the letter with t.** il ouvrit la lettre en tremblant; **he picked up the phone and, not without t., dialled** il saisit l'écouteur et composa le numéro non sans nervosité

trespass¹ ['trespəs] *n* **(a)** *Jur* (*on property*) violation *f* de propriété **(b)** *Rel* offense *f*, péché *m*; **forgive us our trespasses** pardonne-nous nos offenses

trespass² *vi* **(a)** *Jur* **to t. (on sb's property)** entrer sans autorisation dans la propriété de qn; **please leave, you're trespassing** veuillez quitter les lieux, vous n'êtes pas autorisés à être ici; **to t. (up)on sb's rights** violer *ou* enfreindre les droits de qn; **I don't wish to t. on your time** je ne veux pas abuser de votre temps; **I don't wish to t. on your area of responsibility** je ne veux pas empiéter sur vos attributions **(b)** *Rel* pécher (**against** contre); **as we forgive those that t. against us** comme nous pardonnons à ceux qui nous ont offensés

trespasser ['trespəsər] *n Jur* (*on sb's land*) auteur *m* d'une violation de propriété (foncière); **trespassers will be prosecuted** (*on sign*) défense d'entrer sous peine d'amende

trespassing ['trespəsɪŋ] *n* (*on sb's land*) violation *f* de propriété (foncière); **no t.** (*on sign*) défense d'entrer

tress [tres] *n* boucle *f*; (*plait*) tresse *f*; *Lit* **tresses** (*of woman*) chevelure *f*, cheveux *mpl*

trestle ['tres(ə)l] *n* tréteau *m*, chevalet *m*; **t. bridge** pont *m* de *ou* sur chevalets; **t. table** table *f* à tréteaux

trews [truːz] *npl* (*trousers*) *Scot* pantalon *m* en tartan; *Br F* pantalon

triad ['traɪæd] *n* **(a)** (*group of three*) triade *f*; *Mktg* **t. markets** marchés *mpl* de la triade **(b)** *Ch* élément *m* trivalent **(c)** *Mus* accord *m* parfait

trial ['traɪəl] *n* **(a)** *Jur* (*proceedings*) procès *m*; **to bring sb to t.** faire passer qn en jugement; **to be on t. for a crime/for one's life** passer en jugement pour un crime/pour un crime passible de la peine de mort; **they were sent for t.** ils furent renvoyés en jugement; **t. by jury** jugement *m* par jury; *Hist* **t. by combat** combat *m* judiciaire; **famous trials** causes *fpl* célèbres; *US* **t. judge** = juge *m* d'instance

(b) (*test*) épreuve *f*; (*of instrument, vehicle etc*) essai *m* (technique); *Sp* match *m* de sélection; **t. of strength** épreuve de force; **to give sth a t.** faire l'essai de qch; **on t.** à l'essai; **to proceed by t. and error** procéder par tâtonnements *ou* par approximations successives; **sheepdog trials** concours *m* de chiens de berger; **speed t.** essai de vitesse

(c) (*ordeal*) épreuve *f* (douloureuse); **that child is a great t. to his parents** cet enfant met ses parents au martyre; **despite the trials and tribulations** en dépit des caprices de la fortune; **after all your trials and tribulations** après tout ce que vous avez dû souffrir

trial balance *n* (*in bookkeeping*) balance *f* de vérification

trial balloon *n Fig* ballon *m* d'essai

trial flight *n Av* vol *m* d'essai

trial game *n Sp* match *m* de sélection

trial offer *n* offre *f* d'essai

trial order *n Com* commande *f* d'essai

trial period *n* période *f* d'essai; **to be on a t.** (*of employee*) faire une période d'essai

trial run *n* (*of machine*) essai *m*; (*of car*) essai sur route

trial separation *n* séparation *f* à l'essai

triangle ['traɪæŋg(ə)l] *n* **(a)** *Geom etc* triangle *m*; *Phys* **t. of forces** triangle des forces; *F* **the eternal t.** l'éternel triangle **(b)** *Mus* triangle *m*; (*drawing instrument*) équerre *f* (en triangle)

triangular [traɪ'æŋgjʊlər] *adj* (*shape etc*) triangulaire, en triangle; (*contest, relationship etc*) triangulaire

triangulate [traɪ'æŋgjʊleɪt] *vt* (*in surveying*) trianguler

triangulation [traɪæŋgjʊ'leɪʃən] *n* (*in surveying*) triangulation *f*

tribal ['traɪb(ə)l] *adj* (*society, warfare, system*) tribal; (*leader*) de tribu; (*people etc*) qui vit en tribus

tribalism ['traɪbəlɪz(ə)m] *n* tribalisme *m*

tribalistic [traɪbə'lɪstɪk] *adj* tribal

tribe [traɪb] *n* **(a)** tribu *f*; *Fig F* tribu, smala *f*; **the twelve tribes of Israel** les douze tribus d'Israël **(b)** *Biol* tribu *f*

tribesman, *pl* **-men** ['traɪbzmən] *n* membre *m* d'une/de la tribu; **Bedouin t.** membre d'une/de la tribu bédouine

tribulation [trɪbjʊ'leɪʃən] *n Fml* tribulations *fpl*; **I had no wish to add to her tribulations** je ne voulais pas ajouter à ses tourments

tribunal [tr(a)ɪ'bjuːnəl] *n* tribunal *m*, -aux

tribune¹ ['trɪbjuːn] *n* (*platform*), *Fig* tribune *f*

tribune² *n* (*officer in ancient Rome etc*) tribun *m*

tributary ['trɪbjʊt(ə)rɪ] **1** *adj* (*state*) tributaire; (*road*) secondaire **2** *n* **(a)** *Geog* (*of river*) affluent *m* **(b)** (*person, country*) tributaire *m*

tribute ['trɪbjuːt] *n* **(a)** (*homage*) tribut *m*, hommage *m*; **to pay (a) t. to sb** rendre hommage à qn; **it is a t. to her/her determination that the work was finished at all** c'est grâce à elle/à sa détermination que le travail a été terminé; **to pay a last t. to sb** rendre à qn les derniers devoirs; **floral tributes** gerbes *fpl* et couronnes *fpl* (de fleurs) **(b)** *Hist* **t. (money)** tribut *m*

trice [traɪs] *n* **in a t.** en un clin d'œil, en moins de rien

tricentenary, *esp US* **tricentennial** [traɪsen'tiːnərɪ, -'tenɪəl] *adj, n* tricentenaire *m*

triceps ['traɪseps] *n Anat* **t. (muscle)** triceps *m*

triceratops [traɪ'serətɒps] *n* tricératops *m*

trichinosis [trɪkɪ'nəʊsɪs] *n Med* trichinose *f*

trick¹ [trɪk] *n* **(a)** (*ruse*) tour *m*, ruse *f*; (*dishonest*) supercherie *f*; (*practical joke*) farce *f*, tour; (*knack*) truc *m*; (*taught to animal, child etc*) tour d'adresse; (*of conjuror*) tour; **by a t.** (*to obtain sth*) par ruse; **to play a t. on sb** faire une farce *ou* une blague à qn; **my eyes must have been playing tricks on me** *or* **playing me tricks** mes yeux ont dû me jouer des tours, j'ai dû avoir la berlue; **t. of the light** effet *m* de lumière; **that was a nasty** *or* **mean** *or* **dirty t.** ça c'était un vilain tour!; **you've been up to your tricks again** vous avez encore fait des vôtres; **the car's up to its old tricks again** la voiture recommence à faire des siennes; **the tricks of the trade** les trucs *ou* les astuces *fpl* du métier; **that should do the t.** ça devrait faire l'affaire, ça devrait marcher; **he has**

the t. of always being in the right place at the right time il a le chic pour être toujours au bon endroit au bon moment; **to teach a dog tricks** apprendre des tours à un chien; **card t.** tour de cartes; **conjuring t.** tour de prestidigitation *ou* de passe-passe; *F* **the whole bag of tricks** tout le bataclan, tout le tremblement; **she doesn't miss a t.** rien ne lui échappe; *F* **how's tricks?** (*how are you?*) comment vas-tu?; (*what's the news?*) quoi de neuf?; **t. cigarette** fausse cigarette *f*; **t. cyclist** cycliste *mf* acrobate; *Sl* (*psychiatrist*) psy *mf*; *Phot, Cin* **t. photography** truquage *m*, trucage *m*; **t. question** question *f* piège; **t. riding** (*on horseback*) voltige *f*

(b) *Old-fashioned* (*mannerism*) manie *f*; (*habit*) habitude *f*; **he has a t. of repeating himself** il a la manie de se répéter

(c) *Cards* pli *m*; **to take** *or* **make a t.** faire une levée *ou* un pli

(d) *Sl* (*of prostitute*) passe *f*; **to turn a t.** faire une passe

trick² *vt* (*sb*) attraper, duper; **I've been tricked** j'ai été refait, je me suis fait avoir; **to t. sb into doing sth** amener qn à faire qch en usant de ruse; **you won't t. me into doing that again!** tu ne m'y reprendras pas!; **to t. sb out of sth** (*of opportunity etc*) frustrer qn de qch; (*of money etc*) escroquer qch à qn

▶ **trick out** *vtsep esp Lit* (*dress*) attifer (**in, with** de)

trickery ['trɪkərɪ] *n* tricherie *f*, duperie *f*; **piece of t.** supercherie *f*; **by t.** par ruse

trickiness ['trɪkɪnɪs] *n* (*of mechanism, situation*) difficulté *f*

trickle¹ ['trɪk(ə)l] *n* (*of water etc*) filet *m*; **sales were down to a t.** il n'y avait presque plus de ventes; **emigration is down to a t.** l'émigration ne se fait plus qu'au compte-goutte; **we've had a slow but steady t. of contributions** les contributions nous arrivent assez lentement mais de manière régulière; *El* **t. charger** chargeur *m* à régime lent; *Econ* **t.-down theory** théorie *f* selon laquelle les richesses accumulées par un petit nombre bénéficieront à tous les membres de la société

trickle² 1 *vi* couler (goutte à goutte); **water was trickling down the wall** l'eau dégoulinait *ou* coulait le long du mur; **tears were trickling down her cheeks** les larmes coulaient le long de ses joues; **news is beginning to t. through** *or* **out from the devastated area** on commence à recevoir peu à peu des nouvelles de la région sinistrée; **refugees are still trickling across the border** quelques rares réfugiés continuent à passer la frontière; **the ball just trickled into the hole** la balle a roulé tout doucement dans le trou; **the results began to t. in** les résultats commençaient à arriver lentement

2 *vt* (*liquid*) laisser goutter, laisser tomber goutte à goutte

trickster ['trɪkstər] *n* escroc *m*; **confidence t.** voleur, -euse à l'américaine

tricky ['trɪkɪ] *adj* **(a)** (*difficult*) difficile; (*awkward*) compliqué, délicat **(b)** (*deceitful*) rusé; *F* **he's a t. customer** c'est un rusé *ou* un malin

tricolour, *US* **tricolor** ['trɪkələr] *n* (*flag*) drapeau *m* tricolore (*principalement français ou irlandais*)

tricorn(e) ['traɪkɔːn] 1 *adj* (*hat*) tricorne 2 *n* tricorne *m*

tricuspid [traɪ'kʌspɪd] *adj Anat* tricuspide

tricycle ['traɪsɪk(ə)l] *n* tricycle *m*

trident ['traɪdənt] *n* (*Neptune's etc*) trident *m*

tried [traɪd] *adj* **well t.** (*remedy*) éprouvé, qui a fait ses preuves; **t. and tested** (*formula*) éprouvé, qui a fait ses preuves; **t. and trusted** (*friend, employee*) sur qui l'on peut compter

triennial [traɪ'enɪəl] *adj* triennal; (*plant*) trisannuel

triennially [traɪ'enɪəlɪ] *adv* tous les trois ans

trier ['traɪər] *n* **to be a t.** (*persevere*) faire des efforts, s'accrocher; **she might not be the best but she's a t.** ce n'est peut-être pas la meilleure mais elle est persévérante

trifle ['traɪf(ə)l] *n* **(a)** (*insignificant thing*) broutille *f*, bagatelle *f*, vétille *f*; (*money*) petite somme *f* d'argent; (*object, gift*) bricole *f*; **to quarrel over a mere t.** se quereller pour un oui pour un non, se quereller sur des riens; **it was sold for a mere t.** on l'a vendu pour un rien **(b) a t.** (*a little*) un tout petit peu, (un) tant soit peu; **a t. too wide/too short** un tantinet trop large/trop court **(c)** *Br Culin* diplomate *m*

▶ **trifle away** *vtsep* (*waste*) gaspiller; **to t. one's time away** gaspiller son temps

▶ **trifle with** *vipo* (*affections etc*) jouer *ou* badiner avec; **she's not a woman to be trifled with** on ne joue pas *ou* ne plaisante pas avec elle; **to t. with one's food** manger du bout des dents, grignoter

trifling ['traɪflɪŋ] *adj* (*unimportant*) insignifiant, peu important; (*negligible*) négligeable; **t. incidents** menus incidents *mpl*; **that's a t. matter** ce n'est qu'une bagatelle; *Iron* **the t. sum of 10,000 francs** la bagatelle de 10 000 francs

triforium, *pl* **-ia** [traɪ'fɔːrɪəm, -ɪə] *n* triforium *m*

trigger¹ ['trɪgər] *n* (*on gun*) détente *f*, gâchette *f*; (*on camera*), *MecE* déclencheur *m*, poussoir *m* (*à ressort*); *Fig* catalyseur *m*; **to be quick on the t.**, *F* **to be t. happy** ne pas hésiter à tirer, *F* avoir la gâchette facile; **t. action** déclenchement *m*; **t. finger** index *m* (*avec lequel on presse sur la détente*); **my t. finger's itching** j'ai la gâchette qui me démange; **t. mechanism** mécanisme *m* de déclenchement

trigger² *vt also Fig* déclencher

▶ **trigger off** *vtsep Fig* = **trigger²**

trigonometric(al) [trɪgənə'metrɪk, -ɪk(ə)l] *adj* trigonométrique

trigonometrically [trɪgənə'metrɪklɪ] *adv* trigonométriquement

trigonometry [trɪgə'nɒmɪtrɪ] *n* trigonométrie *f*

trike [traɪk] *n* (*abbr* **tricycle**) tricycle *m*

trilateral [traɪ'læt(ə)rəl] *adj* trilatéral

trilby ['trɪlbɪ] *n Br* **t. (hat)** chapeau *m* mou, feutre *m*

trilingual [traɪ'lɪŋgw(ə)l] *adj* trilingue

trill¹ [trɪl] *n* **(a)** *Mus* trille *m* **(b)** (*of birds*) chant *m* perlé, trille *m* **(c)** *Ling* consonne *f* roulée

trill² 1 *vi Mus etc* faire des trilles 2 *vt Mus etc* (*note*) triller; *Ling* **trilled consonant** consonne *f* roulée; **I'm up here, trilled Penelope** je suis en haut, dit Pénélope d'une voix flûtée

trillion ['trɪljən] *n* [①**A70,16,1**] **(a)** *Br* (10^{18}) trillion *m* **(b)** *Am* (10^{12}) billion *m*

trilogy ['trɪlədʒɪ] *n* trilogie *f*

trim¹ [trɪm] *n* **(a)** (*of hair etc*) coupe *f* d'entretien; **just a t.** (*said to hairdresser*) c'est simplement pour rafraîchir **(b) in (good) t.** en bon ordre; (*of person*) (*in good health*) en bonne santé; (*fit*) en (bonne) forme; **in fighting t.** prêt pour le combat **(c)** *Naut* (*of sails*) orientation *f*; **in t.** équilibré; **out of t.** déséquilibré **(d)** (*on car*) habillage *m*; **interior t.** garniture *f* intérieure; **seat t.** garnissage *m* des sièges

trim² *adj* soigné; **a t. little yacht** un joli petit voilier; **to have a t. figure** (*of person*) avoir une silhouette svelte; **a t. little garden** un petit jardin coquet *ou* bien tenu

trim³ *vt* **(-mm-) (a)** (*cut*) (*hedge, tree*) tailler; (*edge of book*) ébarber, rogner; (*beard etc*) tailler; (*sb's hair*) couper, rafraîchir; *Comptr* (*database*) supprimer les espaces blancs inutiles de; **to t. (the wick of) a lamp** moucher une lampe; **to t. the budget** réduire le budget; *Culin* **to t. meat** habiller *ou* parer la viande **(b)** (*ship, plane*) équilibrer; (*load*) arrimer; *Naut* (*sails*) orienter **(c)** *Sewing etc* (*dress etc*) orner, garnir (**with** de); (*hat*) garnir; *Am* (*Christmas tree*) décorer; **trimmed with lace** garni de dentelles

▶ **trim away** *vtsep* (*excess growth, unnecessary details, verbiage*) élaguer

▶ **trim down** 1 *vtsep* (*text, size of company, expenditure etc*) réduire 2 *vi* (*spend less*) réduire ses dépenses; (*shed staff*) réduire ses effectifs

▶ **trim off** *vtsep Culin etc* (*fat*) enlever; **to t. the fat off the meat** enlever le gras de la viande; *Fig* **they've trimmed £200 off the budget** ils ont réduit le budget de 200 livres; **I think we could t. a couple of hours off the journey** je pense que nous pourrions gagner environ deux heures sur le trajet

trimaran ['traɪmərən] *n Naut* trimaran *m*

trimester [tr(a)ɪ'mestər] *n esp Am* trimestre *m*

trimmer ['trɪmər] *n* **(a)** (*machine*) (*for wood etc*) machine *f* à trancher; (*in papermaking, bookbinding etc*) massicot *m* **(b)** *Pej* (*opportunist*) opportuniste *mf*

trimming ['trɪmɪŋ] *n* **(a)** (*cutting*) (*of hedges, trees*) taille *f*; (*of edges of book*) ébarbage *m*, rognage *m*; **trimmings** (*pieces*) (*of iron, wood, paper etc*) rognures *fpl*, ébarbures *fpl* **(b)** (*reduction*) (*of expenses etc*) réduction *f* **(c)** (*decoration*) (*of clothes, curtains etc*) garniture *f*, ornement *m*; **trimming(s)** (*on garment etc*) passementerie *f*; *Culin* **(usual) trimmings** (*of dish*) accompagnements *mpl*, garniture; **roast beef and all the trimmings** du rosbif et tout ce qui l'accompagne; *Fig* **with all the trimmings** avec tout le tralala

trimness ['trɪmnɪs] *n* (*of person, thing*) air *m* soigné; (*of figure*) sveltesse *f*

Trinidad ['trɪnɪdæd] *n* (l'île de) la Trinité

Trinity ['trɪnɪtɪ] *n* **(a)** *Rel* **the (Holy) T.** la (sainte) Trinité; **T. Sunday** (la fête de) la Trinité **(b)** *Univ* **T. term** troisième trimestre *m* (universitaire) (*à Oxford et Cambridge*)

trinket ['trɪŋkɪt] *n* (*jewellery*) petit bijou *m* en toc; (*worthless object*) babiole *f*

trinomial [traɪ'nəʊmɪəl] *adj, n Math* trinôme *m*

trio, *pl* **-os** ['triːəʊ(z)] *n Mus etc* trio *m*

trip¹ [trɪp] *n* **(a)** (*journey*) voyage *m*; (*outing*) excursion *f*; **business/honeymoon t.** voyage d'affaires/de noces; **to go on a shopping t.** aller faire des courses; **the t. takes two hours** le trajet dure deux heures; **he's away on a t. to Italy** il est en voyage en Italie; **I'm afraid I'm going to have to make another t. to the loo** je crois que je vais devoir refaire un tour aux cabinets; **round t.** (*circular journey*) voyage circulaire; *Naut* croisière *f*; (*journey there and back*) voyage d'aller et retour; *Br Sch* **school t.** voyage/excursion scolaire; *Br Sch* **geography field t.** excursion *ou* (*longer*) voyage d'études géographique; **t. computer** ordinateur *m* de bord; **t. recorder** compteur *m* journalier, totalisateur *m* kilométrique journalier

(**b**) (**drug**) **t.** voyage *m*, trip *m*; **to be on a t.** faire un voyage *ou* un trip, être en plein trip

(**c**) (*stumble*) faux pas *m*

(**d**) *Sp* (*foul*) croc-en-jambe *m*, *pl* crocs-en-jambe, croche-pied *m*, *pl* croche-pieds; **that was a t.!** il lui a fait un croc-en-jambe!

trip[2] (-pp-) **1** *vi* (**a**) (*stumble*) trébucher, faire un faux pas; (*of horse*) broncher (**b**) (*step lightly*) aller d'un pas léger; **he tripped merrily into the room** il entra dans la pièce d'un pas léger (**c**) *MecE* (*of catch etc*) se déclencher; (*of part of mechanism*) basculer, culbuter (**d**) *Sl* (*on drugs*) faire un trip; **I was tripping at the time** j'étais en plein trip; **I don't know what she was tripping on** je ne sais pas ce qu'elle avait pris (**e**) **to t. off the tongue** (*of name, jingle etc*) bien couler **2** *vt* (**a**) = **trip up 1** (*a*) (**b**) *MecE* (*part of machine*) déclencher; (*lever etc*) culbuter (**c**) *Hum* **to t. the light fantastic** (*dance*) danser

▶ **trip over 1** *vi* trébucher et tomber **2** *vipo* (*sth*) trébucher sur, buter contre; *Fig* **you can't go anywhere here without tripping over celebrities** par ici on ne peut pas faire un pas sans se heurter à une célébrité; **to t. over one's (own) feet** s'emmêler les pieds

▶ **trip up 1** *vtsep* (**a**) (*cause to fall*) faire un croc-en-jambe *ou* un croche-pied à; (*of obstacle*) faire trébucher, faire tomber (**b**) *Fig* (*catch out*) démonter, désarçonner **2** *vi* (**a**) (*stumble*) trébucher, faire un faux pas; **to t. up over a word** trébucher sur un mot (**b**) (*make mistake*) faire une erreur; **the robbers/fugitives finally tripped up** les voleurs/fugitifs ont fini par commettre une erreur; **that's where we tripped up** (*blundered*) c'est là que nous avons fait une gaffe

tripartite [traɪ'pɑːtaɪt] *adj* tripartite; (*divided into three*) divisé en trois, en trois parties

tripe [traɪp] *n Culin* tripes *fpl*; *F* (*nonsense*) bêtises *fpl*; *F* **that's all** *or* **a lot of t.** tout ça c'est des sottises

triphammer ['trɪphæmər] *n MecE* marteau *m* à bascule *ou* à soulèvement

triphase ['traɪfeɪz] *adj El* (*current*) triphasé

triphthong ['trɪfθɒŋ] *n* triphtongue *f*

triplane ['traɪpleɪn] *n* triplan *m*

triple ['trɪp(ə)l] **1** *adj* triple; **t. glazing** triple vitrage *m*; *Sp* **t. jump** triple saut *m*; *Mus* **t. time** mesure *f* ternaire *ou* à trois temps; *St Exch* **t. A rated** noté triple "A"; *St Exch* **t.-A rating** notation *f* AAA **2** *adv* **t. the number/amount** trois fois le nombre/la quantité **3** *n* triple *m*

triple[2] *vti* tripler

Triple Alliance *n Hist* **the T.** la Triplice, la triple Alliance

triplet ['trɪplɪt] *n* (*child*) triplé, -ée; *Mus* triolet *m*; (*in poetry*) tercet *m*

triplex ['trɪpleks] *adj* (*planche*) de trois épaisseurs

triplicate[1] ['trɪplɪkət] **1** *adj* **t. copies** trois exemplaires *mpl* **2** *n* triple *m*, triplicata *m*; **in t.** en triple *ou* trois exemplaire(s); **invoice in t.** facture en triplicata *ou* en trois exemplaires

triplicate[2] ['trɪplɪkeɪt] *vt Com* (*document*) rédiger en trois exemplaires

triply ['trɪplɪ] *adv* triplement

tripod ['traɪpɒd] *n* trépied *m*

tripos ['traɪpɒs] *n Eng Univ* (*at Cambridge*) = éprenues pour l'obtention de la licence ès lettres/ès sciences

tripper ['trɪpər] *n esp Br* (*person*) excursionniste *mf*; **they're (just) day trippers** ils sont (juste) venus passer la journée

triptych ['trɪptɪk] *n Art* triptyque *m*

trip wire *n* fil *m* tendu (*pour déclencher un mécanisme, pour faire tomber qn ou pour avertir de son arrivée*)

trireme ['traɪriːm] *n* trirème *f*, trière *f*

trisect [traɪ'sekt] *vt Geom etc* (*line, angle*) diviser *ou* couper en trois

trisomy ['traɪsəʊmɪ] *n Med* trisomie *f*

trisyllabic [traɪsɪ'læbɪk] *adj* (*in prosody*) tris(s)yllabe, tris(s)yllabique

trisyllable [traɪ'sɪləb(ə)l] *n* (*in prosody*) tris(s)yllabe *m*

trite [traɪt] *adj* banal, -als; (*theme*) rebattu; **t. remarks** banalités *fpl*, lieux *mpl* communs

tritely ['traɪtlɪ] *adv* banalement

triteness ['traɪtnɪs] *n* banalité *f*

tritium ['trɪtɪəm] *n Ch* tritium *m*

triton ['traɪt(ə)n] *n* (*mollusc*), *Myth* triton *m*

triturate ['trɪtjəreɪt] *vt Tech* triturer, broyer

trituration [trɪtjə'reɪʃən] *n Tech* trituration *f*

triumph[1] ['traɪəmf] *n* triomphe *m* (**over** sur); **to achieve great triumphs** remporter de grands succès; **she came home in t.** elle est rentrée triomphante chez elle; **a look of t.** un air triomphant; **the t. in his voice/eyes** le triomphe dans sa voix/ses yeux

triumph[2] *vi* triompher; **to t. over one's enemies** (*defeat*) triompher de ses ennemis

triumphal [traɪ'ʌmf(ə)l] *adj* triomphal; **to get a t. reception** avoir une arrivée triomphale

triumphant [traɪ'ʌmfənt] *adj* triomphant; (*success*) retentissant; **a t. expression** un air de triomphe; **to be t. over sb/sth** triompher de qn/qch

triumphantly [traɪ'ʌmfəntlɪ] *adv* (*to return etc*) en triomphe; (*to look at etc*) d'un air triomphant; (*to say*) d'un ton triomphant

triumvirate [traɪ'ʌmvɪrɪt] *n Hist* triumvirat *m*; *Fig* (*of people*) trio *m*

triune ['traɪjuːn] *adj Rel* d'une unité triple, en trois parties, trin

trivet ['trɪvɪt] *n Culin* trépied *m*

trivia ['trɪvɪə] *npl* vétilles *fpl*, petits riens *mpl*; **to get bogged down in t.** s'embarrasser de futilités; **he has an amazing memory for t.** il a une mémoire remarquable pour les choses sans importance

trivial ['trɪvɪəl] *adj* (**a**) (*unimportant*) insignifiant, sans importance; **t. matter** bagatelle *f*; **t. offence** peccadille *f* (**b**) (*person*) superficiel, frivole; **he's just being t.** il plaisante (**c**) (*banal*) banal, -als, dépourvu d'originalité

triviality [trɪvɪ'ælɪtɪ] *n* (**a**) (*of loss, offence etc*) caractère *m* insignifiant; (*of remark etc*) banalité *f*, futilité *f* (**b**) **to talk polite trivialities** dire des futilités *ou* des banalités pour être poli

trivialization [trɪvɪəlaɪ'zeɪʃən] *n* banalisation *f*

trivialize ['trɪvɪəlaɪz] *vt* (*sth important*) banaliser

trochaic [trəʊ'keɪɪk] *adj, n* (*in prosody*) trochaïque *m*

trochee ['trəʊkiː] *n* (*in prosody*) trochée *m*

trod, trodden *see* **tread**[2]

trogloditic [trɒglə'dɪtɪk] *adj* troglodytique

troglodyte ['trɒglədaɪt] *n* troglodyte *m*

troilism ['trɔɪlɪz(ə)m] amour *m ou* sexe *m* à trois

Trojan ['trəʊdʒən] **1** *adj Hist* troyen, de Troie; **the T. War** la guerre de Troie; *also Fig* **T. Horse** cheval *m* de Troie **2** *n Hist* Troyen, -enne; **like a T.** (*to work*) sans relâche; (*to fight*) vaillamment

troll[1] [trəʊl] *n Fishing* cuiller *f*; (*of fishing rod*) moulinet *m*

troll[2] *vi Fishing* **to t. for pike** pêcher le brochet à la cuiller

troll[3] *n Myth* troll *m*

trolley ['trɒlɪ] *n* (**a**) *Br* (*cart*) chariot *m*; (*two wheeled*) diable *m*; (*for luggage*) chariot à bagages; **(shopping) t.** (*in supermarket etc*) chariot, caddie *m*; **(dinner** *or* **tea) t.** table *f* roulante (**b**) **t. jack** cric *m* rouleur; **t. (wheel)** (poulie *f* de) trolley *m*; *F* **he's off his t.** (*mad*) il débloque

trolleybus ['trɒlɪbʌs] *n* trolleybus *m*

trolley car *n Am* tramway *m* à trolley

trolling ['trəʊlɪŋ] *n Fishing* pêche *f* à la cuiller

trollop ['trɒləp] *n Old-fashioned, Hum* (**a**) (*dirty woman*) souillon *f* (**b**) (*promiscuous woman*) catin *f*, gourgandine *f*

trombone [trɒm'bəʊn] *n Mus* trombone *m*

trombonist [trɒm'bəʊnɪst] *n* tromboniste *mf*

troop[1] [truːp] *n* (**a**) (*of people*) groupe *m*, bande *f* (**b**) *Mil* (*unit*) (*of cavalry, tanks*) peloton *m*; **troops** troupes *fpl*; **to raise troops** lever des troupes; **shock troops** troupes de choc (**c**) (*in scouting*) troupe *f*

troop[2] **1** *vi* **to t. in/off/past** entrer/partir/passer en groupe *ou* en bande **2** *vt esp Br Mil* **to t. the colour** faire le salut au drapeau

troop carrier *n* (*ship*) transport *m* de troupes; (*vehicle*) véhicule *m* blindé de transport de troupes; (*aircraft*) avion *m* de transport de troupes

trooper ['truːpər] *n* (**a**) *Mil* (*soldier*) cavalier *m*, soldat *m* de la cavalerie; *US, Austr* (*mounted police officer*) membre *m* de la police montée; (*horse*) cheval *m* de cavalerie; *US* **(state) t.** (*policeman*) ≈ C.R.S. *m*; *F* **to swear like a t.** jurer comme un charretier (**b**) *Br* = **troopship**

trooping ['truːpɪŋ] *n esp Br Mil* **t. (of) the colour** salut *m* au drapeau, présentation *f* du drapeau; *Br* **the T. of the Colour** la parade militaire à l'occasion de l'anniversaire de la Reine

troopship ['truːpʃɪp] *n* (navire *m* de) transport *m* de troupes

troop train *n* train *m* militaire

trophic ['trəʊfɪk] *adj Med* trophique

trophy ['trəʊfɪ] *n* (*in hunting*), *Sp, Fig* trophée *m*

tropic ['trɒpɪk] *n Astron, Geog* tropique *m*; **the tropics** les tropiques

tropical ['trɒpɪk(ə)l] *adj* (*climate, heat, fish etc*) tropical; (*illness etc*) des tropiques; **it's absolutely t. in here!** il fait une chaleur torride ici!

tropical rain forest *n* forêt *f* tropicale humide

tropism ['trəʊpɪz(ə)m] *n Biol* tropisme *m*

troposphere ['trɒpəsfɪər] *n Met* troposphère *f*

Trot [trɒt] *n Pol F* trotskyste *mf*

trot¹ [trɒt] *n* **(a)** *Horseriding etc* trot *m*; **at a brisk t.** au grand trot; **to set off at a t.** partir au trot; *F* **they've had 22 wins on the t.** ils ont gagné vingt-deux fois à la file *ou* de suite; *F* **for five days on the t.** pendant cinq jours de suite; *F* **to keep sb on the t.** ne laisser aucun repos à qn **(b)** *Sl* **to have the trots** (*diarrhoea*) avoir la chiasse *ou* la courante

trot² **(-tt-) 1** *vi Horseriding* trotter, aller au trot; (*of person*) trotter; (*of child*) trottiner; *F* **I must be trotting (along)** il faut que je file; *F* **I'll just t. up/down/along to the post office** je vais juste faire un saut à la poste; *F* **I'll just t. round to the shops** je vais faire quelques courses en vitesse; *F* **he trotted off down the road** il s'éloigna en trottinant dans la rue **2** *vt* (*horse*) faire trotter

▶ **trot out** *vtsep F* (*produce*) (*excuses*) débiter; (*one's knowledge etc*) faire étalage de, débiter; (*old grievances*) rabâcher; **he can always t. out excuses** il est toujours prêt à débiter des excuses

troth [trəʊθ] *n Arch, Lit* foi *f*; **by my t.!** sur ma foi!

Trotskyite ['trɒtskɪaɪt] *adj, n* trotskyste *mf*

trotter ['trɒtər] *n* **(a)** (*horse*) cheval *m* de trot, trotteur, -euse **(b)** *Culin* **sheep's/pigs' trotters** pieds *mpl* de mouton/de porc **(c)** *F* **trotters** (*feet*) pieds *mpl*

trotting ['trɒtɪŋ] *n Horseriding* trot *m*; **t. race** course *f* de trot (attelé)

troubadour ['tru:bədʊər] *n Liter* troubadour *m*

trouble¹ ['trʌb(ə)l] *n* **(a)** (*problem, difficulty*) ennui *m*, difficulté *f*, problème *m*; **he told me his troubles** il m'a raconté ses malheurs *ou* ses problèmes; **her troubles are over** ses malheurs *ou* ses ennuis sont finis; **in one's time of t.** quand on a des ennuis; **money troubles** problèmes *mpl* d'argent; **what's the t.?** qu'est-ce qu'il y a?, quel est le problème?; **we must get to the root of the t.** il faut chercher la source du mal; **the t. is that …** l'ennui *ou* le problème c'est que …; **the t. with you** *or* **your t. is you don't think** ton problème *ou* le problème chez toi c'est que tu ne réfléchis pas; **the t. with these machines is (that) they're too complicated** le problème avec ces machines c'est qu'elles sont trop compliquées; **you'll have t. with him** il va vous causer des difficultés *ou* des ennuis; **did you have any t. finding the place?** est-ce que tu as eu du mal à trouver?; **this new machine's/system's more t. than it's worth** cette nouvelle machine/ce nouveau système pose plus de problèmes qu'elle/qu'il n'en résoud; **this machine's been** *or* **given nothing but t.** cette machine ne m'a/ne nous a apporté que des problèmes; **to be in t.** avoir des ennuis *ou* des difficultés; **to get into t.** s'attirer des ennuis *ou* des désagréments; *F* (*become pregnant*) tomber enceinte; **to get into t. with the police** avoir affaire à la police; **to get sb into t., to make t. for sb** créer des ennuis à qn; *F* **to get a girl into t.** (*make her pregnant*) mettre une fille enceinte; **to get sb out of t.** tirer qn d'affaire; **to keep out of t.** éviter les ennuis; **to be looking** *or* **asking for t.** (*cause problems for the future*) se préparer des ennuis; **he was asking for t., the way he drank** il cherchait des ennuis à boire comme ça; **are you looking for t.?** (*said aggressively*) tu cherches des ennuis?; **that's asking for t., not locking the door** ne pas verrouiller la porte, c'est tenter le diable; **to make** *or* **cause t.** semer la discorde; **to make t. for oneself** se créer des ennuis

(b) (*disorder, unrest*) désordre *m*; **there was t. in the streets** il y a eu des violences dans la rue; **the Troubles** (*in N. Ireland*) les troubles *mpl*; **there will be t.** il va y avoir du grabuge; **there'll be t. if he finds out** je vais/tu vas/on va/*etc* avoir des ennuis s'il s'en rend compte; *Hum* **there's t. at mill** la révolte gronde

(c) (*physical, medical, mechanical*) **eye t.** affection *f* de l'œil; (*sight disorder*) troubles *mpl* de vision; **stomach t.** troubles digestifs; **to have heart t.** être malade du cœur; **to locate** *or* **trace the t.** (*in machine, engine etc*) trouver la source de la panne; **my eyes have been giving me some t.** mes yeux me donnent quelques soucis; **the car/engine hasn't given me any t.** je n'ai eu aucun problème avec la voiture/le moteur; *Aut etc* **engine t.** panne *f* de moteur; *F* **he's got woman/she's got man t.** ça ne va pas très bien pour lui/elle côté cœur

(d) (*inconvenience*) dérangement *m*, peine *f*, mal *m*; **to take the t. to do sth, to go to the t. of doing sth** prendre *ou* se donner la peine de faire qch; **to go to** *or* **put oneself to** *or* **to take a great deal of t.** se donner beaucoup de mal *ou* de peine; **it's not worth the t.** cela n'en vaut pas la peine; **nothing's too much t. for him** il est toujours prêt à aider les autres; **(it's) no t.** (ça ne pose) aucun problème; **if it's no t.** si ça ne vous dérange pas; **they've gone to all that t. for nothing** ils se sont donné du mal pour rien

trouble² **1** *vt* **(a)** (*worry*) inquiéter; *Med* affliger; **my back's been troubling me for years** ça fait des années que j'ai des douleurs dans le dos; **I'm troubled about his future** son avenir me préoccupe *ou* m'inquiète; **don't let it t. you!** que cela ne vous inquiète pas!, ne vous tourmentez pas à ce sujet!; **how long has this cough been troubling you?** depuis combien de temps souffrez-vous de cette toux?; **her conscience was troubling her** elle avait des problèmes de conscience

(b) (*disturb*) déranger; **I'm sorry to t. you** excusez-moi de vous déranger; **could I t. you a minute?** excusez-moi, vous auriez une minute?; **may I t. you to shut the door?** cela vous dérangerait-il de fermer la porte?

2 *vi* **don't t.!, you needn't t.!** ne vous dérangez pas!; **he didn't even t. to …** il n'a même pas pris la peine de …

troubled ['trʌb(ə)ld] *adj* (*worried*) (*look*) inquiet, -ète; **t. period** (*of history*) époque *f* troublée; **t. sleep** sommeil *m* agité; **he's got a t. conscience** il n'a pas la conscience tranquille; *Fig* **troubled waters** eaux *fpl* troubles

trouble-free *adj* sans problèmes; **a t. holiday** des vacances qui se déroulent/se sont déroulées sans incidents *ou* sans anicroches

troublemaker ['trʌb(ə)lmeɪkər] *n* fauteur, -trice de troubles

troubleshooter ['trʌb(ə)lʃu:tər] *n Pol, Ind etc* médiateur, -trice, conciliateur, -trice; (*for machinery etc*) dépanneur *m*

troubleshooting ['trʌb(ə)lʃu:tɪŋ] *n Pol, Ind etc* médiation *f*, conciliation *f*; *Comptr* dépannage *m*; **t. section** (*in manual*) section *f* de dépannage

troublesome ['trʌb(ə)lsəm] *adj* (*problem, workforce, child etc*) difficile; (*rival*) gênant; (*cough*) pénible

trouble spot *n* point *m* névralgique

troubling ['trʌblɪŋ] *adj* inquiétant

troublous ['trʌbləs] *adj Arch, Lit* troublé, agité

trough [trɒf] *n* **(a)** **(feeding) t.** auge *f*, mangeoire *f*; **drinking t.** abreuvoir *m*; *Fig F* **to have** *or* **get one's snout in the t.** avoir sa part du gâteau **(b)** *Ch, Phys* (*for mercury, water*) cuve *f*, cuvette *f* **(c)** *Geol* auge *f* **(d)** *Phys, Math, Econ* (*of wave, graph, cycle*) creux *m*; *Met* (*barometric*) dépression *f*, zone *f* dépressionnaire

trounce [traʊns] *vt Sp* (*defeat heavily*) écraser, battre à plate(s) couture(s)

trouncing ['traʊnsɪŋ] *n Sp* (*heavy defeat*) défaite *f* écrasante; **Wales gave France a t.** le pays de Galles a battu la France à plate(s) couture(s)

troupe [tru:p] *n* (*of actors etc*) troupe *f*

trouper ['tru:pər] *n Th* membre *m* d'une/de la troupe; *Fig* **he's an old t.** c'est un vieux de la vieille; *Fig* **she's a real t.** elle s'y connaît

trouser press ['traʊzə] *n* presse *f*

trousers ['traʊzəz] *npl* [①A10,e] *esp Br* **(pair of) t.** pantalon *m*; *F* **she's the one who wears the t.** c'est elle qui porte la culotte; *Fig F* **to be caught with one's t. down** être pris au dépourvu; **short t.** shorts *mpl*; **when I was still in short t.** quand j'étais encore en culottes courtes

trouser suit *n* tailleur-pantalon *m*, *pl* tailleurs-pantalons

trousseau ['tru:səʊ] *n* trousseau *m*

trout [traʊt] *n* **(a)** (*inv in pl*) (*fish*) truite *f*; **t. fishing** pêche *f* à la truite **(b)** *F* (*woman*) **old t.** vieille bique *f*

trove [trəʊv] *n* = **treasure-trove**

trowel ['traʊəl] *n Constr* truelle *f*; (*in gardening*) déplantoir *m*; *Fig F* **to lay it on with a t.** en faire trop

Troy [trɔɪ] *n* Troie *f*

troy [trɔɪ] *n* **t. (weight)** (*for gold, money*) poids *m* troy; **t. ounce** once *f* troy (*31,1g*)

truancy ['tru:ənsɪ] *n Sch* absentéisme *m* scolaire

truant ['tru:ənt] **1** *n* élève *mf* qui fait l'école buissonnière; **to play t.** faire l'école buissonnière **2** *adj attrib* qui fait l'école buissonnière

truce [tru:s] *n* trêve *f*; **to call a t.** demander une trêve; **let's call it a t.!** faisons une trêve!

truck¹ [trʌk] *n* **(a)** (*lorry*) camion *m*; (*big, HGV*) poids *m* lourd; *Min* berline *f*, benne *f*, bac *m*; **fork-lift t.** chariot *m* élévateur à fourche; *Am* **wrecking t.** camion de dépannage, dépanneuse *f* **(b)** *Rail* (*for freight*) wagon *m*; **cattle t.** fourgon *m* à bestiaux

truck² **1** *vt* (*goods*) camionner, acheminer par camion **2** *vi esp Am* (*drive a truck*) être conducteur de camion, être camionneur; *F* **keep on trucking!** bon courage!

truck³ *n* **(a)** *F* (*relations*) (*with sb*) rapports *mpl*, relations *fpl*; **I'll have no t. with him** je ne veux rien avoir à faire avec lui **(b)** *Am* (*vegetables*) produits *mpl* maraîchers

truckdriver ['trʌkdraɪvər], **trucker** ['trʌkər] *n esp Am* camionneur *m*, routier *m*

truck farmer *n Am* maraîcher *m*

truck garden *n Am* jardin *m* maraîcher

truck gardener *n Am* maraîcher *m*

truck gardening *n Am* maraîchage *m*
trucking ['trʌkɪŋ] *n esp Am* camionnage *m*; **t. company** entreprise *f* de transports routiers
truckle¹ ['trʌk(ə)l] *n* **t. bed** lit *m* gigogne
truckle² *vi Lit* ramper, s'abaisser (**to** devant)
truckstop ['trʌkstɒp] *n esp Am* café *m* de routiers, routier *m*
truculence ['trʌkjʊləns] *n* agressivité *f*
truculent ['trʌkjʊlənt] *adj* agressif
truculently ['trʌkjʊləntlɪ] *adv* agressivement
trudge¹ [trʌdʒ] *n* marche *f* pénible; **a long t.** un trajet long et pénible
trudge² **1** *vt* **they trudged the streets looking for a cheap hotel** ils se traînaient péniblement à travers les rues à la recherche d'un petit hôtel bon marché **2** *vi* marcher lourdement *ou* péniblement, se traîner; **we trudged across the sodden fields** nous avancions avec peine à travers les champs détrempés; **I've been trudging around the shops all day** je me suis traîné péniblement dans les magasins toute la journée
▶ **trudge along** *vi* (*walk heavily, with difficulty*) cheminer *ou* avancer péniblement, se traîner
true [tru:] **1** *adj* **(a)** (*according with reality, not fictional*) vrai; (*accurate*) exact; **t. account** récit *m* fidèle *ou* exact; **t. adventures** aventures *fpl* vécues; **it is t. that …** il est vrai que …; **if it were t. that …** s'il était vrai que … + *sub.* ; **to come t.** (*of wish etc*) se réaliser; **this also holds t. for …** il en est de même pour …; **how t.!, how very t.!** c'est bien vrai!; **that's all too t., I'm afraid** ce n'est que trop vrai, malheureusement; **I can't believe it's t.** je n'arrive pas à le croire; **it's getting late – t.** il se fait tard – tu as raison; *Acct* **t. and fair view** (*of accounts*) image *f* fidèle; **t. copie** copie *f* conforme
(b) (*genuine*) véritable; (*real*) vrai, réel; **t. repentance** repentir *m* sincère *ou* véritable; **her t. nature** son véritable caractère; **he's a t. Irishman** (*conforms to stereotype*) c'est bien un Irlandais; (*by birth*) c'est un Irlandais, un vrai; **to get a t. idea of the situation** se faire une idée juste de la situation
(c) *MecE, Carp* juste, droit, rectiligne; **to make a piece t.** ajuster une pièce; **his aim was t.** (*was a good shot*) il était bon tireur; (*hit target*) il a visé juste; **the table isn't t.** la table n'est pas d'aplomb
(d) (*faithful*) fidèle, loyal; **to be t. to a friend** être loyal envers *ou* fidèle à un ami; **to be t. to oneself** être fidèle à soi-même; **to be** *or* **remain t. to one's principles** être fidèle à ses principes; **to be t. to a promise** rester fidèle à une promesse; **t. to life** qui correspond bien à la réalité; **t. to form, he …** fidèle à lui-même, il …; **she was an accountant, and t. to type she …** elle était comptable, et bien entendu elle …; **t. to type, he …** (*of Scotsman, accountant*) en bon Écossais/comptable, il …; *Br* **he's a t. blue** (*Tory*) c'est un Conservateur pur et dur; **t. friend** ami(e) loyal(e), vrai(e) ami(e); **t. love** (*feeling, person*) grand amour *m*; **a jury of twelve good men and t.** un jury de douze citoyens de bonne renommée
(e) (*of voice, instrument*) juste
2 *adv* **(a)** *F* (*truthfully*) **tell me t.** dis-moi la vérité
(b) (*to sing, aim*) juste; **to run t.** (*of wheel*) tourner rond *ou* sans balourd
3 *n MecE etc* **out of t.** (*of vertical post, member etc*) hors d'aplomb; (*of horizontal member etc*) dénivelé; (*of axle etc*) faussé, dévoyé; (*of timber*) déjeté; (*of wheel*) désaxé
▶ **true up** *vtsep* (*sth*) mettre bien en place
true-blue **1** *n Br* (*Conservative*) Conservateur, -trice pur(e) et dur(e) **2** *adj* loyal, convaincu
trueborn ['tru:bɔ:n] *adj Old-fashioned* vrai, véritable; **a t. Englishman** un vrai Anglais d'Angleterre
true-false *adj* **t. test** questionnaire *m* auquel on répond par 'vrai' ou 'faux'
true north *n* nord *m* géographique
truffle ['trʌf(ə)l] *n* truffe *f*; *Br* **(rum) t.** (*sweet*) truffe au rhum; **t. hound** chien *m* truffier
trug [trʌg] *n Br* panier *m ou* corbeille *f* de jardinier
truism ['tru:ɪz(ə)m] *n* truisme *m*, vérité *f* de La Palice, lapalissade *f*; **it is a t. that …** c'est un lieu commun de dire que …
truly ['tru:lɪ] *adv* **(a)** (*really, genuinely*) vraiment, véritablement; **a t. difficult situation** une situation vraiment difficile; **I am t. grateful to her** je lui suis sincèrement reconnaissant; **it's t. tragic** c'est vraiment tragique; **I t. believe that …** je crois vraiment *ou* sincèrement que …; **yours t.** (*letter ending*) = je vous prie d'agréer *ou* de croire à mes sentiments distingués; *F* **yours t.** (*myself*) votre serviteur; *F* **meanwhile yours t. had left** entretemps mézigue *ou* votre serviteur était parti
(b) (*in truth*) en vérité, à vrai dire; **(really and) t.?** vrai de vrai?
(c) (*faithfully*) (*to serve sb*) fidèlement, loyalement
trump¹ [trʌmp] *n Arch, Lit* (*trumpet*) **the last t.** la trompette du jugement dernier
trump² *n Cards* **t. (card)** atout *m*; **spades are trumps** c'est atout pique; **to play trumps** jouer l'atout; **to call no trumps** jouer sans atout; *Fig F* **she turned up trumps** elle a fait des miracles; *Fig* **to play one's t. card** jouer son atout
trump³ *vt Cards* (*card*) couper avec l'atout
▶ **trump up** *vtsep* (*invent*) (*excuse*) inventer; **to t. up a charge against sb** fabriquer une accusation contre qn; **trumped-up story** histoire *f* inventée
trumpery ['trʌmpərɪ] *n* (*worthless objects*) camelote *f*; (*nonsense*) absurdités *mpl*
trumpet¹ ['trʌmpɪt] *n Mus* trompette *f*; *Fig* **to blow one's own t.** chanter ses propres louanges; **t. blast** *or* **call** coup *m ou* sonnerie *f* de trompette; *Mil* **t. major** trompette-major *m*, *pl* trompettes-majors; **t. player** trompettiste *mf*; (*in band*) trompette
trumpet² (-t-) **1** *vi* trompeter, sonner de la trompette; (*of elephant*) barrir **2** *vt esp Lit* (*success*) claironner
trumpeter ['trʌmpɪtər] *n Mil* trompette *m*; *Mus* (*by profession*) trompettiste *mf*
trumpeting ['trʌmpɪtɪŋ] *n* sonnerie *f* de trompette; (*of elephant*) barrissement *m*
truncate [trʌŋ'keɪt] *vt* (*body, text etc*) tronquer; (*meeting etc*) écourter
truncated [trʌŋ'keɪtɪd] *adj* (*body, text*) tronqué; (*meeting etc*) écourté; *Geom* **t. cone** cône *m* tronqué
truncheon ['trʌn(t)ʃən] **1** *n* matraque *f*; (*esp for directing traffic*) bâton *m* **2** *vt* matraquer
trundle¹ ['trʌnd(ə)l] *n* **t. bed** lit *m* gigogne
trundle² **1** *vt* (*hoop etc*) faire rouler; (*wheelbarrow, hand cart*) pousser; **they trundled him in on his bed** ils l'ont fait entrer sur son lit à roulettes **2** *vi* (*of hoop etc*) rouler; (*of vehicle*) rouler péniblement; (*of cart*) rouler lourdement; **the project trundled on** le projet avançait péniblement
▶ **trundle out** *vtsep* (*old bicycle, theory etc*) ressortir
trunk [trʌŋk] *n* **(a)** (*of tree, body, artery*) tronc *m*; *Archit* (*of column*) fût *m* **(b)** (*luggage*) malle *f* **(c)** *Am Aut* coffre *m* **(d)** (*of elephant*) trompe *f* **(e)** **trunks** (*for men, for swimming*) maillot *m* (de bain), slip *m* de bain
trunk call *n Br Tel* appel *m* interurbain
trunk line *n Rail* ligne *f* principale, grande ligne; *Tel* inter *m*
trunk road *n Br* route *f* nationale, nationale *f*; **trunk roads** grandes routes *fpl*
trunnion ['trʌnjən] *n Mil, MecE* tourillon *m*
truss¹ [trʌs] *n* **(a)** *Med* bandage *m* herniaire **(b)** *Constr* (*of beam etc*) armature *f*; (*for roof timbers, bridge*) ferme *f*; (*for vaulting*) cintre *m* **(c)** (*of flowers*) touffe *f*; (*of tomatoes*) grappe *f*
truss² *vt* **(a)** *Constr, Tech* (*beam etc*) armer, renforcer **(b)** *Culin* (*fowl*) trousser, brider
▶ **truss up** *vtsep* (*tie up*) (*sb*) ligoter; **trussed up like a chicken** ficelé comme un poulet
trust¹ [trʌst] *n* **(a)** (*belief*) confiance *f* (**in** en); **to put one's t. in sb** mettre sa confiance en qn; **to put one's t. in sth** se reposer sur qch; **to betray sb's t.** trahir la confiance de qn; **I took what you said on t.** je t'ai cru sur parole, je t'ai fait confiance
(b) (*responsibility*) responsabilité *f*; **to be in a position of t.** occuper un poste de confiance; **he placed his child in my t.** il m'a confié la garde de son enfant
(c) *Jur* fidéicommis *m*, fiducie *f*; **to hold in t.** tenir par fidéicommis; (*property etc*) administrer par fidéicommis; **t. company** société *f* fiduciaire; *Br* **National T.** = société *f* pour la conservation des sites et monuments
(d) *Ind etc* (*group*) trust *m*; **brains t.** brain-trust *m*, *pl* brain-trusts; *Fin* **(investment) t.** société *f* de placement(s); **unit t.** société d'investissement à capital variable; **t. bank** banque *f* de gestion de patrimoine
trust² **1** *vt* **(a)** (*believe in*) (*sb*) faire confiance à, se fier à; (*sth*) se fier à; **she's not to be trusted** on ne peut pas se fier à elle; **are the figures to be trusted?** est-ce que ces chiffres sont fiables?; **she's not to be trusted on the question of …** on ne peut pas lui faire confiance quand il s'agit de …; **I don't t. you with money** je ne te confierais pas mon argent; **you can't t. anyone nowadays** on ne peut faire confiance *ou* se fier à personne de nos jours; **I don't t. you with her!** je ne la laisserais pas seule avec toi!; **I couldn't t. myself not to say anything** je ne pourrais pas résister à l'envie de dire quelque chose; **to t. sb with sth** confier qch à qn; **to t. sb to do sth** laisser à qn le soin de faire qch; *F* **t. him to say that!** c'est bien de lui!; *F* **I've lost it – t. you!** je l'ai perdu – ça c'est tout toi! *ou* c'est typique de toi! *ou* ça ne m'étonne pas de toi!; **she won't t. him out of her sight** elle lui fait si peu confiance qu'elle ne le quitte pas des yeux; **to t. one's**

instincts se fier à son instinct; **to t. sb's judgement** se fier au jugement de qn; *F* **I wouldn't t. her as far as I could throw her** je ne lui ferais pas confiance du tout; **there's no-one's judgement I t. as much as hers** je lui fais confiance comme à personne d'autre

(b) (*entrust*) **to t. sth to sb** confier qch à qn

(c) *esp Fml* **to t. (that) ...** (*hope*) espérer que ...; (*express wish that*) exprimer le vœu que ... + *sub*; **I t. he is not ill** j'espère bien qu'il n'est pas malade

2 *vi* **to t. to luck** s'en remettre au hasard

▶ **trust in** *vipo* (*put one's hopes in*) (*sth*) mettre ses espérances *ou* son espoir en; **to t. in God** croire en Dieu; **I want someone I can t. in** (*have confidence in*) il me faut une personne de confiance

trust-busting ['trʌstbʌstɪŋ] *Am* **1** *n* démantèlement *m* des trusts **2** *adj attrib* qui a trait au démantèlement des trusts

trusted ['trʌstɪd] *adj* (*person*) de confiance; **tried and t.** (*remedy, method*) éprouvé; (*friend*) fidèle, éprouvé

trustee [trʌs'tiː] *n* **(a)** *Jur* fidéicommissaire *m*, fiduciaire *m*; (*with powers of attorney*) mandataire *m* **(b)** (*of museum, charity, company, life assurance policy*) administrateur *m*; **board of trustees** conseil *m* d'administration

trusteeship [trʌs'tiːʃɪp] *n* **(a)** *Jur* fidéicommis *m* **(b)** (*of museum, charity etc*) fonction *f* d'administrateur **(c)** *Pol* (*of territory*) tutelle *f*

trustful ['trʌstfʊl] *adj* plein de confiance, confiant

trustfully ['trʌstfəlɪ] *adv* avec confiance

trustfulness ['trʌstfʊlnɪs] *n* confiance *f*

trust fund *n* fonds *m* en fidéicommis

trusting ['trʌstɪŋ] *adj* confiant; (*look*) plein de confiance; **you're far too t.** tu fais trop confiance aux gens; **it's very t. of you to lend it to them** tu leur fais drôlement confiance pour le leur prêter

trustingly ['trʌstɪŋlɪ] *adv* avec confiance

trust territories *npl Pol* territoires *mpl* sous tutelle

trustworthiness ['trʌstwɜːðɪnɪs] *n* (*person*) loyauté *f*, honnêteté *f*; (*of testimony, account etc*) crédibilité *f*, véracité *f*

trustworthy ['trʌstwɜːðɪ] *adj* (*person*) digne de confiance; (*information*) digne de foi; (*testimony*) irrécusable; (*critic, guidebook etc*) très fiable

trusty ['trʌstɪ] *adj Arch, Lit* fidèle, loyal; *Hum* **my t. typewriter** ma bonne vieille machine à écrire

truth [truːθ, *pl* truːðz] *n* vérité *f*; **in t.** en vérité; **the plain** *or* **honest t.** la pure vérité, la vérité pure et simple; **to speak** *or* **tell the t.** dire la vérité; **the t. (of the matter) is** *or* **to tell the t., I forgot it** pour dire la vérité *ou* à dire vrai je l'ai oublié; **... and that's the t.** ... et voilà la vérité; **there's some t. in what you say** il y a du vrai dans ce que vous dites; **there's not a word of t. in it** il n'y a pas un brin de vérité là-dedans; **I told him a few home truths** je lui ai dit son fait *ou* ses quatre vérités; *Jur* **the t., the whole t., and nothing but the t.** la vérité, toute la vérité, rien que la vérité; *prov* **t. will out** la vérité finit toujours par se faire jour; *prov* **t. is the first casualty (of war)** toute guerre s'accompagne de son cortège de mensonges

truth drug *n* sérum *m* de vérité

truthful ['truːθfʊl] *adj* (*person*) sincère, honnête; (*account etc*) véridique; (*description, portrait etc*) fidèle; **to be t.** (*of person*) dire la vérité, être sincère *ou* honnête

truthfully ['truːθfəlɪ] *adv* (*to speak, answer, claim etc*) en disant la vérité; (*to portray etc*) fidèlement

truthfulness ['truːθfʊlnɪs] *n* (*of statement, claim etc*) véracité *f*; (*of portrait etc*) fidélité *f*

truth function *n* fonction *f* de vérité

truth table *n* table *f ou* matrice *f* de vérité

truth value *n* variable *f* 'vrai' ou 'faux'

try¹ [traɪ] *n* **(a)** (*attempt*) essai *m*, tentative *f*; **to have a t. at doing sth** essayer de faire qch; **to have a t. at sth** (*try out*) s'essayer à qch; **I had a t. at skin-diving** je me suis essayé à la plongée sous-marine; **let's have a t.!** essayons toujours!; **can I have a t.?** (est-ce que) je peux essayer?; **I think I'll have a t. for this job** je crois que je vais me présenter pour ce travail; **you've already had three tries** vous avez déjà essayé trois fois; **OK, you can have one more t.** bon d'accord, tu peux encore essayer une fois *ou* tu as encore un essai; **go on, give it a t.** (*activity*) allez, essaie; (*food*) allez, goûte; **at the first t.** du premier coup; **it won't be easy but it's worth a t.** ça ne va pas être facile mais ça vaut la peine *ou* le coup d'essayer; **worth a t.?** ça vaut le coup d'essayer?

(b) *Rugby* essai *m*; **to score a t.** marquer un essai

try² (*pt, pp* **tried** [traɪd]) **1** *vt* **(a)** (*sample*) essayer; **here, t. my pen** tenez, essayez avec mon stylo; **to t. a dish** goûter (à) un mets; **t. some** (*food*) goûtes-y; **I'll t. anything once** il faut tout essayer dans la vie

(b) (*attempt to do*) essayer, tenter; **to t. an experiment** tenter une expérience; **to t. the door/the window** essayer (d'ouvrir) la porte/la fenêtre; **I'd like to see you trying it!** je voudrais bien t'y voir!

(c) [①A43,b,ii] (*attempt*) **to t. to do sth** essayer de faire qch; **she tried to smile** elle a essayé de sourire; **he was trying hard to keep back the tears** il s'efforçait de retenir ses larmes; **it's worth trying** cela vaut la peine d'essayer; *F* **to t. and do sth** tâcher *ou* essayer de faire qch; *F* **t. and be nice to her** tâche d'être gentil avec elle; **to t. doing sth** essayer de faire qch; **t. (asking) Jane** demande à Jane; **have you tried the chemist's?** tu as essayé le pharmacien?; **I tried the number in the book but there was no reply** j'ai essayé le numéro de l'annuaire mais ça ne répondait pas

(d) (*check*) (*mechanism*) vérifier

(e) *Jur* (*case, person*) juger; *US* (*of advocate*) (*case*) plaider; **to be tried for theft** passer en correctionnelle pour vol

(f) (*test*) (*person*) éprouver, mettre à l'épreuve; (*sb's courage, sb's patience etc*) mettre à l'épreuve; **to t. one's strength against sb** se mesurer avec *ou* à qn; **a people sorely tried** une nation fort *ou* durement éprouvée; **to t. one's eyes (reading)** se fatiguer les yeux (à lire)

2 *vi* faire un effort *ou* des efforts; **to t. again** essayer de nouveau; **you must t. harder** il faut faire de plus grands efforts; **at least you tried** au moins tu as/auras essayé; **he didn't really t.** il n'a pas vraiment essayé; **you weren't really trying** tu n'as pas vraiment essayé; **go on then, t.!** alors vas-y, essaie!; **... and she wasn't even trying** ... et elle l'a fait sans le moindre effort; **just you t.!** essaie un peu pour voir!; **I'd like to see you t.!** (*answer to threat, challenge*) je voudrais bien t'y voir!

▶ **try for** *vipo* (*attempt to obtain*) tâcher d'obtenir; **to t. for a job** poser sa candidature à un emploi; **he's trying for (a place at) music school** il essaie d'obtenir une place à l'école de musique; *Sp etc* **she's trying for the record** elle essaie de battre le record

▶ **try on** *vtsep* **(a)** (*clothes, shoes for size or appearance*) essayer **(b)** *F* **to t. it on (with sb)** tenter le coup (avec qn); **they're just trying it on** ils bluffent, c'est du bluff; **you're (just) trying it on!** ça ne marche pas *ou* ne prend pas!; **she tried it on with my husband** (*attempted to seduce*) elle a essayé de séduire mon mari

▶ **try out** *vtsep* (*test*) faire l'essai de; (*new procedure*) essayer, expérimenter; **to t. sth out on sb** essayer *ou* expérimenter qch sur qn; **they're trying him out in goal** ils l'essaient *ou* l'ont mis à l'essai comme gardien de but

trying ['traɪɪŋ] **1** *adj* (*time, experience*) pénible, difficile; (*person*) pénible **2** *n Jur* (*of case, person*) jugement *m*

try-on *n Br F* bluff *m*; **it's just a t.** c'est du bluff

try-out *n* (*of machine etc*) premier essai *m*, essai préliminaire; *Am Th* audition *f*; *Sp* épreuve *f* de sélection; **to give sb/sth a t.** mettre qn à l'essai/essayer qch

try scorer *n Rugby* **the t.** celui qui a marqué l'essai; **France's leading t.** celui qui a marqué le plus d'essais pour la France

tryst [trɪst] *n Lit* rendez-vous *m* amoureux

tsar [tsɑːr] *n* tsar *m*, czar *m*

tsarevitch ['tsɑːrəvɪtʃ] *n* tsarévitch *m*, czarévitch *m*

tsarina [tsɑː'riːnə] *n* tsarine *f*, czarine *f*

tsarist ['tsɑːrɪst] *adj, n* tsariste *mf*

tsetse ['t(s)etsɪ] *n* **t. (fly)** (mouche *f*) tsé-tsé *f inv*

tsp *Culin* (*abbr* **teaspoon, teaspoonful**) cu. à c. ; **2 t. sugar** (*in recipe*) 2 cu. à c. de sucre

TT [tiː'tiː] *n* **(a)** *Br Sp* (*abbr* **Tourist Trophy**) = course *f* motocycliste **(b)** (*abbr* **teetotal**) **I'm TT** je ne bois pas d'alcool

tub [tʌb] *n* **(a)** (*container*) baquet *m*, bac *m*; (*for flowers, shrubs*) bac, caisse *f*; (*for washing*) baquet; (*in washing machine*) cuve *f*; (*of icecream, cream etc*) pot *m*; **t. chair** (fauteuil *m*) crapaud *m* **(b)** (*bathtub*) baignoire *f*; **a hot t.** (*bath*) un bain chaud **(c)** *F* (*boat*) **old t.** vieux rafiot *m*

tuba ['tjuːbə] *n Mus* tuba *m*

tubby ['tʌbɪ] *adj F* (*person*) dodu, boulot, -otte

tube [tjuːb] *n* **(a)** (*of paint, toothpaste*) tube *m*; (*pipe*) tuyau *m*; *Med etc* (*for deep wound*) drain *m*; *Austr F* (*of beer*) boîte *f*; *Aut etc* **inner t.** (*of tyre*) chambre *f* à air; *Ch, Phys etc* **test t.** éprouvette *f*; **(Fallopian) tubes** trompes *fpl* (de Fallope); **(bronchial) tubes** bronches *fpl*; *F* **that's £500 down the tubes** voilà 500 livres de foutues en l'air; *F* **that's all our efforts (gone) down the tubes** et voilà tous nos efforts réduits à néant; *F* **he watched his marriage/life's work go down the tubes** il a vu son mariage/le travail de toute une vie tourner en eau de boudin

(b) *El, Electron, TV etc* (*electronic, thermionic*) tube *m*; **cathode-ray t.** tube cathodique *ou* à rayons cathodiques; *esp Am F* **the t.** (*television*) la télé

(c) *Br F* **the t.** (*London underground*) ≈ le métro; **t. station** ≈ station *f* de métro
tube-feeding *n Med* gavage *m*
tubeless ['tju:blɪs] *adj* (*tyre*) sans chambre (à air)
tuber ['tju:bər] *n* (*root*) racine *f* tubéreuse; (*on potato*) tubercule *m*
tubercle ['tju:bɜ:k(ə)l] *n Anat, Med, Bot* tubercule *m*
tubercular [tju:'bɜ:kjʊlər] *adj Med, Bot* tuberculeux
tuberculin [tjʊ'bɜ:kjʊlɪn] *n Med* tuberculine *f*; **t. test** épreuve *f* de la tuberculinisation, tuberculino-diagnostic *m*
tuberculin-tested [tjʊbɜ:kjʊlɪn'testɪd] *adj* **t. milk** lait *m* garanti exempt de tuberculose, = lait cru certifié
tuberculosis [tjʊbɜ:kjʊ'ləʊsɪs] *n Med* tuberculose *f*
tuberculous [tjʊ'bɜ:kjʊləs] *adj Med* tuberculeux
tubful ['tʌbfʊl] *n* cuvée *f*, plein baquet *m* (**of** de)
tubing ['tju:bɪŋ] *n* (*no pl*) tubes *mpl*; (*pipework*) tuyauterie *f*; **rubber t.** tuyau(x) *m*(*pl*) en caoutchouc
tub-thumper ['tʌbθʌmpər] *n F* harangueur *m*
tubular ['tju:bjʊlər] *adj* tubulaire; *Mus* **t. bells** carillon *m* (*d'orchestre*)
TUC [ti:ju:'si:] *n Br Ind* (*abbr* **Trades Union Congress**) = confédération *f* des syndicats britanniques
tuck¹ [tʌk] *n* (**a**) *Sewing* (petit) pli *m*, rempli *m*, plissé *m* (**b**) *Br Sch F* (*cakes, sweets*) gâteaux *mpl*, friandises *fpl*, sucreries *fpl*; **t. box** boîte *f* à provisions; **t. shop** annexe *f* de la cantine où se vendent les friandises
tuck² *vt* (**a**) *Sewing* (*garment*) faire des plis à (**b**) (*fold*) replier (**c**) (*put*) mettre; **to t. one's legs under one** replier les jambes; **she tucked her arm in(to) mine** elle a passé son bras sous le mien; **he tucked his briefcase under his arm** il mit *ou* cala son porte-documents sous son bras; **to t. one's trousers into one's socks** mettre son pantalon dans ses chaussettes; **to t. a rug round sb** envelopper qn dans une couverture; **the bird tucked its head under its wing** l'oiseau a caché sa tête sous son aile; **she tucked her hair under her hat** elle a glissé ses cheveux sous son chapeau
▶ **tuck away** *vtsep* (*put away*) ranger; (*hide*) cacher, mettre de côté; **he tucked it away in his bag** il l'a rangé dans son sac; **village tucked away in the valley** village blotti au fond de la vallée; **you are** *or* **your house is a bit tucked away** vous êtes *ou* votre maison est un peu à l'écart; **to have some money tucked away** avoir de l'argent de côté; *F* **she really can t. it away!** (*eat a lot*) qu'est-ce qu'elle peut bouffer!; *Fb F* **he tucked it away nicely** (*scored*) il l'envoya dans les filets
▶ **tuck in 1** *vtsep* (*put in, under*) rentrer; **to t. one's shirt in** rentrer sa chemise dans son pantalon; **to t. in the bedclothes** border le lit; **to t. sb in** border qn **2** *vi F* (*eat heartily*) manger à belles dents; **t. in!** allez-y!, mangez!
▶ **tuck into** *vipo F* (*eat heartily*) (*meal*) manger de bon appétit, avaler; **here, t. into this** allez, attaque!
▶ **tuck up** *vtsep* (**a**) (*one's skirt, sleeves*) relever, retrousser (**b**) (*sb*) (*in bed*) border
tucker¹ ['tʌkər] *n* (**a**) *F* **in one's best bib and t.** endimanché (**b**) *esp Austr F* (*food*) bouffe *f*
tucker² *vt esp Am F* (*tire out*) fatiguer; **tuckered (out)** épuisé, éreinté
tuck-in *n F* **to have a good t.** (*eating session*) s'envoyer un bon repas
Tudor ['tju:dər] **1** *n* **the Tudors** la maison des Tudors **2** *adj* des Tudors; *Archit* **T. house** maison *f* de style Tudor, maison élisabéthaine; *Archit* **T. style** style *m* Tudor *ou* élisabéthain
Tuesday ['tju:zdɪ] *n* (①**A75-6**,B-C; **B58-9**,B-C] mardi *m*; **he comes on Tuesdays** il vient le mardi; **every T.** tous les mardis
tufa ['t(j)u:fə] *n Geol* tuf *m* calcaire
tuft [tʌft] *n* (*of grass, feathers, hair*) touffe *f*; (*small beard*) barbiche *f*; (*of bird*) huppe *f*, aigrette *f*; **t. of bristles** (*in paint etc brush*) loquet *m* de soies
tufted ['tʌftɪd] *adj* (*bird*) huppé; **t. duck** morillon *m*; **t. heron** héron *m* à aigrette, aigrette *f*
tug¹ [tʌg] *n* (**a**) (*pull*) **to give sth a t.** tirer sur qch d'un coup sec; **to give a good t.** tirer fort; **he gave a t. at the bell** il a tiré (sur) la sonnette; **I felt a t. at my sleeve** j'ai senti qu'on me tirait par la manche; *Fig* **to feel a t. at one's heartstrings** avoir un serrement de cœur; **t. of war** *Sp* lutte *f* de traction à la corde; *Fig* lutte acharnée et prolongée; *Journ F* **t. of love** lutte *f* d'un couple pour la garde d'un/des enfant(s); *Journ F* **t.-of-love parents** parents *mpl* qui se disputent la garde de leur(s) enfant(s); **t.-of-love child** enfant *mf* dont les parents se disputent la garde (**b**) (*boat*) remorqueur *m*
tug² (**-gg-**) **1** *vi* **to t. at** (*door, handle, sleeve, one's moustache*) tirer sur; (*sb's ear*) tirer **2** *vt* (**a**) = **tug at** (**b**) *Naut* (*ship*) remorquer
tugboat ['tʌgbəʊt] *n* remorqueur *m*
tuition [tju:'ɪʃən] *n* instruction *f*, enseignement *m*; **maths t., t. in maths** enseignement en mathématiques; **private t.** leçons *fpl* particulières
tulip ['tju:lɪp] *n* tulipe *f*; **t. glass** (verre *m*) tulipe; **t. tree** tulipier *m*
tulle [tju:l] *n Tex* tulle *m*
tum [tʌm] *n* (*in children's language*), *F* ventre *m*
tumble¹ ['tʌmb(ə)l] *n* (*fall*) chute *f*; (*head over heels*) culbute *f*; **to take a t.** tomber, faire la culbute; (*off horse, bike*) faire une chute; **she had a nasty t.** elle a fait une mauvaise chute; *Fig* **the party's popularity took a t.** le parti a beaucoup perdu de sa popularité; **prices have taken a bit of a t.** les prix ont chuté
tumble² 1 *vi* (*fall*) tomber (par terre), faire une chute; (*head over heels*) culbuter, faire la culbute; (*of acrobat*) faire des culbutes; *Fig* (*of prices*) chuter; **to t. down the stairs** (*fall*) tomber dans les escaliers; (*rush*) descendre les escaliers quatre à quatre; **to t. into bed** se jeter dans son lit; **to t. out of bed** tomber du lit; **they were tumbling over one another** ils se bousculaient **2** *vt* (**a**) **they tumbled the snowball down the hill** ils ont fait débouler la boule de neige dans la pente (**b**) (*clothes*) (*in tumble dryer*) mettre dans le sèche-linge (**c**) *F* (*make love to*) culbuter (**d**) *F* (*get wise to*) (*person*) démasquer
▶ **tumble about** *vi* (*of children, kittens*) gambader
▶ **tumble down** *vi* (*of wall etc*) s'écrouler; **the wall came tumbling down** le mur s'est écroulé; **building that is tumbling down** édifice qui s'écroule *ou* qui tombe en ruine
▶ **tumble out** *vi* **the suitcase came open and everything tumbled out** la valise s'est ouverte et tout est tombé par terre; **the van doors flew open and the children came tumbling out** les portes de la camionnette se sont ouvertes et les enfants se sont rués à l'extérieur
▶ **tumble to** *vipo F* (*understand*) piger; **eventually she tumbled to it** elle a fini par piger
tumbledown ['tʌmb(ə)ldaʊn] *adj* (*house*) qui tombe en ruine(s)
tumble-drier *n* sèche-linge *m inv*
tumble-dry *vt* (*clothes*) faire sécher au sèche-linge
tumbler ['tʌmblər] *n* (**a**) (*glass*) verre *m* (*sans pied*) (**b**) (*of lock*) gorge *f*; *El* (*of switch etc*) culbuteur *m*; **t. lock** serrure *f* à gorge(s) (**c**) **t. (pigeon)** (pigeon *m*) culbutant *m* (**d**) (*toy*) poussa(h) *m* (**e**) (*acrobat*) acrobate *mf* (**f**) (*tumble-drier*) sèche-linge *m inv*
tumblerful ['tʌmbləfʊl] *n* plein verre *m* (**of** de)
tumbleweed ['tʌmb(ə)lwi:d] *n* herbes *fpl* roulées par le vent
tumbrel ['tʌmbrəl], **tumbril** ['tʌmbrɪl] *n Hist* = charrette *f* (des condamnés)
tumefaction [tju:mɪ'fækʃən] *n* tuméfaction *f*
tumefy ['tju:mɪfaɪ] **1** *vt* tuméfier **2** *vi* se tuméfier
tumescent [tju:'mesənt] *adj* tumescent
tumid ['tju:mɪd] *adj* (**a**) *Med* enflé, gonflé (**b**) (*style etc*) ronflant
tummy ['tʌmɪ] *n F* ventre *m*; **t. ache** mal *m* de ventre; **t. button** nombril *m*; **to have t. trouble** avoir l'estomac dérangé
tumour, *US* **tumor** ['tju:mər] *n Med* tumeur *f*
tumult ['tju:mʌlt] *n* tumulte *m*; (*of emotions*) trouble *m*, émoi *m*; **the t. of his emotions** son trouble; **to be in a t.** (*of person*) être en émoi; (*of country*) être agité; **her emotions were in a t.** elle était en émoi
tumultuous [tjʊ'mʌltjʊəs] *adj* tumultueux; **t. meeting** réunion *f* orageuse; **t. session** séance *f* mouvementée
tumultuously [tjʊ'mʌltjʊəslɪ] *adv* tumultueusement
tumulus, *pl* **-i** ['tju:mjʊləs, -aɪ] *n* tumulus *m*
tun [tʌn] *n* (*liquid measure*) tonneau *m*, fût *m*; (*vat*) (*in brewing*) cuve *f*
tuna ['tju:nə] *n* (*fish*) thon *m*
tundra ['tʌndrə] *n Geog* toundra *f*
tune¹ [tju:n] *n* (**a**) *Mus* (*melody*) air *m*, mélodie *f*; *F* **give us a t.!** faites-nous un peu de musique!, jouez-nous un air!; **it's got no t.** il n'y a pas de mélodie; *Fig* **to call the t.** commander; **to the t. of the Marseillaise** sur l'air de la Marseillaise; *Fig* **to change one's t.** changer de discours; *Fig* **to be fined to the t. of £50** avoir une amende de 50 livres

(**b**) **the piano is in/out of t.** le piano est accordé/désaccordé; **to get out of t.** se désaccorder; **to be out of t.** (*of singer, player*) chanter/jouer faux, détonner; **to sing in/out of t.** chanter juste/faux; **the trumpet isn't in t.** *or* **is out of t. with the other instruments** la trompette n'est pas en harmonie *ou* en accord avec les autres instruments; *Fig* **to be in t. with sb/with one's surroundings** être en harmonie avec qn/avec son milieu; *Fig* **the government's out of t. with public opinion** le gouvernement n'est pas en harmonie avec l'opinion publique; **perfectly in t.** (*of engine*) parfaitement réglé
tune² 1 *vt* (**a**) *Mus* (*instrument*) accorder; **to t. a string to ...** accorder une corde sur ... (**b**) (*radio*) régler; **to t. one's radio/TV to a station** régler son poste de radio/télévision

sur une station/chaîne; *Rad, TV* **stay tuned (to this station/ channel)** restez avec nous **(c)** *Aut etc* (*engine*) régler; **to be tuned** (*of engine*) être bien réglé **2** *vi Mus* **to t. to a note** s'accorder sur une note

▶ **tune in** *vi esp Rad* **don't forget to t. in again tomorrow** n'oubliez pas de nous rejoindre *ou* de vous mettre à l'écoute demain; **to t. in to a station/programme** se brancher sur *ou* mettre une station *ou TV* une chaîne/une émission

▶ **tune up 1** *vi Mus* (*get in tune*) (*of orchestra*) s'accorder **2** *vtsep Aut etc* = **tune² 1(c)**

tuned-in [tju:nd'ɪn] *adj Sl* (*aware*) branché; **she's very t. to other people's needs** elle est toujours consciente des besoins des gens

tuneful ['tju:nfʊl] *adj* mélodieux, harmonieux

tunefully ['tju:nfəlɪ] *adv* mélodieusement

tunefulness ['tju:nfʊlnɪs] *n* qualité *f* mélodieuse

tuneless ['tju:nlɪs] *adj* (*unpleasant*) discordant; (*without melody*) sans mélodie

tuner ['tju:nər] *n* **(a)** *Mus* (*person*) (*of pianos etc*) accordeur *m* **(b)** *Rad etc* tuner *m*, syntonisateur *m*

tune-up *n* (*of engine*) mise *f* au point

tungsten ['tʌŋstən] *n Ch* tungstène *m*; **t. steel** acier *m* au tungstène

tungsten-halogen *n* tungstène-halogène; **t. lamp** lampe tungstène-halogène

tunic ['tju:nɪk] *n* tunique *f*

tuning ['tju:nɪŋ] *n* **(a)** *Mus* accord *m*; **fine t.** accord précis; **t. fork** diapason *m*; **t. hammer** accordoir *m*, clef *f* d'accordeur **(b)** *Aut etc* réglage *m*, (re)mise *f* au point

Tunisia [tju:'nɪzɪə] *n* Tunisie *f*

Tunisian [tju:'nɪzɪən] **1** *adj* tunisien **2** *n* Tunisien, -ienne

tunnel¹ ['tʌn(ə)l] *n* tunnel *m*; (*dug by mole etc*) galerie *f*; **to drive a t. through a mountain** percer un tunnel à travers *ou* sous une montagne; *Fig* **at last we can see (some** *or* **the) light at the end of the t.** enfin on voit le bout du tunnel; **is there light at the end of the t.?** est-ce qu'un jour on verra le bout du tunnel?; *MecE etc* **wind t.** tunnel aérodynamique, soufflerie *f* (aérodynamique)

tunnel² (**-ll-**, *US* **-l-**) **1** *vi* creuser *ou* percer un tunnel; **to t. through into a hill** percer un tunnel à travers *ou* dans *ou* sous une colline; **rats had tunnelled under the foundations** des rats avaient creusé des galeries sous les fondations **2** *vt* **to t. one's way out (of a prison** *etc*) creuser un tunnel pour s'échapper (d'une prison *etc*)

tunnelling, *US* **tunneling** ['tʌn(ə)lɪŋ] *n* percement *m* d'un tunnel/de tunnels; **t. equipment** équipement *m* pour le percement d'un tunnel

tunnel net *n* verveux *m*

tunnel vision *n* rétrécissement *m* du champ visuel; *Fig* vision *f* étroite des choses; *Fig* **to suffer from t.** avoir une vision limitée des choses, avoir des œillères

tunny ['tʌnɪ] *n* **t. (fish)** thon *m*

tuppence ['tʌp(ə)ns] *n Old-fashioned Br F* = **twopence**

tuppenny ['tʌp(ə)nɪ] *adj Old-fashioned Br F* = **twopenny**; **t. halfpenny** = **twopenny-halfpenny**

turban ['tɜ:bən] *n* turban *m*

turbid ['tɜ:bɪd] *adj* **(a)** (*liquid*) trouble, bourbeux **(b)** *Fig Lit* (*thoughts*) embrouillé

turbidity [tɜ:'bɪdɪtɪ] *n* turbidité *f*

turbine ['tɜ:baɪn] *n* turbine *f*; **gas/steam t.** turbine à gaz/à vapeur; **t. engine** turbomoteur *m*

turbo ['tɜ:bəʊ] *n* turbo *m*

turbo button *n Comptr* bouton *m* de turbo

turbocharged ['tɜ:bəʊtʃɑ:dʒd] *adj* turbo-compressé; **t. engine** moteur *m* turbocompressé

turbocharger ['tɜ:bəʊtʃɑ:dʒər] *n* turbocompresseur *m*, turbo *m*

turbocharging ['tɜ:bəʊtʃɑ:dʒɪŋ] *n* suralimentation *f* par turbocompresseur

turbo diesel *n* turbodiesel; **t. engine** moteur *m* turbo-diesel

turbo-electric [tɜ:bəʊɪ'lektrɪk] *adj* turbo-électrique

turbofan ['tɜ:bəʊfæn] *n Av* turboréacteur *m* à double flux

turbogenerator [tɜ:bəʊ'dʒenəreɪtər] *n El* turbogénérateur *m*, turbogénératrice *f*

turbojet ['tɜ:bəʊdʒet] *n Av* **t. (aircraft)** avion *m* à turbopropulseur; **t. (engine)** turboréacteur *m* (*à simple flux*)

turbomarketing ['tɜ:bəʊ'mɑ:kɪtɪŋ] *n Mktg* turbo-mercatique *f*

turboprop ['tɜ:bəʊprɒp] *Av* **t. (aircraft)** avion *m* à turbopropulseur; **t. (engine)** turbopropulseur *m*

turbo-supercharger ['tɜ:bəʊ'su:pətʃɑ:dʒər] *n* turbo-compresseur *m*

turbot ['tɜ:bət] *n* (*fish*) turbot *m*

turbulence ['tɜ:bjʊləns] *n* agitation *f*; *Met, Av* turbulences *fpl*

turbulent ['tɜ:bjʊlənt] *adj* (*crowd*) agité; *Met, Av* turbulent

turbulently ['tɜ:bjʊləntlɪ] *adv* d'une manière turbulente

turd [tɜ:d] *n Sl* **(a)** (*piece of excrement*) étron *m* **(b)** (*person*) con *m*, conne *f*

tureen [tjʊə'ri:n] *n* soupière *f*

turf¹ *pl* **turves, turfs** [tɜ:f, tɜ:vz, tɜ:fs] *n* (*grass-covered earth*) gazon *m*; (*piece*) motte *f* de gazon; *Sl* (*territory*) territoire *m*; *Horseracing* **the t.** le turf, les courses *fpl* de chevaux; **t. cutting** extraction *f* de la tourbe

turf² *vt* **(a)** (*area*) gazonner **(b)** *Br F* (*throw*) balancer

▶ **turf out** *vtsep Br F* (*eject*) (*person*) virer; (*throw away*) (*thing*) foutre en l'air, bazarder; (*reject*) (*plan etc*) rejeter

▶ **turf over** *vtsep* (*ground*) gazonner

turf accountant *n esp Br Horseracing* bookmaker *m*

turgid ['tɜ:dʒɪd] *adj* **(a)** (*swollen*) enflé, gonflé, *Lit* turgide **(b)** (*style etc*) boursouflé, ampoulé

turgidly ['tɜ:dʒɪdlɪ] *adv* (*written etc*) emphatiquement, pompeusement

Turk [tɜ:k] *n* Turc *m*, Turque *f*; *esp Pol* **he's a young T.** c'est un jeune turc

Turkey ['tɜ:kɪ] *n* Turquie *f*

turkey ['tɜ:kɪ] *n* **(a)** (*bird*) dindon *m*, dinde *f*; *Culin* dinde, dindonneau *m*; **hen t.** dinde **(b)** *esp Am F* **to talk t.** parler franchement; *Sl* **cold t.** état *m* de manque de drogue(s) **(c)** *esp Am Sl* (*failed play, film*) bide *m*, four *m*; (*ineffectual person*) abruti, -ie, crétin, -ine

turkey buzzard *n* vautour *m* aura

turkey cock *n* dindon *m*

Turkish ['tɜ:kɪʃ] **1** *adj* turc, *f* turque; **T. bath** bain *m* turc; **T. delight** loukoum *m*; **T. towel** serviette *f* éponge **2** *n Ling* turc *m*

turmeric ['tɜ:mərɪk] *n* curcuma *m*

turmoil ['tɜ:mɔɪl] *n* trouble *m*, tumulte *m*, agitation *f*; (*of rushing water*) remous *m*; **to be in a t.** (*of country, house*) être en ébullition; (*of person*) être agité; **the whole town is in (a) t.** toute la ville est agitée *ou* est en ébullition; **my mind was in a t.** la confusion régnait dans mon esprit

turn¹ [tɜ:n] *n* **(a)** (*revolution*) (*of wheel*) tour *m*, révolution *f*; **with a t. of the wrist** avec un tour de poignet; *Fig* **to give another t. to the screw** serrer la vis; **the meat is done to a t.** la viande est cuite à point

(b) (*act of changing direction*) changement *m* de direction; *Ski* virage *m*; (*in path etc*) tournant *m*; (*of rope*) tour *m*; (*of spiral*) tour, spire *f*; *Aut* **the next t. on the left** la prochaine (rue/route) à gauche; *Aut* **no right/left t.** défense de tourner à droite/à gauche; **sharp t.** virage serré; **twists and turns** tours et détours *mpl*; (*of events*) tournure *f*; **U turn** demi-tour *m*; **three-point t.** demi-tour en trois manœuvres; *Fig* **at every t.** à tout bout de champ; **to take a tragic t.** (*of events*) tourner au tragique; **to take an unexpected t.** (*of events, conversation etc*) prendre une tournure que l'on n'aurait pas imaginée; **to take a t. for the better/worse** (*of situation etc*) s'améliorer/se détériorer; **the patient has taken a t. for the better/the worse** l'état du malade s'est amélioré/a empiré; **the t. of the tide** le changement *ou* renversement de la marée; *Fig* le renversement de tendances; **the milk is on the t.** le lait est en train de commencer à tourner; **at the t. of the century** au tournant du siècle

(c) *F* (*surprise, shock*) choc *m*, coup *m*; **it gave me quite a t.** ça m'a fait un coup; **you gave me such a t.!** vous m'avez fait une belle peur!

(d) *Med F* **she had one of her turns** elle a eu une de ses crises *ou* attaques

(e) (*short walk*) tour *m*, petite promenade *f*; **to take a t. in the garden** faire un tour *ou* quelques pas dans le jardin

(f) (*at activity*) tour *m*; *Br Th* (*in variety show etc*) numéro *m*; **whose t. is it?** c'est à qui le tour?; **it's your t.** (*in game*) c'est votre tour, c'est à vous (de jouer); **to take turns with sb** se relayer avec qn; **they take it in turns to drive** ils se relaient au volant; **each in (his) t., t. and t. about** chacun son tour; **to do sth t. and t. about** faire qch à tour de rôle; **in t.** (*alternately*) tour à tour, à tour de rôle; **they, in t., contributed food** pour leur part, ils donnèrent de la nourriture; **she was by turns optimistic and downcast** elle était tour à tour optimiste et déprimée; **to speak out of t.** parler mal à propos

(g) (*service*) **to do sb a good t.** rendre (un) service à qn; **to do sb a bad t.** jouer un mauvais tour à qn; *prov* **one good t. deserves another** à beau jeu beau retour, un service en vaut un autre

(h) *Old-fashioned* (*purpose*) **it will serve my t.** cela fera mon affaire (pour le moment)

(i) (*style etc*) **t. of mind** tournure *f* d'esprit; **humorous t. of mind** esprit *m* humoristique; **t. of phrase** tournure *f* de phrase; **to have a good t. of speed** être rapide; (*of horse*) être capable de fournir un effort à grande allure

turn² **1** *vt* **(a)** (*wheel, handle etc*) (faire) tourner; (*steering wheel*) braquer, tourner; (*key in lock*) (faire) tourner, faire jouer; *Fig* **to t. the knife in the wound** retourner le fer *ou* le couteau dans la plaie

(b) (*page etc*) tourner; (*mattress, hay etc*) retourner; **to t. a garment inside out** retourner un vêtement; **to t. everything upside down** mettre tout sens dessus dessous; *F* **he didn't t. a hair** il n'a pas bronché *ou* sourcillé; **the sight/story turned my stomach** ce spectacle/l'histoire m'a soulevé le cœur

(c) (*direct*) **she turned her steps towards home** elle a dirigé ses pas vers la maison; **he never turned anyone from his door** il n'a jamais fermé sa porte à personne; **to t. one's thoughts to God** tourner ses pensées vers Dieu; **to t. one's attention to ...** tourner son attention vers *ou* sur ...; **to t. the conversation to ...** orienter la conversation vers ...

(d) (*head*) tourner; (*gaze*) tourner, diriger (**towards** vers); **t. your face this way** regardez de ce côté; **t. your desk this way** tournez votre bureau dans cette direction

(e) (*go round*) **to t. the corner** tourner au coin de la rue; *Fig* passer le moment critique; **she's turned forty** elle a quarante ans passés, elle a passé la quarantaine; **it's turned seven** il est sept heures passées

(f) (*change*) transformer, changer (**into** en); **to t. water into wine** changer l'eau en vin; **his love has been turned to hate** son amour s'est changé *ou* s'est transformé en haine; **to t. a theatre into a cinema** convertir un théâtre en cinéma; **the witch turned him into a crow** la sorcière l'a transformé en corbeau; **we've turned the attic into a study** nous avons transformé *ou* converti le grenier en bureau

(g) (*cause to become*) faire devenir; **the heat has turned the milk sour** la chaleur a fait tourner le lait; **autumn turns the leaves yellow** l'automne fait jaunir les feuilles; **to t. sth green/black** rendre qch vert/noir, verdir/noircir qch; **the blood turned the water red** le sang a rougi l'eau; **Angus MacKinnon, athlete turned journalist** Angus MacKinnon, athlète reconverti dans le journalisme; **success has turned her head** le succès lui a tourné la tête

(h) (*make on lathe*) (*table leg etc*) tourner, façonner au tour; *Fig* **a well turned sentence** une phrase bien tournée; *Knitting* **to t. a heel** faire le talon

2 *vi* **(a)** (*rotate*) tourner; **to t. a complete circle** faire un tour complet; **the steering wheel won't t.** le volant ne tourne pas; **my head's turning** la tête me tourne

(b) to toss and t. (*in bed*) se tourner et se retourner (dans son lit); **to t. upside down** se retourner

(c) (*turn head, turn round*) se retourner; **he turned to look at the landscape** il s'est retourné pour regarder le paysage; **she turned to me – what do <u>you</u> think?** elle se tourna vers moi – qu'est-ce que tu en penses, toi?; *Mil* **right t.!** à droite!; **left t!** à gauche!

(d) (*change direction*) tourner, se diriger; **to t. to the right/the left** (*of person, path etc*) tourner à droite/à gauche; **he turned towards home** il s'est dirigé vers la maison; **the wind is turning** le vent tourne; **my thoughts often t. to this subject** mes réflexions se portent souvent sur ce sujet; **to t. to another subject** passer à une autre question; **the tide is turning** la marée change; **her luck has turned** sa chance a tourné

(e) (*for help*) **to t. to sb (for help/advice)** s'adresser à qn (pour obtenir de l'aide/des conseils); **I didn't know who to t. to** je ne savais pas à qui m'adresser; **to t. to the dictionary** consulter le dictionnaire; **I don't know where** *or* **which way to t.** je ne sais pas à quel saint me vouer

(f) (*change*) se transformer (**into** en), devenir; **caterpillars t. into butterflies** la chenille se métamorphose en papillon; **she's turned into a very hard-headed businesswoman** c'est devenue une femme d'affaires très réaliste; **everything he touches turns to gold** tout ce qu'il touche se change en or; **to t. (sour)** (*of milk*) tourner; *Fig* **to t. sour** tourner au vinaigre; **it's turning cold** il commence à faire froid; **the crowd turned nasty** la foule est devenue agressive; **the leaves are beginning to t.** les feuilles commencent à jaunir; **he turned red** il a rougi; **to t. red/blue** virer au rouge/bleu; **to t. sulky** devenir maussade; **to t. socialist** devenir socialiste

▶ **turn against 1** *vipo* se retourner contre **2** *vtaspo* (*make opposed to*) retourner contre; **she turns everyone against her** elle se met tout le monde à dos; **they turned his argument against him** ils ont retourné son argument contre lui

▶ **turn around** *vi, vtsep* = **turn round**

▶ **turn aside 1** *vi* se retourner; **to t. aside from the path of righteousness** se détourner du droit chemin **2** *vtsep* **to t. aside a blow** détourner *ou* faire dévier un coup

▶ **turn away 1** *vtsep* **(a)** (*direct elsewhere*) (*head, gaze*) détourner; **police were turning drivers/people away (from the scene of the accident)** la police détournait *ou* écartait les automobilistes/les gens (du lieu de l'accident)

(b) (*refuse entry, help etc to*) (*of hospital, hotel etc*) refuser; **to t. sb away in their hour of need** refuser de venir en aide à qn; *Th etc* **to t. people away** refuser du monde; **we've been turning business away** nous avons refusé du travail

2 *vi* (*look away*) se détourner, détourner son regard; (*go away*) s'écarter; **to t. away from sb** (*turn one's back on*) tourner le dos à qn; (*abandon*) délaisser *ou* abandonner qn

▶ **turn back 1** *vi* **(a)** (*return in same direction*) rebrousser chemin, faire demi-tour; *Fig* **there's no turning back now** on ne peut plus faire marche arrière maintenant

(b) (*in book*) **t. back to page ...** revenez à la page ...

2 *vtsep* **(a)** (*of person*) (*cause to return in same direction*) faire faire demi-tour à, faire revenir sur ses pas; **the refugees were turned back at the border** les réfugiés ont été refoulés à la frontière

(b) (*fold*) (*sheets*) replier

(c) (*adjust to earlier time*) (*watch etc*) retarder; **to t. the clocks back an hour** retarder les pendules d'une heure; *Fig* **you can't t. the clock back** on ne peut pas revenir en arrière *ou* revivre le passé

▶ **turn down** *vtsep* **(a)** (*fold down*) (*collar*) rabattre; (*page of book*) plier, corner; **to t. down the bed** ouvrir le lit **(b)** (*reduce*) (*heat, sound etc*) baisser; **to t. down the TV/radio** baisser le son de la télé/radio **(c)** (*refuse, reject*) (*offer*) repousser, rejeter; (*candidate, claim etc*) refuser; **I've been turned down for that job** je n'ai pas été accepté pour cet emploi; **she turned me down flat** elle a refusé catégoriquement, *F* elle m'a envoyé promener; **they offered him a job but he turned them down** ils lui ont proposé un emploi mais il a rejeté leur offre

▶ **turn in 1** *vtsep* **(a) to t. in one's toes** tourner les pieds en dedans **(b)** *F* (*hand in*) (*object*) rendre, rapporter (*à la police*); (*betray to police*) (*person*) livrer *ou* vendre à la police **(c)** *F* (*give up*) (*one's job*) quitter, abandonner **(d)** *Sp, Th* **to t. in a good score/performance** faire un bon score/une belle performance **2** *vi* **(a)** (*point inwards*) **his toes t. in** il a les pieds tournés en dedans **(b)** (*go through entrance off road etc*) **he turned in at the gate** arrivé à la porte, il est entré **(c)** *F* **I think I'll t. in (for the night)** (*go to bed*) je crois que je vais aller me pieuter

▶ **turn off 1** *vtsep* **(a)** (*switch off*) (*water, tap, gas, electricity*) fermer; (*light, radio, TV etc*) éteindre **(b)** *F* (*take away enthusiasm from*) rebuter, refroidir; (*sexually*) couper l'envie à **2** *vi* **(a)** (*leave road, street*) changer de route; **I turned off to the left** j'ai pris (la route/la rue) à gauche, j'ai tourné à gauche; **he turned off onto the motorway** il s'est engagé sur l'autoroute **(b)** (*of heater etc*) se fermer **3** *vipo* **we turned off the main road** nous avons quitté la grande route; **a small street turning off the High Street** une petite rue qui part de la rue principale

▶ **turn on 1** *vtsep* **(a)** (*switch on*) (*water, tap, gas, electricity*) ouvrir; (*light, radio, TV etc*) allumer; **shall I t. on the light?** voulez-vous que j'allume? **(b)** *F* (*excite*) brancher; (*sexually*) exciter; **she turned me on to Zen Buddhism** elle m'a branché sur le bouddhisme zen **2** *vipo* **(a)** (*attack physically or verbally*) s'attaquer à **(b)** (*depend on*) reposer sur, dépendre de; **everything turns on your answer** tout dépend de votre réponse **3** *vi* (*of heater etc*) se mettre en route *ou* en marche

▶ **turn out 1** *vtsep* **(a)** (*eject*) mettre *ou F* flanquer à la porte; (*tenant*) déloger, évincer; (*cattle*) mettre au vert; *Naut* (*men*) réveiller; *Mil* (*troops*) alerter

(b) (*empty*) (*pockets etc*) vider, retourner; *Culin* (*dessert etc*) démouler; **to t. out a drawer** (*empty*) vider un tiroir; (*empty and tidy*) mettre de l'ordre dans un tiroir; **to t. out a room** nettoyer une pièce à fond

(c) (*switch off*) (*gas*) couper, éteindre; (*light*) éteindre

(d) (*produce*) (*goods*) produire, fabriquer; **the factory turns them out by the thousand** l'usine en fabrique par milliers; **the sort of students that we aim to t. out here** le type d'étudiants que nous voulons former ici

(e) well turned out (*person*) élégant, soigné

(f) (*point outwards*) **to t. one's toes out** tourner les pieds en dehors

2 *vi* **(a)** (*attend*) (*to see parade, hear speech etc*) assister; (*of voters*) aller aux urnes; **the doctor/fire brigade had to t. out in the middle of the night** le docteur/les pompiers a/ont dû se déplacer au milieu de la nuit; **the whole town turned out to see it** toute la ville est allée le voir; **not many people turned out for his funeral/the march** il n'est pas venu beaucoup de monde à son enterrement/à la manifestation

(b) (*point outwards*) **his toes t. out** il a les pieds tournés en dehors

(c) (*end*) **to t. out well/badly** bien/mal tourner; **it'll t. out all right** ça s'arrangera; **how did the cake t. out?** le gâteau était-il réussi?; **I don't know how it will t. out** je ne sais pas comment cela finira; **as it turned out** en l'occurrence; **she's turned out (to be) beautiful** elle est devenue une belle femme/jeune fille

(d) (*transpire*) **he turned out to be the son of an old friend of mine** il s'est trouvé qu'il était le fils d'un de mes anciens amis; **she turned out to be a real idiot** elle s'est avérée une vraie gourde; **it turns out that ...** il se trouve que ...; **as it turns out, we would have had time** en fait, nous aurions eu le temps

(e) *F* (*get out of bed*) se lever, sortir du lit

▶ **turn over 1** *vtsep* **(a)** (*turn*) retourner; (*page*) tourner; **to t. over the pages of a book** feuilleter un livre; **she turned the body over** elle a retourné le corps; *Agr* **to t. over the soil** retourner la terre; **to t. an idea/a plan over (in one's mind)** retourner une idée/un projet dans sa tête; **if you want a bit of time to t. it over ...** (*idea, offer etc*) si vous avez besoin d'un peu de temps pour y réfléchir ...; *Fig* **to t. over a new leaf** tourner la page

(b) (*surrender*) **to t. sth over to sb** remettre qch entre les mains de qn; **the thief was turned over to the police** on a remis le voleur entre les mains de la police

(c) (*of business*) rapporter; **he must be turning over a good £1,000 a week** il doit gagner *ou F* se faire au moins 1 000 livres par semaine

(d) *Sl* (*rob*) (*shop*) dévaliser; (*cheat*) rouler; **£500? you've been turned over!** 500 livres? tu t'es fait rouler!

2 *vi* **(a)** (*change position by turning*) se tourner, se retourner; **to t. over in bed** se retourner dans son lit; **to t. (right) over** (*of car etc*) capoter

(b) *TV* (*change channel*) changer de chaîne

(c) (*in reading*) tourner la page

(d) (*of engine*) tourner au ralenti

▶ **turn round 1** *vi* (*rotate*) tourner; (*of crane etc*) tourner, pivoter; (*face other way*) (*of person*) se retourner; (*of vehicle*) tourner; (*abruptly*) faire volte-face; (*in one's opinions etc*) tourner casaque, virer de bord; **she turned round in her chair** elle se retourna sur sa chaise; **t. round and let me see your face** tournez-vous (un peu) que je voie votre visage; **he just turned round and hit me** tout d'un coup il s'est retourné et m'a frappé; **after eight years of marriage she turned round and said she was leaving** après huit années de mariage elle annonça soudain qu'elle partait

2 *vtsep* **(a)** (*move to face other way*) retourner; **she turned the chair round** elle retourna la chaise; **she turned the car round** elle a fait demi-tour

(b) (*reverse*) (*bad situation*) renverser, retourner; **to t. the economy/a company round** remettre l'économie/une entreprise sur pied

(c) *Com* (*process, deal with*) (*order*) traiter, s'occuper de

3 *vipo* (*go around*) (*corner*) tourner

▶ **turn up 1** *vi* **(a)** (*arrive*) arriver, se présenter; **he turned up ten minutes late** il est arrivé *ou F* s'est amené dix minutes en retard; **she turned up at the party with a new boyfriend** elle est arrivée *ou F* a débarqué à la soirée avec un nouveau petit ami; **he'll t. up one of these days** il reparaîtra un de ces jours

(b) I'm sure your keys will t. up (*be found*) je suis sûr qu'on retrouvera tes clés; **it's bound to t. up** il finira bien par réapparaître; **the pen turned up in his jacket** on a retrouvé le stylo dans sa veste; *Fig* **something is sure to t. up** il se présentera sûrement une occasion; **until something better turns up** en attendant mieux

(c) (*turn upwards*) rebiquer; **her nose turns up** elle a le nez retroussé

2 *vtsep* **(a)** (*fold upwards*) (*collar*) relever; (*sleeves, trouser legs*) retrousser; (*to shorten*) raccourcir en faisant un ourlet; **she turned her nose up at the job** elle a refusé l'emploi avec dédain; **don't t. your nose up like that** (*at food*) arrête de faire le dégoûté

(b) (*uncover*) (*card*) retourner

(c) (*find*) trouver; **the investigation has failed to t. up any new information** l'enquête n'a apporté aucun élément nouveau

(d) (*increase, make louder etc*) augmenter; (*gas*) monter; **to t. the radio/radiator up** mettre la radio/le radiateur plus fort

(e) *Br Sl* **t. it up!** (*stop that*) c'est fini, oui!

turnabout ['tɜːnəbaʊt] *n* retournement *m*, revirement *m*

turnaround ['tɜːnəraʊnd] *n* (*of situation, opinion*) retournement *m*, revirement *m*; (*of ship, aeroplane etc*) rotation *f*; *Com* (*of an order*) traitement *m*; *Com* **they offer a faster t.** leurs délais sont plus courts; **t. time** (*for order*) délai *m* de livraison; (*of ferry*) temps *m* de rotation

turncoat ['tɜːnkəʊt] *n Pol etc* renégat *m*

turndown ['tɜːndaʊn] *adj* (*collar etc*) rabattu

turndown housekeeper *n* (*in hotel*) gouvernante *f* du soir

turned-up ['tɜːndʌp] *adj* (*collar etc*) relevé; (*nose*) retroussé

turner ['tɜːnər] *n Ind* tourneur *m*

turnery ['tɜːnərɪ] *n* atelier *m* de tourneur

turning ['tɜːnɪŋ] *n* **(a) the t. of the tide** le changement *ou* renversement de la marée; *Fig* le renversement de tendances; *Aut etc* **t. circle** rayon *m* de braquage; *Fig* **t. point** tournant *m*, moment *m* critique; **at the t. point of her career** au tournant de sa carrière

(b) (*off road etc*) tournant *m*; **the first t. on the right** la première route/rue à droite; *Prov* **it's a long road that has no t.** après la pluie le beau temps

(c) (*on lathe*) tournage *m*, travail *m* au tour

turnip ['tɜːnɪp] *n* (*plant, vegetable*) navet *m*; *Hum* (*pocket watch*) montre *f* de poche *ou* de gousset

turnkey ['tɜːnkiː] **1** *n Arch* (*jailer*) geôlier, -ière **2** *adj* **t. plant/project** usine *f*/projet *m* clés en main; *Comptr* **t. system** système *m* clés en main

turn-off *n* **(a)** (*on motorway etc*) sortie *f*, embranchement *m*; **the Leeds t.** la sortie pour Leeds **(b)** *Sl* **it's a t.** (*boring*) c'est d'un ennui mortel; (*sexually*) c'est dégoûtant; **it's a t. for me** (*sexually*) cela me coupe l'envie

turn-of-the-century *adj* du début du siècle; **t. London** le Londres du début du siècle

turn-on *n Sl* **it's/he's a real t.** (*sexually*) c'est/il est vachement excitant; **is that a t.?** ça t'excite?

turnout ['tɜːnaʊt] *n* **(a)** (*people present*) assistance *f*; (*at election*) nombre *m* de votants; **a good/poor t.** beaucoup/peu de monde; **there was a large** *or* **good t. at his funeral/the wedding/the meeting** il y avait beaucoup de monde à son enterrement/au mariage/à la réunion; **low turnouts at elections** faible participation *f* aux élections **(b)** (*cleaning*) (*of room etc*) nettoyage *m* à fond; **to give sth a good t.** nettoyer qch à fond **(c)** *Ind* (*production*) production *f*, rendement *m* **(d)** (*clothes*) tenue *f*

turnover ['tɜːnəʊvər] *n* **(a)** *Fin* chiffre *m* d'affaires, CA *m*; **our annual t.** notre chiffre d'affaires annuel; **t. tax** impôt *m ou* taxe *f* sur le chiffre d'affaires **(b)** (*of stock*) écoulement *m*, rotation *f*; **t. of capital** roulement *m* de capitaux; **the (staff) t. there is very high** le taux de renouvellement du personnel y est très élevé **(c)** *Culin* chausson *m*; **apple t.** chausson aux pommes

turnpike ['tɜːnpaɪk] *n US* (*road*) autoroute *f* (à péage); *Br Hist* (*barrier*) barrière *f* de péage

turnround ['tɜːnraʊnd] *n esp Br* = **turnaround**

turnstile ['tɜːnstaɪl] *n* tourniquet(-compteur) *m* (d'entrées)

turntable ['tɜːnteɪb(ə)l] *n* **(a)** *Rail* plaque *f* tournante; *Mil* plate-forme *f* tournante **(b)** (*of record player*) platine *f*

turn(-)up *n* **(a)** *Br* (*on trousers*) revers *m* **(b)** *F* **what a t. (for the book)!** ça c'est une sacrée surprise!

turpentine ['tɜːp(ə)ntaɪn] *n* essence *f* de térébenthine; **t. substitute** white-spirit *m*, *pl* white-spirits

turpitude ['tɜːpɪtjuːd] *n Fml* turpitude *f*

turps [tɜːps] *n Br F* essence *f* de térébenthine

turquoise ['tɜːkwɔɪz, -kwɑːz] **1** *n* **(a)** (*stone*) turquoise *f*; **t. necklace** collier *m* en turquoise **(b)** (*colour*) turquoise *m* **2** *adj* turquoise *inv*

turret ['tʌrɪt] *n Archit* tourelle *f*; *Mil, Naut* **(gun) t.** tourelle *f*

turreted ['tʌrɪtɪd] *adj Archit* (*castle*) à tourelles

turtle ['tɜːt(ə)l] **1** *n* (*reptile*) tortue *f* de mer; **t. dove** tourterelle *f* des bois; *Fig* **a pair of t. doves** (*lovers*) un couple d'amoureux *ou* de tourtereaux; **t. neck** col *m* montant; **t. neck(ed) sweater** chandail *m* à col montant; **t. soup** consommé *m* à la tortue **2** *adv* **to turn t.** (*of boat*) chavirer; (*of car*) capoter

Tuscan ['tʌskən] **1** *adj Geog, Archit* toscan **2** *n* **(a)** (*person*) Toscan, -ane **(b)** *Ling* toscan *m*

Tuscany ['tʌskənɪ] *n* Toscane *f*

tush[1] [tʌʃ] *int Old-fashioned* bah!, taratata!

tush[2] [tʊʃ] *n esp Am F* (*buttocks*) derrière *m*

tusk [tʌsk] *n* (*of boar, elephant etc*) défense *f*

tusker ['tʌskər] *n* (*elephant*) pachyderme *m*

tussle[1] ['tʌs(ə)l] *n* empoignade *f*, lutte *f* au corps-à-corps; *Fig* lutte, bataille *f*; **to have a t.** en venir aux mains **(with sb** avec qn)

tussle[2] *vi* **to t. with sb** lutter avec qn; **to t. over sth** se disputer qch

tussock ['tʌsək] *n* touffe *f* d'herbe

tut[1] [tʌt] *int* **t. (t.)!** allons donc!

tut[2] *vi* faire un bruit désapprobateur, émettre une exclamation désapprobatrice; **to t. t. at sb's behaviour** désapprouver la conduite de qn; **don't you t. t. at me!** je me passe de tes commentaires!

tutelage [ˈtjuːtɪlɪdʒ] *n* tutelle *f*; **to be under sb's t.** être sous la tutelle de qn
tutelar, tutelary [ˈtjuːtɪlər, -lərɪ] *adj* tutélaire
tutor¹ [ˈtjuːtər] *n* **(a)** *Br Univ* directeur, -trice d'études **(b)** **private t.** (*in individual subject*) professeur *m* particulier; (*employed on permanent basis*) précepteur *m*; **music t.** professeur de musique **(c)** *Scot Jur* (*of minor etc*) tuteur, -trice
tutor² *vt* instruire; **to t. a child in French** donner à un enfant des leçons particulières de français
tutorial [tjuːˈtɔːrɪəl] **1** *adj* (*work etc*) de répétiteur; *Comptr* **t. program** didacticiel *m*; *Univ* **the t. system** = le système d'enseignement où les étudiant(e)s sont supervisé(e)s par un directeur d'études **2** *n* **(a)** *Br Univ* cours *m* (individuel) fait par le directeur d'études; **I've got a t. at 3 o'clock** j'ai un cours avec mon directeur d'études à trois heures **(b)** *Comptr* didacticiel *m*
tutti-frutti [ˈtʊtɪˈfruːtɪ] *n Culin* plombières *f*
tutu [ˈtuːtuː] *n* (*garment*) tutu *m*
tu-whit tu-whoo [tʊˈwɪttʊˈwuː] *int* hou hou!
tux [tʌks] *n Am F* smoking *m*
tuxedo [tʌkˈsiːdəʊ] *n Am* smoking *m*
TV [tiːˈviː] *n* (*abbr* **television**) télé *f*, TV *f*; **TV (set)** poste *m* de télévision, téléviseur *m*; **TV dinner** plateau-repas *m* surgelé; **TV lounge** salle *f* de télévision; **TV magazine** hebdo *m* télé; **TV movie** téléfilm *m*; **TV personality** vedette *f* de la télévision; **TV programme** programme *m* télé; **TV screen** écran *m* de télévision; **TV station** station *f* de télévision
TVP [tiːviːˈpiː] *n Culin* (*abbr* **textured vegetable protein**) protéine *f* végétale texturée
twaddle¹ [ˈtwɒd(ə)l] *n F* fadaises *fpl*; **to talk t.** dire *ou* débiter des balivernes *ou* des sottises
twaddle² *vi F* **to t. on about sth** débiter des sottises à propos de qch
twain [tweɪn] *adj, n Arch, Lit* deux *m*; *Hum* **and ne'er the t. shall meet** et ils resteront à jamais inconciliables
twang¹ [twæŋ] *n* **(a)** (*of bowstring*) bruit *m* sec; (*of guitar*) son *m* aigu **(b)** (*in voice*) **nasal t.** ton *m* nasillard, nasillement *m*; **to speak with a t.** nasiller, parler d'une voix nasillarde
twang² **1** *vt* (*drawn bowstring*) lâcher; (*strings etc*) faire vibrer; **to t. a guitar** gratter (une guitare) **2** *vi* **(a)** (*of string etc*) vibrer; **to t. on a guitar** gratter (une guitare) **(b)** (*speak with twang*) nasiller
'twas [twɒz] *Arch, Lit* = **it was**
twat [twæt] *n Br Sl* **(a)** (*vagina*) moule *f*, chatte *f* **(b)** (*idiot*) crétin, -ine
tweak¹ [twiːk] *n* **(a)** (*twist*) **he gave her nose a t.** il lui a doucement tordu le nez **(b)** (*adjustment*) petite modification *f*; **to give sth a little t.** donner un petit coup à qch
tweak² *vt* **(a)** (*pinch*) pincer; (*twist*) tordre (avec les doigts); **to t. a boy's ear** tirer l'oreille à un gamin **(b)** (*adjust*) (*engine*) régler; (*text*) apporter quelques petites modifications à
twee [twiː] *adj Br F Pej* mignard, gentillet
tweed [twiːd] *n Tex* tweed *m*; **t. jacket** veste *f* en *ou* de tweed; **tweeds** (*suit, outfit*) complet *m ou* costume *m* de *ou* en tweed
tweedy [ˈtwiːdɪ] *adj* (*cloth*) qui tient du tweed; *F Pej* (*person*) qui affecte la tenue d'un propriétaire rural
'tween [twiːn] *prep Arch, Lit* entre
'tween decks [ˈtwiːndeks] *Naut* **1** *n* faux-pont *m*, entrepont *m* **2** *adj, adv* dans l'entrepont
tweet¹ [twiːt] *n* (*of bird*) pépiement *m*, gazouillement *m*
tweet² *vi* (*of bird*) pépier, gazouiller
tweeter [ˈtwiːtər] *n* (*loudspeaker*) haut-parleur *m* aigu, tweeter *m*
tweezers [ˈtwiːzəz] *npl* [ⓘ**A10**,e] brucelles *fpl*; (*for hairs*) pince *f* à épiler
twelfth [twelfθ] **1** *adj* douzième; **Louis the T.** Louis Douze **2** *n* **(a)** (*of month*) douze *m*; **(on) the t. (of May)** le douze (mai) **(b)** (*person, thing*) douzième *mf* **(c)** (*fraction*) douzième *m*
twelfth man *n Cr* joueur *m* de réserve
Twelfth Night *n* la fête des Rois
twelve [twelv] *adj, n* douze *m*; **t. o'clock** (*midday*) midi *m*; (*midnight*) minuit *m*
twelvemonth [ˈtwelvmʌnθ] *n Old-fashioned, Lit* année *f*
twelve-tone *adj Mus* dodécaphonique; **t. system** dodécaphonisme *m*
twentieth [ˈtwentɪɪθ] **1** *adj* vingtième **2** *n* **(a)** (*of month*) vingt *m*; **(on) the t. of June** le vingt juin **(b)** (*person, thing*) vingtième *mf* **(c)** (*fraction*) vingtième *m*
twenty [ˈtwentɪ] *adj, n* vingt *m*; **t.-one** vingt et un; **t.-two** vingt-deux; **about t. people** une vingtaine de personnes; **the twenties** les années vingt; **to be in one's twenties** avoir entre vingt et trente ans; **t.-four-hour hotline** ligne *f* directe accessible 24 heures sur 24; **t.-four hour service** service vingt-quatre heures sur vingt-quatre; **we've been working t.-four hours a day** nous avons travaillé jour et nuit; **t.-t. vision** vue *f* parfaite; *Rugby* **t.-two metre line** ligne *f* des vingt-deux mètres
twerp [twɜːp] *n Sl* crétin, -ine
twice [twaɪs] *adv* deux fois; **t. as big as sth** deux fois plus grand que qch; **t. as slow** deux fois plus lent; **t. over** à deux reprises; **to think t. before doing sth** y regarder *ou* réfléchir à deux fois avant de faire qch; **to think t. before saying sth** tourner la langue sept fois dans la bouche avant de parler; **she didn't have to think t. before accepting** elle a accepté sans hésiter; **he did not have to be asked t.** il ne se fit pas prier
twiddle¹ [ˈtwɪd(ə)l] *n F* **to give sth a t.** tourner qch
twiddle² **1** *vt F* jouer avec, tripoter; **to t. a knob** tourner un bouton; **to t. one's thumbs** se tourner les pouces; *Fig* **I've spent the whole day twiddling my thumbs** j'ai passé la journée à me tourner les pouces **2** *vi* **to t. with sth** jouer avec *ou* tripoter qch
twig¹ [twɪg] *n* brindille *f*
twig² *vti* **(-gg-)** *Br F* piger; **I soon twigged his little game** je n'ai pas tardé à voir dans son jeu
twilight [ˈtwaɪlaɪt] *n* crépuscule *m*, demi-jour *m*; **in the (evening) t.** au crépuscule, entre chien et loup, à la brune; *Fig* **in the t. of life** au crépuscule de la vie; **the t. hours** les heures *fpl* crépusculaires; *Fig* **the t. world of the paranormal** l'entre-deux-mondes *m* du paranormal
twilight zone *n* **(a)** (*in inner city*) no man's land *m inv* **(b)** (*illegal activity*) zone *f* d'ombre
twill [twɪl] *n Tex* (tissu *m*) croisé *m*, sergé *m*
'twill [twɪl] *Lit* = **it will**
twin [twɪn] **1** *n* jumeau, -elle; **t. brother** frère *m* jumeau; **t. sister** sœur *f* jumelle **2** *adj* jumeau, jumelé; **t. beds** lits *mpl* jumeaux; *Med* **t. birth** accouchement *m* de jumeaux; **t. columns** colonnes *fpl* géminées; *Mktg* **t. plant** lot *m* de deux; **t. turbo** double turbo *m*; **t. tyres** pneus *mpl* jumelés
twin² *vt* **(-nn-)** (*towns*) jumeler; **Paisley is twinned with ...** Paisley est jumelée avec ...
twin-bedded room [ˈtwɪnbedɪd] *n* chambre *f* à lits jumeaux
twin-cam *n* double arbre *m* à cames
twin camshaft *n* double arbre *m* à cames
twin carburettor *n* double carburateur *m*; (*dual carburettor*) carburateur double corps
twine¹ [twaɪn] *n* (*string*) ficelle *f*
twine² **1** *vt* (*threads*) tordre, tortiller; (*garland, fingers etc*) entrelacer **2** *vi* **the road twined up the mountain** la route montait en lacets dans la montagne
▶ **twine about, twine (a)round** **1** *vtaspo* **to t. sth about** *or* **(a)round sth** enrouler qch autour de qch; **he twined his arms around me** il m'a entouré(e) de ses bras **2** *vipo* s'enrouler *ou* s'enlacer autour de; **the ivy had twined around the tree** le lierre s'était enroulé autour de l'arbre
twin-engine(d) aircraft *n* avion *m* bimoteur
twinge [twɪn(d)ʒ] *n* (*of pain*) élancement *m*; (*of gout etc*) légère crise *f*; **t. of conscience** remords *m*; *F* **my tooth/knee still gives the odd t.** ma dent/mon genou m'élance toujours de temps en temps
twining [ˈtwaɪnɪŋ] *adj* (*plant, stem*) volubile
twinkle¹ [ˈtwɪŋk(ə)l] *n* (*of stars, distant lights*) scintillement *m*, clignotement *m*; (*of eyes*) pétillement *m*; **a mischievous t. in the eye** un éclair de malice dans les yeux; *F* **when you were just a t. in your father's eye** quand tu n'étais pas encore de ce monde; **in a t. (of an eye)** en un clin d'œil
twinkle² *vi* (*of light, star*) scintiller, étinceler, clignoter; (*of eyes*) pétiller; **her eyes twinkled with amusement/mischief** ses yeux pétillaient de rire/malice
twinkling [ˈtwɪŋklɪŋ] **1** *adj* (*star etc*) scintillant, étincelant, clignotant; **t. eyes** yeux *mpl* pétillants **2** *n* scintillement *m*, étincellement *m*, clignotement *m*; **in the t. of an eye** en un clin d'œil
twinning [ˈtwɪnɪŋ] *n* (*of two towns etc*) jumelage *m*; **t. arrangements** arrangements *mpl* en vue d'un jumelage; **t. of companies** jumelage d'entreprises
twin room *n* chambre *f* à deux lits simples
twinset [ˈtwɪnset] *n Br* (*garments*) twin-set *m*, *pl* twin-sets; **she's very t. and pearls** elle est très NAP
twin town *n* ville *f* jumelée; **Stirling's t. is Villeneuve-d'Ascq** Stirling est jumelée avec Villeneuve-d'Ascq
twirl¹ [twɜːl] *n* **(a)** (*movement*) tournoiement *m*; (*of dancer etc*) pirouette *f* **(b)** (*shape*) (*of smoke etc*) volute *f*; *Archit* enroulement *m*, volute; (*of seashell*) spire *f*; (*in writing*) enjolivure *f* en spirale; (*in music*) fioriture *f*; **with a t. of cream on top** avec une spirale de crème dessus
twirl² **1** *vt* (*one's partner, lasso*) faire tournoyer; (*walking stick etc*) faire des moulinets avec; (*one's moustache*)

tortiller **2** *vi* (*turn round quickly*) se retourner d'un mouvement; (*when dancing*) tournoyer

► **twirl round 1** *vtsep* = **twirl**² *1* **2** *vi* se retourner brusquement; (*spin several times*) tournoyer

twist¹ [twɪst] *n* **(a)** (*act of twisting*) (*of lid, cap*) tour *m*; **to give one's ankle a t.** se fouler la cheville; **with a t. of the wrist** en un tour de main; **give the lid another t.** donne encore un tour au couvercle

(b) (*of coil*) spire *f*; **twists and turns** (*of road*) tours et détours *mpl*; (*of events etc*) tournure *f*; **final t. in a story** tour *m* inattendu à la fin d'un récit; **this adds a new t. to events** ça donne une tournure inattendue aux événements; **that's a nice t.** c'est bien trouvé; **by a t. of fate** par un coup du sort; *Br F* **to be round the t.** être fou *ou* cinglé; *F* **to get oneself into a t.** (*upset, nervous*) se mettre dans tous ses états

(c) (*of hair*) torsade *f*, tortillon *m*; (*of wool*) écheveau *m*; (*of paper*) tortillon; **sweet in a t. of paper** bonbon dans une papillote; **a t. of lemon** une rondelle de citron; **t. of tobacco** morceau *m* de tabac; **t. drill** foret *m* hélicoïdal

(d) (*dance*) twist *m*

twist² **1** *vt* (*one's hair, rope etc*) tordre, tortiller; *Tex etc* (*thread*) retordre; (*sb's words, meaning of text*) dénaturer; (*truth, meaning of sth*) altérer; **to t. two wires together** torsader deux fils; **to t. one's ankle** se faire une entorse; (*less serious*) se fouler la cheville; **to t. sb's arm** tordre *ou* retourner le bras à qn; *Fig* exercer une pression sur qn; *Hum* **if you t. my arm** si tu insistes; **to t. one's knee** se déboîter le genou; *Fig* **to t. the knife in the wound** retourner le couteau dans la plaie

2 *vi* se tordre; (*of worm etc*) se tortiller; (*of rope etc*) s'entortiller; (*spiral*) former une spirale; (*of smoke*) former des volutes; (*of road etc*) serpenter, faire des lacets; (*dance*) twister; **to t. and turn** (*of road etc*) serpenter

► **twist off 1** *vi* (*of lid*) se dévisser **2** *vtsep* (*lid*) dévisser

► **twist round 1** *vtaspo* (*wrap around*) **to t. sth round sth** enrouler *ou* entortiller qch autour de qch; *F* **he can t. her round his little finger** il la mène par le bout du nez **2** *vtsep* **she twisted her head round and stared at him** elle tourna la tête et le fixa du regard **3** *vi* (*turn*) se retourner; **to t. round in one's seat** se retourner sur son siège

► **twist up 1** *vi* (*of smoke*) s'élever en spirale **2** *vtsep* emmêler, entortiller; **to get all twisted up** (*of cables etc*) s'emmêler, s'entortiller

twisted ['twɪstɪd] *adj* **(a)** tordu; (*wire etc*) entortillé; (*tree*) tordu; (*limb*) tordu, contourné; **to get all t.** s'entortiller; **face t. with pain** traits *mpl* tordus par la douleur; **the t. wreckage of the plane/car** l'épave *f* enchevêtrée de l'avion/de la voiture; *Archit* **t. pillar** colonne *f* torse **(b)** *Fig* (*disturbed*) (*person, character, logic, reasoning*) tordu; **to have a t. mind** avoir l'esprit tordu; **what a t. thing to do** il faut être tordu pour faire une chose pareille; **a t. way of looking at things** une façon tordue de voir les choses; **he's so bitter and t.** il est tellement amer et désabusé

twisted-pair cable *n* câble *m* en paire torsadée

twister ['twɪstər] *n F* **(a)** *Br* (*swindler*) escroc *m* **(b)** *Am* (*tornado*) tornade *f*

twist grip *n* (*on motorbike*) commande *f* par poignée

twisting ['twɪstɪŋ] *adj* (*path*) tortueux

twisty ['twɪstɪ] *adj* (*road etc*) tortueux

twit¹ [twɪt] *n esp Br F* andouille *f*, imbécile *m*

twit² *vt esp Lit* narguer, taquiner (**about** à propos de)

twitch¹ [twɪtʃ] *n* **(a)** (*jerk*) petit coup *m* sec **(b)** (*tic*) tic *m*; (*of limb*) mouvement *m* convulsif

twitch² **1** *vt* (*jerk*) tirer vivement, tirer d'un petit coup sec; **to t. its tail** (*of cat*) faire de petits mouvements de la queue **2** *vi* (*of face, limb*) se contracter nerveusement; (*of eyelid, lip*) trembler; (*of hands*) se crisper nerveusement

twitter¹ ['twɪtər] *n* **(a)** (*of birds*) gazouillement *m*, gazouillis *m* **(b)** *F* **to be in a t.** (*of person*) être tout en émoi *ou* dans tous ses états

twitter² *vi* (*of bird*) gazouiller; *Fig Pej* (*talk*) jacasser

twittering ['twɪtərɪŋ] **1** *adj* (*bird*) gazouillant; *Fig Pej* (*person, voice etc*) piaillant **2** *n* gazouillement *m*; *Fig Pej* (*talk*) jacassement *m*

'twixt [twɪkst] *prep Arch, Lit* entre

two [tuː] *adj, n* deux *m*; **twenty-t.** vingt-deux; *Gym etc* **one t.! one t.!** une deux! une deux!; **no t. men are alike** il n'y a pas deux hommes qui se ressemblent; **to break/fold sth in t.** casser/plier qch en deux; **to walk in twos** *or* **t. by t.** marcher deux à deux *ou* (deux) par deux; *Fig* **to put t. and t. together** en tirer les conclusions (qui s'imposent), faire le rapprochement; *F* **that makes t. of us** on est deux; **t. fours are eight** deux fois quatre (font) huit; **at t. (o'clock)** à deux heures; **a mother of t.** la mère de deux enfants; **the t. of us/them** nous/eux deux; *Cards* **t. of spades** deux de pique; *Mus* **t. part song** chanson *f* à deux voix; **t.-for-the-price-of-one bonus** prime *f* 'deux pour le prix d'un'

two-bit *adj Am F* de quatre sous; (*person*) à la noix

two-colour *adj* de deux couleurs, bicolore; (*print ribbon*) bicolore; *Typ* **t. process** bichromie *f*

two-dimensional *adj* bidimensionnel; *Fig Pej* (*character, film etc*) simpliste, superficiel

two-door *adj* (*car*) à deux portes

two-edged *adj* (*sword, argument*) à double tranchant; (*remark, answer etc*) ambigu, -uë

two-faced ['tuːfeɪst] *adj* hypocrite

twofer ['tuːfər] *n US F* deux billets *mpl etc* vendus pour le prix d'un

twofold ['tuːfəʊld] **1** *adj* double **2** *adv* doublement; **kindness returned t.** bontés rendues au double

two-four *adj Mus* **t. time** mesure *f* à deux quatre; **in t. time** en deux quatre

two-handed *adj* **(a) t. sword** épée *f* à deux mains, espadon *m*; *Tennis* **t. backhand** revers *m* à deux mains **(b)** *Cards* (*game*) qui se joue à deux

two-headed *adj* bicéphale; *Her* (*eagle*) double, à deux têtes

two-horse *adj* (*carriage*) à deux chevaux; *Fig* **a t. race** une épreuve/élection qui ne comprend que deux concurrents

two-legged *adj* bipède

two-part pricing *n* prix *mpl* à double détente

two-party *adj* (*system, politics etc*) bipartite

twopence ['tʌpəns] *n Br* deux pence *mpl*; *Fig F* **it isn't worth t.** ça ne vaut pas tripette

twopenny ['tʌp(ə)nɪ] *adj Br* à *ou* de deux pence; **a t. piece** une pièce de deux pence

twopenny-halfpenny ['tʌp(ə)nɪ'heɪpnɪ] *adj Br Fig F* (*person, ring etc*) à la noix, à la gomme

two-phase *adj El* (*current*) bi-phasé

two-piece 1 *adj* (*suit, swimsuit*) deux pièces **2** *n* (*suit*) (*for woman*) deux-pièces *m*; (*for man*) costume *m* deux pièces; (*swimsuit*) deux-pièces

two-pin *adj El* **t. plug** prise *f* à deux fiches; **t. socket** prise à deux douilles

two-ply *adj* (*rope*) à deux brins; (*wool*) deux fils; (*tissue*) double épaisseur

two-seater *n* (*car*) voiture *f* à deux places; (*plane*) biplace *m*, avion *m* à deux places

two-sided *adj* (*contract, talks etc*) bilatéral

twosome ['tuːsəm] *n* **(a)** (*game*) jeu *m* *ou* partie *f* à deux joueurs; (*dance*) danse *f* à deux **(b)** (*pair*) paire *f*; (*of friends etc*) couple *m*; **let's just go as a t.** allons-y rien que tous les deux

two-speed *adj* (*Europe*) à deux vitesses; **t. monetary union** union *f* monétaire à deux vitesses; **t. wiper** essuie-glace *m* deux vitesses

two-star 1 *adj* **(a)** (*restaurant, hotel*) deux étoiles **(b)** (*petrol*) ordinaire **2** *n* (*petrol*) **five litres of t.** cinq litres d'(essence) ordinaire

two-step *n Mus* pas *m* de deux

two-stroke *adj* (*motorcycle*) à deux temps; **t. engine** moteur *m* à deux temps; **t. mixture** (mélange *m*) deux-temps *m*

two-tier *adj* (*management structure*) à deux niveaux; (*education system, health service*) à deux vitesses

two-time *vt F* tromper; **she had been two-timing him with his best friend** elle le trompait avec son meilleur ami

two-timer *n F* (*husband, wife, lover*) compagnon *m*/compagne *f* infidèle

two-timing *adj F* infidèle; **you t. bastard!** tu es un salaud fini!

two-tone *adj* (*paint, car*) deux tons; (*klaxon etc*) à deux tons; **t. horn** avertisseur *m* deux tons; **t. printing** bichromie *f*, impression *f* en deux couleurs

two-way *adj* (*street*) à double sens; (*mirror*) sans tain; *El* (*switch*) à deux directions; *Telecom* bilatéral; **any relationship is a t. thing** *or* **street** toute relation ne peut exister que si elle est réciproque; **t. converter** catalyseur *m* à deux voies; **t. radio** poste *m* émetteur-récepteur; **t. trade** commerce *m* dans les deux sens

two-wheel drive *n* deux roues motrices *fpl*

two-wheeler *n* deux-roues *m inv*

tycoon [taɪ'kuːn] *n F* magnat *m*

tying up [taɪɪŋ] *n* (*of capital*) immobilisation *f*

tyke [taɪk] *n F* **(a)** (*dog*) cabot *m* **(b)** (*person*) salaud *m*; (*small child*) môme *mf*; (*mischievous child*) diablotin *m*

tympanum, *pl* **-a, -ums** ['tɪmpənəm, -ə, -əmz] *n Anat, Archit* tympan *m*

type¹ [taɪp] *n* **(a)** [①A13,3,a] (*class, sort, example*) type *m*, genre *m*; **people/books of this t.** des personnes/des livres de ce genre; **people of every t.** des gens de toutes sortes; *F* **he's/she's not my t.** ce n'est pas mon genre; **she's not the t. to ...**

elle n'est pas du genre à ...; *F* **he's an odd t.** (*person*) c'est un drôle de type **(b)** *Typ* (*letters*) caractères *mpl*; **to print in large t.** imprimer en gros caractères; **in t.** composé; **wait till you see it in t.** attend de le voir imprimé *ou* de voir ce que ça rend imprimé

type[2] **1** *vt* (*write on typewriter*) taper (à la machine), dactylographier **2** *vi* taper à la machine, dactylographier; **can you t.?** savez-vous taper à la machine?; **he types well** il tape bien

type[3] *vt Med* **to t. blood** déterminer un groupe sanguin

▶ **type in** *vtsep* taper

▶ **type out** *vtsep* taper à la machine

▶ **type up** *vtsep* taper au propre

type-ahead *n Comptr* frappe *f* en continu; **t. buffer** zone *f* tampon de frappe en continu

typecast ['taɪpkɑːst] *vt* (*pt, pp* **typecast**) *Th, Cin* (*actor*) donner toujours les mêmes rôles à; **she was being typecast as a dumb blonde** elle était cantonnée aux rôles de blondes écervelées

typed [taɪpt] *adj* dactylographié, écrit à la machine

typeface ['taɪpfeɪs] *n* œil *m* (de caractère)

type genus *n Biol* genre *m* type

type library *n* typothèque *f*

typescript ['taɪpskrɪpt] *n* texte *m* dactylographié

typeset ['taɪpset] *vt* (*pt, pp* **typeset**) *Typ* composer; **typeset by MWP** composition MWP

typesetter ['taɪpsetər] *n* (*person*) compositeur *m*; (*machine*) machine *f* à composer

typesetting ['taɪpsetɪŋ] *n Typ* composition *f*; **who did the t.?** qui a fait la composition?; **t. machine** machine *f* à composer, composeuse *f*; **t. techniques** techniques *fpl* de composition

typesize ['taɪpsaɪz] *n* (*of text*) taille *f* des caractères

typewriter ['taɪpraɪtər] *n* machine *f* à écrire; **to write sth on a t.** écrire *ou* taper qch à la machine; *Comptr* **t. mode** mode *m* machine à écrire; **t. ribbon** ruban *m* de machine à écrire; *Br* **t. rubber** gomme *f* pour machine à écrire

typewriting ['taɪpraɪtɪŋ] *n* dactylographie *f*

typewritten ['taɪprɪt(ə)n] *adj* (*document etc*) écrit *ou* tapé à la machine, dactylographié

typhoid ['taɪfɔɪd] **1** *adj Med* (*bacillus*) typhoïdique; **t. fever** (fièvre *f*) typhoïde *f*; **t. patient** malade *mf* atteint(e) de la typhoïde **2** *n* (fièvre *f*) typhoïde *f*

typhoon [taɪ'fuːn] *n Met* typhon *m*

typhus ['taɪfəs] *n Med* typhus *m*

typical ['tɪpɪk(ə)l] *adj* typique **(of** de); **the t. Frenchman** le Français typique; **in a t. day you can earn £300** en une journée normale vous pouvez gagner 300 livres; *F* **isn't that** *or* **that's t. (of him/her)!** c'est bien de lui/d'elle!; **t. man/woman!** c'est bien un homme/une femme!; **your letter took six days to get here – t.!** ta lettre a mis six jours pour arriver – ça c'est typique! *ou* ça ne m'étonne pas!

typically ['tɪpɪklɪ] *adv* typiquement; **he's t. French** il est typiquement français; **the countryside is t. Mediterranean** le paysage est typiquement méditerranéen; **he made one of his t. obscure remarks** il a fait une de ses habituelles remarques obscures; **she was t. late** (*normally*) elle arrivait généralement en retard; (*as on other occasions*) conformément à son habitude elle était en retard; **she was t. rude, she was her t. rude self** comme à son habitude, elle a été très désagréable; **employees t. work a 40-hour week** les employés travaillent en moyenne 40 heures par semaine

typify ['tɪpɪfaɪ] *vt* (*of person*) (*officer etc*) personnifier; (*of specimen etc*) être caractéristique de

typing ['taɪpɪŋ] *n* dactylographie *f*, *F* dactylo *f*; **t. error** faute *f* de frappe; **t. paper** papier *m* machine; **t. pool** pool *m* de dactylos; **t. skills** compétences *fpl* en dactylographie; **t. speed** vitesse *f* de frappe

typist ['taɪpɪst] *n* **(copy) t.** dactylographe *mf*, *F* dactylo *mf*; **audio t.** dactylo audio-magnéto; **I'm no t.** je tape très mal; **t.'s error** faute *f* de frappe

typo ['taɪpəʊ] *n Typ F* coquille *f*, faute *f* de frappe

typographer [taɪ'pɒgrəfər] *n* typographe *mf*

typographic(al) [taɪpə'græfɪk, -ɪk(ə)l] *adj* typographique

typographically [taɪpə'græfɪklɪ] *adv* typographiquement

typography [taɪ'pɒgrəfɪ] *n* typographie *f*

tyrannical [tɪ'rænɪk(ə)l] *adj* tyrannique

tyrannically ['tɪrænɪklɪ] *adv* tyranniquement

tyrannize ['tɪrənaɪz] *vt* tyranniser

tyranny ['tɪrənɪ] *n* tyrannie *f*

tyrant ['taɪrənt] *n* tyran *m*

tyre ['taɪər] *n esp Br* pneu *m*, *pl* pneus, pneumatique *m*; **t. lever** démonte-pneu *m*, *pl* démonte-pneus; **t. marks** (*in mud, snow etc*) empreintes *fpl ou* traces *fpl* de pneu; **t. pressure** pression *f* des pneus *ou* de gonflage; **t. pressure gauge** indicateur *m* de pression de pneu; **t. pump** pompe *f* (pour gonfler les pneus); **t. scrub** ripage *m* des pneus; **t. tread depth gauge** indicateur *m* d'usure (de pneu); **t. valve** valve *f* de gonflage; **t. wear** usure *f* des pneus; **town and country t.** pneu à usage mixte

tyre chain *n* chaîne *f* (de pneu)

tyro ['taɪrəʊ] *n* novice *mf*, débutant, -ante

Tyrol (the) [ðətɪ'rəʊl] *n* le Tyrol

Tyrolean [tɪrə'liːən] *adj* tyrolien; **T. hat** chapeau *m* tyrolien

tzar, tzarist *etc* = **tsar, tsarist** *etc*

U

U¹, u [juː] *n* (*letter*) U, u *m*; *Old-fashioned F* **U and non U** ce qui est bien *ou* comme il faut, et ce qui ne l'est pas; **U bend** (*in pipe*) coude *m*; (*in road*) virage *m* en épingle à cheveux; *Naut, Hist* **U boat** sous-marin *m* allemand; *MecE* **U bolt** étrier *m*; *Geog* **U-shaped valley** vallée *f* (à profil) en U; **U turn** *Aut* demi-tour *m, pl* demi-tours; *Fig* revirement *m*; *Aut* **no U turns** demi-tour interdit; *Fig* **to do a (complete) U turn on sth** faire un virage à 180 degrés sur qch

U² *Br Cin* (*abbr* **universal**) = tous publics

UAE [juːeɪ'iː] *n* (*abbr* **United Arab Emirates**) Émirats *mpl* Arabes Unis, EAU *mpl*

UB40 [juːbiː'fɔːtɪ] *n Br* (*abbr* **unemployment benefit form 40**) = carte *f* de pointage (de demandeur d'emploi); (*person*) chômeur, -euse

ubiquitous [juː'bɪkwɪtəs] *adj* (*substance, theme, muzak*) omniprésent; (*person*) doué d'ubiquité; **the u. fast-food joint** l'inévitable fast-food

ubiquity [juː'bɪkwɪtɪ] *n* omniprésence *f*; (*of person*) ubiquité *f*

UCCA ['ʌkə] *n Br* (*abbr* **Universities Central Council on Admissions**) centre *m* national qui traite les demandes d'entrée à l'université

UDA [juːdiː'eɪ] *n Br* (*abbr* **Ulster Defence Association**) = groupement *m* paramilitaire protestant en Irlande du Nord

udder ['ʌdər] *n* (*of cow etc*) mamelle *f*, pis *m*

UDI [juːdiː'aɪ] *n* (*abbr* **Unilateral Declaration of Independence**) déclaration *f* unilatérale d'indépendance

UDR [juːdiː'ɑːr] *n Br* (*abbr* **Ulster Defence Regiment**) régiment *m* de réservistes de l'armée britannique en Irlande du Nord

UEFA [juː'eɪfə] *n* (*abbr* **Union of European Football Associations**) UEFA *f*

UFO [juːe'fəʊ, 'juːfəʊ] *n* (*abbr* **unidentified flying object**) OVNI *m*

ufologist [juː'fɒlədʒɪst] *n* spécialiste *mf* des ovnis

ufology [juː'fɒlədʒɪ] *n* étude *f* des ovnis

Uganda [juː'gændə] *n* Ouganda *m*

Ugandan [juː'gændən] **1** *adj* ougandais **2** *n* Ougandais, -aise

ugh [ʌg] *int* pouah!, beuh!

ugli, *pl* **ugli(e)s** ['ʌglɪ, -ɪz] *n* (*fruit*) tangelo *m*

uglify ['ʌglɪfaɪ] *vt* enlaidir

ugliness ['ʌglɪnɪs] *n* laideur *f*

ugly ['ʌglɪ] *adj* **(a)** (*in appearance etc*) (*person*) laid; (*building, furniture, pattern, hat, colour*) affreux, laid; (*word*) déplaisant; (*bruise, wound, scar*) vilain, méchant; **to grow u.** (s')enlaidir; **an u. woman** un laideron, une femme laide; **she's as u. as sin** elle est laide comme les sept péchés capitaux *ou* comme un pou *ou* à faire peur; *Fig* **u. duckling** vilain petit canard *m*

(b) *Fig* (*threatening*) (*sky, look*) menaçant; (*incident, scene*) désagréable; *F* **an u. customer** un sale type; *F* **nationalism/racism reared its u. head** le nationalisme/racisme s'est réveillé; *F* **to cut up** *or* **turn u.** (*of person*) devenir agressif; **the situation was starting to turn u.** la situation commençait à mal tourner; **an u. rumour** un bruit sinistre

UHF [juːeɪtʃ'ef] *n* (*abbr* **ultrahigh frequency**) UHF *f*

uh-huh [ʌ'hʌ] *int* (*agreeing, yes*) hmm hmm, oui oui; ['ʌhʌ] (*disagreeing, no, don't*) tut-tut, non non

UHT [juːeɪtʃ'tiː] *adj* (*abbr* **ultra heat treated**) **U. milk** lait *m* UHT, lait longue conservation

UK [juː'keɪ] *n* (*abbr* **United Kingdom**) R.U. *m*, Royaume-Uni *m*; **UK sales/prices** ventes/prix au Royaume-Uni

Ukraine [juː'kreɪn] *n* Ukraine *f*

Ukrainian [juː'kreɪnɪən] **1** *adj* ukrainien **2** *n* **(a)** Ukrainien, -ienne **(b)** *Ling* ukrainien *m*

ukulele [juːkə'leɪlɪ] *n Mus* ukulélé *m*, guitare *f* hawaïenne

ulcer ['ʌlsər] *n Med* ulcère *m*; (*in mouth*) aphte *m*; *Fig* plaie *f*; (*ugly building etc*) verrue *f*; **peptic u.** ulcère simple de l'estomac/du duodénum

ulcerate ['ʌlsəreɪt] *Med* **1** *vt* ulcérer; **ulcerated wound** blessure ulcérée *ou* ulcéreuse **2** *vi* s'ulcérer

ulceration [ʌlsə'reɪʃən] *n Med* ulcération *f*

ulcerative ['ʌls(ə)rətɪv] *adj Med* ulcératif

ulcerous ['ʌls(ə)rəs] *adj Med* ulcéreux

ullage ['ʌlɪdʒ] *n* (*in barrel*) creux *m* du tonneau

ulna ['ʌlnə] *n Anat* cubitus *m*

Ulster ['ʌlstər] *n* **(a)** Ulster *m* **(b) u.** (*coat*) ulster *m*

Ulsterman, *pl* **-men** ['ʌlstəmən] *n* Ulstérien *m*

Ulsterwoman, *pl* **-women** ['ʌlstəwʊmən, -wɪmɪn] *n* Ulstérienne *f*

ult [ʌlt] *Old-fashioned Com abbr* **ultimo**

ulterior [ʌl'tɪərɪər] *adj* ultérieur; **u. designs** desseins *mpl* secrets; **u. motive** arrière-pensée, *pl* arrière-pensées; **without u. motive** sans arrière-pensée

ultimate ['ʌltɪmət] **1** *adj* **(a)** (*final*) final, -als, définitif; **the u. effect of an action** l'effet ultime d'une action; **the u. decision is his** c'est à lui qu'appartient la décision finale; **u. goal** but *m* final; **certain of u. success** certain du succès final; **the u. deterrent** l'arme *f* de dissuasion absolue; **they made the u. sacrifice** ils ont fait l'ultime sacrifice

(b) (*basic, fundamental*) fondamental, -aux; **the u. constituents of matter** les constituants fondamentaux de la matière; **is this the u. physical particle?** est-ce la particule fondamentale?

(c) (*supreme, best etc*) suprême, absolu; **the u. double-glazing/laser printer** le double vitrage/l'imprimante laser absolu(e); **the u. sound system** la meilleure sono qui soit; **that really is the u. cheek!** c'est vraiment le comble du culot!; **he really is the u. incompetent!** on ne fait pas plus incompétent que lui

(d) (*furthest*) le plus lointain; **the u. ends of the universe** les limites externes de l'univers; **we trace our u. origins back to …** nous avons établi nos origines les plus lointaines à …

2 *n* **(a)** *Rel, Phil* **the u.** (*the best*) l'absolu *m*

(b) the u. (*the very best*) le fin du fin; **the u. in luxury** le summum du luxe; **it's the u. in vulgarity/bad taste** c'est le comble de la vulgarité/du mauvais goût

ultimately ['ʌltɪmɪtlɪ] *adv* **(a)** (*finally, in the end*) finalement; **the events which led u. to his downfall** les événements qui ont finalement conduit à sa chute **(b)** (*at bottom, basically*) en fin de compte; **u. it's the same thing** en fin de compte *ou* au fond c'est la même chose

ultimatum, *pl* **-tums, -ta** [ʌltɪ'meɪtəm, -təmz, -tə] *n* ultimatum *m*; **to deliver an u. to sb, to present sb with an u.** adresser un ultimatum à qn

ultimo ['ʌltɪməʊ] *adv Old-fashioned Com* du mois dernier; **on the tenth u.** le dix du mois dernier

ultra- ['ʌltrə] *pref* ultra-, hyper-

ultrafashionable ['ʌltrəfæʃənəb(ə)l] *adj* à la pointe de la mode, *F* hyper-mode *inv*

ultrahigh [ʌltrə'haɪ] *adj Phys* **u. frequency** ondes *fpl* ultra-courtes

ultraleft [ʌltrə'left] *Pol* **1** *adj* d'extrême gauche **2** *n* extrême gauche *f*

ultramarine [ʌltrəmə'riːn] *adj, n* **u. (blue)** (bleu d')outremer *m*

ultramodern [ʌltrə'mɒd(ə)n] *adj* ultramoderne

ultramontane [ʌltrə'mɒnteɪn] *adj, n* ultramontain, -aine

ultraright [ʌltrə'raɪt] *Pol* **1** *adj* d'extrême droite **2** *n* extrême droite *f*

ultrasensitive [ʌltrə'sensɪtɪv] *adj* ultrasensible

ultrashort [ʌltrə'ʃɔːt] *adj Phys* ultracourt

ultrasonic [ʌltrə'sɒnɪk] **1** *adj* ultrasonique; **u. alarm** alarme *f* à ultrasons **2** *n* (①A10,c) **ultrasonics** science *f* des ultrasons

ultrasound (scan) ['ʌltrəsaʊnd] *n Med* échographie *f*, ultra-son *m*

ultraviolet [ʌltrə'vaɪələt] *adj Phys* ultraviolet; **u. rays** rayons *mpl* ultraviolets; *Med* **u. treatment** traitement *m* aux (rayons) ultraviolets

ultra vires [ʌltrə'vaɪəriːz, ʊltrə'viːreɪz] *adj, adv Jur* au delà de ses pouvoirs

ululate ['juːljʊleɪt] *vi Fml* (*of owl etc*) ululer, huer; (*of jackal etc*) hurler; (*of person, mourner*) se lamenter

ululation [juːljʊ'leɪʃən] *n Fml* (*of owl etc*) ululation *f*, ululement *m*; (*of jackal etc*) hurlement *m*; (*of person*) lamentation *f*

Ulysses ['juːlɪsiːz] *n* Ulysse *m*

um [ʌm] **1** *int* (*hesitating in speaking*) heu **2** *vi* **to u. and err** bafouiller

umber [ˈʌmbər] **1** *n Art* terre *f* d'ombre *ou* de Sienne; **burnt u.** terre d'ombre brûlée **2** *adj* couleur *inv* d'ombre

umbilical [ʌmˈbɪlɪk(ə)l, ʌmbɪˈlaɪk(ə)l] *adj Anat* ombilical, -aux; **u. cord** cordon *m* ombilical

umbilicus [ʌmˈbɪlɪkəs, ʌmbɪˈlaɪkəs] *n Anat* ombilic *m*, nombril *m*

umbrage [ˈʌmbrɪdʒ] *n* ombrage *m*, ressentiment *m*; **to take u. at sth** prendre ombrage de qch, se froisser de qch

umbrella [ʌmˈbrelə] *n* **(a)** parapluie *m*; **to put up** *or* **open (up) one's u.** ouvrir son parapluie; **to put down** *or* **to fold (up)** *or* **close (up) one's u.** fermer *ou* replier son parapluie; **beach u.** parasol *m*; **u. stand** porte-parapluies *m inv* **(b) under the u. of the United Nations** sous la protection des Nations Unies; **u. organization** organisation *f* qui en regroupe plusieurs autres **(c)** *Mil, Av* **air** *or* **aerial u.** parapluie *m* aérien; **nuclear u.** parapluie nucléaire **(d)** (*of jellyfish*) ombrelle *f*

Umbria [ˈʌmbrɪə] *n* Ombrie *f*

Umbrian [ˈʌmbrɪən] **1** *n* Ombrien, -ienne **2** *adj* ombrien

umlaut [ˈʊmlaʊt] *n Ling* **(a)** (*vowel change*) inflexion *f* vocalique, métaphonie *f* **(b)** (*sign*) tréma *m*

umph [hm] *int* (*disbelieving, not pleased*) hum!, hmm!

umpire¹ [ˈʌmpaɪər] *n Sp etc* arbitre *m*, juge *m*; **to be an u. at a match** arbitrer un match

umpire² *Sp etc* **1** *vt* (*match*) arbitrer **2** *vi* arbitrer (le/un match)

umpteen [ʌmpˈtiːn] *adj F* je ne sais combien de; **I've told you u. times not to ...** je t'ai dit mille *ou* je ne sais combien de fois de ne pas ...; **she's got u. books on Africa** elle a des tas de livres sur l'Afrique; **to have u. reasons for doing sth** avoir trente-six raisons de faire qch

umpteenth [ʌmpˈtiːnθ] *adj F* **that's the u. time I've told you** c'est la énième fois que je te le dis

UN [juːˈen] *n* (*abbr* **United Nations**) ONU *f*; **UN troops/observers** soldats/observateurs de l'ONU

'un [ən] *pron Sl* (= *one*) **a little 'un** un petit, une petite; **he's a bad 'un** c'est un sale type

unabashed [ʌnəˈbæʃt] *adj* (*person*) aucunement décontenancé; **shocked at his u. confession of guilt** choqué de le voir avouer sa culpabilité sans aucune honte

unabashedly [ʌnəˈbæʃədlɪ] *adv* (*unashamedly*) sans aucune honte; (*without being discouraged*) sans se laisser décontenancer, sans se démonter

unabated [ʌnəˈbeɪtɪd] *adj* non diminué; **for three days the storm continued u.** pendant trois jours l'orage a continué sans répit; **the riots went on u.** les émeutes continuèrent sans faiblir; **the crowd continued to cheer with u. enthusiasm** la foule continuait à pousser des acclamations avec toujours autant d'enthousiasme

unabbreviated [ʌnəˈbriːvɪeɪtɪd] *adj* non abrégé

unable [ʌnˈeɪb(ə)l] *adj* incapable; **to be u. to do sth** ne pas pouvoir faire qch; (*because of external factor*) être dans l'impossibilité de faire qch, ne pas pouvoir faire qch; **he seems u. to understand you** il semble être incapable de vous comprendre; **we are u. to help you** nous ne sommes pas en mesure de vous aider; **I was u. to persuade him** je n'ai pas pu le persuader

unabridged [ʌnəˈbrɪdʒd] *adj* non abrégé, intégral, -aux; **u. text** texte *m* intégral; **u. edition** édition *f* intégrale

unaccented, unaccentuated [ʌnəkˈsentɪd, ʌnəkˈsentjʊeɪtɪd] *adj Ling* (*syllable etc*) non accentué, atone; *Mus* **u. beat** temps *m* faible

unacceptable [ʌnəkˈseptəb(ə)l] *adj* inacceptable; (*theory*) irrecevable; (*behaviour*) inadmissible; **these conditions are u. to us** nous ne pouvons pas accepter ces conditions; **it's quite u. for so many people to be homeless** il est tout à fait inacceptable *ou* inadmissible que tant de gens soient sans foyer

unacceptably [ʌnəkˈseptəblɪ] *adv* **an u. high level of ...** un niveau inadmissible *ou* intolérable de ...; **what they are, quite u., demanding is ...** l'objet tout à fait inadmissible de leur demande est ...

unaccommodating [ʌnəˈkɒmədeɪtɪŋ] *adj* (*person*) peu accommodant

unaccompanied [ʌnəˈkʌmp(ə)nɪd] *adj* **(a)** (*person, baggage*) non accompagné **(b)** *Mus* sans accompagnement; **passage for u. violin** passage pour violon seul

unaccomplished [ʌnəˈkʌmplɪʃt] *adj* **(a)** (*not fulfilled, not completed*) (*an ambition*) non réalisé; (*work*) inachevé **(b)** (*mediocre*) (*person, performance etc*) médiocre

unaccountable [ʌnəˈkaʊntəb(ə)l] *adj* **(a)** (*inexplicable*) inexplicable **(b)** (*not accountable*) **to be u. to sb** ne pas avoir à répondre devant qn

unaccountably [ʌnəˈkaʊntəblɪ] *adv* inexpliquablement

unaccounted [ʌnəˈkaʊntɪd] *adj* **there are still several thousand soldiers who are u. for** il y a encore plusieurs milliers de soldats portés disparus; **these £10 are u. for in the balance sheet** ces 10 livres ne figurent pas au bilan; **five of the passengers are still u. for** on reste sans nouvelles de cinq passagers; **two books are still u. for** il manque toujours deux livres

unaccustomed [ʌnəˈkʌstəmd] *adj* **(a)** inaccoutumé, inhabituel **(b)** (*person*) **u. to sth/to doing sth** peu habitué à qch/à faire qch; **u. as I am to public speaking** n'ayant pas l'habitude de faire des discours

unacknowledged [ʌnəkˈnɒlɪdʒd] *adj* **(a)** (*child, talents*) non reconnu; **to go u.** ne pas être reconnu **(b)** (*quotation*) dont on ne cite pas l'auteur **(c)** (*letter*) resté sans réponse; **you shouldn't let his letter go u.** tu ne devrais pas laisser sa lettre sans réponse

unacquainted [ʌnəˈkweɪntɪd] *adj* **to be u. with sb/sth** ne pas connaître qn/qch; **to be u. with a fact** ignorer un fait; **we are not u. with pressure** nous n'ignorons pas ce que c'est que le stress

unadapted [ʌnəˈdæptɪd] *adj* mal adapté, peu adapté (**to sth** à qch)

unaddressed [ʌnəˈdrest] *adj* (*parcel etc*) sans adresse, qui ne porte pas d'adresse

unadopted [ʌnəˈdɒptɪd] *adj* non adopté; **to remain u.** (*of measure*) rester en souffrance; *Br* **u. road** rue *f* non prise en charge par la municipalité

unadorned [ʌnəˈdɔːnd] *adj* sans ornement, sans fioritures; *esp Lit* **her u. beauty** sa beauté sans parure *ou* sans fard; **the u. truth** la vérité pure *ou* toute nue

unadulterated [ʌnəˈdʌltəreɪtɪd] *adj* pur, sans mélange; (*wine*) non frelaté; **u. joy** joie *f* sans mélange; **the u. truth** la vérité pure et simple; **u. by Western influences** non corrompu par les influences occidentales; **this is pure u. garbage!** ceci est purement et simplement de la foutaise!; **I've never heard such u. rot!** je n'ai jamais entendu de telles foutaises!

unadventurous [ʌnədˈventʃərəs] *adj* (*life, person*) peu aventureux; (*style, performance, director, prose etc*) peu audacieux, conventionnel; **we went to Spain again – that's very u. of you** nous sommes retournés en Espagne – ce n'est pas très aventureux de votre part

unadventurously [ʌnədˈventʃərəslɪ] *adv* (*produced, designed*) peu audacieusement; (*to decide, choose*) sans prendre de risques; **we very u. chose beige carpets again** nous n'avons pas pris de risques et avons encore choisi des moquettes beiges

unadvertised [ʌnˈædvətaɪzd] *adj* (*product, meeting etc*) sans publicité; (*action etc*) discret, -ète

unadvisable [ʌnədˈvaɪzəb(ə)l] *adj* (*action*) peu recommandé, imprudent; **alcohol is u. for people suffering from heart complaints** l'alcool est à déconseiller aux cardiaques

unadvised [ʌnədˈvaɪzd] *adj esp Lit* (*unwise*) imprudent

unaesthetic [ʌniːsˈθetɪk] *adj* inesthétique

unaffected [ʌnəˈfektɪd] *adj* **(a)** (*without affectation*) (*person, behaviour*) sans affectation, naturel, simple; (*style*) sans fioritures, simple; **u. joy** joie *f* qui n'a rien de simulé; **u. modesty** modestie *f* non simulée
(b) (*not touched*) **to be u. by sth** (*of person*) ne pas être affecté par qch; (*of thing*) (*by rain, cold, heat etc*) ne pas être altéré par qch; **she remained u. by his tears** elle ne fut pas émue par ses larmes; **we were u. by the strike/recession** nous n'avons pas été affectés par la grève/récession; **there's snow everywhere, but the north-west is u.** il y a de la neige partout, mais le nord-ouest n'est pas touché; *Med* **u. carrier** porteur *m* sain

unaffectedly [ʌnəˈfektɪdlɪ] *adv* (*to behave, speak*) simplement, sans affectation; (*dressed*) sobrement

unaffiliated [ʌnəˈfɪlɪeɪtɪd] *adj* non affilié (**to** à)

unaffordable [ʌnəˈfɔːdəb(ə)l] *adj* inabordable

unafraid [ʌnəˈfreɪd] *adj* sans peur

unaided [ʌnˈeɪdɪd] **1** *adv* sans aide, sans assistance; **he did it u.** il l'a fait tout seul *ou* à lui seul **2** *adj* **by my own u. efforts** par mes propres moyens; **is this your own u. work?** est-ce que tu as travaillé tout seul?

unaired [ʌnˈeəd] *adj* non aéré; (*opinions etc*) non exprimé

unalike [ʌnəˈlaɪk] *adj* dissemblable, différent; **they are not u.** ils se ressemblent un peu, ils ne sont pas totalement dissemblables

unalleviated [ʌnəˈliːvɪeɪtɪd] *adj* sans répit; **u. boredom** ennui *f* mortel

unallocated [ʌnˈæləkeɪtɪd] *adj* (*rooms, places*) non assigné; (*money, grants*) non alloué

unalloyed [ʌnəˈlɔɪd] *adj Lit* (*happiness*) parfait

unalterable [ʌnˈɔːlt(ə)rəb(ə)l] *adj* immuable; (*character*) inaltérable

unalterably [ʌnˈɔːlt(ə)rəblɪ] *adv* immuablement

unaltered [ʌn'ɔːltəd] *adj* inchangé; **let's leave it u.** n'y touchons pas

unambiguous [ʌnæm'bɪgjʊəs] *adj* non équivoque; (*reply*) sans ambiguïté; **what he meant was quite u.** il a été tout à fait clair; **u. terms** termes *mpl* tout à fait *ou* on ne peut plus clairs

unambiguously [ʌnæm'bɪgjʊəslɪ] *adv* (*worded etc*) sans équivoque, sans ambiguïté; **he told us quite u. to …** il nous a dit tout à fait clairement de …

unambitious [ʌnæm'bɪʃəs] *adj* (*person, project etc*) sans ambition, peu ambitieux

un-American [ʌnə'merɪk(ə)n] *adj* contraire à l'esprit américain; (*in a damaging way*) antiaméricain; **he's so u.** ce n'est vraiment pas un américain type

unamused [ʌnə'mjuːzd] *adj* **she was distinctly u.** visiblement, cela ne l'amusait pas

unanimity [juːnə'nɪmɪtɪ] *n* unanimité *f*

unanimous [jʊ'nænɪməs] *adj* unanime; **they were u. in accusing him** ils étaient unanimes à l'accuser; **to reach a u. decision** se prononcer à l'unanimité; **u. vote** résolution *f* adoptée à l'unanimité

unanimously [jʊ'nænɪməslɪ] *adv* à l'unanimité

unannounced [ʌnə'naʊnst] *adj* sans être annoncé; **he marched in u.** il est entré sans se faire annoncer

unanswerable [ʌn'ɑːns(ə)rəb(ə)l] *adj* (*argument*) incontestable, irréfutable; **u. question** question *f* à laquelle on ne peut pas répondre

unanswered [ʌn'ɑːnsəd] *adj* **(a)** (*letter, question*) sans réponse; **I had to leave two questions u.** j'ai dû laisser deux questions sans réponse; **our letter has remained u.** notre lettre est restée sans réponse **(b)** (*argument*) irréfuté

unappealing [ʌnə'piːlɪŋ] *adj* peu attrayant

unappeased [ʌnə'piːzd] *adj Lit* (*hunger, desire, lust*) inassouvi

unappetizing [ʌn'æpɪtaɪzɪŋ] *adj* peu appétissant; **this dish looks really u.** ce plat n'est pas appétissant du tout

unappreciated [ʌnə'priːʃɪeɪtɪd] *adj* peu apprécié; (*difficulty, scope of task etc*) sous-estimé; (*hard work, capability*) non reconnu; **her efforts go u.** le mal qu'elle se donne n'est pas apprécié à sa juste valeur

unappreciative [ʌnə'priːʃɪətɪv] *adj* (*audience*) insensible; (*report etc*) peu favorable; **she was very u. of everything we had done for her** elle ne montrait aucune gratitude après tout ce qu'on avait fait pour elle; **don't be so u.!** ne sois pas si ingrat!

unapproachable [ʌnə'prəʊtʃəb(ə)l] *adj* (*person, place*) inaccessible; **an u. sort of person** une personne d'un abord difficile

unarguable [ʌn'ɑːgjʊəb(ə)l] *adj* (*case, theory*) indéfendable

unarguably [ʌn'ɑːgjʊəblɪ] *adv* (*indisputably*) incontestablement

unarmed [ʌn'ɑːmd] *adj* (*person*) non armé; **I am u.** je ne suis pas armé; **I'm not going in there u.** je n'entre pas là-dedans sans arme; **u. combat** combat *m* sans armes *ou* à mains nues

unashamed [ʌnə'ʃeɪmd] *adj* (*delight, joy*) non déguisé; (*greed, hypocrisy*) flagrant; **to be u. about doing sth** ne pas avoir honte de faire qch; **his u. nationalism** son nationalisme éhonté; **with u. relief** avec un soulagement non dissimulé

unashamedly [ʌnə'ʃeɪmɪdlɪ] *adv* sans honte; **George was u. in favour of the war** George se déclarait ouvertement en faveur de la guerre; **he was u. open about it all** il s'est exprimé sur cette affaire avec une franchise totale; **she was quite u. relieved about not having to …** elle ne cacha pas son soulagement à l'idée de ne pas devoir …; **he is u. outspoken in his support of …** il affiche (tout à fait ouvertement) son soutien à …

unasked [ʌn'ɑːskt] **1** *adv* (*to do sth*) spontanément; **she came to help us quite u.** elle est venue nous aider sans qu'on le lui ait demandé **2** *adj* **u. for** (*gift etc*) spontané, qu'on n'a pas demandé; (*unwanted*) (*advice*) non sollicité

unaspirated [ʌn'æspɪreɪtɪd] *adj Ling* non aspiré

unassailable [ʌnə'seɪləb(ə)l] *adj* (*fortress, position*) imprenable; (*conclusion, argument*) irréfutable; **his reputation is u.** il a une réputation à toute épreuve

unassimilated [ʌnə'sɪmɪleɪtɪd] *adj* inassimilé; **u. knowledge** connaissances *fpl* mal assimilées

unassisted [ʌnə'sɪstɪd] **1** *adv* sans aide, sans assistance; **he did it u.** il l'a fait tout seul **2** *adj* **by her own u. efforts** sans l'aide de personne

unassuming [ʌnə'sjuːmɪŋ] *adj* sans prétention(s), modeste

unassumingly [ʌnə'sjuːmɪŋlɪ] *adv* modestement, avec modestie

unattached [ʌnə'tætʃt] *adj* **(a)** (*part, wire etc*) qui n'est pas attaché **(to** à) **(b)** (*journalist, group etc*) indépendant **(to** de); *Mil* (*officer*) disponible, en disponibilité **(c)** (*not married etc*) **to be u.** être libre *ou* sans attaches

unattainable [ʌnə'teɪnəb(ə)l] *adj* inaccessible **(by** à)

unattended [ʌnə'tendɪd] *adj* **(a)** (*shop, printer etc*) sans surveillance; **to leave one's car u.** laisser sa voiture sans surveillance; **do not leave your luggage u.** surveillez toujours vos bagages **(b)** (*person, child*) seul; **to leave a child u.** laisser un enfant sans surveillance; **don't leave the guests u. (to)** ne négligez pas les invités, occupez-vous des invités; **the leaking pipe has gone u. (to) for months** ça fait des mois que le tuyau fuit et rien n'a été fait **(c)** (*queen etc*) sans escorte

unattractive [ʌnə'træktɪv] *adj* peu attrayant, sans attrait, peu séduisant; (*character*) peu sympathique; **extremely u.** pas du tout attrayant; **she is not u.** elle ne manque pas de charme

unaudited [ʌn'ɔːdɪtɪd] *adj* (*accounts*) non vérifié

unauthenticated [ʌnɔː'θentɪkeɪtɪd] *adj* dont l'authenticité n'est pas établie; *Jur* (*document*) non légalisé

unauthorized [ʌn'ɔːθəraɪzd] *adj* non autorisé, sans autorisation; **no entry to u. persons, no u. access** accès interdit à toute personne étrangère au service; *Comptr* **u. access** accès *m* non autorisé

unavailability [ʌnəveɪlə'bɪlɪtɪ] *n* indisponibilité *f*

unavailable [ʌnə'veɪləb(ə)l] *adj* (*person, goods*) indisponible, pas disponible; (*sold out etc*) épuisé; **the minister was u. for comment** le ministre s'est refusé à tout commentaire

unavailing [ʌnə'veɪlɪŋ] *adj* inutile, vain; (*effort, attempt*) infructueux

unavailingly [ʌnə'veɪlɪŋlɪ] *adv* inutilement, en vain

unavenged [ʌnə'vendʒd] *adv* **it won't go u.** cela ne restera pas impuni; **the u. death of …** la mort de … qui n'a pas été vengée

unavoidable [ʌnə'vɔɪdəb(ə)l] *adj* inévitable; (*fate*) auquel on ne peut échapper; (*event*) qu'on ne peut prévenir; **my absence was u.** mon absence a été due à un cas de force majeure; **it is u. that …** il est inévitable que … + *sub*

unavoidably [ʌnə'vɔɪdəblɪ] *adv* inévitablement; **u. detained** retenu pour raison majeure

unaware [ʌnə'weər] *adj* ignorant, pas au courant **(of sth** de qch); **to be u. of sth** ignorer qch; **her husband was totally u. of what was going on** son mari ne se rendait absolument pas compte de ce qui se passait; **he was u. that he was being watched** il ne se rendait pas compte qu'on l'observait; **we are not u. of the need for reform** nous avons conscience de la nécessité d'une réforme; **is that so?, I was u. of that** ah oui?, je n'étais pas au courant; **you will surely not be u. of the importance of …** l'importance de … ne vous a certainement pas échappé; **if there are any other problems I am u. of them** s'il y a d'autres problèmes, je ne suis pas au courant; **he is sexually/politically u.** il vit dans un monde où la sexualité/la politique n'existe pas

unawares [ʌnə'weəz] *adv* (*without realizing*) inconsciemment, sans s'en rendre compte; **to take** *or* **catch sb u.** (*by surprise*) prendre qn au dépourvu

unbalance [ʌn'bæləns] *vt* déséquilibrer; (*sb's mind*) déranger

unbalanced [ʌn'bælənst] *adj* **(a)** (*person, mind etc*) déséquilibré, dérangé **(b)** (*distribution*) inéquitable; (*reporting*) partial **(c)** (*steering*) mal équilibré **(d)** *Fin* (*account*) non soldé

unbandage [ʌn'bændɪdʒ] *vt* (*wound*) débander

unbaptized [ʌnbæp'taɪzd] *adj* non baptisé

unbar [ʌn'bɑːr] *vt* (*door*) débarrer

unbearable [ʌn'beərəb(ə)l] *adj* insupportable, intolérable; **the children have been u. all day** les enfants ont été insupportables toute la journée; **in this heat, the office is u.** par cette chaleur le bureau n'est pas tenable

unbearably [ʌn'beərəblɪ] *adv* **it was u. painful/hot** la douleur/chaleur était insupportable; **the last scene was u. moving** la dernière scène était d'une tristesse insupportable; **he's u. arrogant** son arrogance est insupportable

unbeatable [ʌn'biːtəb(ə)l] *adj* imbattable; (*army*) invincible; **we offer u. value** nous offrons de la qualité à des prix imbattables

unbeaten [ʌn'biːt(ə)n] *adj* (*champion, army*) invaincu; (*record*) qui n'a pas encore été battu

unbecoming [ʌnbɪ'kʌmɪŋ] *adj* inconvenant, malséant **(to** de la part de); (*garment*) peu seyant; (*facial hair*) peu esthétique; **it's u. of him to act in this manner** il lui sied mal d'agir de la sorte

unbeknown [ʌnbɪ'nəʊn] *adv* **u. to me/her/***etc* à mon/son/*etc* insu; **to do sth u. to anyone** faire qch à l'insu de tous

unbeknownst [ʌnbɪ'nəʊnst] *adv esp Am* = **unbeknown**

unbelief [ʌnbɪ'liːf] *n* incrédulité *f*; **he looked at me in u.** il me regarda avec incrédulité

unbelievable [ʌnbɪ'liːvəb(ə)l] *adj* incroyable; **it's u. that …** il est incroyable que … + *sub*

unbelievably [ʌnbɪ'liːvəblɪ] *adv* incroyablement; **u. stupid** d'une sottise incroyable

unbeliever [ʌnbɪ'liːvər] *n* incrédule *mf*
unbelieving [ʌnbɪ'liːvɪŋ] *adj* incrédule
unbelievingly [ʌnbɪ'liːvɪŋlɪ] *adv* (*to say, look*) d'une manière incrédule
unbend [ʌn'bend] (*pt, pp* **unbent** [ʌn'bent]) **1** *vt* (*steel rod etc*) redresser; (*leg*) déplier **2** *vi* **(a)** (*relax*) devenir moins strict **(b)** (*straighten out*) se redresser; (*of limb*) se déplier
unbending [ʌn'bendɪŋ] *adj* (*character*) inflexible, rigide; **u. attitude** attitude *f* intransigeante
unbias(s)ed [ʌn'baɪəst] *adj* impartial
unbidden [ʌn'bɪd(ə)n] *adv Old-fashioned* **to do sth u.** faire qch spontanément *ou* sans y avoir été invité
unbind [ʌn'baɪnd] *vt* (*pt, pp* **unbound** [ʌn'baʊnd]) **(a)** (*prisoner, hands*) délier **(b)** (*wound*) débander
unbleached [ʌn'bliːtʃt] *adj* **(a)** écru; **u. linen** toile *f* bise *ou* écrue **(b)** (*coffee filters, nappies etc*) sans chlore
unblemished [ʌn'blemɪʃt] *adj* sans défaut; (*reputation*) sans tache
unblinking [ʌn'blɪŋkɪŋ] *adj* (*person*) impassible; (*gaze, look*) fixe; **with u. eyes** sans ciller
unblock [ʌn'blɒk] *vt* (*road, path*) dégager; (*pipe etc*) déboucher; *Comptr* débloquer
unblushing [ʌn'blʌʃɪŋ] *adj* sans vergogne, éhonté; **he remained u. as she declared her love** il écoutait sa déclaration d'amour sans rougir
unblushingly [ʌn'blʌʃɪŋlɪ] *adv* sans rougir
unbolt [ʌn'bəʊlt] *vt* (*door*) déverrouiller; (*rail etc*) déboulonner
unborn ['ʌnbɔːn] *adj* qui n'est pas (encore) né; **u. child** enfant *mf* à naître; **generations yet u.** [ʌn'bɔːn] générations *fpl* à venir, générations futures
unbosom [ʌn'bʊzəm] *vt Lit* **to u. oneself to sb** ouvrir son cœur à qn
unbound [ʌn'baʊnd] *adj* (*book*) non relié, broché; (*hands*) libre; (*prisoner*) pas attaché
unbounded [ʌn'baʊndɪd] *adj* sans bornes, illimité; (*ambition etc*) démesuré
unbowed [ʌn'baʊd] *adj* invaincu, insoumis; **bloody but u.** vaincu, mais non soumis
unbranded [ʌn'brændɪd] *adj Mktg* sans marque
unbreakable [ʌn'breɪkəb(ə)l] *adj* incassable; (*promise, rule etc*) sacré, inviolable; *Sp* (*record*) imbattable; (*habit*) immuable
unbreathable [ʌn'briːðəb(ə)l] *adj* (*air*) irrespirable
unbribable [ʌn'braɪbəb(ə)l] *adj* incorruptible
unbridled [ʌn'braɪd(ə)ld] *adj* **(a)** (*passion, greed etc*) débridé, effréné; (*capitalism*) effréné **(b)** (*horse*) débridé, sans bride
unbroken [ʌn'brəʊk(ə)n] *adj* **(a)** (*plate, chair etc*) non brisé, non cassé, intact **(b)** (*skin, seal etc*) intact; **u. spirit** optimisme *m* intact **(c)** (*promise*) inviolé; (*rules*) toujours observé *ou* respecté; **the peace remained u. for ten years** la paix n'a pas été troublée pendant dix ans; *Sp* **record still u.** record qui n'a pas été battu **(d)** (*silence, expanse of water, years of government etc*) ininterrompu; **u. sheet of ice** nappe de glace continue **(e)** (*horse*) non rompu, non dressé **(f)** *Agr* **u. ground** terre *f* vierge
unbrotherly [ʌn'brʌðəlɪ] *adj* peu fraternel
unbuckle [ʌn'bʌk(ə)l] *vt* (*belt*) déboucler
unbudgeted [ʌn'bʌdʒɪtɪd] *adj* non prévu au budget
unbuilt [ʌn'bɪlt, 'ʌnbɪlt] *adj* **u. plot, plot of u. ground** terrain *m* vague *ou* non construit
unbundle [ʌn'bʌnd(ə)l] *vt* **(a)** *US* (*itemize*) détailler **(b)** *Comptr* décompresser
unbundling [ʌn'bʌndlɪŋ] *n* **(a)** (*of goods*) séparation *f* **(b)** *Comptr* décompression *f*
unburden [ʌn'bɜːd(ə)n] *vt* **to u. oneself** *or* **one's heart** s'épancher; **to u. oneself to sb** se confier à qn; **to u. oneself of a secret** se soulager du poids d'un secret; **to u. one's sorrows to sb** s'épancher auprès de qn
unburied [ʌn'berɪd] *adj* non enterré
unbusinesslike [ʌn'bɪznɪslaɪk] *adj* (*person*) peu commerçant, qui n'a pas le sens des affaires; (*procedure, handling*) peu professionnel; **to conduct one's affairs in an u. way** mal mener ses affaires
unbutton [ʌn'bʌt(ə)n] *vt* (*one's coat etc*) déboutonner; **to come unbuttoned** se déboutonner
unbuttoned [ʌn'bʌt(ə)nd] *adj F* (*relaxed*) décontracté
uncalled capital [ʌn'kɔːld] *n Fin* capital *m* non appelé
uncalled-for *adj* (*remark*) déplacé; (*rebuke*) immérité, injustifié; (*insult*) gratuit; **that was quite u.** c'était tout à fait injustifié
uncannily [ʌn'kænɪlɪ] *adv* étrangement, bizarrement
uncanny [ʌn'kænɪ] *adj* **(a)** (*strange, inexplicable*) étrange, mystérieux; **it's u. how he knows where I am** c'est vraiment étrange *ou* bizarre qu'il sache où je suis; **with u. accuracy** avec une exactitude surprenante **(b)** (*eerie*) inquiétant
uncared-for [ʌn'keədfɔːr] *adj* négligé; **to leave a garden u.** laisser un jardin à l'abandon
uncaring [ʌn'keərɪŋ] *adj* qui ne se soucie pas (des autres), indifférent
uncarpeted [ʌn'kɑːpɪtɪd] *adj* sans tapis, sans moquette
uncashed [ʌn'kæʃt] *adj* non encaissé
uncatalogued [ʌn'kætəlɒgd] *adj* qui n'est pas catalogué
unceasing [ʌn'siːsɪŋ] *adj* incessant, continuel; (*work*) assidu; (*effort*) soutenu
unceasingly [ʌn'siːsɪŋlɪ] *adv* sans cesse, sans arrêt
uncensored [ʌn'sensəd] *adj* (*scene, version etc*) non expurgé; (*version, edition*) intégral
unceremonious [ʌnserɪ'məʊnɪəs] *adj* **it resulted in his u. ejection from the hall** cela a eu pour conséquence qu'il s'est fait expulser de la salle sans cérémonie; **he was packed off in a very u. way to stay with his uncle in Australia** on l'a envoyé très cavalièrement *ou* sans aucune cérémonie chez son oncle en Australie; **after his u. departure from politics** après qu'il eut peu glorieusement abandonné la politique
unceremoniously [ʌnserɪ'məʊnɪəslɪ] *adv* sans cérémonie, brusquement; **he was u. bundled into the police van** il fut embarqué dans le fourgon de police sans cérémonie
uncertain [ʌn'sɜːt(ə)n] *adj* incertain; **it's u. who will win** on ne sait pas au juste qui gagnera; **I feel u. about him** j'ai des doutes à son sujet; **he told him in no u. terms** il lui a dit sans mâcher ses mots; **to be u. what to do** ne pas savoir quoi faire; **I feel u. whether to trust him or not** je ne sais pas si je dois lui faire confiance
uncertainly [ʌn'sɜːt(ə)nlɪ] *adv* d'une façon incertaine; (*to look at sb*) d'un air un peu inquiet
uncertainty [ʌn'sɜːt(ə)ntɪ] *n* incertitude *f*; **there is some u. about …** l'incertitude règne au sujet de …; **u. about** *or* **as to the future** incertitude quant à l'avenir; **to be in a state of u.** être dans l'incertitude; **to remove any u.** pour dissiper toute équivoque; **there's still some u. as to what was actually said** il reste quelque incertitude sur ce qui s'est réellement dit; **there are still too many uncertainties for my liking** il y a encore trop d'incertitudes à mon goût
uncertified [ʌn'sɜːtɪfaɪd] *adj* non certifié
unchain [ʌn'tʃeɪn] *vt* (*dog*) détacher; (*passions*) déchaîner
unchallengeable [ʌn'tʃælɪndʒəb(ə)l] *adj* (*argument*) irréfutable; (*right*) incontestable; (*evidence, proof*) irrécusable; **to be in an u. position** (*of runner, team, politician etc*) être hors d'atteinte
unchallenged [ʌn'tʃælɪndʒd] *adj* **(a)** (*right*) indisputé, incontesté; **to let sth go** *or* **pass u.** (*statement*) ne pas relever qch; (*right*) ne pas contester qch; (*evidence*) ne pas récuser qch; **I can't let that go u.** je ne peux pas laisser passer cela; **to continue u.** continuer sans être contredit; *Sp* **his record stayed u. for several years** personne ne s'est attaqué à son record pendant plusieurs années **(b)** *Mil* **to let sb pass u.** laisser passer qn sans interpellation
unchangeable [ʌn'tʃeɪndʒəb(ə)l] *adj* immuable
unchanged [ʌn'tʃeɪndʒd] *adj* inchangé; *Med* **his condition remains u.** son état est stationnaire
unchanging [ʌn'tʃeɪndʒɪŋ] *adj* immuable
uncharacteristic [ʌnkærəktə'rɪstɪk] *adj* inhabituel; **it's u. of her** cela ne lui ressemble pas; **it's u. for her to make a mistake like that** ce n'est pas dans son habitude de faire une erreur pareille
uncharacteristically [ʌnkærəktə'rɪstɪklɪ] *adv* (*rude, late, reticent etc*) inhabituellement, anormalement; **u. (for him), he arrived late for the meeting** contrairement à son habitude, il arriva en retard à la réunion
uncharitable [ʌn'tʃærɪtəb(ə)l] *adj* peu charitable; **that's rather u. of you** ce n'est pas très charitable de ta part
uncharted [ʌn'tʃɑːtɪd] *adj* (*unexplored*) inexploré; (*not yet mapped*) non porté sur la carte; *Fig* **these are u. waters** (*of a science etc*) ce sont des domaines inexplorés
unchaste [ʌn'tʃeɪst] *adj esp Lit* (*person*) non chaste, impur; (*thoughts*) impur
unchastened [ʌn'tʃeɪs(ə)nd] *adj* (*person*) aucunement repentant, nullement assagi; **he was u. by his experience** son expérience n'a rien rabattu de ses prétentions
unchecked [ʌn'tʃekt] *adj* **(a)** (*not stopped*) (*advance*) sans (la moindre) opposition; (*passion*) effréné; (*anger*) non contenu; **we can't allow this abuse to go u.** nous ne pouvons pas permettre que ces abus continuent; **if Aids were to spread u. …** si le sida se propageait sans qu'on lui oppose de résistance …; **the enemy advanced u.** l'ennemi progressait sans rencontrer de résistance **(b)** (*not verified*) (*report, assessment*) non vérifié **(c)** **u. baggage** bagages *mpl* non-enregistrés
unchivalrous [ʌn'ʃɪvəlrəs] *adj* peu courtois
unchristian [ʌn'krɪstjən] *adj* peu chrétien; **that's very u. of you** ce sont là des paroles/des pensées peu chrétiennes; *F* **at this u. hour** à cette heure indue

uncircumcised [ʌn'sɜːkəmsaɪzd] *adj* non circoncis
uncivil [ʌn'sɪv(ə)l] *adj* impoli
uncivilized [ʌn'sɪvɪlaɪzd] *adj* non civilisé, barbare; **at this u. hour** à cette heure indue; **very u. of you not to have any whisky in the flat!** ce n'est pas du tout civilisé de ta part de ne pas avoir une goutte de whisky chez toi!; **it's very u. of him to keep us waiting like this** ce n'est pas très correct de sa part de nous faire attendre comme ça
unclaimed [ʌn'kleɪmd] *adj* non réclamé; (*right*) non revendiqué; (*benefit*) non touché *ou* réclamé
unclasp [ʌn'klɑːsp] *vt* (*bracelet*) défaire; (*hand in handshake*) desserrer
unclassifiable [ʌn'klæsɪfaɪəb(ə)l] *adj* inclassable
unclassified [ʌn'klæsɪfaɪd] *adj* (*information*) non (classé), secret, -ète, non confidentiel
uncle ['ʌŋk(ə)l] *n* oncle *m*; *Fig* **rich u.** oncle d'Amérique; *US F* **to cry u.** (*give up*) crier grâce; *US* **U. Sam** l'oncle Sam; *US F* **U. Tom** noir *m* qui s'insinue dans les bonnes grâces des blancs
unclean [ʌn'kliːn] *adj also Rel* (*thoughts etc*) impur; *Iron* (*cup etc*) souillé; **to feel u.** se sentir souillé
unclear [ʌn'klɪər] *adj* (*statement*) peu clair, vague; (*result*) incertain; (*prose, text*) obscur; **it's still u. what has happened** ce qui est arrivé n'est pas toujours très clair; **I'm u. about what is wanted** je ne suis pas sûr de ce qu'on demande
uncleared [ʌn'klɪəd] *adj* **(a) u. ground** terrain *m* non défriché **(b)** (*debt*) non liquidé **(c) u. goods** marchandises *fpl* non dédouanées **(d)** (*cheque*) non compensé, non crédité
unclench [ʌn'klen(t)ʃ] *vt* (*fist*) desserrer
unclimbable [ʌn'klaɪməb(ə)l] *adj* (*mountain*) impossible à escalader
unclimbed [ʌn'klaɪmd] *adj* (*mountain, peak*) invaincu (*par les alpinistes*)
uncloak [ʌn'kləʊk] *vt esp Lit* (*plans*) découvrir; (*impostor*) démasquer
unclog [ʌn'klɒg] *vt* **(-gg-)** (*machine*) débloquer; (*drain*) déboucher
unclothed [ʌn'kləʊðd] *adj* nu
unclouded [ʌn'klaʊdɪd] *adj* (*sky, future, bliss*) sans nuage(s); (*vision, liquid*) clair
uncluttered [ʌn'klʌtəd] *adj* **(a)** (*desk, room*) qui n'est pas encombré **(b)** (*style*) dépouillé; **an u. mind** un esprit clair
unco ['ʌŋkəʊ] *adv Scot Arch* très
uncoil [ʌn'kɔɪl] **1** *vt* dérouler; *Hum* **to u. oneself from sb's arms** se dégager (avec difficulté) des bras de qn **2** *vi* (*of snake, rope*) **to u. (itself)** se dérouler
uncollectable [ʌnkə'lektəb(ə)l] *adj* (*tax*) non percevable
uncollected [ʌnkə'lektɪd] *adj* (*luggage*) non réclamé; **u. taxes** impôts *mpl* non perçus
uncoloured, *US* **uncolored** [ʌn'kʌləd] *adj* non coloré; *Fig* **u. account of sth** rapport *m* impartial sur qch
uncombed [ʌn'kəʊmd] *adj* (*hair, wool*) non peigné
uncomely [ʌn'kʌmlɪ] *adj* peu joli
uncomfortable [ʌn'kʌmf(ə)təb(ə)l] *adj* **(a)** (*house, position etc*) inconfortable; (*armchair, garment*) peu confortable; **this is a very u. armchair** on est très mal (assis) dans ce fauteuil; **I'm u. in this bed** je ne suis pas bien dans ce lit; **I feel u. in this collar** je ne suis pas à l'aise avec ce col
(b) to make things u. for sb attirer *ou* créer des ennuis à qn
(c) to feel *or* **be u.** (*ill at ease*) être mal à l'aise; (*embarrassed*) se sentir gêné; **to be** *or* **feel u. about sth** être mal à l'aise à propos de qch; **to make sb feel u.** mettre qn mal à l'aise; **I'd feel u. (about) asking my parents for money** ça me gênerait de demander de l'argent à mes parents; **it's a very u. feeling, knowing you could easily have been killed** c'est un sentiment très déplaisant de savoir que tu aurais très bien pu mourir; **there was an u. silence** il y eut un silence gêné
uncomfortably [ʌn'kʌmf(ə)təblɪ] *adv* **(a)** (*be sitting*) inconfortablement; (*dressed*) de manière inconfortable; **it was u. stuffy in the plane** il y avait une atmosphère étouffante dans l'avion **(b) to come u. close to sth** (*to bankruptcy, war, disaster etc*) s'approcher dangereusement de qch; **we came u. close to meeting them on holiday!** nous avons bien failli les rencontrer pendant les vacances!; **I was u. aware of him watching me** j'étais désagréablement conscient du fait qu'il me regardait
uncommitted [ʌnkə'mɪtɪd] *adj* (*person*) non engagé; (*reserves, funds, troops*) non affecté; **we are u. to any course of action** nous sommes libres de tout engagement quant à la ligne de conduite à adopter; **to remain u.** ne pas s'engager
uncommon [ʌn'kɒmən] **1** *adj* peu commun; **u. word** mot peu usité; **not u.** assez fréquent **2** *adv Arch F* singulièrement
uncommonly [ʌn'kɒmənlɪ] *adv* **(a) not u.** assez souvent **(b)** *Old-fashioned* (*very*) singulièrement; **he took an u. long time over it** il a mis particulièrement longtemps à le faire; **u. good** excellent
uncommunicative [ʌnkə'mjuːnɪkətɪv] *adj* peu communicatif, renfermé, taciturne; **he was very u. about it** il s'est montré très peu communicatif à ce sujet
uncomplaining [ʌnkəm'pleɪnɪŋ] *adj* qui ne se plaint pas, patient, résigné
uncomplainingly [ʌnkəm'pleɪnɪŋlɪ] *adv* sans se plaindre
uncomplicated [ʌn'kɒmplɪkeɪtɪd] *adj* (*style, person*) simple; (*task*) facile
uncomplimentary [ʌnkɒmplɪ'ment(ə)rɪ] *adj* peu flatteur, -euse; **he was very u. about you** il ne s'est pas montré du tout flatteur à ton égard
uncomprehending [ʌnkɒmprɪ'hendɪŋ] *adj* (*person*) qui ne comprend pas; **to give sb an u. look** regarder qn sans comprendre; **in u. amazement** ahuri
uncomprehendingly [ʌnkɒmprɪ'hendɪŋlɪ] *adv* sans comprendre
uncompromising [ʌn'kɒmprəmaɪzɪŋ] *adj* intransigeant; **a man of u. principles** un homme aux principes très stricts; **we took an u. stance on this** nous avons adopté une position inflexible à ce sujet; **u. honesty** honnêteté absolue; **our u. insistence on quality** notre intransigeance quant à la qualité
uncompromisingly [ʌn'kɒmprəmaɪzɪŋlɪ] *adv* sans faire de concessions; **u. honest** d'une honnêteté absolue
unconcealed [ʌnkən'siːld] *adj* non dissimulé
unconcern [ʌnkən'sɜːn] *n* insouciance *f*, indifférence *f*; **to show u. in the face of danger** se montrer indifférent en face du danger
unconcerned [ʌnkən'sɜːnd] *adj* insouciant, indifférent; **u., he went on speaking** nullement troublé, il continua de parler; **they were quite u. about her well-being** ils ne se souciaient pas du tout de son bien-être; **he seems entirely u. about his results** il ne semble pas du tout s'inquiéter de ses résultats
unconcernedly [ʌnkən'sɜːnɪdlɪ] *adv* d'un air indifférent, sans se (laisser) troubler
unconditional [ʌnkən'dɪʃənəl] *adj* inconditionnel, sans réserve; **u. guarantee** garantie *f* inconditionnelle; **u. surrender** reddition *f* sans condition
unconditionally [ʌnkən'dɪʃənəlɪ] *adv* inconditionnellement; (*accept*) sans réserve; **to surrender u.** se rendre sans condition
unconfirmed [ʌnkən'fɜːmd] *adj* non confirmé; **the report remains u.** la nouvelle n'a pas encore été confirmée
uncongenial [ʌnkən'dʒiːnɪəl] *adj* (*person*) peu sympathique, antipathique; (*climate*) peu favorable (**to** à); (*work, atmosphere*) peu agréable
unconnected [ʌnkə'nektɪd] *adj* (*facts etc*) sans rapport (**with** avec); **the two events are totally u.** les deux événements n'ont aucun rapport entre eux; **this reaction was not u. with the recent ...** cette réaction n'était pas sans rapport avec le récent ...
unconquerable [ʌn'kɒŋkərəb(ə)l] *adj* (*enemy*) invincible; (*courage*) indomptable; (*difficulty*) insurmontable
unconquered [ʌn'kɒŋkəd] *adj* (*people, country*) qui n'a pas été conquis; (*peak*) invaincu, vierge
unconscionable [ʌn'kɒnʃənəb(ə)l] *adj Lit* déraisonnable, excessif; **to take an u. time doing sth** mettre un temps invraisemblable à faire qch
unconscious [ʌn'kɒnʃəs] **1** *adj* **(a)** *Med* sans connaissance; **to become u.** perdre connaissance; **to knock sb u.** assommer qn **(b)** (*unaware*) (*movement etc*) inconscient; (*joke, insult*) involontaire; **to be u. of doing sth** ne pas se rendre compte qu'on fait qch; **to be u. of sth** ne pas avoir conscience de qch, ne pas se rendre compte de qch; **the u. mind** l'inconscient *m* **2** *n Psy* **the u.** l'inconscient *m*
unconsciously [ʌn'kɒnʃəslɪ] *adv* inconsciemment, sans s'en rendre compte
unconsciousness [ʌn'kɒnʃəsnɪs] *n* (*unawareness*), *Med* inconscience *f*
unconsecrated [ʌn'kɒnsɪkreɪtɪd] *adj* non consacré
unconsidered [ʌnkən'sɪdəd] *adj* (*remark, opinion*) inconsidéré
unconstitutional [ʌnkɒnstɪ'tjuːʃən(ə)l] *adj* inconstitutionnel
unconstitutionally [ʌnkɒnstɪ'tjuːʃnəlɪ] *adv* inconstitutionnellement
unconstrained [ʌnkən'streɪnd] *adj* **(a)** (*person*) sans contraintes, libre; **to be u. by convention** ne pas connaître les contraintes des conventions; (*consciously reject them*) faire fi des conventions **(b)** (*act*) spontané; (*passion, joy etc*) débordant; **u. laughter** hilarité *f* débordante
unconsummated [ʌn'kɒnsəmeɪtɪd] *adj* (*marriage*) non consommé
uncontaminated [ʌnkən'tæmɪneɪtɪd] *adj* (*by disease, radiation*), *Fig* non contaminé

uncontested [ʌnkən'testɪd] *adj (right)* incontesté; *(election, seat)* non disputé; **the championship has been** *or* **has gone u. for ...** le championnat n'a pas été disputé depuis ...
uncontrollable [ʌnkən'trəʊləb(ə)l] *adj* incontrôlable; *(movement, twitch)* incontrôlable, irrépressible; *(desire)* irrésistible, irrépressible; *(inflation)* irrésistible, incontrôlable; **u. laughter** fou rire *m*, rire irrépressible; **fits of u. temper** violents accès *mpl* de colère; **I felt an u. urge to ...** je me suis senti irrésistiblement poussé à ...
uncontrollably [ʌnkən'trəʊləblɪ] *adv* **she sobbed/laughed/coughed u.** elle ne pouvait s'arrêter de sangloter/rire/tousser; **as inflation rises u.** alors que l'inflation augmente irrésistiblement; **she was u. jealous** elle était d'une jalousie maladive
uncontrolled [ʌnkən'trəʊld] *adj (anger, weeping, laughter)* incontrôlé; *(style)* débridé; **u. passions** passions *fpl* effrénées; **u. inflation** inflation *f* incontrôlée
uncontroversial [ʌnkɒntrə'vɜːʃəl] *adj (subject)* qui ne soulève *ou* ne provoque pas de controverses
unconventional [ʌnkən'venʃənəl] *adj* peu conventionnel, non-conformiste
unconventionally [ʌnkən'venʃnəlɪ] *adv* de manière peu conventionnelle
unconvinced [ʌnkən'vɪnst] *adj* sceptique (**of** au sujet de); **I am still u.** je ne suis toujours pas convaincu
unconvincing [ʌnkən'vɪnsɪŋ] *adj (evidence etc)* peu convaincant; *(excuse)* peu convaincant *ou* vraisemblable; **he was very u. as Tartuffe** il n'était pas convaincant du tout en Tartuffe
unconvincingly [ʌnkən'vɪnsɪŋlɪ] *adv* d'une manière peu convaincante
uncooked [ʌn'kʊkt] *adj* non cuit
uncool [ʌn'kuːl] *adj Sl* ringard
uncooperative [ʌnkəʊ'ɒp(ə)rətɪv] *adj* peu coopératif; **he's being very u.** il se montre très peu coopératif
uncooperatively [ʌnkəʊ'ɒp(ə)rətɪvlɪ] *adv* de manière peu coopérative
uncooperativeness [ʌnkəʊ'ɒp(ə)rətɪvnɪs] *n* manque *m* de coopération
uncoordinated [ʌnkəʊ'ɔːdɪneɪtɪd] *adj (manoeuvre, attack, undertaking, efforts)* qui manque de coordination *ou* d'organisation; *(movements)* désordonné; **to be u.** *(of person, dancer)* manquer de coordination
uncork [ʌn'kɔːk] *vt (bottle)* déboucher; *Fig (pent-up emotions)* laisser libre cours à
uncorrected [ʌnkə'rektɪd] *adj (exercise, proof)* non corrigé; *(error)* non rectifié *ou* corrigé; *Phys* **result u. for temperature/for pressure** résultat *m* brut
uncorroborated [ʌnkə'rɒbəreɪtɪd] *adj* non corroboré
uncorrupted [ʌnkə'rʌptɪd] *adj (person)* non corrompu
uncountable [ʌn'kaʊntəb(ə)l] *adj* [ⓘA9-11,3] *Gram* indénombrable
uncountably [ʌn'kaʊntəblɪ] *adv Gram* **nouns which can only be used u.** noms qu'on ne peut utiliser que de façon indénombrable
uncounted [ʌn'kaʊntɪd] *adj (not counted)* non compté
uncouple [ʌn'kʌp(ə)l] *vt (carriages, engine)* dételer, découpler
uncouth [ʌn'kuːθ] *adj (person, behaviour)* grossier; **u. manners** manières *fpl* gauches *ou* frustes
uncover [ʌn'kʌvər] *vt* **(a)** *(furniture, swimming pool)* découvrir; *(saucepan)* enlever le couvercle de **(b)** *(evidence, plot, conspiracy)* découvrir **(c)** *Chess (piece)* découvrir, dégarnir
uncovered [ʌn'kʌvəd] *adj* **(a)** non couvert, découvert **(b)** *Fin (purchase, sale)* à découvert; **u. cheque** chèque *m* sans provision; *St Exch* **u. position** position *f* non couverte
uncreasable [ʌn'kriːsəb(ə)l] *adj (fabric)* infroissable
uncritical [ʌn'krɪtɪk(ə)l] *adj* dépourvu de sens *ou* d'esprit critique; *(approach, acceptance)* sans discernement; *(audience)* peu exigeant; **to be u. of sb/sth** ne faire preuve d'aucun sens *ou* esprit critique à l'égard de qn/qch
uncross [ʌn'krɒs] *vt (legs)* décroiser
uncrossed [ʌn'krɒst] *adj (cheque)* non barré
uncrowded [ʌn'kraʊdɪd] *adj (beaches)* presque vide; *(roads)* peu encombré; **I'd never seen Heathrow so u.** je n'avais jamais vu aussi peu de monde à Heathrow
uncrowned [ʌn'kraʊnd] *adj* sans couronne; *Fig* **the u. king/queen of ...** le roi/la reine de ...
uncrunch [ʌn'krʌntʃ] *vt Comptr* décompresser, décompacter
uncrushable [ʌn'krʌʃəb(ə)l] *adj (fabric)* infroissable
unction ['ʌŋkʃən] *n* **(a)** *Rel* onction *f* **(b)** = **unctuousness**
unctuous ['ʌŋktjʊəs] *adj* mielleux, onctueux
unctuously ['ʌŋktjʊəslɪ] *adv* d'un air/d'un ton mielleux *ou* onctueux
unctuousness ['ʌŋktjʊəsnɪs] *n* caractère *m* mielleux
uncultivated [ʌn'kʌltɪveɪtɪd] *adj (land, person)* inculte
uncultured [ʌn'kʌltʃəd] *adj (mind, person)* inculte; *(accent)* peu raffiné
uncurbed [ʌn'kɜːbd] *adj (authority)* sans restriction; *(passion)* déchaîné; **if these tendencies are allowed to go u.** si on ne met pas un frein à ces tendances
uncurl [ʌn'kɜːl] **1** *vt (rope, wire)* dérouler; *(one's legs)* déplier; **to u. oneself** s'étirer **2** *vi (of cat)* s'étirer; *(of snake)* se dérouler
uncut [ʌn'kʌt] *adj* **(a)** *(hedge)* non coupé; *(diamond)* brut, non taillé **(b)** *(play, edition)* sans coupures, intégral
undamaged [ʌn'dæmɪdʒd] *adj* non endommagé, intact; *(reputation)* intact
undamped, undampened [ʌn'dæmpt, ʌn'dæmpənd] *adj (courage)* non affaibli
undated [ʌn'deɪtɪd] *adj* non daté, sans date
undaunted [ʌn'dɔːntɪd] *adj* **to be u. by sth** n'être aucunement intimidé *ou* aucunement ébranlé par qch; *(by difficulty)* n'être aucunement découragé par qch; **we carried on u.** nous avons continué sans nous laisser intimider *ou* décourager
undeceive [ʌndɪ'siːv] *vt Lit (person)* détromper
undecided [ʌndɪ'saɪdɪd] *adj* **(a)** *(question, problem)* non résolu; **that's still u.** aucune décision n'a encore été prise **(b)** *(person)* indécis; **to be u. about sth** être indécis à propos de qch; **he was u. whether he would go or not** il se demandait s'il irait ou non; **to be u. how to act** ne pas savoir comment agir
undeclared [ʌndɪ'kleəd] *adj (war, income)* non déclaré; *(love)* non avoué; **u. goods** *(at Customs)* marchandises *fpl* non déclarées
undefeated [ʌndɪ'fiːtɪd] *adj* invaincu
undefended [ʌndɪ'fendɪd] *adj* **(a)** *Mil etc* sans défense; *(goal)* non défendu; *(king at chess)* non protégé **(b)** *Jur (defendant)* qui n'est pas représenté par un avocat; **u. case** débats *mpl* non contentieux; **u. suit** cause *f* où le défenseur s'abstient de plaider
undefiled [ʌndɪ'faɪld] *adj* sans souillure, immaculé; **u. by any contact with Western society** non corrompu par la civilisation occidentale
undefinable [ʌndɪ'faɪnəb(ə)l] *adj* indéfinissable
undefined [ʌndɪ'faɪnd] *adj (term etc)* non défini; *(vague) (feeling etc)* indéterminé, vague
undelete [ʌndɪ'liːt] *vt Comptr* restaurer
undelivered [ʌndɪ'lɪvəd] *adj* non livré, non remis; *(parcel)* en souffrance; **if u. return to sender** en cas de non-délivrance prière de retourner à l'expéditeur
undemanding [ʌndɪ'mɑːndɪŋ] *adj (job, book, person)* peu exigeant
undemocratic [ʌndemə'krætɪk] *adj* antidémocratique
undemonstrative [ʌndɪ'mɒnstrətɪv] *adj (person)* peu expansif, peu démonstratif
undeniable [ʌndɪ'naɪəb(ə)l] *adj* indéniable, incontestable; *(evidence)* irrécusable; **of u. worth** d'une valeur indéniable
undeniably [ʌndɪ'naɪəblɪ] *adv* incontestablement; **an u. talented man** un homme d'un talent incontestable
undenominational [ʌndɪnɒmɪ'neɪʃənəl] *adj* non confessionnel
undependable [ʌndɪ'pendəb(ə)l] *adj (machine, trains, person)* peu fiable
under ['ʌndər] **1** *prep* **(a)** *(beneath)* sous, au-dessous de; **the dog is u. the table** le chien est sous la table; **u. water** sous l'eau; **he hid u. it** il se cacha dessous; **you have to crawl u. it** il faut ramper dessous; **put it u. that** mettez-le là-dessous; **to wear a waistcoat u. one's jacket** porter un gilet sous son veston; **he pulled a stool out from u. the table** il a tiré un tabouret de sous la table; **visible u. the microscope** visible au microscope; *Agr* **field u. wheat** champ *m* mis en blé

(b) *(less than)* **all their books were u. £5** tous leurs livres coûtaient moins de 5 livres; **salaries u. £5000** salaires inférieurs à 5000 livres; **he's u. thirty** il a moins de trente ans; **people u. thirty, the u. thirties** les moins de trente ans; **children u. ten** les enfants au-dessous de dix ans; **in u. ten minutes** en moins de dix minutes; **to speak u. one's breath** parler à mi-voix

(c) *(according to)* **u. his father's will** d'après le testament de son père; **u. the terms of the agreement** d'après les termes de la convention; **u. the terms of the contract** conformément aux termes du contrat; *Com* **u. usual reserve** sauf bonne fin

(d) *(under control of, subordinate to etc)* **to be u. sb** être sous les ordres de qn; **he had a hundred men u. him** il avait cent hommes sous ses ordres; **he has three sales teams u. him** il est responsable de trois équipes de ventes; **to be** *or* **to come u. the authority of the Home Office** relever du Ministère de l'Intérieur; **u. government control** soumis au contrôle de l'État; **u. Louis XIV** sous Louis XIV; **Britain u.**

Thatcher la Grande-Bretagne sous Thatcher; **to study u. sb** étudier sous la direction de qn; **the orchestra, u. Alexander Gibson** l'orchestre, sous la direction d'Alexander Gibson; **she wrote it u. a pseudonym** elle l'a écrit sous un pseudonyme; **to be u. sentence of death** être condamné à mort; **to be u. orders to do sth** avoir reçu l'ordre de faire qch; **u. these conditions** dans ces conditions; **u. the circumstances** vu les circonstances

(e) (*in the process of*) **u. repair** en réparation; **u. construction** en construction; **to keep sb/sth u. observation** surveiller qn/qch; *Med* **u. observation** en observation; **the question is u. examination** la question est à l'étude

(f) (*in list, directory etc*) **it's entered u. F** cela figure à la lettre F; **we're in the phonebook u. Tomson** nous sommes dans l'annuaire sous le nom de Tomson; **are they u. decorators or painters?** sont-ils sous la rubrique décorateurs ou peintres?; **it's u. biology** (*in library etc*) c'est classé sous la rubrique biologie; **to look for/to file sth u. (the heading) ...** chercher/classer qch sous la rubrique ...

2 *adv* **(a)** (*underneath*) (au-)dessous; **to stay u. for two minutes** (*underwater*) rester deux minutes sous l'eau; **to be u.** (*anaesthetic*) être sous anesthésiant; *F* **to get out from u.** (*from difficult situation*) se tirer d'affaire

(b) (*less*) au-dessous; **children of seven years old and u.** des enfants de sept ans et moins

underachieve [ʌndərəˈtʃiːv] *vi esp Sch* ne pas concrétiser ses possibilités

underachiever [ʌndərəˈtʃiːvər] *n esp Sch* élève *mf*/personne *f* qui n'obtient pas des résultats conformes à ses possibilités

under-age *adj* mineur; **u. drinking** consommation *f* d'alcool par les mineurs

underarm [ˈʌndərɑːm] **1** *adv Cr, Tennis* **to bowl/to serve u.** lancer/servir la balle par en-dessous **2** *adj* **(a)** *Cr, Tennis* (*bowl, shot etc*) par en-dessous **(b) u. deodorant** déodorant *m* pour les aisselles

underbelly [ˈʌndəbelɪ] *n* **(a)** (*of animal*) bas-ventre *m*, *pl* bas-ventres **(b)** *Fig* point *m* faible; **the soft u. of Europe** le ventre mou de l'Europe

underbid [ʌndəˈbɪd] (*pt* **underbid**; *pp* **underbid(den)** [-ˈbɪd(n)]) **1** *vt Com etc* **to u. sb** faire des soumissions *ou* offrir des conditions plus avantageuses que qn **2** *vti Cards* **to u. (one's hand)** demander au-dessous de son jeu

underblanket [ˈʌndəblæŋkɪt] *n* couverture *f* entre le matelas et le drap de dessous

underbody [ˈʌndəbɒdɪ] *n Aut* bas *m* de caisse

underbrush [ˈʌndəbrʌʃ] *n* sous-bois *m*

undercapitalization [ʌndəkæpɪtəlaɪˈzeɪʃən] *n Econ* sous-capitalisation *f*

undercapitalized [ʌndəˈkæpɪtəlaɪzd] *adj* (*industry*) sous-capitalisé

undercarriage [ˈʌndəkærɪdʒ] *n Av* train *m* d'atterrissage

undercharge [ʌndəˈtʃɑːdʒ] **1** *vt* **they undercharged him** on ne lui a pas fait payer assez; **they undercharged her** *or* **she was undercharged by £5** on aurait dû lui faire payer 5 livres de plus **2** *vi* demander trop peu **(for sth** pour qch)

underclass [ˈʌndəklɑːs] *n* (*of society*) sous-prolétariat *m*, quart-monde *m*

undercloth [ˈʌndəklɒθ] *n* (*on table*) sous-nappe *f*

underclothes [ˈʌndəkləʊðz] *npl*, **underclothing** [ˈʌndəkləʊðɪŋ] *n* sous-vêtements *mpl*; (*women's*) lingerie *f*, dessous *mpl*

undercoat [ˈʌndəkəʊt] *n* **(a)** (*of paint*) couche *f* de fond, première couche **(b)** *Am Aut* couche *f ou* revêtement *m* antirouille

undercoating [ˈʌndəkəʊtɪŋ] *n* = **undercoat**

undercook [ʌndəˈkʊk] *vt* ne pas assez cuire

under-correction *n Aut* sous-correction *f*, correction *f* insuffisante

undercover [ˈʌndəkʌvər] **1** *adj* secret, -ète, clandestin; **u. agent** agent *m* secret **2** *adv* clandestinement

undercurrent [ˈʌndəkʌrənt] *n* (*in sea*) courant *m* sous-marin; *Fig* **u. of discontent** vague *f* de fond de mécontentement; *Fig* **but there are undercurrents** (*in relationship etc*) mais il y a des tensions sous-jacentes

undercut¹ [ˈʌndəkʌt] *n Culin* filet *m* (de bœuf)

undercut² *vt* (*pt, pp* **undercut**; *prp* **undercutting**) **(a)** *Sp* (*ball*) couper, lifter **(b)** *Com* (*competitor*) vendre moins cher que; (*prices*) casser

underdeveloped [ʌndədɪˈveləpt] *adj* **(a)** *Phot* insuffisamment développé **(b)** (*child*) retardé; (*muscle*) pas assez développé **(c)** *Econ* (*country*) sous-développé; (*area*) insuffisamment mis en valeur; (*resources*) sous-exploité

underdog [ˈʌndədɒg] *n Sp* outsider *m*; (*socially etc*) défavorisé, -ée; *Pol etc* **to side with the underdog(s)** prendre le parti des plus faibles; *Sp* **the underdogs won 5-2** ceux qui étaient donnés perdants à l'avance ont gagné 5 à 2

underdone [ʌndəˈdʌn] *adj Culin* (*undercooked*) pas assez cuit; **I'd like my steak slightly u.** (*rare*) je voudrais mon steak légèrement saignant

underdrawers [ˈʌndədrɔːəz] *npl US* caleçon *m* (d'homme)

underdressed [ʌndəˈdrest] *adj* **to be u.** (*not warm enough*) ne pas être assez habillé *ou* couvert; (*not formal enough*) ne pas être assez bien habillé

underemployed [ʌndəremˈplɔɪd] *adj* (*person*) sous-employé; (*resources*) sous-exploité

underemployment [ʌndəremˈplɔɪmənt] *n* (*of person*) sous-emploi *m*

underestimate¹, underestimation [ʌndərˈestɪmɪt, -estɪˈmeɪʃən] *n* sous-estimation *f*

underestimate² [ʌndərˈestɪmeɪt] *vt* (*expenses, person*) sous-estimer; (*difficulties, opponent*) méconnaître, mésestimer

underexpose [ʌndəreksˈpəʊz] *vt Phot* (*film*) sous-exposer

underexposure [ʌndəreksˈpəʊʒər] *n Phot* (*of film*) sous-exposition *f*

underfed [ʌndəˈfed] *adj* sous-alimenté, mal nourri

underfeeding [ʌndəˈfiːdɪŋ] *n* sous-alimentation *f*

underfelt [ˈʌndəfelt] *n* (*for carpet*) thibaude *f*

underfinance [ʌndəˈfaɪnæns] *vt* financer insuffisamment

underfloor [ˈʌndəflɔːr] *adj* **u. heating** chauffage *m* par le sol

underfoot [ʌndəˈfʊt] *adv* sous les pieds; **it's wet u.** le sol est mouillé; **the snow crunched u.** la neige crissait sous les pieds; **to trample** *or* **tread sth u.** fouler qch aux pieds

underfunded [ʌndəˈfʌndɪd] *adj* (*project etc*) insuffisamment financé

underfunding [ʌndəˈfʌndɪŋ] *n* (*of industry*) insuffisance *f* de financement; **the project suffered from u.** le projet a souffert d'un financement insuffisant

under(-)gardener *n* aide-jardinier *m*, *pl* aides-jardiniers

undergarment [ˈʌndəgɑːmənt] *n* sous-vêtement *m*

undergo [ʌndəˈgəʊ] *vt* (*pt* **underwent** [-ˈwent]; *pp* **undergone** [-ˈgɒn]) (*change*) passer par, subir; (*hardship, examination, operation*) subir; **to u. a complete change** subir une métamorphose complète; **undergoing repairs** en réparation; *Med* **to u. treatment** suivre un traitement

undergrad [ʌndəˈgræd] *n F* = **undergraduate**

undergraduate [ʌndəˈgrædjʊɪt] *n* étudiant, -ante (*qui prépare le DEUG/la licence*); **in my u. days** lorsque j'étais étudiant; **u. life** la vie d'étudiant; **u. newspaper** journal étudiant

underground [ˈʌndəgraʊnd] **1** *adv* **(a)** (*in mine etc*) sous terre

(b) *Fig* (*secretly*) clandestinement, secrètement; **to go u.** passer dans la clandestinité

2 *adj* **(a)** (*work*) sous terre; (*pipe, lake, cable*) souterrain; **u. railway** chemin *m* de fer souterrain; *US Hist* **u. railroad** *or* **railway** (*network for escaping slaves*) réseau *m* clandestin de libération des esclaves; **u. gallery** *or* **passage** souterrain *m*; **u. workings** chantier *m* souterrain, travaux *mpl* souterrains

(b) *Fig* (*clandestine*) (*organization, press*) clandestin, secret, -ète; **u. movement** mouvement *m* clandestin; (*in occupied country*) résistance *f*

3 *n* **(a)** *Br Rail* métro *m*; **u. station** station *f* de métro; **u. train** rame *f* de métro

(b) (*in occupied country etc*) **the u.** la résistance

undergrowth [ˈʌndəgrəʊθ] *n* broussailles *fpl*, sous-bois *m*

underhand [ˈʌndəhænd] *adj* (*person*) sournois; **to behave in an u. way** agir en sous-main; **u. dealings** manœuvres *fpl* clandestines, *F* magouilles *fpl*

underhanded [ʌndəˈhændɪd] *adj* **(a)** = **underhand (b)** *US* (*short of staff or workers*) à court de personnel/de main-d'œuvre

underhandedly [ʌndəˈhændɪdlɪ] *adv* en sous-main

underinsured [ʌndərɪnˈʃɔːd] *adj* sous-assuré

underinvestment [ʌndərɪnˈvestmənt] *n* insuffisance *f* d'investissement

underlay¹ [ˈʌndəleɪ] *n* (*for carpet*) thibaude *f*; (*for tiling*) assise *f*

underlay² [ʌndəˈleɪ] *vt* (*pt, pp* **underlaid** [-ˈleɪd]) **to u. sth with sth** mettre qch sous qch; **carpet underlaid with felt** moquette *f* sur thibaude

underlie [ʌndəˈlaɪ] *vt* (*pt* **underlay** [-ˈleɪ]; *pp* **underlain** [-ˈleɪn]; *prp* **underlying** [-ˈlaɪɪŋ]) être à la base *ou* à l'origine de; **the reasons which underlay her decision** les raisons qui ont motivé sa décision

underline¹ [ˈʌndelaɪn] *n* souligné *m*; **u. command** commande *f* de soulignement *ou* de soulignage

underline² [ʌndəˈlaɪn] *vt* (*word*) souligner; *Fig* (*fact*) souligner, appuyer sur, insister sur

underling [ˈʌndəlɪŋ] *n Pej* subalterne *mf*, subordonné, -ée

underlining [ʌndəˈlaɪnɪŋ] *n* soulignement *m*, soulignage *m*

underlying [ʌndəˈlaɪɪŋ] *adj* (*rock, principles, causes etc*) sous-jacent

undermanager [ˈʌndəmænɪdʒər] *n* sous-chef *m*, sous-directeur *m*

undermanned [ʌndə'mænd] *adj* à court de personnel; *Ind* à court de main-d'œuvre; **to be u.** manquer de personnel/de main d'œuvre
undermanning [ʌndə'mænɪŋ] *n* manque *m ou* pénurie *f* de main-d'œuvre
undermentioned ['ʌndəmenʃənd] *adj Fml* (cité *ou* mentionné) ci-dessous; **the u. persons** les personnes dont les noms suivent
undermine [ʌndə'maɪn] *vt* **(a)** (*coast, wall*) miner, saper; (*of sea, river*) (*cliffs, banks*) affouiller; **foundations undermined by water** fondements minés par l'eau **(b)** (*principle, authority*) saper; (*sb's health*) miner; (*sb's confidence*) ébranler; **to u. the foundations of society** attaquer les bases de la société; **stop undermining me!** arrête de me faire du tort!
undermost ['ʌndəməʊst] *adj* **the u.** le plus bas, *f* la plus basse
underneath [ʌndə'ni:θ] **1** *prep* au-dessous de, sous; **he pushed the letter u. the door** il a glissé la lettre sous la porte; **he pulled it (out) from u. the blanket** il l'a tiré de dessous la couverture **2** *adv* au-dessous, dessous; **he picked up the book and found the ticket u.** il a soulevé le livre et a trouvé le billet dessous **3** *n* dessous *m*; **the u. of the box is black** le dessous de la boîte est noir **4** *adj* de dessous, d'en dessous
undernourished [ʌndə'nʌrɪʃt] *adj* sous-alimenté
undernourishment [ʌndə'nʌrɪʃmənt] *n* sous-alimentation *f*
underpaid [ʌndə'peɪd] *adj* (*work, worker*) sous-payé, sous-rémunéré
underpants ['ʌndəpænts] *npl* (*for men*) slip *m*; **a pair of u.** un slip
underpart ['ʌndəpɑ:t] *n* partie *f* inférieure
underpass ['ʌndəpɑ:s] *n* (*for cars*) tunnel *m*; (*for pedestrians*) (passage *m*) souterrain *m*
underpay [ʌndə'peɪ] *vt* (*pt, pp* **underpaid** [-'peɪd]) (*worker etc*) sous-payer, sous-rémunérer
underpin [ʌndə'pɪn] *vt* **(-pp-)** (*wall, Fig theory*) étayer; (*organization*) être à la base de; **the principles which u. Marxism-Leninism** les principes de base du marxisme-léninisme
underpinning [ʌndə'pɪnɪŋ] *n* étayage *m*; (*of organization, theory*) base *m*
underplay [ʌndə'pleɪ] *vt* **(a)** (*play down*) minimiser l'importance de **(b)** *Th* **to u. a part** (*with subtlety*) jouer un rôle tout en nuances; (*with lack of force*) jouer un rôle de façon trop plate **(c)** *Fig* **to u. one's hand** ne pas être assez exigeant, ne pas demander assez; (*deliberately*) cacher son jeu
underpopulated [ʌndə'pɒpjʊleɪtɪd] *adj* sous-peuplé
underprice [ʌndə'praɪs] *vt* (*article*) mettre un prix trop bas à
underpriced [ʌndə'praɪst] *adj* trés bon marché (par rapport à sa valeur réelle); **at £15.99 it's definitely u.** à 15,99 livres c'est vraiment donné
underpricing [ʌndə'praɪsɪŋ] *n* fixation *f* de prix trop bas
underprivileged [ʌndə'prɪvɪlɪdʒd] **1** *adj* déshérité, défavorisé **2** *npl* **the u.** les défavorisés, les économiquement faibles
underproduce [ʌndəprə'dju:s] *vi Ind* être en situation de sous-production
underproduction [ʌndəprə'dʌkʃən] *n Ind* sous-production *f*
underproductive [ʌndəprə'dʌktɪv] *adj Ind* sous-productif
underqualified [ʌndə'kwɒlɪfaɪd] *adj* sous-qualifié
underrate [ʌndə'reɪt] *vt* (*opponent, difficulty, importance of sth*) sous-estimer
under-represent *vt* minimiser, ne pas donner assez d'importance à
under-representation *n esp Pol* sous-représentation *f*
under-represented [ʌndəreprɪ'zentɪd] *adj esp Pol* sous-représenté
underscore¹ ['ʌndəskɔ:r] *n* souligné *m*
underscore² [ʌndə'skɔ:r] *vt* (*title etc*) souligner; *Fig* (*fact*) faire ressortir, mettre en évidence; (*importance of sth*) souligner
undersea ['ʌndəsi:] *adj* sous-marin
underseal¹ ['ʌndəsi:l] *n Br Aut* couche *f* antirouille (pour dessous de châssis), couche anticorrosion
underseal² *vt Br Aut* **to u. (the chassis of) a car** traiter le châssis d'une voiture contre la rouille
undersecretary [ʌndə'sekrɪt(ə)rɪ] *n* sous-secrétaire *mf*; *Br* **permanent u.** secrétaire *m* général (*d'un ministère*)
undersell [ʌndə'sel] *vt* (*pt, pp* **undersold** [-'səʊld]) *Com* (*competition etc*) vendre moins cher que; (*goods etc*) vendre au-dessous de sa valeur; *Fig* **don't u. yourself at the interview** essaie de bien te vendre lors de l'entretien; **she tends to u. herself** elle a tendance à ne pas suffisamment se mettre en valeur
undersexed [ʌndə'sekst] *adj* de *ou* à faible libido; **he's u.** il a une faible libido
undersheet ['ʌndəʃi:t] *n* alaise *f*, alèse *f*
undershield ['ʌndəʃi:ld] *n Aut* bouclier *m* inférieur
undershirt ['ʌndəʃɜ:t] *n Am* (*for men*) maillot *m*
undershoot [ʌndə'ʃu:t] *vti* (*pt, pp* **undershot** [-'ʃɒt]) *Av* **to u. (the runway)** se présenter *ou* atterrir trop court (sur la piste); *Fig* **to u. a production target** ne pas atteindre ses objectifs de production
underside ['ʌndəsaɪd] *n* dessous *m*
undersigned [ʌndə'saɪnd] *adj, n* soussigné, -ée; **I, the u.** je soussigné(e); **the u. declare that …** les soussignés déclarent que …
undersize(d) [ʌndə'saɪz(d)] *adj* de (trop) petite taille, trop petit
underskirt ['ʌndəskɜ:t] *n* jupon *m*
underslung [ʌndə'slʌŋ] *adj Aut* (*chassis*) surbaissé; (*car*) à carrosserie surbaissée
understaffed [ʌndə'stɑ:ft] *adj* à court de personnel; **the office is u.** le bureau manque de personnel
understaffing [ʌndə'stɑ:fɪŋ] *n* manque *m ou* pénurie *f* de personnel
understand [ʌndə'stænd] (*pt, pp* **understood** [-'stʊd]) **1** *vt* **(a)** (*comprehend*) comprendre; **I don't u. French** je ne comprends pas le français; **he can't make himself understood in German** il ne peut pas se faire comprendre en allemand; **he understands business matters** il s'y connaît *ou* s'y entend en affaires; **this sentence can be understood in several ways** cette phrase peut s'interpréter de plusieurs façons; **no one understands me** personne ne me comprend; **to u. each other** *or* **one another** se comprendre; (*have same ideas etc*) s'entendre; **I quite u. that he must be tired** je comprends très bien qu'il soit fatigué; **I don't u. why he did it** je ne comprends pas pourquoi il l'a fait; **do you u. what he's talking about?** comprenez-vous quelque chose à ce qu'il raconte?; **what I can't u. is that …** ce que je ne comprends pas, c'est que … + *sub*; **I can u. your being angry** je comprends que vous soyez fâché; **I can't u. it** je ne (le) comprends pas; **I'm at a loss to u. it, I can't u. a word of it, I don't u. the first thing about it** je n'y comprends (absolument) rien; **(is that) understood?** (vous avez *ou* c'est bien) compris?, (c'est) entendu?; **that's easily understood** cela se comprend facilement
(b) (*believe*) **I understood that I was to be paid for my work** j'ai cru comprendre que je devais être payé pour mon travail; **I u. (that) you're coming to work here** j'ai appris que vous veniez travailler ici; **he is understood to be abroad, it is understood that he is abroad** il serait à l'étranger; **it must be understood** *or* **you must u. that …** il doit être (bien) entendu *ou* il faut (bien) comprendre que …; **to give sb to u. that …** laisser entendre à qn que …; **I have made it understood** *or* **I have let it be understood that …** j'ai laissé entendre que …
(c) (*sth implicit*) sous-entendre; **am I to u. that …?** (*deduce*) dois-je en conclure que …?; **in this sentence the verb is understood** dans cette phrase le verbe est sous-entendu; **that's understood** cela va sans dire, cela va de soi
2 *vi* comprendre; **now I u.!** je comprends *ou* j'y suis maintenant!; **you don't u.** vous n'y êtes pas; **do you u.?** vous comprenez?; **he left yesterday, I u.** il est parti hier, si j'ai bien compris *ou* si je ne me trompe (pas); **to u. about sth** comprendre qch
understandable [ʌndə'stændəb(ə)l] *adj* compréhensible; **that's u.** cela se comprend (facilement), c'est bien normal; **it's quite u. that she should be …** il est tout à fait compréhensible qu'elle soit …
understandably [ʌndə'stændəblɪ] *adv* naturellement, forcément; **he was u. disappointed** il était compréhensible qu'il soit déçu
understanding [ʌndə'stændɪŋ] **1** *adj* compréhensif (**about sth** au sujet de qch); (*letter, words, smile*) plein de compréhension
2 *n* **(a)** (*comprehension, conception*) compréhension *f*; **the age of u.** l'âge *m* de raison; **it's beyond all u.** c'est incompréhensible, c'est à n'y rien comprendre; **it's beyond my u.** cela dépasse mon entendement, je n'y comprends rien; **he showed great u.** (*sensitivity*) il s'est montré très compréhensif; **to be lacking in u. of a problem** ne pas bien comprendre un problème; **according to my u. of it** si j'ai bien compris; **my u. was that the venue would be paid for by the organizers** j'avais compris que les organisateurs paieraient pour la location des locaux
(b) (*between nations etc*) entente *f*, accord *m*; (*agreement*) accord, arrangement *m*; **spirit of u.** esprit *m* d'entente; **they had an u., there was an u. between them** ils s'étaient arrangés entre eux; **to come to** *or* **to reach an u. (with sb)** s'entendre *ou* s'arranger (avec qn)
(c) (*condition*) condition *f*; **on the u. that he gives it me**

back à (la) condition qu'il me le rende; **on the firm u. that …** à la condition expresse que …

understandingly [ʌndəˈstændɪŋlɪ] *adv* (*to act*) avec compréhension

understate [ʌndəˈsteɪt] *vt* minimiser; (*problem etc*) ne pas insister sur; **understated** (*make-up etc*) discret, -ète; **the deliberately understated figures in the foreground** les silhouettes volontairement estompées au premier plan

understatement [ʌndəˈsteɪtmənt] *n* **(a)** euphémisme *m*; *Ling* litote *f*; **with typical British u.** avec un euphémisme typiquement britannique; **to say it's expensive is an u.** dire que c'est cher est un euphémisme; **that's an u. if I ever heard one!** c'est un des plus beaux euphémismes que j'aie jamais entendus; *F* **that's the u. of the year!** c'est le moins qu'on puisse dire! **(b)** (*low key presentation*) (*of problem, distinction*) minimisation *f*

understeer [ʌndəˈstɪər] *vi* sous-virer; **a car which understeers** une voiture sous-vireuse

understeer(ing) [ʌndəˈstɪər(ɪŋ)] *n* sous-virage *m*, comportement *m* sous-vireur

understudy[1] [ˈʌndəstʌdɪ] *n Th* doublure *f*

understudy[2] *vt Th* (*actor*) doubler; (*role*) servir de doublure pour

undertake [ʌndəˈteɪk] *vt* (*pt* **undertook** [-ˈtʊk]; *pp* **undertaken** [-ˈteɪk(ə)n]) **(a)** (*journey etc*) entreprendre **(b)** (*task*) entreprendre; (*responsibility*) assumer; **to u. to do sth** s'engager à faire qch **(c) to u. that …** garantir que … **(d)** (*vehicle*) doubler par l'intérieur

undertaker [ˈʌndəteɪkər] *n* entrepreneur *m* des pompes funèbres; **ring the u.'s!** appelle les pompes funèbres!

undertaking [ʌndəˈteɪkɪŋ] *n* **(a)** (*enterprise*) entreprise *f*; **it's quite an u.** c'est toute une affaire, **the u. of this project meant that …** la mise en œuvre de ce projet signifiait que … **(b)** (*promise etc*) engagement *m*, promesse *f*; *Jur* soumission *f*; **he gave an u. to do it** *or* **that he would do it** il s'est engagé à *ou* il a promis de le faire; **I give you my solemn u. never to …** je vous promets solennellement de ne jamais …; **I can't give you that u.** je ne peux vous faire cette promesse **(c)** (*profession of undertaker*) métier *m* d'entrepreneur des pompes funèbres

undertax [ʌndəˈtæks] *vt* (*sth*) taxer insuffisamment; (*sb*) ne pas faire payer assez d'impôts à

under-the-counter 1 *adj* (*sales etc*) clandestin **2** *adv* clandestinement

undertone [ˈʌndətəʊn] *n* **(a) in an u.** (*to talk*) à mi-voix, à voix basse **(b) an u. of menace** une note de menace; **grey with blue undertones** gris nuancé de bleu

undertow [ˈʌndətəʊ] *n* (*in water*) courant *m* (sous-marin) (*lorsqu'une vague se retire*); *Fig* tension *f* sous-jacente

underuse[1] [ʌndəˈjuːs] *n* sous-utilisation *f*

underuse[2] [ʌndəˈjuːz] *vt* sous-utiliser

underutilization [ʌndəjuːtɪlaɪˈzeɪʃən] *n* (*of facilities etc*) sous-utilisation *f*

underutilize [ʌndəˈjuːtɪlaɪz] *vt* (*facilities, equipment*) sous-utiliser

undervalue [ʌndəˈvæljuː] *vt Com* (*goods*) sous-évaluer; *Fig* sous-estimer, mésestimer

undervest [ˈʌndəvest] *n esp Br* = **vest**[1] **(a)**

underwater 1 [ˈʌndəwɔːtər] *adj* sous-marin; **u. camera/photography** caméra *f*/photographie *f* sous-marine; **u. microphone** microphone *m* subaquatique **2** [ʌndəˈwɔːtər] *adv* sous l'eau

underwear [ˈʌndəweər] *n* sous-vêtements *mpl*; (*for women*) lingerie *f*, dessous *mpl*

underweight [ʌndəˈweɪt] *adj* (*article*) d'un poids insuffisant; **to be u.** (*of person*) ne pas peser assez; **I'm 10 lbs u.** il me manque cinq kilos, je devrais peser cinq kilos de plus

underwhelm [ʌndəˈwelm] *vt Hum* **your generosity underwhelms me** votre générosité me renverse; **he was obviously underwhelmed by his present** le cadeau l'avait laissé manifestement indifférent; **the critics were underwhelmed by his next film** son nouveau film fut accueilli avec un enthousiasme très relatif par la critique

underworld [ˈʌndəwɜːld] *n* **(a)** *Myth* **the u.** les enfers *mpl* **(b)** (*of criminals*) pègre *f*, milieu *m*

underwrite [ˈʌndəraɪt] (*pt* **underwrote** [-rəʊt]; *pp* **underwritten** [-rɪt(ə)n]) *vt Fin* (*loan, new issue, policy, risk*) garantir, souscrire; **policy underwritten at Lloyd's** police garantie par Lloyd

underwriter [ˈʌndəraɪtər] *n* **(a)** *Fin* syndicataire *mf*, souscripteur *m*, garant *m*; **the underwriters** le syndicat de garantie **(b)** (*in insurance*) assureur *m*; **marine u.** assureur maritime

underwriting [ˈʌndəraɪtɪŋ] *n Fin* (*of issue, policy, risk*) garantie *f*; **marine u.** assurance *f* maritime; **u. commission** commission *f* de garantie; **u. syndicate** syndicat *m* de prise ferme

undeserved [ʌndɪˈzɜːvd] *adj* (*praise, reproach*) immérité

undeservedly [ʌndɪˈzɜːvɪdlɪ] *adv* à tort, injustement; (*be decorated etc*) sans l'avoir mérité

undeserving [ʌndɪˈzɜːvɪŋ] *adj* (*person*) sans mérite; (*cause etc*) peu méritoire; **u. of attention** indigne d'attention

undesirable [ʌndɪˈzaɪərəb(ə)l] **1** *adj* indésirable; **an u. character** un personnage peu recommandable; **to have an u. influence on sb** avoir une mauvaise influence sur qn; **if you think this is u.** si vous pensez que ce n'est pas souhaitable; **it is u. that he should be sent to an adult prison** il est inadmissible qu'on l'envoie dans une prison pour adultes **2** *n* indésirable *mf*

undetected [ʌndɪˈtektɪd] *adj* non détecté, non décelé; **to go u.** passer inaperçu

undetermined [ʌndɪˈtɜːmɪnd] *adj* **(a)** (*quality, date*) indéterminé, incertain; (*issue*) non résolu, irrésolu **(b)** (*not resolute*) irrésolu, indécis

undeterred [ʌndɪˈtɜːd] *adj* **to carry on u.** continuer sans se laisser décourager **(by** par); **we remained u.** nous ne nous sommes pas laissé décourager; **u. by the weather, he went out for a walk** en dépit du mauvais temps, il est sorti se promener

undeveloped [ʌndɪˈveləpt] *adj* **(a)** (*ideas, suggestions*) non développé; (*land, resources*) inexploité, non exploité; (*mind*) non formé **(b)** (*film*) non développé

undeviating [ʌnˈdiːvɪeɪtɪŋ] *adj* (*course, path*) droit, direct; (*faithfulness*) qui ne se dément pas

undies [ˈʌndɪz] *npl F* lingerie *f*, dessous *mpl*

undifferentiated [ʌndɪfəˈrenʃɪeɪtɪd] *adj* indifférencié

undigested [ʌnd(a)ˈdʒestɪd] *adj* (*food*) non digéré, mal digéré; (*facts*) mal assimilé

undignified [ʌnˈdɪgnɪfaɪd] *adj* peu digne, qui manque de dignité; **to be u.** manquer de dignité; **what an u. way to sit!** quelle manière peu élégante de s'asseoir!; **their business venture came to an u. end** leur entreprise a échoué de façon lamentable

undiluted [ʌndaɪˈluːtɪd] *adj* (*liquid*) non dilué; (*acid*) concentré; (*joy, delight, pleasure*) sans mélange

undiminished [ʌndɪˈmɪnɪʃt] *adj* non diminué, intact; **my respect for him remains u.** mon respect pour lui n'a pas diminué *ou* est resté intact; **thirty years later, the appeal of the film remains u.** trente ans plus tard, le film n'a rien perdu de son intérêt

undiplomatic [ʌndɪpləˈmætɪk] *adj* peu diplomatique, peu diplomate

undiplomatically [ʌndɪpləˈmætɪklɪ] *adv* de manière peu diplomate *ou* peu diplomatique

undipped [ʌnˈdɪpt] *adj Aut* **to drive with u. headlights** conduire en plein phares

undiscerning [ʌndɪˈsɜːnɪŋ] *adj* (*eater, wine-drinker*) peu raffiné, peu connaisseur, -euse; (*mind*) peu pénétrant; **to be u.** (*of person*) manquer de discernement

undischarged [ʌndɪsˈtʃɑːdʒd] *adj* **(a)** (*debtor*) non libéré (d'une obligation); *Jur* **u. bankrupt** failli *m* non réhabilité; **u. debt** dette *f* non liquidée **(b)** (*duty*) inaccompli

undisciplined [ʌnˈdɪsɪplɪnd] *adj* indiscipliné

undisclosed [ʌndɪsˈkləʊzd] *adj* non révélé

undiscountable [ʌndɪsˈkaʊntəb(ə)l] *adj Fin* inescomptable

undiscovered [ʌndɪsˈkʌvəd] *adj* non découvert; **u. country** terre *f* inconnue; **the ruins of Troy went u. for …** l'emplacement des ruines de Troie est resté ignoré pendant …

undiscriminating [ʌndɪsˈkrɪmɪneɪtɪŋ] *adj* sans discernement, qui manque de discernement

undiscriminatingly [ʌndɪsˈkrɪmɪneɪtɪŋlɪ] *adv* sans discernement

undisguised [ʌndɪsˈgaɪzd] *adj* non déguisé; (*feelings*) non dissimulé

undisguisedly [ʌndɪsˈgaɪzɪdlɪ] *adv* ouvertement

undismayed [ʌndɪsˈmeɪd] *adj* non découragé; **he was quite u. by the incident** l'incident ne l'a nullement découragé

undisputed [ʌndɪsˈpjuːtɪd] *adj* (*champion*) incontesté, indiscuté; (*success, failure*) incontestable

undistinguished [ʌndɪsˈtɪŋgwɪʃt] *adj* **(a)** médiocre; (*appearance*) peu distingué **(b) the novel is u. by any great originality** ce roman n'a rien de particulièrement original

undisturbed [ʌndɪsˈtɜːbd] *adj* (*sleep*) paisible, calme; (*peace*) que rien ne vient troubler; (*papers*) non dérangé, non déplacé; **please leave us u. for fifteen minutes** veuillez ne pas nous déranger pendant quinze minutes; **she left his papers u.** elle n'a pas touché à ses papiers; **I could do with an u. night's sleep** une bonne nuit de sommeil me ferait du bien; **he was apparently u. by the news** la nouvelle ne l'a apparemment pas troublé

undivided [ʌndɪˈvaɪdɪd] *adj* non divisé; (*loyalties*) sans partage; **he gave her his u. attention/love** il lui a donné toute son attention/tout son amour

undo [ʌn'du:] (*pt* **undid** [-'dɪd]; *pp* **undone** [-'dʌn]) **1** *vt* **(a)** (*piece of work*) détruire; (*mistake*) réparer; **you can't u. the past** ce qui est fait est fait **(b)** *Comptr* (*command*) annuler, défaire; **can't u.** impossible d'annuler; **u. command** commande *f* 'défaire' *ou* 'annuler' **(c)** (*knot, button, knitting*) défaire; (*fastening*) ouvrir; (*screw*) desserrer; (*parcel*) défaire, déficeler; (*shoes*) délacer; (*one's dress*) dégrafer, déboutonner **2** *vi* (*of dress etc*) se défaire

undocumented [ʌn'dɒkjʊmentɪd] *adj* (*subject, history etc*) sur lequel il n'existe pas de documentation

undoing [ʌn'du:ɪŋ] *n* (*downfall*) ruine *f*, perte *f*; **that man will be her u.** cet homme la conduira à sa perte; **drink was his u.** l'alcool a causé sa perte

undomesticated [ʌndə'mestɪkeɪtɪd] *adj* **he's completely u.** il ne sait rien faire dans la maison

undone [ʌn'dʌn] *adj* **(a)** (*knot, button*) défait; **to come u.** (*of knot, button*) se défaire; (*of hair*) se dénouer; (*of screw*) se desserrer; (*of shoe*) se délacer; (*of dress*) se dégrafer; (*of seam*) se découdre, se défaire; (*of parcel*) se déficeler, se défaire **(b)** *Hum, Arch* **I am u.!** je suis perdu! **(c)** (*not finished, not done*) **we had to leave it u.** nous n'avons pas pu le terminer; *Lit* **we have left u. those things which we ought to have done** nous n'avons pas fait les choses que nous aurions dû faire

undoubted [ʌn'daʊtɪd] *adj* (*fact*) incontestable, indubitable

undoubtedly [ʌn'daʊtɪdlɪ] *adv* indubitablement, incontestablement

undramatic [ʌndrə'mætɪk] *adj* (*lacking in interest*) pas très intéressant; **this seemingly u. incident …** cet incident apparemment anodin …

undrawn [ʌn'drɔ:n] *adj* **the curtains were still u.** les rideaux n'étaient toujours pas tirés

undreamed-of, undreamt-of [ʌn'dri:mdɒv, ʌn'dremtɒv] *adj* (*unsuspected*) insoupçonné; (*beyond one's dreams*) inimaginable

undress[1] [ʌn'dres] **1** *vi* se déshabiller **2** *vt* déshabiller; **to get undressed** se déshabiller

undress[2] *n* **in a state of u.** en petite tenue

undressed [ʌn'drest] *adj* **(a)** (*without clothes*) déshabillé; (*in nightdress*) en déshabillé **(b)** (*cloth*) inapprêté; (*wood*) en grume; **u. stone** pierre *f* non taillée **(c)** *Culin* (*meat*) non accommodé; (*lobster*) nature *inv*; (*salad*) non assaisonné **(d)** **u. wound** blessure *f* non pansée

undrinkable [ʌn'drɪŋkəb(ə)l] *adj* (*because unpleasant*) imbuvable; (*because poisonous etc*) non potable

undue [ʌn'dju:] *adj* **(a)** (*demand*) injustifiable **(b)** (*haste, optimism*) exagéré, excessif; **to pay u. attention to sb** s'empresser auprès de qn

undulate ['ʌndjʊleɪt] *vi* onduler, ondoyer

undulating ['ʌndjʊleɪtɪŋ] *adj* onduleux; (*wheat*) ondoyant; **u. country** pays *m* vallonné; **an u. walk** une démarche chaloupée

undulation [ʌndjʊ'leɪʃən] *n* ondulation *f*

unduly [ʌn'dju:lɪ] *adv* (*excessively*) à l'excès, trop; **not u. expensive/concerned** pas excessivement cher/inquiet; **an u. high price** un prix excessif; **to be u. optimistic** faire preuve d'un optimisme peu justifié; **he worries u.** *or* **he's u. worried about his health** sa santé le préoccupe trop

undying [ʌn'daɪɪŋ] *adj* immortel; (*love*) éternel

unearned [ʌn'ɜ:nd] *adj* **(a)** (*reward, punishment*) immérité **(b)** (*money*) qui ne provient pas du travail; **u. income** rentes *fpl*

unearth [ʌn'ɜ:θ] *vt* **(a)** (*dig out of earth*) déterrer, exhumer **(b)** (*find*) (*old photograph, hat etc*) dénicher, *F* dégot(t)er; (*information*) découvrir, trouver; **wherever did you u. that?** où donc as-tu déniché ça?

unearthly [ʌn'ɜ:θlɪ] *adj* **(a)** (*supernatural*) mystérieux; **an u. pallor** une pâleur mortelle **(b)** *F* **at an u. hour** à une heure impossible; **u. din** vacarme *m* de tous les diables; **for some u. reason** pour une raison absurde

unease [ʌn'i:z] *n* malaise *m*

uneasily [ʌn'i:zɪlɪ] *adv* (*uncomfortably*) d'un air gêné; (*worriedly*) avec inquiétude; (*to sleep*) d'un sommeil agité; **the books were u. balanced on the edge of …** les livres étaient en équilibre instable sur le bord de …

uneasy [ʌn'i:zɪ] *adj* (*ill at ease*) mal à l'aise, gêné; (*worried*) inquiet, -ète; (*sleep*) agité; **an u. truce** une trêve précaire *ou* incertaine; **there was an u. silence** il y a eu un silence gêné; **to be u.** être inquiet *ou* anxieux (**about** au sujet de); **to be u. in one's mind about sth** ne pas avoir l'esprit tranquille au sujet de qch; **I've just got an u. feeling that it won't work** j'ai justement la fâcheuse impression que çe ne marchera pas

uneatable [ʌn'i:təb(ə)l] *adj* (*unpleasant to eat*) immangeable

uneaten [ʌn'i:t(ə)n] *adj* non mangé; **u. food** restes *mpl*

uneconomic [ʌni:kə'nɒmɪk] *adj* (*work*) pas rentable

uneconomical [ʌni:kə'nɒmɪk(ə)l] *adj* (*method, car*) peu économique; **it's u. to do it that way** il est antiéconomique d'agir ainsi

unedifying [ʌn'edɪfaɪɪŋ] *adj* peu édifiant

unedited [ʌn'edɪtɪd] *adj* (*text*) qui n'a pas été rédigé définitivement, à l'état brut; (*unexpurgated*) intégral; *Comptr* (*text*) non édité; (*film*) non monté; (*recording*) à l'état brut

uneducated [ʌn'edjʊkeɪtɪd] *adj* (*person*) sans instruction; (*speech, accent*) populaire; (*handwriting*) qui dénote un manque d'instruction

unelectable [ʌnɪ'lektəb(ə)l] *adj* inéligible

unemotional [ʌnɪ'məʊʃən(ə)l] *adj* (*person*) (*not feeling emotion*) peu émotif; (*not showing emotion*) impassible; (*reaction*) peu émotionnel; (*style*) neutre, dépourvu de passion; **he managed to stay quite u. about it** il a réussi à garder la tête froide

unemotionally [ʌnɪ'məʊʃən(ə)lɪ] *adv* (*to react, look at things*) froidement

unemployable [ʌnɪm'plɔɪəb(ə)l] *adj* **I'm 65 but does that make me u.?** j'ai 65 ans mais est-ce que je suis inapte à travailler pour autant?; **he's u.** (*because of criminal record etc*) personne n'est prêt à l'employer

unemployed [ʌnɪm'plɔɪd] **1** *adj* (*person*) au chômage, sans travail; **she was u. for months** elle est restée au chômage pendant des mois; **u. capital** fonds *mpl* inactifs **2** *npl* **the u.** les chômeurs *mpl*

unemployment [ʌnɪm'plɔɪmənt] *n* chômage *m*; **as the u. rate rises …** alors que le taux de chômage est en augmentation …; *Br* **u. benefit**, *Am* **u. compensation** allocation *f ou* indemnité *f* de chômage; **u. contribution** cotisation *f* chômage; **u. figures** statistiques *fpl* du chômage; **u. insurance** assurance *f* chômage

unencumbered [ʌnɪn'kʌmbəd] *adj* non encombré (**by, with** de); *Jur* **u. estate** propriété *f* franche d'hypothèques

unending [ʌn'endɪŋ] *adj* (*controversy, list of complaints etc*) interminable, qui n'en finit plus; (*bliss etc*) éternel

unendurable [ʌnɪn'djʊərəb(ə)l] *adj* insupportable

unenforceable [ʌnɪn'fɔ:səb(ə)l] *adj* inapplicable

un-English [ʌn'ɪŋglɪʃ] *adj* peu anglais; **he's very u.** ce n'est pas du tout l'Anglais type

unenlightened [ʌnɪn'laɪt(ə)nd] *adj* (*people*) ignorant; **an u. age** une époque où règne/régnait l'ignorance; **I remained completely u.** je suis resté dans l'ignorance la plus totale

unenlightening [ʌnɪn'laɪtnɪŋ] *adj* (*comment*) qui jette peu de lumière (sur une question)

unenterprising [ʌn'entəpraɪzɪŋ] *adj* (*person*) peu entreprenant, qui manque d'initiative; (*plan*) qui manque d'audace; **that was very u. of you** vous avez vraiment manqué d'initiative, vous avez fait preuve d'une absence d'initiative totale

unenthusiastic [ʌnɪnθ(j)u:zɪ'æstɪk] *adj* peu enthousiaste; **he seems rather u. about it** ça n'a pas l'air de l'enthousiasmer

unenthusiastically [ʌnɪnθ(j)u:zɪ'æstɪklɪ] *adv* sans enthousiasme

unenviable [ʌn'envɪəb(ə)l] *adj* peu enviable

unequal [ʌn'i:kwəl] *adj* **(a)** (*size, amount*) inégal; **an u. struggle** un combat inégal **(b)** **he was u. to the task** il n'était pas à la hauteur de la tâche

unequalled [ʌn'i:kwəld] *adj* inégalé

unequally [ʌn'i:kwəlɪ] *adv* inégalement

unequivocal [ʌnɪ'kwɪvək(ə)l] *adj* sans équivoque

unequivocally [ʌnɪ'kwɪvəklɪ] *adv* sans équivoque

unerring [ʌn'ɜ:rɪŋ] *adj* infaillible, sûr; **with u. aim, he hit the target** visant avec précision, il a touché la cible

unerringly [ʌn'ɜ:rɪŋlɪ] *adv* infailliblement

UNESCO [ju:'neskəʊ] *n* (*abbr* **United Nations Educational, Scientific and Cultural Organization**) UNESCO *f*

unescorted [ʌnɪ'skɔ:tɪd] *adj* sans escorte

unessential [ʌnɪ'senʃəl] *adj* non essentiel

unesthetic [ʌni:s'θetɪk] *adj US* = **unaesthetic**

unethical [ʌn'eθɪk(ə)l] *adj* (*behaviour*) contraire à l'éthique

unethically [ʌn'eθɪklɪ] *adv* contrairement à l'éthique

uneven [ʌn'i:v(ə)n] *adj* (*not level, not regular*) inégal; (*terrain*) accidenté; **the floorboards are u.** les lattes du plancher ne sont pas toutes au même niveau; **u. breathing** respiration *f* irrégulière; **u. temper** humeur *f* inégale

unevenly [ʌn'i:v(ə)nlɪ] *adv* inégalement; (*to breathe*) irrégulièrement; **the opponents were u. matched** les adversaires étaient de force inégale; **u. distributed load** charge *f* répartie inégalement

unevenness [ʌn'i:v(ə)nnɪs] *n* inégalité *f*; (*of breathing*) irrégularité *f*

uneventful [ʌnɪ'ventfʊl] *adj* (*journey*) sans incidents, calme; **u. life** vie *f* calme *ou* peu mouvementée

uneventfully [ʌnɪ'ventfəlɪ] *adv* **to pass u.** se passer sans incidents

unexceptionable [ʌnɪk'sepʃənəb(ə)l] *adj* (*behaviour*) irréprochable; (*person*) tout à fait convenable

unexceptional [ʌnɪk'sepʃən(ə)l] *adj* ordinaire, qui n'a rien d'exceptionnel

unexchangeable [ʌnɪks'tʃeɪndʒəb(ə)l] *adj* inéchangeable

unexciting [ʌnɪk'saɪtɪŋ] *adj* (*tale, film, job*) insipide, peu passionnant; (*person*) terne, insipide; (*life*) monotone; **u. day** (*uneventful*) journée *f* calme; (*boring*) journée ennuyeuse; **this restaurant serves very u. food** on sert des repas très ordinaires dans ce restaurant

unexpected [ʌnɪks'pektɪd] **1** *adj* (*visitor, result, success*) inattendu; (*event*) imprévu; (*departure*) inopiné; (*help, happiness*) inespéré; **u. meeting** rencontre *f* inopinée; **it was completely u.** on ne s'y attendait pas du tout; **this is all so u.!** tout est si inattendu! **2** *n* **the u.** l'imprévu *m*

unexpectedly [ʌnɪks'pektɪdlɪ] *adv* de manière inattendue; **to arrive u.** arriver à l'improviste; **they won u.** on ne s'attendait pas à ce qu'ils gagnent; **he died u.** il est mort subitement

unexpired [ʌnɪks'paɪəd] *adj* (*lease*) non expiré; (*passport, ticket*) non périmé, encore valable

unexplained [ʌnɪks'pleɪnd] *adj* inexpliqué

unexploded [ʌnɪks'pləʊdɪd] *adj* (*bomb*) qui n'a pas explosé

unexploited [ʌnɪks'plɔɪtɪd] *adj* inexploité

unexplored [ʌnɪks'plɔːd] *adj* (*country etc*) inexploré

unexposed [ʌnɪks'pəʊzd] *adj* **(a)** *Phot* (*film*) vierge **(b)** (*criminal*) non démasqué **(c)** **u. to the influences of the outside world ...** qui n'est pas en contact avec le monde extérieur ...; **u. to the influence of TV** qui n'est pas soumis à l'influence de la télévision

unexpressed [ʌnɪks'prest] *adj* inexprimé

unexpurgated [ʌn'ekspɜːgeɪtɪd] *adj* (*book, text*) non expurgé; **u. edition** édition *f* intégrale

unfading [ʌn'feɪdɪŋ] *adj* (*memory*) ineffaçable, impérissable; (*hope, love*) impérissable

unfailing [ʌn'feɪlɪŋ] *adj* **(a)** (*loyalty*) à toute épreuve; (*means, remedy*) infaillible; (*zeal*) infatigable; (*memory*) sans défaillance; (*kindness*) inaltérable; (*hope, courage*) inébranlable; **to be u. in one's duty** ne jamais faillir à son devoir; **to have an u. ability to do sth** avoir le don de faire qch **(b)** (*supply etc*) inépuisable

unfailingly [ʌn'feɪlɪŋlɪ] *adv* infailliblement, immanquablement

unfair [ʌn'feər] *adj* injuste (**to sb** envers qn); (*deal, arrangement*) peu équitable; **to be u. to sb** (*of situation*) défavoriser qn; **it's u.!** ce n'est pas juste!; **to have an u. advantage over everybody else** être injustement avantagé par rapport à tous les autres; **he has been put at an u. disadvantage** il a été désavantagé; **u. competition** concurrence *f* déloyale

unfairly [ʌn'feəlɪ] *adv* injustement, peu équitablement; (*to play*) déloyalement; **to be u. dismissed** être victime d'un licenciement abusif; **to act u.** se montrer injuste

unfairness [ʌn'feənɪs] *n* injustice *f*

unfaithful [ʌn'feɪθfʊl] *adj* **(a)** **to be u. to** (*one's wife, husband*) tromper, être infidèle à **(b)** (*report*) inexact, infidèle

unfaithfully [ʌn'feɪθfəlɪ] *adv* (*to betray, desert*) de façon déloyale; **to act u. towards one's wife** se comporter de manière infidèle envers sa femme; **to report sth u.** faire un compte-rendu peu fidèle de qch

unfaithfulness [ʌn'feɪθfʊlnɪs] *n* infidélité *f*

unfaltering [ʌn'fɔːltərɪŋ] *adj* sans défaillance; **u. steps** pas *mpl* assurés; **u. voice** voix *f* ferme

unfalteringly [ʌn'fɔːltərɪŋlɪ] *adv* sans faillir; (*to speak*) d'une voix ferme; (*to walk*) d'un pas bien assuré

unfamiliar [ʌnfə'mɪlɪər] *adj* peu familier, peu connu; **u. face** visage *m* inconnu; **to be u. with sth** ne pas connaître *ou* mal connaître qch, ne pas être au fait de qch; **I'm totally u. with this town** je ne connais pas du tout cette ville; **he is quite u. with this subject** il ne sait absolument rien sur ce sujet; **the u. sounds of the language** les sonorités étranges de cette langue

unfamiliarity [ʌnfəmɪlɪ'ærɪtɪ] *n* **(a)** (*of place*) aspect *m* étrange **(b)** (*lack of knowledge*) ignorance *f* (**with** de); **because of my u. with the city/terrain** parce que je ne connaissais pas très bien la ville/le terrain

unfashionable [ʌn'fæʃənəb(ə)l] *adj* (*clothes*) démodé, passé de mode; (*restaurant, author*) qui n'est pas *ou* plus à la mode; (*ideas*) démodé

unfashionably [ʌn'fæʃ(ə)nəblɪ] *adv* (*to dress etc*) sans se préoccuper de la mode

unfasten [ʌn'fɑːs(ə)n] **1** *vt* (*garment, bracelet*) défaire, dégrafer; (*safety belt*) défaire, détacher; (*tie, knot*) défaire; (*door*) ouvrir, déverrouiller; **to come unfastened** (*of garment*) se dégrafer; (*unbuttoned*) se déboutonner; (*of knot*) se défaire, se dénouer; (*of belt*) se détacher; **to u. sth from sth** détacher qch de qch **2** *vi* se détacher; (*of dress etc*) se dégrafer

unfathomable [ʌn'fæðəməb(ə)l] *adj* (*abyss, mystery*) insondable

unfathomed [ʌn'fæðəmd] *adj* (*abyss, mystery*) insondé; **u. depths** profondeurs *fpl* inexplorées

unfavourable, *US* **unfavorable** [ʌn'feɪv(ə)rəb(ə)l] *adj* défavorable, peu favorable (**to** à); (*moment*) peu propice, inopportun; (*wind*) contraire; (*review*) mauvais; (*weather, report*) défavorable; **to appear in an u. light** se montrer sous un jour défavorable

unfavourably, *US* **unfavorably** [ʌn'feɪv(ə)rəblɪ] *adv* défavorablement; **to be u. disposed towards sb/sth** être mal disposé envers qn/qch; **his work compares u. with his brother's** son travail supporte mal la comparaison avec celui de son frère

unfeeling [ʌn'fiːlɪŋ] *adj* (*person*) insensible, dur

unfeelingly [ʌn'fiːlɪŋlɪ] *adv* (*to act*) sans pitié, impitoyablement; (*to answer*) durement, avec dureté

unfeigned [ʌn'feɪnd] *adj* non simulé, sincère

unfeignedly [ʌn'feɪnɪdlɪ] *adv* sans simulation, sincèrement

unfeminine [ʌn'femɪnɪn] *adj* peu féminin

unfenced [ʌn'fenst] *adj* (*land etc*) sans clôture

unfermented [ʌnfə'mentɪd] *adj* non fermenté

unfertilized [ʌn'fɜːtɪlaɪzd] *adj* (*egg*) non fécondé

unfettered [ʌn'fetəd] *adj* sans entrave(s); (*emotion*) non refoulé

unfilial [ʌn'fɪlɪəl] *adj* peu filial

unfinished [ʌn'fɪnɪʃt] *adj* **(a)** (*task, painting etc*) inachevé; **u. game** partie *f* interrompue; **to leave sth u.** laisser qch inachevé; **to have some u. business** avoir quelques affaires à régler; (*esp menacing*) avoir des comptes à régler **(b)** *Ind* (*article*) semi-fini

unfit [ʌn'fɪt] *adj* **(a)** (*inappropriate*) impropre, peu propre (**for** à); **u. for human consumption** impropre à la consommation; **u. to eat** non comestible; **u. to drink** (*unpleasant*) imbuvable; (*harmful*) non potable; **u. for publication** impubliable; **this house is u. for habitation** cette maison est inhabitable

(b) (*person*) (*not suitable*) **u. for military service** inapte au service militaire; *Mil* **to be discharged as u.** être réformé; **she's u. for this type of job** elle n'est pas faite pour ce genre de travail; **to be u. to govern** ne pas être en état de gouverner

(c) (*physically*) **to be u.** ne pas être en forme; **he's u. to travel** il n'est pas en état de voyager; **he is u. for duty** il n'est pas en état d'assurer ses fonctions

unfitness [ʌn'fɪtnɪs] *n* **(a)** (*unsuitability*) **u. for sth/to do sth** inaptitude *f* à qch/à faire qch **(b)** (*lack of fitness*) mauvaise forme *f*

unfitted [ʌn'fɪtɪd] *adj* **to be u. for sth** (*of equipment*) ne pas être adapté à qch; (*of person*) ne pas convenir à qch; (*morally*) être indigne de qch

unfitting [ʌn'fɪtɪŋ] *adj* peu convenable; (*remark*) mal à propos, déplacé

unfittingly [ʌn'fɪtɪŋlɪ] *adv* (*to behave etc*) de manière peu convenable

unfix [ʌn'fɪks] *vt Mil* **to u. bayonets** remettre la baïonnette

unflagging [ʌn'flægɪŋ] *adj* (*interest*) soutenu; (*vigour*) inlassable; (*optimism, courage*) inébranlable

unflaggingly [ʌn'flægɪŋlɪ] *adv* inlassablement, infatigablement

unflappability [ʌnflæpə'bɪlɪtɪ] *n F* imperturbabilité *f*

unflappable [ʌn'flæpəb(ə)l] *adj F* imperturbable; **he is completely u.** il garde toujours son calme

unflattering [ʌn'flætərɪŋ] *adj* peu flatteur (**to** pour); **her hat was most u.** son chapeau était loin de la mettre en valeur; **it shows him in an u. light** ça le montre sous un jour défavorable; **he was rather u. about your playing** il ne s'est pas montré très flatteur quant à votre jeu

unflatteringly [ʌn'flætərɪŋlɪ] *adv* d'une manière peu flatteuse

unfledged [ʌn'fledʒd] *adj* **(a)** (*bird*) sans plumes **(b)** (*person*) sans expérience

unflinching [ʌn'flɪnʃɪŋ] *adj* (*person*) qui ne bronche pas; (*resolute*) résolu; (*resolve, courage*) inébranlable

unflinchingly [ʌn'flɪnʃɪŋlɪ] *adv* sans broncher; (*resolutely*) résolument; **u. loyal** d'une loyauté à toute épreuve

unfold [ʌn'fəʊld] **1** *vt* **(a)** (*newspaper, serviette*) déplier; (*map*) déployer, déplier; **to u. one's arms** décroiser les bras **(b)** (*reveal*) (*one's intentions, plan*) révéler, exposer; (*one's plans, secret*) dévoiler **2** *vi* se déployer, se dérouler; (*of flower*) s'ouvrir, s'épanouir; (*of story, action*) se dérouler

unforced [ʌn'fɔːst] *adj* qui n'est pas forcé, spontané; **u. laugh** rire *m* franc; *Sp* **u. error** faute *f* directe

unforeseeable [ʌnfɔː'siːəb(ə)l] *adj* imprévisible

unforeseen [ʌnfɔː'siːn] *adj* imprévu, inattendu; **unless something u. happens** sauf imprévu; **u. circumstances** imprévus *mpl*; *Jur* force *f* majeure

unforgettable [ʌnfəˈgetəb(ə)l] *adj* inoubliable
unforgivable [ʌnfəˈgɪvəb(ə)l] *adj* impardonnable, inexcusable; **it's u. of me** je suis impardonnable
unforgivably [ʌnfəˈgɪvəblɪ] *adv* **he was u. rude** il s'est montré d'une impolitesse impardonnable
unforgiven [ʌnfəˈgɪv(ə)n] *adj* impardonné
unforgiving [ʌnfəˈgɪvɪŋ] *adj* implacable, impitoyable
unforgotten [ʌnfəˈgɒt(ə)n] *adj* inoublié
unformatted [ʌnˈfɔːmætɪd] *adj* (*disk*) non formaté; (*text*) non mis en forme; **u. capacity** (*of disk*) capacité *f* brute
unformed [ʌnˈfɔːmd] *adj* (*bone*) qui n'est pas (encore) formé; (*mind*) inculte; (*idea*) en gestation
unformulated [ʌnˈfɔːmjʊleɪtɪd] *adj* informulé
unforthcoming [ʌnfɔːθˈkʌmɪŋ] *adj* réservé; **to be u. about sth** être *ou* se montrer réticent au sujet de qch
unfortified [ʌnˈfɔːtɪfaɪd] *adj* non fortifié, sans fortifications
unfortunate [ʌnˈfɔːtjənɪt] **1** *adj* **(a)** (*unlucky*) malchanceux; **he's been most u.** il n'a vraiment pas eu de chance; **the u. people whose houses were flooded** les malheureux dont les maisons ont été inondées
(b) (*accident, event*) malheureux, malencontreux; (*mistake*) regrettable; **an u. state of affairs** une situation regrettable *ou* fâcheuse; **u. consequences** conséquences regrettables; **u. choice of words** choix de mots peu heureux; **in u. circumstances** dans des circonstances regrettables; **it's u. that she has to leave today** il est dommage qu'elle soit obligée de partir aujourd'hui; **how u.!** quel dommage!
2 *n* malheureux, -euse; **the u.** *pl* les infortunés *mpl*; **a poor u.** un pauvre malheureux, une pauvre malheureuse
unfortunately [ʌnˈfɔːtjənɪtlɪ] *adv* malheureusement; **an u. worded statement** une déclaration formulée d'une façon regrettable; **u. for him** malheureusement pour lui
unfounded [ʌnˈfaʊndɪd] *adj* sans fondement; **u. rumour** bruit *m* dénué de tout fondement; **u. criticism** critique *f* injustifiée
unframed [ʌnˈfreɪmd] *adj* sans cadre
unfreeze [ʌnˈfriːz] (*pt* **unfroze** [ʌnˈfrəʊz]; *pp* **unfrozen** [ʌnˈfrəʊz(ə)n]) **1** *vt* (*credit*) dégeler, débloquer **2** *vi* dégeler
unfreezing [ʌnˈfriːzɪŋ] *n* (*of prices*) déblocage *m*
unfrequented [ʌnfrɪˈkwentɪd] *adj* peu fréquenté
unfriendliness [ʌnˈfrendlɪnɪs] *n* froideur *f* (**towards** envers, à l'égard de)
unfriendly [ʌnˈfrendlɪ] *adj* (*person*) peu sympathique; (*tone, feeling*) peu amical, inamical; **to be u. to(wards) sb** traiter qn avec froideur; *Mil* **u. action** action *f* hostile; **u. reception** accueil *m* froid; **environmentally u.** nuisible à l'environnement; **a very u. user-interface** une interface(-)utilisateur très rébarbative; **written in an u. style** écrit dans un style rébarbatif
unfrock [ʌnˈfrɒk] *vt* (*priest etc*) défroquer
unfrozen [ʌnˈfrəʊz(ə)n] *adj* (*credit*) dégelé, débloqué
unfruitful [ʌnˈfruːtfʊl] *adj* infructueux, vain
unfulfilled [ʌnfʊlˈfɪld] *adj* (*duty*) inaccompli; (*promise*) non tenu; (*desire*) non satisfait, inassouvi; (*ambition*) non réalisé; (*prayer*) inexaucé; **to feel u.** éprouver un sentiment d'insatisfaction
unfunny [ʌnˈfʌnɪ] *adj* qui n'est pas drôle; **I find that distinctly u.** je ne trouve pas ça drôle du tout
unfurl [ʌnˈfɜːl] **1** *vt* (*sail, flag*) déployer; (*umbrella*) ouvrir **2** *vi* se déployer
unfurnished [ʌnˈfɜːnɪʃt] *adj* non meublé
ungainliness [ʌnˈgeɪnlɪnɪs] *n* gaucherie *f*
ungainly [ʌnˈgeɪnlɪ] *adj* gauche
ungallant [ʌnˈgælənt] *adj* peu galant, discourtois
ungenerous [ʌnˈdʒen(ə)rəs] *adj* peu généreux; (*remark*) malveillant; **that was rather u. of you** ce n'était pas très généreux de ta part
ungentlemanly [ʌnˈdʒent(ə)lmənlɪ] *adj* peu galant, discourtois; **u. behaviour** manque *m* de savoir-vivre; *Sp* **u. conduct** manque de courtoisie
ungetatable [ʌngetˈætəb(ə)l] *adj F* inaccessible
ungird [ʌnˈgɜːd] *vt* (*pt, pp* **ungirt** [ʌnˈgɜːt]) (*sword*) détacher
unglazed [ʌnˈgleɪzd] *adj* **(a)** (*window*) sans vitres **(b)** (*paper*) mat, non glacé; *Phot* **u. print** épreuve *f* mate **(c)** *Cer* non verni, non émaillé; (*brick*) non vitrifié; **u. porcelain** biscuit *m*
ungodliness [ʌnˈgɒdlɪnɪs] *n* impiété *f*
ungodly [ʌnˈgɒdlɪ] *adj* **(a)** impie, irréligieux **(b)** *F* **an u. row** un bruit de tous les diables; **he got up at an u. hour** il s'est levé à une heure impossible *ou* indue
ungovernable [ʌnˈgʌv(ə)nəb(ə)l] *adj* **(a)** (*people, country*) ingouvernable **(b)** (*desire, passion*) irrésistible; **he has u. fits of temper** il a des accès de colère incontrôlables
ungraceful [ʌnˈgreɪsfʊl] *adj* sans grâce, gauche
ungracefully [ʌnˈgreɪsfəlɪ] *adv* sans grâce, gauchement
ungracious [ʌnˈgreɪʃəs] *adj* peu élégant; **it would be u. of me to refuse** j'aurais mauvaise grâce à refuser
ungraciously [ʌnˈgreɪʃəslɪ] *adv* (*to refuse*) de manière peu élégante; (*to accept*) de mauvaise grâce
ungraciousness [ʌnˈgreɪʃəsnɪs] *n* mauvaise grâce *f*
ungrammatical [ʌngrəˈmætɪk(ə)l] *adj* (grammaticalement) incorrect
ungrammatically [ʌngrəˈmætɪklɪ] *adv* incorrectement
ungrateful [ʌnˈgreɪtfʊl] *adj* (*person, response, Lit task*) ingrat; **to be u. to sb** être peu reconnaissant envers qn (**for sth** de qch), se montrer ingrat envers qn (**for sth** à propos de qch); **don't be so u.!** ne sois pas si ingrat!
ungratefully [ʌnˈgreɪtfəlɪ] *adv* avec ingratitude
ungratefulness [ʌnˈgreɪtfʊlnɪs] *n* ingratitude *f*
ungratified [ʌnˈgrætɪfaɪd] *adj* (*desire*) inassouvi
ungrudging [ʌnˈgrʌdʒɪŋ] *adj* (*assistance*) donné de bon cœur; (*admiration*) (très) sincère
ungrudgingly [ʌnˈgrʌdʒɪŋlɪ] *adv* de bon cœur, généreusement
unguarded [ʌnˈgɑːdɪd] *adj* **(a)** (*not watched over*) non gardé; (*prisoner etc*) sans surveillance; (*town*) sans défense; *Sp* **to leave the goal u.** laisser le but vide **(b)** (*remark*) inconsidéré, irréfléchi; **in an u. moment** dans un moment d'inattention **(c)** (*mechanism*) sans dispositif protecteur; (*fire*) sans garde-feu
unguent [ˈʌŋgwənt] *n* onguent *m*
ungulate [ˈʌŋgjʊleɪt] *adj, n Zool* ongulé *m*
unhallowed [ʌnˈhæləʊd] *adj* non béni, non consacré
unhampered [ʌnˈhæmpəd] *adj* non entravé (**by** par); (*in one's movements*) libre; **u. by regulations** sans être gêné par la réglementation
unhand [ʌnˈhænd] *vt Arch, Hum* lâcher; **u. me!** lâchez-moi!
unhappily [ʌnˈhæpɪlɪ] *adv* **(a)** (*unfortunately*) malheureusement; **u. worded** rédigé de manière malheureuse *ou* maladroite **(b)** (*sadly, miserably*) tristement, d'un air triste; **to live u.** ne pas être heureux; **they're u. married** ils ne sont pas heureux en ménage
unhappiness [ʌnˈhæpɪnɪs] *n* chagrin *m*, tristesse *f*; **the u. of her childhood** son enfance malheureuse
unhappy [ʌnˈhæpɪ] *adj* **(a)** (*sad*) malheureux, triste; **to make sb u.** causer du chagrin à qn; (*esp intentionally*) rendre qn malheureux; **to be u. at leaving sb** être triste de quitter qn **(b)** (*worried*) inquiet, -ète; **I'm u. about leaving the house empty** je n'aime pas laisser *ou* ça m'inquiète de laisser la maison vide **(c)** (*not pleased*) pas satisfait; **to be u. with sb/sth** être mécontent de qn/qch; **we're u. with the quality** nous ne sommes pas satisfaits de la qualité **(d)** (*remark*) malheureux, malencontreux; **an u. state of affairs** une situation regrettable
unharmed [ʌnˈhɑːmd] *adj* (*person*) sain et sauf, indemne; (*thing*) intact, non endommagé; **to escape u.** s'en sortir indemne
unharness [ʌnˈhɑːnɪs] *vt* (*horse*) dételer
unhealthiness [ʌnˈhelθɪnɪs] *n* (*of person*) mauvaise santé *f*; (*of air, place*) insalubrité *f*; (*of influence, relationship*) caractère *m* malsain
unhealthy [ʌnˈhelθɪ] *adj* (*person*) maladif; (*state of mind, influence, relationship*) malsain; (*air, place*) malsain, insalubre; **u. curiosity** curiosité *f* morbide; **to have an u. fascination with death** avoir une fascination morbide pour la mort; **the car's sounding rather u.** la voiture fait un drôle de bruit; *F* **it can be u. to ask too many questions** (*dangerous*) il peut être dangereux de poser trop de questions
unheard [ʌnˈhɜːd] *adj* **their screams went u.** personne n'a entendu leurs cris; **the opinions of the immigrant population go u.** personne ne tient compte des opinions des immigrés; **to condemn sb u.** condamner qn sans l'avoir entendu
unheard-of *adj* **(a)** (*incredible*) inouï; **that's u.!** c'est vraiment incroyable! **(b)** (*unknown*) inconnu; **it was u. in my day** de mon temps ça n'existait pas
unheated [ʌnˈhiːtɪd] *adj* non chauffé
unheeded [ʌnˈhiːdɪd] *adj* **his warning/advice went u.** on n'a pas tenu compte de son avertissement/ses conseils
unheeding [ʌnˈhiːdɪŋ] *adj* **to be u. of sb's advice** ne pas écouter les conseils de qn, ne pas tenir compte des conseils de qn
unhelpful [ʌnˈhelpfʊl] *adj* (*person*) peu serviable; (*criticism, advice*) peu utile; **that's rather u. of them** ce n'est pas très serviable de leur part; **don't be so u.!** tâche donc un peu de nous/m'/*etc* aider!
unhelpfully [ʌnˈhelpfəlɪ] *adv* de façon peu serviable; **she u. suggested that I go and see a clairvoyant** elle n'a rien trouvé de mieux que de me conseiller d'aller voir un voyant; **someone very u. left the disk on a radiator** quelqu'un de très négligent a laissé la disquette sur un radiateur
unheralded [ʌnˈherəldɪd] *adj esp Lit* qui n'est pas annoncé; (*unexpected*) imprévu, inattendu

unhesitating [ʌnˈhezɪteɪtɪŋ] *adj* (*person*) qui n'hésite pas; **u. reply** réponse *f* immédiate *ou* prompte; **my u. reaction** ma réaction immédiate; **you can count on our u. support** vous pouvez compter sur notre soutien sans faille

unhesitatingly [ʌnˈhezɪteɪtɪŋlɪ] *adv* sans hésiter, sans hésitation

unhindered [ʌnˈhɪndəd] *adj* sans obstacle; (*not disturbed*) sans être dérangé (**by** par); **to go u.** passer librement; **u. by all that luggage** sans être encombré par tous ces bagages; **u. by petty regulations** sans être gêné par des règlements tatillons; **u. by any moral scruples** nullement encombré de scrupules

unhinge [ʌnˈhɪndʒ] *vt* (*door etc*) enlever de ses gonds; (*sb's mind*) déranger, détraquer

unhinged [ʌnˈhɪndʒd] *adj* (*person*) dérangé

unhitch [ʌnˈhɪtʃ] *vt* détacher, décrocher; (*horse*) dételer

unholy [ʌnˈhəʊlɪ] *adj Rel* **(a)** (*place etc*) profane; **u. thoughts** des pensées *fpl* coupables **(b)** *F* (*mess, mix-up etc*) épouvantable, affreux; **there was an u. row** il y a eu une dispute épouvantable

unhook [ʌnˈhʊk] **1** *vt* (*picture*) décrocher; (*trailer*) décrocher, dételer; (*garment*) dégrafer; **to come unhooked** (*of dress*) se dégrafer **2** *vi* (*picture*) se décrocher; (*dress*) se dégrafer

unhoped-for [ʌnˈhəʊptfɔːr] *adj* inespéré

unhorse [ʌnˈhɔːs] *vt* désarçonner

unhurried [ʌnˈhʌrɪd] *adj* (*manner*) posé; **she gave an u. reply** elle a pris son temps pour répondre; **in an u. way** sans se presser

unhurt [ʌnˈhɜːt] *adj* (*person*) indemne, sain et sauf, *f* saine et sauve; **to escape u.** sortir indemne *ou* sain et sauf

unhygienic [ʌnhaɪˈdʒiːnɪk] *adj* non hygiénique; **it's u. to ...** il est peu hygiénique de ..., ... est contraire à l'hygiène

UNICEF [ˈjuːnɪsef] *n* (*abbr* **United Nations International Children's Emergency Fund**) UNICEF *m*, FISE *m*

unicellular [juːnɪˈseljʊlər] *adj Biol* unicellulaire

unicorn [ˈjuːnɪkɔːn] *n Myth* licorne *f*

unicycle [ˈjuːnɪsaɪk(ə)l] *n* monocycle *m*

unidentifiable [ʌnaɪˈdentɪfaɪəb(ə)l] *adj* non identifiable

unidentified [ʌnaɪˈdentɪfaɪd] *adj* non identifié; **u. flying object** objet *m* volant non identifié

unidirectional [juːnɪd(a)ɪˈrekʃən(ə)l] *adj Phys etc* unidirectionnel

unification [juːnɪfɪˈkeɪʃən] *n* unification *f*

uniform [ˈjuːnɪfɔːm] **1** *adj* (*colour, style*) uniforme; (*temperature*) constant; **these boxes are all of u. size** ces boîtes sont toutes de la même grandeur; **to make sth u.** uniformiser qch; **u. rate** taux *m* uniforme **2** *n* uniforme *m*; **in u.** en uniforme, en tenue; **out of u.** *Mil etc* en civil; (*air hostess etc*) sans son uniforme

uniformed [ˈjuːnɪfɔːmd] *adj* en uniforme, en tenue; **the u. branch** = la police en uniforme

uniformity [juːnɪˈfɔːmɪtɪ] *n* (*of style*) uniformité *f*; (*of current*) constance *f*

uniformly [ˈjuːnɪfɔːmlɪ] *adv* uniformément

unify [ˈjuːnɪfaɪ] **1** *vt* unifier **2** *vi* s'unifier

unifying [ˈjuːnɪfaɪɪŋ] *adj* unificateur, -trice

unilateral [juːnɪˈlætərəl] *adj* unilatéral; **u. disarmament** désarmement *m* unilatéral

unilaterally [juːnɪˈlætərəlɪ] *adv* unilatéralement

unilingual [juːnɪˈlɪŋgwəl] *adj* unilingue

unimaginable [ʌnɪˈmædʒɪnəb(ə)l] *adj* inimaginable, inconcevable

unimaginably [ʌnɪˈmædʒɪnəblɪ] *adv* incroyablement

unimaginative [ʌnɪˈmædʒɪnətɪv] *adj* (*person*) qui manque d'imagination, peu imaginatif; (*cooking, solution, use of colours*) peu original; **they're very u. about their holidays** ils ne font preuve d'aucune imagination pour ce qui est de partir en vacances; **you're so u.** vous n'avez aucune imagination!

unimaginatively [ʌnɪˈmædʒɪnətɪvlɪ] *adv* sans imagination, d'une manière peu imaginative

unimaginativeness [ʌnɪˈmædʒɪnətɪvnɪs] *n* manque *m* d'imagination

unimpaired [ʌnɪmˈpeəd] *adj* (*health, hearing, force, quality*) intact; **his mind is u.** il conserve toute sa vigueur d'esprit

unimpeachable [ʌnɪmˈpiːtʃəb(ə)l] *adj* (*reputation*) inattaquable; (*evidence, witness*) irrécusable; (*conduct*) irréprochable; **of u. character** d'un caractère irréprochable; **I have it from an u. source** je le tiens de source sûre

unimpeded [ʌnɪmˈpiːdɪd] *adj* sans entrave; **u. by ...** sans être entravé par ...

unimportant [ʌnɪmˈpɔːtənt] *adj* sans importance; **it's quite u.** cela n'a pas la moindre importance; **it's u. what <u>they</u> think** leur opinion ne compte pas *ou* est sans importance

unimposing [ʌnɪmˈpəʊzɪŋ] *adj* (*air, aspect*) peu imposant, peu impressionnant

unimpressed [ʌnɪmˈprest] *adj* qui n'est pas impressionné, peu impressionné (**by** par); **I was u. by his speech** je n'ai pas été impressionné par son discours; **his colleagues were u. by his explanation** ses collègues n'ont pas été convaincus par son explication

unimpressive [ʌnɪmˈpresɪv] *adj* peu impressionnant; (*speech*) peu convaincant; **the countryside of the region is u.** la campagne de cette région n'a rien d'extraordinaire

uninflammable [ʌnɪnˈflæməb(ə)l] *adj* ininflammable

uninfluential [ʌnɪnflʊˈenʃəl] *adj* sans influence

uninformed [ʌnɪnˈfɔːmd] *adj* mal informé, mal renseigné (**about** sur); (*ignorant*) ignorant; (*mind*) inculte

uninhabitable [ʌnɪnˈhæbɪtəb(ə)l] *adj* inhabitable

uninhabited [ʌnɪnˈhæbɪtɪd] *adj* inhabité

uninhibited [ʌnɪnˈhɪbɪtɪd] *adj* (*person*) sans inhibitions, qui n'a pas d'inhibitions; (*emotion etc*) non refréné; **she's so u.** elle est si naturelle

uninitialized [ʌnɪˈnɪʃəlaɪzd] *adj Comptr* non initialisé

uninitiated [ʌnɪˈnɪʃɪeɪtɪd] **1** *adj* non initié (**in** à) **2** *npl* **the u.** les profanes *mpl*, les non-initiés *mpl*

uninjured [ʌnˈɪndʒəd] *adj* indemne; **he was shaken but u. by the accident** il a été secoué par l'accident mais n'a pas été blessé

uninspired [ʌnɪnˈspaɪəd] *adj* (*person*) qui manque d'inspiration; (*architecture, suggestion, style*) banal, -als; **an u. performance** un spectacle peu passionnant

uninspiring [ʌnɪnˈspaɪrɪŋ] *adj* peu passionnant; **I find the prospect u.** l'idée ne m'inspire pas

uninsured [ʌnɪnˈʃʊəd] *adj* non assuré (**against** contre)

unintelligent [ʌnɪnˈtelɪdʒənt] *adj* inintelligent

unintelligible [ʌnɪnˈtelɪdʒɪb(ə)l] *adj* inintelligible

unintelligibly [ʌnɪnˈtelɪdʒɪblɪ] *adv* inintelligiblement

unintended [ʌnɪnˈtendɪd] *adj* involontaire, non intentionnel; (*result*) inattendu; **the pun was quite u.** le calembour était tout à fait involontaire

unintentional [ʌnɪnˈtenʃən(ə)l] *adj* involontaire, non intentionnel; **it was quite u.** ce n'était pas fait exprès

unintentionally [ʌnɪnˈtenʃ(ə)nəlɪ] *adv* involontairement; (*to annoy sb*) sans le vouloir; **he did it quite u.** il ne l'a pas fait exprès

uninterested [ʌnˈɪnt(ə)restɪd] *adj* indifférent (**in** à); **he was u. in what I was saying** il n'était pas intéressé par ce que je disais, ce que je disais ne l'intéressait pas

uninteresting [ʌnˈɪnt(ə)restɪŋ] *adj* inintéressant, sans intérêt

uninterrupted [ʌnɪntəˈrʌptɪd] *adj* ininterrompu, sans interruption; **u. correspondence** correspondance suivie

uninterruptedly [ʌnɪntəˈrʌptɪdlɪ] *adv* sans interruption

uninvited [ʌnɪnˈvaɪtɪd] *adj* **u. guest** visiteur, -euse inattendu(e); (*intruder*) intrus, -use; **to come u.** venir sans invitation; **to do sth u.** faire qch sans y avoir été invité

uninviting [ʌnɪnˈvaɪtɪŋ] *adj* peu attirant, peu attrayant; (*food*) peu appétissant

union [ˈjuːnjən] *n* **(a)** (*joining, being joined*) union *f* (**with** avec); *esp Fml* (*marriage*) union *f*; *Fig* **a u. of French and British skills** un mariage entre le savoir-faire français et britannique; *MecE* **u. nut** écrou *m* de raccord

(b) (*harmony*) **in perfect u.** (*to live together*) en parfaite harmonie

(c) the (American) U. les États-Unis *mpl*, l'Union *f* (américaine); **customs u.** union douanière

(d) (*trade union*) syndicat *m* (ouvrier); **to join a u.** se syndiquer; **to form a u.** créer un syndicat; **non-u. workers** ouvriers, -ières non syndiqué(e)s; **unions and management** les syndicats et la direction, les partenaires sociaux; **u. branch** section *f* syndicale d'entreprise; **u. demands** revendications *fpl* syndicales; **u. leader** responsable *m ou* dirigeant *m* syndical; **u. member** (*in general*) membre *m* d'un syndicat, syndiqué, -ée; (*of particular union*) membre du syndicat, syndiqué, -ée; **increasing/decreasing u. membership** syndicalisation *f* croissante/décroissante; **u. movement** mouvement *m* syndical; **u. regulations** règles *fpl* syndicales; **u. representative** délégué *m ou* représentant *m* syndical; **u. shop** atelier *m* d'ouvriers syndiqués

(e) *US* **u. suit** combinaison *f*

union bashing *n F* critiques *fpl* constantes des syndicats

unionism [ˈjuːnjənɪz(ə)m] *n* **(a)** *Ind* syndicalisme *m* (ouvrier) **(b)** *Pol* unionisme *m*

unionist [ˈjuːnjənɪst] *n* **(a)** *Ind* syndicaliste *mf* **(b)** *Pol* unioniste *mf*; **the U. party** le parti unioniste

unionize [ˈjuːnjənaɪz] *vt* (*workers*) syndiquer

Union Jack *n* drapeau *m* britannique

uniparous [juːˈnɪpərəs] *adj Biol* unipare

unique [juːˈniːk] *adj* **(a)** (*sole*) unique; **the sport is u. to this region** ce sport se joue exclusivement dans cette région, ce sport n'existe que dans cette région; **to be u. in doing sth**

être le seul à faire qch; **you're not u.** ton cas n'est pas unique, tu n'es pas le seul **(b)** *(exceptional)* *(offer, price)* exceptionnel; *(opportunity)* unique, exceptionnel; *Mktg* **u. proposition** proposition *f* unique; *Mktg* **u. selling proposition** proposition *f* unique de vente

uniquely [juːˈniːklɪ] *adv* **(a)** *(to correspond)* exclusivement **(b)** *(extremely)* *(suited, gifted)* exceptionnellement; **he is u. placed to get this information** il est exceptionnellement bien placé pour obtenir ce renseignement

uniqueness [juːˈniːknɪs] *n* **(a)** caractère *m* unique; **that's his u. as a …** c'est ce qui en fait un … à part **(b)** *(exceptional nature)* *(of offer, price)* caractère *m* exceptionnel

unisex [ˈjuːnɪseks] *adj* *(hairdresser's, clothing)* unisexe

unison [ˈjuːnɪs(ə)n] *n* *Mus, Fig* unisson *m*; **in u.** à l'unisson **(with** de); **they all replied in u.** ils ont tous répondu en même temps; **to act in u.** agir à l'unisson

unit [ˈjuːnɪt] *n* **(a)** *(measure)* unité *f*; *Math* **units and tens** unités et dizaines; *Com, Ind* **each box contains a hundred units** chaque boîte contient cent unités; **u. of account** unité de compte; *MecE* **u. of energy/of work** unité d'énergie/de travail; **u. of velocity** unité de vitesse; *Phys* **u. of mass** unité de masse; *Fin* **monetary u.** unité monétaire; **standard u.** module *m*; **thermal u.** unité thermique; *Tel* **u. charge** prix *m* de l'unité; **u. labour costs** coût *m* unitaire de travail

(b) *Admin* *(division)* division *f*

(c) *(section, department)* *(in hospital)* service *m*; *(in school, university, company)* groupe *m*, section *f*; *Med* **intensive care u.** centre *m* de soins intensifs; **X-ray u.** service de radiologie; **u. manager** directeur *m* de service

(d) *Mil* *(group)* unité *f*; **(fighting) u.**, *US* **(combat) u.** unité de combat; **air force u.** unité *ou* groupe *m* de l'armée de l'air

(e) *MecE* *(element)* unité *f*, élément *m*; **the engine forms a u. with the transmission** le moteur fait bloc avec la transmission; *Comptr* **central processing u.** unité centrale; **input/output u.** élément *ou* dispositif *m* (d')entrée-sortie; **(visual) display u.** console *f* de visualisation, visuel *m*; *Constr* **u. construction** préfabrication *f*; **u. furniture** mobilier *m* par éléments; **(kitchen) u.** élément (de cuisine), placard *m*; **the knives are in the u. there** les couteaux sont dans ce placard

(f) *Austr* *(apartment)* appartement *m*

Unitarian [juːnɪˈteərɪən] *adj, n Rel* unitarien, -ienne, unitaire *mf*

Unitarianism [juːnɪˈteərɪənɪz(ə)m] *n Rel* unitarisme *m*

unitary [ˈjuːnɪt(ə)rɪ] *adj* *(system etc)* unitaire

unit cost *n* coût *m* unitaire

unite [juːˈnaɪt] **1** *vt* **(a)** *(join)* unir; **to u. one country with another** unifier deux pays; **to u. idealism with common sense** allier l'idéalisme au bon sens; **he seemed to u. all the qualities one would wish for** il paraissait réunir toutes les qualités souhaitables

(b) *(unify)* *(people)* mettre d'accord; *(party)* unifier; **if we stay united …** si nous restons unis …; **more unites us than separates us** ce qui nous unit est plus fort que ce qui nous divise; **common interests that u. two countries** intérêts communs qui unissent deux pays

(c) *Fml* *(marry)* unir (en mariage)

2 *vi* s'allier **(with** avec); *(of party, states)* s'unifier; *Ch* *(of atoms)* s'unir, se combiner; **to u. against** s'unir contre; *Pol* *(party)* faire bloc contre; **to u. in doing sth** se mettre d'accord pour faire qch

united [juːˈnaɪtɪd] *adj* uni; *(unified)* unifié; **u. efforts** efforts conjugués; *Prov* **u. we stand, divided we fall** l'union fait la force; **to present a u. front** présenter un front uni

United Arab Emirates *npl* [①**A11**,g,ii] Émirats *mpl* arabes unis

United Arab Republic *n* République *f* arabe unie

United Kingdom (of Great Britain and Northern Ireland) *n* Royaume-Uni *m* (de Grande-Bretagne et de l'Irlande du Nord)

United Nations *npl* Nations *fpl* Unies; **U. troops** soldats des Nations Unies

United States (of America) *npl* [①**A11**,g,ii] États-Unis *mpl* (d'Amérique)

unit price *n* prix *m* unitaire *ou* à l'unité

unit trust *n Fin* ≈ société *f* d'investissement à capital variable, SICAV *f inv*

unity [ˈjuːnɪtɪ] *n* **(a)** *(oneness)* unité *f*; **national/political u.** unité nationale/politique; *Prov* **u. is strength** l'union fait la force **(b)** *(harmony)* **there is no u. in his work** ses œuvres manquent d'unité *ou* d'harmonie; *Th* **u. of time, place and action** unité de temps, de lieu et d'action

univ *(abbr* **university)** université *f*

univalent [juːnɪˈveɪlənt] *adj Ch* univalent

universal [juːnɪˈvɜːs(ə)l] **1** *adj* **(a)** universel; **u. suffrage** suffrage *m* universel; **he's a u. favourite** tout le monde l'aime; **this proposal met with u. rejection** la proposition a été unanimement rejetée; **to meet with u. agreement** faire l'unanimité; **to meet with u. acclaim** être applaudi par tout le monde **(b) u. product** *or* **bar code** code-barres *m*, *pl* codes-barres; *MecE* **u. joint** joint *m* de cardan **2** *n Phil* universel *m*

universality [juːnɪvɜːˈsælɪtɪ] *n* universalité *f*

universalize [juːnɪˈvɜːsəlaɪz] *vt* universaliser

universally [juːnɪˈvɜːsəlɪ] *adv* universellement

universe [ˈjuːnɪvɜːs] *n* univers *m*

university [juːnɪˈvɜːsɪtɪ] *n* [①**A6**,d,i] université *f*; **to go to u.** aller à l'université; **he's been to u., he's had a u. education** il a fait des études supérieures; **to get a place at u.** être admis à l'université; **when I was at u.** quand j'étais à l'université; **London U.** l'université de Londres; **u. professor** professeur *m* d'université; **u. student** étudiant, -ante à l'université; **u. town** ville *f* universitaire; *Fig* **the great u. of life** la grande école de la vie

Unix-based [ˈjuːnɪksbeɪst] *adj Comptr* à base d'Unix

unjust [ʌnˈdʒʌst] *adj* injuste **(to** envers, avec); **my suspicions were u.** mes soupçons n'étaient pas fondés

unjustifiable [ʌndʒʌstɪˈfaɪəb(ə)l] *adj* injustifiable

unjustifiably [ʌndʒʌstɪˈfaɪəblɪ] *adv* sans justification

unjustified [ʌnˈdʒʌstɪfaɪd] *adj* **(a)** *(action etc)* injustifié; **he was absolutely u. in doing that** ce qu'il a fait n'était absolument pas justifié **(b)** *(text)* non justifié

unjustly [ʌnˈdʒʌstlɪ] *adv* injustement

unkempt [ʌnˈkem(p)t] *adj* *(hair)* mal peigné, hirsute; *(beard)* hirsute; *(appearance)* négligé; *(person)* *(with regard to hair)* dépeigné; *(in appearance)* débraillé; *(garden)* mal entretenu

unkind [ʌnˈkaɪnd] *adj* *(person)* dur, méchant; *(less strong)* peu aimable, pas gentil; *(remark)* méchant; **u. fate** sort impitoyable *ou* cruel; **that's very u. of him** ce n'est pas du tout gentil de sa part; **to say u. things to sb** dire des méchancetés à qn; **to be u. to animals** être cruel avec les animaux; **to be u. to sb** être méchant envers *ou* avec qn; **it's u. to one's skin/hair** cela agresse la peau/les cheveux; *Lit* **the unkindest cut of all** la pire des trahisons

unkindly [ʌnˈkaɪndlɪ] **1** *adv* méchamment, durement; *(less strong)* peu aimablement; **to take u. to sth** mal accepter qch **2** *adj* *(person)* peu aimable, peu gentil

unkindness [ʌnˈkaɪndnɪs] *n* *(of person)* manque *m* de gentillesse; *(stronger)* méchanceté *f*; *(of remark)* méchanceté; *(of climate)* rigueur *f*

unknot [ʌnˈnɒt] *vt* **(-tt-)** dénouer

unknowing [ʌnˈnəʊɪŋ] *adj* inconscient; **she was the u. cause of their quarrel** sans le savoir, elle était la cause de leur dispute

unknowingly [ʌnˈnəʊɪŋlɪ] *adv* inconsciemment, sans le savoir

unknown [ʌnˈnəʊn] **1** *adj* inconnu **(to** de); **u. person** inconnu, -ue; **the U. Soldier** le Soldat inconnu; *Jur* **verdict against person or persons u.** verdict contre inconnu; **this is a process u. to us, this process is u. to us** c'est un procédé qui nous est inconnu; **it is far from u. in our country** ceci est fort bien connu dans notre pays; *Math etc* **u. quantity** (quantité *f*) inconnue *f*; **he's an u. quantity** *(of uncertain value)* on ne sait pas ce qu'il vaut; *(unpredictable)* on ne sait pas ce qu'il pense

2 *adv* **he did it u. to me** il l'a fait à mon insu; **u. to us, the bus had already gone** nous ne le savions pas, mais le bus était déjà parti; **u. to everyone but her …** personne à part elle ne savait que …

3 *n* **(a)** *(person)* inconnu, -ue

(b) *Math* inconnue *f*

(c) the u. l'inconnu *m*

unlace [ʌnˈleɪs] *vt* *(one's shoes)* délacer, défaire

unladen [ʌnˈleɪd(ə)n] *adj* *(ship, lorry)* sans charge; **u. weight** poids *m* à vide

unladylike [ʌnˈleɪdɪlaɪk] *adj* indigne d'une femme bien élevée, inélégant; *(manners)* peu distingué, inélégant; **it's u. to do that** une jeune femme qui se respecte ne fait pas cela

unlaid [ʌnˈleɪd] *adj* **(a) the table was still u.** la table n'était pas encore mise **(b)** *Sl* *(virgin)* **to be u.** *(of man)* être puceau; *(of woman)* être pucelle

unlamented [ʌnləˈmentɪd] *adj* non regretté; **he passed away u.** il est mort dans l'indifférence générale

unlatch [ʌnˈlætʃ] **1** *vt* *(door)* ouvrir **2** *vi* se déverrouiller

unlawful [ʌnˈlɔːf(ʊ)l] *adj* *(possession, means, procedure)* illégal; **u. arrest** arrestation *f* abusive; **u. detention** détention *f* abusive

unlawfully [ʌnˈlɔːf(ʊ)lɪ] *adv* illégalement

unleaded [ʌnˈledɪd] **1** *adj* *(petrol)* sans plomb **2** *n* essence *f* sans plomb

unlearn [ʌn'lɜːn] *vt* (*pt, pp* **unlearnt** [-'lɜːnt], *occ* **unlearned** [-lɜːnd]) désapprendre

unlearned [ʌn'lɜːnɪd] *adj* inculte

unleash [ʌn'liːʃ] *vt* **(a)** (*dogs*) lâcher **(b)** (*force of army etc*) déchaîner; (*wave of repression*) provoquer, déclencher; **to u. a nuclear war** déclencher une guerre nucléaire; **to u. one's anger** déchaîner sa colère (**on sb** sur qn)

unleavened [ʌn'levənd] *adj* (*pain*) sans levain, azyme

unless [ʌn'les] *conj* à moins que + *sub*; **he will do nothing u. you ask him to** il ne fera rien à moins que vous ne le lui demandiez; **I would always be back by 6.15, unless I was working late** je rentrais toujours à 6h 15 au plus tard, sauf quand je travaillais tard; **u. I'm mistaken** à moins que je (ne) me trompe; **will you do it? – not u. you pay me** le ferez-vous? – seulement si vous me payez; **there aren't any left, not u. you want this one** il n'y en a plus, à moins que vous ne vouliez celui-ci; **u. I hear to the contrary** sauf avis contraire; **u. otherwise stated** sauf indication contraire

unlettered [ʌn'letəd] *adj Lit* peu lettré, inculte

unliberated [ʌn'lɪbəreɪtɪd] *adj* (*woman*) non libéré, non émancipé; **they're very u. here** les gens ne sont pas du tout émancipés ici; **that's very u. of you** la libération de la femme, tu connais?

unlicensed [ʌn'laɪsənst] *adj* **(a)** (*activity*) non autorisé, illicite; *Br* **u. premises** établissement *m* non habilité à vendre des boissons alcoolisées; **u. taxi** taxi *m* qui opère sans licence **(b)** (*car*) = sans vignette

unlike [ʌn'laɪk] **1** *adj* différent, dissemblable; **they're completely u.** ils ne se ressemblent pas du tout **2** *prep* **to be u. sb/sth** être différent de qn/qch; **he's not u. his sister** il ressemble assez à sa sœur; **a proposal not altogether u. yours** une proposition ne différant pas énormément de la vôtre; **he, u. his father** lui, à la différence de *ou* contrairement à son père; **it's u. him to do such a thing** cela ne lui ressemble pas de faire une chose pareille

unlikeable [ʌn'laɪkəb(ə)l] *adj* (*person*) antipathique, peu sympathique; (*thing*) peu agréable

unlikelihood, unlikeliness [ʌn'laɪklɪhʊd, -'laɪklɪnɪs] *n* improbabilité *f*

unlikely [ʌn'laɪklɪ] *adj* improbable, peu probable; (*explanation*) invraisemblable; **that's most** *or* **very** *or* **highly u.** c'est fort improbable; **it's not (at all) u.** c'est très probable, cela se pourrait bien; **it's u. to happen** il y a peu de chances pour que ça arrive; **in the u. event that they do come** au cas peu probable où ils viendraient vraiment; **he's u. to do it** il est peu probable qu'il le fasse; **he's an u. man for the job** il ne semble pas convenir pour ce travail; **we found the ring in a most u. place** nous avons retrouvé la bague dans un endroit auquel nous n'aurions jamais pensé; *F* **she wears the most u. clothes** elle s'habille d'une façon invraisemblable

unlimited [ʌn'lɪmɪtɪd] *adj* (*time*) illimité; (*patience*) sans borne(s); (*funds*) inépuisable; *Fin* (*cover*) sans limitation de somme; **there was u. coffee** il y avait du café à volonté; **he has an u. fund of stories** il a un stock d'histoires inépuisable; **u. buffet** buffet *m* à volonté; **u. mileage** (*of hired car*) = kilométrage *m* illimité; **u. travel** nombre *m* de voyages illimité

unlined [ʌn'laɪnd] *adj* **(a)** (*face*) sans rides **(b)** (*paper*) non réglé **(c)** (*without lining*) non doublé

unlisted [ʌn'lɪstɪd] *adj* non répertorié; *Fin* (*share*) incoté; (*not in phone directory*) qui n'est pas sur l'annuaire; **she was u. in the standard reference works** son nom ne figurait pas dans les livres de référence classiques; *Fin* **u. market** bourse *f* coulisse; *St Exch* **u. security** valeur *f* non cotée, valeur du second marché; **u. securities market** second marché *m*

unlit [ʌn'lɪt] *adj* non allumé; **the u. streets** les rues obscures

unload [ʌn'ləʊd] **1** *vt* **(a)** (*boat, car, goods*) décharger; (*from ship*) débarquer; *F* (*stolen goods*) fourguer; **to u. sth onto sb** fourguer qch à qn; *Fig* **to u. one's problems onto sb** se décharger de ses problèmes sur qn **(b)** (*gun, camera*) décharger **2** *vi* (*of lorry, ship*) décharger

unloaded [ʌn'ləʊdɪd] *adj* **(a)** (*lorry, ship*) (*with load removed*) déchargé; (*without a load*) non chargé, sans chargement **(b)** (*gun, camera*) non chargé; **don't worry, the gun's u.** n'ai pas peur, le fusil n'est pas chargé

unloading [ʌn'ləʊdɪŋ] *n* déchargement *m*; (*from ship*) débarquement *m*; **u. dock** quai *m* de déchargement; **u. note** *or* **permit** permis *m* de débarquement; **u. platform** plate-forme *f* de déchargement

unlock [ʌn'lɒk] **1** *vt* **(a)** (*door*) déverrouiller **(b)** (*secret*) révéler, découvrir **(c)** (*wheel, nut*) débloquer **(d)** **to u. the steering wheel/keyboard** déverrouiller le système de blocage de la direction/le clavier **2** *vi* se déverrouiller

unlocked [ʌn'lɒkt] *adj* (*door*) qui n'est pas fermé à clef

unlocking [ʌn'lɒkɪŋ] *n Aut, Comptr* déverrouillage *m*

unlooked-for [ʌn'lʊktfɔːr] *adj* imprévu

unloose(n) [ʌn'luːs(n)] *vt* (*bolt, screw, tie*) desserrer; **to u. one's grip** lâcher prise; **to u. sb's tongue** délier la langue à qn

unlovable [ʌn'lʌvəb(ə)l] *adj* peu attachant

unloved [ʌn'lʌvd] *adj* mal-aimé; **to be feeling u.** ne pas se sentir aimé, se sentir mal-aimé

unlovely [ʌn'lʌvlɪ] *adj* (*person*) disgracieux; (*sight*) laid

unloving [ʌn'lʌvɪŋ] *adj* (*person*) peu affectueux, peu aimant; (*behaviour*) froid

unluckily [ʌn'lʌkɪlɪ] *adv* malheureusement, par malheur; **u. for me** malheureusement pour moi

unlucky [ʌn'lʌkɪ] *adj* **(a)** (*person*) malchanceux; **to be u.** ne pas avoir de chance; **talk about u.!** quelle malchance!; **you were u. not to have been chosen** tu n'as pas eu de chance de ne pas avoir été choisi; **to be u. in love** ne pas être heureux en amour; **it was u. for him that she arrived just at that moment** malheureusement pour lui, elle est arrivée à cet instant précis

(b) (*coincidence, decision*) malheureux; **it had been an u. day** cela avait été un jour de malchance; **that's u.** ce n'est pas de chance

(c) (*bringing bad luck*) (*number, colour etc*) qui porte malheur; **it's my u. colour** c'est la couleur qui me porte malheur; **don't walk under a ladder, it's u.** ne passez pas sous une échelle, ça porte malheur

unmade ['ʌnmeɪd] *adj* qui n'est pas fait; (*bed*) défait; (*road*) non goudronné

unmade-up *adj* (*face*) non maquillé

unmake [ʌn'meɪk] *vt* (*pt, pp* **unmade** [-'meɪd]) défaire

unman [ʌn'mæn] *vt* (**-nn-**) *Lit* (*cause to lose courage*) décourager, démoraliser

unmanageable [ʌn'mænɪdʒəb(ə)l] *adj* (*person, child*) rebelle; (*horse*) indocile; (*vehicle, ship*) difficile à manœuvrer; (*large book etc*) difficile à manier, peu maniable; (*situation, problem*) ingérable; (*company*) impossible à diriger; **u. hair** cheveux difficiles à coiffer

unmanly [ʌn'mænlɪ] *adj* **(a)** (*effeminate*) efféminé **(b)** (*cowardly*) lâche

unmanned [ʌn'mænd] *adj* (*ship, spaceship*) sans équipage; *Rail* (*level crossing*) automatique; *Astronaut* **u. flight** vol *m* inhabité *ou* non habité; **all of the ticket-windows were u.** il n'y avait personne derrière les guichets; **the reception desk must never be left u.** il doit toujours y avoir quelqu'un au bureau de réception

unmannerliness [ʌn'mænəlɪnɪs] *n Lit* manque *m* de savoir-vivre, impolitesse *f*

unmannerly [ʌn'mænəlɪ] *adj Lit* (*behaviour, person*) impoli

unmapped [ʌn'mæpt] *adj* **u. territory** territoire pour lequel il n'existe pas de carte

unmarked [ʌn'mɑːkt] *adj* **(a)** (*no scratches etc*) sans marque(s); (*no stains etc*) sans tache(s); **u. (police) car** voiture *f* (de police) banalisée; **his body was bruised but his face was u.** il avait des contusions sur le corps mais son visage était intact **(b)** *Sp* (*player*) démarqué **(c)** **my essay was still u.** ma dissertation n'était toujours pas corrigée

unmarketable [ʌn'mɑːkɪtəb(ə)l] *adj* invendable, non commercialisable

unmarriageable [ʌn'mærɪdʒəb(ə)l] *adj* immariable

unmarried [ʌn'mærɪd] *adj* non marié; **he remained u.** il est resté célibataire, il ne s'est jamais marié; **u. mother** mère *f* célibataire; **u. state** célibat *m*

unmask [ʌn'mɑːsk] **1** *vt* démasquer; *esp Lit* (*plot*) dévoiler **2** *vi* se démasquer

unmatched [ʌn'mætʃt] *adj* (*person, ability*) sans égal, incomparable; **she is u. as a novelist** comme romancière, elle n'a pas sa pareille; **he's u. for courage** son courage est inégalé

unmentionable [ʌn'menʃənəb(ə)l] **1** *adj* (*event, thing*) dont il ne faut pas parler; (*word, name*) qu'il ne faut pas prononcer **2** *npl Old-fashioned, Hum* **unmentionables** sous-vêtements *mpl*

unmerciful [ʌn'mɜːsɪfʊl] *adj* impitoyable, sans pitié

unmercifully [ʌn'mɜːsɪfəlɪ] *adv* impitoyablement, sans pitié

unmerited [ʌn'merɪtɪd] *adj* immérité

unmethodical [ʌnmɪ'θɒdɪk(ə)l] *adj* peu méthodique

unmindful [ʌn'maɪndf(ʊ)l] *adj esp Lit* **to be u. of sth** être peu soucieux de qch; **u. of one's own interests** sans penser à ses propres intérêts

unmistakable [ʌnmɪs'teɪkəb(ə)l] *adj* (*feeling*) clair; (*difference*) marqué, manifeste; (*person, building*) que l'on ne peut pas confondre; (*voice, style*) reconnaissable entre mille, que l'on ne peut pas confondre; **you'll see it all right, it's u.** tu le verras sans problème, on ne peut pas le rater;

the u. smell/symptom of ... l'odeur/le symptôme caractéristique de ...

unmistakably [ʌnmɪs'teɪkəblɪ] *adv* clairement, nettement; **the style is u. French** le style est français, il n'y a pas à s'y tromper

unmitigated [ʌn'mɪtɪgeɪtɪd] *adj* (*evil, horror, severity*) total; (*used as intensifier*) (*idiot, cock-up*) véritable; **the tedium was u. by even the slightest hint of humour** l'ennui n'était même pas allégé par la moindre pointe d'humour; **an u. lie** un pur mensonge; **an u. disaster** un échec total

unmixed [ʌn'mɪkst] *adj* (*joy*) sans mélange

unmolested [ʌnmə'lestɪd] *adj* sans encombre; **to leave sb u.** (*not bother*) laisser qn en paix

unmortgaged [ʌn'mɔːgɪdʒd] *adj* non hypothéqué

unmotivated [ʌn'məʊtɪveɪtɪd] *adj* sans mobile; (*person*) non motivé; (*without ambition*) dépourvu d'ambition; **his actions were u. by any desire for personal glory** ses actes n'étaient pas motivés par un quelconque désir de gloire personnelle

unmounted [ʌn'maʊntɪd] *adj* **(a)** (*gem*) non serti; (*photo*) non encadré **(b)** (*not on horseback*) à pied

unmourned [ʌn'mɔːnd] *adj* non pleuré; **he died u.** personne n'a pleuré sa mort

unmoved [ʌn'muːvd] *adj* impassible; **u. by sth** aucunement ému de *ou* par qch; **he remained u. by all our arguments, all our arguments left him quite u.** tous nos arguments le laissaient indifférent *ou* froid

unmusical [ʌn'mjuːzɪk(ə)l] *adj* peu mélodieux; (*person*) peu musicien, -ienne; **to my u. ear it sounds like ...** pour mon oreille peu musicienne ça ressemble à ...

unnameable [ʌn'neɪməb(ə)l] *adj* innommable

unnamed [ʌn'neɪmd] *adj* (*person*) anonyme; (*thing*) innommé

unnatural [ʌn'nætjərəl] *adj* **(a)** (*not normal*) anormal; (*vice*) contre nature; **it's u. for him** cela ne lui ressemble pas **(to** de) **(b)** (*affected*) (*style, person*) peu naturel, affecté; (*laugh*) forcé

unnaturally [ʌn'nætjərəlɪ] *adv* **(a)** (*to develop etc*) anormalement; **she was u. shy** elle était anormalement timide; **not u. we turned the offer down** comme on pouvait s'y attendre nous avons rejeté cette offre; **not u. in the circumstances ...** ce qui est/était bien naturel étant donné les circonstances, ... **(b)** (*affectedly*) (*to speak*) avec affectation; (*to act, walk*) peu naturellement; **the text reads very u.** ce texte est très forcé

unnavigable [ʌn'nævɪgəb(ə)l] *adj* non navigable

unnecessarily [ʌnnesɪ'serɪlɪ] *adv* inutilement; **you're being u. hard on yourself** tu te fais du mal pour rien

unnecessary [ʌn'nesɪs(ə)rɪ] *adj* (*costs, delay, trouble*) inutile; **it was quite u. of you to say that!** tu n'avais vraiment pas besoin de dire cela!; **it's u. to change it** il n'est pas nécessaire *ou* ce n'est pas la peine *ou* il est inutile de le changer; **it's totally u. for you to come too** il est absolument inutile *ou* il n'est absolument pas nécessaire que tu viennes aussi

unneeded [ʌn'niːdɪd] *adj* inutile

unneighbourly, *US* **unneighborly** [ʌn'neɪbəlɪ] *adj* désobligeant; **to behave in an u. manner** manquer de respect envers ses voisins

unnerve [ʌn'nɜːv] *vt* (*disconcert*) déconcerter; **to be unnerved by sb's presence** se sentir déstabilisé *ou* troublé par la présence de qn

unnerving [ʌn'nɜːvɪŋ] *adj* déconcertant

unnervingly [ʌn'nɜːvɪŋlɪ] *adv* **he can be u. flippant** il est parfois d'une désinvolture déconcertante; **there was something u. peaceful about the village** le calme du village avait quelque chose de troublant

unnoticed [ʌn'nəʊtɪst] *adj* inaperçu, inobservé; **she left the party u.** elle a quitté la soirée sans que personne ne s'en rende compte; **to pass** *or* **go u.** passer inaperçu; **to let an insult pass u.** ne pas relever une insulte

unnumbered [ʌn'nʌmbəd] *adj* **(a)** (*page*) non numéroté; (*house*) sans numéro **(b)** *Lit* (*countless*) innombrable

UNO ['juːnəʊ] *n* (*abbr* **United Nations Organization**) ONU *f*

unobjectionable [ʌnəb'dʒekʃənəb(ə)l] *adj* anodin; (*person*) anodin, inoffensif; **it seems u. enough** il n'y a rien à redire

unobservant [ʌnəb'zɜːvənt] *adj* **to be u.** ne pas être observateur, -trice; **you're so u.!** tu n'es vraiment pas observateur!

unobserved [ʌnəb'zɜːvd] *adj* (*departure etc*) inaperçu; **he went out u.** il est sorti sans que personne ne le voit

unobstructed [ʌnəb'strʌktɪd] *adj* (*road*) non encombré; **u. view** vue dégagée *ou* libre; **they marched on u. to ...** ils ont poursuivi leur chemin sans rencontrer d'obstacles jusqu'à ...

unobtainable [ʌnəb'teɪnəb(ə)l] *adj* impossible à obtenir, impossible à se procurer; *Tel* **the number is u.** le numéro n'est pas en service actuellement

unobtrusive [ʌnəb'truːsɪv] *adj* (*person, building*) discret, -ète; **he always tried to remain u.** il cherchait toujours à s'effacer

unobtrusively [ʌnəb'truːsɪvlɪ] *adv* discrètement

unoccupied [ʌn'ɒkjʊpaɪd] *adj* **(a)** (*not busy*) inoccupé; **could you help me if you're u.?** si tu n'as rien à faire, tu pourrais m'aider? **(b)** (*house*) inoccupé, inhabité **(c)** *Mil* **u. zone** zone libre; **the town was still u.** la ville n'était toujours pas occupée **(d)** (*table, seat*) libre, disponible

unofficial [ʌnə'fɪʃəl] *adj* (*meeting*) non officiel; (*information*) officieux; **in an u. capacity** à titre officieux; **from an u. source** de source officieuse; **it's still u.** on ne l'a pas encore confirmé; **u. strike** grève *f* sauvage

unofficially [ʌnə'fɪʃ(ə)lɪ] *adv* non officiellement

unopened [ʌn'əʊpənd] *adj* non ouvert, qui n'a pas été ouvert

unopposed [ʌnə'pəʊzd] *adj* sans opposition; (*to advance*) sans rencontrer d'opposition *ou* de résistance; **we cannot allow this sort of thing to go u.** on ne peut pas laisser faire ce genre de choses; *Pol* **u. candidate** candidat unique; *Parl* **the bill was given an u. second reading** le projet de loi a été accepté sans opposition à la deuxième lecture

unorganized [ʌn'ɔːgənaɪzd] *adj* **(a)** (*event, group, person etc*) non organisé; (*disorganized*) désorganisé **(b)** *Ind* **u. labour** main-d'œuvre *f* non-syndiquée

unoriginal [ʌnə'rɪdʒɪn(ə)l] *adj* sans originalité, peu original

unorthodox [ʌn'ɔːθədɒks] *adj* peu orthodoxe

unostentatious [ʌnɒsten'teɪʃəs] *adj* (*person, behaviour, house, party*) simple; (*dress*) sobre, simple

unostentatiously [ʌnɒsten'teɪʃəslɪ] *adv* (*to act*) simplement; (*dressed*) simplement, sobrement

unostentatiousness [ʌnɒsten'teɪʃəsnɪs] *n* (*of person, lifestyle, house etc*) manque *m* d'ostentation, simplicité *f*

unpack [ʌn'pæk] **1** *vt* (*objects, books, boxes*) déballer; (*suitcase*) défaire; (*car*) décharger **2** *vi* (*after travelling*) défaire sa valise; (*after moving*) déballer *ou* vider ses cartons

unpacking [ʌn'pækɪŋ] *n* (*after moving house*) déballage *m*; **the u. didn't take long** (*after holiday*) nous n'avons pas mis longtemps à défaire nos bagages

unpaid [ʌn'peɪd] **1** *adj* **(a)** (*work, person*) non payé, bénévole; (*post*) non rétribué, non rémunéré; **u. leave** absence *f* non rémunérée; **u. services** services *mpl* à titre gracieux; **u. workers** (travailleurs *mpl*) bénévoles *mpl*

(b) (*bill*) impayé; (*debt*) impayé, non acquitté; **to leave an account u.** laisser arrérager un compte; **u. bill** impayé *m*

(c) (*money*) non versé; **the money is still u.** l'argent n'a toujours pas été versé

2 *adv* **he refused to work u.** il a refusé de travailler sans être payé; **I'll work u.** je vais travailler bénévolement

unpaid-up share *n* action *f* non libérée

unpalatable [ʌn'pælətəb(ə)l] *adj* **(a)** (*food*) peu appétissant **(b)** *Fig* (*truth, facts*) désagréable, dur à avaler

unparalleled [ʌn'pærəleld] *adj* (*beauty*) incomparable, sans égal; (*action, event*) sans précédent

unpardonable [ʌn'pɑːd(ə)nəb(ə)l] *adj* impardonnable, inexcusable

unpardonably [ʌn'pɑːd(ə)nəblɪ] *adv* de façon impardonnable; **she was u. late** elle est arrivée avec un retard impardonnable; **he was u. harsh** il a été d'une dureté impardonnable

unparliamentary [ʌnpɑːlə'ment(ə)rɪ] *adj Parl* (*language, action*) contraire au règles du parlement

unpatented [ʌn'peɪtəntɪd, -'pæ -] *adj* non breveté

unpatriotic [ʌnpeɪtrɪ'ɒtɪk, -pæ-] *adj* (*person*) peu patriote; (*action*) peu patriotique; **to be u.** (*of person*) être mauvais patriote

unpatriotically [ʌnpeɪtrɪ'ɒtɪklɪ, -pæ-] *adv* (*to act*) en mauvais patriote

unpaved [ʌn'peɪvd] *adj* non pavé, sans pavés

unperceived [ʌnpə'siːvd] *adj* non perçu

unperforated [ʌn'pɜːfəreɪtɪd] *adj* sans perforations

unperson ['ʌnpɜːsən] *n Pol* non-personne *f*, *pl* non-personnes

unperturbable [ʌnpə'tɜːbəb(ə)l] *adj* imperturbable

unperturbed [ʌnpə'tɜːbd] *adj* impassible; **to be u. by sth** ne pas se laisser perturber par qch

unpick [ʌn'pɪk] *vt* (*seam, hem*) défaire; (*garment*) découdre

unpin [ʌn'pɪn] *vt* **(-nn-)** ôter les épingles **(from** de)

unplaced [ʌn'pleɪst] *adj* (*competitor*) non classé; (*horse etc*) non placé

unplanned [ʌn'plænd] *adj* (*event*) imprévu; (*child*) non prévu

unplayable [ʌn'pleɪəb(ə)l] *adj* **(a)** *Sp* (*pitch etc*) impraticable; (*service, shot etc*) injouable; **the ball was in an u. position** la balle n'était pas jouable **(b)** *Mus, Th* injouable

unpleasant [ʌn'plezənt] *adj* (*taste, smell*) désagréable; (*person, tone, manner*) désagréable, déplaisant; **to smell u.**

sentir mauvais; **to taste u.** avoir mauvais goût; **to look u.** (*of thing, person*) être peu ragoûtant; **u. weather** mauvais temps *m*; **he made some u. remarks** il a dit des choses désobligeantes; **she was very u. with** *or* **to me** elle a été très désagréable avec moi; **things are getting rather u. between them** la situation est en train de se dégrader entre eux

unpleasantly [ʌn'plezəntlɪ] *adv* de façon désagréable; **the wine was u. sweet** le vin était trop sucré; **we had u. cold weather** il a fait vraiment trop froid

unpleasantness [ʌn'plezəntnɪs] *n* **(a)** (*of person, thing*) caractère *m* désagréable; (*of place*) aspect *m* déplaisant; (*of food*) caractère peu appétissant **(b)** (*disagreement*) différend *m*; (*argument*) dispute *f*; **the will caused some u.** le testament a provoqué des disputes; **there was some u. between them** il y avait encore des tensions entre eux; **we managed to avoid any u.** nous avons réussi à éviter une dispute

unpleasing [ʌn'pli:zɪŋ] *adj* déplaisant; **a not u. effect** un effet qui n'est pas désagréable

unplug [ʌn'plʌg] *vt* **(-gg-) (a)** (*television etc*) débrancher **(b)** (*opening, pipe*) déboucher

unplumbed [ʌn'plʌmd] *adj* (*depths, mystery, knowledge*) insondé

unpoetic(al) [ʌnpəʊ'etɪk, -ɪk(ə)l] *adj* peu poétique

unpolished [ʌn'pɒlɪʃt] *adj* **(a)** (*surface*) non poli; (*stone*) brut; (*floor, furniture*) non ciré, non astiqué; (*shoes*) non ciré **(b)** (*person*) peu raffiné; (*style*) qui manque de raffinement

unpolluted [ʌnpə'lu:tɪd] *adj* non pollué

unpopular [ʌn'pɒpjʊlər] *adj* (*decision, government*) impopulaire; **an u. make of car** une marque de voiture qui n'a pas de succès; **at school she had been an u. child** quand elle était à l'école les autres enfants ne l'aimaient pas beaucoup; **he makes himself u. with everybody** il se fait mal voir de tout le monde; **he's u. with his employees** ses employés ne l'aiment pas (beaucoup); **this decision was very u.** cette décision a été très mal accueillie *ou* très impopulaire

unpopularity [ʌnpɒpjʊ'lærɪtɪ] *n* impopularité *f*

unpopulated [ʌn'pɒpjʊleɪtɪd] *adj* désert, non peuplé

unpractical [ʌn'præktɪk(ə)l] *adj* **(a)** (*person*) peu pratique; **he's completely u.** il n'a aucun sens pratique **(b)** (*plan*) irréalisable

unpractised, *US* **unpracticed** [ʌn'præktɪst] *adj* inexpérimenté; **to be u. in the art of public speaking** ne pas avoir l'habitude de parler en public; **she's quite u. as a manager** elle n'a pas d'expérience en tant que directrice

unprecedented [ʌn'presɪdentɪd] *adj* (*decision*) sans précédent, exceptionnel; **this was quite u. in the continent's history** c'était du jamais vu dans l'histoire du continent

unpredictable [ʌnprɪ'dɪktəb(ə)l] *adj* (*event, person, effect etc*) imprévisible; (*weather*) incertain

unprejudiced [ʌn'predʒʊdɪst] *adj* sans préjugés

unpremeditated [ʌnprɪ'medɪteɪtɪd] *adj Jur* (*offence*) non prémédité

unprepared [ʌnprɪ'peəd] *adj* **(a)** (*food etc*) non préparé; (*speech*) improvisé, impromptu; **to find everything u.** ne rien trouver de prêt; **the hall was quite u. for the party** la salle n'était pas du tout prête pour la soirée **(b)** (*person*) **to be u. for sth** ne pas s'attendre à qch; **to go into an undertaking u.** faire qch sans être préparé; **I was quite u. for the exam** (*hadn't studied for it*) je n'étais pas du tout préparé à l'examen

unpreparedness [ʌnprɪ'peədnɪs, -'peərɪdnɪs] *n* impréparation *f* **(for** à**)**

unprepossessing [ʌnpri:pə'zesɪŋ] *adj* (*person, building*) peu engageant; **a man of u. appearance** un homme à l'apparence peu engageante *ou* peu avenante

unpresentable [ʌnprɪ'zentəb(ə)l] *adj* pas présentable

unpretentious [ʌnprɪ'tenʃəs] *adj* (*person*) sans prétention, simple; (*tastes, house*) simple

unpretentiously [ʌnprɪ'tenʃəslɪ] *adv* simplement

unpriced [ʌn'praɪst] *adj* (*article*) sans prix

unprincipled [ʌn'prɪnsɪp(ə)ld] *adj* (*person*) dénué de principes, sans scrupules; (*behaviour*) sans scrupules; **what an u. thing to do** il ne faut vraiment pas avoir de scrupules pour faire une chose pareille

unprintable [ʌn'prɪntəb(ə)l] *adj* impubliable; *Fig* (*comment, reply*) qu'on n'oserait pas *ou* qu'on ne peut répéter; **what he actually said is u.** ce qu'il a vraiment dit n'est pas répétable

unproductive [ʌnprə'dʌktɪv] *adj* (*method, capital*) improductif; (*land, conversation*) stérile; **an u. afternoon** une après-midi improductive

unprofessional [ʌnprə'feʃən(ə)l] *adj* (*person, action*) pas professionnel; **it looks u. not to …** ça ne fait pas très professionnel de ne pas …; **it's u. to leave a job unfinished** ce n'est pas professionnel de ne pas terminer un travail; **he's rather u. in his approach** il n'est pas très professionnel

unprofessionally [ʌnprə'feʃ(ə)nəlɪ] *adv* (*to do job, work, carry out contract, behave*) de manière peu professionnelle; **he dealt with the whole situation rather u.** la façon dont il s'est occupé de l'affaire n'était pas très professionnelle

unprofitable [ʌn'prɒfɪtəb(ə)l] *adj* (*operation, meeting*) peu fructueux; (*firm*) peu rentable; **we spent an u. morning/afternoon trying to …** nous avons perdu la matinée/l'après-midi à essayer de …

unprofitably [ʌn'prɒfɪtəblɪ] *adv* sans profit

unpromising [ʌn'prɒmɪsɪŋ] *adj* peu prometteur, -euse; **the weather looks u.** on dirait qu'il ne va pas faire beau; **that's an u. start** c'est un mauvais départ *ou* un départ qui augure mal de la suite

unprompted [ʌn'prɒmptɪd] *adj* spontané; **that was quite u. by any self-interest** ce n'était motivé par aucun intérêt personnel

unpronounceable [ʌnprə'naʊnsəb(ə)l] *adj* imprononçable

unprotected [ʌnprə'tektɪd] *adj* **(a)** (*undefended*) sans protection, sans défense; (*wood*) non traité; **u. wood will rot in this weather** si vous ne traitez pas le bois, il va pourrir avec le temps qu'il fait; **to have u. sex** avoir des rapports sexuels non protégés **(b)** *Tech* (*moving part, blade*) non protégé

unproved, unproven [ʌn'pru:vd, -'pru:v(ə)n] *adj* non prouvé

unprovided-for [ʌnprə'vaɪdɪdfɔ:r] *adj* (*family*) sans ressources; (*eventuality*) non prévu; **he left his family u. in his will** il n'a rien laissé à sa famille dans son testament

unprovoked [ʌnprə'vəʊkt] *adj* (*violence, criticism*) gratuit; **an u. attack** une agression gratuite

unpublicized [ʌnp'ʌblɪsaɪzd] *adj* non publié, inédit

unpublished [ʌn'pʌblɪʃt] *adj* inédit, non publié; **the u. facts** les faits qui n'ont pas été révélés au public

unpunctual [ʌn'pʌŋktjʊəl] *adj* peu ponctuel, inexact

unpunctuality [ʌnpʌŋktjʊ'ælɪtɪ] *n* manque *m* de ponctualité, inexactitude *f*

unpunished [ʌn'pʌnɪʃt] *adj* (*crime, criminal*) impuni; **to go u.** rester impuni

unputdownable [ʌnpʊt'daʊnəb(ə)l] *adj F* **(a)** (*book*) captivant, prenant; **I found it absolutely u.** je ne pouvais pas m'arrêter de lire **(b)** (*person*) indestructible

unqualified [ʌn'kwɒlɪfaɪd] *adj* **(a)** (*person*) non qualifié; (*doctor, teacher*) non diplômé; **she's u. for the job** elle n'est pas qualifiée pour le poste; **to be u. to do sth** ne pas avoir la compétence nécessaire pour faire qch; **I'm quite u. to talk about it** je ne suis nullement qualifié pour en parler **(b)** (*unreserved*) (*accusation, support etc*) sans réserve; **to give sth one's u. support** soutenir qch complètement; **u. denial** dénégation *f* catégorique; **u. praise** éloges *mpl* sans réserve; **an u. disaster** un désastre sans nom; **it was an u. success** cela a été un succès formidable **(c)** *Gram* (*adjective*) non modifié

unquenchable [ʌn'kwenʃəb(ə)l] *adj* (*thirst, fire*) inextinguible; (*thirst, curiosity*) insatiable

unquenched [ʌn'kwenʃt] *adj* (*fire*) non éteint; (*desire, curiosity, passion*) inassouvi; **u. thirst** soif non étanchée

unquestionable [ʌn'kwestjənəb(ə)l] *adj* indiscutable; (*right*) incontestable; **u. fact** fait indiscutable

unquestionably [ʌn'kwestjənəblɪ] *adv* incontestablement, sans aucun doute

unquestioned [ʌn'kwestjənd] *adj* indiscuté, incontesté; **to let a statement pass** *or* **go u.** laisser passer une affirmation sans la relever

unquestioning [ʌn'kwestjənɪŋ] *adj* (*obedience*) aveugle; (*trust, loyalty*) absolu; **to be u. about sth** ne pas se poser de questions au sujet de qch

unquestioningly [ʌn'kwestjənɪŋlɪ] *adv* aveuglément, sans se poser de question; **u. loyal** d'une loyauté absolue

unquiet [ʌn'kwaɪət] *adj esp Lit* inquiet, -ète; **u. times** époque *f* troublée

unquote ['ʌnkwəʊt] *vi* (*used only in imp*) (*in dictation*) fermez les guillemets; (*in report*) fin de citation

unquoted [ʌn'kwəʊtɪd] *adj Fin* (*share*) incoté; **u. securities** valeurs *fpl* non cotées

unratified [ʌn'rætɪfaɪd] *adj* non ratifié

unravel [ʌn'ræv(ə)l] **(-ll-,** *US* **-l-) 1** *vt* **(a)** (*fabric*) effiler, effilocher; (*knitting*) défaire; (*jumper, part of jumper*) détricoter **(b)** (*string*) démêler, débrouiller; (*plot*) dénouer, démêler; (*mystery*) débrouiller **2** *vi* **(a) to u. (itself), to come unravelled** (*of cloth*) s'effiler, s'effilocher; (*of knitting*) se défaire; (*of jumper*) se détricoter; (*of rope*) se détordre; *Fig* (*of plan*) se désagréger **(b)** (*of facts, mystery*) s'éclaircir

unread [ʌn'red] *adj* qui n'a pas été lu; **to leave sth u.** ne pas lire qch; **he left the magazine on the table u.** il a laissé la revue sur la table sans l'avoir lue

unreadable [ʌn'riːdəb(ə)l] *adj* (*book, writing*), *Comptr* illisible

unreadiness [ʌn'redɪnɪs] *n* **(a)** (*lack of preparation*) manque *m* de préparation; **in a state of u.** sans être préparé **(b)** (*unwillingness*) **their u. to contribute** la mauvaise volonté qu'ils ont mise à contribuer; (*refusal*) leur refus *m* à contribuer

unready [ʌn'redɪ] *adj* **(a)** (*unprepared*) **to be u. for sth** ne pas être préparé pour qch **(b)** (*unwilling*) **to be u. to help** n'être pas prêt à aider; **she was u. to admit that she might be wrong** elle n'était pas prête à admettre qu'elle puisse avoir tort

unreal [ʌn'rɪəl] *adj* **(a)** irréel; **everything seemed u. to him** il avait l'impression de rêver **(b)** *F* (*very good, very bad, unbelievable*) (*action, situation*) dingue; (*person*) pas vrai

unrealistic [ʌnrɪə'lɪstɪk] *adj* irréaliste

unreality [ʌnrɪ'ælɪtɪ] *n* irréalité *f*

unrealizable [ʌnrɪə'laɪzəb(ə)l] *adj* irréalisable

unrealized [ʌn'rɪəlaɪzd] *adj* **(a)** (*hope, wish*) irréalisé **(b)** *Fin* (*capital*) non réalisé; **u. gain** gain *m* latent; **u. loss** perte *f* latente

unreasonable [ʌn'riːz(ə)nəb(ə)l] *adj* **(a)** (*person*) (*illogical*) déraisonnable; (*unfair*) injuste; **don't be u.!** sois raisonnable!; **you are being very u.** tu es injuste; **they were quite u. in their demands** leurs exigences étaient tout à fait déraisonnables **(b)** (*assumption*) déraisonnable; (*demand*) immodéré; (*price*) excessif; **this would be a not u. assumption** cette supposition ne serait pas inacceptable; **surely it's not u. to expect that ...** on est bien en mesure de s'attendre à ce que ...; **at this u. hour** à cette heure indue

unreasonably [ʌn'riːz(ə)nəblɪ] *adv* d'une manière peu raisonnable; **that's u. expensive** c'est excessivement cher; **they asked, and not altogether u., that ...** ils ont demandé, plutôt légitimement, que ...

unreasoning [ʌn'riːz(ə)nɪŋ] *adj* (*person*) qui ne raisonne pas; **u. hatred** haine irraisonnée *ou* aveugle; **u. panic** peur panique

unrecognizable [ʌnrekəg'naɪzəbl(ə)] *adj* méconnaissable

unrecognized [ʌn'rekəgnaɪzd] *adj* **(a)** (*not accepted*) (*government*) non reconnu; (*writer, talent etc*) méconnu; **her talent went u.** son talent n'a pas été reconnu *ou* est resté méconnu; *Comptr* **u. command** commande *f* inconnue **(b)** (*by people in street etc*) **to go u.** ne pas être reconnu; **he mingled u. in the crowd** il s'est mêlé à la foule sans qu'on le reconnaisse

unrecorded [ʌnrɪ'kɔːdɪd] *adj* **(a)** (*fact, comment*) non enregistré, non noté; **the details of the case went u.** il n'y a pas eu de trace écrite sur les détails de l'affaire **(b)** (*music, tape*) non enregistré; (*tape*) vierge

unrecoverable [ʌnrɪ'kʌvərəb(ə)l] *adj Comptr* irrécouvrable

unrecovered debt [ʌnrɪ'kʌvəd] *n* créance *f* impayée

unredeemed [ʌnrɪ'diːmd] *adj* **(a)** (*sinner*) non racheté; (*bad character*) non compensé (**by** par); **the film is u. by even a spark of humour** il n'y a même pas un soupçon d'humour pour racheter le film; **the town's ugliness is u. by any charm whatsoever** la ville n'a aucun charme quelconque qui puisse racheter sa laideur; **he led a life of u. evil** il a toujours vécu dans le mal **(b)** (*promise*) non rempli, non tenu **(c)** (*pawned object*) non dégagé; **u. pledge** gage *m* non retiré **(d)** *Fin* (*loan*) non amorti, non remboursé; (*draft*) non honoré; (*mortgage*) non purgé

unreel [ʌn'riːl] **1** *vt* (*film, cable*) dérouler **2** *vi* se dérouler

unrefined [ʌnrɪ'faɪnd] *adj* **(a)** (*sugar, petrol*) brut, non raffiné **(b)** (*person, taste*) peu raffiné, grossier; **u. manners** manières *fpl* frustes

unreformed [ʌnrɪ'fɔːmd] *adj* (*person*) qui ne s'est pas corrigé; (*law*) non amendé; **to remain u.** (*of person*) rester incorrigible

unrefreshed [ʌnrɪ'freʃt] *adj* encore fatigué, non reposé

unregistered [ʌn'redʒɪstəd] *adj* (*person*) non inscrit; (*luggage*) non enregistré; (*parcel*) non recommandé; (*car*) non immatriculé; **u. birth** naissance non déclarée

unregretted [ʌnrɪ'gretɪd] *adj* que l'on ne regrette pas; **she died u.** personne n'a regretté sa mort

unrehearsed [ʌnrɪ'hɜːst] *adj* (*play*) joué sans répétitions; (*speech*) improvisé; **believe me, that was completely u.** crois-moi, ce n'était pas du tout prévu

unrelated [ʌnrɪ'leɪtɪd] *adj* **(a)** (*events*) sans rapport (**to** avec; **to each other** l'un avec l'autre); **these facts are totally u.** il n'y a aucun rapport entre ces faits **(b)** (*people*) **they are u.** il n'y a aucun lien de parenté entre eux

unrelenting [ʌnrɪ'lentɪŋ] *adj* (*struggle, criticism, efforts*) acharné; (*pain*) sans rémission; (*pressure, rain*) incessant; (*person, logic*) implacable (**towards** à l'égard de); **he was u. in his insistence that I should ...** il insistait avec acharnement pour que je ... + *sub*; **he was u.** (*would not be persuaded, influenced*) il restait inflexible

unreliability [ʌnrɪlaɪə'bɪlɪtɪ] *n* (*of undertaking, person*) manque *m* de sérieux; (*of result*) inexactitude *f*; (*of machine, car, computer*) manque *m* de fiabilité

unreliable [ʌnrɪ'laɪəb(ə)l] *adj* (*person*) sur qui on ne peut pas compter; (*character*) instable; (*information, result, source*) douteux; (*machine, car, clock*) non fiable; **he's good but terribly u.** il est compétent mais on ne peut jamais compter sur lui

unrelieved [ʌnrɪ'liːvd] *adj* **(a)** (*unvarying*) (*monotony, ugliness, flatness*) uniforme; **she was dressed in u. black** elle était tout de noir vêtue; **u. boredom** ennui mortel; **vast expanses of grey, u. by any bright colour** de vastes étendues de gris qu'aucune couleur vive ne vient égayer **(b)** (*pain*) sans rémission, sans répit

unremarkable [ʌnrɪ'mɑːkəb(ə)l] *adj* (*person, film, food*) médiocre, quelconque

unremitting [ʌnrɪ'mɪtɪŋ] *adj* constant; **u. boredom** ennui mortel; **u. efforts** efforts soutenus; **he was u. in his attentions** il était sans cesse plein d'attentions

unremittingly [ʌnrɪ'mɪtɪŋlɪ] *adv* sans cesse, inlassablement; (*to work*) sans relâche; **u. dull** d'un ennui mortel

unremunerative [ʌnrɪ'mjuːnərətɪv] *adj* peu rémunérateur, -trice

unrepealed [ʌnrɪ'piːld] *adj* (*law etc*) non abrogé

unrepeatable [ʌnrɪ'piːtəb(ə)l] *adj* **(a)** (*remark*) qu'on ne peut répéter, non répétable; **what he said was quite u.** ce qu'il a dit n'est pas répétable **(b)** *Com* (*price*) exceptionnel; (*offer*) unique, exceptionnel

unrepentant [ʌnrɪ'pentənt] *adj* impénitent; **to die u.** mourir dans le péché; **she was u. about what she had done** elle ne s'était pas repentie de ce qu'elle avait fait

unreported [ʌnrɪ'pɔːtɪd] *adj* (*accident, crime*) non signalé; **to go u.** (*of crime*) ne pas être signalé

unrepresentative [ʌnreprɪ'zentətɪv] *adj* peu représentatif; **it's completely u. of ...** ce n'est pas du tout représentatif de ...

unrepresented [ʌnreprɪ'zentɪd] *adj* non représenté; (*nation*) sans représentant, sans délégué

unrequited [ʌnrɪ'kwaɪtɪd] *adj* (*love, feelings*) non réciproque

unreserved [ʌnrɪ'zɜːvd] *adj* **(a)** (*outgoing*) (*person*) sans réserve **(b)** (*approval*) entier; **to be u. in one's praise of sth** ne pas tarir d'éloges à propos de qch; **u. praise** éloges sans réserve **(c)** (*unbooked*) (*seat, table*) non réservé

unreservedly [ʌnrɪ'zɜːvɪdlɪ] *adv* sans réserve; **to trust sb u.** avoir pleine confiance en qn

unresisting [ʌnrɪ'zɪstɪŋ] *adj* soumis, docile

unresolved [ʌnrɪ'zɒlvd] *adj* **(a)** (*person*) irrésolu, indécis **(b)** (*problem etc*) non résolu

unresponsive [ʌnrɪ'spɒnsɪv] *adj* **(a)** (*engine*) qui manque de nervosité; (*steering*) qui ne répond pas bien; **u. to treatment** qui ne réagit pas au traitement; **she complains that her husband is u. in bed** elle se plaint du fait que son mari manque d'enthousiasme au lit **(b)** (*mentally*) (*to suggestion*) indifférent (**to** à); (*audience etc*) inerte, passif; **to be u. to sb's needs** ne pas répondre aux besoins de qn

unrest [ʌn'rest] *n* troubles *mpl*; **social u.** agitation *f* sociale; **labour** *or* **industrial u.** agitation ouvrière; **there was u. among the workers** il y avait de l'agitation parmi les ouvriers

unrestrained [ʌnrɪ'streɪnd] *adj* non réprimé, effréné; **u. laughter** rires non réprimés

unrestrainedly [ʌnrɪ'streɪnɪdlɪ] *adv* librement, sans contrainte

unrestricted [ʌnrɪ'strɪktɪd] *adj* sans restriction, illimité; (*power*) absolu; (*access*) libre; **u. by regulations** non réglementé

unrevealed [ʌnrɪ'viːld] *adj* non révélé

unrewarded [ʌnrɪ'wɔːdɪd] *adj* non récompensé; **they shouldn't go u.** on ne peut pas les laisser sans récompense

unrewarding [ʌnrɪ'wɔːdɪŋ] *adj* **(a)** (*financially*) peu rémunérateur, -trice **(b)** (*intellectually etc*) (*job, subject etc*) ingrat

unrhythmical [ʌn'rɪðmɪk(ə)l] *adj* (*person*) qui n'a pas le sens du rythme; (*music*) peu rythmé

unrig [ʌn'rɪg] *vt* (**-gg-**) *Naut* (*ship*) dégréer

unrighteous [ʌn'raɪtʃəs] **1** *adj* (*person, action*) impie; (*life*) d'impiété **2** *npl* **the u.** les impies *mpl*

unripe [ʌn'raɪp] *adj* vert, qui n'est pas mûr; (*wheat*) en herbe

unrivalled, *US* **unrivaled** [ʌn'raɪv(ə)ld] *adj* sans rival, hors pair; **our goods are u.** nos articles sont sans concurrence

unroadworthy [ʌn'rəʊdwɜːðɪ] *adj* (*vehicle*) qui n'est pas en état de rouler

unroll [ʌn'rəʊl] **1** *vt* (*map, cloth*) dérouler; (*banner*) déferler **2** *vi* se dérouler

unromantic [ʌnrə'mæntɪk] *adj* peu romantique; **how very u. of you!** tu n'es vraiment pas romantique!, tu manques vraiment de romantisme!

unrope [ʌn'rəʊp] *vi* (*in mountaineering*) se détacher (de la cordée)
unruffled [ʌn'rʌf(ə)ld] *adj* **(a)** (*person*) calme, serein; **u., he continued to speak** impassible, il a continué de parler **(b)** (*sea*) calme; (*hair, feathers*) lisse
unruled [ʌn'ru:ld] *adj* (*paper*) non réglé, sans lignes
unruliness [ʌn'ru:lɪnɪs] *n* (*of child*) indiscipline *f*, turbulence *f*; (*of horse*) caractère *m* fougueux
unruly [ʌn'ru:lɪ] *adj* (*child*) indiscipliné, turbulent; (*horse*) fougueux; (*hair*) difficile à coiffer; **the crowd started getting u.** la foule commença à s'agiter
unsaddle [ʌn'sæd(ə)l] *vt* **(a)** (*horse*) desseller; (*donkey*) débâter **(b)** (*rider*) désarçonner
unsafe [ʌn'seɪf] *adj* **(a)** (*dangerous*) dangereux; (*bridge, structure*) peu sûr; (*chair, rope*) peu solide; (*undertaking*) hasardeux; **the chemicals are u. so close to the fire** il est dangereux de laisser ces produits chimiques si près du feu; **u. sex** rapports sexuels non protégés; **it's u. to leave it near the fire** c'est dangereux de le laisser près du feu **(b)** (*in danger*) (*of person*) en danger; **to feel u.** ne pas se sentir en sécurité **(c)** *Jur* douteux
unsaid [ʌn'sed] *adj* **to leave sth u.** passer qch sous silence; **there was a lot that was left u. between them** il y a eu beaucoup de non-dits entre eux; **it's better left u.** mieux vaut ne rien dire; **if you don't do as I say ..., he muttered, and left the rest u.** si tu ne fais pas ce que je te demande ..., murmura-t-il sans finir sa phrase
unsalaried [ʌn'sælərɪd] *adj* (*position*) non rémunéré; (*person*) non salarié
unsaleable [ʌn'seɪləb(ə)l] *adj* (*goods*) invendable
unsalted [ʌn'sɔ:ltɪd] *adj* (*meat, fish*) sans sel; **u. butter** beurre doux
unsatisfactorily [ʌnsætɪs'fækt(ə)rɪlɪ] *adv* d'une manière peu satisfaisante
unsatisfactory [ʌnsætɪs'fækt(ə)rɪ] *adj* (*conclusion, explanation*) non satisfaisant; (*system*) défectueux; **if this item is u. in any way ...** si cet article ne vous donne pas satisfaction ...; **this situation is most u.** cette situation n'est pas du tout satisfaisante
unsatisfied [ʌn'sætɪsfaɪd] *adj* **(a)** (*not content*) non satisfait (**with** de) **(b)** (*not convinced*) **I was u. with her explanation** je n'étais pas satisfait de son explication **(c)** (*appetite*) non rassasié; (*desire, lust*) insatisfait, inassouvi; **the meal left us u.** le repas ne nous a pas rassasiés; **her desire for novelty was still u.** son désir de nouveauté restait inassouvi
unsatisfying [ʌn'sætɪsfaɪɪŋ] *adj* **(a)** (*novel, ending, explanation*) peu satisfaisant **(b)** (*meal etc*) insuffisant
unsavoury, *US* **unsavory** [ʌn'seɪv(ə)rɪ] *adj* **(a)** (*smell*) désagréable; **the food looked rather u.** la nourriture n'était pas appétissante **(b)** (*person, district, bar, reputation*) louche; (*scandal, details*) abject; **there were some rather u. characters in the bar** il y avait des types plutôt louches dans le bar
unsay [ʌn'seɪ] (*pt, pp* **unsaid** [ʌn'sed]) *vt* rétracter, retirer; **you can't u. it** tu ne peux pas retirer ce que tu as dit; **what's said cannot be unsaid** ce qui est dit est dit
unscathed [ʌn'skeɪðd] *adj* (*person*) indemne, sain et sauf; (*building*) intact; **she came through the trial with her reputation u.** sa réputation n'a pas souffert du procès
unscented [ʌn'sentɪd] *adj* (*soap etc*) sans parfum, non parfumé
unscheduled [ʌn'ʃedju:ld] *adj* (*departure, meeting*) imprévu; (*plane, train*) supplémentaire; (*stop*) non prévu
unscholarly [ʌn'skɒləlɪ] *adj* (*not appropriate for a scholar*) qui n'est pas digne d'un intellectuel; (*not written etc in a scholarly way*) peu académique
unschooled [ʌn'sku:ld] *adj* **(a)** *Old-fashioned* (*person*) sans instruction; **he is u. in such matters** il est ignorant en la matière **(b)** (*horse*) non dressé
unscientific [ʌnsaɪən'tɪfɪk] *adj* non scientifique; **isn't that rather u.?** ce n'est pas très scientifique; **that's very u.** ce n'est pas du tout scientifique
unscientifically [ʌnsaɪən'tɪfɪklɪ] *adv* peu scientifiquement
unscramble [ʌn'skræmb(ə)l] *vt* déchiffrer; *Telecom* désembrouiller
unscrambler [ʌn'skræmblər] *n Telecom* décodeur *m*
unscrew [ʌn'skru:] **1** *vt* dévisser **2** *vi* se dévisser
unscripted [ʌn'skrɪptɪd] *adj* (*dialogue in film*) improvisé; (*remark*) non préparé; **that was quite u.** c'était complètement improvisé
unscrupulous [ʌn'skru:pjʊləs] *adj* (*person*) sans scrupules; (*dealings, methods etc*) peu scrupuleux
unscrupulously [ʌn'skru:pjʊləslɪ] *adv* (*to proceed, exploit*) sans scrupules
unscrupulousness [ʌn'skru:pjʊləsnɪs] *n* (*of person*) absence *f* de scrupules; (*of dealings*) malhonnêteté *f*
unseal [ʌn'si:l] *vt* (*letter*) décacheter
unsealed [ʌn'si:ld] *adj* (*letter*) décacheté
unseasonable [ʌn'si:z(ə)nəb(ə)l] *adj* (*fish, fruit*) hors de saison; **this weather's very u.** ce n'est pas un temps de saison
unseasonably [ʌn'si:z(ə)nəblɪ] *adv* **it was u. warm/cold for the time of year** il faisait extrêmement chaud/froid pour la saison
unseasoned [ʌn'si:z(ə)nd] *adj* (*food*) non assaisonné; (*timber*) vert
unseat [ʌn'si:t] *vt* **(a)** (*rider*) désarçonner **(b)** *Parl* (*Member of Parliament*) faire perdre son siège à
unseaworthy [ʌn'si:wɜ:ðɪ] *n* (*ship*) innavigable
unsecured [ʌnsɪ'kjʊəd] *adj* **(a)** *Fin* (*loan*) non garanti; **u. creditor** créancier *m* ordinaire **(b)** (*load*) mal attaché
unseeded [ʌn'si:dɪd] *adj Tennis* (*player*) non classé
unseeing [ʌn'si:ɪŋ] *adj* **to look at sb/sth with u. eyes** regarder qn/qch sans (le) voir
unseemliness [ʌn'si:mlɪnɪs] *n* (*of conduct*) inconvenance *f*
unseemly [ʌn'si:mlɪ] *adj* (*behaviour*) inconvenant
unseen [ʌn'si:n] **1** *adj* **(a)** (*hands, influence, force*) invisible; **u. by the guards they ...** sans que les gardiens les voient, ils ...; **to do sth u.** faire qch sans être vu; **to slip through u.** (*of person, mistake*) passer inaperçu **(b) to buy sth (sight) u.** acheter qch sans l'avoir vu; *Sch* **u. translation** version *f* non préparée **2** *n Sch* version *f* non préparée
unselfconscious [ʌnself'kɒnʃəs] *adj* (*charm*) naturel; (*laugh*) spontané; **he's got a big scar on his face but he's quite u. about it** il a une grande cicatrice sur le visage mais n'est pas complexé; **he's a very u. sort of person** c'est quelqu'un de très spontané *ou* naturel
unselfconsciously [ʌnself'kɒnʃəslɪ] *adv* naturellement; (*to laugh*) de façon spontanée
unselfish [ʌn'selfɪʃ] *adj* généreux; (*motive, gesture*) désintéressé; **one of the most u. people I've met** une des personnes les plus désintéressées que j'aie connues
unselfishly [ʌn'selfɪʃlɪ] *adv* généreusement; **he acted u. and put his own considerations last** il a agit avec désintéressement et a fait passer ses considérations en dernier
unselfishness [ʌn'selfɪʃnɪs] *n* générosité *f*; (*not putting self first*) désintéressement *m*
unsellable [ʌn'seləb(ə)l] *adj* invendable
unsentimental [ʌnsentɪ'ment(ə)l] *adj* peu sentimental; **the film remains u. throughout** le film ne verse jamais dans le mélo
unserviceable [ʌn'sɜ:vɪsəb(ə)l] *adj* inutilisable
unsettle [ʌn'set(ə)l] *vt* (*sb's ideas*) ébranler; (*sb*) (*less deeply*) troubler
unsettled [ʌn'set(ə)ld] *adj* **(a)** (*unstable, uncertain*) (*country*) troublé, instable; (*stock market*) instable; (*weather*) variable, changeant; (*mind*) inquiet, -ète, troublé; **I feel u. at the moment** je me sens perturbé en ce moment; **to have an u. stomach** avoir l'estomac un peu dérangé; **the u. state of the weather** l'incertitude *f* du temps **(b)** (*question, dispute*) irrésolu **(c)** (*bill*) impayé, non réglé **(d)** (*without settlers*) non colonisé
unsettling [ʌn'setlɪŋ] *adj* troublant, dérangeant
unsex [ʌn'seks] *vt* (*man*) déviriliser; (*woman*) déféminiser
unshackle [ʌn'ʃæk(ə)l] *vt* (*prisoner*) ôter les fers à; *Fig* libérer
unshackled [ʌn'ʃæk(ə)ld] *adj* sans entraves, libre; **to be u. by convention** ne pas porter le poids des conventions
unshakeable [ʌn'ʃeɪkəb(ə)l] *adj* inébranlable
unshaken [ʌn'ʃeɪk(ə)n] *adj* (*conviction*) inébranlable; **his faith was u. by ...** sa foi restait inébranlable malgré ...; **he was u. by the news** la nouvelle ne l'a pas ébranlé
unshaven, unshaved [ʌn'ʃeɪv(ə)n, -'ʃeɪvd] *adj* (*chin, armpits, legs*) non rasé; **he was u.** il n'était pas rasé; **you're looking very u.** ça fait combien de temps que tu ne t'es pas rasé?
unsheathe [ʌn'ʃi:ð] *vt* (*sword etc*) dégainer
unsheltered [ʌn'ʃeltəd] *adj* non abrité, non protégé (**from** contre)
unship [ʌn'ʃɪp] *vt* (**-pp-**) *Naut* décharger, débarquer
unshod [ʌn'ʃɒd] *adj* **(a)** (*person*) sans chaussures; (*having removed shoes*) déchaussé **(b)** (*horse*) déferré
unsighted [ʌn'saɪtɪd] *adj* **(a)** (*not visible*) invisible, qui n'est pas en vue; **he was u. by one of his own team** (*not able to see clearly*) un membre de son équipe lui bouchait la vue **(b)** (*sightless*) aveugle
unsightliness [ʌn'saɪtlɪnɪs] *n* laideur *f*
unsightly [ʌn'saɪtlɪ] *adj* laid; (*scar*) vilain; (*hoardings, buildings*) affreux
unsigned [ʌn'saɪnd] *adj* non signé, sans signature
unsinkable [ʌn'sɪŋkəb(ə)l] *adj* insubmersible
unskilful, *US* **unskillful** [ʌn'skɪlf(ʊ)l] *adj* malhabile,

maladroit (**at sth** à qch); **he's u. at convincing people** il ne sait pas convaincre les gens

unskilled [ʌn'skɪld] *adj* **u. worker** ouvrier *m* non qualifié; **u. labour** main-d'œuvre *f* non spécialisée; **to be u. in** *or* **at doing sth** ne pas être doué pour ce qui est de faire qch

unskimmed [ʌn'skɪmd] *adj* (*milk*) entier

unslept-in [ʌn'sleptɪn] *adj* (*bed*) non défait

unsling [ʌn'slɪŋ] *vt* (*pt, pp* **unslung** [-'slʌŋ]) dégréer; (*hammock*) décrocher; **to u. one's rifle** enlever son fusil de l'épaule

unsmiling [ʌn'smaɪlɪŋ] *adj* sérieux; **he stared at me u.** il me fixait sans sourire

unsmoked [ʌn'sməʊkt] *adj* non fumé

unsociability [ʌnsəʊʃə'bɪlɪtɪ], **unsociableness** [ʌn'səʊʃəblnɪs] *n* manque *m* de sociabilité

unsociable [ʌn'səʊʃəb(ə)l] *adj* sauvage, peu sociable

unsocial [ʌn'səʊʃəl] *adj* **(a) to work u. hours** travailler en-dehors des heures habituelles **(b) = unsociable**

unsold [ʌn'səʊld] *adj* invendu; **u. goods** invendus *mpl*

unsoldierly [ʌn'səʊldʒəlɪ] *adj* peu militaire

unsolicited [ʌnsə'lɪsɪtɪd] *adj* (*comment*) non sollicité; (*contribution*) volontaire; (*application*) spontané; **u. manuscript** manuscrit non commandé; **to do sth u.** faire qch spontanément

unsolvable [ʌn'sɒlvəb(ə)l] *adj* insoluble

unsolved [ʌn'sɒlvd] *adj* (*problem*) non résolu

unsophisticated [ʌnsə'fɪstɪkeɪtɪd] *adj* (*person, tastes, pleasures*) simple, non sophistiqué; (*wine*) sans prétention; (*machine*) non sophistiqué

unsound [ʌn'saʊnd] *adj* **(a)** (*kidney etc*) malade; (*foundations, bridge*) en mauvais état; (*timber*) avarié; **his health was u.** il n'était pas en bonne santé; **to be of u. mind** ne pas avoir toute sa raison

(b) (*theory, argument*) mal fondé, peu solide; (*decision, advice*) peu judicieux; (*investment*) peu sûr, douteux; **it is financially u.** les finances ne sont pas saines; **I know it's (politically) u. to say so, but …** je sais que cela va être mal vu de dire cela mais …; **she regarded him as u. on social policy** elle considérait que ses vues en matière de politique sociale n'étaient pas orthodoxes; **he's still rather u. on the basics** ses bases ne sont pas encore très solides

unsparing [ʌn'speərɪŋ] *adj* **to be u. of one's time/with one's advice** ne pas être avare de son temps/de conseils; **to be u. in one's efforts** ne pas ménager ses efforts

unsparingly [ʌn'speərɪŋlɪ] *adv* (*to give, donate*) sans compter, sans regarder à la dépense; (*to work*) sans ménager ses efforts

unspeakable [ʌn'spiːkəb(ə)l] *adj* **(a)** (*bad*) (*conditions, state, pain*) indicible; **it's u.!** c'est innommable *ou* inqualifiable!; **he's really u.!** il est au-dessous de tout! **(b)** (*joy*) indicible, ineffable

unspeakably [ʌn'spiːkəblɪ] *adv* indiciblement; **u. bad** exécrable; **to behave u.** avoir une conduite inqualifiable

unspecified [ʌn'spesɪfaɪd] *adj* non spécifié; **certain u. persons** certaines personnes, dont on taira les noms

unspectacular [ʌnspek'tækjʊlər] *adj* peu spectaculaire

unspent [ʌn'spent] *adj* (*money*) non dépensé; (*cartridge*) qui n'a pas servi; **to vent one's u. rage on sb** se défouler sur qn

unspoilt [ʌn'spɔɪlt] (*occ* **unspoiled** [ʌn'spɔɪld]) *adj* **(a)** (*untouched*) (*countryside, view*) intact; (*tranquillity*) parfait **(b)** (*child*) qui n'est pas gâté; **she's totally u.** ce n'est pas une enfant gâtée; **he was u. by his success** son succès ne lui a pas tourné la tête

unspoken [ʌn'spəʊk(ə)n] *adj* (*fear, thought, threat*) inexprimé; (*agreement*) tacite; **her u. thought was that …** intérieurement elle pensait que …; **although his name remained u. …** bien que son nom n'ait pas été prononcé …

unsporting [ʌn'spɔːtɪŋ], **unsportsmanlike** [ʌn'spɔːtsmənlaɪk] *adj* peu sportif; **that's u.** ce n'est pas très sportif; **MacEnroe was fined for u. behaviour** MacEnroe a été pénalisé pour manque de sportivité

unstable [ʌn'steɪb(ə)l] *adj* instable

unstained [ʌn'steɪnd] *adj* **(a)** *esp Lit* (*reputation*) sans tache **(b)** (*wood*) non teinté

unstamped [ʌn'stæmpt] *adj* (*letter*) sans timbre, non affranchi; *Admin, Jur* (*document*) non estampillé

unstated [ʌn'steɪtɪd] *adj* inexprimé

unstatesmanlike [ʌn'steɪtsmənlaɪk] *adj* peu digne d'un homme d'État

unsteadily [ʌn'stedɪlɪ] *adv* (*to walk*) d'un pas chancelant, en titubant; (*to hold sth*) d'une main tremblante; (*to write*) d'une main tremblante

unsteadiness [ʌn'stedɪnɪs] *adj* (*of table, person*) déséquilibre *m*; (*of hand*) manque *m* de sûreté; (*of drunk person*) démarche *f* chancelante; (*of dollar etc*) instabilité *f*

unsteady [ʌn'stedɪ] *adj* (*table*) instable, branlant; (*legs, footsteps, person*) chancelant; (*hand, voice*) mal assuré; (*position, foothold*) mal assuré, incertain; (*flame*) tremblant, vacillant; (*economy, the dollar etc*) instable; (*stock market*) irrégulier; **to be u. on one's legs** *or* **feet** ne pas tenir très bien sur ses jambes

unsterilized [ʌn'sterɪlaɪzd] *adj* non stérilisé

unstick [ʌn'stɪk] *vt* (*pt, pp* **unstuck** [-'stʌk]) décoller; **to come unstuck** se décoller; *F* (*plan*) s'effondrer; *F* **that's where they came unstuck** c'est là qu'ils ont cafouillé

unstinted [ʌn'stɪntɪd] *adj* **(a)** (*supplies*) abondant, sans restriction **(b) = unstinting (b)**

unstinting [ʌn'stɪntɪŋ] *adj* **(a)** (*person*) **to be u. in one's praise of sb/sth** ne pas tarir d'éloges au sujet de qn/qch; **to be u. in one's efforts to do sth** faire tous ses efforts pour faire qch **(b)** (*compliments, support*) sans réserve; (*admiration*) sans bornes; **u. efforts** efforts illimités; **to give u. praise** ne pas ménager ses louanges

unstintingly [ʌn'stɪntɪŋlɪ] *adv* généreusement; (*to help, work*) sans se ménager; **to praise sb u.** ne pas tarir d'éloges sur qn

unstitch [ʌn'stɪtʃ] *vt* (*seam*) découdre; **to come unstitched** se découdre

unstop [ʌn'stɒp] *vt* **(-pp-)** (*remove stopper from*) déboucher

unstoppable [ʌn'stɒpəb(ə)l] *adj* (*shot*) imparable; **he's u. now** rien ne pourra l'arrêter désormais

unstressed [ʌn'strest] *adj* non accentué, atone

unstring [ʌn'strɪŋ] *vt* (*pt, pp* **unstrung** [-'strʌŋ]) **(a)** (*bow*) débander; **to u. a violin** ôter les cordes d'un violon **(b)** (*beads etc*) ôter le fil de

unstructured [ʌn'strʌktʃəd] *adj* (*questioning*) non structuré

unstudied [ʌn'stʌdɪd] *adj* spontané, naturel

unsubdued [ʌnsəb'djuːd] *adj* indompté

unsubmissive [ʌnsəb'mɪsɪv] *adj* insoumis, rebelle

unsubsidized [ʌn'sʌbsɪdaɪzd] *adj* non subventionné

unsubstantial [ʌnsəb'stænʃəl] *adj* (*meal*) peu substantiel, peu nourrissant; (*novel*) creux

unsubstantiated [ʌnsəb'stænʃɪeɪtɪd] *adj* (*accusation*) non prouvé; (*rumour*) non corroboré

unsubtle [ʌn'sʌt(ə)l] *adj* peu subtil; **how could anyone be so u.!** comment peut-on manquer de subtilité à ce point!; **u. hints** allusions *fpl* lourdes

unsuccessful [ʌnsək'sesfʊl] *adj* (*effort, attempt*) vain, infructueux; (*outcome, marriage*) malheureux; **u. applications will not be acknowledged** nous ne répondrons pas aux personnes dont les candidatures n'ont pas été retenues; **your application has been u.** votre candidature n'a pas été retenue; **it was completely u.** cela a été un échec complet; **to be u.** (*of person, plan, marriage*) ne pas réussir; **she was u. in practically every undertaking she embarked on** elle échouait dans pratiquement tout ce qu'elle entreprenait; **the festival was u.** le festival a été un échec; **I've tried but have been u. up till now** j'ai essayé mais je n'ai pas réussi jusqu'à présent; **u. candidate** (*at election*) candidat non élu

unsuccessfully [ʌnsək'sesfəlɪ] *adv* sans succès, en vain

unsuitability [ʌns(j)uːtə'bɪlɪtɪ] *n* (*of person*) inaptitude *f* **(for sth** à qch); (*of sth*) inadéquation *f* **(for sth** à qch); **the u. of the clothes he was wearing** les vêtements inadéquats qu'il portait

unsuitable [ʌn's(j)uːtəb(ə)l] *adj* (*tools*) impropre, mal adapté **(for** à); (*friend, people*) peu recommandable; (*music, choice of words*) déplacé; (*time*) inopportun; (*conditions, diet*) inadéquat, non approprié; (*clothes*) inadéquat; (*climate*) peu indiqué; (*couple, partners*) mal assorti; **this is an u. environment for a child** ce n'est pas un environnement approprié pour un enfant; **this is an u. time to bring the matter up** ce n'est pas le moment de parler de cela; **I thought Wednesday was u.** je pensais que mercredi ne vous/lui/*etc* convenait pas; **they're u. for each other** ils ne vont pas ensemble; **he's u. for her** ce n'est pas l'homme qu'il lui faut; **he's quite u. for the job** ce n'est pas la personne qu'il faut pour ce poste; **u. for the occasion** qui ne convient pas à la circonstance; **you have chosen a most u. time to …** vous avez mal choisi le moment de …; **the film is u. for children** ce n'est pas un film pour les enfants; **the climate is u. for wheat** le climat ne convient pas au blé

unsuitably [ʌn's(j)uːtəblɪ] *adv* inadéquatement; (*to behave*) de façon inappropriée; **to be u. dressed** ne pas porter les vêtements qui conviennent; **they're u. matched** (*of couple*) ils sont mal assortis

unsuited [ʌn's(j)uːtɪd] *adj* (*person*) inapte (**for** *or* **to sth** à qch); (*material, clothes, equipment*) inadéquat; **she's clearly u. to this type of work** il est clair qu'elle n'est pas faite pour ce genre de travail; **they are u. (to each other)** ils sont mal assortis

unsullied [ʌn'sʌlɪd] *adj* sans tache; **her reputation was u. by …** sa réputation n'a pas souffert de …

unsung [ʌn'sʌŋ] *adj esp Lit (deed)* non célébré; **u. hero** héros *m* méconnu

unsupported [ʌnsə'pɔːtɪd] *adj* (a) *(statement, charges)* sans preuves; **the theories were u. by any evidence** ces théories n'ont été étayées par aucune preuve (b) *(structure, wall)* sans support, sans appui; **to walk u.** marcher sans se faire aider; **he could walk u. by a stick** il marchait sans canne; **to leave one's family u.** ne pas subvenir aux besoins de sa famille; **more and more students are u. by the state** de plus en plus d'étudiants ne reçoivent pas d'aide de l'État

unsure [ʌn'ʃʊər] *adj (person)* incertain (**about** de); *(position)* peu sûr, précaire; **they were u. what to do next** ils n'étaient pas sûrs de savoir quoi faire après; **I was u. what she meant by this** je n'étais pas sûr de savoir ce qu'elle voulait dire par là; **to be u. of oneself** ne pas être sûr de soi; **I'm u. about it/him** j'ai des doutes là-dessus/en ce qui le concerne

unsurpassable [ʌnsə'pɑːsəb(ə)l] *adj* insurpassable

unsurpassed [ʌnsə'pɑːst] *adj* sans égal

unsurprised [ʌnsə'praɪzd] *adj* non surpris; **I was u. by ...** je n'ai pas été surpris par ...

unsurprising [ʌnsə'praɪzɪŋ] *adj* peu surprenant

unsurprisingly [ʌnsə'praɪzɪŋlɪ] *adv* **u., this suggestion was rejected** comme on pouvait s'y attendre, cette suggestion fut rejetée

unsuspected [ʌnsəs'pektɪd] *adj* insoupçonné (**by** de)

unsuspecting [ʌnsəs'pektɪŋ] *adj* qui ne se doute de rien; *(by nature)* peu soupçonneux; **he's so u.** il est si peu soupçonneux; **when he later, all u., ...** quand plus tard, sans se douter de rien, il ...

unsuspicious [ʌnsəs'pɪʃəs] *adj* peu soupçonneux

unsweetened [ʌn'swiːt(ə)nd] *adj* non sucré

unswerving [ʌn'swɜːvɪŋ] *adj (loyalty)* constant, ferme; **they have been u. in their support (for us)** ils nous ont prêté un appui constant

unswervingly [ʌn'swɜːvɪŋlɪ] *adv* sans s'écarter du but; *(to maintain)* sans relâche; **u. loyal** d'une loyauté absolue

unsympathetic [ʌnsɪmpə'θetɪk] *adj* (a) *(lacking understanding)* peu compatissant; **they were very u. about our problems** nos problèmes les laissaient complètement indifférents; **the idea met with an u. reception** l'idée a reçu un accueil plutôt froid; **he was generally u. to modern art** *(didn't like)* de manière générale il appréciait peu l'art moderne; *(made critical statements about)* il n'était généralement pas tendre avec l'art moderne (b) *(unlikeable)* antipathique; **I find the characters of this novel u.** les personnages de ce roman me sont peu sympathiques

unsympathetically [ʌnsɪmpə'θetɪklɪ] *adv* froidement; **the novel/film was u. reviewed by the critics** les critiques n'ont pas été tendres avec le roman/le film

unsystematic [ʌnsɪstə'mætɪk] *adj* non systématique, sans méthode; **you're too u.** tu n'es pas assez méthodique

unsystematically [ʌnsɪstə'mætɪklɪ] *adv* sans méthode

untainted [ʌn'teɪntɪd] *adj (person, judgment)* non corrompu; *(reputation)* sans tache

untalented [ʌn'tæləntɪd] *adj* peu doué

untam(e)able [ʌn'teɪməb(ə)l] *adj (animal, spirit)* indomptable

untamed [ʌn'teɪmd] *adj (animal, spirit, luxuriance)* indompté

untangle [ʌn'tæŋg(ə)l] *vt (wool, string, hair)* démêler; *(mystery)* éclaircir; *(sth complicated)* débrouiller

untapped [ʌn'tæpt] *adj (resources)* inexploité

untarnished [ʌn'tɑːnɪʃt] *adj (metal), Fig* non terni, sans tache

untasted [ʌn'teɪstɪd] *adj* auquel on n'a pas goûté; **to send a dish away u.** renvoyer un plat sans y goûter

untaught [ʌn'tɔːt] *adj (person)* sans instruction; *(skill)* naturel

untaxable [ʌn'tæksəb(ə)l] *adj* non imposable

untaxed [ʌn'tækst] *adj (income)* exempt *ou* exempté d'impôts; *(product)* non imposé, non taxé; *(car)* = sans vignette

unteachable [ʌn'tiːtʃəb(ə)l] *adj (person)* à qui l'on ne peut rien apprendre, incapable d'apprendre; *(subject, art)* impossible à enseigner

untenable [ʌn'tenəb(ə)l] *adj (position)* intenable; *(theory)* insoutenable

untenanted [ʌn'tenəntɪd] *adj* sans locataire(s); **these flats have been u. for years** ces appartements sont inoccupés depuis des années

untended [ʌn'tendɪd] *adj (sick person)* non soigné, sans soins; *(garden)* non entretenu

untested [ʌn'testɪd] *adj* inéprouvé, non prouvé; *(invention, drug)* non essayé; *(sample)* non analysé

unthinkable [ʌn'θɪŋkəb(ə)l] *adj* inconcevable, impensable; **it's u. that ...** il est inconcevable que ... + *sub*; **if the u. should happen** si l'inconcevable se produisait

unthinking [ʌn'θɪŋkɪŋ] *adj (person)* étourdi

unthinkingly [ʌn'θɪŋkɪŋlɪ] *adv (to do sth)* sans réfléchir, étourdiment

unthought-of [ʌn'θɔːtɒv] *adj* auquel on n'a pas pensé

unthread [ʌn'θred] *vt (beads)* ôter le fil de

untidily [ʌn'taɪdɪlɪ] *adv* en désordre; **she's always u. dressed** elle a toujours l'air débraillé

untidiness [ʌn'taɪdɪnɪs] *n (of room, appearance)* désordre *m*; *(of person) (characteristic)* manque *m* d'ordre

untidy [ʌn'taɪdɪ] *adj* (a) *(room, desk)* en désordre, mal rangé; *(hair)* ébouriffé; *(writing)* brouillon; **u. appearance** tenue *f* débraillée; **his playing is u.** *(of musician)* son jeu manque de netteté; **he brings the novel to an u. end** il termine le roman d'une façon plutôt confuse; **an u. mind** un esprit brouillon; **his room/desk always gets u.** sa chambre/son bureau est toujours en désordre (b) *(person) (as characteristic)* désordonné, qui manque d'ordre; **he's such an u. sort of person** il est tellement désordonné

untie [ʌn'taɪ] *vt (pt, pp* **untied**; *prp* **untying**) *(shoelaces, ribbon)* défaire; *(knot)* dénouer; *(knot, parcel)* défaire, délier; *(parcel)* déficeler; *(one's hair, dog, boat)* détacher; **to u. itself, to come untied** *(of knot)* se défaire, se dénouer

until [ʌn'tɪl] **1** *prep* [①**A65**; **A67**] (a) jusqu'à; **you have u. tomorrow to finish it** tu as jusqu'à demain pour le finir; **until 1989** jusqu'en 1989; **u. now** jusqu'ici, jusque-là; **she didn't arrive u. yesterday** elle n'est arrivée qu'hier; **u. then we'll just have to make do** en attendant il va falloir se débrouiller; *Rad, TV* **u. tomorrow, I wish you a very good night** je vous souhaite une très bonne soirée, à demain

(b) **not u. (after) eight o'clock** pas avant huit heures (passées); **not u. tomorrow** pas avant demain; **it wasn't u. after Easter that ...** ce n'est qu'après Pâques que ...; **I've never seen it u. now** c'est la première fois que je le vois

2 *conj* [①**A69,b,ii**] (a) jusqu'à ce que + *sub*; **u. all the windows are open** jusqu'à ce que toutes les fenêtres soient ouvertes; **we'll wait u. you're ready** nous attendrons que vous soyez prêt; **we waited u. the rain stopped** nous avons attendu jusqu'à ce que la pluie cesse; **wait u. the bus stops** attends que le bus soit arrêté; **he drank u. he was ill** il a bu jusqu'à s'en rendre malade; **we worked u. we dropped** nous avons travaillé jusqu'à n'en plus pouvoir; **he laughed u. he cried** il a pleuré de rire

(b) **he won't come u. he's invited** il ne viendra pas avant d'être invité *ou* sans qu'on l'invite; **I won't leave him u. he's completely recovered** je ne le quitterai pas tant qu'il n'est pas tout à fait guéri; **don't do anything u. I say so** ne fais rien avant que je te le dise; **don't sign u. you've checked everything** ne signe rien avant d'avoir tout vérifié

untilled [ʌn'tɪld] *adj* non cultivé, non labouré

untimely [ʌn'taɪmlɪ] *adj (death)* prématuré; *(question, action)* inopportun, intempestif, mal à propos; **to come to an u. end** mourir avant l'âge

untiring [ʌn'taɪərɪŋ] *adj* infatigable, inlassable

untiringly [ʌn'taɪərɪŋlɪ] *adv* infatigablement, inlassablement

unto ['ʌntʊ, 'ʌntə] *prep Arch, Lit* **to liken sth u. sth** comparer qch à *ou* avec qch; *Bible* **u. us a child is born** un enfant nous est né; *Bible* **and I say u. you ...** en vérité je vous le dis ...; **to turn u. sb** se tourner vers qn

untold [ʌn'təʊld] *adj (riches)* immense, énorme; **u. suffering** souffrances *fpl* inouïes; **u. joy** joie *f* indicible

untouchable [ʌn'tʌtʃəb(ə)l] **1** *adj* intouchable **2** *n (in India)* intouchable *mf*, paria *m*

untouched [ʌn'tʌtʃt] *adj* (a) *(by hand etc)* non touché; **to be u. by the influence of ...** ne pas avoir subi l'influence de ...; **most of the city centre has remained u.** une grande partie du centre ville est resté intact; **u. by human hand** *(food)* non manié; **these artefacts have lain u. by human hand for thousands of years** ces objets sont restés inconnus de l'homme pendant des milliers d'années

(b) **he'd left the meal u.** il n'avait pas touché à son repas

(c) *(safe) (person)* indemne, sain et sauf; *(thing)* intact

(d) *(unmoved) (person)* indifférent, insensible (**by** à)

(e) *(without equal)* sans égal, incomparable

untoward [ʌntə'wɔːd, *Am* ʌn'tɔːd] *adj* fâcheux; **I hope nothing u. has happened** j'espère qu'il n'est pas arrivé un malheur

untraceable [ʌn'treɪsəb(ə)l] *adj* introuvable

untrad(e)able [ʌn'treɪdəb(ə)l] *adj St Exch* incotable

untrained [ʌn'treɪnd] *adj (person)* qui n'a pas reçu de formation professionnelle; *(horse)* non dressé; **u. ear** oreille *f* inexercée

untrammelled [ʌn'træməld] *adj* non entravé (**by** par), libre (**by** de)

untransferable [ʌntræns'fɜːrəb(ə)l] *adj* non transmissible; *Jur (right, property)* incessible

untranslatable [ʌntræns'leɪtəb(ə)l] *adj* intraduisible

untravelled [ʌn'trævəld] *adj (person)* qui n'a pas beaucoup voyagé; *(country)* inexploré, peu fréquenté; **he's relatively u.** il n'a pas beaucoup voyagé

untried [ʌn'traɪd] *adj* **(a)** (*not tried out*) qui n'a pas été essayé, non essayé **(b)** (*untested*) (*engine, system*) non testé; **u. troops** troupes qui n'ont pas encore combattu **(c)** *Jur* (*prisoner, case*) qui n'a pas encore été jugé
untrodden [ʌn'trɒd(ə)n] *adj esp Lit* (*path*) peu fréquenté; **u. snow** neige immaculée *ou* vierge; *Fig* **democracy remains for them an u. path** ils n'ont jamais goûté à la démocratie
untroubled [ʌn'trʌbəld] *adj* calme, tranquille; **the markets have been u. by the interest rate rise** les marchés n'ont pas été troublés par la hausse des taux d'intérêt; **he seemed u. by the news** la nouvelle ne semblait nullement le troubler
untrue [ʌn'tru:] *adj* **(a)** (*incorrect*) faux, *f* fausse **(b)** (*unfaithful*) (*to wife, principles etc*) infidèle (**to** à); (*to comrades*) déloyal (**to** envers); **to be u. to oneself** trahir ses principes
untrustworthiness [ʌn'trʌstwɜ:ðɪnɪs] *n* (*of information, machine*) manque *m* de fiabilité; **he was noted for his u.** il avait la réputation de quelqu'un à qui on ne peut pas faire confiance
untrustworthy [ʌn'trʌstwɜ:ðɪ] *adj* (*person*) indigne de confiance; (*reference book, information*) peu fiable; (*evidence*) récusable
untruth [ʌn'tru:θ, *pl* -'tru:ðz] *n* mensonge *m*; **to tell an u.** dire un mensonge
untruthful [ʌn'tru:θfʊl] *adj* (*person*) menteur; (*story*) mensonger; **he's an u. boy** c'est un garçon qui ne dit jamais la vérité
untruthfully [ʌn'tru:θfəlɪ] *adv* de façon mensongère
untruthfulness [ʌn'tru:θfʊlnɪs] *n* (*of evidence*) caractère *m* mensonger; **he was notorious for his u.** c'était un menteur notoire
untuned [ʌn'tju:nd] *adj* (*instrument*) non accordé; (*engine*) qui n'est pas réglé
untuneful [ʌn'tju:nfʊl] *adj* peu mélodieux
untutored [ʌn'tju:təd] *adj esp Lit* (*person*) peu instruit; (*mind, taste*) non formé
untwine [ʌn'twaɪn] *vt* détordre, détortiller
untwist [ʌn'twɪst] **1** *vt* (*strands*) détordre, détortiller; (*jar lid etc*) dévisser; **to u. itself, to come untwisted** se détordre **2** *vi* se détordre
untypical [ʌn'tɪpɪk(ə)l] *adj* inhabituel; **it's very u. of her** c'est très inhabituel de sa part, cela ne lui ressemble pas
untypically [ʌn'tɪpɪk(ə)lɪ] *adj* inhabituellement
unusable [ʌn'ju:zəb(ə)l] *adj* inutilisable
unused [ʌn'ju:zd] *adj* **(a)** (*system, clothes etc*) dont on ne se sert pas; (*road*) pas fréquenté; (*talent*) non employé; (*building*) désaffecté; **her talents had gone largely u.** ses talents étaient restés inexploités; **our nuclear weapons are still u.** nos armes nucléaires n'ont encore jamais été utilisées **(b)** (*never yet used*) qui n'a jamais servi; (*clothes*) neuf **(c)** [ʌn'ju:st] (*person*) peu habitué (**to sth** à qch); **to be u. to doing sth** ne pas avoir l'habitude de faire qch; **I'm still u. to you being here** je ne suis pas encore habitué à ce que tu sois là; **we're not u. to it** nous y sommes habitués
unusual [ʌn'ju:ʒʊəl] *adj* (*not common*) (*colour, style, design, thing to happen*) inhabituel, peu ordinaire; (*strange, out of the ordinary*) insolite; **an u. case of …** un cas peu commun *ou* peu ordinaire de …; **an u. lapse** une défaillance inhabituelle; **a very u. exception** une exception très inhabituelle; **what do you think of my new haircut? – well, it's certainly u.!** que penses-tu de ma nouvelle coupe de cheveux? – ah pour ça c'est original!; **he has some rather u. tastes** il a des goûts bizarres; **it's u. for her not to notice these things** c'est rare qu'elle ne remarque pas ces choses-là; **you don't want a drink?, that's u. for you** tu ne veux pas prendre un verre?, qu'est-ce qui t'arrive?; **the sort of information which is u. in most dictionaries** le genre d'information qu'on ne trouve habituellement pas dans les dictionnaires; **it's u. to see him at the theatre** il est rare qu'on le voie au théâtre; **it's not u.** ce n'est pas rare; **nothing u.** rien d'anormal; **of u. interest** d'un intérêt exceptionnel
unusually [ʌn'ju:ʒʊəlɪ] *adv* inhabituellement; (*exceptionally*) exceptionnellement; **u., this language …** chose inhabituelle, cette langue …; **she stayed u. quiet** elle est restée inhabituellement calme; **u. tall** exceptionnellement grand; **an u. stupid/clever man** un homme d'une stupidité/ intelligence exceptionnelle; **it's very u. designed** c'est conçu de manière très insolite *ou* inhabituelle; **he was u. attentive** contrairement à son habitude, il a été attentif
unutterable [ʌn'ʌt(ə)rəb(ə)l] *adj* (*misery, stupidity*) innommable; (*boredom*) incroyable
unutterably [ʌn'ʌt(ə)rəblɪ] *adv* **u. bored/miserable** d'un ennui/dans une misère invraisemblable; **u. stupid** d'une stupidité innommable
unvaried [ʌn'veərɪd] *adj* (*landscape, life*) sans variété; (*diet*) qui manque de variété
unvarnished [ʌn'vɑ:nɪʃt] *adj* (*surface*) non verni; (*pottery*) non vernissé; *Fig* **the plain u. truth** la vérité pure et simple
unvarying [ʌ'veərɪɪŋ] *adj* invariable, constant
unveil [ʌn'veɪl] **1** *vt* (*statue, plaque etc*) inaugurer; (*new car etc*) présenter; *Fig* (*secret, plan*) dévoiler **2** *vi* se dévoiler
unveiled [ʌn'veɪld] *adj* sans voile
unveiling [ʌn'veɪlɪŋ] *n* (*of statue, plaque etc*) inauguration *f*; (*of new car etc*) présentation *f*; **u. ceremony** cérémonie *f* d'inauguration
unverifiable [ʌn'verɪfaɪəb(ə)l] *adj* invérifiable
unverified [ʌn'verɪfaɪd] *adj* non contrôlé, non vérifié
unversed [ʌn'vɜ:st] *adj* peu versé (**in** dans)
unvoiced [ʌn'vɔɪst] *adj* **(a)** (*opinion*) non exprimé **(b)** *Ling* (*vowel, consonant*) sourd, muet
unwaged [ʌn'weɪdʒd] *adj* (*unpaid*) non rémunéré
unwanted [ʌn'wɒntɪd] *adj* non voulu; **u. child** enfant non désiré; **u. hair** poils superflus; **his help had been u.** on n'avait pas voulu de son aide; **to give away all one's u. books** se débarrasser de tous les livres dont on n'a plus besoin; **to be feeling u.** (*in the way*) se sentir de trop; (*unloved*) se sentir mal-aimé
unwarlike [ʌn'wɔ:laɪk] *adj* non belliqueux
unwarrantable [ʌn'wɒrəntəb(ə)l] *adj* injustifiable
unwarrantably [ʌn'wɒrəntəblɪ] *adj* de manière injustifiable
unwarranted [ʌn'wɒrəntɪd] *adj* injustifié; **u. insult** insulte gratuite; **u. familiarity** familiarité indue
unwary [ʌn'weərɪ] **1** *adj* imprudent, imprévoyant; **an u. reader** un lecteur non averti **2** *npl* **the u.** les imprudents *mpl*
unwashed [ʌn'wɒʃt] **1** *adj* non lavé **2** *npl F Hum* **the great u.** les prolétaires *mpl*, les prolos *mpl*
unwavering [ʌn'weɪvərɪŋ] *adj* constant; (*support, loyalty*) absolu; (*belief, conviction*) ferme; (*determination*) inébranlable; (*gaze*) soutenu
unwaveringly [ʌn'weɪvərɪŋlɪ] *adv* (*to support, be in favour of*) résolument; (*to look at sb*) sans faiblir
unweaned [ʌn'wi:nd] *adj* (*child, kitten*) non sevré
unwearable [ʌn'weərəb(ə)l] *adj* (*garment*) immettable
unwearying [ʌn'wɪərɪɪŋ] *adj* inlassable, infatigable
unwed [ʌn'wed] *adj Old-fashioned, Lit* qui n'est pas marié; **he remained u.** il ne s'est jamais marié
unweighted [ʌn'weɪtɪd] *adj Econ* (*index*) non pondéré; **u. figures** chiffres bruts
unwelcome [ʌn'welkəm] *adj* (*visitor*) importun; (*news, development*) fâcheux; **to feel u.** ne pas se sentir le/la bienvenu(e); **u. visits** visites importunes; **a not u. visit** une visite opportune; **her news could not have been more u.** les nouvelles qu'elle avait n'auraient pas pu être plus fâcheuses; **to make sb feel u.** faire sentir à qn qu'il n'est pas le bienvenu/qu'elle n'est pas la bienvenue; **the extra £50 was not u.** les 50 livres supplémentaires ne tombaient pas mal du tout
unwell [ʌn'wel] *adj* souffrant; **are you feeling u.?** êtes-vous souffrant?
unwholesome [ʌn'həʊlsəm] *adj* malsain; **u. demand** (*for products*) demande *f* indésirable
unwieldy [ʌn'wi:ldɪ] *adj* (*tool, object*) peu maniable, difficile à manier; (*method, approach*) trop complexe; (*system, bureaucracy*) lourd; (*person*) lourd et gauche
unwilling [ʌn'wɪlɪŋ] *adj* (*helper*) réticent; (*consent*) donné à contrecœur; **an u. accomplice** un complice malgré moi/lui/ *etc*; **to be u. to do sth** être peu disposé à faire qch, ne pas vouloir faire qch; **I was u. that my wife should know** *or* **for my wife to know** je ne voulais pas que ma femme le sache
unwillingly [ʌn'wɪlɪŋlɪ] *adv* à contrecœur
unwillingness [ʌn'wɪlɪŋnɪs] *n* réticence *f*; **they showed such an u. to accept the terms that …** ils ont été tellement réticents à accepter les conditions que …; **their u. to compromise on this issue made agreement impossible** leur refus du compromis sur ce point rendait tout accord impossible
unwind [ʌn'waɪnd] (*pt, pp* **unwound** [-'waʊnd]) **1** *vt* dérouler; (*ball of wool*) défaire, dérouler **2** *vi* **(a)** (*unroll*) se dérouler; (*of ball of wool*) se défaire, se dérouler **(b)** *F* (*relax*) se détendre, se relaxer
unwise [ʌn'waɪz] *adj* (*person*) peu prudent, peu sage; (*action, investment*) peu judicieux; **that was very u. of you** c'était très imprudent de votre part
unwisely [ʌn'waɪzlɪ] *adv* imprudemment
unwitting [ʌn'wɪtɪŋ] *adj* involontaire; **if I have caused you any u. offence** si je vous ai offensé sans le vouloir
unwittingly [ʌn'wɪtɪŋlɪ] *adv* (*without realizing*) sans le savoir; (*without intending to*) involontairement
unwomanly [ʌn'wʊmənlɪ] *adj* peu féminin
unwonted [ʌn'wəʊntɪd] *adj esp Lit* inaccoutumé
unworkable [ʌn'wɜ:kəb(ə)l] *adj* (*plan*) impraticable
unworldliness [ʌn'wɜ:ldlɪnɪs] *n* détachement *m* de ce monde; (*naivety*) simplicité *f*, candeur *f*

unworldly [ʌnˈwɜːldlɪ] *adj* détaché de ce monde; (*naive*) simple, candide; *esp Lit* (*beauty*) qui n'est pas de ce monde, irréel

unworn [ʌnˈwɔːn] *adj* (*clothes*) non porté; **these shoes look u.** on dirait que ces chaussures n'ont jamais été portées

unworthiness [ʌnˈwɜːðɪnɪs] *n* indignité *f*

unworthy [ʌnˈwɜːðɪ] *adj* indigne (**of sth/sb** de qch/qn); **u. of notice** qui ne mérite pas qu'on y fasse attention; **that's u. of you** c'est indigne de vous

unwounded [ʌnˈwuːndɪd] *adj* indemne; **to be u.** ne pas être blessé

unwrap [ʌnˈræp] *vt* (**-pp-**) (*parcel*) défaire; (*sweet, sandwich*) déballer; **to come unwrapped** (*of parcel*) se défaire

unwritten [ʌnˈrɪt(ə)n] *adj* non écrit; (*tradition*) oral; (*agreement*) verbal; **it's an u. law in this office that ...** dans ce bureau on respecte la convention selon laquelle ...; **he had broken one of the u. laws of the gang** il n'avait pas respecté l'une des conventions du gang

unyielding [ʌnˈjiːldɪŋ] *adj* (*material, surface*) qui ne cède pas, résistant; (*frozen ground*) dur; (*person, determination*) inébranlable, ferme; **u. grip** prise *f* de fer

unyoke [ʌnˈjəʊk] *vt* dételer, découpler

unzip [ʌnˈzɪp] (**-pp-**) **1** *vt* descendre la fermeture éclair® de; **will you u. me?** tu veux bien descendre *ou* défaire ma fermeture éclair? **2** *vi* (*of garment*) **it unzips at the side** ça s'ouvre sur le côté

UP [juːˈpiː] *n Com* (*abbr* **unit price**) PU *m*

up¹ [ʌp] (*NOTE: when* **up** *is an integral part of a verb eg.* **come up, go up, get up, take up,** *the user should consult the verb in question*) **1** *adv* **(a)** (*at the top*) en haut; (*to the top*) vers le haut; **all the way up, the whole way up, right up (to the top)** (*of stairs, hill*) jusqu'en haut; **half way up** jusqu'à mi-hauteur; **to live three flights up** habiter *Br* au troisième *ou Am* au quatrième (étage); **to throw sth up in the air** jeter qch en l'air; **to put one's hand up** lever la main; **hands up!** haut les mains!; **what are you doing up there?** qu'est-ce que tu fais là-haut?; **up above** en haut; **up above sth** au-dessus de qch; **before the sun was up** avant le lever du soleil; **would you like the window up a bit?** (*in car*) veux-tu que je remonte un peu la vitre?; **Comet with Thomas up** (*in horseracing*) Comet monté par Thomas; **the river's up** la rivière est en crue; **to lay sth face up** mettre qch à l'endroit; **this side up** (*on packing case*) haut, dessus; **put it the other way up** retournez-le; **he's something quite high up in the civil service** il est haut placé dans l'administration; **to be up in arms** être en révolte; **up with ...!** (*supporting*) vive ...!

(b) (*when travelling etc*) **to walk up and down** se promener de long en large; **to go up north** aller dans le nord; **to go up to London for the day** aller passer la journée à Londres; *Univ* **he's going up to Oxford** il va faire ses études à l'université d'Oxford; **up in London** à Londres; **up in Yorkshire** au nord dans le Yorkshire; *Univ* **up at Oxford** à l'université d'Oxford; **to come up before the judge** être cité devant les magistrats

(c) (*and above*) **from £10 up** à partir de 10 livres; **suitable to children aged seven and up** convient aux enfants âgés de sept ans et plus; **all ranks from sergeant up** tous les rangs à partir de celui de sergent

(d) (*on display, finished*) **to put up the results** afficher les résultats; **are the results up yet?** les résultats sont-ils déjà affichés?; **there's a big notice up at the station saying ...** il y a un grand panneau à la gare disant ...; **our curtains still aren't up** nous n'avons toujours pas accroché nos rideaux; **the new building is up** le nouveau bâtiment est terminé; **when the tent's up** quand la tente sera montée

(e) (*for repair etc*) **this road's always up** cette route est toujours en réparation; **careful, we've got some of the floorboards up** attention au plancher, il manque des lattes; **when we've got the carpet up ...** quand nous aurons enlevé la moquette ...

(f) (*higher*) **prices are 10% up on last year's** les prix ont augmenté de dix pour cent depuis l'année dernière; **bread is up again** le pain a encore augmenté; **the temperature is going up** la température monte; **business is looking up** les affaires sont à la hausse

(g) (*ahead*) *Sp* **to be one goal up** mener par un but; *Golf* **to be one hole up** avoir un trou d'avance; **to be one up on sb** (*in point, score*) avoir un point d'avance sur qn; *Fig* (*have advantage*) avoir l'avantage sur qn; **his blood was up** le sang lui bouillait; **speak up!** parlez plus fort!

(h) (*knowledgeable*) **to be well up in a subject** connaître un sujet à fond; **how well up are you in German?** tu t'y connais en allemand?

(i) (*with proximity*) **lean it up against the wall** appuyez-le contre le mur; **they were standing close up to each other** ils se tenaient tout près l'un de l'autre; **to be up against difficulties** se heurter à des difficultés; *Fig F* **to be up against it** être dans le pétrin

(j) (*out of bed*) debout, levé; **to be up late** veiller tard; **to be up all night** ne pas se coucher de la nuit; **isn't he up yet!** il n'est pas encore levé *ou* debout!; **I was up late this morning** je me suis levé tard ce matin; **he's always up and about by seven** il est toujours debout à sept heures; **to be up and about again** (*after illness*) être de nouveau sur pied

(k) *F* (*wrong*) **what's up?** qu'est-ce qui se passe?, qu'y a-t-il?; **what's up with you/him?** qu'est-ce qui te/lui prend?; **something's up** il y a quelque chose qui ne va pas; **there's something up with him** il y a quelque chose qui ne va pas chez lui

(l) (*finished*) **time is up** il est l'heure; **your time's up** c'est fini; **his time is up** (*of prisoner*) il a purgé sa peine; **his leave is up** sa permission est expirée; *F* **the game's up** (*we've been found out*) nous sommes faits; (*I've found you out*) vous êtes faits; *F* **I thought it was all up with me** j'ai cru que ma dernière heure était arrivée; *F* **it's all up with him** c'en est fait de lui, il a son compte

(m) up to (*as far as*) jusqu'à; **to go up to sb** s'approcher de qn; **covered in mud up to the ears** couvert de boue jusqu'aux oreilles; **what page** *or* **where are you up to?** où en es-tu *ou* à quelle page en es-tu?; **we're up to page 50** nous en sommes à la page 50; **up to now, up to here** jusqu'ici; **up to then** jusqu'alors, jusque-là; **up to £100 a week** jusqu'à 100 livres par semaine; **up to what age?** jusqu'à quel âge?

(n) up to (*good enough for*) **to be up to one's job** être à la hauteur de sa tâche; **he's not up to it** il n'est pas capable de le faire; **he's not up to the journey** il n'est pas à même de faire le voyage; **I don't feel up to it** je ne m'en sens pas le courage; **I don't feel up to much** je ne me sens pas bien; **it's not up to much** ça ne vaut pas grand-chose

(o) up to (*doing, esp Pej*) **he's up to something** il mijote quelque chose; **what are the children up to?** que font les enfants?; **hey you, what do you think you're up to?** eh vous là-bas, qu'est-ce que vous fabriquez?; **what's that guy over there up to?** qu'est-ce qu'il fabrique, ce type là-bas?; **what's he up to with that ladder?** qu'est-ce qu'il a l'intention de faire *ou* qu'est-ce qu'il fabrique avec cette échelle?; **what are you up to with my girlfriend?** qu'est-ce que tu lui veux à ma copine?

(p) (*to be decided by*) **what shall I do? – that's up to you** qu'est-ce que je fais? – c'est à toi de décider; **it's entirely up to you whether you go or not** il ne tient qu'à toi de rester ou de partir

(q) (*be the responsibility of*) **it's up to him to do it** c'est à lui de le faire; **it's up to you to tell her** c'est à toi de lui dire

(r) (*phrases*) **to be up and coming** (*person, team etc*) être plein d'avenir, promettre; **to be up and running** (*of new machine etc*) être en service; (*of project*) être en route; **to get sth up and running** (*new machine*) mettre qch en service; (*project*) mettre qch en route

2 *prep* **to go up the stairs** monter l'escalier; **to climb up a hill** monter *ou* grimper une colline; **to go up the street** remonter la rue; **further up the street** plus loin dans la rue; **they live further up the street** ils habitent plus loin *ou* plus haut dans cette rue; **the smoke went up my nose** la fumée m'est montée par le nez; **the gas goes up this pipe** le gaz monte par ce tuyau; **the cat is up a tree** le chat est (perché) sur un arbre; **the cat went up a tree** le chat a grimpé à un arbre; **it's up river from here** c'est en amont d'ici; **to walk up and down the platform** aller et venir sur le quai; (*nervously etc*) arpenter le quai; **he lives up your way** il habite par chez vous *ou* du côté de chez vous; *Br F* **he's up the pub** il est au pub; *Br F* **I'm going up the shops** je vais faire un tour en courses; *Vulg* **up yours!** va te faire enculer!

3 *adj Comptr* **up arrow** flèche *f* vers le haut; **up arrow key** touche *f* flèche vers le haut; **up escalator** escalator® *m* qui monte; **he ran down the up side** il est descendu en courant du côté où l'on est censé monter; *Rail* **up line** voie *f* en direction d'une grande gare; **up train** train *m* qui va dans une grande gare

4 *n* **(a) ups and downs** (*of life*) hauts et bas *mpl*, vicissitudes *fpl*; (*in politics*) avatars *mpl*; *Com* (*of market*) oscillations *fpl*; (*of terrain*) ondulations *fpl*; **life is full of ups and downs** la vie est faite de hauts et de bas

(b) *F* **to be on the up and up** (*be honest*) être clair *ou* fiable; *Br* (*be improving*) être en train de monter *ou* de faire son chemin

up² (**-pp-**) **1** *vt* **(a)** *F* (*prices etc*) augmenter; **to up the stakes** (*at cards etc*), *Fig* monter la mise; **to up sticks** plier bagages; **he just upped sticks and left** il a plié bagages et est parti (**b**) (*swans*) recenser **2** *vi F* **to u. and leave** *or* **go** partir; **they upped and went** ils sont partis très soudainement; **one day he just upped and left her** un beau jour il l'a quittée sans crier gare; **he just upped and hit him** tout à coup il (s'est levé et) l'a frappé

up-and-coming *adj* (*person, economy, team*) qui est plein d'avenir, prometteur; (*town*) plein d'avenir

up-and-down *adj* **u. movement** mouvement *m* de haut en bas

up-and-over *adj* **u. door** (*of garage etc*) porte *f* basculante

up-and-under *n Rugby* up and under *m*

upbeat ['ʌpbiːt] **1** *n Mus* levé *m* **2** *adj F* (*optimistic, cheerful*) optimiste

upbraid [ʌp'breɪd] *vt* faire des reproches à, réprimander

upbringing ['ʌpbrɪŋɪŋ] *n* éducation *f*; **what sort of (an) u. has she had?** comment a-t-elle été élevée?, quelle éducation a-t-elle eu?

up-change *n* (*of gears*) passage *m* à la vitesse supérieure

upchuck ['ʌptʃʌk] *vti US F* (*vomit*) rendre

upcoming ['ʌpkʌmɪŋ] *adj Am* prochain

upcountry [ʌp'kʌntrɪ] *esp Am, Austr* **1** *n* intérieur *m* (du pays) **2** *adj* de l'intérieur (du pays) **3** *adv* **to go u.** aller vers l'intérieur

update[1] ['ʌpdeɪt] *n* mise *f* à jour; *Comptr* (*of software package*) mise *f* à jour, actualisation *f*; **to give sb an u. on sth** mettre qn au courant de qch; **a dictionary should have an u. at least every 5 years** un dictionnaire devrait être remis à jour au minimum tous les 5 ans

update[2] [ʌp'deɪt] *vt* (*file, record*) mettre à jour, actualiser; (*equipment etc*) moderniser; (*person*) mettre au courant; **could you u. me on what's been happening?** pourriez-vous me mettre au courant de ce qui s'est passé?; **it needs regular updating** une remise à jour régulière est nécessaire; **it hasn't been updated since 1933** il n'a pas été remis à jour depuis 1933

updating [ʌp'deɪtɪŋ] *n* mise *f* à jour

up-draught, *US* **up-draft** *n Av* courant d'air ascendant

upend [ʌp'end] *vt* (*thing*) mettre debout; **to u. sb** (*turn upside down*) mettre qn les pieds en l'air, mettre qn à l'envers

up-front **1** *adj* (**a**) *F* (*honest, frank*) franc, *f* franche, direct (**about sth** à propos de qch) (**b**) (*payment*) à l'avance **2** *adv* (*to be paid etc*) à l'avance; **to ask for some of the cash u.** demander une avance

upgrade[1] ['ʌpgreɪd] *n* (**a**) *Am* (*slope*) pente *f* ascendante; (*of railway line*) montée *f* (**b**) *Am* **to be on the u.** (*of prices*) monter; (*of business*) reprendre, se relever; (*of invalid*) être en voie de guérison (**c**) *Comptr* (*of system*) augmentation *f* de puissance; (*for software*) mise *f* à jour, actualisation *f*; (*for hardware*) (*expansion*) extension *f*; (*new model, processor etc*) nouvelle version *f*; **u. kit** kit *m* d'évolution *ou* d'extension

upgrade[2] [ʌp'greɪd] **1** *vt* (**a**) (*improve*) (*product*) améliorer; (*of user*) (*software*) se procurer la dernière version de; (*hardware*) (*expand*) ajouter une/des extension(s) à; (*buy new and better*) remplacer par une/des nouvelle(s) version(s); (*memory*) augmenter (**b**) (*raise to higher rank*) nommer à un niveau supérieur, surclasser; (*civil servant*) monter en grade **2** *vi* (*expand computer system*) ajouter une/des extension(s); (*buy newer and better model*) acquérir une/des nouvelle(s) version(s); **we've decided to u. to the GT model** nous avons décidé de passer à un modèle supérieur et d'acheter le GT

upgrad(e)ability [ʌpgreɪdə'bɪlɪtɪ] *n* possibilités *fpl* d'extension

upgrad(e)able [ʌp'greɪdəb(ə)l] *adj Comptr* (*system*) évolutif; (*memory*) extensible; **u. architecture** architecture *f* évolutive

upgrading [ʌp'greɪdɪŋ] *n* (**a**) (*of system*) amélioration *f*; *Comptr* (*expansion*) ajout *m* d'une/de plusieurs extension(s) (**of** à); (*replacement by newer and better*) acquisition *f* d'une/de nouvelle(s) version(s); (*of memory*) extension *f* (**b**) (*of person*) avancement *m*; **the u. of the polytechnic to university status** le reclassement de l'IUT au rang d'université

upheaval [ʌp'hiːv(ə)l] *n* bouleversement *m*; **political u.** agitation *f* politique; **an emotional u.** un bouleversement affectif; **moving house is such an u.** déménager est un tel bouleversement *ou* chamboulement; **the u. of moving office** le tumulte qu'entraîne un déménagement dans d'autres bureaux

uphill ['ʌphɪl] **1** *adj* (*road*) qui monte; (*struggle*) pénible, difficile; **it's u. all the way** ça monte tout le long du chemin; *Fig* c'est une lutte permanente; **u. ski** ski *m* amont **2** *adv* **to go u.** monter; **it's a good way u. from here** il faut monter pas mal pour y arriver; **to ski u.** skier en amont

uphold [ʌp'həʊld] *vt* (*pt, pp* **upheld** [-'held]) soutenir; (*opinion, principle*) défendre; *Jur* (*decision*) confirmer; **to u. the law** faire observer la loi

upholder [ʌp'həʊldər] *n* (*of cause*) défenseur *m*

upholster [ʌp'həʊlstər] *vt* (*pad*) capitonner, rembourrer; (*cover*) (*sofa etc*) tapisser, garnir (**with, in** de)

upholstered [ʌp'həʊlstəd] *adj* (*padded*) capitonné, rembourré; (*covered*) (*sofa*) tapissé, garni; **u. in velvet/leather** garni de velours/cuir; *F* **she's well u.** elle est bien rembourrée

upholsterer [ʌp'həʊlstərər] *n* tapissier *m* en ameublement

upholstery [ʌp'həʊlstərɪ] *n* (**a**) (*padding*) (*of armchair etc*) capitonnage *m*, rembourrage *m*; (*covering*) garniture *f*; (*in car*) garniture intérieure; **leather u.** garniture en cuir (**b**) (*trade*) tapisserie *f* d'ameublement

upkeep ['ʌpkiːp] *n* (*of house, building, horse*) entretien *m*; **he paid nothing towards the u. of the children** il ne donnait pas d'argent pour subvenir aux besoins matériels des enfants

upland ['ʌplənd] **1** *n* (*usu pl*) **the uplands** le haut pays, les hauteurs *fpl* **2** *adj* (*village*) de montagne

uplift[1] ['ʌplɪft] *n* (**moral**) **u.** inspiration *f* (morale); **u. bra** soutien-gorge *m* de maintien

uplift[2] [ʌp'lɪft] *vt* (**a**) (*soul, heart*) élever (**b**) *Scot* (*collect*) récupérer

uplifted [ʌp'lɪftɪd] *adj* (**a**) (*of hand*) levé (**b**) (*morally, spiritually*) élevé (**by sth** par qch)

uplifting [ʌp'lɪftɪŋ] *adj* (*experience, sermon etc*) édifiant

uplighter ['ʌplaɪtər] *n* lampe *f* halogène; (*on wall*) applique *f* murale

uplink receiver ['ʌplɪŋk] *n* récepteur *m* de liaison terre/satellite

up-market **1** *adj* (*product*) haut de gamme; (*district, person, accent*) bourgeois **2** *adv* **to go u.** (*of company*) se mettre à faire du haut de gamme; (*of person*) prendre des goûts de luxe

upmost ['ʌpməʊst] *adj* = **uppermost 1**

upon [ə'pɒn] *prep* [①A67] sur; **on** *and* **upon** *are interchangeable in meaning; in modern English* **upon** *is used more formally; in certain phrases, however,* **upon** *is preferable*; **u. my word!** ma parole!; **the enemy was u. us** l'ennemi nous attaquait; **I came u. it by accident** je l'ai trouvé par hasard; **you brought it u. yourself** ne t'en prends qu'à toi-même!

upper ['ʌpər] **1** *adj* (**a**) (*part, storey, deck, branch etc*) supérieur; *Anat* **u. arm** bras *m*; **the u. atmosphere** les couches supérieures de l'atmosphère; **u. jaw/lip** mâchoire/lèvre supérieure; **temperature in the u. twenties** température qui dépasse 25 degrés; **u. ASCII** ASCII *m* supérieur; *Th* **u. circle** deuxième balcon *m*; **u. limit** limite *f* maximale

(**b**) **u. reaches** (*of river*) amont *m*; **the u. Rhine** le haut Rhin

(**c**) **the u. end of the table** le bout de la table; **the u. echelons of the civil service** les plus hauts échelons de l'administration; **the u. classes** la haute société; **the u. middle classes** la haute bourgeoisie; **to gain the u. hand** prendre le dessus; **to let sb get the u. hand** laisser qn prendre le dessus, laisser qn dominer

(**d**) *Mus* (*keyboard*) du côté droit; (*register*) aigu, -uë

2 *n* (**a**) (*of shoe*) empeigne *f*; *F* **to be down on one's uppers** être dans la gêne

(**b**) *Sl* (*drug*) amphétamine *f*, amphé *f*

Upper Canada *n* le haut Canada

upper-case *adj Typ* (*letters*) majuscule

upper-class *adj* (*accent, person*) aristocratique; **to be very u.** être très aristocrate; **u. twit** = stéréotype *m* de l'aristocrate bête et exaspérant

upper crust *n F* (*of society*) la haute, le dessus du panier, la crème

upper-crust *adj F* (*accent, person*) aristo, de la haute; **they're frightfully u.** ils sont très aristos

upper-cut *n Boxing* uppercut *m*

Upper Egypt *n* la Haute-Égypte

Upper House *n Parl* Chambre *f* haute

uppermost ['ʌpəməʊst] **1** *adj* (**a**) (*in position*) le plus haut, le plus élevé (**b**) (*in importance*) de la plus grande importance; **to be u.** tenir le premier rang; **the problem (which is) u. in our minds** le problème qui nous préoccupe au premier chef **2** *adv* en dessus

upper school *n Sch* grandes classes *fpl*

upper sixth *n Br Sch* ≈ terminale *f*

upping ['ʌpɪŋ] *n* **swan u.** recensement *m* des cygnes

uppity ['ʌpɪtɪ], **uppish** ['ʌpɪʃ] *adj F* présomptueux, arrogant; **he's getting very u.** il se croit quelqu'un; **don't you get u. with me!** ne joue pas les arrogants avec moi!

upright ['ʌpraɪt] **1** *adj* (**a**) (*line*) vertical; (*wall, writing*) droit; **u. piano** piano *m* droit; **u. freezer** congélateur *m* armoire (**b**) (*honest*) droit, honnête **2** *adv* debout; **to stand u.** se tenir droit; **sitting u. on his chair** assis droit sur sa chaise; **to put** *or* **stand sth u.** mettre qch debout *ou* d'aplomb **3** *n* **(a)** (*of door, ladder etc*) montant *m*; *Fb* **the uprights** les montants de but **(b)** (*piano*) piano *m* droit

uprightly ['ʌpraɪtlɪ] *adv* droitement, honnêtement

uprightness ['ʌpraɪtnɪs] *n* droiture *f*, honnêteté *f*

uprising [ʌp'raɪzɪŋ] *n* soulèvement *m*, insurrection *f*

uproar ['ʌprɔːr] *n* (*noise*) tapage *m*, vacarme *m*; (*protest*) tollé *m*; **the meeting finished in (an) u.** la réunion s'est terminée dans la confusion; **his suggestion caused an u.** (*shouting, protests*) sa suggestion a provoqué un tollé; **the recent u. in the press about …** la tempête qui a récemment éclaté dans la presse au sujet de …

uproarious [ʌp'rɔːrɪəs] *adj* (*noisy*) tumultueux; (*hilarious*) hilarant; **u. laughter** grands éclats de rire

uproariously [ʌp'rɔːrɪəslɪ] *adv* **to laugh u.** rire à gorge déployée; **u. funny** désopilant

uproot [ʌp'ruːt] *vt* (*plant, evil*) déraciner, extirper; **to u. sb from his home** déraciner qn; **to feel uprooted** se sentir déraciné

UPS [juːpiː'es] *n Comptr* (*abbr* **uninterruptible power supply**) onduleur *m*

upsadaisy ['ʌpsədeɪzɪ] *int F* hop là!

upset[1] ['ʌpset] *n* **(a)** (*disturbance*), *Fig* bouleversement *m*; **the bad news caused quite an u.** les mauvaises nouvelles ont provoqué une grande consternation; **with the fewest possible number of upsets to our plans** avec le moins de bouleversements possibles dans nos projets; **he can't stand upsets in his routine** il ne supporte pas que sa routine soit dérangée; **have you had an u. with her?** (*difficulty, argument etc*) est-ce que tu t'es disputé *ou* as eu un problème avec elle?; **losing 25-3 was something of an u.** se faire battre 25 à 3 a été une sacrée déception; **after the u. at the last match** après la déception du dernier match; **that's going to cause a bit of an u.** cela va faire du bruit

(b) to have a stomach u. avoir une grippe intestinale

upset[2] [ʌp'set] *vt* (*pt, pp* **upset**; *prp* **upsetting**) **(a)** (*knock over, spill*) renverser; (*boat*) (faire) chavirer **(b)** (*plans, schedule, calculations etc*) bouleverser, déranger **(c)** (*emotionally*) (*person*) faire de la peine à, blesser; (*of sight, news, death*) bouleverser; **don't mention that!, you'll u. her again** ne parle pas de ça!, tu vas encore la contrarier; **the least thing upsets him** il est très impressionnable; **don't u. yourself** arrête, tu te fais du mal **(d)** (*stomach*) déranger; (*digestion*) troubler

upset[3] (*before noun* ['ʌpset], *otherwise* [ʌp'set]) *adj* **(a)** (*sad*) triste; (*annoyed*) fâché, ennuyé; (*offended*) vexé, blessé; **she's u. because you called her a …** elle est vexée parce que tu l'as traitée de …; **what are you so u. about?** qu'est-ce qui te met dans cet état?; **are you still u. or are we friends again?** est-ce que tu es toujours fâché ou sommes-nous amis à nouveau?; **we'd be very u. if we missed the deadline** nous serions très ennuyés si nous dépassions l'échéance; **you'd be u. too if you'd just paid …** tu serais aussi fâché que moi si tu venais juste de payer …; **I'm u. about losing it/her** ça me fait mal au cœur de le/la perdre; **she was clearly u. by the pictures** (*distraught, moved*) ces images l'avaient manifestement perturbée; **we're u. about losing the order** ça nous contrarie de perdre cette commande; **I'd be very u. if you didn't come** je serais très triste si tu ne venais pas; **he was so u. he couldn't speak** il était tellement bouleversé qu'il n'arrivait pas à parler; **come on now, there's nothing to be u. about** allons, il n'y a pas de quoi en faire un drame; **don't be** *or* **get u.** ne t'en fais pas

(b) (*stomach*) dérangé

(c) u. price (*at auctions*) mise *f* à prix

upsetting [ʌp'setɪŋ] *adj* (*saddening*) attristant, affligeant; (*annoying*) contrariant, fâcheux; (*offending*) vexant, blessant; (*disturbing*) troublant; (*more seriously*) bouleversant; **I didn't find the experience in the least u.** l'expérience ne m'a pas du tout perturbé; **viewers might find some of these scenes u.** certaines des scènes qui vont suivre peuvent être de nature à perturber les téléspectateurs

upshift ['ʌpʃɪft] *n* (*of gears*) passage *m* à la vitesse supérieure

upshot ['ʌpʃɒt] *n* résultat *m*; **what will be the u. of it?** cela finira comment?; **the u. of it all was that he resigned** le résultat, c'est qu'il a donné sa démission

upside down ['ʌpsaɪd] **1** *adv* **(a)** à l'envers; (*person, animal*) la tête en bas; **to hold sth u.** tenir qch à l'envers; **to turn u.** se retourner **(b)** (*in disorder*) en désordre; **to turn everything u.** tout bouleverser, tout mettre sens dessus dessous **2** *adj* **u.** renversé; **pineapple u. cake** gâteau *m* renversé à l'ananas

upside risk *n St Exch* risque *f* de hausse

upstage[1] [ʌp'steɪdʒ] *Th* **1** *adj* de l'arrière-scène **2** *adv* à l'arrière-scène

upstage[2] *vt* (*person*) éclipser

upstairs ['ʌpsteəz] **1** *adv* en haut; **he's u.** il est en haut; **she has a second living room u.** elle a un deuxième salon en haut *ou* à l'étage; **they live u. from us** ils habitent au-dessus de chez nous; **I'll take your things u.** je vais monter tes affaires; **to come/go u.** venir/monter à l'étage *ou* en haut; **he chased me u.** il m'a poursuivi dans les escaliers; *Fig F* **to kick sb u.** donner de l'avancement à qn pour s'en débarrasser; *F* **he hasn't got much u.** (*is not very clever*) il n'a pas grand-chose dans le crâne

2 *adj* (*room*) d'en haut, du haut; **our u. neighbours** nos voisins du dessus; **we have an u. sitting room** nous avons un salon à l'étage

3 *n* **(the) u.** les pièces *fpl* d'en haut; **the house has no u.** la maison n'a pas d'étage

upstanding [ʌp'stændɪŋ] *adj* **(a)** (*erect*) droit, qui se tient bien; **a fine u. young man** un jeune homme bien comme il faut **(b)** (*honest*) honnête **(c)** *Fml* **please be u. for the toast** veuillez vous lever pour porter le toast

upstart ['ʌpstɑːt] *n* parvenu, -ue

upstate ['ʌpsteɪt] *US* **1** *adj* du nord; **u. New York** la partie nord de l'État de New York **2** *adv* (*to go*) vers le nord

upstream ['ʌpstriːm] **1** *adv* **(a)** (*to be*) en amont **(from** de**)** **(b)** (*to row etc*) en remontant le courant, à contre-fil de l'eau; **the salmon swims u.** le saumon remonte la rivière **2** *adj* d'amont

upstroke ['ʌpstrəʊk] *n* (*in writing*) délié *m*; (*of piston*) course *f* montante *ou* ascendante

upsurge ['ʌpsɜːdʒ] *n* (*of enthusiasm, hatred*) vague *f*; (*of activity, interest*) regain *m*; (*of inflation*) montée *f* soudaine

upswept ['ʌpswept] *adj Aut, Av* profilé; **u. hair(style)** coiffure *f* en hauteur

upswing ['ʌpswɪŋ] *n* **(a)** (*movement*) mouvement *m* ascendant **(b)** (*improvement*) amélioration *f* sensible; **business is on the u.** les affaires sont en train de redémarrer; **the economy is on the u.** il y a un redressement de l'économie

uptake ['ʌpteɪk] *n* **(a)** *F* (*understanding*) **to be quick on the u.** avoir l'esprit vif; **he's a bit slow on the u.** il est un peu lent à comprendre *ou* à la détente **(b)** (*taking up*), *Biol* assimilation *f*; *Admin* **the u. of benefits** la proportion des gens qui font valoir leurs droits aux allocations

uptight [ʌp'taɪt] *adj F* **(a)** (*nervous*) nerveux, tendu; **he's u. about the exams/about meeting them** il est nerveux *ou* tendu à cause des examens/à l'idée de les rencontrer **(b)** (*inhibited*) coincé; (*on particular occasion*) crispé, mal à l'aise; **don't be so u., everyone else is enjoying themselves** ne sois pas aussi crispé, tout le monde s'amuse **(c)** (*conventional*) (*parents, attitude*) dur, strict

up-to-date *adj* (*very recent*) récent; (*method, equipment, technology*) moderne, sophistiqué; (*person*) qui est dans le vent *ou* à la mode; (*information, views*) à jour; **to keep one's files/accounts u.** tenir ses fichiers/comptes à jour; **to bring sb u. on sth** mettre qn à jour sur qch; **to get the figures u.** mettre les chiffres à jour

up-to-the-minute *adj* (*news, information*) de dernière minute; (*style*) dernier cri *inv*

uptown ['ʌp'taʊn] *esp US* **1** *adv* dans les quartiers résidentiels de la ville **2** *n* les quartiers *mpl* résidentiels; **u. society** les milieux chics

upturn[1] ['ʌptɜːn] *n* amélioration *f*; (*in business, economy*) redressement *m*, reprise *f*

upturn[2] [ʌp'tɜːn] *vt* renverser

upturned ['ʌptɜːnd] *adj* **(a)** (*upside down*) (*boat, bowl*) renversé **(b)** (*nose*) retroussé; **he gazed down at her u. face** il contemplait son visage, qu'elle tenait levé vers lui

upward ['ʌpwəd] **1** *adj* montant, ascendant; **u. mobility** (*in society*) mobilité *f* sociale vers le haut; **u. movement** (*of piston*) mouvement *m* ascensionnel; **their u. progress was halted by …** leur ascension fut stoppée par …; **u. slope** pente *f* ascendante; **u. tendency** *or* **movement** (*of prices etc*) tendance *f* à la hausse, mouvement de hausse; **u. trend** tendance ascensionnelle **2** *adv* = **upwards**

upwardly ['ʌpwədlɪ] *adv* **to be u. mobile** (*in society*) avoir la possibilité de s'élever dans la société; **the u. mobile** = les gens qui montent dans l'échelle sociale

upwards ['ʌpwədz] *adv* (*to move, climb etc*) vers le haut; **to look u.** regarder en haut; **to put sth face u. on the table** mettre qch à l'endroit sur la table; **lying face u.** (*person*) couché sur le dos; **from £100 u.** à partir de 100 livres; **it costs u. of £100** ça coûte plus de 100 livres; **u. of 500 pupils** plus de 500 élèves; **children from ten (years) u.** des enfants à partir de dix ans; *Comptr* **u. compatible** compatible avec les versions suivantes, compatible vers le haut

upwind ['ʌpwɪnd] *adv* (*to sail*) contre le vent; (*to be*) contre le vent, au vent; **to be u. of an animal** être au vent d'un animal

Ural [ˈjʊərəl] *n* **the U. (river)** l'Oural *m*; **the U. mountains, the Urals** les monts Ourals, l'Oural
uranium [jʊˈreɪnɪəm] *n Ch* uranium *m*
Uranus [jʊˈreɪnəs, ˈjʊrənəs] *n Astron* Uranus *f*; *Myth* Uranus *m*
urban [ˈɜːbən] *adj* urbain; **u. areas** agglomérations *fpl* urbaines; **u. clearway** rue *f* à stationnement interdit (en ville); *Aut* **u. cycle** cycle *m* urbain; **u. decay** délabrement *m* des villes; **u. expressway** voie *f* rapide urbaine; **u. fuel consumption** consommation *f* en ville; **u. guerilla** guerilla *f* des villes; **u. legend** *or* **myth** légende *f*, faux fait *m* divers; **u. planner** urbaniste *mf*; **u. poster advertising** affichage *m* urbain; **u. renewal** rénovations *fpl* urbaines; **u. sprawl** ville *f* tentaculaire; **the u. sprawl of the London suburbs** la banlieue de Londres interminable
urbane [ɜːˈbeɪn] *adj* (*person*) courtois, d'une politesse raffinée; (*wit, joke*) raffiné
urbanely [ɜːˈbeɪnlɪ] *adv* courtoisement, avec urbanité
urbanism [ˈɜːbənɪz(ə)m] *n* urbanisme *m*
urbanite [ˈɜːbənaɪt] *n esp Am* citadin, -ine
urbanity [ɜːˈbænɪtɪ] *n* urbanité *f*, courtoisie *f*
urbanization [ɜːbənaɪˈzeɪʃən] *n* urbanisation *f*
urbanize [ˈɜːbənaɪz] *vt* urbaniser
urchin [ˈɜːtʃɪn] *n* **(street) u.** galopin *m*; *esp Hum* (*child*) gamin, -ine
Urdu [ˈʊəduː] *n Ling* ourdou *m*
urea [jʊˈriːə] *n Ch* urée *f*
ureter [jʊˈriːtər] *n Anat* uretère *m*
urethra [jʊˈriːθrə] *n Anat* urètre *m*
urge[1] [ɜːdʒ] *n* (*desire*) envie *f*; *Psy* pulsion *f*; **to have an irresistible u. to do sth** avoir une envie irrésistible de faire qch; **to have a powerful u. to succeed** avoir très envie de réussir; **he's lost the u. to win** il a perdu l'envie *ou* la rage de gagner; **I had an u. to hit him** j'ai eu envie de le frapper; **I'll let you know if I ever get the u.** je te le dirai si j'en ai envie *ou* si ça me chante; *F* **when I get the u.** quand j'ai envie; *F* **the bottle's there, help yourself if you get the u.** la bouteille est là, servez-vous si ça vous dit
urge[2] *vt* **(a)** (*try to persuade*) **to u. sb to do sth** conseiller vivement à qn de faire; **he urged me not to do it** il m'a vivement conseillé de ne pas le faire; **I urged him to accept** je lui ai vivement conseillé d'accepter; **they urged us to give up, but in vain** ils ont insisté pour que nous abandonnions, mais en vain
(b) (*recommend earnestly*) **to u. caution** recommander *ou* conseiller la prudence; **to u. peace on the nations of the world** exhorter les nations du monde à la paix; **to u. that sth be done** recommander *ou* conseiller de faire qch
(c) (*goad, encourage etc*) **to u. a horse forward** pousser un cheval; **he urged his men into battle** il poussa ses hommes dans la bataille
▶ **urge on** *vtsep* (*person, team, runner*) encourager; (*horse*) pousser; **to u. sb on to do sth** pousser qn à faire qch
urgency [ˈɜːdʒənsɪ] *n* urgence *f*; **it's a matter of u.** il y a urgence, c'est urgent; **could you do this as a matter of the utmost u.?** pourriez-vous faire ceci de toute urgence?; **there was a note of u. in her voice** il y avait quelque chose de pressant dans sa voix; **what's all the u.?** qu'y a-t-il de si urgent?; **there's no u.** ce n'est pas urgent, il n'y a pas urgence; **he shows no sense of u.** il ne se presse pas
urgent [ˈɜːdʒənt] *adj* (*need, case, delivery*) urgent; (*meeting, treatment, solution, tone*) d'urgence; **to be in u. need of sth** avoir un besoin pressant de qch; **I was in u. need of a drink** il me fallait absolument quelque chose à boire; **the matter is u.** c'est urgent; **this is u.** c'est une urgence, c'est urgent; **just how u. is it?** mais est-ce vraiment urgent?; **just how u. is it that you should be there tomorrow?** qu'y a-t-il de si urgent qui exige que tu y sois demain?; **the doctor had an u. call** le médecin a été appelé d'urgence; *Fml* **at their u. request** sur leurs instances pressantes
urgently [ˈɜːdʒəntlɪ] *adv* d'urgence; **a doctor is u. required** on demande un médecin d'urgence; **to press u. for sth** réclamer qch de façon urgente *ou* instamment; **they u. called a meeting** ils ont convoqué une réunion d'urgence
uric [ˈjʊərɪk] *adj* (*acid*) urique
urinal [ˈjʊərɪn(ə)l, juːˈraɪn(ə)l] *n* urinoir *m*; **the urinals** l'urinoir
urinary [ˈjʊərɪnərɪ] *adj Anat* urinaire; **u. tract infection** infection *f* urinaire
urinate [ˈjʊərɪneɪt] *vi* uriner
urine [ˈjʊərɪn] *n* urine *f*; *Med* urines *fpl*; **u. sample** échantillon *m* d'urine
urn [ɜːn] *n* urne *f*; **(tea) u.** fontaine *f* à thé
urogenital [jʊərəʊˈdʒenɪt(ə)l] *adj Anat* urogénital
urological [jʊərəʊˈlɒdʒɪk(ə)l] *adj* urologique
urologist [jʊˈrɒlədʒɪst] *n* urologue *mf*
urology [jʊˈrɒlədʒɪ] *n Med* urologie *f*
Ursa [ˈɜːsə] *n Astron* **U. Major/Minor** la Grande/la Petite Ourse
urticaria [ɜːtɪˈkeərɪə] *n Med* urticaire *f*
Uruguay [ˈjʊərəgwaɪ] *n* Uruguay *m*
Uruguayan [jʊərəˈgwaɪən] **1** *adj* uruguayen **2** *n* Uruguayen, -enne
US [juːˈes] **1** *n* (*abbr* **United States**) USA *mpl* **2** *adj* (*forces, officials etc*) américain; **US dollar** dollar *m* américain
us *pers pron objective case* **(a)** [ⓘA26; A42,3; B17-18,2] (*unstressed*) [əs] nous; **he sees us** il nous voit; **in front of/behind us** devant/derrière nous; **he gave it to us** il nous l'a donné; **tell us** dis-nous; **he wrote us a letter** il nous a écrit une lettre; **he stayed with us a month** il est resté chez nous pendant un mois; **there are three of us** nous sommes trois; **those of us who were left ...** ceux d'entre nous qui restaient ...
(b) (*stressed*) [ʌs] nous; **that concerns us alone** cela ne regarde que nous; **between them and us** entre eux et nous; **as for us Englishmen** quant à nous autres Anglais; **he couldn't believe that it was us** il ne pouvait pas croire que c'était nous
(c) *F* (*me*) **let's have a look** fais-moi voir; **give us a bit of it** donnez-m'en un peu
USA [juːesˈeɪ] *n* **(a)** (*abbr* **United States of America**) USA *mpl* **(b)** *abbr* **United States Army**
usable [ˈjuːzəb(ə)l] *adj* utilisable, employable
USAF [juːeseɪˈef] *n abbr* **United States Air Force**
usage [ˈjuːsɪdʒ] *n* **(a)** (*use*) utilisation *f*; **the machine wasn't designed for such heavy u.** la machine n'avait pas été conçue pour une utilisation aussi intensive; **this book has had some rough u.** ce livre a été maltraité **(b)** (*custom*) usage *m*; **an old u.** une vieille coutume; **sanctified by u.** consacré par l'usage **(c)** *Ling* usage *m*; **words in everyday u.** mots d'usage courant; **it's not in current u.** ce n'est pas dans l'usage courant; **a book on modern English u.** un livre sur les usages de l'anglais moderne; **it's not a u. I'm familiar with** ce n'est pas un usage que je connais
use[1] [juːs] *n* **(a)** (*utilization*) emploi *m*, utilisation *f*; **the u. of steel in building** l'emploi de l'acier dans la construction; **one of the main uses of steel** un des principaux emplois de l'acier; **to make u. of sth** (*tool, equipment*) se servir de qch; (*word, material*) utiliser *ou* employer qch; **to make good u. of sth, to put sth to good u.** faire bon usage de qch; **I'll find a u. for it** ça peut servir; **a word in everyday u.** un mot d'usage courant; **the word is not in u. any more** ce mot ne s'emploie plus *ou* est désuet; **not in u., out of u.** (*on sign*) hors service; **for u. in case of fire** à employer en cas d'incendie; **for u. in schools** à l'usage des écoles; **directions** *or* **instructions for u.** mode *m* d'emploi; *Pharm* **for external u.** pour usage externe; **to improve with u.** s'améliorer à l'usage
(b) (*ability to use*) jouissance *f*, usage *m*; *Jur* usufruit *m*; **to have full u. of one's faculties** jouir de toutes ses facultés; **to lose the u. of a leg** perdre l'usage d'une jambe; **to have the u. of the bathroom** avoir le droit de se servir de la salle de bain; **you can have the u. of my car while I'm in London** tu pourras te servir de ma voiture pendant que je serai à Londres
(c) (*usefulness*) utilité *f*; **to be of u.** être utile **(for sth** à qch); **can I be of any u. (to you)?** puis-je vous être utile à quelque chose?; **it's of no u. to me** je n'en ai pas besoin; **it's not much u.** cela ne sert pas à grand-chose; *F* **a fat lot of u. that'll be to you!** si tu crois que ça va t'avancer!; *F Iron* **you're a lot of u.!** je te remercie de ton aide!; *F* **he's no u.** c'est un incapable; **he's no u. in bed** au lit, il est nul; **to have no u. for sth** ne savoir que faire de qch; **I've no further u. for it** je n'en ai plus besoin; *F* **I have no u. for people like that** ces gens-là ne m'intéressent pas; **it was no u.** c'était inutile; **it's no u. discussing the question** inutile de discuter la question; **it's no u. crying** cela ne sert à rien de pleurer; **it's no u. my talking** ce que je dis ne sert à rien; **it's no u.(, I can't do it)!** c'est peine perdue(, je ne peux pas le faire)!; **is it any u. writing to him?** est-ce que ça servirait à quelque chose de lui écrire?; **what u. would that be?** à quoi cela servirait-il?; **what's the u. of doing it/of going there?** à quoi bon le faire/y aller?; **what's the u.!, I give up!** à quoi bon! j'abandonne!
(d) = **usage**
use[2] [juːz] **1** *vt* **(a)** (*object*) se servir de, utiliser; (*word*) employer, utiliser; **to be used for sth** servir à qch; **are you using this knife?** est-ce que tu te sers de ce couteau?; **I used the money to rebuild my garage** j'ai utilisé *ou* employé l'argent pour reconstruire mon garage; **the frying pan will last a long time if you u. it carefully** cette poêle à frire durera longtemps si vous en prenez soin; **do you mind if I u.**

the toilet? puis-je utiliser vos toilettes?; **this word is no longer used** ce mot est désuet *ou* n'est plus usité; **the term is used more generally to refer to …** on utilise ce terme de manière plus générale pour désigner …; **word used figuratively** mot employé au (sens) figuré; **to u. one's intelligence/intuition** faire marcher son intelligence/intuition; **u. your head!** fais marcher ta cervelle!; **u. your eyes!** ouvrez les yeux!; **to u. force/violence** avoir recours à la force/la violence; **to u. diplomacy** user de diplomatie; **to u. discretion** agir avec discrétion; **to u. one's influence** user de son influence; **to u. every means (at one's disposal)** employer tous les moyens (à sa disposition); *F* **I could u. some coffee/a holiday** j'ai besoin d'un café/de vacances

(b) (*exploit*) **I feel I've been used** j'ai l'impression qu'on se sert de moi; **she doesn't care about him, she's just using him** elle ne l'aime pas, elle ne fait que se servir de lui

(c) (*consume*) (*petrol, electricity etc*) consommer; **we've been using too much electricity** nous avons consommé trop d'électricité

(d) *Arch* (*treat*) **to u. sb well** bien traiter qn; **to u. sb badly** maltraiter qn; **he had a reputation for using his workers well** il avait la réputation de bien traiter ses employés; *not Arch F* **how's the world been using you?** comment ça va?

2 [①A59,g; B28,2] (*as aux*) [juːst] **when we were children we used to play together** quand nous étions enfants nous jouions ensemble; **my father used to tell me that …** mon père me disait toujours que …; **it used to be a pleasant town to live in** c'était autrefois une ville agréable à habiter; **things aren't what they used to be** les choses ne sont plus ce qu'elles étaient; **she used not** *or* **use(d)n't to like oysters** avant elle n'aimait pas les huîtres; **I used not to like him, I didn't use to** [ˈjuːstə] **like him** avant je ne l'aimais pas; **do you smoke? – I do now, but I didn't u. to** est-ce que vous fumez? – je ne fumais pas mais je m'y suis mis; **do you smoke? – I used to** est-ce que vous fumez? – j'ai arrêté; **do you travel much? – I used to** vous voyagez beaucoup? – autrefois, oui

▶ **use up** *vtsep* (*food, milk*) finir; (*funds, resources*) épuiser; (*energy*) dépenser la totalité de; (*paint, hot water, ideas, money, resources, time*) utiliser la totalité de; **she had used up all her strength** elle avait épuisé toutes ses forces; **u. up the leftovers to make a …** utiliser *ou* accommoder les restes pour faire un …

used [juːzd] *adj* **(a)** (*worn*) usé, usagé; (*stamp*) oblitéré, qui a déjà servi; **u. car** voiture *f* d'occasion; **hardly u.** presque neuf **(b)** [juːst] (*accustomed*) **u. to (doing) sth** habitué à (faire) qch; **to get u. to sth/sb** s'habituer *ou* se faire à qch/qn; **to get sb u. to sth** habituer qn à qch; **I'm not u. to it** je n'en ai pas l'habitude; **you'll get u. to it in time** vous vous y ferez à la longue; **I'm not u. to being spoken to like that!** je n'ai pas l'habitude qu'on me parle comme ça!

useful [ˈjuːsfʊl] *adj* **(a)** (*of use*) utile; **this book was very u. to me** ce livre m'a été très utile *ou* m'a rendu grand service; **it's u. to know** c'est bon à savoir; **it will come in very u.** cela rendra bien service; **a u. man to know** une relation utile, un homme qu'il est bon d'avoir dans ses relations; **to make oneself u.** se rendre utile; *Iron* **that's u.!** formidable!; **u. life** vie *f* utile; **this machine has a u. life of ten years** cette machine a une durée de vie de dix ans

(b) (*skilful*) **he plays a u. game of chess** il joue bien aux échecs; **to be u. with one's fists** savoir se servir de ses poings; **to be u. with a gun** savoir manier un fusil

usefully [ˈjuːsfəlɪ] *adv* utilement; **her time had been u. employed** elle s'était occupée utilement; **one might u. write a book on …** il serait fort utile qu'on écrive un livre sur …; **is there anything I can u. do?** puis-je faire quelque chose pour me rendre utile?

usefulness [ˈjuːsfʊlnɪs] *n* utilité *f*; **it/he has outlived its/his u.** cela/il ne sert plus à rien

useless [ˈjuːslɪs] *adj* **(a)** (*not useful*) inutile; (*unusable*) inutilisable; (*no good*) nul; (*remedy*) inefficace; **I hope I haven't been completely u. to you** j'espère que je ne t'ai pas été complètement inutile; **to be full of u. information** être riche en informations inutiles; **a map without a key is u.** une carte sans légende est inutilisable; *F* **to be worse than u.** (*of person*) être au-dessous de tout; (*of object*) ne rien valoir du tout, *Sl* ne pas valoir un pet de lapin

(b) (*incompetent*) (*person*) bon à rien, incompétent, nul; **I'm u. at languages** je suis nul en langues; **he's u. in bed** au lit, il est nul; **a u. person** un(e) bon(ne) à rien

(c) (*futile*) inutile; **it was u. to resist** il était inutile de résister; **it would be u. to make further requests** cela ne servirait à rien de faire d'autres demandes; **give up, it's u.!** laisse tomber, ça ne sert à rien!; **it's u. even trying to discuss it** ce n'est même pas la peine d'essayer d'en discuter

uselessly [ˈjuːslɪslɪ] *adv* inutilement

uselessness [ˈjuːslɪsnɪs] *n* inutilité *f*; (*of person*) incompétence *f*; (*of remedy*) inefficacité *f*; **his general u.** sa nullité

user [ˈjuːzər] *n* (*of road, means of transport*) usager, -ère; (*of device, computer, dictionary*) utilisateur, -trice; (*of telephone*) abonné, -ée; **bus users** les usagers du bus; *Comptr* **u. group** club *m* d'utilisateurs; **u. guidance** indications *fpl* pour l'utilisateur; **u. identification** identification *f* de l'utilisateur; **u. identification code** code *m* d'identification de l'utilisateur; *Comptr* **u. language** langage *m* utilisateur; **u. manual** manuel *m* d'utilisation; *Mktg* **u. panel** panel *m* d'utilisateurs; **u. software** logiciel *m* utilisateur; **u. support** assistance *f* à l'utilisateur

user-definable *adj Comptr* (*characters, keys*) définissable par l'utilisateur

user-defined [juːzədɪˈfaɪnd] *adj Comptr* défini par l'utilisateur; **u. key** touche *f* personnalisée

user-friendliness *n* (*of software, computer*) convivialité *f*; (*of keyboard*) confort *m* d'emploi; (*of machine, dictionary, manual*) facilité *f* d'utilisation

user-friendly *adj* (*software, computer*) convivial; (*keyboard*) confortable, facile d'emploi; (*machine, technology, instruction manual, dictionary*) facile à utiliser

user-interface *n Comptr etc* interface *f* utilisateur

user-specific *adj* spécifique à l'utilisateur

use-the-user scheme *n Mktg* offre-ami *f*, *pl* offres-ami

usher[1] [ˈʌʃər] *n Jur* (*in court*) (huissier) audiencier *m*; *Th, Cin* placeur *m*; (*at wedding*) garçon *m* d'honneur

usher[2] *vt* **I was ushered into the presence of the boss** je fus introduit auprès du directeur; **they hastily ushered him away/out** ils le firent s'éloigner/sortir à la hâte

▶ **usher in** *vtsep* introduire, faire entrer; **to u. in a new epoch** marquer le début d'une nouvelle époque

usherette [ʌʃəˈret] *n Th, Cin* ouvreuse *f*

USM [juːesˈem] *n* **(a)** (*abbr* **United States Mail**) = service *m* des postes américain **(b)** *Mil abbr* **United States Marines** **(c)** *Fin abbr* **United States Mint** **(d)** *Fin* (*abbr* **unlisted securities market**) second marché *m*

USN [juːesˈen] *n* (*abbr* **United States Navy**) marine *f* nationale américaine

USP [juːesˈpiː] *n Mktg* (*abbr* **unique selling proposition**) proposition *f* unique de vente

USS [juːesˈes] *n* (*abbr* **United States Ship**) **U. Nimitz** le Nimitz

USSR [juːesesˈɑːr] *n* (*abbr* **Union of Soviet Socialist Republics**) URSS *f*

usual [ˈjuːʒʊəl] **1** *adj* habituel; **at the u. time** à l'heure habituelle; **it's the u. practice** c'est la pratique courante; **I didn't get my u. bus this morning** je n'ai pas pris le bus que je prends d'habitude ce matin; **it wasn't the u. postman** ce n'était pas notre facteur habituel *ou F* de d'habitude; **u. time, u. place, OK?** même heure, même endroit, d'accord?; **she's back to her u. self again** elle a retrouvé la forme; **you're not your u. cheery self today** tu as perdu ton sourire aujourd'hui; **it's quite u. for that sort of thing to happen** ces choses-là arrivent fréquemment; **it's u. (for that to happen) with these machines** ça arrive fréquemment avec ces machines; **it's not u. to have to wait this long** d'habitude on n'attend pas aussi longtemps; **it's u. to pay in advance** il est d'usage de payer d'avance; **earlier/later than u.** plus tôt/plus tard que d'habitude; **more/less than u.** plus/moins que d'habitude; **as u.,** *F* **as per u.,** comme d'habitude; **business as u.** (*on sign*) ouvert pendant les réparations; **despite recent events it was business as u.** malgré les récents événements, la vie continuait comme si de rien n'était

2 *n F* (*in bar*) **(are you having) your u.?** (votre demi/votre whisky/*etc*) comme d'habitude?; **the u. please, Jim** comme d'habitude s'il te plaît, Jim

usually [ˈjuːʒʊ(ə)lɪ] *adv* d'habitude, habituellement; **I u. get up at seven** d'habitude je me lève à sept heures, je me lève habituellement à sept heures; **he was more than u. polite** il s'est montré encore plus poli que d'habitude; **it's not u. that difficult** ce n'est pas aussi difficile que ça d'habitude *ou* habituellement; **she's not u. like that** d'habitude elle n'est pas comme ça

usufruct [ˈjuːzjʊfrʌkt] *n Jur* usufruit *m* (**of** de)

usufructuary [juːzjʊˈfrʌktjʊərɪ] *adj, n Jur* usufruitier, -ière; **u. right** droit *m* usufructuaire

usurer [ˈjuːʒərər] *n* usurier, -ière

usurious [juːˈzjʊərɪəs] *adj* (*interest etc*) usuraire

usurp [juːˈzɜːp, -ˈsɜːp] *vt* (*throne, title*) usurper (**from** sur)

usurpation [juːzəˈpeɪʃən, -sɜː-] *n* usurpation *f*

usurper [jʊˈzɜːpər, -sɜː-] *n* usurpateur, -trice

usury [ˈjuːʒʊrɪ] *n* usure *f*; **that's u.!** c'est du vol!

Ut *abbr* Utah
utensil [juːˈtens(ə)l] *n* ustensile *m*; **(set of) kitchen utensils** batterie *f* de cuisine
uterine [ˈjuːtəraɪn] *adj* utérin
uterus [ˈjuːtərəs] *n Anat* utérus *m*
utilitarian [juːtɪlɪˈteərɪən] *adj, n* utilitaire *mf*
utilitarianism [juːtɪlɪˈteərɪənɪz(ə)m] *n* utilitarisme *m*
utility [juːˈtɪlɪtɪ] *n* **(a)** (*usefulness*) utilité *f*; **u. vehicle/car** véhicule *m*/voiture *f* utilitaire; **u. furniture** meubles *mpl* fonctionnels et peu chers; *Fb* **u. player** joueur, -euse polyvalent(e); *Comptr* **u. (program)** programme *m* (utilitaire), utilitaire *m*; **u. room** buanderie *f* **(b) (public) utilities, utilities sector** secteur *m* des services, services *mpl* publics
utilizable [juːtɪˈlaɪzəb(ə)l] *adj* utilisable
utilization [juːtɪl(a)ɪˈzeɪʃ(ə)n] *n* utilisation *f*; **better u. of resources** meilleure utilisation *ou* meilleur emploi des ressources
utilize [ˈjuːtɪlaɪz] *vt* utiliser, se servir de; (*take advantage of*) (*opportunity, situation*) tirer profit de
utmost [ˈʌtməʊst] **1** *adj* **(a)** (*greatest*) **the u.** le plus grand; **the u. poverty** la misère la plus noire; **with the u. contempt** avec le plus grand mépris; **it is of the u. importance that he should be present** il est absolument essentiel qu'il soit présent; **with the u. ease** avec la plus grande facilité, avec une extrême facilité; **it was only with the u. difficulty that we were able to persuade them** nous avons eu toutes les peines du monde à les convaincre

(b) (*furthest*) **the u. ends of the earth** les confins *mpl ou* les extrémités *fpl* de la terre

2 *n* **(a) to live life to the u.** profiter pleinement de la vie; **to enjoy oneself to the u.** s'amuser au plus haut point; **to do sth to the u. of one's abilities** faire qch au maximum de ses capacités; **I'll help you to the u. of my ability** je ferai tout ce qui est en mon pouvoir pour vous aider; **to do one's u. to achieve sth** faire tout son possible pour arriver à qch; **she tried her u. to persuade him** elle a fait tout ce qu'elle a pu pour le persuader

(b) that's the u. we can offer c'est le maximum que nous puissions offrir; **$50,000 at the u.** 50 000 dollars au grand maximum
Utopia [juːˈtəʊpɪə] *n* utopie *f*
Utopian [juːˈtəʊpɪən] **1** *adj* utopique **2** *n* utopiste *mf*
utter¹ [ˈʌtər] *adj* complet, -ète, absolu; **he's an u. stranger to me** il m'est complètement étranger; **u. boredom** ennui *m* mortel; **it's u. madness** c'est de la folie totale *ou* pure; **we were in u. darkness** nous étions dans l'obscurité totale; **u. rubbish** (*goods*) de la pure camelote; (*nonsense*) des absurdités; **what u. rubbish!** quel tas de sottises!; **he's an u. fool** il est complètement idiot; **u. poverty** la misère la plus noire; **to my u. horror** comble de l'horreur; **to her u. amazement** à sa plus grande stupéfaction
utter² *vt* **(a)** (*cry*) jeter, pousser; (*word*) prononcer, dire; (*curse*) lancer; **I didn't u. a word** je n'ai pas desserré les dents; **never u. his name in her presence** il ne faut jamais prononcer son nom devant elle; **if you u. another sound you're going straight to bed!** et si je t'entends encore une fois tu vas directement au lit! **(b)** (*lies*) débiter **(c)** *Fml* (*counterfeit money*) émettre, mettre en circulation
utterance [ˈʌtərəns] *n* **(a)** (*what is said*) paroles *fpl*, propos *mpl*, mots *mpl*; *Ling* énoncé *m*; **what was his last u.?** quels ont été ses derniers mots?; **they taped the child's first utterances** ils ont enregistré les premiers mots de l'enfant; **his recent utterances in the national press** ses récentes déclarations dans la presse nationale **(b)** (*expression*) (*of sound*) expression *f*; **on her u. of his name** au moment où elle prononça son nom; **to give u. to one's feelings/a thought** exprimer ses sentiments/une pensée
utterly [ˈʌtəlɪ] *adv* complètement, absolument; **u. stupid** d'une bêtise extrême
uttermost [ˈʌtəməʊst] *adj, n* = **utmost**
U-tube *n* tube *m* en U
UV [juːˈviː] *adj* (*abbr* **ultra-violet**) UV
uvula, *pl* **-as, -ae** [ˈjuːvjələ, -əs, -iː] *n Anat* uvule *f*, luette *f*
uvular [ˈjuːvjələr] *adj* uvulaire
uxorious [ʌkˈsɔːrɪəs] *adj Fml* (*husband*) soumis
uxoriousness [ʌkˈsɔːrɪəsnɪs] *n Fml* (*of husband*) soumission *f* à sa femme

V

V¹, v¹ [viː] *n* (*letter*) V, v *m*; **to fly in a V formation** (*of birds*) voler en formant un V; **V-neck (sweater), V-necked sweater** pull *m* à col en V; **V-necked dress** robe *f* à encolure en pointe *ou* en V; **V-shaped** en (forme de) V; **V-sign** (*for victory*) V de la victoire; (*insult*) ≈ bras *m* d'honneur; **to give sb the V-sign** ≈ faire un bras d'honneur à qn
V² *El* (*abbr* **volt(s)**) V.
v² **(a)** (*abbr* **verse**) v. **(b)** *Jur, Sp abbr* **versus** **(c)** (*abbr* **very**) t.
Va *abbr* **Virginia**
V & A [viːən'eɪ] *n Br* (*abbr* **Victoria and Albert Museum**) = musée *m* d'arts décoratifs, à Londres
vac [væk] *n Br Univ, Sch F* vacances *fpl*
vacancy ['veɪkənsɪ] *n* **(a)** (*position*) place *f* vacante, poste *m* vacant, vacance *f*; **we have a v. for …** (*job advert*) nous recherchons …; **to fill a v.** pourvoir un poste vacant; **v. on the board** siège *m* à pourvoir au conseil d'administration **(b)** (*at hotel*) chambre *f* libre; (*at camp site*) place *f* libre; **no vacancies** complet **(c)** (*of expression*) caractère *m* absent; **a look of sheer v.** un visage dénué de toute expression
vacant ['veɪkənt] *adj* **(a)** (*empty*) vide; (*hotel room, seat, lavatory*) libre; (*flat*) inoccupé; (*official post*) vacant, à pourvoir; **situations v.** (*newspaper column*) offres *fpl* d'emploi; **v. possession** (*of building*) jouissance *f* immédiate; **v. site,** *Am* **v. lot** terrain *m* vague; (*for sale*) terrain à vendre **(b)** (*mind*) vide; (*look*) (*absent-minded*) distrait, vague, sans expression; (*stupid*) niais, stupide; **with a v. expression** le regard perdu **(c)** (*time*) libre
vacantly ['veɪkəntlɪ] *adv* (*to gaze etc*) (*absentmindedly*) d'un air distrait *ou* absent; (*with lack of intelligence*) d'un regard perdu; (*stupidly*) d'un air stupide
vacate [və'keɪt] *vt* (*seat, flat, hotel room, job*) quitter; (*room*) libérer, quitter; *Jur* **to v. the premises** vider les lieux
vacation¹ [və'keɪʃən] *n* **(a)** (*holiday*) vacances *fpl*; **during** *or* **in the v.** pendant les vacances; **we spent the v. travelling around Europe** nous avons voyagé en Europe pendant nos vacances; *Am* **to take a v.** prendre des vacances; **to be on v.** être en vacances; **the long v.** *Jur* les vacances judiciaires, la vacation; *Univ* les grandes vacances; *Am* **v. bond** (*form of timeshare*) obligation *f* 'vacances'; *Am* **v. center** club *m* de vacances; *Am* **v. home** résidence *f* secondaire; *Am Admin* **v. leave** congé *m* annuel; **v. work** travail *m* effectué pendant les vacances (*par un étudiant*) **(b)** *Fml* (*leaving*) (*of premises*) évacuation *f*; **v. of office** démission *f*
vacation² *vi Am* prendre *ou* passer ses vacances (**at, in** à, en)
vacationist, vacationer [veɪ'keɪʃənɪst, -ər] *n Am* vacancier, -ière; (*in summer*) estivant, -ante
vaccinate ['væksɪneɪt] *vt Med* vacciner (**against** contre); **to get vaccinated** se faire vacciner
vaccination [væksɪ'neɪʃən] *n Med* vaccination *f*; **smallpox v.** vaccination contre la variole
vaccine ['væksiːn] *n Med* vaccin *m*
vaccinee [væksɪ'niː] *n US* personne *f* vaccinée
vacillate ['væsɪleɪt] *vi* hésiter (**between** entre)
vacillating ['væsɪleɪtɪŋ] **1** *adj* (*undecided*) irrésolu, indécis **2** *n* (*indecision*) indécision *f*, irrésolution *f*
vacillation [væsɪ'leɪʃən] *n* indécision *f*
vacuity [væ'kjuːɪtɪ] *n* vacuité *f*; **vacuities** bêtises *fpl*, niaiseries *fpl*
vacuous ['vækjʊəs] *adj* (*look*) hébété, vide d'expression; (*remark, laugh*) niais, bête; (*book, film*) idiot; **he's completely v.** c'est un parfait idiot; **what an utterly v. thing to say** quelle niaiserie, quelle idiotie
vacuously ['vækjʊəslɪ] *adv* bêtement
vacuousness ['vækjʊəsnɪs] *n* (*of laugh*) bêtise *f*, niaiserie *f*; (*of remark, debate*) vacuité *f*
vacuum¹, *pl* **-ua, -uums** ['vækjʊm, -jʊə, -jʊmz] *n* **(a)** *Phys* vide *m*, vacuum *m*; *Fig* vide; **to produce** *or* **create a v.** faire le vide; **nature abhors a v.** la nature a horreur du vide; *Fig* **a cultural/political v.** un vide sur le plan culturel/politique; **to live in a v.** vivre en vase clos; **a v. of ideas** une pénurie d'idées **(b)** (*machine*) aspirateur *m*; **to give the carpet a v.** passer l'aspirateur sur la moquette **(c)** *Aut* (*of venturi*) dépression *f*; **v. advance** avance *f* à dépression; **v. chamber** chambre *f* à dépression; **v. tank** réservoir *m* à dépression
vacuum² *vt* (*carpet*) passer l'aspirateur sur; (*room*) passer l'aspirateur dans
vacuum bottle *n Am* (bouteille *f*) thermos® *mf inv*, bouteille isolante
vacuum cleaner *n* aspirateur *m*
vacuum flask *n Br* (bouteille *f*) thermos® *mf inv*, bouteille isolante
vacuuming ['vækjʊmɪŋ] *n* **to do the v.** passer l'aspirateur
vacuum-packed *adj* emballé sous vide
vacuum packing *n Ind, Com* emballage *m* sous vide
vacuum pump *n* pompe *f* à vide
vacuum tube *n Am El* tube *m* à vide électronique
vade mecum [vɑːdɪ'meɪkəm] *n* vade-mecum *m inv*, aide-mémoire *m inv*
vagabond ['vægəbɒnd] **1** *n* vagabond, -onde **2** *adj* vagabond, errant
vagary ['veɪgərɪ] *n* caprice *m*; **the vagaries of fashion/the weather** les caprices de la mode/du temps
vagina [və'dʒaɪnə] *n Anat* vagin *m*
vaginal [və'dʒaɪn(ə)l] *adj Anat* vaginal; **v. discharge** pertes *fpl* (blanches); **v. examination** examen *m* vaginal; **v. smear** frottis *m* vaginal; **to have a v. smear taken** se faire faire un frottis vaginal
vagrancy ['veɪgrənsɪ] *n Jur* vagabondage *m*; **to be arrested for v.** être arrêté pour vagabondage
vagrant ['veɪgrənt] **1** *n* vagabond, -onde **2** *adj* errant
vague [veɪg] *adj* (*person, look, reply*) vague; (*impression, memory*) vague, imprécis, confus; (*shape, outline*) flou, imprécis; **to bear a v. resemblance to sb/sth** ressembler vaguement à qn/qch; **there's been some v. talk of …** on a parlé vaguement de …; **the conditions were left deliberately v.** les conditions ont été laissées délibérément vagues; **I haven't the vaguest idea** je n'en ai pas la moindre idée; **I had a v. idea that he was dead** j'avais vaguement l'idée qu'il était mort; **he was rather v. about the date** il s'est montré assez vague à propos de la date; **she was v. (about it)** elle est restée vague là-dessus
vaguely ['veɪglɪ] *adv* (*to look*) d'un air vague; (*to remember, express*) vaguement, confusément; (*to agree, resemble*) vaguement; (*slightly*) légèrement; **to be v. reminiscent of …** rappeler vaguement …; **their music sounds v. like the Beatles** leur musique ressemble vaguement aux Beatles
vagueness ['veɪgnɪs] *n* caractère *m* vague, vague *m*, imprécision *f*; (*of shape, outline, photograph*) caractère flou; (*of story, report, memory etc*) manque *m* de précision
vain [veɪn] *adj* **(a)** (*conceited*) vaniteux, orgueilleux; **she was v. about her beauty** elle était fière de sa beauté **(b)** (*unavailing*) vain, inutile, stérile; **v. efforts** efforts *mpl* vains *ou* inutiles **(c)** (*hope*) vain; (*pleasure*) futile; **v. promises** vaines promesses *fpl*, promesses vaines **(d) in v.** en vain, vainement; **to labour in v.** travailler en vain, perdre sa peine; **her efforts were in v.** ses efforts ont été inutiles; **it was all in v.** c'était peine perdue; **to take God's name in v.** invoquer le nom de Dieu en vain; *F* **who's taking my name in v.?** qui est-ce qui parle de moi?
vainglorious [veɪn'glɔːrɪəs] *adj Fml* vaniteux, orgueilleux
vaingloriously [veɪn'glɔːrɪəslɪ] *adv Fml* vaniteusement, orgueilleusement
vainglory [veɪn'glɔːrɪ] *n Fml* vanité *f*, orgueil *m*
vainly ['veɪnlɪ] *adv* **(a)** (*uselessly*) vainement, en vain **(b)** (*conceitedly*) vaniteusement, avec vanité
valance ['væləns] *n* (*on side of bed*) frange *f* de lit; (*for curtains*) cantonnière *f*, lambrequin *m*; (*on vehicle*) tablier *m*, doublure *f* d'aile, bouclier *m*
valanced sheet ['vælənst] *n* housse *f* cache-sommier
vale [veɪl] *n Arch, Lit* vallée *f*; (*small*) vallon *m*; *Fig* **this v. of tears** cette vallée de larmes
valediction [vælɪ'dɪkʃən] *n* **(a)** (*farewell*) adieu(x) *m(pl)* **(b)** *Am Univ, Sch* = **valedictory 2**

valedictorian [vælɪdɪk'tɔːrɪən] *n Am Univ, Sch* membre *m* d'une promotion qui prononce le discours d'adieu
valedictory [vælɪ'dɪktərɪ] **1** *adj* (*address, dinner*) d'adieu **2** *n Am Univ, Sch* (*at graduation*) discours *m* d'adieu
valence ['veɪləns] *n Am* = **valency**
valency ['veɪlənsɪ] *n Br Ch* valence *f*
valentine ['væləntaɪn] *n* **(a) v.** (**card**) carte *f* de la Saint-Valentin; **(St) V.'s Day** (*14 February*) la Saint-Valentin **(b)** (*recipient of card*) = celui/celle qui reçoit une carte envoyée le jour de la Saint-Valentin; **will you be my v.?** = phrase *f* écrite sur les cartes de la Saint-Valentin pour exprimer ses sentimants amoureux à l'égard du/de la destinataire; **George is my v.** c'est George que j'aime
valerian [və'leərɪən] *n Bot, Pharm* valériane *f*
valet¹ ['væleɪ, 'vælɪt] *n* (*servant*) valet *m* de chambre; (*in hotel*) = employé *m* qui s'occupe de l'entretien des vêtements des clients; *Am* (*who parks car*) = employé d'un hôtel ou d'un restaurant qui se charge de garer les voitures des clients; **v. parking** (*at hotel*) service *m* de voiturier; **v. service** (*for clothes*) service de nettoyage des vêtements
valet² *vt* (**valeted** ['vælɪtɪd]) **to v. a car** laver et nettoyer une voiture; **can I have my suit valeted?** puis-je faire nettoyer mon costume?; **valeting service** (*for clothes*) service *m* de nettoyage des vêtements; (*for car*) service de lavage et de nettoyage
valetudinarian [vælɪtjuːdɪ'neərɪən] *adj, n* valétudinaire *mf*
Valhalla [væl'hælə] *n Myth* Walhalla *m*
valiant ['vælɪənt] *adj* courageux, vaillant, valeureux; **to make a v. effort** faire un courageux effort (**to do** pour faire)
valiantly ['vælɪəntlɪ] *adv* courageusement, vaillamment, valeureusement
valid ['vælɪd] *adj* (*contract, document etc*) valide, valable; (*passport*) en règle; (*reason, objection*) valable, recevable; **v. argument** argument *m* valable *ou* solide; **ticket v. for three months** billet bon pour trois mois; **no longer v.** (*ticket, passport etc*) périmé
validate ['vælɪdeɪt] *vt* **(a)** (*act, contract, ticket*) valider, rendre valable; *US* **to v. an election** valider une élection **(b)** (*prove*) (*theory*) confirmer **(c)** *Comptr* valider
validation [vælɪ'deɪʃən] *n* **(a)** (*of act, contract*) validation *f*; **v. stamp** cachet *m* de validation **(b)** (*of theory*) confirmation *f*
validator ['vælɪdeɪtər] *n* (*for tickets*) cachet *m*
validity [və'lɪdɪtɪ] *n* (*of contract, document*) validité *f*; (*of argument*) force *f*, justesse *f*; (*of claim*) bien-fondé *m*; **these objections have no v.** ces objections ne sont pas fondées
validly ['vælɪdlɪ] *adv* validement, valablement
valise [və'liːs, -iːz] *n Old-fashioned* (*suitcase*) valise *f*; (*hand luggage*) sac *m* de voyage
Valium® ['vælɪəm] *n* Valium *m*; **to be on V.** être au Valium; **the doctor has put her on V.** le docteur l'a mise au Valium
Valkyrie ['vælkɪrɪ] *n Myth* Walkyrie *f*, Valkyrie *f*
valley ['vælɪ] *n* **(a)** vallée *f*; (*small*) vallon *m*; **the Rhone V.** la vallée du Rhône **(b)** *Constr* noue *f*; (*of roof*) cornière *f*
valor ['vælər] *n US* = **valour**
valorization [vælərаɪ'zeɪʃən] *n* valorisation *f*
valorize ['vælərаɪz] *vt Com, Fin* valoriser
valorous ['vælərəs] *adj Fml* valeureux, vaillant
valour, *US* **valor** ['vælər] *n* courage *m*, vaillance *f*, bravoure *f*; **to be decorated for v.** (*of soldier, police officer etc*) être décoré pour son courage
valuable ['væljʊəb(ə)l] **1** *adj* (*help, time*) précieux; (*object*) précieux, de valeur, de prix; **nothing v. was taken** aucun objet de valeur n'a été volé; **v. gift** cadeau *m* de valeur; **she has given years of v. service** elle a donné des années de bons et loyaux services **2** *npl* **valuables** objets *mpl* de valeur
valuation [væljʊ'eɪʃən] *n Fin* **(a)** (*setting of value*) évaluation *f*, estimation *f*, appréciation *f*; *Jur* prisée *f* et estimation; (*by expert*) expertise *f*, rapport *m* d'expertise; **to get a v. of sth** faire expertiser qch; **to make a v. of the goods** faire l'expertise des marchandises; *Com* **v. charge** taxation *f* à la valeur

(b) (*value*) (*of painting, house*) valeur *f* estimée; **the v. on the house was £50,000** la valeur estimée de la maison était de 50 000 livres; **to set too high/too low a v. on goods** surestimer/sous-estimer des marchandises; *Fig* **to take** *or* **accept sb at his/her own v.** estimer qn selon l'opinion qu'il a de lui-même/qu'elle a d'elle-même
valuator ['væljʊeɪtər] *n* = **valuer**
value¹ ['væljuː] *n* **(a)** (*worth*) valeur *f*; **to be of v.** (*of jewellery etc*) avoir de la valeur; **of great v.** de grande *ou* haute valeur; **your help/contribution was of great v.** votre aide/ contribution a été très précieuse; **she has been of great v. to the company** elle a apporté une contribution précieuse à l'entreprise; **to be of great sentimental v.** avoir une grande valeur sentimentale; **of little v.** de peu de valeur; **to be of little v.** être sans grande valeur; **her advice/help was of little v.** ses conseils n'ont/son aide n'a pas été très utile(s); **of no v.** sans valeur; **it is nothing of any v.** ce n'est rien qui ait une quelconque valeur; **to lose v., to fall in v.** se dévaluer, s'avilir; *Fin* se dévaloriser; **loss of v., fall in v.** dévalorisation *f*; **to set a v. on sth** (*evaluate*) évaluer qch; *Com* attribuer une cote de valeur à qch; **to set a high/low v. on sth** attribuer une haute/faible valeur à qch; **to set too high a v. on sth** attacher trop de valeur *ou* de prix à qch, surestimer qch; **he sets a very high v. on her** il estime que c'est une personne d'une grande valeur; **goods to the v. of ten pounds** marchandises d'une valeur de dix livres; **what will this do to the v. of property?** quel effet est-ce que ça va avoir sur le prix de l'immobilier?; **commercial** *or* **market v.** (*worth*) valeur marchande; (*price*) cours *m*; **replacement v.** valeur de remplacement; **it's good v.** c'est très avantageux; **at £2 it's very good v.** à 2 livres, c'est une bonne affaire *ou* c'est intéressant; *Fin* **v. for collection** valeur *f* à l'encaissement; **v. for money** (*heading on restaurant or wine review*) rapport *m* qualité/prix; **to get (good) v. for one's money** en avoir pour son argent; **he gives you v. for money** il vous en donne pour votre argent; **it's v. for money** ça vaut le coup, ce n'est pas cher; **the large size gives you better v. (for your money)** le grand format est plus avantageux; **get better v. for your money with Wundapantz** (*advertising slogan*) Wundapantz vous en donne plus pour votre argent; *Mktg* **v. brand** marque *f* de valeur; *Mktg* **v. chain** chaîne *f* de valeur; *Fin* **v. date** date *f* de valeur, jour *m* de valeur; **v. marketing** mercatique *f* de la valeur; *Banking* **v. today trade** transaction *f* valeur jour

(b) *Math, Mus, Ling* valeur *f*; **let y have the v. 15** soit y égale 15; *Th* **to give full v. to each word** donner du poids à chaque mot

(c) values (*standards*) valeurs *fpl*; **sense of values** sens *m* des valeurs; **moral values** valeurs morales; **according to a set of values** selon certains principes
value² *vt* **(a)** (*evaluate*) (*goods*) évaluer, estimer, apprécier; *Com* (*assess value of*) expertiser; (*property, painting*) faire l'expertise de; **to get sth valued** faire expertiser qch, faire évaluer qch; **to v. a house at £50,000** évaluer une maison à 50 000 livres **(b)** (*appreciate*) (*person, thing*) tenir à, faire grand cas de; **to v. sb as a friend** tenir à *ou* apprécier qn en tant qu'ami; **if you v. your life** si vous tenez à la vie
value-add *n Mktg* valeur *f* ajoutée
value-added *adj Fin* (*product, service etc*) à valeur ajoutée; *Comptr* **v. network** réseau *m* à valeur ajoutée; **high v. product** produit *m* à haute valeur ajoutée; *Br* **v. tax** taxe *f* à la valeur ajoutée, taxe sur la valeur ajoutée
valued ['væljuːd] *adj* (*contribution*) précieux; (*colleague, employee*) estimé; **my v. friend, Mr Thomson** M. Thomson, dont l'amitié m'est si précieuse; **v. customer card** carte *f* de fidélité
value judgement *n* jugement *m* de valeur
valueless ['væljʊlɪs] *adj* sans valeur
valuer ['væljʊər] *n* (*of antique etc*) expert *m*; **official v.** commissaire-priseur *m*, *pl* commissaires-priseurs
valve [vælv] *n Tech* soupape *f*; (*tap, cock*) robinet *m*, vanne *f*; *Cycling* (*of inner tube*), *Anat* valve *f*; *Mus* (*of brass instrument*) piston *m*; *El* (*of radio*) lampe *f*, valve; (**sluice**) **v.** vanne de communication; **gas/water v.** vanne à gaz/d'eau; *Aut* **v. clearance** jeu *m* de soupapes; **v. gear, v. train** train *m* de soupapes
valved [vælvd] *adj Tech* à valve(s), à soupape(s); *Mus* (*instrument*) à pistons
valvular ['vælvjʊlər] *adj Med* valvulaire
vamoose [və'muːs] *vi esp Am F* décamper, filer; **let's v.** filons, fichons le camp
vamp¹ [væmp] *n Mus F* accompagnement *m* improvisé
vamp² *vi Mus F* (*improvise*) improviser (au piano)
vamp³ *n Old-fashioned F* (*woman*) femme *f* fatale, vamp *f*
vamp⁴ *Old-fashioned F* **1** *vt* (*of woman*) (*man*) vamper **2** *vi* (*of woman*) jouer la femme fatale
▶ **vamp up** *vtsep F* (*building*) retaper; (*story*) enjoliver, embellir
vampire ['væmpaɪər] *n Myth, Fig* vampire *m*; **v. bat** vampire
vampiric [væm'pɪrɪk] *adj* vampirique
vampirism ['væmpaɪərɪz(ə)m] *n Myth, Fig* vampirisme *m*
vampish ['væmpɪʃ] *adj Old-fashioned F* (*looks, dress*) de vamp, de femme fatale
VAN [væn] *n Comptr* (*abbr* **value-added network**) réseau *m* à valeur ajoutée
van¹ *n* = **vanguard**
van² *n* **(a)** *Aut* (*large*) camion *m*, fourgon *m*; *Br* (*small*) camionnette *f*, fourgonnette *f*; **furniture** *or* **removal v.** camion de déménagement; **delivery v.** camion/camionnette de livraison; **outside broadcasting v.** car *m* de radio-

reportage; **v. driver** chauffeur *m* de camionnette; *Am* **v. pool** = coopérative *f* de transport (*en vertu de laquelle les employés d'une société se rendent sur leur lieu de travail dans une camionnette souvent payée par la société en question*) **(b)** *Br Rail* wagon *m*, fourgon *m*; **luggage v.** fourgon à bagages

van³ *n esp Br Tennis* avantage *m*; **v. in** avantage dedans *ou* au servant; **v. out** avantage dehors *ou* au relanceur

vanadium [vəˈneɪdɪəm] *n Ch* vanadium *m*

vandal [ˈvænd(ə)l] *n* vandale *mf*

vandalism [ˈvændəlɪz(ə)m] *n* vandalisme *m*; **act of v.** acte *m* de vandalisme

vandalize [ˈvændəlaɪz] *vt* (*building, telephone etc*) saccager; **several pictures have been vandalized** plusieurs tableaux ont été mutilés (par des vandales)

vane [veɪn] *n* **(a)** (*for indicating wind direction*) girouette *f* **(b)** (*of windmill*) aile *f*; (*of turbine*) aube *f*, ailette *f*, palette *f*; (*of bomb, torpedo*) ailette; **the vanes** (*of turbine*) l'aubage *m*

vanguard [ˈvængɑːd] *n Mil, Fig* avant-garde *f*; *Fig* **to be in the v. of a movement** être un des pionniers d'un mouvement; **to be in the v. of technological progress** être à la pointe du progrès technologique

vanilla [vəˈnɪlə] *n* (*flavouring*) vanille *f*; **flavoured with v., v. flavoured** vanillé, (parfumé) à la vanille; **v. essence** extrait *m* de vanille; **v. ice** glace *f* à la vanille; **v. plant** vanille, vanillier *m*; **v. pod** gousse *f* de vanille; **v. sugar** sucre *m* vanillé

vanilla swap *n St Exch* swap *m* vanilla

vanillin [vəˈnɪlɪn] *n Ch* vanilline *f*

vanish [ˈvænɪʃ] *vi* disparaître; (*of visions, suspicions*) se dissiper, s'évanouir; (*of difficulties*) s'aplanir; **to make sth v.** faire disparaître qch; (*of magician*) escamoter qch, faire disparaître qch; **elephants are vanishing from the earth** les éléphants sont en voie de disparition; **to v. from sight** disparaître à la vue; **to v. without trace** disparaître sans laisser de trace; **to v. into thin air** se volatiliser; **he's vanished** il a disparu; *F* (*to avoid sth, sb*) il s'est éclipsé; **she saw her last hope v.** elle a vu s'évanouir son dernier espoir

vanishing [ˈvænɪʃɪŋ] **1** *adj* qui disparaît; *Old-fashioned* **v. cream** crème *f* de jour **2** *n* disparition *f*; *Fig* **to do a v. act** s'éclipser; **he's done his famous v. act again** le voilà qui s'est encore éclipsé; *Art* **v. point** point *m* de fuite; *Fig* **profits have dwindled to v. point** les bénéfices se sont trouvés réduits à néant; **to do a v. trick** (*of magician*) faire un tour de passe-passe; *Fig* (*disappear from sight*) s'éclipser

vanity [ˈvænɪtɪ] *n* **(a)** (*conceit*) vanité *f*, orgueil *m*; **to do sth out of v.** faire qch par vanité *ou* pour la gloriole; **v. bag** (petit) sac *m* de dame (pour le soir); **v. case** (*make-up bag*) nécessaire *m* de maquillage; (*small case*) mallette *f* de toilette, vanity-case *m*; **v. mirror** miroir *m* de courtoisie; *Br* **v. unit** table *f* de toilette avec lavabo encastré; *Am* **v. press** maison *f* d'édition qui publie des livres à compte d'auteur **(b)** *Lit* (*futility*) futilité *f*; *Bible* **all is v.** tout est vanité

vanquish [ˈvæŋkwɪʃ] *vt* (*person, one's passions*) vaincre, triompher de

vanquisher [ˈvæŋkwɪʃər] *n* vainqueur *m*; **Alexander, the v. of the Persians** Alexandre, celui qui a triomphé des Perses

vantage [ˈvɑːntɪdʒ] *n* **(a)** **(point of) v., v. point** (*place*) terrain *m* avantageux, position *f* avantageuse; **to take up a v. point** choisir une position avantageuse; **from our v. point we could see …** de la position avantageuse où nous étions nous pouvions voir …; *Fig* **from the v. point of the twentieth century, it is easy to …** avec le recul qui nous est possible au vingtième siècle, il est facile de … **(b)** *Tennis* avantage *m*

Vanuatu [ˈvænuːætuː] *n* Vanuatu

vapid [ˈvæpɪd] *adj* insipide, plat; **v. style** style *m* fade

vapidity [vəˈpɪdɪtɪ] *n* (*of conversation*) fadeur *f*, insipidité *f*; (*of style*) platitude *f*

vapor [ˈveɪpər] *n US* = **vapour**

vaporization [veɪpəraɪˈzeɪʃən] *n* vaporisation *f*

vaporize [ˈveɪpəraɪz] **1** *vt* vaporiser; (*in science fiction*) pulvériser **2** *vi* se vaporiser, se gazéifier

vaporizer [ˈveɪpəraɪzər] *n* (*spray*) atomiseur *m*, vaporisateur *m*

vaporous [ˈveɪpərəs] *adj Fml* (*sky, style*) vaporeux

vapour, *US* **vapor** [ˈveɪpər] *n* **(a)** vapeur *f*; *Constr* **v. barrier** coupe-vapeur *m inv*; **v. bath** *Med* bain *m* de vapeur; (*at Turkish baths*) étuve *f* humide; *Av* **v. trail** traînée *f* de condensation **(b)** *Old-fashioned Med* **to have the vapours** avoir des vapeurs

variability [veərɪəˈbɪlɪtɪ] *n* (*of weather etc*) variabilité *f*; *Biol* (*of type*) inconstance *f*

variable [ˈveərɪəb(ə)l] **1** *adj* (*weather, amounts etc*) variable; **rainfall is v. according to season** les précipitations varient selon les saisons; **the combinations are infinitely v.** les combinaisons peuvent varier à l'infini; **v. (at will)** réglable; **v. costs** frais *mpl ou* coûts *mpl ou* charges *fpl* variables; **v. motion** mouvement *m* varié; *Math* **v. quantity** quantité *f* variable; *Astron* **v. star** étoile *f* variable; **v. unit cost** coût *m* variable unitaire **2** *n Math, Comptr* variable *f*; *Econ* **random v.** variable aléatoire

variable-rate interest *n* intérêt *m* variable

variable-rate security *n* valeur *f* à revenu variable

variably [ˈveərɪəblɪ] *adv* variablement

variance [ˈveərɪəns] *n* **(a)** (*disagreement*) désaccord *m*, discordance *f*; **to be at v. with sb** être en désaccord *ou* en contradiction avec qn; **his views are totally at v. with mine** ses opinions sont totalement différentes des miennes; **historians are at v. on this point** les historiens diffèrent entre eux *ou* ne sont pas d'accord sur ce point; **this theory is at v. with the facts** cette théorie est incompatible *ou* en contradiction avec les faits **(b)** (*difference*) (*in temperature, volume etc*) variation *f*; *Ch, Math* variance *f*

variant [ˈveərɪənt] **1** *adj* différent **(from** de); **v. reading** variante *f*; **v. spelling** variante (orthographique) **2** *n* variante *f*

variation [veərɪˈeɪʃən] *n* **(a)** (*difference*) variation *f*; **there was very little v. in quality** la qualité variait très peu; **v. between two readings** (*using scientific instrument*) écart *m* entre deux lectures **(b)** (*different version*) variation *f*; **another v. on the same theme** une autre variation sur le même thème **(c)** *Mus* variation *f* **(on** sur); **theme and variations** thème *m* et variations

varicoloured, *US* **-colored** [ˈveərɪkʌləd] *adj Fml* aux couleurs variées, versicolore

varicose [ˈværɪkəʊs] *adj Med* variqueux; **v. vein** varice *f*

varied [ˈveərɪd] *adj* **(a)** (*diverse*) varié **(b)** *Biol* (*in colour*) multicolore, versicolore

variegated [ˈveərɪgeɪtɪd] *adj* **(a)** *Fml* (*diverse*) varié **(b)** (*multi-coloured*) bigarré, bariolé, versicolore; *Bot* panaché; **to become v.** (*of flower, leaf*) se panacher

variegation [veərɪˈgeɪʃən] *n* (*in colour*) diversité *f* de couleurs, bigarrure *f*; *Bot* panachure *f*, diaprure *f*

varietal [vəˈraɪətəl] *n* (*wine*) monocru *m*

variety [vəˈraɪətɪ] *n* **(a)** (*diversity*) variété *f*, diversité *f*; **the hillocks give v. to the landscape** les petites collines accidentent le paysage; *Prov* **v. is the spice of life** il faut varier les plaisirs; (*a change is good*) le changement donne du piquant à la vie

(b) (*assortment*) **a v. of patterns** un assortiment de modèles; **a large** *or* **wide v. of materials** (*in shop*) un grand *ou* vaste choix de tissus; **there is a v. of possible causes** il y a diverses causes possibles; **for a v. of reasons** pour des raisons diverses; **an astonishing v. of reasons was given** on a fourni des raisons incroyablement variées; **in a v. of ways** de diverses manières, diversement; *Am* **v. meat** abats *mpl*; *Am* **v. store** grand magasin *m*

(c) *Bot* (*of flower etc*) variété *f*

(d) (*sort*) type *m*

(e) *Th* variétés *fpl*; **to work in v.** travailler dans le monde des variétés

variety artist *n* artiste *mf* de variétés

variety show *n* spectacle *m* de variétés

variety theatre *n* théâtre *m* de variétés

variola [vəˈraɪələ] *n Med* variole *f*, petite vérole *f*

various [ˈveərɪəs] *adj* divers; **of v. kinds** de diverses sortes; **to talk about v. things** parler de chose(s) et d'autre(s) *ou* de choses diverses; **her skills are many and v.** ses aptitudes sont nombreuses et diverses; **known under v. names** connu sous des noms divers; **v. people saw it** plusieurs personnes l'ont vu; **for v. reasons** pour des raisons diverses; **there are v. reasons why you shouldn't go** tu ne dois pas y aller pour plusieurs raisons; **at v. times** à diverses reprises, en diverses occasions; **in v. ways** de diverses *ou* plusieurs manières, diversement

variously [ˈveərɪəslɪ] *adv* diversement, de diverses *ou* plusieurs manières; **v. estimated at …** estimé par diverses sources à …; **she has v. been called …** elle a été tour à tour surnommée …

varlet [ˈvɑːlɪt] *n Arch* (*rascal*) coquin *m*, vaurien *m*

varmint [ˈvɑːmɪnt] *n esp US* **young v.** petit polisson *m*

varnish¹ [ˈvɑːnɪʃ] *n* vernis *m*; *esp Br* **nail v.** vernis à ongles; **v. remover** *Ind etc* décapant *m* pour vernis; (*for nails*) dissolvant *m*; **(coat of) v.** (couche *f* de) vernis; **to give sth a v.** vernir qch

varnish² *vt* (*wood, painting*) vernir; **to v. one's (finger)nails** se mettre du vernis à ongles

▶ **varnish over** *vtsep* vernir; *Fig* (*facts*) déguiser; (*incident*) passer sur; (*person's faults*) glisser sur, jeter un voile complaisant sur

varnisher [ˈvɑːnɪʃər] *n* vernisseur *m*

varnishing [ˈvɑːnɪʃɪŋ] *n* vernissage *m*; **v. day** (*of exhibition*) vernissage

varsity ['vɑːsɪtɪ] **1** *n* **(a)** *Br F* université *f*, *F* fac *f*; **the V. match** le match entre Oxford et Cambridge **(b)** *US Univ* (*team*) équipe *f* universitaire **2** *adj* universitaire

vary ['veərɪ] **1** *vt* (*one's style, diet*) varier, diversifier; (*programme*) apporter de la variété à; **to v. one's methods** changer de méthodes; **to v. one's route** changer d'itinéraire de temps en temps

2 *vi* varier, changer; *Biol* s'écarter du type, présenter une variation; **the ingredients v. from place to place** les ingrédients varient d'un endroit à l'autre; **it varies with the weather** ça change en fonction du temps; **it varies** ça dépend; **to v. in quality/weight** varier en qualité/poids; **to v. from sth** s'écarter de *ou* différer de qch; **as to the date, authors v.** les auteurs ne sont pas d'accord *ou* varient quant à la date; **opinions v.** les avis sont partagés

varying ['veərɪɪŋ] *adj* qui varie, variable, changeant; **I've had v. reports about that restaurant** j'ai entendu des avis divergents sur ce restaurant; **they have v. opinions about this** leurs opinions divergent *ou* diffèrent sur ce point; **with v. results** avec des résultats plus ou moins satisfaisants; **with v. degrees of success** avec plus ou moins de succès

vascular ['væskjʊlər] *adj Biol* vasculaire

vascularization [væskjʊləraɪ'zeɪʃən] *n Med* vascularisation *f*

vas deferens [væz'defərenz] *n Anat* canal *m* déférent

vase [vɑːz, *Am* veɪz] *n* vase *m*; **flower v.** vase à fleurs

vasectomy [və'sektəmɪ] *n Surg* vasectomie *f*; **to have a v.** se faire faire une vasectomie

Vaseline® ['væsəliːn] *n* vaseline *f*

vasoconstricting [veɪzəʊkən'strɪktɪŋ] *adj Med* vasoconstricteur, -trice

vasoconstriction [veɪzəʊkən'strɪkʃən] *n Med* vasoconstriction *f*

vasoconstrictor [veɪzəʊkən'strɪktər] *Med* **1** *n* vasoconstricteur *m* **2** *adj* vasoconstricteur, -trice

vasodilation [veɪzəʊdaɪ'leɪʃən] *n Med* vasodilatation *f*

vasodilator [veɪzəʊdaɪ'leɪtər] *Med* **1** *n* vasodilatateur *m* **2** *adj* vasodilatateur, -trice

vasomotor ['veɪzəʊməʊtər] *adj Anat* vasomoteur, -trice

vassal ['væs(ə)l] *adj, n Hist* vassal *m*, -aux; *Fig* subordonné, -ée, vassal; **v. state** pays *m* vassal

vassalage ['væsəlɪdʒ] *n Hist* vassalité *f*, vasselage *m*; *Fig* sujétion *f*

vast [vɑːst] *adj* immense; **in the v. majority of cases** dans la très grande *ou* l'immense majorité des cas; **a v. number of people** un extrêmement grand nombre de gens; **a v. expanse of territory** une immense *ou* vaste étendue de territoire; **his v. knowledge** son immense savoir; **to spend a v. amount** *or* **v. sums (of money)** dépenser de grosses sommes d'argent; **at v. expense** à grands frais; **there's a v. difference between them** il y a une différence énorme entre eux

vastly ['vɑːstlɪ] *adv* immensément; **to be v. knowledgeable about sth** avoir des connaissances très vastes *ou* très étendues sur qch; **v. different** extrêmement différent; **they're not v. different** ils ne sont pas très différents

vastness ['vɑːstnɪs] *n* immensité *f*

VAT [viːeɪ'tiː, væt] *n Br* (*abbr* **value added tax**) TVA *f*; **V. credit** crédit *m* de TVA; **V. exempt** exonéré de TVA; **V. exemption** franchise *f* de TVA; **V.-man** = inspecteur *m* de la TVA ; **V. rate** taux *m* de TVA; **V. rebate** décote *f* de TVA; **V. reference** *or* **registration number** code *m* assujetti TVA; **V. return** déclaration *f* de TVA, état *m* (de) TVA

vat [væt] *n* (*container*) cuve *f*, bac *m*; **v. dyes** colorants *mpl* de cuve

vatful ['vætfʊl] *n* (*quantity*) cuvée *f*

Vatican ['vætɪkən] *n* **the V.** le Vatican; **V. City** la cité du Vatican; **the V. Council** le concile du Vatican; *F Hum* **V. roulette** = méthode *f* de contraception basée sur l'abstinence périodique

VAT-registered person *n* déclarant *m* de TVA

vaudeville ['vɔːdəvɪl] *n Am Th* variétés *fpl*; **v. artist** artiste *mf* de variétés; **v. show** spectacle *m* de variétés

vault¹ [vɔːlt, vɒlt] *n* **(a)** *Archit* voûte *f*; **tunnel v.** voûte cylindrique; **fan v.** voûte en éventail; **ribbed v.** voûte d'ogives *ou* à nervures; *Fig* **the v. of heaven** la voûte céleste **(b)** (*underground*) (*of country house, castle*) cave *f*; (*of church, for burial*) caveau *m*; **family v.** caveau de famille; **(bank) v.** chambre *f* forte

vault² *Archit* **1** *vt* **to v. (over)** (*cellar*) voûter **2** *vi* (*of roof*) former une voûte

vault³ *n Gym* saut *m* (*en s'aidant d'une ou de deux mains*); (*on vaulting horse*) saut au cheval d'arçons; **(pole) v.** saut à la perche

vault⁴ **1** *vi* (*jump*) sauter (*en s'aidant d'une ou de deux mains*); **he vaulted over the gate** il a sauté la barrière; **to v. into the saddle** sauter en selle **2** *vt* (*barrier*) sauter, franchir d'un saut (*en s'aidant d'une ou deux mains*)

vaulted ['vɔːltɪd, 'vɒl-] *adj Archit* voûté, en (forme de) voûte

vaulting¹ ['vɔːltɪŋ, 'vɒl-] *n Archit* voûte(s) *f(pl)*; **barrel v.** voûte(s) en berceau

vaulting² **1** *n Gym* **v. horse** cheval *m* d'arçons, cheval-arçons *m*, *pl* chevaux-arçons **2** *adj Fig* **v. ambition** ambition *f* démesurée

vaunt [vɔːnt] *vt* se vanter de, se faire gloire de; **our much vaunted justice** notre justice tant vantée *ou* dont on fait tant l'éloge; *esp Lit* **the city vaunts a 13th century castle** la ville s'enorgueillit de son château du 13ème siècle

VC [viː'siː] *n abbr* **(a)** *Br Mil* (**Victoria Cross**) = la plus haute distinction britannique accordée pour récompenser le courage d'un militaire; **to be awarded the VC** recevoir la Victoria Cross; **John Smith VC** = John Smith, titulaire de la Victoria Cross **(b)** *US Hist* **Vietcong (c) vice chairman/ chairwoman/chairperson (d) vice consul**

VCR [viːsiː'ɑːr] *n* (*abbr* **video cassette recorder**) magnétoscope *m*

VD [viː'diː] *n Med* (*abbr* **venereal disease**) maladie *f* vénérienne; **VD clinic** centre *m* de traitement des maladies vénériennes

VDT [viːdiː'tiː] *n Comptr abbr Br* **visual** *or Am* **video display terminal**

VDU [viːdiː'juː] *n Comptr* (*abbr* **visual display unit**) écran *m*, afficheur *m*; **V. operator** personne *f* travaillant sur écran; **V. user** utilisateur *m* d'écran

veal [viːl] *n Culin* veau *m*; **v. cutlet** côtelette *f* de veau

vector ['vektər] *n Math, Phys, Med* vecteur *m*; **v.-borne disease** maladie *f* transmise par (agent) vecteur; **v. function** fonction *f* vectorielle; *Comptr* **v. generator** générateur *m* de vecteurs; **v. graphics** affichage *m* vectoriel; **v. processing** traitement *m* de vecteurs, traitement vectoriel

vectored interrupt ['vektəd] *n Comptr* interruption *f* vectorisée

vectorial [vek'tɔːrɪəl] *adj Math* vectoriel

vee engine [viː] *n* moteur *m* en V

veep [viːp] *n US F* vice-président, -ente, *pl* vice-président(e)s

veer¹ [vɪər] *n* (*of wind*) changement *m* de direction; (*of ship*) virement *m* de bord; *Fig* (*of opinion*) revirement *m*

veer² **1** *vi* (*of wind*) tourner; (*of ship*) virer de bord; (*of car, road*) tourner abruptement, virer; *Naut* **to v. off course** dévier du cap fixé, dévier de sa route; *Aut* **he veered to the right** il a viré à droite; **the car veered off the road** la voiture a fait une embardée et a quitté la route; *Fig* **the conversation veered towards politics** la conversation a tourné à la politique; **to v. between two extremes** alterner entre deux extrêmes **2** *vt* (*ship*) faire virer

▶ **veer round** *vi* (*of vehicle, person*) faire demi-tour; (*of wind*) changer de direction; *Fig* (*of person*) se ranger à l'opinion contraire

veg¹ [vedʒ] *n* (*inv in pl*) *Br F* légume *m*; **meat and two v.** plat *m* comportant de la viande et deux légumes (*typique de la gastronomie britannique traditionnelle*)

veg² *vi esp US Sl* (*relax*) **to v. (out)** paresser

vegan ['viːgən] *n* végétalien, -ienne

veganism ['viːgənɪz(ə)m] *n* végétalisme *m*

vegeburger ['vedʒɪbɜːgər] *n* hamburger *m* végétarien

vegetable ['vedʒtəb(ə)l] **1** *adj* végétal; **the v. kingdom** le règne végétal; **v. life** la vie végétale; **v. matter** matières *fpl* végétales; **v. oils** huiles *fpl* végétales; *Fig* **to lead a v.-like existence** mener une existence végétative

2 *n* **(a)** [①A9,b,ii] *Culin* légume *m*; **to grow vegetables** cultiver *ou* faire pousser des légumes; **green vegetables** légumes verts; **early vegetables** primeurs *fpl*; *Fig* **to live like a v.** végéter, mener une vie végétative; *Fig* **the accident has left her a v.** l'accident l'a privée de toutes ses facultés; **v. dish** (*meal*) plat *m* de légumes; (*container*) légumier *m*, plat à légumes; **v. garden** (jardin *m*) potager *m*; **v. knife** couteau *m* à légumes; **v. marrow** courge *f*; **v. rack** casier *m* à légumes; **v. soup** soupe *f* aux *ou* de légumes

(b) *Bot* végétal *m*

vegetal ['vedʒɪt(ə)l] *adj Bot* végétal

vegetarian [vedʒɪ'teərɪən] *adj, n* végétarien, -ienne; **to be a v.** être végétarien; **v. restaurant** restaurant *m* végétarien

vegetarianism [vedʒɪ'teərɪənɪz(ə)m] *n* végétarisme *m*

vegetate ['vedʒɪteɪt] *vi Pej* végéter; **to v. in an office** végéter *ou* moisir dans un bureau

vegetation [vedʒɪ'teɪʃən] *n* végétation *f*

vegetative ['vedʒɪtətɪv, -teɪtɪv] *adj* végétatif; *Fig* **v. existence** existence *f* végétative

veggie ['vedʒɪ] *n F* **(a)** (*vegetarian*) végétarien, -ienne **(b)** *esp Am* (*vegetable*) légume *m*

veggieburger ['vedʒɪbɜːgər] *n* = **vegeburger**

vehemence ['viːɪməns] *n* (*of orator*) véhémence *f*; **with all the v. of youth** avec l'ardeur de la jeunesse

vehement ['viːɪmənt] *adj* (*orator*) véhément; (*desire*) passionné; (*attack, effort, dislike*) violent; **she was most v. in her insistence** elle a insisté avec une grande véhémence

vehemently ['viːɪməntlɪ] *adv* avec véhémence; (*to dislike*) violemment; **to be v. opposed to sth** être fortement opposé à qch

vehicle ['viːɪk(ə)l] *n* **(a)** (*means of transport*) véhicule *m*; **(extra) long v.** convoi *m* grande longueur, convoi exceptionnel; **heavy goods v.** poids *m* lourd; **v. check-in** (*at ferry*) contrôle *m* des véhicules; **v. frame** châssis *m*; **v. identification number** numéro *m* d'immatriculation du véhicule; **v. registration document** carte *f* grise
(b) *Fig* (*of thought, for propaganda*) véhicule *m*; **the newspaper as a v. for advertising** le journal comme moyen de publicité; **the play is merely a v. for his talents** la pièce n'est qu'un moyen de mettre ses talents en valeur
(c) (*for paint*) véhicule *m*
(d) *Pharm* excipient *m*

vehicular [vɪ'hɪkjʊlər] *adj* des véhicules, des voitures; **v. accident** accident *m* de la circulation; **v. traffic** circulation *f*; **closed to v. traffic** interdit aux véhicules

veil¹ [veɪl] *n* (*of nun, sign of mourning*) voile *m*; (*on hat*) voilette *f*; *Fig* (*of smoke, mist*) voile; (*of politeness, culture*) vernis *m*; **bridal v.** voile de mariée; *Rel* **to take the v.** prendre le voile; *Fig* **to draw** *or* **throw a v. over sth** jeter un voile sur qch; **under a v. of secrecy** sous le voile du secret

veil² *vt* (*face, painting*) voiler; (*one's feelings, intentions*) voiler, cacher, dissimuler; **their plans were veiled in secrecy** leurs plans étaient gardés secrets; **to v. oneself** se voiler; **to v. one's face** se voiler le visage

veiled [veɪld] *adj* voilé, couvert d'un voile; *Fig* voilé, caché, dissimulé; (*comment, threat, allusion*) voilé; **to express oneself in v. terms** s'exprimer en termes voilés; **a thinly v. reference to** une référence à peine voilée à; **thinly v. hostility** hostilité à peine déguisée

vein [veɪn] *n* **(a)** *Anat* veine *f*; *Ent* (*of wing*) nervure *f*; *Bot* (*of leaf*) nervure, veine; **he has noble blood in his veins** il a du sang bleu dans les veines **(b)** *Geol, Min* veine *f*, filon *m*; (*in wood, marble*) veine; *Fig* **a v. of melancholy/humour** une pointe de mélancolie/d'humour **(c)** *Fig* (*manner, style*) veine *f*, disposition *f*, humeur *f*; **the poetic v.** la veine poétique; **other remarks in the same v.** d'autres observations faites dans le même esprit

veined [veɪnd] *adj* (*marble etc*) veiné, à veines; *Bot, Ent* nervuré

veining ['veɪnɪŋ] *n* **(a)** (*streaks*) veinure *f*, marbrure *f* **(b)** *Bot, Ent* nervures *fpl*

velar ['viːlər] *adj, n Ling* vélaire *f*

velcro® ['velkrəʊ] *n* velcro *m*; **v. fastener** (*on shoe, sleeve*) patte *f* velcro; (*full-length, on coat*) fermeture *f* velcro; **v. strip** bande *f* velcro

veld(t) [velt] *n* veld(t) *m*

vellum ['veləm] *n* vélin *m*; **v. paper** papier *m* vélin

velocipede [vɪ'lɒsɪpiːd] *n Hist* vélocipède *m*

velocity [vɪ'lɒsɪtɪ] *n* vélocité *f*, vitesse *f*

velodrome ['viːlədrəʊm] *n* vélodrome *m*

velour(s) [və'lʊər] *n Tex* (*velvet*) velours *m* de laine; (*felt*) feutre *m* taupé

velum, *pl* **-la** ['viːləm, -ə] *n Anat* voile *m* du palais

velvet ['velvɪt] *n Tex* velours *m*; **v. skirt/collar** jupe *f*/col *m* de velours; **to have (a) skin like v.** avoir une peau de pêche; **as smooth as v.** (*skin*) doux comme du *ou* le velours; (*drink*) velouté; **black v.** (*drink*) mélange *m* de champagne et de stout; *Pol* **the V. Revolution** la révolution de velours; *Fig* **to be on v.** mener la vie de château; **with v. tread** à pas feutrés; **an iron hand in a v. glove** une main de fer dans un gant de velours

velveteen [velvɪ'tiːn] *n Tex* velours *m* de coton; **v. jacket** veste *f* en velours de coton

velvety ['velvɪtɪ] *adj* (*appearance, taste*) velouté; (*wine*) velouté, qui a du velouté; (*to the touch*) velouteux, doux comme le velours

venal ['viːn(ə)l] *adj* vénal

venality [vɪ'nælɪtɪ] *n* vénalité *f*

vend [vend] *vt esp Jur, Admin* vendre; **machine that vends coffee** distributeur *m* automatique (payant) de café

vendee [ven'diː] *n Jur* acquéreur *m*

vendetta [ven'detə] *n* vendetta *f*; **to wage a v. against sb** mener une vendetta contre qn

vending ['vendɪŋ] *n* vente *f*; **v. machine** distributeur *m* automatique (payant)

vendor ['vendɔːr] *n* **(a)** (*person*) *Com, Jur* vendeur, -euse; *Comptr* fournisseur *m*; **(street) v.** marchand *m* ambulant **(b)** (*machine*) distributeur *m* automatique (payant)

veneer¹ [və'nɪər] *n* **(a)** (*covering*) placage *m*, revêtement *m*; (*material*) bois *m* de placage, bois à plaquer **(b)** *Fig* masque *m*, apparence *f* extérieure; (*of culture*) vernis *m*; **a v. of politeness/respectability** un vernis de politesse/respectabilité; **beneath the v. of politeness** sous le masque de politesse

veneer² *vt* (*wood*) plaquer (**with** avec)

venerable ['ven(ə)rəb(ə)l] *adj* (*old man etc*) vénérable

venerate ['venəreɪt] *vt* (*sb, sth*) vénérer

veneration [venə'reɪʃən] *n* vénération *f* (**for** pour); **to hold sb in v.** avoir de la vénération pour qn

venereal [vɪ'nɪərɪəl] *adj Med* vénérien; **v. disease** maladie *f* vénérienne

venereology [vɪnɪərɪ'ɒlədʒɪ] *n Med* vénéréologie *f*

Venetian [vɪ'niːʃən] **1** *adj* vénitien; **V. blind** store *m* vénitien; **V. glass** verre *m* de Venise; **V. lace** point *m* de Venise **2** *n* Vénitien, -ienne

Venezuela [vene'zweɪlə] *n* Vénézuéla *m*

Venezuelan [vene'zweɪl(ə)n] **1** *adj* vénézuélien **2** *n* Vénézuélien, -ienne

vengeance ['ven(d)ʒəns] *n* vengeance *f*; **to take v. on sb** se venger de qn; **to take v. for** tirer vengeance de; (*person's death*) venger; *Fig F* **with a v.** (*to set to work*) furieusement; (*to start doing sth again*) de plus belle; (*to rain*) (*more than before*) pour de bon; (*heavily*) à seaux, à verse; **to work with a v.** travailler d'arrache-pied; **the autumn set in with a v.** l'automne a fait une entrée en force

vengeful ['ven(d)ʒfʊl] *adj* (*person*) vindicatif; (*look*) vengeur

vengefully ['ven(d)ʒfʊlɪ] *adv* d'une manière vindicative

vengefulness ['ven(d)ʒfʊlnɪs] *n* (*of action*) caractère *m* vindicatif; (*of person*) esprit *m* de vengeance

venial ['viːnɪəl] *adj* **(a)** *Rel* (*sin*) véniel **(b)** (*error*) sans gravité, véniel

veniality [viːnɪ'ælɪtɪ] *n* caractère *m* véniel

Venice ['venɪs] *n* Venise *f*

venison ['venɪs(ə)n] *n Culin* venaison *f*; **haunch of v.** quartier *m* de chevreuil

venom ['venəm] *n* (*poison*), *Fig* venin *m*; **to say with v.** dire avec méchanceté *ou* malveillance

venomous ['venəməs] *adj* (*snake, spider etc*) venimeux; (*plant*) vénéneux; *Fig* (*criticism*) venimeux, envenimé; **a v. look** un regard venimeux; *Fig* **a v. tongue** une langue de vipère

venomously ['venəməslɪ] *adv* avec venin *ou* méchanceté

venous ['viːnəs] *adj* (*system, blood*) veineux

vent¹ [vent] *n* **(a)** (*for intake*) ouverture *f*, orifice *m*; (*for outlet*) évent *m*; (*for ventilation in car*) aérateur *m*; (*of ventilation shaft*) soupirail *m*, -aux; *Geol* (*of volcano*) cheminée *f*; (*of fish, bird*) orifice anal; *Aut* **v. pipe** tuyau *m* de mise à l'air libre **(b)** *Fig* **to give v. to one's grief/anger/indignation** donner libre cours à sa douleur/sa colère/son indignation; **to give v. to one's spleen** décharger sa bile

vent² *vt* **(a)** (*pipe*) décharger, vider des gaz; (*gas from pipe, steam from boiler*) évacuer **(b)** *Fig* (*one's anger*) donner libre cours à, laisser éclater, exhaler; **to v. one's spleen/anger on sb** décharger sa bile/épancher sa colère sur qn

vent³ *n* (*on jacket*) fente *f*

ventilate ['ventɪleɪt] *vt* **(a)** (*room*) aérer, ventiler; (*tunnel*) ventiler; (*mine*) éventer **(b)** *Fig* (*question, feelings*) mettre au grand jour

ventilated ['ventɪleɪtɪd] *adj* **(a)** (*aired*) aéré **(b)** *Br F* (*over-excited*) **to get v. about sth** se mettre dans tous ses états à propos de qch

ventilation [ventɪ'leɪʃən] *n* (*of room*) aération *f*, ventilation *f*; (*of mine*) aérage *m*; **v. air filter** filtre *m* à air de ventilation; *Min* **v. shaft** puits *m* de ventilation *ou* d'aération *ou* d'aérage; **v. system** système *m* d'aération *ou* de ventilation

ventilator ['ventɪleɪtər] *n* **(a)** *Tech* ventilateur *m*, aérateur *m*; *Naut* manche *f* à air **(b)** *Med* respirateur *m*, poumon *m* artificiel; **to be on a v.** être sur respirateur

venting screw ['ventɪŋ] *n Aut* vis *f* de mise à l'air libre *ou* de purge

ventral ['ventr(ə)l] *adj Anat, Biol* ventral; **v. fins** nageoires *fpl* ventrales

ventricle ['ventrɪk(ə)l] *n Anat* ventricule *m*

ventriloquism [ven'trɪləkwɪz(ə)m] *n* ventriloquie *f*

ventriloquist [ven'trɪləkwɪst] *n* ventriloque *mf*; **v.'s dummy** marionnette *f* de ventriloque

venture¹ ['ventʃər] *n* **(a)** (*risky undertaking*) entreprise *f* hasardeuse *ou* risquée; **this v. into advertising/fiction** cette incursion dans la publicité/fiction; **desperate v.** tentative *f* désespérée **(b)** (*business undertaking*) entreprise *f*; **joint v.** (*undertaking*) affaire *f* en participation; (*company*) entreprise en participation; *Com* **v. team** équipe *f* commando **(c)** *Arch* **at a v.** (*at random*) au hasard

venture² **1** *vt* (*one's life, money*) risquer, aventurer; **to v. to do sth** se hasarder à faire qch, se risquer à faire qch; **I v. to affirm he knew nothing about it** j'ose affirmer qu'il n'en savait rien; **to v. a remark** hasarder une remarque; **I ventured the remark that …** je me suis hasardé à faire la remarque que …; **to v. an opinion** se hasarder *ou* se risquer à donner une opinion; *Prov* **nothing venture(d) nothing gain(ed)** qui ne risque rien n'a rien

2 *vi* **to v. into unknown territory** s'aventurer en terre inconnue; **this is the first time he has ventured into historical fiction** c'est sa première incursion dans la fiction historique; **to v. out of doors** se risquer à sortir; **to v. too far** s'aventurer trop loin
▶ **venture forth** *or* **out** *vi esp Lit* (*after illness, from hiding etc*) s'aventurer à sortir; **they ventured forth into the unknown** ils s'aventurèrent dans l'inconnu; **they ventured forth on their quest for …** ils partirent à la recherche de …
▶ **venture on, venture upon** *vipo* se risquer à, se hasarder à
venture capital *n* capital-risque *m*
venture capitalist *n* pourvoyeur *m* de capital-risque
Venture Scout *n Br* routier *m*
venturesome ['ventʃəsəm] *adj* **(a)** (*person*) aventureux, entreprenant **(b)** (*action*) risqué, hasardeux
venturi throat [ven'tjuːrɪ] *n Aut* col *m* du venturi
venue ['venjuː] *n* **(a)** (*hall*) salle *f*; (*for football match*) terrain *m*; **the v. for the concert will be the Albert Hall/Birmingham** le concert se déroulera à l'Albert Hall/Birmingham; **what is the v. for the match?** où est-ce que le match aura lieu?; **there has been a change of v.** ça n'a plus lieu au même endroit, ça se tiendra ailleurs **(b)** *Jur* lieu *m* du jugement; **to change the v. of a trial** renvoyer une affaire devant une autre cour
venule ['venjuːl] *n Anat* veinule *f*
Venus ['viːnəs] *n Astron, Myth* Vénus *f*; *Bot* **V. flytrap** dionée *f*, attrape-mouches *m inv*
veracious [və'reɪʃəs] *adj Fml* (*person, account*) véridique
veracity [və'ræsɪtɪ], **veraciousness** [və'reɪʃəsnɪs] *n esp Fml* (*of person, report*) véracité *f*
veranda(h) [və'rændə] *n Archit* véranda *f*
verb [vɜːb] *n* [①**A38-63**; **B22-50**] *Gram* verbe *m*
verbal[1] ['vɜːb(ə)l] **1** *adj* (*agreement, promise*) verbal, oral; (*communication, skills*) verbal; **v. agreement** convention *f* verbale, accord *m* verbal; **v. abuse** paroles *fpl* insultantes; *F* **v. diarrhoea** logorrhée *f*; **v. noun** nom *m* verbal **2** *n Br Sl* **to give sb the v.** (*shout at sb*) engueuler qn; **they were given the v.** ils se sont fait engueuler
verbal[2] *vt Br Sl* (*of police*) = impliquer dans un crime en citant devant la cour un prétendu aveu
verbalize ['vɜːbəlaɪz] *vt* **(a)** (*idea*) exprimer par des mots; *Psy* (*experience*) verbaliser **(b)** *Gram* (*noun*) employer comme verbe
verbally ['vɜːbəlɪ] *adv* **(a)** (*orally*) verbalement, oralement, de vive voix; **to be v. abused** se faire insulter verbalement; **to agree v. to do sth** se mettre d'accord verbalement pour faire qch **(b)** (*as a verb*) en tant que verbe
verbatim [vɜː'beɪtɪm] **1** *adv* mot à mot, textuellement; **to report a speech v.** rendre compte mot à mot d'un discours **2** *adj* exact, mot à mot; **to give a v. account of sth** faire un compte-rendu mot à mot de qch
verbena [vɜː'biːnə] *n Bot* verveine *f*; **lemon(-scented) v.** citronnelle *f*
verbiage ['vɜːbɪɪdʒ] *n* verbiage *m*
verbose [vɜː'bəʊs] *adj* (*writer, style*) verbeux, diffus, prolixe
verbosely [vɜː'bəʊslɪ] *adv* avec verbosité, verbeusement; **v. worded** verbeux
verbosity [vɜː'bɒsɪtɪ] *n* verbosité *f*, prolixité *f*
verdant ['vɜːdənt] *adj Fml* vert, verdoyant
verdict ['vɜːdɪkt] *n* **(a)** *Jur* verdict *m*; **to bring in a v. of guilty/not guilty** rendre un verdict de culpabilité/de non-culpabilité; **to return a v.** prononcer *ou* rendre un verdict; **to reach a v.** conclure, décider; **the jury returned a v. of suicide** (*in coroner's court*) le jury a conclu au suicide; **open v.** (*at inquest*) = jugement *m* qui ne formule aucune conclusion sur les circonstances dans lesquelles la mort a eu lieu **(b)** *Fig* jugement *m*, avis *m*; **to give one's v.** se prononcer (**on** sur); **what's your v.?** qu'est-ce que tu en penses?
verdigris ['vɜːdɪgrɪs] *n* vert-de-gris *m*
verdure ['vɜːdʒər] *n Lit* (*colour*) verdure *f*; (*foliage*) verdure, feuillage *m*
verge [vɜːdʒ] *n* **(a)** *Br Aut* (*of road*) bas-côté *m*, accotement *m*; **sitting on the grass v. of the road** assis sur l'herbe du bord de la route; **soft verges** (*road sign*) accotement instable **(b)** *Fig* **on the v. of tears/disaster/a nervous breakdown** au bord des larmes/du désastre/de la crise de nerfs; **on the v. of death** à la frontière de la mort; **on the v. of ruin** à deux doigts de la ruine; **to be on the v. of doing sth** être sur le point de faire qch; **on the v. of manhood** au seuil de l'âge viril **(c)** *esp Lit* (*edge*) (*of river*) bord *m*; (*of forest*) orée *f*
▶ **verge on** *vipo* confiner à, friser; **red verging on pink** rouge qui tire sur le rose; **he was verging on sixty/hysteria** il frisait la soixantaine/l'hystérie
verger ['vɜːdʒər] *n Br Rel* bedeau *m*
Vergil ['vɜːdʒɪl] *n Antiq, Liter* Virgile *m*
verifiable [verɪ'faɪəb(ə)l] *adj* vérifiable
verification [verɪfɪ'keɪʃən] *n* vérification *f*; **v. procedures** procédures *fpl* de vérification; **to produce evidence in v. of a theory** fournir des preuves qui confirment *ou* vérifient une théorie
verify ['verɪfaɪ] *vt* (*check, prove*) vérifier; (*confirm*) vérifier, confirmer; (*information, accounts*) vérifier, contrôler; **this verifies my suspicions/my fears** cela confirme mes soupçons/mes craintes; **I can v. that Gillian Love was present** je peux confirmer que Gillian Love était bien là
verily ['verɪlɪ] *adv Arch, Bible* en vérité, vraiment
verisimilitude [verɪsɪ'mɪlɪtjuːd] *n Fml* vraisemblance *f*
veritable ['verɪtəb(ə)l] *adj* véritable, vrai; **this is a v. disaster** c'est un véritable *ou* vrai désastre
veritably ['verɪtəblɪ] *adv* véritablement
verity ['verɪtɪ] *n Lit* vérité *f*; *Rel* **the (eternal) verities** les vérités éternelles
vermicelli [vɜːmɪ'tʃelɪ] *n Culin* vermicelle(s) *m(pl)*
vermicide ['vɜːmɪsaɪd] *n Pharm* vermicide *m*
vermiculite [vɜː'mɪkjʊlaɪt] *n* vermiculite *f*
vermiform ['vɜːmɪfɔːm] *adj* vermiforme
vermifugal [vɜːmɪ'fjuːg(ə)l] *adj* vermifuge
vermifuge ['vɜːmɪfjuːdʒ] *n* vermifuge *m*
vermilion [və'mɪljən] **1** *n* vermillon *m* **2** *adj* (de) vermillon *inv*, vermeil, -eille
vermin ['vɜːmɪn] *n* [①**A11,f,ii**] (*inv in pl*) (*fleas, lice etc*), *Fig* vermine *f*; (*mice, rats etc*) animaux *mpl* nuisibles; **pigeons are v.** les pigeons sont des animaux nuisibles
verminous ['vɜːmɪnəs] *adj* (*covered with fleas, lice etc*) couvert de vermine; *Fig* (*dirty*) (*coat, flat*) miteux; *Fig* **you v. little creep!** espèce de vermine!
vermouth ['vɜːməθ] *n* vermout(h) *m*
vernacular [və'nækjʊlər] **1** *adj* **(a)** *Ling* vernaculaire, indigène **(b)** *Archit* local **2** *n* **(a)** (*everyday speech*) langue *f* vulgaire; **in the v.** dans la langue vulgaire; **to translate the Bible into the v.** traduire la Bible dans la langue vulgaire **(b)** (*dialect*) langue *f* vernaculaire *ou* indigène **(c)** *Archit* style *m* local **(d)** (*jargon*) jargon *m*; **the sporting v.** le jargon sportif
vernal ['vɜːn(ə)l] *adj Fml* printanier, du printemps; *Astron, Bot* vernal; **v. equinox** équinoxe *m* de printemps
veronal ['verən(ə)l] *n Pharm* véronal *m*
veronica [və'rɒnɪkə] *n Bot* véronique *f*
verruca, *pl* **-ae** [ve'ruːkə, -kiː] *n* verrue *f*
versant ['vɜːsənt] *n* (*of mountain*) versant *m*
versatile ['vɜːsətaɪl] *adj* **(a)** (*person*) aux talents variés, polyvalent; (*dress, jacket*) (*can be worn anywhere*) passe-partout; (*has detachable parts, is reversible etc*) polyvalent; (*tool, machine*) polyvalent, d'une grande souplesse d'emploi, universel; **a v. mind** un esprit souple *ou* universel **(b)** *Biol* versatile
versatility [vɜːsə'tɪlɪtɪ] *n* **(a)** (*of person*) variété *f* de talents *ou* d'aptitudes; (*adaptability*) faculté *f* d'adaption; (*of mind*) souplesse *f*, universalité *f*; (*of tool, machine*) polyvalence *f*, grande souplesse d'emploi; **his v.** la variété de ses talents; **she has v. of mind** c'est un esprit universel **(b)** *Biol* (*of organ*) versatilité *f*
verse [vɜːs] *n* **(a)** (*poetry*) vers *mpl*; **free v.** vers libres; **light v.** poésie *f* légère **(b)** (*stanza*) (*of song*) couplet *m*; (*of poem, hymn*) strophe *f*, stance *f* **(c)** (*of Bible*) verset *m*
versed [vɜːst] *adj* versé (**in** en, dans); **v. in the arts** versé dans les arts; **to be well v. in mathematics** être fort instruit dans les mathématiques; **I am well v. in his ways** je le connais bien, je sais bien comment il est
versification [vɜːsɪfɪ'keɪʃən] *n* **(a)** (*art*) versification *f* **(b)** (*metre*) (*of verse*) facture *f*; (*of author*) métrique *f*
versifier ['vɜːsɪfaɪər] *n Pej* versificateur *m*
versify ['vɜːsɪfaɪ] **1** *vt* (*story etc*) versifier, mettre en vers **2** *vi* versifier, faire des vers
version ['vɜːʃən] *n* **(a)** (*account*) (*of facts*) version *f*; **he gave us a very different v. of the affair** il nous a donné de cette affaire un récit très différent; **according to his v.** d'après sa version des faits; **her v. differs from mine** sa version des faits diffère de la mienne **(b)** (*variation*) (*of car, text, recipe*) version *f*; **the military v. of this aircraft** la version militaire de cet avion; **the TV v. of a novel** l'adaptation *f* d'un roman pour la télévision **(c)** (*translation*) version *f*, traduction *f*; **the English v. of the Bible** la version anglaise de la Bible
verso ['vɜːsəʊ] *n* **(a)** (*of page*) verso *m* **(b)** (*of medal*) revers *m*
versus ['vɜːsəs] *prep Jur, Sp* contre; *Sp* **Martin v. Thomas** Martin contre Thomas; *Fig* **the advantage of a higher salary v. the loss of security** l'avantage d'un salaire plus élevé en contrepartie d'une sécurité moindre; *Fig* **the relative merits of public v. private ownership** les avantages relatifs de la propriété de l'État par opposition à la propriété privée

vertebra, *pl* **-ae** ['vɜːtɪbrə, -iː] *n* vertèbre *f*
vertebral ['vɜːtɪbrəl] *adj* vertébral; **v. column** colonne *f* vertébrale
vertebrate ['vɜːtɪbreɪt, -brɪt] **1** *adj* (*animal*) vertébré; (*characteristic*) des vertébrés **2** *n* vertébré *m*
vertex, *pl* **-ices** ['vɜːteks, -tɪsiːz] *n* **(a)** *Geom* (*of angle, curve*) sommet *m* **(b)** *Anat* vertex *m*
vertical ['vɜːtɪk(ə)l] **1** *adj* vertical; **in a v. position** en position verticale, à la verticale; **v. line** (ligne *f*) verticale *f*; **v. cliff** falaise *f* à pic; **v. elevation** altitude *f*; **v. integration** intégration *f ou* concentration *f* verticale; **v. marketing** mercatique *f* verticale; *St Exch* **v. spread** écart *m* vertical; **v. suspension file** fiche *f* verticale suspendue **2** *n* (*line, position*) verticale *f*
vertical hold *n TV* bouton *m* de commande de synchronisme vertical
verticality [vɜːtɪ'kælɪtɪ] *n* verticalité *f*
vertical landing *n Av* atterrissage *m* vertical
vertically ['vɜːtɪklɪ] *adv* verticalement, à la verticale; *Av* **to take off/land v.** décoller/atterrir à la verticale
vertical take-off *n Av* décollage *m* vertical; **v. aircraft** avion *m* à décollage vertical
vertical takeover *n* prise *f* de contrôle verticale
vertiginous [vɜː'tɪdʒɪnəs] *adj* vertigineux
vertigo ['vɜːtɪgəʊ] *n Med* vertige *m*; **to suffer from/get v.** avoir le vertige; **I had an attack of v.** j'ai été pris de vertige
verve [vɜːv] *n* verve *f*, brio *m*; **to play/act with v.** jouer avec verve *ou* brio
Very ['vɪərɪ] *n Mil* **V. light** fusée *f* éclairante; **V. (light) pistol** pistolet *m* lance-fusée(s)
very ['verɪ] **1** *adv* [①A24-25,d,iv] **(a)** (*extremely*) très; **v. good** (*adj phrase*) très bon, fort bon; (*adv phrase*) très bien, fort bien; **a v. good dictionary** un très *ou* fort bon dictionnaire; **v. good, captain** très bien, mon capitaine; **he is v. well known in Paris** il est très connu à Paris; **that's v. kind of you** c'est très gentil à vous; **you are v. kind** vous êtes bien bon; **so v. little** si peu; **there's v. little one can do to help** on ne peut pas faire grand-chose pour aider; **I took only a v. little** j'en ai pris très peu; **it isn't so v. difficult** ce n'est pas tellement difficile, ce n'est pas si difficile que ça; **he was not v. pleased** il n'était pas très content; **v. (v.) few** très (très) peu; **are you hungry? – yes, v.** avez-vous faim? – oui, très; **he wore a v. pleased expression** il avait l'air très satisfait; **I feel v. much better** je me sens beaucoup mieux; **it is v. much better to wait** il vaut bien mieux attendre; *Comptr* **v. high level language** langage *m* très évolué; **v. large scale integration** intégration *f* à très grande échelle; *Rel* **the V. Reverend ...** le très révérent ...

(b) (*emphatic use*) **the v. first** le tout premier; **we were the v. first to arrive** nous étions les tout premiers à arriver; **the v. last** le tout dernier; **the v. best** tout ce qu'il y a de mieux *ou* de meilleur; **at the v. most/least** tout au plus/au moins; **at the v. latest** au plus tard; **the v. same** exactement le même; **I v. nearly died** j'ai bien failli mourir; **it was the v. last thing I expected** c'était vraiment la dernière chose à laquelle je m'attendais; **the v. next day** dès le lendemain, le lendemain même; **in the v. front row** au tout premier rang; **a room of my v. own** une pièce rien qu'à moi; **it's my v. own** c'est à moi tout seul

2 *adj* **(a)** (*emphatic use*) même; **he lives in this v. house** il habite dans cette maison même; **sitting in this v. room** assis dans cette pièce même; **by its v. nature** par sa nature même; **you are the v. man I wanted to see** vous êtes justement l'homme que je voulais voir; **come here this v. minute!** venez ici à l'instant!; **this v. day** aujourd'hui même; **it was a year ago to the v. day** c'était il y a un an jour pour jour; **these are his v. words** ce sont là ses propres paroles; **at the v. beginning** au tout début; **he knows our v. thoughts** il connaît jusqu'à nos pensées; **the v. idea frightens me** cette pensée suffit à m'effrayer; **I shudder at the v. thought of it** je frémis rien que d'y penser

(b) *Rel, Arch* (*real, true*) vrai, véritable
very high frequency *n Rad* hyperfréquences *fpl*
very low frequency *n Rad* très basse fréquence *f*
VESA ['viːsə] *n Comptr* (*abbr* **video electronics standard association**) VESA *m*
vesical ['vesɪk(ə)l] *adj Anat, Med* vésical
vesicle ['vesɪk(ə)l] *n Biol, Med* vésicule *f*
vesper ['vespər] *n Rel* **vespers** vêpres *fpl*; **to attend vespers** aller aux vêpres; **the v. bell** la cloche des vêpres *ou* du soir
vessel ['ves(ə)l] *n* **(a)** *Naut* bateau *m*; (*large*) navire *m* **(b)** (*receptacle*) récipient *m*; *Phys* **communicating vessels** vases *mpl* communicants **(c)** *Anat, Bot* vaisseau *m*
vest[1] [vest] *n* **(a)** *Br* (*for men*) maillot *m* de corps; (*for women*) chemise *f*, *Can* camisole *f*; (*for baby*) brassière *f*; *Sp* maillot; **string v.** gilet *m* en point noué *ou* en filet maille (aérée) **(b)** *Am* (*waistcoat*) gilet *m*; **v. pocket** poche *f* de gilet
vest[2] *vt* **(a) to v. sb with authority** investir *ou* revêtir qn d'autorité; **to v. property in sb** assigner des biens à qn; **right vested in the Crown** droit dévolu à la Couronne; **by the authority vested in me** en vertu de l'autorité dont je suis investi; **authority vested in the people** autorité exercée par le peuple **(b)** *Rel* (*clothe*) (*dignitary, priest*) vêtir, revêtir
vestal virgin ['vest(ə)l] *n Antiq* vestale *f*
vested interest ['vestɪd] *n* intérêt *m*; (*person*) personne *f* qui a un interêt matériel; **to have a v. in sth** avoir des intérêts dans qch; **to have a v. in sth being done** avoir intérêt à ce que qch soit fait; **I do have a v. in the play's success** j'ai intérêt à ce que la pièce soit un succès
vestibule ['vestɪbjuːl] *n* **(a)** (*entrance hall*) vestibule *m*, antichambre *f*; (*of public building*) hall *m* **(b)** *Am Rail* soufflet *m*; **v. train** train *m* à soufflets **(c)** *Anat* (*of ear*) vestibule *m*
vestige ['vestɪdʒ] *n* **(a)** (*trace*) (*of civilization etc*) vestige *m*; **not a v. of ...** (*truth, common sense*) pas une once de ... **(b)** *Biol* organe *m* rudimentaire
vestigial [ves'tɪdʒɪəl] *adj* **(a)** résiduel; **the v. remains of an abbey/a civilization** les vestiges d'une abbaye/d'une civilisation; **some v. sense of decency prevented him from doing it** le peu de décence qui lui restait l'a empêché de le faire **(b)** *Biol* (*organ*) rudimentaire
vestment ['vestmənt] *n* vêtement *m* (de cérémonie); *Rel* chasuble *f*; **(church) vestments** vêtements sacerdotaux
vest-pocket *adj Am* (*camera, dictionary etc*) de poche; *Fig* **a v. version of Fontainebleau** une version miniature de Fontainebleau; **v. park** parc *m* miniature
vestry ['vestrɪ] *n Rel* **(a)** (*in church*) sacristie *f* **(b)** (*parish council*) conseil *m* paroissial
Vesuvius [vɪ'suːvɪəs] *n* le Vésuve
vet[1] [vet] *n* vétérinaire *mf*; **to take an animal to the v.('s)** emmener un animal chez le vétérinaire
vet[2] *vt* **(-tt-)** (*person*) (*for security purposes*) effectuer un contrôle de sécurité sur; (*purchases, expenditure*) contrôler; (*candidate, proposal, decision*) (*examine*) examiner; (*approve*) approuver; **she's been positively vetted** le contrôle de sécurité dont elle a fait l'objet s'est avéré satisfaisant; **his mother vets his girlfriends** sa mère a un droit de regard sur ses petites amies
vet[3] *n Am Mil F* (*abbr* **veteran**) ancien combattant *m*
vetch [vetʃ] *n Bot* vesce *f*
veteran ['vet(ə)rən] **1** *n* vétéran *m*, *F* vieux *m* de la vieille; *Mil* ancien combattant *m*; **a v. of the First World War, a First World War v.** un ancien combattant de la Première Guerre Mondiale; **I have a real old v. of a typewriter** j'ai une machine à écrire, c'est une antiquité!

2 *adj* (*activist, opponent etc*) de longue date; (*sportsman, actor*) chevronné; **she is a v. campaigner for human rights** elle a fait campagne pour les droits de l'homme depuis très longtemps; **this ten-year-old boy is a v. traveller** ce petit garçon de dix ans est un voyageur aguerri; **v. army** armée *f* de vétérans; *Aut* **v. car** (*in Britain*) voiture *f* d'époque (*d'avant 1905*); (*in international categories*) vétéran *m*; **v. soldier** vieux soldat *m*
Veterans Day *n US* ≈ l'Armistice *f*, *Can* ≈ le Jour du Souvenir
veterinarian [vet(ə)rɪ'neərɪən] *n esp Am* vétérinaire *mf*
veterinary ['vet(ə)rɪn(ə)rɪ] *adj* vétérinaire; **she has a v. practice** elle a un cabinet de vétérinaire; **v. medicine** médecine *f* vétérinaire; *Br* **v. surgeon** vétérinaire *mf*
veto[1], *pl* **-oes** ['viːtəʊ, -əʊz] *n* veto *m*; **right of v.** droit *m* de veto; **to have the right** *or* **power of v.** avoir le droit de veto; **to put a v. on sth** mettre *ou* opposer son veto à qch; **to use one's v.** exercer son droit de veto; *Comptr* **in v. mode** en mode sélectif
veto[2] *vt* mettre *ou* opposer son veto à; **he vetoed it** il y a mis *ou* opposé son veto; **the spending was vetoed** cette dépense a été rejetée par véto
vetting ['vetɪŋ] *n* (*examining*) (*of candidate, proposal, decision*) examen *m*; (*of purchases, expenditure*) contrôle *m*; (*security check*) contrôle de sécurité; **v. procedure** procédure *f* de contrôle
vex [veks] *vt* ennuyer, fâcher, chagriner; **I was vexed by her attitude** son attitude m'ennuyait *ou* me chagrinait
vexation [vek'seɪʃən] *n* **(a)** (*cause*) contrariété *f*, ennui *m* **(b)** (*sadness*) chagrin *m* **(c)** (*anger*) dépit *m*
vexatious [vek'seɪʃəs] *adj esp Fml* (*person, thing*) contrariant, irritant, ennuyeux; (*circumstances*) fâcheux
vexed [vekst] *adj* **(a)** (*cross*) fâché, ennuyé, chagriné **(b) v. question** question *f* controversée *ou* très débattue *ou* non résolue; **it is a v. question whether ...** c'est une question controversée de savoir si ...
vexing ['veksɪŋ] *adj* contrariant, irritant, ennuyeux

VGA [viːdʒiː'eɪ] *n Comptr* (*abbr* **video graphics adaptor**) VGA *m*; **V. monitor** moniteur *m* VGA
VHF [viːeɪtʃ'ef] *adj Rad, TV* (*abbr* **very high frequency**) **V. radio** radio *f* en hyperfréquences; **to broadcast on V.** émettre en hyperfréquences
VHS [viːeɪtʃ'es] *adj TV abbr* **video home system**
via ['vaɪə, 'viːə] *prep* par; (*travelling*) par, *esp Spec* via; **I found out v. Fiona/head office** j'ai découvert ça par l'intermédiaire de Fiona/du siège social
viability [vaɪə'bɪlɪtɪ] *n* (*of foetus, seed, company etc*) viabilité *f*; (*of project etc*) viabilité, chances *fpl* de succès
viable ['vaɪəb(ə)l] *adj* (*foetus, seed, company etc*) viable; (*project etc*) viable, qui a des chances de réussir; **I can see no v. alternative** je ne vois pas d'autre moyen d'y parvenir
viaduct ['vaɪədʌkt] *n* viaduc *m*
vial ['vaɪəl] *n Fml* fiole *f*; (*for drugs*) ampoule *f*
viands ['vaɪəndz] *npl Arch* aliments *mpl*
viaticum [vaɪ'ætɪkəm] *n Rel* viatique *m*
vibes [vaɪbz] *npl F* **(a)** (*atmosphere*) ambiance *f*; **the v. are good** ça marche, ça gaze; **this place gives me bad v.** cet endroit me fait un effet désagréable; **I get good v. from it** ça me branche; **I get good v. from him/her** il/elle me plaît; **I'm getting strange v. from him** je ne le sens pas très bien; **what sort of v. do you get from him?** comment tu le sens? **(b)** *Mus* vibraphone *m*
vibrancy ['vaɪbrənsɪ] *n* animation *f*; (*of colours, style*) vivacité *f*; (*of personality*) flamme *f*, fougue *f*
vibrant ['vaɪbrənt] *adj* (*cultural scene, musical scene*) très actif, dynamique; (*city*) animé, plein de vie; (*new company*) dynamique; (*painting, description*) plein de vie; **city v. with activity** ville palpitante d'activité; **v. colours** couleurs *fpl* vives; **v. personality** personnalité *f* pleine d'entrain
vibraphone ['vaɪbrəfəʊn] *n Mus* vibraphone *m*
vibrate [vaɪ'breɪt] **1** *vi* vibrer; *Phys* vibrer, osciller; **her voice vibrated with emotion** sa voix était vibrante d'émotion; **you're making the house v.** tu fais trembler les murs; **to v. with activity** vibrer d'activité **2** *vt* faire vibrer
vibrating [vaɪ'breɪtɪŋ] *adj* vibrant
vibration [vaɪ'breɪʃən] *n* **(a)** vibration *f*; *Phys etc* oscillation *f*, pulsation *f* **(b)** *Fig F* **vibrations** = **vibes (a)**
vibrato [vɪ'brɑːtəʊ] *n Mus* vibrato *m*
vibrator [vaɪ'breɪtər] *n* **(a)** *El* vibrateur *m*, vibreur *m* **(b)** (*for massage, also sexual*) vibromasseur *m*
vibratory [vaɪ'breɪtərɪ] *adj Phys etc* vibratoire
viburnum [vaɪ'bɜːnəm] *n Bot* viorne *f*
vicar ['vɪkər] *n* **(a)** *Church of Eng* pasteur *m* **(b)** *Cathol* **v. apostolic** vicaire *m* apostolique; **v. general** vicaire général, grand vicaire; **the V. of Christ** le vicaire de Jésus-Christ
vicarage ['vɪkərɪdʒ] *n Church of Eng* presbytère *m* (*d'un pasteur*)
vicarious [vaɪ'keərɪəs, vɪ-] *adj* **(a)** (*at second hand*) indirect; **to lead a v. existence** vivre par procuration; **v. pleasure** (*enjoyed indirectly*) plaisir *m* procuré indirectement; **to take v. pleasure in sth** retirer indirectement du plaisir de qch; **v. sex does nothing for me** le sexe par procuration, ce n'est pas pour moi; **he gets a v. thrill from watching porn films** il trouve son plaisir à regarder des films pornographiques; **v. punishment** (*suffered indirectly*) châtiment *m* indirect; (*suffered on sb's behalf*) châtiment souffert pour un autre/des autres **(b)** (*power, authority*) délégué
vicariously [vaɪ'keərɪəslɪ, vɪ-] *adv* **(a)** (*on sb's behalf*) à la place d'un autre; (*indirectly*) indirectement; **to live v.** vivre par procuration **(b)** (*by delegation*) par délégation, par procuration
vice[1] [vaɪs] *n* (*immorality*) vice *m*; **to lead a life of v.** vivre dans le vice; **to sink into v.** sombrer dans le vice; **avarice is a v.** l'avarice est un vice; *Hum* **it's my only v.** c'est mon seul vice; **there's no v. in him** il n'est pas méchant
vice[2], *US* **vise** *n Tech* étau *m*; **he had a grip like a v.** il avait une poigne de fer; **v. clamp** *or* **jaw** mâchoire *f*
vice[3] *n* **(a)** *F abbr* **vice-chairman, vice president,** *Univ* **vice chancellor (b) v. admiral** *Fr* vice-amiral *m* d'escadre, *Can* vice-amiral
vice-chairman, *pl* **-men** *n* vice-président, *pl* vice-présidents
vice-chairmanship *n* vice-présidence *f*, *pl* vice-présidences
vice chancellor *n Pol* vice-chancelier *m*, *pl* vice-chanceliers; *Univ Br* président *m* d'université; *US* vice-président *m* d'université
vice-chancellorship [vaɪs'tʃɑːnsələʃɪp] *n Pol* fonction *f ou* dignité *f* de vice-chancelier; *Univ Br* présidence *f* d'université; *US* vice-présidence *f* d'université
vice-consul *n* vice-consul *m*, *pl* vice-consuls
vice-consulate *n* (*post or premises*) vice-consulat *m*, *pl* vice-consulats
vicelike ['vaɪslaɪk] *adj* **held in a v. grip** serré dans une poigne de fer, serré comme dans un étau
vice-marshal *n Av* **air v.** général *m* de division aérienne
vice-presidency *n* vice-présidence *f*; **a candidate for the v.** un candidat à la vice-présidence
vice-president *n* vice-président, -ente, *pl* vice-président(e)s
vice-presidential *adj* **v. candidate** candidat *m* à la vice-présidence
vice ring *n* organisation *f* criminelle (*impliquée dans la prostitution/le trafic de drogue/etc*)
viceroy ['vaɪsrɔɪ] *n* vice-roi *m*, *pl* vice-rois
Vice Squad *n* **the V.** la brigade mondaine *ou* des mœurs, *F* la Mondaine, *F* les Mœurs *fpl*
vice versa [vaɪs'vɜːsə] *adv* vice versa
vicinity [vɪ'sɪnɪtɪ] *n* **(a)** (*neighbourhood*) voisinage *m*; **in the v.** dans les alentours *ou* environs; **in the v. of Dover** à proximité de *ou* dans les environs de Douvres; **there was no-one in the immediate v.** il n'y avait personne dans le voisinage immédiat; **in the immediate v. of the factory** aux abords de l'usine; **in the v. of five thousand pounds** environ cinq mille livres, aux alentours de cinq mille livres **(b)** *Fml* (*nearness*) proximité *f* (**to** de)
vicious ['vɪʃəs] *adj* **(a)** (*harsh, violent*) rageur, violent; (*malicious*) méchant, haineux; (*struggle*) acharné; **v. blow/wind** coup *m*/vent *m* violent; **she has a v. tongue** c'est une mauvaise langue; **a v. attack** une attaque brutale; **to make a v. attack on sb's character** lancer une attaque haineuse contre la personne *ou* la réputation de qn; **v. gossip** méchants commérages *mpl* **(b)** *Old-fashioned, Lit* (*depraved*) vicieux, dépravé **(c)** (*horse, dog*) méchant
vicious circle *n* cercle *m* vicieux
viciously ['vɪʃəslɪ] *adv* (*violently*) violemment; (*maliciously*) méchamment, haineusement; (*to attack*), *also Fig* férocement
viciousness ['vɪʃəsnɪs] *n* (*of wind, blow*) violence *f*; (*of attack*) brutalité *f*, férocité *f*; (*of criticism*) méchanceté *f*
vicissitude [vɪ'sɪsɪtjuːd] *n Lit* vicissitude *f*
victim ['vɪktɪm] *n* (*of attack, murder etc*) victime *f*; (*of fire*) sinistré, -ée, incendié, -ée; (*of flood*) sinistré, -ée, inondé, -ée; (*of shipwreck etc*) sinistré, -ée; **to be sb's v.** être la victime de qn; **to be the v. of an attack** être victime d'une attaque; **the v. of sb's trickery** la dupe de la fourberie de qn; **v. of an accident, accident v.** accidenté, -ée; **to fall v. to sb's charm** succomber au charme de qn; **to fall v. to a disease** être frappé d'une maladie; **she was a** *or* **the v. of her own success** elle a été la victime de son propre succès
victimization [vɪktɪmaɪ'zeɪʃən] *n* brimades *fpl* (**of** sur, contre); **this is management v.** c'est un traitement discriminatoire de la part de la direction; **it results in the v. of the lower paid** cela se traduit par la discrimination des petits salaires; **there will be no v. of workers who have gone on strike** les ouvriers qui se sont mis en grève ne souffriront aucune représaille
victimize ['vɪktɪmaɪz] *vt* **it victimizes the lower paid** cela constitue un traitement discriminatoire à l'égard des petits salaires, ce sont les petits salaires qui en souffrent; **he felt that he was being victimized** il se croyait victime d'un traitement discriminatoire; **I'm being victimized** on s'en prend à moi; **strikers thought that they were being victimized** les grévistes se croyaient victimes de représailles
victimless ['vɪktɪmlɪs] *adj* **v. crime** = crime *f* sans victime
victor ['vɪktər] *n Fml* vainqueur *m*; **to emerge the clear v.** sortir grand vainqueur
Victoria [vɪk'tɔːrɪə] *n Hist* **Queen V.** la reine Victoria; *Mil* **V. Cross** = la plus haute distinction britannique, accordée pour récompenser le courage d'un militaire; *Can* **V. Day** fête *f* de la Reine; **V. Falls** Chutes *fpl* Victoria
victoria [vɪk'tɔːrɪə] *n* **v. (plum)** = grosse prune *f* rouge
Victorian [vɪk'tɔːrɪən] **1** *adj* victorien, -ienne, du règne de la reine Victoria; (*values*) victorien **2** *n* Victorien, -ienne
Victoriana [vɪktɔːrɪ'ɑːnə] *n* bric-à-brac *m*/antiquités *fpl* de l'époque victorienne
victorious [vɪk'tɔːrɪəs] *adj* (*army, team etc*) victorieux, vainqueur *m*; (*struggle, campaign*) victorieux; (*day etc*) de victoire; **to be v. over sb** remporter la victoire sur qn
victoriously [vɪk'tɔːrɪəslɪ] *adv* victorieusement, en vainqueur
victory ['vɪktərɪ] *n* victoire *f*; **to claim v.** revendiquer la victoire; **to snatch v. from the jaws of defeat** arracher la victoire; **he described the decision as a v. for common sense** il a décrit la décision comme étant une victoire du bon sens; **to gain a** *or* **the v.** remporter la victoire (**over** sur), être victorieux; **v. celebrations** réjouissances *fpl* occasionnées par une victoire, réjouissances pour célébrer la victoire; **v. parade** parade *f* pour célébrer la victoire; **the Winged V. of Samothrace** la Victoire ailée de Samothrace
victual ['vɪt(ə)l] (**-ll-**, *US* **-l-**) **1** *vt* (*ship, garrison*) ravitailler, approvisionner **2** *vi* s'approvisionner, se ravitailler

victualler, *US* **victualer** [ˈvɪtlər] *n Fml* fournisseur *m* de vivres; *Br Fml* **licensed v.** débitant *m* de boissons

victuals [ˈvɪt(ə)lz] *npl Old-fashioned, Lit* (*food*) vivres *mpl*, victuailles *fpl*

vicuna [vɪˈkjuːnə] *n* (*animal, wool, cloth*) vigogne *f*; **v. coat/jacket** manteau *m*/veste *f* en vigogne

video[1] [ˈvɪdɪəʊ] *n* (a) *TV* (*medium*) vidéo *f*; (*cassette*) vidéocassette *f*, cassette *f* vidéo; (*recorder*) magnétoscope *m*; **a v. of the World Cup** une vidéo de la Coupe du Monde; **to show a v.** passer une vidéo; **to have sth on v.** avoir qch sur vidéo; **v. channel** canal *m* vidéo; **v. clip** vidéo-clip *m*, *pl* vidéo-clips, clip *m* (vidéo); **v. club** vidéoclub *m*; **v. (control) engineer** ingénieur *m* de la vision; **v. film** film *m* vidéo; **v. frequency** vidéofréquence *f*; **v. library** vidéothèque *f*; **v. link** liaison *f* vidéo; **v. playback system** système *m* de lecture de cassettes vidéo; **v. prompter** télésouffleur *m*; **v. recorder camera** caméscope *m*; **v. recording** enregistrement *m* vidéo, enregistrement sur magnétoscope; **v. recording camera** caméscope *m*; **v. rights** droits *mpl* d'exploitation vidéo; **v. shop** ≈ vidéoclub *m*; **v. signal** signal *m* vidéo

(b) *Comptr* **v. accelerator card** carte *f* vidéo accélératrice; **v. card** carte *f* vidéo; **v. controller** contrôleur *m* vidéo; **v. memory** mémoire *f* vidéo; **v. port** port *m* vidéo

video[2] *vt* (a) (*record*) enregistrer (en vidéo), enregistrer sur magnétoscope, magnétoscoper (b) (*using camcorder*) filmer (à la caméra vidéo); **they didn't know they were being videoed** ils ne savaient pas qu'ils étaient filmés

video camera *n* caméra *f* vidéo

video cassette *n* cassette *f* vidéo, vidéocassette *f*; **v. recorder** magnétoscope *m*

video CD *n* vidéodisque *m*

video conference *n* vidéoconférence *f*, visioconférence *f*

video conferencing *n* vidéoconférences *fpl*

videodisc, *US* **videodisk** [ˈvɪdɪəʊdɪsk] *n* disque *m* vidéo, vidéodisque *m*; **v. player** lecteur *m* de vidéodisque

video display terminal *n Am* console *f* de visualisation

video game *n* jeu *m* vidéo

videogram [ˈvɪdɪəʊgræm] *n* vidéogramme *m*

videographic [ˈvɪdɪəʊˈgræfɪk] *adj* vidéographique

video nasty *n F* = film *m* sur vidéocassette à contenu violent et/ou pornographique

video-on-demand *n* vidéo *f* à la demande

videophone [ˈvɪdɪəʊfəʊn] *n* vidéophone *m*, visiophone *m*

video recorder *n* magnétoscope *m*

video-selling *n Mktg* vidéovente *f*

videoshopping [ˈvɪdɪəʊʃɒpɪŋ] *n* vidéoachat *m*

videotape [ˈvɪdɪəʊteɪp] **1** *n* bande *f* vidéo **2** *vt* enregistrer sur magnétoscope

videotex [ˈvɪdɪəʊteks] *n Comptr* vidéotex *m*

vie [vaɪ] *vi* (**vied** [vaɪd]; **vying** [ˈvaɪɪŋ]) rivaliser (**with sb** avec qn); **they are vying for the championship** ils se disputent le championnat; **to v. with each other in doing sth** rivaliser l'un avec l'autre/les uns avec les autres pour faire qch, faire qch à qui mieux mieux; **they v. with each other for cruelty** ils rivalisent de cruauté; **they were vying with one another to impress her** ils rivalisaient l'un avec l'autre pour la séduire

Vienna [vɪˈenə] *n* Vienne *f*

Viennese [vɪəˈniːz] **1** *adj* viennois **2** *n* Viennois, -oise

Vietcong [vjetˈkɒŋ] *n inv, adj* Viêt-cong *mf*; **a prisoner of the V.** un prisonnier des Viêt-congs

Vietnam [vjetˈnɑːm, -ˈnæm] *n* Vietnam *m*

Vietnamese [vjetnəˈmiːz] **1** *adj* vietnamien **2** *n* (a) Vietnamien, -ienne (b) *Ling* vietnamien *m*

Viet Vet [vjetˈvet] *n US Mil F* ancien *m* du Vietnam

view[1] [vjuː] *n* (a) (*sight*) vue *f* (**of** de); **exposed to/hidden from v.** exposé/caché aux regards; **to pass out of** *or* **be lost to v.** disparaître; **in v.** en vue; **in full v. of the crowd** sous les regards de la foule; **keep your hands in full v.** garde tes mains bien en vue; **they did it in full v. of the military guard** ils l'ont fait au nez et à la barbe de la sentinelle militaire; **at last a hotel came into v.** enfin j'ai/il a/*etc* aperçu un hôtel; **we were in v. of land** nous étions en vue de la terre; **to keep sth in v.** ne pas perdre qch de vue; **on v. (to the public)** (*of collection*) ouvert au public; **famous people are permanently on v.** les gens célèbres sont en permanence exposés aux regards; **private v.** (*of exhibition etc*) avant-première *f*, *pl* avant-premières; (*of exhibition of paintings*) vernissage *m*; **field of v.** (*of telescope*) champ *m*; **angle of v.** angle *m* de champ

(b) (*scene, prospect*) vue *f*, perspective *f*; (*photo etc*) vue; **a room with a v.** une chambre avec vue; **front v.** vue de face; **from here you have a good v. of the castle** d'ici on a une très belle vue du château; **you will get a better v. from here** vous verrez mieux d'ici; *Fig* **to take the long v.** adopter une perspective à long terme; *Archit* **front/back v.** élévation *f* du devant/du derrière; **sectional v.** vue en coupe, profil *m*

(c) (*opinion*) opinion *f*, idée *f*, avis *m* (**about** au sujet de; **on** sur); **it's a widely-held v.** c'est une opinion très répandue; **point of v.** point *m* de vue; **to express a v.** exprimer une opinion *ou* un avis; **I support the v. that …** je partage l'opinion selon laquelle …; **to have very decided views on sth** avoir des idées très arrêtées sur qch; **what is your v. on the matter?** quelle est votre opinion sur la question?; **in my v.** à mon avis; **in the v. of many of our colleagues** de l'avis de nombreux de nos collègues; **our views differ** nos opinions diffèrent; **to share sb's views** partager les opinions de qn

(d) (*intention*) **to have sth in v.** avoir qch en vue; **with this in v.** à cette fin; **they bought the house with a v. to letting it** ils ont acheté la maison en vue de *ou* dans le but de *ou* avec l'idée de la louer

(e) (*prep phrase*) **in v. of what has happened** étant donné *ou* compte tenu de ce qui est arrivé; **in v. of these facts** compte tenu de ces faits; **in v. of the great heat** vu la grande chaleur

view[2] **1** *vt* (a) (*look at, watch*) regarder; (*slides*) visionner; *TV* (*programme*) regarder; *Comptr* (*codes*) visualiser; **when viewed from the outside** vu de l'extérieur

(b) (*inspect*) inspecter, examiner; (*exhibition, paintings*) voir; (*house for sale*) visiter, voir

(c) (*consider*) considérer, voir; (*prospect*) envisager; **viewed from a commercial perspective** *or* **standpoint, the proposal …** d'un point de vue commercial, cette proposition …; **how do you v. the situation?** comment voyez-vous la situation?; **when viewed in this light** vu sous cet angle; **to v. sth with horror/delight** envisager qch avec horreur/ravissement; **the proposal was viewed unfavourably by the authorities** la proposition était considérée d'un œil peu favorable par les autorités

2 *vi TV* regarder la télévision

viewdata [ˈvjuːdeɪtə] *n Comptr* vidéotex *m*

viewer [ˈvjuːər] *n* (a) *TV* téléspectateur, -trice; **I'm a a regular v. of your programme** je suis un de vos fidèles téléspectateurs (b) *Phot* (*for slides*) visionneuse *f*

viewership [ˈvjuːəʃɪp] *n Am TV* public *m*

viewfinder [ˈvjuːfaɪndər] *n Phot* viseur *m*

viewing [ˈvjuːɪŋ] *n* (a) (*inspection*) examen *m*, inspection *f*; (*of exhibition, paintings*) visite *f*; **open for v. from seven to nine** (*of house etc*) visites de sept à neuf heures; **v. is by arrangement with the owner** visite sur accord préalable du propriétaire; **v. times** heures *fpl* de visite; **v. window** fenêtre *f* d'observation

(b) *TV* **we've got a good evening's v. tonight** il y a de bonnes choses à la télé ce soir; **this new programme is recommended v.** cette nouvelle émission est à recommander; **the series makes for compulsive v.** c'est une série prenante *ou* captivante; **suitable for home v.** pour tout public; **v. audience** public *m*; **v. habits** habitudes *fpl* d'écoute; **the v. public** les téléspectateurs *mpl*; *TV* **v. room** salle *f* de visionnage; **v. time** temps *m* d'antenne

viewing figures *npl TV* indice *m* d'écoute

viewpoint [ˈvjuːpɔɪnt] *n* (a) (*opinion*) point *m* de vue; **from the international v.** du point de vue international (b) (*lookout*) point *m* de vue

vigil [ˈvɪdʒɪl] *n* veille *f*; (*over sick person or corpse*) veillée *f*; *Rel* vigile *f*; **to keep v.** veiller

vigilance [ˈvɪdʒɪləns] *n* vigilance *f*; *US Pej* **v. committee** milice *f* privée, comité *m* d'autodéfense

vigilant [ˈvɪdʒɪlənt] *adj* vigilant; **under the v. eye of …** sous l'œil vigilant de …; **to be v. for sth** être à l'affût de qch; **to keep a v. watch over sth** surveiller qch avec vigilance

vigilante [vɪdʒɪˈlæntɪ] *n Pej* membre *m* d'une milice privée; **v. justice** justice *f* sommaire, autodéfense *f*

vigilant(e)ism [vɪdʒɪˈlænt(ɪ)ɪz(ə)m] *n esp US Pej* = tendance *f* au développement de l'autodéfense ou des milices privées

vigilantly [ˈvɪdʒɪləntlɪ] *adv* vigilamment, avec vigilance

vignette[1] [vɪˈnjet] *n* (a) (*illustration*) vignette *f*; (*portrait, photo*) buste *m* sur un fond dégradé; *Fig* **this ten-minute v. of city life** cet aperçu de dix minutes de la vie dans une grande ville (b) (*camera matte*) cache *m*

vigor [ˈvɪgər] *n US* = **vigour**

vigorous [ˈvɪgərəs] *adj* (*strong*) vigoureux; **v. in body and mind** robuste de corps et d'esprit; **a v. defence of their case** une défense énergique de leur affaire; **v. denial** dénégation *f* vive *ou* vigoureuse; **v. growth** forte croissance *f*; **v. plant** plante *f* vigoureuse

vigorously [ˈvɪgərəslɪ] *adv* vigoureusement; **she v. denied the allegation** elle a très vivement *ou* vigoureusement dénié l'allégation

vigour, *US* **vigor** [ˈvɪgər] *n* (a) vigueur *f*; **to deny sth with**

great v. nier qch vigoureusement; **the v. of youth** la sève de la jeunesse **(b)** *US* **laws in v.** lois en vigueur

Viking ['vaɪkɪŋ] *Hist* **1** *n* Viking *m* **2** *adj* viking; **V. ship** drakkar *m*

vile [vaɪl] *adj* **(a)** (*nasty, unpleasant*) abominable, exécrable; **the soup was v.** la soupe était infecte; **he's in a v. temper** il est d'une humeur exécrable **(b)** (*base, despicable*) vil, infâme, ignoble; **to be v. to sb** être ignoble envers qn; **it was a v. thing to do/say** c'est ignoble d'avoir fait/dit ça; **a v. calumny** une calomnie infâme; **the vilest of men** le dernier des hommes

vilely ['vaɪllɪ] *adv* **(a)** (*decorated etc*) d'une manière abominable *ou* exécrable **(b)** (*basely, despicably*) vilement, bassement; **to behave v. towards sb** se comporter d'une manière ignoble envers qn

vileness ['vaɪlnɪs] *n* **(a)** (*nastiness*) caractère *m* exécrable; **the v. of the weather** le temps abominable **(b)** (*baseness*) (*of person, feeling*) bassesse *f*, caractère *m* ignoble; **her v. towards her mother** la manière ignoble dont elle traite/traitait sa mère

vilification [vɪlɪfɪ'keɪʃən] *n* dénigrement *m*, diffamation *f*, calomnie *f*

vilify ['vɪlɪfaɪ] *vt* dénigrer, diffamer, calomnier; (*reputation, name*) salir

villa ['vɪlə] *n* (*in country*) maison *f* de campagne; (*in town*) pavillon *m* de banlieue; (*at seaside, Roman*) villa *f*; **to rent a v. in Spain** louer une villa en Espagne

village ['vɪlɪdʒ] *n* **(a)** village *m*; (*large*) bourg *m*; **I'm going into the v.** je vais au village; **the whole v. was talking about it** tout le village en parlait; **the v. church/grocer** l'église/l'épicier du village; **a v. inn** une auberge de campagne; **v. life** vie *f* de village **(b)** *US* (*municipality*) petite municipalité *f*

village green *n* = pelouse *f* située au centre du village, ≈ place *f* du village

village hall *n* salle *f* des fêtes

village idiot *n* idiot *m* du village

villager ['vɪlɪdʒər] *n* villageois, -oise

villain ['vɪlən] *n* (*scoundrel*) scélérat *m*; *Br F* (*criminal*) voyou *m*; *Br F* **the big London villains** les grands criminels de Londres; *F* **you little v.!** petit garnement!, petit coquin!; *Th* **the v. (of the piece)** le traître; *Fig* **so you are the v. of the piece!** alors c'est vous qui êtes responsable de tout ça!; *Fig* **why am I always the v. of the piece?** pourquoi est-ce que c'est toujours moi que l'on blâme?

villainous ['vɪlənəs] *adj* (*behaviour, food etc*) vil, infâme; (*weather*) exécrable; **he gave us a v. look** il nous a regardés d'un sale œil; **v. deed** infamie *f*

villainously ['vɪlənəslɪ] *adv* d'une manière infâme *ou* ignoble

villainy ['vɪlənɪ] *n* infamie *f*

villein ['vɪlən] *n Hist* vilain *m*, serf *m*

villus, *pl* **villi** ['vɪləs, -aɪ] *n Anat* villosité *f*

vim [vɪm] *n F* vigueur *f*, énergie *f*; **full of v. (and vigour)** plein d'entrain; **put a bit more v. into it!** mets-y un peu plus d'entrain!

vinaigrette [vɪnɪ'gret] *n Culin* vinaigrette *f*

vindaloo [vɪndə'lu:] *n* = plat *m* indien très épicé

vindicate ['vɪndɪkeɪt] *vt* (*justify*) (*faith, claim, report*) justifier; (*exonerate*) (*person*) disculper; (*uphold*) (*what one has said*) prouver; (*report*) appuyer; **I was vindicated by the official inquiry** l'enquête officielle m'a donné raison; **to v. one's rights** revendiquer ses droits, faire valoir son bon droit

vindication [vɪndɪ'keɪʃən] *n* justification *f*; **in v. of his conduct** pour justifier sa conduite, en justification de sa conduite; **this is a clear v. of our policy** cela démontre le bien-fondé de notre politique

vindicator ['vɪndɪkeɪtər] *n* défenseur *m*

vindictive [vɪn'dɪktɪv] *adj* (*spiteful*) vindicatif

vindictively [vɪn'dɪktɪvlɪ] *adv* vindicativement; **he had quite v. made sure she would not get the job** par esprit de vengeance, il avait tout mis en œuvre pour qu'elle n'obtienne pas le poste

vindictiveness [vɪn'dɪktɪvnɪs] *n* (*of reprisals, remarks*) caractère *m* vindicatif; **the v. in her voice** son ton vindicatif; **she did it out of (sheer) v.** elle a fait cela par esprit de vengeance

vine [vaɪn] *n* **(a)** (*grapevine*) vigne *f*; **v. growing** viticulture *f*; **v. grower** viticulteur *m*, vigneron, -onne; **v.-growing country/region** pays *m*/région *f* viticole *ou* vinicole; **v. leaf** feuille *f* de vigne; *Fig* **to wither on the v.** ne pas aboutir **(b)** *Am* (*climbing plant*) plante *f* grimpante

vinegar ['vɪnɪgər] *n* **(a)** (*condiment*) vinaigre *m*; **wine/cider v.** vinaigre de vin/de cidre; **tarragon v.** vinaigre à l'estragon; *Culin* **oil and v. dressing** vinaigrette *f* **(b)** *Am F* (*vitality*) vigueur *f*, allant *m*

vinegary ['vɪnɪg(ə)rɪ] *adj* **(a)** (*taste etc*) de vinaigre; (*sauce*) vinaigré; **to turn v.** (*of wine*) tourner en vinaigre **(b)** *F* (*tone*) acerbe, aigre

vinery ['vaɪnərɪ] *n* (*hothouse*) serre *f* où l'on cultive la vigne

vineyard ['vɪnjəd] *n* (*field*) (champ *m* de) vigne *f*; (*establishment*) vignoble *m*; **the best vineyards** les meilleurs crus *mpl*

viniculture ['vɪnɪkʌltʃər] *n* viticulture *f*

vino ['vi:nəʊ] *n F* (*wine*) pinard *m*

vinous ['vaɪnəs] *adj* vineux

vintage ['vɪntɪdʒ] **1** *n* (*year of wine*) année *f*; (*wine*) cru *m*; **what v. is it?** quelle année est-ce que c'est?; **of the 1964 v.** de l'année 1964; **one of the great vintages** un grand cru; **this is a somewhat mediocre v.** c'est un cru plutôt médiocre; *Fig* **bicycle of 1920 v.** bicyclette du modèle de 1920; **we're of the same v.** nous sommes de la même époque

2 *adj* **(a)** (*wine*) millésimé; **v. year** année *f* de bon vin, grande année; **v. port** (*old*) vieux porto *m*

(b) (*film*) classique; *Aut* **v. car** = voiture *f* construite entre 1916 et 1930

(c) (*of high quality*) excellent; **the play is v. Shaw** la pièce est du meilleur Shaw; **it's been a v. year for comedy** ça a été une excellente année pour ce qui est de la comédie

vintner ['vɪntnər] *n Fml* négociant *m* en vins

vinyl ['vaɪnɪl] *n* vinyle *m*; *Mus F* **the album is available on v. and cassette** l'album existe sur vinyle et en cassette; **v. (book) jacket** couverture *f* en vinyle; **v. acetate** acétate *m* de vinyle; **v. resin** résine *f* vinylique

viol ['vaɪəl] *n Mus* viole *f*; **bass v.** basse *f* de viole; *US* (*double bass*) contrebasse *f*

viola¹ [vɪ'əʊlə] *n Mus* **(a)** (*violin*) alto *m*; **v. player** altiste *mf* **(b)** (*viol*) viole *f*; **v. da gamba** viole de gambe; **v. d'amore** viole d'amour

viola² ['vaɪələ] *n Bot* **(a)** (*genus*) violacée *f* **(b)** (*flower*) violette *f* (de jardin)

violate ['vaɪəleɪt] *vt* **(a)** (*disregard*) violer; (*sanctuary*) violer, profaner; (*rule*) manquer à; (*law*) violer, enfreindre; (*sb's trust*) trahir; **to v. sb's privacy** faire intrusion auprès de qn **(b)** *Old-fashioned* (*rape*) violer, outrager

violation [vaɪə'leɪʃən] *n* (*of oath, law, rights*) violation *f*; (*of sanctuary*) viol *m*, profanation *f*; (*of rule*) manquement *m*, infraction *f*; (*of order*) infraction; *Am* **(traffic) v.** infraction au code de la route; **v. of territorial waters** dépassement *m* des eaux territoriales; **v. of sb's privacy** intrusion *f* auprès de qn; **it's a v. of my privacy** c'est une intrusion; **v. of rights** abus *m* de droits; **in v. of the treaty, they ...** ils ont enfreint le traité et ...; **this is in v. of the treaty** c'est une violation du traité

violator ['vaɪəleɪtər] *n* **(a)** (*of law*) violateur, -trice **(b)** *Old-fashioned* (*of woman*) violateur *m*, violeur *m*

violence ['vaɪələns] *n* **(a)** (*roughness*) violence *f*; **v. on television** la violence à la télévision; **to use v.** user de violence; **to resort to v.** recourir *ou* en venir à la violence; *Jur* **to commit acts of v.** se livrer à des voies de fait; **robbery with v.** vol *m* avec agression *f ou* avec coups et blessures; **he had struck his victim with great v.** il avait frappé sa victime avec une grande violence; **to do v. to sth** (*distort*) faire violence à qch; **the translation does considerable v. to the original** la traduction dénature beaucoup le texte original

(b) (*intensity*) violence *f*, intensité *f*; **she said, with some v.** dit-elle avec violence; **the v. of the impact** la violence du choc

violent ['vaɪələnt] *adj* **(a)** (*fierce, rough*) violent; (*braking*) brutal; **v. storm** orage *m* violent, tempête *f*; **to die a v. death** mourir de mort violente; **to be in a v. temper** être furieux; **to become v.** (*of person*) devenir violent *ou* agressif **(b)** (*intense*) violent, vif, fort; (*coughing, fever, pain*) violent; **v. colours** couleurs *fpl* criardes *ou* crues; **to take a v. dislike to sb** se prendre d'une aversion violente *ou* d'une vive aversion à l'égard de qn

violently ['vaɪələntlɪ] *adv* **(a)** (*fiercely, roughly*) violemment, avec violence; (*to die*) de mort violente **(b)** (*intensely*) vivement, extrêmement; **his heart was beating v.** son cœur battait à se rompre; **after supper I became v. ill** après le souper j'ai été terriblement malade; **she was v. sick** elle a été prise de vomissements violents; **to fall v. in love with sb** tomber follement amoureux de qn

violet ['vaɪələt] **1** *n* **(a)** (*plant*) violette *f*; **Parma v.** violette de Parme; *Fig* **shrinking v.** personne *f* timide; **she is no shrinking v.** elle est loin d'être timide **(b)** (*colour*) violet *m* **2** *adj* **v.(-coloured)** violet, de couleur violette

violin [vaɪə'lɪn] *n* violon *m*; **first v.** premier violon, violon principal; **v. case** étui *m* à violon; **v. concerto** concerto *m* pour violon; **v. maker** luthier *m*

violinist [vaɪə'lɪnɪst] *n* violoniste *mf*

violoncellist [vaɪələn'tʃelɪst] *n Fml* violoncelliste *mf*

violoncello [vaɪələn'tʃeləʊ] *n Fml* violoncelle *m*

VIP [vi:aɪ'pi:] *n* (*abbr* **very important person**) personnage *m* de marque, VIP *mf inv*; **to get the V. treatment** être traité comme un personnage de marque; **V. guest** hôte *m* de marque; **V. list** liste *f* des VIP; **V. lounge** (*in airport*) salon *m* réservé aux personnages de marque

viper ['vaɪpər] *n* (*snake*), *Fig* vipère *f*; **to cherish a v. in one's bosom** réchauffer un serpent dans son sein

viperish ['vaɪpərɪʃ] *adj* vipérin, de vipère; **v. tongue** langue *f* venimeuse *ou* de vipère

virago [vɪ'rɑːgəʊ] *n Pej* virago *f*, mégère *f*

viral ['vaɪrəl] *adj Med* viral; **v. pneumonia** pneumonie *f* virale

Virgil ['vɜːdʒɪl] *n Antiq, Liter* Virgile *m*

virgin ['vɜːdʒɪn] **1** *n* vierge *f*; (*man*) *F* puceau *m*; **he/she is a v.** il/elle est vierge; **the (Blessed) V.** la Sainte Vierge; *Astron* **the V.** la Vierge; *Br Hist* **the V. Queen** (*Elizabeth I*) la Reine Vierge; **the V. Islands** les îles *fpl* Vierges **2** *adj* (*woman*) vierge; (*man*) *F* puceau; (*modesty etc*) de vierge, virginal, -aux; *Rel* **v. birth** maternité *f* divine; **v. forest/soil/wool** forêt *f*/sol *m*/laine *f* vierge; **v. snow** neige *f* virginale; **v. (olive) oil** huile *f* d'olives vierge; *Fig* **this market is v. territory for the company** ce marché constitue un territoire vierge pour la société

virginal ['vɜːdʒɪn(ə)l] **1** *adj* virginal, -aux, de vierge **2** *n Mus* **virginal(s), pair of virginals** virginal *m*

Virginia [və'dʒɪnɪə] *n Geog* la Virginie; *Bot* **V. creeper** vigne *f* vierge; **V. (tobacco)** tabac *m* de Virginie, virginie *m*

virginity [və'dʒɪnɪtɪ] *n* virginité *f*; **to lose one's v.** perdre sa virginité; **to lose one's political/professional v.** perdre son innocence sur le terrain politique/professionnel

Virgo ['vɜːgəʊ] *n Astron* la Vierge; *Astrol* **I'm a V.** je suis Vierge; *Astrol* **Virgos should be careful this week** Vierges, soyez prudents cette semaine

virile ['vɪraɪl, *Am* 'vɪrəl] *adj* viril

virility [vɪ'rɪlɪtɪ] *n* virilité *f*; **he's just trying to prove his v.** il essaye simplement de prouver sa virilité

virologist [vaɪ'rɒlədʒɪst] *n* virologiste *mf*, virologue *mf*

virology [vaɪ'rɒlədʒɪ] *n* virologie *f*

virtual ['vɜːtjʊəl] *adj* **(a)** **it's a v. impossibility** c'est quasiment impossible; **he's a v. prisoner** il est quasiment prisonnier; **the v. extinction/monopoly** la quasi-extinction/le quasi-monopole; **he's the v. head of the business** c'est lui le vrai chef de la maison; **it was a v. failure** ce fut en fait un échec; **this was a v. admission of guilt** de fait c'était un aveu de culpabilité **(b)** *Phys, Comptr* virtuel

virtual image *n* image *f* virtuelle

virtually ['vɜːtjʊəlɪ] *adv* virtuellement, pratiquement; **I'm v. certain of it** j'en suis virtuellement *ou* pratiquement certain; **v. all of them came** ils sont pratiquement tous venus

virtual memory *n* mémoire *f* virtuelle

virtual reality *n* réalité *f* virtuelle

virtual storage *n* mémoire *f* virtuelle

virtue ['vɜːtjuː] *n* **(a)** (*goodness, chastity*) vertu *f*; *Prov* **v. is its own reward** la vertu est sa propre récompense; **to make a v. of necessity** faire de nécessité vertu **(b)** (*advantage*) avantage *m*; **the hotel has the v. of being cheap** l'hôtel a l'avantage d'être bon marché; **there's no v. in just going faster** la rapidité n'a aucun mérite en soi **(c)** (*power*) vertu *f*; **the healing virtues of certain plants** les vertus curatives de certaines plantes **(d) by** *or* **in v. of** en vertu de; **by v. of one's office** à titre d'office

virtuosity [vɜːtjʊ'ɒsɪtɪ] *n Mus etc* virtuosité *f*

virtuoso, *pl* **-sos, -si** [vɜːtjʊ'əʊzəʊ, -zəʊz, -ziː] *n Mus etc* virtuose *mf*; **he gave a v. performance** (*of musician, actor*) il a joué en virtuose

virtuous ['vɜːtjʊəs] *adj* vertueux; **to feel v. about doing sth** se sentir vertueux parce qu'on fait/a fait qch; **with that oh-so-v. look on his face** avec son (petit) air de sainte nitouche *ou* de ne pas y toucher; **there's no need to look so v.** ce n'est pas la peine de prendre ton air de petit saint

virtuously ['vɜːtjʊəslɪ] *adv* vertueusement

virulence ['vɪr(j)ʊləns] *n* virulence *f*

virulent ['vɪr(j)ʊlənt] *adj* (*disease, prejudice*) virulent; *Fig* (*colour*) criard; **a particularly v. strain of flu** un type de grippe particulièrement violent; **to make a v. attack on sb** lancer une attaque virulente contre qn; **she was v. in her criticism of the system** elle était virulente dans sa critique du système; **v. satire** satire *f* venimeuse

virulently ['vɪr(j)ʊləntlɪ] *adv* avec virulence

virus, *pl* **-uses** ['vaɪrəs, -əsɪz] *n* **(a)** *Med* virus *m*; **there's a v. going round** il y a un virus qui sévit *ou* qui se promène; **I've got a v. of some kind** j'ai un virus quelconque **(b)** *Comptr* virus *m*; **to disable a v.** désactiver un virus; **to write a v.** concevoir un virus; **v. attack** infection *f* virale; **v. author** créateur *m* de virus; **v. check** détection *f* de virus; **to run a v. check on a disk** faire tourner le programme détecteur de virus sur une disquette; **v. detection** détection *f* de virus; **v. detection program** programme *m* détecteur de virus; **v. detector** détecteur *m* de virus; **v. elimination program** programme *m* d'élimination de virus; **v. program** programme *m* virus

virus-free *adj Comptr* dépourvu de virus

virus-infected *adj Comptr* contaminé par un/des virus

Visa® ['viːzə] *n* carte *f* bleue, carte Visa®

visa[1] ['viːzə] *n* (*on passport, document*) visa *m*; **to apply for a v. for Poland** demander un visa pour la Pologne

visa[2] *vt* (**visaed** ['viːzəd]) (*passport*) viser, apposer un visa à

visage ['vɪzɪdʒ] *n Fml* visage *m*, figure *f*

vis-à-vis ['viːzɑːviː] **1** *prep* (*compared with, in terms of*) par rapport à; (*about*) en ce qui concerne **2** *n* (*counterpart*) homologue *mf*

viscera ['vɪsərə] *npl Anat* viscères *mpl*

visceral ['vɪsər(ə)l] *adj Anat, Fig* viscéral

viscid ['vɪsɪd] *adj* visqueux, gluant

viscidity [vɪ'sɪdɪtɪ] *n* viscosité *f*

viscose ['vɪskəʊs] *n Ch* viscose *f*

viscosity [vɪs'kɒsɪtɪ] *n* viscosité *f*; **v. index** indice *m* de viscosité

viscount ['vaɪkaʊnt] *n* vicomte *m*

viscountcy ['vaɪkaʊntsɪ] *n* vicomté *f*

viscountess ['vaɪkaʊntɪs] *n* vicomtesse *f*

viscounty ['vaɪkaʊntɪ] *n* vicomté *f*

viscous ['vɪskəs] *adj* visqueux; *MecE* **v. coupling** visco-coupleur *m*

vise [vaɪs] *n US* = **vice**[2]

visibility [vɪzɪ'bɪlɪtɪ] *n* visibilité *f*; **good/bad v.** bonne/mauvaise visibilité; **v. was down to a few yards** la visibilité était réduite à quelques mètres; **v. is one hundred yards** la visibilité est de cent mètres; **the car has good front and rear v.** la voiture donne une bonne visibilité avant et arrière

visible ['vɪzɪb(ə)l] *adj* visible; **to become v.** apparaître; **the house was now v.** la maison était en vue; **v. to the naked eye** visible à l'œil nu; *Jur* **to have no v. means of support** n'avoir aucun moyen apparent de subvenir à ses propres besoins; **with v. satisfaction** avec une satisfaction évidente; *Com* **v. defects** défauts *mpl* apparents; **v. horizon** horizon *m* visuel

visibly ['vɪzɪblɪ] *adv* visiblement, manifestement; (*to grow etc*) à vue d'œil; **she was v. moved** elle était visiblement émue

Visigoth ['vɪzɪgɒθ] *n Hist* Wisigoth, -othe

vision ['vɪʒən] *n* **(a)** (*sight*) vision *f*, vue *f*; **to have good/poor v.** avoir une bonne/une mauvaise vue; **the accident had impaired his v.** cet accident avait affaibli sa vue; **field/angle of v.** champ *m*/angle *m* visuel; *Med* **double v.** double vision, diplopie *f*

(b) *Fig* (*foresight, imagination*) clairvoyance *f*, perspicacité *f*; **man/woman of v.** homme *m*/femme *f* d'une grande perspicacité *ou* qui voit loin dans l'avenir

(c) (*dream*) vision *f*; (*apparition*) vision, apparition *f*; **to have** *or* **see visions** avoir des visions; **visions of wealth** visions de richesse(s); **to have visions of doing sth** se voir faire qch; **I had visions of having to walk all the way into town** je me suis vu devoir aller jusqu'en ville à pied; **I had visions of you in a police cell** je te voyais déjà dans une cellule de police; **she always had visions of owning her own business** elle avait toujours rêvé d'avoir sa propre entreprise

(d) *TV* image *f*; **a temporary loss of v.** une perte momentanée de l'image; **v. control** contrôle *m* de l'image; **v. mixer** mélangeur *m* vidéo

visionary ['vɪʒənərɪ] **1** *adj* (*leader*) visionnaire **2** *n* visionnaire *mf*

visit[1] ['vɪzɪt] *n* (*call, tour*) visite *f*; (*stay*) séjour *m*; *Am* (*talk*) causerie *f*, causette *f* (**with sb** avec qn); **(social) v.** visite; **courtesy v.** visite de politesse; **I had a v. from your aunt last week** j'ai eu la visite de ta tante la semaine dernière; **to pay sb a v.** faire une visite à qn, rendre visite à qn; **to return sb's v.** rendre sa visite à qn; *F* **to pay a v.** (*go to lavatory*) aller au petit coin; **to be on a v.** *Br* **to** *or Am* **with friends** être en visite chez des amis; **I'm here on a v.** je suis ici en visite, je suis de passage ici; **the last time I made a v. to London** la dernière fois que je me suis rendu à Londres; **this is my first v. to your country** c'est la première fois que je viens dans votre pays; *Naut* **right of v. (and search)** (*at sea*) droit *m* de visite

visit[2] **1** *vt* **(a)** (*of doctor*) (*patient*) visiter; (*of representative*) (*customer*) passer chez; **to v. sb** (*call on*) rendre visite à qn; (*stay with*) faire un séjour chez qn; **we're visiting relatives** nous sommes en visite dans de la famille; **we visited the museums** nous avons visité les musées; **worth visiting** (*museum etc*) qui vaut la visite *ou* le détour

(b) *Bible* (*punish*) (*person, sin*) punir; **to v. the sins of the fathers upon the children** punir les enfants pour les péchés des pères

2 *vi* **(a)** (*be on a visit*) être en visite; **I don't live here, I'm only visiting** je n'habite pas ici, je ne suis que de passage

(b) *Am* (*talk*) **stay and v. a while** reste à bavarder un petit moment

▶ **visit with** *vipo Am* **(a)** (*stay with*) être en visite chez **(b)** (*talk with*) bavarder avec

visitation [vɪzɪˈteɪʃən] *n* **(a)** (*official visit*) visite *f*; (*of bishop*) visite pastorale; **the restaurant had a v. from the Department of Health** le restaurant a eu une visite d'inspection du ministère de la Santé; *Hum* **we're having a v. from the managing director next week** le directeur général nous fait l'honneur de sa visite la semaine prochaine **(b)** *Rel* **(the Feast of) the V.** (la fête de) la Visitation; **v. (of God)** (*punishment*) châtiment *m*

visiting [ˈvɪzɪtɪŋ] **1** *adj* en visite; *Sp* **the v. team** les visiteurs *mpl*; *US F* **v. fireman** = personnage *m* de marque en visite; **v. lecturer** (*who gives talks*) conférencier, -ière; *US* **v. nurse** infirmière *f* à domicile *ou* visiteuse; **v. professor** (*at university*) professeur *m* invité **2** *n* **to go v.** aller en visites; *Br* **v. card** carte *f* de visite

visiting hours *npl* (*in hospital, prison*) heures *fpl* de visite; **v. are (from) five to seven** les visites ont lieu de cinq à sept heures

visiting rights *npl Jur* (*of divorced parent*) droit *m* de visite

visitor [ˈvɪzɪtər] *n* **(a)** (*guest, tourist*) visiteur, -euse; (*in hospital, prison, museum etc*) visiteur, -euse; **an unexpected v.** un visiteur inattendu; **to have visitors** (*at the moment*) avoir du monde *ou* des invités *ou* de la visite; **I rarely have visitors** c'est rare que j'aie de la visite; **you have a v.** tu as de la visite; **London will have half a million visitors this summer** 500 000 personnes visiteront Londres cette été; **she is a frequent v. to our country** elle se rend regulièrement dans notre pays; **a v. from Mars** un voyageur venu de Mars; *Br* **health v.** infirmière *f* à domicile *ou* visiteuse; **visitors' book** (*at hotel*) registre *m*; (*at exhibition, tourist attraction*) livre *m* d'or; *Br* **v.'s passport** = passeport *m* temporaire; **visitors' tax** taxe *f* de séjour

(b) (*bird*) oiseau *m* migrateur; **this species is a winter v. to Britain** cette espèce vient passer l'hiver en Grande-Bretagne; **it's a rare v. to these shores** c'est une espèce que l'on voit rarement sous ces latitudes

visitor centre *n* (*in park, at tourist attraction etc*) centre *m* d'accueil pour les visiteurs

visor [ˈvaɪzər] *n* (*on helmet, cap*) visière *f*; **to raise/lower one's v.** soulever/baisser sa visière; *Aut* **sun v.** pare-soleil *m inv*

vista [ˈvɪstə] *n* vue *f*, perspective *f*; *Fig* perspective; *Fig* **to open up new vistas** ouvrir de nouvelles perspectives *ou* de nouveaux horizons

vistadome [ˈvɪstədəʊm] *n Am Rail* vistadôme *m*

visual [ˈvɪzjʊəl, ˈvɪʒ-] **1** *adj* visuel; **the v. arts** les arts *mpl* visuels; **to have a v. memory** avoir une mémoire visuelle; **her comedy is very v.** son comique repose sur les effets visuels; **his fabrics have great v. appeal** ses tissus sont très attrayants visuellement; **v. check** contrôle *m* visuel; *Sch* **v. methods (of teaching)** enseignement *m* par l'image; *Anat* **v. nerve** nerf *m* optique; *Mil, Naut* **v. signal/signalling** signal *m*/signalisation *f* optique **2** *n* (*of design*) maquette *f*

visual aid *n* (*in teaching*) support *m* visuel

visual display *n* affichage *m*

visual display unit *n Br Comptr* console *f* de visualisation, afficheur *m*

visualization [vɪzjʊəlaɪˈzeɪʃən, vɪʒ-] *n* visualisation *f*

visualize [ˈvɪzjʊəlaɪz, ˈvɪʒ-] *vt* (*imagine*) se représenter; (*foresee*) envisager; **she had difficulty visualizing him without his beard** elle avait du mal à se le représenter *ou* à l'imaginer sans sa barbe

visually [ˈvɪzjʊəlɪ, ˈvɪʒ-] *adv* visuellement; **v. handicapped** malvoyant; **the v. handicapped** les malvoyants *mpl*; **v. impaired** qui a des problèmes de vue; **the v. impaired** les personnes *fpl* qui ont des problèmes de vue

vital [ˈvaɪt(ə)l] **1** *adj* **(a)** (*essential to life*) vital; **v. force** force *f* vitale; **v. functions** fonctions *fpl* vitales; **v. organ** organe *m* vital; *Med* **v. signs** signes *fpl* de vie **(b)** (*decisive, indispensable*) essentiel, capital, vital; **it is v. that ...** il est indispensable *ou* essentiel que ... + *sub*; **to play a v. role** jouer un rôle capital; **a question of v. importance** une question d'une importance vitale *ou* capitale, une question de toute première importance; *F* **v. statistics** (*of woman*) mensurations *fpl* **(c)** (*full of life, vigorous*) vigoureux, dynamique **2** *n Anat etc* **vitals** organes *mpl* vitaux

vitality [vaɪˈtælɪtɪ] *n* (*of organism*) vitalité *f*; (*of institution*) vitalité, vigueur *f*; (*of person, style*) énergie *f*, vigueur; **I wish I had her v.** j'aimerais bien avoir son énergie

vitalize [ˈvaɪtəlaɪz] *vt* vitaliser, vivifier

vitally [ˈvaɪt(ə)lɪ] *adv* **supplies are v. needed** on a un besoin vital de vivres; **v. important question** question d'une importance vitale *ou* de toute première importance; **it is v. important that ...** il est essentiel *ou* il faut absolument que ... + *sub*; **v. for the British, the European Commission has agreed** la Commission Européenne a accepté, ce qui est vital *ou* capital pour les Britanniques

vitamin [ˈvɪtəmɪn, *Am* ˈvaɪ-] *n Biol, Ch* vitamine *f*; **with added vitamins** vitaminé; **v. C/D** vitamine C/D; *Med* **v. deficiency** carence *f* vitaminique *ou* en vitamines; (*disease*) avitaminose *f*; **v. tablet** comprimé *m* de vitamines

vitiate [ˈvɪʃɪeɪt] *vt* **(a)** *Fml* (*spoil, weaken*) (*blood, air*) vicier **(b)** *Jur* (*contract*) vicier

vitiation [vɪʃɪˈeɪʃən] *n Fml* viciation *f*

viticulture [ˈvɪtɪkʌltʃər] *n* viticulture *f*

vitreous [ˈvɪtrɪəs] *adj* **(a)** *Ch, Geol* vitreux; **v. enamel** émail *m* vitrifié **(b)** *Anat* **v. body** (*in eye*) corps *m* vitré; **v. humour** humeur *f* vitrée

vitrification [vɪtrɪfɪˈkeɪʃən] *n* vitrification *f*

vitrified [ˈvɪtrɪfaɪd] *adj* vitrifié

vitrify [ˈvɪtrɪfaɪ] **1** *vt* vitrifier **2** *vi* se vitrifier

vitriol [ˈvɪtrɪəl] *n Ch, Fig* vitriol *m*; **to throw v. at sb** lancer du vitriol sur qn, vitrioler qn; *Fig* **the v. of her remarks** la virulence *ou* l'acerbité de ses remarques; *Fig* **the article was sheer v.** c'était un article au vitriol

vitriolic [vɪtrɪˈɒlɪk] *adj* (*acid*) vitriolique; *Fig* (*attack, speech*) au vitriol; **v. criticism** critique *f* mordante

vitriolize [ˈvɪtrɪəlaɪz] *vt* vitrioler

vituperate [vɪˈtjuːpəreɪt] *vi Fml* déblatérer, vitupérer (**against sb/sth** contre qn/qch)

vituperation [vɪtjuːpəˈreɪʃən] *n Fml* vitupération *f*

vituperative [vɪˈtjuːpərətɪv] *adj Fml* injurieux

Vitus [ˈvaɪtəs] *n Med F* **Saint V.'s dance** danse *f* de Saint-Guy

viva[1] [ˈviːvə] *int, n* (*cry*) vivat *m*

viva[2] [ˈvaɪvə] *n Br Univ F* = **viva voce 3**

vivacious [vɪˈveɪʃəs] *adj* (*esp woman, girl*) vif, animé, enjoué; **she has a v. laugh** elle a un rire enjoué; **she is v.** elle a de la vivacité; **she was very v. yesterday evening** elle avait beaucoup d'entrain *ou* était très enjouée hier soir

vivaciously [vɪˈveɪʃəslɪ] *adv* avec vivacité *ou* entrain; (*to laugh*) d'un air enjoué

vivacity [vɪˈvæsɪtɪ] *n* vivacité *f*, entrain *m*; **the v. of her laugh** son rire enjoué

vivarium, *pl* **-iums, -ia** [vaɪˈveərɪəm, -ɪəmz, -ɪə] *n* (*for animals, plants*) vivarium *m*

viva voce [ˈvaɪvəˈvəʊsɪ, -ˈvəʊtʃɪ] **1** *adv* de vive voix, oralement **2** *adj* oral **3** *n Univ* (examen *m*) oral *m*; **to take a v.** passer un oral

vivid [ˈvɪvɪd] *adj* (*light, colour*) vif, éclatant, brillant; (*language, terms*) vivant, coloré; (*memory*) très vif, très clair; **v. flash of lightning** éclair *m* aveuglant; **v. imagination** imagination *f* vive; **it left a v. impression on me** ça m'a laissé une forte impression; **I have a v. recollection of the scene** j'ai un souvenir très vif *ou* très net de la scène; **v. description of sth** description *f* vivante de qch

vividly [ˈvɪvɪdlɪ] *adv* vivement, avec éclat; (*to remember*) nettement, clairement; **to describe sth v.** décrire qch d'une manière vivante *ou* sous de vives couleurs

vividness [ˈvɪvɪdnɪs] *n* (*of light, colours*) vivacité *f*, éclat *m*; (*of memory*) netteté *f*; **the v. of his style** la vigueur *ou* le pittoresque de son style

vivify [ˈvɪvɪfaɪ] *vt Fml* vivifier, (r)animer

viviparous [vɪˈvɪpərəs] *adj Bot, Zool* vivipare

vivisect [vɪvɪˈsekt, ˈvɪvɪsekt] *vt Fml* pratiquer des vivisections sur

vivisection [vɪvɪˈsekʃən] *n* vivisection *f*; **the v. debate** le débat sur la vivisection

vivisectionist [vɪvɪˈsekʃənɪst] *n* (*practitioner*) personne *f* qui pratique la vivisection

vixen [ˈvɪks(ə)n] *n* (*animal*) renarde *f*; *Pej* (*woman*) mégère *f*

viz [vɪz] *adv* (*when reading aloud usu* **namely** [ˈneɪmlɪ]) (*abbr* **videlicet**) à savoir, c'est-à-dire

vizier [vɪˈzɪər] *n Hist* vizir *m*; **grand v.** grand vizir

vizor [ˈvaɪzər] *n* = **visor**

VLF [viːelˈef] *n Rad abbr* **very low frequency**

VLSI [viːeleˈsaɪ] *n Comptr abbr* **very large scale integration**

vocab [ˈvəʊkæb] *n F* voca(bulaire) *m*

vocabulary [vəˈkæbjʊlərɪ] *n* **(a)** (*glossary*) vocabulaire *m* **(b)** (*of person*) vocabulaire *m*; (*of language*) vocabulaire, lexique *m*; **a large/small v.** un vocabulaire étendu/limité; **to enlarge one's v.** enrichir son vocabulaire; **v. test** test *m* de vocabulaire

vocal [ˈvəʊk(ə)l] **1 (a)** *adj* (*music*) vocal; (*communication*) verbal, oral; **v. score** partition *f* de chant **(b)** *Fig* (*forthright*) (*person*) qui se fait entendre; **to be v. in one's criticisms** faire clairement entendre ses critiques; **the most v. member of the audience** le membre de l'auditoire qui s'est fait le plus entendre; **he is very v. about ...** il parle beaucoup

de …, il se fait entendre souvent au sujet de … **2** *n Ling* son *m* vocal; *Mus* **vocals** chant *m*, partie *f* vocale; **on vocals** au chant
vocal cords *npl Anat* cordes *fpl* vocales
vocalic [vəˈkælɪk] *adj Ling* vocalique
vocalist [ˈvəʊkəlɪst] *n* chanteur, -euse; **who was the v. on their first album?** qui chantait sur leur premier album?; **backing v.** choriste *mf*
vocalization [vəʊkəlaɪˈzeɪʃən] *n Mus, Ling* vocalisation *f*
vocalize [ˈvəʊkəlaɪz] **1** *vt* **(a)** (*articulate*) (*doubt, complaint*) exprimer **(b)** *Ling* (*consonant*) vocaliser **2** *vi Mus* faire des vocalises, vocaliser
vocally [ˈvəʊk(ə)lɪ] *adv* vocalement, oralement; (*to protest*) à haute voix
vocation [vəʊˈkeɪʃən] *n* vocation *f*; **to have a v.** avoir une vocation; **teaching is a v.** l'enseignement, c'est une vocation; **to miss one's v.** manquer sa vocation
vocational [vəʊˈkeɪʃənəl] *adj* (*teaching, course, training*) professionnel; **v. adviser,** *Am* **v. guidance counselor** orienteur *m* professionnel; **v. guidance** orientation *f* professionnelle; **v. qualification** brevet *m* professionnel; **v. training** formation *f* professionnelle
vocative [ˈvɒkətɪv] *adj, n Gram* **v. (case)** (cas *m*) vocatif *m*; **in the v.** au vocatif
vociferate [vəˈsɪfəreɪt] *vi* (*protest*) vociférer, crier (**against** contre)
vociferation [vəsɪfəˈreɪʃən] *n* (*protest*) vocifération *f*, cri *m*
vociferous [vəˈsɪfərəs] *adj* vociférant, bruyant; **she was most v. in her opposition** elle s'y est opposée bruyamment
vociferously [vəˈsɪfərəslɪ] *adv* bruyamment; (*to protest*) à haute voix
VOD [viːəʊˈdiː] *n* (*abbr* **video on demand**) vidéo *f* à la demande
vodka [ˈvɒdkə] *n* vodka *f*; **v. and orange** vodka orange
vogue [vəʊg] *n* vogue *f*, mode *f* (**for** de); **in v.** en vogue, à la mode; **to come into v.** devenir à la mode; **out of v.** démodé; **v. word** mot *m* à la mode
voice¹ [vɔɪs] *n* **(a)** (*of person*) voix *f*; **to raise/lower one's v.** hausser/baisser la voix; **to keep one's v. down** parler à voix basse; **his v. has broken** sa voix a mué; **his v. was breaking** (*with emotion*) sa voix se brisait; **in a low v.** à voix basse, à mi-voix; **he's got a deep v.** il a une voix grave; **to speak in a loud v.** parler à haute voix *ou* à voix haute; **at the top of one's v.** à tue-tête; **to make one's v. heard** se faire entendre; **he likes the sound of his own v.** il aime à s'entendre parler; **she's not in (good) v.** (*of singer*) elle n'est pas en voix; **to lose one's v.** perdre sa voix; *Comptr* **v. card** carte *f* vocale; *Comptr* **v. chip** puce *f* de reconnaissance vocale; *Comptr* **v. recognition software** logiciel *m* de reconnaissance vocale; **v. synthesizer** synthétiseur *m* de paroles

(b) *Fig* **a dissenting v.** un protestataire; **hers was the only dissenting v.** elle était la seule à protester; **the v. of conscience/reason** la voix de la conscience/de la raison; **a little v. inside her told her it was wrong** (*her conscience told her*) une petite voix en elle lui dit que c'était mal; **the v. of the people** la voix du peuple; **with one v.** tout d'une voix, à l'unanimité; **to give v. to one's indignation** exprimer son indignation

(c) (*right to express opinion*) voix *f*, suffrage *m*; **we have no v. in the matter** nous n'avons pas voix au chapitre; **proportional representation would give small parties a greater v.** la représentation proportionnelle donnerait davantage voix au chapitre aux petits partis

(d) [①**A40**,9; **B36**,J] *Gram* (*of verb*) voix *f*; **in the active/passive v.** à la voix active/passive, à l'actif/au passif
voice² *vt* **(a)** (*opinion, one's anger etc*) exprimer; **to v. the general feeling** exprimer le sentiment général *ou* l'opinion générale **(b)** *Ling* (*consonant*) sonoriser
voice-activated [ˈvɔɪsæktɪveɪtɪd] *adj* (*device*) commandé par la voix, à commande vocale
voice activation *n* commande *f* vocale
voice box *n Anat* larynx *m*
voiced [vɔɪst] *adj Ling* (*consonant*) sonore
-voiced [vɔɪst] *suff* **low/loud-v.** à la voix basse/forte
voice input *n Comptr* entrée *f* vocale
voiceless [ˈvɔɪslɪs] *adj Ling* sourd, non voisé
voicemail [ˈvɔɪsmeɪl] *n* messagerie *f* téléphonique
voice-over *n Cin, TV* voix *f* off, voix hors champ, voix en surimpression; **who did the v.?** qui a fait la voix off *ou* la voix hors champ?
voice recognition *n* reconnaissance *f* vocale
voice response *n* réponse *f* vocale
voice test *n* audition *f*
void¹ [vɔɪd] **1** *adj* **(a)** **v. of** (*lacking in*) dépourvu *ou* dénué de; **the proposal is v. of reason** la proposition est dénuée *ou* dépourvue de raison **(b)** *Jur* (*deed, contract*) **(null and) v.** nul; **to make v.** annuler, frapper de nullité **(c)** *Lit* (*empty*) vide **2** *n* vide *m*; **to fill the v.** combler le vide; **the aching v. in his heart** le vide douloureux qu'il y avait dans son cœur
void² *vt* **(a)** *Jur* (*contract*) résoudre, annuler **(b)** (*one's bowels*) évacuer
voile [vɔɪl] *n Tex* voile *m*
vol **(a)** *Phys* (*abbr* **volume**) vol **(b)** (*abbr* **volume**) (*book in series*) tome, t
volatile [ˈvɒlətaɪl] *adj* **(a)** (*person*) versatile, changeant; (*situation*) explosif; (*prices, market*) volatile; **she's been rather v. recently** elle est d'humeur assez changeante ces temps-ci **(b)** *Ch, Comptr* volatil; *Comptr* **v. random access memory** mémoire *f* vive volatile; **v. oil** huile *f* volatile
volatility [vɒləˈtɪlɪtɪ] *n* **(a)** (*of person*) inconstance *f*, caractère *m* changeant; (*of situation*) caractère explosif; (*of prices, market*) volatilité *f*; **the v. of her moods** ses changements d'humeur **(b)** *Ch* volatilité *f*
volatilize [vɒˈlætɪlaɪz] *Ch* **1** *vt* (*liquid*) volatiliser **2** *vi* se volatiliser
vol-au-vent [ˈvɒləʊvɒn] *n Culin* vol-au-vent *m inv*
volcanic [vɒlˈkænɪk] *adj Geog, Fig* volcanique
volcano, *pl* **-oes** [vɒlˈkeɪnəʊ, -əʊz] *n* volcan *m*
vole [vəʊl] *n* (*animal*) campagnol *m*
volition [vəˈlɪʃən] *n* volition *f*, volonté *f*; **to do sth of one's own v.** faire qch de son propre gré
volley¹ [ˈvɒlɪ] *n* **(a)** (*of gunfire*) volée *f*, salve *f*; (*of blows, stones etc*) volée, grêle *f*; *Fig* (*of insults*) volée, bordée *f*; **to fire** *or* **discharge a v.** tirer une volée *ou* une salve **(b)** *Sp* (balle *f* prise de) volée *f*; *Tennis* **half v.** demi-volée *f*, *pl* demi-volées
volley² **1** *vt* **(a)** *Mil* (*projectiles*) tirer une volée *ou* une salve de **(b)** **to v. the ball** *Tennis* effectuer une volée; *Fb* reprendre la balle de volée; *Tennis* **to half v. the ball** effectuer une demi-volée **2** *vi* **(a)** (*of guns*) partir ensemble **(b)** *Tennis* relancer la balle à la volée; **he is volleying extremely well** sa volée est superbe
volleyball [ˈvɒlɪbɔːl] *n Sp* volley-ball *m*; **v. player** volleyeur, -euse
volt [vəʊlt] *n El* volt *m*
voltage [ˈvəʊltɪdʒ] *n El* tension *f*; **high/low v.** haute/basse tension; **v. adaptor** transformateur *m*; **v. smoother** régulateur *m* de tension
voltaic [vɒlˈteɪɪk] *adj El* voltaïque
volte-face [ˈvɒltfɑːs] *n* volte-face *f inv*; **to make a (complete) v.** faire volte-face
voltmeter [ˈvəʊltmiːtər] *n El* voltmètre *m*
volubility [vɒljʊˈbɪlɪtɪ] *n* volubilité *f*
voluble [ˈvɒljʊb(ə)l] *adj* volubile; **he was v. in his denials** il a nié avec volubilité; **to be a v. talker** parler avec beaucoup de volubilité
volubly [ˈvɒljʊblɪ] *adv* avec volubilité
volume [ˈvɒljuːm] *n* **(a)** (*book*) volume *m*, tome *m*; **work in six volumes, six-v. work** ouvrage *m* en six volumes; **v. one** volume *ou* tome premier, premier volume; *Fig* **to speak volumes** (*of action, remark etc*) être révélateur (**about** de), en dire long (**about** sur)

(b) (*amount*) volume *m*; **v. of business** volume des affaires; **volumes of smoke** nuages *mpl ou* tourbillons *mpl* de fumée; **volumes of water** flots *mpl ou* torrents *mpl* d'eau; **a huge v. of work** une énorme quantité de travail; *Comptr* **v. label** label *m* de volume

(c) *Mus, Rad* volume *m*; **to turn the v. up/down** augmenter/diminuer le volume; *Rad* **at full v.** à fond, à plein volume; **turn the radio up full v.** mets la radio à fond; **v. control** réglage *m* de volume; (*knob, switch*) bouton *m* de (réglage de) volume
volumetric [vɒljʊˈmetrɪk] *adj Ch, Phys* volumétrique; **v. alarm** alarme *f* antivol volumétrique
voluminous [vəˈljuːmɪnəs] *adj* **(a)** (*correspondence, documentation*) volumineux; (*notes*) copieux; **in v. detail** en grands détails **(b)** (*jacket etc*) ample
voluminously [vəˈljuːmɪnəslɪ] *adv* abondamment
voluntarily [vɒlʌnˈteərɪlɪ] *adv* **(a)** (*willingly*) volontairement, de son plein gré **(b)** (*unpaid*) bénévolement
voluntary [ˈvɒlənt(ə)rɪ] **1** *adj* **(a)** (*willing*) volontaire; (*offer*) spontané; **v. confession of guilt** confession *f* volontaire, aveu *m* spontané; **v. export restraint** autolimitation *f* des exportations; **v. foreign credit restraint** restriction *f* facultative *ou* volontaire de crédit à l'étranger; *Com* **v. group** groupe *m* volontaire, commerce *m* associé; **v. standards** normes *fpl* d'application volontaire **(b)** (*involving volunteers*) **v. organization** organisation *f* bénévole **(c)** *Physiol* volontaire **2** *n Rel, Mus* (*on organ*) morceau *m* pour orgue; (*on trumpet*) morceau pour trompette
voluntary redundancy *n* départ *m* volontaire (en échange d'une indemnité); **to take v.** quitter son emploi en échange d'une indemnité

voluntary service *n* service *m* volontaire
voluntary work *n* bénévolat *m*; **to do v.** faire du bénévolat
voluntary worker *n* bénévole *mf*
volunteer[1] [vɒlən'tɪər] **1** *n Mil etc* volontaire *mf*; (*for charity etc*) bénévole *mf*; **to call for volunteers** demander des volontaires; **can I have a v. from the audience?** y a-t-il une personne dans la salle qui voudrait bien venir sur scène?; **as a v.** *Mil* en volontaire; (*for charity*) en bénévole; **v. army** armée *f* de volontaires; **v. service** service *m* volontaire **2** *adj* (*teacher etc*) bénévole
volunteer[2] **1** *vt* (*one's services*) offrir volontairement *ou* spontanément; (*information*) donner spontanément; **to v. advice** offrir des conseils; **she seemed unwilling to v. anything more than this** elle n'avait pas l'air de vouloir en dire plus; **'maybe I will' was as much as he would v.** pour toute réponse il déclara 'peut-être que oui'; **to v. to do sth** se porter volontaire *ou* se proposer pour faire qch; **I wish I'd never volunteered to help** si seulement je ne m'étais pas porté volontaire pour aider!; **he's always volunteering other people** il propose toujours les services des autres sans leur demander leur avis; **they volunteered their son to look after the neighbours' dog** ils ont proposé que leur fils s'occupe du chien des voisins

2 *vi Mil* s'engager comme volontaire (**for** pour); (*for charitable work etc*) proposer ses services (**for** pour); **why don't you v.?** pourquoi est-ce que tu ne te portes pas volontaire?; (*as audience participant*) pourquoi est-ce que tu n'y vas pas?; **I wish I'd never volunteered for this** si seulement je ne m'étais pas porté volontaire!
voluptuary [və'lʌptʊərɪ] *n esp Pej* voluptueux, -euse
voluptuous [və'lʌptjʊəs] *adj* **(a)** (*figure*) sensuel **(b)** (*pleasure*) voluptueux
voluptuously [və'lʌptʊəslɪ] *adv* voluptueusement
voluptuousness [və'lʌptjʊəsnɪs] *n* **(a)** (*of figure*) sensualité *f* **(b)** (*of pleasure*) volupté *f*
vomit[1] ['vɒmɪt] *n* vomissure *f*, vomi *m*; **to choke on one's own v.** s'étouffer avec son propre vomi
vomit[2] **1** *vt* vomir; **to v. blood** vomir du sang; **he vomits up everything he eats** il vomit *ou* rejette *ou* rend tout ce qu'il mange; **to v. (forth) smoke** (*of chimney*) vomir de la fumée **2** *vi* vomir
vomiting ['vɒmɪtɪŋ] *n* vomissements *mpl*
voodoo[1] ['vu:du:] *n* vaudou *m*; **v. priest** prêtre *m* vaudou
voodooism ['vu:du:ɪz(ə)m] *n* vaudou *m*
voracious [və'reɪʃəs, vɒ-] *adj* (*person, appetite*) vorace; (*hunger*) vorace, de loup; (*reader*) avide; **I was feeling quite v.** j'avais une faim de loup
voraciously [və'reɪʃəslɪ, vɒ-] *adv* (*to eat*) voracement, avec voracité; (*to read*) avidement; **to be v. hungry** avoir une faim de loup
voracity [vɒ'ræsɪtɪ] *n* voracité *f*
vortex, *pl* **-ices, -exes** ['vɔ:teks, -ɪsi:z, -eksɪz] *n Lit* (*of dust, smoke*) tourbillon *m*; (*whirlpool*) gouffre *m*; *Fig* **the v. of politics** le tourbillon de la politique
votary ['vəʊtərɪ] *n* fervent, -ente (**of** de); *Rel* dévot, -ote (**of** à)
vote[1] [vəʊt] *n* **(a)** (*by a group*) vote *m*, scrutin *m*; (*of individual*) vote, voix *f*, suffrage *m*; (*right to vote*) droit *m* de vote; **v. by a show of hands** vote à main levée; **popular v.** consultation *f* populaire; **to put a question to the v.** soumettre une question au vote; **let's put it to the v.** votons; **to take the v.** procéder au scrutin; **to take a v. on sth** voter sur qch; **to give one's v. to sb** donner son vote *ou* sa voix à qn; **to count** *or* **tell the votes** compter les votes, dépouiller le scrutin; **they've got my v.** je vote pour eux; **can I count on your v.?** puis-je compter sur votre vote?; **to be elected by one v.** être élu à une voix de majorité; **the motion was adopted by six votes to two** la motion a été adoptée par six voix contre deux; **how many votes did she get?** combien de voix est-ce qu'elle a obtenu?; **to record** *or* **cast one's v.** voter; **the v. went against her** le vote a été en sa défaveur; **one man, one v.** suffrage universel; **to have the v.** avoir le droit de vote; **votes for women!** le droit de vote aux femmes!; **British women got the v. in 1928** les femmes britanniques ont obtenu le droit de vote en 1928; **the Republicans got 52% of the v.** les républicains ont remporté 52% du scrutin; **to increase one's (share of the) v.** obtenir de meilleurs résultats; **they increased their v. by 12%** ils ont amélioré leurs résultats de 12%; **to lose the trade union/black v.** perdre les suffrages des syndicalistes/des Noirs

(b) (*of assembly*) motion *f*, résolution *f*; **v. of censure** *or* **no confidence** motion de censure; **v. of confidence** vote *m* de confiance; **to propose a v. of thanks** faire un discours de remerciement
vote[2] **1** *vi* voter (**for** pour; **against** contre); **to v. by (a) show of hands** voter à mains levées; **to v. in favour of a proposal** voter une proposition; **to v. Communist** voter communiste; **v. for Thomas!** votez Thomas!; *Fig* **to v. with one's feet** (*by leaving*) indiquer sa désapprobation en quittant les lieux; (*by not turning up*) indiquer sa désapprobation en ne venant pas

2 *vt* (*sum of money, credit*) voter; **to v. £50,000 for the victims of the disaster** voter 50 000 livres pour les sinistrés; **the senators voted themselves a pay rise** les sénateurs se sont voté une augmentation de salaire; **I v. (that) we go** je propose que nous y allions; **they voted the holiday a success** ils ont décidé d'un commun accord que les vacances avaient été une réussite
▶ **vote down** *vtsep* (*motion*) rejeter; (*candidate*) (*not elect*) ne pas élire; (*not re-elect*) ne pas réélire
▶ **vote in** *vtsep* (*candidate*) élire (**as** en tant que)
▶ **vote on** *vipo* mettre au vote; **the Chairman refused to let them v. on it** le président a refusé de les laisser mettre la question au vote
▶ **vote out** *vtsep* (*decision, bill etc*) rejeter; (*person*) ne pas réélire
▶ **vote through** *vtsep* ratifier, approuver, accepter
voter ['vəʊtər] *n* (*taking part in vote*) votant, -ante; (*with right to vote*) électeur, -trice; **the voters** l'électorat *m*; **French voters go to the polls tomorrow** les Français vont aux urnes demain; **v. registration** inscription *f* sur les registres électoraux; **v. turnout** (*at election*) taux *m* de participation électorale
voting ['vəʊtɪŋ] **1** *adj* (*assembly, member*) votant **2** *n* (*participation in election*) (participation *f* au) vote *m*; (*polling*) scrutin *m*; **result of the v.** résultat *m* du vote *ou* scrutin; *US* **v. machine** machine *f* à voter; *Com* **v. shares** actions *fpl* donnant droit au vote
voting booth *n* isoloir *m*
voting paper *n* bulletin *m* de vote
voting rights *npl Com* droits *mpl* de vote
votive ['vəʊtɪv] *adj* votif; **v. offering** ex-voto *m inv*
vouch [vaʊtʃ] *vi* **to v. for the truth of sth** témoigner de *ou* répondre de *ou* attester la vérité de qch; **to v. for sb** répondre de qn, se porter garant de qn; **I can v. for his honesty** je peux me porter garant de son honnêteté; **I can v. for the severity of the side effects** je peux témoigner de la sévérité des effets secondaires
voucher ['vaʊtʃər] *n* **(a)** (*receipt as proof of transaction*) pièce *f* justificative; *Com* pièce comptable **(b)** (*giving price reduction*) coupon *m*; (*to exchange for goods, service etc*) bon *m*; **(gift) v.** bon-cadeau *m*, *pl* bons-cadeaux; **luncheon v.** chèque-repas *m*, *pl* chèques-repas, chèque-restaurant *m*, *pl* chèques-restaurant
vouchsafe [vaʊtʃ'seɪf] *vt Fml* **to v. sb sth** accorder *ou* octroyer qch à qn; **to v. to do sth** (*condescend*) daigner faire qch
vow[1] [vaʊ] *n* vœu *m*, serment *m*; **to take one's vows** prononcer *ou* faire ses vœux; **to make a v.** faire un vœu (**to do** de faire); **to take a v. of poverty** faire vœu de pauvreté; **to take a v. of silence** (*of monk etc*) faire vœu de silence; (*refuse to talk about sth*) promettre de ne rien dire; **to break a v.** rompre *ou* transgresser un vœu, rompre un serment; **to keep a v.** respecter un serment
vow[2] *vt* vouer, jurer; **to v. obedience** jurer obéissance; **to v. revenge on sb** faire vœu de se venger sur qn; **to v. to do sth** faire vœu *ou* jurer de faire qch
vowel ['vaʊəl] *n Ling* voyelle *f*; **v. shift** mutation *f* vocalique; **v. sound** son *m* vocalique
vox pop [vɒks] *n* forum *m* populaire
voyage[1] ['vɔɪɪdʒ] *n* (*crossing*) traversée *f*; **(sea) v.** voyage *m* en mer; **a two-day v. away** à deux jours de voyage; **v. by air** voyage en avion; **v. in space** voyage dans l'espace; **v. out/back** voyage d'aller/de retour
voyage[2] *vi Lit* voyager; **to v. across the ocean/the desert** traverser l'océan/le désert
voyager ['vɔɪɪdʒər] *n Lit* voyageur, -euse
voyeur [vwɑ:'jɜ:r] *n* voyeur, -euse
voyeurism [vwɑ:'jɜ:rɪz(ə)m] *n* voyeurisme *m*
voyeuristic [vwɑ:jɜ:'rɪstɪk] *adj* **to take a v. pleasure in sth** prendre un plaisir de voyeur à qch; **it's just v.** ce n'est que du voyeurisme
VP [vi:'pi:] *n abbr* **Vice-President**
VR [vi:'ɑ:r] *Br* (*abbr* **Victoria Regina**) la Reine Victoria
VRAM ['vi:ræm] *n Comptr* (*abbr* **volatile random access memory**) VRAM *f*
vs (*abbr* **versus**) contre, c.
VSO [vi:es'əʊ] *n Br abbr* **Voluntary Service Overseas**
Vt *abbr* **Vermont**
VTOL [vi:ti:əʊ'el] *n* (*abbr* **vertical take-off and landing (aircraft)**) ADAV *m* (avion à décollage et à atterrissage verticaux)

vulcanite ['vʌlkənaɪt] *n* ébonite *f*
vulcanization [vʌlkənaɪ'zeɪʃən] *n Ind* vulcanisation *f*
vulcanize ['vʌlkənaɪz] *vt Ind* (*rubber*) vulcaniser
vulgar ['vʌlgər] *adj* (**a**) (*coarse*) vulgaire; **don't be v.**! ne sois pas vulgaire!; **v. expressions** expressions *fpl* vulgaires; **to make v. remarks** dire des vulgarités *fpl*; **to be v. in one's speech** s'exprimer vulgairement (**b**) *Fml* (*widespread*) vulgaire, commun; **v. errors** erreurs *fpl* très répandues; **v. Latin** latin *m* vulgaire; **the v. tongue** la langue commune, la langue vulgaire
vulgar fraction *n Math* fraction *f* ordinaire
vulgarian [vʌl'geərɪən] *n* (*coarse person*) personne *f* vulgaire
vulgarism ['vʌlgərɪz(ə)m] *n* vulgarisme *m*; (*swearword*) vulgarité *f*, grossièreté *f*
vulgarity [vʌl'gærɪtɪ] *n* vulgarité *f*, grossièreté *f*
vulgarization [vʌlgəraɪ'zeɪʃən] *n* vulgarisation *f*
vulgarize ['vʌlgəraɪz] *vt* vulgariser; *Pej* (*one's style etc*) vulgariser, trivialiser
vulgarly ['vʌlgəlɪ] *adv* (*coarsely*) vulgairement, grossièrement; *Fml* (*informally*) vulgairement
Vulgate ['vʌlgɪt, -eɪt] *n Rel* **the V.** la Vulgate
vulnerability [vʌln(ə)rə'bɪlɪtɪ] *n* vulnérabilité *f*
vulnerable ['vʌln(ə)rəb(ə)l] *adj* vulnérable; **he's at a v. age** il est à un âge vulnérable; **v. to criticism** sensible à la critique; **that's her v. spot** c'est son point faible *ou* son talon d'Achille; **the v. spot in our defences** le point faible de nos défenses; **this left them v. on their eastern border** cela les a laissés dans une position vulnérable sur leur frontière est
vulture ['vʌltʃər] *n* vautour *m*; *Fig* vautour, rapace *m*
vulva ['vʌlvə] *n Anat* vulve *f*
vulvitis [vʌl'vaɪtɪs] *n Med* vulvite *f*
VU meter [vjuː] *n TV* vu-mètre *m*
vv *abbr* **verses**
vying *see* **vie**

W

W[1], **w** ['dʌb(ə)ljuː] *n* *(letter)* W, w *m*
W[2] **(a)** *El* *(abbr* **watt(s)***)* W **(b)** *(abbr* **west***)* O.
wacky ['wækɪ] *adj F (person, sense of humour)* farfelu; *(idea, film)* loufoque
wad[1] [wɒd] *n* **(a)** *(of cotton wool)* tampon *m*, bouchon *m*; *(of chewing gum)* boulette *f* **(b)** *(of bank notes)* liasse *f*; *(of forms, documents)* paquet *m*, pile *f*, tas *m*; *esp Am* **to shoot one's w.** *F (spend all one's money)* claquer tout son fric; *Vulg (of man, have orgasm)* décharger, envoyer la sauce *ou* la purée **(c)** *Mil (for cartridge)* bourre *f*
wad[2] *vt* **(-dd-) (a)** *Sewing* ouater, capitonner **(b)** *(paper)* faire un tampon de; **she wadded (up) the money and stuffed it in her pocket** elle plia les billets et les fourra dans sa poche
▶ **wad up** *vtsep* = **wad**[2] **(b)**
wadding ['wɒdɪŋ] *n (material for clothes)* ouate *f*
waddle[1] ['wɒd(ə)l] *n* dandinement *m*; **to walk with a w.** *(of person)* marcher en se dandinant
waddle[2] *vi* se dandiner, marcher en se dandinant; **to w. along** avancer en se dandinant
wade [weɪd] **1** *vi* **(a)** *(in water)* **the only way to cross the river was by wading** la seule façon de traverser la rivière était à gué; **to w. across a stream** passer un cours d'eau à gué; **he waded out to the island** il est allé jusqu'à l'île à gué; **she waded into the river to rescue him** elle s'avança dans la rivière pour le sauver **(b)** *esp Am (paddle)* patauger dans l'eau **2** *vt (stream)* passer à gué
▶ **wade in** *vi* **(a)** *(go into water)* entrer dans l'eau **(b)** *Fig (to work, task)* s'y mettre; **when the fight started, everybody waded in** quand la bagarre a commencé tout le monde s'en est mêlé; **he always has to w. in with his opinion** il faut toujours qu'il donne son avis; **it would have been much better if you had let them sort it out themselves instead of wading in** tu aurais mieux fait de les laisser se débrouiller entre eux plutôt que de t'y mettre aussi
▶ **wade into** *vipo Fig (attack) (person)* s'attaquer à, s'en prendre à; *(task)* s'attaquer à, se mettre à; **to w. into sb with one's fists** attaquer qn à coups de poings; **when Anne insulted him, he waded into her** quand Anne l'a insulté, il lui a dit ses quatre vérités; **critics have waded into his latest film** la critique a démoli son dernier film
▶ **wade through** *vipo* **to w. through mud** avancer *ou* marcher péniblement dans la boue; **to w. through piles of dirty clothing** *(walk through them)* se tailler un chemin à travers des piles de linge sale; *F (wash them)* venir à bout de piles de linge sale; *F* **I'm wading through his latest novel** j'avance péniblement dans son dernier roman; *F* **we spent two hours wading through the agenda** il nous a fallu deux heures pour venir à bout de l'ordre du jour
wader ['weɪdə(r)] *n* **(a)** *(bird)* échassier *m* **(b) waders** *(boots)* cuissardes *fpl*, bottes *fpl* de pêcheur
wadi ['wɒdɪ] *n Geog* oued *m*
wading ['weɪdɪŋ] **1** *adj* **w. bird** échassier *m* **2** *n esp Am (paddling)* pataugeage *m*; **w. pool** *(for children)* pataugeoire *f*, petit bassin *m*
wafer ['weɪfə(r)] *n* **(a)** *Culin* gaufrette *f*; *Rel* hostie *f* **(b)** *Electron (of silicon)* tranche *f*
wafer-thin *adj (slice)* mince comme du papier à cigarette *ou* comme une pelure d'oignon; *Fig (majority)* infime; **to cut sth w.** couper qch en tranches très fines
waffle[1] ['wɒf(ə)l] *n Culin* gaufre *f*; **w. iron** gaufrier *m*
waffle[2] *n Br F (wordiness)* verbiage *m*; **a load of (pretentious) w.** beaucoup de blabla (prétentieux); **her speech was just the usual w.** son discours n'était que du verbiage, comme d'habitude
waffle[3] *vi Br F* parler pour ne rien dire; *(in writing)* faire du remplissage; **what did you say to that? – I just waffled** qu'est-ce que tu as répondu à ça? – j'ai baratiné; **you won't get away with waffling in this interview** tu ne pourras pas te tirer de cet entretien en faisant du baratin *ou* en parlant dans le vague; **he just waffles on** (il n'a rien à dire mais) il ne sait pas s'arrêter
waft[1] [wɑːft, wɒft] *n (of wind, perfume)* bouffée *f*
waft[2] **1** *vt (of wind)* **to w. a sound/a scent through the air** porter *ou* transporter un son/un parfum dans les airs; **the music was wafted in by the breeze** la musique se faisait entendre, transportée par la brise **2** *vi (of smell, sound)* être porté par le vent *ou* la brise; **the scent of roses wafted in through the window** le parfum des roses entrait par la fenêtre; **her voice wafted gently down the stairs** sa voix douce parvenait jusqu'en bas de l'escalier
wag[1] [wæg] *n (action)* agitation *f*; **with a w. of its tail** *(of dog)* en remuant *ou* en agitant la queue
wag[2] **(-gg-) 1** *vt (finger)* agiter, remuer; **to w. its tail** *(of dog, bird)* remuer *ou* agiter la queue; **to w. one's finger at sb** menacer qn du doigt; **to w. one's head** hocher la tête **2** *vi* s'agiter, se remuer; **its tail was wagging** *(of dog)* sa queue frétillait *ou* remuait; **tongues are wagging** les langues vont bon train (**about** sur, au sujet de); **tongues were wagging about her behaviour** son comportement faisait jaser *ou* parler les gens; **if you carry on like this tongues will begin to w.** si tu continues comme ça, les gens vont jaser; **to set (people's) tongues wagging** faire jaser les gens
wag[3] *n F (person)* plaisantin *m*, farceur, -euse; **what w. left this here?** qui est le petit plaisantin qui a laissé ça ici?
wage[1] [weɪdʒ] *n* [①A10,f] *(pay)* **wage(s)** paie *f*, salaire *m*; *(of domestic servant)* gages *mpl*; **basic w.** salaire de base; **living w.** minimum vital; **that's not even a living w.** c'est un salaire avec lequel on ne peut même pas vivre; **to get one's weekly w.** recevoir son salaire *ou* sa paie de la semaine, *F* toucher sa semaine; **to earn good wages** être bien payé; *Bible* **the wages of sin is death** la mort est le prix du péché; **w. and price spiral** spirale *f* des prix et des salaires; **w. bargaining** négociations *fpl* salariales; **w. bill** dépenses *fpl* salariales; **w. ceiling** salaire *m* plafonné; **w. claim** *or* **demand** revendication *f* salariale; **w.-cost inflation** inflation *f* par les salaires; **wages ledger** grand livre *m* de paie, journal *m* de paie, journal des salaires; **wages policy** politique *f* des salaires; **wages sheet** bordereau *m* de salaires
wage[2] *vt* **to w. war** faire la guerre (**with, on, against** à); **to w. a campaign against smoking** mener une campagne anti-tabac; **to w. a campaign for peace/against homelessness** faire campagne pour la paix/pour les sans-abri
wage cut *n* réduction *f* de salaire, réduction salariale
wage deductions *npl* retenues *fpl* salariales, retenues sur salaire
wage earner *n* salarié, -iée; *(breadwinner)* soutien *m* de famille; **in many cases it is the woman who is the w.** c'est souvent la femme qui travaille
wage freeze *n* blocage *m* des salaires; **to impose a w.** bloquer les salaires
wage increase *n* augmentation *f* de salaire
wage inflation *n* inflation *f* des salaires
wage packet *n (envelope)* paie *f* en espèces; *(money)* paie, salaire *f*
wager[1] ['weɪdʒə(r)] *n Old-fashioned, Fml* pari *m*; **to lay** *or* **make a w.** faire un pari, parier; **he did it for a w.** il l'a fait pour tenir un pari
wager[2] *vt Old-fashioned, Fml (sum of money)* parier; **to w. that ...** parier que ...; **to w. one's reputation** mettre sa réputation en jeu; **I'd w. my life on it** j'en mettrais ma main au feu
wage rise *n* augmentation *f* de salaire
wage slave *n F* = personne *f* qui dépend entièrement de son salaire pour vivre
waggish ['wægɪʃ] *adj Old-fashioned F* facétieux, drôle; *(sense of humour)* blagueur
waggle ['wæg(ə)l] *vti* remuer, bouger; **to w. one's eyebrows/ears** (faire) remuer ses sourcils/ses oreilles
Wag(g)on ['wægən] *n Astron* **the W.** la Grande Ourse
wag(g)on ['wægən] *n* **(a)** *(horse-drawn)* charrette *f* (à quatre roues), chariot *m*; *Am (child's toy)* petit chariot; *Fig* **to be on the w.** être au régime sec; *Fig* **to fall off the w.** *(temporarily)* faire un écart; *(permanently)* se remettre à boire; *US Hist* **w.**

train convoi *m* de chariots bâchés **(b)** *Aut Am* break *m*; *US* **patrol w.** voiture *f* cellulaire, *F* panier *m* à salade **(c)** *Br Rail* wagon *m* (découvert); **goods w.** wagon à marchandises
wag(g)oner ['wægənər] *n* roulier *m*, charretier *m*
wag(g)onette [wægə'net] *n* (*carriage*) break *m* attelé
wag(g)onload ['wægənləʊd] *n* (*of hay etc*) charretée *f*; *Rail* (charge *f* de) wagon *m*
Wagnerian [vɑːg'nɪərɪən] *adj, n Mus* wagnérien, -ienne
wagtail ['wægteɪl] *n* (*bird*) bergeronnette *f*, hochequeue *m*, lavandière *f*
wah-wah pedal ['wɑːwɑː] *n Mus* pédale *f* wah-wah *ou* wa-wa
waif [weɪf] *n* (*child*) enfant *mf* abandonné(e); (*animal*) animal *m* errant; **she looks like a w.** elle a l'air d'une petite malheureuse; **waifs and strays** miséreux *mpl*
waiflike ['weɪflaɪk] *adj* (*appearance*) maigrelet; **the w. look of some models** la maigreur famélique de certains mannequins
wail¹ [weɪl] *n* cri *m* plaintif, plainte *f*, gémissement *m*; (*of new-born baby*) vagissement *m*; (*of siren etc*) hurlement *m*; **she heard a w. from upstairs, the baby had obviously woken up** elle entendit des pleurs venant d'en haut, manifestement, le bébé s'était réveillé; **a w. of complaint** un gémissement plaintif; **the child gave a w.** l'enfant se mit à hurler
wail² *vi* gémir; (*of new-born child*) vagir; (*of siren*) hurler; **what's he wailing about now?** de quoi se plaint-il maintenant?; **to w. over sth** se lamenter sur qch, pleurer sur qch
wailing ['weɪlɪŋ] **1** *adj* (*cry, singing*) plaintif; (*siren*) hurlant, strident; **w. voice** voix gémissante; **a w. saxophone** le son aigu d'un saxophone **2** *n* (*of person*) plainte(s) *f(pl)*, lamentation(s) *f(pl)*; (*of siren*) hurlement(s) *m(pl)*; **the W. Wall** (*in Jerusalem*) le mur des Lamentations
wain [weɪn] *n Arch, Lit* charrette *f*; **hay w.** charrette à foin
wainscot¹ ['weɪnskət] *n* lambris *m*, boiseries *fpl*
wainscot² *vt* (-t(t)-) lambrisser
wainscot(t)ing ['weɪnskətɪŋ] *n* **(a)** (*material*) lambris *m*, boiseries *fpl* **(b)** (*action*) lambrissage *m*
waist [weɪst] *n* **(a)** (*of person, dress*) taille *f*, ceinture *f*; **down/up to the w.** jusqu'à la ceinture, jusqu'à mi-corps; **stripped to the w.** nu jusqu'à la ceinture, torse nu; **it's too tight at the w.** ça serre à la taille; **what w. are these trousers?** quel est le tour de taille de ce pantalon?; **to put one's arm round sb's w.** prendre qn par la taille; **w. lock** (*in wrestling*) ceinture; **w. (measurement)** tour *m* de taille **(b)** (*of hourglass, violin*) étranglement *m*; (*of pipe*) rétrécissement *m* **(c)** *Naut* (*of ship*) embelle *f*, passavant *m* **(d)** *Old-fashioned Am* (*blouse*) corsage *m*
waistband ['weɪstbænd] *n* ceinture *f*
waistcoat ['weɪskəʊt] *n Br* gilet *m*
waist-deep *adj* (*water*) à hauteur de la taille; **the water was almost w.** l'eau arrivait à mi-corps; **to be w. in water** avoir de l'eau jusqu'à la taille *ou* jusqu'à mi-corps; *Fig* **I'm w. in work/files** je croule sous le travail/les dossiers, je suis submergé de travail/dossiers
waisted ['weɪstɪd] *adj* (*coat, jacket*) cintré
waist-high *adj* (*grass*) à hauteur de la taille
waistline ['weɪstlaɪn] *n Sewing* taille *f*; **to watch one's** *or* **think of one's w.** surveiller sa ligne
wait¹ [weɪt] *n* **(a)** attente *f*; **it was quite a w.** il a fallu attendre très longtemps; **we had a long w.** nous avons dû attendre longtemps; **it was worth the w.** ça valait la peine d'attendre; **it will be a long w. before the next train** il va falloir attendre longtemps avant que le prochain train arrive; **to lie in w.** (*ambush*) se tenir en embuscade; **to lie in w. for sb** (*ambush*) attendre qn au passage; (*of military, police*) tendre un guet-apens à qn **(b)** *Old-fashioned Br* **waits** (*door-to-door carol singers*) chanteurs *mpl* de Noël
wait² **1** *vi* **(a)** attendre; **to w. for sb/sth** attendre qn/qch; **w. a moment/a minute/a bit** attendez un moment/un instant/un peu; **to w. for sth to be done** attendre que qch soit fait; **what are you waiting for?** qu'attendez-vous?; **we're waiting to be served** nous attendons qu'on nous serve *ou* qu'on s'occupe de nous; **to keep sb waiting** faire attendre qn; **w. until tomorrow** attendez jusqu'à demain; **I shall w. until she's ready** j'attendrai qu'elle soit prête; **(just) you w.!** (*threat*) attends un peu!, tu vas voir ce que tu vas voir!; **just w. till I tell you what's happened!** attends que je te dise ce qui s'est passé!; **w. for it!** (*not yet, guess what*) attends!; **I can't w. to ...** j'ai hâte de ...; **I can't w. to see him** je brûle d'impatience de le voir; **I can't w. for the weekend** vivement le weekend, j'ai hâte que le weekend arrive; **I can hardly w.** je meurs d'impatience; *Iron* je n'attends que ça, je brûle d'impatience; *Com* **repairs while you w.** réparations minute; *Prov* **everything comes to him** *or* **to he who waits** tout vient à point à qui sait attendre; **we must w. and see** il faudra voir; **w. and see!** attends voir!; **w.-and-see policy** politique *f* attentiste, attentisme *m*; **a w.-and-see approach** une approche attentiste; *Comptr* **w. state** état *m* d'attente
(b) to w. at table servir (à table), faire le service
2 *vt* (*opportunity, signal*) attendre, guetter; **w. your turn!** attendez votre tour!; **don't w. dinner for me** ne m'attendez pas pour vous mettre à table
▶ **wait about** *vi* attendre; **don't keep me waiting about** ne me fais pas attendre
▶ **wait behind** *vi* rester; **could you w. behind?, there's something I'd like to ask you** est-ce que vous pourriez attendre?, j'aimerais vous demander quelque chose
▶ **wait in** *vi* (*stay at home*) rester à la maison; **to w. in for sb** rester à la maison pour attendre qn
▶ **wait on 1** *vipo* (*serve*) servir; *Am* **to w. on table** servir (à table), faire le service; **to w. on sb hand and foot** être aux petits soins pour qn **2** *vi* (*continue to wait*) continuer à attendre
▶ **wait out** *vtsep* (*war, storm*) attendre la fin de; **to w. it out** attendre que qch arrête *ou* soit fini, patienter
▶ **wait up** *vi* **(a)** (*not go to bed*) ne pas aller se coucher, veiller, rester debout; **she always waited up until her daughter was home** elle attendait toujours que sa fille rentre pour se coucher; **I'll w. up for you** j'attendrai que tu arrives *ou* rentres avant d'aller me coucher; **I'll be late so don't w. up for me** je rentrerai tard, couche-toi sans m'attendre **(b)** *Am* (*halt*) attendre; **w. up, I can't walk as fast as you** attends-moi, je ne peux pas marcher aussi vite que toi
waiter ['weɪtər] *n* garçon *m* (de restaurant); **head w.** maître *m* d'hôtel; **w.!** garçon!; **w. service** service *m* à table
waiting ['weɪtɪŋ] *n* attente *f*; **it's all the w. (that) I can't stand** ce que je ne supporte pas, c'est d'avoir à attendre tout le temps; *Aut* **no w.** stationnement interdit; **w. at table** service *m* (à table); **to play a w. game** pratiquer une politique attentiste; **w. list** liste *f* d'attente; **to be on the w. list** être sur la liste d'attente; **there's a two-month w. list for an operation** il faut attendre deux mois pour une opération; **w. period** période *f* d'attente; *Com* délai *m* de carence
waiting chef *n* chef *m* serveur
waiting room *n* (*in station*) salle *f* d'attente, hall *m*; (*at doctor's*) salle d'attente
waitlist ['weɪtlɪst] *vt Am* mettre sur la liste d'attente; **I'm waitlisted for the next flight** je suis sur la liste d'attente pour le prochain vol
wait loop *n Comptr* boucle *f* d'attente
waitperson ['weɪtpɜːs(ə)n] *n Am* (*male*) garçon *m*, serveur *m*; (*female*) serveuse *f*; **w. wanted** (*notice in café etc*) on cherche du personnel
waitress ['weɪtrɪs] *n* serveuse *f*; **w.!** mademoiselle!; **w. service** service *m* à table
waive [weɪv] *vt* (*one's claims, rights*) renoncer à, abandonner; (*principle*) déroger à; (*condition, rule*) ne pas insister sur; **on this occasion, I think we can w. the rules** pour cette fois, je crois que nous pouvons nous permettre d'ignorer le règlement
waiver ['weɪvər] *n Jur* **w. of a right** renonciation *f* à un droit; **w. of a claim** désistement *m* de revendication
wake¹ [weɪk] *n Naut* sillage *m*; *Fig* **in the w. of sth** à la suite de qch; **in the w. of the storm** à la suite de la tempête; **the war brought famine in its w.** la guerre a amené la famine dans son sillage; *Fig* **to follow in sb's w.** marcher sur les traces *ou* dans le sillage de qn; **Steven followed in his father's w. and became a lawyer** Steven a suivi l'exemple de son père et est devenu avocat; **since then many other countries have followed in our w.** depuis lors bon nombre d'autres pays nous ont suivis; **he left the other athletes trailing in his w.** il a laissé les autres athlètes à la traîne *ou* loin derrière lui
wake² *n* (*in Ireland*) (*vigil over body*) veillée *f* de corps; **to have a w. for sb** organiser une veillée de commémoration en souvenir de qn; *Fig* **it is too soon to hold a w. for the ideal of European unity** il est encore trop tôt pour enterrer l'idéal de l'unité européenne
wake³ (*pt* **woke** [wəʊk], **waked** [weɪkt]; *pp* **woke, waked, woken** ['wəʊk(ə)n]) **1** *vi* se réveiller; **to w. with a start** se réveiller en sursaut **2** *vt* (*person*) réveiller; (*from inaction*) tirer de sa torpeur; (*emotion, memory*) éveiller, ranimer; **w. me at six** réveillez-moi à six heures; **to be hard to w.** avoir le sommeil lourd; **to make enough noise to w. the dead** faire un bruit à réveiller les morts
▶ **wake up 1** *vi* **(a)** (*from sleep*) se réveiller; **come on, w. up!** allons, réveillez-vous!; (*be more alert*) remuez-vous!, secouez-vous!
(b) *Fig* (*become aware*) prendre conscience; **it took him a while to w. up to what was going on** il lui fallut un certain temps pour comprendre *ou* réaliser ce qui se passait; **she's gradually waking up to the truth** elle commence à voir les

choses telles qu'elles sont; **come on, w. up!** enfin, ouvre les yeux!

2 *vtsep* (*person*) (*from sleep*) réveiller; (*from inaction*) tirer de sa torpeur, secouer; *Fig* **this country needs waking up** ce pays a besoin de se réveiller; *Fig* **that woke her up to what was going on** ça lui a ouvert les yeux sur ce qui se passait

wakeful ['weɪkfʊl] *adj* **(a)** (*not sleepy*) (*person*) éveillé, peu disposé à dormir; **w. night** nuit blanche; **to have a w. night** passer une nuit blanche **(b)** (*vigilant*) vigilant

wakefulness ['weɪkfʊlnɪs] *n* **(a)** (*insomnia*) insomnie *f* **(b)** (*vigilance*) vigilance *f*

waken ['weɪk(ə)n] **1** *vt* **(a)** éveiller, réveiller; **noise fit to w. the dead** bruit à réveiller les morts **(b)** (*emotion*) réveiller, ranimer **2** *vi esp Lit* se réveiller, s'éveiller

wake-up *adj esp Am* **w. call** réveil *m* téléphonique; **to ask for a w. call** (*in hotel etc*) demander à être réveillé par téléphone

wakey ['weɪkɪ] *int F* **w. (w.)!** debout!, réveillez-vous!

waking ['weɪkɪŋ] *n* **between sleeping and w.** entre la veille et le sommeil; **w. hours** heures *fpl* de veille; **to spend (all) one's w. hours doing sth** passer tout son temps à faire qch

wale [weɪl] *n Fml* (*of whiplash*) marque *f*, trace *f*, zébrure *f*

Wales [weɪlz] *n* pays *m* de Galles; **New South W.** (*in Australia*) la Nouvelle-Galles du Sud

walk¹ [wɔːk] *n* **(a)** (*action*) marche *f*; **it's half an hour's w. from here** c'est à une demi-heure d'ici à pied *ou* une demi-heure de marche d'ici; **it's only a short w. (from here)** c'est à deux pas (d'ici)

(b) (*stroll*) promenade *f* (à pied), tour *m*; **to go for a w.** (aller) se promener, faire un tour *ou* une promenade; **it's a lovely w. from here to the village** c'est une promenade très agréable d'ici jusqu'au village; **to take sb for a w.** emmener qn en promenade *ou* se promener; **to take the dog for a w.** sortir *ou* promener le chien; *Am F* **take a w.!** (*get lost!*) va te faire voir!, disparais!

(c) (*gait*) façon *f* de marcher, démarche *f*, allure *f*; **I know him by his w.** je le reconnais à sa démarche

(d) (*speed*) **to go** *or* **move at a w.** aller *ou* avancer au pas; **to drop into a w.** (*of horse*) se mettre au pas; (*of person*) (*after running*) se remettre à marcher

(e) (*path*) avenue *f*, promenade *f*; (*in garden*) allée *f*; **covered w.** allée couverte; *Archit* péristyle *m*, ambulatoire *m*

(f) *Am* (*sidewalk*) trottoir *m*; *Am* **cross w.** passage *m* clouté (pour piétons)

(g) *Fig* **w. of life** (*social class*) milieu *m*; **people from all walks of life** des gens de tous milieux

walk² **1** *vi* **(a)** (*move on foot*) marcher; **to w. on** *or* **in the road** marcher sur la chaussée; **to w. two paces forward** faire deux pas en avant; **to w. on all fours** marcher à quatre pattes; **is the baby walking yet?** est-ce que le bébé marche maintenant?; **to w. in one's sleep** (*be a sleepwalker*) être somnambule; **I'll w. a little way with you** je vais vous accompagner un bout de chemin; **I can't w. another step** je ne peux pas faire un pas de plus; **to w. with a limp** boiter (en marchant); **he walks five kilometres every day** il fait cinq kilomètres à pied tous les jours; *esp Am* **w.!/don't w.!** (*traffic sign*) (piétons) passez!/attendez!; **to w. up/down the street/the stairs** monter/descendre la rue/l'escalier; **to w. up and down** (*pace the floor*) se promener de long en large, faire les cent pas; **to w. up to sb** s'approcher de qn; **to w. across** *or* **over the street to speak to sb** traverser la rue pour parler à qn; **please w. in** entrez sans frapper; **to w. through the town/the crowd** traverser la ville/la foule (à pied); *Fig* **you should learn to w. before you try to run** chaque chose en son temps; *Fig* **to w. on water** marcher sur l'eau; **as far as the party faithful are concerned, he can w. on water** aux yeux des fidèles du parti, il est capable de miracles; *Fig* **to be walking on air** être aux anges

(b) (*as opposed to riding, driving etc*) aller à pied; (*for exercise, pleasure*) se promener (à pied); **to w. home/back** rentrer/retourner à pied; **I missed the bus so I had to w.** j'ai raté le bus donc j'ai dû marcher; **w.!** (*don't run*) ne cours pas!

(c) (*of horse, rider*) aller au pas

(d) (*of ghost*) revenir

(e) *F* (*disappear, be stolen*) (*of money, object*) disparaître; (*disappear*) (*of suspected criminal*) partir; **the money seems to have walked** l'argent semble s'être envolé

2 *vt* **(a)** (*move along*) **to w. the streets** (*wander*) courir les rues, battre le pavé; (*of prostitute*) faire le trottoir; **to w. one's beat** *or* **one's round** (*of policeman*) faire sa ronde; *Th* **to w. the boards** être sur les planches; *Naut* **to w. the plank** subir le supplice de la planche

(b) (*accompany*) **to w. sb home** raccompagner qn; **to w. sb to the bus stop** accompagner qn jusqu'à l'arrêt de bus; **he walked me halfway home** il m'a accompagné à pied jusqu'à mi-chemin

(c) (*make move*) **John walked me off my feet in London** John m'a fait marcher pendant des kilomètres à Londres; **to w. a horse** (*lead along*) conduire *ou* promener un cheval (au pas); (*bring to a walk*) mettre un cheval au pas; **to w. the dog** promener *ou* sortir le chien; **the physio walked him up and down** le kiné l'aidait à faire quelques pas

▶ **walk away** *vi* s'en aller, partir; *Fig* **to w. away from trouble/a problem** éviter une situation difficile/un problème; *Fig* **to w. away from a situation** se distancier d'une situation; *Fig* **just w. away from it!** laisse tomber!; **you can't just w. away from it** tu ne peux pas te dérober comme ça

▶ **walk away with** *vipo F* **(a)** (*take*) prendre; **I walked away with an antique dressing table for just thirty pounds** j'ai réussi à avoir une coiffeuse ancienne pour seulement trente livres; **he walked away with a small fine** il s'en est tiré avec une petite amende **(b)** (*steal*) faucher **(c)** (*win easily*) (*prize, nomination*) remporter haut la main

▶ **walk in on** *vipo* (*disturb*) déranger; **she walked in on them having sex** elle est entrée sans prévenir et les a trouvés en train de faire l'amour

▶ **walk into** *vipo* **(a)** (*enter*) (*room*) entrer dans; **to w. straight into a job** (*after leaving school etc*) trouver *ou* obtenir facilement un emploi **(b)** (*collide with*) (*person, thing*) rentrer dans; **he walked right into me/it** il m'est rentré en plein dedans/il est rentré en plein dedans

▶ **walk off** **1** *vi* s'en aller, partir **2** *vtsep* **to w. off one's lunch** faire une promenade pour digérer

▶ **walk off with** *vipo F* = **walk away with**

▶ **walk on** *vi* **(a)** (*continue walking*) continuer à marcher **(b)** *Th* (*have minor stage part*) figurer, faire *ou* remplir un rôle de figurant(e)

▶ **walk out** *vi* sortir **(in a rage** en colère); (*go on strike*) débrayer, se mettre en grève; **you can't just w. out as soon as things get a bit difficult** tu ne peux pas disparaître *ou* tout laisser tomber dès que les choses deviennent un peu difficiles; **to w. out on one's commitments** laisser tomber ses engagements, ne pas tenir ses engagements; **the delegates walked out of the meeting** les délégués ont quitté la réunion (en signe de protestation); *F* **to w. out on sb** (*desert*) abandonner qn, plaquer qn; (*leave in anger*) quitter qn en colère, partir en claquant la porte

▶ **walk over** *vipo* **(a)** *F* (*treat badly*) **to w. all over sb** marcher sur les pieds de qn; **you shouldn't let him/her/people w. all over you** tu ne devrais pas te laisser marcher sur les pieds **(b)** *Sp* **to w. over the course** inspecter le terrain (avant l'épreuve)

▶ **walk round** *vipo* (*museum, shops etc*) faire le tour de

▶ **walk through** *vipo* (*one's exams etc*) réussir sans effort, *F* réussir les doigts dans le nez

walkabout ['wɔːkəbaʊt] *n* (*of aborigines*) voyage *m* dans le désert; *Fig* (*of politician, celebrity*) bain *m* de foule; **to go w.** (*of aborigines*) aller faire un voyage dans le désert; *Fig F* (*disappear, be stolen*) (*of missing object, money etc*) disparaître, s'envoler; *Fig* **to go (on a) w.** (*of politician, celebrity*) prendre un bain de foule

walkaway ['wɔːkəweɪ] *n Am Sp F* victoire *f* facile

'walk' button *n Comptr* case *f* 'marche'

walker ['wɔːkər] *n* **(a)** (*person*), *Sp* marcheur, -euse; (*for leisure*) promeneur, -euse; **I'm not much of a w.** je ne suis pas un grand marcheur; **he's a fast/slow w.** il marche vite/lentement **(b)** (*aid*) (*for infirm person*) (dé)ambulateur *m*; (*for baby*) trotte-bébé *m*, *pl* trotte-bébés, youpala *m*

walkie-talkie [wɔːkɪ'tɔːkɪ] *n Rad* talkie-walkie *m*, *pl* talkies-walkies

walk-in **1** *adj* (*customer in hotel*) sans réservation; (*patient*) sans rendez-vous; *Am* (*apartment*) de plain-pied; **w. wardrobe** dressing *m*; **w. cupboard** débarras *m*; **w. fridge** armoire *f* réfrigérante; **the flat is in w. condition** l'appartement est libre d'occupation **2** *n* (*customer in hotel*) client, -ente sans réservation; *esp Am* (*patient*) patient, -ente sans rendez-vous

walking ['wɔːkɪŋ] **1** *adj* (*traveller, ghost*) ambulant; **at a w. pace** au pas; **to slow (down) to a w. pace** (*after running*) se remettre à marcher; **that man's a w. disaster area!** ce type est une catastrophe ambulante!; **she's a w. dictionary/encyclopedia** c'est un dictionnaire/une encyclopédie ambulant(e); *Mil* **w. wounded** blessés *mpl* en état de marcher

2 *n* marche *f*; **w. is the best form of exercise** la marche est le meilleur des exercices; **two hours' w.** deux heures de marche *ou* de promenade; **I like w.** j'aime bien marcher; **it's within w. distance** on peut aisément s'y rendre à pied; **it's not within w. distance** on ne peut pas s'y rendre à pied; **it's ten minutes' w. distance** c'est à dix minutes à pied; *esp Am*

F **to give sb their w. orders** *or* **papers** (*employee*) mettre *ou* flanquer qn à la porte, renvoyer qn; (*lover etc*) plaquer qn; *Sp* **w. race** concours *m* de marche; **w. shoes** chaussures *fpl* de marche; **w. shorts** short *m* de randonnée
walking frame *n Br* (dé)ambulateur *m*
walking holiday *n* randonnée *f*; **we went on a w. in the Basque Country** nous sommes partis en randonnée *ou* nous avons fait une randonnée dans le Pays Basque
walking-out dress *n Mil* tenue *f* de ville
walking stick *n* canne *f*
walking tour *n* randonnée *f*; (*in town*) visite *f* à pied
Walkman® ['wɔːkmən] *n* (*personal stereo*) walkman® *m*, baladeur *m*
walk-on 1 *n Th* **w. (part)** rôle *m* de figurant(e) **2** *adj Av* (*flight, service*) pour lequel il n'est pas nécessaire d'effectuer de réservation
walkout ['wɔːkaʊt] *n* (*going on strike*) débrayage *m*, mise *f* en grève; (*from meeting*) départ *m* (en signe de protestation); **to cause a w.** (*at meeting etc*) provoquer le départ d'un groupe *ou* d'une faction (en signe de protestation); **they staged a w. when their demands were refused** (*went on strike*) ils se sont mis en grève quand leurs revendications ont été refusées
walk-out *n* (*from hotel*) client, -ente qui part sans payer
walkover ['wɔːkəʊvər] *n Sp F* victoire *f* facile; **it was a w.!** c'était facile *ou F* fastoche!
walk-through *n Th* répétition *f* (technique)
walk-up *adj, n Am* **w. (building)** (immeuble *m*) sans ascenseur *m*; **third-floor w.** (*apartment*) appartement *m* au deuxième étage sans ascenseur
walkway ['wɔːkweɪ] *n* allée *f* (couverte), passage *m* (couvert); **(moving) w.** tapis *m* roulant
wall¹ [wɔːl] *n* **(a)** (*of house etc*) mur *m*; (*of town, city*) murs *mpl* (d'enceinte), remparts *mpl*; (*for fortification*) muraille *f*; (*of blood cell, abdomen, cave, tunnel etc*) paroi *f*; **to live outside the city walls** vivre à l'extérieur des remparts; **only the rich lived within the walls of the city** seuls les riches vivaient intra-muros; **to leave only the four walls standing** ne laisser que les quatre murs; **between these four walls** entre ces quatre murs; **what I say now must not go beyond these four walls** ce que je vais vous dire maintenant ne doit pas sortir d'ici; **the Great W. of China** la grande muraille de Chine; **w. bars** (*in gym*) espalier *m*; **w. bracket** console *f* murale; **w. clock** pendule *f* murale; **w. cupboard** placard *m* mural; **w. lamp** applique *f* murale, lampe *f* murale; **w. map** carte *f* murale; **w. paintings** peintures *fpl* murales
(b) (*of tyre*) flanc *m*
(c) *Fig* (*of ice*) muraille *f*; (*of fire*) rideau *m*, mur *m*; (*of silence*) mur; (*of policemen*) barrage *m*; **a w. of flame** un rideau de flammes; **to break down a w. of silence** abattre un mur de silence; **to come up against a blank** *or* **brick w.** se heurter à un mur; **to have one's back to the w.** en être réduit à la dernière extrémité, être au pied du mur; **to drive** *or* **push sb to the w.** acculer qn, mettre qn au pied du mur; **to go to the w.** (*go bankrupt*) faire faillite; **the weakest always go(es) to the w.** le plus faible est toujours battu; **to bang** *or* **beat one's head against a (brick) w.** se cogner la tête contre les murs; *F* **you might as well talk to a brick w.** autant parler à un mur; *F* **to drive** *or* **send sb up the w.** rendre qn fou/*f* folle *ou* dingue; **people like him should be put (up) against the w. (and shot)** les gens comme lui méritent la peine de mort
wall² *vt* murer, entourer de murs
► **wall in** *vtsep* murer, entourer de murs; **the park was walled in on all four sides by giant buildings** le parc était bordé sur les quatre côtés par des immeubles gigantesques; **he felt walled in by the surrounding mountains** il se sentait prisonnier des montagnes qui l'entouraient
► **wall off** *vtsep* séparer par un mur; **part of the garden was walled off from the rest** une partie du jardin était isolée du reste par un mur
► **wall up** *vtsep* (*window, door*) murer, condamner; *Hist* (*prisoner*) emmurer
wallaby ['wɒləbɪ] *n* (*animal*) wallaby *m*
wallah ['wɒlə] *n* (*in India*) employé *m*, garçon *m*; *F* **tea w.** préposé *m* au thé; **punkah-w.** tireur *m* de panka
wallchart ['wɔltʃɑːt] *n* affiche *f*, panneau *m* mural
wallcovering ['wɔːlkʌvərɪŋ] *n* tapisserie *f*, revêtement *m* mural
walled [wɔːld] *adj* (*garden*) clos; **w. city** ville fortifiée
wallet ['wɒlɪt] *n* portefeuille *m*
wall-eyed *adj* (*person, fish*) (*with large amount of white showing*) aux yeux globuleux; (*person*) (*with squint*) à strabisme divergent
wallflower ['wɔːlflaʊər] *n* (*plant*) giroflée *f* jaune; *Fig* **to be a w.** (*at a dance*) faire tapisserie
walling up ['wɔːlɪŋ] *n* (*of window*) murage *m*
wall-mounted *adj* (*clock, telephone*) mural
Walloon [wɒ'luːn] **1** *adj* wallon **2** *n* **(a)** Wallon, -onne **(b)** *Ling* wallon *m*
wallop¹ ['wɒləp] *n* **(a)** *F* (*blow*) gros coup *m*; (*spanking*) fessée *f*; **I'll give you a w. in a minute** je vais te coller une beigne dans une minute; **she gave him a real w. across the face** elle lui a flanqué une sacrée beigne; **give it a w. with the hammer** mets-y un coup de marteau; **to pack quite a w.** (*of boxer etc*) frapper dur; (*of drink*) être fort, arracher **(b)** *Br Sl* (*beer*) bière *f*
wallop² *vt F* (*person*) (*one blow*) filer un gnon à; (*several blows*) battre, flanquer une raclée à; *Sp* (*defeat*) battre à plate(s) couture(s); **to w. the ball** (*with bat, hand*) frapper dans la balle; **she walloped him over the head with the rolling pin** elle lui donna un grand coup sur la tête avec le rouleau à pâtisserie; **w. it with the hammer** tape dessus à coup(s) de marteau; **and w.! it crashed to the ground!** et paf! il est tombé par terre!
walloping ['wɒləpɪŋ] *F* **1** *adj* énorme; **a w. great lie** un gros *ou* énorme mensonge **2** *n* rossée *f*; **to give sb a w.** rosser qn; *Sp* battre qn à plate(s) couture(s); **he got a w. from his mother** il s'est fait coller une raclée par sa mère; *Sp* **we gave them a w. they'll never forget** on leur a flanqué une pâtée qu'ils ne sont pas près d'oublier
wallow¹ ['wɒləʊ] *n* (*pool etc*) trou *m* bourbeux, mare *f* bourbeuse; **there's nothing like a w. in a warm bath to unwind** rien de tel qu'un bon bain pour se détendre; **to have a w. in the mud** se vautrer dans la boue; **we all enjoy a good w. in nostalgia** tout le monde aime se laisser aller à la nostalgie de temps en temps
wallow² *vi* (*of animal*) se vautrer; (*of ship*) être ballotté (par les flots); **to w. in self-pity** s'apitoyer sur son propre sort; **to w. in a bath** se prélasser dans un bain; **to be wallowing in luxury** baigner dans le luxe; **to w. in sin/nostalgia** se complaire dans le péché/la nostalgie
wallpaper¹ ['wɔːlpeɪpər] *n also Comptr* papier *m* peint; **w. paste** colle *f* badigeon; **w. stripper** (*liquid*) produit *m* décollant pour papier peint; (*scraper*) couteau *m* de peintre; (*gadget*) décolleuse *f* à papier peint
wallpaper² *vt* (*room*) tapisser
wallpapering ['wɔːlpeɪpərɪŋ] *n* **w. is easy** poser du papier peint est facile; **w. brush** (*for applying paste*) pinceau *m* à encoller le papier peint; (*for smoothing paper*) balai *m* de colleur
Wall Street *n* Wall Street, la Bourse *ou* le centre financier de New York; **according to W. ...** selon la Bourse de New York ..., selon Wall Street ...; **a W. broker** un courtier de la Bourse de New York
wall-to-wall *adj* **all the rooms have w. carpeting** toutes les pièces ont de la moquette; **the room was w. with people** la pièce était bondée; *Fig* **w. coverage** (*of event etc*) couverture *f* complète; **the sort of party where you get w. trendies** le genre de soirée bourrée de gens branchés
wally ['wɒlɪ] *n Br F* (*idiot*) andouille *f*, imbécile *mf*; **I felt a bit of a w.** je me suis senti un peu idiot; **he looked a real** *or* **right w.** il avait vraiment l'air d'un imbécile
walnut ['wɔːlnʌt] *n* **(a)** (*fruit*) noix *f*; **w. oil** huile *f* de noix; **w. cake** gâteau *m* aux noix **(b) w. (tree)** noyer *m* **(c)** (*wood*) (bois *m* de) noyer *m*; **w. desk/bookcase** bureau *m*/bibliothèque *f* en noyer; **w. stain** brou *m* de noix
walrus ['wɔːlrəs] *n* (*animal*) morse *m*; *F* **w. moustache** moustache *f* à la gauloise
Walter Mitty [wɔːltə'mɪtɪ] *adj* **to be a W. character, to live in a W. world** vivre dans un monde imaginaire
waltz¹ [wɔːls] *n* valse *f*; **to play a w.** jouer une valse; **to dance a w.** danser une valse, valser; **may I have this w.?** voulez-vous danser cette valse avec moi?
waltz² *vi* valser; **to w. with sb** faire valser qn; *Fig* **to w. into a room** faire irruption dans une pièce; **she waltzed through the interview** elle a passé son entretien brillamment *ou F* les doigts dans le nez
► **waltz off** *vi F* (*leave*) partir, s'en aller; **to w. off with first prize** remporter le premier prix haut la main
waltzer ['wɔːlsər] *n* (*dancer*) valseur, -euse
wampum ['wɒmpəm] *n* **(a)** (*beads*) wampum *m* (*ceintures faites de coquillages servant de monnaie à certaines tribus indiennes en Amérique du Nord*) **(b)** *Am F* (*money*) pognon *m*, fric *m*
WAN [wæn] *n Comptr* (*abbr* **wide area network**) réseau *m* longue distance
wan [wɒn] *adj* (*person*) pâlot, -otte, blême; **to grow w.** pâlir, blêmir; **w. light** lumière *f* blafarde; **w. smile** sourire *m* triste
wand [wɒnd] *n* **(a)** (*magic*) baguette *f* **(b)** (*for bar codes*) lecteur *m* de codes barres

wander¹ ['wɒndər] *n* balade *f*; **to go for a w. in the woods** aller se promener dans les bois, faire une balade dans les bois

wander² **1** *vi* **(a)** (*roam, stray*) errer, se promener au hasard; **we weren't allowed to w. too far from the path** nous n'avions pas le droit de nous aventurer trop loin du chemin; **don't w. too far, the bus will be here in ten minutes** ne t'éloigne pas trop, le bus sera là dans dix minutes; **they were allowed to w. wherever they wanted** ils avaient le droit d'aller là où ils voulaient; **they wandered round the town, soaking up the atmosphere** ils flânèrent dans la ville, s'imprégnant de l'atmosphère; **to w. about the house** errer dans la maison; **to w. (about) aimlessly** errer sans but; **to w. about the world** rouler sa bosse (un peu partout); **his eyes wandered over the scene** ses regards se promenaient sur cette scène

(b) (*verbally*) radoter; **to w. (in one's mind)** divaguer; **to w. from the subject** sortir du sujet, digresser; **my thoughts were wandering** j'avais l'esprit ailleurs, j'étais ailleurs; **to let one's thoughts w.** laisser vaguer ses pensées; **his mind wanders at times** *or* **is apt to w.** il a des absences

(c) *F* (*go*) **I think I'll be wandering off now** je crois que je vais y aller *ou* me mettre en route maintenant; **I'll just w. down to the beach later** j'irai faire un tour *ou* je descendrai à la plage plus tard; **could you w. round to the post office for me?** pourriez-vous passer à la poste pour moi?; **he just wandered in to the office at about 10.30** il est tranquillement arrivé au bureau à 10h30; **shall we start wandering back then?** alors, on prend doucement le chemin du retour?

2 *vt* **to w. the streets** traîner dans les rues; **to w. the world** courir le monde; **to w. the hills** se balader dans les collines

wanderer ['wɒndərər] *n* vagabond, -onde; **the w. returns!** voilà un revenant!

wandering ['wɒndərɪŋ] *adj* **(a)** (*person, life*) errant, vagabond; (*tribe*) nomade; *Hum* **w. hands** mains *fpl* baladeuses; **w. Jew** (*plant*) misère *f*; **W. Jew** Juif *m* errant; **w. minstrels** ménestrels *mpl* ambulants **(b)** (*mind, gaze*) distrait; (*thoughts, attention*) vagabond; (*account, speech*) décousu

wanderings ['wɒndərɪŋz] *npl* **(a)** (*roaming*) pérégrinations *fpl* **(b)** (*mental*) **in his w.** dans ses divagations

wanderlust ['wɒndəlʌst] *n* désir *m* de voyager, passion *f* des voyages

wane¹ [weɪn] *n* **to be on the w.** (*of moon*) décroître; (*of person, civilization*) être à *ou* sur son déclin; (*of popularity, enthusiasm*) diminuer; (*of beauty*) être sur le retour; (*of career*) être sur la pente descendante, décliner; *Fig* **his star is on the w.** son étoile pâlit

wane² *vi* (*of moon*) décroître, décliner; (*of beauty*) se faner; (*of enthusiasm*) s'affaiblir, s'attiédir; (*of popularity, power, influence*) diminuer; *Fig* **his star/his glory is waning** son étoile pâlit/sa gloire diminue

wangle¹ ['wæŋg(ə)l] *n F* combine *f*, embrouille *f*, truc *m*

wangle² *vt F* (*get*) carotter, resquiller; **I wangled myself a trip to Rome** je me suis débrouillé pour obtenir un voyage à Rome; **I'll w. it somehow** je me débrouillerai; **he wangled his way onto the delegation/into the hall** il réussit à s'immiscer dans la délégation/à s'introduire dans le hall; **could you w. me a ticket?** est-ce que tu pourrais m'avoir un ticket?; **how did you w. that?** comment est-ce que tu as arrangé ça?

wangler ['wæŋglər] *n F* resquilleur, -euse

wangling ['wæŋglɪŋ] *n F* resquillage *m*, carottage *m*; **with a bit of w. I managed to get myself a ticket** j'ai eu mon ticket en faisant marcher le système D; **it just needs a bit of w.** il suffit de resquiller un peu

waning ['weɪnɪŋ] **1** *adj* (*support, interest*) décroissant; (*health*) déclinant; (*light*) défaillant, faiblissant; **w. moon** lune décroissante; **his w. influence** son influence déclinante *ou* décroissante; **his w. enthusiasm** son enthousiasme en baisse **2** *n* (*of moon*) décroissance *f*, décroissement *m*; (*of beauty*) déclin *m*; (*of empire*) décadence *f*; (*of enthusiasm*) diminution *f*

wank¹ [wæŋk] *n Br Vulg* **(a)** (*masturbation*) branlette *f*; **to have a w.** se branler, se faire une branlette; **to give sb a w.** branler qn **(b)** *Fig* **he was talking a load of w.** il disait beaucoup de conneries

wank² *vi Br Vulg* **(a)** (*masturbate*) se branler **(b)** *Fig* **to w. on about sth** baver à propos de qch; **what's he wanking on about now?** qu'est-ce qu'il bave, maintenant?

▶ **wank off** *Br Vulg* **1** *vi* se branler **2** *vtsep* **to w. oneself off** se branler; **to w. sb off** branler qn

wankel engine ['wæŋk(ə)l] *n Aut* moteur *m* wankel

wanker ['wæŋkər] *n Br* **(a)** *Vulg* branleur *m* **(b)** *Sl* (*fool*) branleur *m*

wanly ['wɒnlɪ] *adv* (*to shine*) faiblement; (*to smile*) tristement

wanna ['wɒnə] *F* = **want to**, *see* **want²**

wannabe ['wɒnəbi:] *n esp Am F* = personne *f* rêvant de devenir célèbre/riche/*etc* (mais qui n'en a pas l'étoffe); **the disco was full of Madonna wannabes** la discothèque était pleine de clones de Madonna; **they're just a bunch of wannabes** ce n'est qu'un tas de rêveurs (qui n'arriveront jamais nulle part)

wanness ['wɒnnɪs] *n* pâleur *f*

want¹ [wɒnt] *n* **(a)** (*need*) besoin *m*; **to minister** *or* **attend to sb's wants** pourvoir aux besoins de qn; **my wants are few** j'ai peu de besoins

(b) (*poverty*) misère *f*, besoin *m*; **to be in w.** être dans le besoin *ou* la gêne; **war on w.** lutte *f* contre la misère

(c) (*lack*) manque *m*, défaut *m*; **there was no w. of volunteers** on ne manquait pas de volontaires; **to be in w. of sth** avoir besoin de qch; **w. of imagination/respect** manque d'imagination/de respect; **for w. of sth** faute de qch, à défaut de qch; **it was not for w. of trying** ce n'a pas été manque d'avoir essayé; **for w. of foresight** par manque de prévoyance; **for w. of something better** faute de mieux; **for w. of something better to do** faute d'avoir quelque chose de mieux à faire; **for w. of a better word** faute d'un mot plus approprié; *Prov* **for w. of a nail the shoe was lost, for w. of a shoe the horse was lost** faute d'un point Martin perdit son âne

want² **1** *vt* **(a)** (*desire*) vouloir; **she knows what she wants** elle sait ce qu'elle veut; **the more you get the more you w.** plus on en a, plus on en veut; **do you w. any?** en voulez-vous?; **is that all you w.?** est-ce tout ce que vous voulez?; **what more do you w.?** que voulez-vous de plus?; **what** *or* **how much do you w. for this armchair?** combien vendez-vous ce fauteuil?, combien voulez-vous pour ce fauteuil?; *Iron* **you don't w. much, do you!** tu es bien exigeant!; **you're wanted** on vous demande; **you're wanted on the phone** on vous demande au téléphone; **the boss wants you (in his office)** le patron veut te voir (dans son bureau); **we're not wanted here** nous sommes de trop ici; **people like you are not wanted round here** on ne veut pas de gens comme vous par ici; **they don't w. (to have) me** ils ne veulent pas de moi; **what does he w. with me?** que me veut-il?; **what does he w. me for?** qu'est-ce qu'il me veut?; **to w. sth from sb** vouloir qch de qn; **what do you w. from her?** que voulez-vous d'elle?; **to w. to do sth** vouloir faire qch; **I w. to tell you that ...** je voudrais vous dire que ...; **I w. to see the manager** je veux voir le directeur; **there's someone here who wants to see the manager** il y a quelqu'un qui veut voir *ou* qui demande le directeur; **he could have done it if he had wanted to** il aurait pu le faire s'il l'avait voulu; **don't come if you don't w. to** *or* **unless you w. to** ne venez pas si ça ne vous dit pas; **I don't w. it known** je ne veux pas que cela se sache; **what do you w. done?** que désirez-vous qu'on fasse?; **I don't w. you turning everything upside down** je ne veux pas que vous mettiez tout sens dessus dessous; **I don't w. any fuss** je ne veux pas d'histoires; **I've had enough criticism from you, I w. no more of it!** j'ai eu assez de critiques de ta part, ça suffit!

(b) (*need*) (*of person*) avoir besoin de; (*of thing*) exiger, réclamer, demander; **you w. good eyesight to be a pilot** il faut avoir une bonne vue pour être pilote; **that child wants taking down a peg or two** cet enfant a besoin d'être remis à sa place; **it wants a bit more red to make it the same shade** il faut un peu plus de rouge pour obtenir le même ton; **to w. rest** avoir besoin de repos; **it's a situation that wants careful handling** cette situation demande du tact *ou* qu'on ait du tact; **I shall w. you** j'aurai besoin de vous; **have you everything you w.?** avez-vous tout ce qu'il vous faut?; **we've more than we w.** nous en avons plus qu'il n'en faut; **you shall have as much as you w.** vous en aurez autant que vous voudrez; **I've had all I want(ed)** j'en ai eu assez; **the goods can be supplied as (and when) they are wanted** on peut fournir les articles au fur et à mesure des besoins; **that's the very thing I w., that's just what I w.** c'est juste ce qu'il me faut, cela fera parfaitement mon affaire; **I have the very thing you w.** j'ai juste ce qu'il vous faut; **the very man we w.** l'homme de la circonstance; **what does she w. with a house?** qu'est-ce qu'elle veut faire d'une maison?; **wanted, a good cook** (*advertisement*) on demande *ou* recherche une bonne cuisinière; **he's wanted by the police** il est recherché par la police; **your hair wants cutting** tu as besoin de te faire couper les cheveux, tu devrais te faire couper les cheveux; **the lawn wants cutting** la pelouse a besoin d'être tondue; **the plants w. watering about once a week** il faut arroser les plantes environ une fois par semaine

(c) (*giving advice, instructions*) **you w. to be on your guard** il faut vous méfier; **you w. to be careful with him** il faut que tu fasses attention avec lui

2 *vi* (*be lacking*) manquer (**for** de); **to w. for nothing** ne manquer de rien; **her family will see to it that she doesn't w. (for anything)** sa famille veillera à ce qu'elle ne manque de rien

▶ **want in** *vi F* (*of cat, dog*) vouloir entrer; *Fig* (*want to be part of sth*) vouloir être inclus; **Big Vern wants in on the deal** Big Vern veut être sur le coup

▶ **want out** *vi F* (*of cat, dog*) vouloir sortir; *Fig* (*no longer want to be part of sth*) vouloir retirer ses cartes du jeu; **this has gone far enough, I w. out!** c'est allé trop loin, je laisse tomber!

want ad *n US Journ* demande *f* (**for** de); (*for job*) offre *f* d'emploi; **to go through the want ads** (*looking for job*) parcourir les annonces d'offre d'emploi

wanted ['wɒntɪd] *adj* (*desired*) désiré, voulu; (*child*) désiré; (*criminal*) recherché par la police; **'w. for murder'** 'recherché pour meurtre'; **a w. poster** un avis de recherche; **to feel w.** (*at work*) se sentir apprécié

wanted ad *n Journ* demande *f*; (*for job*) offre *f* d'emploi

wanting ['wɒntɪŋ] *adj* (**a**) (*missing*) **to be w.** faire défaut; **there is something w.** le compte n'y est pas (**b**) **to be w. in sth** (*of person*) manquer de qch; **to be w. in intelligence** être peu intelligent; **he's not w. in intelligence** il n'est pas bête; *Lit* **to be found w.** se trouver en défaut; **he was tried and found w.** il a été mis à l'épreuve et cela n'a pas été concluant

wanton ['wɒntən] **1** *adj* (**a**) (*unjustified*) gratuit, sans motif; **w. cruelty** cruauté gratuite; **w. destruction** destruction sans raison *ou* gratuite (**b**) *Old-fashioned* (*licentious*) (*person, behaviour*) licencieux, impudique; **w. thoughts** pensées *fpl* impudiques *ou* libertines **2** *n Old-fashioned* (*woman*) femme *f* légère; (*man*) libertin *m*

wantonly ['wɒntənlɪ] *adv* (**a**) (*to injure, insult*) sans motif (**b**) *Old-fashioned* (*licentiously*) de façon dévergondée

wantonness ['wɒntənnɪs] *n* (**a**) (*of insult etc*) gratuité *f* (**b**) *Old-fashioned* (*licentiousness*) libertinage *m*

wapiti ['wɒpɪtɪ] *n* (*deer*) wapiti *m*

War *abbr* **Warwickshire**

war¹ [wɔːr] *n* (**a**) guerre *f*; **a state of w. now exists** l'état de guerre est déclaré (**between** entre); **in (time of) w.** en temps de guerre; **w. establishment** *or* **strength** effectif(s) *m(pl)* de guerre; **to set a unit on a w. footing** mettre une unité sur pied de guerre; **preparations for w.** préparatifs *mpl* de guerre; *Lit* **to let loose the dogs of w.** déchaîner les fureurs de la guerre; **to start a w.** déclencher une guerre; **to be at w. with a country** être en (état de) guerre avec un pays; **to make** *or* **wage w. on** *or* **against a country** faire la guerre à *ou* contre un pays; **to go to w.** se mettre en guerre (**over a territory** pour un territoire); *Fig F* **you look as if you've been in the wars** te voilà dans un drôle d'état; *Am Pol* **w. chest** (*for campaign*) fonds *m* spécial; **the w. effort** l'effort *m* de guerre; **w. film** film *m* de guerre; **w. hero** héros *m* de guerre; **w. paint** (*of Amerindian*) peinture *f* de guerre; *Hum* (*of woman*) maquillage *m*; **w. risk** (*in insurance*) risques *mpl* de guerre; **w. widow** veuve *f* de guerre; **the American Civil W.**, *US* **the W. Between the States** la guerre de Sécession; **the Great W.** (*1914-1918*) la Grande Guerre

(**b**) *Fig* guerre *f*, lutte *f*; **w. of nerves** guerre des nerfs; **class w.** lutte des classes; *Econ* **price w.** guerre des prix; **w. of words** dispute *f*, altercation *f*; **to wage w. on** *or* **against sb/sth** faire la guerre à *ou* contre qn/à qch, lutter *ou* militer contre qn/qch; **the w. on drugs** la lutte contre la drogue

war² *vi* (**-rr-**) **to w. against sb/sth** mener une campagne contre qn/qch, lutter contre qn/qch; **to w. against abuses** faire la guerre aux abus

warble¹ ['wɔːb(ə)l] *n* (*of bird*) gazouillement *m*, gazouillis *m*

warble² **1** *vi* (*of bird*) gazouiller; (*of lark*) grisoller; *Fig* (*of person*) chanter **2** *vt Fig* (*of person*) (*song*) roucouler

warbler ['wɔːblər] *n* (*bird*) fauvette *f*

warbling ['wɔːblɪŋ] **1** *adj* (*bird*) gazouillant; (*sound*) mélodieux **2** *n* = **warble¹**

war cemetery *n* cimetière *m* militaire

war correspondent *n* correspondant, -ante de guerre

war crimes *npl* crimes *mpl* de guerre

war criminal *n* criminel, -elle de guerre

war cry *n* (*of Amerindian*), *Fig* cri *m* de guerre

ward [wɔːd] *n* (**a**) (*person*) pupille *mf*; *Jur* **w. of court** pupille sous tutelle judiciaire; **to be made a w. of court** être placé sous tutelle judiciaire (**b**) *Med* salle *f* d'hôpital; **which w. is she in?** dans quelle salle est-elle?; **to walk the wards** (*of medical student*) assister aux leçons cliniques (**c**) *Pol* (*electoral division*) circonscription *f* électorale

▶ **ward off** *vtsep* (*blow*) parer, écarter; (*danger*) détourner, écarter; (*illness, accusations*) éviter

war dance *n* danse *f* guerrière

warden ['wɔːd(ə)n] *n* (*of institution, hostel, prison*) directeur, -trice; (*of national park*) gardien, -ienne; *Br* **Lord W. of the Cinque Ports** gouverneur *m* des Cinq Ports

warder ['wɔːdər] *n Br* (*in prison*) gardien, -ienne

wardress ['wɔːdrɪs] *n Br* (*in prison*) gardienne *f*

wardrobe ['wɔːdrəʊb] *n* (**a**) (*cupboard*) armoire *f*, garde-robe *f*, *pl* garde-robes; **w. drawer/mirror** tiroir *m*/miroir *m* d'armoire (**b**) (*clothes*) (ensemble *m* de) vêtements *mpl*, garde-robe *f*; **Miss Smith's w. by ...** (*on film credits*) les costumes de Miss Smith ont été fournis par ...; **to have a large w.** avoir une garde-robe importante; **she brought half her w. with her** elle a emporté la moitié de sa garde-robe; **w. trunk** malle *f* penderie (**c**) *Th* **to work in w.** être costumier/costumière, s'occuper des costumes; **w. mistress** costumière *f*, habilleuse *f*

wardroom ['wɔːdruːm] *n Naut* carré *m* des officiers

wardship ['wɔːdʃɪp] *n* tutelle *f*

ware [weər] *n* (**a**) (*manufactured articles*) articles *mpl*; **aluminium w.** ustensiles *mpl* en aluminium; **cast-iron w.** poterie *f* en fonte (**b**) **wares** (*goods for sale*) marchandise(s) *f(pl)*; *Lit* **to cry one's wares** faire l'article de *ou* vanter sa marchandise

warehouse¹ ['weəhaʊs] *n* entrepôt *m*, magasin *m*; (*for furniture*) garde-meuble *m*, *pl* garde-meubles; **bonded w.** entrepôt de la douane; *Com* **ex w.** sortie *f* d'entrepôt; **w. manager** responsable *mf* d'entrepôt; **w. receipt** récépissé *m* d'entreposage; **w. warrant** certificat *m* d'entreposage

warehouse² ['weəhaʊz] *vt* (em)magasiner; (*goods in bond*) entreposer

warehouseman, *pl* **-men** ['weəhaʊsmən] *n* magasinier *m*, entrepositaire *m*, manutentionnaire *m*

warehousing ['weəhaʊzɪŋ] *n* (em)magasinage *m*; (*of goods in bond*) entreposage *m*; **w. company** société *f* d'entrepôts; **w. costs** frais *mpl* d'entreposage

warfare ['wɔːfeər] *n* guerre *f*

war game *n* exercice *m* sur la carte; (*with model soldiers*) jeu *m* de stratégie militaire

war grave *n* sépulture *f* militaire

warhead ['wɔːhed] *n* ogive *f*; (*on torpedo*) cône *m* de charge

warhorse ['wɔːhɔːs] *n* (**a**) (*person*) **an old w.** *Mil* un vieux soldat; *Pol* un vétéran de la politique (**b**) *Hist* (*horse*) destrier *m*, cheval *m* de bataille (**c**) *Mktg* cheval *m* de bataille

warily ['weərɪlɪ] *adv* avec précaution; **the soldiers advanced w. through the forest** les soldats avançaient avec prudence dans la forêt; **they eyed him w. as he continued his explanation** ils le regardaient avec méfiance alors qu'il poursuivait son explication

wariness ['weərɪnɪs] *n* circonspection *f*, prudence *f*; **his w. of computers** sa réticence envers l'informatique

warlike ['wɔːlaɪk] *adj* (*appearance, bearing*) guerrier; (*people*) belliqueux

warlock ['wɔːlɒk] *n* sorcier *m*, magicien *m*

warlord ['wɔːlɔːd] *n* seigneur *m* de la guerre; **the local w.** le chef militaire local

warm¹ [wɔːm] **1** *adj* (**a**) (*garment, colour etc*) chaud; (*iron, oven*) assez chaud; **to be w.** (*of water*) être chaud; (*of person*) avoir chaud; **come inside, it's lovely and w.** viens à l'intérieur, il fait bon; **the water's only just w.** l'eau est à peine chaude; **to get w.** (*of person, room*) se réchauffer; (*of water*) chauffer; **the radiator was getting warmer** le radiateur commençait à chauffer; **you're getting warmer** (*in guessing game etc*) tu chauffes; **you're really w.** (*in guessing game etc*) tu brûles; **make sure you keep w.** ne prends pas froid; **to keep a dish w.** garder un plat au chaud; *Fig* **to keep a place w. for sb** (*job*) garder un emploi pour qn; **I'll do it once the w. weather is here** je le ferai quand il commencera à faire chaud; **it's getting warmer** (*of weather*) il commence à faire plus chaud; **it's w. work** c'est une besogne qui donne soif; *Fig* **to make things** *or* **it w. for sb** mener la vie dure à qn, en faire voir de toutes les couleurs à qn; *Fig* **things were getting a bit too w.** (*dangerous*) ça commençait à chauffer; *Aut, Comptr* **w. start** démarrage *m* à chaud

(**b**) (*enthusiastic, kind*) chaleureux; **to meet with a w. reception** être accueilli chaleureusement; **w. heart** cœur généreux; **w. smile** sourire accueillant; **w. welcome** accueil chaleureux; **to give sb a w. welcome** accueillir qn chaleureusement

2 *n* **to have a w.** se réchauffer; **come into the w.** viens au chaud; **to give sth a w.** réchauffer qch; **to give one's hands a w. at the fire** se réchauffer les mains près du feu

warm² **1** *vt* (faire) chauffer; **to w. oneself by the fire/in the sun** se chauffer près du feu/au soleil; **wine/news that warms the heart** vin/nouvelle qui réchauffe le cœur; **that will w. the cockles of your heart** voilà qui vous réchauffera; **it warms the cockles of my heart to see ...** ça me réchauffe le cœur de voir ...

2 *vi* (se) chauffer, s'échauffer, se réchauffer; *Fig* **to w. to sb** (commencer à) ressentir de la sympathie pour qn; **I didn't w. to him** il ne m'a pas plu; **they warmed to one another immediately** ils se sont pris de sympathie immédiatement; **to w. to an idea** se laisser séduire par une idée; **to w. to one's theme** bien entrer dans son sujet

▶ **warm over** *vtsep* **(a)** *esp Am (soup etc)* (faire) réchauffer **(b)** *Fig (novel etc)* réchauffer

▶ **warm up 1** *vi* **(a)** *(of weather)* faire plus chaud; *Fig (of party, audience)* s'animer; *(of discussion)* s'échauffer, s'animer **(b)** *(of dancer, musician, orchestra), Sp* s'échauffer; *(of engine, radio)* se mettre en route **2** *vtsep (thing)* faire chauffer; *(person)* réchauffer; *Fig (party)* animer; *Aut* **to w. up the engine** (faire) chauffer le moteur; **to w. up the soup** (faire) réchauffer le potage; *Fig* **to w. an audience up** chauffer le public, mettre un public en train

warm-blooded *adj (animal)* à sang chaud; *Fig (person)* passionné, ardent

war memorial *n* monument *m* aux morts

warm front *n Met* front *m* chaud

warm-hearted [wɔːm'hɑːtɪd] *adj (person, welcome)* chaleureux; **we were given a very w. welcome** nous fûmes chaleureusement accueillis; **she is very w.** elle a un grand cœur

warm-heartedly [wɔːm'hɑːtɪdlɪ] *adv* chaleureusement, avec chaleur

warming ['wɔːmɪŋ] **1** *adj* qui réchauffe; *Fig (news, thought)* qui réchauffe le cœur, réconfortant **2** *n* chauffage *m*; **w. pan** bassinoire *f*

warming up *n* **(a)** *(of food)* réchauffage *m* **(b)** *Sp* échauffement *m*; **w. exercises** exercices *mpl* d'échauffement

warmly ['wɔːmlɪ] *adv* **(a)** *(dressed)* chaudement **(b)** *(to applaud)* chaudement; *(to recommend)* vivement, chaudement; *(to welcome, thank sb)* chaleureusement; **his suggestion was not w. received** sa proposition n'a pas été chaudement accueillie; **the film was w. received by the critics** le film a été accueilli par la critique avec enthousiasme

warmonger ['wɔːmʌŋgər] *n* belliciste *mf*

warmongering ['wɔːmʌŋg(ə)rɪŋ] *n* bellicisme *m*, propagande *f* de guerre

warmth [wɔːmθ] *n* **(a)** *(of sun, fire)* chaleur *f*; **we huddled together for w.** nous nous sommes blottis les uns contre les autres pour nous tenir chaud **(b)** *(enthusiasm)* ardeur *f*, chaleur *f*; *(of welcome)* cordialité *f*, chaleur; **to receive sth with w.** *(idea, proposal)* accueillir qch avec enthousiasme **(c)** *(anger)* emportement *m*, vivacité *f*; **... she said with some w.** ... dit-elle d'un ton vif

warm-up *n* **(a)** *(of dancer, musician, orchestra), Sp* échauffement *m*; **to do a w.** s'échauffer; **they get a ten-minute w.** ils ont dix minutes d'échauffement; **w. match** match *m* préparatoire *ou* d'entraînement; *esp US* **w. suit** survêtement *m*; **w. time** *(for machine)* temps *m* d'échauffement **(b) come and have a w. by the fire** viens te réchauffer auprès du feu **(c)** *TV etc* **w. man** chauffeur *m* de salle

warn [wɔːn] **1** *vt* **(a)** *(caution)* avertir, prévenir **(that** que); **he warned me not to do it** il m'a déconseillé de le faire; **to w. sb about** *or* **against sth** mettre qn en garde contre qch; **to w. sb about** *or* **against doing sth** conseiller à qn de ne pas faire qch; **he warned her against going, he warned her not to go** il lui a conseillé (fortement) de ne pas y aller; **to w. sb of a danger** avertir qn d'un danger; **they warned me about you** on m'avait mis en garde contre toi, on m'avait prévenu à ton égard; *Hum* **my parents warned me about people like you!** mes parents m'avaient bien dit de me méfier des gens comme toi!; **you have been warned!** vous voilà averti *ou* prévenu!; **I'm warning you for the last time** je te préviens pour la dernière fois; **I shan't w. you again** tenez-vous-le pour dit

(b) *(alert, inform)* informer, donner l'éveil à; **she had been warned in advance** elle était prévenue; **to w. the police** alerter la police

2 *vi* **he warned of possibly serious consequences** il évoqua les graves conséquences possibles

▶ **warn off 1** *vtsep (tell to leave)* **he warned them off his land** il leur demanda instamment de quitter ses terres; **the signs are meant to w. people off** les panneaux sont là pour interdire aux gens d'entrer **2** *vtaspo (advise against)* **to w. sb off sth** déconseiller qch à qn; **to w. sb off drink/smoking** déconseiller l'alcool/la cigarette à qn; **to w. sb off doing sth** déconseiller à qn de faire qch

warning ['wɔːnɪŋ] *n* **(a)** *(caution)* avertissement *m*; *(alarm)* alerte *f*; **to give sb a w.** mettre qn en garde; **this is your last w.** *(to child)* c'est la dernière fois que je te le dis; *(to worker)* c'est votre dernier avertissement; **in spite of repeated warnings** malgré de nombreux avertissements; **to sound a note of w.** recommander la prudence; **he was let off with a w.** il en a été quitte pour un avertissement; **let this be a w. to you** que cela vous serve de leçon *ou* d'exemple *ou* d'avertissement; **she gave him a w. glance** elle lui lança un regard d'avertissement *ou* pour l'avertir; **w. beep** signal *m* sonore; **w. bell** sonnette *f ou* sonnerie *f* d'alarme; **w. buzzer** avertisseur *m* sonore; **w. device** (appareil *m ou* dispositif *m* d')alarme *f*; **w. light** voyant *m* (lumineux), témoin *m* (lumineux), avertisseur lumineux; *Naut* feu *m* d'avertissement; **w. message** *(on computer screen)* message *m* d'avertissement; *Naut, Fig* **w. shot** coup *m* de semonce, avertissement; *Fig* **to fire a w. shot** tirer sur le signal d'alarme; **w. sign** *(indication)* signe *m* annonciateur; *(notice)* pancarte *f* d'avertissement; *Aut* signal de danger; **w. signal** signal avertisseur, signal d'alarme; *Ind* **w. strike** grève *f* d'avertissement; **w. system** système *m ou* dispositif d'alarme

(b) *(advance notice)* avis *m*, préavis *m*; **we only received a few days' w.** nous n'avons été prévenus que quelques jours à l'avance; **she didn't give him much w.** elle l'a prévenu assez tard; **I'm giving you fair w.** vous voilà averti!; **without w.** sans préavis, sans déclaration préalable; **he just left without w.** il est parti sans crier gare; **it just broke down without w.** elle est tombée en panne d'un seul coup; *Ind* **strike w.** préavis de grève

warning triangle *n Aut* triangle *m* de présignalisation

War Office *n Br Hist* Ministère *m* de la Guerre

warp[1] [wɔːp] *n* **(a)** *(distortion) (of plank)* voilure *f*, gauchissement *m*; *(in time)* brèche *f* **(b)** *Tex* chaîne *f*; *(for tapestry)* lisse *f*, lice *f*

warp[2] **1** *vt (distort) (wood, metal sheet)* gauchir, voiler; *Fig (mind, character, person)* pervertir; *(judgement)* fausser **2** *vi (of cupboard door etc)* se déformer, gauchir; *(of timber)* se voiler, gauchir; *(of sheet metal)* (se) gondoler

warpath ['wɔːpɑːθ] *n* **to be on the w.** *(of Amerindian etc)* être sur le sentier de la guerre; *Fig* en vouloir à tout le monde; *Fig* **the boss is on the w.** le patron est d'une humeur massacrante

warped [wɔːpt] *adj (wood)* gauchi, voilé; *Fig (mind, person)* perverti; *(judgement)* faussé; **that's a very w. way of thinking** c'est une drôle de manière de voir les choses; **w. sense of humour** sens de l'humour tordu; **you must be a bit w. if you think that's funny!** tu dois être un peu tordu pour trouver ça drôle!

warping ['wɔːpɪŋ] *n (of plank)* gauchissement *m*; *(of metal sheet)* gondolement *m*; *(of wheel)* voilure *f*, voilement *m*

warplane ['wɔːpleɪn] *n* avion *m* de guerre

warrant[1] ['wɒrənt] *n* **(a)** *Com (guarantee)* garantie *f*; *Fin* bon *m* de souscription d'actions, Obsa *m inv* **(b)** *Jur* mandat *m*, ordre *m*; *Admin* mandat; **w. of arrest** mandat d'arrêt *ou* d'arrestation; **there's a w. out against him** *or* **for his arrest** il est sous le coup d'un mandat d'arrêt; **warehouse w.** certificat *m* d'entrepôt, warrant *m*, warrant cédule; **w. for payment** ordonnance *f* de paiement; **travel w.** feuille *f* de route

warrant[2] *vt* **(a)** *(justify)* justifier; **nothing can w. such conduct** rien ne justifie une pareille conduite, rien ne peut excuser une telle conduite; **his performance warranted better** sa prestation méritait mieux **(b)** *(guarantee) (sth)* garantir, répondre de; *Old-fashioned* **it won't happen again, I w. you!** cela n'arrivera pas deux fois, je vous le promets! **(c)** *Com* warranter

warrantable ['wɒrəntəb(ə)l] *adj (justifiable)* justifiable

warrantee [wɒrən'tiː] *n* receveur, -euse d'une/de la garantie

warrant officer *n Mil* adjudant *m*

warrantor ['wɒrəntɔːr] *n Jur* garant, -ante

warranty ['wɒrəntɪ] *n Com* garantie *f*; **under w.** sous garantie; **is it still under w.?** est-ce que c'est encore sous garantie?; **the iron has a one-year w.** le fer à repasser est garanti un an; **breach of w.** rupture *f* de garantie; **w. certificate** certificat *m* de garantie

warren ['wɒrən] *n (of rabbit)* garenne *f*, clapier *m*; *Fig* labyrinthe *m*, dédale *m*

warring ['wɔːrɪŋ] *adj (countries)* en guerre; *Fig (ideologies)* en conflit; **w. factions within the Labour Party** des factions adverses au sein du Labour Party

warrior ['wɒrɪər] *n* guerrier, -ière; **w. tribes** tribus guerrières

Warsaw ['wɔːsɔː] *n* Varsovie *f*; *Pol* **W. Pact** pacte *m* de Varsovie; **the W. Pact nations** les nations *fpl* du pacte de Varsovie

war-scarred ['wɔːskɑːd] *adj (city, country)* dévasté par la guerre

warship ['wɔːʃɪp] *n* navire *m ou* vaisseau *m* de guerre

wart [wɔːt] *n* verrue *f*; **a biography of Charles de Gaulle, warts and all** une biographie de Charles de Gaulle écrite sans complaisance *ou* qui ne fait pas de cadeaux; **she'll have to accept him as he is, warts and all** il faudra qu'elle l'accepte comme il est, avec tous ses défauts

warthog ['wɔːthɒg] *n* phacochère *m*

wartime ['wɔːtaɪm] *n* temps *m* de guerre; **in w.** en temps de guerre; **w. conditions** conditions *fpl* de guerre; **w. London** le Londres des années de guerre

warty ['wɔːtɪ] *adj* couvert de verrues, verruqueux

wary ['weərɪ] *adj* avisé, prudent, circonspect; **to be w. of sb/sth** se méfier de qn/qch; **I'm still w. about signing it** j'hésite encore à le signer; **to keep a w. eye on sb** surveiller qn de près

war zone *n* zone *f* de guerre

was *see* **be**

Wash *abbr* **Washington**

wash¹ [wɒʃ] *n* **(a)** (*action*) lavage *m*; **to have a w.** se laver; **give your face a w.** lave-toi le visage; **to have a w. and brush up** faire un brin de toilette; **to give sth a w.** laver qch

(b) (*laundry*) lessive *f*, blanchissage *m*; **to send clothes to the w.** donner du linge à laver *ou* à blanchir; **to do the w.** faire la lessive; **your jeans are in the w.** (*being washed*) ton jean est au lavage; **it'll come out in the w.** ça partira au lavage; *Fig* **it will all come out in the w.** (*become known*) ça finira par se savoir; (*be all right*) ça finira par s'arranger; *Old-fashioned* **w. house** buanderie *f*, lavanderie *f*; (*public*) lavoir *m*; *US* (*laundry*) blanchisserie *f*

(c) *Med* (*for wounds*) lotion *f*; (*for plants*) lessive *f* (insecticide); (*against mildew*) bouillie *f*

(d) *Art* (*of water colour, Indian ink*) lavis *m*; **colour w.** (*for walls*) badigeon *m*

(e) (*of waves, ship*) remous *m*

wash² **1** *vt* **(a)** (*clean*) (*car, clothes, plate, etc*) laver; **w. in cool/hot water** à laver à l'eau tiède/chaude; **hand w. only** laver à la main seulement; **to w. sth in cold water** laver qch à l'eau froide; **to w. oneself** se laver; **to w. one's face/hands/hair** se laver le visage/les mains/les cheveux; *Br Euph* **would you like to w. your hands?** (*go to lavatory*) voulez-vous que je vous montre où est la salle de bain?; *Fig* **to w. one's hands of sb/sth** se laver les mains de qn/qch; *Fig* **I w. my hands of the affair** je me lave les mains de cette affaire; *Rel* **to be washed of one's sins** être lavé de ses péchés

(b) *Med* (*wound*) nettoyer

(c) *Ind* (*mineral, coal*) laver; (*gas*) épurer

(d) *Art* (*drawing*) laver; **to w. the walls** (*paint*) badigeonner les murs (**with** de)

(e) (*of sea*) (*shore*) baigner; **to w. sb/sth ashore** rejeter qn/qch sur le rivage; **he was washed overboard** il fut emporté par une vague

2 *vi* **(a)** (*wash oneself*) se laver; **material that washes well** tissu qui se lave bien; **you w. and I'll dry** (*doing dishes*) tu laves et j'essuie; *Br F* **that won't w.!** ça ne prend pas!, ça ne marche pas!

(b) the waves washed against the cliff les vagues baignaient la falaise

▶ **wash away** **1** *vtsep* **(a)** (*remove by washing*) faire partir; **to w. one's sins away** se laver de ses péchés **(b)** (*of rain, flood etc*) **the flood washed away part of the river bank** l'inondation a érodé une partie de la berge; **the village was washed away by the flood** le village a été emporté par l'inondation; **heavy rains had washed away the topsoil** des pluies abondantes avaient entraîné la terre; **washed away by the tide** emporté *ou* enlevé par la mer **2** *vi* (*of mark, stain*) s'en aller *ou* partir au lavage

▶ **wash down** *vtsep* **(a)** (*walls, car*) laver à grande eau **(b)** (*help to swallow*) (*pill*) faire descendre; **to w. down one's dinner with a glass of beer** boire un verre de bière en dînant

▶ **wash off** **1** *vtsep* (*remove by washing*) enlever, faire partir **2** *vi* (*of mud, dirt*) s'en aller *ou* partir au lavage

▶ **wash out** **1** *vtsep* **(a)** (*remove by washing*) (*stain*) enlever **(b)** (*clean*) (*cup, bottle*) laver, rincer, nettoyer; **to w. out a few clothes** *or* **things** faire une petite lessive; *Fig* **to be completely washed out** (*tired*) être complètement lessivé *ou* vanné *ou* à plat **(c)** *Art* (*colour*) dégrader; **washed out** (*of colour, material*) délavé, déteint **(d)** *Min* **to w. out the gold** extraire l'or **(e)** (*of football match etc*) **to be washed out** être annulé à cause de la pluie **(f)** *Geol* éroder **2** *vi* (*of stain, colour*) partir au lavage; **it will w. out** ça partira au lavage

▶ **wash over** *vipo* (*of waves*) balayer; *Fig* (*have no effect on*) ne faire aucun effet à; **anything I say just washes over her** rien de ce que je lui dis ne lui fait le moindre effet

▶ **wash up** **1** *vtsep* **(a)** *Br* **to w. up the dishes** laver *ou* faire la vaisselle **(b)** (*of sea*) rejeter sur le rivage; **wreckage washed up by the sea** débris rejetés par la mer **2** *vi* **(a)** *Br* (*do dishes*) faire la vaisselle **(b)** *US* (*have a wash*) se débarbouiller **(c)** *Fig* (*end up*) (*of person*) finir, échouer; **he washed up in Australia** il a échoué en Australie

washable ['wɒʃəb(ə)l] *adj* lavable

wash-and-wear *adj* lavé-repassé

washbasin ['wɒʃbeɪs(ə)n] *n* lavabo *m*

washboard ['wɒʃbɔːd] *n* planche *f* à laver

washbowl ['wɒʃbəʊl] *n* lavabo *m*; (*large*) bassine *f*

washcloth ['wɒʃklɒθ] *n Br* (*for washing dishes*) lavette *f*; *Am* (*face cloth*) = gant *m* de toilette

washday ['wɒʃdeɪ] *n* jour *m* de la lessive

washed-out ['wɒʃd'aʊt] *adj* (*faded*) délavé; *Fig* (*tired*) lessivé

washed(-)up [wɒʃd'ʌp] *adj Fig F* **to be (all) w.** (*of person*) être fini *ou F* fichu; (*of plan*) être tombé à l'eau; **he's all w.** c'est un homme fini *ou* liquidé; **he's all w. as a boxer** il est fini comme boxeur

washer¹ ['wɒʃər] *n* **(a)** (*person*) laveur, -euse; **w. up,** *F* **w. upper** laveur, -euse de vaisselle; (*in restaurant*) plongeur, -euse **(b)** *F* (*machine*) (*for clothes*) machine *f* à laver; (*for dishes*) lave-vaisselle *m inv*

washer² *n Tech* rondelle *f*, bague *f*; **the tap needs a new w.** il faut changer la bague du robinet

washer bottle *n Aut* réservoir *m* de lave-glace

washer-dryer *n* machine *f* à laver séchante

washerwoman, *pl* **-women** ['wɒʃəwʊmən, -wɪmɪn] *n* blanchisseuse *f*

wash(-)hand basin *n* lavabo *m*

washing ['wɒʃɪŋ] *n* **(a)** (*action*) (*of car, wall etc*) lavage *m*; (*of clothes*) lessive *f*; (*at laundry*) blanchissage *m*; (*of one's body*) toilette *f*; *Rel* (*of feet, hands*) lavement *m*; **to do the w.** faire la lessive; **Monday is w. day** le lundi est le jour de la lessive **(b)** (*dirty clothes*) linge *m* à laver; (*clean clothes*) linge lavé

washing machine *n* machine *f* à laver

washing powder *n* lessive *f* (en poudre), détergent *m*

washing soda *n* cristaux *mpl* de soude

washing-up *n Br* vaisselle *f*; **to do the w.** faire la vaisselle; (*in restaurant*) faire la plonge; **w. bowl** cuvette *f*, bassine *f*; **w. liquid** produit *m* à vaisselle; **w. water** eau *f* de vaisselle

washleather ['wɒʃleðər] *n* peau *f* de chamois; **w. gloves** gants *mpl* chamois

washout ['wɒʃaʊt] *n F* (*failure*) fiasco *m*; (*person*) raté, -ée, zéro *m*; **the whole thing's a w.** c'est une perte sèche

washrag ['wɒʃræg] *n US* = gant *m* de toilette

washroom ['wɒʃruːm] *n* **(a)** *esp Am* (*lavatory in hotel etc*) toilettes *fpl*; **where's the w.?** où sont les toilettes? **(b)** (*with toilets, washbasins etc*) salle *f* d'eau, cabinet *m* de toilette

washstand ['wɒʃstænd] *n* (*table*) table *f* de toilette; *Am* (*washbasin*) lavabo *m*

washtub ['wɒʃtʌb] *n* (*for clothes*) baquet *m* (à lessive)

washup ['wɒʃʌp] *n* **(a)** *Med F* (*before operating*) stérilisation *f* des mains **(b)** *Am* **to have a w.** se laver (les mains et la figure), se débarbouiller

wash-wipe *n Aut* lavage-balayage *m*

wasn't ['wɒz(ə)nt] = **was not,** *see* **be**

Wasp [wɒsp] *n Am esp Pej* (*abbr* **White Anglo-Saxon Protestant**) = Américain *m* blanc protestant d'origine anglo-saxonne

wasp [wɒsp] *n* (*insect*) guêpe *f*; **wasps' nest** guêpier *m*; **w. waist** (*of person*) taille *f* de guêpe

waspish ['wɒspɪʃ] *adj* méchant, acerbe; (*tone*) hargneux

waspishly ['wɒspɪʃlɪ] *adv* (*to do*) d'une manière acerbe; (*to say*) avec hargne

wassail ['wɒseɪl] *vi Lit* chanter des chants de Noël; **to go wassailing** aller de maison en maison en chantant des chants de Noël

wastage ['weɪstɪdʒ] *n* **(a)** (*loss*) gaspillage *m*; (*of heat*) déperdition *f*, perte *f*; *Com* (*in shipping*) freinte *f* **(b)** (*what is wasted*) déchets *mpl*, rebuts *mpl*; **buy enough material to allow for w.** achetez suffisamment de tissu pour compenser les pertes **(c)** (*reduction of workforce*) départ *m* d'employés; **we hope to achieve this by natural w.** nous pensons y parvenir grâce à des départs volontaires

waste¹ [weɪst] *adj* **(a)** (*uncultivated*) **w. land** *or* **ground** terre *f* inculte *ou* en friche; (*in town*) terrains *mpl* vagues; **to lay w.** (*country*) dévaster, ravager, piller **(b)** (*product*) non utilisé, perdu; **w. heat** chaleur *f* perdue; **w. heat recovery** récupération *f* de la chaleur perdue; **w. products** déchets *mpl*; **w. water** (*domestic*) eaux *fpl* usées; *Ind* eaux résiduaires *ou* usées; **w. water treatment** traitement *m* des eaux usées

waste² *n* **(a)** (*of money, effort*) gaspillage *m*; **it's a terrible w. of food** c'est un terrible gâchis *ou* gaspillage de nourriture; **it's a w. of their skills** c'est gaspiller leurs talents; **w. of time** perte *f* de temps; **it's a w. of time** c'est du temps perdu; **it's a w. of time trying to convince her** je perds mon/tu perds ton/*etc* temps à essayer de la convaincre; **that film is a real w. of time** ce film ne vaut rien, ce film est nul; *F* **he's a w. of space** il est nul; **to go to w.** (*of food, talent*) se perdre; (*of land, garden*) partir à l'abandon

(b) (*rubbish*) déchets *mpl*; (*household waste*) ordures *fpl* ménagères; *Min* déblais *mpl*

(c) (*desert*) région *f* inculte, désert *m*; **the wastes of the Sahara** les étendues désertes du Sahara

waste³ *vt* (a) (*squander*) (*stocks, money*) gaspiller; (*paper*) gâcher; (*fortune*) dissiper, dilapider; (*time*) perdre, gaspiller; (*opportunity*) rater, manquer; **she felt that she had wasted her youth** (*misspent*) elle avait l'impression d'avoir gâché sa jeunesse; **nothing is wasted** rien ne se perd; **I hate wasting food** j'ai horreur de gâcher la nourriture; **to w. one's life** gâcher sa vie; **she's wasted in that job** cet emploi est bien au-dessous de ses capacités; **to w. one's words** *or* **breath** parler en pure perte; **don't w. your breath on him** ne perds pas ta salive, il ne le vaut pas; **you're wasting your breath, he won't understand** ne gaspille pas ta salive pour rien, il ne comprend pas; **you're wasting your energy** vous vous dépensez inutilement; **I haven't any time to w. on him** je n'ai pas de temps à perdre pour lui; **we're wasting time** nous perdons notre temps; **we've already wasted too much time on this** nous avons déjà perdu trop de temps là-dessus; **to w. no time doing sth** ne pas perdre de temps pour faire qch; *F* **you didn't w. any time, did you!** tu n'as pas perdu de temps, hein?; **that would be wasted on me** ce serait trop beau pour moi; **expensive wine is wasted on me** (*not appreciated by*) je suis incapable d'apprécier le bon vin; **a beautiful house like that is wasted on such people** une belle maison comme ça, c'est trop beau pour des gens pareils; **the joke was wasted on him** il n'a pas compris la plaisanterie; *Prov* **w. not, want not** qui épargne gagne

(b) (*consume*) (*person*) consumer, épuiser, faire dépérir; (*body, limb*) décharner, atrophier; **her body was wasted by disease** son corps était décharné par la maladie

(c) *Am Sl* (*murder*) tuer

▶ **waste away** *vi* (*of person*) dépérir, s'affaiblir

wastebasket ['weɪstbɑːskɪt] *n esp Am* corbeille *f* (à papier); *Comptr* corbeille; *Comptr* **w. icon** icône *f* de la corbeille

wastebin ['weɪstbɪn] *n* corbeille *f* à papier

waste collection *n* ramassage *m* des ordures

wasted ['weɪstɪd] *adj* (a) (*sick person, body*) affaibli, amaigri; (*through drug use*) dévasté, ravagé; (*limb*) atrophié (b) (*money*) gaspillé; (*effort*) inutile; (*opportunity*) perdu; **it was a w. journey** c'était un voyage pour rien; **w. life** vie gaspillée; **w. time** temps perdu

waste disposal *n* élimination *f ou* destruction *f* des déchets *ou* des ordures; **w. site** dépôt *m* d'ordures; **w. unit** broyeur *m* d'ordures

wasteful ['weɪstfʊl] *adj* (*person*) gaspilleur, -euse; (*expense*) excessif; (*process*) peu économique; **w. practices** gaspillage *m*; **don't be so w. with the hot water!** ne gaspillez pas l'eau chaude!; **it is w. of human resources** c'est gaspiller les ressources humaines

wastefully ['weɪstfəlɪ] *adv* prodigalement, avec prodigalité; **to spend money w.** gaspiller son argent

wastefulness ['weɪstfʊlnɪs] *n* gaspillage *m*

wasteland ['weɪstlænd] *n* (*desert*) région *f* inculte, désert *m*; (*in city*) terrain *m* vague; *Fig* désert; **an industrial/cultural w.** un désert industriel/culturel

wastepaper ['weɪstpeɪpər] *n* vieux papiers *mpl*; **w. basket** corbeille *f* à papier

waste pipe *n* (*for overflow*) tuyau *m* d'écoulement; (*of bath*) écoulement *m*

waster ['weɪstər] *n* (a) (*wasteful person*) gaspilleur, -euse; **time w.** (*own time*) personne *f* qui perd son temps; (*other people's time*) personne qui fait perdre à qn son temps (b) (*good for nothing*) bon *m*/bonne *f* à rien

wasting ['weɪstɪŋ] *n* (a) (*of resources, time*) gaspillage *m* (b) (*of body*) dépérissement *m*, amaigrissement *m*; (*of limb*) atrophie *f*; *Med* **w. of muscle** fonte *f* musculaire; **w. disease** maladie *f* qui ronge

wasting away *n* (*of body*) dépérissement *m*, amaigrissement *m*; (*of limb*) atrophie *f*

wastrel ['weɪstrəl] *n* (*useless person*) vaurien, -ienne, bon *m*/bonne *f* à rien

watch¹ [wɒtʃ] *n* (a) (*observation*) garde *f*, surveillance *f*; **to keep w.** monter la garde; **to keep a close w. on** *or* **over sb** surveiller qn de près; **to put** *or* **set a w. on sb** faire surveiller qn; **to be on the w. for sb** épier *ou* guetter qn

(b) (*timepiece*) montre *f*; **it's six o'clock by my w.** il est six heures à ma montre; **w. chain** chaîne *f* de montre *ou* de gilet; *Comptr* **w. pointer** pointeur-montre *m*, *pl* pointeurs-montres; **w. spring** ressort *m* de montre

(c) *Naut* (*shift*) quart *m*; (*men*) bordée *f*; **to be on w.** être de quart; **the officer of the w.** l'officier *m* du quart

(d) *Hist* (*guard*) **the w.** la garde, le guet; **w. committee** comité *m* qui veille au maintien de l'ordre de la commune

(e) (*vigil*) veille *f*; *Lit* **in the watches of the night** pendant les heures de veille; **to keep w. at sb's bedside** veiller au chevet de qn

watch² **1** *vi* (a) (*look on*) regarder; **they watched helplessly as the wall came tumbling down** ils regardèrent, impuissants, le mur qui s'écroulait; **they're watching to see if you make a mistake** ils surveillent pour voir si tu fais une erreur

(b) (*keep vigil*) veiller; **to w. by a sick person** veiller auprès d'un malade

2 *vt* (a) (*observe*) observer, regarder attentivement; **I'm not going to stand back and w. him make a fool of himself** je ne vais pas juste le regarder se ridiculiser; **I want to w. what happens when you tell him the news** je veux voir ce qui se passe quand tu lui annonceras la nouvelle; **to w. sb closely** ne pas quitter qn des yeux; (*of police, secret service*) surveiller qn de près; **to have sb watched** faire surveiller qn; **we are being watched** on nous observe; **to w. birds** observer les oiseaux; **you're not doing it properly, w. me** tu t'y prends mal, regarde-moi faire; *Prov* **a watched pot never boils** plus on désire une chose plus elle se fait attendre

(b) [①**A40**,C,1,a; **B33**,2,b,i] (*look at, monitor*) regarder; **I watched her working** je la regardais travailler; **to w. television** regarder la télévision; **is there anything worth watching on TV?** est-ce qu'il y a quelque chose de bien (à regarder) à la télévision?; **to w. a football match** (*attend*) assister à un match de football; (*on television*) regarder un match de football; **to w. the course of events/sb's career** suivre le cours des événements/la carrière de qn; *Pej* **to w. the clock** avoir les yeux rivés à *ou* fixés sur l'heure; **to w. the world go by** regarder passer la foule

(c) (*be careful of*) faire attention à; **we shall have to w. the expenses** il nous faudra faire attention aux dépenses; **we'll have to w. the time** (*so as not to be late*) il va falloir que nous fassions attention à l'heure; **w. what you say about …** fais attention à ce que tu dis au sujet de …; **w. you don't say anything stupid** fais attention à ne pas dire quelque chose de stupide; **w. where you're going!** (*or you'll fall*) regarde où tu vas!; (*or you'll bump into somebody*) regarde devant toi!; **w. your language!** surveille ton langage!; **to w. one's weight** surveiller sa ligne; **w. the step!** (fais) attention à la marche!; **w. your step!** (*don't fall*) fais attention de ne pas tomber!; (*step carefully*) fais attention où tu mets les pieds!; (*be careful*) fais attention!; *F* **w. it!** fais gaffe!

(d) (*keep an eye on*) (*children, luggage etc*) surveiller; **our neighbour is watching the flat while we're away** notre voisin s'occupe de notre appartement pendant que nous sommes en voyage

(e) (*be mindful of*) **to w. one's opportunity/time** guetter l'occasion/le moment propice

▶ **watch for** *vipo* **something to w. for this month is the London marathon** la chose à ne pas rater ce mois, c'est le marathon de Londres; **w. for the moment when he realizes she may be the killer** regarde bien la scène où il comprend qu'elle est peut-être l'assassin

▶ **watch out** *vi* faire attention; **you'd better w. out, the boss knows** tu devrais te méfier, le patron est au courant; **w. out!** attention!, prenez garde!

▶ **watch out for** *vipo* (a) (*look for*) **ask the garage to w. out for a decent second-hand car** demande au garage d'essayer de trouver une bonne voiture d'occasion; **w. out for trouble when Fred gets out of prison** méfiez-vous quand Fred sortira de prison (b) *Am* (*take care of*) (*person*) s'occuper de (c) (*keep watch*) (*for return of*) attendre; (*for approach of*) guetter (d) (*be careful of*) faire attention à; **w. out for Ronnie!** gare à Ronnie!

▶ **watch over** *vipo* (*guard, protect*) (*person*) veiller sur; (*person's interest, welfare*) veiller à

watchband ['wɒtʃbænd] *n* bracelet *m* de montre

watchdog ['wɒtʃdɒg] *n* chien *m* de garde; *Fig* (*person*) contrôleur *m*; (*organization*) organisme *m* de surveillance *ou* de contrôle; (**consumer**) **w.** protecteur *m* des intérêts du consommateur; (*organization*) organisme protégeant les intérêts du consommateur; *Fig* **w. committee** comité *m* de surveillance; *Comptr* **w. program** programme *m* sentinelle

watcher ['wɒtʃər] *n* (*of political etc scene*) observateur, -trice; **Downing Street/Kremlin watchers** les observateurs de Downing Street/du Kremlin; **to be a weight w.** surveiller son poids

watchful ['wɒtʃfʊl] *adj* vigilant, alerte, attentif; **to be w.** être sur ses gardes; **to keep a w. eye on** *or* **over sb** surveiller qn de près; **under the w. eye of his grandmother** sous l'œil vigilant de sa grand-mère; **we're keeping a w. eye on the**

situation nous suivons la situation de près; **to be w. of sb** observer *ou* épier qn d'un œil méfiant *ou* jaloux
watchfully [ˈwɒtʃfəlɪ] *adv* avec vigilance, d'un œil attentif
watching brief [ˈwɒtʃɪŋ] *n* **to have a w.** avoir un mandat de contrôle
watchmaker [ˈwɒtʃmeɪkər] *n* horloger, -ère
watchmaking [ˈwɒtʃmeɪkɪŋ] *n* horlogerie *f*
watchman, *pl* **-men** [ˈwɒtʃmən] *n* gardien *m*
watch night service *n Rel* veillée *f* du 31 décembre
watchstrap [ˈwɒtʃstræp] *n* bracelet *m* de montre
watchtower [ˈwɒtʃtaʊər] *n* tour *f* d'observation *ou* de guet; (*in prison camp*) mirador *m*
watchword [ˈwɒtʃwɜːd] *n* mot *m* de passe; (*slogan*) mot d'ordre
water[1] [ˈwɔːtər] *n* **(a)** eau *f*; **is the w. safe to drink?** est-ce que l'eau est potable?; **to take** *or* **drink the waters** (*mineral springs*) prendre les eaux, faire une cure; *Fig* **to get into hot w.** se mettre dans de mauvais draps; **to drink a glass of cold w.** boire un verre d'eau fraîche; *Fig* **to pour cold w. on a scheme** se montrer très négatif à l'égard d'un projet; **to put w. in one's wine** couper son vin d'eau; **the wine flowed like w.** le vin a coulé à flots; *Fig* **to spend money like w.** jeter l'argent par les fenêtres; *Prov* **you can lead a horse to w. but you cannot make him drink** on ne saurait faire boire un âne qui n'a pas soif; *Fig* **to hold w.** (*of argument etc*) tenir debout; **my shoes let in w.** mes chaussures prennent l'eau; **to take w. on** (*of ship*) embarquer son eau, faire de l'eau; **the waters of the Danube** les eaux du Danube; **to feel like a fish out of w.** se sentir perdu *ou* hors de son élément; *Prov* **still waters run deep** il faut se méfier de l'eau qui dort; **the steeple of the church was all that remained above w.** seul le clocher de l'église était hors de *ou* au-dessus de l'eau; **to keep oneself** *or* **one's head above w.** se maintenir à la surface *ou* sur l'eau; *Fig* garder la tête hors de l'eau; (*financially*) faire face à ses engagements; **by w.** en bateau; (*to transport goods*) par voie d'eau; **under w.** (*land, roots*) inondé; (*submarine*) en plongée; (*to swim*) sous l'eau; *Fig* **that's all w. under the bridge now** c'est du passé tout ça; *Fig* **a lot of w. has flowed under the bridge since then** il y a de l'eau qui a coulé sous les ponts depuis; **she's a real w. baby** c'est un vrai petit poisson; **high/low w.** marée *f* haute/basse; **w. bottle** gourde *f*; **hot w. bottle** bouillotte *f*; **w. butt** citerne *f*; **w. carrier** porteur, -euse d'eau; *Old-fashioned* **w. closet** waters *mpl*, toilettes *fpl*; **w. cooling** refroidissement *m* par eau; **w. cures** thermalisme *m*, cures *fpl* thermales; **w. damage** dégâts *mpl* des eaux; **w. hammer** (*in pipes*) cognements *mpl* dans la canalisation; **w. hole** (*for animals*) mare *f*; *Culin* **w. ice** sorbet *m*; *Tech* **w. jacket** chemise *f* d'eau; *Aut* **w. jet** gicleur *m* d'eau; *Sp* **w. jump** douve *f*, brook *m*; **w. mattress** matelas *m* à eau; **w. meadow** champ *m* souvent inondé; **w. plant** plante *f* aquatique; *Admin* **w. rate** taxe *f* sur l'eau; **w. shortage** pénurie *f* d'eau; *Ch* **w. soluble** hydrosoluble; *Myth* **w. sprite** ondin, -ine; **w. sterilizing tablet** pastille *f* pour purifier l'eau; **w. table** niveau *m* hydrostatique; **w. temperature gauge** jauge *f* de température d'eau; **w. temperature warning light** témoin *m* d'alerte de température d'eau
(b) *Med* **w. on the brain** hydrocéphalie *f*; **w. on the knee** hydarthrose *f* du genou, épanchement *m* de synovie; *Obst* **breaking of the waters** perte *f* des eaux; **her waters have broken** elle a perdu les eaux; **to pass** *or* **make w.** uriner
(c) (*of diamond*) **a diamond of the first w.** un diamant de première eau; *Old-fashioned Fig* **a villain of the first w.** une canaille de premier ordre
water[2] **1** *vt* **(a)** (*plant, garden*) arroser; **an area watered by many rivers** une région arrosée par de nombreuses rivières **(b)** (*liquid*) diluer, délayer; **to w. one's wine** couper son vin **(c)** (*animals*) faire boire, donner à boire à, abreuver **(d)** *Tex* **watered silk** soie *f* moirée **2** *vi* (*of eyes*) pleurer, larmoyer; **it makes my mouth w.** cela me fait venir l'eau à la bouche
► **water down** *vtsep* **(a)** (*liquid*) diluer, délayer **(b)** *Fig* (*expression, remark, accusation*) atténuer; **to w. down one's claims** en rabattre, mettre de l'eau dans son vin; **to w. down an article** rendre un article moins virulent; **a watered-down version of sth** une version édulcorée de qch
water bed *n* matelas *m* d'eau
water bird *n* oiseau *m* aquatique
water biscuit *n* = petit biscuit *m* croustillant
water blister *n* ampoule *f*
water board *n Br Admin* service *m* des eaux
water boatman *n* (*insect*) notonecte *mf*
waterborne [ˈwɔːtəbɔːn] *adj* **(a)** (*vessel*) à flot, flottant **(b)** (*goods*) transporté par voie d'eau **(c)** (*disease*) d'origine hydrique
water buffalo *n* kérabau *m*
water cannon *n* canon *m* à eau; **police turned water cannons on the crowd** la police a arrosé la foule avec des canons à eau
water chestnut *n* châtaigne *f* d'eau
water chute *n* (*in swimming pool*) toboggan *m*
watercolour, *US* **watercolor** [ˈwɔːtəkʌlər] *n* (*picture*) aquarelle *f*; (*paint*) couleur *f* pour aquarelle, peinture *f* à l'eau; **to paint in watercolours** faire de l'aquarelle; **a w. artist** un/une aquarelliste
water-cooled [ˈwɔːtəkuːld] *adj* refroidi par eau; **w. engine** moteur *m* à refroidissement d'eau
watercourse [ˈwɔːtəkɔːs] *n* cours *m* d'eau
water cracker *n Am* = petit biscuit *m* croustillant
watercress [ˈwɔːtəkres] *n Bot, Culin* cresson *m* de fontaine
waterfall [ˈwɔːtəfɔːl] *n* chute *f* d'eau, cascade *f*
waterfowl [ˈwɔːtəfaʊl] *n* **(a)** (*bird*) oiseau *m* aquatique **(b)** (*no pl*) (*birds*) gibier *m* d'eau, sauvagine *f*
waterfront [ˈwɔːtəfrʌnt] *n* bord *m* de l'eau; (*docks*) quais *mpl*; **to live on the w.** vivre au bord des quais/au bord de l'eau; **w. house** maison sur les quais/au bord de l'eau
water gun *n Am* pistolet *m* à eau
water heater *n* chauffe-eau *m inv*
water hen *n* poule *f* d'eau
wateriness [ˈwɔːtərɪnɪs] *n* (*of soup, sth boiled*) insipidité *f*, fadeur *f*; (*of colour*) ton *m* délavé
watering [ˈwɔːtərɪŋ] *n* **(a)** (*of plant*) arrosage *m*; (*of fields*) irrigation *f*; **w. can** arrosoir *m* **(b)** (*of animals*) abreuvage *m*; **w. place** (*for cattle*) abreuvoir *m*; *Old-fashioned Br* (*spa*) ville *f* d'eau, station *f* thermale; **w. hole** (*for animals*) mare *f*, point *m* d'eau; *Fig F* (*bar*) bar *m*; *F* **this was my favourite w. hole** c'est là que j'allais régulièrement me rincer le gosier **(c)** (*of eyes*) larmoiement *m* **(d)** *Tex* (*of silk*) moirage *m*
water level *n* niveau *m* de l'eau
water lily *n* nénuphar *m*
water line *n* ligne *f* de flottaison
waterlogged [ˈwɔːtəlɒgd] *adj* (*boat, carpet*) plein d'eau; (*wood*) imprégné d'eau; (*shoes, clothes*) trempé; (*land*) détrempé, imbibé d'eau; (*subsoil*) détrempé
Waterloo [wɔːtəˈluː] *n* **the Battle of W.** la bataille de Waterloo; *Fig* **to meet one's W.** (*come up against unresolvable situation*) avoir son compte; (*come up against unbeatable opponent*) trouver son maître; **it's like W. station here** (*noisy and busy*) c'est une vraie maison de fous ici
water main *n* conduite *f* d'eau
watermark[1] [ˈwɔːtəmɑːk] *n* **(a)** *Naut* (*for high or low water*) laisse *f* **(b)** (*on paper, bank note*) filigrane *m*
watermark[2] *vt* filigraner
watermelon [ˈwɔːtəmelən] *n* pastèque *f*, melon *m* d'eau
water meter *n* compteur *m* d'eau
water mill *n* moulin *m* à eau
water park *n* parc *m* aquatique
water pipe *n* tuyau *m* d'eau
water pistol *n* pistolet *m* à eau
water polo *n Sp* water-polo *m*
water power *n* énergie *f* hydraulique
waterproof[1] [ˈwɔːtəpruːf] **1** *adj* imperméable; (*watch, joint, seal*) étanche; **w. sheet** bâche *f* étanche **2** *n* imperméable *m*; **waterproofs** vêtements *mpl* imperméables
waterproof[2] *vt* imperméabiliser
waterproofing [ˈwɔːtəpruːfɪŋ] *n* (*action*) imperméabilisation *f*; (*substance*) imperméabilisant *m*
water pump *n* pompe *f* à eau
water rat *n* rat *m* d'eau; *Fig* **she's a real w.** c'est un vrai petit poisson
water-repellent **1** *adj* imperméable, hydrofuge; (*product, spray*) imperméabilisant **2** *n* imperméabilisant *m*
water-resistant *adj* qui résiste à l'eau, résistant à l'eau
watershed [ˈwɔːtəʃed] *n* **(a)** *Geog* (*line*) ligne *f* de partage des eaux; *Am* (*area*) bassin *m* hydrographique **(b)** *Fig* point *m* décisif, tournant *m*; *TV* **the (nine o'clock) w.** = l'heure après laquelle l'émission de programmes destinés aux adultes est autorisée; **at this w. in her life** à ce moment critique de sa vie; **the decision proved to be a w.** la décision s'est avérée marquer un grand tournant
waterside [ˈwɔːtəsaɪd] *n* bord *m* de l'eau; (*quays*) quais *mpl*; **on** *or* **by** *or* **at the w.** au bord de l'eau; **w. flowers** fleurs du bord de l'eau; *US* **w. workers** dockers *mpl*
water ski *vi Sp* faire du ski nautique
water skiing *n Sp* ski *m* nautique
water snail *n* hélice *f* aquatique
water sports *npl* sports *mpl* nautiques
waterspout [ˈwɔːtəspaʊt] *n* **(a)** *Met* trombe *f* **(b)** (*pipe*) tuyau *m*, descente *f* (d'eau)
water supply *n* alimentation *f* en eau; (*intake point*) arrivée *f* d'eau

water tank *n* réservoir *m* d'eau
watertight ['wɔːtətaɪt] *adj* **(a)** étanche (à l'eau); **to be w.** (*keep water in*) retenir l'eau; *Naut* **w. bulkhead** cloison *f* étanche **(b)** *Fig* (*alibi*) en béton; (*system of checks and balances etc*) infaillible; (*argument, case*) irréfutable
water tower *n* château *m* d'eau
water transport *n* transport *m* par voie d'eau
waterway ['wɔːtəweɪ] *n* voie *f* navigable
water wheel *n* roue *f* à eau, roue hydraulique
water wings *npl* (*for swimming*) flotteurs *mpl*
waterworks ['wɔːtəwɜːks] *npl* **(a)** (*establishment*) usine *f* de distribution d'eau **(b)** *Br Med F* (*urinary system*) voies *fpl* urinaires; **he's having a bit of trouble with his w.** il a des problèmes de vessie **(c)** *F* **to turn on the w.** (*start to cry*) se mettre à pleurer, ouvrir la fontaine
watery ['wɔːtərɪ] *adj* **(a)** (*full of water*) **w. cabbage/vegetables** chou/légumes insipide(s); **w. soup** potage trop clair; **w. tea** thé trop léger; **w. coffee** café trop léger, lavasse *f*; **w. beer** bière insipide; **w. eyes** (*because of wind, dust etc*) yeux qui pleurent; **she gave a w. smile** elle sourit à travers ses larmes **(b)** (*colour*) déteint, délavé **(c)** (*sky*) chargé de pluie; **w. moon** lune entourée d'un halo **(d)** *Lit* **to find a w. grave** être enseveli par les eaux
watt [wɒt] *n El* watt *m*
wattage ['wɒtɪdʒ] *n El* puissance *f ou* consommation *f* en watts
watt-hour *n El* wattheure *m*
wattle[1] ['wɒt(ə)l] *n* **(a) w.-and-daub wall** mur *m* en clayonnage revêtu de boue *ou* d'argile **(b)** *Austr* (*tree*) acacia *m*
wattle[2] *n* (*of bird*) caroncule *f*; (*of fish*) barbillon *m*
wave[1] [weɪv] *n* **(a)** *Naut* vague *f*, lame *f*; *Fig* vague; **the pain came in waves** la douleur venait par vagues; *Art* **new w.** nouvelle vague; **w. of crime/refugees/enthusiasm** vague de criminalité/de réfugiés/d'enthousiasme; **w. of anger** bouffée *f* de colère; **a w. of bitterness swept over her** un flot d'amertume l'envahit; *F* **to make waves** (*cause trouble*) créer des remous

(b) *Phys* (*electric, magnetic*) onde *f*; **radio waves** ondes radio; **long waves** grandes ondes; **medium/short waves** ondes moyennes/courtes

(c) (*in hair*) ondulation *f*; **to have a natural w. (in one's hair)** avoir les cheveux qui ondulent naturellement; **her hair fell in waves to her waist** ses cheveux ondulaient jusqu'à sa taille

(d) (*movement*) balancement *m*, ondoiement *m*; (*of hand, hat*) geste *m*, signe *m*; **with a w. of his hand** d'un geste *ou* d'un signe de la main; **the Queen gave them a w. from the car** la Reine les salua de la main depuis la voiture; **with a w. of her magic wand** d'un coup de baguette magique
wave[2] **1** *vi* **(a)** (*of person*) faire signe; (*of flag*) flotter (au vent); (*of corn, grass, plume*) ondoyer, onduler; **to w. to sb** (*signal to*) faire signe à qn; (*greet*) saluer qn de la main; **the kids went to the window to w.** (*goodbye/hello*) les gosses sont allés à la fenêtre pour faire au revoir/bonjour de la main; **the President stepped onto the balcony to w. to the crowd** le président est sorti sur le balcon pour saluer la foule; **he waved to us as he left** il nous fit au revoir de la main en partant; **I waved to him to stop** je lui ai fait signe d'arrêter

(b) my hair waves naturally mes cheveux ondulent naturellement

2 *vt* **(a)** (*arm, handkerchief*) agiter; (*umbrella, walking stick*) brandir; **to w. a flag** agiter un drapeau; **to w. one's hand** faire signe de la main; **to w. one's arms about** agiter les bras; **stop waving that gun about** cesse d'agiter ce pistolet dans tous les sens; **to w. a magic wand** agiter une baguette magique; *Fig* **to do sth by waving a magic wand** faire qch d'un coup de baguette magique; **to w. goodbye to sb** agiter la main en signe d'adieu à (l'adresse de) qn, faire au revoir de la main à qn; **w. Mummy goodbye** fais au revoir à maman; *Fig* **you can w. your money goodbye** tu peux abandonner tout espoir de récupérer ton argent

(b) (*hair*) **to have one's hair waved** se faire faire une mise en plis
▶ **wave aside** *vtsep* **to w. sb aside** faire signe à qn de s'écarter; **to w. aside an objection** écarter une objection
▶ **wave down** *vtsep* **to w. a car/sb down** faire signe à une voiture/qn de s'arrêter
▶ **wave on** *vtsep* **to w. a car on** faire signe à une voiture de continuer; **he waved us on** de la main il nous a fait signe de continuer
waveband ['weɪvbænd] *n Rad* gamme *f* d'ondes, plage *f* (d'ondes)
wavelength ['weɪvleŋθ] *n Rad, Fig* longueur *f* d'onde; *Fig* **we weren't on the same w.** nous n'étions pas sur la même longueur d'onde
wave machine *n* machine *f* à vagues
wave power *n* énergie *f* des vagues
waver ['weɪvər] *vi* (*falter*) (*of person*) vaciller; (*of voice*) trembler; (*of courage*) faiblir; (*of gaze*) flotter; (*of troops*) fléchir; (*of flame*) vaciller; **they never wavered in their support, their support never wavered** leur soutien n'a jamais faibli; **to w. in one's resolution** chanceler dans sa résolution; **the price wavered around the £46 per kilo mark** le prix tournait autour des 46 livres le kilo; **to w. between** hésiter entre; **to w. over** hésiter sur; **they wavered over whether to tell their parents** ils se demandèrent s'ils allaient en parler à leurs parents
waverer ['weɪvərər] *n* indécis, -ise
wavering ['weɪvərɪŋ] **1** *adj* (*person, mind*) irrésolu, indécis, vacillant; (*voice*) tremblant; (*courage*) faiblissant; (*flame*) vacillant, tremblotant; **their w. resolution** leur détermination chancelante **2** *n* (*of person*) hésitation *f*, irrésolution *f*; (*of voice*) tremblement *m*; (*of courage*) défaillance *f*; (*of flame*) tremblement, vacillement *m*
waviness ['weɪvɪnɪs] *n* (*of surface*) caractère *m* onduleux *ou* ondulé; (*of hair*) ondulations *fpl* naturelles
waving ['weɪvɪŋ] *adj* (*fields, corn*) ondulant, ondoyant
wavy ['weɪvɪ] *adj* onduleux, ondulé; **w. hair** cheveux *mpl* ondulés; **w. line** ligne *f* tremblée
wax[1] [wæks] *n* cire *f*; (*for skis*) fart *m*; (*in ears*) cérumen *m*; **(paraffin) w.** cire (minérale), paraffine *f*; **to mould sb like w.** façonner *ou* former (le caractère de) qn comme de la cire; *esp Am* **w. beans** haricots *mpl* beurre; **w. crayons** crayons *mpl* gras pour enfants
wax[2] *vt* **(a)** (*floor, furniture*) cirer, encaustiquer; (*furniture*) astiquer; *Ski* farter **(b)** (*in order to remove hairs*) épiler (à la cire); **to w. one's legs** s'épiler les jambes (à la cire)
wax[3] *vi* **(a)** (*of the moon*) croître; **to w. and wane** croître et décroître **(b)** *esp Fml* (*be, become*) **to w. eloquent in support of sth** déployer toute son éloquence en faveur de qch; **he waxed indignant** il s'indigna; **to w. lyrical/poetical** devenir lyrique/poétique (**about** à propos de)
waxed [wækst] *adj* (*floor, tablecloth*) ciré; (*thread*) poissé; (*moustache*) gominé; **w. cotton** coton *m* ciré; **a w. cotton jacket** une veste en coton ciré
waxen ['wæks(ə)n] *adj* **(a)** (*of wax*) de cire, en cire **(b)** (*like wax*) cireux; (*complexion*) de cire; **w. pallor** pâleur cireuse
waxing[1] ['wæksɪŋ] *n* (*of floor, furniture*) cirage *m*, encaustiquage *m*; (*of skis*) fartage *m*
waxing[2] *n* **(a)** (*of moon*) croissance *f* **(b)** *Aut* (*of diesel*) paraffinage *m*
waxwing ['wækswɪŋ] *n* (*bird*) jaseur *m*
waxwork ['wækswɜːk] *n* **w. (dummy)** figure *f* de cire; **waxworks** (*place*) musée *m* de cire
waxy ['wæksɪ] *adj* cireux; (*complexion*) de cire; (*potato*) ferme, non farineux
way[1] [weɪ] *n* **(a)** (*street*) rue *f*; (*path*) chemin *m*; **over** *or* **across the w.** de l'autre côté du chemin *ou* de la rue; **the house/the people over** *or* **across the w.** la maison/les gens d'en face; *US Rail* **w. station** gare *f* intermédiaire; *US Rail* **w. train** (train *m*) omnibus *m*

(b) (*route*) chemin *m*; **the w. to the station** le chemin qui mène *ou* qui conduit à la gare, le chemin de la gare; **to show sb the w.** montrer la route *ou* le chemin à qn; **to ask one's w.** demander son chemin; **to lose one's w.** s'égarer, se perdre; **that's the w. to ruin** c'est le chemin de la ruine; **the right w.** le bon chemin, la bonne route; **to go the wrong w.** se tromper de chemin, faire fausse route; **to go the nearest** *or* **shortest w.** prendre le plus court chemin; **to know one's w. about a place** connaître un endroit; **you'll soon find your w. about** tu trouveras bientôt ton chemin tout seul; *Fig* **he knows his w. about** *or* **around** il sait se débrouiller, il est débrouillard; **to prepare the w.** préparer la voie; **on the w.** en cours de route, en chemin, chemin faisant; **to stop on the w.** s'arrêter en chemin; **to start on one's w.** se mettre en route; **to be on one's** *or* **the w. to Paris** être en route pour Paris; **on my** *or* **the w. home** en revenant chez moi, en rentrant; **I must be on my w.** je dois partir; **I'm on my w.** (*coming*) j'arrive; (*going*) je pars; **he's well on the w. to doing it** il est en bonne voie de le faire; **the building is well on the w. to completion** l'édifice est bien avancé; *F* **there's a baby on the w.** elle attend un bébé; **to lead the w. in research** être à la pointe de la recherche; **to lead the w. in fighting inflation** être le chef de file dans la lutte contre l'inflation; **to go the w. of all things** *or* **of all flesh** aller où va toute chose, mourir; **we went our separate ways** nous avons suivi chacun notre chemin; **to go one's own w.** (*follow own wishes*) faire à sa guise; (*differ from others*) faire bande à part, suivre son chemin; **to go out of one's w.** s'écarter de son chemin, dévier de sa route, faire un détour; *Fig* **to go out of one's w. to oblige sb** se donner de la peine pour être agréable à qn; **the w. to a man's heart is through his stomach** = pour conquérir le cœur d'un homme, il faut lui faire de bons petits plats; **the village is rather out of the w.** le village est un peu isolé; **that's nothing out of the w.** rien d'extraordinaire à cela; *Rel* **the W. of the Cross** le chemin de la Croix; **w. in/out** entrée *f*/sortie *f*; **w. through** passage *m*; **to find a w. out/in** trouver moyen de sortir/d'entrer; **to find a w. out of a deadlock** trouver une issue à une impasse; **to find a w. out of a problem** trouver une solution à un problème; **to leave sb a w. out** laisser à qn le moyen de sortir d'une difficulté; **easy w. out** solution *f* de facilité; **to find one's w. to a place** se rendre quelque part; **can you find your w. there?** est-ce que tu sais y aller tout seul?; **I can't find my w. back to the hotel** je n'arrive pas à retrouver l'hôtel; **can you find your w. out?** vous connaissez le chemin pour sortir?; **I can find my own w. out** (*out of house etc*) je trouverai mon chemin; **however did it find its w. into print?** comment en est-on venu à l'imprimer?; **she made her w. to the door/the bar** elle se dirigea vers la porte/se rendit au bar; **to make one's w. towards sb** se diriger vers qn; **to make** *or* **work** *or* **push one's w. through the crowd** se frayer un chemin à travers la foule; **she made her w. into the house** elle a pénétré dans la maison; **to make one's w. back/out/home** revenir/sortir/rentrer; **how to make one's w. (in the world)** comment réussir; **to work one's w. up** s'élever (à force de travail); **to pay one's w.** (*of company*) se suffire; (*contribute to expenses*) payer sa part; **to see one's w. (clear) to doing sth** être à même de faire qch; **couldn't you see your w. (clear) to doing it?** ne trouveriez-vous pas moyen de le faire?; **to stand in sb's w.** être dans le chemin de qn, barrer le passage à qn; **I don't wish to stand in the w. of your happiness** je ne voudrais pas faire obstacle à votre bonheur; **to stand in the w. of a scheme** s'opposer à un projet; **the obstacles that stand in our w.** les obstacles qui se dressent sur notre chemin; **to put difficulties in sb's w.** opposer *ou* créer des difficultés à qn; **to get in one another's w.** se gêner (les uns les autres); **work gets in the w. of my social life** le travail m'empêche de sortir autant que je voudrais; **to be in sb's w.** gêner qn; **this table is in the w.** cette table gêne le passage *ou* est encombrante; **you're in the w.** tu gênes le passage; *Fig* tu gênes, tu me/nous/*etc* déranges; **to get out of the w.** (*to let sb pass*) se ranger, s'ôter du chemin, s'écarter; **(get) out of the w.!** poussez-vous!, ôtez-vous de là *ou* de mon chemin!; **to get out of sb's w.** s'ôter *ou* s'écarter du chemin de qn; *Fig* (*in relationship*) laisser le champ libre à qn; **to get sb out of the w.** se débarrasser de qn, écarter *ou* éloigner qn; **to get sth out of the w.** enlever *ou* pousser qch; *Fig* **let's get the subject of holidays out of the w. first** réglons d'abord la question des vacances; **to keep out of the w.** se tenir à l'écart; **to keep out of sb's w.** éviter qn; **to make w. for sb** laisser passer qn, faire place à qn; **clear the w.!** poussez-vous!; **the agreement will clear the w. for the company's expansion** l'accord déblaiera le terrain pour permettre l'expansion de la société; *Fig* **the w. is clear** la voie est libre; **he is retiring to make w. for a younger man** il prend sa retraite pour céder la place à un plus jeune; **the cinema is going to be demolished to make w. for a supermarket** le cinéma va être démoli et sera remplacé par un supermarché

(c) (*distance*) **to go a little w.** *or* **part of the w. with sb** faire un bout de chemin avec qn; **all the w.** tout le long du chemin; (*to the end*) jusqu'au bout; **he talked the entire** *or* **whole w.** il a parlé pendant tout le trajet; *F* **to go the whole w.** *or* **all the w.** (*sexually*) aller jusqu'au bout; *Fig* **I'm with you all the w.** (*agree*) je suis tout à fait d'accord (avec toi); **I flew most of the w.** j'ai fait la plupart du voyage en avion; **I've come a long w.** j'ai fait un long voyage, j'arrive de loin; *Fig* **she's come a long w.** (*been successful*) elle a bien réussi (dans la vie); *Fig* **she'll go a long w.** elle ira loin; **it's a long w. to London, London's a long w. from here** Londres est bien loin d'ici; **it's a long w. from Paris to Rome** la route est longue de Paris à Rome; **to have a long w. to go** avoir un long chemin à faire; **a little** *or* **short w. off** à peu de distance; **it's only a short w. (off)** c'est assez proche; **Christmas is still a long w. off** Noël est encore loin; **a little understanding goes a long w.** un peu de compréhension facilite bien les choses; **a little of it goes a long w.** (*it's very economical, strong-tasting*) il en faut très peu; **I like it but a little goes a long w.** (*of rich food*) j'aime ça mais à petites doses; **a little of him goes a long w.** on en a vite assez de lui; **you can make a little meat go a long w. by doing this** utilisez au mieux un petit morceau de viande en faisant ceci; **to make one's money go a long w.** savoir ménager ses sous; **by a long w.** de beaucoup; **not by a long w.** il s'en faut de beaucoup; **you're a long w. out** *or* **out by a long w.** vous êtes loin du compte, vous vous trompez de beaucoup

(d) (*direction*) côté *m*, direction *f*, sens *m*; **which w. is the wind blowing?** d'où vient *ou* souffle le vent?; **which w. does the tap turn?** dans quel sens faut-il tourner le robinet?; *Fig* **so that's the w. the wind's blowing!** ça se passe donc comme ça!; **this w.** de ce côté-ci, par ici; **that w.** de ce côté-là, par là; **(step) this w.!** venez *ou* passez par ici!; **is this the w.?** c'est par ici?; **which w. is the library from here?** par où faut-il passer pour aller à la bibliothèque?; **which w. did you come?** par où êtes-vous venu?; **which w. did she go?** par où est-elle passée?; **which w. do we go?** de quel côté *ou* par où allons-nous?; **this w. and that** de-ci de-là, de tous (les) côtés; **he didn't know which w. to look** il ne savait pas où regarder; **to look the other w.** détourner les yeux; **I've nothing to say one w. or the other** je n'ai rien à dire pour ou contre; **they set off, each going his own w.** ils sont partis chacun de leur côté; **I'm going your w.** je vais de votre côté; **the next time you're that w.** la prochaine fois que vous passerez par là; *F* **down our w.** chez nous; *F* **she lives out Hampstead w.** elle habite du côté de Hampstead; **if the chance comes your w.** si l'occasion se présente à vous; **that works both ways** ça vaut *ou* marche dans les deux sens; *Fig F* **to swing both ways** (*be bisexual*) être *ou* marcher à voile et à vapeur; **the wrong w.** à contresens; *Fig F* **to rub sb up the wrong w.** prendre qn à rebrousse-poil; **the wrong w. up** sens dessus dessous, à l'envers; **to hold sth (the) right w. up** tenir qch dans le bon sens; **to split a sum of money three ways** partager une somme en trois; *Am* **every which w.** dans tous les sens

(e) (*means*) moyen *m*; **to find a w. of doing sth** trouver (le) moyen de faire qch; *Admin* **ways and means** voies et moyens; **there are ways and means** il y a des moyens; *Parl* **Committee of Ways and Means** Commission *f* du Budget

(f) (*manner*) façon *f*, manière *f*; **in this w.** de cette façon; **in a friendly w.** amicalement; (*to treat sb*) en ami; **speaking in a general w.** (parlant) d'une façon générale; **in such a w. as to ...** de façon à ..., de telle sorte que ...; *F* **no w.!** jamais de la vie!, pas question!, *F* des clous!; *F* **there's no w. he'll ...** il est absolument impossible qu'il ... + *sub*; *F* **there's no w. that's Jeanne Moreau!** tu rigoles?, ce n'est pas Jeanne Moreau!; **without in any w. wishing to criticize** sans aucunement vouloir critiquer; **either w.** (*whatever you decide*) quoi que tu décides; (*whatever happens*) quoi qu'il arrive; **that's the w.!** ça y est!, voilà!, à la bonne heure!; **in such and such a w.** de telle et telle façon; **to go** *or* **set about it the right w.** s'y prendre de la bonne manière *ou* comme il faut; **you're going the right w. to make her angry** ça, c'est la meilleure manière de la mettre en colère; **the best w. is to say nothing** le mieux est de ne rien dire; **in one w. or another** d'une façon ou d'une autre; **there are no two ways about it** il n'y a pas à discuter; **we can't go on in the same old w.** nous ne pouvons pas (toujours) continuer comme ça; **I don't like the w. things are going** je n'aime pas la tournure que prennent les choses; **they'll never finish it the w. things are going** ils n'en finiront jamais, au train où vont les choses; **w. of doing sth** manière *ou* façon de faire qch; **w. of speaking/writing** façon de parler/d'écrire; **w. of living** style *m* de vie; **her w. of looking at things** sa manière de voir (les choses); **it isn't what he says, it's the w. he says it** ce n'est pas ce qu'il dit mais la manière dont il le dit; **I don't like the w. you talk to her** je n'aime pas la manière dont tu lui parles; **to my w. of thinking** selon moi, à mon sens; **that's not my w. (of doing things)** ce n'est pas mon genre, ce n'est pas ma façon de faire; **that's her w.** c'est sa façon de faire; **that's always the w. when you're in a hurry** c'est toujours comme ça quand on est pressé; **that's always the w. with him** il est toujours comme ça, c'est toujours comme ça avec lui; **to do things in one's own w.** faire les choses à sa façon *ou* à sa manière; **to have a w. of one's own** *or* **one's own w. of doing sth** avoir une façon à soi de faire qch, avoir sa méthode pour faire qch; **he's a genius in his w.** c'est un génie dans son genre; **she does what she can for them in her small w.** elle les aide dans la mesure de ses moyens; **the restaurant is doing quite well in a small w.** le restaurant marche bien à son échelle; **he started out in a small w.** (*of businessman*) il a commencé petit; **one's ways** (*behaviour*) ses manières; **you'll soon get into our ways** vous vous ferez bientôt à nos habitudes; **engaging ways** petites façons engageantes; **I know his little ways** je connais ses petites manies; **to get** *or* **fall into the w. of doing sth** (*through habit*) prendre l'habitude de faire qch, s'habituer à faire qch; (*through practice*) apprendre à faire qch; **you'll get into the w. of it** vous vous y ferez; **that's one w. of looking at it!** c'est une façon de voir!; **he has a w. with children** il sait s'y prendre avec les enfants; **to have one's (own) w.** en faire à sa tête; **to get one's (own) w.** arriver à ses fins; **she wants her (own) w.** elle veut n'en faire qu'à sa tête; **if I had my w.** si on me laissait faire; **have it your (own)**

w. (*do as you like*) faites ce que vous voulez *ou* à votre guise; (*if you insist*) soit; **she had it all her (own) w.** elle a fait exactement ce qu'elle a voulu; **you can't have it both ways** on ne peut pas avoir le beurre et l'argent du beurre; *Old-fashioned, Hum* **he had his w. with her** (*sexually*) il a obtenu ses faveurs

(g) (*respect*) égard *m*; **in many ways** à bien des égards; **in some ways** à certains points de vue; **in every w.** sous tous les rapports, en tous points; **in one w.** d'un certain point de vue; **you're right in a w.** d'une certaine manière vous avez raison; **in no w.** en aucune façon, nullement; **she is in no w.** *or* **not in any w. to blame** elle n'est aucunement *ou* elle n'est en aucune façon responsable; **this should in no w. be regarded as a victory** cela ne doit en aucune façon être considéré comme une victoire

(h) (*sphere*) **I met him in the ordinary w. of business** je l'ai rencontré dans le courant de mes affaires

(i) (*progress*) *Naut* erre *f*; **to get under w.** (*of person*) se mettre en route; (*of ship*) appareiller; (*of meeting*) commencer; (*of campaign etc*) démarrer; **the ship was under w.** le navire était en marche *ou* en route; **an important experiment is under w.** une expérience importante est en cours; **the project is well under w.** le projet est bien avancé

(j) (*state, condition*) état *m*; **to be in a good/bad w.** être bien/mal en point; **things seem in a bad w.** les choses ont l'air d'aller mal; **his business is in a bad w.** ses affaires vont mal *ou* périclitent; **to be in a fair w. to do sth** être en bonne voie de *ou* en (bonne) passe de faire qch; **to put sb in the w. of earning a few pounds** donner à qn l'occasion de gagner quelques livres

(k) by the w., … au fait …, à propos …; **to mention sth by the w.** mentionner qch en passant *ou* incidemment; **(let it be said) by the w.** soit dit en passant; **all this is by the w.** tout ceci est entre parenthèses; **by the w., did you see him yesterday?** à propos, l'avez-vous vu hier?; **by w. of** (*via*) par, via; (*with the intention of*) à titre de; **by w. of introduction/warning** à titre d'introduction/d'avertissement; **he asked after her dog by w. of changing the conversation** il a demandé des nouvelles de son chien, histoire de changer de sujet; **what do you have by w. of** *or* **in the w. of fruit?** qu'est-ce que vous avez comme fruits?

way² *adv F* (*a lot*) très; **w. ahead** très avancé (**of** sur); **it was w. back in the twenties** cela remonte aux années vingt; **Mary and I go w. back** *or* **are friends from w. back** Mary et moi sommes amies de longue date; **w. down south** là-bas dans le sud; **to be w. out** (*mistaken*) (*of person*) faire une grosse erreur, se tromper sérieusement; **your guess was w. out** vous étiez très loin de la vérité; **it's w. more than I can afford** c'est beaucoup plus que je ne peux payer

waybill ['weɪbɪl] *n Com* feuille *f* de route, connaissement *m*, bulletin *m ou* bordereau *m* d'expédition

wayfarer ['weɪfeərər] *n* voyageur, -euse (à pied)

wayfaring ['weɪfeərɪŋ] *n* voyages *mpl* (à pied); **w. man** voyageur *m* (à pied); **a w. life** une vie de voyages

waylay [weɪ'leɪ] *vt* (*pt, pp* **waylaid** [weɪ'leɪd]) **(a)** (*attack*) attaquer, agresser; **to be waylaid** se faire agresser **(b)** (*in order to speak to*) arrêter au passage

way-out *adj* **(a)** *F* (*weird, eccentric*) dingue **(b)** *Old-fashioned Sl* (*great*) géant

wayside ['weɪsaɪd] *n* bord *m* de la route; **to fall by the w.** (*not keep up*) rester en chemin; (*become dishonest*), *Hum* s'écarter du droit chemin; **w. chapel/inn** chapelle/auberge au bord de la route; **w. flowers** fleurs qui poussent en bordure de route

wayward ['weɪwəd] *adj* capricieux; **to be w.** (*of person*) n'en faire qu'à sa tête

waywardness ['weɪwədnɪs] *n* caractère *m* difficile; **a certain w. became apparent in his character** il est apparu comme quelqu'un qui n'en faisait qu'à sa tête

WC [dʌb(ə)lju:'si:] *n* (*abbr* **water closet**) WC *mpl*; **where is the WC?** où sont les WC?

we [wi:] *pers pron pl* [①A26-27] **(a)** (*unstressed*) nous; **we were playing** nous jouions; **here we are!** nous voilà!; **we both thank you** nous vous remercions tous (les) deux **(b)** (*stressed*) nous; **we are English, they are French** nous, nous sommes anglais, eux, ils sont français; **you don't think that we did it!** vous ne pensez pas que c'est nous qui l'avons fait?; **we English** nous autres Anglais **(c)** [①A27,e; f,ii] (*indefinite*) on; **how are we this morning, Mrs Smith?** comment ça va ce matin, Mme Smith?; **as we say in England** comme on dit en Angleterre; **we all make mistakes sometimes** tout le monde peut se tromper **(d)** [①A27,f,i] (*plural of majesty, editorial* **we**) nous; **we are convinced that …** nous sommes convaincus que …

w/e (*abbr* **week ending**) semaine se terminant …

weak [wi:k] *adj* **(a)** (*person, currency*) faible; (*in character*) faible (mentalement), mou, *f* molle; (*health*) fragile, délicat; (*body*) fragile; (*argument*) faible, peu convaincant; (*style*) mou; (*decision*) qui dénote de la faiblesse; **to grow w.** (*of person*) s'affaiblir, faiblir; **to be w. in body** être physiquement faible; **to have a w. heart** avoir le cœur faible; **to have w. (eye)sight** avoir une mauvaise vue; **to have a w. stomach** avoir un estomac délicat; **w. with hunger** affaibli par la faim; **to feel as w. as a kitten** se sentir mou comme une chiffe; *F* **to be w. in the head** être faible d'esprit; *F* **you must be w. in the head if you believe that** tu dois être dérangé pour croire ça; *Old-fashioned* **the weaker sex** le sexe faible; **in a w. moment** dans un moment de faiblesse; **his w. side** *or* **spot** son point faible; **to find sb's w. spot** trouver le point faible de qn; **she gave a w. smile** elle a eu un faible sourire; **the weaker pupils** les élèves moins doués; **to be w. in French** être faible en français; **the play is w. in character analysis** la pièce est faible du point de vue de l'analyse des personnages; **to have a w. chin/mouth** avoir le menton fuyant/la bouche tombante; **I feel all w. at the knees** j'ai les jambes en coton; **he makes me go all w. at the knees** j'ai les jambes en coton rien que de le voir; *Mus* **w. beat** temps *m* faible; *Rad* **w. signal** signal *m* faible

(b) (*solution*) dilué, étendu; **w. tea** thé léger, *Pej* thé pas assez fort; *Aut* **w. mixture** mélange *m* pauvre

(c) *Gram* (*verb*) faible; *Ling* (*syllable*) non accentué

weaken ['wi:k(ə)n] **1** *vt* affaiblir; (*foundations of house*) miner; *Aut* **to w. the mixture** appauvrir le mélange **2** *vi* (*of person, authority, argument*) s'affaiblir, faiblir; (*of sound*) fléchir; (*of currency*) s'affaiblir; **don't w.** ne faiblis pas; **her courage weakened** son courage a fléchi *ou* faibli; **the pound has weakened against the dollar** la livre est en baisse par rapport au dollar

weakening ['wi:k(ə)nɪŋ] **1** *adj* (*makes lose strength*) affaiblissant; (*losing strength*) faiblissant **2** *n* affaiblissement *m*; (*of will, resistance*) fléchissement *m*; (*of current, currency*) affaiblissement, fléchissement

weakhearted [wi:k'hɑ:tɪd] *adj* sans courage

weak-kneed [wi:k'ni:d] *adj Fig* (*person*) lâche, mou, *f* molle; (*decision*) lâche

weakling ['wi:klɪŋ] *n* (*morally*) mauviette *f*, faible *mf*; (*physically*) gringalet *m*

weakly ['wi:klɪ] **1** *adj* (*person*) débile, chétif **2** *adv* **(a)** (*lacking strength*) faiblement **(b)** (*lacking energy*) sans énergie, mollement; **she protested w.** elle protesta mollement

weak-minded *adj* **(a)** (*unintelligent*) faible d'esprit **(b)** (*lacking character*) irrésolu, indécis, qui manque de résolution

weakness ['wi:knɪs] *n* **(a)** (*of body, character, link, argument*) faiblesse *f*; *Aut* (*of mixture*) pauvreté *f* **(b)** (*fault*) point *m* faible; **we all have our own weaknesses** nous avons tous nos faiblesses; **to have a w. for sth/sb** (*like*) avoir un faible pour qch/qn

weak-willed [wi:k'wɪld] *adj* faible, sans volonté

weal¹ [wi:l] *n* (*from whip*) marque *f ou* trace *f* de coup

weal² *n Arch* **the common w.** le bien commun

wealth [welθ] *n* **(a)** (*riches*) richesse(s) *f(pl)*; **he was a man of great w.** il était très riche **(b)** (*abundance*) (*of details etc*) abondance *f*, profusion *f*; **a w. of information** une mine d'informations; **this job offers a w. of opportunity for travel** cet emploi offre de nombreuses occasions de voyage; **she has had a w. of opportunities to prove it** elle a eu une quantité d'occasions de le prouver

wealth-creating ['welθkri:eɪtɪŋ] *adj* générateur, -trice de richesses

wealth creation *n* création *f* de richesses

wealth tax *n* impôt *m* sur la fortune

wealthy ['welθɪ] **1** *adj* riche, opulent; **w. heiress** riche héritière **2** *npl* **the w.** les riches *mpl*

wean [wi:n] *vt* (*baby*) sevrer; *Fig* **youngsters today are being weaned on computers** les jeunes d'aujourd'hui sont nourris d'informatique; **she had been weaned on Mozart** elle a grandi sur les airs de Mozart; *Fig* **to w. sb from** *or* **off a bad habit** détacher *ou* détourner qn d'une mauvaise habitude; *Fig* **he was trying to w. himself off cigarettes** il essayait de se passer peu à peu de la cigarette

weaner ['wi:nər] *n* (*pig*) = porcelet *m* venant d'être sevré et pesant moins de 40 kg

weaning ['wi:nɪŋ] *n* sevrage *m*

weapon ['wepən] *n Mil, Fig* arme *f*; **the carrying of weapons is illegal** le port d'armes est prohibé; **he was carrying a w.** il avait une arme sur lui; **it is an important w. in the fight against inflation** c'est une arme importante dans la lutte contre l'inflation

weaponry ['wepənrɪ] *n* (*weapons*) armes *fpl*, armement *m*

wear¹ [weər] *n* **(a)** (*clothing*) vêtements *mpl*; **children's w.** vêtements pour enfants; **for country w.** pour la campagne

(b) (*use, deterioration*) usure *f*, détérioration *f* (par usure); (*of machine*) fatigue *f*; (*of road*) dégradation *f*; **to stand hard** *or* **heavy w.** (*of material*) être d'un bon usage; **those shoes still have some w. in them** ces chaussures sont toujours mettables; **my shoes are showing signs of w.** mes chaussures commencent à s'user; **you'll get lots of w. out of it** (*it will last for a long time*) vous le porterez longtemps; (*it is versatile, can be worn often*) vous le porterez beaucoup; **they get very heavy w.** (*of shoes etc*) ils ont la vie dure; **to be the worse for w.** (*of garment, sofa etc*) être usé *ou* défraîchi; (*of machine*) être abîmé; *Fig* (*of person*) (*tired*) être épuisé; (*bruised*) être amoché; (*hung over*) avoir la gueule de bois; **the next morning he was looking a bit the worse for w.** le lendemain matin il avait l'air plutôt en travers

wear[2] (*pt* **wore** [wɔːr]; *pp* **worn** [wɔːn]) **1** *vt* **(a)** (*garment, glasses, watch, beard etc*) (*have on*) porter; (*put on*) mettre; (*look, smile*) avoir; **he was wearing glasses/his new jacket** il portait des lunettes/son nouveau veston; **w. your glasses/ your new jacket** mets tes lunettes/ton nouveau veston; **she wasn't wearing make-up** elle n'était pas maquillée; **she never wears make-up** elle ne se maquille pas; **she was wearing eye-shadow/lipstick** elle avait de l'ombre à paupières/du rouge à lèvres; **I never w. eye-shadow/ lipstick** je ne mets jamais d'ombre à paupières/de rouge à lèvres; **his face wore a smile** il souriait; **his face wore a dubious look** son visage affichait un air dubitatif, il avait un air dubitatif; **skirts are being worn long this year** les jupes sont longues cette année; **to w. black** porter du noir; **I've nothing (fit) to w.** je n'ai rien à me mettre, je n'ai rien de mettable; **he was wearing his slippers** il était en pantoufles; **to w. one's hair long** avoir les cheveux longs; **to w. one's hair in pigtails/in a bun** porter des nattes/un chignon; **you must w. your seat belt** tu dois attacher ta ceinture de sécurité; **she wears her age well** elle porte bien son âge; *Br Fig F* **they won't w. it** ça ne marchera pas avec eux; *Br Fig F* **she won't w. that argument** on ne lui fera pas avaler cet argument

(b) (*use, rub etc*) user; **to w. holes in sth** faire des trous à qch (à force d'usage); **to w. a hole/a track in sth** faire un trou/creuser un sillon dans qch; **the water had worn grooves in the rock** l'eau avait creusé des rigoles dans le rocher; **worn with anxiety** usé par les soucis; **the surface has been worn smooth** la surface est devenue lisse (à force d'usure); **to be worn to a shadow** (*of person*) ne plus être que l'ombre de soi-même; **to w. a surface flat** araser une surface; **a path had been worn across the lawn** des centaines d'allées et venues avaient fait un chemin dans la pelouse

2 *vi* **(a)** (*become rubbed etc*) s'user; **to w. smooth** (*of stone*) devenir lisse (par frottement); **my patience is wearing thin** je suis bientôt à bout de patience; **his jokes are wearing a bit thin** ça commence à bien faire avec ses blagues

(b) (*last*) **to w. well** (*of material*) être de bon usage, faire bon usage; *F* (*of person*) bien porter son âge; **jeans w. well** (*look good after much use*) les jeans vieillissent bien; **this coat has worn well** ce manteau m'a bien servi *ou* m'a fait de l'usage; **the film has not worn well** le film n'a pas bien vieilli; **it will w. for ever** c'est inusable

(c) to w. to a close *or* **an end** toucher à sa fin

▶ **wear away 1** *vtsep* user, ronger; **much of the detail has been worn away** les détails ont été en grande partie effacés; **the pattern on the carpet has been worn away** le motif du tapis s'est effacé **2** *vi* (*of material*) s'user; (*of pattern*) s'effacer; **the stone has worn away** la pierre s'est érodée

▶ **wear down 1** *vtsep* user; **to w. one's heels down** user ses talons; **to w. down the enemy's resistance** user *ou* épuiser peu à peu la résistance de l'ennemi; *Fig* **to w. sb down** faire céder qn, *F* avoir qn à l'usure **2** *vi* s'user

▶ **wear off** *vi* **(a)** (*be removed*) (*of colour, pattern*) s'effacer, disparaître **(b)** (*decrease*) (*of pain*) se calmer; (*of anaesthetic*) cesser de faire effet; **the novelty soon wore off** l'attrait de la nouveauté a vite passé; **it'll w. off** ça passera

▶ **wear on** *vi* (*of time*) s'écouler (lentement), avancer (lentement); **as the evening wore on** à mesure que la soirée avançait

▶ **wear out 1** *vtsep* **(a)** (*one's clothes etc*) user **(b)** (*exhaust*) (*person, sb's patience*) épuiser; **I'm worn out** je suis crevé; **to w. oneself out** s'user, s'épuiser; **to w. oneself out with work** se tuer au travail *ou* à travailler **2** *vi* **(a)** (*of material*) s'user; **this material will never w. out** ce tissu ne s'use pas *ou* est inusable **(b)** (*of patience*) s'épuiser

wearable ['weərəb(ə)l] *adj* (*garment*) mettable

wear and tear *n* usure *f*; (*of building*) dégradation *f*; **the cost of w.** les frais d'entretien; *Jur* **fair** *or* **reasonable w.** (*of rented goods etc*) usure naturelle *ou* normale

wearer ['weərər] *n* **a jacket that is too heavy for the w.** une veste trop lourde à porter; **designed with the w.'s comfort in mind** conçu pour le confort de celui qui le portera

wearily ['wɪərɪlɪ] *adv* **(a)** (*to answer, to smile etc*) d'un air las, avec lassitude; (*to answer*) d'un ton las **(b)** (*to walk etc*) péniblement

weariness ['wɪərɪnɪs] *n* **(a)** (*tiredness*) fatigue *f*, lassitude *f*; **a general air of w. has settled over the country** un sentiment général de morosité s'est emparé du pays **(b)** (*discontent*) ennui *m*, lassitude *f*

wearing ['weərɪŋ] **1** *adj* fatigant, lassant; (*stronger*) épuisant; **their company is rather w.** je trouve leur présence assez pénible; **a very w. day** une journée très fatigante **2** *n Fml* **w. apparel** vêtements *mpl*, habits *mpl*

wearisome ['wɪərɪs(ə)m] *adj* fatigant, ennuyeux; **his w. insistence on ...** sa façon pénible d'insister sur ...

weary[1] ['wɪərɪ] *adj* **(a)** (*tired*) (*physically*) fatigué, las, *f* lasse; (*mentally*) las, dégoûté (**of** de); **in their present w. state** dans l'état de fatigue où ils sont pour le moment; **he had grown w. of listening to their complaints** il s'était lassé de les écouter se plaindre; **to feel w.** se sentir las; **to look w.** avoir l'air fatigué; **to be w. of war/solitude** être las de la guerre/de la solitude; **to be w. of life** être dégoûté de la vie; **to grow w. of waiting** se lasser d'attendre; **w. smile** sourire las **(b)** (*tiring*) fatigant, ennuyeux; **a w. day** une journée fatigante; **it was a w. climb** la montée était pénible

weary[2] **1** *vi* se lasser, se fatiguer (**of** de); **to w. of doing sth** se lasser de faire qch **2** *vt* lasser, fatiguer; **he wearies me with all his complaints** je suis las de l'entendre se plaindre, il me lasse avec ses plaintes

wearying ['wɪərɪɪŋ] *adj* fatigant, ennuyeux; **I find her quite w.** je la trouve très pénible; **I find it very w.** cela me fatigue beaucoup

weasel ['wiːz(ə)l] *n* (*animal*) belette *f*; *Fig F* (*person*) personne *f* sournoise; *F* **w. word** parole *f* ambiguë

▶ **weasel out** *vi F* **to w. out of an obligation** se débrouiller pour éviter une obligation; **you're not going to w. out of it this time!** tu ne vas pas te défiler cette fois!

weather[1] ['weðər] *n* [①B27,E,2,a] temps *m*; **in all weathers** par tous les temps; **in (the) hot/cold w.** par temps chaud/froid; **the w. is settled, we're in for a spell of fine w.** le temps est au beau; **we had good w. for the time of year** nous avons eu du beau temps pour la saison; **what kind of w. did you have on your holiday?** quel temps avez-vous eu pendant vos vacances?; **what's the w. like?** quel temps fait-il?; **in spite of bad w.** en dépit du mauvais temps; **in this** *or* **such w.** par un temps pareil; **w. permitting** si le temps le permet; *Fig* **to make heavy w. (of doing sth)** (*make a fuss*) faire un tas d'histoires (pour faire qch); (*find difficulty*) avoir toutes les peines du monde (à faire qch); **to make heavy w.** (*of ship*) bourlinguer; *Fig* **to keep one's w. eye open** veiller au grain; *Fig* **to be under the w.** (*ill*) ne pas se sentir bien, ne pas être très bien; (*depressed*) être déprimé; **w. (situation), state of the w.** état *m* du temps; **w. side** (*of house etc*) côté exposé au vent; *Naut* bord du vent; **w. strip** (*for door, window*) bourrelet *m* isolant, calfeutrage *m*; **w. vane** (*on roof*) girouette *f*; **w. warning** (*announcement*) alerte *f* météorologique; **to issue a w. warning** lancer une alerte météorologique

weather[2] **1** *vt* **the rocks had been weathered by wind and rain** le vent et la pluie avaient érodé les rochers; *Naut* **to w. a storm** étaler une tempête; *Fig* **to w. the storm** tenir le coup; *Pol* tenir le coup, surmonter la crise

2 *vi* (*of rock*) s'éroder; (*of copper*) se couvrir de patine, se patiner; (*fade*) (*of paintwork, stonework etc*) vieillir; **the brickwork has weathered to a pleasant shade of pink** la brique a pris une jolie couleur rose avec le temps; **a stone that weathers well** une pierre qui supporte bien le passage du temps; *Fig* **he has weathered well** il a bien vieilli; **the theory has weathered well** la théorie a bien résisté au temps

weatherbeaten ['weðəbiːt(ə)n] *adj* (*person, face*) hâlé, basané; (*cliffs, rocks, castle*) battu par le vent et la pluie

weatherboarding ['weðəbɔːdɪŋ] *n Constr* planches *fpl* à recouvrement

weatherbound ['weðəbaʊnd] *adj* retenu *ou* arrêté par le mauvais temps

weather bulletin *n* bulletin *m* météorologique

weather chart *n* carte *f* météorologique

weathercock ['weðəkɒk] *n* (*on roof*), *Fig* girouette *f*

weather forecast *n* prévisions *fpl* météorologiques, météo *f*; **what's the w. for tomorrow?** quelle est la météo pour demain?

weathering ['weðərɪŋ] *n* (*of rocks*) érosion *f*; (*fading*) (*of paintwork, stonework*) vieillissement *m*

weatherman, *pl* **-men** ['weðəmæn, -men] *n TV, Rad* monsieur *m* météo; **what did the w. say?** qu'est-ce qu'ils ont dit à la météo?

weather map *n* carte *f* météorologique

weatherproof¹ ['weðəpru:f] *adj* (*paint, coating*) résistant à l'eau; (*fabric*) imperméable; (*windows, house*) étanche; (*equipment, machinery*) qui résiste aux intempéries

weatherproof² *vt* (*fabric*) imperméabiliser; (*house*) rendre étanche

weather report *n* bulletin *m* météorologique

weather satellite *n* satellite *m* météo

weather ship *n* navire-météo *m*, *pl* navires-météo

weather station *n* station *f* météorologique

weatherstrip ['weðəstrɪp] *vt* (*window*) calfeutrer

weave¹ [wi:v] *n Tex* (*pattern*) tissage *m*; **a tight/loose w.** un tissage serré/lâche

weave² (*pt* **wove** [wəʊv]; *pp* **woven** ['wəʊv(ə)n]) **1** *vt Tex* tisser; (*garland, basket*) tresser; (*strands, small branches*) entrelacer; **to w. yarn into cloth** tisser du fil; **to w. a garland out of flowers** tresser une guirlande de fleurs; *Fig* **skilfully woven plot** intrigue bien tissée *ou F* ficelée; **to w. a spell** composer un charme; **to w. one's way through sth** se faufiler entre *ou* parmi qch; **she weaves the various strands of the story into a satisfying whole** elle tisse les différents fils de l'histoire en un tout satisfaisant; **political elements have been woven into the plot** des éléments politiques ont été introduits dans *ou* intégrés à l'intrigue
2 *vi* **(a)** *Tex* tisser
(b) *Fig* **to w. through the traffic** se frayer un chemin parmi les voitures; **to w. in and out of the crowd** se faufiler dans la foule *ou* parmi la foule
(c) *F* **to get weaving** (*start*) s'y mettre; **get weaving!** vas-y!

weaver ['wi:vər] *n Tex* tisserand, -ande, tisseur, -euse

weaver(bird) ['wi:və(bɜ:d)] *n* tisserin *m*

weaving ['wi:vɪŋ] *n Tex* tissage *m*

web [web] *n* **(a)** (*fabric*) tissu *m*; **w. of lies** tissu de mensonges; **a w. of intrigue** un nid d'intrigues **(b)** (*of spider*) toile *f* **(c)** *Biol* (*of duck, frog etc*) palmure *f* **(d)** *Comptr* **the W.** le Web

webbed [webd] *adj* palmé; **w. foot** pied *m* palmé

webbing ['webɪŋ] *n* **(a)** (*of chair, bed etc*) sangles *fpl* **(b)** (*fabric*) toile *f* à sangles **(c)** *Biol* palmure *f* **(d)** *Mil* sangles *fpl*

web-footed, web-toed *adj* palmipède, aux pieds palmés

web-offset printing *n* impression *f* (offset) continue

wed [wed] (*pt, pp* **wedded**, *occ* **wed**; *prp* **wedding**) **1** *vt* **(a)** (*get married to*) épouser; *Fig* **to be wedded to one's work** faire passer son travail avant tout; **they're wedded to the idea of …** ils tiennent absolument à l'idée de …; **the fate of the project was wedded to that of the Chairman** la destinée du projet était liée à celle du Président **(b)** (*of priest*) (*couple*) marier; **he wanted to see all his daughters wed before he died** il voulait voir toutes ses filles mariées avant sa mort **2** *vi* se marier

we'd [wi:d] **(a)** = **we had,** *see* **have²** **(b)** = **we would,** *see* **would**

wedded ['wedɪd] *adj* (*person*) marié; **my (lawful) w. wife/husband** mon épouse/époux légitime; **w. bliss** bonheur *m* conjugal

wedding ['wedɪŋ] *n* mariage *m*, noce(s) *f(pl)*; **I've been invited to a w.** j'ai été invité à un mariage; **w. anniversary** anniversaire *m* de mariage; **w. band** alliance *f*; **w. breakfast** repas *m* de noces; **w. cake** gâteau *m* de noces; **w. day** jour *m* de mariage; **on my w. day** le jour de mon mariage; **w. dress** robe *f* de mariée; **the w. guests** les invités *mpl* (au mariage); **w. invitation** invitation *f* au mariage; **w. list** liste *f* de mariage; *Mus* **w. march** marche *f* nuptiale; **w. night** nuit *f* de noces; **w. present** cadeau *m* de mariage; **w. ring** alliance *f*; *Hum Sl* **w. tackle** (*man's genitals*) bijoux *mpl* de famille

wedge¹ [wedʒ] *n* **(a)** *Tech* (*for keeping sth in place*) cale *f*; (*for cutting wood*) coin *m*; **to drive in a w.** enfoncer un coin; *Fig* **it has driven a w. between them** ça a mis une distance entre eux; *Fig* **it's the thin end of the w.** c'est s'engager sur une mauvaise pente; **w.-heeled shoes** chaussures à semelles compensées **(b)** **w. of cake** morceau *m* (triangulaire) de gâteau, part *f* (de gâteau); **a w. of cheese** un morceau de fromage

wedge² *vt Tech* coincer; **to w. a door open** maintenir une porte ouverte avec une cale; **to w. a piece of paper in a crack** coincer *ou* enfoncer un bout de papier dans une fente; **I was wedged (in) between two large women** je me suis trouvé coincé entre deux grosses femmes

wedge-shaped *adj* en (forme de) coin; **a w. piece of cheese/land** un triangle de fromage/de terre

wedlock ['wedlɒk] *n Jur* mariage *m*; **to be born out of w.** être un enfant illégitime

Wednesday ['wenzdɪ] *n* [ⓘA75-6,B-C; B58-9,B-C] mercredi *m*; **on Wednesdays** le mercredi; **every W.** tous les mercredis

wee¹ [wi:] *adj esp Scot F* petit; **a w. bit** un petit peu; **a w. drop of whisky** un doigt *ou* une larme de whisky

wee² *n, vi Br F* = **wee(-)wee**

weed¹ [wi:d] *n* **(a)** (*in garden*) mauvaise herbe *f*; **the garden was overgrown with weeds** le jardin était envahi par les mauvaises herbes **(b)** *Old-fashioned F* **the w.** (*tobacco*) le tabac; (*marijuana*) la marijuana, l'herbe *f*; **to give up the w.** arrêter de fumer **(c)** *Pej* (*person*) (*in build*) personne *f* chétive, gringalet *m*; (*in character*) mauviette *f*; **don't be such a w.!** arrête de faire la mauviette!

weed² **1** *vt* (*garden*) désherber; (*path*) arracher les mauvaises herbes de; *Fig* **to w. the files** faire le nettoyage dans les fichiers **2** *vi* arracher *ou* enlever les mauvaises herbes; (*with hoe*) sarcler

► **weed out** *vtsep Fig* (*weak candidates*) éliminer; **to w. out the bad (from the good)** éliminer *ou* rejeter ce qui est de mauvaise qualité

weeding ['wi:dɪŋ] *n* désherbage *m*; (*with hoe*) sarclage *m*

weedkiller ['wi:dkɪlər] *n* herbicide *m*, désherbant *m*

weeds [wi:dz] *npl Old-fashioned* (*widow's*) vêtements *mpl* de deuil

weedy ['wi:dɪ] *adj* **(a)** (*garden etc*) couvert de mauvaises herbes **(b)** *Pej* (*person, arms*) malingre, chétif **(c)** (*feeble*) (*sound of instrument*) faible

week [wi:k] *n* semaine *f*; **what day of the w. is it?** quel jour de la semaine sommes-nous?; **next/last w.** la semaine prochaine/dernière; **the w. before last** pas la semaine dernière, celle d'avant; **the w. after next** pas la semaine prochaine, celle d'après; **w. in w. out** toutes les semaines que Dieu nous envoie; **I haven't seen her for** *or* **in weeks** ça fait des semaines que je ne l'ai pas vue, je ne l'ai pas vue depuis des semaines; *Rel* **Holy W.** la semaine sainte; **once/twice a w.** une/deux fois par semaine; **every w.** tous les huit jours; **within a w.** sous huitaine; **a w. from now, today w., in a w.'s time** aujourd'hui en huit, dans une huitaine; **tomorrow/Tuesday w.** demain/mardi en huit; **yesterday w.** il y a eu hier huit jours; **in a w. or so** dans une huitaine; **it'll take a w. to get there** il faudra une semaine pour arriver là-bas; **in six weeks' time** dans six semaines; **a w. ago today** il y a (aujourd'hui) huit jours; **I'm taking a w.'s holiday** *or* **a w. off** je vais prendre huit jours de congé; *Ind etc* **forty-hour w.** semaine de quarante heures; **a w.'s wages** le salaire d'une semaine, une semaine de salaire, *F* une semaine; **this dress cost me a w.'s wages** cette robe m'a coûté une semaine de salaire; **to be paid by the w.** être payé à la semaine

weekday ['wi:kdeɪ] *n* jour *m* ouvrable; **on weekdays** en semaine; **weekdays only** en semaine uniquement, tous les jours sauf samedi et dimanche

weekend¹ [wi:k'end] *n* week-end *m*, *pl* week-ends, *Can* fin *f* de semaine; **to have one's weekends free** être libre le week-end; **have a good w.!** bon week-end!, *Can* bonne fin de semaine!; **I'll do it at** *or esp Am* **on the w.** je le ferai pendant ce week-end; *Br* **what do you do at the weekend(s)?**, *esp Am* **what do you do (on) weekends?** qu'est-ce que vous faites le week-end?; **what are you doing at the w.?** qu'est-ce que vous faites ce week-end?; **to make a w. visit to relations** rendre visite à de la famille pendant le week-end; **w. cottage** résidence *f* secondaire (*où on passe le week-end*)

weekend² *vi* passer le week-end *ou Can* la fin de semaine

weekend break *n* séjour *m* qui dure un week-end; **to take a w. in Paris** passer un week-end à Paris

weekender [wi:k'endər] *n* **they're weekenders** ils viennent/vont y passer le week-end

weekly ['wi:klɪ] **1** *adj* (*magazine, visit, payment*) hebdomadaire; (*pay*) de la semaine; (*tenant*) à la semaine; **these incidents were an almost w. occurrence** ces incidents avaient lieu presque chaque semaine **2** *n* (journal *m*/revue *f*) hebdomadaire *m*; **the weeklies** la presse hebdomadaire **3** *adv* (*every week*) toutes les semaines, tous les huit jours, chaque semaine; **twice w.** deux fois par semaine; **to be paid w.** être payé à la semaine

weeknight ['wi:knaɪt] *n* soir *m* de semaine; **at seven on weeknights** à sept heures les soirs de semaine; **I'm not letting you go to a party on a w.** je ne vais pas te permettre d'aller à une soirée pendant la semaine

weenie ['wi:nɪ] *n Am* = **wiener**

weeny ['wi:nɪ] *adj F* minuscule

weeny-bopper *n F* = très jeune fan *f* de musique pop

weep¹ [wi:p] *n* **to have a good w.** pleurer un bon coup; **a good w. would help you** pleure un bon coup, ça ira mieux; **to have a little w.** verser quelques larmes

weep² (*pt, pp* **wept** [wept]) **1** *vi* **(a)** (*of person*) pleurer; **to w. bitterly** pleurer à chaudes larmes; **to w. for joy** pleurer de joie; **to w. for sb** (*mourn*) pleurer (la mort de) qn; (*feel sorry for*) pleurer sur le sort de qn; **to w. for one's lost youth** pleurer sa jeunesse perdue; **it's enough to make you w.** c'est à faire pleurer; **I could have wept to see it** j'en aurais pleuré (en le voyant) **(b)** (*of wall, rock*) suinter, suer; (*of sore*) couler, exsuder; **the smoke was making my eyes w.** la fumée me faisait pleurer les yeux **2** *vt* **to w. tears of joy** pleurer de joie; **to w. one's heart** *or* **one's eyes out** pleurer à chaudes larmes

weeping ['wi:pɪŋ] **1** *adj* **(a)** (*child*) qui pleure **(b)** *Med* (*eczema*) suintant **2** *n* (*of person*) pleurs *mpl*, larmes *fpl*; **we could hear w. from the next room** on pouvait entendre quelqu'un qui pleurait dans la pièce d'à côté; **the sound of w.** des pleurs; **a fit of w.** une crise de larmes

weeping willow *n* (*tree*) saule *m* pleureur

weepy ['wi:pɪ] *F* **1** *adj* **(a)** (*book, film*) larmoyant, mélo; **there's a w. bit coming next** il y a un passage mélo après **(b) to feel w.** avoir envie de pleurer; **it makes me go all w.** ça me fait pleurer **2** *n* (*book, film*) mélo *m*, livre *m*/film *m* à faire pleurer dans les chaumières

weevil ['wi:vɪl] *n* (*beetle*) charançon *m*

wee(-)wee¹ *n Br F* (*in children's language*) pipi *m*; **to have a w.** faire pipi; **do you want to go w.?** tu veux faire pipi?

wee(-)wee² *vi Br F* (*in children's language*) faire pipi

weft [weft] *n Tex* trame *f*

weigh [weɪ] **1** *vt* **(a)** (*package etc*) peser; **to w. sth in one's hand** soupeser qch; **to w. oneself** se peser

(b) (*consider*) (*one's words*) peser, mesurer, ménager; **to w. sth in one's mind** considérer qch; **to w. the consequences** calculer les conséquences (**of sth** de qch); **to w. the pros and (the) cons** peser le pour et le contre; **to w. the risks/the evidence** évaluer les risques/les preuves; **to w. one thing against another** mettre deux choses en balance

(c) *Naut* **to w. anchor** lever l'ancre, appareiller

2 *vi* **(a)** (*of person, parcel etc*) peser; **it weighs two kilos** ça pèse deux kilos; *F* **this case weighs a ton** cette valise pèse une tonne; **how much do you w.?** combien est-ce que tu pèses?

(b) it's weighing on my mind cela me trouble *ou* me tracasse; **it weighed heavy on his conscience** cela pesait sur sa conscience

(c) (*have influence*) **her qualifications weighed in her favour** ses qualifications ont fait pencher la balance en sa faveur *ou* ont joué en sa faveur; **his past record weighed against him** son passé a joué en sa défaveur

▶ **weigh down** *vtsep* surcharger; **in order to w. the body down** pour alourdir le corps; **branch weighed down with fruit** branche surchargée de fruits; *Fig* **weighed down by** *or* **with heavy responsibilities** accablé de grosses responsabilités; *Fig* **to be weighed down by** *or* **with grief** être accablé par la tristesse

▶ **weigh in** *vi* **(a)** (*of jockey, boxer*) (*before race or match*) se faire peser; **he weighed in at 75 kilos** il faisait 75 kilos à la pesée **(b)** *F* (*enter fight, debate*) intervenir; **to w. in (with an argument)** intervenir (en présentant un argument)

▶ **weigh out** *vtsep* peser; **w. out 200 grams of flour for me** pèse-moi 200 grammes de farine

▶ **weigh up** *vtsep* **to w. up the situation** peser la situation; **to w. sb up** (*their character*) estimer la valeur de qn; (*their intentions*) estimer les intentions de qn; **to w. up one's chances of doing sth** calculer ses chances de faire qch; **to w. up the advantages and disadvantages of sth** peser le pour et le contre de qch

weighbridge ['weɪbrɪdʒ] *n* pont-bascule *m*, *pl* ponts-bascules

weigh-in *n Boxing, Horseracing* pesée *f*

weighing ['weɪɪŋ] *n Com* pesage *m*; **w. machine** balance *f*

weighing in *n* (*of jockey, boxer*) pesage *m*; **w. room** pesage

weight¹ [weɪt] *n* **(a)** (*of person, parcel etc*) poids *m*; **to feel the w. of sth** (*in hand*) soupeser qch; **that case must be quite a w.** cette valise doit être drôlement lourde; **to sell by w.** vendre au poids; **to give short w.** tricher sur le poids; **it's ten pounds in w.** cela pèse dix livres; **it's twice the w. of the other one** ça pèse deux fois plus que l'autre; **they're the same w.** ils font le même poids; **it's worth its w. in gold** cela vaut son pesant d'or; **what a w.!** que ça pèse lourd!, que c'est lourd!; **to lose w.** perdre du poids; **to gain** *or* **put on w.** prendre du poids; **to watch one's w.** surveiller son poids; **to have a w. problem** avoir un problème de poids; *Fig* **to pull one's w.** y mettre du sien; *Fig* **you're not pulling your w.** tu ne fais pas assez d'effort; *Horseracing* **to carry w.** être handicapé; **to be a w. watcher** surveiller son poids; **w. charge** taxation *f* au poids; *Med* **w. loss** amaigrissement *m*

(b) (*for weighing*) poids *m*; **set of weights** série *f* de poids; **weights and measures** poids et mesures *fpl*

(c) (*object*) (*of clock*) poids *m*; (*for fishing net*) lest *m*; **to do w. training** faire des haltères; **don't lift any heavy weights** ne soulève pas de poids trop lourds

(d) (*load*) charge *f*; **this pillar bears the w. of the whole building** cette colonne soutient tout le bâtiment; **to give way under the w. of sth** fléchir sous le poids de qch; **he feels the w. of his responsibilities** ses responsabilités lui pèsent; **that is** *or* **takes a w. off my mind** cela me soulage, ça m'ôte un poids; *F* **I'm going to take the w. off my feet for a bit** je vais me reposer un peu

(e) (*of blow*) force *f*; **his blow had no w. behind it** son coup était sans force; **you'll feel the w. of my hand, my lad!** tu vas recevoir une claque, mon gars!

(f) *Fig* (*importance*) importance *f*; **to give w. to an argument** donner du poids à un argument; **what he says carries w.** sa parole a du poids *ou* de l'autorité; **she doesn't carry much w. with the committee** elle n'a pas beaucoup d'influence auprès du comité; **the w. of the evidence was against him** les témoignages pesaient contre lui; **he threw his w. behind the other candidate** il a soutenu l'autre candidat à fond; *F* **to throw one's w. about** *or* **around** faire l'important; **they won the battle by sheer w. of numbers** ils ont gagné la bataille parce qu'ils avaient l'avantage numérique

weight² *vt* **(a)** (*fix a weight to*) attacher un poids à; (*net, rope*) lester, plomber; (*walking stick*) plomber **(b)** *Econ* (*index, average etc*) pondérer; *Fig* **the circumstances are weighted in his favour** les circonstances pèsent en sa faveur *ou* lui sont favorables; **the electoral system is weighted against small parties** le système électoral défavorise les petits partis

▶ **weight down** *vtsep* (*hold down*) retenir *ou* maintenir avec un poids; **the body had been weighted down with stones** le corps avait été alourdi de pierres

weighted ['weɪtɪd] *adj* **(a)** (*with a weight*) chargé d'un poids; (*balloon*) lesté; (*walking stick*) plombé **(b)** (*average, index*) pondéré; **w. average unit cost** coût *m* unitaire moyen pondéré

weightily ['weɪtɪlɪ] *adv* (*to reason*) puissamment, avec force

weighting ['weɪtɪŋ] *n Econ* (*of index etc*) pondération *f*, coefficient *m*; *Admin* **London w.** indemnité *f* de résidence à Londres

weightless ['weɪtlɪs] *adj Astronaut* **w. conditions** état *m* d'apesanteur

weightlessness ['weɪtlɪsnɪs] *n Astronaut* apesanteur *f*

weightlifter ['weɪtlɪftər] *n* haltérophile *mf*

weightlifting ['weɪtlɪftɪŋ] *n* haltérophilie *f*

weight limit *n* limitation *f ou* limite *f* de poids

weighty ['weɪtɪ] *adj* **(a)** (*heavy*) pesant, (très) lourd **(b)** *Fig* (*motive*) grave, important, sérieux; (*reasoning*) puissant, d'un grand poids; (*argument*) de poids

weir [wɪər] *n* (*across river etc*) barrage *m*

weird [wɪəd] *adj* **(a)** (*eerie*) mystérieux, inquiétant **(b)** (*odd*) étrange, bizarre; **he went a bit w. after his parents died** il est devenu un peu bizarre après la mort de ses parents; **that's w.** c'est bizarre

weirdie ['wɪədɪ] *n F* = **weirdo**

weirdly ['wɪədlɪ] *adv* (*oddly*) étrangement, bizarrement

weirdness ['wɪədnɪs] *n* (*oddness*) (*of person, clothing*) caractère *m* étrange *ou* bizarre

weirdo, weirdy ['wɪədəʊ, -dɪ] *n F* excentrique *mf*, drôle d'oiseau *m*; (*frightening etc*) type *m* bizarre

welcome¹ ['welkəm] *adj* **(a)** (*person*) bienvenu; **to make sb w.** faire bon accueil à qn; **you're always w.** vous êtes toujours le bienvenu; **any friend of Bob's is always w. here** les amis de Bob sont toujours les bienvenus ici; **I did not feel w.** je ne me suis pas senti le bienvenu; **the card is w. in over 1,000 outlets** la carte est acceptée dans plus de 1000 points de vente; **w.!** soyez le bienvenu (chez nous)!; **w. to England!** bienvenue en Angleterre!; **w. back!** nous sommes heureux de vous revoir!; *Rad, TV* (*after commercial*) re-bonjour!/re-bonsoir!; **w. home!** bienvenue à la maison!

(b) (*agreeable*) agréable; **a w. cup of coffee** une bonne tasse de café; **this is a very w. development** c'est un grand progrès; **this is w. news** je me réjouis/nous nous réjouissons de cette nouvelle; **the hotel was a w. sight** on a aperçu l'hôtel avec plaisir; **that would be most w.** (*coffee, brandy, sandwich*) ça me ferait le plus grand bien; **this cheque is most w.** ce chèque est vraiment bienvenu *ou* tombe à merveille; **a w. change** un changement opportun; **the laid-back atmosphere of Little Piddlington made a w. change from London** l'atmosphère détendue de Little Piddlington nous changeait en bien de Londres

(c) (*free*) **to be w. to do sth** être le bienvenu à faire qch; **you're w. to ask any questions** vos questions seront les bienvenues; **anybody is w. to attend** c'est ouvert à tous;

you're w. to borrow any of my books ma bibliothèque est à votre disposition; **they're w. to stay with us** ils peuvent venir chez nous; **you're w. to it** je t'en prie (ne te gêne pas); *Iron* je te le/la laisse; **you're w. to try** libre à vous d'essayer; **you're w.!** (*on being thanked*) je vous en prie!, de rien!, ce n'est rien!; **tell her she's w.** dis-lui que ce n'est rien

welcome² *n* accueil *m*; **we were given a wonderful w.** nous avons été merveilleusement bien accueillis; **the whole town prepared a w. for him** la ville entière se préparait à l'accueillir; **to extend a w. to sb** souhaiter la bienvenue à qn; **to give sb a warm w.** faire un accueil chaleureux à qn; **he gave us a very poor** *or* **cold w.** il nous a reçus froidement, il nous a mal reçus; **w. bouquet** bouquet *m* d'accueil; **w. drink** cocktail *m* d'accueil, pot *m* d'accueil

welcome³ *vt* **(a)** (*person*) (*wish welcome*) souhaiter la bienvenue à; (*greet*) faire bon accueil à, bien accueillir, accueillir *ou* recevoir avec plaisir; **to w. the/an opportunity to do sth** se réjouir de *ou* saluer l'occasion de faire qch; **I w. every chance of getting out of the house** je suis content de sortir de la maison chaque fois que c'est possible; **his efforts weren't welcomed** ses efforts ont reçu peu d'encouragement; *Rad, TV* **I am pleased to w. back Sharon McTeir** j'ai le plaisir d'accueillir à nouveau Sharon McTeir

(b) (*receive*) accueillir; **to w. sb warmly** faire un accueil chaleureux à qn; **the announcement was welcomed with indifference** la nouvelle a été accueillie avec indifférence

welcome committee *n Am* comité *m* d'accueil

welcome mat *n Am* paillasson *m*; *Am Fig* **to put out the w. for sb** accueillir qn à bras ouverts

welcome pack *n* (*in hotel, at conference*) lot *m* d'accueil

welcome reception *n* réception *f* de bienvenue

welcoming ['welkəmɪŋ] *adj* (*smile, person, atmosphere*) accueillant; (*speech, committee*) d'accueil

weld¹ [weld] *n* (*joint*) soudure *f*; **w. spot** point *m* de soudure

weld² *vt* **to w. (together)** (*pieces of metal*) souder; (*pieces of plastic*) unir à chaud; *Fig* **to w. employees into a team** réunir des employés en une équipe bien soudée; **he has welded his players into a formidable unit** il a soudé ses joueurs pour former une équipe formidable

welder ['weldər] *n* soudeur, -euse; **w.'s mask** masque *m* protecteur pour la soudure

welding ['weldɪŋ] *n* soudure *f*, soudage *m*; **arc w.** soudure à l'arc; **w. torch** chalumeau *m* soudeur

welfare ['welfeər] *n* **(a)** (*wellbeing*) bien-être *m*; **to have sb's w. at heart** avoir à cœur le bonheur *ou* le bien-être de qn; **w. centre** = centre *m* d'assistance sociale; **w. work** = assistance *f* sociale; **w. worker** = assistant, -ante social(e) **(b)** *Am* (*social security*) **to be on w.** toucher les allocations; **w. benefits** allocations *fpl* de sécurité sociale; **w. check** chèque *m* d'allocations; **the w. lines are lengthening** la masse des gens qui touchent le chômage augmente; **to stand in the w. line** recevoir les allocations chômage

Welfare State *n Br* **the W.** l'État *m* providence

well¹ [wel] *n* **(a)** (*of water, oil*) puits *m*; **we get our water from a w.** notre eau vient d'un puits; **to drive/sink a w.** forer/creuser un puits; **w.-digger** puisatier *m*; **w. water** eau *f* de puits **(b)** (*shaft*) (*for lift*) puits *m*, cage *f*; (*stairwell*) cage, jour *m*; (*sump*) fond *m* de carter; (*on fishing boat*) vivier *m*, réservoir *m*; *Br Jur* **the w. of the court** le barreau; *Culin* **make a w. in the flour** faire une fontaine dans la farine **(c)** *Arch* (*spring*) source *f*, fontaine *f*

well² (*comp* **better**; *superl* **best**) **1** *adj* **(a)** (*in good health*) **to be w.** être bien portant *ou* en bonne santé, se porter *ou* aller bien; **to sound w.** avoir l'air en forme; **are you okay?, you don't sound very w.** ça va?, tu n'as pas l'air bien; **how are you? – w., thank you** comment allez-vous? – bien, merci; **he's not very w.** il n'est pas très bien; **to get w.** guérir, se rétablir, se remettre; **you look w.** tu as l'air en forme; **he's not a w. man** il ne se porte pas bien, il n'a pas une bonne santé

(b) it is w. to ... (*advisable*) il est opportun de ...; **it would be w. to ...** il serait bon *ou* utile *ou* recommandable de ...; **it would be w. not to mention it again** il vaudrait mieux ne plus en reparler; **it would be just as w. if you were present** ce serait mieux si vous étiez présent, vous feriez mieux d'être présent; **it is just as w. we did leave without her** c'est aussi bien que nous soyons partis sans elle; **it might be as w. to ...** il faudrait peut-être ..., il serait peut-être bon de ...; **it was w. for him that nobody saw him** heureusement pour lui que personne ne l'a vu; *Prov* **all's w. that ends w.** tout est bien qui finit bien; **all's w.!** tout va bien!; **that's all very w., but ...** c'est bien beau *ou* joli, tout ça, mais ...; **it is all very w. for you to say that** tu peux bien dire ça, toi; **w. and good!** soit!, bon!; **that's all very w. and good, but ...** c'est très bien, tout ça, mais ...

2 *adv* **(a)** (*satisfactorily etc*) bien; **to work w.** bien travailler; **to do as w. as one can** faire de son mieux; **this boy will do w.** ce garçon ira loin; **to be doing w.** (*after operation etc*) aller bien; **mother and baby are both doing w.** la mère et l'enfant se portent bien; **w. done!** bravo!, très bien!; **w. played!** bien joué!; **the government hasn't come out of it very w.** le gouvernement n'en est pas sorti grandi; **to do oneself w.** (*indulge oneself*) bien se soigner; (*in restaurant etc*) bien manger (et bien boire); **it wouldn't look w. if we refused** si on refusait cela ferait mauvaise impression; **you would do w. to be quiet (about it)** vous feriez bien *ou* le mieux serait de vous taire; **I know her w.** je la connais bien; **I know only too w. what patience it needs** je ne sais que trop quelle patience cela exige; **I can't very w. do it** il ne m'est guère possible de le faire; **he apologized, as w. he might** il s'est excusé, ce qui était la moindre des choses; **one might as w. say that black is white** autant dire que blanc est noir; **you might as w. stay** (*there's no point in going now*) tu ferais aussi bien de rester; **I might (just) as w. do it myself** je ferais aussi bien de le faire moi-même; **very w.!** (*OK*) (très) bien!, entendu!; **everyone speaks w. of him** tout le monde dit du bien de lui; **she is very w. thought of** on pense beaucoup de bien d'elle; **to do w. by sb** se montrer généreux envers qn; **he meant w.** il voulait bien faire; **he means w.** ses intentions sont bonnes; **you're w. out of it** soyez heureux d'en être quitte; **the fête went off w.** la fête s'est bien passée; *Arch* **w. met!** heureuse rencontre!, vous arrivez bien à propos!

(b) (*intensive*) bien; **it is w. known that ...** tout le monde sait que ...; **it's w. worth trying** cela vaut bien la peine *ou F* le coup d'essayer; **she's w. able to look after herself** elle est tout à fait capable de se débrouiller toute seule; **I can w. believe it** je veux bien le croire; **I am w. aware of that** j'en suis bien conscient; **we'll be w. away by the time she wakes up** nous serons déjà loin quand elle se réveillera; *Br F* **w. away** (*drunk*) parti; **it's w. after six** il est six heures bien sonnées; **buy your tickets w. ahead of time** *or* **w. in advance** achetez vos billets bien à l'avance; **he's w. over fifty** il a largement dépassé la cinquantaine; **to be w. up in a subject** bien posséder un sujet; **leave w. enough alone** ne t'en mêle pas; *Br F* **w. and truly** bel et bien; *Hum* **w. padded** *or* **upholstered** (*plump*) bien rembourré

(c) pretty w. all presque tout; **it's pretty w. finished** c'est presque *ou* pratiquement terminé; *F* **it serves him damn w.** *or* **jolly w. right!** il l'a bien cherché *ou* mérité!, c'est bien fait pour lui!

(d) as w. (*also*) aussi; **take me as w.** emmenez-moi aussi; **I need some as w.** il m'en faut également; **as w. as** (*in addition to*) de même que, comme, ainsi que; **by day as w. as by night** de jour comme de nuit, le jour comme la nuit

(e) (*introducing remark*) eh bien, donc; (*exclamatory*) ça alors!, pas possible!; **w., as I was telling you** eh bien *ou* donc comme je vous disais; **w., who was it?** eh bien, qui était-ce?; **w., here we are (at last)!** enfin nous voilà!; **you told her?, (oh** *or* **ah) w.!** vous le lui avez dit?, eh bien!; **w., w.!** (*expressing resignation*) tant pis!, que voulez-vous!; (*surprise*) tiens, tiens!; **w. I never!** ça alors!; **w., that's life!** c'est la vie!; **w. then** eh bien, alors; **w. then, why worry about it?** eh bien *ou* alors, pourquoi se faire du mauvais sang?

3 *n* **(a) the w. and the sick** (*pl*) les bien portants *mpl* et les malades

(b) to wish sb w. vouloir du bien à qn; (*in attitude*) être bien disposé envers qn

► **well out** *vi* (*of liquid*) jaillir

► **well over** *vi* (*of tears*) jaillir

► **well up** *vi* (*of water, spring*) jaillir, *Lit* monter; **tears welled up in her eyes** les larmes lui sont montées aux yeux

we'll [wi:l] **(a)** = **we shall,** *see* **shall (b)** = **we will,** *see* **will³**

well-adjusted *adj* équilibré

well-advised *adj* sage, prudent, judicieux; **you would be w. to say yes** tu aurais (tout) intérêt à dire oui; **it was not very w. of you to annoy her like that** ce n'était pas très malin de l'ennuyer comme ça

well-appointed *adj* (*house*) bien aménagé

well-argued *adj* bien argumenté

well-attended *adj* bien suivi; **the classes were not w.** les cours étaient peu suivis

well-balanced *adj* (*person, debate*) équilibré; (*coverage*) impartial; **I think she's fairly w.** je pense qu'elle est plutôt bien équilibrée

well-behaved *adj* (*child*) sage; (*animal*) bien dressé

wellbeing ['welbi:ɪŋ] *n* bien-être *m*; **physical and moral w.** santé *f* physique et morale

well-born *adj* de bonne famille; **she was not sufficiently w. to marry him** elle n'était pas assez bien née pour l'épouser

well-bred *adj* (*polite*) bien élevé; (*of good family*) de bonne famille
well-built *adj* (*building*) bien construit, solide; (*machine, car*) de bonne fabrication; (*person*) solide, bien bâti
well-chilled *adj* (*wine*) frais, *f* fraîche
well-chosen *adj* bien choisi; **a few w. words** quelques mots bien choisis
well-connected *adj* **to be w.** avoir des relations
well-defined *adj* bien défini
well-developed *adj* bien développé
well-disposed *adj* (*person*) bien disposé (**towards** envers)
well-documented *adj* bien documenté
well-done *adj Culin* bien cuit
well-dressed *adj* bien habillé
well-earned *adj* bien mérité
well-educated *adj* instruit, cultivé
well-endowed *adj* (*physically*) (*man*) bien monté; (*woman*) bien roulé
well-equipped *adj* bien équipé
well-established *adj* bien implanté
well-fed *adj* bien nourri
well-fixed *adj Am F* riche
well-founded *adj* (*suspicion*) fondé
well-groomed *adj* (*person*) soigné; (*horse*) bien pansé
well-grounded *adj* fondé
wellhead ['welhed] *n Petr* tête *f* de puits
well-heeled *adj F* riche, cossu
well-hung *adj Sl* (*man*) bien monté
well-in *adj F* (**a**) *Br* **to be w. with sb** être bien avec qn (**b**) *Austr* (*rich*) riche
well-informed *adj* (*about specific event etc*) informé; (*generally*) (*person, mind*) au courant; **to be w. on a subject** bien posséder un sujet
wellington ['welɪŋtən] *n Br* **wellingtons, w. boots** bottes *fpl* en caoutchouc
well-intentioned *adj* bien intentionné
well-judged *adj* judicieux; (*shot, pass*) bien visé, bien vu
well-kept *adj* (*garden*) bien (entre)tenu, soigné; (*hands*) soigné; (*secret*) bien gardé
well-known *adj* (bien) connu, célèbre; (*expert*) réputé; **a w. liar** un fameux menteur; **it is w. that …** il est bien connu que …
well-liked *adj* apprécié
well-loved *adj* très aimé
well-made *adj* (*furniture*) bien fait, de fabrication soignée; (*garment*) de coupe soignée; (*play*) bien construit
well-mannered *adj* poli, bien élevé
well-matched *adj* (*couple*) bien assorti; (*teams*) de force égale; **Bob can't possibly be as boring as Sarah – oh yes he is, they're very w.** Bob ne peut pas être aussi ennuyeux que Sarah – et pourtant si, ils se sont bien trouvés
well-meaning *adj* (*person*) bien intentionné; (*remark*) fait avec les meilleures intentions; **she's very w.** elle est pleine de bonnes intentions
well-nigh *adv* presque, pratiquement; **w. impossible** quasiment impossible
well-off 1 *adj* riche; **to be very w.** avoir de la fortune, *F* avoir de quoi; **you don't know when you're w.** vous ne connaissez pas votre bonheur; **to be w. for books/cupboards/paper** avoir beaucoup de livres/placards/papier **2** *npl* **the w.** les riches *mpl*
well-oiled *adj Fig F* (*drunk*) soûl, parti
well-paid *adj* bien payé, bien rétribué
well-preserved *adj* bien conservé; *Fig* **she's w.** elle est bien conservée
well-proportioned *adj* bien proportionné
well-read *adj* (*person*) instruit, cultivé
well-respected *adj* respecté
well-rounded *adj* (*education, course etc*) complet
well-spent *adj* (*money, time*) bien utilisé, bien employé; **it was time w.** je n'ai/il n'a/*etc* pas perdu mon/son/*etc* temps; **I'm not sure this is time w.** je crains que ça ne soit une perte de temps
well-spoken *adj* qui parle bien
well-stacked *adj Br Sl* (*woman*) bien balancé, bien roulé, bien foutu; **she's w.!** il y a du monde au balcon!
well-stocked *adj* (*shop*) bien approvisionné
well-thought-of *adj* apprécié
well-thought-out *adj* (*plan etc*) bien pensé
well-thumbed *adj* (*book, magazine*) qui a fait de l'usage, écorné
well-timed *adj* opportun, bien calculé
well-to-do 1 *adj* aisé, riche, cossu **2** *npl* **the w.** les riches *mpl*, les fortunés *mpl*
well-tried *adj* (*remedy*) éprouvé, qui a fait ses preuves
well-trodden *adj* **a w. path** un chemin très fréquenté; *Fig* **a w. path to fame** une voie très fréquentée qui mène vers la célébrité
well-turned *adj* (*speech*) bien tourné; (*ankle*) galbé
well-versed *adj* versé (**in** dans)
wellwisher ['welwɪʃər] *n* (*of cause etc*) partisan, -ane; **a w.** (*at end of anonymous letter*) un ami qui vous veut du bien; **surrounded by wellwishers** entouré d'admirateurs
well-woman clinic *n* clinique *f* pour femmes; (*session*) consultations *fpl* dans la clinique pour femmes
well-worn *adj* (*garment*) très usé; (*argument*) rebattu, usé jusqu'à la corde
well-written *adj* bien écrit
welly ['welɪ] *n Br F* (*boot*) botte *f* en caoutchouc; **he really gave the ball some w.** il a tapé dans le ballon de toutes ses forces
Welsh [welʃ] **1** *adj* gallois, du pays de Galles; **W. dresser** vaisselier *m*; **W. rabbit** *or* **rarebit** ≈ croque-monsieur *m, pl* croque monsieurs **2** *n* (**a**) **the W.** (*pl*) les Gallois *mpl* (**b**) *Ling* gallois *m*
▶ **welsh on** *vipo F* **to w. on sb** faire faux bond à qn; **to w. on a bet** ne pas tenir un pari
Welshman, *pl* **-men** ['welʃmən] *n* Gallois *m*
Welshwoman, *pl* **-women** ['welʃwʊmən, -wɪmɪn] *n* Galloise *f*
welt [welt] *n* (**a**) (*of shoe*) trépointe *f* (**b**) (*left by blow*) marque *f ou* trace *f* de coup
welter[1] ['weltər] *n* **a w. of** (*details, statistics*) une pléthore de; (*forms*) une masse de; **a w. of blood and guts** une marée de sang
welter[2] *vi Lit* (*in mud*) se vautrer, se rouler; (*in blood*) nager, baigner
welterweight ['weltəweɪt] *n Boxing* poids *m* mi-moyen, poids welter; **to fight as a** *or* **at w.** boxer dans la catégorie des poids welters; **w. match** match *m* de poids welters
wen [wen] *n Med* kyste *m* sébacé, *F* loupe *f*
wench[1] [wentʃ] *n* (**a**) *Hum F* (*young woman*) (jeune) fille *f*, jeune femme *f*; **great strapping w.** grande gaillarde *f* (**b**) *Arch* (**serving**) **w.** (*in inn*) serveuse *f*; **kitchen w.** fille *f* de cuisine
wench[2] *vi Arch, Hum* **to go wenching** courir le jupon
wencher ['wentʃər] *n Arch, Hum* coureur *m* de jupons
wend [wend] *vt* **to w. one's way** se diriger, s'acheminer (**to** vers); **to w. one's way homeward** prendre le chemin du retour
Wendy house ['wendɪ] *n Br* = maison *f* en modèle réduit pour enfants
Wensleydale ['wenzlɪdeɪl] *n* **W.** (**cheese**) fromage *m* de Wensleydale
went *see* **go[2]**
wept *see* **weep[2]**
were *see* **be**
we're [wɪər] = **we are,** *see* **be**
weren't [wɜːnt] = **were not,** *see* **be**
werewolf, *pl* **-wolves** ['wɪəwʊlf, -wʊlvz] *n Myth* loup-garou *m, pl* loups-garous
Wesleyan ['wesliən] *adj, n* wesleyen, -enne
west [west] **1** *n* ouest *m*; **the house faces (the) w.** la maison fait face à l'ouest; **on the w., to the w.** à l'ouest (**of** de); **the W.** *Pol* l'Occident *m*; (*in United States*) les États *mpl* occidentaux; (*in Canada*) les provinces *fpl* de l'ouest; *US* **the Far W.** le Far-West; *US* **the Mid(dle) W.** les États de la Prairie

2 *adv* à l'ouest; **to travel w.** voyager vers l'ouest; **to go w.** partir pour l'ouest; *Old-fashioned F* (*die*) casser sa pipe, passer l'arme à gauche; *F* **there's another plate gone w.!** encore une assiette de cassée!

3 *adj* ouest *inv*; (*wind*) d'ouest; (*wall*) qui fait face *ou* qui est exposé à l'ouest
West Africa *n* Afrique *f* occidentale
West Bank *n* (*in Middle East*) Cisjordanie *f*
West Berlin *n* Berlin *m* Ouest
westbound ['westbaʊnd] *adj* allant vers l'ouest; *Rail* (*on underground*) en direction de la banlieue ouest; **the w. lane of the motorway** la voie de l'autoroute qui va vers l'ouest; **w. traffic** les véhicules allant vers l'ouest; **w. traffic is subject to delays** la circulation est ralentie dans le sens ouest
West Coast *n US* côte *f* ouest
West Country *n Br* sud-ouest *m* de l'Angleterre
West End *n Br* quartier *m* du centre-ouest de Londres; *F* **to go up the W.** sortir en ville (à Londres); **the W. theatres** les théâtres du centre-ouest de Londres, les théâtres des quartiers chics de Londres
westerly ['westəlɪ] **1** *adj* (*wind*) d'ouest, qui vient de l'ouest; (*current*) qui se dirige vers l'ouest; **w. point** point situé à *ou* vers l'ouest **2** *adv* vers l'ouest **3** *npl Met* **westerlies** vents *mpl* d'ouest

western ['westən] **1** *adj* ouest *inv*, de l'ouest; *esp Pol* occidental; *Pol* **the W. powers** les puissances occidentales; **w. roll** (*high jump*) rouleau *m* costal **2** *n Cin* western *m*; (*novel*) roman-western *m*, *pl* romans-westerns
Western Australia *n* Australie *f* occidentale
westerner ['westənər] *n* **(a)** *Pol* occidental, -ale, -aux **(b)** *Geog* habitant, -ante de l'ouest
Western Europe *n* Europe *f* occidentale
Western Islands, Western Isles *npl* (*of Scotland*) Hébrides *fpl*
westernization [westənaɪ'zeɪʃən] *n* occidentalisation *f*
westernize ['westənaɪz] *vt* (*people*) occidentaliser; **to become westernized** s'occidentaliser
westernmost ['westənməʊst] *adj* le plus à l'ouest
West German **1** *adj* ouest-allemand **2** *n* Ouest-Allemand, -ande
West Germany *n* Allemagne *f* de l'Ouest
West Indian **1** *adj* des Antilles, antillais **2** *n* Antillais, -aise
West Indies *npl* Antilles *fpl*
Westminster ['westmɪnstər] *n* Westminster (*siège du gouvernement britannique*)
West Point *n US* = collège *m* militaire
West Side *n US* quartiers *mpl* ouest de New York
westward ['westwəd] **1** *adj* (*journey*) vers l'ouest **2** *adv* = **westwards**
westwards ['westwədz] *adv* à l'ouest; (*to travel*) vers l'ouest
wet¹ [wet] *adj* (*comp* **wetter**; *superl* **wettest**) **(a)** (*soaked*) mouillé; (*damp*) humide; (*weather*) pluvieux; **to get w.** se mouiller; **to get one's feet w.** se mouiller les pieds; **to be w. through** *or* **w. to the skin** être trempé *ou* mouillé jusqu'aux os; **her cheeks were w. with tears** ses joues étaient baignées de larmes; **the ink/paint was still w.** l'encre/la peinture n'était pas encore sèche; *Fig* **he's (still) w. behind the ears** il manque de maturité, il n'est pas mûr; **when you're a bit less w. behind the ears** quand tu seras un peu plus mûr; **three w. days** trois jours de pluie; **the wettest summer on record** l'été le plus humide dont on se souvienne; **when it's w.** (*raining*) quand il pleut; **the w. season** la saison des pluies; *Br* **w. fish** poisson frais; **a w.-look hair-do** une coiffure à l'aspect mouillé; **a w.-look coat** un manteau moiré *ou* brillant; **w. paint** (*notice*) peinture fraîche
(b) *Br F* (*silly*) bête, idiot; (*excuse*) faible; (*weak, pathetic*) lamentable; *Pol* modéré; **don't be so w.!** (*stupid*) ne sois pas si bête!; (*lacking in physical courage*) du nerf!; **he thinks it's w. to discuss emotions** il trouve ça mièvre de parler des sentiments
(c) (*allowing alcohol sales*) (*country, state*) qui permet la vente des boissons alcoolisées
(d) **w. lease** (*for aircraft*) location *f* d'avion avec équipage
wet² *n* **(a)** (*dampness*) humidité *f* **(b)** (*rain*) pluie *f*; *Austr* **the w.** (*season*) la saison des pluies; **to go out in the w.** sortir sous la pluie **(c)** *Br Pol F* modéré, -ée
wet³ *vt* (**-tt-**) mouiller, humecter; (*sponge*) imbiber; (*pastry*) mouiller; (*clay*) humidifier, mouiller; **to w. the bed** (*of child*) faire pipi au lit; **to w. one's pants** *or* **oneself** mouiller sa culotte, faire pipi dans sa culotte; *Fig F* pisser dans sa culotte; *Hum F* **to w. one's whistle** se rincer *ou* s'humecter le gosier; *Fig F* **we'll have to w. the baby's head** il faudra qu'on arrose la naissance du bébé
wetback ['wetbæk] *n US Pej* = ouvrier *m* agricole mexicain entré illégalement aux États-Unis
wet blanket *n Fig* rabat-joie *m inv*, trouble-fête *mf inv*
wet cell *n El* pile *f* à élément humide
wet dock *n* bassin *m* à flot
wet dream *n* pollution *f ou* éjaculation *f* nocturne
wether ['weðər] *n* (*ram*) bélier *m* châtré
wetlands ['wetləndz] *npl* marais *mpl*
wetness ['wetnɪs] *n* humidité *f*; **renowned for the w. of its climate** connu pour son climat pluvieux
wet nurse *n* nourrice *f*
wet rot *n* moisissure *f* humide
wet suit *n* combinaison *f* de plongée
wetting ['wetɪŋ] *n* **to get a w.** se faire mouiller; **w. the bed can be a sign that ...** l'incontinence nocturne peut indiquer que ...; *Ch* **w. agent** (agent *m*) mouillant *m*
wet-weather tyre *n* pneu *m* pluie
WEU [dʌb(ə)ljuːiː'uː] *n Pol* (*abbr* **Western European Union**) UEO *f*
we've [wiːv] = **we have**, *see* **have²**
WFP [dʌb(ə)ljuːef'piː] *n* (*abbr* **World Food Programme**) PAM *m*
whack¹ [wæk] *F* **1** *n* **(a)** (*blow*) (*with stick*) coup *m* retentissant *ou* bien appliqué; (*with hand*) claque *f*, taloche *f*; **to give sb a w.** donner un grand coup à qn; *Fig* **to have a w. at sth** (*try*) essayer de faire qch, tenter le coup **(b)** (*share*) part *f*; **all I want is a fair w.** tout ce que je veux, c'est ma part; **he didn't get his w.** il n'a pas eu sa part; **you're already earning (the) top w. for this job** tu gagnes déjà le maximum pour ce travail; **we can offer you £50,000, top w.** (*no more*) nous pouvons vous offrir 50 000 livres, dernier prix *ou* grand maximum **2** *int* v'lan!, vlan!
whack² *F* **1** *vt* **(a)** (*hit*) (*person*) (*one blow*) filer un gnon à; (*several blows*) battre, *F* cogner; (*ball*) (*of tennis player, golf player*) donner un grand coup dans; (*of football player*) donner un grand coup de pied dans; **to w. sb over the head** frapper qn sur la tête; **to w. sb with a stick/ruler** donner un coup de bâton/de règle à qn; **Pele whacked the ball into the net** Pele a envoyé le ballon d'un grand coup de pied dans le filet **(b)** *Sp* (*defeat*) (*one's opponents*) battre à plate(s) couture(s), piler **2** *vi* **to w. at sth with a stick** donner un coup de bâton à qch
▶ **whack off** *vi Sl* (*masturbate*) se branler
whacked [wækt] *adj Br F* (*exhausted*) vanné, crevé
whacker [wækər] *n F* **(a)** (*large thing*) **what a w.!, isn't it a w.!** (*piece of meat, vegetable, fish*) quel morceau!, c'est un sacré morceau!; **that's a bit of a w.!** (*alcoholic drink*) quelle dose! **(b)** *Old-fashioned* (*lie*) gros mensonge *m*
whacking ['wækɪŋ] *F* **1** *adj* énorme **2** *adv* **w. great** énorme; **a w. great cabbage** un chou énorme *ou* monstrueux; **a w. great lie** un gros mensonge **3** *n* **(a)** (*beating*) rossée *f*, raclée *f*; **his father gave him a w.** son père lui a donné une raclée **(b)** *Sp* (*defeat*) **we gave them a w.** on leur a mis la pâtée
whacko ['wækəʊ] **1** *adj F* = **wacky** **2** *int Old-fashioned Br Sl* magnifique!
whacky ['wækɪ] *adj esp Am F* = **wacky**
whale¹ [weɪl] *n* **(a)** baleine *f*; **blue w.** baleine bleue; **white w.** bél(o)uga *m*; **w. calf** baleineau *m*; **w. hunter** baleinier *m*; **w. oil** huile *f* de baleine **(b)** *F* **we had a w. of a time** on s'est drôlement bien amusé
whale² *vi* pêcher la baleine, aller à la pêche à la baleine
whaleboat ['weɪlbəʊt] *n* baleinier *m*
whalebone ['weɪlbəʊn] *n* (*in corset*) busc *m*, baleine *f*
whaler ['weɪlər] *n* (*person, vessel*) baleinier *m*
whaling ['weɪlɪŋ] *n* pêche *f ou* chasse *f* à la baleine; **w. fleet** baleiniers *mpl*; **w. ship** baleinier *m*
wham¹ ['wæm] *int F* v'lan!, vlan!
wham² (**-mm-**) *F* **1** *vi* rentrer (**into** dans); *Fb* **the ball whammed into the back of the net** le ballon a filé dans les buts; **her fist whammed into his face** son poing s'est écrasé sur son visage; **she whammed into the wall** elle s'est écrasée contre le mur; **the car whammed into the lamppost** la voiture est rentrée dans le réverbère **2** *vt* enfoncer; *Fb* **to w. the ball into the net** envoyer le ballon dans le filet à toute volée
wharf, *pl* **-s, wharves** [wɔːf, -s, wɔːvz] *n* quai *m*; *Com* **ex w.** à prendre sur quai
wharfage ['wɔːfɪdʒ] *n* droits *mpl* de quai *ou* de bassin
what [wɒt] **1** *adj* **(a)** [①**A33**,g] (*rel*) **he took w. little I had left** il m'a pris le peu qui me restait; **I'll give you w. money I have** je vais vous donner ce que j'ai comme argent
(b) [①**A31**,c-d; **B15**,C,1] (*interr direct or indirect*) quel, quelle, *pl* quels, quelles; **w. time is it?** quelle heure est-il?; **w. date is it (today)?** quelle est la date (d'aujourd'hui)?; **tell me w. books you want** dites-moi quels livres vous désirez; **w. right has she to give orders?** de quel droit donne-t-elle des ordres?; **w. good** *or* **use is this?** à quoi ça sert?; **w. sort of (a) book is it?** quelle sorte de livre est-ce?; **w. colour/size is it?** c'est de quelle couleur/de quelle taille?
(c) [①**A5**; **B15**,C,2] (*exclamatory*) **w. an idea!** quelle idée!; **w. a fool he is!** qu'il est bête!, comme il est bête!; **w. a fuss about nothing!** voilà bien du bruit pour rien!; **w. a question!** quelle question!; **w. a man!** quel homme!; **w. a pity!** quel dommage!; **w. a (long) time you are taking to get dressed!** qu'est-ce que vous êtes long à vous habiller!; **w. a lot of people!** que de gens!, que de monde!
2 *pron* **(a)** [①**B21-22**,F,g] (*rel*) (*subject*) ce qui; (*object*) ce que; **w. is done cannot be undone** ce qui est fait est fait; **I don't know w. has happened** je ne sais pas ce qui est arrivé; **w. I like is a detective story** moi, ce que j'aime, ce sont les romans policiers; **w. is most remarkable is that ...** ce qu'il y a de plus remarquable c'est que ...; **this is w. it's all about** voici ce dont il s'agit; **but that's not w. I said** mais ce n'est pas ce que j'ai dit; **come w. may** advienne que pourra; **he never talks about w. he has gone through** il ne parle jamais de ce qu'il a enduré; **w. with golf and tennis I have no time to write** entre le golf et le tennis je n'ai pas le temps d'écrire; *Sl* **to give sb w. for** (*scold*) passer un savon à qn; (*beat*) flanquer une bonne raclée à qn
(b) [①**A31**,c-d; **B16**,3,c-f] (*interr direct*) (*subject*) qu'est-ce qui; (*object*) qu'est-ce que, que, quoi; **w. has happened?** qu'est-ce qui est arrivé?; **w.'s happening?** que se passe-t-il?; **w. do**

you want? qu'est-ce que vous voulez?; **w. on earth are you doing here?** qu'est-ce que vous pouvez bien faire ici?; **w. is it?** (*identify it*) qu'est-ce?, qu'est-ce que c'est?; (*what is wrong*) qu'est-ce qu'il y a?; **w.'s that?** (*identify it*) qu'est-ce que c'est que ça?; (*what did you say*) quoi?; **w.'s that you're telling me?** qu'est-ce que vous me dites?; **w. will become of her?** que deviendra-t-elle?; **w.'s the matter?** qu'est-ce qu'il y a?, qu'y a-t-il?; **w.'s the date (today)?** quel jour sommes-nous?; **w.'s her address?** quelle est son adresse?; **w.'s his name?** quel est son nom?, comment s'appelle-t-il?; **w.'s that to you?** qu'est-ce que cela vous fait?, est-ce que ça vous regarde?; **w. is she to you that you're so concerned about her?** il faut qu'elle soit bien importante pour toi pour que tu sois aussi inquiet à son sujet; **w. is there to see in this town?** qu'y a-t-il à voir dans cette ville?; **w.'s the good** *or* **the use?** à quoi bon?; **w.'s to be done?** que faire?; **w. did I tell you?** qu'est-ce que je vous avais dit?, je vous l'avais bien dit!; **w. will people say?** que dira-t-on?, que vont dire les gens?; **w.'s the French for 'dog'?** comment dit-on 'dog' en français?; **w. else could bring me here?** quoi d'autre pourrait me faire venir ici?; **w. could be more beautiful?** quoi de plus beau?; **w. do seven and eight make?** combien font sept plus huit?; **w. is the rent?** à combien s'élève le loyer?; **w. do I owe you?** qu'est-ce que je vous dois?; (*in shop*) c'est combien?, ça fait combien?; **w. is he like?** comment est-il?; **w. do you take me for?** pour qui me prenez-vous?; **w.'s it made of?** en quoi est-ce que c'est fait?, c'est fait en quoi?; **w. are you thinking of?** à quoi pensez-vous?; **w. were you thinking of, letting her go out on her own?** qu'est-ce qui t'a pris de la laisser sortir toute seule?; **w. about the ten pounds I lent you?** et les dix livres que je vous ai prêtées?; **w. about a game of bridge?** si on faisait une partie de bridge?; **w. about you?** et vous?; **w. about that coffee?** et ce café?; **w.'s that for?** à quoi cela sert-il?, à quoi ça sert?; **w. did he do that for?** pourquoi a-t-il fait cela?; **what for?** pourquoi?; **w. on earth for?** mais pourquoi donc?; **and w. if she hears about it?** et si elle l'apprend?; **w. then?** et après?; *F* **so w.?** et alors?; *F* **d'you think I'm mad or w.?** tu crois que je suis fou ou quoi?; **w. did you say?** vous disiez?, pardon?; **w. of it?** qu'est-ce que cela fait?, eh bien, et après?; **well, w. of it?** et bien?, et après?

(c) (*indirect*) (*subject*) ce qui; (*object*) ce que; **tell me w.'s happened** dites-moi ce qui s'est passé; **I don't know w. you want** je ne sais pas ce que vous désirez; **he didn't know w. to say/do** il ne savait que dire/faire; **there were books and I don't know w.** il y avait des livres et je ne sais quoi d'autre *ou* encore; *F* **paper, pens, pencils, and w. not** *or* **and w. have you** du papier, des stylos, des crayons et d'autres choses encore *ou* et je ne sais quoi encore; **tell me w. you're crying for** dites-moi pourquoi vous pleurez; **tell me w.'s to be done** dis-moi ce qu'il y a à faire; **I'll tell you w.** je vais vous dire, écoutez; **he knows w.'s w.** (*in a subject*) il s'y connaît; **I've still to find out w.'s w.** (*how things work etc*) il faut que je trouve comment ça marche; (*what the situation is*) il faut que je me mette au courant de la situation; **I'll show him w.'s w.!** je vais lui montrer de quel bois je me chauffe!

(d) (*exclamatory*) **w. she has suffered!** ce qu'elle a souffert!; **w. next (I ask myself)!** ça par exemple!, et puis quoi encore!; **w.! you can't come!** comment! vous ne pouvez pas venir!; **w.! no eggs!** quoi! pas d'œufs!; *Old-fashioned F* **nice girl, w.!** joli brin de fille, hein!

what-d'ye-call-'em, -her, -him, -it ['wɒtjəkɔːləm, -ər, -ɪm, -ɪt] *n F* (*thing*) machin *m*, truc *m*; (*person*) chose *mf*, machin *m*, machine *f*; **Miss W.-d'ye-c.-her** mademoiselle Chose *ou* Machine

whate'er [wɒt'eər] *pron Lit* = **whatever 1**

whatever [wɒt'evər] [①A31,e; A33,h] **1** *pron* **(a)** (*rel*) (*subject*) tout ce qui; (*object*) tout ce que; **w. you like** tout ce qui vous plaira, tout ce que vous voudrez

(b) (*no matter what*) quoi que + *sub*; **w. it is** *or* **may be** quoi que ce soit; **w. happens, keep calm** quoi qu'il survienne, restez calme; **he shall have w. he wants** quoi qu'il désire, il l'aura; **w. she says** *or* **may say** en dépit de ce qu'elle dit; **use w. you can find** utilise ce que tu trouveras; **w. can she have said to make him so angry?** qu'est-ce qu'elle a bien pu dire pour le mettre dans une telle colère?

(c) *F* **pens, pencils, paper and w.** des stylos, des crayons, du papier et tout ce que vous voulez; **... or w.** (*something similar*) ... ou quelque chose de ce genre; (*anything you like*) ... ou tout ce que vous voulez

2 *adj* **(a)** (*no matter what*) **w. price they are asking** quel que soit le prix qu'ils demandent; **w. mistakes I (may) have made** quelles que soient les erreurs que j'ai faites

(b) (*emphatic*) **under any pretext w.** sous quelque prétexte que ce soit; **no hope w.** pas le moindre espoir, pas l'ombre d'un espoir; **is there any hope w.?** y a-t-il l'ombre d'un espoir?; **none w.** pas un seul; **nothing w.** absolument rien

what-ho *int Old-fashioned Br* **(a)** eh bien!, tiens! **(b)** (*greeting*) bonjour!, salut!

whatnot ['wɒtnɒt] *n* **(a)** (*for ornaments*) étagère *f* **(b)** *F* (*thing*) machin *m*, truc *m*; (*person*) chose *mf*, machin *m*, machine *f* **(c)** *F* **... and w.** ... et ainsi de suite, ... et tout ce qui s'ensuit; **there was champagne, caviar and w.** il y avait du champagne, du caviar et tout le tralala

what's-her-, -his-, -its-name ['wɒtsə-, -ɪz-, -ɪtsneɪm] *n F* = **what-d'ye-call-'em** *etc*

whatsit ['wɒtsɪt] *n F* machin *m*, truc *m*

whatsoever [wɒtsəʊ'evər] **1** *pron Lit* **w. it may be** quoi que ce soit **2** *adj* (*emphatic*) = **whatever 2 (b)**

wheat [wiːt] *n* blé *m*, froment *m*; **to plant land with w.** mettre une terre en blé; *Agr, Fig* **to divide the w. from the chaff** séparer le bon grain de l'ivraie; **w. field** champ *m* de blé

wheatear ['wiːtɪər] *n* (*bird*) traquet *m* (motteux), cul-blanc *m*, *pl* culs-blancs

wheaten ['wiːt(ə)n] *adj* (*bread*) de froment, de blé

wheatgerm ['wiːtdʒɜːm] *n* germes *mpl* de blé

wheatmeal ['wiːtmiːl] *n* farine *f* grossière, grosse farine de froment; **w. bread** pain *m* de froment

wheatsheaf ['wiːtʃiːf] *n* gerbe *f* de blé

wheedle ['wiːd(ə)l] *vt* **(a) to w. sb into doing sth** faire faire qch à qn à force de cajoleries; **she wheedled me into agreeing** elle m'a cajolé tant et si bien que j'ai fini par accepter **(b) to w. sth out of sb** obtenir *ou* soutirer qch de qn par des cajoleries; **he wheedled his way into the old lady's confidence** il s'est assuré la confiance de la vieille dame à force de cajoleries

wheedling ['wiːd(ə)lɪŋ] **1** *adj* (*manner etc*) enjôleur, cajoleur; **w. voice** voix pateline **2** *n* cajoleries *fpl*

wheel[1] [wiːl] *n* **(a)** (*on car, printer etc*) roue *f*; (*small*) roulette *f*; **on wheels** sur roues/roulettes; *Br* **meals on wheels** repas livrés à domicile (*aux personnes âgées etc*); *F* **my wheels** (*my car*) ma bagnole; *Fig* **the fifth w.** la cinquième roue du carrosse; *Am F* **to feel like a fifth w.** être la cinquième roue du carrosse; *Av* **landing wheels** roues (du train) d'atterrissage; *Av* **nose w.** roue (d'atterrisseur) avant; **the wheels** (*of mechanism, watch*) les rouages *mpl*; *Fig* **the wheels of government** les rouages du gouvernement; *Fig* **there are wheels within wheels** c'est une affaire très compliquée *ou* dont il faut connaître les dessous, c'est plus compliqué que cela n'en a l'air; *Fig* **the w. has come full circle** la boucle est bouclée; *Hist* **to condemn a criminal to the w.** condamner un criminel à la roue; *Hist* **to break sb on the w.** rouer qn; **big w.** (*at fair*) grande roue; *Am F* (*important person*) gros bonnet *m*, huile *f*; **the w. of fortune** la roue de la fortune; **w. alignment** parallélisme *m* des roues; *Aut* **w. arch** passage *m* de roue; *Aut* **w. bolt** boulon *m* de roue; *Aut* **w. brace** clé *f* en croix; *Aut* **w. chain** chaîne *f* (de pneu); *Aut* **w. cover** enjoliveur *m*; *Aut* **w. cylinder** cylindre *m* de roue; *Aut* **w. disc** enjoliveur *m*; *Aut* **w. hop** rebond *m* des roues; *Aut* **w. lock(-up)** blocage *m* des roues; *Aut* **w. nut** écrou *m* de roue; *Aut* **w. rim** jante *f* de roue; *Aut* **w. shimmy** phénomène *m* de shimmy; *Aut* **w. spin** patinage *m* de roues; *Aut* **w. track** alignement *m* des roues; *Aut* **w. trim** enjoliveur *m* de roues; *Aut* **w. wobble** flottement *m* des roues

(b) (*for steering*) *Aut* volant *m* (de direction); *Naut* roue *f* du gouvernail, barre *f*; **to be at the w.** *Aut* être au volant; *Naut* tenir la barre *ou* le gouvernail; *Fig* tenir la barre; **the man at the w.** *Aut* le conducteur, l'homme au volant; *Naut* l'homme de barre; *Fig* l'homme qui mène la barque, *F* le grand patron; **do you want to take a turn at the w.?** tu veux me remplacer au volant *ou Naut* à la barre?

(c) *Mil etc* (*movement*) (mouvement *m* de) conversion *f*; **left/right w.** conversion à gauche/à droite

wheel[2] **1** *vt* (*barrow, bicycle*) pousser; **to w. sth in a barrow** transporter qch en brouette; **to w. a child in a pram** promener un enfant dans son landau **2** *vi* **(a)** (*circle*) (*of birds*) tournoyer; (*of plane*) tourner **(b)** *Mil* opérer *ou* effectuer une conversion; **left w.!** par file à gauche, gauche! **(c)** *F* **to w. and deal** brasser des affaires (plus ou moins louches); **after spending the whole week wheeling and dealing** après une semaine complète de tractations

▶ **wheel about, wheel around 1** *vi* **(a)** (*turn*) faire demi-tour *ou* se retourner (brusquement); **she wheeled around to face him** elle s'est retournée brusquement pour lui faire face **(b)** (*circle*) tourner en rond *ou* en cercle, tournoyer; **vultures wheeling about in the sky** des vautours qui tournoient dans le ciel **2** *vtsep* (*turn*) tourner; (*dancing partner*) faire tourner

▶ **wheel in** *vtsep* **(a)** (*in wheelchair*) faire entrer en fauteuil roulant **(b)** *Br F* (*show in*) faire entrer; **w. him in as soon as he arrives** faites-le entrer dès qu'il arrive
▶ **wheel round** *vi, vtsep* = **wheel about**
wheelbarrow ['wi:lbærəʊ] *n* brouette *f*
wheelbase ['wi:lbeɪs] *n Aut* empattement *m*
wheelchair ['wi:ltʃeər] *n* fauteuil *m* roulant; **she'll be in a w. for the rest of her life** elle sera dans un fauteuil roulant pour le reste de ses jours; **w. access** facilité *f* d'accès pour fauteuils roulants; **access is difficult for people in wheelchairs** l'accès est difficile pour les personnes en fauteuil roulant
wheelclamp¹ ['wi:lklæmp] *n Aut* sabot *m* de Denver
wheelclamp² *vt Aut* mettre un sabot de Denver à; **I got wheelclamped last week** je me suis pris un sabot la semaine dernière
wheeled [wi:ld] *adj* à roues; (*on castors*) à roulettes
-wheeled [-wi:ld] *suff* **two/three-w.** à deux/trois roues
-wheeler [-wi:lər] *suff* **two/three-w.** voiture *f*/bicyclette *f* à deux/trois roues, véhicule *m* à deux/trois roues
wheeler-dealer *n F* brasseur *m* d'affaires, *Pej* magouilleur, -euse
wheelhouse ['wi:lhaʊs] *n Naut* abri *m* de navigation
wheelie ['wi:lɪ] *n Br F* **to do a w.** = rouler sur la roue arrière d'une bicyclette/d'une moto
wheeling ['wi:lɪŋ] *n* **(a)** (*of birds etc*) tournoiement *m* **(b)** **w. and dealing** brassage *m* d'affaires, *Pej* tractations *fpl*, magouilles *fpl*
wheelwright ['wi:lraɪt] *n* charron *m*
wheeze¹ [wi:z] *n* **(a)** (*noise*) respiration *f* sifflante **(b)** *Br F* (*trick*) ruse *f*, truc *m*; **a good w.** une bonne astuce, une bonne combine
wheeze² *vi* respirer péniblement
wheezing ['wi:zɪŋ] *n* (*of person*) respiration *f* difficile; *Med* sibilance *f* respiratoire
wheezy ['wi:zɪ] *adj* (*person, voice*) asthmatique, poussif; **she's still a little bit w. after her cold** elle a encore un peu de mal à respirer après son rhume; *Fig* **a w. old barrel organ** un vieil orgue de Barbarie asthmatique
whelk [welk] *n* buccin *m*
whelp¹ [welp] *n* (*dog*) jeune chien *m*, chiot *m*; (*of big cat*) petit *m*; *Old-fashioned F* (*youth*) garnement *m*
whelp² *vi* (*of animals*) mettre bas
when [wen] **1** *adv* **(a)** (*interr*) quand; **w. will you come?** quand viendrez-vous?; **w. will the wedding be?** à quand le mariage?; **w. ever** *or* **w. on earth will he come?** quand donc *ou* quand diable viendra-t-il?; *F* **say w.!** (*when pouring drink*) dites-moi stop!
(b) (*rel*) **the day w. I first met her** le jour où je l'ai rencontrée pour la première fois; **one day w. I was on duty** un jour que j'étais de service; **at the very time w. ...** au moment même où ..., alors même que ...
2 *conj* [①**A69**,b,ii; **B29-30**,11] **(a)** (*at the time that*) quand, lorsque; **w. I came into the room** quand *ou* lorsque je suis entré dans la pièce; **w. I think of what she must have suffered!** quand je pense à ce qu'elle a dû souffrir!; **I get very irritated w. talking to her** je m'énerve chaque fois que je lui parle; *Culin* **w. cool, turn out onto a dish** une fois refroidi, démouler sur un plat
(b) (*at which time*) **the prince will arrive on the 10th, w. he will open the new university** le prince arrivera le dix et inaugurera la nouvelle université; **I had just gone to bed w. the phone rang** je venais de me mettre au lit quand le téléphone sonna
(c) (*though*) **he walked there w. he could have taken the car** il y est allé à pied, alors qu'il aurait pu prendre la voiture
(d) (*since*) **what's the good of telling you w. you won't listen to me?** à quoi bon vous le dire puisque vous ne voulez pas m'écouter?
3 *pron* **(a)** (*interr*) **until w. can you stay?** jusqu'à quand pouvez-vous rester?; **since w. have you been living in Paris?** depuis quand habitez-vous Paris?; *Iron* **since w. have you been interested in opera?** depuis quand est-ce que tu t'intéresses à l'opéra?
(b) (*rel*) **since w. I have always bought a car of that make** depuis lors je n'achète que des voitures de cette marque; **until w. I shall stay in Paris** d'ici là je reste à Paris
4 *n* **the w. and the how of it** quand et comment cela s'est-il passé/se passera-t-il
whence [wens] *adv Arch, Lit* d'où; **no one knows w. he comes** personne ne sait d'où il vient; **w. I conclude that ...** d'où je conclus que ...
whenever, *Lit* **whene'er** [wen'evər, -'eər] *conj, adv* [①**A69**,b,ii] **(a)** (*every time*) toutes les fois *ou* chaque fois que; **w. I see it I think of you** chaque fois que je le vois je pense à vous; **I go w. I can** j'y vais aussi souvent que possible
(b) (*any time*) à n'importe quel moment; **come w. you like** venez quand vous voudrez *ou* à n'importe quel moment; **Sunday, Monday or w.** dimanche, lundi, ou n'importe quel jour; **next month or w.** le mois prochain ou n'importe quand
(c) (*interr*) quand; **w. did you find (the) time to do all that?** quand avez-vous trouvé le temps de faire tout cela?
where [weər] **1** *interr adv* **(a)** (*in what place or direction*) où; **w. am I?** où suis-je?; **tell me w. she is** dites-moi où elle est; **w. did you put it?** où l'avez-vous mis?; **w. are you going to?** où allez-vous?; **w. does he come from?** d'où vient-il?; **w. have you got to?, w. are you?** (*in work, book etc*) où en êtes-vous?; (*when looking for someone*) où êtes-vous passé?, où êtes-vous?; **w. should I be if I had followed your advice?** qu'est-ce que je serais devenu si j'avais suivi vos conseils?
(b) w. is the use *or* **the good of it?** à quoi bon (faire) cela?
2 *rel conj, rel adv* [①**A69**,b,iii] (*in, at, to the place which*) (là) où; **I'll stay w. I am** je resterai (là) où je suis; **go w. you like** allez où vous voudrez; **that's w. we've got to** voilà où nous sommes; **that is w. you are mistaken** c'est là que vous vous trompez, voilà où vous vous trompez; **he came to (the place) w. I was fishing** il est venu à l'endroit où je pêchais; **I can see it from w. we are** je le vois d'où nous sommes; **delete w. inapplicable** (*on form*) rayer les mentions inutiles; **the house w. I was born** la maison où *ou* dans laquelle je suis né; **they went to Paris, w. they stayed a week** ils sont allés à Paris et y sont restés huit jours
3 *n* **the w. and the when** le lieu et la date/l'heure
whereabouts **1** [weərə'baʊts] *adv* où; **do you know w. the town hall is?** savez-vous de quel côté se trouve l'hôtel de ville?; **w. in France do you live?** où est-ce que tu habites en France? **2** ['weərəbaʊts] *npl* **nobody knows her w., her w. are unknown** personne ne sait où elle est; **we are still unsure of his exact w.** on ignore encore le lieu où il se trouve exactement; **the precise w. of the control centre** le lieu précis où se trouve le centre de contrôle
whereafter [weə'rɑ:ftər] *rel adv Arch, Lit* après quoi, à la suite de quoi
whereas [weə'ræz] *conj* **(a)** *Jur etc* (*introducing preamble*) attendu que, vu que, puisque **(b)** (*on the other hand*) alors que, tandis que
whereat [weə'ræt] *adv, conj Arch, Lit* à quoi, sur quoi; **w. he replied that ...** (ce) à quoi il a répondu que ...
whereby [weə'baɪ] *adv Arch, Fml* par quoi, par quel moyen; **we have a situation here w. ...** nous sommes ici en présence d'une situation dans laquelle ...; **a scheme w. we can ...** un plan par lequel nous pouvons ...
wherefore ['weəfɔ:r] **1** *adv Arch, Lit* **(a)** (*interr*) pourquoi, pour quelle raison **(b)** (*rel*) donc, pour cette raison **2** *n* **the why and the w.** le pourquoi et le comment
wherein [weə'rɪn] *adv Arch, Lit* en quoi; **w. the difficulty lies** où se trouve la difficulté
whereof [weə'rɒv] *adv Arch, Lit* (*interr*) en quoi, de quoi; (*rel*) dont; **a matter w. I know nothing** une affaire dont j'ignore tout
whereon [weə'rɒn] *adv Arch, Lit* sur lequel; **the day w. ...** le jour où ...; **w. he left us** sur quoi il nous a quittés
wheresoever, wheresoe'er [weəsəʊ'evər, -'eər] *adv, conj esp Lit* = **wherever**
whereupon [weərə'pɒn] *adv, conj Lit* (*at which point*) sur quoi, après quoi; **w. he left us** sur quoi il nous a quittés
wherever [weə'revər] *conj, adv* [①**A69**,b,iii] **(a)** (*every place*) partout où, n'importe où; **I shall remember it w. I go** où que j'aille, je m'en souviendrai; **I'll go w. you want (me to)** j'irai partout où vous voudrez (que j'aille); **w. possible** partout où cela est possible; *F* **at home, in the office or w.** à la maison, au bureau ou n'importe où **(b)** (*whichever place*) **w. they come from** d'où qu'ils viennent; **he comes from Glossop, w. that may be** il est originaire d'un bled appelé Glossop, et ne me demandez pas où cela se trouve **(c)** (*interr*) où; **w. can he be?** où peut-il bien être?
wherewithal ['weərwɪðɔ:l] *n* **the w.** l'argent *m*, le nécessaire, les moyens *mpl*; **I haven't the w. to buy it** je n'ai pas de quoi l'acheter
whet [wet] *vt* **(-tt-)** **(a)** (*sharpen*) (*tool, blade*) aiguiser, affûter, repasser **(b)** (*stimulate*) (*appetite*) stimuler, aiguiser; **the weekend break in Florence had whetted her appetite for travel** ce week-end à Florence lui avait donné soif de voyages
whether ['weðər] *conj* [①**A68-9**,2,a] **(a)** (*indirect question*) si; **I don't know w. it's true** je ne sais pas si c'est vrai; **it's doubtful** *or* **uncertain w. ...** il est douteux *ou* peu certain que ... + *sub*; **I doubt w. he'll come** je doute qu'il vienne; **I want to know w. ... or w. ...** je voudrais savoir si ... ou si ...; **it depends on w. you're in a hurry or not** cela dépend (de) si vous êtes pressé ou non

(b) (*conditional*) **w. it rains or (w. it) snows, he always goes out** qu'il pleuve ou qu'il neige, il sort toujours; **w. she comes or not we shall leave** qu'elle vienne ou non *ou* qu'elle vienne ou qu'elle ne vienne pas, nous partirons; **w. or not this is true** qu'il en soit ainsi ou non; **everyone, w. rich or poor, needs it** chacun, qu'il soit riche ou pauvre, en a besoin; **you'll listen to me w. you like it or not** tu vas m'écouter, que tu le veuilles ou non; **w. he likes it or not** que cela lui plaise ou non

whetstone ['wetstəʊn] *n* pierre *f* à aiguiser *ou* à repasser

whew [hju:] *int* **(a)** (*relief, fatigue*) ouf! **(b)** (*astonishment*) mon Dieu!

whey [weɪ] *n* petit-lait *m*

which [wɪtʃ] [①**A31**,c] **1** *adj* **(a)** [①**B15**,C,1] (*interr*) quel, *f* quelle, *pl* quels, quelles; **w. colour do you like best?** quelle couleur aimez-vous le mieux?; **w. way do we go?** par où allons-nous?; **w. way is the wind blowing?** d'où vient le vent?; **w. one?** lequel?, laquelle?; **w. ones?** lesquels?, lesquelles?; **I know w. one you want** je sais lequel vous désirez

(b) [①**A33**,f,ii] (*rel*) lequel, laquelle, *pl* lesquels, lesquelles; **he stayed here two weeks, during w. time he never left the house** il est resté ici deux semaines, et pendant (tout) ce temps il n'a pas quitté la maison; **she came at noon, at w. time I'm usually in the garden** elle est venue à midi, heure à laquelle je suis habituellement au jardin

2 *pron* **(a)** [①**B16**,3,a] a (*interr*) lequel, laquelle, *pl* lesquels, lesquelles; **w. have you chosen?** lequel/laquelle/lesquels/lesquelles avez-vous choisi(e)(s)?; **w. of you?** lequel d'entre vous?; **w. of the two (girls) is the prettier?** laquelle des deux (filles) est la plus jolie?; **w. would you rather have?** lequel préfériez-vous (avoir)?; **I can never tell w. is w.** je ne sais jamais les distinguer, je ne sais jamais lequel est l'un et lequel est l'autre; **I don't know w. to choose** je ne sais (pas) lequel choisir; **I don't mind w.** n'importe (lequel)

(b) [①**A32-33**,d-g; **B20-21**,F] (*rel*) (*subject*) qui; (*object*) que; (*referring to whole clause*) (*subject*) ce qui; (*object*) ce que; **the house w. is for sale** la maison qui est à vendre; **the book w. I bought yesterday** le livre que j'ai acheté hier; **he looked like a retired colonel, w. in fact he was** il avait l'air d'un colonel en retraite, ce qu'il était en effet; **she was back in London, w. I didn't know** elle était de retour à Londres, fait que *ou* ce que j'ignorais

(c) (*with prepositions*) lequel, laquelle, *pl* lesquels, lesquelles; **to w., at w.** auquel, à laquelle, *pl* auxquels, auxquelles; **of w., from w.** duquel, de laquelle, *pl* desquels, desquelles; **the house of w. I am speaking** la maison dont je parle; **the countries to w. we are going** *or* **w. we're going to** les pays où nous allons; **the pen with w. I'm writing, the pen w. I'm writing with** le stylo avec lequel j'écris; **the town in w. we live, the town w. we live in** la ville où nous habitons *ou* que nous habitons *ou* dans laquelle nous habitons; **he insists that actors should have talent, in w. he is right** il exige que les acteurs aient du talent, (ce) en quoi il a raison; **there are no trains on Sunday, w. I hadn't thought of** il n'y a pas de trains le dimanche, ce à quoi je n'avais pas pensé; **after w. he went out** après quoi il est sorti

whichever [wɪtʃ'evər] [①**A33**,h] **1** *pron* **(a)** (*any*) (*subject*) celui qui, *f* celle qui, *pl* ceux qui, celles qui; (*object*) celui que *etc*; **take w. you like best** prenez celui que vous préférez; **w. of you comes in first** celui (d'entre vous) qui arrive le premier; **the 30th or the last Friday in the month, w. comes first** le 30 ou le dernier vendredi du mois, suivant lequel de ces deux jours survient le premier

(b) (*no matter which*) **w. of the measures they adopt ...** (*one*) quelle que soit la mesure qu'ils adoptent ..., quelque mesure qu'ils adoptent ..., qu'ils adoptent une mesure ou une autre ..., ils peuvent adopter n'importe quelle mesure ...; (*more than one*) quelles que soient les mesures qu'ils adoptent ..., quelques mesures qu'ils adoptent ..., ils peuvent adopter n'importe quelles mesures ...; **w. you choose, you will have a good bargain** quel que soit celui/quelle que soit celle/*etc* que vous choisissiez *ou* vous pouvez choisir n'importe lequel/laquelle/*etc*, vous ferez une bonne affaire

(c) [①**A31**,e] (*interr*) lequel, laquelle, *pl* lesquels, lesquelles; **w. shall I choose?** lequel vais-je choisir?

2 *adj* **(a)** (*the one/ones which*) **buy w. model is cheapest** achète le modèle qui est le moins cher(, peu importe lequel); **take w. ties you prefer** prends les cravates que tu préfères(, peu importe lesquelles); **I'll have w. cake Mary doesn't want** je prendrai le gâteau que Mary ne veut pas; **you should write to w. organization you think best** vous devriez écrire à l'organisme qui vous paraît le meilleur

(b) (*no matter which*) **w. candidate wins the election, he will have to ...** quel que soit le candidat qui remporte l'élection, il lui faudra ...; **w. road you take, it'll take you two hours** quelle que soit la route que tu prennes *ou* quelque route que tu prennes *ou* que tu prennes une route ou une autre *ou* tu peux prendre n'importe quelle route, tu mettras deux heures; **in w. company you work ...** quelle que soit l'entreprise dans laquelle tu travailles ..., dans quelque entreprise que tu travailles ..., que tu travailles dans une entreprise ou dans une autre ..., tu peux travailler dans n'importe quelle entreprise ...; **w. way you turn ...** de quelque côté que vous vous tourniez ..., que vous vous tourniez d'un côté ou d'un autre ..., vous pouvez vous tourner de n'importe quel côté ...

whiff [wɪf] *n* (*smell*) (*of wine, socks, incense etc*) odeur *f*; *Fig* **a w. of scandal** un parfum de scandale; **to catch a w. of sth** (*smell*) sentir qch; *Fig* (*hear rumours about*) avoir vent de qch; **he had caught a w. of something suspicious** il avait senti que quelque chose de louche était dans l'air; **there mustn't be the slightest w. of suspicion that I'm involved** rien ne doit laisser penser que je suis impliqué; **to go out for a w. of fresh air** sortir pour respirer un peu *ou* pour prendre l'air; *F* **what a w.!** (*bad smell*) qu'est-ce que ça pue!

whiffy ['wɪfɪ] *adj Br F* puant, qui pue; **the dog's a bit w.** ce chien sent fort; **it's a bit w. in here, don't you think?** ça schlingue par ici, tu ne trouves pas?

Whig [wɪg] *n Pol Hist* whig *m*

while¹ [waɪl] *n* **(a)** (*time*) (espace *m* de) temps *m*; **a short w.** un petit moment; **some w. later** (*soon after*) un moment plus tard; (*longer*) quelque temps plus tard; **after a w.** au bout de quelque temps, quelque temps après; **after a little w., a little w. later** peu de temps après; **for a (short) w.** pendant un moment; **in a short** *or* **little w.** sous peu, avant peu; **a short** *or* **little w. ago** il y a peu de temps; **a long w.** longtemps; **a long w. ago** il y a longtemps; **a good w.** pas mal de temps; **it lasted a good w.** ça a duré un bon moment; **it will be a good w. before you see him again** vous ne le reverrez pas de si tôt; **it will take me quite a w.** cela me prendra un certain temps *ou* pas mal de temps; **it took me a w. to realize what she meant** j'ai mis un certain temps à comprendre ce qu'elle voulait dire; **stay a little w. longer** restez encore un peu; **all the w.** tout le temps; **once in a w.** de temps en temps, de temps à autre; *Arch* **the w.** en attendant, pendant ce temps

(b) to be worth (one's) w. valoir la peine, *F* valoir le coup; **it's not worth our w. waiting** cela ne vaut pas *ou* ce n'est pas la peine que nous attendions; **it is perhaps worth w. pointing out that ...** cela vaut peut-être la peine de faire remarquer que ...; **I'll make it worth your w.** vous serez bien récompensé de votre peine

while² *conj* **(a)** [①**B29-30**,11] (*during the time that*) pendant que, tandis que; **don't speak w. the performance is in progress** ne parlez pas pendant le spectacle; **he drowned w. he was having a bath** il s'est noyé en prenant un bain; **w. (he was) here** pendant qu'il était ici; **w. in Paris** pendant mon/son/*etc* séjour à Paris; **w. reading I fell asleep** tout en lisant, je me suis endormi; **w. this was going on** sur ces entrefaites; **w. you're at** *or* **about it, could you photocopy this too?** pendant que tu y es, peux-tu aussi me photocopier cela?

(b) (*as long as*) tant que; **w. there's life there's hope** tant qu'il y a de la vie il y a de l'espoir

(c) (*although*) quoique + *sub*, bien que + *sub*; **w. I admit it's difficult** quoique j'admette que c'est difficile

(d) (*whereas*) tandis que; **one of the sisters was in white, w. the other was all in black** une des sœurs était vêtue de blanc, tandis que l'autre était tout en noir

► **while away** *vtsep* (*time*) faire passer, tuer; (*hour*) tuer; **we whiled away the hours by playing cards** on faisait passer le temps en jouant aux cartes; **I played patience to w. away the time** j'ai fait des réussites pour m'occuper

whilst [waɪlst] *conj esp Br* = **while²**

whim [wɪm] *n* caprice *m*, fantaisie *f*, lubie *f*; **passing w.** toquade *f*; **to do sth on a w.** faire qch sur un coup de tête; **it was just a w.** ce n'était qu'un caprice; **it was a sudden w. of his** c'était un de ses caprices; **she indulges his every w.** elle lui passe tous ses caprices

whimper¹ ['wɪmpər] *n* (*crying*) pleurnicherie *f*, pleurnichement *m*; (*of dog*) petit cri *m* plaintif; *Fig* (*complaint*) geignement *m*, plainte *f*; **without so much as a w.** sans se plaindre

whimper² *vi* (*of person*) pleurnicher, geindre; (*of dog*) pousser de petits cris plaintifs; **the dog's whimpering to be let in** le chien gémit pour qu'on le laisse entrer

whimpering ['wɪmpərɪŋ] **1** *adj* pleurnicheur, gémissant; (*dog*) qui pousse de petits cris plaintifs **2** *n* (*crying*) pleurnichement *m*, pleurnicheries *fpl*; (*of dog*) petits cris *mpl* plaintifs; *Fig* (*complaints*) plaintes *fpl*

whimsey ['wɪmzɪ] *n* = **whimsy**
whimsical ['wɪmzɪk(ə)l] *adj (person)* capricieux, fantasque; *(playful)* malicieux; *(behaviour, sense of humour, story, remark)* farfelu; *(smile)* malicieux
whimsicality [wɪmzɪ'kælɪtɪ] *n (of person)* caractère *m* capricieux *ou* fantasque; *(playfulness)* malice *f*; *(of behaviour, sense of humour, story, remark)* caractère farfelu
whimsically ['wɪmzɪklɪ] *adv (capriciously)* capricieusement; *(playfully)* malicieusement; *(directed, written)* de façon farfelue; *(to smile)* malicieusement
whimsy ['wɪmzɪ] *n* **(a)** *(capricious idea)* fantaisie *f*; **she dismissed the idea as a mere piece of w.** elle rejeta cette idée qui lui parut de la plus haute fantaisie **(b)** *(playfulness)* malice *f*
whin [wɪn] *n (plant)* ajonc *m*, genêt *m* épineux
whine¹ [waɪn] *n* **(a)** *(crying) (of child)* gémissement *m*; *(of dog)* gémissement *m*, geignement *m* **(b)** *(of engine etc)* bruit *m* strident
whine² *vi* **(a)** *(cry) (of child)* pleurnicher; *(of person, dog)* gémir; *(in pain etc)* geindre **(b)** *(complain)* se plaindre; **she's always whining about something** elle est toujours en train de se lamenter à propos d'une chose ou d'une autre; **you've nothing to w. about** il n'y a pas de quoi vous plaindre; **stop whining!** assez de jérémiades!
whinge¹ [wɪndʒ] *n F (complaint)* plainte *f*; **to have a w. about sth** se plaindre (à propos) de qch
whinge² *vi F* **(a)** *(cry) (of child)* pleurnicher, gémir **(b)** *(complain)* se plaindre; **stop whingeing!** assez de jérémiades!; *Austr* **a whingeing pom** un Anglais qui se plaint toujours
whining ['waɪnɪŋ] **1** *adj (voice)* geignard; *(child)* pleurnicheur; *(tone)* plaintif **2** *n* **(a)** *(of person, dog)* gémissement *m*; *(in pain etc)* geignement *m* **(b)** *(complaining)* jérémiades *fpl*, plaintes *fpl*; **stop your w.!** assez de jérémiades!; **I've had enough of his w.** j'en ai assez de ses jérémiades
whinny¹ ['wɪnɪ] *n (of horse)* hennissement *m*
whinny² *vi (of horse)* hennir; *Fig (of person)* brailler
whinnying ['wɪnɪɪŋ] *adj* **a w. laugh** un rire qui ressemble à un hennissement; **he gave a w. laugh** il se mit à rire en hennissant
whip¹ [wɪp] *n* **(a)** *(lash)* fouet *m*; *Fig F* **to give sb a fair crack of the w.** donner toutes ses chances à qn; *Fig F* **to get a fair crack of the w.** avoir toutes ses chances; *Fig* **to have** *or* **hold the w. hand** avoir l'avantage, avoir le dessus; *Fig* **to have the w. hand over sb** avoir barre(s) sur qn **(b)** *Parl (person)* chef *m* de file, whip *m*; *(order)* appel *m* aux membres d'un groupe **(c)** *(movement) (of cable etc)* mouvement *m* brusque **(d)** *Culin* = mousse *f*; **strawberry/raspberry w.** = mousse aux fraises/framboises
whip² **(-pp-) 1** *vt* **(a)** *(horse)* fouetter; *(child)* donner le fouet à; *Culin (egg whites)* battre en neige; *(cream)* fouetter, battre; **to w. a top** fouetter *ou* faire aller un sabot; **whipped cream** crème fouettée; *Fig* **he whipped the crowd into a frenzy with his speech** son discours rendit la foule frénétique; **the rain was whipping the window panes** la pluie fouettait *ou* cinglait les vitres
(b) *F (defeat)* battre à plate(s) couture(s); **I know when I'm whipped** je sais quand déclarer forfait
(c) *Sewing* **to w. a seam** surjeter une couture, faire un surjet
(d) *F (move quickly)* **she whipped it out of sight** elle l'a caché d'un mouvement rapide; **she's been whipped into hospital** elle a été transportée à l'hôpital de toute urgence
(e) *F (steal)* faucher, piquer; **someone's whipped my wallet** on m'a piqué mon portefeuille
2 *vi* fouetter; **the rain was whipping against the panes** la pluie fouettait *ou* cinglait les vitres
► **whip away** *vtsep F (remove quickly)* enlever brusquement *ou* d'un geste rapide
► **whip back** *vi F (return)* retourner rapidement; **w. back and get it** retournez-y en vitesse le chercher
► **whip in 1** *vi F (go in, drop in)* **I'll just w. in and buy ...** je vais juste passer acheter ... **2** *vtsep (of huntsman)* rassembler
► **whip off** *vtsep F (remove) (clothes)* ôter *ou* enlever rapidement, se débarrasser de
► **whip out** *F* **1** *vtsep (extract)* sortir rapidement; **he whipped out a revolver** il a sorti brusquement un revolver; **to w. out sb's appendix** enlever l'appendice de qn **2** *vi (go out)* sortir en vitesse; **I'm just whipping out to the library** je file à la bibliothèque
► **whip round** *vi F* **(a)** *(turn)* se retourner vivement **(b)** *(go quickly)* **w. round to the chemist's for me** fais un saut à la pharmacie pour moi **(c)** *Br (collect money)* faire une collecte; **we whipped round to get a present for her** nous avons fait une collecte pour lui acheter un cadeau
► **whip up** *vtsep* **(a)** *(arouse) (horse)* toucher (du fouet); *Fig* **to w. up an audience** galvaniser *ou* exalter un public **(b)** *Parl (summon) (members of party)* faire passer un appel urgent à; **to w. up support for sth** susciter un soutien en faveur de qch **(c)** *Culin (egg whites)* battre en neige; *(cream)* battre, fouetter; *F* **I'll w. you up something to eat** je vais te préparer *ou* te faire quelque chose à manger en vitesse; *F* **I'll see what I can w. up** je vais voir ce que je peux préparer en vitesse
whipcord ['wɪpkɔːd] *n* **(a)** *(on whip)* mèche *f* de fouet **(b)** *Tex* whipcord *m*; **w. trousers** pantalon *m* en whipcord
whiplash ['wɪplæʃ] *n* **(a)** *(from whip)* coup *m* de fouet; *Fig* **tongue like a w.** langue cinglante **(b)** *Med* **w. (injury)** coup *m* du lapin, *Spec* lésion *f* traumatique des cervicales, syndrome *m* cervical traumatique
whipper-in [wɪpər'ɪn] *n (of hounds)* piqueur *m*
whippersnapper ['wɪpəsnæpər] *n F* petit malin *m*
whippet ['wɪpɪt] *n (dog)* whippet *m*
whipping ['wɪpɪŋ] *n* correction; **to give sb a w.** donner une correction à qn; *Fig* **w. boy** bouc *m* émissaire; **w. cream** crème *f* fraîche à fouetter
whippoorwill ['wɪpʊwɪl] *n Am (bird)* engoulevent *m* de Virginie, *Can* engoulevent bois-pourri
whipround ['wɪpraʊnd] *n Br F* quête *f*, collecte *f*; **to have a w. for sb** organiser une collecte pour qn
whir [wɜːr] *n, vi* = **whirr**
whirl¹ [wɜːl] *n (of wheel)* mouvement *m* giratoire; *(of leaves, dust)* tourbillon *m*, tournoiement *m*; *Fig F* **would you like to give it a w.?** tu veux essayer?; *Fig F* **I'll have a w. at it** je vais tenter le coup; **a w. of activity** un tourbillon d'activités; **my head's in a w.** la tête me tourne; **the social w.** les tourbillons de la vie mondaine
whirl² 1 *vi (of dead leaves etc)* tourbillonner, tournoyer; *(of propeller etc)* tourner; *(of top)* tournoyer; **whirling dervish** derviche *m* tourneur; **my head's whirling** la tête me tourne; **the thoughts that were whirling through my head** les pensées qui tourbillonnaient dans ma tête **2** *vt (dead leaves etc)* faire tournoyer, faire tourbillonner; **to w. sb/sth around** *(of person)* faire tournoyer qn/qch autour de soi; **he whirled her onto the dance floor** il l'a entraînée en tournoyant sur la piste de danse
► **whirl along 1** *vi* filer à toute vitesse *ou* à toute allure **2** *vtsep* entraîner à toute vitesse *ou* à fond de train; **the train whirled us along** le train nous emportait à grande allure
► **whirl round 1** *vi (of person)* se retourner brusquement; *(of dancer)* pirouetter; *(of leaves)* tourbillonner, tournoyer; **she whirled round and round in the middle of the dance floor** elle tournait et tournait au milieu de la piste de danse **2** *vtsep* **to w. sb round** faire tournoyer qn
whirligig ['wɜːlɪgɪg] *n (top)* tourniquet *m*; *(merry-go-round)* manège *m* de chevaux de bois
whirlpool ['wɜːlpuːl] *n* tourbillon *m* (d'eau), gouffre *m*; *Fig* **a w. of violence** un tourbillon de violence; **w. bath** Jacuzzi® *m*, bain *m* à remous
whirlwind ['wɜːlwɪnd] *n* tourbillon *m* (de vent), trombe *f* (de vent); **to come in like a w.** entrer comme une tornade; **w. romance** aventure *f* enivrante; **w. tour** visite *f* éclair
whirlybird ['wɜːlɪbɜːd] *n Old-fashioned F (helicopter)* hélico *m*
whirr¹ [wɜːr] *n (of machines)* ronflement *m*, ronronnement *m*; *(of propeller etc)* vrombissement *m*
whirr² *vi (of machinery etc)* ronfler, ronronner; *(of propeller)* vrombir
whisk¹ [wɪsk] *n* **(a)** *(for beating eggs)* fouet *m*, batteur *m* **(b)** *(action)* **give the eggs a w.** battre les œufs; **a w. of the tail/the duster** un coup de queue/de chiffon
whisk² 1 *vt* **(a)** **to w. its tail** *(of cow etc)* agiter sa queue; **to w. a duster over the table** donner un coup de chiffon sur la table **(b)** *(move quickly)* **he was whisked to hospital** il a été transporté à l'hôpital de toute urgence; **she whisked it out of sight** elle l'a caché d'un mouvement rapide **(c)** *Culin (eggs)* battre; *(cream)* fouetter **2** *vi* **she whisked past me** elle est passée devant moi comme un éclair
► **whisk away, whisk off** *vtsep (thing)* enlever d'un geste rapide; *(person)* emporter très rapidement; **to w. away a fly** chasser une mouche; **the president was whisked away in a helicopter** le président a été emmené à toute vitesse en hélicoptère; **he was whisked away to hospital in an ambulance** il a été transporté de toute urgence en ambulance à l'hôpital
► **whisk up** *vtsep Culin (eggs)* battre; *(cream)* fouetter
whisker ['wɪskər] *n* **whiskers** *(of man)* favoris *mpl*; *(of cat, mouse etc)* moustache(s) *f(pl)*; *Sp Fig* **to win by a w.** gagner d'un poil *ou* de justesse; *Fig* **to escape death by a w.** frôler la mort, échapper de justesse à la mort

whiskered [ˈwɪskəd] *adj* (*man*) qui porte des favoris

whisky, *Irish, US* **whiskey** [ˈwɪskɪ] *n* whisky *m*; **two whiskies** deux whiskies; **a w. and soda** un whisky soda; **w. on the rocks** whisky avec des glaçons, *Can* whisky sur glace *ou* aux glaçons; **w. company** société *f* de fabrication de whisky; **w. distillery** distillerie *f* de whisky; **w. glass** verre *m* à whisky; *esp Br* **w. mac** = whisky mélangé à du vin de gingembre; *esp Am* **w. sour** = whisky avec du jus de citron/de citron vert

whisper¹ [ˈwɪspər] *n* **(a)** (*of person speaking*) chuchotement *m*; *esp Lit* (*of wind in leaves*) bruissement *m*; **to speak in a w.** *or* **in whispers** chuchoter, parler en chuchotant; **to say sth in a w.** chuchoter qch, dire qch tout bas; **... she said in a loud w.** ... chuchota-t-elle assez fort **(b)** (*rumour*) rumeur *f*, bruit *m*; **I've heard whispers** *or* **a w. that ...** j'ai entendu dire que ...; **and remember, not a w. of it to anyone!** et souviens-toi, pas un mot à qui que ce soit!

whisper² **1** *vi* (*of person speaking*) chuchoter, parler bas; *esp Lit* (*of wind in leaves*) bruire; **to w. to sb** chuchoter à l'oreille de qn, parler à voix basse à qn; **stop whispering, Evans!** ça suffit les messes basses, Evans! **2** *vt* **(a) to w. sth to sb** chuchoter qch à qn, dire qch à voix basse à qn; **what were you whispering to her?** qu'est-ce que tu lui disais à l'oreille?; **whispered conversation** conversation à voix basse **(b)** (*as rumour*) **it is being whispered that ...** le bruit court que ..., on dit que ...

whispering [ˈwɪspərɪŋ] *n* **(a)** (*of person speaking*) chuchotement *m*; *esp Lit* (*of wind*) bruissement *m*; *Archit* **w. gallery** voûte *f* acoustique, galerie *f* à écho; **stop that w.!** ça suffit les messes basses! **(b)** *Pej* (*rumours*) rumeur *f*; **w. campaign** campagne *f* de diffamation

whist [wɪst] *n Cards* whist *m*; **to have a game of w.** faire une partie de whist; **to play w.** jouer au whist; **w. drive** tournoi *m* de whist; **w. player** joueur, -euse de whist

whistle¹ [ˈwɪs(ə)l] *n* **(a)** (*noise*) sifflement *m*; (*blow on a whistle*) coup *m* de sifflet; **she gave a w. of surprise** elle a sifflé de surprise; *Sp* **final w.** coup de sifflet final **(b)** (*object*) sifflet *m*; **to blow a w.** donner un coup de sifflet; *Sp* **to blow the w. for a foul/for half-time** siffler une faute/la mi-temps; *Fig F* **to blow the w. on sth** révéler *ou* dévoiler qch; *Fig F* **to blow the w. on sb** dénoncer qn; *Fig F* **who blew the w.?** qui a vendu la mèche?

whistle² **1** *vi* (*of person, bird, wind etc*) siffler; (*on whistle*) donner un coup de sifflet; **she whistled in surprise** elle a sifflé de surprise; **the bullet whistled past his ear** la balle a passé en sifflant tout près de son oreille; *Fig* **to w. in the dark** essayer de se rassurer; **to w. for one's dog/a taxi** siffler son chien/un taxi; *Fig F* **he can w. for his money** il peut courir après son argent; *Fig F* **you can w. for it!** tu peux toujours courir! **2** *vt* (*tune*) siffler, siffloter; *Sp* **to w. half-time** siffler la mi-temps

▶ **whistle up** *vtsep F* **I'll w. up a few friends to help us** je vais trouver quelques amis pour nous aider; **can you w. up some more sandwiches?** peux-tu nous avoir *ou* dégoter encore quelques sandwichs?

whistle-blower *n Fig, F* personne *f* qui vend la mèche; **we need a few more whistle-blowers like her** il faudrait d'autres personnes comme elle pour tirer sur la sonnette d'alarme

whistler [ˈwɪslər] *n* **(a)** (*person*) siffleur, -euse **(b)** (*bird*) oiseau *m* siffleur **(c)** (*animal*) siffleur *m*, marmotte *f* canadienne, *Can* siffleux *m*

whistle-stop *n Am* **(a)** *Rail* halte *f* (à arrêt facultatif); *Pol* **w. tour** tournée *f* électorale rapide; **a w. tour of Europe** un tour rapide en Europe **(b)** *F* (*village*) patelin *m*, bled *m*

whistling [ˈwɪslɪŋ] *n* sifflement *m*

Whit [wɪt] *adj, n* **W. (Sunday)** (le dimanche de) la Pentecôte; **W. Monday** le lundi de la Pentecôte

whit [wɪt] *n* (*usu in neg*) brin *m*; **it won't make a w. of difference** ça ne changera rien à rien; **it doesn't matter a w.** ça n'a aucune espèce d'importance; **she doesn't care a w. about him or anyone else** elle se fiche de lui comme du reste; **he's not a w. the better for it** il ne s'en porte nullement mieux; **I don't care a w.** je m'en moque comme de ma première chemise *ou* comme de l'an quarante

white¹ [waɪt] **1** *adj* (*bread, hair, wine etc*) blanc, *f* blanche; **as w. as snow** blanc comme la neige; **we had a w. Christmas** on a eu de la neige à Noël; **to turn** *or* **go w.** (*of face*) devenir blanc *ou* pâle *ou* blême; (*of hair*) blanchir; **he's going w.** (*hair*) il commence à blanchir; **he went w. overnight** ses cheveux sont devenus blancs du jour au lendemain; **w. with fear** blanc de peur; **w. as a ghost/sheet** pâle comme la mort/un linge; *Fig* **whiter than w.** (*person*) blanc comme neige; **w. alloy** = **w. metal**; **w. blood-cell** globule *m* blanc, leucocyte *m*; **w. chocolate** chocolat *m* blanc; **w. coffee** café *m* au lait; **do you take your coffee w.?** tu prends du lait dans ton café?; *Br Hist* **w. feather** = symbole *m* de lâcheté; **w. flag** drapeau *m* blanc; **w. flour** farine *f* de ménage; **w. gold** (*platinum*) or *m* blanc; *Com* **w. goods** (*linen*) articles *mpl* de blanc; (*refrigerators, washing machines etc*) appareils *mpl* ménagers; **w. horses** (*waves*) moutons *mpl*; **a w. man** un blanc; **the w. man's burden** = obligation *f* pour les blancs d'assurer l'instruction des habitants noirs de leurs colonies; **w. meat** (*of chicken*) blanc *m*; (*as opposed to red*) viande blanche; **w. metal** métal *m* blanc, antifriction *f*; *Am* **w. sale** solde *m* des articles de blanc; *Culin* **w. sauce** sauce *f* blanche; **w. space** (*on page*) espace *m* blanc; **w. stick** (*of blind person*) canne *f* blanche; *Av Sl* **w. tail, w.-tail plane** avion *m* n'appartenant encore à aucune compagnie aérienne; **w. tie** (*evening dress*) habit *m*; **w.-tie occasion** occasion *f* mondaine *ou* officielle; **w. wedding** mariage *m* en blanc; **she's having a w. wedding** elle se marie en blanc

2 *n* **(a)** (*colour*) blanc *m*; **dressed in w.** habillé en blanc *ou* de blanc; **whites** *Com* linge blanc; *Sp* tenue blanche; **wash your whites with Jizmo** lavez votre linge avec Jizmo
(b) (*person*) blanc *m*, blanche *f*
(c) (*of egg, eyes*) blanc *m*

white² *vt Rel, Fig* **whited sepulchre** sépulcre *m* blanchi

▶ **white out** *vtsep* (*delete*) masquer au vernis correcteur blanc

white ant *n* fourmi *f* blanche, termite *m*

whitebait [ˈwaɪtbeɪt] *n* (*fish*) blanchaille *f*; **a dish of w.** un plat de friture

whiteboard [ˈwaɪtbɔːd] *n* tableau *m* blanc

whitecaps [ˈwaɪtkæps] *npl* (*waves*) moutons *mpl*

white-collar *adj* **w. worker** employé *m* de bureau, col *m* blanc; **w. union** syndicat *m* d'employés de bureau; **w. crime** délits *mpl* financiers

white dwarf *n Astron* naine *f* blanche

white elephant *n Fig* **this is turning into something of a w.** (*of project etc*) cela devient un gouffre sans utilité apparente; **the fear is that the National Library will turn out to be another w.** on craint que la Bibliothèque Nationale ne soit une nouvelle construction coûteuse et peu utile

white ensign *n Naut* pavillon *m* blanc

white-faced [ˈwaɪtˈfeɪst] *adj* au visage pâle

whitefish [ˈwaɪtfɪʃ] *n* corégone *m*

white fish *n Br* (*generic term*) poisson *m* à chair blanche et non huileuse

white-haired *adj* aux cheveux blancs; *Am Fig* **w. boy** chouchou *m*

Whitehall [ˈwaɪthɔːl] *n* (*British government*) l'Administration *f* britannique

white-headed *adj* **(a)** (*animal*) à tête blanche **(b)** (*person*) aux cheveux blancs; *Am Fig* **w. boy** chouchou *m*

white hope *n Sp* grand espoir *m*; **she's our w. for the Olympics** elle est notre espoir pour les jeux Olympiques

white-hot *adj* chauffé *ou* porté à blanc

White House *n* Maison *f* Blanche

white knight *n St Exch* chevalier blanc

white-knuckle *adj F* **I'm a w. flyer** j'ai la trouille en avion; **a w. ride** (*at fair etc*) un tour de manège qui fait peur

white lie *n* pieux mensonge *m*; **I told a w.** j'ai dit un pieux mensonge

white-livered [ˈwaɪtlɪvəd] *adj Fig* (*person*) poltron

white magic *n* magie *f* blanche

white meter heating *n Br* = système *m* de chauffage permettant d'accumuler la chaleur pendant les heures creuses

whiten [ˈwaɪt(ə)n] **1** *vt* **(a)** (*hair, linen, shoes*) blanchir **(b)** (*with whitewash*) blanchir à la chaux, badigeonner de chaux **2** *vi* blanchir; (*with fear etc*) pâlir, blêmir

whiteness [ˈwaɪtnɪs] *n* (*of snow, skin*) blancheur *f*; (*of face*) pâleur *f*

white noise *n* bruit *m* de fond

white-on-black *n Typ* noir au blanc *m*

whiteout [ˈwaɪtaʊt] *n* visibilité *f* nulle (à cause de la neige); **in w. conditions** dans des conditions de visibilité nulle

white paper *n Parl* livre *m* blanc

white pepper *n* poivre *m* blanc

white pudding *n Culin* boudin *m* blanc

White Russia *n Hist* Russie *f* Blanche

white shark *n* requin *m* blanc

white-slaver *n* personne *f* qui se livre à la traite des blanches

white slavery *n* traite *f* des blanches

white spirit *n* white-spirit *m*, *pl* white-spirits

whitethorn [ˈwaɪtθɔːn] *n* (*tree*) aubépine *f*

whitethroat [ˈwaɪtθrəʊt] *n* (*bird*) fauvette *f* grisette

whitewall [ˈwaɪtwɔːl] *n* **w. (tyre** *or US* **tire)** pneu *m* à flanc blanc

whitewash¹ ['waɪtwɒʃ] *n* **(a)** (*paint*) blanc *m ou* lait *m* de chaux, badigeon *m* à la chaux, **to give a wall a coat of w.** badigeonner un mur (à la chaux) **(b)** *Fig* (*dishonest exoneration*) blanchiment *m*; **a w. (job)** une opération de blanchiment **(c)** *Sp F* défaite *f* à zéro, raclée *f*

whitewash² *vt* **(a)** (*paint*) peindre *ou* blanchir à la chaux, badigeonner en blanc **(b)** *Fig* (*exonerate dishonestly*) blanchir; (*events, episode*) maquiller **(c)** *Sp F* (*one's opponents*) battre à plate couture, donner une raclée à

whitewashing ['waɪtwɒʃɪŋ] *n* **(a)** (*painting*) peinture *f* à la chaux, badigeonnage *m* **(b)** *Fig* (*of sb's reputation*) blanchiment *m*

white water *n* eau *f* vive; **white-water rafting** descente *f* en eau vive

white whale *n* bél(o)uga *m*

whitewood ['waɪtwʊd] *n* bois *m* blanc

whitey ['waɪtɪ] *n US Pej* blanc *m*, blanche *f*; (*npl*) les blancs

whither ['wɪðər] *adv, conj Arch, Lit* **(a)** (*interr*) où, vers quel lieu; **w. Britain?** où va la Grande-Bretagne? **(b)** (*rel*) (là) où; **I shall go w. fate leads me** j'irai là où me mènera le destin

whiting ['waɪtɪŋ] *n* (*fish*) merlan *m*

whitish ['waɪtɪʃ] *adj* blanchâtre

whitlow ['wɪtləʊ] *n Med* panaris *m*

Whitney system *n* (*in hotel*) planning *m* Whitney

Whitsun(tide) ['wɪtsən(taɪd)] *n* (la fête *ou* la saison de) la Pentecôte

whittle ['wɪt(ə)l] *vt* (*stick*) tailler (au couteau)

▶ **whittle away** *vtsep* (*one's capital*) rogner, manger; (*resistance*) faire tomber petit à petit; **our capital/lead has been whittled away** notre capital/avance a été réduit(e) à presque rien

▶ **whittle down** *vtsep* (*one's capital*) rogner, manger; **we've whittled down the number of candidates** nous avons réduit le nombre des candidats; **can you w. it down by another 5%?** peux-tu le réduire d'encore 5%?

Whitworth thread [wɪtwəθ] *n MecE* filetage *m* Whitworth

whizz¹ [wɪz] **1** *int* pan! **2** *n* **(a)** (*of bullet*) sifflement *m* **(b)** *F* (*expert*) as *m*, crack *m* **(at** en**)**; **he's a real w. in the kitchen** il cuisine comme un chef; **she's a real w. with computers** c'est un as en informatique

whizz² *vi* **(a)** (*of bullet etc*) siffler **(b)** *F* (*move quickly*) **we were whizzing along at top speed** on fonçait; **the cars whizzed past** les voitures passaient à toute allure; **she whizzed back into the house to get some money** elle retourna dare-dare à la maison chercher de l'argent

▶ **whizz by** *vi F* (*of traffic*) passer à toute vitesse; (*of holiday, time etc*) passer à toute vitesse, filer

▶ **whizz through** *vipo F* (*work*) faire à toute vitesse; (*meal*) avaler; (*book*) lire à toute vitesse

whizz kid *n F* jeune prodige *m*

WHO [dʌb(ə)ljuːeɪtʃ'əʊ] *n* (*abbr* **World Health Organization**) OMS *f*

who [huː] *pron* **(a)** [①**A31**,a; **B16**,3,b] (*interr*) (*subject*) qui, qui est-ce qui; (*object*) qui, qui est-ce que; **w. is it?** qui est-ce?; **w. with?** avec qui?; **w. is that woman?** qui est cette femme?; **w. on earth told you that?** qui diable vous a dit cela?; *Tel* **w.'s speaking?** qui est à l'appareil?; *Tel* **may I ask w.'s speaking?** (*when taking call for another*) c'est de la part de qui?; **w. is this?** (*on telephone*) qui êtes-vous?; **w. did you say?** qui ça?; **w. does he think he is?** pour qui se prend-il?; **w. of us can still remember it?** qui parmi nous *ou* lesquels d'entre nous se le rappelle(nt) encore?; **w. do you want?** qui voulez-vous?; **w. were you talking to?** à qui parliez-vous?; **to know w.'s w.** (*the right people*) avoir des relations; **you'll soon find out w.'s w.** (*who people are*) tu connaîtras très vite tout le monde; **tell me w.'s w.** dites-moi qui est qui

(b) [①**A32**,a-d; **B20**,F,1-3d] (*rel*) qui; (*to avoid ambiguity*) *Fml* lequel, laquelle, *pl* lesquels, lesquelles; (*independent rel*) (celui/celle/*etc*) qui; **the friends w. came yesterday** les amis qui sont venus hier; **Louise's father, w. is very rich** le père de Louise, qui *ou Fml* lequel est très riche; **deny it w. will** le nie qui voudra

whoa [wəʊ] *int* (*to horse*) ho!, holà!; *F* (*to person*) doucement!, attendez!

whodun(n)it [huː'dʌnɪt] *n F* (*novel*) roman *m* policier; (*film*) film *m* policier

whoever [huː'evər] *pron* **(a)** (*anyone that*) celui/celle/*etc* qui, quiconque; **w. finds it may keep it** celui qui le trouvera pourra le garder **(b)** [①**A33**,h] (*no matter who*) qui que + *sub*; **w. you are, speak!** qui que vous soyez, parlez!; **w. wrote that letter** qui que ce soit qui ait écrit cette lettre; *F* **... or w. ...** ou qui que ce soit; **w. she marries** qui que ce soit qu'elle épousera, celui qu'elle épousera; **w. you like** qui vous voudrez **(c)** [①**A31**,e] (*intensive*) **w. can that be at this time of night?** qui cela peut-il bien être à cette heure tardive?

whole [həʊl] **1** *adj* **(a)** [①**A36**,d,iii] (*entire*) entier, complet, -ète; **cook the fish w.** faites cuire le poisson entier; **he swallowed it w.** (*food*) il l'a avalé sans le mâcher; *Fig* il a pris ça pour de l'argent comptant; **a w. loaf** un pain entier; **to tell the w. truth** dire toute la vérité; **the w. world** le monde entier; **do you have to tell the w. world?** est-ce que tu tiens à ce que tout le monde le sache?; **to last a w. week** durer toute une semaine; **I never saw her the w. evening** je ne l'ai pas vue de (toute) la soirée; **w. families died of it** des familles entières en sont mortes; *F* **to go the w. hog** aller jusqu'au bout; **they went the w. hog for the party** ils n'ont pas fait les choses à moitié pour la fête; **w. milk** lait *m* entier; *Math* **w. number** nombre *m* entier

(b) (*emphatic*) tout, entier, tout entier; **I don't think it will make a w. lot of difference** je ne pense pas que ça fasse une énorme différence; **we've had a w. heap of problems** nous avons eu tout un tas de problèmes; **the w. lot of you** vous tous; **there's still a w. lot left** il en reste encore plein; **for a w. lot of reasons** pour tout un tas de raisons

(c) (*intact*) (*thing*) intact; *Bible* **his hand was made w.** sa main fut guérie

2 *n* tout *m*, totalité *f*, ensemble *m*; **the w. of the school** l'école entière, toute l'école; **nearly the w. of our resources** la presque totalité de nos ressources; **he spent the w. of that year in London** il a passé toute cette année-là à Londres; **the w. amounts to ...** le total se monte à ...; **to buy/sell sth as a w.** acheter/vendre qch en bloc; **taken as a w.** pris dans sa totalité; **on the w.** dans l'ensemble; **the w. is greater than the sum of its parts** le tout est plus grand que la somme des parties

wholefood ['həʊlfuːd] *n* aliments *mpl* complets; **w. restaurant** restaurant *m* biologique

wholehearted [həʊl'hɑːtɪd] *adj* (*enthusiasm, support etc*) sans réserve; (*laugh*) qui vient du cœur; **she was less than w. in her endorsement of him** elle ne l'approuvait qu'à moitié; **a w. admirer** un admirateur inconditionnel; **she had never really been w. in her commitment to Europe** elle n'a jamais été convaincue à 100% par l'Europe

wholeheartedly [həʊl'hɑːtɪdlɪ] *adv* de bon *ou* de grand *ou* de tout cœur; (*to agree*) de tout cœur; **to support sb w.** soutenir qn sans réserve *ou* inconditionnellement; **I admire you w.** je vous admire sans réserve

wholemeal ['həʊlmiːl] *adj Br* **w. bread** pain *m* complet; **w. flour** farine *f* complète

wholeness ['həʊlnɪs] *n* intégralité *f*, intégrité *f*

wholesale ['həʊlseɪl] **1** *n* (vente *f* en) gros *m*; **w. and retail** gros et détail

2 *adj* **(a)** *Com* de gros, en gros; **w. bank** banque *f* de gros; **w. co-operative** coopérative *f* d'achats; **w. dealer** *or* **merchant** grossiste *mf*, commerçant, -ante en gros; *Banking* **w. market** marché *m* de gré à gré entre banques; **w. price index** indice *m* des prix de gros; **w. price** prix *m* de *ou* en gros; **w. trade** commerce *m* de *ou* en gros

(b) *Fig* **by w. borrowing** en empruntant de tous côtés; **a w. slaughter** un massacre, une tuerie en masse

3 *adv* **(a) to sell/buy w.** vendre/acheter en gros; **I can get it for you w.** je peux vous l'avoir au prix de gros

(b) *Fig* en masse, en bloc; **communities have been destroyed w.** des communautés entières ont été détruites

wholesaler ['həʊlseɪlər] *n* grossiste *mf*, commerçant, -ante en gros; **w. margin** marge *f* du grossiste

wholesaling ['həʊlseɪlɪŋ] *n* vente *f* en gros

wholesome ['həʊlsəm] *adj* (*food*) sain; (*air, climate*) salubre; (*person, appearance*) comme il faut; **a very w. young man** un petit jeune homme propre sur lui; **she has a w. appearance** elle a l'air rangé, elle a l'air (bien) comme il faut

wholesomeness ['həʊlsəmnɪs] *n* (*of food*) nature *f* saine; (*of air*) salubrité *f*; **the w. of her appearance** son côté rangé *ou* (bien) comme il faut

whole-wheat *adj Am* **w. bread** pain *m* complet

wholly ['həʊllɪ] *adv* tout à fait, complètement, entièrement

wholly-owned subsidiary *n* filiale *f* à 100%

whom [huːm] *pron* (*objective case*) *often Fml* **(a)** [①**A31**,a; **B16**,3,b] (*interr*) qui, qui est-ce que; **w. did you see?** qui avez-vous vu?, qui est-ce que vous avez vu?; **to w./of w. are you speaking?** à qui/de qui parlez-vous?; **I don't know to w. to turn** je ne sais à qui m'adresser

(b) [①**A32**,a-c; **B20-21**,F,1-3d] (*rel*) (*direct object*) que, lequel, laquelle, *pl* lesquels, lesquelles; (*indirect object and after prep*) qui; **the woman w. you saw** la femme que vous avez vue; **somebody to w. he could talk** quelqu'un à qui il pouvait parler; **the friend of w. I speak** l'ami dont je parle; **these two men, both of w. were quite young** ces deux hommes, qui l'un et l'autre étaient tout jeunes

(c) (*independent rel*) celui/celle/*etc* que, qui; **those w. the gods love die young** qui est aimé des dieux meurt jeune

whomsoever [hu:msəʊ'evər] *pron Fml* (a) (*any person whom*) celui (quel qu'il soit) que; **w. they choose** celui qu'ils choisiront (b) (*no matter whom*) qui que ce soit que

whoop[1] *n* (a) [wu:p] (*shout*) cri *m* (de joie); *Am* (*of owl*) (h)ululement *m* (b) [hu:p] *Med* (*in whooping cough*) quinte *f*

whoop[2] *vi* (a) [wu:p] (*shout*) crier, pousser des cris (de joie); *Am* (*of owl*) (h)ululer; *F* **to w. it up** (*have good time, celebrate*) faire la noce (b) [hu:p] *Med* tousser convulsivement à cause d'une coqueluche; **she's been whooping all night** elle a eu des quintes de toux toute la nuit

whoopee 1 [wʊ'pi:] *int* youpi **2** ['wʊpi:] *n Old-fashioned F* **to make w.** (*enjoy oneself*) faire la noce *ou* la bombe; (*sexually*) faire l'amour

whooper ['hu:pər] *n* **w. swan** cygne *m* chanteur *ou* sauvage

whooping cough ['hu:pɪŋ] *n* coqueluche *f*

whoops [wʊps] *int* houp-là!

whop [wɒp] *vt* (**-pp-**) *F* (a) (*hit*) battre, rosser (b) (*defeat*) battre à plates coutures, massacrer

whopper ['wɒpər] *n F* (a) (*huge thing*) quelque chose de colossal *ou* d'énorme; **a w. of a fish** un poisson énorme *ou* maous(se); **it's a real w.!** il est énorme! (b) (*lie*) énorme *ou* gros mensonge *m*

whopping ['wɒpɪŋ] *F* **1** *adj* énorme; **w. great** *or* **huge** énorme; **a w. great lie** un énorme *ou* gros mensonge **2** *n* rossée *f*, raclée *f*

whore[1] [hɔ:r] *n* prostituée *f*, *Sl* putain *f*; *Sl* **w. house** bordel *m*

whore[2] *vi Old-fashioned, Lit* (*of man*) **to w., to go whoring** fréquenter les prostituées

whoremonger ['hɔ:mʌŋgər] *n Arch* habitué *m* des lieux de débauche; **he was a w.** il fréquentait les filles de petite vertu

whoring ['hɔ:rɪŋ] *n Old-fashioned, Lit* (a) (*by woman*) prostitution *f* (b) (*by man*) **because of all his w.** parce qu'il n'arrêtait pas de fréquenter les prostituées

whorl [wɜ:l] *n* (a) *Bot* verticille *m* (b) (*turn of spiral*) spire *f*, volute *f*; (*of shell*) spire, enroulement *m*; (*of fingerprint*) sillon *m*

whorled [wɜ:ld] *adj* (*flower*) verticillé; (*shell*) convoluté

whortleberry ['wɜ:t(ə)lberɪ] *n* (*fruit*) airelle *f* myrtille

whose [hu:z] *poss pron* (a) (*interr*) [①**A31**,b] de qui; (*ownership*) à qui; **w. are these gloves?** à qui sont ces gants?; **w. daughter are you?** de qui êtes-vous la fille?; **w. fault is it?** à qui la faute?; **w. book did you borrow?** à qui avez-vous emprunté un livre?; **w. is this?** à qui est-ce? (b) [①**A32**,e; **B21**,e,ii] (*rel*) dont; (*after prep*) de qui, duquel, de laquelle, *pl* desquels, desquelles; **the pupil w. work I showed you** l'élève dont je vous ai montré le travail; **the man to w. wife I gave the money** l'homme à la femme de qui *ou* duquel j'ai donné l'argent

whosoever [hu:səʊ'evər] *pron Arch, Fml* = **whoever**

Who's Who *n Br* ≈ Bottin *m* Mondain

why [waɪ] **1** *adv, conj* (a) [①**A40**,C,1,a] (*interr*) pourquoi, pour quelle raison; **w. (ever) didn't you say so?** pourquoi ne l'avez-vous pas dit?; **w. not?** pourquoi pas?; **w. not agree?** pourquoi ne pas accepter?; **w. bother?** à quoi bon (s'en donner la peine)?; **w. get angry?** à quoi bon se mettre en colère?

(b) (*rel*) pourquoi; **that is (the reason) w. ...** voilà pourquoi ..., c'est pourquoi ...; **w. he should always be late I do not understand** qu'il soit toujours en retard, je ne me l'explique pas; **I'll tell you w.** je vais vous dire pourquoi

2 *n* (*pl* **whys**) pourquoi *m*, raison *f*; **I like to know the whys and wherefores of things** j'aime connaître le pourquoi et le comment des choses

3 *int* (a) (*surprise*) **w., it's David!** tiens, mais c'est David!; **w., you're not afraid, are you?** vous n'avez tout de même pas peur, si?

(b) (*protest*) **w., it's simple** allons, c'est simple; **w., what's the harm?** mais quel mal y a-t-il?

(c) (*hesitation*) **w., I really don't know** vraiment *ou* franchement je ne sais pas

(d) (*introducing consequence*) **if this doesn't do, w. we must try something else** si ceci ne réussit pas, alors *ou* eh bien il faudra essayer autre chose

WI [dʌb(ə)lju:'aɪ] *n* (a) *Br abbr* **Women's Institute** (b) *abbr* **West Indies**

wick [wɪk] *n* (a) (*of lamp, candle*) mèche *f* (b) *Br Sl* **she gets on my w.** elle me tape sur les nerfs; **it gets on my w. that he's always there** ça me tape sur les nerfs qu'il soit toujours là

wicked ['wɪkɪd] **1** *adj* (a) (*evil*) mauvais, méchant; (*crime*) atroce, affreux; **what a w. thing to do!** qu'est-ce que c'est méchant!; **a w. lie** un affreux mensonge; *F* **you w. little thing!** (*to child*) petit vilain!/petite vilaine!

(b) *Fig* (*dreadful*) (*weather*) affreux, atroce; (*pain*) cruel, atroce; **he's got a w. temper** il a très mauvais caractère; **it's w. to waste so much food** c'est un crime de gaspiller tant de nourriture; **they're asking a w. price for their house** ils ont mis leur maison en vente à un prix exorbitant; **it's a w. shame that ...** il est scandaleux que ... + *sub*

(c) *Fig* (*mischievous*) malicieux, espiègle

(d) *Sl* (*good*) génial, super; **she makes a w. curry** elle fait un curry d'enfer

2 *npl* **the w.** les méchants *mpl*; *Hum* **(there's) no rest for the w.** pas de répit pour les braves

wickedly ['wɪkɪdlɪ] *adv* (a) (*evilly*) méchamment (b) *Fig* (*extremely*) terriblement, affreusement; **w. expensive** hors de prix; **w. funny** à mourir de rire; **she makes a w. good curry** elle fait un curry extra (c) (*mischievously*) malicieusement; **she was smiling w.** elle souriait d'un air malicieux

wickedness ['wɪkɪdnɪs] *n* méchanceté *f*, perversité *f*; (*of crime*) atrocité *f*

wicker ['wɪkər] *n* osier *m*; **a w. basket/chair** un panier/une chaise en osier

wickerwork ['wɪkəwɜ:k] *n* (*objects*) vannerie *f*, objets *mpl* en osier; **w. chair** chaise en osier *ou* en vannerie

wicket ['wɪkɪt] *n* (a) (*beside large door etc*) **w. (door)** porte *f* à piétons; **w. (gate)** petite porte à claire-voie; (*at level crossing*) portillon *m* (b) *Am* (*in bank, post office etc*) guichet *m* (c) *Cr* (*sticks*) guichet *m*; (*area*) terrain *m* entre les guichets; **to take/lose a w.** prendre/perdre un guichet; **to keep w.** garder les guichets

wicketkeeper ['wɪkɪtki:pər] *n Cr* gardien *m* de guichet

wide [waɪd] **1** *adj* (a) (*broad*) (*road, river*) large; (*desert, ocean*) vaste; (*garment*) ample, large; **the road gets wider after the village** la route s'élargit après le village; **to be five metres w.** faire cinq mètres de large *ou* de largeur; **how w. is the room?** quelle est la largeur de la pièce?, combien est-ce que la pièce fait de large?; **to travel the w. world** parcourir le vaste monde; **in the whole w. world** dans le monde entier; **to give a w. yawn** bâiller en ouvrant largement la bouche; *Phot* **w. angle of view** grand angle de champ; *Aut* **w. load** (*notice on vehicle*) = convoi exceptionnel; *Cin* **w. screen** grand écran

(b) (*extensive*) (*range, experience, knowledge*) étendu, vaste, ample; (*influence*) répandu; **there is a w. difference between ...** il y a une grande différence entre ...; **in a wider sense** dans un sens plus large, par extension; **in the widest sense of the word** dans l'acception la plus large du mot

(c) *Br F* **a w. boy** un fricoteur

2 *adv* (a) (*far*) loin; **w. apart** espacé; **with one's legs w. apart** les jambes très écartées

(b) (*to open etc*) largement, grandement; **to fling the door open w.** *or* **w. open** ouvrir la porte toute grande; **w.-open door** porte toute grande ouverte; **to open one's eyes w.** ouvrir les yeux tout grands; **to be w. awake** être complètement *ou* bien éveillé; *Fig* avoir l'esprit vif; *Boxing* **to leave oneself w. open** se découvrir; *Fig* **to leave oneself w. open to criticism** prêter le flanc à *ou* s'exposer à la critique; **this town is w. open (to attack)** cette ville est très exposée (aux attaques); *Aut* **to take a bend w.** prendre un virage large

(c) (*to fall, shoot*) loin du but; **w. of the mark** (*far from target*) loin du but; (*far from truth*) loin de la réalité *ou* de la vérité

3 *n Cr* balle *f* écartée *ou* qui passe hors de la portée du batteur

wide-angle *adj Phot* **w. lens** objectif *m* grand angle; *Cin* **w. shot** panoramique *m*

wide area network *n Comptr* grand réseau *m*, réseau longue distance

wide-body *adj Av* **w. plane** avion *m* à fuselage élargi

wide-eyed *adj* les yeux grands ouverts, les yeux écarquillés; **he looked at me in w. amazement** il m'a regardé avec des yeux grands comme des soucoupes, il m'a regardé les yeux écarquillés

widely ['waɪdlɪ] *adv* (a) (*extensively*) largement; **she has travelled w.** elle a beaucoup voyagé; **it is w. thought** *or* **believed that ...** on pense couramment *ou* communément que ...; **w. known** très connu, connu partout; **w. different versions of what happened** des versions très différentes des événements (b) (*at a distance*) **w. spaced** très espacé

widely-read *adj* **to be w.** (*of person*) avoir beaucoup lu; (*of author*) avoir un public très étendu; (*of book, newspaper*) être très lu; **the Bible remains the most w. of all books** la Bible demeure le livre le plus lu

widen ['waɪd(ə)n] **1** *vt* (a) (*road, channel, garment, hole*) élargir (b) (*influence, limits of sth*) étendre **2** *vi* (a) s'élargir;

the breach is widening la rupture s'accentue **(b)** (*of influence*) s'étendre
▶ **widen out** *vi* (*of road, river, valley*) s'élargir
wideness ['waɪdnɪs] *n* largeur *f*
widening ['waɪd(ə)nɪŋ] *n* **(a)** (*of road, channel*) élargissement *m* **(b)** (*of influence*) extension *f*
widespread ['waɪdspred] *adj* (*belief, poverty*) répandu; **w. opinion** opinion largement répandue *ou* généralement admise; **w. damage** des dégâts importants
widgeon ['wɪdʒən] *n* (*bird*) canard *m* siffleur
widget ['wɪdʒɪt] *n Br F* truc *m*
widow[1] ['wɪdəʊ] *n also Typ* veuve *f*; **she was left a w. at (the age of) thirty** elle a été veuve à l'âge de trente ans; *F* **golf w.** femme *f* délaissée par son mari qui joue constamment au golf; *Bible, Fig* **w.'s mite** denier *m* de la veuve; **w.'s peak** pointe *f* sur le front que forme la racine des cheveux; **w.'s pension** pension *f* de veuve; **w.'s weeds** deuil *m* de veuve
widow[2] *vt* **to be widowed** (*of man*) devenir veuf; (*of woman*) devenir veuve
widowed ['wɪdəʊd] *adj* (*man*) veuf; (*woman*) veuve; **his w. mother** sa mère qui est/était veuve
widower ['wɪdəʊər] *n* veuf *m*
widowhood ['wɪdəʊhʊd] *n* veuvage *m*
width [wɪdθ] *n* **(a)** (*of road, chest*) largeur *f*; (*of garment*) ampleur *f*; (*of tyre*) grosseur *f*; (*of cloth, wallpaper*) lé *m*, laize *f*, largeur *f*; **to be three metres in w.** avoir trois mètres de large **(b)** (*of knowledge, Mktg of product range*) largeur *f* **(c)** (*of swimming pool*) largeur *f*; **to swim six widths (of the pool)** nager six largeurs
widthways ['wɪdθweɪz], **widthwise** ['wɪdθwaɪz] *adv* dans la largeur, en largeur
wield [wi:ld] *vt* **(a)** (*handle*) (*sword, pen*) manier; *Fig* (*power, influence*) exercer **(b)** (*brandish*) (*weapon, stick*) brandir
Wiener ['vi:nər] *n Culin* **W. schnitzel** escalope *f* viennoise
wiener ['wi:nər] *n Am* **(a)** saucisse *f* de Frankfort; **w. roast** barbecue *m* de saucisses de Frankfort **(b)** *Sl* (*penis*) zizi *m*
wife, *pl* **wives** [waɪf, waɪvz] *n* **(a)** femme *f* (mariée); *esp Admin* épouse *f*; **Mr Martin and his w.** M. Martin et sa femme; **she was his second w.** c'était sa deuxième femme; **the baker's w.** (*who is also a baker*) la boulangère; (*who is not a baker*) la femme du boulanger; *Br F* **the w.** ma/ta/*etc* moitié **(b)** *Arch* (*woman*) femme *f*
wifely ['waɪflɪ] *adj* de bonne épouse
wife-swapping ['waɪfswɒpɪŋ] *n* échangisme *m*; **w. party** soirée *f* échangiste
wig [wɪg] *n* (*full length*) perruque *f*; (*hairpiece*) postiche *m*; *Br* (*for lawyers*) perruque; **she's wearing a w.** elle porte une perruque
wigeon ['wɪdʒən] *n* (*bird*) canard *m* siffleur
wigged [wɪgd] *adj* (*judge etc*) à perruque
wigging ['wɪgɪŋ] *n Old-fashioned Br F* réprimande *f*; **to give sb a good w.** attraper qn; **to get a good w.** se faire passer un savon
wiggle[1] ['wɪg(ə)l] *n* (*of body etc*) tortillement *m*; **to give sth a w.** agiter *ou* remuer qch; **she gave her hips a seductive w.** elle marchait en tortillant les fesses
wiggle[2] **1** *vt* agiter, remuer; **he wiggled his backside** il remuait du derrière; **to w. one's toes** remuer ses orteils; **to w. one's hips** tortiller les hanches; **to w. one's way out of a difficulty** se tirer *ou* s'extraire d'une position difficile **2** *vi* (*of person, snake*) se remuer, se tortiller; (*of fish*) frétiller; **stop wiggling!** arrête de te tortiller!; *Fig* **to try to w. out of it** chercher une échappatoire; **don't try to w. out of it!** n'essaie pas de t'en tirer comme ça!; **to w. out of a difficulty** se tirer *ou* s'extraire d'une position difficile
wiggly ['wɪglɪ] *adj F* (*snake etc*) qui se remue *ou* se tortille; **w. line** trait ondulé
wigmaker ['wɪgmeɪkər] *n* perruquier, -ière
wigwam ['wɪgwæm] *n* wigwam *m*
wilco ['wɪlkəʊ] *int esp Rad* (= **will comply**) j'exécute
wild[1] [waɪld] **1** *adj* **(a)** (*animal, plant*) sauvage; **w. and woolly** (*untamed*) frustre, rustre; (*not thought out*) irréfléchi; **w. country** pays *m* inculte *ou* sauvage; **w. cherry (tree)** merisier *m*; **w. dog** chien *m* sauvage; **w. flowers** fleurs *fpl* des champs *ou* sauvages; **w. goose** oie *f* sauvage; *Fig* **w. horses wouldn't drag it out of me** rien au monde ne me le ferait dire; **w. man** sauvage *m*; *Pol* extrémiste *m*; *Fig* **to sow one's w. oats** jeter sa gourme; **w. rice** riz *m* sauvage

(b) (*wind*) furieux, violent; **the weather's been pretty w.** les éléments se sont déchaînés; *Naut* **in w. weather** par gros temps; **w. sea** mer agitée; **a w. (and stormy) night** une nuit de tempête

(c) (*unrestrained*) (*person*) dissipé, dissolu; (*adolescent*) indiscipliné; (*behaviour*) déréglé; (*idea*) délirant, abracadabrant; (*project*) insensé, extravagant; (*party*) fou, *f* folle, déchaîné; **he's got some pretty w. friends** certains de ses amis sont de vrais casse-cou; **what a w. thing to do!** quelle inconscience!; **I'm worried by all his w. talk** tous ses propos irréfléchis m'inquiètent; **having so much money is beyond my wildest dreams** même dans mes rêves les plus fous je n'aurais jamais espéré posséder autant d'argent; **to make a w. rush at sth** se ruer sur qch; **w. applause** applaudissements frénétiques; **w. enthusiasm** enthousiasme délirant *ou* débordant; **w. eyes** yeux égarés; **w. with joy/rage** fou de joie/rage; **it makes me w. to think that ...** j'enrage *ou* cela me met en rage quand je pense que ...; **to drive sb w.** mettre qn en fureur; **w. promises** promesses extravagantes *ou* insensées; **w. rumour** bruit extravagant *ou* sans fondation

(d) (*random*) **it was just a w. guess** c'était un coup au hasard; **to make a w. guess (at the answer)** répondre à tout hasard *ou* à l'aveuglette; **some of the estimates were pretty w.** certaines des estimations étaient complètement à côté

(e) *Cards* libre; **the Joker is w.** le joker peut être joué n'importe quand; *Fig* **w. card** élément *m* imprévisible

(f) *F* (*enthusiastic*) **to be w. about sb/sth** être emballé par qn/qch, être dingue de qn/qch; **I'm not w. about it** ça ne m'emballe pas

2 *adv* **to grow w.** (*of plant*) pousser à l'état sauvage; **to run w.** (*of children*) mener une vie sans discipline; (*of hooligans*) se livrer à des actes de violence; (*of escaped bull etc*) s'emballer; (*of garden*) être laissé à l'abandon, être abandonné; **their children are allowed to run w.** leurs enfants peuvent faire tout et n'importe quoi

3 *n* **in the w.** (*of animal*) à l'état sauvage; **the call of the w.** l'appel de la nature; **in the wilds** dans une région sauvage *ou* déserte; **he lives in the wilds of Africa/Ealing** il habite au fin fond de l'Afrique/d'Ealing
wild[2] *vi Am Sl* = effectuer, en bande, des actes de violence extrême contre des personnes
wildcard ['waɪldkɑ:d] *n Comptr* joker *m*; **w. character** caractère *m* joker
wildcat[1] ['waɪldkæt] *n* **(a)** (*animal*) chat *m* sauvage; *Fig* **she's a w.** c'est une tigresse; *Am Fig* **w. scheme** projet *m* extravagant *ou* risqué; *Fig* **w. strike** grève *f* sauvage **(b)** *Am Petr* **w. (well)** forage *m* d'exploration **(c)** *Mktg* **wildcats** dilemmes *mpl*
wildcat[2] *vi Am Petr* faire un forage d'exploration
wildcatter ['waɪldkætər] *n Am Petr* (*company*) entrepreneur *m* de forage d'exploration; (*driller*) ouvrier *m* qui effectue des forages d'exploration
wildebeest ['wɪldɪbi:st, 'vɪl-] *n* (*animal*) gnou *m*
wilder ['waɪldər] *n Am Sl* = membre *m* d'une bande de jeunes voyous effectuant des actes de violence extrême contre des personnes
wilderness ['wɪldənɪs] *n* **(a)** (*desert*) désert *m*; **an economic w.** un désert économique; **a voice in the w.** une voix qui prêche dans le désert; *Fig* **to be in the w.** (*of politician, party*) faire sa traversée du désert; *Fig* **during his w. years** pendant sa traversée du désert; **the party believes that the w. years may be about to end** le parti pense que sa traversée du désert touche à sa fin **(b)** (*overgrown garden*) jungle *f*; **the garden is turning into a w.** le jardin est en train de se transformer en jungle
wildfire ['waɪldfaɪər] *n* **to spread like w.** (*of news*) se répandre comme une traînée de poudre; (*of disease*) se propager très rapidement
wildfowl ['waɪldfaʊl] *n* gibier *m* d'eau, sauvagine *f*
wild-goose chase *n* fausse piste *f*; **the search for the information was a real w.** on a cherché en vain les renseignements; **I've been on a w. round town trying to get the fabric** j'ai couru toute la ville pour rien à la recherche du tissu; **to go on a w.** faire fausse piste; **to send sb on a w.** mettre qn sur une fausse piste
wilding ['waɪldɪŋ] *n Am Sl* = actes *mpl* de violence extrême effectués par une bande de voyous contre des personnes
wildlife ['waɪldlaɪf] *n* faune *f* (et flore *f*); **w. film** film *m* animalier; *esp Br* **w. park** parc *m* naturel; **w. programme** émission *f* sur les animaux; **w. reserve** *or* **sanctuary** réserve *f* naturelle
wildly ['waɪldlɪ] *adv* **(a)** (*without control*) (*to behave*) sans contraintes; (*to cheer*) frénétiquement; (*to applaud*) à tout rompre; **to talk w.** dire des folies; **to talk w. of suicide** tenir des propos insensés de suicide; **the children had been behaving w. all afternoon** les enfants ont été intenables toute l'après-midi; **to rush about w.** courir comme un fou; **her heart was beating w.** son cœur battait à tout rompre; **prices have been fluctuating w.** les prix ont subi des fluctuations violentes

(b) (*at random*) (*to answer, guess*) au hasard, au petit bonheur; **by now it was clear that he was guessing w.** il était clair qu'il répondait au hasard; **to hit out w.** lancer des coups au hasard

(c) (*as intensifier*) (*expensive, funny etc*) extrêmement; **w. inaccurate** dramatiquement inexact; **w. happy** follement heureux, aux anges; **to be w. excited** être surexcité; **w. exaggerated** follement exagéré; **it's not w. encouraging** ça n'est pas franchement encourageant; **I'm not w. enthusiastic about it** je ne suis pas franchement emballé

wildness ['waɪldnɪs] *n* **(a)** (*of country, animal*) état *m* sauvage; (*of region*) état inculte **(b)** (*of wind, waves*) fureur *f*, violence *f*; (*of storm*) violence **(c)** (*of applause*) frénésie *f*; (*of ideas, words*) extravagance *f*

Wild West *n* Far West *m*

wiles [waɪlz] *npl* ruses *fpl*, artifices *mpl*; **he used all of his w. to persuade her** il l'a persuadée à force de ruse(s) *ou* d'artifice(s); **to fall a victim to sb's w.** succomber aux séductions de qn

wilful, *US* **willful** ['wɪlfʊl] *adj* **(a)** (*stubborn*) obstiné, entêté, volontaire **(b)** (*deliberate*) délibéré, intentionnel, volontaire; *Jur* **w. murder** homicide *m* volontaire *ou* prémédité; **w. damage** bris *m*, dommage *m* délibéré; **with w. intent** délibérément

wilfully, *US* **willfully** ['wɪlfəlɪ] *adv* **(a)** (*stubbornly*) obstinément, avec entêtement; **she has behaved quite w. over this issue** elle n'en a fait qu'à sa tête pour cette question **(b)** (*deliberately*) délibérément; **are you being w. obtuse?** est-ce que tu fais exprès de faire l'idiot?

wilfulness, *US* **willfulness** ['wɪlfʊlnɪs] *n* **(a)** (*stubbornness*) obstination *f*, entêtement *m*; **the sheer w. of his refusal** son refus obstiné *ou* entêté **(b)** (*deliberateness*) caractère *m* délibéré

wiliness ['waɪlɪnɪs] *n* astuce *f*, caractère *m* rusé

will[1] [wɪl] *n* **(a)** (*faculty, determination*) volonté *f*; **to have a strong/weak w.** avoir beaucoup/peu de volonté; **w. of iron, iron w.** volonté de fer; **he has a w. of his own** il sait ce qu'il veut, il est volontaire; **strength of w.** force *f* de volonté; **the w. to live** la volonté de survivre; **she seems to have lost the w. to live** elle semble avoir perdu sa volonté de vivre; **good/ill w.** bienveillance *f*/malveillance *f*; **to show good w.** faire preuve de bonne volonté; **I bear her no ill w.** (*have no wish for revenge*) je ne lui en veux pas; (*do not dislike her*) je ne lui veux aucun mal; **to work with a w.** travailler de bon cœur *ou* avec détermination; **with the best w. in the world** avec la meilleure volonté du monde; *Prov* **where there's a w. there's a way** vouloir c'est pouvoir

(b) (*desire, wish*) volonté *f*, désir *m*; **the w. of the people** la volonté du peuple; **to impose one's w. on sb** imposer sa volonté à qn; **at w.** (*to choose, fire*) à volonté; (*to depart etc*) quand on veut; **free w.** libre arbitre *m*; **to do sth of one's own free w.** faire qch de son plein gré; **to do sth against one's w.** faire qch contre son gré *ou* à contrecœur; *Bible* **Thy w. be done** que ta volonté soit faite

(c) *Jur* testament *m*; **the last w. and testament of ...** les dernières volontés de ...; **to make one's w.** faire son testament; **to mention sb in one's w.** mettre *ou* coucher qn sur son testament

will[2] *vt* **(-ll-) (a) to w. sb to do** *or* **into doing sth** faire faire qch à qn (par la volonté), souhaiter ardemment que qn fasse qch; (*by hypnotism*) suggestionner à qn de faire qch; **the crowd was willing him to win** la foule voulait absolument qu'il gagne; **she was willing her child to live** elle souhaitait de toutes ses forces que son enfant survive; **you can't just w. these things to happen** on ne peut pas faire arriver ces choses par un simple acte de volonté; **to w. oneself to do sth** faire un effort de volonté pour faire qch; *Arch, Lit* **God so willed it** Dieu l'a voulu ainsi

(b) *Jur* (*leave in one's will*) **to w. sth** léguer qch, disposer de qch par testament; **to w. sth to sb** léguer qch à qn

will[3] *modal, aux v* [①A55-56,18,a] **(I will, you/he/we/***etc* **will;** *Arch* **thou wilt**; *pt, cond* **would** [wʊd]; **I will, he will** *etc are often contracted into* **I'll** [aɪl], **he'll** [hiːl] *etc*; **I would, they would** *etc to* **I'd** [aɪd], **they'd** [ðeɪd] *etc*; **will not** *and* **would not** *to* **won't** [wəʊnt], **wouldn't** ['wʊd(ə)nt])

(a) [①A49,12] (*expressing future*) **I'll do it tomorrow** je le ferai demain; **he won't do it again** il ne le fera plus; **w. he be there? – he w.** y sera-t-il? – oui (il y sera); **w. he be there? – no, he won't** y sera-t-il? – non (il n'y sera pas); **but I shall starve! – no, you won't** mais je vais mourir de faim! – mais non!; **you won't forget, w. you?** vous n'oublierez pas, hein?; **you'll write to me, won't you?** vous m'écrirez, n'est-ce pas?; **we w. be there** nous serons là; **Mr Long w. explain the situation to you** (*immediate future*) M. Long va vous expliquer la situation

(b) (*consent*) **I w. not do it** je refuse de le faire; **I w. not have that said of me** je ne veux pas qu'on dise cela de moi; *F* **w. do!** d'accord!; **the engine won't start** le moteur ne veut pas démarrer; **it won't open** ça ne s'ouvre pas, ça ne veut pas s'ouvrir; **just wait a moment, w. you?** pouvez-vous attendre un instant?; (*emphatic*) voulez-vous bien attendre un instant?; **won't you sit down?** asseyez-vous, je vous en prie

(c) (*emphatic*) **accidents will happen** on ne peut pas éviter les accidents; **she will go out in spite of her cold** elle persiste à sortir malgré son rhume; **he will get in my way** il est toujours dans mon chemin; **the doctor will have his little joke** il aime (à) plaisanter, le docteur; **I will not have it!** je ne permettrai pas cela!; **will you be quiet!** voulez-vous bien vous taire!

(d) (*habit*) **this hen w. lay up to six eggs a week** cette poule pond jusqu'à six œufs par semaine

(e) (*conjecture*) **you'll be tired** vous devez être fatigué

(f) (*wish*) vouloir; **do as you w.** faites comme vous voudrez; **say what you w., you won't be believed** quoi que vous disiez, on ne vous croira pas

(g) (*injunction*) **you'll be here at three** soyez ici à trois heures

willful *etc US* = **wilful** *etc*

William the Conqueror ['wɪlɪəm] *n* Guillaume le Conquérant

willie ['wɪlɪ] *n Br F* (*penis*) zizi *m*

willies ['wɪlɪz] *npl F* **to have the w.** avoir le trac *ou* la frousse; **this place gives me the w.** cet endroit me fiche la frousse *ou* me donne les chocottes; **I had a bad case of the w.** j'avais une frousse incroyable

willing ['wɪlɪŋ] *adj* **(a)** (*compliant*) de bonne volonté, bien disposé; **w. men** hommes de bonne volonté; **w. hands** mains secourables; *Fig* **w. horse** bonne poire

(b) (*ready*) **to be w. to do sth** bien vouloir faire qch, être disposé à faire qch; **w. to help** prêt à rendre service, serviable; **she's always w. to lend a hand** elle est toujours prête à rendre service; **I am more than w. to come with you** je ne demande pas mieux que de vous accompagner; **I am w. and able to help them** je peux les aider et je le ferai très volontiers; **she wasn't very w. to tell me what had happened** elle ne tenait pas vraiment à me dire ce qui s'est passé; **w. or not** bon gré mal gré; **God w.** s'il plaît à Dieu; *F* **to show w.** faire preuve de bonne volonté

willingly ['wɪlɪŋlɪ] *adv* **(a)** (*voluntarily*) volontairement; **he came along quite w.** il est venu de son plein gré; **she had not gone there w.** elle n'y était pas allée de son plein gré **(b)** (*with pleasure*) volontiers, avec plaisir

willingness ['wɪlɪŋnɪs] *n* **(a)** (*compliance*) bonne volonté *f*; **with the utmost w.** de très bon cœur **(b)** (*readiness*) empressement *m* **(to do sth** à faire qch)

will-o'-the-wisp [wɪləðə'wɪsp] *n also Fig* feu *m* follet

willow ['wɪləʊ] *n* **(a) w. (tree)** saule *m*; **w. pattern plate** assiette *f* chinoise à motifs bleus **(b)** *Old-fashioned Cr F* **the w.** la batte

willowy ['wɪləʊɪ] *adj* (*person*) souple, svelte, élancé

willpower ['wɪlpaʊər] *n* volonté *f*; **through w. alone** par ma/sa/*etc* seule volonté; **lack of w.** manque *m* de volonté

willy-nilly ['wɪlɪ'nɪlɪ] *adv* **(a)** (*without order, randomly*) au hasard; **the editor just altered a few words w.** le rédacteur a simplement changé quelques mots au hasard **(b)** (*willingly or not*) bon gré mal gré

wilt[1] [wɪlt] **1** *vi* **(a)** (*of plant*) se flétrir, se faner **(b)** *Fig* (*of person*) (*with heat, fatigue*) dépérir, languir; (*at reproach*) perdre contenance; (*lose courage*) se dégonfler; **I'm beginning to w.** (*become tired*) je commence à fatiguer; **he tends to w. under pressure** il ne résiste pas à la pression **2** *vt* (*of heat*) (*flowers*) faner, dessécher

wilt[2] *see* **will[3]**

Wilts *abbr* **Wiltshire**

wily ['waɪlɪ] *adj* rusé, astucieux, malin, *f* -igne, roublard; **he's a w. old bird** *or* **fox** c'est un vieux roublard

wimp [wɪmp] *n F* poule *f* mouillée, mauviette *f*

▶ **wimp out** *vi F* se défiler

wimpish ['wɪmpɪʃ] *adj F* (*behaviour, attitude*) de poule mouillée, de mauviette; **you didn't go because it was raining?, how w.!** tu n'y es pas allé à cause de la pluie?, quelle mauviette!

wimple ['wɪmp(ə)l] *n* (*worn by nun*) guimpe *f*

win[1] [wɪn] *n Sp etc* victoire *f*; **to have three wins in succession** emporter trois victoires consécutives; **to back a horse for a w.** jouer un cheval gagnant

win[2] (*pt, pp* **won** [wʌn]; *prp* **winning) 1** *vt* **(a)** (*be successful in*) (*battle, race, bet*) gagner; **to w. an election** remporter une élection; **to w. an argument** avoir le dessus dans une discussion; *F* **you can't w. them all, you w. some you lose some** on ne peut pas toujours gagner

(b) (*obtain*) (*prize*) remporter, gagner; **to w. a contract** remporter un marché; **I won 500 pounds off him at poker**

j'ai gagné 500 livres en jouant au poker contre lui; **the Greens have won ten seats** les Verts ont gagné dix sièges; **they won the seat from Labour** ils ont enlevé le siège aux Travaillistes

(c) (*acquire*) (*popularity, sb's good will*) acquérir; (*sb's attention*) captiver; (*sb's confidence*) gagner; **to w. fame** trouver la gloire; **she was desperate to w. his favour** elle cherchait désespérément à attirer ses bonnes grâces; **to w. a reputation for sth** se faire une réputation de qch; **to w. the right to do sth** obtenir le droit de faire qch; **to w. sb's love** se faire aimer de qn; **to w. recognition** parvenir à être reconnu; **he has finally won recognition for his work** son travail a finalement été reconnu; **she was gradually winning recognition as a talented young poet** elle commençait à se faire connaître en tant que jeune poète; **you've just won yourself a friend** tu viens juste de te faire un ami; **how to w. friends and influence people** comment se faire des amis et influencer les gens; **to w. sb away from sth** détourner *ou* détacher qn de qch; **she won her way to the top of her profession** elle a réussi à atteindre le sommet de sa profession

2 *vi* gagner; *Sp* **to w. by a length** gagner d'une longueur; **to back a horse to w.** jouer un cheval gagnant; *F* **you (just) can't w.** j'aurai/tu auras/*etc* toujours tort; *F* **to w. hands down** gagner les doigts dans le nez *ou* les mains dans les poches; **w. or lose, I'm sure I'll enjoy this match** que je gagne ou que je perde je suis certain que je vais m'amuser pendant ce match

▶ **win back** *vtsep* (*territory, championship*) reprendre (**from** à), reconquérir (**from** sur); (*esteem, friendship*) reconquérir; (*money*) regagner

▶ **win out** *vi* (*succeed*) y arriver, réussir

▶ **win over, win round** *vtsep* **I think we should manage to w. her over** *or* **round in the end** je pense qu'on devrait finir par la persuader; **to w. sb round** *or* **over to one's position** gagner qn à sa cause; **see whether you can w. him over** essayez de le persuader de se mettre avec nous; **I won him round to my point of view** j'ai réussi à le rallier à mon point de vue

▶ **win through** *vi* (*succeed*) y arriver, réussir; *Sp* **to w. through to the second round** passer le premier tour

wince[1] [wɪns] *n* (*of pain etc*) crispation *f*

wince[2] *vi* (*with pain*) tressaillir; (*with embarrassment*) se crisper; **the remark made him w.** il s'est crispé en entendant cette remarque

winceyette [wɪnsɪ'et] *n Br Tex* flanelle *f* de coton, flanellette *f*, pilou *m*; **w. sheet** drap *m* en flanelle de coton

winch [wɪntʃ] *n* treuil *m*; (*on boat*) winch *m*

▶ **winch in** *vtsep* amener *ou* rentrer à l'aide d'un treuil

▶ **winch up** *vtsep* soulever *ou* hisser *ou* monter à l'aide d'un treuil; **the crew were winched up by helicopter** l'équipage a été hissé à l'aide d'un hélicoptère *ou* a été hélitreuillé

wind[1] [wɪnd] *n* **(a)** (*air*) vent *m*; **strong winds** vents forts *ou* violents; **there's quite a w.** il y a beaucoup de vent; *Naut* **to sail against the w.** avoir le vent debout; *Naut* **to sail** *or* **run before the w.** avoir *ou* être vent arrière; *Naut* **to sail with w. and tide** avoir vent et marée; **in the teeth of the w.** contre le vent; **to sail into the w.** venir *ou* aller au lof; *Fig* **to sail close to the w.** (*when telling joke*) friser l'indécence; (*in business dealings*) friser la malhonnêteté; *Fig* **my friends are all scattered to the four winds** mes amis sont dispersés aux quatre coins du monde; *Fig* **to throw caution to the w.** oublier toute prudence; *Fig* **to see** *or* **find out which way the w. blows** voir d'où vient le vent; *Fig* **there's something in the w.** il se prépare *ou* se mijote quelque chose; *Fig* **a w.** *or* **the winds of change** un vent de changement; *Fig* **to go like the w.** aller comme le vent; *Old-fashioned F* **to raise the w.** rassembler des fonds; *Fig F* **to put the w. up sb** faire une peur bleue à qn; *Fig F* **to have** *or* **get the w. up** avoir le trac *ou* la frousse; (*stronger*) avoir une peur bleue; *Fig* **to take the w. out of sb's sails** déjouer les projets de qn, couper l'herbe sous le pied à qn; **w. gag** (*on microphone*) anti-vent *m*; *Av* **w. indicator** indicateur *m* de direction du vent; *Th, Cin* **w. machine** machine *f* à faire le vent; *Aut* **w. noise** bruit *m* aérodynamique; *Aut* **w. roar** bruit *m* du vent

(b) (*scent*) vent *m*; *Fig* **to get w. of sth** avoir vent de qch

(c) *Med* (*flatulence*) vent(s) *m*(*pl*), flatuosité *f*; **to break w.** lâcher un vent; **to have w.** avoir des gaz; **beans give you w.** les haricots donnent des gaz; **the baby's got w.** le bébé n'a pas fait son rot; **to get the baby's w. up** faire faire son rot au bébé; *F* **to be full of w.** (*useless talk*) parler à tort et à travers *ou* pour ne rien dire; (*boastful talk*) être vantard

(d) (*breath*) souffle *m*, respiration *f*; **let me get my w.** laissez-moi souffler *ou* reprendre mon souffle

(e) *Mus* **the w.** (*in orchestra*) les instruments *mpl* à vent; **w. instrument** instrument à vent; **w. ensemble** ensemble *m* d'instruments à vent

(f) *Ind* vent *m*, air *m ou* vent de soufflerie; *Mus* **w. chest** (*of organ*) laie *f*, sommier *m*

wind[2] *vt* (*of blow*) (*person*) couper la respiration *ou* le souffle à; (*of race*) (*person, horse*) essouffler; (*baby*) faire faire son rot à; **I was badly winded** (*by blow*) j'avais le souffle coupé; (*by race*) j'étais très essoufflé

wind[3] [waɪnd] *n* **to give the clock a w.** remonter la pendule

wind[4] (*pt, pp* **wound** [waʊnd]) **1** *vi* tourner; (*of path, river*) serpenter; (*of staircase*) monter en colimaçon; **the road winds up/down the hill** le chemin monte/descend en serpentant **2** *vt* **(a)** (*roll*) enrouler; *Tex* (*thread, silk*) dévider; **to w. wool into a ball** enrouler de la laine (pour en faire une pelote); **to w. cotton on a reel** bobiner du coton; *Fishing* **to w. in the line** ramener la ligne; **to w. a bobbin** enrouler le fil sur une bobine; *El* **to w. a dynamo** armer une dynamo **(b)** (*clock*) remonter **(c)** (*handle*) tourner

▶ **wind down 1** *vtsep* **(a)** (*car window*) baisser **(b)** (*reduce*) réduire progressivement *ou* graduellement **2** *vi* **(a)** (*of party, meeting etc*) tirer à sa fin; **the party didn't begin to w. down until nearly 4 am** la fête n'a commencé à diminuer en intensité que vers 4 heures du matin **(b)** *F* (*relax*) décompresser, se détendre

▶ **wind round 1** *vtaspo* enrouler autour de; **to w. a scarf round one's neck** enrouler une écharpe autour de son cou; **she wound her arms round the child** elle a entouré l'enfant de ses bras **2** *vipo* (*of thread*) s'enrouler autour de

▶ **wind up 1** *vtsep* **(a)** (*car window*) remonter

(b) (*rope etc*) enrouler

(c) (*clock*) remonter; (*spring*) bander; *Fig* **to be all wound up** (*of person*) être excité *ou* énervé

(d) (*end*) finir, terminer; *Com* (*company*) liquider, dissoudre; (*account*) régler, clôturer; **she wound up her speech by announcing that ...** elle a terminé son discours en annonçant que ...; **she winds up the book with a chapter on ...** elle boucle son livre par un chapitre sur ...

(e) *Br F* (*tease*) faire marcher; **they're only winding you up** ils te font marcher, ils essaient seulement de te mettre en boîte; **don't you know when you're being wound up?** tu ne te rends même pas compte quand on te fait marcher *ou* quand on essaie de te mettre en boîte?

2 *vi* **(a)** (*end speech etc*) conclure

(b) *F* (*end up*) **he'll w. up in prison** il finira en prison; **we usually w. up back at my place** généralement nous finissons chez moi; **we wound up working for the same company** nous nous sommes retrouvés à travailler pour la même compagnie

windbag ['wɪndbæg] *n F* moulin *m* à paroles; **what a w.!** quel bavard!

windblown ['wɪndbləʊn] *adj* **w. hair** cheveux décoiffés par le vent; **you're looking a bit w.** tu es un peu décoiffé

wind-borne *adj* porté par le vent

windbreak ['wɪndbreɪk] *n* brise-vent *m inv*

windcheater ['wɪndtʃiːtər] *n* (*jacket*) blouson *m*, *Can* coupe-vent *m inv*

wind-chill *adj* **w. factor** facteur *m* d'abaissement de la température provoqué par le vent

wind chimes *npl* carillon *m* éolien

wind energy *n* énergie *f* éolienne

winder ['waɪndər] *n* **(a)** (*device*) *Tex* bobinoir *m*, dévidoir *m*; (*on clock, watch*) remontoir *m* **(b)** *Aut* (*on car door*) lève-glace *m inv* **(c)** (*person*), *Tex* bobineur, -euse, dévideur, -euse; (*of clocks*) remonteur, -euse

windfall ['wɪndfɔːl] *n* **(a)** (*in garden, orchard etc*) fruit *m* abattu par le vent, fruit tombé **(b)** *Fig* aubaine *f*, bonne fortune *f*; (*legacy*) héritage *m* inattendu; **I've had a bit of a w. from my aunt** j'ai eu la chance d'hériter d'un peu d'argent de ma tante; **w. profits** (*of company*) bénéfices *mpl* inattendus

wind gauge *n* anémomètre *m*

winding ['waɪndɪŋ] **1** *adj* (*path, stream*) sinueux, qui serpente; (*road*) en lacets; **w. streets** rues tortueuses; **w. staircase** escalier *m* tournant *ou* en vis *ou* en colimaçon **2** *n* **(a)** mouvement *m* sinueux, cours *m* sinueux; **windings** (*of river*) replis *mpl*, méandres *mpl*; (*of road*) zigzags *mpl* **(b)** *Tex* bobinage *m*, embobinage *m*; *El* enroulement *m*, bobinage; **w. gear** (*of lift*) treuil *m*; *Min* appareils *mpl ou* machine *f* d'extraction; *Arch* **w. sheet** linceul *m*, suaire *m*

winding-up *n* (*of business etc*) liquidation *f*, dissolution *f*; (*of speech*) fin *f*, conclusion *f*; (*of account*) clôture *f*

windjammer ['wɪnddʒæmər] *n Naut* grand voilier *m*

windlass ['wɪndləs] *n* treuil *m*

windmill ['wɪndmɪl] *n* moulin *m* à vent; *Fig* **to tilt at windmills** se battre contre des moulins à vent

window ['wɪndəʊ] *n* **(a)** (*of house etc*) fenêtre *f*; **to look in at/**

out of the w. regarder par/à la fenêtre; **to break a w.** casser une vitre *ou* un carreau; *Fig F* **to throw money out of the w.** jeter l'argent par les fenêtres; *Fig F* **that's my holiday out of the w.** voilà mes vacances fichues en l'air; **that's her chances of qualifying out of the w.** voilà ses chances de qualification qui partent en fumée; *Fig* **a w. on sth** un aperçu de qch; **w. of opportunity** ouverture *f*
(b) *Comptr* fenêtre *f*
(c) (*of ticket office*) guichet *m*
(d) (*of shop*) vitrine *f*, devanture *f*; **w. display** étalage *m*
(e) (*of car, train*) vitre *f*, glace *f*
(f) (*on envelope*) fenêtre *f*; **w. tab** (*on suspension file*) onglet *m* à fenêtre

window box *n* (*for flowers*) jardinière *f*
window cleaner *n* (*person*) laveur, -euse de vitres *ou* de carreaux; (*product*) produit *m* pour nettoyer les vitres
window-dress *vt* (*accounts, balance sheet*) camoufler, habiller
window-dresser *n* étalagiste *mf*
window-dressing *n* (art *m* de l')étalage *m*; *Fig* façade *f*, décor *m* de théâtre, camouflage *m*; **w. of a balance sheet** habillage *m ou* camouflage de bilan; **no amount of w. can hide the fact that the party is in crisis** rien ne pourra camoufler l'état de crise dans lequel se trouve le parti; *Fig* **it's just w.** ce n'est qu'une façade
window envelope *n* enveloppe *f* à fenêtre
window frame *n* cadre *m* de fenêtre; (*around glass*) châssis *m* de fenêtre
windowing ['wɪndəʊɪŋ] *n Comptr* fenêtrage *m*
window ledge *n* (*outside*) rebord *m* de fenêtre; (*inside*) appui *m ou* tablette *f* de fenêtre
windowless ['wɪndəʊlɪs] *adj* sans fenêtres
windowpane ['wɪndəʊpeɪn] *n* vitre *f*, carreau *m*
window seat *n* (*in house*) banquette *f* située dans l'embrasure d'une fenêtre; (*in aircraft*) place *f* côté hublot; (*in train, bus*) place côté fenêtre
window-shop *vi* faire du lèche-vitrines; **to w. for a coat** faire du lèche-vitrines pour trouver un manteau
window-shopper *n* personne *f* qui fait du lèche-vitrines; **the streets were full of window-shoppers** les rues étaient pleines de gens en train de faire du lèche-vitrines
window-shopping *n* lèche-vitrines *m*; **to go w.** faire du lèche-vitrines
windowsill ['wɪndəʊsɪl] *n* (*outside*) rebord *m* de fenêtre; (*inside*) appui *m ou* tablette *f* de fenêtre
window winder *n Aut* lève-vitre *m inv*, lève-glace *m inv*
windpipe ['wɪndpaɪp] *n Anat* trachée *f*
wind-pollinated ['wɪndpɒlɪneɪtɪd] *adj* pollinisé par le vent
wind-pollination *n* pollinisation *f* par le vent
wind power *n* énergie *f* éolienne
windscreen ['wɪndskriːn] *n* (a) *Br Aut* pare-brise *m inv*; **w. cleaner** lave-glace *m inv*; **w. pillar** montant *m* de pare-brise (b) (*of microphone*) bonnette *f* (anti-vent)
windscreen washer *n* lave-glace *m inv*; **w. bottle** réservoir *m* du lave-glace; **w. jet** gicleur *m* de lave-glace
windscreen wiper *n* essuie-glace *m inv*
windshield ['wɪndʃiːld] *n Am* = **windscreen (a)**
wind sleeve *n Av* manche *f* à air, *Sl* biroute *f*
windsock ['wɪndsɒk] *n Av* manche *f* à air, *Sl* biroute *f*
windstorm ['wɪndstɔːm] *n* tempête *f* de vent
windsurf ['wɪndsɜːf] *vi* faire de la planche à voile
windsurfer ['wɪndsɜːfər] *n Sp* (a) (*board*) planche *f* à voile (b) (*person*) véliplanchiste *mf*
windsurfing ['wɪndsɜːfɪŋ] *n* (*sport*) planche *f* à voile; **to go w.** faire de la planche à voile
windswept ['wɪndswept] *adj* balayé par le vent; **w. hair** cheveux décoiffés par le vent
wind tunnel *n* soufflerie *f*, tunnel *m* aérodynamique; **w. test** essai *m* en soufflerie
wind-up ['waɪndʌp] *n Br F* **is this a w.?** tu me fais marcher?
windward ['wɪndwəd] **1** *adj* au vent; **the W. Islands** les îles *fpl* du Vent **2** *adv* contre le vent; **to sail w.** avoir le vent debout **3** *n* côté *m* au vent; **lying to (the) w. of ...** situé au vent de ...
windy[1] ['wɪndɪ] *adj* (a) (*day*) de grand vent; **it's very w.** il fait beaucoup de vent; **March is usually a w. month** en général il y a du vent au mois de mars (b) (*place*) venteux, balayé par le vent, exposé au vent *ou* aux quatre vents; **the W. City** = Chicago (c) *Old-fashioned Br F* **to be w.** (*afraid*) avoir le trac *ou* la frousse
windy[2] ['waɪndɪ] *adj* (*road etc*) sinueux
wine[1] [waɪn] *n* (a) vin *m*; **wines and spirits** (*shop sign*) vins et spiritueux; **w. producing district** pays *m* vinicole *ou* de vignobles; **w. bottle** bouteille *f* de vin (vide); **w. box** cubitainer *m*; **w. cellar** cave *f* (à vin); **w. cooler** rafraîchissoir *m*, rafraîchisseur *m* (à vin); **w. list** (*in restaurant*) carte *f* des vins; **w. route** route *f* des vins; *Am* **w. steward** sommelier *m*; **w. vinegar** vinaigre *m* de vin; **w. waiter** sommelier *m* (b) (*colour*) lie *f* de vin
wine[2] *vt* **to w. and dine sb** fêter qn
wine bar *n* bar *m* à vin
wine-coloured *adj* lie de vin *inv*
wineglass ['waɪnglɑːs] *n* verre *m* à vin
wine merchant *n* (*dealer*) négociant *m* en vins; (*shopkeeper*) marchand *m* de vin
winepress ['waɪnpres] *n* pressoir *m*
wine tasting *n* dégustation *f*; **I'm going to a w.** je vais à une dégustation de vins
wing[1] [wɪŋ] *n* (a) (*of bird, insect, plane*) aile *f*; *Fig* **to take sb under one's w.** prendre qn sous son aile *ou* sous sa protection; *Lit* **fear lent him wings** la peur lui donnait des ailes; **to shoot a bird on the w.** tirer un oiseau au vol *ou* à la volée; **to be on the w.** (*of bird*) voler; **to take w.** s'envoler, prendre son vol *ou* son essor; *Fig* **to spread** *or* **stretch one's wings** élargir son horizon; *Av* **wings** (*insignia*) insigne *m* de pilote; **w. flap** (*of plane*) volet *m* (d'aile)
(b) (*of building*) aile *f*; (*of hospital*) pavillon *m*; (*of door*) battant *m*; *Th* **the wings** la coulisse, les coulisses; **to be standing** *or* **waiting in the wings** *Th* attendre dans les coulisses; *Fig* rester dans les coulisses
(c) *Mil* (*of army*) aile *f*, flanc *m*; *Sp* aile; (*player*) ailier *m*; **the w. halves** les demis *mpl* aile; *Rugby* **w. forward** avant-aile *m*, *pl* avant-ailes; *Rugby* **w. threequarter** trois-quarts *m inv* aile; **she plays on the w.** elle est ailier; *Pol* **the left w. (of the party)** l'aile gauche (du parti)
(d) (*of nut*) oreille *f*, ailette *f*; **w. bolt/screw** boulon *m*/vis *f* à ailettes; **w. chair** fauteuil *m* à oreilles; **w. collar** col *m* cassé
(e) *Br* (*of car*) aile *f*
(f) *Mil Av* (*unit*) escadre *f* aérienne; *US* brigade *f* aérienne
wing[2] *vt* (a) (*injure*) (*bird*) frapper *ou* blesser à l'aile; **I've winged him** je lui ai mis du plomb dans l'aile (b) *esp Am F* **to w. it** improviser (c) **to w. its/one's way towards** (*of bird, Fig of person*) voler vers; **while the letters were winging their way over the ocean** pendant que les lettres survolaient l'océan; **my report should be winging its way towards you now** mon rapport devrait te parvenir incessamment sous peu
wing commander *n Br Mil Av* (*Am* = **lieutenant colonel**) lieutenant-colonel *m* (de l'armée de l'air)
wingding ['wɪŋdɪŋ] *n US F* **w. (party)** soirée *f*, fête *f*, surprise-partie *f*, *pl* surprises-parties
winged [wɪŋd, *Lit often* 'wɪŋɪd] *adj* (*with wings*) ailé; **w. insects** insectes ailés
-winged [wɪŋd] *suff* **red/white/***etc***-w.** aux ailes rouges/blanches/*etc*
winger ['wɪŋər] *n Fb, Rugby* ailier *m*
wingless ['wɪŋlɪs] *adj* sans ailes, aptère
wing mirror *n* rétroviseur *m* latéral *ou* extérieur
wingspan ['wɪŋspæn], **wingspread** ['wɪŋspred] *n* (*of bird, plane*) envergure *f*; **the eagle has a w. of two metres** l'aigle a une envergure de deux mètres
wink[1] [wɪŋk] *n* clignement *m* d'œil, clin *m* d'œil; **to give sb a w.** faire un clin d'œil à qn; **with a w.** en clignant de l'œil; *Fig F* **to tip sb the w.** prévenir *ou* avertir qn (**about** de); **I didn't sleep a w.** *or* **didn't get a w. of sleep all night** je n'ai pas fermé l'œil *ou* dormi de toute la nuit; **it was all over in the w. of an eye** tout était fait en un clin d'œil; **a nod's as good as a w. to him** il comprend à demi-mot
wink[2] **1** *vi* cligner de l'œil *ou* des yeux; (*of star, light*) clignoter; **it's as easy as winking** c'est simple comme bonjour **2** *vt* **she winked an eye** elle a fait un clin d'œil
▶ **wink at** *vipo* (*person*) faire un clin d'œil à; *Fig* (*abuse, illegal practice*) fermer les yeux sur
▶ **wink away** *vtsep* (*tear, dust*) cligner des yeux pour chasser
winker ['wɪŋkər] *n Br Aut F* clignotant *m*
winking ['wɪŋkɪŋ] *adj* (*light*) clignotant
winkle ['wɪŋk(ə)l] *n* (a) (*mollusc*) bigorneau *m* (b) *Br F* **w. pickers** chaussures *fpl* à bout pointu
▶ **winkle out** *vtsep Br F* (*sth*) extraire; **I finally winkled the information out of him** j'ai fini par lui tirer les vers du nez; **it's no good trying to w. any money out of me** ce n'est pas la peine d'essayer de me soutirer de l'argent; **go and w. them out of the pub** va les déloger du pub
winner ['wɪnər] *n* (a) (*person*) vainqueur *m*, gagnant, -ante; (*horse*) (cheval *m*) gagnant; **the w. of the big prize** (*in lottery*) le gagnant du gros lot; **to back a w.** *Horseracing* jouer un cheval gagnant; *Fig* jouer gagnant, bien miser; **every one's a w.!** (*at fair, in raffle etc*) à tous les coups (l')on gagne! (b) *Fig* (*successful novel, play*) roman *m*/pièce *f* à grand succès; **this book will be a w.** ce livre a un succès assuré; **to be on to a w.** jouer gagnant *ou* la bonne carte

winning ['wɪnɪŋ] **1** *adj* **(a)** (*victorious*) gagnant; **w. number** (*in lottery*) numéro *m* gagnant *ou* sortant; **w. post** poteau *m* d'arrivée; **he was first past the w. post** il était le premier à atteindre le poteau d'arrivée; **the w. side** les vainqueurs *mpl*; *Sp* **w. streak** série *f* de victoires; **to be on a w. streak** (*when gambling*) être dans une série gagnante **(b)** (*attractive*) attrayant, séduisant; (*smile*) engageant, charmant; **that child has a w. way with her** cette enfant est très gracieuse **2** *n* **(a)** (*of sth*) acquisition *f* **(b)** (*usu pl*) **winnings** (*at races etc*) gains *mpl*

winnow ['wɪnəʊ] *vt Agr* (*grain*) vanner; **to w. the chaff from the grain** séparer le bon grain de l'ivraie; *Fig* **to w. the evidence** passer les témoignages au crible *ou* au peigne fin

winnowing ['wɪnəʊɪŋ] *n Agr* vannage *m*; *Fig* examen *m* minutieux; **w. basket** van *m*; **winnowings** (*of grain*) vannure *f*

wino ['waɪnəʊ] *n F* ivrogne *mf*, soûlard, -arde

winsome ['wɪnsəm] *adj* charmant, séduisant

winsomely ['wɪnsəmlɪ] *adv* d'une manière séduisante, de façon charmante

winter¹ ['wɪntər] *n* [①A6-7,d,v] hiver *m*; **in w.** en hiver; *Lit* **he has seen sixty winters** il compte soixante hivers; **W. Olympic Games, W. Olympics** Jeux *mpl* Olympiques d'hiver; **w. break** (petites) vacances *fpl* d'hiver; **w. clothing** vêtements *mpl ou Can* linge *m* d'hiver; **w. corn** semis *m* d'hiver; *Aut* **w. driving mode** mode *m* de conduite hiver; **w. holiday** vacances *fpl* d'hiver; **w. quarters** quartiers *mpl* d'hiver; *Aut* **w. setting** (*for transmission*) réglage *m* hiver; **w. visitor** (*tourist*) hivernant, -ante; **a w. visitor to these shores** (*bird*) un visiteur hivernal de nos régions

winter² **1** *vi* (*of people*) passer l'hiver (**at** à); (*of cattle*) hiverner **2** *vt* (*livestock*) hiverner

winter-flowering *adj* (*plant*) hibernal, hiémal

winter garden *n* (*conservatory*) jardin *m* d'hiver

wintergreen ['wɪntəgriːn] *n* (*plant*) gaulthérie *f*

winterize ['wɪntəraɪz] *vt esp Am* (*car, house etc*) mettre en état pour passer l'hiver, *Can* hivériser

winter resort *n* station *f* de sports d'hiver

winter season *n* saison *f* d'hiver

winter solstice *n* solstice *m* d'hiver

winter sports *npl* sports *mpl* d'hiver; **w. resort** station *f* de sports d'hiver; **w. tourism** tourisme *m* blanc

wintertime ['wɪntətaɪm], *Lit* **wintertide** [-taɪd] *n* hiver *m*

winterweight ['wɪntəweɪt] *adj* (*coat etc*) d'hiver

wint(e)ry ['wɪnt(ə)rɪ] *adj* (*weather etc*) d'hiver; (*cold*) hivernal; **it's quite w. this morning** c'est presque un jour d'hiver, ce matin; **because of the w. conditions** parce qu'il fait/faisait un temps d'hiver; **w. smile** sourire glacial

wipe¹ [waɪp] *n* **(a)** (*action*) (*with cloth, handkerchief, sponge*) coup *m* de torchon/de mouchoir/d'éponge; **to give sth a w. (over/round)** essuyer qch, donner un coup de torchon/ d'éponge à qch **(b)** (*moist tissue*) lingette *f* **(c)** *TV, Cin* volet *m*

wipe² **1** *vt* **(a)** (*table, plate*) essuyer; **to w. one's face/hands/ eyes** s'essuyer la figure/les mains/les yeux; **to w. oneself, to w. one's bottom** s'essuyer les fesses, se torcher; *Vulg* **it's not fit to w. your arse with** tu peux te torcher avec; *Fig F* **we wiped the floor with them** nous n'en avons fait qu'une bouchée **(b)** (*erase recording etc from*) effacer; **the tape has been wiped** la bande a été effacée **2** *vi* **(a)** (*when washing up, dusting*) essuyer **(b) the windscreen wiper isn't wiping** l'essuie-glace ne marche pas

▶ **wipe away** *vtsep* (*tears*) essuyer; (*mark*) enlever, ôter; *Fig* (*memories*) effacer

▶ **wipe off** **1** *vtsep* **(a)** (*splash*) enlever, essuyer **(b)** (*sth from blackboard*) effacer; (*marks*) enlever; *F* **that'll w. the smile off his face** ça va lui enlever le sourire; *F* **w. that smile off your face!** arrête de sourire comme ça!; **to w. a town off the map** *or* **off the face of the earth** rayer une ville de la carte **2** *vi* (*of stain etc*) s'enlever

▶ **wipe out** *vtsep* **(a)** (*bath etc*) nettoyer

(b) (*debt*) liquider, amortir; **his gambling debts wiped out his entire fortune** ses dettes de jeu ont eu raison de toute sa fortune; **many small traders were wiped out in the recession** de nombreux petits commerçants ont été balayés par la récession

(c) (*memory, one's past*) effacer

(d) (*army*) exterminer; **whole families were wiped out by the disease** des familles entières ont été exterminées par la maladie; **the fire wiped out the whole district** l'incendie a détruit tout le quartier

(e) *F* (*exhaust*) épuiser; **I feel wiped out after interviewing so many people** ça m'a crevé *ou* lessivé de faire passer tous ces entretiens

▶ **wipe up** **1** *vtsep* (*dirt*) nettoyer, enlever; (*liquid*) essuyer; (*dishes*) essuyer **2** *vi* essuyer la vaisselle

wiper ['waɪpər] *n Aut* (*for windscreen*) essuie-glace *m inv*; **w. arm** porte-raclette *m*, *pl* porte-raclettes; **w. blade** raclette *f* de balai

wiping out ['waɪpɪŋ] *n* **(a)** (*of debt*) liquidation *f*, amortissement *m* **(b)** (*of memory*) effacement *m*

wire¹ ['waɪər] *n* **(a)** fil *m* métallique, fil de fer; *El* fil (électrique); **cheese w.** fil à couper le beurre; **the high w.** (*in circus*) la corde raide; *Fig* **to get one's wires crossed** se tromper, s'embrouiller; *esp Am F* **to pull the wires** tirer les ficelles, faire jouer ses pistons; *Mil* **w. entanglements** barbelés *mpl*; **w. fence** clôture *f* en fil de fer; **w. mesh** toile *f* métallique; **w. meshing** treillis *m* métallique *ou* en fil de fer; **w. netting** grillage *m*; **w. rope** câble *m* métallique; *Am* **w. service** agence *f* de presse; *Aut* **w. wheel** roue *f* fil; **w. wool** paille *f* de fer

(b) *esp Am* (*finishing line*) ligne *f* d'arrivée; *Fig* **down to the w.** jusqu'à la dernière minute; **to get an application in under the w.** soumettre une demande juste à temps; *Fig* **to (just) get in under the w.** (*of application etc*) arriver de justesse

(c) *Am F* (*hidden microphone*) **he agreed to wear a w.** il accepta de porter un micro

(d) *Old-fashioned* (*telegram*) télégramme *m*

wire² *vt* **(a)** (*fix with wire*) attacher avec du fil de fer; (*jaw*) mettre en place avec du fil de fer; (*flowers etc*) monter sur fil de fer; (*close off with wire*) (*opening*) grillager; **wired glass** verre armé **(b)** *El* (*house*) faire l'installation électrique de; **to w. a hall for sound** sonoriser une salle **(c)** *esp Am F* (*police officer*) munir d'un micro **(d)** (*send telegram to*) envoyer un télégramme à; (*message*) télégraphier; **he wired that he would arrive at twelve** il a télégraphié qu'il arriverait à midi

▶ **wire into** *vipo F* **he wired into his colleagues about their failure to keep him informed** il est rentré dans ses collègues en leur reprochant leur mauvaise communication avec lui; **they wired into the food as if they hadn't eaten for days** ils ont attaqué la nourriture comme s'ils n'avaient pas mangé depuis des jours; **they got wired into the backlog of work** ils ont attaqué le *ou* se sont attelés au travail en retard

▶ **wire up** *vtsep El* (*devices*) brancher (**to** sur); (*put electronic bugs in*) (*room*) installer des micros dans

wire brush *n* brosse *f* métallique

wirecutter ['waɪəkʌtər] *n* coupe-fil *m inv*; **(pair of) wirecutters** pince(s) coupante(s)

wire-haired *adj* (*terrier*) à poil dur

wireless ['waɪəlɪs] **1** *adj* sans fil **2** *n Old-fashioned* **w. (set)** poste *m* de T.S.F., radio *f*; **they communicated by w.** ils communiquaient par radio

wirepuller ['waɪəpʊlər] *n esp Am F* personne *f* qui a du piston

wirepulling ['waɪəpʊlɪŋ] *n esp Am F* intrigues *fpl*; **a bit of w. would help his cousin get the job** un peu de piston pourrait aider son cousin à avoir le poste

wiretap¹ ['waɪətæp] *n* **they've put a w. on him** *or* **his telephone** on a mis sa ligne sur écoute

wiretap² *vt* (*telephone line*) mettre sur écoute

wiretapping ['waɪətæpɪŋ] *n* mise *f* sur écoute d'une ligne téléphonique

wireworm ['waɪəwɜːm] *n* (*pest*) larve *f* de taupin; (*millipede*) iule *m*

wiring ['waɪərɪŋ] *n* **(a)** (*action*) (*of flowers etc*) montage *m* sur fil de fer; *El* installation *f* éléctrique **(b)** *El* (*system*) (*in house etc*) installation *f* électrique

wiring diagram *n* schéma *m* de branchement, schéma de câblage

wiry ['waɪərɪ] *adj* **(a)** (*hair*) raide **(b)** (*person*) vigoureux, (sec et) nerveux

Wis *abbr* **Wisconsin**

wisdom ['wɪzdəm] *n* (*knowledge*) sagesse *f*; (*advisability*) sagesse, prudence *f*; **the received** *or* **conventional w.** l'opinion communément admise; **to question the w. of a decision** mettre en cause la sagesse d'une décision; **w. tooth** dent *f* de sagesse

wise¹ [waɪz] *adj* (*knowledgeable*) sage; (*advisable*) prudent; **a w. man** un sage; **the Three W. Men** les (Rois) Mages *mpl*; **to get** *or* **grow wise(r)** (*learn more*) s'assagir; (*gain experience*) acquérir de l'expérience; **it wouldn't be w. to do it** ça ne serait pas sage *ou* prudent (de le faire); **w. after the event** sage après coup; **everyone can be w. after the event** c'est facile d'avoir raison après coup; **I'm no wiser than you** je n'en sais pas plus long que vous; **she's none** *or* **not any the wiser (for it)** elle n'est pas plus avancée; **without anyone being (any) the wiser** à l'insu de tout le monde, sans que personne ne sache; **no one will be any the wiser** personne n'en saura rien; *F* **to get w. to a fact** se rendre compte d'un fait; *F* **to get w. to sb** se rendre compte de *ou* réaliser ce que qn fait; *F* **I'm w. to his tricks** je connais ses combines; *F* **to put sb w. to sth** avertir qn de qch; *F* **to put sb w. to sb** prévenir qn contre qn; *F* **w. guy** petit malin *m*

wise² *n Lit* (*way*) manière *f*, façon *f*; **in no w.** en aucune manière *ou* façon, nullement, aucunement

▶ **wise up** *esp Am F* **1** *vtsep* mettre à la page; **w. me up about it** mets-moi au courant **2** *vi* **to w. up to sb** se rendre compte du petit jeu de qn; **to w. up to the fact that ...** se rendre compte du fait que ...; **w. up!** ouvre les yeux!

-wise [waɪz] *suff* **(a)** (*indicating direction*) dans le sens de ...; **lengthw.** dans le sens de la longueur **(b)** [①A22,e] *F* (*with reference to*) en ce qui concerne ..., du point de vue de ..., côté ...; **healthw. /salaryw.** en ce qui concerne la santé/le salaire, côté santé/salaire

wiseacre [ˈwaɪzeɪkər] *n* (*person who thinks he's smart*) petit malin *m*

wisecrack¹ [ˈwaɪzkræk] *n F* vanne *f*, blague *f*; **to make a w.** faire *ou* lancer une vanne; **I don't want any more wisecracks** je ne veux plus entendre une seule vanne

wisecrack² *vi F* sortir une/des vanne(s), faire de l'esprit

wisecracking [ˈwaɪzkrækɪŋ] *adj F* blagueur

wisely [ˈwaɪzlɪ] *adv* **(a)** sagement, prudemment **(b) to shake one's head w.** secouer la tête d'un air entendu

wish¹ [wɪʃ] *n* **(a)** (*desire*) désir *m*; **I have no w. to go/to see it** je n'ai pas envie d'y aller/de le voir; **I have no w. to offend you, but ...** je n'ai aucune envie de te blesser, mais ...; **to express a w. to do sth** exprimer le désir de faire qch; **the w. to please** le désir de plaire; **by my father's w.** sur le désir de mon père; *Hum* **your w. is my command** vos désirs sont des ordres; **it was done against** *or* **contrary to my wishes** cela s'est fait à l'encontre de mon désir *ou* contre mon gré; **to make a w.** faire un vœu; **your w. will come true** ton vœu se réalisera; *Psy* **w. fulfilment** réalisation *f* du désir

(b) (*what is desired*) **you shall have your w.** votre vœu sera exaucé; **his great w. was to see his son become president** son plus grand souhait *ou* désir était de voir son fils président

(c) (*greeting*) **they send you their best wishes** ils te font leurs amitiés; **please give your parents my best wishes** (*said verbally*) fais toutes mes amitiés à tes parents; (*in writing*) transmets mes meilleures pensées à tes parents; **with best wishes** (*at end of letter*) (bien) amicalement; **with best wishes for a speedy recovery** avec tous mes/nos meilleurs vœux de prompt rétablissement; **to send all good wishes to sb** présenter ses souhaits à qn

wish² **1** *vi* **to w. for sth** désirer *ou* vouloir *ou* souhaiter qch; **to w. for happiness/peace** désirer *ou* souhaiter le bonheur/la paix; **to have everything one can** *or* **could w. for** avoir tout pour être heureux; **I couldn't w. for anything better** je ne pourrais désirer mieux; **what more can** *or* **could you w. for?** que souhaiter de plus?; **as you w.** comme vous voulez

2 *vt* **(a)** (*want*) vouloir; **to w. to do sth** désirer *ou* vouloir faire qch; **I w. it to be done** je désire *ou* je veux que cela soit fait; **I w. them to be here tomorrow** je désire *ou* je souhaite qu'ils soient là demain; **it is to be wished that ...** il est à souhaiter que ...

(b) (*want sth impossible, unlikely*) **I w. I were a bird!** je voudrais être un oiseau!; **I w. I were in your place** je voudrais bien être à votre place; **I w. I had seen it!** j'aurais bien voulu voir cela!, si seulement j'avais pu le voir!; **I w. I hadn't left so early** je regrette d'être parti si tôt, si seulement je n'étais pas parti si tôt; **I w. she would come** j'aimerais bien qu'elle vienne; **how I w. I could (do it)!** si seulement je pouvais (le faire)!; **I w. he wouldn't say things like that!** il ne pourrait pas éviter de dire des choses pareilles!; **w. you were here!** (*on postcard*) je pense à vous

(c) (*have feelings towards, greet*) **he wishes me well** il est bien disposé envers moi; **he wishes nobody ill** il ne veut de mal à personne; **w. me luck** souhaite-moi bonne chance; **to w. sb a pleasant journey** souhaiter bon voyage à qn; **to w. sb goodnight** souhaiter bonne nuit à qn, dire bonsoir à qn; *Iron* **I w. you joy of it** je te souhaite bien du plaisir

▶ **wish away** *vtsep* faire disparaître comme par enchantement; **you can't w. your problems away** tu ne vas pas te débarrasser de tes problèmes d'un coup de baguette magique; **to w. one's life away** souhaiter que sa vie soit différente

▶ **wish on** *vtaspo* **to w. sth on sb** obliger qn à accepter qch; **it was wished on me by my boss** j'ai été obligé de l'accepter à cause de mon patron, mon patron m'a obligé à l'accepter; **the boss wished his son on the head of marketing** le patron a imposé son fils au directeur du marketing; **I wouldn't w. this on my worst enemy** je ne souhaiterais pas cela à mon pire ennemi; **it's not an experience I would w. on anyone** c'est une expérience que je ne souhaiterais à personne; **can we w. the children on you for the day?** est-ce qu'on peut vous laisser les enfants pour la journée?

wishbone [ˈwɪʃbəʊn] *n* fourchette *f*, bréchet *m*; *esp Am* (*on surfboard*) wishbone *m*; **to pull a w. with sb** = faire un vœu avec qn en essayant de casser le bréchet du poulet

wishbone suspension *n Aut* suspension *f* triangulée

wishful [ˈwɪʃfʊl] *adj* **that's a bit of w. thinking** c'est prendre ses désirs pour des réalités

wishy-washy [ˈwɪʃɪwɒʃɪ] *adj F* (*style*) fade, insipide; (*person*) indécis; (*compromise*) insatisfaisant; **a w. liberal** un libéral mou

wisp [wɪsp] *n* (*strand*) (*of straw, wool*) brin *m*; **w. of smoke** traînée *f* de fumée; **w. of hair** mèche *f* de cheveux; **a little w. of a girl** un tout petit bout de fille; **a w. of cloud** un filet de nuage

wispy [ˈwɪspɪ] *adj* (*beard, hair*) fin; (*cloud*) vaporeux

wisteria [wɪsˈtɪərɪə] *n* (*plant*) glycine *f*

wistful [ˈwɪstfʊl] *adj* nostalgique; (*look, air, smile*) mélancolique; **he sounded w. when he spoke of her** il parlait d'elle avec une nuance de regret dans la voix

wistfully [ˈwɪstfəlɪ] *adv* avec nostalgie, avec regret; **she looked w. at the children playing in the street** (*wanting to join them*) elle regardait avec envie les enfants qui jouaient dans la rue; (*thinking of the baby she never had*) elle regardait avec regret les enfants qui jouaient dans la rue

wit¹ [wɪt] *n* **(a)** (*intelligence*) (*often pl*) esprit *m*, entendement *m*, intelligence *f*; **he hasn't the w. to see it** il n'est pas assez intelligent pour s'en apercevoir; **he didn't have the w. to come and tell me** il n'a pas eu la présence d'esprit de me le dire; **he hasn't the w. he was born with!** il n'a pas inventé la poudre!; **to have quick wits** avoir l'esprit vif; **to have lost one's wits** avoir perdu l'esprit *ou* la raison; **to collect** *or* **gather one's wits** se ressaisir, reprendre ses esprits; **to have/keep one's wits about one** avoir/conserver toute sa présence d'esprit; **you need your wits about you in this job** il faut avoir de la présence d'esprit dans ce métier; **she has all her wits about her** c'est une maligne *ou* une fine; **to be at one's w.'s end** ne plus savoir que faire; **to have** *or* **engage in a battle of wits** jouer au plus fin; **to live by one's wits** vivre d'expédients; **to scare sb out of his/her wits** faire une peur bleue à qn; **to put one's wits to work on a problem** s'attaquer à un problème

(b) (*humour*) esprit *m*, vivacité *f* d'esprit; **in a speech full of his usual w.** dans un de ses discours très spirituels; **flash of w.** trait *m* d'esprit; **sparkling with w.** étincelant d'esprit

(c) (*person*) bel esprit *m*, homme *m*/femme *f* d'esprit; **what a w.!** toujours le mot pour rire!

wit² *adv Jur* **to w.** à savoir ..., c'est-à-dire ...

witch [wɪtʃ] *n* sorcière *f*; *Fig Pej* **old w.** vieille sorcière; **w. doctor** sorcier *m* guérisseur; **w. hazel** (*plant*) hamamélis *m*

witchcraft [ˈwɪtʃkrɑːft] *n* sorcellerie *f*; **to practise w.** pratiquer la sorcellerie

witchery [ˈwɪtʃərɪ] *n* **(a)** (*practice*) ensorcellement *m*, enchantement *m* **(b)** (*influence, charm*) envoûtement *m*, fascination *f*

witch-hunt *n Pol* chasse *f* aux sorcières

witch-hunting *n Pol* chasse *f* aux sorcières

witching [ˈwɪtʃɪŋ] *adj Lit, Hum* **the w. hour** minuit *m*, l'heure *f* du crime

with [wɪð] *prep* **(a)** (*expressing accompaniment*) avec; **to travel/work w. sb** voyager/travailler avec qn; **he is staying w. friends** il est chez des amis; **to mingle w. the crowd** se mêler à la foule; **I have nobody to go out w.** je n'ai personne avec qui sortir; **here I am w. nobody to talk to** me voilà sans personne à qui parler; **I'll be w. you in a moment** je serai à vous dans un instant; **some cheese to eat w. it** du fromage pour manger avec; **this is a problem that will always be w. us** ce problème sera toujours d'actualité; **she came in w. a suitcase** elle est entrée avec une valise; **I'm sorry I don't have a handkerchief w. me** je suis désolé, je n'ai pas de mouchoir; **do you have a pencil w. you?** avez-vous un crayon sur vous?; **to leave a child w. sb** laisser un enfant à la garde de qn; **the decision rests** *or* **lies w. you** c'est à vous de décider; **what will happen to her w. both her parents dead?** (*now that they are dead*) que va-t-elle devenir maintenant que son père et sa mère sont morts?

(b) (*having*) à; **a knife w. a silver handle** un couteau à manche d'argent; **a girl w. blue eyes** une jeune fille aux yeux bleus; **a child w. a cold** un enfant enrhumé; **w. his/her hat on** le chapeau sur la tête; **w. his (over)coat on** en pardessus; **w. your intelligence you'll easily guess what followed** intelligent comme vous l'êtes vous devinerez facilement la suite; *Arch* **w. child** (*of woman*) enceinte

(c) (*expressing association*) avec; **to correspond w. sb** correspondre avec qn; **to have to do w. sb** avoir à faire avec qn; **to have nothing to do w. sb** n'avoir rien à faire avec qn; **to part w. sth** se dessaisir *ou* se défaire de qch; **the next move is w. him** c'est à lui d'agir maintenant; **w. him all men are equal** tous les hommes sont égaux à ses yeux *ou* pour lui; **to be patient w. sb** être patient avec qn; **to be honest w. oneself** être honnête envers *ou* avec soi-même; **it's a habit w. me** c'est une habitude chez moi; **to use one's influence w. sb** agir auprès de qn; **all is well w. her** elle va bien; **I sympathize w. you** je vous plains; **I don't agree w. you** je ne suis pas d'accord avec vous; **I'm w. you** (*I support you*) je suis de votre côté; (*I understand*) je vous suis, je comprends; **I'm not w. you** (*I don't understand*) je ne (vous) suis pas, je ne comprends pas; *F* **to be w. it** (*fashionable*) être à la page *ou* dans le vent; *F* **I'm not w. it today** je n'y suis pas aujourd'hui; **to rise w. the lark** se lever au chant du coq; **w. these words/w. that he dismissed me** sur ces mots/là-dessus, il m'a congédié; **she said this w. a smile** elle a dit ça avec un sourire *ou* en souriant; **w. a cry** en poussant un cri; **to compete w. sb** concourir avec qn; **to fight w. sb** se battre contre *ou* avec qn; *F* **get w. it** (*become alert*) réveille-toi; (*realize what's happening*) ouvre les yeux

(d) (*despite*) malgré; **w. all his faults** malgré tous ses défauts; **w. the best will in the world** avec la meilleure volonté du monde

(e) (*expressing instrument, agent*) **to cut sth w. a knife** couper qch avec un couteau *ou* au couteau; **to walk w. (the aid of) a stick** marcher avec une canne; **to fight w. swords** se battre à l'épée; **to take sth w. both hands** prendre qch à deux mains; **to strike w. all one's might** frapper de toutes ses forces; **to tremble w. rage** trembler de rage; **to be stiff w. cold** être engourdi par le froid; **to be ill w. measles** avoir la rougeole; **to fill a vase w. water** remplir un vase d'eau; **lorry loaded w. timber** camion chargé de bois; **it's pouring w. rain** il pleut à verse

(f) (*forming adv phrase*) **to work w. a will** travailler avec courage *ou* ardeur; **to receive/welcome sb w. open arms** recevoir/accueillir qn à bras ouverts; **w. all due respect** avec tout le respect que je vous dois; **w. your permission** avec votre permission; **w. this object (in view)** dans ce but; **I say it w. regret** je le dis à regret; **w. a few exceptions** à part quelques exceptions, quelques exceptions mises à part; **away w. care!** plus de soucis!, ça suffit, les soucis!; **down w. the police!** à bas les flics!; *F* **to hell w. him!** qu'il aille au diable!, qu'il aille se faire voir!

withal [wɪ'ðɔːl] *adv Arch* de plus

withdraw [wɪð'drɔː] (*pt* **withdrew** [-'druː]; *pp* **withdrawn** [-'drɔːn]) **1** *vt* **(a)** (*one's hand, support*) retirer; **the government has withdrawn funding from the project** le gouvernement a arrêté de financer le projet

(b) (*troops*) retirer

(c) (*money*) retirer; **to w. coins from circulation** retirer des pièces de la circulation, démonétiser des pièces

(d) (*offer, remark, candidacy*) retirer; (*promise*) retirer, revenir sur; (*claim*) renoncer à; **to w. a charge** se rétracter; **to w. an order** *Com* annuler une commande; *Admin* rapporter un décret; *Jur* **to w. one's action** retirer sa plainte; *Fml* **to w. one's labour** faire la grève; **the right to w. one's labour** le droit de grève

2 *vi* **(a)** (*also after sex act*) se retirer (**from** de); **he withdrew ten paces** il a reculé de dix pas; **to w. in favour of sb** (*of candidate*) se désister en faveur de qn; **to w. into oneself** se replier sur soi-même; **to w. into silence** se renfermer dans le silence

(b) *Mil* se retirer

withdrawal [wɪð'drɔː(ə)l] *n* **(a)** (*of one's troops*) retrait *m*; (*by troops*) retraite *f*; **to make a w.** (*of troops*) se retirer, battre en retraite; *Fig* **to make a w. from one's position** battre en retraite

(b) *Banking* retrait *m*; **cash w.** décaissement *m*; **to make a w.** faire un retrait; **w. of capital** retrait de fonds; **w. from circulation** démonétisation *f*; **w. limit** plafond *m* de retrait *ou* d'autorisation; **w. notice** avis *m* de retrait de fonds; **w. slip** bordereau *m* de retrait

(c) *Psy* repli *m* sur soi; **the boy is showing signs of w.** le jeune garçon présente des signes de repli sur lui-même; *Med* **w. symptoms** (*from alcohol*) symptômes *mpl* d'abstinence; (*from drugs*) (état *m ou* crise *f* de) manque *m*; **to suffer w. symptoms** (*of alcoholic, drug addict*) être en manque; *Fig* se sentir perdu

(d) (*of decree, order*) rappel *m*; (*of promise, accusation*) rétractation *f*; (*of complaint*) retrait *m*; **w. of a candidate** désistement *m* d'un candidat

(e) (*after sex act*) retrait *m*; **w. method** méthode *f* du retrait

withdrawn [wɪð'drɔːn] *adj* (*reserved*) replié sur soi-même

wither ['wɪðər] **1** *vi* (*of plant*) se dessécher, se flétrir, se faner; (*of limb*) s'atrophier; *Fig* (*of beauty*) passer, (se) faner; (*of hope*) s'évanouir; (*of person, company*) dépérir; **without the steel industry the region will simply w. and die** sans l'industrie sidérurgique, la région va mourir lentement; **the party gradually withered and died** le parti s'est peu à peu éteint **2** *vt* (*of wind, heat*) (*plant*) dessécher, flétrir, faner; (*limb*) atrophier; *Fig* **to w. sb with a look** foudroyer qn du regard

▶ **wither away, wither up** *vi* = wither 1

withered ['wɪðəd] *adj* (*plant*) desséché, flétri, fané; **w. arm** bras atrophié

withering ['wɪðərɪŋ] *adj* (*heat*) qui dessèche, qui flétrit; *Fig* (*look*) foudroyant; (*tone*) de mépris; **w. sarcasm** sarcasme cinglant; **to give sb a w. look** foudroyer qn du regard

witheringly ['wɪðərɪŋlɪ] *adv* (*to look at*) avec mépris; (*to say*) d'un ton méprisant

withers ['wɪðəz] *npl* (*of horse*) garrot *m*

withershins ['wɪðəʃɪnz] *adv Scot* à contre-sens

withhold [wɪð'həʊld] *vt* (*pt, pp* **withheld** [-'held]) **(a)** (*not give*) (*consent, help*) refuser; (*money*) retenir; (*taxes*) prélever; **to w. recognition of a country** ne pas reconnaître un pays **(b)** (*suppress*) (*fact etc*) taire, supprimer; (*information*) retenir, bloquer; **I managed to w. my indignation/laughter** j'ai réussi à contenir mon indignation/rire; **to w. the truth from sb** cacher la vérité à qn **(c)** *Jur* (*property*) détenir

withholding [wɪð'həʊldɪŋ] *n* **(a)** (*of help, aid, loan*) refus *m*; (*of taxes*) prélèvement *m*, retenue *f* **(b)** (*of information, facts*) rétention *f*

within [wɪð'ɪn] **1** *adv* **from w.** de l'intérieur; **seen from w.** vu de l'intérieur *ou* du dedans; **staff required, apply w.** (*notice in shop window*) on recherche du personnel, se présenter à l'intérieur

2 *prep* **(a)** (*not beyond*) **w. reason** dans des limites raisonnables; **to keep w. the law** rester dans (les limites de) la légalité; **it is quite w. the realms of possibility** c'est dans les limites du possible; **to keep** *or* **live w. one's income** vivre selon ses moyens; **w. sight** en vue; **to keep sb/sth w. sight** avoir qn/qch à portée de vue; **to be w. sight of the shore** avoir la côte en vue; **w. call** à portée de (la) voix; **w. two miles of the town** à moins de deux milles de la ville; **w. a radius of ten kilometres** dans un rayon de dix kilomètres; **I live w. walking distance of the office** je peux aller au travail à pied; **is it w. walking distance?** est-ce qu'on peut y aller à pied?; **we were w. an inch of death** nous étions à deux doigts de la mort

(b) (*in expressions of time*) **w. an hour** en moins d'une heure; **it will be ready w. an** *or* **the hour** ça sera prêt d'ici une heure; **w. a week** (*in the space of*) en moins d'une semaine; (*by the time a week has passed*) d'ici une semaine; **w. the week** avant la fin de la semaine, dans la semaine; **w. a year of his death** (*after he died*) moins d'un an après sa mort; (*before he died*) moins d'un an avant sa mort; **w. the next week** dans le courant de la semaine prochaine; **w. the next five years, w. five years from now** d'ici cinq ans; **w. the required time** dans le délai prescrit; **w. twenty-four hours** dans les vingt-quatre heures; **w. ten days of receipt of your order** dans un délai de dix jours à compter de la réception de votre commande; **w. a short time** (*soon*) à court délai; (*soon after*) peu de temps après; **her time was w. a few seconds of the world record** son temps était à quelques secondes du record du monde

(c) *Old-fashioned, Lit* (*inside*) à l'intérieur de, en dedans de; **w. these four walls** entre ces quatre murs; **the enemy is w. our frontiers** l'ennemi est dans nos frontières; **a voice w. me** une voix intérieure

without [wɪð'aʊt] **1** *prep* **(a)** sans; **she did it w. asking/being asked** elle l'a fait sans demander/sans qu'on le lui demande; **to be w. a care in the world** n'avoir aucun souci; **w. a tail/coat/hope** sans queue/manteau/espoir; **to be w. food** manquer de nourriture; **he came back w. any money** il est revenu sans argent; **w. any difficulty** sans aucune difficulté; **the rumour is w. foundation** la rumeur est dénuée de fondement *ou* n'est pas fondée; **not w. difficulty** non sans difficulté; **w. end** sans fin; **he passed by w. seeing me/being seen** il est passé sans me voir/être vu; **it goes w. saying that ...** il va sans dire *ou* de soi que ...; **can you do it w. her knowing about it?** pouvez-vous le faire sans qu'elle le sache?; **they are w. any knowledge of French** ils n'ont aucune connaissance du français; **to do** *or* **go w. sth** se passer de qch; **I don't want her to go w. anything** je ne veux pas qu'elle manque de quoi que ce soit; **w. so much as saying goodbye/asking permission** sans même dire au revoir/demander la permission

(b) *Arch* (*outside*) en dehors de

2 *adv Arch* à l'extérieur, au dehors; **from w.** de l'extérieur; **seen from w.** vu de l'extérieur *ou* du dehors
with-pack premium *n Mktg* prime *f* directe
withstand [wɪð'stænd] *vt* (*pt, pp* **withstood** [-'stʊd]) (*person, pain, pressure*) résister à; **to w. the heat** supporter la chaleur; *Mil etc* **to w. an attack** soutenir une attaque
withy ['wɪðɪ] *n* brin *m ou* lien *m* d'osier
witless ['wɪtlɪs] *adj* stupide, sot, *f* sotte; *F* **to scare sb w.** faire une peur bleue à qn
witness[1] ['wɪtnɪs] *n* **(a)** (*person*) témoin *m*; (*to will*) témoin testamentaire; **will you act as a w. at our wedding?** est-ce que vous voulez bien être témoin à notre mariage?; **I gave my name as a w.** j'ai donné mon nom en tant que témoin; *Jur* **w. to a document** *or* **a deed** témoin instrumentaire, témoin à un acte; *Jur* **to call sb as w.** citer qn comme témoin; *Jur* **w. for the defence/prosecution** témoin à décharge/charge
(b) (*testimony*) témoignage *m*; **to give w. on behalf of the accused** rendre témoignage pour l'accusé, témoigner en faveur de l'accusé; **to bear w. to sth** rendre *ou* porter témoignage de qch, témoigner de qch, attester qch; **this situation bears w. to the need to ...** cette situation témoigne de la nécessité de ...; *Rel* **to bear false w.** porter un faux témoignage; **I call you to w.** j'en appelle à votre témoignage
witness[2] **1** *vt* (*scene*) être spectateur *ou* témoin de; (*interview etc*) assister à; *Jur* (*deed*) attester; *Jur* (*signature*) certifier; **I witnessed the whole thing** j'ai assisté à tout ce qui s'est passé; **this house has witnessed many deaths** cette maison a vu de nombreux décès; **we are witnessing a historic event** nous assistons à un événement historique; **he had witnessed the entire scene from his window** il avait vu *ou* assisté à toute la scène depuis sa fenêtre; **never in my entire life have I witnessed such stupidity** je n'ai jamais, de ma vie entière, vu une telle stupidité
2 *vi Jur* **to w. to sth** témoigner de qch; **to w. against/for sb** témoigner contre/en faveur de qn
witness box *n Br Jur* barre *f* des témoins; **to go into the w.** paraître à la barre
-witted [-'wɪtɪd] *suff* **slow/quick/***etc***-w.** qui a l'esprit lent/vif/*etc*
witter[1] ['wɪtər] *n Br F* = **wittering**
witter[2] *vi Br F* **to w. (on)** parler interminablement, parler pour ne rien dire; **to w. (on) about sth** parler interminablement de qch; **what's he wittering (on) about now?** qu'est-ce qu'il est encore en train de raconter?
wittering ['wɪtərɪŋ] *n Br F* bavardage *m*; **his constant w. gets on my nerves** son papotage me tape sur les nerfs
witticism ['wɪtɪsɪz(ə)m] *n* mot *m* d'esprit, bon mot
wittily ['wɪtɪlɪ] *adv* spirituellement, avec esprit
wittiness ['wɪtɪnɪs] *n* (*of remark etc*) esprit *m*, sel *m*
wittingly ['wɪtɪŋlɪ] *adv* (*intentionally*) sciemment, en connaissance de cause, intentionnellement
witty ['wɪtɪ] *adj* spirituel, plein d'esprit
wizard ['wɪzəd] **1** *n* sorcier *m*, magicien *m*; *Fig* génie *m*; **he's a real w. with figures/computers** c'est un as des chiffres/des ordinateurs; **to be a financial w.** avoir le génie de la finance *ou* des affaires; **she's a w. on the violin** c'est une violoniste géniale *ou* de génie; **to be a w. with a sewing needle** avoir des doigts de fée (pour la couture) **2** *adj Old-fashioned Br F* épatant, excellent
wizardry ['wɪzədrɪ] *n* sorcellerie *f*, magie *f*; *Fig* génie *m*, habileté *f*; **her financial w.** son talent génial en matière de finance; **that was sheer w. with the ball** c'était un jeu purement et simplement génial
wizened ['wɪzənd] *adj* ratatiné; (*cheeks*) parcheminé; (*apple*) ratatiné, ridé; **to become w.** (*of person, apple*) se ratatiner; (*of skin*) se parcheminer
wk *abbr* **week**
WO [dʌb(ə)ljuː'əʊ] *n Br Mil abbr* **warrant officer**
wo(a) ['wəʊ(ə)] *int* (*to horse*) ho!, holà!
woad [wəʊd] *n* guède *f*
wobble[1] ['wɒb(ə)l] *n* **(a)** (*swaying*) **the chair/desk has got a bit of a w.** la chaise/le bureau est légèrement bancal(e) *ou* branlant(e); **there is a slight w. in the front wheel of the bike** la roue avant du vélo a un léger jeu; **in order to stop the w.** (*of chair leg*) pour la caler; **I can still detect a slight w. when she moves off** (*of inexperienced cyclist*) on voit qu'elle n'est pas encore très sûre sur son vélo; *Aut* **front-wheel w.** shimmy *m* **(b)** (*of voice*) tremblement *m*
wobble[2] *vi* **(a)** (*sway*) (*of flame*) vaciller, osciller; (*of jelly, thighs etc*) trembler; (*of table*) branler; (*of person*) chanceler; (*of building, tooth*) bouger; (*of wheel*) avoir du jeu **(b)** (*of voice etc*) trembler, chevroter **(c)** *F* (*hesitate*) hésiter
wobbly ['wɒblɪ] **1** *adj* **(a)** (*table, chair*) branlant; (*flame*) vacillant; (*person*) chancelant; **the whole structure is slightly w.** toute la structure bouge légèrement; **my legs** *or* **I feel w.** j'ai les jambes en coton; *F* **I'm a bit w. on irregular verbs** je ne maîtrise pas vraiment les verbes irréguliers **(b)** (*voice etc*) chevrotant, tremblotant **2** *n F* **to throw a w.** piquer une *ou* sa crise
wodge [wɒdʒ] *n Br F* (*of bread*) gros morceau *m*; (*of money*) gros paquet *m*; **a huge w. of time** un bon bout de temps
woe [wəʊ] *n Lit* malheur *m*, chagrin *m*, peine *f*; **to tell a tale of w.** raconter ses malheurs; **to recount one's woes** égréner ses malheurs; **w. is me!** pauvre de moi!, malheureux que je suis!; **w. betide you if you're late** malheur à toi si tu es en retard
woebegone ['wəʊbɪgɒn] *adj* (*look, face*) désolé, abattu; **to look w.** avoir l'air désolé
woeful ['wəʊfʊl] *adj* **(a)** (*bad*) déplorable, mauvais; **w. standard of workmanship** qualité *f* de travail déplorable **(b)** *Lit* (*look*) affligé, malheureux; (*news*) attristant, affligeant; **the Knight of the W. Countenance** le chevalier à la Triste Figure
woefully ['wəʊfəlɪ] *adv* **(a)** (*bad, ill-equipped, inadequate etc*) terriblement; (*low*) déplorablement; **a w. inadequate husband** un très mauvais mari **(b)** (*to say, to look at*) tristement
wog [wɒg] *n Br Offensive Sl* métèque *m*
wok [wɒk] *n* wok *m*, poêle *f* chinoise
wold [wəʊld] *n Geog* plateau *m*
wolf, *pl* **wolves** [wʊlf, wʊlvz] *n* **(a)** loup *m*; **she w.** louve *f*; **w. cub** louveteau *m*; **to be as hungry as a w.** avoir une faim de loup; *Fig* **that will keep the w. from the door** cela vous/nous/*etc* mettra à l'abri du besoin; *Fig* **to throw sb to the wolves** sacrifier qn; **a w. in sheep's clothing** un loup déguisé en brebis; **to cry w.** crier au loup **(b)** *F* (*womanizer*) coureur *m* de jupons
► **wolf down** *vtsep* engloutir, dévorer
wolfhound ['wʊlfhaʊnd] *n* chien-loup *m*, *pl* chiens-loups; **Irish w.** lévrier *m* d'Irlande
wolfish ['wʊlfɪʃ] *adj* de loup; (*appetite*) vorace; **a w. grin** un sourire aux dents longues
wolfram ['wʊlfrəm] *n Miner* wolfram *m*
wolfsbane ['wʊlfsbeɪn] *n* (*plant*) aconit *m*
wolf whistle *n* = sifflement *m* admiratif (*au passage d'une jolie fille*); **he gave her a w.** il l'a sifflée
wolf-whistle *vti* siffler; **to be wolf-whistled** se faire siffler
wolverine ['wʊlvəriːn] *n* glouton *m*
woman, *pl* **women** ['wʊmən, 'wɪmɪn] *n* [①A14,12,c] femme *f*; **an old w.** une vieille femme, *Pej* une vieille; *F* (*man*) un chipoteur; **the other w.** l'autre femme; **they have a w. in to do the cleaning** ils ont quelqu'un qui vient faire le ménage; **she's his w.** c'est sa compagne; **he's got women all over the place** il a des maîtresses partout; *Old-fashioned, F* **the little w.** (*my wife*) ma femme; *F* **get in the car, w.!** allez femme, en voiture!; **to run after women** courir le jupon; **a w.'s place is in the home** une femme doit rester à la maison; *prov* **a w.'s work is never done** = les femmes sont constamment occupées (à la maison); **the women's movement**, *F* **women's lib** le Mouvement pour la libération de la femme (M.L.F.); *F Pej* **women's libber** (*member*) membre *m* du M.L.F.; (*supporter*) partisan, -ane du M.L.F. ; *Journ* **women's page** page *f* des lectrices; **women's magazines** magazines féminins, revues féminines; **women's problems** ennuis *ou* problèmes de femmes *ou* féminins; **w. artist** femme peintre; **w. chaser** coureur *m* de jupons; **w. doctor** femme médecin; **women doctors** femmes médecins; **w. driver** femme au volant, conductrice *f*; **it was a w. driver** c'était une femme qui conduisait; **w. friend** amie *f*
womanhater ['wʊmənheɪtər] *n* misogyne *m*
womanhood ['wʊmənhʊd] *n* féminité *f*; **to grow to w.** devenir femme
womanish ['wʊmənɪʃ] *adj Pej* (*characteristic of a woman*) de femme; (*man*) efféminé
womanize ['wʊmənaɪz] *vi* courir les femmes, courir le jupon
womanizer ['wʊmənaɪzər] *n* coureur *m* (de femmes)
womanizing ['wʊmənaɪzɪŋ] *n* aventures *fpl*; **she was fed up with his w.** elle en avait assez qu'il coure le jupon
womankind ['wʊmənkaɪnd] *n* (*no pl*) les femmes *fpl*
womanliness ['wʊmənlɪnɪs] *n* féminité *f*
womanly ['wʊmənlɪ] *adj* féminin
womb [wuːm] *n Anat* utérus *m*; **the child she carried in her w.** l'enfant qu'elle portait dans son ventre *ou Lit* sein; **while still in his mother's w.** quand il était encore dans le ventre de sa mère
wombat ['wɒmbæt] *n* wombat *m*, phascolome *m*
women ['wɪmɪn] *npl see* **woman**
womenfolk ['wɪmɪnfəʊk] *n* (*no pl*) les femmes *fpl*; **the settlers**

brought their w. les colons ont amené leurs femmes et leurs filles

won *see* **win²**

wonder¹ ['wʌndər] *n* **(a)** *(miracle)* merveille *f*, miracle *m*, prodige *m*; **to work** *or* **do wonders** faire des merveilles *ou* des miracles; **the seven wonders of the world** les sept merveilles du monde; **a nine-day(s') w.** la merveille d'un jour; **one of the wonders of the world** une des merveilles du monde; **it's a w. (that) he hasn't lost it** c'est un miracle qu'il ne l'ait pas perdu; **no** *or* **little** *or* **small w. that the plan failed** il n'est guère *ou* pas étonnant que le projet n'ait pas réussi; **she's angry and no** *or* **little w.** elle est en colère et ce n'est pas étonnant; **w. cure** traitement *m* miracle; **w. drug** remède *m* miracle

(b) *(astonishment)* étonnement *m*, surprise *f*; *(admiration)* émerveillement *m*, admiration *f*; **in w.** émerveillé; **to look at sb in w.** regarder qn avec émerveillement; **to fill sb with w.** émerveiller qn; **an expression** *or* **look of w.** un air émerveillé, une expression d'émerveillement; **I looked at it with a sense of w.** je l'ai regardé, émerveillé; **he has no sense of w.** il n'a aucune capacité d'émerveillement

wonder² **1** *vi* *(be amazed)* s'étonner, s'émerveiller (**at** de); *Iron* **I really w. at you sometimes!** tu me surprendras toujours!; **I w. at how he manages to do it** je suis étonné par sa façon de s'y prendre; **I w. about her sometimes** je me pose des questions à son sujet parfois; **I was wondering about buying a new car** je songeais à acheter une nouvelle voiture; **I don't w. at it** cela ne m'étonne pas *ou* ne me surprend pas; **it's not to be wondered at that she left** il n'est pas étonnant qu'elle soit partie, rien d'étonnant à ce qu'elle soit partie

2 *vt* **(a)** *(be amazed)* **to w. that ...** s'étonner que ... + *sub*; **I w. that nobody thought of it before** je m'étonne que personne n'y ait pensé avant; **can you w. that he refused?** comment s'étonner qu'il ait refusé?

(b) *(ask oneself)* se demander; **I w.** *(if he/she/etc will do that)* je me le demande; **one wonders!** c'est à se demander!; **it makes you w. how safe these power stations are** on en vient à se demander si ces centrales électriques sont vraiment sûres; **I w. whether he'll come** je me demande *ou* je voudrais bien savoir s'il viendra; **one wonders whether ...** c'est à se demander si ...; **I shouldn't w. if he were already married** cela ne m'étonnerait pas *ou* ne me surprendrait pas qu'il soit déjà marié; **she knows a lot more, I shouldn't w.** cela ne m'étonnerait pas qu'elle en sache beaucoup plus long que ça; **I w. who invented that** je suis curieux de savoir qui a inventé cela; **I w. why!** je voudrais bien savoir pourquoi!; **their son will help them – I w.!** leur fils leur viendra en aide – vous croyez?; **I was wondering if you were free tonight** je me demandais si vous étiez libre ce soir; **oh, I just wondered** *(answering question 'why do you ask?')* oh, pour rien, comme ça; **I was just wondering where you'd got to** j'étais en train de me demander où tu étais

wonderful ['wʌndəfʊl] *adj* merveilleux, prodigieux, admirable; *(film, book)* remarquable, formidable; **it's w. weather** il fait un temps fantastique; **a w. meal** un excellent *ou* délicieux repas; **she's a w. mother** c'est une mère merveilleuse; **she's a w. person** elle est fantastique; **it was w.!** c'était merveilleux *ou* magnifique!; **we had a w. time** nous nous sommes très bien amusés

wonderfully ['wʌndəfəlɪ] *adv* merveilleusement; **he sings w.** il chante merveilleusement *ou* remarquablement (bien); **it was w. hot** il faisait délicieusement chaud; **w. well** merveilleusement bien, à merveille; **a w. good book** un livre absolument génial; **we had some w. good food** nous avons très bien mangé

wondering ['wʌndərɪŋ] *adj* *(amazed)* étonné, émerveillé; **the child's w. eyes** les yeux émerveillés de l'enfant

wonderingly ['wʌndərɪŋlɪ] *adv* avec étonnement, d'un air étonné

wonderland ['wʌndəlænd] *n* pays *m* des merveilles; **Alice in W.** Alice au Pays des Merveilles

wonderment ['wʌndəmənt] *n* *Lit* émerveillement *m*; **she looked at him with** *or* **in w.** elle l'a regardé avec émerveillement

wondrous ['wʌndrəs] *Arch, Lit* **1** *adj* merveilleux **2** *adv* **w. wise** très sage

wondrously ['wʌndrəslɪ] *adv Arch, Lit* merveilleusement

wonky ['wɒŋkɪ] *adj Br F* *(machine)* détraqué, déglingué; *(gadget, zip, switch etc)* qui débloque; *(collar, picture etc)* de travers; *(wardrobe, shelves)* branlant; *(one leg short)* *(chair, table)* boiteux; *(idea)* fumeux; **to feel w.** *(of person)* se sentir patraque; **this sentence is a bit w.** il y a quelque chose qui cloche dans cette phrase; **my grammar's a bit w.** ma grammaire cloche un peu; **the floorboards are a bit w.** le plancher n'est pas dans un état merveilleux

wont¹ [wəʊnt] *adj Lit* **to be w. to do sth** avoir coutume *ou* l'habitude de faire qch; **he is w. to panic** il a tendance à paniquer, il panique facilement

wont² *n Lit* coutume *f*, habitude *f*; **according to his w., as is/was his w.** selon sa coutume, à *ou* selon *ou* suivant son habitude

won't [wəʊnt] = **will not**, *see* **will³**

wonted ['wəʊntɪd] *adj Lit* habituel, accoutumé

woo [wuː] *vt* **(a)** *Fig* *(potential employee, supporter, company)* courtiser; *(fame)* rechercher; **they wooed voters with promises of reforms** *(tried to attract)* ils ont essayé d'attirer des électeurs avec des promesses de réforme; *(succeeded in attracting)* ils se sont assuré les voix des électeurs avec des promesses de réforme; **they wooed him away from their rivals by promising him more money** ils lui ont fait quitter leurs concurrents en lui promettant plus d'argent **(b)** *Arch, Lit* *(court)* *(woman)* faire la cour à, courtiser

wood [wʊd] *n* **(a)** *(group of trees)* bois *m*; **a walk in the woods** une promenade en forêt; *Fig* **you can't see the w. for the trees** les arbres cachent la forêt; **his problem is that he can't see the w. for the trees** son problème, c'est que les arbres lui cachent la forêt; *Fig* **we're not out of the w. yet** nous ne sommes pas encore tirés d'affaire

(b) *(material)* bois *m*; **made of w.** fait de bois, en bois; *Fig* **touch w.!**, *US* **knock on w.!** touchons du bois!; **w. ash** cendre *f* de bois; **w. block** planche *f*, bois; **w. carver** sculpteur *m* sur bois; **w. carving** sculpture *f* sur bois; **w. chisel** ciseau *m* à bois; **w. fire** feu *m* de bois; **w. floor** plancher *m* en bois; **w. panelling** boiserie *f*; **w. pulp** pâte *f* à papier; **w. stove** poêle *m* à bois

(c) *(in wine making)* **the w.** le tonneau, le fût; **wine in the w.** vin *m* en tonneau *ou* en fût; **beer (drawn) from the w.** bière tirée au fût

(d) *Golf* bois *m*; **a number 4 w.** un bois numéro 4

(e) *Bowls* boule *f*

(f) *Mus* = **woodwind**

wood alcohol *n* alcool *m* méthylique

wood anemone *n* anémone *f* des bois

woodbine ['wʊdbaɪn] *n* *(honeysuckle)* chèvrefeuille *m* des bois; *US* *(Virginia creeper)* vigne *f* vierge

woodchuck ['wʊdtʃʌk] *n* marmotte *f* d'Amérique

woodcock ['wʊdkɒk] *n* *(usu inv in pl)* bécasse *f* (des bois)

woodcraft ['wʊdkrɑːft] *n* **(a)** *(knowledge of forest)* connaissance *f* de la forêt **(b)** *(woodwork)* (pratique *f* du) travail *m* sur bois

woodcut ['wʊdkʌt] *n* gravure *f* sur bois

woodcutter ['wʊdkʌtər] *n* bûcheron *m*

woodcutting ['wʊdkʌtɪŋ] *n* **(a)** *Art* *(process, object)* gravure *f* sur bois **(b)** *(in forest)* abattage *m* du bois

wooded ['wʊdɪd] *adj* boisé; **w. country** pays boisé

wooden ['wʊd(ə)n] *adj* **(a)** *(made of wood)* de bois, en bois; **w. pallet** palette *f* en bois; **w. shoes** sabots *mpl*; **w. spoon** *Culin* cuiller *f* en *ou* de bois; *Fig* prix *m* de consolation **(b)** *Fig* *(movement, manner)* raide, gauche; *(look)* impassible; *(performance, actor)* peu naturel; **w. smile** sourire *m* forcé

wooden-headed *adj F* *(stupid)* stupide, bouché

Wooden Horse *n Myth* Cheval *m* de Troie

woodenness ['wʊdənnɪs] *n Fig* *(of manner)* raideur *f*; *(of actor, performance)* manque *m* de naturel

woodland ['wʊdlənd] *n* région *f* boisée, bois *mpl*; **w. scenery** paysage boisé; **w. flowers** fleurs de bois

woodlark ['wʊdlɑːk] *n* alouette *f* des bois

woodlouse, *pl* **-lice** ['wʊdlaʊs, -laɪs] *n* cloporte *m*

woodman, *pl* **-men** ['wʊdmən] *n* *(logger)* bûcheron *m*

wood nymph *n Myth* dryade *f*

woodpecker ['wʊdpekər] *n* pic *m*

wood pigeon *n* (pigeon *m*) ramier *m*

woodpile ['wʊdpaɪl] *n* tas *m ou* monceau *m* de bois

woodshed ['wʊdʃed] *n* remise *f* à bois; *Fig* **there's something nasty in the w.** il se passe du vilain

woodsman, *pl* **-men** ['wʊdzmən] *n esp US* *(hunter)* chasseur *m* (en forêt); *(for skins)* trappeur *m*; *(in forestry)* forestier *m*

woodstack ['wʊdstæk] *n* = **woodpile**

woodwind ['wʊdwɪnd] *n Mus* **the w.** les bois *mpl*; **w. instrument** instrument *m* à vent en bois

woodwork ['wʊdwɜːk] *n* **(a)** *(action)* travail *m* du bois; *(smaller scale)* menuiserie *f*, ébénisterie *f*; *(school subject)* menuiserie **(b)** *(carved wood)* bois *m* travaillé; *(ornamental)* boiserie *f*; *(structural)* charpente *f*; **that's a fine piece of w.** c'est de la belle menuiserie; *Fig Pej* **to come out of the w.** sortir d'on ne sait où; *Sp* **to hit the w.** heurter les bois

woodworm ['wʊdwɜːm] *n* ver *m* à bois; **this table's got w.** cette table est vermoulue; **it's full of w.** c'est rongé par les vers

woody ['wʊdɪ] *adj* **(a)** (*countryside*) boisé **(b)** *Bot* ligneux **(c)** (*smell, texture*) de bois
wooer ['wu:ər] *n Old-fashioned, Lit* prétendant *m*
woof[1] [wu:f] *n Tex* trame *f*
woof[2] [wʊf] *n* (*of dog*) aboiement *m*; **the doggie goes w. (w.)** (*in children's language*) le toutou fait oua-oua
woof[3] [wʊf] *vi* (*of dog*) aboyer, faire oua-oua
woofer ['wu:fər] *n* (*in stereo equipment*) haut-parleur *m* de basses, boomer *m*, woofer *m*
wool [wʊl] *n* **(a)** (*material*) laine *f*; **the w. industry** l'industrie lainière; **the w. trade** le commerce des laines; **pure** *or* **all w. suit** complet *m* pure laine; **a ball of w.** une pelote de laine; *Fig* **to pull the w. over sb's eyes** jeter de la poudre aux yeux de qn; *Fig* **you can't pull the w. over my eyes** tu ne peux pas me faire croire n'importe quoi; **w. cloth** tissu de laine; **w. grower** éleveur, -euse de moutons; **w. shop** magasin de laines **(b)** (*of animal*) pelage *m* **(c)** *Tech* **steel** *or* **wire w.** paille *f* de fer
woolen, wooly *etc US* = **woollen, woolly** *etc*
woolgathering ['wʊlgæð(ə)rɪŋ] *n F* **(a)** (*daydreaming*) rêvasserie *f* **(b)** (*used as a verb*) **to be w.** rêvasser, être dans les nuages; **he's always w.** il a toujours l'esprit ailleurs, il est toujours ailleurs
woollen, *US* **woolen** ['wʊlən] **1** *adj* (*dress etc*) en laine; **w. materials** laines *fpl*, lainages *mpl* **2** *npl* **woollens** lainages *mpl*
woolliness, *US* **wooliness** ['wʊlɪnɪs] *n* **(a)** (*of reasoning, style*) imprécision *f*; (*of ideas*) caractère *m* confus; (*of outline*) manque *m* de netteté, flou *m* **(b)** (*resemblance to wool*) nature *f* laineuse (**of** de)
woolly, *US* **wooly** ['wʊlɪ] **1** *adj* **(a)** (*resembling wool*) laineux, de laine; **w. clouds** nuages ouatés; **w. hair** cheveux crépus **(b)** *Fig* (*vague*) peu net; (*outline*) flou; **w. ideas** idées vagues *ou* nébuleuses; **w.-minded** aux idées imprécises *ou* vagues; **w. style** style qui manque de précision; **a w. liberal** un libéral aux idées vagues **2** *n F* (*garment*) tricot *m*, laine *f*; **winter woollies** vêtements chauds d'hiver
Woolsack ['wʊlsæk] *n Br Parl* **the W.** = le siège du Lord Chancellor (à la Chambre des Lords)
woozy ['wu:zɪ] *adj F* (*person*) dans les vapes, patraque; **I feel a bit w.** je me sens un peu patraque, je me sens tout chose
wop [wɒp] *n Offensive Sl* macaroni *m*, rital *m*
Worcs *abbr* **Worcestershire**
word[1] [wɜ:d] *n* **(a)** mot *m*; **w. for w.** (*to repeat sth*) mot pour mot; (*to translate sth*) mot à mot, textuellement; **in a w.** en un mot, (en) bref; **in a w., no** en un mot, non; **in a few words** en quelques mots; **in other words** en d'autres termes, autrement dit; **those were her very words** ce sont ses propres mots; **I told him what I thought of him in so many words** je lui ai dit clairement ce que je pensais de lui; **did she say you could take it? – well, not in so many words** est-ce qu'elle a dit que tu pouvais le prendre? – eh bien, pas exactement; **in the strict sense of the w.** au sens strict du mot; **he doesn't know a w. of German** il ne sait pas un mot d'allemand; **'robbery' would be a better w. for it** 'vol' serait un mot plus approprié; **'bad' isn't the w. for it** 'mauvais' n'est pas le mot; **that's the wrong** *or* **not the right w. (for it)** ce n'est pas le mot qui convient; **there's a w. for it in Russian** il y a un mot pour exprimer cela en russe; **the Spanish w. for 'mouse'** 'souris' en espagnol; **he was reserved – that's one w. for it!** il était réservé – c'est le moins qu'on puisse dire!; **there's a w. for people like you, it's 'thief'** les gens dans ton genre, on les appelle des voleurs; **she used a less flattering w.** elle a utilisé un terme moins flatteur; **what's the w. I'm looking for?** quel est le mot que je cherche?; **there's no other w. for it** il n'y a pas d'autre mot; **the spoken/written w.** la parole/les écrits *mpl*; **in the words of Voltaire** selon (l'expression de) Voltaire, comme l'a dit Voltaire; **that is your w., not mine** c'est toi qui as dit cela, pas moi; **in your own words** selon tes propres mots; **a 600-w. article** un article de 600 mots; **I can't put it into words** je n'arrive pas à l'exprimer par des mots; **he's a man of few words** c'est un homme qui parle peu *ou* qui ne parle pas beaucoup; **I can't get a w. out of her** je ne peux pas en tirer un mot; **I couldn't get a w. in (edgeways)** je n'ai pas pu placer un mot; **he didn't say a w.** il n'a rien dit, il n'a pas soufflé mot; **not a w.!** pas un mot!, bouche cousue!; **without a w.** sans mot dire; **with these words, he went** sur ces mots *ou* là-dessus, il est parti; **words fail me!** j'en perds la parole!; **too ridiculous for words** d'un ridicule sans nom; **too stupid for words** d'une bêtise indicible; **too beautiful for words** d'une beauté ineffable; **fine words, but we'll see if their actions match them** belles paroles, mais nous verrons si l'on peut en dire de même de leurs actes; **kind words** des mots aimables; **w. picture** description *f* imagée *ou* pittoresque; (*of person*) portrait *m* en prose; **words per minute** (*of printer, typist*) mots par minute; **to be w. perfect** (*of actor*) savoir son rôle sur le bout du doigt

(b) (*remarks, conversation*) **may I have a w. with you?, I'd like a w. with you** puis-je vous parler un instant?; **I'll have a w. with her about it** je lui en toucherai deux mots; **I have been asked to say a few words of introduction** on m'a demandé de dire quelques mots d'introduction; **you're putting words into my mouth** vous me faites dire des choses que je ne veux pas dire; **you've taken the words (right) out of my mouth** tu me l'as retiré de la bouche; **to put in a good w. for sb** dire *ou* glisser un mot en faveur de qn; **he never has a good w. for anyone** il ne peut pas s'empêcher de dire du mal des gens; **a w. in/out of season** un conseil opportun/inopportun; **a w. of warning** une mise en garde; **I gave him a w. of warning** je l'ai mis en garde; **can I offer you a w. (or two) of advice?** puis-je vous donner un petit conseil?; **they had few words of comfort for her** ils ne lui ont pas dit grand-chose pour la consoler; **a w. of sympathy** un mot de condoléances

(c) (*no pl*) (*message*) nouvelle *f*; (*official etc*) avis *m*, déclaration *f*; **to send sb w. of sth** faire part à qn de qch; (*officially, formally*) faire savoir qch à qn; **they sent w. that ...** ils ont fait savoir que ...; **we received w. that ...** on nous a apporté la nouvelle que ...; **have you had any w. yet?** (*of how they are etc*) est-ce que tu as eu des nouvelles?; **there's (been) no w. from Moscow** on n'a pas de nouvelles de Moscou; **by w. of mouth** (*to tell sb sth*) verbalement; (*to spread*) (*of rumours*) de bouche à oreille; **the w. is that he's retiring** on raconte qu'il va prendre sa retraite; **the w. on the street is that Fingers Fred did it** le bruit court que c'est Fingers Fred qui l'a fait; **she left w. with George for them to join her** elle a demandé à George de leur dire de la rejoindre

(d) (*promise*) parole *f*; **one's w. of honour** sa parole d'honneur; **to give sb one's w.** donner sa parole à qn; **to keep one's w.** tenir (sa) parole; **to break one's w.** manquer à sa parole; **to go back on one's w.** revenir sur sa parole; **I give you my w., (you can) take my w. for it** je vous en donne ma parole, je vous en réponds; **I'll take your w. for it** je vous crois sur parole, je m'en rapporte à vous; **we've only got her w. for it** du moins, c'est ce qu'elle nous a dit; **it's your w. against his** c'est votre parole contre la sienne; **he's a man of his w.** c'est un homme de parole; **she's as good as her w.** elle tient parole; **she was better than her w.** elle a fait mieux que tenir ses promesses; **his w. is as good as his bond** sa parole vaut sa signature; **they took her at her w.** ils l'ont prise au mot; **we will hold you to your w.** nous vous obligerons à tenir parole; **my w.!** ma parole!

(e) to have words with sb (*argue*) se disputer *ou* se quereller avec qn; **they had words** ils ont eu des mots

(f) (*order*) **w. of command** ordre *m*; **to give the w. to do sth** (*give order*) donner l'ordre de faire qch; (*give signal*) donner le signal de faire qch; **if you want any more paper just say the w.** si tu veux encore du papier, dis-le

(g) *Rel* **the w. of God** la parole de Dieu; **the W.** (*Christ*) le Verbe; **to spread the w.** (*proselytize*) annoncer la bonne parole

(h) *Comptr* mot *m*

(i) (*lyrics*) **words and music by Ian Smith** paroles *fpl* et musique *f* par Ian Smith; **listen to the words** écoute les paroles
word[2] *vt* (*document etc*) formuler, rédiger; (*comment*) formuler, exprimer; **it could have been better worded** il aurait/tu aurais/*etc* pu mieux le formuler; **be careful how you w. it** fais attention à la manière dont tu le formules; **a cleverly worded contract** un contrat habilement formulé
word association *n* association *f* de mots
word blindness *n* dyslexie *f*
wordbook ['wɜ:dbʊk] *n* vocabulaire *m*, lexique *m*
word count *n esp Comptr* nombre *m* de mots; **to do a w.** compter les mots; **w. facility** fonction *f* de comptage de mots
word group *n* groupe *m* de mots, membre *m* de phrase
wordiness ['wɜ:dɪnɪs] *n* verbosité *f*, prolixité *f*
wording ['wɜ:dɪŋ] *n* **(a)** (*choice of words*) (*of article, document*) formulation *f*, (choix *m* de) termes *mpl*; (*of problem*) énoncé *m*; (*of banker's draft, bill of exchange*) libellé *m*; **the w. was ambiguous** les termes étaient ambigus, la formulation était ambiguë; **it is important to get the w. right** il est important de choisir les termes appropriés **(b)** (*action*) (*of document*) rédaction *f*
wordless ['wɜ:dlɪs] *adj esp Lit* sans paroles, muet
wordlessly ['wɜ:dlɪslɪ] *adv* sans dire un mot
word list *n* liste *f* de mots; (*content of dictionary*) nomenclature *f*

word order *n* [ⓘA72-3,17; B59-60,A] *Gram* ordre *m* des mots

word-process *vt* rédiger par traitement de texte; **word-processed text** texte *m* écrit au traitement de texte

word processing *n* traitement *m* de texte; **w. package, w. software** logiciel *m* de traitement de texte; **w. skills** compétences *fpl* en matière de traitement de texte

word processor *n* (*hardware*) machine *f* de traitement de texte; (*software*) (logiciel *m* de) traitement *m* de texte, texteur *m*

wordsmith ['wɜːdsmɪθ] *n* **he's a real w.** il sait manier les mots

word split *n Typ* coupure *f* de mot

wordwrap ['wɜːdræp] *n Comptr* passage *m* automatique à la ligne suivante

wordy ['wɜːdɪ] *adj* verbeux, prolixe, diffus

work[1] [wɜːk] *n* **(a)** (*labour*) travail *m*, -aux; **to be at w.** être au travail; **they are at w. on a new book** ils sont en train de travailler à un nouveau livre; **the forces at w.** les forces en jeu; **there are evil forces at w.** des forces maléfiques sont à l'œuvre; **to be hard at w.** être en plein travail; **he was hard at w. gardening** il était en plein jardinage; **to start w., to set** *or* **get to w.** se mettre au travail; **they set to w. digging the hole** ils se sont mis à creuser le trou; **they put him to w. in the kitchen** ils l'ont mis au travail dans la cuisine; **she was set to w. cataloguing the collection** on lui a donné pour tâche de répertorier la collection; **to stop w.** cesser le travail; (*for the day*) suspendre le travail; **w. environment** milieu *m* de travail; **w. method** méthode *f* de travail; **w. standard** norme *f* de travail

(b) (*task*) travail *m*, -aux, ouvrage *m*, besogne *f*, tâche *f*; **I've (got) w. to do** j'ai (du travail) à faire; **to have too much w. to do** avoir trop de travail à faire; **to get through a lot of w.** abattre de la besogne; **to give sb some w. to do** donner du travail à faire à qn; **there's a lot of w. to be done** il y a beaucoup (de travail) à faire; **it will take a lot of w. to make a team out of them** ça va être un drôle de travail de faire d'eux une équipe; **she put a lot of w. into her exams** elle a beaucoup travaillé à ses examens; **they're doing some w. for an American firm** (*of subcontractor*) ils travaillent pour une firme américaine; **very little w. has been done on this disease** peu de travail a été effectué sur cette maladie; **let's get down to w.!** mettons-nous au travail!; **a fine piece of w.** un beau travail; **the brandy had done its w.** l'eau-de-vie avait fait son effet; **I'll have my w. cut out to finish in time** je vais en baver pour finir à l'heure; **you'll have your w. cut out with him** il vous donnera du fil à retordre; **he made quick w. of the ironing** il est rapidement venu à bout du repassage; **to make w. for sb** compliquer la vie à qn; **day's w.** (travail d'une) journée *f*; **it's all in a day's w.** ça n'a rien d'exceptionnel; **good w.!** bien fait!; **it was thirsty w.** c'était un travail qui donnait soif; **the w. of a professional** le travail *ou* l'œuvre *f* d'un professionnel; **this break-in is the w. of a professional** cette effraction est l'œuvre d'un professionnel

(c) (*product, achievement*) ouvrage *m*, œuvre *f*; **the works of God** les œuvres de Dieu; **good works** bonnes œuvres; **the (complete) works of Shakespeare** les œuvres *ou* l'œuvre *m ou f* de Shakespeare; **a w. of art/genius** une œuvre d'art/de génie; **his early works** ses premières œuvres; **w. of fiction** ouvrage de fiction; **is this all your own w.?** est-ce que vous avez fait ça tout seul?; **her w. sells well** ses ouvrages se vendent bien; **very detailed/delicate w.** (*embroidery, carving etc*) ouvrage très détaillé/délicat

(d) (*employment*) travail *m*, emploi *m*; **I need w.** il me faut du travail; **what kind of w. are you looking for?** quel genre de travail recherchez-vous?; **cleaning w.** nettoyage *m*; **I'm looking for translation w.** je cherche des traductions (à faire); **office w.** travail de bureau; **manual w.** travail manuel; **skilled w.** travail qualifié; **the factory will provide w. for a hundred people** l'usine fournira du travail à cent personnes; **to be off w.** ne pas travailler (*parce qu'on est malade*); **to be out of w.** (*unemployed*) être en *ou* au chômage; **she's not in w. at the moment** elle ne travaille pas en ce moment; *F* **nice w. if you can get it** il y en a qui ne s'embêtent pas!; *Br F* **he's a nasty bit** *or* **piece of w.** c'est un sale type; *Br F* **their daughter is a nasty bit** *or* **piece of w.** leur fille est une sale gosse

(e) (*workplace*) (lieu *m* de) travail *m*; **works** (*factory*) usine *f*; **he's not at w. today** il ne travaille pas aujourd'hui; **on my way to w.** en allant travailler *ou* au travail; **someone at w. told me** quelqu'un au travail me l'a dit; **someone from w.** quelqu'un du travail; **someone from your w. called** quelqu'un de ton travail a appelé; **works council** comité *m* d'entreprise; **works outing** sortie *f* annuelle des employés *ou* des ouvriers

(f) *Mil* (*usu pl*) **works** ouvrages *mpl*, travaux *mpl*; **field works** travaux de campagne

(g) *Constr* (*usu pl*) **works** travaux *mpl*; **public works** travaux publics; **road works ahead!** attention travaux!; *US* **w. zone!** travaux!, chantier!

(h) (*mechanism*) (*usu pl*) **works** (*of watch etc*) rouages *mpl*, mécanisme *m*

(i) *F* **they had eggs, bacon, toast, the works** ils avaient des œufs, du bacon, du pain grillé, tout, quoi!; *F* **the whole works** tout le bataclan, tout le tralala; **in his autobiography we are given the full works** (*full details of life*) son autobiographie nous livre tous les dessous de sa vie; **I treated myself to the full works at the beauty parlour** je me suis payé une séance de luxe chez l'esthéticienne; *Sl* **to give sb the works** (*beating*) passer qn à tabac; (*luxury treatment*) jouer le grand jeu à qn; *esp US F* **to shoot the works** (*spend all one's money*) claquer tout son fric; **to be in the works** (*in preparation*) être en cours

work[2] (*pt, pp* **worked** [wɜːkt], *Arch and in a few expressions* **wrought** [rɔːt]) **1** *vi* **(a)** (*of person*) travailler; (*for good of other people*) œuvrer; **to w. hard** travailler dur; **to w. like a slave** *or* **a dog** *or* **a Trojan** *or* **a beaver** travailler comme un forçat *ou* comme un bœuf; **to w. a 40-hour week** faire une semaine de 40 heures; **to w. long hours** faire de grandes journées de travail; *Ind* **to w. to rule** faire la grève du zèle; **to w. in leather/brass** travailler dans le cuir/cuivre; **she works in publishing** elle travaille dans l'édition; **to w. on** *or* **for a newspaper** collaborer à un journal; **to w. for a good cause** travailler pour une bonne cause; **he worked with the poor and the sick** il travaillait avec les pauvres et les malades; **the city council, working to improve the quality of life** le conseil municipal, à l'œuvre pour l'amélioration de la qualité de la vie; **all her life she worked for peace/to bring the two countries together** toute sa vie elle a œuvré pour la paix/pour unir les deux pays; **we are working towards a peaceful solution** nous œuvrons en vue d'une solution pacifique; **to w. against sb** intriguer *ou* travailler contre qn; **their earlier popularity was now working against them** leur popularité des débuts jouait maintenant en leur défaveur; **let your body weight w. for you rather than against you** laisse ton poids jouer en ta faveur plutôt que contre toi; **her age worked in her favour** son âge a joué en sa faveur; **working from the principle that ...** partant du principe que ...; **I am working on the assumption that you can type** je pars du principe que vous savez taper à la machine

(b) (*be employed*) travailler, avoir un emploi; **who do you w. for?** chez qui est-ce que vous travaillez?; **she works for Smith and Wilson** elle travaille chez Smith and Wilson; **she works for the water board** elle travaille au service des eaux

(c) (*function*) (*of machine, system*) fonctionner, marcher; **the pump isn't working** la pompe ne marche *ou* ne fonctionne pas; **the lift isn't working** l'ascenseur est hors de service *ou* est en panne; **the system works well** le système fonctionne bien; **I can't get this machine to w.** je n'arrive pas à faire marcher cette machine; **they soon got** *or* **had it working** ils sont vite parvenus à le faire fonctionner; **can you show me how the photocopier works?** est-ce que tu peux me faire voir comment marche la photocopieuse?; **it works like this, here's how it works** (*of machine, system*) cela marche de la façon suivante, voilà comment ça marche; **it works both ways** ça marche dans les deux sens; **to w. as sth** (*serve the function of*) faire office de qch; **high unemployment works as a brake on wage claims** le taux élevé de chômage freine la hausse des salaires; **the clock works off electricity** la pendule marche à l'électricité; **these tools w. by compressed air** ces outils sont actionnés par *ou* marchent à l'air comprimé

(d) (*have effect, succeed*) (*of drug, cleaning product*) faire effet; (*of plan, method*) marcher, y faire; (*of yeast*) fermenter; **the drug works in most cases** le médicament fait de l'effet dans la plupart des cas; **rubbing the stain won't w.** frotter la tache ne servira à rien; **she tried everything she could think of but nothing worked** elle a essayé tout ce à quoi elle pouvait penser mais rien n'a marché; **this isn't working** (*not succeeding*) ça ne marche pas; **his plan didn't w.** son projet a échoué *ou* n'a pas réussi; **that/flattery won't w. with me** ça/la flatterie ne prend pas avec moi

(e) (*of face, features*) remuer, s'agiter

(f) (*move*) **to w. upstream** remonter le courant; **a band of rain working across the country** un front de pluie qui traverse le pays; **the infection has worked downwards** l'infection a progressé vers le bas; **I knew what he was trying to w. round to** je savais où il voulait en venir; **he finally worked round to asking her out** il l'a finalement invitée à sortir; **I haven't done it yet but I'm working round**

to it je ne l'ai pas encore fait, mais je vais m'en occuper; **to w. loose** (*of nut etc*) se desserrer

2 *vt* **(a)** (*person, horse etc*) faire travailler; **he works his employees/himself very hard** il exige beaucoup de travail de son personnel/lui-même; **to w. oneself to death** se tuer à force de travailler; **don't w. yourself to death!** ne va pas te tuer à la tâche *ou* à l'ouvrage!; *Iron* ne te fais pas trop mal, surtout!

(b) (*operate*) (*machine etc*) faire travailler, faire fonctionner, faire marcher; **it is worked by steam/electricity** cela marche à la vapeur/à l'électricité

(c) (*bring about*) (*miracle, cure*) opérer; (*change*) amener; **the beauty of the place was beginning to w. its magic on her** la beauté de l'endroit commençait à exercer sa magie sur elle; **the destruction wrought by the fire** la dévastation causée par l'incendie; **I'll w. it** *or* **things so that they pay in advance** je ferai de sorte qu'ils paient à l'avance; **his keys had worked a hole in his pocket** ses clefs avaient fini par faire un trou dans sa poche

(d) (*move*) **to w. one's hands free** parvenir à dégager ses mains; **she worked the ropes loose** elle a réussi à desserrer les cordes petit à petit; **to w. one's way down/up** descendre/monter petit à petit *ou* avec précaution; **his hand worked its way up my leg** sa main remontait progressivement sur ma jambe; **he worked his way towards her** il s'est avancé vers elle petit à petit; **they worked their way through the crowd** ils se sont frayé un chemin à travers la foule; **they worked their way through the list** ils ont traité chaque élément de la liste tour à tour; **we're working our way through the French subjunctive** nous sommes en train d'étudier le subjonctif en français; **he's worked his way through the whole grant** il a épuisé toute la subvention; **they have worked themselves into a corner** ils se sont mis dans une impasse

(e) (*mine, quarry*) exploiter; (*land*) travailler; *Com* **to w. the south-east** (*of representative*) couvrir le sud-est

(f) *Naut* **to w. one's passage** payer son passage par son travail; **he worked his passage to Rio** il a payé son passage à Rio en travaillant; **to w. one's way through university** (*of student*) travailler pour payer ses études

(g) *Sewing* (*design, initials*) broder; **the flowers are worked in silk** les fleurs sont brodées en soie

▶ **work in** *vtsep* (*include, introduce*) (*incident in novel etc*) introduire; (*mix in*) incorporer, mélanger; **to w. in a reference to unemployment** faire une allusion au chômage; **to w. the other ingredients in** incorporer les autres ingrédients

▶ **work into** *vtaspo* **gently w. the cream into your hands** massez-vous les mains pour faire pénétrer la crème; **w. the dye into the surface of the leather** faites pénétrer la teinture dans le cuir; **he worked several references to her into his speech** il a glissé plusieurs allusions à elle dans son discours; **she worked the clay into the shape of a giraffe** elle modela l'argile pour en faire une girafe; **his oratory had them worked into a frenzy** sa virulence oratoire les avait rendus frénétiques; **it takes a while to w. yourself into the right frame of mind** il faut un certain temps pour se mettre dans le bon état d'esprit

▶ **work off** *vtsep* (*one's anger, bad mood*) évacuer (**by doing** en faisant); **to w. off one's anger on sb** passer sa colère sur qn; **I want to w. off some fat** je veux perdre du poids

▶ **work on 1** *vi* (*continue to work*) continuer à travailler

2 *vipo* **(a)** (*be involved in*) travailler à *ou* sur; **he's working on an edition of Hamlet** il travaille à *ou* prépare une édition de Hamlet; **we're working on it** nous travaillons là-dessus; **a detective is working on this case** un détective est sur cette affaire; **he's been working on his breaststroke/emotional problems** il a travaillé sa brasse/essayé de résoudre ses problèmes sentimentaux

(b) (*use as basis*) **have you any data to w. on?** avez-vous des données sur lesquelles vous fonder?

(c) (*sb*) (*persuade*) influencer, agir sur (l'esprit de); (*attempt to persuade*) travailler

▶ **work out 1** *vtsep* **(a)** (*calculate*) (*cost, distance, sum*) calculer; **from this information, w. out the answer** à partir de cette information, déduisez la réponse; **it took me ages to w. out the right answer** j'ai mis un temps fou pour trouver la réponse exacte; **to w. out the total** faire la somme; **I w. it out at £22** d'après mes calculs, ça fait 22 livres; **the dog had worked out how to open the door** le chien avait compris comment ouvrir la porte; **he's a strange person – I'd worked that out!** il est bizarre – je m'en étais rendu compte!; **well, you can w. it out for yourself** alors, pas besoin que je te fasse un dessin

(b) (*devise*) (*way of doing sth*) trouver, mettre au point; (*scientific method etc*) élaborer

(c) (*resolve*) (*problem*) résoudre; **we must try to w. out our differences** nous devons essayer de résoudre nos désaccords; **I'm sure we can w. this thing out** (*your problem*) je suis sûr que nous pouvons arranger ça; (*our argument*) je suis sûr que nous finirons par nous mettre d'accord

(d) (*understand*) comprendre; **I can't w. her out** je n'arrive pas à la comprendre; **she couldn't w. it out** elle n'y comprenait rien

(e) (*of mine, seam*) **to be worked out** être épuisé

2 *vi* **(a)** (*be resolved*) **I wonder how it will all w. out** je me demande comment cela finira *ou* va finir; **it** *or* **things worked out very well for me** ça a *ou* les choses ont très bien marché pour moi; **it worked out well** *or* **all right for us** ça s'est bien passé pour nous, les choses ont bien tourné pour nous; **but it didn't w. out that way** mais il en a été tout autrement; **it worked out badly for them** les choses ont mal tourné pour eux

(b) (*succeed*) (*of marriage, arrangement*) marcher; **they started a business together, but it didn't w. out** ils ont monté une affaire ensemble, mais ça n'a pas marché; **I don't like my job, but things may w. out** je n'aime pas mon travail, mais ça va peut-être s'arranger; **how is the new system working out?** est-ce que le nouveau système marche?; **are things working out for you OK?** est-ce que ça se passe bien pour toi?; **how's the new manager working out?** comment est-ce que le nouveau directeur se débrouille?

(c) (*amount to*) **how much does it all w. out at?** ça fait combien en tout?; **it** *or* **the cost works out at £150 a head** cela fait 150 livres par personne; **it'll w. out more expensive like that** ça reviendra plus cher comme ça

(d) *Sp* s'entraîner

▶ **work up 1** *vtsep* **(a)** (*develop*) **to w. up an appetite** s'ouvrir l'appétit; **I can't w. up much enthusiasm/interest for the idea** j'ai du mal à m'enthousiasmer pour/à m'intéresser à cette idée

(b) (*arouse*) **he worked the crowd up into a frenzy** il a rendu la foule frénétique; **she had worked herself up into a dreadful rage** elle s'était mise dans une rage terrible; **to get worked up** (*upset*) se rendre malade (**about** au sujet de); (*angry*) se fâcher (**about** au sujet de); (*excited*) se mettre dans tous ses états (**about** au sujet de); **he's all worked up** il est dans tous ses états; **I'm too worked up to do it now** je suis trop énervé *ou* trop à cran pour le faire maintenant

2 *vi* (*of skirt*) remonter

▶ **work up to** *vipo* (*move towards*) (*sth*) avancer par degrés à; **what are you working up to?** où voulez-vous en venir?; **he was working up to a discussion of his salary** il amenait progressivement la discussion sur le sujet de son salaire; **the symphony was working up to its finale** la symphonie allait crescendo, annonçant le finale

workability [wɜːkə'bɪlɪtɪ] *n Tech* maniabilité *f*

workable ['wɜːkəb(ə)l] *adj* **(a)** *Tech* (*material*) maniable **(b)** (*mine*) exploitable **(c)** (*project*) réalisable, possible; **it isn't a w. proposition** ce n'est pas une proposition réalisable

workaday ['wɜːkədeɪ] *adj* de tous les jours; (*explanation*) simple; **w. clothes** habits de tous les jours; **the w. world of the office** la routine du bureau

workaholic [wɜːkə'hɒlɪk] *n F* bourreau *m* de travail

work area *n Comptr* zone *f* de travail

workbag ['wɜːkbæg] *n Sewing* sac *m* à ouvrage

workbasket ['wɜːkbɑːskɪt] *n Sewing* corbeille *f* à ouvrage

workbench ['wɜːkbentʃ] *n* établi *m*

workbook ['wɜːkbʊk] *n* cahier *m* d'exercices

workbox ['wɜːkbɒks] *n Sewing* boîte *f* à ouvrage

workday ['wɜːkdeɪ] *n* (*weekday*) jour *m* ouvrable; (*day of work*) journée *f* de travail

worker ['wɜːkər] *n* **(a)** travailleur, -euse; *Ind* ouvrier, -ière; **hard w.** travailleur assidu; **to be a hard w.** être un bon travailleur; **Workers of the world unite!** travailleurs de tous les pays, unissez-vous!; **the workers** (*as opposed to management*) le personnel; **workers and management** partenaires *mpl* sociaux; **workers' control** autogestion *f*; **w. director** ouvrier siégeant au conseil d'administration; **w. participation** participation *f* des ouvriers **(b)** *Ent* **w. (bee/ant)** ouvrière *f*

worker-priest *n* prêtre-ouvrier *m*, *pl* prêtres-ouvriers

work file *n Comptr* fichier *m* de travail

workflow ['wɜːkfləʊ] *n* rythme *m* de travail; **w. schedule** plan *m* de travail

workforce ['wɜːkfɔːs] *n* main-d'œuvre *f*; (*non-industrial*) personnel *m*

work group *n* groupe *m* de travail

workhorse ['wɜːkhɔːs] *n* cheval *m* de labour; *Fig* **to be a w.** travailler comme un cheval *ou* une bête; **she's a willing w.** elle est toujours prête à faire n'importe quelle tâche

workhouse ['wɜːkhaʊs] *n* **(a)** *Br Hist* (*for the poor*) asile *m* des pauvres **(b)** *Old-fashioned US* (*prison*) maison *f* de correction

working ['wɜːkɪŋ] **1** *adj* **(a)** (*person*) qui travaille; **w. man/woman/people** ouvrier *m*/ouvrière *f*/ouvriers; **w. wife/mother** femme mariée/mère *f* de famille qui travaille; **he's very hard-w.** il est très travailleur, il travaille très dur; **a relaxed w. environment** un milieu professionnel détendu; **throughout her w. life** tout au long de sa vie active *ou* de sa vie professionnelle; **the w. class** *or* **classes** la classe ouvrière; **w. clothes** vêtements *mpl* de travail; **w. day** (*weekday*) jour *m* ouvrable; (*day of work*) journée *f* (de travail); *Comptr* **w. file** fichier *m* de travail; **w. lunch** déjeuner *m* d'affaires *ou* de travail; **the w. week** la semaine de travail

(b) (*machine etc*) qui fonctionne; **in w. order** en état de fonctionnement *ou* marche; **to be in good w. order** bien fonctionner; **w. parts of a machine** mécanisme *m* d'une machine; **w. model** modèle *m* qui fonctionne; **w. speed** vitesse *f* de régime

(c) w. agreement modus vivendi *m*; **to have a w. knowledge of French/the law** posséder une connaissance suffisante du français/du droit; **the two leaders have a good w. relationship** les deux dirigeants ont une bonne relation de travail; **w. majority** majorité suffisante; **w. theory** théorie qui donne des résultats

2 *n* **(a)** (*work*) travail *m*; **w. at home** le travail à domicile

(b) (*of mine, forest*) exploitation *f*; *Min* **workings** chantiers *mpl* d'exploitation; **old mine workings** anciens chantiers d'exploitation d'une mine

(c) (*operation*) (*of machine etc*) manœuvre *f*

(d) (*mechanism*) (*usu pl*) **workings** mécanisme *m*, rouages *mpl*; (*of organization, system*) rouages; **I can't fathom the workings of her mind** je ne comprends pas ce qui se passe dans sa tête

working capital *n Fin* capital *m* d'exploitation, fonds *m ou* capital de roulement, capital roulant; **w. requirements** besoins *mpl* en fonds de roulement

working-class *adj* (*family etc*) ouvrier; (*accent*) prolétaire, *F* prolo; **he's very w.** il fait très prolétaire; **w. district** quartier *m* populaire

working conditions *npl* conditions *fpl* de travail

working copy *n* (*of document, text*) copie *f* de travail

working girl *n* (*prostitute*) professionnelle *f*

working hours *npl* heures *fpl* de travail; (*of doctor, nurse*) service *m*; **we keep normal w.** nous faisons des journées normales de travail

working men's club *n Br* = club *m* pour ouvriers

working out *n Math* (*of problem*) résolution *f*; **show all w.** faire apparaître un raisonnement

working party *n Pol, Ind* groupe *m* de travail; *Mil* atelier *m*, équipe *f*

work in progress *n* **(a)** *Acct* produits *mpl* en cours **(b)** (*actual work*) travaux *mpl* en cours

workload ['wɜːkləʊd] *n* quantité *f* de travail; **to have a heavy w.** avoir beaucoup de travail

workman, *pl* **-men** ['wɜːkmən] *n* ouvrier *m*; **he's a good/bad w.** c'est un bon/mauvais ouvrier; *Prov* **a bad w. blames his tools** les mauvais ouvriers ont toujours de mauvais outils; **workmen's compensation** indemnité *f* d'invalidité (pour les ouvriers)

workmanlike ['wɜːkmənlaɪk] *adj* (*job*) bien fait, de professionnel; **to do sth in a w. manner** faire qch de façon professionnelle; **w. performance** représentation honnête

workmanship ['wɜːkmənʃɪp] *n* (*of sth made*) travail *m*; (*of clothes*) façon *f*; **sound w.** fabrication *ou* exécution soignée; **fine (piece of) w.** beau travail; **the w. on this furniture is superb** ce meuble est fait de façon superbe; **poor w.** travail de mauvaise qualité; **he was famous for his w.** il était connu pour la finesse de son travail; **Swiss w. is second to none** la fabrication suisse est la meilleure du monde; **you don't get any w. these days** la qualité n'est plus ce qu'elle était

workmate ['wɜːkmeɪt] *n esp Br* collègue *mf* de travail

work-out *n Sp* séance *f* d'entraînement

workpeople ['wɜːkpiːp(ə)l] *npl* ouvriers *mpl*

work permit *n* permis *m* de travail

workplace ['wɜːkpleɪs] *n* lieu *m* de travail

workroom ['wɜːkruːm] *n* atelier *m ou* salle *f* de travail

workshare ['wɜːkʃeər] *n* travail *m* en temps partagé; (*person*) travailleur, -euse en temps partagé; **workshares are becoming more common** le partage du travail devient de plus en plus courant

worksharing ['wɜːkʃeərɪŋ] *n* partage *m* du travail; **we have a w. arrangement** nous avons un système de partage du travail; **w. is becoming popular** le partage du travail est de plus en plus courant

workshop ['wɜːkʃɒp] *n* atelier *m*; **a music/an acting w.** un atelier de musique/de théâtre; *Aut* **w. manual** manuel *m* d'entretien

workshy ['wɜːkʃaɪ] *adj* fainéant; **to be w.** bouder *ou* renâcler à la besogne

workspace ['wɜːkspeɪs] *n Comptr* espace *m* de travail

workstation ['wɜːksteɪʃən] *n Comptr* station *f ou* poste *m* de travail

worktable ['wɜːkteɪb(ə)l] *n* table *f* de travail; *Sewing* table à ouvrage

worktop ['wɜːktɒp] *n* (*in kitchen*) plan *m* de travail

work-to-rule *n Ind* grève *f* du zèle; **to operate a w.** faire une grève du zèle

workweek ['wɜːkwiːk] *n esp Am* semaine *f* de travail; **a four-day w.** une semaine (de travail) de quatre jours; **the forty-hour w.** la semaine de quarante heures

world [wɜːld] *n* **(a)** monde *m*; **in this w.** en ce monde; **the other** *or* **next w., the w. to come** l'autre monde; *Rel* **the w., the flesh and the devil** le monde, la chair et le diable; **he's not long for this w.** il n'en a pas pour longtemps à vivre; **to bring a child into the w.** (*of mother, midwife, doctor*) mettre un enfant au monde; **she came into the w. on 22nd May 1953** elle est venue au monde le 22 mai 1953; **he wants the best of both worlds** il veut tout avoir; **the end of the w.** la fin du monde; *F* **it's not the end of the w.** ce n'est pas la fin du monde, ce n'est pas une catastrophe; *Rel* **w. without end** pour les siècles des siècles; **the whole w.** le monde entier; **there isn't a nicer spot in the whole w.** il n'y a pas d'endroit plus agréable au monde; **to be alone in the w.** être seul au monde; **you're not the only person in the w.!** tu n'es pas seul au monde!; **the happiest man in the w.** l'homme le plus heureux du monde; **he's the w.'s worst letter-writer** il n'y a pas pire correspondant que lui au monde; **you're the w.'s worst!** il n'y a pas pire que toi!; **she lives in a w. of her own** elle vit dans un monde à part; **you live in a dream** *or* **fantasy w.** tu vis dans un monde imaginaire; **the w. we live in is not like that** le monde dans lequel nous vivons n'est pas comme ça; **it's a different w. up north** c'est complètement différent au nord; **the book takes us into a w. of corruption and intrigue** le livre nous entraîne dans un monde de corruption et d'intrigues; *F* **it's out of this w.** c'est (quelque chose d')extraordinaire *ou* épatant; *F* **it was out of this w.** (*of experience, holiday etc*) c'était fabuleux; *F* **the mountains were out of this w.** les montagnes étaient d'une beauté extraordinaire; **what in the w. is the matter with you?** que pouvez-vous bien avoir?; **where in the w. is that?** où est-ce que ça peut bien être?; **I wouldn't do it for (anything in) the w.** je ne le ferais pour rien au monde; **nothing in the w. could make me leave** rien au monde ne pourrait me faire partir; **what I want most of all in the w. is for you to be happy** ce que je souhaite le plus au monde, c'est que tu sois heureux; **it's been happening ever since the w. began** ça se passe comme ça depuis que le monde est monde; **to go round the w.** faire le tour du monde; **(round-the-)w. trip** *or* **tour** voyage autour du monde; **he has seen the w.** il a vu du pays; **map of the w., w. map** carte du monde; (*in two hemispheres*) mappemonde *f*; **(all) the w. over, all over the w.** dans le monde entier; **people are the same the w. over** les gens sont partout pareils; **to the end of the w.** jusqu'au bout du monde; **it's a small w.!** (que) le monde est petit!; **the Old/New W.** l'ancien/le nouveau monde; **the ancient** *or* **classical w.** l'antiquité *f*; **the English-speaking w.** le monde anglophone; **the richest nation in the w.** la nation la plus riche au monde; **w. champion** champion *m* du monde; **w. championship** championnat *m* du monde; **w. domination** domination *f* du monde; **they have w. domination in gymnastics** ils dominent le monde de la gymnastique; **w. history** histoire *f* universelle; **w. market** marché *m* mondial; **w. opinion** l'opinion *f* internationale; **w. politics** politique *f* mondiale; *Pol* **w. power** puissance *f* mondiale; **w. rights** droits *mpl* d'exploitation pour le monde entier; **w. trade** commerce *m* international

(b) (*society*) monde *m*; **it's the way of the w.** ainsi va le monde; **what is the w. coming to?** où allons-nous?; **man of the w.** homme *m* qui connaît la vie *ou* qui a l'expérience du monde; **she doesn't care what the w. thinks** elle se moque de ce que les gens pensent; **he's gone up in the w.** il a fait du chemin; **to come down in the w.** déchoir; **all the w. knows** c'est bien connu, tout le monde le sait; *F* **the w. and his wife seemed to be there** tout le monde sans exception semblait être présent; **the singer had the w. at her feet** la chanteuse avait tout le monde à ses pieds

(c) (*circle, field*) **the w. of literature** *or* **of letters, the literary w.** le milieu *ou* monde littéraire; **the theatrical w.** le milieu *ou* monde du théâtre

(d) (*great deal*) **that will do you a w. of good** cela vous fera le plus grand bien; **there's a w. of difference between ...** il y a une différence énorme entre ...; **their opinions are worlds apart** leurs opinions sont totalement différentes; **she**

thinks the w. of him elle l'admire énormément; **she means the w. to them** elle compte énormément à leurs yeux; **I'd give the w. to know what he's thinking** je donnerais n'importe quoi pour savoir ce qu'il pense; **they kept on talking, for all the w. as if nothing had happened** ils ont continué à parler comme s'il ne s'était rien passé

World Bank *n* Banque *f* Mondiale

world-beater *n* **a w.** le meilleur/la meilleure du monde, le leader mondial; **we've got a real w. here** c'est le nouveau leader mondial

world-beating [biːtɪŋ] *adj* meilleur du monde; **of w. quality** d'une qualité inégalée; **the new w. X52** le X52, nouveau leader mondial

World Cup *n Fb* coupe *f* du monde

World Fair *n* exposition *f* internationale

world-famous *adj* de renommée mondiale, célèbre dans le monde entier

World Health Organization *n* Organisation *f* mondiale de la santé

worldliness ['wɜːldlɪnɪs] *n* **(a)** (*knowledge of world*) connaissance *f* du monde; **there was an air of w. about her** elle avait l'air de quelqu'un qui a l'expérience du monde **(b)** (*materialism*) matérialisme *m*, attachement *m* aux biens de ce monde

worldly ['wɜːldlɪ] *adj* **(a)** (*of this world*) de ce monde, matériel; **all his w. goods** toute sa fortune; **w. matters** les choses matérielles; **he's a child in w. matters** il n'a aucune expérience du monde; **w. pleasures** les plaisirs de ce monde; **w. wisdom** la sagesse du monde *ou* du siècle **(b)** (*knowledgeable*) qui a l'expérience du monde, qui connaît le monde; **she was very w. for one so young** elle avait une bien grande expérience du monde pour quelqu'un d'aussi jeune **(c)** (*materialistic*) matérialiste; **w. clerics** clergé attaché aux biens matériels

worldly-wise *adj* qui a l'expérience du monde, qui connaît le monde; **with a w. air** avec l'air de quelqu'un qui connaît le monde

world record *n* record *m* mondial

World Series *n US* = championnat *m* du monde de base-ball

world television *n* mondovision *f*

world war *n* guerre *f* mondiale; **World War One/Two, First/Second World War** première/deuxième guerre mondiale

world-weary *adj* las/*f* lasse de ce monde

worldwide ['wɜːldwaɪd] **1** *adj* mondial; **w. rights** droits *mpl* d'exploitation pour le monde entier *Comptr* **W. Web** réseau *m* mondial de serveurs multimédias, Web *m* **2** *adv* dans le monde entier; **the Olympics are watched w.** on regarde les Jeux Olympiques dans le monde entier

WORM [wɜːm] *Comptr* (*abbr* **write once read many times**) WORM

worm¹ *n* **(a)** ver *m*; (*maggot*) asticot *m*; *Fig* **the w. has turned** j'en ai/elle en a/*etc* assez de se laisser mener par le bout du nez; *Fig* **even a w. will turn** il y a une limite à tout; **he's a w.** c'est un minable; **w.'s-eye view** (*from below*) perspective vue d'en bas; (*from lowly position*) perspective au ras des pâquerettes; **to get a w.'s-eye view of the theatre/catering industry** voir le monde du théâtre/de la restauration au ras des pâquerettes *ou* d'un point de vue restreint; *Fig* **the w. in the bud** le ver dans le fruit; *F* **that's opening a real can of worms** nous allons nous fourrer dans un véritable guêpier; *Med, Vet* **to have worms** avoir des vers; *F* **to be food for worms** bouffer les pissenlits par la racine; **meal w.** ver de farine; *Pharm* **w. powder** poudre *f* à vers, poudre vermifuge

(b) *Tech* (*of screw*) filet *m*; **w. (screw)** vis *f* sans fin; **w. and roller steering** direction *f* à vis et galet

worm² *vt* **(a) he wormed himself** *or* **his way along the tunnel** il a avancé dans le tunnel en rampant *ou* en se tortillant; **to w. one's way out of/into sth** se faufiler hors de/dans qch; *Fig* **I'd like to see her w. her way out of that one** j'aimerais bien voir comment elle va s'en tirer; **to w. oneself into sb's favour/confidence** s'insinuer dans les bonnes grâces de qn/la confiance de qn; **to w. a secret out of sb** tirer un secret de qn, arracher un secret à qn; **I'll w. it out of him** je saurai lui tirer les vers du nez **(b)** *Vet* **to w. a dog** débarrasser un chien de ses vers

wormcast ['wɜːmkɑːst] *n* déjection *f* de ver de terre

wormeaten ['wɜːmiːtən] *adj* (*wood*) vermoulu; (*fruit*) véreux; *Fig* (*hat, slippers*) miteux

worm gear *n* engrenage *m* à vis sans fin

wormhole ['wɜːmhəʊl] *n* (*in wood, ground*) trou *m* de ver; (*in cloth, wood*) piqûre *f* (de ver)

wormwood ['wɜːmwʊd] *n Bot* armoise *f* (amère); *Lit* **life to him was gall and w.** la vie pour lui n'était qu'amertume et dégoût

wormy ['wɜːmɪ] *adj* (*furniture*) infesté *ou* plein de vers; (*fruit*) véreux; (*wood, cloth*) piqué des vers

worn [wɔːn] **1** *pp see* **wear² 2** *adj* **(a)** (*weary*) las, *f* lasse; **w. with anxiety** usé par les soucis **(b)** (*with use*) (*shoes, edges etc*) usé

worried ['wʌrɪd] *adj* **(a)** (*look, expression, letter*) inquiet, -ète; (*person*) tracassé, soucieux; **I'm w. about this** cela m'inquiète *ou* me tracasse; **he was w. by these developments** ces développements l'inquiétaient; **she's w. about the car** elle est inquiète au sujet de la voiture; **they're w. sick about her** ils sont malades d'inquiétude à son sujet; **he looks w.** il a l'air préoccupé *ou* soucieux **(b)** (*weaker sense*) **I was w. it would be the wrong size** j'avais peur que ce ne soit pas la bonne taille

worriedly ['wʌrɪdlɪ] *adv* avec inquiétude

worrier ['wʌrɪər] *n* anxieux, -ieuse; **he's such a w.** il se fait tellement de soucis; **don't be such a w.** arrête de t'inquiéter comme ça

worrisome ['wʌrɪsəm] *adj* tracassant, inquiétant

worry¹ ['wʌrɪ] *n* souci *m*, tracas *m*; **financial worries** soucis d'argent; **it's causing me a lot of w.** cela m'inquiète beaucoup; **that's the least of my worries** c'est le moindre *ou* le dernier de mes soucis; *F* **what's your w.?** qu'est-ce qui ne va pas?; **w. beads** chapelet *m* (*pour s'occuper les mains*)

worry² **1** *vt* **(a)** (*cause anxiety to*) inquiéter; **these events worried her greatly** ces événements l'ont beaucoup inquiétée; **that boiler worries me, suppose it blows up?** la chaudière m'inquiète, si elle explosait?; **Janet worries me sometimes, she's not like other little girls** Janet m'inquiète parfois, elle n'est pas comme les autres petites filles; **something is worrying her** il y a quelque chose qui la préoccupe *ou* qui la travaille; **tell me what's worrying you** dites-moi ce qui vous préoccupe; **it doesn't w. me what other people think** je ne me soucie pas de ce que les autres pensent; **it worried him that he was getting older** le fait de vieillir le préoccupait; **it doesn't seem to w. you if other people get hurt** que d'autres souffrent ne semble pas te préoccuper; **doesn't it w. you, your daughter being out this late?** ça ne vous inquiète pas que votre fille ne soit pas rentrée à cette heure tardive?; **it doesn't w. her who she upsets** elle ne se préoccupe pas des gens qu'elle froisse; **it worries me to think of them all on their own** ça m'inquiète de penser qu'ils sont tout seuls; **to w. oneself sick** *or* **to death about sb/sth** se rendre malade d'inquiétude *ou* mourir d'inquiétude au sujet de qn/qch

(b) (*bother, disturb*) ennuyer; **he doesn't want to be worried with these minor details** il ne veut pas être embêté par ces petits détails; **don't w. him about it, I'll do it** ne l'ennuie pas avec ça, je m'en occuperai; **don't w. yourself about it** ne t'embête pas avec ça; **don't you w. your pretty little head about it** ne te fais pas de soucis, mignonne!

(c) (*of dog, wolf*) (*harass*) (*sheep*) attaquer, harceler; (*bite*) secouer entre ses dents

2 *vi* se tracasser, s'inquiéter, se faire du souci *ou* de la bile *ou* du mauvais sang; **don't tell them, they'll only w.** ne le leur dis pas, ça ne fera que les inquiéter; **he keeps worrying about that business** cette affaire lui travaille l'esprit; **don't (you) w.! not to w.!** ne vous tracassez *ou* inquiétez pas!, ne vous en faites pas!; **sorry, I forgot the milk – don't w. (about it)** je suis désolée, j'ai oublié le lait – ne vous inquiétez pas (pour ça); **not to w.! it'll wash out** ce n'est rien, ça partira au lavage; **don't (you) w. about me** ne t'inquiète pas pour moi; **there's plenty more beer, don't you w.** il reste plein de bière, ne t'en fais pas; **you'll find out soon enough, don't you w.** vous n'allez pas tarder à le savoir, ne vous en faites pas; **there's** *or* **it's nothing to w. about** il n'y a pas de quoi se faire du souci; **it's only a scratch, nothing to w. about** ce n'est qu'une égratignure, pas de quoi s'inquiéter; **what's the use of worrying?** à quoi bon se tourmenter?; *F* **I should w.!** ce n'est pas mon affaire!

worryguts ['wʌrɪgʌts] *n Br F* bileux, -euse; **don't be such a w.** arrête de te tracasser autant

worrying ['wʌrɪɪŋ] **1** *adj* tracassant, inquiétant **2** *n* tracas *m*, tourment *m*, inquiétude *f*; **all this w. will get you nowhere** à quoi bon se tourmenter?

worrywart ['wʌrɪwɔːt] *n Am F* = **worryguts**

worse [wɜːs] **1** *adj* (*comp of* **bad**) pire, plus mauvais **(than** que); **I'm a w. player than he is** *or* **him** *or Fml* **he** je joue plus mal que lui; **your problems are w. than ours** vos problèmes sont pires que les nôtres; **the situation was w. than (it had been) before** la situation était pire qu'avant; **there's nothing w. than arriving too early** il n'y a rien de pire que d'arriver trop tôt; **you're bad at French but he's w.** tu es mauvais en français mais il est plus mauvais que toi; **in w. condition** dans un plus mauvais état; **this is getting w. and w.** c'est *ou* ça va de mal en pis; **how are things? – no w. than before** comment ça va? – pas plus mal qu'avant; **things could be w.** ça pourrait être pire; **you're only**

making things *or* **matters w.** vous ne faites qu'aggraver les choses; **to make things** *or* **matters w. ...** par *ou* pour surcroît de malheur ...; **it'll just make it w. if you tell them** ça ne va faire qu'empirer les choses si tu le leur dis; **you'll only make matters w. for yourself by offending them** tu ne feras qu'aggraver ton cas en les blessant; **it will be even w. for them if she finds out** ça va être encore pire pour eux si elle l'apprend; **it might** *or* **could have been w.** ça aurait pu être pire; **he escaped with nothing w. than a fright** il en fut quitte pour la peur; **what is w. ...** ce qui est plus grave ...; **to go from bad to w.** aller de mal en pis; **to get w.** (*deteriorate*) s'altérer; (*of illness*) s'aggraver, empirer; **the situation is getting w.** la situation s'aggrave; **his memory's got a lot w.** sa mémoire s'est beaucoup amoindrie; **how do you feel today? – w.** comment ça va aujourd'hui? – pire; **things will get w. before they get better** les choses vont empirer avant de s'améliorer; **I'm none the w. for it** je ne m'en trouve pas plus mal; **they were none the w. for their experience** ils ne s'en sont pas trouvés plus mal pour autant; **I think none the w. of him because he accepted** ce n'est pas parce qu'il a accepté que j'ai une moins bonne opinion de lui; **so much the w. for them!** tant pis pour eux!; **she was the w. for drink** elle était éméchée; **a sofa somewhat the w. for wear** un sofa un peu défraîchi; **he was rather the w. for wear** il était en mauvais état; **she was looking the worse for w.** elle avait l'air en travers; *F* **w. things happen at sea** ce n'est pas la fin du monde; **w. luck!** hélas!

2 *n* **there was w. to follow** *or* **to come** le pire était encore à venir; **I have seen w.** j'en ai vu bien d'autres, j'ai vu pire; **to change for the w.** s'altérer; **a change for the w.** un changement en mal; **he has taken a sudden turn for the w.** son état s'est subitement aggravé

3 *adv* (*comp of* **badly**) plus mal, *Lit* pis; **w. still** pire encore; **you could do (a lot) w.** (*than accept offer*) ce n'est vraiment pas si mal; (*than marry him or her*) tu aurais pu tomber plus mal; **he could do w. than accept their offer** il pouvait faire pire que d'accepter leur proposition; **to think w. of sb for doing sth** estimer qn moins pour avoir fait qch; **I don't think any w. of her for it** je n'ai pas une plus mauvaise opinion d'elle pour autant; **he is w. off than before** (*in worse situation*) sa situation a empiré; (*even poorer*) il est encore plus pauvre qu'avant; **the noise went on w. than ever** le vacarme a repris de plus belle

worsen ['wɜːs(ə)n] **1** *vt* (*situation*) empirer; (*crisis, infection, bad mood*) aggraver; (*relations, driving conditions*) rendre plus difficile; **you'll only w. things** tu ne feras que rendre les choses plus difficiles **2** *vi* (*of situation*) empirer, devenir pire; (*of health*) s'aggraver, empirer; **the situation has since worsened** la situation a empiré depuis; **the worsening situation** la situation qui est en train de s'aggraver; **her worsening memory** sa mémoire faiblissante

worsening ['wɜːs(ə)nɪŋ] *n* aggravation *f*

Worship ['wɜːʃɪp] *n esp Br* (*title*) **His W. the Mayor** monsieur le maire; **yes, your W.** oui, Votre Honneur

worship[1] ['wɜːʃɪp] *n* **(a)** *Rel* culte *m*; **divine w.** le culte divin; **hours of w.** heures *fpl* des offices; **place of w.** lieu *m* consacré au culte; **to be an object of w.** être un objet d'adoration **(b)** (*love, adoration*) adoration *f*

worship[2] **(-pp-) 1** *vt* **(a)** *Rel* (*god, idol*) rendre *ou* vouer un culte à, adorer; **to w. the golden calf** adorer le veau d'or **(b)** (*love, adore*) adorer, vouer un culte à; **she worshipped her mother** elle adorait sa mère; **he worships Elvis Presley** il voue un culte à Elvis Presley; **he worships the ground she walks on** il vénère jusqu'au sol qu'elle foule; **to w. money** vouer un culte à l'argent **2** *vi* **the church where his family has worshipped for years** l'église où sa famille fait ses dévotions depuis des années; **where does he w.?** à quelle église/à quel temple/à quelle synagogue/à quelle mosquée va-t-il?

worshipful ['wɜːʃɪpfʊl] *adj esp Br* honorable (*titre des membres des Corporations de Londres, des juges de paix*)

worshipper ['wɜːʃɪpər] *n* adorateur, -trice; **the worshippers** (*in church*) les fidèles *mpl*

worst[1] [wɜːst] **1** *adj* (*superl of* **bad**) (le) pire, (le) plus mauvais; **that was his w. mistake** c'était sa plus grave erreur; **his w. enemy** son pire ennemi; **you're your own w. enemy** tu es ton plus grand ennemi; **the w. thing about it was the heat** le pire c'était la chaleur; **the w. weather was in the south** c'était dans le sud qu'il faisait le plus mauvais temps; **the w. possible situation** la pire situation possible

2 *n* **the w. that could happen** le pire *ou* la pire chose qui puisse arriver; **the w. of it is that ...** le pire c'est que ...; **that's the w. of cheap shoes** c'est l'inconvénient des chaussures bon marché; **when things are at their** *or* **the w.** quand les choses vont au plus mal; **to get the w. of it** (*in a fight*) avoir le dessous; **he's prepared for the w.** il s'attend au pire; **at the w., if it comes to the w., if the w. comes to the w.** au pire; **if it comes to the w., we can always take the train** dans le pire des cas, nous pouvons toujours prendre le train; **at the w. there's still the possibility of finding another actor** au pire, il y a toujours la possibilité de trouver un autre acteur; **the w. is yet to come** on n'a pas encore vu le pire, et ce n'est pas fini; **do your w.!** allez-y!, essayez toujours!; **the w. is over** le plus mauvais moment est passé; **the w. of the storm is over** le plus fort de l'orage est passé; **the w. has happened!** c'est la catastrophe!; **and that's not the w. of it!** et ce n'est pas le pire!, et il y a pire encore!; **I'm at my w. in the morning** le matin est mon plus mauvais moment de la journée; **you haven't seen her at her w.** tu ne l'as pas vue dans ses mauvais moments; **even at her w. she is still a brilliant player** même quand elle joue mal, elle reste une joueuse fantastique

3 *adv* (*superl of* **badly**) (le) plus mal, *Lit* (le) pis; **out of all of us I played w.** j'ai joué le plus mal de nous tous; **that frightened me w. of all** c'est ce qui m'a fait le plus peur; **the w. possible situation** la pire situation possible; **the elderly are the w. off** les personnes âgées sont les plus mal loties; **they are the w. paid** ce sont les plus mal payés; **the w. dressed men in Europe** les hommes les plus mal habillés d'Europe

worst[2] *vt Old-fashioned* battre, vaincre, défaire; **to be worsted** avoir le dessous

worst-case *adj* **w. scenario** scénario *m* catastrophe; **w. projection** prévision *f* qui envisage le pire; **what's the w. scenario?** quel est le pire qui puisse se produire?

worsted ['wʊstɪd] *n Tex* laine *f* peignée, peigné *m*

worth [wɜːθ] **1** *adj* **(a)** (*having a value of*) valant; **to be w. ...** valoir ...; **to be w. a lot of money** (*of thing*) valoir cher, avoir beaucoup de valeur; (*of person*) être riche; **this ring is w. $500** cette bague vaut 500 dollars; **how much** *or* **what is this painting w.?** combien vaut ce tableau?; **it's not w. anything** cela ne vaut pas quatre sous; **the house isn't w. what they paid for it** la maison ne vaut pas le prix qu'ils ont payé pour l'avoir; **this cheque/contract isn't w. the paper it's printed on** ce chèque/contrat n'a aucune valeur; **she's w. ten of you** elle en vaut dix comme toi; **to be w. nothing** ne rien valoir; **what is the franc w.?** combien vaut le franc?; **it's not w. much** cela ne vaut pas grand-chose; **to be w. sth to sb** valoir qch pour qn; **this old book is w. a lot to me** ce vieux livre a beaucoup de valeur pour moi; **what's my silence w. to you?** tu donnerais combien pour que je me taise?; **whatever it may be w.** quoi que cela vaille; **I'll tell you this for what it's w.** je vous dis ça pour ce que ça vaut; **she's a lawyer, for what that's w.** elle est avocate, pour ce que cela vaut; **for what it's w., I think they're wrong** pensez-en ce que vous voulez mais je crois qu'ils ont tort; **that's my advice, for what it's w.** c'est mon conseil, il vaut ce qu'il vaut; **it would be as much as my life is w.** ce serait risquer ma vie; **it would be more than my job's w.** ça me coûterait mon emploi; *Fig* **it's not w. the candle** le jeu ne vaut pas la chandelle

(b) (*meriting*) **it's not w. the trouble** cela ne *ou* n'en vaut pas la peine; **is it w. while?, is it w. it?** cela (en) vaut-il la peine?; **it's not w. my/your/*etc* while doing it** ça ne vaut pas la peine que je le fasse/tu le fasses/*etc*; **it isn't w. it** ça ne vaut pas le coup; **don't get upset, he isn't w. it** ne te rends pas malade, il n'en vaut pas la peine; **you're w. it** tu en vaux la peine; **this novel is not w. reading** ce roman ne vaut pas la peine *ou* ne mérite pas d'être lu; **it's so late, it's not w. going** il est si tard, ça ne vaut pas la peine *ou F* le coup d'y aller; **something w. having** une chose précieuse; **without you, life wouldn't be w. living** sans toi, la vie ne vaudrait pas la peine d'être vécue; **your life won't be w. living** (*if you get on the wrong side of him etc*) ça sera invivable pour toi; **it's the only thing that makes their lives w. living** c'est la seule chose qui donne de la valeur à leur vie; **it's w. thinking about** cela mérite réflexion; **it's w. knowing** c'est bon à savoir; **the castle is w. a visit** le château vaut la visite; **your friendship/opinion is w. a lot to me** ton amitié/ton opinion représente beaucoup pour moi

(c) (*having money*) **he's w. millions** il est riche à millions; **that is all I am w.** voilà toute ma fortune; *Fig* **he was pulling for all he was w.** il tirait de toutes ses forces

2 *n* valeur *f*; **of great/little/no w.** de grande/de peu de/d'aucune valeur; **give me £4 w. of petrol** donnez-moi (pour) 4 livres d'essence; **to have/want one's money's w.** en avoir/en vouloir pour son argent; **a day's w. of food/water** un jour de vivres/d'eau; **an hour's w. of my time** une heure de mon temps; **she has no sense of her own w.** elle n'est pas consciente de sa propre valeur

worthily ['wɜ:ðɪlɪ] *adv* (*to live*) dignement, honorablement; (*to donate, sacrifice*) honorablement

worthiness ['wɜ:ðɪnɪs] *n* mérite *m*

worthless ['wɜ:θlɪs] *adj* (**a**) (*object*) sans valeur, qui ne vaut rien (**b**) **he's completely w.** c'est un vaurien

worthlessness ['wɜ:θlɪsnɪs] *n* (**a**) (*of object*) peu *m* de valeur (**b**) (*of person*) nature *f* méprisable

worthwhile [wɜ:θ'waɪl] *adj* qui en vaut la peine *ou F* le coup; **at last I've found a w. job** j'ai enfin trouvé un poste qui me donne satisfaction; **she didn't think it w. replacing the van** elle ne pensait pas que cela valait la peine de remplacer la camionnette

worthy ['wɜ:ðɪ] **1** *adj* (**a**) (*distinguished, meriting respect*) digne; **a w. man** un homme respectable *ou* estimable; **a w. life** une vie honorable *ou* vertueuse

(**b**) **w. of** (*deserving, meriting*) digne de; **surely my letter was at least w. of an answer?** ma lettre méritait quand même une réponse, non?; **w. of respect** digne de respect; **you're not w. of your father** tu n'es pas digne de ton père; **her remarks are w. of contempt** ses remarques sont dignes de mépris; **he is a w. winner** il a mérité sa victoire; **to be w. to do sth** être digne de faire qch; **I am not w. to kiss your hand** je ne suis pas digne de baiser ta main; **it is w. of note that ...** il est à noter que ...; **the town has no museum w. of the name** la ville n'a aucun musée digne de ce nom

2 *n* (*of place*) personnage *m*; *Hum* **the village worthies** les notables *mpl* du village

wotcher ['wɒtʃər] *int Br F* (*hello!*) salut!

would [wʊd] *modal aux v* [ⓘA55-56] (**I would, they would** *etc are often contracted to* **I'd** [aɪd], **they'd** [ðeɪd] *etc*; **would not** *to* **wouldn't** ['wʊd(ə)nt]) (**a**) (*expressing future*) **she told me she w. be there** elle m'a dit qu'elle serait là

(**b**) (*consent*) **I wouldn't do it for anything** je ne le ferais pour rien au monde; **w. you pass the mustard please?** voudriez-vous bien me passer la moutarde?; **the wound wouldn't heal** la blessure ne voulait pas se cicatriser, la blessure ne se cicatrisait pas

(**c**) (*emphatic*) **I quite forgot! – you would!** j'ai oublié! – c'est bien de vous! *ou* ça ne m'étonne pas de vous!; **you would insist on going** évidemment, il a fallu que tu insistes pour y aller; *F* **I wouldn't know** (*I don't know*) je ne saurais dire

(**d**) (*habit*) **she w. often return home exhausted** elle rentrait souvent très fatiguée

(**e**) (*conjecture*) **w. that be your cousin you have in mind?** c'est à votre cousin que vous pensez?; **that w. be your job, am I right?** et ce serait toi qui t'occuperais de cela, non?

(**f**) (*wish*) vouloir; **what w. you have me do?** que voulez-vous que je fasse?; **he w. if he could** il le ferait s'il le pouvait; *Lit* **w. (that) I were a bird!** je voudrais être un oiseau!; **w. to God it wasn't true!** plût à Dieu que cela ne fût pas vrai!

(**g**) [ⓘA50-1,13; B31-2] (*conditional*) **she w. come if you invited her** elle viendrait si vous l'invitiez; **had he** *or* **if he had let go, he w. have fallen** s'il avait lâché prise il serait tombé

would-be *adj* prétendu; *Pej* soi-disant; (*housebuyer, student*) potentiel; (*musician, actor*) en herbe; **troops seized the w. assassin** les militaires ont attrapé l'assassin avant qu'il ne commette le crime; **the w. burglar was tied up to a chair** le cambrioleur, pris sur le fait, était attaché à une chaise

wound[1] [wu:nd] *n* (**a**) *Med* blessure *f*; **bullet w.** blessure par balle (**b**) *Fig* plaie *f*; **to reopen a w.** *or* **an old w.** rouvrir une plaie; **to rub salt in the w.** retourner le fer *ou* le couteau dans la plaie

wound[2] **1** *vt* (**a**) blesser; **to be badly wounded** être gravement blessé; **wounded in the shoulder** blessé *ou* atteint à l'épaule (**b**) *Fig* (*of accusation etc*) blesser; **to w. sb's pride** blesser qn dans son amour-propre; **to w. sb's feelings** blesser les susceptibilités de qn, froisser *ou* heurter qn; **my feelings were wounded** j'ai été froissé *ou* heurté **2** *vi* causer une blessure

wound[3] [waʊnd] *pt, pp see* **wind**[4]

wounded ['wu:ndɪd] **1** *adj* blessé; **the w. man** le blessé; *Fig* **w. pride** orgueil froissé **2** *npl* **the w.** les blessés *mpl*

wounding ['wu:ndɪŋ] *adj* blessant; **he found it w. to his pride** cela a blessé son amour-propre

wow[1] [waʊ] *F* **1** *int* oh là là! **2** *n* (*success*) succès *m* fou; **it's a w.** c'est sensationnel; **this is a w. of a show** c'est un spectacle sensationnel

wow[2] *vt F* emballer

wow[3] *n* (*in sound system*) pleurage *m*

WP [dʌb(ə)lju:'pi:] *n Comptr* (**a**) *abbr* **word processing** (**b**) *abbr* **word processor**

wp (*abbr* **weather permitting**) si le temps le permet

WPC [dʌb(ə)lju:pi:'si:] *n Br* (*abbr* **woman police constable**) femme-agent *f*, *pl* femmes-agents

wpm [dʌb(ə)lju:pi:'em] (*abbr* **words per minute**) mots par minute

WRAC [ræk] *n Br* (*abbr* **Women's Royal Army Corps**) ≈ AFAT

wrack[1] [ræk] *n* (*seaweed*) varec(h) *m*

wrack[2] *n* = **rack**[1]

WRAF [ræf] *n Br Mil* (*abbr* **Women's Royal Air Force**) = section *f* féminine de l'armée de l'air britannique

wraith [reɪθ] *n* apparition *f*

wraithlike ['reɪθlaɪk] *adj* (*appearance*) semblable à une apparition *ou* un spectre, spectral

wrangle[1] ['ræŋg(ə)l] *n* dispute *f*, querelle *f*

wrangle[2] **1** *vi* se disputer, se quereller, se chamailler (**over** à propos de) **2** *vt Am* (*livestock*) garder

wrangler ['ræŋglər] *n* (**a**) (*quarreller*) querelleur, -euse (**b**) *Am* (*cowboy*) cowboy *m*

wrangling ['ræŋglɪŋ] *n* (*quarrelling*) disputes *fpl*, querelles *fpl*; **there has been a lot of w. over who to give the job to** il y a eu beaucoup de querelles pour décider à qui donner le poste

wrap[1] [ræp] *n* (*blanket*) (*for journey*) couverture *f*; (*shawl*) châle *m*; (*cloak*) pèlerine *f*, manteau *m*; *Fig* **to keep sth under wraps** garder qch secret; *Fig* **the wraps were taken off the new car today** la voiture a été montrée au public pour la première fois aujourd'hui; *F* **it's a w.!** (*is complete*) ça y est, c'est fini!

wrap[2] (**-pp-**) **1** *vt* envelopper, emballer; **to w. sth in paper** envelopper *ou* empaqueter qch dans du papier; **the cheese was wrapped in plastic** le fromage était emballé *ou* enveloppé sous plastique; **would you like it wrapped?** (*of gift*) c'est pour offrir?; **to w. a baby in a shawl** emmitoufler un bébé dans un châle; *Fig* **wrapped in mystery** enveloppé *ou* entouré de mystère **2** *vi Comptr* (*of lines*) se boucler

▶ **wrap round** *vtaspo* **to w. sth round sth** enrouler *ou* entortiller qch autour de qch; **w. this blanket round you/your shoulders** enroule cette couverture autour de toi/de tes épaules; **he wrapped the bandage round my finger** il a enroulé le bandage autour de mon doigt; **the cable wrapped itself round the ...** le câble s'est enroulé autour du ...; *F* **he wrapped his car round a tree** il a encadré un arbre

▶ **wrap up 1** *vtsep* (**a**) (*parcel, present*) envelopper; **to w. sth up in sth** envelopper qch dans qch; **w. yourself up well** (*dress warmly*) emmitoufle-toi bien; **wrapped up** (*person*) emmitouflé

(**b**) *Fig* **to be wrapped up in sth** (*absorbed*) être uniquement préoccupé de qch; **he is wrapped up in his work** il est entièrement absorbé par son travail; **she is too wrapped up in herself/in her own problems** elle est trop préoccupée par elle-même/par ses propres problèmes; **they are wrapped up in each other** ils sont uniquement préoccupés l'un par l'autre

(**c**) *F* (*bring to an end*) (*deal, negotiations, discussion*) conclure; **well that about wraps it up for today** voilà, c'est à peu près tout pour aujourd'hui

2 *vi* (**a**) (*put on warm clothes*) (bien) s'emmitoufler

(**b**) *Br F* (*stop talking*) se taire; **w. up!** ferme-la!, écrase!

wraparound ['ræpəraʊnd] *n* = **wrapround 1**

wrap-around bumper *n* pare-chocs *m* enveloppant

wrapover ['ræpəʊvər] **1** *n* (*skirt*) jupe *f* portefeuille **2** *adj* **w. skirt** jupe *f* portefeuille; **w. top** cache-cœur *m inv*

wrapped [ræpt] *adj* (*bread, sweets etc*) emballé

wrapper ['ræpər] *n* (**a**) (*packaging*) (papier *m* d')emballage *m*; (*of sweet*) papier *m*; (*of cigar*) emballage *m*; **her pocket was full of old sweet wrappers** sa poche était pleine de vieux papiers de bonbons (**b**) (*of book*) couverture *f*, couvre-livre *m*, *pl* couvre-livres; (*to protect jacket*) liseuse *f*; (*of newspaper being mailed*) bande *f* (**c**) *Old-fashioned* (*dressing gown*) saut-de-lit *m*, *pl* sauts-de-lit

wrapping ['ræpɪŋ] *n* (*material*) emballage *m*; **w. paper** papier *m* d'emballage

wrapround ['ræpraʊnd] **1** *n* (*in word processing*) bouclage *m*, renouement *m* (des mots) **2** *adj Aut* **w. rear window** lunette *f* arrière panoramique; **w. windscreen** pare-brise *m* panoramique

wrath [rɒθ] *n Lit* courroux *m*; **the w. of God** la colère de Dieu

wrathful ['rɒθfʊl] *adj Lit* courroucé, en colère

wreak [ri:k] *vt* (*havoc*) entraîner; **to w. (one's) vengeance upon sb** exercer *ou* assouvir sa vengeance sur qn; **the hurricane wreaked terrible destruction on the island** l'ouragan a entraîné de terribles destructions sur l'île

wreath [ri:θ, *pl* ri:ðz, ri:θs] *n* (**a**) (*of flowers*) couronne *f*, guirlande *f*; (**funeral**) **w.** couronne mortuaire; **w. of poppies** couronne de coquelicots; **he laid a w. on her grave** il a déposé une couronne sur sa tombe (**b**) (*of smoke, mist*) volute *f*

wreathe [ri:ð] **1** *vt* (**a**) (*encircle*) enguirlander; (*sb's head*) couronner; **the mountain was wreathed with mist** la montagne était entourée de brouillard; **her face was**

wreathed in smiles son visage était rayonnant **(b)** (*entwine*) (*flowers*) enrouler (**round** autour de) **2** *vi* (*of smoke*) tourbillonner

wreck[1] [rek] *n* **(a)** (*ship*) navire *m* naufragé, épave *f*; (*car, lorry, train, plane*) voiture *f*/camion *m*/train *m*/avion *m* accidenté(e), épave; **my car's a total w.** ma voiture est bonne pour la casse; **the burnt-out w. of a bus** les restes calcinés d'un bus; **human wrecks** épaves (humaines); *Fig* **to be a physical/nervous w.** avoir la santé détraquée/les nerfs détraqués; **the man's an emotional w.** le type est une loque, au niveau émotionnel; *Fig* **after two hours with those kids I was a total w.** après deux heures avec ces gamins j'étais complètement épuisé

(b) (*destruction*) (*of ship*) naufrage *m*; **to be saved from the w.** échapper au naufrage

wreck[2] *vt* **(a)** (*ship*) faire faire naufrage à, causer le naufrage de; **to be wrecked** (*of ship, person*) faire naufrage; **the ship was wrecked on these rocks** le bateau a fait naufrage sur ces rochers

(b) (*car*) démolir; (*building*) démolir, détruire; **vandals have wrecked the building/train** les vandales ont abîmé le bâtiment/le train; **to w. one's health** se ruiner la santé

(c) *Fig* (*undertaking*) faire échouer, saboter; (*person's hopes*) détruire, ruiner, briser; (*chances*) ruiner; **to w. sb's plans** faire échouer les projets de qn; **to w. sb's marriage** ruiner *ou* détruire le mariage de qn; **this defeat has wrecked the team's chances** cette défaite a anéanti les chances de l'équipe; **the accident wrecked her hopes** l'accident a anéanti ses espoirs; **you wrecked his life/career** tu as brisé sa vie/sa carrière

wreckage ['rekɪdʒ] *n* (*no pl*) (*of ship*) épave *f*; (*of aircraft, train, car*) débris *mpl*; **piece of w.** épave; **documents were found in the w.** on a trouvé des documents parmi les débris; *Fig* **she hoped to salvage something from the w. of her career** elle espérait sauver quelque chose de ce qui restait de sa carrière

wrecker ['rekər] *n* **(a)** *Constr* (*of buildings*) démolisseur *m* **(b)** (*salvager*) sauveteur *m* d'épaves **(c)** *Am Aut* (*vehicle*) dépanneuse *f*, camion *m* de dépannage; (*person*) dépanneur *m* **(d)** *Hist* (*person who causes shipwrecks*) naufrageur *m*, pilleur *m* d'épave

wrecking truck *or* **car** ['rekɪŋ] *n Am* camion *m* de dépannage, dépanneuse *f*

Wren [ren] *n Br F* = membre *m* du Women's Royal Naval Service; **the Wrens** = section *f* féminine de la marine britannique

wren [ren] *n* troglodyte *m*

wrench[1] [rentʃ] *n* **(a)** (*twist*) mouvement *m* violent de torsion; **to give sth a w.** tordre qch violemment; **he gave his ankle a w.** il s'est fait une entorse; (*less serious*) il s'est foulé la cheville **(b)** *Fig* (*emotional*) **the separation was a terrible w.** la séparation fut un déchirement affreux; **it will be a w. to leave the old house** il m'en/nous en/*etc* coûtera de quitter la vieille maison **(c)** (*tool*) clef *f*; **adjustable w.** clef à ouverture variable, clef universelle

wrench[2] *vt* (*twist*) tordre *ou* tourner violemment; **to w. one's ankle/shoulder** se fouler la cheville/l'épaule; **to w. the lid open** forcer le couvercle; **to w. off/out** arracher *ou* enlever (avec un violent effort de torsion); **to w. sth (away) from sb** arracher qch à qn; **she wrenched herself free** d'une secousse elle se dégagea; *Fig* **nothing could w. her away from her book** rien ne pouvait l'arracher à son livre

wrest [rest] *vt* arracher (**from** à); **she wrested the knife from him** *or* **his grip** elle lui a arraché le couteau; **to w. a confession from sb** arracher un aveu à qn; **we could w. no meaning from the coded message** nous n'avons pu tirer aucun sens du message codé; **I managed to w. her attention away from the tennis** j'ai réussi à l'arracher au tennis qui occupait toute son attention

wrestle[1] ['res(ə)l] **1** *vi* **(a)** (*physically*) lutter (**with** avec, contre); **to w. together** lutter, se prendre corps à corps; **the two men wrestled briefly** les deux hommes ont brièvement lutté; *Fig* **to w. with one's umbrella** se (dé)battre avec son parapluie; *Fig* **he wrestled with the zip/knot in the darkness** il s'est débattu avec la fermeture éclair®/le nœud dans le noir

(b) *Fig* **to w. with** (*difficulties, temptation*) lutter contre; (*adversity*) être aux prises avec; (*problem*) s'attaquer à; **they've been wrestling with the problem for years** ils sont aux prises avec ce problème depuis des années; **to w. with one's conscience** être aux prises avec sa conscience

2 *vt* lutter avec *ou* contre; **he wrestled his attacker to the ground** il a jeté son attaquant au sol dans la lutte

wrestle[2] *n* (*fight*), *Fig* lutte *f* (corps à corps), corps à corps *m* (**with** contre); **after a w. with the knot, she was free** après s'être débattue avec le nœud, elle était libre; *Fig* **after a w. with his conscience, he agreed** après une lutte avec sa conscience, il a accepté

▶ **wrestle down** *vtsep* (*one's opponent*) terrasser (*à la lutte*)

wrestler ['reslər] *n* lutteur, -euse

wrestling ['reslɪŋ] *n* lutte *f*; (*professional*) catch *m*; **Sumo w.** lutte *f* Sumo; **w. match** match *m* de catch

wretch [retʃ] *n* **(a)** (*pitiable person*) malheureux, -euse; **poor w.** pauvre diable *m* **(b)** (*despicable person*) misérable *mf*; **you w.!** misérable!; **you little w.!** petit fripon!

wretched ['retʃɪd] *adj* **(a)** (*miserable*) misérable; **to feel w.** (*ill*) être mal en train; (*depressed*) avoir le cafard; (*guilty*) s'en vouloir; **to lead a w. existence** mener une existence misérable; **to be in w. poverty** être dans une misère affreuse

(b) (*bad, pitiful*) pitoyable, lamentable; (*meal*) triste, pauvre; **the animal/house was in a w. state** l'animal/la maison était dans un état lamentable; **this coffee is w. stuff!** ce café est abominable; **what w. weather!** quel temps abominable!, quel temps de chien!; **it's a w. business** c'est une affaire *ou* une histoire lamentable; **she's a w. singer** c'est une piètre chanteuse; **w. hovel** taudis *m*

(c) (*despicable*) misérable; **it was a w. thing to do/say** c'est immonde d'avoir fait/dit ça

(d) *F* (*expressing anger, contempt etc*) fichu, *Old-fashioned* damné, sacré; **I can't find that w. umbrella** je ne retrouve pas ce fichu parapluie

wretchedly ['retʃɪdlɪ] *adv* **(a)** (*as intensifier*) (*cold, poor, unhappy*) terriblement, affreusement; **to be w. poor** être dans une misère affreuse; **to be w. ill** être malade à faire pitié **(b)** (*in an unhappy fashion*) de façon pitoyable, pitoyablement

wretchedness ['retʃɪdnɪs] *n* **(a)** (*misfortune*) misère *f* **(b)** (*sadness*) tristesse *f* **(c)** (*of clothes, living conditions*) extrême pauvreté *f*

wrick[1] [rɪk] *n Br* = **rick[3]**

wrick[2] *vt Br* = **rick[4]**

wriggle[1] ['rɪg(ə)l] *n* tortillement *m* du corps; **to give a w.** se tortiller, se trémousser

wriggle[2] **1** *vi* **(a)** (*of worm, person*) se tortiller; (*of fish*) frétiller; **stop wriggling!** arrête de t'agiter!; **to w. through a hedge** se faufiler à travers une haie (en se tortillant); **he managed to w. into the sweater** il a réussi à enfiler le pull en se tortillant; **to w. free** se libérer en se faufilant

(b) *Fig* **to w. out of a difficulty** se tirer d'affaire; **I'd like to see him w. out of this one!** j'aimerais savoir comment il va s'en sortir!; **w. out of that one if you can!** à toi de t'en sortir!; **to try to w. out of it** chercher une échappatoire; **he tried to w. out of his promise** il a essayé de se dégager de sa promesse

2 *vt* (*fingers*) tortiller; (*legs*) agiter; **she wriggled her way along the tunnel** elle s'est faufilée le long du tunnel; *Fig* **to w. one's way out of a situation/a problem/a commitment** se dérober devant *ou* se dégager d'une situation/d'un problème/d'un engagement; *Fig* **I'd like to see him w. his way out of that!** j'aimerais bien voir comment il va se sortir de cette situation!

wriggler ['rɪglər] *n* **he's a terrible w.** il gigote tout le temps

wriggling ['rɪg(ə)lɪŋ] **1** *adj* = **wriggly** **2** *n* tortillement *m*; **a w. movement** un tortillement

wriggly ['rɪglɪ] *adj* (*person*) qui gigote; **the children started getting w.** les enfants commençaient à gigoter; **the fish was wet and w.** le poisson était humide et frétillant; **a w. worm** un ver qui se tortille

wring[1] [rɪŋ] *n* **to give the clothes a w.** tordre le linge; (*by machine*) essorer le linge; **he gave my hand a w.** il m'a donné une vigoureuse poignée de main

wring[2] *vt* (*pt, pp* **wrung** [rʌŋ]) tordre; (*washing*) tordre; (*by machine*) essorer; **do not w.** (*on garment label*) ne pas essorer; **to w. sb's hand** serrer (longuement) la main de qn; **to w. one's hands (in despair)** se tordre les mains (de désespoir); **to w. a bird's neck** tordre le cou à une volaille; *F* **I'd like to w. his neck** j'ai envie de lui tordre le cou; **to w. a secret from sb** arracher un secret à qn; **to w. money from sb** arracher *ou* extorquer de l'argent à qn; **to w. tears from sb** arracher des larmes à qn; **to w. the last drop of pathos from a situation** extraire la dernière goutte de pathos d'une situation

▶ **wring out** *vtsep* (*washing*) tordre; (*by machine*) essorer; **to w. the water out** (*from clothes*) exprimer l'eau; **to feel wrung out** se sentir lessivé *ou* moulu

wringer ['rɪŋər] *n* essoreuse *f* (à rouleaux); **he put the clothes through the w.** il passa les vêtements à l'essoreuse; *Fig F* **to put sb through the w.** faire passer un mauvais quart d'heure à qn

wringing ['rɪŋɪŋ] **1** *adj* **w. (wet)** (*clothes*) trempé, à tordre **2** *n* (*of washing*) tordage *m*; (*by machine*) essorage *m*; **she told us the news, with much w. of hands** elle nous a annoncé la nouvelle, en se tordant les mains

wrinkle¹ [ˈrɪŋk(ə)l] *n* **(a)** (*on skin*) ride *f*; (*in cloth, paper, carpet*) faux pli *m* **(b)** *Old-fashioned F* (*tip*) renseignement *m* utile, tuyau *m*

wrinkle² **1** *vt* (*skin*) rider, plisser; (*dress*) froisser, chiffonner, faire des plis à; **to w. one's forehead** froncer les sourcils; **to w. one's nose** froncer le nez; **her stockings were wrinkled** ses bas faisaient des plis **2** *vi* (*of skin*) se rider, se plisser; (*of dress*) se plisser, faire des plis; (*of apple*) se rider, se ratatiner

wrinkled [ˈrɪŋk(ə)ld] *adj* (*forehead*) plissé; (*skin*) ridé; (*dress*) froissé, chiffonné; (*fruit*) ridé, ratatiné; **a w. old man** un vieil homme (tout) fripé

wrinkly [ˈrɪŋklɪ] **1** *adj* (*skin*) (*after bath*) fripé; (*with old age*) ridé, fripé; (*blouse*) froissé; **to go all w.** (*of apple etc*) se ratatiner; (*of skin, fingers*) se friper, devenir tout fripé **2** *n esp Br F Pej, Hum* (*old person*) croulant, -ante

wrist [rɪst] *n* (*of hand, dress etc*) poignet *m*

wristband [ˈrɪstbænd] *n* **(a)** (*on shirt*) poignet *m*, manchette *f* **(b)** (*sweatband*) bracelet *m* en éponge; *Gym* (*of leather*) bracelet de force (en cuir) **(c)** (*of watch*) bracelet *m*

wristbone [ˈrɪstbəʊn] *n Anat* os *m* du carpe

wristlet [ˈrɪstlɪt] *n* bracelet *m*

wristlock [ˈrɪstlɒk] *n* (*in wrestling*) clef *f* de poignet; **to put a w. on sb** faire une clef de poignet à qn

wristwatch [ˈrɪstwɒtʃ] *n* montre-bracelet *f*, *pl* montres-bracelets, bracelet-montre *m*, *pl* bracelets-montres

writ¹ [rɪt] *n Jur* acte *m* judiciaire, mandat *m*, ordonnance *f*; (*summons*) assignation *f*; **w. of attachment** ordre *m* de saisie; **w. of possession** envoi *m* en possession; **to serve a w. on sb, to issue a w. against sb** assigner qn (en justice); **his w. no longer runs in this part of the country** cette région n'est plus sous son pouvoir; *Rel* **Holy W.** les saintes Écritures *fpl*, l'Écriture sainte

writ² *see* **write**

write [raɪt] (*pt* **wrote** [rəʊt]; *pp* **written** [ˈrɪt(ə)n], *Arch* **writ** [rɪt]) **1** *vt* **(a)** (*one's name, novel, letter, piece of music etc*) écrire; (*article*) rédiger; (*cheque*) faire, écrire; *Com* libeller; **can I w. you a cheque for it?** est-ce que je peux vous faire un chèque?; **w. the answer in the space provided** écrivez la réponse dans l'espace réservé à cet effet; **that was not written by me** cela n'est pas écrit de ma main; **do you w. it with a capital?** ça s'écrit avec une majuscule?, ça prend une majuscule?, tu l'écris avec une majuscule?; **the paper is written all over** la feuille est couverte d'écritures; **embarrassment was written all over her (face)** la gêne se lisait sur son visage; **his guilt was written on his face** sa culpabilité se lisait sur son visage; *F* **he's got journalist written all over him** on voit tout de suite que c'est un journaliste; *Fig* **writ large** (*obvious*) écrit en gros, écrit en grosses lettres; **this is Conservative policy writ large** c'est la politique conservatrice toute crachée; **it is written that …** il est écrit que …; *Comptr* **to w. sth to disk** écrire qch sur disque

(b) *esp Am* (*write a letter to*) écrire à

2 *vi* écrire; **w. and tell me what you think** écris pour me dire ce que tu en penses; **she writes well** (*of author*) elle écrit bien; (*expresses herself well in writing*) elle a un beau style; (*has good handwriting*) elle a une belle écriture; **he can w. in Italian** il sait écrire l'italien; **they can read and w.** ils savent lire et écrire; **please w. in black ink** prière d'écrire en noir; **this pen won't w.** ce stylo ne marche pas *ou* n'écrit pas; **she writes** (*is an author*) elle écrit; **to w. for children** écrire des livres pour enfants; **to w. for a paper** écrire dans *ou* collaborer à un journal; **he writes on** *or* **about gardening** il écrit des articles sur le jardinage; **to w. to sb** écrire à qn; **I wrote (to them) to complain** je leur ai écrit pour me plaindre; **we still w.** (*to each other*) nous nous écrivons toujours; **he writes home regularly** il écrit à sa famille régulièrement; *Fig* **that's nothing to w. home about** il n'y a pas de quoi s'en relever la nuit *ou* s'extasier; **w. for our catalogue/more information** nous écrire pour obtenir un catalogue/plus d'informations

▶ **write away for** *vipo* écrire pour demander; **w. away for a free sample** écrire pour obtenir un échantillon gratuit

▶ **write back** *vi* répondre; **she wrote back to say that …** elle a répondu (à la lettre) pour dire que …

▶ **write down** *vtsep* **(a)** (*in order to remember*) noter; (*one's name*) écrire; **to w. down one's thoughts/ideas** mettre ses pensées/ses idées par écrit **(b)** *Fin* (*capital*) réduire; *Acct* déprécier

▶ **write in** **1** *vtsep* (*enter in writing*) (*correction*) insérer; **w. in the correct answer** mettez *ou* écrivez la bonne réponse; *Am* **to w. in a complaint** envoyer une plainte à la direction; *US Pol* **to w. sb in** inscrire qn **2** *vi* (*send letter*) écrire; **many (of our) viewers wrote in with suggestions** de nombreux téléspectateurs nous ont envoyé leurs suggestions; **to w. in for** (*catalogue, free gift etc*) demander par courrier

▶ **write off** **1** *vtsep* **(a)** *Fin* (*capital*) réduire, amortir; (*debt*) amortir; **to w. so much off for wear and tear** déduire tant pour l'usure; *Com* **to w. off a bad debt** défalquer une mauvaise créance, passer une créance aux profits et pertes **(b)** *F* **my car was written off** ma voiture était bonne pour la casse; **she wrote off her father's car** elle a bousillé la voiture de son père; *F* **the critics wrote the play off** les critiques ont démoli la pièce; **they had written her off as a has-been** ils l'avaient cataloguée comme une ringarde **2** *vi* (*send letter*) écrire; **to w. off for a catalogue** demander *ou* commander un catalogue par courrier

▶ **write out** *vtsep* **(a)** (*write in full*) transcrire; (*copy*) mettre au net; **w. this out neatly** écris *ou* recopie cela au propre; **to w. sth out in full** écrire qch en toutes lettres **(b)** (*write*) (*cheque*) faire; *Med* (*prescription*) rédiger **(c)** *TV, Rad* (*remove from script*) (*character*) supprimer (le rôle de)

▶ **write up** *vtsep* **(a)** (*prepare*) (*news item, report*) écrire, rédiger; **w. up your notes** mettez vos notes au propre **(b)** (*praise*) faire l'éloge de **(c)** (*update*) (*diary, accounts*) mettre à jour **(d)** *Fin* (*value of stocks*) augmenter

write access *n Comptr* accès *m* en écriture

write area *n Comptr* zone *f* d'écriture

write-back *n Acct* **w. of provisions** reprises *fpl* sur provisions

write density *n Comptr* densité *f* d'écriture

write-down *n Fin* dépréciation *f*

write head *n Comptr* tête *f* d'écriture

write-off *n* **(a)** *Acct* annulation *f* par écrit; **w. of expenditure** amortissement *m* de dépenses **(b)** (*car*) épave *f*; *F* (*project etc*) perte *f* sèche; **my car was a (complete) w.** ma voiture a été complètement détruite *ou* n'était plus qu'une épave

write-protect *vt Comptr* protéger contre l'écriture

write-protected *adj Comptr* protégé en écriture

write protection *n Comptr* protection *f* contre l'écriture

write-protect notch *n Comptr* encoche *f* de protection contre l'écriture

writer [ˈraɪtər] *n* **(a)** (*professional*) écrivain *m*; (*of novel, scenario, letter etc*) auteur *m* **(of** de); **woman w.** femme *f* écrivain; **w.'s block** vertige *m* de la page blanche; **w.'s cramp** crampe *f* des écrivains; **the present w., the w. (of this letter)** celui qui écrit, l'auteur (de cette lettre); **I'm not a good letter w.** (*I don't write often*) la correspondance n'est pas mon fort; (*I don't write well*) je n'ai pas la plume facile; **to be a good/bad w.** bien/mal écrire **(b)** *Scot Jur* notaire *m*; **W. to the Signet** = avoué *m*

write speed *n Comptr* vitesse *f* d'écriture

write-up *n* **(a)** *Journ* article *m*; **the play got a good w.** la pièce a eu une bonne critique **(b)** *Fin* (*of stock*) augmentation *f* de la valeur comptable

writhe [raɪð] *vi* (*of person*) se contorsionner; (*with pain*) se tordre; (*of snakes, worms*) grouiller; **to w. in agony** se tordre dans des souffrances atroces; **the remark made him w.** (*with shame, embarrassment*) en entendant la remarque, il ne savait plus où se mettre; (*with indignation, anger*) en entendant la remarque, il s'est raidi d'indignation/de colère; **the memory still makes me w. with embarrassment** ce souvenir me fait encore rougir

writing [ˈraɪtɪŋ] *n* **(a)** (*action*) écriture *f*; **the art of w.** l'art de l'écriture; **I'm very bad about letter w.** je suis très mauvais correspondant; **at the time of w.** au moment où j'écris/il écrit/*etc*; *Journ* à l'heure où nous rédigeons ceci; **that's my w.** (*handwriting*) c'est mon écriture; **his w. is bad** (*illegible*) il écrit mal; *Fig* **the w. is on the wall** la catastrophe est imminente; **the w. was on the wall for the Roman Empire** la fin de l'empire romain était imminente; **I could see the w. on the wall** je savais à quoi m'attendre; **in w.** (*to put sth, answer*) par écrit; **I won't be satisfied until I see it in w.** je ne serai pas satisfait tant que ce ne sera pas écrit noir sur blanc; **can I have that in w.?** est-ce que vous pouvez me mettre cela par écrit?; **to commit the facts to w.** consigner les faits par écrit; **to take up w.** (*of author*) commencer à écrire

(b) (*work*) littérature *f*, œuvre *f* littéraire; **the writings of an author** les écrits *mpl ou* l'œuvre *m* d'un auteur; **selected writings** morceaux *mpl* choisis; **a fine piece of w.** (*passage*) un beau passage; (*book, article*) quelque chose de très bien écrit

(c) (*style*) style *m*; **his w. has matured** son style a mûri

writing case *n* correspondancier *m*

writing desk *n* pupitre *m*, bureau *m*, secrétaire *m*

writing off *n Acct* (*of debt*) amortissement *m*

writing pad *n* bloc-correspondance *m*, *pl* blocs-correspondance

writing paper *n* papier *m* à lettres
writing table *n* pupitre *m*, bureau *m*, secrétaire *m*
written ['rɪt(ə)n] **1** *pp see* **write 2** *adj* écrit; (*in writing*) par écrit; **w. confirmation** confirmation *f* écrite *ou* par écrit; **the w. word** le mot écrit; **w. consent** consentement *m* par écrit; **w. law** loi *f* écrite; *Sch etc* **w. examination** épreuve *f* écrite
WRNS [renz] *n Br Mil* (*abbr* **Women's Royal Naval Service**) = section *f* féminine de la marine britannique
wrong[1] [rɒŋ] **1** *adj* **(a)** (*morally bad*) (*judgement etc*) mauvais; **it is w. to steal, stealing is w.** c'est mal de voler; **it was w. of you not to tell me!** c'était très mal de votre part de ne pas m'en parler!; **it is w. for people to have to pay for hospital care** il n'est pas normal que les gens doivent payer les soins hospitaliers; **it's w. that they should suffer because of other people's incompetence** il n'est pas normal qu'ils pâtissent de l'incompétence des autres
(b) (*incorrect, mistaken*) faux, *f* fausse; (*attitude, sort, key, bus, road*) mauvais; (*answer*) mauvais, incorrect; **my watch is w.** ma montre n'est pas à l'heure; **w. use of a word** emploi abusif d'un mot; **don't get the w. idea** ne te fais pas de fausses idées; **his ideas are all w.** il a des idées tout de travers; **to be in the w. place** ne pas être à sa place; **to drive on the w. side of the road** conduire du mauvais côté de la route; *Fig* **to get out of bed on the w. side** se lever du pied gauche; *esp Br Fig* **to get on the w. side of sb** se faire mal voir de qn; **your sock is the w. side out** ta chaussette est à l'envers; **to be (the) w. side up** être à l'envers; **to be on the w. side of forty** avoir (dé)passé la quarantaine; **to take the w. train** se tromper de train; *also Fig* **to back the w. horse** miser sur le mauvais cheval; **to take the w. road** se tromper de chemin *ou* de direction; **this is the w. road for Munich** ce n'est pas la bonne route pour aller à Munich; **she gave me the w. address** elle ne m'a pas donné la bonne adresse, elle m'a donné une mauvaise adresse; **to put sb on the w. track** mettre qn sur une fausse piste; **to be on the w. scent** *or* **track** suivre une mauvaise piste, faire fausse piste; **you've got the w. man, Jack Taylor isn't a murderer** vous faites erreur, Jack Taylor n'est pas un meurtrier; **to come at the w. time** venir à un mauvais moment *ou* mal à propos; **to do/say the w. thing** commettre un impair, dire/faire ce qu'il ne faut pas, *F* faire une gaffe, mettre les pieds dans le plat; **I'm the w. person to ask** il ne faut pas me demander ça à moi; **you're talking to the w. person** (*ask sb else*) ce n'est pas à moi qu'il faut demander ça; *Tel* **w. number** mauvais numéro *m*; **to dial the w. number** composer un mauvais numéro; **I think you've got the w. number** je crois que vous n'avez pas fait le bon numéro; **it was the w. number** (*I didn't dial correctly*) ce n'était pas le bon numéro; **who was that? – nobody, it was a w. number** qui était-ce? – personne, c'était une erreur de numéro *ou* un mauvais numéro; *Mus* **w. note** fausse note; *Fig* **her speech hit the w. note** son discours n'était pas dans la note
(c) to be w. (*of person*) avoir tort, se tromper, être dans l'erreur; **they were w. to assume** *or* **in assuming that ...** ils ont eu tort de supposer que ...; **that's just where you are w.** c'est justement ce qui vous trompe, c'est justement là que vous vous trompez; **to be w. about sb/sth** se tromper sur le compte de qn/sur qch; **you were w. about the price** tu avais tort en ce qui concerne le prix; **I was w. about her** je me suis trompé sur son compte *ou* sur elle; **you were w. to contradict him** vous avez eu tort de le contredire
(d) we went the w. way nous nous sommes trompés de chemin; **I was sent the w. way** on m'a mal dirigé; **if you want to impress him you're going the w. way about it!** si tu veux l'impressionner tu t'y prends mal!; **you're setting about it in the w. way** vous vous y prenez mal *ou* de travers; **to take sth the w. way** prendre quelque chose à contre-pied; **it went down the w. way** (*of food*) je l'ai/il l'a/*etc* avalé de travers; **to stroke a cat the w. way** caresser un chat à rebrousse-poil
(e) (*amiss*) **what's w.?** qu'est-ce qui ne va pas?; **is there something** *or* **anything w.?** quelque chose ne va pas?; **what's w. with you?** qu'avez-vous?, qu'est-ce qui ne va pas?; **what's w. with these people?** (*that they don't understand*) qu'est-ce qu'ils ont qui ne va pas, ces gens?; **there's something w. with me** (*ill*) j'ai quelque chose qui ne va pas; **there must be something w. with me** (*that people don't like me*) il doit y avoir quelque chose qui ne va pas chez moi; *F* **he's w. in the head** il a quelque chose qui ne tourne pas rond dans sa tête, il est un peu timbré; **there was something w. with our car** nous avons eu des ennuis avec la voiture; **there's nothing w. with the engine** le moteur fonctionne normalement; **there's something w. somewhere** il y a quelque chose qui cloche *ou* qui ne tourne pas rond; **I hope there's nothing w.** j'espère qu'il n'est rien arrivé; *F* **what's w. with that?** qu'avez-vous à redire à cela?; **there's nothing w. about wanting a holiday without the kids** il n'y a pas de mal à vouloir des vacances sans les enfants; **what's w. with going to France?** quel mal y a-t-il à aller en France?; **what's w. with my idea?** qu'est-ce qu'elle a qui ne va pas, mon idée?
2 *n* **(a)** (*immoral action*) mal *m*; **to know right from w.** distinguer le bien du mal; **in her eyes he can do no w.** il trouve toujours grâce à ses yeux; **the president can do no w.** le président ne peut pas mal faire
(b) (*unjust action*) tort *m*, injustice *f*; **to right a w.** réparer une injustice; **two wrongs do not make a right** on ne répare pas le mal par le mal; **to do sb w., to do w. to sb** faire tort à qn; **you do her great w. in accusing her of not caring** tu lui as fait beaucoup de tort en l'accusant de s'en moquer
(c) (*mistake*) **to be in the w.** (*because of an action*) être dans son tort; (*be mistaken*) avoir tort; **to put sb in the w.** mettre qn dans son tort
3 *adv* **(a)** (*morally*) mal; **you did w.** vous avez mal agi
(b) (*incorrectly*) mal, incorrectement; **to guess w.** mal deviner; **you've added it up w.** vous avez mal calculé; **you have spelt my name w.** vous avez mal orthographié mon nom; **she got the time/address/name w.** (*was mistaken about*) elle s'est trompée d'heure/d'adresse/de nom; (*misunderstood*) elle a mal compris l'heure/l'adresse/le nom; *F* **don't get me w., I'm not saying ...** comprenez-moi bien, je ne dis pas ...; *F* **you've got me w.** vous m'avez mal compris; *esp Am* **to get in w. with sb** se faire mal voir de qn
(c) to go w. (*of mechanism*) se déranger, se dérégler, se détraquer; (*of business*) aller mal, aller de travers; (*mistake route*) se tromper de chemin; *Fig* se fourvoyer, faire fausse route; (*go morally astray*) se dévoyer, mal tourner; (*be mistaken*) se tromper, commettre une erreur; **then things started to go terribly w.** et puis les choses ont commencé à aller très mal; **his son went w.** son fils a mal tourné; **we went w. at that crossroads** nous nous sommes trompés à ce carrefour; **it's at the end of this road, you can't go w.** c'est au bout de cette route, vous ne pouvez pas vous tromper; **where I went w. was in being too kind to him** là où j'ai commis une erreur, c'est en me montrant trop gentil avec lui; **you can't go w. buying secondhand** vous ne faites pas d'erreur en achetant d'occasion, vous faites forcément le bon choix en achetant d'occasion; **the clock's gone w. again** la pendule s'est déréglée encore une fois; **something went w. with the lighting** nous avons/il a/*etc* eu un problème avec l'éclairage; **all our plans went w.** tous nos projets ont échoué; **things have gone w.** les choses ont mal tourné; **she used to be a normal, happy little girl, but something went w.** c'était une petite fille normale et heureuse mais quelque chose a mal tourné; **the space flight went disastrously w.** le vol spatial a tourné à la catastrophe
wrong[2] *vt* faire (du) tort à, léser, être injuste pour *ou* envers; **he feels wronged** il se sent lésé
wrongdoer ['rɒŋdu:ər] *n* **(a)** (*of immoral action*) auteur *m* d'une injustice; **they did not regard themselves as wrongdoers** ils ne se considéraient pas comme coupables **(b)** (*of illegal action*) malfaiteur *m*
wrongdoing ['rɒŋdu:ɪŋ] *n* **(a)** (*immoral action*) (*usu pl*) **wrongdoings** méfaits *mpl* **(b)** (*illegal action*) infraction *f* à la loi
wrong-foot *vt* (*sb*) *Sp* prendre à contre-pied; *Fig* prendre à l'improviste *ou* au dépourvu *ou* au pied levé
wrongful ['rɒŋfʊl] *adj* **w. arrest** arrestation *f* injustifiée *ou* arbitraire; **w. dismissal** (*of employee*) renvoi *m* injustifié; **w. imprisonment** emprisonnement *m* injustifié *ou* arbitraire
wrongfully ['rɒŋfəlɪ] *adv* injustement, à tort, de façon arbitraire
wrong-headed *adj* buté
wrongly ['rɒŋlɪ] *adv* **(a)** (*unjustly*) à tort, à faux; **I've been w. accused** on m'a accusé injustement *ou* à tort *ou* à faux; **rightly or w.** à tort ou à raison **(b)** (*incorrectly*) mal, incorrectement; **to choose w.** mal choisir
wrongness ['rɒŋnɪs] *n* **(a)** (*incorrectness*) erreur *f*, inexactitude *f* **(b)** (*injustice*) (*of accusation etc*) injustice *f*
wrote *see* **write**
wrought [rɔ:t] **1** *pt, pp see* **work**[2] **2** *adj* (*silver, gold*) travaillé, ouvragé, façonné; (*metal*) ouvré, forgé; **w. iron** fer forgé; **w.-iron gate** portail en fer forgé; *Fig* **finely w. phrase** phrase finement ciselée
wrought-up *adj* (*nervous, anxious*) anxieux; (*angry, upset*) en colère, dans tous ses états; **there's no need to get so w. about it!** pas la peine de vous faire de soucis pour ça!; **she's still pretty w. over her son's death** elle est encore très affectée par la mort de son fils
WRVS [dʌb(ə)lju:ɑ:vi:'es] *n Br abbr* **Women's Royal Voluntary Service**
wry [raɪ] *adj* (*comp* **wrier, wryer**) (*smile, comment*) ironique;

(*humour*) pince-sans-rire; **to pull a w. face** faire la grimace; **she is w. but never bitter** elle est désabusée mais jamais amère

wryly ['raɪlɪ] *adv* (*to remark etc*) avec ironie; **to smile w.** avoir un sourire ironique; **her w. observed portrait** son portrait ironique

wt (*abbr* **weight**) p.

wulfenite ['wʊlfənaɪt] *n* wulfénite *f*

wunderkind ['wʌndəkɪnd, 'vʊndəkɪnt] *n* enfant *mf* prodige

WVa *abbr* **West Virginia**

WW *abbr* **World War**

WWW [dʌb(ə)lju:dʌb(ə)lju:'dʌb(ə)lju:] *n* (*abbr* **world wide web**), réseau *m* mondial de serveurs multimédias, Web *m*

wych-elm ['wɪtʃelm] *n* orme *m* blanc *ou* de(s) montagne(s)

wynd [waɪnd] *n Scot* venelle *f*

Wyo *abbr* **Wyoming**

WYSIWYG ['wɪzɪwɪg] *n Comptr* (*abbr* **what you see is what you get**) tel écran-tel écrit *m*, tel-tel *m*, Wysiwyg *m*; **W. display** affichage *m* tel écran-tel écrit *ou* tel-tel *ou* Wysiwyg

X, x [eks] *n* (*letter*) X, x *m*; **X marks the spot** l'endroit est marqué d'une croix; **for x number of years** pendant x années; *formerly Cin* **X (certificate) film** = film *m* interdit aux moins de 18 ans; **the film was an X** le film a été interdit aux moins de 18 ans; *Math* **x-axis** abscisse *f*; *Biol* **X-chromosome** chromosome *m* x.

xenon ['zenɒn] *n Ch* xénon *m*

xenophobe ['zenəfəʊb] *n* xénophobe *mf*

xenophobia [zenə'fəʊbɪə] *n* xénophobie *f*

xenophobic [zenə'fəʊbɪk] *adj* xénophobe

xerography [zɪə'rɒgrəfɪ] *n* xérographie *f*

Xerox®¹ ['zɪərɒks] *n* photocopie *f*

Xerox®² *vt* photocopier

XL ['ek'sel] (*abbr* **extra large**) XL

Xmas ['krɪsməs, 'eksməs] *n* (*abbr* **Christmas**) Noël *m*

X-rated *adj formerly Cin* interdit aux moins de 18 ans; *Fig* obscène, indécent

X-ray¹ *n* (**a**) (*radiation*) rayon *m* X; *Fig F* **you must have X. eyes!** tu es médium!; **X. examination** examen *m* radiographique *ou* radioscopique, radioscopie *f*; **X. diagnosis** radiodiagnostic *m*; **X. machine** machine *f* à rayon X; **X. photograph** radio(graphie) *f*, cliché *m* radiographique; **X. photography** radio(graphie); **X. treatment** radiothérapie *f*; **X. unit** service *m* de radiologie (**b**) (*picture*) radio *f*; *Med* **to have/take an X.** passer/faire une radio

X-ray² *vt Med* (*person, chest*) radiographier; **to be X-rayed** se faire radiographier, *F* passer à la radio

xylograph ['zaɪləʊgrɑːf] *n* xylographie *f*

xylographic [zaɪləʊ'græfɪk] *adj* xylographique

xylography [zaɪ'lɒgrəfɪ] *n* xylographie *f*

xylophone ['zaɪləfəʊn] *n Mus* xylophone *m*

xylophonist [zaɪ'lɒfənɪst] *n Mus* joueur, -euse de xylophone

Y

Y, y, *pl* **y's, ys** [waɪ, waɪz] *n* (*letter*) Y, y *m*, i *m* grec; *Math* **y-axis** ordonnée *f*; *Biol* **Y-chromosome** chromosome *m* y; **Y-shaped** en fourche, en Y
yacht¹ [jɒt] *n* yacht *m*; **(sailing) y.** voilier *m*; **racing y.** yacht de course; **y. club** yacht-club *m*, *pl* yacht-clubs; **y. race** régate *f*
yacht² *vi* faire de la voile
yachting [ˈjɒtɪŋ] *n* voile *f*; **to go y.** faire de la voile; **y. cap** casquette *f* de yachtman
yachtsman, *pl* **-men** [ˈjɒtsmən] *n* yacht(s)man *m*, *pl* yacht(s)men; (*in yacht race*) régatier *m*; (*for amusement*) plaisancier *m*; **round-the-world y.** navigateur *m* qui fait/a fait/*etc* le tour du monde
yachtswoman, *pl* **-women** [ˈjɒtswʊmən, wɪmɪn] *n* yacht(s)woman *f*, *pl* yacht(s)women; (*in yacht race*) régatière *f*; (*for amusement*) plaisancière *f*; **round-the-world y.** navigatrice *f* qui fait/a fait/*etc* le tour du monde
yack¹ [jæk] *n F* jacasserie *f*; **to have a y. about sth/sb** jacasser au sujet de qch/qn; **it's ages since we've had a really good y.** ça fait longtemps qu'on ne s'est pas taillé une bonne bavette
yack² *vi F* jacasser; **it's y., y., y. all day long!** elle n'arrête/els n'arrêtent/*etc* pas de jacasser toute la journée!
yackety-yack [ˈjækətɪˈjæk] *adv F* **to go y.** jacasser
yah [jɑː] **1** *int* (*in affirmation*) oui (évidemment) **2** *n F* (*loud upper-class person*) snob *mf*
yahoo [jəˈhuː] *n F* brute *f*
yak¹ [jæk] *n* (*animal*) ya(c)k *m*
yak² *n, vi F* = **yack**
yam [jæm] *n* (*plant, tuber*) igname *f*
yammer¹ [ˈjæmər] *n F* boucan *m*; **a terrible y. of voices** un brouhaha terrible
yammer² *vi F* (*complain*) pleurnicher, geindre; **what's he yammering on about?** (*going on about*) qu'est-ce qu'il raconte?
yang [jæŋ] *n Phil* yang *m*
Yank, Yankee [jæŋk, ˈjæŋkɪ] *F* **1** *n* **(a)** (*from the US*) Ricain, -aine, Amerloque *mf*, Yankee *mf* **(b)** *US esp Pej* (*from the Northern US*) habitant, -ante des États du Nord **2** *adj* **(a)** (*from the US*) ricain, amerloque **(b)** *US esp Pej* (*from the Northern US*) qui habite les États du Nord
yank¹ [jæŋk] *n F* **to give sth a y.** tirer qch un bon coup; **she gave his hair a y.** elle lui a tiré les cheveux
yank² *vt F* tirer (d'un coup sec); **to y. the door open** ouvrir la porte d'un coup sec; **to y. sth loose/out/off** arracher qch d'un coup sec; **to y. out a tooth** arracher une dent (d'un seul coup)
yap¹ [jæp] *n* (*of dog*) jappement *m*
yap² *vi* (-pp-) **(a)** (*of dog*) japper **(b)** *Fig F* (*of person*) jacasser; **what's he yapping on about now?** qu'est-ce qu'il est encore en train de raconter?
yapping [ˈjæpɪŋ] **1** *adj* (*dog*) jappeur **2** *n* (*no pl*) **(a)** (*of dog*) jappement *m*; **I wish that dog would stop its y.!** si ce chien pouvait arrêter ses jappements! **(b)** *Fig F* (*of person*) jacasseries *fpl*
yappy [ˈjæpɪ] *adj F* (*dog*) jappeur
yard¹ [jɑːd] *n* **(a)** (*measurement*) yard *m* (*0,914m*); (*in Canada*) verge *f*; **square y.** yard carré (*0,836m²*); *Fig* **his face was a y. long** il faisait une tête de trois pieds de long; *Fig* **yards of statistics, statistics by the y.** des statistiques à n'en plus finir **(b)** *Naut* (*spar*) vergue *f*
yard² *n* **(a)** (*of house, farm, stable etc*) cour *f*; *Am* (*garden*) jardin *m*; *Sch* cour, préau *m*; *Austr* (*cattle enclosure*) parc *m* à bétail *ou* à bestiaux **(b)** *Ind* (*for working*) chantier *m*; **timber** *or* **lumber y.** chantier de bois; **builder's y.** chantier (de construction); *Naut* **repair y.** chantier de radoub; **(ship) y.** chantier naval; **naval (dock)y.**, *US* **navy y.** chantier naval de l'État, arsenal *m* maritime *ou* de la marine **(c)** (*for storage*) dépôt *m* de marchandises **(d)** *Br F* **the Y.** (*Scotland Yard*) ≈ la Sûreté
yardage [ˈjɑːdɪdʒ] *n* = métrage *m*
yardarm [ˈjɑːdɑːm] *n Naut* bout *m* de vergue
yardstick [ˈjɑːdstɪk] *n* (*ruler*) yard *m*; *Fig* (*standard of comparison*) critère *m*, point *m* de référence; *Fig* **to measure others by one's own y.** mesurer les autres selon ses propres valeurs
yarmulka [ˈjɑːməlkə] *n* (*Jewish skullcap*) kippa *f*
yarn¹ [jɑːn] *n* **(a)** *Tex* fil *m*; (*cotton*) filé *m* **(b)** *F* (*unbelievable story*) histoire *f* à dormir debout; (*long story*) longue histoire; **to spin a y.** raconter *ou* débiter une histoire
yarn² *vi F* débiter des histoires, bavasser
yarrow [ˈjærəʊ] *n* (*plant*) achillée *f*, mille-feuille *f*
yashmak [ˈjæʃmæk] *n* (*Muslim veil*) litham *m*
yaw¹ [jɔː] *n Naut* embardée *f*; *Av* (mouvement *m* de) lacet *m*
yaw² *vi Naut* faire une embardée; *Av* faire un (mouvement de) lacet
yawl [jɔːl] *n Naut* (*sailing vessel*) sloop *m*, yawl *m*; (*small boat*) yole *f*
yawn¹ [jɔːn] *n* **(a)** bâillement *m*; **to give a y.** bâiller; **to let out a y.** laisser échapper un bâillement **(b)** *Fig* (*boring thing*) plaie *f*; **the book/film is one long y.** le livre/film est ennuyeux à mourir
yawn² **1** *vi* **(a)** (*with tiredness etc*) bâiller (**with** de) **(b)** *Fig* (*of chasm etc*) être béant, béer; **the gulf yawned at his feet** le gouffre s'ouvrait *ou* béait à ses pieds **2** *vt F* **to y. one's head off** bâiller à se décrocher la mâchoire
yawning [ˈjɔːnɪŋ] **1** *adj* **(a)** (*person*) qui bâille **(b)** *Fig* (*chasm*) béant, ouvert; (*difference, gap*) énorme **2** *n* bâillement *m*
yaws [jɔːz] *npl Med* pian *m*
ye¹ [jiː] *def art* (*pseudo-archaic*), *Arch* le, la, les; **Ye Olde Shoppe** la Vieille Boutique
ye² *pers pron* **(a)** *pl Arch, Lit* vous; **seek and ye shall find** cherchez et vous trouverez; *F* **ye gods!** grand Dieu! **(b)** *sing F, Dial* tu, vous; **how d'ye do?** comment vas-tu?, comment allez-vous?
yea [jeɪ] **1** *adv Bible, Lit* **(a)** (*yes*) oui **(b)** (*truly, indeed*) en vérité **2** *n* oui *m*; *US Pol* **yeas and nays** voix *fpl* pour et contre
yeah [jeə] *adv F* ouais; **oh y.?** (*disbelief, challenging*) vraiment?, ah ouais?; **y. y.!** (*implying disbelief*) ouais, c'est ça!
year [jɪər] *n* (①B58,B,3) **(a)** an *m*, année *f*; **in the y.** (*Arch* **of our Lord** *or* **of grace**) **1850** en l'an *ou* en l'année (du Seigneur *ou* de grâce) 1850; **a ticket valid for one** *or* **a y.** un billet valable (pour) un an; **I have known him for ten years** je le connais depuis dix ans; *Hist* **the Thirty Years' War** la Guerre de Trente Ans; **sentenced to ten years' imprisonment** condamné à dix ans de prison; **he got five years** (*prison sentence*) il en a pris pour cinq ans; **a y.'s work/salary** un an de travail/de salaire; **a y. last/next September** il y a eu/il y aura un an en septembre; **it will be a y. in April** (*answering question 'how long?'*) ça va faire un an en avril; **we're going/we went to Greece this y.** nous allons/nous sommes allés en Grèce cette année; **last y.** l'an dernier, l'année dernière; **next y.** l'an prochain, l'année prochaine; **this day next y.** dans un an jour pour jour; **every y.** tous les ans, chaque année, *Fml* annuellement; **twice a y.** deux fois par an; **to earn £10,000 a y.** gagner 10 000 livres par an; **a y.-old child, a one-y.-old (child)** un enfant (âgé) d'un an; **to be ten years old** avoir dix ans; *Fml* **she's in her eightieth y.** elle est dans sa quatre-vingtième année; **new y.** nouvel an; **we'll see you in the new y.** nous vous verrons au début de l'année prochaine; **New Y.'s Day** le jour de l'An, le 1er de l'An; *Am* **New Y's** (*New Year's Day*) le jour de l'An, le 1er de l'An; (*New Year's Eve*) le 31 décembre, la Saint-Sylvestre; **Happy New Y.!** bonne année!; **to see the old y. out** *or* **the new y. in** faire la veillée *ou* le réveillon de la Saint-Sylvestre, réveillonner; **for many long years** pendant de longues années; **for many years now we have been promised a new road** ça fait maintenant de nombreuses années qu'on nous promet une nouvelle route; **all (the) y. round** (pendant) toute l'année; **y. in (and) y. out** une année après l'autre; **y. by y.** d'année en année; **over the years** au fil des ans *ou* années; **in the early years of the century/their marriage** au cours des premières années de ce siècle/de leur mariage;

years ago il y a bien des années; **this is where I met him, all those years ago** c'est ici que je l'ai rencontré il y a tant d'années; **it's years since I saw him, I haven't seen him for** *or* **in years** (*for many years*) ça fait des années que je ne l'ai pas vu, je ne l'ai pas vu depuis des années; *F* (*for a long time*) il y a une éternité que je ne l'ai vu; **it seemed like years rather than hours** les heures m'ont semblé des années; **years and years** des années et des années; **the best years of our lives** les plus belles années de notre vie; **from his earliest years** dès son plus jeune âge; **to be old for one's years** (*of child*) être précoce; (*of adult*) faire plus vieux que son âge; **to be young for one's years** faire jeune pour son âge; **to be getting on in years** prendre de l'âge; **advanced in years** âgé; **smoking can take years off your life** fumer peut raccourcir la durée de votre vie; *F* **those kids have taken years off my life!** ces gamins m'ont fait prendre dix ans d'un coup!; **working there put years on him** le fait de travailler là l'a vieilli; **that dress takes years off her** cette robe la fait paraître des années plus jeune *ou* la rajeunit beaucoup; **calendar** *or* **civil y.** année civile; **financial** *or* **fiscal** *or* **tax y.** année budgétaire, exercice *m* (financier); **leap y.** année bissextile; *Astron* **light y.** année-lumière *f*, *pl* années-lumière, année de lumière; **school y.** année scolaire; **solar/lunar y.** année solaire/lunaire

(**b**) (*at school, university etc*) année *f*; **third-y. student** étudiant, -ante de troisième année; **he was in my y.** (*at school*) il était dans ma classe; (*at university*) il est de ma promotion; **she was in the y. above/below me** elle était dans la classe au-dessus/en dessous de la mienne

(**c**) (*of wine*) millésime *m*, année *f*; **a good y. for claret** une bonne année *ou* un bon millésime pour le bordeaux rouge; *Fig* **it was a good y. for apples/French cinema** ça a été une bonne année pour les pommes/le cinéma français

yearbook ['jɪəbʊk] *n* annuaire *m*, almanach *m*

year-end *n Acct* de fin d'exercice; **y. accounts** compte *m* de résultats; **y. closing of accounts** clôture *f* annuelle des livres

yearling ['jɪəlɪŋ] **1** *n* (*in general*) animal *m* d'un an; (*horse*) poulain *m* d'un an; (*thoroughbred*) yearling *m* **2** *adj* d'un an

yearlong ['jɪəlɒŋ] *adj* qui dure/a duré un an *ou* toute l'année; **they had a y. wait** ils ont attendu une année entière *ou* toute une année

yearly ['jɪəlɪ] **1** *adj* annuel **2** *adv* (*once a year*) annuellement, une fois par an; (*every year*) annuellement, tous les ans

yearn [jɜːn] *vi* **to y. for** *or* **after sb/sth** languir après qn/qch; **they y. for their own country** ils ont la nostalgie de leur propre pays; **to y. to do sth** brûler de faire qch

yearning ['jɜːnɪŋ] *n* désir (**for** de); **he felt a great y. to ...** il ressentait un désir ardent de ...

yearningly ['jɜːnɪŋlɪ] *adv* avec un désir ardent

year-round *adj* ininterrompu; **California enjoys y. sun** en Californie il y a du soleil toute l'année

yeast [jiːst] *n* levure *f*; **brewer's y.** levure de bière

yeasty ['jiːstɪ] *adj* de levure

yell¹ [jel] *n* (**a**) hurlement *m*, grand cri *m*; **to give a y.** pousser un grand cri *ou* un hurlement; **yells of laughter** hurlements de rire (**b**) *Am* (*organized shout*) (*of students etc*) cri *m* de guerre *ou* de bataille

yell² **1** *vi* hurler, crier à tue-tête; **to y. at sb** hurler après qn; **to y. with pain/laughter** hurler de douleur/de rire **2** *vt* **to y. (out)** (*song*) hurler, beugler; (*order*) hurler, *F* gueuler

yelling ['jelɪŋ] *n* hurlements *mpl*; **there was a lot of y. going on next door** ça hurlait *ou F* gueulait pas mal à côté

yellow¹ ['jeləʊ] **1** *adj* (**a**) (*in colour*) jaune; **to turn** *or* **go y.** jaunir; *Br Aut* **y. line** ligne *f* jaune; *Br* **to park on a double y. line** = se garer sur une zone de stationnement interdit; **y. metal** cuivre *m* jaune, laiton *m* (**b**) *F* (*cowardly*) trouillard, lâche; **he says you're y.!** il dit que tu n'es qu'un trouillard *ou* un lâche!; **to turn** *or* **go y.** se dégonfler; **to have a y. streak** être un peu trouillard sur les bords (**c**) *Old-fashioned Pej* **the y. peril** le péril jaune **2** *n* jaune *m*

yellow² *vti* jaunir; **papers yellowed with age** papiers jaunis par le temps

yellowbelly ['jeləʊbelɪ] *n F* (*coward*) froussard, -arde, trouillard, -arde

yellow card *n Fb* carton *m* jaune

yellow fever *n* fièvre *f* jaune

yellowhammer ['jeləʊhæmər] *n* (*bird*) bruant *m* jaune

yellowish ['jeləʊɪʃ] *adj* jaunet, -ette, *Pej* jaunâtre

yellowness ['jeləʊnɪs] *n* (**a**) (*colour*) ton *m* jaune, teinte *f* jaune; (*of person*) teint *m* jaune; **judging by the y. of her skin** à en juger par son teint jaune (**b**) (*cowardice*) lâcheté *f*

yellow pages *npl* (*of telephone directory*) pages *fpl* jaunes

yelp¹ [jelp] *n* jappement *m*, glapissement *m*; **to let out a y.** laisser échapper un jappement *ou* un glapissement

yelp² *vi* japper, glapir; **to y. with pain** gémir de douleur

yelping ['jelpɪŋ] *n* (*no pl*) jappements *mpl*, glapissements *mpl*

Yemen (the) [ðə'jemən] *n* le Yémen

Yemeni(te) ['jemənɪ, -aɪt] **1** *adj* yéménique, yéménite **2** *n* Yéménite *mf*

yen¹ [jen] *n* (*currency*) yen *m*

yen² *n* (*desire*) envie *f*; **to have a y. for sth/to do sth** avoir envie de qch/de faire qch

yeoman, *pl* **-men** ['jəʊmən] *n* (**a**) *Hist* (*small freeholder*) franc-tenancier *m*, *pl* francs-tenanciers; *Fig* **to do y. service** rendre des services inestimables (**b**) *Br Mil, Hist* soldat *m* du yeomanry; **Y. of the Guard** = hallebardier *m* à la Tour de Londres

yeomanry ['jəʊmənrɪ] *n* (*no pl*) (**a**) *Hist* (*small freeholders*) francs-tenanciers *mpl* (**b**) *Br Mil Hist* = corps *m* de cavalerie composé de volontaires

yep [jep] *adv esp Am F* ouais

yes [jes] **1** *adv* (**a**) [①B61,D] oui; (*contradicting negation*) si; **to answer y. or no** répondre par oui ou (par) non; **to say y.** dire oui, dire que oui; **y., certainly!, oh y.!** mais oui!; **are you hungry? – y. (I am)** avez-vous faim? – oui; **you didn't hear me? – y., I did** vous ne m'avez pas entendu? – (mais) si; **would you like some cake? – y. please** *or esp Am* **thanks** est-ce que vous voulez du gâteau? – oui, s'il vous plaît; **could I have a glass of water? – y., of course** est-ce que je pourrais avoir un verre d'eau? – oui, bien sûr; **y. sir/madam** (*I'm coming*) voilà, monsieur/madame

(**b**) (*interrogatively*) **y.?** (*are you sure*) vraiment?; (*go on*) et puis après?; (*to sb waiting to speak*) oui?, vous désirez?

2 *n* (*pl* **yeses** ['jesɪz]) oui *m inv*; **an emphatic y.** un oui énergique

yes-man, *pl* **-men** ['jesmæn, -men] *n F* béni-oui-oui *m inv*

yesterday ['jestəd(e)ɪ] *adv, n* hier *m*; **the day before y.** avant-hier; **a week ago y.** il y a eu hier huit jours; **y. week, a week (from) y.** d'hier en huit; **y.'s paper/milk** le journal/le lait d'hier; **y. morning/evening** hier matin/soir; **I can remember it as clearly as if it had happened y.** je m'en souviens comme si c'était hier; *Pej* **y.'s men/designers** les hommes/designers qui appartiennent au passé; **y.'s heroes** les héros *mpl* de jadis; *Lit* **our yesterdays** les jours *mpl* d'autrefois *ou* d'antan

yesteryear ['jestəjɪər] *n Lit* **of y.** d'antan; **the snows of y.** les neiges *fpl* d'antan

yet [jet] **1** *adv* (**a**) (*still*) encore; **we've got ten minutes y.** nous avons encore dix minutes; **jobs y. to be done** tâches encore à faire; **y. more** encore plus; **y. again** encore une fois; **y. greater advantages** des avantages encore plus grands; **y. another mistake** encore une erreur; **y. one more** encore un(e) autre

(**b**) (*in neg phrases*) encore; (*in questions*) (*already*) déjà; **I haven't finished y.** je n'ai pas encore fini; **we're not ready y.** nous ne sommes pas encore prêts; **have they decided y.?** est-ce qu'ils ont déjà décidé?; **are you ready y.?** tu es prêt?; **not y.** pas encore; **don't go y.** ne partez pas encore; **it will not happen just y.** cela n'arrivera pas tout de suite; **we're not going just y.** nous ne partons pas tout de suite; **as y. nothing has been done** jusqu'à présent *ou* jusqu'ici rien n'a été fait; **not as y.** pas encore; **as y. unexplored jungle** jungle pas encore explorée

(**c**) (*in spite of everything*) malgré tout; **I shall catch him y.!** je finirai bien par l'attraper!; **I'll do it y.!** j'y arriverai!

(**d**) *Old-fashioned* (*even*) **not finished nor y. started** pas achevé ni même commencé

2 *conj* néanmoins, cependant, tout de même; **and y. I like him** et cependant *ou* et malgré tout *ou* néanmoins il me plaît, mais il me plaît tout de même

yeti ['jetɪ] *n* yeti *m*

yew [juː] *n* (*tree*) if *m*; (*wood*) (bois *m* d')if

Y-fronts® ['waɪfrʌnts] *npl* slip *m* ouvert

YHA [waɪeɪtʃ'eɪ] *n* (*abbr* **Youth Hostels Association**) FUAJ *f*

Yid [jɪd] *n Offensive Sl* youpin, -ine

Yiddish ['jɪdɪʃ] *adj, n Ling* yiddish *m*

yield¹ [jiːld] *n* (*of field, machine*) rendement *m*; (*of fruit tree, capital outlay, land etc*) rapport *m*; (*of mine*) production *f*, produit *m*, débit *m*; **this tree gives a better/poor y.** cet arbre donne un meilleur/un faible rapport; *Fin* **the y. on these shares is large** ces actions rapportent beaucoup

yield² **1** *vt* (**a**) (*give*) rapporter, produire, donner; **shares that y. high interest** actions à gros rendement; **to y. a profit** rapporter *ou* dégager un bénéfice; **these remarks y. an insight into his motives** ces remarques donnent une idée de ses motifs; **further investigations yielded no new information** des recherches supplémentaires n'ont fourni aucune information nouvelle

(**b**) (*concede*) (*fortress to enemy, right etc*) céder; **to y. ground** céder du terrain; **to y. a point to sb** céder à qn sur un point; *also Sp* concéder un point à qn; **divers have made the ocean y. (up) its treasures** les plongeurs ont fait livrer ses trésors à l'océan; *Lit* **to y. (up) the ghost** *or* **one's soul** rendre l'âme

2 *vi* **(a)** *(surrender)* céder **(to** à); *(of army, enemy)* se rendre; **to y. to force** céder devant la force; **to y. to reason** se rendre à la raison; **we shall not y. to threats** nous ne céderons pas aux menaces; **I had to y. to them on that point** j'ai dû leur céder sur ce point; **to y. to temptation** succomber *ou* céder à la tentation; **to y. to sb's wishes** consentir *ou* céder aux désirs de qn

(b) *(of rope etc)* céder; *(of beam etc)* s'affaisser, fléchir; **the plank yielded under our weight** la planche a manqué *ou* cédé sous notre poids

(c) *Am Aut* **y.!** *(on sign)* vous n'avez pas la priorité!

yielding ['ji:ldɪŋ] *adj* **(a)** *(person)* facile, complaisant, accommodant; **the management hasn't been very y.** la direction n'a pas été très accommodante **(b)** *(substance)* souple, élastique, flexible

yikes [jaɪks] *int F* mince!

yin [jɪn] *n Phil* yin *m*; **y. and yang** le yin et le yang

yippee [jɪ'pi:] *int F* hourra!, bravo!

Y-junction *n* fourche *f*

YMCA [waɪemsi:'eɪ] *n* *(abbr* **Young Men's Christian Association)** Union *f* chrétienne de jeunes gens

yo [jəʊ] *int* hé!, eh!

yob [jɒb], **yobbo** ['jɒbəʊ] *n Br F* voyou *m*, loubar(d) *m*; **y. culture** *expression datant de la période thatchérienne utilisée pour désigner une attitude et un comportement agressifs et anti-intellectuels, par ex.* this yob culture - beer-swilling, violent and self-centred

yobbish ['jɒbɪʃ] *adj Br F* de voyou; **it makes you look y.** ça te donne l'air d'un voyou; **don't be so y.** arrête de jouer les voyous

yodel[1] ['jəʊd(ə)l] *n Mus* (chant *m* à la) tyrolienne *f*

yodel[2] *vi* **(-ll-**, *US* **-l-)** *Mus* jodler, iodler

yod(el)ler, *US* **yod(e)ler** ['jəʊd(ə)lər] *n* jodleur, -euse, iodleur, -euse

yoga ['jəʊgə] *n* yoga *m*

yoghurt, yoghourt ['jɒgət, 'jəʊ-] *n* yaourt *m*, yog(h)urt *m*; **y. drink** yaourt à boire

yogi ['jəʊgɪ] *n* yogi *m*

yogurt *n* = **yoghurt**

yoke[1] [jəʊk] *n* **(a)** *(for ox)*, *Fig* joug *m*; *Fig* **the y. of convention** le joug des conventions; *Fig* **to throw off the y.** secouer le joug, s'affranchir du joug **(b)** *(for carrying)* palanche *f* **(c)** *Sewing* empiècement *m* **(d)** *El (of dynamo)* carcasse *f*, bâti *m*

yoke[2] *vt* **(a)** *(oxen)* accoupler, atteler **(to the plough** à la charrue); *Fig* lier; *Fig* **to y. together** *(in marriage)* unir **(b)** *Tech (pieces of equipment)* accoupler

yokel ['jəʊk(ə)l] *n Pej* rustre *m*, campagnard, -arde

yolk [jəʊk] *n* **(a)** *Culin (of egg)* jaune *m*; **take the y. of an egg** prenez un jaune d'œuf **(b)** *Biol* vitellus *m*; **y. bag** *or* **sac** membrane *f* vitelline

Yom Kippur [jɒmkɪ'pʊər] *n Jewish Rel* Yom Kippour *m*

yomp [jɒmp] *vi Mil* crapahuter, crapaüter; **a group of hikers was yomping towards us** un groupe de marcheurs se dirigeait vers nous avec tout leur chargement

yon [jɒn] *adj, adv Arch, Dial* = **yonder**

yonder ['jɒndər] *Lit* **1** *adv* **(down/over) y.** là-bas **2** *adj* ce … -là, cette … -là, *pl* ces … -là; **y. elms** ces ormes là-bas, ces ormes-là

yonks [jɒŋks] *npl F* une éternité; **we've been waiting for y.** ça fait une éternité qu'on attend; **I haven't been there in y.** ça fait une paye que je n'y suis pas allé; **that was y. ago** ça fait une paye

yoohoo ['ju:hu:] *int* ohé!

yore [jɔ:r] *n Arch, Lit* **of y.** (d')autrefois, d'antan; **in days of y.** au temps jadis, autrefois

Yorkshire ['jɔ:kʃɪər] *n* le comté d'York; *Br Culin* **Y. pudding** = pâte *f* à choux cuite servie avec du rosbif; **Y. terrier** yorkshire(-terrier) *m*, *pl* yorkshire(-terriers)

Yoruba ['jɒrʊbə] **1** *n* **(a)** *(person)* Yor(o)uba *mf* **(b)** *Ling* yor(o)uba **2** *adj* yor(o)uba

you [ju:] *pers pron* [①**B64**,6] **(a)** [①**A26**,A; **A42**,3; **B17**,1,b] *(subject) sing, pl* vous; *sing (when addressing relatives, intimate friends, children, animals, deities)* tu; **y. are very kind** vous êtes bien aimable(s)/tu es bien aimable; **how are y.?** comment allez-vous?/comment vas-tu?; **there y. are** *(here's what you wanted, it's done, see what I mean)* et voilà; *(I was looking/waiting for you)* vous voilà/te voilà; **y. all know who I mean** vous savez tous de qui je veux parler

(b) [①**B17**,2,a-b] *(as object of verb)* vous/te, *pl* vous; **I hope to see y. tomorrow** j'espère vous/te voir demain; **I'll give y. some** je vous en/t'en donnerai; **I told y. so!** je vous/te l'avais bien dit!

(c) *(after preposition)* vous/toi, *pl* vous; **between y. and me** *(when confiding)* entre vous et moi/entre toi et moi, entre nous soit dit; **I gave them to y.** je te/vous les ai donnés; **away with y.!** allez-vous-en!/va-t'en!; **all of y.** vous tous; **to/for y. and yours** à/pour toi et les tiens/vous et les vôtres; **now there's a singer for y.!** ah, voilà un chanteur!; **now there's a typical politician for y.** voilà un politicien type; **now there's manners for y.!** ça au moins c'est quelqu'un de bien élevé/ce sont des gens bien élevés!; *Iron* en voilà des manières!

(d) *(stressed)* vous/toi, *pl* vous; **y. and I will go by train** vous et moi/toi et moi nous irons par le train; **is that y.?** c'est vous/toi?; **oh, it's y.** ah, c'est vous/toi; **I am older than y.** je suis plus âgé que vous/que toi; **if I were y.** (si j'étais) à votre/ta place; **hey! y. there!** eh! dites donc, là-bas!; **poor old y.!** mon pauvre vieux!, ma pauvre vieille!; **silly/lucky (old) y.!** quel gros bêta/veinard tu fais!; *F* **that jacket/job wasn't y.** cette veste/ce travail n'était pas ton style; **y. two are very different** vous êtes très différents tous les deux; **y. four! come with me** vous quatre! venez avec moi; **where are y. two going?** où est-ce que vous allez, tous les deux?; **how long have y. two been married?** cela fait combien de temps que vous êtes mariés tous les deux?; *F* **y. lot** vous

(e) *(in the imperative)* **don't y. cry!** ne pleure pas!; **don't y. dare!** ne t'avise surtout pas de faire ça!; **y. sit down and eat your lunch!** toi, assieds-toi et mange ton déjeuner!; **never y. mind!** ne t'occupe pas de ça, toi!; **now <u>you</u> tell a joke** à ton tour *ou* à toi de raconter une blague maintenant; **don't <u>you</u> start!** ne commence pas, toi!, ne t'y mets pas, toi!; **just y. try!** essaye un peu pour voir!

(f) *(in apposition)* **y. lawyers/Englishmen** vous autres avocats/Anglais; **y. idiot(, y.)!** idiot que tu es!, espèce d'idiot!; **y. darling(, y.)!** tu es un amour!

(g) [①**A27**,e; **B15**,2,c] *(indefinite)* on; **y. never can tell** on ne sait jamais; **the joy y. feel when …** la joie qu'on ressent quand …; **exercise is good for y.** (prendre de) l'exercice est bon pour la santé

you-all [j(ə)'ɑ:l] *pers pron Southern US F* vous tous; *(speaking to one person)* vous

you'd [ju:d] **(a)** = **you had**, *see* **have**[2] **(b)** = **you would**, *see* **will**[3]

you-know-who *n* qui-vous-savez *mf*; **yesterday I had a telephone call from y.** hier, j'ai reçu un coup de téléphone de qui-vous-savez

you'll [ju:l] **(a)** = **you will**, *see* **will**[3] **(b)** = **you shall**, *see* **shall**

young [jʌŋ] **1** *adj* **(a)** *(person, animal)* jeune; *(baby animal)* petit; **younger** plus jeune; **younger son/daughter** fils cadet/fille cadette; **my younger brother** mon frère cadet; **the youngest** le/la plus jeune, le cadet/la cadette; **this is my youngest, Vicki** voici ma cadette *ou* ma dernière, Vicki; **he's younger than me** *or* **I (am)** il est plus jeune *ou* moins âgé que moi, il est mon cadet; **she's two years younger than me** elle est plus jeune que moi *ou* elle est ma cadette de deux ans; **they wanted someone younger** ils voulaient quelqu'un de plus jeune; **when I was twenty years younger** quand j'avais vingt ans de moins; **if I were twenty years younger!** si j'avais vingt ans de moins!; **you're only y. once** on n'est jeune qu'une fois, la jeunesse ne dure qu'un temps; **she's too y. for alcohol/to get married** elle est trop jeune pour boire de l'alcool/se marier; **don't be too hard on him, he's only y.** ne sois pas trop sévère avec lui, il est encore bien jeune; **I am not as y. as I used to be** je n'ai plus mes jambes de vingt ans; **y. man** jeune homme; **y. woman** jeune femme; **now you listen to me, y. man/woman** écoute-moi un peu jeune homme/ma petite dame; **he's her y. man** c'est son petit ami; **a y. couple/mother** un jeune couple/une jeune mère; **a y. family** des enfants en bas âge; **y. people** jeunes gens *mpl*, jeunes *mpl*; **Pliny the Younger** Pline le Jeune; **the younger generation** la jeune génération; **in his younger days** dans son jeune temps, dans sa jeunesse; **in my young(er) days** dans ma jeunesse; **a y. country/company** un pays/une société de création récente; **a y. wine** un vin vert; **the night is y.!** j'ai/nous avons toute la soirée devant moi/nous!

(b) *(youthful)* jeune; **y. for his age** *or* **years** jeune pour son âge; **y. in spirit** *or* **at heart** jeune d'esprit; **to grow** *or* **get y. again, to grow younger** rajeunir; **you look younger than ever!** tu parais plus jeune que jamais!; **she's a y. forty** elle ne fait pas ses quarante ans; **thirty's still y.!** trente ans c'est encore jeune!

2 *n* **(a)** *(people)* **the y.** *pl* les jeunes (gens) *mpl*, la jeunesse; **books for the y.** livres pour la jeunesse; **it appeals to y. and old alike** ça plaît aux jeunes comme aux moins jeunes

(b) an animal and its y. un animal et ses petits; **a mare with y.** *(pregnant)* une jument pleine

Young Conservatives *npl* jeunes conservateurs *mpl*

youngish ['jʌŋɪʃ] *adj* assez jeune, *F* jeunet, -ette; **he's a y. fifty** il ne fait pas tout à fait ses cinquante ans
Young Liberals *npl* jeunes libéraux *mpl*
young offenders' institution *n Br* maison *f* de correction
youngster ['jʌŋstər] *n* **(a)** (*young person*) jeune *mf*, jeune personne *f* **(b)** (*child*) petit, -ite, *F* gosse *mf*
your [jɔːr] *poss adj* **(a)** [①**A30**,8; **A42**,3; **B19-20**,E,1] *sing, pl* votre, *pl* vos; *sing* (*when addressing relatives, intimate friends, children, animals, deities*) ton, ta, *pl* tes; **y. house** votre/ta maison; **y. friends** vos/tes ami(e)s; **y. father and mother** votre père et votre mère/ton père et ta mère; (*formal*) vos père et mère; **the most recent of y. books, y. most recent book** votre/ton livre le plus récent; **have you hurt y. hand?** vous vous êtes/tu t'es fait mal à la main?; **turn y. head(s)** tourne(z) la tête; **y. turn!** (*to play etc*) à vous/toi!; **Y. Majesty** votre Majesté; **I like y. London buses** j'aime bien les bus que vous avez à Londres; **I object to y. visiting the children** je m'oppose à ce que tu rendes visite aux enfants
(b) (*indefinite*) son, sa, *pl* ses; **you cannot alter y. nature** on ne peut pas changer son caractère
(c) *F* **y.** (**typical** *or* **average**) **Frenchman** le Français moyen; **of course, y. kings and queens don't do that** bien sûr, les rois et les reines ne font pas ça
you're [jɔːr] = **you are,** *see* **be**
yours [jɔːz] *poss pron* [①**A30**,8; **B20**,E,2] *sing, pl* le vôtre, la vôtre, *pl* les vôtres; *sing* (*when addressing relatives, intimate friends, children*) le tien, la tienne, *pl* les tiens, les tiennes; **this is y.** ceci est à vous/à toi, c'est le vôtre/le tien; **these are y.** ceux-ci sont à toi/à vous, ceux-ci sont les tiens/les vôtres; **you and y.** vous et les vôtres/toi et les tiens; **the bathroom's all y.** la salle de bains est libre maintenant; **can I use your telephone? – it's all y.** est-ce que je peux utiliser ton téléphone? – vas-y; **y.** (**sincerely**) (*in informal letter*) bien amicalement; (*in formal letter*) veuillez agréer l'expression de mes sentiments distingués *ou* respectueux; *Com, Fml* **in reply to y. of the 14th November** en réponse à votre lettre en date du 14 novembre; **y. is a nation of travellers** vous êtes une nation de voyageurs; **y. was no easy task** ta tâche n'était pas facile; **he is a friend of y.** c'est un de vos/tes amis, c'est un ami à vous/toi; **that's no business of y.** cela ne vous/te regarde pas, ce n'est pas votre/ton affaire; *Pej* **that dog of y.** votre/ton sacré *ou* fichu *ou* foutu chien
yourself [jɔː'self], *pl* **yourselves** [jɔː'selvz] *pers pron* [①**A29**] **(a)** (*emphatic*) *sing, pl* vous-même(s); *sing* (*when addressing relatives, intimate friends, children, deities*) toi-même; **you said y.** *or* **you y. said it was cheap** tu as dit toi-même/vous avez dit vous-même que ce n'était pas cher; **tell her y.** dis-lui toi-même/dites-lui vous-même; **you don't look quite y.** vous avez/tu as l'air mal en train; **just be y.** contente-toi d'être toi-même/contentez-vous d'être vous-même
(b) [①**B26**,D] (*reflexive*) vous/te, *pl* vous; **are you enjoying y.?** tu t'amuses/vous vous amusez bien?; **have you hurt y.?** vous êtes-vous/tu t'es fait mal?; **I see you've got y. a wife/you've bought y. a car** je vois que tu t'es trouvé une femme/que tu t'es acheté une voiture; *F* **have y. a good time** amuse-toi bien; **and you call y. a Christian/socialist!** et vous vous dites/tu te dis chrétien/socialiste!
(c) (*after preposition*) **see for y.** vois toi-même/voyez vous-même; **see for yourselves** voyez vous-mêmes; **tell us something about y.** parle-nous de toi/parlez-nous de vous; **what about y.?** et toi/vous?; **speak for y.!** parle pour toi!/parlez pour vous!; **keep it for y.** garde-le pour toi/gardez-le pour vous; **do you live by y.?** vous vivez/tu vis (tout) seul?; **did you do this by y.?** est-ce que vous avez/tu as fait ça tout seul?; **among yourselves** (*reciprocal*) entre vous
(d) (*used impersonally*) soi-même; (*reflexive*) se; **you have to do it y.** il faut le faire soi-même; **you can't take y. too seriously** il ne faut pas se prendre trop au sérieux
youth [juːθ, *pl* juːðz] *n* [①**A11**,f,ii] **(a)** (*no pl*) (*period*) jeunesse *f*, jeune âge *m*; **in his early y.** dans sa première jeunesse; **she is not in the first flush of y., she is past her first y.** elle n'est pas de la première jeunesse; **lost y.** jeunesse perdue; *Myth* **the fountain of Y.** la Fontaine de Jouvence; **y. will have its way** *or* **its fling** il faut que jeunesse se passe
(b) (*male teenager*) jeune homme *m*, adolescent *m*
(c) (*no pl*) (*young people*) (*of village etc*) jeunes gens *mpl*, jeunesse *f*; **inner-city y.** la jeunesse des quartiers déshérités; **the y. of today** la jeunesse *ou* les jeunes d'aujourd'hui; **y. fare** tarif *m* jeune; **y. market** marché *m* de la jeunesse; **y. orchestra** orchestre *m* de jeunes
youth club *n* centre *m* (de loisirs) pour les jeunes
youth culture *n* la culture jeune
youthful ['juːθfʊl] *adj* **(a)** (*person, face, fashion etc*) jeune; **to look y.** avoir l'air jeune; **y. good looks** (*of men*) air *m* de jeune homme; **he is a y. fifty-two** il est jeune pour ses cinquante-deux ans **(b)** (*error*) de jeunesse; (*enthusiasm, impetuousness*) juvénile
youthfulness ['juːθfʊlnɪs] *n* jeunesse *f*; (*youthful appearance*) air *m* de jeunesse, air jeune
youth hostel *n* auberge *f* de jeunesse
youth hostelling *n* **to go y. in France** visiter la France en séjournant dans des auberges de jeunesse
Youth Hostels Association *n* association *f* des auberges de jeunesse
you've [juːv] = **you have,** *see* **have**[2]
yowl[1] [jaʊl] *n* (*of dog*) hurlement *m*; (*of cat*) miaulement *m*; **there was a y. of protest/pain from him** il a émis un cri de protestation/douleur
yowl[2] *vi* (*of dog, person*) hurler; (*of cat*) miauler
yo-yo® ['jəʊjəʊ] *n* **(a)** yo-yo® *m inv F* **he was jumping up and down like a y.** il sautait sur place comme s'il était monté sur un ressort; *F* **I've been up and down the stairs like a y. all day** je n'ai pas arrêté de monter et de descendre l'escalier toute la journée **(b)** *Am F* (*fool*) abruti, -ie
yr (*abbr* **year**) a.
YTS [waɪtiː'es] *n Br* (*abbr* **Youth Training Scheme**) (*person*) TUC *mf*; (*job*) TUC *m*
yucca ['jʌkə] *n* (*plant*) yucca *m*; **a y. plant** un yucca
yuck [jʌk] *int F* pouah!, berk!
yucky ['jʌkɪ] *adj F* dégoûtant; **to feel y.** (*not well*) se sentir patraque
Yugoslav ['juːgəʊslɑːv] **1** *adj* yougoslave **2** *n* Yougoslave *mf*
Yugoslavia [juːgəʊ'slɑːvɪə] *n* Yougoslavie *f*; **the ex-Y.** l'ex-Yougoslavie
Yugoslavian [juːgəʊ'slɑːvɪən] *adj* yougoslave
yule [juːl] *n Arch, Lit* Noël *m*; **y. log** bûche *f* de Noël
yuletide ['juːltaɪd] *n Arch, Lit* période *f* de Noël; **y. festivities** fêtes *fpl* de Noël
yummy ['jʌmɪ] *adj F* délicieux; (*person*) sexy *inv*; **y.!** miam-miam!
yum-yum [jʌm'jʌm] *int F* miam-miam!
yup [jʌp] *adv US F* ouais
yuppie ['jʌpɪ] *n usu Pej* (*abbr* **young upwardly mobile professional**) yuppie *mf*; **y. area/restaurant** quartier/restaurant chic et branché; *F* **y. flu** encéphalomyélite *f* myalgique
yuppify ['jʌpɪfaɪ] *vt F* rendre chic et branché; **the area/pub has become rather yuppified** ce quartier/pub est plein de yuppies maintenant
YWCA [waɪdʌb(ə)ljuːsiː'eɪ] *n* (*abbr* **Young Women's Christian Association**) Union *f* chrétienne de jeunes femmes

Z

Z, z, *pl* **zs, z's** [zed, *US* ziː, *pl* zedz, *US* ziːz] *n* (*letter*) Z, z *m*
Zaire [zɑːˈɪər] *n* Zaïre *m*
Zairean [zɑːˈɪərɪən] **1** *adj* zaïrois **2** *n* Zaïrois, -oise
Zambezi (the) [ðəzæmˈbiːzɪ] *n* le Zambèze
Zambia [ˈzæmbɪə] *n* Zambie *f*
Zambian [ˈzæmbɪən] **1** *adj* zambien **2** *n* Zambien, -ienne
zaniness [ˈzeɪnɪnɪs] *n F* loufoquerie *f*
zany [ˈzeɪnɪ] *adj F* loufoque
zap¹ [zæp] *F* **1** *int* (*esp in comic books*) paf! **2** *n* (*energy*) punch *m*; **to be full of z.** avoir une pêche d'enfer
zap² *F* **1** *vt* **(a)** (*destroy, stun, disable*) (*with ray gun, by bombing etc*) détruire; (*person*) éliminer
(b) (*put, send*) **z. it in the microwave** balance-le au micro-ondes; **we'll z. it across to you by courier** on vous l'enverra *ou* expédiera vite fait par courrier; **they zapped him off to the TV studios** ils l'ont emmené vite fait *ou* sur les chapeaux de roues aux studios de la télé
(c) *Comptr* (*delete*) effacer
(d) (*hit*) donner un coup à, cogner
2 *vi* **(a)** (*change channel on TV*) zapper, *Can* pitonner
(b) (*move fast*) **he's been zapping in and out of his office all morning** il n'arrête pas d'entrer et de sortir de son bureau depuis ce matin; **the project's really zapping along** le projet avance vraiment à fond de train; **z., z. and it's done!** tac tac et c'est fini!
▶ **zap up** *vtsep F* (*make more exciting*) **to z. up one's style** rendre son style plus coloré *ou* vivant; **to z. up the colour scheme** (*in house etc*) rehausser les couleurs
zapped [zæpt] *adj F* (*exhausted*) crevé, claqué
zapper [ˈzæpər] *n F* (*for TV*) télécommande *f*
zapping [ˈzæpɪŋ] *n* (*changing TV channels*) zapping *m*
zappy [ˈzæpɪ] *adj F* (*fast*) (*car, computer*) rapide; (*stylish, punchy*) (*prose, manager, style*) énergique, qui a du punch
Z chart *n* tableau *m* en Z
zeal [ziːl] *n* zèle *m*, ardeur *f*; (*religious*) zèle, ferveur *f*; **to show excessive z.** faire preuve d'un zèle excessif
zealot [ˈzelət] *n* **(a)** *Bible, Hist* **Z.** zélote *mf* **(b)** *Fig* fanatique *mf*, *Lit* zélateur, -trice (**for** de)
zealotry [ˈzelətrɪ] *n* fanatisme *m*, ferveur *f*
zealous [ˈzeləs] *adj* zélé; (*campaigner, advocate*) fervent; **z. to do sth** empressé de faire qch; **to be z. in doing sth** faire qch avec zèle
zealously [ˈzeləslɪ] *adv* avec zèle
zebra [ˈzebrə, ˈziːbrə] *n* zèbre *m*; *Br Aut* **z. crossing** passage *m* clouté *ou* pour piétons
zebu [ˈziːbuː] *n* (*animal*) zébu *m*
zed [zed] *n Br* (*letter*) z *m*
zee [ziː] *n US* (*letter*) z *m*; **z. chart** tableau *m* en Z
Zen [zen] *n Rel* **Z. (Buddhism)** (bouddhisme *m*) zen *m*
zenith [ˈzenɪθ] *n Astron, Fig* zénith *m*; *Fig* **at the z. of his fame** à l'apogée *ou* au sommet de sa gloire
zephyr [ˈzefər] *n Lit* zéphyr *m*
zeppelin [ˈzepəlɪn] *n Av, Hist* zeppelin *m*
zero¹ [ˈzɪərəʊ] **1** *n* [①A71,3] *Math, Comptr* zéro *m*; **z. point two (0.2)** zéro virgule deux (0,2); **z. hour** l'heure *f* H; **I'd put your chances at z.** je dirais que tes chances sont nulles; *Comptr* **with z. wait states** sans état d'attente; **z. (point)** (*on graduated scale*) zéro; **the thermometer is at z./four below z.** le thermomètre est à zéro/à quatre au-dessous de zéro; **the temperature fell below z.** la température est tombée au-dessous de zéro; **exports are down to z.** les exportations sont tombées à zéro; **z. altitude** altitude *f* zéro; *Mktg* **z. defects purchasing** achat *m* de qualité à 100%, achat zéro défaut; **z. (economic) growth** croissance *f* zéro, croissance économique nulle; **z. gravity** apesanteur *f*; *Pol* **z. option** option *f* zéro; *Admin* **z. rating** imposition *f* nulle
2 *adj F* **he's got z. intelligence/charm** il n'a aucun(e) intelligence/charme
zero² *vt* (*instrument etc*) (re)mettre à zéro
▶ **zero in 1** *vtsep Mil* (*gun*) régler le tir de **2** *vi* (*of missile etc*) se régler sur une/la cible
▶ **zero in on** *vipo Mil* (*target*) régler le tir sur; (*of missile etc*) se régler sur; *Fig* (*concentrate on*) (*subject, problem*) se concentrer sur; (*identify*) aller droit sur; **they zeroed in on the one weak point of the argument** ils ont été droit sur le seul point faible de l'argument
zeroed [ˈzɪərəʊd] *adj* (*milometer*) à zéro
zeroing [ˈzɪərəʊɪŋ] *n Comptr* initialisation *f* du compteur
zero-rated *adj* (*without VAT*) exempt *ou* exonéré de TVA
zero-rating *n Fin* franchise *f* de TVA, taux *m* zéro, taux nul
zest [zest] *n* **(a)** (*enjoyment*) enthousiasme *m*, entrain *m*; (*in speaking*) verve *f*; **with z.** (*to fight etc*) avec élan, avec entrain; (*to eat*) avec appétit, de bon appétit; **her z. for life** sa joie de vivre **(b)** (*interest*) saveur *f*, goût *m*; **to add z. to the adventure** donner du piquant à l'aventure **(c)** (*of orange, lemon*) zeste *m*
zestful [ˈzestfʊl] *adj* (*person*) plein d'enthousiasme *ou* d'entrain; (*in speaking*) plein de verve; (*approach*) enthousiaste; (*performance*) plein de vie
zeugma [ˈzjuːgmə] *n* zeugma *m*, zeugme *m*
zigzag¹ [ˈzɪgzæg] **1** *n* zigzag *m*; **in zigzags** en zigzag **2** *adj* **z. marking** (*on road*) marquage *m* en zig-zag; **z. path** sentier *m* en zigzag; **z. pattern** dessin *m* à zigzags **3** *adv* **the road runs z.** la route fait des zigzags
zigzag² *vi* **(-gg-)** (*of road, line*) zigzaguer, faire des zigzags
zigzagging [ˈzɪgzægɪŋ] *n* zigzags *mpl*
zilch [zɪltʃ] *n esp Am Sl* zéro *m*, que dalle
zillion [ˈzɪljən] *n F* des millions *mpl* (et des millions)
Zimbabwe [zɪmˈbɑːbweɪ] *n* Zimbabwe *m*
Zimbabwean [zɪmˈbɑːbweɪən] **1** *adj* zimbabwéen **2** *n* Zimbabwéen, -éenne
Zimmer® [ˈzɪmər] *n* **Z. (frame)** déambulateur *m*
zinc [zɪŋk] *n* zinc *m*; **z.-bearing** zincifère; **z. oxide** oxyde *m* de zinc; **z. white** (*paint*) blanc *m* de zinc; *Pharm* **z. ointment** pommade *f* à l'oxyde de zinc
zincblende [ˈzɪŋkblend] *n Miner* blende *f*
zing [zɪŋ] *n F* **(a)** (*zest*) punch *m* **(b)** (*sound*) sifflement *m*
zinnia [ˈzɪnɪə] *n* (*flower*) zinnia *m*
Zion [ˈzaɪən] *n* Sion *m*
Zionism [ˈzaɪənɪz(ə)m] *n Pol* sionisme *m*
Zionist [ˈzaɪənɪst] *adj, n Pol* sioniste *mf*
zip¹ [zɪp] *n* **(a)** *Br* **z. (fastener)** fermeture *f* éclair® *inv*, fermeture à glissière, *Belg* tirette *f* **(b)** *F* (*vigour*) énergie *f*, vitesse *f*; **put some z. into it!** mets-y du nerf!; **your style needs more z.** ton style a besoin d'un peu plus de punch **(c)** (*of bullet*) sifflement *m*
zip² *vi* **(-pp-)** (*like bullet*) siffler; **to z. past** (*of car etc*) passer en trombe
▶ **zip along** *vi* fonçer, aller à fond de train
▶ **zip in 1** *vtsep* (*lining*) attacher à l'aide d'une fermeture éclair® *ou* à glissière **2** *vi* s'attacher à l'aide d'une fermeture éclair® *ou* à glissière
▶ **zip into 1** *vipo* **to z. into the chemist's** faire un saut à la pharmacie **2** *vtaspo* **they zipped themselves into their sleeping bags** ils ont fermé leurs sacs de couchage; **to z. oneself into one's tent/overalls** fermer la fermeture éclair® de sa tente/combinaison; **she zipped the baby into his anorak** elle a enfilé le bébé dans son anorak et a fermé la fermeture éclair®
▶ **zip on 1** *vtsep* attacher à l'aide d'une fermeture éclair® *ou* à glissière **2** *vi* s'attacher à l'aide d'une fermeture éclair®
▶ **zip through** *vipo F* (*do quickly*) faire à toute vitesse; (*read quickly*) lire à toute vitesse
▶ **zip up 1** *vtsep* (*clothes*) remonter *ou* fermer la fermeture éclair® *ou* à glissière de; **z. me up** remonte ma fermeture **2** *vi* se fermer à l'aide d'une fermeture éclair® *ou* à glissière
zip code *n Am* code *m* postal
zip gun *n Am* pistolet *m* de fabrication artisanale
zipper [ˈzɪpər] *n esp Am* fermeture *f* éclair® *inv ou* à glissière; **z. bag** (sac *m*) fourre-tout *m inv* à fermeture éclair® *ou* à glissière
zipping [ˈzɪpɪŋ] *n* (*with tape*) avance *f* rapide
zippy [ˈzɪpɪ] *adj F* plein d'énergie *ou* d'entrain *ou* de punch; **a z. little car** une petite voiture nerveuse; **look z.!** grouille-toi!

zircon [ˈzɜːkɒn] *n Miner* zircon *m*
zit [zɪt] *n Am F* (*pimple*) bouton *m*
zither [ˈzɪðər] *n Mus* cithare *f*
zizz [zɪz] *n Br F* somme *m*; **to have a z.** faire un petit somme
zodiac [ˈzəʊdɪæk] *n Astrol* zodiaque *m*; **the signs of the z.** les signes *mpl* du zodiaque
zodiacal [zəʊˈdaɪək(ə)l] *adj* zodiacal
zombi(e) [ˈzɒmbɪ] *n Rel, Fig* zombi *m*; **he walks about like a z.** il a tout le temps l'air abruti *ou* l'air d'un zombi; **I feel like a z.** je me sens complètement abruti
zonal [ˈzəʊn(ə)l] *adj* zonal
zone¹ [zəʊn] *n* **(a)** zone *f*; *Admin* **no parking z.** zone d'interdiction de stationner; **parking meter z.** ≈ zone bleue; *Mil* **battle/war z.** zone de l'avant/de guerre; **danger z.** zone dangereuse; **z. of vision** (*when driving*) périmètre *m* de vision **(b)** *US* **(postal delivery) z.** zone *f* (de distribution) postale
zone² *vt* (*town etc*) répartir en zones
zoning [ˈzəʊnɪŋ] *n* répartition *f* en zones; (*in town planning*) zonage *m*
zonked (out) [zɒŋkt(ˈaʊt)] *adj Sl* (*drugged*) défoncé; (*drunk*) pété, bourré; (*exhausted*) crevé, vanné
zoo [zuː] *n* jardin *m* zoologique, *F* zoo *m*; **z. park** parc *m* zoologique
zookeeper [ˈzuːkiːpər] *n* gardien, -ienne de zoo
zoological [zəʊəˈlɒdʒɪk(ə)l, zuːə-] *adj* zoologique; **z. garden(s)** jardin *m* zoologique
zoologist [zəʊˈɒlədʒɪst, zuː-] *n* zoologiste *mf*
zoology [zəʊˈɒlədʒɪ, zuː-] *n* zoologie *f*
zoom¹ [zuːm] *n* **(a)** (*noise*) bourdonnement *m*; (*louder*) vrombissement *m* **(b)** *Cin, TV* (*shot*) zoom *m*; *Comptr* **z. box** case *f* zoom; *Phot* **z. lens** zoom, objectif *m* à distance focale variable, objectif zoom
zoom² *vi* **(a) to z. along** *or* **past/through** passer/traverser en trombe *ou* comme une flèche; **the cars are zooming along the road** les voitures passent en trombe sur la route; **children were zooming around on skateboards** des enfants passaient à toute vitesse sur des planches à roulettes **(b)** *Av* (*climb steeply*) monter en chandelle
▶ **zoom in** *vi Cin, TV* faire un zoom avant
▶ **zoom in on** *vipo Cin, TV* faire un zoom avant sur; *Fig* se concentrer sur; **the camera zoomed in on her face** la caméra a pris son visage en zoom avant
▶ **zoom off** *vi* déguerpir, partir en vitesse
▶ **zoom out** *vi Cin, TV* faire un zoom arrière
▶ **zoom up** *vi* (*of plane*) monter en chandelle; (*of rocket etc*) s'élever; (*of hit record etc*) monter comme une flèche; (*of prices etc*) monter en flèche
zooming [ˈzuːmɪŋ] *n Phot* changement *m* de focale
zoophyte [ˈzəʊəfaɪt] *n Biol* zoophyte *m*
zoot suit [ˈzuːtsuːt] *n* = costume *m* tapageur des années 40, rembourré aux épaules
zounds [zaʊndz] *int Arch* morbleu!, sacrebleu!
zucchini [zʊˈkiːnɪ, zuː-] *n Am* courgette *f*; **z. bread/lasagne** gâteau *m*/lasagnes *fpl* aux courgettes
Zulu [ˈzuːluː] **1** *adj* zoulou *inv in f*, *pl* zoulous **2** *n* **(a)** Zoulou *mf* **(b)** *Ling* zoulou *m*
Zululand [ˈzuːluːlænd] *n* Zoulouland *m*
zwieback [ˈzwiːbæk] *n Am* = biscotte *f*
zygote [ˈzaɪgəʊt] *n Biol* zygote *m*

GRAMMAIRE ANGLAISE

ENGLISH GRAMMAR

Table des Matières

1 Glossaire des Termes Grammaticaux

ABSTRAIT Un nom abstrait est un nom qui ne désigne pas un objet physique ou une personne, mais une qualité ou un concept. *Bonheur, vie, longueur* sont des exemples de noms abstraits.

ACTIF L'actif ou la voix active est la forme de base du verbe, comme dans *je le surveille*. Elle s'oppose à la forme passive (*il est surveillé par moi*).

ADJECTIF C'est un mot qui décrit un nom. Parmi les adjectifs on distingue les adjectifs qualificatifs (*une* ***petite*** *maison*), les adjectifs démonstratifs (***cette*** *maison*), les adjectifs possessifs (***ma*** *maison*), etc.

ADJECTIF SUBSTANTIVE C'est un adjectif employé comme nom. Par exemple l'adjectif *jeune* peut aussi s'employer comme nom, comme dans *il y a beaucoup de jeunes ici*.

ADVERBE Les adverbes accompagnent normalement un verbe pour ajouter une information supplémentaire en indiquant **comment** l'action est accomplie (adverbe de manière), **quand**, **où** et **avec quelle intensité** l'action est accomplie (adverbes de temps, de lieu et d'intensité), ou **dans quelle mesure** l'action est accomplie (adverbes de quantité). Certains adverbes peuvent aussi s'employer avec un adjectif ou un autre adverbe (par exemple *une fille* **très** *mignonne*, ***trop*** *bien*).

APPOSITION On dit qu'un mot ou une proposition est en apposition par rapport à un autre mot ou une autre proposition lorsque l'un ou l'autre est placé directement après le nom ou la proposition, sans y être relié par aucun mot (par exemple *M. Duclos,* ***notre directeur****, a téléphoné ce matin*).

ARTICLE DEFINI Les articles définis sont *le, la, les* en français. Ils correspondent tous à **the** en anglais.

ARTICLE INDEFINI Les articles indéfinis sont *un, une* en français. Ils correspondent à **a** (ou **an**) en anglais.

ASPECT L'aspect correspond à la manière dont on envisage l'action et son déroulement dans le temps. On distingue l'aspect simple, l'aspect progressif (ou continu) et le 'perfect'.

ATTRIBUT Groupe nominal placé juste après le verbe 'être'. Dans la phrase *he is a school teacher, a school teacher* est l'attribut.

AUXILIAIRE Les auxiliaires sont employés pour former les temps composés d'autres verbes, par exemple dans **he has gone** (il est parti), **has** et 'est' sont les auxiliaires. En anglais on distingue les 'auxiliaires ordinaires' (**have**, **be**, **do**), et les 'auxiliaires modaux', ou 'défectifs' (**can**, **could**, **may**, etc.). Voir MODAL.

CARDINAL Les nombres cardinaux sont *un, deux, trois*, etc. On les oppose aux nombres ordinaux. Voir ORDINAL.

COLLECTIF Un collectif est un nom qui désigne un groupe de gens ou de choses, mais qui est au singulier. Par exemple **flock** (troupeau) et **fleet** (flotte) sont des collectifs.

COMPARATIF Le comparatif des adjectifs et des adverbes permet d'établir une comparaison entre deux personnes, deux choses ou deux actions. En français on emploie *plus ... que, moins ... que* et *aussi ... que* pour exprimer une comparaison.

COMPLEMENT D'OBJET DIRECT Groupe nominal ou pronom qui accompagne un verbe sans préposition entre les deux. Par exemple *j'ai rencontré* ***un ami***.

COMPLEMENT D'OBJET INDIRECT Groupe nominal ou pronom qui suit un verbe, normalement séparé de ce dernier par une préposition (en général **à**) : *je parle* ***à mon ami***. Vous noterez qu'en français comme en anglais on omet souvent la préposition devant un pronom. Par exemple dans *je lui ai envoyé un cadeau, lui* est l'équivalent de *à lui* : c'est le complément d'objet indirect.

CONDITIONNEL Mode verbal employé pour exprimer ce que quelqu'un ferait ou ce qui arriverait si une condition était remplie, par exemple ***il viendrait*** *s'il le pouvait*; *la chaise* ***se serait cassée*** *s'il s'était assis dessus*.

CONJONCTION Les conjonctions sont des mots qui relient deux mots ou propositions. On distingue les conjonctions de coordination, comme *et, ou, or*, et les conjonctions de subordination comme *parce que, après que, bien que*, qui introduisent une proposition subordonnée.

CONJUGAISON La conjugaison d'un verbe est l'ensemble des formes d'un verbe à des temps et des modes différents.

CONTINU Voir FORME PROGRESSIVE.

DEFECTIF Voir MODAL.

DEMONSTRATIF Les adjectifs démonstratifs (*ce, cette, ces*, etc.) et les pronoms démonstratifs (*celui-ci, celui-là*, etc.) s'emploient pour désigner une personne ou un objet bien précis.

DENOMBRABLE Un nom est dénombrable s'il peut avoir un pluriel et si on peut l'employer avec un article indéfini. Par exemple **house** (maison), **car** (voiture), **dog** (chien).

EXCLAMATION Mots ou phrases employés pour exprimer une surprise, une joie ou un mécontentement, etc. (*quoi !, comment !, quelle chance !, ah non !*).

FAMILIER Le langage familier est le langage courant d'aujourd'hui employé dans la langue parlée, mais pas à l'écrit, comme dans les lettres officielles, les contrats, etc.

FORME PROGRESSIVE La forme progressive d'un verbe se forme avec **to be + participe présent**, comme dans : *I am thinking, he has been writing all day, will she be staying with us?* On l'appelle aussi forme continue.

GERONDIF Le gérondif est aussi appelé 'verbe substantivé'. En anglais, il a la même forme que le **participe présent** d'un verbe, c.-à-d. radical + **ing**. Par exemple ***skiing is fun*** *le ski, c'est amusant*, ***I'm fed up with waiting*** *j'en ai assez d'attendre*.

IDIOMATIQUE Les expressions idiomatiques (ou idiomes) sont des expressions qui ne peuvent normalement pas se traduire mot à mot dans une autre langue. Par exemple *he thinks he's the cat's whiskers* correspond en français à *il se croit sorti de la cuisse de Jupiter*.

IMPERATIF On emploie ce mode pour exprimer un ordre (par exemple *va-t'en, tais-toi !*) ou pour faire des suggestions (*allons-y*).

INDENOMBRABLE Les noms indénombrables sont des noms qui n'ont normalement pas de pluriel, par exemple *le beurre, la paresse*.

INDICATIF C'est le mode le plus courant, celui qui décrit l'action ou l'état, comme dans *j'aime, il est venu, nous essayons*. Il s'oppose au subjonctif, au conditionnel et à l'impératif.

INFINITIF L'infinitif en anglais est la forme de base, comme on la trouve dans les dictionnaires précédée ou non de **to** : **to eat** ou **eat**. On appelle cette forme sans **to** le radical.

INTERROGATIF Les mots interrogatifs sont employés pour poser des questions, par exemple *qui ? pourquoi ?* La forme interrogative d'une phrase est la question, par exemple *le connaît-il ?, dois-je le faire ?, peuvent-ils attendre un peu ?*

MODAL Les auxiliaires modaux en anglais sont **can/could, may/might, must/had to, shall/should, will/would**, de même que **ought to, used to, dare** et **need**. Une de leurs caractéristiques est qu'aux formes interrogative et négative, ils se construisent sans **do**.

MODE Le mode représente l'attitude du sujet parlant vis-à-vis de l'action dont il est question dans la phrase. Voir INDICATIF, SUBJONCTIF, CONDITIONNEL, IMPERATIF.

NOM Mot servant à désigner une chose, un être animé, un lieu ou des idées abstraites. Par exemple *passeport, chat, magasin, vie*. On distingue aussi les dénombrables, les indénombrables et les collectifs. Voir DENOMBRABLE, INDENOMBRABLE et COLLECTIF.

NOMBRE Le nombre d'un nom indique si celui-ci est **singulier** ou **pluriel**. Un nom singulier fait référence à une seule chose ou à une seule personne (*train, garçon*), et un nom pluriel à plusieurs (*trains, garçons*).

OBJET DIRECT Voir COMPLEMENT.

OBJET INDIRECT Voir COMPLEMENT.

ORDINAL Les nombres ordinaux sont *premier, deuxième, troisième*, etc.

PARTICIPE PASSE En français c'est la forme *mangé, vendu*, etc. Le participe passé anglais est la forme verbale employée après *have*, comme dans *I have* ***eaten***, *I have* ***said***, *you have* ***tried***, *it has been* ***rained on***.

PARTICIPE PRESENT Le participe présent en anglais est la forme verbale qui se termine en *-ing*.

PASSIF Un verbe est au passif ou à la voix passive lorsque le sujet ne fait pas l'action mais la subit : *les tickets sont vendus à l'entrée*. En anglais, la voix passive est formée avec le verbe **to be** et le participe passé du verbe, par exemple ***he was rewarded*** *il fut récompensé*.

PAST PERFECT Voir PERFECT.

PERFECT C'est l'aspect qui peut exprimer une action accomplie ou une action du passé qui se poursuit dans le présent. On distingue le *present perfect*, comme dans **I have seen** (j'ai vu), le *past perfect* (ou *pluperfect*) comme dans **I had seen** (j'avais vu).

PERSONNE Pour chaque temps, il y a trois personnes du singulier (1ère : *je*, 2ème : *tu*, 3ème : *il/elle/on*) et trois personnes du pluriel (1ère : *nous*, 2ème : *vous*, 3ème : *ils/elles*).

PHRASE Une phrase est un groupe de mots qui peut être composé d'une ou de plusieurs propositions (voir PROPOSITION). La fin d'une phrase est en général indiquée par un point, un point d'exclamation ou un point d'interrogation.

PLUPERFECT Voir PERFECT.

PLURIEL Voir NOMBRE.

POSSESSIF Les adjectifs ou les pronoms possessifs s'emploient pour indiquer la possession ou l'appartenance. Ce sont des mots comme *mon/le mien, ton/le tien, notre/le nôtre*, etc.

PRESENT PERFECT Voir PERFECT.

PRONOM Un pronom est un mot qui remplace un nom. Il en existe différentes catégories :

* **pronoms personnels** (*je, me, moi, tu, te, toi, etc.*)

* **pronoms démonstratifs** (*celui-ci, celui-là*, etc.)

* **pronoms relatifs** (*qui, que*, etc.)

* **pronoms interrogatifs** (*qui ?, quoi ?, lequel ?*, etc.)

* **pronoms possessifs** (*le mien, le tien*, etc.)

* **pronoms réfléchis** (*me, te, se*, etc.)

* **pronoms indéfinis** (*quelque chose, tout*, etc.)

PROPOSITION Une proposition est un groupe de mots qui contient au moins un sujet et un verbe : *il chante* est une proposition. Une phrase peut être composée de plusieurs propositions : *il chante/quand il prend sa douche/et qu'il est content*.

PROPOSITION SUBORDONNEE	Une proposition subordonnée est une proposition qui dépend d'une autre. Par exemple dans *il a dit qu'il viendrait, qu'il viendrait* est la proposition subordonnée.
QUESTIONS	Il existe deux types de questions : les questions au style **direct**, qui sont des questions telles qu'elles ont été posées, avec un point d'interrogation (par exemple, *quand viendra-t-il ?*) ; les questions au style **indirect**, qui sont introduites par une proposition et ne nécessitent pas de point d'interrogation (par exemple *je me demande quand il viendra*).
RADICAL	Voir INFINITIF.
REFLECHI	Les verbes réfléchis 'renvoient' l'action sur le sujet (par exemple *je me suis habillé*). Ils sont moins nombreux en anglais qu'en français.
SINGULIER	Voir NOMBRE.
SUBJONCTIF	Par exemple *il faut que je* ***sois*** *prêt,* ***vive*** *le Roi*. Le subjonctif est un mode qui n'est pas très souvent employé en anglais.
SUJET	Le sujet d'un verbe est le nom ou le pronom qui accomplit l'action. Dans les phrases *je mange du chocolat* et *Pierre a deux chats, je* et *Pierre* sont des sujets.
SUPERLATIF	C'est la forme d'un adjectif ou d'un adverbe qui, en français, se construit avec *le plus ..., le moins ....*
TEMPS	Le temps d'un verbe indique quand l'action a lieu, c'est-à-dire le présent, le passé, le futur.
TEMPS COMPOSE	Les temps composés sont les temps qui se construisent avec plus d'un élément. En anglais, ils sont formés par l'**auxiliaire** et le participe **présent** ou **passé** du verbe conjugué. Par exemple *I am reading, I have gone*.
VERBE	Le verbe est un mot qui décrit une action (*chanter, marcher*). Il peut aussi décrire un état (*être, paraître, espérer*).
VERBE COMPOSE	Un verbe composé (en anglais) est un verbe comme *ask for* ou *run up*. Son sens est généralement différent de la somme des sens des deux parties qui le composent, par exemple ***he goes in for skiing in a big way*** *il adore faire du ski* (différent de : ***he goes in for a medical next week*** *il va se faire examiner la semaine prochaine*), ***he ran up an enormous bill*** *ça lui a fait une note énorme* (différent de : ***he ran up the road*** *il a monté la rue en courant*).
VOIX	Il existe deux voix pour les verbes : la voix active et la voix passive. Voir ACTIF et PASSIF.

2 Les Articles

A LES FORMES

a) L'article indéfini 'un/une' se traduit par **a** devant une consonne et par **an** devant une voyelle :

a cat	un chat
an owl	une chouette
a dog	un chien
an umbrella	un parapluie

Il est cependant important de se souvenir que l'on emploie **a/an** selon que l'initiale du mot qui suit se prononce comme une voyelle ou non. Ainsi le 'h' muet est précédé de **an** :

an hour	une heure
an heir	un héritier
an honest man	un honnête homme

Il en est de même pour les abréviations commençant phonétiquement par une voyelle :

an MP	un député

En revanche, la diphtongue se prononçant 'iou' et qui s'écrit 'eu' ou 'u' est précédée de **a** :

a university	une université
a eucalyptus tree	un eucalyptus
a union	un syndicat

Avec le mot **hotel**, on peut employer soit **a** ou **an**, bien que dans le langage parlé, on préfère l'emploi de **a**.

b) L'article défini 'le', 'la', 'les' se traduit toujours par **the** :

the cat	le chat
the owl	la chouette
the holidays	les vacances

On peut prononcer le **e** de **the** un peu comme un 'i' français lorsque le mot qui suit commence phonétiquement par une voyelle (voir a) ci-dessus), comme pour **the owl**, ou lorsqu'il est accentué :

he's definitely *the* man for the job
voilà vraiment l'homme qu'il faut pour ce travail

B LA POSITION DE L'ARTICLE

L'article précède le nom et tout adjectif (avec ou sans adverbe) placé devant un nom :

a smart hat/the smart hat
un chapeau élégant/le chapeau élégant

a very smart hat/the very smart hat
un chapeau très élégant/le chapeau très élégant

Cependant **all** et **both** précèdent l'article défini :

they had all the fun
ce sont eux qui se sont bien amusés

both the men (= both men) **were guilty**
les deux hommes étaient tous les deux coupables

Et les adverbes **quite** et **rather** précèdent normalement l'article :

it was quite/rather a good play
c'était une assez bonne pièce

it was quite the best play I've seen
c'était vraiment la meilleure pièce que j'aie jamais vue

Cependant, **quite** et **rather** se placent parfois *après* l'article indéfini comme dans :

that was a rather unfortunate remark to make
c'était une remarque plutôt regrettable

that would be a quite useless task
ce serait une tâche tout à fait inutile

Les adverbes **too**, **so** et **as** précèdent l'adjectif et l'article indéfini. On a donc la construction :

too/so/as + adjectif + article + nom :

if that is not too great a favour to ask
si ce n'est pas trop vous demander

never have I seen so boring a film
je n'ai jamais vu de film aussi ennuyeux

I have never seen as fine an actor as Olivier
je n'ai jamais vu d'acteur aussi bon qu'Olivier

On peut aussi trouver **many a** (plus d'un), **such a** (un tel) et **what a** (quel !) :

many a man would do the same
plus d'un homme ferait la même chose

she's such a fool
elle est tellement idiote

what a joke!
quelle blague !

Remarquez qu'avec **such**, l'adjectif suit l'article indéfini, tandis qu'avec **so**, il le précède (voir aussi ci-dessus) :

I have never seen such a beautiful painting
je n'ai jamais vu une peinture aussi belle

I have never seen so beautiful a painting
je n'ai jamais vu une peinture aussi belle

Half (la moitié de) aussi précède habituellement l'article :

half the world knows about this
presque tout le monde est au courant

I'll be back in half an hour
je serai de retour dans une demi-heure

Mais si **half** et le nom forment un mot composé, l'article se place en premier :

why don't you buy just a half bottle of rum?
pourquoi n'achètes-tu pas juste une demi-bouteille de rhum ?

C'est-à-dire une petite bouteille de rhum. Comparez :

he drank half a bottle of rum
il a bu la moitié d'une bouteille de rhum

C L'EMPLOI DES ARTICLES

1 L'article indéfini (a, an)

Normalement l'article défini s'emploie uniquement pour les noms dénombrables, mais comme nous le verrons p A9, on peut discuter le fait qu'un nom soit dénombrable ou pas.

a) Devant un nom générique, pour faire référence à une catégorie ou à une espèce :

a mouse is smaller than a rat
une souris est plus petite qu'un rat

A mouse et **a rat** représentent les souris et les rats en général. Avec une légère différence de sens, l'article défini peut aussi s'employer devant un terme générique. Voir ci-dessous p A6.

Remarquez que le terme générique **man** représentant l'humanité (à la différence de **a man, a male human being** 'un homme') ne prend pas l'article :

a dog is man's best friend
le chien est le meilleur ami de l'homme

b) Avec des noms attributs du sujet ou dans des appositions, ou bien après **as**, en particulier avec des noms de métiers à la différence du français :

he is a hairdresser
il est coiffeur

she has become a Member of Parliament
elle est devenue député

Miss Behrens, a singer of formidable range, had no problems with the role
Miss Behrens, chanteuse au registre de voix extraordinaire, n'a eu aucun problème à tenir le rôle

John Adams, a real tough guy, was leaning casually on the bar
John Adams, un vrai dur, était appuyé négligemment au bar

he used to work as a skipper
il travaillait comme capitaine

L'article indéfini s'emploie dans de tels cas lorsque le nom fait partie d'un groupe. S'il n'y a pas appartenance à un groupe, on omet l'article, comme dans l'exemple suivant, où la personne mentionnée est unique :

she is now Duchess of York
elle est maintenant duchesse d'York

Professor Draper, head of the English department
le Professeur Draper, chef du département d'anglais

Si le nom fait référence à une caractéristique plutôt qu'à une appartenance à un groupe, on omet aussi l'article (on l'omet toujours après **turn**) :

he turned traitor
il s'est vendu à l'ennemi

surely you're man enough to stand up to her
tu es sûrement homme à lui tenir tête

mais: **be a man!**
sois un homme !

Si on a une liste de mots en apposition, on peut omettre l'article :

Maria Callas, opera singer, socialite and companion of Onassis, died in her Paris flat yesterday
Maria Callas, cantatrice, membre de la haute société et compagne d'Onassis, est morte hier à Paris, dans son appartement

On emploie l'article défini **the** pour une personne célèbre (ou pour distinguer une personne d'une autre ayant le même nom) :

Maria Callas, the opera singer
Maria Callas, la cantatrice

c) Comme préposition

L'article indéfini peut s'employer dans le sens de 'par', comme dans les exemples suivants :

haddock is £1.80 a kilo
le haddock est à 1,80 livres le kilo

take two tablets twice a day
prenez deux comprimés deux fois par jour

d) Avec **little** ('peu de' + *sing.*) et **few** ('peu de' + *pl.*)

L'article indéfini qui accompagne ces deux mots indique un sens positif (un peu de). Employés seuls, **little** et **few** ont un sens négatif :

she needs a little attention (= some attention)
elle a besoin d'un peu d'attention

she needs little attention (= hardly any attention)
elle a besoin de peu d'attention

they have a few paintings (= some)
ils ont quelques tableaux

they have few paintings (= hardly any)
ils ont peu de tableaux

Cependant **only a little/few** signifient plus ou moins la même chose que **little/few**, qui sont moins courants :

I have only a little coffee left (= hardly any)
il ne me reste presque plus de café

I can afford only a few books (= hardly any)
je ne peux me permettre d'acheter que quelques livres

Remarquez aussi l'expression **a good few**, qui équivaut à 'pas mal de' en français :

there are a good few miles to go yet
il y a encore pas mal de miles à parcourir

he's had a good few (to drink)
il a pas mal bu

2 L'article défini (the)

a) L'article défini s'emploie avec des noms dénombrables et des noms indénombrables :

the butter (indénombrable)	le beurre
the cup (sing. dénombrable)	la tasse
the cups (pl. dénombrable)	les tasses

b) Comme l'article indéfini, l'article défini peut s'employer devant un nom générique. Il paraît alors plus scientifique :

the mouse is smaller than the rat (comparez avec 1a) ci-dessus)
la souris est plus petite que le rat

when was the potato first introduced to Europe?
quand est-ce que la pomme de terre fut introduite en Europe pour la première fois ?

c) Un groupe prépositionnel après un nom peut avoir pour fonction soit de définir ou préciser le nom, soit de le décrire. S'il définit le nom, il faut employer l'article défini :

I want to wear the trousers on that hanger
je veux mettre le pantalon qui est sur ce cintre

she has just met the man of her dreams
elle vient juste de rencontrer l'homme de sa vie

the parcels from Aunt Mary haven't arrived yet
les paquets de tante Mary ne sont pas encore arrivés

Si par contre le groupe prépositionnel sert à décrire ou à classifier plutôt qu'à définir, on omet normalement l'article :

everywhere we looked we saw trousers on hangers
partout où nous regardions nous voyions des pantalons sur des cintres

knowledge of Latin and Greek is desirable
des connaissances en latin et en grec sont souhaitées

presence of mind is what he needs
ce qu'il lui faut, c'est de la présence d'esprit

I always love receiving parcels from Aunt Mary
j'aime toujours recevoir des paquets de tante Mary

Dans la phrase :

the presence of mind that she showed was extraordinary
la présence d'esprit dont elle a fait preuve était extraordinaire

l'emploi de **the** est obligatoire parce que l'on fait référence à un exemple de présence d'esprit bien précis, comme le fait apparaître la proposition relative qui suit.

Cependant, quand le complément du nom introduit par **of** sert à la fois à décrire et à définir le nom, c'est-à-dire que le nom n'est ni totalement général, ni totalement spécifique, on emploie l'article défini :

the women of Paris (= women from Paris, in general)
les femmes de Paris

the children of such families (= children from such families)
les enfants de telles familles

d) L'omission de l'article défini

A la différence du français, l'omission de l'article défini en anglais est très fréquente. Ainsi un grand nombre de noms ne sont pas précédés de l'article s'ils font référence à une fonction ou à des caractéristiques en général, plutôt qu'à l'objet. Ces catégories de noms comprennent :

i) les institutions, par exemple :

church	l'église
prison	la prison
college	le collège d'enseignement supérieur
school	l'école
court	le tribunal
university	l'université
hospital	l'hôpital

Exemples:

do you go to church?
tu vas à la messe (tous les dimanches) ?

she's in hospital again and he's in prison
elle est encore une fois à l'hôpital et il est en prison

aren't you going to school today?
tu ne vas pas à l'école aujourd'hui ?

Joan is at university
Joan est à l'université

Cependant, en anglais américain on préfère l'emploi de l'article défini devant **hospital** :

Wayne is back in the hospital
Wayne est de retour à l'hôpital

Si le nom fait référence à un objet physique (le bâtiment) plutôt qu'à sa fonction, on emploie alors **the** :

walk up to the church and turn right
allez jusqu'à l'église, puis tournez à droite

the taxi stopped at the school
le taxi s'est arrêté devant l'école

The s'emploie aussi pour désigner un nom défini ou précisé par le contexte :

at the university where his father studied
à l'université où son père a étudié

she's at the university
elle est à l'université (dans cette ville, etc.)

Pour faire référence à l'institution en général, on emploie l'article :

the Church was against it
l'Eglise était contre

ii) les moyens de transport précédés de **by** :

we always go by bus/car/boat/train/plane
nous partons toujours en bus/en voiture/en bateau/par le train/par avion

iii) les repas :

can you meet me before lunch?
tu peux me voir avant le déjeuner ?

buy some haddock for tea, will you?
achète du haddock pour le dîner, veux-tu ?

Mais si l'on fait référence à une occasion précise, on emploie l'article. Ainsi il existe une grande différence entre :

I enjoy lunch j'aime le déjeuner

et :

I am enjoying the lunch j'apprécie ce déjeuner

Dans le premier cas, on fait référence au plaisir de manger à midi ; dans le second cas à un repas particulier.

iv) les moments de la journée et de la nuit après une préposition autre que **in** et **during** :

I don't like going out at night
je n'aime pas sortir le soir/la nuit

these animals can often be seen after dusk
on peut souvent voir ces animaux après le crépuscule

they go to bed around midnight
ils vont se coucher vers minuit

mais :

see you in the morning!
à demain matin !

if you feel peckish during the day, have an apple
si tu as faim dans la journée, mange une pomme

v) les saisons, en particulier pour exprimer un contraste par rapport à une autre saison plutôt que pour faire référence à une période de l'année. Ainsi :

spring is here! (winter is over)
le printemps est là (l'hiver est fini)

it's like winter today
on se croirait en hiver aujourd'hui

mais :

the winter was spent at expensive ski resorts
on passait l'hiver dans des stations de ski de luxe

he needed the summer to recover
il avait besoin de l'été pour récupérer

Après **in**, on emploie parfois l'article défini, avec très peu de différence de sens entre les deux cas :

most leaves turn yellow in (the) autumn
la plupart des feuilles deviennent jaunes en automne

En anglais américain, on préfère l'emploi de **the**.

vi) dans les combinaisons **next/last** dans les expressions de temps :

Si de telles expressions sont envisagées par rapport au présent, on n'emploie normalement pas l'article :

can we meet next week?
est-ce qu'on peut se voir la semaine prochaine ?

he was drunk last night
il était ivre hier soir/la nuit dernière

Dans les autres cas on emploie l'article :

we arrived on March 31st and the next day was spent relaxing by the pool
nous sommes arrivés le 31 mars et on a passé le jour suivant à se relaxer près de la piscine

vii) avec des noms abstraits :

a talk about politics
un discours sur la politique

a study of human relationships
une étude sur les relations humaines

suspicion is a terrible thing
le soupçon est une chose terrible

Mais, bien sûr, lorsque le mot est précisé, on emploie l'article (voir 2c) ci-dessus) :

the politics of disarmament
la politique de désarmement

viii) avec certaines maladies :

he has diabetes	**I've got jaundice**
il a du diabète	j'ai la jaunisse

Cependant, pour certaines maladies communes, on peut employer l'article dans un anglais un peu plus familier :

she has (the) flu	**he's got (the) measles**
elle a la grippe	il a la rougeole

ix) avec les noms de couleurs :

red is my favourite colour
le rouge est ma couleur préférée

x) avec les noms de matériaux, d'aliments, de boissons, et de corps chimiques, etc. :

oxygen is crucial to life
l'oxygène est indispensable à la vie

concrete is used less nowadays
on emploie moins le béton de nos jours

I prefer corduroy
je préfère le velours côtelé

it smells of beer
ça sent la bière

xi) devant les noms de langues et de matières scolaires :

German is harder than English
l'allemand est plus difficile que l'anglais

Remarquez ici l'emploi des majuscules en anglais.

I hate maths
je déteste les maths

xii) devant les noms pluriels à sens général :

he loves antiques	**he's frightened of dogs**
il adore les antiquités	il a peur des chiens

e) L'article défini n'est normalement pas employé lorsque l'on fait référence à des noms de pays, de comtés, d'états :

Switzerland	la Suisse
England	l'Angleterre
Sussex	le Sussex
Texas	le Texas
in France	en France
to America	en Amérique

i) mais il existe quelques exceptions :

the Yemen	le Yémen
(the) Sudan	le Soudan
(the) Lebanon	le Liban

et lorsque le nom du pays est qualifié :

the People's Republic of China
la République Populaire de Chine

the Republic of Ireland
la République d'Irlande

ii) les noms de lieux au pluriel prennent l'article :

the Philippines	les Philippines
the Shetlands	les Shetlands
the Azores	les Açores
the Midlands	les Midlands
the Borders	la région des Borders
the Netherlands	les Pays-Bas
the United States	les Etats-Unis

Il en est de même pour les noms de famille :

the Smiths
les Smith

iii) les fleuves, les rivières et les océans prennent l'article :

the Thames	la Tamise
the Danube	le Danube
the Pacific	le Pacifique
the Atlantic	l'Atlantique

iv) les noms de régions prennent l'article :

the Tyrol	le Tyrol
the Orient	l'Orient
the Ruhr	la Ruhr
the Crimea	la Crimée
the City (of London)	la Cité de Londres
the East End	le East End

v) les noms de montagnes et de lacs ne prennent pas l'article :

Ben Nevis	le Ben Nevis
K2	le K2
Lake Michigan	le lac Michigan

mais les chaînes de montagnes sont précédées de l'article :

the Himalayas	l'Himalaya
the Alps	les Alpes

Il existe cependant des exceptions :

the Matterhorn	le mont Cervin
the Eiger	l'Eiger

vi) les noms de rues, de parcs et de places, etc. ne prennent normalement pas l'article :

he lives in Wilton Street
il habite Wilton Street

they met in Hyde Park
ils se sont rencontrés à Hyde Park

there was a concert in Trafalgar Square
il y avait un concert à Trafalgar Square

Mais il existe des exceptions. Parfois l'article fait partie intégrante du nom :

the Strand	le Strand

et parfois on trouve des exceptions fondées sur un usage purement local :

the Edgware Road	l'Edgware Road

f) On omet l'article dans les énumérations (même à deux termes) :

the boys and girls
les garçons et les filles

the hammers, nails and screwdrivers
les marteaux, les clous et les tourne-vis

g) Les noms d'hôtels, de pubs, de restaurants, de théâtres, de cinémas, de musées sont normalement précédés de **the** :

the Caledonian (Hotel), the Red Lion, the Copper Kettle, the Old Vic, the Odeon, the Tate (Gallery)

Mais vous noterez **Covent Garden** (l'opéra royal) et **Drury Lane** (un théâtre du West End à Londres).

h) Les journaux et quelques magazines prennent **the** :

the Observer, the Independent, the Daily Star

et par exemple les magazines :

the Spectator, the Economist

Cependant la plupart des magazines ne sont pas précédés de l'article :

Woman's Own, Punch, Private Eye, etc.

et les deux magazines de télévision et de radio, que l'on appelait autrefois **The Radio Times** et **The TV Times** (et que certains appellent encore ainsi) sont aujourd'hui mentionnés sans article lorsqu'on en fait la publicité à la télévision :

Radio Times et **TV Times**

i) Les instruments de musique

L'article défini s'emploie lorsqu'on fait référence à une aptitude :

she plays the clarinet
elle joue de la clarinette

Cependant lorsqu'on fait référence à une occasion précise plutôt qu'à une aptitude d'ordre général, on omet l'article :

in this piece he plays bass guitar
il joue de la basse dans ce morceau

j) Les noms de titres sont normalement précédés de l'article défini :

the Queen la reine
the President le président

Cependant lorsque le titre est suivi du nom de la personne on omet l'article défini :

Doctor MacPherson le docteur MacPherson
Queen Elizabeth la reine Elizabeth
Prime Minister le Premier Ministre
Churchill Churchill

Remarquez : **Christ** le Christ

k) L'omission de l'article défini pour produire un effet spécial :

i) On omet parfois l'article défini pour produire un effet particulier ; soit pour dénoter une importance, un statut ou parfois dans un jargon :

all pupils will assemble in hall
tous les élèves se rassembleront dans le hall

the number of delegates at conference
le nombre des délégués à la conférence

ii) les gros titres de journaux (omission de l'article indéfini aussi) :

Attempt To Break Record Fails
La tentative pulvériser le record échoue

New Conference Centre Planned
Projet pour un nouveau Palais des Congrès

iii) les instructions (omission de l'article indéfini aussi) :

break glass in emergency
casser la vitre en cas d'urgence

Pour la traduction de l'article partitif voir pp A34-5. Pour les articles avec les parties du corps voir p A30.

3 Les Noms

A LES TYPES DE NOMS

Les noms anglais n'ont pas de genre grammatical ('le/la' est toujours **the**).

1 Les noms concrets et les noms abstraits

On peut classer les noms de différentes manières. On peut ainsi les diviser en **(1)** noms 'concrets', c'est-à-dire des noms faisant référence à des êtres animés ou à des choses : **woman** (femme), **cat** (chat), **stone** (pierre) et en **(2)** noms 'abstraits', c'est-à-dire des noms qui expriment un concept qui n'est pas physique, des caractéristiques ou des activités : **love** (l'amour), **ugliness** (la laideur), **classification** (la classification).

Un grand nombre de noms abstraits sont formés en ajoutant une terminaison (suffixe) à un adjectif, à un nom ou à un verbe. Cependant beaucoup de noms abstraits ne prennent pas cette terminaison. C'est le cas de **love** (l'amour), **hate** (la haine), **concept** (le concept) par exemple. Voici quelques terminaisons de noms abstraits couramment employées (certaines peuvent aussi s'employer pour des noms concrets).

a) *Les noms abstraits formés à partir d'autres noms*

-age	**percent + -age**	**percentage**	pourcentage
-cy	**democrat + -cy**	**democracy**	démocratie
-dom	**martyr + -dom**	**martyrdom**	martyre
-hood	**child + -hood**	**childhood**	enfance
-ism	**alcohol + -ism**	**alcoholism**	alcoolisme
-ry	**chemist+ -ry**	**chemistry**	chimie

b) *Les noms abstraits formés à partir d'adjectifs*

-age	**short+ -age**	**shortage**	pénurie
-cy	**bankrupt + -cy**	**bankruptcy**	faillite
	normal + -cy (anglais américain)	**normalcy**	normalité
-hood	**likely + -hood**	**likelihood**	probabilité
-ism	**social + -ism**	**socialism**	socialisme
-ity	**normal+ -ity**	**normality**	normalité
-ness	**kind+ -ness**	**kindness**	gentillesse

c) *Les noms abstraits formés à partir de verbes*

-age	**break + -age**	**breakage**	rupture
-al	**arrive + -al**	**arrival**	arrivée
-ance	**utter + -ance**	**utterance**	déclaration
-(at)ion	**starve + -ation**	**starvation**	famine
	operate+ -ion	**operation**	opération
-ing	voir p A39 le gérondif		
-ment	**treat + -ment**	**treatment**	traitement

Remarquez que la terminaison du nom, de l'adjectif ou du verbe doit parfois subir quelques changements avant d'ajouter le suffixe.

2 Les noms communs et les noms propres

On peut aussi classer les noms en noms 'communs' et en noms 'propres', ces derniers faisant référence à des noms de personnes ou à des noms géographiques, de jours et de mois.

Communs		*Propres*	
cup	tasse	**Peter**	Pierre
palace	palais	**China**	la Chine
cheese	fromage	**Wednesday**	mercredi
time	le temps	**August**	août
love	l'amour	**Christmas**	Noël

Remarquez que les noms propres s'écrivent avec une majuscule en anglais.

3 Les noms dénombrables et indénombrables

Une classification, déterminante pour l'absence ou la présence de l'article indéfini, permet de distinguer les noms en 'dénombrables' et 'indénombrables'. Un nom dénombrable à part entière peut, bien sûr, être considéré comme une unité (c'est-à-dire qu'il peut être précédé d'un nombre), et doit avoir une forme au singulier aussi bien qu'au pluriel. Les noms indénombrables à part entière ne sont quant à eux ni au singulier, ni au pluriel, puisque par définition on ne peut les compter, bien qu'ils soient suivis d'un verbe au singulier. On dit qu'ils représentent une 'totalité' :

Dénombrables

a/one pen/three pens	un crayon/trois crayons
a/one coat/three coats	un manteau/trois manteaux
a/one horse/three horses	un cheval/trois chevaux
a/one child/three children	un enfant/trois enfants

Indénombrables

furniture	les/des meubles
spaghetti	les/des spaghettis
information	les/des informations
rubbish	les/des ordures
progress	les/des progrès
fish	les/des poissons
fruit	les/des fruits
news	les/des nouvelles
violence	la violence

Lorsque l'on veut faire référence à une unité de chacun de ces noms indénombrables, il faut faire précéder le nom indénombrable d'un autre nom qui soit dénombrable. Ainsi on emploie, par exemple, **piece** pour indiquer une ou plusieurs unités :

a piece of furniture/two pieces of furniture
un meuble/deux meubles

De même on dira **an act of violence** (un acte de violence), **an item of news** (une nouvelle), **a strand of spaghetti** (un spaghetti) où **act**, **item** et **strand** sont des dénombrables tout à fait normaux. Le dénombrable qui accompagne **cattle** est **head**, qui ne prend jamais **-s** dans ce sens : **ten head of cattle** (dix têtes de bétail).

Voici d'autres exemples de noms indénombrables à part entière : **baggage** (les bagages), **luggage** (les bagages), **garbage** (les ordures), **advice** (les conseils). Pour un mot comme **knowledge** (la/les connaissance(s)), voir p A10. Pour **accommodation**, voir p A11.

a) *Les noms qui sont soit dénombrables, soit indénombrables*

i) Certains noms peuvent être dénombrables ou indénombrables, suivant que leur sens fait référence à une 'unité' ou une 'totalité'. De tels noms font souvent référence à la nourriture ou aux matériaux :

Dénombrables	*Indénombrables*
that sheep has only one lamb ce mouton n'a qu'un agneau	**we had lamb for dinner** nous avions de l'agneau pour le dîner
what lovely strawberries! quelles belles fraises !	**there's too much strawberry in this ice-cream** cette glace a trop le goût de fraise
do you like my nylons? tu aimes mes bas ?	**most socks contain nylon** la plupart des chaussettes contiennent du nylon
he bought a paper il a acheté un journal	**I'd like some writing paper** je voudrais du papier à lettres
she's a beauty c'est une beauté	**love, beauty and truth** l'amour, la beauté et la vérité
she has a lovely voice elle a une jolie voix	**she has no voice in the making of decisions** elle n'a pas voix au chapitre lorsqu'il s'agit de prendre des décisions

ii) Comme en français, les noms indénombrables deviennent dénombrables lorsqu'ils représentent 'une partie de' ou 'une variété de' :

I'd like a coffee
je voudrais un café

two white wines, please
deux vins blancs, s'il vous plaît

Britain has a large selection of cheeses
la Grande-Bretagne a une grande sélection de fromages

a very good beer
une très bonne bière

iii) Certains noms dénombrables sont parfois employés au pluriel pour indiquer une immensité, en général dans un style littéraire :

The Snows of Kilimanjaro
les Neiges du Kilimanjaro

still waters run deep (proverbe)
il faut se méfier de l'eau qui dort

Cependant, il est tout à fait normal d'employer **waters** pour faire référence aux eaux territoriales d'un pays (**the territorial limit of Danish waters**), ou aux eaux ayant une vertu médicale : **he has been to take the waters at Vichy** (il a pris les eaux à Vichy).

Weather est considéré comme une 'totalité', sauf dans l'expression **in all weathers** (par tous les temps).

b) *Quelques problèmes que posent les dénombrables*

Un nom totalement dénombrable peut être précédé de l'article indéfini, ou de tout adjectif numéral, d'un adjectif démonstratif pluriel (**these**), ou d'un adjectif indéfini (**few, many**), et peut être accompagné d'un verbe au pluriel :

a/one table
three/these/those/few/many tables are ...

Mais certains mots ont un statut ambiguë :

i) Par exemple, le mot **data**, 'données' (du latin **datum** (sing.), **data** (pl.)). On peut dire **these/those data are** mais rarement **many/few data** (on préfère **much/little data**) et en aucun cas **seven data** car on ne peut pas compter les '**data**'. **Data** n'a donc pas de singulier, et l'on devra dire **seven pieces of data**. En fait, ce mot est en passe de devenir indénombrable : **this/that/much/little data is** s'entend et s'écrit aujourd'hui plus fréquemment que **these/those/many/few data are**.

ii) **Vegetable** est un autre cas intéressant. En effet on peut dire **many vegetables** (et **a/one vegetable**). Cependant, on peut aussi dire **much vegetables** lorsque l'on fait référence à l'ensemble de la catégorie d'aliments 'légumes' et non pas à des légumes en particulier :

the Japanese still eat twice as much vegetables, including beans, as the British
les Japonais mangent encore deux fois plus de légumes, dont des haricots, que les Britanniques

Dans cette phrase, on a choisi **much** et non pas **many**, car **many** aurait mis l'accent sur chacun des légumes : **many vegetables** tend à signifier 'beaucoup de sortes de légumes' (**many kinds of vegetables**), alors que l'on se réfère ici à la quantité. On aurait aussi pu éviter ce problème en écrivant **a lot of vegetables**. **Much** accompagne donc certains noms au pluriel, indiquant clairement que l'on insiste sur la totalité.

iii) Les mots qui modifient la 'quantité' de noms pluriels posent aussi un problème : les plus courants d'entre eux étant **less** et **fewer** (moins de). Nombreux sont ceux qui n'emploient plus **fewer** à l'oral avec les noms au pluriel. Ainsi l'usage le plus répandu du comparatif de **few** à l'oral (et souvent à l'écrit) est **less**. **Fewer** a tendance à être soutenu et trop précis, et il est parfaitement normal d'entendre par exemple **less books/students/crimes** (moins de livres/d'étudiants/de crimes) dit par n'importe qui, quel que soit leur niveau d'éducation.

iv) l'article indéfini et le pluriel avec des indénombrables:

Certains noms abstraits sont dénombrables à part entière (**possibility**) et certains sont normalement indénombrables à part entière (**indignation, hate, anger**). Certains de ces noms abstraits indénombrables prennent souvent l'article indéfini, en particulier s'ils sont accompagnés par un adjectif ou un groupe adjectival, tel qu'un groupe prépositionnel ou une proposition relative. C'est parce que le groupe adjectival individualise le nom :

candidates must have a good knowledge of English
les candidats doivent avoir des bonnes connaissances en anglais

he expressed an indignation so intense that people were taken aback
il exprima une indignation si véhémente que les gens en furent stupéfaits

On peut parfois trouver des noms abstraits comme ceux-ci au pluriel. Ainsi **fears** et **doubts** sont fréquents :

he expressed his fears
il exprima ses craintes

I have my doubts
j'ai mes doutes

Dans d'autres cas, le pluriel indique des manifestations individuelles d'un concept abstrait :

the use of too many adjectives is one of his stylistic infelicities
l'une de ses maladresses stylistiques réside dans l'emploi d'un trop grand nombre d'adjectifs

c) *Les noms en* ***-ics***

Lorsque ces noms sont considérés comme des concepts abstraits, ils sont suivis d'un verbe au singulier :

mathematics is a difficult subject
les mathématiques sont un sujet difficile

On préférera en revanche un verbe au pluriel lorsque l'on met l'accent sur les manifestations pratiques du concept :

his mathematics are very poor
il est très faible en mathématiques

what are your politics?
quelles sont vos opinions politiques ?

d) *Les maladies, les jeux et les nouvelles*

Certains noms se terminant par ce qui semble être le **-s** du pluriel sont indénombrables. Le mot **news** par exemple, les maladies telles que **measles** (rougeole), **mumps** (oreillons), **rickets** (rachitisme), **shingles** (zona) et quelques noms des jeux :

the news hasn't arrived yet
la nouvelle n'est pas encore arrivée

mumps is not a dangerous disease
les oreillons ne sont pas une maladie dangereuse

darts is still played in many pubs
on joue encore aux fléchettes dans beaucoup de pubs

billiards is preferred to dice in some countries
on préfère jouer au billard plutôt qu'aux dés dans certains pays

Il en est de même pour **bowls** (boules), **dominoes** (dominos), **draughts** (dames) et **checkers** ('dames' en anglais américain).

e) *Noms de 'paires'*

Certain noms au pluriel faisant référence à des objets composés de deux parties égales n'ont pas de forme au singulier, et doivent être précédés de **a pair of** si l'on veut mettre l'accent sur leur nombre :

my trousers are here
mon pantalon est ici

this is a good pair of trousers
c'est un bon pantalon

two new pairs of trousers
deux pantalons neufs

de même :

bellows (soufflet), **binoculars** (jumelles), **glasses** (lunettes), **knickers** (culotte, slip), **pants** (culotte), **pincers** (tenailles), **pyjamas** (**pajamas** en anglais américain) (pyjama), **pliers** (pinces, tenailles), **scales** (balance), **scissors** (ciseaux), **shears** (cisailles), **shorts** (short), **spectacles** (lunettes), **tights** (bas), **tongs** (fer à friser), **tweezers** (pince à épiler)

f) *Noms que l'on ne trouve normalement qu'au pluriel et qui sont suivis d'un verbe au pluriel*

i) **arms** (armes), **arrears** (arriéré(s)), **auspices** (auspices), **banns** (bans (de mariage)), **clothes** (vêtements), **customs** (douane(s)), **dregs** (la lie), **earnings** (revenus), **entrails** (entrailles), **goods** (marchandise(s)), **greens** (légumes verts), **guts** (boyaux, courage), **lodgings** (logement(s)), **looks** (apparence(s)), **manners** (manières), **means** (moyens (financiers)), **odds** (cote(s)), **outskirts** (environs, banlieue(s)), **pains** (peine, effort), **premises** (locaux), **quarters** (résidence(s)), **remains** (restes), **riches** (richesse(s)), **spirits** (humeur, alcool), **(soap) suds** (mousse de savon), **surroundings** (environs, cadre), **tropics** (tropiques), **valuables** (objets de valeur)

et le nom italien au pluriel **graffiti** (qui est aussi accompagné d'un verbe au singulier)

Ces noms sont normalement accompagnés d'un verbe au pluriel, mais ils ont parfois aussi une forme au singulier, ce qui entraîne souvent un changement de sens :

ashes (cendres en général) mais **cigar(ette) ash, tobacco ash** (la cendre de cigar(ette)/tabac)

contents (le contenu) mais **content** (la quantité qui peut être contenue) :

show me the contents of your purse
montre-moi le contenu de ton porte-monnaie

mais :

what exactly is the lead content of petrol?
quelle est la teneur exacte du plomb dans l'essence ?

funds (des fonds) mais **fund** (un fonds) :

I'm short of funds
je suis à court de fonds

mais :

we started a church roof repair fund
nous avons commencé à faire une collecte pour réparer le toit de l'église

stairs : plus courant que **stair** au sens de **flight of stairs** ((volée d')escalier). **Stair** peut aussi faire référence à une marche dans un escalier.

thanks : vous noterez la possibilité d'employer l'article indéfini devant un adjectif (pas de singulier dans ce cas) :

a very special thanks to ...
un grand merci à ...

wages : souvent au singulier aussi, particulièrement lorsqu'il est précédé d'un adjectif :

all we want is a decent wage
tout ce que nous voulons c'est un salaire correct

Accommodations (logement) est employé en anglais américain. En anglais britannique, on emploie **accommodation** comme indénombrable représentant une totalité.

ii) Quelques noms ne portent jamais la marque du pluriel :

> **cattle** (bétail), **clergy** ((membres du) clergé), **livestock** ((têtes de) bétail), **police** (police, policiers), **vermin** (vermine, parasites)

Mais même **clergy** et **police** peuvent parfois être accompagnés d'un article indéfini, s'ils sont qualifiés par un adjectif, par un groupe prépositionnel ou par une proposition relative. Dans de tels cas il existe une différence de sens importante entre **clergymen** (écclésiastiques) et **body of clergymen** (ensemble du clergé), et **policemen** (policiers) et **police force** (la police). Comparez :

> **seventy-five clergy were present**
> 75 membres du clergé étaient présents

> **the problem is whether the country needs a clergy with such old-fashioned views**
> le problème est de savoir si le pays a besoin d'un clergé aux opinions aussi dépassées

> **at least thirty police were needed for that task**
> on a eu besoin d'au moins 30 policiers pour cette tâche

> **the country needed a semi-military police**
> le pays avait besoin d'une police semi-militaire

Folk dans le sens de 'gens', 'personnes', ne prend normalement pas de **-s** en anglais britannique :

> **some folk just don't know how to behave**
> certaines personnes ne savent pas se tenir

tandis qu'en anglais américain on dit **folks**, ce qui en anglais britannique est normalement employé lorsqu'on s'adresse familièrement à des personnes et qui signifie aussi 'famille, parents' :

> **sit down, folks** (anglais britannique)
> asseyez-vous mes amis

> **I'd like you to meet my folks** (anglais britannique)
> j'aimerais que vous rencontriez ma famille

Youth 'la jeunesse' (génération) peut être suivi aussi bien d'un verbe au singulier que d'un verbe au pluriel :

> **our country's youth has/have little to look forward to**
> la jeunesse de notre pays a peu de perspectives d'avenir

mais il est dénombrable dans le sens de 'jeune homme' :

> **they arrested a youth/two youths**
> ils ont arrêté un jeune/deux jeunes

g) *Les noms collectifs*

i) Ce sont des noms qui, au singulier, sont accompagnés d'un verbe au singulier quand le nom désigne un totalité, ou d'un verbe au pluriel si l'on désire mettre l'accent sur les membres du groupe :

> **the jury is one of the safeguards of our legal system** (sing.)
> le jury est garant de notre système législatif

> **the jury have returned their verdict** (pluriel)
> le jury a rendu son verdict

Remarquez **their** (leur) dans le second exemple. Les pronoms faisant référence à de tels noms s'accordent normalement en nombre avec le verbe :

> **as the crowd moves forward it becomes visible on the hill-top**
> à mesure que la foule avance, on la voit apparaître au sommet de la colline

> **the crowd have been protesting for hours; they are getting very impatient**
> la foule proteste depuis des heures ; elle commence à s'impatienter

L'emploi du verbe au pluriel est plus répandu en anglais britannique qu'en américain.

Les mots suivants sont des exemples typiques de noms collectifs :

> **army** (armée), **audience** (public), **choir** (chorale), **chorus** (refrain, chœur), **class** (classe), **committee** (comité), **enemy** (ennemi), **family** (famille), **firm** (firme), **gang** (gang), **(younger and older) generation** (génération (jeune, ancienne)), **government** (gouvernement), **group** (groupe), **majority** (majorité), **minority** (minorité), **orchestra** (orchestre), **Parliament** (Parlement), **proletariat** (prolétariat), **public** (public), **team** (équipe).

Les noms de nations faisant référence à une équipe (sportive) sont normalement accompagnés d'un verbe au pluriel en anglais britannique :

> **France have beaten England**
> la France a battu l'Angleterre

bien que le singulier et le pluriel soient tout aussi corrects.

ii) Remarquez que les noms de pays au pluriel se comportent comme des noms collectifs :

> **the Philippines has its problems like any other country** (sing.)
> les Philippines ont leurs problèmes comme tout autre pays

> **the Philippines consist of a group of very beautiful islands** (pluriel)
> les Philippines se composent d'un groupe de très belles îles

Il en est de même pour **the Bahamas**, **the United States**, etc.

iii) Les mots **crew** (équipage), **staff** (personnel), **people** (peuple) sont souvent des noms collectifs, comme dans :

> **the crew is excellent** (sing.)
> l'équipage est excellent

> **the crew have all enjoyed themselves** (pluriel)
> l'équipage s'est bien amusé

> **the staff of that school has a good record** (sing.)
> le personnel de cette école a obtenu de bons résultats

> **the staff don't always behave themselves** (pluriel)
> le personnel ne se conduit pas toujours bien

> **it is difficult to imagine a people that has suffered more** (sing.)
> il est difficile d'imaginer un peuple qui ait plus souffert

> **the people have not voted against the re-introduction of capital punishment** (pluriel)
> le peuple n'a pas voté contre le rétablissement de la peine capitale

Ces trois mots diffèrent des autres noms collectifs par le fait qu'ils peuvent être des dénombrables à part entière, avec ou sans la terminaison **-s** au pluriel, suivant leur sens. Si le pluriel est en **-s**, il est le même que le pluriel en **-s** d'autres noms collectifs :

> **five crews/staffs/peoples** (nations)**/armies/ governments**, etc.

Cependant, le pluriel sans **-s** fait référence à des membres individuels :

> **the captain had to manage with only fifteen crew**
> le capitaine devait se débrouiller avec seulement quinze membres d'équipage

> **the English Department had to get rid of five staff**
> le département d'anglais a dû renvoyer cinq personnes

> **he spoke to six people about it**
> il a parlé à six personnes à ce sujet

On peut tout aussi bien dire **crew members**, **staff members** or **members of staff** au pluriel.

Pour **clergy** et **police**, voir f) ii) ci-dessus.

B LES FORMES

1 Les pluriels en -(e)s

a) La marque du pluriel est normalement **-(e)s** en anglais :

soup : soups soupe(s)
peg : pegs pince(s) à linge
bus : buses bus
quiz : quizzes jeu(x) télévisé(s)
bush : bushes buisson(s)
match : matches allumette(s)
page : pages page(s)

-es s'emploie pour des mots en **-s**, **-x**, **-z**, **-ch** ou **-sh**. On le prononce alors /ɪz/.

b) Pour les noms se terminant par une consonne plus **-y**, le **-y** se transforme en **-ies** :

lady : ladies dame(s), demoiselle(s)
loony : loonies cinglé(s)

Mais le pluriel régulier en **-s** s'emploie lorsque le **-y** est précédé par une voyelle :

trolley : trolleys chariot(s)

Une exception à cela : l'usage de **monies** (sommes d'argent) dans un registre soutenu ou juridique :

all monies currently payable to the society
toutes les sommes d'argent maintenant dues à la société

Pour plus de détails, voir la section **L'Orthographe**, p A74.

c) Les noms en **-o** prennent parfois un **-s**, parfois **-es** au pluriel. Il est difficile d'établir des règles précises dans ce cas, cependant on peut dire que l'on ajoute seulement un **-s** si (1) le **-o** suit une autre voyelle (**embryo - embryos** embryons, **studio - studios** studios) ; ou si (2) le nom est une abréviation (**photo - photos, piano - pianos** (de **pianoforte**)). Dans d'autres cas, il est difficile de généraliser, bien que l'on puisse observer une préférence pour le **-s** avec des mots qui ont encore une connotation étrangère pour les britanniques :

(avec **-es**) **echo**, **cargo** (cargaison), **hero**, **mosquito** (moustique), **negro**, **potato** (pomme de terre), **tomato**, **torpedo** (torpille)

(avec **-s**) **canto** (chant), **memento**, **proviso** (stipulation), **quarto**, **solo**, **zero**, **zoo**

(avec **-s** ou **-es**) **banjo**, **buffalo** (buffle), **commando**, **flamingo** (flamand rose), **motto**, **volcano**

d) Pour certains noms en **-f(e)**, le **-f** se transforme en **-ve** au pluriel :

calf : calves veau(x)

Il en est de même pour : **elf**, **half** (moitié), **knife** (couteau), **leaf** (feuille d'arbre), **life** (vie), **loaf** (pain), **self** (soi), **sheaf** (gerbe), **shelf** (étagère), **thief** (voleur), **wife** (épouse), **wolf** (loup).

Certains peuvent avoir un pluriel en **-ves** ou en **-s** :

dwarf : dwarfs/dwarves nain(s)
hoof : hoofs/hooves sabot(s)
scarf : scarfs/scarves écharpe(s)
wharf : wharfs/wharves quai(s)

Un grand nombre de ces mots conservent le **-f** :

belief : beliefs croyance(s)

Il en est de même pour **chief** (chef), **cliff** (falaise), **proof** (preuve), **roof** (toit), **safe** (coffre-fort), **sniff** (reniflement), etc.

e) Quelques mots français se terminant avec un **-s** muet au singulier ne changent pas leur pluriel à l'écrit; on ajoute cependant le son /**z**/ au pluriel à l'oral :

corps - le pluriel se prononce avec /**z**/.

f) Les mots français en **-eu** ou **-eau** prennent un **-s** ou un **-x** (que l'on prononce tous les deux /**z**/), par exemple :

adieu, bureau, tableau

gateau prend normalement un **-x**.

g) *Les noms d'animaux*

Certains noms d'animaux, notamment les noms de poissons, se comportent (ou se comportent presque toujours) comme les noms mentionnés dans la section 3a) ci-dessous, c'est-à-dire qu'ils ne prennent pas de marque du pluriel :

cod (morue), **hake** (colin), **herring** (hareng), **mackerel** (maquereau), **pike** (brochet), **salmon** (saumon), **trout** (truite) (mais on dit **sharks** (requins)), **deer** (cerf), **sheep** (mouton), **grouse** (coq de bruyère).

D'autres noms d'animaux prennent un **-s** ou rien. Dans le contexte de la chasse, on omet souvent le **-s**. Comparez :

these graceful antelopes have just been bought by the zoo
le zoo vient juste d'acheter ces antilopes gracieuses

they went to Africa to shoot antelope
ils sont allés en Afrique pour chasser l'antilope

Il en est de même pour :

buffalo (buffle), **giraffe**, **lion**, **duck** (canard), **fowl** (volaille), **partridge** (perdrix), **pheasant** (faisan), et bien d'autres.

Le pluriel régulier de **fish** est **fish**, mais **fishes** s'emploie pour faire référence à des espèces de poissons.

h) *Les adjectifs numéraux*

i) **hundred** (cent), **thousand** (mille), **million**, **dozen** (douzaine), **score** (vingt) et **gross** (douze douzaines) n'ont pas de pluriel en **-s** lorsqu'ils sont précédés par un autre adjectif numéral. Remarquez la différence de construction avec le français pour 'million', 'milliard' et 'douzaine' :

five hundred/thousand/million people
cinq cents/mille/millions *de* gens

two dozen eggs
deux douzaines *d'*œufs

we'll order three gross
nous commanderons trente-six douzaines

mais :

there were hundreds/thousands/millions of them
il y en avait des centaines/milliers/millions

I've told you dozens of times
je te l'ai dit des dizaines de fois

Peter and Kate have scores of friends
Peter et Kate ont des tas d'amis

ii) Les unités de mesure le **foot** et le **pound** peuvent être soit au pluriel, soit au singulier :

Kate is five foot/feet eight
Kate mesure un mètre soixante-douze

that comes to three pound(s) fifty
ça fait trois livres cinquante

2 Les pluriels avec un changement de voyelle

Il existe un petit groupe de mots dont le pluriel se forme au moyen d'un changement de voyelle :

foot : feet pied(s)
goose : geese oie(s)
louse : lice pou(x)
man : men homme(s)
mouse : mice souris
tooth : teeth dent(s)
woman : women femme(s)
/wɪmɪn/

3 Les pluriels invariables

a) *singulier et pluriel sans* ***-s*** :

(air)craft (avion), **counsel** (avocat), **offspring** (progéniture), **quid** ('balle' (argent)), par exemple :

we saw a few aircraft
nous avons vu quelques avions

both counsel asked for an adjournment
les deux avocats ont demandé un renvoi

these are my offspring
c'est ma progéniture

this will cost you ten quid (familier = pound(s))
ça te coûtera cent balles

(Mass) media prend parfois un verbe au singulier, parfois un verbe au pluriel, sans qu'il y ait de différence de sens.

Les mots **kind, sort, type** (genre, sorte, type) apparaissant dans une phrase du type **these/those** + nom + **of** très souvent ne prennent pas de **-s** :

these kind of people always complain
ce genre de personne se plaint toujours

she always buys those sort of records
elle achète toujours ce genre de disque

Il est aussi possible de dire :

this kind of record

où les deux noms sont au singulier.

b) *singulier et pluriel en* ***-s***

barracks (caserne), **crossroads** (carrefour), **innings** (tour de batte), **means** (moyens, ressources) (comparez avec **means** (= moyens financiers) p A10), **gallows** (potence), **headquarters** (quartier général), **series** (série), **shambles** (désordre), **species** (espèce), **-works** (usine), par exemple :

every means was tried to improve matters
on a usé de tous les moyens pour améliorer les choses

this is a dreadful shambles
c'est un désordre abominable

they have built a new gasworks north of here
ils ont construit une nouvelle usine à gaz au nord d'ici

Certains de ces noms, en particulier **barracks**, **gallows**, **headquarters**, **-works** peuvent aussi s'employer dans un sens singulier avec un verbe au pluriel :

these are the new steelworks
c'est la nouvelle aciérie

On fait référence ici à une seule usine.

c) ***dice*** *et* ***pence***

Ce sont à proprement parler les pluriels irréguliers de **die** (dé) et **penny**, mais ils commencent à remplacer rapidement le singulier.

Die ne s'emploie pratiquement jamais que dans les expressions figées telles que **the die is cast** (les dés sont jetés) ou **straight as a die** (d'une grande honnêteté). Et il est normal d'entendre **one pence** (un pence) plutôt que **one penny** (un penny) lorsque l'on parle du coût de quelque chose. En revanche on parle encore de la pièce de monnaie en disant **a penny**, donnant au pluriel plusieurs **pennies**, comme dans la phrase suivante : **these are 18th-century pennies** (ce sont des pennies du XVIIIe siècle). Comme **die**, on emploie **penny** dans certaines expressions figées : **to spend a penny** (aller aux toilettes).

4 Les pluriels en -en

Il n'en existe que trois, et un seul est commun :

child : children enfant(s)

Les autres sont :

ox : oxen bœuf(s)
brother : brethren frère(s)

ce dernier faisant référence aux membres d'une congrégation religieuse, comme dans :

our Catholic brethren from other countries
nos frères catholiques d'autres pays

Le pluriel normal de **brother** est, bien entendu, **brothers**.

5 Les pluriels en -a ou -s

Ce sont des noms latins au singulier en **-um** ou des noms grecs au singulier en **-on**. Beaucoup d'entre eux ont un pluriel en **-s**, en particulier s'ils sont employés couramment, par exemple :

museum (musée), **stadium** (stade), **demon**, **electron**

Certains, souvent employés dans un langage scientifique et dont le singulier est **-um/-on**, ont un pluriel en **-a**, par exemple :

an addendum un addenda (*ou* addendum)

numerous addenda de nombreux addenda

De même on a **bacterium** (bactérie), **curriculum** (programme d'étude), **erratum**, **ovum** (ovule), **criterion** (critère), **phenomenon**

Certains varient entre le pluriel en **-s** et en **-a** :

memorandum, **millennium** (millénaire), **symposium**, **automaton** (automate)

Le pluriel de **medium** est toujours **mediums** lorsque ce mot fait référence à un extra-lucide. Lorsqu'il signifie 'moyen', le pluriel est soit **media** ou **mediums**. Pour **(mass) media**, voir **Les Pluriels invariables**, ci-dessus, section 3. Pour **data**, voir p A9.

Il apparaît que **strata** (pluriel de **stratum**) remplacera bientôt **stratum** au singulier.

6 Les pluriels en -e ou -s

Ces noms sont latins ou grecs et ont une terminaison en **-a** au singulier. Ceux qui sont fréquemment employés ont un pluriel en **-s**, comme **arena** et **drama**. Les noms plus techniques ou scientifiques ont tendance à avoir un pluriel en **-e** (on obtient alors la terminaison **-ae** prononcée /i:/ ou /aɪ), par exemple **alumna** et **larva**. La terminaison de certains varie selon le niveau de langue employé dans le contexte. Ainsi **antenna** prend toujours un **-e** lorsqu'il fait référence aux insectes, mais un **-s** lorsqu'il signifie antenne de télévision en américain. Il en est de même pour **formula** et **vertebra**.

7 Les pluriels en -i ou -s (mots italiens)

Quelques mots empruntés de l'italien, notamment **libretto**, **tempo** et **virtuoso**, conservent parfois leur pluriel italien en **-i** /i:/. C'est plus particulièrement le cas de **tempo**. Parfois ils prennent le **-s** du pluriel régulier anglais. Vous noterez que **confetti** et les pâtes **macaroni, ravioli, spaghetti** et d'autres, sont des indénombrables, c'est-à-dire qu'ils sont suivis d'un verbe au singulier. Pour **graffiti**, voir p A10.

8 Les pluriels en -i ou -es (mots latins)

Ceux qui sont courants prennent normalement la terminaison **-es** au pluriel, comme :

campus, **chorus** (refrain, chœur), **virus**

Ceux qui appartiennent au langage plus érudit, gardent en général leur pluriel latin en **-i** (que l'on prononce /i:/ ou /aɪ) comme par exemple :

alumnus, **bacillus**, **stimulus**.

D'autres prennent les deux formes au pluriel : **cactus**, **fungus** (champignon, fongus), **nucleus**, **syllabus** (programme d'université). Il en est de même pour les noms grecs latinisés : **hippopotamus** et **papyrus**. Le pluriel de **genius** est **geniuses** au sens de 'personne extrêmement intelligente', mais **genii** lorsqu'il signifie '(bon/mauvais) esprit'.

9 Les pluriels des noms en -ex ou -ix

Ces noms latins peuvent conserver leur pluriel d'origine, leur singulier en **-ex/-ix** se transforme alors en **-ices** au pluriel, ou bien ils prennent **-es**, par exemple :

> **index** : pluriel **indices** ou **indexes**

Il en est de même pour **appendix**, **matrix**, **vortex**.

Mais remarquez que **appendixes** est le seul pluriel pour la partie du corps, tandis que **appendixes** et **appendices** peuvent s'employer pour désigner les parties d'un livre ou d'une thèse.

10 Le pluriel des noms grecs en -is

Ces derniers changent le **-is** /ɪs/ en **-es** /i:z/ au pluriel, par exemple :

an analysis	une analyse
various different analyses	différentes analyses

Il en est de même pour : **axis**, **basis**, **crisis**, **diagnosis**, **hypothesis**, **oasis**, **parenthesis**, **synopsis**, **thesis**.

Mais remarquez : **metropolis** : **metropolises**

11 Les pluriels en -im ou -s

Les trois mots hébreux **kibbutz**, **cherub** (chérubin) et **seraph** (séraphin) peuvent soit prendre **-(e)s** (pluriel régulier) ou **-im** au pluriel.

12 Les pluriels des noms composés

a) *Le pluriel porte sur le deuxième élément*

Lorsque le deuxième élément est un nom (et qu'il n'est pas précédé d'une préposition) :

> **boy scouts**, **football hooligans**, **girl friends** (petites amies), **road users** (usagers de la route), **man-eaters** (mangeurs d'hommes, cannibales) (comparez à **menservants** dans c) ci-dessous)

et lorsque le mot composé est formé d'un verbe + adverbe :

> **lay-bys** (aires de stationnement), **lie-ins** (grasses matinées), **sit-ins**, **stand-bys**, **tip-offs** (tuyaux)

Remarquez que les noms de mesures se terminant par **-ful** peuvent avoir un **-s** à la fin de l'un ou l'autre de leurs éléments : **spoonfuls** ou **spoonsful**.

b) *Le pluriel porte sur le premier élément*

Lorsque le deuxième élément est un groupe prépositionnel :

editors-in-chief	rédacteurs en chef
fathers-in-law	beaux-pères
men-of-war	bâtiments de guerre
aides-de-camp	

Mais si le premier élément n'est pas considéré comme une personne, on place le **s** en final, comme dans :

will-o'-the-wisps	**jack-in-the-boxes**
feux follets	diables à ressort

Les noms composés formés à partir d'un verbe et d'un adverbe prennent eux aussi un **-s** à la fin du premier élément (à la différence de ceux composés d'un verbe + adverbe, qui ont un **-s** en finale. voir a) ci-dessus) :

hangers-on	**passers-by**
parasites	passants

Les noms composés avec **-to-be** prennent un **-s** à la fin du premier élément :

brides-to-be	**mothers-to-be**
futures mariées	futures mamans

Le premier élément porte aussi la marque du pluriel si le second élément est un adjectif :

> **Lords temporal and spiritual**
> membres laïques et ecclésiastiques de la Chambre des Lords

Mais beaucoup peuvent aussi porter la marque du pluriel sur le deuxième élément (ce qui est de plus en plus courant) :

> **attorneys general** ou **attorney generals** (Procureurs Généraux)
> **directors general** ou **director generals**
> **poets laureate** ou **poet laureates**
> **courts-martial** ou **court-martials**

c) *Les deux éléments portent la marque du pluriel*

Lorsque le nom composé avec **man** ou **woman** sert à distinguer le genre (mais le premier élément peut aussi être au singulier) :

menservants	domestiques (comparez **man-eaters** dans a) ci-dessus)
gentlemen farmers	gentlemen-farmers
women doctors	femmes médecins

C USAGE : PLURIEL OU SINGULIER ?

a) *Le pluriel distributif*

i) type 1, dans un groupe nominal

Dans beaucoup de cas l'anglais préfère le pluriel :

> **between the ages of 30 and 45**
> entre l'âge de 30 et 45 ans
>
> **the reigns of Henry VIII and Elizabeth I**
> le règne d'Henri VIII et celui d'Elisabeth Ire

ii) type 2, dans une proposition

Dans ce cas, le nom au pluriel (souvent précédé d'un adjectif possessif) fait référence à un nom ou pronom possessif au pluriel mentionné auparavant, par exemple :

> **we changed our minds**
> nous avons changé d'avis
>
> **many people are unhappy about their long noses**
> beaucoup de gens ne sont pas satisfaits de leur long nez
>
> **cats seem to spend their lives sleeping**
> les chats semblent passer leur vie à dormir
>
> **they deserve a kick up their backsides**
> ils méritent un coup de pied au derrière
>
> **we respectfully removed our hats**
> nous avons respectueusement retiré notre chapeau
>
> **can we change places?**
> on peut changer de place ?

Mais ce n'est pas une règle bien définie. Certaines personnes ont de l'eau jusqu'à la ceinture : **up to their waists** ou **up to the waist**, et ils ont de l'eau ou des dettes jusqu'au cou : **up to their necks** and **up to the neck**. Les conducteurs changent de vitesse (**change gear** ou **gears**) et ils peuvent risquer la vie de leurs passagers : **the death** ou **deaths of their passengers**.

Il y a des situations où des gens **have egg on their face** ou **faces**, c'est-à-dire l'air ridicule, mais seul **faces** est employé s'il s'agit d'un vrai œuf !

Et il y a des choses que certains **turn their nose(s) up at**, c'est-à-dire qu'ils considèrent inférieures. Il semble que si l'expression est employée dans un sens figuré, on emploie le plus souvent le singulier, parfois précédé d'un article défini plutôt que d'un pronom possessif. Ainsi **we pay through the nose** (payer quelque chose la peau des fesses), **we take children under our wing** (on prend des enfants sous son aile), et **we are sometimes at the end of our tether** (on est parfois à bout de nerfs) - autant d'exemples dans lesquels aucune image concrète n'apparaît.

b) *Le complément du nom placé avant ou après le nom*

Lorsqu'un nom est déterminé par une préposition + un nom au pluriel placés après ce nom, comme dans :

a collection of bottles
une collection de bouteilles

le nom au pluriel se transformera en singulier lorsqu'il est placé devant le nom qu'il détermine :

a bottle collection
une collection de bouteilles

Il existe beaucoup d'exemples de ce genre : **record dealer** (disquaire), **letter box** (boîte à lettres), **foreign language teaching** (enseignement des langues étrangères).

Cependant, il y a des cas où l'on préfère un complément du nom au pluriel placé avant le nom, parfois parce que le singulier aurait un sens différent. Ainsi on dirait :

a problems page courrier du cœur

parce que le mot **problem** au singulier signifie normalement 'qui cause des problèmes', comme dans :

a problem student
un étudiant à problèmes/qui pose des problèmes

a problem case
un cas à problèmes/problématique

Il en est de même pour :

a singles bar
un bar pour les célibataires

an explosives investigation
une enquête sur les explosifs

étant donné que :

a single bar un seul bar
an explosive investigation une enquête explosive

signifient quelque chose de complètement différent.

Mais souvent ou le singulier ou le pluriel est possible :

in this noun(s) section dans cette section des noms
a Falkland(s) hero un héros des Falkland

D LE GENITIF

1 Les formes

a) *Le génitif singulier se forme en ajoutant* **-'s** *après le nom :*

the cat's tail la queue du chat

et le génitif pluriel en ajoutant seulement l'apostrophe au pluriel :

the cats' tails la queue des chats

Il y a souvent confusion au sujet de la position de l'apostrophe. Comparez ces deux exemples :

the boy's school l'école du garçon
the boys' school l'école de garçons

Dans le premier exemple, **boy** est au singulier, on parle donc de l'école d'un garçon. Dans le deuxième exemple le nom **boys** est au pluriel, on parle donc de l'école où vont plusieurs garçons.

Si le pluriel ne se termine pas en **-s**, le génitif pluriel se forme avec le **-'s** comme le singulier :

the men's toilet les toilettes des hommes
the children's room la chambre des enfants

b) *Exceptions*

i) Beaucoup de noms classiques (en particulier les noms grecs) se terminant en **-s** prennent normalement juste une apostrophe, en particulier s'ils sont formés de plus d'une syllabe :

Socrates' wife l'épouse de Socrate
Aeschylus' plays les pièces d'Eschyle

On pourrait même trouver des noms modernes ayant la même caractéristique, comme dans :

Dickens' (ou **Dickens's**) **novels**
les romans de Dickens

ii) Avant le mot **sake** (amour de/nom de) le génitif singulier est normalement indiqué par l'apostrophe seule avec des noms se terminant en **-s** :

for politeness' sake par politesse

c) Pour les types de noms composés mentionnés p A14, on ajoute le **-'s** du génitif au deuxième élément, même si c'est le premier élément qui porte la marque du pluriel **-s** :

she summoned her ladies-in-waiting
elle convoqua ses dames de compagnie

the lady-in-waiting's mistress
la maîtresse de la dame de compagnie

2 Le génitif et la construction avec 'of'

a) *Les êtres animés (personnes, animaux)*

Le génitif est plus courant avec les personnes qu'avec les objets :

John's mind l'esprit de John
my mother's ring la bague de ma mère

Of n'est normalement pas employé dans ces deux exemples, mais on peut l'employer pour faire référence à des animaux :

the wings of an insect/the insect's wings
les ailes d'un insecte/de l'insecte

the movements of the worm/the worm's movements
les mouvements du ver de terre

Cependant, les animaux supérieurs sont considérés comme des personnes pour ce qui concerne la formation du génitif :

the lion's paw shot out from the cage
la patte du lion surgit de la cage

b) *Les objets inanimés*

La construction normale se forme avec **of** :

the size of the coat
la taille du manteau

the colour of the telephone
la couleur du téléphone

Mais avec certains noms d'inanimés, le génitif est aussi possible :

the mind's ability to recover
la capacité de l'esprit à guérir

the poem's capacity to move
la capacité du poème à émouvoir

en particulier si de tels noms font référence à des lieux ou à des institutions :

England's heritage (= the heritage of England)
l'héritage de l'Angleterre

the University's catering facilities (= the catering facilities of the University)
le service de restauration de l'université

Les noms faisant référence au temps et à la valeur sont souvent accompagnés du génitif :

today's menu le menu du jour
two months' work deux mois de travail
you've had your money's worth tu en as eu pour ton argent

Remarquez que la construction avec **of** pour des noms faisant référence au temps implique souvent une qualité de premier ordre ou une distinction particulière, comme dans :

our actor of the year award goes to ...
le prix du meilleur acteur de l'année est attribué à ...

ou bien elle peut impliquer que la durée ne doit pas être prise littéralement, comme dans :

the University of tomorrow
l'université de demain

Ici **tomorrow** ne peut signifier que l'avenir.

Un génitif peut avoir un sens ou littéral ou métaphorique :

Tomorrow's World (métaphorique)
le monde de demain

tomorrow's phone call (littéral)
le coup de téléphone de demain

tomorrow's food (soit littéral, soit métaphorique)
la nourriture de demain

Les mesures de distances sont parfois au génitif, en particulier dans des expressions figées :

a stone's throw (away)	**at arm's length**
à deux pas (d'ici)	à distance

3 Le génitif sans nom

a) Si le nom que le génitif détermine est assez clair de par le contexte, on peut alors l'omettre :

it's not my father's car, it's my mother's
ce n'est pas la voiture de mon père, c'est celle de ma mère

b) Le 'double génitif' (c'est-à-dire la construction avec **of** et le génitif dans la même phrase) est fréquent si le génitif fait référence à une personne *bien définie*. Mais le premier nom est normalement précédé d'un article *indéfini*, d'un pronom *indéfini* ou d'un adjectif numéral :

he's a friend of Peter's
c'est un ami de Peter

he's an acquaintance of my father's
c'est une connaissance de mon père

he's no uncle of Mrs Pitt's
ce n'est pas l'oncle de Madame Pitt

here are some relatives of Miss Young's
voici des parents de Mademoiselle Young

two sisters of my mother's came to visit
deux sœurs de ma mère sont venues nous rendre visite

Un pronom démonstratif peut parfois précéder le premier nom. Ceci implique un certain degré de familiarité :

that car of your father's - how much does he want for it?
cette voiture, ton père, combien est-ce qu'il la vend ?

L'article défini ne peut normalement pas s'employer avec le premier nom, à moins qu'une proposition relative (ou autre déterminatif) ne suive le génitif :

the poem of Larkin's (that) we read yesterday is lovely
le poème de Larkin que nous avons lu hier est magnifique

this is the only poem of Larkin's to have moved me
c'est le seul poème de Larkin qui m'ait ému

c) Le nom sous-entendu après un génitif fait souvent référence à des locaux :

at the baker's (= baker's shop)
chez le boulanger

at Mary's (= at Mary's place)
chez Mary

Il est important de souligner que si un établissement (commercial) est particulièrement bien connu, on omet souvent l'apostrophe. Ainsi on a tendance à écrire **at Smiths** (chez Smiths) ou **in Harrods** (chez Harrods), le premier représentant une chaîne de magasins qui couvre la Grande-Bretagne, le second étant le célèbre grand magasin de Londres. Mais on trouverait habituellement **he bought it at Bruce Miller's** (il l'a acheté chez Miller's), étant donné que cet établissement n'est pas fermement implanté dans l'esprit des gens sur une échelle nationale.

d) On trouve souvent le 'groupe génitif' dans deux types de constructions : **(1)** nom + déterminatif introduit par une préposition, et **(2)** noms reliés par **and.** Dans de telles combinaisons, on peut ajouter le **-'s** au dernier élément :

the Queen of Holland's yacht
le yacht de la reine de Hollande

the head of department's office
le bureau du chef de département

John and Kate's new house
la nouvelle maison de John et de Kate

an hour and a half's work
un travail d'une heure et demie

Si le nom est au pluriel, on emploie normalement la construction avec **of** :

the regalia of the Queens of Holland
les insignes royaux des reines de Hollande

Cependant, si les deux noms ne forment pas une unité, ils prennent chacun la marque du génitif **-'s** :

Shakespeare's and Marlowe's plays
les pièces de Shakespeare et de Marlowe

E LE FEMININ

En anglais, il est courant de ne pas employer de mot ou de terminaison distincts pour déterminer le genre d'un nom. Beaucoup de noms s'emploient à la fois pour un homme et pour une femme :

artist (artiste), **banker** (banquier(-ère)), **cousin** (cousin(e)), **friend** (ami(e)), **lawyer** (avocat(e)), **neighbour** (voisin(e)), **novelist** (romancier(-ère)), **teacher** (enseignant(e)), **zoologist** (zoologiste).

Mais il existe certains cas où l'on emploie différentes terminaisons pour distinguer le féminin du masculin :

Féminin	*Masculin*
actress (actrice)	**actor** (acteur)
duchess (duchesse)	**duke** (duc)
goddess (déesse)	**god** (dieu)
heroine (héroïne)	**hero** (héros)
princess (princesse)	**prince** (prince)
widow (veuve)	**widower** (veuf)
businesswoman (femme d'affaires)	**businessman** (homme d'affaires)

bien que dans beaucoup de cas il s'agisse d'une distinction de *termes*, tout comme **daughter/son** (fille/fils), **cow/bull** (vache/taureau), etc.

Mais on peut aussi dire **she is a good actor** (elle est très bonne actrice), ou bien **she was the hero of the day** (elle était le héros du jour).

S'il est nécessaire d'identifier le sexe d'une personne, on emploie soit :

a female friend (une amie)	**a male friend** (un ami)
a female student (une étudiante)	**a male student** (un étudiant)

soit : **a woman doctor** (une femme médecin)
a man doctor (un médecin)

Lorsqu'il n'est pas nécessaire ou pas possible de distinguer ou d'identifier le sexe d'une personne, il est courant d'employer le mot **person** :

a chairperson	un(e) président(e)
a salesperson	un(e) représentant(e) de commerce
a spokesperson	un porte-parole

bien que certaines femmes soient satisfaites d'être **chairman.**

L'emploi du mot **person** devient de plus en plus courant, par exemple dans les petites annonces :

security person required
on cherche garde de sécurité

4 Les Adjectifs

1 Généralités

★ Les adjectifs anglais ne s'accordent jamais avec le nom.

★ L'adjectif se place toujours devant le nom en dehors de certaines exceptions (voir 3. b) ci-dessous).

2 Epithète et attribut

Les termes 'épithète' et 'attribut' font référence à la position de l'adjectif par rapport au nom. Si l'adjectif est placé devant le nom, il est épithète (***this old car*** cette vieille voiture). S'il est placé tout seul après un verbe, il est attribut (***this car is old*** cette voiture est vieille).

Si un adjectif a plusieurs sens, chacun de ces sens peut entrer dans une catégorie différente.

a) *Epithète seulement*

i) Certains adjectifs qui ont un rapport fort avec le nom auquel ils se rapportent dans des constructions toutes faites sont uniquement épithètes, comme dans :

he's a moral philosopher
c'est un philosophe spécialiste en éthique

ii) Les participes passés sont parfois employés de cette manière :

a disabled toilet (toilet for disabled people)
des toilettes pour handicapés

iii) Très souvent en anglais on emploie des noms avec une fonction d'adjectif :

a cardboard box
une boîte en carton

a polystyrene container
un emballage en polystyrène

a foreign affairs correspondent
un correspondant étranger

a classification problem
un problème de classification

b) *Attribut seulement*

Les adjectifs qui sont uniquement attributs qualifient généralement une condition physique ou un état mental, comme ***afraid*** (effrayé), ***ashamed*** (honteux), ***faint*** (= sur le point de perdre conscience), ***fond*** (attaché), ***poorly*** (souffrant), ***(un)well*** (en mauvaise/bonne santé) :

the girl is afraid
la fille a peur

the children need not feel ashamed
les enfants n'ont pas besoin d'avoir honte

my uncle is fond of me
mon oncle m'aime bien

he suddenly felt faint
il se sentit tout à coup sur le point de s'évanouir

our mother has been unwell for some time
notre mère ne se sent pas bien depuis un certain temps

Mais remarquez l'expression :

he's not a well man
il n'est pas dans le meilleur de sa forme (= il est très malade)

De même, ***ill*** et ***glad*** sont le plus souvent attributs, mais sont parfois épithètes lorsqu'ils ne font pas référence à une personne :

his ill health may explain his ill humour
cette mauvaise santé peut expliquer sa mauvaise humeur

these are glad tidings (vieilli)
ce sont de bonnes nouvelles

3 La position

a) Si plus d'un adjectif précède le nom, celui ou ceux qui peuvent aussi être attributs se placent en premier. Les adjectifs qui peuvent être épithètes uniquement ont un rapport trop étroit avec le nom pour qu'un autre mot puisse se placer entre eux et le nom :

he is a young parliamentary candidate
c'est un jeune candidat parlementaire

they have employed a conscientious social worker
ils ont employé une assistante sociale consciencieuse

a big old red brick house
une grande et vieille maison de brique rouge

Remarquez que les adjectifs ***old*** et ***little*** changent de sens selon leur position. Comparez (a-d) avec (e-h) :

(a) **they only have old worn-out records**
ils n'ont que des vieux disques usés

(b) **up the path came a very old (and) dirty man**
sur le chemin est apparu un homme très vieux et très sale

(c) **I think I left a little black book behind**
je crois que j'ai laissé un petit cahier noir

(d) **I want the little round mirror over there**
je veux le petit miroir rond par ici

(e) **silly old me!**
suis-je donc bête !

(f) **you dirty old man, you!**
espèce de vieux cochon !

(g) **this is my cute little sister**
c'est mon adorable petite sœur

(h) **what an adorable, sweet little cottage!**
quelle petite maison adorable et mignonne !

En (a-d) ***old*** et ***little*** ont leur premier sens et pourraient, avec ces sens, prendre une position d'attribut. Mais en (e-h) le caractère littéral des expressions est perdu : ***a dirty old man*** (un obsédé sexuel) n'est pas forcément âgé. Dans ce cas, on fait plus une allusion au comportement qu'à l'âge de la personne. ***My little sister*** en (g) signifie 'ma sœur plus jeune'; on ne s'intéresse pas du tout à la taille de la personne. Et ***little*** en (h) donne plus une description des émotions du locuteur que des dimensions de la maison. De même, en (e), ***old*** ne veut pas du tout dire 'vieux'.

b) Parfois, quand il est mis en apposition, l'adjectif se place après le nom sans qu'un verbe soit nécessaire. Ces adjectifs (et toute qualification supplémentaire éventuelle) sont similaires en fonction et en usage aux propositions relatives :

this is a custom peculiar to Britain
c'est une coutume propre à la Grande-Bretagne

this is a man confident of success
c'est un homme sûr de réussir

Les adjectifs ne peuvent être en apposition que s'ils peuvent aussi être attributs, et sont très fréquents lorsqu'ils sont qualifiés par un groupe prépositionnel, comme on le voit dans les exemples ci-dessus. Mais on trouve aussi des adjectifs en apposition employés dans un but emphatique, toujours employés par deux et plus :

her jewellery, cheap and tawdry, was quickly removed
ses bijoux, pas chers et clinquants, furent rapidement enlevés

he looked into a face sympathetic but firm
il vit un visage sympathique mais décidé

books, new or secondhand, for sale
livres, neufs ou d'occasion, à vendre

Cette fonction est assez fréquente (mais non obligatoire) après des mots imprécis comme ***things*** et ***matters*** :

his interest in matters linguistic
son intérêt pour tout ce qui touche à la linguistique

she has an abhorrence of things English
elle a en horreur tout ce qui est anglais

et pour les adjectifs en ***-able*** ou ***-ible***, surtout si le nom est précédé de **only** (seul, unique) ou d'un superlatif :

they committed the worst atrocities imaginable
ils commirent les pires atrocités imaginables

he's the only person responsible
il est la seule personne responsable

this is the most inexpensive model available
c'est le modèle disponible le moins cher

c) Certains adjectifs d'origine française ou latine se placent après le nom auquel ils se rapportent comme en français, et dans des expressions toutes faites comme ***poet laureate*** (le poète lauréat), ***the Princess Royal*** (la Princesse Royale), ***Lords Spiritual*** (membres ecclésiastiques de la Chambre des Lords), ***Lords Temporal*** (membres temporels), ***letters patent*** (lettres patentes), ***lion rampant*** (lion rampant), ***devil incarnate*** (diable incarné).

4 La comparaison

Les Formes

a) Il y a trois degrés de comparaison : ***la forme de base***, ***le comparatif*** et ***le superlatif*** :

sweet doux	***beautiful*** beau	*(forme de base)*
sweeter plus doux	***more beautiful*** plus beau	*(comparatif)*
sweetest le plus doux	***the most beautiful*** le plus beau	*(superlatif)*

Pour les changements d'orthographe résultant de l'addition de ***-er***, ***-est*** (***happy - happier*** ou ***big - bigger***) voir p A74.

b) ***-er/-est*** *ou* ***more/most*** *?*

i) Plus l'adjectif est court, plus il est probable que son comparatif et son superlatif se formeront en ajoutant ***-er*** et ***-est***. Ceci concerne particulièrement les adjectifs monosyllabiques, comme ***keen***, ***fine***, ***late***, ***wide***, ***neat***, etc. Des adjectifs très courants comme ***big*** ou ***fast*** prennent toujours la forme ***-er/-est***.

Si les adjectifs ont deux syllabes, on trouve ***-er/-est*** et ***more/most***, ***-er/-est*** étant particulièrement courants avec les adjectifs qui se terminent en ***-y***, ***-le***, ***-ow***, ***-er*** :

(noisy) ***this is the noisiest pub I've ever seen***
c'est le pub le plus bruyant que j'aie jamais vu

(feeble) ***this is the feeblest excuse I've heard***
c'est la plus mauvaise excuse que j'aie entendue

(shallow) ***the stream is shallower up there***
le ruisseau est moins profond en amont

(clever) ***she's the cleverest***
c'est la plus intelligente

On tend à employer ***more*** et ***most*** d'une façon de plus en plus générale au lieu de ***-er/-est***. ***Commoner*** et ***pleasanter*** étaient plus courants qu'ils ne le sont maintenant ; de même que ***politer*** et ***handsomer*** par rapport à ***more polite*** et ***more handsome***, ces derniers étant maintenant tout à fait acceptés.

ii) Les adjectifs de plus de deux syllabes utilisent ***more*** et ***the most*** :

this is the most idiotic thing I ever heard!
c'est la chose la plus idiote que j'aie entendue !

I prefer a more traditional Christmas
je préfère un Noël plus traditionnel

she's getting more and more predictable
il devient de plus en plus facile de deviner ce qu'elle va faire

Mais il existe des exceptions à cette règle :

she's unhappier than she has ever been
elle est plus malheureuse que jamais

he's got the untidiest room in the whole house
il a la chambre la plus désordonnée de toute la maison

Dans ces cas, on peut aussi employer ***more/the most***.

iii) Les adjectifs qui sont formés à partir des participes passés prennent ***more*** au comparatif et ***the most*** au superlatif :

she's more gifted than her sister
elle est plus douée que sa sœur

the most advanced students
les étudiants les plus avancés

that's the most bored I've ever been!
je ne me suis jamais autant ennuyé !

Tired peut prendre les terminaisons ***-er/-est***.

iv) Si la comparaison se fait entre deux adjectifs (comme choix de mots) on ne peut employer que ***more*** :

this sauce is more sweet than sour
cette sauce est plus douce qu'aigre

c) *Les comparaisons irrégulières*

Quelques adjectifs ont un comparatif et un superlatif irréguliers.

bad mauvais	**worse** pire	**worst** le pire
far loin	**further/** **farther** plus loin	**furthest/** **farthest** le plus loin
good bon	**better** meilleur	**best** le meilleur
little peu	**less/lesser** moins	**least** le moins
many beaucoup	**more** plus	**most** le plus
much beaucoup	**more** plus	**most** le plus

Remarquez aussi ***late, latter, last*** (dernier, deuxième, le dernier) (mais ***later*** (plus tard), ***latest*** (le dernier)) et ***old***, ***elder***, ***eldest*** (vieux, plus vieux, aîné) (mais ***older*** (plus vieux), ***oldest*** (le plus vieux)).

Pour l'emploi du comparatif et du superlatif (et les variantes), voir ci-dessous et p A19.

d) *La comparaison d'infériorité*

Pour former les comparatifs d'infériorité, on place les adverbes ***less/the least*** devant les adjectifs :

it's less interesting than I thought it would be
c'est moins intéressant que je ne le pensais

this was the least interesting of his comments
c'était son commentaire le moins intéressant

Il existe une autre façon d'exprimer le comparatif :

it's not as/so interesting as I thought it would be
ce n'est pas aussi intéressant que je ne le pensais

L'Emploi

i) Dans les comparaisons ***than*** se traduit par 'que' :

it's hotter here than in Spain
il fait plus chaud ici qu'en Espagne

ii) Le comparatif est employé quand deux personnes ou deux choses sont comparées :

of the two, she is the cleverer
des deux, elle est la plus intelligente

Dans l'anglais parlé d'aujourd'hui, certains emploient aussi le superlatif :

of the two, she is the cleverest
des deux, elle est la plus intelligente

sauf, bien sûr, quand ***than*** suit (***she is cleverer than her brother*** elle est plus intelligente que son frère).

iii) Quand plus de deux personnes ou choses sont comparées on emploie le superlatif :

she is the cleverest in the class
elle est la plus intelligente de la classe

iv) Dans les annonces publicitaires, il n'y a souvent qu'un terme dans la comparaison :

Greece - for a better holiday
La Grèce - pour de meilleures vacances

v) Dans certains cas, le comparatif est employé non pas pour marquer le degré, mais le contraste. Cela s'applique surtout pour les adjectifs qui n'ont pas de forme de base :

former: latter	**inner: outer**
premier : dernier	intérieur : extérieur
upper: nether	**lesser: greater**
supérieur : inférieur	petit : grand

Ces adjectifs dans ce sens sont toujours épithètes.

Nether est maintenant remplacé dans la plupart des cas par ***lower*** et il est limité essentiellement au registre de la plaisanterie :

he removed his nether garments
il a enlevé son pantalon

f) Le superlatif absolu : il exprime que quelque chose est à un 'très haut degré' au lieu d'être au 'plus haut degré'. Habituellement, on emploie ***most*** au lieu de ***-est***, même avec des adjectifs monosyllabiques :

this is most kind!
c'est très gentil !

I thought his lecture was most interesting
j'ai trouvé que sa conférence était des plus intéressantes

mais parfois un superlatif en ***-est*** est employé comme épithète :

she was rather plain but had the sweetest smile
elle n'était pas très jolie, mais elle avait un sourire magnifique

please accept my warmest congratulations!
acceptez, je vous en prie, mes très chaleureuses félicitations

g) *Cas particuliers*

i) further/farther *et* ***furthest/farthest***

Further est d'un usage plus courant que ***farther*** quand on fait référence à la distance (et lorsqu'il est employé comme adverbe) :

this is the furthest (farthest) point
c'est le point le plus éloigné

(En tant qu'adverbe : ***I can't go any further (farther)*** je ne peux pas aller plus loin)

Si on fait référence au temps, à un nombre, on ne peut employer que ***further*** :

any further misdemeanours and you're out
une autre incartade et tu sors

this must be delayed until a further meeting
ceci doit être reporté à un prochain meeting

anything further can be discussed tomorrow
pour le reste, on verra demain

et comme un adverbe :

they didn't pursue the matter any further
ils ont décidé d'en arrêter là pour cette affaire

ii) later/latter *et* ***latest/last***

Later et ***latest*** font référence au temps, ***latter*** et ***last*** à l'ordre, à la série :

(a) ***his latest book is on war poetry***
son dernier livre en date est sur la poésie en temps de guerre

(b) ***his last book was on war poetry***
son dernier livre était sur la poésie en temps de guerre

Latest en (a) a le sens de 'le plus récent', alors que ***last*** en (b) fait référence au dernier d'une série de livres.

Pour ***latter***, voir **Les Nombres**, p A72. Notez, de plus, que ***latter*** sous-entend une division en deux, comme dans ***the latter part of the century*** (la dernière moitié du siècle).

iii) less/lesser

Less est quantitatif, ***lesser*** est qualitatif :

use less butter
prenez moins de beurre

the lesser of two evils
le moindre de deux maux

you'll lose less money if you follow my plan
tu perdras moins d'argent si tu suis mes plans

there's a lesser degree of irony in this novel
il y a moins d'ironie dans ce roman

Mais remarquez ***the lesser*** (opposé à ***the great(er)***) comme un adjectif de catégorie dans un registre technique ou scientifique :

the Lesser Black-backed Gull (nom scientifique)
le goéland à tête noire

Pour ***less*** avec les noms dénombrables, voir **Les Noms**, p A10.

iv) older/elder *et* ***oldest/eldest***

Elder et ***eldest*** font en général référence aux liens familiaux uniquement :

this is my elder/eldest brother
c'est mon frère aîné

bien que ***older*** soit aussi utilisable dans ce contexte. Si ***than*** (que) suit, seul ***older*** est possible :

my brother is older than I am
mon frère est plus vieux que moi

Remarquez l'emploi de ***elder*** comme nom :

listen to your elders
écoute tes aînés

she is my elder by two years
elle est mon aînée de deux ans

the elders of the tribe
les anciens de la tribu

5 Les adjectifs employés comme noms

a) Les adjectifs peuvent s'employer comme noms. Cet emploi concerne en général les ***concepts abstraits*** et les ***classes ou groupes de gens*** (en général ou dans un contexte particulier) :

i) Concepts abstraits :

you must take the rough with the smooth
il faut prendre les choses comme elles viennent

the use of the symbolic in his films
l'utilisation du symbolique dans ses films

ii) Classes ou groupes de gens :

we must bury our dead
nous devons enterrer nos morts

the poor are poor because they have been oppressed by the rich
les pauvres sont pauvres parce qu'ils ont été opprimés par les riches

the blind, the deaf	**the young, the old**
les aveugles, les sourds	les jeunes, les vieux

Et la célèbre description des chasseurs de renards par Oscar Wilde :

the unspeakable in full pursuit of the uneatable
l'innommable à la poursuite de l'immangeable

Remarquez qu'en anglais ces mots ont un sens de pluriel collectif. Pour désigner une personne dans un groupe, on ajoute **man**, **woman**, **person**, etc. selon le cas :

a blind woman	**three deaf people**
une aveugle	trois sourds

b) Normalement, un adjectif ne peut pas remplacer un nom singulier dénombrable. Dans ce cas, il est nécessaire d'employer **one** (mais voir aussi ***one***, p A37) :

> **I don't like the striped shirt; I prefer the plain one**
> je n'aime pas la chemise à rayures, je préfère l'unie

> **of all the applicants, the French one was the best**
> de tous les candidats, le Français était le meilleur

Cependant, il existe un certain nombre de participes passés que l'on peut utiliser (avec l'article défini) pour remplacer un nom dénombrable. Par exemple :

> **the accused**
> l'accusé/les accusés

> **the deceased/the departed**
> le mort/les morts

> **the deceased's possessions were sold**
> les biens du mort furent vendus

Ces adjectifs substantivés ne prennent pas de **-s** au pluriel.

c) Pour les exemples au pluriel en a), on n'ajoutait pas de **-s** à l'adjectif, mais parfois la conversion d'un adjectif en nom est totale et l'adjectif prend un **-s** au pluriel :

> **the Blacks against the Whites in South Africa**
> les Noirs contre les Blancs en Afrique du Sud

> **the Reds**
> les Rouges (les Communistes)

> **here come the newly-weds**
> voilà les nouveaux mariés

> **please put all the empties in a box**
> s'il te plaît, mets les vides dans un carton (les bouteilles vides)

d) *Nationalités*

i) En anglais, les adjectifs et les noms de nationalité prennent une majuscule (ainsi que les noms de langues) :

an American car	**an American**
une voiture américaine	un Américain

ii) On peut rendre la nationalité de quatre façons différentes :

(1) adjectif ordinaire

(2) nom et adjectif identiques

(3) comme le groupe (2) mais le nom prend un **-s** au pluriel

(4) nom et adjectif différents (mais, au pluriel, le nom + **-s** est aussi possible)

Groupe 1

adjectif : ***English Literature***
la littérature anglaise

employé comme nom (lorsqu'il se réfère à la nation) :

> **the English are rather reserved**
> les Anglais sont plutôt réservés

Les adjectifs du Groupe 1 ne peuvent pas être utilisés comme noms pour faire référence à des individus. Dans ce cas, la terminaison ***-man*** (ou ***-woman***) est utilisée :

> **we spoke to two Englishmen/Englishwomen**
> nous avons parlé à deux Anglais/Anglaises

D'autres exemples appartenant au Groupe 1 sont ***Irish*** (irlandais), ***Welsh*** (gallois), ***French*** (français), ***Dutch*** (hollandais).

Groupe 2

adjectif : ***Japanese art***
l'art japonais

employé comme nom lorsqu'il se réfère à une nation :

> **the Japanese are a hardworking nation**
> les Japonais sont un peuple de travailleurs

et lorsqu'il se réfère à des individus (sans **-s** au pluriel) :

> **it's hard to interpret the smile of a Japanese**
> il est difficile d'interpréter le sourire d'un Japonais

> **I've got six Japanese in my class**
> il y a six Japonais dans ma classe

D'autres adjectifs comme ***Japanese*** se terminent en ***-ese*** : ***Chinese*** (chinois), ***Burmese*** (birman), ***Vietnamese*** (vietnamien), ***Portuguese*** (portugais), et aussi ***Swiss*** (suisse).

Groupe 3

adjectif : ***German institutions***
les institutions allemandes

employé comme nom (au pluriel avec un **-s**) lorsqu'il fait référence à une nation :

> **the Germans produce some fine cars**
> les Allemands produisent de belles voitures

et lorsqu'il se réfère à des individus (avec un **-s** au pluriel) :

> **he was having a conversation with a German**
> il était en conversation avec un Allemand

> **we met quite a few Germans on our holiday**
> nous avons rencontré un bon nombre d'Allemands pendant nos vacances

De même, ceux qui se terminent en **-an**, par exemple :

> ***African*** (africain), ***American*** (américain), ***Asian*** (asiatique), ***Australian*** (australien), ***Belgian*** (belge), ***Brazilian*** (brésilien), ***Canadian*** (canadien), ***European*** (européen), ***Hungarian*** (hongrois), ***Indian*** (indien), ***Iranian*** (iranien), ***Italian*** (italien), ***Norwegian*** (norvégien), ***Russian*** (russe)

(mais notez que ***Arabian*** (arabe) appartient au Groupe 4 ci-dessous) et ceux qui se terminent en ***-i*** :

> ***Iraqi*** (iraquien), ***Israeli*** (israélien), ***Pakistani*** (pakistanais)

Remarquez que l'on emploie ***Bangladesh*** comme adjectif (***the Bangladesh economy*** l'économie bengalaise), et ***Bangladeshi*** pour les personnes (***a Bangladeshi/three Bangladeshis came to see me*** un Bengalais est venu me voir/trois Bengalais sont venus me voir).

On trouve aussi dans ce groupe ***Czech*** (tchèque), ***Cypriot*** (chypriote), ***Greek*** (grec).

Groupe 4

adjectif : ***Danish furniture***
les meubles danois

employé comme nom lorsqu'il fait référence à une nation :

> **the Danish know how to eat**
> les Danois savent bien manger

Mais il y a un nom différent qui peut aussi être utilisé pour faire référence à la nation :

> **the Danes know how to eat**
> les Danois savent bien manger

et qui est la *seule* forme admise pour désigner les individus :

> **a Dane will always ask you what something costs**
> un Danois vous demandera toujours combien ça coûte

> **there were two Danes in the cast**
> il y avait deux Danois dans la distribution

De même pour : ***British/Briton*** (Britannique), ***Finnish/Finn*** (Finlandais), ***Polish/Pole*** (Polonais), ***Spanish/Spaniard*** (Espagnol), ***Swedish/Swede*** (Suédois).

Remarquez ***Arabian/Arab*** : l'adjectif courant est ***Arabian*** (***Arabian Nights*** les Milles et Une Nuits) sauf si l'on parle de la langue ou des chiffres :

> **the Arabic language is difficult – do you speak Arabic?**
> la langue arabe est difficile – parlez-vous l'arabe ?

> **thank God for Arabic numerals, I can't cope with the Roman ones**
> heureusement qu'il y a les chiffres arabes, je ne m'en sors pas avec les chiffres romains

Arab est employé pour désigner les individus, sauf si ***Saudi*** le précède. Dans ce cas ***Saudi Arabian*** ou ***Saudi*** est employé :

> **he's worked a lot with Arabs**
> il a beaucoup travaillé avec des Arabes

> **the hotel has been hired by Saudi Arabians** (ou ***Saudis***)
> l'hôtel a été loué par des Saoudiens

ii) Remarques sur ***Scottish, Scots*** et ***Scotch*** (écossais) :

Aujourd'hui ***Scotch*** est d'un usage rare, sauf dans des locutions (concernant souvent la nourriture ou les boissons), par exemple ***Scotch egg*** (= une sorte de rissole qui contient un œuf dur), ***Scotch whisky***, ***Scotch broth*** (potage d'orge, de légumes et d'agneau) et ***Scotch terrier***.

Dans les autres cas, l'adjectif est normalement ***Scottish*** comme dans ***a Scottish bar*** (un bar écossais), ***Scottish football supporters*** (supporters de football écossais), même si ***Scots*** est parfois utilisé pour les personnes : ***a Scots lawyer*** (un avocat écossais). Les linguistes font maintenant la distinction entre le ***Scottish English*** (= l'anglais parlé avec un accent écossais) et le ***Scots*** (= le dialecte écossais).

Pour désigner la nation, on emploie ***the Scots*** (les Ecossais) (parfois ***the Scottish***). L'individu est ***a Scot*** (au pluriel ***Scots***) ou ***a Scotsman*** (au pluriel ***Scotsmen***).

e) En général, un adjectif français se traduira par un adjectif anglais et pourtant, ce n'est pas toujours le cas. Voici une liste de cas où les adjectifs de nationalité anglais seront traduits par un génitif français :

the French embassy	l'ambassade de France
the French rugby team	l'équipe de France de rugby
the Nantes team	l'équipe de Nantes, l'équipe nantaise
the Glasgow team, the Glaswegian team	l'équipe de Glasgow
the French league	le championnat de France
the French cup	la Coupe de France
the Brazilian Grand Prix	le Grand Prix du Brésil
French soil	la terre de France
the French crown	la couronne de France
the French coastline	les côtes de France
an English grammar	une grammaire de l'anglais

5 Les Adverbes

Par adverbe on entend un seul mot (par exemple **happily**) et par groupe adverbial ou proposition adverbiale on entend un groupe de mots ayant une fonction adverbiale.

A LES DIFFERENTS TYPES

a) *Adverbes en tant que tels et dérivés*

On peut distinguer deux sortes d'adverbes suivant leur forme : les adverbes 'en tant que tels' ou les adverbes 'dérivés'.

Les adverbes 'dérivés' sont ceux dérivés d'une autre classe de mots, par exemple :

happily (heureusement)	de l'adjectif ***happy***
hourly (par heure)	du nom ***hour*** ou de l'adjectif ***hourly***
moneywise (en ce qui concerne l'argent)	du nom ***money***

Parmi les adverbes en tant que tels on trouve :

here ici	**often** souvent
there là-bas	**never** jamais
now maintenant	**soon** bientôt
then alors	**very** très

b) *Sens*

Les adverbes peuvent se diviser en divers types selon leur sens. Les adverbes suivants sont particulièrement courants :

i) Adverbes de temps :

now (maintenant), ***then*** (alors), ***once*** (une fois), ***soon*** (bientôt), ***always*** (toujours), ***briefly*** (brièvement)

I saw her once	je l'ai vue une fois
you always say that	tu dis toujours ça

ii) Adverbes de lieu :

here (ici), ***there*** (là-bas), ***everywhere*** (partout), ***up*** (en haut), ***down*** (en bas), ***back*** (derrière)

> **come here**
> viens ici

iii) Adverbes de manière :

well (bien), ***clumsily*** (maladroitement), ***beautifully*** (merveilleusement)

> **what's worth doing is worth doing well**
> ce qui vaut la peine d'être fait vaut la peine d'être bien fait

iv) Adverbes d'intensité :

rather (plutôt), ***quite*** (assez), ***very*** (très), ***hardly*** (à peine), ***extremely*** (extrêmement)

> **this gravy is rather good**
> cette sauce est plutôt bonne

B LES DIFFERENTES FORMES

a) *Les adverbes en **-ly***

On ajoute normalement cette terminaison directement à l'adjectif correspondant :

> **sweet : sweetly**
> gentil : gentiment

Mais si l'adjectif se termine en ***-ic***, on ajoute ***-ally*** :

> **intrinsic : intrinsically**
> intrinsèque : intrinsèquement

drastic : drastically
radical : radicalement

Les seules exceptions sont :

public : publicly
publique : publiquement

et ***politic : politicly*** (judicieux : judicieusement) employé assez rarement.

Pour les changements d'orthographe (comme dans ***happy : happily*** heureux : heureusement ou ***noble: nobly*** noble : noblement), voir p A74.

Remarquez que l'on prononce toujours la voyelle de ***-ed*** à l'intérieur d'un adverbe, qu'on la prononce dans l'adjectif correspondant ou pas :

assured : assuredly (**-e** prononcé dans l'adverbe)
assuré : assurément

offhanded : offhandedly (**-e** prononcé dans les deux cas)
désinvolte : avec désinvolture

b) *Même forme que l'adjectif*

Certains adverbes ont la même forme que l'adjectif correspondant, par exemple :

a fast car une voiture rapide	**he drives too fast** il conduit trop vite
a hard punch un coup dur	**he hit him hard** il l'a frappé fort

D'autres adverbes peuvent soit avoir la même forme que l'adjectif soit avoir la terminaison ***-ly*** :

why are you driving so slow(ly)?
pourquoi conduis-tu si lentement ?

he speaks a bit too quick(ly) for me
il parle un peu trop vite pour moi

La forme sans ***-ly*** est parfois considérée comme appartenant au langage familier.

c) *La comparaison*

On forme le comparatif et le superlatif des adverbes ayant un degré de signification (voir 1b) ci-dessus) avec ***-er/-est*** ou ***more/the most*** de la même manière que les adjectifs.

Les adverbes formés à partir de l'adjectif + ***-ly*** ont un comparatif et un superlatif construits avec ***more*** et ***the most*** :

the most recently published works in this field
les ouvrages publiés le plus récemment dans ce domaine

Mais ***early***, qui n'est pas dérivé d'un adjectif sans ***-ly***, prend ***-er/-est*** :

he made himself a promise to get up earlier in future
il s'est promis de se lever plus tôt à l'avenir

Les adverbes qui ont la même forme que l'adjectif correspondant prennent ***-er/-est*** :

I can run faster than you think
je peux courir plus vite que tu crois

we arrived earlier than we expected
nous sommes arrivés plus tôt que prévu

Aux adjectifs ***slow*** et ***quick*** on peut ajouter soit ***-ly*** ou ne pas ajouter de terminaison du tout (ce que certains considèrent familier) pour former l'adverbe. Ils ont donc deux types de comparatifs :

you ought to drive more slowly
tu devrais conduire plus lentement

could you drive a little slower please
pourriez-vous conduire un peu plus lentement, s'il vous plaît ?

letters are arriving more quickly than they used to
les lettres arrivent plus vite qu'avant

letters are getting through quicker than before
les lettres arrivent plus vite qu'avant

Les adverbes suivants sont irréguliers :

badly mal	**worse** pire	**worst** le pire
far loin	**further, farther** plus loin	**furthest, farthest** le plus loin
little peu	**less** moins	**least** le moins
much beaucoup	**more** plus	**most** le plus
well bien	**better** mieux	**best** le mieux

Le comparatif de ***late*** est ***later*** (régulier) : le superlatif est ***latest*** (régulier = le plus récent) et ***last*** (irrégulier = le dernier). Pour les différences de sens et d'usage entre ***latest*** et ***last***, ***further/furthest*** et ***farther/farthest***, comparez les adjectifs correspondants, p A19.

d) *Pour exprimer l'idée de 'plus/moins ... plus/moins ...'*

the hotter it gets, the more she suffers
plus il fait chaud, plus elle souffre

the less I see of him the better!
moins je le vois, mieux je me porte !

the sooner the better
le plus tôt sera le mieux

the more the merrier
plus on est de fous, plus on rit

e) ***-wise***

On peut ajouter le suffixe ***-wise*** à des noms pour former un adverbe qui a le sens général de 'en ce qui concerne' (quel que soit le nom) :

how's he feeling? – do you mean mentally or healthwise?
comment se sent-il ? – tu veux dire mentalement ou en ce qui concerne sa santé ?

Bien que cette construction soit très courante, elle a tendance à être employée à l'oral plus qu'à l'écrit, et elle n'est pas toujours considérée comme particulièrement élégante, surtout pour un usage plus 'créatif' :

things are going quite well schedule-wise
les choses se passent assez bien en ce qui concerne nos prévisions

we're not really short of anything furniture-wise
nous ne manquons pas de grand-chose en ce qui concerne les meubles

the town's quite well provided restaurant-wise
la ville a pas mal de restaurants

C L'EMPLOI

1 Fonctions de l'adverbe et des constructions adverbiales

Les adverbes et les groupes adverbiaux s'emploient pour modifier:

(1) des verbes :

he spoke well il a bien parlé	**he spoke in a loud voice** il a parlé d'une voix forte

(2) des adjectifs :

that's awfully nice of you c'est vraiment gentil à vous	**this isn't good enough** ça n'est pas assez bien

(3) d'autres adverbes :

she didn't sing well enough
elle n'a pas assez bien chanté

it happened extremely quickly
ça s'est passé extrêmement vite

(Remarquez que **enough** suit l'adjectif ou l'adverbe qu'il modifie.)

(4) des noms qui sont employés comme des adjectifs attributs :

this is rather a mess c'est plutôt en désordre

he's quite a hero c'est un vrai héros

(5) toute la phrase :

fortunately they accepted the verdict
par bonheur ils ont accepté le verdict

this is obviously a problem
c'est de toute évidence un problème

amazingly enough, it was true
aussi incroyable que cela puisse paraître, c'était vrai

2 Les adverbes ayant la même forme que l'adjectif

Parmi ceux-ci on trouve :

far (lointain - loin), ***fast*** (rapide - vite), ***little*** (petit - peu), ***long*** (long - longtemps), ***early*** (en avance - tôt), ***only*** (seul - seulement)

et un certain nombre en **-ly** dérivés de noms (faisant souvent référence au temps), par exemple :

daily (quotidien - tous les jours), ***monthly*** (mensuel - tous les mois), ***weekly*** (hebdomadaire - toutes les semaines), ***deathly*** (cadavérique - comme la mort), ***leisurely*** (tranquille - sans se presser)

he travelled to far and distant lands (adjectif)
il a voyagé dans des pays lointains

he travelled far and wide (adverbe)
il a voyagé par monts et par vaux

this is a fast train (adjectif)
c'est un train rapide

you're driving too fast (adverbe)
vous roulez trop vite

he bought a little house (adjectif)
il a acheté une petite maison

little do you care! (adverbe)
ça t'importe peu !

Churchill loved those long cigars (adjectif)
Churchill aimait ces longs cigares

have you been here long? (adverbe)
vous êtes ici depuis longtemps ?

you'll have to catch the early plane (adjectif)
il faudra que tu prennes le premier avion

they arrived early (adverbe)
ils sont arrivés tôt

she's an only child (adjectif)
elle est fille unique

I've only got 10p (adverbe)
j'ai seulement 10p.

do you get a daily newspaper? (adjectif)
vous achetez un quotidien ?

there's a flight twice daily (adverbe)
il y a un vol deux fois par jour

you'll receive this in monthly instalments (adjectif)
vous le recevrez en versements mensuels

the list will be updated monthly (adverbe)
la liste sera mise à jour tous les mois

a deathly silence fell on the spectators (adjectif)
un silence de mort s'abattit sur les spectateurs

she was deathly pale (adverbe)
elle avait le teint blafard

we took a leisurely stroll after dinner (adjectif)
nous avons fait une promenade tranquille après le dîner

his favourite pastime is travelling leisurely along the Californian coast (adverb)
son passe-temps favori est de voyager à loisir le long de la côte californienne

3 La position de l'adverbe

a) *Les adverbes de temps*

i) S'ils font référence à un moment précis, on les place normalement en fin de phrase :

the shops close at 8 tonight
les magasins ferment à 8 heures ce soir

tonight the shops close at 8
ce soir les magasins ferment à 8 heures

will I see you tomorrow?
est-ce que je te vois demain ?

tomorrow it'll be too late
demain il sera trop tard

Mais le mot ***now*** (maintenant) précède souvent le verbe :

I now see the point
je vois maintenant ce que vous voulez dire

now I see the point
maintenant je vois ce que vous voulez dire

I see the point now
je vois ce que vous voulez dire maintenant

now is the time to make a decision
c'est maintenant le moment de prendre une décision

ii) Si l'on fait référence à un moment imprécis, on place normalement l'adverbe avant le verbe principal :

I always buy my shirts here
j'achète toujours mes chemises ici

we soon got to know him
on a bientôt appris à le connaître

we have often talked about it
on en a souvent parlé

they have frequently discussed such matters
ils ont fréquemment discuté de tels sujets

Mais de tels adverbes suivent normalement les formes du verbe ***to be*** :

he's never late
il n'est jamais en retard

he was frequently in trouble with the police
il avait souvent des problèmes avec la police

S'il y a plus d'un auxiliaire, ces adverbes ont tendance à précéder le deuxième. Pour les accentuer on peut les placer après le deuxième auxiliaire :

she has frequently been visited by distant relatives
des parents lointains lui ont fréquemment rendu visite

she has been frequently visited by distant relatives
fréquemment des parents lointains lui ont rendu visite

b) *Les adverbes de lieu*

Ils suivent le verbe (et le complément d'objet) :

they travelled everywhere
ils/elles ont voyagé partout

they have gone back
ils/elles sont retourné(e)s

I saw you there
je vous ai vu là-bas

Mais remarquez la position à l'initiale devant ***be*** :

there's the postman voilà le facteur

here are your books voici tes livres

et devant des pronoms personnels employés avec ***be, come*** et ***go*** :

there he is le voilà
here she comes la voilà (qui arrive)

c) *Les adverbes de manière*

i) Très souvent la position d'un adverbe de manière ne changera aucunement le sens de la phrase. On peut donc le placer où bon nous semble, suivant les nuances, ou le ton que l'on veut donner au discours :

they stealthily crept upstairs
they crept stealthily upstairs
they crept upstairs stealthily
ils ont monté les escaliers furtivement

steathily, they crept upstairs
furtivement, ils ont monté les escaliers

she carefully examined the report
she examined the report carefully
elle examina le rapport avec attention

it was beautifully done
it was done beautifully
ce fut très bien fait

Mais, dans certains cas, si l'on veut mettre l'accent sur l'adverbe, la position où il aura plus d'impact est en fin de phrase. Comparez par exemple :

he quickly wrote a postcard (and left)
il a rapidement écrit une carte (et il est parti)

he wrote a postcard quickly (which nobody could read)
il a écrit une carte en vitesse (qui était illisible)

Plus on met l'accent sur la manière, plus l'adverbe a des chances de suivre le verbe.

Dans la phrase suivante, une seule position est possible :

they fought the war intelligently
ils ont mené la guerre avec intelligence

ii) Si le complément d'objet direct est extrêmement long, on évite de placer l'adverbe en fin de phrase :

she carefully examined the report sent to her by the Minister
elle examina attentivement le rapport envoyé par le Ministre

iii) La position en tête de phrase est très descriptive et emphatique :

clumsily, he made his way towards the door
maladroitement, il se dirigea vers la porte

iv) Les adverbes modifiant les phrases et les adverbes modifiant les verbes :

Suivant la place qu'il a dans la phrase, l'adverbe va modifier la phrase entière ou bien le verbe seul :

Comparez les phrases suivantes :

she spoke wisely at the meeting
elle a parlé avec sagesse durant la réunion

she wisely spoke at the meeting
elle a eu la sagesse de parler à la réunion

Voici des exemples analogues :

she spoke naturally and fluently (modifie le verbe)
elle parla avec naturel et aisance

she naturally assumed it was right (modifie la phrase)
elle supposa naturellement que c'était vrai

naturally, she assumed it was right (modifie la phrase)
naturellement elle supposa que c'était vrai

she understood it clearly (modifie le verbe)
elle comprit cela clairement

she clearly understood it (modifie la phrase ou le verbe)
de toute évidence elle comprit cela
elle comprit cela clairement

clearly, she understood it (modifie la phrase)
de toute évidence elle le comprit

Le mot ***enough*** peut aussi s'employer après un adverbe pour marquer le fait que l'adverbe est employé pour modifier la phrase :

funnily (enough), they both spoke at the meeting
aussi drôle que cela puisse paraître, ils ont parlé tous les deux à la réunion

d) *Les adverbes d'intensité*

i) Si ceux-ci modifient des adverbes, des adjectifs ou des noms, ils précèdent ces mots :

she played extremely well
elle a joué extrêmement bien

this is very good
c'est très bien

it's too difficult to define
c'est trop difficile à définir

it's rather a shame
c'est bien dommage

ii) Sinon ils précèdent normalement le verbe principal :

I nearly forgot your anniversary
j'ai failli oublier ton anniversaire

I could hardly remember a thing
je pouvais à peine me souvenir de quoi que ce soit

I merely asked
j'ai tout simplement demandé

we just want to know the time of departure
nous voulons juste connaître l'heure du départ

we very much enjoyed your book
nous avons beaucoup apprécié votre livre

they also prefer white wine
ils/elles préfèrent aussi le vin blanc

Mais ***too*** (dans le sens de 'aussi') suit normalement les mots qu'il modifie :

you too should go and see the exhibition
toi aussi, tu devrais aller voir cette exposition

you should try to see that exhibition too
tu devrais aussi aller voir cette exposition

iii) only (seulement)

Cet adverbe pose rarement des difficultés en anglais parlé, car l'accentuation et l'intonation révèlent son sens :

(a) ***Bill only saw Bob today***
Bill a seulement vu Bob (mais il ne lui a pas parlé)

(b) ***Bill only saw Bob today***
Bill n'a vu que Bob aujourd'hui (il n'a vu personne d'autre)

(c) ***Bill only saw Bob today***
Bill n'a vu Bob qu'aujourd'hui (il l'a vu seulement aujourd'hui/aujourd'hui seulement)

Mais de telles différences sont obscures dans la langue écrite, à moins que le contexte ne soit clair. Ainsi dans (b) dans la langue écrite, on changerait la place de l'adverbe de la façon suivante :

Bill saw only Bob today
Bill n'a vu que Bob aujourd'hui

et (c) deviendrait :

it was only today that Bill saw Bob
ce n'est qu'aujourd'hui que Bill a vu Bob

Dans (a), on écrirait probablement le mot accentué en italique :

Bill only *saw* Bob today
Bill n'a fait que voir Bob aujourd'hui

iv) very ou ***much*** ? (très/beaucoup)

★ Devant des adjectifs dans leur forme de base, on emploie ***very*** :

these are very fine
ils sont très beaux

ainsi que devant des superlatifs en ***-est*** :

these are the very finest copies I've seen
ce sont les plus belles copies que j'aie jamais vues

Cependant, dans la construction au superlatif qui suit, ***much*** s'emploie devant ***the*** du superlatif :

this is much the best example in the book
c'est de loin le meilleur exemple du livre

★ Le comparatif est accompagné de ***much*** :

she's much taller than you
elle est bien plus grande que toi

she's much more particular
elle est beaucoup plus pointilleuse

★ Il en est de même avec les adverbes :

you do it very well, but I do it much better
tu le fais très bien, mais je le fais bien mieux

★ Les verbes sont accompagnés de ***much*** (qui est lui-même modifié par ***very***) :

I love you very much
je t'aime énormément

★ Avant les participes passés :

S'ils ont la fonction d'adjectif, on emploie ***very*** :

I'm very tired
je suis très fatigué

we're very interested in this house
nous sommes très intéressés par cette maison

they became very offended
ils se sont beaucoup offensés

they sat there, all very agitated
ils étaient assis là, tous très agités

I'm very pleased to meet you
je suis très heureux de vous rencontrer

these suitcases are looking very used
ces valises paraissent très usagées

Mais s'ils ne sont pas considérés comme adjectifs en tant que tels, ou s'ils gardent leur fonction verbale, on emploie alors ***much*** :

this has been much spoken about (pas ***very***)
on en a beacoup parlé

these suitcases haven't been much used (pas ***very***)
ces valises n'ont pas été très utilisées

he has been much maligned (pas ***very***)
on l'a beaucoup diffamé

they were much taken aback by the reception they received (aussi ***very***)
ils ont été époustouflés par l'accueil qu'on leur a réservé

his new house is much admired by people round here (pas ***very***)
les gens du coin ont beaucoup d'admiration pour sa nouvelle maison

Dans un langage familier, on préfère employer ***a lot*** que ***much***, en particulier à la forme affirmative :

these haven't been used a lot
ceux-ci n'ont pas été beaucoup utilisés

v) enough

Lorsqu'il est employé comme adverbe, ***enough*** se place après l'adjectif :

he isn't big enough for that yet
il n'est pas encore assez grand pour ça

On l'emploie aussi après un nom employé comme adjectif attribut :

he isn't man enough for the job
il n'a pas la carrure suffisante pour ce travail

Remarquez que ***enough*** peut séparer l'adjectif du nom :

it's a decent enough town
c'est pas mal comme ville

e) *Les adverbes modifiant toute la phrase*

i) On a beaucoup de choix quant à la position dans la phrase. Voir plus haut sous ***les adverbes de manière***, pp A23-4. Voici quelques exemples de phrases modifiées par des adverbes qui ne sont pas des adverbes de manière :

probably that isn't true
that probably isn't true
ceci n'est probablement pas vrai

fortunately, he stopped in time
heureusement, il s'est arrêté à temps

he fortunately stopped in time
il s'est heureusement arrêté à temps

he stopped in time, fortunately
il s'est arrêté à temps, heureusement

f) *La place de* ***not***

i) Not précède le groupe adverbial qu'il modifie :

is he here? – not yet
est-il ici ? – pas encore

do you mind? – not at all
ça ne te dérange pas ? – pas du tout

he speaks not only English, but also French
il parle non seulement anglais, mais aussi français

he lives not far from here
il n'habite pas loin d'ici

Dans l'exemple suivant, c'est ***absolutely*** (absolument) qui qualifie ***not***, et pas le contraire :

have you said something to her? – absolutely not
tu lui a dit quelque chose ? – absolument pas

ii) Not suit le verbe ***be*** :

he is not hungry
il n'a pas faim

iii) Puisque ***do*** s'emploie lorsque le verbe principal est à la forme négative, il y a toujours au moins un auxiliaire à cette forme. ***Not*** (ou ***-n't***) suit normalement le premier auxiliaire :

he does not smoke/he doesn't smoke
il ne fume pas

they would not have seen her/they wouldn't have seen her
ils ne l'auraient pas vue

Mais dans des questions, la forme complète de ***not*** suit le sujet, tandis que ***-n't*** le précède, étant lié à l'auxiliaire :

did they not shout abuse at her?
didn't they shout abuse at her?
est-ce qu'ils ne lui ont pas lancé des insultes ?

have they not shouted abuse at her?
haven't they shouted abuse at her?
est-ce qu'ils ne lui ont pas lancé des insultes ?

iv) En américain, ***not*** peut précéder un subjonctif :

it is important that he not be informed of this
il est important qu'il ne soit pas informé de cela

v) Remarquez aussi ce qui suit :

did you do it? – not me
tu l'as fait ? – non, c'est pas moi

will she come? – I hope not
est-ce qu'elle viendra ? – j'espère que non

Ici ***not*** est la négation de ***will come*** (***I hope she won't come*** j'espère qu'elle ne viendra pas)

6 Les Pronoms Personnels

	Singulier	*Pluriel*
1ère	**I/me**	**we/us**
2ème	**you**	**you**
3ème	**he/him, she/her, it**	**they/them**

Voir p A73 pour l'ordre des pronoms personnels dans une phrase.

Dans le tableau ci-dessus la première forme de chaque paire est la forme du sujet, la seconde celle des autres emplois :

she's not here yet (sujet)
elle n'est pas encore là

Jane didn't see her (complément d'objet direct)
Jane ne l'a pas vue

Jane wrote her a letter (complément d'objet indirect)
Jane lui a écrit une lettre

it's her! — c'est elle !
with/for her — avec/pour elle

You correspond à toutes les formes de la deuxième personne française 'tu, vous' au singulier et au pluriel.

a) *Sujet ou complément ?*

i) Habituellement, les formes sujets (**I**, **you**, **he**, **she**, **we**, **they**) sont utilisées comme sujets. Des phrases comme :

me and the wife are always there
ma femme et moi, nous sommes toujours là

sont incorrectes, bien qu'elles soient souvent entendues. Mais en anglais, on utilise souvent la forme complément (**me**, **him**, **her**, **us**, **them**) là où en français on utilise les formes 'moi, toi', etc. :

who is it? – it's me
qui est-ce ? – c'est moi

who did it? – me (ou **I did**)
qui a fait cela ? – moi

It is I/he/she, etc. seraient considérés d'une politesse presque ridicule.

Cependant, si une proposition relative suit, les formes sujets sont assez courantes à condition que le pronom relatif ait une fonction de sujet; on dira :

it was I who did it

ou :

it was me that did it (familier)
c'est moi qui l'ai fait

mais toujours :

it was me (that) you spoke to
c'est à moi que vous avez parlé

La forme sujet **I** est fréquente dans la phrase **between you and I** (entre vous et moi). Cet emploi incorrect est décrié par les puristes qui lui préfèrent **between you and me**. Voir plus loin à **Pronoms réfléchis**, p A29.

ii) On place généralement la forme complément après **than** et **as** (si aucun verbe ne suit) :

she's not as good as him, but better than me
elle n'est pas aussi bonne que lui, mais meilleure que moi

mais, si un verbe suit :

she's not as good as he is, but better than I am
elle n'est pas aussi bonne que lui, mais meilleure que moi

Cependant, dans un style plus soutenu, la forme sujet peut être placée en position finale après **than** et **as**, et surtout après **than** :

he is a better man than I
c'est un homme meilleur que moi

b) *Omission du pronom sujet*

En général on n'omet pas le pronom sujet en anglais - il existe cependant, comme partout, quelques exceptions :

i) Omission de ***it*** :

Dans un registre familier, le pronom à la troisième personne du singulier **it** peut être omis dans des usages comme :

looks like rain this afternoon
on dirait qu'il va pleuvoir cet après-midi

what do you think of it? – sounds/smells good
qu'est-ce que tu en penses ? – ça a l'air/sent bon

Mais ce n'est pas une caractéristique que l'on peut appliquer à n'importe quel autre exemple.

ii) Emplois particuliers :

Les pronoms peuvent être omis quand plus d'un verbe suit le sujet :

I know the place well, go there once a week, even thought about moving there
je connais bien cet endroit, j'y vais une fois par semaine, j'ai même pensé m'y installer

iii) Impératif :

A l'impératif, bien sûr, on omet les pronoms sujets :

don't do that!
ne fais pas cela !

Mais on peut les utiliser pour renforcer le sens de l'impératif (par exemple, pour proférer une menace) :

don't you do that!
ne fais donc pas ça, toi !

c) ***He, she*** *ou* ***it*** *?*

He (**him**, **his**) ou **she** (**her**) sont parfois employés pour désigner autres choses que des personnes, c.-à-d. des animaux et certains objets. Dans ce cas, on montre que le locuteur a une relation assez intime avec la chose ou l'animal en question, ou qu'il montre un intérêt tout particulier envers cette chose ou envers cet animal. Autrement, on emploie **it**.

i) Animaux :

Fluffy is getting on: she probably won't give birth to any more kittens
Fluffy vieillit, elle n'aura sans doute plus de chatons

the poor old dog, take him for a walk, can't you!
le pauvre vieux toutou, tu veux bien l'emmener faire une promenade ?

mais :

a dog's senses are very keen; it can hear much higher frequencies than we can

les sens des chiens sont très développés; ils peuvent percevoir des fréquences bien plus élevées que nous

ii) Moyens de transport :

On utilisera en général le féminin **she**, à moins d'une raison particulière (qui peut être tout à fait personnelle) :

she's been a long way, this old car
elle en a fait du chemin, cette vieille voiture

there she is! - the Titanic in all her glory!
le voilà - le Titanic dans toute sa splendeur !

mais :

this ship is larger than that one, and it has an extra funnel
ce bateau est plus grand que celui-là, et il a une cheminée de plus

The Flying Scotsman will soon have made his/her last journey
le 'Flying Scotsman' fera bientôt son dernier voyage (à propos du train)

iii) Pays :

and Denmark? - she will remember those who died for her
et le Danemark ? - il se souviendra de ceux qui sont morts pour lui

mais :

Denmark is a small country; it is almost surrounded by water
le Danemark est un petit pays ; il est presque entièrement entouré d'eau

d) ***It*** *sans référence*

i) Comme en français, on peut utiliser en anglais le pronom impersonnel ***it*** pour parler du temps, donner des jugements et décrire des situations, etc. :

it's raining
il pleut

it's freezing in here
on se gèle ici

what's it like outside today?
il fait quel temps dehors aujourd'hui ?

it's very cosy here
c'est très confortable ici

it's wrong to steal
il ne faut pas voler

it's not easy to raise that sort of money
ce n'est pas facile de trouver une telle somme d'argent

it's clear they don't like it
il est clair que ça ne leur plaît pas

it looks as if/seems/appears that they've left
on dirait qu'ils sont partis

Et aussi pour faire référence à un point précis dans l'espace ou dans le temps :

it's ten o'clock
il est dix heures

it's June the tenth
c'est le 10 Juin

it's time to go
il est temps de partir

it's at least three miles
ça fait au moins 4 kilomètres

Mais si on évoque la durée, on emploie ***there*** :

there's still time to mend matters
il reste du temps pour réparer les choses

Remarquez aussi la phrase ***it says*** (on dit) pour faire référence à un texte :

it says in today's Times that a hurricane is on its way
on dit dans le 'Times' d'aujourd'hui qu'un ouragan se dirige sur nous

ii) It peut aussi être utilisé d'une façon impersonnelle, surtout dans des expressions toutes faites :

that's it! (that's right)
c'est ça !

she thinks she's it (familier)
elle s'y croit

beat it! (familier)
va-t'en !

she has it in for him (familier)
elle a une dent contre lui

e) *Emploi collectif*

You, **we** et **they** sont souvent employés d'une façon collective pour désigner 'les gens en général'. La différence entre ces trois termes se résume au fait que si **you** est employé, la personne à laquelle on s'adresse fait normalement partie des 'gens', alors que si le locuteur emploie **we**, il renforce le fait qu'il est lui-même inclus dans ces 'gens'. **They** fait référence aux *autres* gens en général :

you don't see many prostitutes in Aberdeen any more
on ne voit plus beaucoup de prostituées à Aberdeen

I'm afraid we simply don't treat animals very well
j'ai bien peur qu'on ne traite pas les animaux très bien

they say he beats his wife
on dit qu'il bat sa femme

***i)* You** employé pour faire une remarque sur une situation :

you never can find one when you need one
on n'en trouve jamais quand on en a besoin

you never can be too careful
on n'est jamais trop prudent

***ii)* You** employé pour donner des instructions :

you first crack the eggs into a bowl
cassez d'abord les œufs dans un saladier

you must look both ways before crossing
il faut regarder des deux côtés de la route avant de traverser

Voir aussi **one** p A28.

f) *Emplois particuliers de* **we**

En dehors de l'emploi collectif de **we** (voir e) ci-dessus), il convient de noter deux autres emplois :

i) le 'nous' de majesté (= je), comme on le trouve dans la célèbre remarque de la Reine Victoria :

we are not amused
nous ne trouvons pas cela drôle

ii) le 'nous' de condescendance ou ironique (= tu, vous), très fréquemment utilisé par les professeurs et par les infirmières :

and how are we today, Mr Jenkins?, could we eat just a teeny-weeny portion of porridge?
et comment nous portons-nous aujourd'hui, M.Jenkins ? allons-nous manger un tout petit peu de porridge ?

I see, Smith, forgotten our French homework, have we?
alors, Smith, on a oublié ses exercices de français, n'est-ce pas ?

g) *Emploi de* ***they***

i) L'emploi de **they** collectif est devenu très courant, pour renvoyer à **somebody**, **someone**, **anybody**, **anyone**, **everybody**, **everyone**, **nobody**, **no one**. Le **they** collectif évite le **he or she** maladroit (parfois écrit **s/he**).

Certains considèrent malheureux l'emploi de **he** seul comme pronom collectif mis pour 'les gens'. Le **they (their, them(selves))** collectif est maintenant courant dans l'anglais parlé et parfois écrit (même si on ne fait référence qu'à un sexe) et offre un moyen pratique d'éviter de s'exprimer d'une façon qui pourrait être jugée sexiste :

if anybody has anything against it, they should say so
si certains sont contre, qu'ils le disent

everybody grabbed their possessions and ran
tout le monde a ramassé ses affaires et s'est enfui

somebody has left their bike right outside the door
quelqu'un a laissé son vélo juste devant la porte

Cet emploi est de plus en plus courant avec des noms précédés non seulement par **any**, **some** ou **no**, mais aussi par l'article indéfini collectif :

some person or other has tampered with my files - they'll be sorry
quelqu'un a touché à mes dossiers sans permission - il va le regretter

no child is allowed to leave until they have been seen by a doctor
aucun enfant ne pourra sortir avant d'avoir été examiné par un médecin

a person who refuses to use a deodorant may find themselves quietly shunned at parties
les gens qui refusent de se mettre du déodorant risquent de se trouver un peu seul pendant des soirées

Pour l'emploi de **one**, voir h) ci-dessous.

ii) **They** est employé pour faire référence à une (ou à plusieurs) personne(s) que l'on ne connaît pas, mais qui représente(nt) l'autorité, le pouvoir, le savoir :

they will have to arrest the entire pit
on va devoir arrêter la mine toute entière

they should be able to repair it
ils devraient pouvoir le réparer

they will be able to tell you at the advice centre
on pourra vous renseigner au bureau d'information

when you earn a bit of money they always find a way of taking it off you
quand on gagne un peu d'argent, ils trouvent toujours un moyen pour vous en prélever

De cet emploi est née l'expression 'them and us' (eux et nous) qui fait référence à ceux qui ont le pouvoir (eux), et ceux qui ne l'ont pas (nous).

h) ***One*** *collectif*

One est employé comme un sujet et comme un complément d'objet. La forme possessive est **one's**.

i) Si **one** est collectif, le locuteur s'inclut dans 'les gens en général' :

well, what can one do?
eh bien, qu'est-ce qu'on peut faire ?

one is not supposed to do that
on n'est pas censé faire ça

One offre un moyen pratique d'éviter les erreurs d'interprétation de **you** comme dans :

you need to express yourself more clearly
tu dois t'exprimer plus clairement

Pour être plus précis, un locateur désirant énoncer une généralité, et non pas faire référence à un individu en particulier, préferera utiliser la phrase suivante :

one needs to express oneself more clearly
il faut s'exprimer plus clairement

Cependant, on évite habituellement d'employer ce pronom d'une façon excessive ou répétitive.

ii) L'emploi de **one** pour la première personne, c.-à-d. à la place de **I** (je) ou **we** (nous), est maintenant considéré précieux :

seeing such misery has taught one to appreciate how lucky one is in one's own country
le spectacle de tant de misère nous a appris à apprécier la chance que nous avons de vivre dans notre pays

one doesn't like to be deprived of one's little pleasures, does one?
on ne se prive de rien, n'est-ce pas ?

En anglais américain, le pronom à la troisième personne au masculin peut suivre un **one** collectif :

one shouldn't take risks if he can avoid it
on ne devrait pas prendre de risques si on peut l'éviter

i) ***It*** *ou* ***so*** *?*

Comparez :

(a) **she managed to escape – I can quite believe it**
elle a réussi à s'échapper – je le crois bien

(b) **did she manage to escape? – I believe so**
est-elle parvenue à s'échapper ? – oui, je le pense

La conviction est plus forte en (a) où on est presque convaincu. En (b) la croyance est plus vague et on pourrait remplacer **believe** (croire) par **think** (penser). De même, **it** représente quelque chose de précis, mais **so** est plus vague. Voici d'autres exemples où **it/so** font référence à une affirmation précédente :

it's a difficult job, but I can do it
c'est difficile, mais je peux le faire

you promised to call me but didn't (do so)
tu avais promis de m'appeler, mais tu ne l'as pas fait

you're a thief ! there, I've said it
tu es un voleur ! voilà, je l'ai dit

you're a thief ! – if you say so
tu es un voleur ! – puisque tu le dis

D'autres verbes qui prennent souvent **so** : **expect**, **hope**, **seem**, **suppose**, **tell** :

has he left? – it seems so
il est parti ? – on dirait bien

I knew it would happen, I told you so
je savais que ça arriverait, je vous l'avais dit

7 Les Pronoms Réfléchis

	Singulier	*Pluriel*
1ère	**myself** (moi-même)	**ourselves**
2ème	**yourself**	**yourselves**
3ème	**himself, herself, itself, oneself**	**themselves**

a) Employé comme attribut, complément d'objet direct, complément d'objet indirect et après des prépositions pour renvoyer au sujet :

I am not myself today (attribut)
je ne me sens pas bien aujourd'hui

she has burnt herself (complément d'objet direct)
elle s'est brûlée

we gave ourselves a little treat (complément d'objet indirect)
nous nous sommes offert une petite gâterie

why are you talking to yourself? (après une préposition)
pourquoi parles-tu tout seul ?

Mais lorsqu'on évoque l'espace ou la direction, (au sens propre ou au sens figuré) les pronoms personnels sont souvent préférés après une préposition :

we have a long day in front of us
nous avons une longue journée devant nous

she put her bag beside her
elle a posé son sac à côté d'elle

have you got any cash on you?
avez-vous du liquide sur vous ?

she married beneath her
elle s'est déclassée en se mariant

he has his whole life before him
il a toute la vie devant lui

mais toujours **beside + -self** dans un sens figuré :

they were beside themselves with worry
ils étaient dévorés d'inquiétude

b) *Emploi d'intensité*

Lorsque le locuteur souhaite donner une certaine intensité à quelque chose dont il parle, il emploie souvent un pronom réfléchi :

you're quite well-off now, aren't you? – you haven't done so badly yourself
tu es plutôt riche, n'est-ce pas ? – tu ne t'es pas si mal débrouillé toi-même

only they themselves know whether it is the right thing to do
eux seuls savent si c'est la bonne chose à faire

get me a beer, will you? – get it yourself
tu vas me chercher une bière, s'il te plaît ? – va te la chercher tout seul

for the work to be done properly, one has to do it oneself
pour bien faire ce travail, il faut le faire soi-même

La position du pronom réfléchi peut modifier le sens de la phrase :

the Prime Minister wanted to speak to him herself
le Premier Ministre a voulu lui parler elle-même

mais :

the Prime Minister herself wanted to speak to him
le Premier Ministre elle-même a voulu lui parler (c.-à-d. que pas moins qu'elle a voulu lui parler)

c) *Après **as**, **like**, **than** et **and***

Après ces mots, il est très courant qu'on utilise les pronoms réfléchis au lieu des pronoms personnels, parfois parce qu'on hésite entre la forme de sujet et la forme de complément (voir **Les Pronoms Personnels** p A26) :

he's not quite as old as myself
il n'est pas aussi âgé que moi

like yourself, I also have a few family problems
comme vous, j'ai aussi mes problèmes familiaux

this job needs people more experienced than ourselves
ce travail demande des gens plus qualifiés que nous

he said it was reserved specially for you and myself
il a dit que ça nous était spécialement réservé, a toi et à moi

d) *Verbes réfléchis*

i) Quelques rares verbes ne sont que réfléchis, par exemple : **absent oneself** (s'absenter), **avail oneself of** (utiliser), **betake oneself** (se rendre), **demean oneself** (s'abaisser), **ingratiate oneself** (se faire bien voir), **perjure oneself** (se parjurer), **pride oneself** (se fier).

ii) D'autres ont des significations totalement différentes lorsqu'ils sont réfléchis et lorsqu'ils ne le sont pas :

he applied for the post
il a posé sa candidature pour le poste

he should apply himself more to his studies
il devrait se consacrer davantage à ses études

iii) Et il existe plusieurs verbes dont le sens demeure le même que le verbe soit réfléchi ou non :

they always behave (themselves) in public
ils se conduisent toujours bien en public

we found it very difficult to adjust (ourselves) to the humid climate
nous avons trouvé très difficile de nous adapter au climat humide

Notez que l'élément réfléchi peut ajouter un sens de détermination. Comparez :

(a) **he proved to be useful**
il a fini par être utile

(b) **so as not to face redundancy, he'll have to prove himself more useful**
pour éviter le licenciement, il devra se montrer plus utile

(c) **the crowd pushed forward**
la foule avançait

(d) **the crowd pushed itself forward**
la foule s'avançait

Dans l'exemple (d), il y a plus de détermination que dans l'exemple (c).

8 Les Possessifs

a) *Les adjectifs*

	Singulier	*Pluriel*
1ère	**my** (mon, ma, mes)	**our** (notre, nos)
2ème	**your** (ton, ta, tes; votre, vos)	**your** (votre, vos)
3ème	**his** (son, sa, ses)	**their** (leur, leurs)
	her (son, sa, ses)	
	its (son, sa, ses)	

Les pronoms

	Singulier	*Pluriel*
1ère	**mine** (le mien, etc.)	**ours**
2ème	**yours**	**yours**
3ème	**his, hers, its**	**theirs**

Remarquez qu'à la troisième personne du singulier il y a trois formes que l'on utilise selon que le possesseur est du sexe masculin ou féminin ou qu'il est neutre. Il est important de se souvenir qu'il n'existe pas de genres grammaticaux en anglais et que le choix entre **his/her** dépend uniquement du sexe du possesseur. Pour les objets et les animaux on emploie **its** (voir ci-dessous) :

who is that man? what is his name?
qui est cet homme ? quel est son nom ?

who is that woman? what is her name?
qui est cette femme ? quel est son nom ?

what street is this? what is its name?
quelle est cette rue ? quel est son nom ?

Dans les cas où l'on emploie **he** ou **she** pour des animaux ou pour des objets (voir **Les Pronoms Personnels** pp A26-7), on emploie les possessifs correspondants :

our dog's hurt his/its paw
notre chien s'est fait mal à la patte

the lion is hunting its prey
le lion chasse sa proie

Voici d'autres exemples :

they've bought their tickets/they've bought theirs
ils/elles ont acheté leurs tickets/ils/elles ont acheté les leurs

ours is much older/ours are much older
le/la nôtre est beaucoup plus vieux/vieille/les nôtres sont beaucoup plus vieux/vieilles

Remarquez le 'double génitif' (comparez à p A16) :

he's an old friend of mine
c'est un de mes anciens amis

that mother of hers is driving me mad
sa mère à elle me rend fou

b) *Adjectif possessif ou article ?*

On utilise en anglais un adjectif possessif où, très souvent, en français on préfère utiliser l'article défini. C'est souvent le cas lorsqu'on parle du corps ou des vêtements :

he put his hands behind his back
il a mis les mains derrière le dos

she's broken her leg **my head is spinning**
elle s'est cassé la jambe j'ai la tête qui tourne

what have you got in your pockets?
qu'est-ce que tu as dans les poches ?

Dans une phrase utilisant une préposition, l'article défini est généralement employé (bien que l'adjectif possessif soit aussi possible) :

he grabbed her by the waist
il l'a attrapée par la taille

he was punched on the nose
il a reçu un coup de poing dans le nez

Mais si le mot qui désigne une certaine partie du corps est lui-même qualifié par un adjectif, alors l'adjectif possessif, et non l'article, est utilisé :

he grabbed her by her slim little waist
il l'a attrapée par sa petite taille mince

Voir aussi **Le Pluriel Distributif** dans la section **Les Noms**, p A14.

9 Les Démonstratifs

Singulier	*Pluriel*
this, that	**these, those**

Les formes sont les mêmes pour l'adjectif démonstratif (ce, cette, ces, etc.) et le pronom démonstratif (celui-ci, celle-ci, celle-là, etc.).

a) This et **these** renvoient à quelque chose qui se trouve **près** du locuteur, ou qui a un rapport **immédiat** avec le locuteur, alors que **that** et **those** ont un rapport plus distant avec lui. **This/these** sont à **here/now** ce que **that/those** sont à **there/then** :

(a) **this red pen is mine; that one is yours**
ce crayon rouge-ci est le mien ; celui-là est le tien

(b) **that red pen is mine; this one is yours**
ce crayon rouge-là est le mien ; celui-ci est le tien

En (a) le crayon rouge se trouve plus près du locuteur que l'autre crayon ; en (b) c'est le contraire.

Autres exemples :

I want to go – you can't mean that
je veux partir – tu ne veux pas dire ça !

this is what I want you to do ...
voici ce que je veux que tu fasses ...

in those days it wasn't possible
à cette époque-là ce n'était pas possible

what are these (knobs) for?
à quoi servent ceux-ci/ces boutons ?

this is Christine, is that Joanna? (au téléphone)
ici Christine, c'est Joanna ?

Quand ils sont pronoms, les démonstratifs ne peuvent pas renvoyer à des personnes, sauf s'ils sont sujets ou attributs :

this is Carla **who is this?**
c'est Carla qui est-ce ?

Ainsi dans :

would you take this?
tu veux bien prendre ça ?

this ne peut pas désigner une personne.

b) ***this/these*** *indéfinis*

L'emploi de **this/these** comme pronoms indéfinis est très courant en l'anglais familier parlé, quand on raconte une histoire, une blague par exemple :

this Irishman was sitting in a pub when ...
un Irlandais était assis dans un pub quand ...

the other day these guys came up to me ...
l'autre jour, des types se sont approchés de moi ...

c) ***that/this*** *adverbes*

En anglais parlé, **that/this** sont souvent utilisés comme des adverbes, dans un sens proche de **so** (si), avant un adjectif ou avant un autre adverbe :

I like a red carpet but not one that red
j'aime bien les tapis rouges, mais pas aussi rouge que ça

I don't like doing it that/this often
je n'aime pas le faire si souvent

now that we've come this far, we might just as well press on
puisqu'on est allé jusque là, autant continuer

I don't want that/this much to eat!
je veux pas manger autant que ça !

she doesn't want to marry him, she's not that stupid
elle ne veut pas se marier avec lui, elle n'est pas si stupide

10 Les Interrogatifs

who/whom/whose, which, what et toutes les formes combinées avec **-ever**, par exemple : **whichever**

On distingue l'emploi adjectif de l'emploi pronom :

which do you want? (pronom)
lequel veux-tu ?

which flavour do you want? (adjectif)
quel parfum veux-tu ?

Remarquez qu'ils sont invariables. Le premier exemple pourrait tout aussi bien se traduire par 'laquelle/lesquels/lesquelles veux-tu ?'

a) *Who et whom*

Who et **whom** sont toujours des pronoms (c.-à-d. qu'ils ne sont jamais suivis par un nom) et ils renvoient à des personnes :

who are you?
qui êtes-vous ?

to whom were your remarks addressed?
à qui s'adressaient vos remarques ?

Whom est utilisé dans un style soutenu, lorsqu'il est complément d'objet (direct ou indirect) ou qu'il suit une préposition :

whom did she embrace?
qui a-t-elle embrassé ?

to whom did he give his permission?
à qui a-t-il donné la permission ?

I demanded to know to whom he had spoken
ou :
I demanded to know whom he had spoken to
j'ai exigé de savoir à qui il avait parlé

En anglais parlé d'aujourd'hui, **who** est normalement utilisé pour toutes les fonctions. (**Whom** est obligatoire directement **après** une préposition, mais ce genre de tournure n'est pas très employé en anglais parlé d'aujourd'hui.) Par exemple :

who did you see at the party?
qui as-tu vu à la soirée ?

I want to know who you spoke to just now
I want to know to whom you spoke just now (style soutenu)
je veux savoir avec qui tu étais en train de parler

b) *whose*

C'est la forme au génitif de **who**. Il peut être pronom ou adjectif :

whose are these bags?	**whose bags are these?**
à qui sont ces sacs ?	ce sont les sacs de qui ?

c) *which/what*

Au contraire de **who(m)**, **which** peut être adjectif ou pronom, et peut renvoyer à une personne ou à un objet :

which actor do you mean?
de quel acteur parles-tu ?

which of the actors do you mean?
duquel des acteurs parles-tu ?

of these two recordings, which do you prefer?
de ces deux enregistrements, lequel préfères-tu ?

which recording do you prefer?
quel enregistrement préfères-tu ?

La différence entre **which** et **who/what** est que **which** est limitatif : il invite celui à qui on parle à faire un choix parmi un certain nombre de choses précises.

Comparez :

what would you like to drink?
qu'est-ce que tu veux boire ?

I've got coffee or tea – which would you like?
j'ai du café ou du thé – qu'est-ce que tu veux ?

Si l'objet du choix n'est pas identifié avant la question, on ne peut employer que **what** :

what would you like to drink? I've got sherry or vermouth or Campari
qu'est-ce que tu veux boire ? j'ai du sherry, du vermouth ou du Campari

d) *what*

Lorsqu'il est un pronom, **what** ne renvoie jamais à une personne :

what is this object?
qu'est-ce que c'est que cet objet ?

don't ask me what I did
ne me demande pas ce que j'ai fait

sauf si on fait référence à des caractéristiques personnelles :

and this one here, what is he? - he's German
et celui-ci, qu'est-ce qu'il est ? - c'est un Allemand

Lorsqu'il est adjectif, **what** peut renvoyer à une personne, à un animal ou à une chose :

what child does not like sweets?
quel enfant n'aime pas les bonbons ?

what kind of powder do you use?
quelle sorte de lessive utilisez-vous ?

Pour la différence entre **which** et **what**, voir c) ci-dessus.

Remarquez l'emploi de **what** dans les exclamations :

what awful weather!
quel temps affreux !

what a dreadful day!
quelle journée épouvantable !

what must they think!
qu'est-ce qu'ils doivent penser !

e) *Avec -ever*

Le suffixe **-ever** exprime la surprise, la confusion ou l'ennui, l'agacement :

whatever do you mean? (confusion ou ennui)
qu'est-ce que tu veux dire ?

whoever would have thought that? (surprise)
qui donc aurait pu penser cela ?

whatever did you do that for? (ennui, agacement)
pourquoi as-tu donc fait ça ?

11 Les Relatifs

who/whom/whose, **which**, **what**, **that** et toutes les formes combinées avec **-ever**, par exemple : **whichever**.

a) Les pronoms relatifs (sauf **what**) ont en général un antécédent auquel ils se rapportent. Dans :

> **she spoke to the man who/that sat beside her**
> elle a parlé à l'homme qui s'était assis à côté d'elle

who/that est le pronom relatif et **the man** l'antécédent.

b) *Déterminative et explicative*

Une proposition relative peut être déterminative ou explicative. Si elle est déterminative, elle est **nécessaire** au sens de la phrase complète par le lien qui l'unit à l'antécédent. Si elle est explicative, elle a un rapport moins étroit avec l'antécédent. Une proposition explicative a un rôle similaire à une parenthèse. Par exemple :

> **he helped the woman who had called out**
> il aida la femme qui avait appelé au secours

Cette phrase peut vouloir dire deux choses : (1) 'il aida la femme qui avait appelé au secours et non celle qui ne l'avait pas fait' ; ou (2) 'il aida la femme (qui, par ailleurs, avait appelé au secours)'.

Dans le sens (1), on a une proposition relative déterminative : on définit la femme comme celle qui avait appelé au secours.

Dans le sens (2), la femme a déjà été évoquée et définie dans la conversation, et la proposition relative n'apporte pas d'éléments majeurs à la phrase ; elle ne fait que donner une information supplémentaire, mais pas nécessaire.

Il n'est pas tout à fait exact, cependant, de dire que la phrase comme on l'a donnée plus haut peut avoir deux significations : les propositions relatives explicatives *devraient* être précédées d'une virgule, les propositions relatives déterminatives jamais. Ainsi, dans cette phrase, la proposition relative est déterminative. La proposition explicative serait :

> **he helped the woman, who had called out**
> il aida la femme, qui avait appelé au secours

Il est évident que l'emploi des propositions déterminatives n'a de sens que s'il existe deux possibilités ou plus. C'est-à-dire qu'une proposition relative qui a un antécédent exclusif comme **my parents** (je n'ai que deux parents, et je n'ai pas besoin de préciser ou déterminer lesquels) est toujours explicative :

> **my parents, who returned last night, are very worried**
> mes parents, qui sont rentrés hier soir, sont très inquiets

> **he went to Godalming, which is a place I don't much care for**
> il est allé à Godalming, qui n'est pas un endroit que j'apprécie particulièrement

Le pronom relatif **that** est employé uniquement avec des propositions relatives déterminatives. **Who** et **which** peuvent être utilisés dans les deux cas.

c) ***who/whom/that***

Who ou **that** sont utilisés comme sujets (qui) :

> **the girl who/that rescued him got a medal**
> la fille qui l'a sauvé a reçu une médaille

Who(m) ou **that** sont utilisés comme compléments (que) :

> **the man who(m)/that she rescued was a tourist**
> l'homme qu'elle a sauvé était un touriste

Whom est utilisé dans un style plus soutenu. Pour plus de renseignements, voir **Les Interrogatifs**, p A31.

d) ***who/which/that***

***i)* who/that**

Ces formes renvoient à des personnes ou à des animaux dont il a été question dans la section **Les Pronoms Personnels** c) ci-dessus, p A26 :

> **we ignored the people who/that were late**
> nous n'avons pas tenu compte des gens qui étaient en retard

> **the mouse did not get past Fluffy, who had it in her jaws in no time**
> la souris ne put pas s'échapper à Fluffy, qui la prit dans sa gueule en un éclair

Remarquez que **who** uniquement et non **that** peut être employé dans le second exemple, qui est une proposition relative explicative, voir b) ci-dessus.

Pour les noms collectifs, si l'on veut leur donner un caractère individuel, on emploie **who** ou **that**. Si l'on considère le groupe d'une manière moins personnelle, on emploie **which** ou **that** :

> **the crowd who/that had gathered were in great spirits** (aspect personnalisé)
> la foule qui s'était rassemblée était très enthousiaste

> **the crowd which/that had gathered was enormous** (aspect collectif)
> la foule qui s'était rassemblée était énorme

De même pour les noms de sociétés et ceux des grands magasins :

> **try Harrods who, I'm sure, will order it for you** (aspect personnalisé)
> va voir chez Harrods qui, j'en suis sûr, le commandera pour toi

> **you'll find it in Harrods, which is a gigantic store** (aspect non personnalisé)
> tu le trouveras chez Harrods, qui est un magasin gigantesque

***ii)* which/that**

Which ou **that** ne sont pas utilisés pour désigner des personnes :

> **the car which/that drove into me**
> la voiture qui m'est rentrée dedans

> **the disks which/that I sent you**
> les disquettes que je t'ai envoyées

Attention : bien que les pronoms personnels puissent être utilisés pour des moyens de transport, comme on l'a vu pp A26-7, cette possibilité de personnalisation ne s'applique pas aux pronoms relatifs.

e) ***whose***

La forme au génitif **whose** renvoie à des personnes et à des animaux. Elle est souvent employée, quand elle renvoie à une chose, à la place de **of which** :

> **this is the girl whose mother has just died**
> c'est la fille dont la mère vient juste de mourir

> **oh, that's that new machine whose cover is damaged**
> oh, c'est la nouvelle machine dont le couvercle est abîmé

> **the department, whose staff are all over 50, is likely to be closed down**
> ce service, dont le personnel a plus de 50 ans, risque de fermer

> **these are antiques whose pedigree is immaculate**
> ce sont des objets anciens dont l'authenticité est irréprochable

> **the vehicles, the state of which left a good deal to be desired, had been in use throughout the year**
> les véhicules, dont l'état laissait à désirer, avaient été en service pendant toute l'année

f) ***which***

i) **Which** ne renvoie jamais aux personnes :

> **I received quite a few books for Christmas, which I still haven't read**
> j'ai reçu un bon nombre de livres pour Noël, que je n'ai pas encore lus

sauf quand on évoque un trait de caractère :

> **she accused him of being an alcoholic, which in fact he is**
> elle l'a accusé d'être alcoolique, ce que d'aillleurs il est

ii) On ne trouve **which** utilisé comme adjectif qu'après une préposition ou lorsque son antécédent est une chose. **Which** quand il est adjectif est d'un style un peu soutenu, même après une préposition :

> **he returned to Nottingham, in which city he had been born and bred**
> il revint à Nottingham, ville dans laquelle il avait grandi

et il est très soutenu quand il n'est pas accompagné d'une préposition :

> **he rarely spoke in public, which fact only added to his obscurity**
> il parlait très peu en public, particularité qui contribuait à le laisser dans l'ombre

ou archaïque ou légal si l'antécédent est une personne :

> **Messrs McKenzie and Pirie, which gentlemen have been referred to above ...**
> MM. McKenzie et Pirie, lesquels messieurs ont été évoqués plus haut ...

g) ***what***

i) **What** est le seul relatif qui ne prend pas d'antécédent. Il peut être pronom ou adjectif. Quand il est pronom, il fait référence normalement à une chose, et a souvent le sens de **that which** (ce qui/que), ou, au pluriel, **the things which** (les choses qui/que) :

> **show me what did the damage**
> montre-moi ce qui a causé les dégâts

Quand il est adjectif, il peut renvoyer à une personne ou à une chose, et il correspond à **the** (+ nom) **who/which** :

> **show me what damage was done**
> montre-moi quels dégâts ont été faits

> **with what volunteers they could find, they set off for the summit**
> avec les volontaires qu'ils ont pu trouver, ils sont partis à la conquête du sommet

> **what money they had left, they spent on drink**
> l'argent qu'il leur restait, ils le dépensèrent en alcool

ii) **what** ou **which**?

Seul **which** peut renvoyer à une proposition complète alors que **what** n'a pas d'antécédent. Mais **what** peut annoncer ou anticiper une proposition. Comparez les deux exemples suivants :

> **she left the baby unattended, which was a silly thing to do**
> elle a laissé le bébé tout seul, ce qui était idiot

mais :

> **she left the baby unattended and what's more, she smacked it when it cried**
> elle a laissé le bébé tout seul, et pire encore, elle lui a donné une fessée quand il s'est mis à pleurer

h) *Avec* ***-ever***

Au contraire des pronoms interrogatifs, (voir ci-dessus, p A31) **-ever** n'exprime pas la surprise, la confusion ou l'agacement quand il est associé avec un relatif ; il permet seulement de les renforcer dans le sens de **no matter (who, which, what)** (qui que ce soit qui/que) :

> **tell it to whoever you want to**
> dis-le à qui tu veux

> **take whichever (tool) is best**
> prend celui (des outils) qui convient le mieux

> **do whatever you like**
> fais ce que tu veux

> **I'll do it whatever happens**
> je le ferai quoi qu'il arrive

> **whatever problems we may have to face, we'll solve them**
> quels que soient les problèmes que nous ayons à affronter, nous les résoudrons

i) *Omission du relatif*

Le pronom relatif peut être omis (et il l'est très souvent en anglais parlé) dans les propositions relatives déterminatives sauf s'il est sujet ou s'il est précédé par une préposition :

> **these are the things (which/that) we have to do**
> ce sont les choses que nous devons faire

> **I saw the boy (who/that) you met last night**
> j'ai vu le garçon que tu as rencontré hier soir

> **is this the assistant (who/that) you spoke to?**
> est-ce à cette assistante que tu as parlé ?

> **who's the girl you came to the party with?**
> qui est la fille avec qui tu es venu à la soirée ?

> **she's not the woman (that) she was**
> elle n'est plus la femme qu'elle était

Remarquez que **that** seulement pourrait être utilisé dans cette dernière phrase.

Remarquez aussi que la construction assez soutenue :

> **who are the people with whom you are doing business?**
> qui sont les gens avec qui vous travaillez ?

peut être évitée si l'on change de place la préposition (**with**) :

> **who are the people you are doing business with?**

En anglais familier parlé, le pronom relatif sujet est souvent omis après **there is, here is, it is, that is** :

> **there's a man wants to speak to you**
> il y a un monsieur qui veut te parler

> **it isn't everybody gets a chance like that**
> ce n'est pas tout le monde qui a une chance comme ça

> **that was her husband just walked by**
> c'est son mari qui vient juste de passer

12 Les Pronoms et les Adjectifs Indéfinis

a) *some* et *any*

i) Lorsqu'ils sont combinés avec **-body**, **-one**, **-thing**, ce sont des pronoms, alors que **some** et **any** seuls peuvent être pronoms ou adjectifs, singulier ou pluriel :

did you speak to anybody?
as-tu parlé à quelqu'un ?

tell me something
dis-moi quelque chose

I have some (sugar)
j'ai du sucre/j'en ai

do you have any (friends)?
avez-vous des amis ?/en avez-vous ?

ii) Si le locuteur emploie **some**, il considère que la chose, l'animal ou la personne dont il parle existe ou, au moins, il s'attend à ce qu'ils existent. S'il emploie **any**, il ne formule aucune condition concernant cette éventualité d'existence. C'est pourquoi **any** est utilisé dans les propositions négatives, et avec des mots qui ont un sens négatif, comme **hardly** (à peine) :

I haven't got any money, but you have some
je n'ai pas d'argent, mais toi, tu en as

I have got hardly any money
je n'ai presque pas d'argent

De même, **any** est fréquent dans les propositions interrogatives et conditionnelles, car ces propositions sont par définition non-affirmatives :

have you got any money?
avez-vous de l'argent ?

if you have any money, give it to me
si tu as de l'argent, donne-le-moi

Cependant, c'est une erreur de dire (comme le font d'autres grammaires) que **some** est rare dans les propositions interrogatives et conditionnelles. Tout dépend de ce que le locuteur veut dire ou de ce qu'il sous-entend. Comparez :

(a) **have you got some brandy for the pudding?**
avez-vous du brandy pour le pudding ?

(b) **did you bring some sweets for the kids?**
avez-vous apporté quelques bonbons pour les enfants ?

(c) **if you had some milk, you'd feel better**
si vous preniez du lait, vous vous sentiriez mieux

(d) **if they leave some ice- cream behind, can I have it?**
s'ils laissent de la glace, je peux la manger ?

(e) **have we got any brandy in the house?**
est-ce qu'on a du brandy quelque part ?

(f) **did you give any sweets to that donkey?**
avez-vous donné des bonbons à cet âne ?

(g) **if you've had any milk, please tell me**
si vous avez pris du lait, dites-le-moi

(h) **if they left any ice-cream behind, I didn't see it**
s'ils ont laissé de la glace, je ne l'ai pas vue

En (a)-(d) **some** veut dire 'un peu de' ou 'quelques', alors que en (e)-(h) **any** veut dire 'du tout'. Par exemple, en (e) le locuteur veut savoir s'il y a du brandy à la maison ou s'il n'y en a pas. Il ne s'intéresse pas à la quantité, comme c'est le cas du locuteur en (a), qui en veut juste assez pour le pudding.

De même, **some milk** en (c) veut dire 'un verre de lait' ou une quantité semblable, alors que le médecin qui parle en (g) veut savoir si le malade a pris la moindre quantité de lait (parce que le lait pourrait expliquer certains symptômes).

iii) **Some/any** et leur combinaisons :

Comparez :

(a) **have they produced any?**
est-ce qu'ils en ont fait ?

(b) **have they produced anything?**
est-ce qu'ils ont fait quelque chose ?

En (a) le nom auquel **any** fait référence est sous-entendu et a été évoqué un peu plus tôt ; mais en (b) on ne fait pas de référence directe à quelque chose en particulier. Un exemple typique pour (a) serait :

they're always going on about how much they like children - have they produced any yet?
ils disent toujours qu'ils adorent les enfants; est-ce qu'ils en ont déjà fait un ?

et pour (b) :

the think-tank have been locked away for a week - have they produced anything yet?
le groupe de réflexion est enfermé depuis une semaine - est-ce qu'ils ont trouvé quelque chose ?

Les pronoms **some** et **any** peuvent aussi renvoyer à des noms indénombrables (dans l'exemple ci-dessus, **any** fait référence à un nom dénombrable (**children**), qui doit être au pluriel) :

I've run out of coffee, have you got any?
je n'ai plus de café, tu en as ?

Mais remarquez que **some** est pronom quand il a le sens de 'les gens qui' ou 'ceux qui' :

there are some who will never learn
il y a des gens qui n'apprendront jamais

iv) **some(thing)/any(thing)** + **of** + nom :

Some/any avant une locution qui commence par **of** est **quantitatif** par son sens, alors que **something/ anything** + locution qui commence par **of** est **qualitatif**. Comparez :

(a) **give me some of that cheese**
donne-moi (un peu) de ce fromage

(b) **he hasn't got any of her qualities**
il n'a aucune de ses qualités

(c) **he hasn't got anything of her qualities**
il n'a en rien ses qualités

(d) **there is something of the artist in her**
il y a quelque chose d'artistique chez elle

En (a) et en (b) **some** et **any** font référence à 'une part de, un peu de' alors que en (c) et en (d) ils renvoient à 'quelque chose dans la manière de' ou 'quelque chose qui relève de'.

v) **some** = un(e) certain(e) :

On a vu plus haut (en ii) ci-dessus) que **some** est utilisé dans un contexte positif avec des noms au pluriel (**would you like some biscuits?**) ou des noms indénombrables (**he stayed here for some time**). Lorsqu'il est placé devant un nom dénombrable au **singulier**, il veut souvent dire 'un certain' :

some person (or other) must have taken it
quelqu'un l'aura pris

he's got some fancy woman in London, it seems
il semble qu'il a une certaine bonne amie à Londres

come and see me some time
il faudra que tu viennes me voir un jour (emploi de **time** différent de celui dans l'exemple ci-dessus)

vi) **some** = 'un mauvais' ou 'un bon' :

En anglais familier, on utilise souvent **some** dans ces deux sens :

> **some husband you are! - always in the pub with your mates!**
> quel mauvais mari tu fais, toujours au pub avec tes copains !

> **this really is some party!**
> c'est vraiment une soirée fantastique !

vii) Les adverbes **some/any, something, anything** :

Some : devant des nombres = à peu près, autour de :

> **some fifty people were present**
> une cinquantaine de personnes étaient présentes

avec **more** :

> **talk to me some more**
> parle-moi encore un peu

en anglais américain :

> **we talked some**
> on a un peu parlé

Any est utilisé comme un adverbe devant les comparatifs :

> **he isn't any less of a friend in spite of this**
> il n'en est pas moins mon ami pour autant

> **I refuse to discuss this any further**
> je refuse de parler de cela davantage

Avant **like**, **something** ou **anything** sont aussi employés comme adverbes dans le sens de 'plutôt' ou 'environ' (**something**) et 'rien' (**anything**) :

> **it looks something like a Picasso**
> ça ressemble à du Picasso

> **something like fifty or sixty people were present**
> environ cinquante à soixante personnes étaient présentes

> **it wasn't anything like I had imagined**
> ça n'avait rien à voir avec ce que j'avais imaginé

Autrement **something** employé comme adverbe d'intensité est familier ou régional :

> **that baby howls something terrible!**
> ce bébé hurle d'une façon terrible

> **he fancies her something rotten**
> elle lui plaît un maximum

b) *no* et *none*

i) **No** est adjectif :

> **he has no house, no money, no friends**
> il n'a pas de maison, pas d'argent, pas d'amis

sauf s'il est employé comme un adverbe, dans le sens de 'pas' devant les comparatifs :

> **we paid no more than 2 pounds for it**
> nous ne l'avons pas payé plus de deux livres

> **I want £2 for it, no more, no less**
> j'en veux deux livres, ni plus, ni moins

La différence entre **not** et **no** dans ce cas est que **not** est plus précis, **no** ayant un caractère émotionnel. **No more than** peut être remplacé par **only** (seulement). Mais si le locuteur dit :

> **I wish to pay not more than £2**
> j'aimerais ne pas payer plus de deux livres

il précise que le prix ne doit pas dépasser deux livres.

ii) **None** est un pronom :

> **do you have any cigarettes? – no, I've none left**
> avez-vous des cigarettes ? – non, je n'en ai plus

> **I tried a lot but none (of them) fitted**
> j'en ai essayé beaucoup, mais aucun ne m'allait

Remarquez qu'en anglais parlé courant, une phrase comme :

> **I have none**
> je n'en ai pas

peut paraître formelle ou d'un ton dramatique ou est employée pour marquer l'emphase. La construction normale serait :

> **I don't have any**
> je n'en ai pas

Quand on fait référence à des gens, **none of them/us/you** (aucun d'eux/de nous/de vous) est plus courant que **none** (aucun, personne) en anglais parlé :

> **none of us knew where he had filed it**
> aucun de nous ne savait où il l'avait classé

> **I waited for them for hours, but none of them came**
> je les ai attendus pendant des heures, mais aucun d'eux n'est venu

> **many have set out to climb this mountain but none have ever returned**
> nombreux sont ceux qui sont partis à la conquête de cette montagne, mais aucun n'en est jamais revenu

Quand on veut donner à une phrase un ton emphatique, on peut employer la construction **not one** :

> **not one (of them) was able to tell me the answer!**
> pas un (d'entre eux) n'a été capable de me répondre

iii) **None** : singulier ou pluriel ?

Le sens littéral de **none** étant **no one** (pas un), on trouve souvent logique de le faire suivre par un verbe au singulier, comme :

> **none of them has seen it before**
> aucun d'entre eux ne l'a déjà vu

Cependant, un verbe au pluriel est d'un emploi tout à fait courant en anglais parlé (et écrit) d'aujourd'hui :

> **none of them have seen it before**

iv) **None** est un adverbe :

Il est utilisé devant **the** + un comparatif (comparez avec **any** en a) vii ci-dessus) :

> **none the less** (= nevertheless) néanmoins

> **you can scratch a CD and it is none the worse for it**
> même si vous rayez un CD, vous pouvez quand même l' écouter

> **he took the medicine but is feeling none the better**
> il a pris les médicaments, mais il ne se sent pas mieux pour autant

> **after his explanation we were all none the wiser**
> malgré ses explications, nous n'étions pas plus avancés

c) *every* et *each*

i) **Each** peut être un pronom ou un adjectif ; **every** est toujours un adjectif. Ils font référence tous les deux à des noms dénombrables uniquement :

> **each (of them) was given a candle**
> on a donné une bougie à chacun (d'eux)

> **each (child) was given a candle**
> on a donné une bougie à chacun (chaque enfant)

> **every child needs a good education**
> tous les enfants doivent recevoir une bonne éducation

Every et **each** sont différents car **every** sous-entend la totalité (il n'y a pas d'exception) alors que **each** individualise. Dans les deux premiers exemples, **each** implique 'l'un après l'autre'. C'est pourquoi **each** fait souvent référence à un plus petit nombre qu'**every**, qui est plus général, comme on le voit dans le dernier exemple.

Remarquez que **every** peut être précédé d'une forme au génitif (nom ou pronom) :

Wendy's every move was commented on
on commenta chacun des faits et gestes de Wendy

her every move was commented on
on commenta chacun de ses faits et gestes

et notez son emploi avec les nombres :

she goes to the dentist every three months
elle va chez le dentiste tous les trois mois

every other day there's something wrong
un jour sur deux, il y a quelque chose qui ne va pas

the clock seems to stop every two days
l'horloge semble s'arrêter tous les deux jours

La différence entre **every other** et **every two** est que **every other** sous-entend une irritation devant le fait que quelque chose est répétitif tandis que **every two** est plus objectif et précis.

Remarquez aussi son emploi adverbial :

every now and then
every now and again
every so often

qui veulent tous dire 'de temps en temps'.

Everybody/everyone et **everything** sont des pronoms, et ils sont toujours suivis d'un verbe au singulier mais, comme les autres pronoms indéfinis, **everybody** peut être suivi de **they**, **them(selves)** ou **their** (voir **Les Pronoms Personnels**, p A26).

d) *all*

i) **All** est un adjectif ou un pronom et renvoie à des noms dénombrables ou indénombrables. Remarquez que lorsqu'un article défini ou un pronom personnel est utilisé, il se place entre **all** et le nom :

all coins are valuable to me
toutes les pièces ont de la valeur pour moi

I want all the/those/their coins
je veux toutes les/ces/leurs pièces

all his energy was spent
il a dépensé toute son énergie

I want them all/all of them
je les veux tous

I want it all/all of it
je le veux en entier

ii) **all** et **everything** :

La différence entre ces deux mots est souvent assez légère. **All** sera employé si le locuteur évoque quelque chose qui n'est pas précis. Seul **all** peut renvoyer à des noms indénombrables.

we ate everything that was on the table
nous avons mangé tout ce qui était sur la table

all that was on the table was a single vase
tout ce qu'il y avait sur la table était un vase

did you eat the ice-cream? – not all (of it)
as-tu mangé la glace ? – pas tout

they believed everything/all he said
ils croyaient tout ce qu'il disait

did he say anything? – all that he said was 'do nothing'
a-t-il dit quelque chose ? – il n'a dit que 'ne faites rien'

iii) **all** et **whole** :

La différence principale entre **all** et l'adjectif **whole** réside dans le fait que **whole** accentue parfois un aspect précis de ce que l'on exprime :

don't interrupt me all the time
ne m'interromps pas tout le temps

he sat there the whole time without moving
il est resté là pendant tout le temps sans bouger

he ate all of the pie
il a mangé tout le gâteau

he ate the whole pie
il a mangé le gâteau en entier

Mais l'emploi de **whole** est limité aux noms dénombrables :

the whole town (ou **all the town**)
toute la ville

mais seulement :

all the butter (indénombrable)
tout le beurre

Remarquez que **whole** ne s'emploie pas avec un nom au pluriel. On emploie alors, par exemple :

all the books in their entirety
tous les livres en entier

iv) **all** adverbe :

L'emploi adverbial de **all** est clair dans les exemples ci-dessous, où **all** signifie **completely** (complètement) :

he was all covered in mud
il était complètement couvert de boue

should we teach her a lesson? – I'm all in favour (of that)
on devrait lui donner une leçon ? – je suis tout à fait d'accord (avec ça)

it's all over
c'est fini

Voici d'autres exemples de l'adverbe **all** :

I've told you all along not to eat the cat's food
je t'ai toujours dit de ne pas manger la nourriture du chat

he was covered in mud all over
il était couvert de boue de la tête aux pieds

Devant des comparatifs :

I've stopped smoking and feel all the better for it
j'ai arrêté de fumer et je m'en sens tellement mieux

your remark is all the more regrettable since the Principal was present
votre remarque est d'autant plus regrettable que le Proviseur était présent

e) *other(s)* et *another*

i) **Another** est suivi de, ou remplace, un nom singulier dénombrable. Un nom pluriel peut suivre **other** uniquement, tandis que **others** est toujours un pronom :

I want another (hamburger)
j'en veux un autre/je veux un autre hamburger

other children get more money
les autres enfants ont plus d'argent

I like these colours – don't you like the others?
j'aime ces couleurs – tu n'aimes pas les autres ?

ii) Si **than** suit un nom, **other** suivra, et ne précédera pas, ce nom :

there are difficulties other than those mentioned by the government
il y a d'autres difficultés que celles qui sont mentionnées par le gouvernement

Dans cette phrase, **other** pourrait aussi précéder **difficulties**, mais il est toujours placé après **none** :

who should arrive? none other than Jimbo himself
et qui est arrivé ? Jimbo en personne

iii) Parfois **no other** est utilisé à la place de **not another** :

he always wears that coat; he has no other (coat)
il porte toujours ce manteau ; il n'en a pas d'autre

iv) Remarquez la construction avec **some** et ses combinaisons, quand **some** veut dire 'un(e) certain(e) ...' (comparez avec a) v ci-dessus). On ajoute **or other** pour intensifier l'aspect vague de la chose dont on parle :

somebody or other must have betrayed her
quelqu'un a dû la trahir

we'll get there somehow or other (emploi adverbial)
on y arrivera d'une manière ou d'une autre

he married some girl or other from the Bahamas
il s'est marié avec une fille des Bahamas

v) Avec **one** :

One ... another et **one ... the other** ont habituellement la même signification :

one week after another went by
one week after the other went by
les semaines sont passées les unes après les autres

Mais si le locuteur ne fait référence qu'à deux choses, alors **one ... the other** est préféré :

the two brothers worked well together: one would sweep the yard while the other chopped the wood
les deux frères travaillaient bien ensemble : l'un balayait la cour pendant que l'autre coupait le bois

cependant, si le second élément est précédé d'une préposition, **one ... another** est aussi employé dans ce cas :

they would sit there and repeat, one after another, every single word of the lesson
ils s'asseyaient là et répétaient, l'un après l'autre, chaque mot de la leçon

On trouve parfois la combinaison **the one ... the other**, qui aurait pu être employée dans l'exemple des deux frères ci-dessus. Dans la locution utilisant **hand, the one** est obligatoire :

on the one hand, you'd earn less, on the other your job satisfaction would be greater
d'un côté tu gagnerais moins d'argent, mais d'un autre côté, tu aurais une plus grande satisfaction professionnelle

f) *either* et *neither*

i) **Either** a souvent le sens de 'l'un ou l'autre' en parlant de deux choses (on utilisera **any** s'il y en a plus de deux). Il peut être adjectif ou pronom :

'bike' or 'bicycle': either (word) will do
'vélo' ou 'bicyclette' : l'un ou l'autre ira

either parent can look after the children
l'un ou l'autre des parents peut s'occuper des enfants

Either peut aussi vouloir dire 'chaque' ou 'les deux', et dans ce cas, c'est un adjectif :

he was sitting in a taxi with a girl on either side
il était assis dans un taxi, une fille de chaque côté

ii) **Neither** est la forme négative de **either** :

he's in love with both Tracy and Cheryl, but neither of them fancies him
il est amoureux de Tracy et de Cheryl, mais il ne plaît à aucune des deux

neither kidney is functioning properly
aucun des reins ne fonctionne correctement

iii) **Either** et **neither** prennent souvent un verbe au pluriel, s'ils sont suivis de **of** et d'un nom au pluriel :

(n)either of the boys are likely to have done it

bien qu'on emploie un verbe au singulier dans un langage soutenu :

neither of the boys is likely to have done it
il est peu probable que l'un des deux garçons l'ait fait

either of the boys is likely to have done it
il est probable que l'un des deux garçons l'ait fait

iv) **(N)either** adverbe :

L'adverbe **either** n'est utilisé que dans des propositions négatives. Il correspond à **too** dans les propositions affirmatives :

I can't do it either
je ne peux pas le faire non plus (comparez avec **I can do it too**)

L'adverbe **neither** (= **nor**) est utilisé dans une proposition **qui suit** une proposition négative :

I can't swim and neither can she
je ne sais pas nager, et elle non plus

I can't swim – neither can I
je ne sais pas nager – moi non plus

ou dans un style familier :

I can't swim – me neither
je ne sais pas nager – moi non plus

Voir aussi **Les Conjonctions**, p A68.

g) *Both*

Both fait référence à deux choses ou à deux personnes, mais dans le sens de 'l'un et l'autre'. Comme pour **all**, l'article défini ou le pronom personnel (éventuel) suit **both**, qui peut être un pronom ou un adjectif :

I like both (those/of those) jackets
j'aime ces deux vestes ; j'aime l'une et l'autre de ces vestes

I love both my parents
j'aime mon père et ma mère

I love both (of them)/them both
je les aime tous les deux

both (the/of the) versions are correct
les deux versions sont correctes

h) *One*

i) Ce pronom est employé dans le sens de 'une seule chose/personne' en référence à ce qui a été évoqué dans une phrase ou une proposition précédente :

do you like dogs? I bet you haven't ever owned one
vous aimez les chiens ? je suis sûr que vous n'en avez jamais eu

we've a lot of Elvis records – we have only one
nous avons beaucoup de disques d'Elvis – nous n'en avons qu'un

his case is a sad one
son cas est triste

this solution is one of considerable ingenuity
c'est une solution remarquablement ingénieuse

Il peut aussi être employé au pluriel (**ones**) :

I like silk blouses, especially black ones
j'aime bien les chemisiers de soie, surtout ceux qui sont noirs

ii) L'emploi restrictif :

which girl do you prefer? – the tall one
quelle fille préférez-vous ? – la grande

I prefer the pen you gave me to the one my aunt gave me
je préfère le stylo que vous m'avez donné à celui que ma tante m'a donné

these are the ones I meant
ce sont celles dont je parlais

these burgers are better than the ones you make
ces hamburgers sont meilleurs que ceux que tu fais

iii) **One(s)** est habituellement employé après des adjectifs qui font référence à des noms dénombrables :

I asked for a large whisky and he gave me a small one
je lui ai demandé un grand whisky, et il m'en a donné un petit

which shoes do you want? the grey ones?
quelles chaussures voulez-vous ? les grises ?

Cependant, si deux adjectifs en contraste sont placés près l'un de l'autre, on peut parfois se dispenser d'utiliser **one(s)** :

I like all women, both (the) tall and (the) short
j'aime toutes les femmes, les grandes et les petites

she stood by him in good times and bad
elle fut à ses côtés pour le meilleur et pour le pire

today I wish to talk about two kinds of climate, the temperate and the tropical
aujourd'hui je vais vous parler de deux sortes de climats, le climat tempéré et le climat tropical

Si aucun nom n'a été mentionné ou évoqué, l'adjectif fonctionne comme un nom, et **one(s)** n'est pas employé :

the survival of the fittest
la persistance du plus apte

fortune favours the brave
la chance sourit aux braves

Il est évident que **one** ne peut pas référer à un nom indénombrable :

do you want white sugar or brown?
voulez-vous du sucre blanc ou du roux ?

iv) **One** est parfois employé dans un sens proche de 'quelqu'un' ou 'une personne', comme dans :

she screamed her head off like one possessed
elle hurlait comme une (femme) possédée

I'm not one for big parties
je ne suis pas quelqu'un qui aime les grandes soirées

I'm not one to complain
je ne suis pas du genre à me plaindre

v) **One** collectif, voir p A28.

7 Les Verbes

A LES DIFFERENTS TYPES

On peut distinguer trois types de verbes : les verbes réguliers, les verbes irréguliers et les auxiliaires.

1 Les verbes réguliers

Ces verbes forment leur prétérit et leur participe passé en ajoutant **-(e)d** au radical du verbe :

		Prétérit	*Participe Passé*
seem	(sembler)	**seemed**	**seemed** /d/
kiss	(embrasser)	**kissed**	**kissed** /t/
plant	(planter)	**planted**	**planted** /ɪd/
manage	(diriger)	**managed**	**managed** /d/

Voir p A74 pour les changements d'orthographe.

2 Les verbes irréguliers

Les verbes irréguliers se caractérisent par leurs formes particulières au prétérit et au participe passé, qui font apparaître parfois un changement de voyelle :

(parler)	**speak, spoke, spoken**
(voir)	**see, saw, seen**
(aller)	**go, went, gone**
(gâter)	**spoil, spoilt, spoilt**
(couper)	**cut, cut, cut**

Vous trouverez une liste des verbes irréguliers p A61.

3 Les auxiliaires

Un auxiliaire modifie le verbe principal dans la phrase. Dans **he can sing** (il sait chanter) l'auxiliaire est **can** et le verbe principal est **sing**. On fait la distinction entre les auxiliaires 'ordinaires' et les auxiliaires modaux (ou défectifs).

a) *Les auxiliaires ordinaires*

Ce sont :

be (être), **have** (avoir) et **do** (faire).

Voir aussi sections 9, 17 et 23.

On les appelle 'ordinaires' parce qu'ils peuvent parfois avoir fonction de verbe ordinaire :

he does not sing (**does** = auxiliaire, **sing** = verbe principal)
il ne chante pas

he does the washing up (**does** = verbe principal)
il fait la vaisselle

b) Les **auxiliaires modaux** sont appelés ainsi car ils remplacent le mode du subjonctif dans de nombreux cas (voir pp A51-2). En voici la liste :

can - could	pouvoir (capacité)
may - might	pouvoir (possibilité - permission)
shall - should	futur - devoir (moral), conseil, etc.
will - would	futur - conditionnel, ordre, etc.
must	devoir (obligation)
ought to	devoir (moral)

Lorsqu'ils ne sont pas accompagnés d'un verbe ordinaire, ce dernier est sous-entendu :

can you get some time off? – yes, I can
est-ce que tu peux te libérer ? – oui

Vous trouverez l'emploi des auxiliaires p A55.

B LES FORMES

1 L'infinitif

On distingue l'infinitif complet (avec **to** : **to be**) et l'infinitif sans **to** :

he can sing	**he is trying to sing**
il sait chanter	il essaie de chanter

Dans ces deux phrases le mot **sing** est à l'infinitif. Pour l'infinitif passé et la voix passive, voir p A40.

2 Le participe présent

Il se forme à partir du radical + **-ing** :

they were whispering
ils murmuraient

Voir **Notes sur l'Orthographe** p A74.

3 Le participe passé

Le participe passé des verbes réguliers est identique à leur prétérit (radical du verbe + **-ed**) :

they have gone
ils/elles sont parti(e)s

Les verbes irréguliers ont un grand nombre de formes différentes au participe passé. Voir A2 ci-dessus, ainsi que la liste des verbes irréguliers p A6.

4 Le gérondif

Le gérondif a la même forme que le participe présent :

I don't like *picking* strawberries
je n'aime pas cueillir les fraises

***sailing* is a very popular sport in Greece**
la voile est un sport très populaire en Grèce

5 Le présent

Il se construit avec le radical + **-(e)s** à la 3ème personne du singulier (pour les changements d'orthographe, voir p A74) :

	Singulier		
1ère	*I*	**sing**	je chante
2ème	*you*	**sing**	tu chantes
3ème	*he/she/it*	**sings**	il/elle chante
	Pluriel		
1ère	*we*	**sing**	nous chantons
2ème	*you*	**sing**	vous chantez
3ème	*they*	**sing**	ils/elles chantent

Les auxiliaires modaux ne changent pas de forme à la troisième personne du singulier. Il en est de même pour les verbes **dare** et **need** lorsqu'ils sont employés comme auxiliaires :

he may come
il se peut qu'il vienne

how dare he come here!
comment ose-t-il venir ici ?!

Les auxiliaires ordinaires ont des formes irrégulières, voir la liste p A63.

6 Le prétérit

Le prétérit des verbes réguliers est identique à leur participe passé (radical du verbe + **-ed**) :

they kicked the ball
ils ont donné un coup de pied dans le ballon

Pour les verbes irréguliers et les auxiliaires, voir A2 et 3 ci-dessus, ainsi que la liste des verbes irréguliers et des auxiliaires de la page A61 à la page A63. La forme du verbe est la même à toutes les personnes :

		Régulier (embrasser)	*Irrégulier* (chanter)	*Auxiliaire* (pouvoir)
	Singulier			
1ère	*I*	**kissed**	**sang**	**could**
2ème	*you*	**kissed**	**sang**	**could**
3ème	*he/she/it*	**kissed**	**sang**	**could**
	Pluriel			
1ère	*we*	**kissed**	**sang**	**could**
2ème	*you*	**kissed**	**sang**	**could**
3ème	*they*	**kissed**	**sang**	**could**

7 Les temps et les aspects

L'infinitif, le présent et le passé peuvent avoir différents aspects, considérant un événement dans le temps de trois manières différentes.

Dans la liste ci-dessous les traductions sont données A TITRE INDICATIF.

Simple, progressif et perfect (ou passé) :

infinitif	**(to) watch** (regarder)
infinitif progressif	**(to) be watching** (être en train de regarder) (**be** + participe présent)
infinitif passé	**(to) have watched** (avoir regardé) (**have** + participe passé)
infinitif passé progressif	**(to) have been watching** (avoir été en train de regarder)
présent simple	**(I/you/he,** etc.) **watch(es)** (je/tu/il, etc.) regarde(s)
passé simple (ou prétérit)	**" watched** (je regardai, etc.)
présent progressif	**" am/are/is watching** (" suis/es/est en train de regarder)
passé progressif	**" was/were watching** (j'étais, etc. en train de regarder)
present perfect	**" have/has watched** (j'ai regardé, etc.)
past perfect	**" had watched** (j'avais regardé, etc.)
present perfect progressif	**" have/has been watching** (j'ai, etc. été en train de regarder)
past perfect progressif	**" had been watching** (j'avais, etc. été en train de regarder)

Pour les formes employées au futur, voir p A49.

8 Les modes

Les modes font référence à l'attitude d'une personne par rapport aux propos qu'elle rapporte. Il existe trois modes :

'l'indicatif' pour exprimer des faits réels

le 'subjonctif' pour exprimer un souhait, une incertitude ou une possibilité, etc.

'l'impératif' pour exprimer des ordres et des suggestions.

La seule différence de forme entre l'indicatif et le subjonctif réside dans la présence de **-(e)s** à la 3ème personne du singulier au présent de l'indicatif :

God save the Queen! Vive la reine !

Le subjonctif de **to be** est **be** à toutes les personnes du présent et **were** à toutes les personnes du passé :

be they for or against, they all have to pay
qu'ils soient pour ou qu'ils soient contre, ils doivent tous payer

if I were you, I'd leave him
si j'étais toi, je le quitterais

Pour le mode impératif on emploie le radical du verbe seul :

ring the bell!
sonne (la cloche) !

somebody go and get it!
que quelqu'un aille le chercher !

9 Les voix

Les deux 'voix' sont la voix active et la voix passive. Elles indiquent si c'est le sujet d'un verbe qui fait l'action de ce verbe :

we always listen to him
nous l'écoutons toujours (voix active)

ou si le sujet subit l'action :

he was always listened to
il a toujours été écouté (voix passive)

Le passif se forme avec le verbe **be** + participe passé :

infinitif	**(to) be watched** (être regardé)
infinitif passé	**(to) have been watched** (avoir été regardé)
présent simple	**are/is watched** (es/est, etc. regardé)
passé simple (ou prétérit)	**was/were watched** (j'étais, etc. regardé)
présent progressif	**am/are/is being watched** (suis/es/est, etc. en train d'être regardé)
passé progressif	**was/were being watched** (j'étais, etc. en train d'être regardé)
present perfect	**have/has been watched** (a/ont, etc. été regardé)
past perfect	**had been watched** (j'avais, etc. été regardé)
present perfect progressif	**have/has been being watched** (j'ai, etc. été en train d'être regardé)
past perfect progressif	**had been being watched** (j'avais, etc. été en train d'être regardé)

Le passif de l'infinitif progressif (par exemple **to be being driven**) est assez inhabituel en anglais (bien que parfaitement possible) :

I wouldn't like to be being filmed looking like this
je ne voudrais pas être filmé dans cet état

Il en est de même pour le passif du present perfect progressif :

he may have been being operated on by then
il était peut-être en train de se faire opérer à ce moment-là

C EMPLOIS

1 L'infinitif

a) *Sans* ***to***

i) après les auxiliaires modaux et après **do** :

I must go il faut que je m'en aille
I don't know je ne sais pas

ii) après **dare** et **need** lorsqu'ils sont employés comme auxiliaires :

how dare you talk to me like that!
comment oses-tu me parler ainsi !

you needn't talk to me like that
tu n'as pas besoin de me parler comme ça

iii) après **had better** et **had best** (aussi **would best** en anglais américain) :

you had better apologize
tu ferais mieux de t'excuser

you had (you'd) best ask the porter
tu ferais mieux de demander au portier

iv) avec ce que l'on appelle la construction 'accusatif avec infinitif' (nom/pronom + infinitif ayant fonction de complément d'objet direct). Comparez avec b)ii ci-dessous :

★ après **let** (laisser), **make** (faire) et **have** (faire *dans ce cas*) (voir aussi p A55) :

we let him smoke nous l'avons laissé fumer
I made him turn round je l'ai fait tourner

we had him say a few words
nous lui avons fait dire quelques mots

★ après les verbes de perception suivants :

feel (sentir), **hear** (entendre), **see** (voir), **watch** (regarder) :

I felt the woman touch my back
j'ai senti la femme me toucher le dos

we heard her tell the porter
on l'a entendu le dire au portier

they saw him die
ils l'ont vu mourir

we watched the train approach the platform
on a regardé le train s'approcher du quai

Pour **feel** (sembler à quelqu'un), voir b) ii ci-dessous.

Ces verbes peuvent aussi être suivis du participe présent pour mettre l'accent sur la durée de l'action :

I felt her creeping up behind me
je sentais qu'elle s'approchait de moi à pas de loup

we heard her crying bitterly in the next room
nous l'avons entendue pleurer amèrement dans l'autre pièce

she saw smoke coming from the house
elle a vu de la fumée venir de la maison

they watched him slowly dying
ils l'ont vu mourir petit à petit

★ on peut trouver deux formes de l'infinitif après **help** :

we helped him (to) move house
nous l'avons aidé à déménager

L'infinitif sans **to** est aussi particulièrement employé dans le langage publicitaire :

our soap helps keep your skin supple and healthy-looking
notre savon aide à garder votre peau souple et vous donnera bonne mine

Pour les constructions passives correspondantes employées avec ces verbes, voir b) ii ci-dessous.

v) après **why (not)** (pourquoi (pas)) :

why stay indoors in this lovely weather?
pourquoi rester à l'intérieur par ce beau temps ?

why not try our cream cakes?
pourquoi ne pas essayer nos gâteaux à la crème ?

b) *Avec* ***to***

i) L'infinitif avec **to** peut s'employer comme sujet, comme attribut ou comme complément d'objet direct dans une phrase. La phrase suivante contient les trois emplois (dans cet ordre) :

to die is to cease to exist
mourir est cesser d'exister

ii) Comme complément d'objet direct, comparez a) iv ci-dessus.

★ Après des verbes exprimant un désir ou une antipathie, en particulier **want** (vouloir), **wish** (souhaiter), **like** (aimer), **prefer** (préférer), **hate** (ne pas aimer/hair) :

I want/wish you to remember this
je veux/souhaite que tu te souviennes de cela

John would like you to leave
John aimerait que vous partiez

we prefer your cousin to stay here
nous préférons que votre cousin reste ici

we would hate our cat to suffer
nous n'aimerions pas que notre chat souffre

★ Dans un langage assez soutenu, après des verbes exprimant des points de vue, des croyances, un jugement, une supposition ou une affirmation :

we believe this to be a mistake
nous croyons que c'est une erreur

we supposed him to be dead
nous supposions qu'il était mort

we considered/judged it to be of little use
nous considérions/jugions cela peu utile

I felt/knew it to be true
j'avais l'impression/je savais que c'était vrai

these accusations he maintained to be false
il soutenait que ces accusations étaient fausses

Un langage moins soutenu préférerait une proposition introduite par **that** :

we believe (that) this is a mistake
nous croyons que c'est une erreur

I know (that) it's true
je sais que c'est vrai

he maintained that these accusations were false
il a soutenu que ces accusations étaient fausses

★ Dans la construction passive correspondante, on garde **to** :

this was believed to be a mistake
on pensait que c'était une erreur

★ Remarquez l'expression courante **be said to**, pour laquelle il n'existe pas d'équivalent à la voix active en anglais :

it is said to be true
il paraît que c'est vrai

he's said to be rich
il paraît qu'il est riche

★ La forme **to** + infinitif doit aussi être employée dans des constructions passives avec les verbes mentionnés dans a) iv ci-dessus :

she was made to do it
on l'a forcée à le faire

he was seen to remove both jacket and tie
on l'a vu enlever sa veste et sa cravate

iii) Employé à la suite de noms, de pronoms et d'adjectifs :

she has always had a tendency to become hysterical
elle a toujours eu tendance à avoir des crises d'hystérie

we shall remember this in years to come
on se rappellera de cela pendant des années

there are things to be done
il y a des choses à faire

there is that to take into consideration
il y a ça à prendre en considération

glad to meet you!
heureux de faire votre connaissance !

we were afraid to ask
nous avions peur de demander

this game is easy to understand
ce jeu est facile à comprendre

De telles constructions sont particulièrement courantes après des superlatifs et après **only** :

this is the latest book to appear on the subject
c'est le livre le plus récent qui soit paru sur ce sujet

she's the only person to have got near him
elle est la seule personne à avoir pu l'approcher

iv) Correspondant à une proposition subordonnée :

★ Exprimant un but ou une conséquence (parfois accompagné de **in order** ou **so as** (but) ou **only** (conséquence) pour souligner ses propos) :

he left early (in order/so as) to get a good seat for the performance
il est parti tôt afin d'/pour avoir une bonne place au spectacle

they arrived (only) to find an empty house
à leur arrivée, la maison était vide

try to be there
essaie d'être là

Remarquez qu'en anglais parlé, on peut remplacer **to** après **try** par **and** :

try and be there

★ Dans des propositions interrogatives indirectes :

tell me what to do
dis-moi quoi faire

I didn't know where to look
je ne savais pas où regarder

we didn't know who to ask
nous ne savions pas à qui demander

we weren't sure whether to tell him or not
nous ne savions pas si nous devions le lui dire ou non

★ Pour exprimer le temps ou la circonstance :

I shudder to think of it
j'en tremble (rien que) d'y penser

to hear him speak, one would think he positively hates women
à l'entendre parler, on dirait vraiment qu'il déteste les femmes

v) Equivalent d'une principale, dans des exclamations exprimant la surprise :

to think she married him!
dire qu'elle l'a épousé !

vi) Dans des phrases elliptiques exprimant des événements à venir. On les trouve particulièrement dans le langage journalistique :

MAGGIE TO MAKE GREEN SPEECH
MAGGIE FERA UN DISCOURS VERT

GORBACHEV TO VISIT DISASTER ZONE
GORBACHEV VISITERA LA ZONE SINISTREE

vii) On peut aussi trouver l'infinitif avec césure, où un adverbe est placé entre **to** et le radical du verbe. Cette forme est devenue très courante, mais peu appréciée de beaucoup, qui soutiennent qu'il ne faut jamais séparer **to** de l'infinitif :

nobody will ever be able to fully comprehend his philosophy
personne ne sera jamais capable de comprendre complètement sa philosophie

Cela peut cependant être la place que l'on choisirait instinctivement pour un adverbe :

the way out of this is to really try and persuade him
le moyen de s'en sortir, c'est de vraiment essayer de le persuader

Ici **really** signifie 'beaucoup' et il modifie **try**, tandis que dans la phrase suivante, **really** signifie 'en fait', et modifie ainsi toute la phrase :

the way out of this is really to try and persuade him
le moyen de s'en sortir, c'est en fait d'essayer de le persuader

viii) On emploie souvent **to** sans le radical du verbe dans une répétition, plutôt que l'infinitif complet :

why haven't you tidied your room? I told you to
pourquoi n'as-tu pas rangé ta chambre ? je t'ai dit de le faire

I did it because she encouraged me to
je l'ai fait parce qu'elle m'y a encouragé

ix) **For** + nom/pronom et l'infinitif avec **to** :

there has always been a tendency for our language to absorb foreign words
notre langue a toujours eu tendance à absorber des mots étrangers

he waited for her to finish
il attendit qu'elle ait fini

La construction idiomatique qui suit exprime souvent une condition ou un but :

for the university to function properly, more money is needed
afin que l'université fonctionne bien, il faut plus d'argent

ou elle peut exprimer une circonstance et même être le sujet de la phrase :

for me to say nothing would be admitting defeat
ne rien dire serait admettre ma défaite

for a man to get custody of his children used to be difficult
c'était difficile à l'époque pour un homme d'obtenir la garde de ses enfants

2 Le gérondif

Le gérondif (ou le verbe substantivé) possède des caractéristiques propres aux noms et aux verbes.

a) *Caractéristiques nominales*

i) Un gérondif peut être sujet, attribut ou complément d'objet :

skating is difficult (sujet)
le patin à glace, c'est difficile

that's cheating (attribut)
c'est de la triche

I hate fishing (complément)
je déteste pêcher

Comme on l'a vu, ce sont des fonctions qui sont communes à l'infinitif ; pour les différences d'emploi, voir 4 ci-dessous.

ii) Il peut être placé après une préposition :

he's thought of leaving
il a pensé partir

L'infinitif ne peut pas occuper cette place.

iii) Il peut être modifié par un article, par un adjectif ou par un possessif, ou par une proposition commençant par **of** :

he has always recommended the reading of good literature
il a toujours encouragé la lecture des bons auteurs

there was a knock on the door
on frappa à la porte

careless writing leaves a bad impression
une écriture peu soignée donne une mauvaise impression

the soprano's singing left us unmoved
le chant du soprano nous a laissé totalement froid

there was no end to his trying to be difficult
il prenait un malin plaisir à créer des problèmes

the timing of his remarks was unfortunate
il a mal choisi son moment pour faire des remarques

b) *Caractéristiques verbales*

i) Un gérondif peut être suivi d'un complément d'objet ou d'un attribut :

hitting the dog was unavoidable
il était inévitable de rentrer dans le chien

becoming an expert took him more than twenty years
il lui a fallu plus de vingt ans pour devenir expert en la matière

ii) Il peut être modifié par un adverbe :

she was afraid of totally disillusioning him
elle avait peur de lui enlever toute illusion

iii) Il peut avoir un sujet :

the idea of John going to see her is absurd
l'idée que John aille/soit allé la voir est absurde

3 Le possessif et le gérondif

Il existe souvent une incertitude concernant la présence ou l'absence d'un adjectif possessif :

do you remember him/his trying to persuade her?
tu te souviens qu'il a essayé de la persuader ?

Les deux formes sont correctes. Mais cela ne signifie pas qu'il n'existe pas parfois des différences d'emploi entre les deux. Il faut noter les exemples suivants :

a) *Le gérondif sujet ou attribut*

Dans ce cas, l'emploi du possessif est normal :

your trying to persuade me will get you nowhere
tes tentatives de me persuader ne te mèneront nulle part

it was John's insisting we went there that saved the situation
c'est grâce à l'insistance de John qui voulait que nous y allions que la situation fut sauvée

b) *Le gérondif complément ou placé après une préposition*

Dans ces cas, les deux emplois sont possibles :

they spoke at great length about him/his being elected president
ils parlèrent longtemps de son élection comme président

you don't mind me/my turning up so late, do you?
ça ne te dérange pas que j'arrive si tard, n'est-ce pas ?

they spoke at great length about Richard/ Richard's being elected president
ils parlèrent longtemps de l'élection de Richard comme président

Mais il y a des cas où l'emploi du possessif présenterait un problème de style dans un langage parlé ou familier :

they laughed their heads off at him falling into the river
ils riaient à n'en plus pouvoir parce qu'il était tombé dans la rivière

L'emploi de l'adjectif possessif **his** serait ici d'un langage trop soutenu dans cet exemple.

Dans ces constructions, le gérondif ne doit pas être confondu avec le participe présent. La phrase :

I hate people trying to get in without paying
je déteste les gens qui essaient d'entrer sans payer

est ambiguë. Si **trying** est un gérondif, le sens de la phrase est : **I hate the fact that (some) people try to get in without paying** (je déteste le fait que certaines personnes essaient d'entrer sans payer). Si c'est un participe présent, le sens devient : **I hate people who try to get in without paying** (je déteste les gens qui essaient d'entrer sans payer).

Mais la forme en **-ing** est, bien sûr, très clairement un gérondif dans une phrase comme :

I hate their trying to get in without paying
je déteste qu'ils essaient d'entrer sans payer

On a plus tendance à employer le possessif devant le gérondif en anglais américain qu'en anglais britannique.

c) *Le facteur d'emphase*

Si le sujet du gérondif est particulièrement accentué, le possessif a moins de chance d'être employé :

just to think of HER marrying John!
que ce soit elle qui épouse John, je n'arrive pas à le croire !

4 Comparaison entre le gérondif et l'infinitif

a) *Peu ou pas de différence*

On a vu que l'infinitif et le gérondif ont des caractéristiques nominales du fait que l'un et l'autre peuvent fonctionner comme sujet, complément d'objet ou attribut. Il y a souvent peu ou pas de différence de sens entre eux :

we can't bear seeing you like this
we can't bear to see you like this
nous ne pouvons pas supporter de vous voir comme ça

bien que dans les dictons ou les citations, les expressions soient 'figées', comme dans les exemples suivants :

seeing is believing
voir, c'est croire

to err is human, to forgive divine
l'erreur est humaine, le pardon est divin

b) *Différents sens*

i) Le général contre le particulier : le gérondif indique souvent un fait général, l'infinitif indique un fait plus particulier :

I hate refusing offers like that (général)
je déteste refuser des offres comme ça

I hate to refuse an offer like that (particulier)
je déteste refuser une offre comme celle-ci

Mais il existe des exceptions :

I prefer being called by my Christian name
I prefer to be called by my Christian name
je préfère être appelé par mon prénom

En anglais américain, l'infinitif est souvent utilisé dans des cas où en anglais britannique on emploierait un gérondif :

I like cooking (anglais britannique)
I like to cook (anglais américain)
j'aime faire la cuisine

Ces deux exemples font référence à un penchant général. Si on voulait faire référence à une occasion particulière, on dirait en anglais britannique et en anglais américain :

I'd like to cook something for you
je voudrais vous préparer un repas

ii) Si le verbe **try** signifie 'tenter, essayer', on peut employer l'infinitif ou le gérondif :

I once tried to make a film, but I couldn't
I once tried making a film, but I couldn't
j'ai essayé de faire un film une fois, mais je n'ai pas réussi

try to speak more slowly
try speaking more slowly
essaie de parler plus lentement

Mais si **try** est employé avec le sens de 'connaître par l'expérience', alors seul le gérondif est employé :

I've never tried eating shark
je n'ai jamais mangé du requin

Comparez avec ceci :

I once tried to eat shark, but couldn't
j'ai essayé de manger du requin une fois, mais je n'ai pas pu

iii) Après **forget** (oublier) et **remember** (se souvenir) l'infinitif fait référence au futur, le gérondif au passé, en relation avec 'l'oubli' ou 'le souvenir' :

I won't forget to dance with her (dans le futur)
je n'oublierai pas de danser avec elle

I won't forget dancing with her (dans le passé)
je n'oublierai pas que j'ai dansé avec elle

will she remember to meet me? (dans le futur)
se souviendra-t-elle de son rendez-vous avec moi ?

will she remember meeting me? (dans le passé)
se souviendra-t-elle d'avoir fait ma connaissance ?

c) *L'infinitif seulement ou le gérondif seulement*

i) L'infinitif seulement :

Certains verbes ne peuvent être suivis que de l'infinitif, par exemple **want** (vouloir), **wish** (souhaiter), **hope** (espérer), **deserve** (mériter) :

I want/wish to leave
je veux/souhaite partir

we hope to be back by five
nous espérons être de retour vers cinq heures

he deserves to be punished
il mérite d'être puni

ii) Le gérondif seulement :

D'autres verbes ne sont suivis que du gérondif, par exemple : **avoid** (éviter), **consider** (considérer), **dislike** (ne pas aimer), **enjoy** (apprécier), **finish** (finir), **keep** (continuer), **practise** (faire, pratiquer), **risk** (risquer) :

he avoided answering my questions
il évitait de répondre à mes questions

won't you consider travelling by air?
vous ne voulez pas y aller en avion ?

I dislike dressing up for the theatre
je n'aime pas devoir m'habiller pour aller au théâtre

we enjoy having friends round to dinner
nous aimons recevoir des amis pour le dîner

she finished typing her letter
elle a fini de taper sa lettre

why do you keep reminding me?
pourquoi continues-tu à me le rappeler ?

would you mind stepping this way, Sir?
voulez-vous bien venir par ici, Monsieur ?

you must practise playing the piano more often
tu dois travailler ton piano plus souvent

I don't want to risk upsetting Jennifer
je ne veux pas risquer de contrarier Jennifer

iii) Dans les exemples des deux sections ci-dessus, l'infinitif et le gérondif sont les compléments d'objet direct des verbes précédents. Il en est de même pour le gérondif dans la phrase suivante :

I stopped looking at her
je me suis arrêté de la regarder

Mais l'infinitif n'est pas complément d'objet direct dans :

I stopped to look at her
je me suis arrêté pour la regarder

Ici, l'infinitif fonctionne comme un complément circonstanciel de but, ce qui explique la différence considérable de sens entre les deux phrases. La différence est de la même importance entre :

he was too busy talking to her
il était trop occupé à lui parler

et :

he was too busy to talk to her
il était trop occupé pour lui parler

Il faut noter ici que les adjectifs **worth** et **like** ne peuvent être suivis que par le gérondif :

that suggestion is worth considering
cette proposition vaut la peine d'être considérée

that's just like wishing for the moon
c'est comme demander la lune

iv) Il est aussi important de faire la distinction entre **to**, marque de l'infinitif et **to**, préposition. Le gérondif doit suivre une préposition, comme dans :

I'm tired of watching television
j'en ai assez de regarder la télévision

what do you think about getting a loan?
qu'est-ce que tu dirais de faire un emprunt ?

Ceci, bien sûr, concerne aussi la préposition **to** :

they are committed to implementing the plan
ils se sont engagés à réaliser le projet

we're looking forward to receiving your letter
nous attendons votre lettre avec impatience

I object to raising money for that purpose
je ne trouve pas cela normal que l'on rassemble des fonds pour ça

we're not used to getting up at this hour
nous ne sommes pas habitués à nous lever à cette heure

Be accustomed to est parfois employé avec l'infinitif, bien qu'on le trouve aussi avec le gérondif :

they've never been accustomed to pay(ing) for anything
ils n'ont jamais eu l'habitude de payer pour quoi que ce soit

5 Le participe présent

Le participe présent fonctionne normalement comme une forme verbale ou comme un adjectif.

a) *Comme une forme verbale*

i) Le participe présent est employé avec **be** pour former le progressif :

he is/was/has been/had been running
il court/courait/a couru/avait couru

ii) Le participe présent fonctionne fréquemment comme une proposition relative sans pronom relatif :

they went up to the people coming from the theatre (= who were coming)
ils allèrent vers les gens qui venaient du théâtre

iii) Cependant, le participe présent peut partager son sujet avec le verbe au présent ou au passé. Dans ce cas, le participe présent est précédé d'une virgule :

she turns/turned towards the man, looking pleasantly surprised
elle se tourne/tourna vers l'homme, l'air agréablement surpris

Ici, le sujet de **looking** est **she** ; mais si on omet la virgule, on comprendra que le sujet de **looking** est **the man**, et la phrase appartient alors au type ii) ci-dessus.

Ce participe présent relativement lâche peut précéder son sujet :

looking pleasantly surprised, she turned towards the man
l'air agréablement surpris, elle se tourna vers l'homme

Il exprime souvent une cause, une condition ou le temps, étant équivalent à une proposition subordonnée :

living alone, she often feels uneasy at night (= because/since/as she lives alone ...)
vivant seule, elle se sent souvent inquiète le soir

you'd get more out of life, living alone (= ... if you lived alone)
tu profiterais plus de la vie, si tu vivais seule

driving along, I suddenly passed my old school (= as/while I was driving along ...)
j'étais en train de conduire, quand soudain je me suis aperçu que je venais de passer devant mon ancienne école

Mais parfois aussi il est équivalent à une proposition indépendante :

she went up to him, asking for his advice (= ... and (she) asked for his advice)
elle s'approcha, pour lui demander conseil

living in the Scottish Highlands, he is a sensitive musician who helped organize the Bath Orchestra (= he lives in the Highlands and (he) is ...)
vivant dans les Highlands en Ecosse, c'est un musicien sensible qui contribua à l'organisation de l'Orchestre de Bath

iv) Le participe présent 'non-rattaché' :

Un participe présent est considéré comme 'non-rattaché' si son sujet est différent de celui du verbe de la principale au présent ou au passé :

coming down the staircase carrying an umbrella, one of the cats tripped him up
un des chats le fit trébucher, alors qu'il descendait l'escalier, un parapluie à la main

Il est assez peu probable que le sujet de **coming** soit **one of the cats** ! Les participes présents 'non-rattachés' doivent normalement être évités car ils causent souvent un amusement non intentionnel. Cependant, si un sujet indéfini est sous-entendu comme le **we** indéfini ou le 'on' français, alors un participe présent est acceptable :

generally speaking, British cooking leaves a good deal to be desired
d'une manière générale, la cuisine britannique laisse à désirer

judging by the way she dresses, she must have a lot of confidence
à voir sa façon de s'habiller, elle doit avoir une grande confiance en elle

the work will have to be postponed, seeing that only two of us have tools
le travail devra être remis à plus tard, puisque seulement deux d'entre nous ont des outils

v) Dans les autres circonstances, pour éviter un participe présent 'non-rattaché', le sujet du participe (différent du sujet de l'autre verbe) peut le précéder dans ce qu'on appelle la 'construction absolue' :

the lift being out of order, we had to use the stairs
l'ascenseur étant en panne, nous avons dû monter par les escaliers

she being the hostess, any kind of criticism was out of the question
étant donné que c'était elle qui recevait, il était hors de question de faire quelque critique que ce soit

we'll do it on Sunday, weather permitting
nous le ferons dimanche, si le temps le permet

God willing, we can do it
si Dieu le veut, nous pouvons le faire

b) *Comme un adjectif*

she has always been a loving child
elle a toujours été une enfant aimante

her appearance is striking
son allure est frappante

she finds Henry very charming
elle trouve Henry vraiment charmant

De cette fonction dérive la fonction adverbiale :

he is strikingly handsome
il est remarquablement beau

Remarquez que cette structure est bien plus courante en anglais qu'en français :

a self-adjusting mechanism
un mécanisme à auto-réglage

the falling birthrate
le taux de natalité en baisse

increasing sales
des ventes en hausse

6 Comparaison du participe présent et du gérondif

a) *La phrase suivante :*

I can't get used to that man avoiding my eyes all the time

est ambiguë, car **avoiding** peut être compris comme un gérondif ou un participe présent.

Si c'est un gérondif, la phrase équivaut à **I can't get used to the fact that that man is avoiding my eyes** (je ne peux pas m'habituer au fait que cet homme fuit mon regard).

Mais si c'est un participe présent, le sens est **I can't get used to that man who is avoiding my eyes** (je ne peux pas m'habituer à cet homme qui fuit mon regard).

Dans la phrase suivante, il ne fait aucun doute que la forme en **-ing** est un gérondif :

children suffering like that is on our conscience (= the suffering of children)
la souffrance de ces enfants pèse sur notre conscience

et il n'y a pas de d'ambiguïté sur le participe présent dans :

children suffering like that are on our conscience (= children who suffer)
les enfants qui souffrent comme cela pèsent sur notre conscience

b) Quand un gérondif modifie un nom, seul le gérondif est accentué dans le discours, et non pas le nom :

a living room un salon

mais quand l'élément modificateur est un participe présent, celui-ci et le nom sont accentués de la même manière :

a living animal un animal vivant

7 Le participe passé

Beaucoup des emplois suivants peuvent être comparés avec ceux du participe présent. Voir 5 ci-dessus.

a) *Comme forme verbale*

i) Le participe passé s'emploie avec **have** pour former le present perfect et le past perfect :

he has/had arrived
il est/était arrivé

et avec **be** pour former la voix passive :

she is/was admired
elle est/était admirée

et avec les deux auxiliaires pour former le passif au present perfect et au past perfect :

she has/had been admired
elle a/avait été admirée

ii) Le participe passé est fréquemment employé pour former une proposition relative elliptique :

they ignore the concerts given by the local orchestra (= which are given)
ils ne vont pas aux concerts donnés par l'orchestre local

they ignored the concerts given by the local orchestra (= which were/had been given)
ils ne sont pas allés aux concerts donnés par l'orchestre local

Il peut aussi avoir la fonction d'une subordonnée de cause, de condition ou de temps. Une conjonction (en particulier **si** et **quand**) peut parfois rendre son sens explicite :

watched over by her family, Monica felt safe but unhappy
surveillée par sa famille, Monica se sentait en sécurité, mais malheureuse

(if) treated with care, records should last for years and years
si l'on en prend soin, les disques devraient durer des années et des années

records should last for years and years if treated with care
les disques devraient durer des années et des années si l'on en prend soin

(when) asked why, he refused to answer
quand on lui demanda pourquoi, il refusa de répondre

he refused to answer when asked why
il refusa de répondre lorsqu'on lui demanda pourquoi

Ou il peut avoir valeur de principale :

born in Aberdeen, he now lives in Perth with his wife and children
né à Aberdeen, il habite maintenant à Perth avec sa femme et ses enfants

iii) La phrase est parfois déséquilibrée de manière inacceptable lorsque le participe passé n'est pas rattaché au sujet de la phrase :

told to cancel the meeting, his project was never discussed

On pourrait exprimer ceci de manière plus élégante :

his project was never discussed as he was told to cancel the meeting
son projet ne fut jamais examiné car on lui demanda d'annuler la réunion

iv) La 'construction absolue' (voir 5a) v ci-dessus) :

the problems solved, they went their separate ways
les problèmes résolus, ils sont partis chacun de leur côté

that done, he left
cela fait, il est parti

b) *Comme adjectif*

I am very tired
je suis très fatigué(e)

the defeated army retreated
l'armée vaincue battit en retraite

Remarquez que dans le premier exemple l'adverbe est **very**, puisqu'il se place devant un adjectif. Si l'adverbe est **much**, c'est que l'on insiste plus sur le caractère verbal du participe passé :

I am much obliged
je vous suis très obligé(e)

Lorsque **aged** (âgé), **beloved** (bien-aimé), **blessed** (sacré), **cursed** (maudit) et **learned** (érudit) sont des adjectifs, on prononce normalement **-ed** /ɪd/. Mais lorsque ce sont des verbes, on adopte la prononciation régulière /d/ et /t/ :

he has aged
il a vieilli

an aged man /ɪd/
un homme âgé

8 Les questions

a) *Phrases complètes*

i) **Do** s'emploie pour des questions à moins que (a) la phrase ne contienne un autre auxiliaire (**have**, **will**, etc.), auquel cas l'auxiliaire précède le sujet, ou que (b) le sujet ne soit un pronom interrogatif. **Do** est au présent ou au passé, le verbe conjugué à l'infinitif :

do you come here often?
tu viens souvent ici ?

how do we get to Oxford Street from here?
comment on fait pour aller d'ici à Oxford Street ?

did you see that girl?
tu as vu cette fille ?

what did you say?
qu'est-ce que tu as dit ?

mais (quand d'autres auxiliaires sont employés) :

are they trying to speak to us?
est-ce qu'ils essaient de nous parler ?

where are you taking me?
où est-ce que tu m'emmènes ?

have they seen us?
est-ce qu'ils nous ont vu(e)s ?

can you come at eight?
tu peux venir à huit heures ?

will you help us?
tu pourras nous aider ?

et quand on a un pronom interrogatif sujet :

who said that?
qui a dit ça ?

what happened?
qu'est-ce qui s'est passé ?

what have they said to you?
qu'est-ce qu'ils t'ont dit ?

what shall we eat tonight?
qu'est-ce qu'on va manger ce soir ?

Pour **dare** et **need**, voir p A59. Pour **have**, voir p A54.

ii) En anglais parlé, où l'on distingue une proposition interrogative d'une proposition affirmative par l'intonation, on peut employer l'ordre des mots d'une affirmative dans une interrogative (bien que ce soit un emploi moins fréquent en anglais qu'en français) :

you just left him standing there?
tu l'as laissé planté là ?

you're coming tonight?
tu viens ce soir ?

Dans des propositions interrogatives indirectes, on emploie normalement l'ordre des mots de la proposition affirmative directe :

when are you leaving? (style direct)
quand est-ce que tu pars ?

et :

he asked her when she was leaving (style indirect)
il lui a demandé quand elle partait

b) *Les question-tags*

Ce sont des phrases courtes qui suivent une phrase affirmative ou négative, et qui normalement ont pour but d'ammener une confirmation.

i) Une proposition affirmative est suivie d'un tag à la forme négative et vice versa :

you can see it, can't you?
tu le vois, n'est-ce pas ?

you can't see it, can you?
est-ce que tu peux le voir ?

à moins que le tag n'exprime une attitude emphatique plutôt qu'une question. Dans de tels cas, un tag à la forme affirmative suit une proposition affirmative :

so you've seen a ghost, have you? (incrédulité ou ironie)
alors, tu as vu un fantôme, c'est ça ?

you think that's fair, do you? (ressentiment)
tu crois que c'est juste, hein ?

you've bought a new car, have you? (surprise ou intérêt)
alors, tu as acheté une nouvelle voiture ?

Remarquez que le question-tag reprend le temps employé dans la principale :

you want to meet him, don't you?
tu veux le rencontrer, n'est-ce pas ?

you wanted to meet him, didn't you?
tu voulais le rencontrer, n'est-ce pas ?

you'll want to meet him, won't you?
tu voudras le rencontrer, n'est-ce pas ?

ii) Si la proposition qui précède a un auxiliaire, il faut le répéter dans le tag :

you have seen it before, haven't you?
tu l'as déjà vu, n'est-ce pas ?

they aren't sold yet, are they?
ils n'ont quand même pas déjà été vendus ?

you will help me, won't you?
tu m'aideras, n'est-ce pas ?

you oughtn't to say that, ought you?
tu ne devrais pas dire ça, d'accord ?

S'il n'y a pas d'auxiliaire dans la proposition précédente, on emploie normalement **do** dans le tag :

he sleeps in there, doesn't he?
il dort là, n'est-ce pas ?

your cousin arrived last night, didn't she?
ta cousine est arrivée hier soir, n'est-ce pas ?

à moins que le tag ne suive un impératif, auquel cas on emploie un auxiliaire à la forme affirmative (en particulier **will/would**). Ces tags permettent souvent de nuancer l'impératif :

leave the cat alone, will you?
laisse le chat tranquille, d'accord ?

take this to Mrs Brown, would you?
tu veux bien apporter ça à Mme Brown ?

Dans de tels cas la forme négative **won't** indique une invitation :

help yourselves to drinks, won't you?
servez-vous en boisson, je vous en prie

9 Les négations

a) *La négation des formes conjuguées*

i) **Do** avec **not** s'emploie à moins que la proposition ne contienne un autre auxiliaire (**should, will**, etc.). En anglais courant à l'oral ou à l'écrit, il est normal de trouver la contraction de l'auxiliaire (**don't, won't, can't**, etc.) :

we do not/don't accept traveller's cheques
nous n'acceptons pas les chèques de voyage

mais (avec un autre auxiliaire) :

the matter should not/shouldn't be delayed
il ne faudrait pas tarder à s'occuper de ça

ii) Dans la question négative **not** suit le sujet, à moins qu'il ne soit contracté :

do they not accept traveller's cheques?
(mais : **don't they accept ...?**)
est-ce qu'ils n'acceptent pas les chèques de voyage ?

should you not try his office number?
(mais : **shouldn't you try ...?**)
ne devrais-tu pas essayer son numéro au bureau ?

iii) Les verbes exprimant un point de vue **believe, suppose, think**, etc. sont normalement à la forme négative, même si la négation porte logiquement sur le verbe dans la proposition complément d'objet :

I don't believe we have met
je ne crois pas que nous nous soyons déjà rencontrés

I don't suppose you could lend me a fiver?
ça t'embêterait de me prêter un billet de 5 livres ?

I didn't think these papers were yours
je ne pensais pas que ces papiers étaient à toi

mais **hope** est plus logique :

I hope it won't give me a headache
j'espère que ça ne me donnera pas mal à la tête

et il n'est même pas accompagné de **do** lorsqu'il est employé seul :

is she ill? – I hope not
elle est malade ? – j'espère que non

De nombreuses formes sont possibles pour des réponses courtes avec **believe, suppose** et **think** :

will she marry him?
va-t-elle l'épouser ?

I don't believe/think so (couramment employé)
je ne crois pas/ne pense pas

I believe/think not (moins courant, plus soigné)
I don't suppose so (couramment employé)
I suppose not (couramment employé)

b) *La négation des infinitifs et des gérondifs*

On la forme en plaçant **not** devant l'infinitif ou le gérondif :

we tried not to upset her
nous avons essayé de ne pas la contrarier

I want you to think seriously about not going
je veux que tu songes sérieusement à ne pas partir

not eating enough vegetables is a common cause of ...
le fait de ne pas manger assez de légumes est une cause fréquente de ....

L'exemple avec l'infinitif ci-dessus a bien sûr un sens différent de :

we didn't try to upset her
nous n'avons pas essayé de la contrarier

où l'auxiliaire est à la forme négative.

Remarquez l'expression idiomatique **not to worry = don't worry** :

I won't manage to finish it by tomorrow – not to worry
je n'arriverai pas à terminer avant demain – ce n'est pas grave

En anglais de tous les jours, on peut intercaler **not** entre le **to** de l'infinitif et le verbe (**we tried to not upset her**), bien que cela soit considéré incorrect par beaucoup, voir p A41.

c) *La négation des impératifs*

i) Avec **do**. **Do not** a pour forme contractée **don't** :

don't worry	ne t'inquiète pas
don't be silly	ne sois pas bête

L'emploi de la forme complète **do not** est couramment employé dans des déclarations officielles, sur des modes d'emploi, des panneaux, etc. :

do not fill in this part of the form
ne pas remplir cette partie du formulaire

do not feed the animals
défense de nourrir les animaux

do not exceed the stated dose
ne pas dépasser la dose prescrite

La forme complète peut aussi s'employer pour rendre un impératif plus emphatique en anglais parlé :

I'll say it again - do not touch!
je le redis encore - ne touche pas !

Dans la forme de l'impératif **let's**, employée pour des suggestions, l'ordre des mots est le suivant :

don't let's wait any longer
n'attendons pas davantage

ii) Il existe une autre manière d'exprimer la négation à l'impératif, en employant **not** seul après le verbe. Ceci est de l'anglais comme il est employé, par exemple, dans la Bible ou dans les œuvres de Shakespeare. Il peut aussi être employé pour produire un effet comique ou sarcastique :

worry not, I'll be back soon
ne t'inquiète pas, je reviendrai bientôt

fear not, the situation is under control
n'aie pas peur, je maîtrise la situation

Mais cet emploi est tout à fait normal avec **let's** :

let's not wait any longer
n'attendons pas davantage

d) **Never** n'est normalement pas accompagné de **do** :

we never accept traveller's cheques
nous n'acceptons jamais les chèques de voyage

I never said a word
je n'ai rien dit

Mais si l'on veut mettre l'accent sur **never**, on peut alors employer **do** ou **did** :

you never did like my cooking, did you?
tu n'as jamais aimé ma cuisine, hein ?

S'il y a une inversion auxiliaire/sujet, on emploie **do** :

never did it taste so good!
ça n'a jamais été aussi bon !

never did their courage waver
à aucun moment leur courage n'a faibli

Dans le premier de ces deux exemples, la phrase est plus une exclamation qu'une négation, et dans la seconde, le style est poétique ou rhétorique.

e) *La traduction des formes négatives en français*

i) ne ... jamais

he never speaks to me/he doesn't ever speak to me
il ne me parle jamais

ii) ne ... rien

I saw nothing/I didn't see anything
je n'ai rien vu

iii) ne ... personne

she agrees with nobody (no-one)/she doesn't agree with anybody (anyone)
elle n'est d'accord avec personne

iv) ne ... plus

I don't smoke any more/any longer
je ne fume plus

words which are no longer used/words which aren't used any longer
des mots qui ne sont plus employés

10 Pour exprimer le présent

On peut exprimer le présent de différentes façons selon que l'on se réfère à des événements habituels ou généraux, ou à des événements précis, et selon que ceux-ci sont considérés comme des actions en cours ou comme des événements ponctuels. Cette section décrit les emplois des formes verbales appropriées.

a) *Le présent simple*

i) Pour des événements habituels ou généraux, ou pour des vérités universelles :

I get up at seven o'clock every morning
je me lève à sept heures tous les matins

Mrs Parfitt teaches French at the local school
Madame Parfitt enseigne le français dans l'école du quartier

the earth revolves round the sun
la terre tourne autour du soleil

ii) Avec des verbes qui n'impliquent pas d'idée de progression dans le temps. Ces verbes sont parfois appelés 'statiques' et ils expriment souvent le désir, le dégoût, l'opinion ou font référence aux sens :

I (dis)like/love/hate/want that girl
j'aime (je n'aime pas)/j'adore/je déteste/je veux cette fille

I believe/suppose/think you're right
je crois/suppose/pense que vous avez raison

we hear/see/feel the world around us
nous entendons/voyons/sentons le monde autour de nous

it tastes good/it smells good
c'est bon/ça sent bon

Remarquez que ces verbes 'statiques' peuvent devenir des verbes 'dynamiques', si le sens sous-entend le 'déroulement' ou qu'une action dure. Dans de tels cas, on emploie le présent progressif :

what are you thinking about?
à quoi penses-tu ?

we're not seeing a lot of him these days
on ne le voit pas beaucoup ces jours-ci

are you not feeling well today?
est-ce que vous ne vous sentez pas bien aujourd'hui ?

we're tasting the wine to see if it's all right
nous goûtons le vin pour voir s'il est bon

b) *Le présent progressif*

i) Le présent progressif est employé avec des verbes 'dynamiques', c.-à-d. des verbes qui renvoient à des événements en cours et normalement temporaires :

don't interrupt while I'm talking to somebody else
ne m'interromps pas quand je parle à quelqu'un d'autre

please be quiet; I'm watching a good programme
tais-toi, s'il te plaît ; je regarde une émission intéressante

he's trying to get the car to start
il essaie de faire démarrer la voiture

not now, I'm thinking
pas maintenant, je réfléchis

Comparez :

I live in London (présent simple)
je vis à Londres

I'm living in London (présent progressif)
je vis à Londres (maintenant)

La deuxième phrase implique que le locuteur n'est pas installé à Londres d'une façon permanente, que c'est d'une manière temporaire qu'il vit à Londres.

ii) Si l'on fait référence à a) i ci-dessus, il est clair que les adverbes de temps absolu ou d'habitude sont fréquents avec le présent simple, comme dans :

he always goes to bed after midnight
il va toujours se coucher après minuit

Cet emploi du présent simple s'applique pour donner les états de fait. Mais on emploie parfois le présent progressif avec de tels adverbes, en particulier avec **always** et **forever**, lorsque l'on souhaite exprimer non seulement le fait lui-même, mais une attitude vis-à-vis de celui-ci, en particulier une attitude d'irritation, d'amusement ou de surprise :

you're always saying that! (irritation)
tu dis toujours ça !

he's always criticizing me (ressentiment)
il me critique tout le temps

John is forever forgetting his car keys (légère ironie)
John oublie toujours ses clés de voiture

I'm always finding you here at Betty's (surprise)
tiens, je te trouve toujours ici chez Betty !

11 Pour exprimer le passé

a) *Le prétérit*

On l'emploie lorsque l'on veut mettre l'accent sur l'accomplissement d'une action, souvent à un moment précis indiqué par un adverbe :

he caught the train yesterday
il a pris le train hier

he didn't say a word at the meeting
il n'a pas dit un mot pendant la réunion

Maria Callas sang at the Lyric Opera only a few times
Maria Callas ne chanta/n'a chanté à l'Opéra qu'en de rares occasions

b) ***used to/would***

Lorsque l'on veut faire référence à un événement habituel au passé, on emploie souvent **used to** ou **would** :

on Sundays we used to go to my grandmother's
on Sundays we would go to my grandmother's
le dimanche on allait chez ma grand-mère

c) *Le passé progressif*

Ce temps a pour but d'insister sur la continuité d'une action ou d'un événement :

what were you doing last night around 9 o'clock? – I was repairing the garage door
qu'est-ce que tu faisais hier soir vers 9 heures ? – je réparais la porte du garage

I was watching my favourite programme when the phone rang
je regardais mon émission préférée, quand le téléphone a sonné

Dans le deuxième exemple, **was watching** (passé progressif) s'oppose à **rang** (prétérit). Les deux verbes sont en contraste de manière différente dans l'exemple suivant, où les formes des verbes ont été inversées :

I watched his face while the phone was ringing
j'ai regardé son visage pendant que le téléphone sonnait

Ici le locuteur insiste sur le fait que 'regarder' s'est produit à un certain moment. Il ne prend donc pas en compte l'idée de continuité que le verbe pourrait exprimer, en revanche il met l'accent sur la continuité de 'sonner'. Les deux exemples illustrent l'emploi du passé progressif pour des événements servant de toile de fond à d'autres événements de courte durée, pour lesquels on préfère l'aspect simple.

d) *Le present perfect (progressif)*

On emploie le present perfect pour des actions du passé ou des événements qui ont un lien avec le présent :

she has read an enormous number of books (c'est-à-dire qu'elle est érudite)
elle a lu énormément de livres

Comparez le present perfect avec le prétérit dans les deux phrases qui suivent :

have you heard the news this morning? (c'est encore la matinée)
tu as entendu les informations ce matin ?

did you hear the news this morning? (c'est maintenant l'après-midi ou le soir)
tu as entendu les informations ce matin ?

he has just arrived (il est là maintenant)
il vient d'arriver

he arrived a moment ago (accent sur le moment du passé)
il est arrivé il y a un instant

Mrs Smith has died (elle est morte maintenant)
Mme Smith est morte

Mrs Smith died a rich woman (au moment où elle est morte, elle était riche)
Mme Smith est morte riche

Pour insister sur le fait qu'une action est continue, on peut employer l'aspect progressif :

I've been living in this city for 10 years
cela fait dix ans que je vis dans cette ville

Cependant, ici on peut aussi employer la forme simple dans le même sens :

I've lived in this city for 10 years

Remarquez que l'on emploie **since** pour traduire 'depuis' pour faire référence à un moment précis dans le temps :

I've been living here since 1971
je vis ici depuis 1971

Dans certains cas, cependant, l'emploi de l'aspect progressif et l'emploi de la forme simple impliquent des idées différentes. Comparez :

I've been waiting for you for three whole hours!
cela fait trois bonnes heures que je t'attends !

I've waited for you for three whole hours!
je t'ai attendu pendant trois heures !

On ne dirait pas la deuxième phrase directement à la personne que l'on attend lorsque cette personne finit par arriver. Mais on pourrait le dire à cette personne au téléphone, sous-entendant ainsi que l'on va maintenant cesser d'attendre.

On pourrait aussi bien dire la première phrase à la personne lorsqu'elle arrive qu'au téléphone.

e) *Le past perfect (progressif)*

Le past perfect permet de décrire des actions et des événements passés survenus avant d'autres événements passés. Il exprime un passé par rapport à un autre passé :

she had left when I arrived
elle était partie lorsque je suis arrivé

she left when I arrived
elle est partie lorsque je suis arrivé

L'aspect progressif permet d'insister sur le fait que l'action est continue :

she had been trying to get hold of me for hours when I finally turned up
cela faisait des heures qu'elle essayait de me contacter lorsque je suis enfin arrivé

I had been meaning to contact him for ages
cela faisait très longtemps que j'avais l'intention de le contacter

Pour le past perfect dans les propositions conditionnelles, voir p A51.

12 Pour exprimer le futur

a) ***will** et **shall***

i) Lorsque le locuteur fait référence au futur à la 1ère personne, on peut employer **will** ou **shall**. Ces deux formes se contractent en **'ll**. Cependant l'emploi de **shall** est peu fréquent ailleurs qu'en Grande Bretagne :

I will/I'll/I shall inform Mr Thompson of her decision
je ferai part de sa décision à Mr Thompson

we won't/shan't be long
ça ne nous prendra pas longtemps

I will/I'll/I shall be in Rome when you're getting married
je serai à Rome quand vous vous marierez

ii) Aux autres personnes, on emploie **will** :

you will/you'll be surprised when you see him
vous serez surpris quand vous le verrez

he will/he'll get angry if you tell him this
il se mettra en colère si tu lui dis cela

Remarquez qu'après **when** l'anglais emploie un présent pour faire référence au futur, comme dans l'exemple ci-dessus. Ceci s'applique aussi pour d'autres conjonctions de temps, par exemple :

I'll do it as soon as I get home
je le ferai dès que j'arriverai à la maison

life will be easier once you learn to accept ... (ou **once you have learnt to accept ...**)
la vie sera plus facile une fois que tu auras appris à accepter ...

iii) Si le locuteur exprime une intention à la deuxième ou à la troisième personne (souvent une promesse ou une menace), on rencontre alors parfois **shall**, mais cet emploi n'est plus de nos jours aussi courant que celui de **will** :

you shall get what I promised you
tu auras ce que je t'ai promis

they shall pay for this!
ils/elles vont me le payer !

Si l'intention ou la volonté n'est pas celle du locuteur, on emploie alors **will ('ll)** :

he will/he'll do it, I'm sure
il le fera, j'en suis sûr(e)

iv) On emploie **shall** pour exprimer des suggestions :

shall we go?
on y va ?

shall I do it for you?
tu veux que je te le fasse ?

Dans ces deux exemples, on n'emploierait pas **will**.

v) On emploie **will** pour demander à quelqu'un de faire quelque chose :

will you step this way, please?
voulez-vous venir par ici, s'il vous plaît ?

vi) pour proposer de faire quelque chose, pour affirmer quelque chose en ce qui concerne l'avenir immédiat :

Dans les exemples suivants, en emploie **will** de préférence à **shall** (bien que la forme contractée soit de loin la plus courante) :

leave that, I'll do it
laisse ça, je vais le faire

what's it like? – I don't know, I'll try it
c'est bon ? – je ne sais pas, je vais y goûter

try some, you'll like it
goûtez-y, vous aimerez ça

there's the phone – ok, I'll answer it
le téléphone sonne – bon, je réponds

b) *Le futur simple et le futur progressif*

i) la continuité de l'action :

Will et **shall** peuvent être suivis de la forme progressive, si le locuteur veut insister sur l'aspect continu de l'action :

I'll be marking essays and you'll be looking after the baby
je corrigerai des dissertations et tu t'occuperas du bébé

ii) les demandes ou les questions :

On peut aussi employer la forme progressive pour indiquer que le locuteur parle de façon neutre d'un état de choses et souhaite atténuer la nuance de volonté que pourrait sous-entendre l'aspect simple. C'est pourquoi on rencontre souvent **will/shall** + forme progressive de l'infinitif dans des phrases qui sous-entendent un arrangement préalable :

she'll be giving two concerts in London next week
(= she is due to give ...)
elle donnera deux concerts à Londres la semaine prochaine

will you be bringing that up at the meeting?
est-ce que tu comptes en parler à la réunion ?

La question :

will you bring that up at the meeting?
tu en parleras à la réunion ?

est plus susceptible d'être interprétée comme une demande ou une prière que comme une question quant à ce que vous avez l'intention de faire.

c) ***be going to***

i) Bien souvent, il n'y a aucune différence entre **be going to** et **will** :

I wonder if this engine is ever going to start (... will ever start)
je me demande si le moteur va finir par démarrer

you're going to just love it (you'll just love it)
tu vas adorer ça

what's he going to do about it? (what'll he do about it?)
qu'est-ce qu'il va faire ?

ii) Pour indiquer une intention, **be going to** est plus couramment employé que **will** ou **shall** :

we're going to sell the house after all
en fin de compte, nous allons vendre la maison

he's going to sue us
il va nous faire un procès

I'm going to go to London tomorrow
je vais aller à Londres demain

Mais dans une phrase plus longue comprenant d'autres locutions adverbiales et d'autres propositions, on peut aussi employer **will** :

look, what I'll do is this, I'll go to London tomorrow, talk to them about it and ...
écoute, voilà ce que je vais faire, je vais aller à Londres demain, je vais leur en parler et ...

iii) **be going to** s'emploie de préférence à **will** lorsque les raisons justifiant les prévisions sont directement liées au présent :

it's going to rain (look at those clouds)
il va pleuvoir (regarde ces nuages)

I know what you're going to say (it's written all over your face)
je sais ce que tu vas dire (en voyant ton expression)

d) *Le présent simple*

i) Dans les principales, le présent simple exprime le futur lorsque l'on fait référence à un programme établi, en particulier lorsque l'on fait référence à un horaire :

when does university start? – classes start on October 6th
quand a lieu la rentrée universitaire ? – les cours reprennent le 6 octobre

the train for London leaves at 11 am
le train qui va à Londres part à 11 heures

ii) On emploie généralement le présent simple dans les propositions temporelles ou conditionnelles :

you'll like him when you see him
il te plaira quand tu le verras

if he turns up, will you speak to him?
tu lui parleras s'il vient ?

Ne confondez pas les propositions de ce type commençant par **when** et **if** et les propositions compléments d'objet interrogatives. Dans ces dernières, **when** signifie 'quand ?, à quel moment ?' et **if** signifie 'si' (adverbe interrogatif), et la forme du verbe est la même que celle du verbe de l'interrogation directe correspondante :

do you know when dad's taking the dog out?
est-ce que tu sais quand Papa va sortir le chien ? (quand est-ce que Papa va sortir le chien ?)

I wonder if she'll be there
je me demande si elle sera là

e) *Le présent progressif*

i) Le présent progressif est souvent très semblable à **be going to**, servant à exprimer l'intention :

I'm taking this book with me (I'm going to take this book with me)
j'emporte ce livre (je vais emporter ce livre)

what are you doing over Christmas? (what are you going to do over Christmas?)
qu'est-ce que tu fais à Noël ? (qu'est-ce que tu vas faire ... ?)

ii) Mais lorsque l'idée d'intention est moins importante, le présent progressif a tendance à sous-entendre l'idée d'arrangement préalable, et son usage est alors similaire à celui de **will** + infinitif progressif ou du présent simple :

she's giving two concerts in London next week
elle donne deux concerts à Londres la semaine prochaine

the train for London is leaving soon
le train pour Londres part bientôt

f) ***be to***

On emploie souvent **be to** pour faire référence à des projets d'avenir spécifiques, en particulier des projets qu'ont pour nous d'autres personnes, le hasard ou la destinée :

the President is to visit the disaster zone (pour le style employé dans les grands titres voir p A41)
le président doit visiter la zone sinistrée

we are to be there by ten o'clock
nous devons y être pour dix heures

are we to meet again, I wonder?
nous reverrons-nous un jour, je me le demande ?

g) ***be about to***

Be about to exprime le futur très proche :

you are about to meet a great artist (very shortly you will meet a great artist)
vous êtes sur le point de rencontrer un grand artiste

the play is about to start (any second now)
la pièce est sur le point de commencer

Be about to peut aussi s'employer pour exprimer des intentions quant au futur, mais c'est là un usage plus courant en anglais américain :

I'm not about to let him use my car after what happened last time
je ne vais pas lui laisser prendre ma voiture après ce qui s'est produit la dernière fois

En anglais britannique on aurait davantage tendance à employer **be going to**.

h) *Le futur antérieur (progressif)*

On emploie le futur antérieur pour faire référence à une action qui aura été achevée avant une autre action dans le futur :

by the time we get there he will already have left
d'ici à ce que nous arrivions, il sera déjà parti

by then we'll have been working on this project for 5 years
nous aurons alors travaillé pendant cinq ans sur ce projet

On emploie aussi le futur antérieur pour exprimer des suppositions quant au présent ou au passé :

you'll have been following developments on this, no doubt
vous aurez, sans aucun doute, suivi les développements de cette affaire

13 Pour exprimer la condition

Dans les phrases conditionnelles, on exprime la condition dans une proposition subordonnée placée avant ou après la proposition principale et commençant normalement par **if** :

if the train is late, we'll miss our plane
si le train a du retard, nous raterons notre avion

we'll miss our plane if the train is late
nous raterons notre avion si le train a du retard

Pour les conditions négatives **unless** (si...ne, à moins que) est parfois employé :

unless the train is on time, we'll miss our plane
if the train isn't on time, we'll miss our plane
si le train n'est pas à l'heure, nous raterons notre avion

Etant donné que l'action de la principale dépend de la condition de la subordonnée, cette action doit être au futur (pour les exceptions voir a)i ci-dessous). L'auxiliaire qui se rapproche le plus d'un futur pur est **will**, qui, de même que sa forme du passé **would**, est employé dans les exemples illustrant les emplois des phrases au conditionnel.

a) *Pour faire référence au présent/futur*

i) possibilité vraisemblable :

Le verbe de la proposition subordonnée est au présent ou au present perfect. La proposition principale comprend la construction **will** + infinitif (quelquefois **shall** + infinitif à la 1ère personne) :

if you see her, you will not recognize her
si tu la vois, tu ne la reconnaîtras pas

if you are sitting comfortably, we will begin
si vous êtes assis confortablement, nous allons commencer

if you have completed the forms, I will send them off
si vous avez rempli les formulaires, je les enverrai

if he comes back, I shall ask him to leave
s'il revient, je lui demanderai de partir

Il y a trois exceptions importantes :

★ Si le verbe de la principale est aussi au présent, cela sous-entend généralement un résultat automatique ou habituel. Dans ces phrases, **if** a presque le sens de **when(ever)** (lorsque, à chaque fois que) :

if the sun shines, people look happier
quand le soleil brille, les gens ont l'air plus heureux

if people eat rat poison, they often die
souvent, quand les gens mangent de la mort-aux-rats, ils en meurent

if you're happy, I'm happy
si ça te va, ça me va

if you don't increase your offer, you don't get the house
si vous n'offrez pas plus, vous n'aurez pas la maison

★ Lorsque **will** est aussi employé dans la subordonnée, le locuteur fait alors référence à la bonne volonté d'une personne ou à son intention de faire quelque chose :

if you will be kind enough to stop singing, we will/shall be able to get some sleep
si vous vouliez bien arrêter de chanter, que nous puissions dormir

if you will insist on eating all that fatty food you will have to put up with the consequences
si tu continues à manger aussi gras, tu devras en supporter les conséquences

Lorsque cette forme est employée pour demander à quelqu'un de faire quelque chose, on peut ajouter à la phrase un nuance de politesse en employant **would** :

if you would be kind enough to stop playing the trombone, we would/should be able to get some sleep
si vous aviez la bonté d'arrêter de jouer du trombone, nous pourrions dormir

★ Lorsque l'on emploie **should** dans la subordonnée (à toutes les personnes), cela sous-entend que la condition est moins probable. Ces propositions avec **should** sont souvent suivies de l'impératif, comme cela est le cas dans les deux premiers exemples :

if you should see him, ask him to call
au cas où vous le verriez, demandez-lui de m'appeler

if he should turn up, try and avoid him
s'il venait, essayez de l'éviter

if they should attack you, you will have to fight them
s'ils en venaient à vous attaquer, il vous faudrait vous défendre

Dans un style légèrement plus soutenu, on peut omettre **if** et faire commencer la phrase par la proposition subordonnée avec **should** :

should the matter arise again, telephone me at once
si le problème devait se présenter de nouveau, téléphonez-moi immédiatement

ii) possibilité peu probable ou irréelle :

L'expression 'possibilité peu probable ou irréelle' signifie que l'on s'attend à ce que la condition ne se réalise pas ou qu'on l'oppose à des faits connus. Le verbe de la proposition subordonnée est au passé ; la principale comprend la construction **would** (également **should** à la première personne) + infinitif :

if you saw her, you would not recognize her
si tu la voyais, tu ne la reconnaîtrais pas

if she had a car, she would visit you more often
si elle avait une voiture, elle te rendrait visite plus souvent

if I won that amount of money, I would/should just spend it all
si je gagnais une telle somme d'argent, je dépenserais tout

if the lift was working properly, there would not be so many complaints
si l'ascenseur marchait correctement, il n'y aurait pas autant de réclamations

Ce type de phrase n'exprime pas nécessairement une possibilité peu probable ou irréelle. Elle présente souvent peu de différence par rapport à la construction du type a)i ci-dessus :

if you tried harder, you would pass the exam (if you try harder, you will pass the exam)
si tu faisais plus d'efforts, tu réussirais ton examen

L'emploi du passé peut donner à la phrase un ton un peu plus 'amical' et poli.

b) *Pour faire référence au passé*

i) Dans ces cas-là la condition n'est pas réalisée, puisque ce qui est exprimé dans la proposition commençant par **if** ne s'est pas produit. Le verbe de la subordonnée est au past perfect ; la principale comprend la construction **would** (également **should** à la première personne) + infinitif passé :

if you had seen her, you would not have recognized her
si tu l'avais vue, tu ne l'aurais pas reconnue

if I had been there, I would/should have ignored him
si j'avais été là, j'aurais fait semblant de ne pas le voir

Dans un style légèrement plus soutenu, on peut omettre **if** et faire commencer la subordonnée par **had** :

had I been there, I would/should have ignored him

ii) exceptions :

★ Si la proposition principale fait référence à la non réalisation dans le présent d'une condition dans le passé, on peut aussi employer **would** + infinitif :

if I had studied harder, I would be an engineer today
si j'avais étudié davantage, je serais ingénieur maintenant

★ On emploie le passé dans les deux propositions si, comme cela est le cas dans a) i ci-dessus, on sous-entend un résultat automatique ou habituel (**if** = when(ever)) :

if people had influenza in those days, they died
si les gens attrapaient la grippe en ce temps-là, ils en mouraient

if they tried to undermine the power of the Church, they were burned at the stake
s'ils essayaient de saper le pouvoir de l'Eglise, ils mouraient au bûcher

★ Si on s'attend à ce que la condition se soit réalisée, les restrictions quant à la concordance des temps indiquées dans a) et b) ci-dessus ne s'appliquent plus. Dans ces cas-là, **if** signifie souvent 'comme' ou 'puisque'. Remarquez, par exemple, la diversité des formes verbales employées dans les propositions principales qui suivent les propositions commençant par **if** (qui sont toutes au passé) :

if he was rude to you, why did you not walk out?
s'il a été grossier avec toi, pourquoi est-ce que tu n'es pas parti(e) ?

if he was rude to you, why have you still kept in touch?
if he was rude to you, why do you still keep in touch?
s'il a été grossier avec toi, pourquoi est-ce que tu es resté(e) en contact avec lui ?

if he told you that, he was wrong
s'il t'a dit ça, il a eu tort

if he told you that, he has broken his promise
s'il t'a dit ça, il a manqué à sa promesse

if he told you that, he is a fool
s'il t'a dit ça, c'est un imbécile

14 Le subjonctif

Par opposition à l'indicatif, qui est le mode du réel, le subjonctif est le mode du non-réel, et exprime, par exemple, le souhait, l'espoir, la possibilité, etc. (Voir **Les Modes** p A39).

Le présent du subjonctif est identique par sa forme à l'infinitif (sans **to**) aux trois personnes du singulier et du pluriel. Autrement dit, la seule différence entre les formes du présent du subjonctif et celles du présent de l'indicatif est l'omission du **-s** à la troisième personne du singulier.

L'imparfait du subjonctif n'est marqué du point de vue de la forme qu'à la première et à la troisième personne du singulier du verbe **to be**, qui est **were**. Cependant, dans le langage de tous les jours, on emploie de préférence **was** (voir aussi b) vi ci-dessous).

a) *Le subjonctif dans les propositions principales*

Ici, l'emploi du subjonctif est limité à des locutions fixes exprimant l'espoir ou le souhait, par exemple :

God save the Queen!
Vive la reine !

Long live the King!
Vive le roi !

Heaven be praised!
Dieu soit loué !

b) *Le subjonctif dans les propositions subordonnées*

i) Dans les propositions conditionnelles, le subjonctif passé est d'un emploi très courant; voir 13a) ii ci-dessus. L'emploi du présent du subjonctif appartient à un niveau de langue très soutenu ou à un style littéraire :

if this be true, old hopes are born anew
si c'était vrai, tous les espoirs renaîtraient

sauf dans l'expression consacrée **if need be** = 's'il le faut, si besoin est' :

if need be, we can sell the furniture
s'il le faut, nous pouvons vendre les meubles

Remarquez aussi l'emploi dans les tournures concessives :

they are all interrogated, be they friend or foe
ils sont tous interrogés, qu'ils soient amis ou ennemis

ii) Les propositions comparatives, introduites par **as if** ou **as though** contiennent souvent, mais certainement pas dans tous les cas, un subjonctif passé :

he treats me as if I was/were a child
il me traite comme si j'étais un gamin

iii) Le subjonctif passé est employé après **if only** et dans les propositions compléments d'objet direct après **wish** et **had rather**, toutes ces propositions exprimant le souhait ou le désir :

if only we had a bigger house, life would be perfect
si seulement nous avions une maison plus grande, tout serait parfait

are you going abroad this year? – I wish I were/was
est-ce que tu pars à l'étranger cette année ? – si seulement je pouvais !

I wish he was/were back at school
si seulement il avait repris l'école

where's your passport? – I wish I knew
où est ton passeport ? – si je le savais !

do you want me to tell you? – I'd rather you didn't
tu veux que je te le dise ? – je n'aime mieux pas !

iv) Dans un langage soutenu (par exemple, le langage juridique), on rencontre parfois le présent du subjonctif dans les propositions complément d'objet direct après les verbes ou les expressions impersonnelles (telles que : 'il est souhaitable', 'il est important') indiquant une suggestion ou un souhait :

we propose that the clause be extended to cover such eventualities
nous proposons que la clause soit élargie pour couvrir ces éventualités

it is important that he take steps immediately
il est important qu'il prenne des mesures immédiatement

it is imperative that this matter be discussed further
il est impératif de discuter davantage de cette affaire

Dans ces propositions, le subjonctif est d'un emploi plus courant en anglais américain qu'en anglais britannique et n'est en aucun cas rare en dehors du langage des négociations ou du langage juridique. Bien que l'anglais américain influence rapidement l'anglais britannique, ce dernier préfère toujours l'emploi de **should** + infinitif :

we suggest that the system (should) be changed
nous suggérons que le système soit changé

I am adamant that this (should) be put to the vote
j'insiste pour que cela soit soumis au vote

it is vital that he (should) start as soon as possible
il est primordial qu'il commence aussitôt que possible

v) Après **it's time**, lorsque le locuteur veut insister sur le fait que quelque chose devrait être fait, on emploie le subjonctif passé :

it's time we spoke to him
il est temps que nous lui parlions

it's high time they stopped that
il est grand temps qu'ils arrêtent cela

tandis que dans les exemples suivants, on ne fait qu'exprimer l'opportunité du moment :

it's time to speak to him about it
c'est le moment de lui en parler

***vi)* if I was/if I were**

Les confusions sont fréquentes quant à l'emploi correct de **if I was/if I were**.

Il existe des cas dans lesquels on ne peut employer que **if I was**, c'est-à-dire les cas dans lesquels la condition à laquelle on fait référence n'est en aucun cas une condition irréelle :

if I was mistaken about it then it certainly wasn't through lack of trying
si je me suis trompé(e), ce n'est certainement pas faute d'avoir fait de mon mieux

Le locuteur ne met pas en cause le fait que l'erreur soit réelle, mais il se contente d'en expliquer la cause.

Par contre dans la phrase suivante :

if I were mistaken about it, surely I would have realized
si je m'étais trompé(e), je m'en serais certainement aperçu(e)

le locuteur exprime un doute quant à la réalité de l'erreur et l'emploi du subjonctif **were** est donc approprié. Mais il ne serait pas non plus faux d'employer **was** dans ce contexte; il s'agit simplement là d'une expression appartenant à un langage moins soutenu.

15 Un emploi particulier du passé

Nous avons vu dans les sections 13 et 14 comment le subjonctif passé peut faire référence au présent dans des propositions conditionnelles ou autres. Outre ces emplois du subjonctif passé, le passé peut faire référence au présent dans les propositions principales exprimant une attitude plus hésitante et donc plus polie et respectueuse. Ainsi :

did you want to see me?
vous vouliez me voir ?

est plus poli, plus hésitant, ou moins sec que :

do you want to see me?
vous voulez me voir ?

Mais dans l'expression usuelle :

I was wondering if you could help me do this
est-ce que vous pourriez m'aider à faire cela ?

l'emploi du passé exprime maintenant toujours la nuance de politesse et n'est pour ainsi dire pas différent de :

I wonder if you could help me with this

L'expression usuelle :

I was hoping you could help me here
j'ai un problème, est-ce que vous pourriez m'aider ?

pour formuler une demande polie, n'a pas de construction correspondante au présent.

16 La voix passive

En ce qui concerne les différences de forme entre la voix active et la voix passive, voir p A40.

a) *Le passif direct et indirect*

Dans la phrase à la voix active :

they sent him another bill
ils lui ont envoyé une autre facture

another bill est le complément d'objet direct et **him** est le complément d'objet indirect. Si dans une construction correspondante à la voix passive, le complément d'objet direct de la phrase à la voix active devient le sujet de la phrase à la voix passive, on a alors un 'passif direct' :

another bill was sent (to) him
une autre facture lui a été envoyée

alors qu'un 'passif indirect' aurait pour sujet le complément d'objet indirect de la phrase à la voix active :

he was sent another bill
on lui a envoyé une autre facture

b) *Le passif d'état et le passif d'action*

Dans la phrase suivante, le verbe exprime un état :

the shop is closed
la boutique est fermée

tandis que dans l'exemple suivant, cela ne fait aucun doute qu'il exprime une action :

the shop is closed by his mother at 4 pm every day
la boutique est fermée par sa mère tous les jours à 16 heures

Dans la première phrase le verbe est appelé 'verbe d'état', dans la deuxième phrase le verbe est appelé 'verbe d'action'. C'est le contexte qui nous l'apprend et non pas la forme. La forme du verbe reste la même. L'absence de formes distinctes peut parfois donner lieu à des ambiguïtés comme par exemple :

his neck was broken when they lifted him

signifiant soit (passif d'état) 'son cou était cassé quand ils l'ont soulevé', soit (passif d'action) 'son cou fut cassé quand ils l'ont soulevé'. Cependant si l'on souhaite insister sur l'aspect de passif d'action (souvent plus vivant), on peut employer **get** comme auxiliaire à la place de **be**, dans le language de tous les jours en particulier :

his neck got broken when they lifted him
il a eu le cou cassé quand ils l'ont soulevé

they finally got caught
ils ont fini par se faire prendre

he got kicked out of the pub
il s'est fait mettre à la porte du pub

On peut aussi employer le verbe **have** pour exprimer un passif d'action :

he had his neck broken when they lifted him
il a eu le cou cassé quand ils l'ont soulevé

they've had their house burgled three times
ils se sont fait cambrioler trois fois

c) *Voix passive ou voix active ?*

i) Si ce qui fait l'action est moins important que l'action accomplie, on préfère souvent la voix passive à la voix active. Ainsi dans :

his invitation was refused
son invitation a été refusée

d'après le locuteur l'identité de la personne qui refuse n'a évidemment pas d'importance. Si, dans le langage scientifique en particulier, on emploie de très nombreuses tournures passives, c'est parce que l'on considère que mentionner l'agent ou celui qui fait l'action manque d'objectivité. On écrit :

the experiment was conducted in darkness
l'expérience a été effectuée dans le noir

plutôt que :

I conducted the experiment in darkness
j'ai effectué l'expérience dans le noir

ii) Si celui qui fait l'action n'a aucune importance ou si on ne le connaît pas, de nombreux verbes apparaissent à la voix active mais ont un sens passif. Il y a peu de différence entre :

the theatre runs at a profit
le théâtre fait des bénéfices

et :

the theatre is run at a profit

ou entre

her eyes were filled with tears
ses yeux étaient remplis de larmes

et :

her eyes filled with tears

Ces formes actives à sens passif sont d'un emploi relativement fréquent en anglais et souvent l'emploi d'une forme passive serait maladroit, voire impossible :

a cloth which feels soft
un tissu qui est doux au toucher

silk blouses do not wash well
les chemisiers en soie ne se lavent pas bien

this essay reads better than your last one
cette dissertation se lit mieux que la dernière que vous avez écrite

it flies beautifully
il se pilote très bien

where is the film showing?
où est-ce que le film passe ?

he photographs well
il est photogénique

iii) Quelquefois, la voix active à sens passif se limite à l'infinitif :

the house is to let
la maison est à louer

I am to blame
je suis à blâmer

mais de tels cas sont rares. Cependant, dans les constructions du type **there is** + (pro)nom avec infinitif, l'infinitif actif à sens passif est courant :

there is work to do (= ... to be done)
il y a du travail à faire

when we get home there'll be suitcases to unpack
quand nous rentrerons à la maison, il y aura les valises à défaire

there was plenty to eat
il y avait beaucoup de choses à manger

have you got anything to wash?
est-ce que tu as quelque chose à laver ?

Dans certains cas, on peut employer indifféremment l'infinitif actif ou l'infinitif passif :

> **there's nothing else to say/to be said**
> il n'y a rien d'autre à dire
>
> **is there anything to gain/to be gained from it?**
> est-ce qu'il y a quelque chose à y gagner ?

Mais quelquefois dans ces constructions après les pronoms **something**, **anything**, **nothing**, il peut y avoir une différence entre l'infinitif actif (à sens passif) et l'infinitif passif de **do**. Par exemple :

> **there is always something to do**

signifie généralement (mais pas nécessairement) 'on trouve toujours à s'occuper', tandis que :

> **there is always something to be done**

signifie 'il y a toujours du travail à faire'.

iv) 'on'

Le passif est bien plus employé en anglais qu'en français. Souvent le français préfère une construction avec 'on' :

> **he was spotted leaving the bar**
> on l'a vu sortant du bar
>
> **that's already been done**
> on l'a déjà fait
>
> **I hadn't been told that**
> on ne m'avait pas dit ça

17 Be, have, do

a) *be*

i) **Be** est employé comme auxiliaire avec le participe passé afin de former un passif, et avec le participe présent pour exprimer l'aspect progressif du passif (p A40). Parfois **be** peut remplacer **have** en tant qu'auxiliaire pour l'aspect 'perfect' (ou passé) (voir p A40), comme dans :

are you finished? est-ce que tu as fini ?	**our happiness is gone** notre bonheur s'est enfui

Dans ces cas-là, on insiste particulièrement sur l'état actuel plutôt que sur l'action.

ii) Comme les autres auxiliaires modaux, **be** n'est pas accompagné de **do** dans les négations et les interrogations. Cependant, lorsque **be** se comporte comme un verbe indépendant et non pas comme un auxiliaire, on emploie **do** dans les impératifs à la forme négative :

> **don't be silly**
> ne fais pas l'idiot

iii) Lorsque **be** est un verbe ordinaire (c'est-à-dire pas un auxiliaire), il n'est pas employé à l'aspect progressif, sauf lorsqu'il fait exclusivement référence au comportement. Ainsi il y a une différence entre :

> **he is silly**
> il est sot (= de nature)

et :

> **he is being silly**
> il fait le sot

et entre :

> **he's American**
> il est américain

et :

> **if you said it that way, I'd assume you were deliberately being American**
> si tu disais ça de cette façon, je penserais que tu t'exprimes exprès à l'américaine

b) *have*

i) **Have** est employé avec le participe passé pour former l'aspect 'perfect' (p A39).

En tant que verbe ordinaire, il exprime quelquefois une activité ou une expérience, comme dans les expressions suivantes :

to have dinner dîner/ déjeuner	**to have difficulty** avoir du mal à
to have a chat bavarder	**to have a good time** s'amuser/passer un bon moment

Lorsque **have** n'exprime pas une activité, il fait normalement référence à la possession, à un état, ou à quelque chose organisé à l'avance :

to have a farm avoir une ferme	**to have an appointment** avoir un rendez-vous
to have toothache avoir mal aux dents	**to have time (**for or **to do something)** avoir le temps (de faire quelque chose)

Donc :

> **she'll have the baby in August**

appartient au premier type si la phrase signifie qu'elle donnera naissance au bébé. Par contre, si la phrase signifie qu'elle 'recevra' le bébé (si elle l'adopte, par exemple), elle appartient au deuxième type.

On peut appeler les types **have 1** (**activité +**) et **have 2** (**activité -**).

ii) **have 1** :

★ Il se comporte comme les verbes ordinaires normaux dans les interrogations et dans les négations, c'est-à-dire qu'il est accompagné de **do**, ainsi que dans les question-tags :

> **did you have the day off yesterday?**
> est-ce que tu a pris un jour de congé hier ?
>
> **we don't have conversations any more**
> nous ne nous parlons plus
>
> **we had a marvellous time, didn't we?**
> nous avons vraiment passé un très bon moment, n'est-ce pas ?

★ **Have 1** peut s'employer à l'aspect progressif :

> **he telephoned as we were having lunch**
> il a téléphoné pendant que nous déjeunions
>
> **I'm having trouble with Carol these days**
> j'ai des problèmes avec Carol ces temps-ci

iii) **have 2** :

★ Au lieu de **have 2**, l'anglais britannique emploie souvent **have got**, particulièrement dans le langage parlé, et surtout au présent :

> **he has/he has got/he's got a large garden**
> il a un grand jardin

Au passé, on emploie normalement **had** ou **used to have**, ce dernier insistant sur l'idée de possession prolongée, la répétition ou l'habitude :

> **they all had flu in July last year**
> ils ont tous eu la grippe en juillet l'année dernière
>
> **he had/used to have a large garden once**
> autrefois, il avait un grand jardin
>
> **we had/used to have lots of problems in those days**
> en ce temps-là, nous avions beaucoup de problèmes

★ Dans les interrogations, le sujet et **have** peuvent être inversés :

> **have you any other illnesses?**
> avez-vous d'autres maladies ?

Dans les négations, **not** peut s'employer sans **do** :

> **he hasn't a garden**
> il n'a pas de jardin

On considère parfois ces phrases comme appartenant à un niveau de langue plutôt soutenu, et dans le langage de tous les jours, on préfère employer **have ... got** ou une construction avec **do** :

> **have you got/do you have any other illnesses?**
> **he hasn't got/doesn't have a garden**

La tournure en **do** est récemment devenue d'un emploi plus fréquent du fait de l'influence de l'anglais américain où il est normal de l'employer. Notez que si le locuteur souhaite faire passer l'idée de quelque chose qui se produit habituellement, régulièrement ou de façon générale, alors on emploie particulièrement fréquemment la tournure en **do** :

have you got/do you have any food for the dog?
est-ce que tu as de la nourriture pour le chien ?

mais :

do you always have dog-food in the sideboard ?
est-ce que tu as toujours de la nourriture pour chiens dans ton buffet ?

lorsque **have** a un sens très voisin de 'avoir en permanence'. De même :

have you got/do you have a pain in your chest?
est-ce que vous ressentez une douleur dans la poitrine ?

mais :

do you frequently have a pain in your chest?
est-ce que vous ressentez souvent une douleur dans la poitrine ?

Dans les question-tags après **have**, on peut employer **have** ou **do** puisque, comme nous l'avons vu, **have** peut s'employer avec ou sans **do** dans les interrogations. **Do**, de plus en plus fréquemment employé à cause de l'usage américain, est particulièrement courant au passé :

he has a Rolls, hasn't/doesn't he?
il a une Rolls, n'est-ce pas ?

they had a large garden once, hadn't they/didn't they?
ils avaient un grand jardin autrefois, n'est-ce pas ?

Mais après **have got**, on ne peut employer que **have** dans les questions-tags :

he's got a Rolls, hasn't he?
il a une Rolls, n'est-ce pas ?

Remarquez la différence suivante entre l'anglais britannique et l'anglais américain :

have you a minute? – no, I haven't (britannique)
have you a minute? – no, I don't (américain)
tu as une minute? – non

★ L'aspect progressif n'est pas possible avec **have 2** à moins qu'il fasse référence au futur. Ainsi :

they are having a baby

ne signifie en aucun cas 'ils ont un bébé', mais 'ils vont avoir un bébé'. Dans la phrase :

today I'm having the car
aujourd'hui je prends la voiture

am having = type **have 1**.

iv) L'emploi causatif de ***have*** :

Le verbe **have** est employé dans des constructions du type 'faire faire quelque chose'. Par exemple :

they're having a new porch built
ils se font construire une nouveau porche

could you have these photocopied?
est-ce que vous pouvez faire photocopier cela ?

I'll have it done immediately
je vais le faire faire immédiatement

we'll have to have the loo fixed
il va falloir que nous fassions réparer les W.-C.

what on earth have you had done to your hair?
qu'est-ce qui est arrivé à tes cheveux ?

Remarquez que **get** peut s'employer à la place de **have** dans tous les exemples ci-dessus, sauf le dernier.

★ Dans une construction américaine, l'idée de 'faire faire quelque chose' a en majeure partie disparu :

Mr Braithwaite is here – ah, have him come in
M. Braithwaite est là – ah, faites-le entrer

Ceci équivaut simplement à prier quelqu'un de demander à M. Braithwaite d'entrer.

★ On peut aussi employer le verbe **have** ou **get** avec un complément d'objet direct :

I'll have the kitchen send it up to your room, madam
je vais demander à la cuisine de vous le monter à votre chambre, madame

Notez que **have** est employé sans **to**. Cependant avec **get**, qui a le même sens, on emploi **to** :

I'll get the kitchen to send it up to your room, madam

v) Constructions à la voix passive :

Le verbe **have** s'emploie aussi pour former un type de construction passive, particulièrement pour sous-entendre que le sujet de la phrase a souffert d'une manière ou d'une autre (voir aussi 16 b) :

he's had all his money stolen
il s'est fait voler tout son argent

he's had both his wives killed in car crashes
ses deux femmes se sont fait tuer dans des accidents de voiture

c) *do*

On a déjà vu l'emploi de **do** dans les interrogations et les négations - voir p A46. Voir p A72 pour son emploi dans les autres cas d'inversion.

i) Le **do** emphatique :

Dans les phrases qui ne sont ni des interrogations, ni des négations, on peut, pour marquer l'emphase, employer un **do** (que l'on accentue à l'oral) avant le verbe principal :

oh, I do like your new jacket!
oh, j'aime beaucoup ta nouvelle veste !

do try to keep still !
essaye de rester tranquille

he doesn't know any German but he does know a little French
il ne sait pas l'allemand, mais par contre il sait un peu de français

I didn't manage to get tickets for ..., but I did get some for...
je n'ai pas réussi à avoir de billets pour ..., mais par contre, j'en ai pour ...

Et le verbe **do** lui-même peut s'employer avec **do** en tant qu'auxiliaire emphatique :

well, if you don't do that, what do you do?
bon, si tu ne fais pas ça, qu'est-ce que tu fais, alors ?

we don't do much skiing, but what we do do is go hill-walking
nous ne faisons pas beaucoup de ski, mais par contre nous faisons des promenades en montagne

ii) **do** pour remplacer le verbe :

On a déjà donné des exemples de cet emploi dans la section traitant des question-tags (voir p A46). En voici d'autres exemples :

she never drinks! – oh yes, she does
elle ne boit jamais ! – bien sûr que si

can I help myself to another cream cake? – please do
est-ce que je peux avoir un autre gâteau à la crème ? – je vous en prie !

do you both agree? – I do, but she doesn't
vous êtes tous les deux d'accord ? – moi oui, mais elle, non

18 Les auxiliaires modaux

Ce sont les auxiliaires **will-would**, **shall-should**, **can-could**, **may-might**, **must-had to**, **ought to**.

a) *will-would*

Les formes négatives contractées sont **won't-wouldn't**.

i) Pour les phrases au conditionnel voir pp A50-1.

ii) Pour une étude générale de l'expression du futur, voir p A49.

iii) Pour exprimer les ordres plutôt qu'un futur pur :

you will do as you are told!
tu feras ce qu'on te dit !

new recruits will report to headquarters on Tuesday at 8.30 am
les jeunes recrues se présenteront au quartier général mardi à 8 heures 30

will you stop that right now!
arrête tout de suite !

iv) Pour faire appel, sur un ton plutôt cérémonieux, aux souvenirs ou aux connaissances de quelqu'un :

you will recall last week's discussion about the purchase of a computer
vous vous souvenez certainement de notre discussion de la semaine dernière concernant l'achat d'un ordinateur

you will all know that the inspector has completed his report
vous savez certainement tous que l'inspecteur a terminé son procès-verbal

v) Pour exprimer une supposition, plutôt qu'un futur :

there's the telephone, Mary! – oh, that will be John
le téléphone sonne, Mary ! – oh, ça doit être John

they'll be there by now
ils/elles doivent être arrivé(e)s maintenant

how old is he now? – he'll be about 45
quel âge a-t-il maintenant ? – il doit avoir à peu près 45 ans

vi) Pour insister sur la notion de capacité ou d'inclination naturelle ou inhérente, ou sur la notion de comportement caractéristique, plutôt que pour exprimer un futur :

cork will float on water
le liège flotte sur l'eau

the Arts Centre will hold about 300 people
le centre culturel peut contenir environ 300 personnes

John will sit playing with a matchbox for hours
John peut rester assis à jouer avec une boîte d'allumettes pendant des heures

it's so annoying, he will keep interrupting! (accent sur 'will' à l'oral)
c'est énervant, il n'arrête pas de m'interrompre !

the car won't start
la voiture ne veut pas démarrer

well, if you will drive so fast, what do you expect?
ben ! il fallait t'y attendre, à conduire aussi vite !

De même **would**, pour faire référence au passé :

when he was little, John would sit playing with a matchbox for hours
quand il était petit, John restait assis à jouer avec une boîte d'allumettes pendant des heures

she created a scene in public – she would!
elle a fait une scène en public – c'est bien elle !

vii) Pour poser des questions ou proposer quelque chose :

will you have another cup?
vous en voulez une autre tasse ?

won't you try some of these?
vous ne voulez pas y goûter ?

viii) Pour demander à quelqu'un de faire quelque chose :

will you move your car, please?
est-ce que vous pouvez déplacer votre voiture, s'il vous plaît ?

On peut poser la même question d'une façon légèrement plus polie :

would you move your car, please?
est-ce que vous pourriez déplacer votre voiture, s'il vous plaît ?

ix) Pour exprimer la détermination :

I will not stand for this!
je ne le supporterai pas !

I will be obeyed!
je veux qu'on m'obéisse !

b) *shall-should*

Les formes négatives contractées sont **shan't-shouldn't**.

i) Pour les phrases au conditionnel, voir p A50.

ii) Pour **should**, équivalent du subjonctif, voir p A52.

iii) Pour **shall** exprimant le futur, voir p A49.

iv) (**shall** uniquement) Dans le langage juridique ou officiel, **shall** s'emploie fréquemment pour exprimer une obligation. Ce sens de **shall** est très semblable à celui de **must** :

the committee shall consist of no more than six members
le comité sera constitué de six membres au plus

the contract shall be subject to English law
le contrat sera régi par la loi anglaise

v) (**should** uniquement) obligation (souvent obligation morale) :

you should lose some weight
tu devrais perdre du poids

he shouldn't be allowed to
il ne devrait pas y être autorisé

you really should see this film
tu devrais essayer de voir ce film

is everything as it should be?
est-ce que tout va comme il faut ?

something was not quite as it should be
il y avait quelque chose qui n'allait pas

vi) (**should** uniquement) déduction, probabilité :

it's ten o'clock, they should be back any minute
il est dix heures, ils devraient rentrer d'un moment à l'autre

John should have finished putting up those shelves by now
John devrait avoir fini d'installer ces étagères maintenant

are they there? – I don't know, but they should be
ils/elles sont là ? – je ne sais pas, mais ils/elles devraient

vii) (**should** uniquement) affirmations hésitantes :

I should just like to say that ...
j'aimerais simplement dire que ...

I should hardly think that's right
je ne pense pas que ça soit vrai

will he agree? – I shouldn't think so
est-ce qu'il sera d'accord ? – je ne pense pas

viii) **Should** est souvent employé pour faire référence à la **notion** (par opposition à la **réalité concrète**) d'une action. Cet emploi de **should** est quelquefois qualifié de 'putatif' :

that she should want to take early retirement is quite understandable
il est tout à fait compréhensible qu'elle veuille prendre sa retraite anticipée

Comparez ce dernier exemple avec :

it is quite understandable that she wanted to take early retirement
il est tout à fait compréhensible qu'elle ait voulu prendre sa retraite anticipée

La différence est subtile. Dans le premier cas, la proposition subordonnée est au présent. Dans le second cas, elle est au passé.

Il est important de remarquer que ce **should** est neutre pour ce qui est du temps. Le premier exemple ci-dessus pourrait tout aussi bien faire référence au passé (**she has taken early**

retirement) ou au futur (**she will be taking early retirement**) suivant le contexte. Le second exemple ne peut bien sûr que faire référence au passé.

L'emploi putatif de **should** peut être comparé à l'emploi de **should** lorsqu'il est employé après les constructions ou après les verbes impersonnels de suggestion, de souhait ou d'ordre, dont il est question dans la section sur le subjonctif, pp A51-2.

Dans l'exemple ci-dessus, l'emploi putatif de **should** est apparu dans une proposition subordonnée, mais il peut aussi apparaître dans des propositions principales :

> **where have I put my glasses? – how should I know?**
> où est-ce que j'ai mis mes lunettes ? – comment veux-tu que je le sache ?

> **as we were sitting there, who should walk by but Joan Collins!**
> nous étions assis, là, et devine qui passe ? ... Joan Collins !

> **there was a knock at the door, and who should it be but ...**
> on frappe à la porte, et qui c'est ? ...

c) *can-could*

Les formes négatives contractées de **can-could** sont **can't-couldn't**. La forme négative non contractée au présent est **cannot**.

i) capacité (= be able to) :

> **I can't afford it**
> je ne peux me le permettre

> **I can swim**
> je sais nager

> **when I was young, I could swim for hours**
> quand j'étais jeune, je pouvais nager pendant des heures

La troisième phrase fait référence à une capacité passée. Cependant, dans les propositions conditionnelles, **could** + infinitif fait référence au présent et au futur (comparez avec **would** dans la section **Pour Exprimer la Condition** pp A50-1) :

> **if you try/tried harder, you could lose weight**
> si tu faisais plus d'efforts, tu arriverais à perdre du poids

ii) permission :

> **can/could I have a sweet?**
> je peux avoir un bonbon ?

Remarquez que **could** fait autant référence au présent ou au futur que **can**. La seule différence est que **could** est un peu plus hésitant ou poli. Cependant, **could** peut quelquefois s'employer pour exprimer une permission au passé lorsque le contexte est incontestablement passé :

> **for some reason we couldn't smoke in the lounge yesterday; but today we can**
> pour une raison ou une autre, nous ne pouvions pas fumer dans le salon hier, mais aujourd'hui nous pouvons

Il existe souvent une légère nuance de sens entre **can** et **may** lorsqu'ils signifient 'avoir le droit de', dans la mesure où **can** est moins cérémonieux que **may**.

iii) possibilité :

> **what shall we do tonight? – well, we can/could watch a film**
> qu'est-ce qu'on va faire ce soir ? – ben ... on pourrait voir un film

Là encore, on peut remarquer que **could** ne fait pas référence au passé mais au présent ou au futur. Pour faire référence au passé, on doit employer **could** suivi de l'infinitif passé :

> **instead of going to the pub, we could have watched a film**
> au lieu d'aller au pub, nous aurions pu voir un film

> **I could have (could've) gone there if I'd wanted to, but I didn't**
> j'aurais pu y aller si j'avais voulu, mais je ne voulais pas

Il y a quelquefois une différence importante entre **can** et **may** quant à la façon dont ils font référence à la possibilité : **can** exprime fréquemment la possibilité logique pure et simple, tandis que **may** sous-entend souvent l'incertitude, le hasard ou un certain degré de probabilité d'un événement :

> (a) **your comments can be overheard**
> on peut entendre vos remarques

> (b) **your comments may be overheard**
> on pourrait entendre vos remarques

Dans (a) on dit qu'il est possible d'entendre les remarques, par exemple parce qu'elles sont faites à voix très haute, qu'il soit ou non probable que quelqu'un les entende effectivement. Dans (b) on dit qu'il est dans une certaine mesure probable que quelqu'un entende effectivement les remarques.

On peut aussi voir la différence dans les propositions à la forme négative :

> **he can't have heard us** (= it is impossible for him to have heard us)
> il ne peut pas nous avoir entendus

> **he may not have heard us** (= it is possible that he did not hear us)
> il se peut qu'il ne nous ait pas entendus

iv) suggestions (**could** uniquement) :

> **you could always try Marks & Spencers**
> tu peux toujours essayer à Marks & Spencers

> **he could express himself more clearly**
> il pourrait s'exprimer plus clairement

Cette construction peut parfois traduire une sorte de reproche :

> **you could have let us know!**
> tu aurais pu nous le dire !

> **he could have warned us!**
> il aurait pu nous prévenir !

d) *may-might*

La forme négative contractée **mayn't** exprimant la permission négative, c'est-à-dire l'interdiction, disparaît progressivement et est remplacée par **may not** ou **must not/mustn't** ou encore **can't**. La forme négative contractée de **might** est **mightn't**, mais elle n'est pas employée pour exprimer l'interdiction.

i) permission :

> **you may sit down** (comparer avec **can** dans c) ii ci-dessus, ici langage plutôt soutenu)
> vous pouvez vous asseoir

> **may I open a window? – no, you may not!**
> est-ce que je peux ouvrir une fenêtre ? – non, pas question

> **you must not/mustn't open the windows in here**
> tu ne dois pas ouvrir les fenêtres ici

Il est extrêmement poli d'employer **might** pour exprimer la permission :

> **I wonder if I might have another wee glass of sherry**
> pourrais-je avoir un autre petit verre de sherry ?

> **might I suggest we adjourn the meeting?**
> puis-je me permettre de suggérer que nous ajournions la réunion ?

Notez que **might** fait référence au présent et au futur, et fait très rarement référence au passé lorsqu'il est employé dans une proposition principale. Comparez :

> **he then asked if he might smoke** (langage plutôt soutenu)
> **he then asked if he was allowed to smoke**
> il a alors demandé s'il pouvait fumer

et :

he wasn't allowed to smoke
il n'avait pas le droit de fumer, il ne pouvait pas fumer

On ne peut pas employer **might** dans le dernier exemple. On ne peut employer **might** comme passé dans une principale que dans certains cas spéciaux :

in those days we were told not to drink; nor might we smoke or be out after 10 o'clock
en ce temps-là, nous n'avions pas le droit de boire, pas plus que de fumer ou de rentrer après dix heures

Une manière plus courante et moins littéraire de formuler cette phrase serait :

in those days we were told not to drink; nor were we allowed to smoke or be out after 10 o'clock

ii) possibilité :

it may/might rain
il pleuvra, peut-être

they may/might be right
il se peut qu'ils aient raison

it mayn't/mightn't be so easy as you think
ce ne sera peut-être pas aussi facile que vous le pensez

she may/might have left already
elle est peut-être déjà partie

Might exprime généralement un moindre degré de possibilité.

Remarquez la tournure idiomatique :

and who may/might you be?
à qui ai-je l'honneur ?

dans laquelle l'emploi de **may/might** introduit une nuance de surprise, d'amusement ou peut-être d'ennui dans la question :

and who may/might you be to give out orders?
et pour qui est-ce que tu te prends pour donner des ordres ?

iii) Notez l'emploi de **might** pour formuler des suggestions :

you might help me dry the dishes
tu pourrais m'aider à essuyer la vaisselle

well, you might at least try!
tu pourrais au moins essayer, enfin !

you might have a look at chapter 2 for next Wednesday
vous voudrez bien lire le chapitre 2 pour mercredi prochain

he might be a little less abrupt
il pourrait être un peu moins brusque

L 'usage suivant exprime souvent une pointe de reproche :

you might have warned us what would happen!
vous auriez pu nous prévenir de ce qui allait se produire !

he might have tried to stop it!
il aurait pu essayer d'arrêter cela !

iv) souhaits :

may the best man win!
que le meilleur gagne !

may you be forgiven for telling such lies!
que le Bon Dieu te pardonne de dire de tels mensonges !

might I be struck dumb if I tell a lie!
que le diable m'emporte si je mens !

Cet usage est normalement réservé à des expressions consacrées (comme dans les deux premiers exemples) ou considérées comme étant d'un style quelque peu ampoulé ou littéraire (comme dans le dernier).

e) *must-had to*

i) obligation :

you must try harder
tu dois faire un effort

we must park the car here and walk the rest of the way
il faut que nous garions la voiture ici et que nous fassions le reste du chemin à pied

Remarquez que l'on emploie **had to** pour le passé. On ne peut employer **must** pour le passé qu'au discours indirect, et même alors **had to** est beaucoup plus courant :

you said the other day that you had to/must clean out the garden shed
tu as dit l'autre jour qu'il faudrait que tu nettoies la cabane du jardin

On peut aussi employer **have to**, ou **have got to** dans un niveau de langue moins soutenu, au présent. La différence entre **must** et **have (got) to** réside généralement dans le fait que **must** exprime des sentiments personnels d'obligation ou de contrainte tandis que **have (got) to** exprime une obligation extérieure. Comparez :

I must go and visit my friend in hospital
il faut que je rende visite à mon amie à l'hôpital (= je pense qu'il est nécessaire que j'y aille)

you must go and visit your friend in hospital
il faut que tu rendes visite à ton ami à l'hôpital (je pense qu'il est nécessaire que tu y ailles)

I have (got) to be at the hospital by 4 pm
je dois être à l'hôpital pour 4 heures de l'après-midi (c'est-à-dire j'y ai un rendez-vous)

ii) négations :

Les tournures négatives exigent une vigilance toute particulière. On ne peut employer **must not/mustn't** que pour exprimer l'interdiction (= une obligation de ne pas faire quelque chose) :

we mustn't park the car here (= we're not allowed to park here)
nous ne devons pas nous garer ici (= nous n'avons pas le droit de nous garer ici)

you mustn't take so many pills (= do not take so many pills)
il ne faut pas que tu prennes autant de cachets

Mais si l'obligation négative signifie, non pas par exemple qu'il est interdit de faire quelque chose, mais qu'il n'est pas nécessaire ou obligatoire de faire quelque chose, alors ont doit employer **don't have to** ou **haven't got to** :

we don't have to park here, we could always drive a little further
nous ne sommes pas obligés de nous garer ici, nous pourrions aller un peu plus loin

you don't have to take so many pills (= you needn't take ...)
tu n'as pas besoin de prendre autant de comprimés

we haven't got to be there before 9
nous n'avons pas besoin d'y être avant neuf heures

iii) déduction, probabilité :

if they're over 65, they must be old age pensioners
s'ils ont plus de 65 ans, ils doivent être retraités

you must be joking!
tu veux rire !

they must have been surprised to see you
ils ont dû être surpris de te voir

Have to s'emploie souvent dans ce sens :

you have to be kidding!
c'est une blague !

de même que **have got to**, en anglais britannique en particulier :

well if she said so, it's got to be true (it's = it has)
si elle l'a dit, c'est que c'est vrai

A la forme négative, on emploie **can** :

he can't be that old!
il ne peut pas être si vieux que ça !

f) ***ought to***

La forme négative contractée de **ought to** est **oughtn't to**, et l'infinitif placé après **ought** est précédé de **to**, ce qui n'est pas le cas des autres auxiliaires modaux.

i) obligation :

Ought to et **should**, lorsqu'ils expriment l'obligation, ont des significations similaires :

you oughtn't to speak to her like that
tu ne devrais pas lui parler de cette façon

I ought to be going now
il faudrait que je m'en aille maintenant

I know I really ought (to), but I don't want to
je sais bien que je devrais, mais je n'en ai pas envie

ii) déduction, probabilité :

they ought to have reached the summit by now
ils devraient avoir atteint le sommet maintenant

20 square metres? – that ought to be enough
20 mètres carrés ? – ça devrait suffire

Comparez la différence entre **ought to** et **must** dans la phrase suivante :

if they possess all these things, they must be rich
(déduction logique)
ils doivent être riches s'ils possèdent tout ça

if they possess all these things, they ought to be happy (prévision ou probabilité logique - ou obligation morale)
ils devraient être heureux s'ils possèdent tout ça

g) ***used to***

Puisqu'il est possible de former des phrases interrogatives et négatives contenant **used to** sans employer **do**, certains considèrent **used to** comme une sorte de semi-auxiliaire. Cependant, l'emploi de **do** est au moins aussi courant que le fait de l'omettre :

he used not/usedn't to visit us so often
he didn't use to visit us so often
(autrefois), il ne nous rendait pas visite aussi souvent

A la forme interrogative, la forme sans **do** est moins courante et appartient davantage au langage écrit qu'au langage parlé :

used you to live abroad?
did you use to live abroad?
est-ce que vous habitiez à l'étranger (autrefois) ?

On emploie souvent **never** à la place de **not** :

he never used to visit us so often
(autrefois), il ne nous rendait pas visite aussi souvent

Used to exprime une action habituelle dans le passé, mais sans cependant exprimer l'idée de comportement typique ou caractéristique que traduirait **would**, voir (a) vi ci-dessus :

John used to play badminton when he was younger
John jouait au badminton lorsqu'il était plus jeune

I used to live abroad
autrefois, je vivais à l'étranger

do you smoke? – I used to
est-ce que tu fumes ? – plus maintenant

19 Dare, need

Ces verbes peuvent se comporter soit comme des verbes ordinaires, soit comme des auxiliaires modaux. Lorsqu'ils sont auxiliaires :

- ils ne prennent pas de **-s** à la troisième personne du singulier du présent
- on n'emploie pas **do** dans les phrases interrogatives ou négatives
- s'ils sont suivis d'un infinitif, celui-ci n'est pas précédé de **to**.

a) *Lorsqu'ils sont verbes ordinaires*

he didn't dare to speak
il n'osait pas parler/il n'a pas osé parler

does he really dare to talk openly about it?
est-ce qu'il ose vraiment en parler ouvertement ?

I dare you
je t'en défie

he needs some money
il a besoin d'argent

you don't need to pay for them now
ce n'est pas la peine que tu les paies maintenant

all he needs to do now is buy the tickets
tout ce qu'il a à faire maintenant, c'est d'acheter les billets

Cependant, **dare** peut être en partie un verbe ordinaire (par exemple avec **do** dans les phrases interrogatives ou négatives) et en partie un auxiliaire (suivi d'un infinitif sans **to**) :

does he really dare talk openly about it?
est-ce qu'il ose vraiment en parler ouvertement ?

mais on doit employer l'infinitif avec **to** après le participe présent :

not daring to speak to her, he quietly left the room
n'osant pas lui parler, il sortit de la pièce silencieusement

Dans les propositions **principales** à la forme affirmative (c'est-à-dire les propositions principales qui ne sont ni interrogatives ni négatives), **need** ne peut qu'avoir le statut de verbe ordinaire :

the child needs to go to the toilet
l'enfant a besoin d'aller aux toilettes

b) *Lorsqu'ils sont auxiliaires modaux*

he dared not speak
il n'osait pas parler/il n'a pas osé parler

dare he talk openly about it?
est-ce qu'il ose en parler ouvertement ?

this is as much as I dare spend on it
je ne peux pas me permettre de dépenser plus

you needn't pay for them right now
ce n'est pas la peine que tu les paies maintenant

need I pay for this now?
est-ce qu'il faut que je paie ça maintenant ?

all he need do now is buy the tickets
tout ce qu'il a à faire maintenant, c'est d'acheter les billets

Notez que **I dare say** = 'probablement' :

I dare say he's going to fail
il va probablement échouer

is it going to rain, do you think? – I dare say it will
est-ce que tu crois qu'il va pleuvoir ? – probablement

20 Les verbes composés

a) *Les verbes composés inséparables*

i) Il est important de faire une distinction entre un 'verbe + préposition introduisant un complément' ((a) et (c) ci-dessous) et un 'verbe composé + complément d'objet direct' ((b) et (d)). Dans le dernier cas, la préposition fonctionne comme une **particule** faisant partie du verbe, c'est-à-dire comme un prolongement du verbe. Comparez les deux phrases :

(a) **they danced after dinner**
ils ont dansé après le dîner

(b) **they looked after the child**
ils se sont occupé de l'enfant

Au premier abord, ces deux phrases semblent avoir la même structure, et cependant, lorsqu'on y regarde de plus près, on se rend compte que les deux mots **look after** forment une seule unité verbale (comparez avec **they nursed the child** ils ont soigné l'enfant), tandis que cela n'est pas le cas pour **danced after** : **after dinner** est un complément introduit par une préposition distincte du verbe et qui fonctionnent comme groupe adverbial de temps dans (a), tandis que **the child** est le complément d'objet direct de **look after** dans (b). On peut observer la même différence dans les deux exemples suivants :

(c) **they went through Germany**
ils sont passés par l'Allemagne

(d) **they went through the accounts** (= examined)
ils ont examiné la comptabilité

ii) **Look after** et **go through** (= examiner) sont des verbes composés. Ceux-ci sont souvent très idiomatiques, c'est-à-dire qu'on ne peut pas déduire leur sens du sens des différents éléments qui les composent, car ceux-ci peuvent rarement se traduire littéralement. Voici d'autres exemples :

go by (= suivre – des instructions)
pick on (= chercher querelle à, s'en prendre à)
get at (= attaquer ; graisser la patte à)

you can't do your own thing; you have to go by the book
tu ne peux pas faire ce que tu veux ; il faut agir selon les règles

the teacher's always picking on him
le professeur s'en prend toujours à lui

my mother is always getting at me
ma mère est toujours sur mon dos

I'm sure the jury have been got at
je suis sûr qu'on a graissé la patte au jury

iii) Certaines structures que l'on pourrait former avec un verbe + préposition introduisant un complément ne peuvent en aucun cas être formées avec les verbes composés. Par exemple, les interrogations avec les verbes composés admettent l'emploi des pronoms **who** et **what**, mais pas l'emploi des adverbes **where, when, how** :

they looked after the girl/who(m) did they look after?
ils se sont occupé de la petite fille/de qui se sont-ils occupé ?

they went through the accounts/what did they go through?
ils ont examiné la comptabilité/qu'est-ce qu'ils ont examiné ?

the police officer grappled with the thug/who(m) did he grapple with?
l'agent de police a lutté avec le voyou/avec qui a-t-il lutté ?

Mais les interrogations **where did they look?/where did they go?/how** (ou **where**) **did he grapple?** n'ont aucun sens. Par contre le verbe + préposition introduisant un complément admet souvent des interrogations introduites par un adverbe :

they went through Germany/where did they go?
ils sont passés par l'Allemagne/par où est-ce qu'ils sont passés ?

they worked with great care/how did they work?
ils ont travaillé avec beaucoup de soin/comment ont-ils travaillé ?

they danced after dinner/when did they dance?
ils ont dansé après le dîner/quand ont-ils dansé ?

iv) Un verbe composé étant considéré comme une seule unité, on peut souvent (mais pas toujours) l'employer dans une construction passive :

the child has been looked after very well indeed
on s'est vraiment très bien occupé de l'enfant

the accounts have been gone through
la comptabilité a été examinée

do you feel you're being got at?
est-ce que tu as l'impression que tout le monde est après toi ?

On ne peut pas employer le passif avec un verbe + préposition introduisant un complément. On ne peut pas dire **the dinner was danced after** ou **great care has been worked with**.

b) *Les verbes composés séparables*

i) Une différence importante entre les verbes composés inséparables et les verbes composés séparables réside dans la possibilité qu'ont les verbes composés séparables d'admettre un complément d'objet direct avant la particule :

look up these words/look these words up
cherche ces mots (dans le dictionnaire)

turn down the television/turn the television down
baisse la télévision

have you switched on the computer?/have you switched the computer on?
est-ce que tu as mis l'ordinateur en marche ?

have you tried on any of their new line of shoes?/have you tried any of their new line of shoes on?
est-ce que tu as essayé leurs nouveaux modèles de chaussures ?

Et si le complément d'objet direct est un pronom, la particule **doit** être placée après celui-ci :

look them up/turn it down/switch it on
cherche-les/baisse-la/mets-le en marche

ii) Tandis que les verbes composés inséparables sont toujours transitifs (lorsqu'on les considère comme unités complètes), certains verbes composés séparables sont toujours transitifs et d'autres peuvent être transitifs ou intransitifs :

back up (= soutenir - seulement transitif) :
he always backs her up
il la soutient toujours

cool down (= faire refroidir - transitif) :
cool the rolls down in the fridge
fais refroidir les petits pains dans le frigidaire

cool down (= se refroidir - intransitif) :
let the rolls cool down
laisse les petits pains refroidir

iii) Avec les verbes composés séparables, la particule ne peut pas précéder un pronom relatif, alors que cela est la seule position possible avec les verbes composés inséparables. Nous pouvons ainsi dire :

this is a man on whom you can rely
c'est un homme sur lequel vous pouvez compter

parce que **rely on** est un verbe composé inséparable, tandis qu'on ne peut en aucun cas dire :

this is his wife up whom he has always backed

car **back up** est un verbe composé séparable.

iv) Comme de nombreux verbes composés inséparables (voir a) ii ci-dessus), de nombreux verbes composés séparables sont très idiomatiques :

square up (= régler - des dettes, etc.)
bring round (= faire reprendre connaissance à ; convertir à un point de vue)
set back (= coûter - de l'argent à quelqu'un) :

if you pay now, we can square up later
si tu payes maintenant, nous pourrons régler nos comptes plus tard

give him a brandy; that'll bring him round
donne-lui un cognac, ça lui fera reprendre connaissance

do you think anything will bring him round to our point of view?
est-ce que tu crois qu'on pourrait l'amener à penser comme nous ?

that car must have set you back at least £10,000
cette voiture doit vous avoir coûté au moins 10 000 livres

c) *Les verbes composés seulement intransitifs*

Il y a aussi des verbes composés intransitifs (qui ne sont bien entendu jamais séparables) :

poor people often lose out
les pauvres sont souvent perdants

the entire species is on the verge of dying out
l'espèce entière est sur le point de disparaître

A la différence des verbes composés inséparables, ces verbes n'ont jamais de forme passive.

d) *Les verbes composés, transitifs, jamais séparables, à complémentation*

Ils sont composés de trois mots et non pas deux, par exemple :

come up with
trouver, concocter

Avec ces verbes, le complément d'objet ne peut jamais séparer le verbe et ses particules, c'est-à-dire que des phrases du type **have you come it up with?** sont impossibles. Le complément d'objet direct doit suivre la dernière particule.

we've come up with a great solution
nous avons trouvé une solution idéale

Les deux particules ne peuvent pas non plus précéder un pronom relatif. Ainsi on dira :

is there anything else (which) you can come up with?
est-ce que tu peux trouver quelque chose d'autre ?

Mais on ne peut PAS mettre les deux particules avant un pronom relatif comme dans la phrase (agrammaticale) : **is there anything else up with which you can come?**

Autres exemples de verbes composés, transitifs, jamais séparables, à complémentation (idiomatiques) :

make off with (voler)
make up to (essayer de se faire bien voir par)
live up to (se montrer à la hauteur de)
stand up for (prendre le parti de)
crack down on (sévir contre)

somebody made off with her suitcase
quelqu'un lui a volé sa valise

this is the teacher Fiona has been making up to throughout term, but her marks are no better
c'est le professeur dont Fiona a essayé de se faire bien voir tout le trimestre, mais ses notes n'en sont pas meilleures pour autant

it was difficult for him to live up to this reputation
il lui était difficile d'être à la hauteur de cette réputation

why didn't you stand up for me if you knew I was right?
pourquoi est-ce que tu n'as pas pris mon parti si tu savais que j'avais raison ?

every Christmas police crack down on drink-and-drive offenders
chaque année à Noël la police sévit contre ceux qui prennent le volant après avoir bu

21 Le temps au discours indirect

Le discours indirect permet de rapporter les paroles de quelqu'un. La concordance des temps en anglais dans le discours indirect a les mêmes caractéristiques qu'en français :

Henry said/had said, 'I am unhappy' (direct)
Henry a dit/avait dit : 'je suis malheureux'

Henry said/had said (that) he was unhappy (indirect)
Henry a dit/avait dit qu'il était malheureux

22 Liste des verbes irréguliers

Les américanismes sont indiqués par *. Les formes peu courantes, archaïques ou littéraires sont données entre parenthèses. Les traductions ci-dessous ne sont pas restrictives et ne donnent qu'un des sens de base.

Infinitif		Prétérit	Participe Passé
abide	(*supporter*)	**(abode)** [1]	**abided**
arise	(*surgir*)	**arose**	**arisen**
awake	(*s'éveiller*)	**awoke, awaked**	**awoken, (awaked)**
bear	(*porter*)	**bore**	**borne** [2]
beat	(*battre*)	**beat**	**beaten** [3]
become	(*devenir*)	**became**	**become**
befall	(*arriver*)	**befell**	**befallen**
beget	(*engendrer*)	**begot**	**begotten**
begin	(*commencer*)	**began**	**begun**
behold	(*apercevoir*)	**beheld**	**beheld**
bend	(*courber*)	**bent**	**bent** [4]
bereave	(*priver*)	**bereaved**	**bereft** [5]
beseech	(*implorer*)	**besought**	**besought**
bestride	(*chevaucher*)	**bestrode**	**bestridden**
bet	(*parier*)	**bet, betted**	**bet, betted**
bid	(*offrir*)	**bid**	**bid**
bid	(*commander*)	**bade**	**bidden**
bind	(*attacher*)	**bound**	**bound**
bite	(*mordre*)	**bit**	**bitten**
bleed	(*saigner*)	**bled**	**bled**
blow	(*souffler*)	**blew**	**blown**
break	(*casser*)	**broke**	**broken** [6]
breed	(*élever*)	**bred**	**bred**
bring	(*apporter*)	**brought**	**brought**
broadcast	(*diffuser*)	**broadcast**	**broadcast**
build	(*construire*)	**built**	**built**
burn	(*brûler*)	**burnt, burned**	**burnt, burned**
burst	(*éclater*)	**burst**	**burst**
buy	(*acheter*)	**bought**	**bought**
cast	(*jeter*)	**cast**	**cast**
catch	(*attraper*)	**caught**	**caught**
chide	(*gronder*)	**chid, chided**	**chid, (chidden), chided**
choose	(*choisir*)	**chose**	**chosen**
cleave	(*fendre*)	**clove, cleft,**	**cloven, cleft** [7]
cleave	(*adhérer*)	**cleaved, (clave)**	**cleaved**
cling	(*s'accrocher à*)	**clung**	**clung**
clothe	(*habiller*)	**clothed, (clad)**	**clothed, (clad)**
come	(*venir*)	**came**	**come**
cost	(*coûter*)	**cost**	**cost**
creep	(*ramper*)	**crept**	**crept**
crow	(*chanter*)	**crowed, (crew)**	**crowed**
cut	(*couper*)	**cut**	**cut**
dare	(*oser*)	**dared, (durst)**	**dared, (durst)**
deal	(*traiter*)	**dealt**	**dealt**
dig	(*fouiller*)	**dug**	**dug**
dive	(*plonger*)	**dived, dove***	**dived**
draw	(*dessiner, tirer*)	**drew**	**drawn**

[1] Régulier dans la construction **abide by** 'se conformer à, suivre' : **they abided by the rules**.

[2] Mais **born** au passif = 'né' ou comme un adjectif : **he was born in France/a born gentleman**.

[3] Remarquez la forme familière **this has me beat/you have me beat there** *cela me dépasse/tu m'as posé une colle* et **beat** dans le sens de 'très fatigué, épuisé' : **I am (dead) beat**.

[4] Remarquez la phrase **on one's bended knees** *à genoux*.

[5] Mais **bereaved** dans le sens de 'endeuillé' comme dans **the bereaved received no compensation** *la famille du disparu ne reçut aucune compensation*. Comparez : **he was bereft of speech** *il en perdit la parole*.

[6] Mais **broke** quand il s'agit d'un adjectif = 'fauché' : **I'm broke**.

[7] **cleft** n'est employé qu'avec le sens de 'coupé en deux'. Remarquez **cleft palate** *palais fendu* et **(to be caught) in a cleft stick** *(être) dans une impasse*, mais **cloven foot/hoof** *sabot fendu*.

Infinitif		Prétérit	Participe Passé
dream	*(rêver)*	**dreamt,dreamed**	**dreamt, dreamed**
drink	*(boire)*	**drank**	**drunk** [8]
drive	*(conduire)*	**drove**	**driven**
dwell	*(demeurer)*	**dwelt, dwelled**	**dwelt, dwelled**
eat	*(manger)*	**ate**	**eaten**
fall	*(tomber)*	**fell**	**fallen**
feed	*(nourrir)*	**fed**	**fed**
feel	*(sentir)*	**felt**	**felt**
fight	*(battre)*	**fought**	**fought**
find	*(trouver)*	**found**	**found**
fit	*(aller à)*	**fit*, fitted**	**fit*, fitted**
flee	*(s'envoler)*	**fled**	**fled**
fling	*(lancer)*	**flung**	**flung**
fly	*(voler)*	**flew**	**flown**
forbear	*(s'abstenir)*	**forbore**	**forborne**
forbid	*(interdire)*	**forbad(e)**	**forbidden**
forget	*(oublier)*	**forgot**	**forgotten**
forgive	*(pardonner)*	**forgave**	**forgiven**
forsake	*(abandonner)*	**forsook**	**forsaken**
freeze	*(geler)*	**froze**	**frozen**
get	*(obtenir)*	**got**	**got, gotten*** [9]
gild	*(dorer)*	**gilt, gilded**	**gilt, gilded** [10]
gird	*(ceindre)*	**girt, girded**	**girt, girded** [10]
give	*(donner)*	**gave**	**given**
go	*(aller)*	**went**	**gone**
grind	*(grincer)*	**ground**	**ground**
grow	*(pousser)*	**grew**	**grown**
hang	*(pendre)*	**hung, hanged** [11]	**hung, hanged** [11]
hear	*(entendre)*	**heard**	**heard**
heave	*(lever)*	**hove, heaved** [12]	**hove, heaved** [12]
hew	*(tailler)*	**hewed**	**hewn, hewed**
hide	*(cacher)*	**hid**	**hidden**
hit	*(frapper)*	**hit**	**hit**
hold	*(tenir)*	**held**	**held**
hurt	*(blesser)*	**hurt**	**hurt**
keep	*(garder)*	**kept**	**kept**
kneel	*(s'agenouiller)*	**knelt, kneeled**	**knelt, kneeled**
knit	*(tricoter)*	**knit, knitted** [13]	**knit, knitted** [13]
know	*(savoir, connaître)*	**knew**	**known**
lay	*(coucher)*	**laid**	**laid**
lead	*(mener)*	**led**	**led**
lean	*(s'appuyer)*	**leant, leaned**	**leant, leaned**
leap	*(sauter)*	**leapt, leaped**	**leapt, leaped**
learn	*(apprendre)*	**learnt, learned**	**learnt, learned**
leave	*(laisser)*	**left**	**left**
lend	*(prêter)*	**lent**	**lent**

Infinitif		Prétérit	Participe Passé
let	*(laisser)*	**let**	**let**
lie	*(coucher)*	**lay**	**lain**
light	*(allumer)*	**lit, lighted**	**lit, lighted** [14]
lose	*(perdre)*	**lost**	**lost**
make	*(faire)*	**made**	**made**
mean	*(signifier)*	**meant**	**meant**
meet	*(rencontrer)*	**met**	**met**
melt	*(fondre)*	**melted**	**melted, molten** [15]
mow	*(faucher)*	**mowed**	**mown, mowed**
pay	*(payer)*	**paid**	**paid**
plead	*(plaider)*	**pled*, pleaded**	**pled*, pleaded** [16]
put	*(poser)*	**put**	**put**
quit	*(quitter)*	**quit, (quitted)**	**quit (quitted)** [17]
read	*(lire)*	**read**	**read**
rend	*(déchirer)*	**rent**	**rent**
rid	*(débarrasser)*	**rid (ridded)**	**rid**
ride	*(monter à)*	**rode**	**ridden**
ring	*(sonner)*	**rang**	**rung**
rise	*(se lever)*	**rose**	**risen**
run	*(courir)*	**ran**	**run**
saw	*(scier)*	**sawed**	**sawn, sawed**
say	*(dire)*	**said**	**said**
see	*(voir)*	**saw**	**seen**
seek	*(chercher)*	**sought**	**sought**
sell	*(vendre)*	**sold**	**sold**
send	*(envoyer)*	**sent**	**sent**
set	*(mettre)*	**set**	**set**
sew	*(coudre)*	**sewed**	**sewn, sewed**
shake	*(secouer)*	**shook**	**shaken**
shear [18]	*(tondre)*	**sheared**	**shorn, sheared**
shed	*(perdre)*	**shed**	**shed**
shine	*(briller)*	**shone** [19]	**shone** [19]
shoe	*(chausser)*	**shod, shoed**	**shod, shoed** [20]
shoot	*(abattre, tirer)*	**shot**	**shot**
show	*(montrer)*	**showed**	**shown,showed**
shrink	*(rétrécir)*	**shrank, shrunk**	**shrunk, shrunken** [21]
shut	*(fermer)*	**shut**	**shut**
sing	*(chanter)*	**sang**	**sung**
sink	*(couler)*	**sank**	**sunk, sunken**[22]
sit	*(s'asseoir)*	**sat**	**sat**
slay	*(tuer)*	**slew**	**slain**
sleep	*(dormir)*	**slept**	**slept**
slide	*(glisser)*	**slid**	**slid**

[8] Quand c'est un adjectif placé avant le nom, **drunken** 'ivre, ivrogne' est parfois employé (**a lot of drunk(en) people** *beaucoup de gens ivres*) et il **doit** toujours être employé devant les noms représentant des objets inanimés (**one of his usual drunken parties** *une de ses nombreuses soirées bien arrosées.*

[9] Mais **have got to** se dit aussi en américain avec le sens de 'devoir, être obligé de' : **a man has got to do what a man has got to do** *un homme doit faire ce qu'il doit faire.* Comparez avec : **she has gotten into a terrible mess** *elle s'est fourrée dans une sale situation.*

[10] Les formes du participe passé **gilt** et **girt** sont très couramment employées comme adjectif placé avant le nom : **gilt mirrors** *des miroirs dorés,* **a flower-girt grave** *une tombe entourée de fleurs* (mais toujours **gilded youth** *la jeunesse dorée,* dans lequel **gilded** signifie 'riche et bienheureux').

[11] Régulier quand il a le sens de 'mettre à mort par pendaison'.

[12] **Hove** est employé dans le domaine nautique comme dans la phrase **heave into sight** : **just then Mary hove into sight** *et Mary pointa à l'horizon/apparut.*

[13] Irrégulier quand il a le sens de 'unir' (**a close-knit family** *une famille unie*), mais régulier lorsqu'il a le sens de 'fabriquer en laine' et quand il fait référence aux os = 'se souder'.

[14] Lorsque le participe passé est employé comme un adjectif devant un nom, **lighted** est souvent préféré à **lit** : **a lighted match** *une allumette allumée* (mais : **the match is lit, she has lit a match** *l'allumette est allumée, elle a allumé une allumette*). Dans les noms composés, on emploie généralement **lit** : **well-lit streets** *des rues bien éclairées.* Au sens figuré (avec **up**), **lit** uniquement est employé au prétérit et au participe passé : **her face lit up when she saw me** *son visage s'illumina lorsqu'elle me vit.*

[15] On emploie **molten** uniquement comme un adjectif devant les noms, et seulement lorsqu'il signifie 'fondu à une très haute température', par exemple : **molten lead** *du plomb fondu* (mais **melted butter** *du beurre fondu*).

[16] En anglais d'Ecosse et en américain, on emploie **pled** au passé et au participe passé.

[17] En américain, les formes régulières ne sont pas employées, et elles sont de plus en plus rares en anglais britannique.

[18] Le participe passé est normalement **shorn** devant un nom (**newly-shorn lambs** *des agneaux tout juste tondus*) et toujours dans la phrase **(to be) shorn of** *(être) privé de* : **shorn of his riches he was nothing** *privé de ses richesses, il n'était plus rien.*

[19] Mais régulier quand il a le sens de 'cirer, astiquer' en américain.

[20] Quand c'est un adjectif, on n'emploie que **shod** : **a well-shod foot** *un pied bien chaussé.*

[21] **Shrunken** n'est employé que lorsqu'il est adjectif : **shrunken limbs/her face was shrunken** *des membres rabougris/son visage était ratatiné.*

[22] **Sunken** n'est employé que comme un adjectif : **sunken eyes** *des yeux creux.*

Infinitif		Prétérit	Participe Passé
sling	*(lancer)*	**slung**	**slung**
slink	*(s'en aller furtivement)*	**slunk**	**slunk**
slit	*(fendre)*	**slit**	**slit**
smell	*(sentir)*	**smelt, smelled**	**smelt, smelled**
smite	*(frapper)*	**smote**	**smitten** [23]
sneak	*(entrer, etc. à la dérobée)*	**snuck*, sneaked**	**snuck*,sneaked**
sow	*(semer)*	**sowed**	**sown, sowed**
speak	*(parler)*	**spoke**	**spoken**
speed	*(aller vite)*	**sped, speeded**	**sped, speeded**
spell	*(écrire)*	**spelt, spelled**	**spelt, spelled**
spend	*(dépenser)*	**spent**	**spent**
spill	*(renverser)*	**spilt, spilled**	**spilt, spilled**
spin	*(filer)*	**spun**	**spun**
spit	*(cracher)*	**spat, spit***	**spat, spit***
split	*(se briser)*	**split**	**split**
spoil	*(abîmer)*	**spoilt, spoiled**	**spoilt, spoiled**
spread	*(étendre)*	**spread**	**spread**
spring	*(bondir)*	**sprang**	**sprung**
stand	*(se tenir)*	**stood**	**stood**
steal	*(voler)*	**stole**	**stolen**
stick	*(enfoncer, coller)*	**stuck**	**stuck**
sting	*(piquer)*	**stung**	**stung**
stink	*(puer)*	**stank**	**stunk**
strew	*(répandre)*	**strewed**	**strewn, strewed**
stride	*(avancer à grands pas)*	**strode**	**stridden**
strike	*(frapper)*	**struck**	**struck, stricken**[24]
string	*(enfiler)*	**strung**	**strung**
strive	*(s'efforcer)*	**strove**	**striven**
swear	*(jurer)*	**swore**	**sworn**
sweat	*(suer)*	**sweat*, sweated**	**sweat*, sweated**
sweep	*(balayer)*	**swept**	**swept**
swell	*(gonfler)*	**swelled**	**swollen, swelled**[25]
swim	*(nager)*	**swam**	**swum**
swing	*(se balancer)*	**swung**	**swung**
take	*(prendre)*	**took**	**taken**
teach	*(enseigner)*	**taught**	**taught**
tear	*(déchirer)*	**tore**	**torn**
tell	*(dire)*	**told**	**told**
think	*(penser)*	**thought**	**thought**
thrive	*(fleurir)*	**thrived, (throve)**	**thrived, (thriven)**
throw	*(jeter)*	**threw**	**thrown**
thrust	*(pousser)*	**thrust**	**thrust**
tread	*(marcher)*	**trod**	**trodden**
understand	*(comprendre)*	**understood**	**understood**
undertake	*(s'engager)*	**undertook**	**undertaken**
wake	*(se réveiller)*	**woke, waked**	**woken, waked**
wear	*(porter)*	**wore**	**worn**
weave	*(tisser)*	**wove** [26]	**woven** [26]
weep	*(pleurer)*	**wept**	**wept**
wet	*(mouiller)*	**wet*, wetted** [27]	**wet*, wetted** [27]
win	*(gagner)*	**won**	**won**
wind	*(remonter)*	**wound**	**wound**
wring	*(tordre)*	**wrung**	**wrung**
write	*(écrire)*	**wrote**	**written**

23 Les auxiliaires be, have, do: leurs formes

a) BE

Présent		*Prétérit*		*Participe Passé*
1ère	**I am**	1ère	**I was**	**been**
2ème	**you are**	2ème	**you were**	
3ème	**he/she/it is**	3ème	**he was**	
1ère	**we are**	1ère	**we were**	
2ème	**you are**	2ème	**you were**	
3ème	**they are**	3ème	**they were**	

Contracté avec le mot précédant :

I'm = I am ; you're = you are ; he's/John's = he is/ John is ; we're/you're/they're = we are/you are/ they are

Contracté avec **not** :

aren't I? (questions seulement) **= am I not? ; you/we/ they aren't ; he isn't ; I/he wasn't ; you/we/they weren't**

On a aussi : **I'm not ; you're not**, etc.

Pour le subjonctif, voir pp A51-2.

b) HAVE

Présent		*Prétérit*		*Participe Passé*
1ère	**I have**	1ère	**I had**	**had**
2ème	**you have**	2ème	**you had**	
3ème	**he/she/it has**	3ème	**he had**	
1ère	**we have**	1ère	**we had**	
2ème	**you have**	2ème	**you had**	
3ème	**they have**	3ème	**they had**	

Contracté avec le mot précédant :

I've/you've/we've/they've = I have, etc. **he's = he has**
I'd/you'd/he'd/we'd/they'd = I had, etc.

Vous noterez que **he's/she's** ne sont normalement pas contractés lorsqu'ils sont employés comme verbes en tant que tels et non comme auxiliaires au présent :

I've two cars	**he has two cars**
j'ai deux voitures	il a deux voitures

Contracté avec **not** :

haven't ; hasn't ; hadn't

c) DO

Présent		*Prétérit*		*Participe Passé*
1ère	**I do**	1ère	**I did**	**done**
2ème	**you do**	2ème	**you did**	
3ème	**he/she/it does**	3ème	**he did**	
1ère	**we do**	1ère	**we did**	
2ème	**you do**	2ème	**you did**	
3ème	**they do**	3ème	**they did**	

Contracté avec **not** :

don't ; doesn't ; didn't

[23] Verbe archaïque dont le participe passé **smitten** s'emploie encore comme adjectif : **he's completely smitten with her** *il est complètement fou d'elle.*

[24] **Stricken** n'est utilisé que dans le sens figuré (**a stricken family/stricken with poverty** *une famille accablée/accablée par la pauvreté*). Il est très courant dans les noms composés (accablé par) : **poverty-stricken**, **fever-stricken**, **horror-stricken** (aussi **horror-struck**), **terror-stricken** (aussi **terror-struck**), mais on dit toujours **thunderstruck** *frappé par la surprise, abasourdi de surprise.*

C'est aussi un emploi américain **the remark was stricken from the record** *la remarque a été rayée du procès-verbal.*

[25] **Swollen** est plus courant que **swelled** comme verbe (**her face has swollen** *son visage a gonflé)* et comme adjectif (**her face is swollen/a swollen face**). **A swollen head** *une grosse tête*, pour quelqu'un qui a une haute opinion de soi-même, devient **a swelled head** en américain.

[26] Mais il est régulier lorsqu'il a le sens de 'se faufiler' : **the motorbike weaved elegantly through the traffic** *la moto se faufilait avec agilité entre les voitures.*

[27] Mais irrégulier aussi en anglais britannique lorsqu'il a le sens de 'mouiller par de l'urine' : **he wet his bed again last night** *il a encore mouillé son lit la nuit dernière.*

14 Les Prépositions

1 Les prépositions servent à exprimer des relations de temps, de lieu, de possession, etc. Elles sont normalement suivies d'un nom ou d'un pronom comme :

after - after the show après le spectacle
on - on it là-dessus
of - of London de Londres

Cependant, dans certaines constructions les prépositions anglaises peuvent se placer en fin de proposition :

the people I came here with
les gens avec lesquels je suis venu

something I had never dreamed of
quelque chose dont je n'avais jamais rêvé

Voir aussi **Les Verbes Composés**, p A59, ainsi que **Les Pronoms Interrogatifs et Relatifs**, pp A31-2.

2 Voici une liste des prépositions les plus couramment employées. Etant donné que la plupart des prépositions ont toute une richesse de sens et d'emplois, seuls les usages les plus importants et ceux particulièrement intéressants ou susceptibles de poser des problèmes à ceux qui apprennent l'anglais sont mentionnés ci-dessous.

★ **about** et **around**

i) 'lieu' (dans les environs, en tous sens) :

Souvent il n'y a pas de différence entre **about** et **around**, bien qu'en anglais américain on préfère **around** :

they walked about/around town
ils se sont promenés dans la ville

he must be about/around somewhere
il doit être dans les parages

the dog was racing about/around in the garden
le chien courait en tous sens dans le jardin

ii) 'autour de' :

he lives just (a)round the corner
il habite au coin de la rue

she put the rope (a)round his chest
elle a mis la corde autour de sa poitrine

iii) 'environ' :

I have about £1 on me
j'ai environ une livre sur moi

it'll cost you around £20
ça te coûtera environ 20 livres

iv) 'au sujet de', 'sur' (seulement **about**) :

what's the book about? – it's a story about nature
de quoi parle le livre ? – c'est une histoire sur la nature

on peut être plus technique, plus académique :

he gave a paper on Verdi and Shakespeare
il a donné une conférence sur Verdi et Shakespeare

a book on English grammar
un livre sur la grammaire anglaise

★ **above** (au-dessus de)

Comparez **above** avec **over**. Il y a en général peu de différence entre les deux :

he has a lovely mirror above/over the mantelpiece
il a un très joli miroir au-dessus de la cheminée

Mais **above** exprime normalement le fait d'être 'situé au-dessus de' dans un sens purement physique :

the shirts had been placed in the wardrobe above the socks and underwear
les chemises avaient été placées dans l'armoire au-dessus des chaussettes et des sous-vêtements

mais :

he flung his coat over a chair
il a jeté son manteau sur une chaise

★ **across** (à travers)

Across et **over** ont souvent un sens très proche, cependant **across** a tendance à indiquer une dimension horizontale (sur la largeur de) :

he walked across the fields to the farm
il a traversé les champs jusqu'à la ferme

he laid out his suit across the bed
il étendit son costume en travers du lit

★ **after** (après)

i) Dans un sens figuré, remarquez la différence entre **ask after** et **ask for** :

he asked after you
il m'a demandé de tes nouvelles

he asked for you
il a demandé à te parler

ii) dans un sens figuré impliquant un but :

they keep striving after the happiness which eludes them
ils sont à la recherche d'un bonheur qui toujours leur échappe

iii) Dans un sens temporel on pourrait comparer **after** et **since**. La différence entre les deux apparaît dans l'emploi des temps : prétérit (**after**) et present perfect (**since**). Comparez :

he wasn't well after his journey
il ne se sentait pas bien après son voyage

he hasn't been well since his journey
il ne se sent pas bien depuis son voyage

Voir aussi **to**

La même différence existe sans verbe dans la proposition. Ainsi il y a une grande différence entre :

Britain after the war
La Grande-Bretagne après la guerre

et :

Britain since the war
La Grande-Bretagne depuis la guerre

★ **against** (contre)

i) Ceci implique normalement un obstacle :

they didn't fight against them, they fought with them
ils n'ont pas combattu contre eux, ils ont combattu avec eux

we're sailing against the current
nous naviguons à contre-courant

ii) Mais il peut impliquer un choc, comme dans :

he knocked his head against the wall
il s'est cogné la tête contre le mur

iii) pour dénoter une opposition par rapport à un fond :

she held the picture against the wall
elle a tenu l'image contre le mur

she was silhouetted against the snow
sa silhouette se découpait sur la neige

★ **among(st)** (parmi)

Alors que **between** (entre) implique deux éléments, **among(st)** implique une multitude :

he sat between John and Joan
il s'est assis entre John et Joan

he sat among(st) the flowers
il s'est assis parmi les fleurs

Remarquez que les 'deux éléments' ne sont pas toujours mentionnés avec **between** (à la différence de l'exemple ci-dessus). Il signifie seulement qu'une division entre deux choses, deux personnes ou deux groupes est impliquée. Ainsi il est parfaitement correct de dire :

the road ran between the houses
la route passait entre les maisons

même s'il y en a 250. Ici on indique que la route sépare les maisons en deux groupes. Mais notez qu'on dirait :

the cats were running to and fro among the houses
les chats couraient en tous sens entre les maisons

Ici on n'indique plus une séparation entre deux groupes de maisons. Bien sûr s'il n'y a que deux maisons, on dirait :

the cats were running to and fro between the houses

★ **at** (à)

Voir aussi **to**.

At ou **in** ? : **at** fait référence à un point précis (souvent sur une échelle réelle ou imaginaire). Ainsi on dirait :

the big hand stopped at six o'clock
la grande aiguille s'est arrêtée sur le six

et :

the train stops at Dundee, Edinburgh and York
le train s'arrête à Dundee, Edimbourg et York

Ces villes ne sont pas considérées comme villes dans la phrase ci-dessus, mais comme des étapes sur un itinéraire. On dirait :

he lives in Dundee
il vit à Dundee

Dans la phrase :

he is at Dundee
il est à Dundee

une fois de plus **Dundee** ne fait pas référence à la ville ; mais à une institution, comme l'université de Dundee, par exemple.

Cependant on peut employer **at** avec des noms de petites villes et de villages :

there's still a pier at Tighnabruaich
il y a toujours une jetée à Tighnabruaich

En revanche, on ne dit pas :

he lives at Tighnabruaich

mais **in**.

Avec le verbe **arrive**, **at** est aussi employé pour marquer la un point précis :

they finally arrived at the foot of the hill
ils sont finalement arrivés au pied de la colline

sinon on emploie **in** :

when we arrived in London, we ...
lorsque nous sommes arrivés à Londres, nous ...

Dans un sens figuré, on emploie toujours **arrive at** :

have they arrived at any decision yet?
est-ce qu'ils sont déjà parvenus à une décision ?

at ou **by** ? :

i) pour exprimer un lieu, comparez :

(a) **he was sitting at the table**
il était assis à la table

(b) **he was sitting by the table**
il était assis près de la table

ii) pour exprimer le temps, comparez :

(a) **be there at six o'clock**
sois là à six heures

(b) **be there by six o'clock**
sois là avant six heures

At fait référence à un point dans le temps, tandis que **by** signifie 'pas plus tard que'.

★ **before** (devant, avant)

Il fait référence au temps et à l'espace :

be there before six o'clock
sois là avant six heures

he knelt before the Queen
il s'agenouilla devant la reine

i) Dans un sens spatial, il y a parfois une différence entre **before** et **in front of**. **In front of** est plus littéral en ce qui concerne la position. C'est le terme que l'on emploie le plus souvent en anglais courant :

he was standing in front of the judge in the queue
il se tenait devant le juge dans la file

tandis que **before** implique souvent une relation qui n'est pas purement locative :

he stood before the judge
il se tenait devant le juge

Remarquez aussi que dans les exemples ci-dessus, **in front of** n'implique pas que les deux personnes sont face à face. **Before**, lui, implique cette idée.

ii) Dans le sens temporel de **before**, comparez son emploi avec des verbes à la forme négative et celui de **until**. **Before** signifie 'plus tôt que' et **until** 'jusqu'à (un certain temps)' :

(a) **you will not get the letter before Monday**
tu ne recevras pas la lettre avant lundi

(b) **you will not get the letter until Monday**
tu ne recevras pas la lettre avant lundi

Dans (a) la lettre arrivera lundi ou n'importe quel jour après lundi (mais pas avant), dans (b) la lettre arrivera lundi.

★ **below** (au-dessous de)

Below est le contraire de **above** (au-dessus de), et **under** (sous) est le contraire de **over**. Voir **above** ci-dessus. Exemples :

50 metres below the snow-line
à 50 mètres au-dessous de la limite des neiges éternelles

he was sitting under the bridge
il était assis sous le pont

below the bridge the water gets deeper
au-dessous du pont l'eau est plus profonde

his shoes were under the bed
ses chaussures étaient sous le lit

★ **beside** et **besides**

beside = à côté de :

sit beside me
assieds-toi à côté de moi

besides = en plus de, à part :

there were three guests there besides him and me
il y avait trois invités à part lui et moi

★ **between** (entre), voir **among** (parmi)

★ **but**

But employé comme préposition signifie 'sauf', 'excepté'. On peut aussi employer **except** pour remplacer **but** dans pratiquement tous les cas, mais l'inverse n'est pas possible. Quand on emploie **but**, il est pratiquement toujours placé après des pronoms indéfinis ou interrogatifs, ou des adverbes comme **anywhere**, **where**, etc. :

nobody but/except you would think of that
personne à part toi ne penserait à ça

where else but/except in France would you ...?
où, sinon en France, est-ce qu'on pourrait ... ?

mais seul **except** est possible dans la phrase suivante :

we can all swim except Lorna
nous savons tous nager sauf Lorna

★ **by**

Voir aussi **at** et **from**.

i) Il est utile de comparer **by** avec **on** dans son usage avec des mots faisant référence à des moyens de transport :

he goes by train
il prend le train

is there only one conductor on this train?
y-a-t-il un seul contrôleur dans ce train ?

By met l'accent sur le moyen de transport, et le nom qui suit n'a normalement pas d'article, sauf dans des cas comme :

I'll be coming on/by the three-thirty
j'arriverai par (le train/bus/l'avion) de trois heures trente

où l'on ne fait pas directement référence au moyen de transport.

On peut employer **in** à la place de **on** si l'idée d'intérieur domine :

it's often cold in British trains
il fait souvent froid dans les trains britanniques

Remarquez aussi **live by** et **live on. Live by** signifie 'gagner sa vie d'une occupation', tandis que **live on** signifie 'vivre avec un revenu de/de nourriture'. L'emploi de **by** insiste sur le moyen :

he lives by acting in commercials
il gagne sa vie en jouant dans des pubs

he lives by his pen
il vit de sa plume

he lives on £100 a month
il vit avec 100 livres par mois

he lives on fruit
il se nourrit de fruits

Live by signifie aussi 'vivre selon les règles de' :

it is difficult to live by such a set of doctrines
il est difficile de vivre en appliquant un tel ensemble de doctrines

ii) passif :

By s'emploie pour introduire le complément d'agent (celui par qui l'action est accomplie) dans des constructions passives :

his reaction surprised us
sa réaction nous a surpris

we were surprised by his reaction
nous avons été surpris par sa réaction

★ **due to** (à cause de, grâce à)

Il a le même emploi que **owing to** (à cause de/en raison de) :

this was due to/owing to his alertness of mind
c'était grâce à sa vivacité d'esprit

Etant donné que **due** est un adjectif, certaines personnes soutiennent qu'il devrait se placer, comme un adjectif attribut, après une des formes du verbe **be** comme dans l'exemple ci-dessus, et qu'il est mal employé dans l'exemple ci-dessous. Cependant, il est de plus en plus courant d'employer **due to** dans des structures adverbiales dans lesquelles on le considère comme une locution prépositionnelle comme **because of, in front of**, etc. :

the train is late, due to an accident near Bristol
le train est en retard, à cause d'un accident près de Bristol

★ **during** (pendant), voir **for**

★ **except** (sauf), voir **but**

★ **for** (pour, pendant)

i) Lorsque **for** est employé comme préposition de temps, il est utile de la comparer avec **during** (pendant) et **in** (en). **For** insiste sur l'idée de durée (pendant combien de temps ?), tandis que **during** indique la période au cours de laquelle des actions se produisent (quand ?) :

for the first five months you'll be stationed at Crewe
pendant les cinq premiers mois, vous serez basés à Crewe

during the first five months you're likely to be moved
au cours des cinq premiers mois, vous serez vraisemblablement transférés

he let the cat out for the night
il a fait sortir le chat pour la nuit

he let the cat out during the night
il a fait sortir le chat pendant/dans la nuit

L'accent mis sur la durée par **for** est aussi parfois opposé à **in**, qui signifie 'dans une période' :

I haven't seen her for five years
je ne l'ai pas vue depuis cinq ans

he didn't see her once in five years
il ne l'a pas vue une seule fois en cinq ans

Cependant, en anglais américain, on emploierait normalement **in** dans le premier exemple :

I haven't seen her in five years
ça fait cinq ans que je ne l'ai pas vue

et cet usage s'est étendu à l'anglais britannique.

Pour l'emploi de **for/since** avec des expressions de temps, voir p A48.

ii) Lorsque **for** est préposition de lieu, il est utile de la comparer avec **to** :

(a) **the flight for/to Dublin is at 3 o'clock**
le vol de Dublin est à 3 heures

(b) **nothing went wrong on the flight to Dublin**
aucun incident ne s'est produit sur le vol de Dublin

La différence entre les deux est que **to** implique l'arrivée à destination, tandis que **for** exprime uniquement le projet ou l'intention d'aller dans la direction de cette destination.

★ **from** (de (provenance))

i) Comme nous l'avons vu plus haut, (voir **by** ci-dessus), **by** insiste sur le moyen, et **from** indique la provenance, le point de départ. Comparez :

judging by experience, this is unlikely to happen
si l'on en juge par l'expérience, il y a peu de chances que cela se produise

judging from earlier experiences, he had now learnt not to be so easily led astray
ses expériences antérieures lui avaientes appris à ne pas se laisser si facilement détourner du droit chemin

Bien sûr, il existe parfois peu ou pas de différence étant donné que la distinction entre le moyen et la provenance n'est pas pertinente :

judging by his clothes, he must be poor
si l'on en juge par ses vêtements, il doit être pauvre

judging from these figures, business is good
si l'on en juge par ces chiffres, les affaires se portent bien

L'idée de provenance évoquée par **from** apparaît aussi lorsqu'on l'oppose à **of, by** et **with** dans les exemples suivants :

the cat died from eating too much fish
le chat est mort d'avoir mangé trop de poisson

he died of cancer/by drowning
il est mort d'un cancer/par noyade

the cat is trembling with fear
le chat tremble de peur

from what I have heard
d'après ce que j'ai entendu

ii) avec **different** :

different se construit avec **from**, bien qu'on puisse le trouver suivi de **to**, cette dernierè construction étant incorrecte.

that's different to/from mine
c'est différent du mien

that's different to/from what he said before
c'est différent de ce qu'il a dit auparavant

Mais **than**, bien qu'on l'entende souvent, est à l'origine un américanisme.

★ **in** et **into** (dans)

Pour **in**, voir aussi **at**, **by**, **for**.

En principe **in** signifie 'dans un espace', tandis que **into** implique un mouvement d'un endroit à l'intérieur d'un autre :

he was sitting in the living room
il était assis dans la salle de séjour

he went into the living room
il est entré dans la salle de séjour

Le problème se complique si l'action implique un mouvement d'un endroit à l'intérieur d'un autre (et où l'on pourrait s'attendre à trouver **into**), on emploie souvent **in** si l'accent est mis sur le **résultat** plutôt que sur le mouvement :

did you put sugar in my coffee?
est-ce que tu as mis du sucre dans mon café ?

Et réciproquement, on emploie parfois **into** lorsqu'il n'y a pas de verbe de mouvement, mais seulement si l'on implique le mouvement :

you've been in the bathroom for an hour
tu es dans la salle de bain depuis une heure

the kitchen is awful, have you been into the bathroom yet?
la cuisine est affreuse, est-ce que tu es allé dans la salle de bain ?

De même, dans un sens figuré :

he's into fast cars at the moment
il est branché voitures de sport en ce moment

this will give you an insight into how it works
cela vous donnera une idée sur la manière dont il fonctionne

★ **in front of** (devant), voir **before**

★ **of** (de), voir **about** et **from**

★ **on** (sur), voir **about**, **by** et **upon**

★ **opposite** (en face de)

Il est parfois accompagné de **to**, parfois pas :

the house opposite (to) ours is being pulled down
on est en train de démolir la maison en face de la nôtre

★ **outside** (dehors, en dehors de)

Il est souvent accompagné de **of** en américain, mais pas souvent en anglais britannique :

he reads a lot outside (of) his main subject area
il lit beaucoup en dehors de sa spécialité

★ **over** (par dessus), voir **above** et **across**

★ **owing to** (en raison de), voir **due to**

★ **since** (depuis), voir **after**.

★ **till** (jusqu'à + complément de temps), voir **to**

★ **to** (jusqu'à, vers, à)

Voir aussi **for**, **from**.

Lorsqu'il est opposé à **until/till** (jusqu'à), **to** (jusqu'à) fait référence à un aboutissement dans le temps. **Until** et **till** font eux aussi référence à un aboutissement dans le temps, mais on insiste plus particulièrement sur l'activité exprimée dans la phrase :

he has one of those nine to five jobs
il a un des ces emplois de bureau routiniers

the shop is closed from 1 to 2 pm
le magasin ferme de 13 heures à 14 heures

he played his flute until 10 o'clock
il jouait de sa flûte jusqu'à 10 heures

last night I worked from eight till midnight
hier soir j'ai travaillé de huit heures jusqu'à minuit

Il n'y a pas de différence de sens entre **until** et **till**.

To dans un sens différent peut avoir des similarités avec **at** après certains verbes. Dans de tels cas, **to** indique tout simplement une direction vers un but, tandis que **at** a un sens plus fort, car il dénote un désir de rapport plus étroit de la part de celui qui fait l'action :

will we manage to get to the station in time?
est-ce qu'on va arriver à la gare à temps ?

those boxes on top of the wardrobe - I can't get at them!
ces boîtes sur l'armoire - je n'arrive pas à les attraper !

Remarquez l'expression **get at** dans un sens figuré :

why are you getting at me?
pourquoi est-ce que tu es toujours sur mon dos ?

what are you getting at?
où voulez-vous en venir ?

★ **toward(s)** (vers)

Voir aussi **against**.

Toward s'emploie normalement en anglais américain, **towards** en anglais britannique.

★ **under** (sous), voir **below**

★ **until** (jusqu'à + complément de temps), voir **before** et **to**

★ **upon** (sur)

Il existe peu de différences de sens entre **upon** et **on**, mais **upon** est bien plus livresque ou soutenu :

what are your views upon ...?
quelle est votre opinion sur ... ?

upon having, with great difficulty, reached Dover, he immediately set sail for France
après avoir atteint Douvres avec grande difficulté, il s'embarqua immédiatement pour la France

Mais on trouve aussi **upon** dans certaines expressions (assez désuètes) où **on** n'est pas possible :

upon my word! par exemple !
upon my soul! grand Dieu !

Upon ne peut remplacer **on** pour exprimer (a) une date, (b) un moyen (voir **by** ci-dessus), (c) un état, (d) 'avec', 'sur' :

(a) **can you come on Saturday?**
tu peux venir samedi ?

(b) **he lives on fruit; our heaters run on gas**
il vit de fruits ; nos radiateurs fonctionnent au gaz

(c) **he's on the phone; it's on TV; he's on edge**
il est au téléphone ; c'est à la télé ; il est à cran

(d) **have you got any money on you?**
tu as de l'argent sur toi ?

En cas de doute, **on** n'est jamais faux (à part dans les exceptions mentionnées ci-dessus).

★ **with** (avec), voir **from**

★ **without** (sans)

En anglais on emploie l'article :

without a/his hat sans chapeau
without (any) butter sans beurre

15 Les Conjonctions

Les conjonctions sont des mots qui relient deux mots ou deux propositions. On distingue les conjonctions de 'coordination' et les conjonctions de 'subordination'. Les conjonctions de coordination relient des mots ou des propositions qui ont une même fonction dans la proposition. Les conjonctions de subordination relient des propositions qui dépendent d'autres structures (normalement d'autres propositions). Voir plus loin **La Structure de la Phrase** p A72.

1 Les conjonctions de coordination

Elles peuvent être 'simples' :

and	**but**	**or**	**nor**	**neither**
et	mais	ou	ni	ni

ou 'corrélatives' :

both ... and
à la fois ...

either ... or
soit ... soit

neither ...nor
ni ... ni

a) *Exemples de conjonctions de coordination simples*

i) **you need butter and flour**
tu as besoin de beurre et de farine

she's old and fragile
elle est âgée et frêle

they ate and drank a great deal
ils ont beaucoup mangé et beaucoup bu

they finished their work and then they went out to dinner
ils ont terminé leur travail et puis ils sont sortis dîner

ii) **but** et **or** offrent les mêmes possibilités de combinaison que **and**, par exemple :

she's plain but rich
elle n'est pas très jolie mais elle est riche

trains to or from London have been delayed
les trains en partance et en provenance de Londres ont du retard

Remarquez aussi l'usage suivant :

we can but try
on ne peut qu'essayer

iii) **Nor** s'emploie devant le second élément (ou le troisième, etc.), après un **not** apparu plus tôt dans la phrase :

I don't eat sweets, nor chocolate, nor any kind of sugary thing
je ne mange pas de bonbons, ni de chocolat, ni aucunes sucreries

On peut aussi employer **or** dans cette même construction :

I don't eat sweets, or chocolate, or any kind of sugary thing

Nor s'emploie aussi pour relier des propositions. Il est parfois accompagné de **and** ou **but**. Remarquez l'inversion sujet-auxiliaire du verbe :

I don't like coffee, nor do I like tea
je n'aime pas le café et je n'aime pas le thé non plus

I don't like coffee, (and) nor does she
je n'aime pas le café, et elle non plus

I don't understand it, (but) nor do I need to
je ne comprend pas ça, mais ça n'est pas nécessaire

iv) **Neither** s'emploie seulement pour relier deux propositions :

I don't like coffee, neither does she
je n'aime pas le café, elle non plus

I don't understand it, (and/but) neither do I need to
je ne comprends pas, et/mais ça n'est pas nécessaire

v) Si **(n)either ... (n)or** relie deux noms, le verbe s'accorde en nombre avec le nom le plus proche du verbe :

either the record player or the speakers have to be changed
either the speakers or the record player has to be changed
il faut changer soit les enceintes, soit la platine

b) *Exemples de conjonctions de coordination corrélatives*

you need both butter and flour
vous avez besoin de beurre et de farine

she's both old and fragile
elle est (à la fois) âgée et frêle

they both laughed and cried
ils ont à la fois ri et pleuré

you need either butter or margarine
tu as besoin soit de beurre, soit de margarine

she'll be either French or Italian
ce sera une Française ou une Italienne

she was travelling either to or from Aberdeen
elle allait à Aberdeen ou bien elle en revenait

you need neither butter nor margarine
tu n'as besoin ni de beurre, ni de margarine

she's neither old nor fragile
elle n'est ni âgée, ni frêle

c) **or** recouvre quatre sens de base

i) Un sens exclusif ou alternatif :

he lives in Liverpool or Manchester
il habite à Liverpool ou à Manchester

ii) Dans le même sens que **and** :

you could afford things like socks or handkerchiefs or ties
vous pourriez vous offrir des choses comme des chaussettes ou des mouchoirs ou des cravates

iii) Pour relier deux synonymes :

acquired immune deficiency syndrome, or Aids
le syndrome immuno déficitaire acquis, ou sida

iv) Lorsqu'il relie deux propositions dans le sens de 'sinon' :

apologize to her, or she'll never speak to you again
excusez-vous auprès d'elle, ou elle ne vous parlera plus jamais

2 Les conjonctions de subordination

Il existe un grand nombre de conjonctions de subordination. Certaines sont 'simples', comme **because** (parce que) ou **so that** (si bien que) ; d'autres sont corrélatives (comparez avec 1 ci-dessus), comme **as ... as** (aussi ... que), **so ... that** (afin ... que), **more ... than** (plus ... que).

a) *Introduisant une proposition substantive*

Les propositions substantives ont la même fonction que les (pro)noms et les groupes nominaux dans la phrase :

(a) **I told him that they had done it**
je lui ai dit qu'ils l'avaient fait

(b) **I told him the facts**
je lui ai dit les faits

Dans (a), une proposition substantive est le complément d'objet direct de **told**, dans (b), c'est un groupe nominal.

Les conjonctions qui introduisent des propositions substantives sont **that** (que), **if** (si), **whether** (si + *choix*) et

how (comment). **That** est parfois omis si la proposition subordonnée est le complément d'objet direct de la phrase, mais pas si elle en est le sujet :

he said (that) he wanted to see me (complément d'objet)
il a dit qu'il voulait me voir

that such people exist is unbelievable (sujet)
que de tels personnes existent est incroyable

he asked me if/whether I had any money (complément d'objet)
il m'a demandé si j'avais de l'argent (ou pas)

whether I have any money or not is none of your business (sujet)
que j'aie de l'argent ou non ne te regarde pas

he said how it was done (complément d'objet)
il a dit comment c'était fait

how it's done is immaterial (sujet)
la manière dont c'est fait est sans importance

That, **if**, **whether** et **how** employés comme ci-dessus ne doivent pas être confondus avec leur rôle lorsqu'ils introduisent un groupe adverbial (voir ci-dessous).

b) *Introduisant une proposition adverbiale*

i) Voir **Les Adverbes**, p A21. Il existe un grand nombre de conjonctions qui introduisent des propositions adverbiales ; parmi celles-ci on trouve beaucoup d'exemples de noms ou de verbes ayant fonction de conjonction, ce qui est le cas de **the minute** (à la minute où) et de **the way** (de la manière dont) dans :

he arrived the minute the clock struck twelve (= conjonction de temps, comparez avec **when**)
il est arrivé à la minute où la pendule sonnait midi

he didn't explain it the way you did (= conjonction de manière, comparez avec **how**)
il ne l'a pas expliqué de la manière dont tu l'as fait

ou **provided** (du moment que) et **considering**, comme dans :

provided you keep quiet, you can stay (= conjonction de condition, comparez avec **if**)
du moment que tu restes sage, tu peux rester

he's doing well considering he's been here for only a week (= conjonction de concession, comparez avec **although**)
il se débrouille bien si l'on considère qu'il n'est ici que depuis une semaine

Les conjonctions adverbiales principales :

ii) Conjonctions de temps : **after** (après que), **as** (alors que), **before** (avant que), **since** (depuis que), **until** (jusqu'à ce que), **when** (lorsque), **whenever** (chaque fois que), **while** (tandis que). L'idée de futur dans les subordonnées introduites par une de ces conjonctions est exprimée par un présent en anglais (voir p A49) :

he came back after the show had finished
il est revenu après que le spectacle fût/soit terminé

the phone rang as he was having a bath
le téléphone a sonné alors qu'il prenait son bain

before you sit down, you must see the bedroom
avant que tu ne t'asseyes, il faut que tu voies la chambre

they've been crying (ever) since their parents left
ils pleurent depuis que/le moment où leurs parents sont partis

he talked non-stop until it was time to go home
il a parlé sans s'arrêter jusqu'à ce qu'il fût/soit l'heure de partir

when he's ready we'll be able to get going at last
quand il sera prêt, on pourra enfin se mettre en route

you don't have to go upstairs whenever the baby cries
tu n'es pas obligé de monter chaque fois que le bébé pleure

while I'm asleep, will you drive?
tu conduiras, pendant que je dors ?

iii) Conjonctions de lieu : **where** (où), **wherever** (où que) :

plant them where there is a lot of shade
plante-les là où il y a beaucoup d'ombre

wherever she goes, he follows
où qu'elle aille, il suit

iv) Conjonctions de manière, de comparaison ou d'intensité : **as** (comme), **as if** (comme si), **as though** (comme si), **how** (comment), **however** (cependant) :

he does it as he's always done it
il le fait comme il l'a toujours fait

he behaved as if/as though there was (were) something wrong
il s'est comporté comme s'il y avait quelque chose qui clochait

you can pay how you want
tu peux payer comme tu veux

however hard you try, you won't manage
même si tu fais tout ton possible, tu n'y arriveras pas

however exciting it may be, he won't be interested
si passionnant que ce soit, il ne sera pas intéressé

v) Conjonctions de cause : **as** (étant donné que), **because** (parce que), **only** (cependant, mais), **since** (puisque) :

as there was nothing but biscuits in the house, we went out to eat
comme il n'y avait rien dans la maison à part des biscuits, nous sommes allés dîner dehors

I love you because you are you
je t'aime parce que tu es telle que tu es

I would have done it really, only I didn't think there was time
je l'aurais fait volontiers, mais je ne pensais pas qu'on avait le temps

since you've been so kind to me, I want to give you a present
puisque tu as été si gentil avec moi, je veux te faire un cadeau

vi) Conjonctions de concession : **(al)though** (bien que), **even if** (même si), **even though** (bien que), **whether** (soit que) :

we let him come (al)though he was a nuisance
nous l'avons laissé venir, bien qu'il nous ait apporté des ennuis

you can stay, even if/even though you haven't paid your rent
tu peux rester, même si tu n'as pas payé ton loyer

I'm doing it whether you like it or not
je le fais que ça te plaise ou non

vii) Conjonctions de but : **in order to** (afin de), **lest** (de peur/crainte que/de), **so that** (afin que) :

they went to the stage door in order to get a glimpse of him
ils sont allés à la sortie des artistes afin de pouvoir l'apercevoir

I apologized lest she should be offended
je me suis excusé(e) de peur qu'elle ne fût/soit blessée

he did it so that she would be happy
il l'a fait afin qu'elle soit heureuse

Remarquez que **lest** a tendance à être employé dans un usage littéraire. Il est toujours possible d'employer **so that ... not** à la place :

I apologized so that she shouldn't be offended
je me suis excusé(e) afin qu'elle ne fût/soit pas blessée

viii) Conjonctions de conséquence : **so that** (si bien que) :

if you can arrange things so that we're all there at the same time
si tu peux t'organiser pour qu'on soit tous là en même temps

ix) Conjonctions de condition: **if** (si), **so/as long as** (tant que), **unless** (à moins que) :

only tell me if you want to
dis-le moi seulement si tu veux

so long as you promise to be careful
tant que tu promets d'être prudent

tell me, unless you don't want to
dis-moi, à moins que tu ne le veuilles pas

c) But est une conjonction de subordination dans les sens suivants :

i) 'sans que' (après **never** et **hardly**) :

it never rains but it pours (proverbe)
un malheur n'arrive jamais seul

hardly a day goes by but something happens
il ne se passe presque jamais un jour sans que quelque chose ne se produise

ii) employé avec **that** (après certains noms négatifs) :

there's no doubt but that he's responsible
il n'y a aucun doute qu'il est responsable

d) *Introduisant des propositions comparatives*

Les propositions subordonnées comparatives ne modifient pas d'autres propositions (comme le font les propositions adverbiales). Elles modifient des éléments de la proposition : groupes nominaux, groupes adverbiaux et adjectivaux.

Les conjonctions comparatives sont corrélatives (comparez avec **conjonctions de coordination**, p A68): **more ... than** (plus ... que), **less ... than** (moins ... que), et **as ... as** (autant ...que).

i) Modifiant un nom :

they killed more people than we can imagine
ils ont tué plus de gens que nous ne pouvons l'imaginer

they killed as many people as the other side (did)
ils ont tué autant de gens que les autres

ii) Modifiant un adjectif :

it was less comfortable than we'd thought
c'était moins confortable que nous n'avions pensé

it was as comfortable as we thought
c'était aussi confortable que nous le pensions

iii) Modifiant un adverbe :

you did it better than I could have done
tu l'as mieux fait que je n'aurais pu le faire

you did it as well as I could have done
tu l'as fait aussi bien que j'aurais pu le faire

Remarquez l'absence de négation dans les exemples anglais.

16 Les Nombres

1 Les nombres cardinaux et les nombres ordinaux

	Cardinaux		*Ordinaux*
1	**one**	1st	**first**
2	**two**	2nd	**second**
3	**three**	3rd	**third**
4	**four**	4th	**fourth**
5	**five**	5th	**fifth**
6	**six**	6th	**sixth**
7	**seven**	7th	**seventh**
8	**eight**	8th	**eighth**
9	**nine**	9th	**ninth**
10	**ten**	10th	**tenth**
11	**eleven**	11th	**eleventh**
12	**twelve**	12th	**twelfth**
13	**thirteen**	13th	**thirteenth**
14	**fourteen**	14th	**fourteenth**
15	**fifteen**	15th	**fifteenth**
16	**sixteen**	16th	**sixteenth**
17	**seventeen**	17th	**seventeenth**
18	**eighteen**	18th	**eighteenth**
19	**nineteen**	19th	**nineteenth**
20	**twenty**	20th	**twentieth**
21	**twenty-one**	21st	**twenty-first**
30	**thirty**	30th	**thirtieth**
40	**forty**	40th	**fortieth**
50	**fifty**	50th	**fiftieth**
60	**sixty**	60th	**sixtieth**
70	**seventy**	70th	**seventieth**
80	**eighty**	80th	**eightieth**
90	**ninety**	90th	**ninetieth**
100	**a/one hundred**	100th	**(one) hundredth**
101	**a/one hundred and one**	101st	**(one) hundred and first**
200	**two hundred**	200th	**two hundredth**
1,000	**a/one thousand**	1,000th	**(one) thousandth**
1,345	**a/one thousand three hundred and forty-five**	1,345th	**one thousand three hundred and forty-fifth**

1,000,000	**a/one million**	**millionth**
1,000,000,000 (^{9})	**a/one billion**	**billionth**
1,000,000,000,000 (^{10})	**a/one trillion**	**trillionth**

Remarquez qu'en anglais britannique, **a billion** était (et est encore parfois) 10^{12} (dix à la puissance douze) et **a trillion** 10^{18}. Les nombres donnés dans la liste sont des valeurs américaines, qui sont maintenant aussi employées en anglais britannique. 10^9 (un milliard) était (et est encore parfois) appelé **a thousand million** en anglais britannique.

Remarquez l'emploi de la virgule pour indiquer les milliers.

2 Les fractions

a) *Les fractions ordinaires*

On écrit les fractions avec un nombre cardinal (ou parfois **a** à la place de **one**) + un nombre ordinal :

$^1/_5$ = **a/one fifth**

$^3/_8$ = **three eighths**

$3^4/_9$ = **three and four ninths**

$^1/_2$ = **a/one half**

$^1/_4$ = **a quarter**

$^3/_4$ = **three quarters**

Remarquez que $1^1/_4$ hours = **an/one hour and a quarter** ou **one and a quarter hours** (une heure et quart).

Remarquez que le **-s** est maintenu lorsque les fractions sont employées comme adjectifs :

they had a two-thirds majority
ils ont eu une majorité de deux tiers

L'emploi des fractions ordinaires est beaucoup plus courant en anglais qu'en français.

b) *Les nombres décimaux*

Alors que dans les autres pays européens on utilise une virgule pour les nombres décimaux, les anglophones se servent du point :

25.5 = twenty-five point five

Les décimales sont énumérées une à une après le point :

25.552 = twenty-five point five five two

3 Nought, zero, '0', nil

a) *Anglais britannique*

Nought et **zero** sont utilisés pour le chiffre 0. Dans les calculs, **nought** est habituel :

add another nought (ou **zero**) **to that number**
ajoute un autre zéro à ce chiffre

put down nought and carry one
je pose zéro et je retiens un

0.6 = nought point six
zéro virgule six

Pour un nombre sur une échelle, on préfère **zero** :

it's freezing - it's 10 below zero
il gèle - il fait moins 10

comme en anglais scientifique :

given zero conductivity
étant donné une conductivité de zéro

a country striving for zero inflation
un pays qui se bat pour atteindre une inflation nulle

Lorsqu'on prononce le chiffre comme la lettre 'o', il s'agit normalement d'un numéro de téléphone.

Nil est toujours utilisé pour les points ou les buts en sports :

Arsenal won four nil (= 4-0)
ou :
Arsenal won by four goals to nil
Arsenal a gagné quatre buts à zéro

sauf au tennis, où l'on utilise 'love' :

Lendl leads forty-love
Lendl mène quarante zéro

(mot dérivé du français 'l'œuf' à cause de sa ressemblance graphique)

Nil est aussi utilisé dans le sens de **nothing** (rien) (qui se dit aussi parfois **zero**) :

production was soon reduced to nil (ou **zero**)
la production fut rapidement réduite à zéro

b) *Anglais américain*

Zero est utilisé dans presque tous les cas :

how many zeros are there in a billion?
combien y a-t-il de zéros dans un milliard ?

my telephone number is 721002 (seven two one zero zero two)

Chicago Cubs zero (au basket)

Cependant, au tennis on utilise le mot **love**, voir 3 a) ci-dessus.

4 Les dates

a) *Années*

1989 se dit :

nineteen eighty-nine

ou, plus rarement :

nineteen hundred and eighty-nine

1026 se dit :

ten twenty-six

Dans cet exemple, l'utilisation de **hundred** n'est pas habituel.

b) *Mois et jours*

On peut écrire la date de différentes manières :

12(th) May	**May 12(th)**
the twelfth of May	**May the twelfth**

En anglais américain parlé, il est plus courant d'omettre le mot **the** quand on fait commencer la date par le mois :

May 12 (dit : May twelfth/May twelve)

En anglais britannique, on écrit les dates en mettant le jour en premier, et en anglais américain, on met le mois en premier :

10/4/92 (= 10th April 1992, anglais britannique)
4/10/92 (= 10th April 1992, anglais américain)

5 Les numéros de téléphone

On lit les numéros de téléphone comme des chiffres séparés (voir aussi 3 ci-dessus) :

1567 = one five six seven
40032 = four double 'o' three two (anglais britannique)
four zero zero three two (anglais américain)

Mais à l'écrit, il est normal de les regrouper par groupes de chiffres pour faire apparaître les différents codes régionaux en opération :

0141-221-5266

6 Les adresses

En Amérique du Nord les numéros à quatre chiffres se lisent :

3445 Sherbrooke Street
thirty-four forty-five Sherbrooke Street

7 Les opérations

Il existe plusieurs façons d'exprimer les opérations arithmétiques. Voici certaines des plus courantes :

12 + 19 = 31
twelve and/plus nineteen is/equals thirty-one

19 – 7 = 12
nineteen minus seven is/equals twelve
seven from nineteen is/leaves twelve
nineteen take away seven is/leaves twelve (emploi enfantin)

2 x 5 = 10
twice five is ten
two fives are ten

4 x 5 = 20
four times five is/equals twenty
four fives are twenty

36 x 41 = 1476
thirty-six times forty-one is/equals one thousand four hundred and seventy-six
thirty-six multiplied by forty-one is/equals one thousand four hundred and seventy-six

10÷2 = 5
ten divided by two is/equals five
two into ten goes five (emploi plus familier)

8 Hundred, thousand, million

Pour **hundred**, **thousand**, **million** (**billion**, **trillion**) avec ou sans **-s**, voir **Les Noms**, p A8. Comparez aussi:

first they came in ones and twos, but soon in tens - at last in tens of thousands
ils sont d'abord arrivés par petits groupes, mais bientôt par dizaines - puis par dizaines de milliers

in the 1950s (= nineteen fifties)
dans les années cinquante

she's now in her eighties
elle est maintenant octogénaire (elle a entre 80 et 90 ans)

9 The former et the latter

Au lieu d'employer **the first** on emploie **the former** si on fait référence à une personne/chose parmi deux qui viennent juste d'être évoquées ; et **the latter** (au lieu de **the last**) quand on fait référence à la dernière de deux personnes/ choses :

trains and coaches are both common means of transport - the former are faster, the latter less expensive
le train et le car sont deux moyens de transport couramment utilisés - l'un est plus rapide, l'autre moins cher

De ces expressions, **the latter** est plus souvent utilisé, et il peut aussi faire référence à la dernière chose d'une énumération qui en comprend plus de deux :

Spain, Italy, Greece: of these countries the latter is still the most interesting as regards ...
l'Espagne, l'Italie, la Grèce : de tous ces pays, le dernier est le plus intéressant en ce qui concerne ...

Des noms peuvent suivre **the former/the latter** :

of the dog and the cat, the former animal makes a better pet in my opinion
du chien ou du chat, c'est le premier qui, à mon avis, fait le meilleur animal domestique

10 Once et twice

Once est utilisé pour 'une fois', **twice** pour 'deux fois'. **Thrice** (trois fois) est archaïque :

if I've told you once, I've told you a thousand times
je te l'ai déjà dit mille fois

I've only seen her twice
je ne l'ai vue que deux fois

17 La Structure de la Phrase

a) *Le sujet*

i) En général, le sujet précède l'auxiliaire et le verbe :

he may smoke
il peut fumer

L'inversion du sujet et du verbe a lieu dans les cas suivants (s'il y a plus d'un auxiliaire, seul le premier auxiliaire précède le sujet) :

ii) dans les questions :

may I?	**(when) can you come?**
puis-je ?	(quand) peux-tu venir ?

would you have liked to have the chance?
auriez-vous voulu avoir la possibilité ?

iii) dans les propositions conditionnelles, lorsque **if** est omis :

had I got there in time, she'd still be alive
si j'étais arrivé à temps, elle serait encore en vie

should that be true, I'd be most surprised
si c'était vrai, je serais vraiment surpris

iv) quand la phrase commence avec un mot qui a un sens négatif (comme **never, seldom**) :

never did I think this would happen
je n'aurais jamais pensé que cela allait se passer

I can't swim – nor/neither can I
je ne sais pas nager – moi non plus

little did I think this would happen
je ne me doutais pas du tout que cela pourrait arriver

hardly had he entered the room, when the ceiling caved in
à peine etait-il entré dans la pièce, que le plafond s'écroula

seldom have I enjoyed a meal so much
j'ai rarement autant apprécié un repas

Mais **nevertheless, nonetheless** et **only**, qui font tous les trois référence à un affirmation précédente, sont suivi par les mots dans leur ordre normal :

I know he smokes, nevertheless/nonetheless he should be invited
je sais qu'il fume, mais on devrait quand même l'inviter

we'd like you to come, only we haven't got enough room
nous aimerions que vous veniez, mais nous n'avons pas assez de place

v) souvent quand une phrase commence avec un adverbe de degré :

so marvellously did he play, that it brought tears to the eyes of even a hardened critic like me
son jeu était si merveilleux qu'il a même fait monter les larmes aux yeux d'un critique aussi endurci que moi

only too well do I remember those words
je m'en souviens trop bien, de ces paroles

vi) parfois lorsque la phrase commence avec un adverbe, si le verbe n'a pas un sens descriptif fort, et si le sujet a une certaine importance :

in that year came the announcement that the space shuttle would be launched
cette année-là fut annoncé le lancement de la navette spatiale

on the stage stood a little dwarf
sur la scène se tenait un petit nain

out came a scream so horrible that it made my hair stand on end
on entendit tout à coup un cri si horrible que mes cheveux se dressèrent sur ma tête

to his brave efforts do we owe our happiness (assez littéraire)
c'est à son grand courage que nous devons notre bonheur

pour donner un effet dramatique lorsqu'un adverbe est placé en position initiale :

a big black car pulled up and out jumped Margot
une grosse voiture noire s'arrêta et Margot en sortit avec précipitation

vii) après **so** placé en position initiale (= aussi) :

I'm hungry – so am I
j'ai faim – moi aussi

viii) au discours direct :

Après le discours direct, le verbe d'expression précède parfois son sujet, surtout si c'est un nom (plus le nom a une signification forte dans la phrase, plus on aura tendance à inverser l'ordre des mots) :

'you're late again', said John/John said
'tu es encore en retard', dit John

'you're late again !', boomed the furious sergeant (ou **the furious sergeant boomed)**
'tu es encore en retard', hurla le sergent furieux

Mais l'ordre normal est obligatoire quand on utilise les temps composés :

'you're late again', John had said
'tu es encore en retard', avait dit John

Si le sujet est un pronom, alors le sujet se met habituellement en première place :

'you're late again', he said
'tu es encore en retard', dit-il

Quand le verbe précède le pronom, c'est fréquemment parce qu'une proposition relative suit ou parce qu'on veut donner un caractère de plaisanterie à la phrase :

'you're late again', said I, who had been waiting for at least five hours
'tu es encore en retard', ai-je dit ; ça faisait au moins cinq heures que j'attendais

Les journalistes ont tendance à concentrer un grand nombre d'informations sur un sujet (**vivacious blonde Mary Lakes from Scarborough said : '...'** la blonde et enjouée Marie Lakes de Scarborough dit : '...'). Vu qu'il est plutôt étrange en anglais de placer un mot à signification descriptive si faible comme **said** en dernière position dans la phrase, les journalistes changent souvent l'ordre de la phrase dans de tels cas :

said vivacious blonde Mary Lakes from Scarborough :
comme le dit la blonde et enjouée Mary Lakes de Scarborough ...

S'il y a un adverbe, l'inversion est moins courante, mais possible :

'you're back again', said John tentatively
'tu es de retour', dit John avec hésitation

Mais s'il y a un complément d'objet, après **ask** ou **tell** par exemple, on ne fait pas l'inversion :

'she is late again', John told the waiting guests
'elle est encore en retard', dit John aux invités qui attendaient

b) *Le complément d'objet*

Le complément d'objet suit normalement le verbe, mais il est en position initiale dans les cas suivants :

i) dans les questions qui commencent par un pronom interrogatif qui est complément d'objet :

who(m) did you meet?
qui as-tu rencontré ?

ii) dans les propositions subordonnées interrogatives et relatives :

(please ask him) what he thinks
(demande-lui, s'il te plaît,) ce qu'il pense

(can we decide) which position we're adopting?
(pouvons-nous décider) quelle attitude nous adoptons ?

(he brought back) what she'd given him
(il a ramené) ce qu'elle lui avait donné

iii) pour renforcer un objet, surtout quand l'objet est **that** :

that I couldn't put up with
cela, je ne pouvais pas l'accepter

that I don't know
ça, je ne sais pas

but his sort I don't like at all
son genre, je ne l'aime pas du tout

iv) si la phrase contient un complément d'objet direct et un complément d'objet indirect, le complément d'objet indirect précède le complément d'objet direct si un des deux (ou les deux) est un nom :

he gave her a kiss
il lui a donné un baiser

Mais si, au lieu du complément indirect, on a une locution prépositionnelle adverbiale, cette locution se place en dernière position :

he gave the old tramp a fiver

ou :

he gave a fiver to the old tramp
il a donné un billet de cinq livres au vieux mendiant

v) Quand les deux compléments sont tous les deux des pronoms, alors le complément d'objet indirect précède le complément d'objet direct :

could you please send her these in the mail tonight?
tu peux les lui envoyer par le courrier de ce soir ?

would you give me one?
tu veux bien m'en donner un ?

well, tell them that then
et bien, dis-le leur

he wouldn't sell me one
il ne voulait pas m'en vendre un

that secretary of yours, will you lend me her?
cette secrétaire que tu as, tu veux bien me la prêter ?

On fait une exception à cette règle dans l'emploi de **it** avec **give** ou **lend**, etc. pour lesquels il y a deux possibilités :

could you give it him when you see him?
could you give him it when you see him?
tu veux bien le lui donner quand tu le verras ?

Il est aussi possible de dire :

could you give it to him when you see him?

Si **to** est employé, alors l'ordre des mots est semblable à celui dans l'exemple ci-dessus :

he wouldn't sell one to me
il ne voulait pas m'en vendre un

18 Notes Concernant l'Orthographe

1 *y en i*

Un **y** placé après une consonne se change en **i** devant les terminaisons suivantes :

-able, **-ed**, **-er** (adjectifs ou noms)
-est, **-es** (noms et verbes)
-ly et **-ness**

ply : plies : pliable
cry : cried : cries : crier
happy : happier : happiest : happily : happiness

Exceptions :

shyly (timidement) et **slyly** (sournoisement) (on évite d'employer **slily** qui est rare). Par contre, **drily** est plus courant que **dryly** :

Les noms propres qui se terminent en **-y** prennent seulement **-s** :

there were two Henrys at the party
il y avait deux Henri à la soirée

Les composés en **-by** prennent **-s** :

standbys

De même **dyer** (teinturier) et parfois **flyer** (aviateur) (aussi **flier**).

Mais **y** précédé par une voyelle ne change pas et la terminaison des noms ou des verbes est **-s** au lieu de **-es** :

play : plays : playable : player
coy : coyer : coyest : coyly : coyness

Mais remarquez **lay : laid**, **pay : paid**, **say : said**, et **daily**, **gaily** (aussi **gayly**).

2 *ie en y*

Ce changement a lieu devant **-ing** :

die : dying, **lie : lying**

3 *Chute de la voyelle finale -e*

Normalement **-e** est omis si une syllabe qui commence par une voyelle est ajoutée :

love : loving : lovable
stone : stony

Mais il existe un certain nombre d'exceptions, comme **matey** (copain), **likeable** (aimable), **mileage** (distance parcourue en miles), **dyeing** (= teinture - à ne pas confondre avec **dying** = mourir), **hoeing** (binage), **swingeing** (= énorme, à ne pas confondre avec **swinging** = dans le vent).

Si le mot se termine en **-ce** ou en **-ge**, alors le **-e** est maintenu devant **-a** et **-o** :

irreplaceable, **changeable**, **outrageous**

Si la syllabe suivante commence avec une consonne, le **-e** est conservé habituellement :

love : lovely
bore : boredom

Mais encore, il existe des exceptions importantes, surtout :

due : duly **true : truly**
whole : wholly **argue : argument**

4 *-our ou -or*

Quand un suffixe est ajouté à certains des mots se terminant en **-our**, on fait tomber le **-u** :

humour : humorist
vigour : vigorous

Mais il y a une exception importante concernant cela pour le mot **colour** :

colour : colourful : colourlessness : colourist

Cela ne pose pas de problèmes pour les Américains qui ont définitivement laissé tomber le **-u** :

humor : humorist

5 *Doublement des consonnes*

Après une voyelle courte accentuée, on double la consonne finale lorsqu'elle est placée devant **-er**, **-est**, **-ed**, **-ing** :

fit : fitter : fittest : fitted : fitting
begin : beginner : beginning

Aussi après **-ur** ou **-er** :

occur : occurred : occurring
refer : referred : referring

mais :

keep : keeper : keeping

ou :

cure : cured : curing

parce que la voyelle dans ce mot est longue

et :

vomit : vomited : vomiting

parce que le **-i** n'est pas accentué.

En anglais britannique **-l** est doublé même dans une syllabe non-accentuée :

revel : revelled : reveller : revelling
travel : travelled : traveller : travelling

Ce phénomène concernant le **-l** n'a pas lieu en anglais américain :

travel : traveled : traveler : traveling

Remarquez aussi :

kidnap : kidnapped : kidnapper (anglais britannique)
kidnap : kidnaped : kidnaper (anglais américain)

6 *c en ck*

Les mots qui se terminent en **-c** changent le **-c** en **-ck** avant **-ed**, **-er**, **-ing** :

frolic : frolicked : frolicking
picnic : picnicked : picnicker : picnicking

7 *Variantes américaines*

En plus des variantes américaines données en 4 et 5 ci-dessus, il faut noter les suivantes :

a) anglais britannique **-gue**, anglais américain **-g** :

catalogue : catalog

b) anglais britannique **-tre**, anglais américain **-ter** :

centre : center

c) anglais britannique **-nce**, anglais américain **-nse** :

defence : defense
offence : offense
pretence : pretense

d) Quelques mots différents. Le premier de chaque paire est en anglais britannique :

cheque : check,
cigarette (aussi américain) **: cigaret**
pyjamas : pajamas
practise (pratiquer) **: practice** (le nom a **-ce** des deux côtés de l'Atlantique)
programme : program (mais en informatique aussi **program** en anglais britannique)
tyre : tire (pneu)

19 Les Expressions de Temps

A L'HEURE

what's the time?, what time is it? quelle heure est-il ?

what time do you make it? quelle heure avez-vous ?

a) *les heures*

it's 12 noon (midday)/ midnight il est midi/minuit

it's one/two o'clock il est une heure/deux heures

b) *les demi-heures*

it's half past midnight il est minuit et demi(e)

it's half past twelve (in the afternoon) il est midi et demi(e)

it's half past one, it's one thirty
it's half one *(familier)*
il est une heure et demie

c) *les quarts d'heure*

it's (a) quarter past two il est deux heures et quart

at (a) quarter to two à deux heures moins le quart

d) *les minutes*

it's twenty-three minutes past four, it's 4.23
il est 4 heures 23

it's twenty to five, it's 4.40
il est 5 heures moins 20

Remarquez qu'en anglais américain on peut aussi employer **after** au lieu de **past** et **of** au lieu de **to**.

e) ***a.m.*** *et* ***p.m.***

a.m. du matin

p.m. de l'après-midi/du soir

it is 7.10 p.m. il est 7 heures 10 du soir

it's ten to seven, it's 6.50 il est sept heures moins dix

Les expressions du type 'quinze heures', etc. (à la place de 'trois heures', etc.) ne s'emploient pas dans l'anglais de tous les jours. On les rencontre cependant parfois dans les horaires et surtout dans le langage militaire (souvent suivis de **hours**) :

'o' five hundred hours 5 heures du matin

fifteen hundred hours quinze heures

fifteen thirty hours quinze heures trente

we took the sixteen-twenty to Brighton
nous avons pris le train de 16h20 pour Brighton

Remarquez les abréviations : **7.15** = 7h15.

B LA DATE

1 Les mois, les jours et les saisons

a) *Les mois (**months**)*

January	janvier
February	février
March	mars
April	avril
May	mai
June	juin
July	juillet
August	août
September	septembre
October	octobre
November	novembre
December	décembre

b) *Les jours de la semaine (**the days of the week**)*

Monday	lundi
Tuesday	mardi
Wednesday	mercredi
Thursday	jeudi
Friday	vendredi
Saturday	samedi
Sunday	dimanche

c) *Les saisons (**the seasons**)*

spring (le printemps) **summer** (l'été)
autumn (l'automne) **winter** (l'hiver)

En anglais américain on dit aussi **fall** pour 'l'automne'. Pour l'emploi de l'article voir p A7.

2 Les dates

a) On emploie les nombres ordinaux pour les dates (à la différence du français) :

the fourteenth of July le quatorze juillet

the second of November le deux novembre

I wrote to you on the third of March
je vous ai écrit le trois mars

Voir aussi **Les Nombres** p A70.

C EXPRESSIONS IDIOMATIQUES

at 5 o'clock	à cinq heures
(a) about 11 o'clock	à onze heures environ
(at) about midnight	vers minuit
(at about 10 o'clock	vers (les) dix heures
it's past six o'clock	il est six heures passées
at exactly four o'clock	à quatre heures précises *ou* pile
on the stroke of three	sur le coup de trois heures
from 9 o'clock onwards	à partir de neuf heures
shortly before seven	peu avant sept heures
shortly after seven	peu après sept heures
it's late	il est tard
he's late	il est en retard
the train is twenty minutes late	le train a vingt minutes de retard
my watch is six minutes slow	ma montre retarde de six minutes
my watch is six minutes fast	ma montre avance de six minutes
one day/morning/evening	un jour/matin/soir
this evening, tonight	ce soir
tomorrow evening, tomorrow night	demain soir
yesterday evening, last night	hier soir
Saturday evening	samedi soir
I'm going out on Saturday night *or* evening	je sors samedi soir
on Saturday evening	dans la soirée de samedi
during Saturday night	dans la nuit de samedi (à dimanche)
tomorrow morning	demain matin
yesterday morning	hier matin
Monday morning	lundi matin
I'm going (on) Monday morning	j'y vais lundi matin
the next day	le lendemain
the next morning	le lendemain matin
a week on Monday, Monday week	lundi en huit
a fortnight on Monday	lundi en quinze
next week	la semaine prochaine
this (coming) week	la semaine qui vient
last week	la semaine dernière

I saw him the other Saturday	je l'ai vu l'autre samedi
I'm starting on Monday	je commence lundi
he comes on Mondays, he comes on a Monday	il vient le lundi
come one Monday	viens un lundi
he comes in the afternoon(s)	il vient l'après-midi
come one afternoon	viens un après-midi
every other Monday, every second Monday	un lundi sur deux
every Saturday	tous les samedis
every Saturday evening *or* night	tous les samedis soirs
I spent the whole Sunday doing the cleaning	j'ai passé tout mon dimanche à faire le ménage
all her Sundays	tous ses dimanches
in the early afternoon/ evening	au début de l'après-midi/ de la soirée, en début d'après-midi/de soirée
I'll phone him first thing in the morning	je lui téléphonerai en tout début de la matinée
in the middle of June, mid-June	au milieu (du mois de) juin, (à la) mi-juin
in the middle of winter, mid-winter	au milieu de l'hiver
I've a meeting late morning	j'ai une réunion à la fin de la matinée ou en fin de matinée
at the end of winter	à la fin de l'hiver
we'll talk about it again at the end of January	on en reparlera fin janvier *ou* à la fin du mois de janvier
what day is it today?	quel jour sommes-nous aujourd'hui ?
what's the date?	le combien sommes-nous ?
it's the third of April	c'est le trois avril
in February	en/au mois de février
in 1996	en 1996
in the summer of 1996, in summer 1996	l'été 1996
in the sixties, in the 60s, in the 1960s	dans les années soixante
in the early/late sixties	au début/à la fin des années soixante
in the seventeenth century	au dix-septième siècle
in the 17th C	au XVIIe

FRENCH GRAMMAR

GRAMMAIRE FRANÇAISE

Contents

1 Glossary of Grammatical Terms

ADJECTIVE A describing word, which adds information about a noun, telling us what something is like (eg *a* ***small*** *house, a* ***red*** *car, an* ***interesting*** *pastime*).

ADVERB Adverbs are normally used with a verb to add extra information by indicating **how** the action is done (adverbs of manner), **when, where** and **with how much intensity** the action is done (adverbs of time, place and intensity), or **to what extent** the action is done (adverbs of quantity). Adverbs may also be used with an adjective or another adverb (eg *a* ***very*** *attractive girl,* ***very*** *well*).

AGREEMENT In French, words such as adjectives, articles and pronouns are said to agree in number and gender with the noun or pronoun they refer to. This means that their spelling changes according to the **number** of the noun (singular or plural) and according to its **gender** (masculine or feminine).

ANTECEDENT The antecedent of a relative pronoun is the word or words to which the relative pronoun refers. The antecedent is usually found directly before the relative pronoun (eg in the sentence *I know* ***the man*** *who did this, the man* is the antecedent of *who*).

APPOSITION A word or a clause is said to be in apposition to another when it is placed directly after it without any joining word (eg *Mr Jones,* ***our bank manager****, rang today*).

ARTICLE See DEFINITE ARTICLE, INDEFINITE ARTICLE and PARTITIVE ARTICLE.

AUXILIARY The French auxiliary verbs, or 'helping' verbs, are **avoir** (*to have*) and **être** (*to be*). They are used to make up the first part of compound tenses, the second part being a past participle (eg *I* ***have*** *eaten*).

CARDINAL Cardinal numbers are numbers such as *one, two, ten, fourteen,* as opposed to **ordinal** numbers (eg *first, second*).

CLAUSE A clause is a group of words which contains at least a subject and a verb: *he said* is a clause. A clause often contains more than this basic information, eg *he said this to her yesterday*. Sentences can be made up of several clauses, eg *he said/ he'd call me / if he were free*. See SENTENCE.

COMPARATIVE The comparative forms of adjectives and adverbs allow us to compare two things, persons or actions. In English, *more ... than, ...er than, less ... than* and *as ... as* are used for comparison.

COMPOUND Compound tenses are verb tenses consisting of more than one element. In French, the compound tenses of a verb are formed by the **auxiliary** verb and the **past participle**: *j'ai visité, il est venu.*

CONDITIONAL This mood is used to describe what someone would do, or something that would happen if a condition were fulfilled (eg *I* ***would come*** *if I were well; the chair* ***would have broken*** *if he had sat on it*).

CONJUGATION The conjugation of a verb is the set of different forms taken in the particular tenses of that verb.

CONJUNCTION Conjunctions are linking words. They may be coordinating or subordinating. Coordinating conjunctions are words like *and, but, or*; subordinating conjunctions are words like *because, after, although*.

DEFINITE ARTICLE The definite article is *the* in English and *le, la* and *les* in French.

DEMONSTRATIVE Demonstrative adjectives (eg *this, that, these*) and pronouns (eg *this one, that one*) are used to point out a particular person or object.

DIRECT OBJECT A noun or a pronoun which in English follows a verb without any linking preposition, eg *I met* ***a friend***.

ELISION Elision consists in replacing the last letter of certain words (*le, la, je, me, te, se, de, que*) with an apostrophe (') before a word starting with a **vowel** or a **silent h** (eg *l'eau, l'homme, j'aime*).

ENDING The ending of a verb is determined by the **person** (1st/2nd/3rd) and **number** (singular/plural) of its subject. In French, most tenses have six different endings.
See PERSON and NUMBER.

EXCLAMATION Words or sentences used to express surprise, wonder (eg *what!, how!, how lucky!, what a nice day!*).

FEMININE See GENDER.

GENDER The gender of a noun indicates whether the noun is **masculine** or **feminine** (all French nouns are either masculine or feminine).

IDIOMATIC Idiomatic expressions (or idioms), are expressions which cannot normally be translated word for word. For example, *it's raining cats and dogs* is translated by *il pleut des cordes*.

IMPERATIVE A mood used for giving orders (eg *eat!, don't go!*).

INDEFINITE Indefinite pronouns and adjectives are words that do not refer to a definite person or object (eg *each, someone, every*).

INDEFINITE ARTICLE The indefinite article is *a* in English and *un, une* and *des* in French.

INDICATIVE The normal form of a verb as in *I like, he came, we are trying*. It is opposed to the subjunctive, conditional and imperative.

INDIRECT OBJECT A pronoun or noun which follows a verb indirectly, with a linking preposition (usually **to**), eg *I spoke to* ***my friend/him***.

INFINITIVE The infinitive is the basic form of the verb as found in dictionaries. Thus *to eat, to finish, to take* are infinitives. In French, the infinitive is recognized by its ending: *mang**er**, fin**ir**, prend**re***.

INTERROGATIVE Interrogative words are used to ask a question. This may be a direct question (***when*** *will you arrive?*) or an indirect question (*I don't know* ***when*** *he'll arrive*).
See QUESTION.

MASCULINE See GENDER.

MOOD The name given to the four main areas within which a verb is conjugated.
See INDICATIVE, SUBJUNCTIVE, CONDITIONAL, IMPERATIVE.

NOUN A naming word, which can refer to living creatures, things, places or abstract ideas, eg *postman, cat, shop, passport, life*.

NUMBER The number of a noun indicates whether the noun is **singular** or **plural**. A singular noun refers to one single thing or person (eg *boy, train*) and a plural noun to several (eg *boys, trains*).

ORDINAL Ordinal numbers are *first, second, third, fourth* and all other numbers which end in **-th**. In French, all ordinal numbers, except for *premier* (first) and *second* (second), end in **-ième**.

PARTITIVE ARTICLE The partitive articles are *some* and *any* in English and *du, de la* and *des* (as in *du pain, de la confiture, des bananes*) in French.

PASSIVE A verb is used in the passive when the subject of the verb does not perform the action but is subjected to it. The passive is formed with the verb **to be** and the past participle of the verb, eg *he was rewarded*.

PAST PARTICIPLE The past participle of a verb is the form which is used after **to have** in English, eg *I have* ***eaten****, I have* ***said****, you have* ***tried***.

PERSON In any tense, there are three persons in the singular (1st: *I ...*; 2nd: *you ...*; 3rd: *he/she ...*), and three in the plural (1st: *we ...*; 2nd: *you ...*; 3rd: *they ...*).
See also ENDING.

PERSONAL PRONOUN Personal pronouns stand for a noun. They usually accompany a verb and can be either the subject (*I, you, he/she/it, we, they*) or the object of the verb (*me, you, him/her/it, us, them*).

PLURAL See NUMBER.

POSSESSIVE Possessive adjectives and pronouns are used to indicate possession or ownership. They are words like *my/mine, your/yours, our/ours*.

PREPOSITION Prepositions are words such as *with, in, to, at, of*. They are followed by a noun or a pronoun.

PRESENT PARTICIPLE The present participle is the verb form which ends in **-ing** in English (**-ant** in French).

PRONOUN A word which stands for a noun. The main categories of pronouns are:

* **Relative pronouns** (eg *who, which, that*)
* **Interrogative pronouns** (eg *who?, what?, which?*)
* **Demonstrative pronouns** (eg *this, that, these*)
* **Possessive pronouns** (eg *mine, yours, his*)
* **Personal pronouns** (eg *you, him, us*)
* **Reflexive pronouns** (eg *myself, himself*)
* **Indefinite pronouns** (eg *something, all*)

QUESTION There are two question forms: **direct** questions stand on their own and require a question mark at the end (eg *when will he come?*); **indirect** questions are introduced by a clause and require no question mark (eg *I wonder when he will come*).

REFLEXIVE Reflexive verbs 'reflect' the action back onto the subject (eg *I dressed myself*). They are always found with a reflexive pronoun and are much more common in French than in English.

SENTENCE A sentence is a group of words made up of one or more clauses (see CLAUSE). The end of a sentence is indicated by a punctuation mark (usually a full stop, a question mark or an exclamation mark).

SILENT H The name 'silent **h**' is actually misleading since an **h** is never pronounced in French. The point is that, when a silent **h** occurs, any preceding vowel is not pronounced either. For example, the **h** in *j'habite* is silent (note the *j'*). The **h** in *je hurle* is not silent (note the *je*).

SIMPLE TENSE Simple tenses are tenses in which the verb consists of one word only, eg *j'habite, Maurice partira.*

SINGULAR See NUMBER

SUBJECT The subject of a verb is the noun or pronoun which performs the action. In the sentences *the train left early* and *she bought a record, the train* and *she* are the subjects.

SUBJUNCTIVE The subjunctive is a verb form which is rarely used in English (eg *if I were you, God save the Queen*), but common in French.

SUPERLATIVE The form of an adjective or an adverb which, in English, is marked by *the most ..., the ...est* or *the least ....*

TENSE Verbs are used in tenses, which tell us when an action takes place, eg in the present, the imperfect, the future.

VERB A 'doing' word, which usually describes an action (eg *to sing, to work, to watch*). Some verbs describe a state (eg *to be, to have, to hope*).

2 Articles

A THE DEFINITE ARTICLE

1 Forms

In English, there is only one form of the definite article: **the.** In French, there are three forms, depending on the gender and number of the noun following the article:

- with a masculine singular noun: **le**
- with a feminine singular noun: **la**
- with a plural noun (masc or fem): **les**

Masc Sing	*Fem Sing*	*Plural*
le chauffeur the driver	**la secrétaire** the secretary	**les étudiants** the students
le salon the lounge	**la cuisine** the kitchen	**les chambres** the bedrooms

Note: **le** and **la** both change to **l'** before a vowel or a silent **h**:

	Masculine	*Feminine*
before vowel	**l'avion** the plane	**l'odeur** the smell
before silent h	**l'homme** the man	**l'hôtesse** the hostess

Pronunciation: the **s** of **les** is pronounced **z** when the noun following it begins with a vowel or a silent **h**.

2 Forms with the prepositions à and de

When the definite article is used with **à** or **de**, the following spelling changes take place:

a) *with **à** (to, at)*

à + le → au
à + les → aux

à + la and **à + l'** do not change

au restaurant at/to the restaurant	**aux enfants** to the children
à la plage at/to the beach	**à l'aéroport** at/to the airport

Pronunciation: the **x** of **aux** is pronounced **z** when the noun following it begins with a vowel or a silent **h**.

b) *with **de** (of, from)*

de + le → du
de + les → des

de + la and **de + l'** do not change

du directeur of/from the manager	**des chômeurs** of/from the unemployed
de la région of/from the area	**de l'usine** of/from the factory

Pronunciation: the **s** of **des** is pronounced **z** when the noun following it begins with a vowel or a silent **h**.

3 Use

As in English, the definite article is used when referring to a particular person or thing, or particular persons or things:

les amis dont je t'ai parlé the friends I told you about	**le café est prêt** the coffee is ready

However, the definite article is used far more frequently in French than in English. It is used in particular in the following cases where English uses no article:

a) *when the noun is used in a general sense*

i) to refer to all things of a kind:

vous acceptez les chèques ?
do you accept cheques?

le sucre est mauvais pour les dents
sugar is bad for the teeth

ii) to refer to abstract things:

le travail et les loisirs	**la musique classique**
work and leisure	classical music

iii) when stating likes and dislikes:

j'aime la viande, mais je préfère le poisson
I like meat, but I prefer fish

je déteste les tomates
I hate tomatoes

b) *with geographical names*

i) continents, countries and areas:

le Canada	**la France**	**l'Europe**
Canada	France	Europe
la Bretagne	**l'Afrique**	**les Etats-Unis**
Brittany	Africa	the United States

But: the article **la** is omitted with the prepositions **en** and **de** when used with feminine country names:

j'habite en France	**il vient d'Italie**
I live in France	he comes from Italy

With masculine country names, the corresponding prepositions **à** and **de** follow the normal rules:

j'habite au Portugal/aux Etats-Unis
I live in Portugal/in the United States

je viens du Japon/des Etats-Unis
I come from Japan/from the United States

A very few country names do not require an article (eg **Panama**).

Articles are not used with country names on maps.

ii) mountains, lakes and rivers:

le mont Everest	**le lac de Genève**
Mount Everest	Lake Geneva

c) *with names of seasons*

l'automne	autumn
l'hiver	winter
le printemps	spring
l'été	summer

But: **en automne/été/hiver**
in autumn/summer/winter

au printemps	**un jour d'été**
in spring	a summer's day

d) *with names of languages*

j'apprends le français
I'm learning French

But: **ce film est en anglais**
this film is in English

e) *with parts of the body*

j'ai les cheveux roux	**ouvrez la bouche**
I've got red hair	open your mouth
les mains en l'air !	**l'homme à la barbe noire**
hands up!	the man with the black beard

f) *with names following an adjective*

le petit Pierre	**la pauvre Isabelle**
little Peter	poor Isabelle

g) *with titles*

le docteur Coste	**le commandant Cousteau**
Doctor Coste	Captain Cousteau

h) *with days of the week to express regular occurrences*

que fais-tu le samedi ?
what do you do on Saturdays?

i) *with names of subjects or leisure activities*

les maths	**l'histoire et la géographie**
maths	history and geography

la natation, la lecture, le football
swimming, reading, football

j) *in expressions of price, quantity etc*

c'est combien le kilo/la douzaine/la bouteille ?
how much is it for a kilo/dozen/bottle?

B THE INDEFINITE ARTICLE

1 Forms

In French, there are three forms of the indefinite article, depending on the number and gender of the noun it accompanies:

- with a masculine singular noun:	**un**	a
- with a feminine singular noun:	**une**	a
- with a plural noun (masc or fem):	**des**	some

Note: **des** is often not translated in English:

il y a des nuages dans le ciel
there are clouds in the sky

2 Use

a) On the whole, the French indefinite article is used in the same way as its English equivalent:

un homme	**une femme**	**des hommes/femmes**
a man	a woman	(some) men/women
un livre	**une tasse**	**des livres/tasses**
a book	a cup	(some) books/cups

b) However, the English indefinite article is not always translated in French:

i) when stating someone's profession or occupation:

mon père est architecte
my father is an architect

elle est médecin
she is a doctor

But: the article is used after **c'est**, **c'était** etc:

c'est un acteur célèbre
he's a famous actor

ce sont des fraises
these are strawberries

ii) with nouns in apposition:

Madame Leclerc, employée de bureau
Mrs Leclerc, an office worker

iii) after **quel** in exclamations:

quel dommage !	**quelle surprise !**
what a pity!	what a surprise!

c) In negative sentences, **de** (or **d'**) is used instead of **un**, **une**, **des**:

je n'ai pas d'amis	**je n'ai plus de voiture**
I don't have any friends	I don't have a car any more

d) In French (but not in English), the indefinite article is used with abstract nouns followed by an adjective:

avec une patience remarquable
with remarkable patience

elle a fait des progrès étonnants
she's made amazing progress

But: the article is not used when there is no adjective:

avec plaisir	**sans hésitation**
with pleasure	without hesitation

C THE PARTITIVE ARTICLE

1 Forms

There are three forms of the French partitive article, which corresponds to 'some'/ 'any' in English:

- with a masculine singular noun:	**du**
- with a feminine singular noun:	**de la**
- with plural nouns (masc or fem):	**des**

du vin	**de la bière**	**des fruits**
some wine	some beer	some fruit

Note: **de l'** is used in front of masculine or feminine singular nouns beginning with a vowel or a silent **h**:

de l'argent	**de l'eau**
some money	some water

2 Use

a) On the whole, the French partitive article is used as in English. However, English tends to omit the partitive article where French does not:

achète du pain buy (some) bread	**vous avez du beurre ?** do you have (any) butter?
je voudrais de la viande I'd like some meat	**tu veux de la soupe ?** do you want (any) soup?

tu dois manger des légumes
you must eat (some) vegetables

as-tu acheté des poires ?
did you buy (any) pears?

b) The partitive article is replaced by **de** (or **d'**) in the following cases:

i) in negative expressions:

il n'y a plus de café there isn't any coffee left	**je n'ai pas de verres** I don't have any glasses

But: **ce n'est pas du cuir, c'est du plastique**
it's not leather, it's plastic

je n'ai que de l'argent français
I have only French money

ii) after expressions of quantity (see also p B57):

il boit trop de café he drinks too much coffee	**il gagne assez d'argent** he earns enough money

iii) after **avoir besoin de**:

j'ai besoin d'argent I need (some) money	**tu as besoin de timbres ?** do you need (any) stamps?

iv) where an adjective is followed by a plural noun:

de grands enfants (some) tall children	**de petites villes** (some) small towns

But: if the adjective comes after the noun, **des** does not change:

des résultats encourageants
encouraging results

3 Partitive or definite article?

When no article is used in English, be careful to use the right article in French: **le/la/les** or **du/de la/des.**

If **some/any** can be inserted before the English noun, the French partitive article should be used. But if the noun is used in a general sense and inserting **some/any** in front of the English noun does not make sense, the definite article must be used:

did you buy fish? (*ie any fish*)
tu as acheté *du* poisson ?

yes, I did; I like fish (*ie fish in general*)
oui ; j'aime *le* poisson

3 Nouns

Nouns are naming words, which refer to persons, animals, things, places or abstract ideas.

A GENDER

All French nouns are either masculine or feminine; there is no neuter as in English. Though no absolute rule can be stated, the gender can often be determined either by the meaning or the ending of the noun.

1 Masculine

a) *by meaning*

i) names of people and animals:

un homme a man	**le boucher** the butcher	**le tigre** the tiger

ii) names of common trees and shrubs:

	le chêne the oak	**le sapin** the fir tree	**le laurier** the laurel
But:	**une aubépine** a hawthorn		**la bruyère** the heather

iii) days, months, seasons:

lundi Monday	**mars** March	**le printemps** spring

iv) languages:

le français French	**le polonais** Polish	**le russe** Russian

v) rivers and countries not ending in a silent **e**:

	le Nil the Nile	**le Portugal** Portugal	**le Danemark** Denmark
But:	**le Danube** the Danube	**le Rhône** the Rhone	**le Mexique** Mexico

b) *by ending*

-acle	**le spectacle** (show) ***But:* une débâcle** (shambles)
-age	**le fromage** (cheese) ***But:* la cage** (cage), **une image** (picture), **la nage** (swimming), **la page** (page), **la plage** (beach), **la rage** (rage, rabies)
-é	**le marché** (market) *But:* nouns ending in **-té** and **-tié** (see p B6)
-eau	**le chapeau** (hat) ***But:* l'eau** (water), **la peau** (skin)
-ège	**le piège** (trap), **le collège** (secondary school)
-ème	**le thème** (theme, topic) ***But:* la crème** (the cream)
-isme, -asme	**le communisme** (communism), **le tourisme** (tourism), **l'enthousiasme** (enthusiasm)
-o	**le numéro** (the number) ***But:* la dynamo** (dynamo) and most abbreviated expressions: **une auto** (car), **la météo** (weather forecast), **la photo** (photograph), **la radio** (radio), **la sténo** (shorthand), **la stéréo** (stereo)

Nouns ending in a *consonant* are usually *masculine*.

Notable exceptions are:

i) most nouns ending in **-tion**, **-sion**, **-ation**, **-aison**, **-ison**

ii) most abstract nouns ending in **-eur** (see p B6)

iii) the following nouns ending in a consonant:

la clef (key)	**la nef** (nave)
la soif (thirst)	**la faim** (hunger)
la fin (end)	**la façon** (manner)
la leçon (lesson)	**la boisson** (drink)
la moisson (harvest)	**la rançon** (ransom)
la mer (sea)	**la cuiller** (spoon)
la chair (flesh)	**la basse-cour** (farmyard)
la cour (yard)	**la tour** (tower)
la brebis (ewe)	**une fois** (once)
la vis (screw)	**la souris** (mouse)
la part (share)	**la plupart** (majority, most)
la dent (tooth)	**la dot** (dowry)
la forêt (forest)	**la jument** (mare)
la mort (death)	**la nuit** (night)
la croix (cross)	**la noix** (nut)
la paix (peace)	**la perdrix** (partridge)
la toux (cough)	**la voix** (voice)

2 Feminine

a) *by meaning*

i) names of females (people and animals):

la mère	**la bonne**	**la génisse**
the mother	the maid	the heifer

ii) names of rivers and countries ending in a silent **e**:

la Seine	**la Russie**	**la Belgique**
the Seine	Russia	Belgium

iii) saints days and festivals:

la Toussaint	**la Pentecôte**
All Saints' Day	Whitsun

But: **Noël** (Christmas) is masculine except with the definite article: **à la Noël** (at Christmas)

b) *by ending*

-ace	**la place** (square, seat) ***But:*** **un espace** (space)
-ade	**la salade** (salad) ***But:*** **le grade** (degree, rank), **le stade** (stadium)
-ance, -anse	**la puissance** (power), **la danse** (dancing)
-ée	**la soirée** (evening) ***But:*** **le musée** (museum), **le lycée** (secondary school)
-ence, -ense	**une évidence** (evidence), **la défense** (defence) ***But:*** **le silence** (silence)
-ère	**la lumière** (light) ***But:*** **le mystère** (mystery), **le caractère** (character)
-eur	**la peur** (fear) ***But:*** **le bonheur** (happiness), **le chœur** (choir), **le cœur** (heart), **un honneur** (honour), **le labeur** (toil), **le malheur** (misfortune)
-ie	**la pluie** (rain) ***But:*** **le génie** (genius), **un incendie** (fire), **le parapluie** (umbrella)
-ière	**la bière** (beer) ***But:*** **le cimetière** (cemetery)
-oire	**la gloire** (glory) ***But:*** **le laboratoire** (laboratory), **le pourboire** (tip)
-tion, -sion, -ation, -aison, -ison	**la fiction** (fiction), **la nation** (nation), **la raison** (reason), **la prison** (prison)
-té	**la bonté** (goodness) ***But:*** **le côté** (side), **le comté** (county), **le traité** (treaty), **le pâté** (pâté)
-tié	**la moitié** (half), **la pitié** (pity)

Most nouns ending in a silent **e** following two consonants:

la botte (boot), **la couronne** (crown), **la terre** (earth), **la masse** (mass), **la lutte** (struggle)

But: **le verre** (glass), **le parterre** (flower-bed), **le tonnerre** (thunder), **un intervalle** (interval), **le carosse** (carriage)

3 Difficulties

a) some nouns may have either gender depending on the sex of the person to whom they refer:

un artiste	**une artiste**
a (male) artist	a (female) artist
le Russe	**la Russe**
the Russian (man)	the Russian (woman)

similarly:

un aide/une aide	an assistant
un camarade/une camarade	a friend
un domestique/une domestique	a servant
un enfant/une enfant	a child
un malade/une malade	a patient
un propriétaire/une propriétaire	an owner

b) others have only one gender for both sexes:

un ange	**un amateur**	**un auteur**
an angel	an amateur	an author(ess)
une connaissance	**la dupe**	**un écrivain**
an acquaintance	the dupe	a writer
Sa Majesté	**le médecin**	**le peintre**
His/Her Majesty	the doctor	the painter
une personne	**le poète**	**le professeur**
a person	the poet(ess)	the teacher
la recrue	**le sculpteur**	**la sentinelle**
the recruit	the sculptor (sculptress)	the sentry
le témoin	**la victime**	**la vedette**
the witness	the victim	the (film) star

c) the following nouns change meaning according to gender:

	Masculine	*Feminine*
aide	male assistant	assistance, female assistant
crêpe	mourning band	pancake
critique	critic	criticism
faux	forgery	scythe
livre	book	pound
manche	handle	sleeve
manœuvre	labourer	manoeuvre
mémoire	memorandum	memory
mode	method, way	fashion
mort	dead man	death
moule	mould	mussel
page	pageboy	page
pendule	pendulum	clock
physique	physique	physics
poêle	stove	frying pan
poste	post (*job*), set	post office
somme	nap	sum
tour	trick, tour	tower
trompette	trumpeter	trumpet
vapeur	steamer	steam
vase	vase	silt
voile	veil	sail

d) **gens** is regarded as feminine when it follows an adjective, and masculine when it precedes it:

de bonnes gens	**des gens ennuyeux**
good people	bores

e) city names

Some city names are traditionally feminine:

La Rochelle, La Haye (The Hague)

Alger la Blanche
Algiers, the white city

Others are masculine in everyday usage:

le Paris des années 30
Paris in the 30s

le Londres de mon souvenir
the London I remember

le vieux Nice
old Nice

Berlin fut totalement détruit
Berlin was completely destroyed

In literary French, however, city names are feminine:

Caen fut prise après de terribles bombardements
Caen was taken after a terrible bombardment

B THE FORMATION OF FEMININES

The feminine of nouns may be formed in the following ways:

1 Add an e to the masculine:

un ami a (male) friend — **une amie** a (female) friend

un Hollandais a Dutchman — **une Hollandaise** a Dutch woman

a) nouns which end in **-e** in the masculine do not change:

un élève a (male) pupil — **une élève** a (female) pupil

b) the addition of **e** often entails an alteration of the masculine form:

i) nouns ending in **-t** and **-n** double the final consonant:

le chien — **la chienne** (dog/bitch)
le chat — **la chatte** (cat)

ii) nouns ending in **-er** add a grave accent to the **e** before the silent **e**:

un ouvrier — **une ouvrière** (workman/female worker)

iii) nouns ending in **-eur** change into **-euse**:

le vendeur — **la vendeuse** (male/female shop assistant)

a few nouns ending in **-eur** change into **-eresse**:

le pécheur — **la pécheresse** (sinner)

iv) nouns ending in **-teur** change into **-teuse** or **-trice** according to the following guidelines:

if the stem of the word is also that of a present participle the feminine form is in **-euse**:

le chanteur — **la chanteuse** (male/female singer)

but if the stem is not that of a present participle, the feminine form is in **-trice**:

le lecteur — **la lectrice** (male/female reader)

v) nouns ending in **-f** change to **-ve**:

le veuf — **la veuve** (widower/widow)

vi) nouns ending in **-x** change to **-se**:

un époux — **une épouse** (husband/wife)

vii) nouns ending in **-eau** change to **-elle** :

le jumeau — **la jumelle** (male/female twin)

2 Use a different word (as in English):

le beau-fils — **la belle-fille** (son/daughter-in-law)
le beau-père — **la belle-mère** (father/mother-in-law)
le bélier — **la brebis** (ram/ewe)
le bœuf — **la vache** (ox/cow)
le canard — **la cane** (drake/duck)
le cheval — **la jument** (horse/mare)
le cerf — **la biche** (stag/hind)
le coq — **la poule** (cock/hen)
le fils — **la fille** (son/daughter)
le frère — **la sœur** (brother/sister)
un homme — **une femme** (man/woman)
un jars — **une oie** (gander/goose)
le mâle — **la femelle** (male/female)
le neveu — **la nièce** (nephew/niece)
un oncle — **une tante** (uncle/aunt)
le parrain — **la marraine** (godfather/godmother)
le père — **la mère** (father/mother)
le porc — **la truie** (pig/sow)
le roi — **la reine** (king/queen)

3 Add the word 'femme' (or 'femelle' for animals):

une femme poète (poetess)
un perroquet femelle (female parrot)

4 Irregular feminines:

un abbé — **une abbesse** (abbot/abbess)
un âne — **une ânesse** (donkey)
le comte — **la comtesse** (count/countess)
le dieu — **la déesse** (god/goddess)
le duc — **la duchesse** (duke/duchess)
un Esquimau — **une Esquimaude** (Eskimo)
le fou — **la folle** (madman/mad woman)
un héros — **une héroïne** (hero/heroine)
un hôte — **une hôtesse** (host/hostess)
le maître — **la maîtresse** (master/mistress)
le prêtre — **la prêtresse** (priest/priestess)
le prince — **la princesse** (prince/princess)
le tigre — **la tigresse** (tiger/tigress)
le Turc — **la Turque** (Turk)
le vieux — **la vieille** (old man/old woman)

C THE FORMATION OF PLURALS

1 Most nouns form their plural by adding s to the singular:

le vin	**les vins**	wine
un étudiant	**des étudiants**	student

2 Nouns ending in -s, -x or -z remain unchanged:

le bras	**les bras**	arm
la voix	**les voix**	voice
le nez	**les nez**	nose

3 Nouns ending in -au , -eau and -eu add x to the singular:

	le tuyau	**les tuyaux**	drain-pipe
	le bateau	**les bateaux**	boat
	le jeu	**les jeux**	game
But:	**le landau**	**les landaus**	pram
	le bleu	**les bleus**	bruise
	le pneu	**les pneus**	tyre

4 Nouns ending in -al change to -aux :

	le journal	**les journaux**	newspaper
But:	**le bal**	**les bals**	dance
	le carnaval	**les carnavals**	carnival
	le festival	**les festivals**	festival

5 Nouns ending in -ail change to -aux:

le bail	**les baux**	lease
le travail	**les travaux**	work
le vitrail	**les vitraux**	stained-glass window

Common exceptions in which the plural is formed in **-ail**:

le chandail	**les chandails**	sweater
le détail	**les détails**	detail
l'épouvantail	**les épouvantails**	scarecrow
l'éventail	**les éventails**	fan
le rail	**les rails**	rail

6 Nouns ending in -ou:

a) seven nouns ending in **-ou** add **x** in the plural:

le bijou	**les bijoux**	jewel
le caillou	**les cailloux**	pebble
le chou	**les choux**	cabbage
le genou	**les genoux**	knee
le hibou	**les hiboux**	owl
le joujou	**les joujoux**	toy
le pou	**les poux**	louse

b) other nouns ending in **-ou** add **s**:

le clou	**les clous**	nail

7 Plural of compound nouns

Each noun ought to be checked individually in a dictionary:

eg	**le chou-fleur**	**les choux-fleurs**	cauliflower
	le beau-père	**les beaux-pères**	father-in-law
But:	**un essuie-glace**	**des essuie-glaces**	windscreen wiper
	le tire-bouchon	**les tire-bouchons**	corkscrew

8 Irregular plurals

un œil	**des yeux**	eye
le ciel	**les cieux**	sky
Monsieur	**Messieurs**	Mr
Madame	**Mesdames**	Mrs
Mademoiselle	**Mesdemoiselles**	Miss

9 Collective nouns

a) *singular in French but plural in English:*

le bétail cattle
la famille family
la police police

la police *a* arrêté certains grévistes
the police *have* arrested some strikers

b) *plural in French but singular in English:*

les nouvelles sont bonnes
the news is good

10 Proper nouns

a) Ordinary family names are invariable:

j'ai rencontré les Leblanc
I met the Leblancs

b) Historical names add **-s**:

les Stuarts	**les Bourbons**	**les Tudors**
the Stuarts	the Bourbons	the Tudors

4 Adjectives

Adjectives are describing words which usually accompany a noun (or a pronoun) and tell us what someone or something is like:

une *grande* ville
a *large* city

un passe-temps *intéressant*
an *interesting* pastime

elle est *espagnole*
she is *Spanish*

c'était *ennuyeux*
it was *boring*

A AGREEMENT OF ADJECTIVES

In French, adjectives agree in number and gender with the noun or pronoun they refer to. This means that, unlike English adjectives, which don't change, French adjectives have four different forms which are determined by the noun they go with:

- **masculine singular** for masculine singular words (basic form, found in the dictionary)
- **feminine singular** for feminine singular words
- **masculine plural** for masculine plural words
- **feminine plural** for feminine plural words

un passeport *vert*
a green passport

une voiture *verte*
a green car

des gants *verts*
green gloves

des chaussettes *vertes*
green socks

Note: If two singular words share the same adjective, the adjective will be in the plural:

un foulard et un bonnet *rouges*
a red scarf and (a red) hat

If one of these words is feminine, one masculine, the adjective will be masculine plural:

une robe et un manteau *noirs*
a black dress and (a black) coat

B FEMININE FORMS OF ADJECTIVES

1 General rule

Add the letter **e** to the masculine singular form:

Masculine	*Feminine*
grand	**grande**
amusant	**amusante**
anglais	**anglaise**
bronzé	**bronzée**

un livre amusant
an amusing book

une histoire amusante
an amusing story

il est bronzé
he is suntanned

elle est bronzée
she is suntanned

2 Adjectives already ending in -e

These do not change:

Masculine	*Feminine*
rouge	**rouge**
jaune	**jaune**
pauvre	**pauvre**
brave	**brave**
jeune	**jeune**
malade	**malade**

mon père est malade
my father is ill

ma mère est malade
my mother is ill

3 Others

The spelling of some adjectives changes when the **e** is added:

a) The following masculine endings generally double the final consonant before adding **e**:

Masculine ending	*Feminine ending*
-el	**-elle**
-eil	**-eille**
-en	**-enne**
-on	**-onne**
-as	**-asse**
-et	**-ette**

Masculine		*Feminine*
réel	(real)	**réelle**
cruel	(cruel)	**cruelle**
pareil	(similar)	**pareille**
ancien	(old)	**ancienne**
italien	(Italian)	**italienne**
bon	(good)	**bonne**
gras	(greasy)	**grasse**
bas	(low)	**basse**
muet	(dumb)	**muette**
net	(clear)	**nette**

un problème actuel — a topical problem
la vie actuelle — present-day life

un bon conseil — good advice
c'est une bonne recette — it's a good recipe

But: the feminine ending of some common adjectives in **-et** is **-ète** instead of **-ette**:

Masculine		*Feminine*
complet	(complete)	**complète**
incomplet	(incomplete)	**incomplète**
concret	(concrete)	**concrète**
discret	(discreet)	**discrète**
inquiet	(worried)	**inquiète**
secret	(secret)	**secrète**

b)

Masculine in **-er**		*Feminine in* **-ère**
cher	(dear)	**chère**
fier	(proud)	**fière**
dernier	(last)	**dernière**

c)

Masculine in **-x**		*Feminine in* **-se**
heureux	(happy)	**heureuse**
malheureux	(unhappy)	**malheureuse**
sérieux	(serious)	**sérieuse**
jaloux	(jealous)	**jalouse**

But:

doux	(soft)	**douce**
faux	(false)	**fausse**
roux	(red-haired)	**rousse**
vieux	(old)	**vieille**

d)

Masculine in **-eur**		*Feminine in* **-euse**
menteur	(lying)	**menteuse**
trompeur	(deceitful)	**trompeuse**

But: This rule applies only when the stem of the adjective is also the stem of a present participle (eg **mentant**, **trompant**). The following five adjectives simply add an **e** to the feminine, **-eur** becoming **-eure**:

Masculine		*Feminine*
extérieur	(external)	**extérieure**
intérieur	(internal)	**intérieure**
inférieur	(inferior)	**inférieure**
supérieur	(superior)	**supérieure**
meilleur	(better)	**meilleure**

The feminine ending of the remaining adjectives in **-teur** is **-trice**:

Masculine		*Feminine*
protecteur	(protective)	**protectrice**
destructeur	(destructive)	**destructrice**

e)

Masculine in **-f**		*Feminine in* **-ve**
neuf	(new)	**neuve**
vif	(lively)	**vive**
naïf	(naive)	**naïve**
actif	(active)	**active**
passif	(passive)	**passive**
positif	(positive)	**positive**
bref	(brief)	**brève** (note the **è**!)

f)

Masculine in **-c**		*Feminine in* **-che** *or* **-que**
blanc	(white)	**blanche**
franc	(frank)	**franche**
sec	(dry)	**sèche** (note the **è**!)
public	(public)	**publique**
turc	(Turkish)	**turque**
grec	(Greek)	**grecque** (note the **c**!)

g) The following five common adjectives have an irregular feminine form and two forms for the masculine singular: the second masculine form, based on the feminine form, is used before words starting with a vowel or a silent **h**:

Masculine	*Feminine*	*Masculine 2*
beau (beautiful)	**belle**	**bel**
nouveau (new)	**nouvelle**	**nouvel**
vieux (old)	**vieille**	**vieil**
fou (mad)	**folle**	**fol**
mou (soft)	**molle**	**mol**

un beau lac a beautiful lake	**une belle vue** a beautiful view	**un bel enfant** a beautiful child
un nouveau disque a new record	**la nouvelle année** the new year	**un nouvel ami** a new friend
un vieux tableau an old painting	**la vieille ville** the old town	**un vieil homme** an old man

h) Other irregular feminines:

Masculine		*Feminine*
favori	(favourite)	**favorite**
gentil	(nice)	**gentille**
nul	(no)	**nulle**
frais	(fresh)	**fraîche**
malin	(shrewd)	**maligne**
sot	(foolish)	**sotte**
long	(long)	**longue**
aigu	(sharp)	**aiguë**
ambigu	(ambiguous)	**ambiguë**
chic	(elegant)	**chic**
châtain	(chestnut)	**châtain**

C PLURALS OF ADJECTIVES

1 General rule

The masculine and feminine plural of adjectives is formed by adding an **s** to the singular form:

un vélo neuf — a new bike
des vélos neufs — new bikes

une belle fleur — a beautiful flower
de belles fleurs — beautiful flowers

2 Adjectives ending in -s or -x

If the masculine singular ends in **-s** or **-x**, there is obviously no need to add the **s**:

il est heureux — he's happy
ils sont heureux — they are happy

un touriste anglais an English tourist	**des touristes anglais** English tourists

3 Others

A few masculine plurals are irregular (the feminine plurals are all regular):

a)	*Singular* *in* **-al**		*Plural* *in* **-aux**
	normal	(normal)	**normaux**
	brutal	(brutal)	**brutaux**
	loyal	(loyal)	**loyaux**
But:	**fatal**	(fatal)	**fatals**
	final	(final)	**finals**
	natal	(native)	**natals**
	naval	(naval)	**navals**
b)	*Singular* *in* **-eau**		*Plural* *in* **-eaux**
	beau	(beautiful)	**beaux**
	nouveau	(new)	**nouveaux**

D POSITION OF ADJECTIVES

1 Unlike English adjectives, French adjectives usually follow the noun:

un métier intéressant an interesting job	**des parents modernes** modern parents

Adjectives of colour and nationality always follow the noun:

des chaussures rouges red shoes	**le drapeau britannique** the British flag

2 However, the following common adjectives generally come before the noun:

beau	beautiful
bon	good
court	short
gentil	nice
grand	big, tall
gros	fat
haut	high
jeune	young
joli	pretty
long	long
mauvais	bad
méchant	nasty, naughty (*child*)
meilleur	better
moindre	lesser, least
petit	small
pire	worse
vieux	old
vilain	nasty, ugly

3 Some adjectives have a different meaning according to their position:

	Before noun	*After noun*
ancien	former	ancient
brave	good	brave
certain	some	sure
cher	dear	expensive
dernier	last	last (= *latest*)
grand	great (*people only*)	big, tall
même	same	very
pauvre	poor (*pitiable*)	poor (*not rich*)
propre	own	clean
seul	single, only	alone, lonely
simple	mere	simple
vrai	real	true

mon ancien métier my former job	**un tableau ancien** an old painting
un brave type a nice fellow	**un homme brave** a brave man
un certain charme a certain charm	**un fait certain** a definite fact
chère Brigitte dear Brigitte	**un cadeau cher** an expensive present
la dernière séance the last performance	**le mois dernier** last month
une grande vedette a great star	**un homme assez grand** a fairly tall man
le même endroit the same place	**la vérité même** the truth itself
mon pauvre ami ! my poor friend!	**des gens pauvres** poor people
mon propre frère my own brother	**une chambre propre** a clean room
mon seul espoir my only hope	**un homme seul** a lonely man
un simple employé an ordinary employee	**des goûts simples** simple tastes
un vrai casse-pieds a real bore	**une histoire vraie** a true story

4 If a noun is accompanied by several adjectives, the same rules apply to each of them:

le bon vieux temps
the good old days

un joli foulard rouge
a pretty red scarf

E COMPARATIVE AND SUPERLATIVE OF ADJECTIVES

Persons or things can be compared by using:

i) the comparative form of the adjective:

more ... than, ...er than, less ... than, as ... as

ii) the superlative form of the adjective:

the most ... , the ...est, the least ...

1 The comparative

The comparative is formed as follows:

plus ... (que) more ... (than)	**plus long** longer	**plus cher** more expensive
moins ... (que) less ... (than)	**moins long** less long	**moins récent** less recent
aussi ... (que) as ... (as)	**aussi bon** as good	**aussi important** as important

une plus grande maison a larger house	**un village plus ancien** an older village

le football est-il plus populaire que le rugby ?
is football more popular than rugby?

ces gants sont moins chauds que les autres
these gloves are less warm than the other ones

elle est beaucoup/bien moins patiente que lui
she's far less patient than he is

le problème de la pollution est tout aussi grave
the pollution problem is just as serious

2 The superlative

a) *Formation*

le/la/les plus ...	the most ...., the ...est
le/la/les moins ...	the least ...

le plus grand pays the largest country	**la plus grande ville** the largest city
les plus grands acteurs the greatest actors	**les plus grandes voitures** the largest cars

b) *Word order*

i) The normal rules governing word order of adjectives apply. When a superlative adjective comes after the noun, the article is used twice, before the noun and before the adjective:

le plat le plus délicieux the most delicious dish	**l'histoire la plus passionnante** the most exciting story

ii) When a possessive adjective is used, there are two possible constructions, depending on the position of the adjective:

ma plus forte matière
my best subject

or:

son besoin le plus urgent est de trouver un emploi
his most urgent need is to find a job

c) *'in' is normally translated by* **de**:

la plus jolie maison du quartier/de la ville
the prettiest house in the area/town

le restaurant le plus cher de France
the most expensive restaurant in France

Note: Verbs following the superlative usually take the subjunctive (see p B31).

3 Irregular comparatives and superlatives

Adjective	*Comparative*	*Superlative*
bon good	**meilleur** better	**le meilleur** best
mauvais bad	**pire** **plus mauvais** worse	**le pire** **le plus mauvais** the worst
petit small	**moindre** **plus petit** smaller, lesser	**le moindre** **le plus petit** the smallest, the least

Note: - **plus mauvais** is used in the sense of worse in quality, taste etc

- **moindre** usually means 'less in importance', and **plus petit** means 'less in size':

le moindre de mes soucis
the least of my worries

elle est plus petite que moi
she is smaller than I (am)

F ADJECTIVES OF NATIONALITY

i) French, unlike English, does not use capital letters for adjectives of nationality (only nouns indicating nationality are written with a capital letter in French):

une voiture anglaise an English car	**une Anglaise** an English woman

ii) An English nationality adjective is sometimes best translated by a French genitive construction:

l'ambassade de France	the French embassy
l'équipe de France de rugby	the French rugby team
l'équipe de Nantes	the Nantes team
l'équipe de Glasgow	the Glasgow or Glaswegian team
le championnat de France	the French league
la Coupe de France de football	the French football cup
le Grand Prix du Brésil	the Brazilian Grand Prix
la terre de France	French soil
la couronne de France	the French crown, the crown of France
les côtes de France	the French coastline
une grammaire de l'anglais	an English grammar, a grammar of English

5 Adverbs

Adverbs are normally used with a verb to express:

		Adverbs of
how	(an action is done)	manner
when		time
where		place
with how much intensity		intensity
to what extent		quantity

A ADVERBS OF MANNER

These are usually formed by adding **-ment** to the adjective (like **-ly** in English):

1 If the adjective ends in a consonant, -ment is added to its feminine form:

Adjective (masc, fem)	*Adverb*
doux, douce (soft)	**doucement** (softly)
franc, franche (frank)	**franchement** (frankly)
final, finale (final)	**finalement** (finally)

2 If the adjective ends in a vowel, -ment is added to its masculine form:

	Adjective	*Adverb*
	absolu (absolute)	**absolument** (absolutely)
	désespéré (desperate)	**désespérément** (desperately)
	vrai (true)	**vraiment** (truly)
	simple (simple)	**simplement** (simply)
But:	**gai** (cheerful)	**gaiement** *or* **gaîment** (cheerfully)
	nouveau (new)	**nouvellement** (newly)
	fou (mad)	**follement** (madly)

3 Many adverbs have irregular forms:

a) Some change the **e** of the feminine form of the adjective to **é** before adding **-ment**:

Adjective	*Adverb*
commun (common)	**communément** (commonly)
précis (precise)	**précisément** (precisely)
profond (deep)	**profondément** (deeply)
énorme (enormous)	**énormément** (enormously)
aveugle (blind)	**aveuglément** (blindly)

b) Adjectives which end in **-ent** and **-ant** change to **-emment** and **-amment**

Note: both endings are pronounced **-amant**:

	Adjective	*Adverb*
	prudent (careful)	**prudemment** (carefully)
	évident (obvious)	**évidemment** (obviously)
	brillant (brilliant)	**brillamment** (brilliantly)
But:	**lent** (slow)	**lentement** (slowly)

4 Some adverbs are completely irregular, including some of the most commonly used ones:

Adjective	*Adverb*
bon (good)	**bien** (well)
bref (brief)	**brièvement** (briefly)
gentil (kind)	**gentiment** (kindly)
mauvais (bad)	**mal** (badly)
meilleur (better)	**mieux** (better)

5 Some adjectives are also used as adverbs in certain set expressions, eg:

parler bas/haut *or* **fort** to speak softly/loudly

coûter/payer cher	to cost/pay a lot
s'arrêter court	to stop short
couper court	to cut short
voir clair	to see clearly
marcher droit	to walk straight
travailler dur	to work hard
chanter faux/ juste	to sing off key/in tune
sentir mauvais/ bon	to smell bad/good
refuser net	to refuse point blank

6 After verbs of saying and looking in French, an adverbial phrase is often preferred to an adverb:

'tu m'écriras ?' dit-il ***d'une voix triste***
'will you write to me?' he said *sadly*

elle nous a regardés ***d'un air dédaigneux***
she looked at us *disdainfully*

7 English adverbs may be expressed in French by a preposition followed by a noun, eg:

sans soin	carelessly
avec fierté	proudly
avec amour	lovingly

B ADVERBS OF TIME

These are not usually formed from adjectives. Here are the commonest ones:

alors	then
après	afterwards
aujourd'hui	today
aussitôt	at once
bientôt	soon
d'abord	first
déjà	already
demain	tomorrow
encore	still, again
pas encore	not yet
enfin	at last, finally
hier	yesterday
parfois	sometimes
rarement	seldom
souvent	often
tard	late
tôt	early
toujours	always
tout de suite	immediately

c'est déjà Noël !
it's Christmas already!

tu as déjà essayé ?
have you tried before?

il mange encore !
he's still eating!

elle n'est pas encore arrivée
she hasn't arrived yet

C ADVERBS OF PLACE

Here are the commonest ones:

ailleurs	somewhere else
ici	here
là	there
loin	far away
dessus	on top, on it
au-dessus	over, above
dessous	underneath
au-dessous	below
dedans	inside
dehors	outside
devant	in front, ahead
derrière	behind
partout	everywhere

ne restez pas dehors !
don't stay outside!

mon nom est marqué dessus
my name is written on it

qu'est-ce qu'il y a dedans ?
what's inside?

passez devant
go in front

D ADVERBS OF INTENSITY AND QUANTITY

These may be used with a verb, an adjective or another adverb. Here are the commonest ones:

à peine	hardly
assez	enough, quite
autant	as much/many
beaucoup	a lot, much/many
combien	how much/many
comme	how
moins	less
plus	more
presque	nearly
peu	little
seulement	only
si	so
tant	so much/many
tellement	so much/many
très	very
trop	too, too much/many
un peu	a little

vous avez assez bu !
you've had enough to drink!

il ne fait pas assez chaud
it's not warm enough

nous avons beaucoup ri
we laughed a lot

comme c'est amusant !
how funny!

je vais un peu mieux
I'm feeling a little better

c'est si fatigant !
it's so tiring!

elle parle trop
she talks too much

il est très timide
he's very shy

Note: All of these adverbs, except **à peine**, **comme**, **presque**, **si**, **très**, **seulement**, may be followed by **de** and a noun to express a quantity (see p B57).

E POSITION OF ADVERBS

1 Adverbs usually follow verbs:

je vais rarement au théâtre
I seldom go to the theatre

comme vous conduisez prudemment !
you do drive carefully!

2 With compound tenses, shorter adverbs usually come between the auxiliary and the past participle:

j'ai enfin terminé
I have finished at last

nous y sommes souvent allés
we've often gone there

il me l'a déjà dit
he's already told me

elle avait beaucoup souffert
she had suffered a lot

3 But adverbs of place and many adverbs of time follow the past participle:

je l'ai rencontré hier
I met him yesterday

elle avait cherché partout
she had looked everywhere

mettez-le dehors
put it outside

tu t'es couché tard ?
did you go to bed late?

4 Adverbs usually come before adjectives or other adverbs:

très rarement
very seldom

trop vite
too quickly

elle est vraiment belle
she is really beautiful

F COMPARATIVE AND SUPERLATIVE OF ADVERBS

1 The comparative and superlative of adverbs are formed in the same way as those of adjectives:

Adverb	*Comparative*	*Superlative*
souvent often	**plus souvent (que)** more often (than)	**le plus souvent** (the) most often
	moins souvent (que) less often (than)	**le moins souvent** (the) least often
	aussi souvent (que) as often (as)	

Note: The superlative of the adverb always takes the masculine singular article **le**:

je le vois plus souvent qu'avant
I see him more often than I used to

il conduit moins prudemment que moi
he drives less carefully than I do

c'est lui qui conduit le moins prudemment
he's the one who drives the least carefully

je sais cuisiner aussi bien que toi !
I can cook as well as you!

Note:

a) **as ... as possible** is translated either by **aussi ... que possible** or by **le plus ... possible:**

as far as possible **aussi loin que possible**
le plus loin possible

b) after a negative, **aussi** is often replaced by **si**:

pas si vite !
not so fast!

c) In French, the idea of **not so**, **not as** is often expressed by **moins** (less):

parle moins fort !
don't talk so loud!

2 Irregular comparatives and superlatives

Adverb	*Comparative*	*Superlative*
beaucoup much, a lot	**plus** more	**le plus** (the) most
bien well	**mieux** better	**le mieux** (the) best
mal badly	**pis** *or* **plus mal** worse	**le pis** *or* **le plus mal** (the) worst
peu little	**moins** less	**le moins** (the) least

Note:

a) **mieux/le mieux** must not be confused with **meilleur/le meilleur**, which are adjectives, used in front of a noun.

b) **pis/le pis** are only found in certain set expressions:

tant pis
so much the worse, too bad

de mal en pis
from bad to worse

6 Pronouns and Corresponding Adjectives

A DEMONSTRATIVES

1 Demonstrative adjectives

a) ***CE***

ce is often used to point out a particular person or thing, or persons or things. It is followed by the noun it refers to and agrees in number and gender with that noun.

- with a masculine singular noun: **ce (cet)** this/that
- with a feminine singular noun: **cette** this/that
- with a plural noun (masc or fem): **ces** these/those

ce roman m'a beaucoup plu
I really liked this novel

il a neigé ce matin
it snowed this morning

cette chanson m'énerve
that song gets on my nerves

cette fois, c'est fini !
this time, it's over!

tu trouves que ces lunettes me vont bien ?
do you think these glasses suit me?

cet is used instead of **ce** in front of a word that begins with a vowel or a silent **h**:

cet après-midi
this afternoon

cet hôtel
that hotel

b) ***-CI** and **-LA***

French does not have separate words to distinguish between 'this' and 'that'. However, when a particular emphasis is being placed on a person or object, or when a contrast is being made between persons or objects, **-ci** and **-là** are added to the noun:

-ci translates the idea of this/these

-là translates the idea of that/those

je suis très occupé ces jours-ci
I'm very busy these days

que faisiez-vous ce soir-là ?
what were you doing that evening?

d'où vient ce fromage-là ? – ce fromage-ci, Monsieur ?
where does that cheese come from? – this cheese, sir?

2 Demonstrative pronouns

Demonstrative pronouns are used instead of a noun with **ce/cette/ces**. They are:

a) **celui, celle, ceux, celles**

b) **ce**

c) **ceci, cela, ça**

a) ***CELUI***

i) **celui** agrees in number and gender with the noun it refers to. It has four different forms:

	Masc	*Fem*
Sing	**celui**	**celle**
Plur	**ceux**	**celles**

ii) use of **celui**

celui, celle, ceux and **celles** cannot be used on their own. They are used:

★ with **-ci** or **-là**, for emphasis or for contrast:

celui-ci	**celle-ci**	this (one)
celui-là	**celle-là**	that (one)
ceux-ci	**celles-ci**	these (ones)
ceux-là	**celles-là**	those (ones)

j'aime bien ce maillot, mais celui-là est moins cher
I like this swimsuit, but that one is cheaper

je voudrais ces fleurs – lesquelles ? celles-ci ou celles-là ?
I'd like these flowers – which ones? these or those?

★ with **de** + noun, to express possession:

je préfère mon ordinateur à celui de Jean-Claude
I prefer my computer to Jean-Claude's

range ta chambre plutôt que celle de ta sœur
tidy your own bedroom rather than your sister's

mes parents sont moins sévères que ceux de Nicole
my parents aren't as strict as Nicole's

les douches municipales sont mieux que celles du camping
the public showers are better than those at the campsite

★ with the relative pronouns **qui**, **que**, **dont** to introduce a relative clause (for use of these relative pronouns, see pp B20-2).

celui/celle/ ceux/ celles qui	the one(s) who/which
celui/ celle/ ceux/ celles que	the one(s) whom/which
celui/ celle/ ceux/ celles dont	the one(s) of which/ whose

lequel est ton père ? celui qui a une moustache ?
which one is your father? the one with the moustache?

regarde cette voiture ! celle qui est garée au coin
look at that car! the one which is parked at the corner

deux filles, celles qu'il avait rencontrées la veille
two girls, the ones he had met the day before

voilà mon copain, celui dont je t'ai parlé l'autre jour
here's my friend, the one I told you about the other day

b) ***CE***

i) **ce** (meaning 'it', 'that') is mostly found with the verb **être**:

c'est	**ce serait**	**c'était**
it's/that's	it/that would be	it/that was

Note: **ce** changes to **c'** before an **e** or an **é**.

ii) use of **ce**

★ with a noun or pronoun, **ce** is used to identify people or things, or to emphasize them; it is translated in a variety of ways:

qu'est-ce que c'est ? – c'est mon billet d'avion
what's that? – it's my plane ticket

qui est-ce ? – c'est moi
who is it? – it's me

ce doit être lui
that must be him

c'est un artiste bien connu
he's a well-known artist

c'était une bonne idée
it was a good idea

ce sont mes amis
they're my friends

c'est la dernière fois !
it's the last time!

c'est elle qui l'a fait
she's the one who did it

c'est celui que j'ai vu
he's the one I saw

★ before an adjective, **ce** is used to refer to an idea, an event or a fact which has already been mentioned; it does not refer to any specific noun:

c'était formidable
it was great

ce serait amusant
it would be funny

oui, c'est vrai
yes, that's true

c'est sûr ?
is that definite?

ce n'est pas grave
it doesn't matter
or it's not serious

c'est bon à entendre
that's good to hear

Note: the translation of **it** is an area of some difficulty for students of French, as it is sometimes translated by **ce** and sometimes by **il/elle**; see the section on p B63.

3 *ceci, cela, ça*

ceci (this), **cela** (that) and **ça** (that) are used to refer to an idea, an event, a fact or an object. They never refer to a particular noun already mentioned.

non, je n'aime pas ça !
no, I don't like that!

ah, bon ? cela m'étonne
really? that surprises me

ça, c'est un acteur !
that's what I call an actor!

souvenez-vous de ceci
remember this

ça m'est égal
I don't mind

cela ne vous regarde pas
that's none of your business

buvez ceci, ça vous fera du bien
drink this, it'll do you good

ça alors !
well, really!

cela s'appelle comment, en anglais ?
what do you call this in English?

Note: **ceci** is not very common in French; **cela** and **ça** are often used to translate 'this' as well as 'that'; **ça** is used far more frequently than **cela** in spoken French.

B INDEFINITE ADJECTIVES AND PRONOUNS

1 Indefinite adjectives

They are:

Masculine	*Feminine*	
autre(s)	**autre(s)**	other
certain(s)	**certaine(s)**	certain
chaque	**chaque**	each, every
même(s)	**même(s)**	same
plusieurs	**plusieurs**	several
quelque(s)	**quelque(s)**	some
tel(s)	**telle(s)**	such
tout (tous)	**toute(s)**	all, every

a) ***CHAQUE** and **PLUSIEURS***

chaque (each) is always singular, **plusieurs** (several) always plural; the feminine form is the same as the masculine form:

j'y vais chaque jour
I go there every day

chaque personne
each person

plusieurs années
several years

il a plusieurs amis
he's got several friends

b) ***AUTRE, MEME** and **QUELQUE***

autre (other), **même** (same) and **quelque** (some) agree in number with the noun that follows; the feminine is the same as the masculine:

je voudrais un autre café
I'd like another coffee

d'autres couleurs
other colours

la même taille
the same size

les mêmes touristes
the same tourists

quelque temps après
some time later

à quelques kilomètres
a few kilometres away

Note: **même** has a different meaning when placed after the noun (see p B10).

c) ***CERTAIN, TEL** and **TOUT***

certain (certain, some), **tel** (such) and **tout** (all) agree in number and gender with the noun; they have four different forms:

un certain charme
a certain charm

une certaine dame
a certain lady

à certains moments
at (certain) times

certaines personnes
some people

un tel homme
such a man

une telle aventure
such an adventure

de tels avantages
such advantages

de telles difficultés
such difficulties

quoi ! tu as mangé tout le fromage et tous les fruits ?
what! you've eaten all the cheese and all the fruit?

toute la journée
all day long

toutes mes matières
all my subjects

Note:

i) **tel**: the position of the article **un/une** with **tel** is not the same as in English: **un tel homme** = such a man.

ii) **tel** cannot qualify another adjective; when it is used as an adverb, 'such' is translated by **si** or **tellement** (so):

c'était un si bon repas/un repas tellement bon !
it was such a good meal!

iii) **tous les/toutes les** are often translated by 'every':

tous les jours	**toutes les places**
every day	all seats, every seat

2 Indefinite pronouns

a) These are:

Masculine	*Feminine*	
aucun	**aucune**	none, not any
autre(s)	**autre(s)**	another one, other ones
certains	**certaine(s)**	certain, some
chacun	**chacune**	each one, everyone
on		one, someone, you, they, people, we
personne		nobody
plusieurs	**plusieurs**	several (ones)
quelque chose		something, anything
quelqu'un		someone
quelques-uns	**quelques-unes**	some, a few
rien		nothing
tout (tous)	**toute(s)**	everything, every one, all

pas celui-là, l'autre
not that one, the other one

où sont les autres ?
where are the others?

certains disent que ...
some say that...

personne n'est venu
no one came

qui est là ? – personne
who's there? – nobody

qu'as-tu ? – rien
what's wrong? – nothing

plusieurs d'entre eux
several of them

chacun pour soi !
every man for himself!

il manque quelque chose ?
is anything missing?

dis quelque chose !
say something!

quelqu'un l'a averti
someone warned him

il y a quelqu'un ?
is anyone in?

j'ai tout oublié
I've forgotten everything

c'est tout, merci
that's all, thanks

elles sont toutes arrivées
they've all arrived

allons-y tous ensemble
let's all go together

b) *Points to note*

i) **aucun(e)**, **personne** and **rien**: these can be used on their own, but they are more often used with a verb and the negative word **ne** (see negative expressions, p B60):

personne n'habite ici
no one lives here

il n'y a rien à manger
there's nothing to eat

ii) **aucun(e)**, **un(e) autre**, **d'autres**, **certain(e)s**, **plusieurs** and **quelques-un(e)s**: when these pronouns are used as direct objects, the pronoun **en** must be used before the verb:

je n'en ai lu aucun
I haven't read any (of them)

donne-m'en une autre
give me another one

j'en ai vu d'autres qui étaient moins chers
I saw other ones which were cheaper

j'en connais certains
I know some of them

il y en a plusieurs
there are several

tu m'en donnes quelques-uns
will you give me a few?

achètes-en quelques-unes
buy a few

iii) **personne**, **quelque chose**, **rien**, **plusieurs**: when these are followed by an adjective, the preposition **de (d')** must be used in front of the adjective:

il n'y a personne de libre
there's no one available

quelque chose de mieux
something better

il y en avait plusieurs de cassés
several of them were broken

rien de grave
nothing serious

iv) **autre** is commonly used in the following expressions:

quelqu'un d'autre	**quelque chose d'autre**	**rien d'autre**
someone else	something else	nothing else

c) *ON*

This pronoun is used in a variety of ways in French. It can mean:

i) *one/you/they/people* in a general sense

en France, on roule à droite
in France, they drive on the right

on ne sait jamais
you/one never know(s)

on ne doit pas mentir
you shouldn't lie

ii) *someone* (an undefined person)

In this sense, **on** is often translated by the passive (see p B36):

on me l'a déjà dit
someone's already told me
I've already been told

on vous l'apportera
someone will bring you it
it will be brought to you

iii) *we*

In spoken French, **on** is increasingly used instead of **nous**; although it refers to a plural subject, it is followed by the third person singular:

qu'est-ce qu'on fait ?
what shall we do?

fais vite, on t'attend !
hurry up, we're waiting for you!

Note: in compound tenses with the auxiliary **être**, the agreement of the past participle with **on** is optional:

on est allé au cinéma
on est allés au cinéma
we went to the pictures

on est rentré en taxi
on est rentrées en taxi
we got home by taxi

C INTERROGATIVE AND EXCLAMATORY ADJECTIVES AND PRONOUNS

1 The interrogative adjective QUEL ?

a) *Forms*

quel (which, what) agrees in number and gender with the noun it refers to. It has four forms:

- with a masc sing noun: **quel ?**
- with a fem sing noun: **quelle ?**
- with a masc plur noun: **quels ?**
- with a fem plur noun: **quelles ?**

b) *Direct questions*

quel est votre passe-temps favori ?
what's your favourite pastime?

quelle heure est-il ?
what time is it?

quels jours as-tu de libres ?
which days have you got free?

quelles affaires comptes-tu prendre avec toi ?
what/which things do you intend to take with you?

c) *Indirect questions*

je ne sais pas quel disque choisir
I don't know which record to choose

il se demande quelle veste lui va le mieux
he's wondering which jacket suits him best

2 The exclamatory adjective QUEL !

quel ! has the same forms as the interrogative adjective **quel ?**:

quel dommage !
what a pity!

quelle belle maison !
what a beautiful house!

quels imbéciles !
what idiots!

3 Interrogative pronouns

These are:

lequel/ laquelle/ lesquel(le)s ?	which (one)?
qui ?	who?, whom?
que ?	what?
quoi ?	what?
ce qui	what
ce que	what

ce qui and **ce que** are used only in indirect questions; all other interrogative pronouns can be used both in direct and indirect questions.

a) *LEQUEL ?*

i) *forms*

lequel (which?, which one?) agrees in gender and in number with the noun it stands for:

- with a masc sing noun:	**lequel ?**	which (one)?
- with a fem sing noun:	**laquelle ?**	which (one)?
- with a masc plur noun:	**lesquels ?**	which (ones)?
- with a fem plur noun:	**lesquelles ?**	which (ones)?

after the prepositions **à** and **de**, the following changes occur

à + lequel ?	❹	**auquel ?**
à + lesquels ?	❹	**auxquels ?**
à + lesquelles ?	❹	**auxquelles ?**
de + lequel ?	❹	**duquel ?**
de + lesquels ?	❹	**desquels ?**
de + lesquelles ?	❹	**desquelles ?**

à/de + laquelle? do not change

ii) *direct questions*

je cherche un hôtel; lequel recommandez-vous ?
I'm looking for a hotel; which one do you recommend?

nous avons plusieurs couleurs; vous préférez laquelle ?
we have several colours; which one do you prefer?

lesquels de ces livres sont à toi ?
which of these books are yours?

je voudrais essayer ces chaussures – lesquelles ?
I would like to try these shoes on – which ones?

iii) *indirect questions*

demande-lui lequel de ces ordinateurs est le moins cher
ask him which (one) of these computers is the cheapest

c'est dans une de ces rues, mais je ne sais plus laquelle
it's in one of these streets, but I can't remember which one

b) *QUI ?*

qui (who?, whom?) is used to refer to people; it can be both subject and object and can be used after a preposition:

qui t'a accompagné ?
who accompanied you?

qui as-tu appelé ?
who did you call?

tu y vas avec qui ?
who are you going with?

c'est pour qui ?
who is it for?

pour qui vous prenez-vous ?
who do you think you are?

à qui l'as-tu donné ?
who did you give it to?

Note: **que** (not **qui**!) changes to **qu'** before a vowel or a silent **h**:

qui est-ce qu'elle attend ?
who is she waiting for?

qui ? can be replaced by **qui est-ce qui ?** (subject) or **qui est-ce que ?** (object) in direct questions:

qui est-ce qui veut du café ?
who wants coffee?

qui est-ce que tu as vu?
who did you see?

avec qui est-ce que tu sors ce soir ?
who are you going out with tonight?

But: **qui** cannot be replaced by **qui est-ce qui** or **qui est-ce que** in indirect questions:

j'aimerais savoir qui vous a dit ça
I'd like to know who told you that

elle se demandait de qui étaient les fleurs
she was wondering who the flowers were from

For more details on the use of **qui/que** as relative pronouns, see p B20.

c) *QUE ?*

que (what?) is used to refer to things; it is only used in direct questions; it is always a direct object and cannot be used after prepositions:

que désirez-vous ?
what do you wish?

qu'a-t-il dit ?
what did he say?

que ? is rather formal and is usually replaced by **qu'est-ce que ?** in spoken French.

Note: **que** becomes **qu'** before a vowel or a silent **h**.

d) *QU'EST-CE QUI ?*

qu'est-ce qui ? (what?) is used as the subject of a verb; it cannot refer to a person:

qu'est-ce qui lui est arrivé ?
what happened to him?

qu'est-ce qui la fait rire ?
what makes her laugh?

e) *QU'EST-CE QUE ?*

qu'est-ce que ? (what?) replaces **que ?** as the object of a verb; it becomes **qu'est-ce qu'** before a vowel or a silent **h**:

qu'est-ce que tu aimes lire ?
what do you like reading?

qu'est-ce qu'il va faire pendant les vacances ?
what's he going to do during the holidays?

f) *QUOI ?*

quoi ? (what?) refers to things; it is used:

i) instead of **que** or **qu'est-ce que** after a preposition:

à quoi penses-tu ?
what are you thinking about?

dans quoi l'as-tu mis ?
what did you put it in?

ii) in indirect questions:

demandez-lui de quoi il a besoin
ask him what he needs

je ne sais pas à quoi ça sert
I don't know what it's for

g) *CE QUI, CE QUE*

ce qui and **ce que** (what) are only used in indirect questions; they replace **qu'est-ce qui** and (**qu'est- ce**) **que**.

They are used in the same way as the relative pronouns **ce qui** and **ce que** (see p B21).

i) **ce qui** is used as the subject of the verb in the indirect question (**ce qui** is the subject of **s'est passé** in the following example):

nous ne saurons jamais ce qui s'est passé
we'll never know what happened

ii) **ce que** (**ce qu'** before a vowel or a silent **h**) is used as the object of the verb in the indirect question (**ce que** is the object of **il faisait** in the following example):

je n'ai pas remarqué ce qu'il faisait
I didn't notice what he was doing

D PERSONAL PRONOUNS

There are four categories of personal pronouns:

- **subject** pronouns
- **object** pronouns
- **disjunctive** pronouns
- **reflexive** pronouns

For reflexive pronouns, see p B26.

1 Subject pronouns

Person	Singular		Plural	
1st	**je (j')**	I	**nous**	we
2nd	**tu**	you	**vous**	you
3rd	**il**	he, it	**ils**	they
	elle	she, it	**elles**	they
	on	one, we, they		

Note:

a) **je** changes to **j'** before a vowel or a silent **h**:

j'ai honte I'm ashamed — **j'adore les frites** I love chips

j'habite en Ecosse I live in Scotland

b) **tu** and **vous**

vous can be plural or singular; it is used when speaking to more than one person (plural), or to a stranger or an older person (singular):

vous venez, les gars ? are you coming, lads? — **vous parlez l'anglais, Monsieur ?** do you speak English(, sir)?

tu is used when speaking to a friend, a relative, a younger person, or someone you know well:

tu viens, Marc ? are you coming, Marc?

c) **il/ils, elle/elles** may refer to people, animals or things, and must be of the same gender as the noun they replace:

ton stylo ? *il* est là your pen? there *it* is — **ta montre ? *elle* est là** your watch? there *it* is

tes gants ? *ils* sont là your gloves? there *they* are — **tes lunettes ? *elles* sont là** your glasses? there *they* are

When referring to several nouns of different genders, French uses the masculine plural **ils**:

tu as vu *le* stylo et *la* montre de Marie ? – oui, *ils* sont dans son sac
have you seen Marie's pen and watch? – yes, *they*'re in her bag

d) **on**: see p B15.

2 Object pronouns

These include:
- direct object pronouns
- indirect object pronouns
- the pronouns **en** and **y**

a) *Forms*

	Person	Direct	Indirect
Sing	1st	**me (m')** me	**me (m')** (to) me
	2nd	**te (t')** you	**te (t')** (to) you
	3rd	**le (l')** him, it	**lui** (to) him
		la (l') her, it	**lui** (to) her
Plur	1st	**nous** us (to)	**nous** us
	2nd	**vous** you	**vous** (to) you
	3rd	**les** them	**leur** (to) them

Note:

i) **me, te, le** and **la** change to **m', t'** and **l'** before a vowel or a silent **h**:

il m'énerve ! he gets on my nerves! — **je m'habituerai à lui** I'll get used to him

ii) **te** and **vous**: the same distinction should be made as between the subject pronouns **tu** and **vous** (see section 1 b).

iii) **le** is sometimes used in an impersonal sense, when it refers to a fact, a statement or an idea which has already been expressed; it is usually not translated in English:

j'irai en Amérique un jour ; en tout cas je *l'*espère
I'll go to America one day; I hope so anyway

elle a eu un bébé – je *le* sais, elle me *l'*a dit
she's had a baby – I know, she told me

iv) **moi** and **toi** are used instead of **me** and **te**, except when **en** follows:

écris-*moi* bientôt write to me soon — **donne *m'*en** give me some

b) *Position*

In French, object pronouns come immediately before the verb they refer to. With a compound tense, they come before the auxiliary:

on *t'*attendra ici we'll wait for you here — **je *l'*ai rencontrée en ville** I met her in town

Note: When there are two verbs, the pronoun comes immediately before the verb it refers to:

j'aimerais lui demander I'd like to ask him — **tu l'as entendu chanter ?** have you heard him sing?

In positive commands (affirmative imperative) the pronoun follows the verb and is joined to it by a hyphen:

regarde-*les* ! look at them! — **parle-*lui* !** speak to him!

dis-*nous* ce qui s'est passé tell us what happened

c) *Direct pronouns and indirect pronouns*

i) Direct object pronouns replace a noun which follows the verb directly. They answer the question 'who(m)?' or 'what?':

WHO(M) did you see? **qui as-tu vu ?** — I saw *my friend*; I saw *him* **j'ai vu *mon ami* ; je *l'*ai vu**

tu *me* connais you know *me* — **j'aime *le* voir danser** I like to see *him* dance

je *les* ai trouvés I found *them* — **ne *nous* ennuie pas !** don't bother *us*!

ii) Indirect object pronouns replace a noun which follows the verb with a linking preposition (usually **à** = 'to'). They answer the question 'who(m) to?':

WHO did you speak to? **à qui as-tu parlé ?** — I spoke *to Marc*; I spoke *to him* **j'ai parlé *à Marc* ; je *lui* ai parlé**

elle *lui* a menti she lied *to him* — **je *te* donne ce disque** I'm giving this record *to you*

je ne *leur* parle plus I'm not talking *to them* any more

iii) **le/la/les** or **lui/leur**?

Direct pronouns differ from indirect pronouns only in the 3rd person and great care must be taken here:

★ English indirect object pronouns often look like direct objects; this becomes obvious when the object is placed at the end of the sentence:

I showed him your photo = I showed your photo to him
je *lui* ai montré ta photo

This is particularly the case with the following verbs:

acheter	to buy	**offrir**	to offer
donner	to give	**prêter**	to lend
montrer	to show	**vendre**	to sell

je *lui* ai acheté un livre I bought him a book = I bought a book *for him* — **ne *leur* prête pas mes affaires** don't lend them my things = don't lend my things *to them*

★ Some verbs take a direct object in English and an indirect object in French (see p B50):

je ne *lui* ai rien dit I didn't tell *him* anything — **je *leur* demanderai** I'll ask *them*

tu *lui* ressembles you look like *him* — **téléphone-*leur*** phone *them*

★ Some verbs take a direct object in French and an indirect object in English (see pp B49-50):

je *l'*attends — I'm waiting *for him*

écoutez-*les* ! — listen *to them*!

d) *Order of object pronouns*

When several object pronouns are used together, they come in the following order:

i) Before the verb:

1 **me te nous vous**
2 **le la les**
3 **lui leur**

il *me l'*a donné — he gave *me it*

je vais *vous les* envoyer — I'll send *them to you*

ne *la leur* vends pas — don't sell *it to them*

je *le lui* ai acheté — I bought *it for him*

ii) After the verb:

With a positive command (affirmative imperative), the order is as follows:

1 **le la les**
2 **moi (m') toi (t') nous vous**
3 **lui leur**

apporte-*les-moi* ! — bring *them to me*!

prête-*la-nous* ! — lend *us it*!

dites-*le-lui* ! — tell *him*!

rends-*la leur* ! — give *it* back *to them*!

3 The pronoun EN

a) *Use*

en is used instead of **de** + noun. Since **de** has a variety of meanings, **en** can be used in a number of ways:

i) It means 'of it/them', but also 'with it/them', 'about it/them', 'from it/there', 'out of it/there':

tu es sûr *du prix* ? – j'*en* suis sûr
are you sure of the price? – I'm sure *of it*

je suis content *de ce cadeau* ; j'*en* suis content
I'm pleased with this present; I'm pleased *with it*

elle est folle *des animaux* ; elle *en* est folle
she's crazy about animals; she's crazy *about them*

il est descendu *du train* ; il *en* est descendu
he got off the train; he got *off it*

il revient *de Paris* ; il *en* revient
he's coming back from Paris; he's coming *from there*

ii) Verb constructions

Particular care should be taken with verbs and expressions which are followed by **de** + noun. Since **de** is not always translated in the same way, **en** may have a number of meanings:

il a envie *de ce livre* ; il *en* a envie
he wants this book; he wants *it*

je te remercie *de ta carte* ; je t'*en* remercie
I thank you for your card; I thank you *for it*

tu as besoin *de ces papiers* ? tu *en* as besoin ?
do you need these papers? do you need *them*?

elle a peur *des chiens* ; elle *en* a peur
she's afraid of dogs; she's afraid *of them*

tu te souviens *de ce film* ? tu t'*en* souviens ?
do you remember this film? do you remember *it*?

iii) 'some'/'any'

en replaces the partitive article (**du**, **de la**, **des**) + noun; it means 'some'/'any':

tu veux *du café* ? – non, je n'*en* veux pas
do you want (any) coffee? – no, I don't want *any*

j'achète *des fruits* ? – non, j'*en* ai chez moi
shall I buy (some) fruit? – no, I've got *some* at home

il y a *de la place* ? – *en* voilà là-bas
is there any room? – there's *some* over there

iv) Expressions of quantity

en must be used with expressions of quantity not followed by a noun. It replaces **de** + noun and means 'of it/them', but is seldom translated in English:

tu as pris assez *d'argent* ? — did you take enough money?

tu *en* as pris assez ? — did you take enough?

vous avez *combien de frères* ? – j'*en* ai deux
how many brothers do you have? – I've got two

j'ai fini *mes cigarettes* ; je vais *en* acheter un paquet
I've finished my cigarettes; I'm going to buy a packet

b) *Position*

Like object pronouns, **en** comes immediately before the verb, except with positive commands (affirmative imperative), where it comes after the verb and is linked to it by a hyphen:

j'en veux un kilo — I want a kilo (of it/them)

j'en ai marre ! — I'm fed up (with it)!

prends-en assez ! — take enough (of it/them)!

laisses-en aux autres ! — leave some for the others!

When used in conjunction with other object pronouns, it always comes last:

ne *m'en* parlez pas ! — don't tell me about it!

je *vous en* donnerai — I'll give you some

prête-*lui-en* ! — lend him some!

gardez-*nous-en* ! — keep some for us!

4 The pronoun Y

a) *Use*

y is used instead of **à** + noun (not referring to a person). It is used:

i) As the indirect object of a verb. Since the preposition **à** is translated in a variety of ways in English, **y** may have various meanings (it, of it/them, about it/them etc):

tu joues *au tennis* ? – non, j'*y* joue rarement
do you play tennis? – no, I seldom play (*it*)

je pense *à mes examens* ; j'*y* pense souvent
I'm thinking *about* my exams; I often think *about them*

il s'intéresse *à la photo* ; il s'*y* intéresse
he's interested *in* photography; he's interested *in it*

ii) Meaning 'there':

j'ai passé deux jours *à Londres* ; j'*y* ai passé deux jours
I spent two days *in* London; I spent two days *there*

il est allé *en Grèce* ; il *y* est allé
he went *to* Greece; he went *there*

Note: **y** must always be used with the verb **aller** (to go) when the place is not mentioned in the clause. It is often not translated in English:

comment vas-tu *à l'école* ? – j'*y* vais en bus
how do you go to school? – I go (there) by bus

allons-*y*! — let's go!

on *y* va demain — we're going (there) tomorrow

iii) Replacing the prepositions **en**, **dans**, **sur** + noun; **y** then means 'there', 'in it/them', 'on it/them':

je voudrais vivre *en France* ; je voudrais *y* vivre
I'd like to live in France; I'd like to live *there*

je les ai mis *dans ma poche* ; je les *y* ai mis
I put them in my pocket; I put them *there*

***sur la table* ? non, je ne l'*y* vois pas**
on the table? no, I don't see it *there*

b) *Position*

Like other object pronouns, **y** comes immediately before the verb, except with a positive command (affirmative imperative), where it must follow the verb:

j'*y* réfléchirai — I'll think about it

il s'*y* est habitué — he got used to it

pensez-*y* ! think about it!	**n'*y* allez pas !** don't go!

When used with other object pronouns, **y** comes last:

il va *nous y* rencontrer he'll meet us there	**je *l'y* ai vu hier** I saw him there yesterday

5 Disjunctive pronouns

a) *Forms*

Person		*Singular*	*Plural*
1st		**moi** me	**nous** us
2nd		**toi** you	**vous** you
3rd	(*Masc*)	**lui** him	**eux** them
	(*Fem*)	**elle** her	**elles** them
	(*Impersonal*)	**soi** oneself	

Note:

i) **toi/vous**: the same difference should be made as between **tu** and **vous** (see p B17).

ii) **soi** is used in an impersonal, general sense to refer to indefinite pronouns and adjectives (**on**, **chacun**, **tout le monde**, **personne**, **chaque** etc); it is mainly found in set phrases, such as:

chacun pour soi
every man for himself

b) *Use*

Disjunctive pronouns, also called emphatic pronouns, are used instead of object pronouns (only when referring to persons) in the following cases:

i) In answer to a question, alone or in a phrase without a verb:

qui est là ? – moi who's there? – me	**j'aime les pommes ; et toi ?** I like apples; do you?

qui préfères-tu, lui ou elle ? – elle, bien sûr
who do you prefer, him or her? – her, of course

ii) After **c'est/ce sont**, **c'était/étaient** etc:

ouvrez, c'est moi ! open up, it's me!	**non, ce n'était pas lui** no, it wasn't him

iii) After a preposition:

vous allez chez lui ? are you going to his place?	**tu y vas avec elle ?** are you going with her?
regarde devant toi ! look in front of you!	**oh, c'est pour moi ?** oh, is that for me?

iv) Verb constructions: special care should be taken with verbs followed by a preposition:

tu peux compter sur moi you can count on me	**quoi ! tu as peur de lui ?** what! you're afraid of him?
il m'a parlé de toi he told me about you	**je pense souvent à vous** I often think about you

Note: Emphatic pronouns are only used when referring to persons. Otherwise, use **y** or **en**.

v) For emphasis, particularly when two pronouns are contrasted. The unstressed subject pronoun is usually included:

vous, vous m'énervez ! *you* get on my nerves!	**lui, il joue bien ; elle, non** *he* plays well; *she* doesn't
moi, je n'aime pas l'hiver *I* don't like winter	**eux, ils sont partis** *they*'ve left

vi) In the case of multiple subjects (two pronouns or one pronoun and one noun):

lui et son frère sont dans l'équipe
he and his brother are in the team

ma famille et moi allons très bien
my family and I are very well

vii) As the second term of comparisons:

il est plus sympa que toi he is nicer than you	**elle chante mieux que lui** she sings better than he does

viii) Before a relative pronoun:

c'est lui que j'aime he's the one I love	**c'est toi qui l'as dit** you're the one who said it

lui qui n'aime pas le vin blanc en a bu six verres
he, who doesn't like white wine, had six glasses

ix) With **-même(s)** (-self, -selves), **aussi** (too), **seul** (alone):

faites-le vous-mêmes do it yourselves	**j'irai moi-même** I'll go myself
lui aussi est parti he too went away	**elle seule le sait** she alone knows

x) To replace a possessive pronoun (see p B20):

c'est *le mien* ; il est à moi
it's mine; it belongs to me

E POSSESSIVE ADJECTIVES AND PRONOUNS

1 Possessive adjectives

a) *Forms*

Possessive adjectives always come before a noun. Like other adjectives, they agree in gender and number with the noun; the masculine and feminine plural are identical

Singular *Masc*	*Fem*	*Plural* *Masc and Fem*	
mon	**ma**	**mes**	my
ton	**ta**	**tes**	your
son	**sa**	**ses**	his/her/its/one's
notre	**notre**	**nos**	our
votre	**votre**	**vos**	your
leur	**leur**	**leurs**	their

j'ai mis mon argent et mes affaires dans mon sac
I've put my money and my things in my bag

comment va ton frère ? et ta sœur ? et tes parents ?
how's your brother? and your sister? and your parents?

notre rue est assez calme our street is fairly quiet	**ce sont vos amis** they're your friends

Note: **mon/ton/son** are used instead of **ma/ta/sa** when the next word starts with a vowel or silent **h**:

mon ancienne maison my old house	**ton amie Christine** your friend Christine

son haleine sentait l'alcool
his breath smelled of alcohol

b) *Use*

i) The possessive adjective is repeated before each noun and agrees with it:

mon père et ma mère sont sortis
my mother and father have gone out

***ii)* son/sa/ses**

son, **sa** and **ses** can all mean 'his', 'her' or 'its'. In French, the form of the adjective is determined by the gender and number of the noun that follows, and not by the possessor:

il m'a prêté sa mobylette et son casque
he lent me his moped and his helmet

elle s'entend bien avec sa mère, mais pas avec son père
she gets on well with her mother, but not with her father

il cire ses chaussures ; elle repasse ses chemisiers
he's polishing his shoes; she's ironing her shirts

***iii)* ton/ta/tes** and **votre/vos**

The two sets of words for 'your', **ton/ta/tes** and **votre/vos**, correspond to the two different forms **tu** and **vous**; they must not be used together with the same person:

Papa, tu as parlé à ton patron ?
have you spoken to your boss, Dad?

Monsieur ! votre brochure ! vous ne la prenez pas ?
Sir! your brochure! aren't you taking it?

iv) In French, the possessive adjective is replaced by the definite article (**le/la/les**) with the following:

★ parts of the body:

il s'est essuyé les mains	**elle a haussé les épaules**
he wiped his hands	she shrugged (her shoulders)

★ descriptive phrases tagged on to the end of a clause, where English adds 'with':

il marchait lentement, les mains dans les poches
he was walking slowly, with his hands in his pockets

elle l'a regardé partir les larmes aux yeux
she watched him leave with tears in her eyes

2 Possessive pronouns

Singular		*Plural*	
Masc	*Fem*	*Masc and Fem*	
le mien	**la mienne**	**les mien(ne)s**	mine
le tien	**la tienne**	**les tien(ne)s**	yours
le sien	**la sienne**	**les sien(ne)s**	his/hers/its
le nôtre	**la nôtre**	**les nôtres**	ours
le vôtre	**la vôtre**	**les vôtres**	yours
le leur	**la leur**	**les leurs**	theirs

Possessive pronouns are used intead of a possessive adjective + noun. They agree in gender and in number with the noun they stand for, and not with the possessor (it is particularly important to remember this when translating 'his' and 'hers'):

j'aime bien ton chapeau, mais je préfère le mien
I quite like your hat, but I prefer mine

on prend quelle voiture ? la mienne ou la tienne ?
which car shall we take? mine or yours?

comment sont vos profs ? les nôtres sont sympas
what are your teachers like? ours are nice

j'ai pris mon passeport, mais Brigitte a oublié le sien
I brought my passport, but Brigitte forgot hers

j'ai gardé ma moto, mais Paul a vendu la sienne
I've kept my motorbike but Paul has sold his

à or **de** + possessive pronoun

The prepositions **à** or **de** combine with the articles **le** and **les** in the usual way:

à + le mien	→	**au mien**
à + les miens	→	**aux miens**
à + les miennes	→	**aux miennes**
de + le mien	→	**du mien**
de + les miens	→	**des miens**
de + les miennes	→	**des miennes**

demande à tes parents, j'ai déjà parlé aux miens
ask your parents, I've already spoken to mine

leur appartement ressemble beaucoup au nôtre
their flat is very similar to ours

j'aime bien les chiens, mais j'ai peur du tien
I like dogs, but I'm afraid of yours

Note: after the verb **être**, the possessive pronoun is often replaced by **à** + emphatic (disjunctive) pronoun (see p B19):

à qui est cette écharpe ? – elle est à moi
whose scarf is this? – it's mine

ce livre est à toi ? – non, il est à elle
is this book yours? – no, it's hers

c'est à qui ? à vous ou à lui ?
whose is this? yours or his?

F RELATIVE PRONOUNS

1 Definition

Relative pronouns are words which introduce a relative clause. In the following sentence:

I bought the book which you recommended

'which' is the relative pronoun, 'which you recommended' is the relative clause and 'the book' is the antecedent (ie the noun the relative pronoun refers to).

2 Forms

Relative pronouns are:

qui	who, which	**lequel**	which
que	who(m), which	**dont**	of which, whose
quoi	what	**ce qui**	what
où	where	**ce que**	what

qui, que, quoi, lequel, ce qui and **ce que** can also be used as interrogative pronouns (see p B16) and must not be confused with them.

3 Use

a) *QUI*

qui is used as the subject of a relative clause; it means:

i) 'who', 'that' (referring to people):

connaissez-vous le monsieur qui habite ici ?
do you know the man who lives here?

ce n'est pas lui qui a menti
he's not the one who lied

ii) 'which', 'that' (referring to things):

tu as pris le journal qui était sur la télé ?
did you take the paper which/that was on the telly?

b) *QUE*

que (written **qu'** before a vowel or a silent **h**) is used as the object of a relative clause; it is often not translated and means:

i) 'who(m)', 'that' (referring to people):

la fille que j'aime ne m'aime pas
the girl (that) I love doesn't love me

ii) 'which', 'that' (referring to things):

j'ai perdu le briquet qu'il m'a offert
I've lost the lighter (which/that) he gave me

c) *QUI* or *QUE?*

qui (subject) and **que** (object) are translated by the same words in English (who, which, that). To use the correct pronoun in French, it is essential to know whether a relative pronoun is the object or the subject of the relative clause:

i) when the verb of the relative clause has its own subject, the object pronoun **que** must be used:

c'est un passe-temps que j'adore
it's a pastime (that) I love (*the subject of 'adore' is 'je'*)

ii) otherwise the relative pronoun is the subject of the verb in the relative clause and the subject pronoun **qui** must be used:

j'ai trouvé un manteau qui me plaît
I found a coat that I like (*the subject of 'plaît' is 'qui'*)

d) *LEQUEL*

i) forms

lequel (which) has four different forms, as it must agree with the noun it refers to:

	Singular	*Plural*
Masculine	**lequel**	**lesquels**
Feminine	**laquelle**	**lesquelles**

lequel etc combines with the prepositions **à** and **de** as follows:

à + lequel	→	**auquel**
à + lesquels	→	**auxquels**
à + lesquelles	→	**auxquelles**

de + lequel	→	**duquel**
de + lesquels	→	**desquels**
de + lesquelles	→	**desquelles**

à + laquelle and **de** + laquelle do not change.

quels sont les sports auxquels tu t'intéresses ?
what are the sports (which) you are interested *in*?

voilà le village près duquel on campait
here's the village near which we camped

***ii)* qui** or **lequel** with a preposition?

When a relative pronoun follows a preposition, the pronoun used is either **qui** or **lequel**. In English, the relative pronoun is seldom used and the preposition is frequently placed after the verb or at the end of the sentence.

qui is generally used after a preposition when referring to people:

où est la fille *avec* qui je dansais ?
where's the girl I was dancing *with*?

montre-moi la personne *à* qui tu as vendu ton vélo
show me the person you sold your bike *to*

lequel is often used after a preposition when referring to things:

l'immeuble *dans* lequel j'habite est très moderne
the building (which) I live *in* is very modern

je ne reconnais pas la voiture *avec* laquelle il est venu
I don't recognize the car (which) he came *in*

lequel is also used when referring to persons after the prepositions **entre** (between) and **parmi** (among):

des touristes, parmi lesquels il y avait des Japonais
tourists, among whom were (some) Japanese people

il aimait deux filles, entre lesquelles il hésitait
he loved two girls, between whom he was torn

e) *DONT*

dont (of which, of whom, whose) is frequently used instead of **de qui**, **duquel** etc. It means:

i) 'of which', 'of whom':

un métier dont il est fier
a job (which) he is proud of

Care must be taken with verbs that are normally followed by **de** + object: **de** is not always translated by 'of' in English, and is sometimes not translated at all (see section on verb constructions p B50):

voilà les choses *dont* j'ai besoin
here are the things (*which*) I need

les gens *dont* tu parles ne m'intéressent pas
I'm not interested in the people you're talking about

l'enfant *dont* elle s'occupe n'est pas le sien
the child she is looking after is not hers

ii) 'whose'

dont is also used to translate the English pronoun 'whose'. In French, the construction of the clause that follows **dont** differs from English in two ways:

★ the noun which follows **dont** is used with the definite article (**le, la, les, l'**):

mon copain, dont *le* père a eu un accident
my friend, whose father had an accident

★ the word order in French is **dont** + subject + verb + object:

je te présente Hélène, dont tu connais déjà le frère
this is Helen, whose brother you already know

c'était dans une petite rue dont j'ai oublié le nom
it was in a small street the name of which I've forgotten

Note: **dont** cannot be used after a preposition:

une jolie maison, *près* de laquelle il y a un petit lac
a pretty house, *next* to which there is a small lake

f) *OU*

***i)* où** generally means 'where':

l'hôtel où on a logé était très confortable
the hotel where we stayed was very comfortable

***ii)* où** often replaces a preposition + **lequel**, meaning 'in/to/on/at which' etc:

c'est la maison où je suis né
that's the house in which/where I was born

une surprise-partie où il a invité tous ses amis
a party to which he invited all his friends

***iii)* où** is also used to translate 'when' after a noun referring to time:

le jour où	**la fois où**	**le moment où**
the day when	the time when	the moment when

tu te rappelles le soir où on a raté le dernier métro ?
do you remember the evening when we missed the last train?

g) *CE QUI, CE QUE*

ce is used before **qui** and **que** when the relative pronoun does not refer to a specific noun. Both **ce qui** and **ce que** mean 'that which', 'the thing which', and are usually translated by 'what':

***i)* ce qui**

ce qui is followed by a verb without a subject (**qui** is the subject):

ce qui s'est passé ne vous regarde pas
what happened is none of your business

ce qui m'étonne, c'est sa patience
what surprises me is his patience

Note: the comma and the **c'**

***ii)* ce que**

ce que (**ce qu'** before a vowel or a silent **h**) is followed by a verb with its own subject (**que** is the object):

fais ce que tu veux	**c'est ce qu'il a dit?**
do what you want	is that what he said?

ce que vous me demandez est impossible
what you're asking me is impossible

***iii)* tout ce qui/que**

tout is used in front of **ce qui/que** in the sense of 'all that', 'everything that':

c'est tout ce que je veux	**tout ce que tu as fait**
that's all I want	everything you did

tu n'as pas eu de mal ; c'est tout ce qui compte
you weren't hurt; that's all that matters

***iv)* ce qui/que** are often used in indirect questions (see p B16):

je ne sais pas ce qu'ils vont dire
I don't know what they'll say

v) when referring to a previous clause, **ce qui** and **ce que** are translated by 'which':

elle est en retard, ce qui arrive souvent
she's late, which happens often

***vi)* ce que/qui** are used with a preposition (when the preposition refers to **ce**):

ce n'est pas étonnant, après ce qui lui est arrivé
it's not surprising, after what happened to him

il y a du vrai dans ce que vous dites
there is some truth in what you say

But: **QUOI** is used instead of **ce que** after a preposition when the preposition refers to **que**, and not to **ce**:

c'est ce à quoi je pensais
that's what I was thinking about

***vii)* ce que** is used with the preposition **de** when **de** refers to **ce**:

je suis fier de ce qu'il a fait
I'm proud of what he did

But: **ce dont** is used instead of **de + ce que** when **de** refers to **que**, and not to **ce**:

> **c'est ce dont j'avais peur**
> that's what I was afraid of
>
> **tu as trouvé ce dont tu avais besoin ?**
> did you find what you needed?

7 Verbs

A REGULAR CONJUGATIONS

1 Conjugations

There are three main conjugations in French, which are determined by the infinitive endings. The first conjugation verbs, by far the largest category, end in **-er** (eg aim**er**) and will be referred to as **-er** verbs; the second conjugation verbs end in **-ir** (eg fin**ir**) and will be referred to as **-ir** verbs; the third conjugation verbs, the smallest category, end in **-re** (eg vend**re**) and will be referred to as **-re** verbs.

2 Simple tenses

The simple tenses in French are:

a) present

b) imperfect

c) future

d) conditional

e) past historic

f) present subjunctive

g) imperfect subjunctive

For the use of the different tenses, see pp B28-32.

3 Formation of tenses

The tenses are formed by adding the following endings to the stem of the verb (mainly the stem of the infinitive) as set out in the following section:

a) *PRESENT:* stem of the infinitive + the following endings:

-er Verbs	**-ir** Verbs	**-re** Verbs
-e, -es, -e, -ons, -ez, -ent	**-is, -is, -it, -issons, -issez, -issent**	**-s, -s, -, -ons, -ez, -ent**
AIMER	FINIR	VENDRE
j'aim**e**	je fin**is**	je vend**s**
tu aim**es**	tu fin**is**	tu vend**s**
il aim**e**	il fin**it**	il vend
elle aim**e**	elle fin**it**	elle vend
nous aim**ons**	nous fin**issons**	nous vend**ons**
vous aim**ez**	vous fin**issez**	vous vend**ez**
ils aim**ent**	ils fin**issent**	ils vend**ent**
elles aim**ent**	elles fin**issent**	elles vend**ent**

b) *IMPERFECT:* stem of the first person plural of the present tense (ie the '**nous**' form minus **-ons**) + the following endings:

-ais, -ais, -ait, -ions, -iez, -aient

j'aim**ais**	je finiss**ais**	je vend**ais**
tu aim**ais**	tu finiss**ais**	tu vend**ais**
il aim**ait**	il finiss**ait**	il vend**ait**
elle aim**ait**	elle finiss**ait**	elle vend**ait**
nous aim**ions**	nous finiss**ions**	nous vend**ions**
vous aim**iez**	vous finiss**iez**	vous vend**iez**
ils aim**aient**	ils finiss**aient**	ils vend**aient**
elles aim**aient**	elles finiss**aient**	elles vend**aient**

Note: the only irregular imperfect is **être**: **j'étais** etc.

c) *FUTURE:* infinitive + the following endings:

-ai, -as, -a, -ons, -ez, -ont

Note: Verbs ending in **-re** drop the final **e** of the infinitive

j'aimer**ai**	je finir**ai**	je vendr**ai**
tu aimer**as**	tu finir**as**	tu vendr**as**
il aimer**a**	il finir**a**	il vendr**a**
elle aimer**a**	elle finir**a**	elle vendr**a**
nous aimer**ons**	nous finir**ons**	nous vendr**ons**
vous aimer**ez**	vous finir**ez**	vous vendr**ez**
ils aimer**ont**	ils finir**ont**	ils vendr**ont**

elles aimer**ont**	elles finir**ont**	elles vendr**ont**

d) *CONDITIONAL:* infinitive + the following endings:

-ais, -ais, -ait, -ions, -iez, -aient

Note: Verbs ending in **-re** drop the final **e** of the infinitive

j'aimer**ais**	je finir**ais**	je vendr**ais**
tu aimer**ais**	tu finir**ais**	tu vendr**ais**
il aimer**ait**	il finir**ait**	il vendr**ait**
elle aimer**ait**	elle finir**ait**	elle vendr**ait**
nous aimer**ions**	nous finir**ions**	nous vendr**ions**
vous aimer**iez**	vous finir**iez**	vous vendr**iez**
ils aimer**aient**	ils finir**aient**	ils vendr**aient**
elles aimer**aient**	elles finir**aient**	elles vendr**aient**

e) *PAST HISTORIC:* stem of the infinitive + the following endings:

-er Verbs	**-ir** Verbs	**-re** Verbs
-ai, -as, -a, -âmes, -âtes, -èrent	**-is, -is, -it, -îmes, -îtes, -irent**	**-is, -is, -it, -îmes, -îtes, -irent**
j'aim**ai**	je fin**is**	je vend**is**
tu aim**as**	tu fin**is**	tu vend**is**
il aim**a**	il fin**it**	il vend**it**
elle aim**a**	elle fin**it**	elle vend**it**
nous aim**âmes**	nous fin**îmes**	nous vend**îmes**
vous aim**âtes**	vous fin**îtes**	vous vend**îtes**
ils aim**èrent**	ils fin**irent**	ils vend**irent**
elles aim**èrent**	elles fin**irent**	elles vend**irent**

f) *PRESENT SUBJUNCTIVE:* stem of the first person plural of the present indicative + the following endings:

-e, -es, -e, -ions, -iez, -ent

j'aim**e**	je finiss**e**	je vend**e**
tu aim**es**	tu finiss**es**	tu vend**es**
il aim**e**	il finiss**e**	il vend**e**
elle aim**e**	elle finiss**e**	elle vend**e**
nous aim**ions**	nous finiss**ions**	nous vend**ions**
vous aim**iez**	vous finiss**iez**	vous vend**iez**
ils aim**ent**	ils finiss**ent**	ils vend**ent**
elles aim**ent**	elles finiss**ent**	elles vend**ent**

g) *IMPERFECT SUBJUNCTIVE:* stem of the first person singular of the past historic + the following endings:

-er Verbs	**-ir** Verbs	**-re** Verbs
-asse, -asses, -ât, -assions, -assiez, -assent	**-isse, -isses, -ît, -issions, -issiez, -issent**	**-isse, -isses, -ît, -issions, -issiez, -issent**
j'aim**asse**	je fin**isse**	je vend**isse**
tu aim**asses**	tu fin**isses**	tu vend**isses**
il aim**ât**	il fin**ît**	il vend**ît**
elle aim**ât**	elle fin**ît**	elle vend**ît**
nous aim**assions**	nous fin**issions**	nous vend**issions**
vous aim**assiez**	vous fin**issiez**	vous vend**issiez**
ils aim**assent**	ils fin**issent**	ils vend**issent**
elles aim**assent**	elles fin**issent**	elles vend**issent**

B STANDARD SPELLING IRREGULARITIES

Spelling irregularities only affect **-er** verbs.

1 Verbs ending in -cer and -ger

a) Verbs ending in **-cer** require a cedilla under the **c** (**ç**) before an **a** or an **o** to preserve the soft sound of the **c**: eg **commencer** (to begin).

b) Verbs ending in **-ger** require an **-e** after the **g** before an **a** or an **o** to preserve the soft sound of the **g**: eg **manger** (to eat).

Changes to **-cer** and **-ger** verbs occur in the following tenses: present, imperfect, past historic, imperfect subjunctive and present participle.

	COMMENCER	MANGER
Present		
	je commence	je mange
	tu commences	tu manges
	il commence	il mange
	elle commence	elle mange
	nous **commençons**	nous **mangeons**
	vous commencez	vous mangez
	ils commencent	ils mangent
	elles commencent	elles mangent
Imperfect		
	je **commençais**	je **mangeais**
	tu **commençais**	tu **mangeais**
	il **commençait**	il **mangeait**
	elle **commençait**	elle **mangeait**
	nous commencions	nous mangions
	vous commenciez	vous mangiez
	ils **commençaient**	ils **mangeaient**
	elles **commençaient**	elles **mangeaient**
Past Historic		
	je **commençai**	je **mangeai**
	tu **commenças**	tu **mangeas**
	il **commença**	il **mangea**
	elle **commença**	elle **mangea**
	nous **commençâmes**	nous **mangeâmes**
	vous **commençâtes**	vous **mangeâtes**
	ils commencèrent	ils mangèrent
	elles commencèrent	elles mangèrent
Imperfect Subjunctive		
	je **commençasse**	je **mangeasse**
	tu **commençasses**	tu **mangeasses**
	il **commençât**	il **mangeât**
	elle **commençât**	elle **mangeât**
	nous **commençassions**	nous **mangeassions**
	vous **commençassiez**	vous **mangeassiez**
	ils **commençassent**	ils **mangeassent**
	elles **commençassent**	elles **mangeassent**
Present Participle		
	commençant	**mangeant**

2 Verbs ending in -eler and -eter

a) Verbs ending in **-eler**

Verbs ending in **-eler** double the **l** before a silent **e** (ie before **-e**, **-es**, **-ent** of the present indicative and subjunctive, and throughout the future and conditional): eg **appeler** (to call).

Present Indicative	*Present Subjunctive*
j'**appelle**	j'**appelle**
tu **appelles**	tu **appelles**
il **appelle**	il **appelle**
elle **appelle**	elle **appelle**
nous appelons	nous appelions
vous appelez	vous appeliez
ils **appellent**	ils **appellent**
elles **appellent**	elles **appellent**

Future	*Conditional*
j'**appellerai**	j'**appellerais**
tu **appelleras**	tu **appellerais**
il **appellera**	il **appellerait**
elle **appellera**	elle **appellerait**
nous **appellerons**	nous **appellerions**
vous **appellerez**	vous **appelleriez**
ils **appelleront**	ils **appelleraient**
elles **appelleront**	elles **appelleraient**

But: some verbs in **-eler** including the following are conjugated like **acheter** (see p B24):

celer	to conceal
congeler	to (deep-)freeze
déceler	to detect, reveal
dégeler	to defrost
geler	to freeze

harceler	to harass
marteler	to hammer
modeler	to model
peler	to peel

b) Verbs ending in **-eter**

Verbs ending in **-eter** double the **t** before a silent **e** (ie before **-e, -es, -ent** of the present indicative and subjunctive, and throughout the future and conditional): eg **jeter** (to throw).

Present Indicative	*Present Subjunctive*
je **jette**	je **jette**
tu **jettes**	tu **jettes**
il **jette**	il **jette**
elle **jette**	elle **jette**
nous jetons	nous jetions
vous jetez	vous jetiez
ils **jettent**	ils **jettent**
elles **jettent**	elles **jettent**

Future	*Conditional*
je **jetterai**	je **jetterais**
tu **jetteras**	tu **jetterais**
il **jettera**	il **jetterait**
elle **jettera**	elle **jetterait**
nous **jetterons**	nous **jetterions**
vous **jetterez**	vous **jetteriez**
ils **jetteront**	ils **jetteraient**
elles **jetteront**	elles **jetteraient**

But: some verbs in **-eter** including the following are conjugated like **acheter** (see section e):

crocheter	to pick (*lock*)
fureter	to ferret about
haleter	to pant
racheter	to buy back

c) Verbs ending in **-oyer** and **-uyer**

In verbs ending in **-oyer** and **-uyer** the **y** changes to **i** before a silent **e** (ie before **-e, -es, -ent** of the present indicative and subjunctive, and throughout the future and conditional): eg **employer** (to use) and **ennuyer** (to bore).

Present Indicative	*Present Subjunctive*
j'**emploie**	j'**emploie**
tu **emploies**	tu **emploies**
il **emploie**	il **emploie**
elle **emploie**	elle **emploie**
nous employons	nous employions
vous employez	vous employiez
ils **emploient**	ils **emploient**
elles **emploient**	elles **emploient**

Future	*Conditional*
j'**emploierai**	j'**emploierais**
tu **emploieras**	tu **emploierais**
il **emploiera**	il **emploierait**
elle **emploiera**	elle **emploierait**
nous **emploierons**	nous **emploierions**
vous **emploierez**	vous **emploieriez**
ils **emploieront**	ils **emploieraient**
elles **emploieront**	elles **emploieraient**

Note: **envoyer** (to send) and **renvoyer** (to dismiss) have an irregular future and conditional: **j'enverrai**, **j'enverrais**; **je renverrai**, **je renverrais**.

d) Verbs ending in **-ayer**

In verbs ending in **-ayer**, eg **balayer** (to sweep), **payer** (to pay), **essayer** (to try), the change from **y** to **i** is optional:

eg	je **balaie**	*or*	je **balaye**
	je **paie**	*or*	je **paye**
	j'**essaie**	*or*	j'**essaye**

e) Verbs in **e** + consonant + **er**

Verbs like **acheter**, **enlever**, **mener**, **peser** change the (last) **e** of the stem to **è** before a silent **e** (ie before **-e**, **-es**, **-ent** of the present indicative and subjunctive and throughout the future and conditional):

Present Indicative	*Present Subjunctive*
j'**achète**	j'**achète**
tu **achètes**	tu **achètes**
il **achète**	il **achète**
elle **achète**	elle **achète**
nous achetons	nous achetions
vous achetez	vous achetiez
ils **achètent**	ils **achètent**
elles **achètent**	elles **achètent**

Future	*Conditional*
j'**achèterai**	j'**achèterais**
tu **achèteras**	tu **achèterais**
il **achètera**	il **achèterait**
elle **achètera**	elle **achèterait**
nous **achèterons**	nous **achèterions**
vous **achèterez**	vous **achèteriez**
ils **achèteront**	ils **achèteraient**
elles **achèteront**	elles **achèteraient**

Verbs conjugated like **acheter** include:

achever to complete	**haleter** to pant
amener to bring	**harceler** to harass
celer to conceal	**lever** to lift
crever to burst	**marteler** to hammer
crocheter to pick (*lock*)	**mener** to lead
élever to raise	**modeler** to model
emmener to take away	**peler** to peel
enlever to remove	**peser** to weigh
étiqueter to label	**se promener** to go for a walk
fureter to ferret about	**semer** to sow
geler to freeze	**soulever** to lift

f) Verbs in **é** + consonant + **er**

Verbs like **espérer** (to hope) change **é** to **è** before a silent **e** in the present indicative and subjunctive. BUT in the future and conditional **é** is retained.

Present Indicative	*Present Subjunctive*
j'**espère**	j'**espère**
tu **espères**	tu **espères**
il **espère**	il **espère**
elle **espère**	elle **espère**
nous espérons	nous espérions
vous espérez	vous espériez
ils **espèrent**	ils **espèrent**
elles **espèrent**	elles **espèrent**

Future	*Conditional*
j'**espérerai**	j'**espérerais**
tu **espéreras**	tu **espérerais**
il **espérera**	il **espérerait**
elle **espérera**	elle **espérerait**
nous **espérerons**	nous **espérerions**
vous **espérerez**	vous **espéreriez**
ils **espéreront**	ils **espéreraient**
elles **espéreront**	elles **espéreraient**

Verbs conjugated like **espérer** include verbs in **-éder**, **-érer**, **-éter** etc:

accéder	to accede to
céder	to yield
célébrer	to celebrate
compléter	to complete
considérer	to consider
décéder	to die
digérer	to digest
gérer	to manage
inquiéter	to worry
libérer	to free
opérer	to operate
pénétrer	to penetrate
persévérer	to persevere
posséder	to possess
précéder	to precede
préférer	to prefer
protéger	to protect
récupérer	to recover
refréner	to curb
régler	to rule

régner	to reign
répéter	to repeat, to rehearse
révéler	to reveal
sécher	to dry
succéder	to succeed
suggérer	to suggest
tolérer	to tolerate

C AUXILIARIES AND THE FORMATION OF COMPOUND TENSES

1 Formation

a) The two auxiliary verbs **AVOIR** and **ETRE** are used with the past participle of a verb to form compound tenses.

b) *The past participle*

The regular past participle is formed by taking the stem of the infinitive and adding the following endings:

-er	-ir	-re
aim(**er**) + **é**	fin(**ir**) + **i**	vend(**re**) + **u**
aim**é**	fin**i**	vend**u**

For the agreement of past participles see pp B35-6.

c) *Compound tenses*

In French there are seven compound tenses: perfect, pluperfect, future perfect, past conditional (conditional perfect), past anterior, perfect subjunctive, pluperfect subjunctive.

2 Verbs conjugated with AVOIR

a) *Perfect*	b) *Pluperfect*
present of **avoir** + past participle	imperfect of **avoir** + past participle
j'ai aimé	**j'avais aimé**
tu as aimé	**tu avais aimé**
il a aimé	**il avait aimé**
elle a aimé	**elle avait aimé**
nous avons aimé	**nous avions aimé**
vous avez aimé	**vous aviez aimé**
ils ont aimé	**ils avaient aimé**
elles ont aimé	**elles avaient aimé**

c) *Future Perfect*	d) *Past Conditional*
future of **avoir** + past participle	conditional of **avoir** + past participle
j'aurai aimé	**j' aurais aimé**
tu auras aimé	**tu aurais aimé**
il aura aimé	**il aurait aimé**
elle aura aimé	**elle aurait aimé**
nous aurons aimé	**nous aurions aimé**
vous aurez aimé	**vous auriez aimé**
ils auront aimé	**ils auraient aimé**
elles auront aimé	**elles auraient aimé**

e) *Past Anterior*

past historic of **avoir** + past participle

j'eus aimé
tu eus aimé
il eut aimé
elle eut aimé
nous eûmes aimé
vous eûtes aimé
ils eurent aimé
elles eurent aimé

f) *Perfect Subjunctive*	g) *Pluperfect Subjunctive*
present subjunctive of **avoir** + past participle	pluperfect subjunctive of **avoir** + past participle
j'aie aimé	**j'eusse aimé**
tu aies aimé	**tu eusses aimé**
il ait aimé	**il eût aimé**
elle ait aimé	**elle eût aimé**
nous ayons aimé	**nous eussions aimé**
vous ayez aimé	**vous eussiez aimé**
ils aient aimé	**ils eussent aimé**
elles aient aimé	**elles eussent aimé**

3 Verbs conjugated with ETRE

a) *Perfect*	b) *Pluperfect*
present of **être** + past participle	imperfect of **être** + past participle
je suis arrivé(e)	**j'étais arrivé(e)**
tu es arrivé(e)	**tu étais arrivé(e)**
il est arrivé	**il était arrivé**
elle est arrivée	**elle était arrivée**
nous sommes arrivé(e)s	**nous étions arrivé(e)s**
vous êtes arrivé(e)(s)	**vous étiez arrivé(e)(s)**
ils sont arrivés	**ils étaient arrivés**
elles sont arrivées	**elles étaient arrivées**

c) *Future Perfect*	d) *Past Conditional*
future of **être** + past participle	conditional of **être** + past participle
je serai arrivé(e)	**je serais arrivé(e)**
tu seras arrivé(e)	**tu serais arrivé(e)**
il sera arrivé	**il serait arrivé**
elle sera arrivée	**elle serait arrivée**
nous serons arrivé(e)s	**nous serions arrivé(e)s**
vous serez arrivé(e)(s)	**vous seriez arrivé(e)(s)**
ils seront arrivés	**ils seraient arrivés**
elles seront arrivées	**elles seraient arrivées**

e) *Past Anterior*

past historic of **être** + past participle

je fus arrivé(e)
tu fus arrivé(e)
il fut arrivé
elle fut arrivée
nous fûmes arrivé(e)s
vous fûtes arrivé(e)(s)
ils furent arrivés
elles furent arrivées

f) *Perfect Subjunctive*	g) *Pluperfect Subjunctive*
present subjunctive of **être** + past participle	imperfect subjunctive of **être** + past participle
je sois arrivé(e)	**je fusse arrivé(e)**
tu sois arrivé(e)	**tu fusses arrivé(e)**
il soit arrivé	**il fût arrivé**
elle soit arrivée	**elle fût arrivée**
nous soyons arrivé(e)s	**nous fussions arrivé(e)s**
vous soyez arrivé(e)(s)	**vous fussiez arrivé(e)(s)**
ils soient arrivés	**ils fussent arrivés**
elles soient arrivées	**elles fussent arrivées**

4 AVOIR or ETRE?

a) *Verbs conjugated with* ***avoir***

The compound tenses of most verbs are formed with **avoir**:

j'ai marqué un but	**elle a dansé toute la nuit**
I scored a goal	she danced all night

b) *Verbs conjugated with* ***être***

i) all reflexive verbs (see p B26):

je me suis baigné
I had a bath

ii) the following verbs (mainly of motion):

aller	to go
arriver	to arrive
descendre	to go/come down
entrer	to go/come in
monter	to go/come up
mourir	to die

naître	to be born
partir	to leave
passer	to go through, to drop in
rester	to remain
retourner	to return
sortir	to go/come out
tomber	to fall
venir	to come

and most of their compounds:

revenir	to come back
devenir	to become
parvenir	to reach, to manage to
rentrer	to return home
remonter	to go up again
redescendre	to go down again

But: **prévenir** (to warn) and **subvenir** (to provide for) take a direct object and are conjugated with **avoir**.

Note: **passer** can also be conjugated with **avoir**:

il a passé par Paris
he went via Paris

Some of the verbs listed above can take a direct object. In such cases they are conjugated with **avoir** and can take on a different meaning:

descendre	to take/bring down, to go down (*the stairs, a slope*)
monter	to take/bring up, to go up (*the stairs, a slope*)
rentrer	to take/bring/put in
retourner	to turn over
sortir	to take/bring out

les élèves sont sortis à midi
the pupils came out at midday

les élèves ont sorti leurs livres
the pupils took out their books

elle n'est pas encore descendue
she hasn't come down yet

elle a descendu un vieux tableau de l'atelier
she brought an old painting down from the loft

elle a descendu l'escalier
she came down the stairs

les prisonniers sont montés sur le toit
the prisoners climbed on to the roof

le garçon a monté les bouteilles de vin de la cave
the waiter brought the bottles of wine up from the cellar

nous sommes rentrés tard
we returned home late

j'ai rentré la voiture dans le garage
I put the car in the garage

je serais retourné à Paris
I would have returned to Paris

le jardinier a retourné le sol
the gardener turned over the soil

ils sont sortis de la piscine
they got out of the swimming pool

le gangster a sorti un revolver
the gangster pulled out a revolver

D REFLEXIVE VERBS

1 Definition

Reflexive verbs are so called because they 'reflect' the action back onto the subject. Reflexive verbs are always accompanied by a reflexive pronoun; eg in the following sentence:

I looked at myself in the mirror

'myself' is the reflexive pronoun.

je lave la voiture
I'm washing the car

je *me* lave
I'm washing *myself*

j'ai couché le bébé
I put the baby to bed

je *me* suis couché
I went to bed (I put *myself* to bed)

2 Reflexive pronouns

They are:

Person	*Singular*	*Plural*
1st	**me (m')** myself	**nous** ourselves
2nd	**te (t')** yourself	**vous** yourself/selves
3rd	**se (s')** himself, herself, itself, oneself	**se (s')** themselves

Note:

a) **m', t'** and **s'** are used instead of **me, te** and **se** in front of a vowel or a silent **h**:

tu t'amuses ? – non, je m'ennuie
are you enjoying yourself? – no, I'm bored

il s'habille à la salle de bain
he gets dressed in the bathroom

b) French reflexive pronouns are often not translated in English:

je me demande si ...
I wonder if ...

ils se moquent de moi
they're making fun of me

c) Plural reflexive pronouns can also be used to express reciprocal actions; in this case they are translated by 'each other' or 'one another':

nous nous détestons
we hate one another

ils ne se parlent pas
they're not talking to each other

d) **se** can mean 'ourselves' or 'each other' when it is used with the pronoun **on** meaning 'we' (see p B15):

on s'est perdu
we got lost

on se connaît
we know each other

3 Position of reflexive pronouns

Reflexive pronouns are placed immediately before the verb, except in positive commands, where they follow the verb and are linked to it by a hyphen:

tu te dépêches ?
will you hurry up?

dépêchons-nous !
let's hurry!

ne t'inquiète pas
don't worry

ne vous fiez pas à lui
don't trust him

Note: reflexive pronouns change to emphatic (disjunctive) pronouns in positive commands:

elle doit se reposer
she needs to rest

repose-toi
have a rest

4 Conjugation of reflexive verbs

a) *Simple tenses*

These are formed in the same way as for non-reflexive verbs, except that a reflexive pronoun is used.

b) *Compound tenses*

These are formed with the auxiliary **être** followed by the past participle of the verb.

A full conjugation table is given on p B44.

5 Agreement of the past participle

a) In most cases, the reflexive pronoun is a direct object and the past participle of the verb agrees in number and in gender with the reflexive pronoun:

il s'est trompé
he made a mistake

elle s'est endormie
she fell asleep

ils se sont excusés
they apologized

elles se sont assises
they sat down

b) When the reflexive pronoun is used as an indirect object, the past participle does not change:

nous nous sommes écrit
we wrote to each other

elle se l'est acheté
she bought it for herself

When the reflexive verb has a direct object, the reflexive pronoun is the indirect object of the reflexive verb and the past participle does not agree with it:

Caroline s'est tordu la cheville
Caroline sprained her ankle

vous vous êtes lavé les mains, les filles ?
did you wash your hands, girls?

6 Common reflexive verbs

s'en aller to go away	**s'éloigner (de)** to move away (from)	**se moquer de** to laugh at
s'amuser to have fun	**s'endormir** to fall asleep	**s'occuper de** to take care of
s'appeler to be called	**s'ennuyer** to be bored	**se passer** to happen
s'approcher (de) to come near	**s'étonner (de)** to be surprised at	**se passer de** to do without
s'arrêter to stop	**s'excuser (de)** to apologize (for)	**se promener** to go for a walk
s'asseoir to sit down	**se fâcher** to get angry/ fall out	**se rappeler** to remember
s'attendre à to expect	**s'écrier** to cry out/exclaim	**se raser** to shave
se baigner to have a bath	**s'habiller** to get dressed	**se renseigner** to make enquiries
se battre to fight	**se hâter** to hurry	**se ressembler** to look alike
se blesser to hurt oneself	**s'inquiéter** to worry	**se retourner** to turn round
se coucher to go to bed	**s'installer** to settle down	**se réveiller** to wake up
se débarrasser de to get rid of	**se laver** to wash	**se sauver** to run away
se demander to wonder	**se lever** to get up	**se souvenir (de)** to remember
se dépêcher to hurry	**se mêler de** to meddle with	**se taire** to be/keep quiet
se déshabiller to undress	**se mettre à** to start	**se tromper** to be mistaken
se diriger vers to move towards	**se mettre en route** to set off	**se trouver** to be (situated)

E IMPERSONAL VERBS

1 Conjugation

Impersonal verbs are used only in the third person singular and in the infinitive. The subject is always the impersonal pronoun **il** = it.

il neige
it's snowing

il y a du brouillard
it's foggy

2 List of impersonal verbs

a) *verbs describing the weather*

i) **faire** + adjective:

il fait beau/chaud
it's fine/warm

il fait frais/froid
it's cool/cold

il fera beau demain
the weather will be good tomorrow

il va faire très froid
it will be very cold

ii) **faire** + noun:

il fait beau temps
the weather is nice

il fait mauvais temps
the weather is bad

Note: **il fait jour**
it's day(light)

il fait nuit
it's dark

iii) other impersonal verbs and verbs used impersonally to describe the weather:

il gèle	**(geler)**	it's freezing
il grêle	**(grêler)**	it's hailing
il neige	**(neiger)**	it's snowing
il pleut	**(pleuvoir)**	it's raining
il tonne	**(tonner)**	it's thundering

Note: some of these verbs may be used personally:

je gèle I am freezing

iv) **il y a** + noun:

il y a des nuages	it's cloudy
il y a du brouillard	it's foggy
il y a du verglas	it's icy

b) ***être***

i) **il est** + noun:

il est cinq heures	it's five o'clock
il était une fois un géant	there was once a giant

ii) **il est** + adjective + **de** + infinitive:

il est difficile de	it's difficult to
il est facile de	it's easy to
il est nécessaire de	it's necessary to
il est inutile de	it's useless to
il est possible de	it's possible to

il est difficile d'en parler
it is difficult to speak about it

Note: the indirect object pronoun in French corresponds to the English 'for me, for him' etc:

il m'est difficile d'en parler
it is difficult for me to speak about it

iii) **il est** + adjective +**que**:

il est douteux que	it's doubtful that
il est évident que	it's clear that
il est possible que	it's possible that
il est probable que	it's probable that
il est peu probable que	it's unlikely that
il est vrai que	it's true that

Note: **que** may be followed by the indicative or the subjunctive (see p B30):

il est probable qu'il ne viendra pas
he probably won't come

il est peu probable qu'il vienne
it's unlikely that he'll come

c) ***arriver, se passer*** *(to happen)*

il est arrivé une chose curieuse
a strange thing happened

que se passe-t-il ?
what's happening

d) ***exister*** *(to exist)*, ***rester*** *(to remain)*, ***manquer*** *(to be missing)*

il existe trois exemplaires de ce livre
there are three copies of this book

il me restait six francs
I had six francs left

il me manque vingt francs
I am twenty francs short

e) ***paraître, sembler*** *(to seem)*

il paraîtrait/semblerait qu'il ait changé d'avis
it would appear that he has changed his mind

il paraît qu'il va se marier
it seems he's going to get married

il me semble que le professeur s'est trompé
it seems to me that the teacher has made a mistake

f) *other common impersonal verbs*

i) ***s'agir*** *(to be a matter of)*

may be followed by a noun, a pronoun or an infinitive:

il s'agit de ton avenir
it's about your future

de quoi s'agit-il ?
what is it about?

il s'agit de trouver le coupable
we must find the culprit

ii) falloir (*to be necessary*)

may be followed by a noun, an infinitive or the subjunctive:

il faut deux heures pour aller à Paris it takes two hours to get to Paris	**il me faut plus de temps** I need more time

il faudra rentrer plus tôt ce soir
we'll have to come home earlier tonight

il faut que tu parles à Papa
you'll have to speak to your Dad

iii) suffire (*to be enough*)

may be followed by a noun, an infinitive or the subjunctive:

il suffit de peu de choses pour être heureux
it takes little to be happy

il suffit de passer le pont
you only have to cross the bridge

il suffira qu'ils te donnent le numéro de téléphone
they will only have to give you the telephone number

iv) valoir mieux (*to be better*)

may be followed by an infinitive or the subjunctive:

il vaudrait mieux prendre le car
it would be better to take the coach

il vaut mieux que vous ne sortiez pas seule le soir
you'd better not go out alone at night

F TENSES

For the formation of the different tenses, see pp B22-3 and B25.

Note: French has no continuous tenses (as in 'I am eating', 'I was going', 'I will be arriving'). The 'be' and '-ing' parts of English continuous tenses are not translated as separate words. Instead, the equivalent tense is used in French:

I am eating	**je mange**
I will be eating	**je mangerai**

1 Present

The present is used to describe what someone does/ something that happens regularly, or what someone is doing/ something that is happening at the time of speaking.

a) *regular actions*

il travaille dans un bureau he works in an office	**je lis rarement le journal** I seldom read the paper

b) *continuous actions*

ne le dérangez pas, il travaille
don't disturb him, he's working

je ne peux pas venir, je garde mon petit frère
I can't come, I'm looking after my little brother

Note: the continuous nature of the action can also be expressed by using the phrase **être en train de** (to be in the process of) + infinitive:

je suis en train de cuisiner
I'm (busy) cooking

c) *immediate future*

je pars demain
I'm leaving tomorrow

But: the present cannot be used after **quand** and other conjunctions of time when the future is implied (see pp B29-30):

je le ferai quand j'aurai le temps
I'll do it when I have the time

d) *general truths*

la vie est dure
life is hard

2 Imperfect

The imperfect is a past tense used to express what someone was doing or what someone used to do or to describe something in the past. The imperfect refers particularly to something that *continued* over a period of time, as opposed to something that happened at a specific point in time.

a) *continuous actions*

The imperfect describes an action that was happening eg when something else took place (imperfect means unfinished):

il prenait un bain quand le téléphone a sonné
he was having a bath when the phone rang

excuse-moi, je pensais à autre chose
I'm sorry, I was thinking of something else

Note: the continuous nature of the action can be emphasized by using **être en train de** + infinitive:

j'étais en train de faire le ménage
I was (busy) doing the housework

b) *regular actions in the past*

je le voyais souvent quand il habitait dans le quartier
I used to see him often when he lived in this area

quand il était plus jeune il voyageait beaucoup
when he was younger he used to travel a lot

c) *description in the past*

il faisait beau ce jour-là the weather was fine that day	**c'était formidable !** it was great!
elle portait une robe bleue she wore a blue dress	**elle donnait sur la rue** it looked onto the street

3 Perfect

The perfect tense is a compound past tense, used to express *single* actions which have been completed, ie what someone did or what someone has done/has been doing or something that has happened or has been happening:

je l'ai envoyé lundi I sent it on Monday	**on est sorti hier soir** we went out last night
tu t'es bien amusé ? did you have a good time	**je ne l'ai pas vu** I didn't see him
j'ai lu toute la journée I've been reading all day	**tu as déjà mangé ?** have you eaten?

Note: *Perfect or imperfect?*

In English, the simple past ('did', 'went', 'prepared') is used to describe both single and repeated actions in the past. In French, the perfect only describes single actions in the past, while repeated actions are expressed by the imperfect (they are sometimes signposted by 'used to'). Thus 'I went' should be translated 'j'allais' or 'je suis allé' depending on the nature of the action:

après dîner, je suis allé en ville
after dinner I went to town

l'an dernier, j'allais plus souvent au théâtre
last year, I went to the theatre more often

4 Past Historic

This tense is used in the same way as the perfect tense, to describe a single, completed action in the past (what someone did or something that happened). It is a literary tense, not common in everyday spoken French; it is found mainly as a narrative tense in written form:

le piéton ne vit pas arriver la voiture
the pedestrian didn't see the car coming

5 Pluperfect

This compound tense is used to express what someone had done/had been doing or something that had happened or had been happening:

il n'avait pas voulu aller avec eux
he hadn't wanted to go with them

elle était essoufflée parce qu'elle avait couru
she was out of breath because she'd been running

However, the pluperfect is not used as in English with **depuis** (for, since), or with **venir de** + infinitive (to have just done something). For details see sections **9** and **10**.

il neigeait depuis une semaine
it had been snowing for a week

les pompiers venaient d'arriver
the firemen had just arrived

6 Future

This tense is used to express what someone will do or will be doing or something that will happen or will be happening:

je ferai la vaisselle demain	**j'arriverai tard**
I'll do the dishes tomorrow	I'll be arriving late

Note: the future and not the present as in English is used in time clauses introduced by **quand** (when) or other conjunctions of time where the future is implied (see section **11**):

il viendra quand il le pourra
he'll come when he can

French makes frequent use of **aller** + infinitive (to be about to do something) to express the immediate future:

je vais vous expliquer ce qui s'est passé
I'll explain (to you) what happened

il va déménager la semaine prochaine
he's moving house next week

7 Future Perfect

This compound tense is used to describe what someone will have done/will have been doing in the future or to describe something that will have happened in the future:

j'aurai bientôt fini
I will soon have finished

In particular, it is used instead of the English perfect in time clauses introduced by **quand** or other conjunctions of time where the future is implied (see section **11**):

appelle-moi quand tu auras fini
call me when you've finished

on rentrera dès qu'on aura fait les courses
we'll come back as soon as we've done our shopping

8 Past Anterior

This tense is used instead of the pluperfect to express an action that preceded another action in the past (ie a past in the past). It is usually introduced by a conjunction of time (translated by 'when', 'as soon as', 'after' etc) and the main verb is in the past historic:

il se coucha dès qu'ils furent partis
he went to bed as soon as they'd left

à peine eut-elle raccroché que le téléphone sonna
she'd hardly hung up when the telephone rang

9 Use of tenses with depuis ('for', 'since')

a) The present must be used instead of the perfect to describe actions which started in the past and have continued until the present:

il habite ici depuis trois ans
he's been living here for three years

elle l'attend depuis ce matin
she's been waiting for him since this morning

But: The perfect, not the present, is used when the clause is negative or when the action has been completed:

il n'a pas pris de vacances depuis longtemps
he hasn't taken any holidays for a long time

j'ai fini depuis un bon moment
I've been finished for quite a while

Note:

i) **il y a ... que** or **voilà ... que** are also used with the present tense to translate 'for':

it's been ringing for ten minutes
ça sonne depuis dix minutes
il y a dix minutes que ça sonne
voilà dix minutes que ça sonne

ii) **depuis que** is used when 'since' introduces a clause, ie when there is a verb following **depuis**:

elle dort depuis que vous êtes partis
she's been sleeping since you left

iii) do not confuse **depuis** (for, since) and **pendant** (for, during): **depuis** refers to the starting point of an action which is still going on and **pendant** refers to the duration of an action which is over and is used with the perfect:

il vit ici depuis deux mois	**il a vécu ici pendant deux mois**
he's been living here for two months	he lived here for two months

b) the imperfect must be used instead of the pluperfect to describe an action which had started in the past and was still going on at a given time:

elle le connaissait depuis son enfance
she had known him since her childhood

il attendait depuis trois heures quand on est arrivé
he had been waiting for three hours when we arrived

But: if the sentence is negative or if the action has been completed, the pluperfect and not the imperfect is used:

je n'étais pas allé au théâtre depuis des années
I hadn't been to the theatre for years

il était parti depuis peu
he'd been gone for a short while

Note:

i) **il y avait ... que** + imperfect is also used to translate 'for':

she'd been living alone for a long time
elle habitait seule depuis longtemps
il y avait longtemps qu'elle habitait seule

ii) **depuis que** is used when 'since' introduces a clause; if it describes an action which was still going on at the time, it can be followed by the imperfect, otherwise it is followed by the pluperfect:

il pleuvait depuis que nous étions en vacances
it had been raining since we had been on holiday

il pleuvait depuis que nous étions arrivés
it had been raining since we arrived

iii) do not confuse **depuis** and **pendant**: **depuis** refers to the starting point of an action which is still going on and **pendant** refers to the duration of an action which is over; **pendant** is used with the pluperfect:

j'y travaillais depuis un an
I had been working there for a year

j'y avais travaillé pendant un an
I had worked there for a year

10 Use of tenses with venir de

venir de + infinitive means 'to have just done'.

a) if it describes something that has just happened, it is used in the present instead of the perfect:

l'avion vient d'arriver	**je viens de te le dire !**
the plane has just arrived	I've just told you!

b) if it describes something that had just happened, it is used in the imperfect instead of the pluperfect:

le film venait de commencer	**je venais de rentrer**
the film had just started	I'd just got home

11 Use of tenses after conjunctions of time

quand	when
tant que	as long as
dès/aussitôt que	as soon as
lorsque	when
pendant que	while

Verbs which follow these conjunctions must be used in the following tenses:

a) *future instead of present*

je te téléphonerai quand je serai prêt
I'll phone you when I am ready

on ira dès qu'il fera beau
we'll go as soon as the weather is fine

b) *future perfect instead of perfect* when the future is implied

on rentrera dès qu'on aura fini les courses
we'll come back as soon as we've done our shopping

je t'appellerai dès qu'il sera arrivé
I'll call you as soon as he has arrived

c) *conditional present/perfect instead of perfect/pluperfect* in indirect speech

il a dit qu'il sortirait quand il aurait fini
he said that he would come out when he had finished

For the tenses of the subjunctive and conditional, see below and p B31.

G MOODS

1 The Subjunctive

In spoken everyday French, the only two subjunctive tenses that are used are the present and the perfect. The imperfect and the pluperfect subjunctive are found mainly in literature or in texts of a formal nature.

The subjunctive is always preceded by the conjunction **que** and is used in subordinate clauses when the subject of the subordinate clause is different from the subject of the main verb.

Some clauses introduced by **que** take the indicative. But the subjunctive must be used after the following:

a) *Verbs of emotion*

être content que	to be pleased that
être déçu que	to be disappointed that
être désolé que	to be sorry that
être étonné que	to be surprised that
être fâché que	to be annoyed that
être heureux que	to be happy that
être surpris que	to be surprised that
être triste que	to be sad that
avoir peur que ... ne	to be afraid/to fear that
craindre que ... ne	to be afraid/to fear that
regretter que	to be sorry that

ils étaient contents que j'aille les voir
they were pleased (that) I went to visit them

je serais très étonné qu'il mente
I would be very surprised if he was lying

on regrette beaucoup que tu n'aies pas pu vendre ta voiture
we're very sorry (that) you couldn't sell your car

Note: **ne** is used after **craindre que** or **avoir peur que**, but does not have a negative meaning in itself and is not translated in English:

je crains que l'avion *ne* soit en retard
I'm afraid (that) the plane will be late

b) *Verbs of wishing and willing*

aimer que	to like
désirer que	to wish (that)
préférer que	to prefer (that)
souhaiter que	to wish (that)
vouloir que	to want

Note: In English, such verbs are often used in the following type of construction: verb of willing + object + infinitive (eg I'd like you to listen); this type of construction is impossible in French, where a subjunctive clause has to be used:

je souhaite que tu réussisses
I hope you will succeed

il aimerait que je lui écrive plus souvent
he'd like me to write to him more often

voulez-vous que je vous y amène en voiture ?
would you like me to drive you there?

préférez-vous que je rappelle demain ?
would you rather I called back tomorrow?

c) *Impersonal constructions* (expressing necessity, possibility, doubt, denial, preference)

il faut que	it is necessary (that) (*must*)
il est nécessaire que	it is necessary that (*must*)
il est important que	it is important (that)
il est possible que	it is possible that (*may*)
il se peut que	it is possible that (*may*)
il est impossible que	it is impossible (that) (*can't*)
il est douteux que	it is doubtful whether
il est peu probable que	it is unlikely that
il semble que	it seems (that)
il est préférable que	it is preferable (that)
il vaut mieux que	it is better (that) (*had better*)
c'est dommage que	it is a pity (that)

Note: these expressions may be used in any appropriate tense:

il faut qu'on se dépêche
we must hurry

il était important que tu le saches
it was important that you should know

il se pourrait qu'elle change d'avis
she might change her mind

il est peu probable qu'ils s'y intéressent
they're unlikely to be interested in that

il semble qu'elle ait raison
she appears to be right

il vaudrait mieux que tu ne promettes rien
you'd better not promise anything

c'est dommage que vous vous soyez manqués
it's a pity you missed each other

d) *Some verbs and impersonal constructions expressing doubt or uncertainty* (mainly used negatively or interrogatively)

douter que	to doubt (that)
(ne pas) croire que	(not) to believe (that)
(ne pas) penser que	(not) to think (that)
(ne pas) être sûr que	(not) to be sure that
il n'est pas certain que	it isn't certain that
il n'est pas évident que	it isn't obvious that
il n'est pas sûr que	it isn't certain that
il n'est pas vrai que	it isn't true that

je doute fort qu'il veuille t'aider
I very much doubt whether he'll want to help you

croyez-vous qu'il y ait des places de libres ?
do you think there are any seats available?

on n'était pas sûr que ce soit le bon endroit
we weren't sure that it was the right place

il n'était pas certain qu'elle puisse gagner
it wasn't certain whether she could win

e) ***attendre que*** (to wait until, to wait for someone to do something)

attendons qu'il revienne
let's wait until he comes back

f) *Some subordinating conjunctions*

bien que	although
quoique	although
sans que	without
pour que	so that
afin que	so that
à condition que	provided that
pourvu que	provided that
jusqu'à ce que	until
en attendant que	until
avant que ... (ne)	before
à moins que ... (ne)	unless
de peur que ... ne	for fear that
de crainte que ... ne	for fear that
de sorte que	so that
de façon que	so that
de manière que	so that

Note: When **ne** is shown in brackets, it may follow the conjunction, although it is seldom used in spoken French; it does not have a negative meaning, and is not translated in English.

il est allé travailler bien qu'il soit malade
he went to work although he was ill

elle est entrée sans que je la voie
she came in without me seeing her

voilà de l'argent pour que tu puisses aller au cinéma
here's some money so that you can go to the pictures

d'accord, pourvu que tu me promettes de ne pas le répéter
all right, as long as you promise not to tell anyone

tu l'as revu avant qu'il (ne) parte ?
did you see him again before he left?

je le ferai demain, à moins que ce (ne) soit urgent
I'll do it tomorrow, unless it's urgent

elle n'a pas fait de bruit de peur qu'il ne se réveille
she didn't make any noise, in case he would wake up

parle moins fort de sorte qu'elle ne nous entende pas
talk more quietly so that she doesn't hear us

Note: when **de façon/manière que** (so that) express a result, as opposed to a purpose, the indicative is used instead of the subjunctive:

il a fait du bruit, de sorte qu'elle l'*a entendu*
he made some noise, so that she heard him

g) *A superlative or adjectives like **premier** (first), **dernier** (last), **seul** (only) followed by **qui** or **que***

c'était le coureur le plus rapide que j'aie jamais vu
he was the fastest runner I ever saw

But: the indicative is used with a statement of fact rather than the expression of an opinion:

c'est le coureur le plus rapide qui a gagné
it was the fastest runner who won

h) *Negative and indefinite pronouns (eg **rien**, **personne**, **quelqu'un**) followed by **qui** or **que***

je ne connais personne qui sache aussi bien chanter
I don't know anyone who can sing so well

il n'y a aucune chance qu'il réussisse
he hasn't got a chance of succeeding

ils cherchent quelqu'un qui puisse garder le bébé
they're looking for someone who can look after the baby

2 Avoiding the subjunctive

The subjunctive can be avoided, as is the tendency with modern spoken French, provided that both verbs in the sentence have the same subject. It is replaced by an infinitive introduced by the preposition **de**, the preposition **à** or by no preposition at all (see pp B32-3).

a) ***de*** *+ infinitive replaces the subjunctive after*

i) verbs of emotion:

j'ai été étonné d'apprendre la nouvelle
I was surprised to hear the news

il regrette de ne pas avoir vu cette émission
he's sorry he didn't see this programme

tu as peur de ne pas avoir assez d'argent ?
are you worried you won't have enough money?

ii) **attendre** (to wait) and **douter** (to doubt):

j'attendrai d'avoir bu mon café
I'll wait until I've drunk my coffee

iii) most impersonal constructions:

il serait préférable de déclarer ces objets
it would be better to declare these things

il est important de garder votre billet
it's important that you should keep your ticket

iv) most conjunctions:

il est resté dans la voiture afin de ne pas se mouiller
he stayed in the car so as not to get wet

j'ai lu avant de m'endormir
I read before falling asleep

tu peux sortir, à condition de rentrer avant minuit
you can go out, as long as you're back before midnight

b) ***à*** *+ infinitive replaces the subjunctive after*

i) **de façon/manière:**

mets la liste sur la table, de manière à ne pas l'oublier
put the list on the table so that you won't forget it

ii) **premier, seul, dernier:**

il a été le seul à s'excuser
he was the only one who apologised

c) *the infinitive without any linking preposition replaces the subjunctive after*

i) verbs of wishing and willing:

je voudrais sortir avec toi
I'd like to go out with you

ii) **il faut, il vaut mieux:**

il vous faudra prendre des chèques de voyage
you'll have to take some traveller's cheques

il lui a fallu recommencer à zéro
he had to start all over again

il vaudrait mieux lui apporter des fleurs que des bonbons
it would be better to take her flowers than sweets

Note: an indirect object pronoun is often used with **il faut** to indicate the subject (who has to do something)

iii) verbs of thinking:

je ne crois pas le connaître
I don't think I know him

tu penses être chez toi à cinq heures ?
do you think you'll be home at five?

iv) **pour** and **sans**:

le car est reparti sans nous attendre
the coach left without waiting for us

j'économise pour pouvoir acheter une moto
I'm saving up to buy a motorbike

3 The Conditional

a) *The conditional present*

i) The conditional present is used to describe what someone would do or would be doing or what would happen (if something else were to happen):

si j'étais riche, j'*achèterais* un château
if I were rich, I *would buy* a castle

Note: when the main verb is in the conditional present, the verb after **si** is in the imperfect.

ii) It is also used in indirect questions or reported speech instead of the future:

il ne m'a pas dit s'il *viendrait*
he didn't tell me whether he *would come*

b) *The conditional perfect (or past conditional)*

The conditional perfect or past conditional is used to express what someone would have done or would have been doing or what would have happened:

si j'avais su, je n'aurais rien dit
if I had known, I wouldn't have said anything

qu'aurais-je fait sans toi ?
what would I have done without you?

Note: if the main verb is in the conditional perfect, the verb introduced by **si** is in the pluperfect.

c) *Tenses after **si***

The tense of the verb introduced by **si** is determined by the tense of the verb in the main clause:

Main verb		following '**SI**' Verb
conditional present	❹	imperfect
conditional perfect	❹	pluperfect

je te le dirais si je le savais
I would tell you if I knew

je te l'aurais dit si je l'avais su
I would have told you if I had known

Note: never use the conditional (or the future) with **si** unless **si** means whether (ie when it introduces an indirect question):

je me demande si j'y serais arrivé sans toi
I wonder if (= *whether*) I would have managed without you

4 The Imperative

a) *Definition*

The imperative is used to give commands, or polite instructions, or to make requests or suggestions; these can be positive (affirmative imperative: 'do!') or negative ('don't!'):

mange ta soupe !
eat your soup

n'aie pas peur !
don't be afraid!

partons !
let's go!

entrez !
come in!

faites attention !
be careful!

n'hésitez pas !
don't hesitate!

tournez à droite à la poste
turn right at the post office

b) *Forms*

The imperative has only three forms, which are the same as the **tu, nous** and **vous** forms of the present tense, but without the subject pronoun:

	-ER *Verbs*	**-IR** *Verbs*	**-RE** *Verbs*
'tu' form:	**regarde** watch	**choisis** choose	**attends** wait
'nous' form:	**regardons** let's watch	**choisissons** let's choose	**attendons** let's wait
'vous' form:	**regardez** watch	**choisissez** choose	**attendez** wait

Note:

i) the **-s** of the **tu** form of **-er** verbs is dropped, except when **y** or **en** follow the verb:

parle-lui !
speak to him!

But **parles-en avec lui**
speak to him about it

achète du sucre !
buy some sugar!

But **achètes-en un kilo**
buy a kilo (of it)

ii) the distinction between the subject pronouns **tu** and **vous** (see p B17) applies to the **tu** and **vous** forms of the imperative:

prends ta sœur avec toi, Alain
take your sister with you, Alain

prenez le plat du jour, Monsieur ; c'est du poulet rôti
have today's set menu, sir; it's roast chicken

les enfants, prenez vos imperméables ; il va pleuvoir
take your raincoats, children; it's going to rain

c) *Negative commands*

In negative commands, the verb is placed between **ne** and **pas** (or the second part of other negative expressions):

ne fais pas ça !
don't do that!

ne dites rien !
don't say anything!

d) *Imperative with object pronouns*

In positive commands, object pronouns come after the verb and are attached to it by a hyphen. In negative commands, they come before the verb (see pp B17-18):

dites-moi ce qui s'est passé
tell me what happened

attendons-les !
let's wait for them

prends-en bien soin, ne l'abîme pas !
take good care of it, don't damage it!

ne le leur dis pas !
don't tell them (that)!

ne les écoutez pas
don't listen to them

e) *Imperative of reflexive verbs*

The position of the reflexive pronoun of reflexive verbs is the same as that of object pronouns:

tais-toi !
be quiet!

levez-vous !
get up!

méfiez-vous de lui
don't trust him

arrêtons-nous ici
let's stop here

ne nous plaignons pas
let's not complain

ne t'approche pas plus !
don't come any closer!

f) *Alternatives to the imperative*

i) infinitive

the infinitive is often used instead of the imperative in written instructions and in recipes:

s'adresser au concierge
see the caretaker

ne pas fumer
no smoking

verser le lait et bien mélanger
pour in the milk and stir well

ii) subjunctive

as the imperative has no third person (singular or plural), **que** + subjunctive is used for giving orders in the third person:

que personne ne me dérange !
don't let anyone disturb me!

qu'il entre !
let him (come) in!

qu'elle parte, je m'en fiche !
I don't care if she goes!

g) *Idiomatic usage*

The imperative is used in spoken French in many set phrases. Here are some of the most common ones:

allons donc !
you don't say!
hey! (*protest*)

dis/ dites donc !
by the way!

tiens/tenez !
here you are!

tiens ! voilà le facteur
ah! here comes the postman

tiens (donc) !
(oh) really?

tiens ! tiens !
well, well! (fancy that!)

voyons !
come (on) now!

voyons donc !
let's see now

H THE INFINITIVE

1 The infinitive is the basic form of the verb. It is recognized by its ending, which is found in three forms corresponding to the three conjugations: -er, -ir, -re.

These endings give the verb the meaning 'to ...':

acheter
to buy

choisir
to choose

vendre
to sell

Note: although this applies as a general rule, the French infinitive will often be translated by a verb form in *-ing* (see p B62).

2 Uses of the infinitive

The infinitive can follow a preposition, a verb, a noun, a pronoun, an adverb or an adjective.

a) *After a preposition*

The infinitive can be used after some prepositions (**pour, avant de, sans, au lieu de, afin de** etc):

sans attendre
without waiting

avant de partir
before leaving

b) *After a verb*

There are three main constructions when a verb is followed by an infinitive:

i) with no linking preposition

ii) with the linking preposition **à**

iii) with the linking preposition **de**

i) Verbs followed by the infinitive with no linking preposition:

★ verbs of wishing and willing, eg:

vouloir	to want
souhaiter	to wish
désirer	to wish, to want
espérer	to hope

voulez-vous manger maintenant ou plus tard ?
do you want to eat now or later?

je souhaite parler au directeur
I wish to speak to the manager

★ verbs of seeing, hearing and feeling, eg:

voir	to see
écouter	to listen to
regarder	to watch
sentir	to feel, to smell
entendre	to hear

je l'ai vu jouer
I've seen him play

tu m'as regardé danser ?
did you watch me dance?

j'ai entendu quelqu'un crier
I heard someone shout

★ verbs of motion, eg:

aller	to go
monter	to go/come up
venir	to come
entrer	to go/come in
rentrer	to go/come home
sortir	to go/come out
descendre	to go/come down

je viendrai te voir demain
I'll come and see you tomorrow

il est descendu laver la voiture
he went down to wash the car

va acheter le journal
go and buy the paper

Note: in English, 'to come' and 'to go' may be linked to the verb that follows by 'and'; 'and' is not translated in French.

aller + infinitive can be used to express a future action, eg what someone is going to do:

qu'est-ce que tu vas faire demain ?
what are you going to do tomorrow?

★ modal auxiliary verbs (see pp B36-7)

★ verbs of liking and disliking, eg:

aimer	to like
adorer	to love
aimer mieux	to prefer
détester	to hate
préférer	to prefer

tu aimes voyager ?
do you like travelling?

j'aime mieux attendre
I'd rather wait

je déteste aller à la campagne
I hate going to the country

j'adore faire la grasse matinée
I love having a long lie in

★ some impersonal verbs (see p B27)

★ a few other verbs, eg:

compter	to intend to
sembler	to seem
laisser	to let, to allow
faillir	'to nearly' (do)
oser	to dare

ils l'ont laissé partir
they let him go

je n'ose pas le lui demander
I daren't ask him

tu sembles être malade
you seem to be ill

je compte partir demain
I intend to leave tomorrow

j'ai failli manquer l'avion
I nearly missed the plane

★ in the following set expressions:

aller chercher	to go and get, to fetch
envoyer chercher	to send for
entendre dire (que)	to hear (that)
entendre parler de	to hear about
laisser tomber	to drop
venir chercher	to come and get
vouloir dire	to mean

va chercher ton argent
go and get your money

j'ai entendu dire qu'il était journaliste
I've heard that he is a journalist

tu as entendu parler de ce film ?
have you heard about this film?

ne le laisse pas tomber !
don't drop it!

ça veut dire 'demain'
it means 'tomorrow'

ii) Verbs followed by **à** + infinitive:

A list of these is given on p B49:

je dois aider ma mère à préparer le déjeuner
I must help my mother prepare lunch

il commence à faire nuit
it's beginning to get dark

alors, tu t'es décidé à y aller ?
so you've made up your mind to go?

je t'invite à venir chez moi pour les vacances de Noël
I invite you to come to my house for the Christmas holidays

je passe mon temps à lire et à regarder la télé
I spend my time reading and watching TV

cela sert à nettoyer les disques
this is used for cleaning records

iii) Verbs followed by **de** + infinitive:

A list of these is given on p B49:

je crois qu'il s'est arrêté de pleuvoir
I think it's stopped raining

tu as envie de sortir ?
do you feel like going out?

le médecin a conseillé à Serge de rester au lit
the doctor advised Serge to stay in bed

j'ai décidé de rester chez moi
I decided to stay at home

essayons de faire du stop
let's try and hitch-hike

tu as fini de m'ennuyer ?
will you stop annoying me?

demande à Papa de t'aider
ask your Dad to help you

je t'interdis d'y aller
I forbid you to go

n'oublie pas d'en acheter !
don't forget to buy some!

j'ai refusé de le faire
I refused to do it

je vous prie de m'excuser
please forgive me

il vient de téléphoner
he's just phoned

c) *After a noun, a pronoun, an adverb or an adjective*

There are two possible constructions: with **à** or with **de**.

i) with the linking preposition **à**:

il avait plusieurs clients à voir
he had several customers to see

c'est difficile à dire
it's difficult to say

ii) with the linking preposition **de**:

je suis content de te voir
I am pleased to see you

iii) **à** or **de** with pronouns, adverbs or nouns?

★ **à** conveys the idea of something to do or to be done after the following:

beaucoup	a lot
plus	more
tant	so much
trop	too much
assez	enough
moins	less
rien	nothing
tout	everything
quelque chose	something

une maison à vendre
a house for sale

j'ai des examens à préparer
I've got exams to prepare

il nous a indiqué la route à suivre
he showed us the road to follow

il y a trop de livres à lire
there are too many books to read

il n'y a pas de temps à perdre
there's no time to lose

c'était une occasion à ne pas manquer
it was an opportunity not to be missed

★ **de** is used after nouns of an abstract nature, usually with the definite article, eg:

l'habitude de	the habit of
l'occasion de	the opportunity to
le temps de	the time to
le courage de	the courage to
l'envie de	the desire to
le besoin de	the need to
le plaisir de	the pleasure of
le moment de	the time to

il n'avait pas l'habitude d'être seul
he wasn't used to being alone

je n'ai pas le temps de lui parler
I don't have time to talk to him

avez-vous eu l'occasion de la rencontrer ?
did you have the opportunity to meet her?

ce n'est pas le moment de le déranger
now is not the time to disturb him

je n'ai pas eu le courage de le lui dire
I didn't have the courage to tell him

iv) **à** or **de** with adjectives?

★ **à** is used in a passive sense (something to be done) and after **c'est**:

un livre agréable à lire
a pleasant book to read

il est facile à satisfaire
he is easily satisfied

c'est intéressant à savoir
that's interesting to know

c'était impossible à faire
it was impossible to do

★ **de** is used after **il est** in an impersonal sense (see p B27):

il est intéressant de savoir que ...
it is interesting to know that ...

Note: for the use of **c'est** and **il est**, see p B63.

★ **de** is used after many adjectives, in particular those where the idea of 'of' is present in English, eg:

certain/sûr de	certain of/to
capable de	capable of
incapable de	incapable of
coupable de	guilty of

j'étais sûr de réussir
I was sure of succeeding

il est incapable d'y arriver seul
he is incapable of managing on his own

de is also used with adjectives of emotion, feeling and generally with adjectives denoting a state of mind, eg:

content de	pleased/happy to
surpris/étonné de	surprised to
fier de	proud to
heureux de	happy to
fâché de	annoyed to/at
triste de	sad to
gêné de	embarrassed to
désolé de	sorry for/to

j'ai été très content de recevoir ta lettre
I was very pleased to get your letter

elle sera surprise de vous voir
she will be surprised to see you

nous avons été très tristes d'apprendre la nouvelle
we were very sad to hear the news

But: **à** is used with **prêt à** (ready to) and **disposé à** (willing to):

es-tu prête à partir ?
are you ready to go?

je suis tout disposé à vous aider
I'm very willing to help you

d) ***faire*** + infinitive

faire is followed by an infinitive without any linking preposition to express the sense of 'having someone do something' or 'having something done'; two constructions are possible:

i) with one object

ii) with two objects

i) when only one object is used, it is a direct object:

je dois le faire réparer
I must have it fixed

il veut faire repeindre sa voiture
he wants to have his car resprayed

je ferai nettoyer cette veste ; je la ferai nettoyer
I'll have this jacket cleaned; I'll have it cleaned

tu m'as fait attendre !
you made me wait!

je le ferai parler
I'll make him talk

Note: the following set expressions:

faire entrer	to show in
faire venir	to send for

faites entrer ce monsieur
show this gentleman in

je vais faire venir le docteur
I'll send for the doctor

ii) when both **faire** and the following infinitive have an object, the object of **faire** is indirect:

elle lui a fait prendre une douche
she made him take a shower

je leur ai fait ranger leur chambre
I made them tidy their room

e) *Infinitive used as subject of another verb:*

trouver un emploi n'est pas facile
finding a job isn't easy

3 The perfect infinitive

a) *Form*

The perfect or past infinitive is formed with the infinitive of the auxiliary **avoir** or **être** as appropriate (see pp B25-6), followed by the past participle of the verb, eg:

avoir mangé	**être allé**	**s'être levé**
to have eaten	to have gone	to have got up

b) *Use*

i) after the preposition **après** (after):

après avoir attendu une heure, il est rentré chez lui
after waiting for an hour, he went back home

il s'en est souvenu après s'être couché
he remembered after going to bed

ii) after certain verbs:

se souvenir de	to remember
remercier de	to thank for
regretter de	to regret, to be sorry for
être désolé de	to be sorry for

je vous remercie de m'avoir invité
I thank you for inviting me

il regrettait de leur avoir menti
he was sorry for lying to them

tu te souviens d'avoir fait cela ?
do you remember doing this ?

I PARTICIPLES

1 The present participle

a) *Formation*

Like the imperfect, the present participle is formed by using the stem of the first person plural of the present tense (the **nous** form less the **-ons** ending):

-ons is replaced by **-ant** (= English *-ing*)

Exceptions:

Infinitive	*Present Participle*
avoir to have	**ayant** having
être to be	**étant** being
savoir to know	**sachant** knowing

b) *Use as an adjective*

Used as an adjective, the present participle agrees in number and in gender with its noun or pronoun:

un travail fatigant tiring work	**la semaine suivante** the following week
ils sont très exigeants they're very demanding	**des nouvelles surprenantes** surprising news

c) *Use as a verb*

The present participle is used far less frequently in French than in English, and English present participles in *-ing* are often not translated by a participle in French (see p B62).

i) used on its own, the present participle corresponds to the English present participle:

ne voulant plus attendre, ils sont partis sans moi
not wanting to wait any longer, they left without me

pensant bien faire, j'ai insisté
thinking I was doing the right thing, I insisted

ii) **en** + present participle:

When the subject of the present participle is the same as that of the main verb, this structure is often used to express simultaneity (ie 'while doing something'), manner (ie 'by doing something') or to translate English phrasal verbs.

★ simultaneous actions

In English this structure is translated by:

- while/when/on + present participle (eg 'on arriving')
- while/when/as + subject + verb (eg 'as he arrived')

il est tombé en descendant l'escalier
he fell as he was going down the stairs

en le voyant, j'ai éclaté de rire
when I saw him, I burst out laughing

elle lisait le journal en attendant l'autobus
she was reading the paper while waiting for the bus

Note: the adverb **tout** is often used before **en** to emphasize the fact that both actions are simultaneous, especially when there is an element of contradiction:

elle écoutait la radio tout en faisant ses devoirs
she was listening to the radio while doing her homework

tout en protestant, je les ai suivis
under protest, I followed them

★ manner

when expressing how an action is done, **en** + participle is translated by: 'by' + participle, eg:

il gagne sa vie en vendant des voitures d'occasion
he earns his living (by) selling second-hand cars

j'ai trouvé du travail en lisant les petites annonces
I found a job by reading the classified ads

★ phrasal verbs of motion

en + present participle is often used to translate English phrasal verbs expressing motion, where the verb expresses the means of motion and a preposition expresses the direction of movement (eg 'to run out', 'to swim across').

In French, the English preposition is translated by a verb, while the English verb is translated by **en** + present participle:

il est sorti du magasin *en courant*
he *ran* out of the shop

elle a traversé la route *en titubant*
she *staggered* across the road

2 The past participle

a) *Forms*

For the formation of the past participle see p B25.

b) *Use*

The past participle is mostly used as a verb in compound tenses or in the passive, but it can also be used as an adjective. In either case, there are strict rules of agreement to be followed.

c) *Rules of agreement of the past participle*

i) When it is used as an adjective, the past participle always agrees with the noun or pronoun it refers to:

un pneu crevé a burst tyre	**une pomme pourrie** a rotten apple
ils étaient épuisés they were exhausted	**trois assiettes cassées !** three broken plates!

Note: in French, the past participle is used as an adjective to describe postures or attitudes of the body, where English uses the present participle. The most common of these are:

accoudé	leaning on one's elbows
accroupi	squatting
agenouillé	kneeling
allongé	lying (down)
appuyé (contre)	leaning (against)
couché	lying (down)
étendu	lying (down)
penché	leaning (over)
(sus)pendu	hanging

il est allongé sur le lit he's lying on the bed	**une femme assise devant moi** a woman sitting in front of me

ii) In compound tenses:

★ with the auxiliary **avoir**:

the past participle only agrees in number and gender with the direct object when the direct object comes before the participle, ie in the following cases:

- in a clause introduced by the relative pronoun **que**:

le jeu vidéo que j'ai acheté the video-game I bought	**la valise qu'il a perdue** the suitcase he lost

- with a direct object pronoun:

ta carte ? je l'ai reçue hier
your card? I got it yesterday

zut, mes lunettes ! je les ai laissées chez moi
blast, my glasses! I've left them at home

- in a clause introduced by **combien de**, **quel** (**quelle, quels, quelles**) or **lequel** (**laquelle, lesquels, lesquelles**):

combien de pays as-tu visités ?
how many countries have you visited?

laquelle avez-vous choisie ?
which one did you choose?

Note: if the direct object comes after the past participle, the participle remains in the masculine singular form:

on a rencontré des gens très sympathiques
we met some very nice people

★ with the auxiliary **être**

- the past participle agrees with the subject of the verb:

quand est-elle revenue ? when did she come back?	**elle était déjà partie** she'd already left
ils sont passés te voir ? did they come to see you?	**elles sont restées là** they stayed here

Note: this rule also applies when the verb is in the passive:

elle a été arrêtée
she's been arrested

- reflexive verbs

in most cases, the past participle of reflexive verbs agrees with the reflexive pronoun if the pronoun is a direct object; since the reflexive pronoun refers to the subject, the number and gender of the past participle are determined by the subject:

Jacques s'est trompé Jacques made a mistake	**Marie s'était levée tard** Marie had got up late
ils se sont disputés ? did they have an argument?	**elles se sont vues** they saw each other

Michèle et Marie, vous vous êtes habillées?
Michèle and Marie, have you got dressed yet?

But: the past participle does not agree when the reflexive pronoun is an indirect object:

elles se sont écrit
they wrote *to* each other

This is the case in particular where parts of the body are mentioned:

elle s'est lavé les cheveux she washed her hair	**ils se sont serré la main** they shook hands

J THE PASSIVE

1 Formation

The passive is used when the subject does not perform the action, but is subjected to it, eg:

the house has been sold   he was made redundant

Passive tenses are formed with the corresponding tense of the verb **être** ('to be', as in English), followed by the past participle of the verb, eg:

j'ai été invité
I was invited

The past participle must agree with its subject, eg:

elle a été renvoyée
she has been dismissed

ils seront déçus they will be disappointed	**elles ont été vues** they were seen

2 Avoidance of the passive

The passive is far less common in French than in English. In particular, an indirect object cannot become the subject of a sentence in French, ie the following sentence where 'he' is an indirect object has no equivalent in French: he was given a book (*ie a book was given to him*)

In general, French tries to avoid the passive wherever possible. This can be done in several ways:

a) *Use of the pronoun* **on**

on m'a volé mon portefeuille
my wallet has been stolen

on construit une nouvelle piscine
a new swimming pool is being built

en France, on boit beaucoup de vin
a lot of wine is drunk in France

b) *Agent becomes subject of the verb*

If the agent, ie the real subject, is mentioned in English, it can become the subject of the French verb:

la nouvelle va les surprendre
they will be surprised by *the news*

mon correspondent m'a invité
I've been invited by *my penfriend*

mon cadeau te plaît ?
are you pleased with *my present?*

c) *Use of a reflexive verb*

Reflexive forms can be created for a large number of verbs, particularly in the third person:

elle s'appelle Anne she is called Anne	**ton absence va se remarquer** your absence will be noticed
ce plat se mange froid this dish is eaten cold	**cela ne se fait pas ici** that isn't done here

d) *Use of* ***se faire*** + infinitive (when the subject is a person)

il s'est fait renverser par une voiture
he was run over by a car

je me suis fait voler (tout mon argent)
I've been robbed (of all my money)

3 Conjugation

For a complete conjugation table of a verb in the passive, see **être aimé** (to be loved) p B38.

K MODAL AUXILIARY VERBS

The modal auxiliary verbs are always followed by the infinitive. They express an obligation, a probability, an intention, a possibility or a wish rather than a fact.

The five modal auxiliary verbs are: **DEVOIR, POUVOIR, SAVOIR, VOULOIR** and **FALLOIR**.

1 Devoir (conjugation see p B41)

Expresses: a) obligation, necessity
b) probability
c) intention, expectation

a) *obligation*

nous devons arriver à temps we must arrive in time	**demain tu devras prendre le bus** tomorrow you'll have to take the bus
nous avions dû partir we had (had) to go	**j'ai dû avouer que j'avais tort** I had to admit that I was wrong

In the conditional, **devoir** may be used for advice, ie to express what should be done (conditional present) or should have been done (past conditional):

vous devriez travailler davantage
you ought to/should work harder

tu ne devrais pas marcher sur l'herbe
you shouldn't walk on the grass

tu aurais dû tout avouer
you should have admitted everything

tu n'aurais pas dû manger ces champignons
you shouldn't have eaten those mushrooms

Note: the French infinitive is translated by a past participle in English: **manger** eat*en*.

b) *probability*

il doit être en train de dormir
he must be sleeping (he's probably sleeping)

j'ai dû me tromper de chemin
I must have taken the wrong road

Note: in a past narrative sequence in the distant past 'must have' is translated by a pluperfect in French:

il dit qu'il avait dû se tromper de chemin
he said he must have taken the wrong road

c) *intention, expectation*

je dois aller chez le dentiste
I am supposed to go to the dentist's

le train doit arriver à 19h30
the train is due to arrive at 7.30 p.m.

2 Pouvoir (conjugation see p B45)

Expresses: a) capacity, ability
b) permission
c) possibility

a) *capacity/ability*

Superman peut soulever une maison
Superman can lift a house

cette voiture peut faire du 150
this car can go up to 93 mph

il était si faible qu'il ne pouvait pas sortir de son lit
he was so weak that he couldn't get out of bed

b) *permission*

puis-je entrer ? may I come in? **puis-je vous offrir du thé ?** may I offer you some tea?

c) *possibility*

cela peut arriver
it can happen

Note: **pouvoir** + the infinitive is usually replaced by **peut-être** and the finite tense: eg **il s'est peut-être trompé de livres** (he may have taken the wrong books).

In the conditional, **pouvoir** is used to express something that could or might be (conditional present) or that could or might have been (past conditional):

tu pourrais t'excuser
you might apologize

j'aurais pu vous prêter mon magnétophone
I could have lent you my tape-recorder

Note: with verbs of perception (eg **entendre** to hear, **sentir** to feel, to smell, **voir** to see), **pouvoir** is often omitted:

j'entendais le bruit des vagues
I could hear the sound of the waves

3 Savoir (conjugation see p B46)

Means: 'to know how to'

je sais/savais conduire une moto
I can/used to be able to ride a motorbike

4 Vouloir (conjugation see p B48)

Expresses: a) desire
b) wish
c) intention

a) *desire*

je veux partir I want to go **voulez-vous danser avec moi ?** will you dance with me?

b) *wish*

je voudrais être riche
I wish I were rich

je voudrais trouver un travail intéressant
I should like to find an interesting job

j'aurais voulu lui donner un coup de poing
I would have liked to punch him

c) *intention*

il a voulu sauter par la fenêtre
he tried to jump out of the window

Note: **veuillez**, the imperative of **vouloir**, is used as a polite form to express a request ('would you please'):

veuillez ne pas déranger
please do not disturb

5 Falloir (conjugation see p B43)

Expresses: necessity

il faut manger pour vivre
you must eat to live

il faudrait manger plus tôt ce soir
we should eat earlier tonight

il aurait fallu apporter des sandwichs
we should have brought sandwiches

Note: some of the above verbs can also be used without infinitive constructions. They then take on a different meaning (eg **devoir** = to owe, **savoir** = to know).

L CONJUGATION TABLES

The following verbs provided the main patterns of conjugation including the conjugation of the most common irregular verbs. They are arranged in alphabetical order.

-er verb (*see p B22*)		AIMER
-ir verb (*see p B22*)		FINIR
-re verb (*see p B22*)		VENDRE
Reflexive verb (*see pp B26-7*)		SE MEFIER
Verb with auxiliary **être** (*see pp B25-6*)		ARRIVER
Verb in the passive (*see p B36*)		ETRE AIME
Auxiliaries (*see pp B25-6*)		AVOIR
		ETRE
Verb in **-eler/-eter** (*see pp B23-4*)		APPELER
Verb in **e** + consonant + **er** (*see p B24*)		ACHETER
Verb in **é** + consonant + **er** (*see p B24*)		ESPERER
Modal auxiliaries (*see pp B36-7*)		DEVOIR
		POUVOIR
		SAVOIR
		VOULOIR
		FALLOIR
Irregular verbs	ALLER	METTRE
	CONDUIRE	OUVRIR
	CONNAITRE	PRENDRE
	CROIRE	RECEVOIR
	DIRE	TENIR
	DORMIR	VENIR
	ECRIRE	VIVRE
	FAIRE	VOIR

ACHETER to buy

Present
j'achète
tu achètes
il achète
nous achetons
vous achetez
ils achètent

Past Historic
j'achetai
tu achetas
il acheta
nous achetâmes
vous achetâtes
ils achetèrent

CONDITIONAL

Past Anterior
j'eus acheté etc

Future Perfect
j'aurai acheté etc

Imperfect
j'achetais
tu achetais
il achetait
nous achetions
vous achetiez
ils achetaient

Perfect
j'ai acheté
tu as acheté
il a acheté
nous avons acheté
vous avez acheté
ils ont acheté

Present
j'achèterais
tu achèterais
il achèterait
nous achèterions
vous achèteriez
ils achèteraient

Future
j'achèterai
tu achèteras
il achètera
nous achèterons
vous achèterez
ils achèteront

Pluperfect
j'avais acheté
tu avais acheté
il avait acheté
nous avions acheté
vous aviez acheté
ils avaient acheté

Past
j'aurais acheté
tu aurais acheté
il aurait acheté
nous aurions acheté
vous auriez acheté
ils auraient acheté

SUBJUNCTIVE

Present
j'achète
tu achètes
il achète
nous achetions
vous achetiez
ils achètent

Imperfect
j'achetasse
tu achetasses
il achetât
nous achetassions
vous achetiez
ils achetassent

Perfect
j'aie acheté
tu aies acheté
il ait acheté
nous ayons acheté
vous ayez acheté
ils aient acheté

IMPERATIVE
achète
achetons
achetez

INFINITIVE

Present
acheter

Past
avoir acheté

PARTICIPLE

Present
achetant

Past
acheté

AIMER to like, to love

Present
j'aime
tu aimes
il aime
nous aimons
vous aimez
ils aiment

Past Historic
j'aimai
tu aimas
il aima
nous aimâmes
vous aimâtes
ils aimèrent

CONDITIONAL

Past Anterior
j'eus aimé etc

Future Perfect
j'aurai aimé etc

Imperfect
j'aimais
tu aimais
il aimait
nous aimions
vous aimiez
ils aimaient

Perfect
j'ai aimé
tu as aimé
il a aimé
nous avons aimé
vous avez aimé
ils ont aimé

Present
j'aimerais
tu aimerais
il aimerait
nous aimerions
vous aimeriez
ils aimeraient

Future
j'aimerai
tu aimeras
il aimera
nous aimerons
vous aimerez
ils aimeront

Pluperfect
j'avais aimé
tu avais aimé
il avait aimé
nous avions aimé
vous aviez aimé
ils avaient aimé

Past
j'aurais aimé
tu aurais aimé
il aurait aimé
nous aurions aimé
vous auriez aimé
ils auraient aimé

SUBJUNCTIVE

Present
j'aime
tu aimes
il aime
nous aimions
vous aimiez
ils aiment

Imperfect
j'aimasse
tu aimasses
il aimât
nous aimassions
vous aimassiez
ils aimassent

Perfect
j'aie aimé
tu aies aimé
il ait aimé
nous ayons aimé
vous ayez aimé
ils aient aimé

IMPERATIVE
aime
aimons
aimez

INFINITIVE

Present
aimer

Past
avoir aimé

PARTICIPLE

Present
aimant

Past
aimé

ETRE AIME to be loved

Present
je suis aimé(e)
tu es aimé(e)
il (elle) est aimé(e)
nous sommes aimé(e)s
vous êtes aimé(e)(s)
ils (elles) sont aimé(e)s

Past Historic
je fus aimé(e)
tu fus aimé(e)
il (elle) fut aimé(e)
nous fûmes aimé(e)s
vous fûtes aimé(e)(s)
ils (elles) furent aimé(e)s

CONDITIONAL

Past Anterior
j'eus été aimé(e) etc

Future Perfect
j'aurai été aimé(e) etc

Imperfect
j'étais aimé(e)
tu étais aimé(e)
il (elle) était aimé(e)
nous étions aimé(e)s
vous étiez aimé(e)(s)
ils (elles) étaient aimé(e)s

Perfect
j'ai été aimé(e)
tu as été aimé(e)
il a (elle) été aimé(e)
nous avons été aimé(e)s
vous avez été aimé(e)(s)
ils (elles) ont été aimé(e)s

Present
je serais aimé(e)
tu serais aimé(e)
il (elle) serait aimé(e)
nous serions aimé(e)s
vous seriez aimé(e)(s)
ils (elles) seraient aimé(e)s

Future
je serai aimé(e)
tu seras aimé(e)
il (elle) sera aimé(e)
nous serons aimé(e)s
vous serez aimé(e)(s)
ils (elles) seront aimé(e)s

Pluperfect
j'avais été aimé(e)
tu avais été aimé(e)
il (elle) avait été aimé(e)
nous avions été aimé(e)s
vous aviez été aimé(e)(s)
ils (elles) avaient été aimé(e)s

Past
j'aurais été aimé(e)
tu aurais été aimé(e)
il (elle) aurait été aimé(e)
nous aurions été aimé(e)s
vous auriez été aimé(e)(s)
ils (elles) auraient été aimé(e)s

SUBJUNCTIVE

Present
je sois aimé(e)
tu sois aimé(e)
il (elle) soit aimé(e)
nous soyons aimé(e)s
vous soyez aimé(e)(s)
ils (elles) soient aimé(e)s

Imperfect
je fusse aimé(e)
tu fusses aimé(e)
il (elle) fût aimé(e)
nous fussions aimé(e)s
vous fussiez aimé(e)(s)
ils (elles) fussent aimé(e)s

Perfect
j'aie été aimé(e)
tu aies été aimé(e)
il (elle) ait été aimé(e)
nous ayons été aimé(e)s
vous ayez été aimé(e)(s)
ils (elles) aient été aimé(e)s

IMPERATIVE
sois aimé(e)
soyons aimé(e)s
soyez aimé(e)(s)

INFINITIVE

Present
être aimé(e)(s)

Past
avoir été aimé(e)(s)

PARTICIPLE

Present
étant aimé(e)(s)

Past
été aimé(e)(s)

ALLER to go

Present
j'vais
tu vas
il va
nous allons
vous allez
ils vont

Imperfect
j'allais
tu allais
il allait
nous allions
vous alliez
ils allaient

Future
j'irai
tu iras
il ira
nous irons
vous irez
ils iront

Past Historic
j'allai
tu allas
il alla
nous allâmes
vous allâtes
ils allèrent

Perfect
je suis allé(e)
tu es allé(e)
il (elle) est allé(e)
nous sommes allé(e)s
vous êtes allé(e)(s)
ils (elles) sont allé(e)s

Pluperfect
j'étais allé(e)
tu étais allé(e)
il (elle) était allé(e)
nous étions allé(e)s
vous étiez allé(e)(s)
ils (elles) étaient allé(e)s

Past Anterior
je fus allé(e) etc

Future Perfect
je serai allé(e) etc

CONDITIONAL

Present
j'irais
tu irais
il irait
nous irions
vous iriez
ils iraient

Past
je serais allé(e)
tu serais allé(e)
il (elle) serait allé(e)
nous serions allé(e)s
vous seriez allé(e)(s)
ils (elles) seraient allé(e)s

SUBJUNCTIVE

Present
j'aille
tu ailles
il aille
nous allions
vous alliez
ils aillent

Imperfect
j'allasse
tu allasses
il allât
nous allassions
vous allassiez
ils allassent

Perfect
je sois allé(e)
tu sois allé(e)
il (elle) soit allé(e)
nous soyons allé(e)s
vous soyez allé(e)(s)
ils (elles) soient allé(e)s

IMPERATIVE
va
allons
allez

INFINITIVE

Present
aller

Past
être allé(e)(s)

PARTICIPLE

Present
allant

Past
allé

APPELER to call

Present
j'appelle
tu appelles
il appelle
nous appelons
vous appelez
ils appellent

Imperfect
j'appelais
tu appelais
il appelait
nous appelions
vous appeliez
ils appelaient

Future
j'appellerai
tu appelleras
il appellera
nous appellerons
vous appellerez
ils appelleront

Past Historic
j'appelai
tu appelas
il appela
nous appelâmes
vous appelâtes
ils appelèrent

Perfect
j'ai appelé
tu as appelé
il a appelé
nous avons appelé
vous avez appelé
ils ont appelé

Pluperfect
j'avais appelé
tu avais appelé
il avait appelé
nous avions appelé
vous aviez appelé
ils avaient appelé

Past Anterior
j'eus appelé etc

Future Perfect
j'aurai appelé etc

CONDITIONAL

Present
j'appellerais
tu appellerais
il appellerait
nous appellerions
vous appelleriez
ils appelleraient

Past
j'aurais appelé
tu aurais appelé
il aurait appelé
nous aurions appelé
vous auriez appelé
ils auraient appelé

SUBJUNCTIVE

Present
j'appelle
tu appelles
il appelle
nous appelions
vous appeliez
ils appellent

Imperfect
j'appelasse
tu appelasses
il appelât
nous appelassions
vous appelassiez
ils appelassent

Perfect
j'aie appelé
tu aies appelé
il ait appelé
nous ayons appelé
vous ayez appelé
ils aient appelé

IMPERATIVE
appelle
appelons
appelez

INFINITIVE

Present
appeler

Past
avoir appelé

PARTICIPLE

Present
appelant

Past
appelé

ARRIVER to arrive, to happen

Present
j'arrive
tu arrives
il arrive
nous arrivons
vous arrivez
ils arrivent

Imperfect
j'arrivais
tu arrivais
il arrivait
nous arrivions
vous arriviez
ils arrivaient

Future
j'arriverai
tu arriveras
il arrivera
nous arriverons
vous arriverez
ils arriveront

Past Historic
j'arrivai
tu arrivas
il arriva
nous arrivâmes
vous arrivâtes
ils arrivèrent

Perfect
je suis arrivé(e)
tu es arrivé(e)
il (elle) est arrivé(e)
nous sommes arrivé(e)s
vous êtes arrivé(e)(s)
ils (elles) sont arrivé(e)s

Pluperfect
j'étais arrivé(e)
tu étais arrivé(e)
il (elle) était arrivé(e)
nous étions arrivé(e)s
vous étiez arrivé(e)(s)
ils (elles) étaient arrivé(e)s

Past Anterior
je fus arrivé(e) etc

Future Perfect
je serai arrivé(e) etc

CONDITIONAL

Present
j'arriverais
tu arriverais
il arriverait
nous arriverions
vous arriveriez
ils arriveraient

Past
je serais arrivé(e)
tu serais arrivé(e)
il (elle) serait arrivé(e)
nous serions arrivé(e)s
vous seriez arrivé(e)(s)
ils (elles) seraient arrivé(e)s

SUBJUNCTIVE

Present
j'arrive
tu arrives
il arrive
nous arrivions
vous arriviez
ils arrivent

Imperfect
j'arrivasse
tu arrivasses
il arrivât
nous arrivassions
vous arrivassiez
ils arrivassent

Perfect
je sois arrivé(e)
tu sois arrivé(e)
il (elle) soit arrivé(e)
nous soyons arrivé(e)s
vous soyez arrivé(e)(s)
ils (elles) soient arrivé(e)s

IMPERATIVE
arrive
arrivons
arrivez

INFINITIVE

Present
arriver

Past
être arrivé(e)(s)

PARTICIPLE

Present
arrivant

Past
arrivé

AVOIR to have

Present
j'ai
tu as
il a
nous avons
vous avez
ils ont

Imperfect
j'avais
tu avais
il avait
nous avions
vous aviez
ils avaient

Future
j'aurai
tu auras
il aura
nous aurons
vous aurez
ils auront

Past Historic
j'eus
tu eus
il eut
nous eûmes
vous eûtes
ils eurent

Perfect
j'ai eu
tu as eu
il a eu
nous avons eu
vous avez eu
ils ont eu

Pluperfect
j'avais eu
tu avais eu
il avait eu
nous avions eu
vous aviez eu
ils avaient eu

Past Anterior
j'eus eu etc

Future Perfect
j'aurai eu etc

CONDITIONAL

Present
j'aurais
tu aurais
il aurait
nous aurions
vous auriez
ils auraient

Past
j'aurais eu
tu aurais eu
il aurait eu
nous aurions eu
vous auriez eu
ils auraient eu

SUBJUNCTIVE

Present
j'aie
tu aies
il ait
nous ayons
vous ayez
ils aient

Imperfect
je eusse
tu eusses
il eût
nous eussions
vous eussiez
ils eussent

Perfect
j'aie eu
tu aies eu
il ait eu
nous ayons eu
vous ayez eu
ils aient eu

IMPERATIVE
aie
ayons
ayez

INFINITIVE

Present
avoir

Past
avoir eu

PARTICIPLE

Present
ayant

Past
eu

CONDUIRE to lead, to drive

Present
je conduis
tu conduis
il conduit
nous conduisons
vous conduisez
ils conduisent

Imperfect
je conduisais
tu conduisais
il conduisait
nous conduisions
vous conduisiez
ils conduisaient

Future
je conduirai
tu conduiras
il conduira
nous conduirons
vous conduirez
ils conduiront

Past Historic
je conduisis
tu conduisis
il conduisit,
nous conduisîmes
vous conduisîtes
ils conduisirent

Perfect
j'ai conduit
tu as conduit
il a conduit
nous avons conduit
vous avez conduit
ils ont conduit

Pluperfect
j'avais conduit
tu avais conduit
il avait conduit
nous avions conduit
vous aviez conduit
ils avaient conduit

Past Anterior
j'eus conduit etc

Future Perfect
j'aurai conduit etc

CONDITIONAL

Present
je conduirais
tu conduirais
il conduirait
nous conduirions
vous conduiriez
ils conduiraient

Past
j'aurais conduit
tu aurais conduit
il aurait conduit
nous aurions conduit
vous auriez conduit
ils auraient conduit

SUBJUNCTIVE

Present
je conduise
tu conduises
il conduise
nous conduisions
vous conduisiez
ils conduisent

Imperfect
je conduisisse
tu conduisisses
il conduisît
nous conduisissions
vous conduisissiez
ils conduisissent

Perfect
j'aie conduit
tu aies conduit
il ait conduit
nous ayons conduit
vous ayez conduit
ils aient conduit

IMPERATIVE
conduise
conduisons
conduisez

INFINITIVE

Present
conduire

Past
avoir conduit

PARTICIPLE

Present
conduisant

Past
conduit

CONNAITRE to know

Present
je connais
tu connais
il connaît
nous connaissons
vous connaissez
ils connaissent

Imperfect
je connaissais
tu connaissais
il connaissait
nous connaissions
vous connaissiez
ils connaissaient

Future
je connaîtrai
tu connaîtras
il connaîtra
nous connaîtrons
vous connaîtrez
ils connaîtront

Past Historic
je connus
tu connus
il connut
nous connûmes
vous connûtes
ils connurent

Perfect
j'ai connu
tu as connu
il a connu
nous avons connu
vous avez connu
ils ont connu

Pluperfect
j'avais connu
tu avais connu
il avait connu
nous avions connu
vous aviez connu
ils avaient connu

Past Anterior
j'eus connu etc

Future Perfect
j'aurai connu etc

CONDITIONAL

Present
je connaîtrais
tu connaîtrais
il connaîtrait
nous connaîtrions
vous connaîtriez
ils connaîtraient

Past
j'aurais connu
tu aurais connu
il aurait connu
nous aurions connu
vous auriez connu
ils auraient connu

SUBJUNCTIVE

Present
je connaisse
tu connaisses
il connaisse
nous connaissions
vous connaissiez
ils connaissent

Imperfect
je connusse
tu connusses
il connût
nous connussions
vous connussiez
ils connussent

Perfect
j'aie connu
tu aies connu
il ait connu
nous ayons connu
vous ayez connu
ils aient connu

IMPERATIVE
connais
connaissons
connaissez

INFINITIVE

Present
connaître

Past
avoir connu

PARTICIPLE

Present
connaissant

Past
connu

CROIRE to believe

Present
je crois
tu crois
il croit
nous croyons
vous croyez
ils croient

Past Historic
je crus
tu crus
il crut
nous crûmes
vous crûtes
ils crurent

Imperfect
je croyais
tu croyais
il croyait
nous croyions
vous croyiez
ils croyaient

Perfect
j'ai cru
tu as cru
il a cru
nous avons cru
vous avez cru
ils ont cru

Future
je croirai
tu croiras
il croira
nous croirons
vous croirez
ils croiront

Pluperfect
j'avais cru
tu avais cru
il avait cru
nous avions cru
vous aviez cru
ils avaient cru

CONDITIONAL

Past Anterior
j'eus cru etc

Future Perfect
j'aurai cru etc

Present
je croirais
tu croirais
il croirait
nous croirions
vous croiriez
ils croiraient

Past
j'aurais cru
tu aurais cru
il aurait cru
nous aurions cru
vous auriez cru
ils auraient cru

SUBJUNCTIVE

Present
je croie
tu croies
il croie
nous croyions
vous croyiez
ils croient

Imperfect
je crusse
tu crusses
il crût
nous crussions
vous crussiez
ils crussent

Perfect
j'aie cru
tu aies cru
il ait cru
nous ayons cru
vous ayez cru
ils aient cru

IMPERATIVE
crois
croyons
croyez

INFINITIVE

Present
croire

Past
avoir cru

PARTICIPLE

Present
croyant

Past
cru

DEVOIR to have to

Present
je dois
tu dois
il doit
nous devons
vous devez
ils doivent

Past Historic
je dus
tu dus
il dut
nous dûmes
vous dûtes
ils durent

Imperfect
je devais
tu devais
il devait
nous devions
vous deviez
ils devaient

Perfect
j'ai dû
tu as dû
il a dû
nous avons dû
vous avez dû
ils ont dû

Future
je devrai
tu devras
il devra
nous devrons
vous devrez
ils devront

Pluperfect
j'avais dû
tu avais dû
il avait dû
nous avions dû
vous aviez dû
ils avaient dû

CONDITIONAL

Past Anterior
j'eus dû etc

Future Perfect
j'aurai dû etc

Present
je devrais
tu devrais
il devrait
nous devrions
vous devriez
ils devraient

Past
j'aurais dû
tu aurais dû
il aurait dû
nous aurions dû
vous auriez dû
ils auraient dû

SUBJUNCTIVE

Present
je doive
tu doives
il doive
nous devions
vous deviez
ils doivent

Imperfect
je dusse
tu dusses
il dût
nous dussions
vous dussiez
ils dussent

Perfect
j'aie dû
tu aies dû
il ait dû
nous ayons dû
vous ayez dû
ils aient dû

IMPERATIVE
dois
devons
devez

INFINITIVE

Present
devoir

Past
avoir dû

PARTICIPLE

Present
devant

Past
dû

DIRE to say

Present
je dis
tu dis
il dit
nous disons
vous dites
ils disent

Past Historic
je dis
tu dis
il dit
nous dîmes
vous dîtes
ils dirent

Imperfect
je disais
tu disais
il disait
nous disions
vous disiez
ils disaient

Perfect
j'ai dit
tu as dit
il a dit
nous avons dit
vous avez dit
ils ont dit

Future
je dirai
tu diras
il dira
nous dirons
vous direz
ils diront

Pluperfect
j'avais dit
tu avais dit
il avait dit
nous avions dit
vous aviez dit
ils avaient dit

CONDITIONAL

Past Anterior
j'eus dit etc

Future Perfect
j'aurai dit etc

Present
je dirais
tu dirais
il dirait
nous dirions
vous diriez
ils diraient

Past
j'aurais dit
tu aurais dit
il aurait dit
nous aurions dit
vous auriez dit
ils auraient dit

SUBJUNCTIVE

Present
je dise
tu dises
il dise
nous disions
vous disiez
ils disent

Imperfect
je disse
tu disses
il dît
nous dissions
vous dissiez
ils dissent

Perfect
j'aie dit
tu aies dit
il ait dit
nous ayons dit
vous ayez dit
ils aient dit

IMPERATIVE
dis
disons
dites

INFINITIVE

Present
dire

Past
avoir dit

PARTICIPLE

Present
disant

Past
dit

DORMIR to sleep

Present
je dors
tu dors
il dort
nous dormons
vous dormez
ils dorment

Imperfect
je dormais
tu dormais
il dormait
nous dormions
vous dormiez
ils dormaient

Future
je dormirai
tu dormiras
il dormira
nous dormirons
vous dormirez
ils dormiront

Past Historic
je dormis
tu dormis
il dormit
nous dormîmes
vous dormîtes
ils dormirent

Perfect
j'ai dormi
tu as dormi
il a dormi
nous avons dormi
vous avez dormi
ils ont dormi

Pluperfect
j'avais dormi
tu avais dormi
il avait dormi
nous avions dormi
vous aviez dormi
ils avaient dormi

Past Anterior
j'eus dormi etc

Future Perfect
j'aurai dormi etc

CONDITIONAL

Present
je dormirais
tu dormirais
il dormirait
nous dormirions
vous dormiriez
ils dormiraient

Past
j'aurais dormi
tu aurais dormi
il aurait dormi
nous aurions dormi
vous auriez dormi
ils auraient dormi

SUBJUNCTIVE

Present
je dorme
tu dormes
il dorme
nous dormions
vous dormiez
ils dorment

Imperfect
je dormisse
tu dormisses
il dormît
nous dormissions
vous dormissiez
ils dormissent

Perfect
j'aie dormi
tu aies dormi
il ait dormi
nous ayons dormi
vous ayez dormi
ils aient dormi

IMPERATIVE
dors
dormons
dormez

INFINITIVE

Present
dormir

Past
avoir dormi

PARTICIPLE

Present
dormant

Past
dormi

ECRIRE to write

Present
j'écris
tu écris
il écrit
nous écrivons
vous écrivez
ils écrivent

Imperfect
j'écrivais
tu écrivais
il écrivait
nous écrivions
vous écriviez
ils écrivaient

Future
j'écrirai
tu écriras
il écrira
nous écrirons
vous écrirez
ils écriront

Past Historic
j'écrivis
tu écrivis
il écrivit
nous écrivîmes
vous écrivîtes
ils écrivirent

Perfect
j'ai écrit
tu as écrit
il a écrit
nous avons écrit
vous avez écrit
ils ont écrit

Pluperfect
j'avais écrit
tu avais écrit
il avait écrit
nous avions écrit
vous aviez écrit
ils avaient écrit

Past Anterior
j'eus écrit etc

Future Perfect
j'aurai écrit etc

CONDITIONAL

Present
j'écrirais
tu écrirais
il écrirait
nous écririons
vous écririez
ils écriraient

Past
j'aurais écrit
tu aurais écrit
il aurait écrit
nous aurions écrit
vous auriez écrit
ils auraient écrit

SUBJUNCTIVE

Present
j'écrive
tu écrives
il écrive
nous écrivions
vous écriviez
ils écrivent

Imperfect
j'écrivisse
tu écrivisses
il écrivît
nous écrivissions
vous écrivissiez
ils écrivissent

Perfect
j'aie écrit
tu aies écrit
il ait écrit
nous ayons écrit
vous ayez écrit
ils aient écrit

IMPERATIVE
écris
écrivons
écrivez

INFINITIVE

Present
écrire

Past
avoir écrit

PARTICIPLE

Present
écrivant

Past
écrit

ESPERER to hope

Present
j'espère
tu espères
il espère
nous espérons
vous espérez
ils espèrent

Imperfect
j'espérais
tu espérais
il espérait
nous espérions
vous espériez
ils espéraient

Future
j'espérerai
tu espéreras
il espérera
nous espérerons
vous espérerez
ils espéreront

Past Historic
j'espérai
tu espéras
il espéra
nous espérâmes
vous espérâtes
ils espérèrent

Perfect
j'ai espéré
tu as espéré
il a espéré
nous avons espéré
vous avez espéré
ils ont espéré

Pluperfect
j'avais espéré
tu avais espéré
il avait espéré
nous avions espéré
vous aviez espéré
ils avaient espéré

Past Anterior
j'eus espéré etc

Future Perfect
j'aurai espéré etc

CONDITIONAL

Present
j'espérerais
tu espérerais
il espérerait
nous espérerions
vous espéreriez
ils espéreraient

Past
j'aurais espéré
tu aurais espéré
il aurait espéré
nous aurions espéré
vous auriez espéré
ils auraient espéré

SUBJUNCTIVE

Present
j'espère
tu espères
il espère
nous espérions
vous espériez
ils espèrent

Imperfect
j'espérasse
tu espérasses
il espérât
nous espérassions
vous espérassiez
ils espérassent

Perfect
j'aie espéré
tu aies espéré
il ait espéré
nous ayons espéré
vous ayez espéré
ils aient espéré

IMPERATIVE
espère
espérons
espérez

INFINITIVE

Present
espérer

Past
avoir espéré

PARTICIPLE

Present
espérant

Past
espéré

ETRE to be

Present
je suis
tu es
il est
nous sommes
vous êtes
ils sont

Imperfect
j'étais
tu étais
il était
nous étions
vous étiez
ils étaient

Future
je serai
tu seras
il sera
nous serons
vous serez
ils seront

Past Historic
je fus
tu fus
il fut
nous fûmes
vous fûtes
ils furent

Perfect
j'ai été
tu as été
il a été
nous avons été
vous avez été
ils ont été

Pluperfect
j'avais été
tu avais été
il avait été
nous avions été
vous aviez été
ils avaient été

CONDITIONAL

Past Anterior
j'eus été etc

Future Perfect
j'aurai été etc

Present
je serais
tu serais
il serait
nous serions
vous seriez
ils seraient

Past
j'aurais été
tu aurais été
il aurait été
nous aurions été
vous auriez été
ils auraient été

SUBJUNCTIVE

Present
je sois
tu sois
il soit
nous soyons
vous soyez
ils soient

Imperfect
je fusse
tu fusses
il fût
nous fussions
vous fussiez
ils fussent

Perfect
j'aie été
tu aies été
il ait été
nous ayons été
vous ayez été
ils aient été

IMPERATIVE
sois
soyons
soyez

INFINITIVE

Present
être

Past
avoir été

PARTICIPLE

Present
étant

Past
été

FAIRE to do, to make

Present
je fais
tu fais
il fait
nous faisons
vous faites
ils font

Imperfect
je faisais
tu faisais
il faisait
nous faisions
vous faisiez
ils faisaient

Future
je ferai
tu feras
il fera
nous ferons
vous ferez
ils feront

Past Historic
je fis
tu fis
il fit
nous fîmes
vous fîtes
ils firent

Perfect
j'ai fait
tu as fait
il a fait
nous avons fait
vous avez fait
ils ont fait

Pluperfect
j'avais fait
tu avais fait
il avait fait
nous avions fait
vous aviez fait
ils avaient fait

CONDITIONAL

Past Anterior
j'eus fait etc

Future Perfect
j'aurai fait etc

Present
je ferais
tu ferais
il ferait
nous ferions
vous feriez
ils feraient

Past
j'aurais fait
tu aurais fait
il aurait fait
nous aurions fait
vous auriez fait
ils auraient fait

SUBJUNCTIVE

Present
je fasse
tu fasses
il fasse
nous fassions
vous fassiez
ils fassent

Imperfect
je fisse
tu fisses
il fît
nous fissions
vous fissiez
ils fissent

Perfect
j'aie fait
tu aies fait
il ait fait
nous ayons fait
vous ayez fait
ils aient fait

IMPERATIVE
fais
faisons
faites

INFINITIVE

Present
faire

Past
avoir fait

PARTICIPLE

Present
faisant

Past
fait

FALLOIR to be necessary

Present
il faut

Imperfect
il fallait

Future
il faudra

Past Historic
il fallut

Perfect
il a fallu

Pluperfect
il avait fallu

CONDITIONAL

Past Anterior
il eut fallu

Future Perfect
il aura fallu

Present
il faudrait

Past
il aurait fallu

SUBJUNCTIVE

Present
il faille

Imperfect
il fallût

Perfect
il ait fallu

IMPERATIVE

INFINITIVE

Present
falloir

Past
avoir fallu

PARTICIPLE

Present

Past
fallu

FINIR to finish

Present
je finis
tu finis
il finit
nous finissons
vous finissez
ils finissent

Past Historic
je finis
tu finis
il finit
nous finîmes
vous finîtes
ils finirent

Imperfect
je finissais
tu finissais
il finissait
nous finissions
vous finissiez
ils finissaient

Perfect
j'ai fini
tu as fini
il a fini
nous avons fini
vous avez fini
ils ont fini

Future
je finirai
tu finiras
il finira
nous finirons
vous finirez
ils finiront

Pluperfect
j'avais fini
tu avais fini
il avait fini
nous avions fini
vous aviez fini
ils avaient fini

CONDITIONAL

Past Anterior
j'eus fini etc

Future Perfect
j'aurai fini etc

Present
je finirais
tu finirais
il finirait
nous finirions
vous finiriez
ils finiraient

Past
j'aurais fini
tu aurais fini
il aurait fini
nous aurions fini
vous auriez fini
ils auraient fini

SUBJUNCTIVE

Present
je finisse
tu finisses
il finisse
nous finissions
vous finissiez
ils finissent

Imperfect
je finisse
tu finisses
il finît
nous finissions
vous finissiez
ils finissent

Perfect
j'aie fini
tu aies fini
il ait fini
nous ayons fini
vous ayez fini
ils aient fini

IMPERATIVE
finis
finissons
finissez

INFINITIVE

Present
finir

Past
avoir fini

PARTICIPLE

Present
finissant

Past
fini

SE MEFIER to be suspicious

Present
je me méfie
tu te méfies
il se méfie
nous nous méfions
vous vous méfiez
ils se méfient

Past Historic
je me méfiai
tu te méfias
il se méfia
nous nous méfiâmes
vous vous méfiâtes
ils se méfièrent

Imperfect
je me méfiais
tu te méfiais
il se méfiait
nous nous méfiions
vous vous méfiiez
ils se méfiaient

Perfect
je me suis méfié(e)
tu t'es méfié(e)
il (elle) s'est méfié(e)
nous nous sommes méfié(e)s
vous vous êtes méfié(e)(s)
ils (elles) se sont méfié(e)s

Future
je me méfierai
tu te méfieras
il se méfiera
nous nous méfierons
vous vous méfierez
ils se méfieront

Pluperfect
je m'étais méfié(e)
tu t'étais méfié(e)
il (elle) s'était méfié(e)
nous nous étions méfié(e)s
vous vous étiez méfié(e)(s)
ils (elles) s'étaient méfié(e)s

CONDITIONAL

Past Anterior
je me fus méfié(e) etc

Future Perfect
je me serai méfié(e) etc

Present
je me méfierais
tu te méfierais
il se méfierait
nous nous méfierions
vous vous méfieriez
ils (elles) se méfieraient

Past
je me serais méfié(e)
tu te serais méfié(e)
il (elle) se serait méfié(e)
nous nous serions méfié(e)s
vous vous seriez méfié(e)(s)
ils (elles) se seraient méfié(e)s

SUBJUNCTIVE

Present
je me méfie
tu te méfies
il se méfie
nous nous méfiions
vous vous méfiiez
ils se méfient

Imperfect
je me méfiasse
tu te méfiasses
il se méfiât
nous nous méfiassions
vous vous méfiassiez
ils se méfiassent

Perfect
je me sois méfié(e)
tu te sois méfié(e)
il (elle) se soit méfié(e)
nous nous soyons méfié(e)s
vous vous soyez méfié(e)(s)
ils (elles) se soient méfié(e)s

IMPERATIVE
méfie-toi
méfions-nous
méfiez-vous

INFINITIVE

Present
se méfier

Past
s'être méfié(e)(s)

PARTICIPLE

Present
se méfiant

Past
méfié

METTRE to put

Present
je mets
tu mets
il met
nous mettons
vous mettez
ils mettent

Past Historic
je mis
tu mis
il mit
nous mîmes
vous mîtes
ils mirent

Imperfect
je mettais
tu mettais
il mettait
nous mettions
vous mettiez
ils mettaient

Perfect
j'ai mis
tu as mis
il a mis
nous avons mis
vous avez mis
ils ont mis

Future
je mettrai
tu mettras
il mettra
nous mettrons
vous mettrez
ils mettront

Pluperfect
j'avais mis
tu avais mis
il avait mis
nous avions mis
vous aviez mis
ils avaient mis

CONDITIONAL

Past Anterior
j'eus mis etc

Future Perfect
j'aurai mis etc

Present
je mettrais
tu mettrais
il mettrait
nous mettrions
vous mettriez
ils mettraient

Past
j'aurais mis
tu aurais mis
il aurait mis
nous aurions mis
vous auriez mis
ils auraient mis

SUBJUNCTIVE

Present
je mette
tu mettes
il mette
nous mettions
vous mettiez
ils mettent

Imperfect
je misse
tu misses
il mît
nous missions
vous missiez
ils missent

Perfect
j'aie mis
tu aies mis
il ait mis
nous ayons mis
vous ayez mis
ils aient mis

IMPERATIVE
mets
mettons
mettez

INFINITIVE

Present
mettre

Past
avoir mis

PARTICIPLE

Present
mettant

Past
mis

OUVRIR to open

Present
j'ouvre
tu ouvres
il ouvre
nous ouvrons
vous ouvrez
ils ouvrent

Imperfect
j'ouvrais
tu ouvrais
il ouvrait
nous ouvrions
vous ouvriez
ils ouvraient

Future
j'ouvrirai
tu ouvriras
il ouvrira
nous ouvrirons
vous ouvrirez
ils ouvriront

Past Historic
j'ouvris
tu ouvris
il ouvrit
nous ouvrîmes
vous ouvrîtes
ils ouvrirent

Perfect
j'ai ouvert
tu as ouvert
il a ouvert
nous avons ouvert
vous avez ouvert
ils ont ouvert

Pluperfect
j'avais ouvert
tu avais ouvert
il avait ouvert
nous avions ouvert
vous aviez ouvert
ils avaient ouvert

Past Anterior
j'eus ouvert etc

Future Perfect
j'aurai ouvert etc

CONDITIONAL

Present
j'ouvrirais
tu ouvrirais
il ouvrirait
nous ouvririons
vous ouvririez
ils ouvriraient

Past
j'aurais ouvert
tu aurais ouvert
il aurait ouvert
nous aurions ouvert
vous auriez ouvert
ils auraient ouvert

SUBJUNCTIVE

Present
j'ouvre
tu ouvres
il ouvre
nous ouvrions
vous ouvriez
ils ouvrent

Imperfect
j'ouvrisse
tu ouvrisses
il ouvrît
nous ouvrissions
vous ouvrissiez
ils ouvrissent

Perfect
j'aie ouvert
tu aies ouvert
il ait ouvert
nous ayons ouvert
vous ayez ouvert
ils aient ouvert

IMPERATIVE

ouvre
ouvrons
ouvrez

INFINITIVE

Present
ouvrir

Past
avoir ouvert

PARTICIPLE

Present
ouvrant

Past
ouvert

POUVOIR to be able to

Present
je peux
tu peux
il peut
nous pouvons
vous pouvez
ils peuvent

Imperfect
je pouvais
tu pouvais
il pouvait
nous pouvions
vous pouviez
ils pouvaient

Future
je pourrai
tu pourras
il pourra
nous pourrons
vous pourrez
ils pourront

Past Historic
je pus
tu pus
il put
nous pûmes
vous pûtes
ils purent

Perfect
j'ai pu
tu as pu
il a pu
nous avons pu
vous avez pu
ils ont pu

Pluperfect
j'avais pu
tu avais pu
il avait pu
nous avions pu
vous aviez pu
ils avaient pu

Past Anterior
j'eus pu etc

Future Perfect
j'aurai pu etc

CONDITIONAL

Present
je pourrais
tu pourrais
il pourrait
nous pourrions
vous pourriez
ils pourraient

Past
j'aurais pu
tu aurais pu
il aurait pu
nous aurions pu
vous auriez pu
ils auraient pu

SUBJUNCTIVE

Present
je puisse
tu puisses
il puisse
nous puissions
vous puissiez
ils puissent

Imperfect
je pusse
tu pusses
il pût
nous pussions
vous pussiez
ils pussent

Perfect
j'aie pu
tu aies pu
il ait pu
nous ayons pu
vous ayez pu
ils aient pu

IMPERATIVE

INFINITIVE

Present
pouvoir

Past
avoir pu

PARTICIPLE

Present
pouvant

Past
pu

PRENDRE to take

Present
je prends
tu prends
il prend
nous prenons
vous prenez
ils prennent

Imperfect
je prenais
tu prenais
il prenait
nous prenions
vous preniez
ils prenaient

Future
je prendrai
tu prendras
il prendra
nous prendrons
vous prendrez
ils prendront

Past Historic
je pris
tu pris
il prit
nous prîmes
vous prîtes
ils prirent

Perfect
j'ai pris
tu as pris
il a pris
nous avons pris
vous avez pris
ils ont pris

Pluperfect
j'avais pris
tu avais pris
il avait pris
nous avions pris
vous aviez pris
ils avaient pris

Past Anterior
j'eus pris etc

Future Perfect
j'aurai pris etc

CONDITIONAL

Present
je prendrais
tu prendrais
il prendrait
nous prendrions
vous prendriez
ils prendraient

Past
j'aurais pris
tu aurais pris
il aurait pris
nous aurions pris
vous auriez pris
ils auraient pris

SUBJUNCTIVE

Present
je prenne
tu prennes
il prenne
nous prenions
vous preniez
ils prennent

Imperfect
je prisse
tu prisses
il prît
nous prissions
vous prissiez
ils prissent

Perfect
j'aie pris
tu aies pris
il ait pris
nous ayons pris
vous ayez pris
ils aient pris

IMPERATIVE

prends
prenons
prenez

INFINITIVE

Present
prendre

Past
avoir pris

PARTICIPLE

Present
prenant

Past
pris

RECEVOIR to receive

Present
je reçois
tu reçois
il reçoit
nous recevons
vous recevez
ils reçoivent

Imperfect
je recevais
tu recevais
il recevait
nous recevions
vous receviez
ils recevaient

Future
je recevrai
tu recevras
il recevra
nous recevrons
vous recevrez
ils recevront

Past Historic
je reçus
tu reçus
il reçut
nous reçûmes
vous reçûtes
ils reçurent

Perfect
j'ai reçu
tu as reçu
il a reçu
nous avons reçu
vous avez reçu
ils ont reçu

Pluperfect
j'avais reçu
tu avais reçu
il avait reçu
nous avions reçu
vous aviez reçu
ils avaient reçu

Past Anterior
j'eus reçu etc

Future Perfect
j'aurai reçu etc

CONDITIONAL

Present
je recevrais
tu recevrais
il recevrait
nous recevrions
vous recevriez
ils recevraient

Past
j'aurais reçu
tu aurais reçu
il aurait reçu
nous aurions reçu
vous auriez reçu
ils auraient reçu

SUBJUNCTIVE

Present
je reçoive
tu reçoives
il reçoive
nous recevions
vous receviez
ils reçoivent

Imperfect
je reçusse
tu reçusses
il reçût
nous reçussions
vous reçussiez
ils reçussent

Perfect
j'aie reçu
tu aies reçu
il ait reçu
nous ayons reçu
vous ayez reçu
ils aient reçu

IMPERATIVE
reçois
recevons
recevez

INFINITIVE

Present
recevoir

Past
avoir reçu

PARTICIPLE

Present
recevant

Past
reçu

SAVOIR to know

Present
je sais
tu sais
il sait
nous savons
vous savez
ils savent

Imperfect
je savais
tu savais
il savait
nous savions
vous saviez
ils savaient

Future
je saurai
tu sauras
il saura
nous saurons
vous saurez
ils sauront

Past Historic
je sus
tu sus
il sut
nous sûmes
vous sûtes
ils surent

Perfect
j'ai su
tu as su
il a su
nous avons su
vous avez su
ils ont su

Pluperfect
j'avais su
tu avais su
il avait su
nous avions su
vous aviez su
ils avaient su

Past Anterior
j'eus su etc

Future Perfect
j'aurai su etc

CONDITIONAL

Present
je saurais
tu saurais
il saurait
nous saurions
vous sauriez
ils sauraient

Past
j'aurais su
tu aurais su
il aurait su
nous aurions su
vous auriez su
ils auraient su

SUBJUNCTIVE

Present
je sache
tu saches
il sache
nous sachions
vous sachiez
ils sachent

Imperfect
je susse
tu susses
il sût
nous sussions
vous sussiez
ils sussent

Perfect
j'aie su
tu aies su
il ait su
nous ayons su
vous ayez su
ils aient su

IMPERATIVE
sache
sachons
sachez

INFINITIVE

Present
savoir

Past
avoir su

PARTICIPLE

Present
sachant

Past
su

TENIR to hold

Present
je tiens
tu tiens
il tient
nous tenons
vous tenez
ils tiennent

Imperfect
je tenais
tu tenais
il tenait
nous tenions
vous teniez
ils tenaient

Future
je tiendrai
tu tiendras
il tiendra
nous tiendrons
vous tiendrez
ils tiendront

Past Historic
je tins
tu tins
il tint
nous tînmes
vous tîntes
ils tinrent

Perfect
j'ai tenu
tu as tenu
il a tenu
nous avons tenu
vous avez tenu
ils ont tenu

Pluperfect
j'avais tenu
tu avais tenu
il avait tenu
nous avions tenu
vous aviez tenu
ils avaient tenu

Past Anterior
j'eus tenu etc

Future Perfect
j'aurai tenu etc

CONDITIONAL

Present
je tiendrais
tu tiendrais
il tiendrait
nous tiendrions
vous tiendriez
ils tiendraient

Past
j'aurais tenu
tu aurais tenu
il aurait tenu
nous aurions tenu
vous auriez tenu
ils auraient tenu

SUBJUNCTIVE

Present
je tienne
tu tiennes
il tienne
nous tenions
vous teniez
ils tiennent

Imperfect
je tinsse
tu tinsses
il tînt
nous tinssions
vous tinssiez
ils tinssent

Perfect
j'aie tenu
tu aies tenu
il ait tenu
nous ayons tenu
vous ayez tenu
ils aient tenu

IMPERATIVE
tiens
tenons
tenez

INFINITIVE

Present
tenir

Past
avoir tenu

PARTICIPLE

Present
tenant

Past
tenu

VENDRE to sell

Present
je vends
tu vends
il vend
nous vendons
vous vendez
ils vendent

Imperfect
je vendais
tu vendais
il vendait
nous vendions
vous vendiez
ils vendaient

Future
je vendrai
tu vendras
il vendra
nous vendrons
vous vendrez
ils vendront

Past Historic
je vendis
tu vendis
il vendit
nous vendîmes
vous vendîtes
ils vendirent

Perfect
j'ai vendu
tu as vendu
il a vendu
nous avons vendu
vous avez vendu
ils ont vendu

Pluperfect
j'avais vendu
tu avais vendu
il avait vendu
nous avions vendu
vous aviez vendu
ils avaient vendu

CONDITIONAL

Past Anterior
j'eus vendu etc

Future Perfect
j'aurai vendu etc

Present
je vendrais
tu vendrais
il vendrait
nous vendrions
vous vendriez
ils vendraient

Past
j'aurais vendu
tu aurais vendu
il aurait vendu
nous aurions vendu
vous auriez vendu
ils auraient vendu

SUBJUNCTIVE

Present
je vende
tu vendes
il vende
nous vendions
vous vendiez
ils vendent

Imperfect
je vendisse
tu vendisses
il vendît
nous vendissions
vous vendissiez
ils vendissent

Perfect
j'aie vendu
tu aies vendu
il ait vendu
nous ayons vendu
vous ayez vendu
ils aient vendu

IMPERATIVE
vends
vendons
vendez

INFINITIVE

Present
vendre

Past
avoir vendu

PARTICIPLE

Present
vendant

Past
vendu

VENIR to come

Present
je viens
tu viens
il vient
nous venons
vous venez
ils viennent

Imperfect
je venais
tu venais
il venait
nous venions
vous veniez
ils venaient

Future
je viendrai
tu viendras
il viendra
nous viendrons
vous viendrez
ils viendront

Past Historic
je vins
tu vins
il vint
nous vînmes
vous vîntes
ils vinrent

Perfect
je suis venu(e)
tu es venu(e)
il (elle) est venu(e)
nous sommes venu(e)s
vous êtes venu(e)(s)
ils (elles) sont venu(e)s

Pluperfect
j'étais venu(e)
tu étais venu(e)
il (elle) était venu(e)
nous étions venu(e)s
vous étiez venu(e)(s)
ils (elles) étaient venu(e)s

CONDITIONAL

Past Anterior
je fus venu(e) etc

Future Perfect
je serai venu(e) etc

Present
je viendrais
tu viendrais
il viendrait
nous viendrions
vous viendriez
ils viendraient

Past
je serais venu(e)
tu serais venu(e)
il (elle) serait venu(e)
nous serions venu(e)s
vous seriez venu(e)(s)
ils (elles) seraient venu(e)s

SUBJUNCTIVE

Present
je vienne
tu viennes
il vienne
nous venions
vous veniez
ils viennent

Imperfect
je vinsse
tu vinsses
il vînt
nous vinssions
vous vinssiez
ils vinssent

Perfect
je sois venu(e)
tu sois venu(e)
il (elle) soit venu(e)
nous soyons venu(e)s
vous soyez venu(e)(s)
ils (elles) soient venu(e)s

IMPERATIVE
viens
venons
venez

INFINITIVE

Present
venir

Past
être venu(e)(s)

PARTICIPLE

Present
venant

Past
venu

VIVRE to live

Present
je vis
tu vis
il vit
nous vivons
vous vivez
ils vivent

Imperfect
je vivais
tu vivais
il vivait
nous vivions
vous viviez
ils vivaient

Future
je vivrai
tu vivras
il vivra
nous vivrons
vous vivrez
ils vivront

Past Historic
je vécus
tu vécus
il vécut
nous vécûmes
vous vécûtes
ils vécurent

Perfect
j'ai vécu
tu as vécu
il a vécu
nous avons vécu
vous avez vécu
ils ont vécu

Pluperfect
j'avais vécu
tu avais vécu
il avait vécu
nous avions vécu
vous aviez vécu
ils avaient vécu

CONDITIONAL

Past Anterior
j'eus vécu etc

Future Perfect
j'aurai vécu etc

Present
je vivrais
tu vivrais
il vivrait
nous vivrions
vous vivriez
ils vivraient

Past
j'aurais vécu
tu aurais vécu
il aurait vécu
nous aurions vécu
vous auriez vécu
ils auraient vécu

SUBJUNCTIVE

Present
je vive
tu vives
il vive
nous vivions
vous viviez
ils vivent

Imperfect
je vécusse
tu vécusses
il vécût
nous vécussions
vous vécussiez
ils vécussent

Perfect
j'aie vécu
tu aies vécu
il ait vécu
nous ayons vécu
vous ayez vécu
ils aient vécu

IMPERATIVE
vis
vivons
vivez

INFINITIVE

Present
vivre

Past
avoir vécu

PARTICIPLE

Present
vivant

Past
vécu

VOIR to see

Present
je vois
tu vois
il voit
nous voyons
vous voyez
ils voient

Past Historic
je vis
tu vis
il vit
nous vîmes
vous vîtes
ils virent

Past Anterior
j'eus vu etc

Future Perfect
j'aurai vu etc

Imperfect
je voyais
tu voyais
il voyait
nous voyions
vous voyiez
ils voyaient

Perfect
j'ai vu
tu as vu
il a vu
nous avons vu
vous avez vu
ils ont vu

Future
je verrai
tu verras
il verra
nous verrons
vous verrez
ils verront

Pluperfect
j'avais vu
tu avais vu
il avait vu
nous avions vu
vous aviez vu
ils avaient vu

CONDITIONAL

Present
je verrais
tu verrais
il verrait
nous verrions
vous verriez
ils verraient

Past
j'aurais vu
tu aurais vu
il aurait vu
nous aurions vu
vous auriez vu
ils auraient vu

SUBJUNCTIVE

Present
je voie
tu voies
il voie
nous voyions
vous voyiez
ils voient

Imperfect
je visse
tu visses
il vît
nous vissions
vous vissiez
ils vissent

Perfect
j'aie vu
tu aies vu
il ait vu
nous ayons vu
vous ayez vu
ils aient vu

IMPERATIVE
vois
voyons
voyez

INFINITIVE

Present
voir

Past
avoir vu

PARTICIPLE

Present
voyant

Past
vu

VOULOIR to want

Present
je veux
tu veux
il veut
nous voulons
vous voulez
ils veulent

Past Historic
je voulus
tu voulus
il voulut
nous voulûmes
vous voulûtes
ils voulurent

Past Anterior
j'eus voulu etc

Future Perfect
j'aurai voulu etc

Imperfect
je voulais
tu voulais
il voulait
nous voulions
vous vouliez
ils voulaient

Perfect
j'ai voulu
tu as voulu
il a voulu
nous avons voulu
vous avez voulu
ils ont voulu

Future
je voudrai
tu voudras
il voudra
nous voudrons
vous voudrez
ils voudront

Pluperfect
j'avais voulu
tu avais voulu
il avait voulu
nous avions voulu
vous aviez voulu
ils avaient voulu

CONDITIONAL

Present
je voudrais
tu voudrais
il voudrait
nous voudrions
vous voudriez
ils voudraient

Past
j'aurais voulu
tu aurais voulu
il aurait voulu
nous aurions voulu
vous auriez voulu
ils auraient voulu

SUBJUNCTIVE

Present
je veuille
tu veuilles
il veuille
nous voulions
vous vouliez
ils veuillent

Imperfect
je voulusse
tu voulusses
il voulût
nous voulussions
vous voulussiez
ils voulussent

Perfect
j'aie voulu
tu aies voulu
il ait voulu
nous ayons voulu
vous ayez voulu
ils aient voulu

IMPERATIVE
veuille
veuillons
veuillez

INFINITIVE

Present
vouloir

Past
avoir voulu

PARTICIPLE

Present
voulant

Past
voulu

M VERB CONSTRUCTIONS

There are two main types of verb constructions: verbs can be followed:

1 by another verb in the infinitive
2 by an object (a noun or a pronoun)

1 Verbs followed by an infinitive

There are three main constructions when a verb is followed by an infinitive:

a) verb + infinitive (without any linking preposition)
b) verb + **à** + infinitive
c) verb + **de** + infinitive

For examples of these three types of constructions, see pp B32-3 and B34-5.

a) *Verbs followed by an infinitive without preposition*

These include verbs of wishing and willing, of movement and of perception:

adorer to love	**aimer** to like	**aimer mieux** to prefer
aller to go (and)	**compter** to intend to	**descendre** to go down (and)
désirer to wish	**détester** to hate	**devoir** to have to
écouter to listen to	**entendre** to hear	**entrer** to go in (and)
envoyer to send	**espérer** to hope to	**faire** to make
falloir to have to	**laisser** to let	**monter** to go up (and)
oser to dare	**pouvoir** to be able to	**préférer** to prefer to
regarder to watch	**rentrer** to go in/back (and)	**savoir** to know how to to
sembler to seem to	**sentir** to feel	**sortir** to go out (and)
souhaiter to wish to	**valoir mieux** to be better to	**venir** to come (and)
voir to see	**vouloir** to want to	

b) *Verbs followed by **à** +* infinitive

aider à	to help (to do)
s'amuser à	to enjoy (doing)
apprendre à	to learn (to do)
s'apprêter à	to get ready (to do)
arriver à	to manage (to do)
s'attendre à	to expect (to do)
autoriser à	to allow (to do)
chercher à	to try (to do)
commencer à	to start (doing)
consentir à	to agree (to do)
consister à	to consist in (doing)
continuer à	to continue (to do)
se décider à	to make up one's mind (to do)
encourager à	to encourage (to do)
enseigner à	to teach how (to do)
forcer à	to force (to do)
s'habituer à	to get used (to doing)
hésiter à	to hesitate (to do)
inciter à	to prompt (to do)
s'intéresser à	to be interested in (doing)
inviter à	to invite (to do)
se mettre à	to start (doing)
obliger à	to force (to do)
parvenir à	to succeed (in doing)
passer son temps à	to spend one's time (doing)
perdre son temps à	to waste one's time (doing)
persister à	to persist in (doing)
pousser à	to urge (to do)
se préparer à	to get ready (to do)
renoncer à	to give up (doing)
rester à	to be left (to do)
réussir à	to manage (to do)
servir à	to be used for (doing)
songer à	to think of (doing)
tarder à	to delay/be late in (doing)
tenir à	to be keen (to do)

c) *Verbs followed by **de*** + infinitive

accepter de	to agree (to do)
accuser de	to accuse of (doing)
achever de	to finish (doing)
s'arrêter de	to stop (doing)
avoir besoin de	to need (to do)
avoir envie de	to feel like (doing)
avoir peur de	to be afraid (to do)
cesser de	to stop (doing)
se charger de	to undertake (to do)
commander de	to order (to do)
conseiller de	to advise (to do)
se contenter de	to make do with (doing)
craindre de	to be afraid (to do)
décider de	to decide (to do)
déconseiller de	to advise against (doing)
défendre de	to forbid (to do)
demander de	to ask (to do)
se dépêcher de	to hasten (to do)
dire de	to tell (to do)
dissuader de	to dissuade from (doing)
s'efforcer de	to strive (to do)
empêcher de	to prevent (from doing)
s'empresser de	to hasten (to do)
entreprendre de	to undertake (to do)
essayer de	to try (to do)
s'étonner de	to be surprised (at doing)
éviter de	to avoid (doing)
s'excuser de	to apologize for (doing)
faire semblant de	to pretend (to do)
feindre de	to pretend (to do)
finir de	to finish (doing)
se garder de	to be careful not to (do)
se hâter de	to hasten (to do)
interdire de	to forbid (to do)
jurer de	to swear (to do)
manquer de	'to nearly' (do)
menacer de	to threaten (to do)
mériter de	to deserve (to do)
négliger de	to fail (to do)
s'occuper de	to undertake (to do)
offrir de	to offer (to do)
omettre de	to omit (to do)
ordonner de	to order (to do)
oublier de	to forget (to do)
permettre de	to allow (to do)
persuader de	to persuade (to do)
prier de	to ask (to do)
promettre de	to promise (to do)
proposer de	to offer (to do)
recommander de	to recommend (to do)
refuser de	to refuse (to do)
regretter de	to be sorry (to do)
remercier de	to thank for (doing)
résoudre de	to resolve (to do)
risquer de	to risk (doing)
se souvenir de	to remember (doing)
suggérer de	to suggest (doing)
supplier de	to implore (to do)
tâcher de	to try (to do)
tenter de	to try (to do)
venir de	to have just (done)

2 Verbs followed by an object

In general, verbs which take a direct object in French also take a direct object in English, and verbs which take an indirect object in French (ie verb + preposition + object) also take an indirect object in English.

There are however some exceptions:

a) *Verbs followed by an indirect object in English but not in French* (the English preposition is not translated)

attendre	to wait for
chercher	to look for

demander	to ask for
écouter	to listen to
espérer	to hope for
payer	to pay for
regarder	to look at
reprocher	to blame for

on a demandé l'addition
we asked for the bill

j'attendais l'autobus
I was waiting for the bus

je cherche mon frère
I'm looking for my brother

tu écoutes la radio ?
are you listening to the radio?

b) *Verbs which take a direct object in English, but an indirect object in French*

convenir à	to suit
se fier à	to trust
jouer à	to play (*game, sport*)
jouer de	to play (*musical instrument*)
obéir à	to obey
désobéir à	to disobey
pardonner à	to forgive
renoncer à	to give up
répondre à	to answer
résister à	to resist
ressembler à	to resemble (to look like)
téléphoner à	to phone

tu peux te fier à moi
you can trust me

tu joues souvent au tennis ?
do you often play tennis?

il joue bien de la guitare
he plays the guitar well

tu as répondu à sa lettre ?
did you answer his letter?

téléphonons au médecin
let's phone the doctor

obéis à ton père !
obey your father!

c) *Verbs which take a direct object in English but* **de** *+ indirect object in French*

s'apercevoir de	to notice
s'approcher de	to come near
avoir besoin de	to need
changer de	to change
douter de	to doubt
se douter de	to suspect
s'emparer de	to seize, to grab
jouir de	to enjoy
manquer de	to lack, to miss
se méfier de	to mistrust
se servir de	to use
se souvenir de	to remember
se tromper de ...	to get the wrong ...

je dois changer de train ?
do I have to change trains?

il ne s'est aperçu de rien
he didn't notice anything

méfiez-vous de lui
don't trust him

je me servirai de ton vélo
I'll use your bike

tu te souviens de Jean ?
do you remember Jean?

il s'est trompé de numéro
he got the wrong number

d) *Some verbs take* **à** *or* **de** *before an object, whereas their English equivalent uses a different preposition*

i) Verb + **à** + object:

croire à	to believe in
s'intéresser à	to be interested in
penser à	to think of/about
songer à	to think of
rêver à	to dream of/about
servir à	to be used for

je m'intéresse au football et à la course automobile
I'm interested in football and in motor-racing

à quoi penses-tu ?
what are you thinking about?

ça sert à quoi ?
what is this used for?

ii) Verb + **de** + object:

dépendre de	to depend on
être fâché de	to be annoyed at
féliciter de	to congratulate for
parler de	to speak of/about
remercier de	to thank for
rire de	to laugh at
traiter de	to deal with, to be about
vivre de	to live on

cela dépendra du temps
it'll depend on the weather

il m'a parlé de toi
he told me about you

tu l'as remercié du cadeau qu'il t'a fait ?
did you thank him for the present he gave you?

3 Verbs followed by one direct object and one indirect object

a) In general, these are verbs of giving or lending, and their English equivalents are constructed in the same way, eg

donner quelque chose à quelqu'un
to give something to someone

il a vendu son ordinateur à son voisin
he sold his computer to his neighbour

Note: After such verbs, the preposition 'to' is often omitted in English but **à** cannot be omitted in French, and particular care must be taken when object pronouns are used with these verbs (see p B17).

b) With verbs expressing 'taking away', **à** is translated by 'from' (**qn** stands for 'quelqu'un' and **sb** for 'somebody')

acheter à qn	to buy from sb
cacher à qn	to hide from sb
demander à qn	to ask sb for
emprunter à qn	to borrow from sb
enlever à qn	to take away from sb
ôter à qn	to take away from sb
prendre à qn	to take from sb
voler à qn	to steal from sb

à qui as-tu emprunté cela ?
who did you borrow this from?

il l'a volé à son frère
he stole it from his brother

4 Verb + indirect object + de + infinitive

Some verbs which take a direct object in English are followed by **à** + object + **de** + infinitive in French (**qn** stands for 'quelqu'un' and **sb** for 'somebody'):

commander à qn de faire	to order sb to do
conseiller à qn de faire	to advise sb to do
défendre à qn de faire	to forbid sb to do
demander à qn de faire	to ask sb to do
dire à qn de faire	to tell sb to do
ordonner à qn de faire	to order sb to do
permettre à qn de faire	to allow sb to do
promettre à qn de faire	to promise sb to do
proposer à qn de faire	to offer to do for sb, to suggest to sb to do

je lui ai conseillé de ne pas essayer
I advised him not to try

demande à ton fils de t'aider
ask your son to help you

j'ai promis à mes parents de ne jamais recommencer
I promised my parents never to do this again

8 Prepositions

Prepositions in both French and English can have many different meanings, which presents considerable difficulties for the translator. The following guide to the most common prepositions sets out the generally accepted meanings on the left, with a description of their use in brackets, and an illustration. The main meanings are given first. Prepositions are listed in alphabetical order.

à

at	(place)	**au troisième arrêt** at the third stop
	(date)	**à Noël** at Christmas
	(time)	**à trois heures** at three o'clock
	(idiom)	**au hasard, au travail** at random, at work
in	(place)	**à Montmartre** in Montmartre **à Lyon** in Lyons **au supermarché** in the supermarket **à la campagne** in the country **au lit** in bed **au loin** in the distance
	(manner)	**à la française** in the French way **à ma façon** (in) my way
to	(place)	**aller au théâtre** to go to the theatre **aller à Londres** to go to London
	(+ infinitive)	**c'est facile à faire** it is easy to do (*see p B33*)
away from	(distance)	**à 3 km d'ici** three kms away
by	(means)	**aller à bicyclette/ à vélo** to go by bike **je l'ai reconnu à ses habits** I recognized him by his clothing
	(manner)	**fait à la main** made by hand
	(rate)	**à la centaine** by the hundred **100 km à l'heure** 60 mph
for/ up to	(+ pronoun)	**c'est à vous de jouer** it's your turn **c'est à nous de le lui dire** it's up to us to tell him
	(purpose)	**une tasse à café** a coffee cup
his/her/my etc	(possessive)	**son sac à elle** her bag
on	(means)	**aller à cheval/à pied** to go on horseback/ on foot
	(place)	**à la page 12** on page 12 **à droite/à gauche** on/to the right/left
	(time)	**à cette occasion** on this occasion
with	(descriptive)	**une maison à cinq pièces** a house with five rooms **un homme aux cheveux blonds** a man with blond hair **l'homme à la valise** the man with the case
	(idiom)	**à bras ouverts** with open arms

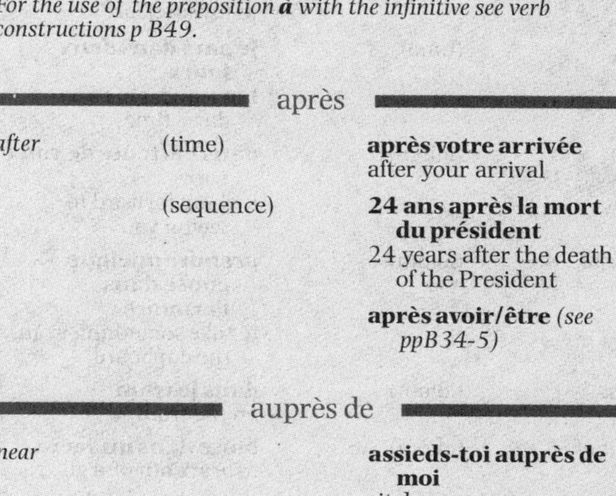

*For the use of the preposition **à** with the infinitive see verb constructions p B49.*

après

after	(time)	**après votre arrivée** after your arrival
	(sequence)	**24 ans après la mort du président** 24 years after the death of the President **après avoir/être** (*see ppB34-5*)

auprès de

near		**assieds-toi auprès de moi** sit down near me
compared to		**ce n'est rien auprès de ce que tu as fait** it's nothing compared to what you've done

avant

before	(time)	**avant cet après-midi** before this afternoon **avant ce soir** before tonight **avant de s'asseoir** before sitting down
	(preference)	**la famille avant tout** the family first (before everything)

avec

with	(association)	**aller avec lui** to go with him
	(means)	**il a tondu le gazon avec une tondeuse** he cut the lawn with a lawnmower

chez

at	(place)	**chez moi/toi** at/to my/your house **chez mon oncle** at my uncle's **chez le pharmacien** at the chemist's
among		**chez les Ecossais** among the Scots
about		**ce qui m'énerve chez toi, c'est ...** what annoys me about you is ...

in — **chez Sartre**
in Sartre's work

contre

against (place) — **contre le mur**
against the wall

with (after verb) — **je suis fâché contre elle**
I'm angry with her

for — **échanger des gants contre un foulard**
to exchange gloves for a scarf

dans

in (position) — **dans ma serviette**
in my briefcase

(time) — **je pars dans deux jours**
I'm leaving in two days' time

(idiom) — **dans l'attente de vous voir**
looking forward to seeing you

from (idiom) — **prendre quelque chose dans l'armoire**
to take something from the cupboard

on (idiom) — **dans le train**
on the train

out of (idiom) — **boire dans un verre**
to drink out of a glass

de

from (place) — **je suis venu de Glasgow**
I have come from Glasgow

(date) — **du 5 février au 10 mars**
from February 5th to March 10th
d'un weekend à l'autre
from one weekend to another

of (adjectival) — **un cri de triomphe**
a shout of triumph

(contents) — **une tasse de café**
a cup of coffee

(cause) — **mourir de faim**
to die of hunger

(measurement) — **long de 3 mètres**
3 metres long

(time) — **ma montre retarde de 10 minutes**
my watch is 10 minutes slow

(price) — **le montant est de 200 francs**
the total is 200 francs

(possessive) — **la mini-jupe de ma sœur**
my sister's miniskirt

(adjectival) — **les vacances de Pâques**
the Easter holidays

(after 'quelque chose') — **quelque chose de bon**
something good

(after 'rien') — **rien de nouveau**
nothing new

(after 'personne') — **personne d'autre**
nobody else

(quantity) — **beaucoup de, peu de**
many, few

by (idiom) — **je le connais de vue**
I know him by sight

in (manner) — **de cette façon**
in this way

(after superlatives) — **la plus haute montagne d'Ecosse**
the highest mountain in Scotland

on — **de ce côté**
on this side

than (comparative) — **moins de 5 francs**
less than 5 francs
plus de trois litres
more than three litres

to (after adjectives) — **ravi de vous voir**
delighted to see you
il est facile de le faire
it is easy to do it

(after verbs) — **s'efforcer de**
to try to

with (cause) — **tomber de fatigue**
to drop with exhaustion

depuis

for (time) — **j'étudie le français depuis 3 ans**
I have been studying French for 3 years
j'étudiais le français depuis 3 ans
I had been studying French for 3 years
je n'ai pas vu de lapins depuis des années
I haven't seen a rabbit for years

from (place) — **depuis ma fenêtre, je vois la mer**
from my window I can see the sea

(time) — **depuis le matin jusqu'au soir**
from morning till evening

since — **depuis dimanche**
since Sunday

derrière

behind (place) — **derrière la maison**
behind the house

dès

from (time) — **dès six heures**
from six o'clock onwards
dès 1934
as far back as 1934
dès le début
from the beginning
dès maintenant
from now on

(place) — **dès Edimbourg**
from (the moment of leaving) Edinburgh

devant

before/in front of (place) — **devant l'école**
in front of the school

en

in	(place)	**être en ville** to be in town **en Angleterre** in England
	(colour)	**un mur peint en jaune** a wall painted yellow
	(material)	**une montre en or** a gold watch
	(dates etc)	**en quelle année ?** in what year? **en 1986** in 1986 **en été, en juillet** in the summer, in July
	(dress)	**en bikini** in a bikini
	(language)	**en chinois** in Chinese
	(time)	**j'ai fait mes devoirs en 20 minutes** I did my homework in 20 minutes
by	(means)	**en auto/en avion** by car/by plane
like, as		**il s'est habillé en femme** he dressed as a woman
on	(idiom)	**en vacances** on holiday **en moyenne** on average
	(+present participle)	**en faisant** on/while/by doing

***Note: en** is not used with the definite article except in certain expressions: **en l'an 2000** (in the year 2000), **en l'honneur de** (in honour of) and **en la présence de** (in the presence of).*

en tant que

as/in (my) capacity as		**en tant que professeur** as a teacher

entre

among		**être entre amis** to be among friends
between	(place)	**entre Londres et Douvres** between London and Dover
	(time)	**entre 6 et 10 heures** between 6 and 10
	(idiom)	**entre toi et moi** between you and me
in	(punctuation)	**entre guillemets** in inverted commas **entre parenthèses** in brackets

d'entre

of/from among		**certains d'entre eux** some of them

envers

to/towards		**être bien disposé envers quelqu'un** to be well-disposed towards someone

hors de

out of		**hors de danger** out of danger

jusque

up to/ as far as	(place)	**jusqu'à la frontière espagnole** as far as the Spanish border
	(time)	**jusqu'ici/ jusque-là** up to now/up till then
till		**jusqu'à demain** till tomorrow

malgré

in spite of		**malgré la chaleur** in spite of the heat

par

by	(agent)	**la lettre a été envoyée par mon ami** the letter was sent by my friend
	(means of transport)	**par le train** by train
	(distributive)	**trois fois par semaine** three times a week
by		**deux par deux** two by two
	(place)	**par ici/là** this/that way
in/on	(weather)	**par un temps pareil** in such weather **par un beau jour d'hiver** on a beautiful winter's day
out of	(place)	**regarder par la fenêtre** to look out of the window **jeter du pain par la fenêtre** to throw bread out of the window
to/on		**tomber par terre** to fall to the ground **étendu par terre** lying on the ground
	(+ infinitive)	**commencer/finir par faire** to begin/end by doing

parmi

among		**parmi ses ennemis** among his enemies

pendant

for	(time)	**il l'avait fait pendant 5 années** he had done it for 5 years
during		**pendant l'été** during the summer

pour

for		**ce livre est pour vous** this book is for you **mourir pour la patrie** to die for one's country

	(purpose)	**c'est pour cela que je suis venu** that's why I have come
	(emphatic)	**pour moi, je crois que** personally, I think that
	(time)	**j'en ai pour une heure** it'll take me an hour **je serai là pour 2 semaines** I'll be here for 2 weeks

(**pour** stresses intention and future time: see **depuis** and **pendant** pp B52 and B5)

	(idiom)	**c'est bon pour la santé** it's good for your health
to	(+ infinitive)	**il était trop paresseux pour réussir aux examens** he was too lazy to pass the exams

près de

near	(place)	**près du marché** near the market
nearly	(time)	**il est près de minuit** it's nearly midnight
	(quantity)	**près de cinquante** nearly fifty

quant à

as for		**quant à moi** as for me

sans

without	(+ noun)	**sans espoir** without hope
	(+ pronoun)	**je n'irai pas sans vous** I'll not go without you
	(+ infinitive)	**sans parler** without speaking **sans s'arrêter** without stopping

sauf

except for		**ils sont tous partis, sauf John** everyone left except John
barring		**sauf accidents/ sauf imprévu** barring accidents/ the unexpected

selon

according to		**selon le président** according to the President **selon moi** in my opinion

sous

under	(physical)	**sous la table** under the table
	(historical)	**sous Elisabeth II** under Elizabeth II
in	(weather)	**sous la pluie** in the rain
	(idiom)	**sous peu** shortly/before long **sous la main** to hand **sous tous les rapports** in all respects **sous mes yeux** before my eyes

sur

on/upon	(place)	**le bol est sur la table** the bowl is on the table
off		**prendre sur le rayon** to take off the shelf
out of	(proportion)	**neuf sur dix** nine out of ten **une semaine sur trois** one week in three
over	(place)	**le pont sur la Loire** the bridge over the Loire
about	(idiom)	**une enquête sur ...** an enquiry about ...
at		**sur ces paroles** at these words **sur ce, il est sorti** at this /whereupon he went out
by		**quatre mètres sur cinq** four metres by five
in		**sur un ton amer** in a bitter tone (of voice)
over		**l'emporter sur quelqu'un** to prevail over someone

vers

towards	(place)	**vers le nord** towards the north
	(time)	**vers la fin du match** towards the end of the match
about	(time)	**vers 10 heures** about 10 o'clock

voici/voilà

here	(is)	**le voici qui vient** here he comes
there	(is)	**voilà où il demeure** that is where he lives

9 Conjunctions

Conjunctions are words or expressions which link words, phrases or clauses. They fall into two categories:

A coordinating
B subordinating

A COORDINATING CONJUNCTIONS

1 Definition

These link two similar words or groups of words (eg nouns, pronouns, adjectives, adverbs, prepositions, phrases or clauses). The principal coordinating conjunctions (or adverbs used as conjunctions) are:

et and	**mais** but	**ou** or
ou bien or (else)	**soit** or (either)	**ni** neither
alors then	**aussi** therefore	**donc** then, therefore
puis then (next)	**car** for (because)	**or** now
cependant however	**néanmoins** nevertheless	**pourtant** yet, however
toutefois however		

il est malade, mais il ne veut pas aller au lit
he's ill but he won't go to bed

il faisait beau, alors il est allé se promener
it was fine so he went for a walk

2 Repetition

a) Some coordinating conjunctions are repeated:

soit ... soit either ... or

prenez soit l'un soit l'autre
take (either) one or the other

ni ... ni neither ... nor

le vieillard n'avait ni amis ni argent
the old man had neither friends nor money

b) **et** and **ou** can be repeated in texts of a literary nature:

et ... et both ... and
ou ... ou whether ... or

3 aussi

aussi means 'therefore' only when placed before the verb. The subject pronoun is placed after the verb (see p B59).

il pleuvait, aussi Pascal n'est-il pas sorti
it was raining, so Pascal didn't go out

when **aussi** follows the verb it means 'also':

j'ai aussi mis mon imperméable
I also put my raincoat on

B SUBORDINATING CONJUNCTIONS

These join a subordinate clause to another clause, usually a main clause. The principal subordinating conjunctions are:

comme	as	**parce que**	because
puisque	since	**ainsi que**	(just) as
à mesure que	as	**tant que**	as long as
avant que	before	**après que**	after
jusqu'à ce que	until	**depuis que**	since
si	if	**à moins que**	unless
pourvu que	provided that	**quoique**	although
bien que	although	**quand**	when
lorsque	when	**dès que**	as soon as
aussitôt que	as soon as	**pour que**	in order that
afin que	so that	**de sorte que**	so that
de façon que	so that	**de peur que (+ ne)**	for fear that, lest

Note: some subordinating conjunctions require the subjunctive (see pp B30-1).

C QUE

que can be coordinating or subordinating

1 coordinating in comparisons (see pp B10 and B12-13)

il est plus fort que moi
he is stronger than I

2 subordinating

a) *meaning 'that'*

elle dit qu'elle l'a vu
she says she has seen him

je pense que tu as raison
I think you're right

il faut que tu viennes
you'll have to come

b) *replacing another conjunction*

When a conjunction introduces more than one verb, **que** usually replaces the second (and subsequent) subordinating conjunctions to avoid repetition:

comme il était tard et que j'étais fatigué, je suis rentré
as it was late and I was tired, I went home

Note: the mood after **que** is the same as that taken by the conjunction it replaces, except in the case of **si** in which **que** requires the subjunctive:

s'il fait beau et que tu sois libre, nous irons à la piscine
if it's fine, and you are free, we'll go to the swimming pool

10 Numbers and Quantity

A CARDINAL NUMBERS

0	**zéro**	40	**quarante**
1	**un (une)**	50	**cinquante**
2	**deux**	60	**soixante**
3	**trois**	70	**soixante-dix**
4	**quatre**	71	**soixante et onze**
5	**cinq**	72	**soixante-douze**
6	**six**	80	**quatre-vingt(s)**
7	**sept**	90	**quatre-vingt-dix**
8	**huit**	99	**quatre-vingt dix-neuf**
9	**neuf**	100	**cent**
10	**dix**	101	**cent un(e)**
11	**onze**	102	**cent deux**
12	**douze**	121	**cent vingt et un(e)**
13	**treize**	122	**cent vingt-deux**
14	**quatorze**	200	**deux cents**
15	**quinze**	201	**deux cent un(e)**
16	**seize**	1000	**mille**
17	**dix-sept**	1988	**mille neuf cent quatre-vingt-huit**
18	**dix-huit**		
19	**dix-neuf**	2000	**deux mille**
20	**vingt**	10 000	**dix mille**
30	**trente**	1 000 000	**un million**

Note:

a) **un** is the only cardinal number which agrees with the noun in gender

un kilo a kilo	**une pomme** an apple

b) hyphens are used in compound numbers between 17 and 99 except where **et** is used (this also applies to compound numbers after 100: **cent vingt-trois** 123).

c) **cent** and **mille** are not preceded by **un** as in English (one hundred).

d) **vingt** and **cent** multiplied by a number take an **s** when they are not followed by another number.

e) **mille** is invariable.

B ORDINAL NUMBERS

		abbreviation
1st	**premier/ première**	**1**er/**1**ère
2nd	**deuxième/ second**	**2**e
3rd	**troisième**	**3**e
4th	**quatrième**	**4**e
5th	**cinquième**	**5**e
6th	**sixième**	**6**e
7th	**septième**	**7**e
8th	**huitième**	**8**e
9th	**neuvième**	**9**e
10th	**dixième**	**10**e
11th	**onzième**	**11**e
12th	**douzième**	**12**e
13th	**treizième**	**13**e
14th	**quatorzième**	**14**e
15th	**quinzième**	**15**e
16th	**seizième**	**16**e
17th	**dix-septième**	**17**e
18th	**dix-huitième**	**18**e
19th	**dix-neuvième**	**19**e
20th	**vingtième**	**20**e
21st	**vingt et unième**	**21**e
22nd	**vingt-deuxième**	**22**e
30th	**trentième**	**30**e
100th	**centième**	**100**e
101st	**cent unième**	**101**e
200th	**deux centième**	**200**e
1000th	**millième**	**1 000**e
10 000th	**dix millième**	**10 000**e

Note:

a) ordinal numbers are formed by adding **-ième** to cardinal numbers, except for **premier** and **second**; **cinq**, **neuf** and numbers ending in **e** undergo slight changes: **cinquième**, **neuvième**, **onzième**, **douzième** etc.

b) ordinal numbers agree with the noun in gender and number

le premier ministre the Prime Minister	**la première fleur du printemps** the first flower of spring

c) there is no elision with **huitième** and **onzième**

le huitième jour the eighth day	**du onzième candidat** of the eleventh candidate

d) cardinal numbers are used for monarchs, except for 'first'

Charles deux Charles II	**Charles premier** Charles I

C FRACTIONS AND PROPORTIONS

1 Fractions

Fractions are expressed as in English: cardinal followed by ordinal:

deux cinquièmes
two fifths

But: $^1/_4$ **un quart** $^1/_2$ **un demi, une demie; la moitié**
$^1/_3$ **un tiers** $^3/_4$ **trois quarts**

2 Decimals

The English decimal point is conveyed by a comma in French:

un virgule huit (1,8)
one point eight (1.8)

3 Approximate numbers

une huitaine about eight	**une dizaine** about ten
une trentaine about thirty	**une centaine** about a hundred

But: **un millier**
about a thousand

Note: **de** is used when the approximate number is followed by a noun:

une vingtaine d'enfants
about twenty children

4 Arithmetic

Addition	**deux plus quatre**	2 + 4
Subtraction	**cinq moins deux**	5 -2
Multiplication	**trois fois cinq**	3 x 5
Division	**six divisé par deux**	6 ÷ 2
Square	**deux au carré**	2^2

D MEASUREMENTS AND PRICES

1 Measurements

a) *Dimensions*

la salle de classe est longue de 12 mètres
la salle de classe a/fait 12 mètres de longueur/de long
the classroom is 12 metres long

Similarly:

profond(e)/de profondeur/de profond deep
épais(se)/d'épaisseur thick
haut(e)/de hauteur/de haut high

ma chambre fait quatre mètres sur trois
my bedroom is about 4 metres by three

b) *Distance*

à quelle distance sommes-nous du lycée ?
how far are we from the secondary school?

nous sommes à deux kilomètres du lycée
we are 2 kilometres from the secondary school

combien y a-t-il d'ici à Blois ?
how far is it to Blois?

2 Price

ce chandail m'a coûté 110 francs
this sweater cost me 110 francs

j'ai payé ce chandail 110 francs
I paid 110 francs for this sweater

des pommes à 10 francs le kilo
apples at 10 francs a kilo

du vin blanc à 12 francs la bouteille
white wine at 12 francs a bottle

cela fait/revient à 42 francs
that comes to 42 francs

ils coûtent 25 francs pièce
they cost 25 francs each

E EXPRESSIONS OF QUANTITY

Quantity may be expressed by an adverb of quantity (eg 'a lot', 'too much') or by a noun which names the actual quantity involved (eg 'a bottle', 'a dozen').

1 Expression of quantity + de + noun

Before a noun, expressions of quantity are followed by **de** (**d'** before a vowel or a silent **h**) and never by **du**, **de la** or **des**, except for **bien des** and **la plupart du/des**:

assez de
enough

autant de
as much/many

beaucoup de
a lot of, much, many

combien de
how much/many

moins de
less, fewer

plus de
more

peu de
little, few

un peu de
a little

tant de
so much/many

tellement de
so much/many

trop de
too much/many

bien du/de la/des
many, a lot of

la plupart du/de la/des
most

il y a assez de fromage ?
is there enough cheese?

j'ai beaucoup d'amis
I've got a lot of friends

je n'ai pas beaucoup de temps
I haven't got much time

il y a combien de pièces ?
how many rooms are there

tu as combien d'argent ?
how much money have you you got?

mange plus de légumes !
eat more vegetables!

il y avait peu de choix
there was little choice

peu de gens le savent
not many people know that

tu veux un peu de pain ?
would you like a little bread?

il y a tant d'années
so many years ago

j'ai trop de travail
I've got too much work

il y a trop de voitures
there are too many cars

bien des gens
a good many people

la plupart des Français
most French people

2 Noun expressing quantity + de + noun

une boîte de
a box/tin/jar of

une bouteille de
a bottle of

une bouchée de
a mouthful of (*food*)

une cuillerée de
a spoonful of

une douzaine de
a dozen

une gorgée de
a mouthful of (*drink*)

un kilo de
a kilo of

un litre de
a litre of

une livre de
a pound of

un morceau de
a piece of

un paquet de
a packet of

une paire de
a pair of

une part de
a share/helping of

une tasse de
a cup of

une tranche de
a slice of

un verre de
a glass of

je voudrais une boîte de thon et un litre de lait
I'd like a tin of tuna fish and a litre of milk

il a mangé une douzaine d'œufs et six morceaux de poulet
he ate a dozen eggs and six pieces of chicken

3 Expressions of quantity used without a noun

When an expression of quantity is not followed by a noun, **de** is replaced by the pronoun **en** (see p B18):

il y avait beaucoup de neige ; il y en avait beaucoup
there was a lot of snow; there was a lot (of it)

elle a mangé trop de chocolats ; elle en a trop mangé
she's eaten too many chocolates; she's eaten too many (of them)

11 Expressions of Time

A THE TIME

quelle heure est-il? what time is it?

a) *full hours*

il est midi/minuit it is 12 noon *or* midday/ midnight

il est une heure it is 1 o'clock

b) *half-hours*

il est minuit et demi(e) it is 12.30 a.m.

il est midi et demi(e) it is 12.30 p.m.

il est une heure et demie it is 1.30

c) *quarter-hours*

il est deux heures et/un quart it is a quarter past two

il est deux heures moins le quart it is a quarter to two

d) *minutes*

il est quatre heures vingt-trois it 23 minutes past 4

il est cinq heures moins vingt it is 20 to 5

Note: **minutes** is usually omitted; **heures** is never omitted.

e) *a.m. and p.m.*

du matin a.m.

de l'après-midi/ du soir p.m.

il est sept heures dix du soir it is 7.10 p.m.

il est sept heures moins dix du matin it is 6.50 a.m.

The 24 hour clock is commonly used:

dix heures trente 10.30 a.m.

quatorze heures trente-cinq 2.35 p.m.

dix-neuf heures dix 7.10 p.m.

Note: times are often abbreviated as follows:

dix-neuf heures dix **19h10**

B THE DATE

1 Names of months, days and seasons

a) *Months* (**les mois**)

janvier	January
février	February
mars	March
avril	April
mai	May
juin	June
juillet	July
août	August
septembre	September
octobre	October
novembre	November
décembre	December

b) *Days of the week* (**les jours de la semaine**)

dimanche	Sunday
lundi	Monday
mardi	Tuesday
mercredi	Wednesday
jeudi	Thursday
vendredi	Friday
samedi	Saturday

c) *Seasons* (**les saisons**)

le printemps (spring) **l'été** (summer)
l'automne (autumn) **l'hiver** (winter)

For prepositions used with the seasons see p B4.

Note: in French the months and days are masculine and do not have a capital letter, unless they begin a sentence.

2 Dates

a) cardinals (eg **deux, trois**) are used for the dates of the month except the first:

le quatorze juillet the fourteenth of July

le deux novembre the second of November

But: **le premier février** the first of February

The definite article is used as in English; French does not use prepositions ('on' and 'of' in English):

je vous ai écrit le trois mars
I wrote to you on the third of March

b) **mil** (a thousand) is used instead of **mille** in dates from 1001 onwards:

mil neuf cent quatre-vingt sept
nineteen hundred and eighty-seven

3 année, journée, matinée, soirée

Année, journée, matinée, soirée (the feminine forms of **an, jour, matin** and **soir**) are usually found in the following cases:

a) *when duration is implied* (eg the whole day):

pendant une année	for a (whole) year
toute la journée	all day long
dans la matinée	in the (course of the) morning
passer une soirée	to spend an evening
l'année scolaire/universitaire	the school/academic year

b) *with an ordinal number (eg* **première***) or an indefinite expression:*

la deuxième année	the second year
dans sa vingtième année	in his twentieth year
plusieurs/quleques années	several/a few years
bien des/de nombreuses années	many years
environ une année	about a year

c) *with an adjective:*

de bonnes/mauvaises années	good/bad years

C IDIOMATIC EXPRESSIONS

à cinq heures	at 5 o'clock
à onze heures environ	(at) about 11 o'clock
vers minuit	(at) about midnight
vers (les) dix heures	(at) about 10 o'clock
il est six heures passées	it's past 6 o'clock
à quatre heures précises *ou* **pile**	at exactly 4 o'clock
sur le coup de trois heures	on the stroke of three
à partir de neuf heures	from 9 o'clock onwards
peu avant sept heures	shortly before seven
peu après sept heures	shortly after seven
tôt ou tard	sooner or later
au plus tôt	at the earliest
au plus tard	at the latest
il est tard	it is late
il est en retard	he is late
le train a vingt minutes de retard	the train is twenty minutes late
ma montre retarde de six minutes	my watch is six minutes slow
ma montre avance de six minutes	my watch is six minutes fast
ce soir	this evening, tonight
demain soir	tomorrow evening, tomorrow night
hier soir	yesterday evening, last night
samedi soir	Saturday evening
je sors samedi soir	I'm going out on Saturday night *or* evening
dans la soirée de samedi	on Saturday evening

dans la nuit de samedi (à dimanche)	during Saturday night
demain matin	tomorrow morning
hier matin	yesterday morning
lundi matin	Monday morning
j'y vais lundi matin	I'm going there on Monday morning
le lendemain matin	the next morning
lundi en huit	a week on Monday, Monday week
lundi en quinze	a fortnight on Monday
la semaine prochaine	next week
la semaine qui vient	this coming week
je l'ai vu l'autre samedi	I saw him the other Saturday
je commence lundi	I'm starting (on) Monday
il vient le lundi	he comes on Mondays, he comes on a Monday
viens un lundi	come one Monday
il vient l'après-midi	he comes in the afternoon(s)
viens un après-midi	come one afternoon
un lundi sur deux	every other Monday, every second Monday
tous les samedis	every Saturday
tous les samedis soirs	every Saturday evening *or* night
j'ai passé tout mon dimanche à faire le ménage	I spent my whole Sunday doing the housework
tous ses dimanches	all her Sundays
au début de l'après-midi/de la soirée, en début d'après-midi/de soirée	in the early afternoon/evening
je lui ai téléphonerai au début de la matinée	I'll phone him first thing in the morning
au début du mois	at the beginning of the month
j'ai une réunion au milieu de la matinée *ou* en milieu de matinée	I have a meeting mid-morning
au milieu (du mois) de juin, (à la) mi-juin	in the middle of June, mid-June
au milieu de l'hiver	in the middle of winter, midwinter
j'ai une réunion à la fin de la matinée *ou* en fin de matinée	I have a meeting late morning
à la fin de l'hiver	at the end of the winter
on en reparlera fin janvier *ou* à la fin du mois de janvier	we'll talk about it again at the end of January
quel jour sommes-nous aujourd'hui ?	what day is it today?
le combien sommes-nous aujourd'hui ?	what's today's date, what's the date today?
nous sommes/c'est le 3 avril	it's the third of April
aujourd'hui, nous sommes samedi	today is Saturday, it's Saturday today
vendredi 12 juillet 1996	Friday, July 12th 1996
nous nous sommes vus le vendredi 12 juillet	we saw each other on Friday, July 12th
en février, au mois de février	in February
en février 1996	in February 1996
en 1996	in 1996
l'été 1996	in the summer of 1996, in summer 1996
dans les années soixante	in the sixties, in the 60s, in the 1960s
au début/à la fin des années soixante	in the early/late sixties
au dix-septième siècle	in the seventeenth century
au XVIIe	in the 17th Century

12 The Sentence

A WORD ORDER

Word order is usually the same in French as in English, except in the following cases:

1 Adjectives

Many French adjectives follow the noun (see p B10):

de l'argent *italien*
(some) *Italian* money

j'ai les yeux *bleus*
I've got *blue* eyes

2 Adverbs

In simple tenses, adverbs usually follow the verb (see p B12):

j'y vais *rarement*
I *seldom* go there

il fera *bientôt* nuit
it will *soon* be dark

3 Object pronouns

Object pronouns usually come before the verb (see p B17):

je *t'*attendrai
I'll wait *for you*

il *la* lui a vendue
he sold *it* to him

4 Noun phrases

Noun phrases are formed differently in French (see p B64):

une chemise en coton
a cotton shirt

le père de mon copain
my friend's father

5 Exclamations

The word order is not affected after **que** or **comme** (unlike after 'how' in English):

que tu es bête !
you *are* silly!
(how silly you are!)

qu'il fait froid !
it's so cold!

comme il chante mal !
he sings so badly!

comme c'est beau !
that's so beautiful!

6 DONT

dont must be followed by the subject of the clause it introduces; compare:

l'agence d'emploi dont j'ai perdu la lettre
the employment agency whose letter I lost

l'agence d'emploi dont la lettre est arrivée hier
the employment agency whose letter arrived yesterday

7 Inversion

In certain cases, the subject of a French clause is placed after the verb. Word order is effectively that of an interrogative sentence (see p B61). This occurs:

a) *after the following, but only when they start a clause*

à peine	**aussi**	**peut-être**
hardly	therefore	maybe, perhaps

à peine Alain était-il sorti qu'il a commencé à pleuvoir
Alain had hardly gone out when it started raining

il y avait une grève du métro, aussi a-t-il pris un taxi
there was an underground strike, so he took a taxi

peut-être vont-ils téléphoner plus tard
maybe they'll phone later

But: **Alain était à peine sorti qu'il a commencé à pleuvoir**

ils vont peut-être téléphoner plus tard

b) *when a verb of saying follows direct speech*

'si tu veux', a répondu Marie 'if you want', Marie replied	**'attention !' a-t-elle crié** 'watch out!', she shouted
'j'espère que non', dit-il 'I hope not', he said	**'répondez !' ordonna-t-il** 'answer!', he ordered

B NEGATIVE EXPRESSIONS

1 Main negative words

a)

ne ... pas	not
ne ... point	not (*literary*)
ne ... plus	no more/longer, not ... any more
ne ... jamais	never
ne ... rien	nothing, not ... anything
ne ... guère	hardly

b)

ne ... personne	nobody, no one, not ... anyone
ne ... que	only
ne ... ni (ni ... ni)	neither ... nor
ne ... aucun(e)	no, not any, none
ne ... nul(le)	no
ne ... nulle part	nowhere, not ... anywhere

Note:

i) **ne** becomes **n'** before a vowel or a silent **h**.

ii) **aucun** and **nul**, like other adjectives and pronouns, agree with the word they refer to; they are only used in the singular.

2 Position of negative expressions

a) *with simple tenses and with the imperative*

negative words enclose the verb: **ne** comes before the verb, and the second part of the negative expression comes after the verb:

je ne la connais pas I don't know her	**n'insistez pas !** don't insist!
je n'ai plus d'argent I haven't any money left	**tu ne le sauras jamais** you'll never know
ne dis rien don't say anything	**il n'y a personne** no one's here
je n'avais que dix francs I only had ten francs	**il n'est nulle part** it isn't anywhere
tu n'as aucun sens de l'humour you have no sense of humour	**ce n'est ni noir ni bleu** it's neither black nor blue

b) *with compound tenses*

with **ne ... pas** and the other expressions in list 1a, the word order is: **ne** + auxiliary + **pas** + past participle:

il n'est pas revenu he didn't come back	**je n'ai plus essayé** I didn't try any more
je n'avais jamais vu Paris I had never seen Paris	**on n'a rien fait** we haven't done anything

with **ne ... personne** and the other expressions in list 1b, the word order is: **ne** + auxiliary + past participle + **personne/ que/ni** etc:

il ne l'a dit à personne he didn't tell anyone	**tu n'en as acheté qu'un ?** did you only buy one?
je n'en ai aimé aucun I didn't like any of them	**il n'est allé nulle part** he hasn't gone anywhere

c) *with the infinitive*

i) **ne ... pas** and the other expressions in list 1a are placed together before the verb:

je préfère ne pas y aller I'd rather not go	**essaye de ne rien perdre** try not to lose anything

ii) **ne ... personne** and the other expressions in list 1b enclose the infinitive:

il a été surpris de ne voir personne
he was surprised not to see anybody

j'ai décidé de n'en acheter aucun
I decided not to buy any of them

d) *at the beginning of a sentence*

when **personne**, **rien**, **aucun** and **ni ... ni** begin a sentence, they are followed by **ne**:

personne ne le sait nobody knows	**rien n'a changé** nothing has changed
ni Paul ni Simone ne sont venus neither Paul nor Simone came	**aucun secours n'est arrivé** no help arrived

3 Combination of negative expressions

Negative expressions can be combined:

ne ... plus jamais	
ne ... plus rien	**ne ... jamais rien**
ne ... plus personne	**ne ... jamais personne**
ne ... plus ni ... ni	**ne ... jamais ni... ni**
ne ... plus que	**ne ... jamais que**

on ne l'a plus jamais revu we never saw him again	**il n'y a plus rien** there isn't anything left
plus personne ne viendra no one will come any more	**tu ne dis jamais rien** you never say anything
je ne bois jamais que de l'eau I only ever drink water	**je ne vois jamais personne** I never see anybody

4 Negative expressions without a verb

a) ***PAS***

pas (not) is the most common of all negatives; it is frequently used without a verb:

tu l'aimes ? – pas beaucoup do you like it? – not much	**ah non, pas lui !** oh no, not him!
non merci, pas pour moi no thanks, not for me	**un roman pas très long** not a very long novel
lui, il viendra, mais pas moi he will come, but I won't	**j'aime ça ; pas toi ?** I like that; don't you?

b) ***NE***

ne is not used when there is no verb:

qui a crié ? – personne who shouted? – nobody	**jamais de la vie !** not on your life!
rien ! je ne veux rien ! nothing! I want nothing!	**rien du tout** nothing at all

c) ***NON***

non (no) is always used without a verb:

tu aimes la natation ? – non, pas du tout
do you like swimming? – no, not at all

tu viens, oui ou non ? – je crois que non
are you coming, yes or no? – I don't think so

Note: **non plus** = 'neither':

je ne le crois pas – moi non plus
I don't believe him – neither do I

je n'ai rien mangé – nous non plus
I haven't eaten anything – neither have we

C DIRECT AND INDIRECT QUESTIONS

1 Direct questions

There are three ways of forming direct questions in French:

a) subject + verb (+ question word)
b) (question word) + **est-ce que** + subject + verb
c) (question word) + verb + subject = inversion

a) *subject + verb (+ question word)*

The word order remains the same as in statements (subject + verb) but the intonation changes: the voice is raised at the end of the sentence. This is by far the most common question form in conversational French:

tu l'as acheté où ?
where did you buy it?

je peux téléphoner d'ici ?
can I phone from here?

vous prendrez quel train ?
which train will you take?

tu lui fais confiance ?
do you trust him?

c'était comment ?
what was it like?

la gare est près d'ici ?
is the station near here?

le train part à quelle heure ?
what time does the train leave?

cette robe me va ?
does this dress suit me?

b) *(question word) + est-ce que + subject + verb*

This question form is also very common in conversation:

qu'est-ce que tu as ?
what's the matter with you?

est-ce qu'il est là ?
is he in?

est-ce que ton ami s'est amusé ?
did your friend have a good time?

où est-ce que vous avez mal ?
where does it hurt?

c) *inversion*

This question form is the most formal of the three, and the least commonly used in conversation.

i) if the subject is a pronoun, word order is as follows:

(question word) + verb + hyphen + subject

où allez-vous ?
where are you going?

voulez-vous commander ?
do you wish to order?

quand est-il arrivé ?
when did he arrive?

avez-vous bien dormi ?
did you sleep well?

ii) if the subject is a noun, a pronoun referring to the noun is inserted after the verb, and linked to it with a hyphen:

(question word) + noun subject + verb + hyphen + pronoun

où ton père travaillait-il ?
where did your father work?

Nicole en veut-elle ?
does Nicole want any?

iii) **-t-** is inserted before **il** and **elle** when the verb ends in a vowel:

comment va-t-il voyager ?
how will he travel?

aime-t-elle le café ?
does she like coffee?

pourquoi a-t-il refusé ?
why did he refuse?

Marie viendra-t-elle ?
will Marie be coming?

Note: when a question word is used, modern French will often just invert verb and noun subject, without adding a pronoun; no hyphen is then necessary:

où travaille ton père ?
where does your father work?

2 Indirect questions

a) *Definition*

Indirect questions follow a verb and are introduced by an interrogative (question) word, eg:

ask him when he will arrive
I don't know why he did it

b) *Word order*

i) The word order is usually the same as in statements: question word + subject + verb:

je ne sais pas s'il voudra
I don't know if he'll want to

dis-moi où tu l'as mis
tell me where you put it

il n'a pas dit quand il appellerait
he didn't say when he would phone

ii) If the subject is a noun, verb and subject are sometimes inverted:

demande-leur où est le camping
ask them where the campsite is

But: **je ne comprends pas comment l'accident s'est produit**
I don't understand how the accident happened

il ne savait pas pourquoi les magasins étaient fermés
he didn't know why the shops were closed

3 Translation of English question tags

a) Examples of question tags are: isn't it? aren't you? doesn't he? won't they? haven't you? is it? did you? etc.

b) French doesn't use question tags as often as English. Some of them can however be translated in the following ways:

i) **n'est-ce pas ?**

n'est-ce pas ? is used at the end of a sentence when confirmation of a statement is expected:

c'était très intéressant, n'est-ce pas ?
it was very interesting, wasn't it?

tu voudrais trouver un emploi stable, n'est-ce pas ?
you would like to find a secure job, wouldn't you?

vous n'arriverez pas trop tard, n'est-ce pas ?
you won't be arriving too late, will you?

ii) **hein ?** and **non ?**

In conversation **hein ?** and **non ?** are often used after affirmative statements instead of **n'est-ce pas** :

il fait beau, hein ?
it's nice weather, isn't it?

il est amusant, non ?
he's funny, isn't he?

D ANSWERS ('YES' AND 'NO')

1 Oui, Si and Non

a) **oui** and **si** mean 'yes' and are equivalent to longer positive answers such as: 'yes, it is', 'yes, I will', 'yes, he has' etc:

tu m'écriras ? – oui, bien sûr !
will you write to me? – (yes) of course I will

b) **non** means 'no' and is equivalent to longer negative answers such as: 'no, it isn't', 'no, I didn't' etc:

c'était bien ? – non, on s'est ennuyé(s)
was it good? – no, it wasn't; we were bored

2 Oui or Si ?

oui and **si** both mean 'yes', but **oui** is used to answer an affirmative question, and **si** to contradict a negative question:

cette place est libre ? – oui
is this seat free? – yes (it is)

tu n'aimes pas lire ? – si, bien sûr !
don't you like reading? – yes, of course (I do)

13 Translation Problems

A GENERAL TRANSLATION PROBLEMS

1 French words not translated in English

Some French words are not translated in English, particularly:

a) *Articles*

Definite and indefinite articles are not always translated (see pp B3-4):

dans *la* société moderne, *les* prix sont élevés
in modern society, prices are high

ah non ! encore *du* riz ! je déteste *le* riz !
oh no! rice again! I hate rice!

b) *que*

que meaning 'that' as a conjunction (see p B55) or 'that'/'which'/'whom' as a relative pronoun (see p B20) cannot be omitted in French:

j'espère *que* tu vas mieux — I hope you're better
elle pense *que* c'est vrai — she thinks it's true

celui *que* j'ai vu — the one I saw
c'est un pays *que* j'aime — it's a country I like

c) *Prepositions*

Some French verbs are followed by a preposition (+ indirect object) when their English equivalent takes a direct object (without preposition) (see p B50):

elle a téléphoné *au* médecin — she phoned the doctor
tu l'as dit *à* ton père ? — did you tell your father?

d) *le*

When **le** (it) is used in an impersonal sense (see p B17), it is not translated:

oui, je *le* sais — yes, I know
dis-*le*-lui — tell him

2 English words not translated in French

Some English words are not translated in French, for example:

a) *Prepositions*

i) with verbs which take an indirect object in English, but a direct object in French (see pp B49-50):

tu l'as payé combien ? — how much did you pay *for* it?
écoutez cette chanson — listen *to* this song

ii) in certain expressions (see pp B58-9):

je viendrai te voir lundi soir
I'll come and see you *on* Monday night

b) *'can'*

'can' + verb of hearing or seeing (see p B37):

je ne vois rien ! — I can't see anything
tu entends la musique ? — can you hear the music?

3 Other differences

a) *English phrasal verbs*

Phrasal verbs are verbs which, when followed by a preposition, take on a different meaning, eg 'to give up', 'to walk out'. They do not exist in French and are translated by simple verbs or by expressions:

to give up	to run away	to run across
abandonner	**s'enfuir**	**traverser en courant**

b) *English possessive adjectives*

English possessive adjectives (my, your etc) are translated by the French definite article (**le/la/les**) when parts of the body are mentioned (see p B20):

brush *your* teeth — **brosse-toi *les* dents**
he hurt *his* foot — **il s'est fait mal *au* pied**

c) *'from'*

'from' is translated by **à** with verbs of 'taking away' (see p B50):

he hid it *from* his parents — **il l'a caché *à* ses parents**
borrow some *from* your dad — **empruntes-en *à* ton père**

B SPECIFIC TRANSLATION PROBLEMS

1 Words in -ing

The English verb form ending in **-ing** is translated in a number of ways in French:

a) *by the appropriate French tense* (see p B28)

he's speaking (present tense)	**il parle**
he was speaking (imperfect)	**il parlait**
he will be speaking (future)	**il parlera**
he has been speaking (perfect)	**il a parlé**
he had been speaking (pluperfect)	**il avait parlé**
he would be speaking (conditional)	**il parlerait**

b) *by a French present participle* (see p B35)

i) as an adjective:

un livre amusant — a funny book
c'est effrayant — it's frightening

ii) as a verb, with **en** (while/on/by doing something; see p B35):

'ça ne fait rien', dit-il en souriant
'it doesn't matter', he said smiling

j'ai vu mes copains en sortant du lycée
I saw my friends while (I was) coming out of school

But: **en** + present participle cannot be used when the two verbs have different subjects, eg:

I saw my brother coming out of school
j'ai vu mon frère sortir du lycée/qui sortait du lycée

c) *by a present infinitive* (see pp B32-4)

i) after a preposition:

au lieu de rire — instead of laughing
avant de traverser — before crossing

ii) after verbs of perception:

je l'ai entendu appeler — I heard him calling
je l'ai vue entrer — I saw her going in

iii) after verbs of liking and disliking:

j'adore faire du camping — I love camping
tu aimes lire ? — do you like reading?

iv) after verbs followed by **à** or **de**:

tu passes tout ton temps à ne rien faire
you spend all your time doing nothing

il a commencé à neiger — it started snowing
continuez à travailler — go on working

tu as envie de sortir ? — do you feel like going out?
il doit finir de manger — he must finish eating

v) when an English verb in **-ing** is the subject of another verb:

attendre serait inutile — waiting would be pointless
écrire est une corvée ! — writing is a real chore!

vi) when an English verb in **-ing** follows 'is' or 'was' etc:

mon passe-temps favori, c'est d'aller à la discothèque
my favourite pastime is going to the disco

d) *by a perfect infinitive* (see pp B34-5)

i) after **après** (after):

j'ai pris une douche après avoir nettoyé ma chambre
I had a shower after cleaning my room

ii) after certain verbs:

regretter to regret	**remercier de** to thank for	**se souvenir de** to remember

e) *by a noun*

particularly when referring to sports, activities, hobbies etc:

le ski skiing	**la natation** swimming	**l'équitation** horse-riding
la voile sailing	**le patinage** skating	**le canoë** canoeing
la lecture reading	**la planche à voile** windsurfing	**la cuisine** cooking
la boxe boxing	**la lutte** wrestling	**la marche à pied** walking

2 It is (It's)

'it is' (it's) can be translated in three ways in French:

a) il/elle + être
b) ce + être
c) il + être

a) ***il*** or ***elle*** (see p B17)

il or **elle** are used with the verb **être** to translate 'it is', 'it was' etc (+ adjective) when referring to a particular masculine or feminine noun (a thing, a place etc):

merci de ta carte ; elle était très amusante
thanks for your card; it was very funny

regarde ce blouson ; il n'est vraiment pas cher
look at that bomber jacket; it really isn't expensive

b) ***ce*** (see p B14)

ce (**c'** before a vowel) is used with the verb **être** to translate 'it is', 'it was' etc in two cases:

i) if **être** is followed by a word which is not an adjective on its own, ie by a noun, a pronoun, an expression of place etc:

c'était sa voix it was his voice	**c'est une grande maison** it's a big house
c'est moi ! c'est Claude ! it's me! it's Claude!	**c'est le tien ?** is it yours?
c'est en France que tu vas ? is it France you're going to?	**c'est pour lundi** it's for Monday

ii) if **être** is followed by an adjective which refers to something previously mentioned, an idea, an event, a fact, but not to a specific noun:

l'homme n'ira jamais sur Saturne ; ce n'est pas possible
man will never go to Saturn; it's not possible

j'ai passé mes vacances en Italie ; c'était formidable !
I spent my holidays in Italy; it was great!

oh, je m'excuse ! – ce n'est pas grave
oh, I'm sorry! – it's all right

c) ***il*** (see pp B27-8)

il is used to translate 'it is', 'it was' etc in three cases:

i) with **être** followed by an adjective **+ de** or **que** (ie referring to something that follows, but not to a specific noun):

il est impossible de connaître l'avenir
it's impossible to know the future

il est évident que tu ne me crois pas
it's obvious you don't believe me

ii) to describe the weather (see p B27):

il y a du vent it's windy	**il faisait très froid** it was very cold

iii) with **être** to tell the time and in phrases relating to the time of day, or in such expressions as **il est temps de** (it's time to):

il est deux heures du matin it's two a.m.	**ah bon ! il est tard !** really! it's late!
il est temps de partir it's time to go	

Note: with other expressions of time, **c'est** is used:

c'est lundi ou mardi ? is it Monday or Tuesday?	**c'était l'été** it was summer

3 To be

Although 'to be' is usually translated by **être**, it can also be translated in the following ways:

a) ***avoir***

i) **avoir** is used instead of **être** in many set expressions:

avoir faim/soif	to be hungry/thirsty
avoir chaud/froid	to be warm/cold
avoir peur/honte	to be afraid/ashamed
avoir tort/raison	to be wrong/right

ii) **avoir** is also used for age:

quel âge as-tu ? how old are you?	**j'ai vingt- cinq ans** I'm twenty five

b) ***aller***

aller is used for describing health:

je vais mieux I am/feel better	**tout le monde va bien** everyone's fine

c) ***faire***

faire is used in many expressions to describe the weather (see p B27):

il fait beau it's fine	**il fera chaud** it will be hot

Note: **il y a** can also be used to describe the weather, but only before **du/de la/des**:

il y a du vent/des nuages/de la tempête
it's windy/cloudy/stormy

d) *untranslated*

'to be' is not translated when it is the first part of an English continuous tense; instead, the appropriate tense is used in French (see p B28):

I'm having a bath **je prends un bain**	he was driving slowly **il conduisait lentement**

4 Any

'any' can be translated in three different ways:

a) ***du/de la/des*** *or* ***de*** (see pp B4-5)

the partitive article is used with a noun in negative and interrogative sentences:

il ne mange jamais de viande he never eats any meat	**tu veux du pain ?** do you want any bread?

b) ***en*** (see p B18)

en is used to translate 'any' without a noun in negative and interrogative sentences:

je n'en ai pas I haven't got any	**il en reste ?** is there any left?

c) ***n'importe quel(le)/quel(le)s*** *or* ***tout(e)/tou(te)s***

these are used to translate 'any' (and 'every') when they mean 'no matter which':

il pourrait arriver à n'importe quel moment
he could be arriving any time

prends n'importe quelle couleur, je les aime toutes
take any colour, I like them all

5 Anyone, anything, anywhere

Like 'any', these can be translated in different ways:

a) in interrogative sentences

il y a quelqu'un ?
is anyone in?

tu l'as vu quelque part ?
did you see it anywhere?

il a dit quelque chose ?
did he say anything?

b) in negative sentences

il n'y a personne
there isn't anyone

je ne le vois nulle part
I can't see it anywhere

je n'ai rien fait
I didn't do anything

c) in the sense of 'any' (and 'every'), 'no matter which'

n'importe qui peut le faire
anyone can do that

il croit n'importe quoi
he believes anything

j'irai n'importe où
I'll go anywhere

n'importe quand
anytime

6 You, your, yours, yourself

French has two separate sets of words to translate 'you', 'your', 'yours', 'yourself':

a) tu, te (t'), toi, ton/ta/tes, le tien etc
b) vous, votre/vos, le vôtre etc

For their respective meanings and uses, see pp B17, B19, B20.

a) ***tu*** *etc*

tu, te, ton etc correspond to the **tu** form of the verb (second person singular) and are used when speaking to one person you know well (a friend, a relative) or to someone younger. They represent the familiar form of address:

***tu* viens au concert avec *ton* copain, Annie ? alors, je *t'*achète deux places : une pour *toi* et une pour lui**
are *you* coming to the concert with *your* boyfriend, Annie? well, then, I'll get *you* two seats: one for *you* and one for him

b) ***vous*** *etc*

vous, vos etc correspond to the **vous** form of the verb (second person plural) and are used:

i) when speaking to more than one person:

dépêchez-*vous*, les gars ! *vous* allez manquer le train
hurry up, boys! *you*'ll miss the train

ii) when speaking to one person you do not know well or to someone older. They represent the formal or polite form of address:

je regrette, Monsieur, mais *vous* ne pouvez pas garder *votre* chien avec *vous* dans ce restaurant
I'm sorry, sir, but *you* can't keep *your* dog with you in this restaurant

c) when speaking or writing to one person, you must not mix words from both sets, but decide whether you are being formal or familiar, and use the same form of address throughout:

Cher Michel,
Merci de *ta* lettre. Comment vas-*tu* ?...

Dear Michel,
Thanks for *your* letter. How are *you*? ...

Monsieur,
Pourriez-*vous* me réserver une chambre dans *votre* hôtel pour le huit juin ?

Dear Sir,
Could *you* book a room for me in *your* hotel for the eighth of June?

vous etc and **tu** etc can only be used together when **vous** is plural (ie when it refers to more than one person):

***tu* sais, Jean, *toi* et *ta* sœur, *vous vous* ressemblez**
you know, Jean, *you* and *your* sister look like *each other*

7 Noun phrases

A noun phrase is a combination of two nouns used together to name things or people. In English, the first of these nouns is used to describe the second one, eg 'a love story'. In French, however, the position of the two nouns is reversed, so that the describing noun comes second and is linked to the first one by the preposition **de** (or **d'**):

une histoire d'amour
a love story

un magasin de disques
a record shop

un acteur de cinéma
a film actor

un arrêt d'autobus
a bus stop

un film d'aventure
an adventure film

un coup de soleil
sunstroke

une boule de neige
a snowball

un roman de science-fiction
a science fiction novel

un match de football
a football game

le château d'Edimbourg
Edinburgh castle

un conte de fées
a fairy tale

un joueur de rugby
a rugby player

un employé de bureau
an office clerk

Note: *when the describing noun refers to a material, the preposition* ***en*** *is often used instead of* ***de***:

un pull en laine
a woollen jumper

un pantalon en cuir
leather trousers

une bague en or
a gold ring

un sac en plastique
a plastic bag

8 Possession

In English, possession is often expressed by using a noun phrase and tagging **'s** at the end of the first word, eg:

my friend's cat

This is translated in French by: object + **de** + possessor:

le chat de mon ami

Note: *the use of the article* ***le/la/les***.

le fiancé de ma sœur
my sister's fiancé

les amis de Chantal
Chantal's friends

les événements de la semaine dernière
last week's events

When **'s** is used in the sense of 'someone's house' or 'shop' etc, it is translated by the preposition **chez**:

je téléphone de chez Paul
I'm telephoning from Paul's

chez le dentiste
at/to the dentist's

FRENCH-ENGLISH

FRANÇAIS-ANGLAIS

A, a [ɑ] *nm* (the letter) A, a; **connaître un sujet de A (jusqu')à Z** to know a subject inside out *or* from A to Z *or* from beginning to end; **prouver qch par A plus B** to prove sth in a logical *or* scientific fashion

à [a] *prép* [①**A65-67**] (*contracts with the article* **le** *into* **au**, *with the article* **les** *into* **aux**) **(a)** (*direction*) **il est venu à moi** he came (up) to me; **revenir à la surface** to come back (up) to the surface, to resurface; **aller à l'église/au collège/au cinéma/au marché** to go to church/to school/to the cinema/to the market; **se mettre** *ou* **s'asseoir au piano** to sit down at the piano; **monter au premier étage** to go up to the first floor; **partir à la recherche de ses ancêtres** to begin a search for one's ancestors; **de Paris à Lyon** from Paris to Lyons; **se rendre au Japon/aux Antilles/à la Guadeloupe/à Terre-Neuve** to travel to Japan/to the West Indies/to Guadeloupe/to Newfoundland; **au lit!** off to bed!; **au feu!** fire!; **au voleur!** stop thief!; **courir à sa perte** to head for disaster; **(de) vingt à trente personnes** between twenty and thirty people

(b) (*position*) **au coin de la rue** at the corner of the street, at the street corner; **vivre à Montpellier/à la campagne** to live in Montpellier/in the country; **à l'horizon** on the horizon; **à la page deux** on page two; **à l'ombre** in the shade; **au grenier** in the attic; **à la maison** at home; **au théâtre** at the theatre; **au Canada** in Canada; **aux États-Unis** in the United States; **à la Jamaïque** in Jamaica; **à Cuba** in Cuba; **à Paris** in Paris; **se tenir à la fenêtre** to stand at the window; **à deux kilomètres d'ici** two kilometres (away) from here; **avoir mal aux dents/yeux/pieds/au ventre** to have toothache/sore eyes/sore feet/stomach ache; **à la télévision/à la radio** on (the) television/on the radio; **le sourire aux lèvres** with a smile on his/her/*etc* lips; **un livre à la main** with a book in his/her/*etc* hand; **au fond** basically, fundamentally; **au fond, il n'est pas méchant** deep down, he's not a bad person

(c) (*dans le temps*) **du matin au soir** from morning to *or* till night; **remettre une affaire à plus tard** to put something off (until later), to postpone something; **à jamais** for ever; **à demain!/mardi!** see you tomorrow!/on Tuesday!; **du lundi au vendredi** from Monday to Friday, *US* Monday to *or* thru Friday; **je serai chez elle de lundi à vendredi** I'll be at her house from Monday to Friday; **il sera là à 8 heures/à la tombée de la nuit/au petit matin** he'll be there at 8 o'clock/at nightfall/in the early hours; **à temps** on time; **à un certain moment** at some moment; **au printemps** in (the) spring; **le 2 au soir** on the evening of the 2nd; **à Noël** at Christmas; **au revoir** goodbye (for now); **à ces mots** at these words; **au premier mot** at the first word; **à première vue** on first sight; **à mon arrivée** on my arrival; **à deux heures** at two o'clock; **à toute heure du jour et de la nuit** at all hours of the day and night; **au vingtième siècle** in the twentieth century; **à l'avenir** in (the) future; **à l'aube** at dawn

(d) (*distribution*) **faire du 10 litres aux 100 (km)** to do 100 kilometres on 10 litres; **faire du 90 km à l'heure** to do 90 km an *or* per hour; **payé au mois/au forfait** paid monthly *or* by the month/at a fixed rate; **travailler à la pièce** to do piecework; **vendre des oranges à la pièce** to sell oranges separately *or* individually; **vendre des huîtres à la douzaine** to sell oysters by the dozen; **entrer deux à deux** to come in two by two; **se battre d'homme à homme** to fight man to man; *Tennis* **quinze à** fifteen all; **monter l'escalier quatre à quatre** to go upstairs four (steps) at a time; **peu à peu, petit à petit** little by little, gradually

(e) (*avec complément d'objet indirect*) **attacher un cheval à un arbre** to tie a horse to a tree; **aspirer au calme** to long for peace and quiet; **échapper à qch** to escape from sth; *Fig* **avoir un fil à la patte** to be tied down; **attacher de l'importance à qch** to attach importance to sth; **s'adresser à qn** to address sb, to speak to sb; **lettre ouverte à ...** open letter to ...; **donner qch à qn** to give sth to sb, to give sb sth; **parler à qn** to speak to sb; **dire qch à qn** to say sth to sb, to tell sb sth; **penser à qn/qch** to think of *or* about sb/sth; **s'habituer à qch** to become used to sth; **à quoi cela sert-il?** what's that used for?; (*quel intérêt?*) what's the good of that?; **survivre à qn/qch** to survive *or* outlive sb/sth; **prendre qn à témoin** to call sb to witness *or* as a witness; **s'opposer à qch** to oppose sth; **résister à qn/qch** to resist sb/sth; **cacher/voler qch à qn** to hide/steal sth from sb; **prendre qch à qn** to take sth from sb; **boire à (même) la bouteille** to drink (straight) from the bottle; **faire faire qch à qn** to make sb do sth, to get sb to do sth; **faire savoir qch à qn** to tell sb about sth, to inform sb of sth; **laisser croire à qn que ...** to let sb think *or* believe that ...; **c'est à vous de décider** it's for you *or* up to you to decide; **c'est à vous** (*de jouer etc*) it's your turn; *Rad* **à vous** over (to you); **la parole est à M. Dupont** Mr Dupont will now speak; **c'est aimable à vous d'être venu** it's kind *or* good of you to have come

(f) (*possession, attributs etc*) **ce livre est à Paul** this book is Paul's, this is Paul's book, this book belongs to Paul; **un ami à moi** a friend of mine; **la sœur à Anne** Anne's sister; **enfant aux yeux bleus** child with blue eyes, blue-eyed child; **homme à barbe noire** man with a black beard; **une expression bien à Anne** a typically Anne expression; **chambre à deux lits** room with twin beds; **voiture à toit ouvrant** car with a sun roof

(g) [①**B34**,c,iii] (*destination, usage*) for; **affaire à suivre** something worth watching *or* keeping an eye on; **c'est à voir** it remains to be seen; **bon à jeter** fit for the dustbin; **une machine à coudre** a sewing machine; **j'ai une veste à nettoyer** I have a jacket to be cleaned; (*c'est moi qui vais le faire*) I have a jacket to clean; **j'ai une lettre à écrire** I have a letter to write; **je voudrais quelque chose à boire** I'd like something to drink; **maison à vendre** house for sale; **tasse à thé** teacup; **brosse à dents** toothbrush; **moulin à vent** windmill; **moulin à café** coffee grinder; **pompe à vélo** bicycle pump; **poudre à récurer** scouring powder; **pompe à eau** water pump

(h) (*manière*) **à pied** on foot; **écrire à la machine** to type; **montre à quartz** quartz watch; **ça fonctionne à l'électricité** it runs on electricity; **à la main** by hand; **fait à la main** handmade; **peint à la main** hand painted; **jouer un air au violon** to play a tune on the violin; **arriver à l'improviste** to arrive unexpectedly; **à toute allure** at top speed; **à ce rythme, nous y sommes encore demain** the way we're going *or* at this rate we'll still be at it tomorrow; **recevoir qn à bras ouverts** to receive sb with open arms; **cuisine à l'huile** cooking with oil; **à l'espagnole** in the Spanish manner *or* way; **un repas à l'anglaise** a typical(ly) English meal; *F* **encore une histoire à la Marie** another one of Marie's typical stories; **manger à sa faim** to eat one's fill; (*autant que possible*) to eat as much as one can; **faire qch à sa manière** *ou* **façon** to do sth (in) one's own way; **nous l'avons fait à trois** there were three of us doing it; **se mettre à plusieurs pour faire qch** to team up *or* to get together with several people to do sth; *Sp* **rugby à quinze/treize** Rugby Union/League

(i) à mon avis in my opinion; **à ce qu'il dit** according to him *or* to what he says, from what he says; **au reste** moreover, besides; **à cette condition** on this condition; **cela se fera à une seule condition** that will be done on one condition; **à la demande générale** by popular request; **à ma grande surprise** to my great surprise

(j) (*expression du prix*) **vendre qch à dix francs le kilo** to sell sth for *or* at ten francs a kilo; **à quel prix vendez-vous cela?** how much are you asking for that?; **un timbre à deux francs** a two-franc stamp; **à ce prix, on ne peut pas se plaindre** at that price you can't complain

(k) (*après adjectif*) **indispensable à qn/qch** indispensable *or* essential to sb/for sth; **parallèle à** parallel to; **hostile à** hostile to; **utile à** useful for

(l) (*avec le verbe à l'infinitif*) [①**B31**,2,b; **B33**,b,ii] **penser à faire qch** (*envisager*) to think of doing sth; (*se souvenir*) to remember to do sth; **songer à faire qch** to dream of *or* about doing sth; **consentir à faire qch** to consent *or* agree to do sth; **encourager qn à faire qch** to encourage sb to do sth;

c'est à refaire it will have to be done again; **il me reste à faire une dissertation de philo** I still have to do a philosophy essay; **il ne me reste qu'à vous remercier** it only remains for me to thank you; **commencer à faire qch** to begin to do sth, to start doing sth; **apprendre à lire** to learn to read

(m) *(conséquence)* **laid à faire peur** frightfully ugly; **s'ennuyer à mourir** to be bored to death; **c'était à mourir de rire** it was hilarious; **jolie à croquer** pretty as a picture; **il est à croquer dans son petit costume de marin** he looks good enough to eat in his little sailor suit; **c'est à se demander si elle sait de quoi elle parle** you begin to wonder if she knows what she's talking about; **geler à pierre fendre** to freeze hard; **à quoi bon le lui dire?** what's the good *or* use of telling him?

(n) je suis prêt à vous écouter I'm willing to listen to you; **facile à comprendre** easy to understand; **il est homme à se défendre** he's the kind of man who will hit back; **elle est à plaindre** she is *or* deserves to be pitied; **être le seul à faire qch** to be the only one to do sth; **le troisième à arriver** the third to arrive

(o) à partager les mêmes périls ils ont appris à s'estimer by *or* through sharing the same dangers they gained respect for each other; **à rouler trop vite, tu vas finir par avoir un accident** if you go on driving too fast, you're going to end up having an accident; **à en juger par …** judging by…, to judge by …; **à les en croire** according to them, if we are to believe them

A3 [atrwa] *nm* A3

A4 [akatr] *nm* A4

abaissant [abɛsɑ̃] *adj* degrading

abaisse [abɛs] *nf Culin* thinly rolled pastry

abaisse-langue *nm inv Méd* spatula, tongue depressor

abaissement [abɛsmɑ̃] *nm* **(a)** *(d'un store etc)* lowering, pulling down; *(du niveau d'un fleuve etc)* lowering **(b)** *(chute)* fall; *(du sol, d'un bâtiment)* subsidence, sinking; *(de la température, des prix)* fall, drop; *(des prix)* reduction **(c)** *Litt (humiliation)* abasement, humiliation

abaisser [abese] **1** *vt* **(a)** to lower; *(store)* to pull down; *(pont-levis)* to let down; **a. son regard** to look down; **a. un mur** to pull down a wall

(b) *(prix)* to lower; *(prix, coût, pression etc)* to reduce

(c) *Litt (humilier)* to humble, to abase

(d) *Math* **a. une perpendiculaire à une ligne** to drop a perpendicular to a line; **a. le chiffre des dizaines** *(dans une division)* to bring down the figure in the tens column

(e) *Culin* **a. une pâte** to roll out pastry

2 s'abaisser *vpr* **(a)** to fall away, to dip, to slope down, to go down; *(s'effondrer)* to subside; **la fenêtre s'abaisse quand on appuie sur ce bouton** the window slides down when you press this button

(b) *(chuter)* to drop, to fall

(c) s'a. jusqu'à faire qch *(consentir)* to stoop so low as to do sth; *(d'une personne orgueilleuse)* to condescend to do sth; **s'a. à des compromissions** to stoop to compromise

(d) s'a. devant Dieu to humble oneself before God

abaisseur [abesœr] **1** *nm Anat* depressor **2** *adj Él (transformateur)* step-down

abandon [abɑ̃dɔ̃] *nm* **(a)** *(de biens, de droits etc)* surrender; *(de droits)* renunciation; *Fin* **a. de créances** debt forgiveness; **faire a. de qch à qn** to make over *or* relinquish *or* surrender sth to sb

(b) *Sp (au cours d'une épreuve)* retirement, withdrawal; *(avant la course)* withdrawal

(c) *Jur (d'enfants)* desertion, abandonment; *(de fonction)* desertion, dereliction; **a. du domicile conjugal** desertion

(d) *(état)* neglect; **finir sa vie dans l'a.** to end one's life alone; **à l'a.** *(jardin)* (completely) neglected; *Naut* adrift, derelict

(e) *(détente)* lack of restraint; **parler avec un complet a.** to speak quite freely *or* without restraint; **dans un moment d'a.** in a moment of abandon *or* freedom

(f) *Ordinat* abort

abandonné, -ée [abɑ̃dɔne] **1** *adj (personne)* abandoned, deserted; *(air)* untidy; **navire a. en mer** derelict; **maison abandonnée** deserted house **2** *n* **les abandonnés** waifs and strays

abandonner [abɑ̃dɔne] **1** *vt* **(a)** *(qn)* to desert, to abandon, *Litt* to forsake; *Naut* **a. un homme** to maroon a man; *Naut* **a. le bâtiment** to abandon ship; *Av* **a. le bord** *ou* **un avion en vol** to bale out; *Mil* **a. son poste** to desert one's post

(b) *(délaisser) (voiture)* to abandon; *(village)* to abandon, to desert; **mes forces m'abandonnent** my strength is failing me

(c) *(renoncer à) (qch)* to surrender, to renounce, to give up; **a. la course** to abandon *or* withdraw from the race; **a. un projet** to abandon a project; **il a abandonné les études à quatorze ans** he dropped out (of school) when he was fourteen; **a. la partie** to throw in one's hand; **a. sa part d'héritage (à sa sœur)** to forgo one's share of an inheritance (in favour of one's sister); **a. ses prétentions** to renounce *or* surrender one's claims

(d) *Ordinat* to abort

2 *vi* to give up; *Sp* to give up, to retire; *F* **c'est trop dur, j'abandonne** it's too hard, I give up

3 s'abandonner *vpr* **(a)** *(se laisser aller)* to let oneself go, *Fml* to be unconstrained; **s'a. au chagrin** to give oneself up to *or* to abandon oneself to grief; **s'a. au sommeil** to abandon oneself to sleep

(b) *(s'en remettre à)* **s'a. à son sort** to resign oneself to one's fate

(c) *(se confier)* to open up

abaque [abak] *nm* **(a)** *(boulier)* abacus, counting frame **(b)** *Math* chart, graph **(c)** *Archit* abacus

abasourdir [abazurdir] *vt* to deafen; *Fig* to astound, to stun; *Fig* **nous sommes restés abasourdis par la nouvelle** we were flabbergasted *or* astounded *or* stunned by the news

abasourdissant [abazurdisɑ̃] *adj (bruit)* deafening; *Fig (nouvelle)* stunning, astounding

abasourdissement [abazurdismɑ̃] *nm* bewilderment, stupefaction

abat [aba] *nm* **(a) abats** offal, *Am* variety meat; *(de volaille)* giblets **(b)** *Arch* slaughter **(c) pluie d'a.** sudden shower

abâtardi [abɑtardi] *adj* degenerate

abâtardir [abɑtardir] **1** *vt (espèce)* to cause to degenerate; *(qualité)* to debase **2 s'abâtardir** *vpr* to degenerate, to deteriorate

abâtardissement [abɑtardismɑ̃] *nm* degeneracy

abat-jour *nm inv* lampshade; *Fig* **mettre la main en a.** to shade one's eyes with one's hand

abattage [abataʒ] *nm* **(a)** *(de bâtiments)* knocking down, pulling down; *(d'arbres etc)* felling, cutting down, clearing; *Min* cutting, working; *Min* **face d'a.** working face; *Naut* **a. en carène** careening; **avoir de l'a.** *Vieilli* to be full of energy; *Fig (d'un acteur, d'un politicien etc)* to have charisma **(b)** *(d'animal)* slaughtering, killing; **grand a. de gibier** heavy bag of game **(c)** *Com* **vente à l'a.** sale at knock-down prices

abattant [abatɑ̃] **1** *adj* **siège a.** tip-up seat **2** *nm (d'un comptoir, d'une table)* flap

abattement [abatmɑ̃] *nm* **(a)** *(physique)* exhaustion, *Fml* prostration **(b)** *(moral)* despondency, dejection, depression, low spirits **(c)** *Fin (d'impôts)* allowance

abatteur, -euse [abatœr, -øz] *n* **(a) a. de besogne** hard worker, *F* slogger **(b)** *(d'arbres)* feller **(c)** *(d'animaux)* slaughterer

abattis [abati] *nm* **(a)** *(des arbres)* felling, clearing **(b)** *Région* heap of felled trees; **a. de maisons** heap of fallen houses **(c)** *Culin pl* giblets **(d)** *Arg pl* limbs, hands and feet; **si tu viens te battre avec moi, commence par numéroter tes a.!** if you're going to pick a fight with me, you can say your prayers right now!

abattoir [abatwar] *nm* slaughterhouse, abattoir; *Fig* **envoyer des hommes à l'a.** to send men to the slaughter *or* to be slaughtered *or* butchered

abattre [abatr] *(conj like* **battre***)* **1** *vt* **(a)** *(faire tomber)* to knock down, to throw down, to pull down; *(régime)* to overthrow; **a. son rival** to floor *or* fell one's opponent, to knock down one's opponent; **a. une maison/un mur** to pull *or* knock down a house/a wall; **a. de la besogne** to get through a lot of work

(b) *(arbres)* to fell, to cut down, to clear; **a. du minerai** to break down *or* to stope ore

(c) *(tuer) (personne, cochon, bœuf)* to slaughter, to kill; *(animal malade ou dangereux)* to destroy; *Arg (qn)* to bump off; **a. un avion** to bring down *or* shoot down an aircraft; **c'est un homme à a.** this man is on the hit-list

(d) *(poussière, vent)* to lay; *Prov* **petite pluie abat grand vent** a soft answer will turn away wrath

(e) *(du vent) (arbre)* to blow down; *(blé)* to flatten; *Naut* **a. navire en carène** to careen a ship

(f) *Fig (fatiguer) (de la chaleur)* to drain of energy; *(d'une maladie)* to lay low

(g) *(démoraliser)* to dishearten, to depress; **ne vous laissez pas a.!** keep your chin *or* spirits up!; **cette nouvelle l'a profondément abattu** this news has really crushed *or* demoralized him

(h) *Cartes* **a. ses cartes** *ou* **son jeu** to lay one's cards on the table, to lay down one's hand; *Fig* to lay one's cards on the table

(i) *Naut* to pay off

2 s'abattre *vpr* **(a)** *(tomber)* to fall, to crash down, to collapse; **le pilier s'abattit** the pillar came crashing down

(b) s'a. sur qch to pounce on sth; (*d'un oiseau*) to swoop down on(to) sth; **les précipitations qui se sont abattues sur la région** the torrential rain which has been falling on the region; **les injures n'ont pas cessé de s'a. sur l'orateur** insults rained down constantly on the speaker; **le malheur s'abattra sur toi et ta descendance!** misfortune will descend upon you and your offspring!

abattu [abaty] **1** *adj* dejected, dispirited, low-spirited; **a. par la chaleur** limp with the heat; **a. par l'échec** depressed *or* demoralized by the failure; **visage a.** drawn face **2** *nm* **fusil à l'a.** uncocked rifle

abbatial, -ale, -aux, -ales [abasjal, -o] **1** *adj* **terres abbatiales** abbey lands; **église abbatiale** abbey (church) **2** *nf* **abbatiale** abbey (church)

abbaye [abei] *nf* abbey

abbé [abe] *nm* **(a)** (*supérieur d'une abbaye*) abbot **(b)** (*prêtre*) **j'en parlerai à monsieur l'a.** I'll mention it to the priest; **(Monsieur) l'a. Constantin** Father Constantin

abbesse [abɛs] *nf* abbess

abc [abese] *nm inv* **(a)** (*livre pour apprendre à lire*) ABC, alphabet (book); (*livre scolaire*) primer **(b)** *Fig* (*d'une science*) rudiments; **apprendre l'a. du métier** to learn the rudiments *or* basics of the job

abcès [apsɛ] *nm* abscess; **a. à la gencive** gumboil; *Fig* **crever** *ou* **vider l'a.** to resolve the situation

abdication [abdikasjɔ̃] *nf* (*d'un monarque, d'une autorité*) abdication; (*d'une autorité, de droits*) renunciation, surrender

abdiquer [abdike] **1** *vt* (*trône, autorité*) to abdicate; (*droits etc*) to renounce, to surrender **2** *vi* to abdicate

abdomen [abdɔmɛn] *nm Anat* abdomen

abdominal, -ale, -aux, -ales [abdɔminal, -o] **1** *adj* abdominal **2** *nmpl* **abdominaux** abdominal *or* stomach muscles; **faire des abdominaux** *ou F* **des abdos** to do stomach muscle exercises

abducteur [abdyktœr] *Anat* **1** *adj* (*muscle*) abductor **2** *nm* abductor muscle

abécédaire [abesedɛr] **1** *adj Vieilli* alphabetical **2** *nm* ABC, alphabet book

abeille [abɛj] *nf* (*insecte*) bee; **a. mâle** drone; **a. mère** queen bee; **nid d'abeilles** bees' nest, honeycomb; *Aut* **radiateur nid d'abeilles** honeycomb radiator; *F* **elle ne cesse de travailler, c'est une vraie petite a.** she never stops working, she's a real busy bee

▶ **abeille: a. domestique** hive *or* honey bee; **a. neutre** *ou* **ouvrière** worker (bee)

aber [abɛr] *nm Géog* deep estuary

aberrant [abɛrɑ̃] *adj* **(a)** *Biol* aberrant **(b)** (*absurde*) (*comportement*) aberrant, illogical; (*remarque*) nonsensical; **avoir une conduite aberrante** to behave illogically; **c'est a.!** it's absurd

aberration [abɛrasjɔ̃] *nf* (*de l'esprit, du comportement*), *Astron, Biol, Math, Opt* aberration; **a. chromosomique** chromosome abnormality; **dans un moment d'a.** in a moment of aberration; **c'est une a.!** it's absurd!

abêtir [abɛtir] **1** *vt* **a. qn** to make sb stupid; **la télévision abêtit les enfants** television deadens *or* stultifies children's minds **2** *vi* to addle the brain **3 s'abêtir** *vpr* to grow *or* become stupid

abêtissant [abetisɑ̃] *adj* mind-destroying, mindless

abhorrer [abɔre] *vt Litt* to abhor, to loathe

abîme [abim] *nm* **(a)** (*de l'océan*) abyss, chasm, depth(s); *Fig* gulf; *Géol* swallowhole; **les abîmes de l'océan** the ocean depths; *Fig* **un a. nous sépare** we are separated by a gulf, there is a gulf between us; **plonger dans les abîmes de l'angoisse** to plunge into the depths of anguish; *Fig* **le livre est un a. d'ennui** this book is extremely boring *or* deadly dull; *Fig* **un a. de science** a person of immense learning; (*qui peut fournir beaucoup de renseignements*) a mine of information; *Litt* **les abîmes de l'histoire** the earliest beginnings of history, the mists of time

(b) (*moral*) despair; **il est au bord de l'a.** he is on the brink *or* verge of depression *or* despair

(c) (*financier*) ruin; **courir à l'a.** to be on the road to ruin, to be heading for ruin

abîmer [abime] **1** *vt* (*qch*) to spoil, to damage; *F* (*qn*) to injure; **livre abîmé par la pluie** book spoilt by the rain; **a. ses affaires** to damage one's belongings; **abimé en cours de transit** damaged in transit; *F* **se faire a. (le portrait)** to get beaten up *or* knocked about **2 s'abîmer** *vpr* **(a)** *Litt* **s'a. dans les flots** to sink, *Litt* to be engulfed by *or* swallowed up by the sea; *Fig* **s'a. dans la douleur/dans ses pensées** to be sunk in grief/lost in thought **(b)** (*d'un fruit*) to spoil, to go bad; (*de chaussures*) to wear out; **s'a. facilement** not to wear well **(c) s'a. la santé** to damage one's health; **tu t'abîmes les yeux** you're ruining your eyes *or* eyesight

abject [abʒɛkt] *adj Litt* (*pauvreté*) abject; *Péj* (*personne, comportement*) mean, contemptible, despicable

abjectement [abʒɛktəmɑ̃] *adv Litt* abjectly; *Péj* contemptibly, despicably

abjection [abʒɛksjɔ̃] *nf Litt* abjectness, abjection; **se conduire avec a.** to behave abjectly

abjuration [abʒyrasjɔ̃] *nf* abjuration; (*d'un serment*) renunciation; (*d'une menace, d'une hérésie*) recantation

abjurer [abʒyre] *vt* to abjure, to forswear; (*serment*) to renounce; (*hérésie*) to recant; (*insulte, confession*) to retract

ablatif, -ive [ablatif, -iv] *Gram* **1** *adj* ablative **2** *nm* ablative case; **à l'a.** in the ablative; **a. absolu** ablative absolute

ablation [ablasjɔ̃] *nf* ablation; *Méd* **a. des amygdales** removal of the tonsils, tonsillectomy

ablette [ablɛt] *nf* (*poisson*) bleak

ablution [ablysjɔ̃] *nf* washing, *Fml* ablution; *F* **faire ses ablutions** to wash, *Hum* to perform one's ablutions

abnégation [abnegasjɔ̃] *nf* abnegation, self-sacrifice

aboi [abwa] *nm* (*used in*) **aux abois** (*cerf, ennemi*) at bay; *Fig* (*dans un état désespéré*) hard pressed, with one's back to *or* against the wall; *Fig* **ils sont aux abois** they are in desperate *or* dire straits

aboiement [abwamɑ̃] *nm* (*d'un chien*) barking; (*des chiens de la meute*) baying; **il fit entendre un a. timide** he gave a timid little bark; **les aboiements de votre chien** your dog's barking; *Fig Péj* **les aboiements de la presse** the rantings of the press

abolir [abɔlir] *vt* to abolish, to suppress; (*dette etc*) to cancel; **le téléphone abolit les distances** the telephone makes distances irrelevant

abolissement [abɔlismɑ̃] *nm*, **abolition** [abɔlisjɔ̃] *nf* abolition, suppression; (*d'un décret*) repeal, annulment; **l'a. de l'esclavage** the abolition of slavery

abolitionnisme [abɔlisjɔnism] *nm Hist* abolitionism

abolitionniste [abɔlisjɔnist] *adj, n Hist* abolitionist

abominable [abɔminabl] *adj* abominable, foul; (*crime*) heinous; (*odeur*) foul; **une fin** *ou* **mort a.** a horrible death; **l'a. homme des neiges** the abominable snowman; **temps a.** abominable *or* filthy weather

abominablement [abɔminabləmɑ̃] *adv* abominably

abomination [abɔminasjɔ̃] *nf* **(a)** abomination, abhorrence; **avoir qch/qn en a.** to loathe sth/sb **(b)** (*chose atroce*) abomination; **ne l'écoute pas, elle ne dit que des abominations** don't listen to her, she has a foul tongue; **ce café est une a.** this coffee is abominable; **c'est une a.!** it's abominable!, it's atrocious!

abominer [abɔmine] *vt* to abominate, to loathe

abondamment [abɔ̃damɑ̃] *adv* abundantly, plentifully, copiously; **manger/boire a.** to eat/drink in copious amounts; **se servir a. de pain/dans la caisse du magasin** to help oneself to plenty of bread/from the till; **il a plu a. toute la nuit** it rained heavily all night; **peu a.** scantily; **dossier a. documenté** well-researched file; **se documenter a.** to gather large amounts of information *or* material; **parler a.** to talk a great deal

abondance [abɔ̃dɑ̃s] *nf* **(a)** (*profusion*) abundance, plenty; **on trouve des pommes en a. sur le marché** there is an abundant *or* a plentiful supply of apples on the market; **il y a une a. de fautes** there are numerous mistakes; **une a. de fruits** an abundance of fruit; **corne d'a.** cornucopia, horn of plenty **(b)** (*d'informations, de détails*) wealth; **vivre dans l'a.** to live in affluence; **parler avec a.** to speak volubly; *Litt* **parler d'a.** to speak off the cuff, to speak extempore

abondant [abɔ̃dɑ̃] *adj* abundant, copious, plentiful; (*style, vocabulaire*) rich; (*feuillage*) luxuriant; (*repas*) copious, hearty; (*excuses, saignement*) profuse; (*pluie*) heavy; **une chevelure abondante** a thick head of hair; **chevelure peu abondante** thin hair; **une récolte peu abondante** a poor *or* scanty harvest; **elle m'a donné d'abondants conseils** she gave me a great deal of advice

abonder [abɔ̃de] *vi* **(a)** (*foisonner*) to be plentiful, to abound **(en** in); **le raisin abonde cet automne** the grapes are plentiful this autumn **(b) rivière qui abonde de** *ou* **en poissons** river that abounds in fish; **votre texte abonde en images** your text abounds *or* is rich in imagery; **a. de biens** to be blessed with riches **(c) a. dans le sens de qn** to be entirely of sb's opinion, to agree entirely *or* thoroughly with sb

abonné, -ée [abɔne] **1** *n* (*à un journal etc*) subscriber; *Rail, Th* season-ticket holder; *Admin* **abonnés du gaz/de l'électricité** gas/electricity consumers; *Tél* **il n'y a pas d'a. au numéro que vous avez demandé** = the number you have dialled has not been recognized **2** *adj* (*à un journal*) subscribing; *Rail, Th* holding a season ticket; **les membres abonnés au théâtre** members holding a season ticket for the theatre; *Admin* **être a. au téléphone/gaz** to be a telephone subscriber/gas consumer; *Fig* **j'ai l'habitude de ce genre d'ennui, j'y suis a.!** I'm used to this kind of problem, it's the story of my life!

abonnement [abɔnmɑ̃] *nm* **(a)** (*à un journal etc*) subscription; **prendre un a. au Figaro** to subscribe to *or* take out a subscription to the Figaro **(b)** *Admin* **a. au téléphone** (telephone) line rental; **a. à l'eau** water rates; *Rail, Th* **(carte d')a.** season ticket; **a. collectif** group subscription; **a. saisonnier** season ticket; **prendre un a.** to take out a season ticket

abonner [abɔne] **1** *vt* (*à une revue etc*) to take out a subscription for; **je vais vous a. à cette revue** I'll take out a subscription to that magazine for you **2 s'abonner** *vpr* **(a) s'a. à une revue** to take out a subscription to a magazine **(b)** *Rail etc* to take out a season ticket; *Admin* **s'a. au téléphone** to be a telephone subscriber

abord [abɔr] **1** *nm* **(a)** (*à terre*) access, approach; **île d'un a. difficile** island that is difficult to approach; *Fig* **un auteur d'un a. difficile** an author who is difficult to get to grips with *or* not very accessible

(b) abords approaches **(d'un endroit** to a place); (*d'une ville*) outskirts

(c) (*façon d'accueillir*) approachability; **être d'un a. rude/chaleureux** to have a rough/welcoming manner (with people); **être d'un a. facile/difficile** to be approachable/unapproachable

2 *adv* **d'a., tout d'a.** at first, to begin with; (*tout de suite*) straight away, at once; (*premièrement*) first, in the first place, first and foremost; **dès l'a.** from the (very) first, from the outset; **au premier a., de prime a.** at first sight; **d'a., elle ne dit jamais merci** for a start, she never says thank you; **toi, d'a., je ne te parle plus** I'm not talking to you, so there!

abordable [abɔrdabl] *adj* **(a)** (*piste d'atterrissage etc*) easy to land on; (*côte, rivage*) easy to approach; (*lieu*) easy of access, accessible **(b)** (*prix*) reasonable, affordable; **vos prix ne sont pas abordables** your prices are unreasonable **(c)** (*personne*) approachable; **peu a.** aloof, standoffish; (*grincheux*) grumpy

abordage [abɔrdaʒ] *nm Naut* **(a)** (*manœuvre de guerre*) boarding; **monter** *ou* **sauter à l'a. (d'un navire)** to board a ship; **à l'a.!** get ready to board! **(b)** (*collision*) collision; **il y a eu un a. causé par le brouillard** two ships collided in the fog **(c)** (*pour attaquer*) (*autre bateau*) boarding; (*pour s'amarrer*) coming alongside

aborder [abɔrde] **1** *vi* to land, to make land; (*dans un port*) to berth; *Vieilli* **a. un port** to reach a port **2** *vt* **(a)** (*person*) to accost; **se faire a. dans la rue** to be approached in the street **(b)** (*question, difficulté*) to tackle **(c)** (*navire dans un combat*) to board, to grapple; (*se mettre côte à côte de*) (*bateau*) to come alongside **(d)** (*rentrer en collision avec*) (*bateau*) to collide with *or* run foul of *or* run down

aborigène [abɔriʒɛn] **1** *adj* native, indigenous (**de** to); (*relatif aux peuplades australiennes*) Aboriginal **2** *n* (*d'un pays*) native; **les aborigènes d'Australie** the (Australian) Aborigines

abortif, -ive [abɔrtif, -iv] **1** *adj* **(a)** abortive **(b)** *Méd* **pilule abortive** abortion pill; *Jur* **manœuvres abortives** (procuring of) abortion **2** *nm Méd* abortifacient

aboucher [abuʃe] **1** *vt* **(a)** (*faire rencontrer*) (*qn avec qn*) to put in touch *or* contact **(b)** *Tech* **a. le tuyau au robinet** to connect the pipe (up) to the tap **2 s'aboucher** *vpr* **(a)** (*rencontrer*) **s'a. avec qn** to get in touch with sb, to contact sb **(b)** *Tech* **le tuyau s'abouche sur l'aspirateur** the tube is connected *or* connects to the vacuum cleaner

Aboukir [abukir] *nm* Ab(o)ukir; *Hist* **la bataille d'A.** the battle of the Nile

abouler [abule] *Arg* **1** *vt* to bring; (*donner*) to hand over; **aboule ça ici!** bring it here!, hand it over! **2 s'abouler** *vpr* (*arriver*) to turn up, to show up

about [abu] *nm Tech* butt

abouter [abute] *vt Tech* (*poutres etc*) to join end to end, to butt(-joint)

aboutir [abutir] *vi* **(a) a. à qch** (*mener à*) (*d'un chemin, escalier*) to lead to sth; (*de différentes directions*) to converge on sth, to lead to sth; *Fig* (*d'une tentative, d'efforts*) to result in sth; **n'a. à rien** (*d'un projet*) to come to nothing, *F* to go up in smoke; **leur raisonnement aboutit à une évidence** their reasoning leads to an obvious conclusion; **pour a. aux fins que nous poursuivons** to attain the end (which) we have in view; **a. dans un champ/sur la place du village** (*d'une personne*) to end up in a field/in *or* at the village square; *Fig* **j'ai abouti à la conclusion que ...** I finally concluded that ...; *Fig* **nous n'avons abouti à aucun résultat** in the end we didn't get any result **(b)** (*d'un projet etc*) to succeed; **ne pas a.** to fail, to fall through; **faire a. qch** to bring sth to a successful conclusion

aboutissants [abutisɑ̃] *nmpl* **connaître les tenants et les a. d'une affaire** to know the ins and outs of an affair, to know all there is to know about an affair

aboutissement [abutismɑ̃] *nm* (*d'un effort etc*) result, outcome

aboyer [abwaje] *vi* **(j'aboie; j'aboierai)** (*d'un chien*) to bark; (*chien de meute*) to bay; *Fig* **a. après qn** to shout *or* yell at sb

aboyeur, -euse [abwajœr, -øz] **1** *adj* (*chien*) barking **2** *n F* tout, *US* barker **3** *nm* (*oiseau*) sandpiper

abracadabra [abrakadabra] *nm* abracadabra

abracadabrant [abrakadabrɑ̃] *adj F* (*histoire*) cock-and-bull

abraser [abraze] *vt Tech* to abrade

abrasif, -ive [abrazif, -iv] *adj, nm Tech* abrasive

abrasion [abrazjɔ̃] *nf Tech* abrasion; *Géol* **a. de la roche par l'eau** abrasion of the rock by the water

abrégé [abreʒe] *nm* précis, summary; (*d'un roman*) abridg(e)ment; (*d'une thèse*) abstract; **a. d'histoire de France** short history of France; **a. de philosophie** a short guide to philosophy; **voici les faits en a.** here are the facts in a few words *or* in brief; **en a.** in abridged *or* abbreviated form; **écrire en a.** to write in abbreviated form

abrégement [abrɛʒmɑ̃] *nm* **(a)** (*d'un discours etc*) summarizing; (*d'une syllabe*) shortening; **a. d'un délai** shortening of the amount of time allowed for sth **(b)** (*texte*) summary, précis; (*d'un roman*) abridg(e)ment; (*d'un mot*) abbreviation; **a. (d'un ouvrage)** abridged edition (of a work)

abréger [abreʒe] **(j'abrège, n. abrégeons; j'abrégerai) 1** *vt* **(a)** (*vie, travail etc*) to shorten, to cut short; **pour a. votre attente** so as not to keep you waiting **(b)** (*article*) to abridge, to cut down; (*mot*) to abbreviate **2** *vi* to be brief; **pour a.** to be brief, to cut it short; *F* **allez, abrège!** come on, get *or* come to the point!

abreuvement [abrœvmɑ̃] *nm* (*des animaux*) watering

abreuver [abrœve] **1** *vt* **(a)** (*chevaux, bétail etc*) to water **(b)** (*pré etc*) to flood, to irrigate; (*pompe*) to prime; (*tonneaux*) to season; **l'Égypte est abreuvée par le Nil** Egypt is watered by the Nile; *Fig* **a. qn d'injures** to shower *or* cover sb with insults, to heap insults on sb; *Fig* **les téléspectateurs sont abreuvés de publicité** the viewers are swamped *or* bombarded with advertising **2 s'abreuver** *vpr* (*d'un cheval*) to drink; *F* (*d'une personne*) to knock it back

abreuvoir [abrœvwar] *nm* **(a)** (*dans une rivière etc*) watering place; **mener les chevaux à l'a.** to lead the horses to water **(b)** (*baquet*) drinking trough

abréviation [abrevjasjɔ̃] *nf* abbreviation

abri [abri] *nm* shelter, cover; (*écran, paravent*) screen; (*pour les plantes*) (tent) cloche; **a. à outils/à vélos** tool/bike shed; **a. public** public shelter; **a. de sous-marins** submarine pen; **a. bétonné** bunker; **a. sous roche** rock shelter; **prendre a.** to take cover; **famille sans a.** homeless family; **à l'a.** sheltered, under shelter, under cover; **mettre qch à l'a.** to shelter *or* screen sth; **se mettre à l'a.** to take shelter; **à l'a. de qch** sheltered *or* screened from sth; **se mettre à l'a. de la pluie** to (take) shelter from the rain; **se mettre à l'a. de l'auvent** to shelter in the doorway; **a. contre le vent** windscreen; *Fig* **à l'a. de toute suspicion** free from (all) suspicion; *Fig* **personne n'est à l'a. d'une erreur** anybody can make a mistake; **il sera toujours à l'a. du besoin** he will always be protected from hardship, he will never experience hardship; *Naut* **à l'a. de la côte** under the lee of the shore

▶ **abri: a. anti-nucléaire** (nuclear) bunker; **a. fiscal** tax shelter; **a. souterrain** air-raid shelter

abribus [abribys] *nm* bus shelter

abricot [abriko] **1** *nm* apricot **2** *adj inv* apricot-coloured

abricoté [abrikɔte] *adj* apricot flavoured

abricotier [abrikɔtje] *nm* apricot tree

abrier (s') [sabrije] *vpr Can* to cover oneself up (well)

abri-garage, *pl* **abris-garages** *nm* carport

abriter [abrite] **1** *vt* **(a)** (*protéger*) to shelter, to screen, to shield, to protect; (*yeux*) to shade; **a. ses yeux du soleil** to shade one's eyes from the sun; **cet auvent nous abrite des regards indiscrets** the awning shields us from prying eyes **(b)** (*héberger*) to house; **cet hôtel peut a. cent personnes** the hotel can accommodate a hundred people **2 s'abriter** *vpr* (*de la pluie*) to (take) shelter (**contre** from); (*des tirs*) to take cover; **s'a. derrière qn** to shelter behind sb; *Fig* **il s'abrite derrière le règlement** he shelters *or* hides behind the rules

abrivent [abrivɑ̃] *nm* windbreak

abrogation [abrɔgasjɔ̃] *nf* (*de la loi etc*) abrogation, rescinding, repeal

abrogeable [abrɔʒabl] *adj* repealable

abroger [abrɔʒe] *vt* **(j'abrogeai(s); n. abrogeons)** (*loi etc*) to abrogate, to rescind, to repeal

abrupt [abrypt] **1** *adj* **(a)** (*rocher, pente*) sheer, steep **(b)** *Fig* (*manière*) abrupt, blunt; **répondre d'un ton a.** to give an abrupt *or* short answer, to answer abruptly *or* shortly **2** *nm* steep slope

abruptement [abryptəmɑ̃] *adv* **(a)** steeply, abruptly **(b)** *Fig* abruptly

abruti, -ie [abryti] **1** *adj* **(a)** stupefied, dazed; (*par la chaleur*) exhausted; **j'étais complètement a. après cette séance** my mind *or* brain was totally dead after that session; **a. par l'alcool** stupefied *or* sodden with drink **(b)** *F* stupid, idiotic, moronic; **avoir un air a.** to look stupid *or* moronic **2** *n F* idiot, fool

abrutir [abrytir] **1** *vt* **(a)** (*abêtir*) (*qn*) to exhaust; **ce travail m'abrutit** this work's addling my brain; **la chaleur m'abrutissait** my brain couldn't work in that heat; **je suis abruti de travail** my brain's dead from too much work

(b) (*de l'alcool etc*) to stupefy; **les buveurs, que l'alcool abrutit** drinkers whose minds are (being) numbed *or* deadened by alcohol

2 s'abrutir *vpr* **(a)** (*se fatiguer*) **s'a. de travail/de discussions** to work oneself to the point of exhaustion/to wear oneself out with discussion

(b) (*devenir stupide*) to become dazed *or* stupefied; **on s'abrutit à trop regarder la télévision** too much television addles the brain

abrutissant [abrytisɑ̃] *adj* **(a)** (*fatigant*) exhausting, wearing; (*bruit*) deafening **(b)** (*abêtissant*) mind-destroying

abrutissement [abrytismɑ̃] *nm* (*abêtissement*) **a. de qn** reducing of sb to a mindless state; **propagande qui cause l'a. des masses** propaganda that stops people thinking for themselves

ABS [abeɛs] *nm Aut* **système A.** ABS

abscisse [apsis] *nf* abscissa

abscons, -onse [apskɔ̃, -ɔ̃s] *adj Péj* obscure, abstruse

absence [apsɑ̃s] *nf* **(a)** (*de personne*) absence; **en** *ou* **pendant mon a.** in *or* during my absence, when I am/was/*etc* away; **en l'a. de ma secrétaire** while *or* when my secretary is away; **nous avons regretté votre a.** we were sorry that you weren't with us; **nous regrettons tous les jours son a.** (*d'un mort*) we miss him every day; **briller par son a.** to be conspicuous by one's absence; **a. de l'école** non-attendance at *or* absence from school; **comment expliquez-vous toutes ces absences?** how do you explain all these absences?

(b) (*manque*) (*de meubles, de principes, du père etc*) lack; **a. de demande** absence *or* lack of demand; **a. de goût** lack of taste, tastelessness; **a. d'imagination** lack of imagination; **a. d'esprit** absent-mindedness; **j'ai eu une a. d'esprit et j'ai oublié …** I absentmindedly forgot …; **il a des absences** he's apt to be absent-minded, he has *or* is prone to memory lapses; **dans un moment d'a.** in a moment of absent-mindedness, in an absent-minded moment; (*de négligence, de manque d'attention*) without thinking

(c) *Méd* **a. (épileptique)** epileptic vertigo

▶ **absence**: *Mil etc* **a. illégale** absence without leave; **a. non rémunérée** unpaid leave; **a. rémunérée** paid leave

absent, -ente [apsɑ̃, -ɑ̃t] **1** *adj* **(a)** absent, away; **il est a. de Paris en ce moment** he isn't in Paris at the moment; **quand ma femme est absente** when my wife's away; *Mil* **a. sans permission** absent without leave, AWOL

(b) (*qui n'existe pas*) absent, missing; **une déclaration d'où tout humour était a.** a statement totally lacking in humour; **chez cet animal les dents sont absentes** this animal has no teeth

(c) (*distrait, rêveur*) absent; **son esprit est a.** his mind is far away, *F* he's miles away; **il avait un air a.** he was miles away

2 *n* (*à une réunion etc*) absentee; **les Français ont été les grands absents lors de la Coupe du Monde** the French were the most notable absentees from the World Cup; *Prov* **les absents ont toujours tort** it's always the people who are not there that get blamed; **il ne faut pas dire du mal des absents** you shouldn't say bad things about people when they're not there to defend themselves

absentéisme [apsɑ̃teism] *nm* absenteeism

absentéiste [apsɑ̃teist] **1** *adj* (regularly) absent; **propriétaire a.** absentee landlord **2** *n* (regular) absentee

absenter (s') [sapsɑ̃te] *vpr* (*de chez soi*) to go away; (*de l'école*) to stay away; **je ne me suis pas absentée de toute la journée** I haven't been out all day; **il a dû s'a. pour quelques heures** he had to go somewhere for a few hours, *F* he had to pop out for a few hours; **son mari s'absente beaucoup** her husband is away a lot

absidal, -ale, -aux, -ales [apsidal, -o] *adj* apsidal

abside [apsid] *nf Archit* apse

absidiole [apsidjɔl] *nf Archit* apsidal chapel

absinthe [apsɛ̃t] *nf* **(a)** (*boisson*) absinthe **(b)** (*plante*) wormwood

absolu [apsɔly] **1** *adj* **(a)** absolute; **zéro a.** absolute zero; **poser une règle absolue** to lay down a hard and fast rule; **refus a.** flat refusal; **majorité absolue** absolute majority **(b)** (*total*) absolute; **nous sommes dans l'impossibilité absolue de vous donner des réponses définitives** we are quite unable to give you any definite answers; **pouvoir a.** absolute power; **caractère a.** autocratic nature; **liberté absolue** absolute *or* total freedom **(c)** (*ton, voix*) peremptory **(d)** *Gram* absolute **2** *nm Phil* **l'a.** the absolute; **juger qch dans l'a.** to judge sth in the absolute *or* out of context

absolument [apsɔlymɑ̃] *adv* **(a)** (*complètement*) absolutely; **a.!** absolutely!; **a. pas!** absolutely not!; **a. rien** nothing whatsoever **(b)** (*strictement*) (*parler*) peremptorily; **c'est a. défendu** it is absolutely *or* strictly forbidden; **je le veux a.** I insist on it; **nier a. qch** to deny sth flatly **(c)** (*sans faute*) simply, absolutely; **vous devez a. y aller!** you simply *or* absolutely must go! **(d)** (*sans limite*) **régner a.** to reign as an absolute monarch; **a. parlant** speaking generally **(e)** *Gram* absolutely

absolution [apsɔlysjɔ̃] *nf* **(a)** *Rel* absolution **(b)** *Jur* discharge, acquittal

absolutisme [apsɔlytism] *nm Pol* absolutism

absorbant [apsɔrbɑ̃] *adj* **(a)** (*matériau, qualités*) absorbent **(b)** (*livre, tâche*) absorbing, engrossing

absorber [apsɔrbe] **1** *vt* **(a)** (*d'une éponge etc*) (*eau etc*) to absorb, to soak up; *Ch* (*gaz*) to occlude; **le noir absorbe la lumière** black absorbs light

(b) (*nourriture*) to consume; (*boisson*) to drink; (*médicament*) to take; *Écon* **la multinationale va a. cette entreprise** the multinational is going to take over *or F* swallow up the firm; **les travaux ont absorbé toutes mes économies** the repairs have used up all my savings

(c) (*d'une lecture*) to absorb, to engross; **son travail l'absorbe** he/she is completely wrapped up in his/her work; **cette pensée m'absorbe complètement** I think about it constantly; **être absorbé dans ses pensées** to be lost in thought

2 s'absorber *vpr* to become absorbed *or* engrossed (**dans** in); **s'a. dans la lecture d'un livre** to be absorbed *or* lost in a book

absorption [apsɔrpsjɔ̃] *nf* absorption; **a. de médicaments** (the) taking of medicines; *Écon* **a. d'une petite société par une grosse** the takeover of a small company by a large one

absoudre [apsudr] *vt* (*prp* **absolvant**; *pp* **absous,** *f* **absoute**; *pr ind* **j'absous, il absout, n. absolvons, ils absolvent**; *pr sub* **j'absolve**; *p hist & pr sub are lacking*; *fu* **j'absoudrai**) **(a) a. qn de qch** to forgive sb sth; *Rel* **a. qn de ses péchés** to absolve sb from his sins, to forgive sb his sins; *Rel* **je vous absous** I absolve you **(b)** *Jur* (*qn*) to absolve, to acquit

abstenir (s') [sapstənir] *vpr* (*conj like* **tenir**) to stand aside *or* aloof; *Pol* to abstain (from voting); **s'a. de qch** to abstain from sth, to forgo sth; **s'a. de faire qch** to refrain *or* abstain from doing sth; **s'a. de commentaires** to refrain from comment; **s'a. de manger du chocolat/de boire de l'alcool** to keep off chocolate/alcohol; **dans le doute abstiens-toi** when in doubt, don't

abstention [apstɑ̃sjɔ̃] *nf* abstention (**de** from)

abstentionnisme [apstɑ̃sjɔnism] *nm Pol* (*de vote etc*) abstention

abstentionniste [apstɑ̃sjɔnist] *n Pol* abstainer; **le nombre des abstentionnistes** the number of abstentions

abstinence [apstinɑ̃s] *nf* abstinence; (*qualité d'une personne*) abstemiousness; *Rel* **jour d'a.** day of abstinence; **faire a. le vendredi** to abstain from eating meat on Fridays; **a. (sexuelle)** (sexual) abstinence

abstinent, -ente [apstinɑ̃, -ɑ̃t] **1** *adj* abstemious **2** *n* abstainer; (*qui ne boit pas d'alcool*) teetotaller; *Rel* person who practises abstinence

abstraction [apstraksjɔ̃] *nf* **(a)** *Phil* abstraction; **un esprit capable d'a.** a mind capable of abstract thought **(b) faire a. de qch** to disregard sth; **a. faite du style** style apart **(c)** (*idée abstraite*) abstract idea, abstraction; **se perdre dans des abstractions** to lose oneself in abstractions

abstraire [apstrɛr] (*conj like* **traire**) **1** *vt* to separate, to isolate; *Phil* to abstract **2 s'abstraire** *vpr* **s'a. dans qch** to become engrossed in sth

abstrait [apstrɛ] **1** *adj* (*idée, art etc*) abstract; (*question*) abstruse, deep **2** *nm* **(a)** (*abstraction*) abstract, abstraction; **dans l'a.** in the abstract, in theory **(b)** *Beaux-Arts* abstract art; (*artiste*) abstract artist; (*tableau*) abstract (painting)

abstraitement [apstrɛtmɑ̃] *adv* **(a)** (*en théorie*) in the abstract; **parler a.** to talk in the abstract *or* in abstract terms **(b)** (*distraitement*) abstractedly, absent-mindedly

abstrus, -use [apstry, -yz] *adj* abstruse, recondite
absurde [apsyrd] **1** *adj* absurd, preposterous; **votre conduite est totalement a.!** your behaviour is totally preposterous; **elle est complètement a.** she's completely ridiculous **2** *nm* **l'a.** absurdity; *Phil* the absurd; **réduire une théorie à l'a.** to reduce a theory ad absurdum; *Phil* **démonstration par l'a.** reductio ad absurdum; **l'a. de la situation** the absurdity *or* absurdness of the situation, the absurd thing about the situation; **le théâtre de l'a.** the theatre of the absurd
absurdement [apsyrdəmɑ̃] *adv* absurdly, preposterously
absurdité [apsyrdite] *nf* **(a)** (*caractère absurde*) absurdity, preposterousness; **l'a. de l'existence** the absurdity of existence **(b)** (*chose absurde*) absurdity, piece of nonsense; **cette réaction est une a.** this reaction is completely absurd; **dire des absurdités** to talk nonsense
abus [aby] *nm* **(a)** (*mauvais emploi*) abuse, misuse (**de** of); (*excès*) overindulgence (**de** in); **l'a. des médicaments** the misuse of pharmaceutical drugs; **l'a. de boissons** alcohol abuse; **faire a. de qch** to indulge too freely in sth; **faire a. de son autorité** to abuse one's authority; **employer un terme par a.** to misuse a term

(b) *Jur* (*de droits*) violation; **a. de confiance** breach of trust; **a. d'autorité/de pouvoir** abuse *or* misuse of (one's) authority/power; **a. de biens sociaux** misuse of a company's assets; **a. de droits sociaux** misappropriation of corporate funds

(c) (*pratique*) abuse, corrupt practice; **un écrivain connu pour ses a. de langage** a writer known his abuse of the language *or F* for murdering the language; **réformer un a.** to remedy an abuse; **je ne supporte plus ses a.!** I can't stand his/her outrageous behaviour any longer!; **faire quelques a.** to overdo it, to overindulge; **c'est un a. (que) de croire que ...** it is a mistake to suppose that ...; *F* **il y a de l'a.!** that's going too far!
abuser [abyze] **1** *vi* **a. de qch** to misuse sth; (*exploiter*) to take (unfair) advantage of sth; **vous abusez de vos forces** you're overtaxing yourself; **a. du tabac** to smoke too much; **il ne faut pas a. des bonnes choses** good things should be enjoyed in moderation, enough is as good as a feast; **a. de l'amabilité de qn** to impose on sb *or* on sb's kindness; **a. de la confiance de qn** to abuse sb's confidence; **j'abuse de votre temps** I am taking up too much of your time; **n'abusez point** be moderate; **je ne voudrais pas a., j'ai peur d'a.** I don't want to cause you any inconvenience; **c'est un peu fort, elle abuse!** she's going a bit (too) far!; **vous abusez!** that's a bit much!; **a. d'une femme** to abuse a woman sexually

2 *vt* to deceive; **il ne nous abusera pas par de belles paroles** he will not deceive us with fine words

3 s'abuser *vpr* to be mistaken; **je vous ai déjà rencontré, si je ne m'abuse** I've met you before, if I'm not mistaken
abusif, -ive [abyzif, -iv] *adj* **(a)** (*emploi d'un mot*) incorrect; **il serait a. de l'affirmer** it would be an exaggeration to say that **(b)** (*excessif*) excessive; **emploi a. de la force** excessive *or* unwarranted use of force; **mère abusive** possessive *or* domineering mother
abusivement [abyzivmɑ̃] *adv* incorrectly, wrongly; **employer un mot a.** to use a word incorrectly *or* wrongly; **elle a profité a. de la situation** she took unfair advantage of the situation
abuter [abyte] *vt* **a. un camion à un quai** to back a lorry against a platform
abyme [abim] *nm* **tableau/film/pièce avec structure en a.** painting within a painting/film within a film/play within a play
abyssal, -ale, -aux, -ales [abisal, -o] *adj* (*faune etc*) abyssal; *Fig* (*profondeurs*) unfathomable; **les fosses abyssales** the troughs of the ocean depths
abysse [abis] *nm Géog* abyssal zone; *Fig* **les abysses du désespoir** the depths of despair
Abyssinie [abisini] *nf* Abyssinia
abyssinien, -ienne [abisinjɛ̃, -jɛn] **1** *adj* Abyssinian **2** *n* **A.** Abyssinian
A.C. [ase] *abrév* **appellation contrôlée**
acabit [akabi] *nm Péj* **ils sont du même a.** they're tarred with the same brush; **je me méfie des gens de cet a.** I don't trust people like that; **des drogués, des dealers et autres paumés de cet a.** drug addicts, dealers and other dropouts of the same type
acacia [akasja] *nm* (*arbre*) **a. vrai** acacia; (*robinier*) **a. vulgaire, faux a.** locust tree, false acacia
académicien, -ienne [akademisjɛ̃, -jɛn] *n* academician; member of the Académie française
académie [akademi] *nf* **(a)** (*des lettres, des sciences, d'art*) society; **l'A. française** the French Academy **(b)** (*école*) school, academy; **a. de musique** music school, school of music; **a. de danse** dancing school; **a. de dessin** school of art, art school **(c)** *Admin* (*en France*) educational district **(d)** (*de Platon etc*) academy **(e)** (*étude*) nude
académique [akademik] *adj* **(a)** academic; **les palmes académiques** = insignia of decoration granted by the French Ministry of Education; **séance a.** sitting *or* meeting of an Academy; **occuper un fauteuil a.** (*de l'Académie française*) to be a member of the French Academy; *Littér Péj* **style a.** pedantic style; **débat a.** academic discussion **(b)** *Admin* **inspection a.** board of school inspectors **(c)** *Beaux-Arts* **figure a.** nude
académisme [akademism] *nm Beaux-Arts souvent Péj* academicism
Acadie [akadi] *nf Hist* Acadia
acadien, -ienne [akadjɛ̃, -jɛn] **1** *adj* Acadian **2** *nm Ling* Acadian **3** *n* **A.** Acadian
acajou [akaʒu] **1** *nm* **(a)** mahogany; **table en a.** mahogany table **(b) noix d'a.** cashew nut; **a. à noix** cashew nut tree **2** *adj inv* reddish-brown, auburn
acanthe [akɑ̃t] *nf Bot, Archit* acanthus
a capella [akapɛla] *adv Mus* a capella; **chanter a.** to sing a capella
acariâtre [akarjɑtr] *adj* bad-tempered, cantankerous; **être d'humeur a.** to be bad-tempered
acarien [akarjɛ̃] *nm* (*insecte*) dust mite
accablant [akɑblɑ̃] *adj* **(a)** (*malchance, témoignage, responsabilités*) overwhelming; (*chaleur*) overpowering, oppressive **(b)** (*témoignage*) damning
accablé [akɑble] *adj* (*de travail etc*) overwhelmed; (*de peine*) overcome, weighed down; **a. de fatigue** overwhelmed with fatigue; **a. par la chaleur** overwhelmed *or* overcome by the heat; **a. de dettes** burdened with debt
accablement [akɑbləmɑ̃] *nm* dejection, despondency, depression
accabler [akɑble] *vt* **(a)** to overpower, to overwhelm; **être accablé de douleur** to be grief-stricken; **il m'accable de travail** he piles work on me; **il m'accable de questions** he bombards me with questions; **a. qn d'injures** to heap abuse on sb; **elle nous accable de recommandations** she heaps advice on us **(b)** (*fournir des preuves contre*) to damn
accalmie [akalmi] *nf* lull; **dans un moment d'a.** in a calm moment, in a moment of respite
accaparant [akaparɑ̃] *adj* demanding; **un emploi a.** a demanding job; **leurs enfants sont très accaparants** their children take up a lot of their time
accaparement [akaparmɑ̃] *nm* monopolizing; (*des stocks*) buying up; (*des marchandises*) cornering
accaparer [akapare] *vt* (*stocks*) to buy up; (*marchandises*) to corner, to hoard; (*pouvoir*) to seize; **a. le marché de l'automobile** to corner the automobile market; **a. la conversation** to monopolize the conversation; **a. les meilleures places** to secure *or* corner the best seats; **son travail l'accapare trop** his/her work takes up too much of his/her time; **je ne voudrais pas vous a. toute la soirée** I don't want to monopolize you for the whole evening
accapareur, -euse [akaparœr, -øz] **1** *n* (*de nourriture etc*) buyer-up; (*société*) monopolist, *Péj* grabber **2** *adj* (*personne*) possessive
accastillage [akastijaʒ] *nm Naut* (*d'un navire*) fittings
accastiller [akastije] *vt Naut* (*navire*) to fit out
accéder [aksede] *vi* **(j'accède, n. accédons; j'accéderai) (a)** (*atteindre*) to have access (**à** to); **on accède à la porte par un escalier** a flight of steps leads to the door; *Ordinat* **a. à un programme** to access a program

(b) (*accepter*) to comply, to agree; **a. à une requête** to comply with a request; **a. à une condition** to agree *or* assent to a condition

(c) (*parvenir*) to accede; **a. à de hautes responsabilités** to acquire important responsibilities; **a. à un poste important** to obtain *or* to get an important job; **a. au trône** to accede to the throne; **a. à la propriété** (*d'un appartement, d'une maison*) to be a first-time buyer; **pour permettre aux jeunes ménages d'a. à la propriété** to allow young couples to buy their first home
accélérateur, -trice [akseleratœr, -tris] **1** *adj* accelerating **2** *nm Aut, Ordinat* accelerator; *Nucl* **a. de particules** particle accelerator; **a. d'électrons** betatron; *Aut* **appuyer sur l'a.** to accelerate; *Ordinat* **a. graphique** graphic(s) accelerator
accélération [akselerasjɔ̃] *nf* acceleration; (*du travail*) speeding up; **a. de la pesanteur** gravitational acceleration; *Aut* **pédale d'a.** accelerator (pedal); *Aut* **en a. partielle** part-throttle; **avoir une bonne a.** to have good acceleration
accéléré [akselere] **1** *adj* quick, fast, rapid; (*mouvement*) accelerated; **un cours a.** a crash course **2** *nm Cin* accelerated motion

accélérer [akselere] **(j'accélère, n. accélérons; j'accélérai) 1** *vt* to accelerate, to speed up; **a. le mouvement** to speed up **2** *vi* **dépêche-toi, accélère!** hurry up, get a move on!; *Aut* **passe en seconde et accélère** go into second and accelerate; **a. à vide** to rev the engine **3 s'accélérer** *vpr* to accelerate, to speed up; (*du pouls*) to go faster, to speed up

accent [aksɑ̃] *nm* **(a)** (*phonétique*) accent, stress; **a. d'intensité** *ou* **tonique** tonic accent

(b) *Gram* accent; **a. aigu/grave** acute/grave (accent); **e a. circonflexe** e circumflex

(c) (*prononciation*) accent; **parler le français avec un a. anglais** to speak French with an English accent; **il n'a pas l'accent** *ou* **d'accent** he doesn't have an accent

(d) (*inflexion*) tone of voice; *Fig* **son récit a l'a. de la vérité** his account rings true; *Ling* **a. de phrase** sentence stress; *Fig* **mettre l'a. sur la présentation du produit** to put the emphasis on *or* to emphasize the presentation of the product

(e) les accents du désespoir the accents of despair; **il parlait avec des accents de rage/de terreur dans la voix** his voice was angry/terror-stricken; **les accents de la Marseillaise** the strains of the Marseillaise

accentuation [aksɑ̃tɥasjɔ̃] *nf* **(a)** (*des syllabes etc*) stressing; **les règles de l'a. espagnole** the stress rules in Spanish **(b)** *Gram* accentuation, placing of the grammatical accents; **faire des fautes d'a.** to put accents in the wrong place **(c)** (*d'un phénomène*) growth

accentué [aksɑ̃tɥe] *adj* stressed, accented; *Fig* pronounced, marked; **traits fortement accentués** pronounced *or* strongly marked features; **les traits accentués par la fatigue** features drawn with fatigue

accentuer [aksɑ̃tɥe] **1** *vt* **(a)** (*syllabes etc*) to stress; **syllabe non accentuée** unstressed syllable **(b)** *Gram* **a. une voyelle** to mark a vowel with an accent **(c)** *Fig* to emphasize, to accentuate; **son conseil/cet incident n'a fait qu'a. leurs problèmes** his advice/this incident has only added to their problems; **a. le chômage** to increase *or* add to unemployment **2 s'accentuer** *vpr* to become more pronounced *or* marked

acceptabilité [akseptabilite] *nf Gram* acceptability; *Mktg* **a. de la marque** brand acceptability

acceptable [akseptabl] *adj* **(a)** acceptable **(à** to**)**; **offre a.** reasonable offer **(b)** (*voiture, maison, machine*) in fair condition; (*performance*) reasonably good

acceptablement [akseptabləmɑ̃] *adv* acceptably, in an acceptable manner

acceptant, -ante [akseptɑ̃, -ɑ̃t] *adj, n Com, Jur* acceptant

acceptation [akseptasjɔ̃] *nf* acceptance

accepter [aksepte] *vt* to accept; (*défi*) to take up; (*pari*) to take on; **il n'accepte pas l'échec/la difficulté** he refuses to acknowledge failure/the existence of problems; **elle n'arrive pas à a. le mariage de sa fille** she can't come to terms with her daughter's marriage; **je n'accepte pas votre conduite d'hier soir** I find your behaviour last night unacceptable; **je n'accepte pas cette théorie** I don't accept that theory, I don't agree with that theory; **a. de faire qch** to agree to do sth; **elle n'accepte pas que son mari soit au chômage** she can't *or* won't accept the fact that her husband is unemployed; **a. qn comme** *ou* **pour arbitre** to accept sb as an arbitrator; **il a été accepté dans la famille** he was accepted into the family; **acceptez-vous Jean-Guy Pierre pour époux?** ≈ do you take this man, Jean-Guy Pierre, as your lawfully wedded husband?

accepteur [akseptœr] *nm* **(a)** *Com* (*d'une facture*) acceptor, drawee **(b)** *Ch, Électron* acceptor

acception [aksepsjɔ̃] *nf Fml* **(a)** (*d'un mot etc*) meaning, sense, *Fml* acceptation **(b) sans a. de race/de sexe** (*dans une offre d'emploi*) open to candidates of all races/of both sexes, irrespective of race/sex

accès [aksɛ] *nm* **(a)** (*approche*) access, approach; **les a. de la gare** the station approaches, the approaches to the station; **le refuge est facile d'a.** the shelter is easily accessible *or* easy to reach; **avoir a. à qch** to have access to sth; **donner a. à qch** to give access *or* to lead to sth; **ce diplôme donne a. à toute une gamme de professions passionnantes** this diploma opens the door to a wide range of exciting professions; **trouver a. auprès de qn** to be admitted to sb's presence; **être d'a. facile/difficile** (*d'une personne*) to be approachable/unapproachable; (*d'un auteur, d'un livre etc*) to be accessible/not very accessible; **facile/difficile d'a.** (*lieu*) easy/hard to reach, easy/hard to get to; **l'a. à la profession de médecin devient de plus en plus difficile** entry into the medical profession is becoming more and more difficult; *Rail* **a. aux quais** to the trains

(b) (*poussée*) fit, attack, outburst; **a. de fièvre** attack *or* bout of fever; **des a. de toux** fits of coughing, coughing fits; **a. de faiblesse** fainting fit; **a. d'enthousiasme** burst *or* fit of enthusiasm; **a. de tristesse/découragement** wave of sadness/discouragement; **a. de colère/folie** fit of anger/madness; **travailler par a.** to work by *or* in fits and starts

(c) *Ordinat* access; **avoir a. à** to be able to access; **code d'a.** access code; **à a. multiple** multi-access; **temps d'a.** access time; **a. aléatoire** random access; **a. au bus local** local bus access; **a. direct à la mémoire** direct memory access; **a. à distance** remote access; **a. en écriture** write access; **a. rapide** high-speed access, fast access; **a. sécurisé par mot de passe** password-protected access; **a. sélectif** selective access; **a. au système** system access

accessibilité [aksesibilite] *nf* accessibility

accessible [aksesibl] *adj* **(a)** (*où l'on peut arriver*) accessible; **séminaire a. à tous les licenciés** seminar open to all graduates; **endroit a.** accessible place, place that can be reached easily; **parc a. à tous** park open to everybody; *Fig* **les prix sont très accessibles** the prices are within everyone's reach, the prices are very affordable; **un livre tout à fait a.** a wholly accessible book **(b)** (*personne*) approachable; **a. à la pitié** open to pity; **a. à la flatterie** susceptible to flattery

accession [aksesjɔ̃] *nf* **(a)** (*au pouvoir etc*) accession; **faciliter l'a. des femmes à la politique** to make it easier for women to enter politics; **l'a. à la propriété est rendue possible à tous** home ownership is within everyone's reach; **a. au trône** accession to the throne; **l'a. du pays à l'indépendance a eu lieu en 1968** the country became independent *or* gained independence in 1968 **(b)** (*à un contrat, un parti*) adherence, adhesion

accessit [aksesit] *nm* (*dans un examen*) honourable mention; **remporter un a. en musique** to get an honourable mention in music

accessoire [akseswar] **1** *adj* accessory; *Compta* (*frais*) incidental; **jouer un rôle a.** to play a subordinate role; **c'est un détail a.** it's an incidental detail **2** *nm* **(a)** (*objet*) accessory, *Fml* appurtenance; *Th etc* **accessoires** properties, *F* props; **voiture vendue sans accessoires** car sold without accessories; **magasin des accessoires** property room; **chapeau et accessoires coordonnés** hat and matching accessories; **a. d'objectif** lens attachment; *Ordinat* **a. de bureau** desk accessory **(b)** (*ce qui est accessoire*) (minor) details; **on s'occupera de l'a. plus tard** we'll take care of the (minor) details later

accessoirement [akseswarmɑ̃] *adv* (*si besoin est*) if necessary, if need be; **je m'occupe a. de la comptabilité** I look after the accounts in addition to my main duties

accessoiriser [akseswarize] *vt* (*vêtements etc*) to accessorize

accessoiriste [akseswarist] *n Th etc* props (man/*f* woman), property man *or f* mistress; *TV* props buyer

accident [aksidɑ̃] *nm* **(a)** (*événement imprévisible*) accident; (*contretemps*) mishap; **je l'ai retrouvé par a.** I found it by accident, I found it accidentally; **nous sommes arrivés sans a.** we arrived safely *or* safe and sound; **la cérémonie s'est déroulée sans a.** the ceremony went off without a hitch

(b) (*collision, malheur*) **a. de chemin de fer** railway accident; **a. d'avion** plane *or* air crash; **a. de voiture** car accident *or* crash; **a. de la route** road accident; **a. de la circulation** traffic accident; **a. mortel** fatal accident, fatality; **être victime d'un a.** to meet with an accident

(c) *Méd* **a. cardiaque** cardiac arrest, heart attack; **a. vasculaire** vascular accident

(d) *Mus* accidental

(e) a. de terrain unevenness *or* irregularity of the ground

▶ **accident**: **a. de parcours** hitch; *Fig* **son échec n'est qu'un a. de parcours** his failure is just a temporary hitch *or* setback; **a. du travail** industrial accident, accident in the workplace

accidenté, -ée [aksidɑ̃te] **1** *adj* **(a)** (*terrain*) uneven, broken **(b) voiture accidentée** damaged car **2** *n* victim of an accident; **les accidentés** the injured, the casualties; **accidentés de la route** road accident victims; **les accidentés du travail** victims of industrial accidents

accidentel, -elle [aksidɑ̃tɛl] *adj* **(a)** (*imprévu*) accidental; **une rencontre accidentelle** a chance *or* an accidental meeting; **je le rencontrai de façon purement accidentelle** I met him quite by accident; **mort accidentelle** (*dans un accident*) accidental death **(b)** *Mus* **signes accidentels** accidentals; (*armature constante*) key signature

accidentellement [aksidɑ̃tɛlmɑ̃] *adv* accidentally; (*mourir*) in an accident, as a *or* the result of an accident

accidenter [aksidɑ̃te] *vt* (*voiture*) to damage, *F* to prang

acclamation [aklamasjɔ̃] *nf* acclamation, cheering; **les acclamations de la foule** the cheers *or* acclamations of the crowd; **discours salué d'acclamations** speech greeted with cheers; **elle fut élue par a.** she was elected by acclamation

acclamer [aklame] *vt* (*qn, discours*) to acclaim, to cheer; (*en tapant dans les mains*) to applaud; (*saluer qn, discours*) to greet with cheers; **a. qn empereur** to acclaim sb emperor

acclimatable [aklimatabl] *adj* acclimatizable, *US* acclimatable

acclimatation [aklimatasjɔ̃] *nf* acclimatization, *US* acclimation; **jardin d'a.** zoological gardens

acclimatement [aklimatmɑ̃] *nm* acclimatization, *US* acclimation

acclimater [aklimate] **1** *vt* to acclimatize, *US* to acclimate (**à** to); *Fig* (*usages*) to introduce **2 s'acclimater** *vpr* to become *or* get acclimatized *or US* acclimated

accointance [akwɛ̃tɑ̃s] *nf Péj* **accointances** dealings, relations; **avoir des accointances dans le milieu des affaires** to have contacts in the business world

accointer (s') [sakwɛ̃te] *vpr Péj Vieilli* **s'a. avec qn** to take up with sb

accolade [akɔlad] *nf* (**a**) (*embrassade*) (formal) embrace; **donner/recevoir l'a.** to embrace/to be embraced (**b**) *Hist* accolade; **recevoir l'a.** ≈ to be knighted (**c**) *Mus* brace; *Typ* curly bracket, brace (**d**) *Archit* (**arc en**) **a.** ogee arch

accolement [akɔlmɑ̃] *nm* joining, bracketing

accoler [akɔle] **1** *vt* (**a**) (*joindre côte à côte*) to join side by side, to couple; *Typ* to brace, to bracket; **le nom de l'épouse est accolé à celui du mari** the wife's surname is joined *or* added to that of the husband; **accolé aux murs** built on the walls (**b**) (*vigne*) to tie up **2 s'accoler** *vpr* (*de plantes*) to intertwine, to cling

accommodant [akɔmɔdɑ̃] *adj* accommodating; **a. en affaires** easy to do business with

accommodation [akɔmɔdasjɔ̃] *nf* (**a**) (*adaptation*) adapting; **a. d'une pièce aux usages d'un bureau** adaptation *or* conversion of a room for office use (**b**) *Physiol* (*des yeux*) accommodation

accommodement [akɔmɔdmɑ̃] *nm* compromise, arrangement, agreement; **en venir à un a.** to come to a compromise *or* arrangement, to come to terms (**avec** with); **politique d'a.** give-and-take policy; *Com* **a. avec ses créanciers** composition with one's creditors

accommoder [akɔmɔde] **1** *vt* (**a**) *Culin* (*nourriture*) to prepare; **a. les restes** to use up the leftovers; **a. une salade** to dress a salad

(**b**) **a. qch à qch** to fit *or* adapt sth to sth; **a. une pièce à un usage particulier** to adapt a room to *or* for a particular purpose; *Opt* **a. l'objectif sur l'infini** to set *or* adjust the lens to infinity

2 s'accommoder *vpr* (**a**) *Litt* **s'a. à qch** to adapt to sth; **il s'accommode à toutes les circonstances** he's very adaptable; **je m'accommode à tout** anything will do for me

(**b**) **s'a. de qch** to make the best of sth, to put up with sth; **il vous faudra vous a. de cette pièce pour dormir** you'll have to make do with sleeping in this room

(**c**) **s'a. avec qn** to come to an agreement with sb; (*par un compromis*) to compromise with sb; (*créancier*) to compound with

(**d**) *Arch* (*dans un fauteuil etc*) to make oneself comfortable, to settle down

accompagnateur, -trice [akɔ̃paɲatœr, -tris] *n* (**a**) *Mus* accompanist (**b**) (*d'un voyage organisé*) courier, tour guide, tour leader; (*de sortie scolaire*) accompanying adult

accompagnement [akɔ̃paɲmɑ̃] *nm* (**a**) *Mus* accompaniment; **chanter sans a.** to sing unaccompanied (**b**) *Mil etc* close support; **tir d'a.** supporting fire; *Av* **chasseur d'a.** escort fighter (**c**) *Culin* (*servi avec la viande etc*) accompaniment, trimmings; **qu'y a-t-il comme a.?** what does it come with?, what is it served with?; **servi avec des frites en a.** served with chips

accompagner [akɔ̃paɲe] **1** *vt* (**a**) (*venir avec, aller avec*) (*qn*) to go *or* come with, *surtout Fml* to accompany; **il est arrivé accompagné de ses amis** he arrived with his friends; **accompagné de sa secrétaire** accompanied by his secretary; **est-ce que tu vas m'a.?** are you coming with me?; **a. qn jusqu'à la gare** to see sb to the station; **a. qn un bout de chemin** to go part of the way with sb; **l'angoisse qui accompagne ses pensées** the anguish which accompanies his thoughts

(**b**) (*escorter*) to escort; (*groupe de touristes*) to act as courier *or* tour guide to; (*groupe d'enfants*) to accompany; **accessible aux enfants accompagnés uniquement** children must be accompanied by an adult

(**c**) *Mus* **a. qn au piano** to accompany sb on the piano

(**d**) (*ajouter à*) **il a accompagné ses mots d'un sourire** he said it with a smile; **il a accompagné le bouquet de fleurs d'une carte** he enclosed a card with the bouquet of flowers; *Culin* **a. une viande de pommes de terre** to serve potatoes with meat

2 s'accompagner *vpr* (**a**) *Mus* **elle s'accompagne elle-même** she plays her own accompaniment

(**b**) *Culin* (*avec des légumes etc*) to be served; **le porc s'accompagne bien de pommes** apples go well with pork

(**c**) (*advenir en même temps que*) to be accompanied by, to come with; **ces maux de tête s'accompagnent souvent de saignements de nez** these headaches are often accompanied by nose bleeds

accompli [akɔ̃pli] *adj* (*musicien, linguiste, menteur etc*) accomplished; **fait a.** fait accompli, accomplished fact; **on le mit devant le fait a.** he was presented with a fait accompli; **il a quarante ans accomplis** he's turned forty; **à quarante ans accomplis, il serait temps que tu prennes une décision** now you've turned forty, it's time you made a decision

accomplir [akɔ̃plir] **1** *vt* (**a**) (*but etc*) to accomplish, to achieve; (*tâche*) to carry out; (*souhait, promesse*) to fulfil (**b**) (*apprentissage etc*) to complete, to finish; **c'est une mauvaise action que tu as accomplie là** it was very wrong of you to do that; **a. un geste** to make a gesture **2 s'accomplir** *vpr* to be realized, to come true; **notre souhait s'est accompli** our wish came true; *Rel* **que la volonté du Seigneur s'accomplisse** the Lord's will be done

accomplissement [akɔ̃plismɑ̃] *nm* (**a**) (*d'une tâche, d'une fonction*) accomplishment, performance, carrying out; (*d'un souhait*) fulfilment; **c'était l'a. de plusieurs années de travail** it was the result of several years' work (**b**) (*d'un apprentissage*) completion

accord [akɔr] *nm* (**a**) (*traité*) agreement; (*non formel*) understanding; (*transaction commerciale*) bargain; (*pour résoudre un conflit*) settlement; **conclure un a.** to enter into an agreement; **a. de principe** agreement in principle; **arriver** *ou* **parvenir à un a.** to come to an agreement, to reach (an) agreement; **un a. est intervenu d'après lequel ...** an agreement has been reached by which ...

(**b**) (*entente*) agreement (**sur** on); **vivre en** *ou* **de bon a.** to live in harmony; **l'a. parfait qui règne entre nous deux** the perfect harmony between us; **être en a. avec la nature** to be in harmony *or* at one with nature; **vivre en a. avec ses principes** to live by one's principles; **être en a. avec soi-même** to be true to oneself; **en a. avec qn** in agreement with sb; **mettre d'a. deux points de vue** to reconcile two points of view; **se mettre d'a.** *ou* **tomber d'a. avec qn** to come to an agreement with sb; **être d'a. avec qn** to agree with sb; **les témoins ne sont pas d'a.** the witnesses disagree *or* differ; **mes comptes sont d'a.** my accounts balance; **tout est d'a.** everything is settled *or* arranged; **c'est d'a., d'a.!** all right!, OK!; **d'un commun a.** by common consent, by mutual agreement

(**c**) (*autorisation*) consent; **il a donné son a.** he gave his consent; **la décision doit être prise en a. avec les différents intéressés** the decision must be made with the agreement *or* the consent of the different parties involved

(**d**) *Gram* [①B8,4,B; B35-36,2] agreement, concordance (**avec** with); **l'a. de l'adjectif avec le nom** the agreement of the adjective with the noun; **les règles d'a.** the rules of agreement

(**e**) *Mus* chord; **a. parfait** common chord; **faux a.** discord; **a. arpégé** *ou* **brisé** *ou* **figuré** broken chord; **a. de sensible** dominant seventh (chord)

(**f**) (*réglage*) *Mus* pitch; *Tech* tuning; *Mus* **tenir l'a.** (*d'un piano etc*) to keep *or* stay in tune

▶ **accord**: *Électron* **a. d'antenne** alignment input; *Com, Pol* **a. bilatéral** bilateral agreement; *Com* **a. de clearing** clearing agreement; **a. commercial** trade agreement; *Com* **a. de compensation** offset agreement; *Com* **a. de distribution exclusive** exclusive distribution agreement; *Com* **a. d'exclusivité** exclusivity arrangement; **a. de franchise** franchise agreement; **A. général sur les tarifs et le commerce** General Agreement on Tariffs and Trade; **accords d'Helsinki** Helsinki Agreement *or* Accord; *Com* **a. de libre-échange** Free Trade Agreement; *Com* **a. de licence** licensing agreement; *Com* **a. multilatéral** multilateral agreement; **a. de partenariat** partnership agreement; *Rad* **a. précis** fine tuning; *Com* **a. de représentation** agency agreement; *Com* **a. de reprise** buyback arrangement; **a. verbal** verbal agreement

accordage [akɔrdaʒ] *nm*, **accordement** [akɔrdəmɑ̃] *nm Mus* tuning

accordéon [akɔrdeɔ̃] *nm* accordion; **a. à touches** *ou* **à boutons/diatonique** piano/diatonic accordion; *Fig* **en a.** (*chaussettes*) wrinkled, coming down; **plissé** *ou* **plissage a.** accordion pleats; *Fig* **voiture en a.** concertinaed car

accordéoniste [akɔrdeɔnist] *n* accordionist, accordion player

accorder [akɔrde] **1** *vt* (**a**) (*ennemis*) to reconcile

(**b**) *Gram* **a. le verbe avec le sujet** to make the verb agree with the subject

(**c**) *Mus* (*instrument de musique*) to tune; **a. les violons au**

ton du piano to tune the violins to the pitch of the piano; *Fig* **il faudrait a. vos violons** (*de deux personnes ou plus*) you'd better get your story straight

(**d**) (*faveur, pardon etc*) to grant; (*découvert bancaire*) to allow, to give; **a. des dommages-intérêts** to award damages; **a. un escompte** to allow a discount; *Com* **a. une licence à qn** to license sb; **pouvez-vous m'a. quelques minutes?** can you spare me a few minutes?; **je n'ai pas essayé très longtemps, je vous l'accorde** I didn't try for very long, I grant you *or* I admit; **je t'accorde qu'il a tout pour plaire** he's very attractive, I('ll) grant you that; **a. à qn de faire qch** to give sb permission to do sth; **elle accorde la plus grande importance à ce travail** she attaches the greatest importance to this job; **il n'accorde pas la moindre valeur à ce que je dis** he doesn't attach the slightest value to anything I say; **c'est à peine s'il m'a accordé un regard** he barely glanced my way; **on m'a accordé huit jours de congé** I have been given a week's leave

(**e**) (*harmoniser*) to match (up)

2 s'accorder *vpr* (**a**) (*se mettre d'accord*) (*sur qch*) to agree, to come to an agreement (**avec qn** with sb); **s'a. sur le prix** to agree on (the) price; **s'a. à** *ou* **pour faire qch** to agree to do sth; **on s'accorde à penser que la maladie sera curable d'ici là** there is a general belief *or* it is generally believed that the disease will be curable by then; **tout le monde s'accorde à dire qu'elle est stupide** everyone agrees that she's stupid

(**b**) (*s'entendre*) to get on (**avec qn** with sb); **ils s'accordent mal** they don't get on (at all) well; **ils s'accordent très bien** they get on very well (together)

(**c**) (*aller avec, correspondre*) to correspond; (*de couleurs etc*) to harmonize; (*de chiffres*) to tally; (*de témoignages*) to square; (*d'un projet*) to fit in (**avec** with); **cette action ne s'accorde pas avec son caractère** this action is not in keeping *or* in line with his/her character; **cela ne s'accorde pas avec mes idées** it doesn't fit in with my ideas; *Com* **faire a. les livres** to agree the books; **il faut que la pratique s'accorde avec la théorie** the practice should correspond to *or* with the theory; **cette ceinture s'accorde à toutes les tenues** this belt goes with *or* can be worn with everything

(**d**) *Gram* to agree; **le verbe s'accorde avec le sujet** the verb agrees with the subject

(**e**) (*se donner*) to allow *or* grant oneself; **s'a. dix minutes de repos** to allow *or* give oneself ten minutes' rest

accordeur [akɔrdœr] *nm* (piano) tuner

accordoir [akɔrdwar] *nm* (piano) tuning key

accort [akɔr] *adj Litt* winsome

accostable [akɔstabl] *adj Naut* **plage a.** beach suitable for mooring

accostage [akɔstaʒ] *nm* (**a**) *F* (*de qn*) accosting (**b**) *Naut* (*du quai*) drawing alongside (**c**) *Astronaut* docking

accoster [akɔste] **1** *vt* (**a**) (*qn*) to go *or* come up to, to accost; (*pour l'agresser*) to accost (**b**) *Naut* **a. un bateau le long du quai** to bring a boat alongside (the quay); **le bateau/la navette spatiale nous a accostés** the boat/the space shuttle came alongside us **2** *vi Naut* (*navire*) to come on board; (*d'un navire*) to berth, to dock; *Astronaut* to dock

accotement [akɔtmɑ̃] *nm* (**a**) (*de la route*) verge; **a. non stabilisé** soft verge *or* shoulder (**b**) *Rail* shoulder

accoter [akɔte] **1** *vt* (*qch contre qch*) to lean; (*navire, mur etc*) to shore up; **accoté contre qch** leaning against sth; **a. une échelle à** *ou* **contre un mur** to lean a ladder against a wall **2 s'accoter** *vpr* to lean; **s'a. à** *ou* **contre un mur** to lean against a wall

accotoir [akɔtwar] *nm* armrest, elbow rest; (*pour la tête*) headrest

accouchée [akuʃe] *nf* mother (*of newborn child*); *Méd* **salle des accouchées** maternity ward

accouchement [akuʃmɑ̃] *nm* childbirth; **elle a eu un a. difficile** she had a difficult birth; **ce médecin fait plusieurs accouchements par jour** this doctor carries out *or* performs several deliveries a day; **on a dû provoquer l'a.** she had to be induced; *Fig* **il a enfin fini son texte, ce fut un véritable a.!** he really laboured to finish his text

▶ **accouchement: a. avant terme** premature delivery *or* birth; **a. aux forceps** forceps delivery; **a. naturel** natural childbirth; **a. prématuré** premature delivery *or* birth; **a. à terme** full-term delivery; **a. sans douleur** natural childbirth; **cours d'a. sans douleur** natural childbirth classes

accoucher [akuʃe] **1** *vi* (**a**) to give birth; **a. d'un garçon** to give birth to a boy; **elle doit a. dans un mois** her baby's due in a month's time; **a. chez soi** to have a home birth *or* confinement (**b**) *F* **mais accouche donc!** come on, out with it! *or* spit it out!; **il a accouché de ce recueil de nouvelles** he has laboured to produce this collection of short stories **2** *vt* to deliver

accoucheur, -euse [akuʃœr, -øz] **1** *n* (*médecin*) obstetrician **2** *nf* (*sage-femme*) **accoucheuse** midwife

accouder (s') [sakude] *vpr* to lean on one's elbow(s); **s'a. à la fenêtre** to lean out of the window; **s'a. sur son bureau** to be sitting with one's elbows on one's desk, to lean (one's elbows) on one's desk

accoudoir [akudwar] *nm* (**a**) (*de fauteuil*) armrest, elbow rest (**b**) *Archit* balustrade

accouple [akupl] *nf* leash

accouplement [akupləmɑ̃] *nm* (**a**) coupling, join(ing), link(ing); *Él* connecting; (*de bœufs*) yoking; (**b**) (*d'animaux*) pairing, mating

▶ **accouplement**: *Av* **a. bendix** bendix drive; *Tech* **a. à débrayage** disengaging gear, clutch coupling; *Aut* **a. direct** direct drive; **a. à glissement** slip clutch; *Av* **a. à griffe(s)** dog clutch, coupling

accoupler [akuple] **1** *vt* (**a**) (*unir par deux*) to couple, to join; (*pièces*) to couple (up); *Él* (*batteries etc*) to connect, to group; (*bœufs*) to yoke; **a. un moteur à une batterie** to connect an engine up to a battery (**b**) (*animaux*) to mate **2 s'accoupler** *vpr* to mate, to pair; (*avoir des relations sexuelles*) to copulate

accourir [akurir] *vi* (*conj like* **courir**; *aux* **avoir** *or* **être**) to run (up), to rush up; **à mes cris, ils ont accouru** *ou* **sont accourus** they came running when they heard my cries; **ils ont accouru** *ou* **sont accourus à mon secours** they ran *or* came running to help me

accoutrement [akutrəmɑ̃] *nm Péj* dress, garb, *F* get-up

accoutrer [akutre] **1** *vt souvent Péj* to rig out (**de** in); **accoutré d'une vieille capote** rigged out in an old army greatcoat; **tu ne peux pas l'a. ainsi, il est ridicule!** you can't rig him out like that, it looks ridiculous! **2 s'accoutrer** *vpr* to rig oneself out (**de** in)

accoutumance [akutymɑ̃s] *nf* (**a**) (*adaptation*) familiarization (**à** with); (*à la douleur etc*) inurement (**à** to); *Méd* **a. (à une drogue)** tolerance (to a drug); **l'effet d'a. des drogues dures** the habit-forming effect of hard drugs (**b**) *Litt* (*habitude*) habit, usage

accoutumé [akutyme] **1** *adj* usual, habitual; **à l'heure accoutumée** at the usual time **2** *adv* **à l'accoutumée** usually; **il est arrivé à huit heures comme à l'accoutumée** he arrived at eight o'clock as usual

accoutumer [akutyme] **1** *vt* **a. qn à qch** to accustom sb to sth, to get sb used to sth; **être accoutumé à qch** to be accustomed *or* used to sth **2 s'accoutumer** *vpr* **s'a. à** to get *or* become used *or* accustomed to; **s'a. à la fatigue** to become accustomed *or* used *or* hardened to fatigue; **je ne peux pas m'y a.** I can't get used to it

accouvage [akuvaʒ] *nm* artificial incubation

accréditation [akreditasjɔ̃] *nf* (*d'un ambassadeur, d'un journaliste*) accreditation, accrediting

accrédité, -ée [akredite] **1** *adj* of good standing, accredited; **notre représentant a.** our authorized representative **2** *n* agent; *Fin* beneficiary, payee

accréditer [akredite] **1** *vt* (**a**) (*ambassadeur, journaliste*) to accredit; (*dans le générique d'un film etc*) to acknowledge; **je suis accrédité pour mener les négociations** I have been appointed to lead the negotiations; *Fin* **a. un client** to open an account for a client; *Fin* **être accrédité auprès d'une banque** to have credit facilities at a bank (**b**) (*rendre plausible*) to substantiate, to give credence to; **cette rumeur est accréditée par ses dernières actions** this rumour is substantiated *or* backed up by his latest actions **2 s'accréditer** *vpr* (*d'une rumeur etc*) to gain ground, to spread

accréditif [akreditif] *nm* credential; (*lettre de crédit*) letter of credit

accro [akro] *F* **1** *adj* (*à la drogue*); *Fig* addicted (**à** to), hooked (**à** on); **il va à tous les matchs de foot, il est a.** he goes to all the football matches, he's a real addict **2** *n* (*à une activité*) addict

accroc [akro] *nm* (**a**) (*dans les vêtements etc*) tear, *Fml* rent (**b**) *Fig* hitch, difficulty, snag; **la cérémonie s'est déroulée sans a.** the ceremony went off without a hitch; **faire un a. à sa réputation** to spoil one's reputation, *F* to blot one's copybook

accrochage [akrɔʃaʒ] *nm* (**a**) *Aut* minor accident; *Boxe* clinch (**b**) *Rail* hitching on, coupling (**c**) (*d'un tableau etc*) hanging (up); (*dans un musée*) (small) exhibition (**d**) *Rad* (*d'une station*) picking up (**e**) (*dispute*) altercation, squabble; *Mil* brush, skirmish

accroche [akrɔʃ] *nf* (*titre d'appel*) blurb; (*verbale*) striking (publicity) slogan, catch phrase

accroche-casseroles [akrɔʃkasrɔl] *nm inv* saucepan rack
accroche-cœur, *pl* **accroche-cœurs** *nm* kiss curl; **se faire des accroche-cœurs** to put one's hair into kiss curls
accrocher [akrɔʃe] **1** *vt* **(a)** (*retenir*) to hook, to catch; **a. un asticot à son hameçon** to attach a maggot to one's fishing hook; **a. sa robe à des ronces** to catch one's dress on brambles; *Aut* **il a accroché mon pare-choc** he caught *or* hit my bumper; **titre qui accroche le lecteur** striking *or* eye-catching title; **vitrine qui accroche le regard** eye-catching display in a shop-window; *F* **a. qn** to buttonhole *or* corner sb
(b) *Rail* (*wagon*) to hitch on, to couple
(c) (*navire*) to grapple
(d) (*suspendre*) to hang up; *Constr* (*porte*) to hang; **a. son manteau** to hang up one's coat; *Fig* **il faut avoir le cœur bien accroché** you need a strong stomach *or* strong nerves, *Arg* **a. sa montre** to put one's watch in hock, to pop one's watch
(e) *Rad* **a. une station** to tune in to a station
2 *vi* (*aux vêtements etc*) to stick, to catch; *Fig* **les négociations ont accroché** there has been a hitch in the negotiations; **ça ne marche pas très bien entre eux, ça accroche souvent** things aren't very good between them, they argue a lot; **ça n'a pas du tout accroché** (*entre deux personnes*) they didn't get on, *F* they didn't click
3 s'accrocher *vpr* **(a) s'a. à qn/qch** to hold on to sb/sth; (*ne pas lâcher, aussi Fig*) to cling on to sb/sth; **accroche-toi à la rampe** hold on tight *or* hang on to the handrail; *Fig* **elle s'accroche à lui, il est son seul espoir** she's clinging to him as her only hope; *Fig* **s'a. à des illusions** to cling to illusions; *Fig F* **accroche-toi, tu n'as pas tout entendu!** brace yourself, you haven't heard everything yet!
(b) (*se fixer*) **ça s'accroche au mur par un clou** you fasten *or* attach it to the wall with a nail
(c) (*tenir*) to stick at it, *F* to hang in there
(d) *Boxe* to clinch; *Fig* **les deux voitures se sont accrochées** the two cars clipped each other
(e) *F* (*se disputer*) to have a row; **s'a. avec qn** to have a row with sb, to clash with sb
(f) tu peux te l'a.! you can kiss goodbye to that!, you've had it!
accrocheur, -euse [akrɔʃœr, -øz] **1** *adj* **(a)** (*tenace*) tenacious, stubborn **(b)** (*titre, slogan etc*) eye-catching, catchy **2** *n* **c'est un a.** he's a fighter
accroire [akrwar] *vt* **faire a. à qn que ...** to make sb believe that ...; **elle veut nous en faire a.** (*abuser de notre crédulité*) she's trying to fool us; (*se faire valoir*) she's trying to impress us
accroissement [akrwasmɑ̃] *nm* **(a)** increase (**de** in); **taux d'a.** rate of increase; *Math* **a. d'une fonction** increment of a function **(b)** (*d'une plante etc*) growth
accroître [akrwatr] (*prp* **accroissant**; *pp* **accru**; *pr ind* **j'accrois, il accroît, n. accroissons, ils accroissent**; *impf* **j'accroissais**; *p hist* **j'accrus**; *fu* **j'accroîtrai**) **1** *vt* to increase, to enlarge, to add to; (*réputation*) to enhance **2 s'accroître** *vpr* to increase, to grow
accroupir (s') [sakrupir] *vpr* to squat (down), to crouch (down); **accroupi** squatting, crouching
accroupissement [akrupismɑ̃] *nm* crouching, squatting
accru [akry] *nm Bot* sucker
accu [aky] *nm Él* battery; *Fig* **recharger ses accus** to recharge one's batteries
accueil [akœj] *nm* (*façon d'accueillir*) reception, welcome, greeting; (*lieu*) reception; **tenir l'a.** to be on reception; **hôtesse d'a.** receptionist; **centre d'a.** reception centre; **passez à l'a.** go to the reception desk, go to reception; **a. handicapés** services for the disabled; **faire bon a. à qn/qch** to welcome sb *or* give sb a warm welcome/to welcome sth; **faire mauvais a. à qn** to give sb a cool reception; **ils ont fait un a. très mitigé à notre proposition** they gave our proposal a very mixed reception; **a. hostile** *ou* **défavorable** hostile reception; **discours/cérémonie d'a.** welcoming speech/ceremony; *Com* **faire (bon) a. à une traite** to honour a bill
accueillant [akœjɑ̃] *adj* welcoming
accueillir [akœjir] *vt* (*conj like* **cueillir**) (*qn, nouvelle idée*) to receive, to greet; **(bien) a. qn** to welcome sb, to give sb a warm welcome; **mal a. qn** to give sb a bad reception; **a. qn à bras ouverts** to welcome sb with open arms; **cet hôtel peut a. jusqu'à 500 visiteurs** the hotel can accommodate up to 500 visitors; **j'ai un ami qui pourrait vous a. pendant un certain temps** I have a friend who could put you up for a while; **se faire a. par des volées de pierre** to be greeted with *or* by volleys of stones; **le film a été mal accueilli par le public** the film got a bad reception from the public; *Com* **a. une traite** to meet *or* honour a bill
acculer [akyle] *vt* (*qn*) to drive back (**contre** against); (*animal*) to bring to bay *or* to a stand; *Fig* (*qn*) to drive to the wall; *Fig* **être acculé aux aveux/à la ruine** to be forced into a confession/into bankruptcy
acculturation [akyltyrasjɔ̃] *nf* acculturation
accumulateur [akymylatœr] *nm Él* battery, accumulator; *Aut* **a. de carburant** fuel accumulator
accumulation [akymylasjɔ̃] *nf* **(a)** (*action*) accumulation; (*d'énergie*) storage; (*d'argent*) hoarding; (*en magasin*) stockpiling; **chauffage par a.** storage heating; **chauffage à a. nocturne** (night) storage heating **(b)** (*stock*) accumulation; (*d'argent, de nourriture*) hoard; (*d'objets*) collection; (*d'erreurs*) series
accumuler [akymyle] **1** *vt* to accumulate, to amass; (*nourriture, argent*) to hoard; (*énergie*) to accumulate, to store; (*entasser*) to heap up, to pile up; (*en magasin*) to stockpile; **a. les médailles** to accumulate medals; **a. les preuves/renseignements** to gather evidence/information; **a. les gaffes/erreurs** to make a series of blunders/mistakes; **quand je suis fatigué, j'accumule les erreurs** I make lots of mistakes when I'm tired; *F* **tu les accumules!** you're making quite a habit of it!
2 s'accumuler *vpr* to accumulate; (*de nuages*) to gather, to build up; *Fin* (*des intérêts*) to accrue; **les plaintes s'accumulent sur mon bureau** complaints are piling up on my desk; **les preuves s'accumulent contre elle** the evidence is building up against her
accusateur, -trice [akyzatœr, -tris] **1** *adj* (*regard, doigt*) accusing, *Fml* accusatory; (*preuve*) incriminating; **j'ai pointé vers lui un index a.** I pointed an accusing finger at him **2** *n* accuser; (*d'un officiel*) impeacher, arraigner; *Hist* **a. public** public prosecutor
accusatif [akyzatif] *nm Gram* accusative (case); **mot à l'a.** word in the accusative
accusation [akyzasjɔ̃] *nf* **(a)** (*condamnation*) accusation; **lancer** *ou* **porter une a. contre qn** to bring an accusation against sb **(b)** *Jur* **mettre qn en a.** to commit sb for trial; **quels sont les chefs** *ou* **les sujets d'a.?** what are the charges? **(c)** *Pol* impeachment, arraignment; **faire une a. contre la politique extérieure actuelle** to deliver an indictment against current foreign policy
accusé, -ée [akyze] **1** *adj* (*trait etc*) prominent, pronounced, bold; **rides très accusées** very deep wrinkles **2** *n* (*d'un crime*) accused; (*au tribunal*) defendant, prisoner at the bar **3** *nm* **a. de réception** (*pour une lettre*) acknowledgement (of receipt); *Ordinat* acknowledge, acknowledgement
accuser [akyze] **1** *vt* **(a)** (*incriminer*) to accuse; **a. qn de (faire) qch** to accuse sb of (doing) sth; **on l'accuse de meurtre** he is (being) accused of murder; *Fig* **a. le sort** to blame fate
(b) (*tendance, baisse etc*) to show; **paroles qui accusent une grande ignorance** words that betray *or* show *or* reveal great ignorance; **elle accuse trente ans** she looks (at least) thirty; **il commence à a. son âge** he's starting to look his age; **il accuse le coup** *Boxe* he's feeling that one; *Fig* he's obviously shaken
(c) (*faire ressortir*) to define, to show up, to accentuate; **esquisse qui accuse tous les muscles** sketch that brings out every muscle; **le temps a accusé son avarice** he has got meaner with time
(d) a. réception de qch to acknowledge (receipt of) sth
2 s'accuser *vpr* **(a)** (*se rendre coupable*) to admit, to confess; **il s'est accusé du crime pour protéger son frère** he confessed to the crime to protect his brother
(b) (*se renforcer*) to become more pronounced *or* marked
acerbe [asɛrb] *adj* sharp, harsh, acerbic; **réprimande a.** sharp reprimand; **discussion a.** ill-tempered discussion; **parler d'un ton a.** to speak sharply
acéré [asere] *adj* (*lame etc*) sharp; *Fig* (*remarque*) cutting, scathing; **langue acérée** sharp tongue; **il écrit des satires d'une plume acérée** he writes satire with a scathing pen
acérer [asere] *vt* (**j'acère**; **j'acérerai**) (*rare*) to sharpen, to give a keen edge to
acétate [asetat] *nm Ch* acetate; **a. de cuivre** copper acetate; *Tex* **a. de cellulose** cellulose acetate
acétique [asetik] *adj Ch* acetic; **odeur a.** vinegary smell
acétocellulose [asetɔselyloz] *nf Ch* cellulose acetate
acétone [asetɔn] *nf Ch* acetone
acétylène [asetilɛn] *nm Ch* acetylene; **lampe à a.** acetylene lamp *or Am* torch
acétylsalicylique [asetilsalisilik] *adj Pharm* **acide a.** acetylsalicylic acid
ACF [aseɛf] *nm* (*abrév* **Automobile Club de France**) = automobile association of France
achalandage [aʃalɑ̃daʒ] *nm Jur, Com* custom, customers, clientele; (*fonds de commerce*) goodwill

achalandé [aʃalɑ̃de] *adj* **magasin bien a.** well stocked shop; *Vieilli* (*ayant nombreux clients*) well patronized shop

achalander [aʃalɑ̃de] *vt F* (*magasin*) to stock

achaler [aʃale] *vt Can* to annoy, to bother

achards [aʃar] *nmpl Culin* relish

acharné [aʃarne] *adj* (*enragé, furieux*) (*lutte*) desperate, bitter; (*concurrence*) cut-throat; (*travail*) relentless; (*joueur*) inveterate; **meute acharnée à la poursuite** pack in hot *or* eager pursuit; **hommes acharnés les uns contre les autres** men fighting desperately against each other; **ils sont acharnés à se faire du mal** they're bent on hurting each other, they're desperately trying to hurt each other

acharnement [aʃarnəmɑ̃] *nm* relentlessness; **a. au** *ou* **pour le travail** passion for work; **avec a.** relentlessly; **se battre avec a.** to fight tooth and nail; *Pharm* **a. thérapeutique** = use of intensive medication (*to keep a person alive*)

acharner [aʃarne] **1 s'acharner** *vpr* **s'a. après** *ou* **contre** *ou* **sur qn** (*persécuter*) to be always after sb; **le meurtrier s'est acharné sur sa victime** the murderer savaged his victim; **les examinateurs se sont acharnés sur le candidat** the examiners really stuck the knife into the candidate; **pourquoi t'acharnes-tu à essayer de le lui faire comprendre?** why are you so determined to try to make him understand?; **le malheur s'acharne après lui** he is dogged by misfortune; **s'a. à** *ou* **sur qch** to work desperately hard at sth, to slave (away) at sth; **il s'acharne à vous nuire** he is set on harming you; **elle ne se décourage pas, elle s'acharne** she doesn't let herself be discouraged, she just keeps at it *or F* keeps plugging away

2 *vt Vieilli* **a. la meute après une bête** to set the pack on (the track of) a quarry; **a. un chien** to flesh *or* blood a hound

achat [aʃa] *nm* **(a)** (*action*) purchase, buying; **faire un a.** to make a purchase, to buy something; **faire l'a. de qch** to buy sth; **aller faire ses achats** to go shopping; **pouvoir d'a.** purchasing power; **prix d'a.** purchase price; **centrale d'a.** central purchasing office; *Can* **agent d'a.** procurement officer **(b)** (*ce qu'on a acheté*) purchase; **ses achats** one's shopping, *surtout Fml* one's purchases; **tu me montres tes achats?** show me what you've bought

▸ **achat**: **a. au comptant** *ou* **contre espèces** cash purchase; **a. à crédit** purchase on credit, credit purchase; **a. impulsif** impulse buy; *Com* **a. juste à temps** just-in-time purchasing; **a. non prémédité** impulse buy; **a. renouvelé** repeat purchase; **a. spontané** impulse buy; *Com* **a. de système** systems buying; *Fin* **a. à terme** forward purchase; **achats centralisés** centralized purchasing; *Mktg* **achats comparatifs** comparison shopping; **achats directs** direct purchasing; **achats à domicile** teleshopping; **achats hors taxes** tax-free shopping; **achats regroupés** one-stop buying *or* shopping

acheminement [aʃminmɑ̃] *nm* **(a)** (*progrès*) step, progress **(à, vers** towards) **(b)** (*de marchandises, paquets*) forwarding, shipment; **a. du courrier** mail delivery *or* handling

acheminer [aʃmine] **1** *vt* **(a)** (*conduire*) (*qn*) to set on his way **(sur, vers** towards) **(b)** (*marchandises etc*) to dispatch, to convey, to forward **(sur, vers** to); (*courrier*) to handle

2 s'acheminer *vpr* **s'a. vers** to set out for, to make one's way towards; **s'a. vers le succès** to be heading for success; **nous nous acheminons vers de grands changements structurels** we are moving towards great structural changes

acheter [aʃte] **(j'achète, n. achetons; j'achèterai) 1** *vt* **(a) a. qch** to buy sth, *Fml* to purchase sth; **a. qch à qn** to buy sth from sb; **a. qch à** *ou* **pour qn** to buy sth for sb; **je vais lui a. un livre** I'm going to buy him/her a book; **a. en gros/au détail** to buy wholesale/retail; **a. qch à crédit/au comptant** to buy sth on credit/for cash; **a. à tempérament** to buy by instalments; *Fin* **a. à terme** to buy forward; **j'ai acheté ce livre 50 francs** I bought this book for 50 francs; **je ne l'ai pas acheté cher** I didn't pay much for it *or* a high price for it; **a. qch (à) bon marché** to buy sth cheap; *Fig* **a. qch chèrement** to pay a high price for sth; *Fig* **c'est une façon bien basse d'a. votre pardon** it's a very low way of buying forgiveness; **a. chat en poche** to buy a pig in a poke

(b) *F* (*qn*) to bribe, to buy off; **a. la complicité de qn** to buy sb's silence; **se faire a.** to be bribed

2 s'acheter *vpr* **ça s'achète en pharmacie** you can buy it/them in any pharmacy; **ces choses-là ne s'achètent pas** such things cannot be bought *or* are not for sale; *Fig* **s'a. une conduite** to turn over a new leaf

acheteur, -euse [aʃtœr, -øz] *n* buyer, purchaser; *Jur* vendee; *Com* **elle est acheteuse pour Prisunic®** she is a buyer for Prisunic; *Mktg* **a. impulsif** impulsive buyer, impulse buyer; **a. industriel** business buyer; **je suis acheteur!** I'm in the market!, I'm interested!

achevé [aʃve] *adj* (*artiste, style etc*) accomplished; (*travail*) perfect; (*perfection*) absolute; **il est d'un ridicule a.** he's utterly ridiculous; *F* **sot a.** utter *or* absolute fool; **menteur a.** (*accompli*) consummate *or* accomplished liar; (*sans honte*) out and out liar

achèvement [aʃɛvmɑ̃] *nm* (*de travaux*) completion, finishing; **date d'a.** target *or* completion date

achever [aʃve] **(j'achève, n. achevons; j'achèverai) 1** *vt* **(a)** (*finir*) (*discours*) to end, to conclude; (*travail etc*) to finish (off), to complete; **laisse-lui le temps d'a. sa phrase** let him finish what he's saying; **toutes nos peines sont loin d'être achevées** our troubles are all far from over; **avant d'a. ma lettre** before closing *or* finishing my letter; **a. ses jours** *ou* **sa vie** to end one's days; **a. de faire qch** to finish doing sth; **achève de boire ton café** drink up *or* finish your coffee

(b) (*mettre à mort*) (*personne*) to finish off; (*animal*) to put out of its misery *or* out of pain; *F* **cette grosse perte l'a achevé** this heavy loss was the end of him; *F* **ça m'a achevé** that really finished me (off)

2 s'achever *vpr* **(a)** (*finir*) to draw to a close, to end; **c'est ainsi que l'histoire s'achève** that's how the story finishes *or* ends; **le jour s'acheva tristement** the day closed *or* ended sadly *or* on a sad note

(b) (*d'un travail*) to reach completion

achigan [aʃigɑ̃] *nm Can* (*poisson*) (black) bass

Achille [aʃil] *nm* Achilles

achoper [aʃɔpe] *vi Can Fig* **a. sur qch** to stumble over sth

achoppement [aʃɔpmɑ̃] *nm Litt* obstacle, difficulty; **pierre d'a.** stumbling block

achopper [aʃɔpe] *vi* **c'est là que ça achoppe** that's the stumbling block; **a. au problème de …** to come to grief over the problem of …; **a. sur un mot** to stumble over a word

achromatique [akrɔmatik] *adj* achromatic

acide [asid] **1** *adj* acid(ic); (*au goût*) tart, sour; *Fig* (*personne*) witty; *Fig* (*propos, remarques*) acid, cutting; **une pomme a.** a sour apple; *Biol* **milieu a.** acidic environment; **savon a.** acidic soap **2** *nm* (*drogue*), *Ch* acid; **a. désoxyribonucléique** deoxyribonucleic acid; **a. folique** folic acid; **a. gras** fatty acid

acidificateur [asidifikatœr] *nm* acidifier, acidifying agent

acidification [asidifikasjɔ̃] *nf* acidification

acidifier [asidifje] **1** *vt* to acidify **2 s'acidifier** *vpr* to become acid, to turn sour

acidité [asidite] *nf* acidity; (*d'une pomme etc*) sourness, tartness; *Fig* (*d'un commentaire*) wittiness; *Ch* **l'a. d'une solution** the acidity of a solution; *Méd* **a. gastrique** acid stomach, hyperacidity

acidose [asidoz] *nf Méd* acidosis

acidulé [asidyle] *adj* acidulous; **bonbons acidulés** acid drops

acier [asje] *nm* steel; **lame d'a.** *ou* **en a.** steel blade; **a. au chrome/au nickel** chrome/nickel steel; *Fig* **avoir un moral d'a.** to be very resilient, *F* to be a tough cookie; *Fig* **regard d'a.** steely look

▸ **acier**: **a. au carbone** carbon steel; **a. cémenté** case-hardened steel; **a. embouti** pressed steel; **a. galvanisé** galvanized steel; **a. inoxydable** stainless steel; **a. à ressort** spring steel; **a. trempé** hardened *or* tempered steel

aciérie [asjeri] *nf* steel works

aciériste [asjerist] *nm* steel maker *or* manufacturer

acmé [akme] *nf Litt* acme, peak; *Méd* crisis

acné [akne] *nf* acne; **a. juvénile** *ou* **vulgaire** teenage acne; **avoir de l'a.** to have *or* suffer from acne; **traitement contre l'a.** acne treatment

acolyte [akɔlit] *nm* **(a)** *Péj* confederate, accomplice **(b)** *Rel* acolyte

acompte [akɔ̃t] *nm* instalment, *US* installment; (*avance, premier versement*) payment on account, down payment; **payer par acomptes** to pay by *or* in instalments; **recevoir un a.** to receive something on account; **verser un a.** to make a down payment; **a. de** *ou* **sur dividende** interim dividend; *Fin* **a. provisionnel** interim payment; **a. mensuel** monthly instalment, monthly payment; *Fig* **j'ai pris un petit a.** I had a little taster

aconit [akɔnit] *nm* (*plante*) aconite

a contrario [akɔ̃trarjo] *adv* **raisonnement a.** converse reasoning

acoquiner (s') [sakɔkine] *vpr Péj* to team up, to fall in **(avec** with)

Açores (les) [lezasɔr] *nfpl* the Azores

à-côté [akote] *nm* **(a)** (*verbal*) aside **(b)** (*élément secondaire*) **les à-côtés d'une question** the side issues of a question; **les à-côtés de l'histoire** sidelights on history; **il a quelques à-côtés** he makes a bit on the side **(c)** *F* (*financier etc*) extra

à-coup [aku] *nm* jerk, jolt, jar, shock; *Él* surge (of current); **il y eut des à-coups au départ de la voiture** the car jerked *or* jolted as it set off; **il travaille par à-coups** he works by *or* in fits and starts; *Aut* **le moteur a des à-coups** the engine judders; **sans à-coups** smoothly

acousticien, -ienne [akustisjɛ̃, -jɛn] *n* acoustician

acoustique [akustik] **1** *adj* acoustic; **cornet a.** ear trumpet; **tuyau a.** speaking tube; **voûte a.** whispering gallery; **les phénomènes acoustiques** acoustics **2** *nf Phys* acoustics; **a. d'une salle** acoustics of a hall

acquéreur [akerœr] *nm* purchaser, buyer; *Jur* vendee; **notre voiture n'a pas trouvé a.** we couldn't find a buyer for our car

acquérir [akerir] (*prp* **acquérant**; *pp* **acquis**; *pr ind* **j'acquiers, il acquiert, n. acquérons, ils acquièrent**; *pr sub* **j'acquière, n. acquérions**; *impf* **j'acquérais**; *p hist* **j'acquis**; *fu* **j'acquerrai**) **1** *vt* **(a)** (*obtenir*) to acquire, to obtain, to get; (*habitude*) to get into; (*expérience, confiance*) to acquire, to gain; **nous avons acquis la certitude de son innocence** we have established beyond doubt that he/she is innocent; **l'expérience acquise au long d'une carrière** the experience gained in the course of one's career; **a. de mauvaises habitudes** to get into bad habits; *Prov* **un bien en acquiert un autre** money attracts money

(b) (*prendre*) to acquire; **a. de la valeur** to go up *or* increase in value

(c) (*devenir propriétaire de*) to acquire; (*acheter*) to purchase, to buy; **a. une terre d'un voisin** to purchase *or* buy land from a neighbour; **a. un bien par héritage** to come into *or* to inherit some property

(d) a. qch à qn to bring sth to sb, to bring sb sth

2 s'acquérir *vpr* **(a)** (*se prendre*) **cette habitude s'acquiert facilement** it's easy to get into the habit; **une fortune peut s'a. de différentes manières** there are different ways of making one's fortune

(b) (*s'attirer*) to win, to gain

acquêt [akɛ] *nm Jur* acquisition; (*fortuit*) windfall; **communauté réduite aux acquêts** = marriage settlement whereby only goods acquired since the marriage are deemed to be held in common

acquiescement [akjɛsmɑ̃] *nm* acquiescence; *Jur* **a. licite/conditionnel** lawful/conditional consent; **hocher la tête en signe d'a.** to nod one's agreement

acquiescer [akjese] *vi* (**j'acquiesçai(s); n. acquiesçons**) **a. à qch** (*se résigner*) to acquiesce in sth; (*consentir*) to agree *or* assent to sth; **a. d'un signe de tête** to agree with a nod of the head, to nod one's approval; **elle a acquiescé d'un sourire** she gave a smile of agreement, she smiled her agreement; *Jur* **a. à un acte** to consent (fully) to an act

acquis [aki] **1** *adj* (*savoir, caractères etc*) acquired; **fait a.** established *or* accepted fact; **tenir pour a.** to take for granted; **son aide nous est acquise** we can take it for granted that he will help us; **droits a.** vested interests; **cela est a.** that's been established; **ce droit lui est a.** he/she has an established right in this respect; **je vous suis tout a.** I entirely agree **2** *nm* (*connaissances*) knowledge; (*réussite*) attainments, achievements; **a. sociaux** social benefits that have been won

acquisitif, -ive [akizitif, -iv] *adj Jur* acquisitive

acquisition [akizisjɔ̃] *nf* **(a)** (*fait*) acquisition; **faire l'a. de qch** to acquire sth; (*acheter*) to purchase sth **(b)** (*bien acquis*) acquisition; (*bien acheté*) purchase; **c'est ma dernière a.** it's my latest acquisition

acquit [aki] *nm* **(a)** *Com* receipt; **donner a. de qch** to give a receipt for sth; **pour a.** received (with thanks), paid; **a. de douane** customs receipt; **a. de paiement** receipt; **a. de transit** transshipment note **(b)** (*d'un navire*) clearance **(c)** (*d'une promesse*) discharge, release; **par a. de conscience** to ease one's conscience, to put one's mind at rest; **faire qch par manière d'a.** to do sth as a matter of form **(d)** *Jur* **sentence** *ou* **ordonnance d'a.** order of acquittal

acquit-à-caution, *pl* **acquits-à-caution** [akiakosjɔ̃] *nm* bond note

acquittement [akitmɑ̃] *nm* **(a)** (*d'une dette etc*) discharge, payment; (*d'effet*) acquittal **(b)** *Jur* acquittal; **verdict d'a.** verdict of not guilty

acquitter [akite] **1** *vt* **(a) a. qn** (*d'une obligation etc*) to release sb **(b)** *Jur* **a. un accusé** to acquit *or* discharge a defendant **(c)** (*obligation*) to fulfil; (*dette*) to discharge **(d)** (*facture*) to receipt, to pay **2 s'acquitter** *vpr* **s'a. d'une obligation/d'un devoir** to fulfil *or* carry out *or* discharge an obligation/a duty; **s'a. de son devoir** to do one's duty; **comment pourrai-je m'a. envers vous?** how can I repay you?

acre [akr] **1** *nf Hist* = acre **2** *nm Can* acre

âcre [ɑkr] *adj* (*goût*) bitter; (*odeur*) pungent, acrid; *Fig* (*souvenir*) bitter; (*propos, humeur*) caustic

âcreté [ɑkrəte] *nf* (*d'un goût*) bitterness; (*d'une odeur*) pungency; *Fig* (*de la jalousie, la douleur*) bitterness; (*de propos*) caustic nature

acrimonie [akrimɔni] *nf* (*mauvaise humeur*) acrimony; (*d'un discours, d'une querelle*) acrimoniousness, bitterness

acrimonieux, -euse [akrimɔnjø, -øz] *adj* (*mots, querelle etc*) acrimonious, bitter

acrobate [akrɔbat] **1** *n* acrobat; *Fig* **c'est un a.** he can wriggle out of anything **2** *nm* (*mammifère*) flying squirrel

acrobatie [akrɔbasi] *nf* **(a)** (*art*) acrobatics; **numéro** *ou* **tour d'a.** acrobatic feat; **faire des acrobaties** to do *or* perform acrobatics; **a. aérienne** stunt flying, aerobatics **(b)** *Fig* (*virtuosité*) clever trick; **a. intellectuelle** intellectual acrobatics; **il s'en sortira par une a.** he'll wriggle out of it somehow

acrobatique [akrɔbatik] *adj* acrobatic

acronyme [akrɔnim] *nm Ling* acronym

acropole [akrɔpɔl] *nf* acropolis; **l'A.** the Acropolis

acrostiche [akrɔstiʃ] *nm* acrostic

acrylique [akrilik] **1** *adj Ch, Tex* acrylic **2** *nm Tex* acrylic; **pull en a.** acrylic pullover

ACT [asete] (*abrév* **arbre à cames en tête**) ohc

acte [akt] *nm* **(a)** (*action*) action, act, deed; **moins de paroles, des actes!** let's have less talk and more action!; **a. de courage** act of bravery *or* courage, brave *or* courageous act *or* action; **faire a. de bonne volonté** to show willing *or* good will; **faire a. d'autorité** to use *or* exercise one's authority; **passer aux actes** to take action; **il menace de se suicider, j'ai peur qu'il passe aux actes** I'm scared that he'll carry out his threats of suicide; **faire a. de présence** to put in an appearance; **faire a. de candidature à un emploi** to submit an application *or* to apply for a job; **faire a. de souverain** to exercise the royal prerogative; **faire a. d'héritier** to come forward as an heir; **a. de terrorisme** act of terrorism; **a. de guerre** act of war; **être facturé à l'a.** to be billed on a usage basis

(b) *Jur* = instrument; (*establishing ownership*) deed, title; **a. authentique** *ou* **notarié, a. sur papier timbré** deed executed and authenticated by a notary; **dont a.** duly noted *or* acknowledged

(c) (*certificat*) record; **prendre a. de qch** to record *or* note *or* take a note of *or* set down sth; *Fml* **nous prenons a. de votre candidature** we acknowledge your application; **donner a. de qch** to grant sth, to admit sth

(d) actes (*de procès etc*) records; (*d'un organisme scientifique etc*) transactions; (*d'un colloque*) proceedings

(e) *Th* act; **tragédie en trois actes** three-act tragedy, tragedy in three acts; **dans le second a.** in the second act

▶ **acte**: **a. d'accusation** bill of indictment, charges; *Bible* **Actes des Apôtres** Acts of the Apostles; **a. d'association** partnership deed; *Jur* **a. de cession** deed *or* certificate of transfer; **a. de contrition** act of contrition; **a. de décès** death certificate; **a. de dernière volonté** last will and testament; **a. d'état civil** = certificate of birth/marriage/death; *Rel* **a. de foi** act of faith; **a. judiciaire** writ; **a. de mariage** marriage certificate; **a. médical** medical treatment; **a. de naissance** birth certificate; *Jur* **a. notarié** notarized deed; *Jur* **a. de propriété** title deed; **a. sous seing privé** private agreement; **a. unique européen** Single European Act; **a. de vente** bill of sale, deed of sale

acteur, -trice [aktœr, -tris] *n* **(a)** *Th, Cin* actor, *f* actress; **a. de cinéma/de théâtre** film/stage actor; **se faire a.** to go on the stage; **a. à transformations** quick-change artist **(b)** (*d'un événement*) participant; (*sur le marché*) player; **les différents acteurs de la négociation** the different participants in *or* parties involved in the negotiation

actif, -ive [aktif, -iv] **1** *adj* **(a)** (*défenseur, participation, substance, Gram verbe, voix*) active; (*substance etc*) potent; **le principe a. d'un produit** the active ingredient of a product; *Écon* **population active** labour force; **femme active** working woman; *Mil* **armée active** regular army; **service a.** (active) service; **citoyen a.** person with the right to vote

(b) (*personne*) active; **sa grand-mère est très active pour son âge** his grandmother is very sprightly for her age; **faire un commerce a.** to do a brisk trade

(c) *Com, Jur* **dettes actives** accounts receivable

(d) *Ordinat* active; **rendre a.** (*unité etc*) to activate

2 *nm* **(a)** *Com* assets; (*moyens financiers*) credit (account); **mettre qch à l'a. de qn** to credit sb with sth; *Fig* **il faut mettre sa patience à son a.** you have to give him credit for patience; *Fig* **avoir plusieurs prix à son a.** to have several prizes to one's name *or* credit; *Fig* **avoir plusieurs infractions à son a.** to have several offences to one's name

(b) *Gram* [①A40,9] **verbe à l'a.** verb in the active voice

3 *n* active person; **c'est un a.!** he likes to do things, he's a doer

▶ **actif**: *Compta* **a. circulant** circulating *or* floating *or* current assets; **a. corporel** tangible asset; **a. fictif** fictitious asset; **a.**

immobilisé fixed *or* capital asset; **a. incorporel** intangible asset; **a. net** net assets *or* worth; **a. soustractif** depreciated credit balance; **a. stable** fixed *or* long-term asset

action [aksjɔ̃] *nf* **(a)** (*acte*) action, act; **l'a. de marcher** the act of walking; **commettre** *ou* **faire une a. insensée** to commit a senseless act; **commettre** *ou* **faire une bonne/mauvaise a.** to do a good/bad deed; **a. d'éclat** brilliant feat

(b) (*influence, effet*) (*d'une substance*) action, effect; **a. sur qch** action *or* effect on sth; **ce désherbant n'a aucune a. sur le liseron** this weedkiller has no effect on bindweed; **exercer une a. sur qn** to have influence over sb; **sans a.** ineffectual, ineffective; **a. de l'eau** effect of water; **par l'a. personnelle d'un membre du club** through the personal intervention of a club member

(c) (*activité*) (*d'une machine etc*) action, motion, working, functioning; **entrer en a.** (*d'une loi etc*) to come into force *or* effect; *Pol* **recourir à l'a. directe** to resort to direct action; **hors d'a.** out of action; **développer son champ d'a.** to expand one's sphere of activity *or* field of operations, to expand the scope of one's activities; **homme d'a.** man of action, action man; **passer à l'a.** to take action, to act; **mettre qch en a.** to set sth in motion, to put sth into operation

(d) (*d'un orateur etc*) action, gesture

(e) (*intrigue*) action; (*d'une pièce, d'un roman*) plot; **scène qui retarde l'a.** scene that delays the action; **un film d'a.** action-packed movie; (*genre*) action movie; *TV, Cin* **a.!** action!; **l'a. se déroule à Prague** the action is set in Prague

(f) *Fin* share; (*document*) share certificate; **actions** shares, *esp Am* stock; **avoir des actions dans** to have shares *or* a shareholding in; **détenir des actions d'une société** to have shares in a company; **compagnie par actions** joint-stock company; **hausse/baisse des actions** rise/fall in the value of shares; *Fig* **les actions du ministre montent/baissent** the minister's stock is rising/falling

(g) *Jur* action, lawsuit, trial; **intenter une a. judiciaire** *ou* **en justice** to take legal action; **mener une a. contre qch** to take action against sth; (*pour de l'argent*) to sue sb; **a. en divorce** divorce suit

(h) *Mil* action, fight, engagement; **dans le feu de l'a.** (*pendant la guerre*) in the heat of battle; *Fig* in the heat of the moment

(i) *Suisse* **vente a.** bargain offer

▶ **action**: *Fin* **a. de jouissance** dividend share; *Ordinat* **a. logique** logical operation; *Fin* **a. nominative** bearer registered share; *Fin* **a. ordinaire** ordinary share, *US* common stock; *Fin* **a. au porteur** bearer stock share; *Fin* **a. privilégiée** preference share, *US* preferred stock; *Mktg* **a. de stimulation** sales stimulation campaign; *Mktg* **a. de vente** sales campaign *or* drive *or* action

actionnaire [aksjɔnɛr] *n Fin* shareholder; **a. majoritaire/minoritaire** majority/minority shareholder

actionnariat [aksjɔnarja] *nm* shareholding; **a. ouvrier** workers owning shares in their company

actionnement [aksjɔnmɑ̃] *nm* activation; **a. à distance** remote-control operation

actionner [aksjɔne] *vt* **(a)** (*mettre en marche*) to start up, to turn on; (*faire fonctionner*) to operate, to drive, to run; *MecE* to actuate; **actionné à la main** hand operated; **a. les freins** to put on *or* apply the brakes **(b)** *Jur* to sue, to bring an action against; **a. qn en dommages-intérêts** to sue sb for damages

actionneur [aksjɔnœr] *nm MecE* actuator

activation [aktivasjɔ̃] *nf* activation

activé [aktive] *adj Ch* activated; *Ordinat* active

activement [aktivmɑ̃] *adv* actively, briskly, busily; **prendre a. qch en charge** to take an active responsibility for sth; **s'occuper a. de qch** to be actively engaged in sth; **vivre a.** to lead an active life

activer [aktive] **1** *vt* **(a)** (*presser*) to stimulate, to rouse; (*accélérer*) to speed up; (*feu*) to stoke; **a. un ouvrage** to press on with *or* to speed up a piece of work; *F* **activez!** get a move on! **(b)** *Ch, Nucl etc* to activate **(c)** *Ordinat* to activate; **a. une option** to select an option **2 s'activer** *vpr* to be busy, to busy oneself, to bustle about; **s'a. (à qch)** to get on *or* press on (with sth)

activisme [aktivism] *nm Pol* activism

activiste [aktivist] *adj, n Pol* activist

activité [aktivite] *nf* activity; (*d'une substance*) potency; **l'a. d'une ville** the (amount of) activity in a city; **elle déploie une grande a. au travail** she invests a lot of energy in her work; **maintenir l'a. industrielle** to keep industry going; **une région reconnue pour son a.** a region known for its industrial/cultural/*etc* activity; **en a.** in action, in operation, in progress; (*personne*) working, employed; **en pleine a.** (*entreprise*) in full operation *or* production, fully operational; (*personne*) very busy; (*secteur économique, hôtel etc*) very busy, bustling; **un moment de grande a.** a very busy time; **marché sans a.** dull market; **l'usine est en a.** the factory is working *or* is in production; **volcan en a.** active volcano; **le temps d'a. d'un employé** the length of (active) service of an employee; **être en a. (de service)** to be on active duty *or* on the active list; **je ne connais pas ses activités** I know nothing about his activities; **le centre de jeunes propose les activités suivantes** the following activities are available at the youth centre

▶ **activité**: **a. économique** economic activity; **a. de plein air** outdoor activity; **a. professionnelle** occupation; **a. solaire** solar activity; **a. sportive** sport, sporting activity; *Scol etc* **activités dirigées** project work, projects

actrice [aktris] *nf* actress (*voir aussi* **acteur (a)**)

actuaire [aktɥɛr] *nm* actuary

actualisation [aktɥalizasjɔ̃] *nf* **(a)** (*de textes etc*) updating, update; **(b)** *Écon* discounting; **taux d'a.** rate of discount **(c)** *Phil* actualization

actualiser [aktɥalize] **1** *vt* **(a)** (*texte, méthode de travail*) to update **(b)** *Écon* to discount **(c)** *Phil* **a. qch** to turn sth into a reality, to actualize sth **2 s'actualiser** *vpr* **(a)** (*se moderniser*) to become more up to date **(b)** *Phil* to become a reality, to come into being

actualité [aktɥalite] *nf* **(a)** topicality; **l'a. politique française** the current French political scene; **cette question est toujours d'a.** this is still a topical question; **question d'une a. brûlante** burning question; **les actualités** (*dans la presse*) current events *or* affairs; *TV, Rad* news; **actualités filmées** newsreel; **actualités télévisées** television news **(b)** *Phil* actuality, reality

actuariat [aktɥarja] *nm* actuarial profession

actuariel [aktɥarjɛl] *adj* actuarial

actuel, -elle [aktɥɛl] *adj* present, current; **le gouvernement a.** the present government; **l'état a. du pays** the present *or* current state of the country; **valeur actuelle** present *or* current value; **à l'heure actuelle** at the present time; **dans la situation actuelle** as things are *or* stand at the moment; **cette question est toujours actuelle** this is still a topical question, the question is still relevant today

actuellement [aktɥɛlmɑ̃] *adv* (just) now, at present, at the present time

acuité [akɥite] *nf* (*de la douleur etc*) acuteness, sharpness, keenness; (*d'un argument*) sharpness; **il a analysé le problème avec une a. remarquable** his analysis of the problem was remarkably shrewd; **a. d'un son** high pitch of a sound; **a. visuelle** keenness of vision *or* eyesight; **a. intellectuelle** sharpness of intellect

acuponcteur, -trice, acupuncteur, -trice [akypɔ̃ktœr, -tris] *n Méd* acupuncturist

acuponcture, acupuncture [akypɔ̃ktyr] *nf Méd* acupuncture; **se soigner à l'a.** to have acupuncture treatment

acutangle [akytɑ̃gl] *adj Math* acute-angled

ADAC [adak] *nm* (*abrév* **avion à décollage et atterrissage courts**) STOL

adage [adaʒ] *nm* adage, (common) saying; **selon l'a.** as the saying goes

adagio [adadʒjo] *adv, nm Mus* adagio

Adam [adɑ̃] *nm* Adam; *F* **en costume d'A.** in one's birthday suit; **pomme d'A.** Adam's apple

adaptabilité [adaptabilite] *nf* adaptability (**to** à)

adaptable [adaptabl] *adj* adaptable

adaptateur, -trice [adaptatœr, -tris] **1** *nm* **(a)** *El, MecE, Phot, Ordinat* adapter; **a. (secteur)** (mains) adaptor; *Ordinat* **a. graphique amélioré** enhanced graphics adapter, EGA; **a. femelle/mâle** female to male adaptor; **a. vidéo** video adaptor **(b)** *Rad* convertor **2** *n* (*d'un roman pour le cinéma etc*) adapter

adaptation [adaptasjɔ̃] *nf* **(a)** adaptation (**à** to); **faire un effort d'a.** to make an effort to adapt; **faculté d'a.** adaptability **(b)** *TV, Cin, Th* adaptation; **a. d'une nouvelle au théâtre/pour la télévision** adaptation of a short story for the stage/for television; *TV, Cin* **a. à l'écran** screen adaptation; *TV* **a. en feuilleton** (*d'un roman etc*) serialization; **faire une nouvelle a. de 'Macbeth'** to do a new adaptation of 'Macbeth'; **a. théâtrale** stage adaptation

adapter [adapte] **1** *vt* **(a)** **a. qch à qch** to adapt sth to sth; **a. un règlement à un cas personnel** to adapt a rule to (fit) individual circumstances; **est-ce vraiment adapté à la situation?** is it really suitable for the situation?; **a. un tube à un autre** to make one tube fit another **(b)** *TV, Cin, Th* **a. un roman à la scène** to adapt a novel for the stage; *TV* **a. en feuilleton** to serialize **2 s'adapter** *vpr* to adapt; **la prise s'adapte à toutes les télévisions** the plug fits all types of television; **s'a. aux conditions nouvelles** to adapt (oneself) *or* adjust to new conditions; **il sait s'a.** he's very adaptable *or* flexible

ADAV [adav] *nm* (*abrév* **avion à décollage et atterrissage verticaux**) VTOL

addenda [adɛ̃da] *nm inv* [①A13,5] addendum (**à** to)

additif, -ive [aditif, -iv] **1** *adj* additive **2** *nm* (**a**) supplement, addition; (*à un texte*) additional clause; **a. à un budget** addition to a budget (**b**) *Ch etc* additive; **sans additifs** additive free; **a. anti-détonant** anti-knock additive; **a. antigivre** antifreeze additive; **a. anti-mousse** anti-foam additive; **a. anti-oxydant** oxidation inhibitor; **a. détergent** detergent additive

addition [adisjɔ̃] *nf* (**a**) (*fait d'ajouter*) addition, adding (to); (*pour faire un total*) adding up; **apprendre à faire les additions** to learn how to do addition *or* how to add up; **faire l'a. des chiffres** to add up *or F* tot up the figures; **l'a. d'un paragraphe à un texte** the addition *or* adding of a paragraph to a text; **l'a. de thym améliorera le ragoût** adding some thyme will improve the stew (**b**) (*extension*) addition, extension; **faire une a. à une maison** to build an extension to a house; **en a. à** in addition to (**c**) [①A71,7; B56,C,4] *Math* addition (**d**) (*au restaurant etc*) bill, *Am* check (**e**) *Typ* note

additionnel, -elle [adisjɔnɛl] *adj* additional, extra; *Ordinat* add-on

additionner [adisjɔne] **1** *vt* to add (up), *F* to tot up; **a. un alcool d'un peu d'eau** to add a little water to a drink; **lait additionné d'eau** watered down milk; **café additionné d'eau-de-vie** coffee laced with spirits **2** *vi* to add (up) **3 s'additioner** *vpr* to add up; **aux longues heures de travail s'additionnent celles passées dans le métro** along with the long working hours, there are those spent on the underground

additionneur [adisjɔnœr] *nm Ordinat* adder

additionneuse [adisjɔnøz] *nf* adding machine, adder

adducteur, -trice [adyktœr, -tris] **1** *adj Anat etc* adducent; **canal a.** feeder canal **2** *nm* (**a**) *Anat* adductor (**b**) *Constr* supply main

adduction [adyksjɔ̃] *nf* (**a**) *Anat* adduction (**b**) *Tech* admission, intake; *Constr* **a. d'eau** canalization; **adductions d'eau** water supply

adénoïde [adenɔid] *adj Méd* **végétations adénoïdes** adenoids

adent [adɑ̃] *nm Menuis* dovetail

adepte [adɛpt] *n* (**a**) (*partisan*) follower, adherent; **un a. de la non-violence** a supporter of non-violence; **les adeptes de la marche à pied** walking enthusiasts; **a. du cinéma** film fan *or* buff; **a. des ordinateurs** computer buff; **c'est une a. du ski** she loves skiing; **faire des adeptes** to attract followers *or* a following (**b**) (*rare*) (*personne initiée*) adept, initiate

adéquat [adekwa] *adj* (*personne, lieu, expression, méthode*) appropriate, suitable; (*montant, quantité*) adequate

adéquation [adekwasjɔ̃] *nf* appropriateness, suitability

adhérence [aderɑ̃s] *nf* adhesion, adherence; **a. des pneus (à la route)** grip of the tyres (on the road); **cette voiture a une excellente a. à la route** this car has excellent road-holding

adhérent, -ente [aderɑ̃, -ɑ̃t] **1** *adj* (*substance, propriétés*) adhesive **2** *n* member; **a. d'un parti** member of a party; (*partisan*) supporter of a party; **carte d'a.** membership card

adhérer [adere] *vi* (**j'adhère, n. adhérons; j'adhérerai**) (**a**) to adhere, to stick (**à** to); **a. à la route** (*des pneus*) to grip the road (**b**) (*à une opinion, un idéal etc*) to adhere, to hold, to subscribe (**à** to) (**c**) (*s'inscrire*) **a. (à un parti)** to join (a party)

adhésif, -ive [adezif, -iv] **1** *adj* adhesive, sticky; **pansement a.** sticking plaster; **papier a.** sticky(-backed) paper **2** *nm* adhesive

adhésion [adezjɔ̃] *nf* (**a**) (*fait de coller*) adhesion, sticking; (*des pneus*) grip(ping), road-holding; **force d'a.** adhesiveness (**b**) (*accord*) agreement, approval; **donner son a. à un projet** to support *or* give one's support to a plan (**c**) (*inscription*) adhesion, adherence (**à** to); (*d'un parti*) membership; **après leur a. à la UE** after joing the EU; **le nombre des adhésions augmente** the number of new members is increasing

ad hoc [adɔk] *adj, adv* ad hoc

adieu, *pl* **-eux** [adjø] **1** *int* (**a**) *Arch* goodbye!, *Arch* farewell!; **dire a. à qn** to say goodbye to sb; *Fig F* **dire a. à qch** to kiss sth goodbye, to say goodbye to sth (**b**) *Région* (*bonjour*) hello!, hi!; **allez a.!, à demain** bye then, see you tomorrow **2** *nm* farewell; **des adieux déchirants/émouvants** heart-rending/emotional farewells *or* partings; **faire ses adieux** to make one's farewells, to say one's goodbyes; **faire ses adieux à qn** to say goodbye to sb; **faire ses adieux à la scène** to make one's final appearance on stage; **baiser d'a.** goodbye kiss; (*à tout jamais*) parting *or* farewell kiss

adipeux, -euse [adipø, -øz] *adj* (*tissu etc*) adipose, fatty; **un visage pâle et a.** a pale, bloated face

adiposité [adipozite] *nf* adiposity

adjacent [adʒasɑ̃] *adj* adjacent (**à** to); *Math* **angles adjacents** adjacent angles

adjectif, -ive [adʒɛktif, -iv] **1** *adj* (*expression, locution etc*) adjectival **2** *nm* [①A17-21; B8-11] adjective; **a. attribut** predicative adjective; **a. épithète** attributive adjective; **a. déterminatif** determiner; **a. verbal** present participle; **a. substantivé** adjective used as a noun

adjectival, -ale, -aux, -ales [adʒɛktival, -o] *adj* adjectival

adjectiver [adʒɛktive] *vt* to use as an adjective

adjoindre [adʒwɛ̃dr] (*conj like* **joindre**) **1** *vt* (**a**) **a. qch à qch** to unite *or* associate sth with sth; **a. un mode d'emploi à un appareil** to include *or* enclose an instruction booklet with an appliance (**b**) **a. qn à qn** to give sb to sb as an assistant; **a. qn à un comité** to add sb to a committee **2 s'adjoindre** *vpr* (*assistant*) to engage; **s'a. à d'autres** to join (in) with others

adjoint, -ointe [adʒwɛ̃, -wɛ̃t] **1** *adj* assistant, deputy; (*directeur etc*) associate, *Can* **Sous-ministre a.** Assistant Deputy Minister **2** *n* assistant; **a. au maire** deputy mayor

adjonction [adʒɔ̃ksjɔ̃] *nf* (**a**) (*fait d'ajouter*) adding, addition; **produit sans a. de sucre** product with no added sugar (**b**) (*élément adjoint*) (*à un texte etc*) addition; (*d'un hôpital*) annexe

adjudant [adʒydɑ̃] *nm* (**a**) *Mil* warrant officer class II, *US* warrant officer (junior grade); **a-chef** warrant officer class I, *US* chief warrant officer; **(capitaine) a-major** adjutant, *US* executive officer (**b**) (*oiseau*) adjutant bird

adjudicataire [adʒydikatɛr] *n* (*à un contrat*) successful tenderer; (*aux enchères*) highest bidder, purchaser; **être l'a.** to be awarded the contract

adjudicateur, -trice [adʒydikatœr, -tris] *n* adjudicator; (*d'un contrat etc*) awarder

adjudication [adʒydikasjɔ̃] *nf* adjudication, allocation; (*d'un contrat*) award; (*vente aux enchères*) selling *or* sale by auction; **mettre qch en a.** (*marché administratif*) to invite tenders for sth; (*aux enchères*) to put sth up for (sale by) auction; **a. forcée** compulsory sale

adjuger [adʒyʒe] (**j'adjugeai(s); n. adjugeons**) **1** *vt* **a. qch à qn** to award sth to sb; (*allouer*) to allocate sth to sb; (*aux enchères*) to knock sth down to sb; **une fois! deux fois! trois fois! adjugé! vendu!** going! going! gone! **2 s'adjuger** *vpr* **s'a. qch** to appropriate sth, to take possession of sth; **elle s'est adjugée la plus belle part** she took the biggest share for herself

adjuration [adʒyrasjɔ̃] *nf* entreaty, plea

adjurer [adʒyre] *vt* **a. qn de faire qch** to implore *or* entreat sb to do sth

adjuvant [adʒyvɑ̃] *nm* (**a**) *Méd* adjuvant (**b**) *Ch, Tech* additive (**de** to); *Pétr* dope (**c**) *Fig* stimulus

admettre [admɛtr] *vt* (*conj like* **mettre**) (**a**) (*accueillir*) **a. qn** to admit sb, to let sb in; **les chiens ne sont pas admis** (*sur la porte d'un magasin etc*) no dogs allowed; **a. qn chez soi** to let sb into one's house; **être admis à un club** to be admitted to a club; **être admis à l'université** to be accepted for university; **être admis à un examen** to pass an examination

(**b**) (*accepter*) **a. qn à siéger** to admit sb as a (new) member; **a. qch** to admit *or* admit of *or* permit *or* allow sth; **je n'admets pas qu'on me mente** I won't tolerate being lied to; **il n'admet pas mes explications** he doesn't *or* won't accept my explanations; **elle n'admet pas la discussion** she won't allow *or* permit any discussion; **cette règle n'admet aucune exception** the rule admits of *or* allows no exceptions, there can be no exceptions to the rule; **l'usage admis** the accepted custom; **non, cela je ne l'admets pas!** no, I don't agree with that!; **cela je ne l'admettrai pas** I won't allow it, I'm not having it

(**c**) (*reconnaître*) to admit, to acknowledge; **il admet que c'est vrai** he admits *or* acknowledges that it is true; **admettons que j'aie tort** assuming *or* supposing (that) I'm wrong

(**d**) *Jur* **a. un appel** to grant leave to appeal

(**e**) (*laisser entrer*) (*vapeur, pétrole*) to let in; **l'essence est admise dans le moteur par ce conduit** the petrol enters the engine through this pipe

administrateur, -trice [administratœr, -tris] *n* (**a**) administrator; **a. foncier** land agent; (*qui vend des maisons, des appartements*) estate agent (**b**) (*d'une société, d'une banque etc*) director (**c**) (*de fondation*) trustee

▶ **administrateur**: **a. délégué** executive director; **a. judiciaire** official receiver; *TV, Cin* **a. de la production** production director; *Ordinat* **a. du réseau** network manager

administratif, -ive [administratif, -iv] *adj* administrative

administration [administrasjɔ̃] *nf* (**a**) (*d'affaires etc*) administration, direction, management; (*d'un pays*) governing; **conseil d'a.** board of directors; **elle a confié l'a. de son affaire à des collaborateurs** she entrusted the handling of her business to colleagues; **mauvaise a.** (*d'une société*) mismanagement

(**b**) (*ensemble des directeurs*) board of directors; (*d'une institution*) governing body; **l'a. est en délibération** the board is meeting

(**c**) (*service public*) government service; (*fonctionnaires*) authorities, officials; **l'a. publique, l'A.** ≈ the Civil Service; **entrer dans l'a.** to become a civil servant; **travailler dans l'a.** to work in the Civil Service

▶ **administration**: **a. des Douanes** Customs and Excise; **l'a. des Eaux et Forêts** *Br* ≈ the Forestry Commission; **a. fiscale** tax authorities; **a. du personnel** personnel management; **a. portuaire** port authorities; *Ordinat* **a. de réseau** network management

administrativement [administrativmɑ̃] *adv* administratively

administré, -ée [administre] *n* citizen

administrer [administre] *vt* (**a**) (*affaire, propriété*) to administer, to manage; (*affaire*) to conduct; (*pays*) to govern (**b**) (*justice*) to dispense; *Rel* (*sacrements*) to administer; **a. un malade** to administer *or* give the last rites to a sick person; **a. un remède à un malade** to administer medication to a patient; **je vais lui a. une bonne correction** I'm going to give him/her a good hiding (**c**) *Jur* **a. des preuves** to produce proofs

admirable [admirabl] *adj* admirable; (*très bon*) (*cuisinière, père de famille*) wonderful; **elle a été a. de courage/volonté** she showed admirable courage/willpower

admirablement [admirabləmɑ̃] *adv* admirably; (*très bien*) (*chanter, cuisiner*) wonderfully; **ça fonctionne a. bien** it's working perfectly

admirateur, -trice [admiratœr, -tris] *n* admirer; (*d'une vedette de variété etc*) fan

admiratif, -ive [admiratif, -iv] *adj* (*geste etc*) admiring

admiration [admirasjɔ̃] *nf* admiration; **avoir de l'a. pour qn** to admire sb, to be full of *or* filled with admiration for sb; **être en a. devant qch** to be filled with admiration for sth; **il est en a. devant sa fille** he is full of *or* filled with admiration for his daughter; **tomber en a.** to be filled with admiration for; **tu fais l'a. de plus d'un** many people admire you; **cette peinture a fait l'a. de tout le monde** this painting was admired by everybody; **soulever l'a. de qn** to be admired by sb

admirer [admire] *vt* to admire; **admiré de tous** admired by all; *Iron* **j'admire la légèreté avec laquelle tu parles de la famine dans ton pays!** I admire the way you speak so casually about famine in your country!

admis, -ise [admi, -iz] **1** *adj* (**a**) (*reçu*) accepted (**b**) (*autorisé à entrer*) admitted, allowed (in) (**c**) (*accepté*) allowed, acceptable; **c'est chose communément admise ici** it's a widely accepted fact here; **c'est l'opinion communément admise** it's the commonly held opinion (**d**) **il a été a. à passer les épreuves à la session de septembre** (*autorisé à*) he was allowed *or* permitted to take the tests in September **2** *n Univ* (*à un examen*) successful candidate

admissibilité [admisibilite] *nf* admissibility; (*à un emploi*) eligibility; *Scol* **épreuves d'a. (à l'examen oral)** written examinations (to gain admission to the oral examination)

admissible [admisibl] *adj* (*excuse, preuve, conduite*) admissible, allowable; *Jur* (*preuve*) admissible; **a. à un emploi** eligible for a job; *Scol* **(candidats) admissibles** candidates who have qualified for the oral examination

admission [admisjɔ̃] *nf* (**a**) admission (**à, dans** to); **demande d'a. dans un club** club membership application; **a. à un club** admission to a club; **cotisation d'a.** entrance *or* admission fee

(**b**) *Com* (*de marchandises*) entry; **a. en franchise** duty-free entry; **a. temporaire** temporary entry

(**c**) (*entrée*) *Tech* intake; *Aut* induction; (*temps moteur*) induction *or* intake stroke; **période d'a.** induction stroke; **soupape d'a.** inlet valve

(**d**) *Bourse* **a. à la cote** admission to quotation

(**e**) *Univ* pass; **le nombre des admissions à un concours** the number of passes *or* successful candidates at a competitive examination; **il a eu son a. à Centrale** he was accepted into Centrale

admixtion [admiksjɔ̃] *nf* admixture (**à** with)

admonestation [admɔnɛstasjɔ̃] *nf* admonishing

admonester [admɔnɛste] *vt* to admonish

admonition [admɔnisjɔ̃] *nf* admonition

ADN [adeɛn] *nm* (*abrév* **acide désoxyribonucléique**) DNA

ado [ado] *n F* (*adolescent*) teenager; **magazine/club/musique pour ados** teenage magazine/club/music

adobe [adɔb] *nm* (*brique, maison*) adobe

adolescence [adɔlesɑ̃s] *nf* adolescence; **pendant l'a.** during adolescence *or* one's teenage years *or* one's teens

adolescent, -ente [adɔlesɑ̃, -ɑ̃t] **1** *adj* adolescent, teenage **2** *n* adolescent, teenager; (*jeune homme*) youth; (*jeune fille*) girl (in her teens) *or* teenage girl

adon [adɔ̃] *nm Can F* coincidence

Adonis [adɔnis] *nm Myth* Adonis

adonis [adɔnis] *nm* (**a**) (*bel homme*) Adonis; **je ne suis pas vraiment un a.!** I'm no Adonis!, I'm no oil painting! (**b**) (*insecte*) adonis

adonner (s') [sadɔne] *vpr* **s'a. à qch** to give oneself up to sth; **s'a. à l'étude** to devote oneself to study; **s'a. à une profession** to take up a profession; **s'a. à la boisson** to take to drink; **s'a. à une vie de plaisirs** to abandon oneself to a life of pleasure

adoptant, -ante [adɔptɑ̃, -ɑ̃t] **1** *adj* adoptive **2** *n* adoptive parent

adopté, -ée [adɔpte] **1** *adj* adopted **2** *n* adopted child

adopter [adɔpte] *vt* (**a**) (*prendre sous sa tutelle*) (*enfant*) to adopt; *Fig* **nous l'avons adopté comme un fils** we treated him like a son

(**b**) (*accepter*) **a. qn pour ami** to choose sb as a friend, to befriend sb; **il a très vite été adopté par ses nouveaux collègues** he was very quickly accepted by his new colleagues

(**c**) (*choisir*) (*produit*) to adopt; (*nom*) to adopt, to assume; (*cause*) to adopt, to take up, to embrace; **a. un produit comme norme** to standardize on a product

(**d**) (*approuver, voter*) **a. un projet de loi/une résolution** to adopt *or* pass *or* carry a bill/a resolution; **adopté à l'unanimité** carried unanimously

adoptif, -ive [adɔptif, -iv] *adj* (*enfant, pays*) adopted; (*parent*) adoptive

adoption [adɔpsjɔ̃] *nf* (*d'un enfant, d'une proposition, d'une idée, d'une mode*) adoption; **procédure d'a.** adoption procedure; *Parl* (*d'un projet de loi*) adoption, carrying; **mon pays d'a.** my country of adoption, my adopted country

adorable [adɔrabl] *adj* adorable, charming; **vous êtes a. dans cette robe** you look charming in that dress

adorablement [adɔrabləmɑ̃] *adv* adorably

adorateur, -trice [adɔratœr, -tris] *n* (**a**) (*d'une religion*) worshipper (**b**) (*d'un chanteur*) ardent admirer, fan; (*d'une femme*) admirer

adoration [adɔrasjɔ̃] *nf* (**a**) (*d'une divinité*) adoration, worship (**b**) (*attachement très profond*) profound admiration (**de** for); **vouer une véritable a. à qn** to nurse a feeling of adoration for sb; **être en a. devant son bébé** to worship one's baby

adorer [adɔre] **1** *vt* (**a**) (*divinité*) to adore, to worship (**b**) (*qn, qch*) to love; (*plus fort*) to adore; (*star du cinéma, petit ami etc*) to idolize; *Euph* **Joseph Beuys?, bof, je n'adore pas** Joseph Beuys?, well, I wouldn't call him my favourite; **j'adore monter à cheval** I adore *or* love riding **2 s'adorer** *vpr* to adore each other

adossé [adose] *adj* (**a**) (*dos contre dos*) back to back (**b**) **a. à qch** (*personne*) with one's back against sth, leaning against sth; (*édifice etc*) backed on to sth

adosser [adose] **1** *vt* (**a**) **a. deux choses** to place two things back to back (**b**) **a. qch à** *ou* **contre qch** to place *or* lean *or* rest sth (with its back) against sth; **a. une chaise à qch** to put a chair with its back against sth **2 s'adosser** *vpr* **s'a. à** *ou* **contre qch** to lean (up) against sth; **le village s'adosse à la colline** the village is built against the hillside

adouber [adube] *vt* (**a**) *Échecs* (*pièce*) to adjust (**b**) *Arch* (*chevalier*) to dub

adoucir [adusir] **1** *vt* (**a**) (*voix, eau, tissu, peau*) to soften; (*contraste, couleur*) to tone down; (*lumière*) to subdue; (*boisson, goût*) to sweeten; **sa nouvelle coiffure adoucit son expression** her new haircut softens her face

(**b**) (*tempérer*) (*douleur, chagrin etc*) to alleviate, to relieve, to ease; **a. une situation tendue** to ease *or* alleviate a tense situation; *Prov* **la musique adoucit les mœurs** music hath charms to soothe the savage breast

(**c**) (*qn*) to pacify, to mollify

(**d**) (*surface, bois etc*) to smooth, to soften; (*angle*) to smooth off; (*verre*) to (rough-)polish

(**e**) *Métal* to temper; (*fonte de fer*) to soften

2 s'adoucir *vpr* (**a**) (*d'une voix*) to grow softer, to soften, to mellow

(**b**) (*du temps*) to get *or* grow milder

(**c**) (*de la douleur*) to decrease

(**d**) (*du caractère*) to mellow; **il s'est adouci avec l'âge** he has mellowed with age; **ce cognac s'adoucit avec le temps** this brandy mellows with age

adoucissage [adusisaʒ] *nm* (**a**) *Métal* tempering; (*de fonte de fer*) softening (**b**) (*de glace, de marbre*) polishing (**c**) (*des couleurs*) toning down

adoucissant [adusisɑ̃] **1** *adj* softening; **crème adoucissante pour les mains** hand cream; **produit a. pour le linge** fabric softener **2** *nm* (*pour le linge*) fabric softener
adoucissement [adusismɑ̃] *nm* **(a)** (*de la voix etc*) softening; (*du caractère*) calming; (*de la température*) rise; **on prévoit un a.** milder weather is forecast **(b)** (*de la douleur etc*) alleviation **(c)** (*de surfaces, d'angles*) smoothing **(d)** sweetening; (*de l'eau*) (water) softening **(e)** *Métal* annealing
adoucisseur [adusisœr] *nm* (water) softener
ad patres [adpatrɛs] *adv* **envoyer qn a.** to send sb to meet his maker
ad(r). *abrév* **adresse**
adrénaline [adrenalin] *nf Méd* adrenalin(e)
adressable [adrɛsabl] *adj Ordinat* addressable
adressage [adrɛsaʒ] *nm Ordinat* addressing; **mode d'a.** address mode; **a. direct** direct addressing
adresse [adrɛs] *nf* **(a)** [①A71,6] address; **nom, profession et a.** name, address and occupation; **nous avons échangé nos adresses** we exchanged addresses; **a. personnelle** home address; **a. au bureau** office address; **a. de facturation** invoicing address, address for invoicing; **a. de livraison** delivery address; (*d'objets volumineux*) shipping address; **a. du siège social** head office *or* registered office address; **a. électronique** e-mail address; **carnet d'adresses** address book; **changer d'a.** to change one's address; **faire son changement d'a.** (*à la poste*) to have one's mail redirected; *Fig* **tu te trompes d'a.** you've come to the wrong person, you're knocking at the wrong door; **il m'a donné une bonne a.** (*de restaurant, de magasin etc*) he recommended a good restaurant/shop/*etc*; **inconnu à cette a.** not known at this address; *Fig* **une observation à votre a.** (*intention*) a remark aimed at *or* meant for you; **je l'ai dit à l'a. de ceux qui ...** I said it for the benefit of those who ...
(b) (*dans une assemblée*) (formal) address
(c) (*habileté*) skill, dexterity; (*savoir faire*) diplomacy; **jongler avec a.** to juggle skilfully *or* with dexterity; **faire des tours d'a.** to perform tricks; **dénué d'a.** bungling; **il lui faudra une sacrée a. pour se tirer de cette situation** he'll have to be damn clever to get out of this situation
(d) *Ordinat* address; **a. absolue** absolute *or* specific address; **a. de mémoire** memory address; **a. virtuelle** virtual address
adresser [adrese] **1** *vt* **(a)** (*lettre etc*) to address; **la lettre lui fut adressée dans sa résidence d'été** the letter was addressed to (him at) his summer residence; **lettre mal adressée** incorrectly addressed letter
(b) (*envoyer*) to send *or* to refer (**qn à qn** sb to sb); **on m'a adressé à vous** (*par le biais d'un médecin etc*) I have been recommended to come and see you, I have been referred to you; **le médecin m'a adressé à un spécialiste** the doctor sent *or* referred me to a specialist
(c) (*remarques etc*) to address, to aim; **a. des remerciements à qn** to deliver thanks to sb; **cette remarque était adressée à Martin** this remark was aimed at *or* meant for Martin; **a. un sourire à qn** to smile at sb; **elle ne m'adresse plus la parole depuis notre dispute** she hasn't spoken to me since our argument
2 s'adresser *vpr* **s'a. à qn** (*d'une remarque, recommandation etc*) to apply to sb; (*d'une personne*) to speak to sb; **s'a. ici** apply within; (*pour des renseignements*) enquire within; **adressez-vous à l'agent** ask the policeman; **s'a. à l'imagination/au bon sens de qn** to appeal to sb's imagination/common sense; **le livre s'adresse aux enfants** the book is aimed at children
Adriatique [adriatik] **1** *adj* Adriatic **2** *nf* **l'A.** the Adriatic
Adrien [adriɛ̃] *nm* Adrian; *Rom Hist* Hadrian
adroit [adrwa] *adj* **(a)** (*habile*) dexterous, deft, skilful, handy; **être a. de ses mains** to be clever *or* good with one's hands **(b)** (*réponse, diplomate*) shrewd, clever, skilful, *US* skillful; **il le lui a annoncé de but en blanc, ce qui n'est pas très a.** he informed him quite bluntly, which wasn't very tactful; **phrase adroite** neatly turned phrase, neat turn of phrase
adroitement [adrwatmɑ̃] *adv* (*fabriqué*) skilfully, *US* skillfully, cleverly; (*juger*) shrewdly; (*finir un discours etc*) neatly; **se défendre a.** to defend oneself skilfully *or* adroitly
adr. tél. *abrév* **adresse télégraphique**
adsorber [atsɔrbe] *vt Phys, Biol* to adsorb
adsorption [atsɔrpsjɔ̃] *nf Phys, Biol* adsorption
adulateur, -trice [adylatœr, -tris] *n Litt* adulator; (*flatteur*) sycophant
adulation [adylasjɔ̃] *nf Arch* adulation, flattery (**de** of); *Péj* sycophancy
aduler [adyle] *vt* to idolize
adulte [adylt] **1** *adj* (*personne*) adult, grown-up; (*plante, animal*) mature, fully-grown; **l'âge a.** adulthood; **atteindre l'âge a.** to reach adulthood; **à l'âge a.** when fully grown; **ça n'est pas très a. cette réaction** that is not a very mature way to react **2** *n* adult, grown-up
adultère[1] [adyltɛr] **1** *adj* adulterous **2** *n* adulterer, *f* adulteress
adultère[2] *nm* adultery; **commettre un a.** to commit adultery; **pour cause d'a.** for reasons of adultery, on grounds of adultery
adultérin, -ine [adylterɛ̃, -in] *adj Jur* **enfant a.** child conceived in adultery, adulterine child
ad valorem [advalɔrɛm] *adj & adv* ad valorem
advenir [advənir] *v impers* (*conj like* **venir**) (*used only in the third person*) to occur, to happen, *Litt* to befall, to chance; **or, il advint que ...** now it came to pass that ...; **quoi qu'il advienne** no matter what happens; **advienne que pourra** come what may
adventice [advɑ̃tis] *adj* (*imprévu*) adventitious; (*sans cause ou but précis*) casual
adventif, -ive [advɑ̃tif, -iv] *adj Bot* (*racine etc*) adventitious; *Géol* (*cône*) parasitic
adverbe [advɛrb] *nm* [①A21-25; B11-13] adverb; **a. de manière/de temps** adverb of manner/time
adverbial, -ale, -aux, -ales [advɛrbjal, -o] *adj* adverbial; **locution adverbiale** adverbial phrase
adversaire [advɛrsɛr] *n* adversary, opponent; (*dans un conflit, une guerre*) enemy
adverse [advɛrs] *adj* (*hostile*) adverse, unfavourable, *US* unfavorable; **fortune a.** bad luck; **critique a.** unfavourable criticism; *Jur* **la partie a.** the opposing party, the other side; *Sp* **le camp a.** the opposing side
adversité [advɛrsite] *nf Litt* **(a)** (*sort*) adversity, adverse circumstances **(b)** (*malheur*) misfortune, trial; **lutter contre l'a.** to fight in the face of adversity
ad vitam aeternam [advitametɛrnam] *adv F* from here to eternity, till kingdom come
AELE [aəɛlə] *nf* (*abrév* **Association européenne de libre-échange**) EFTA
aérage [aeraʒ] *nm* **(a)** (*d'une pièce etc*) ventilation, airing **(b)** (*de l'eau*) aeration
aérateur [aeratœr] *nm* ventilator, (air) vent
aération [aerasjɔ̃] *nf* = **aérage**
aéré [aere] *adj* airy, well-ventilated
aérer [aere] (**j'aère, n. aérons; j'aérerai**) **1** *vt* **(a)** (*mine*) to ventilate; (*pièce, linge*) to air **(b)** (*eau*) to aerate **(c)** (*rendre moins dense*) (*texte, exposé etc*) to lighten **2 s'aérer** *vpr* to get some fresh air; **avoir besoin de s'a.** to need some fresh air *or* a breath of fresh air
aérien, -ienne [aerjɛ̃, -jɛn] *adj* **(a)** air; (*plante, racine*) aerial; (*phénomène etc*) atmospheric; *Mil* **les forces aériennes** the air force; **défense/attaque aérienne** air defence/raid; *Av* **compagnie aérienne** airline; **poste aérienne** air mail; **expédier par fret a.** to airfreight **(b)** (*texture etc*) (light and) airy; (*grâce, allure, démarche etc*) light, floating; **marcher d'un pas a.** to have a spring in one's step **(c)** (*câble etc*) overhead; (*voie ferrée*) elevated
aérium [aerjɔm] *nm* (open air) sanatorium
aéro- [aerɔ, -o] *préf* aero-
aérobic [aerobik] *nm* aerobics; **professeur/cours d'a.** aerobics teacher/class; **faire de l'a.** to do aerobics
aérocâble [aerokɑbl] *nm* cableway
aéro-club, *pl* **aéro-clubs** *nm* flying *or* aero club
aérodrome [aerodrom] *nm* aerodrome, airfield, *US* airdrome
aérodynamique [aerodinamik] **1** *adj* aerodynamic; (*forme, voiture*) streamlined **2** *nf* aerodynamics
aérodynamisme [ærodinamism] *nm* aerodynamics
aérodyne [aerodin] *nm* aerodyne
aérofrein [aerofrɛ̃] *nm Av* air brake
aérogare [aerogar] *nf* air terminal, terminal building
aérogastrie [aerogastri] *nf Méd* aerogastria
aéroglisseur [aeroglisœr] *nm* hovercraft
aérogramme [aerogram] *nm* air mail letter
aérographe [aerograf] *nm* airbrush
aérologie [aerolɔʒi] *nf* aerology
aéromodélisme [aeromɔdelism] *nm* model aircraft making
aéromoteur [aeromɔtœr] *nm* wind engine
aéronaute [aeronot] *n* aeronaut
aéronautique [aeronotik] **1** *adj* aeronautic(al) **2** *nf* aeronautics; **ingénieur d'a.** aeronautical engineer
aéronaval, -ale, -als, -ales [aeronaval] **1** *adj* (*forces etc*) air and sea **2** *nf* **l'Aéronavale** ≈ *Br* the Fleet Air Arm, *US* the Naval Air Service
aéronef [aeronɛf] *nm* aircraft; (*dirigeable*) airship
aérophagie [aerofaʒi] *nf* **avoir** *ou* **faire de l'a.** to suffer from flatulence
aérophotographie [aerofotografi] *nf* aerial photography
aéroplane [aeroplan] *nm Vieilli* aeroplane, *US* airplane

aéropoint [ærɔpwɛ̃] *nm Av* ≈ airmile; **accumuler des aéropoints** to collect airmiles
aéroport [aerɔpɔr] *nm* airport; **a. de destination** airport of destination, destination airport; **a. de départ** airport of departure, departure airport; **a. de déroutement** diverting airport; **a. de remplacement** alternative airport; **Aéroports de Paris** Paris Airports Authority
aéroporté [aerɔpɔrte] *adj* airborne
aéroportuaire [aerɔpɔrtɥɛr] *adj (équipement, installations etc)* airport
aéropostal, -ale, -aux, -ales [aerɔpɔstal, -o] **1** *adj* airmail **2** *nf Hist* **l'Aéropostale** the (French) airmail service
aérosol [aerɔsɔl] **1** *nm* aerosol; **vendu en a.** sold in aerosol *or* spray form **2** *adj inv* aerosol; **bombe a.** aerosol (can)
aérospatial, -ale, -aux, -ales [aerɔspasjal, -o] *adj (équipement etc)* aerospace
aérostat [aerɔsta] *nm* balloon, aerostat
aérostatique [aerɔstatik] **1** *adj* aerostatic **2** *nf* aerostatics
aérostier [aerɔstje] *nm* balloonist
Aérotrain® [aerɔtrɛ̃] *nm* hovertrain
aérotransporté [aerɔtrɑ̃spɔrte] *adj (marchandises, passagers, troupes)* airborne
AF *abrév* **(a) allocations familiales (b) Air France**
affabilité [afabilite] *nf* graciousness, affability (**avec, envers** to, towards); **être d'une grande a.** to be very gracious *or* affable
affable [afabl] *adj* gracious, affable (**envers, avec** to, towards, with)
affablement [afabləmɑ̃] *adv* graciously, affably
affabulateur, -trice [afabylatœr, -tris] **1** *adj* **qu'est-ce que tu peux être a.** you're too fond of telling tall stories **2** *n* fibber, storyteller
affabulation [afabylasjɔ̃] *nf* fabrication(s), distortion(s); **les résultats publiés ne sont qu'une a.** the published results are pure invention
affabuler [afabyle] *vi* to invent things, to make things up
affacturage [afaktyraʒ] *nm Com* factoring
affadir [afadir] **1** *vt (nourriture etc)* to make insipid *or* tasteless; *(couleur, style, personnalité etc)* to make dull *or* uninteresting **2 s'affadir** *vpr (nourriture etc)* to become insipid; *(couleur, style, personnalité etc)* to become dull *or* uninteresting
affaiblir [afeblir] **1** *vt* **(a)** *(réduire)* to lessen, to reduce; **l'usage a affaibli le sens du mot** the meaning of the word has become weakened through overuse; **a. le courage de qn** to dampen sb's courage; *Phot* **a. un cliché** to reduce (the contrasts of) a negative

(b) *(d'une maladie)* to weaken, *Fml* to enfeeble, to debilitate; **affaibli par la maladie** weakened by illness

2 s'affaiblir *vpr* **(a)** *(devenir faible)* to grow *or* become weak(er) *or* feeble(r), to lose one's strength; *(d'un son)* to become *or* grow fainter; **ma vue s'affaiblit rapidement** my eyesight is deteriorating *or* failing rapidly; **mes forces s'affaiblissaient** my strength was failing; **la tempête s'affaiblit** the storm is abating

(b) *(s'atténuer)* **le sens du mot s'affaiblit au XVIe siècle** the word took on a weaker meaning in the 16th century
affaiblissement [afeblismɑ̃] *nm* **(a)** weakening; *(de la force etc)* diminution; *(du sens d'un mot)* weakening; *TV (de signaux)* attenuation; **a. de la lumière** dimming (of the light) **(b)** *(faiblesse)* weakness; *Méd* debility
affaire [afɛr] *nf* **(a)** business, concern; **ce n'est pas votre a.** it's not your business, it's none of your business; **occupez-vous de vos affaires** mind your own business; **ça, c'est mon a.** that's my business; *(je m'en occupe)* (you can) leave that to me; **mettre le nez dans les affaires de qn** to stick one's nose into sb's business; **mettre de l'ordre dans ses affaires** to put one's affairs in order; **ce n'est pas l'a. de tout le monde** not everybody can do that; **c'est l'a. d'un médecin** it's a case for a doctor; **a. d'argent** money matter; **a. de cœur** love affair; **a. d'honneur** duel; **a. de conscience** matter of conscience; **a. difficile** difficult question *or* matter; **c'est (une) a. de goût** it's a matter *or* question of taste; **ce n'est que l'a. d'un instant** it won't take a minute; **ça, c'est une autre a.** that's another question *or* another matter; **avoir a. à** to deal with; **nous avons eu a. à un homme charmant** we were dealt with by a charming man; **s'il continue à mentir, il aura a. à moi!** if he keeps on lying, he'll have me to contend with *or* me to answer to!

(b) *(compte)* **ça fait mon a.** that's just what I need *or* what I was looking for; **cela ne fera pas l'a.** that won't do; **il fera votre a.** he's just the man for you; **cela devrait tout à fait faire mon a.** that should do the trick; **faire son a. à qn** *F* to give sb what he deserves *or* what he's asking for *or* what was coming to him; *Arg (le tuer)* to do sb in, to bump sb off

(c) *(ennui)* (difficult *or* serious) business; **c'est une a. de pots-de-vin qui a fait la une des journaux** it's a case of bribery which made the headlines; **c'est une sale/drôle a.** it's a nasty/funny business; **il cherche à étouffer l'a.** he's trying to hush up the whole affair; **ce n'est pas une petite a., c'est toute une a.** it's quite a business; **je n'en fais pas une a.** I'm not making an issue of it; **en voilà une a.!** here's a nice mess *or* a nice kettle of fish!; *(ce n'était pas la peine)* it's a lot of fuss about nothing!; **la belle a.!** is that all?, so what?; **se tirer d'a.** to get out of a difficulty; **tirer qn d'a.** to get sb out of trouble *or* out of the woods; **les médecins vont pouvoir le tirer d'a.** the doctors will be able to pull him through; **se faire une a. de qch** to get all worked up about sth; *Pol* **l'a. de Suez** the Suez Crisis; **l'a. est encore chaude** *(toute la presse en parle)* it's still very much in the news, it's still hot news

(d) *(transaction)* (business) transaction, deal; *(achat à bon marché)* bargain; **une bonne/mauvaise a.** a good/bad deal; **on fait des affaires dans ce magasin** you get good bargains in this shop; **être dur en affaires** *(homme)* to be a hard-headed businessman; *(femme)* to be a hard-headed businesswoman; **ils font des affaires en or** they're coining it, they're making money hand over fist, they're raking it in; **faire des affaires avec qn** to do business with sb; **il est sur une a. avec le Mozambique** he's doing a deal with Mozambique; **chiffre d'affaires** turnover; **homme d'affaires** businessman; *(d'un sportif etc)* business manager; **femme d'affaires** businesswoman; **voyage d'affaires** business trip; **déjeuner d'affaires** business *or* working lunch; **droit des affaires** corporate law; **avocat d'affaires** corporate lawyer

(e) les affaires business; **comment vont les affaires?** how's business?; **parler affaires** to talk business *or F* shop; **les affaires sont les affaires (et on ne fait de cadeaux à personne)** business is business (and nobody gets any favours *or* anything for nothing)

(f) *(entreprise)* firm, business; **une grosse a.** a large firm

(g) affaires *(effets personnels)* things, possessions, belongings; **tu peux mettre tes affaires dans le vestibule** you can put your things in the hall; **ranger ses affaires** to put one's things away, to tidy up one's things; **mettre de l'ordre dans ses affaires** to tidy up; **mets tes petites affaires dans ce sac** put your small things in this bag; *Hum* **il est en train de préparer ses petites affaires** he's sorting out his bits and pieces

(h) *Pol* **les affaires de l'État** affairs of State; **ce n'est pas une a. d'État** it's of no great importance; **on ne va pas en faire une a. d'État** we're not going to make a big issue of it; **le ministère des Affaires étrangères** ≈ *Br* the Foreign (and Commonwealth) Office, *US* the State Department; **ministre des Affaires étrangères** *Br* Foreign (and Commonwealth) Secretary, *US* Secretary of State; *Can* **Ministère des Affaires Extérieures** External Affairs Department
affairé [afere] *adj* busy; **ils entraient et sortaient d'un air a.** they were bustling in and out; **être a. à faire qch** to be busy doing sth
affairement [afɛrmɑ̃] *nm* bustle, bustling activity
affairer (s') [safere] *vpr* to be busy, to busy oneself; **s'a. autour de qn** to fuss (a)round sb; **s'a. à tout remettre en place** to be busy tidying up
affairisme [aferism] *nm Péj* wheeling and dealing
affairiste [aferist] *n Péj* wheeler-dealer; **ce n'est qu'un a.** he thinks of nothing but making money *or* getting rich *or Am* making a fast buck
affaissement [afɛsmɑ̃] *nm* **(a)** *(de terrain)* subsidence, sinking; *(d'une fondation)* settling; *(du plancher, d'une poutre)* sagging; **il y a eu un a. de terrain** there was (land) subsidence **(b)** *(accablement)* depression, dejection, despondency; *Méd* prostration, collapse; **l'a. de l'enthousiasme** the waning of enthusiasm; **l'a. du moral** the collapse of morale
affaisser (s') [safɛse] *vpr* **(a)** *(du terrain)* to subside; *(d'une poutre, d'un fauteuil etc)* to sag **(b)** *(tomber, s'écrouler)* *(dans une chaise)* to sink down *or* back; *(de fatigue etc)* to collapse **(c)** *Fig Litt (décliner)* to decline, to sink; **il s'affaisse de jour en jour** he is declining *or* sinking day by day
affaler [afale] **1** *vt (objet)* to lower; *Naut* **a. la voile** to lower the sail; **affale!** lower away! **2 s'affaler** *vpr* to collapse; **s'a. par terre** to sink to the ground; **s'a. dans un fauteuil** to sink *or F* flop into an armchair
affamé, -ée [afame] **1** *adj* hungry, *F* starving, ravenous, famished; *(mourant de faim)* starving; **regarder qch d'un œil a.** to look hungrily at sth; *Fig* **être a. de succès/d'argent** to be hungry for success/money **2** *n* **les affamés** the hungry, the starving
affamer [afame] *vt* to starve
affectation [afɛktasjɔ̃] *nf* **(a)** *Péj (pose)* affectation, affectedness;

(*simulacre*) pretence, affectation; **parler avec a.** to speak affectedly; **être sans a.** to be without affectation, to be unaffected; **sans a.** (*dire etc qch*) without affectation, unaffectedly; **avec une a. de générosité** with a show of generosity

(b) (*fait de désigner*) assignment, allocation, allotment; **l'a. de subventions à une association** the allocation of subsidies to an association; **a. des places** seating plan

(c) *Mil etc* assignment, posting; **avoir une** *ou* **être en a. spéciale** ≈ to be in a reserved occupation

(d) *Ordinat* (*de touche*) assignment; **a. de mémoire** memory allocation

▸ **affectation**: **a. de fonds** appropriation of funds; **a. hypothécaire** mortgage charge

affecté [afɛkte] *adj Péj* (*personne, manière*) affected

affecter [afɛkte] **1** *vt* **(a)** (*destiner*) to assign (**à** to), to allocate, to earmark; **a. des fonds à** to allocate funds to

(b) (*désigner*) (*employé*) to assign, to appoint; *Mil* (*soldat, détachement*) to detail, to post, to draft; *Naut* **être affecté à un navire** to be posted to a ship

(c) (*feindre*) to feign, to affect; **a. de faire qch** to pretend to do sth; **a. la désinvolture la plus complète** to feign *or* affect an extremely offhand attitude

(d) (*toucher*) (*qn*) to affect, to move; **vivement affecté par la nouvelle** greatly moved by the news

(e) (*agir sur*) (*carrière, santé etc*) to affect, to have an effect on; **la grève a affecté plusieurs usines** the strike has affected *or* hit several factories; **les pluies qui affectent le nord de l'Europe** the rain affecting *or* over northern Europe

(f) (*prendre*) (*forme, couleur etc*) to assume, to take on

2 s'affecter *vpr* to be troubled *or* unsettled; **elle s'affecte de la moindre dispute** she is upset by the slightest argument

affectif, -ive [afɛktif, -iv] *adj*, emotional, *Spéc* affective; **sa vie affective** his emotional life

affection [afɛksjɔ̃] *nf* **(a)** (*attachement*) affection, fondness, liking (**pour** for); **une preuve d'a.** a show of affection; **en manque d'a.** in need of affection; **prendre qn en a.** to become attached to *or* fond of sb; **terme d'a.** term of affection; **avoir de l'a. pour qn** to feel *or* have affection for sb, to be fond of sb; **avec a.** affectionately **(b)** *Méd* disease, complaint, ailment; **a. cutanée** skin disorder *or* complaint

affectionné [afɛksjɔne] *adj* affectionate, loving; **votre cousin(e) affectionné(e)** (*dans une lettre*) your affectionate cousin

affectionner [afɛksjɔne] *vt* (*ami, connaissance etc*) to be attached to, to be fond of; (*chiens etc*) to like; **affectionné de tous** loved by all; **le genre de petits plats qu'il affectionne** the type of food he likes *or* is fond of

affectivité [afɛktivite] *nf* affectivity

affectueusement [afɛktɥøzmɑ̃] *adv* affectionately; **a. à tous** (*dans une lettre*) love to all

affectueux, -euse [afɛktɥø, -øz] *adj* affectionate, loving

afférent [aferɑ̃] *adj* **(a)** *Jur* **la part afférente à** the portion accruing to **(b) a. à** (*concernant*) relating to, relevant to, pertaining to **(c)** *Méd* afferent

affermer [afɛrme] *vt* (*ferme etc*) to lease, to rent; (*terre etc*) to take on lease

affermir [afɛrmir] **1** *vt* **(a)** (*fondations etc*) to strengthen, to make firm; **crème pouvant a. les chairs** toning *or* firming cream **(b)** (*pouvoir, croyance*) to strengthen, to consolidate; (*santé*) to improve; **a. sa voix** to strengthen one's voice; **a. qn dans sa position** to strengthen *or* consolidate sb in his/her position **2 s'affermir** *vpr* to become stronger, to strengthen; (*du ciment*) to harden; (*des chairs, des muscles*) to firm up

affermissement [afɛrmismɑ̃] *nm* strengthening; (*du pouvoir etc*) consolidation; (*d'un ciment*) hardening; (*des chairs, des muscles*) firming up

affichage [afiʃaʒ] *nm* **(a)** (*pose d'affiches*) billsticking, billposting; **a. interdit** stick *or Am* post no bills; **tableau** *ou* **panneau d'a.** notice board, *Am* bulletin board; (*dans aéroport, gare*) arrivals and departures (board) **(b)** *Ordinat* display; **horloge/montre à a. digital** *ou* **numérique** digital clock/watch **(c)** *Av* visual indicator

▸ **affichage**: **a. à cristaux liquides** liquid crystal display; **a. digital** digital display *or* readout; **a. dynamique** (*publicité*) mobile advertising; *Ordinat* **a. graphique** graphics display; *Ordinat* **a. inversé** reverse video; **a. mobile** (*publicité*) mobile advertising; *Ordinat* **a. non entrelacé** non-interlaced display; *Ordinat* **a. numérique** digital display; *Ordinat* **a. à plasma** plasma display; **a. des prix** price display; **a. routier** (*publicité*) roadside advertising; **a. rural** (*publicité*) rural advertising; *Ordinat* **a. tel écran-tel écrit** WYSIWYG; **a. transport** (*publicité*) public transport advertising, transportation advertising; **a. urbain** (*publicité*) urban (poster) advertising; *Ordinat* **a. vectoriel** vector graphics

affiche [afiʃ] *nf* poster, bill; (*de protestation*) placard; (*de publicité*) advertisement; **colleur d'affiches** billsticker, bill poster; **a. à la main** handbill; **a. électorale** election poster; **affiches publicitaires** advertisements; **a. de théâtre** playbill; **être à l'a.** (*de spectacle*) to be on, to be showing; **les pièces à l'a.** the plays now on *or* now showing; **la pièce a tenu l'a.** *ou* **est restée à l'a. pendant deux ans** the play ran for two years; **tenir longtemps l'a.** to have a long run; **qui tient l'a.** long-running; **mettre à l'a.** to put on, to stage; **quitter l'a.** to close; **être en tête d'a.** to be top of the bill, to have top billing

afficher [afiʃe] **1** *vt* **(a)** (*annonce, affiche*) to stick (up), to post (up); (*prix*) to display; **a. une vente** to advertise a sale; **défense d'a.** stick *or Am* post no bills; **a. complet** (*d'un spectacle*) to be sold out

(b) (*montrer, étaler*) to parade, to show off, to flaunt, to make a display of; (*mépris, indifférence*) to put on; **a. son savoir** to air *or* flaunt one's knowledge; **a. son ignorance** to display *or* expose *or* betray one's ignorance; **a. sa pauvreté** to plead poverty; **derrière cette nonchalance affichée** behind this outwardly casual air; **a. son nouvel amant** to flaunt *or* parade one's latest lover; *Com* **a. un déficit/un excédent** to show a deficit/a surplus

(c) *Ordinat* (*message*) to display; **l'écran affiche ...** the on-screen message appears ..., the screen displays the message ...

2 s'afficher *vpr* **(a)** (*d'une personne*) **elle s'affiche avec un homme plus âgé qu'elle** she's flaunting herself with an older man **(b)** (*sur un écran*) to be displayed

affichette [afiʃɛt] *nf* small poster *or* advertisement

afficheur [afiʃœr] *nm* **(a)** billsticker, billposter **(b)** *Ordinat* VDU, visual display unit; **a. LCD** LCD display; **a. à cristaux liquides** liquid crystal display

affichiste [afiʃist] *n* poster designer

affidavit [afidavit] *nm Jur* affidavit

affidé, -ée [afide] *n Péj* accomplice

affilage [afilaʒ] *nm* sharpening, whetting

affilée (d') [dafile] *adv* **cinq heures d'a.** five hours at a stretch *or* at a time *or* on end; **lire vingt chapitres d'a.** to read twenty chapters in one go *or* straight off *or* at one sitting

affiler [afile] *vt* (*lame etc*) to sharpen, to whet, to put an edge on; *Fig* **avoir la langue bien affilée** (*être méchant*) to have a sharp *or* wicked tongue

affiliation [afiljasjɔ̃] *nf* affiliation; **demander son a. à un club** to apply for membership to a club; **l'a. d'un membre à un club** a member's affiliation to a club

affilié, -ée [afilje] **1** *adj* affiliated **2** *n* affiliated member

affilier [afilje] **1** *vt* to affiliate (**à** to, with) **2 s'affilier** *vpr* to join; (*d'une organisation*) to become affiliated; **s'a. à un parti** to join a party

affin [afɛ̃] *adj Ling* related, cognate; *Math* affine

affinage [afinaʒ] *nm Métal* refining; (*de l'acier, du fer*) smelting; (*du vin, du fromage*) maturing

affinement [afinmɑ̃] *nm* refinement

affiner [afine] **1** *vt* **(a)** (*purifier*) to improve, to refine, to make better; (*fer, or*) to refine; (*fromage etc*) to ripen, to mature **(b)** (*intelligence*) to sharpen; (*goût, plaisir etc*) to refine; **ces livres ont affiné son jugement** these books have sharpened his judgment **2 s'affiner** *vpr* **(a)** (*d'une personne*) to become more refined; (*des traits*) to become finer; (*de l'intelligence*) to become sharper; **elle s'est affinée en suivant un nouveau régime** she has lost weight *or* slimmed down on her new diet **(b)** (*du fromage etc*) to ripen, to mature

affinité [afinite] *nf* **(a)** (*entre personnes*) affinity (**entre** between); (*physique*) resemblance; (*de caractère*) similarity of character; **nous avons une grande a. de goûts** we have many tastes in common **(b)** *Ch* attraction; **a. pour un corps** affinity for a body

affirmatif, -ive [afirmatif, -iv] **1** *adj* **(a)** affirmative, positive; **réponse affirmative** affirmative answer, answer in the affirmative; **signe a.** nod (of agreement); **faire un signe a. de la tête** to nod in agreement **(b)** (*personne*) assertive, positive; **il a été très a.** he was very definite **2** *nf* **l'affirmative** the affirmative; **dans l'affirmative** if so, if the answer is yes, if you can; **répondre par l'affirmative** to answer in the affirmative, to say *or* answer yes **3** *adv* **affirmatif** affirmative

affirmation [afirmasjɔ̃] *nf* affirmation, assurance, assertion, statement; **a. trop générale** sweeping statement; **a. de soi** self-assertion; **a. de la personnalité** assertion of one's personality

▸ **affirmation**: *Jur* **a. de créance** proof of debt; **a. sous serment** affidavit; (*lors d'un procès etc*) statement on oath

affirmativement [afirmativmɑ̃] *adv* in the affirmative

affirmer [afirme] **1** *vt* **(a)** (*soutenir*) to maintain; **il affirme vous connaître** he maintains that he knows you; **je ne peux**

rien a. I can't say anything for certain; **je n'affirmerais pas que …** I wouldn't swear to it that …; **a. qch sous serment** to state sth on oath *or* on affidavit

(**b**) (*manifester, prouver*) to assert; **a. son autorité** to assert one's authority, to make one's authority felt; **a. son amitié** to declare one's friendship

2 s'affirmer *vpr* (**a**) (*s'exprimer pleinement*) (*d'une personne*) to assert oneself (**b**) (*se révéler*) **son talent s'affirme peu à peu** his talent is gradually expressing itself *or* becoming apparent; **beaucoup de vos observations se sont affirmées justes** many of your observations have proved correct *or* have been confirmed; **cet ordinateur s'est affirmé le plus performant de tous** this computer has established itself as the best performer

affleurement [aflœrmɑ̃] *nm Géol* outcrop

affleurer [aflœre] **1** *vt* (*bois de charpente etc*) to bring to the same level, to make flush; **a. à qch** to be level *or* even *or* flush with sth **2** *vi aussi Fig* to float *or* rise to the surface; *Géol* (*d'un filon*) to outcrop; *Fig* **l'espace d'une seconde il laissa a. ses sentiments** for a second he let his feelings show through

affliction [afliksjɔ̃] *nf* affliction, sorrow; **plongé dans l'a.** deeply distressed

affligeant [afliʒɑ̃] *adj* (*nouvelle, vision*) distressing, painful; **manque d'imagination a.** pitiful *or* appalling lack of imagination

affligé, -ée [afliʒe] **1** *adj* (**a**) (*atteint*) afflicted, troubled (**de** with) (**b**) (*peiné*) grieved, distressed **2** *n* **les affligés** the afflicted

affliger [afliʒe] (**j'affligeai(s); n. affligeons**) **1** *vt* (**a**) (*atteindre*) to afflict (**de** with); **région que le choléra afflige** area afflicted with cholera; **la nature l'a affligé d'un grand nez** nature has cursed him with a big nose (**b**) (*peiner*) to pain, to distress, to grieve; **la nouvelle l'a profondément affligé** the news deeply distressed him *or* caused him great distress **2 s'affliger** *vpr* to be grieved *or* distressed (**de qch** about sth); **ne vous affligez pas ainsi** don't take it so much to heart

affluence [aflyɑ̃s] *nf* (*de personnes*) crowd; (*de marchandises*) abundance; **heures d'a.** (*transports*) rush hours; (*dans les magasins etc*) peak hours

affluent [aflyɑ̃] *nm* (*d'une rivière*) tributary

affluer [aflye] *vi* (*d'un liquide*) to flow (**vers** towards; **dans** into); (*du sang*) to rush, to flow (**à** to); **a. à** *ou* **dans un endroit** to crowd *or* flock to a place

afflux [afly] *nm Méd etc* (*de sang*) rush; *Él* (*de courant*) surge; (*de visiteurs*) crowd; *Compta* **a. de capitaux** inflow *or* influx of capital

affolant [afɔlɑ̃] *adj* (*spectacle, nouvelle*) distressing, horrifying; *F* **c'est a.** (*ce qu'elle a grandi etc*) it's frightening *or* incredible

affolé [afɔle] *adj* (**a**) demented, frantic, panic-stricken; **il était a.** he was scared out of his wits (**b**) *Tech* (*aiguille du compas*) spinning, crazy

affolement [afɔlmɑ̃] *nm* (**a**) (*de personne*) panic, *F* flap; **voyons, pas d'a.** come on, there's no need to panic; **dans un moment d'a.** in a moment of panic, in a panic-stricken moment (**b**) (*d'une aiguille magnétique*) perturbation, unsteadiness, spinning (**c**) (*d'un moteur, d'une hélice etc*) racing; (*d'une poulie etc*) disconnecting

affoler [afɔle] **1** *vt* (**a**) (*qn*) to madden, to drive crazy *or* to distraction; (*foule*) to throw into a panic (**b**) (*aiguille de compas*) to disturb, to perturb **2 s'affoler** *vpr* (**a**) (*paniquer*) to panic, to get in(to) a panic, *F* to lose one's head; **s'a. pour un rien** to get into a flap about nothing (**b**) (*d'une aiguille de compas*) to spin (**c**) (*d'une machine*) to begin to race

affouiller [afuje] *vt* (*de l'eau*) (*rive, fondation etc*) to undermine, to erode, to wash away, to lay bare

affranchi, -ie [afrɑ̃ʃi] **1** *adj* (**a**) (*esclave*) free(d), emancipated; *Fig* **un esprit a.** an open mind; **un esprit a. des préjugés** a mind free from prejudice (**b**) (*lettre*) stamped, with a stamp on; **lettre bien/mal affranchie** letter with/without enough stamps on it **2** *n* (**a**) (*esclave*) emancipated slave (**b**) (*marginal*) free spirit

affranchir [afrɑ̃ʃir] **1** *vt* (**a**) (*esclave etc*) to free, to set free, to emancipate; **a. qn/qch de qch** to free *or* release sb/sth from sth; **par son attitude très cordiale il nous a affranchis de toute gêne** his friendly attitude ensured that we didn't feel in the least awkward

(**b**) (*envoi*) to pay the postage on; (*tamponner*) (*lettre*) to frank, to stamp; **colis affranchi** pre-paid parcel; **machine à a.** (**les lettres**) franking machine, franker

(**c**) *Cartes* (*couleur*) to unblock

(**d**) *F* (*renseigner*) **a. qn** to put sb in the picture

2 s'affranchir *vpr* **s'a. du joug** to cast off the yoke; **s'a. d'une habitude** to break (oneself of) a habit; **s'a. d'idées préconçues** to rid oneself of preconceived ideas

affranchissement [afrɑ̃ʃismɑ̃] *nm* (**a**) (*d'un esclave etc*) emancipation, setting free (**b**) (*de lettre*) prepayment; (*fait de tamponner*) stamping, franking; (*montant payé*) (*de lettre, de paquet etc*) postage, carriage; **tarif d'a.** postage rate

affranchisseuse [afrɑ̃ʃisøz] *nf* franking machine, franker

affres [afr] *nfpl Litt* (*angoisse*) (spasm of) anguish; (*du doute etc*) agonies, horrors; **a. de la mort** death throes; **a. de la faim** pangs of hunger, hunger pangs; **découvrir toutes les a. de l'humiliation** to discover the agonies of humiliation

affrètement [afrɛtmɑ̃] *nm* charter, *Fml* affreightment; **a. au voyage** trip charter; **a. à temps** time charter

affréter [afrete] *vt* (**j'affrète, n. affrétons; j'affréterai**) (*navire, avion*) to charter

affréteur [afretœr] *nm Naut* charterer; *Aut* **a. routier** road haulier

affreusement [afrøzmɑ̃] *adv* (*en retard*) terribly, frightfully; (*blessé, torturé*) horribly; (*défiguré*) horribly, shockingly; **je suis a. coiffée** my hair's a mess; **il parle a. mal l'anglais** his English is awful

affreux, -euse [afrø, -øz] **1** *adj* (**a**) (*laid*) horrible, hideous, dreadful, ghastly; **un visage a.** a horrible *or* hideous face; **il est a.** he's terribly *or* horribly ugly; **un a. petit chapeau/chien** a horrible *or* an ugly little hat/dog

(**b**) (*atroce*) (*nouvelles, pauvreté, crime etc*) awful, horrible, dreadful, shocking

(**c**) *F* (*détestable*) awful, dreadful; **mal de tête a.** splitting headache; **qu'est-ce que ça a augmenté, c'est a.!** it's dreadful *or* shocking how the price has gone up; **c'est a. ce qu'il y a comme monde!** it's dreadfully *or* awfully busy; **ce gamin est un a. jojo** that child is a (frightful) little horror; **temps a.** filthy *or* shocking weather

2 *n* (**a**) *Mil F* white mercenary (*usu in Africa*)

(**b**) *F* (*vilain personnage*) **c'est un a.** he's a nasty piece of work

affriander [afrijɑ̃de] *vt Litt* to entice, to allure

affriolant [afrijɔlɑ̃] *adj* (*décolleté, vêtement*) alluring, tantalising; **ce travail n'a rien d'a.** it's not the world's most exciting job

affrioler [afrijɔle] *vt* to excite, to tempt

affriquée [afrike] *nf Ling* affricate (consonant)

affront [afrɔ̃] *nm* affront, insult, *F* slap in the face; **subir un a.** to be affronted *or* insulted; **faire** *ou* **infliger un a. à qn** to affront *or* insult sb; (*snober qn*) to snub sb; **doubler ses torts d'un a.** to add insult to injury

affrontement [afrɔ̃tmɑ̃] *nm* (**a**) (*de l'ennemi, du danger etc*) confrontation, confronting, clash; **l'a. de deux personnalités différentes** the clash *or* conflict of two different personalities (**b**) (*de deux choses*) joining edge to edge; *Chir* bringing into apposition

affronter [afrɔ̃te] **1** *vt* (**a**) (*qn, qch*) to face, to confront, to brave, to tackle; **a. une épreuve avec courage** to face *or* meet an ordeal bravely; **a. la colère de qn** to brave the wrath of sb (**b**) (*mettre de front*) to join face to face *or* edge to edge; (*plaques de métal etc*) to bring together; *Chir* to bring into apposition (**c**) *Sp* to meet, to clash with **2 s'affronter** *vpr* (*d'ennemis etc*) to clash, to confront each other; *Sp* (*de deux équipes, joueurs etc*) to meet, to clash; **leurs personnalités s'affrontent constamment** their personalities clash constantly; **deux thèses s'affrontent** there are two conflicting theories

affubler [afyble] *Péj* **1** *vt* **a. qn de qch** to dress sb up in sth, to deck *or* rig sb out in sth; **elle m'affublait toujours des pires guenilles** she always made me wear the most awful old rags **2 s'affubler** *vpr* to rig *or* deck oneself out, to get oneself up (**de** in); **il s'affuble souvent des vêtements les plus ridicules** he often gets himself all rigged out in the most ridiculous clothes

affût [afy] *nm* (**a**) (*guêt*) hiding place; (*pour observatoire d'oiseaux etc*) hide; **chasse au cerf à l'a.** deer stalking; **être** *ou* **se mettre à l'a. de** (*qn*) to lie in wait for; (*être vigilant*) (*vis-à-vis de qn, qch*) to be on the watch *or* lookout for; *Fig* **être à l'a. de qch** to be on the lookout for sth (**b**) *Mil* carriage; (*d'un télescope etc*) mounting

affûtage [afytaʒ] *nm* (**a**) (*d'outils*) sharpening, grinding; (*d'une scie*) setting (**b**) set of bench tools

affûter [afyte] *vt* (*outil*) to grind, to sharpen, to whet; (*scie*) to set; *Fig* (*esprit*) to sharpen; *Courses de chevaux* **a. un cheval** to bring a horse to the top of its form

affûteur [afytœr] *nm* (tool)grinder, sharpener; (*de scies*) setter

affûteuse [afytøz] *nf* grinding machine

afghan, -ane [afgɑ̃, -an] **1** *adj* Afghan **2** *n* **A.** Afghan **3** *nm Ling* Afghan

Afghanistan [afganistɑ̃] *nm* Afghanistan

aficionado, -os [afisjɔnado, -os] *nm* aficionado; **les aficionados du vélo** cycling enthusiasts

afin [afɛ̃] *adv* **(a) a. de faire qch** (in order) to, so as to do sth **(b)** [①A68,2; B55,B] **a. que +** *sub* so that, in order that, *Fml, Litt* that; **a. que les autres puissent le voir** so that the others may see it

AFNOR [afnɔr] *nf* (*abrév* **Association française de normalisation)** French industrial standards authority, *Br* ≈ BSI, *US* ≈ ANSI

a fortiori [afɔrsjɔri] *adv* a fortiori, all the more so; *Phil* a fortiuri

A.F.P. [aɛfpe] *abrév* **Agence France Presse**

A.F.P.A. [aɛfpea] *abrév* **Association pour la formation professionnelle des adultes**

africain, -aine [afrikɛ̃, -ɛn] **1** *adj* African **2** *n* **A.** African

africanisation [afrikanizasjɔ̃] *nf Pol* Africanization

africaniser [afrikanize] **1** *vt* to Africanize **2** *vpr* **s'africaniser** to become Africanized

africaniste [afrikanist] *n* student of African races and languages

afrika(a)ns [afrikɑ̃s] *nm Ling* Afrikaans

Afrikander [afrikɑ̃dɛr] *n* Afrikaner

Afrique [afrik] *nf* Africa; **l'A. du Nord** North Africa; **l'A. du Sud** South Africa

afro [afro] *adj* (*coupe de cheveux*) Afro; **avoir une coiffure a.** to have an Afro; **à l'a.** Afro (style); **les cheveux à l'a.** Afro hair

afro-américain, -aine 1 *adj* Afro-American, Black American **2** *n* **A.** Afro-American, Black American

afro-asiatique 1 *adj* Afro-Asian **2** *n* **A.** Afro-Asian

afro-cubain, -aine 1 *adj* Afro-Cuban **2** *n* **A.** Afro-Cuban

after-shave [aftœrʃɛv] **1** *nm* after-shave **2** *adj* **lotion a.** after-shave (lotion)

A.G. [aʒe] *abrév* **assemblée générale**

agaçant [agasɑ̃] *adj* annoying, irritating, aggravating

agacement [agasmɑ̃] *nm* irritation, annoyance; **dire/témoigner son a.** to express/show one's annoyance *or* irritation

agacer [agase] *vt* **(j'agaçai(s); n. agaçons) (a)** (*dents, nerfs*) to set on edge; (*nerfs, oreilles*) to grate on **(b)** (*énerver*) **a. qn** to annoy sb, to irritate sb, to aggravate sb, to get on sb's nerves; **ça m'agace de t'entendre dire encore la même chose** it annoys me *or* gets on my nerves to hear you saying the same thing again; **a. un chien** to tease a dog; **il m'agace avec ses questions** he's getting on my nerves, asking all those questions; **elle m'agace, avec sa façon de faire l'enfant tout le temps** she gets on my nerves, the way she acts so childishly all the time

agaceries [agasri] *nfpl* charms, wiles; **faire des a.** to use one's charm(s) *or* wiles

agape [agap] *nf Hum* **agapes** feast, spread; **nous allons faire des agapes chez Jeannot** we're going to have a real feast *or F* slap-up meal at Jeannot's

agar-agar [agaragar] *nm* agar-agar

agaric [agarik] *nm* (*champignon*) agaric

agate [agat] *nf* **(a)** *Minér* agate; **a. noire** *ou* **d'Islande** obsidian; **a. onyx** sardonyx **(b)** (*bille*) glass marble

agave, agavé [agav, agave] *nm* (*plante*) agave; **a. d'Amérique** American aloe, sisal hemp

âge [ɑʒ] *nm* **(a)** (*d'une personne*) age; **quel â. avez-vous?** how old are you?; **quand j'avais votre â.** when I was your age; **à ton â., je travaillais** when I was your age, I was working; **à ton â., on ne pleure plus** you're old enough now not to cry, at your age, you shouldn't be crying; **nous avons le même a., nous sommes du même â.** we are the same age; **à l'â. de six ans** at the age of six; **quel â. lui donnez-vous?** how old do you think he is *or* would you say he was?; **on ne lui donne pas du tout son â.** he doesn't look his age at all; **je ne sais pas quel â. lui donner** I don't know how old he can be; **accuser** *ou* **faire son â.** to look one's age; **dès son â. le plus tendre** *ou* **dès son plus jeune â.** from his earliest years; **un homme d'un certain â.** a middle-aged man; **en dépit de son grand â.** in spite of his great age; **mourir à un grand â.** *ou* **à un â. avancé** *ou* **à un bel â.** to die at a ripe old age; **un homme d'un grand â.** a very old man; **faire plus jeune que son â.** to look younger than one really is, not to look one's age; **il n'a pas d'â., on ne peut pas dire quel â. il a** it is difficult to tell how old he is; **être d'â. légal** to be of age; **être en â. de faire qch, être d'â. à faire qch** to be old enough to do sth; **j'ai passé l'â. de ce genre de choses** I've grown out of that kind of thing; **fréquenter des gens de son â.** to see people of one's own age; **ce n'est plus de mon â.** I'm too old for that type of thing; **être en â. de se marier** to be old enough *or* of an age to marry; **un whisky de 15 ans d'â.** a 15-year-old whisky; **hors d'â.** (*cheval*) aged; **le bas â.** infancy; **enfant en bas â.** infant; **le premier â.** childhood; (*tout premier*) infancy; **couches premier/deuxième â.** nappies for children up to 12 months old/between 12 and 18 months old; **le bel â.** youth; **l'â. ingrat** the awkward *or* difficult age; **sans â.** ageless; **avoir l'â. de raison** to have reached the age of reason; **l'â. d'homme** manhood; **l'â. adulte** adulthood; **être d'â. mûr** *ou* **entre deux âges** *ou* **d'un certain â.** to be middle-aged; **elle est bien pour son â.** she's marvellous for her age; **les maux qui viennent avec l'â.** the aches and pains that come with old age; **un homme d'â.** an old man; **le troisième â.** retirement age; (*personnes*) the over sixties; **les gens du troisième â.** the elderly, senior citizens, *Am* golden agers; **à l'â. que j'ai, à mon â.** at my age, at my time of life; **mourir avant l'â.** to die before one's time, to die young; **â. mental** mental age; **avoir un â. mental de six ans** to have a mental age of six; *Fig* **être dans** *ou* **à la fleur de l'â.** to be in the bloom *or* flower of youth; *Fig* **être dans la force de l'â.** to be in one's prime *or* the prime of life; *Fig* **le retour d'â.** the change of life

(b) generation; **d'â. en â.** from generation to generation

(c) *Hist* age, period, epoch; *Archéol* **l'â. de (la) pierre** the Stone Age; **l'â. de la pierre taillée** the palaeolithic age; **l'â. de la pierre polie** the neolithic age; **l'â. de** *ou* **du bronze** the Bronze Age; **l'â. de** *ou* **du fer** the Iron Age; *Hist* **le moyen â.** the Middle Ages; **costumes du moyen â.** medi(a)eval costumes; *Myth* **l'â. d'or** the golden age; **l'â. d'or du cinéma muet** the golden age of silent movies; **c'est une tradition qui est venue du fond des âges** it's a tradition which has come down through the ages

âgé [ɑʒe] *adj* **(a)** (*qui a tel âge*) old, aged; **â. de dix ans** ten years old, ten years of age, aged ten; **je suis plus/moins â. que vous** I am older/younger than you **(b)** (*vieux*) old, *Litt* aged ['eidʒid]; **assez â.** elderly; **les personnes âgées** old *or* elderly people, senior citizens

agence [aʒɑ̃s] *nf* **(a)** agency, bureau; **a. de publicité/de traduction** advertising/translation agency; **a. de renseignement(s)** information bureau; **a. de placement** employment agency *or* bureau; **a. de presse** press *or* news agency; **a. commerciale** (*d'agence de voyages etc*) public sales office; **a. conseil en communication** public relations *or* PR consultancy; *Com* **a. de distribution physique** physical distribution agency; **A. nationale pour l'emploi** ≈ Job Centre, *Can* ≈ CEC; **a. de promotion des ventes** sales promotion agency; **a. de réceptif** ground handling agency, ground operator; **a. de réservation** booking agency; **a. de voyages de discompte** discount travel agency, bucket shop; **a. distributrice** (*d'agence de voyages*) retail travel agency; **a. photographique** photographic agency; **a. réceptive** ground handling agency; **a. de presse de télévision** television news agency; **a. de tourisme** *ou* **de voyages** travel agency *or* agent's; **a. immobilière** estate agent's *or* agency

(b) (*de banque*) branch office

agencement [aʒɑ̃smɑ̃] *nm* **(a)** arrangement; (*des pièces d'une machine etc*) fitting (together); (*d'une maison, d'une radio, d'un embrayage etc*) layout; **a. de l'intrigue** (*d'un roman etc*) construction of the plot; **l'a. d'un spectacle** the way a show is put together **(b) agencements** fixtures, fittings

agencer [aʒɑ̃se] **1** *vt* **(j'agençai(s); n. agençons)** (*maison etc*) to lay out, to design; (*pièces de machine etc*) to fit (together), to adjust; **local bien agencé** well designed premises; **phrases mal agencées** badly constructed sentences **2 s'agencer** *vpr* to be laid out; **les parties du discours s'agencent bien/mal** the different parts of the speech go/don't hang well together

agencier [aʒɑ̃sje] *nm Journ* news agency journalist

agenda [aʒɛ̃da] *nm* (*pour noter des rendez-vous, journal*) diary; *Ordinat* organizer, planner; **a. de poche/de bureau** pocket/desk diary; **a. organisateur** personal organizer, Filofax®; **a. de réservation** book *or* hotel register, reservations book; **a. électronique** personal organizer

agenouiller (s') [saʒnuje] *vpr* to kneel (down); **s'a. devant un autel** to kneel at *or* before an altar

agenouilloir [aʒnujwar] *nm* prie-Dieu; (*coussin*) hassock; (*planche*) kneeling bench

agent [aʒɑ̃] *nm* **(a)** (*facteur*) agent, agency, medium; **a. économique/atmosphérique** economic/atmospheric factor; **a. chimique** chemical agent; **a. monétaire** circulating medium

(b) *Gram* agent; **complément d'a.** agent

(c) (*personne*) agent; **un a. de la CIA** a CIA agent; **a. (de police)** police officer *or* constable; **a. de la circulation** traffic policeman; **pardon, monsieur l'a.** excuse me, officer

▶ **agent**: **a. d'affaires** business agent; **a. agréé** registered agent; **a. d'assurance(s), a. de change** *Fin* stockbroker, exchange broker; *Com* mercantile broker; *Com* **a. autorisé** authorized representative; **a. commercial** sales agent, sales representative, sales rep; **a. commissionnaire** commission agent; *Com* **a. de contact** contact; *Com* **a. direct** commission agent; **a. de distribution à l'export** export distribution agent; **a. en douanes** customs broker; **a. double** double agent; **a. exclusif** sole agent; **a. exportateur** export agent; *Com* **a. de fret** freight forwarder, forwarding agent; *Com* **a. général** agent; **a. immobilier/de publicité** estate/advertising agent; **a. importateur** importer; *Com* **a. indépendant** free agent; *Com* **a. intermédiaire** agent middleman; *Com* **a. de liaison** contact; *Mil* liaison officer; *Com* **a. de ligne** forwarding agent; **a. littéraire** literary agent; **a. de maîtrise** foreman; *Com* **a. mandataire** authorized representative; **a. maritime** shipping agent; **a. de réceptif** ground handling agent; **a. de recouvrements** debt collector; **a. de réservation** reservation agent; **a. secret** secret agent; **a. de sécurité** security officer; *Com* **a. technico-commercial** sales technician; **a. de transmission** runner, dispatch rider, messenger; **a. de voyages** travel agent

AGETAC [aʒetak] (*abrév* **Accord général sur les tarifs et le commerce**) *nm* GATT

aggiornamento [a(d)ʒjɔrnamɛnto] *nm* adaptation to new circumstances; **le parti doit faire son a.** the party has to move with the times

agglomérant [aglɔmerɑ̃] **1** *adj* (*matériau*) binding **2** *nm* binding material, binder

agglomérat [aglɔmera] *nm* agglomerate

agglomération [aglɔmerasjɔ̃] *nf* **(a)** (*de ville*) agglomeration, built-up area; **vitesse limitée dans les agglomérations** speed restriction in built-up areas; **les grandes agglomérations** the great urban centres; **l'a. lyonnaise/parisienne** Lyons/Paris and its suburbs; **l'a. londonienne** Greater London **(b)** (*de fuel etc*) caking

aggloméré [aglɔmere] **1** *adj* conglomerate; **panneau de fibres agglomérées** fibreboard **2** *nm* **(a)** *Géol, Constr* conglomerate **(b)** (*briquette*) compressed fuel, briquette **(c)** (*de bois*) fibreboard; **a. de liège** agglomerated cork

agglomérer [aglɔmere] **(j'agglomère, n. agglomérons; j'agglomérerai) 1** *vt* to agglomerate; **toute la population est agglomérée dans ...** the entire population is packed together in ... **2 s'agglomérer** *vpr* to agglomerate; (*d'un mélange, de substances différentes*) to cohere, to bind; (*de fuel etc*) to cake; **les populations pauvres s'agglomèrent dans les favelas** the poor population is packed together in the shanty towns

agglutinant [aglytinɑ̃] **1** *adj* **(a)** (*adhésif*) agglutinant, adhesive **(b)** *Ling* (*langues*) agglutinative **2** *nm* (*de conglomérats*) bond

agglutination [aglytinasjɔ̃] *nf* **(a)** (*action*) agglutination, caking; (*d'un mélange, de substances différentes*) binding **(b)** (*de microbes*) clump **(c)** *Ling* **phénomène d'a.** agglutination

agglutiner [aglytine] **1** *vt* to agglutinate; (*mélange etc*) to bind **2 s'agglutiner** *vpr* **(a)** (*de personnes*) to congregate, to gather **(b)** *Méd* (*des bords d'une plaie*) to join, to unite

aggravant [agravɑ̃] *adj Méd, Jur etc* (*symptôme, circonstances*) aggravating

aggravation [agravasjɔ̃] *nf* **(a)** (*d'une maladie etc*) aggravation; (*du temps, d'un conflit etc*) worsening **(b)** (*d'une peine*) increase

aggraver [agrave] **1** *vt* **(a)** (*maladie, crime*) to worsen, to make worse, to aggravate; **pour a. les choses** to make matters worse **(b)** (*peine*) to increase, to augment; (*difficultés, imposition*) to increase **2 s'aggraver** *vpr* to worsen, to become worse, to deteriorate; **la situation s'aggrave de jour en jour** the situation is getting *or* becoming worse by the day; **son état s'est aggravé** his condition has deteriorated, he has taken a turn for the worse; **les choses s'aggravent** things are getting worse

agile [aʒil] *adj aussi Fig* agile, nimble; (*démarche*) nimble; **elle est a. de ses doigts** she has nimble fingers

agilement [aʒilmɑ̃] *adv* agilely, nimbly

agilité [aʒilite] *nf* (*physique, mentale*) agility; **a. d'un raisonnement** agility of an argument

agios [aʒjo] *nmpl Fin* premium; (*dans un échange*) agio; (*quand on est à découvert*) bank charges; (*d'un emprunt*) interest payments

agiotage [aʒjɔtaʒ] *nm Bourse* stock jobbing, agiotage; (*truquage*) rigging the market; (*en prenant des risques financiers*) speculating, gambling

agioter [aʒjɔte] *vi Bourse* to speculate, to gamble

agioteur, -euse [aʒjɔtœr, -øz] *n Bourse* speculator, gambler

agir [aʒir] **1** *vi* **(a)** (*faire quelque chose*) to act; **a. de soi-même** to act on one's own initiative; **a. sur le conseil de qn** to act on sb's advice; **maintenant agissons** now let's get going, now let's get down to it; **il est temps d'a.** it's time to take action *or* to act; **faire a. qn** to get sb to act *or* to take action; **je vais a. en votre faveur (auprès du ministre)** I am going to intervene on your behalf (with the minister); **faire a. qch** to set sth going *or* working, to put sth in motion; **a. en connaisseur** to know what one is doing; **a. en sage** to act wisely; **bien/mal a. envers qn** to act *or* behave well/badly towards sb; **je n'aime pas sa façon** *ou* **manière d'a.** I don't like the way he goes about things; **est-ce ainsi que vous agissez envers moi?** is this how you treat me?

(b) (*produire un effet*) to act, to operate, to take effect; **médicament qui agit vite** quick-acting medicine, medicine that acts *or* takes effect quickly; **a. sur qch** to act on sth; **les mauvaises conditions de travail finissent par a. sur le moral/la santé** bad working conditions will end up affecting one's morale/health; **a. sur qn** to exercise an influence on sb; **a. sur les sentiments de qn** to work on sb's feelings; *Bourse* **a. sur le marché** to rig the market

(c) *Jur* **a. au nom de qn** to act on behalf of sb; **a. civilement contre qn** to sue sb; **a. au criminel/civil** to prosecute/to sue

2 s'agir (de) *v impers* [①B27,E,2,f] **(a)** (*être question de*) **de quoi s'agit-il?** what's the matter?, what's it all about?, *F* what's up?; **il ne veut pas me dire de quoi il s'agit** he won't tell me what the matter is; **je ne sais pas vraiment de quoi il s'agit** I don't really know what it's about; **l'affaire dont il s'agit** the matter in hand; **il ne s'agit pas d'argent** it's not a question of money; **il ne s'agit pas de cela** that is not the question *or* not the point, that's neither here nor there; **il s'agit de lui** it concerns him, it is about him; **quand il s'agit d'aider, il est toujours occupé** when it comes to helping, he always seems to be busy!; **s'agissant de ...** as for ..., as far as ... is concerned

(b) (*falloir*) it is a question of ...; **il ne s'agit que de les rendre heureux** it is only a question of making them happy; **il s'agirait de savoir si ...** the question is whether ...; **il s'agirait de se dépêcher** we've got to hurry; (*c'est notre dernière chance*) it's a case of now or never; **il s'agit de savoir ce que tu veux!** make up your mind!

agissant [aʒisɑ̃] *adj* effective, efficient; **un remède a.** an effective remedy

agissements [aʒismɑ̃] *nmpl souvent Péj* dealings, manoeuvres, machinations

agitateur, -trice [aʒitatœr, -tris] **1** *n Pol* agitator **2** *nm* **(a)** *Ch* stirring *or* glass rod **(b)** (*appareil*) stirring machine, agitator, mixer

agitation [aʒitasjɔ̃] *nf* **(a)** (*de la mer*) roughness, choppiness **(b)** (*inquiétude*) agitation; (*bougeotte*) restlessness, agitation, fidgeting; (*excitation*) excitement; *Pol* unrest; *Psy* (state of) perturbation *or* disturbance; **l'a. de la ville** the bustle of the city; **ville en pleine a.** bustling town; **il l'a trouvée dans un état de grande a.** he found her greatly excited; **cette nouvelle a provoqué l'a. des esprits** the news greatly upset *or* worried people; **l'a. ouvrière** (labour) unrest; **a. sociale** civil commotion

agité, -ée [aʒite] **1** *adj* **(a)** (*mer*) choppy, rough; (*ciel*) wild **(b)** *Méd* (*patient*) feverish, restless; (*nuit*) restless, sleepless; (*sommeil*) broken, fitful **(c)** (*foule*) agitated, tumultuous; (*personne*) restless, excited, fidgety; (*esprit*) perturbed, troubled; (*époque*) unsettled; **vie agitée** hectic life **2** *n* restless *or* unsettled person; *Méd* **pavillon des agités** security wing, wing for dangerous patients

agiter [aʒite] **1** *vt* **(a)** (*mouchoir, drapeau, bras*) to wave; (*bouteille*) to shake; (*aile, éventail*) to flutter; (*du vent*) (*arbre, branches*) to sway; (*mer*) to rouse; (*mélange*) to stir; (*air*) to fan; **a. la queue** (*d'un chien*) to wag his tail; (*d'un cheval*) to flick its tail; **a. avant usage/de consommer** shake before use

(b) (*inquiéter*) to perturb, to trouble; (*malade*) to agitate, to excite; **cette nouvelle risque de l'a. encore plus** this news could upset him even more; **malade agité par la fièvre** patient restless with fever; **elle est agitée par cette rencontre** the meeting has upset her *or* has got her (all) worked up; **a. le peuple** *ou* **les masses** to stir up the masses

(c) (*idée*) to discuss, to debate

2 s'agiter *vpr* **(a)** to be agitated; (*s'affairer*) to bustle around; **s'a. dans l'eau** to splash about in the water; **s'a. dans son sommeil** to toss (about) *or* thrash around in one's sleep

(b) (*s'énerver*) to become agitated *or* excited, to get upset *or* worked up; (*de la mer*) to get rough; **il ne faut pas que le malade s'agite** care should be taken not to upset *or* excite the patient

agit-prop [aʒitprɔp] *nf inv* (*abrév* **agitation-propagande**) agit-prop

agneau, -eaux [aɲo] *nm* lamb; **(peau d')a.** lambskin; **laine d'a.** lamb's wool; *Fig* **c'est un a.** he is as meek as a lamb; *Fig* **mon a.** my (pet) lamb; **doux comme un a.** as gentle as a lamb; *Rel* **l'A. sans tache** the Lamb (of God); *Culin* **côtelette d'a.** lamb chop; *Culin* **gigot d'a.** leg of lamb

agnelage [aɲəlaʒ] *nm* **(a)** *(mise à bas)* lambing **(b)** *(saison)* lambing season
agneler [aɲəle] *vi* **(elle agnèle; elle agnèlera)** to lamb
agnelet [aɲəlɛ] *nm* lambkin, young lamb
agneline [aɲəlin] *nf* lamb's wool
agnelle [aɲɛl] *nf* ewe lamb
agnosticisme [agnɔstisism] *nm* agnosticism
agnostique [agnɔstik] *adj, n* agnostic
à gogo [agogo] *adv F* galore; **avoir de l'argent à.** to have money galore *or* to burn
agonie [agɔni] *nf* death agony *or* struggle, pangs of death; **être à l'a.** to be at one's last gasp *or* at death's door; *Fig* to be suffering agonies; **lente a.** lingering death; *Fig* **l'a. d'un régime** the death throes of a regime
agonir [agɔnir] *vt* **a. qn d'injures/d'insultes** to heap insults *or* abuse on sb, to hurl insults *or* abuse at sb; **se faire a.** to be loudly insulted *or* abused
agonisant, -ante [agɔnizɑ̃, -ɑ̃t] **1** *adj* dying, in the throes of death; **de sa voix agonisante** with his dying breath; *Fig* **un règne a.** a reign in its dying moments *or* death throes **2** *n* dying person; **prières pour les agonisants** prayers for the dying
agoniser [agɔnize] *vi* to be dying *or* at the point of death; *Fig* *(d'une entreprise)* to be on its last legs
agoraphobe [agɔrafɔb] *adj Méd* agoraphobic
agoraphobie [agɔrafɔbi] *nf Méd* agoraphobia; **souffrir d'a.** to be agoraphobic
agrafage [agrafaʒ] *nm* fastening; *(de feuilles de papier)* stapling; *(d'un objet sur un établi etc)* clamping; *Tech* dowelling; *(de vêtements)* fastening, hooking
agrafe [agraf] *nf* **(a)** fastener; *(d'une médaille, d'un album)* clasp; *(d'une sangle)* buckle; *(de bureau)* staple; *Chir etc* suture clip; **a. de diamants** diamond clasp; **agrafes et portes (de couturière)** hooks and eyes **(b)** *Constr* clamp, cleat, cramp iron **(c)** *(d'une fenêtre etc)* hasp, catch **(d)** *Archit (d'une voûte)* keystone
agrafer [agrafe] *vt* **(a)** *(accrocher)* to fasten, to clip together; *(avec une agrafeuse)* to staple; *(robe)* to hook up; *(ceinture)* to buckle; **j'ai tellement grossi que je n'arrive plus à a. mes vêtements!** I've put on so much weight that I can't do up *or* fasten my clothes!; *F* **aide-moi à a. ma robe!** do me up! **(b)** *Constr* to clamp, to cramp **(c)** *F (de la police) (arrêter)* to nab, to nick; **il va finir par se faire a.** he's going to end up getting nabbed *or* nicked
agrafeuse [agraføz] *nf* stapler
agraire [agrɛr] *adj* agrarian; **réforme a.** land reform; **mesures agraires** land measures; *Jur* **loi a.** land act
agrammatical, -ale, -aux, -ales [agramatikal, -o] *adj Ling* ungrammatical
agrandir [agrɑ̃dir] **1** *vt* **(a)** *(rendre plus grand)* to make larger, to enlarge; *(photographie etc)* to enlarge; *(influence, cercle de relations)* to increase, to extend; **a. une maison/un appartement** to extend a house/flat; **a. qch en long/en large** to lengthen/widen sth

(b) *(faire paraître plus grand)* to make appear larger, to magnify; **a. sa taille** to make oneself look taller; **ce papier peint agrandit la pièce** this wallpaper makes the room look larger

(c) *(développer) (affaire)* to expand

(d) *(esprit etc)* to uplift

2 s'agrandir *vpr (devenir plus grand)* to grow larger; *(en quantité)* to become greater, to increase; *(prendre du volume)* to expand; **nous allons nous a.** we are going to enlarge our premises; **elle veut s'a.** *(dans son appartement)* she wants more space
agrandissement [agrɑ̃dismɑ̃] *nm* **(a)** *(extension)* enlargement, extension, expansion; **a. en long/en large** lengthening/widening; **travaux d'a.** extension work **(b)** *(d'une entreprise etc)* extension; *(d'un holding etc)* increase **(c)** *Phot* enlargement
agrandisseur [agrɑ̃disœr] *nm Phot* enlarger
agrarien, -ienne [agrarjɛ̃, -jɛn] *adj, n Pol* agrarian
agréable [agreabl] **1** *adj* pleasant, agreeable; *(apparence, arrangement)* pleasing; *(manière etc)* nice, pleasant; **un jeune homme très a.** a very pleasant *or* nice young man; **se rendre a. à qn** to be pleasant to sb; **a. au goût** pleasant to the taste; **a. à voir** pleasing to the eye; *F (femme)* easy on the eye; **peu a.** disagreeable **2** *nm* **joindre l'utile à l'a.** to combine business with pleasure **3** *n* **faire l'a.** to make oneself pleasant **(auprès de** to)
agréablement [agreabləmɑ̃] *adv* pleasantly, agreeably; **nous avons été a. surpris par ta décision** we were pleasantly surprised by your decision
agréé [agree] **1** *adj (échantillon etc)* approved; *Com* recognized, authorized; *Can* **comptable a.** chartered *or US* certified accountant **2** *nm Jur (devant un tribunal de commerce)* counsel
agréer [agree] **1** *vt (fournisseur, équipement)* to approve; **a. un contrat** to approve an agreement; **veuillez a. l'assurance de mes salutations distinguées** *(dans une lettre) (à une personne dont on connaît le nom)* yours sincerely; *(à une personne dont on ne connaît pas le nom)* yours faithfully **2** *vi* to please; **si cela vous agrée** if that suits you
agreg [agrɛg] *nf Univ F* = **agrégation 1**
agrégat [agrega] *nm* aggregate
agrégation [agregasjɔ̃] *nf* **(a)** *Univ* **(concours de) l'a.** = competitive examination for posts on the teaching staff of lycées and universities **(b)** *Constr* aggregation, binding; **matière d'a.** *(pour une route etc)* binding material
agrégé, -ée [agreʒe] *Univ* **1** *adj* who has passed the agrégation examination **2** *n* graduate who has passed the agrégation examination
agréger [agreʒe] **1** *vt* **(a)** *(rassembler)* **les cristaux agrégés dans la roche** the crystals incorporated in the rock **(b)** *(admettre) (société)* to incorporate; *(individu)* to admit **2 s'agréger** *vpr* **(a)** to combine, to merge **(b) s'a. à un groupe** to join a group
agrément [agremɑ̃] *nm* **(a)** *(plaisir)* pleasure, amusement; **voyage d'a.** pleasure trip; **arts d'a.** amateur artistic pursuits; **livres d'a.** light reading

(b) *(charme)* attractiveness, pleasantness, charm; **une ville sans a.** an unattractive town; **agréments** *(d'un lieu)* amenities; *(d'une personne)* charm

(c) *Mus* **notes d'a.** grace notes

(d) *(accord)* approval, consent; **nous avons besoin de l'a. de la sécurité sociale pour commencer à vous soigner** the social security must give us their approval *or* consent before we can begin to treat you

(e) *Com (d'agence de voyages)* agency appointment; *(garantie financière)* bonding scheme
agrémenter [agremɑ̃te] *vt* to ornament, to decorate; *(robe etc)* to trim; **texte agrémenté de citations** text laced with quotations
agrès [agrɛ] *nmpl* **(a)** *Naut* tackle **(b)** *Sp* (gymnastics) apparatus; **faire des a.** to do exercises on the apparatus
agresser [agrese] *vt* to attack (without provocation), to assault; *(yeux, tympans)* to assault; **le soleil agresse la peau** the sun damages the skin *or* has a damaging effect on the skin; **se faire a.** to be attacked; *(dans un lieu public et pour son argent)* to be mugged; **arrête de m'a., ce n'est pas de ma faute!** stop being so aggressive towards me, it's not my fault!; *F* **ne te sens pas agressé** don't think you're being got at
agresseur [agrɛsœr] *nm* attacker, aggressor, assailant
agressif, -ive [agresif, -iv] *adj (ton, personne, couleur etc)* aggressive
agression [agrɛsjɔ̃] *nf* **(a)** *(agressivité)* aggression **(b)** *(acte) (sur un passant etc)* mugging **(de** of); *(d'un pays)* act of aggression **(de** against); **ce genre de publicité est une véritable a.** this kind of advertising is extremely aggressive; **être victime d'une a.** to be attacked; *(dans un lieu public et pour son argent)* to be mugged; **a. de la peau par les intempéries** damaging effects of bad weather on the skin; **le bruit est une réelle a.** noise is a real act of aggression; **les agressions de la vie moderne** the stresses of modern life
agressivement [agresivmɑ̃] *adv* aggressively
agressivité [agresivite] *nf* aggressiveness
agreste [agrɛst] *adj Litt* **(a)** rustic; *(site)* rural **(b)** *(personne, manières)* uncouth
agricole [agrikɔl] *adj (produit, nation etc)* agricultural; **comice(s) agricole(s)** agricultural show; **exploitation a.** farming; *(ferme)* farm; **petite exploitation a.** small farm, smallholding; **travail a.** farmwork, farming; **ouvrier a.** farm worker *or* hand; **la population a.** the farming population
agriculteur, -trice [agrikyltœr, -tris] *n* farmer
agriculture [agrikyltyr] *nf* agriculture, farming
agripper [agripe] **1** *vt (qn, qch)* to clutch (at), to grip; *(saisir) (qch)* to seize (hold of) **2 s'agripper** *vpr* to cling; **il s'agrippait au bord de la fenêtre** he was clinging to the window sill
agro [agrɔ] *nm F abrév* **Institut national agronomique**
agro-alimentaire [agroalimɑ̃tɛr] **1** *adj (industrie, secteur)* food **2** *nm* agribusiness
agrochimie [agroʃimi] *nf* agro-chemistry
agronome [agrɔnɔm] *nm* agronomist, agricultural economist; **ingénieur a.** agricultural engineer *or* scientist
agronomie [agrɔnɔmi] *nf* agronomy; *Écon* agronomics
agronomique [agrɔnɔmik] *adj* agronomic(al); **l'Institut national a.** = (university level) college for students of agronomics
agrume [agrym] *nm* citrus fruit
agrumicole [agrymikɔl] *adj* citrus fruit-producing
aguerrir [agerir] **1** *vt (qn)* to harden, to toughen; *(troupes)* to train (for battle) **2 s'aguerrir** *vpr* **s'a. à** *ou* **contre qch** to

become hardened to sth; (*apprendre à accepter, se débrouiller*) to learn to take sth in one's stride; **ça va te permettre de t'a.** (*d'aller en pension etc*) it will toughen you up a bit

aguets [agɛ] *adv* **aux a.** on the watch, on the lookout; **être** *ou* **se tenir aux a.** to be on the watch *or* on the lookout; **avoir l'oreille aux a.** to keep one's ears open

aguichant [agiʃɑ̃] *adj* seductive, provocative

aguiche [agiʃ] *nf* (*publicité*) teaser

aguicher [agiʃe] *vt* to excite, to arouse, *F* to lead on

aguicheur, -euse [agiʃœr, -øz] **1** *adj* seductive, provocative; **une fillette aguicheuse** a little tease, a nymphet **2** *nf* **aguicheuse** provocative woman, tease

Ah (*abrév* **ampère-heure**) Ah

ah [ɑ] **1** *int* ah!; (*exprimant la surprise*) oh!; **ah, que c'est beau!** isn't it beautiful!; **ah oui!** well yes, of course!; **ah ça non/oui!** certainly not/certainly!; *Iron* **ah ah, je savais bien que tu me cachais quelque chose** aha! I knew that you were hiding something from me **2** *nm inv* **pousser des oh et des ah** to ooh and aah

ahaner [aane] *vi Litt* to puff and pant

ahuri, -ie [ayri] **1** *adj* (*regard*) astounded; (*personne*) stupefied, *F* flabbergasted; **avoir l'air a.** to look astounded *or* stupefied **2** *n* idiot, numbskull

ahurir [ayrir] *vt* to astound, to stupefy

ahurissant [ayrisɑ̃] *adj* astounding, incredible, stupefying; *F* **il a un culot a.** he's got one hell of a cheek

ahurissement [ayrismɑ̃] *nm* stupefaction; **il ne revient pas de son a.** he can't get over it

aï [ai] *nm* (*mammifère*) three-toed sloth

AIDA [aida] *abrév Mktg* **(attention-intérêt-désir-action)** AIDA

aide[1] [ɛd] *nf* help, assistance; (*humanitaire*) aid; **j'ai dû lui demander de l'a.** I had to ask him for help; **appeler à l'a.** to call for help; **donner son a. à qn** to help sb; **venir en a. à qn, apporter son a. à qn** to help sb, to come to sb's assistance *or* aid; **recourir à l'a. d'un médecin** to call in a doctor; **à l'a.!** help!; **à l'a. de qch** with the help *or* assistance of sth; **avec l'a. de qn** with the help *or* assistance of sb; **faire qch sans a.** to do sth without help *or* on one's own

▶ **aide[1]:** *Ordinat* **a. à la césure** hyphenation help; *Ordinat* **a. contextuelle** context-sensitive help; *Econ* **a. au développement** foreign aid (to developing countries); **a. de l'État** = national assistance; *Compta* **a. fiscale** tax credit; **a. gouvernementale** government aid; **a. judiciaire** legal aid; *Ordinat* **a. en ligne** on-line help; **a. au logement** accommodation allowance; **a. publique au développement** official development assistance; **a. au retour** repatriation assistance; **a. sociale** *Br* social security, *Am* welfare

aide[2] *n* assistant, helper; *Naut* mate; (*de géomètre*) chainman

▶ **aide[2]: a. de camp** aide-de-camp; **a. de cuisine** assistant cook, kitchen hand; **a.** *nf* **familiale** *ou* **maternelle** mother's help; **a. de laboratoire** laboratory assistant; **a.** *nf* **ménagère** home help

aidé [ede] *adj* **(a)** (*assisté*) **elle n'est pas très aidée** she doesn't have much help (around the house); **elle est très aidée par cette femme** she gets a lot of help from this woman **(b)** *Admin* **contrat a.** = employment contract whereby part of an employee's salary is paid by the state **(c)** *Fig* **il n'est pas très a.** (*pas très intelligent*) he's not very smart, he's a bit of a dimwit

aide-comptable, *pl* **aides-comptables** *n* assistant accountant, accounts clerk

aide-cuisinier, *pl* **aides-cuisiniers** *n* kitchen assistant

aide-gouvernante, *pl* **aides-gouvernantes** *nf* assistant housekeeper

aide-mécanicien, *pl* **aide-mécaniciens** *nm* garage hand

aide-mémoire *nm inv* aide-memoire; *TV* prompt card; *Ordinat* quick reference guide **j'ai besoin d'un a.** I need someting to jog my memory

aider [ede] **1** *vt* [①A40,B,1,a] to help, to assist, to aid; **attends, je vais t'a.** hold on, I'll help you *or* I'll give you a hand; **que puis-je faire pour vous a.?** how may I help you?; **je me suis fait a. par un ami** I got a friend to help me *or* to give me a hand; **tu ne peux pas t'occuper de ta maison toute seule, fais-toi a.** you can't look after the house on your own, get some help *or* get someone to help you; **a. qn à faire qch** to help sb to do sth; **a. qn à monter/descendre/entrer/sortir** to help sb up/down/in/out; **a. qn à mettre/ôter son pardessus** to help sb on/off with his/her coat; **Dieu aidant** with God's help; *Iron* **tu veux que je t'aide?** stop that

2 *vi* **a. à qch** to contribute to(wards) sth; **elle n'aide jamais!** she never helps (out), she never lends a hand

3 s'aider *vpr* **(a)** *Prov* **aide-toi et le ciel t'aidera** God helps those who help themselves; **il faut s'a. les uns les autres** we must help one another

(b) s'a. de qch to make use of sth; **s'a. d'un dictionnaire** to consult a dictionary; **marcher en s'aidant d'une canne/de béquilles** to walk with the aid of a stick/crutches

aide-serveur, *pl* **aides-serveurs** *nm* waiter's assistant, *Am* busboy

aide-soignant, -ante, *pl* **aides-soignant(e) s** *n* nursing auxiliary, auxiliary nurse

aïe [aj] *int* (*cri de douleur*) ow!, ouch!; *Fig* **a.! j'ai fait une gaffe!** oh no *or* oh dear, I've put my foot in it!; **a. a. a.!** boy oh boy!

AIEA [aiəa] *nf Nucl* (*abrév* **Agence internationale de l'énergie atomique**) IAEA

aïeul, -eule, *pl* **aïeux** [ajœl, ajø] *n* **(a)** (*ancêtre*) ancestor; *F* **mes aïeux!** goodness me! **(b)** *Vieilli pl* **aïeuls** grandfather, *f* grandmother

aigle [ɛgl] **1** *nm* **(a)** (*oiseau*) eagle; **a. royal** *ou* **fauve** *ou* **doré** golden eagle; **grand a. des mers** erne, sea eagle; *Fig* **un œil d'a.** a keen *or* penetrating glance; *Fig* **avoir un œil d'a.** to be eagle-eyed; **nez en bec d'a.** hook *or* aquiline nose

(b) *Fig* genius, mastermind; **ce n'est pas un a.** he's no genius

(c) (*lutrin*) lectern

(d) (*poisson*) **a. de mer** eagle ray

(e) eagle; *Mil* **l'a. noir de Prusse** the black eagle of Prussia

(f) (*en patinage*) **grand a.** spread-eagle

2 *nf* **(a)** *Hér* eagle; **a. de sable éployée** eagle displayed sable; **double a., a. à deux têtes** double-headed eagle

(b) *Mil* eagle, standard; **les aigles romaines** the Roman eagles; **l'a. impérial (des armées napoléoniennes)** the imperial eagle

aiglefin [ɛgləfɛ̃] *nm* (*poisson*) haddock

aiglette [ɛglɛt] *nf Hér* eaglet

aiglon, -onne [ɛglɔ̃, -ɔn] *n* (*oiseau*) eaglet, young eagle; *Hist* **L'A.** Napoleon II

aigre [ɛgr] **1** *adj* (*goût etc*) sour, sharp, acid, tart; (*lait*) sour; *Fig* (*propos*) cutting; (*personne*) sour; (*éprouvant du ressentiment*) bitter; (*vent, froid*) bitter; (*son*) harsh, shrill; **parler d'un ton a.** to speak sharply **2** *nm* **tourner à l'a.** (*d'un aliment etc*) to turn sour; *Fig* (*d'une discussion*) to turn nasty

aigre-doux, -douce *adj* (*sauce*) sweet and sour; *Fig* (*remarque*) snide, *F* catty

aigrefin[1] [ɛgrəfɛ̃] *nm* (*poisson*) haddock

aigrefin[2] *nm Péj* swindler, (financial) shark

aigrelet, -ette [ɛgrəlɛ, -ɛt] *adj* (*vin, goût*) (rather) sour; (*son, voix*) harsh, reedy

aigrement [ɛgrəmɑ̃] *adv* acrimoniously, bitterly

aigrette [ɛgrɛt] *nf* **(a)** (*d'un héron*) aigrette; (*d'un perroquet etc*) crest; (*d'une chouette*) horn; (*de cheveux, de fourrure*) tuft **(b)** (*panache*) aigrette, plume; **a. de diamants** spray of diamonds **(c)** *Bot* egret; (*du maïs*) tassel **(d)** *Él* (*décharge*) aigrette, brush **(e)** (*oiseau*) egret

aigreur [ɛgrœr] *nf* **(a)** (*d'un goût*) sourness, tartness, acidity; *Fig* (*du tempérament*) sourness; (*d'une remarque*) sharpness, bitterness; **il en parle encore avec a.** he's still very bitter about it **(b)** *Méd* **aigreurs (d'estomac)** acidity, excess stomach acid

aigri [egri] *adj* embittered, soured

aigrir [egrir] **1** *vt* **a. qch** to turn sth sour; *Fig* **a. qn** to embitter sb, to make sb bitter **2** *vi* to turn *or* grow sour; (*du lait*) to turn **3 s'aigrir** *vpr* (*devenir acide*) to turn sour; *Fig* **son caractère s'est aigri** he has become embittered

aigu, -uë [egy] *adj* **(a)** (*douleur*) acute, sharp; (*curiosité*) intense; (*conflit, jalousie*) bitter; (*regard*) penetrating; (*esprit, sensation, intelligence*) keen, sharp; **elle a un sens a. du rôle de chacun** she has a keen sense of what everybody's role should be **(b)** (*instrument*) sharp, pointed; *Math* **angle a.** acute angle **(c)** (*son*) shrill, sharp, high-pitched **(d)** *Gram* **accent a.** acute (accent)

aigue-marine, *pl* **aigues-marines** [ɛgmarin] *nf* aquamarine

aiguillage [egɥijaʒ] *nm* **(a)** *Rail* (*manœuvre*) switching *or* shifting of points; (*d'un train*) shunting; **poste d'a.** signal box **(b)** *Rail* (*appareil*) points, *US* switches; **a. à deux voies** two-way switch **(c)** *Fig* orientation; **faire une erreur d'a.** to take the wrong turning *or* course

aiguille [egɥij] *nf* **(a)** needle; **a. à coudre/repriser/tricoter** sewing/darning/knitting needle; **travail à l'a.** needlework; **a. à passer** *ou* **à lacet** bodkin; *Méd* **a. hypodermique** hypodermic needle; *Fig* **chercher une a. dans une botte de foin** to look for a needle in a haystack; *Fig* **de fil en a. nous en sommes venus à parler de notre enfance** one thing led to another and we got talking about our childhood

(b) *Ordinat* pin; **imprimante à aiguilles** 24 pin printer

(c) a. de glace icicle; *Géol* **a. (rocheuse)** needle; (*d'un sommet*) spine; **a. de pin** pine needle; **a. de mer** (*poisson*) pipe fish, garfish; **a. à tracer** scriber; **a. de graveur** etching needle

(d) *Rail* tongue rail, point rail, blade; **a. de raccordement** points, *Am* switches

(e) (*d'une obélisque, d'un pic etc*) needle, point; (*d'une église*) (church) spire

(f) (*de boussole, de compteur de vitesse etc*) needle; (*d'une montre, d'une horloge*) hand; **petite a.** hour hand; **grande a.** minute hand; **a. trotteuse** second hand

aiguillée [egɥije] *nf* (short) piece of thread

aiguiller [egɥije] *vt Rail* (*train*) to shunt, *Am* to switch; *Fig* **a. la police sur une fausse piste** to put the police on a false scent; *Fig* **on l'a aiguillé vers la profession de banquier** he was steered *or* guided into banking; *Fig* **il a été mal aiguillé dans ses études** he was badly advised about his studies; *Fig* **a. ses recherches vers un certain domaine** to orient(ate) *or* direct one's research towards a particular field

aiguilleur [egɥijœr] *nm Rail* pointsman, *Am* switchman; *Av* **a. du ciel** air traffic controller

aiguillon [egɥijɔ̃] *nm* **(a)** (*pique-bœuf*) goad; *Fig* incentive, spur, stimulus; *Fig* **sa remarque me fit l'effet d'un a.** his remark spurred me on **(b)** *Bot* prickle, thorn; (*d'une guêpe*) sting

aiguillonner [egɥijɔne] *vt* (*bœufs*) to goad; *Fig* (*qn*) (*de la jalousie, de l'ambition*) to spur on; (*d'une personne*) to urge on; *Fig* **l'appât du gain l'aiguillonne** the lure of money spurs him on

aiguisé [egize] *adj* (*couteau*) sharp; *Fig* (*appétit, intérêt*) keen

aiguiser [egize] *vt* **(a)** (*couteau etc*) to sharpen, to put an edge on, to grind; (*scie, rasoir*) to set; (*faux*) to whet; (*outil*) to sharpen to a point **(b)** *Fig* (*curiosité, jalousie*) to arouse; (*appétit*) to whet; (*intelligence*) to sharpen

aiguiseur, -euse [egizœr, -øz] *n* (*d'outils etc*) grinder, sharpener

aiguisoir [egizwar] *nm* (*outil*) (knife) sharpener, steel; (*pierre à aiguiser*) whetstone

aïkido [ajkido] *nm Sp* aikido; **faire de l'a.** to do aikido

ail, *pl* **ails** [aj] *Vieilli* **aulx** [o] *nm* **(a)** *Culin* garlic; **une gousse d'a.** a clove of garlic; **un bulbe** *ou F* **une tête d'a.** a head of garlic **(b)** (*plante*) allium

aile [ɛl] *nf* **(a)** (*d'oiseau, de papillon etc*) wing; (*de manchot*) flipper; **battre des ailes** to beat *or* flap its wings; **battre de l'a.** (*d'un oiseau*) to flutter; *Fig* (*d'une personne*) to be flustered *or* embarrassed; **l'entreprise bat de l'a.** the firm is struggling (to survive) *or* is in a bad way; **avoir du plomb dans l'a., en avoir dans l'a.** (*d'un oiseau*) to be winged; *Fig* (*d'une personne*) to be hard hit; *Fig* **la théorie a du plomb dans l'a.** the theory doesn't stand up; *Fig* **la peur nous donnait des ailes** fear lent us wings; *Fig* **voler de ses propres ailes** to stand on one's own (two) feet; *Fig* **vouloir voler avant d'avoir ses ailes** to want to run before one can walk; *Fig* **rogner les ailes à qn** to clip sb's wings; *Fig F* **avoir un coup dans l'a.** to have had a bit too much to drink; *Fig* **prendre qn sous son a.** to take sb under one's wing; *Fig* **travailler sous l'a. d'un grand professeur** to be the protégé of an eminent professor

(b) *Aut* wing, *Am* fender; (*d'un bâtiment, de la scène*) wing; (*d'une armée*) wing, flank; (*d'un moulin*) sail; (*d'un sémaphore*) arm; (*d'une hélice, d'une turbine*) blade; (*d'une oreille*) helix; (*du nez*) wing; (*d'une poutre*) flange

(c) *Av* wing, aerofoil, *Am* airfoil; **a. courbe** cambered wing; **a. en flèche** swept-back wing; **a. à fente** slotted wing; **a. en delta** delta wing; **a. cantilever, a. en porte à faux** cantilever wing

(d) *Fb* wing; **les demi ailes** the wing halves; *Rugby, Fb* **jouer trois quarts a.** to play wing three-quarters; **à l'a. gauche** on the left wing

(e) *Sp* **a. volante** *ou* **libre** (*sport*) hang-gliding; (*objet*) hang-glider; **faire de l'a. volante** to hang-glide, to go hang-gliding

ailé [ele] *adj* winged, feathered, *Spéc* alate

aileron [ɛlrɔ̃] *nm* **(a)** (*d'oiseau*) pinion; (*de requin etc*) fin **(b)** *Av* aileron **(c)** *Av etc* fin; **a. stabilisateur** stabilizer fin; **stabilisateur à a.** fin stabilizer **(d)** *Aut* wing, *Am* fender; (*de voiture de course*) aerofoil; **a. arrière** rear wing **(e)** (*de roue à eau*) paddle board **(f)** (*d'un sous-marin*) fin keel; (*d'une planche à voile*) skeg

ailette [ɛlɛt] *nf* **(a)** (*d'un radiateur*) radiating plate, fin; *Aut* **a. de refroidissement** cooling fin; **tube à ailettes** fanned *or* gilled tube **(b)** (*d'une pièce de machine*) lug, tenon; (*d'un coquillage*) stud; **vis à ailettes** wing nut, thumbscrew **(c)** (*d'une torpille, d'un éventail, d'un ventilateur etc*) vane; (*d'une bombe, d'une missile*) wing, fin; (*d'un avion*) fin; (*d'une turbine*) blade; **à ailettes** (*roue etc*) bladed; (*bombe, missile*) winged

ailier [elje] *nm Sp* winger

ailler [aje] *vt Culin* to put garlic in

ailleurs [ajœr] *adv* **(a)** (*à un autre endroit*) elsewhere, somewhere else; **elle vient d'a.** she's not from here, she's not from these parts; **c'est dit a. dans le texte** it's mentioned somewhere else in the text; **on a dû passer par a.** we had to come a different way; *Fig* **être a.** to be miles away; **partout a.** everywhere else; (*n'importe où*) anywhere else; **nulle part a.** nowhere else; **vous mangerez ici comme nulle part a.** you'll eat better here than you will anywhere else; *F* **va voir a. si j'y suis** take a walk

(b) **d'a.** besides, anyway, *surtout Fml* moreover; (*quoi qu'il en soit*) however; (*au fait*) come to that, for that matter; **d'a., j'avais quelque chose à te dire à ce sujet** by the way, I had something to tell you about this

(c) **par a.** in other respects; (*par qn d'autre etc*) from another source; (*d'ailleurs*) moreover

ailloli [ajɔli] *nm* = aïoli

aimable [ɛmabl] *adj* **(a)** (*gentil*) kind, pleasant, agreeable; **vous êtes bien a., c'est très a. de votre part** it's very kind of you, it's very good of you; **peu a.** disagreeable; (*remerciements, propos etc*) ungracious; **échanger quelques mots aimables avec qn** to exchange a few kind words with sb **(b)** *Arch* (*que l'on peut aimer facilement*) lovable, attractive

aimablement [ɛmabləmɑ̃] *adv* kindly, pleasantly

aimant[1] [ɛmɑ̃] *nm* magnet; **a. supraconducteur** superconducting magnet

aimant[2] [ɛmɑ̃] *adj* (*parent etc*) loving

aimantation [ɛmɑ̃tasjɔ̃] *nf* magnetization

aimanter [ɛmɑ̃te] *vt* to magnetize

aimer [eme] **1** *vt* **(a)** (*d'amour*) to love; **a. qn (d'amour)** to love sb, to be in love with sb; **tu crois qu'il m'aime?** do you think he loves me?

(b) (*apprécier, avoir de l'affection pour*) (*qn, qch*) to like, to be fond of; **il te téléphone encore, ouh, je n'aime pas ça!** he's calling you again, oh I don't like that at all!; **elle n'aime pas la viande crue** she doesn't like raw meat; **a. qn d'amitié** to be good friends with sb; **je n'aime guère Pierre** I don't like Pierre very much, I don't care for Pierre very much; **j'aime beaucoup Pierre** I like Pierre very much, I'm very fond of Pierre; **j'aime beaucoup la musique** I'm very fond of music; **je t'aime bien** I like you a lot; **se faire a. de qn** to win sb's affection; **plante qui aime un sol calcaire** plant that likes a chalky soil; **tu sais que nous n'aimons pas ce genre de choses** you know we don't like that sort of thing; **a. (à) faire qch** to like doing sth; **j'aurais aimé le voir** I would like to have seen him; *prov* **qui m'aime aime mon chien** love me, love my dog; **je vais prendre un pot — qui m'aime me suive!** I'm going for a drink — anyone want to join me?; **j'aime autant le cidre que le vin** I like cider just as much as wine; **j'aime(rais) autant rester ici** I would just as soon stay here **(que de ...** as ...); **j'aime autant qu'il ne m'attende pas** I would just as soon he didn't wait for me; **a. mieux** to prefer; **ah, j'aime mieux ça, j'ai cru que tu avais oublié de les inviter** now that's more like it, I thought you'd forgotten to invite them; **j'aime** *ou* **j'aimerais mieux rester ici** I would rather *or* sooner stay here; *F* **j'aime mieux pas** I'd rather not

2 s'aimer *vpr* **(a)** (*être attaché par amour*) to love each other, to be in love (with each other); (*avoir des relations sexuelles*) to make love; **ils s'aiment** they are in love (with each other)

(b) (*être fier de soi*) to think a lot of oneself; (*à une occasion particulière*) to be pleased with oneself; **je ne m'aime pas dans cette veste** (*ne me plais pas*) I don't like myself in this jacket

aine [ɛn] *nf Anat* groin

aîné, -ée [ene] **1** *adj* [①A19,g,iv] (*de deux personnes*) elder; (*de plus que deux personnes*) eldest; **mon frère a.** my elder brother; (*plus de deux frères*) my eldest brother; **la branche aînée de la famille** the elder *or* senior branch of the family **2** *n* elder *or* eldest (child); **l'a. ne va pas encore à l'école** the eldest doesn't go to school yet; **nos aînés** our elders; **il est mon a.** he is older than me; **il est mon a. de deux ans** he is two years older than me

aînesse [ɛnɛs] *nf* **droit d'a.** law of primogeniture

ainsi [ɛ̃si] **1** *adv* **(a)** (*de cette façon*) like this, like that, in this *or* that way, *Fml* thus; **c'est a. que commence la chanson** the song starts like this, this is how the song starts; **c'est a. qu'il est devenu soldat** and that is *or* was how he became a soldier; **s'il en est a.** if that is the case, if (it is) so; **puisqu'il en est a. je n'ai plus rien à dire** under the circumstances I have nothing more to say; **les choses étant a.** if that's the way *or* how things are; **et a. de suite** and so on, and so forth; **pour a. dire** so to speak, as it were; **a. soit-il** so be it; *Rel* amen; **a. donc** so; **a. donc tu nous quittes** so you're leaving us then?; **a. partait Zarathustra** thus spake Zarathustra

(b) (*par exemple*) for example, for instance; **il m'arrive des aventures, a., l'autre jour ...** things happen to me, for instance, the other day ...

2 *conj* **(a)** so; **a. vous ne venez pas?** so you're not coming?

(b) as well as, and; **cette règle a. que la suivante me paraît** *ou* **paraissent inutile(s)** this rule, as well as *or* and the next, seems to me to be unnecessary

AIO [aio] *abrév Mktg* **(activités, intérêts et opinions)** AIO

aïoli [ajɔli] *nm Culin* garlic mayonnaise

air [ɛr] *nm* **(a)** (*gaz*) air, atmosphere; **une bouffée d'a. pur** a breath of fresh air; *Fig* **cette discussion a été comme une bouffée d'a. pur** this discussion has been like a breath of fresh air; **privé d'a., sans a.** airless; **cela manque d'a. ici** it's stuffy in here; **j'ouvre la porte pour faire de l'a.** I'll open the door to let some air in; **l'a. de la mer/des montagnes** (the) sea/mountain air; **donner de l'a. à** (*pièce*) to ventilate, to air; (*qn*) to give some (fresh) air; **à a. conditionné** air conditioned; **avoir l'a. conditionné** to have air conditioning; **sortir prendre l'a.** to go out for some fresh air; *Fig* **vivre de l'a. du temps** to live on (next to) nothing *or* on fresh air; **ne pas laisser à l'a.** not to be exposed to the air; **allez, de l'a.!** go on, clear off!; **au grand a., en plein a., à l'a. libre** in the fresh air, in the open air; **vie au grand a.** open-air life; **vie de plein a.** outdoor life; **concert en plein a.** open-air concert; **libre comme l'a.** free as a bird; *Typ* **donner de l'a. à la composition** to lead out *or* space out the type

(b) (*ciel*) **l'a.** the air; **la conquête de l'a.** the conquest of the air; **prendre l'a.** (*d'un avion*) to take off; **la navette spatiale s'éleva dans les airs** the space shuttle rose into the air; **tenir l'a.** to keep flying; (*être en état de voler*) to be airworthy; **ministère de l'A.** = ministry responsible for air defence; **Armée de l'A.** Air Force; **École de l'A.** ≈ R.A.F. College, U.S.A.F. Academy; **hôtesse de l'a.** air hostess; **jouer les filles de l'a.** to vanish into thin air; **mal de l'a.** air sickness; **en l'a.** in the air; **regarder en l'a.** to look up; *Fig* **être en l'a.** (*en désordre*) to be in a mess; **il a mis toute la maison/mon bureau en l'a.** he made an awful mess of the house/my office; *Fig* **ficher qch en l'a.** to mess sth up; **mes projets sont fichus en l'a. à cause de lui** my plans have all gone up in smoke because of him; *Fig* **elle veut tout envoyer** *ou F* **foutre en l'a.** she wants to throw it all up *or F* chuck *or* jack it all in; *Fig* **paroles en l'a.** idle talk; *Fig* **parler en l'a.** to talk wildly *or* rashly; *Fig* **j'ai dit ça en l'a.** I was talking off the top of my head; *Fig* **c'est une tête en l'a.** he's got his head in the clouds

(c) *Fig* (*atmosphère*) **elle est passée prendre l'a. de l'atelier** she looked in at the workshop to see how things were; **changer d'a.** to have a change of scene; **il y a quelque chose dans l'a.** there's something in the air *or* wind, there's something brewing; **il y a de la dispute/de l'orage dans l'a.** there's an argument/a storm brewing; **c'est dans l'a. du temps** (*de se préoccuper de l'environnement etc*) it's the in thing

(d) (*vent*) wind; **courant d'a.** draught; **il ne fait pas d'a.** there's not a breath of air

(e) (*allure*) appearance, look; **avoir bon** *ou* **grand a.** (*d'une personne*) to look distinguished; (*d'une robe etc*) to be smart; (*être seyant*) to be becoming; **a. de famille** family likeness; **un jeune homme à l'a. très comme il faut** a very respectable-looking young man; **avoir un faux a. de ...** to have a vague *or* slight resemblance to ..., to look vaguely like ...; **il a un drôle d'a.** he looks odd *or* funny; **cette fillette a un petit a. malin** that little girl looks very mischievous; **la ville a un a. de fête** the town is looking festive, the town has a festive look about it; **elle, avec son a. de ne pas y toucher** her with her innocent look; **se donner** *ou* **prendre des airs** to give oneself *or* to put on airs, to (try to) look important; **prendre des airs entendus** to have a knowing look; **ne prends pas tes grands airs!** don't get on your high horse!

(f) avoir l'a. to look, to seem; **avoir l'a. fatigué/déçu/de s'ennuyer/d'être intéressé** to look tired/disappointed/bored/interested; **sa voiture a l'a. ancienne** his car looks old; **Marie a l'a. contente** Marie looks happy; *F* **avoir l'a. fin** to look daft; **il a l'a. d'un étranger** he looks like a foreigner; **ils ont l'a. d'avoir peur** they look as if they're afraid; **tu as l'a. de ne pas comprendre le problème** you look as if you don't understand the problem; **cela en a tout l'a.** it looks like it; **n'avoir l'a. de rien** (*d'une personne*) to seem *or* appear insignificant, to seem *or* appear of no importance; (*d'une maison etc*) to be unpretentious, to look nothing much (from the outside); (*d'un travail*) to look (deceptively) easy; **il n'a l'a. de rien, mais il est d'une force extraordinaire** he doesn't look much, but he's unbelievably strong; **le temps a l'a. d'être à la pluie** it looks like rain

(g) *Mus* tune, air, melody; **un a. à la mode** a popular tune; **a. varié** theme with variations; **un a. d'opéra** an (operatic) aria

(h) *Équitation* **les airs du manège** the paces of a horse

▶ **air**: **a. comprimé** compressed air; **a. liquide** liquid air; **a. recyclé** recirculated air; **a. refroidi** cooled air

airain [ɛrɛ̃] *nm* (*cuivre et étain*) bronze; (*cuivre et zinc*) brass; *Écon* **la loi d'a.** (Lassalle's) iron law of wages

air-air [ɛrɛr] *adj inv Mil* air-to-air; **missile a.** air-to-air missile

airbus® [ɛrbys] *nm Av* airbus

aire [ɛr] *nf* **(a)** (*surface plane*) (plane) surface; (*plancher*) floor; (*d'un pont*) roadway, floor; **a. (d'une grange)** threshing floor **(b)** (*d'un champ, d'un triangle, d'un bâtiment etc*) area; *Fig* **a. d'influence** sphere of influence; **a. linguistique** linguistic region; *Géog* **a. de drainage** drainage area, basin **(c)** (*d'un aigle*) eyrie **(d)** *Naut* **les aires de vent** the points of the compass

▶ **aire**: *Av* **a. d'atterrissage** landing area; *Géog* **a. continentale** continental shield; **a. de dédouanement** customs clearance area; **a. de jeux** play area; *Astronaut* **a. de lancement** launching site; **a. de lavage** *Aut* car wash, washing bay, *Am* wash rack; *Av* washdown; *Av* **a. de manœuvre** apron; **a. de pique-nique** picnic site *or* area; **a. de repos** (*sur l'autoroute*) parking *or* picnic area; **a. de services (principale)** service area; (*panneau indicateur*) services; **a. de stationnement** *Av* tarmac, apron; *Aut* parking area, lay-by

airedale [ɛrdɛl] *nm* Airedale (terrier)

airelle [ɛrɛl] *nf* (*plante*) **a. myrtille** bilberry, blaeberry, *Am* blueberry, huckleberry; **a. coussinette** cranberry

air-sol [ɛrsɔl] *adj inv Mil* air-to-ground; **missile a.** air-to-ground missile

aisance [ɛzɑ̃s] *nf* **(a)** (*facilité*) ease; (*de mouvement etc*) freedom; **faire qch avec a.** to do sth easily *or* with ease; **donner de l'a. à qch** to ease sth; **parler** *ou* **s'exprimer avec a.** to speak *or* express oneself with great ease *or* facility; **jouir de l'a., être dans l'a.** to be well off *or* comfortably off; **vivre dans l'a.** to live comfortably **(b) fosse d'aisances** cesspool; *Vieilli* **lieu** *ou* **cabinet d'aisances** public convenience *or* lavatory

▶ **aisance**: *Jur* **a. de voirie** easement

aise [ɛz] **1** *nf* ease, comfort; **être à l'a.** *ou* **à son a.** (*bien installé*) to be comfortable; (*avoir beaucoup de place*) to have (elbow) room; (*financièrement*) to be well off; **tu serais plus à l'a. si tu lui en parlais une bonne fois pour toutes** you'd feel more comfortable *or* more at ease if you told him once and for all; **tu seras bien plus à l'a. dans cette pièce** you'll be much more comfortable in this room; **on tient à l'a. à six dans cette voiture** this car holds six comfortably; *F* **à l'a.!** easy!, no problem!, it's a piece of cake *or Br* a doddle!; **à ton a.!** suit yourself!; **ne pas être à son a., se sentir mal à l'a.** to feel awkward, to feel uncomfortable, to feel ill at ease; (*physiquement*) to feel indisposed *or* off colour; **être (très) à l'a.** to be relaxed; **je l'ai mis à l'a. en l'appelant Roger** I put him at his ease by calling him Roger; *Iron* **elle peut en parler à son a.!** it's easy (enough) *or* it's all right for her to talk!; **mettez-vous à votre a.** make yourself comfortable; **il en prend à son a. avec ses collègues** he takes his colleagues for granted; **faire qch à son a.** to do sth at one's own convenience; **aimer ses aises** to like one's comforts; **il prend ses aises** he makes himself at home

2 *adj Litt* **je suis bien** *ou* **tout a. de l'entendre parler ainsi** I'm delighted to hear him talk this way

aisé [eze] *adj* **(a)** (*manière*) easy, free; (*vêtement, situation*) comfortable; (*personne*) (*financièrement*) comfortably off, well-to-do, *F* well heeled; **parler d'un ton a.** to speak in a natural way **(b)** (*tâche*) easy

aisément [ezemɑ̃] *adv* **(a)** comfortably, freely; **vivre a.** to be comfortably off **(b)** (*facilement*) easily, readily

aisselle [ɛsɛl] *nf* **(a)** *Anat* armpit **(b)** *Bot* axilla

A.I.T.A. [aitea] *nf* (*abrév* **Association internationale des transports aériens**) IATA

Aix-la-Chapelle [ɛkslaʃapɛl] *nf* Aachen, Aix-la-Chapelle

ajiste [aʒist] *n* (youth) hosteller

ajointer [aʒwɛ̃te] *vt* to join up; (*planches, tuyaux etc*) to fit end to end

ajonc [aʒɔ̃] *nm* (*plante*) furze, gorse

ajour [aʒur] *nm* (*laissant passer la lumière*) opening, hole, orifice; (*en sculpture etc*) (ornamental) perforation, openwork; *Couture* **ajours** hemstitching; (*dans une dentelle etc*) openwork

ajouré [aʒure] *adj* perforated; (*motif*) openwork; **travail a.** *Menuis* fretwork; *Couture* drawn-thread work

ajourer [aʒure] *vt* **(a)** (*pour laisser passer la lumière*) to pierce an opening; **a. une mansarde** to make a window in an attic **(b)** (*d'un ornement*) to perforate, to pierce; *Couture* to hemstitch

ajournement [aʒurnəmɑ̃] *nm* **(a)** (*d'une réunion*) postponement; (*après le début de la séance*) adjournment; *Scol* (*d'un* *candidat*) referring; *Mil* (*d'un conscrit*) deferment **(b)** *Jur* writ of summons (to appear), subpoena

ajourner [aʒurne] *vt* **(a)** (*réunion, décision, voyage etc*) to postpone, to put off, to defer; (*après le début de la séance*) to adjourn; (*projet*) to delay; *Pol* (*projet de loi*) to table; *Scol* (*candidat*) to refer; *Mil* (*conscrit*) to grant deferment to **(b)** *Jur* (*qn*) to subpoena

ajout [aʒu] *nm* (*à un texte*) addition; (*à un bâtiment*) extension; *Mktg* **a. à la gamme** range addition; *Mktg* **a. à la ligne** line addition

ajouté [aʒute] *nm* (*à un manuscrit, un contrat*) addition

ajouter [aʒute] **1** *vt* **(a)** to add; *Ordinat* (*à une base de données*) to append; **a. qch à qch** to add sth to sth; **sans a. que** ... not to mention the fact that ...; **a. aux embarras de qn** to add to sb's difficulties; **'venez aussi,' ajouta-t-il** 'you come too,' he added; **nous devons a. que** ... it should also be stated that ...; **je dois a. qu'il m'a été très utile** I must add *or* I must also say that he has been very useful to me

(b) a. foi à qch to believe sth, to have faith in sth

2 *vi* **ajouter à** to add to

3 s'ajouter *vpr* to be added (**à** to); **à ceci viennent s'a. les frais de déplacement** on top of this there are travel expenses (to be added)

ajustable [aʒystabl] *adj* adjustable

ajustage [aʒystaʒ] *nm* **(a)** (*d'une robe etc*) fitting **(b)** (*d'une machine*) assembly; **atelier d'a.** fitting shop; **a. mécanique** machining **(c)** fit; **a. serré** tight fit; **a. lâche** *ou* **à jeu** loose fit

ajustement [aʒystəmɑ̃] *nm* **(a)** (*d'un appareil, des prix etc*) adjusting, adjustment; (*fait de régler*) arrangement; **a. des salaires** wage adjustment; *Com* **a. fret** bunker adjustment factor; *Mktg* **a. stratégique** strategic *or* marketing fit **(b)** **ajustements** fittings

ajuster [aʒyste] **1** *vt* **(a)** (*appareil, outil*) to adjust; (*monter*) (*machine*) to set up; (*pièce*) to gauge; **nous ajustons la moquette aux dimensions de la pièce** we're altering the carpet to fit the dimensions of the room; **a. son fusil** to aim one's gun; **feu bien ajusté** well aimed fire; **a. son coup** to have a precise target (in mind); **a. qch à qch** to fit *or* adjust *or* adapt sth to sth; *Couture* **a. un vêtement à qn** to fit a garment on sb; **on a fait a. la veste à la taille de ma sœur** we had the jacket altered to fit my sister; **veste (bien) ajustée** close- *or* tight-fitting jacket; **a. son chapeau devant le miroir** to adjust one's hat in front of the mirror; *F* **comme vous voilà ajusté!** what a sight you look!

(b) (*mettre au point*) to put right *or* straight; **a. la théorie à la pratique** to adapt the theory to the practice

2 s'ajuster *vpr* **(a)** (*de personne*) to straighten one's clothes, to tidy oneself up

(b) l'embout s'ajuste sur le tuyau the nozzle fits the pipe; **cette clef s'ajuste à chacune des serrures** this key fits each of the locks

ajusteur [aʒystœr] *nm* **a. sur métaux, a. mécanicien** (metal) fitter, filer, bench hand; **a. de tubes (de chaudières)** tube setter

alacrité [alakrite] *nf Litt* liveliness, alacrity

Aladin [aladɛ̃] *nm* Aladdin

alaire [alɛr] *adj Av* **charge a.** wing load(ing); **surface a.** wing area

alaise [alɛz] *nf* drawsheet

alambic [alɑ̃bik] *nm Ch, Ind* still; **passer qch par** *ou* **à l'a.** to distil *or US* distill sth

alambiqué [alɑ̃bike] *adj* (*texte*) abstruse, overcomplicated; (*esprit*) oversubtle; (*explication, système etc*) convoluted, involved

alangui [alɑ̃gi] *adj* languid

alanguir [alɑ̃gir] **1** *vt* to make languid; (*affaiblir*) to enfeeble, to make feeble; **la chaleur alanguit les ouvriers** the heat is making the workers lethargic *or* listless **2 s'alanguir** *vpr* to grow languid, to flag, to droop, to wilt

alanguissement [alɑ̃gismɑ̃] *nm* languor

alarmant [alarmɑ̃] *adj* alarming, frightening; **son état est a.** his condition is giving serious cause for concern

alarme [alarm] *nf* (*alerte*) alarm; **donner/sonner l'a.** to give/sound the alarm; **signal d'a.** alarm; *Rail* **tirer la sonnette d'a.** to pull the communication cord; *Fig* **prendre l'a.** to take fright; *Fig* **à la prochaine a. il faudra vous amener à l'hôpital** if there's another scare *or* alarm you'll have to be taken to hospital; *Fig* **une fausse a.** a false alarm; **état d'a.** state of alarm

▸ **alarme**: **a. antivol** anti-theft alarm; **a. incendie** fire alarm; **a. lumineuse** warning light; *Aut* **a. d'oubli des feux** lights-on warning buzzer; *Aut* **a. périmétrique** perimeter alarm; **a. sonore** beep; **a. télécommandée** remote-control alarm; **a. à ultrasons** ultrasonic alarm

alarmer [alarme] **1** *vt* to alarm, to frighten; (*d'un bruit*) to startle; **la nouvelle ne nous a pas alarmés** we were not alarmed at *or* by the news **2 s'alarmer** *vpr* to take fright; **il s'alarme pour un rien** the least thing frightens him; **il n'y a pas lieu de s'a.** there is no cause for alarm *or* concern

alarmisme [alarmism] *nm* alarmism

alarmiste [alarmist] **1** *adj* alarmist; **la presse a.** the sensational press **2** *n* alarmist

Alaska [alaska] *nm* Alaska; **en A.** in Alaska

albanais, -aise [albanɛ, -ɛz] **1** *adj* Albanian **2** *nm Ling* Albanian **3** *n* **A.** Albanian

Albanie [albani] *nf* Albania

albâtre [albɑtr] *nm* alabaster; **peau d'a.** alabaster skin, skin like alabaster

albatros [albatrɔs] *nm* (*oiseau*) albatross

albigeois, -oise [albiʒwa, -waz] *npl Hist* **les A.** the Albigenses, the Albigensians

albinisme [albinism] *nm* albinism

albinos [albinos] **1** *adj inv* albino; **un lapin a.** an albino rabbit **2** *n inv* albino

Albion [albjɔ̃] *nf Hist* Albion, Britain; *Litt* **la perfide A.** perfidious Albion

album [albɔm] *nm Phot, Mus etc* album; **a. de timbres/de photos** stamp/photo album

albumen [albymɛn] *nm Biol* albumen

albumine [albymin] *nf Ch* albumin

alcali [alkali] *nm Ch* alkali

alcalin, -ine [alkalɛ̃, -in] *adj Ch* alkaline

alcaloïde [alkalɔid] *nm Ch* alkaloid

alchimie [alʃimi] *nf* alchemy

alchimiste [alʃimist] *nm* alchemist

alcool [alkɔl] *nm* **(a)** alcohol; **lampe à a.** spirit lamp, *US* alcohol lamp **(b)** (*boisson*) alcohol; (*whisky, eau-de-vie etc*) spirits, hard liquor, *F* the hard stuff; **je ne bois jamais d'a.** (*de liqueurs etc*) I never drink spirits; (*rien d'alcoolisé*) I don't drink (anything alcoholic); **il ne tient pas l'a.** he can't hold his drink; **l'a. au volant accroît considérablement les risques d'accidents** drink-driving greatly increases the risk of accidents; **a. de poire** pear brandy; **vous prendrez bien un petit a.?** would you like a liqueur or a brandy or something?

▸ **alcool**: **a. à 90°** = surgical spirit, *US* rubbing alcohol; **a. absolu** pure *or* absolute alcohol; **a. blanc** (*kirsch etc*) clear spirits; **a. à brûler** methylated spirits; *Ind* **a. dénaturé** methylated spirits; **a. éthylique** ethyl alcohol

alcoolémie [alkɔlemi] *nf Méd* presence of alcohol in the blood; **taux d'a.** level of alcohol in the blood

alcoolique [alkɔlik] **1** *adj* alcoholic **2** *n* alcoholic; **être un a.** to be an alcoholic

alcoolisation [alkɔlizasjɔ̃] *nf* alcoholization

alcoolisé [alkɔlize] *adj* (*boisson*) alcoholic

alcooliser [alkɔlize] **1** *vt* (*vin*) to fortify **2 s'alcooliser** *vpr* to drink too much, to get drunk

alcoolisme [alkɔlism] *nm* alcoholism

alco(o)lo [alkɔlo] *n F* alcoholic, drunk

alcoomètre [alkɔmɛtr] *nm* alcohol(o)meter

alcootest [alkɔtest] *nm* breathalyser test; **faire passer** *ou* **subir un a. à un conducteur** to breathalyze *or* breath-test a motorist

alcôve [alkov] *nf* alcove; **a. de dortoir** cubicle; **secrets d'a.** pillow talk

aldéhyde [aldeid] *nm Ch* aldehyde; **a. formique** formaldehyde

al dente [aldɛnte] *adj Culin* (*pâtes*) al dente

aldin [aldɛ̃] *adj Typ* (*édition, caractère*) Aldine

ale [ɛl] *nf* (light) ale

aléa [alea] *nm* risk, hazard, chance; **l'affaire présente trop d'aléas** it's too risky a business; **les aléas de la vie** the hazards of life

aléatoire [aleatwar] *adj* (*échantillon*) random; (*résultat*) unpredictable, chancy, uncertain; *Jur* (*contrat etc*) aleatory; *Math* **fonction/variable a.** random function/variable; *Ordinat* **accès a.** random access

alémanique [alemanik] *adj Ling* **Suisse a.** German-speaking Switzerland

alêne [alɛn] *nf* awl; **a. plate** bradawl

alentour [alɑ̃tur] **1** *adv* around, round about; **les villages a.** the surrounding *or* neighbouring villages; **le pays d'a.** the surrounding *or* neighbouring countryside **2** *nmpl* **alentours** surroundings, vicinity; **aux alentours de la ville/300F** in the vicinity of the town/300 francs; **il n'y avait personne aux alentours** there was no-one around *or* in the vicinity; **il est arrivé aux alentours de midi** he arrived (some time) around mid-day

aléoute [aleut], **aléoutien, -ienne** [aleusjɛ̃, -jɛn] **1** *adj* Aleutian; **les (îles) Aléoutiennes** the Aleutian Islands **2** *n* **A.** Aleut(ian)

alerte [alɛrt] **1** *nf* alarm; **donner/sonner l'a.** to give/sound the alarm; **fausse a.** false alarm; **a. (aérienne)** air-raid warning;

à la première a. as soon as the alarm goes; **en cas d'a.** if the alarm sounds; **état d'a.** state of alert; **l'état d'a. est déclaré** a state of alert has been declared; **être en a.** to be on the alert; *Mil* **fin d'a.** all clear; *Av* **a. en piste** scramble; **côte d'a.** danger level; **l'a. fut chaude** it was a narrow escape; *Méd* **nous avions eu une a. en septembre** we had a warning sign *or* a scare in September

2 *adj* **(a)** alert; (*promenade*) brisk; (*personne*) sprightly, alert; **style a.** (*écrit*) lively style; **il est paralysé mais son esprit est très a.** he's paralysed but his mind is (still) very alert

(b) *Arch* vigilant, watchful

3 *int* look out! *Arch* to arms!

▶ **alerte: a. à la bombe** bomb scare; **a. rouge** red alert

alerter [alɛrte] *vt* (*troupes, opinion publique etc*) to alert; **a. qn sur qch** to alert sb to sth

alésage [alezaʒ] *nm Métal* **(a)** (*opération*) boring (out); (*d'un cylindre*) reaming **(b)** (*diamètre*) (*d'un canon de fusil*) bore; (*d'un moteur à combustion*) bore; (*d'un cylindre etc*) internal diameter

alèse [alɛz] *nf Méd* drawsheet, undersheet

aléser [aleze] *vt Métal* to bore (out); (*élargir*) to ream

aléseuse [alezøz] *nf Métal* borer; (*pour élargir*) reamer

alester [alɛste], **alestir** [alɛstir] *vt Naut* (*gréement*) to trim up, to tidy up

alevin [alvɛ̃] *nm* alevin, fry, young fish

alevinage [alvinaʒ] *nm* (*d'une rivière etc*) stocking with young fish

aleviner [alvine] *vt* to stock a river with young fish

alevinier [alvinje] *nm*, **alevinière** [alvinjɛr] *nf* breeding pond, nursery

Alexandrie [alɛksɑ̃dri] *nf* Alexandria

alexandrin, -ine [alɛksɑdrɛ̃, -in] **1** *adj* **(a)** *Littér* alexandrine; **poème en vers alexandrins** poem in alexandrine verse *or* in alexandrines **(b)** *Géog* Alexandrian; *Fig* **des discussions alexandrines** convoluted discussions **2** *nm Littér* alexandrine (verse)

alexie [alɛksi] *nf Méd* word blindness, alexia

alezan, -ane [alzɑ̃, -an] **1** *adj* (*cheval*) chestnut **2** *nm* **a. châtain** chestnut sorrel; **a. roux** red bay

alfa [alfa] *nm Bot* esparto (grass); **papier d'a.** esparto paper; **tiré sur a.** printed on esparto paper

algarade [algarad] *nf* row, quarrel; **nous avons eu une a.** we've had a row

algèbre [alʒɛbr] *nf* algebra; **a. booléenne** Boolean algebra; **résoudre un problème par l'a.** to solve a problem algebraically; *Fig* **c'est de l'a. pour moi** it's all Greek to me

algébrique [alʒebrik] *adj* algebraic

Alger [alʒe] *nf* Algiers; *Hist* (the Department of) Alger

Algérie [alʒeri] *nf* Algeria; **en A.** in Algeria

algérien, -ienne [alʒerjɛ̃, -jɛn] **1** *adj* Algerian **2** *n* **A.** Algerian

algérois, -oise [alʒerwa, -waz] **1** *adj* of *or* from Algiers **2** *n* **A.** inhabitant *or* native of Algiers

algie [alʒi] *nf* ache, pain

algol [algɔl] *nm Ordinat* ALGOL

algonkien, -ienne [algɔ̃kjɛ̃, -jɛn] *Géol* **1** *adj* Algonkian **2** *nm* Algonkian

Algonquin, -ine [algɔ̃kɛ̃, -in] **1** *adj* (*peuple*) Algonquin **2** *nm Ling* Algonquian **3** *n* Algonquin

algorithme [algɔritm] *nm Math, Ordinat* algorithm; *Ordinat* **a. de chiffrement** coding *or* encryption algorithm; *Ordinat* **a. de tri** sorting algorithm

algorithmique [algɔritmik] *adj Math, Ordinat* algorithmic

algue [alg] *nf* **algues** seaweed, *Spéc* algae

alias [aljɑs] *adv* alias, otherwise *or* also known as; *Ordinat* alias; **Joe Balance, a. le Braqueur** Joe Balance, alias *or* a. k. a. the Robber

alibi [alibi] *nm* alibi; **il a invoqué un a. absurde pour justifier son absence** he gave an absurd alibi to explain his absence

aliénable [aljenabl] *adj Jur* alienable, transferable

aliénant [aljenɑ̃] *adj* alienating

aliénation [aljenasjɔ̃] *nf* **(a)** (*de l'esprit*) alienation; **conditions d'a.** alienating conditions; *Psy* **a. mentale** insanity **(b)** *Jur* (*des droits, de biens etc*) alienation, transfer; (*de liberté*) loss

aliéné, -ée [aljene] *Psy* **1** *adj* mad, insane **2** *n* insane person; **les aliénés** the insane; **hospice d'aliénés** mental hospital

aliéner [aljene] **(j'aliène; n. aliénerons) 1** *vt* **(a)** (*sentiments etc*) to alienate, to estrange; **ce commentaire vous a aliéné la sympathie de l'auditoire** that comment lost you the audience's sympathy; **ces conditions de vie ne peuvent qu'a. les jeunes** such living conditions can only alienate young people

(b) *Jur* (*biens, droits etc*) to alienate, to transfer; **a. sa liberté** to give up one's freedom

(c) (*psychisme*) to derange, to unhinge

2 s'aliéner *vpr* (*qch*) to lose; (*qn*) to alienate (oneself from); **s'a. la sympathie de l'électorat** to lose the goodwill of the electorate; **s'a. un ami** to alienate a friend; **s'a. l'amitié de qn** to lose sb's friendship; **s'a. par le travail** to be alienated by work

aliéniste [aljenist] *n Méd* alienist

alignement [aliŋ(ə)mɑ̃] *nm* **(a)** (*opération*) alignment, aligning; *Mil* (*d'une ligne*) dressing; *Compta* (*d'un compte etc*) making up, balancing; (*de son, image*) tracking; **être dans l'a.** to be in a line; **maison frappée d'a.** house scheduled for realignment; **se mettre à l'a.** to fall into line, to line up; *Mil* **à droite a.!** right dress!; *Écon* **a. monétaire** alignment of currencies; *Com* **a. des prix** alignment of prices, price alignment; *Pol* **l'a. du parti sur la politique de l'URSS** the party's alignment with the policy of the USSR

(b) (*d'un mur etc*) alignment, line; **un a. de menhirs** a line of menhirs; *Constr* **déborder** *ou* **dépasser l'a.** to project beyond the building line; **prendre des alignements** to get one's bearings

(c) *Rail* (*ligne droite*) straight stretch

aligner [aliɲe] **1** *vt* **(a)** (*mettre en ligne*) to align, to line up, to put in a line; (*arranger*) to lay out; *Mil* to dress (a line); *Compta* (*compte*) to balance; **a. un terrain** to mark out a plot (of ground); *Typ* **a. des caractères** to align *or* range type; *Pol* **a. sa politique sur celle des États voisins** to fall into line with the policy of neighbouring states; *Econ* **a. une monnaie** to align a currency

(b) (*dire, faire à la suite*) (*arguments*) to marshal; **a. des phrases** to string sentences together; **je passe ma journée à a. des chiffres** I spend my day producing lists of figures; *F* **les a.** (*payer*) to pay out, to cough up

2 s'aligner *vpr* (*d'une politique, d'une action*) (*sur qch*) to be in line with sth; (*d'un pays, d'une personne*) to fall into line; *Mil* to dress; **les enfants s'alignent dans la cour** the children are lining up in the playground; *Pol* **la Hongrie s'alignait sur l'URSS** Hungary used to follow the Soviet line; *Arg* **tu peux toujours t'a.!** (*tu n'es pas à la hauteur*) just you try it!

aliment [alimɑ̃] *nm* **(a)** food; **a. pauvre/riche** food that is low/high in nutritional value; **des aliments en conserve/surgelés** tinned/frozen food; **a. périssable** perishable food; *Physiol* **a. complet** complete food; *Fig* **cette histoire a servi d'a. à la presse** the press made a meal out of the story **(b)** *Jur* **aliments** alimony

alimentaire [alimɑ̃tɛr] *adj* **(a)** (*denrée, plante etc*) nutritious; **produits alimentaires** food, foodstuffs; **conserves alimentaires** tinned *or* canned food(s); **régime a.** diet; *Admin, Hist* **carte a.** ration card; **surveiller son bol a.** to watch what one eats; **mauvaises habitudes alimentaires** bad eating habits

(b) *Jur* **pension** *ou* **provision a.** alimony, maintenance; **payer** *ou* **verser une pension a.** to pay alimony *or* maintenance; **il est en retard dans le paiement de la pension a.** he's late with his *or* the alimony; *Fig* **travail** *ou* **occupation a.** job that keeps body and soul together

(c) *Physiol* **canal** *ou* **tube a.** alimentary canal; **pompe a.** feed pump

alimentation [alimɑ̃tasjɔ̃] *nf* **(a)** (*régime alimentaire*) food, nourishment; *Biol* nutrition; **avoir une a. équilibrée** to have a balanced diet; **a. défectueuse** malnutrition; **surveillez votre a.** watch what you eat, watch your diet; **article d'a.** foodstuff; **(magasin d')a.** grocer's shop; **(rayon d')a.** grocery department, food counter

(b) (*action*) (*de plantes, d'animaux etc*) feeding; (*de ville, de marché etc*) supply; **l'a. d'une ville en eau** the water supply to a town

(c) *Tech* (*d'une chaudière etc*) feed(ing); (*d'un fusil*) feed mechanism; (*en électricité*) power supply; **pompe d'a.** feed pump; **a. par pesanteur** *ou* **par gravité** gravity feed; *Aut* **a. par injection** fuel injection; *Él* **bloc d'a.** power supply; **câble** *ou* **fil d'a.** feeder; **a. papier** (*d'une imprimante*) sheetfeed, paper feed; **a. feuille à feuille** *ou* **page par page** (*d'une imprimante*) cut sheet *or* single sheet feed; *Ordinat* **a. ininterruptible** uninterruptible power supply

alimenter [alimɑ̃te] **1** *vt* (*qn*) to feed, to nourish; (*marché*) to supply with food; (*chaudière*) to feed; **ruisseaux qui alimentent une rivière** streams that feed a river; *Él* **a. une usine en courant** to supply a factory with power; *Fig* **a. la curiosité de qn** to feed sb's curiosity; *Fig* **a. la conversation par des anecdotes** to keep the conversation going with anecdotes; *Fig* **ces petits incidents risquent d'a. la discorde entre elles** these little incidents are likely to fuel the discord between them; **a. un compte** to pay money into an account

2 s'alimenter *vpr* to eat; (*d'un malade*) to take (solid) food

alinéa [alinea] *nm Typ* (**a**) (*renfoncement*) paragraph indent, indent; **mettre à l'a.** to indent; **a. négatif** hanging indent (**b**) (*texte*) paragraph, *F* para
alité [alite] *adj* confined to (one's) bed, *F* laid up; (*infirme*) bedridden
alitement [alitmɑ̃] *nm* confinement to bed; **trois jours d'a.** three days in bed
aliter [alite] **1** *vt* **a. qn** to confine sb to bed, to keep sb in bed **2 s'aliter** *vpr* (*se mettre au lit*) to take to one's bed; (*rester au lit*) to stay in bed
alizé [alize] *adj, nm* **les (vents) alizés** the trade winds
allaitant [alɛtɑ̃] *adj* suckling, nursing; **mère allaitante** nursing mother
allaitement [alɛtmɑ̃] *nm* feeding, nursing, suckling; **a. au biberon** bottle-feeding; **a. mixte** mixed feeding; **a. naturel** breast-feeding; **durant l'a.** during breast-feeding
allaiter [alete] *vt* (*enfant*) to breast-feed, to nurse; (*enfant, petit*) to suckle
allant [alɑ̃] **1** *adj* (*personne*) active, busy, lively; (*personne âgée*) active, mobile, able to move *or* walk about **2** *nm* initiative, drive, energy; **avoir de l'a., être plein d'a.** to be full of go *or* (drive and) energy; **elle travaille avec a.** she works energetically *or* with gusto
alléchant [aleʃɑ̃] *adj* (*offre, plat*) attractive, alluring, enticing, tempting; (*odeur etc*) appetizing
allécher [aleʃe] *vt* (**j'allèche, n. alléchons**; **j'allécherai**) to attract, to entice, to tempt, to allure; **j'étais alléché par cette proposition** I was tempted by the proposal
allée [ale] *nf* (**a**) (*dans un jardin, menant à une maison*) path; (*permettant le passage de voitures*) drive; (*entre deux immeubles*) passage, alley; (*dans une ville*) street, avenue; (*longée d'arbres*) walk; **a.** (**cavalière**) bridle path; **a. des Acacias** Acacia Avenue; **a. de circulation** (*d'un magasin*) aisle
(**b**) **allées et venues** coming(s) and going(s), running about; **j'ai dû faire de nombreuses allées et venues pour obtenir ce visa** I had to run all over the place to get this visa; **qu'est-ce que signifient ces allées et venues à cette heure tardive?** what's the meaning of all these comings and goings at this time of night?
allégation [alegasjɔ̃] *nf* allegation
allégé [aleʒe] *adj* (*beurre etc*) low-fat, diet; (*confiture etc*) low-sugar
allège [alɛʒ] *nf* (**a**) *Naut* lighter, hopper, barge; *Com* **frais d'a.** lighterage; **franco a.** free over side (**b**) (*de fenêtre*) window breast, (window) sill
allégeance¹ [aleʒɑ̃s] *nf* (**a**) (*nationalité*) nationality; **avoir la double a.** to have dual nationality (**b**) *Hist* **serment d'a.** oath of allegiance; **faire a. à ...** to pledge one's allegiance to ...
allégeance² *nf Sp* (*de bateaux*) handicapping
allégement [alɛʒmɑ̃] *nm* (**a**) (*d'impôts, charges etc*) reduction; **a. fiscal** tax relief (**b**) (*de véhicule, fardeau*) lightening
alléger [aleʒe] *vt* (**j'allège, n. allégeons**; **j'allégeai(s)**; **j'allégerai**) (**a**) (*impôts, charges etc*) to reduce; (*douleur, chagrin*) to alleviate, to relieve, to soothe (**b**) (*véhicule, fardeau etc*) to lighten; (*poutres de charpente etc*) to ease the strain on; *Scol* **a. un programme scolaire** to lighten a school syllabus (**c**) *Tech* (*qch*) to reduce the volume of; (*bois*) to plane down; (*métal*) to file down, to fine down
allégorie [alegɔri] *nf* allegory; **par a.** allegorically
allégorique [alegɔrik] *adj* allegorical
allégoriquement [alegɔrikmɑ̃] *adv* allegorically
allègre [alɛgr] *adj* lively, jolly, cheerful; (*musique*) lively; **parler d'un ton a.** to speak cheerfully *or* light-heartedly; **caractère a.** cheerful disposition; **avoir le cœur a.** to be light-hearted; **marcher d'un pas a.** to walk with a spring in one's step
allégrement [alɛgrəmɑ̃] *adv* cheerfully; *Iron* blithely; (*marcher*) with a spring in one's step; **il s'est a. moqué de nous** he has been quite blithely making fools of us
allégresse [alegrɛs] *nf* joy, cheerfulness, liveliness; **plein d'a.** full of joy; **a. générale** general rejoicing; **cris d'a.** cries of joy
allegretto [alegrɛtto] *adv, nm Mus* allegretto
allegro [alegro] *adv, nm Mus* allegro
alléguer [alege] *vt* (**j'allègue, n. alléguons**; **j'alléguerai**) (**a**) (*invoquer*) to allege, to plead; **a. l'ignorance** to plead ignorance; **a. une excuse/raison** to put forward *or* offer *or* give an excuse/reason; **a. comme raison que le temps manquait** to give lack of time as one's reason; **il allégua que personne ne l'avait informé de ce projet** he alleged that no-one had informed him of the plan (**b**) (*auteur, texte etc*) to cite, to quote
alléluia [aleluja] *int, nm Rel* alleluia, hallelujah
Allemagne [almaɲ] *nf* Germany; **l'A. de l'ouest/de l'est** West/East Germany; **les deux Allemagnes** the two Germanies; **l'ambassadeur d'A.** the German ambassador
allemand, -ande [almɑ̃, -ɑ̃d] **1** *adj* German; **la langue allemande** the German language, German **2** *nm Ling* German, the German language **3** *n* **A.** German; **A. de l'Est/de l'Ouest** East/West German **4** *nf Mus* **allemande** allemande
aller¹ [ale] **1** *vi* (*prp* **allant**; *pp* **allé**; *pr ind* **je vais,** (*Arch, Dial* **je vas**), **tu vas, il va, n. allons, v. allez, ils vont**; *pr sub* **j'aille, n. allions, ils aillent**; *imp* **va (vas-y), allons, allez**; *impf* **j'allais**; *p hist* **j'allai**; *fu* **j'irai**; *the aux is* **être**) (**a**) (*se rendre*) to go; **a. à Paris** to go to Paris; **navire allant à Bordeaux** ship bound for Bordeaux; **a. chez le coiffeur/médecin/au marché** to go to the hairdresser's/to the doctor/to the market; **a. en course/à la chasse/à la pêche/à cheval/en voiture/au galop/au trot** *voir ces mots*; **a. aux champignons** to go mushroom-picking; **on va sur Lyon** we're going to *or* as far as Lyons; **a. de ville en ville** to go from town to town; **a. devant/derrière/à côté de qn** to go in front of/behind/beside sb; **a. chez qn** to go to sb's house, to call on *or* visit sb, to go and see sb; **je vais chez lui pour dîner ce soir** I'm going to his house for dinner this evening; **je vais chez ma grand-mère quand je suis à Paris** I call on *or* visit my grandmother whenever I'm in Paris; **nous allons toujours chez Maxim's** we always go to Maxim's; **a. jusqu'à qch/qn** to go as far as sth/to go up to sb; **qui va là?** who goes there?; **ne faire qu'a. et venir** to be always on the go *or* on the move; **je n'ai fait qu'a. et venir ce matin pour obtenir les papiers** I did nothing but run all over the place this morning to get the papers; **je ne ferai qu'a. et revenir** I shall come straight back; **où allons-nous?** where are we going?; *Fig* (*qu'est-ce qu'on va devenir?*) what are things coming to?; **je suis allé aux nouvelles** I went to find out what was happening; **il va sur ses quarante ans** he is getting on for forty, he is nearly forty (years old); **il ira loin** he will go far *or* will distinguish himself; **insulter un agent de police? ça peut a. loin, ça** insulting a policeman can have serious consequences; **vous allez trop loin** you're going too far; **vous n'irez pas loin avec 50 francs** 50 francs won't get you very far, you won't get very far on 50 francs; **soyez tranquille, cela n'ira pas plus loin** don't worry, it won't go any further; **cette vieille voiture n'ira pas loin** this old car won't get very far; **a. jusqu'au bout** to see it through; (*avoir des rapports sexuels*) to go the whole way; **nous irons jusqu'au bout** we shall carry on to the end; **a. au fond des choses** to get to the bottom of things; **décontractez-vous, laissez-vous a.** relax, let yourself go; **il faut apprendre à laisser a. les choses** you must learn to let things take their course; **reprends-toi, tu ne dois pas te laisser a.** pull yourself together, you mustn't let yourself go; **se laisser a. à la tendresse/à de meilleurs sentiments** to give way to tenderness/better feelings; **sa remarque m'est allée droit au cœur** his remark went straight to my heart; **l'eau va jusqu'à la taille** the water is waist-deep; **l'eau lui allait jusqu'à la taille** the water came up to his waist; **ses cheveux vont jusqu'à la taille** her hair goes down to her waist, she has waist-length hair
(**b**) (*se déplacer*) to go, to move; (*à pied*) to walk; **on y va à pied** we're walking there; **a. en vélo/voiture/avion/bateau** to go by bike/car/plane/boat; **on va à la catastrophe** we're heading for disaster; **j'y suis allé très lentement** I went very slowly; **j'y suis allé en deux heures** it took me two hours to get there
(**c**) (*with adv*) **a. bon train** to go at a good pace; **a. grand train** to race along; **la voiture va vite** the car goes fast
(**d**) (*mener*) to lead, to go; **chemin qui va à la gare** road leading to the station; *Prov* **tous les chemins vont à Rome** all roads lead to Rome
(**e**) (*être conçu pour*) **ces ciseaux vont bien pour couper les roses** these scissors are good for cutting roses; **plat qui va au feu** *ou* **allant au feu** *ou* **au four** fireproof *or* ovenproof dish
(**f**) (*marcher*) (*bien, mal*) to go; **tout va bien** everything is going well *or* is fine; **tout va mal** things are going badly, things aren't going at all well; **non, ça ne va pas du tout** (*ce n'est pas ce que j'ai demandé*) no, that won't do at all; **ça va!** (*d'accord*) OK!; **ça va, ça va, on te pardonne** OK, OK, you're forgiven; *F* **non mais ça va pas (la tête)?!** are you crazy?!, what's wrong with you?!; **ça ira!** we'll/I'll/*etc* manage!; **ça va comme ça** it's all right *or* it's fine *or* that will do (as it is); **merci, ça va comme ça, j'ai eu assez à manger** that will do *or* that's fine, thanks, I've had enough to eat; **faire a.** to get by, to struggle along; **ça n'irait pas du tout** that would never do; **ça va a. mal si tu me mens** if you've been lying to me, there'll be trouble; **il y a quelque chose qui ne va pas**

there's something wrong; **tout a l'air d'aller bien entre eux** everything seems to be fine between them; **je vous en offre cent francs, ça va?** I'll give you 100 francs for it, OK?; **ça va tout seul** it's a piece of cake; **cela ne va pas tout seul** it's not (that) easy, it's not an easy job

(g) (*d'un appareil, d'une horloge etc*) to go, to work, to run; **la pendule va bien/mal** the clock is/isn't working (properly); **quand le bâtiment va, tout va** what's good for the construction industry is good for us all; **les affaires vont/ne vont pas** business is good/slack; **faire a. un commerce** to run a business; **tout va comme sur des roulettes** everything is going like clockwork

(h) (*être de la bonne taille etc*) to fit; **ce veston ne va pas bien** this jacket doesn't fit well

(i) (*tenir*) **c'est trop grand pour a. dans le panier** it's too big to go *or* get *or* fit into the basket; **je ne sais pas où vont les assiettes** I don't know where the plates go

(j) (*se porter*) **comment allez-vous?** how are you?; **je vais bien,** *F* **ça va** I'm well, I'm all right, I'm fine; **cela va mieux** I'm better; **cela ne va pas** I'm not feeling very well

(k) a. à qn (*de couleurs etc*) to suit sb; (*de vêtements*) to fit sb; (*de climat, de denrées*) to agree with sb; (*d'un projet etc*) to suit sb; **cela vous va comme un gant** (*d'une robe etc*) it fits you like a glove; (*d'une situation etc*) it suits you down to the ground; **cette robe te va mal** (*elle te grossit*) that dress doesn't suit you; **la chemise ne me va pas** (*elle est trop petite*) the shirt doesn't fit me; **ça me va!** (*d'accord*) agreed!, done!; **ça te va bien de me conseiller** you're a fine one to give me advice

(l) (*être assorti*) **a. avec qch** (*de couleurs etc*) to go well with sth, to match sth; **a. (bien) ensemble** to go well together; **chaussettes qui ne vont pas ensemble** odd socks

(m) (aller + *inf*) **a. voir qn** to go and *or* to see sb, to call on sb; **a. trouver qn** to go and find sb; **va voir si quelqu'un n'a pas sonné à la porte** go and see if that was someone ringing the doorbell; **a. se promener** to go for a walk; **va donc le lui dire!** go and tell him then!; **n'allez pas vous imaginer que ...** don't imagine that ..., don't go imagining that ..., don't get it into your head that ...; **allez donc savoir!** how are you (supposed) to know?; *F* **allez vous faire voir!** go to hell!

(n) (*used as an auxiliary*) to be going, to be about (to do sth); **il va s'en occuper** he is going to see about it, he'll deal with it; **je vais te dire quelque chose** let me tell you something; **je sais ce que tu vas me dire** I know what you're about to tell me; **il va venir** he'll be coming; **je vais devoir prendre une décision** I'm going to have to make a decision; **il va pouvoir acheter la voiture dont il rêve** he's going to be able to buy the car of his dreams; **elle allait tout avouer** she was about to confess everything; **sa santé va (en) empirant** his/her health is steadily deteriorating

(o) (*avec y*) **j'y vais!, on y va!** coming!; **j'y vais** (*ouvrir la porte*) I'll get it; **est-ce comme ça que vous y allez?** is that how you go about it *or* do it?; **allez-y doucement!** easy *or* gently (does it)!; **il y va fort** he's going a bit too far, he's going a bit over the top; **y a. de tout son cœur** to put one's heart and soul into it; **y a. carrément** *ou* **franchement** to make no bones about it; **vas-y, dis-moi ce que tu as à dire!** go on then, say what you've got to say!; **maintenant allons-y!** now (let's get down) to it!; **allons-y!** well, here goes!; **vas-y!/allez-y!** go!, on you go!; (*au travail etc*) get on with it!; (*pose-moi ces questions*) fire away!; *F* **y a. de qch** to lay *or* stake sth; **il y est allé de ses économies** he staked his savings; **y a. de son reste** to stake one's all; **y a. de sa personne** to take a hand in it oneself, *F* to do one's bit; **il y est allé de son histoire/sa petite chanson** he gave us his story/little song

(p) (*interjection*) **allons, dépêchez-vous!** come on, hurry up!; **allez, s'il te plaît, viens avec moi!** oh go on, come with me, please!; **allons donc!** (*c'est vrai?*) (well I) never!; **allez, je vous écoute** go ahead, I'm listening; **allez, c'est oublié** don't worry, it's all forgotten; **allons bon!** there now!; (*exprimant de l'irritation*) oh no!; **allons, sois un peu raisonnable!** come on now, be reasonable!; **allons, allons, calme-toi** come on now, calm down; **va pour une soirée au cinéma** OK then, a night out at the cinema it is; **allez, allez, débarrasse la table** come on *or* along (now), clear the table!; *F* **va donc, eh patate!** if you don't like it, you can lump it!; **va donc eh vieux crétin** get lost, you idiot!

2 s'en aller *vpr* (*pr ind* **je m'en vais**; *imp* **va-t'en, allons-nous-en, allez-vous-en, ne t'en va pas, ne nous en allons pas**; *perf* **je m'en suis allé(e)**, **nous nous en sommes allé(e)s) (a)** (*partir*) to go away, to leave; **les voisins s'en vont** the neighbours are moving; **s'en a. en vacances** to go away on holiday; **elle s'en est allée** *ou F* **s'est en allée assez satisfaite** she went away fairly satisfied; **allez-vous-en!** go away!; **allons-nous-en!** let's go!; **s'en aller en fumée** to go up in smoke; **à demain, je m'en vais** I'm off, see you tomorrow; **il faut que je m'en aille** I must be going; **ses forces s'en allaient** his strength was failing

(b) (*mourir*) to pass away, to die; **le malade s'en va** the patient is sinking (fast)

(c) (*disparaître*) **les taches ne veulent pas s'en a.** the stains won't come off *or* out

(d) (+ *inf*) **s'en a. faire qch** to go off and *or* to do sth; **je m'en vais lui dire ce que je pense** I'm going to tell him exactly what I think; **va-t-en voir si il ne ment pas!** how am I/are we/*etc* supposed to know if he's telling the truth or not!; **je m'en vais vous raconter ça** I'll tell you all about it

3 *v impers* **il va sans dire** *ou* **il va de soi que ...** it stands to reason *or* it goes without saying that ...; **il va sans dire qu'elle a refusé** it goes without saying that she refused, needless to say, she refused; **il en va de même pour lui/moi** it's the same with him/me; **il n'en va pas de même pour eux** things are different for them; **il en va de sa réputation** his reputation is at stake; **il y va de vingt mille francs** it's a matter of twenty thousand francs; **il y allait de sa vie** it was a matter of life and death (for him), his life was at stake; **il y va de sa place** his job is at stake; **il y va de votre santé** your health is at risk, you're risking your health

aller² *nm* going; (*d'un aller retour*) outward journey; **a. retour, voyage d'a. (et) retour** round trip, return journey, journey there and back; *Naut* voyage out and home; **billet a. retour** return ticket; *F* **un a.** a single ticket, *Am* a one-way ticket; **deux allers et un aller retour pour Marseille, s'il vous plaît** two singles and a return to Marseilles, please; **à l'a.** on the way there; **je me suis arrêté en route à l'a.** I stopped on my *or* the way (there); **cargaison d'a.** outward cargo; *Sp* **match a.** away match; **a. retour du piston** up and down stroke; *F* **si tu continues, tu vas recevoir un a. et retour dont tu te souviendras** if you carry on you'll get a clip round the ear that you won't forget in a hurry

allergène [alɛrʒɛn] *nm Méd* allergen

allergénique [alɛrʒenik] *adj Méd* allergenic

allergie [alɛrʒi] *nf Méd* allergy; **avoir** *ou* **faire une a. au poil de chat** to have an allergy *or* to be allergic to cat hair; *Fig* **elle a fini par faire** *ou* **avoir une véritable a. au travail** she eventually became completely allergic to work

allergique [alɛrʒik] *adj Méd* allergic **(à** to); *Fig* **il est a. aux maths** he's allergic to maths

allergologiste [alɛrgɔlɔʒist], **allergologue** [alɛrgɔlɔg] *n Méd* allergist

alliage [aljaʒ] *nm Métal* alloy; **sans a.** pure, unalloyed; *Fig* **un a. d'idées fausses** a mish-mash *or* hotchpotch of mistaken ideas

alliance [aljɑ̃s] *nf* **(a)** (*entente*) alliance; (*d'un couple*) marriage, union; **conclure une a.** to enter into *or* forge an alliance; **faire a. avec/contre qn** to ally *or* team up with/against sb; **entrer par a. dans une famille** to marry into a family; **faire a. avec une autre famille** to be joined to another family by marriage; **parent par a.** relation by marriage; **traité d'a.** treaty of alliance **(b)** (*bague*) wedding ring **(c)** (*combinaison*) (*de parfums etc*) combination; **une a. de termes très réussie** a very effective juxtaposition of terms

allié, -ée [alje] **1** *adj* **(a)** (*nation etc*) allied **(b)** (*dans une famille*) related by marriage; **être bien a.** to be well connected **2** *n* ally; (*de famille*) relation by marriage; (*moins précis*) family connection; **invitation lancée aux parents et alliés** invitation sent out to immediate family and close relatives; **il est d'accord avec nous, c'est un a.** he agrees with us, he's on our side; *Hist* **les Alliés** the Allies

allier [alje] (*impf & pr sub* **n. alliions, v. alliiez) 1** *vt* **(a)** (*unir*) to ally, to unite; **intérêts communs qui allient deux pays** common interests that unite two countries; **a. une famille à** *ou* **avec une autre** to unite one family with another by marriage

(b) (*métaux*) to alloy, to mix; (*couleurs*) to harmonize, to blend, to match; (*qualités, mots etc*) to combine **(à** with); **a. l'intelligence à la beauté** to combine intelligence and beauty

2 s'allier *vpr* **(a)** (*s'unir*) to form an alliance, to become allies, to ally **(avec qn** with sb); **s'a. à une famille** to marry into a family; **s'a. contre qch/qn** to unite against sth/sb

(b) (*de liquides*) to mix; (*de métaux*) to alloy; (*de couleurs*) to harmonize, to blend; (*de goûts, de qualités*) to combine

alligator [aligatɔr] *nm* alligator

allitératif, -ive [aliteratif, -iv] *adj* alliterative

allitération [aliterasjɔ̃] *nf* alliteration; **a. en s** alliteration of (the letter) s

allô, allo [alo] *int Tél* hello!
alloc [alɔk] *nf F* benefit
allocataire [alɔkatɛr] *n* beneficiary; (*à la sécurité sociale etc*) claimant, recipient
allocation [alɔkasjɔ̃] *nf* **(a)** (*d'argent, de terres, de marchandises etc*) allocation, granting; *Fin* (*de titres etc*) allotment **(b)** (*prestation financière*) allowance, grant; **elle touche les allocations (familiales)** she gets child benefit
▶ **allocation**: **a. (de) chômage** unemployment benefit; **a. (de) logement** housing benefit; **a. (de) maternité** maternity benefit; **allocations familiales** child benefit, family allowance(s), *US* dependents' allowances
allocution [alɔkysjɔ̃] *nf* **(a)** short speech, address; **prononcer une a.** to make a speech **(b)** *Rel, Jur* (*par un évêque, un juge aux jurés*) charge
allogène [alɔʒɛn] *adj* (*population etc*) non-indigenous, non-native
allogreffe [alɔgrɛf] *nf Chir* allograft, homograft
allonge [alɔ̃ʒ] *nf* **(a)** (*d'une table*) (extension) leaf; (*d'un tuyau, d'une cornue etc*) adaptor, lengthening tube; (*de machine*) coupling rod; **mettre une a. à qch** to put an extension to sth, to lengthen sth; **a. de tige** extension rod; **a. de boucher** meathook **(b)** *Boxe* reach; **il a une bonne a.** he has a long reach
allongé, -ée [alɔ̃ʒe] **1** *adj* long; (*forme, silhouette*) elongated; **avoir le visage allongé** to have a long face; *Méd* **les malades allongés** recumbent patients; *Anat* **la moelle allongée** the medulla oblongata; *Sp* **coup a.** follow through
2 *n Méd* recumbent patient
allongement [alɔ̃ʒmɑ̃] *nm* **(a)** (*d'un canal etc*) lengthening, extension; (*d'une robe*) lengthening; (*de métaux etc*) elongation, strain; *Mil* (*des tirs*) lifting **(b)** (*de temps*) protraction, extension; **a. de la journée de travail** lengthening *or* extension of the working day; **a. de l'espérance de vie des femmes** increase in women's life expectancy **(c)** *Av* (*des ailes*) aspect ratio
allonger [alɔ̃ʒe] **(j'allongeai(s); n. allongeons) 1** *vt* **(a)** (*rendre plus long*) to lengthen; (*forme, silhouette*) to elongate; (*vêtement*) to let down; *Mil* (*tirs*) to lift; **cette robe allonge votre silhouette** this dress makes you look taller; *Culin* **a. la sauce** to thin (down) the sauce; *Fig* to spin it out
(b) (*bras*) to stretch out; (*cou*) to crane; (*cordage etc*) to extend, to draw out; **a. le pas** to quicken one's pace *or* step(s); *Sp* **a. l'allure** to increase the pace
(c) a. un malade to lay a sick person down; *F* **a. qn** to knock sb down, to floor sb; **a. un coup à qn** to aim a blow at sb; *F* **je lui ai allongé une gifle dont il se souviendra** I gave him a slap he'll remember for a long time; *F* **a. l'argent** (*payer*) to hand over *or* fork out the money
(d) (*conversation, période, délai etc*) to protract, to prolong
2 s'allonger *vpr* **(a)** (*des jours etc*) to grow longer, to lengthen; (*d'un enfant*) to get taller, to grow; **elle a changé de corps, elle commence à s'a.** her body has changed, she's starting to stretch out
(b) (*se coucher*) to stretch (oneself) out, to lie down; *F* **s'a. (par terre)** (*tomber*) to fall flat on the ground, to come a cropper
3 *vi* to extend; *Sp* **le peloton des coureurs allonge derrière** the field is strung out behind; **les jours commencent à a.** the days are starting to get longer, the days are drawing out
allopathe [alɔpat] *Méd* **1** *adj* allopathic **2** *n* allopath, allopathist
allopathie [alɔpati] *nf Méd* allopathy
allouer [alwe] *vt Admin* (*salaire etc*) to award; (*actions, rations etc*) to allocate, to apportion; **on lui a alloué un délai supplémentaire de deux jours** he was granted *or* allowed a two-day extension; **a. une dépense/un budget** to allow *or* pass an item of expenditure/a budget; *Jur* **a. une somme à qn à titre de dommages-intérêts** to award sb damages; **pendant le temps alloué** (*faire qch*) within the allotted time, within the time allowed
allumage [alymaʒ] *nm* (*d'une lampe, d'un feu*) lighting; (*d'une lampe électrique*) switching on; (*d'un moteur à combustion*) ignition; (*d'une mine*) firing; *Aut* **a. par bobine batterie** battery-coil ignition; **a. par compression** compression ignition; **a. à déclenchement statique** breakerless ignition; **a. défectueux** misfiring; **a. électronique** electronic *or* breakerless ignition; **a. par magnéto haute tension** high-tension magneto ignition; **a. prématuré** pre-ignition; **a. sans rupteur** breakerless ignition; **a. à rupteur transistorisé** transistorized ignition; **a. statique** breakerless ignition; **a. transistorisé** transistorized ignition
allumé, -ée [alyme] **1** *adj* **(a)** alight, burning; (*d'un haut fourneau*) in blast **(b)** *F* (*ivre*) tiddly, tipsy **(c)** *F* (*dingue*) crazy, off one's head *or* rocker **2** *n F* nutcase, nutter
allume-cigare, *pl* **allume-cigares** [alymsigar] *nm* cigar lighter
allume-gaz [alymgaz] *nm inv* (*pour cuisinière*) gas lighter
allumer [alyme] **1** *vt* **(a)** (*lampe à pétrole, feu, pipe*) to light; (*lampe, télévision, électricité*) to switch on, to turn on; *Aut* to ignite; **tu pourrais a. la chambre?** could you switch on *or* turn on *or* put on the light in the bedroom?; **veux-tu a. la lumière?** will you switch on *or* turn on *or* put on the lights?; **a. une pompe** to prime a pump
(b) *Fig* (*passions, personnes*) to inflame, to excite, to stir up, to arouse; **a. l'imagination** to fire the imagination; **elle allume les hommes** she excites men, she turns men on; **se faire a.** (*séduire*) to get aroused, *F* to get turned on; (*reprendre*) to get a ticking *or* telling off
2 s'allumer *vpr* (*de la lumière*) to come on; *Fig* (*des yeux*) to light up; *Aut* to fire; **ça ne s'allume pas** the light's not working; **où est-ce que ça s'allume?** where does it switch *or* turn on?; **ça s'allume et ça s'éteint** the light's going on and off; **s'a. prématurément** (*d'un moteur*) to backfire
3 *vi* to switch on *or* turn on *or* put on the light(s)
allumette [alymɛt] *nf* **(a)** match; **a. de sûreté** safety match; **pochette/boîte d'allumettes** book/box of matches; **frotter une a.** to strike a match; *F* **des jambes comme des allumettes** legs like matchsticks **(b)** *Culin* **a. au fromage** cheese straw; **pommes allumettes** game chips
allumeur [alymœr] *nm* **(a)** (*appareil*) lighter, igniting device; (*de moteur*) distributor; *Aut* **allumeur-distributeur** distributor unit **(b)** *Arch* lighter, igniter; **a. de réverbère** lamplighter
allumeuse [alymøz] *nf F* (*femme séductrice*) tease
allure [alyr] *nf* **(a)** (*vitesse*) pace, speed; **marcher à (une) vive a.** to walk at a brisk pace; **à toute a.** at full *or* top speed; *Sp* at full stretch; **pleine a.** maximum speed
(b) (*démarche*) walk, gait; (*manière de se tenir*) bearing, appearance; **allures d'un cheval** paces of a horse; **cela lui donne une belle a.** that makes her look nice
(c) (*manière de se présenter*) manner; (*manière d'agir*) way(s) of doing things; (*d'une personne, d'événements etc*) appearance, look; **il prend** *ou* **se donne des allures de roi quand il est en visite** he acts *or* behaves like royalty when he's visiting; **elle/la voiture a de l'a.** she's/the car's got (real) style; **l'a. des affaires** the way things are going; **prendre bonne a.** to look promising, to look well
(d) (*d'un fourneau, d'un moteur etc*) working; **a. régulière** smooth running; **a. de marche** rating; **a. normale** normal speed; **a. économique de croisière** cruising speed
allusif, -ive [alyzif, -iv] *adj* allusive; **sois moins a.** be more specific!
allusion [alyzjɔ̃] *nf* allusion **(à** to); *Péj* innuendo; **faire a. à qn/qch** to refer to *or* to allude to *or* to make an allusion to sb/sth; **c'est à vous que s'adresse cette a.** that's a dig at you, that's meant for you; **cette a. m'échappe** I can't see what he's/she's/you're/*etc* getting at
allusivement [alyzivmɑ̃] *adv* allusively
alluvial, -iale, -iaux, -iales [alyvjal, -jo] *adj Géol* alluvial
alluvions [alyvjɔ̃] *nfpl Géol* alluvium
almanach [almana] *nm* (*calendrier*) almanac, yearbook
aloès [alɔɛs] *nm* (*plante*) aloe; *Pharm* **amer d'a.** bitter aloes
aloi [alwa] *nm* **(a)** (*de chose, de personnes*) **de bon a.** genuine; **une plaisanterie de mauvais a.** an unsavoury joke, a joke in bad taste; **des résultats de mauvais a.** unpromising results; **un succès de bon a.** a well-deserved *or* worthy success **(b)** (*titre*) = proportion of precious metal in an alloy
alopécie [alɔpesi] *nf Méd* alopecia
alors [alɔr] **1** *adv* **(a)** (*à cette époque-là*) (*dans le passé*) then, at that time, at the time; (*dans le futur*) then; **elle était a. institutrice** she was a teacher then *or* at the time; **a. nous nous marierons** then we'll get married; **que faisiez-vous a.?** what were you doing then *or* at the time?; **jusqu'a.** until then; **la vie d'a.** life then *or* in those days; **le ministre d'a.** the minister at the time, the then minister
(b) (*dans ce cas*) (well) then, in that case, in such a case; **s'il mourrait, a., elle devrait reprendre son travail** if he died, then she would have to go back to work; **a. vous viendrez?** well then, you're coming?; **et (puis) a.?, a. quoi?** and what then?; (*qu'est-ce que ça peut faire?*) so what?; *F* **non mais a., pour qui te prends-tu?** really!, just who do you think you are?; **je ne suis pas le banquier de tout le monde, non mais a.!** honestly! I'm not made of money, you know!; **a., tu viens?** are you coming then?; **merde a.!** shit!; **a., …** right …, now then …; **a. Sophie, tu es prête?** OK *or* right Sophie, are you ready?, are you ready then, Sophie
(c) (*donc*) therefore, so; **il n'était pas là, a. je suis revenu** he wasn't there, so I came back
2 *conj* **a. (même) que** (at the very time) when, even when; (*bien que*) even though; **vous économisez, a. qu'il faudrait**

dépenser you're saving, when you should be spending; **a. même que je le pourrais** even though I could
alouette [alwɛt] *nf* **(a)** *(oiseau)* lark; **a. des champs** skylark; **a. des bois** woodlark; **a. de mer** summer snipe, sea lark, dunlin **(b)** *Culin* **a. sans tête** veal olive
alourdi [alurdi] *adj* heavy, dull; **a. de sommeil** drowsy; **a. par le sommeil** heavy with sleep; **style a. par trop de tournures compliquées** style weighed down by too many complicated expressions; *Fin* **le marché est alourdi** the market is dull
alourdir [alurdir] **1** *vt (qch)* to make heavy; *(qn, qch)* to weigh down; *Fig (sens)* to dull; *(phrase)* to make cumbersome *or* unwieldy; **les abus de toutes sortes ont alourdi ses traits** overindulgence has thickened his features **2 s'alourdir** *vpr* to grow *or* become heavy
alourdissement [alurdismɑ̃] *nm* (process of) growing heavy; *(des membres etc)* growing heaviness; *(des sens)* dulling; **sensation d'a.** feeling of heaviness
aloyau, -aux [alwajo] *nm Culin (de bœuf)* sirloin; **bifteck d'a.** T-bone (steak)
alpaga [alpaga] *nm Zool, Tex* alpaca
alpage [alpaʒ] *nm (pâturage)* alp, mountain pasture; *(droit) (dans les pâturages)* right of pasture; *(saison)* = season spent by livestock in mountain pastures
alpaguer [alpage] *vt F* to nab, to collar; **se faire a. par la police** to get nabbed *or* collared by the police
alpe [alp] *nf* **(a)** *Région (pâturage)* alp, mountain pasture **(b)** **Les Alpes** the Alps; **les Alpes suisses** the Swiss Alps; **cor des Alpes** alpenhorn
alpestre [alpɛstr] *adj (paysage, climat etc)* alpine; **plante a.** alpine (plant)
alpha [alfa] *nm* **(a)** *(lettre de l'alphabet grec)* alpha; *Fig* **l'a. et l'oméga** Alpha and Omega, the beginning and the end; *Fig* **connaître l'a. et l'oméga de qch** to know sth from beginning to end **(b)** *(particule, rayons, radiation)* alpha
alphabet [alfabɛ] *nm* **(a)** alphabet; **apprendre son a. à un enfant** to teach a child the alphabet **(b)** *Scol* spelling book
alphabétique [alfabetik] *adj* alphabetical; **par ordre a.** in alphabetical order, alphabetically; **index a.** index in alphabetical order
alphabétiquement [alfabetikmɑ̃] *adv* alphabetically
alphabétisation [alfabetizasjɔ̃] *nm* **l'a. de la population** teaching the population to read and write; **taux d'a.** literacy rate
alphabétiser [alfabetize] *vt* to teach to read and write
alphanumérique [alfanymerik] *adj* alphanumeric
alphapage [alfapaʒ] *nm* bleeper
alpha-test *nm Ordinat* alphatest; **alpha-tests** alpha testing
alpin [alpɛ̃] *adj (plante, chasseurs)* alpine; **la chaîne alpine, le massif a.** the Alps; **ski a.** downhill skiing
alpinisme [alpinism] *nm Sp* mountaineering, climbing; **faire de l'a.,** to go mountaineering *or* climbing
alpiniste [alpinist] *n* mountaineer, climber
Alsace [alzas] *nf* Alsace
alsacien, -ienne [alzasjɛ̃, -jɛn] **1** *adj* from Alsace, Alsatian **2** *nm Ling* Alsatian (dialect) **3** *n* **A.** inhabitant of Alsace, Alsatian
altérable [alterabl] *adj* liable to deterioration; **marchandise a.** perishable goods
altéragène [alteraʒɛn] *adj (substance)* harmful to the environment, noxious
altérant [alterɑ̃] *adj* thirst-producing, thirst-making
altération [alterasjɔ̃] *nf* **(a)** change (for the worse); *(de la santé etc) (par un agent extérieur)* impairment; *(de denrées, de la santé etc)* deterioration; *Ordinat (de fichier)* corruption; **a. de la voix** breaking of the voice **(b)** *(falsification) (de monnaie, document etc)* falsification; *(de denrées)* adulteration; *(de texte)* garbling; *(de faits)* misrepresentation **(c)** *Mus* sharp/flat sign, inflection; *(dans le courant du morceau)* accidental **(d)** *(soif)* great thirst
altercation [altɛrkasjɔ̃] *nf* altercation, dispute; **avoir une a. avec qn** to have a quarrel *or* a row with sb
altéré [altere] *adj* **(a)** *(couleur)* faded; *(visage)* drawn, haggard; **voix altérée par l'émotion** voice strained *or* faltering with emotion; **les faits sont altérés** the facts have been distorted **(b)** *Ordinat* corrupt **(c)** *Litt (assoiffé)* thirsty; **a. de sang** thirsting for blood, bloodthirsty; **être a. de pouvoir** to thirst *or* hunger for power
alter ego [altɛrego] *nm inv* alter ego
altérer [altere] **(j'altère, n. altérons; j'altérerai) 1** *vt* **(a)** *(détériorer)* to change (for the worse); *(viande, vin; Fig tempérament)* to spoil, to taint; *(vin, alimentation)* to adulterate; *(santé)* to impair **(b)** *Ordinat* to corrupt **(c)** *(fausser) (qch)* to tamper with; *(document)* to falsify; *(texte, histoire)* to garble; *(monnaie)* to falsify; **a. la vérité** to twist the truth **(d)** *Mus* **a. une note** to inflect a note **(e) a. qn** to make sb thirsty **2 s'altérer** *vpr* to deteriorate; *(de couleurs)* to fade; *Ordinat* to go corrupt
altérité [alterite] *nf Phil* otherness
alternance [altɛrnɑ̃s] *nf* **(a)** *(des saisons, des feuilles etc)* alternation; **a. des cultures** crop rotation; **en a.** alternately; **nous venons en a. un jour sur deux** we come on alternate days **(b)** *Pol (des membres du gouvernement)* alternation **(c)** *Él* alternation; **redresseur à deux alternances** full-wave rectifier
alternateur [altɛrnatœr] *nm Él* alternating-current generator, alternator
alternatif, -ive [altɛrnatif, -iv] **1** *adj* **(a)** *(successif, périodique)* alternative **(b)** *Él (courant)* alternating; *(moteur, scie, mouvement)* reciprocating **(c)** *(projet, médecine etc)* alternative **2** *nf* **alternative (a)** *(succession)* alternation, succession; **des alternatives de lumière et d'obscurité** alternation(s) of light and shade **(b)** *(choix)* alternative, option, choice; **vous pouvez accepter ou refuser, voilà l'a.** take it or leave it, there's no other choice; **être dans une a.** to have to choose one way or the other; **l'a. verte** *ou* **écologique** the green alternative *or* option
alternativement [altɛrnativmɑ̃] *adv* alternately, in turn
alterne [altɛrn] *adj (feuilles, angles etc)* alternate
alterner [altɛrne] **1** *vi* **(a)** *(se succéder)* to alternate **(b)** *(avec qn)* to take turns, to take it in turns **(pour** to + *inf*); **ils alternent pour veiller** they take it in turns to sit up; **a. à la surveillance** to take (it in) turns to keep watch **2** *vt (cultures)* to rotate
altesse [altɛs] *nf* highness; **son A. impériale** his/her Imperial Highness
altier -ière [altje, -jɛr] *adj (ton, port)* haughty, proud, arrogant
altimètre [altimɛtr] *nm* altimeter, altitude indicator; *Av* **a. à contact** altitude switch
altiport [altipɔr] *nm* high altitude airport
altiste [altist] *nm Mus* viola player
altitraceur [altitrasœr] *nm* altitude recorder
altitude [altityd] *nf* altitude; **à basse/haute a.** at low/high altitude; **à cent mètres d'a.** at an altitude of 100 metres; **en a.** at (a high) altitude; *Av* **prendre de l'a.** to climb; **vol à haute a.** altitude flight; **a. limite** ceiling; *Méd* **cure d'a.** high-altitude treatment; **mal d'a.** altitude sickness; **ivresse d'a.** altitude narcosis
alto [alto] *nm Mus* **(a)** alto, counter-tenor (voice) **(b)** *(instrument à cordes)* viola; *(saxophone)* alto
altocumulus [altɔkymylys] *nm inv Météo* altocumulus
altostratus [altɔstratys] *nm inv Météo* altostratus
altruisme [altrɥism] *nm* altruism
altruiste [altrɥist] **1** *adj* altruistic **2** *n* altruist
altuglas® [altyglas] *nm* = thick form of Perspex®
alumine [alymin] *nf Ch* alumina, aluminium oxide
aluminé [alymine] *adj* aluminized
aluminium [alyminjɔm] *nm* aluminium, *Am* aluminum; **sulfate d'a.** aluminium sulphate
alun [alœ̃] *nm* alum; **pierre d'a.** styptic pencil
alunir [alynir] *vi* to land on the moon
alunissage [alynisaʒ] *nm* moon landing
alvéolaire [alveɔlɛr] *adj* cellular; *(motif)* honeycomb; *(nerf, veine, consonne)* alveolar
alvéole [alveɔl] *nm* **(a)** *(pulmonaire)* alveolus; *(de cire d'abeilles etc)* cell; *(d'un bureau etc)* pigeonhole; *(d'un revolver)* chamber; **alvéoles pulmonaires** alveoli of the lungs **(b)** *(de dent)* socket; *(de diamant)* socket, seat(ing) **(c)** *(de pierre etc)* cavity, pit; *Él* **alvéoles d'un grillage** interstices of an accumulator grid **(d)** *Mil* gun pit
alvéolé [alveɔle] *adj* honeycomb(ed), *Spéc* alveolate; **carton a.** corrugated cardboard
amabilité [amabilite] *nf* friendliness, amiability; *(bonté)* kindness; **dans un ton plein d'a.** in a friendly tone (of voice); **auriez-vous l'a. de me dire ...?** would you be good *or* kind enough to tell me ...?; **faites mes amabilités à ...** give my kindest regards to ...
amadou [amadu] *nm* tinder
amadouement [amadumɑ̃] *nm (fait d'enjôler)* wheedling, coaxing; *(apaisement)* softening
amadouer [amadwe] *vt (enjôler, gagner)* to coax, to wheedle, to persuade; *(apaiser)* to soften; **elle essaie de l'a. pour qu'il accepte** she's trying to coax *or* to wheedle him into accepting
amagnétique [amaɲetik] *adj* non-magnetic
amaigrir [amɛgrir] **1** *vt* **(a)** to make thin; **la maladie l'a amaigri** his illness has made him lose weight **(b)** *Agr (sol)* to impoverish **(c)** *Constr (colonne, poutre etc)* to thin down, to reduce **2 s'amaigrir** *vpr* to grow thin, to lose weight
amaigrissant [amɛgrisɑ̃] *adj (régime)* slimming

amaigrissement [amɛgrismɑ̃] *nm* **(a)** *(non volontaire)* weight loss, growing thin; *(volontaire)* slimming; **cure d'a.** slimming cure **(b)** *(dans l'épaisseur)* reducing; *(d'une poutre etc)* thinning down

amalgamation [amalgamasjɔ̃] *nf* amalgamation

amalgame [amalgam] *nm* **(a)** *(dentaire), Ch* amalgam; *Fig* confusion; **il est tentant de faire l'a. de ces deux idées** these two ideas are easily confused **(b)** *(alliage)* mixture

amalgamer [amalgame] **1** *vt* **(a)** *(or, argent, Él plaque de zinc)* to amalgamate **(b)** *(banques, sociétés etc)* to amalgamate, to merge; **il a tendance à a. les deux partis** *(il ne voit pas la différence)* he tends to get confused between the two parties; *(il les considère comme un seul parti)* he tends to think of the two parties as one **2 s'amalgamer** *vpr* to merge, to amalgamate

amande [amɑ̃d] *nf (fruit)* almond; *(dans un noyau d'abricot etc)* kernel; **amandes amères/douces** bitter/sweet almonds; **amandes pilées** ground almonds; **pâte d'amandes** almond paste; *Fig* **les yeux en a.** almond(-shaped) eyes

amandier [amɑ̃dje] *nm (arbre)* almond tree

amanite [amanit] *nf (champignon)* **a. phalloïde** death cap; **a. tue-mouches** fly agaric

amant, -ante [amɑ̃, -ɑ̃t] **1** *n* lover; **a. de la nature** nature-lover **2** *nm* lover; **prendre un a.** to take a lover

amarante [amarɑ̃t] *nf (fleur)* amarant(h); **a. commune** *ou* **à fleurs en queue** love-lies-bleeding

amariner [amarine] **1** *vt Naut* **(a)** *(navire ennemi)* to man **(b)** *(homme, équipage)* to accustom to life at sea **2 s'amariner** *vpr* to find *or* get one's sea legs

amarrage [amaraʒ] *nm Naut* **(a)** mooring, fastening; *(lieu)* berth, moorings; **droits d'a.** berthing dues **(b) faire un a. sur une corde** to lash a rope

amarre [amar] *nf* **(a)** (mooring) rope; *(d'avant)* painter; **navire sur ses amarres** ship at her moorings; **rompre ses amarres** *(d'un navire)* to break adrift, to break its moorings; **larguer les amarres** to cast off; *Fig* to break one's moorings **(b)** *(câble)* cable, hawser; **a. de retenue** guy

amarrer [amare] *vt Naut etc* **(a)** *(navire etc)* to make fast, to moor; **navire amarré à quai** boat berthed *or* lying at the quay **(b)** *(cordage, chaîne)* to make fast **(c)** *(haussières etc)* to seize, to lash

amaryllis [amarilis] *nf (fleur)* amaryllis; **a. belle-dame** belladonna lily

amas [ama] *nm* **(a)** *(tas)* heap, pile, accumulation; **des a. de glace** packs of ice; *Anat* **a. graisseux** lump of fat **(b)** *Astron* cluster, constellation; **a. globulaire** globular cluster **(c)** *(de cristal)* colony **(d)** *Min* lode

amasser [amase] **1** *vt* **(a)** *(amonceler)* to amass, to heap up, to pile up **(b)** *(de l'argent)* to hoard (up); **a. une belle somme** to amass a tidy sum **(c)** *(rassembler)* to collect; *(troupes etc)* to gather together **2 s'amasser** *vpr* to build up, to pile up; **une foule s'amassait** a crowd was gathering; **les preuves s'amassent contre vous** the evidence is building up *or* piling up against you

amateur [amatœr] *nm* **(a)** *(passionné)* lover; **a. de vieux meubles/de vieilles photos** lover of old furniture/ old photos; **a. d'art** art lover; **a. d'oiseaux** bird fancier; **édition d'a.** collector's *or* booklover's edition; **a. de cinéma** film buff; **être a. de qch** to be fond of *or* to have a taste for sth

(b) *(dans une vente)* bidder; **est-ce qu'il y a des amateurs?** any takers?

(c) *(non-professionnel)* amateur; **photographe/théâtre a.** amateur photographer/theatre; **elle joue bien pour un a.** she plays well for an amateur; *Sp* **championnat d'amateurs** amateur championship; **faire qch en a.** to do sth as a hobby, to dabble in sth; **il fait de la photo en a.** he's an amateur photographer; **travail d'a.** work done by an amateur; *Péj* amateurish work

amateurisme [amatœrism] *nm Sp etc* amateurism; *Péj* amateurishness, amateurism

amazone [amazon] *nf* **(a)** *Myth* Amazon **(b) l'A.** the (river) Amazon **(c)** *(cavalière)* horsewoman; **monter en a.** to ride side-saddle **(d)** *(jupe)* riding habit

Amazonie [amazɔni] *nf* Amazonia

ambages [ɑ̃baʒ] *nfpl (seulement dans l'expression)* **parler sans a.** to speak plainly, not to beat about the bush; **il me l'a dit sans ambages** he told me quite plainly *or* without beating about the bush

ambassade [ɑ̃basad] *nf* **(a)** *(mission)* embassy; *(moins importante)* mission; **envoyer une a. extraordinaire** to send a special mission; **être envoyé en a. auprès de qn** to be sent on a mission to sb **(b)** *(édifice)* embassy; *(personnel)* ambassador's staff, embassy; **l'a. de France/du Canada** the French/Canadian embassy; **a. de Tunisie en France** the Tunisian embassy in France; **obtenir une a.** to be appointed ambassador

ambassadeur [ɑ̃basadœr] *nm* ambassador; *(représentant)* envoy; **a. extraordinaire** ambassador extraordinary; **l'a. de Grande-Bretagne** the British ambassador; **a. auprès du roi/ de la reine d'Angleterre** Ambassador to *or* at the Court of St James; *Fig* **l'a. de la poésie indienne** the ambassador of Indian poetry; *Fig* **vous êtes les ambassadeurs de votre pays** you are ambassadors for your country

ambassadorial, -iale, -iaux, -iales [ɑ̃basadɔrjal, -jo] *adj* ambassadorial

ambassadrice [ɑ̃basadris] *nf* **(a)** *(diplomate)* (woman) ambassador; *Fig* ambassadress **(b)** *(femme de l'ambassadeur)* ambassador's wife

ambiance [ɑ̃bjɑ̃s] *nf (environnement)* surroundings, environment; *(atmosphère)* atmosphere, ambiance; **une a. de travail** a working atmosphere; **l'a. au travail** the atmosphere at work; **musique d'a.** atmospheric music; *Péj* Muzak®; **régulateur d'a.** thermostat; *Fin* **l'a. générale** the prevailing tone; *F* **il y a de l'a. ici** there's a cheerful *or* good atmosphere here; **il y a beaucoup d'a.** it's very lively, there's a very good atmosphere; **mettre de l'a.** to liven things up, to create a good atmosphere

ambiant [ɑ̃bjɑ̃] *adj (atmosphère etc)* surrounding; **milieu a.** environment; **température ambiante** room temperature; *Tech* ambient temperature

ambidextre [ɑ̃bidɛkstr] *adj* ambidextrous

ambigu, -uë [ɑ̃bigy] *adj* ambiguous

ambiguïté [ɑ̃bigɥite] *nf* ambiguity; **répondre sans a.** to give an unambiguous *or* unequivocal answer

ambigument [ɑ̃bigymɑ̃] *adv* ambiguously

ambitieusement [ɑ̃bisjøzmɑ̃] *adv* ambitiously; *Péj* pretentiously

ambitieux, -ieuse [ɑ̃bisjø, -jøz] **1** *adj* ambitious **2** *n* ambitious person; *Péj* careerist

ambition [ɑ̃bisjɔ̃] *nf* ambition **(de faire** to do); **elle manque d'a.** she lacks ambition; **être dévoré par l'a.** to be consumed with ambition; **un homme sans a.** an unambitious man; **mettre toute son a. à un travail** to put everything one has into a piece of work, *F* to give it one's all; **avoir de l'a.** to have ambition, to be ambitious

ambitionner [ɑ̃bisjɔne] *vt* to set one's heart on **(qch** sth; **de faire qch** doing sth)

ambivalence [ɑ̃bivalɑ̃s] *nf* ambivalence

ambivalent [ɑ̃bivalɑ̃] *adj* ambivalent

amble [ɑ̃bl] *nm Équitation* amble, pace, *US* single-foot; **a. rompu** rack; **aller l'a.** to amble

ambler [ɑ̃ble] *vi (d'un cheval etc)* to amble (along)

ambre [ɑ̃br] **1** *nm* **(a) a. gris** ambergris; **pomme d'a.** pomander **(b) a. jaune** (yellow) amber; **un collier en a.** an amber necklace **2** *adj inv* amber

ambré [ɑ̃bre] *adj* **(a)** perfumed with amber(gris) **(b)** amber-coloured, *US* -colored; *(complexion, couleur)* warm; **un vin a.** an amber-coloured wine

ambroisie [ɑ̃brwazi] *nf* ambrosia; *Fig* **c'est de l'a.!** it's like nectar!

ambulance [ɑ̃bylɑ̃s] *nf* ambulance

ambulancier, -ière [ɑ̃bylɑ̃sje, -jɛr] *n* ambulance man, ambulance woman; *(conducteur, -trice)* ambulance driver

ambulant [ɑ̃bylɑ̃] **1** *adj* itinerant, travelling; **épicier a.** mobile grocer; **comédiens ambulants** strolling players; **marchand a.** itinerant dealer, hawker; **cirque a.** travelling circus; *Méd* **érysipèle a.** migrant erysipelas; *F* **c'est un cadavre a.** he's a walking corpse, he looks like death warmed up; **c'est un dictionnaire a.** he's a walking dictionary **2** *nm Admin (de taxes, de douanes etc)* itinerant collector

ambulatoire [ɑ̃bylatwar] *adj* ambulatory; *Méd* **malade a.** out-patient; **(fièvre) typhoïde a.** ambulant typhoid; **traitement a.** outpatient treatment

âme [ɑm] *nf* **(a)** *Rel, Phil* soul; *(motif) (d'une entreprise)* inspiration, soul, life; **se donner corps et â. à qch** to give oneself body and soul to sth; **rendre l'â.** to give up the ghost; **de toute mon â.** with all my heart; **elle a l'â. d'une artiste** she has the soul of an artist; **il est peintre dans l'â.** he's a painter through and through *or* to the core; **il jouait de la flûte avec â.** he played the flute with great feeling; **une déclaration sans â.** an unfeeling *or* a soulless declaration; **Dieu ait son â.** God rest his soul; **les âmes en peine** the souls in Purgatory; **aller comme une â. en peine** to wander around like a lost soul; **avoir l'â. chevillée au corps** to have nine lives; **chercher la paix de l'â.** to seek spiritual peace; **â. sœur** kindred soul *or* spirit, soul mate; **en mon â. et conscience** to the best of my knowledge and belief; **cet homme est d'une grandeur d'â. extraordinaire** that man has an extraordinary nobility of spirit; **état d'â.** state of mind, mood; **elle était l'â. de notre organisation** she was the heart and soul of our organization

(**b**) (*personne*) **une bonne â.** a well-meaning person, a good soul; **ne pas rencontrer â. qui vive** not to meet a (living) soul; **un hameau de 50 âmes** a hamlet of some 50 inhabitants; *Iron* **il y a toujours de bonnes âmes pour conseiller quand c'est trop tard** there are always plenty of people ready with helpful advice when it's too late!; **c'est une â. généreuse** he has great generosity of spirit; **je connais quelques grandes âmes** I know a few high-minded people; **avoir charge d'âmes** *Rel* to have the cure of souls; (*d'enfants, de passagers etc*) to have lives in one's care

(**c**) (*d'un fusil, d'une pompe*) bore; (*d'une statue, d'un câble*) core; (*d'une poutre de bois ou métallique*) web; (*de rail*) centre rib; *Av* (*des ailes*) web; *Mus* (*d'un violon*) sound post

améliorable [ameljɔrabl] *adj* capable of being improved, improvable; **le système est a.** the system could be improved

améliorant [ameljɔrɑ̃] *adj Agr* **culture** *ou* **plante améliorante** cover crop

amélioration [ameljɔrasjɔ̃] *nf* (**a**) improvement, change for the better; **on note une nette a. dans les relations des deux pays** there has been a distinct improvement in the relations between the two countries; **l'a. de son état de santé** the improvement in his condition; **il y a de l'a.** there's some improvement; **il y a de l'a. dans les affaires** business is improving; **faire des améliorations dans qch** to make improvements to sth; **travaux d'a.** improvements; *Mktg* **a. du produit** product augmentation *or* improvement (**b**) *Jur* (*de biens etc*) appreciation

amélioré [ameljɔre] *adj* improved; (*modèle, version*) enhanced; **un petit mousseux a.** a very good quality sparkling wine

améliorer [ameljɔre] **1** *vt* (*propriété, sol, traduction etc*) to improve; (*service, chambre d'hôtel*) to upgrade; **a. son état** to improve one's situation **2 s'améliorer** *vpr* to get better, to improve; **sa santé/le temps s'améliore** his health/the weather is improving; **ça ne s'améliore pas** it's not getting any better

amen [amɛn] *nm inv* amen; *Fig* **il s'attend à ce que je dise a. à tout ce qu'il dit!** he expects me to agree with everything he says!

aménagement [amenaʒmɑ̃] *nm* (**a**) (*disposition*) arrangement, layout, *Can* **a. paysager** open-plan offices

(**b**) **aménagements** fittings, fixtures, installations; *Naut, Av* accommodation, berthing; **les nouveaux aménagements dans un quartier** new developments in a district

(**c**) (*action*) equipping, arranging; (*d'un navire*) fitting out; **a. d'une usine** equipping *or* fitting out of a factory

(**d**) *Écon, Admin* **a. urbain et rural** town and country planning; *Écon, Admin* **a. du territoire** regional development, physical planning; **a. forestier** forest management

(**e**) (*amendement*) adjustment; **un a. dans un contrat** an adjustment to a contract; **a. fiscal** tax adjustment

(**f**) *Ordinat* housekeeping

aménager [amenaʒe] *vt* (**j'aménageai(s); n. aménageons**) (**a**) (*maison, navire etc*) to fit out; **étable aménagée** converted cowshed; **a. une cuisine en salle à manger** to convert a kitchen into a dining-room; **a. une douche dans une salle de gymnastique** to install a shower in a gymnasium; **route aménagée** made-up road; **a. un emploi du temps** to adjust a timetable (**b**) (*ville*) to plan; (*approvisionnement etc*) to divide, to distribute; **a. une forêt** to manage a forest

amende [amɑ̃d] *nf* (**a**) fine, penalty; **mettre une a. à qn** to fine sb; **être condamné à l'a.** *ou* **à une a.** to be fined; *F* **mettre qn à l'a.** to fine sb; **200F d'a.** a 200 franc fine; **défense d'entrer sous peine d'a.** trespassers will be prosecuted; **a. fiscale** tax penalty; **a. pour stationnement interdit** parking fine; **a. immédiate** on-the-spot fine (**b**) **faire a. honorable** to make amends

amendement [amɑ̃dmɑ̃] *nm* (**a**) (*du sol etc*) improvement (**b**) (*engrais*) (soil) conditioner (**c**) *Pol* (*à un projet de loi etc*) amendment; (*clause*) additional clause

amender [amɑ̃de] **1** *vt* (**a**) to make better; (*sol etc*) to improve (**b**) *Pol etc* (*projet de loi etc*) to amend **2 s'amender** *vpr* to turn over a new leaf

amène [amɛn] *adj* pleasing, agreeable; **peu a.** unpleasant, disagreeable

amenée [amne] *nf* (**a**) **tuyau** *ou* **conduite d'a.** *Constr* branch pipe; (*d'eau*) supply pipe; *Él* lead (**b**) (*d'air*) inlet, intake

amener [amne] (**j'amène, n. amenons; j'amènerai**) **1** *vt* (**a**) (*qn*) to bring; *Mil* (*réserves etc*) to bring up; (*eau, gaz etc*) to lay on; **amenez votre ami/chien avec vous** bring your friend/dog (with you); **quel bon vent vous amène?** what brings you here?; **les oléoducs amènent le pétrole à la raffinerie** the pipelines carry the oil to the refinery; *Culin* **a. l'eau à ébullition** to bring the water to the boil; **a. qn à faire qch** to get *or* induce sb to do sth; **et ceci nous amène à parler de la ponctualité** which brings us to the question of punctuality; **a. qn à son opinion** to bring sb round to one's point of view; **a. un sujet** to bring up *or* raise a subject; **a. la conversation sur un sujet** to bring the conversation round to a subject; **un bon auteur sait a. le dénouement de son récit** a good author knows how to bring his story to a conclusion; **a. une querelle** to bring about *or* lead to a quarrel; **a. une mode** to bring in a fashion

(**b**) *Naut* (*signal*) to haul down; (*couleurs*) to strike; (*bateau, drapeau, voile*) to lower

(**c**) (*tirer à soi*) to draw in, to bring in; **le pêcheur amène les filets** the fisherman draws in the nets

2 s'amener *vpr F* to turn up; **amène-toi ici!** come (over) here!

aménité [amenite] *nf* (**a**) (*de manières, d'un accueil etc*) charm, graciousness; (*de style*) charm, grace; **nous avons été traités sans a.** we were treated ungraciously (**b**) *Iron* **aménités** insults, uncomplimentary remarks

aménorrhée [amenɔre] *nf Méd* amenorrhoea

amenuisement [amənɥizmɑ̃] *nm* (*des ressources*) diminishing, dwindling; (*des espoirs*) dwindling

amenuiser [amənɥize] **1** *vt* to reduce, to thin (down), to whittle down; **a. ses économies/ses réserves** to whittle down one's savings/supplies **2 s'amenuiser** *vpr* (*d'une valeur*) to decline; (*de l'espoir, des chances*) to fade; (*économies, provisions*) to dwindle, to run low

amer[1], -ère [amɛr] **1** *adj* (*goût, Fig souvenirs, personne*) bitter **2** *nm* (*boisson*) bitters

amer[2] *nm Naut* seamark, landmark

amèrement [amɛrmɑ̃] *adv* bitterly

américain, -aine [amerikɛ̃, -ɛn] **1** *adj* American; **cuisine américaine** = kitchen with a bar separating the cooking and eating areas **2** *n* **A.** American **3** *nm Ling* American (English) **4** *nf* **américaine** (**a**) **vivre à l'a.** to live American-style (**b**) *Culin* **homard à l'a.** lobster américaine (**c**) *Cyclisme* track relay (race) (**d**) *Aut* **une a.** an American car

américanisation [amerikanizasjɔ̃] *nf* Americanization

américaniser [amerikanize] **1** *vt* to Americanize **2 s'américaniser** *vpr* to become Americanized

américanisme [amerikanism] *nm Ling* Americanism

américaniste [amerikanist] *n* specialist in American studies

amérindien, -ienne [amerɛ̃djɛ̃, -jɛn] **1** *adj* Amerindian, American Indian **2** *n* **A.** Amerindian, American Indian

Amérique [amerik] *nf* America; **l'A. du Nord/du Sud** North/South America; **l'A. latine** Latin America; **l'A. centrale** Central America; **les Amériques** the Americas

Amerlo(t) [amɛrlo], **Amerloque** [amɛrlɔk] *n F* Yank

amerrir [amerir] *vi* (**a**) *Av* to land on the sea, to make a sea landing (**b**) (*d'un vaisseau spatial*) to splash down

amerrissage [amerisaʒ] *nm Av* landing on the sea, sea landing; (*d'un vaisseau spatial*) splashdown; *Av* **a. forcé** ditching

amertume [amɛrtym] *nf* bitterness

améthyste [ametist] *nf* amethyst

ameublement [amœbləmɑ̃] *nm* (**a**) (*action de meubler*) furnishing (**b**) (*meubles*) set *or* suite of furniture; **un a. très simple** very simple furniture; **magasin d'a.** furniture store; **tissu d'a.** furnishing fabric

ameublir [amœblir] *vt* (**a**) *Agr* (*sol*) to loosen, to break up (**b**) *Jur* (*biens immobiliers*) to convert into personalty, to bring into the communal estate

ameublissement [amœblismɑ̃] *nm* (**a**) *Agr* (*du sol*) loosening, breaking up (**b**) *Jur* (*biens immobiliers*) conversion into personalty, inclusion in the communal estate

ameuter [amøte] **1** *vt* (**a**) (*gens*) to bring out; **a. une foule** to draw a crowd; **elle va a. tout le voisinage si elle continue à hurler comme ça!** she'll have the whole neighbourhood out if she carries on shouting like that! (**b**) (*chiens*) to form into a pack, to pack **2 s'ameuter** *vpr* to form a mob

ami, -ie [ami] **1** *n* friend; **un de mes meilleurs amis** one of my best friends; **a. intime** close friend; **a. d'enfance** childhood friend; **un a. de la maison** a friend of the family; **en a.** as a friend; **mon a.** (*entre amis*) my dear fellow; (*entre époux*) my dear; **mon amie** my dear, my love; **être sans amis** to be friendless, to have no friends; **faire a.-a.** (*de deux personnes*) to decide to be pals; (*se réconcilier*) to make up (**avec** with); **son a.** her boyfriend; (*amant*) her lover; *F* **sa petite amie** his girlfriend; **son amie** (*sa maîtresse*) his mistress; **eh l'a.! viens donc m'aider!** hey, you (over) there, come and give me a hand!; **un a. des arts** a patron of the arts; **les amis de la nature/de bêtes** nature/animal lovers; *Ling* **faux amis** false friends, faux amis; *Géog* **les îles des Amis** the Friendly

Islands, Tonga; **société des amis** Society of Friends, Quakers

2 *adj* friendly (**de** to); (*vent*) favourable; **un visage a.** a friendly face; **peuple a.** ally, friendly state

amiable [amjabl] **1** *adj Jur* friendly, conciliatory, amicable; **partage a.** amicable sharing arrangement; **a. compositeur** arbitrator **2** *adv* **à l'a.** amicably; *Jur* **arranger une affaire à l'a.** to settle a difference out of court; **s'arranger à l'a.** to settle out of court; **divorce à l'a.** no-fault divorce; **arrangement à l'a.** amicable arrangement; **vente à l'a.** private sale, sale by private contract

amiante [amjɑ̃t] *nm Minér* asbestos; **plaque d'a.** asbestos mat; **fibres d'a.** asbestos fibres

amibe [amib] *nf* amoeba, *US* ameba

amibiase [amibjaz] *nf Méd* amoebiasis, *US* amebiasis

amibien, -ienne [amibjɛ̃, -jɛn] *adj Méd* amœbic, *US* amebic; **dysenterie amibienne** amœbic dysentery

amical, -ale, -aux, -ales [amikal, -o] **1** *adj* (*conseil, ton etc*) friendly; (*relations*) amicable; **être a. avec qn** to be friendly towards sb; **peu a.** unfriendly; *Sp* **match a.** friendly (match); **association amicale** association **2** *nf* **amicale** association; *Br Scol* old-boys'/-girls' *or* former pupils' association; *US Univ* alumni association

amicalement [amikalmɑ̃] *adv* in a friendly way; **discuter a.** to have a friendly chat; **bien a. à vous** (*dans une lettre*) yours (ever)

amide [amid] *nm Ch* amide

amidon [amidɔ̃] *nm* starch

amidonnage [amidɔnaʒ] *nm* starching

amidonner [amidɔne] *vt* to starch

amincir [amɛ̃sir] **1** *vt* (*qch*) to make thinner; (*bois*) to fine down, to thin down; (*métal*) to machine down; **cette robe t'amincit** that dress makes you look thinner *or* slimmer **2 s'amincir** *vpr* to get thinner **3** *vi* to get slimmer

amincissant [amɛ̃sisɑ̃] *adj* slimming; **régime a.** (slimmer's *or* slimming) diet

amincissement [amɛ̃sismɑ̃] *nm* (*de choses*) thinning down; (*du métal*) machining down; (*d'une personne*) growing thinner *or* slimmer; **a. rapide** rapid loss of weight

amine [amin] *nf Ch, Pharm* **a. de réveil** amphetamine

aminé [amine] *adj Ch* **acide a.** amino acid

aminoacide [aminoasid] *nm Ch* amino acid

amiral, -ale, -aux, -ales [amiral, -o] **1** *adj* **vaisseau a.** (*en mer*) flagship; (*dans un port*) guardship **2** *nm* **(a)** *Mil* admiral, flag officer; **a. de la flotte** admiral of the fleet **(b)** (*coquillage*) admiral shell

amirale [amiral] *nf* admiral's wife

amirauté [amirote] *nf* **(a)** *Mil* Admiralty; **conseil d'a.** ≈ *Br* Admiralty Board; *Jur* High Court of Admiralty **(b) îles de l'A.** the Admiralty Islands; **île de l'A.** (*Colombie Britannique*) Admiralty Island

amitié [amitje] *nf* **(a)** (*sentiment*) friendship; **éprouver de l'a.** *ou* **un sentiment d'a. pour** *ou* **envers qn** to have friendly feelings towards sb; **étroite a.** close friendship; **concevoir de l'a. pour qn, prendre qn en a.** to take a liking to sb, to take to sb; **se lier d'a. avec qn** to make friends with sb, to become friendly with sb; **par a.** out of friendship; **une très ancienne a.** a long-standing friendship; **a. particulière** homosexual relationship; *Pol* **l'a. qui existe entre nos deux pays** the friendship between our two countries

(b) (*marque*) kindness, favour; **faites-moi l'a. de le lui dire** do me the favour of telling him so; **mes amitiés à votre sœur** my best wishes to your sister; **sincères amitiés de ...** best wishes from ...

ammoniac, -iaque [amɔnjak] *Ch* **1** *adj* **gaz a.** ammonia; **sel a.** sal ammoniac **2** *nm* ammonia

ammoniacal, -ale, -aux, -ales [amɔnjakal -o] *adj Ch* of ammonia

ammoniaque [amɔnjak] *nf Ch* ammonia

ammoniaqué [amɔnjake] *adj* ammoniated

ammonite [amɔnit] *nf* (*fossile*) ammonite

amnésie [amnezi] *nf Méd* amnesia; **souffrir d'a.** to have amnesia

amnésique [amnezik] *Méd* **1** *adj* amnesic; **être a.** to have amnesia **2** *n* amnesia case, amnesiac

amniocentèse [amnjosɛ̃tɛz, amnjosɑ̃tɛz] *nf Méd* amniocentesis; **se faire faire une a.** to have an amniocentesis

amnioscopie [amnjɔskɔpi] *nf Méd* amnioscopy

amniotique [amnjɔtik] *nf Physiol* amniotic; **liquide a.** amniotic fluid

amnistie [amnisti] *nf* amnesty; **accorder une a.** to grant an amnesty

amnistier [amnistje] *vt* (*pr sub & impf* **n. amnistiions, v. amnistiiez**) to grant amnesty to, to pardon

amocher [amɔʃe] *Arg* **1** *vt* **a. qn** to knock *or* bash sb about, to beat sb up; **la voiture est sérieusement amochée** the car's really been bashed up, the car's (in) one hell of a mess; **se faire a.** to get bashed up *or* beaten up **2 s'amocher** *vpr* **elle s'est bien amochée en tombant** she smashed herself up when she fell

amoindrir [amwɛ̃drir] **1** *vt* to decrease, to lessen, to diminish; (*affaiblir*) to weaken; (*mal*) to mitigate; (*déconsidérer*) (*qn*) to belittle; **la fièvre amoindrit ses forces** the fever is sapping his strength; **a. la puissance de qn** to curtail sb's power **2 s'amoindrir** *vpr* to diminish, to grow less

amoindrissement [amwɛ̃drismɑ̃] *nm* lessening, decrease, diminution

amollir [amɔlir] **1** *vt* (*substance etc*) to soften; **pareille chaleur m'amollit** heat like this makes me feel weak **2 s'amollir** *vpr* to soften, to become soft; (*du courage etc*) to flag, to weaken

amollissement [amɔlismɑ̃] *nm* (*du courage etc*) softening, weakening, flagging; **pareille chaleur entraîne l'a. général** heat like this makes everyone feel weak

amonceler [amɔ̃sle] **(j'amoncelle, n. amoncelons; j'amoncellerai) 1** *vt* to pile up, to heap up, to accumulate, to amass; **a. des preuves** to pile up *or* amass evidence **2 s'amonceler** *vpr* to pile up, to accumulate

amoncellement [amɔ̃sɛlmɑ̃] *nm* **(a)** (*action*) heaping (up), piling (up), accumulation; (*des nuages*) banking up **(b)** (*pile*) heap, pile; **a. de neige** covering of snow

amont [amɔ̃] **1** *nm* (*d'une rivière*) upper waters; **en a., vers l'a.** upstream, up river; **la Seine en a. de Paris** the Seine above Paris; **vent d'a.** off-shore wind; *Écon* **activités d'a.** upstream activities **2** *adj inv* uphill; **ski a.** uphill skiing

amoral, -ale, -aux, -ales [amɔral, -o] *adj* amoral

amoralité [amɔralite] *nf* amorality

amorçage [amɔrsaʒ] *nm* **(a)** (*d'une pompe, d'un moteur, d'une cartouche etc*) priming; (*d'un champ magnétique*) building up; *Ordinat* booting; *Méd* (*du sommeil*) induction; **le système d'a. d'une bombe** the detonating system of a bomb **(b)** (*d'un crochet, d'un cordage*) baiting

amorce [amɔrs] *nf* **(a)** beginning; (*d'une route etc en travaux*) initial section; **a. de négociations** preliminary talks **(b)** (*détonateur*) primer, fuse, detonator; (*d'une petite arme*) percussion *or* cartridge cap; *Él* fuse; (*d'une pompe*) priming; (*d'une soudure*) scarf; **pistolet à amorces** cap gun **(c)** *Pêche* bait **(d)** *Cin* leader

amorcer [amɔrse] **(j'amorçai(s); n. amorçons) 1** *vt* **(a)** (*bâtiment, route, attaque, discours etc*) to begin, to start; **a. des négociations** to initiate negotiations **(b)** *Ordinat* to boot (up); **a. de nouveau** to reboot **(c)** (*pompe*) to prime, to fetch; (*coquillage*) to cap; *Él* (*dynamo*) to start, to excite; (*arc*) to strike; (*soudure*) to scarf; (*bombe*) to fuse **(d)** (*cordage, piège etc*) to bait **(e)** *Vieilli* (*animal, personne*) to entice **2 s'amorcer** *vpr* to begin; *Ordinat* to boot (up); **une baisse des cours s'amorce** stocks and shares are showing a downward trend

amorçoir [amɔrswar] *nm* **(a)** *Pêche* ground-baiting appliance **(b)** (*vrille*) auger, twist bit, boring bit

amorphe [amɔrf] *adj* **(a)** *Ch, Minér, Biol* amorphous **(b)** (*sans énergie*) lifeless, apathetic; **cette chaleur me rend totalement a.** this heat is making me lethargic *or* listless

amorti [amɔrti] **1** *adj* **(a)** *Phys* (*vague*) damped **(b) marteau a.** cushioned hammer **(c)** *Fin* (*bien*) depreciated; (*capital*) amortized **2** *nm Tennis etc* drop shot; *Fb* trap

amortir [amɔrtir] **1** *vt* **(a)** (*bruit*) to deaden, to muffle; (*lumière*) to subdue; (*douleur*) to dull; (*ardeur*) to damp; (*passion*) to damp, to cool; (*couleur*) to tone down; (*chute*) to break; (*choc*) to absorb, to deaden; (*coup*) to break the force of; *Fb* (*ballon*) to trap; *Tennis* (*balle*) to kill; *Aut* (*secousses*) to damp

(b) *Fin* (*rembourser*) (*dette*) to redeem, to pay off, to amortize; *Compta* to write off, to amortize

(c) *Fin* (*rentabiliser*) **il a amorti sa nouvelle voiture en six mois** he recouped the cost of his new car in six months; **le matériel a été amorti dès la première année** the equipment paid for itself from the first year onwards

(d) *Phys* (*oscillations*) to damp down *or* out

(e) *Constr* to slack, to slake (lime)

2 s'amortir *vpr* **(a)** (*dépenses, investissement etc*) to pay for itself

(b) (*de bruits etc*) to fade, to die down

amorti-sacrifice *nm Baseball* squeeze-bunt

amortissable [amɔrtisabl] *adj Fin* redeemable

amortissant [amɔrtisɑ̃] *adj Aut* shock-absorbent

amortissement [amɔrtismɑ̃] *nm* **(a)** *Fin* (*d'une dette*) redemption, paying off, liquidation; **l'a. est plus rapide** (*d'une voiture*) it pays for itself faster; **fonds** *ou* **caisse d'a.** sinking fund; *Compta* **amortissement-dépenses** amortization *or* write-off of expenditure

(b) *Compta* (*perte de valeur*) depreciation; **provision pour a.**

depreciation allowance; **a. dégressif** accelerated depreciation; **a. dérogatoire** excess tax depreciation over normal; **a. linéaire** straightline depreciation; **amortissements cumulés** cumulative depreciation; **amortissements différés** deferred depreciation

(c) *(d'une chute)* breaking; *(d'un choc)* absorption; *Aut* damping; *(du son)* deadening

amortisseur [amɔrtisœr] *nm* **(a)** *Aut etc* shock absorber, *US* snubber; **a. de commande sur carburateur** carburettor damper; **a. de vibrations** vibration damper; **a. hydraulique** hydraulic shock absorber, hydraulic damper; **a. à gaz** gas strut; **a. hydro-élastique** hydrolastic displacer unit **(b)** *MecE* **a. à moulinet** air brake; **a. pneumatique** air cushion **(c)** *Él* damper

amour [amur] *nm (f in pl)* **(a)** *(sentiment)* love; **aimer qn d'a.** to be in love with sb; **ils filent le parfait a.** they are completely in love (with each other); **l'a. d'une mère** a mother's love; **l'a. maternel/paternel/filial** a mother's/father's/child's love; **l'a. du prochain** love of one's neighbour; **avec a.** lovingly; *(traiter, soigner)* with loving care; **a. platonique** platonic love; **s'aimer d'a. platonique** to love each other platonically; **l'a. libre** free love; **elle est folle d'a. pour lui** she's madly in love with him; **a. intéressé** cupboard love; **alors, c'est le grand a.?** so, it's true love then?, *F* so, it's the real thing then?; **chanson d'a.** love song; **enfant de l'a.** love child; **se marier par a.** to marry for love; **faire qch par a.** to do sth out of love; **mariage d'a.** love match; **roman/film d'a.** romantic novel/film; **histoire d'a.** love story; *Fig* **c'est une véritable histoire d'a. qui me lie à cette ville** I have a love affair with this city; **faire l'a.** to make love **(avec** with); **l'a. de Dieu** the love of God; **pour l'a. du Ciel, tiens-toi bien!** for heaven's sake, sit up straight!

(b) amours *(vie amoureuse)* love life; **les premières amours** first love, calf love; **à tes amours!** *(en buvant)* your health!, cheers!; *(à qn qui éternue)* bless you!; **où en sont tes amours?** how's your love life?

(c) *(personne)* **mon a.** my love, my darling; **une de mes anciennes amours** an old flame of mine; **les voitures sont ses seul(e) s amours** cars are his sole passion

(d) A. Cupid, Eros, the god of Love; **beau comme l'A.** handsome as a Greek god; **quel a. d'enfant!** what an adorable child!; **tu es un a.!** you('re an) angel!; **sois un a.!** be a dear, be an angel!; **tu serais un a. si tu voulais me chercher mes cigarettes** be an angel and fetch my cigarettes; **un a. d'histoire** a very sweet story

(e) *(goût)* **l'a. (pour qch)** love (of sth), passion (for sth); **l'a. de la nature** love of nature; **l'a. de la justice** passion for justice; **faire qch avec a.** to do sth lovingly *or* with love

amouracher (s') [samuraʃe] *vpr* **s'a. de qn** to become infatuated with sb

amourette [amurɛt] *nf* **(a)** *(entre deux personnes)* little fling **(b)** *Culin* **amourettes** spinal marrow

amoureusement [amurøzmɑ̃] *adv (avec tendresse)* lovingly; *(avec passion)* amorously

amoureux, -euse [amurø, -øz] **1** *adj* **(a)** *(soin, regard, geste)* loving; **vie amoureuse** love life; **tomber a.** to fall in love; **être a. de qn** to be in love with sb; *Fig* **il est a. de cette petite maison** he's in love with this little house; **être a. de qch** to be a lover of sth; **je suis a. de cette région** I love that part of the country; **je suis a. de la nature** I'm a nature-lover **(b)** *(passionné) (regard, geste)* amorous **2** *n* lover, man/woman in love; **pour les amoureux de la nature** for nature-lovers *or* lovers of nature; **c'est mon a.** he's my boyfriend

amour-propre [amurprɔpr] *nm (dignité)* self-respect, pride; **il n'a aucun a.** he has no self-respect *or* pride; **blesser l'a. de qn** to hurt *or* wound sb's pride; **elle est blessée dans son a.** her pride is hurt; **pétri d'a.** eaten up with conceit

amovible [amɔvibl] *adj* **(a)** detachable; *Ordinat (disque dur)* removable; **siège a.** sliding seat **(b)** *Jur (fonctionnaire)* removable; **fonction a.** = office that may be withdrawn from the holder (and given to another person)

ampérage [ɑ̃peraʒ] *nm Él* amperage

ampère [ɑ̃pɛr] *nm Él* ampere

ampère-heure, *pl* **ampères-heures** *nm* ampere-hour

ampèremètre [ɑ̃pɛrmɛtr] *nm Él* ammeter

amphé [ɑ̃fe] *nf F (amphétamine)* speed

amphétamine [ɑ̃fetamin] *nf* amphetamine

amphi [ɑ̃fi] *nm F Univ (salle)* lecture hall; *(cours)* lecture

amphibie [ɑ̃fibi] **1** *adj Biol (plante, animal)* amphibious; **appareil** *ou* **voiture a.** amphibian; *Mil* **opération a.** combined operation **2** *nm (véhicule etc), Biol* amphibian

amphibiens [ɑ̃fibjɛ̃] *nmpl Zool* amphibians, Amphibia

amphithéâtre [ɑ̃fiteɑtr] *nm* **(a)** *Univ* lecture hall **(b)** *Th* gallery, *F* the gods **(c)** *Archit* amphitheatre, *US* amphitheater; **en a.** in tiers, tier upon tier

amphore [ɑ̃fɔr] *nf* jar; *Archéol* amphora

ample [ɑ̃pl] *adj* **(a)** *(robe, jupe etc)* full **(b)** *(magasin, théâtre etc)* roomy, spacious **(c)** *(récit)* full; *(approvisionnement)* plentiful, ample; **jusqu'à plus a. informé** until fuller *or* more information is available; **le sujet est a.** the subject is a wide one; **je vais vous donner de plus amples détails** I will give you fuller *or* more details

amplement [ɑ̃pləmɑ̃] *adv* amply, fully; **nous avons a. le temps** we have plenty of time; **je vous ai a. servi** I have given you plenty; **il nous a a. renseigné/conseillé** he has given us plenty of information/advice; **c'est a. suffisant** it's more than enough

ampleur [ɑ̃plœr] *nf* **(a)** *(d'un vêtement)* width, fullness; *(de la voix)* volume, fullness; **ça manque un peu d'a. au bras** it's not quite full enough in the arm **(b)** *(importance)* scale, extent; **le mouvement politique prend de l'a.** the (political) movement is growing in size *or* is taking on new dimensions; **devant l'a. du désastre** in view of the extent *or* the scope of the disaster; *Mktg* **a. de gamme** breadth of range; *Mktg* **a. de la ligne de produits** product-line length

ampli [ɑ̃pli] *nm F* amplifier

amplificateur, -trice [ɑ̃plifikatœr, -tris] **1** *adj Rad etc* amplifying; *Opt* magnifying **2** *nm* amplifier

amplification [ɑ̃plifikasjɔ̃] *nf* **(a)** *(d'un sujet)* amplification, development; *(d'un mouvement politique, phénomène)* growth; *(exagération)* exaggeration **(b)** *Rad etc* amplification; *Opt* magnification

amplifier [ɑ̃plifje] *(impf & pr sub* **n. amplifiions, v. amplifiiez)** **1** *vt* **(a)** *(bruit, son, idée etc)* to amplify; *(histoire)* to embroider on; *(scandale)* to magnify, to blow up; **a. les échanges commerciaux** to increase trade **(b)** *Opt* to magnify; *Él* to amplify **2 s'amplifier** *vpr (en taille, en étendue etc)* to grow; **le bruit s'amplifie** the noise is growing *or* getting louder; **les revendications ouvrières s'amplifient** the workers' demands are increasing, the workers are increasing their demands

amplitude [ɑ̃plityd] *nf* **(a)** *(d'une oscillation)* amplitude; *Rad* **modulation d'a.** amplitude modulation **(b)** *(variation)* range; **a. thermique** temperature range **(c)** *Litt (de l'espace etc)* amplitude, vastness; *(d'un désastre, d'une catastrophe)* magnitude, scale

ampoule [ɑ̃pul] *nf* **(a)** *(d'une lampe électrique)* (light) bulb; *(d'un thermomètre)* bulb; *(d'un thermos)* container; **une a. de 75 watts** a 75 watt bulb; **a. à baïonnette/vis** bayonet/screw-in (light) bulb; *Aut* **a. de détection de chaleur** heat-sensing bulb **(b)** *(de la peau, du métal etc)* blister; *Hum* **il ne risque pas de se faire des ampoules** he's not going to die of exhaustion **(c)** *(fiole)* phial

ampoulé [ɑ̃pule] *adj Péj (discours)* inflated, bombastic

amputation [ɑ̃pytasjɔ̃] *nf* **(a)** *(d'un membre etc)* amputation **(b)** *Fig (d'un livre etc)* cutting down; *(d'une revendication)* reduction; **cet article a subi de sérieuses amputations** this article has been drastically cut; **c'est une sérieuse a. à sa fortune** it has cut into his fortune

amputé, -ée [ɑ̃pyte] *n* amputee

amputer [ɑ̃pyte] *vt* **(a)** *(membre)* to amputate; **il fut amputé du bras gauche** his left arm was amputated **(b)** *Fig (article etc)* to cut down; *(revendication)* to cut, to reduce **(de** by); **a. un capital** to make inroads into one's/sb's capital

amulette [amylɛt] *nf* amulet, charm

amusant [amyzɑ̃] **1** *adj* amusing, funny; *(divertissant)* entertaining; **comme c'est a., je n'avais pas remarqué …** that's funny, I hadn't noticed …; **je ne trouve pas ça très a.** I don't find that very funny *or* amusing, *Hum* I am not amused; **c'était très a.** it was great fun **2** *nm* **le plus a., c'est que …** the funniest *or* most amusing thing is that …; **l'a. de l'histoire** the amusing part of the story, what was funny *or* amusing about the story

amuse-gueule [amyzgœl] *nm inv* cocktail snack, nibble; *Fig* appetizer

amusement [amyzmɑ̃] *nm* amusement; **avoir besoin d'a.** to need amusement *or* entertainment; **faire qch pour son a.** to do sth for one's own amusement; *Iron* **tu parles d'un a.!** what fun!

amuser [amyze] **1** *vt* to amuse; *(divertir)* to entertain; **l'histoire m'a beaucoup amusé** I found the story really funny; *(divertissante)* I found the story really entertaining; **en attendant il faut a. la salle** in the meantime we must keep the audience amused; **si tu penses que ça m'amuse!** if you think I enjoy (doing) it!; **tu crois que ça m'amuse, ce genre de situations!** do you think I enjoy this kind of situation?; **ah ça t'amuse, toi!** you think that's funny, do you?; **fais-le si ça t'amuse** do it if it amuses you; **il avait un regard amusé quand il nous a dit bonjour** he looked amused *or* as if something was amusing him when he said hello to us

2 s'amuser *vpr* (*se distraire*) to enjoy oneself, to have a good time; **je ne me suis jamais aussi bien amusé** I've had the time of my life; **les enfants s'amusent dans le jardin** the children are playing in the garden; **amusez-vous bien!** have fun!, enjoy yourselves!; **s'a. aux dépens de qn** to amuse oneself at sb's expense; **s'a. avec qn** to have fun with sb; **s'a. de qn/de qch** to make fun of sb/sth; **s'a. à faire qch** to have fun doing sth; **faire qch pour s'a.** to do sth for fun *or* for the fun of it; *F* **ne t'amuse pas à recommencer** don't you dare do that again; **si tu crois que je vais m'a. à faire ça** if you think I've nothing better to do than that; **nous n'avons pas le temps de nous a. en chemin/à faire ça** we can't afford to waste time on the way/doing that

amusette [amyzɛt] *nf* **(a)** *Vieilli* pastime, diversion **(b)** *Belg* frivolous person

amuseur, -euse [amyzœr, -øz] *n* entertainer

amygdale [ami(g)dal] *nf* tonsil; **inflammation des amygdales** tonsillitis; **se faire opérer des amygdales** to have one's tonsils out; *F* **se sucer les amygdales** to snog (furiously)

amygdalectomie [ami(g)dalɛktɔmi] *nf Chir* tonsillectomy

amygdalite [ami(g)dalit] *nf Méd* tonsillitis; **faire une a.** to have tonsillitis

an [ɑ̃] *nm* year; **tous les trois ans** every three years; **dans trois ans** in three years' time, three years from now; **l'an passé** *ou* **dernier** last year; **l'an prochain** next year; **par an** per year; *Fin* per annum; **j'ai deux semaines de vacances par an** I have two weeks' holiday per *or* a year; **deux fois par an** twice a year; **tous les ans** every year; **avoir dix ans** to be ten (years old); (*d'une machine*) to be ten years old; **je gagne tant par an** I earn so much a year; **ami de vingt ans** friend of twenty years' standing; **bon an, mal an** on average over the years; **le jour** *ou* **le premier de l'an, le nouvel an** New Year's day; **l'an II de la République** Year Two of the Republic; **en l'an 2000** in the year 2000; **je m'en moque comme de l'an 40** I couldn't give a damn about it, I couldn't care less

anabaptisme [anabatism] *nm* Anabaptism

anabaptiste [anabatist] *adj, n* Anabaptist

anabolisant [anabɔlizɑ̃] **1** *nm Méd* anabolic steroid **2** *adj* anabolic

anabolisme [anabɔlism] *nm Méd* anabolism

anacarde [anakard] *nm* cashew nut

anacardier [anakardje] *nm* cashew tree

anachorète [anakɔrɛt] *nm* recluse; *Rel* anchorite; *Fig* **il mène une vie d'a.** he lives the life of a recluse

anachronique [anakrɔnik] *adj* anachronistic

anachronisme [anakrɔnism] *nm* anachronism

anacoluthe [anakɔlyt] *nf* anacoluthia

anaconda [anakɔ̃da] *nm* anaconda

anaérobie [anaerɔbi] *adj* anaerobic

anagrammatique [anagramatik] *adj* anagrammatic(al)

anagramme [anagram] *nf* anagram

A.N.A.H. [ana] *nf* (*abrév* **Agence nationale pour l'amélioration de l'habitat**) = housing department

anal, -ale, -aux, -ales [anal, -o] *adj Anat, Psy* anal

analeptique [analɛptik] *adj, nm Pharm* analeptic

analgésie [analʒezi] *nf Méd* analgesia

analgésique [analʒezik] *adj, nm Pharm* analgesic

anallergique [analɛrʒik] *adj* (*produit cosmétique*) hypoallergenic

analogie [analɔʒi] *nf* analogy; **raisonner par a.** to argue from analogy; **par a. avec** by analogy with

analogique [analɔʒik] *adj* **(a)** analogical; **dictionnaire a.** analogical dictionary **(b)** *Électron* analogue, *US* analog; **calculatrice a.** analog computer; **montre a.** analogue watch

analogue [analɔg] **1** *adj* analogous (**à** to, with), similar (**à** to); **dans des conditions analogues** in similar conditions **2** *nm* analogue, *US* analog, parallel; **ce mot anglais n'a pas d'a. en français** this English word has no equivalent in French

analphabète [analfabɛt] *adj, n* illiterate (person)

analphabétisme [analfabetism] *nm* illiteracy

analysable [analizabl] *adj* analysable, surtout *US* analyzable

analyse [analiz] *nf* **(a)** [①**A14,10**] (*étude*) analysis; **en dernière a.** in the last *or* final analysis, when all is said and done, all things considered; **avoir l'esprit d'a.** to have an analytical mind; **faire l'a. de qch** to analyse sth; **roman/film d'a.** psychological novel/film; **a. de la situation** situation(al) analysis

(b) *Méd* test; **laboratoire d'analyses** pathology laboratory; **a. de sang/d'urine** blood/urine test; **faire des analyses de sang** to undergo blood tests

(c) *Psy* (psycho)analysis; **être en a.** to be in analysis; **commencer/finir son a.** to begin *or* go into analysis/to finish *or* come out of analysis

▶ **analyse**: *Mktg* **a. des attraits et des atouts** opportunity and issue analysis; *TV Rad* **a. de l'audience** audience research *or* analysis; **a. des besoins** needs analysis; **a. du chemin critique** critical path analysis; **a. des coûts** cost analysis; **a. de la demande** demand analysis; **a. de données** data analysis; *Écon* **a. économique** economic analysis; *Ordinat* **a. factorielle** factor analysis; **a. fonctionnelle** systems analysis; *Mktg* **a. des forces et faiblesses** strengths and weaknesses analysis; *Mktg* **a. des forces, faiblesses, opportunités et menaces** SWOT analysis; *Ling* **a. grammaticale** parsing; *Ling* **faire l'a. grammaticale d'une phrase** to parse a sentence; *Math* **a. infinitésimale** (*différentielle et intégrale*) calculus; *Ling* **a. logique** analysis; *Ling* **faire l'a. logique d'une phrase** to analyse a sentence; **a. du marché** market analysis; **a. des médias** media analysis; *Mktg* **a. d'un modèle de décision en arborescence** decision-tree analysis; *Mktg* **a. des opportunités et des menaces** opportunity and threat analysis; **a. prévisionnelle** predictive analysis; **a. qualitative** qualitative analysis; *Ch* **a. quantitative** quantitative analysis; **a. du rendement** rate-of-return analysis; **a. des risques** risk analysis; **a. par segment** cluster analysis; **a. de séries temporelles** time-series analysis; **a. statistique** statistical analysis; **a. du style de vie** lifestyle analysis; *Ordinat* **a. syntaxique** parsing; **a. du ton de la voix** voice pitch analysis; **a. de la valeur** value analysis; **a. de la valeur perçue** perceived value analysis; **a. vectorielle** vector analysis; **a. des ventes** sales analysis; **a. volumétrique** volumetric analysis

analyser [analize] **1** *vt* **(a)** (*faits etc*) to analyse, *esp US* to analyze; *Méd* (*sang, urine etc*) to test; *Ordinat* to parse; **a. une phrase** *Gram* to parse a sentence; (*en propositions*) to analyse a sentence **(b)** *Psy* to (psycho)analyse; **se faire a.** to be (psycho)analysed **2 s'analyser** *vpr* to analyse one's feelings; **elle s'a. trop** she goes in for too much self-analysis

analyseur [analizœr] *nm* analyser, surtout *US* analyzer; *TV* scanner; *Ordinat* **a. syntaxique** parser; *Ordinat* **a. logique** logic analyzer

analyste [analist] *n Ordinat etc* analyst; *Psy* (psycho)analyst; **être un bon a. de ses sentiments** to be good at analysing one's feelings; *Mktg* **a. du marché** market analyst; *Mktg* **a. mercaticien** marketing analyst; *Fin* **a. en placements financiers** investment analyst

analyste-programmeur, *pl* **analystes programmeurs** *nm Ordinat* systems analyst

analytique [analitik] **1** *adj* analytical; **géométrie a.** analytic geometry; **un esprit a.** an analytical mind; *Psy* **suivre un traitement a.** to have psychoanalytical treatment **2** *nf* analytics

analytiquement [analitikmɑ̃] *adv* analytically

anamnèse [anamnɛz] *nf Méd* anamnesis

anamorphose [anamɔrfoz] *nf* anamorphosis

ananas [anana(s)] *nm* (*fruit*) pineapple; (*plante*) pineapple plant; **serre à a.** pinery; **a. frais/en conserve** fresh/tinned *or* canned pineapple

anaphore [anafɔr] *nf* anaphora

anaphorique [anafɔrik] *adj* anaphoric

anar [anar] *n F* = **anarchiste**

anarchie [anarʃi] *nf Pol; Fig* anarchy

anarchique [anarʃik] *adj* (*comportement*) anarchic(al); (*philosophie, système*) anarchistic

anarchiquement [anarʃikmɑ̃] *adv* anarchically, in an anarchic(al) manner; *Fig* chaotically, in a chaotic manner

anarchisant [anarʃizɑ̃] *adj* with anarchist tendencies *or* leanings

anarchisme [anarʃism] *nm* anarchism

anarchiste [anarʃist] *Pol* **1** *adj* anarchist; *Fig* chaotic, disorderly; (*personne*) rebellious, non-conformist **2** *n* anarchist; *Fig* rebel, non-conformist

anarcho-syndicaliste, *pl* **anarcho-syndicalistes** [anarkosɛ̃dikalist] *n* anarchosyndicalist

anathématiser [anatematize] *vt* to curse, *Fml* to anathematize

anathème [anatɛm] *nm* anathema

anatife [anatif] *nm* (*crustacé*) barnacle

anatomie [anatɔmi] *nf* anatomy; *Méd* **a. pathologique** morbid anatomy; *F* **une belle a.** a great body *or* figure; **pièce d'a.** anatomical figure; **avoir une a. d'athlète** to have the body of an athlete

anatomique [anatɔmik] *adj* anatomical

anatomiquement [anatɔmikmɑ̃] *adv* anatomically

anatomiste [anatɔmist] *n* anatomist

ancestral, -ale, -aux, -ales [ɑ̃sɛstral, -o] *adj* ancestral

ancêtre [ɑ̃sɛtr] *nm* ancestor; *F* (*vieillard*) old man; **la maison de ses ancêtres** his family home; (*château etc*) his ancestral home; **être sur les traces de ses ancêtres** to be tracking down one's ancestors; **nos ancêtres les Gaulois** our ancestors *or* forefathers the Gauls; **Bartok est l'a. de la musique contemporaine** Bartok is the father of contemporary music; **c'est l'a. de la vidéo** it's the forerunner of the video

anche [ɑ̃ʃ] *nf Mus* (*de hautbois, de clarinette etc*) reed, tongue; **jeu d'anches** (*d'un orgue*) reed-stop

anchois [ɑ̃ʃwa] *nm* (*poisson*) anchovy; **a. de Norvège** sprat; **beurre d'a.** /**sauce aux a.** anchovy paste/sauce; **filets d'a.** anchovy fillets; *F* **serrés comme des a.** packed like sardines

ancien, -ienne [ɑ̃sjɛ̃, -jɛn] **1** *adj* [ⓘB10,D3] **(a)** (*vieux*) ancient, old, antique; **monument a.** ancient monument; **meubles anciens** antique furniture; **anciens meubles** old furniture

(b) *Hist* ancient, old(en), early, bygone, past; **les peuples anciens** people of antiquity; **le grec a.** ancient *or* classical Greek; **dans l'a. temps** in the old(en) days, in bygone days, in days gone by; **l'A. Testament** the Old Testament; **c'est de l'histoire ancienne** (*c'est oublié*) that's ancient history

(c) (*révolu*) (*professeur, élève etc*) former, old, ex; (*d'avant*) (*voiture, maison etc*) old; **a. président** former *or* past president; **a. élève** (*d'une école*) old pupil, old boy; *US Univ* alumnus; **je suis un de vos anciens élèves** I'm a former pupil of yours; **anciens combattants** ex-servicemen, *Am* veterans; **mon a. époux** my ex-husband; **c'est un a. boxeur** he's a former boxer, he used to be a boxer

(d) (*capitaine, officier etc*) senior; **je suis plus a. que vous dans la profession** I've been in the profession longer than you; **il est votre a.** he is senior to you

2 *nm* **(a)** *Hist* **les anciens** the ancients

(b) *Rel, Pol* elder; **les anciens du village** the older inhabitants of the village; **les anciens de la tribu** the elders of the tribe; **respecter les anciens** to respect one's elders; *F* **l'a.** (*père*) the old man

(c) **aimer l'a.** (*meubles*) to like antique furniture *or* antiques; (*architecture*) to like old buildings

(d) *Vieilli* (*de scouts*) patrol leader

3 *n* (*par l'expérience*) **c'est une ancienne dans la maison** she's been with the firm a long time; **les anciens de l'entreprise** the company's long-time *or* long-serving employees

anciennement [ɑ̃sjɛnmɑ̃] *adv* formerly

ancienneté [ɑ̃sjɛnte] *nf* **(a)** (*d'un monument, d'une race etc*) age, antiquity; **de toute a.** from time immemorial **(b)** (*par l'expérience*) seniority, length of service; **a. de grade** seniority in rank; **avoir 15 ans d'a. dans une entreprise** to have 15 years' service with a firm; **avancer à l'a.** to be promoted by seniority; **il a plus d'a. que moi** he's been with the company longer than I have

ancillaire [ɑ̃silɛr] *adj* ancillary; **amours ancillaires** love affairs with a servant/servants

ancolie [ɑ̃kɔli] *nf* (*fleur*) aquilegia, columbine

ancrage [ɑ̃kraʒ] *nm* **(a)** *Naut* anchoring; (*attache*) anchorage; **(droits d')a.** anchorage dues **(b)** *Constr etc* (*action*) anchoring, anchorage, fixing; (*d'un mur*) bracing, staying; (*dispositif*) wall tie; **plaque/tige d'a.** anchor plate/tie; **point d'a.** (*d'un câble*) cable anchorage; *Fig* base; *Fig* **ce studio à Londres est son point d'a., c'est à partir de là qu'il rayonne** this studio in London is his base for touring around; *Fig* **l'a. de nouvelles idées** the taking root of new ideas **(c)** *Ordinat* justification; **a. à droite/gauche** right/left justification

ancre [ɑ̃kr] *nf* **(a)** anchor; **a. de veille** sheet anchor; **lever l'a.** to weigh anchor; *Fig F* (*partir*) to get moving, to hit the road; **jeter l'a.** to anchor; *Fig* to settle down; *Av* **a. de ballon** balloon anchor, grapnel; *Naut Arch* **a. de miséricorde** sheet anchor **(b)** *Constr etc* (*d'un mur, d'un fourneau etc*) anchor, cramp iron, tie (plate); (*d'une chaudière*) brace, stay

ancrer [ɑ̃kre] **1** *vt* **(a)** (*navire, montgolfière*) to anchor; *Fig* **il faut lui a. cette idée dans la tête** we/you/*etc* have to get that into his head; *Fig* **je ne sais pas qui lui a ancré cette idée dans la tête mais il n'en démord pas** I don't know who put that idea in his head but he won't let go of it; **cette idée est profondément ancrée en lui** this idea is firmly rooted in his mind

(b) *Constr* (*cheminée, moteur, chaudière etc*) to brace, to tie, to stay, to anchor

2 s'ancrer *vpr* (*d'anémone de mer etc*) to attach itself; *Fig* (*d'une idée, d'un concept*) to stick, to become rooted; *Fig* **elle a décidé de s'a. dans cette région** she has decided to put down roots in the region; *Fig* **je m'ancrais dans mon intention première** I stuck fast to my original intention; *Fig* **celui en qui s'ancre la foi ...** he whose faith is steadfast ...

andain [ɑ̃dɛ̃] *nm* swathe

andalou, -ouse [ɑ̃dalu, -uz] **1** *adj* Andalusian **2** *nm* **(a)** *Ling* Andalusian (dialect) **(b)** (*cheval*) Andalusian horse **3** *n* **A.** Andalusian

Andalousie [ɑ̃daluzi] *nf* Andalusia

andante [ɑ̃dɑ̃t(e)] *adv, nm Mus* andante

andantino [ɑ̃dɑ̃tino] *adv, nm Mus* andantino

Andes [ɑ̃d] *nfpl* **les A.** the Andes; **la Cordillère des A.** the Andean *or* the Great Cordillera

andin [ɑ̃dɛ̃] *adj* Andean

andorran, -ane [ɑ̃dɔrɑ̃, -an] **1** *adj* Andorran **2** *n* **A.** Andorran

Andorre [ɑ̃dɔr] *n* Andorra; **le val/la principauté d'A.** the Vale/Principality of Andorra

andouille [ɑ̃duj] *nf* **(a)** *Culin* chitterlings sausage **(b)** *F* (*imbécile*) fool, twit; **faire l'a.** to play the fool

andouiller [ɑ̃duje] *nm* (*d'un cervidé*) antler

andouillette [ɑ̃dujɛt] *nf Culin* = small chitterlings sausage (for frying)

androgène [ɑ̃drɔʒɛn] **1** *adj* androgenic **2** *nm* androgen, male hormone

androgyne [ɑ̃drɔʒin] **1** *adj* androgynous **2** *n* androgyne

androïde [ɑ̃drɔid] *nm* android

Andromaque [ɑ̃drɔmak] *nf* Andromache

Andromède [ɑ̃drɔmɛd] *nf* Andromeda

andropause [ɑ̃drɔpoz] *nf* male menopause

âne [ɑn] *nm* **(a)** donkey, *Litt, Vieilli* ass; **â. mâle** jackass; **promenade à dos d'â.** donkey ride; **se promener à dos d'â.** to go for a donkey ride; *Prov* **on ne saurait faire boire un â. qui n'a pas soif** you may lead a horse to water but you cannot make him drink; **être comme l'â. de Buridan** to be unable to make up one's mind between two things; *Fig* **le coup de pied de l'â.** the final insult, the last straw **(b)** *F* (*idiot*) ass; (*ignare*) dunce; **bonnet d'â.** dunce's cap; **espèce d'â. bâté!** stupid ass!

anéantir [aneɑ̃tir] **1** *vt* to annihilate; **a. les espérances de qn** to dash sb's hopes, to put an end to sb's hopes; *Fig* **la nouvelle l'a anéantie** she was staggered by the news **2 s'anéantir** *vpr* **(a)** (*disparaître*) (*d'espoir, de chances de succès*) to be dashed **(b)** *Rel* (*devant Dieu*) to humble *or* abase oneself

anéantissement [aneɑ̃tismɑ̃] *nm* **(a)** (*de l'espoir etc*) destruction; (*d'un empire etc*) annihilation, destruction; **l'a. de l'individu/de la personnalité** the annihilation of the individual/the personality **(b)** (*abattement*) **dans un état d'a. total** completely shattered

anecdote [anɛkdɔt] *nf* anecdote

anecdotique [anɛkdɔtik] *adj* anecdotal

anémie [anemi] *nf Méd* anaemia, *US* anemia; **faire de l'a.** to have anaemia; **a. pernicieuse** pernicious anaemia; *Fig* **l'a. d'un secteur** the enfeebled state of an industrial sector

anémier [anemje] **1** *vt* **a. qn** to make sb anaemic *or US* anemic; *Fig* **la crise a anémié la sidérurgie** the crisis has severely weakened the steel industry **2 s'anémier** *vpr* to become anaemic *or US* anemic; *Fig* **un secteur qui s'anémie** an industrial sector that is falling into decline

anémique [anemik] *adj* (*personne*) anaemic, *US* anemic; *Fig* feeble, weak

anémomètre [anemɔmɛtr] *nm* anemometer, wind gauge; **a. badin** airspeed indicator

anémone [anemɔn] *nf* anemone; **a. sylvie** wood anemone; **a. de mer** sea anemone

ânerie [ɑnri] *nf F* **(a)** (*stupidité, bêtise*) stupidity; **il est d'une â.!** what an idiot!; **quelle â.!** (*ta décision etc*) how idiotic! **(b)** (*action, propos*) **je crois que je viens de dire/faire une â.** I think I've just said/done something silly; **faire des âneries** to make an ass *or* a fool of oneself; **dire des âneries** to talk tripe *or* rubbish

anéroïde [anerɔid] *adj Météo* (*baromètre*) aneroid

ânesse [ɑnɛs] *nf* she ass, jenny; **lait d'â.** ass's milk

anesthésiant [anɛstezjɑ̃] *adj, nm Méd* anaesthetic, *US* anesthetic

anesthésie [anɛstezi] *nf Méd* anaesthesia, *US* anesthesia; **a. générale/locale** general/local anaesthetic; **on va vous faire une a. locale/générale** we're going to give you a local/general anaesthetic; **mettre un malade sous a.** to anaesthetize a patient, to put a patient under anaesthetic; **elle est encore sous a.** she's still under (the) anaesthetic

anesthésier [anɛstezje] *vt Méd* to anaesthetize, *US* to anesthetise; *Fig* (*crainte*) to deaden; (*opinion publique*) to an(a)esthetize

anesthésiologie [anɛsteziɔlɔʒi] *nf Méd Br* anaesthetics, *US* anesthesiology

anesthésique [anɛstezik] *adj, nm Méd* anaesthetic, *US* anesthetic

anesthésiste [anɛstezist] *n Méd* (*médecin*) *Br* anaesthetist, *US* anesthetologist; *US* (*infirmière*) anesthetist

aneth [anɛt] *nm* (*plante*) dill

anévrisme, anévrysme [anevrism] *nm Méd* aneurism, aneurysm

anfractuosité [ɑ̃fraktɥozite] *nf* crevice, crack

ange [ɑ̃ʒ] *nm Rel* angel; **un visage d'a.** an angelic face; *Beaux-Arts* **a. joufflu** chubby little cherub; **être le bon a. de qn** to be sb's good angel; **être le mauvais a. de qn** to be a bad influence on sb; **être aux anges** to be in seventh heaven, to be walking on air; **rire aux anges** to smile contentedly; *F* **faiseuse d'anges** backstreet abortionist; *F* **un a. passe** silence is wonderful; **un a. passa** there was a sudden silence in the conversation; *Fig* **discuter du sexe des anges** to talk round in circles; **oui, mon a.** yes (my) angel; **tu es un a.** you're an angel; **tu serais un a. si tu allais me chercher mes cigarettes** be an angel and fetch me my cigarettes; **beau comme un a.** pretty as a picture; **sage comme un a.** (as) good as gold; **une patience d'a.** the patience of a saint; **une douceur d'a.** angelic sweetness

▶ **ange**: **a. déchu** fallen angel; **a. gardien** guardian angel; *Iron* bodyguard; *Vieilli* **a. tutélaire** guardian angel

angéiologie [ɑ̃ʒejolɔʒi] *nf Méd* angiology

angélique [ɑ̃ʒelik] **1** *adj* angelic(al); *Rel* **la salutation a.** the Hail Mary; **être d'une patience a.** to have the patience of a saint **2** *nf Culin* angelica

angélisme [ɑ̃ʒelism] *nm* saintliness

angelot [ɑ̃ʒlo] *nm* **(a)** little angel, cherub **(b)** (*poisson*) monkfish, angel fish *or* ray *or* shark

angélus [ɑ̃ʒelys] *nm Rel* angelus (bell)

angevin, -ine [ɑ̃ʒvɛ̃, -in] **1** *adj* Angevin, (of *or* from) Angers/Anjou **2** *n* **A.** Angevin, person from Angers/Anjou

angine [ɑ̃ʒin] *nf Méd* sore throat, *AM* strep throat; (*amygdales*) tonsillitis, **avoir une a.** to have a sore throat/to have tonsillitis; **a. de poitrine** angina (pectoris)

angiographie [ɑ̃ʒjografi] *nf Méd* angiography

angiome [ɑ̃ʒjom] *nm Méd* angioma

angioplastie [ɑ̃ʒjoplasti] *nf Méd* angioplasty

anglais, -aise [ɑ̃glɛ, -ɛz] **1** *adj* English; (*incorrect au sens strict*) (*armée, marchandises etc*) British **2** *nm* English (language); **l'a. correct** the King's *or* Queen's English; **a. britannique/américain** British/American English **3** *n* **A.** Englishman, Englishwoman; (*incorrect au sens strict*) Briton; **les A.** the English; (*incorrect au sens strict*) the British; **les A. ont débarqué,** *Can* **j'ai la visite des A.** I have my period **4** *nf* **anglaise** *F* **filer à l'anglaise** to slip away; *Culin* **pommes de terre à l'anglaise** boiled potatoes **5** *fpl* **anglaises** ringlets

angle [ɑ̃gl] *nm* **(a)** (*d'un mur, d'une pièce etc*) corner, angle; **la maison qui fait l'a. appartient à mon oncle** the house on the corner belongs to my uncle; **armoire d'a.** corner cupboard; **l'a. de la rue** the street corner; **à l'a. du chemin** at the bend of the road; **l'a. de la table** the corner of the table; *Fig* **arrondir les angles** to soften one's approach; (*d'une réglementation etc*) to make more flexible; **c'est toujours elle qui arrondit les angles** she's always the one who smooths things over

(b) (*point de vue*) angle, point of view; **nous ne voyons pas les choses sous le même a.** we don't see things from the same angle *or* in the same way; **sous cet a.-là** from that angle, from that point of view; **vu sous cet a.** seen from that angle; **a. d'attaque** (*d'un sujet*) line of attack, approach

(c) *Géom* angle; **a. aigu/obtus** acute/obtuse angle; **a. plat/droit** straight angle/right angle; **les rues se coupent à angles droits** the roads cross at right angles; **former un a. avec qch** to be at right angles to sth

(d) *Menuis etc* **abattre les angles de qch** to chamfer sth; **soudure d'a.** fillet weld; **roue d'a.** bevel wheel, mitre wheel; **a. oblique** bevel rule, mitre square; **engrenage d'a.** bevel gear; **fer d'a.** angle iron

(e) (*d'un outil*) edge; **à angles vifs** with sharp edges

▶ **angle**: *Aut* **a. de braquage** turning circle; **a. de cap** track course; *Aut* **a. de chasse** caster angle; *Av* **a. critique** stalling angle; *Opt* **a. d'incidence** angle of incidence; *Mil* **a. de mire** angle of sight; **a. mort** (*au tir*) dead angle; (*dans un rétroviseur etc*) blind spot; *TV, Cin* **a. plongée** high angle; *TV, Cin* **a. de prise de vue** shooting *or* camera angle; *Opt* **a. de réfraction** angle of refraction; *TV, Cin* **a. de vue** angle of view

angledozer [ɑ̃glədɔzɛr] *nm* angledozer

Angleterre [ɑ̃glətɛr] *nf* England; (*incorrect au sens strict*) Britain; **la bataille d'A.** (*1940*) the Battle of Britain; *Couture* **point d'A.** Brussels (bobbin) lace

anglican, -ane [ɑ̃glikɑ̃, -an] *Rel* **1** *adj* Anglican; **l'Église anglicane** the Church of England, the Anglican Church **2** *n* Anglican

anglicanisme [ɑ̃glikanism] *nm Rel* Anglicanism

anglicisant, -ante [ɑ̃glisizɑ̃, -ɑ̃t] *n* student of English, English scholar

angliciser [ɑ̃glisize] **1** *vt* (*mot etc*) to anglicize **2** **s'angliciser** *vpr* to become anglicized

anglicisme [ɑ̃glisism] *nm Ling* Anglicism

angliciste [ɑ̃glisist] *n* (*étudiant*) student of English; (*spécialiste*) specialist in English, Anglicist

anglo- [ɑ̃glo] *préf* Anglo-

anglo-américain **1** *adj* Anglo-American **2** *nm Ling* American English **3** *n* **A.** Anglo-American

anglo-catholique *Rel* **1** *adj* Anglo-Catholic **2** *n* Anglo-Catholic

anglo-irlandais, -aise **1** *adj* Anglo-Irish; **l'Accord a.** the Anglo-Irish Agreement **2** *n* **A.** Anglo-Irishman, -woman

anglomane [ɑ̃gloman] *n* anglomaniac

anglomanie [ɑ̃glomani] *nf* anglomania

anglo-normand, -ande **1** *adj* **(a)** **les îles anglo-normandes** the Channel Islands **(b)** *Hist* Anglo-Norman **2** *nm Ling* Anglo-Norman

anglophile [ɑ̃glofil] **1** *adj* anglophile, pro-English **2** *n* anglophile

anglophilie [ɑ̃glofili] *nf* anglophilia

anglophobe [aglofɔb] **1** *adj* anglophobic **2** *n* anglophobe

anglophobie [ɑ̃glofɔbi] *nf* anglophobia

anglophone [ɑ̃glofɔn] **1** *adj* English-speaking, *Can* anglophone **2** *n* English-speaking person, *Can* Anglophone

anglo-saxon, -onne [ɑ̃glosaksɔ̃, -ɔn] **1** *adj* Anglo-Saxon; **les pays anglo-saxons** the English-speaking countries **2** *n Ling* Anglo-Saxon **3** *n* **A.** English speaker; *Hist* Anglo-Saxon

angoissant [ɑ̃gwasɑ̃] *adj* (*nouvelles*) distressing; (*attente*) agonizing; (*film, livre*) frightening; (*moment*) tense, anxious; (*situation, expérience*) alarming; **le fait d'être au chômage peut être très a.** being out of work can be very distressing

angoisse [ɑ̃gwas] *nf* anguish, distress; (*douleur*) agony; *Méd* **une crise d'a.** an anxiety attack; **les angoisses de la mort** the pangs of death; **vivre dans l'a. de la mort** to live in fear of dying; **considérer qch avec a.** (*à l'avenir*) to dread sth; (*au passé*) to look back on sth with anguish; *F* **quelle a.!** what a drag!

angoissé [ɑ̃gwase] **1** *adj* distressed, anxious; **j'étais a.** my heart was in my mouth **2** *n* person who suffers from anxiety, anxiety-sufferer

angoisser [ɑ̃gwase] **1** *vt* **a. qn** to fill sb with anxiety *or* distress *or* anguish; *F* **ça m'angoisse d'entrer dans un supermarché/d'être seul avec lui** I can't face going into a supermarket/being alone with him; **ce n'est tout de même pas ça qui t'angoisse!** you're not getting all worked up over a thing like that, are you! **2** *vi F* to worry, to get worked up; **j'angoisse à mort** I'm worried to death, I'm worried stiff **3** **s'angoisser** *vpr* to get anxious, *F* to get worked up; **elle s'angoisse pour un rien** she gets worked up over nothing

Angola [ɑ̃gɔla] *nm* Angola

angolais, -aise [ɑ̃gɔlɛ, -ɛz], **angolan, -ane** [ɑ̃gɔlɑ̃, -an] **1** *adj* Angolan **2** *n* **A.** Angolan

Angora [ɑ̃gɔra] **1** *adj* (*souvent inv*) (*laine, pull*) angora; **poil de chèvre a.** mohair **2** *nm* **(a)** (*lapin*) angora rabbit; (*chat*) Persian cat; (*chèvre*) angora **(b)** *Tex* angora (wool)

angstrœm, angström [ɑ̃gstrœm] *nm Phys* angström

anguille [ɑ̃gij] *nf* (*poisson*) eel; **a. de mer** conger eel; *Fig* **il y a a. sous roche** there's something brewing *or* in the wind; (*qch de louche*) there's something fishy going on, I smell a rat; *F* **elle a filé comme une a.** she ran off like greased lightning; **être souple comme une a.** to be (as) flexible as rubber, to be made of rubber

angulaire [ɑ̃gylɛr] **1** *adj* angular; *Constr* **pierre a.** cornerstone; *Fig* **la pierre a. d'une théorie/de la société** the cornerstone of a theory/of society **2** *nm Phot* **grand a.** wide-angle lens

anguleux, -euse [ɑ̃gylø, -øz] *adj* (*visage, silhouette etc*) angular, bony; (*contours etc*) rough, rugged; *Fig* **caractère a.** awkward disposition

anicroche [anikrɔʃ] *nf* difficulty, hitch, snag; **se passer sans a.** to go smoothly *or* without a hitch

aniline [anilin] *nf Ch* aniline

animal, -ale, -aux, -ales [animal, -o] **1** *nm* [①**A12**,1,g; **A15**,D,2,a; **A26**,C,i] animal; **société protectrice des animaux** society for the prevention of cruelty to animals; **a. domestique** pet; **l'homme est un a. social** man is a social animal; **il en a de la chance, cet a.-là!** what a lucky beggar *or* brute!; **c'est un drôle d'a.** he's a funny old beggar; *F* **quel a.!** what a brute!, what a beast!; **espèce d'a.!** you pig! **2** *adj* **(a)** (*règne, question etc*) animal; **chaleur animale** animal warmth **(b)** (*instinct etc*) animal; **avoir une confiance animale en qn** to trust sb instinctively

animalerie [animalri] *nf* animal room; (*bâtiment séparé*) animal house

animalier [animalje] **1** *adj* (*peinture etc*) animal; **peintre a.** animal painter **2** *nm* **(a)** (*peintre*) painter *or* sculptor of animals **(b)** (*dans un laboratoire*) animal keeper

animalité [animalite] *nf* animality, animal nature; (*des êtres humains*) animal side

animateur, -trice [animatœr, -tris] **1** *adj* (*énergie, pouvoir*) life-giving

2 *n* **(a)** *TV* presenter; (*d'émission de variétés*) host, compère, MC, *US* emcee; (*de jeu télévisé ou radiophonique*) quiz *or* question master; *Rad* presenter, radio personality; (*d'une émission de musique pop*) disc jockey, DJ, deejay; (*d'un débat*) moderator

(b) (*sur un bateau*) entertainments officer; (*de centre aéré*) organizer; **l'animatrice d'un centre de jeunes** the organizer *or* youth leader of a youth club; *Mktg* **a. d'une réunion de groupe** group discussion moderator

(c) *Cin* animator

(d) (*personne qui a de l'entrain*) stimulating person; **il a d'excellents talents d'a.** he's extremely good at livening things up

▶ **animateur**: **a. socioculturel** community worker in social and cultural activities; **a. sportif** sports presenter; *TV* **a. vedette** star presenter

animation [animasjɔ̃] *nf* **(a)** (*vie*) animation, liveliness; **l'a. des rues** the bustle in the streets; **mettre de l'a. dans une soirée** to liven up a party; **il parle avec beaucoup d'a.** he speaks with great animation; **ville pleine d'a.** town full of life; *Fin* **a. du marché** buoyancy of the market; *Com* **a. des ventes** sales drive *or* promotion

(b) (*divertissements*) activities; **faire de l'a.** to organize activities in a community

(c) *Cin* animation; **film d'a.** animated film; **a. de photos** photo-animation; **a. par ordinateur** computer animation

(d) *Météo* **a. satellite** satellite picture

animatique [animatik] *nf Ordinat* animation; *TV, Cin* animatic

animé [anime] *adj* **(a)** (*personne, discussion etc*) animated, spirited, lively; (*agité*) (*discussion*) heated; (*rue, quartier etc*) busy, bustling; *Fin* **marché a.** brisk *or* buoyant market **(b)** *Cin* **dessin a.** cartoon

animer [anime] **1** *vt* **(a)** (*stimuler*) (*qn, qch*) to animate, to give life to; **la passion du travail l'anime** he is driven by his passion for work; **animé par un nouvel espoir** buoyed up with new hope

(b) (*mener, diriger*) to move, to propel; (*discussion*) to lead, to conduct; (*entreprise*) to lead, to mastermind; (*machine*) to drive; **animé d'un sentiment de jalousie** prompted by feelings of jealousy; **animé de bonnes intentions** motivated by good intentions

(c) (*rendre plus vivant*) (*conversation*) to enliven; (*quartier, pièce*) to liven up; (*pièce*) to brighten up

(d) *TV, Rad* **a. une émission** to present a programme

2 s'animer *vpr* to come to life; **la conversation s'animait** the conversation was getting more lively *or* was warming up; **la ville s'anime avec le marché** the town comes to life on market day; **la rue s'anime le soir** the street wakes up at night; **son visage s'anima** his face lit up; **les esprits s'animent, il va y avoir de la bagarre** people are getting worked up, there's going to be trouble

animisme [animism] *nm* animism

animiste [animist] *adj, n* animist

animosité [animozite] *nf* animosity (**contre** for, towards), hostility (**contre** towards); **être plein d'a. envers** *ou* **contre** *ou* **pour qn** to feel great hostility towards sb; **avoir de l'a. contre** *ou* **pour qn** to feel animosity towards sb; **garder de l'a. contre qn** to nurse a grudge against sb; **agir par a.** to act out of spite

anion [anjɔ̃] *nm Phys* anion

anis [ani(s)] *nm* (*plante*) anise; (*boisson*) (**sirop d'**)**a.** aniseed cordial; *Culin* (**graine d'**)**a.** aniseed; **à l'a.** aniseed-flavoured

aniser [anize] *vt Culin* to flavour with aniseed

anisette [anizɛt] *nf* anisette

ankylose [ɑ̃kiloz] *nf* stiffness; *Méd* ankylosis; **une sorte d'a. gagne peu à peu tous ses membres** his limbs are gradually stiffening up

ankyloser [ɑ̃kiloze] **1** *vt Méd* to ankylose; **être ankylosé** to be stiff **2 s'ankyloser** *vpr* to become *or* get stiff; *Fig* (*dans un métier etc*) to get into a rut

annal, -ale, -aux, -ales [anal, -o] *adj Jur* valid for one year; **location annale** yearly letting

annales [anal] *nfpl* annals, (public) records; **les a. du crime** the annals of crime; **les a. du bac** = past examination papers (with annotations); **a. de géographie/littéraires** geographical/literary review; *Fig* **ça restera dans les a.** it will go down in (the annals of) history

annamite [anamit] **1** *adj* Annamese, Annamite **2** *nm Ling* Annamese **3** *n* **A.** person from Annam

anneau, -eaux [ano] *nm* **(a)** (*cercle*) ring; (*bague*) ring; **a. de rideau** curtain ring; **avoir des petits anneaux d'or aux oreilles** to have little gold rings *or* hoops in one's ears; **toutes ses clés sont sur un même a.** (*d'un porte-clé*) all his keys are on the same ring; *Gym* **les anneaux** the rings; *Gym* **exercices aux anneaux** ring exercises; **jeu des anneaux** hoop-la

(b) *Bot* annulus

(c) (*de chaîne*) link; (*de cheveux*) ringlet, curl; (*d'un serpent*) coil; (*d'une clé*) bow

(d) *Tech* ring, collar; (*d'un moyeu etc*) hoop; (*d'un cordage*) sling; **a. brisé** key *or* split ring; **a. à fiche** ring-bolt, eye-bolt; *Aut* **a. de retenue de charge** load restraining eye

(e) *Naut* **a. de port** = berth with facilities for hooking up to land-based power and water supplies

▶ **anneau**: **a. épiscopal** episcopal *or* bishop's ring; **a. nuptial** *ou* **de mariage** wedding ring; *Astron* **a. de Saturne** ring of Saturn

année [ane] *nf* [①B58,B3] year; **Bonne A.!** Happy New Year!; **fin d'a.** end of the year; **une a. de vacances** a year's holiday; **payer à l'a.** to pay by the year; **a. après a.** year after year; **d'a. en a.** year by year; **une a. après l'autre** year in year out; **nous nous connaissons depuis bien des années** we've known each other for years; **il y a des années que je ne l'ai pas vue** I haven't seen her for years; **les années 80** the eighties, the 80s; **en quelle a. Charlemagne a-t-il été couronné?** in what year was Charlemagne crowned?; **l'a. prochaine/dernière** next/last year; **pendant les années de guerre/d'occupation** during the war years/the years of occupation; **quelle est son a. de naissance?** what year was he/she born?; **elle entre dans sa trentième a.** she'll be 30 (on her) next birthday; *Univ* **entrer en troisième a. de médecine** to go into one's third year of medicine; *Univ* **les classes de deuxième a.** the second year students, *US* the sophomores

▶ **année**: **a. bissextile** leap year; **a. budgétaire** financial year; **a. civile** calendar year; **a. comptable** accounting *or* financial year, *Am* fiscal year

année-lumière *nf* light year; **à des années-lumière** (*étoile etc*) light years away; *Fig* **nous sommes à des années-lumière l'un de l'autre** we're light years away from each other, we're worlds apart

annelé [anle] *adj* (*colonne, ver etc*) ringed

annexe [anɛks] **1** *nf* **(a)** (*bâtiment*) annex(e); (*de ferme, château*) outbuilding **(b)** (*de projet de loi*) rider; (*de loi*) schedule; (*de livre, rapport*) appendix; (*de lettre*) enclosure; **en a. à ma lettre** enclosed with my letter; **en a. veuillez trouver ...** please find enclosed ...; **annexes** *Compta* notes to the accounts; (*d'un livre*) back matter, appendices **(c)** *Rel* chapel of ease **(d)** (*d'un état*) dependency **(e)** *Naut* (*d'un bateau*) dinghy **2** *adj* **établissement a.** annex(e); **lettre a.** covering letter; **industries annexes** subsidiary industries; **revenus annexes** supplementary income

annexer [anɛkse] **1** *vt* **(a)** *Pol* (*territoire*) to annex **(b)** (*document etc*) to append, to attach; **pièces annexées (à une lettre)** enclosures **2 s'annexer** *vpr* **s'a. qch** to acquire sth for oneself; **il s'est annexé la meilleure place** he grabbed the best seat for himself

annexion [anɛksjɔ̃] *nf* annexation

Annibal [anibal] *nm Antiq* Hannibal

annihilation [aniilasjɔ̃] *nf* annihilation; (*des efforts, effets etc*) destruction

annihiler [aniile] *vt* **(a)** (*armée etc*) to annihilate, to destroy; (*efforts, travail etc*) to destroy; **toute forme d'agressivité l'annihile** he goes to pieces when faced with any form of aggressive behaviour **(b)** *Jur* to annul, to cancel

anniversaire [aniversɛr] **1** *adj* (*cérémonie*) anniversary; **la date a.** (*de la Libération etc*) the anniversary **2** *nm* (*d'une naissance*) birthday; (*d'une victoire, d'une mort etc*) anniversary; (*d'un mariage*) (wedding) anniversary; **le cinquantième a. de leur mariage** their 50th wedding anniversary; **c'est mon a.** it's my birthday; **mon vingtième a., l'a. de mes vingt ans** my twentieth birthday; **bon a.!** happy birthday!; **gâteau/carte d'a.** birthday cake/card

annonce [anɔ̃s] *nf* **(a)** announcement; (*surtout par écrit*) notification, notice; *Cartes* declaration, bid; *Fig* sign, indication; *Rel* **faire l'a. d'un mariage** to publish the banns; **faire une a.** to make an announcement; **les annonces de la semaine** the weekly notices; *Fig* **le retour des hirondelles est l'a. du printemps** it's a sign of spring when the swallows return; *TV, Rad* **a. de continuité** continuity announcement; *TV* **a. de programme** programme trail

(b) (*de publicité etc*) advertisement; **passer une (petite) a. dans un journal/sur Minitel** to put an ad(vert) in a newspaper/on Minitel; **petites annonces** classified advertisements, small ads; **annonces classées** classified ads

annoncer [anɔ̃se] (**j'annonçai(s); n. annonçons**) **1** *vt* **(a)** (*déclarer*) to announce, to give notice of; **a. une mauvaise nouvelle à qn** to break bad news to sb; **a. ses fiançailles en public** to announce one's engagement publicly

(b) (*dans journal*) (*soldes etc*) to advertise

(c) (*indiquer*) to promise, to foretell, to herald; **tout**

semble a. le succès everything points to success; cela n'annonce rien de bon it looks unpromising, no *or* nothing good will come of that; le rire des enfants dans la cour annonce la fin des classes the sound of children laughing in the playground means that *or* is a sign that classes have finished; l'hirondelle annonce le printemps the swallow is a sign that spring is on its way, the swallow heralds the approach of spring

(d) a. qn to show sb in; (*lors d'une occasion officielle*) to announce sb; se faire a. to give one's name

(e) (*être l'indice de*) (*intelligence, caractéristiques, qualités*) to be a sign of, to point to; (*qch qui va arriver*) to herald; ce recueil de poèmes annonce un caractère tourmenté the collection of poems points to a soul in torment

2 s'annoncer *vpr* (a) (*prévenir de sa visite*) to give notice of one's arrival (b) (*se présenter*) (*de la situation*) cela s'annonce bien it looks promising; cela s'annonce mal it looks unpromising, no good *or* nothing good will come of that; l'avènement de la démocratie s'annonce partout en Europe there are signs all over Europe of the advent of democracy

annonceur [anɔ̃sœr] *nm* (a) (*de publicité*) advertiser (b) *Rad, TV* (*speaker*) announcer

annonciateur, -trice [anɔ̃sjatœr, -tris] *adj* signes annonciateurs du printemps signs that spring is on the way, signs that herald the approach of spring

annonciation [anɔ̃sjasjɔ̃] *nf Rel* annunciation; fête de l'A. Feast of the Annunciation, Lady Day

annotateur, -trice [anɔtatœr, -tris] *n* (*d'un texte etc*) annotator, commentator

annotation [anɔtasjɔ̃] *nf* (a) (*action*) annotating, making notes (b) (*note*) annotation, note; faire des annotations dans un texte to annotate a text

annoter [anɔte] *vt* (*texte*) to annotate; (*livre*) to write notes in

annuaire [anɥɛr] *nm* annual; (*d'un organisme international*) yearbook; l'a. du téléphone *ou* téléphonique telephone directory, *F* the phone book; je suis dans l'a. I'm in the book; je ne suis pas dans l'a., je suis sur la liste rouge I'm not in the (phone) book, I'm ex-directory; a. du commerce trade directory; a. papier printed directory; a. électronique electronic directory; a. des marées tide table; l'A. militaire the Army list, *US* the Army Register; l'A. de la Marine the Navy List; a. de l'université university calendar

annuel, -elle [anɥɛl] *adj* annual, yearly; congé a. annual leave; plante annuelle annual; rente annuelle annuity; magistrature annuelle = judicial office held only for one year

annuellement [anɥɛlmɑ̃] *adv* annually, yearly

annuité [anɥite] *nf* (a) (*dans le remboursement d'un emprunt*) annual instalment *or* repayment; *Compta* a. constante (*de remboursement*) fixed annual payment; *Compta* a. d'amortissement annual depreciation *or* writedown (b) (*rente*) annuity

annulaire [anylɛr] 1 *adj* annular, ring-shaped 2 *nm* ring finger, third finger

annulation [anylasjɔ̃] *nf* (a) (*d'un contrat, d'une commande, de vacances etc*) cancelling, cancellation; *Jur etc* (*d'un mariage*) annulment; (*d'un jugement*) quashing, setting aside; (*d'un acte judiciaire*) annulment, repeal; (*d'un contrat*) voidance; (*d'un testament*) setting aside; *Com* a. rétroactive retroactive cancellation; a. de dernière minute late cancellation (b) *Ordinat* deletion; a. d'entrée (*commande*) cancel entry; a. des révisions (*commande*) undo changes

annuler [anyle] 1 *vt* (a) (*contrat, commande etc*), *Ordinat* to cancel; (*dette*) to cancel, to write off; (*marché*) to call off; *Jur* (*mariage*) to annul; (*loi, jugement*) to render void, to repeal, to rescind; (*testament*) to set aside; a. un ordre de grève to call off a strike (b) *Banque* (*chèque etc*) to cancel (c) (*remplacer*) to supersede, to cancel; ce catalogue annule les précédents this catalogue supersedes all previous issues (d) *Fb* (*but*) to disallow 2 s'annuler *vpr* to cancel each other out

anoblir [anɔblir] *vt* a. qn to ennoble sb, to raise sb to the peerage

anoblissement [anɔblismɑ̃] *nm* ennoblement (de of); lettres d'a. letters patent of nobility

anode [anɔd] *nf Él* anode

anodin [anɔdɛ̃] *adj* harmless, innocuous; (*blessure, changement*) slight, minor; (*infection*) mild; cette remarque n'était pas anodine this remark was not as innocent as it might seem; une personne tout à fait anodine a totally insignificant person; *Méd* remèdes anodins painkillers; *Fig* moyen/remède a. ineffective method/remedy; mensonge a. white lie

anodique [anɔdik] *adj Él* anodic, anodal; (*courant*) anode

anomalie [anɔmali] *nf Gram, Astron, Biol* anomaly; *Méd* disorder; si vous remarquez la moindre a. dans la comptabilité if you should notice the slightest irregularity in the accounting; il y a une a. dans le fonctionnement de la machine the machine has a malfunction

ânon [ɑnɔ̃] *nm* little donkey; (*très jeune*) baby donkey

ânonnement [ɑnɔnmɑ̃] *nm* mumbling, faltering tone

ânonner [ɑnɔne] 1 *vt* (*paroles*) to stumble *or* blunder through; â. une récitation to recite sth falteringly 2 *vi* to mumble

anonymat [anɔnima] *nm* anonymity; garder l'a. to remain anonymous; faire qch dans l'a. le plus complet to do sth anonymously

anonyme [anɔnim] *adj* (*écrivain, lettre etc*) anonymous; *Fig* (*décor, intérieur*) impersonal, anonymous

anonymement [anɔnimmɑ̃] *adv* anonymously

anophèle [anɔfɛl] *nm Zool* anopheles mosquito

anorak [anɔrak] *nm* anorak

anorexie [anɔrɛksi] *nf Méd* anorexia; a. mentale anorexia nervosa; faire de l'a. to suffer from anorexia

anorexique [anɔrɛksik] *adj, n Méd* anorexic

anormal, -ale, -aux, -ales [anɔrmal, -o] 1 *adj* (a) (*non-conforme*) abnormal; personne d'une maigreur anormale abnormally thin person; évolution anormale d'une maladie unexpected development of an illness; enfants anormaux (*en intelligence*) educationally subnormal children; il fait un temps a. the weather is abnormal, *F* the weather is all wrong for this time of year; il fait une chaleur anormale it's abnormally hot

(b) (*injuste*) unjust, unfair; il est a. que … + *sub* it is unfair that …

(c) (*extraordinaire*) extraordinary; ce qu'il y a d'a., c'est que … the strange *or* extraordinary thing is that …

2 *n Méd, Psy* mentally defective person; *F* c'est un a. he's round the bend

3 *nm* l'a., c'est que … (*injuste*) what's unjust is that …; (*extraordinaire*) what's unusual is that …

anormalement [anɔrmalmɑ̃] *adv* abnormally

anormalité [anɔrmalite] *nf* abnormality

ANPE [aɛnpeø] *nf* (*abrév* Agence nationale pour l'emploi) *Br* ≈ Jobcentre, *Can* ≈ CEC; être à l'A. ≈ to be registered with the Jobcentre

ANRS [aɛnɛrɛs] *nf* (*abrév* Agence nationale de recherches sur le sida) Aids research institute

anse [ɑ̃s] *nf* (a) (*d'une cruche, d'un panier*) handle; (*d'un cadenas*) shackle; *Fig* faire danser *ou* valser l'a. du panier (*d'un domestique etc*) to fiddle the books; *Archit* voûte en a. de panier basket-handle arch; *Fig* faire le pot *ou* le panier à deux anses to have someone on each arm (b) (*d'une corde etc*) loop, bight; *Anat* loop; a. à vis screw eye(bolt) (c) *Géog* cove

antagonique [ɑ̃tagɔnik] *adj* (*forces, personnes etc*) antagonistic; (*interêts, influences*) conflicting

antagonisme [ɑ̃tagɔnism] *nm* (*de personne*), *Physiol* antagonism

antagoniste [ɑ̃tagɔnist] 1 *adj* antagonistic, opposed; avoir des positions antagonistes to have opposing *or* conflicting opinions; les partis antagonistes the opposing parties; force a. antagonistic force; (*de contrôle*) controlling force, countercheck; *Anat* muscles antagonistes antagonists; couple a. opposing couple 2 *n* antagonist, opponent

antalgique [ɑ̃talʒik] *adj, nm Pharm* analgesic

antan [ɑ̃tɑ̃] *adv Arch, Litt* d'a. of yesteryear; où sont les neiges d'a.? where are the snows of yesteryear?

antarctique [ɑ̃tarktik] *Géog* 1 *adj* Antarctic; cercle a. Antarctic circle 2 *nm* l'A. Antarctica, the Antarctic; une expédition dans l'A. an Antarctic expedition

anté- [ɑ̃te] *préf* ante-, pre-

antécédence [ɑ̃tesedɑ̃s] *nf Phil, Géog* antecedence

antécédent [ɑ̃tesedɑ̃] 1 *adj* previous, antecedent, anterior (à to) 2 *nm* (a) [①A32-33; B20-22,F] *Ling, Phil* antecedent (b) antécédents previous history, past record, *Fml* antecedents; antécédents médicaux medical history; il y a des antécédents cancéreux dans ma famille my family has a history of cancer; avoir de bons/mauvais antécédents to have a good/bad record

antéchrist [ɑ̃tekrist] *nm* antichrist

antédiluvien, -ienne [ɑ̃tedilyvjɛ̃, -jɛn] *adj* antediluvian; *F* ma télévision est antédiluvienne my television is an antique; *F* c'est une relation antédiluvienne I've known him for donkey's years

antémémoire [ɑ̃tememwar] *nf Ordinat* cache (memory)

anténatal, -ale, -aux, -ales [ɑ̃tenatal, -o] *adj Méd* antenatal

antenne [ɑ̃tɛn] *nf* [①A13,6] (a) *Rad* aerial, antenna; (*d'un satellite, d'un robot*) antenna; a. de télévision television aerial; à l'a. on-air; être à l'a. to be on the air; on est à l'a. dans cinq minutes we'll be on the air in five minutes; prendre/garder l'a. to go/stay on the air; passer à l'a. (*d'une *émission*) to be broadcast *or* televised; (*d'une personne*) to be on television/radio; **rendre l'a.** (*d'un présentateur etc*) to go back, to return (to the studio *etc*); **je dois rendre l'a.** I have to hand over now; **je vous passe l'a., à vous l'a.!** (I'll hand) over to you; **hors a.** off-air; **déclarer hors a. que ...** to declare off the air that ...

(**b**) (*d'un insecte*) antenna, feeler; *Fig* **avoir des antennes** to have a sixth sense, to be perceptive, to pick up on things; *Fig* **avoir ses antennes quelque part** to have one's feelers out, to have informers

(**c**) *Mil* **a. chirurgicale** advanced surgical unit

(**d**) (*de société*) branch

▶ **antenne**: **a. en cadre** loop aerial; *TV* **a. collective** shared aerial; *Aut* **a. électrique** electric aerial; **a. d'émission** broadcast antenna; **a. fermée** loop aerial; *Aut* **a. manuelle** manual aerial; **a. parabolique** (satellite) dish, dish antenna; *Av* **a. pendante** trailing aerial; **a. de réception** receiver aerial, receiving aerial *or* antenna; **a. satellite** satellite antenna; **a. télescopique** telescopic mast; **a. terrestre** ground antenna; **a. en V** rabbit's ears

antépénultième [ɑ̃tepenyltjɛm] *adj* antepenultimate, third (from) last

antérieurement [ɑ̃terjœrmɑ̃] *adv* previously, earlier; **cela s'est passé a. à notre rencontre** that happened before we met

antérieur, -eure [ɑ̃terjœr] *adj* (**a**) (*période*) former; (*date*) earlier; (*année*) previous; (*engagement*) prior; **tous ces événements sont antérieurs à la révolution** all these events took place before the revolution; **cela est a. à ma naissance** that was before I was born; **a. au mariage** premarital; **dans une vie antérieure** in a previous life *or* existence; [①A50,12,h; B29,7-8] *Gram* **futur a.** future perfect; *Gram* **passé a.** past anterior (**b**) (*muscle*) anterior; (*membre etc*) fore; (*mur, voyelle etc*) front

antériorité [ɑ̃terjɔrite] *nf* precedence; *Gram* anteriority

anthère [ɑ̃tɛr] *nf Bot* anther

anthologie [ɑ̃tɔlɔʒi] *nf* anthology

anthracite [ɑ̃trasit] **1** *nm* (**a**) *Minér* anthracite (**b**) (*couleur*) charcoal grey **2** *adj inv* charcoal grey

anthrax [ɑ̃traks] *nm Méd* carbuncle; **a. malin** anthrax

anthropique [ɑ̃trɔpik] *adj* anthropogenic

anthropocentrique [ɑ̃trɔpɔsɑ̃trik] *adj* anthropocentric

anthropocentrisme [ɑ̃trɔpɔsɑ̃trism] *nm* anthropocentrism

anthropoïde [ɑ̃trɔpɔid] **1** *adj* anthropoid **2** *nm* anthropoid ape

anthropologie [ɑ̃trɔpɔlɔʒi] *nf* anthropology

anthropologique [ɑ̃trɔpɔlɔʒik] *adj* anthropological

anthropologiste [ɑ̃trɔpɔlɔʒist], **anthropologue** [ɑ̃trɔpɔlɔg] *n* anthropologist

anthropométrie [ɑ̃trɔpɔmetri] *nf* anthropometry

anthropométrique [ɑ̃trɔpɔmetrik] *adj* anthropometric(al); *Admin* **service a.** criminal anthropometry department, *Br* ≈ Criminal Records Office; **fiche a.** = record containing fingerprints and details of height, weight *etc*

anthropomorphe [ɑ̃trɔpɔmɔrf] *adj* anthropomorphic

anthropomorphisme [ɑ̃trɔpɔmɔrfism] *nm* anthropomorphism

anthropophage [ɑ̃trɔpɔfaʒ] **1** *adj* cannibalistic, man-eating **2** *n* cannibal

anthropophagie [ɑ̃trɔpɔfaʒi] *nf* cannibalism

anti[1] [ɑ̃ti] *préf* anti-

anti[2] *préf* ante-

antiadhésif [ɑ̃tiadezif] **1** *adj* (*revêtement etc*) nonstick **2** *nm* antiadhesive; **casserole recouvert d'un a.** nonstick saucepan

antiaérien, -ienne [ɑ̃tiaerjɛ̃, -jɛn] *adj* (*arme, défense*) anti-aircraft; **abri a.** air-raid shelter

anti-âge *adj inv* (*traitement, crème*) anti-ageing

antialcoolique [ɑ̃tialkɔlik] *adj* (*ligue etc*) temperance

antialcoolisme [ɑ̃tialkɔlism] *nm* temperance, teetotalism

antiallergique [ɑ̃tialɛrʒik] *adj* hypoallergenic

antiasthénique [ɑ̃tiastenik] *adj Méd* antiasthenic

antiatomique [ɑ̃tiatɔmik] *adj* antinuclear; **abri a.** fall-out shelter; **manifestation a.** ban-the-bomb *or* anti-nuclear demonstration

antibactérien [ɑ̃tibakterjɛ̃] **1** *adj* antibacterial **2** *nm* antibacterial product

antibiogramme [ɑ̃tibjɔgram] *nm Méd* antibiogram

antibiotique [ɑ̃tibjɔtik] *Pharm* **1** *adj* antibiotic; **un traitement a.** a course of antibiotics **2** *nm* antibiotic; **être sous antibiotiques** to be on antibiotics

antiblocage [ɑ̃tiblɔkaʒ] *nm Aut* **a. de freins** anti-lock braking system, anti-lock brakes; **a. des roues** anti-lock brakes

antibrouillage [ɑ̃tibrujaʒ] *nm Rad etc* anti-jamming

antibrouillard [ɑ̃tibrujar] *adj, nm Aut* (**phare**) **a.** fog lamp

antibruit [ɑ̃tibrɥi] *adj inv* (*mur*) soundproof; **lutte a.** noise abatement campaign

antibuée [ɑ̃tibɥe] *adj, nm Aut* (**dispositif**) **a.** demister

anticalcaire [ɑ̃tikalkɛr] *nm* (*qui empêche les dépôts*) scale preventer; (*qui détartre*) scale remover

anticancéreux, -euse [ɑ̃tikɑ̃serø, -øz] *adj* **centre/sérum a.** cancer hospital/serum

anticasseurs [ɑ̃tikasœr] *adj inv Pol* **Loi a.** = law banning violent behaviour during demonstrations

anticathode [ɑ̃tikatɔd] *nf* anticathode

antichambre [ɑ̃tiʃɑ̃br] *nf* waiting room, antechamber; **pilier d'a.** (*d'un ministre etc*) hanger-on; **faire a.** to hang around in the waiting room; *Fig* to wait patiently to see sb

antichar [ɑ̃tiʃar] *Mil* **1** *adj* anti-tank **2** *nm* anti-tank device

antichoc [ɑ̃tiʃɔk] *adj inv* shock-proof; *Méd* **traitement a.** anti-shock treatment

anticipatif, -ive [ɑ̃tisipatif, -iv] *adj* anticipatory, anticipative; **paiement a.** prepayment

anticipation [ɑ̃tisipasjɔ̃] *nf* anticipation; **payer par a.** to pay in advance; **demander l'a. d'un paiement** to ask for payment in advance; **littérature d'a.** science fiction; **film d'a.** science-fiction film

anticipé [ɑ̃tisipe] *adj* (*paiement*) advance; (*départ, retour*) early; **prendre sa retraite anticipée** to take early retirement; **avec mes remerciements anticipés** thanking you in advance

anticiper [ɑ̃tisipe] **1** *vt* to forecast; (*réaction, réponse*) to anticipate; (*action*) to forestall; **plaisir anticipé** anticipated pleasure; **j'anticipais déjà le pire** I was expecting the worst; *Fin* **dividende anticipé** advance dividend; **remboursement anticipé** redemption before due date; **a. un paiement** to pay in advance **2** *vi* to anticipate, to look *or* think ahead; *Sp etc* to anticipate one's opponent's moves; **n'anticipons pas** let's not look *or* think too far ahead; **a. sur les événements** to anticipate events; **je ne voudrais pas a. sur ce qui sera dit plus tard** I don't wish to anticipate *or* guess what will be said later; **a. sur ses revenus** to spend one's income in advance

anticlérical, -ale, -aux, -ales [ɑ̃tiklerikal, -o] *adj, n* anticlerical

anticléricalisme [ɑ̃tiklerikalism] *nm* anti-clericalism

anticlinal, -aux [ɑ̃tiklinal, -o] *nm Géol* anticline

anticoagulant [ɑ̃tikɔagylɑ̃] *adj, nm Pharm* anticoagulant

anticolonialisme [ɑ̃tikɔlɔnjalism] *nm* anti-colonialism

anticolonialiste [ɑ̃tikɔlɔnjalist] *adj* anti-colonialist

anticommunisme [ɑ̃tikɔmynism] *nm Pol* anticommunism; **faire de l'a. primaire** to be a dyed-in-the-wool anticommunist

anticommuniste [ɑ̃tikɔmynist] *adj, n Pol* anticommunist

anticonceptionnel, -elle [ɑ̃tikɔ̃sɛpsjɔnɛl] *adj* (*pilule*) contraceptive; (*mesures etc*) contraceptive, birth-control

anticonformisme [ɑ̃tikɔ̃fɔrmism] *nm* non-conformism; **faire de l'a.** to be a non-conformist

anticonformiste [ɑ̃tikɔ̃fɔrmist] *adj, n* non-conformist

anticonstitutionnel, -elle [ɑ̃tikɔ̃stitysjɔnɛl] *adj* anticonstitutional, unconstitutional

anticonstitutionnellement [ɑ̃tikɔ̃stitysjɔnɛlmɑ̃] *adv* unconstitutionally

anticorps [ɑ̃tikɔr] *nm* antibody; **a. monoclonal** monoclonal antibody

anti-corrosion *adj* corrosion-resistant

anti-crevaison *adj Aut* (*pneu*) run-flat

anticyclique [ɑ̃tisiklik] *adj* anticyclic

anticyclonal, -ale, -aux, -ales [ɑ̃tisiklɔnal, -o] *adj Météo* anticyclonic; **aire anticyclonale** high-pressure area

anticyclone [ɑ̃tisiklon] *Météo* **1** *nm* anticyclone **2** *adj* **abri a.** cyclone cellar

anticyclonique [ɑ̃tisiklɔnik] *adj Météo* anticyclonic

antidate [ɑ̃tidat] *nf* antedate

antidater [ɑ̃tidate] *vt* to backdate; (*contrat etc*) to antedate

antidéflagrant [ɑ̃tideflagrɑ̃] *adj* explosion-proof

antidémarrage [ɑ̃tidemaraʒ] *nm Aut* engine immobilizer; **a. codé** (security-coded) immobilizer

antidémocratique [ɑ̃tidemɔkratik] *adj* antidemocratic, undemocratic

antidépresseur [ɑ̃tidepresœr] *adj, nm* anti-depressant

antidérapant [ɑ̃tiderapɑ̃] *Aut* **1** *adj* (*pneu, route*) non-skid; (*semelle, tapis*) non-slip **2** *nm* (*pneu*) non-skid tyre; (*revêtement*) non-slip coating

antidétonant [ɑ̃tidetɔnɑ̃] *adj, nm* anti-knock

antidiphtérique [ɑ̃tidifterik] *adj* **vaccin a.** diphtheria vaccine

antidopage [ɑ̃tidɔpaʒ] *nm*, **antidoping** [ɑ̃tidɔpiŋ] *nm Sp* **contrôle a.** drug(s) test; **être positif au contrôle a.** to fail a drugs test

antidote [ɑ̃tidɔt] *nm Méd, Fig* antidote (**contre** for)

anti-éblouissant *adj Aut* (*phares*) anti-dazzle

antiéconomique [ɑ̃tiekɔnɔmik] *adj* (*mesure*) uneconomic

antiémétique [ɑ̃tiemetik] *adj, nm Méd* antiemetic

antienne [ɑ̃tjɛn] *nf* antiphon; *Fig* **c'est toujours la même a.** he says that all the time, it's always the same old tune; *Fig* **chanter toujours la même a.** to be always harping on the same subject

antiesclavagisme [ɑ̃tiɛsklavaʒism] *nm Pol* anti-slavery movement, abolitionism
antiesclavagiste [ɑ̃tiɛsklavaʒist] **1** *adj* anti-slavery, abolitionist **2** *n* person opposed to slavery, abolitionist
antifading [ɑ̃tifadiŋ] *nm inv* automatic volume control
antifasciste [ɑ̃tifasist, -ʃist] *adj, n Pol* anti-fascist
antifongique [ɑ̃tifɔ̃ʒik] **1** *adj Méd* fungicidal **2** *nm* fungicide
anti-friction *nm inv* babbit, bearing *or* white metal
anti-g [ɑ̃tiʒe] *adj inv Av* **vêtement** *ou* **combinaison a.** (anti) G suit
antigang [ɑ̃tigɑ̃g] *adj* **brigade a.** = police squad concerned with combating terrorism and organized crime
antigaz [ɑ̃tigɑz] *adj* anti-gas
antigel [ɑ̃tiʒɛl] *nm* antifreeze
antigène [ɑ̃tiʒɛn] *nm Méd* antigen
antigivre [ɑ̃tiʒivr] **1** *adj Av* anti-icing; *Aut* de-icing **2** *nm Av* anti-icer; *Aut* de-icer
antiglisse [ɑ̃tiglis] *adj inv* **vêtements/tissu a.** non-slip clothing/material
antigrippal, -ale, -aux, -ales [ɑ̃tigripal] *adj* (*médicament, remède etc*) anti-flu
antihalo [ɑ̃tialo] *nm Photo* anti-halo
antihéros [ɑ̃tiero] *nm* antihero
antihistaminique [ɑ̃tiistaminik] *adj, nm Méd* antihistamine
antihygiénique [ɑ̃tiiʒjenik] *adj* unhygienic, insanitary
anti-inflammatoire *adj Méd* anti-inflammatory
anti-inflationniste *adj Écon* anti-inflation(ary)
antillais, -aise [ɑ̃tijɛ, -ɛz] **1** *adj* West-Indian **2** *nm Ling* creole **3** *n* **A.** West-Indian
Antilles [ɑ̃tij] *nfpl* **les A.** the (French) West Indies; **la Mer des A.** the Caribbean (Sea)
antilog [ɑ̃tilɔg] *nm Math F* antilog
antilogarithme [ɑ̃tilɔgaritm] *nm Math* antilogarithm
antilope [ɑ̃tilɔp] *nf* [ⓘA12,1,g] antelope
antimagnétique [ɑ̃timaɲetik] *adj* antimagnetic
antimatière [ɑ̃timatjɛr] *nf* antimatter
antimilitarisme [ɑ̃timilitarism] *nm* antimilitarism
antimilitariste [ɑ̃timilitarist] *adj, n* antimilitarist
antimissile [ɑ̃timisil] *adj* anti-missile; **missile a.** anti-missile missile
antimite(s) [ɑ̃timit] **1** *adj* (*vêtement*) mothproof; (*produit*) moth-repellent; **bombe a.** mothkiller **2** *nm* **antimite** mothkiller, moth-repellent
antimoine [ɑ̃timwan] *nm Ch* antimony
antimonarchique [ɑ̃timɔnarʃik] *adj* antimonarchic(al)
antimonarchisme [ɑ̃timɔnarʃism] *nm* antimonarchism
antimonarchiste [ɑ̃timɔnarʃist] *n* antimonarchist
anti-mousse *adj inv* (*pouvoir, agent*) anti-foam
antimycosique [ɑ̃timikɔzik] *adj, nm Méd* antimycotic
antinazi, -e [ɑ̃tinazi] *adj, n* anti-Nazi
antinévralgique [ɑ̃tinevralʒik] *adj, nm Pharm* antineuralgic
antinomie [ɑ̃tinɔmi] *nf* antinomy
antinomique [ɑ̃tinɔmik] *adj* antinomic
antinucléaire [ɑ̃tinykleɛr] *adj* anti-nuclear
antioxydant [ɑ̃tiɔksidɑ̃] *nm* anti-oxidant
anti-paludéen *adj, nm Pharm* antimalarial
antipaludique [ɑ̃tipalydik] *Pharm* **1** *adj* antimalaria(l) **2** *nm* antimalarial (drug)
antipape [ɑ̃tipap] *nm Hist, Rel* antipope
antiparasitage [ɑ̃tiparazitaʒ] *nm Rad, Él* suppression
antiparasite [ɑ̃tiparazit] *Rad Aut etc* **1** *nm* suppressor, interference eliminator **2** *adj* **dispositif a.** suppressor, interference eliminator
antiparlementaire [ɑ̃tiparləmɑ̃tɛr] *adj Pol* antiparliamentary
antiparlementarisme [ɑ̃tiparləmɑ̃tarism] *nm* antiparliamentarianism
antipathie [ɑ̃tipati] *nf* antipathy; **avoir** *ou* **éprouver de l'a. pour qn** to have antipathy for *or* feel antipathy towards sb; **éprouver une grande a. pour qn** to have great antipathy for *or* feel great antipathy towards sb
antipathique [ɑ̃tipatik] *adj* unpleasant; **je le trouve très a.** I don't like him at all; **je ne le trouve pas du tout a.** I quite like him
antipelliculaire [ɑ̃tipelikylɛr] *adj* **shampooing a.** (anti-) dandruff shampoo
antipersonnel [ɑ̃tipɛrsɔnɛl] *adj inv Mil* antipersonnel
antiphone [ɑ̃tifɔn] *nm Rel* antiphon
antiphrase [ɑ̃tifraz] *nf Ling* antiphrasis; **dire qch par a.** to say sth ironically
antipodal, -ale, -aux, -ales [ɑ̃tipɔdal, -o] *adj* antipodean
antipode [ɑ̃tipɔd] *nm Géog* antipodes; **la Nouvelle-Zélande est l'a.** *ou* **aux antipodes de la France** New Zealand is on the other side of the world from France; **aux antipodes** at *or* in the antipodes; *Fig* diametrically opposed, poles apart; *Fig* **son opinion est à l'a.** *ou* **aux antipodes de la mienne** his opinion is quite the opposite of mine *or* is poles apart from mine
antipoétique [ɑ̃tipɔetik] *adj* unpoetic
antipoison [ɑ̃tipwazɔ̃] *adj Méd* **centre a.** poisons unit
antipoliomyélite [ɑ̃tipɔljɔmjelit] *adj* **vaccination a.** polio vaccination
antipollution [ɑ̃tipɔlysjɔ̃] *adj inv* (*mesures*) anti-pollution
antiprogressif, -ive [ɑ̃tiprɔgrɛsif, -iv] *adj* reactionary
antiprotectionniste [ɑ̃tiprɔtɛksjɔnist] **1** *adj* (*ligne d'action*) free-trade **2** *n* antiprotectionist, free trader
antipsychiatrie [ɑ̃tipsikjatri] *nf* anti-psychiatry
antipyrétique [ɑ̃tipiretik] *adj, nm Méd* antipyretic, antifebrile
antipyrine [ɑ̃tipirin] *nf Méd* antipyrine
antiquaille [ɑ̃tikaj] *nf Péj* worthless old junk
antiquaire [ɑ̃tikɛr] *n* antique dealer
antique [ɑ̃tik] **1** *adj* old, ancient; (*mobilier*) antique, *Péj* old-fashioned, antiquated; **la Grèce a.** ancient *or* classical Greece **2** *nm* **(a)** (*art*) art from the antiquity; (*objets d'art de l'Antiquité*) works of art from the antiquity **(b) l'a.** the antique, classical antiquity **(c)** *Typ* antique
antiquité [ɑ̃tikite] *nf* **(a)** (*ancienneté*) antiquity **(b)** (*temps anciens*) ancient times, antiquity; **ça remonte à la plus haute a.** that goes back *or* dates back to time immemorial; **connu de toute a.** known (about) since time immemorial **(c)** *Hist* **l'a. grecque** ancient Greek civilization **(d) antiquités** (*meubles etc anciens*) antiques; **magasin d'antiquités** antique shop **(e) les antiquités** the works of classical antiquity
antirabique [ɑ̃tirabik] *adj Méd* (*vaccin*) anti-rabies
antirachitique [ɑ̃tiraʃitik] *adj Méd* antirachitic
antiracisme [ɑ̃tirasism] *nm* antiracialism, anti-racism
antiraciste [ɑ̃tirasist] *adj, n* antiracist, antiracialist
antiradar [ɑ̃tiradar] **1** *adj* anti-radar **2** *nm* anti-radar device
antireflet [ɑ̃tirəflɛ] *adj inv* nonreflective; *Ordinat* non-reflecting, antiglare
antiréglementaire [ɑ̃tireglәmɑ̃tɛr] *adj* against regulations
antireligieux, -euse [ɑ̃tirəliʒjø, -øz] *adj* antireligious
antirépublicain, -aine [ɑ̃tirepyblikɛ̃, -ɛn] *adj, n* antirepublican
antirévolutionnaire [ɑ̃tirevɔlysjɔnɛr] *adj, n* antirevolutionary
antirides [ɑ̃tirid] *adj inv* (*crème*) anti-wrinkle
anti-roman, *pl* **anti-romans** *nm Littér* anti-novel
antirouille [ɑ̃tiruj] **1** *nm* rust preventive **2** *adj inv* (*métal*) rustproof, non-rusting; (*produit, traitement*) rust-preventing
antiroulis [ɑ̃tiruli] *nm Naut, Av* (gyro) stabilizer; *Aut* anti-roll bar
anti-scintillements *adj Ordinat* flicker-free
antiscorbutique [ɑ̃tiskɔrbytik] *adj, nm Pharm* antiscorbutic
antisèche [ɑ̃tisɛʃ] *nf F* crib sheet
antiségrégationniste [ɑ̃tisegregasjɔnist] *adj, n* antisegregationist
antisémite [ɑ̃tisemit] **1** *adj* anti-semitic **2** *n* anti-semite
antisémitique [ɑ̃tisemitik] *adj* anti-semitic
antisémitisme [ɑ̃tisemitism] *nm* anti-semitism
antisepsie [ɑ̃tisɛpsi] *nf Méd* antisepsis
antiseptique [ɑ̃tisɛptik] *adj, nm Méd* antiseptic
antisérum [ɑ̃tiserɔm] *nm Méd* antiserum
antisionisme [ɑ̃tizjɔnism] *nm* anti-Zionism
antisioniste [ɑ̃tizjɔnist] *adj, n* anti-Zionist
antisocial, -ale, -aux, -ales [ɑ̃tisɔsjal, -o] *adj* antisocial
antisolaire [ɑ̃tisɔlɛr] *adj* sun-reflective
anti-sous-marin *adj Mil* anti-submarine
antisoviétique [ɑ̃tisɔvjetik] *adj* anti-Soviet
antispasmodique [ɑ̃tispasmɔdik] *adj, nm Pharm* antispasmodic
antisportif, -ive [ɑ̃tispɔrtif, -iv] *adj* (*opposé au sport*) anti-sport; (*contraire à l'esprit du sport*) unsportsmanlike, unsporting
antistrophe [ɑ̃tistrɔf] *nf* antistrophe
antisudoral, -aux [ɑ̃tisydɔral, -o] *adj, nm* anti-perspirant
antitabac [ɑ̃titaba] *adj inv* (*lutte, campagne*) anti-smoking
antiterroriste [ɑ̃titerɔrist] *adj* anti-terrorist, anti-terrorism
antitétanique [ɑ̃titetanik] *Méd* **1** *adj* antitetanus **2** *nm* antitetanus serum
antithèse [ɑ̃titɛz] *nf* antithesis; *Fig* **je suis l'a. de ma sœur** I'm the opposite of my sister
antithétique [ɑ̃titetik] *adj* antithetic(al)
antitoxine [ɑ̃titɔksin] *nf Méd* antitoxin
antitoxique [ɑ̃titɔksik] *adj Méd* antitoxic
antitrust [ɑ̃titrœst] *adj inv Br* anti-monopoly, *surtout US* antitrust; **lois a.** anti-monopoly laws
antituberculeux, -euse [ɑ̃titybɛrkylø, -øz] *adj Méd* antitubercular; **centre a.** tuberculosis centre
antitussif, -ive [ɑ̃titysif, -iv] *adj, nm Méd* **sirop a.** cough mixture *or* syrup *or* medicine
antivariolique [ɑ̃tivarjɔlik] *adj Méd* **vaccin a.** smallpox vaccine

antivénérien [ɑ̃tivenerjɛ̃] *adj Méd* antivenereal
antivenimeux, -euse [ɑ̃tivənimø, -øz] *adj* antivenin
anti-vent *nm* (*pour microphone*) wind gag
antiviral, -ale, -aux, -ales [ɑ̃tiviral, -o] *adj Méd* antivirus
antivirus [ɑ̃tivirys] *nm* antivirus
antivivisection(n)iste [ɑ̃tivivisɛksjɔnist] **1** *n* antivivisectionist **2** *adj* antivivisection(ist); **société a.** antivivisection society
antivol [ɑ̃tivɔl] **1** *adj inv* (*équipement*) anti-theft; (*serrure*) thief-proof; *Aut* **alarme a.** car alarm **2** *nm* (*pour les cycles*) lock; (*pour les voitures*) steering lock; *Aut* **a. de direction** steering column lock; *Aut* **a.-contact** ignition lock
antonomase [ɑ̃tɔnɔmaz] *nm Litt* antonomasia
antonyme [ɑ̃tɔnim] **1** *adj* antonymous **2** *nm* antonym
antre [ɑ̃tr] *nm* **(a)** (*caverne*) cave, cavern; (*d'animaux, de brigands*); *Fig* (*d'une personne*) den, lair; **un a. de voleurs** a den of thieves **(b)** *Anat* antrum, sinus
anurie [anyri] *nf Méd* anuria
anus [anys] *nm Anat* anus; *Chir* **a. artificiel** colostomy
Anvers [ɑ̃vɛr(s)] *nm* Antwerp
anversois, -oise [ɑ̃vɛrswa, -waz] **1** *adj* of *or* from Antwerp **2** *n* **A.** (*natif*) native of Antwerp; (*habitant*) inhabitant of Antwerp
anxiété [ɑ̃ksjete] *nf* anxiety; **éprouver de l'a.** to feel anxious; **avec a.** anxiously
anxieusement [ɑ̃ksjøzmɑ̃] *adv* anxiously
anxieux, -ieuse [ɑ̃ksjø, -jøz] **1** *adj* **(a)** (*inquiet*) anxious, uneasy **(b) a. de faire qch** anxious *or* impatient to do sth; **il est a. de partir** he's anxious *or* impatient to leave **2** *n* worrier
anxiogène [ɑ̃ksjɔʒɛn] *adj* causing anxiety
anxiolytique [ɑ̃ksjɔlitik] **1** *adj* anxiolitic **2** *nm* tranquilizer
aorte [aɔrt] *nf Anat* aorta
aortique [aɔrtik] *adj Anat* aortic, aortal
août [u(t)] *nm* [①**A75-6,**B-C; **B58-9,**B-C] August; **en a., au mois d'a.** in (the month of) August; **le premier/le sept a.** (on) the first/the seventh of August, (on) August the first/the seventh, *US* (on) August first/seventh; **le quinze a.** the Assumption, Assumption Day; **à la mi-a.** in mid-August
aoûtat [auta] *nm* harvest mite, *Am* chigger
aoûtien, -ienne [ausjɛ̃, -jɛn] *n* August holidaymaker *or Am* vacationer
apache [apaʃ] *nm* **A.** Apache
apaisant [apɛzɑ̃] *adj* (*geste, paroles*) appeasing; (*nouvelles, effet etc*) soothing, calming
apaisement [apɛzmɑ̃] *nm* (*d'une personne en colère, des dieux*) appeasement, appeasing; (*d'une personne en colère ou inquiète*) calming (down); (*de la douleur*) alleviation; **donner des apaisements à qn** (*paroles*) to give (re)assurance to sb, to (re)assure sb
apaiser [apeze] **1** *vt* (*personne en colère, dieux*) to appease, to pacify; (*personne en colère ou inquiète*) to calm (down); (*douleur, enfant*) to soothe; (*faim*) to appease, to satisfy; (*soif*) to quench; (*craintes*) to calm, to allay **2 s'apaiser** *vpr* (*d'une personne*) to calm down; (*du vent*) to drop, to subside; (*de la douleur, des craintes*) to subside; **la foule s'apaisait** the crowd was calming down *or* becoming quieter
apanage [apanaʒ] *nm* prerogative; **elle croit avoir l'a. de la sagesse** she thinks she has a monopoly on wisdom
aparté [aparte] *nm* **(a)** *Th* aside, stage whisper; **en a.** aside, in a stage whisper **(b)** (*entre deux personnes*) private conversation; **en a.** in private, as an aside; **il le lui a dit en a.** he took him/her aside *or* to one side to tell him/her
apartheid [apartɛd] *nm* apartheid
apathie [apati] *nf* apathy, listlessness; **le malade est dans une a. totale** the patient is completely listless; **il sombra dans une complète a.** he sank into a state of complete apathy
apathique [apatik] *adj* apathetic, listless
apatride [apatrid] *adj, n Jur* stateless (person)
apatridie [apatridi] *nf Jur* statelessness
Apennins [apenɛ̃] *nmpl* Apennines
aperception [apersɛpsjɔ̃] *nf Phil* apperception
apercevoir [apɛrsəvwar] (*prp* **apercevant**; *pp* **aperçu**; *pr ind* **j'aperçois, n. apercevons, ils aperçoivent**; *pr sub* **j'aperçoive, n. apercevions**; *impf* **j'apercevais**; *p hist* **j'aperçus**; *fu* **j'apercevrai**) **1** *vt* to perceive, to see; (*soudain, rapidement*) (*qn, qch*) to catch sight of, to catch a glimpse of; **je n'ai fait que l'a.** I caught only a glimpse of him/her; **elle cherche à ne pas laisser a. sa fatigue** she's trying not to let her tiredness show; **je commence à a. ses raisons** I'm starting to see his reasons; **si on y pense bien, on aperçoit des difficultés** if you think about it, you start to see difficulties
2 s'apercevoir *vpr* **(a)** (*être visible*) to be noticeable; **cela ne s'aperçoit pas** it isn't visible *or* noticeable
(b) (*comprendre, réaliser*) **s'a. de qch** to realize *or* notice sth, to become aware *or* conscious of sth; **il s'est aperçu qu'il n'avait pas ses clés** he realized that he hadn't got his keys with him; **sans s'en a.** without being aware of it, without noticing it
(c) (*se voir*) (*de deux personnes*) to catch a glimpse of each other; (*soi-même*) to catch sight of oneself
aperçu [apɛrsy] *nm* **(a)** (*coup d'œil*) glimpse; **a. sur la campagne** glimpse of the countryside **(b)** (*idée générale*) general idea, outline, summary; **par a.** at a rough estimate; **ça te donnera un a. du travail à faire** that'll give you an idea of the work to be done; *Ordinat* **a. avant impression** print preview **(c)** (*intuition*) insight (**sur** into)
apériodique [aperjɔdik] *adj Él* aperiodic
apéritif [aperitif] **1** *nm* aperitif; **viens prendre l'a. chez moi demain soir** come round and have an early evening drink tomorrow **2** *adj Litt* (*promenade etc*) pre-prandial
apéro [apero] *nm F* = **apéritif**
aperture [apɛrtyr] *nf Ling* aperture
apesanteur [apəzɑ̃tœr] *nf* weightlessness; **en état d'a.** in weightless conditions
à-peu-près *nm inv* approximation, rough estimate, guess; **calculer une somme par à.** to make a rough calculation; **il y a trop d'à. dans votre exposé** there is too much woolliness in your report
apeuré [apœre, -øre] *adj* scared, frightened
apeurer [apœre] *vt* to frighten, to scare
APEX [apɛks] *nm* (*ticket*) APEX
apex [apɛks] *nm* apex
aphasie [afazi] *nf Méd* aphasia
aphasique [afazik] *Méd* **1** *adj* aphasi(a)c **2** *n* aphasic
aphis [afis] *nm* aphis, greenfly
aphone [afɔn] *adj Méd* voiceless; **elle était a. pour avoir trop crié** she'd lost her voice through shouting too much
aphonie [afɔni] *nf Méd* loss of voice; **être atteint d'a.** to have lost one's voice
aphorisme [afɔrism] *nm* aphorism; *Péj* **s'exprimer par aphorismes** to speak in platitudes
aphrodisiaque [afrɔdizjak] *adj, nm Pharm* aphrodisiac
aphte [aft(ə)] *nm Méd* mouth ulcer
aphteux, -euse [aftø, -øz] *adj Méd, Vét* **fièvre aphteuse** foot-and-mouth disease
à-pic [apik] *nm inv* cliff, bluff
apicole [apikɔl] *adj* apiarian; **exploitation a.** honey farm
apiculteur, -trice [apikyltœr, -tris] *n* beekeeper, apiarist
apiculture [apikyltyr] *nf* beekeeping, apiculture
apitoiement [apitwamɑ̃] *nm* pity, compassion; **porté à l'a.** compassionate; **pas d'a.!** (*à mon égard*) don't commiserate (with me), don't be sympathetic; **leurs apitoiements** their pity *or* compassion
apitoyant [apitwajɑ̃] *adj* pitiful, *Litt* piteous
apitoyer [apitwaje] (**j'apitoie, n. apitoyons; j'apitoierai**) **1** *vt* **a. qn** to move sb (to pity), to incite sb to pity **2 s'apitoyer** *vpr* **s'a. sur qn** to pity sb, to feel pity for sb; **s'a. sur (le sort de) qn** to commiserate with sb; **s'a. sur soi-même** *ou* **sur son sort** to feel sorry for oneself; **ça ne sert à rien de s'a. sur soi-même** feeling sorry for yourself/himself/*etc* won't help, self-pity won't help
aplanir [aplanir] **1** *vt* (*surface*) to flatten, to smooth; (*bois*) to plane; (*métal*) to planish; (*route etc*) to level; (*imperfections*) to smooth out; *Fig* (*difficultés*) to iron out; *Fig* (*conflit*) to settle **2 s'aplanir** *vpr* (*du sol*) to become level; **les problèmes se sont aplanis d'eux-mêmes** the problems have ironed *or* smoothed themselves out
aplanissement [aplanismɑ̃] *nm* (*du sol*) levelling; (*des difficultés*) ironing out
aplat [apla] *nm Ordinat* solid (figure)
aplati [aplati] *adj* **(a)** flattened, flat; (*nez*) flat **(b)** (*sphère etc*) oblate
aplatir [aplatir] **1** *vt* (*qch*) to flatten, to make flat; (*angle*) to blunt; *Métal* (*rivet*) to clench; (*tête de rivet*) to hammer down; **a. au fer** to press; **a. qch à coups de marteau** to hammer sth flat; *Fig F* **a. qn** (*casser la figure à qn*) to flatten sb; **il l'a aplati d'un coup de poing** he knocked him down *or* flattened him with one punch
2 *vi Rugby* to score a try, to touch down
3 s'aplatir *vpr* (*de coiffure*) to go flat; (*d'un chapeau*) to get flattened; **s'a. par terre** to lie down flat on the ground; *F* (*tomber*) to come a cropper; **s'a. contre un mur** to flatten oneself against a wall; *Fig* **s'a. devant qn** to grovel to sb
aplatissage [aplatisaʒ] *nm Tech* pressing; (*d'une surface, d'une couture*) flattening; (*d'un rivet*) hammering down
aplatissement [aplatismɑ̃] *nm* **(a)** flatness; **l'a. de la Terre aux pôles** the flattening of the earth at the poles **(b)** *Fig* (*abaissement*) grovelling

aplomb [aplɔ̃] *nm* (**a**) perpendicularity; **d'a.** upright, vertical(ly), plumb; **mets la bouteille d'a., elle va tomber** straighten up the bottle, it's going to fall; **les étagères ne sont pas d'a.** the shelves are out of plumb *or* off plumb; **bien d'a. sur ses pieds** steady on one's feet; *Fig F* **je ne suis pas d'a. aujourd'hui** I'm out of sorts *or* off colour today; *Fig* **voilà qui vous remettra d'a.** that will revive you, *F* that will buck you up; *Fig* **il me faut dix mille francs pour me remettre d'a.** I need ten thousand francs to set me back on my feet; **hors d'a.** out of plumb, out of true; **à l'a. de qch** straight above/below sth; *Tech* plumb with sth
(**b**) (*assurance*) (self-)assurance, coolness; **perdre son a.** to lose one's self-assurance; *Péj* **avoir l'a. de dire/de faire qch** to have the cheek *or* nerve to say/do sth; **il ne manque pas d'a.** he's got a nerve *or* a cheek

apnée [apne] *nf Méd* apnea; **plonger en a.** to dive without breathing apparatus

apocalypse [apɔkalips] *nf* apocalypse, revelation; *Bible* **l'A.** the Book of Revelation, the Apocalypse; **les quatre cavaliers de l'A.** the four horsemen of the Apocalypse; *Fig* **vision d'a.** apocalyptic vision; *Fig* **un paysage d'a.** a post-holocaust landscape

apocalyptique [apɔkaliptik] *adj* apocalyptic(al); *Fig* **silence/paysage a.** doom-laden silence/post-holocaust landscape

apocope [apɔkɔp] *nf Ling* apocope

apocryphe [apɔkrif] **1** *adj* apocryphal, *Péj* of doubtful authenticity **2** *npl Bible* **les Apocryphes** the Apocrypha

apogée [apɔʒe] *nm Astron* apogee; **la lune est à son a.** the moon is at its apogee; *Fig* **à l'a. de sa gloire** at the height of one's fame; *Fig* **être à l'a. de sa carrière** to be at the height *or* pinnacle of one's career; *Fig* **atteindre son a.** to reach one's peak

apolitique [apɔlitik] *adj* apolitical

apolitisme [apɔlitism] *nm* apolitical attitude

Apollon [apɔlɔ̃] *nm Myth* Apollo; *Beaux-Arts* **A. du Belvédère** Apollo Belvedere

apollon [apɔlɔ̃] *nm Fig* Adonis, Greek god; **ce n'est pas vraiment un a.!** he's no Adonis!, he's no oil painting!

apologétique [apɔlɔʒetik] **1** *adj* apologetic **2** *nf Rel* apologetics

apologie [apɔlɔʒi] *nf* (*défense*) apologia (**de** for), defence; **faire l'a. de qn/qch** to justify *or* defend sb/sth; (*éloge*) encomium, eulogy; (*louer*) to eulogize sb/sth

apologiste [apɔlɔʒist] *n* apologist

apologue [apɔlɔg] *nm* apologue

apophyse [apɔfiz] *nf Phys* apophysis

apoplectique [apɔplɛktik] *adj, n Méd* apoplectic

apoplexie [apɔplɛksi] *nf Méd* apoplexy; **attaque d'a.** apoplectic seizure, stroke

apostasie [apɔstazi] *nf Rel* apostasy; **faire acte d'a.** to apostatize, to become an apostate; *Fig* to renounce one's party *or* principles, to desert the cause

apostasier [apɔstazje] *vi* (*pr sub, impf* **n. apostasiions, v. apostasiiez**) to apostatize, to become an apostate; *Fig* to renounce one's party *or* principles, to desert the cause

apostat, -ate [apɔsta, -at] **1** *adj* apostate, renegade; **curé a.** renegade priest **2** *n* apostate; *Fig* **ce politicien est un a.** that politician has renounced his principles

a posteriori [apɔsterjɔri] **1** *adv* with hindsight, after the event; *Phil* a posteriori; **a. je me suis rendu compte que c'était moi qui avais raison** with hindsight, I realized that I was right **2** *adj inv* **méthode a.** a posteriori method

apostolat [apɔstɔla] *nm Rel* apostolate; *Fig* **cette profession est un a.** this job is a real vocation

apostolique [apɔstɔlik] *adj* (*temps, église etc*) apostolic; **vicaire a.** vicar apostolic; **pères apostoliques** apostolic fathers

apostrophe[1] [apɔstrɔf] *nf* (**a**) *Ling, Gram* apostrophe; **mot mis en a.** word used in apostrophe; **le vocatif est le cas de l'a.** the vocative is the case of direct address (**b**) (*interpellation*) reproach, reprimand; **les apostrophes des conducteurs énervés** the rude remarks of angry motorists

apostrophe[2] *nf Gram* (*signe*) apostrophe

apostropher [apɔstrɔfe] **1** *vt* **a. qn** (*pour attirer son attention*) to shout to sb; (*être impoli envers lui*) to address sb rudely, to shout at sb; (*l'insulter vivement*) to hurl abuse at sb **2 s'apostropher** *vpr* to shout at one another; **les supporters des équipes de foot s'apostrophent** the football supporters hurl abuse at each other

apothéose [apɔteoz] *nf* (**a**) apotheosis, deification; *Fig* (*consécration*) crowning moment *or* glory; **cette promotion est l'a. de sa carrière** this promotion is the crowning moment of his/her career; **l'a. du cinéma français** the supreme achievement *or* the crowning glory of French cinema; **finir en a.** to end in triumph (**b**) *Th* grand finale

apothicaire [apɔtikɛr] *nm Vieilli* apothecary; *Fig* **tenir des comptes d'a.** to know where every penny goes

apôtre [apotr] *nm* apostle; *Fig* **se faire l'a. du recyclage** to become an advocate of recycling; *Fig* **il fait toujours le bon a.** he always puts on such a saintly air

Appalaches [apalaʃ] *nmpl* **les (monts) Appalaches** the Appalachian Mountains, the Appalachians

appalachien, -ienne [apalaʃjɛ̃, -jɛn] *adj* Appalachian; **relief a.** Appalachian relief

apparaître [aparɛtr] (*conj like* **paraître**; *the auxiliary is* **être**, *sometimes* **avoir**) **1** *vi* (**a**) (*devenir visible*) to appear; **il lui est apparu en rêve** he came *or* appeared to her in a dream; **a. à travers le brouillard** to loom out of the fog; **un spectre lui était apparu** a ghost had appeared to him
(**b**) (*se révéler*) to become evident *or* apparent; **cette décision m'est apparue évidente** it seemed the obvious decision
(**c**) (*sembler*) **le projet lui apparaissait impossible** the plan seemed impossible to him; **il m'apparaît comme le seul capable d'y parvenir** he seems to me to be the only person capable of doing it
2 *vi impers* **il apparaît que vous avez été souvent absent** it appears that you have frequently been absent; **selon les statistiques, il apparaîtrait que ...** according to the statistics, it would appear that ...

apparat [apara] *nm* pomp, show, display; **tenue d'a.** ceremonial dress; **en grand a.** with great pomp and ceremony; **dîner d'a.** banquet; **discours d'a.** ceremonial speech; **lettres d'a.** illuminated letters

apparatchik [aparatʃik] *nm* apparatchik

apparaux [aparo] *nmpl* (**a**) *Naut* tackle, gear; **les gros a.** the purchase (**b**) *Gym* apparatus

appareil [aparɛj] *nm* (**a**) (*instrument*) apparatus, equipment; *Ind* (*sing or pl*) plant; **appareils ménagers** household appliances; **appareils de laboratoire** laboratory apparatus; **a. auxiliaire** *ou* **de secours** stand-by equipment; **a. de pêche** fishing tackle; *Min* **a. de forage** drilling rig; **a. d'enregistrement** recorder; **a. de lecture** (*de microfilm*) reader; *MecE* **a. de levage** lifting tackle; *Cin* **a. de projection** film projector; **a. à gaz** gas appliance; *Rail* **a. de voie** switch gear; **a. de prothèse** prosthesis, artificial limb *etc*; **a. (dentaire)** (*correctif*) brace; (*dentier*) dentures; **a. à sous** slot machine, fruit machine, one-armed bandit
(**b**) *Tél* telephone; **Marcelline à l'a.** Marcelline speaking *or* here; **qui est à l'a.?** who's speaking?
(**c**) *Av* aircraft, plane; **a. de chasse** fighter; **a. d'école** training aircraft, trainer
(**d**) *Phot* **a. (photographique), a-photo** camera; **a. reflex** reflex camera
(**e**) (*administration etc*) bodies, authorities; **mettre en jeu l'a. de la justice** to put the machinery of the law in motion; **l'a. du parti** the party machine *or* apparatus; *Ind* **a. de production** production facilities; **a. commercial** commercial structure
(**f**) *Méd* dressing; (*pour fracture*) splint, plaster
(**g**) *Anat* system, apparatus; **a. digestif** digestive system; **a. respiratoire** respiratory system
(**h**) *Constr* (*de pierres*) height; (*agencement*) bond; **assise de grand a.** course of large stones
(**i**) (*d'un texte*) **a. critique** critical apparatus
(**j**) *Litt* display, magnifence, pomp; *Fig* **dans le plus simple a.** in the nude

appareillage [aparɛjaz] *nm* (**a**) *Naut* getting under way, weighing (anchor), setting sail (**b**) (*matériel*) fittings, equipment, accessories; *Ind* plant; **a. électrique** electrical equipment (**c**) (*d'un atelier etc*) installation, fitting (up), setting up (**d**) *Constr* (*de pierres, de briques*) bonding

appareillement [aparɛjmɑ̃] *nm* (*d'animaux pour la reproduction*) pairing, mating; (*de bœufs*) pairing

appareiller [apareje] **1** *vt* (**a**) *Naut* **a. un navire** to rig a boat out (**b**) *Constr* (*pierres, briques*) to bond (**c**) (*filet*) to spread (**d**) (*atelier etc*) to install, to fit up *or* out (**e**) *Méd* (*handicapé*) to fit up; **a. un sourd** to fit a deaf person with a hearing aid (**f**) (*assortir*) **a. une lampe** to find a match for a lamp **2** *vi Naut* to get under way

appareilleur [aparɛjœr] *nm* (*de pierres etc*) trimmer, fitter, dresser; *Constr* foreman mason

apparemment [aparamɑ̃] *adv* apparently; **a. tout allait bien** everything seemed to be going well

apparence [aparɑ̃s] *nf* (**a**) (*air, aspect extérieur*) appearance, look; **cette maison/voiture a une belle a.** this house/car looks nice; **donner une belle a. à sa maison en la repeignant** to make one's house look nice by repainting it; **quelque a. de (la) vérité** some semblance of truth; **un homme à l'a. négligée/soignée** an untidy-looking *or* an unkempt(-looking) man/a tidy-looking *or* a neat(-looking) man; **selon toute a.** to all appearances; **contre toute a.** against all expectations

(b) (*aspect trompeur*) **il ne faut pas se fier aux apparences** appearances can be deceptive; **prendre l'a. pour réalité** to confuse appearance with reality; **sous de fausses apparences** under false pretences; **sous une a. de douceur se cache une grande fermeté** beneath a mild-mannered exterior there lies great strength of will; **il a l'air gentil, mais ce n'est qu'une (fausse) a.** he seems nice, but it's only a façade; **il ne faut pas juger sur les apparences** you shouldn't judge by *or* on appearance(s) (alone); **il ne faut pas s'arrêter à l'a.** you should look beyond the façade; **en a.** outwardly, on the surface; **plus difficile en a. qu'en réalité** less difficult than it looks; **pour sauver les apparences** for the sake of appearances; (*pour éviter une humiliation*) to save face

(c) (*trace*) semblance, vestige; **elle n'a plus la moindre a. de respect pour lui** she no longer has the slightest vestige of respect for him

apparent [aparɑ̃] *adj* **(a)** (*visible*) visible, apparent; **peu a.** hardly noticeable; **sans raison apparente** for no apparent reason **(b)** (*prétendu*) apparent, not real; **c'est la raison apparente, mais la vérité est autre** that's the ostensible reason, but the truth is quite different; **mouvement a. du soleil** apparent movement of the sun; **sous cette apparente bonté se cache un grand égoïsme** beneath that kind exterior there lies great selfishness; **piété apparente** outward piety **(c)** *Jur* **héritier a.** heir apparent

apparenté [aparɑ̃te] **(a)** *adj* (*par le mariage*) related; (*qui a des liens avec*) related, connected; **bien a.** well connected **(b)** *Pol* **candidat a. au Parti socialiste** *etc* = candidate who, though not a member of the Socialist *etc* Party, can count on its support in an election **(c)** *Ch* **éléments apparentés** related *or* affinitive elements

apparentement [aparɑ̃təmɑ̃] *nm Pol* = practice of forming electoral alliances (under proportional representation)

apparenter (s') [saparɑ̃te] *vpr* **(a)** to marry (**à une famille** into a family) **(b)** *Pol* to form an alliance (**à** with) **(c)** *Fig* to have sth in common (**à** with); **les deux tendances s'apparentent en de nombreux points** the two trends have many things in common

apparier [aparje] (*impf & pr sub* **n. appariions, v. appariiez**) **1** *vt* **(a)** (*oiseaux pour la reproduction*) to couple, to pair, to mate **(b)** (*chaussettes, chevaux etc*) to match, to pair; (*adversaires*) to pair off **2 s'apparier** *vpr* (*des oiseaux*) to mate

appariteur [aparitœr] *nm* (*d'université*) mace bearer

apparition [aparisjɔ̃] *nf* **(a)** appearance; (*d'une fièvre*) outbreak; **l'a. des boutons/des symptômes** the appearance of the spots/symptoms; **faire une courte a.** (*d'une personne*) to make a brief appearance; *TV, Cin* **brève a.** short *or* cameo appearance, cameo; **la star a finalement fait son a. vers 18 heures** the star finally appeared *or* made his/her appearance around six o'clock **(b)** (*de fantôme*) apparition; (*d'un ange*) appearance; **avoir des apparitions** to see things

appartement [apartəmɑ̃] *nm* **(a)** flat, *Am* apartment; (*dans un hôtel etc*) suite, set of rooms; **a. de passage** pied-à-terre; **a. de fonction** company flat; **vivre en a.** to live in a flat; **plantes d'a.** indoor *or* house *or* pot plants **(b)** (*dans un château etc*) **les grands appartements** the state apartments

appartenance [apartənɑ̃s] *nf* **(a) a. à qch** (the fact of) belonging to sth *or* being part of sth; *Math* **a. à un ensemble** membership of a set; **a. à un parti** membership of a party **(b) appartenances** (*d'une maison, d'un château*) appurtenances

appartenir [apartənir] (*conj like* **tenir**) **1** *vi* **(a)** (*être la possession de*) to belong (**à** to), to be owned (**à** by); **cette maison lui appartient en propre** this house is his own personal property

(b) (*dépendre*) **pour des raisons qui t'appartiennent** for your own private reasons; **cela n'appartient pas à mes fonctions** this does not come within the scope of my duties

(c) (*par famille etc*) **a. à qch** to be part of sth, to belong to sth, to be a member of sth; *Math* **a. à un ensemble** to be a member of a set; **elle appartient à une famille très riche** she comes from a very wealthy family

2 s'appartenir *vpr* **je ne m'appartiens pas** I'm not my own master; (*je n'ai pas de temps à moi*) I've no time to call my own

3 *v impers* **à tous ceux qu'il appartient** to all whom it may concern; **il appartient au comité de prendre la décision** it is for the committee *or* up to the committee to decide, the decision lies with the committee; **il ne m'appartient pas de le critiquer** it is not for me to criticize him; *Iron* **il vous appartient bien de me critiquer** you're a fine one to criticize me

appas [apɑ] *nmpl Litt* charms

appât [apɑ] *nm* **(a)** (*de pêche*) bait; *Fig* (*du succès*) lure; **a. de fond** ground bait; **mettre l'a. à la ligne** to bait the line; **mordre à l'a.** (*d'un poisson, Fig d'une personne*) to rise to the bait; *Fig* **animé par l'a. du gain** driven by the lure of money **(b)** (*pour la volaille*) soft food

appâter [apɑte] *vt* **(a)** (*poissons, oiseaux etc*) to lure with bait; *Fig* (*personne*) to entice; *Fig* **a. qn par des promesses** to entice sb with promises **(b)** (*hameçon etc*) to bait **(c)** *Vieilli* (*volaille*) to force-feed

appauvrir [apovrir] **1** *vt* to impoverish; *Méd* **a. le sang** to thin the blood; **a. la constitution de qn** to weaken sb's constitution **2 s'appauvrir** *vpr* to grow poorer; (*du sol*) to lose its fertility, to become impoverished; **la langue risque de s'a.** there is a risk that the language will become impoverished

appauvrissement [apovrismɑ̃] *nm* (*d'un pays, du sol etc*) impoverishment; (*d'une race*) degeneration; (*de la santé, des stocks*) deterioration; (*du sang*) thinning; (*d'une entreprise*) decline in the financial position

appeau, *pl* **appeaux** [apo] *nm* bird call; *Fig* **servir d'a. à qn** to act as a decoy for sb

appel [apɛl] *nm* **(a)** (*invitation, sollicitation*) appeal; (*d'un spécialiste etc*) calling in; **faire a. à qn** to call on sb; (*faire venir*) (*plombier etc*) to send for; **faire a. à la générosité de qn** to appeal to sb's generosity; **cette formation fait a. à des connaissances commerciales** this training course calls for *or* requires some knowledge of business; **faire a. à tout son courage** to summon up all one's courage; **il faut faire a. à tous vos souvenirs** you have to search your memory; **l'a. à la révolte** the call to revolt; **l'a. du Général de Gaulle** General de Gaulle's appeal *or* call to the French nation; *Rad* **nous lançons un a. à tous les automobilistes sur la R.N. 7** here is a message for all motorists on the RN 7

(b) *Jur* appeal (at law); **avis d'a.** notice of appeal; **Cour d'a.** Court of Appeal; **faire a. d'une décision** to appeal (against) a decision; **juger en a. (d'une décision)** to hear an appeal (from a decision); **casser un jugement en a.** to quash a sentence on appeal; **jugement sans a.** final judgment; *Fig* **c'est ce que j'ai décidé, et c'est sans a.** that's my decision and it's final *or F* that's that

(c) (*attirance*) call; (*voix*) voice; **l'a. du printemps** the call of spring; **l'a. du large** *ou* **de la mer** the call of the sea; **l'a. de la nature** the call of the wild; **l'a. de la conscience** the voice of conscience

(d) (*cri*) call, shout; **cri d'a.** call for help; **entendre un a. au secours** to hear a cry for help; **a. d'incendie** fire alarm; **accourir à un a.** to run in answer to sb's call; *Fig* **il m'a fait un a. du regard pour que je lui vienne en aide** his eyes pleaded with me to help; *Fig* **faire un a. du coude à qn** (*pour attirer son attention sur qch*) to nudge sb; *Aut* **faire un a. de phares** to flash one's headlights (**à qn** at sb)

(e) *Fin* **faire un a. de fonds** to call up capital; *Com* **faire un a. d'offres** to invite bids *or* tenders; *Mktg* **a. à froid** cold call; *Com* **produit d'a.** loss leader

(f) *Mil* **l'a. aux armes** the call to arms; **devancer l'a.** to join up before being enlisted; **a. de mobilisation** mobilization order

(g) [①A71,5] *Tél* **touche d'a.** call key; **signal d'a.** call waiting service; **numéro d'a.** (telephone) number; **a. téléphonique** (tele)phone call; **a. de réveil** wake-up *or* alarm call; **a. interurbain** trunk call; **a. matinal** early morning call; **a. gratuit** freecall; **il y a eu un a. pour vous** there was a (telephone) call for you; **a. avec préavis** person to person call; *Rad* **indicatif d'a.** call sign

(h) *Av* **a. particulier** selective calling

(i) (*pour vérifier*), *Scol* roll call, register; **faire l'a. (des écoliers)** to take *or* call the register; **répondre à l'a.** to be present; **feuille/cahier d'a.** roll, register; *Mil* **l'a. du soir** tattoo; **manquant à l'a.** missing

(j) *Tech* **a. d'air** intake of air; **vitesse d'a.** inflow; **a. d'un aimant** pull of a magnet; **le moteur part au premier a.** the engine starts at the first touch of the switch

(k) *Typ* **a. de note** footnote reference, superior figure

(l) *Sp* take-off; **quel est le pied d'a.?** which is the take-off foot?; **un bon coup d'a. sur le tremplin** a good kick off from the springboard

(m) (*signal*) signal, call; **l'a. à la prière** (Muslim) call to prayer

(n) *Ordinat* call; (*de commande*) selection; **a. automatique** automatic dial

appelant, -ante [aplɑ̃, -ɑ̃t] *Jur* **1** *adj* (*partie etc*) appealing **2** *n* **(a)** *Jur* appellant (against a judgment); **se porter a.** to appeal **(b)** *Télécom* caller

appelé [aple] *nm* **(a)** *Mil* conscript; *Fig* **il y a beaucoup d'appelés, mais peu d'élus** many are called, but few are chosen **(b)** *Télécom* party called

appeler [aple] **(j'appelle, n. appelons; j'appellerai) 1** *vt* **(a)** *(qn, chien)* to call (to); *(taxi)* to call, to hail; **a. au secours** to call for help; **a. qn dans la rue** to call to sb in the street; **a. qn de la main** *ou* **du geste** to beckon (to) sb; **les noms sont appelés un à un** the names are called out one by one; *Jur* **a. une cause** to call (out) a case

(b) *Tél* **a. qn (au téléphone)** to ring sb (up), to call sb; **a. Paris** to call Paris; **a. un taxi/un médecin** to phone for a taxi/a doctor

(c) *(convoquer)* to call in, to send for, to summon; *Jur* **a. qn (en justice)** to summon(s) sb; *(poursuivre)* to sue sb; **a. qn à témoin** to call sb to witness; **a. les pompiers** to call the fire brigade; **faire a. un médecin** to call in *or* send for a doctor; **a. l'ascenseur** to call the lift; **elle a été appelée auprès de son père mourant** she was called to her dying father's bedside; *Mil* **a. qn sous les drapeaux** to call sb up, to conscript sb; *aussi Hum* **le devoir t'appelle** duty calls; *Fin* **capital appelé** called-up capital

(d) a. qn à *(fonction etc)* to appoint *or* assign sb to; **être appelé à qch** to be destined for sth; **cette technique est appelée à se développer partout dans le monde** the technique is destined *or* set to spread throughout the world; **son courage l'appelle à ce genre d'action** his courage inspires him to that kind of action; **il fut appelé à travailler à l'étranger** he was called to work overseas

(e) *(donner un nom à)* to call; **nous l'avons appelé David** we have called him David; **tu l'appelles par son prénom?** do you call him by his first name?; **j'appelle cela une bêtise** I call that *or* that's what I call a stupid mistake; **voilà ce que j'appelle un homme** now that's what I call a man; **vous appelez cela danser?** (do) you call that dancing?; **a. un chat un chat, a. les choses par leur nom** to call a spade a spade

(f) *(demander, réclamer)* to call for; *(critique)* to invite; **ce problème appelle une solution immédiate** the problem calls for an immediate solution; **a. qn à faire qch** to call on *or* invite sb to do sth; **je vous appelle tous à y réfléchir** I call on *or* invite you all to think about it

(g) *(entraîner)* to provoke, to arouse, to attract; *Prov* **un malheur en appelle un autre** misfortunes never come singly; **la violence appelle la violence** violence breeds *or* begets violence

(h) *Ordinat (fichier)* to call up

2 *vi* **(a)** *(crier)* to call, to shout; **il arrive qu'il appelle la nuit** he sometimes calls out *or* shouts out in the night; **elle appelait à l'aide** *ou* **au secours** she was calling *or* shouting for help; **si tu as un problème, tu appelles** if you have a problem, just shout

(b) *Tél* to call, to phone; **laisse-la a. la première** wait for her to call *or* phone you

(c) en a. à qn to appeal to sb; **j'en appelle à votre bon sens** I appeal to your common sense; **j'en appelle de votre décision** I challenge your decision; *Jur* **a. d'un jugement** to appeal against a sentence; **en a.** to appeal

3 s'appeler *vpr* **(a)** *(avoir pour nom)* to be called; **comment vous appelez-vous?** what is your name?; **je m'appelle David** my name is David; **cela s'appelle un plaqueminier** it's called a persimmon; *F* **voilà qui s'appelle pleuvoir!** it's raining with a vengeance!; **nous nous appelons par nos prénoms** we call each other by our first names, we're on first-name terms **(b)** *Tél (entre plusieurs individus)* **alors, on s'appelle, hein?** talk to you on the phone

appellation [apɛlasjɔ̃] *nf* **(a)** name; *(de produit)* designation, *Fml* appellation; **vin sans a.** non-vintage wine; **a. injurieuse** abusive term

▶ **appellation**: **a. contrôlée** *(de vin)* guaranteed vintage; **a. d'origine** designation *or* label of origin

appendice [apɛ̃dis] *nm* [①A14,9] **(a)** *Anat* appendix; *Zool, Bot* appendage; **se faire enlever l'a.** to have one's appendix out; *Hum* **quel a. nasal!** what a conk *or* hooter! **(b)** *(d'un livre)* appendix, supplement **(c)** *Vieilli (d'un bâtiment)* annex(e) **(d)** *(d'un ballon)* neck

appendicectomie [apɛ̃disɛktɔmi] *nf Chir* append(ic)ectomy

appendicite [apɛ̃disit] *nf Méd* appendicitis; **crise d'a.** appendicitis; **a. chronique** grumbling appendix; **se faire opérer de l'a.** to have an operation for appendicitis, to have one's appendix out

appentis [apɑ̃ti] *nm Constr (bâtiment)* lean-to; *(toit)* lean-to, sloping roof; *(remise)* outhouse, shed

appesantir [apəzɑ̃tir] **1** *vt (rendre moins agile)* to slow down, to weigh down; **l'âge a appesanti sa démarche** old age has slowed his step; **paupières appesanties par le sommeil** eyes heavy with sleep

2 s'appesantir *vpr* to grow heavier; **son pas s'appesantit avec la fatigue** his step grew slower *or* heavier through fatigue; *Fig* **la main de fer de l'Inquisition s'appesantit sur** ... the iron fist of the Inquisition weighed down on ...; *Fig* **la nuit s'appesantit sur la ville** black night fell over the town; *Fig* **s'a. sur un sujet** to dwell on a subject; *Fig F* **pas la peine de s'a., passons à autre chose** there's no point in dwelling on it, let's get on to something else

appesantissement [apəzɑ̃tismɑ̃] *nm (de la marche, des recherches)* slowing (down); *(des pas)* (growing) heaviness

appétence [apetɑ̃s] *nf Litt* penchant, partiality; **une a. d'aventure** a penchant for adventure

appétissant [apetisɑ̃] *adj (nourriture)* appetizing, tempting; *Fig (femme)* alluring

appétit [apeti] *nm* **(a)** *(de nourriture)* appetite; **couper l'a. à qn** to spoil *or* take away sb's appetite; **donner de l'a. à qn** to give sb an appetite; **mettre qn en a.** to give sb an appetite; **manger de bon a.** *ou* **avec a.** to eat heartily *or* with relish, *F* to tuck in; **avoir un a. d'oiseau** to have a small *or* poor appetite, to peck at one's food; **avoir bon** *ou* **un gros a.** to have a hearty appetite; **bon a.!** enjoy your meal!, bon appetit!; **manger sans a.** *(sans plaisir)* not to enjoy one's food; *(picorer)* to pick at one's food; **je n'ai plus d'a.** I've lost my appetite, I'm off my food; *Prov* **l'a. vient en mangeant** only when you start eating do you realize you're hungry; *Fig* the more you get the more you want

(b) *(désir)* desire, craving **(de** for); **a. sexuel** sexual desire; **a. du gain** craving for money; **l'a. de la connaissance** a thirst *or* hunger for knowledge

applaudimètre [aplodimɛtr] *nm* clapometer

applaudir [aplodir] **1** *vt* to applaud; **se faire a. à tout rompre** to get tremendous applause, to bring the house down; *Fig* **je vous applaudis de tout cœur** I congratulate you with all my heart **2** *vi* to applaud, to clap; **a. à tout rompre** to applaud *or* clap thunderously; *Fig* **nous applaudissons à la reprise des relations entre nos deux pays** we welcome the resumption of relations between our two countries; *Fig* **a. à une décision/un changement** to applaud *or* welcome a decision/a change **3 s'applaudir** *vpr* **s'a. (de qch)** to congratulate oneself, to pat oneself on the back (for having done sth)

applaudissement [aplodismɑ̃] *nm (souvent pl)* **(a)** applause, clapping; **un tonnerre** *ou* **une tempête d'applaudissements** thunderous applause; **soulever des applaudissements** to be applauded **(b)** *Litt* approval

applicable [aplikabl] *adj* applicable; **cette règle est a. à tous les cas** this rule applies to all cases; **a. à partir du premier janvier** to take effect from the first of January

applicateur [aplikatœr] **1** *nm (device)* applicator; **tampon avec a.** applicator tampon **2** *adj* **pinceau a.** applicator

application [aplikasjɔ̃] *nf* **(a)** *(de peinture etc)* application, applying; **première a. de peinture** first coat of paint; *Couture* **broderie d'a.** appliqué (work); **bois d'a.** veneer

(b) *(d'un règlement)* application; *(de la loi)* enforcement; **mettre une théorie en a.** to put a theory into practice; **mettre une loi en a.** to enforce *or* implement a law; **entrer en a.** to come into force; **a. d'une somme d'argent à un projet** use of a sum of money for a project; **en a. de ce décret** in pursuance of this decree; *Mil etc* **école d'a.** school of instruction

(c) *(débouché)* application; *(de la matière première)* use

(d) *(assiduité)* application (to one's work), industriousness; **travailler avec a.** to apply oneself to one's work, to work diligently

(e) *Ordinat* **a. bureautique** business application; **a. en service** current application; **a. graphique** graphics application; **logiciel d'a.** application software

applique [aplik] *nf* **(a)** *(lampe)* wall light **(b)** *Couture* appliquéd ornament

appliqué [aplike] *adj* **(a)** *(personne)* hard working, diligent; *(écriture)* careful **(b)** *(sciences)* applied; **informatique appliquée à la gestion** computer technology applied to management

appliquer [aplike] **1** *vt* **(a)** *(mettre)* to apply **(sur** to); **a. une couche de peinture sur qch** to put a coat of paint on sth, *esp Fml* to apply a coat of paint to sth; **a. une oreille au mur** to put one's ear to the wall, to listen through the wall; **un coup bien appliqué** a well-planted *or* well-aimed blow; **elle lui fit une bise bien appliquée** she planted a kiss on his cheek

(b) *(utiliser)* to apply; **a. une loi à un cas particulier** to apply a law to a particular case; **a. (les dispositions de) la loi** to apply the law; **a. un traitement à une maladie** to apply a treatment to an illness; **a. une recette particulière** to use a particular recipe; *Jur* **a. le maximum de la peine** to impose the maximum penalty

(c) (*concentrer*) to apply; **a. toute son attention à un problème** to devote *or* apply all one's attention to a problem; **a. son esprit à ses études** to apply one's mind to one's studies

2 s'appliquer *vpr* (a) (*se concentrer*) to apply oneself, to take pains; **elle doit s'a. davantage** she has to apply herself more; **s'a. à qch** to apply oneself to sth, to take pains over sth; **il s'applique à vérifier toutes les dates** he's taking pains to check all the dates; **elle s'applique à me contredire** she is making a point of contradicting me; **il s'applique à apprendre le français** he is making a serious effort to learn French

(b) (*d'un réglement etc*) to apply (**à** to); **à qui s'applique cette remarque?** who is that remark intended for?; **le règlement s'applique pour tous** the rule applies to everybody

(c) (*se placer*) to be applied; **le cataplasme s'applique directement sur la peau** the poultice should be applied directly (on)to the skin

appoint [apwɛ̃] *nm* (a) *Com, Fin* exact money *or* change; **faire l'a.** (*ajouter le reste*) to make up the full amount, to give the exact change; (*donner la somme exacte*) to pay the exact amount; **ressources d'a.** additional (sources of) income; **ce travail à mi-temps lui fait un petit a.** this part-time job brings him a little extra income; **chauffage/éclairage d'a.** additional heating/lighting; **siège d'a.** extra chair; **un travail d'a.** a second job (b) (*contribution*) contribution; **apporter son a. à qch** to contribute to sth, to take part in sth

appointements [apwɛ̃tmɑ̃] *nmpl* salary; **toucher ses a.** to draw one's salary

appointer [apwɛ̃te] *vt* (a) (*payer*) (*qn*) to pay (a salary to); **être appointé à la semaine** to be paid weekly *or* by the week (b) (*crayon etc*) to sharpen

appontage [apɔ̃taʒ] *nm* (*d'un porte-avion*) landing (on an aircraft carrier); **officier d'a.** landing officer; **crosse** *ou* **crochet d'a.** arrester hook

appontement [apɔ̃tmɑ̃] *nm Naut* (*de bois*) jetty, pier, landing stage

apponter [apɔ̃te] *vi* (*sur un porte-avion*) to land (on an aircraft carrier)

apport [apɔr] *nm* (a) (*fait d'apporter*) contribution, contributing; *Écon* inflow, influx; **a. de capitaux** contribution of capital; *Compta* **a. en capital** capital contribution; *Compta* **a. en numéraire** cash contribution; **a. d'argent frais** injection of new money; *Compta* **apports libérés** fully paid-up capital; **capital d'a.** initial capital; **actions d'a.** founder's *or* promoter's shares; **l'a. du tourisme dans une région** the financial contribution made by tourism to a region; **sans a. extérieur nous étions perdus** without outside (financial) help we'd have been ruined; *Jur* **a. de pièces** (*dans une enquête*) deposit(ing) of documents; *Jur* **biens d'a.** estate brought in by husband/wife on marriage; **a. en communauté** = goods contributed by husband and wife to the joint estate; **terres d'a.** earthworks; **l'a. de la civilisation grecque** the contribution made by Greek civilization

(b) (*chose ajoutée, Fin dans une entreprise*) initial share; **un a. en nature** a contribution in kind; **les fruits donnent un a. de vitamines indispensable** fruit provides essential vitamins; **l'a. en vitamines du foie** the vitamins provided by liver, the vitamins present in liver; *Agr* **un gros a. d'engrais** a heavy dressing of manure; **a. de chaleur, a. calorifique** heat supply *or* input

(c) *Tech* coating, layer, deposit

▶ **apport**: *Jur* **a. dotal** dowry, marriage portion

apporter [apɔrte] *vt* (a) to bring (**qch à qn** sth to sb); **je t'ai apporté la cassette vidéo** I've brought you the video; *Fin* **a. des capitaux** to bring in capital

(b) **a. du soin/un grand intérêt à faire qch** to do sth carefully/with great interest

(c) (*donner*) (*bonheur, soulagement etc*) to bring; **cette démonstration n'apporte aucune preuve supplémentaire** this demonstration gives *or* provides no additional proof; **cette expérience lui a beaucoup apporté** the experience has been very beneficial for him; **qu'est-ce que ça peut t'a.?** what good can that do you?; **notre relation ne m'apporte plus rien** I'm not getting anything out of our relationship any more, our relationship doesn't do anything for me any more; **tu me m'apportes plus rien** you've got nothing to offer me any more, I've outgrown you; **ce travail ne m'apporte pas grand-chose** I don't get very much out of this work

(d) (*changements etc*) to cause, to bring about; **ce que l'avenir apportera** what the future has in store

apposer [apoze] *vt* to place, to put, *Fml* to affix; **a. une affiche sur un mur** to stick a poster on a wall; *Jur* **a. les scellés** (*pour interdire tout accès*) to affix the seals; **a. sa signature à** to put one's signature to; *Jur* **a. sa signature à un acte** to append *or* affix one's signature to a deed; **a. une clause à un acte** to insert a clause in *or* add a clause to an act

apposition [apozisjɔ̃] *nf* (a) *Admin* (*d'un sceau, de scellés, de signature etc*) affixing, appending (b) [①**A5**,C,1,b; **B4**,b,b,ii] *Gram* apposition; **mot en a.** word in apposition

appréciable [apresjabl] *adj* (a) (*par les sens*) perceptible

(b) (*évolution, changement etc*) appreciable, noticeable; **une différence à peine a.** a barely perceptible difference; **la différence est difficilement a.** it's difficult to tell the difference

(c) (*non négligeable*) considerable, appreciable (*usu attrib*); **à une distance a.** at an appreciable *or* considerable distance

(d) (*louable*) (*motivations*) praiseworthy; **ses qualités de dirigeant ont été fort appréciables** his leadership qualities were greatly appreciated; **le changement de temps est tout à fait a.** (*bienvenu*) the change in the weather is very welcome

appréciateur, -trice [apresjatœr, -tris] *n* appreciator (**de** of); *Com etc* appraiser, valuer; **a. du talent** person who recognizes talent, good judge of talent

appréciatif, -ive [apresjatif, -iv] *adj* (*regard, silence*) appreciative; *Com* **devis a.** estimate

appréciation [apresjasjɔ̃] *nf* (a) (*évaluation*) valuation, estimation, estimate; (*d'une distance*) judging; **faire l'a. des marchandises** to value *or* to make a valuation of goods; (b) (*opinion*) judgement, opinion; (*d'une œuvre d'art, d'un repas etc*) appreciation; **les appréciations sont notées dans la marge** the comments are in the margin; **je laisse cette tapisserie/ce problème à votre a.** I'll leave you to form an opinion on this piece of tapestry/this problem (c) (*augmentation de valeur*) appreciation, rise in value

apprécier [apresje] (*pr sub, impf* **n. appréciions, v. appréciiez**) **1** *vt* (a) (*évaluer*) to appraise; (*peinture etc*) to estimate the value of, to value; **tu ne l'apprécies pas à sa juste valeur** you don't appreciate his/her true worth

(b) (*déterminer*) to determine; (*approximativement*) (*température, distance, son*) to estimate; (*distance*) to judge; (*différences, nuances*) to appreciate, to judge

(c) (*aimer*) to appreciate; **un bon repas entre amis, voilà ce que j'apprécie le plus** having a good meal with friends is what I enjoy doing most *or* is what I like most; **je n'apprécie pas ce genre de plaisanterie** I don't appreciate *or* I don't much care for that kind of joke; **elle ne l'apprécie pas du tout** she doesn't like him at all; **elle l'apprécie, sans plus** she just likes him; (*ils ne sont pas amants*) she's just good friends with him

2 *vi F* **elle n'a pas apprécié** she didn't appreciate that, she wasn't very amused *or* pleased

3 s'apprécier *vpr* (a) (*de personnes*) to like each other

(b) (*de monnaie*) to appreciate

appréhender [apreɑ̃de] **1** *vt* (a) *Jur* **a. qn (au corps)** to arrest *or* apprehend sb (b) (*qch*) to dread, to fear; **j'appréhende de rentrer** *ou* **le retour** I'm dreading going back; **j'appréhende toujours un peu les voyages en avion** I'm always a bit apprehensive about travelling by air (c) (*notion*) to grasp **2** *vi* to be apprehensive

appréhensif, -ive [apreɑ̃sif, -iv] *adj* apprehensive

appréhension [apreɑ̃sjɔ̃] *nf* (a) (*crainte*) apprehension (**de** of); **avoir des appréhensions** to be apprehensive (b) (*d'une notion*) grasp

apprendre [aprɑ̃dr] (*conj like* **prendre**) **1** *vt* (a) (*leçon, commerce, langue, méthode etc*) to learn; **il n'a jamais rien appris à l'école** he didn't learn a thing at school

(b) (*nouvelles etc*) to learn, to hear (of), to get to know of; **comment l'avez-vous appris?** how did you hear *or* find out?; **nous l'avons appris à la radio/aux informations** we heard it on the radio/on the news; **j'ai appris que tu allais te marier** I've heard that you're getting married; **je l'ai appris de bonne source** I have it on good authority

(c) (*enseigner*) **a. qch à qn** to teach sb sth; **a. à qn à faire qch** to teach *or* show sb how to do sth; **il m'a tout appris** he taught me everything I know

(d) (*informer*) **a. qch à qn** to inform sb of sth, to tell sb sth; *F* **vous ne m'apprenez rien!** you're telling me!, you're not telling me anything new!; **il faut tout lui a., il ne sait rien** he has to be told everything, he hasn't a clue

2 *vi* to learn; **a. facilement** to find learning easy; **a. vite/lentement** to be a fast/slow learner; **a. à faire qch** to learn how to do sth; **a. à lire/skier** to learn to read/(how) to ski, *Prov* **on apprend à tout âge** it is never too late to learn, you're never too old to learn; *F* **je vous apprendrai à me parler de la sorte!** I'll teach you to speak to me like that!; *F* **ça vous apprendra!** serve(s) you right!, that'll teach you!; *F* **je vais lui a. à vivre** I'm going to teach him a few manners

3 **s'apprendre** *vpr* **ça s'apprend vite** it's easy to learn, it can be learned quickly; **le chinois ne s'apprend pas facilement** it isn't easy to learn Chinese

apprenti, -ie [aprɑ̃ti] *n* apprentice; *Jur* articled clerk; **une apprentie couturière** an apprentice dressmaker; **a. menuisier** carpenter's apprentice; **je ne suis qu'un a.** I'm only a beginner *or* a novice

▶ **apprenti**: **a. conducteur** learner (driver); **a. sorcier** sorcerer's apprentice; *Fig* **cesse donc de jouer les apprentis sorciers!** stop meddling with things that you know nothing about!

apprentissage [aprɑ̃tisaʒ] *nm* training; (*chez un artisan*) apprenticeship; **centre d'a.** training school; **contrat d'a.** contract of apprenticeship; **mettre qn en a. chez un patron** to apprentice sb to an employer; **être en a. chez qn** to be apprenticed to sb; **faire l'a. de la vie** to gain some experience of life, *F* to go through the university of life; **faire l'a. de la douleur** to become acquainted with grief

apprêt [aprɛ] *nm* **(a)** (*opération*) (*de tissus, de cuirs etc*) dressing, finishing **(b)** (*substance*) (*de tissu etc*) finish, dress; (*de peinture*) primer, size; **a. anti-corrosion** anti-corrosion primer **(c)** (*affectation*) affectation, affectedness; **style sans a.** unaffected style

apprêtage [aprɛtaʒ] *nm Tech* **(a)** (*de tissu*) dressing, finishing **(b)** (*de peinture*) priming, sizing

apprêté [aprete] *adj* **(a)** (*style, attitude etc*) affected, stiff; **coiffure apprêtée** fussy hairstyle **(b) papier a.** glossy paper

apprêter [aprete] **1** *vt* **(a)** (*repas etc*) to prepare; **a. un enfant** to get a child ready, to dress a child; **les femmes apprêtent la mariée** the women help the bride to dress *or* get ready **(b)** (*tissus etc*) to dress, to finish, to stiffen; (*cuir*) to finish **(c)** (*surface*) to prime **2 s'apprêter** *vpr* (*s'habiller*) to get dressed; (*se donner un coup de peigne etc*) to tidy oneself (up); **s'a. à faire qch** to be getting ready *or* preparing to do sth, to be on the point of doing sth

apprivoisable [aprivwazabl(ə)] *adj* tameable

apprivoisé [aprivwaze] *adj* tame

apprivoisement [aprivwazmɑ̃] *nm* taming, domestication

apprivoiser [aprivwaze] **1** *vt* (*animal*) to tame; *Fig* (*qn*) to win over; *Fig* **je veux a. cette peur** I want to conquer this fear **2 s'apprivoiser** *vpr* (*d'un animal*) to become domesticated *or* tame; *Fig* (*d'une personne*) to become more sociable; *Fig* **s'a. à une idée** to get used to *or* come round to an idea

approbateur, -trice [aprɔbatœr, -tris], **approbatif, -ive** [aprɔbatif, -iv] *adj* (*geste, sourire etc*) approving; **regard a.** look of approval

approbation [aprɔbasjɔ̃] *nf* approval (**de qch** of sth); (*de documents officiels, de comptes rendus*) certifying, approval; **donner son a. à qch** to give one's approval to sth, to approve sth; **le film a reçu l'a. du public** the film was well received by the public; **a. tacite** tacit approval; **votre conduite est digne d'a.** your behaviour is commendable; **cette étude mérite l'a. de tous** this study merits general approval; *Com* **pour a.** for approval; **a. des comptes** approval of the accounts

approchable [aprɔʃabl] *adj* (*endroit, personne*) approachable, accessible; **le refuge n'est pas a. en voiture** the shelter is not accessible *or* cannot be reached by car; **elle n'est pas a. aujourd'hui** (*elle est de mauvaise humeur*) she's not very approachable today

approchant [aprɔʃɑ̃] *adj* similar, approximate (**de** to); **offre approchante** near offer; **je n'ai jamais rien vu d'a.** I've never seen anything like it *or* anything approaching it; **voilà ce qu'il a dit ou quelque chose d'a.** that is what he said, or something like it; **je cherche qch d'a.** I'm looking for something similar

approche [aprɔʃ] *nf* **(a)** approach; **l'a. de l'hiver** the approach of winter; **à l'a. de la vieillesse** as old age draws/drew near; **aux approches de la trentaine** as you/*etc* near *or* approach thirty; **à son a.** as he came up, as he approached; **d'une a. difficile** (*lieu*) hard to get to, not easily accessible; (*personne*) unapproachable; (*livre etc*) hard to understand; **à l'a. de la difficulté, elle abandonne** she gives up whenever a difficulty arises; **un homme d'a. facile** an approachable man

(b) (*manière d'aborder*) **une nouvelle a. du problème** a new approach to the problem; **travail d'a.** manoeuvre, *US* maneuver; **cette étude a nécessité un long travail d'a.** the study required a great deal of preliminary work; *Mktg* **a. bayésienne** Bayesian theory; *Av* **a. à vue** visual approach; **chasse à l'a.** deerstalking

(c) (*environs*) **les approches d'une ville** the approaches of a town; **aux approches du village** on the outskirts of the village

(d) *Typ* (*faute*) = extra space wrongly inserted between two letters; (*signe*) close-up sign *or* mark

(e) *Zool* mating

approché [aprɔʃe] *adj* (*résultat, valeur*) approximate

approcher [aprɔʃe] **1** *vt* (*qn, qch*) to approach, to come near, to come close to; **a. qch de qn/qch** to bring *or* draw sth near (to) sb/sth; **approchez votre chaise** pull up your chair; **a. sa chaise de la lampe** to move one's chair nearer the lamp; **ne m'approchez pas** don't come near me; **elle approche les plus grands noms du spectacle** she rubs shoulders with the biggest names in showbusiness; **a. des lions d'assez près** to get quite close to some lions; **on ne peut pas l'a.** you can never see him; (*parce qu'il ne le veut pas*) you can't get near him, he's unapproachable; **le président? on ne peut pas l'a. comme ça!** you can't just walk up to the President!

2 *vi* **(a)** to approach, to draw near(er), to come nearer; **l'heure** *ou* **le moment approche** it will soon be time; **la nuit approchait** night was falling, it was beginning to get dark; **faites-le a.** ask him to come closer; **approche! je vais te montrer quelque chose!** come (over) here! I've something to show you!; **a. de qn/qch** to approach sb/sth; **nous approchons de Paris** we are approaching *or* getting near Paris; **a. du but** to be nearing one's goal; **il approche de la trentaine** he's getting on for *or* nearing *or* approaching thirty; **nous approchions alors des 200 km/heure** we were going at almost 200 km an hour

(b) a. de qch to be *or* to come close to sth; **ça en approche** it's close, it's getting close (to it); **son art approche de la perfection** his art comes close to perfection; **tu approches de la vérité** you're getting close to the truth; **son comportement approche de la folie** his behaviour borders on insanity

(c) *Zool* to mate

3 s'approcher *vpr* to come *or* go closer *or* nearer, to draw near(er), to approach; **je n'ai pas pu m'a. de la scène, il y avait trop de monde** I couldn't get near the stage, there were too many people; **je me suis approché pour voir** I went closer to have a look; **s'a. de qn/qch** to come *or* go up to sb/sth; **ne t'approche pas du chien** don't go near the dog; **il faut t'a.!, viens!** come on!, come closer!; **le navire s'approchait de la terre** the ship was nearing land; **s'a. de la perfection** to be almost perfect, to be close to perfection

approfondi [aprɔfɔ̃di] *adj* (*recherche*) elaborate, detailed, extensive; (*enquête*) detailed, in-depth; (*connaissances*) thorough, in-depth

approfondir [aprɔfɔ̃dir] **1** *vt* **(a)** (*lit de la rivière etc*) to deepen, to excavate **(b)** (*examiner*) (*problème*) to go deeply *or* thoroughly into; (*sujet*) to study thoroughly; **a. une affaire** to get to the root of a matter; **sans a. la question** *ou* **le sujet** without going into too much detail; **laisse-moi le temps d'a. la question** give me time to examine the question in detail **2 s'approfondir** *vpr* to become deeper, to deepen

approfondissement [aprɔfɔ̃dismɑ̃] *nm* **(a)** (*d'un canal etc*) deepening, excavating, excavation **(b)** (*d'une question*) in-depth analysis; (*d'une étude*) further development

appropriation [aprɔprijasjɔ̃] *nf* **(a)** (*de biens etc*) appropriation; **a. par violence** forcible seizure; **a. de fonds** embezzlement, misappropriation of funds **(b)** *Arch, Belg* cleaning, tidying up

approprié [aprɔprije] *adj* appropriate (**à** for)

approprier [aprɔprije] (*pr sub, impf* **n. appropriions, v. appropriiez**) **1** *vt* **(a)** (*adapter*) **a. qch** to arrange sth, to suit sth; **a. qch à qch** to adapt sth to sth; **a. son style à un public** (*nettoyer*) to adapt one's style to (suit) an audience **(b)** *Arch, Belg* to clean; (*ranger*) to tidy **2 s'approprier** *vpr* **(a)** (*s'adjuger*) **s'a. qch** to appropriate sth **(b)** (*s'adapter*) **s'a. à qch** to be suitable *or* appropriate for sth, to be in keeping with sth, to suit sth; **cette musique s'approprie à la situation** this music is suitable for the occasion

approuver [apruve] *vt* **a. qch** to approve of sth; **a. qch de la tête** to nod approval; **a. qn** to agree with sb; **a. qn de faire/d'avoir fait qch** to think sb is right for doing/having done sth; **elle approuve tout ce qu'il dit/fait** she agrees with everything he says/does; **nous vous approuvons dans votre choix** we approve of your choice; **a. qch officiellement** to agree formally to sth; *Com* **a. une facture** to pass an invoice; **a. un contrat** to ratify a contract; *Com* **a. et contre-argumenter** to agree and counter; *Admin* **a. une nomination** to confirm an appointment; **a. un appel** to endorse an appeal; **lu et approuvé** read and approved; **lessive approuvée par un grand nombre de fabriquants** washing powder recommended by a large number of manufacturers; *Méd* **médicament approuvé** approved drug *or* medicine

approvisionné [aprɔvizjɔne] *adj* stocked, supplied (**de, en** with); **bien a.** well-stocked; **magasin bien/mal a. en …** shop with a good/poor stock of …

approvisionnement [aprɔvizjɔnmɑ̃] *nm* **(a)** (*ravitaillement*) (*d'une ville, d'une armée*) supplying; (*d'une personne*) catering; (*d'un magasin*) stocking; **l'a. de la ville en produits frais** the supply(ing) of fresh produce to the town **(b)**

(*provisions*) supply, stock, provisions; **faire un a. de qch** to lay in a supply of sth

approvisionner [aprɔvizjɔne] **1** *vt* **(a)** (*ravitailler, fournir*) to supply (**de** with); (*qn*) to cater for; (*magasin*) to stock; **a. une île en produits frais** to supply an island with fresh produce **(b)** *Banque* **a. son compte** to pay money into one's account; **son compte en banque n'est plus approvisionné** his bank account is no longer in credit **2 s'approvisionner** *vpr* to lay in provisions, to get a stock *or* a supply (**en, de** of); **s'a. chez (qn)** to get one's supplies from (sb); (*d'une ménagère etc*) to shop at (sb's); **s'a. au marché** to shop *or* to do one's shopping *or* to buy one's provisions at the market; **s'a. en qch** to stock up on sth

approximatif, -ive [aprɔksimatif, -iv] *adj* [①B56,C3] (*calcul, estimation*) approximate, rough; **nous nous sommes exprimés dans un anglais a.** we expressed ourselves in broken English

approximation [aprɔksimasjɔ̃] *nf* approximation, rough estimate; *Math* approximation

approximativement [aprɔksimativmɑ̃] *adv* approximately, roughly; **dans une heure a.** in an hour or so

appt *abrév* **appartement**

appui [apɥi] *nm* **(a)** (*support*) support, prop; *Archit* balustrade; **mur d'a.** supporting *or* retaining wall; **barre d'a.** handrail; **point d'a.** (*d'un levier*) fulcrum; *Mil* (*d'opérations*) base; **à hauteur d'a.** elbow high; **mettre un a. à un mur** to shore up a wall; **prendre a. sur qch** to be supported by *or* on sth; (*d'une personne*) to support oneself on sth; **prendre a. sur le pied gauche** (*pour sauter*) to take off from the left foot; **a. de fenêtre** window ledge *or* sill; **a. de porte** door sill

(b) (*moral etc*) support, backing; **a. moral** moral support; **prêter son a. à qn** to support *or* lend support to sb, to back sb up; **vous avez mon a.** you have my support *or* backing; **être sans appui(s)** to be friendless; **avoir des appuis en haut lieu** to have friends in high places; **à l'a.** (*de qch*) in support; **à l'a. il me montra tes lettres** to support *or* to back up what he said he showed me your letters; **avec preuves à l'a.** with supporting evidence; **à l'a. d'un témoignage** in support of testimony

(c) *Mil* **a. direct** close *or* *US* direct support; **tir d'a.** covering fire; **a. tactique/aérien** tactical/air support

(d) *Ordinat* **a. droite** flush right; **texte en appui droite** right justified text

appui-bras, *pl* **appuis-bras** *nm* armrest

appuie- [apɥi] (*compound nouns of which the first element is* **appui-** *have an alternative form* **appuie-**, *in which case they are invariable*)

appui-jambes, *pl* **appuis-jambes** *nm* leg rest

appui-nuque, *pl* **appuis-nuque** *nm* headrest

appui-queue, *pl* **appuis-queue** *nm Billard* (cue) rest, *F* jigger

appui-tête *pl* **appuis-tête** *nm* headrest, head restraint

appuyé [apɥije] *adj* (*plaisanterie, ironie*) laboured, *US* labored, heavy; **regard a.** (fixed) stare; **il lui lançait des regards appuyés** he stared at him intently

appuyer [apɥije] **(j'appuie, n. appuyons; j'appuierai) 1** *vt* **(a)** (*mettre contre*) to lean, to rest; **(qch contre qch** sth against sth); **a. sa tête contre la fenêtre** to lean one's head against the window; **a. sa tête sur l'épaule de qn** to rest one's head on sb's shoulder; *Fig* **a. son opinion sur qch** to base one's opinion on sth; *Fig* **théorie appuyée sur des faits** theory supported by facts

(b) (*exercer une pression sur*) **a. qch sur qch** to press sth on sth; **a. son pied sur la pédale de frein** to put one's foot on the brake; *Fig* **a. son regard sur qn** to stare intently at sb

(c) (*mur, solive etc*) to support, to prop (up)

(d) *Fig* (*soutenir*) **a. une pétition** to support a petition (**par** by); **a. une proposition** to second a proposal; **a. un candidat** to back *or* support a candidate; **a. la demande de qn** to support sb's request

2 *vi* **(a)** (*reposer*) to bear (**sur** on); **poutre qui appuie sur deux montants** beam resting *or* bearing on two uprights

(b) (*presser*) to depress; **a. sur la valise pour la fermer** to press down on the suitcase to close it; **a. sur le point sensible** to press the sore spot; **a. sur son stylo** to press on one's pen; **a. sur le bouton** to press the button; *Aut F* **a. sur le champignon** (*accélérer*) to step on it, to put one's foot down; **a. sur une syllabe** to stress a syllable; *Mus* **a. sur une note** to hold a note; **a. sur l'urgence d'un problème** to stress the urgency of a problem; *F* **inutile d'a. là-dessus, on a compris** you don't need to keep going on about it, we understand; **appuyez à droite à la sortie du village** bear right as you leave the village

3 s'appuyer *vpr* **(a)** (*reposer*) **s'a. sur** *ou* **contre** *ou* **à qch** to lean *or* rest on *or* against sth; **s'a. sur** *ou* **contre le bras de qn** to lean on sb's arm; **s'a. sur qn** to lean on sb; *Fig* to lean *or* to rely *or* depend on sb; **s'a. sur son expérience pour conseiller qn** to draw on *or* to use one's experience to advise sb; **ses recherches s'appuient sur des découvertes récentes** his research is based on recent discoveries

(b) *F* **s'a. une corvée** to be lumbered with a chore; **c'est toujours moi qui m'appuie la vaisselle** it's always me who gets lumbered with the dishes!; **s'a. un bon dîner/un gentil petit voyage** to treat oneself to *or* stand oneself a good dinner/a nice little trip

âpre [ɑpr] *adj* **(a)** (*aigre*) rough, harsh; **voix â.** rasping voice; **goût â.** sour taste; **vin â.** rough wine **(b)** (*temps, vent*) raw **(c)** (*dégoût*) bitter, biting, sharp; (*ironie*) scathing **(d)** (*lutte*) bitter **(e)** (*concurrence etc*) keen; **homme â. (au gain)** grasping man; **être â. au gain** to be grasping *or* money-grabbing

âprement [ɑprəmɑ̃] *adv* (*défendu*) fiercely; (*se disputer*) violently

après [aprɛ] **1** *prép* **(a)** (*dans le temps, dans l'espace*) after; **il est arrivé a. moi** he arrived after me; **a. tout** after all; **fermé a. 20 heures** closed from 8 o'clock (onwards); **a. bien des discussions, nous avons décidé de ...** after a great deal of discussion, we decided to ...; **jour a. jour** day after day; **a. vous, monsieur/madame!** after you!; **et a. cela, madame?** (*au restaurant*) and to follow, madam?; **a. quoi** after which; **je suis** *ou* **viens a. lui** I am *or* come after him; **tourner à droite a. la poste** turn right just past the post office; *F* **courir a. qn** to run after sb; **les chiens risquent de nous courir a.** the dogs might run after us; *Fig F* **ces garçons qui te courent a.** those boys who are (always) chasing (after) you; *Fig F* **tout le monde leur court a.** everybody runs after them; **jurer/maugréer a. qn** to swear/grumble at sb; **il est toujours a. moi** he's always nagging at me *or* getting at me; *F* **en avoir a. qn** to have it in for sb; **les jeux passent a. le travail** work comes before play; **ça passe a. tout le reste** everything else comes first

(b) d'a. according to; **d'a. ce qu'elle a dit** going by *or* according to what she said; **d'a. l'horloge il est trois heures** according to the clock it's three; **peint d'a. nature** painted from life; **paysage d'a. Turner** landscape after Turner; **texte d'a. Cicéron** text adapted from Cicero; **d'a. l'article 12** under article 12; **d'a. vos instructions** in accordance with your instructions

(c) (+ *inf*) **a. avoir dîné** after dinner; **a. manger** after eating

2 *adv* afterwards, later; **parlez d'abord, je parlerai a.** you speak first, I'll speak afterwards; **six semaines a.** six weeks later; **les vacances, ça passe a.** holidays are not a priority; **avec lui, la famille, ça passe a.** his family takes second place; **le jour (d')a.** the next *or* following day, the day after; **la page d'a.** the next *or* following page; **nous eûmes des huîtres et a. du saumon** we had oysters followed by salmon; **et a.?** what then?; **et a., qu'est-ce qu'il a dit?** and then what did he say?; *F* **eh bien, et puis a.?** well, what of it?, what about it?, so what?

3 *conj* **a. que** after, when; **a. que je fus** *ou F* **sois parti** after I had gone; *vieilli* **a. que j'aurai fini** when I have finished

après- [aprɛ] *préf* post-...; **la période de l'a.-soixante-huit** the period after 1968, the post-1968 period; **le Moscou de l'a.-Gorbatchev** Moscow in the post-Gorbachev era; **les jeunes de l'a.-sida** the post-Aids generation

après-demain *adv* the day after tomorrow

après-dîner, *pl* **après-dîners** *nm* evening; **discours d'a.** after-dinner speech

après-guerre, *pl* **après-guerres** *nm* post-war period

après-midi *nm ou f inv* afternoon; **trois heures de l'a.** three (o'clock) in the afternoon, three pm

après-rasage, *pl* **après-rasages 1** *adj inv* **lotion a.** aftershave (lotion) **2** *nm* aftershave

après-ski *nm inv* (*chaussure*) snowboot

après-vente *adj inv Com* **service a.** aftersales service

âpreté [ɑprəte] *nf* **(a)** (*du vin, de la voix, de l'hiver etc*) roughness, harshness; (*du froid*) sharpness; (*d'un fruit*) sourness, tartness **(b)** (*du ton etc*) bitterness; (*des reproches*) sharpness, bitterness; (*de la concurrence*) fierceness

a priori [apriɔri] **1** *adj inv* a priori; **raisonnement a.** a priori reasoning **2** *adv* a priori; **a. ça me paraît possible** in principle, I think it's possible **3** *nm inv* preconception, apriorism; **avoir des a. (contre/en faveur de qch)** to be biased *or* prejudiced (against/in favour of sth); **être sans a.** to be impartial

ap(r). J.-C. (*abrév* **après Jésus-Christ**) AD

à-propos *nm* (*d'une expression etc*) aptness, appropriateness, relevance; **avoir l'esprit d'à.** to have presence of mind; **répondre avec à.** to give a suitable *or* an appropriate reply;

il fait des commentaires sans le moindre à. he makes comments that aren't the slightest bit relevant; **votre observation manque d'à.** your remark is not to the point *or* is irrelevant; **son manque d'à. lui jouera des tours** the fact that he always does/says the wrong thing is going to cause him problems

apte [apt] *adj* **a. à faire qch/à qch** fit *or* suited *or* qualified to do sth/for sth; **peu a.** (**à faire qch**) unsuitable, ill-equipped (to do sth); **a. à accomplir une tâche** well suited *or* qualified to carry out a task; **a. à naviguer** seaworthy; *Mil* **a. au service** fit for military service; *Jur* **a. à hériter** entitled to inherit

aptère [aptɛr] *adj* wingless; *Beaux-Arts* **victoire a.** wingless victory

aptéryx [apteriks] *nm* (*oiseau*) kiwi

aptitude [aptityd] *nf* **(a)** (*capacité*) aptitude, ability (**à, pour** to); **il a des aptitudes manuelles** he's good with his hands; **avoir des aptitudes intellectuelles** to have intellectual skills; **avoir une a. à (faire qch)** to have the capacity (for doing sth); (*être doué*) to have a gift (for sth); **test d'a.** aptitude test; **certificat d'a. professionnelle** = vocational training certificate **(b)** *Jur* capacity

apurement [apyrmɑ̃] *nm* **(a)** (*d'un compte*) auditing, agreeing **(b)** (*d'une dette*) discharge

apurer [apyre] *vt* **(a)** (*comptes*) to audit **(b)** (*dette*) to discharge

aquaculteur, -trice [akwakyltœr, -tris] *n* fish farmer

aquaculture [akwakyltyr] *nf* aquaculture; (*de poissons*) fish farming

aquaplanage [akwaplanaʒ] *nm Aut* aquaplaning

aquaplane [akwaplan] *nm Sp* aquaplaning; (*planche*) aquaplane

aquaplaning [akwaplaniŋ] *nm Aut* = **aquaplanage**

aquaplaniste [akwaplanist] *n Sp* aquaplaner

aquarelle [akwarɛl] *nf Beaux-Arts* watercolour, *US* watercolor; **peindre à l'a.** to paint in watercolours; **une a. de Matisse** a watercolour by Matisse, a Matisse watercolour

aquarelliste [akwarɛlist] *n* watercolourist, *US* watercolorist

aquarium [akwarjɔm] *nm* aquarium; **a. d'eau de mer** oceanarium

aquatinte [akwatɛ̃t] *nf* aquatint

aquatique [akwatik] *adj* **(a)** (*oiseau, plante, sport*) aquatic **(b)** (*sol*) marshy, watery

aqueduc [ak(ə)dyk] *nm* **(a)** (*construction*) aqueduct **(b)** *Anat* aqueduct, canal

aqueux, -euse [akø, -øz] *adj* **(a)** (*boisson, fruit etc*) watery; (*sol*) waterlogged **(b)** *Anat, Ch etc* aqueous, water; **humeur aqueuse** aqueous humour

à quia [akɥija] *adv Litt* **être à.** to be at a loss for words *or* a reply; **mettre qn à.** to render sb speechless, to nonplus sb

aquiculture [akɥikyltyr] *nf* = **aquaculture**

aquifère [akɥifɛr] *adj Géol* **nappe a.** aquifer

aquilin, -ine [akilɛ̃, -in] *adj* (*profil etc*) aquiline; **nez a.** aquiline *or* hook *or* Roman nose

aquilon [akilɔ̃] *nm* north wind

Aquin [akɛ̃] *nm* **Saint Thomas d'A.** St Thomas Aquinas

aquitain, -aine [akitɛ̃, -ɛn] **1** *adj* of *or* from Aquitaine **2** *n* **A.** (*natif*) native of Aquitaine; (*habitant*) inhabitant of Aquitaine

Aquitaine [akitɛn] *nf Hist* (province of) Aquitaine; **bassin d'A.** Basin of Aquitaine

A.R. (*abrév* **aller retour**) return

ara [ara] *nm* (*oiseau*) macaw

arabe [arab] [①**A20-21**,d] **1** *adj* (*monde, littérature, pays*) Arab, Arabic; (*chiffres, langue etc*) Arabic; (*cheval*) Arab; (*coutumes, civilisation etc*) Arabian, Arabic **2** *nm Ling* Arabic **3** *n* **A.** Arab

arabesque [arabɛsk] **1** *adj* (*architecture etc*) arabesque, Arabian **2** *nf* (*danse, ornement*) arabesque; **la fumée monte en arabesques** the smoke curls up

arabica [arabika] *nm* (*café*) arabica

Arabie [arabi] *nf* Arabia; **A. saoudite** Saudi Arabia; **le désert d'A.** the Arabian desert

arabique [arabik] *adj* **gomme a.** gum arabic

arabisant, -ante [arabizɑ̃, -ɑ̃t] *n* Arabic scholar, Arabist

arabisation [arabizasjɔ̃] *nf* Arabization

arabiser [arabize] *vt* to Arabize

arable [arabl] *adj* (*terre etc*) arable

arabophone [arabɔfɔn] **1** *adj* Arabic-speaking **2** *n* Arabic speaker

arachide [araʃid] *nf* (*plante*) peanut, groundnut, *Br F* monkey nut; **huile d'a.** groundnut oil; **beurre d'a.** peanut butter

arachnéen, -enne [arakneɛ̃, -ɛn] *adj* (*de l'araignée*) of spiders, *Litt* **légèreté arachnéenne** gossamer lightness; **être d'une légèreté arachnéenne** to be as light as thistledown

arachnides [araknid] *nmpl Zool* Arachnida

arachnoïde [araknɔid] *nf Anat* arachnoid (membrane)

araignée [areɲe] *nf* spider; **toile d'a.** cobweb, spider's web; *F* **avoir une a. au plafond** to have a screw loose, to have bats in the belfry; *Fig* **a. du matin, chagrin, a. du soir, espoir** = seeing a spider in the morning will bring bad luck, seeing one in the evening will bring good luck

▶ **araignée**: *Zool* **a. d'eau** water spider; **a. de mer** (*crustacé*) spider crab; (*poisson*) weever (fish)

araire [arɛr] *nm Agr* swing *or* ard plough

araméen, -enne [arameɛ̃, -ɛn] *adj, nm Ling* Aramaic

arasé [arɑze] *adj* flush; **armoire arasée** built-in cupboard

araser [arɑze] *vt* **(a)** *Constr* **a. un mur** to level (off) a wall; **a. deux pierres** to make two stones flush; **a. une planche** to plane a plank down **(b)** *Géol* (*roche*) to erode, to weather

aratoire [aratwar] *adj* (*outils, instruments*) agricultural

araucaria [arokarja] *nm* (*arbre*) araucaria, *F* monkey puzzle (tree)

arbalète [arbalɛt] *nf* crossbow

arbalétrier [arbaletrije] *nm* **(a)** *Constr* (*d'un toit etc*) principal rafter **(b)** (*soldat*) crossbowman

arbitrage [arbitraʒ] *nm* **(a)** *Sp* (*au tennis*) umpiring; (*au football*) refereeing; (*dans un conflit social*) arbitration; **conseil d'a.** (*dans un conflit social*) conciliation *or* arbitration board; **soumettre un litige à l'a. d'un tiers** to take a dispute to arbitration by a third party; *Sp* **erreur d'a.** mistake by the referee *or* umpire **(b)** *Banque etc* arbitrage

▶ **arbitrage**: **a. de change** arbitration of exchange; *Bourse* **a. en reports** jobbing in contango(e)s

arbitragiste [arbitraʒist] *n Bourse* arbitrager

arbitraire [arbitrɛr] **1** *adj* **(a)** (*nom, choix etc*) arbitrary; (*punition etc*) discretionary **(b)** (*gouvernement, pouvoir, action etc*) arbitrary, despotic, high-handed; (*ordre*) arbitrary **2** *nm* arbitrariness, arbitrary nature; **laisser qch à l'a. de qn** to leave sth to sb's discretion

arbitrairement [arbitrɛrmɑ̃] *adv* arbitrarily

arbitral, -ale, -aux, -ales [arbitral, -o] *adj Jur* arbitration; **tribunal a.** tribunal, court of arbitration; **solution arbitrale, règlement a.** settlement by arbitration; **commission arbitrale** board of referees

arbitre [arbitr] *nm* **(a)** *Jur* arbitrator, referee, adjudicator **(b)** *Sp* referee; *Tennis* umpire; **a. de touche** *Fb* linesman; *Rugby* touch judge **(c)** *Fig* (*de la mode, dans une dispute etc*) arbiter **(d)** *Phil* **libre a.** free will

▶ **arbitre**: **a. rapporteur** (*dans un conflit commercial*) arbitrator

arbitrer [arbitre] *vt* **(a)** *Jur* to arbitrate **(b)** *Sp* (*match de football*) to referee; (*match de tennis*) to umpire **(c)** *Bourse* **a. des valeurs** to do arbitrage trading

arboré [arbɔre] *adj* planted with trees

arborer [arbɔre] *vt* **(a)** (*dresser*) to raise, to erect, to set up; (*drapeau*) to hoist; *Naut* (*mât*) to step; **a. l'étendard de la révolte** to raise the standard of revolt **(b)** (*porter, exhiber*) **a. une cravate rouge/une rose à la boutonnière** to wear *or* sport a red tie/a rose in one's buttonhole; **elle arbore un sourire triomphant** she is wearing a triumphant smile; **a. un air de mépris** to affect an air of disdain; **a. certaines idées** to parade certain ideas

arborescence [arbɔresɑ̃s] *nf* **(a)** *Bot* arborescence **(b)** *Ordinat* (*structure*) tree diagram *or* structure, directory structure; (*chemin*) directory path

arborescent [arbɔresɑ̃] *adj* **(a)** *Bot* arborescent; **fougère arborescente** tree fern **(b)** *Math, Ordinat* **structure arborescente** tree diagram *or* structure, directory structure

arborétum [arbɔretɔm] *nm Bot* arboretum

arboricole [arbɔrikɔl] *adj* **(a)** (*technique etc*) arboricultural **(b)** (*animal*) tree-dwelling, arboreal

arboriculteur, -trice [arbɔrikyltœr, -tris] *n* nurseryman, nurserywoman

arboriculture [arbɔrikyltyr] *nf* arboriculture; **a. fruitière** fruit growing

arborisation [arbɔrizasjɔ̃] *nf* (*de cristaux*) arborization; (*du givre sur les vitres*) tree-like markings

arborisé [arbɔrize] *adj Minér* dendritic

arbouse [arbuz] *nf* arbutus-berry

arbousier [arbuzje] *nm* (*arbre*) arbutus; **a. commun** strawberry tree

arbre [arbr] *nm* **(a)** [①**B5**,1a,ii] (*végétal*) tree; **jeune a.** sapling; **a. fruitier** fruit tree; **arbres d'agrément** ornamental trees; **a. à feuille(s) caduque(s)** deciduous tree; **a. résineux** softwood (tree); **a. feuillu** hardwood (tree); **a. vert** evergreen (tree); *Fig* **faire l'a. fourchu** to do a headstand (*with one's legs apart*); *Prov* **entre l'a. et l'écorce, il ne faut point mettre le doigt** don't get involved in other people's affairs; *Fig* **les arbres cachent la forêt** you can't see the wood for the trees; *Fig* **les arbres lui cachent la forêt** he can't see the wood for the trees; *Fig* **couper l'a. pour avoir le fruit** to kill the goose that lays the golden egg (**b**) *Ordinat* tree; *Math, Ordinat* **structure en a.** tree diagram

(**c**) *MecE* shaft, spindle, axle; (*d'horloge etc*) arbor

▶ **arbre**: **a. d'accouplement** coupling shaft; *Aut* **a. arrière** back axle shaft; **a. à cames** camshaft; *Aut* **a. à cames en tête** overhead camshaft; **a. à caoutchouc** rubber tree; **a. à cardan** *ou* **de cardan(s)** cardan shaft; **a. coudé** *ou* **vilebrequin, a-manivelle** crankshaft; **a. creux** hollow spindle, tubular shaft; **l'a. de la Croix** the Rood; **a. de culbuteur** rocker shaft; *Mktg* **a. de décision** decision tree; *Aut* **a. de distribution** distributor shaft, camshaft; *Aut* **a. d'entrée** input *or* primary shaft; **a. d'entraînement** drive shaft; *Aut* **a. d'essieu** axle shaft; **a. à excentrique(s), a. excentré** *ou* **excentrique** eccentric shaft; **a. fou** loose shaft; **a. généalogique** family tree; **faire son a. généalogique** to trace one's family tree; **a. de l'hélice, a. porte-hélice** propeller shaft; *Él* **a. d'induit** armature shaft; *Aut* **a. intermédiaire** layshaft, countershaft; **a. de Jessé** tree of Jesse; **a. de Judée** Judas tree; **a. de la liberté** tree of liberty; **a. moteur** *ou* **de commande** main *or* driving shaft; **a. de Noël** Christmas tree; **a. à pain** bread(fruit) tree; **a. de plein vent** standard; *Aut* **a. de pompe** pump shaft; *Aut* **a. primaire** primary *or* input shaft; *Aut* **a. principal** mainshaft, third motion shaft; *Aut* **a. de renvoi** layshaft; *Anat* **a. respiratoire** respiratory system; *Aut* **a. de roue** axle shaft; *Aut* **a. secondaire** secondary shaft, layshaft; *Aut* **a. de sortie** output shaft; **a. de tour** lathe spindle, mandrel; **a. de transmission** line shaft; *Aut* propeller *or* transmission shaft, propshaft; **a. de vie** tree of life

arbrisseau, -eaux [arbriso] *nm* shrub; **plantation d'arbrisseaux** shrubbery

arbuste [arbyst] *nm* bush, shrub; **plantation d'arbustes** shrubbery

arc [ark] *nm* (**a**) (*arme*) bow; **tir à l'a.** archery; **tirer à l'a.** to do archery; **tu sais tirer à l'a.?** can you use a bow and arrow?; **à la portée de l'a.** within bowshot; **corde de l'a.** bowstring; *Fig* **avoir plusieurs cordes à son a.** to have more than one string to one's bow; **ressort à a.** bow spring; **scie à a.** bow saw (**b**) *Archit, Anat* arch; **l'a. des sourcils/de l'aorte** the arch of the eyebrows/of the aorta; **a. dentaire** dental arch (**c**) *Geom* **a. de cercle** arc of a circle; **assis en a. de cercle** sitting in a semicircle (**d**) *Él* **a. voltaïque** voltaic arc; **a. électrique** electric arc; **soudure en a.** arc welding; **lampe à a.** arc lamp

▶ **arc**: **a. brisé** *ou* **aigu** gothic arch; **a. en fer à cheval** horseshoe arch; **a. en plein cintre, a. roman** semicircular arch; **a. de triomphe** triumphal arch

arcade [arkad] *nf* (**a**) *Archit* archway; **a. feinte** blind arch; **arcades** arcade; **se promener sous les arcades** to walk through the arcade (**b**) *Anat* **a. dentaire/orbitaire** dental/orbital arch; **a. sourcilière** the arch of the eyebrows

arcadé [arkade] *adj* (*allée, promenade etc*) arcaded

arcane [arkan] *nf* mystery; **les arcanes de la politique/du pouvoir** the arcane mysteries of politics/of power

arcature [arkatyr] *nf Archit* arcature, blind arcade

arc-boutant, *pl* **arcs-boutants** [arkbutɑ̃] *nm* (**a**) *Archit* flying buttress (**b**) *Constr* abutment pier

arc-bouter [arkbute] **1** *vt* (**a**) (*mur*) to buttress, to support with flying buttresses (**b**) (*étayer*) (*mur etc*) to prop up, to shore up **2 s'arc-bouter** *vpr* to brace oneself; **s'a. sur ses jambes** to brace one's legs

arc-doubleau, *pl* **arcs-doubleaux** [arkdublo] *nm Archit* transverse rib

arceau, -eaux [arso] *nm* (**a**) (*d'une voûte*) arch (**b**) (croquet) hoop; *Méd* (bed)-cradle; *Aut* **a. de sécurité** roll bar, roll-over framework

arc-en-ciel, *pl* **arcs-en-ciel** [arkɑ̃sjɛl] *nm* rainbow

archaïque [arkaik] *adj* (*style, expression etc*) archaic

archaïsant [arkaizɑ̃] *adj* archaistic

archaïsme [arkaism] *nm* archaism

archange [arkɑ̃ʒ] *nm* archangel

arche[1] [arʃ] *nf Rel* ark; **l'a. de Noé** Noah's ark; **l'a. d'alliance, l'a. sainte** the Ark of the Covenant

arche[2] *nf* (*d'un pont etc*) arch; *Géol* **a. naturelle** natural arc

archéologie [arkeɔlɔʒi] *nf* arch(a)eology

archéologique [arkeɔlɔʒik] *adj* arch(a)eological

archéologue [arkeɔlɔg] *n* arch(a)eologist

archer [arʃe] *nm* archer, bowman

archet [arʃɛ] *nm* (**a**) (*de violon etc*) bow; **scie à a.** bow saw; **avoir un bon coup d'a.** (*d'un violoniste*) to be a good violinist; (*d'un violoncelliste*) to be a good cellist (**b**) *Rail* pantograph

archétype [arketip] **1** *adj* archetypal **2** *nm* archetype, prototype; **c'est l'a. du père de famille** he is the archetypal father figure

archevêché [arʃəveʃe] *nm* (**a**) (*territoire*) archbishopric, archdiocese (**b**) (*fonction*) archbishopric (**c**) (*résidence*) archbishop's palace

archevêque [arʃəvɛk] *nm* archbishop

archiconnu [arʃikɔny] *adj F* very well known; **c'est a.** everybody knows that

archicube [arʃikyb] *nm Scol F* graduate of the École Normale Supérieure

archidiacre [arʃidjakr] *nm Rel* archdeacon

archidiocèse [arʃidjɔsɛz] *nm Rel* archdiocese, archbishopric

archiduc [arʃidyk] *nm* archduke

archiduchesse [arʃidyʃɛs] *nf* archduchess

archiépiscopal, -ale, -aux, -ales [arʃiepiskɔpal, -o] *adj* archiepiscopal

archiépiscopat [arʃiepiskɔpa] *nm* archiepiscopate, archiepiscopacy

archifaux, -fausse [arʃifo, -fos] *adj F* dead wrong

Archimède [arʃimɛd] *nm Hist* Archimedes; *Phys* **le principe d'A.** Archimedes' principle; **vis d'A.** *HydE* Archimedean screw

archimillionnaire [arʃimiljɔnɛr] *adj, n F* multimillionaire

archipel [arʃipɛl] *nm Géog* archipelago

archisec, -sèche [arʃisɛk, -sɛʃ] *adj F* bone-dry

archisecret, -ète [arʃisəkrɛ, -ɛt] *adj F* top secret, hush-hush

architecte [arʃitɛkt] *n* (*d'un immeuble; Fig d'une réforme*) architect; **a. paysagiste** landscape architect; **a. naval** naval architect; **a. urbaniste** town planner

architectonique [arʃitɛktɔnik] **1** *adj* architectonic **2** *nf* architectonics

architectural, -ale, -aux, -ales [arʃitɛktyral, -o] *adj* architectural

architecture [arʃitɛktyr] *nf* (*d'une ville, d'un ordinateur etc*) architecture; **a. navale/industrielle/religieuse** naval/industrial/religious architecture; **cette maison a une très belle a.** this house is beautifully designed; *Fig* **l'a. du corps** the way the body is designed, the structure of the body; *Ordinat* **a. client-serveur** client-server architecture; *Ordinat* **a. évolutive** upgradeable architecture; *Ordinat* **a. à micro-canaux** microchannel architecture

architecturer [arʃitɛktyre] *vt* (*discours, roman, texte*) to structure; *Ordinat* **architecturé autour de ...** with its architecture built around ...

architrave [arʃitrav] *nf Archit* architrave

archivage [arʃivaʒ] *nm* archiving, filing

archive [arʃiv] *nf Ordinat* archive

archiver [arʃive] *vt* to archive, to file

archives [arʃiv] *nfpl* archives, records; **exemplaire des a.** file copy; **les a. nationales** ≈ the (Public) Record Office; **a. audiovisuelles/sonores** audiovisual/sound archives; **a. de coupures de presse** cuttings library; **a. photographiques** photographic archives; *F* **ça restera dans les a.** that'll go down in history, wonders will never cease

archiviste [arʃivist] *n* archivist; (*fonction publique*) keeper of public records; *Com etc* clerk (in charge of records), filing clerk

arçon [arsɔ̃] *nm* (**a**) (*de selle*) saddle bow; **vider les arçons** to fall off one's horse; **être ferme sur ses arçons** to be steady in the saddle; *Fig Vieilli F* to have fixed opinions; *Gym* **cheval d'arçons** (vaulting) horse (**b**) *Tex* bow

arçonner [arsɔne] *vt Tex* (*coton, laine etc*) to card *or* clean with a bow

arctique [arktik] **1** *adj* arctic; **cercle a.** arctic circle **2** *nm* **l'A.** the Arctic

ardemment [ardamɑ̃] *adv* (*aimer*) ardently, passionately; (*travailler*) enthusiastically, eagerly; **désirer qch a.** to crave sth; **désirer a. faire qch** to yearn to do sth

Ardennes (les) [lezardɛn] *nfpl* the Ardennes; **la Bataille des A.** the Battle of the Bulge

ardent [ardɑ̃] *adj* (**a**) (*feu etc*) burning hot, scorching, blazing; **soleil a.** scorching *or* blazing sun; **soif ardente** raging thirst; **cheveux d'un blond/roux a.** strawberry *or* reddish blond/fiery red hair; **rouge a.** fiery red

(**b**) (*passionné*) fiery, passionate, ardent; **désir a.** burning desire; **jeune homme a.** a hot-blooded *or* passionate young man; **ardente conviction** deep-seated conviction; **j'en ai l'ardente conviction** I am firmly convinced of it; **socialiste a.** red-hot Socialist; **a. sportif** keen sportsman

(**c**) (*vif*) (*intérêt*) keen; (*imagination*) vivid; (*curiosité*) burning; *F* (*lutte*) fierce; **être dans une colère ardente** to be in a furious rage

ardeur [ardœr] *nf* (**a**) (*du soleil, du feu etc*) heat (**b**) (*enthousiasme*) eagerness, ardour, *US* ardor, fervour, *US* fervor; **cheval plein d'a.** high-spirited *or* high-mettled horse; **travailler avec a.** to work hard *or* enthusiastically; **soutenir son opinion avec a.** to argue one's case with passion *or* passionately; **modère tes ardeurs!** calm down!, don't get excited!; **les ardeurs de la passion** the heat of passion; **son a. à lire** his passion for reading

ardoise [ardwaz] **1** *nf* **(a)** *Minér* slate; **(feuille d')a.** slate; **maison au toit d'ardoises** house with a slate roof; **couvrir un toit d'a.** to slate a roof **(b) a. (à écrire)** (writing) slate; *F* *(compte)* bill, cost; **crayon d'a.** slate pencil; *F* **mets ça sur mon a.** put it on my slate *or* bill *or* tab; *F* **il a des ardoises dans tous les bars de la ville** he owes money in all the bars in town; *F* **j'ai quelques ardoises à régler** I've got a few bills to pay; *TV, Cin* **a. d'identification** identifying head slate; *Ordinat* **a. électronique** notepad computer **2** *adj* **(couleur) gris a.** slate grey (colour)
ardoisé [ardwaze] *adj* slate-colour(ed), bluish-grey
ardoisier, -ière [ardwazje, -jɛr] **1** *adj* slaty; **schiste a.** slate clay, shale **2** *nm* *(exploitant)* owner of a slate quarry; *(ouvrier)* slate worker *or* quarryman **3** *nf* **ardoisière** slate quarry
ardt *abrév* **arrondissement**
ardu [ardy] *adj* **(a)** *(tâche etc)* difficult, hard, arduous **(b)** *Rare* *(pente etc)* steep
are [ar] *nm Agr* are (= 100 square metres)
arec [arɛk] *nm* **(a)** areca palm (tree) **(b) (noix d')a.** areca *or* betel nut
areligieux, -ieuse [arəliʒjø, -øz] *adj* not religious
aréna [arena] *nf Can* arena
arène [arɛn] *nf* **(a)** *(d'amphithéâtre)* arena; *(de tauromachie)* bullring; **les arènes d'Arles** the amphitheatre of Arles; *Fig* **descendre dans l'a.** to enter the ring *or* the fray, to take up the challenge; *Fig* **l'a. politique** the political arena **(b)** *Arch, Litt* sand
arénicole [arenikɔl] *adj* that lives in sand
aréole [areɔl] *nf Anat, Bot, Méd* areola
aréomètre [areɔmɛtr] *nm* hydrometer
aréométrie [areɔmetri] *nf* hydrometry
aréopage [areɔpaʒ] *nm Fig* learned gathering *or* assembly
arête [arɛt] *nf* **(a)** *(de poisson)* (fish) bone; **c'est du poisson pané, garanti sans arêtes** it's breaded fish, guaranteed boneless; **enlever toutes les arêtes d'un poisson** to bone a fish; **poisson plein d'arêtes** bony fish; **grande a.** *(d'un poisson)* backbone; **dessin en a. de hareng** *ou Archit* **de poisson** herringbone pattern **(b)** *(du nez)* bridge **(c)** *Constr etc* line; **a. d'un comble** hip of a roof; **pierre d'a.** quoin stone; **a. de voûte** groin **(d)** *Av* **a. dorsale** *(du fuselage)* dorsal fin **(e)** *Géog* ridge **(f)** *(de graminés etc)* beard **(g)** *(de la lame d'une épée, d'une baïonnette)* ridge, rib
argent [arʒɑ̃] *nm* **(a)** *(métal)* silver; **vaisselle d'a.** (silver) plate; **couverts en a.** silver cutlery; **a. en feuille** silver foil, silver leaf; **bijoux en a.** silver jewellery; *Prov* **la parole est d'a., le silence est d'or** speech is silver, silence is golden; *Sp* **gagner la médaille d'a.** to win the silver (medal); *Fig* **cheveux d'a.** silvery(-grey) hair; **reflets d'a. sur le lac** silvery glints on the lake

(b) *Fin* money; **avoir de l'a.** *(être riche)* to have money; *(sur soi)* to have some money; *Compta* **a. en caisse** cash in hand; *(recettes)* takings; **payer a. comptant** to pay (in) cash; *F* **se faire un a. fou** to make lots *or* loads of money; **les puissances de l'a.** the rich and powerful; *Fig* **l'a. lui fond entre les mains** money just slips through his fingers; **elle le fait pour l'a.** she does it for the money; **attendre une rentrée d'a.** to be waiting for money to come in; *Fig* **jeter de l'a. par les fenêtres** to throw money down the drain, to throw money away; **en avoir pour son a.** to have *or* get one's money's worth, to get good value for (one's) money; *Fig* **plaie d'a. n'est pas mortelle** money isn't everything, it's only money; *Fig* **prendre tout pour a. comptant** to take everything at face value; **le temps, c'est de l'a.** time is money

▶ **argent**: **a. liquide** cash (in hand), ready money *or* cash; **a. de poche** pocket money
argenté [arʒɑ̃te] *adj* **(a)** *(couleur)* silver, silvery; **gris a.** silver-grey; **reflet a.** silvery glint, glint of silver; **renard a.** silver fox **(b)** *(plaqué, couvert)* silver-plated **(c)** *F* *(riche)* well-heeled, loaded; **je ne suis pas très a. en ce moment** I'm not in funds at the moment, I'm a bit hard up at the moment, I'm a bit strapped at the moment
argenter [arʒɑ̃te] *vt* to silver(-plate); *Fig* **la lune argente le lac de ses reflets** the moon gives the lake a silvery sheen
argenterie [arʒɑ̃tri] *nf* (silver) plate, silverware
argenteur [arʒɑ̃tœr] *nm* silverer, silver plater
argentin[1], -ine [arʒɑ̃tɛ̃, -in] *adj* *(voix, rire, vagues)* silvery; *(cloche)* tinkling
argentin[2], -ine **1** *adj* Argentinian, Argentine; **la République Argentine** Argentina, the Argentine (Republic) **2** *n* **A.** Argentinian, Argentine **3** *nf* **l'Argentine** Argentina, the Argentine (Republic)
argile [arʒil] *nf* clay; **a. à blocaux** boulder clay; **a. schisteuse** shale; **traitement par l'a.** mud-pack treatment; **masque d'a.** mud-pack; **a. cuite** terracotta, earthenware; *Fig* **une statue** *ou* **un colosse aux pieds d'a.** an idol with feet of clay
argileux, -euse [arʒilø, -øz] *adj* clayey
argon [argɔ̃] *nm Ch* argon
argonaute [argɔnot] *nm* **(a)** *Myth, Fig* Argonaut **(b)** *(mollusque)* argonaut, paper nautilus
argot [argo] *nm* slang; **parler a.** to talk (in) slang; **mot d'a.** slang word; **l'a. (parisien)** Paris(ian) slang; **a. des voleurs** thieves' cant; **a. du milieu** underworld slang; **a. scolaire** school slang
argotique [argɔtik] *adj* *(langue)* slangy; **expression a.** *(propre à un milieu)* cant phrase; *(familière)* slang expression
argotisme [argɔtism] *nm* slang expression
arguer [arg(ɥ)e] **(j'argue** [ʒargy]; **n. arguions** [nuzargyjɔ̃]**)** **1** *vt* **(a)** *Litt* to infer, to assert, to deduce; **que peut-il a. de ce fait?** what can he deduce *or* infer from this fact?, what conclusion(s) can he draw from this fact?; **il argue qu'on ne l'avait pas prévenu** his excuse is that he was not informed **(b)** *Jur* **a. une pièce de faux** to assert a deed to be forged **2** *vi* **a. de** to argue that, to give as a reason; **elle argua du manque d'informations fournies** she argued that insufficient information had been provided
argument [argymɑ̃] *nm* **(a)** *(démonstration)* argument; **tirer a. de qch** to use sth as an argument; **a. de vente** selling point; **arguments de vente** sales pitch **(b)** *(d'un livre etc)* outline, summary; *(d'un article, d'un film)* synopsis **(c)** *Math* argument
argumentaire [argymɑ̃tɛr] *nm* (sales) blurb; *Com* **rédiger un a.** to draw up a list of selling points; **l'a. est très convainquant** the sales pitch is very convincing
argumentateur, -trice [argymɑ̃tatœr, -tris] *Péj* **1** *adj* argumentative **2** *n* arguer
argumentation [argymɑ̃tasjɔ̃] *nf* **(a)** argument; **une a. serrée** a series of closely argued points **(b)** *Com* sales pitch
argumenter [argymɑ̃te] *vi* to argue **(contre** against**)**; *F* to be argumentative; **on ne peut pas a. de ce fait** you can't base an argument on that fact; **discours/démonstration bien argumenté(e)** well-argued speech/demonstration
Argus [argys] *nm* **(a)** *Myth* Argus **(b) l'A. (de l'Automobile)** ≈ Glass's Guide
argutie [argysi] *nf* quibble; **mettre fin à des arguties** to stop quibbling
aria [arja] *nf Mus* aria
aride [arid] *adj* *(pays, sujet)* arid, dry, barren; *(œuvre)* dry; *(cœur)* unfeeling; **une imagination a.** an unfertile imagination
aridité [aridite] *nf* aridity, aridness, barrenness; **l'a. d'un sujet** the dryness *or* aridity of a topic
arien, -ienne [arjɛ̃, -jɛn] **1** *adj* Aryan **2** *n* **A.** Aryan
ariette [arjɛt] *nf Mus* arietta, ariette
aristo [aristo] *n F* nob, toff
aristocrate [aristɔkrat] *n* aristocrat
aristocratie [aristɔkrasi] *nf* aristocracy
aristocratique [aristɔkratik] *adj* aristocratic
Aristote [aristɔt] *nm Phil* Aristotle; **la logique d'A.** Aristotelian logic
aristotélicien, -ienne [aristɔtelisjɛ̃, -jɛn] *adj, n Phil* Aristotelian
arithméticien, -ienne [aritmetisjɛ̃, -jɛn] *n* arithmetician
arithmétique [aritmetik] **1** *adj* arithmetical **2** *nf* **(a)** [①A71,7; B56,C4] *(matière, calculs)* arithmetic; **a. en virgule fixe** fixed point arithmetic; **a. en virgule flottante** floating point arithmetic **(b)** *(livre)* arithmetic book
arlequin [arlɔkɛ̃] *nm Th* Harlequin; **habillé en a.** in Harlequin costume; **manteau d'a.** proscenium arch
arlequinade [arlɔkinad] *nf Th* harlequinade; *Fig* (piece of) buffoonery
arlésien, -ienne [arlezjɛ̃, -jɛn] **1** *adj* Arlesian, of *or* from Arles **2** *n* **A.** *(natif)* native of Arles; *(habitant)* inhabitant of Arles; *Fig* **c'est l'Arlésienne!** *(d'une femme)* does this girl really exist?; *(d'un homme)* does this man really exist?
armada [armada] *nf Hist* armada; **l'Invincible A.** the Invincible Armada; *Fig F* **une a. de photographes** an army of photographers
armagnac [armaɲak] *nm* Armagnac
armateur [armatœr] *nm Naut* *(d'un navire, d'une expédition)* fitter-out; *(propriétaire)* shipowner
armature [armatyr] *nf* **(a)** *(dans le béton)* reinforcement; *(d'une poutre etc)* truss; *(d'une fenêtre etc)* frame, brace; **soutien-gorge à a.** underwired bra; *Fig* **l'a. de nos principes moraux** the basis *or* the underpinnings of our moral principles **(b)** *(d'un câble électrique)* armouring, sheathing **(c)** *Él* *(d'un aimant, d'une petite dynamo, d'un magnétophone)* armature; *(d'un condensateur)* plate; **a. de soupape/de pompe** valve/pump gear **(d)** *Mus* key signature
arme [arm] *nf* **(a)** arm, weapon; *(en escrime)* sword; **salle d'armes** armoury; *(d'escrime)* fencing school; **l'a. du crime**

the murder weapon; **port d'a.** carrying of weapons; **porter une a. sur soi** to carry a weapon; **prendre le pouvoir par les armes** to take power by force; **nation en** *ou* **sous les armes** nation in arms; **prendre les armes** to take up arms, to rise up in arms (**contre** against); *Mil* to parade under arms; **déposer les armes** to lay down one's arms, to surrender; **porter les armes** to be a soldier; *Mil* **aux armes!** to arms! guard turn out!; **le métier** *ou* **la carrière des armes** the military profession, soldiering; **suspension d'armes** cessation of hostilities; **frères d'armes** brothers in arms; **place d'armes** parade ground; **passer qn par les armes** to send sb to the firing squad; **sans armes** unarmed; *Fig* **passer l'a. à gauche** to snuff it, to kick the bucket; (*dans un accident*) to cop it; *Fig* **il fait ses premières armes** he's earning his spurs; *Fig* **fournir des armes à qn** to provide sb with ammunition; *Fig* **le cynisme est son a. favorite** cynicism is his favourite weapon; *Fig* **l'indépendance est une a. à double tranchant** independence is a two-edged sword; *Fig* **la télévision est l'a. absolue des politiciens** television is the politician's ultimate weapon; *Fig* **à armes égales** on equal terms; *Fig* **avec armes et bagages** (with) bag and baggage

(**b**) (*section de l'armée*) arm, branch, service; **a. de l'infanterie** infantry; **douze mille hommes de toutes armes** twelve thousand men of all arms *or* services

(**c**) *Hér* **armes** (coat of) arms

▶ **arme**: **a. atomique** atomic weapon; **a. biologique** biological weapon; **combat à l'a. blanche** knife fight; **a. blanche** knife; **a. chimique** chemical weapon; **armes classiques** conventional weapons; **armes conventionnelles** conventional weapons; **a. de dissuasion** deterrent; **a. à feu** firearm; **a. non classique** non-conventional weapon, advanced weapon; **a. non conventionnelle** non-conventional weapon, advanced weapon; **a. nucléaire** nuclear weapon; **armes portatives** small arms; **armes traditionnelles** conventional weapons

armé [arme] **1** *adj* (**a**) armed; **troupe armée** body of troops; **vol à main armée** hold-up, armed robbery; **animal a. de piquants/d'une carapace** animal with spines/a shell; **a. d'une canne/d'un dictionnaire/d'un guide touristique** armed with a stick/a dictionary/a guidebook; **a. jusqu'aux dents** armed to the teeth; **sortir a. de chez soi** to go out carrying a weapon; *Fig* **être bien/mal a. pour partir dans la vie** to be well/badly equipped to make one's way in the world; *Fig* **mes enfants partiront armés dans le monde du travail** my children will be well qualified to find a job

(**b**) (*renforcé*) fortified, strengthened; **poutre armée** trussed beam; **béton a.** reinforced concrete; **verre a.** wired glass

(**c**) (*arme à feu*) cocked; **pistolet à demi a.** pistol at half cock

2 *nm* **à l'a.** (*arme à feu*) cocked

armée [arme] *nf* (**a**) [①**A11**,g,i] *Mil* army; **partir à l'a.** to join the army; (*pour faire son service militaire*) to start one's military service; **a. de métier** professional *or* regular army; **a. d'occupation** army of occupation; **lever une a.** to raise an army; **a. permanente** standing army; **a. régulière** *ou* **active** regular army; **l'a. de terre** the army, the land forces; **l'a. de l'air** the air force; **l'a. de mer** the navy, the naval forces; **a. de secours** relieving army; **les armées alliées** the allied armies *or* forces; **être dans l'a.** to be in the army; **la 8ème a.** the 8th army; **le Dieu des armées** the Lord of Hosts; **groupe d'a.** army group

(**b**) **l'A. du Salut** the Salvation Army

(**c**) (*foule*) **quelle a. d'incapables!** what a shower (of incompetents)!; **toute une a. de fonctionnaires** a whole army of officials; **une a. d'insectes ravageurs** an army of marauding insects

armement [arməmɑ̃] *nm* (**a**) (*d'une armée*) (*action*) arming, equipping; (*équipement*) armament, equipment; (*armes*) **armements** armaments, weaponry; **officier d'a.** ordnance officer; **vente d'armements** sale of arms; **la vente d'armements a diminué** arms sales have decreased; **réduction des armements** arms reduction; **course aux armements** arms race

(**b**) (*d'une poutre etc*) strengthening, bracing; (*d'un câble etc*) sheathing

(**c**) *Naut* (*action*) commissioning, fitting out; (*équipement*) equipment, gear, stores; **mettre un navire en a.** to put a ship in commission; **port d'a.** port of registry

(**d**) (*en personnel*) manning

(**e**) *Com* (*profession*) merchant shipping

(**f**) (*d'un fusil*) loading; (*d'un fusible*) arming; (*d'un appareil photo etc*) setting; (*d'une arme à feu chargée*) cocking; (*d'une machine etc*) mounting, fitting up

Arménie [armeni] *nf* Armenia

arménien, -ienne [armenjɛ̃, -jɛn] **1** *adj* Armenian **2** *nm Ling* Armenian **3** *n* **A.** Armenian

armer [arme] **1** *vt* (**a**) (*munir d'armes*) (*soldats*) to arm (**de** with); **je sors toujours armé** I always carry a weapon when I go out; *Fig* **a. qn contre les difficultés de la vie** to equip sb to deal with the difficulties of life; *Fig* **il est armé d'un solide bagage universitaire** he's equipped with a good university education; *Fig* **cette position l'arme de tous les pouvoirs** this job puts him in a position of real power

(**b**) (*ville*) to fortify; (*solive*) to strengthen, to brace; (*dynamo*) to wind; (*câble*) to sheathe, to armour; **a. du béton** to reinforce concrete

(**c**) *Naut* (*navire*) to equip, to fit out, to commission; (*bateau etc*) to man; (*cabestan*) to rig; **a. les avirons** to ship the oars

(**d**) (*fusible*) to arm; (*appareil*) to set; (*arme à feu*) to cock; (*canons, pompe*) to man; (*machine, artillerie*) to mount; (*machine*) to fit up; **a. son appareil photo** to set one's camera

(**e**) *Hist* **a. qn chevalier** to knight sb

(**f**) *Mus* **a. la clef** (*d'un morceau de musique*) to put the key signature

2 *vi Naut* **le navire arme à Brest** the ship is being commissioned at Brest; **a. sur un navire** to serve on a vessel

3 s'armer *vpr* to arm oneself; *Fig* **je me suis armé de mon livre préféré pour attendre** I armed myself with my favourite book to read while I waited; *Fig* **s'a. de courage/de patience** to summon up (one's) courage/patience

armistice [armistis] *nm* armistice; (*temporaire*) truce; **journée** *ou* **anniversaire de l'A.** Armistice Day, Remembrance Day, *US* Veterans' Day

armoire [armwar] *nf* (*placard*) cupboard, *surtout Am* closet; (*pour les vêtements*) wardrobe, *surtout Am* closet; **a. à linge** linen cupboard; **a. à provisions** store cupboard; **a. à pharmacie** medicine chest *or* cabinet; **a. frigorifique** cold store; **a. de toilette** *ou* **de salle de bain** bathroom cabinet; **a. ignifugée** fireproof cabinet; **a. à fournitures** stationery supplies cupboard; **a. de cuisine** kitchen cupboard; **a. normande** large wardrobe; **a. à glace** mirrored wardrobe; *Fig Hum* **c'est une a. à glace** he's built like a tank

armoiries [armwari] *nfpl Hér* (coat of) arms, armorial bearings

armorial, -ale, -aux, -ales [armɔrjal, -o] *adj* armorial

armoricain, -aine [armɔrikɛ̃, -ɛn] **1** *adj* Armorican; **massif a.** Armorican massif **2** *n Hist* **A.** Armorican, ancient Breton

Armorique [armɔrik] *nf* Armorica

armoriste [armɔrist] *nm* heraldic artist

armure [armyr] *nf* (**a**) (*cuirasse etc*) armour; (*d'animaux*) defence; **a. complète** suit of armour; **a. d'un navire de guerre** armour (plating) of a warship; *Fig* **cette insolence est une a., elle s'en protège** she uses insolence as a defence mechanism (**b**) *Tex* weave, pattern, design; **a. toile** plain weave (**c**) *Él* (*d'une dynamo*) pole piece, armouring; (*d'un câble*) sheathing (**d**) *Mus* key signature

armurier [armyrje] *nm* (**a**) (*fabriquant etc*) arms manufacturer; (*de pistolets etc*) gunsmith; (*vendeur*) gun dealer (**b**) *Mil etc* armourer

A.R.N. [aɛrɛn] *nm* (*abrév* **acide ribonucléique**) RNA

arnaque [arnak] *nf F* swindle, rip-off; **attention à l'a.!** be careful you don't get ripped off!; **c'est de l'a.!** what a rip-off!

arnaquer [arnake] *vt F* to cheat, to swindle, to rip off; **se faire a.** to get ripped off

arnaqueur, -euse [arnakœr, -øz] *n F* swindler, rip-off merchant

arnica [arnika] *nf Bot, Pharm* arnica

aromate [arɔmat] *nm* (*herbe*) herb; (*épice*) spice

aromathérapie [arɔmaterapi] *nf Méd* aromatherapy

aromatique [arɔmatik] *adj* (**a**) aromatic; (*saveur*) spicy; **plantes aromatiques** aromatic plants (**b**) *Ch* **carbures aromatiques** aromatics

aromatisation [arɔmatizasjɔ̃] *nf Ch* aromatization

aromatiser [arɔmatize] *vt* (**a**) *Culin* to flavour, *US* to *flavor* (**b**) *Ch* to aromatize

arome, arôme [arom] *nm* aroma; (*goût*) flavour, *US* flavor; **crème glacée, a. vanille** vanilla flavour ice-cream

aronde [arɔ̃d] *nf Menuis* **queue d'a.** dovetail; **assembler qch en queue d'a.** to dovetail sth

arpège [arpɛʒ] *nm Mus* arpeggio

arpéger [arpeʒe] *vt Mus* **a. un accord** to play a chord in *or* as an arpeggio

arpent [arpɑ̃] *nm Hist* arpent (= *one acre*)

arpentage [arpɑ̃taʒ] *nm* surveying, land measuring; **faire l'a. d'un terrain** to measure a piece of ground

arpenter [arpɑ̃te] *vt* (**a**) (*terre*) to survey, to measure (**b**) (*parcourir rapidement*) **a. le terrain** to stride over the ground; **il arpentait le quai** he was pacing up and down the platform

arpenteur [arpɑ̃tœr] *nm* (land) surveyor

arpion [arpjɔ̃] *nm Arg* (*pied*) hoof; (*orteil*) toe

arqué [arke] *adj* arched, curved; (*poutre etc*) cambered; (*nez*) high-bridged; (*cheval*) bandy-legged; **jambes arquées** bow legs

arquebuse [arkəbyz] *nf* (h)arquebus

arquebusier [arkəbyzje] *nm* (*soldat*) (h)arquebusier

arquer [arke] **1** *vt* (*bois, fer etc*) to bend, to arch, to curve; (*surface*) to camber; **a. le dos** to arch one's back **2** *vi* **(a)** (*fléchir*) to bend, to sag, to buckle **(b)** *F* (*marcher*) to walk; **je ne pouvais plus a.** (*j'étais épuisé*) I couldn't walk another step, I couldn't put one foot in front of the other **3 s'arquer** *vpr* to bend, to become bent *or* arched

arrachage [araʃaʒ] *nm* (*des plantes etc*) pulling up, uprooting; (*des pommes de terre*) lifting; (*d'une dent, d'un clou etc*) pulling out, extraction

arraché [araʃe] *nm Sp* (*en haltérophilie*) snatch; *Fig* **obtenir un accord à l'a.** to obtain a deal after much effort; *Fig* **gagner à l'a.** to snatch a victory

arrache-agrafes [araʃagraf] *nm inv* staple remover

arrache-clou, *pl* **arrache-clous** [araʃklu] *nm* claw hammer

arrachement [araʃmɑ̃] *nm* **(a)** (*d'un arbre etc*) uprooting **(b)** *Fig* (*déchirure*) wrench; **l'a. du départ** the wrench of leaving; **nous ne pouvons quitter Paris sans a.** it will be a wrench leaving Paris **(c)** *Constr* toothing **(d)** (*en mécanique*) tearing, wrenching, stripping; **effort d'a.** wrenching force **(e)** *Méd etc* wrench

arrache-moyeu, *pl* **arrache-moyeux** [araʃmwajø] *nm Aut* **a. universel** universal hub puller

arrache-pied (d') [daraʃpje] *adv* without interruption, relentlessly; **travailler d'a.** to work steadily; (*excessivement*) to slave away

arracher [araʃe] **1** *vt* **(a)** (*enlever*) to pull out; (*arbre*) to pull up, to uproot; (*pommes de terre*) to lift; *Fig* (*argent, promesse, secret*) to extract (**de** from); (*dent*) to extract, to pull out; (*affiche*) to tear down, to pull down; **a. qch à qn/des mains de qn** to snatch sth from sb/from sb's hands; *Fig* **on est quand même parvenu à lui a. quelques paroles** we did manage to get a few words out of him; *Fig* **nous sommes parvenus à lui a. cet aveu** we managed to extract that confession from him; **se faire a. une dent** to have a tooth extracted *or* out; **a. les yeux à qn** to tear sb's eyes out; *Fig* **j'avais envie de lui a. les yeux** I wanted to strangle him; *Fig* **il faut a. son masque** we/they/*etc* must unmask him

(b) (*déchirer*) **cela m'arrache le cœur** it breaks my heart, *Arg* **la tequila pure, ça arrache la gueule!** pure tequila will blow your head off

(c) *Fig* (*personne*) **a. qn de son foyer** (*armée d'occupation, police*) to drag *or* uproot sb from his home; **a. qn à la mort** to snatch *or* rescue sb from the jaws of death; **a. qn au sommeil** to rouse sb from (his) sleep; **la sonnerie du réveil m'a arraché du lit** the alarm dragged me out of bed; **a. qn à son travail/à la télé** to tear *or* drag sb away from his work/ the TV

2 *vi* **(a)** *Arg* (*alcool fort, piment*) **ça arrache!** that's dynamite!

(b) *Can* **en a.** to have difficulties

3 s'arracher *vpr* (*se déchirer*) **elle s'est arrachée (sa robe) dans la grille** she tore *or* ripped her dress on the railings; *Fig* **je n'y comprends rien, je m'arrache les cheveux!** I don't understand it at all, I'm tearing my hair out!; *Fig* **c'est à s'a. les cheveux!** it's enough to make you tear your hair out!; *Fig* **tu t'arraches les yeux à lire dans le noir!** you'll ruin your eyesight reading in the dark!; *Fig* **tout le monde la demande, on se l'arrache** she's very much in demand, they're even fighting over her; **on se l'arrache** (*d'un livre etc*) copies are being snatched up; *Fig* **impossible de m'a. de ce pays** I could never tear myself away from this country; *Fig* **s'a. à sa rêverie** to wake from one's day-dream; *Arg* **alors? on s'arrache?** time to go?

arrache-roulement, *pl* **arrache-roulements** [araʃrulmɑ̃] *nm Aut* **a. universel** universal bearing puller

arracheur, -euse [araʃœr, -øz] **1** *n* (*de pommes de terre etc*) lifter; *Fig* **mentir comme un a. de dents** to lie through one's teeth **2** *nf Agr* **arracheuse** (*outil*) grubbing plough, grubber; (*de pommes de terres*) (potato) lifter; (*de betteraves*) (beet) puller

arrachoir [araʃwar] *nm Agr* (*de pommes de terre*) (potato) lifter; (*de betteraves*) (beet) puller

arraisonnement [arɛzɔnmɑ̃] *nm Naut* (*d'un navire*) boarding; **a. de la patente (d'un navire)** examination of the bill of health, sanitary report

arraisonner [arɛzɔne] *Naut* **1** *vt* **a. un navire** to hail a vessel; (*l'aborder*) to stop and examine a ship **2** *vi* **a. avec les autorités du port** to report to the port authorities

arrangeant, -ante [arɑ̃ʒɑ̃, -ɑ̃t] *adj* accommodating, helpful

arrangement [arɑ̃ʒmɑ̃] *nm* **(a)** (*fait d'arranger*) arranging, putting in order; (*manière d'être arrangé*) (*du mobilier etc*) arrangement; **l'a. des fleurs dans un vase** the arrangement of flowers in a vase; **l'a. de ses cheveux demande un soin constant** his hairstyle demands constant attention; **l'a. des mots dans une phrase** the word order in a sentence

(b) *Mus* **a. pour violon** arrangement for violin

(c) (*accord*) agreement, settlement; (*officieux*) understanding; **mal prendre ses arrangements** to arrange *or* plan things badly; **sauf a. contraire** unless otherwise agreed; **essayer de trouver un a. financier avec son banquier** to try to come to (some kind of) arrangement with one's banker; *Jur* **a. à l'amiable** out of court settlement

arranger [arɑ̃ʒe] (**j'arrangeais; n. arrangeons**) **1** *vt* **(a)** (*meubles etc*) to arrange; (*livres, pièce*) to put in order; (*pièce*) to tidy (up); (*cravate etc*) to straighten; *F* **le voilà bien arrangé!** what a mess he looks!; **ils l'ont drôlement arrangé, il a des bleus partout** they've given him a good going over, he's covered in bruises; **a. qn de la belle manière** (*physiquement, en dire du mal*) to have a go at sb; *F* **on vous a arrangé** (*volé*) you've been had *or* done, you've been ripped off; **voilà un bouge où on vous arrange le client** it's a rip-off joint; *Sl* **se faire a.** (*tuer*) to get bumped off

(b) (*voiture, montre etc*) to repair, to overhaul; (*montre*) to mend; **je vais t'a. ça** I'll fix it for you

(c) (*concert etc*) to arrange, to organize; **a. qch d'avance** to arrange *or* plan sth in advance; **il arrange bien sa vie** he's got his life well organized; **je vous ai arrangé un entretien avec lui** I've arranged a meeting with him for you; **ne t'en fais pas, j'ai tout arrangé** don't worry, I've made all the arrangements

(d) (*conflit etc*) to settle; **je vais essayer d'a. les choses** I'll try to put things right; **cela n'arrangera rien** that won't (be much) help; **cela n'arrange pas nos affaires** that's no good (to us), that doesn't help (us)

(e) (*plaire à, satisfaire*) (*qn*) to suit, to be convenient for; **ça t'arrangerait que je vienne te chercher?** would it suit you *or* would it be convenient if I came to collect you?; **faire qch pour a. qn** to do sth to help sb; **on ne peut pas a. tout le monde** you can't please everybody; **tu ne fais que ce qui t'arrange** you only do what suits you; **ça t'arrange?** does that suit you?

(f) *Mus* (*morceau pour violon etc*) to arrange

2 s'arranger *vpr* **(a)** (*s'organiser etc*) to manage; **si vous pouvez vous a. pour le voir** if you can manage to see him *or* make the time to see him; **arrangez-vous pour être là** make sure you're there; *F* **je ne sais pas comment tu t'arranges, mais tu es toujours en retard** I don't know how you manage it, but you're always late

(b) (*se contenter*) **il s'arrange de tout** he's very adaptable; **s'a. d'un vieux lit** to make do with an old bed

(c) (*sa tenue, son apparence*) to tidy oneself up; **tu as vu comment tu t'es arrangé!** have you seen the state you're in?!

(d) (*se mettre d'accord*) **s'a. avec qn** to come to an agreement *or* to terms with sb; **arrange-toi avec elle, elle peut peut-être te prêter sa voiture** sort things out with her, maybe she can lend you her car; **arrangez-vous** settle it among yourselves; **on s'est arrangé à l'amiable** we came to an amicable arrangement *or* agreement

(e) (*s'améliorer*) to work out; **cela s'arrangera** things will turn out all right; **cela s'arrangera tout seul** that will sort itself out; **ça ne s'arrange pas!** it's not getting any better!; **elle ne fait rien pour s'a.** she doesn't do anything to make the most of herself; **ça n'a pas l'air de s'a. entre eux** things don't seem to have got any better between them

arrangeur, -euse [arɑ̃ʒœr, -øz] *n Mus* arranger

arrérages [areraʒ] *nmpl* **(a)** (*de salaires, du loyer etc*) arrears **(b)** (*intérêt*) back interest; **coupon d'a.** interest *or* dividend warrant

arrestation [arɛstasjɔ̃] *nf* arrest; **procéder à l'a. de qn** to arrest sb; **mettre qn en état d'a.** to place sb under arrest; **en état d'a.** under arrest; **a. préventive/provisoire** custodial/ conditional arrest

arrêt [arɛ] *nm* **(a)** (*interruption*) stop, stoppage, stopping; **a. de travail** stoppage; **véhicule à l'a.** stationary vehicle; **a. d'urgence** emergency stop; **point d'a.** stopping place *or* point; *Mus* (*pendant une pause*) pause; **faire un a. au cours de son voyage** to break one's journey, to stop over; **nous avons fait plusieurs arrêts pendant le voyage** we made several stops during the journey; **a. en cours de route** break of journey, stopover; **trajet sans a.** non-stop journey; **New**

York est un a. obligatoire New York is an absolute must; **il neige sans a. depuis mercredi** it's been snowing non-stop *or* continuously since Wednesday; **la machine tombe sans a. en panne** the machine is constantly *or* continually breaking down; **c'est ce que je lui dis sans a.** that's what I tell him over and over again; **dix minutes d'a.** ten minutes' stop; (*pour café, repos etc*) ten minutes' break; **temps d'a.** pause, halt; **chien d'a.** setter, pointer; *Fig* **rester** *ou* **tomber en a. devant qn/qch** to stop and stare at sb/sth; **marquer un temps d'a.** to pause, to halt, to mark time; **a. de paiement** stoppage of payment(s); **a. des comptes** closing (off) the accounts; *Méd* **a. du cœur** heart failure; **a. (inopiné)** breakdown; *Rad, TV* **a. d'émission** break in transmission; *TV, Cin* **a. sur image** freeze frame, stop frame; **robinet d'a.** stopcock; *Rail* **signal d'a.** stop signal; *Ordinat* shutdown; *Ordinat* **a. anormal du système** system crash; *Ordinat* **a. de défilement** scroll lock; *Ordinat* **a. de l'impression** (*commande*) stop printing

(b) (*de bus etc*) **a. de bus** bus stop; **a. facultatif** request stop; **ne pas descendre avant l'a.** do not get off before the bus/train/*etc* has come to a complete stop; **le train est sans a. jusqu'à l'aéroport** the train goes non-stop to the airport

(c) (*d'une porte etc*) stop, catch; (*d'un verrou*) tumbler; **cran d'a.** safety catch; **a. de pied** toeclip

(d) *Jur* (*prononcé par la cour d'assises, cour d'appel ou cour de cassation*) judgement, adjudication; **prononcer** *ou* **rendre un a.** to pronounce *or* deliver judgement; **a. par défaut** judgement by default; **a. de défense** stay of execution; **a. de mort** death sentence; *Fig* **les arrêts de la Providence** the decrees of Providence; *Fig* **les arrêts de la mode** the dictates of fashion

(e) (*arrestation*) arrest; **ordre** *ou* **mandat d'a.** (*d'une personne*) warrant for the arrest; **mettre un officier aux arrêts** to put an officer under arrest; **arrêts à la chambre, arrêts domestiques** house arrest; **être en maison d'a.** to be in prison, to be under *or* to be held in detention

(f) (*saisie*) seizure, impounding, attachment; **faire a. sur des marchandises** to impound *or* seize goods

(g) *Fb* tackle; *Rugby,* **a. de volée** mark; **faire un a. de volée** to make a mark

(h) *Naut* (*d'un navire*) detention

arrêt-court [arεkur] *nm Can Baseball* shortstop

arrêté [arete] **1** *adj* **(a)** (*idées etc*) fixed, decided; **homme aux opinions arrêtées** dogmatic man, man with set ideas; (*décidé*) man with decided views; **c'est une chose arrêtée** it's already been decided; **dessein a.** settled design **(b)** *Sp* **départ a.** standing start **2** *nm* **(a)** *Admin* decision, order, decree; **a. ministériel** departmental order (signed by a minister); **a. municipal** by-law; **a. préfectoral** by-law; **a. d'exécution** decree providing for the enforcement of a law **(b)** *Com* **a. de compte(s)** closing off of an account

arrêter [arete] **1** *vt* **(a)** (*stopper*) (*qn, qch*) to stop; (*véhicule*) to bring to a stop *or* to a standstill; (*fuite*) to stem; *Ordinat* to halt; (*système*) to shut down; **là je vous arrête, je ne suis pas d'accord** stop right there, I don't agree!; **tu pourrais m'a. au bureau de tabac?** could you drop me off at the tobacconist's?; **a. un cheval** to pull up a horse; **rien ne l'arrêtera** nothing will stop him, he will stop at nothing; **quel obstacle vous arrête?** what's stopping you?; **a. le vent** to break (the force of) the wind; *Aut* **a. le moteur** to switch off the engine; **a. la croissance** to arrest growth; **le brouillard/la neige a complètement arrêté toute circulation** fog/snow has brought traffic to a (complete) standstill; *Fb* **a. un tir** to save *or* stop a shot; **a. le gibier** (*d'un chien*) to point game

(b) (*fixer*) (*volet, planche etc*) to fix, to fasten, to secure; *Fig* **a. l'attention** to draw *or* catch attention; *Fig* **je voudrais a. votre attention sur ce point** I'd like to draw your attention to this point; *Fig* **ce détail arrêta mon attention** this detail caught my attention; *Couture* **a. un point** to fasten off a stitch; *Tricot* **a. les mailles** to cast off

(c) (*criminel*) to arrest, to seize; (*contrebande, livres etc*) to seize; **l'assassin n'a pas encore été arrêté** the murderer is still at large

(d) (*déterminer*) to decide; **a. un jour** to fix *or* appoint a day; **la date n'a pas encore été arrêtée** the date has not yet been decided on *or* fixed; **a. un prix** to fix a price; **a. un programme/un projet** to draw up a programme/plan; **il a été arrêté que la séance débuterait à 14 heures** it has been decided that the meeting will begin at 2 o'clock; **a. un marché** to close a deal

(e) *Com* (*compte*) to make up, to close (off)

2 *vi* to stop, to halt; **dites au chauffeur d'a. devant l'hôtel de ville** tell the driver to stop at *or* in front of the town hall; **elle n'arrête jamais de parler** she never stops talking; **elle est toujours occupée à laver, elle n'arrête pas** she's always washing something or other, she never stops; **arrête!, arrêtez!** stop (it)! that's enough!

3 s'arrêter *vpr* **(a)** (*s'immobiliser*) to stop, to come to a stop *or* a standstill; (*d'un corps mobile*) to come to rest; *Ordinat* (*système*) to shut down; **s'a. court** to stop short; **ma montre s'est arrêtée** my watch has stopped; **la voiture s'est arrêtée** the car stopped *or* pulled up; (*en s'approchant*) the car drew up; **s'a. en route** to break one's journey; **nous nous sommes arrêtés dans un village pittoresque** we stopped in a picturesque village; **s'a. chez qn** to call at sb's house/*etc*; **passer sans s'a.** to pass without stopping

(b) (*cesser*) to stop; **la pluie va s'a.** the rain will stop *or* it will stop raining soon; **s'a. de faire qch** to stop doing sth; **s'a. de fumer** to give up smoking

(c) (*faire attention à*) to fix one's attention (**à qch** on sth), to dwell, to insist (**à qch** on sth); **il ne faut pas s'a. aux apparences** one should not go by appearances

arrhes [ar] *nfpl* deposit; **verser des a.** to pay a deposit; **stipulation d'a.** right to annul a sale by paying a fine

arriération [arjerasjɔ̃] *nf Psy* **a. mentale** retardation; (*d'un enfant etc*) backwardness

arrière [arjεr] **1** *adv* **(a) en a.** (*à une certaine distance*) behind; **rester en a.** (*ne pas aller, sortir*) to remain *or* stay behind; (*en se promenant avec d'autres personnes*) to lag behind; *Naut* **avoir le vent en a.** to have the wind astern; **en a. de qn/qch** behind sb/sth; **il est resté en a. de sa classe** he stayed at the bottom of the class; **en a. de son siècle** *ou* **de son temps** behind the times

(b) (*en retard*) **locataire en a. pour ses loyers** tenant in arrears with his/her rent

(c) (*derrière*) backwards; **a.!** (stand) back!; **a., Satan!** back, Satan!; **cheveux en a.** hair brushed *or* combed back, hair swept back; **revenir en a.** to come back; *Fig* **j'ai l'impression de revenir en a., c'est tout à fait comme dans mon enfance** I feel like I've gone *or* stepped back in time, it's exactly how it was in my childhood; **pencher la tête en a.** to lean one's head back; **retourner en a.** to go *or* turn back; *Fig* **il faut remonter loin en a. pour trouver une épidémie de ce genre** you have to go back a long way (in history) to find such an epidemic; *Fig* **vous revenez en a., nous avons déjà parlé de ça** you're going (back) over previous ground, we've already talked about *or* covered that; *Fig* **pas la peine de revenir en a., c'est oublié** there's no point in looking back, it's all been forgotten; **regarder en a.** to look back; *Naut* **en a. (à) toute (vitesse)!** full speed astern!

2 *adj inv* back; **faire marche a.** to reverse, to back; *Naut* **faire marche** *ou* **machine a.** to go astern; *Fig* to back down, to backtrack; *Aut* **où est la marche a.?** where is reverse (gear)?; *Aut* **essieu a.** back *or* rear axle; **lunette a.** rear window; **feu a.** rear light; **à moteur a.** rear-engined; **siège** *ou* **banquette a.** (*d'une voiture*) back seat; **siège a. (de motocyclette)** pillion seat; *Couture* **point a.** backstitch

3 *nm* **(a)** (*d'une maison etc*) back, back part, rear; *Aut* tail; **assis à l'a. de la voiture** sitting in the back of the car; *Aut* **un modèle tout à l'a.** a rear-engined model

(b) *Naut* (*d'un navire*) stern; **vers l'a.** aft; **sur l'a.** astern; **aller à l'a.** to go aft

(c) *Mil* **l'a.** the rear; *Fig* **protéger ses arrières** to protect one's rear, to leave oneself a way out

(d) *Fb* (full) back; *Rugby* full back; *Fb* **a. gauche** left back; **à l'a.** at full back

arriéré, -ée [arjere] **1** *adj* **(a)** (*dû*) late, behind, in arrears; **paiement a.** overdue *or* outstanding payment **(b)** (*dépassé, démodé*) **être a.** (*d'une personne*) to be behind the times; **idées arriérées** old-fashioned ideas; *Écon* **pays arriérés** under-developed *or* backward countries **(c)** (*attardé*) (*enfant*) backward **2** *nm* (*d'un compte etc*) arrears; (*de travail, d'une correspondance etc*) backlog; **a. du loyer** rent arrears, arrears of rent; **il y a un a. de cinq mille livres** £5000 is still outstanding; *Mil* **a. de solde** back pay; **a. de permissions** accumulated leave **3** *n* backward *or* retarded person

arrière-ban *nm Fig* **tout le monde était là, le ban et l'a.** they were all there, the world and his wife; **le ban et l'a. de LVMH** the entire LVMH clan

arrière-bassin, *pl* **arrière-bassins** *nm* inner dock

arrière-bouche, *pl* **arrière-bouches** *nf* back of the mouth, *Spéc* fauces

arrière-boutique, *pl* **arrière-boutiques** *nf* back shop, *US* back store

arrière-cour, *pl* **arrière-cours** *nf* backyard

arrière-cuisine, *pl* **arrière-cuisines** *nf* scullery, back kitchen

arrière-défense, *pl* **arrière-défenses** *nf Fb* (the) back four (defence), the backs

arrière-fond, *pl* **arrière-fonds** *nm* innermost depth(s)

arrière-garde, *pl* **arrière-gardes** *nf Mil* rearguard; *Naut* rear squadron; *Fig* **c'est un professeur d'a.** he's a teacher of the old guard
arrière-gorge, *pl* **arrière-gorges** *nf* back of the throat; **voix d'a.** throaty voice
arrière-goût, *pl* **arrière-goûts** *nm aussi Fig* aftertaste (**de** of); **ce vin a un a. de fruit** this wine leaves a fruity aftertaste
arrière-grand-mère, *pl* **arrière-grand-mères** *nf* great-grandmother
arrière-grand-oncle, *pl* **arrière-grand-oncles** [arjɛrgrɑ̃tɔ̃kl] *nm* great-great-uncle
arrière-grand-père, *pl* **arrière-grands-pères** *nm* great-grandfather
arrière-grands-parents *nmpl inv* great-grandparents
arrière-grand-tante, *pl* **arrière-grand-tantes** *nf* great-great-aunt
arrière-main, *pl* **arrière-mains** *nm* **(a)** *Tennis etc* **(coup d')a.** backhand (stroke) **(b)** *(d'un cheval)* (hind)quarters
arrière-neveu, -nièce, *pl* **arrière-neveux, -nièces** *n* great-nephew, -niece
arrière-pays *nm inv* hinterland
arrière-pensée, *pl* **arrière-pensées** *nf* ulterior motive
arrière-petit-fils, -petite-fille, *pl* **arrière-petits-fils, -petites-filles** *n* great-grandson, -granddaughter
arrière-petit-neveu, -petite-nièce, *pl* **arrière-petits-neveux, -petites-nièces** *n* great-great-nephew, -niece
arrière-petits-enfants [arjɛrpətizɑ̃fɑ̃] *nmpl* great-grandchildren
arrière-plan, *pl* **arrière-plans** *nm* background; **à l'a.** in the background; *(derrière, en arrière)* at the back; *Th* upstage; *Fig* **ce projet est passé à l'a.** this plan has been put on the back burner; *Fig* **mettre qch à l'a.** to put sth on the back burner; *Fig* **rester à l'a.** to remain in the background; **se trouver relégué à l'a.** to be pushed into the background; *Th Fig* to be upstaged
arrière-pont, *pl* **arrière-ponts** *nm Naut* after deck
arrière-port, *pl* **arrière-ports** *nm* inner harbour
arriérer [arjere] **(j'arrière, n. arriérons; j'arriérerai) 1** *vt (paiement etc)* to postpone, to delay, to defer **2 s'arriérer** *vpr* to fall into arrears
arrière-saison, *pl* **arrière-saisons** *nf* **(a)** late season, late autumn *or Am* fall **(b)** *Agr* **les pêches sont chères dans l'a.** peaches are expensive at the end of the season
arrière-salle, *pl* **arrière-salles** *nf* back room
arrière-train, *pl* **arrière-trains** *nm (d'un animal)* (hind)quarters; *F (d'une personne)* rump, rear
arrimage [arimaʒ] *nm Naut etc* **(a)** *(du chargement d'un navire etc)* stowing; **bois d'a.** dunnage **(b)** *(chargement)* stowage **(c)** *(d'une navette spatiale)* docking
arrimer [arime] **1** *vt* **(a)** *Naut etc (cargaison etc)* to stow **(b)** *(fixer)* to secure *or* fasten; **a. un chargement sur le toit d'une voiture** to secure *or* fasten a load to the roof of a car **2** *vi Astronaut* to dock
arrimeur [arimœr] *nm Naut* stevedore
arrivage [arivaʒ] *nm (de marchandises)* consignment; **nous attendons un a. (de produits) venant de France** we're expecting a consignment *or* delivery from France; *Iron, Pej* **t'as vu le nouvel a.?** *(vacanciers etc)* have you seen the new arrivals *or* the new lot?; *Fin* **a. de fonds de l'étranger** accession of funds from abroad
arrivant, -ante [arivɑ̃, -ɑ̃t] *n* arrival; **le dernier a.** the last person to arrive; **les nouveaux arrivants** the new arrivals, the newcomers
arrivé, -ée [arive] **1** *adj* **être a.** *(socialement)* to have made it in society; **il fait très quadragénaire a.** he looks a real forty-something nouveau riche **2** *n (personne)* **un nouvel a.** a newcomer, a new arrival; **le dernier a.** the last (person) to arrive; **le dernier a. a un gage!** = last one there's a cissy!
arrivée [arive] *nf* **(a)** *(de personne etc)* arrival, coming; *(d'une situation, d'une nouvelle étape)* advent; **on attend son a. pour la semaine prochaine** he/she is expected to arrive next week; **depuis son a. au pouvoir** since his coming to power; **depuis son a. à la direction** since he joined the management; **a. matinale** early morning arrival; **a. tardive** late arrival; **à mon a.** when I arrived; **arrivées** arrivals; **tableau des arrivées** arrivals board; **heures d'a.** *(du courrier)* times of delivery; **l'a. du printemps** the coming *or* arrival *or* onset of spring; **l'a. de nouveaux produits sur le marché** the arrival of new products onto the market
(b) *Tech* inlet; *(pour la vapeur etc)* intake, admission; **a. (d'huile)** (oil) feed; *Aut* **a. d'essence** petrol inlet; *Aut* **a. de carburant** fuel inlet
(c) *Sp* (winning) post, finish; **ligne d'a.** finishing line
arriver [arive] *vi (aux* **être***)* **(a)** *(parvenir à destination)* to arrive, to come; *(dans un hôtel)* to arrive, to check in; **a. en voiture** to come by car; **a. par le train/le bateau** to come by train/boat; **il est arrivé en courant** he came running up; **il arrive de voyage** he is just back from a journey; **a. chez soi** to arrive home, to get back home; **a. à temps** to arrive *or* to be on *or* in time; **a. en retard** to be late; **a. le premier** to be the first to arrive, to come *or* be first; **a. dans les premiers** to be among the first to finish; **le printemps est arrivé** spring is here!, spring has arrived!; **l'avion devait a. à midi** the plane was due at midday; **j'arrive!** (I'm) coming!, I'll be with you in a moment!, I'll be right there!; **c'est à cette heure-là que tu arrives?** and what time do you call this to be turning up?; **arrivez (vite)!** hurry up!; **nous sommes presque arrivés** we're almost there; **mangeons, ça la fera peut-être a.** let's start eating, maybe that'll make her come
(b) a. à un endroit to reach *or* get to *or* arrive at a place; **a. à quai** to berth, to dock; **a. à bon port** to arrive safely; **le paquet m'est arrivé trop tard** the parcel reached me too late; **l'eau m'arrive aux chevilles** the water comes up to my ankles; **ma fille m'arrive déjà à l'épaule** my daughter comes up to my shoulder already; **ses cheveux lui arrivent aux épaules** her hair comes down to her shoulders *or* is shoulder-length; **le bruit arrivait jusqu'à ma chambre** the noise reached my bedroom; *Fig* **elle ne lui arrive pas à la cheville** she's not in the same class as him, he's head and shoulders above her
(c) j'en étais arrivé là lorsque ... I had got to that point when ...; **j'en arrive à me demander s'il n'est pas stupide** I'm beginning to wonder whether he's stupid or something; *F* **si c'est pas malheureux d'en a. là!** it's such a pity to be reduced to that!, what a pity it's come to that!; **en a. aux coups** to come to blows
(d) *(socialement)* to succeed; **c'est un homme qui arrivera** he is a man who will succeed *or* get on *or* do well
(e) *(parvenir à un but)* to succeed; **a. à ses fins** to succeed in one's aims *or* plans; **avec du courage on arrive à tout** with courage one can achieve anything; **a. à faire qch** to succeed in doing sth; **je n'arrive pas à le faire toute seule** I can't do *or* manage it on my own; **pour a. à le lui faire accepter, tu devras être patient** to get him to accept it, you'll just have to be patient; **je n'arrive pas à y croire** I just can't believe it; **j'arrive au même résultat que tout à l'heure** I get the same result as before; *Fig* **a. à la vérité** to arrive at *or* get at the truth; *Fig* **a. au fait** to come to the point; **et pour ma voiture? – j'y arrive** what about my car? – I'm (just) coming to that; **tu n'y arriveras pas!** you'll never do it!; **comment y a.?** how can it be done?; **tu n'arriveras jamais à rien!** you'll never amount to anything!, you'll never get anywhere in life!; *F* **tu y arrives?** can you do *or* manage *or* get *or* make it?; **a. à échéance** to fall due; *(d'un bail)* to expire; *(d'un prêt)* to mature
(f) [①B27,E,2,c] *(se produire)* to happen, to occur; **ça t'est déjà arrivé?** has that ever happened to you (before)?; **cela arrive tous les jours** it happens every day; *Prov* **un malheur n'arrive jamais seul** misfortunes never come singly; **ça n'arrive qu'aux autres** it's something that happens to other people; **cela ne nous arrivera jamais** it will never happen to us; **cela n'arrive qu'à nous!** just our luck!; **il lui est arrivé un accident** he had an accident; **je ne voudrais pas qu'il lui arrive quelque chose** I don't want anything to happen to him; **cela arrive à tout le monde** it can happen to anyone; **quoi qu'il arrive** whatever happens, whatever may happen, come what may; **devine ce qu'il m'arrive!** guess what!, guess what's happened (to me)!; **mais qu'est-ce qu'il t'arrive en ce moment?** what's wrong with you at the moment?; **il m'arrive souvent d'oublier** I often forget, I'm apt to forget; **il nous arrive rarement d'aller au restaurant** we rarely go to restaurants; **il pourrait a. qu'il se trompe** he might have made a mistake, it could be that he's made a mistake; **s'il vous arrivait de la voir, dites-le-lui** if you (should) happen to see her, tell her
arrivisme [arivism] *nm Péj* unscrupulous ambition
arriviste [arivist] *n Péj* (social) climber, careerist
arrogance [arɔgɑ̃s] *nf* arrogance; **parler avec a.** to speak arrogantly
arrogant, -ante [arɔgɑ̃, -ɑ̃t] **1** *adj* arrogant, overbearing **2** *n* arrogant person
arroger (s') [sarɔʒe] *vpr* **(je m'arrogeai(s); n. n. arrogeons) s'a. un droit/un privilège** to assume *or* claim a right/a privilege
arrondi [arɔ̃di] **1** *adj* **(a)** rounded, round; **visage a.** round face; **chiffre a.** rounded-off number **(b)** *Ling* **voyelle arrondie** rounded vowel **2** *nm* **(a)** roundness, rounded form; *(d'une bordure etc)* round-off; *Av* fillet, fillet radius; **l'a. du visage** the round shape *or* roundness of the face **(b)** *Av* flare out; **atterrissage avec a.** flared landing **(c)** *(d'une jupe)* hemline

arrondir [arɔ̃dir] **1** *vt* **(a) a. qch** to round sth (off), to make sth round; **la grossesse commence à a. son ventre** her pregnancy is beginning to make her stomach swell; **cette coupe de cheveux arrondit ton visage** that haircut makes your face look round(er); **a. une jupe** to level a skirt; **a. son bras** to flex one's (arm) muscles; **les yeux arrondis par l'étonnement** in wide-eyed astonishment; *Fig* **a. les angles** to smooth down the rough edges, to smooth things over

(b) *Ling* **a. une voyelle** to round a vowel

(c) *Fin etc* (*vers le haut*) to round up; (*vers le bas*) to round down; **a. sa fortune** to amass a considerable sum of money; *F* **a. ses fins de mois** to supplement one's income; **a. une somme/un poids** to round off a sum/a weight; **vous pouvez a. à deux cents francs** you can round it up to two hundred francs; **a. au franc supérieur/inférieur** to round up/down to the nearest franc; **a. son champ** to add to *or* to round off one's land; *Math* **a. un résultat** to correct a result (to the nearest whole number *or* to so many decimal places)

(d) *Naut* **a. un cap** to round *or* double a cape

(e) *Av* (*avant l'atterrissage*) to flare out

2 s'arrondir *vpr* to become rounded; (*du visage*) to round out, to fill out; **pendant la grossesse, elle s'est arrondie** she swelled up during her pregnancy; **son visage s'est arrondi** his face has become round(er) *or* has filled out; **sa fortune s'arrondit** his fortune is growing

arrondissement [arɔ̃dismɑ̃] *nm* **(a)** *Admin* (*à Paris, Marseille, Lyon*) =administrative district **(b)** (*d'un territoire etc*) rounding (off)

arrosage [arozaʒ] *nm* **(a)** (*des plantes*) watering; (*d'une pelouse etc*) sprinkling, spraying; *Culin* (*de la pâte etc*) wetting, moistening; *F* **un bon a.** a good soaking; **a. des rues** watering of the streets; **voiture d'a.** water cart; **tuyau d'a.** hose **(b)** (*publicité*) bombardment, flood; **l'a. continuel par les médias** the constant media bombardment **(c)** (*d'un pré*) irrigation **(d)** (*du vin etc*) watering, diluting **(e)** *Mil* heavy bombing *or* shelling

arroser [aroze] **1** *vt* **(a)** (*rues, plantes*) to water; (*pelouse*) to sprinkle, to spray; *Culin* **a. un rôti** to baste a joint; *F* **j'ai été bien arrosé** I got soaking wet; **vous allez vous faire a.** you're going to get soaked; **ville très peu arrosée** town with little rainfall; **repas (abondamment) arrosé de vin** meal washed down with (plenty of) wine; **café arrosé** laced coffee, *Vieilli* **visage arrosé de larmes** face bathed in tears

(b) a. une prairie to irrigate a meadow; **rivière qui arrose une région** river that waters a district; **la Seine arrose Paris** the Seine flows through Paris

(c) (*vin, lait*) to water down, to dilute

(d) (*de la publicité*) to bombard

(e) *Mil* **a. une ville** to bomb *or* shell a town; **a. des troupes de projectiles** to spray the troops with missiles

(f) *Fig F* (*soudoyer*) **a. qn pour obtenir qch de lui** to grease sb's palm to get sth from him; **on a dû l'a. pour qu'il accepte** we had to bribe him into accepting

2 s'arroser *vpr* **(a) ça ne s'arrose pas** (*plantes*) it doesn't need watering

(b) ça s'arrose! that calls for a drink!

arroseur [arozœr] *nm* (*appareil*) sprinkle; *Fig* **c'est (le gag de) l'a. arrosé** the boot's on the other foot

arroseuse [arozøz] *nf* (*de rue*) water(ing) cart, street sprinkler

arrosoir [arozwar] *nm* watering can

arr(t) *abrév* **arrondissement**

arsenal, -aux [arsənal, -o] *nm* **(a)** *Mil* arsenal; **a. maritime** *ou* **de la marine** naval dockyard **(b)** (*dépôt d'armes*) **a. d'artillerie** gun factory; **découverte d'un a. chez un particulier** discovery of an arsenal of weapons in sb's house **(c)** *F* (*attirail*) gear, paraphernalia; **un a. d'outils** a whole range of tools; **il emporta son a. de drogues** he took his whole stock of drugs with him; **l'a. des lois** the weight of the law

arsenic [arsənik] *nm Ch* arsenic

art [ar] *nm* **(a)** (*technique*) art, craft; **l'a. militaire** *ou* **de la guerre** the art of war; **l'a. oratoire** (the art of) public speaking; **l'a. culinaire** the art of (good) cooking; **dans les règles de l'a.** by the book, according to the rules

(b) (*esthétique*) art; **l'a. pour l'a.** art for art's sake; **pour l'amour de l'a.** for art's sake; **a. égyptien/italien** Egyptian/ Italian art; **l'a. antique/baroque/de la Renaissance** antique/ baroque/Renaissance art; **musée d'a. contemporain** museum of modern art; **beaux-arts** fine arts; *Beaux-Arts, Fig* **œuvre d'a.** work of art; **l'a. poétique** poetics; **ville d'a.** city of artistic interest; **livre d'a.** art book; **histoire de l'a.** history of art; **c'est du grand a.!** it's a work of art!

(c) le septième/le huitième/le neuvième a. cinema/ television/cartoons; **cinéma d'a. et d'essai** art cinema

(d) (*savoir-faire*) **l'a. de ...** the art of ...; **elle a l'a. des soirées réussies** she's got a flair *or* a knack for organizing successful parties; **les Français ont l'a. de vivre** French people know how to live *or* how to enjoy life; **il a l'a. et la manière pour parler aux femmes** he has a way with women; *F* **il a l'a. de m'énerver** he's got a gift for getting up my nose

(e) (*adresse*) skill; **faire qch avec a.** to do sth skilfully

(f) *Scol Can* **maître ès arts** master of arts

(g) *Constr* **travaux** *ou* **ouvrages d'a.** civil engineering structures *or* works

▶ **art**: **a. déco** art deco; **a. dramatique** dramatic art; **a. du feu** ceramics; **a. nouveau** art nouveau; **l'a. sacré** *ou* **religieux** religious art; **arts décoratifs** decorative arts; **arts graphiques** graphic arts; **arts martiaux** martial arts; **arts plastiques** fine arts

Arte [arte] *n* = French-German TV channel

artefact [artefakt] *nm* artefact, artifact

artère [artɛr] *nf* **(a)** *Anat* artery; **a. aorte** aorta; **a. pulmonaire** pulmonary artery; **on a l'âge de ses artères** you're as old as you feel **(b)** *Fig* artery; (*route etc*) main highway, arterial road; (*en ville*) main thoroughfare

artériel, -ielle [arterjɛl] *adj Physiol* arterial; **tension artérielle** blood pressure

artériole [arterjɔl] *nf Anat* arteriole

artériosclérose [arterjɔskleroz] *nf Méd* arteriosclerosis, hardening of the arteries

artésien, -ienne [artezjɛ̃, -jɛn] *adj* (*puits*) Artesian

arthrite [artrit] *nf Méd* arthritis; **a. sèche** *ou* **déformante** rheumatoid arthritis

arthritique [artritik] *Méd* **1** *adj* arthritic **2** *n* arthritic (patient), sufferer from arthritis

arthro- [artrɔ] *préf* arthro-

arthropode [artrɔpɔd] *nm* arthropod

arthrose [artroz] *nf Méd* osteoarthritis

Arthur [artyr] *nm F* **je vais me faire appeler A.!** I'll catch it!

artichaut [artiʃo] *nm* (*légume*) globe artichoke; *Culin* **fonds d'artichauts** artichoke hearts; *Fig* **c'est un cœur d'a.** he/she flits from one affair to another

article [artikl] *nm* **(a)** *Com* article, commodity; **articles** goods, wares; **articles de luxe** luxury goods; **a. en réclame** special offer; **nous ne suivons** *ou* **faisons plus cet a.** we don't stock that item any more; **articles de voyage** travel goods; **articles de ménage** household requisites; **articles de bureau** office supplies; **articles de toilette** toiletries; **a. pour hommes/femmes** menswear/ladies' wear; **a. bas de gamme** bottom of the range item; **a. démarqué** markdown; **a. haut de gamme** top of the range item; **a. à forte rotation** fast mover; **articles de consommation** consumables, consumer goods; **faire l'a.** to make a sales pitch; *Mktg* **a. d'appel** traffic builder; *Mktg* **a. de caisse** check-out display item

(b) (*d'une facture etc*) item; (*de compte*) entry; **articles divers** sundries

(c) (*dans un journal etc*) article; *Journ* **a. de tête** editorial, leader, leading article; **un a. de dictionnaire** a dictionary entry; *Journ* **a. clé en main** rip n' read article; *Journ* **a. d'appel** lead(ing) story; *Journ* **a. de fond** feature (article); *Journ* **a. nécrologique** obituary; *Journ* **a. principal** lead(ing) story, main feature

(d) (*d'un traité etc*) article, clause; (*sujet*) point; **il est très ferme sur cet a.** he's very strict about that *or* on that point; **a. de foi** article of faith

(e) (*point critique*) critical point; **ce qu'il a dit à l'a. de la mort** what he said just before he died; **être à l'a. de la mort** to be at the point of death

(f) *Ent* joint

(g) [①**A4-8; B3-5**] *Gram* **a. défini/indéfini** definite/indefinite article

(h) *Ordinat* (*dans base de données*) record; (*commande*) command; **a. 'annuler'** undo command; **a. contrasté** highlighted command; **a. de menu** command, menu item

articulaire [artikylɛr] *adj Anat* articular, articulatory; *Méd* **rhumatisme a.** rheumatoid arthritis

articulation [artikylasjɔ̃] *nf* **(a)** *Anat etc* joint, *Spéc* articulation; *Bot* node; *Anat* **a. du doigt** knuckle; **a. à** *ou* **par emboîtement** ball and socket joint **(b)** *Tech* connection, joint; **accouplement à a.** jointed coupling; **a. à rotule** ball-and-socket joint **(c)** (*prononciation*) articulation **(d)** (*organisation*) **l'a. des idées d'un texte** the structuring of ideas in a text **(e)** *Jur* (*des faits*) numeration

articulé [artikyle] *adj* **(a)** articulate(d), jointed; (*membre, articulation etc*) hinged; **poupée articulée** doll with movable joints; *MecE* **courroie articulée** chain *or* link belt **(b)** *Ling* (*discours*) articulate

articuler [artikyle] **1** *vt* **(a)** *(assembler)* to articulate, to hinge, to link, to joint; **a. des idées dans un texte** to organize ideas in a text

(b) *Ling* to articulate; *Fig (dire)* **il n'a même pas pu a. son nom tant il était terrorisé** he was so afraid he couldn't even say his own name

(c) *Jur (faits)* to enumerate, to set forth; *(fait)* to state clearly *or* definitely

2 s'articuler *vpr* to be joined together; **la façon dont les os s'articulent** the way the bones are joined together; **ces deux parties s'articulent assez bien** the two parts of the text hang together well; **son raisonnement s'articule autour d'un point central** his argument is based on a central point; *Ling* **le j espagnol s'articule dans le fond de la gorge** the Spanish j is pronounced in the back of the throat

3 *vi* to articulate; **mal a.** to mumble; **articule!** speak clearly!, *Fml* articulate!

artifice [artifis] *nm* **(a)** *(ruse)* trick, contrivance; **user de tous les artifices pour ...** to resort to every trick (in the book) in order to ...; **les artifices de la toilette** the little tricks women use to make themselves (look) beautiful **(b)** *(pyrotechnique)* **pièce d'a.** firework

artificialité [artifisjalite] *nf* artificiality

artificiel, -ielle [artifisjɛl] *adj* **(a)** *(non naturel) (lumière, fleurs, goût etc)* artificial; *(lac)* artificial, manmade; *(perle etc)* imitation; *(dent etc)* false; *Fig (personne)* artificial, false; **jambe artificielle** artificial leg; **colorant a.** artificial colouring; **rire a.** forced laugh **(b)** *(arbitraire)* arbitrary; **classification artificielle** arbitrary classification

artificiellement [artifisjɛlmɑ̃] *adv* artificially; *(arbitrairement)* arbitrarily

artificier [artifisje] *nm (fabricant)* firework manufacturer; *(dans un feu d'artifice)* master of ceremonies

artificieusement [artifisjøzmɑ̃] *adv Litt* deceitfully, craftily

artificieux, -ieuse [artifisjø, -jøz] *adj Litt* deceitful, wily

artillerie [artijri] *nf* **(a)** artillery, ordnance; **a. de campagne** field artillery; **a. légère/lourde** light/heavy artillery; **a. navale** naval artillery; **a. motorisée** motorised artillery; **a. anti-chars**; *Belg* **a. anti-blindés** anti-tank artillery; **a. anti-aérienne** anti-aircraft artillery; **a. d'assaut** assault artillery *or* guns; **tir d'a.** artillery fire; **pièce d'a.** artillery cannon; *Aut* **roue type a.** artillery type wheel **(b)** *(collectif)* gunnery

artilleur [artijœr] *nm* artilleryman, gunner

artimon [artimɔ̃] *nm Naut* **(mât d')a.** mizzenmast; **voile d'a.** mizzen (sail); **a. de cape** storm mizzen

artisan, -ane [artizɑ̃, -an] *n* artisan, craftsman; *Fig* **il est l'a. de sa réussite** he brought about his own success, he's the author *or* architect of his own success

artisanal, -ale, -aux, -ales [artizanal, -o] *adj* **métier a.** craft; **production artisanale** small-scale production (by craftsmen); **magasin a.** craft shop; **poterie artisanale** hand-made pottery; **fait de façon artisanale** made in the traditional way; **leur maison d'édition est restée très artisanale** their publishing house has remained very small-scale

artisanalement [artizanalmɑ̃] *adv* **fait a.** hand-crafted, made by craftsmen

artisanat [artizana] *nm (profession)* craft industry; **l'a. indigène** the native craftsmen; **encourager l'a.** to encourage small-scale industry *or* the craft industries; **a. d'art** arts and crafts; **produits d'a. régional** local handicrafts

artiste [artist] **1** *n* **(a)** *(esprit créatif)* artist; *Fig* **avoir une sensibilité d'a.** to have an artistic temperament, to be artistic; **c'est un a., il a une mentalité d'a.** he's a real eccentric; *Fig* **eh l'a.!, viens par là!** hey, smarty pants, come over here! **(b)** *Th, Mus* performer; *Th* actor, *f* actress; *(chanteur)* singer; *(danseur)* dancer; **a. peintre** painter; **entrée des artistes** stage door **2** *adj (tempérament, style)* artistic; **se donner un genre a.** to try to look all arty

artistement [artistəmɑ̃] *adv* artistically

artistique [artistik] *adj* artistic

artistiquement [artistikmɑ̃] *adv* artistically

arum [arɔm] *nm (fleur)* arum

aryen, -enne [arjɛ̃, -ɛn] **1** *adj* Aryan **2** *n* **A.** Aryan

AS *abrév* **assurances sociales**

as [ɑs] *nm* **(a)** *Cartes etc* ace; **amener deux as** to throw two aces; **as de pique** ace of spades; *F Culin (dans la volaille)* parson's nose; *Fig F* **être ficelé** *ou* **fichu comme l'as de pique** to be dressed any old how; *Fig F* **être coiffé comme l'as de pique** to have hair like a bird's nest; *Arg Fig* **être aux as** *ou* **plein aux as** to be rolling (in it); *F* **ma prime est passée à l'as** my bonus never materialized; *F* **les vacances sont passées à l'as** that's the holidays out of the window

(b) *(dominos)* one; **l'as blanc** one blank

(c) *F (champion)* ace; *(aux jeux)* crack player, star; **au tennis c'est un as** he's an ace at tennis; **as du volant** *ou* **de la route** crack (racing) driver, ace driver; **Pierre c'est un a., il sait tout faire** Pierre's wonderful *or Sl* Pierre's ace, he can do anything

a/s *(abrév* **aux soins de)** c/o

asbeste [azbɛst] *nm Minér* asbestos

asbestose [azbɛstoz] *nf Méd* asbestosis

ASBL [aɛsbeɛl] *(abrév* **association sans but lucratif)** *nf* non-profit-making organization, *Am* not-for-profit organization

ascendance [asɑ̃dɑ̃s] *nf* **(a)** *Astron* ascent **(b)** *(de famille etc)* ancestry; **l'une et l'autre famille avaient une a. canadienne** both families were of Canadian ancestry *or* descent; **a. maternelle** ancestry on his/her/*etc* mother's side; **être d'a. noble** to be of noble ancestry **(c)** *Phys* **a. thermique** thermal (current)

ascendant [asɑ̃dɑ̃] **1** *adj (mouvement, courant, échelle, série)* ascending; *(mouvement etc)* upward; *Av* **vol a.** climbing flight; **course ascendante** *(d'un piston)* up stroke; **tuyau a.** standpipe **2** *nm* **(a)** *Astron etc* ascendant; **astre qui est à l'a.** star in the ascendant **(b)** *(influence)* ascendancy, influence; **avoir de l'a. sur qn** to have influence over sb; **elle subit l'a. de son mari** she's dominated by her husband **(c) ascendants** *(famille)* ancestry **(d)** *Astrol* rising sign; **Verseau a. Cancer** Aquarius with Cancer as his rising sign *or* with Cancer in the ascendant

ascenseur [asɑ̃sœr] *nm* **(a)** lift, *Am* elevator; **a. de marchandises** goods hoist; **a. de service** service lift; **a. à bagages** baggage lift; **a. à tous les étages** lift to all floors; **a. à sas** canal lift; *Fig* **renvoyer l'a.** to return the favour **(b)** *Ordinat* scroll box

ascension [asɑ̃sjɔ̃] *nf* **(a)** *(montée, escalade)* ascent; *Av* climb; **faire l'a. d'une montagne** to climb a mountain; **une a. facile** an easy climb; **l'a. du Mont Blanc** the climbing *or* ascent of Mont Blanc; *Av* **angle d'a.** climbing angle; *Av* **a. verticale** vertical climb; *Astron* right ascension; *Rel* **fête** *ou* **jeudi de l'A.** Ascension Day; **l'île de l'A.** Ascension Island **(b)** *Astron* **a. d'un astre** ascension of a star; **a. verticale** right ascension **(c)** *Fig* progress, ascent, rise; **l'a. professionnelle de qn** sb's climb up the professional ladder; **l'a. de Bonaparte** the rise of Bonaparte

ascensionnel, -elle [asɑ̃sjɔnɛl] *adj (mouvement)* upward; *Av* **force ascensionnelle** lifting power, lift; **vitesse ascensionnelle** rate of climb, climbing speed; **mouvement a.** up-stroke; *Sp* **parachutisme a.** parascending

ascensionner [asɑ̃sjɔne] *vi* to climb

ascensionniste [asɑ̃sjɔnist] *n* climber, mountaineer

ascèse [asɛz] *nf* asceticism; **mener une vie d'a.** to live an ascetic life

ascète [asɛt] *n* ascetic

ascétique [asetik] *adj* ascetic; **vie a.** ascetic life

ascétisme [asetism] *nm* asceticism

ASCII [aski] *abrév Ordinat* **A. inférieur** lower ASCII; **A. supérieur** upper ASCII

ascorbique [askɔrbik] *adj (acide)* ascorbic

asdic [asdik] *nm Naut* **(Allied Submarine Detection Investigation Committee)** asdic

asepsie, aseptie [asɛpsi] *nf Méd* asepsis

aseptique [asɛptik] *adj Méd* aseptic

aseptisation [asɛptizasjɔ̃] *nf (d'une blessure, d'un pansement)* sterilization, asepsis; *(d'une pièce)* disinfection

aseptiser [asɛptize] *Méd vt (blessure)* to sterilize; *(pièce)* to disinfect; *Fig Péj* **un univers aseptisé** a sterile *or* sanitized environment

asexué [asɛksɥe], **asexuel, -elle** [asɛksɥɛl] *adj Biol* asexual

asiatique [azjatik] **1** *adj* Asian, Asiatic; **grippe a.** Asian flu **2** *n* **A.** Asian, Asiatic

Asie [azi] *nf* Asia; **l'A. Mineure** Asia Minor; **A. du Sud-Est** South-East Asia

asile [azil] *nm* **(a)** *Jur* sanctuary; **droit d'a.** right of sanctuary; **a. politique/diplomatique** political/diplomatic asylum; **demander l'a. politique** to ask for political asylum **(b)** *(abri)* shelter, refuge; retreat; **lieu d'a.** (place of) refuge; **sans a.** without refuge, *Arch* **a. des pauvres** ≈ workhouse; **a. de nuit** night shelter, *F* dosshouse; **a. des marins** sailors' home; **a. (d'aliénés)** mental hospital, *Vieilli* lunatic asylum; *F* **il faut le mettre à l'a.!** he belongs in the loony bin *or* at the funny farm!, he ought to be locked away!; *Litt* **a. de paix** haven of peace; **le dernier a.** the grave

asinien, -ienne [azinjɛ̃, -jɛn] *adj* asinine

asocial, -ale, -aux [asɔsjal, -o] *adj, n* asocial, maladjusted (person)

asparagus [asparagys] *nm* asparagus fern

aspartam(e) [aspartam] *nm* aspartame

aspect [aspɛ] *nm* **(a)** *(vue)* sight, *Fml* aspect

(b) (*air*) appearance, look; **avoir un a. imposant** to look imposing; **je n'aime pas l'a. de cette affaire** I don't like the look of the thing; **un démon qui pouvait prendre tous les aspects** a demon who could take on any appearance

(c) (*angle*) angle, point of view; **considérer une affaire sous tous ses aspects** to look at a problem from every angle *or* from all points of view; **vu sous cet a.** seen from this angle *or* point of view; **sous tous ses aspects** from every angle, from all points of view

(d) *Astrol* (*des étoiles*) aspect, relative positions

(e) [①A39,7] *Gram* aspect; **a. perfectif** perfective

asperge [aspɛrʒ] *nf* **(a)** (*plante*) asparagus; **a. plumeuse** asparagus fern; **une botte d'asperges** a bunch of asparagus; **pointe** *ou* **tête d'a.** asparagus tip; **plant d'asperges** asparagus bed **(b)** *F* (*personne*) beanpole

asperger [aspɛrʒe] *vt* (**j'aspergeai(s); n. aspergeons**) (*linge etc*) to sprinkle with water; **a. qn d'eau bénite** to sprinkle sb with holy water; **une voiture nous a aspergés d'eau** a (passing) car sprayed us with water; **se faire a.** to get splashed

aspergès [aspɛrʒɛs] *nm Rel* **(a)** (*goupillon*) aspergillum, holy-water sprinkler **(b)** (*rite*) Asperges

aspérité [asperite] *nf* **(a)** (*d'une surface etc*) unevenness, ruggedness, roughness **(b)** (*d'un caractère, d'une voix*) asperity, harshness, sharpness

asperme [aspɛrm] *adj Bot* seedless

aspersion [aspɛrsjɔ̃] *nf* sprinkling; *Agr* drench

aspersoir [aspɛrswar] *nm* **(a)** *Rel* aspergillum **(b)** (*d'un arrosoir*) rose

asphaltage [asfaltaʒ] *nm Constr etc* asphalting

asphalte [asfalt] *nm Minér* asphalt; **a. minéral** pitch, bitumen; **route en a.** asphalt road; *F* **arpenter l'a.** to pace up and down the streets

asphalter [asfalte] *vt* (*route etc*) to asphalt

asphodèle [asfɔdɛl] *nm* (*plante*) asphodel; **a. rameux** branched lily, king's rod; **a. blanc** king's spear

asphyxiant [asfiksjɑ̃] **(a)** asphyxiating, suffocating; **gaz a.** poison gas **(b)** *Fig* (*atmosphère etc*) stifling, suffocating

asphyxie [asfiksi] *nf* asphyxia, asphyxiation, suffocation; *Min etc* gassing; **mourir d'a.** *ou* **par a.** to die of asphyxiation; *Fig* **a. économique** economic strangulation

asphyxié, -ée [asfiksje] *adj* (*personne*) asphyxiated, suffocated; *Min etc* gassed; **mourir a.** to die of asphyxiation

asphyxier [asfiksje] (*pr sub, impf* **n. asphyxiions, v. asphyxiiez**) **1** *vt* to asphyxiate, to suffocate; *Min etc* to gas; *Fig* **elle se sent asphyxiée par sa famille** she feels suffocated *or* stifled by her family **2 s'asphyxier** *vpr* (*accidentellement*) to be asphyxiated, to suffocate; (*au gaz*) to be gassed; (*pour se suicider*) to suffocate oneself; (*au gaz*) to gas oneself

aspic[1] [aspik] *nm* (*serpent*) asp

aspic[2] *nm Culin* aspic

aspidistra [aspidistra] *nm* (*plante*) aspidistra

aspirant, -ante [aspirɑ̃, -ɑ̃t] **1** *adj* sucking; **pompe aspirante** suction pump; **ventilateur a.** suction fan; **course aspirante** induction *or* admission stroke **2** *n* candidate (**au** for) **3** *nm Naut* midshipman; *Mil* = officer cadet; *Naut* **a. pilote** apprentice pilot

aspirateur, -trice [aspiratœr, -tris] **1** *adj* aspiratory; (*mécanisme*) suction **2** *nm* (*pour la maison*) vacuum (cleaner), hoover®; *Ch, Ind, Méd* (*de gaz, d'air*) exhauster, aspirator; **passer l'a. dans la maison** to vacuum(-clean) *or* hoover® the house; **passer une pièce/moquette à l'a.** to vacuum(-clean) *or* hoover® a room/rug; **un coup d'a.** a quick once-over with the vacuum (cleaner) *or* hoover®; **a. à céréales** grain elevator; **a. de buées** extractor fan

aspiration [aspirasjɔ̃] *nf* **(a)** *Physiol* inhaling (of air into the lungs), *Spéc* inspiration; *Tech* (*d'eau dans pompe etc*) suction, sucking up; *Aut* aspiration; *Aut* **à a. naturelle** naturally aspirated, unblown; **ventilateur à a.** exhaust fan; (*d'un moteur à combustion interne*) admission, induction; **clapet d'a.** intake valve **(b)** (*désir, ambition*) aspiration, yearning (**à, vers** for, after); **aspirations à la scène** ambitions to go on the stage **(c)** *Ling* aspiration

aspiré [aspire] *adj Ling* aspirate(d)

aspirée [aspire] *nf Ling* aspirate

aspirer [aspire] **1** *vi* **(a)** (*inspirer*) to breathe in, to inhale **(b)** (*ambitionner*) to aspire (**à** to); **a. à la gloire/la célébrité** to aspire to glory/fame; **a. à un poste** to covet a post; **a. à faire qch** to long to do sth; **elle aspire à devenir actrice** she longs to become an actress **2** *vt* **(a)** (*air, parfum etc*) to inhale, to breathe (in); (*poudre etc*) to sniff up **(b)** (*eau etc*) (*d'une pompe*) to suck up, to suck in, to draw (up) **(c)** *Ling* (*un son*) to aspirate, to breathe; **l'h est aspiré en allemand** the h is aspirated in German

aspirine [aspirin] *nf Pharm* aspirin; **un cachet d'a.** an aspirin; **prenez deux aspirines** take two aspirin(s)

aspiro-batteur, *pl* **aspiro-batteurs** [aspirobatœr] *nm* beating vacuum cleaner

assagir [asaʒir] **1** *vt* to quieten down; **le mariage l'a assagi** marriage has calmed him down; **voilà qui l'assagira** that will knock some sense into him; **le temps assagit les passions** passions will cool with time **2 s'assagir** *vpr* to settle down

assagissement [asaʒismɑ̃] *nm* quietening (down), calming (down); (*des esprits*) calming (down)

assaillant, -ante [asajɑ̃, -ɑ̃t] *n* assailant, attacker

assaillir [asajir] *vt* (*prp* **assaillant**; *pp* **assailli**; *pr ind* **j'assaille, n. assaillons, ils assaillent**; *impf* **j'assaillais**; *p hist* **j'assaillis**; *fu* **j'assaillirai**) to assault, to attack; *Fig* (*de difficultés, remords etc*) to beset; **à mon retour j'ai été assailli de questions** when I came back I was bombarded with questions

assainir [asɛnir] **1** *vt* (*maison, murs*) to clean up; (*atmosphère etc*) to cleanse, to purify; (*étable*) to clean, to disinfect; (*marais*) to drain; (*ville*) to improve the sanitation of; (*monnaie, marché etc*) to stabilize; **a. les finances/l'administration** to reorganize finance/administration; **a. une rivière** to clean up a river **2 s'assainir** *vpr* (*d'atmosphère, Fig de marché*) to become healthier; *Fig* **la situation s'est assainie** the situation has improved

assainissant [asɛnisɑ̃] *adj* cleansing, purifying

assainissement [asɛnismɑ̃] *nm* (*d'atmosphère*) cleansing, purifying; (*de terrain*) drainage; (*de ville*) improving of the sanitation; *Fin* stabilization; **a. monétaire** stabilization of the currency; **travaux d'a.** drainage work

assaisonnement [asɛzɔnmɑ̃] *nm* **(a)** (*de plat*) seasoning, flavouring; (*de salade*) dressing; **je n'aime pas ce plat, l'a. est trop fade** I don't like this dish, it's under-seasoned **(b)** (*aromate etc*) seasoning, flavouring

assaisonner [asɛzɔne] *vt* **(a)** *Culin* to season, to flavour (**de** with); (*salade*) to dress; *Fig F* **se faire a.** (*réprimander*) to get a good telling-off; **le président a vraiment été assaisonné dans le journal de ce matin** the president really got it in the paper this morning **(b)** *F* (*faire payer plus*) to rip off; **je me suis fait assaisonné** I got ripped off

assassin, -ine [asasɛ̃, -in] **1** *nm* murderer, *f* murderess; (*d'une personnalité politique etc*) assassin; **à l'a.!** murder!; **l'a. est Madame Duval** the murderer is Mrs Duval **2** *adj* **(a)** (*horde etc*) murderous **(b)** *Fig* (*sourire*) provocative, bewitching; **elle lance des œillades assassines à tous les hommes** she's always making eyes at men

assassinat [asasina] *nm* murder; (*d'une personnalité politique etc*) assassination; *Jur* premeditated murder, *US* murder in the first degree

assassiner [asasine] *vt* to murder; (*homme politique etc*) to assassinate; *F* (*chanson etc*) to murder; *Fig* **si je rentre en retard, je vais me faire a. par mes parents** if I get home late, my parents will murder me; *Fig* **je ne vais pas vous a., c'est seulement 100 francs** I'm not going to charge you the earth, it's only 100 francs

assaut [aso] *nm* **(a)** (*attaque*) assault, attack; *surtout Mil* charge, onslaught; **canon d'a.** assault gun; **troupes d'a.** assault *or* storm troops; **a. à la baïonnette** bayonet charge; **donner l'a. à** to storm, to launch an attack on; *Fig* **partir à l'a. du Mont Blanc/d'une entreprise** to set out to conquer Mont Blanc/to take over a firm; **les meilleures places ont été prises d'a.** everybody made a rush for the best seats; **les assauts répétés d'une maladie** the repeated attacks *or* onslaughts of a disease

(b) (*combat*) match, bout; **a. de lutte** wrestling bout; **a. de boxe** boxing match; **faire a. d'élégance/de zèle/de courtoisie** to (try to) outdo each other in elegance/zeal/politeness

assèchement [asɛʃmɑ̃] *nm* (*de route*) drying; (*de terrain, mare etc*) draining, drainage; (*de mine*) pumping dry

assécher [aseʃe] (**j'assèche, n. asséchons; j'assècherai**) **1** *vt* to dry; (*marais etc*) to drain; (*mine etc*) to pump dry *or* out **2 s'assécher** *vpr* to become dry, to dry up

ASSEDIC [asedik] *nfpl* (*abrév* **Associations pour l'emploi dans l'industrie et le commerce**) French unemployment benefits department (≈Unemployment Benefit Office); **toucher les A.** to get unemployment benefit; **faire un dossier aux A.** to apply for unemployment benefit

assemblage [asɑ̃blaʒ] *nm* **(a)** (*de personnes*) gathering; (*d'objets*) collection, combination; **a. de circonstances** combination of circumstances

(b) (*d'éléments de machine etc*) assembling, assembly; *Menuis* joint, joining; *Couture* sewing together; *Tricot* making up; (*de feuillets*) gathering, collating

(c) (*structure*) assembly; **un a. de tiges métalliques** an assembly *or* structure of metal shafts; **a. à queue d'aronde** dovetail joint; **a. par vis/à rivets** screw/rivet assembly; **a. à tenon et mortaise** mortise-and-tenon joint

(d) *Ordinat* **programme d'a.** assembler

(e) *Él* connection; **a. en quantité** parallel connection

(f) (*par soudure*) bond

assemblée [asɑ̃ble] *nf* (a) (*réunion*) assembly; (*plus petite*) meeting; **se réunir en a.** to assemble (for a meeting) (b) *Pol* **A. nationale** National Assembly, *Br* ≈ House of Commons, *US* ≈ House of Representatives; **A. parlementaire européenne** European Parliamentary Assembly (c) (*foule*) gathering; **une nombreuse a.** a large gathering; **l'a. des fidèles** the congregation

▶ **assemblée**: **a. des actionnaires** shareholders' meeting; **a. annuelle/extraordinaire** annual/extraordinary general meeting; **a. générale** annual general meeting; **a. générale d'actionnaires** general meeting of shareholders; **a. générale extraordinaire** extraordinary general meeting; **a. générale ordinaire** annual general meeting

assembler [asɑ̃ble] **1** *vt* (a) to assemble; (*personnes*) to call together, to assemble; (*comité etc*) to convene; (*ingrédients, idées, ce dont on a besoin etc*) to collect, to gather (together); *Naut* **a. l'équipage** to muster the crew

(b) (*machine, meuble en kit etc*) to assemble, to put *or* fit together; (*documents*) to collate; (*feuillets*) to collate, to gather

(c) *Menuis, Tech etc* to join (up), to joint; **a. deux morceaux à plat** to butt-joint two pieces; **a. deux pièces par soudure/collage** to weld/glue two parts together

(d) *Ordinat* (*programme*) to assemble; (*modules*) to link

(e) *Él* (*cellules*) to connect, to join up

2 s'assembler *vpr* to assemble, to meet, to gather; (*d'une foule*) to gather; **s'a. devant un spectacle insolite** to gather in front of an unusual sight; **les membres s'assemblent deux fois par an** the members meet twice a year; *Prov* **qui se ressemble s'assemble** birds of a feather flock together

assembleur, -euse [asɑ̃blœr, -øz] **1** *n* assembler; (*de machines etc*) fitter **2** *nf* **assembleuse** (*machine*) gatherer **3** *nm Ordinat* assembler

asséner [asene] *vt* (**j'assène, n. assénons; j'assènerai**) (*coup*) to strike; **coup bien asséné** telling *or* well-aimed blow; **a. une réplique** to answer back like a shot; **la façon dont la propagande est assénée** the way propaganda is thrust at you; **on nous assène des publicités toute la journée** we are bombarded with adverts all day long; **c'est là qu'il lui a asséné l'argument final** that's when he hurled the final argument at him

assentiment [asɑ̃timɑ̃] *nm* assent, consent, agreement; **avoir l'a. de tous** to be supported unanimously; **sourire d'a.** smile of agreement

asseoir [aswar] (*prp* **asseyant**; *pp* **assis**; *pr ind* **j'assieds** [asje], **il assied, n. asseyons, ils asseyent** *or* **j'assois, il assoit, ils assoient**; *pr sub* **j'asseye, n. asseyions** *or* **j'assoie**; *imp* **assieds, asseyons, asseyez**; *impf* **j'asseyais** *or* **j'assoyais**; *p hist* **j'assis**; *p sub* **j'assisse**; *fu* **j'assiérai** *or* **j'assoirai**) **1** *vt* (a) (*installer*) to seat, to sit; **asseyez-le sur le gazon** sit him down on the grass; **faire a. qn** to ask sb to sit down *or* to take a seat

(b) (*fondations etc*) to place, to lay; **a. une pierre** to bed a stone; **a. une statue sur un piédestal** to stand a statue on a pedestal; **a. une tente/un camp** to pitch a tent/(a) camp; *Fig* **a. son autorité/sa réputation** to establish one's authority/reputation; *Fig* **a. une théorie sur des résultats scientifiques** to base a theory on scientific results; *Fin* **a. l'impôt sur le revenu** to base taxation on income

(c) *F* (*étonner*) to amaze, to stagger; **ça m'assoit complètement de voir qu'il réussit aussi vite** I'm staggered to see him succeeding so quickly

2 s'asseoir *vpr* to sit (down); **asseyez-vous** (*à de nombreuses personnes*) sit down, be seated; (*à une ou deux personnes*) sit down, have *or* take a seat; **asseyez-vous, je vous en prie** please sit down *or* take a seat; **vous permettez que je m'asseye** *ou* **m'assoie?** may I sit down?; **s'a. sur une chaise/dans un fauteuil** to sit on a chair/in an armchair; **s'a. (sur son séant)** (*d'une position allongée*) to sit up; *Fig F* **s'a. sur qn** to ignore sb; *Fig F* **les ordres du patron, moi, je m'assois dessus** I don't give a damn about the boss's orders!

assermenté [asɛrmɑ̃te] *adj* sworn (in); (*témoin etc*) on oath; **fonctionnaire a.** sworn official; *Hist* **(prêtre) non a.** non-juring (priest)

assermenter [asɛrmɑ̃te] *vt* (*qn*) to swear in; (*témoin etc*) to administer the oath to

assertion [asɛrsjɔ̃] *nf* assertion

asservi [asɛrvi] *adj* (*appareil*) servo; **moteur a.** servomotor

asservir [asɛrvir] **1** *vt* (a) (*assujettir*) to enslave, to subjugate, to subdue; (*nation*) to reduce to slavery; **a. ses instincts** to control one's instincts, to keep one's instincts under control; **être asservi à la mode** to be a slave to fashion (b) (*de mécanisme de commande etc*) (*pièce*) to control **2 s'asservir** *vpr* to submit, to bow (**à** to)

asservissant [asɛrvisɑ̃] *adj* enslaving; **avoir un emploi a.** to be a slave to one's job

asservissement [asɛrvismɑ̃] *nm* (a) (*assujettissement*) (*d'un pays*) subjection (**à** to), reduction to slavery, enslavement; (*envers qn plus fort*) subservience; **vivre dans l'a. des médias** to believe everything the newspapers and television say (b) *Tech* control; (*de mécanisme*) servo control

assesseur [asɛsœr] *nm* (a) *Jur* (**juge**) **a.** (*auprès d'un magistrat etc*) assessor (b) **être secondé par ses assesseurs** to be supported by one's assistants

assez [ase] *adv* (a) [①A25,d,v] (*suffisamment*) enough; **vous travaillez bien a.** you work quite enough; **elle parle a. bien l'anglais pour ce poste** she speaks English well enough for the job; **(c'est) a. parlé!** that's enough talking!; **nous sommes a. de trois, nous n'avons pas besoin de toi** three's enough, we don't need you; **il est a. bête pour la croire!** he's stupid enough to believe her; **il n'est pas a. bête pour dire oui** he's not so stupid as to say yes; **être a. près pour voir** to be near enough to see; **il n'avait pas a. pour vivre/pour acheter des cigarettes** he hadn't enough to live on/enough (money) to buy cigarettes; **a.!** that's enough!, stop!; **a.!, je ne veux plus t'entendre** that's enough! I don't want to hear another sound out of you; **j'en ai a.!** I've had enough (of it)!, I'm sick *or* tired of it!, I'm fed up!; **en voilà a. (sur ce sujet)!** that's enough (about that)!; **c'en est a.!** that's enough of that!; **j'en ai plus qu'a. de ses sautes d'humeur!** I've had more than enough of his moods

(b) (**a. de** + *n*) enough; **il y a a. de pain pour tous** there's enough bread for everybody; **avez-vous a. d'argent?** have you enough money?; **a. de promesses! des actes!** enough (of) promises! let's see some action!

(c) [①A4,B] (*plutôt*) quite, rather, fairly; **elle est a. jolie** she's quite pretty; **je suis a. de votre avis** I'm rather inclined to agree with you; **je suis a. content de ma carrière** I'm quite *or* fairly happy with my career; **arriver a. tard** to arrive rather *or* fairly late; **j'ai dû attendre a. longtemps** I had to wait quite a long time; **il parle a. peu** he doesn't talk much

assidu [asidy] *adj* assiduous; (*employé, élève etc*) industrious, hard-working; (*soin, attention*) constant; (*visiteur*) regular, constant; **efforts assidus** untiring efforts; **travailleur a.** hard worker; **présence assidue aux cours** regular attendance at classes; **le médecin est a. auprès de ses malades** the doctor takes good care of *or* is very attentive to his patients; **faire une cour assidue à qn** to court sb persistently; *Vieilli* **un amoureux a.** a persistent suitor

assiduité [asidɥite] *nf* (a) assiduity, perseverance; *Scol etc* regular attendance; **a. à (faire) qch** assiduity in (doing) sth; **a. au travail** devotion to work (b) (*fréquence*) constant attention(s), constant care; **fréquenter qn avec a.** to be a frequent visitor at sb's house (c) **il la poursuit de ses assiduités depuis des années** he's been forcing his attentions on her for years

assidûment [asidymɑ̃] *adv* assiduously, unremittingly; (*fréquenter un lieu*) regularly; **il y travaille a.** he is hard at work on it

assiégé, -ée [asjeʒe] **1** *adj* besieged **2** *npl* **les assiégés** the besieged

assiégeant, -ante [asjeʒɑ̃, -ɑ̃t] **1** *adj* (*armée etc*) besieging **2** *n* besieger

assiéger [asjeʒe] *vt* (**assiégeant; j'assiège, n. assiégeons; j'assiégerai**) (*ville, château*) to besiege, to lay siege to; (*personne*) to surround, to crowd round; *Fig* **les journalistes ont assiégé l'hôtel** journalists besieged *or* laid siege to the hotel; *Fig* **assiégé par l'inondation** hemmed in by flood water; *Fig* **la ville est assiégée par les touristes** the town is overrun with *or* by tourists; *Fig* **a. qn de demandes** to pester sb with requests

assiette [asjɛt] *nf* (a) (*vaisselle*) plate; **manger dans une a.** to eat off *or* from a plate; **ne mange pas avec le nez dans ton a.** don't eat like that with your nose right in your plate

(b) (*fondation*) (*de bâtiment etc*) situation, site; (*de camp*) disposition; (*du terrain*) lie; (*de pierre, poutre etc*) set; (*d'un impôt, d'un taux*) base; (*d'une route*) foundation, bottom, bed

(c) (*d'un cavalier*) seat; (*de bateau*) trim; *Av, Naut* **angle d'a.** trim angle; **avoir une bonne a.** *Équitation* to have a good seat; *Naut* to be in good trim; *F* **ne pas être dans son a.** to be out of sorts *or* off colour *or* under the weather; **prendre**

son a. (*de fondation, canon etc*) to set, to settle, to bed down

▶ **assiette**: *Culin* **a. anglaise** assorted cold meat(s), cold cuts; *F* **a. au beurre** cushy job; **a. des coupes** felling plan; **a. creuse** soup dish; **a. à dessert** dessert plate; **a. d'impôts** tax base; **a. plate** dinner plate; **a. à soupe** soup dish *or* plate

assiettée [asjete] *nf* plate(ful)

assignable [asiŋabl] *adj* (*limite*) assignable; (*cause, raison*) ascribable, attributable

assignataire [asiŋatɛr] *adj* **banque a.** warrant bank

assignation [asiŋasjɔ̃] *nf* **(a)** *Fin* (*de parts, fonds*) assignment, transfer (**à** to) **(b)** *Jur* (*action*) serving of a writ *or* summons *or* process; (*acte*) (writ of) summons, subpoena; **signifier** *ou* **faire** *ou* **donner** *ou* **envoyer une a. à** to serve a writ on, to issue a summons to; (*témoin*) to subpoena

▶ **assignation**: **a. à comparaître** summons; **a. à résidence** house arrest

assigner [asiŋe] *vt* **(a)** to assign; (*heure etc*) to fix, to appoint; (*cause*) to attribute, to ascribe (**à** to); **a. une tâche à qn** to assign *or* allot a job to sb; **a. une somme à un paiement** to earmark a sum for a payment, to allocate a sum to a payment; **a. une dépense sur le trésor public** to charge an expense to public funds **(b)** *Jur* (*témoin etc*) to summon, to subpoena, to cite; **a. qn en justice** (*de la cour*) to issue a writ against sb; (*d'un demandeur*) to have a writ issued against sb; (*d'un huissier*) to serve a writ on sb; **a. qn à résidence** to place sb under house arrest

assimilable [asimilabl] *adj* **(a)** (*absorbable*) (*connaissances, aliment*) easily assimilated *or* absorbed; **population très a.** a population that assimilates *or* integrates easily **(b)** (*comparable*) **une maladie a. à une autre** an illness comparable to another

assimilation [asimilasjɔ̃] *nf* **(a)** (*absorption, Fig*) assimilation; **l'a. chlorophyllienne** photosynthesis; *Ling* **a. de phonèmes** assimilation of phonemes; **politique d'a.** policy of assimilation **(b)** (*comparaison*) comparison

assimilé [asimile] **1** *adj* **(a)** (*immigrés etc*) assimilated **(b)** (*de même nature*) related; **le sucre et produits assimilés** sugar and related products **(c)** *Mil, Naut* **être a. à ...** to rank as *or* with ..., to be ranked as ...; **a. au grade de capitaine** ranking *or* ranked as a captain **2** *nm Journ* press employee entitled to carry a press card; **cadres et assimilés** executives and those in the same category; **officiers et assimilés** officers and equivalent

assimiler [asimile] **1** *vt* **(a)** (*absorber*) (*aliment, Fig connaissances, immigrés etc*) to assimilate **(b)** (*comparer*) to assimilate, to compare (**à** to, with); **a. qch à** to class sth as, to put sth in the same category as **2 s'assimiler** *vpr* **(a)** (*des aliments etc*) to be assimilated; (*d'immigrants etc*) to assimilate, to become assimilated; **ces minéraux s'assimilent facilement** these minerals are easily assimilated **(b)** (*être comparable*) to be comparable (**à** to)

assis [asi] *adj* sitting, seated; **nous étions a. auprès du feu** we were sitting *or* seated round the fire; *Fig F* **en rester a.** to be flabbergasted; *Fig* **il a une situation bien assise** he has a secure job; *Rail, Th etc* **places assises** seats; **il n'y a plus de places assises** standing room only; *Jur* **magistrature assise** the bench

Assise [asiz] *nf* Assisi; **St François d'A.** St Francis of Assisi

assise [asiz] *nf* **(a)** (*des fondations*) bed; (*de moteur etc*) bed(plate); *Géol* bed, stratum; *Fig* (*d'un raisonnement, d'une théorie*) basis, foundation; **ajuster l'a. d'une soupape** to seat a valve **(b)** *Constr* (*de maçonnerie*) course; (*de ciment*) layer **(c)** *Jur* **les assises** the assizes; **cour d'assises** Assize Court; **être envoyé devant la cour d'assises** to be committed for trial; **avocat d'assises** criminal lawyer **(d) assises** (*d'un congrès*) sittings; (*d'un syndicat*) conference; **tenir ses assises** (*d'un parti*) to hold a conference; (*d'un club*) to hold a general meeting

assistanat [asistana] *nm* **(a)** (*aide*) aid **(b)** *Univ* assistantship

assistance [asistɑ̃s] *nf* **(a)** (*assemblée*) audience; *Sp* spectators; (*lors d'une manifestation etc*) onlookers; *Rel* congregation; **je demande un peu de calme à l'a.** could the audience please be quiet; **y a-t-il un médecin dans l'a.?** is there a doctor in the house?

(b) (*aide*) assistance, help, aid; **demander l'a. de qn** to ask for sb's assistance *or* help; **prêter (son) a.** to assist; **faire qch sans a.** to do sth unaided *or* without help

(c) elle est à l'A. (publique) depuis l'âge de trois ans she's been in care since she was three; **les enfants de l'A. (publique)** children in care

(d) (*de magistrat, prêtre*) presence, attendance

▶ **assistance**: **a. dépannage** roadside assistance; *Aut* **a. des freins** power braking; **a. judiciaire** *ou* **juridique** legal aid; *Com* **a. maritime** salvage; **a. médicale** (*à un pays du Tiers Monde*) medical aid *or* assistance; *Méd* **a. respiratoire** artificial respiration; **a. sanitaire** medical care; **a. sociale** welfare work; **a. technique** (*à un pays du Tiers Monde*) technical aid *or* assistance; **a. technique aux véhicules** roadside assistance

assistant, -ante [asistɑ̃, -ɑ̃t] *n* **(a)** (*aide*) assistant; (*à l'école*) language assistant; *Univ* (*de travaux pratiques*) demonstrator, laboratory assistant; **l'a. du metteur en scène** assistant producer; **maître a.** ≈ senior lecturer, *US* assistant professor **(b) assistants** members of the audience; *Sp* spectators

▶ **assistant** *TV, Cin* **a. cadreur, a. caméraman** focus puller; **a. du chef de cuisine** sous chef; **a. de direction** deputy *or* assistant manager; **a. opérateur** camera assistant; **a. de production** production *or* producer's assistant, PA; **assistante sociale** social worker, welfare worker *or* officer; (*à l'hôpital*) medical social worker

assisté [asiste] **1** *adj* **(a)** *Admin* (*personne*) on social security; **enfants assistés** children in care **(b)** *Aut* **freins assistés** power-assisted brakes; **direction assistée** power steering **(c)** *Ordinat* **a. par ordinateur** (*enseignement, fabrication etc*) computer-aided *or* -assisted **2** *n* person on social security, *Péj* person living on hand-outs; **avoir une mentalité d'a.** to expect everything to be handed to one on a plate

assister [asiste] **1** *vi* **a. à qch** to be (present) at sth; (*cérémonie*) to attend sth; **je ne peux pas vous répondre, je n'ai pas assisté à la scène** I can't give you an answer, I wasn't at the scene **2** *vt* (*qn*) to help, to assist; **dans cette entreprise, je ne me sens pas assisté du tout** I don't feel I'm getting any help in this company at all; **tu devrais te faire a.** you ought to get help, you ought to get somebody to help you; **a. qn de ses conseils** to give sb some helpful advice; **prêtre assisté de deux enfants de chœur** priest attended by two altar boys

associatif, -ive [asɔsjatif, -iv] *adj Math* **loi associative** associative law; **mouvement a.** association; **mémoire associative** involuntary memory

association [asɔsjasjɔ̃] *nf* **(a)** (*groupe, société*) society, association; *Com* partnership **(b)** (*réunion*) (*de mots, d'idées*) association; **cette a. a été très bénéfique pour les deux entreprises** this association has been very beneficial for both companies; **l'a. de ces deux aliments** the combination of these two foods

▶ **association**: **a. d'automobilistes** motoring organization; **a. de bienfaisance** charity, charitable organization *or* institution; **a. à but non lucratif** non-profit-making *or Am* not-for-profit organization; **a. commerciale** trade association; **a. de défense des consommateurs** consumer protection association; **A. européenne de libre-échange** European Free Trade Association; **A. internationale des transports aériens** International Air Transport Association; *Jur* **a. de malfaiteurs** conspiracy; **a. de parents d'élèves** parent-teacher association; **a. professionnelle** trade association; **a. sportive** sports club; **a. syndicale** trade union; **a. d'utilité publique** public utility

associé, -ée [asɔsje] **1** *adj* associated; *surtout Fin Bourse* joint; *Fin* **porteurs** *ou* **souscripteurs associés** joint holders (of stock); *Admin* **territoires associés** associated territories **2** *n* associate, honorary member; *Com* partner, business associate; **a. principal** senior partner; **a. commandité** acting partner; **a. commanditaire** sleeping partner

associer [asɔsje] (*pr sub, impf* **n. associions, v. associiez**) **1** *vt* **(a)** (*joindre, lier*) to associate, to unite, to join; **comment peux-tu a. deux thèses aussi différentes?** how can you compare two such different theories?; **a. les travailleurs aux profits de leur entreprise** to allow workers to share in their firm's profits; **il a associé son frère à son expédition** he brought his brother in on his expedition

(b) (*mentalement*) to associate; **j'ai toujours associé la neige à Noël** I've always associated snow with Christmas; **a. des idées** to associate ideas

2 s'associer *vpr* **(a) s'a. à qch** to share *or* participate *or* join in sth; **s'a. à un voyage** to come *or* go along on a trip; **je m'associe à votre douleur** I share (in) your grief; **s'a. à un crime** to be a party to a crime

(b) s'a. à *ou* **avec qn** (*dans une lutte etc*) to join forces with sb; *Com etc* to enter into partnership with sb; **s'a. qn** to take sb on as a partner; **les deux pays se sont associés** the two countries have joined forces

(c) (*s'allier*) to combine; **les deux parfums s'associent merveilleusement bien** these two fragrances combine wonderfully *or* go wonderfully well together

assoiffant [aswafɑ̃] *adj* (*travail*) thirsty

assoiffé [aswafe] *adj* thirsty; *Fig* **a. de sang** bloodthirsty; *Fig* **a. de savoir/de vengeance** thirsty *or* hungry for knowledge/revenge

assoiffer [aswafe] *vt* to make thirsty
assolement [asɔlmɑ̃] *nm Agr* (*des cultures*) rotation; **a. triennal** three course system
assoler [asɔle] *vt Agr* to rotate
assombrir [asɔ̃brir] **1** *vt* to darken, to obscure; *Fig* to cast a shadow over; **cette triste nouvelle a assombri le repas** the sad news cast a shadow over the meal; **nous avons passé des vacances merveilleuses sans rien qui vienne les a.** nothing spoiled *or* marred our wonderful holidays; **ciel assombri** cloudy *or* overcast sky; **visage assombri** gloomy face **2 s'assombrir** *vpr* (*du ciel*) to become dark; (*du ciel, d'un visage*) to cloud over; **il s'assombrit en me voyant** he glowered when he saw me
assombrissement [asɔ̃brismɑ̃] *nm* (*du ciel, de l'humeur*) darkening, clouding over; (*d'une pièce*) darkening
assommant [asɔmɑ̃] *adj F* boring, tedious, deadly dull; **il est a., cet enfant-là!** that child is a real pain!
assommer [asɔme] *vt* **(a) a. un bœuf** to fell an ox; **a. qn** (*l'étourdir*) to knock sb senseless, to stun sb; *Fig* **arrête ou je t'assomme!** stop that or I'll knock your block off!; **la chaleur m'assomme** the heat's overpowering **(b)** *F* (*ennuyer*) to bore (to death); (*harceler*) to pester; **tu m'assommes à toujours demander la même chose** you're getting on my nerves always asking the same thing
assommeur, -euse [asɔmœr, -øz] *nm* slaughterer
assommoir [asɔmwar] *nm* **(a)** (*arme*) club, bludgeon; (*plus petit*) cosh, *US* blackjack; *F* **porter un coup d'a. à qn** to deal sb a knock-out blow **(b)** (*bar*) dive
assomption [asɔ̃psjɔ̃] *nf* **(a)** *Rel* **(fête de) l'A. (de la Vierge Marie)** (feast of) the Assumption (of the Blessed Virgin) **(b)** *Géog* **A.** Asuncion **(c)** (*hypothèse*) assumption
assonance [asɔnɑ̃s] *nf Ling* assonance
assorti [asɔrti] *adj* **(a)** (*en harmonie*) matched, matching; **bien a.** well-matched; **couple mal a.** ill-matched *or* ill-assorted couple; **couleurs assorties** colours that match, matching colours; **pull avec jupe assortie** jumper with matching skirt
(b) (*bonbons, clous etc*) assorted, mixed; **fromages assortis** choice of cheeses; (*au restaurant*) cheese board *or* platter
(c) bien a. (*magasin etc*) well-stocked
(d) (*accompagné*) **a. de** accompanied by, along with; **une peine de prison assortie d'une amende de 10 000 francs** a prison sentence accompanied by a fine of 10, 000 francs; **un accord a. de plusieurs conditions** an agreement with several conditions
assortiment [asɔrtimɑ̃] *nm* **(a)** (*ensemble*) (*de marchandises etc*) assortment, variety, collection; (*d'outils*) set; (*de produits*) mix, selection; **ample a. d'échantillons** wide range of patterns; **a. de charcuterie** assorted cold meats **(b)** (*action*) matching; **a. parfait de couleurs** perfect match(ing) of colours
assortir [asɔrtir] **(j'assortis, n. assortissons) 1** *vt* **(a)** (*couleurs etc*) to match; **a. les accessoires à sa robe** to match one's accessories to *or* with one's dress; **elle n'a pas su a. les invités** she didn't manage to choose a good mix of guests; **nos mentalités sont bien/mal assorties** we think/don't think the same way **(b)** *Com* to restock **2 s'assortir** *vpr* **(a)** (*être en harmonie*) to match, to blend, to go well together; **la ceinture s'assortit à la robe** the belt goes well with the dress **(b)** (*s'accompagner*) **le texte s'assortit d'illustrations** the text is accompanied with *or* by illustrations
assoupi [asupi] *adj* dozing, *Fml* somnolent; (*volcan, passion*) dormant
assoupir [asupir] **1** *vt* (*personne*) to make drowsy *or* sleepy, to send to sleep; (*la douleur, les sens*) to calm, to deaden, to dull; **a. une dispute** to calm a dispute **2 s'assoupir** *vpr* to drop off to sleep, to doze off; (*de la douleur, du chagrin*) to die down
assoupissant [asupisɑ̃] *adj* soporific
assoupissement [asupismɑ̃] *nm* (*somnolence*) drowsiness
assouplir [asuplir] **1** *vt* to soften; (*cuir*) to make supple; *Fig* (*réglementation*) to relax, to make less strict; **cette lessive va a. votre linge** this washing powder will make your clothes feel soft; *Fig* **cela va finir par a. son caractère** it'll eventually make him more flexible **2 s'assouplir** *vpr* (*du cuir, d'une personne*) to become supple; (*du caractère*) to become more flexible; **s'a. les muscles** to limber up
assouplissant [asuplisɑ̃] **1** *adj* **liquide a. (pour le linge)** fabric softener **2** *nm* fabric softener
assouplissement [asuplismɑ̃] *nm* softening; *Fig* (*de la réglementation*) relaxing; **exercices d'a., assouplissements** limbering-up exercises
assouplisseur [asuplisœr] *nm* (fabric) softener
assourdir [asurdir] **1** *vt* **(a)** (*personne*) to make deaf, to deafen **(b)** (*son*) to deaden, to muffle; (*tambour, cloche, oreilles*) to muffle; (*violon*) to mute; *Ling* (*consonne*) to unvoice **(c)** (*lumière, couleur*) to soften, to subdue, to tone down **2 s'assourdir** *vpr Ling* to become unvoiced *or* voiceless
assourdissant [asurdisɑ̃] *adj* (*bruit etc*) deafening
assourdissement [asurdismɑ̃] *nm* (*de personne*) (*processus*) deafening; (*résultat*) temporary deafness; (*de son*) deadening; (*de tambour*) muffling; *Ling* (*de consonne*) unvoicing
assouvir [asuvir] **1** *vt* (*faim, désir*) to satisfy, to appease, to assuage; **a. sa soif** to quench one's thirst; **a. sa curiosité** to satisfy one's curiosity **2 s'assouvir** *vpr* (*faim*) to be satisfied *or* assuaged; (*passions*) to be assuaged
assouvissement [asuvismɑ̃] *nm* (*de la faim, du désir etc*) satisfying, satisfaction; (*de la soif*) quenching; **un sentiment d'a.** a feeling of satisfaction, a satisfied feeling
assuétude [asyetyd] *nf Méd* addiction
assujetti, -ie [asuʒeti] **1** *adj* (*peuple*) subject, subjugated **(à** to); **tous les citoyens sont assujettis à l'impôt** all citizens are subject *or* liable to tax **2** *n* person liable for tax
assujettir [asyʒetir] **1** *vt* **(a)** (*province etc*) to subdue, to subjugate **(b)** (*qn*) to subject, to make liable **(à** to); **a. qn à faire qch** to compel *or* oblige sb to do sth; **a. une population à des lois** to subject a population to laws; **a. une population à l'impôt** to make a population liable for tax **(c)** (*objet*) to fix, to fasten **(à** to), to make secure; **les planches sont assujetties par des clous** the planks are held in place with nails **2 s'assujettir** *vpr* to submit **(à** to)
assujettissant [asyʒetisɑ̃] *adj* (*travail*) exacting, demanding
assujettissement [asyʒetismɑ̃] *nm* **(a)** (*action*) subjection, subjugation **(b)** (*état*) subjection, subservience **(à** to) **(c)** (*contrainte*) tie **(d)** (*à l'impôt*) liability **(à** for)
assumer [asyme] **1** *vt* **(a)** (*droit, responsabilité etc*) to assume, to take on, to take upon oneself; **a. les frais** to meet the costs *or* expenses, to bear the costs; **a. un risque** to take a risk; **a. un poste** to hold a post; **a. son service** to take up one's duties **(b)** (*accepter*) (*conséquences*) to bear, to take on board; **a. la perte de qn de cher** to come to terms with the loss of a loved one **2** *vi F* **il va falloir que tu assumes** you'll have to live with it **3 s'assumer** *vpr* to come to terms with oneself
assurable [asyrabl] *adj* insurable
assurance [asyrɑ̃s] *nf* **(a)** (*confiance*) (self-)assurance, (self-) confidence; **parler avec a.** to speak confidently *or* with confidence; **perdre son a.** to lose one's self-assurance; **vous pouvez l'acheter en toute a.** you can buy it with complete confidence
(b) (*garantie*) security, pledge; **elle vivait dans l'a. de la réussite** she was assured of success; **je vous donne l'a. que tout sera fait d'ici demain** I assure you *or* I guarantee (you) that everything will be done by tomorrow; **demander/recevoir des assurances** to ask for/to receive assurance; **recevez l'a. de mes sentiments distingués** (*dans une lettre*) yours faithfully
(c) *Com* insurance; **police d'a.** insurance policy; **prime d'a.** insurance premium; **compagnie** *ou* **société d'assurances** insurance company; **agent d'assurance(s)** insurance agent; **courtier d'assurance(s)** insurance broker; *F* **je vais écrire à mon a.** I'll write to my insurance company; **contracter une a.** to take out insurance, to take out an insurance policy
(d) (*en alpinisme*) **(point d')a.** (*d'alpiniste*) belay
▶ **assurance**: **a.-accident, a. contre les accidents** accident insurance; **a. 'ad valorem'** replacement value insurance; **a. automobile** car *or* motor insurance; **a. bagage(s)** baggage insurance; *Aut Suisse* **a. casco** comprehensive *or* all-risks insurance; *Com* **a. catalogue coface** standard export guarantee insurance; **a. catalogue évolutif** upgradeable standard insurance; **a. chômage** (*payé par le patron et le salarié*) ≈ unemployment insurance; (*reçu par le chômeur*) ≈ unemployment benefit(s); **a. collective** group insurance; **a. confiscation** confiscation insurance; **a. contre les accidents du travail** employers' liability insurance; **a. crédit** credit *or* loan insurance; **a. décès-invalidité** whole life and disability insurance; **a. dépannage** car breakdown and recovery insurance; **a. foire** exhibition insurance; **a. garantie constructeur** manufacturer's guarantee insurance; **a.-incendie, a. contre l'incendie** fire insurance; **a. invalidité** ≈ disability pension; **a. maintenance étendue** extended maintenance insurance; **a. maintenance visite** callout maintenance insurance; **a. maladie** health insurance; **a. maritime** marine insurance; **a. maternité** ≈ maternity benefit(s); **a. médicale** medical insurance; **a. multirisque** comprehensive insurance; **a. offre** tender insurance; **a. offre coface** Export Credit Guarantee tender insurance; **a. panne mécanique** mechanical breakdown insurance; **a. perte de l'exploitation** insurance for loss of trade; **a. prospection**

market exploration insurance; **a. responsabilité civile** public liability insurance; **a. responsabilité produit** product-liability insurance; *Admin* **assurances sociales** ≈ national insurance; **a. au tiers** third-party insurance; **a. tous risques** comprehensive *or* all-risks insurance; **a. tous risques chantiers** comprehensive site insurance; **a. transport** transportation insurance; **a. vacances** holiday insurance; **a. vieillesse** ≈ retirement pension; **a. sur la vie, a.-vie** life insurance *Br* life assurance; **prendre une a.-vie** to take out life insurance; **a. vol** theft insurance

assuré, -ée [asyre] **1** *adj* **(a)** (*plein d'assurance*) (*pas, voix etc*) firm, sure; (*air, personne*) assured, confident; **voix mal assurée** unsteady *or* quavering voice; **d'une main assurée** with a steady hand **(b)** (*certain*) (*remède*) certain; (*retraite*) secure, safe; **il n'y a encore rien d'a.** there is nothing fixed yet; **tenez pour a. qu'il vous écrira** rest assured that he will write to you; **la victoire est assurée** we/they/*etc* are certain of victory

2 *n* **l'a.** the policy holder, the insured; *Admin* **les assurés sociaux** ≈ national insurance contributors, those who pay national insurance

assurément [asyremɑ̃] *adv* assuredly, surely, undoubtedly, certainly; **il le fera a.** he's certain to do it; **a. non!** certainly not!; **oui, a.!** yes, of course!

assurer [asyre] **1** *vt* **(a)** (*immobiliser*) to make firm *or* steady; (*attacher*) to fix, to secure, to fasten; (*échelle*) to steady; (*mur*) to prop up; (*corde*) to make fast; (*alpiniste*) to belay; **a. qn sec** to give sb a tight rope; **a. ses arrières** *Mil* to protect one's rear; *Fig* to protect oneself against any eventuality; **a. la sécurité d'un pays** to make a country secure; **a. sa fortune** to consolidate one's fortune

(b) (*se charger de*) to look after; **le courrier littéraire sera assuré par M. Leclerc** the literary column will looked after by Mr Leclerc; **la France assure le rapatriement des touristes** the French government is repatriating the tourists; **un service régulier est assuré entre Paris et Londres** there is a regular service between Paris and London; **la sécurité est assurée par des soldats de métier** professional soldiers are providing the security cover *or* are responsible for security; **la secrétaire assurera la permanence de 9 à 12** the secretary will be there from 9 till 12; **a. la défense de qn** to defend sb; **a. une rente à qn** to settle an annuity on sb

(c) (*garantir*) to ensure, to guarantee; **cette formation vous assure un avenir brillant** this type of training will ensure *or* guarantee you a brilliant future; **ma retraite m'assure de quoi vivre** my pension gives me enough to live on; **ce but assure la victoire des Allemands** this goal assures the Germans of victory; **a. une créance** to stand security for *or* to guarantee a debt

(d) (*certifier*) **a. qch à qn, a. qn de qch** to assure sb of sth; **il m'a assuré qu'il voulait bien le faire** he assured me that he was willing to do it; **il m'a assuré de son amitié** he assured me of his friendship; **c'est bien vrai, je te l'assure** *ou F* **je t'assure** it's quite true, I (can) assure you; **je t'assure que ce n'est pas amusant** I (can) assure you, it's not funny; **il vient de nous a. de sa participation** he's just assured us that he will be taking part

(e) (*par contrat d'assurance*) **a. qn** to insure sb; **se faire a. sur la vie** to take out a life insurance (policy); **a. un immeuble contre l'incendie** to insure a building against fire; **êtes-vous assuré?** are you insured?

2 *vi F* to be good at, to cope well with; **j'assure pas du tout en maths** I'm hopeless at maths, I'm no good at maths; **elle assure, cette nana, avec les mecs** she has a real way with the men, that girl; **t'as pas amené les sandwichs? vraiment, t'assure pas** didn't you bring the sandwiches? honestly, you're hopeless!; **ça assure!** brilliant!, wicked!; **a. comme une bête** to do brilliantly *F* **à l'entretien j'ai assuré un max** I did brilliantly at the interview

3 s'assurer *vpr* **(a)** (*vérifier*) **s'a. de qch** to make sure *or* certain of sth; **je vais m'en a.** (*le vérifier*) I'll check; (*faire en sorte que ça soit fait*) I'll make sure of it; **assurez-vous que c'est encore possible** make sure *or* check that it's still possible; **s'a. du transport** to make sure one has transport; **il faut que nous nous assurions de la véracité de ses dires** we must ensure that he is speaking the truth

(b) (*par contrat d'assurance*) to take out insurance, to insure oneself (**contre** against); **s'a. au tiers/sur la vie** to take out third-party/life insurance

(c) (*se pourvoir*) **tu aurais dû t'a. de l'aide** you should have got help; **s'a. la collaboration de qn** to secure sb's collaboration; **s'a. du silence de qn** to secure sb's silence; **les Allemands se sont assuré la victoire** the Germans have ensured themselves of victory

(d) (*s'affermir*) to settle oneself firmly; (*d'un alpiniste*) to belay oneself; **s'a. sur ses pieds** to steady oneself on one's feet

assureur [asyrœr] *nm* insurer

Assyrie [asiri] *nf* Assyria

assyrien, -ienne [asirjɛ̃, -jɛn] **1** *adj* Assyrian **2** *nm Ling* (ancient) Assyrian **3** *n* **A.** Assyrian

aster [aster] *nm* aster; **a. de Chine** China aster; **a. œil-du-Christ** Michaelmas daisy, *US* aster

astérisque [asterisk] *nm Typ* asterisk

astéroïde [asterɔid] *nm Astron* asteroid

asthénie [asteni] *nf Méd* tiredness, *Spéc* asthenia

asthmatique [asmatik] *adj, n Méd* asthmatic

asthme [asm] *nm Méd* asthma; **être atteint d'a., avoir** *ou* **faire de l'a.** to suffer from *or* to have asthma; **crise d'a.** attack of asthma, asthma attack

asticot [astiko] *nm* maggot; *F* (*type*) bloke, geezer

asticoter [astikɔte] *vt F* to needle, to bug, to bait

astigmate [astigmat] *adj, n Méd, Opt* astigmatic

astigmatisme [astigmatism] *nm Méd, Opt* astigmatism

astiquage [astikaʒ] *nm* polishing

astiquer [astike] *vt* (*maison*) to clean; (*sol*) to polish; (*casserole*) to scour

astragale [astragal] *nm* **(a)** *Anat* ankle bone **(b)** *Archit* (*de colonne etc*) astragal

astrakan [astrakɑ̃] *nm* astrakhan (fur); **manteau d'a.** astrakhan coat

astral, -ale, -aux, -ales [astral, -o] *adj* (*influence, corps etc*) astral; **esprits astraux** astral spirits; **thème a.** (astrological) star chart

astre [astr] *nm* star, heavenly body; **contempler les astres** to look at the stars, to stargaze; **consulter les astres** to consult the stars; **beau comme un a.** (as) handsome as a Greek god; **né sous un a. favorable** born under a lucky star

astreignant [astrɛɲɑ̃] *adj* exacting, demanding

astreindre [astrɛ̃dr] (*prp* **astreignant**; *pp* **astreint**; *pr ind* **j'astreins, il astreint, n. astreignons**; *impf* **j'astreignais**; *p hist* **j'astreignis**; *fu* **j'astreindrai**) **1** *vt* to compel, to oblige (**à faire qch** to do sth), to tie down (**à un devoir** to a duty); **astreint au service militaire** liable for military service **2 s'astreindre** *vpr* **s'a. à un régime sévère** to keep to a strict diet; **s'a. à faire du sport** to force oneself to do sport

astreinte [astrɛ̃t] *nf* obligation; **les astreintes de la vie moderne** the pressures of modern life

astringence [astrɛ̃ʒɑ̃s] *nf* astringency

astringent [astrɛ̃ʒɑ̃] *adj, nm* astringent

astro- [astrɔ] *préf* astro-

astrolabe [astrɔlab] *nm* spacelab

astrologie [astrɔlɔʒi] *nf* astrology

astrologique [astrɔlɔʒik] *adj* astrological

astrologue [astrɔlɔg] *n* astrologer

astronaute [astrɔnot] *n* astronaut

astronautique [astrɔnotik] *nf* astronautics

astronef [astrɔnɛf] *nm* spaceship

astronome [astrɔnɔm] *n* astronomer

astronomie [astrɔnɔmi] *nf* astronomy

astronomique [astrɔnɔmik] *adj Astron, Fig* astronomical; **heure a.** sidereal time; *Fig F* **pratiquer des prix astronomiques** (*d'un magasin*) to charge astronomical prices

astronomiquement [astrɔnɔmikmɑ̃] *adv* astronomically

astrophysicien, -ienne [astrɔfizisjɛ̃, -jɛn] *n* astrophysicist

astrophysique [astrɔfizik] **1** *adj* astrophysical **2** *nf* astrophysics

astuce [astys] *nf* **(a)** (*finesse*) astuteness, shrewdness; **elle a répondu avec beaucoup d'a.** she answered very astutely *or* shrewdly; **c'est un enfant plein d'a.** he/she is a very sharp child **(b)** (*truc*) trick; (*conseil*) tip; **il doit y avoir une a.** there must be a trick to it; **l'a., c'est de ne pas pointer en sortant** the trick is not to clock off when you leave; **les astuces du métier** the tricks of the trade; **a. du vendeur** sales acumen; **Windows 95: 50 astuces** Windows 95: 50 tips **(c)** (*plaisanterie*) witticism; (*jeu de mots*) pun; **je ne saisis pas l'a.** I don't get it

astucieusement [astysjøzmɑ̃] *adv* astutely, shrewdly; **il a arrangé sa petite chambre très a.** he has arranged his little room very cleverly

astucieux, -ieuse [astysjø, -jøz] *adj* (*personne, comportement*) astute, shrewd, clever; (*solution, méthode*) clever, cunning; **réponse astucieuse** crafty *or* clever answer

asymétrie [asimetri] *nf* asymmetry

asymétrique [asimetrik] *adj* asymmetrical

asymptomatique [asɛ̃ptɔmatik] *adj Méd* (*maladie*) asymptomatic; **porteur a.** carrier without symptoms

asynchrone [asɛ̃kron] *adj Ordinat* asynchronous

asyntaxique [asɛ̃taksik] *adj Gram* asyntactic

atavique [atavik] *adj* atavistic; *Biol* **retour a.** throwback

atavisme [atavism] *nm* atavism; **faire qch par a.** to do sth because it's in one's genes

atchoum [atʃum] *int (éternuement)* atishoo!

atelier [atəlje] *nm* **(a)** (work)shop; *(dans une maison)* workroom; *(d'artiste)* studio; **a. de réparations** repair shop; *Tech* **a. de montage** *ou* **d'assemblage** assembly shop; **a. d'ajustage** fitting shop; **a. de constructions mécaniques** machine shop; **a. de tissage** weaving shed; **a. de constructions navales** shipyard; *Aut* **a. de carrosserie** bodyshop; *Aut* **a. de peinture** paint shop; *TV, Cin* **a. de décors** scenic workshop; *TV, Cin* **a. de production** production workshop, graphics studio; *Ordinat* **a. de flashage** bromide bureau; **chef d'a.** foreman; **il est devenu contremaître après cinq ans d'a.** he became a foreman after five years on the factory *or* shop floor; **camion a.** repair van

(b) *(ensemble du personnel d'un atelier)* staff

(c) *(groupe de travail)* (work-)group; **les enfants travaillent en ateliers de trois** the children work in groups of three

(d) *(loge maçonnique)* lodge

atemporel, -elle [atɑ̃pɔrɛl] *adj* timeless

atermoiement [atɛrmwamɑ̃] *nm* **(a)** *Com, Jur* = arrangement with creditors for extension of time for payment; **a. d'une lettre de change** renewal of a bill **(b)** *F* **atermoiements** delays, procrastination, shillyshally(ing); **après mille atermoiements, elle a dit oui** after much shillyshallying, she said yes; **sans atermoiements** without a moment's hesitation

atermoyer [atɛrmwaje] *vi* to procrastinate

athée [ate] **1** *adj (personne, argument)* atheistical **2** *n* atheist

athéisme [ateism] *nm* atheism

athénée [atene] *nm* **(a)** athenaeum **(b)** *Belg, Suisse* (state) secondary school

Athènes [atɛn] *nf* Athens

athénien, -ienne [atenjɛ̃, -jɛn] **1** *adj* Athenian **2** *n* **A.** Athenian; *Hum* **et c'est là que les Athéniens s'atteignirent** and at that point things started to get rather complicated

athlète [atlɛt] *n* athlete; **avoir un corps d'a.** to have the body of an athlete *or* an athletic body

athlétique [atletik] *adj* athletic

athlétiquement [atletikmɑ̃] *adv* athletically

athlétisme [atletism] *nm* athletics, track and field; **épreuves d'a.** athletic events, track and field events

Atlantide [atlɑ̃tid] *nf* Atlantis

atlantique [atlɑ̃tik] **1** *adj* Atlantic; **l'océan A.** the Atlantic (Ocean) **2** *nm* **l'A.** the Atlantic (Ocean); **Organisation du Traité de l'A. Nord** North Atlantic Treaty Organization

atlas [atlas] *nm* **(a)** *(recueil de cartes)* atlas **(b)** *Myth, Géog* **A.** Atlas **(c)** *Anat* atlas

atmosphère [atmɔsfɛr] *nf* **(a)** atmosphere; **humidité de l'a.** atmospheric humidity; *Fig* **vivre dans l'a. de qn** to breathe the same air as sb; *Fig* **une a. de vacances** a holiday atmosphere *or* feeling; *Fig* **avoir besoin de changer d'a.** to need a change of atmosphere *or* scene(ry) **(b)** *Phys (pression de 760 mm de mercure)* atmosphere

atmosphérique [atmɔsferik] *adj* atmospheric; *Rad* **parasites atmosphériques** atmospherics; **perturbations atmosphériques** atmospheric disturbances

atoca [atɔka] *nm Can (plante)* cranberry

atoll [atɔl] *nm Géog* atoll

atome [atom] *nm* particle, bit; *Phys* atom; **atomes de poussière** specks of dust; *Fig* **avoir des atomes crochus avec qn** to hit it off with sb, to get on very well with sb; *Fig* **nous n'avons aucun a. crochu** we have nothing in common; *Fig* **pas un a. de vérité** not an ounce *or* iota of truth

atome-gramme, *pl* **atomes-grammes** *nm Phys* gram-atom

atomicité [atɔmisite] *nf Ch* atomicity

atomique [atɔmik] *adj (théorie, poids etc)* atomic; **masse a.** atomic mass; **nombre** *ou* **numéro a.** atomic number; **sciences atomiques** atomics; **bombe a.** atom(ic) bomb; **guerre a.** atomic war(fare); **énergie a.** atomic energy; **sous-marin à propulseur** *ou* **propulsion a.** nuclear(-powered *or* -propelled) submarine; **pile a.** atomic reactor; **centre a.** atomic research station; **usine a.** atomic energy plant; **l'époque a.** the nuclear *or* atomic age; **Commissariat à l'énergie a.** ≈ Atomic Energy Authority, *US* Atomic Energy Commission

atomisation [atɔmizasjɔ̃] *nf* atomization; *Pol Péj* **a. du pouvoir** the dispersal of power

atomisé, -ée [atɔmize] **1** *n* victim of a nuclear attack **2** *adj Aut* atomized

atomiser [atɔmize] *vt* **(a)** *(pulvériser)* to atomize; **a. de l'eau sur les fleurs** to mist the flowers **(b)** *Mil* to destroy with nuclear warheads, *F* to nuke; *(à la bombe)* to drop a nuclear bomb on; *Fig* to smash to smithereens

atomiseur [atɔmizœr] *nm* atomizer, spray; *Aut* atomizer; *(injecteur)* sprayer; **parfum en a.** spray perfume

atomisme [atɔmism] *nm Phil* atomism

atomiste [atɔmist] *nm* **(a)** *(savant etc)* nuclear *or* atomic physicist **(b)** *Phil* atomist

atomistique [atɔmistik] **1** *nf* nucleonics, nuclear engineering, atomic science **2** *adj* atomic; *Phil* **théorie a.** atomistic theory

atonal, -ale, -aux, -ales [atɔnal] *adj (musique)* atonal

atonalité [atɔnalite] *nf* atonality

atone [atɔn] *adj* **(a)** *(regard)* dull, vacant, lacklustre; **un individu a.** a lacklustre individual **(b)** *Méd* atonic **(c)** *Ling* unstressed, unaccented

atonie [atɔni] *nf* **(a)** *(mollesse)* lethargy, listlessness, lack of vitality **(b)** *Méd* poor physical condition, *Spéc* atony

atours [atur] *nmpl* adornments, finery; **parée de ses plus beaux a.** in all her finery

atout [atu] *nm Cartes* trump; *Fig* asset, advantage; **a. maître** master trump; **a. carreau** diamonds are trumps; **jouer a.** to play a trump, to play trumps; **avoir tous les atouts dans son jeu** *Cartes; Fig* to hold all the winning cards; *Fig* **ce candidat a des atouts** this candidate has a lot going for him; *Fig* **c'est un a. que de savoir l'anglais** a knowledge of English is an asset

atoxique [atɔksik] *adj Biol* non-poisonous, non-toxic

âtre [ɑtr] *nm* **(a)** *(cheminée)* fireplace, hearth; **au coin de l'â.** by *or* round the fireplace **(b)** *Ind (de forge etc)* hearth; *(du forgeron)* (blacksmith's) forge

atroce [atrɔs] *adj (crime etc)* atrocious, heinous; *(terrible)* dreadful, horrible; **douleur a.** excruciating *or* agonizing pain; **j'avais une peur a. de le rencontrer** I dreaded meeting him; **d'une laideur a.** hideously ugly; **une odeur a.** a foul *or* an awful *or* a horrible smell; **il fait un temps a.** the weather is shocking *or* dreadful; **elle a fait un a. cauchemar** she had an awful nightmare

atrocement [atrɔsmɑ̃] *adv (cruellement)* atrociously, shockingly; *(horriblement)* dreadfully, awfully, horribly, terribly; **elle a été a. torturée** she was hideously tortured; **elle a a. mal** she's in dreadful *or* terrible pain; **ça sentait a. mauvais** it smelled awful *or* horrible; **il a fait a. froid** it was dreadfully cold

atrocité [atrɔsite] *nf* **(a)** *(cruauté)* atrociousness; *(d'un crime)* atrocity; **leurs exactions sont d'une a. indescriptible** their acts of violence are indescribably atrocious **(b)** *(acte)* atrocity; **les atrocités commises pendant la guerre** the atrocities committed during the war; *F* **on m'a raconté des atrocités sur votre compte** I have been hearing dreadful things about you; *F* **ce tableau est une a.** this picture is a real horror *or* an atrocity

atrophie [atrɔfi] *nf Méd (d'un membre, du foie)* atrophy; **a. intellectuelle** intellectual atrophy

atrophié [atrɔfje] *adj (foie, intelligence)* atrophied; *(membre)* wasted, withered

atrophier [atrɔfje] **1** *vt (membre, intelligence)* to atrophy **2** **s'atrophier** *vpr (d'un membre)* to wither away; *Fig (de l'intelligence)* to atrophy

atropine [atrɔpin] *nf Ch* atropin(e)

attabler (s') [atable] *vpr* to sit down at the (dinner *etc*) table; **veuillez vous a. pour que nous commencions à dîner** please sit down at the table so that we can begin to eat

attachant [ataʃɑ̃] *adj* **(a)** *(livre)* captivating **(b)** *(personnalité)* engaging, attractive

attache [ataʃ] *nf* **(a)** *(fixation)* **point d'a.** connection; **pièce d'a.** fastening; **rivets d'a.** jointing rivets; *Naut* **droit d'a.** mooring right; **droits d'a.** *(frais)* mooring dues, moorage; **port d'a.** home port, port of registry; *Fig* home base; **borne d'a.** *Naut* bollard; *Él* terminal

(b) *(lien)* tie, fastener, fastening; *(pour réparer la porcelaine)* rivet; *Él* (wire) clamp; *(sur les vêtements)* loop, tab; **a. de diamants** diamond clasp; *Rail* **a. de rail** rail fastening; **a. de bureau** clip; *Fig* **nos attaches dans ce pays** our close ties *or* links with this country; *Fig* **sans attaches** unattached, unconnected; *Fig* **je n'avais plus aucune a. dans cette ville** there was nothing to keep me in the town; *Fig* **j'ai gardé beaucoup d'attaches en France** I have kept many ties with France

(c) *Anat (de muscle)* origin, attachment; **a. de la main/du pied** wrist/ankle joint; **avoir les attaches fines** to have delicate wrists and ankles

(d) *Constr etc* connection, bond, brace; *(de poutre en béton armé)* binder

(e) *Bot* tendril

attaché, -ée [ataʃe] **1** *adj* **(a)** *(enchaîné)* fastened, tied up; *(chien)* chained up; **on l'a laissé a. au radiateur pendant une semaine** he was left tied (up) to the radiator for a week

(b) (*lié affectivement*) attached; **être a. à qn/qch** to be attached *or* devoted to sb/sth; **être très a. à une région/à ses responsabilités** to be very attached to a region/very devoted to one's duties

(c) (*dépendant*) linked, attached; **les avantages attachés à une fonction** the benefits going with a post; **mon bonheur est a. au vôtre** my happiness is bound up with yours; *Bourse* **coupon a.** cum dividend

2 *n* attaché; **a. militaire** military attaché; **a. commercial** commercial attaché; *Com* sales representative **a. de presse** press attaché *or* officer; **a. d'administration** junior civil servant

attaché-case, *pl* **attachés-cases** [ataʃekɛs] *nm* attaché case

attachement [ataʃmɑ̃] *nm* **(a)** (*pour qn, qch*) attachment **(pour** to), affection **(pour** for) **(b)** *Constr* = daily statement of work carried out and expenses incurred

attacher [ataʃe] **1** *vt* **(a)** (*fixer, enchaîner*) to attach, to fasten **(qch à qch** sth to sth); (*avec ficelle, corde*) to tie (up), to do up; (*avec une chaîne*) to chain (up); **a. un cheval** to tie up *or* tether a horse; **a. qch avec une boucle** to buckle sth; **a. qch avec des clous/épingles** to nail/pin sth on; **a. deux choses avec des clous/épingles** to nail/pin two things together; **a. ses cheveux avec un ruban** to tie a ribbon in one's hair; **a. ses cheveux** to tie one's hair back; **a. une étiquette à un paquet** to stick a label on a parcel; **il faut bien a. le paquet** you should tie up the parcel securely; **a. un prisonnier au poteau** to tie a prisoner to the stake; **attachez vos ceintures** fasten your seat belts; **tu peux m'a. ma robe?** can you fasten my dress?, can you do up my dress?, can you do me up?; **a. ses lacets** *ou* **chaussures** to do up *or* tie (up) *or* fasten one's shoelaces

(b) (*accorder*) **a. de l'importance à qch** to attach importance to sth; **a. du prix** *ou* **de la valeur à** to attach great value to; **a. une signification à un fait/un acte** to read into a fact/an act

(c) a. un nouveau secrétaire à une ambassade to attach a new secretary to an embassy; **ce domestique est attaché au service de la famille depuis cinquante ans** this servant has been in the family's employment for fifty years

(d) (*lier sentimentalement*) to attach; **ce qui m'attache à lui** what attaches me to him; **tout ce qui nous attache à la vie** everything we hold dear in life

(e) a. ses yeux *ou* **ses regards sur** to fix one's eyes on

2 *vi Culin F* **les pommes de terre ont attaché** the potatoes have stuck (to the pan); **casserole qui n'attache pas** non-stick saucepan

3 s'attacher *vpr* **(a)** (*d'une chose*) to cling, to stick **(à** to); (*ne pas s'enlever*) to be attached *or* stuck **(à** to); (*avec une agrafe etc*) to be fastened **(à** to); (*avec ficelle, corde etc*) to be tied **(à** on, to); **les protestants se sont attachés aux grilles avec des menottes et des chaînes** the protesters handcuffed and chained themselves to the railings; **la sangsue s'attacha à son mollet** the leech clung *or* stuck to his calf; **le lierre s'attache aux arbres** ivy clings to trees; **collier qui s'attache avec une agrafe** necklace that fastens with a clip; **la jupe s'attache par derrière** the skirt fastens (up) *or* does up at the back; *Fig* **s'a. aux pas de qn** to follow sb closely

(b) (*se lier sentimentalement*) **tu t'attaches trop aux gens que tu rencontres** you get too attached to the people you meet; **elle s'est beaucoup attachée à cette vieille dame** she has got *or* become very attached to that old lady; **s'a. à qn** to become *or* grow fond of *or* attached to sb; **s'a. à une région** to become attached to a region; **je ne veux pas m'a.** I don't want to tie myself down *or* get involved *or* to commit myself; **elle sait s'a. ses élèves** she knows how to gain her pupils' affection

(c) (*se concentrer sur*) **s'a. aux faits** to stick to the facts; **ce n'est pas la peine de s'a. aux détails** there's no point getting caught up in details; **s'a. à une tâche** to apply oneself to a job; **s'a. à qch** to pay particular attention to sth; **s'a. à bien faire son travail** to take particular care over one's work; **s'a. à l'honnêteté/l'éducation** to attach great importance to *or* to set great store by honesty/education

attaquable [atakabl] *adj* **(a)** *Mil* open to attack, attackable **(b)** (*fait, opinion etc*) contestable; (*testament etc*) open to attack

attaquant, -ante [atakɑ̃, -ɑ̃t] **1** *adj* attacking **2** *n* assailant, attacker; *Sp* striker

attaque [atak] *nf* **(a)** *Mil etc* attack, assault; (*d'une voiture, d'un train etc*) hold-up **(de** of); **à l'a.!** attack!; **a. concertée** concerted attack; **reprise d'a.** renewed attack; **corps d'a.** attacking party; *aussi Fig* **passer à l'a.** to go on to the offensive; *Fig* **il a attendu de la connaître un peu mieux pour passer à l'a.** he waited until he knew her a bit better before he moved in for the kill; **repasser à l'a.** to return to the attack; **monter une a.** to mount an attack; **a. frontale** *ou* **de front** frontal *or* head-on attack; **subir une a.** to be attacked; *Fig* **les attaques de la presse** attacks by the press; *Fig* **diriger de violentes attaques contre qn** to attack sb violently; **a. de côté** flank attack; **a. latérale** flank attack; **a. par encerclement** encirclement attack

(b) *Sp* attack; (*à l'aviron*) catch; *Cartes* lead

(c) d'a. vigorously; **se sentir d'a.** to feel in good shape, *Am* to feel bright-eyed and bushy-tailed; **se sentir d'a. pour faire qch** to feel up to *or* ready to do sth; **être d'a.** (*en pleine forme*) to be on top form; **il est toujours d'a.** he is still going strong; **il n'est plus assez d'a. pour faire de longues marches** he's no longer up to going for long walks

(d) *Méd* (*de maladie douloureuse*) attack; (*de fièvre, grippe*) bout; **a. d'épilepsie** epileptic fit; **a. d'apoplexie** (apoplectic) stroke; **a. de nerfs** fit of hysterics; **une a.** (*crise cardiaque*) a heart attack

(e) *MecE* **a. directe** (*de moteur*) direct drive; **pignon d'a.** driving pinion; *Av, Naut* **bord d'a.** (*d'aile, d'hélice*) leading edge; **angle d'a.** leading angle

(f) (*d'un article*) intro; *Mus* (*d'un instrument*) entry; (*d'une note*) attack; **chef d'a.** (*de l'orchestre*) first violin, leader

▸ **attaque**: *Av* **a. aérienne** air raid *or* strike; **a. à la bombe** bomb attack, bombing; **a. à main armée** armed robbery

attaquer [atake] **1** *vt* **(a)** (*qn, ennemi, place forte etc*) to attack; (*qn, ennemi*) to set upon, to assault; (*de l'acide*) (*métal*) to attack, to eat into, to corrode; *Mil* **a. de front** to make *or* to launch a frontal attack on; **attaquez!** engage!; **être attaqué par les moustiques** to be attacked by mosquitoes; **a. qn à coup de poings** to lay into sb, to go for sb with one's fists; *Fig* **a. les abus/les préjugés** to attack injustice/prejudices; *Fig* **a. qn sur un sujet** to tackle sb on a subject; *Jur* **a. (la validité d')un testament** to contest a will; *Jur* **a. qn en justice** to prosecute sb, to bring an action against sb; *Fig* **a. la réputation/l'honneur de qn** to attack sb's reputation/honour; *Méd* **le poumon droit est attaqué** the right lung is affected

(b) (*repas, sujet, travail etc*) to tackle, to get to work on; **nous attaquons demain l'ascension du Mont Blanc** tomorrow we('ll) attack *or* tackle Mont Blanc; **attaquons le repas avant que ça ne refroidisse** let's tuck in *or* get stuck in before it gets cold

(c) *Mus* (*note*) to attack; (*morceau*) to strike up; **bien a. la note** to hit the note well *or* clearly

2 *vi* **(a)** to attack; **qui a attaqué le premier?** (*à deux enfants qui se battent*) who started it?; *Mktg* **a. de front** to launch a frontal attack; *Mktg* **a. latéralement** to launch a flank attack

(b) *Mus* **a. faux** to hit the wrong note

(c) *Cartes* **a. trèfle/de la reine** to lead clubs/the queen

(d) (*d'acides etc*) to corrode

3 s'attaquer *vpr* **s'a. à qn/qch** to attack *or* make an attack on *or* tackle sb/sth; **elle s'attaque à tout le monde** she's always having a go at people; **s'a. à une difficulté/un problème** to grapple with *or* to tackle a difficulty/a problem

attardé, -ée [atarde] **1** *adj* **(a) il ne restait plus que quelques passants attardés** there were only a few people out late; **il profite de la pénombre pour attaquer les promeneurs attardés** he takes advantage of the dim light to attack people who are out walking late

(b) (*dans le temps*) behind the times; **ma grand-mère est complètement attardée** my grandmother is completely behind the times *or* old-fashioned; **idées** *ou* **conceptions attardées** old-fashioned *or* outmoded ideas

(c) *Psy* (*mentalement*) (*enfant*) (mentally) retarded

2 *n* **(a)** *Psy* **a. (mental)** (mentally) retarded person

(b) (*dans une course etc*) **les attardés** the laggards, those that bring up the rear

attarder [atarde] **1** *vt* to keep late, to delay; **une crevaison nous a attardés** we were delayed by a puncture

2 s'attarder *vpr* to linger, to loiter; (*en se promenant*) to lag behind, to dawdle; **s'a. en route** to dawdle on the way; **ne nous attardons pas** let's not linger; *F* let's not hang about; **nous nous sommes attardés chez nos amis** we stayed on late at our friends' house; **elle s'est attardée au travail** she stayed late at work; **s'a. pour regarder le paysage** to linger to look at the scenery; **s'a. à qch** to linger over sth; *Péj* to waste one's time on sth; **ne nous attardons pas sur ce point** let's not dwell on this point; **inutile de s'a. là-dessus** there's no point in dwelling on it

atteindre [atɛ̃dr] (*prp* **atteignant**; *pp* **atteint**; *pr ind* **j'atteins, il atteint, n. atteignons**; *impf* **j'atteignais**; *p hist* **j'atteignis**; *fu* **j'atteindrai) 1** *vt* **(a)** (*parvenir à*) to reach, *Fml* to attain; **a. la ville** to reach the town, to get to the town; **a. la plus haute étagère** to reach the top shelf; **je ne peux pas l'a.** I can't reach it; **a. qn** to catch sb up; **a. l'ennemi** to catch up with the enemy; **a. son but** to attain *or* achieve one's aim; **a. l'âge de soixante ans** to reach the age of sixty

(b) (*s'élever à*) to reach; **le nombre des participants atteint le millier** the number of participants is nearing *or* reaching the thousand mark; **très peu de montagnes atteignent 8 000 mètres** very few mountains reach (a height of) 8,000 metres; **la pollution atteint la cote d'alerte** pollution is reaching danger level; **a. un prix élevé** to reach *or* fetch a high price

(c) (*toucher*) to hit, to reach; **a. le but** to hit the target *or* the mark; **ne pas a. le but** to fall short of the mark; **a. une couche pétrolifère** to strike oil; **être atteint (par une balle) à la jambe** to be shot in the leg; **être atteint d'une maladie** to be struck down by a disease; (*d'arbres etc*) to be attacked by a disease; **le poumon est atteint** the lung is affected; **un malade très atteint** a seriously ill patient; *F* **il est complètement atteint** (*fou*) he's completely cracked *or* potty; *Fig* **tu peux le lui dire, mais cela ne l'atteint pas** you can tell him, but it doesn't have any effect; *Fig* **rien ne l'atteint** nothing affects him, he's impervious to everything; *Fig* **elle est atteinte dans son amour-propre** her pride has been wounded *or* hurt; *Fig* **une perte qui m'a profondément atteinte** a loss which affected me very badly

2 *vi* **a. à qch** to reach *or* attain sth; **a. à son but** to achieve one's aim; **son travail atteint à la perfection** his work is close to *or* is nearing perfection

atteinte [atɛ̃t] *nf* **(a)** (*portée*) reach; **hors d'a.** (*fuyard etc*) beyond reach, out of reach; *Fig* **sa réputation est hors d'a.** his reputation is beyond attack *or* is unassailable; **se dérober** *ou* **se soustraire à l'a. de la loi** to circumvent *or* get round *or F* dodge the law; (*s'échapper*) to get out of the clutches of the law

(b) (*attaque*) blow, stroke, attack; **légère a. au bras** slight blow on the arm; **les premières atteintes d'une maladie** the first attacks of an illness; **a. au crédit de qn** blow to sb's credit; **porter a. à l'autorité de qn** to undermine sb's authority; **a. portée aux privilèges** breach of privilege; **porter a. aux intérêts de qn** to interfere with sb's interests, to affect sb's interests; **je considère que c'est une a. à mon honneur** I consider it an attack on *or* a blow to my honour; **porter a. à la réputation de qn** to damage sb's reputation

attelage [atlaʒ] *nm* **(a)** (*action d'atteler*) harnessing; (*de bœufs*) yoking; *Constr etc* attachment; (*de remorques etc*) tying, fastening; (*avec un crochet*) hooking on; *Rail* coupling; (*Astronaut*) **l'a. d'engins spatiaux** the docking of spacecraft **(b)** (*animaux*) team; (*de chevaux*) pair; (*de bœufs*) yoke; (*voiture*) carriage (and horses)

atteler [atle] **(j'attelle, n. attelons; j'attellerai) 1** *vt* **(a)** (*chevaux etc*) to harness; (*bœufs*) to yoke; *Fig* **toujours attelé à son travail** always hard at work *or* hard at it

(b) a. une voiture to attach horses to a carriage; **voiture attelée de quatre chevaux** carriage drawn by four horses; *Sp* **course de trot attelé** trotting race; *Rail* **a. des wagons** to couple (up) wagons

2 s'atteler *vpr* **le gouvernement doit s'a. au problème du chômage** the government must tackle the problem of unemployment; **s'a. à une tâche/un travail** to buckle down *or* get down to a task/a job; **je m'y attelle tous les jours** I force myself to do it every day

attelle [atɛl] *nf Méd* splint

attenant [at(ə)nɑ̃] *adj* adjacent (**à** to), adjoining, bordering; **deux chemins attenants** two intersecting paths

attendre [atɑ̃dr] **1** *vt* to wait for, *Fml, Litt* to await; **qu'attendez-vous?** what are you waiting for?; **le déjeuner nous attend** lunch is ready; **une surprise vous attend** there's a surprise in store for you, you've got a surprise waiting for you; **l'avenir nous attend** the future lies before us; **j'attends midi pour lui téléphoner** I'll wait until twelve o'clock before I telephone him; **aller a. qn à la gare** to go to meet *or* to go and meet sb at the station; **a. la fin de l'histoire** to wait for *or* until the end of the story; **il se fait a.** he's keeping us waiting; **la réponse ne s'est pas fait attendre** the reply wasn't long in coming; **tu t'es fait a.!** and about time too!; **nous n'attendions que toi** now you're here we can start/go/*etc*; **on l'attend la semaine prochaine** he is expected next week; **je l'attends d'un moment à l'autre** I'm expecting him any minute now; **nous l'attendions tous avec impatience** we were all looking forward to seeing him; **nous attendons les résultats avec impatience** we can't wait to get the results; **j'attends des explications** I'm waiting for an explanation; **je n'en attends rien de bon** I'm not expecting anything good to come of it; **a. un bébé** to be expecting (a baby); **attendez voir** just wait, wait and see; (*laissez-moi réfléchir*) let me see; **on ne t'attendait plus** we'd given up on you; **qu'attend-il de moi?** what does he want *or* expect from me?; **elle n'attend que ça** that's (just) what she wants *or* is waiting for; **je n'attends qu'une chose, les vacances** I (just) can't wait for the holidays to begin; **a. que qn fasse qch** to wait for sb to do sth; **j'attendrai (jusqu'à ce) qu'il soit prêt** I shall wait until he's ready; *Fig* **a. qn au tournant** to be waiting to catch sb out; **a. son tour** to wait one's turn; **qu'est-ce tu attends pour aller porter plainte?** what are you waiting for? go and complain

2 *vi* **(a)** to wait; **perdre son temps à a.** to waste one's time waiting; **désolé de vous avoir fait a.** sorry to have kept you waiting; **le train n'attendra pas** the train won't wait; **j'attends de voir pour juger** I'll wait and see before I pass judgment; **a. de faire qch** to wait (until it is time) to do sth; **attendons jusqu'à demain** let's wait until tomorrow; *F* **on ne va pas a. 107 ans** we're not going to wait forever; *Iron* **j'ai failli a.!** nice of you to turn up!; **attends un peu que je t'attrape!** just you wait till I catch you!; **attendez (donc)!** hang *or* hold on! wait (a bit)!, just a moment *or* a minute!; **sans plus a.** without further ado; *Prov* **tout vient à point à qui sait a.** everything comes to him who waits; **il vaut mieux a. encore un peu** it would be better to wait a bit longer; **a. une heure** to wait (for) an hour; **il ne perd rien pour a.** he's got it coming to him; **un plat qui n'attend pas** a dish that won't wait, a dish you have to eat straight away

(b) *F* **a. après qn/qch** to wait for *or* to need sb/sth; **porte-lui ce livre, il attend après** take this book to him, he is waiting for it

(c) en attendant meanwhile, in the meantime; **un remplaçant va arriver, mais en attendant, c'est nous qui devons tout faire** a replacement will arrive, but in the meantime, we have to do everything; **en attendant son arrivée** until he arrives, while waiting for him to arrive; **en attendant de vous voir** until I/we/*etc* see you; **il te dit peut-être qu'il t'aime, mais en attendant il vit avec une autre** maybe he does say he loves you, but he's living with somebody else all the same

3 s'attendre *vpr* **s'a. à qch** to expect sth; **il ne faut pas s'a. à des miracles** you can't expect miracles; **il faut s'a. à tout** one must be prepared *or* ready for anything; **je m'y attendais** I expected as much; **il fallait s'y a.** it was only to be expected; **je m'attendais à ce que tu me le dises** I was expecting you to tell me; **je ne m'attendais pas à ça** I wasn't expecting *or* hadn't expected that

attendri [atɑ̃dri] *adj* **regard a.** fond *or* tender look

attendrir [atɑ̃drir] **1** *vt* **(a)** (*le cœur de qn*) to soften; (*personne*) to move, to touch; **cela attendrirait un cœur de pierre** it would melt a heart of stone; **s'il espère m'a. avec ses cadeaux, il se trompe** if he's hoping to soften me up with his presents, he's got another think coming

(b) (*meat*) to make tender, to tenderize

2 s'attendrir *vpr* to be moved *or* touched; **les médecins ne peuvent se permettre de s'a.** doctors cannot allow themselves to get emotionally involved; **s'a. sur qch** to be moved (to tears) *or* touched by sth; **s'a. sur un bébé** to gush over a baby; **s'a. sur soi-même** *ou* **sur son propre sort** to feel sorry for oneself; **il s'attendrit facilement** he is very emotional

attendrissant [atɑ̃drisɑ̃] *adj* moving, touching; **sa crédulité est attendrissante** his naivety is touching

attendrissement [atɑ̃drismɑ̃] *nm* tenderness; **allons!, pas d'a.!** come on, let's not get emotional; **larmes d'a.** tender tears of emotion

attendrisseur [atɑ̃drisœr] *nm* (meat) tenderizer

attendu [atɑ̃dy] **1** *adj* expected; **le jour tant a. est arrivé** the long-awaited *or* much-awaited day arrived; **le train est a. pour cinq heures** the train is expected at five o'clock **2** *prép* (*les circonstances*) considering; (*les événements*) owing to; (*ses services*) in consideration of; **a. son attitude envers moi** considering *or* in view of his attitude towards me **3** *conj* **a. que** + *ind* considering that, seeing that; *Jur* whereas

attentat [atɑ̃ta] *nm* attack; **a. contre la vie de qn** attempted murder, attempt on sb's life; *Pol* assassination attempt; **victime d'un a.** victim of an attack

▶ **attentat**: **a. à la liberté** violation *or* infringement of liberty; *Jur* **a. aux mœurs** indecent behaviour, public indecency; **a. à la pudeur** indecent assault; **a. à la sûreté de l'État** high treason

attentatoire [atɑ̃tatwar] *adj Jur* **action a. à l'autorité** action that is a challenge to *or* in contempt of authority; **mesure a. à la liberté** measure that constitutes an infringement of *or* an attack on liberty

attente [atɑ̃t] *nf* **(a)** (*fait d'attendre*) waiting; (*période*) wait; **je ne supporte plus cette a.** I can't stand this waiting any longer; **vous devez compter une a. de quatre heures** you should expect a four-hour wait; **être dans l'a. de qch** to be waiting for sth; **salle d'a.** waiting room; **rester en a.** to be held over; **liste d'a.** waiting list; **file d'a.** *Br* queue, *Am* line; *Ordinat* **liste de fichiers à imprimer en a.** print queue; *Mil* **combat d'a.** delaying action; *Chir* **ligature d'a.** temporary ligature; *Av* **circuit d'a.** holding pattern, stack

(**b**) (*espoir*) expectation(s), anticipation; **contre toute a.** contrary to all expectations; **remplir l'a. de qn, répondre à l'a. de qn** to come up *or* live up to sb's expectations; **dans l'a. de votre réponse/de vous rencontrer** (*dans une lettre*) awaiting your reply/looking forward to meeting you

attenter [atɑ̃te] *vi* to make an attempt (**à** on, against); **a. à la vie de qn** to make an attempt on sb's life; **a. à ses jours** to attempt suicide; **a. à la liberté de qn** to infringe upon sb's liberty

attentif, -ive [atɑ̃tif, -iv] *adj* (**a**) (*en alerte*) **soyez attentifs!** pay attention!; **il n'est pas a.** he doesn't pay attention; **être (très) a. aux autres** to be (very) attentive to others; **écouter d'un air a. /d'une oreille attentive** to listen attentively; **être a. à qch** to look after sth, to see to sth; **être a. à ses intérêts** to look after one's (own) interests; **être a. à sa santé** to look after oneself *or* one's health; **a. aux prix** price-conscious (**b**) (*appliqué*) careful; **examen a.** careful examination

attention [atɑ̃sjɔ̃] *nf* (**a**) attention; **appliquer toute son a. à qch** to devote one's undivided attention to sth; **faute d'a.** through not paying attention; **faire un effort d'a.** to try to be more attentive, to try to concentrate; **écouter avec a.** to listen attentively; **porter** *ou* **tourner** *ou* **diriger son a. vers** *ou* **sur qch** to turn one's attention to sth; **attirer l'a.** (*d'un objet ou d'un fait*) to attract attention; **c'est ce détail qui a attiré mon a.** it's this detail which attracted *or* caught my attention; **attirer l'a. de qn sur qch** to draw sb's attention to sth; **puis-je avoir votre a. s'il vous plaît** (may I have) your attention please; **faire a. à sa santé** to take care of one's health; **ne faire aucune a. à qn/qch, ne pas prêter la moindre a. à qn/qch** to take no *or* to take not the slightest notice of sb/sth; **il a fait très a. de ne pas la blesser** he took great care not to hurt her; **(faites) a.!** take care!, look out!, watch it!; **a. à la peinture** mind the paint; (*écriteau*) wet paint; **a. à la fermeture des portières, a. au départ!** *Rail* ≈ stand clear of the doors!, mind the doors!; **a. au train** beware of (the) trains; **a., verglas** caution, ice; **a. aux travaux** caution, road works ahead; **faites a. à** *ou* **de ne pas vous perdre** be careful not to get lost; **faites a. (à ce) que personne ne sorte** take care *or* be sure that no one leaves (the house); **à l'a. de Marie Berne** for the attention of Marie Berne

(**b**) (*amabilité*) attention(s), consideration; **être plein d'attention(s) envers qn** to be full of consideration for sb, to be very attentive towards sb; **il a eu l'a. de m'avertir** he was considerate enough to warn me

attentionné [atɑ̃sjɔne] *adj* attentive; **être a. envers qn** to be full of consideration for sb, to be very attentive towards sb

attentisme [atɑ̃tism] *nm* wait-and-see policy

attentivement [atɑ̃tivmɑ̃] *adv* attentively, carefully; (*regarder*) closely

atténuant [atenɥɑ̃] *adj Jur* (*circonstances*) mitigating, extenuating

atténuateur [atenɥatœr] *nm* attenuator

atténuation [atenɥasjɔ̃] *nf* (**a**) diminishing, reducing, lessening; (*de lumière*) dimming, subduing; (*de couleur*) toning down; (*d'une chute*) breaking; (*d'un châtiment, d'une sentence*) mitigation, reduction; (*de la douleur*) easing, relief (**b**) *Phot* (*de négatif*) reduction; (*des contrastes*) softening (**c**) (*d'un crime*) extenuation

atténué [atenɥe] *adj* attenuated, diminished; *Jur* **responsabilité atténuée** diminished responsibility

atténuer [atenɥe] **1** *vt* (**a**) to diminish, to reduce, to lessen; (*couleur*) to tone down; (*lumière*) to dim, to subdue; (*châtiment, conséquences*) to mitigate; (*douleur*) to ease, to relieve; **a. une chute** to break a fall (**b**) *Phot* (*négatif etc*) to reduce; (*contrastes*) to soften, to tone down (**c**) (*offense*) to extenuate; (*crime etc*) to make less serious; **sa situation n'atténue en rien la gravité de ce qu'il a fait** his situation in no way lessens *or* reduces the seriousness of what he has done **2 s'atténuer** *vpr* to lessen; (*de la lumière*) to fade

atterrant [aterɑ̃] *adj* overwhelming; (*nouvelle*) shattering

atterrer [atere] *vt* to appal; **sa naïveté m'atterre** I am appalled *or* staggered by his naivety; **ils se regardent atterrés** they look at each other aghast

atterrir [aterir] *vi* (**a**) *Naut* (*voir la terre*) to make *or* sight land, to make a landfall; (*toucher le fond*) to ground, to run ashore (**b**) *Av* to land; **l'avion a dû a. en catastrophe** the aeroplane had to make an emergency landing; **a. trop court** to undershoot; **a. trop long** to overshoot; **a. brutalement** to crash (land), to make a rough *or* bumpy landing; *F* **a. dans un bar/dans un fossé/à l'hôpital** to land up *or* end up *or* finish up in a bar/a ditch/hospital; *F* **atterris, mon vieux!** you dozy thing!

atterrissage [aterisaʒ] *nm* (**a**) *Av* landing, touchdown; *Fig F* **elle a cru qu'il l'aimait et l'a. a été difficile** she thought he loved her but she came down to earth with a bump; **a. trop long** overshoot; **a. trop court** undershoot; **a. forcé** forced landing; **a. à vue** visual landing; **a. aux instruments** instrument landing; **a. sans visibilité** blind landing; **a. brutal** rough *or* bumpy landing; **a. en catastrophe** emergency landing; **terrain d'a.** (*ensemble des pistes*) landing strip *or* field; **pont d'a.** (*de porte-avions*) landing deck; **a. en douceur** soft landing

(**b**) *Naut* making (the) land, landfall; (*en touchant le fond*) grounding, running ashore

(**c**) *Télécom* (*de câble marin*) landing

attestation [atɛstasjɔ̃] *nf* (*action*) attestation; (*certificat*) certificate; **demander l'a. du professeur** to ask for a reference from the teacher; **a. du médecin/de l'employeur** doctor's/employer's certificate; **a. d'assurance** certificate of insurance; **a. de rejet** (*de chèque*) notification of returned cheque; *Jur* **a. du titre** warranty of title; **a. sous serment** *ou* **sur l'honneur** affidavit

attester [atɛste] *vt* (**a**) **a. qch** to attest *or* certify sth, to testify to sth; (*la réputation de qn*) to vouch for; (*sortie d'argent*) to confirm; **a. que qch est vrai** to attest *or* certify that sth is true; **c'est un fait attesté** it is an established fact, it is beyond doubt; **sa réponse atteste sa mauvaise foi** his reply bears witness to *or* demonstrates his bad faith; **nous pensons tous qu'il a menti et la bande enregistrée en atteste** we all think he lied and the tape recording proves it; *Ling* **forme attestée** attested form; **ce mot n'est attesté dans aucun dictionnaire** this word isn't attested *or* doesn't occur in any dictionary

(**b**) (*prendre à témoin*) **a. qn (de qch)** to call sb to witness (to sth); **a. l'autorité de qn en faveur d'une affirmation** to advance a statement on the authority of sb

attiédir [atjedir] **1** *vt* (*eau chaude etc*) to cool; (*eau froide*) to warm, to take the chill off; *Fig* **a. les passions de qn** to calm *or* cool sb's passions **2 s'attiédir** *vpr* (*de l'eau chaude*) to cool down, to become tepid *or* lukewarm; (*de l'eau froide*) to warm up; *Fig* (*des passions*) to cool

attiédissement [atjedismɑ̃] *nm* (*de l'eau chaude*) cooling down; (*de l'eau froide*) warming up; *Fig* (*des passions*) cooling

attifer [atife] **1** *vt F* to rig out, to get up, to deck out (**de** in); **elle est toujours attifée de manière impossible** she's always rigged out in the most ridiculous fashion; **elle attife ses enfants n'importe comment** she dresses her children any old how; **comme le voilà attifé** what a sight he looks! **2 s'attifer** *vpr* **elle s'attife toujours bizarrement** she's always wearing strange rig-outs

attiger [atiʒe] *vi* (**j'attigeais; n. attigeons**) *Arg, Vieilli* (*exagérer*) to go over the top, to go too far; **tu attiges!** come off it!

attique [atik] **1** *adj Antiq* Attic, Athenian **2** *nm Archit* (*étage*) attic

attirail [atiraj] *nm* (**a**) equipment, gear; (*d'outils etc*) set; (*de cuisine*) utensils; (*de jardin*) tools; **a. de pêche** fishing tackle (**b**) *F* paraphernalia; **avant d'acheter la moto, il s'est acheté tout l'a.** before buying the motorbike, he bought himself all the right gear; **elle est arrivée avec tout un a. de photographe** she arrived with a lot of photographer's paraphernalia

attirance [atirɑ̃s] *nf* attraction (**vers** to); (*du plaisir, d'un endroit etc*) lure, fascination; **éprouver de l'a. pour qn** to be drawn *or* attracted to sb; **je n'ai aucune a. vers** *ou* **pour les mathématiques** maths does not appeal to me in the least

attirant [atirɑ̃] *adj* attractive; (*force etc*) drawing; (*manières, sourire*) alluring, engaging

attirer [atire] **1** *vt* (**a**) (*d'un aimant, du soleil etc*) to attract, to draw; **quelque chose les attire l'un vers l'autre** something draws them together, there is some kind of attraction between them; **ce qui m'attire dans ce projet** what attracts me *or* what I find attractive about this project; **je ne sais pas ce qui m'attire en** *ou* **chez elle** I don't know what attracts me to her; **la Grèce, ça ne vous attire pas?** doesn't Greece appeal to you?; **sa pièce attire un grand public** his play draws a large audience; **a. qn dans un coin** to draw *or* take sb into a corner; **a. qch à** *ou* **sur qn** to bring sth on sb; **cela risque de vous a. des ennuis/des ennemis** that may cause you problems/make enemies for you; **avec ton insolence, tu vas nous a. des ennuis** your insolence is going to cause us problems; **a. la colère de qn sur qn** to bring down sb's wrath on sb; **je voudrais a. votre attention sur ce point** I'd like to draw your attention to this point; **c'est vraiment quelqu'un qui attire la sympathie** he/she is someone who gains a lot of sympathy; **son roman a attiré de violentes critiques** his novel has come in for *or* has attracted harsh criticism; **affiche qui attire les regards** eye-catching poster

(**b**) (*séduire*) to attract; **elle attire les hommes d'un certain âge/paumés** she attracts middle-aged men/losers; **a. qn dans un piège** to lure sb into a trap; **a. qn par des promesses** to entice sb with promises

2 s'attirer *vpr* (**a**) (*mutuellement*) to attract each other; **ils s'attirent** they're attracted to each other; **les contraires s'attirent** opposites attract (each other)

(**b**) (*sur soi*) **s'a. des critiques/des éloges** to come in for criticism/praise; **je me suis attiré la colère de mon père** I incurred my father's anger; **il s'est attiré la reconnaissance du patron** he earned his boss's gratitude; **s'a. des sympathies/des ennemis** to gain sympathy/to make enemies

attiser [atize] *vt* (**a**) (*feu*) to stir (up), to poke; *Ind etc* to stoke (**b**) *Fig* (*désir, mécontentement*) to fan the flames of, to fuel; **a. les haines/le racisme** to stir up hatred/racism

attitré [atitre] *adj* (*chargé d'une fonction*) appointed, recognized; (*journaliste*) accredited; **fournisseurs attitrés de sa Majesté** purveyors by appointment to his/her Majesty; (*habituel*) **mon marchand de légumes a.** my usual *or* regular greengrocer; **mon fauteuil a.** my chair, the chair I sit in

attitrer [atitre] *vt* (*ambassadeur*) to appoint

attitude [atityd] *nf* (**a**) (*disposition*) attitude; **a. hostile/intransigeante** hostile/uncompromising attitude (**envers, à l'égard de, pour, en face de** towards); **quelle est votre a. vis à vis de ce problème?** what is your stance *or* position on this problem?, how do you stand on this problem?

(**b**) (*conduite*) attitude; **je n'aime pas son a.** I don't like his attitude; **tu as eu une a. déplorable au cours de cette réunion** you behaved appallingly during the meeting, your behaviour during the meeting was appalling; **ce n'est qu'une a.** it's only an act *or* a pose

(**c**) (*port*) attitude; **il prit une a. décontractée** he struck a casual pose

attouchement [atuʃmɑ̃] *nm* (**a**) (*pour guérir*) laying on of hands (**b**) (*sexuel*) **se livrer à des attouchements sur qn** to fondle sb; *Jur* to interfere with sb

attractif, -ive [atraktif, -iv] *adj* (**a**) *Phys* (*pouvoir*) attractive, drawing; (*force*) gravitational (**b**) *Fig* (*prix, vertu*) attractive

attraction [atraksjɔ̃] *nf* (**a**) (*d'un aimant etc*) attraction, pull; *Phys* **a. universelle** gravitation; **a. moléculaire** molecular attraction

(**b**) (*d'un endroit, d'une personne etc*) attraction; **l'a. de deux personnes l'une pour l'autre** the attraction between two people; **exercer une a. sur qn** to attract sb; **l'a. qui me porte vers cet endroit** the attraction this place has for me

(**c**) (*de cabaret*) number; *F* **c'est la grosse a.** he/she is the big attraction

(**d**) **attractions** attractions; (*à la foire*) sideshows; *Th* variety show; (*au restaurant*) cabaret show; **parc d'attractions** amusement park; **les attractions passent à 21 heures** the show starts at 9 o'clock; **a. touristique** tourist *or* visitor attraction

attrait [atrɛ] *nm* (**a**) (*chose*) attraction, lure; (*état*) attractiveness; (*de la jeunesse etc*) charm; **l'a. de la mer** the call of the sea; **a. touristique** (*charme*) tourist appeal; **l'a. de l'aventure** the lure of adventure; **les attraits d'une carrière dans le commerce** the attraction of a business career; *Mktg* **a. commercial** market appeal; **dépourvu d'a.** unattractive, devoid of attraction; **ressentir de l'a. pour qn** to feel attracted by sb (**b**) **attraits** (*d'une femme*) charms

attrapade [atrapad] *nf*, **attrapage** [atrapaʒ] *nm F* (**a**) (*dispute*) quarrel, set-to (**b**) (*réprimande*) ticking-off, telling-off; **j'ai eu droit à un(e) bon(ne) a.** I got a right telling-off

attrape [atrap] *nf* (**a**) (*farce*) trick, hoax; **faire une a. à qn** to play a trick *or* a practical joke on sb; (*tromper*) to take sb in; **c'est une a.** there's a catch in it; **magasin de farces et attrapes** joke shop (**b**) *Arch* (*à oiseaux etc*) trap, gin snare

attrape-couillon, *pl* **attrape-couillon(s)** *nm F* gimmick

attrape-mouche(s) *nm inv* (**a**) (*piège*) flypaper (**b**) (*fleur*) Venus flytrap, Venus's-flytrap

attrape-nigaud, *pl* **attrape-nigaud(s)** *nm* trick

attraper [atrape] **1** *vt* (**a**) (*capturer*) (*personne, animal*) to catch

(**b**) (*saisir*) (*ballon, voleur etc*) to catch; (*se saisir de*) to grab; **les voleurs se sont fait a.** the thieves were caught; **attention si je t'attrape!** if I catch you there'll be trouble!; **il l'attrapa par le poignet** he grabbed *or* caught her (by the) wrist; **tu peux m'a. le torchon?** could you grab that cloth for me?; **a. un autobus/un train** to catch a bus/a train; **je n'ai pu a. que quelques secondes/bribes de leur conversation** I could only catch a few seconds/snatches of their conversation

(**c**) (*prendre, contracter*) **a. froid** to catch a chill; **a. un bon coup de soleil** to get badly sunburned; **a. un rhume** to catch (a) cold; **j'ai attrapé mal à la tête** I've got a headache; **a. mal** to catch a cold; **en a. pour dix ans** to get ten years' (imprisonment); *Aut etc* **a. une contravention** to get a ticket, to pick up a ticket; **a. un accent** to pick up an accent

(**d**) (*tromper*) **a. qn** to trick *or* cheat sb, to take sb in; **là, vous êtes bien attrapé** you fell for it hook, line and sinker *or* good and proper

(**e**) (*surprendre*) to catch; *F* **a. qn à faire qch** to catch sb doing sth; **et méfie-toi, si je t'y attrape encore une fois ...!** don't let me catch you (at it) again, or else ...!; **a. qn sur le fait** to catch sb in the act, to catch sb red-handed

(**f**) *F* (*gronder*) **a. qn** to scold sb, to give sb a good talking to; **se faire a.** to get told off, to catch it

2 s'attraper *vpr* (**a**) (*d'une maladie etc*) to be caught; **le sida ne s'attrape pas par la salive** you can't catch AIDS through saliva; **ça s'attrape facilement** it's very catching

(**b**) *se disputer* to scold each other

attrape-touristes *nm inv F* tourist trap

attrayant [atrɛjɑ̃] *adj* attractive, appealing; **peu a.** unattractive

attribuable [atribɥabl] *adj* attributable, ascribable (**à** to)

attribuer [atribɥe] **1** *vt* (**a**) (*allouer*) to assign, to allot (**à** to), to confer (**à** (up)on); (*prix, récompense*) to award; *Fin* (*actions*) to allot; **a. des rôles** *ou* **des fonctions** to allocate duties (**à** to); *Th* **a. un rôle à qn** to cast sb for a part; **a. le rôle de Cyrano à qn** to cast sb as Cyrano

(**b**) (*fait, livre etc*) to attribute, to ascribe (**à** to); (*crime, erreur*) to blame (**à** on); (*de l'importance à qch*) to attach; **on attribue l'incendie à une inattention** the fire has been blamed on carelessness; **ne m'attribue pas des motivations qui sont les tiennes** don't project your motives onto me; **a. un projet à qn** to give sb the credit for a plan; **tableau attribué à Hogarth** painting attributed to Hogarth

2 s'attribuer *vpr* (*un devoir*) to take upon oneself; **s'a. qch** to claim *or* lay claim to sth; **il s'est attribué tout le mérite** he claimed *or* took all the credit

attribut [atriby] [①A17,2-3] **1** *nm* attribute; *Mktg* **a. du produit** product attribute; *Ordinat* **a. de fichier** file attribute; *Ordinat* **a. de mise en forme** formatting parameter **2** *adj Gram* attributive; **nom a.** attributive noun

attribution [atribysjɔ̃] *nm* (**a**) assigning, attribution, attributing (**à** to); (*des tâches*) allocation, allocating; (*de bourses d'étude etc*) awarding; *Th* (*des rôles*) casting; *Fin* (*d'actions*) allotment; *Bourse* **actions d'a.** bonus shares; **avis d'a.** letter of allotment; **a. (d'essence/de sucre)** quota, ration (of petrol/sugar); **attributions** prerogative, competence, powers; (*de fonction*) duties, functions, responsibilities; **cela entre dans ses attributions** this comes within his competence *or* is part of his duties (**b**) (*d'une œvre*) attribution; **l'a. de cette œuvre à Maillol est inexacte** this work is wrongly attributed to Maillol (**c**) *Gram* **complément d'a.** indirect object

attriqué [atrike] *adj Can* **mal a.** badly dressed

attristant [atristɑ̃] *adj* (*nouvelle etc*) saddening, depressing

attristé [atriste] *adj* (*visage*) sad; (*regard*) sorrowful; **contempler qch d'un œil a.** to gaze sadly at sth

attrister [atriste] **1** *vt* to sadden, to grieve; **cette décision m'attriste** I am saddened by this decision; **cela m'attriste de voir ...** it makes me sad *or* saddens me to see ...

2 s'attrister *vpr* to be sad (**de qch** about sth); **je m'attriste de les voir si démunis** I'm sad *or* saddened to see them so helpless

attroupement [atrupmɑ̃] *nm* (*de manisfestants etc*) crowd; *Jur* unlawful *or* riotous assembly; **leur éclat dans la rue a provoqué un a.** their scene in the street drew a crowd; **la loi contre les attroupements** ≈ the Riot Act; **un a. pacifique** a peaceful assembly

attrouper [atrupe] **1** *vt* (*foule etc*) to gather together; **arrêtez de crier, vous allez a. les passants** stop shouting, you'll draw a crowd **2 s'attrouper** *vpr* to gather, to assemble; **les manifestants s'attroupaient** the demonstrators were gathering

atypique [atipik] *adj* atypical

au [o] *voir* **à**

aubade [obad] *nf* dawn serenade; **donner l'a. à qn** to serenade sb

aubaine [obɛn] *nf* (**a**) (*chance etc*) windfall, godsend; **c'était vraiment une a. de vendre ton salon à ce prix-là** it was a real godsend to be able to sell your suite for that price; **profiter de l'a.** to take advantage of one's good luck; **quelle a.!** what a stroke of luck! (**b**) *Can* (*occasion*) bargain, good buy

aube[1] [ob] *nf* **(a)** *(matin)* dawn; **à l'a. (du jour)** at dawn, at daybreak; **partir dès l'a.** to leave at dawn; *Fig* **l'a. de la civilisation** the dawn of civilization **(b)** *Rel* alb

aube[2] *nf* **(a)** *Naut (de roue)* paddle, blade; **roue à aubes** paddle (wheel); **vapeur à roue à aubes** paddleboat **(b)** *(de turbine)* blade, vane; *(de ventilateur)* vane

aubépine [obepin] *nf (arbuste)* hawthorn, may (tree); **fleurs d'a.** may (blossom)

aubère [obɛr] **1** *adj* red roan **2** *nm* red roan (horse)

auberge [obɛrʒ] *nf* inn; **a. rurale** *ou* **de campagne** country inn; **tenir a.** to keep an inn; *Fig* **c'est un peu une a. espagnole** what you get out of it depends on what you put in; **a. de jeunesse** youth hostel; **il prend notre maison pour une a.** he treats our house like a hotel; *Fig F* **on n'est pas sorti de l'a.** we're not out of the wood(s) yet

aubergine [obɛrʒin] **1** *nf* **(a)** *(plante)* aubergine, *Am* egg-plant **(b)** *Vieilli Fig F (contractuelle)* (female) traffic warden **2** *adj inv* aubergine

aubergiste [obɛrʒist] *n* innkeeper

aubette [obɛt] *nf surtout Belg* newspaper kiosk; *(abribus)* bus shelter

aubriétie [obriesi] *nf (plante)* aubrietia

auburn [obœrn] *adj inv* auburn

aucun, -une [okɛ̃, -yn] **1** *pron* [①A35,b; B15,B2; B60,B] **(a)** *(avec négation exprimée ou sous-entendue, accompagné de ne ou sans) (être humain)* no one, nobody; *(chose)* none, not any; **lequel des deux veux-tu? – a.** which of the two do you want? – neither; **je ne me fie à a. d'entre eux** I don't trust any of them; **a. (des deux) ne viendra** neither (of them) will come; **de tous ces élèves a. n'a répondu** not one of these pupils answered

(b) *(avec négation implicite)* **de tous vos soi-disant amis, a. interviendra-t-il?** will any of your so-called friends intervene?

(c) *(positif)* anyone; **il travaille plus qu'a.** he works more than anyone (else)

(d) *Litt* **d'aucuns** some people; **d'aucuns prétendent qu'il est encore en vie** there are some who maintain that he is still alive

2 *adj* **(a)** *(positif, interrogatif)* any; **un des plus beaux livres qui aient été écrits sur a. sujet** one of the finest books written on any subject; **plus rapide qu'a. autre coureur** faster than any other runner; **avez-vous aucune intention de le faire?** have you any intention of doing it?

(b) *(négatif)* no, not any; **je n'ai aucune idée** I don't have any idea, I have no idea; **sans aucune exception** without any exception; **le fait n'a aucune importance** the fact is of no importance; **oui, sans a. doute** yes, without a *or* any doubt; **en aucune façon je ne l'aiderai** I will not help him in any way (at all); **sans mentionner a. nom** mentioning no names, without mentioning any names; **réparer qch sans a. mal** to repair sth with no difficulty at all *or* without any difficulty at all; **il n'a jamais fait a. mal à personne** he never did anyone any harm

aucunement [okynmɑ̃] *adv* in no way, not at all, by no means, not in the slightest, not in the least; **je n'en suis a. étonné** I am not the slightest surprised; **je ne la connais a.** I don't know her at all; **je ne m'attendais a. à ce qu'il vînt** I never expected him to come

audace [odas] *nf* **(a)** *(courage, assurance)* audacity, boldness, daring; **il faut beaucoup d'a. pour le faire/réussir** you need to be very bold *or* very daring to do it/to succeed **(b)** *(culot)* audacity, impudence; **vous avez l'a. de me dire cela!** you have the audacity *or* impudence *or* cheek *or* nerve to tell me that!; **ah! tu ne manques pas d'a.!** you've got the cheek of the Devil! **(c)** *(action audacieuse)* **elle est jeune, elle a toutes les audaces** she is young and daring; **une a. de style** daring unconventionality of style, stylistic daring

audacieusement [odasjøzmɑ̃] *adv* **(a)** *(avec courage)* audaciously, boldly, daringly; **elle a a. demandé un rendez-vous avec le grand patron** she boldly requested a meeting with the big boss **(b)** *(avec culot)* impudently

audacieux, -euse [odasjø, -øz] *adj* **(a)** *(courageux)* audacious, bold, daring; **il fait des harmonies de couleurs très audacieuses** he uses very bold combinations of colour **(b)** *(culotté)* impudent; *(mensonge etc)* brazen

au-deçà *Arch* **1** *adv* on this side **2** *prép* **a. de** on this side of

au-dedans **1** *adv* inside **2** *prép* **a. de** inside, within

au-dehors **1** *adv* outside **2** *prép* **a. de** outside, beyond

au-delà **1** *adv* beyond; **il est très connu dans la région et même a.** he is very well-known in the region and even further afield; **jusqu'à une certaine somme mais pas a.** up to a certain sum but no further **2** *nm* **l'a.** the next world, the hereafter **3** *prép* **a. de** beyond, on the other side of; **n'allez pas a. de cent francs** don't go above *or* beyond a hundred francs

au-dessous [odəsu, otsu] **1** *adv* below, underneath; **sur la table et a.** on the table and under it; **les locataires a.** the tenants below *or* downstairs; **les enfants âgés de sept ans et a.** children of seven (years) and under; **on en trouve à 50 francs et même a.** you can get them for 50 francs or even less; **musique transposée deux tons a.** music transposed two tones lower *or* two tones down

2 *prép* [①A65] **a. de** below, under **cinquante kilomètres a. de Paris** fifty kilometres south of Paris; **a. du genou** below the knee; **les locataires a. de nous** the tenants below *or* underneath us; **quinze degrés a. de zéro** fifteen degrees below zero; **a. de la moyenne/du pair** below average/par, *Litt* **il est a. de lui de se plaindre** it is beneath him to complain; **a. de cinq ans** under five (years of age); **quantités a. de 30 kilos** quantities of less than 30 kilos; **a. de 100 francs** less than *or* under *or* below 100 francs; **acheter qch a. de sa valeur** to buy sth for less than it is worth; **son travail était a. de mon attente** his work fell short of what I expected; **je suis a. de la tâche** I'm not up to the job; **être a. de tout** to be beneath contempt

au-dessus [odəsy, otsy] **1** *adv* above; **une terrasse avec une marquise a.** a terrace with an awning over it *or* above (it); **la salle de bains est a.** the bathroom is upstairs; **mille francs et a.** a thousand francs and up(wards); **la qualité a.** the next grade up; **tout ce qui est a. est bien meilleur** everything up-market of this is a lot better; **musique transposée un ton a.** music transposed a tone higher *or* up a tone

2 *prép* [①A64] **a. de** above; **le château est situé a. du village** the castle stands above the village; **il a son nom a. de la porte** his name is above *or* over the door; **les avions volaient a. de nos têtes** the planes were flying overhead; **l'eau leur montait jusqu'a. des genoux** the water came up above their knees; **deux degrés a. de zéro** two degrees above zero; **a. de cinquante francs** more than fifty francs, over fifty francs; **cinquante kilomètres a. de Paris** fifty kilometres north of Paris; **a. de la moyenne** above average; **a. de cinq ans** over five (years of age); **le colonel est a. du commandant** a colonel is higher than a major; **la tâche est a. de leurs forces** the job is too much for them *or* is beyond them; **vivre a. de ses moyens** to live beyond one's means; **je suis a. de ça** I'm above that, I wouldn't stoop to that

au-devant [odvɑ̃] *(utilisé uniquement dans les propositions telles que* **aller** *ou* **courir** *ou* **se jeter** *ou* **se précipiter a.)** **1** *adv* **quand il y a du danger, je vais a.** when there is danger ahead, I go to meet it; **quand je prévois une objection je vais a.** when I anticipate an objection, I take steps in advance **2** *prép* **aller/courir a. de qn** to go/run to meet sb; **aller a. des désirs de qn** to anticipate sb's wishes; **aller a. d'un danger** to anticipate a danger; **aller a. d'un complot** to forestall a plot; **aller a. du danger/d'une défaite** to court danger/failure

audibilité [odibilite] *nf* audibility

audible [odibl] *adj* audible

audience [odjɑ̃s] *nf* **(a)** *Jur* hearing, session, court; **plaider en pleine a.** *ou* **en a. publique** to plead in open court; **a. à huis clos** hearing in camera; **tenir a.** to hold a court *or* a sitting; **l'a. est suspendue** the case is adjourned; **l'a. est reprise** the case is resumed

(b) *(intérêt du public)* following; **ce cinéaste a trouvé a. auprès des jeunes** this film-maker has gained a following among young people

(c) *(public)* audience; **a. captive** captive audience; **a-cible** target audience; **a. cumulée** cumulative audience (size); **a. utile** *(d'un support, d'un média)* addressable audience; **a. utile nette** *(d'un support, d'un média)* net addressable audience reached

(d) *(entrevue)* audience, hearing; **recevoir qn sur lettre d'a.** to interview sb by appointment; **tenir une a.** *(roi)* to hold an audience; **donner une a. à qn** to grant sb an audience

audiencier [odjɑ̃sje] *nm Jur* **huissier a.** court crier, usher

audimat® [odimat] *nm (appareil)* = device installed in homes for calculating television audience ratings; *(résultats)* audience ratings, audience viewing figures; **cette émission a un bon a.** this programme attracts a large audience

audimètre [odimɛtr] *nm* audiometer, people meter, setmeter

audimétrie [odimetri] *nf* = calculation of audience ratings

audioconférence [odjokɔ̃ferɑ̃s] *nf* audioconference; **a. multipoint** multipoint audioconference; **a. point à point** point-to-point audioconference

audiofréquence [odjofrekɑ̃s] *nf* audiofrequency

audiomètre [odjomɛtr] *nm* audiometer

audionumérique [odjonymerik] *adj* digital audio; **disque a.** compact disc; **a. DAB** digital audio broadcasting, DAB

audio-oral, -ale, -aux, -ales [odjɔɔral, -o] *adj (méthode, exercice)* audio

audiophone [odjofɔn] *nm* hearing aid
audioprothésiste [odjoprɔtezist] *n* hearing-aid specialist
audiotypie [odjotipi] *nf* audiotyping
audiotypiste [odjotipist] *n* audiotypist
audio(-)visuel, -elle [odjɔvizɥɛl] **1** *adj* **(a)** *Scol etc* (*méthodes etc*) audiovisual **(b)** *TV, Rad* television and radio **2** *nm* **(a)** *Scol etc* audiovisual aids **(b)** *TV, Rad* television and radio
audiphone [odifɔn] *nm Tél* pre-recorded telephone message service
audit [odit] *nm* audit; **cabinet d'a.** firm of auditors; **être chargé de l'a. d'une société** to audit a company; **a. social** = management consultancy report; **a. de diagnostic** diagnostic audit; **a. de qualité** quality audit; **a. de vente** sales audit; *Mktg* **a. des détaillants** retail audit; **a. marketing** *ou* **mercatique** marketing audit; **a. consommateur** consumer audit
auditer [odite] *vt* (*entreprise*) to audit
auditeur, -trice [oditœr, -tris] *n* **(a)** listener; **les auditeurs** the audience; *Rad, TV* **programme des auditeurs** request programme; *Univ* **suivre un cours en a. libre** = to follow a university course without being officially registered as a student, *Am* to audit a course **(b)** *Admin* **a. à la Cour des comptes** = Commissioner of Audit **(c)** (*chargé de l'audit*) auditor; **a. mercatique** marketing auditor
auditif, -ive [oditif, -iv] *adj* (*nerf*) auditory; **avoir des problèmes auditifs** to have hearing problems; **prothèse** *ou* **aide auditive** hearing aid; **mémoire auditive** aural memory
audition [odisjɔ̃] *nf* **(a)** (*de chanteur etc*) audition; **passer une a.** to have an audition **(b)** (*écoute*) hearing; **juger d'un opéra à la première a.** to judge an opera at the first hearing **(c)** *Jur* **a. des témoins** hearing *or* examination of the witnesses; **nouvelle a.** rehearing **(d)** (*concert*) **a. de piano** (private) piano recital
auditionner [odisjɔne] **1** *vt* **(a)** *Th* to audition **(b)** *Jur* to hear **2** *vi Th etc* to have an audition, to audition (**pour un rôle** for a part)
auditoire [oditwar] *nm* **(a)** audience **(b)** *Jur* court; *Belg, Suisse* auditorium
auditorium [oditɔrjɔm] *nm* auditorium; *Rad, TV* (broadcasting, television) studio; **a. d'enregistrement** sound studio
auge [oʒ] *nf* **(a)** (*pour animaux*) trough; **a. d'écurie** manger; *F* **amène ton a.!** (*assiette*) pass me your plate **(b)** (*pour mener l'eau au moulin*) flume, channel; *HydE* = **auget** **(c)** (*d'un concasseur*) hopper
auget [oʒɛ] *nm* **(a)** (small) trough; (*d'une cage d'oiseau*) seed *or* water trough **(b)** (*de roue à eau*) bucket; **roue à augets** bucket *or* overshot wheel
augmentation [ɔgmɑ̃tasjɔ̃] *nf* **(a)** increase, growth; *Admin* (*de salaire*) increment; **a. des dépenses/du chômage/de la consommation** increase in expenditure/unemployment/consumption; **a. de salaire** (pay-)rise, rise *or* increase in wages, *Am* raise; **a. du capital** increase in capital; **demander une a.** to ask for a (pay-)rise *or Am* a raise; **a. de prix** price increase; **a. du prix de vente** mark-up; **être en a.** to be rising, to be on the increase; **les chiffres du chômage sont en nette a.** there is a marked increase in the unemployment figures
(b) *Ordinat* **a. de puissance** upgrade, upgrading
(c) *Mus* augmentation
(d) *Tricot* **faire une a.** to make a stitch, to make one
augmenter [ɔgmɑ̃te] **1** *vt* to increase; **a. la durée de cuisson** to increase the cooking time; **édition augmentée** enlarged edition; **a. une douleur** to aggravate a pain; **cela risque d'a. sa colère** that is liable to make him even more angry; **a. le prix de qch** to put up *or* increase *or* raise the price of sth; **a. qn** to raise *or* increase sb's salary *or* wages
2 *vi* **(a)** to increase; **la criminalité augmente** crime is increasing *or* on the increase; **empêcher les frais d'a.** to keep expenses down; **tout augmente!** everything's going up!; **le prix a augmenté de 10% par rapport à l'année dernière** the price is up 10% on last year; **la douleur augmente** the pain is worsening; **la chaleur augmente** it is getting hotter; **un conflit qui va en augmentant** an escalating conflict
(b) *Tricot* to make a stitch, to make one; **a. de deux mailles au commencement du rang suivant** increase two at the beginning of the next row
(c) *Mus* **en augmentant** crescendo
3 s'augmenter *vpr* **notre société s'est augmentée d'une nouvelle part de capital/de trois nouveaux cadres/de filiales à l'étranger** our firm has acquired new capital/three new managers/branches abroad
augure [ɔgyr] *nm* **(a)** *Antiq* (*devin*) augur; **consulter les augures** to consult the oracle; **le Collège des augures** the College of Augurs **(b)** (*présage*) augury, omen; **de bon a.** auspicious; **ce beau temps me paraît de bon a.** this nice weather seems to be a good omen; **de mauvais a.** ominous; **prendre les augures** to take the auguries; *Fig* **oiseau de mauvais a.** bird of ill omen
augurer [ɔgyre] *vt* to augur, to forecast; **a. l'avenir** to forecast *or* foresee the future; **a. bien/mal de qch** to bode well/not to bode well for sth, to augur well/ill for sth; **une querelle le premier jour, voilà qui augure mal de leur mariage** a quarrel on the first day doesn't bode well for their marriage; **que peut-on a. de cette rencontre prochaine?** what does this next meeting hold in store?; **je n'augure rien de bon de tout cela** I don't see any good coming of all this
Auguste [ɔgyst] *nm* **(a)** *Hist* Augustus; **le siècle d'A.** the Augustan Age **(b) l'a.** (*au cirque*) the 'funny man'
auguste [ɔgyst] *adj* august, majestic; **une a. assemblée** an august *or* illustrious assembly
Augustin [ɔgystɛ̃] **1** *adj Rel* Augustinian **2** *nm* **(a)** Augustine **(b)** *Rel* Augustinian (friar); **les Augustins** the Augustin friars
augustinien, -ienne [ɔgystinjɛ̃, -jɛn] *adj Phil* Augustinian
auj *abrév* **aujourd'hui**
aujourd'hui [oʒurdɥi] *adv* **(a)** (*ce jour*) today; **quel jour sommes-nous a.?** what day is it today, what's today?; **c'est a. le cinq/dimanche** today is the fifth/is Sunday, it's the fifth/Sunday today; **le journal d'a.** today's paper; **ce sera tout pour a.** that's all for today; **(d')a. en huit/en quinze** a week/two weeks today, *Br* today week/fortnight; **il y a a. huit jours** a week ago today; **ce n'est pas d'a. que je la connais** I have known her for a long time; *F* **c'est pour a. ou pour demain?** I/we haven't got all day! **(b)** (*à l'heure actuelle*) nowadays, these days; **les jeunes gens d'a.** (the) young people (of) today; **l'Europe d'a.** modern-day *or* present-day Europe, the Europe of today
aulne [on] *nm* (*arbre*) alder
aulx *voir* = **ail**
aumône [omon] *nf* alms; **demander l'a.** to beg *or* ask for charity; **faire l'a. à qn** to give money to sb; **donner qch en a. à qn** to give sb sth out of charity; **réduit à l'a.** reduced to begging; *Fig* **faire l'a. d'un regard à qn** to spare sb a glance, to condescend *or* deign to look at sb
aumônier [omonje] *nm* chaplain; **aumônier militaire** army chaplain
aune¹ [on] *nm* (*arbre*) alder
aune² *nf Arch* ell (1.188 m); *Vielli Fig* **figure longue d'une a.** face as long as a fiddle
auparavant [oparavɑ̃] *adv* before(hand), previously; **a. il faut s'assurer de ...** first we/you must make sure of ...; **l'année a.** the preceding year, the year before; **comme a.** as before; **mais a. nous devons parler** but we must have a talk first *or* beforehand
auprès [oprɛ] *prép* **a. de** **(a)** (*près de*) close to, (close) by, beside, near; **tout a. de qn/qch** close to *or* beside sb/sth; **il a toujours une garde-malade a. de lui** he always has a nurse with him *or* at hand
(b) (*indiquant une relation*) **agir a. de qn** to use one's influence with sb; **se renseigner a. de qn** to ask sb; **se renseigner a. d'un service** to enquire at a department; **être bien a. de qn** to be in favour with sb, to be in sb's good books; **trouver grâce a. de qn** to be in favour with sb, to find favour with sb; **je sais que je passe pour un idiot a. d'eux** I know that they take me for an idiot; **ambassadeur a. du roi de Suède** ambassador to the King of Sweden; **avocat a. du tribunal** advocate attached to the tribunal
(c) (*en comparaison de*) compared with, in comparison with, next to
auquel [okɛl] *voir* = **lequel**
aura [ɔra] *nf* aura; *Méd* **a. épileptique** epileptic aura
auréole [ɔreɔl] *nf* **(a)** (*de saint, de la lune*) halo; (*du soleil*) corona; *Fig* **il pare son épouse d'une a.** he puts his wife on a pedestal; **entouré de l'a. de la gloire/réussite** bathed in glory/flushed with success **(b)** (*trace*) ring, mark; **le tableau a laissé une a. sur le mur** the picture has left a ring on the wall; **son matelas est couvert d'auréoles** his mattress is covered in dirty marks; **détachant qui ne laisse pas d'a.** stain remover that doesn't leave rings
auréoler [ɔreɔle] **1** *vt* (*d'un peintre*) to surround with a halo; *Fig* to exalt, to glorify; **elle est auréolée de génie** she positively radiates genius **2 s'auréoler** *vpr* to be crowned (**de** with)
auréomycine [ɔreɔmisin] *nf Méd* aureomycin
auriculaire [ɔrikylɛr] **1** *adj* (*confession etc*) auricular; *Anat* **appendice a.** auricular appendix; *Mil etc* **protecteur a.** ear protector **2** *nm* **l'a.** the little finger
auricule [ɔrikyl] *nf* **(a)** *Anat* (*du cœur*) auricle; **a. de l'oreille** lower lobe of the ear **(b)** *Bot, Zool* auricula, auricle; (*de mollusque*) auricula
auriculothérapie [ɔrikyloterapi] *nf Méd* aural acupuncture

aurifère [ɔrifɛr] *adj* gold-bearing; **champ** *ou* **gisement a.** goldfield
aurifier [ɔrifje] *vt* (*une dent*) to put a gold filling in
Aurigny [ɔriɲi] *nm* Alderney; **vache d'A.** Alderney (cow)
auriol [ɔriɔl] *nm* (*oiseau*) oriole
aurique [ɔrik] *adj Naut* **voile a.** gaffsail; **gréement a.** gaff rig; **à gréement a.** gaff-rigged
aurochs [ɔrɔks] *nm* aurochs, wild ox
aurore [ɔrɔr] **1** *nf* **(a)** dawn, daybreak, break of day; **aux aurores** at the crack of dawn; **l'a. commence à paraître** *ou* **à poindre** dawn is breaking; *Fig* **l'a. de la civilisation** the dawn of civilization **(b)** (*papillon*) orange tip **2** *adj inv* (saffron *or* golden) yellow
▶ **aurore**: **a. australe** aurora australis, southern lights; **a. boréale** aurora borealis, northern lights; **a. polaire** aurora polaris, polar light
auscultation [ɔskyltasjɔ̃] *nf Méd* auscultation
ausculter [ɔskylte] *vt Méd* (*patient etc*) to auscultate, to sound
auspices [ɔspis] *nmpl* **(a)** (*présage*) auspice, omen; **mauvais a.** ill *or* bad omen; **l'année commence sous d'heureux/de fâcheux a.** the year begins auspiciously/inauspiciously **(b)** (*appui*) **sous les a. de qn** under the auspices of sb
aussi [osi] [①B55,A3] **1** *adv* **(a)** (*également*) also, too; **c'est a. ce que je pense** that's what I think too; **vous venez a.** you are coming too; **elle fait du grec, et a. du latin** she's doing Greek and Latin too; **je suis fatigué – toi a.?** I'm tired – you too?; **gardez a. ceux-là** keep those too, keep those as well; **moi a.** me too, so am I/so can I/so do I/so shall I/so did I/so was I/*etc*; **et moi a. je suis peintre** I'm a painter too *or* as well; **j'écoute du classique a. bien que du jazz** I listen to classical music as well as jazz, I listen to (both) classical music and jazz

(b) [①A5,B] (*tellement*) so; **après avoir attendu a. longtemps** after waiting so long *or* for such a long time; **je ne pensais pas que tu étais a. sensible** I didn't think you were so *or* that sensitive; **une a. bonne affaire, ça ne se manque pas** a deal as good as that shouldn't be passed up; **un homme a. travailleur que vous** a man as hardworking as you; **d'a. belles journées** such nice days; **avez-vous jamais entendu une symphonie a. bizarre?** have you ever heard such a peculiar symphony?

(c) (*dans les phrases comparatives*) as; **pas a. gros que** not so big as, not as big as; **il est a. grand que son frère** he is as tall as his brother; **tout a. au sud/à l'est que Paris** as far south/east as Paris; **ma méthode est tout a. bonne que la vôtre** my method is just *or* every bit as good as yours; **on pourrait a. bien rester là ce soir** we might as well stay here this evening; **je le connais a. peu que son frère** I don't know him any better than I know his brother

(d) (*quelque*) however; **a. bizarre que cela soit/semble** however odd it may be/seem, (as) strange as it my be/seem

2 *conj* [①B59,12,7] therefore, consequently, so; **la vie est chère ici, a. nous devons** *ou* **devons-nous économiser** the cost of living is high here, so we have to economize; **il ne regarde pas où il met les pieds, a. il tombe tout le temps** he doesn't watch where he's going, so he falls over all the time; *F* **a., c'est ta faute** after all, it's your fault
aussitôt [osito] **1** *adv* immediately, straight away, at once; **a. dit, a. fait** no sooner said than done; **a. l'argent reçu je vous paierai** as soon as I get the money I will pay you; **a. après** immediately after; **a. après son retour je suis parti** as soon as *or* the minute he returned I left **2** *conj* [①B29-30,11] **a. que +** *ind* as soon as; **il se repentit de ses paroles a. qu'il les eut prononcées** he regretted his words as soon as he had said them; **a. que le train est parti, je me suis rendu compte que ...** no sooner had the train left than I realized ...
austère [ostɛr] *adj* (*vie*) austere; (*jeûne*) strict; (*style*) severe, austere; (*expression*) stern; (*robe*) plain, severe
austèrement [ostɛrmɑ̃] *adv* austerely; **elle s'habille a.** she dresses very austerely *or* plainly
austérité [osterite] *nf* **(a)** austerity; **vivre dans l'a.** to live in austerity; **la période d'a.** the days of austerity; **mesures d'a.** austerity measures **(b) austérités** asceticism, mortification of the flesh
austral, -als *ou* **-aux** [ostral, -o] *adj* (*hemisphere*) southern
Australasie [ostralazi] *nf* Australasia
australasien, -ienne [ostralazjɛ̃, -jɛn] **1** *adj* Australasian **2** *n* **A.** Australasian
Australie [ostrali] *nf* Australia
australien, -ienne [ostraljɛ̃, -jɛn] **1** *adj* Australian **2** *n* **A.** Australian
austro-hongrois, -oise [ostroɔ̃grwa, -waz] *Hist* **1** *adj* Austro-Hungarian **2** *n* **A.** Austro-Hungarian
autant [otɑ̃] *adv* **(a)** (*intensité*) **je ne savais pas qu'il avait a. souffert** I did not know he had suffered so *or* as much; **je ne le savais pas a. respecté** I did not know he was so greatly respected; **travailles-tu toujours a.?** (*qu'aujourd'hui*) do you always work so *or* as *or* this hard?; (*qu'avant*) are you working as hard as ever?; **a. en emporte le vent** it's all idle talk; **a. vous l'aimez, a. il vous hait** he hates you as much as you love him; **tout a.** quite as much; **il m'en veut, mais je lui en veux tout a.** he's angry with me, but I'm just as angry with him; **encore a.** as much again

(b) (*quantité*) **tout a.** quite as much; (*de choses individuelles*) quite as many; **encore a.** as much/many again; **je n'en ai pas assez, remettez m'en encore a.** I don't have enough, give me as much/many again *or* the same again; **tous les salariés ont été augmentés d'a.** all the employees received the same pay rise, everybody's salary went up by the same amount; **le coût de la vie a augmenté de 5% mais les salaires n'ont pas augmenté d'a.** the cost of living has increased by 5% but salaries have not risen accordingly *or* have not risen in line; **a. pour moi!** I stand corrected!

(c) (*de même*) the same, likewise; **on ne peut pas en dire a. de tout le monde** you can't say as much *or* the same for everybody; **essaie un peu d'en faire a.** try to do the same; **peux-tu en dire a.?** can you say as much?

(d) ils disent qu'ils réfléchissent, a. dire qu'ils ont accepté they say they're thinking about it, in other words they've accepted; **j'aime a. vous dire que je n'apprécie pas vos manières!** I don't mind telling you that I don't care for your manners!; **j'aime a. vous le dire tout de suite** I might as well tell you right away; **j'aimerais a. aller au cinéma** I would just as soon go to the cinema; **a. le faire tout de suite** better do it right away; **a. ne rien faire du tout** we might as well do nothing at all; **a. rester ici** we may as well stay here; **a. dire que ...** one might as well say that ...; **a. dire que c'était difficile/que je n'étais pas content** as you can imagine, it was difficult/I wasn't happy

(e) a. que as much as; (*de choses individuelles*) as many as; **a. que possible** as far as possible; **sois à l'heure a. que possible** do your best to be on time; **faites a. que vous pourrez** do as much as you can; **(pour) a. que je sache** as far as I know, to the best of my knowledge; **j'en sais a. que toi** your guess is as good as mine, I know as much (about it) as you do; **c'est a. ta faute que la mienne** it is as much your fault as mine, you're as much to blame as I am; **il est a. à craindre qu'elle** he is as much to be feared as she is; *F* **a. ça qu'autre chose** it's all the same to me; **a. que j'en puis(se) juger** as far as I can judge; **pour a. qu'il est en mon pouvoir** to the best of my ability; **a. que faire se peut** as much as possible, as much as can be; **je me suis dépêché a. que faire se peut** I hurried as fast as I could

(f) a. de as much, so much; (*de choses individuelles*) as many, so many; **a. de filles que de garçons** as many girls as boys; **ils ont a. de terrain/d'amis que vous** they have as much land/as many friends as you; *Litt* **ce sont a. de (voleurs** *etc*) they are nothing better than (a pack of thieves *etc*); **ce sera a. de moins à payer** it will be so much the less to pay; **c'est a. de gagné** that's so much gained, that's so much to the good

(g) d'a. (plus) que especially *or* particularly since; **d'a. plus/moins (que)** all the more/less (because); **j'en suis surpris, d'a. plus qu'au fond il est honnête** I am all the more surprised because basically he is honest; **elle travaille d'a. mieux qu'elle se sait surveillée** she works all the better for knowing that someone's keeping an eye on her; **cela vous sera d'a. plus facile que vous êtes jeune** it will be all the easier for you since you are young

(h) pour a. for all that; **j'ai plus de travail mais ce n'est pas pour a. que j'ai plus d'argent** just because I have more work doesn't mean that I have more money; **elle est très riche, elle n'est pas plus heureuse pour a.** she's very rich, but she isn't any the happier for it *or* but that doesn't mean she's any the happier; **elle ne s'en fait pas pour a.** she doesn't worry about it
autarcie [otarsi] *nf Pol* autarky; **une communauté qui vit en a.** a self-sufficient community
autarcique [otarsik] *adj Pol* autarkic
autel [otɛl] *nm aussi Fig* altar; **maître a.** high altar; **a. latéral** side altar; **nappe d'a.** altar cloth; **pierre d'a.** altar stone *or* table; **tableau d'a.** altarpiece; **conduire sa fille à l'a.** to give one's daughter away (in marriage); **suivre qn à l'a.** to walk up the aisle with sb, to marry sb
auteur [otœr] *nm* **(a)** (*de livre*) author, writer; (*de chanson*) composer; (*de tableau*) painter; **droit d'a.** copyright; **droits d'a.** royalties; **un droit d'a. de 10%** a 10% royalty; *Fig* **citer ses auteurs** to quote one's authorities **(b)** (*responsable*)

author; (*d'une race*) founder; (*d'un crime*) perpetrator; (*d'un projet*) promoter, sponsor; *Jur* principal; **a. d'un accident** party at fault in an accident; *Fig* **être l'a. de la ruine de qn** to be the cause of sb's downfall; **qui est l'a. de cette plaisanterie?** whose idea was that joke?; *Hum* **je vous présente l'a. de mes jours** this is my beloved father/mother

authenticité [otɑ̃tisite] *nf* authenticity; **on conteste l'a. de ce tableau** the authenticity of this painting is in doubt

authentification [otɑ̃tifikasjɔ̃] *nf* authentication; **cachet d'a.** approved stamp

authentifier [otɑ̃tifje] *vt* to authenticate

authentique [otɑ̃tik] *adj* authentic, genuine; **c'est un fait a.** it's a true fact; **bourgogne a.** genuine burgundy; *Jur* **acte a.** instrument drawn up by a solicitor; **copie a.** certified copy; *F* **je ne te mens pas, c'est a.!, c'est ce qu'il a dit!** I'm not lying to you, it's true! that's what he said!

authentiquement [otɑ̃tikmɑ̃] *adv* authentically, genuinely

authentiquer [otɑ̃tike] *vt Vieilli* (*document etc*) to authenticate, to certify, to legalize

autisme [otism] *nm Psy* autism

autiste [otist] *adj, n Psy* autistic

autistique [otistik] *adj Psy* autistic

auto [oto] **1** *nf* (motor) car; **les autos tamponneuses** dodgems, bumper cars; **jouer avec des petites autos** to play with toy cars **2** *adj inv* **assurance a.** car insurance; **budget a.** car budget

auto- *préf* auto-, self-

auto-accusation *nf* self-accusation

auto-adhésif, -ive *adj* self-adhesive; **bande auto-adhésive** adhesive tape

auto-allumage *nm* running-on, self-ignition, post-ignition

auto-amorçage *nm* automatic *or* self priming

auto-antigène *nm Physiol* autoantigen

autoberge [otobɛrʒ] *nf* = highway running along a river embankment

autobiographie [otobjografi] *nf* autobiography

autobiographique [otobjografik] *adj* autobiographical

autobronzant [otobrɔ̃zɑ̃] **1** *adj* self-tanning **2** *nm* self-tanning cream; *F* fake tan

autobus [otobys] *nm* bus

autocar [otokar] *nm* coach, bus; **a. de luxe** luxury coach

autocariste [otokarist] *nm* coach tour operator

autocassable [otokasabl] *adj* **ampoule a.** easy-to-open *or* break-open phial

auto-censure *nf* self-censorship; **faire de l'a.** to practise self-censorship

autocensurer(s') [sotosɑ̃syre] *vpr* to practise self-censorship

autochenille [otoʃnij] *nf* half-track vehicle

autochrome [otokrom] *adj* (*pellicule, film*) colour

autochtone [otɔkton] **1** *adj* aboriginal, *Can* native; *Géol* **terrain a.** autochthonous rock **2** *n* native, *Admin* non-alien, *Spéc* autochthon; *Can* **Conseil national des autochtones du Canada** Native Council of Canada; *Hum* **les autochtones ne sont pas très accueillants** the natives aren't very friendly

autocinétique [otosinetik] *adj* autokinetic

autoclave [otoklav] **1** *adj* hermetically-sealed, pressure-sealed; **marmite a.** autoclave, digester **2** *nm* **(a)** *Ch, Ind* **a.** autoclave, digester **(b)** *Méd* sterilizer **(c)** *Culin Vieilli* pressure cooker

autocode [otokɔd] *nm Ordinat* assembly language

autocollant [otokɔlɑ̃] **1** *adj* self-adhesive; (*enveloppe*) self-sealing **2** *nm* sticker

autocommutateur [otokɔmytatœr] *nm Ordinat* autoswitch; **a. privé** PBX, private branch exchange

autoconduction [otokɔ̃dyksjɔ̃] *nf Électron* mutual induction

autoconsommation [otokɔ̃sɔmasjɔ̃] *nf* subsistence farming; **économie d'a.** subsistence economy

autocopiant [otokɔpjɑ̃] *adj* self-copying

autocopie [otokɔpi] *nf* (*de documents*) duplicating

autocopier [otokɔpje] *vt* (*pr sub, impf* **n. autocopiions, v. autocopiiez**) to duplicate

autocorrecteur [otokɔrɛktœr] *adj Ordinat* self-correcting

autocorrection [otokɔrɛksjɔ̃] *nf* self-correction; **faire de l'a.** to do one's own correction

auto-couchettes *adj inv* **train a.** ≈ motorail train

autocrate [otokrat] *n Pol* autocrat

autocratie [otokrasi] *nf Pol* autocracy

autocratique [otokratik] *adj* autocratic

autocratiquement [otokratikmɑ̃] *adv* autocratically

autocritique [otokritik] *nf* self-criticism; **faire son a.** to criticize oneself

autocuiseur [otokɥizœr] *nm* pressure cooker

autodafé [otodafe] *nm Hist* auto-da-fé; **faire un a. de livres rares** to burn rare books

autodébrayage [otodebrɛjaʒ] *nm Aut* automatic clutch

autodéfense [otodefɑ̃s] *nf* self-defence

autodestructeur, -trice [otodɛstryktœr, -tris] *adj* self-destructive

autodestruction [otodɛstryksjɔ̃] *nf* self-destruction

autodétermination [otodetɛrminasjɔ̃] *nf Pol* self-determination

autodidacte [otodidakt] **1** *adj* self-taught, self-educated **2** *n* autodidact

autodrome [otodrom] *nm* motor-racing track; (*pour les essais*) car-testing track

auto-école *pl* **auto-écoles** *nf* school of motoring, driving school

auto-érotique *adj Psy* autoerotic

auto-érotisme *nm Psy* autoeroticism

auto-fécondation *nf Bot* self-pollination

autofinancé [otofinɑ̃se] *adj Fin* financed from cashflow

autofinancement [otofinɑ̃smɑ̃] *nm Fin* self-financing, financing from cashflow

autofinancer (s') [sotofinɑ̃se] *vpr Fin* to be self-financing

autofocus [otofɔkys] **1** *Phot nm* autofocus **2** *adj* autofocus; **appareil a.** autofocus camera

autogène [otoʒɛn] *adj* **(a)** *Physiol* **faire du training a.** to learn how to relax **(b)** *Tech* **soudure a.** autogenous weld

autogenèse [otoʒənɛz] *nf Biol* autogenesis

autogéré [otoʒere] *adj* self-managed

autogestion [otoʒɛstjɔ̃] *nf* self-management

autogestionnaire [otoʒɛstjɔnɛr] *adj* self-managing

autogire [otoʒir] *nm Av* autogyro

autograissage [otogrɛsaʒ] *nm MecE* self-lubrication

autograisseur, -euse [otogrɛsœr, -øz] *adj* (*roulement, palier etc*) self-lubricating

autographe [otograf] **1** *adj* autograph; (*lettre etc*) handwritten **2** *nm* autograph

autogreffe [otogrɛf] *nf Chir* autograft

autoguidage [otogidaʒ] *nm* **(retour par) a.** homing; **cellule d'a.** homing eye

autoguidé [otogide] *adj* (*missile*) self-directional, homing

auto-immune *adj Méd* autoimmune

auto-immunisation *nf Méd* autoimmunization

auto-induction *nf Électron* self-induction

auto-intoxication *nf* autointoxication, autotoxaemia

autolubrifiant [otolybrifjɑ̃] *adj* self-lubricating

autolubrification [otolybrifikasjɔ̃] *nf* self-lubrication

autolyse [otoliz] *nf* autolysis

auto-marché *pl* **auto-marchés** *nm* car mart

automate [otɔmat] *nm* [①**A13,5**] automaton, robot; **marcher comme un a.** to walk like a robot; **vivre comme un a.** to live like a automaton

automation [otɔmajɔ̃] *nf* automation

automatique [otɔmatik] **1** *adj* (*action*) automatic; (*appareil*) self-acting; **'attention à la fermeture a. des portières'** 'danger, automatically closing doors'; **à mise en marche a.** self-starting; **réflexe a.** automatic reflex; *Méd* involuntary reflex; **payer l'électricité par prélèvement a.** to pay one's electricity bill by direct debit; *F* **votre dossier est envoyé à Paris, c'est a.** your file has been sent to Paris, that's the usual procedure; **il va vouloir te voir, c'est a.** he'll want to see you, it's a dead cert

2 *nm* **(a)** (*téléphone*) automatic; **il faut passer par l'a.** you have to go through the switchboard

(b) (*pistolet*) automatic

3 *nf* **(a)** *Tech* automatics, automation **(b)** *Aut* automatic

automatiquement [otɔmatikmɑ̃] *adv* automatically; **votre nom est inséré a. dans le fichier** your name is automatically entered in the file; *F* **si vous ne payez pas vos impôts, vous agissez a. contre la loi** by not paying your tax you are automatically breaking the law

automatisable [otɔmatizabl] *adj* automatable

automatisation [otɔmatizasjɔ̃] *nf* automation

automatiser [otɔmatize] *vt* to automate

automatisme [otɔmatism] *nm* **(a)** *Physiol, Méd* automatism; **agir par a.** to act automatically; **fermer la porte à double tour est devenu un a.** double-locking the door has become automatic **(b)** (*fonctionnement*) automatic working *or* functioning **(c)** (*dispositif*) automatic device

automédication [otomedikasjɔ̃] *nf* self-medication

automitrailleuse [otomitrajøz] *nf* armoured car

automnal, -ale, -aux, -ales [otɔ(m)nal, -o] *adj* autumnal

automne [otɔn] *nm* [①**A6,d,v**] autumn, *Am* fall; **l'équinoxe d'a.** the autumnal equinox; **en a., à l'a.** in autumn; **une soirée d'a.** an autumn evening; *Fig* **à l'a. de sa vie** in the autumn of his/her life

automobile [otomɔbil] **1** *adj* **(a)** (*à moteur*) self-propelling, automotive; **voiture a.** motor vehicle; **canot a.** motor boat **(b)** (*relatif à la voiture*) **club a.** automobile club; **assurance**

a. car *or* motor insurance; **industrie a.** automobile *or* car industry; **accessoires automobiles** car accessories **2** *nf* (motor) car, *Am* automobile; *Mil* **a. blindée** armoured car; **salon de l'a.** motor show; **l'a. marche bien en France** the car industry is doing well in France

automobilisme [otomɔbilism] *nm* motoring

automobiliste [otomɔbilist] *n* motorist

automoteur, -trice [otomɔtœr, -tris] **1** *adj* (*véhicule*) self-propelling, automotive; (*valve etc*) self-acting; **train a.** multiple unit (Diesel) train **2** *nf* **automotrice** railcar **3** *nm Naut* self-propelled barge

automutilation [otomytilasjɔ̃] *nf* self-mutilation

autoneige [otonɛʒ] *nf Can* snowmobile

autonettoyant [otonetwajɑ̃] *adj* **four a.** self-cleaning oven

autonome [otɔnɔm] *adj* autonomous, self-governing; (*état, région etc*) independent; (*appareil*) self-contained; (*personne*) self-sufficient; *Ordinat* **calculateur a.** stand-alone (computer)

autonomie [otɔnɔmi] *nf* (**a**) *Pol* autonomy, self-government (**b**) (*de personne*) self-sufficiency; **ma fille veut avoir son a.** my daughter wants her independence (**c**) *Av* cruising radius, range; (*de voiture*) range; **l'avion a deux heures/800km d'a.** the aircraft has a range of two hours/800km (**d**) (*de batterie*) battery life, life

autonomiste [otɔnɔmist] *n Pol* autonomist

autopalpation [otopalpasjɔ̃] *nf Méd* self-examination

autopont [otopɔ̃] *nm* flyover

autoportant [otopɔrtɑ̃], **autoporteur[1], -euse** [otopɔrtœr, -øz] *adj Archit* self-supporting

autoporteur[2] [otopɔrtœr] *adj Aut* integral, integrated; (*carrosserie*) frameless

autoportrait [otopɔrtrɛ] *nm* self-portrait

autopropulsé [otoprɔpylse] *adj* self-propelled

autopropulsion [otoprɔpylsjɔ̃] *nf* self-propulsion

autopsie [otɔpsi] *nf* autopsy; **a. (cadavérique)** post mortem (examination); **pratiquer une a.** to carry out a post mortem (examination); *Fig* **faire l'a. d'une œuvre** to examine a work critically

autopsier [otopsje] *vt* to perform a post mortem (examination) on, to autopsy

autopunition [otopynisjɔ̃] *nf Psy* self-punishment

autoradio [otoradjo] *nm* car radio

autorafraîchissement [otorafrɛʃismɑ̃] *nm Ordinat* auto-refresh

autorail [otoraj] *nm* railcar

auto-régénérateur, -trice [otoreʒeneratœr, -tris] *adj Nucl* (*réacteur etc*) breeder

autoréglage [otoreglaʒ] *nm Tech* self-regulation

autorégulateur, -trice [otoregylatœr, -tris] **1** *adj* self-regulating **2** *nm* self-acting regulator

autorégulation [otoregylasjɔ̃] *nf* self-regulation

autoreverse [otorəvɛrs] **1** *adj* **appareil a.** auto-reverse **2** *nm* auto-reverse

autorisation [otɔrizasjɔ̃] *nf* (**a**) authorization, authority, permission; **donner à qn l'a. de faire qch** to authorize sb to do sth, to give sb permission to do sth; **demander l'a. de faire qch** to ask permission to do sth; *surtout Mil, Admin etc* to request authority to do sth; **je n'ai pas eu l'a. de sortir ce soir** I didn't get permission to go out tonight; **il nous manque encore l'a. du conseil municipal pour ouvrir le restaurant** we still need the council's authorization to open the restaurant; **avoir l'a. de bâtir** to have planning permission (**b**) (*document*) licence; **montrez-moi votre a.** show me your permit

▶ **autorisation**: *Ordinat* **a. d'accès** access authorization; **a. de dédouanement** customs clearance authorization; *TV, Cin* **a. d'exploitation** rights; **a. d'exporter** export permit; *Admin* **a. de sortie du territoire** = parental authorization for a minor to travel abroad; *Av* **a. de vol** flight clearance

autorisé [otɔrize] *adj* (**a**) (*qualifié*) authorized; **tenir qch d'une source autorisée** to have sth from an authoritative source; **les milieux autorisés** (the) official circles (**b**) (*permis*) permitted, permissible, allowed; **tournure autorisée par l'usage** turn of phrase sanctioned *or* hallowed by usage; **il se croit tout a.** he thinks he can get away with anything (**c**) (*étalon*) approved

autoriser [otɔrize] **1** *vt* (**a**) **a. qn à faire qch** to authorize *or* permit sb to do sth, to give sb the authority to do sth; **je vous autorise à sortir de table** you may have my permission to leave the table; **l'alcool ne lui est pas autorisé** he is not allowed (to drink) alcohol; **a. la pêche** to allow fishing

(**b**) (*justifier*) (*une action*) to justify, to authorize, to sanction; **ces découvertes autorisent à penser que ...** these discoveries entitle us to believe that ...; **rien ne nous autorise à le croire** nothing entitles us to believe that

2 s'autoriser *vpr* **je m'autorise de ces résultats pour ...** on the basis of these results I feel entitled to ...

autoritaire [otɔritɛr] *adj* authoritative, *Pej* authoritarian

autoritairement [otɔritɛrmɑ̃] *adv* authoritatively, *Pej* in an authoritarian manner

autoritarisme [otɔritarism] *nm* authoritarianism

autorité [otɔrite] *nf* (**a**) (*domination*) authority; **exercer son a. sur qn** to exercise authority over sb; **il n'a aucune a. sur ses élèves** he can't keep order *or* he has no control over his pupils; **a. parentale** parental authority; **être sous l'a. de qn** to be under sb's authority; **il veut tout emporter d'a.** he wants his own way in everything, *F* he wants to run the whole show; **agir de pleine a.** to act with full powers; **faire qch d'a.** to do sth on one's own (responsibility), to take it upon oneself to do sth; **de sa propre a.** on one's own authority; **territoire soumis à l'a. de ...** area within the jurisdiction of ...; *Jur* **l'a. de la loi** the force of the law

(**b**) *poids* authority; **avoir de l'a. sur qn** to have influence *or* authority over sb; **faire a. en qch** to be an authority on sth; **il fait a. en matière de physique nucléaire** he is an authority on nuclear physics; **ce livre fait a. dans le milieu** this book is taken as the authority here; *Jur* **cas d'espèce qui font a.** leading cases; **parler avec a.** to speak authoritatively *or* with authority

(**c**) (*gouvernement*) **l'a.** the authorities; **les représentants de l'a.** the representatives of authority; **l'a. fiscale** the tax authorities; **les autorités** the authorities, the powers that be; **les autorités locales/religieuses** the local/religious authorities; **autorités portuaires** port authorities

(**d**) (*personne*) **citer une a.** to quote an authority; **c'est une a., elle est très écoutée** she's an authority, people take a lot of notice of what she says

autoroute [otorut] *nf* (**a**) *Aut* motorway, *US* freeway, *US* thruway; **prendre l'a.** to take the motorway; **a. à péage** toll motorway, *US* turnpike (road) (**b**) *Ordinat* **a. de l'information** information (super)highway; **a. interactive** interactive highway; **a. électronique** electronic highway, superhighway

autoroutier, -ière [otorutje, -jɛr] *adj* **système a.** motorway *or US* freeway system *or* network

autosatisfaction [otosatisfaksjɔ̃] *nf* self-satisfaction

auto-stop *nm* hitch-hiking, *F* hitching; **faire de l'a.** to hitch-hike, *F* to hitch, to thumb a lift; **prendre qn en a.** to pick up a hitch-hiker; **je ne voyage qu'en a.** I hitch-hike everywhere I go; **faire le tour de l'Europe en a.** to hitch-hike around Europe

auto-stoppeur, -euse *pl* **auto-stoppeurs, -euses** *n* hitch-hiker, *F* hitcher

autosuffisance [otosyfizɑ̃s] *nf Écon* self-sufficiency

autosuggestion [otosygʒɛstjɔ̃] *nf* auto-suggestion

autotest [ototɛst] *nm Ordinat* self-test

autotester(s') [sototɛste] *vpr Ordinat* to self-test, to auto-test

autour[1] [otur] **1** *adv* around; **une ville avec des murs tout a.** a town with walls all around it **2** *prép* [**①A64**] **a. de** around, *esp Br* round, about; **nous nous sommes assis a. de la table** we sat down round the table; **discuter qch a. d'un verre** to discuss sth over a drink; **enrouler qch a. de son cou** to coil sth round one's neck; **ce qui se passe a. de nous** what is going on around *or* round about us; *F* **il a a. de vingt ans** he is (somewhere) about twenty, he's twentyish; **tourner a. de la question** *ou* **du pot** to beat about the bush; **tout a. de ...** all around ...

autour[2] *nm* (*oiseau*) **a.** (**des palombes**) goshawk

autovaccin [otovaksɛ̃] *nm Méd* autovaccine

autre [otr] [**①A36-7**,e; **B14-15**,B] **1** *adj* (**a**) other; **l'a. côté** the other side; **une a. semaine/un a. jour** another week/another day; **une a. fois** another time; **toute a. femme aurait agi de la même façon** any other woman would have acted in the same way; **les choux et autres légumes** cabbages and (all) other vegetables; **des choux et d'autres légumes** cabbages and some other vegetables; **tous les autres verbes que ceux en -er** all verbs other than those in -er; **je ne pourrai pas y aller, entre autres raisons je suis à court d'argent** I can't go, for one thing I'm short of money; **l'a. monde** the next world; **sans faire d'a. observation** without making any further observation; **sans a. perte de temps** without further loss of time; **l'a. lundi** the other Monday; (*prochain*) Monday week; **je l'ai vu l'a. jour/soir** I saw him the other day/evening

(**b**) **vous autres hommes vous êtes seuls coupables** it is you men alone who are to blame; **nous autres Anglais** we English (people); **vous autres** you others, all of you; **eh, vous autres! venez par ici!** hey, you lot! come over here!

(**c**) (*second*) **il se croit un a. Napoléon** he thinks he is a second *or* another Napoleon; **mon frère, c'est un a. moi-même** my brother is just another me (**d**) (*différent*) other, different; **donnez-moi un a. torchon** give me another cloth; *Prov* **autres temps autres mœurs** other days other ways; **il est a. que je ne le pensais** he is different from what I thought; **elle est devenue a.** she has changed, she has become different; **cela a fait de lui un a. homme** it made a new man of him; **une tout a. femme** quite a different woman; **j'ai des idées autres** I have different ideas, my ideas are different; **être d'une a. opinion** to think otherwise *or* differently

(**e**) **a. chose** (*en plus*) something else; (*en remplacement*) something different; **j'ai a. chose d'important à vous dire** I have something else of importance to tell you; **avez-vous a. chose à faire?** have you anything else to do?; **ce qu'il éprouve pour elle, ce n'est pas a. chose que de l'amour** what he feels for her is nothing other than love; *F* **a. chose, ma mère est partie hier** not only that, but my mother left yesterday; **c'est tout a. chose!** that's quite a different thing!; **une chose est de parler, a. chose est d'agir** it's one thing to talk, it's another to act; **a. part** somewhere else

2 *pron* (**a**) **les défauts des autres** the failings of others; **d'autres vous diront que ...** others *or* other people will tell you that ...; **tous les autres sont là** all the others are there; **encore un a.** one more, another (one); **encore bien d'autres** many more besides

(**b**) **cela peut arriver d'un jour à l'a.** it may happen any day; **je l'attends d'un moment à l'a.** I expect him any moment; **je le vois de temps à a.** I see him from time to time *or* now and again *or* now and then; **un jour ou l'a.** one day or another, one of these days; **d'un bout à l'a.** from one end to the other, from start to finish, from end to end; **il a menti d'un bout à l'a.** he lied from start to finish

(**c**) **la science est une chose, l'art en est une a.** science is one thing, art is another; **il parle d'une façon et agit d'une a.** he says one thing and does another

(**d**) **l'un et l'a.** both; **les uns et les autres** (*tout le monde*) all (and sundry), one and all; (*deux groupes*) both parties; **il a parlé aux uns et aux autres** he spoke to them all; **l'un et l'a. ont été punis** both were punished; **il passe son temps chez l'un ou l'a.** he spends his time with one friend or another

(**e**) **l'un ou l'a.** either; **c'est l'un ou l'autre!** it's either or, it's one thing or the other; **c'est tout l'un ou tout l'a.** there is no happy medium, it's either one extreme or the other; **ni l'un ni l'a.** neither; **ni l'un ni l'a. ne sont venus** neither of them came; **je ne les connais ni l'un ni l'a.** I don't know either of them; **je n'ai vu ni les uns ni les autres** I didn't see any of them

(**f**) **l'un ..., l'a. ...** one ..., the other ...; **l'un dit ceci, l'a. dit cela** one says this and the other says that; **les uns ..., les autres ...** some ..., others ..., some ..., some ...; **ils s'en allèrent, les uns par ci les autres par là** they went off some one way, some another; **sans prendre parti ni pour les uns ni pour les autres** without taking either side; **l'un ne va pas sans l'a.** you can't have one without the other, the two go hand in hand; **qui voit l'un voit l'a.** there's no difference between them, you can't tell the two apart; **l'un vaut l'a.** there's no difference between them, the one's just as good/bad as the other

(**g**) **l'un l'a.** each other, one another; **on va s'aider l'un l'a.** we'll help each other; **elles se moquent les unes des autres** they make fun of each other; **vivre l'un pour l'a.** to live for each other; **aller l'un à côté de l'a.** to walk side by side; **ils dépendent l'un de l'a.** they depend on each other; **l'un auprès de l'a., auprès l'un de l'a.** near each other, near one another

(**h**) **l'un dans l'a., il se fait mille francs** with one thing and another he earns a thousand francs; **une année dans l'a.** taking one year with another

(**i**) **d'a.** else; **il y a quelque chose d'a. dans la boîte? – non, rien d'autre** is there anything else in the box? – no, nothing else; **il n'y en a pas d'a.** there's no other; **parler de choses et d'autres** to talk about this and that; **personne d'a. ne le sait** nobody else knows; **quelqu'un d'a.** somebody else; **je ne demande rien d'a.** I don't ask for anything more, I ask for nothing more; **c'est de la stupidité et rien d'a.** it's stupidity and nothing else, it's nothing but stupidity, it's sheer stupidity; **que pouvait-il faire d'a.?** what else could he do?; **que pouvaient-ils faire d'a. que de l'inviter?** what else could they do but invite him?; **qui d'a. que lui aurait pu le faire?** who else (but him) could have done it?; (**dites cela**) **à d'autres!** who do you think you're kidding?, get away!; *F* **j'en ai vu bien d'autres** I've been through worse than that

(**j**) (*personne*) someone *or* somebody else; **adressez-vous à un a.** ask someone else *or* somebody else; **je l'ai pris pour un a.** I mistook him for someone else; **c'était un touriste comme un a.** he was just an ordinary tourist; **c'est une raison comme une a.** it's as good a reason as any; **c'est un homme pas comme les autres** he is not like other men; **peut m'importe ce que pensent les autres** I don't care what anyone else thinks *or* what other people think; *F* **comme dit l'a.** as the saying goes, as they say; *F* **dis donc! t'as vu l'a.?** God! did you see him/her there?; *F* **et l'a. qui fait encore son cirque!** and that one making his/her usual scene!; **il n'est pas plus bête qu'un a.** he is no more stupid than anyone else; **nul a. ne l'a vu** no one else *or* nobody else saw him; **tout a. le comprendrait** anyone else would understand it; **il y avait des Écossais, entre autres** there were some Scots, among others

autrefois [otrəfwa] *adv* formerly, in the past; (*à une époque particulière*) once; **c'est ce qu'on faisait a. à la maison, avant l'accident** that's what we used to do at home, before the accident; **a., il était plus bavard** he was more talkative before *or* in the past, he used to be more talkative; **il y avait a. un roi** once upon a time there was a king; **c'était l'usage a.** it was the custom in former times *or* in olden days; **d'a.** of long ago; **sa vie d'a.** his past life; **les hommes d'a.** men of old *or* of olden times; **des chants d'a.** old-time songs

autrement [otrəmɑ̃] *adv* (**a**) (*différemment*) otherwise, differently; **il me l'a raconté a. que vous** the way he told it was different from the way you told it; **faisons a.** let's do *or* set about it (in) another way; **Alain, a. appelé Jojo** Alain, otherwise known as Jojo; **le bouton d'or, a. appelé ...** the buttercup, otherwise known as ..., the buttercup or ...; **a. dit** in other words, put differently; **tu ne viendras pas demain? a. dit, tu ne veux plus me voir!** so you're not coming tomorrow? in other words, you don't want to see me any more!; **il ne put faire a. que d'obéir** he had no alternative but to obey; **à chaque fois que je le vois, je pleure, je n'arrive pas à faire a.** every time I see him I cry, I can't help myself; *F* **pas moyen de faire a.** there's no alternative, there's no other way; **pas moyen de faire a. que de l'emmener** there's no alternative *or* there's nothing else to do *or* nothing else for it but to take him along

(**b**) (*plus*) (far) more; **elle est a. intelligente** she is far more intelligent, she is more intelligent by far; **c'est bien a. sérieux** that is far more serious

(**c**) (*sinon*) otherwise, or (else); **venez demain, a. il sera trop tard** come tomorrow, otherwise it will be too late; **explique-lui, a. elle n'arrivera pas à le faire** explain it to her, otherwise *or* or (else) she won't be able to do it; **les verres n'étaient pas propres, a. c'était pas mal** the glasses weren't clean, but otherwise it wasn't bad

(**d**) **pas a.** not particularly; **cela ne me surprend pas a.** that does not particularly surprise me

Autriche [otriʃ] *nf* Austria

autrichien, -ienne [otriʃjɛ̃, -jɛn] **1** *adj* Austrian **2** *n* **A.** Austrian

autruche [otryʃ] *nf* (*oiseau*) ostrich; **œuf d'a.** ostrich egg; **chaussures/sac en a.** ostrich-skin shoes/handbag; *Fig F* **avoir un estomac d'a.** to have a cast-iron stomach; *Fig* **pratiquer la politique de l'a., faire l'a.** to bury one's head in the sand

autrui [otrɥi] *pron indéf* others, other people; **convoiter le bien d'a.** to covet one's neighbour's property; **ne fais pas à a. ce que tu ne voudrais pas qu'on te fît** do as you would be done by

auvent [ovɑ̃] *nm* (**a**) porch roof; **un toit en a.** a sloping roof; **s'abriter sous l'a.** to shelter in the porch (**b**) (*de tente*) canopy, awning (**c**) *Ind* (*au-dessus de l'âtre etc*) hood; *Aut* **auvents de capot** bonnet louvres

auvergnat, -ate [ovɛrɲa, at] **1** *adj* of Auvergne **2** *nm Ling* Auvergne dialect **3** *n* **A.** (*natif*) native of Auvergne; (*habitant*) inhabitant of Auvergne

aux [o] *voir* = **à**

auxiliaire [ɔksiljɛr, o-] **1** *adj* (*verbe, troupes etc*) auxiliary; **machine a.** auxiliary engine; **bureau a.** sub-office; **services auxiliaires de l'armée** non-combatant services; **maître a.** supply teacher **2** *n* (*aide*) auxiliary, helper, assistant; *Admin* temporary civil servant; (*aux PTT*) non-permanent employee; *Com* facilitator; **c'est un a. précieux** he's a valuable helper **3** *nm* (**a**) *Naut* auxiliary cruiser (**b**) *Av, Naut* **les auxiliaires** the auxiliary engines (**c**) *Mil* **auxiliaires** auxiliaries (**d**) [①**A38,3; A54-9; B25-6**] *Gram* auxiliary verb

▶ **auxiliaire**: **a. familiale** ≈ mother's help; **a. de justice** representative of the law; **a. médical** medical auxiliary

auxquels [okɛl] *voir* = **lequel**

AV (*abrév* **avant**) front

av. *abrév* **avenue**

avachi [avaʃi] *adj* (**a**) (*vêtements, bottes etc*) (*déformé par l'usage*) out of shape, shapeless; **elle traîne toujours son**

vieux manteau tout a. she wears her shapeless old coat everywhere she goes **(b)** (*posture*) sloppy; (*personne, muscles*) flabby; **être a. dans un fauteuil** to be slumped in an armchair

avachir [avaʃir] **1** *vt* **(a)** (*vêtements etc*) to make shapeless; (*cuir*) to soften **(b)** (*personne, muscles*) to make flabby; **la chaleur m'avachit** the heat makes me feel quite limp *or* floppy **2 s'avachir** *vpr* **(a)** (*du cuir*) to soften, to become soft; (*des vêtements*) to become shapeless, to lose its shape **(b)** (*de personne*) to become flabby; (*se laisser aller*) to let oneself go, to go to seed; **s'a. dans un fauteuil** to flop into an armchair

avachissement [avaʃismɑ̃] *nm* (*de cuir*) softening; (*des vêtements*) losing shape; (*de posture*) sloppiness; (*de personne, muscles*) flabbiness

aval[1], -als [aval] *nm Fin* (*d'un effet de commerce*) endorsement; **a. bancaire** bank guarantee, aval; **pour a.** guaranteed by; **donner son a. à un billet** to endorse *or* back a bill; **donneur d'a.** guarantor, backer; *Fig* **donner son a. à un projet** to give a project one's backing *or* support

aval[2] *nm* **(a)** downstream side; **les villages d'a.** the villages downstream; **canal d'a.** (*d'écluse*) tail race; **porte d'a.** tail *or* aft gate; **en a.** downstream, down-river; *Rail* down the line; **en a. du village/du torrent** downstream of the village/torrent; **le ski a.** the downhill ski **(b)** *Écon* **stade a.** (*de la production*) downstream **(c)** *Télécom* down side

avalanche [avalɑ̃ʃ] *nf* avalanche; **a. de pierres** avalanche of stones; **a. boueuse** avalanche of mud; **couloir d'a.** avalanche corridor; **a. électronique/ionique** avalanche of electrons/ions; *Fig* **a. d'injures/de compliments** shower of insults/compliments; *Fig* **ce fut une a. de lettres** letters came pouring in, there was a flood of letters

avalancheux, -euse [avalɑ̃ʃø, -øz] *adj* prone to avalanches; **couloir a.** avalanche corridor

avaler [avale] **1** *vt* **(a)** (*absorber*) to swallow (down); **a. son repas sans mâcher** to swallow down one's meal without chewing it; **a. son repas** to bolt one's meal; **j'avale mon repas et j'arrive** I'll just get my food down, then I'll be along; **a. son vin d'un trait** to swallow one's wine in one gulp; **j'ai avalé de travers** it went down the wrong way; **a. qch tout rond** to swallow sth whole; **je meurs de faim, je n'ai rien avalé depuis hier** I'm starving, I haven't had a thing to eat since yesterday; *Fig* **a. ses mots** to swallow one's words; **a. la fumée** to inhale; *Fig* **j'ai cru qu'elle allait m'a. tout cru** I thought she was going to bite my head off; **a. une carte de crédit** (*d'un distributeur automatique*) to eat *or* swallow a credit card; **je préfère a. ma salive et penser à autre chose** I prefer to grin and bear it and think of something else; **on dirait qu'il a avalé son parapluie!** he's as stiff as a poker!; **a. les kilomètres** to eat up the miles; **il a avalé 'Vol de Nuit' en une soirée** he read *or* devoured 'Vol de Nuit' in an evening

(b) *Fig* **a. le morceau** *ou* **la pilule** to take one's medicine *or* one's punishment; **celle-là est dure à a.** that's a tall story, I can hardly swallow that; **tu auras du mal à leur faire a. ça** you'll have a job getting them to swallow that; **on peut lui faire a. n'importe quoi, il est tellement naïf** he's so naive he'll swallow anything; *F* **tu as avalé ta langue?** have you lost your tongue?, has the cat got your tongue?; *F* **a. son acte de naissance** to kick the bucket, to pop one's clogs

2 *vi* to swallow; *F* **qu'est-ce qu'il avale!** he doesn't half put it away!

avaleur [avalœr] *nm* **a. de sabres** sword-swallower

avaliser [avalize] *vt Fin* to avalize; *Com* (*effet de commerce*) to endorse, to back; *Fig* **a. un projet** to back a project

à-valoir *nm inv* (*paiement*) advance

avance [avɑ̃s] *nf* **(a)** (*marche*) advance; **l'a. d'une armée/d'un mouvement indépendantiste** the advance of an army/of an independence movement; **l'a. rapide de l'indice du coût de la vie** the rapid rise *or* climb of the cost of living index; *Él* **a. d'une magnéto** magneto lead; **a. rapide** (*sur magnétophone*) fast-forwarding, zipping; **mettre une cassette en a. rapide** to fast-forward a cassette, to put a cassette on fast forward

(b) (*dans le temps, l'espace, avantage*) lead; **avoir de l'a. sur qn** to be ahead of sb; **avoir une a. de 2 minutes/2 km** to have a 2-minute/2-km lead; **avoir 2 minutes/2 km d'a. sur qn** to have a 2-minute/2 km lead over sb; (*en début de course*) to have a 2-minute/2 km head start on sb; *Sp* **un trou/but/set d'a.** one hole/goal/set up; **j'ai fini le projet avec deux jours d'a. sur le programme** I finished the project two days ahead of schedule; **j'ai fini le contrôle avec un quart d'heure d'a.** I finished the test a quarter of an hour ahead of time; **arriver avec cinq minutes d'a.** to arrive five minutes early; **il vaut toujours mieux arriver à la gare avec quelques minutes d'a.** it's always better to arrive at the station a few minutes early *or* with a few minutes to spare; **nous avons pris de l'a. sur nos poursuivants/concurrents** we've pulled away from our pursuers/competitors; **accentuer/conserver/perdre son a. sur qn** to increase/maintain/lose one's lead over sb; *Sp* **donner de l'a. à qn** to give sb a head start; **je vais le laisser prendre de l'a. dans la ligne droite** I'll let him get ahead in the straight; **grâce à l'a. acquise pendant les deux premières heures de la course** thanks to the lead he/she/*etc* established *or* built up during the first two hours of the race; **Paris-St-Germain cherche à préserver son a. au classement** Paris-St-Germain are trying to hold on to *or* maintain their lead in the league; **l'a. des Français au niveau de la recherche** the French lead in the sphere of research; **une mauvaise gestion peut nous faire perdre notre a.** we may lose our lead through bad management; *F* **la belle a.!** much good that will do/did/is doing you!

(c) *Tech* (*d'un outil*) feed movement, travel; **mécanisme d'a.** feed mechanism

(d) *Aut* **a. à l'allumage** ignition advance; **mettre de l'a. à l'allumage** to advance the ignition; **réduire l'a.** to retard the ignition; **levier d'a.** ignition lever; **a. à l'échappement** exhaust lead

(e) *Fin* **a. (de fonds)** advance; **par a., à titre d'a.** as an advance; **faire une a. de mille francs à qn** to give sb an advance of a thousand francs; **demander une a. sur salaire** to ask for an advance on one's salary; **faire les avances d'une entreprise** to advance funds for an enterprise; *Cin* **a. sur recette(s)** (*d'acteur*) advance payment; (*de metteur-en-scène*) = money invested in the production of a film to be recouped from the box office takings

(f) faire des avances à qn to approach sb; (*sexuellement*) to make advances to sb; **ne réponds jamais aux avances de ce monsieur!** don't ever respond to that man's advances!

(g) d'a., à l'a., par a. in advance; **payer qn d'a.** *ou* **à l'a.** to pay sb in advance; **payable à l'a.** payable in advance; **retenir** *ou* **louer une place huit jours à l'a.** to book a seat a week in advance; **et pourtant, je les ai prévenus deux mois à l'a.** I did warn them two months in advance *or* beforehand; **entrer à l'école primaire avec un an d'a.** to go to primary school a year early; *Scol* **avoir un an d'a.** to be a year ahead; **je vous remercie d'a.; par a., merci** (*dans une lettre*) thanking you in advance *or* in anticipation; **je m'en réjouis d'a.** I'm greatly looking forward to it; **je savourais à l'a. le plaisir de ...** I was relishing (in anticipation) the thought of ..., I was relishing the prospect of ...

(h) en a. early; **je suis en a. d'une demi-heure** I am half an hour early; **je suis arrivé très en a.** I arrived very early; **elle sait déjà lire, elle est très en a. pour son âge** she can already read, she's very advanced for her age; **être en a. sur son temps** to be ahead of one's time; **la moisson est en a. cette année** the harvest is early this year; *F* **je vous préviens, nous ne sommes pas en a.!** I'm warning you, we're not exactly running on time!

avancé [avɑ̃se] *adj* **(a)** (*dans l'espace*) advanced; **position avancée** advanced *or* forward position; *Rail* **signal a.** distant signal; **j'étais trop a. sur ma route pour pouvoir faire demi-tour** I had gone too far along the road to be able to turn back

(b) (*précoce*) forward; **les pommiers sont bien avancés cette année** the apple trees are early this year; **c'est un esprit a.** he's a progressive thinker; **élève a.** pupil ahead of his class; **opinions avancées** advanced *or* progressive ideas

(c) (*dans le temps*) **à une heure avancée de la nuit** late in the night, well on in the night; **à une heure peu avancée** quite early on; *Can* **heure avancée** daylight saving time; **l'été est bien a.** summer is well advanced; **à un âge a.** late in life, at an advanced age

(d) (*fruit*) overripe; **viande avancée** rotten meat

(e) (*presque à terme*) (far) advanced; **à un stade a. du projet** at an advanced stage in the project; **je ne suis pas assez a. dans mon travail pour pouvoir sortir ce soir** I'm not far enough ahead with my work to be able to go out tonight; *F* **vous voilà bien a.!** a lot of good that's done you!; **tu es bien a. maintenant que tu l'as renvoyé: tu n'as personne pour le remplacer!** a lot of good it's done you firing him, you've got no one to replace him!; **vous n'en êtes pas plus a.** you're no further forward

avancée [avɑ̃se] *nf* **(a)** (*saillie*) bulge, projection, protuberance; *Constr* **a. du toit** eaves **(b)** (*de la mer, du désert, Fig des nationalistes etc*) advance **(c)** (*d'une ligne de pêche*) leader, trace

avancement [avɑ̃smɑ̃] *nm* **(a)** (*mouvement*) advancing, putting forward **(b)** *Ordinat etc* **a. automatique** automatic feed; **a. ligne par ligne** line feed; **a. du papier** paper feed; **a. par friction** friction feed **(c)** (*de projet*) advancement, furtherance; **état d'a. des travaux** progress report **(d)**

(*promotion*) promotion; **a. à l'ancienneté** promotion by seniority; **avoir** *ou* **obtenir de l'a.** to be promoted **(e)** (*progrès*) advance(ment), progress; **l'a. des sciences** the advance *or* progress of science **(f)** *Jur* **a. d'hoirie** = part of inheritance given in advance

avancer [avɑ̃se] **(j'avançai(s); n. avançons) 1** *vt* **(a)** (*mettre en avant*) to move forward; (*la main*) to stretch out, to hold out; **avance un peu ton pied, tu écrases la queue du chien** move your foot (forward) a bit, you're crushing the dog's tail; **a. sa chaise pour mieux voir** to pull up *or* forward one's chair to see better; **il avança son verre** he held out his glass; **elle avança son petit visage vers moi** she moved her little face towards me; **a. une voiture jusqu'au portail** to drive a car up to the door; *Fml, Hum* **l'automobile de Monsieur est avancée** Sir's carriage awaits; *F* **laisse-moi t'a. jusqu'au métro** let me take you as far as the underground; *Échecs* **a. un pion** to advance a pawn

(b) *Fig* **a. une proposition** to put forward *or* advance a proposal; **a. ses raisons** to produce *or* set out one's reasons; **comment peut-il prouver ce qu'il avance?** how can he prove his assertion?; **comme l'ont avancé certains chercheurs …** as some researchers have proposed …

(c) (*dans le temps*) to bring forward; **la réunion a été avancée du 14 au 7** the meeting has been brought forward from the 14th to the 7th; **a. l'heure du dîner** to put dinner forward; **a. une montre d'une heure** to put a watch forward one hour

(d) a. de l'argent à qn to advance money to sb; (*prêter*) to lend sb money; **tu peux m'a. (l'argent de) mon train?** could you lend me my train fare?

(e) (*promouvoir*) to further; **être avancé** to be promoted, to get promotion; **faire a. la cause de la démocratie** to advance the cause of democracy, to further democracy; **faire a. la science** to bring about scientific progress; **a. ses recherches** to push on with *or* get ahead with one's research; **a. une plante** to bring on *or* force a plant; **est-ce que ça t'avancerais si je faisais les courses?** would it help you along if I did the shopping?; **à quoi cela vous avancera-t-il?** what good will that do you?, how much better (off) will you be for it?; **ça ne t'avancera à rien de te mettre en colère** losing your temper won't get you anywhere; **je lui ai posé des questions, mais ses réponses ne m'ont pas beaucoup avancé** I asked him some questions, but his answers got me no further forward *or* left me none the wiser

2 *vi* **(a)** (*aller de l'avant*) to move *or* go forward; (*d'un bateau*) to make headway; (*d'une armée*) to advance; **a. à grands pas** to stride along; **a. à pas de loup** to creep along; **a. à tâtons** to feel *or* grope one's way; **a. d'un pas** to take a *or* one step forward; **avancez vers moi** come towards me; **chaque année, la mer avance un peu plus sur notre terrain** each year the sea encroaches a little further on our land; **faire a. qn** to help sb along; (*en le poussant*) to push sb along; **faire a. une chaise roulante** to push a wheelchair; *Mil* **faire a. les troupes** to advance the troops, to move the troops forward; **faire a. sa voiture jusqu'à la porte** to drive one's car up to the door; **vous ne pouvez pas a., s'il vous plaît? je ne peux pas passer** could you move please? I can't get past; **tu n'avances pas assez vite, on ne sera jamais à l'heure** you're not going fast enough, we'll never be on time; **allez avance! on va être en retard** come on, move! we're going to be late; **aux heures de pointe, on n'avance pas sur cette route** during the rush hours, you can't move on this road; **nous n'avancions pas d'un centimètre** we weren't moving an inch; **nous avancions péniblement dans les marais** we struggled our way through the swamp; **le vieil homme avançait en traînant les pieds** the old man shuffled along

(b) (*faire des progrès*) to progress, to get on; **le travail avance** the work is progressing *or* getting on *or* coming along; **depuis sa démission, ça n'avance plus** since he/she resigned, things have been at a standstill *or* have ground to a halt; *F* **alors, ça avance?** so how's it coming along?; **je n'avance pas dans mon livre** I'm not making any headway with this book; **mon livre n'avance pas** my book isn't coming along at all; **on sentait en lui le désir de faire a. les choses** you could tell he wanted to get things moving (along); **a. en âge** to be getting on; **la nuit avance** it's getting late; **la matinée avançait péniblement** the morning was dragging on *or* wore on

(c) (*dans une carrière etc*) to advance; **a. en grade** to get promoted; *Mil* to rise in rank

(d) (*dans le temps*) (*d'une montre*) to be fast; **l'horloge avance** the clock is fast; **montre qui avance d'une minute par jour** watch that gains a minute a day; **vous avancez de dix minutes** your watch is ten minutes fast

(e) (*de promontoire, toit etc*) to jut out, to project, to protrude; **les rochers avançaient sur la mer** the rocks jutted out into the sea; **le balcon avançait sur la baie** the balcony jutted out over the bay

3 s'avancer *vpr* **(a)** (*aller devant*) to move forward; **s'a. vers qch** to make one's way *or* to head towards sth; **s'a. d'un pas** to take a *or* one step forward; **avance-toi si tu veux voir** move forward if you want to see; **s'a. péniblement** to drag oneself along

(b) (*dans une tâche*) to make headway; **elle en a profité pour s'a. dans son travail** she made use of this to get ahead in her work

(c) *Fig* **il s'est trop avancé pour reculer** he has gone too far to take it back; **elle refuse de s'a. sur ce point** she won't be drawn on this matter; **je crois que je me suis trop avancé en disant que mes parents leur prêteraient leur maison** I think I went too far when I said my parents would lend them their house; **tu t'avances un peu en disant que je vais avoir ce boulot** you're getting ahead of yourself a bit in saying that I'm going to get this job

(d) (*de promontoire etc*) to jut out; **une langue de terre s'avance dans la mer** a strip of land juts out *or* runs out into the sea

avanie [avani] *nf Litt* snub; **subir** *ou* **essuyer une a.** to be snubbed

avant [avɑ̃] **1** *prép* [①A65] **(a)** (*dans le temps*) before; **venez a. midi** come before twelve o'clock; **il sera ici a. une heure** he will be here by one o'clock; (*dans moins d'une heure*) he will be here within an *or* the hour; **je le verrai a. quinze jours** I shall see him within *or* in less than a fortnight; **pas a. lundi** not before Monday; **pas a. de nombreuses années** not for many years to come; **il a terminé la course a. moi** he finished the race before me *or* ahead of me; **a. son arrivée** before he arrives/arrived, before his arrival; **juste a. la pluie** just before it started to rain, just before the rain started; **800 a. Jésus-Christ** 800 BC; **a. imposition** *ou* **impôt** before tax

(b) (*dans l'espace*) before; **la maison est a. la boucherie** the house is before the butcher's; **l'article se place a. le nom** the article is placed before the noun *or* in front of the noun

(c) (*priorité*) **a. la ceinture noire, il y a la ceinture bleue** the blue belt comes before the black belt; **mettre** *ou* **faire passer la santé a. le reste** to put one's health above *or* before all else; **pour lui, la famille passe a. tout** for him, (the) family comes first; **a. tout** first of all, above all; **a. toute chose** before anything else, in the first place; **a. tout, il faut que tu sois satisfait** above all (else) *or* first and foremost, we want you to be satisfied

(d) (**a. de +** *inf*) **je vous reverrai a. de partir** I shall see you before I leave; **ne fais rien a. d'être tout à fait sûr** do not do anything until you are quite certain; **lave-toi les mains a. de manger** wash your hands before eating *or* you eat; *Litt* **a. que de mourir** before dying

(e) (**a. que +** *sub*) **je vous reverrai a. que vous (ne) partiez** I shall see you again before you leave; **je serai parti a. que vous ayez fini** I shall be gone by the time (that) you have finished; **ne partez pas a. qu'on vous le dise** don't go until you are told; *F* **celle-là, a. qu'elle arrive!** the time it takes (for) her to get here!

(f) il est à quelques mètres en a. de nous he's a few metres in front of us; **en a. du village se trouvait une petite église** there was a little church just before the village; *Litt* **avec rien que la mort en a. de nous** with nothing but death awaiting *or* before us

2 *adv* **(a)** (*auparavant*) before; (*par rapport à un événement futur*) beforehand; **a. j'avais les cheveux longs** I used to have long hair; **a. je voulais être prof** I wanted to be a teacher before, I used to want to be a teacher; **il était arrivé quelques mois a.** he had arrived some months before *or* earlier; **réfléchis a., tu parleras après** think first, speak later; **on commencera mardi, que tout le monde ait lu la pièce a.** we'll start on Tuesday, (so) everyone make sure you've read the play beforehand; **tu ferais mieux de téléphoner a.** you'd better phone beforehand; **du pain comme on le faisait a.** bread the way they used to make it; **bien/peu a.** well/shortly before; **juste a.** just before; **il l'a mentionné a. dans la préface** he mentioned it before *or* earlier in the preface; **le jour d'a., tout était calme** the day before, everything was quiet

(b) (*dans l'espace*) **n'allez pas jusqu'à l'église, sa maison est a.** don't go as far as the church, his house is before (you come to) it

(c) (*loin*) far, deep; **pénétrer très a. dans les terres** to penetrate far inland; **le harpon pénétra très a. dans les chairs** the harpoon sank deep into the flesh; *Fig* **tu t'es**

engagé trop a. you've got too involved, you're in too deep; **on l'a empêché de pousser plus a. son enquête** he was prevented from taking his investigation(s) any further

(d) (*tard*) far, late; **très a. dans la journée** very late in the day; *Litt* **on dut attendre fort a. dans le siècle la diffusion du vaccin** vaccinations did not become readily available until well on into the century

(e) en a. in front, ahead; *Mil* **en a.!** forward!; *Mil* **en a., marche!** forward march!; **en a. toute!** *Naut* full steam ahead!; *Fig* forward march!; **en a. la musique!** (*on y va*) let's be off!; (*ça recommence*) here we go again!; **il est parti en a. pour reconnaître le chemin** he set off ahead to reconnoitre the route; **envoyer qn en a.** to send sb ahead *or* on (in front); **aller en a.** to go to the front; **elle marche toujours quelques mètres en a.** she always walks a few yards in front *or* ahead; **se pencher en a.** to lean forward(s); **tomber en a.** to fall forwards; **faire deux pas en a.** to take two steps forward, to move forward two steps; *Fig* **mettre qn en a.** to push sb forward; *Fig* **mettre le règlement/la loi en a.** to hide behind the rule book *or* the law; *Fig* **mettre en a. une question** to bring up a question

3 *adj inv* front; **la partie a. du navire** the fore part of the ship; **roue a.** front wheel; *Aut* **à traction a.** with front-wheel drive

4 *nm* **(a)** *Aut, Rail, Av* front; *Naut* bow; (*de piston*) crank end; **l'a. de la voiture est complètement défoncé** the front of the car is completely smashed in; **les enfants ne doivent pas s'asseoir à l'a.** children may not sit in (the) front; **tu seras mieux à l'a.** you'll be better in (the) front; **le logement de l'équipage est à l'a.** the crew's quarters are forward; *Naut* **présenter l'a. à la lame** to be head to sea; **aborder un navire par l'a.** to collide with a ship head on; **par tribord a.** on the starboard bow; **sur** *ou* **à l'a. du mât** before the mast; **aller de l'a.** to go *or* forge ahead; *Fig* **lui, au moins, il allait de l'a.** at least he always forged ahead

(b) *Fb etc* forward; **la ligne des avants** the forward line; *Rugby* **a. de deuxième ligne** second-row forward, lock (forward); **il joue a.** he plays up front

(c) *Mil* **l'a.** the front

avantage [avɑ̃taʒ] *nm* **(a)** (*profit*) advantage; **a. pécuniaire** monetary gain; **a. en nature** benefit in kind, *F* perk; **a. concurrentiel** competitive advantage; **a. fiscal** tax benefit; **a. matériel/personnel** material/personal gain; **avantages sociaux** social security benefits; **il ne m'en revient aucun a.** I'm not getting any advantage *or* benefit from it; **être à l'a. de qn** to be to sb's advantage; **la situation tourne à votre a.** the situation is turning to your advantage; **et voilà que Vincent cherche encore à tirer a. de la situation** there's Vincent trying to turn the situation to his advantage again; **trouver de l'a. à faire qch** to find it an advantage *or* advantageous to do sth

(b) (*atout*) advantage; **présenter un a.** to have an advantage; **cette solution a l'a. d'être rapide et efficace** this solution has the advantage of being quick and effective; **les avantages que vous procure un appartement en ville** the benefits *or* advantages gained from having a flat in town; **posséder un ordinateur est un a. certain** owning a computer is a definite advantage; **sa connaissance du français lui est un a. précieux** his knowledge of French is a great asset to him; **avoir un a. sur qn** to have an advantage over sb; **avoir (sur qn) l'a. du nombre/de l'âge** to have the advantage of number/age (over sb)

(c) *Jur* gift, donation; **à titre d'a.** as a gift

(d) *Sp, Tennis, Fig* advantage; **donner l'a. à qn** to give sb a head start; **je vais lui donner l'a. dans la ligne droite** I'll let him go in front of me in the straight; **c'est tout à ton a. d'être arrivé en avance** it's to your advantage that you arrived early; **il a changé à son a.** he has changed for the better; **s'habiller à son a.** to dress to one's best advantage; **paraître à son a.** (*physiquement*) to look one's best; (*à un entretien*) to be at one's best; **il est à son a. en uniforme** he looks his best in uniform; **parler à l'a. de qn** to speak in sb's favour; **avoir l'a. sur qn** to have the advantage of *or* over sb; **prendre l'a.** *Sp* to go into the lead; (*sur un marché*) to become the leader; **conserver l'a.** *Sp* to stay in the lead; (*sur un marché*) to hold onto one's lead; **prendre l'a. sur qn** to take the lead from sb; **il a l'a.** the odds are in his favour; *Tennis* **a. (au) service** (*Leconte au service*) advantage Leconte; *Tennis* **a. dehors** (*Leconte au service, Noah en face*) advantage Noah; *Tennis* **a. Navratilova** advantage Navratilova

(e) il y a a. à + *inf* it is best to, it is worth one's while to + *inf*; **il y aura a. à ce que vous soyez présent** it will be a good thing *or* just as well if you are present; **tu aurais a. à être poli la prochaine fois** you would do well to be polite next time

(f) *Fml* **à quoi dois-je l'a. de votre venue?** to what do I owe the honour of your visit?; **je n'ai pas l'a. de vous connaître** I have not had the honour of making your acquaintance

avantagé [avɑ̃taʒe] *adj* **être fort a. par rapport aux autres** to enjoy many advantages over others; **a. par la nature** (*physiquement*) well endowed; *Péj* **la pauvre, elle n'a pas été avantagée par la nature** the poor thing, nature hasn't been too kind to her!; *Sp* **joueur a.** player who has been given a start

avantager [avɑ̃taʒe] *vt* **(j'avantageai(s); n. avantageons) (a)** (*favoriser*) to favour, to give an advantage; **ton expérience t'avantage par rapport aux autres candidats** your experience gives you an advantage over the other candidates; **son bégaiement ne l'avantage pas** his stammer doesn't help him **(b)** (*physiquement*) **l'uniforme l'avantage** he looks his best in uniform; **cette coiffure ne l'avantage vraiment pas** that hairstyle really doesn't flatter her

avantageusement [avɑ̃taʒøzmɑ̃] *adv* advantageously, to advantage; **elle sait mettre a. son décolleté en valeur** she knows how to show off her cleavage to advantage; **parler de qn a.** to speak favourably of sb

avantageux, -euse [avɑ̃taʒø, -øz] *adj* **(a)** (*intéressant*) advantageous, favourable; (*bon marché*) good value; *Com* **prix a.** reasonable price **(b)** (*flatteur*) **parler de qn en termes a.** to speak favourably of sb; **robe avantageuse** becoming dress; **portrait a.** flattering portrait **(c) poitrine avantageuse** well-developed bust **(d)** *Péj* (*vaniteux*) conceited, vain; **prendre un ton a.** to adopt a superior tone

avant-aile, *pl* **avant-ailes** *nm Rugby* wing-forward, flanker

avant-bassin, *pl* **avant-bassins** *nm Naut* outer basin, dock

avant-bras *nm inv Anat* forearm

avant-cale, *pl* **avant-cales** *nf Naut* fore hold

avant-centre, *pl* **avant-centres** *nm Fb* centre forward

avant-corps *nm inv Archit* (*d'un bâtiment*) projecting part

avant-cour, *pl* **avant-cours** *nf Archit* forecourt

avant-coureur, *pl* **avant-coureurs 1** *nm* forerunner, precursor; *Mil* scout **2** *adj* (*symptôme*) warning; **choc a. (de séisme)** preliminary tremor; **les signes avant-coureurs du changement** the harbingers of change

avant-dernier, -ière, *pl* **avant-derniers, -ières 1** *adj* last but one, second (to) last, *Fml* penultimate; **l'avant-dernière fois** the time before last **2** *n* last but one, second (to) last, next to last

avant-garde, *pl* **avant-gardes** *nf* **(a)** *Mil* advance(d) guard; **détachement d'a.** advance(d) party **(b) hommes d'a.** men in the van, pioneers; *Pol* **les éléments d'a.** the avant-garde; **livre d'a.** avant-garde book; **les découvertes de l'a.** the discoveries of the avant-garde; **technique d'a.** avant-garde technique; **être à l'a. de la mode/du progrès** to be in the vanguard *or* at the forefront of fashion/progress

avant-gardisme [avɑ̃gardism] *nm* avant-gardism

avant-gardiste, *pl* **avant-gardistes** [avɑ̃gardist] **1** *adj* avant-garde **2** *n* avant-gardiste

avant-goût, *pl* **avant-goûts** *nm* foretaste, anticipation, first impression; **cela m'a donné un a. de ce qu'allait être ma vie/mon travail** it gave me a taste *or* foretaste of my life to come/of what my work would be like

avant-guerre, *pl* **avant-guerres** *nm ou F* pre-war period; **la mode d'a.** pre-war fashion

avant-hier [avɑ̃tjɛr] *adv* the day before yesterday; **a. au soir** the night *or* evening before last

avant-main, *pl* **avant-mains** *nm* **(a)** (*de cheval*) forequarters, forehand **(b)** *Tennis* **coup d'a.** forehand (stroke)

avant-plan, *pl* **avant-plans** *nm Beaux-Arts, Phot etc* foreground

avant-pont, *pl* **avant-ponts** *nm Naut* foredeck

avant-port, *pl* **avant-ports** *nm Naut* outer harbour

avant-poste, *pl* **avant-postes** *nm Mil* outpost

avant-première, *pl* **avant-premières** *nf* private view *or* viewing, preview; *Th* dress rehearsal; **présenté en a.** (*film, pièce etc*) previewed, given an advanced showing

avant-propos *nm inv* (*de livre*) preface, foreword; *Fig* **après quelques a.** after a few preliminary remarks; **en a. à cette conférence** before the lecture gets underway, as a prelude to this lecture

avant-scène, *pl* **avant-scènes** *nf Th* **(a)** *Antiq* proscenium, apron, forestage **(b) (loge d')a.** stage box

avant-spectacle, *pl* **avant-spectacles** *nm* pre-show performance; **en a.** as a curtain-raiser

avant-titre, *pl* **avant-titres** *nm* (*d'un livre*) half-title

avant-toit, *pl* **avant-toits** *nm* eaves; **comble avec a.** umbrella roof

avant-train, *pl* **avant-trains** *nm* **(a)** *Aut* front-axle unit **(b)** (*d'une charrue*) wheels **(c)** *Mil* limber

avant-veille, *pl* **avant-veilles** *nf* two days before; **l'a. de Noël** two days before Christmas
avare [avar] **1** *adj* **(a)** (*mesquin*) mean, miserly, *F* tight **(b) il n'est pas a. de compliments** he's generous *or* lavish with his compliments; **il n'est pas a. de ses conseils** he's only too happy to offer advice **2** *n* miser
avarice [avaris] *nf* avarice, miserliness; **au diable l'a.!** you can't take it with you!, to hell with the expense!
avaricieux, -ieuse [avarisjø, -jøz] **1** *adj* miserly, avaricious, *F* stingy **2** *n* miser, skinflint; **un vieil a.** an old miser
avarie [avari] *nf* **(a)** (*à un bateau, moteur etc*) damage; **subir une a.** to be damaged; **faire subir une a. à qch** to damage sth **(b) déclaration d'avaries** (ship's) protest; **avaries matérielles de mer** damage done by sea water **(c) avaries-frais** average; **règlement d'avaries** adjustment of average; **répartiteur d'avaries** average adjuster
avarié [avarje] *adj* (*marchandises etc*) damaged, spoiled; (*viande, poisson etc*) rotten
avarier [avarje] (*pr sub & impf* **n. avariions, v. avariiez**) **1** *vt* (*marchandises etc*) to damage **2 s'avarier** *vpr* (*nourriture etc*) to go off, to go bad, to rot; (*denrées non comestibles*) to be damaged
avatar [avatar] *nm* **(a)** (*transformation*) transformation, change, metamorphosis; **avatars** (*de la vie politique etc*) ups and downs, vicissitudes **(b)** (*mésaventure*) mishap, misadventure **(c)** (*incarnation*) avatar, incarnation
Ave [ave] *nm* Ave; **l'A. Maria** the Hail Mary
avec [avɛk] **1** *prép* **(a)** with; **je vous ai vu a. lui** I saw you with him; **je crois a. vous que ...** like you, I believe that ...; **le public est a. nous** the public is with *or* behind us; **a. qui viendras-tu?** who are you coming with, *Fml* with whom are you coming?; **être bien/mal a. qn** to be getting on well/badly with sb; **un pavillon a. garage** a detached house with a garage; **elle ressemble à sa sœur, a. des traits plus réguliers** she is like her sister, but with more regular features

(b) (*manière*) **a. enthousiasme/tristesse** enthusiastically/sadly, with enthusiasm/sadness; **a. beaucoup de gentillesse** very kindly, with great kindness; **a. beaucoup de franchise** very candidly; **elle danse a. beaucoup de grâce** she dances very gracefully; **c'est a. émotion que j'accepte le poste** I'm thrilled to accept the job; **mots dits a. colère** words spoken in anger

(c) (*simultanéité*) **la capacité pulmonaire diminue a. l'âge** lung capacity decreases with age; **l'oxygène se rarefie avec l'altitude** air becomes thinner with altitude; **cela viendra a. le temps** that will come in *or* with time; **il se lève a. le soleil** he gets up at sunrise; **il est arrivé a. la nuit** he arrived when it was getting dark, he arrived at nightfall; **le paysage change a. les saisons** the countryside changes with the seasons

(d) (*à cause de*) **a. tous les ennuis qu'il a eus, il ne sait plus où donner de la tête** with all the problems he's had, he doesn't know whether he's coming or going; **a. cette sécheresse, rien ne pousse** nothing will grow with this drought; **impossible de sortir a. cette pluie/ce temps** it's impossible to go out in *or* with this rain/weather

(e) (*malgré*) **a. tous ses défauts, il a quand même réussi à se faire accepter** with *or* in spite of all his faults, he has still managed to become accepted; **a. tout le respect que je vous dois** with all due respect

(f) (*moyen*) **a. l'aide de qn** with sb's help; **ouvrir une porte a. une clef** to open a door with a key; **a. 10000 francs par mois, on s'en sort très bien** you can get by *or* manage perfectly well on *or* with 10,000 francs per month; **je fais toujours mes devoirs a. de la musique** I always have music on when I'm doing my homework; **aujourd'hui, on va faire notre gymnastique a. de la musique** today we're going to do our gymnastics to music; **je m'endors mieux a. de la musique** I fall asleep more quickly with music on; **je préfère travailler a. la lumière du jour** I prefer to work in daylight; **j'ai eu un accident a. cet avion** I had an accident in this plane

(g) (*contre*) **lutter a. qch** to struggle with sth; **se battre a. qn** to fight (with) sb

(h) (*à l'égard de*) **elle est toujours gentille a. moi/les enfants** she's always nice to me/children; **c'est un amour a. sa femme** he's a darling to his wife; **être dur a. qn** to be hard on sb; **être franc a. qn** to be frank with sb

(i) (*en ce qui concerne*) **a. elle, on ne sait jamais** you never can tell with her; **a. toi, c'est toujours pareil** it's always the same with you, it's always the same old story with you; **tu sais bien qu'a. lui, on peut avoir confiance** you know that he can be trusted; **a. le caractère qu'elle a** with her character; *F* **il nous embête a. ses problèmes de famille!** he's driving us mad with all his family problems!

(j) *F* **elle est grande, mince, athlétique, et sympa a. ça** she's tall, slim, athletic, and what's more, she's nice; **et avec (tout) ça, il n'est pas content!** and he still isn't happy!; **... et ne me dis pas a. (tout) ça qu'il n'a pas triché!** ... and don't tell me after all that that he didn't cheat!; **et a. cela** *ou* **ceci, madame?** anything else, madam?

(k) d'a. from; **distinguer** *ou* **séparer le bon d'a. le mauvais** to distinguish (the) good from (the) bad; **divorcer d'a. sa femme** to divorce one's wife

2 *adv F* with it; with them; **il a pris la caisse et s'est sauvé a.** he ran off with the takings; **j'espérais qu'il laisserait sa femme à la maison, malheureusement, il est venu a.** I was hoping he'd leave his wife at home, unfortunately he brought her with him; **nous n'avions qu'un vieux tourne-disque, il a bien fallu faire a.** we only had an old record player so we had to make do (with it); *Dial* **tu viens a.?** are you coming too?
aveline [avlin] *nf* (*fruit*) hazel nut, cob (nut)
avelinier [avlinje] *nm* (*arbre*) hazel
aven [avɛn] *nm Géol* swallowhole
avenant [avnɑ̃] **1** *adj* (*personne, manières etc*) pleasant, gracious **2** *nm* **(a) à l'a.** in keeping, correspondingly; **ils se sont conduits à l'a.** they acted accordingly; **le bâtiment est beau et le jardin est à l'a.** the building is beautiful and the garden is in keeping with it **(b)** (*de traité*) codicil **(c)** (*de police d'assurance*) additional clause, endorsement **(d)** (*de verdict*) rider
avènement [avɛnmɑ̃] *nm* **(a)** (*du Christ etc*) advent; (*d'un messie*) coming; **depuis l'a. de l'automobile** since the advent of the (motor) car **(b)** (*accession*) advent, coming, arrival; **a. au trône** accession to the throne
avenir[1] [av(ə)nir] *nm* future; **qu'est-ce que l'a. nous réserve?** what does the future hold for us?, what has the future in store for us?; **prédire l'a.** to predict the future; **jeune homme d'un grand a.** *ou* **de beaucoup d'a.** young man with a great future ahead of him; **c'est un homme d'a.** he's an up-and-coming man *or* a man with a (promising) future; *Sp* **un joueur d'a.** a coming player; **un métier d'a.** a career with good prospects; **un avocat d'a.** a lawyer with a great future (ahead of him), an up-and-coming lawyer; **situation sans a.** job with no future *or* prospects, dead-end job; **assurer l'a. de qn** to make provision for sb; **dans l'a.** in the future, at some future date; **dans un a. très prochain** in the very near *or* in the immediate future; **à l'a. je serai plus circonspect** in future I shall be more cautious
avenir[2] *nm inv Jur* (*à l'avocat de la partie adverse*) writ of summons; **signifier un a. à la partie adverse** to serve a writ on the other party
Avent [avɑ̃] *nm Rel* Advent
aventure [avɑ̃tyr] *nf* **(a)** adventure; **tu ne peux pas savoir l'a. qui m'est encore arrivé** you can't imagine the adventure I've just had *or* what's just happened to me; **homme d'aventures** adventurous man, adventurer; **film d'aventures** adventure film; **a. effrayante** terrifying experience; **pour trouver des fruits en hiver, c'est tout une a.** it's quite a business *or F* a heck of a job finding fruit in winter

(b) (*liaison*) (love) affair; **il collectionne les aventures (amoureuses)** he has one affair after another

(c) l'a. chance, luck; **tenter l'a.** to try one's luck; **vie d'a.** life of adventure; **l'a. est au coin de la rue** the unexpected is always round the corner; **à l'a.** at random; **aller** *ou* **errer à l'a.** to wander about aimlessly; **partir à l'a.** to set off in search of adventure; **vivre à l'a.** to live in a happy-go-lucky fashion; *Litt* **par a., d'a.** by chance

(d) la bonne a. fortune-telling; **dire** *ou* **tirer la bonne a. (à qn)** to tell (sb's) fortune; **diseuse de bonne a.** fortune teller
aventuré [avɑ̃tyre] *adj* risky, chancy
aventurer [avɑ̃tyre] **1** *vt* (*sa vie etc*) to risk; **a. une grosse somme d'argent** to risk *or* venture a large sum of money **2 s'aventurer** *vpr* to venture (**dans** into); **s'a. en pays inconnu** to venture into an unknown country; *Fig* **s'a. en terrain glissant** to venture into dangerous territory; **je ne m'aventurerai pas à dire que ...** I won't go so far as to say ...
aventureusement [avɑ̃tyrøzmɑ̃] *adv* adventurously
aventureux, -euse [avɑ̃tyrø, -øz] *adj* adventurous; **homme a. au jeu** reckless gambler; **projet a.** hazardous *or* risky plan
aventurier, -ière [avɑ̃tyrje, -jɛr] *n* adventurer, *f* adventuress
aventurisme [avɑ̃tyrism] *nm Pol* adventurism
avenue [avny] *nf* (*de ville*) avenue; (*menant à une maison*) drive(way); **les avenues du pouvoir** the paths to power
avéré [avere] *adj* (*fait*) recognized, established; **ennemi a.** avowed enemy; **marxistes avérés** professed Marxists; **il est a. que ...** it is confirmed that ...
avérer [avere] (**j'avère, n. avérons; j'avérerai**) **1** *vt Jur Vieilli* (*fait*) to aver **2 s'avérer** *vpr* to be proved (correct), to be

confirmed; **elle s'est avérée indispensable dans l'équipe** she's proved to be *or* turned out to be an essential member of the team; **il s'est avéré que ...** it's turned out that ..., as it's turned out, ...

avers [avɛr] *nm (de monnaie)* obverse

averse [avɛrs] *nf* sudden shower, downpour; **essuyer une a.** to be caught in a shower; *Fig* **une a. de félicitations** a flood *or* stream of congratulations

aversion [avɛrsjɔ̃] *nf* aversion (**pour** to, for), dislike (**pour** for, of); **avoir une a.** *ou* **de l'a. pour** *ou* **contre qn** to have an aversion to *or* for sb, to have a dislike for sb; **prendre qn en a.** to take a dislike to sb

averti [avɛrti] *adj (bien informé)* (well-)informed; *(expérimenté)* experienced; **un homme a.** an experienced man, an expert; *Prov* **un homme a. en vaut deux** forewarned is forearmed; **a. de qch** aware *or* warned of sth; **se tenir pour a.** to take a warning; **vous voilà a.!** I give you fair warning!, don't say I haven't warned you!

avertir [avɛrtir] *vt* **a. qn de qch** to inform sb of sth; **a. qn du danger d'une situation** to warn *or* tell sb of *or* about the danger(s) of a situation; **je l'en avais averti** I had warned him of *or* against it; **je vous en avertis!** I give you fair warning!; **je vais me mettre en colère, je t'avertis!** I'm going to get angry, I'm warning you!; *Ordinat* **a. de la réception de** to acknowledge

avertissement [avɛrtismɑ̃] *nm* **(a)** *(avis préalable)* warning; **renvoyer qn sans a. préalable** to discharge sb at a moment's notice; **lettre envoyée à titre d'a.** letter sent as a reminder; *(avis)* warning letter

(b) *(réprimande)* warning, reprimand; *Sp (de l'arbitre)* warning, caution

(c) *(signal)* danger signal *or* sign, warning signal; **a. de tempête** gale warning; **a. (au lecteur)** foreword (to book); *Ordinat* **a. de réception** *(de message)* acknowledgement; *Ordinat* **a. à réception d'un courrier** mail received message

(d) *Jur* **billet d'a.** summons to appear before a magistrate

(e) *Admin* demand note

avertisseur, -euse [avɛrtisœr, -øz] **1** *nm* **(a)** *(dispositif)* warning signal, alarm; *Aut* horn; *Ind* hooter; *Rail* signal; **a. d'incendie** fire alarm; **a. sonore** warning buzzer; *(klaxon)* horn; **avertisseurs sonores interdits après 22.00 heures** no sounding of horns after 10 pm; *Aut* **a. de marche arrière** reversing beeper; *Aut* **a. deux tons** two-tone horn; **a. lumineux** warning light; **a. optique** warning light **(b)** *Th* callboy **2** *adj* **signal a.** warning signal

aveu, -eux [avø] *nm* **(a)** *(confession)* confession, acknowledgement; *Jur* admission; **faire l'a. d'une erreur** to own up *or* confess to a mistake; **passer aux aveux** to make a confession; **faire des aveux complets** to make a full confession; **de son a. même, il est ruiné** on his own admission, he's bankrupt; **je dois vous faire un a., je n'y étais pas non plus** I must confess *or* admit, I wasn't there either, I have to tell you, I wasn't there either; **arracher des aveux à un accusé** to drag *or* wring *or* wrest a confession out of *or* from a defendant; **il est certain, de l'a. de tout le monde, que ...** it is commonly acknowledged that ...

(b) *Jur* consent, authorization; **obtenir l'a. de qn pour faire qch** to obtain sb's consent to do sth

(c) *Hist* recognition between a vassal and his overlord; **homme sans a.** vagabond, vagrant

aveuglant [avœglɑ̃] *adj* blinding, dazzling; *Fig* **une évidence/preuve aveuglante** a glaringly *or* patently *or* blindingly obvious fact/proof

aveugle [avœgl] **1** *adj* **(a)** *(atteint de cécité)* blind; **devenir a.** to go blind; **a. d'un œil** blind in one eye; **être a. de naissance, naître a.** to be born blind, to be blind from birth; *Opt* **point a.** blind spot

(b) *Fig Archit* **fenêtre/arcade a.** blind window/arch; **mur a.** blind wall; *Tech* **écrou a.** blind nut; **trou a.** dead hole; **bout a. (d'un tuyau)** blind end

(c) *(haine)* blind, unreasoning; *(confiance)* implicit; **avoir une confiance a. en qn** to trust sb implicitly *or* unreservedly; **obéissance a.** blind *or* unquestioning obedience; **son amour pour elle le rend a.** he's blinded by his love for her

2 *n* blind man; blind woman; **les aveugles** the blind; *Fig* **suivre qn en a.** to follow sb blindly; *Vieilli* **aller à l'a.** to grope one's way

aveuglement [avœgləmɑ̃] *nm* **(a)** *(moral, mental)* blindness; **l'a. de la passion/de la colère** the blindness of passion/of anger **(b)** *Arch* blinding; **depuis son a.** since his blindness

aveuglément [avœglemɑ̃] *adv* blindly; **obéir a.** to obey blindly

aveugle-né, -née, *pl* **aveugles-né(e)s** **1** *adj (homme, femme)* blind from birth **2** *n* congenitally blind person, person blind from birth

aveugler [avœgle] **1** *vt* **(a)** *(rendre aveugle)* to blind **(b)** *(de la lumière etc)* to blind, to dazzle; *Fig* **aveuglé par la colère** blind with rage; *Fig* **son amour pour elle l'aveugle** he's blinded by his love for her **(c)** *Naut* **a. une voie d'eau** to stop a leak **(d)** *(boucher)* to plug, to stop (up), to block up; **a. une fenêtre** to wall up *or* block a window **2 s'aveugler** *vpr Fig* to be blind, to shut one's eyes (**sur** to sth); **il ne faut pas t'a., ça ne sera pas facile** don't delude yourself *or F* kid yourself, it won't be easy; **s'a. sur les défauts de qn** to shut one's eyes *or* turn a blind eye to sb's faults

aveuglette (à l') [alavœglɛt] *adv* blindly; **aller à l'a.** to feel *or* grope one's way; **avancer à l'a. vers qch** to feel *or* grope one's way to(wards) sth; *Fig* **choisir qch à l'a.** to choose sth at random *or* in the dark *or* blindly; **lancer des coups à l'a.** to hit out blindly; *Av* **voler à l'a.** to fly blind

aveulir [avølir] **1** *vt Litt* to enervate; *(sentiments)* to deaden **2 s'aveulir** *vpr* to be effete

aveulissement [avølismɑ̃] *nm* effeteness

aviaire [avjɛr] *adj* **peste a.** fowl plague *or* pest

aviateur, -trice [avjatœr, -tris] *n* aviator

aviation [avjasjɔ̃] *nf* **(a)** *(activité)* flying, aviation; **aimer l'a.** to like flying; **il fait de l'a. le week-end** he goes flying at the weekends; **école d'a.** flying school, school of aviation **(b)** *(secteur)* aviation; **a. civile/commerciale** civil/commercial aviation; **a. de tourisme** civil aviation; **champ** *ou* **terrain d'a.** airfield; **usine d'a.** aircraft factory; **compagnie d'a.** airline **(c)** *(Mil)* air force; **base d'a.** air base

avicole [avikɔl] *adj* **élevage a.** *(activité)* poultry farming; *(établissement)* poultry farm

aviculteur, -trice [avikyltœr, -tris] *nm* poultry farmer,

aviculture [avikyltyr] *nf* **(a)** *(d'oiseaux)* aviculture **(b)** *(de volailles)* poultry farming

avide [avid] *adj* **(a)** *(passionné)* eager, avid, greedy; **a. de qch** *(âpre)* greedy for sth; *(plein d'enthousiasme)* eager for sth; **espérances avides** eager hopes; **a. de sang** bloodthirsty; **a. de tout savoir** eager for knowledge **(b)** *Péj* greedy, covetous (**de** of); *(mains, nature)* grasping

avidement [avidmɑ̃] *adv* greedily, hungrily; **écouter a.** to listen eagerly *or* avidly

avidité [avidite] *nf* avidity, greed(iness); *(de nourriture)* greed, gluttony; **manger avec a.** to eat greedily; **écouter avec a.** to listen eagerly *or* avidly

avili [avili] *adj* **(a)** *(personne)* degraded, debased, demeaned **(b)** *Com (monnaie, système monétaire)* debased; *(biens)* depreciated

avilir [avilir] **1** *vt* **(a)** *(dégrader)* to degrade, to debase, to lower **(b)** *Com (monnaie, prix etc)* to depreciate, to lower, to bring down **2 s'avilir** *vpr* **(a)** *(d'une personne)* to lower *or* demean oneself **(b)** *(de biens)* to depreciate, to come down (in value)

avilissant [avilisɑ̃] *adj* debasing, degrading

avilissement [avilismɑ̃] *nm* **(a)** *(dégradation)* debasement, degradation **(b)** *Com* depreciation; *(de prix)* fall

aviné [avine] *adj (attrib)* intoxicated, inebriated; **haleine avinée** breath reeking of wine

aviner [avine] *vt (tonneau)* to impregnate with wine

avion [avjɔ̃] *nm* aeroplane, aircraft, plane, *Am* airplane; **j'ai fait une partie du trajet en a.** I flew part of the way; **par a.** (by) airmail; **voyager en a.** to travel by plane *or* air, to fly; **prendre l'a. pour aller à Londres** to get *or* take the plane to London, to fly to London; **accident d'a.** plane crash; **détournement d'a.** hijacking, hijack, skyjacking

► **avion**: **a. d'attaque au sol** ground attack aircraft; **a. bimoteur** twin-engine aircraft; **a. de bombardement** bomber; **a. charter** charter plane; **a. de chasse** fighter (plane); **a. commercial** commercial aircraft; **a. à décollage et atterrissage courts** short take-off and landing aircraft; **a. à décollage et atterrissage verticaux** vertical take-off and landing aircraft; **a. furtif** stealth bomber; **a. à géometrie variable** swing-wing aircraft; **a. gros porteur** jumbo jet, wide bodied aircraft; **a. à hélices** prop jet; **a. de ligne** airliner, passenger aircraft; **a. mixte** passenger and cargo plane; **a. moyen porteur** regular bodied aircraft; **a. de pénétration** intruder; **a. petit porteur** narrow bodied aircraft; **a. ravitailleur** tanker; **a. à réaction** jet, jet plane, jet aircraft; **a. de reconnaissance** reconnaissance aircraft; **a. supersonique** supersonic aircraft; **a. de tourisme** private aircraft; **a. transbordeur** air ferry; **a. de transport** transport aircraft

avion-cargo, *pl* **avions-cargos** *nm* freight plane, cargo plane

avion-citerne, *pl* **avions-citernes** *nm Av* tanker (aircraft)

avion-école, *pl* **avions-écoles** [avjɔ̃ekɔl] *nm* trainer, training aircraft

avionique [avjɔnik] *nf Av* avionics

avionneur [avjɔnœr] *nm* **(a)** *(concepteur)* airframe designer **(b)** *(constructeur)* airframe manufacturer

avion-taxi, *pl* **avions-taxis** *nm* air taxi, taxiplane
aviron [avirɔ̃] *nm* **(a)** (*rame*) oar, *Can* (canoe) paddle; **a. de couple** scull; **avirons de couple** *ou* **accouplés** double-banked oars; **avirons de** *ou* **en pointe** single-banked oars; **a. de galère** sweep; **les avirons dans l'eau!** hold water!; **engager son a.** to catch a crab; **coup d'a.** stroke **(b)** *Sp* **l'a.** rowing; **cercles d'a.** rowing clubs; **faire de l'a.** to row
avironner [avirɔne] *vi Can* (*en canoë*) to paddle
avis [avi] *nm* **(a)** (*opinion*) opinion, judg(e)ment; **a. d'expert** expert advice *or* opinion; **exprimer** *ou* **émettre un a.** to express a view *or* an opinion; **être du même a. que qn** to be of the same opinion as sb; **ne pas être du même a. que qn** to disagree with sb; **sauf meilleur a. je crois que …** with all due deference I think that …; *Prov* **deux a. valent mieux qu'un** two heads are better than one; **à** *ou* **selon mon a.** in my opinion; **à mon humble a. …** in my humble opinion …; *F* **on ne t'a pas demandé ton a.!** nobody asked you!, mind your own business!, nobody asked your opinion!; **de l'a. de tous** in the opinion *or* judgment of all; **on dit qu'il est riche mais ce n'est pas l'a. de tout le monde** he's said to be rich but not everyone would agree with that; **je suis tout à fait de votre a.** I entirely agree with you; **j'ai changé d'a.** I have changed my mind; *Hum* **elle change d'a. comme de chemise** she changes her mind like she changes her underwear; **être d'a. de faire qch** to be of a mind to do sth; **êtes-vous d'a. de rester ici?** are you for staying here?
(b) (*conseil*) advice; **donner des a. à qn sur qch** to give sb some advice; **prendre** *ou* **demander l'a. de qn** to ask sb's advice
(c) (*avertissement*) notice, announcement; **a. (au public)** public notice, notice (to the public); **donner a. de qch** to give notice of sth; **donner a. à qn de qch** to advise sb of sth; **a. par écrit** notice in writing; **jusqu'à nouvel a.** until further notice, until you hear further; **à moins d'a. contraire** unless I/you/*etc* hear to the contrary; *Com* **note** *ou* **lettre d'a.** advice note; **suivant a.** as per advice
▶ **avis**: **a. de la banque** bank notification *or* advice; **a. de crédit** credit advice; **a. de débit** debit advice; *Com* **a. de domiciliation** domiciliation advice; *Journ* **a. éditorial** editorial opinion; *Bourse* **a. d'exécution** contract note; **a. d'expédition** (*de marchandises*) dispatch *or* consignment note; **a. d'expédition standard** (*de marchandises*) standard shipping note; **a. d'imposition** tax assessment; **a. de livraison** delivery note; **a. de paiement** payment advice; **a. de prélèvement** direct debit advice; **a. de réception** acknowledgement (of receipt); **a. de rejet** (*de chèque*) notice of returned cheque; *Banque* **a. de virement** (bank) transfer advice
avisé [avize] *adj* sensible, wise, prudent; **être trop a. pour faire qch** to be too sensible *or* cautious *or* wary to do sth; **il est trop a. pour …** he knows better than to …; **acheteur a.** discriminating purchaser; **bien a.** well-advised; **mesures mal avisées** ill-advised measures; **tu serais mal a. de …** you'd be ill-advised to …
aviser [avize] **1** *vt* **(a)** (*informer*) to inform, to notify, to advise; **a. qn de qch** to inform *or* warn *or Com* advise sb of sth; **a. qn de faire qch** to give sb notice to do sth; **a. qn que + *ind*** to warn sb that …
(b) *Arch, Litt* (*entrevoir*) to perceive, to catch a glimpse of
2 *vi* **a. à** (*situation etc*) to decide what to do about, to see about *or* to; **vous ferez bien d'y a.** you had better look into it; **a. à faire qch** to see about doing sth; **a. à ce que qch se fasse** to take steps to have sth done; **il est temps d'a.** it is time to decide *or* to make up one's mind; **j'aviserai en temps voulu** I'll see to that when it's necessary
3 s'aviser *vpr* **(a) s'a. de qch** to think of sth; **il ne s'avise de rien** he's not aware of anything; **s'a. que** to notice that, to become aware that, to realize that
(b) s'a. de faire qch to take it upon oneself to do sth; **ne vous en avisez pas!** don't dare to do such a thing!, don't you dare!, you'd better not!; **et ne t'avise pas de recommencer!** don't (you) dare start again!
aviso [avizo] *nm Naut* sloop; **a.-torpilleur** torpedo gunboat; **a. d'escorte** corvette; **canonnière-a.** gunboat
avitaminose [avitaminoz] *nf* vitamin deficiency, avitaminosis
aviver [avive] **1** *vt* **(a)** (*couleurs etc*) to revive, to brighten; (*couleurs, image*) to touch up; (*plaie, blessure*) to irritate; (*passion*) to excite, stir up; (*feu*) to fan, to revive, to stir up; (*appétit*) to sharpen; (*querelle*) to stir up; **a. d'anciennes rancunes** to revive ancient grudges **(b)** (*ferronnerie*) to burnish; (*marbre*) to polish **(c)** (*surfaces à souder*) to clean up **(d)** (*outil etc*) to put a keen edge on, to whet **2 s'aviver** *vpr* (*souvenirs, controverse etc*) to be stirred up, to be revived; (*couleur*) to become brighter
av. J.-C. (*abrév* **avant Jésus-Christ**) BC

avocat¹, -ate [avɔka, -at] *n* **(a)** *Jur* lawyer, *esp Am* attorney; (*à la barre*) *Br* barrister; **plaider par a.** to be represented by counsel; **elle est a.** *ou* **avocate** she's a barrister **(b)** *Fig* advocate; **a. du diable** devil's advocate
▶ **avocat**: **a. conseil** consulting barrister; **a. consultant** counsel in chambers; **a. général** assistant public prosecutor (in a court of appeal)
avocat² *nm* (*fruit*) avocado (pear)
avocat-avoué, *pl* **avocats-avoués** *nm* ≈ attorney
avocatier [avɔkatje] *nm* (*arbre*) avocado (tree)
avocette [avɔsɛt] *nf* (*oiseau*) avocet
avoine [avwan] *nf* **(a)** oats; **a. commune** common oats; **farine d'a.** oatmeal; **flocons d'a.** porridge oats; **bouillie d'a.** (oatmeal) porridge; **galette d'a.** oatcake **(b)** *Arg* (*argent*) dosh, dough
avoir¹ [avwar] (*prp* **ayant**; *pp* **eu**; *pr ind* **j'ai, tu as, il a, n. avons, v. avez, ils ont**; *pr sub* **j'aie, tu aies, il ait, n. ayons, v. ayez, ils aient**; *imp* **aie, ayons, ayez**; *impf* **j'avais**; *p hist* **j'eus, tu eus, il eut, n. eûmes, v. eûtes, ils eurent**; *impf sub* **j'eusse**; *fu* **j'aurai**; **avoir** *is the auxiliary of all transitive and of many intransitive verbs*) **1** *vt* [①A54-5,b] **(a)** (*maison, télévision, sœur, enfant, animal domestique*) to have; **tu ne veux pas a. d'enfant?** do you not want to have children?; **elle vient d'a. un enfant** she's just had a child; **quel diplôme avez-vous?** what degree have you got, what degree do you have?; **il donnerait tout ce qu'il a pour …** he'd give everything he's got *or* he has to …; **on a 4 heures d'anglais par semaine** we have *or* we've got 4 hours (of) English a week; *F* **faut que j'y aille, j'ai math!** I've got to go, I've got maths!; **j'ai Monsieur Lê comme professeur de math** I've (got) Mr Lê for maths; **j'ai Bill pour ami/voisin** Bill is a friend/neighbour of mine; **a. un entretien/une dispute/une conversation avec qn** to have an interview/an argument/a conversation with sb; **j'ai rendez-vous chez le médecin** I have *or* I've got a doctor's appointment; **a. des amis à dîner** to have friends to *or* for dinner; **je te rappelle que nous avons des amis à dîner ce soir** remember we're having friends to *or* for dinner tonight; **as-tu de quoi manger/vivre?** have you (got) enough to eat/live on?, do you have enough to eat/live on?; **ça coûte cher d'avoir une voiture** it's expensive to run a car; **qu'est-ce que vous avez là?** what have you (got) there?; **c'est un joli collier que vous avez là** that's a pretty necklace you have *or* you've got there; **il a encore son père** his father is still alive, he's still got his father; **Dieu ait son âme** God rest his/her soul
(b) (*obtenir*) to get; **j'ai eu sa réponse ce matin** I had *or* got his answer this morning; **pourriez-vous m'a. ce renseignement?** could you get that information for me?; **j'ai eu du mal à a. Paris/le numéro** (*au téléphone*) I've had trouble getting (through to) Paris/the number; **c'est lui que j'ai eu au téléphone hier** he's the one I talked to *or* had on the phone yesterday; **j'ai bien eu mon train ce matin** I caught my train all right this morning; **j'ai eu ce réfrigérateur à bon marché** I got *or* bought this refrigerator cheap; **celui-là, je l'aime et je l'aurai!** (*je le séduirai*) I love that man and I'll get him! *or* I'm going to have him!
(c) (*mesure, âge*) **a. dix ans** to be ten (years old); **le mur a trois mètres de haut** the wall is three metres high; **a. plusieurs centaines de mètres de profondeur/de longueur/de largeur** to be several hundred metres deep/long/broad
(d) (*dans les descriptions physiques et morales*) to have; **a. les yeux bleus** to have blue eyes; **a. de grandes mains/de beaux yeux** to have big hands/beautiful eyes; **a. les cheveux longs** to have long hair; **je commence à a. des cheveux blancs** I'm starting to get a few grey hairs; **a. du charme** to have charm, to be full of charm; **elle a du talent** she has (got) talent; **il a beaucoup d'ambition** he's got a lot of ambition; **elle a beaucoup d'humour** she has (got) a good sense of humour; **elle avait un foulard sur les cheveux** she had a scarf in her hair; **elle avait une jolie robe bleue** she had a pretty blue dress on; **il avait un bébé dans les bras** he had a baby in his arms
(e) (*toucher*) to hit, to get; *F* (*duper*) to take for a ride, to con; **je crois que je l'ai eue (la cible)** I think I hit *or* got it; **on les aura!** we'll get them!; **il finira par se faire a. (par la police)** he'll end up getting done (by the police); **on l'a eu!** (*dupé*) he's been had!, he's been taken for a ride!; **je t'ai eu!** got you!; **tu m'as bien eu cette fois-ci!** you really got me that time!, I really fell for it that time!; **se faire a.** to be had, to be taken for a ride; **je veux acheter une voiture d'occasion mais je ne veux pas me faire a.** I want to buy a second hand car, but I don't want to get ripped off *or* done *or* conned; **je me suis fait a. de 100 francs** I got done out of 100 francs
(f) (*faire*) **il eut un mouvement brusque** he made a

sudden movement; **il eut un sourire** he gave a smile; **il eut un cri de surprise** he gave a cry of surprise; **il eut un petit rire moqueur** he gave a mocking little laugh; **il eut un regard étrange** he gave a strange look

(g) (*souffrir de*) to have; **a. un rhume/la grippe/le hoquet** to have a cold/(the) flu/(the) hiccups; **a. du diabète/du cholestérol** to have diabetes/excess cholesterol; **a. mal au cœur** to feel sick; **a. de la fièvre** to have a *or* be running a temperature; **a. la rougeole** to have measles

(h) (*éprouver*) **qu'avez-vous?, qu'est-ce que vous avez?** what's wrong *or* the matter *or* up (with you)?; **je ne sais pas ce que j'ai, je ne me sens pas bien du tout** I don't know what's wrong *or* the matter with me, I don't feel at all well; **mais qu'est-ce qu'elle a, cette auto?** what's wrong *or* the matter with this car?; **qu'est-ce que tu as? – j'ai que je suis en colère!** what's wrong with you? – I'm angry, that's what's wrong with me!; **mais qu'est-ce qu'elle a à râler tout le temps?** what's the matter with her, moaning all the time?; **a. de la peine** to be upset; **a. des soucis** to be worried; **a. des doutes** to have misgivings; **a. des remords** to feel remorse

(i) (*après* **en**) **nous en avons pour deux heures** it will take us two hours, we'll be two hours; **j'en ai pour une minute** I won't be a minute; **tu en auras pour combien de temps?** how long will you be?, how long will it take you?; **j'en ai assez, je n'en veux plus** I've had enough, I don't want any more; **j'en ai assez** *ou F* **marre** *ou F* **ras-le-bol** I've had enough *or F* I've had it up to here *or F* I'm sick (to the back teeth) of it; **j'en ai eu pour 100 francs** (*c'est le prix*) it cost me 100 francs; (*en quantité*) I had 100 francs' worth; **en a. contre** *ou* **après qn** to have it in for sb

(j) a. qch à faire to have sth to do; **pourquoi tu t'en vas? – parce que j'ai à faire** why are you leaving? – because I have things to do; **je n'ai rien à faire** I have nothing to do; **j'ai à travailler** I've work to do; **vous n'avez pas à vous inquiéter** you have no need to worry; **tu n'as pas à te mêler de cette histoire** you shouldn't get mixed up in this matter; **je n'ai que faire de cela** I don't need that

(k) [①**B63**,3] *for the verbal phrases* **a. affaire, faim, froid, pitié, raison** *etc see under these words*

2 *v impers* **il y a (a)** (*être présent*) **il y a un problème** there is a problem; **il y a des problèmes** there are problems; **qu'est-ce qu'il peut (bien) y a. dans ce tiroir?** I wonder what's in this drawer?; **qu'est-ce qu'il y a à voir?** what is there to see?; **combien y a-t-il de blessés?** how many wounded are there?; **il n'y en a qu'un** there is only one; **il n'y en aura pas assez pour tout le monde** there won't be enough for everyone; **il n'y en a que pour elle** she gets all the attention; **un homme comme il y en a peu** a man in a million; **une petite fille tout ce qu'il y a de gentil** the nicest little girl you've ever seen; **il y a du soleil aujourd'hui** it's sunny today, the sun is shining today; **il n'y a pas de quoi** please don't mention it, you're welcome!; *F* **quand (il) y en a pour deux, (il) y en a pour trois** there's more than enough to go round; *F* **quand (il n')y en a plus, (il) y en a encore** there'll be plenty more when that's finished; (*comme on apporte encore de la nourriture*) as soon as one lot is finished, another one is on its way!; **il y a hôpital et hôpital!** there are hospitals and hospitals; **il y en a qui disent que …** there are people who say that …, some people say that …; **il y en a un qui va être surpris** someone is in for a surprise; **il n'y a que lui qui …** (*+subj*) he's the only one who …, it's only him that …; **il n'y a qu'à demander** you only have to ask, just ask; **il n'y a pas à hésiter, il faut lui parler** there's no point in hanging about, I/you/we/*etc* have to talk to him; *F* **il n'y a pas à dire, tu es plus fort que moi** there's no denying it *or* there's no question, you're stronger than I am; **à l'entendre, y'a qu'à faire ceci, y'a qu'à faire cela, c'est trop simple** listening to him and his just do this, just do that, it's all too easy

(b) (*se passer*) **il doit y a. quelque chose** there must be something wrong; **qu'y a-t-il à présent?** what now?; **qu'est-ce qu'il y a?** what's the matter?, what's up?; **il y a qu'on t'attendait hier** we were expecting you yesterday, that's what's wrong *or* that's what's the matter

(c) (*temps*) **il y a deux ans** two years ago; **il y avait six mois que j'attendais** I had been waiting for six months; **il y des années qu'on ne s'est pas vus** we haven't seen each other for years; *F* **il y a une éternité** ages ago

(d) (*distance*) **combien y a-t-il d'ici Londres?** how far is it (from here) to London?; **il y a 5 km d'ici à Londres** it's 5 km (from here) to London

3 *v aux* [①**B25**,C; **B35-36**,2c,ii] **j'ai fini** I have *or* I've finished; **j'ai fini ce matin** I finished this morning; **je n'ai pas compris** I did not *or* didn't understand; **je l'ai déjà vu** I have already seen him, I have seen him before; **l'avez-vous lu?** have you read it?; **je l'ai vu/vue hier** I saw him/her yesterday; **attendez que nous ayons fini** wait until we've finished; **j'ai eu vingt ans hier** I was twenty yesterday; **j'ai eu bientôt fini de m'habiller** I (had) soon finished dressing; **quand il eut** *ou* **a eu fini de parler** when he had finished speaking; **j'aurai bientôt fini** I shall soon have finished

avoir² *nm* (*biens*) property, possessions; (*de société*) assets *pl*; (*capital*) capital; (*sur compte*) credit; (*attestation de crédit*) credit note; **a. de compte** account credit; **a. en banque** bank credit; *Compta* **avoir-client** customer credit; *Compta* **avoir-fournisseur** supplier credit; **a. en devises** foreign currency holding; **a. fiscal** tax credit; **tout mon a.** all I possess *or* have; *Com* **doit et a.** debit and credit; **obtenir un a.** to be given credit, to obtain *or* to get credit; **je ne peux pas vous rembourser mais je peux vous faire un a.** I can't give you your money back, but I can give you a credit note

avoirdupoi(d)s [avwardypwa] *nm* avoirdupois

avoisinant [avwazinɑ̃] *adj* neighbouring, nearby; **il a cinquante ans ou un âge a.** he's fifty or thereabout(s); **il a volé une somme avoisinante de 500 francs** he has stolen a sum of around 500 francs *or* close to 500 francs

avoisiner [avwazine] *vt* **a. qch** to be near *or* close to *or* adjacent to sth, to border on sth; **il a volé une somme avoisinant les 500 francs** he has stolen a sum of around 500 francs *or* close to 500 francs; **cela avoisine la malhonnêteté** it's bordering on dishonesty

avortement [avɔrtəmɑ̃] *nm* **(a)** (*chez une femme*) **a. spontané** miscarriage; **a. provoqué** abortion; **a. thérapeutique** termination *or* abortion (for medical reasons) **(b)** (*chez un animal*) casting **(c)** *Fig* (*de projet etc*) failure, falling through

avorter [avɔrte] *vi* **(a)** (*d'une femme*) (*faire une fausse couche*) to miscarry; **elle veut (se faire) a.** she wants (to have) an abortion; **faire a. qn** to give sb an abortion; (*d'une injection etc*) to bring on a miscarriage **(b)** (*d'un animal*) to cast **(c)** *Bot* to develop imperfectly, to fail to ripen, to abort; **arbres avortés** stunted trees **(d)** *Fig* **projet qui a avorté** plan that fell through

avorteur, -euse [avɔrtœr, -øz] *n* abortionist

avorton [avɔrtɔ̃] *nm* (*personne, animal*) runt; (*plante*) stunted plant, *Péj* **espèce d'a.!** you little shrimp *or* squirt!

avouable [avwabl] *adj* (*fait, motif*) avowable; **c'est un métier plus a.** it's a more respectable trade

avoué¹ [avwe] *nm Jur* ≈ solicitor, *US* attorney

avoué² *adj* **(a)** (*fait*) acknowledged, admitted **(b)** (*auteur de …*) confessed; **il est le père a. de cette petite fille** he admits he's the father of this little girl **(c)** (*but*) ostensible; **il est allé là-bas dans le but a. de se venger** he went there ostensibly *or* supposedly for revenge

avouer [avwe] **1** *vt* (*faute etc*) to confess, to admit, to own up to; **elle ne veut pas a. que c'est elle qui a pris l'argent** she won't admit that she took the money; **elle avoue avoir trente ans** she admits to being thirty; **ceci me surprend, je l'avoue** this surprises me, I must confess *or* admit *or* say; **il faut bien a. que c'est lui qui avait raison** it must be admitted *or* said that he was right; **a. avoir fait qch** to confess *or* to own up to having done sth

2 *vi* to confess

3 s'avouer *vpr* to admit (to being *+adj*); **s'a. coupable** to admit one's guilt; **s'a. vaincu** to acknowledge oneself beaten, to acknowledge defeat

avril [avril] *nm* [①**A75-6**,B-C; **B58-9**,B-C] April; **en a.** in April; **au mois d'a.** in the month of April; **pluie d'a.** April showers; **le sept a.** (on) the seventh of April, (on) April (the) seventh; **le premier a.** the first of April; April Fools' Day; **poisson d'a.!** April fool!

avunculaire [avɔ̃kylɛr] *adj* avuncular

axe [aks] *nm* **(a)** [①**A14**,10] (*Géom de plante, de la terre, d'ellipse etc*) axis; **grand/petit a.** major/minor axis; **a. de rotation** axis of rotation; *Constr* **a. d'une route/d'un pont** centre line of a road/bridge; *Aut* **a. routier** trunk road; **les grands axes de la circulation** trunk *or* major roads; *Fig* **les grands axes de sa politique** the main thrust of his policy; *Math* **a. des x/des y** x-axis/y-axis; **a. des abscisses/des ordonnées** x/y axis; **axes de coordonnées** co-ordinate axes; *Tech* **axes principaux d'un corps** principal axes of a body; **cristal à deux axes** biaxial crystal

(b) *MecE etc* axle, spindle, pin; (*de roue de vélo*) axle (pin); **a. de pompe** pump spindle; **a. d'une grue** pin of a crane; **a. du piston** (*d'un moteur*) gudgeon pin; *Aut* **a. de fusée** king pin; **a. transversal** cross-shaft; **a. roulis** roll axis

(c) *Hist* axis; **les Puissances de l'A.** the Axis powers

(d) *Mil* **a. de progression** main direction of advance; **a. (principal) de ravitaillement** main line of supply, main supply route

(e) *Av* **a. de sustentation** lift axis; **a. de descente** glide path, line of descent; **a. balisé** radio range course; **a. balisé**

d'atterrissage radio landing beam; **a. de référence** datum line

axer [akse] *vt* to centre; **être axé sur** *ou* **autour de** to centre on; **sa philosophie est axée sur le don de soi** his philosophy is centred *or* based on self-denial; **toute sa vie est axée là-dessus** it's his whole life, his whole life revolves around it; **il a toujours été axé sur le travail/l'argent** he has always been work-oriented/money-oriented; **il a toujours été axé sur la religion/la recherche du plaisir** for him everything has always revolved around religion/pleasure-seeking; **une visite touristique axée sur ...** a guided tour focusing on ...; **axé sur le profit** profit-oriented; **l'expansion de la compagnie sera axée sur ...** the central thrust of company expansion will be ...

axial, -ale, -aux, -ales [aksjal, -o] *adj* (*ligne, plan*) axial; **effort de compression axiale** collapsible load; *Géol* **plan a.** axial plane; **éclairage a.** (*des rues*) central overhead lighting

axillaire [aksilɛr] *adj Anat, Bot* axillary

axiomatique [aksjɔmatik] *adj* axiomatic

axiome [aksjom] *nm* axiom

axis [aksis] *nm Anat* axis

ayant [ɛjɑ̃] *nm* **(a)** *Jur* **a. cause,** *pl* **ayants cause** (*bénéficiaire de testament*) legal successor, successor in title, legatee; (*bénéficiaire de cadeau*) donee; (*bénéficiaire de transfert*) assignee; (*acheteur*) vendee; (*agent désigné*) executor, trustee **(b) a. droit**, *pl* **ayants droit** (= **ayant cause**) eligible party, entitled beneficiary

ayant-compte, *pl* **ayants-comptes** *nm Banque* account holder

ayatollah [ajatɔla] *nm* ayatollah

azalée [azale] *nf* (*plante*) azalea

azimut [azimyt] *nm Astron etc* azimuth; *Naut etc* **prendre un a.** to take a bearing; *F* **dans tous les azimuts** everywhere, all over the place; *Fig F* **y aller tous azimuts** to go flat out *or* all out, to go at it hammer and tongs; *Fig* **une campagne électorale tous azimuts** an all-out electoral campaign

azimutal, -ale, -aux, -ales [azimytal, -o] *adj* azimuth(al); **cercle a.** azimuth circle; **compas a.** azimuth compass

azimuté [azimyte] *adj F* crazy, round the bend

azotate [azɔtat] *nm Ch* nitrate; **a. de potasse** nitre, saltpetre

azote [azɔt] *nm Ch* nitrogen

azoté [azɔte] *adj* nitrogenous; **engrais azotés** nitrate fertilizers, nitrates

azoter [azɔte] *vt* to nitrogenize

azotique [azɔtik] *adj Ch* nitric

azotite [azɔtit] *nm Ch* nitrite

AZT [azɛdte] *abrév Pharm* (**azydothymidine**) AZT

aztèque [aztɛk] **1** *adj* Aztec **2** *n* **A.** Aztec

azur [azyr] *nm* **(a)** (*couleur*) azure, sky-blue **(b)** *Géog* **la Côte d'A.** the French Riviera **(c)** *Hér* **champ d'a.** field azure **(d) pierre d'a.** lapis lazuli **(e)** *Com* (*pour linge*) blue

azuré [azyre] *adj* **(a)** (sky-)blue, azure **(b)** *Litt* tinged with blue

azurer [azyre] *vt* **(a)** (*linge etc*) to blue **(b)** *Litt* to tinge with blue

azyme [azim] **1** *adj* **pain a.** unleavened bread **2** *nm Jewish, Rel* **fête des azymes** feast of unleavened bread, Passover

B

B, b [be] *nm* **(a)** *(lettre)* B, b **(b)** *Ch (symbole du bore)* B

B.A. [bea] *nf (abrév* **bonne action***)* good deed; **faire sa/une B.A.** to do one's good deed for the day/a good deed

B. A-Ba [beaba] *nm F* ABC, *Am* ABCs, rudiments; **je ne connais que le B. de la comptabilité** I only know the rudiments of accountancy; **c'est le B. de la physique quantique** *(livre)* it's the kiddies' guide to quantum physics

baba¹ [baba] *nm Culin* **b. au rhum** (rum) baba; *F* **elle l'a eu dans le b.** she came unstuck

baba² *adj inv F* dumbfounded, flabbergasted; **j'en suis resté b.** I was absolutely flabbergasted; **j'en suis complètement b.** I'm absolutely flabbergasted

baba cool *n* hippie

Babel [babɛl] *nf* Babel; **la tour de B.** the Tower of Babel; *Fig* **c'est une vraie tour de B.** it's absolute Babel, it's pandemonium

babeurre [babœr] *nm* buttermilk

babil [babi(l)] *nm* *(d'un enfant)* prattle, prattling; *(des oiseaux)* twittering; *(d'un ruisseau)* babbling

babillage [babijaʒ] *nm* **(a)** = **babil** **(b)** *Psy* lallation

babillard, -arde [babijar, -ard] **1** *adj* *(personne)* chattering; *(enfant)* prattling; *(bébé)* babbling; *Fig* **ruisseau b.** babbling brook **2** *n* *(personne)* chatterbox **3** *nm* **(a)** *Can Scol* flannel board **(b)** *Ordinat* bulletin board, BBs

babillement [babijmɑ̃] *nm* = **babil**

babiller [babije] *vi* *(d'une personne)* to chatter; *(d'un enfant)* to prattle; *(d'un ruisseau)* to babble; *(d'un oiseau)* to twitter

babines [babin] *nfpl Zool* chops; *F* *(d'une personne)* chops, lips; **s'essuyer les b.** to wipe one's chops *or* lips; **d'avance, je m'en lèche les b.** my mouth's watering in anticipation

babiole [babjɔl] *nf* **(a)** *(bibelot)* knick-knack, trinket **(b)** *(incident)* trifle

bâbord [babɔr] *nm Naut* port (side); **la barre à b. toute!, b. toute!** hard a-port!; **la terre par b.!** land on the port side!; **aviron de b.** stroke side-oar

babouche [babuʃ] *nf* Turkish slipper

babouin [babwɛ̃] *nm* baboon

baboune [babun] *nf Can F* **faire la b.** to sulk

baby [bebi] **1** *adj inv* **taille b.** baby-size(d); **whisky b.** small whisky **2** *nm* small whisky

baby-boom, *pl* **baby-booms** *nm* baby boom; **enfants du b.** baby-boomers

baby-foot [babifut] *nm inv* table football; *(table)* football table

Babylone [babilɔn] *nf Antiq* Babylon

Babylonie [babilɔni] *nf Antiq* Babylonia

babylonien, -ienne [babilɔnjɛ̃, -jɛn] *Antiq* **1** *adj* Babylonian **2** *n* **B.** Babylonian

babyphone [babifɔn] *nm* baby-listening microphone

baby-sitter, *pl* **baby-sitters** [bebisitœr, babi-] *n* baby-sitter

baby-sitting [bebisitiŋ, babi-] *nm* baby-sitting; **faire du b.** to baby-sit

bac¹ [bak] *nm* **(a)** *(bateau)* ferry (boat); **b. à piétons** passenger ferry; **passer qn dans un b.** to ferry sb across; *Jur* **droit de b.** ferry (right)

(b) *(récipient)* *(pour liquides)* tank, vat; *(d'une cellule électrique)* pot; *(d'un accumulateur)* box, container; *(pour la nourriture etc)* box, container; *(de mineur)* truck, tub; *(d'imprimeur, de photographe)* tray

▶ **bac**: *Ordinat* **b. d'alimentation** sheet feed; *Aut* **b. à cartes** map pocket; **b. à correspondance** correspondence tray; **b. à douche** shower tray; *Ordinat* **b. feuille à feuille** cut sheet feeder; *Ordinat* **b. de feuilles** paper tray; **b. à glace** ice tray; **b. introducteur** *(de feuillets)* sheet feed; **b. à laver** wash tub; **b. à légumes** salad drawer *or* crisper; *Belg* **b. à ordures** *Br* dustbin, *Am* garbage *or* trash *or* ash can; **b. de** *ou* **à papier** *(d'imprimante)* paper tray; **b. de papier A4** A4 paper tray; *Aut* **b. de rangement** stowage bin; **b. roulant** file trolley; **b. à sable** sandpit

bac² *nm F* = **baccalauréat**; **passer le b.** to take *or Br* sit one's baccalauréat; **préparer le b.** to study for one's baccalauréat

baccalauréat [bakalɔrea] *nm* **(a)** = secondary school examination qualifying for entry to university, *Br* ≈ A levels, *(in Scotland)* ≈ Scottish Higher Certificate of Education, *(in Eire)* ≈ School Leaving Certificate **(b)** *Hist* **b. en droit** = degree granted when a student has passed his first two examinations for the Licence en Droit **(c)** *Can Univ* bachelor's degree; **b. ès arts/ès sciences** Bachelor of Arts/Science

baccara(t)¹ [bakara] *nm Cartes* baccarat

baccarat² *nm* *(cristal)* Baccarat crystal

bacchanale [bakanal] *nf* **(a)** *(orgie)* orgy; *(débauche)* drunken revel; *(danse)* bacchanalian dance **(b)** *Antiq* **les bacchanales** the bacchanalia

bacchante [bakɑ̃t] *nf* **(a)** *Antiq* bacchante **(b)** *F* **bacchantes** moustache

bâche [bɑʃ] *nf* **(a)** *Tech* *(réservoir)* tank, cistern **(b)** *(serre)* forcing frame **(c)** *(toile)* tarpaulin, canvas cover; **b. de campement** ground sheet

▶ **bâche**: **b. d'alimentation** feed tank; **b. goudronnée** tarpaulin

bachelier, -ière [baʃəlje, -jɛr] *n Scol* student who has passed the baccalauréat

bâcher [bɑʃe] *vt* **b. qch** to cover sth (with a tarpaulin)

bachi-bouzouk, *pl* **bachi-bouzouks** [baʃibuzuk] *nm Hist* bashi-bazouk; *F* **espèce de b.!** you crackpot!

bachique [baʃik] *adj* Bacchic; **scène b.** bacchanalian scene; **chanson b.** drinking song

bachot¹ [baʃo] *nm Naut* skiff, wherry

bachot² *nm F* = **baccalauréat**; **boîte à b.** crammer

bachotage [baʃɔtaʒ] *nm Scol F* cramming, *Br* swotting; **faire du b.** to do some cramming

bachoter [baʃɔte] *vi Scol F* to cram, *Br* to swot

bachoteur, -euse [baʃɔtœr, -øz] *n Scol F* student cramming *or Br* swotting for an exam

bacillaire [basilɛr] **1** *adj* bacillary **2** *n* tubercular patient

bacille [basil] *nm* **(a)** [①A13,8] *Biol* bacillus **(b)** *(insecte)* stick insect

bacillose [basiloz] *nf Méd* bacillosis, bacillus infection; **b. pulmonaire** pulmonary tuberculosis

background [bakgrawnd] *nm* background

back-office [bakɔfis] *nm Banque* back office

bâclage [bɑklaʒ] *nm F* *(d'un travail)* botching (up)

bâcle [bɑkl] *nf* *(d'une porte, fenêtre)* bar

bâclé [bɑkle] *adj* *(travail etc)* botched (up), slapdash

bâcler [bɑkle] **1** *vt* **(a)** *F* *(travail)* to botch (up); **b. sa toilette** to give oneself a quick wash **(b)** *Arch* *(porte, fenêtre)* to bar **2** *vi* to do a botched job

bacon [bekɔn] *nm Culin* bacon; **œufs au b.** bacon and eggs

bactéricide [bakterisid] **1** *adj* bactericidal **2** *nm* bactericide

bactérie [bakteri] *nf* bacterium, *pl* -ia

bactérien, -ienne [bakterjɛ̃, -jɛn] *adj* bacterial

bactériologie [bakterjɔlɔʒi] *nf* bacteriology

bactériologique [bakterjɔlɔʒik] *adj* bacteriological; **guerre b.** bacteriological *or* germ warfare

bactériologiste [bakterjɔlɔʒist], **bactériologue** [bakterjɔlɔg] *n* bacteriologist

bactériophage [bakterjɔfaʒ] *nm* bacteriophage

badaboum [badabum] *int F* **et b., il est tombé** he fell down, crash, bang, wallop

badaud, -aude [bado, -od] **1** *adj* gawping, *Am* rubbernecking **2** *n* *(promeneur)* stroller; *(curieux)* gawper, *Am* rubberneck

badauder [badode] *vi Vieilli* *(se promener)* to stroll about (idly); *(regarder)* to gawp, *Am* to rubberneck

baderne [badɛrn] *nf F Péj* **une (vieille) b.** an old fogey, an old fossil, an old stick-in-the-mud

badge [badʒ] *nm* badge, *Am* button; *(pour scouts)* badge

badigeon [badiʒɔ̃] *nm* *(pour les murs etc)* (colour)wash, distemper; **b. à la chaux** whitewash; *Méd* **faire un b. de teinture d'iode sur une blessure** to paint a wound with tincture of iodine

badigeonnage [badiʒɔnaʒ] *nm* **(a)** *(de mur etc)* colourwashing, distempering; *(à la chaux)* whitewashing **(b)** *Méd* *(avec de l'iode etc)* painting

badigeonner [badiʒɔne] *vt* (**a**) **b. une surface de qch** to daub a surface with sth; **b. un mur en blanc/en couleur** to whitewash/to colourwash, to distemper a wall; **b. la tourte de jaune d'œuf** to brush the pie with egg yolk (**b**) *Méd* to paint (**d'iode, à l'iode** with iodine)

badin[1] [badɛ̃] *adj* playful, light-hearted

badin[2] *nm Av* airspeed indicator

badinage [badinaʒ] *nm* banter, jesting; **sur un ton de b.** in a bantering *or* playful tone

badine [badin] *nf* cane, switch

badiner [badine] *vi* to jest, to joke; **b. de tout** to turn everything into a joke; **on ne badine pas avec l'amour** love is not something to be trifled with; **il ne faut pas b. avec ce genre de choses** these things are no laughing matter; **il ne badine pas avec la ponctualité** he's very strict about *or* he's a real stickler for punctuality

badinerie [badinri] *nf* jest

badlands [badlɑ̃ds] *nfpl* badlands

badminton [badmintɔn] *nm Sp* badminton

bâdrant [bɑdrɑ̃] *adj Can* bothersome

baffe [baf] *nf F* (*gifle*) slap, clout, clip on the ear; **recevoir/donner une paire de baffes** to get/give a couple of slaps; **tu veux une b. ou quoi?** do you want a clip on the ear?

Baffin [bafɛ̃] *nm* **la terre de B.** Baffin Island

baffle [bafl] *nm Électron* baffle

bafouer [bafwe] *vt* (*qn*) to ridicule, to jeer at; (*règlement, autorité*) to flout; **mari bafoué** cuckold

bafouillage [bafujaʒ] *nm F* (*défaut de prononciation*) stammering, spluttering; (*propos incohérents*) gibberish, nonsense; (*de moteur*) misfiring, missing

bafouille [bafuj] *nf Arg* letter

bafouiller [bafuje] **1** *vi F* (*mal prononcer*) to stammer, to splutter; (*être incohérent*) to talk gibberish *or* nonsense; (*d'un moteur*) to misfire, to miss **2** *vt* to stammer (out), to splutter (out); **je ne sais pas ce qu'il m'a bafouillé** I don't know what he was babbling about

bâfrer [bɑfre] *Arg* **1** *vi* to stuff oneself, to guzzle, *Am* to pig out **2** *vt* (*nourriture*) to guzzle, to wolf

bâfreur, -euse [bɑfrœr, -øz] *n Arg* glutton, *Br* greedy-guts

bagage [bagaʒ] *nm* (**a**) (*équipement*) kit; **plier b.** to pack one's bags *or Mil* one's kit (**b**) **bagages** luggage, *surtout Am* baggage; **retrait des bagages** baggage (re)claim; **fourgon à bagages** luggage van, *Am* baggage car; **voyager avec peu de bagages** to travel light; **faire ses bagages** to pack one's bags (**c**) *Fig* (*connaissance*) knowledge (**en** of); **avoir un bon b. en science éco** to know a lot about economics; **son b. en physique est nul** he doesn't know any physics

▶ **bagage**: **bagages accompagnés** accompanied luggage/baggage; **bagages non accompagnés** unaccompanied luggage/baggage, luggage/baggage in advance; **bagages enregistrés** checked luggage/baggage; **bagages non-enregistrés** unchecked luggage/baggage; **bagages à main** hand luggage/baggage, cabin *or* carry-on baggage; **bagages de soute** hold luggage/baggage

bagagiste [bagaʒist] *nm* luggage *or* baggage handler

bagarre [bagar] *nf* fight, brawl; **b. de rue** street fight; **il va y avoir de la b.** there's going to be a fight; **il cherche la b.** he's looking *or* spoiling for a fight; *Fig* **entre eux, c'est la b.** they've got it in for each other, they're at daggers drawn

bagarrer [bagare] *F* **1** *vi* to fight, to battle (**pour** for); **aimer b.** to like a fight; *Fig* **il faudra b. pour l'avoir** you'll have to fight *or* battle to get it **2** *vpr* **se bagarrer** (*physiquement*) to fight, to scrap, to brawl; (*se quereller*) to quarrel, to argue

bagarreur, -euse [bagarœr, -øz] *F* **1** *adj* (*personne, caractère*) aggressive; *Fig* **elle est bagarreuse** (*elle ne se laisse pas faire*) she's a fighter **2** *n* brawler; *Fig* **c'est une bagarreuse** she's a fighter

bagatelle [bagatɛl] *nf* (**a**) (*chose sans importance*) trifle, bagatelle; **se fâcher pour une b.** to take offence at a (mere) trifle; **elle perd son temps à des bagatelles** she's frittering away her time, she's wasting her time on trifles; **pour la b. de deux mille francs** for a mere two thousand francs (**b**) (*plaisir sexuel*) lovemaking; **il ne pense qu'à la b.** he's got a one-track mind

bagnard [baɲar] *nm* convict

bagne [baɲ] *nm Hist* (*prison*) convict prison; **b. flottant** hulks; **condamné à cinq ans de b.** sentenced to five years' penal servitude; *Fig F* **c'est le b., la vie avec elle!** life with her is torment *or* a real nightmare!

bagnole [baɲɔl] *nf*; *F* car; *Péj* (**vieille**) **b.** (old) jalopy, *Br* (old) banger; **ça, c'est de la b.!** that's some car!

bagou(t) [bagu] *nm F* glibness (of tongue); **avoir du b.** to have the gift of the gab

baguage [bagaʒ] *nm* (*des oiseaux, des arbres*) ringing

bague [bag] *nf* (**a**) (*bijou*) ring; **porter des bagues** to wear rings; **b. en argent/en or** silver/gold ring; **avoir la b. au doigt** to be married; **passer à qn la b. au doigt** to put a ring on sb's finger (**b**) (*d'une boîte de conserve*) ring-pull; (*de cigare*) band (**c**) *Tech, MecE* bush, ring (**d**) (*d'oiseau*) ring

▶ **bague**: **b. d'appui** washer; **b. d'assemblage** collar, sleeve; **b. à bride** adapter; **b. d'espacement** sleeve; **b. de fiançailles** engagement ring; **b.** (**de garniture**) **de piston** piston ring, packing ring; **b. rallonge** (*d'une caméra*) extender lens; **b. de réglage** setting ring; **b. de roulement** ball race, bearing race; **b. de serrage** jubilee clip

baguenauder [bagnode] *F* **1** *vi* to stroll *or* wander around **2** *vpr* **se baguenauder** to stroll *or* wander around

baguer[1] [bage] *vt* (*oiseau, arbre*) to ring; **cigare bagué d'or** cigar with a gold band

baguer[2] *vt Couture* (*plis etc*) to tack, to baste

baguette [bagɛt] *nf* (**a**) (*tige*) switch, stick; (*pain*) French stick; **baguettes** (*pour manger*) chopsticks; **tu ne crois pas que tout va changer, comme ça, d'un coup de b.?** surely you don't believe everything's going to change, just like that, as if by magic *or* as if by the wave of a magic wand?; *Fig* **avoir les cheveux raides comme des baguettes** (**de tambour**) to have hair that's as straight as a poker; *F* **commander** *ou* **mener** *ou* **faire marcher qn à la b.** to rule sb with a rod of iron *or* with an iron hand; **être sous la b. de qn** to be under someone's thumb; **passer par les baguettes** to run the gauntlet

(**b**) *Menuis etc* moulding, beading

(**c**) (*de bas, chaussette*) clock

(**d**) *Aut* **b. de pavillon** roof bar; **b. de protection latérale** side-impact bar

▶ **baguette**: **b. de chef d'orchestre** conductor's baton; **b. magique** magic wand; **d'un coup de b. magique** with a wave of my/his/*etc* magic wand; **baguettes de tambour** drumsticks

baguier [bagje] *nm* ring case

bah [bɑ] *int* bah!, pooh!

Bahamas [baamas] *nfpl* [ⓘA11,g,ii] **les** (**îles**) **B., l'archipel des B.** the Bahamas

Bahreïn [barajn], **Bahrain** [barɛ̃] *nm* Bahrain, Bahrein

bahut [bay] *nm* (**a**) (*coffre*) (round-topped) chest; (*buffet*) sideboard (**b**) *Arg* (*collège, lycée*) school (**c**) *Arg* (*taxi*) cab, taxi

bai [bɛ] *adj* (*cheval*) bay; **b. châtain** chestnut bay

baie[1] [bɛ] *nf Géog* bay; **une petite b. abritée** a sheltered cove; **la grande b. australienne** the Great Australian Bight; **la b. d'Hudson** Hudson Bay

baie[2] *nf Archit* opening; **b. vitrée** picture window

baie[3] *nf Bot* berry

baignade [bɛɲad] *nf* (**a**) (*activité*) swimming, *Br* bathing; **b. interdite** no swimming *or* bathing; (**b**) (*endroit*) swimming *or Br* bathing place

baigner [beɲe] **1** *vt* (*pieds, doigt etc*) to bathe; (*bébé, chien etc*) to bath *or Am* bathe; (*de la mer*) (*côte etc*) to wash; (*d'une rivière*) (*région*) to water; *Fig* **baigné de soleil** bathed in sunlight; **pièce baignée de lumière** room flooded with *or* bathed in light; **il était baigné de sueur** he was dripping with *or* bathed in sweat; **son visage est baigné de larmes** his face is bathed in tears

2 *vi* (*tremper*) to soak, to steep (**dans** in); **les légumes baignent dans une sauce à la tomate** the vegetables are swimming in a tomato sauce; *F* **ça baigne** (**dans l'huile**)! everything's great *or* fine!; **OK, ça baigne!** OK, no problem!; **il baignait dans son sang** he was lying in a pool of his own blood; **la ville baigne dans la brume** the town is shrouded *or* swathed in mist; **maison qui baigne dans la lumière** house that is flooded with *or* bathed in light; **cette histoire/maison baigne dans le mystère** this story/house is shrouded in mystery

3 *vpr* **se baigner** (**a**) (*se laver*) to have *or* take a bath, *Br* to bath, *Am* to bathe

(**b**) (*nager*) (*dans la mer, un lac etc*) to have a swim, *Br* to (have a) bathe; (*dans une piscine*) to have a swim, to swim; **on va se b.?** shall we go for a swim?, shall we go swimming?

baigneur, -euse [beɲœr, -øz] **1** *n Vieilli* swimmer, *Br* bather **2** *nm* (*en porcelaine ou en plastique*) doll

baignoire [bɛɲwar] *nf* (**a**) (*dans la salle de bains*) bath, (bath)tub (**b**) *Th* ground-floor box (**c**) *Naut* (*de sous-marin*) upper part of the conning tower

▶ **baignoire**: **b. encastrée** sunken bath; **b. sabot** hip bath

bail, *pl* **baux** [baj, bo] *nm* lease; **b. commercial** commercial lease; **b. à ferme** farming lease; **b. emphytéotique** long lease; **prendre une maison à b.** to take a lease on *or* to lease a house; **donner une maison à b.** to lease (out) a house; **renouveler un b.** to renew a lease; *F* **ça fait un b. que je ne l'ai pas vu** I haven't seen him for ages

baille [bɑj] *nf Naut* (*baquet*) bucket; (*mauvais bateau*) tub; *F*

la (grande) b. the drink, the sea; **tomber à la b.** to fall into the drink

bâillement [bɑjmɑ̃] *nm* **(a)** (*de personne*) yawn; **étouffer un b.** to stifle a yawn; **bâillements** yawning, yawns **(b)** (*d'une couture etc*) gaping; **b. des rideaux** gap between the curtains

bâiller [bɑje] *vi* **(a)** (*d'une personne*) to yawn; **b. de sommeil/d'ennui/de fatigue** to yawn drowsily/with boredom/with tiredness; *Fig* **son histoire me fait b.** his story is one big yawn; *F* **b. à s'en** *ou* **se décrocher la mâchoire** to yawn one's head off **(b)** (*des coutures, d'un col etc*) to gape; (*d'une porte*) to be *or* stand ajar

bailleur, -eresse [bajœr, bajrɛs] *n* **(a)** *Jur* lessor **(b)** *Com* **b. de fonds** (financial) backer

bailli [baji] *nm Hist* bailiff

bailliage [bajaʒ] *nm Hist* (*district*) bailiwick; (*tribunal*) bailiff's court

bâillon [bɑjɔ̃] *nm* gag; **mettre un b. à qn** to gag sb; **mettre un b. à la presse/l'opposition** to gag *or* muzzle the press/the opposition

bâillonner [bɑjɔne] *vt* to gag; **b. la presse/l'opposition** to gag *or* muzzle the press/the opposition

bain [bɛ̃] *nm* **(a)** (*pour se laver*) bath; (*baignoire*) bath(tub); **prendre un b.** to have *or* take a bath, *Br* to bath, *Am* to bathe; **donner un b. à qn** to give sb a bath, to bath *or* bathe sb; **salle de bain(s)** bathroom; **peignoir** *ou* **sortie de b.** bathrobe; **le b. est rempli/vidé** the bath is full/empty; **fais-moi couler un b.** run me a bath; *Fig F* **être dans le b.** (*être compromis*) to be implicated; (*être habitué*) to be in the swing of things; **elle n'a pas eu de mal à se mettre dans le b.** she had no trouble getting into the swing of things; *Fig* **ils sont dans le même b.** they're in the same boat; **on peut les mettre dans le même b.** you can lump them all together; **je déteste les bains de foule** I hate crowds; **prendre un b. de foule** (*d'une personne célèbre*) to go on a walkabout; (*d'un politicien*) to press the flesh; **petit b.** (*à la piscine*) small *or* children's pool; **grand b.** (*à la piscine*) large pool

(b) (*à la mer etc*) swim, *Br* bathe; **bains de mer** swimming in the sea, *Br* sea bathing; *Vieilli* (*lieu*) seaside resort; **b. en piscine** swimming *or Br* bathing in a pool

(c) *Phot* bath; **b. révélateur** *ou* **de développement** developing bath; **b. de fixage** *ou* **fixateur** fixing bath

(d) *Tex* dye; **ce n'est pas le même b.** it's not the same dye lot

(e) (*pour moutons*) (sheep) dip

▶ **bain**: **b. de bouche** mouthwash; **faire un b. de bouche** to use a mouthwash; **b. de boue** mud bath; **b. bouillonnant** spa bath; *Fig* **b. de jouvence** rejuvenating experience; **ça m'a fait l'effet d'un b. de jouvence** it rejuvenated me, it made me feel years younger; **b. moussant** bubble bath; **b. de pieds** footbath; **prendre un b. de pieds** to soak *or* bathe one's feet; **b.-de-soleil** (*corsage*) sun top, halter top; **b. de soudure** solder bath; **b. turc** Turkish bath; **b. de vapeur** steam bath; **bains (publics)** (public) baths, *Am* bathhouse; **bains romains** Roman baths; **bains de soleil** sunbathing; **prendre un b. de soleil** *ou* **des bains de soleil** to sunbathe

bain-marie, *pl* **bains-marie** [bɛ̃mari] *nm* bain-marie, double saucepan *or Am* boiler; **faire cuire qch au b.** to cook sth in a bain-marie

baïonnette [bajɔnɛt] *nf* bayonet; **mettre/remettre la b.** to fix/unfix bayonets; **charge à la b.** bayonet charge; *Tech* **joint en b.** bayonet joint; *Él* **douille à b.** bayonet socket; *Él* **ampoule à b.** bulb with a bayonet fitting

baïram, beïram [bairam, beiram] *nm* Bairam

baise [bɛz] *nf Vulg* screwing; **il ne pense qu'à la b.** all he ever thinks of is screwing

baise-en-ville *nm inv F* overnight bag; (*pochette*) (man's) handbag

baisemain [bɛzmɛ̃] *nm* hand kissing, kissing of hands; **faire le b. à qn** to kiss sb's hand

baiser[1] [beze] **1** *vt* **(a)** (*embrasser*) to kiss; **b. qn au front** to kiss sb on the forehead; **elle lui baisa les pieds** she kissed his feet **(b)** *Vulg* (*coucher avec*) to fuck, to screw **(c)** *Arg* (*tromper*) to screw; **il m'a bien baisé** he screwed me good and proper; **se faire b.** to be *or* get screwed **(d)** *Arg* (*comprendre*) **qu'est-ce qu'il dit? on n'y baise rien** what's he saying? you can't make head nor tail of it **2** *vi Vulg* **elle baise bien** she's a good screw *or* fuck

baiser[2] *nm* kiss; **gros baisers** (*dans une lettre*) love and kisses; **b. de paix** kiss of peace; **b. d'adieu** parting *or* goodbye *or* farewell kiss; **b. de Judas** Judas kiss; **faire un b. à qn** to give sb a kiss

baiseur, -euse [bezœr, -øz] *n Vulg* **c'est un sacré b./une sacrée baiseuse** he's/she's a great screw

baisse [bɛs] *nf* fall, drop, downturn; (*de la marée*) ebb; **la b. de la natalité** the fall *or* drop in the birthrate; **la b. du niveau scolaire** the fall in educational standards; **b. des prix** fall *or* drop in prices, price cut; (*action*) price cutting; *Bourse* **b. sensible (des cours)** sharp fall (in prices); **être en b.** (*de la température, du nombre des adhésions etc*) to be falling *or* dropping; (*de la popularité de qn*) to be on the decline *or* the wane; (*d'une rivière*) to subside; **le moral du malade est en b.** the patient's morale is sinking; *Bourse* **spéculations à la b.** bear speculations; **jouer à la b.** to bear; **actions en b.** falling shares

baisser [bese] **1** *vt* (*rideau*) to lower; (*store*) to lower, to pull down; (*vitre de voiture*) to open, to lower; **b. une étagère d'un cran** to lower a shelf by one notch; *Aut* **b. ses phares** to dip *or Am* dim one's headlights; **le store est baissé** the blind is down *or* lowered; **b. la lumière** to turn down *or* dim the light; **b. la radio/le chauffage** to turn down the radio/the heating; **b. pavillon** *Naut* to strike one's flag, to surrender; *Fig* (*céder*) to admit defeat, to give in; **b. la tête** *ou* **le front** to bend *or* lower one's head; (*de honte, découragement etc*) to hang one's head; **b. brusquement la tête** to duck; **donner tête baissée dans un piège** to fall headlong into a trap; **b. les yeux** to look down, to lower one's eyes; **les yeux baissés** with downcast eyes; **b. le nez** to hang one's head in shame; *Fig* **il ne faut pas b. les bras, battez-vous!** don't give in, fight!; **b. la voix** to lower one's voice; **b. le ton** (*après une dispute*) to climb down; **je vous prie de b. le ton!** please keep your voice down!; **b. le prix de qch** to lower *or* reduce *or* cut the price of sth; **faire b. les prix** to bring down prices

2 *vi* **(a)** (*de la température*) to fall, to go *or* come down; (*de la marée*) to ebb; (*du feu*) to burn low, to burn down; (*de la vue, de la mémoire*) to fail; *Th* **les lumières baissent** the lights are going down; **le baromètre baisse** the barometer is falling; **le jour baisse** night is falling, it's getting dark

(b) (*s'affaiblir*) (*d'un malade*) to get weaker, to deteriorate; (*de l'enthousiasme*) to fall off, to decline, to weaken; **il a beaucoup baissé dernièrement** (*physiquement*) he has got a lot weaker lately, he has deteriorated a lot lately; (*intellectuellement*) his mind has been going *or* deteriorating a lot lately; **le moral baisse** morale is sinking; **elle a baissé dans mon estime** she's gone down in my estimation

(c) (*des prix*) to fall, to come *or* go down; **la valeur de ces maisons a baissé** these houses have gone down in value; **le niveau scolaire a beaucoup baissé** educational standards have fallen a lot

3 *vpr* **se baisser** to bend down, to stoop; (*pour éviter un coup etc*) to duck; **c'est en se baissant qu'il s'est cogné** he banged himself as he bent down; *Fig* **il n'y a qu'à se b. pour les ramasser** there are loads of them around

baissier [besje] *Bourse* **1** *nm* bear **2** *adj* bearish

bajoues [baʒu] *nfpl* (*d'animal*) chops; *Péj* (*d'une personne*) flabby cheeks

bakélite® [bakelit] *nf* Bakelite®; **téléphone en b.** Bakelite telephone

baklava [baklava] *nm Culin* baklava, baclava

bal, *pl* **bals** [bal] *nm* **(a)** (*fête*) (*populaire*) dance; (*chic*) ball, dance; **b. costumé** *ou* **masqué** *ou* **travesti** fancy dress ball; **donner un b.** to give a dance; **aller au b.** to go dancing; **robe de b.** ball gown, evening dress **(b)** (*endroit*) dance hall

▶ **bal**: **b. populaire** = free, open-air dance to popular music; **b. public** public dance

balade [balad] *nf F* (*à pied*) walk, stroll; (*en voiture*) drive, run; **faire une b.** (*à pied*) to go for a walk *or* stroll; (*en voiture*) to go for a drive *or* run (in the car); **être/partir en b.** (*à pied*) to be out for/go off for a walk; (*en voiture*) to be out for/go off for a drive

balader [balade] *F* **1** *vt* (*personne, chien*) to take (out) for a walk; (*avoir avec soi*) (*qch*) to carry *or* drag around; **il balade toujours cette vieille valise avec lui** he always carries *or* drags that old suitcase around with him **2** *vpr* **se balader** (*à pied*) to go for a walk; (*en voiture*) to go for a drive; **se b. en montagne** to walk in the mountains; **tu ne vas pas te b. en ville avec cette casquette?** surely you're not going to walk around town in that cap?; **ses affaires se baladent dans la maison** his things are lying around all over the house

baladeur, -euse [baladœr, -øz] **1** *adj* (*instinct*) wandering, roving; **j'ai l'âme baladeuse** I'm a wanderer at heart; (*en ce moment*) I want to be up and away; *F* **avoir les mains baladeuses** to have wandering hands; *Tech* **train b.** sliding gear **2** *nf* **baladeuse** (*lampe*) portable lamp, inspection lamp **3** *nm* personal stereo, Walkman®

baladin [baladɛ̃] *nm* strolling player, wandering actor

baladisque [baladisk] *nm* portable compact disc player, Discman®

balafre [balafr] *nf* **(a)** (*coupure*) gash, slash, cut; (*au sabre*) sabre cut **(b)** (*cicatrice*) scar

balafré [balafre] *nm* scarface

balafrer [balafre] *vt* to slash, to gash, to cut; **les agresseurs**

lui ont balafré le visage the attackers slashed his face; **visage balafré** scarred face

balai [balɛ] *nm* **(a)** (*de ménage*) broom; **passer le b.** to sweep the floor, to give the floor a sweep; **donner un coup de b. dans** *ou* **à la cuisine** to give the kitchen a sweep, to sweep the kitchen; *Fig* **donner un coup de b.** (*dans une enteprise*) to have a shake-out; *Fig* **il y a eu un coup de b.** there's been a shake-out; **(allez,) du b.!** clear off!, scram!; *Arg* **con comme un b.** as stupid as they come, bloody stupid, *Br* as daft as a brush **(b)** *F* **(voiture-)b.** (*autobus*) last bus; (*métro*) last underground *or Am* subway **(c)** *Él* brush **(d)** *Aut* (*d'essuie-glace*) blade

▶ **balai**: **b-brosse,** *pl* **balais-brosses** (long-handled) scrubbing-brush; **b. mécanique** carpet sweeper

balaise [balɛz] *adj, n F* = **balèze**

balalaïka [balalaika] *nf Mus* balalaika

balance [balɑ̃s] *nf* **(a)** [ⓘ**A10**,e] (*appareil*) (pair of) scales; (*publique*) weighing machine; **monter sur la b.** to stand on the scales

(b) *Astron, Astrol* **la B.** Libra, the Scales; **être (du signe de la) B.** to be Libra *or* a Libran

(c) *Fig* **candidat mis en b.** candidate who is still being considered; **la victoire/la décision restait en b.** victory/the decision hung in the balance; **mettre qch en b.** to weigh up the pros and cons of sth; **il faut mettre ces deux arguments en b.** you have to weigh each argument against the other; **ce facteur pèse dans la b.** this is an important factor; **cet argument est un poids dans la b.** this argument has great weight; **il y a divers facteurs à mettre dans la b.** there are various factors to take into account; **faire pencher** *ou* **incliner** *ou* **emporter la b.** to tip the scales *or* balance; **votre qualification fera pencher la b. en votre faveur** your qualification will tip the balance in your favour

(d) *Compta, Com* **b. d'un compte** balance *or* balancing of an account; **faire la b.** to make up the balance (sheet); **la b. de l'actif et du passif** the balance of assets and liabilities; **compte en b.** account that balances; **la b. est en excédent** there is a trade surplus

(e) *Pêche* shrimp net

(f) *F* (*mouchard*) squealer, *Br* grass

▶ **balance**: **b. automatique** shop scales; **b. avant inventaire** pre-inventory balance; **b. à bascule** weighbridge; **b. du commerce** *ou* **commerciale** trade balance, balance of trade; **b. créditrice** credit balance; **b. de cuisine** *ou* **de ménage** kitchen scales; **b. déficitaire** trade deficit; *Pol* **b. des forces** *ou* **des pouvoirs** balance of power; **b. d'inventaire** inventory balance; **b. du main courantier de nuit** (*dans un hôtel*) night auditor's report; **b. des paiements** balance of payments; **b. de Roberval** Roberval's balance; **b. romaine** steelyard; **b. de salle de bains** bathroom scales; **b. de vérification** trial balance

balancé [balɑ̃se] *adj* **(bien) b.** (*phrase, tournure*) well-balanced; *F* **elle est bien balancée** she's got a great figure

balance créditrice *nf* credit balance

balancelle [balɑ̃sɛl] *nf* (*de jardin*) *Br* garden *or* swing hammock, *Am* glider

balancement [balɑ̃smɑ̃] *nm* **(a)** (*de bateau, de train, des arbres etc*) swaying, rocking; (*des hanches*) swaying; **balancements** (*en politique*) wavering, shilly-shallying **(b)** *Beaux-Arts, Littér* (*équilibre*) balance

balancer [balɑ̃se] **(je balançai(s); n. balançons) 1** *vt* **(a)** (*bras, jambes, trompe*) to swing; (*qn dans un hamac*) to rock; (*hanches*) to sway; **tu pourrais me b.?** (*sur la balançoire*) can you push me *or* give me a push?; **b. un enfant sur ses genoux** to rock a child on one's knees

(b) *F* (*lancer*) (*pierres, stylo etc*) to chuck, to throw; **tu pourrais me b. le journal** can you chuck *or* throw me the paper?; **b. des pierres à qn** to chuck *or* throw stones at sb; **il est toujours en train de b. des vannes** he's always making snide remarks

(c) *Com* **b. un compte** to balance an account; *Fig* **b. le pour et le contre** to weigh up the pros and cons; **tout bien balancé, c'est d'accord** all things considered, I agree

(d) *F* (*se débarrasser de*) (*qch*) to chuck *or* throw out *or* away; **b. qn** to give sb the push *or Br* the elbow; **elle a tout balancé** (*tout abandonné*) she's given it all up

(e) *F* (*moucharder*) to squeal on, *Br* to grass on, *Br* to shop

2 *vi Litt* (*hésiter*) to waver, to hesitate

3 *vpr* **se balancer (a)** (*d'arbres, de blés etc*) to sway; **se b. sur ses ancres** (*d'un navire*) to ride at anchor; **se b. sur sa chaise** to rock (backwards and forwards) on one's chair; **se b. d'un pied sur l'autre** to rock from one foot to the other

(b) (*sur une balançoire*) to swing; (*sur une bascule*) to see-saw

(c) *Arg* **je m'en balance!** I don't give a damn!, I couldn't care less!; **je me balance complètement de ce qu'ils pensent** I really don't give a damn *or* I really couldn't care less what they think

(d) *F* **il s'est balancé du haut de la tour Eiffel** he chucked *or* threw himself off the top of the Eiffel Tower

balancier [balɑ̃sje] *nm* **(a)** (*d'un funambule*) balancing pole **(b)** (*dans une horloge*) pendulum; (*d'une montre*) balance wheel **(c)** (*d'une pompe*) handle

balançoire [balɑ̃swar] *nf* (*bascule*) seesaw; (*suspendue*) swing; (*dans une foire*) swing-boat; **faire de la b.** to have a go on the seesaw/the swing

balayage [balɛjaʒ] *nm* **(a)** (*d'une pièce etc*) sweeping; (*de la saleté etc*) sweeping up; **b. intermittent** (*d'essuie-glace*) intermittent wipe; **b. unique** (*d'essuie-glace*) flick wipe **(b)** *Rad, Électron, TV* scan(ning), sweep; **fréquence de b.** sweep frequency **(c)** (*de cheveux*) streaks; **se faire faire un b.** to have streaks put in one's hair, to have one's hair streaked

balayer [baleje] *vt* **(je balaie, je balaye; je balaierai, je balayerai) (a)** (*pièce etc*) to sweep (out); (*saleté etc*) to sweep up; **le vent a balayé les nuages** the wind has swept the clouds away; **b. l'ennemi** to drive away the enemy; **b. les critiques/objections/obstacles** to brush aside criticism/objections/obstacles; **les communistes ont été balayés aux dernières élections** the Communists were swept from power *or* were swept out at the last elections; *Fig* **b. devant sa porte** to put one's (own) house in order; **cette nouvelle a balayé tous mes soucis** this news has swept away all my worries

(b) *Rad, Électron, TV* to scan, to sweep; **le radar balaie jusqu'à 100 km** the radar has a sweep of 100 kilometres; **les projecteurs de la prison balaient les champs tout autour** the prison searchlights sweep the fields all around

(c) *Aut* to scavenge

balayette [balɛjɛt] *nf* (small) brush

balayeur, -euse [balɛjœr, -øz] **1** *n* (*personne*) (road) sweeper **2** *nf* **balayeuse (a)** (*machine*) road sweeper **(b)** *Can* (*aspirateur*) vacuum cleaner

balayures [balɛjyr] *nfpl* sweepings

balbutiant [balbysjɑ̃] *adj* (*voix*) stuttering, stammering; **il répondit, tout b.** he stammered an answer; *Fig* **la psychanalyse, encore toute balbutiante** psychoanalysis, still in its infancy *or* still in its early stages

balbutiement [balbysimɑ̃] *nm* stuttering, stammering; (*dans sa barbe*) mumbling, muttering; **les balbutiements d'un jeune enfant** the babbling of a young child; *Fig* **l'informatique n'était alors qu'à ses balbutiements** data processing was then only in its infancy *or* in its early stages

balbutier [balbysje] (*pr sub & impf* **n. balbutiions, v. balbutiiez) 1** *vi* to stutter, to stammer; (*parler dans sa barbe*) to mumble, to mutter **2** *vt* (*des excuses*) to stammer (out); (*en parlant dans sa barbe*) to mumble, to mutter

balcon [balkɔ̃] *nm* **(a)** *Archit* balcony; *F* **il y a du monde au b.** she's well endowed, she's a big girl **(b)** *Th* circle; **premier b.** dress circle; **nous étions placés au deuxième b.** we were in the upper circle

balconnet [balkɔnɛ] *nm* half-cup bra

baldaquin [baldakɛ̃] *nm* (*de lit*) tester, canopy; (*de trône*) canopy, baldachin; **lit à b.** tester bed

Bâle [bɑl] *nf* Basle, Basel

Baléares [balear] *nfpl* **les B.** the Balearic Islands, the Balearics

baleine [balɛn] *nf* **(a)** *Zool* whale; **b. à bosse** humpbacked whale; **b. blanche** white whale; **blanc de b.** spermaceti; *Fig* **rire comme une b.** to laugh like a drain **(b)** (*d'un corset etc*) (whale)bone; (*d'un parapluie*) rib

baleiné [balene] *adj* (*soutien-gorge*) boned; (*col*) stiffened

baleineau, -eaux [balɛno] *nm* whale calf

baleinier, -ière [balenje, -jɛr] **1** *adj* (*bateau, industrie*) whaling **2** *nf* **baleinière** whaleboat, whaler; **baleinière de sauvetage** lifeboat

balèze [balɛz] *F* **1** *adj* (*grand et fort*) hefty, brawny; *Fig* **elle est vraiment b.** (*intelligente*) she's so brainy!; **b. en maths** brilliant at maths **2** *n* (*personne grande et forte*) hefty *or* brawny sort; (*personne intelligente*) brainy sort

balisage [balizaʒ] *nm* **(a)** (*signaux*), *Naut* beacons, buoys; *Av* lights; *Rad* beacons; **projecteur de b.** direction beacon **(b)** (*action*), *Naut* beaconing, buoying; *Av* lighting; *Rad* marking out with beacons

balise [baliz] *nf Naut* beacon, buoy; *Av* light; *Rad* beacon; (*de piste de ski, d'épave*) marker; *Naut* **b. flottante** buoy; *Rad* **b. radar** radar beacon; *Ordinat* **traitement de texte à balises** word processing with embedded visible commands

baliser [balize] **1** *vt Naut* (*chenal*) to beacon, to buoy, to mark out; *Av* (*aéroport*) to equip with lights; (*route*) to mark out with beacons; **b. une piste de ski** to mark out a ski run **2** *vi F* (*avoir peur*) to have the jitters (**pour qch** about sth); **ne m'en parle pas, ça me fait b.** don't talk to me about it, it gives me the jitters

baliseur [balizœr] *nm* **(a)** (**bateau**) **b.** buoy-laying boat **(b)** (*personne*) person who lays buoys

balistique [balistik] **1** *adj* ballistic; **engin b.** ballistic missile **2** *nf* ballistics

baliverne [balivɛrn] *nf* stupid remark; **balivernes** twaddle, nonsense; **débiter des balivernes** to talk twaddle *or* nonsense

balkanique [balkanik] *adj* Balkan

balkanisation [balkanizasjɔ̃] *nf Pol, Fig* Balkanization

ballade [balad] *nf* (*poème court*) ballade; (*poème long*), *Mus* ballad

ballant [balɑ̃] **1** *adj* (*bras, jambes*) swinging, dangling; **assis les pieds ballants** sitting with one's feet dangling **2** *nm* **(a)** (*mouvement*) (*d'un véhicule*) sway, roll **(b)** *Naut* (*d'un cordage*) slack

ballast [balast] *nm* **(a)** *Constr* (*d'une route, d'une voie ferrée*) ballast **(b)** *Naut* ballast tank

ballaster [balaste] *vt* **(a)** *Constr* (*voie ferrée etc*) to ballast **(b)** *Naut* (*remplir*) to ballast; (*vider*) to unballast

balle[1] [bal] *nf* **(a)** (*pour jouer*) ball; **b. de golf/de tennis/de ping-pong** golf/tennis/table-tennis ball; **jouer à la b.** to play ball; **b. au mur** ≈ fives, *Am* handball; *Sp* **renvoyer/lancer la b.** to return the ball/to serve; *Sp F* **c'est une belle b.!** good shot *or* ball!; *Tennis* **faire des** *ou* **quelques balles** to have a knock-up; *Fig* **prendre** *ou* **saisir la b. au bond** to seize the opportunity *or* chance; *Fig* **se renvoyer la b.** to pass the buck; *Fig* **renvoyer la b. à qn** (*dans un débat*) to answer sb back; *Fig* **la b. est dans votre camp** the ball's in your court

(b) (*d'arme*) bullet; **b. de fusil** rifle bullet; *F* **recevoir douze balles dans la peau** to go before the firing squad; **à l'épreuve des balles** bullet-proof

▶ **balle**: **b. de filet** net (ball); **b. de match** match point; **b. morte** spent bullet; **b. perdue** stray bullet; **b. plastique** plastic bullet, baton round; **b. de set** set point; **b. traçante** tracer bullet

balle[2] *nf* **(a)** *Com* (*de coton, laine etc*) bale **(b)** *Arg* (*visage*) mug, *Br* dial; **il a une drôle de b.** he's an odd-looking guy; **quelle b.!** what an ugly mug!

balle[3] *nf* (*de blé*) husk, chaff; *Bot* (*de fleur*) glume

baller [bale] *vi* (*de bras, jambes*) to dangle; (*de tête*) to hang

ballerine [balrin] *nf* **(a)** *Th* ballerina, ballet dancer **(b)** (*chaussure*) pump

balles [bal] *nfpl F* francs; **je te le vends pour deux cents b.** I'll sell it to you for two hundred francs; **t'as pas cent b.?** (*dit dans la rue etc*) ≈ have you got any (spare) change?

ballet [balɛ] *nm Th* ballet; **maître de b.** ballet master; **les ballets du Bolshoi** the Bolshoi Ballet; *Fig Pol* **le b. de ministres** the ministerial merry-go-round; **le b. diplomatique** diplomatic to-ings and fro-ings

ballon [balɔ̃] *nm* **(a)** (*aéronef, vessie*) balloon; **faire un voyage en b.** to make a balloon journey; **monter en b.** to go up in a balloon; **envoyer** *ou* **lancer un b. d'essai** to send up a pilot balloon; *Fig* to put out feelers, to fly a kite; **marchand de ballons** balloon-seller

(b) *Sp etc* (*pour jouer*) ball; *Baseball* (*chandelle*) highball; **b. de football/de rugby/de volley** football/rugby ball/volleyball; **jouer au b.** to play with a ball; **b. d'entraînement (pour boxeurs)** punchball

(c) (*de bande dessinée*) balloon

(d) (*pour boire*) (**verre**) **b.** round wine glass; **un b. de vin blanc** a glass of white wine

(e) *Ch* balloon flask; *Ind* carboy

(f) **b. (d'alcooltest)** (breathalyser) bag; **souffler dans le b.** to blow into the bag

▶ **ballon**: **b. de barrage** barrage balloon; **b. dirigeable** airship, dirigible; **b. gonflable** balloon; (*de football etc*) inflatable ball; **b. d'observation** observation balloon; **b. ovale** rugby ball; (*sport*) rugby; *Méd* **b. d'oxygène** oxygen bottle; **b. de protection** barrage balloon; **b. rond** football; (*sport*) football

ballonné [balɔne] *adj* (*bombé, arrondi*) (*joues*) chubby, round; (*nuages*) puffy; (*ventre*) bloated, distended

ballonnement [balɔnmɑ̃] *nm* (*du ventre, de l'estomac*) distending; **avoir des ballonnements** to feel bloated

ballonner [balɔne] *vt* (*gonfler*) (*cape, jupe, joues*) to puff out; (*ventre, estomac*) to distend; **manger ce genre de choses me ballonne** eating that kind of thing makes me feel bloated *or* gives me wind; **cette herbe risque de b. les bêtes** this grass is liable to bloat the livestock

ballon-panier *nm inv Can Sp* basketball

ballon-sonde, *pl* **ballons-sondes** *nm Météo* sounding balloon

ballot [balo] **1** *nm* **(a)** (*paquet*) bundle, package **(b)** *F* (*imbécile*) twit, wally **2** *adj F* **t'es pas b.?** are you mad?, *Br* are you daft?; **c'est vraiment b. de l'avoir prévenu** it's really crazy to have warned him

ballotin [balɔtɛ̃] *nm* sweet *or Am* candy box; **b. de chocolats** small box of chocolates

ballottage [balɔtaʒ] *nm Pol etc* **scrutin de b.** second ballot, run-off; **il y a b.** there will be a second ballot *or* a run-off; **M. Martin est en b.** Mr Martin has to stand again *or Am* run again in a second ballot

ballottement [balɔtmɑ̃] *nm* (*de train*) rocking, swaying; (*des passagers*) shaking, jolting; (*de porte*) swinging to and fro; (*de navire*) tossing

ballotter [balɔte] **1** *vt* (*bateau*) to toss (about); (*passagers*) to shake *or* jolt (about); **être ballotté par des sentiments opposés** to be pulled this way and that by contradictory feelings; **un enfant ballotté entre ses parents** a tug-of-love child; **un enfant ballotté entre des écoles/villes** a child that has been moved around from school to school/from town to town **2** *vi* (*de bagages*) to be tossed about; (*de porte*) to swing to and fro; (*de bateau*) to toss (about); (*de poitrine*) to bounce (up and down)

ballottine [balɔtin] *nf Culin* meat roll

balloune [balun] *nf Can F* **être en b.** (*enceinte*) to be in the (pudding) club

ball-trap, *pl* **ball-traps** [baltrap] *nm* (*sport*) clay-pigeon shooting, skeet shooting; (*appareil*) trap

balluchon [balyʃɔ̃] *nm F* (*de vêtements*) bundle; **faire son b.** to pack one's bags

balnéaire [balneɛr] *adj* **station b.** seaside resort

balnéothérapie [balneoterapi] *nf Méd* balneotherapy

balourdise [balurdiz] *nf* **(a)** (*manque de finesse*) awkwardness, clumsiness **(b)** (*gaffe*) stupid blunder, *F* clanger

balourd, -ourde [balur, -urd] **1** *adj* (*personne*) awkward, clumsy; (*peu délicat*) loutish, uncouth **2** *n* (*maladroit*) clumsy oaf; **un grand b.** (*grand gars*) a great hulking fellow; **c'est le roi des balourds** he's a great oaf **3** *nm MecE* unbalance

balsa [balza] *nm* balsa (wood)

balsamier [balzamje] *nm* balsam tree

balsamine [balzamin] *nf* (*plante*) balsam

balte [balt] *adj* Baltic; **les pays baltes** the Baltic States

balthazar [baltazar] *nm* (*de champagne*) Balthazar

Baltique [baltik] *nf* **la (mer) B.** the Baltic (Sea)

baluchon [balyʃɔ̃] *nm F* = **balluchon**

balustrade [balystrad] *nf* **(a)** *Archit* balustrade **(b)** (*clôture*) railing

balustre [balystr] *nm Archit* baluster

balzacien, -ienne [balzasjɛ̃, -jɛn] *adj Littér* typical of Balzac; **une description très balzacienne** a description very typical of Balzac; **dans le plus pur style b.** in a style that is pure Balzac

balzan [balzɑ̃] *adj* **cheval b.** horse with white stockings

balzane [balzan] *nf* (*de cheval*) white stocking

bambin, -ine [bɑ̃bɛ̃, -in] *n F* toddler

bamboche [bɑ̃bɔʃ] *nf F* spree, lark; **faire b.** to live it up

bambocher [bɑ̃bɔʃe] *vi F* to live it up

bambocheur, -euse [bɑ̃bɔʃœr, -øz] *n F* reveller; **c'est un b.** he likes living it up

bambou [bɑ̃bu] *nm* (*plante*) bamboo; *Culin* **pousses de b.** bamboo shoots; *Fig F* **coup de b.** (*insolation*) sunstroke; *F* **il a le coup de b.** (*fou*) he's nuts *or* crazy; (*épuisé*) he's shattered *or* whacked; *F* **c'est le coup de b.** (*très cher*) it's a rip-off

bamboula [bɑ̃bula] *nf F* spree, lark; **faire la b.** to live it up

ban [bɑ̃] *nm* **(a)** (*bannissement*) banishment; **mettre qn au b.** to banish sb; **pratique mise au b.** outlawed practice; **être au b. de la société** to be outlawed by society; **être en rupture de b.** to have illegally returned from banishment; *Fig* **être en rupture de b. avec** to have broken with

(b) **bans** (*de mariage*) banns; **publier les bans** to publish the banns

(c) **le b. et l'arrière-b.** *Hist* the ban and the arrière-ban; *Fig* (*tout le monde*) the world and his wife

(d) (*applaudissements*) round of applause; **faire un b. pour qn** to give sb a round of applause, to applaud sb; **un b. pour Monsieur le maire!** a round of applause for the mayor!, = three cheers for the mayor!

(e) (*avant une annonce officielle*) drum roll; *Arch* (*d'un événement*) (public) proclamation

banal [banal] **1** *adj* **(a)** (*pl* **banals**) (*objet*) ordinary, commonplace; (*gens, occupation*) ordinary, run-of-the-mill; (*idée, remarque, style*) trite, banal; (*accident, exemple, excuse*) common; **parler de choses banales** to engage in small talk; **ça, c'est peu b.!** that's unusual, that's a bit out of the ordinary! **(b)** (*pl* **banaux**) *Hist* (*moulin, fournil*) communal **2** *nm* **c'est d'un b.!** it's dead ordinary!; (*idée*) it's so trite!

banalement [banalmɑ̃] *adv* in an ordinary manner; **notre rencontre s'est passée très b.** our meeting took place in very ordinary circumstances

banalisation [banalizasjɔ̃] *nf* **(a)** (*de la violence, du sexe dans les médias*) trivialization; **la b. des transports aériens** the fact that air travel has become commonplace *or* has become an everyday phenomenon; **la b. des voitures de police** the use of unmarked police cars **(b)** *Rail* (*pour une voie à deux sens*) signalling for two-way working; **la b. d'une locomotive** the manning of an engine by several crews

banaliser [banalize] **1** *vt* **(a)** (*sexe, violence etc*) to trivialize; **voiture** *ou* **véhicule banalisé(e)** unmarked police car **(b)** *Rail* (*voie ferrée*) to signal for two-way working; **b. une locomotive** to have an engine manned by several crews **2** *vpr* **se banaliser** to become commonplace

banalité [banalite] *nf* **(a)** (*caractère*) (*d'objet, de gens, d'occupation*) ordinariness; (*d'idée, de remarque, de style*) triteness, banality; (*d'accident, d'exemple*) commonness **(b)** **banalités** small talk, *Péj* platitudes; **un tissu** *ou* **ramassis de banalités** a collection of platitudes

banane [banan] *nf* **(a)** (*fruit*) banana **(b)** *Mil F* (*médaille*) medal, *Br* gong **(c)** *Av F* (*hélicoptère*) chopper **(d)** (*coiffure*) quiff; **porter la b.** to have a quiff **(e)** (*petit sac*) bum-bag, *Am* fanny pack

bananier, -ière [bananje, -jɛr] **1** *nm* **(a)** (*arbre*) banana tree **(b)** *Naut* banana boat **2** *adj* (*plantation, production*) banana; **république bananière** banana republic

banc [bɑ̃] *nm* **(a)** (*siège*) bench, seat

(b) (*de rocher etc*) layer, bed; *Min* (*de charbon*) seam; *Naut* **toucher au b.** to run aground

(c) (*colonie*) (*de poissons*) shoal, school; **b. d'huîtres** oyster bed

(d) (*de brume*) bank; **b. de brouillard** fog bank

(e) *Tech* (work)bench; (*d'un tour*) bed

▶ **banc**: *Jur* **b. des accusés** dock; *Géog* **b. continental** continental shelf; **b. à coulisses** (*à l'aviron*) sliding seat; **b. d'école** school bench; **ils se sont connus sur les bancs de l'école** they got to know each other at school; **b. d'église** pew; *Ind* **b. d'essai** test bed; *Ordinat* benchtest; *Fig* testing ground; **faire passer au b. d'essai** to benchtest; **mettre qch au b. d'essai** to test sth (out); **b. de glace** ice floe, ice field; **b. de jardin** garden bench *or* seat; *Jur* **b. des magistrats** magistrates' bench; *Ordinat* **b. de mémoire** memory bank; *Pol* **le b. des ministres** *Br* ≈ the (government) front bench; *TV, Cin* **b. de montage** editing desk, edit controller; *Can* **b. de neige** snowbank; **b. d'œuvre** churchwardens' pew; *Jur* **b. des prévenus** dock; **b. de roches** reef; **b. de sable** sandbank; **b. des témoins** witness box *or US* witness stand; **le B. de Terre-Neuve** the Banks (of Newfoundland); **b. de vase** mudbank

bancable [bɑ̃kabl] *adj Fin* bankable, negotiable

bancaire [bɑ̃kɛr] *adj* bank(ing); **opérations bancaires** bank(ing) transactions; **chèque b.** bank cheque; **compte b.** bank account; **informatique b.** computerized banking

bancal, -ale, -als, -ales [bɑ̃kal] *adj* (*personne*) lame; (*meuble etc*) wobbly, rickety; *Fig* (*raisonnement, idée*) shaky, unsound; (*projet*) unsound

bancarisation [bɑ̃karizasjɔ̃] *nf* **la b. de l'économie** the growing role of banks in the economy; **la b. de la population française** the spread of the use of banking services amongst the French population

bancarisé [bɑ̃karize] *adj* **presque toutes les PME sont bancarisées** almost all small businesses have accounts with a bank *or* use the banking system

bancassurance [bɑ̃kasyrɑ̃s] *nf Banque* bancassurance

bancassureur [bɑ̃kasyrœr] *nm* insurance banker

bancatique [bɑ̃katik] *nf* electronic *or* computerized banking

banco [bɑ̃ko] *nm Cartes* banco; **faire b.** to go banco

bandage [bɑ̃daʒ] *nm* **(a)** (*pansement*) bandage; (*action*) (*d'une blessure*) bandaging, binding up; **b. herniaire** truss **(b)** (*d'une roue*) (*en caoutchouc*) tyre, *US* tire; (*en métal*) hoop, band **(c)** (*d'un ressort*) tightening; (*d'un arc*) bending

bandagiste [bɑ̃daʒist] *n Méd* truss manufacturer *or* supplier

bandana [bɑ̃dana] *nm* bandan(n)a

bandant [bɑ̃dɑ̃] *adj Vulg* sexy; *Fig* orgasmic; *Fig* **une proposition bandante** a turn-on; **ce n'est pas très b., comme idée de vacances** it doesn't really turn me on as holiday ideas go

bande¹ [bɑ̃d] *nf* **(a)** (*de tissu, de papier, de métal etc*) strip, band; (*de terre*) strip, stretch, belt; (*motif*) stripe; *Fig* **par la b.** in a roundabout way, indirectly; **mettre un journal sous b.** to put a wrapper round a newspaper; **b. de téléimprimeur** ticker tape; *Agr* **culture en bandes de niveau** strip contour farming

(b) *Méd* bandage; **mettre une b. à qn** to put a bandage on sb, to bandage sb

(c) (*magnétique*) tape; (*pellicule*) film; **tourner une b. d'essai** to have a screen test; **faire tourner une b. d'essai à qn** to give sb a screen test

(d) (*de roue*) hoop, band

(e) *Billard* cushion

(f) *Opt* (*du spectre*) band

(g) (*d'une mitrailleuse*) (feeding) belt

(h) *Hér* bend

(i) *Naut* (*de navire*) side; (*inclinaison*) list; **donner de la b.** to list, to have a list

▶ **bande**: **b. d'arrêt d'urgence** hard shoulder; **b. en bobine** open-reel tape, reel-to-reel tape; *Ordinat* **b. en cassettes** cassette tape; **b. cyclable** cycle path *or* lane; *Ordinat* **b. de défilement** scroll bar; **b. dessinée** comic strip, strip cartoon; *Ordinat* **b. de données** data tape; **b. enregistrée** recorded tape; *Av* **b. d'envol** airstrip, landing strip; **b. ferrique** ferric tape; *Ordinat* **b. sans fin** endless tape; *Rad* **b. de fréquences** frequency band; **b. illustrée** comic strip, strip cartoon; *TV, Cin* **b. internationale** music and effects track, M&E track; **b. magnétique** magnetic tape; **b. magnétique audio** audio tape; **b. maîtresse** master tape; *Aut* **b. médiane** (*sur la route*) central (white) line; *Mil* **b. molletière** puttee; **b. noire** terrorist gang; **b. originale (d'un film)** original (film) soundtrack; *Ordinat* **b. de papier** paper tape; *Aut* **b. pare-soleil** shadeband; **b. passante** *Électron* bandwidth; *Ordinat* (video) bandwidth; **b. de présentation** (*d'une chanson etc*) demo tape; *Aut* **b. de protection latérale** side-impact bar; **b. de roulement** (*de pneu*) tread; **b. son** *ou* **sonore** sound reel *or* track; *Aut* **b. de stationnement** layby, *Am* rest stop; **b. Velpeau®** crepe bandage; **b. vidéo** video tape; **b. vidéo promotionnelle** promotional video; **b. vierge** blank tape; **bandes vierges** (film) stock

bande² *nf* **(a)** (*de personnes*) band, group; **b. d'amis** group of friends; **b. de voleurs** gang *or* band of thieves; **b. armée** armed gang; **elle fait b. à part** she keeps (herself) to herself; **viens avec nous, ne fais pas b. à part** come with us, don't stay all on your own *or* all by yourself; **cet artiste fait un peu b. à part dans le mouvement minimaliste français** this artist is rather a special case *or* is something of an exception in the French minimalist movement; **faire qch en b.** to do sth in a group; **être de la b. de qn** to belong to sb's gang; **toute la b.** the whole gang, the whole lot of them; **une b. de fous/d'incapables** a bunch of madmen/incompetents; **b. d'imbéciles!** you bunch of idiots!

(b) (*d'oiseaux*) flock, flight; (*de loups*) pack; (*de buffles*) herd; (*de marsouins*) school; (*de lions*) pride

bandé [bɑ̃de] *adj* **(a)** (*main, cheville etc*) bandaged; **les yeux bandés** blindfold(ed) **(b)** *Hér* bendy

bande-annonce, *pl* **bandes-annonces** *nf Cin* trailer, promo **(de** for)

bandeau, -eaux [bɑ̃do] *nm* **(a)** (*pour les cheveux*) headband; **cheveux en bandeaux** hair parted in the middle and swept back round the sides **(b)** (*sur les yeux*) blindfold; **mettre un b. à qn** to blindfold sb, to put a blindfold on sb; *Fig* **avoir un b. sur les yeux** to be blind **(c)** *Archit* string course **(d)** *Journ* streamer

bandelette [bɑ̃dlɛt] *nf* (*de tissu*) strip, band; **bandelettes** (*de momies*) bandages, wrappings; **b. réactive** *Méd* testing strip; (*pour analyse d'urine*) dipstick; *Aut* **b. talon** chafer strip

bander [bɑ̃de] **1** *vt* **(a)** (*blessure, main etc*) to bandage (up), to put a bandage on; **b. les yeux à** *ou* **de qn** to blindfold sb, to put a blindfold on sb **(b)** (*ressort*) to tighten; **b. un arc** to bend a bow; **b. ses muscles** to tense one's muscles **2** *vi Vulg* to have a hard-on *or* an erection; *Fig* **faire b. qn** to thrill *or* excite sb; **le théâtre, ça la fait b.** she gets a real buzz from the theatre

banderille [bɑ̃drij] *nf* (*en tauromachie*) banderilla

banderole [bɑ̃drɔl] *nf* banderole; (*publicitaire*) streamer; (*de manifestant*) banner

bandit [bɑ̃di] *nm* (*escroc*) crook, swindler, rogue; *Vieilli* (*brigand*) bandit, brigand; **b. de grand chemin** highwayman

banditisme [bɑ̃ditism] *nm* crime; **recrudescence du b.** crime wave; **le grand b.** organized crime

bandoulière [bɑ̃duljɛr] *nf* **(a)** (*d'un sac etc*) shoulder strap; **porter/mettre qch en b.** to carry/sling sth over *or* across one's shoulder; **le sac en b.** with one's bag slung over *or* across one's shoulder **(b)** *Mil* bandolier

bang [bɑ̃g] *nm inv Av* (super)sonic boom

Bangladesh [bɑ̃gladɛʃ, bɛ̃gladɛʃ] *nm* Bangladesh

banian [banjɑ̃] *nm* banyan (tree)

banjo [bɑ̃n(d)ʒo] *nm* [①A12,1,c] *Mus* banjo

banlieue [bɑ̃ljø] **1** *nf* suburbs *pl*; **la grande/petite b.** the outer/inner suburbs; **vivre en b.** to live in the suburbs *or* in suburbia; **maisons de b.** suburban houses; *Rail* **ligne/gare de b.** suburban line/station; **b. rouge** communist-voting suburb **2** *nm Belg* stopping train

banlieusard, -arde [bɑ̃ljøzar, -ard] *n F* suburbanite

banne [ban] *nf* **(a)** (*pour le charbon etc*) cart **(b)** (*panier*) (wicker) basket **(c)** (*de magasin etc*) awning, canopy

banneret [banrɛ] *nm Hist* banneret; **chevalier b.** knight banneret

banneton [bantɔ̃] *nm* **(a)** (*pour le pain*) basket **(b)** (*pour la pêche*) corf

banni, -ie [bani] **1** *adj* (*personne*) banished, exiled **2** *n* exile

bannière [banjɛr] *nf* (*étendard*) banner; **il s'est rangé sous la b. des écologistes** he's joined the ranks of the ecologists; **la b. étoilée** the Star-Spangled Banner; *Fig* **c'est la croix et la b. pour le faire manger** it's a devil of a job *or* a heck of a job getting him to eat; **c'est la croix et la b., ce job!** this job is a real devil!

bannir [banir] *vt* (*personne*) to banish, to exile; **bannissez les pensées négatives de votre esprit** banish negative thoughts from your mind; **il a complètement banni la cigarette** he has completely given up smoking; **vous devez b. le sucre de votre alimentation** you must exclude sugar from your diet, you must cut sugar out of your diet

bannissement [banismɑ̃] *nm* banishment

banquable [bɑ̃kabl] *adj Fin* bankable, negotiable

banque [bɑ̃k] *nf* **(a)** (*commerce*) banking; (*établissement*) bank; **avoir de l'argent à la b.** to have money in the bank; **porter un chèque à la b.** to bank a cheque; **opération de b.** bank(ing) transaction; **billet de b.** banknote, *US* bank bill; **chèque de b.** *Br* bank cheque; **carnet** *ou* **livret de b.** bankbook; **travailler dans la b.** to be in banking; **avoir un compte en b. chez ...** to have an account *or* to bank with ...; **employé/directeur de b.** bank clerk/manager; **b. privée/de l'État** privately-owned/State bank

(b) *Cartes* bank; **tenir la b.** to be (the) banker; **faire sauter la b.** to break the bank

▶ **banque**: **b. d'affaires** *Br* merchant bank, investment bank; **b. centrale** central bank; **b. commerciale** commercial bank; **b. compensatrice** clearing bank; **b. confirmatrice** confirming bank; **b. de crédit** credit bank; **b. de dépôt** clearing bank; **b. de détail** retail bank; (*activité*) retail banking; **b. à distance** direct banking; **b. à domicile** telebanking, home banking; *Ordinat* **b. de données** data bank; **b. d'émission** bank of issue; **b. d'entreprise** corporate banking; **b. d'épargne** savings bank; **B. européenne d'investissement** European Investment Bank; **B. de France** Bank of France; **b. de gestion de patrimoine** trust bank; **b. de gros** wholesale bank; **b. d'images** *Ordinat* image bank; *TV* television archives, image bank; **la B. Mondiale** the World Bank; **b. notificatrice** advising bank; *Méd* **b. de** *ou* **du sang** blood bank; **b. du sperme** sperm bank; **b. statistique** statistics bank; **b. des yeux** eye bank

banquer [bɑ̃ke] *vi F* to cough up, *Br* to stump up; **c'est toujours moi qui banque** it's always me that has to cough up

banqueroute [bɑ̃krut] *nf Jur* bankruptcy; **faire b.** to go bankrupt

banqueroutier, -ière [bɑ̃krutje, -jɛr] *n* bankrupt

banquet [bɑ̃kɛ] *nm* banquet, feast; **salle de b.** banqueting hall

banquette [bɑ̃kɛt] *nf* **(a)** (*siège*) seat; **b. de piano** piano stool; *Aut* **la b. arrière** the back seat **(b)** *Constr* (*de terre etc*) bank; (*de pont, de tunnel*) (foot)path; *Archit* **b. de fenêtre** window seat

banquier, -ière [bɑ̃kje, -jɛr] *n Fin, Cartes* banker; *Fig* **crois-tu que je vais être ton b.?** do you think I'm going to finance *or Am* bankroll you?; **je ne suis pos le b. de tout le monde** I'm not made of money

▶ **banquier**: **b. d'affaires** merchant banker; **b. prêteur** lending bank

banquise [bɑ̃kiz] *nf* ice floe, pack ice, ice pack

bantou, -oue [bɑ̃tu] **1** *adj* Bantu **2** *n* **B.** Bantu

baobab [baɔbab] *nm* baobab (tree)

baptême [batɛm] *nm* **(a)** *Rel* baptism, christening; **conférer** *ou* **donner le b. à qn** to baptize *or* christen sb; **recevoir le b.** to be baptized *or* christened; **nom de b.** Christian name, first *or US* given name **(b)** (*d'une cloche*) blessing; (*d'un navire*) naming, christening

▶ **baptême**: **b. de l'air** first flight; *Mil* **b. du feu** baptism of fire; *Naut* **b. de la ligne** crossing of the line

baptiser [batize] *vt* **(a)** *Rel* (*qn*) to baptize, to christen; (*surnommer*) to christen, to nickname; **ses parents l'ont baptisée Léa** her parents christened her Léa; **on l'avait baptisé le 'Balafré'** they had christened *or* nicknamed him 'Scarface'; **b. son vin/son lait** to water down one's wine/milk **(b)** *Rel* (*cloche*) to bless; (*navire*) to name

baptismal, -ale, -aux, -ales [batismal, -o] *adj* baptismal

baptisme [batism] *nm* baptism

baptistaire [batistɛr] *adj* **registre b.** register of baptisms; **extrait b.** certificate of baptism

baptiste [batist] *adj, n Rel* Baptist

baptistère [batistɛr] *nm Rel* baptist(e)ry

baquet [bakɛ] *nm* **(a)** (*cuve*) tub **(b)** *Aut* (**siège en**) **b.** bucket seat

bar[1] [bar] *nm* (*poisson*) bass; **b. commun** sea perch

bar[2] *nm* (*café, comptoir*) bar; **le b. du coin** the bar on the corner, the local; **prendre une consommation au b.** to have a drink at the bar; **b. américain** (*dans une cuisine*) bar; **b-tabac** = bar that sells tobacco; **b. à vin** wine bar

bar[3] *nm Météo* bar

barachois [baraʃwa] *nm Can* (*dans une rivière*) sandbar

baragouin [baragwɛ̃] *nm F* gibberish, gobbledegook

baragouinage [baragwinaʒ] *nm F* jabbering

baragouiner [baragwine] *F* **1** *vt* (*langue étrangère*) to speak badly; **b. l'anglais** to talk broken English; **qu'est-ce qu'il baragouine?** what's he jabbering (on) about? **2** *vi* to jabber (on)

baragouineur, -euse [baragwinœr, -øz] *n F* jabberer

baraka [baraka] *nf F* (good) luck; **avoir la b.** to be lucky

baraque [barak] *nf* **(a)** (*logement provisoire*) hut, shack, shed **(b)** *F* (*foyer*) place; *Péj* (*lieu*) hole, dump; **casser la b.** to bring the house down; **il n'y a rien à manger dans cette b.!** there's nothing to eat in this joint! **(c)** (*de foire etc*) stall, stand

baraqué [barake] *adj F* hefty

baraquement [barakmɑ̃] *nm* shacks; *Mil* camp

baraquer [barake] *vi* (*d'un chameau*) to kneel down

baratin [baratɛ̃] *nm F* (*bavardage*) chatter; (*d'un vendeur*) sales talk, patter, spiel; (*pour draguer*) sweet *or* smooth talk; **b. publicitaire** blurb; **quel b.!** (*je n'y comprends rien*) what gibberish!; **faire du b. (à qn)** to spin (sb) a yarn, to shoot (sb) a line; **ce type me fait du b.** (*pour draguer*) this bloke's chatting me up; **faire son b. à un client** to give a customer the patter *or* sales talk *or* spiel; **avoir du b.** to be a smooth talker

baratiner [baratine] *F* **1** *vi* (*parler beaucoup*) to chatter; (*parler sans sincérité*) to shoot a line, to spin a yarn; (*d'un vendeur*) to give one's patter *or* sales talk *or* spiel **2** *vt* to sweet-talk; **b. un client** to give a client the patter *or* sales talk *or* spiel; **b. une fille** to chat up a girl

baratineur, -euse [baratinœr, -øz] *n F* smooth talker, smoothie

baratte [barat] *nf* churn

baratter [barate] *vt* (*lait*) to churn

barbacane [barbakan] *nf* **(a)** (*ouvrage*) barbican, outwork; (*meurtrière*) loop(hole) **(b)** (*canalisation*) drainage channel

Barbade [barbad] *nf* Barbados

barbant [barbɑ̃] *adj F* boring

barbaque [barbak] *nf F* meat; (*de mauvaise qualité*) lousy meat

barbare [barbar] **1** *adj* (*cruel, sauvage*) barbaric, barbarous; *F* **il écoute de la musique b.** he's listening to that awful racket he calls music **2** *n* barbarian

barbaresque [barbarɛsk] *Vieilli* **1** *adj* Berber; **les États barbaresques** the Barbary States **2** *n* **B.** Berber

Barbarie [barbari] *nf Vieilli* **la B.** the Barbary States

barbarie [barbari] *nf* **(a)** (*cruauté, action cruelle*) barbarity **(b)** (*manque de civilisation*) barbarism

barbarisme [barbarism] *nm Gram* barbarism

barbe[1] [barb] *nf* **(a)** (*d'homme*) beard; **sans b.** (*adulte*) clean-shaven; (*jeune adolescent*) beardless; **avoir de la b.** (*d'un homme*) to need a shave; (*d'un adolescent*) to have some hairs on one's chin; **se faire pousser la b.** to grow a beard, to let one's beard grow; **faire la b. à qn** to shave sb; **il avait une b. de huit jours** he had a week's beard *or* growth; **tu n'as pas encore de b. au menton et tu crois tout savoir** you're still in short pants and you think you know everything; **brosse/savon à b.** shaving brush/soap; **parler dans sa b.** to mutter, to mumble; **femme à b.** bearded lady; *Fig* **faire qch à la b. de qn** to do sth right under sb's nose; **rire dans sa b.** to laugh up one's sleeve; *F* **quelle b.!** what a drag!, what a bore!; *F* **la b.!** shut it!, shut up!; *F* **vieille b.** old fogey

(b) (*de chèvre, d'oiseau etc*) beard; (*de chat*) whiskers; (*de poisson*) barbel, wattle; (*de plume, d'hameçon*) barb; (*du blé*) beard

(c) *Tech* (*sur moulage etc*) bur(r); **barbes** (*sur papier*) deckle edge

▶ **barbe**: **b. à papa** *Culin* candy floss, *Am* cotton candy

barbe² *nm* **(cheval) b.** barb, Barbary horse
barbeau¹, -eaux [barbo] *nm* **(a)** *(poisson)* **b. commun** barbel; **b. de mer** red mullet **(b)** *Arg (souteneur)* pimp
barbeau² **1** *nm Bot* cornflower **2** *adj inv* **(bleu) b.** cornflower blue
Barbe-Bleue *nm* Bluebeard
barbecue [barbəkju] *nm* barbecue; **faire un b.** to have a barbecue
barbelé [barbəle] **1** *adj (flèche)* barbed; **fil de fer b.** barbed wire **2** *nmpl* **barbelés** barbed wire; *Mil* barbed wire entanglement; **être derrière les barbelés** to be in a prison camp
barber [barbe] *F* **1** *vt (qn)* to bore stiff, to bore to death **2** *vpr* **se barber** to be bored stiff *or* bored to death
barbiche [barbiʃ] *nf* goatee (beard)
barbichette [barbiʃɛt] *nf F* small goatee (beard)
barbier [barbje] *nm* **(a)** *Vieilli (qui rase le visage)* barber **(b)** *Can (coiffeur pour hommes)* (men's) hairdresser, barber; **salon de b.** (men's) hairdresser's, barber's, barbershop
barbillon [barbijɔ̃] *nm* **(a)** *(d'un poisson)* barbel; **barbillons** *(de cheval, bœuf)* barbs **(b)** *(poisson)* barbel; **b. de mer** red mullet
barbital, *pl* **barbitals** [barbital] *nm Pharm* barbitone, *US* barbital
barbiturique [barbityrik] *Pharm* **1** *adj* barbituric **2** *nm* barbiturate
barbiturisme [barbityrism] *nm Méd* barbiturate poisoning; *(dépendance)* barbiturism, addiction to barbiturates
barbon [barbɔ̃] *nm Litt* **vieux b.** greybeard
barbotage [barbɔtaʒ] *nm (dans l'eau)* paddling, splashing (about); *Ch (d'un gaz dans un liquide)* bubbling
barboter [barbɔte] **1** *vi (dans l'eau)* to paddle, to splash (about); *(du gaz)* to bubble *(through liquid)*; **les enfants barbotent dans la piscine** the children are splashing about in the swimming pool **2** *vt Arg (voler)* to pinch, *Br* to nick; **quelqu'un m'a barboté mon stylo** someone's pinched my pen
barboteur, -euse [barbɔtœr, -øz] **1** *n* **(a)** *(dans l'eau)* paddler **(b)** *Arg (voleur)* thief **2** *nm Ch* bubbler, blower **3** *nf* **barboteuse** playsuit, rompers
barbotin [barbɔtɛ̃] *nm Tech* sprocket wheel
barbouillage [barbujaʒ] *nm* **(a)** *(action de peindre)* daubing, smearing; *(action d'écrire)* scrawling, scribbling **(b)** *(mauvaise peinture)* daub; *(griffonnage)* scrawl, scribble
barbouiller [barbuje] *vt* **(a)** *(avec de la peinture)* to daub, to smear; *(salir) (visage)* to smear; *(papier avec de l'encre)* to blot; **visage barbouillé de larmes/de chocolat** tear-stained face/face smeared with chocolate; **b. des toiles** to do a bit of painting **(b)** *(griffonner)* to scribble, to scrawl; **b. un article** to dash off an article **(c)** *F* **ça me barbouille l'estomac** *ou* **le cœur** it makes me feel sick, it turns my stomach; **avoir l'estomac barbouillé** to feel queasy
barbouilleur, -euse [barbujœr, -øz] *n* **(a)** *(de peinture)* dauber, so-called artist **(b) b. (de papier)** scribbler, hack
barbouze [barbuz] *nf F* **(a)** *(barbe)* beard **(b)** *(agent secret)* secret agent
barbu, -ue [barby] **1** *adj* bearded **2** *nm* **(a)** bearded man **(b)** *F* Islamic fundamentalist **3** *nf* **barbue** *(poisson)* brill
barcarolle [barkarɔl] *nf Mus* barcarol(l)e
barcasse [barkas] *nf Naut* launch, boat
Barcelone [barsəlɔn] *nf* Barcelona
barda [barda] *nm Arg* gear, kit, stuff; *Mil* kit
bardage [bardaʒ] *nm* **(a)** *(de matériaux lourds)* hand transport **(b)** *(pour protéger un tableau etc)* boarding; *(d'un bâtiment)* weatherboarding, *Am* siding
bardane [bardan] *nf (plante)* burdock
bardas [bardas] *nm Can (pagaille)* shambles; **être de b.** *(déranger)* to be a nuisance
barde¹ [bard] *nf* **(a)** *Culin (sur un rôti)* bard **(b)** *Hist (protégeant les chevaux de bataille)* bard
barde² *nm* bard, poet
bardeau, -eaux [bardo] *nm* **(a)** *Constr* shingle; **toit de bardeaux** shingle roof **(b)** *Zool* hinny
barder¹ [barde] *v impers F* **ça va b.!** there's going to be trouble!; **c'est là que ça a commencé à b.!** and then the fun began!, and then the sparks flew!
barder² *vt* **(a)** *Culin (volaille etc)* to bard **(b)** *Hist (cheval)* to bard; **chevalier bardé de fer** steel-clad knight; **malle bardée d'étiquettes** trunk stuck all over with labels; **il est bardé de diplômes/décorations** he's got a whole string of qualifications/decorations
bardot [bardo] *nm Zool* hinny
barème [barɛm] *nm* **(a)** *(de notes, de salaires)* scale; *(de prix etc)* list, schedule; **b. de prix** price scale **(b)** *(pour calcul rapide)* ready reckoner
barge¹ [barʒ] *nf Naut* barge, lighter
barge² *adj voir* **barjo**
baril [baril] *nm (de vin)* cask, barrel; *(de poudre)* keg; *(d'anchois)* barrel; *Pétr* barrel *(42 gallons)*; **b. de lessive** drum of washing powder
barillet [barijɛ] *nm* **(a)** *(petit baril)* small barrel *or* cask **(b)** *(d'une pompe)* barrel piston chamber; *(d'un revolver, d'une serrure)* cylinder, barrel; **il n'y avait rien dans le b.** the gun was empty; **b. (de ressort)** *(dans une horloge)* spring box, spring drum; **serrure à b.** cylinder lock, Yale® lock
bariolage [barjɔlaʒ] *nm (de peinture)* painting *or* daubing with bright colours; *Fig (de couleurs)* medley, riot; *Péj (motif)* gaudy colour scheme
bariolé [barjɔle] *adj (tissu)* multicoloured, *Péj* gaudy; **audience bariolée** colourfully dressed audience
barioler [barjɔle] *vt* to paint *or* daub in bright *or Péj* gaudy colours
bariolure [barjɔlyr] *nf* bright *or Péj* gaudy colours
barjo [barʒo] *F* **1** *n* nut, *Br* nutter **2** *adj* nutty, crazy
barmaid [barmɛd] *nf* barmaid
barman, *pl* **barmen, barmans** [barman, -mɛn] *nm* barman
barn [barn] *nm Phys* barn
barographe [barɔgraf] *nm Météo* barograph
baromètre [barɔmɛtr] *nm Météo, Fig* barometer; **b. anéroïde** aneroid barometer; **b. enregistreur** recording barometer
barométrique [barɔmetrik] *adj* barometric
baron [barɔ̃] *nm* **(a)** *(seigneur)* baron; *Fig* **les barons de la finance/de l'industrie** financial/industrial tycoons **(b)** *Arg (protecteur)* protector **(c)** *Culin* **b. d'agneau** baron of lamb
baronnage [barɔnaʒ] *nm (titre)* barony, baronage
baronne [barɔn] *nf* baroness; **bonjour madame la b.** good morning, Lady Smith/*etc*; *(paroles d'un domestique)* good morning, your ladyship *or* my lady
baronnet [barɔnɛ] *nm* baronet
baronnie [barɔni] *nf Hist* barony
baroque [barɔk] **1** *adj (idées etc)* bizarre, odd, strange; *Archit, Beaux-Arts, Mus* baroque; *(perle)* tear-shaped **2** *nm* Baroque
baroud [barud] *nm Mil F* fighting; **b. d'honneur** last-ditch battle, last stand
barouder [barude] *vi F (voyager)* to knock about
baroudeur [barudœr] *nm Mil F (qui aime le combat)* (keen) fighter; **c'est un b.** *(voyageur)* he's knocked about a bit
barouf(le) [baruf(l)] *nm F* din, row, racket; **faire du b.** to make a din *or* row *or* racket
barque [bark] *nf Naut* **(a)** *(embarcation)* boat; **b. de pêcheur** fishing boat; **patron de b.** skipper; *Fig* **bien mener** *ou* **bien conduire sa b.** to manage one's affairs well; *Fig* **c'est elle qui mène la b.** she's the boss, she's in charge **(b) trois-mâts b.** barque
barquette [barkɛt] *nf* **(a)** *(récipient) (pour plat à emporter etc)* container; *(de fraises, framboises etc)* punnet **(b)** *(gâteau)* pastry boat
barracuda [barakyda] *nm* barracuda
barrage [baraʒ] *nm* **(a)** *(fait de bloquer) (d'une route, rue)* blocking (off), closing; *(d'un port)* blocking; *(d'une vallée)* damming; **faire b. à qn/qch** to block sb/sth **(b)** *(fermeture)* barrier, obstruction; *(d'un port)* boom; **b. routier** *ou* **de route** roadblock; **b. de police** police roadblock, police cordon; **b. (de retenue)** dam, barrage; *(de petite taille)* weir; *Mil* **b. aérien** anti-aircraft barrage; **(tir de) barrage** barrage (fire)
barre [bar] *nf* **(a)** *(de métal)* bar, rod; *(de bois etc)* rod; *Sp* bar; *(de danse)* barre; *F* **c'est le coup de b.** it's a rip-off; *Fig F* **avoir un coup de b.** to be shattered *or* whacked; **s'exercer à la b., faire des exercices à la b.** to do exercises at the barre; **avoir barre(s) sur qn** to have an advantage over sb; **passer la b. /sous la b. de 2 000 francs** to rise above/drop below the 2,000 franc mark

(b) *Naut (de bateau)* tiller; *(de navire)* helm; **homme de b.** helmsman; **être à** *ou* **tenir la b.** to be at the helm; **prendre la b.** to take the helm; *Fig* **à partir d'aujourd'hui je prends la b.** as from today, I'm in charge

(c) *Jur* **b. d'un tribunal** bar of a lawcourt; **b. des témoins** witness box, *or US* stand; **paraître à la b.** to appear before the court *or* at the bar; **être appelé à la b.** to be called to the witness box *or* stand

(d) *(d'une rivière, d'un port)* (sand)bar; *(artificielle)* boom; **b. d'eau** (tidal) bore; **b. de flot** tidal wave; **b. de plage** surf

(e) *(trait)* line, dash, stroke; **b. d'un t** cross(bar) of a t; **mettre une b. à un t** to cross a t; *Mus* **b. de mesure** bar (line); **double b.** double bar

(f) *(de cheval)* bar

(g) *Hér* bend sinister

(h) jeu de barres = prisoners' base

▶ **barre**: **b. d'accouplement** tie rod, coupling bar; *(de direction)* steering rod; *Aut* **b. antidevers** *ou* **anti-roulis** anti-roll bar; *Aut* **b. antivol** locking bar; **b. d'appui** (*d'une fenêtre*) rail; **barres asymétriques** asymmetric bars; *Aut* **b. de calandre** nudge bar; **b. de chocolat** bar of chocolate, chocolate bar; *Aut* **b. de connexion** (*de la boîte de direction*) crossbar, tie rod; *Typ, Ordinat* **b. d'espacement** spacebar; *Gym* **b. fixe** horizontal bar; *Ordinat* **b. d'icônes** icon bar; *Aut* **b. latérale de protection anti-intrusion** anti-intrusion side-impact bar; *Ordinat* **b. de menu** menu bar; *Typ* **b. oblique** oblique, slash; *Typ* **b. oblique inversée** backslash; *Ordinat* **b. d'outils** tool bar; **barres parallèles** parallel bars; *Aut* **b. de remorquage** towing rod, towbar; *Aut* **b. de renfort latéral** side-impact bar; **b. de savon** bar of soap, cake of soap; *Ordinat* **b. de sélection** menu bar; *Aut* **b. stabilisatrice** stabilizer bar; *Ordinat* **b. de style** style bar; *Ordinat* **b. de titre** title bar; *Aut* **b. de toit** roof bar; *Aut* **b. de torsion** torsion bar, torque strut

barré [bare] *adj* **(a)** (*chemin, passage, route*) closed; **'route barrée'** 'road closed' **(b) chèque b.** crossed cheque *or US* check; **chèque non b.** open cheque **(c) dent barrée** impacted tooth **(d)** (*à l'aviron*) **un deux b.** a coxed pair **(e)** *F* **on est mal b.** things don't look good

barreau, -eaux [baro] *nm* **(a)** (*d'une fenêtre, cage*) bar; (*d'une échelle*) rung; (*d'une chaise*) rung, crosspiece; *Fig* **b. de chaise** fat cigar; **fenêtre garnie de barreaux** barred window, window with bars; **être derrière les barreaux** to be behind bars **(b)** *Jur* **le b.** the bar; **être reçu** *ou* **admis au b.** to be called to the bar; **rayer qn du b.** to disbar sb

barrement [barmɑ̃] *nm* (*d'un chèque*) crossing

barrer [bare] **1** *vt* **(a)** (*porte, fenêtre*) to bar; *Can* (*fermer à clef*) to lock; (*route, passage, chemin*) to block (off), to close; **b. le passage** *ou* **la route à qn** to block *or* bar sb's way; *Fig* to stand in sb's way, to block sb, to thwart sb **(b)** (*chèque*) to cross; **b. un t** to cross a t **(c)** (*mot etc*) to cross out, to strike out; **je vais pouvoir b. ça de ma liste** I can cross that off my list **(d)** *Naut* (*bateau*) to steer; (*à l'aviron*) to cox **2** *vpr* **se barrer** *F* to clear off, to beat it, to scram

barrette[1] [barɛt] *nf Rel* biretta

barrette[2] *nf* **(a)** (*pour les cheveux*) (hair) slide, *Am* barrette **(b)** (*broche*) brooch; (*de médaille*) bar

▶ **barrette**: *Ordinat* **b. de mémoire vive** RAM module; *Aut* **b. verticale** overrider

barreur [barœr] *nm* **(a)** *Naut* helmsman **(b)** (*à l'aviron*) cox; **un deux sans b.** a coxless pair

barricade [barikad] *nf* **b. (de rue)** (street) barricade; *Fig* **de l'autre côté de la b.** on the opposing side, on the other side of the fence

barricader [barikade] **1** *vt* (*route, porte etc*) to barricade **2 se barricader** *vpr* to barricade oneself in; **se b. dans une chambre** to barricade oneself in a room **(contre** against); (*pour ne pas être dérangé*) to shut *or* lock oneself up in a room

barrière [barjɛr] *nf* **(a)** (*obstacle*) barrier; (*clôture*) fence; (*dans le métro*) gate, barrier; (*d'un passage à niveau*) gate; **barrières culturelles/sociales** cultural/social barriers; *Géog* **b. naturelle** natural barrier; **la Grande B.** the Great Barrier Reef **(b)** *Hist* (*d'une ville, d'un château etc*) gate; (*péage*) toll gate, turnpike

▶ **barrière**: *Com* **b. d'accès** access barrier; *Av* **b. antisouffle** blast wall; **b. à bascule** drop-arm barrier; **b. commerciale** trade barrier; *Aut* **b. de dégel** = ban on the use of a road by heavy traffic during a thaw; *Com* **barrières douanières** trade barriers; *Com* **b. à l'entrée** entry barrier; *Com* **b. non tarifaire** non-tariff barrier; *Phys* **b. de potentiel** potential barrier; *Com* **b. à la sortie** exit barrier; *Phys* **b. thermique** thermal barrier, heat barrier

barrique [barik] *nf* barrel, cask (*containing approx 200 litres*); *F* **il est gros comme une b.** he's as round as a barrel; *Fig F* **plein** *ou* **rond comme une b.** blind drunk, (as) drunk as a lord

barrir [barir] *vi* (*d'un éléphant*) to trumpet

barrissement [barismɑ̃], **barrit** [bari] *nm* (*d'un éléphant*) trumpeting

bartavelle [bartavɛl] *nf* **(perdrix) b.** rock partridge

barycentre [barisɑ̃tr] *nm Math* barycentre

baryte [barit] *nf Ch, Minér* baryta, barium oxide

baryté [barite] *adj Méd* **bouillie barytée** barium meal

baryton [baritɔ̃] *Mus* **1** *adj* (*voix*) baritone **2** *nm* baritone

baryum [barjɔm] *nm Ch, Minér* barium

barzoï [barzɔj] *nm* (*chien*) borzoi

bas[1] [bɑ], **basse** [bɑs] **1** *adj* **(a)** (*de peu de hauteur, d'altitude*) low; (*station de ski etc*) low(-lying); (*baromètre, température, prix*) low; **maison basse de toit** *ou* **à toit b.** low-roofed house, house with a low roof; **b. de plafond** low-ceilinged, with a low ceiling; **b. sur pattes** short-legged; *Boxe, Fig* **coup b.** blow below the belt; **enfant en b. âge** infant; **avoir la vue basse** to be short-sighted *or* near-sighted; **voix basse** low *or* deep voice; **parler à voix basse** to speak in a low voice *or* in a whisper *or* under one's breath; **une note basse** a low note; **une clarinette basse** a bass clarinet; **basse saison** low season; **à b. prix** cheaply, for a low price; **maintenir les prix b.** to keep prices down *or* low; **prix les plus b.** rock-bottom prices, lowest possible prices; **en ce b. monde** here on earth; **au b. mot** at the very least, at the lowest estimate; **le soleil est b.** the sun is low; *Météo* **plafond b.** low ceiling (of cloud); **mer basse** low water *or* tide; **quand la mer est basse** when it's low tide, when the tide is low *or* out; **la marée est basse** the tide is out *or* low; **à marée basse** at low tide; *Fig* **la tête basse** with a hang-dog look; **le moral est très b.** morale is very low; **elle est au plus b.** she's really low, she's at a very low ebb; **terres** *ou* **régions basses** lowlands; **le b. Rhin** the lower Rhine; **la basse Normandie** Lower Normandy; **les Bas Bretons** the inhabitants of Lower Britanny

(b) (*dans hiérarchie*) lower; **les basses classes** (*de la société*) the lower classes; *Pol* **la Chambre basse** the Lower House; **la partie basse d'une ville, la basse ville** the lower (part of a) town

(c) (*dans le temps*) late; **le b. Moyen-Age** the late Middle Ages; **le B-Empire** the Late Empire

(d) *Péj* (*acte*) mean, base, low; (*besognes*) menial; **motif b.** base *or* contemptible motive; **terme/style b.** vulgar expression/style; **c'est une basse vengeance** that was a petty revenge; **c'est vraiment b. de sa part** it's really mean of him; **de basse naissance** of low(ly) birth; **de basse condition** from a poor family

2 *adv* **(a)** (*dans l'espace*) low (down); **être assis trop b.** to be sitting too low (down); **mettre une étagère plus b.** to put a shelf lower (down); **quelques marches plus b.** a few steps lower down *or* farther down; **plus b. dans la rue** farther down the street; **dix lignes plus b.** ten lines (further) down; **les hirondelles volent b.** the swallows are flying low; **voir plus b.** see below; *Fig* **mettre qn plus b. que terre** to treat sb like dirt; *Bourse* **les cours sont tombés très b.** shares are well down; **la température est tombée b. pendant la nuit** the temperature plummeted during the night; **comment a-t-elle pu tomber si b.?** how could she sink so low?; **le malade est bien b.** the patient is very low

(b) chapeau b.! (*bravo*) bravo!; *F* **b. les mains** *ou* **les pattes!** hands off!, keep your paws off!; **b. les pattes!** (*à un chien*) paws (down)!; *Naut* **mettre b. une voile** to haul down a sail; **mettre pavillon b.** *Naut* to lower *or* strike the colours; *Fig F* to climb down

(c) (*des animaux*) **mettre b.** to give birth, *Spéc* to drop (its young); (*d'une jument*) to foal; (*d'une brebis*) to lamb; (*d'une chèvre*) to kid; (*d'une chienne*) to pup, to whelp; (*d'une truie*) to farrow; **mettre b. avant terme** to cast *or* slip its young

(d) (*en intensité*) low; **vous chantez trop b.** (*dans le registre*) you are singing too low; (*doucement*) you are singing too softly; **parler (tout) b.** to (speak in a) whisper; **parlez plus b., je vous prie** please speak more quietly, please lower your voice; **rire tout b.** to chuckle *or* laugh to oneself; **tu pourrais mettre la télévision/le chauffage plus b.?** could you turn down the television/the heating?

(e) en b. (*à l'étage inférieur*) downstairs; **aller en b.** to go downstairs *or* down; **les gens d'en b.** the people below *or* downstairs; **ça a l'air de venir d'en b.** it seems to come from below *or* from downstairs; **agiter les bras de haut en b.** to move one's arms up and down; **de haut en b.** from top to bottom, downwards; **regarder qn de haut en b.** to look sb up and down, to look at sb from head to foot *or* toe; **il est vêtu de neuf de haut en b.** he's dressed from head to toe in new clothes; **de b. en haut** upwards; **la tête en b.** upside down; **ce vase est plus large en b.** this vase is wider at the bottom; **la jupe tombe mal en b.** the skirt hangs wrong at the bottom; **en** *ou* **au b. de** at the bottom of; (*escalier, page*) at the foot *or* bottom of; **en b. du village** at the lower end of the village

(f) à b. la dictature/la police! down with dictatorship/the police!; **à b. Martin!** down with Martin!; **mettre** *ou* **jeter à b.** (*maison*) to pull down, to demolish; (*qn, gouvernement*) to bring down, to overthrow; **mettre b. les armes** *Mil* to lay down one's arms; *Fig* (*dans une dispute*) to give in

3 *nm* **(a)** (*partie inférieure*) bottom; (*d'une colline, échelle, page*) foot, bottom; **les gens du b.** the people below *or* downstairs; **l'étagère du b.** the bottom shelf; **la boulangerie du b.** the bakery at the bottom (*of street, village*); **b. du dos** small of the back; **le** *ou* **les b. du navire** the ship's bottom

(b) *Aut* **b. de caisse** underbody; **b. de marche** sill; **b. de porte** doorsill (**c**) **les hauts et les b.** (*de la vie etc*) the ups and downs; **avoir des hauts et des b.** to have ups and downs *or* highs and lows

▶ **bas**: **b. allemand** low German; *Typ* **b. de casse** lower case; **caractère en b. de casse** lower-case character; **le b. clergé** the lower clergy; **b. de gamme** bottom-of-the-range, down-market; **b. latin** low Latin; *Culin* **b. morceaux** (*de viande*) cheap cuts; *Typ* **b. de page** footer; **les b. quartiers** (*d'une ville*) the poor districts

bas² *nm* (*de femme*) stocking; **b. de soie/de nylon** silk/nylon stocking; **b. fin** *ou* **voile** sheer stocking; **b. mousse** stretch stocking; **b. 15 deniers** 15 denier stocking; **b. sans couture** seamless stocking; **b. filet** *ou* **résille** fishnet *or* mesh stocking; *Méd* **b. de contention** elastic stocking; *Méd* **b. élastique** elastic *or* support stocking; **b. de laine** woollen stocking; *Fig* nest egg; *Méd* **b. à varices** elastic *or* support stocking

basalte [bazalt] *nm Géol* basalt

basaltique [bazaltik] *adj Géol* basaltic

basané [bazane] *adj* (*bronzé*) (sun)tanned, sunburnt; (*tanné*) weatherbeaten; (*naturellement*) swarthy

basaner [bazane] *vt* (*visage etc*) to tan

bas-bleu, *pl* **bas-bleus** *nm Péj* bluestocking

bas-côté *nm* (**a**) (*d'une route etc*) verge, shoulder, side; **défense de stationner sur les bas-côtés** no parking on the verge (**b**) (*d'une église*) (side) aisle

basculant [baskylɑ̃] *adj* **benne basculante** (*de camion*) tipping *or* dump body; **pont b.** drawbridge, bascule bridge; **siège b.** tip-up seat; **fenêtre basculante** tilt window

bascule [baskyl] *nf* (**a**) (*pièce mobile*) rocker; **mouvement de b.** rocking motion; **(jeu de) b.** seesaw; **fauteuil/cheval à b.** rocking chair/horse; *Fig* **politique de b.** balancing act (**b**) **(balance à) b.** weighbridge, weighing machine; **b. automatique** *ou* **du pharmacien** weighing machine; **wagon à b.** tip wagon (**c**) *Aut* toggle; *Ordinat* toggle; (*circuit*) flipflop (circuit); *Électron* **(montage en) b.** bistable trigger circuit, flip-flop circuit

basculement [baskylmɑ̃] *nm* (*renversement*) knocking over; (*des intentions de vote*) swing, reversal

basculer [baskyle] **1** *vt* (**a**) (*culbuter*) to rock; **levier basculé par une came** lever rocked by a cam

(**b**) (*renverser*) (*charrette etc*) to tip (up); (*fardeau, chargement*) to tip off

2 *vi* (**a**) (*tomber*) to fall over, to topple over; **faire b.** (*personne*) to knock over, to knock off balance; (*chargement*) to tip over; **ce pays pourrait b. dans une économie de marché** the country could shift to a market economy; **il a basculé dans l'opposition** he moved over *or* went over to the opposition; *Pol* **b. dans l'extrême droite** to swing (over) to the far right; *Fig* **nous étions heureux, et puis tout a basculé** we were happy, then everything turned upside down

(**b**) *Ordinat* to toggle

basculeur [baskylœr] *nm* (**a**) (*de wagon etc*) tipper (**b**) *Él* rocker switch; *Ordinat* toggle (key)

base [bɑz] *nf* (**a**) (*d'une montagne*) base, foot, bottom; (*d'un bâtiment*) base, foundation(s); *Anat, Math* (*du cœur, d'un triangle etc*) base; (*en arpentage*) base (line); (*d'une machine*) base plate; **jeter** *ou* **poser les bases de qch** to lay the foundations for sth

(**b**) *Mil etc* (*d'opérations*) base; **b. de ravitaillement** supply base; **b. aérienne/navale** air/naval base; **b. de lancement (d'engins)** (missile) launch(ing) site

(**c**) [①A14,10] (*principe*) basis; **être à la b. de qch** to be at the root *or* heart of sth; **argument qui pèche par la b.** fundamentally unsound argument; **sur la b. de qch** on the basis of sth; **vocabulaire/l'anglais de b.** basic vocabulary/English; **les produits de b. pour la maison** basic household goods, basics; **denrées de b.** staple commodities, staples; **avoir des connaissances de b. en informatique** to have an elementary *or* a basic knowledge of information technology; **traitement de b.** basic salary; **produits à b. d'amidon** starch-based products; **boisson à b. de gin** gin-based drink; **alimentation à b. de légumes** vegetable-based diet; **à b. d'Unix** Unix-based; **ordinateur à b. de 486** 486-based computer; **documents/données de b.** source documents/data; *Pol etc* **la b.** (*d'un syndicat etc*) the rank and file, the grassroots; **militant de b.** grassroots activist

(**d**) *Math* (*d'un système de notation*) base, radix; (*d'un logarithme*) radix, root, basis; **calculer en b. 3** to do calculations in base 3

(**e**) *Ch* base

(**f**) *Électron* (*d'un transistor*) base (electrode); *Ordinat* (*d'imprimante laser*) engine

▶ **base**: *Compta* **b. amortissable** basis for depreciation; *Compta* **b. de calcul** basis of calculations; *Ordinat* **b. de connaissances** knowledge base; *Ordinat* **b. de données** database; **mettre qch dans une b. de données** to enter sth into a database, to database sth; **b. de données de consommateurs** customer database; **b. de données relationnelle** relational database; **b. hors taxe** (*de TVA*) amount exclusive of VAT; **b. de loisirs** country park; **b. de maquillage** foundation cream, (makeup) base; **b. de vernis à ongles** nail varnish *or Am* polish base

base-ball [bɛzbol] *nm Sp* baseball

baser [bɑze] **1** *vt* to base (**sur** on); **cette opinion n'est pas basée sur la réalité** this opinion is not based on reality; **entièrement basée sur le commerce** based wholly on trade, wholly trade-based; **avions américains basés en Grande-Bretagne** American aircraft based in Great Britain **2 se baser** *vpr* **se b. sur qch** to base one's argument on sth; **sur quoi te bases-tu pour dire que ...?** what basis do you have *or* what's your basis for saying that ...?

bas-fond, *pl* **bas-fonds** *nm* (**a**) (*creux*) low ground, hollow; *Fig* **les bas-fonds de la société** the dregs of society; **les bas-fonds d'une ville** the seedy districts of a town; **les bas-fonds du journalisme** the gutter press (**b**) (*dans la mer, la rivière*) shallow, shoal

Basic [bazik] *nm Ordinat* BASIC

basilic¹ [bazilik] *nm* (*plante*) basil

basilic² *nm Zool, Myth* basilisk

basilical, -ale, -aux, -ales [bazilikal, -o] *adj Archit* basilical

basilique [bazilik] *nf Archit* basilica

basin [bazɛ̃] *nm Tex* cotton damask

basique [bɑzik] *adj* (**a**) *Ch, Métal* (*sel, procédé etc*) basic; **scorie b.** basic slag (**b**) (*faits etc*) basic; *F* **des connaissances/produits basiques** basic knowledge/products

basket [baskɛt] **1** *nf* **une paire de baskets** a pair of basketball boots; *F Fig* **lâche-moi les baskets** don't hassle me, get off my back **2** *nm Sp* basketball

basket-ball [baskɛtbol] *nm Sp* basketball

basketteur, -euse [baskɛtœr, -øz] *n Sp* basketball player

bas-mât, *pl* **bas-mâts** *nm Naut* lower mast

basquais, -aise [baskɛ, -ɛz] **1** *adj* Basque **2** *nf Culin* **poulet (à la) basquaise** Basque chicken (*cooked with onion, tomato etc*)

basque¹ [bask] **1** *adj* Basque; **le Pays b.** the Basque country **2** *nm Ling* Basque **3** *n* **B.** Basque

basque² *nf* (*d'une veste etc*) skirt, tail; *Fig* **être toujours pendu aux basques de qn** to be always at sb's heels

bas-relief, *pl* **bas-reliefs** *nm Archit etc* bas relief, low relief

basse [bɑs] **1** *adj voir* **bas¹ 2** *nf* (**a**) *Mus* (*partie*) bass part; (*voix, chanteur*) bass; **b. chiffrée** *ou* **continue** *ou* **figurée** figured bass, basso continuo; **b. chantante, b-taille** basso cantante, singing bass; **b. profonde, b-contre, b. noble** basso profundo; **voix de b.** bass voice (**b**) (*contrebasse*) (double) bass; (*saxophone*) bass saxophone; (*guitare*) bass (guitar); (*d'un instrument*) bass strings (**c**) *Naut* shoal, flat, sandbank

▶ **basse**: **b. de hautbois** bassoon; **b. de viole** bass viol

basse-cour, *pl* **basses-cours** *nf* (**a**) (*cour*) farmyard (**b**) (*volaille*) poultry

basse-fosse, *pl* **basses-fosses** *nf* dungeon

bassement [bɑsmɑ̃] *adv* basely, meanly; **elle s'est b. vengée** she took a petty revenge

bassesse [bɑsɛs] *nf* (**a**) (*d'une expression, d'une action, du caractère de qn etc*) baseness; **c'est d'une b.!** how low can you get?; **il est d'une b. sans nom** he's the lowest of the low; *Vieilli* **on lui reproche la b. de sa naissance** his low(ly) birth is held against him (**b**) (*action*) base *or* mean *or* contemptible action; **faire des bassesses** to behave contemptibly; **homme prêt à toutes les bassesses** man who would stoop to anything

basset¹ [basɛ] *nm* (*chien*) basset (hound); **b. allemand** dachshund

basset² *nm Mus* **cor de b.** tenor clarinet in F, basset horn

basse-taille, *pl* **basses-tailles** *nf Mus* basso cantante, singing bass

bassin [basɛ̃] *nm* (**a**) (*récipient*) basin, bowl; (*d'une balance*) pan; *Méd* **b. (de lit)** bedpan

(**b**) (*dans un jardin*) ornamental lake; (*plus petit*) pond; (*de fontaine*) basin; (*réservoir*) tank; **petit b.** (*de la piscine*) small *or* children's pool; **grand b.** (*de la piscine*) large pool; **les bassins du Luxembourg** the pools in the Luxembourg Gardens

(**c**) (*d'un port*) dock, basin; **entrer au b.** to dock; **b. à flot** wet dock; **b. à marée** tidal dock; **b. de radoub** dry dock, graving dock; **b. naturel/artificiel** natural/artificial basin; **b. de décantation** settling tank; **b. filtrant** filter bed

(**d**) *Géol* basin; (*dépression*) depression; **le b. parisien** the

Paris basin; **le b. de la Tamise** the Thames basin; **b. de réception** catchment area

(e) *Anat* pelvis

▶ **bassin**: **b. houiller** coal basin; **b. minier** mining area

bassinant [basinɑ̃] *adj F* boring

bassine [basin] *nf* (*en cuivre*) pan; (*en plastique*) bowl; **b. à confitures** preserving pan; **b. (à vaisselle)** washing-up bowl; **une (pleine) b. de confiture** a panful of jam

bassiner [basine] *vt* **(a)** (*blessure etc*) to bathe; (*plate-bande, fleurs*) to spray lightly **(b)** *Arg* (*qn*) to bore; **elle nous bassine avec ses histoires de bureau** we're bored stiff hearing about her work at the office **(c) b. un lit** to warm a bed (with a warming pan)

bassinet [basinɛ] *nm* **(a)** *Anat* (*du rein*) pelvis **(b)** (*d'armure*) basinet **(c)** *F* **cracher au b.** to cough up, *Br* to stump up

bassinoire [basinwar] *nf* **(a)** (*instrument*) warming pan **(b)** *Arg* (*importun*) bore, pain in the neck

bassiste [bɑsist] *n Mus* (*contrebassiste*) (double) bass player; (*joueur de guitare basse*) bass guitarist

basson [bɑsɔ̃] *nm Mus* **(a)** (*instrument*) bassoon **(b)** (*joueur*) bassoonist

bassoniste [bɑsɔnist] *n* bassoonist

basta [basta] *int F* that's enough!

bastide [bastid] *nf* **(a)** (*en Provence*) (*maison*) country house; (*ferme*) farm **(b)** *Hist* (*en Provence*) (*ville fortifiée*) fortified town

bastille [bastij] *nf* fortress; *Hist* **la B.** the Bastille; **la prise de la B.** the storming of the Bastille

bastingage [bastɛ̃gaʒ] *nm Naut* **(a)** (*garde-corps*) rail; **accoudé aux bastingages** leaning over the rails **(b)** *Hist* bulwark

bastion [bastjɔ̃] *nm* bastion; *Fig* (*de la liberté etc*) bastion, stronghold

baston [bastɔ̃] *nm ou f F* fight, *Br* punch-up

bastonnade [bastɔnad] *nf* beating (with sticks), bastinado

bastos [bastos] *nm Arg* (*balle*) slug, bullet

bastringue [bastrɛ̃g] *nm F* **(a)** (*lieu*) (cheap) dance hall; (*orchestre*) (dance) band; (*bruit*) din, racket **(b)** (*affaires*) gear, stuff, *Br* clobber; **prendre tout son b.** to pack up all one's gear *or* stuff; **et tout le b.** and the whole bag of tricks, and the whole caboodle

bas-ventre, *pl* **bas-ventres** *nm Anat* lower abdomen

BAT [beate] *abrév Typ* (**bon à tirer**) ready to go to press

bât [bɑ] *nm* packsaddle; **cheval de b.** packhorse; *Fig* **c'est là que le b. blesse** that's where the shoe pinches

bataclan [bataklɑ̃] *nm F* paraphernalia, *Br* clobber; **et tout le b.** and the whole caboodle, and whatever else; **vendez tout le b.!** sell the whole lot!

bataille [bataj] *nf* **(a)** (*combat*) battle, fight; **b. de rue** street fight; **b. terrestre/aérienne/navale** land/air/naval battle; **au (plus) fort de la b.** in the thick of the battle; **champ de b.** *Mil* battlefield; *Fig* mess; **cheval de b.** warhorse; *Fig* hobbyhorse; **livrer b. à** to give battle to, to join battle with; *Fig* **c'est une b. constante** it's a constant battle, it's an endless struggle; **la vie est une dure b.** life is a struggle; **la b. contre l'inflation** the battle *or* fight against inflation; **une b. d'idées** a battle of ideas; **une b. politique/électorale** a political/an electoral contest; *Mil* **en b.** in battle order *or* formation, *Arch* in battle array; **stationnement en b.** angled parking; **voitures garées en b.** cars parked at an angle; *Fig* **il portait son chapeau en b.** his hat was all crooked *or* askew; **cheveux en b.** dishevelled hair

(b) *Cartes* beggar-my-neighbour

batailler [bataje] *vi* to fight, to battle; **il est toujours prêt à b.** he's always spoiling for a fight; *F* **j'ai dû b. pendant une heure pour ouvrir la porte** I had to battle (away) for an hour to get the door open

batailleur, -euse [batajœr, -øz] **1** *adj* aggressive, quarrelsome, pugnacious **2** *n* fighter, battler

bataillon [batajɔ̃] *nm Mil* battalion; *F* (*grand nombre*) crowd, swarm (**de** of); **commandant de b.** battalion commander; **b. d'Afrique** = French disciplinary battalion (formerly stationed in North Africa); *F* **elle a un b. de petits chats** she has a whole load of kittens

bâtard, -arde [bɑtar, -ard] **1** *adj* (*enfant*) illegitimate, *Péj* bastard; (*architecture, produit, solution etc*) hybrid; **chien b.** mongrel; **écriture bâtarde** slanting round-hand writing; *Typ* **format b.** bastard size; **pain b.** = short stick of French bread **2** *nm* (*chien*) mongrel; (*pain*) = short stick of French bread **3** *n* (*enfant*) illegitimate child, *Péj* bastard

bâtardise [bɑtardiz] *nf* illegitimacy, *Péj* bastardy; **la b. de cette solution** the hybrid nature of this solution

batavia [batavja] *nf* batavia lettuce

bateau, -eaux [bato] **1** *nm* **(a)** boat; **b. à voiles** sailing boat, *Am* sailboat; **b. à vapeur** steamboat, steamer; **b. à moteur** motorboat; **b. à rames** rowing boat, *Am* rowboat; **b. de plaisance** pleasure boat; **b. de pêche** fishing boat; **b. de sauvetage** lifeboat; **b. pneumatique** rubber dinghy; **b. de guerre** warship, battleship; **faire du b.** to go boating; **faire du b. à voiles/à rames** to go sailing/rowing; **b. d'excursion** pleasure boat; **b. de croisière** cruise ship; **b. mixte** passenger and cargo ship; **b. à fond de verre** glass-bottomed boat; *Rail* **le train du b.** the boat train; **prendre le b.** to take the boat, to go by boat; **je suis venu en** *ou* **par b.** I came by boat; *F* **monter un b. à qn** to have *or Am* put sb on, to pull sb's leg; **encolure b.** (*d'une robe, d'un pull etc*) boat neck, scoop neck

(b) (*sur le trottoir*) driveway entrance

2 *adj F* hackneyed; **un sujet b.** a subject that's been done to death, a hackneyed subject

▶ **bateau**: **b.-citerne**, *pl* **bateaux-citernes** tanker; **b.-école**, *pl* **bateaux-écoles** training ship; **b.-feu**, *pl* **bateaux-feux** lightship; **b.-hôtel**, *pl* **bateaux-hôtels** botel; *Hist* **b.-lavoir**, *pl* **bateaux-lavoirs** wash-house; **b.-mouche**, *pl* **bateaux-mouches** river boat (*on the Seine*); **b.-phare**, *pl* **bateaux-phares** lightship; **b.-pilote**, *pl* **bateaux-pilotes** pilot boat; **b.-pompe**, *pl* **bateaux-pompes** fire boat

batelage[1] [batlaʒ] *nm Naut* **(frais de) b.** lighterage, *Br* waterage (charges)

batelage[2] *nm* (*art du jongleur*) juggling; (*acrobatique*) tumbling, acrobatics

bateleur, -euse [batlœr, -øz] *n Arch* (*jongleur*) juggler; (*acrobate*) tumbler, acrobat

batelier, -ière [batəlje, -jɛr] *n* boatman, waterman, *f* boatwoman; (*sur un bac*) ferryman, *f* ferrywoman; **b. de chaland** bargeman, bargee, lighterman

batellerie [batɛlri] *nf* **(a)** (*transport*) inland water transport **(b)** (*ensemble de bateaux*) small craft

bat-flanc [baflɑ̃] *nm inv* **(a)** (*dans un dortoir, une prison*) wooden partition **(b)** (*d'une stalle*) swinging bail

bath [bat] *adj inv Arg Vieilli* super, fantastic, fabulous

bathymètre [batimɛtr] *nm* bathometer, bathymeter

bathymétrie [batimetri] *nf* bathymetry

bathyscaphe [batiskaf] *nm* bathyscape, bathyscaph(e)

bathysphère [batisfɛr] *nf* bathysphere

bâti [bɑti] *nm* **(a)** *Menuis* frame(work); **b. de fenêtre** window frame; **b. moteur** engine mounting **(b)** *Couture* tacking, basting

batifolage [batifolaʒ] *nm F* **(a)** (*jeu*) larking *or* playing about *or* around **(b)** (*flirt*) flirting

batifoler [batifole] *vi F* to lark *or* play about *or* around; (*flirter*) to flirt

batik [batik] *nm* batik; **une jupe en b.** a batik skirt

bâtiment [bɑtimɑ̃] *nm* **(a) le b., l'industrie du b.** building, the building trade; **être dans le b.** to be in the building trade, to be a builder; **peintre en b.** (house) painter; *Fig* **il est du b.** he's in the same line of business; (*il s'y connaît*) he knows what he's doing; **quand le b. va, tout va** when the building trade is doing well, the whole economy is doing well

(b) (*construction*) building; **b. d'habitation** residential building; **bâtiments de ferme** farm buildings; **usine en trois corps de b.** factory in three main buildings; **elle habite dans ces grands bâtiments** she lives in one of those high-rise blocks *or Br* tower blocks

(c) *Naut* ship, vessel; **b. de guerre** warship, battleship

▶ **bâtiment**: *Naut* **b-école**, *pl* **bâtiments-écoles** training ship

bâtir [bɑtir] **1** *vt* **(a)** (*construire*) (*maison etc*) to build; **(se) faire b. une maison** to have a house built; **terrain à b.** building land *or* site; **b. une fortune** to build up a fortune; *Fig* **b. sur le sable** to build on sand; **b. une théorie/une hypothèse** to build up *or* develop a theory/a hypothesis; **b. une interprétation sur qch** to build up *or* construct an interpretation on sth; **terrain bâti** developed *or* built-up site; **maison bien/mal bâtie** well/poorly built *or* constructed house; **homme bien bâti** well-built man; **un homme bâti comme moi** a man of my build

(b) *Couture* to tack, to baste; **coton à b.** tacking thread

2 *vpr* **se bâtir** to be built; **ces maisons se sont bâties en moins d'un mois** these houses were built *or* were put up *or* went up in less than a month

bâtisse [bɑtis] *nf* **(a)** (*partie en maçonnerie*) masonry **(b)** (*bâtiment*) big building; **ce n'est qu'une grande b.** it's a great (ugly) barracks of a place

bâtisseur, -euse [bɑtisœr, -øz] *n* builder; *Fig* **un b. d'empires** an empire-builder

batiste [batist] *nf Tex* batiste, lawn, cambric

bâton [bɑtɔ̃] *nm* **(a)** (*en bois etc*) stick; (*d'agent de police*) truncheon, *Am* nightstick; **b. d'une croix** staff of a cross; **b. de pavillon** flagstaff, flagpole; **son fils est son b. de vieillesse** his son is the support *or* prop of his old age; *Can*

aller au b. to face the music; **donner des coups de b. à qn** to beat sb (with a stick); *F* **il faut le faire travailler à coup de b.** he won't work unless he's pushed; **il va goûter du b.** he'll get a beating; *Fig* **mettre des bâtons dans les roues** to throw a spanner *or Am* (monkey) wrench in the works; **mettre des bâtons dans les roues à qn** to put a spoke in sb's wheel; *Can* **tenir le mauvais bout du b.** to get the short end of the stick; **travailler à bâtons rompus** to work by fits and starts; **parler à bâtons rompus** to talk about this and that, to make small talk; **conversation à bâtons rompus** rambling conversation

(**b**) (*de colle, de craie, de réglisse, de dynamite*) stick; **b. de rouge (à lèvres)** lipstick

(**c**) (*trait*) (*de crayon etc*) (vertical) line; **apprendre à un enfant à faire des bâtons** to teach a child to write; *Typ* **capitale b.** block letter

▶ **bâton**: **b. d'agent de police** truncheon, *Am* nightstick; **b. de chaise** chair rung *or* crosspiece; *F* **mener une vie de b. de chaise** to lead a wild life; **b. de chef d'orchestre** conductor's baton; **b. ferré** alpenstock; **b. de maréchal** marshal's baton; *Fig* **ce poste fut son b. de maréchal** this post was the peak *or* high point of his career; **b. d'oranger** orange stick; **b. de pélerin** pilgrim's staff; *Fig* **prendre son b. de pélerin** to set out on *or* go on a crusade; **bâtons de ski** ski sticks *or* poles

bâtonner [bɑtɔne] *vt Vieilli* to beat, to cudgel, to cane

bâtonnet [bɑtɔnɛ] *nm* (**a**) (*petit bâton*) small stick; **b. (d'oranger)** orange stick; **b. d'encens** stick of incense (**b**) *Biol* rod bacterium; *Anat* rodlike cell; **bâtonnets de la rétine** retinal rods (**c**) *Ordinat* **b. magnétique** magnetic stripe

bâtonnier [bɑtɔnje] *nm* = leader of the barristers attached to a French lawcourt, ≈ President of the Bar

batraciens [batrasjɛ̃] *nmpl Zool* batrachians

battage [bataʒ] *nm* (**a**) (*d'un tapis etc*) beating; (*du beurre*) churning; (*du blé*) threshing; **b. de l'or** gold beating; **b. des pieux** pile driving (**b**) *F* (*d'un produit, d'une personne*) hype, publicity (campaign); **faire du b. autour de qch** to hype sth (up); **il faudra faire beaucoup de b. pour vendre le livre** it will take a lot of hype *or* publicity to sell the book; **un grand b. publicitaire** a major publicity *or* promotional campaign; **b. médiatique** media hype

battant, -ante [batɑ̃, -ɑ̃t] **1** *adj* **pluie battante** driving *or* pelting *or* lashing rain; **porte battante** (*qui claque*) banging door; (*automatique*) swing door; **le cœur b.** with a pounding heart; *Fig* **faire qch tambour b.** to do sth at the double; **mener les choses tambour b.** to hurry *or* hustle things along; (**tout**) **b. neuf** brand new; **à onze heures b.** *ou* **battantes** on the stroke of eleven

2 *nm* (**a**) (*d'une cloche*) clapper, tongue; (*d'un loquet*) lift; *Naut* (*d'un drapeau*) fly; (*d'une voile*) slab

(**b**) (*d'une table, d'un comptoir etc*) flap; (*d'une porte, d'un volet*) leaf; (*d'un placard*) door; **porte à deux battants** double door; **ouvrir la porte à deux battants** to open both sides of the door

3 *n Sp etc* fighter, battler; **c'est une battante, elle va réussir** she's a fighter, she'll succeed

batte [bat] *nf* (**a**) (*action*) beating; **b. de l'or** gold beating (**b**) (*instrument*) (*de tapis etc*) beater; (*maillet*) mallet; (*massue*) club (**c**) *Sp* bat; **une b. de baseball/cricket** a baseball/cricket bat

battement [batmɑ̃] *nm* (**a**) (*de tambour*) beat(ing); (*de pieds*) tap(ping); (*de mains*) clapping; (*d'ailes*) flapping, flutter(ing); (*de voiles*) flapping; (*de porte*) banging; (*de volets*) banging, rattling; (*d'un pendule*) swing(ing); (*d'une horloge*) ticking; (*d'un danseur*) high kick; *Cartes* shuffling; *Phys* (*d'oscillations*) beating, pulsation; **chaque b. de cœur** every heartbeat; **avoir des battements de cœur** to suffer from palpitations; *Fig* to be in a flutter; *Fig* **donner des battements de cœur à qn** to make sb's heart pound

(**b**) (*entre deux événements etc*) interval; **il y a quelques jours de b. avant d'attaquer le projet** we have a few days' break *or* there are a few days clear before we get stuck into the project; **deux heures de b.** two clear hours; **b. de cinq minutes entre les deux trains** five minutes' wait between the two trains

(**c**) (*sur une fenêtre*) shutter catch

batterie [batri] *nf* (**a**) *Mus* (*de tambour*) beat; (*de caisse claire*) roll; (*suite de notes*) quick succession of notes; (*instruments*) (*dans orchestre classique*) percussion instruments; (*dans orchestre de jazz, de rock*) drums; **tenir la b.** to be on drums; **il joue de la b.** he plays the drums; **à la b., Jean-Pierre!** Jean-Pierre on drums

(**b**) *Mil* battery; **b. antiaérienne/antichars** anti-aircraft/antitank battery; **pièces en b.** guns in firing position *or* in action; **en b.!** action!; **b. d'instruction** training battery; *Fig* **dévoiler ses batteries** to show one's hand; *Fig* **changer de batteries** to change one's plan of attack

(**c**) (*ensemble, groupe*) battery; **b. de chaudières/de fours à coke** battery *or* range *or* bank of boilers/of coke ovens; **b. de projecteurs** bank *or* battery of spotlights; **poulet de b.** battery hen; **élevage en b.** (*de poulets etc*) battery farming; **b. de cuisine** (set of) kitchen utensils; *Fig F* medals, *Br* gongs; **on lui a fait passer toute une b. de tests** he was subjected to a whole battery of tests; **il a dû répondre à toute une b. de questions** he had to answer a whole battery of questions

(**d**) *Él* battery; **b. de rechange** (*pour torche etc*) replacement battery; **fonctionnant sur b.** battery-operated, battery-powered; **b. au cadmium-nickel** nickel cadmium battery; **b. au plomb** lead-acid battery; **b. de cellules photoélectriques** photoelectric cell battery; **b. de secours** emergency battery; **b. sans entretien** no-maintenance battery, maintenance-free battery; **b. à entretien réduit** low-maintenance battery

batteur, -euse [batœr, -øz] **1** *nm* (**a**) *Mus* (*dans un groupe de rock etc*) drummer; *Cr* batsman; *Baseball* batter, striker; (*de chasse*) beater; **b. d'or** gold beater; **b. en grange** thresher; *F* **b. de pavé** loafer, idler (**b**) *Agr* (*d'une batteuse*) beater drum; *Culin* **b. électrique** electric mixer; **b. (à œufs)** (egg) whisk (**c**) **b. de coton** cotton breaker *or* shaker **2** *nf* **batteuse** *Agr* threshing machine, thresher; *Métal* beater

battoir [batwar] *nm* (*pour les tapis*) (carpet) beater; *Vieilli* (*pour le linge*) beetle; *F* (*grande main*) great paw *or* mitt

battre [batr] (*prp* **battant**; *pp* **battu**; *pr ind* **je bats** [ba], **tu bats, il bat, n. battons, v. battez, ils battent**; *p hist* **je battis**; *fu* **je battrai**) **1** *vt* (**a**) (*frapper*) (*personne, chien*) to beat, to hit; (*tapis, or*) to beat; (*blé*) to thresh; (*beurre*) to churn; (*œufs, préparation culinaire*) to beat, to whisk; **b. qn à coups de poings/avec une canne** to punch/cane sb; **b. qn à mort** to beat *or* batter sb to death; **b. qn comme plâtre** to beat the living daylights out of sb; **il bat sa femme** he beats his wife, he is a wife-beater; **il me donne envie de le b. parfois!** I want to hit him sometimes!; **b. le tambour** to beat the drum; **b. le fer (avec un marteau)** to hammer iron; **b. le fer à froid** to cold-hammer iron; **la cape lui bat les talons** his cloak is flapping round his heels; *Prov* **b. le fer quand** *ou* **pendant il est chaud** to strike while the iron is hot; **b. monnaie** to mint coins; *Culin* **b. les blancs en neige** to beat the whites stiffly; **b. l'air en agitant les mains** to saw the air (with one's hands); **la pluie bat les carreaux** the rain is beating *or* lashing against the windowpanes; **la mer bat les rochers** the sea breaks against *or* batters the rocks; **île battue par les flots/les vents** island battered by the waves/the winds; **il avançait, le visage battu par le vent** he moved forward, his face whipped by the wind; *Mil* **b. une position** to fire on a position; *Mus* **b. la mesure** to beat time; **b. la semelle** to stamp one's feet (to keep warm); *Mil* **b. le réveil/la retraite** to beat *or* sound the reveille/retreat; **b. le rappel** to call to arms; *Fig* to call everyone together; *Rel* **b. sa coulpe** to beat one's breast; **b. la campagne** to scour *or* comb the countryside; *Fig* **son esprit commence à b. la campagne** his mind is beginning to wander; **b. un bois/les buissons** to beat a wood/the bushes; *Naut* **b. un pavillon** to fly a flag; **b. pavillon français** to fly the French flag; *Cartes* **b. les cartes** to shuffle the cards; **la nouvelle nous fit b. le cœur** we were thrilled at the news

(**b**) (*vaincre*) (*adversaire*) to beat, to defeat; (*record*) to beat; **battre qn à plate(s) couture(s)** to beat sb hollow; *F* **je te bats, je gagne 1 500F de plus que toi** I earn 1,500 francs more than you, that's one up to me!

2 *vi* (**a**) (*de cœur*) to beat; (*de porte*) to bang; (*de volet*) to bang, to rattle; (*de voile*) to flap; **il a le cœur qui bat quand il la voit** his heart pounds whenever he sees her; **le vent faisait b. les volets** the shutters were banging *or* rattling in the wind

(**b**) **b. des mains** to clap one's hands; (*applaudir*) to clap, to applaud; **b. du pied** (*en cadence*) to tap (with) one's foot; **l'oiseau battait des ailes** the bird was flapping *or* beating its wings; **b. des paupières** to blink

3 se battre *vpr* to fight; **se b. avec** *ou* **contre qn** (*physiquement*) to fight (with *or* against) sb; (*verbalement*) to argue *or* fight with sb; **se b. comme des chiffonniers** to fight like demons; **se b. au couteau** to fight with knives; **se b. en duel** to fight a duel; **se b. contre qch** to fight against sth; **il faut se b. pour réussir** you've got to fight if you want to succeed; **voyons, ne vous battez pas, il y en a pour tout le monde** now don't quarrel *or* fight (over it), there's enough for everyone; **je me suis battu pour obtenir ce visa/avec ce tournevis** I had a lot of trouble getting this visa/with that screwdriver; **il se bat avec ses devoirs** he's struggling *or* having trouble with his homework; *très F* **je m'en bats l'œil** I don't give a damn, I couldn't care less; *très F* **tout le monde s'en bat de ces histoires** nobody gives a damn about these stories; *Vulg* **je m'en bats les couilles jusqu'au plafond** I couldn't give a monkey's (fart)

battu [baty] *adj* beaten; **enfant/femme battu(e)** battered child/wife; **chien b.** mistreated dog; **un air** *ou* **regard de chien b.** a hangdog look; **S.O.S. femmes battues** ≈ battered wives' helpline; **avoir les yeux battus** to have rings *or* circles round one's eyes; **armée battue** defeated *or* beaten army; **ne pas se tenir pour b.** not to admit defeat, not to admit oneself beaten; **fer b.** wrought iron; **or b.** beaten gold; *Tennis* **court en terre battue** clay court; **jouer sur la terre battue** to play on clay; **chemin b.** well-trodden path; **suivre les sentiers battus** *ou* **le chemin b.** to follow the beaten track; **hors des sentiers battus** off the beaten track; **œufs battus en neige** stiffly beaten egg whites; **pas b.** (*en danse*) pas battu

battue [baty] *nf* (*à la chasse*) battue, beat; *Fig* (*pour retrouver qn*) search

batture [batyr] *nf Can* sandbank

bau, -aux [bo] *nm Naut* beam; **maître b.** midship beam

baud [bo(d)] *nm Télécom, Ordinat* baud; **à (une vitesse de) 1200 bauds** at (a speed of) 1200 baud

baudet [bodɛ] *nm* **(a)** (*âne*) ass, donkey; **chargé comme un b.** loaded down, weighed down **(b)** *Menuis* sawhorse, trestle

baudrier [bodrije] *nm* shoulder belt; (*pour épée*) baldric; *Sp* **b. d'escalade** climbing harness; *Astron* **le B. d'Orion** Orion's belt

baudroie [bodrwa] *nf* (*poisson*) monkfish, anglerfish

baudruche [bodryʃ] *nf* bladder; *Fig Péj* (*homme*) empty windbag; **ballon de b.** balloon

bauge [boʒ] *nf* **(a)** (*d'un sanglier*) wallow; *Fig F* **c'est une vraie b.** it's a real pigsty **(b)** *Constr* clay and straw mortar

baume [bom] *nm* **(a)** (*substance*) balm, balsam; **b. de** *ou* **du Canada** Canada balsam; *Pharm* **b. de benjoin** friar's balsam **(b)** *Fig Litt* balm, consolation; **mettre du b. au cœur de qn** (*des propos, l'arrivée de qn etc*) to be a consolation for sb; (*d'une personne*) to console sb **(c)** (*plante*) **b. sauvage** *ou* **des champs** wild mint; **b. vert** garden mint, spearmint

baumier [bomje] *nm* balsam (tree)

baux [bo] *voir* **bail, bau**

bauxite [boksit] *nf Minér* bauxite

bavard, -arde [bavar, -ard] **1** *adj* **(a)** (*qui parle beaucoup*) talkative, garrulous, gabby; **il est b. comme une pie** he'd talk the hind legs off a donkey; **une analyse bavarde** a wordy analysis **(b)** (*indiscret*) indiscreet **2** *n* **(a)** (*qui parle beaucoup*) chatterbox **(b)** (*personne indiscrète*) gossip, *F* blabbermouth

bavardage [bavardaʒ] *nm* **(a)** (*action*) chattering, *Br* nattering; (*commérage*) gossiping; **envoyé au coin pour b.** sent into the corner for talking in class **(b)** (*paroles*) chatter; (*commérage*) gossip, tittle-tattle; **ce ne sont que des bavardages** that's just gossip

bavarder [bavarde] *vi* **(a)** (*parler*) to chatter, *Br* to natter **(b)** (*commérer*) to gossip **(c)** (*être indiscret*) to talk, *F* to blab

bavarois, -oise [bavarwa, -waz] **1** *adj* Bavarian **2** *n* **B.** Bavarian **3** *nf Culin* **bavaroise** Bavarian cream

bavasser [bavase] *vi très F* to gossip

bave [bav] *nf* (*de personne*) dribble, slobber; (*de chien*) slobber, slaver; (*de cheval, de chien enragé*) froth, foam; (*d'escargot*) slime; (*de crapaud*) spittle; *Fig* spiteful *or* malicious talk

baver [bave] **1** *vi* (*d'une personne*) to dribble, to slobber; (*d'un chien*) to slobber, to slaver; (*d'un chien enragé*) to foam at the mouth; (*d'un stylo*) to leak, to run; (*de l'encre*) to smudge; *F* **cela me fait b. de jalousie/de rage/d'admiration** it makes me green with envy/makes me hopping mad/leaves me speechless with admiration; *F* **il en bave d'envie** he's drooling over it; *F* **en b.** to have a rough time of it; **elle m'en a fait b.!** she gave me a rough time **2** *vt F* **en b. des ronds de chapeaux** to have a rough time of it; *Vieilli* (*être étonné*) to have eyes like saucers

bavette [bavɛt] *nf* **(a)** (*d'un bébé, d'un tablier*) bib **(b)** *Culin* skirt (of beef); **b. d'aloyau** undercut of the sirloin; **dans la b. s'il vous plaît** from the flank please **(c)** *F* **tailler une b.** to have a chat *or Br* a natter **(d)** *Aut* mud flap, mud guard

baveux, -euse [bavø, -øz] **1** *adj* (*bouche*) dribbling, slobbery; (*enfant*) dribbling; (*chien*) slobbering, slavering; **omelette baveuse** runny omelette; *Typ* **lettres baveuses** blurred *or* smeared letters **2** *n Can* (*morveux*) pain, pest

Bavière [bavjɛr] *nf* Bavaria

bavocher [bavɔʃe] *vi* to smear

bavochure [bavɔʃyr] *nf* smear

bavoir [bavwar] *nm* bib

bavure [bavyr] *nf* **(a)** *Métal* (*de moulage etc*) burr, wire edge; (*de métal*) barb **(b)** (*tache*) smudge, smear; (*erreur*) slip-up, mistake; **sans bavure(s)** (*emploi adjectival*) faultless; *Fig* impeccable; (*emploi adverbial*) faultlessly; *Fig* impeccably; **un coup sans b.** (*cambriolage etc*) a perfect job; **les bavures de la police** police misconduct

bayer [baje] *vi* **(je baye, je baie, n. bayons; je bayerai, je baierai) b. aux corneilles** to stand gaping

bazar [bazar] *nm* **(a)** (*marché*) (oriental) bazaar **(b)** (*magasin*) general shop *or* store; **de b.** shoddy, (of) poor quality; **littérature de b.** pulp literature **(c)** *F* (*désordre*) shambles; (*bruit*) din, racket; **tout son b.** (*affaires*) all one's things *or* gear; **et tout le b.** and the whole caboodle; **il a mis un sacré b. dans mes papiers** he made a hell of a mess of my papers; **quel b., cette chambre!** this room is a shambles!

bazarder [bazarde] *vt F* (*se débarrasser de*) to get rid of; (*jeter*) to chuck out; (*vendre*) to sell off, *Br* to flog

bazooka [bazuka] *nm Mil* bazooka

BCBG [besebeʒe] *adj* (*abrév* **bon chic bon genre**) ≈ Sloany, *Am* preppy

BCG [beseʒe] *nm Méd* BCG

BD [bede] *nf* **(a)** (*abrév* **bande dessinée**) comic strip, strip cartoon; **lire des BD** to read comics; **aimer la BD** to like comic strips **(b)** *Ordinat* (*abrév* **base de données**) dbase

bd *abrév* **boulevard**

B. de F. *abrév* **Banque de France**

bê [bɛ] *int* baa!

beagle [bigl] *nm* beagle

béant [beɑ̃] *adj* (*bouche, porte*) wide open; (*blessure*) gaping, open; (*gouffre, entrée de grotte*) yawning, gaping

béarnais, -aise [bearnɛ, -ɛz] **1** *adj* Béarn; (*personne*) from the Béarn; *Culin* **sauce béarnaise** béarnaise (sauce) **2** *nf Culin* **béarnaise** béarnaise (sauce) **3** *n* **B.** (*natif*) native of the Béarn; (*habitant*) inhabitant of the Béarn

béat [bea] *adj Rel* blessed; (*heureux*) blissfully happy; *Péj* (*très satisfait*) self-satisfied, smug; **sourire b.** self-satisfied *or* smug smile; **être b. d'admiration** to be open-mouthed in admiration; **elle nous observait d'un air b.** she watched us open-mouthed

béatement [beatmɑ̃] *adv* (*sourire*) smugly

béatification [beatifikasjɔ̃] *nf Rel* beatification

béatifier [beatifje] *vt* (*pr sub & impf* **n. béatifiions, v. béatifiiez**) *Rel* to beatify

béatifique [beatifik] *adj Rel* (*vision*) beatific

béatitude [beatityd] *nf* **(a)** *Rel* beatitude; **les (huit) béatitudes** the Beatitudes **(b)** (*bonheur parfait*) bliss

beatnik [bitnik] *adj, n* beatnik; **la génération b.** the beat generation

beau [bo], **bel** [bɛl], *f* **belle** [bɛl] (*the form* **bel** *is used before m sing nouns beginning with a vowel or a mute h, in the expressions* **bel et bien, Charles le Bel** *and* **Philippe le Bel**) **1** *adj* **(a)** (*physiquement*) (*femme, enfant*) beautiful, good-looking; (*homme*) handsome, good-looking; (*objet, produit, maison, arbre etc*) lovely, beautiful; **un bel homme** a fine figure of a man; **une belle femme** a beautiful *or* good-looking woman; (*sculpturale*) a fine figure of a woman, a handsome woman; **ça n'est pas b. à voir** that's not a pretty *or* an attractive sight; **mettre ses plus beaux habits** to put on one's best *or* finest clothes; *Hist* **Philippe le Bel** Philip the Fair; **la mer est belle** the sea is beautiful; (*calme*) the sea is calm; **le temps est b.** the weather is fine; **nous avons eu (du) b. temps** we had fine weather; **ami des beaux jours** fairweather friend; **un (de ces) beau(x) jour(s)** one (of these) fine day(s); **et un b. jour, il est arrivé** then one (fine) day, he arrived; **oh la belle bleue!** (*de feu d'artifice*) what a lovely blue!; (*jeune fille*) hi, gorgeous!

(b) (*moralement*) fine; **de beaux sentiments** fine *or* noble feelings; **belle action** fine deed; **une belle vie** a full life; **trouver une belle mort** to die a glorious death; *F* **elle a le b. rôle** she's got it *or* things easy, she's sitting pretty; **cela n'est pas b. de votre part** that wasn't very nice of you; **ce n'est pas b. de mentir** it isn't nice to tell lies; *F* **ce n'est pas b. de parler la bouche pleine** it isn't polite *or* nice to speak with your mouth full; **il est b. joueur** he's a good loser

(c) (*excellent*) (*œuvre, artiste, film, match etc*) fine, excellent; (*occasion*) wonderful; **une belle page de littérature** a fine piece of writing; **un b. talent** a talented *or* gifted artist/writer/*etc*; **il a un b. talent de peintre** he has a great gift as a painter, he's a very gifted painter; **20 ans! le bel âge!** twenty! a great age (to be)!; **avoir une belle santé** to be very healthy; **il a une belle situation** he has an excellent job; **ils font un b. couple** they make a fine couple; **oh la belle balle!** what a good *or* lovely shot *or* ball!; **c'est trop b. pour être vrai** it's too good to be true; **ce serait trop b.!** that would be too much (to hope for)!; **le plus b. jour de**

ma vie the best day of my life; *Cartes* **avoir (un) b. jeu** to have good cards *or* a good hand

(d) (*élégant*) (*monsieur, dame*) smart, elegant; **se faire b.** to smarten oneself up; **sois belle et tais-toi** = women should be seen but not heard; **vous voilà b.!** you do look smart!

(e) *Iron* **le bel avantage, ma foi!** well, that's a great advantage!; **tout cela est fort b. mais ...** that's all very fine *or* well but ...; **vous avez fait du b. travail!** you have done well!

(f) (*intensif*) **au b. milieu de la rue** right *or* bang in the middle of the road; **il y a b. temps qu'il est parti** he left a long time ago *or* ages ago; **une belle tranche de tarte** a nice slice of tart; **une belle paie** a good salary, good wages; **c'est une belle sole** that's a lovely piece of sole; **belle fortune** large *or* tidy fortune; **b. poulet** good-sized *or* sizeable chicken; **un b. kilo** a good kilo

(g) (*mauvais*) **une belle congestion pulmonaire** a bad attack of pneumonia; **belle correction** good thrashing; **b. tapage** terrific din *or* racket; **il a fait un b. désordre** he made a terrible mess; **un b. gâchis** a fine mess; **son bras est dans un bel état** his arm is in an awful *or* a terrible state; **j'ai eu une belle peur** I had an awful *or* a terrible fright; *Arg* **un b. salaud** a real *or* right bastard

(h) bel et bien well and truly; **il est bel et bien venu** he really did come; **tu l'avais bel et bien dit** you definitely said so; **vous voilà bel et bien grand-père!** so you've actually become a grandfather!

(i) tout b.! steady (on)!, gently!

(j) de plus belle with a vengeance; **il reprit l'entraînement de plus belle** he resumed training with a vengeance, more enthusiastically than ever; **les discussions/batailles ont recommencé de plus belle** the arguing/fighting has started again with a vengeance, worse than ever

(k) je l'ai échappé belle I had a narrow escape *or* a close shave

(l) il ferait b. voir cela that would be a fine thing to see

(m) j'ai b. le lui dire, il ne veut rien entendre it's no good my trying *or* however much I try to tell him, he just won't listen; **j'avais b. chercher, je ne trouvais rien** however hard I looked *or* no matter how hard I looked *or* look as I might, I found nothing; **vous avez b. parler ...** you can talk until you're blue in the face ...

2 *n* **beau, belle (a) belle** (*jolie femme*) beauty, belle; (*amie, amante*) lady friend; **la Belle et la Bête** Beauty and the Beast; **la Belle au bois dormant** Sleeping Beauty; **allez ma belle, ça suffit** now that's quite enough, my dear

(b) un vieux b. an old roué; **faire le b.** (*d'un chien*) to sit up and beg; *Arch* **un b.** a dandy, a beau, a buck

3 *nm* **(a)** (*beauté*) **le b.** the beautiful, beauty; **l'amour du b.** the love of beauty; **le b., le bien et le vrai** beauty, goodness and truth

(b) le b. de l'histoire c'est que ... the best bit *or* part of the story is that ...; **mais le plus b., c'est que ...** but the best bit *or* part is that ...; *F Iron* **c'est du b.!** that's great!

(c) *Météo* **le temps est au b. (fixe)** the weather is set fair; *Fig* **avoir l'humeur au b. fixe** to be permanently in a good mood

(d) (*beaux objets*) **le b.** beautiful things; **ne vouloir/vendre que du b.** to want/sell only *or* nothing but the best

4 *nf* **belle** *voir* **belle**

▶ **beau**: **un bel âge** a ripe old age; **le b. monde** fashionable society; *Iron* **pour satisfaire tout ce b. monde** in order to satisfy all these fine people; **beaux quartiers** fashionable *or* smart districts; **le b. sexe** the fair sex

beaucoup [boku] *adv* [①**A24-5**,d,iv] (*une grande quantité*) a lot, a great deal; **il reste encore b. à faire** there's still a lot *or* a great deal *or* much to do; **b. de** (*nombre*) a lot of, (a great) many; (*quantité*) a lot of, a great deal of, much; **b. de monde** a lot of people; **b. de vin/chance** a lot of *or* a great deal of wine/luck; **avoir b. d'argent** to have plenty of *or* a lot of money; **ils n'ont pas b. d'argent** they don't have much *or* a lot of *or* a great deal of money; **je n'ai pas eu b. d'occasions** *ou* **l'occasion de le faire** I haven't had much (of an) opportunity to do it; **avec b. de soin** very carefully; **avoir besoin de b. d'attention/d'eau** to need a lot of attention/water; **j'en veux b., 20!** I want a lot, 20!; **il n'en reste pas b.** (*de la tarte etc*) there's not much left; (*des bonbons etc*) there aren't many left; **y a-t-il b. de champignons cette année? – oui, b. /non, pas b.** are there many *or* a lot of mushrooms this year? – yes, there are/no, there aren't; **b. plus/moins de temps/de sel** a lot *or* much more/less time/salt; **b. plus/moins d'enfants/de livres** a lot *or* many more/fewer children/books; **elle veut b.** she wants a lot out of life; **c'est déjà b. s'il veut bien** *ou* **qu'il veuille bien vous parler** it's (quite) something that he condescended to speak to you; **b. pensent que ...** a lot of *or* many people think that ...; **il y est pour b.** he has had a great deal to do with it; **b. d'entre nous/d'entre vous** many *or* a lot of us/you; **de b.** by far; **c'est de b. le meilleur** it's by far *or* it's far and away the best, it's the best by a long chalk; **il s'en faut de b. que je sois riche** I'm far from being rich; **elle vous aime b.** she is very fond of you, she likes you a lot *or* a great deal; **il parle b.** he talks a lot *or* a great deal; **il a b. voyagé/lu** he has travelled/read a lot *or* a great deal; **elle ne lit pas b.** she doesn't read much *or* a lot *or* a great deal; **il parle b. trop** he talks far too much; **je me sens b. mieux** I feel a lot better; **ambitieuse, elle l'est, et b.** she's ambitious, very ambitious; **b. moins/plus vite** a lot *or* much slower/faster; **il est b. plus âgé que sa femme** he is much *or* a lot older than his wife; **ça te plaît? – pas b.** do you like it? – not much *or* not a lot; **j'y tiens b.** it means a lot to me

beauf [bof] *F* **1** *nm* **(a)** (*beau-frère*) brother-in-law **(b)** *Fig Péj* narrow-minded middle-class type **2** *adj Fig Péj* **il est un peu b.** he's a bit of a narrow-minded middle-class type

beau-fils, *pl* **beaux-fils** *nm* **(a)** (*gendre*) son-in-law **(b)** (*après remariage*) stepson

beau-frère, *pl* **beaux-frères** *nm* brother-in-law

beaujolais [boʒɔlɛ] *nm* Beaujolais

beau-père, *pl* **beaux-pères** *nm* **(a)** (*père du conjoint*) father-in-law **(b)** (*après remariage*) stepfather

beaupré [bopre] *nm Naut* bowsprit

beauté [bote] *nf* **(a)** (*de femme, paysage etc*) beauty; **apparaître dans toute sa b.** to appear in all one's beauty; **être en b.** to be looking one's best; **une femme/une vue de toute b.** a magnificent woman/view; *F* **finir en b.** to end with a flourish *or* on a high note; **faire qch pour la b. du geste** to do sth for its own sake; **grain de b.** beauty spot, mole; **institut de b.** beauty parlour; **produits de b.** beauty products, cosmetics; **la b. du diable** youthful beauty; *F* **se (re)faire une b.** to do one's face, to put one's face on

(b) (*femme*) beauty

(c) les beautés artistiques de l'Italie the art treasures of Italy; **les beautés touristiques** the sights

beaux-arts [bozar] *nmpl* fine arts; *Univ* **l'École des b.**, *F* **les B.** the Art School

beaux-parents *nmpl* parents-in-law, *F* in-laws

bébé [bebe] *nm* **(a)** (*nourrisson*) baby; **avoir/vouloir un b.** to have/want a baby; **attendre un b.** to be expecting (a baby); *Fig* **c'est un vrai b., il ne sait rien faire seul** he's a real baby *or* he's just like a child, he can't do anything for himself; **faire le b.** to behave childishly *or* like a baby; **il/elle est très b.** he/she is very childish *or* babyish **(b)** *Com* (*poupée*) (baby) doll **(c)** *Zool* **b. gazelle/lapin** baby gazelle/rabbit

bébé-éprouvette, *pl* **bébés-éprouvette** *nm* test-tube baby

bébelle [bebɛl] *nf Can* (*gadget*) gadget; (*bibelot*) ornament

bébelleux, -euse [bebɛlø, -øz] *adj Can* gadget mad; (*bibelots*) ornament mad

bébête [bebɛt] *F* **1** *adj* silly; **rire b.** giggle, titter **2** *nf* little insect, *Br* creepy-crawly

bec [bɛk] *nm* **(a)** (*d'oiseau*) beak, bill; (*de tortue, pieuvre etc*) beak; **au b. long/court/jaune** long-/short-/yellow-billed; **coup de b.** peck; **donner un coup de b. à qn** to peck sb; *Fig F* to have a dig at sb; **l'oiseau se fait le b.** the bird is sharpening its beak

(b) *F* (*bouche*) mouth, *Br F* gob; **claquer du b.** to be starving; **fin b.** gourmet; **être** *ou* **rester le b. dans l'eau** to be left high and dry; **il n'a pas ouvert le b. de la journée** he hasn't said a single word all day, there hasn't been a peep out of him all day; **il n'ouvre pas beaucoup le b., ton copain** your friend hasn't got much to say for himself, not the world's greatest talker, your friend, is he?; **avoir la cigarette/pipe au b.** to have a cigarette/one's pipe in one's mouth; **ferme ton b.!** shut up!, shut your mouth *or* gob!; **clouer** *ou* **clore le b. à qn** to shut sb up; **avoir bon b.** to have the gift of the gab; **prise de b.** quarrel, slanging match

(c) (*d'outil*) nose; (*de tube*) nozzle; (*de pot*) lip; (*de cafetière*) spout; (*de selle de bicyclette*) peak; (*de clarinette, flûte etc*) mouthpiece; *Arg* **tomber sur un b.** to come a cropper; *Av* **b. d'attaque** (*d'une aile*) leading edge; **b. de plume** pen nib;

(d) *Géog* (*nom de localité*) bill; **le B. de Portland** Portland Bill

▶ **bec**: **b. Bunsen** Bunsen burner; **b. à gaz** gas jet *or* burner; **b. de gaz** (*de cuisinière*) gas ring; **Arg tomber sur un b. de gaz** to come a cropper; **b. verseur** lip

bécane [bekan] *nf F* (*vélo*) bike; (*machine, ordinateur*) machine

bécarre [bekar] *Mus* **1** *adj* (*signe*) natural; **mi b.** E natural **2** *nm* natural

bécasse [bekas] *nf* **(a)** *(oiseau)* **b. (des bois)** woodcock; **b. de mer** oystercatcher **(b)** *F (idiote)* silly woman/girl, silly goose
bécasseau, -eaux [bekaso] *nm (échassier)* sandpiper; *(petit de la bécasse)* young woodcock
bécassine [bekasin] *nf* **(a)** *(oiseau)* snipe **(b)** *F (fille niaise)* silly naive girl
bec-croisé, *pl* **becs-croisés** *nm (oiseau)* crossbill
bec-de-cane, *pl* **becs-de-cane** *nm* **(a)** *(serrure)* catch **(b)** *(poignée)* (door) handle
bec-de-lièvre, *pl* **becs-de-lièvre** *nm Méd* harelip
becfigue [bɛkfig] *nm (oiseau)* (garden) warbler; *(fauvette)* blackcap; *(jaseur)* waxwing; *(pipi)* pipit
bêchage [bɛʃaʒ] *nm (de la terre)* digging (over), turning over
béchamel [beʃamɛl] *adj, nf Culin* **(sauce) b.** béchamel sauce, white sauce
bêche [bɛʃ] *nf* spade
bêcher [beʃe] **1** *vt* **(a)** *(terre)* to dig (over), to turn over; *(plate-bande)* to dig (over) **(b)** *F (qn)* to run down, to pull to pieces **2** *vi F* **depuis que ... elle bêche** since ... she's gone all stuck-up *or* all snooty
bêcheur, -euse [beʃœr, -øz] *n F* **(a)** *(critiqueur)* knocker **(b)** *(snob)* stuck-up person
bécot [beko] *nm F* kiss, peck; **gros b.** smacker
bécoter [bekɔte] *F* **1** *vt* to kiss **2 se bécoter** *vpr* to smooch, to kiss (and cuddle)
becquée [beke] *nf* beakful; *F* **encore une b.!** *(à un enfant)* another little mouthful!; **donner la b. à son bébé** to feed one's baby
becquerel [bɛk(ə)rɛl] *nm Nucl* becquerel
becquet [bekɛ] *nm Aut* spoiler
becquetance [bɛktɑ̃s] *nf Arg* grub, *Br* nosh
becqueter [bɛkte] *vt* **(je becquète, n. becquetons; je becquèterai)** *(d'un oiseau)* to peck at; *Arg (d'une personne)* to eat, *Br* to nosh; **il n'y a rien à b.** there's no grub *or Br* nosh; **on a bien becqueté** we had a good feed *or* nosh
bectance [bɛktɑ̃s] *nf Arg* grub, *Br* nosh
becter [bɛkte] *vt* = **becqueter**
bedaine [bədɛn] *nf F* pot(belly), paunch; **avoir de la b.** to be pot-bellied *or* paunchy; **prendre de la b.** to get a paunch
bédane [bedan] *nm* mortise, (cold) chisel
bédé [bede] *nf F* comic strip
bedeau, -eaux [bədo] *nm Rel* verger
bédéphile [bedefil] *n F* comic-strip freak
bedon [bədɔ̃] *nm F* pot(belly), paunch
bedonnant [bədɔnɑ̃] *adj F* pot-bellied, paunchy
bedonner [bədɔne] *vi F* to get a paunch
bédouin, -ouine [bedwɛ̃, -win] **1** *adj* Bedouin **2** *n* **B.** Bedouin
bée [be] *adj* **bouche b.** gaping, open-mouthed; **rester bouche b. devant qch** to stand gaping *or* open-mouthed in front of sth; **j'en suis resté bouche b.** I was flabbergasted (by it) *or* gobsmacked, it staggered me; **son culot me laisse bouche b.** I am staggered *or* flabbergasted by his cheek; **regarder qch bouche b.** to gape at sth
béer [bee] *vi Litt* **(a) b. d'étonnement/d'admiration** to gape in astonishment/admiration **(b)** *(être grand ouvert)* to be wide open
beffroi [befrwa] *nm* **(a)** *(tour)* belfry **(b)** *(cloche)* **entendre sonner le b.** to hear the bell sound
bégaiement [begɛmɑ̃] *nm* **(a)** *(pathologique)* stuttering, stammering **(b)** *(des petits enfants)* lispings **(c)** *Fig* **bégaiements** hesitant *or* tentative beginnings
bégayant [begɛjɑ̃] *adj* *(involontairement)* stuttering, stammering; *Fig Litt* hesitant, faltering
bégayer [begeje] **(je bégaye, je bégaie, n. bégayons; je bégayerai, je bégaierai) 1** *vi* **(a)** *(pathologiquement)* to stutter, to stammer **(b)** *(des petits enfants)* to lisp **2** *vt* to stammer (out); **b. une excuse** to stammer out an excuse
bégayeur, -euse [begɛjœr, -øz] *adj* stuttering, stammering
bégonia [begɔnja] *nm (plante)* begonia
bègue [bɛg] **1** *adj* stuttering, stammering **2** *n* stutterer, stammerer
bégueule [begœl] **1** *adj* prudish; **ne sois pas b.** don't be prudish, don't be a prude **2** *nf* prude
béguin [begɛ̃] *nm* **(a)** *F* **avoir le b. pour qn/qch** to have a crush on sb/to have taken a fancy to sth; **voilà son nouveau b.** that's his latest crush **(b)** *(pour un petit enfant)* bonnet; *Rel* hood
béguinage [beginaʒ] *nm Rel* Beguine convent
béguine [begin] *nf Rel* Beguine (nun)
bégum [begɔm] *nf* begum
behaviorisme [biavjɔrism, biev-] *nm Psy* behaviourism, *US* behaviorism
behavioriste [biavjɔrist, biev-] *Psy* **1** *adj* behaviourist(ic), *US* behaviorist(ic) **2** *n* behaviourist, *US* behaviorist, behavioural scientist
BEI [beəi] *nf (abrév* **Banque européenne d'investissement***)* EIB
beige [bɛʒ] *adj, nm* beige
beigne¹ [bɛɲ] *nf Arg* slap, clout; **filer** *ou* **flanquer une b. à qn** to give sb a clout, to clout sb one
beigne² *nm Région, Can* doughnut, *US* donut
beignet [bɛɲɛ] *nm* fritter; *(au sucre, à la confiture)* doughnut, *US* donut; **b. de** *ou* **aux pommes** apple fritter; **b. de crevettes** prawn cracker; *(avec de la pâte)* prawn fritter
bel¹ [bɛl] *nm Phys* bel
bel² *adj voir* **beau**
bélandre [belɑ̃dr] *nf* canal barge
bêlant [bɛlɑ̃] *adj aussi Fig* bleating
bel canto [bɛlkɑ̃to] *nm Mus* bel canto
bêlement [bɛlmɑ̃] *nm Zool, Fig* bleating
bélemnite [belɛmnit] *nf (fossile)* belemnite
bêler [bɛle] *vi Zool, Fig* to bleat; *Fig* **qu'est-ce que vous avez à b. comme ça?** what on earth are you bleating about?
belette [bəlɛt] *nf* weasel
belge [bɛlʒ] **1** *adj* Belgian; **une histoire b.** *Br* ≈ an Irish joke, *US* ≈ a Polish joke, *Can* ≈ a Newfie joke **2** *n* **B.** Belgian
belgicisme [bɛlʒisism] *nm (mot)* Belgian-French word; *(tournure)* Belgian-French expression
Belgique [bɛlʒik] *nf* Belgium
bélier [belje] *nm* **(a)** *(animal)* ram **(b)** *Mil* battering ram **(c)** *Constr* **b. (à pilotage)** pile driver, ram(mer); **b. mécanique** bulldozer **(d) b. hydraulique** hydraulic ram; **coup de b.** water hammer **(e)** *Astron, Astrol* **le B.** Aries, the Ram; **être (du signe du) B.** to be (an) Aries
bélière [beljɛr] *nf* **(a)** *(d'une cloche)* clapper ring; *(d'une montre etc)* ring **(b)** *(du bélier qui conduit le troupeau)* (sheep) bell
belladone [beladɔn] *nf (plante)* belladonna, deadly nightshade
bellâtre [belɑtr] *nm Péj* smoothie
belle [bɛl] **1** *adj voir* **beau 2** *nf* **(a)** *Sp* decider, deciding game; *Cartes* rubber game; **jouer** *ou* **faire la b.** *Sp* to play the decider *or* the deciding game; *Cartes* to play the rubber game **(b)** *Naut (d'un navire)* waist; **en b.** abeam **(c)** *F* **se faire la b.** *(de prison)* to break out, to escape **(d)** *F* **il en dit de belles!** he comes out with some good ones!, he really comes out with them!; **j'en ai entendu de belles sur votre compte!** I've heard some nice things about you!; **vous en avez fait une b.!** you've put your foot in it!
belle-dame, *pl* **belles-dames** *nf* **(a)** *(plante)* deadly nightshade **(b)** *(papillon)* painted lady
belle-de-jour, *pl* **belles-de-jour** *nf (plante)* convolvulus, bindweed
belle-de-nuit, *pl* **belles-de-nuit** *nf* **(a)** *(plante)* marvel of Peru, four o'clock **(b)** *F (prostituée)* lady of the night
belle-doche, *pl* **belles-doches** [bɛldɔʃ] *nf F* mother-in-law
belle-famille, *pl* **belles-familles** *nf (de l'époux)* wife's family, *F* in-laws; *(de l'épouse)* husband's family, *F* in-laws
belle-fille, *pl* **belles-filles** *nf* **(a)** *(épouse du fils)* daughter-in-law **(b)** *(après remariage)* stepdaughter
bellement [bɛlmɑ̃] *adv Arch* well and truly; **voilà la vérité, tout b.** that's the simple truth
belle-mère, *pl* **belles-mères** *nf* **(a)** *(mère du conjoint)* mother-in-law **(b)** *(après remariage)* stepmother
belle-sœur, *pl* **belles-sœurs** *nf* sister-in-law
bellicisme [belisism] *nm* bellicosity, warmongering
belligérance [beliʒerɑ̃s] *nf* belligerence
belligérant, -ante [beliʒerɑ̃, -ɑ̃t] **1** *adj* belligerent **2** *n* belligerent, combatant
belliqueux, -euse [bel(l)ikø, -øz] *adj (nation, pays, peuple)* warlike, bellicose; *(personne etc)* aggressive, quarrelsome; *(humeur, tempérament)* aggressive; **tenir des propos b.** to speak aggressively
belote [bəlɔt] *nf Cartes* belote, = pinochle; *F* **faire une b.** to have a game of belote
belouga [beluga] *nm,* **beluga** [belyga] *nm (mammifère)* beluga, white whale
belvédère [bɛlvedɛr] *nm* **(a)** *(construction)* belvedere, gazebo **(b)** *(sur un site naturel)* viewpoint
Belzébuth [bɛlzebyt] *nm Bible* Beelzebub
bémol [bemɔl] *nm Mus* flat; **clarinette en si b.** B-flat clarinet; *Fig* **mettre un b. à ses critiques** to tone down one's criticism; *Fig F* **mettre un b.** to tone it down
bémoliser [bemɔlize] *vt Mus (note)* to flatten, *Am* to flat
ben [bɛ̃] *adv Arg* = **bien**; **b. oui!** why, yes!; **b. voilà, euh ...** yeah, well, er ...
bénarde [benard] *nf* pin key lock, double-sided lock
bénédicité [benedisite] *nm (avant le repas)* grace; **dire le b.** to say grace
bénédictin, -ine [benediktɛ̃, -in] *Rel* **1** *adj (moine, sœur)*

Benedictine **2** *n* Benedictine; *Fig* **un vrai b.** a painstaking scholar; **un travail de b.** a work of painstaking scholarship **3** *nf* **bénédictine** (*liqueur*) Benedictine

bénédiction [benediksjɔ̃] *nf Rel* blessing, benediction; *Fig* blessing; (*d'une église, des couleurs*) consecration; **donner la b.** (*d'un prêtre*) to give *or* pronounce the blessing; *Fig* **vous avez ma b.** you have my blessing; **il a donné sa b. au projet** he gave the plan his blessing; **quelle b.!** what a blessing!, what a godsend!; **il a dit oui, c'est une b.!** it's a blessing he said yes!

bénef [benɛf] *nm Arg* profit; **petits bénefs** perks; **faire 200 francs de b.** to make 200 francs' profit

bénéfice [benefis] *nm* **(a)** (*gain*) profit; **b. brut/net** gross/net profit; **b. non commerciaux** non-trading profits; **réaliser de gros bénéfices** to make large *or* handsome profits; **faites-vous du b.?** do you make a *or* any profit?; **participation aux bénéfices** profit-sharing; **être intéressé aux bénéfices** to share in the profits; **petits bénéfices** perquisites, *F* perks; **avec b.** (*investir*) profitably

(b) (*avantage*) benefit, advantage; **tirer un certain b. de qch** to derive some benefit *or* advantage from sth; **c'est tout à son b. de suivre cette formation** it's wholly to his benefit *or* advantage to do this training; **quel b. aurais-je à te mentir?** what good would it do me to lie to you?, what advantage *or* benefit would I get from lying to you?; **avoir le b. de l'âge** to have the benefit of age; *Jur* **b. du doute** benefit of the doubt; **on peut lui accorder** *ou* **laisser le b. du doute** we can give him the benefit of the doubt; *Th, Sp* **représentation/match à b.** benefit performance/match; **concert donné au b. de la Croix-Rouge** concert given in aid of the Red Cross

(c) *Rel* living, benefice

▶ **bénéfice**: **b. brut d'exploitation** gross operating profit; *Mktg* **b. consommateur** (*d'un produit*) consumer benefit; **b. cumulé** cumulative profit; **b. escompté** desired profit; **b. d'exploitation** operating profit; **b. imposable** taxable profit; **b. transféré** profit transferred

bénéficiaire [benefisjɛr] **1** *adj Com* **solde b.** profit balance; **compte b.** account in credit, account showing a credit balance; **marge b.** profit margin **2** *n* (*d'un chèque etc*) recipient, payee; *Rel, Jur etc* beneficiary

bénéficier [benefisje] *vt* (*impf & pr sub* **n. bénéficiions, v. bénéficiiez**) to benefit (**de** from); **faire b. qn de son expérience** to give sb the benefit of one's experience; **cette carte d'abonnement vous fait b. d'une remise de 20%** this season ticket entitles you to a 20 per cent reduction; **cet article bénéficie d'une remise de dix pour cent** this article carries a ten per cent discount, there is a discount of ten per cent on this article; *Jur* **il a bénéficié d'une ordonnance de non-lieu** he was discharged

bénéfique [benefik] *adj* beneficial (**à** to); *Astrol* (*planète*) beneficent; **ce séjour à la montagne vous sera b.** this stay in the mountains will do you good *or* will be beneficial to you

Bénélux [benelyks] *nm* Benelux

benêt [bənɛ] **1** *adj* silly, stupid **2** *nm* simpleton

bénévolat [benevɔla] *nm* voluntary work; **faire du b.** to do voluntary work

bénévole [benevɔl] **1** *adj* **(a)** (*service, travail, conseiller, infirmière*) voluntary, unpaid; **aide b.** voluntary help; **organisation b.** voluntary organization **(b)** *Litt* (*bienveillant*) (*personne*) benevolent, kindly **2** *n* volunteer, voluntary worker

bénévolement [benevɔlmɑ̃] *adv* **(a)** (*sans être payé*) voluntarily, without pay, unpaid; **il travaille b.** he does voluntary work **(b)** *Litt* (*avec bienveillance*) benevolently, kindly

Bengale [bɛ̃gal] *nm* **(a)** Bengal **(b)** **feu de B.** Bengal light

Bengali [bɛ̃gali] **1** *adj* Bengali, Bengalese **2** *nm Ling* Bengali **3** *n* Bengali

bénignité [beniɲite] *nf* **(a)** (*du climat, d'une maladie*) mildness **(b)** *Litt* (*d'une personne*) benignity, kindness

bénin, -igne [benɛ̃, -iɲ] *adj* **(a)** (*accident*) slight, minor; (*opération*) minor; **tumeur bénigne** benign *or* non-malignant tumour; **forme bénigne de (la) rougeole** mild form of measles **(b)** *Litt* (*personne, tempérament, critique etc*) benign, kindly

béni-oui-oui [beniwiwi] *nm inv F* yes-man

bénir [benir] *vt aussi Fig* to bless; (*église, pain etc*) to consecrate; **(que) Dieu vous bénisse!** (may) God bless you!; **le ciel en soit béni!** thank heaven(s)!; **je bénis cette journée où …** I bless the day when …; **b. la mémoire de qn** to glorify sb's memory; **je bénis cette occasion de parler avec elle** I'm thankful *or* grateful for this opportunity of speaking to her

bénit [beni] *adj* consecrated; **pain b.** consecrated bread, holy bread; **eau bénite** holy water

bénitier [benitje] *nm* **(a)** *Rel* stoup, stoop, holy-water basin; (*pour le baptême*) font **(b)** (*mollusque*) giant clam

benjamin, -ine [bɛ̃ʒamɛ̃, -in] *n* youngest child; **le b. de la famille** the youngest of the family

benjoin [bɛ̃ʒwɛ̃] *nm Com* (gum) benzoin, benjamin

benne [bɛn] *nf Min etc* tub, truck; (*d'une grue*) scoop; (*d'une dragueuse*) bucket; (*de ski etc*) (cable) car; (*de camion*) tipping *or* dump body; **camion à b. (basculante)** tip(per) truck, dump(er) truck

Benoist, Benoît [bənwa] *nm F* **j'te crois, B!** tell me about it!

benoît [bənwa] *adj* ingratiating

benthique [bɛ̃tik] *adj* (*faune etc*) benthic

benthos [bɛ̃tɔs] *nm* benthos

benzène [bɛ̃zɛn] *nm Ch* benzene

benzine [bɛ̃zin] *nf* benzine

benzol [bɛ̃zɔl] *nm Ch* benzol(e)

benzolisme [bɛ̃zɔlism] *nm Méd* benzole poisoning

béotien, -ienne [beɔsjɛ̃, -jɛn] *adj Péj* philistine

BEP [beəpe] *nm Scol abrév* **brevet d'études professionnelles**

BEPC [beəpese] *nm Scol abrév* **brevet d'études du premier cycle**

béquille [bekij] *nf* **(a)** *Méd* crutch; *Fig* prop; **marcher avec des béquilles** to walk on crutches **(b)** (*d'une moto*) stand; *Av* tail skid; *Naut* shore, prop; (*du gouvernail*) tiller **(c)** (*de serrure*) catch; (*poignée*) (door) handle

béquiller [bekije] **1** *vt Naut* (*bateau*) to shore up, to prop up **2** *vi F Arch* to walk on crutches

berbère [bɛrbɛr] **1** *adj* Berber **2** *nm Ling* Berber **3** *n* **B.** Berber

bercail [bɛrkaj] *nm* (*de l'Eglise etc*) fold; **ramener au b. la brebis égarée** to bring the lost sheep back to the fold; *F* **rentrer au b.** to go (back) home; (*d'un mari etc qui a abandonné le foyer*) to return to the fold

berçante [bɛrsɑ̃t] *adj, nf Can* **(chaise) b.** rocking chair

berce [bɛrs] *nf* **(a)** (*plante*) **b. commune** hogweed **(b)** *Belg, Suisse* (*berceau*) cradle

berceau, -eaux [bɛrso] *nm* **(a)** (*de bébé*) cradle; **dès le b.** from the cradle, from birth; *Fig* **le b. d'un mouvement populaire** the birthplace *or* cradle of a popular movement; *F* **il les prend au b.** he's a baby- *or* cradle-snatcher **(b)** *Typ* cradle, bed, support; *Mil* (*d'un fusil*) cradle; (*treillage*) bower, arbour, *US* arbor; *Aut, Av* **b. (du) moteur** engine cradle; *Archit* **voûte en b.** barrel vault; **b. de verdure** leafy bower

bercelonnette [bɛrsəlɔnɛt] *nf* rocking cradle

bercement [bɛrsəmɑ̃] *nm* rocking

bercer [bɛrse] (**je berçai(s), n. berçons**) **1** *vt* **(a)** (*bébé, passager*) to rock; **bateau bercé par la houle** boat rocked by the waves; *Fig* **j'ai été bercé là-dedans dès le plus jeune âge** I was brought up with it from an early age **(b)** *Litt* (*calmer*) (*chagrin*) to soothe **(c)** **b. qn de promesses/de belles paroles** to delude sb with promises/fine words **2 se bercer** *vpr* **se b. d'illusions** to delude oneself, to give oneself false hopes; **se b. d'un espoir** to indulge in a hope

berceur, -euse [bɛrsœr, -øz] **1** *adj* soothing, lulling **2** *nf* **berceuse** (*fauteuil*) rocking chair; (*chanson*) lullaby, cradle song; *Mus* berceuse

béret [berɛ] *nm* **b. (basque)** beret

bergamasque [bɛrgamask] *nf* bergamask

bergamote [bɛrgamɔt] *nf* bergamot; **thé à la b.** Earl Grey tea, tea with bergamot

berge[1] [bɛrʒ] *nf* (*de rivière, de voie ferrée, de route*) bank; (*d'une vallée*) slope, side; **voie sur b.** embankment road

berge[2] *nf F* **il a quarante berges** he's forty; **un type de trente-cinq berges** a guy of thirty-five

berger, -ère [bɛrʒe, -ɛr] **1** *n* shepherd, *f* shepherdess; *Rel* shepherd, pastor; **chien de b.** sheepdog; **l'étoile du b.** the evening star **2** *nm* **(chien) b. allemand** German shepherd, *Br* Alsatian **3** *nf* **bergère** (*fauteuil*) wing chair

bergerette [bɛrʒərɛt] *nf* (*oiseau*) wagtail

bergerie [bɛrʒəri] *nf* **(a)** (*pour moutons etc*) sheepfold, sheep pen; *Fig* **enfermer le loup dans la b.** to set the fox to mind the geese **(b)** *Beaux-Arts, Littér* (*tableau, poème etc*) pastoral

bergeronnette [bɛrʒərɔnɛt] *nf* (*oiseau*) wagtail

béribéri [beriberi] *nm Méd* beriberi; **avoir le b.** to have beriberi

berk [bɛrk] *int* yuk!

berkélium [bɛrkeljɔm] *nm Ch* berkelium

berlander [bɛrlɑ̃de] *vi Can* to dawdle, to waste time

Berlin [bɛrlɛ̃] *n* Berlin; **B-Ouest/-Est** West/East Berlin

berline [bɛrlin] *nf Min* truck, tub; *Aut* (four-door) saloon, *Am* (four-door) sedan; *Arch* (*voiture à cheval*) berlin(e); **b. familiale** family saloon; **b. trois/cinq portes** (three/five door) hatchback

berlingot [bɛrlɛ̃go] *nm* **(a)** *(bonbon)* boiled sweet, *Am* hard candy; *(à la menthe)* humbug **(b)** *(de lait)* (pyramid-shaped) carton; *(de shampoing)* sachet; *(de liquide ménager)* pack
berlinois, -oise [bɛrlinwa, -waz] **1** *adj* of/from Berlin **2** *n* **B.** Berliner
berlue [bɛrly] *nf* **avoir la b.** to be seeing things; *(se faire des illusions)* to delude *or* deceive oneself
berme [bɛrm] *nf (ouvrage)* berm; *(le long d'un canal, d'un fossé etc)* (foot)path, verge
bermuda(s) [bɛrmyda] *nm(pl)* Bermuda shorts, Bermudas
Bermudes [bɛrmyd] *nfpl* **les (îles) B.** Bermuda
bernache [bɛrnaʃ], **bernacle** [bɛrnakl] *nf* **(a)** *(crustacé)* barnacle **(b)** *(oiseau)* barnacle goose
bernardin, -ine [bɛrnardɛ̃, -in] *n Rel* Bernardine, Cistercian
bernard-l'(h)ermite [bɛrnarlɛrmit] *nm inv (crustacé)* hermit crab
Berne [bɛrn] *n* Bern
berne [bɛrn] *nf* **(a)** *Naut* **pavillon en b.** flag at half mast *or Am* half staff **(b)** *Mil* **drapeau en b.** furled flag
berner [bɛrne] *vt* **(a)** *(duper)* to fool, to hoax; *(ridiculiser)* to ridicule **(b)** *Arch (brimer)* to toss in a blanket
bernicle [bɛrnikl] *nf,* **bernique**[1] [bɛrnik] *nf (mollusque)* limpet
bernique[2] *int F* nothing doing!
bernois, -oise [bɛrnwa, -waz] **1** *adj* Bernese **2** *n* **B.** Bernese
bertillonnage [bɛrtijɔnaʒ] *nm (en anthropométrie)* Bertillon system
béryl [beril] *nm Minér* beryl
béryllium [beriljɔm] *nm Ch* beryllium
besace [bəzas] *nf Arch (de mendiant)* bag; *(de pèlerin)* scrip
bésef [bezɛf] *adv F* = **bézef**
besicles, bésicles [bezikl] *nfpl F* specs; *Hist* spectacles
bésigue [bezig] *nm Cartes* bezique
besogne [bəzɔɲ] *nf* (piece of) work, task, job; **se mettre à la b.** to set to work; **rude b.** hard job; **aller vite en b.** to get things done quickly; *F Péj* to rush things; **il est allé vite en b.!** he didn't hang about *or* mess about!; **abattre de la b.** to get through a lot of work; **voilà de la belle b.!** here's a fine mess!; *Fig* **mâcher la b. à qn** to spoon-feed sb
besogner [bəzɔɲe] *vi Péj* to slave away, to toil away
besogneux, -euse [bəzɔɲø, -øz] **1** *adj* **(a)** *(travailleur lent)* plodding; **faire son travail de façon besogneuse** to plod away (at one's work) **(b)** *Arch (dans le besoin)* poor **2** *n* **(a)** *(travailleur lent)* plodder **(b)** *Arch (dans le besoin)* poor person
besoin [bəzwɛ̃] *nm* **(a)** [①A40,C,1,a] *(nécessité)* need; **un b. de chaleur humaine** a need for human warmth; **éprouver le b. de faire qch** to feel the need to do sth; **b. d'appartenance** need to belong; **pourvoir** *ou* **subvenir aux besoins de qn** to provide for sb's needs; **si le b. s'en faisait sentir** if the need *or* necessity arose; **pour les besoins de la cause** for the sake of the cause; **cet enfant a de grands besoins** this child is very demanding; *F* **faire ses besoins** *(d'une personne)* to relieve oneself, to spend a penny, to go to the loo *or Am* john; *(d'un animal)* to do its business; **au b.** if necessary, if need(s) be; **en cas de b.** in an emergency; **avoir b. de qch/qn** to need sth/sb; **j'en ai b. pour lundi** I need it for Monday; **j'ai grand b. de son aide** I'm badly in need of *or* I really need his help; **avoir b. de faire qch** to need to do sth; **il n'a pas b. de venir lundi** he needn't come *or* there's no need for him to come on Monday; **cette maison a grand b. d'être nettoyée** this house really needs to be cleaned *or* is badly in need of a clean; **(il n'y a** *ou* **je n'ai) pas b. de dire qu'elle était là** needless to say (that) *or* it goes without saying (that) she was there; **j'ai b. que tu me laisses tranquille maintenant** I need to be left alone now; **elle a b. qu'on lui parle** she needs someone to talk to; **vous aviez bien b. d'aller lui parler de cela!** you would go and tell him about that!; **tu n'as pas b. de me parler sur ce ton!** there's no need to talk to me in that tone of voice!; *Litt* **il n'est b. d'insister** there is no need to insist; **s'il (en) est b., si b. (en) est** if necessary, if need(s) be; *Compta* **b. en fonds de roulement** working capital requirements

(b) *(misère)* need, poverty, indigence; **être dans le b.** to be in need; **vieillards dans le b.** needy *or* impoverished old people, old people in need
bessemer [bɛsmɛr] *nm Tech* **(convertisseur) b.** Bessemer converter
bestiaire [bɛstjɛr] *nm Litt* bestiary
bestial, -iale, -iaux, -iales [bɛstjal, -o] *adj (personne, colère, air)* brutish; **sensualité bestiale** animal sensuality
bestialement [bɛstjalmɑ̃] *adv* brutishly
bestialité [bɛstjalite] *nf* brutishness; *(perversion)* bestiality
bestiaux [bɛstjo] *nmpl* livestock; **parqués comme des b.** herded together like cattle
bestiole [bɛstjɔl] *nf (bête)* small *or* tiny animal *or* creature; *(insecte)* insect, bug
best-seller, *pl* **best-sellers** [bɛstsɛlœr] *nm* best-seller
bêta[1]**, -asse** [bɛta, -ɑs] *F* **1** *adj* silly, stupid **2** *n* twit, idiot; **oh le gros b.!** *(à un enfant)* you sillybilly!
bêta[2] [bɛta] *nm* **(a)** *(lettre de l'alphabet grec)* beta **(b)** *Phys Nucl* **particules/rayons b.** beta particles/rays
bêtabloquant [bɛtablɔkɑ̃] *nm Pharm* beta-blocker
bétail [betaj] *nm* [①A11,f,ii] livestock; **gros b.** livestock *(including cattle, horses, asses, mules)*; **menu** *ou* **petit b.** smaller livestock; *Fig* **on était traité comme du b.** we were treated like cattle
bétaillère [betajɛr] *nf* cattle truck
bêta-test, *pl* **bêta-tests** *nm Ordinat* beta test; **bêta-tests** beta testing
bêtatron [bɛtatrɔ̃] *nm Nucl* betatron
bête [bɛt] **1** *nf* **(a)** *(animal)* animal, *Litt* beast; **b. à cornes** horned animal; **b. de trait** draught animal; **les bêtes** *(à la ferme)* the animals, the livestock; *F* **reprendre du poil de la b.** *(reprendre le dessus)* to perk up, to pick up; **les bêtes féroces** wild animals; **une b. sauvage** a wild animal; **nos amies les bêtes** our animal friends, our four-legged friends; **sale b.** nasty little animal; **elle m'a regardé comme une b. curieuse** she looked at me as if I was from another planet; *F* **c'est une b. en maths!** he/she's a genius *or* a wiz at maths!; **travailler comme une b.** to work all out *or* flat out; **c'est une bonne b.** he/she's a good sort; **grosse b.!** you silly(billy)!

(b) *(insecte)* insect, bug; **petites bêtes** insects; *(nocives)* vermin; *Fig* **chercher la petite b.** to be over-critical, *F* to nit-pick; **jouer à la b. qui monte, qui monte** = to play round and round the garden like a teddy bear

(c) *(idiot)* fool, idiot, twit; **faire la b.** to act stupid, to pretend to be stupid; *(sans le vouloir)* to act stupidly *or* foolishly

2 *adj* stupid, silly, foolish; **que je suis b.!** how silly *or* stupid of me!; **ce que tu peux être b. parfois!** you can be really stupid sometimes!; **pas si b.!** I'm/she's/*etc* not such a fool (as all that)!; **c'est vraiment b., j'ai oublié mes clés** how stupid, I've forgotten my keys; **c'est trop b., tu aurais dû venir** that's a pity *or* a shame, you should have come; **c'est b., on a loupé le film!** what a pity *or* a shame, we've missed the film!; **il n'est pas si b. qu'il en a l'air** he's not as stupid *or* silly as he looks; **elle est loin d'être b.** she's no fool; *F* **elle est b. comme un âne** *ou* **comme ses pieds** *ou* **à manger du foin** she's as thick as a brick *or Br* as two short planks; **une histoire/une fille b. à pleurer** a pitifully stupid story/girl, a story/girl that is too stupid for words; **mon Dieu qu'il est b.!** God he's stupid!; **l'âge b.** the difficult age; **b. et méchant** stupid and nasty; **c'est b. comme chou, c'est tout b.** it's as easy as pie *or* as anything; **ce n'est pas b.** that's not a bad idea, *Br* that's not daft; *Can* **rester tout b.** *(décontenancé)* to be stupefied; **une mort b.** a stupid *or* senseless death

▶ **bête: b. à bon Dieu** ladybird, *Am* ladybug; *Péj* **b. à concours** swot, *Am* grind; **b. noire:** *Fig* **c'est sa b. noire** *(personne)* he's/she's his bête noire; **les maths, c'est ma b. noire** maths are my pet aversion *or* hate *or* my bête noire; **b. de scène** complete performer; **b. de somme** beast of burden
bétel [betɛl] *nm (plante)* betel
bêtement [bɛtmɑ̃] *adv* stupidly, foolishly, idiotically; **mourir b.** to die senselessly; **tout b.** quite simply, purely and simply
Bethléem [betleɛm] *nm Bible* Bethlehem
bêtifiant [betifjɑ̃] *adj* idiotic
bêtifier [betifje] *(pr sub & impf* **n. bêtifiions, v. bêtifiiez) 1** *vt* to make stupid **2 se bêtifier** *vpr* **ils se bêtifient à trop regarder la télévision** too much television is bad for their minds **3** *vi* to talk nonsense; *(faire l'idiot)* to act *or* play the fool; **quand il parle à un enfant, il bêtifie** he uses baby-talk to children
bêtise [betiz] *nf* **(a)** *(imbécillité)* stupidity, silliness; **être d'une rare b.** to be exceptionally stupid; **elle a eu la b. de dire oui** she was stupid enough to say yes; **tu ne crois pas que c'est de la b. de l'acheter?** don't you think it's a stupid idea *or* it's stupid to buy it?

(b) *(action idiote)* stupid thing (to do); *(parole idiote)* stupid remark, stupid thing to say; **dire des bêtises** to talk nonsense *or Br* rubbish; **quelle b.!** what nonsense!, how ridiculous!; **faire des bêtises** to do silly things; **ne faites pas de bêtises, les petits** don't do anything silly, children; **faire une (grosse) b.** to do something (very) stupid *or* silly; **ça c'est une grosse b.** that is/was very stupid; **il ne faudrait pas qu'elle fasse une b.** we don't want her to do anything silly; **se disputer pour des bêtises** to argue over nothing; **perdre son temps à des bêtises** to waste one's time on trifles; **dépenser tout son argent en bêtises** to fritter away one's money; **elle achète énormément de bêtises** she buys lots of rubbish *or Am* trash

(c) *Can* **bêtises** (*injures*) insults
(d) **bêtises de Cambrai** ≈ mint humbugs, *Am* ≈ hard mint candies

béton [betɔ̃] *nm* (a) *Constr* concrete; **b. armé** reinforced concrete; *Fig* **des muscles en b.** rock-hard muscles; *F* **un alibi en b.** a cast-iron alibi; **il est b., leur dossier** their dossier is watertight (b) *Fb* **faire le b.** to pack the defence (c) *F* **laisse b.** let it drop!, drop it!

bétonnage [betɔnaʒ] *nm* (a) *Constr* concreting (b) *Fb* packing the defence

bétonner [betɔne] 1 *vt Constr* to concrete 2 *vi Fb* to pack the defence

bétonneuse [betɔnøz] *nf*, **bétonnière** [betɔnjɛr] *nf* cement mixer, concrete mixer

bette [bɛt] *nf* (spinach) beet; **b. à carde (blanche), b. à côtes** seakale beet, Swiss chard

betterave [bɛtrav] *nf* **b. (rouge)** beetroot, *Am* beet; **b. sucrière** sugar beet; **b. fourragère** mangel-wurzel

betteravier, -ière [bɛtravje, -jɛr] 1 *adj* **l'industrie betteravière** the beet industry 2 *nm* sugar beet grower

beuglante [bøglɑ̃t] *nf F* (*cri*) yell; (*chanson*) song; **pousser une b.** (*crier*) to shout one's head off; (*chanter*) to bawl out a song

beuglement [bøgləmɑ̃] *nm* (*du bétail*) lowing; (*du taureau*) bellow(ing); *F* (*d'une personne*) bawling, bellowing; (*de la radio etc*) blaring; **pousser des beuglements** to bawl, to bellow

beugler [bøgle] 1 *vi* (*du bétail*) to low; (*d'un taureau*) to bellow; *F* (*d'une personne*) to bawl, to bellow; (*de la radio etc*) to blare; **pas la peine de b., je t'entends!** no need to yell, I can hear you!; **les voisins font b. leur télévision** the neighbours have got their television blaring away 2 *vt F* **b. une chanson** to bawl out *or* bellow out a song

beur [bœr] 1 *n* = North African born in France of immigrant parents 2 *adj inv* (*culture, mode, musique*) = of North Africans born in France of immigrant parents

beurre [bœr] *nm* butter; **b. salé/demi-sel** salted/slightly salted butter; **b. fondu** melted butter; **une motte de b.** a lump of butter; *Culin* **au b.** (*pâtisserie*) made with butter; (*légumes*) with melted butter; **faire la cuisine au b.** to cook with butter; **crème au b.** butter cream; **au b. noir** with black butter; **avoir un œil au b. noir** to have a black eye; **c'est entré comme dans du b.** it went in very easily; *F* **cela compte pour du b.** that doesn't count; *F* **il a fait son b.** he's made a packet; **ça mettra du b. dans les épinards** that will improve matters *or* ease the situation; **elle veut le b. et l'argent du b.** she wants to have her cake and eat it
▶ **beurre**: **b. d'anchois** anchovy butter; **b. de cacahouètes** peanut butter; **b. de cacao** cocoa butter

beurrée [bœre] *nf Can* (*tartine*) slice of bread and butter

beurre-frais *adj inv* buttercup-yellow

beurrer [bœre] 1 *vt* (*pain, plat etc*) to butter; *Arg* **être complètement beurré** to be plastered *or* smashed 2 **se beurrer** *vpr Arg* to get plastered *or* smashed

beurrerie [bœrri] *nf* (a) (*laiterie*) dairy (b) (*industrie*) butter industry

beurrier, -ière [bœrje, -jɛr] 1 *adj* **l'industrie beurrière** the butter industry; **région beurrière** butter-producing region 2 *nm* butter dish

beuverie [bøvri] *nf* binge, drinking session, *Br F* booze-up

bévatron [bevatrɔ̃] *nm Phys Nucl* bevatron

bévue [bevy] *nf* blunder, mistake, slip; **commettre une b.** to blunder, to make a blunder

bey [bɛ] *nm* bey

Beyrouth [berut] *n* Beirut

bézef [bezɛf] *adv F* **il n'y en a pas b.** (*non comptable*) there's not much *or* a lot (of it); (*comptable*) there aren't many *or* a lot (of them)

BFCE [beɛfseə] *nf* (*abrév* **Banque française du commerce extérieur**) French foreign trade bank

bi [bi] *nm Can* **donner** *ou* **faire un bi** to lend a hand

bi- [bi-] *préf* bi-; **bilatéral/bipartisan/***etc* bilateral/bipartisan/*etc*

biacide [biasid] *adj, nm Ch* diacid

biais [bjɛ] 1 *adj Archit* oblique, slanting; **voûte biaise** skew(ed) arch 2 *nm* (a) (*d'un outil, d'une arche*) skew; (*d'un mur*) slant; **en b.** at an angle, slantwise; *Couture* **tailler un tissu dans le b.** to cut material on the bias (b) (*moyen*) way; (*détour*) expedient; **par le b. de son voisin** through his neighbour; **aborder** *ou* **prendre de b. une personne/une question** to approach a person/a question indirectly *or* in a roundabout way; **regarder qn de b.** to look sideways *or* askance at sb (c) (*aspect*) angle; **par quel b. envisager la chose?** from what angle should we look at the issue? (d) *Couture* bias binding

biaiser [bjeze] 1 *vi* (a) (*obliquer*) to be on the slant; (*vers qch*) to veer off (b) *Fig* to dodge the issue; **pour éviter cela, il va falloir b.** we'll have to manœuvre to avoid that 2 *vt* **l'échantillon a été biaisé** the sample has been distorted

biannuel, -elle [bianɥɛl] *adj* biannual

biathlon [biatlɔ̃] *nm Sp* biathlon

bibasique [bibɑzik] *adj Ch* dibasic

bibelot [biblo] *nm* curio, knick-knack; **bibelots sans valeur** trinkets

biberon [bibrɔ̃] *nm* (baby's *or* feeding) bottle; **nourrir** *ou* **élever un enfant au b.** to bottle-feed a child; **il est encore au b.?** is he still being bottle-fed?; **il prend trois biberons par jour** he has three feeds a day; **le moment de b.** feeding time

biberonner [bibrɔne] *vi F* to booze, to tipple

bibi [bibi] *nm* (a) *Arg* (*moi*) yours truly; **et ça, c'est pour b.** that's for yours truly (b) *F* (*chapeau*) (woman's) hat

bibine [bibin] *nf F* (*boisson*) dishwater; **c'est de la b., cette bière** this beer is (like) dishwater

bibite [bibit] *nf Can Arg* bug, insect

bible [bibl] *nf* bible; **la B.** the Bible; **la b. du bricoleur** the do-it-yourselfer's bible; *Ordinat* **b. de paragraphes** library of standard paragraphs

bibliobus [bibliɔbys] *nm* mobile library, *Am* bookmobile

bibliographe [bibliɔgraf] *n* bibliographer

bibliographie [bibliɔgrafi] *nf* bibliography

bibliographique [bibliɔgrafik] *adj* bibliographical

bibliomane [bibliɔman] *n* book lover, *Fml* bibliomaniac

bibliomanie [bibliɔmani] *nf* love of books, *Fml* bibliomania

bibliophile [bibliɔfil] *n* bibliophile, book lover

bibliophilie [bibliɔfili] *nf* love of books, *Fml* bibliophily

bibliothécaire [bibliɔtekɛr] *n* librarian

bibliothéconomie [bibliɔtekɔnɔmi] *nf* library science

bibliothèque [bibliɔtɛk] *nf* (a) (*bâtiment, salle*) library; **b. de prêt** lending library; **b. municipale** municipal *or* public library; **b. universitaire** university library (b) (*meuble*) bookcase (c) (*série*), *Ordinat* library; **la b. verte/rose** = series of books aimed at 7 to 15 year olds/at 5 to 7 year olds; *F* **c'est une b. ambulante** *ou* **vivante** he's a walking encyclopaedia; *Ordinat* **b. de programmes** program library

biblique [biblik] *adj* biblical

Bic® [bik] *nm* **pointe B.** ballpoint pen, *F* Biro®

bic® 1 *adj* **stylo b., pointe b.** ballpoint pen, *Br* Biro® 2 *nm* ballpoint, *Br* Biro®

bicaméral, -ale, -aux, -ales [bikameral, -o] *adj Pol* (*système etc*) bicameral

bicaméralisme [bikameralism], **bicamérisme** [bikamerism] *nm Pol* bicameral system

bicarbonate [bikarbɔnat] *nm Ch* bicarbonate; **b. de soude** bicarbonate of soda, sodium bicarbonate

bicentenaire [bisɑ̃tnɛr] *nm* bicentenary, *US* bicentennial

bicéphale [bisefal] *adj* (*animal*) two-headed, *Spéc* bicephalous

biceps [bisɛps] *Anat* 1 *adj* (*muscle*) biceps 2 *nm* biceps; *F* **avoir des b.** to have muscles

biche [biʃ] *nf* (a) (*mammifère*) hind, doe; **ventre de b.** (*couleur*) reddish-white; **table à pieds de b.** table with cabriole legs; **aux yeux de b.** doe-eyed (b) *F* **ma b.** my darling, my dear

bicher [biʃe] *vi F* (a) (*aller bien*) **ça biche?** how's things? (b) (*se réjouir*) to be tickled pink, *Br* to be as pleased as Punch

bichette [biʃɛt] *nf* (a) (*mammifère*) young *or* small hind (b) *F* **ma b.** my darling, my dear

bichlorure [biklɔryr] *nm Ch* bichloride, dichloride

bichon, -onne [biʃɔ̃, ɔn] *n* (a) (*chien*) lap-dog, toy dog (b) *F* **mon b.** my darling, my love, my dear

bichonner [biʃɔne] 1 *vt* (a) (*préparer*) (*qn*) to make spruce *or* smart (b) (*soigner*) (*qn*) to pamper, to mollycoddle 2 *vpr* **se bichonner** to spruce oneself up

bichromate [bikrɔmat] *nm Ch* bichromate, dichromate

bichromie [bikrɔmi] *nf Typ* two-colour *or* two-tone printing

biclic [biklik] *nm Ordinat* double click

bicliquer [biklike] *vi Ordinat* to double-click

bicolore [bikɔlɔr] *adj or US* two-colour(ed) -color(ed), bicolour(ed), two-tone

biconcave [bikɔ̃kav] *adj* biconcave

biconvexe [bikɔ̃vɛks] *adj* biconvex

bicoque [bikɔk] *nf* (*maison*) shack

bicorne [bikɔrn] 1 *adj Biol, Anat* two-horned, *Spéc* bicorn(u)ate 2 *nm* cocked hat

bicot [biko] *nm* (a) (*biquet*) kid (b) *F* (*terme injurieux*) (*Arabe*) Arab, *Br* wog

bicross [bikrɔs] *nm Sp* cyclo-cross bicycle; **faire du b.** to cyclo-cross, to go cyclo-crossing

biculturalisme [bikyltyralism] *nm* biculturalism

biculturel, -elle [bikyltyrel] *adj* bicultural

bicyclette [bisiklɛt] *nf* bicycle; **aller en ville à** *ou F* **en b.** to cycle to town, to go to town by bicycle; **faire de la b. tous les week-ends** to go cycling *or* to cycle every weekend; **il ne sait pas faire de la b.** he doesn't know how to ride a bicycle
bidasse [bidas] *nm Mil Arg* squaddie, *US* G.I.
bide [bid] *nm Arg* **(a)** (*ventre*) belly; **avoir/prendre du b.** to have/develop a belly; *Fig* **c'est du b.** it's a load of baloney *or Br* codswallop **(b) la pièce/le film a fait un b.** the play/film flopped *or Am* bombed; **un b. complet** a total flop
bidet [bidɛ] *nm* **(a)** (*de toilette*) bidet **(b)** *Vieilli* (*cheval*) nag
bidimensionnel, -elle [bidimɑ̃sjɔnɛl] *adj* bidimensional
bidirectionnel, -elle [bidirɛksjɔnɛl] *adj* bidirectional
bidoche [bidɔʃ] *nf Arg* meat
bidon [bidɔ̃] **1** *nm* **(a)** (*d'huile, d'essence*) can; *Mil etc* (*gourde*) water bottle; **b. d'essence** petrol can, jerry can; **b. à lait** milk churn **(b)** *très F* (*ventre*) belly; **se remplir le b.** to stuff oneself; **c'est du b.** it's a load of baloney *or Br* codswallop; **c'est pas du b.** it's the honest truth **2** *adj F* phoney, fake; (*élections*) rigged
bidonnant [bidɔnɑ̃] *adj Arg* hilarious, screamingly funny; **c'est b.** it's a scream
bidonner (se) [səbidɔne] *vpr Arg* to laugh one's head off, to split one's sides (laughing)
bidonville [bidɔ̃vil] *nm* shantytown
bidouillage [bidujaʒ] *nm Ordinat* patching
bidouiller [biduje] *vt* to patch up; *Ordinat* (*programme*) to patch; (*radio*) to edit
bidule [bidyl] *nm Arg* thingy, thingummy, whatsit; **j'ai vu B.** I saw whatshisname, *f* whatshername *or* thingummy
bief [bjɛf] *nm* **(a)** (*portion du cours d'eau*) reach **(b)** (*d'un moulin*) millcourse, millrace
bielle [bjɛl] *nf Aut* connecting rod, conrod; *Tech* (*sous tension*) (tie) rod; (*sous compression*) push rod, crank arm; *Aut* **b. d'accouplement** track link; **tête de b.** crank head; (*de moteur*) big end; **pied de b.** crosshead; (*de moteur*) little end; *Aut* **b. de connexion** track rod; *Aut* **b. pendante** drop arm, drag link bar
biellette [bjɛlɛt] *nf MecE* (*petite bielle*) small rod; *Aut* **b. de direction** drag link, track rod
biélorusse [bjelorys] **1** *adj* B(y)elorussian **2** *n* **B.** B(y)elorussian
Biélorussie [bjelorysi] *nf* B(y)elorussia
bien [bjɛ̃] **1** *adv* **(a)** (*convenablement*) well; **livre b. écrit** well-written book; **c'est du travail b. fait** it's a fine *or* well-executed piece of work; **j'aime le travail b. fait** I like work that's done well; **il parle b.** he is a good speaker, he speaks well; **on y mange très b.** the food there is very good, you eat very well there; **cette couleur/ce rôle lui va b.** this colour/ this role suits him well; **ça te va b. de critiquer le travail des autres sans rien faire** you're a fine one to criticize the work of others without doing anything yourself; **aller** *ou* **se porter b.** to be well *or* in good health; **tout va b.** all's well, everything's OK *or* fine; **s'y prendre b.** to go about it the right way; *Iron* **voilà qui commence b.** that's a good *or* fine start!; **vous arrivez b.** you've come just at the right moment; **b.!** good!; (*ça suffit*) that's enough!, that will do!; (*entendu*) all right!; **très b.!, fort b.!** very good!, well done!; (*signalant son accord avec le locuteur*) hear, hear!; **écoutez b. ceci** now, listen carefully to this; **il faut b. les soigner** they must be well looked after

(b) (*moralement*) **vous avez b. fait** you did the right thing, you did right; **se conduire** *ou* **se tenir b.** to behave (well); **veux-tu te conduire b.?** will you behave!; **c'est b. fait (pour lui)** it serves him right; **voilà qui est b. dit** well said!; **tu fais b. de me le dire** it's a good thing *or* job you've told me, you've done well to tell me; **tu ferais b. de te méfier** you would do well to beware

(c) (*emphatique*) **est-ce b. raisonnable?** is that really reasonable?; **c'est b. cela** that's right; **il y a b. deux ans que je ne l'ai vue** it's at least *or* it must be two years since I (last) saw her; **j'ai b. dû lire dix de ses livres** I must have read at least ten of his books; **je l'ai regardé b. en face** I looked him full *or* right in the face; **j'irais b. avec vous mais …** I'd love to go with you but …; **j'y suis b. obligé** I just *or* really have to; **conduis b. à droite** drive well over on the right; **b. au milieu** right *or F* bang in the middle; **être b. d'accord** to be entirely *or* completely in agreement, to be in complete agreement; **c'est b. d'accord/compris?** is that agreed/ understood?; **b. à vous** (*dans une lettre*) yours; **je veux b. le croire** I can quite believe it; **je sais b.** I know full well, I'm well aware of it; **qu'est-ce que ça peut b. être/vouloir dire?** whatever can it be/mean?, what on earth can it be/mean?; **je me demande b. ce qu'il pouvait en penser** I really wonder what he might think of it; **c'est b. lui** it is him; **ce sont b. mes lunettes** those are my glasses; **c'est b. une erreur** that's definitely a mistake; **c'est b. de lui** it's just like him, that's typical of him; *F* **c'est b. à moi, ça?** that's really mine?; **est-ce b. le train pour Paris?** is this the right train for Paris?, is this train OK for Paris?; **c'est b. Apollinaire qui a écrit ces poèmes?** am I right in thinking Apollinaire wrote these poems?, Apollinaire did write these poems, didn't he?; **je l'avais b. dit!** didn't I say so?; **on vous avait b. dit que tous les magasins seraient fermés** you were told all the shops would be shut; **voulez-vous b. vous taire!** do shut up!, will you please be quiet!; **il est b. entendu que …** it is understood of course that …; **b. entendu, b. sûr, b. évidemment** of course; **je m'en doutais b.** I thought as much; **c'est b. ce que je pensais** that's just what I thought; **il faut b. qu'on mange quelque chose** we really must eat something; **il est b. venu, mais j'étais occupé** he did come, but I was busy; **je ne veux pas que tu fasses cela – mais vous le faites b., vous!** I don't want you to do that – but you do it, don't you?; *Iron* **c'est b. le moment de parler comme ça!** a fine time *or* what a time to talk like that!; **c'est b. ma chance!** (it's) just my luck!; **c'était b. la peine** it wasn't worth the trouble; **voilà b. les hommes!** just like men!, that's men all over!

(d) (*très*) very; **b. malheureux** very unhappy; **vous venez b. tard** you're very late; **b. souvent** quite often; **c'est b. loin de Paris** it's a long way (away) from Paris; **b. loin de moi l'idée de vous accuser** far be it from me to accuse you; **c'est b. gentil, mais …** that's very kind, but …; **c'est b. simple** it's quite *or* very simple; **je voudrais que ce soit b. clair entre nous** I want us to be quite clear on this

(e) (*beaucoup*) (*souffrir, réfléchir, changer etc*) a lot, a great deal; **b. plus** much *or* a lot more; **b. moins** much *or* a lot less; **tu t'es b. amusé?** did you have a good time?, did you enjoy yourself?; **b. de …** a lot of …, a great deal of …; **b. des …** a lot of …, a good many …; **j'ai eu b. de la peine** *ou* **du mal à la convaincre** I had a lot of *or* a great deal of trouble convincing her; **j'ai reçu b. des lettres** I received a lot of *or* a good many letters; **nous avons eu b. des inquiétudes à son sujet** he caused us a lot of *or* a great deal of worry; **je l'ai vu b. des fois** I have seen him many times; **b. d'autres** many others, lots more

(f) aussi b. just as well, just as easily; **on fera aussi b. d'y aller par nous-mêmes** we can just as well *or* just as easily go there by ourselves

(g) tant b. que mal somehow (or other), after a fashion; **je m'en suis acquitté tant b. que mal** I got through

(h) [①B30-31,f] **b. que** + *sub* although, though; **je le respecte, b. qu'il ne me soit pas sympathique** I respect him (even) though I don't like him

(i) si b. que + *ind* and so; **il ne reparut plus, si b. qu'on le crut mort** he failed to come back, and so he was thought dead

(j) ou b. or else, otherwise; **il faut le lui dire ou b. il l'apprendra par quelqu'un d'autre** we'll have to tell him or else *or* otherwise he'll hear about it from someone else; **viens à la maison ou b. on se retrouve dans un café** come to my place, or (else) we could meet in a café; **ou b. … ou b. …** either … or …

(k) *int* **eh b.!** well!; **eh b. donc!** well then!; **eh b. ça alors!** well, fancy that!

2 *adj inv* **(a)** (*satisfaisant*) good; *Scol* (*sur un devoir*) good; **c'est b.!** good!; **ce serait b. si …** it would be good if …; **comme c'est b. à vous d'être venu!** how good of you to come!; **ce n'est pas b. de vous moquer de lui** it's not nice *or* kind of you to make fun of him; **des gens b.** nice *or* decent people; **il est très b., le nouvel assistant** the new assistant is very good; **il est très bien, ce petit gars** he's a nice fellow; **il me faut quelque chose de b.** I'm looking for something good

(b) (*à l'aise*) **êtes-vous b. dans ce fauteuil/ces chaussures?** are you comfortable in that armchair/those shoes?; **qu'est-ce qu'on serait b., dans une maison comme la tienne!** I'd really feel at home in a house like yours!; **se sentir b. dans un pays** to like it *or* to feel at home in a country; **je suis b. partout** I'm at home anywhere; **ne t'occupe pas de moi, je suis b. comme ça** don't worry about me, I'm fine *or* all right as I am; **nous voilà b.!** we're in a right mess!; **être b. avec qn** to be on good terms with sb, to be well in with sb; **se mettre b. avec qn** to get into sb's good books, to get well in with sb

(c) (*en forme*) well; **je ne me sens pas très b.** I don't feel very well; **vous vous sentez b. maintenant?** do you feel better now?; **il est moins b.** he's not as well (as he was)

(d) (*beau*) (*personne*) good-looking, attractive; **il est b. de sa personne** he's a fine figure of a man; **tu es très b. dans cette robe** you look very good in that dress, that dress suits you very well; **elle est b. sur cette photo** she looks good in this photo

3 *nm* **(a)** *Phil, Rel etc* good; **le b. et le mal** good and evil, right and wrong; **faire le b.** to do good; **homme de b.** good *or* upright man; **le b. public** the public good; **c'est pour votre b.** it's for your own good; **cela m'a fait beaucoup de b.** it did me a lot of good; **ça pourrait peut-être faire du b. à mes rhumatismes** that could perhaps do my rheumatism some good; **faire le plus grand b. à qn** to do sb a great deal of good; **grand b. vous fasse!** much good may it do you!; **vouloir du b. à qn, vouloir le b. de qn** to wish sb well; **je ne veux que votre b.** I only want the best for you; **un ami qui vous veut du b.** a well-wisher; **tout le monde dit du b.** *ou* **parle en b. de lui** everyone speaks well of him; **on m'a dit beaucoup de b. de vous/de ce produit** I've heard a lot of good things about you/about this product; **je trouve qu'il a changé en b.** I think he's changed for the better; **mener une affaire à b.** to bring a matter to a satisfactory conclusion

(b) (*chose matérielle*) possession, property; *Jur* assets; (*argent*) wealth, fortune; **biens** possessions, property; **il a du b. (au soleil)** he's a man of property, he has property; **c'est mon b. le plus cher** it's my dearest possession; **biens et services** goods and services

(c) *F* **en tout b. (et) tout honneur** with the best of intentions

▸ **bien**: **biens capitaux** capital goods *or* items; **biens consommables** consumables; **b. de consommation** consumer product; **b. de consommation durable** consumer durable; **biens de consommation** consumer goods; **biens dotaux** dowry; **b. durable** durable good; **biens durables** (consumer) durables; **biens d'équipement** capital equipment *or* goods; **biens fonciers** landed property; **biens immobiliers** real estate *or* property; **b. industriel** industrial good; **biens intermédiaires** semi-finished goods; **biens meubles** *ou* **mobiliers** personal property *or* estate; **biens de première nécessité** staples; **biens de production** capital goods; *Compta* **biens sociaux** corporate assets *or* funds; **biens successoraux** hereditaments; **biens tangibles** physical goods; **biens vacants** ownerless property

bien-aimé, -ée, *pl* **bien-aimé(e)s** [bjɛ̃neme] **1** *adj* beloved; **mon ami b.** my very dear friend **2** *n* beloved; *Hist* **(Louis) le B.** Louis XV

bien-être [bjɛ̃nɛtr] *nm* (*no pl*) well-being; (*d'une population etc*) welfare; **sentiment de b.** feeling of well-being; **b. du consommateur** consumer welfare

bienfaisance [bjɛ̃fəzɑ̃s] *nf* (*générosité*) benevolence; (*charité*) charity; **bureau de b.** welfare office; **organisation** *ou* **œuvre de b.** charitable organization, charity

bienfaisant [bjɛ̃fəzɑ̃] *adj* **(a)** (*personne*) charitable, kindly **(b)** (*remède etc*) beneficial, salutary; (*vent, pluie*) refreshing

bienfait [bjɛ̃fɛ] *nm* **(a)** (*avantage*) benefit; **les bienfaits de la technique/du traitement** the benefits of technology/of the treatment **(b) un b. du ciel** a godsend; *Prov* **un b. n'est jamais perdu** a good deed will have its reward

bienfaiteur, -trice [bjɛ̃fɛtœr, -tris] *n* benefactor, *f* benefactress; **b. du peuple** people's friend

bien-fondé, *pl* **bien-fondés** *nm* (*d'une opinion, d'un argument, d'une revendication*) validity, merits; *Jur* cogency

bien-fonds, *pl* **biens-fonds** *nm* real estate, landed property

bienheureux, -euse [bjɛ̃nørø, -øz] **1** *adj* **(a)** (*heureux*) blissful, happy **(b)** *Rel* blessed **2** *n Rel* blessed person; **dormir comme un b.** to sleep the sleep of the just; **les b.** the blessed, the blest

bien-jugé *nm* (*no pl*) *Jur* just and lawful decision

biennal, -ale, -aux, -ales [bjenal, -o] **1** *adj* biennial, two-yearly; **contrat b.** two-year contract; **fonction biennale** two-year post; **exposition biennale** biennial exhibition **2** *nf* **biennale** biennial

bien-pensant, -ante, *pl* **bien-pensants, -antes 1** *adj* (*personne*) right-thinking, right-minded, *Péj* self-righteous **2** *n Péj* self-righteous person, prig

bienséance [bjɛ̃seɑ̃s] *nf* propriety, decorum; **respecter les bienséances** to observe the proprieties

bienséant [bjɛ̃seɑ̃] *adj* decorous, proper; **il est b. aux jeunes gens de respecter la vieillesse** it is right and proper for young people to respect old age; **il n'est pas b. de manger avec ses doigts** it is not proper *or* it is not the done thing to eat with your fingers

bientôt [bjɛ̃to] *adv* [①**A23,3,a,ii**] soon, before long; **on est b. arrivé?** are we nearly there?, will we soon be there?; **il est b. deux heures** it'll soon be two o'clock; **tu vas b. arrêter de répéter la même chose?** will you please stop repeating the same thing?; **à b.!** see you soon!, goodbye for now!; **on s'est dit à b.** we said we'd see each other soon; **on se dit adieu ou on se dit à b.?** is it goodbye or just au revoir?; **les beaux jours seront b. là** the fine days will soon be here; **c'est pour b., ce bébé?** is the baby due soon?; *Litt* **b. après** soon after(wards); *Vieilli* **c'est b. dit!** that's easier said than done!

bienveillance [bjɛ̃vɛjɑ̃s] *nf* benevolence, kindness **(envers, pour** to); **avec b.** kindly

bienveillant [bjɛ̃vɛjɑ̃] *adj* kind, kindly, benevolent **(envers, pour** to); **examinateur b.** lenient examiner

bienvenu, -ue [bjɛ̃vny] **1** *adj* (*remarque*) opportune, apposite; (*repas, explication etc*) welcome **2** *n* **soyez le b. /la bienvenue!** welcome!; **vous êtes toujours le b.** you're always welcome; **votre proposition est la b.** your suggestion is welcome

bienvenue [bjɛ̃vny] **1** *nf* welcome; **souhaiter la b. à qn** to welcome sb; **b. à nos amis de Russie!** welcome to our Russian friends!; **b. à Nice!** welcome to Nice!; **allocution de b.** welcoming speech **2** *int Can* you're welcome!

bière[1] [bjɛr] *nf* (*boisson*) beer; **b. blonde** lager; **b. brune** brown ale, *Am* dark beer; **b. pression** draught *or US* draft beer; *Fig* **ce n'est pas de la petite b.** it's no small matter; **c'est de la petite b.** it's small beer

bière[2] *nf* (*cercueil*) coffin, *Am* casket; **assister à la mise en b.** to be present when the body is placed in the coffin

biffe [bif] *nf Mil Arg* infantry

biffer [bife] *vt* (*mot etc*) to cross out, to strike out, to put a line through; **tu peux b. ce nom de ta liste** you can cross *or* strike this name off your list

biffin [bifɛ̃] *nm* **(a)** *Arg* (*chiffonnier*) ragman, *Br* rag-and-bone man **(b)** *Mil F* infantryman

biffure [bifyr] *nf* crossing out, striking out

bifide [bifid] *adj* bifid

bifidus [bifidys] *nm Biol* live culture

bifocal, -ale, -aux, -ales [bifɔkal, -o] *adj* (*lentille etc*) bifocal; **lunettes bifocales** bifocals

bifteck [biftɛk] *nm* (beef)steak; **b. de cheval** horse(meat) steak; *F* **gagner son b.** to earn a living

bifurcation [bifyrkasjɔ̃] *nf* (*d'une route*) junction; (*d'une route, d'un tronc d'arbre etc*) fork; (*professionnelle*) change of direction; **tournez à droite à la b.** take the right fork

bifurquer [bifyrke] *vi* (*d'une route, d'un chemin*) to fork, to divide, to branch off; **nous avons bifurqué vers** *ou* **sur la ville** we turned *or* forked off towards the town; **bifurquez à droite** take the right fork; **b. vers la politique/dans la recherche** to branch out into politics/research

bigame [bigam] **1** *adj* bigamous **2** *n* bigamist

bigamie [bigami] *nf* bigamy

bigarade [bigarad] *nf* (*fruit*) bitter *or* Seville orange

bigarré [bigare] *adj* (*tissu, chemise etc*) multicoloured, *US* multicolored; (*groupe, société etc*) mixed; (*foule*) motley, mixed

bigarreau, -eaux [bigaro] *nm* (*cerise*) bigarreau

bigarrer [bigare] *vt* to colour *or US* to color with (lots of) different colours *or* colors

bigarrure [bigaryr] *nf* mixture *or* medley of colours *or US* colors; (*d'un groupe, style etc*) variety, motley nature; **les bigarrures du costume d'Arlequin** Harlequin's multicoloured *or* motley costume; **une b. de gens** a motley collection of people

big band [bigbɑ̃d] *nm Mus* big band

big(-)bang [bigbɑ̃g] *nm Astron* big bang

bigle [bigl] *Vieilli, Hum* **1** *adj* cross-eyed **2** *n* cross-eyed person

bigler [bigle] *F* **1** *vi* (*loucher*) to squint, to have a squint; **b. sur qch** to squint at sth **2** *vt* (*qch*) to squint at; (*fille*) to eye (up)

bigleux, -euse [biglø, -øz] *F* **1** *adj* (*personne*) (*qui louche*) cross-eyed; (*myope*) short-sighted; **t'es b.?** are you blind? **2** *n F* (*qui louche*) cross-eyed person; (*qui est myope*) short-sighted person

bigophone [bigɔfɔn] *nm F* (*téléphone*) phone, *Br* blower; **passer un coup de b. à qn** to give sb a buzz *or Br* a ring

bigorneau, -eaux [bigɔrno] *nm* (*mollusque*) winkle

bigorner [bigɔrne] **1** *vt Métal* to work on an anvil; *Arg* (*abîmer*) to smash up **2 se bigorner** *vpr Arg* to have a punch-up, to scrap

bigot, -ote [bigo, -ɔt] *Péj* **1** *adj* sanctimonious, holier-than-thou **2** *n* (religious) bigot

bigoterie [bigɔtri] *nf Péj* (religious) bigotry

bigoudi [bigudi] *nm* (hair) curler, (hair) roller; **se mettre des bigoudis** to put one's hair in curlers *or* rollers; **tu ne vas pas sortir en bigoudis!** you're not going out in (your) curlers!

bigre [bigr] *int F Vieilli* gosh!, *Br* crikey!

bigrement [bigrəmɑ̃] *adv F* **vous avez b. raison!** you're dead right!; **il fait b. froid** it's awfully cold; **il a b. changé/grandi** he's changed/grown a heck of a lot; **il était b. surpris** he was dead surprised; **tu étais content? – oui, et b.!** were you satisfied? – yes, and how!

biguine [bigin] *nf Mus* beguine

bihebdo [biɛbdo] *nm* biweekly
bihebdomadaire [biɛbdɔmadɛr] *adj* (*magazine etc*) twice-weekly, biweekly
bijection [biʒɛksjɔ̃] *nf Math* bijection
bijou, -oux [biʒu] *nm* jewel; **bijoux** jewellery, *US* jewelry, jewels; **un b. fantaisie** a piece of costume jewellery; *Fig* **c'est un b.** it's a gem; **cette montre est un b. d'exactitude/de précision** this watch is a marvel of accuracy/precision; **bijoux de famille** family jewels; *Fig Arg* (*sexe masculin*) family jewels, *Br* wedding tackle; *F* **mon b.!** my precious!, my pet!
bijouterie [biʒutri] *nf* **(a)** (*boutique*) jeweller's *or US* jeweler's (shop); (*commerce, fabrication*) jeweller's trade *or* business **(b)** (*bijoux*) jewellery, *US* jewelry, jewels **(c)** (*art*) jewellery-making, *US* jewelry-making
bijoutier, -ière [biʒutje, -jɛr] *n* jeweller, *US* jeweler
bikini [bikini] *nm* bikini
bilabial, -iale, -iaux, -iales [bilabjal, -jo] *Ling* **1** *adj* bilabial **2** *nf* **bilabiale** bilabial
bilan [bilɑ̃] *nm* **(a)** *Fin* (*état*) balance sheet; **faire** *ou* **dresser un b.** to draw up a balance sheet; **déposer son b.** to file one's petition (in bankruptcy); **un dépôt de b.** a petition in bankruptcy
(b) (*appréciation*) (*d'une situation, de faits*) assessment, evaluation; (*résultats*) results; **faire le b. de la situation** to take stock of *or* assess *or* evaluate the situation; **arrivé à 40 ans, on fait souvent le b.** you often stop to take stock, when you reach 40; **'accident sur l'autoroute, b. quatre morts'** 'motorway accident, four dead'; **le b. d'une tremblement de terre** the toll of an earthquake
▶ **bilan**: *Mktg* **b. commercial** market report; **b. comptable** balance sheet; *Compta* **b. condensé** summary balance sheet; **b. financier** financial statement; *Compta* **b. intérimaire** interim statement; *Compta* **b. d'ouverture** opening balance sheet; *Compta* **b. prévisionnel** forecast balance sheet; **b. de santé** complete (medical) check-up; **votre b. de santé est excellent** your state of health is excellent, you are in excellent health; **faire le b. de santé de qn** to give sb a (medical) check-up; **faire le b. de santé d'une entreprise** to assess *or* evaluate the state of a company; *Compta* **b. social** social report
bilantiel [bilɑ̃sjɛl] *adj* balance-sheet
bilatéral, -ale, -aux, -ales [bilateral, -o] *adj* (*paralysie, traité, discussions etc*) bilateral, two-sided; **stationnement b.** parking on both sides (of the road)
bilboquet [bilbɔkɛ] *nm* **(a)** (*jouet*) = cup-and-ball; (*poussah*) tumbler **(b)** *Typ* (piece of) job work
bile [bil] *nf* **(a)** *Physiol* bile **(b)** (*colère*) **échauffer la b. de** *ou* **à qn** to rouse sb's anger; **décharger sa b. sur qn** to vent one's spleen on sb **(c)** (*inquiétude*) **se faire de la b.** to fret, to be worried sick (**pour** about); **elle ne se fait pas de b.** she doesn't let things get on top of her; **ne te fais pas de b.!** don't fret!; **ses humeurs de b. noire** his black moods
biler (se) [səbile] *vpr F* to get worked up, to get all hot and bothered; (*être inquiet*) to be worried sick, to fret; **ne te bile pas!** don't fret!; **elle ne se bile pas, elle!** she's not bothered
bileux, -euse [bilø, -øz] *adj F* easily upset; **elle n'est pas bileuse** she doesn't let things worry her *or* get on top of her
biliaire [biljɛr] *adj Anat* (*vaisseaux etc*) biliary; *Méd* **calcul b.** gallstone, *Spéc* biliary calculus; **vésicule b.** gall bladder; **cirrhose b.** cirrhosis (of the liver)
bilieux, -ieuse [biljø, -jøz] *adj* **(a)** (*tempérament, teint*) bilious **(b)** (*personne*) (*colérique*) irritable, irascible; (*inquiet*) sick with worry
bilingue [bilɛ̃g] *adj* (*personne, dictionnaire etc*) bilingual
bilinguisme [bilɛ̃gɥism] *nm* bilingualism
billard [bijar] *nm* **(a)** [ⓘ**A10**,d] (*jeu*) billiards; **jouer au b.** to play billiards; **faire un b.** *ou* **une partie de b.** to play *or* have a game of billiards **(b)** (*table*) billiard table; *Fig F* **monter** *ou* **passer sur le b.** to have an operation, to be operated on **(c)** (*salle*) billiard saloon; (*dans une maison*) billiard room
▶ **billard**: **b. américain** pool; **b. électrique** pinball; **b. russe** bar billiards
bille¹ [bij] *nf* **(a)** (*pour le billard*) (billiard) ball
(b) *Arg* (*visage*) mug, face; **il a une bonne b.** he looks pleasant enough; **une b. de clown** a funny face; **quelle b., il ne comprend rien!** what a mug, he just doesn't twig!
(c) (*de verre*) marble; **jouer aux billes** to play marbles; *Fig* **reprendre ses billes** to pull out; *F* **elle touche sa b. en informatique** she knows a thing or two about computers; *F* **il ne touche pas une b. au flippeur** he's hopeless *or* lousy *or* zilch at pinball; *Fig* **savoir placer ses billes** to play one's cards right
(d) *Tech* ball; **roulement à billes** ball bearing; **stylo (à) b.** ballpoint (pen), *Br* biro®; **flacon (à) b.** roll-on (bottle); **déodorant à b.** roll-on deodorant
bille² *nf* (*pièce de bois*) billet
billet [bijɛ] *nm* **(a) b. (de banque)** (bank)note, *Am* bill; **un faux b.** a forged banknote; **un b. de cent francs** a hundred-franc note; *F* **je te fiche mon b. qu'il pleuvra!** I bet my bottom dollar it'll rain!
(b) *Com, Fin* (*effet*) note, bill
(c) (*pour voyager*) ticket; **prendre un b. pour Valence** to buy a ticket for Valence
(d) *Th etc* ticket; **b. de théâtre** theatre ticket
(e) *Litt* (*lettre*) note, short letter
(f) *Journ* diary column
▶ **billet**: *Scol* **b. d'absence** absence slip; **b. d'aller** single *or Am* one-way ticket; **b. d'aller (et) retour** return *or Am* round-trip ticket; **b. d'avion** plane ticket; **b. bradé** discounted ticket; **b. circulaire** round-trip ticket; **billets complémentaires** conjunction tickets; **b. demi-tarif** half-fare ticket; **b. doux** love letter, billet doux; *Vieilli* **b. de faire part** = card announcing a birth/wedding/death in the family; **b. 'famille nombreuse'** special SNCF rates for families with 3 children or more; **b. de faveur** complimentary ticket; *Mil* **b. de logement** billet; **b. de naissance** birth certificate; **b. neutre** blank ticket; **b. open** open(-date) ticket; *Fin* **b. à ordre** promissory note; **b. ouvert** open ticket; *Fin* **b. au porteur** bill payable to bearer; **b. de première** first class ticket; *Scol* **b. de retard** = note given to pupil who is late, specifying the time of arrival; **b. de retour** return *or Am* round-trip ticket; **b. sans condition** flexible ticket; **b. de santé** certificate *or* bill of health; **b. de seconde** second class ticket; **b. simple** single *or Am* one-way ticket; *Scol* **b. de sortie** pass, *Br Fml* exeat; **b. souple** flexible ticket; **b. de train** train ticket; **b. de transport** ticket; *Fin* **b. de trésorerie** commercial paper; **b. vert** dollar, *Am F* greenback
billétique [bijetik] *nf Banque, Ordinat* cash dispenser technology
billette [bijɛt] *nf* **(a)** (*du bois de chauffage, du métal*) billet **(b)** *Archit* billet (moulding)
billetterie [bijɛtri] *nf* **(a)** (*opérations*) ticketing; (*lieu*) ticket office **(b)** (*distributeur de billets de banque*) cash dispenser; **b. automatique** automatic ticket machine
billettiste [bijetist] *nmf* ticketing clerk; *Journ* diary column writer
billevesées [bilvəze] *nfpl* nonsense, *F* twaddle; **b. que tout cela!** that's absolute nonsense!
billion [biljɔ̃] *nm* [ⓘ**A70**,16,1] **(a)** (*million de millions*) trillion, *Br Vieilli* billion **(b)** *Arch* (*milliard*) billion, *Br Vieilli* milliard
billot [bijo] *nm* (*de boucher, bourreau*) block; (*dans la cuisine*) butcher's block table; (*de cordonnier*) last; **b. d'enclume** anvil block *or* stock; **périr** *ou* **mourir sur le b.** to be beheaded, to die on the block; *F* **j'en mettrais ma tête sur le b.** I'd stake my life on it
bilobé [bilɔbe] *adj Archit, Biol* bilobate, bilobed
bimane [biman] *Zool* **1** *adj* bimanous **2** *n* bimanous animal
bimbeloterie [bɛ̃blɔtri] *nf* **(a)** (*fabrication, commerce*) fancy goods business *or* trade **(b)** (*objets*) fancy goods, knick-knacks, odds and ends
bimbelotier [bɛ̃blɔtje] *nm* (*fabricant*) maker of fancy goods; (*vendeur*) dealer in fancy goods
bimensuel, -elle [bimɑ̃sɥɛl] **1** *adj* bimonthly, *Br* fortnightly, *Am* semimonthly **2** *nm* bimonthly (magazine), *Br* fortnightly magazine
bimestriel, -elle [bimɛstriɛl] **1** *adj* bimonthly **2** *nm* bimonthly
bimétallique [bimetalik] *adj* bimetallic
bimétallisme [bimetalism] *nm Écon* bimetallism
bimillénaire [bimilenɛr] *adj* bimillenary
bimoteur [bimɔtœr] *adj, nm* **(avion) b.** twin-engine (aircraft)
binage [binaʒ] *nm Agr* harrowing, hoeing; (*de jardin*) hoeing
binaire [binɛr] *adj Math etc* binary; **langage b.** binary notation
biner [bine] **1** *vt Agr* (*sol*) to harrow, to hoe; (*jardin*) to hoe **2** *vi Rel* to celebrate mass twice in one day
binette¹ [binɛt] *nf Agr* hoe
binette² *nf Arg* (*visage*) mug, face
bineuse [binøz] *nf Agr* cultivator
bing [biŋ] *int* bam!, wham!
bingo [biŋgo] *nm* bingo; **jouer au b.** to play bingo
biniou [binju] *nm* **(a)** *Mus* Breton bagpipes **(b)** *F* (*téléphone*) phone, *Br* blower; **donner un coup de b. à qn** to give sb a buzz *or* a call *or Br* a ring
binoclard, -arde [binɔklar, -ard] *n F* specs wearer; **hé b.!** hey four-eyes!
binocle [binɔkl] *nm* pince-nez; *F* **binocles** (*lunettes*) specs
binoculaire [binɔkylɛr] *adj* (*vision, microscope etc*) binocular
binôme [binom] *nm* **(a)** *Math* binomial; **le b. de Newton** the

binomial theorem **(b)** **travailler en b.** (*d'étudiants etc*) to work in twos
binomial, -iale, -iaux, -iales [binɔmjal, -o] *adj Math* binomial
binot [bino] *nm Agr* = **bineuse**
biocarburant [bjokarbyrɑ̃] *nm* biofuel
biochimie [bjoʃimi] *nf* biochemistry
biochimique [bjoʃimik] *adj* biochemical; **demande b. en oxygène** biochemical oxygen demand
biochimiste [bjoʃimist] *n* biochemist
bioclimat [bjoklima] *nm* bioclimate
bioclimatique [bjoklimatik] *adj* bioclimatic
bioclimatologie [bjoklimatɔlɔʒi] *nf* bioclimatology
biodégradable [bjodegradabl] *adj* biodegradable
bioénergétique [bjoenɛrʒetik] **1** *adj* bioenergetic **2** *nf* bioenergetics
bioéthique [bjoetik] *nf Méd* bioethics
biogenèse [bjoʒənɛz] *nf Biol* biogenesis
biographe [bjɔgraf] *n* biographer
biographie [bjɔgrafi] *nf* biography
biographique [bjɔgrafik] *adj* biographical
bio-industrie [bjoɛ̃dystri] *nf* biotechnology industry
biologie [bjɔlɔʒi] *nf* biology
biologique [bjɔlɔʒik] *adj* biological; **horloge b.** biological clock; **parents biologiques** biological parents; **agriculture/jardinage b.** organic farming/gardening; **aliments biologiques** organic food
biologiste [bjɔlɔʒist] *n* biologist
biomasse [bjomas] *nf* biomass
biomatériau [bjomaterjo] *nm* biomaterial
biomédical, -ale, -aux, -ales [bjomedikal, -o] *adj* biomedical
biométrie [bjomètri] *nf* biometrics
bionique [bjɔnik] *nf* bionics
biophysicien, -ienne [bjofizisjɛ̃ -jɛn] *n* biophysicist
biophysique [bjofizik] *nf* biophysics
biopsie [bjɔpsi] *nf Chir* biopsy
biorythme [bjoritm] *nm* biorhythm
BIOS [bjɔs] *nm Ordinat* BIOS
biosphère [bjosfɛr] *nf* biosphere
biosynthèse [bjosɛ̃tɛz] *nf* biosynthesis
biotechnique [bjotɛknik], **biotechnologie** [bjotɛknolɔʒi] *nf Pharm, Ch* biotechnology
biothérapie [bjoterapi] *nf* biotherapy
biotope [bjɔtɔp] *nm* biotope
bioxyde [biɔksid] *nm Ch* dioxide
bip [bip] **1** *int* beep **2** *nm* **(a)** (*son*) beep; **après le b. sonore** after the beep; **faire b.** to beep; *TV, Rad* **b. de censure** censor bleep **(b)** (*appareil*) beeper, pager, bleeper
bipale [bipal] *adj* (*hélice*) twin-bladed
biparti, -ie [biparti], **bipartite** [bipartit] *adj* bipartite
bipartisme [bipartism] *nm Pol* bipartite system
bip-bip, *pl* **bips-bips** *nm* beep
bipède [bipɛd] *adj, nm* biped
biphasé [bifɑze] *Él* **1** *adj* (*courant*) two-phase, diphase **2** *nm* two-phase *or* diphase current
biplace [biplas] *adj, nm Aut, Av* two-seater
biplan [biplɑ̃] *adj, nm* **(avion) b.** biplane
bipolaire [bipɔlɛr] *adj Él, Phys etc* bipolar, two-pole
bipolarisation [bipɔlarizasjɔ̃] *nf Pol* separation into two blocs
bipolarité [bipɔlarite] *nf* bipolarity
biquadratique [bikwadratik] *Math* **1** *adj* (*équation*) biquadratic **2** *nf* biquadratic
bique [bik] *nf F* **(a)** (*chèvre*) nanny goat; **peau de b.** goatskin **(b)** *Péj* (*femme*) **vieille b.** old bag *or* hag
biquet, -ette [bikɛ, -ɛt] *n* **(a)** (*petit de la chèvre*) kid **(b)** *F* **mon b.** my pet, my love
biquotidien, -ienne [bikɔtidjɛ̃, -jɛn] *adj* twice-daily
birbe [birb] *nm F* **vieux b.** old fogey, old fuddy-duddy
biréacteur [bireaktœr] *nm* twin-jet (aircraft)
biréfringence [birefrɛ̃ʒɑ̃s] *nf Opt* double refraction, birefringence
biréfringent [birefrɛ̃ʒɑ̃] *adj Opt* doubly refractive, birefringent
birman, -ane [birmɑ̃, -an] **1** *adj* Burmese **2** *nm Ling* Burmese **3** *n* **B.** Burmese
Birmanie [birmani] *nf* Burma
biroute [birut] *nf* **(a)** *Mil, Av F* (wind) sock, wind sleeve **(b)** *Arg* (*pénis*) dick, cock
bis¹ [bi] *adj* greyish-brown, brownish-grey; **teint b.** dark *or* swarthy complexion; **toile bise** unbleached linen; **pain b.** brown bread
bis² [bis] *adv* **(a)** *Th* encore; *Mus* repeat **(b)** (*dans une adresse*) **10 b.** 10A **(c)** **itinéraire b.** alternative route
bisaïeul, -eule, *pl* **bisaïeul(e)s** [bizajœl] *n Litt* great-grandfather, *f* great-grandmother
bisannuel, -elle [bizanɥɛl] *adj* biennial; **plante bisannuelle** biennial (plant)
bisbille [bisbij] *nf F* squabble, petty quarrel, tiff; **être en b. avec qn** not to see eye to eye with sb, to be at odds with sb
Biscaye [biskaj] *n* Biscay; **le golfe de B.** the Bay of Biscay
biscornu [biskɔrny] *adj* **(a)** (*de forme*) (*chapeau*) crooked; (*personne, nain*) crooked, misshapen; (*sac, maison, bâtiment, cactus*) oddly shaped **(b)** *F* (*idées*) bizarre, weird, cranky; (*raisonnement, esprit*) tortuous
biscoteaux [biskɔto] *nmpl F* biceps; **avoir des b.** to have bulging biceps
biscotte [biskɔt] *nf* rusk
biscuit [biskɥi] *nm* **(a)** *Culin* biscuit, *Am* cookie; **b. au chocolat** chocolate biscuit; **b. au fromage** cheese biscuit **(b)** *Cér* biscuit, bisque; **un b.** a piece of biscuitware
▶ **biscuit**: **b. de fourrage** (*d'avoine etc*) cake; **b. à la cuiller** sponge finger, *Am* lady finger; **b. de mer** ship's biscuit; **b. pour chien** dog biscuit; **b. de Savoie** sponge cake; **biscuits salés** crackers
biscuiterie [biskɥitri] *nf* **(a)** (*usine*) biscuit *or Am* cookie factory **(b)** (*commerce*) biscuit *or Am* cookie trade **(c)** (*fabrication*) biscuit *or Am* cookie making
bise¹ [biz] *nf* (*vent*) north wind
bise² *nf F* (*baiser*) kiss; **donner** *ou* **faire une b. à qn** to give sb a kiss, to kiss sb; **on se fait la b.** we give each other a kiss, we kiss each other; **grosses bises** (*sur une lettre*) love and kisses
biseau, -eaux [bizo] *nm* **(a)** *Menuis etc* (*bord*) chamfer, bevel, chamfered *or* bevelled edge; **taillé en b.** bevel-edged, bevelled, chamfered **(b)** (*d'horloge etc*) bezel; *Mus* (*d'instrument à vent*) lip **(c)** (*outil*) bevel
biseautage [bizotaʒ] *nm* **(a)** *Menuis etc* bevelling, chamfering **(b)** (*de cartes à jouer*) marking
biseauter [bizote] *vt* **(a)** *Menuis etc* to bevel, to chamfer **(b)** (*cartes à jouer*) to mark
biser¹ [bize] *vi Agr* (*du grain*) to darken, to deteriorate
biser² *vt F* to kiss
biset [bizɛ] *nm* (*oiseau*) rock pigeon
bisexualité [bisɛksɥalite] *nf* bisexuality
bisexué [bisɛksɥe] *adj* bisexual; **animal b.** hermaphrodite
bisexuel, -elle [bisɛksɥɛl] *adj* bisexual; **personne bisexuelle** bisexual (person)
bismuth [bismyt] *nm* bismuth
bison [bizɔ̃] *nm* [①A12,1,g] *Zool* bison, buffalo
Bison Futé *nm Aut* 'Crafty Bison', body which advises drivers of congestion on French motorways
bisou [bizu] *nm F* kiss; **faire un b. à son papa** to give Daddy a kiss
bisque [bisk] *nf Culin* bisque; **b. de homard** lobster bisque
bisquer [biske] *vi F* to be riled; **ça va le faire b.** that'll rile him, *Br* that'll get right up his nose
bissecteur, -trice [bisɛktœr, -tris] **1** *adj* (*ligne etc*) bisecting **2** *nf* **bissectrice** bisector, bisecting line
bissection [bisɛksjɔ̃] *nf Math* bisection
bisser [bise] *vt* **(a)** (*d'un artiste*) (*chanson etc*) to give an encore of, to repeat **(b)** (*d'un spectateur*) (*chanson, artiste etc*) to call on to give an encore
bissextile [bisɛkstil] *adj* **année b.** leap year
bistouri [bisturi] *nm Chir* lancet, *Spéc* bistoury
bistre [bistr] **1** *adj* bistre, blackish-brown; **teint b.** swarthy *or* dark complexion **2** *nm* bistre
bistré [bistre] *adj* (*peau*) swarthy, dark
bistrer [bistre] *vt* (*teint*) to darken, to tan
bistro(t) [bistro] *nm F* = café
bisulfate [bisylfat] *nm Ch* bisulphate
bisulfite [bisylfit] *nm Ch* bisulphite
bisulfure [bisylfyr] *nm Ch* disulphide, bisulphide
BIT [beite] *nm* (*abrév* **bureau international du travail**) ILO
bit [bit] *nm Ordinat* bit; **b. d'arrêt** stop bit; **bit de départ** start bit; **b. de contrôle** control bit, check bit; **b. de parité** parity bit; **bits par seconde** bits per second
bite [bit] *nf Vulg* (*pénis*) cock, prick, dick
biterrois, -oise [biterwa, -az] **1** *adj* of/from Béziers **2** *n* (*natif*) native of Béziers; (*habitant*) inhabitant of Béziers
bitonal, -ale, -aux, -ales [bitɔnal, -o] *adj Tel* **sonnerie bitonale** two-tone ring
bitoniau [bitɔnjo] *nm F* thingy, whatsit
bitte¹ [bit] *nf Vulg* = **bite**
bitte² *nf Naut* (*sur un bateau*) bitt; **b. d'amarrage** bollard
bitter [bitɛr] *nm* bitters
bitture [bityr] *nf* **(a)** *Naut* range of cable **(b)** *Arg* **prendre une b.** to get plastered *or* canned; **il tient une sacrée b.** he's absolutely plastered, *Br* he's paralytic
bitturer (se) [səbityre] *vpr Arg* to get plastered *or* canned
bitumage [bitymaʒ] *nm* **(a)** (*de route*) asphalting **(b)** (*de papier etc*) tarring

bitume [bitym] *nm Minér* **(a)** (*asphalte*) bitumen, asphalt; *F* **arpenter le b.** to walk the streets **(b)** (*goudron*) bitumen, tar
bitumer [bityme] *vt* **(a)** (*route*) to asphalt **(b)** (*goudronner*) to tar; **carton bitumé** tarred felt
bitum(in)eux, -euse [bitym(in)ø, -øz] *adj Minér* bituminous
biture [bityr] *nf* = **bitture**
biturer (se) [səbityre] *vpr Arg* = **bitturer (se)**
biunivoque [biɥnivɔk] *adj Math* one-to-one
bivalent [bivalɑ̃] *adj Ch etc* bivalent, divalent
bivalve [bivalv] *adj, nm* bivalve
bivouac [bivwak] *nm* bivouac; **faire un b.** to bivouac; **feu de b.** watchfire; **cet endroit sera un excellent b.** this will be an excellent place to bivouac
bivouaquer [bivwake] *vi* to bivouac
bizarre [bizar] **1** *adj* odd, strange, peculiar, bizarre; **c'est b., ce n'est pas ce qu'elle m'avait dit** that's odd *or* strange, that's not what she told me; **le plus b., c'est que ...** the strangest *or* oddest *or* funniest thing of all is that ...; **b., b., comme c'est b.** curiouser and curiouser **2** *nm* **le b.** the bizarre; **le b. de l'affaire, c'est que ...** the strange *or* odd *or* funny thing is that ...
bizarrement [bizarmɑ̃] *adv* strangely, oddly, peculiarly; **et b., elle est venue toute seule** and for some strange reason she came all alone
bizarrerie [bizarri] *nf* (*de situation, d'idée, d'attitude etc*) strangeness, oddness, peculiarity; (*de personne*) eccentricity; **bizarreries** oddities; (*de personne*) eccentricities
bizarroïde [bizarɔid] *adj F* weird; **ce type est b.** that guy's a weirdo
bizut [bizy] *nm Univ F* freshman, fresher
bizutage [bizytaʒ] *nm Univ F* (*des nouveaux arrivés*) ragging, *Am* hazing
bizuter [bizyte] *vt Univ F* (*nouvel arrivé*) to rag, *Am* to haze
bizuth [bizy] *nm F* = **bizut**
blabla(bla) [blabla(bla)] *nm F* claptrap, boloney; (*dans un discours, texte etc*) padding, waffle; **et b. et ça discute** blah blah
blackboulage [blakbulaʒ] *nm* blackballing; *F* (*d'un candidat à un examen*) failing
blackbouler [blakbule] *vt* to blackball; *F* (*à un examen*) to fail; **se faire b. d'un bureau à l'autre** to get shunted from one office to another
black-out [blakawt] *nm inv* blackout; *Fig* **faire le b. sur un scandale** to hush up *or* cover up a scandal; **c'est le b. total, on ne sait rien** there's a complete blackout, we don't know a thing
blafard [blafar] *adj* (*lune, lumière, teint etc*) pallid, wan, pale
blague [blag] *nf* **(a)** (*plaisanterie*) joke; (*tour*) (practical) joke, trick, hoax; **faire une b. (à qn)** to play a joke *or* trick (on sb); **il m'a fait une sale b.** he played a dirty trick on me; **tout ça c'est de la b.** it's all bunkum *or* nonsense; **ne racontez pas de blagues** you're kidding (me), you're having *or Am* putting me on; **b. à part** seriously, joking apart; **sans b.?** really?, no kidding? **(b) b. (à tabac)** (tobacco) pouch **(c)** *Vieilli* (*erreur*) mistake, blunder
blaguer [blage] *F* **1** *vi* to joke; **il aime bien b.** he likes a joke; **là, tu es en train de b.!** you're joking *or* kidding!, you're having *or Am* putting me on! **2** *vt* (*qn*) to tease, to make fun of
blagueur, -euse [blagœr -øz] *F* **1** *n* (*qui dit des blagues*) joker, comedian; (*qui fait des blagues*) practical joker, prankster **2** *adj* (*remarque*) teasing, bantering; **il est très b.** he really likes a joke
blair [blɛr] *nm Arg* (*nez*) conk, *Br* hooter
blaireau, -eaux [blɛro] *nm* **(a)** (*mammifère*) badger **(b)** (*pour se raser*) shaving brush **(c)** *Beaux-Arts* (badger-hair) brush **(d)** *F* (*imbécile*) nerd, prat
blairer [blere] *vt Arg* **je ne peux pas le b.** I can't stick *or* stand *or* stomach him
blâmable [blɑmabl] *adj* blameworthy; **vous n'êtes pas b.** you're not to blame
blâme [blɑm] *nm* **(a)** (*reproche*) blame; **rejeter le b. de qch sur qn** to lay the blame for sth on sb; **s'attirer le b. de ses parents** to incur one's parents' disapproval **(b)** *Admin* (*sanction*) reprimand; **donner un b. à qn** to reprimand sb, to give sb a reprimand; **recevoir un b.** to be reprimanded
blâmer [blɑme] **1** *vt* **(a)** (*condamner*) (*qn, gouvernment, acte etc*) to blame; **b. qn de faire/d'avoir fait qch** to blame sb for doing/having done sth **(b)** *Admin* (*réprimander*) to reprimand **2** *vpr* **se blâmer** to blame oneself; **je ne peux que me b. d'avoir dit oui** I can't forgive myself for having said yes
blanc, blanche [blɑ̃, blɑ̃ʃ] **1** *adj* **(a)** (*drap, pain, vin, chocolat etc*) white; **b. comme (la) neige** (*tissu, drap etc*) white as snow, snow-white; *Fig* **il est sorti du procès b. comme neige** he came out of the trial whiter than white; **vieillard à cheveux blancs** white-haired old man, old man with white hair; **fromage b.** cream cheese; **verre b.** colourless *or US* colorless glass; **bruit b.** white noise
(b) (*peau*) pale, light-coloured, *US* light-colored; (*pas bronzé*) white; **la race blanche** the white race; **b. de peur** white with fear; **b. de colère** livid with anger; **b. comme un linge** as white as a sheet; **b. comme un cachet d'aspirine** completely white; **il a la peau blanche** (*fragile*) he has a pale skin
(c) *Litt* (*innocent*) innocent, pure; **j'ai les mains blanches** my hands are clean, I'm innocent
(d) (*vierge*) (*page etc*) blank; (*papier*) plain, unlined; **j'ai besoin d'une feuille blanche** I need a clean piece of paper; **nuit blanche** sleepless night; **examen b.** mock (examination); *Scol* **rendre copie blanche** to hand in a blank paper; **mariage b.** unconsummated marriage; **voix blanche** toneless voice; **vers blancs** blank verse; *Tennis* **jeu b.** love game
2 *nm* **(a)** (*couleur*) white; **b. éclatant** brilliant white; **robe d'un b. sale** dingy white dress; **peint en b.** painted white; **être habillé de b., être en b.** to be dressed in white; **mariage en b.** white wedding; **le b. est très à la mode** white is very fashionable; **je vous l'écris noir sur b.** I'm putting it in black and white for you
(b) b. d'une cible bull's-eye of a target; **donner** *ou* **mettre dans le b.** to hit the bull's-eye
(c) (*espace*) blank, space, gap; *Ordinat* blank; **laisser des blancs** to leave blanks *or* spaces *or* gaps; **chèque en b.** blank cheque
(d) (*aux dominos*) blank; **double b.** double blank
(e) saigner qn à b. to bleed sb white; **chauffer un métal à b.** to bring a metal to a white heat; **chauffé à b.** white-hot; **cartouche à b.** blank (cartridge); **tirer à b.** to fire a blank/blanks
(f) *Culin* **b. de poulet** breast of chicken, chicken breast; **tu veux le b. ou la cuisse?** would you like breast or leg *or Am* white meat or dark?
(g) (*colorant*) **b. de billard** billiard chalk; **b. de chaux** whitewash; **b. de zinc** zinc white, oxide of zinc; **b. de céruse** *ou* **d'argent** *ou* **de plomb** white lead; **b. d'Espagne** whiting, whitening
(h) (*linge*) **(articles de) b.** linen; **il est préférable de laver le b. séparément** it is preferable to wash whites separately; **magasin de b.** linen shop; **vente de b.** sale of linen, white sale; *Com* **la grande quinzaine du b.** the great two-week-long linen sale
(i) (*vin*) white wine; **du rouge ou du b.?** red or white?; **b. de b.** = white wine made from white grapes
(j) b. du rosier/de la vigne rose/vine mildew
(k) *TV, Rad* drop-out
3 *nf* **blanche (a)** *Billard* white (ball)
(b) *Mus* minim, *Am* half note
4 *n* **B.** White (man); **Blanche** White (woman); **réservé aux Blancs** reserved for Whites
▶ **blanc**: **b. cassé** off-white; **b. d'œuf** egg white; **le b. des yeux** the whites of the eye; **regarder qn dans le b. des yeux** to look sb straight in the eye
blanc-bec, *pl* **blancs-becs** *nm Péj* greenhorn; (*adolescent*) callow youth
blanchaille [blɑ̃ʃaj] *nf* **(a)** *Pêche* (*poisson*) small fry, bait **(b)** *Culin* whitebait
blanchâtre [blɑ̃ʃatr] *adj* whitish, off-white
Blanche-Neige [blɑ̃ʃnɛʒ] *nf* Snow White; **B. et les Sept Nains** Snow White and the Seven Dwarves
blancheur [blɑ̃ʃœr] *nf* whiteness; *Fig* purity, innocence; **d'une b. de perle** pearl-white; **sa peau est d'une telle b.!** his skin is so white!
blanchiment [blɑ̃ʃimɑ̃] *nm* **(a)** (*d'un plafond, mur etc*) whitewashing **(b)** *Culin* (*de légumes*) blanching **(c)** *Tex* bleaching **(d)** (*de l'argent*) laundering
blanchir [blɑ̃ʃir] **1** *vt* **(a)** (*dents etc*) to whiten, to make white; **b. (à la chaux)** (*plafond, mur etc*) to whitewash; **la neige qui blanchit les sommets** the snow that turns the peaks white; *Typ* **b. la composition** to space out the matter
(b) (*linge*) to launder; *Tex* to bleach; **donner du linge à b.** to send clothes to the laundry; *Fig* **cette déclaration l'a blanchi complètement** this statement has completely exonerated him *or* completely cleared his name; **b. de l'argent** to launder money
(c) *Culin* (*légumes*) to blanch; *Ind* (*sucre*) to refine
(d) *Can Sp* (*équipe*) to shut out
2 *vi* **(a)** (*devenir blanc*) to turn *or* go white
(b) (*pâlir*) to blanch, to turn pale
3 se blanchir *vpr* to clear oneself *or* one's name, to

exonerate onself; **se b. d'une accusation** to clear oneself of *or* exonerate oneself from a charge

blanchissage [blɑ̃ʃisaʒ] *nm* **(a)** *(du linge etc)* laundering; **liste de b.** laundry list **(b)** *Ind (du sucre)* refining **(c)** *Can Sp* shutout

blanchissant [blɑ̃ʃisɑ̃] *adj* **(a)** *(chevelure)* whitening; *(peau etc)* paling; **l'aube blanchissante** the brightening dawn **(b)** **agent b.** whitener

blanchissement [blɑ̃ʃismɑ̃] *nm* **(a)** *(des cheveux)* whitening **(b)** *(de la peau)* blanching, turning pale **(c)** *(de l'argent)* laundering

blanchisserie [blɑ̃ʃisri] *nf* **(a)** *Com* laundry **(b)** *Tex* bleachery

blanchisseur, -euse [blɑ̃ʃisœr, -øz] *n* launderer, laundryman, *f* laundress, *Vieilli* washerwoman

blanc-manger, *pl* **blancs-mangers** *nm Culin* = blancmange

blanc-seing, *pl* **blancs-seings** *nm* signature to a blank document; *Fig* **donner un b. à qn** to give sb a free hand

blanquette[1] [blɑ̃kɛt] *nf Culin (de veau)* blanquette

blanquette[2] *nf* **b. de Limoux** =·sparkling white wine from Limoux

blasé, -ée [blɑze] **1** *adj* blasé **2** *n* blasé person; **faire le b.** to act all blasé

blaser [blɑze] **1** *vt (qn)* to make blasé; **être blasé de qch** to be indifferent to sth **2 se blaser** *vpr* to become blasé; **se b. de qch** to become indifferent to sth

blason [blazɔ̃] *nm Hér* **(a)** *(armes)* coat of arms, armorial bearings, blazon **(b)** *(héraldique)* heraldry

blasonner [blazɔne] *vt Hér* **b. un écu** to blazon an escutcheon

blasphémateur, -trice [blasfematœr, -tris] **1** *n* blasphemer **2** *adj* blaspheming, blasphemous

blasphématoire [blasfematwar] *adj* blasphemous

blasphème [blasfɛm] *nm* blasphemy; **dire** *ou* **prononcer des blasphèmes** to blaspheme

blasphémer [blasfeme] **(je blasphème, n. blasphémons; je blasphémerai) 1** *vi* to blaspheme **(contre** against**) 2** *vt Vieilli* to blaspheme; **b. le nom de Dieu** to take the Lord's name in vain

blastoderme [blastɔdɛrm] *nm Biol* blastoderm

blatérer [blatere] *vi* **(il blatère; il blatérera)** *(d'un chameau)* to roar; *(d'un bélier)* to bleat

blatte [blat] *nf (insecte)* cockroach, black beetle

blaze [blaz] *nm Arg (nez)* conk, *Br* hooter

blazer [blazœr] *nm* blazer

bld *abrév* **boulevard**

blé [ble] *nm* **(a)** *(céréale)* wheat, *Br* corn; **b. dur** hard *or* durum wheat; **b. tendre** soft wheat; **champ de b.** wheatfield; **grenier à b.** granary; **halle aux blés** corn exchange; **b. en herbe** wheat in the blade; *Fig* **manger son b. en herbe** to eat one's seed corn **(b)** *F Fig (argent)* bread, dough, *Br* lolly

▶ **blé**: *Can* **b. d'Inde** maize, *Am* (Indian) corn; **b. noir** buckwheat

bled [blɛd] *nm (en Afrique du Nord)* inland country, interior; *F (région ou village reculé(e))* backwater, place in the middle of nowhere; *(petite ville)* one-horse town; *F* **dans mon b.** in my part of the country; *F Péj* **un sale b., un b. perdu** a godforsaken place, a dump, a hole

blême [blɛm] *adj* **(a)** *(personne, visage, teint)* pallid, wan; **b. de peur** white with fear; **un visage b. de fatigue** a tired, wan face; **b. de rage/colère** white with rage/anger; **elle est devenue b. quand je le lui ai dit** she went white *or* she blanched when I told her **(b)** *Fig* **lueur b.** pale *or* wan light; **matin b.** pale morning

blêmir [blemir] *vi* **(a)** *(de personne)* to turn *or* go pale; **b. de rage/colère** to turn *or* go livid *or* white with rage/anger **(b)** *Fig (de la lumière)* to grow dim *or* faint *or* wan

blêmissement [blemismɑ̃] *nm* paling, turning pale

blennorragie [blɛnɔraʒi] *nf Méd* gonorrhoea

blennorragique [blenɔraʒik] *Méd* **1** *adj* gonorrhoeal **2** *n* gonorrhoea sufferer

blépharite [blefarit] *nf Méd* blepharitis

blèsement [blɛzmɑ̃] *nm* lisping, lisp

bléser [bleze] *vi* **(je blèse, n. blésons; je bléserai)** to lisp

blésité [blezite] *nf* lisping

blessant [blesɑ̃] *adj (remarque etc)* hurtful, cutting; *(personne)* hurtful

blessé, -ée [blese] **1** *adj (par arme)* wounded; *(dans un accident)* injured, hurt; *(moralement)* hurt, upset **2** *n (victime d'une agression)* wounded person, casualty; *(victime d'un accident)* injured person, casualty; **les blessés** the wounded/injured, the casualties; **les blessés légers** the slightly wounded/injured; **les grands blessés** the severely wounded/injured; **un mort et trois blessés** one dead and three wounded/injured; **les blessés de guerre** the war wounded; **b. de la face** person with facial wounds/injuries

blesser [blese] **1** *vt* **(a)** *(par arme)* to wound; *(dans un accident)* to injure, to hurt; **la chute l'a grièvement blessée** she was severely injured *or* hurt in the fall; **vous êtes blessé?** are you hurt?; **ces souliers me blessent** these shoes hurt me; **il a été b. au bras** *(par arme)* he was wounded in the arm; *(dans un accident)* his arm was injured; **être b. à mort** *(par arme)* to be fatally wounded; *(dans un accident)* to be fatally injured

(b) *(moralement) (qn)* to offend, to hurt, to upset; **b. la vue** *ou* **les yeux/l'oreille** to offend the eye/to grate on the ear; **b. qn au vif** to cut sb to the quick; **b. l'amour-propre de qn, b. qn dans son orgueil** *ou* **amour-propre** to hurt *or* injure sb's pride *or* self-esteem; **cette suspicion de ta part me blesse** I resent your suspiciousness; **cela blesse notre sens des convenances** that offends (against) our sense of propriety

2 *vpr* **se blesser** *(physiquement) (avec une arme)* to wound oneself; *(dans un accident)* to hurt *or* injure oneself **(avec** with**)**; **il s'est blessé à la tête** *(avec une arme)* he's wounded himself in the head; *(dans un accident)* he's hurt *or* injured his head

blessure [blesyr] *nf (par arme)* wound; *(dans un accident)* injury; **faire une b. à qn** to wound sb; **b. légère** *ou* **superficielle** slight *or* flesh wound; **b. profonde** deep wound; *Jur* **coups et blessures** assault and battery; **une b. d'amour-propre** a blow to one's pride *or* self-esteem; *Fig* **rouvrir une b.** to open an old wound

blet, blette[1] [ble, blɛt] *adj (fruit)* overripe, soft

blette[2] [blɛt] *nf* = **bette**

blettir [bletir] *vi (d'un fruit)* to become overripe, to go soft

blettissement [bletismɑ̃] *nm (d'un fruit)* overripeness

bleu [blø] **1** *adj* blue; *(bifteck)* very rare; **avoir les yeux bleus** to have blue eyes, to be blue-eyed; **b. de froid** blue with cold; **colère bleue** towering rage; **j'en suis resté b.** I was flabbergasted; *Méd* **maladie bleue** blue disease, *Spéc* cyanosis; *Méd* **enfant b.** blue baby; *Aut* **zone bleue** restricted parking area

2 *nm* **(a)** *(couleur)* blue; *Fig* **n'y voir que du b.** not to catch on, *Br* not to twig; **le b. du ciel** the blue(ness) of the sky; *Mil* **tirer dans le b.** to fire at random; **b. (de lessive)** blue, blueing; **passer du linge au b.** to blue laundry; *Tex* **b. de teinturier** blue, blueing

(b) *(ecchymose)* bruise; **j'ai le bras couvert de bleus** my arm's covered with bruises, my arm's black and blue; **se faire un b.** to bruise oneself

(c) *F (novice)* novice, greenhorn, *Am* tenderfoot; *Mil* raw recruit, rookie

(d) *(fromage)* blue cheese

(e) *Culin* **truite au b.** trout au bleu *(boiled alive in vinegar bouillon)*

(f) **bleu(s) (de chauffe** *ou* **de travail)** *(combinaison)* overalls, *Br* boiler suit; *(salopette)* dungarees; *(à deux pièces)* overalls

(g) *Tech* blueprint

(h) *Vieilli* **petit b.** telegram

▶ **bleu: b. ciel** sky blue; **b. clair** light blue; **b. foncé** dark blue; **b. horizon** sky blue; **b. marine** navy (blue); **b. d'outremer** ultramarine; **b. de Prusse** Prussian blue; **b. roi** royal blue; **b-noir** bluish-black; **encre b-noir** blue-black ink; **b-nuit** midnight blue

bleuâtre [bløɑtr] *adj* bluish

bleuet [bløɛ] *nm* **(a)** *(plante)* cornflower **(b)** *Can (baie)* blueberry

bleuir [bløir] **1** *vt (qch)* to turn *or* make blue **2** *vi* to turn *or* go blue

bleuissement [bløismɑ̃] *nm* turning blue

bleuté [bløte] *adj (lumière, couleur etc)* bluish, blue-tinged; *(verres de lunettes etc)* blue-tinted

bleuter [bløte] *vt (verre, acier etc)* to give a blue tinge to

blindage [blɛ̃daʒ] *nm* **(a)** *Constr, Min (d'une tranchée)* timbering, sheeting **(b)** *Mil etc* armour(-plate *or* -plating), *US* armor(-plate *or* -plating); **plaque de b.** armour-plate **(c)** *Él (d'une valve etc)* screen(ing); *(d'un transformateur etc)* shrouding; *Ordinat* shield

blindé [blɛ̃de] **1** *adj* **(a)** *Mil etc* armoured, armour-plated, *US* armored, *US* armor-plated; *(division, train)* armoured; **porte blindée** steel security door; **abri b.** bombproof shelter; **non b.** *(véhicule)* soft-skinned **(b)** *F* **je suis b.** *(ce n'est pas la première fois que ça m'arrive)* I'm hardened *or* immune to it; **b. contre qch** hardened *or* immune to sth **(c)** *Arg (ivre)* blind drunk, plastered **(d)** *Él (valve)* screened; *(transformateur)* shrouded **2** *nmpl Mil* **les blindés** the armour, *US* the armor

blinder [blɛ̃de] **1** *vt* **(a)** *Constr, Min (tranchée, puits de mine etc)* to sheet, to timber **(b)** *Mil etc* to armour(-plate), *US* to armor(-plate); *(abri)* to make bombproof; **b. sa porte** to reinforce one's door (with steel) **(c)** *Él* to screen, to shroud

(**d**) *F* (*qn*) to harden, to make immune (**contre qch** to sth) **2 se blinder** *vpr* to harden oneself, to become thick-skinned
blinis [blini(s)] *nm Culin* blini
blister [blistɛr] *nm Com* blister pack; **marchandise vendue sous b.** goods sold in blister packs
blizzard [blizar] *nm* blizzard
bloc [blɔk] *nm* (**a**) (*de bois, de pierre etc*) block, lump; **taillé d'un seul b.** cut from a solid block; **elle s'est retournée tout d'un b. et l'a giflé** she turned round smartly and slapped him in the face; **coulé en b.** cast in one piece; **acquérir des droits en b.** to buy rights outright; **il a tout refusé/critiqué en b.** he rejected/criticized everything in its entirety; **visser** *ou* **serrer qch à b.** to screw sth (up) as tightly as possible; **serrer les freins à b.** to jam the brakes on hard; *F* **gonflé à b.** full of beans, raring to go
(**b**) (*de maisons*) block; **il habite dans ce b.** he lives in this block
(**c**) *Pol etc* bloc, group, coalition; **faire b.** to join forces, to unite (**avec** with, **contre** against); **les deux partis font b.** the two parties have formed a bloc *or* group *or* coalition; **former un b.** to make up *or* form a group; **le b. occidental** the Western bloc; **le b. des gauches** the left-wing bloc *or* group *or* coalition
(**d**) (*de papier*) pad; **b. à dessin** sketch pad, drawing pad; **b. de papier à lettre** writing pad; **b. de bureau** office pad, desk pad
(**e**) (*ensemble d'éléments*) unit; *Cin* **b. sonore** sound unit; **former un b.** to make up *or* form a unit
(**f**) *F* (*prison*) clink, *Br* nick; **être au b.** to be in the clink *or* the nick
(**g**) *Ordinat* block; **quelle commande faut-il utiliser pour déplacer un b.?** what's the command for moving a block?; **b. d'alimentation secteur** mains power unit; **b. de données** data block; **b. numérique** numeric keypad; **b. de texte** text block, block of text; **b. de touches** keypad
▶ **bloc**: **b. adresse** address block; *Sp* **b. de départ** starting block; *Aut* **b. des feux arrière** rear light cluster; **b. logique** package; *Aut* **b. moteur** engine block; **b. opératoire** theatre block, operating theatre *or Am* room; *Aut* **b. optique** sealed beam unit; **b. sanitaire** toilet block; **b. technique** (*d'une usine etc*) technical services block
blocage [blɔkaʒ] *nm* (**a**) (*de mécanismes etc*) jamming, sticking; (*des freins*) locking, seizing; *Écon, Fin* freezing; *Sp* (*du ballon*) blocking; *Psy* block; **b. des prix et des salaires** wage and price freeze; *Psy* **il a** *ou* **fait un b.** he's got a (mental) block; *Aut* **b. des roues** wheel lock, wheel lock-up; *Aut* **b. du volant** steering wheel clamp; *Aut* **b. de maintien du corps** bodylock seat restraints; **vis de b.** locking screw (**b**) *Constr* rubble (stone); *Typ* (*des lettres*) turning; *Ordinat* **b. majuscule** caps lock (**c**) *Ordinat* (*dans réseau*) lockout
blocaille [blɔkaj] *nf Constr* rubble (stone)
bloc-cuisine, *pl* **blocs-cuisines** *nm* kitchen unit
bloc-cylindres, *pl* **blocs-cylindres** *nm Aut* cylinder block
bloc-diagramme, *pl* **blocs-diagrammes** *nm Géog* block diagram
bloc-évier, *pl* **blocs-éviers** *nm* sink unit
blockhaus [blɔkos] *nm* (**a**) *Mil* blockhouse, pillbox (**b**) *Naut* armoured *ou US* armored tower; **b. de commandement** conning tower
bloc-moteur, *pl* **blocs-moteurs** *nm Aut* engine block
bloc-notes, *pl* **blocs-notes** *nm* notepad, memo pad; *Ordinat* notepad, scratchpad; **mémoire b.** scratchpad memory; **b. électronique** electronic notepad
bloc-sièges *nm inv* block of seats
bloc-système, *pl* **blocs-systèmes** *nm Rail* block system
blocus [blɔkys] *nm* blockade; **faire le b. d'un port** to blockade a port; **lever/forcer le b.** to raise/to run the blockade
blond, -onde [blɔ̃, -ɔ̃d] **1** *adj* (*cheveux*) fair, blond; (*personne*) fair(-haired), blond; (*sable, blés*) golden; **être b. comme les blés** (*des cheveux*) to be golden(-blond), *Litt* to be corn-coloured; (*d'une personne*) to have golden(-blond) hair, to be golden-haired; **bière blonde** lager; **un demi de blonde** = a half of lager; (**cigarette**) **blonde** Virginia cigarette; **tabac b.** Virginia tobacco
2 *n* (**a**) (*personne*) **un b.** a fair(-haired) man; **une blonde** a blonde, a fair(-haired) woman; **blonde décolorée** peroxide blonde; *Can F* **il va voir sa blonde** he's off to see his girl(friend)
(**b**) *TV, Cin* (*lumière*) blonde
3 *nm* **cheveux** (**d'un**) **b. doré** golden(-blond) hair; **se teindre (les cheveux) en b.** to dye one's hair blond
▶ **blond**: **b. ardent** auburn; **b. cendré** ash blond; **b. platine** platinum blond; **b. vénitien** strawberry blond, Titian red
blondasse [blɔ̃das] *adj* (*cheveux*) washed-out blond
blondeur [blɔ̃dœr] *nf* (*des cheveux*) blondness, fairness; (*du sable, des blés*) goldenness, gold
blondin[1], -ine [blɔ̃dɛ̃, -in] *n* fair-haired child
blondin[2] *nm Tech* cableway
blondinet, -ette [blɔ̃dinɛ, -ɛt] *n* fair-haired child
blondir [blɔ̃dir] **1** *vi* (*des cheveux*) to go *or* turn blond, to get fairer *or* lighter; (*d'une personne*) to go *or* turn blond; **il faut faire b. les oignons dans du beurre** cook the onions in butter until they turn pale yellow **2** *vt* (*cheveux*) to bleach; **l'eau de mer blondit les cheveux** sea water bleaches the hair **3 se blondir** *vpr* **elle s'est blondi les cheveux** she's bleached her hair
bloquer [blɔke] **1** *vt* (**a**) (*mécanisme etc*) to jam; (*porte*) to jam, to wedge; (*port etc*) to blockade; **b. les roues** to lock (up)the wheels; **b. les freins** to jam the brakes on; **bloqué par la neige/le brouillard** snowbound/fogbound; **il m'a bloqué contre un mur** he jammed me up against a wall; *F* **me voilà bloqué à l'hôpital** here I am stuck in hospital
(**b**) (*réunir*) to group together; **les cours sont bloqués sur six jours** the classes are grouped together over six days; **b. ses jours de congés** to lump together one's days off
(**c**) *Constr* (*mur*) to block up *or* fill up (with rubble); *Typ* **b. une lettre** to turn a letter
(**d**) (*chèque*) to stop; (*compte en banque*) to block; (*prix, salaires*) to freeze; (*négociations*) to hold up, to block
(**e**) (*route etc*) to block; *Sp* (*ballon*) to block; **b. le chemin** *ou* **le passage à qn** to block *or* be in sb's way
(**f**) *Belg F* (*sujet*) to bone up on, *Br* to swot up
(**g**) *Psy* **ça me bloque de me sentir observé** I get a (mental) block if I feel I'm being watched; **être bloqué** to have a (mental) block
2 se bloquer *vpr* (**a**) (*de machine, d'ascenseur etc*) to get stuck; (*d'une carte à puce*) to be automatically invalidated; (*de papier*) to jam
(**b**) *Psy* to have *or* get a (mental) block
blottir (se) [səblɔtir] *vpr* to snuggle up, to curl up; **se b. dans son lit** to curl up *or* snuggle up *or* snuggle down in bed; **se b. contre qn/dans les bras de qn** to snuggle up to sb/in sb's arms; **blottis les uns contre les autres** huddled up *or* snuggled up together; **blotti dans un coin** huddled *or* huddling in a corner; **village blotti au fond de la vallée** village tucked away *or* nestling in the valley
blousant [bluzɑ̃] *adj* loose-fitting
blouse [bluz] *nf* (**a**) (*d'écolier, de femme de ménage, de mécanicien etc*) overall; (*de médecin*) (white) coat; (*de paysan*) smock; **b.** (**de laboratoire**) (lab) coat (**b**) *Vieilli* (*de femme*) blouse
blouser [bluze] **1** *vt F* (*qn*) to con, to take in, to cheat **2** *vi* (*d'un corsage etc*) to be loose-fitting **3 se blouser** *vpr F* to make a mistake *or* a blunder
blouson [bluzɔ̃] *nm* (lumber)jacket; (*plus léger*) blouson; **b. en** *ou* **de cuir** leather jacket; **b. d'aviateur** bomber jacket; *F* **b. noir** young hoodlum (*wearing a black leather jacket*) *Br* rocker
blue-jean(s), *pl* **blue-jeans** [blu(d)ʒin(z)] *nm* jeans
blues [bluz] *nm Mus* blues
bluff [blœf] *nm* bluff; **faire du b.** to bluff; **c'est un coup de b.** it's all bluff, he's/they're/*etc* bluffing *or Br* trying it on; **il faut y aller au b.** you'll have to try and bluff
bluffer [blœfe] **1** *vt F* to take in, to trick; *Cartes* to bluff **2** *vi* to bluff; **il ne fait que b.** he's only bluffing, *Br* he's just trying it on
bluffeur, -euse [blœfœr, -øz] *n* bluffer
blush [blœʃ] *nm* (*fard*) blusher
blutage [blytaʒ] *nm* (*de la farine*) bolting
bluter [blyte] *vt* (*farine*) to bolt
BN [beɛn] *nf abrév* **Bibliothèque Nationale**
boa [bɔa] *nm* (**a**) (*serpent*) boa; **b. constricteur** boa constrictor (**b**) (*tour de cou*) boa
boat people [botpipəl] *nmpl* boat people
bob [bɔb] *nm* (**a**) *Sp F* bob(sleigh) (**b**) *F* (*chapeau*) sun hat
bobard [bɔbar] *nm F* tall story
bobinage [bɔbinaʒ] *nm* (**a**) (*opération*) winding, reeling (**b**) *Él* coil
bobine [bɔbin] *nf* (**a**) (*de ruban, fil etc*) reel; (*dans une machine à coudre*) bobbin; (*de machine à écrire, d'appareil photo etc*) spool; (*de film, de papier etc*) roll (**b**) *Él* coil; **b. de dérivation** shunt coil; **b. d'allumage** ignition coil; **b. HT** ht coil; **b. d'induction** induction coil; **b. exploratrice** pick-up coil; **b. haute tension** high-tension coil; **b. magnétique** magnet coil; **b. réceptrice** pick-up coil; **b. à faible inductance** low-inductance coil (**c**) *Arg* (*visage*) mug, face; **elle a fait une drôle de b.** she pulled a (funny) face
bobiner [bɔbine] *vt* (*fil de coton etc*) to wind, to reel; (*fil de fer etc*) to coil

bobineur, -euse [bɔbinœr, -øz] **1** *n Tex, Él* winder **2** *nf* **bobineuse** winding machine, winder

bobinoir [bɔbinwar] *nm Tex, Él* winding machine, winder

bobo [bobo] *nm Enf (blessure légère)* cut; **ça fait b.?** does it hurt?, is it sore?; **j'ai un b. au doigt** my finger hurts; **se faire b.** to hurt oneself

bobonne [bɔbɔn] *nf Arg Péj* missus, old girl; **il est toujours accompagné de b.** he always has his missus *or* old girl with him

bobsleigh [bɔbslɛ(g)] *nm Sp* bobsleigh

bobtail [bɔbtɛjl] *nm (chien)* bobtail

bocage [bɔkaʒ] *nm* **(a)** *Litt (bois)* copse **(b)** *Géog* bocage *(countryside with many hedges, trees and small fields)*

bocager, -ère [bɔkaʒe, -ɛr] *adj* wooded

bocal, -aux [bɔkal, -o] *nm* jar; **mettre des fruits en bocaux** to bottle fruit; **b. à poissons rouges** goldfish bowl

bocard [bɔkar] *nm Métal* ore crusher, stamping mill

Boccace [bɔkas] *nm* Boccaccio

boche [bɔʃ] *F Péj* **1** *adj* Boche, Kraut **2** *n* **B.** Boche, Kraut

bock [bɔk] *nm* **(a)** *(verre)* beer glass **(b)** *(contenu)* glass of beer *(approx 4 l. or 2 pt)*

bocson [bɔksɔ̃] *nm F* **quel b.!** what a shambles!; **ils ont mis le b. dans la chambre** they make a real mess in the room

body [bɔdi] *nm (vêtement)* body

body-building *nm Sp* body building; **faire du b.** to do body building

Boer [bur] *adj, n* Boer

boët(t)e [bwɛt] *nf Pêche* bait

bœuf, *pl* **bœufs** [bœf, bø] **1** *nm* **(a)** [①A13,4] *(mammifère)* bullock, steer; *(de trait)* ox; **bœufs à l'engrais** beeves; **b. gras** fatted ox, prize ox; **bœufs de boucherie** beef cattle; **fort comme un b.** as strong as an ox; *F* **on n'est pas des bœufs** I'm/we're not superhuman; **avoir un b. sur la langue** to keep mum

(b) *(viande)* beef

(c) *Mus* jam session; **faire un b.** to have a jam session, to jam

2 *adj inv F* fantastic, tremendous, amazing; **il a eu un succès b.** he was incredibly successful; **ça a fait un effet b.** it made a really big impression

▶ **bœuf**: *Zool* **b. à bosse** zebu; **b. bourguignon** bœuf bourguignon; **b. gros sel** boiled beef; *Culin* **b. (à la) mode** stewed beef; **b. musqué** musk ox

bof [bɔf] *int* **ça te plaît? – b., pas tellement** do you like it? – not really, no; **ça te dirait de venir avec nous? – b.** would you like to come with us? – I don't know *or* I'm not bothered; **il est chouette, hein, mon nouveau pull? – b.** my new sweater's great, isn't it? – I suppose so

bogie [bɔʒi], **boggie** [bɔgi] *nm Rail* bogie, bogy

bogue [bɔg] *nf* **(a)** *Bot* chestnut bur, *Am* shuck **(b)** *Ordinat* bug; **dépourvu/plein de bogues** bug-free/-ridden; **b. de logiciel** software bug

bohème [bɔɛm] **1** *adj* bohemian; **un esprit b.** an unconventional thinker **2** *n* bohemian; **mener une vie de b.** to lead a bohemian *or* an unconventional life **3** *nf* **la bohème** *(milieu)* bohemia

Bohême [bɔɛm] *nf* Bohemia

bohémien, -ienne [bɔemjɛ̃, -jɛn] **1** *adj* Bohemian **2** *n* gipsy

boire[1] [bwar] *nm* **le b. et le manger** food and drink, eating and drinking; *Fig* **il était si triste qu'il en a perdu le b. et le manger** he was so upset that he couldn't eat or drink; *Can* **c'est l'heure de son b.** *(tétée)* it's his feeding time

boire[2] *(prp* **buvant**; *pp* **bu, bue**; *pr ind* **je bois** [bwa], **il boit, n. buvons, ils boivent**; *pr sub* **je boive, n. buvions**; *impf* **je buvais**; *p hist* **je bus, n. bûmes**; *fu* **je boirai)** **1** *vt* **(a)** *(avaler)* to drink; **b. qch à petits coups** to sip sth; **b. qch d'un (seul) trait** *ou* **d'un seul coup** to drink sth at one gulp, to swig sth down, *Br* to knock sth back; **je ne bois pas d'alcool** I don't drink (alcohol); **b. une bouteille à quatre** to drink a bottle between four; **b. un verre jusqu'à la dernière goutte** to drain a glass; *F* **b. un coup** to have a drink; **il a bu un coup (de trop)** he's had one too many; **tu viens b. un verre?** are you coming for a drink?; *Fig* **b. les paroles de qn** to drink in sb's every word; *F* **b. la** *ou* **une tasse** *(en nageant)* to get a mouthful; *Fig F* **ce n'est pas la mer à b.** it's not that bad, it's no big deal; **b. un bouillon** *(en nageant)* to get a mouthful; *Fin* to make a big loss, to come a cropper; *Fig* **il boit du petit lait** *(il est content)* he's as pleased as Punch; **quand on le flatte, il boit du petit lait** when people flatter him he laps it up

(b) *(des plantes, des matières poreuses etc) (eau)* to soak up, to absorb

2 *vi* **(a)** *(d'une personne)* to drink; *(des plantes)* to soak up *or* absorb water; *Can (d'un bébé)* to feed; **b. à la bouteille** to drink from the bottle; **b. à sa soif, b. jusqu'à plus soif** to drink one's fill; **b. à la santé de qn** to drink (to) sb's health; **b. au succès de qch** to drink to the success of sth; **faire b. qn** to give sb a drink *or* something to drink; **faire b. les chevaux** to water the horses; *Fig* **il y a à b. et à manger là-dedans** it's got its good and its bad points, it's a bit of a mixed bag; *Prov* **qui a bu boira** old habits die hard; **il a commandé à boire** *(pour lui)* he ordered a drink; *(pour deux, trois etc)* he ordered the drinks; **vous avez commandé à b.?** have you ordered something to drink?

(b) *(d'un alcoolique)* to drink; **tu bois trop** you drink too much; **elle boit comme un trou** she drinks like a fish; **je ne sais pas b.** I'm not much of a drinker

3 se boire *vpr (de boisson)* to be drunk; **les vins sucrés se boivent au dessert** sweet wines are drunk with dessert; **ce vin se boit bien** *ou* **se laisse b.** this wine is very drinkable *or* goes down well

bois [bwa] *nm* **(a)** *(forêt)* wood; **petit b.** grove, *Br* spinney; **b. de chênes/sapins** oak/fir wood; **Robin des B.** Robin Hood; **je n'aimerais pas le rencontrer un soir au coin d'un b.** I wouldn't like to meet him in a dark alley

(b) *(arbres)* timber (trees); **abattre** *ou* **couper le b.** to cut down *or* fell timber; *F* **casser du b.** *(d'un avion)* to crash-land

(c) *(matériau)* wood; **petit b.** kindling; **chantier de b.** timber yard; **travail du b.** woodwork; **train de b.** float *or* raft of timber; **jambe de b.** wooden leg; **meubles en b.** wooden furniture; *Can* **maison en b. rond** log house; *Fig* **elle n'est pas de b.** she's only human; *Fig* **être du b. dont on fait les flûtes** to be easy-going; *Fig* **je leur ferai voir de quel b. je me chauffe** I'll show them (what I'm made of); *F* **touchez du b.!** touch wood!, *Am* knock on wood!; *F* **chèque en b.** rubber cheque, cheque that bounces

(d) *(gravure)* woodcut

(e) *(de chaise, raquette etc)* frame; *Tennis* **faire un b.** to hit the ball off the wood *or* the frame

(f) *Mus* **les b.** the woodwind

(g) les bois *(d'un cerf)* the antlers

▶ **bois**: **b. blanc** deal, whitewood; **b. à brûler** firewood; **b. de charpente** timber, *Am* lumber; **b. de chauffage** firewood; *surtout Can* **b. debout** standing timber; **b. dur** hardwood; *Can* **b. franc** hardwood; **b. des îles** West Indian hardwood; **b. de lit** bedstead; **b. de mai** hawthorn; **b. mort** deadwood; **b. d'œuvre** timber, *Am* lumber; **b. de rose** rosewood; **b. de sapin** deal, whitewood; **b. tendre** softwood; **b. vert** unseasoned *or* green timber

boisage [bwazaʒ] *nm Min* **(a)** *(action) (d'un puits, d'une galerie etc)* timbering **(b)** *(ensemble des bois)* timbering, timber work

boisé [bwaze] *adj (région)* wooded; **pays b.** woodland(s), wooded country

boisement [bwazmɑ̃] *nm (d'une région)* afforestation

boiser [bwaze] *vt* **(a)** *(planter d'arbres)* to afforest, to plant with trees **(b)** *(mine, galerie)* to timber

boiserie [bwazri] *nf Constr* woodwork, wainscot(ing), panelling

boisseau, -eaux [bwaso] *nm* **(a)** *Arch, Can (mesure)* bushel; *Fig* **mettre la lumière sous le b.** to keep things hidden **(b)** *Tech (tuyau)* drain tile; *(de cheminée)* chimney (flue) tile; *(de moteur)* throttle chamber

boisson [bwasɔ̃] *nf* **(a)** *(liquide à boire)* drink, *Fml* beverage; **b. gazeuse** fizzy drink; **b. fraîche** cold drink; **boissons alcoolisées/non alcoolisées** alcoholic/soft drinks; **b. chaude** hot drink **(b)** *(alcool)* drink; **il s'est adonné à la b.** he's taken to drink; **pris de b.** inebriated, intoxicated; **débit de boissons** bar **(c)** *Can (spiritueux)* hard liquor, spirits

boîte [bwat] *nf* **(a)** *(récipient)* box; *(de conserves)* can, *Br* tin; **b. à bijoux** jewel box; **b. à couture** *ou* **ouvrage** sewing box; **b. en fer** tin; **une b. de chocolats** a box of chocolates; **des haricots en b.** canned *or Br* tinned beans; *TV, Cin* **en b.** in the can; **mettre en b.** *(marchandises)* to box; *(sardines, légumes etc)* to can, *Br* to tin; *Fig F* **mettre qn en b.** to pull sb's leg; **b. à violon** violin case; *Fig F* **fermer sa b.** to shut one's trap *or* mouth

(b) *Tech (de serrure)* case

(c) *F (entreprise)* firm; *(école)* school; **je travaille dans une b. d'informatique** I work for a computer firm *or* company; **sale b.** rotten hole

(d) b. (de nuit) nightclub; **aller** *ou* **sortir en b.** to go (out) to a nightclub

▶ **boîte**: **b. d'allumettes** *(pleine)* box of matches; *(vide)* matchbox; **b. à bachot** crammer; **b. de conserve** can, *Br* tin; **ils se nourrissent de boîtes de conserve** they live on canned *or Br* tinned food; *Anat* **b. crânienne** *ou* **du crâne** cranium; **b. de dérivation** junction box; **b. de l'embrayage** clutch casing; *Rail* **b. de l'essieu** axle box; **b. à feu** firebox;

Él **b. à fusibles** fuse box; *Aut* **b. à gants** glove compartment; **b. à** *ou* **aux lettres** (*pour envoyer*) letterbox, postbox, pillarbox, *Am* mailbox; (*chez soi*) letterbox, *Am* mailbox; **b. à lettres électronique** electronic mailbox, e-mail box; **b. à malice** secret toy box; **b. à musique**, music box, *Br* musical box; *Av* **b. noire** flight recorder, black box; **b. à outils** toolbox; **b. à pain** bread bin; **b. postale** Post Office Box; **b. à rythmes** drum machine; **b. de secours** first-aid box; **b. à vapeur** steam chest; *Aut* **b. de vitesses** gearbox

boîte-pont, *pl* **boîtes-ponts** *nf Aut* transaxle

boiter [bwate] *vi* (*en marchant*) to limp, to walk with a limp; **b. d'un pied** to be lame in one foot; **b. bas** to limp badly

boiterie [bwatri] *nf* lameness

boiteux, -euse [bwatø, -øz] **1** *adj* (*personne, cheval*) lame; *Fig* (*meuble*) wobbly, rickety; (*explication*) lame; (*raisonnement, projet*) shaky; (*traduction, phrase*) iffy; (*paix*) fragile, uncertain; (*période*) uncertain; **le facteur est b.** the postman walks with *or* has a limp; **vers b.** limping verses; **cette phrase est un peu boiteuse** this sentence doesn't hang together very well *or* doesn't work very well **2** *n* lame man, *f* woman

boîtier [bwatje] *nm* case, casing, housing; *Phot* (camera) body; **b. de montre** watch case; **b. de chirurgien** surgeon's instrument case

▶ **boîtier**: *Ordinat* **b. de commande** command box; *Ordinat* **b. commutateur** data switch; *Ordinat* **b. compact** compact case; *Aut* **b. de direction** steering box; *Aut* **b. de direction à crémaillère** rack and pinion steering box; *Ordinat* **b. grande tour** large tower case; *Ordinat* **b. mini-tour** minitower case; *Ordinat* **b. moyenne tour** miditower case; *Ordinat* **b. de partage** (*pour imprimante*) data switch; *Aut* **b. de raccordement** junction box; **b. de télécommande** remote control; *Ordinat* **b. vertical** vertical case

boitillement [bwatijmɑ̃] *nm* slight limp

boitiller [bwatije] *vi* to limp slightly, to have a slight limp

boit-sans-soif [bwa-] *nm inv Arg* boozer, tippler

bol[1] [bɔl] *nm* **(a)** *Physiol* **b. alimentaire** (alimentary) bolus **(b)** *Pharm, Vét* bolus, pellet

bol[2] *nm* **(a)** (*pièce de vaisselle*) bowl **(b)** *Arg* (*chance*) luck; **manque de b.** bad luck; **coup de b.** stroke of luck; **ne pas avoir de b.** to be unlucky, to be out of luck; **pas de b.!** what rotten luck! **(c)** (*contenu*) bowl(ful); **avaler son b. de café** to drink one's coffee; **on a pris un b. d'air frais** *ou* **pur** we got a good breath of fresh air

bolchevik [bɔlʃəvik, bɔlʃevik] *adj, n* Bolshevik, Bolshevist

bolchevisme [bɔlʃəvism, bɔlʃevism] *nm* Bolshevism

bolcheviste [bɔlʃəvist, bɔlʃevist] *adj, n* Bolshevik, Bolshevist

bolduc [bɔldyk] *nm* gift-wrap ribbon

bolée [bɔle] *nf* (*de cidre etc*) bowl(ful)

boléro [bɔlero] *nm* (*vêtement*), *Mus* bolero

bolet [bɔlɛ] *nm* (*champignon*) boletus

bolide [bɔlid] *nm* (*voiture de course*) racing car; *Astron* meteor, fireball, *Spéc* bolide; **lancé comme un b. sur la route** hurtling along the road; **s'éloigner** *ou* **partir comme un b.** to shoot off like a rocket; **il est arrivé comme un bolide** he arrived at top speed

bolivar [bolivar] *nm* (*monnaie*) bolivar

Bolivie [bɔlivi] *nf* Bolivia

bolivien, -ienne [bɔlivjɛ̃, -jɛn] **1** *adj* Bolivian **2** *n* **B.** Bolivian

bolognais, -aise [bɔlɔɲɛ, -ɛz] **1** *adj* Bolognese; *Culin* **spaghetti bolognaise** spaghetti bolognese; **sauce bolognaise** bolognese sauce **2** *n* **B.** Bolognese

Bologne [bɔlɔɲ] *nf* Bologna

bombage [bɔ̃baʒ] *nm F* (aerosol) graffiti; **faire des bombages sur un mur** to spray-paint a wall with graffiti

bombance [bɔ̃bɑ̃s] *nf F* feast; **faire b.** to go on a spree *or* a binge; (*manger*) to feast

bombardement [bɔ̃bardəmɑ̃] *nm* **(a)** (*avec des obus*) bombardment, shelling; (*avec des bombes*) bombing, bombardment; (*avec des pierres etc*) pelting; (*avec des questions etc*) bombarding; **b. de questions** flood of questions; **b. aérien** air raid; **avion de b.** bomber; **le b. atomique d'Hiroshima** the dropping of the atomic bomb on Hiroshima **(b)** *Phys* bombardment

bombarder [bɔ̃barde] *vt* **(a)** (*avec des obus*) to bombard, to shell; (*avec des bombes*) to bomb, to bombard; **maison bombardée** shelled/bombed house; **b. qn de pierres** to pelt sb with stones; **b. qn de questions** to fire questions at sb, to bombard sb with questions; **être bombardé de lettres/coups de téléphone** to be bombarded *or* inundated with letters/phone calls **(b)** *Phys* (*de neutrons etc*) to bombard **(de** with) **(c)** *F* **on l'a bombardé ministre** he's been pitchforked into the post of minister *or* made a minister out of the blue

bombardier [bɔ̃bardje] *nm Mil* **(a)** *Av* (*avion*) bomber; (*aviateur*) bombardier **(b)** *Arch* bombardier

bombe [bɔ̃b] *nf* **(a)** *Mil etc* bomb; **b. de fabrication artisanale** homemade bomb; **attaque** *ou* **attentat à la b.** bomb attack; **lâcher** *ou* **larguer une b.** to release *or* drop a bomb; *F* **entrer en** *ou* **comme une b.** to come bursting in; *Fig* **cela a fait l'effet d'une b.** it was a real bombshell **(b)** (*atomiseur*) spray, aerosol; **b. de peinture/d'insecticide** paint/fly spray; **déodorant en b.** deodorant spray **(c)** *Équitation* riding hat *or* cap **(d)** *F* **faire la b.** to live it up

▶ **bombe**: **b. A** A bomb; **b. atomique** atom(ic) bomb; *Méd* **b. au cobalt** cobalt bomb; **b. à eau** water bomb; **b. à fragmentation** fragmentation *or* scatter bomb; **b. fumigène** smoke bomb; *Culin* **b. glacée** bombe glacée; **b. H** H bomb; **b. à hydrogène** hydrogen bomb; **b. incendiaire** fire bomb, incendiary bomb; **b. lacrymogène** tear-gas grenade; **b. au plastic** plastic bomb; **b. à retardement** time bomb, delayed-action bomb; **b. volante** flying bomb, *F* doodlebug

bombé [bɔ̃be] *adj* bulging; (*forme*) rounded, curved; **avoir le front b.** to have a bulging forehead; **se tenir droit, la poitrine bombée** to stand up straight with one's chest thrown out; **chaussée bombée** cambered road

bombement [bɔ̃bmɑ̃] *nm* bulge, bulging; (*d'une route*) camber

bomber [bɔ̃be] **1** *vt* **(a)** (*gonfler*) to cause to bulge; (*route*) to camber; **b. la poitrine** *ou* **le torse** to throw out one's chest; *Fig* to swagger (around) **(b)** (*écrire à la bombe*) to spray; **b. des graffiti/des slogans** to spray graffiti/slogans **2** *vi* (*d'un mur etc*) to bulge (out)

bombonne [bɔ̃bɔn] *nf* = **bonbonne**

bôme [bom] *nf Naut* boom

bon[1], bonne [bɔ̃, bɔn] **1** *adj* **(a)** (*moralement*) good; **le b. M. Seguin** good old Mr Seguin; **mon b. monsieur** my dear sir; **défendre la bonne cause** to fight the good fight; **bonne action** good deed; *F* **b. chic b. genre** ≈ Sloany, *Am* ≈ preppy; **la bonne société** polite society

(b) (*agréable*) (*livre, histoire, odeur, ambiance, travail etc*) good; **bonne soirée** pleasant evening; **installé dans un b. fauteuil** settled in a nice *or* comfortable armchair; **j'ai trouvé b. le rôti** I enjoyed the roast, I thought the roast was good; **je ne trouve pas ça très b.** I don't think it's very good, I don't much like it; **qu'est-ce que c'est b.!** that's really good!; **l'eau est bonne** (*en se baignant*) the water's great; **elle est bonne?** (*en se baignant*) what's the water like?; **ils aiment les bonnes choses** they like the good things in life; **elle lui fait de bons petits plats** she makes him nice little meals; **être en bonne compagnie** to be in good company; **être de bonne compagnie** to be good company

(c) (*capable, apte*) good; **un b. médecin/père** a good doctor/father; **les bons élèves** the good *or* bright pupils; **b. en anglais** good at English; *Fin* **b. pour aval** guaranteed by

(d) (*correct*) (*travail, qualité etc*) good; (*réponse, clé, côté, bus etc*) right; **si j'ai bonne mémoire** if my memory serves me (well); **c'est de la bonne qualité** it's good quality; **oui, c'est b.** yes, that's right; **maintenant, c'est b.** (*à qn qui fixe une étagère etc*) it's right *or* fine now; **pour le b. fonctionnement de l'appareil** to ensure the appliance functions correctly; **pour lui, tous les moyens sont bons pour réussir** he'll do anything to succeed, he'll stop at nothing to succeed; **prends le marteau par le b. bout** hold the hammer the right way round; **tourner dans le b. sens** to turn in the right direction; **un intellectuel, dans le b. sens du terme** an intellectual in the true sense of the term; **en b. état** in good condition; *Fig* **frapper/ne pas frapper à la bonne porte** to come to the right/wrong person; *Fig* **la bonne voie** *ou* **route** the right path *or* track; **il a encore de bonnes jambes** he still has a good pair of legs; **avoir une bonne vue** to have good eyesight; **sa vue n'est plus très bonne** he doesn't see too well any more; *Tennis* **la balle est bonne** the ball is in *or* good; **les yaourts sont-ils encore bons?** are the yoghurts still good *or* all right?; **le fusible n'est plus b., il faut le changer** the fuse has gone, we'll have to change it

(e) (*généreux*) good, kind (**pour, envers, avec** to); **c'est un b. garçon** *ou F* **type** *ou* **gars** he's a good sort, he's all right; **tu es trop bonne pour moi** you're too good to me; **être b. avec** *ou* **envers les animaux** to be kind to animals; **c'est parti d'une bonne intention, l'intention était bonne** the intention was good; **être b. public** to be a good audience; **vous êtes bien b. de m'inviter** it's very good *or* kind of you to invite me; *Iron F* **tu es b.!** oh very funny!

(f) (*profitable, utile*) (*investissement etc*) good; **bonne affaire** bargain; **c'est b. à savoir/à se rappeler** it's worth knowing/remembering; **c'est toujours b. à avoir** it's always worth having; **à quoi b.?** what's the point?, what's the good of it?; **à quoi b. se plaindre?** what's the use *or* the good *or* the point of complaining?; **c'est un b. conseil** it's a good piece of advice; **quelle bonne idée!** what a good idea!; **puis-**

je vous être b. à quelque chose? can I do anything for you?, can I be of any help (to you)?; **cet exercice est b. pour le dos** this exercise is good for the back; **ce qui est b. pour les uns n'est pas toujours b. pour les autres** what is good for some is not necessarily good for others

(g) **b. à manger** good to eat; (*comestible*) fit *or* safe to eat; **b. pour le service** *Mil* fit for duty; *Fig* serviceable; **c'est b. pour les nerfs** it's good for your nerves; **il n'est b. qu'à cela** that's all he's fit for; **elle n'est bonne à rien** she's useless, she's good for nothing, she's no good at anything; **c'est b. à jeter** you can throw that away, *F* chuck it out

(h) (*souhaitable*) **si b. vous semble** if you think it advisable; **il est b. de s'en informer tout de suite** it's best to get information straightaway; **il est b. que vous le sachiez** it's just as well that you should know; **juger** *ou* **croire** *ou* **trouver b. de faire qch** to think it best *or* advisable to do sth

(i) (*présage*) good, favourable, *US* favorable; **souhaiter une** *ou* **la bonne année à qn** to wish sb a happy New Year; **b. Noël** Merry Christmas; **b. anniversaire!** happy birthday!; **avoir la bonne vie** to have it easy; **b. week-end!**, *Can* **bonne fin de semaine!** have a good weekend!; **bonne chasse!** good hunting!; **b. voyage!** have a good trip!, bon voyage!; **bonne journée!** have a good *or* nice day!; **b. appétit!** bon appetit!; (*surtout dans un restaurant*) enjoy your meal, *Am F* enjoy!; **bonne nuit** good night; **bonnes vacances!** have a good *or* enjoy your holiday

(j) (*caution, crédit etc*) good; **billet b. pour trois mois** ticket valid *or* good for three months; **ta carte d'étudiant n'est plus bonne** your student card isn't valid any more *or* is out of date; *Com* **b. pour une entrée gratuite/cinq francs de réduction sur votre prochain achat** this entitles you to free admission/to five francs off your next purchase; **son affaire est bonne!, son compte est b.!** he's in for it!; **elle est bonne pour deux mois de prison** she's looking at *or* she's going to get two months in prison; **tu es b. pour la contravention** you're in for a fine; *F* **on est b.!** (*c'est raté*) we've had it!

(k) (*intensif*) good; **j'ai attendu deux bonnes heures** I waited a full *or* a good two hours, I waited (for) two solid hours; **deux bons kilos** two good kilos; **il m'a fallu un b. moment pour comprendre** it took me a (good *or* little) while to understand; **arriver b. premier** to come in an easy first; **il était b. dernier** he was way behind all the others, he brought up the rear; **b. nombre de** a number of, a good many; **prendre une bonne moitié de qch** to take a good half of sth; **donner bonne mesure** to give good *or* full measure; **elle a reçu une bonne fessée** she got a good spanking; **b. gros rire** big resounding laugh; **un b. rhume** a bad cold; **il faudrait qu'on ait une bonne discussion** we must have a good *or* proper discussion *or* talk; **une bonne fois pour toutes** once and for all

(l) *Litt* **tout de b.** in earnest, really; **est-ce pour de b.?** are you serious?; **on se quitte pour de b.** we're splitting up for good; **il pleut pour de b.** it's raining in real earnest; **cette fois, elle pleure pour de b.** this time she's really crying

(m) **b.!** right!, good!, fine!; **b., je viendrai** right *or* good *or* fine, I'll come; **il est malade, allons b.?** he's ill, eh?; **ah b., je ne le savais pas** oh, I didn't know; **b., b., d'accord** all right, all right, OK, OK; **c'est b., j'ai compris** all right *or* OK, I understand

2 *adv* **tenir b.** (*résister*) to stand fast, to hold one's own; **tenez b.!** hold tight!, hold on (tight)!; (*ne lâchez pas*) don't give up *or* in; **sentir b.** to smell good; **il fait b. vivre** it's good to be alive; **un pays où il fait b. vivre** a country that's good to live in; **il ne fait pas b. se promener dans ce quartier** it's not safe to walk in this district

3 *n* **les bons** the good, the righteous; *F* (*dans un film etc*) the goodies; **une histoire de bons et de méchants** a goodies and baddies story; **un b. /une bonne à rien** a good-for-nothing

4 *nm* **cela a du b.** it has its good points, it has some advantages, there's some good in it; **il y a du b. à ne pas travailler** there's something to be said for not working; **le b. de l'histoire** the best part of the story

5 bonne *nf voir* **bonne**

bon² *nm* (a) (*billet*) voucher, coupon, slip (b) *Fin* bond, bill; **b. d'exécution de contrôle** performance bond

▶ **bon: b. d'achat** gift voucher; **b. d'agence** (*d'une agence de voyages*) travel agent's voucher; **b. d'annulation** cancellation form; **b. de caisse** (*justifiant sortie de fonds*) cash voucher; *Compta* interest-bearing note; *Typ* **b. à clicher** machine proof; **b. de commande** order form; *Typ* **b. à copier** machine proof; **b. de débours** (*pour services aux clients d'un hôtel*) visitors paid out voucher, VPO voucher; **b. de décaissement** disbursement voucher, paid out voucher; **b. d'échange** (*d'une agence de voyages*) (travel agent's) voucher; *Com* **b. d'entrée** stock received docket/form; **b. d'épargne** savings certificate; **b. d'essence** petrol coupon; *Com* **b. d'expédition** dispatch note, consignment note; **b. de garantie** guarantee; *Com* guarantee slip; *Com* **b. de livraison** delivery note; **b. au porteur** bearer bond; **b. de réception des marchandises** receipt note; **b. de réduction** money-off coupon *or* voucher, discount voucher; *Com* **b. de remboursement** money-off voucher; **b. de réservation** reservation form; *Com* **b. de sortie** stock issued docket/form; *Fin* **b. de souscription d'actions** warrant; *Tex* **b. teint** *adj* colourfast; (*couleur*) fast; *Fig* (*syndicaliste, socialiste etc*) dyed-in-the-wool, staunch; **b. à tirer 1** *nm* final proof; **donner le b. à tirer** to pass the proofs for press **2** *adj* ready to go to press; **b. du Trésor** treasury bond, exchequer bill; **b. vacances** voucher supplied by holiday associations to less well-off families to help cover holiday expenses

bonace [bɔnas] *nf* lull, calm (*before or after a storm*)

bonapartisme [bɔnapartism] *nm* Bonapartism

bonapartiste [bɔnapartist] *adj, n* Bonapartist

bonard [bɔnar] *adj F* great

bonasse [bɔnas] *adj Péj* soft, mild; **il est b.** he's too easy-going *or* too soft; **répondre d'un ton b.** to answer mildly

bonbon [bɔ̃bɔ̃] *nm* (a) sweet, *Am* candy, *Austr* lolly; **b. anglais** fruit drop; **b. acidulé** acid drop; **b. à la menthe** mint (b) *Belg* (*biscuit*) biscuit

bonbonne [bɔ̃bɔn] *nf* (a) *Ind* carboy (b) (*récipient*) demijohn; **b. en verre** glass demijohn; **une b. de vin** a demijohn of wine

bonbonnière [bɔ̃bɔnjɛr] *nf* (a) (*pour les bonbons*) sweet *or Am* candy box, bonbonnière (b) *Fig* bijou residence

bond [bɔ̃] *nm* (a) (*saut*) leap, bound, spring, jump; **faire un b.** to leap up, to jump up; **franchir qch d'un b.** to clear sth at one bound *or* leap *or* jump; **se lever d'un b.** to spring *or* to leap *or* to jump to one's feet; **les loyers/prix ont fait un b.** rents/prices have shot up; **progresser par bonds** to advance by leaps and bounds; **je fais un b. en ville** I'm just dashing *or Br* nipping into town; **b. en avant** (*technologique etc*) breakthrough

(b) (*d'une balle etc*) bounce, rebound; **saisir** *ou* **prendre la balle au b.** to catch the ball on the bounce *or* the rebound; *Fig* to seize *or* grasp the opportunity; **faire faux b. à qn** to leave sb in the lurch, to let sb down

bonde [bɔ̃d] *nf* (a) (*bouchon*) (*d'un évier, d'une baignoire*) plug; (*d'un tonneau*) bung; (*d'un bassin*) sluice gate; **lâcher** *ou* **lever la b.** to pull the plug out; *Fig* **lâcher la b. à sa colère** to give vent to one's anger (b) (*trou d'évacuation*) (*d'un évier, d'une baignoire*) plughole; (*d'un tonneau*) bunghole; (*d'un bassin*) drainage hole, outlet

bondé [bɔ̃de] *adj* (*bus, cinéma, ville etc*) packed, jam-packed; **des trains bondés de vacanciers** trains packed *or* crammed with holiday makers; *Th* **salle bondée** packed house

bondieuserie [bɔ̃djøzri] *nf Péj* (a) (*bigoterie*) religiosity, over-religious zeal (b) (*objet*) devotional object, religious knick-knack

bondir [bɔ̃dir] *vi* (a) (*sauter*) to leap (up), to spring (up), to jump (up); **b. en avant/arrière** to leap *or* spring *or* jump forward/back; **b. sur qch/qn** to pounce on sth/sb; *Fig* **il a bondi de colère** he flew into a rage; *Fig* **cela me fait b.** it makes me mad, it makes me see red

(b) (*courir*) to rush (off), to dash (off); **j'ai bondi jusqu'à la poste la plus proche** I rushed (off) *or* dashed (off) to the nearest post office; **b. au secours de qn** *ou* **pour aider qn** to spring *or* leap to sb's assistance

(c) (*gambader*) to gambol, to leap (about), to skip (about)

(d) (*d'une balle etc*) to bounce

bondissement [bɔ̃dismɑ̃] *nm* (a) (*saut*) bound, leap (b) (*des agneaux etc*) gambolling, frisking

bon enfant [bɔnɑ̃fɑ̃] *adj inv* (*personne, manières etc*) easy-going, good-natured; (*atmosphère*) easy-going

bonheur [bɔnœr] *nm* (a) (*chance*) good fortune, (good) luck; **j'ai eu le b. de la connaître** I had the good fortune to know her; **porter b. à qn** to bring sb (good) luck; **il ne connaît pas son b.** he doesn't know how lucky he is, he doesn't know his luck; **quel b.!** how marvellous!; **par b.** luckily, fortunately, as luck would have it; **au petit b. (la chance)** at random

(b) (*bien-être*) happiness; **la recherche du b.** the quest for happiness; **le b. de vivre** the joy of living; **faire le b. de qn** to make sb happy; **ces chocolats font mon b.** I adore these chocolates; **l'argent ne fait pas le b.** money can't buy you happiness; **il fait tout pour mon b.** he does everything he can to make me happy; **j'ai eu le b. de voir ma fille naître** I had the joy of seeing my daughter being born; **quel b. de voyager en avion** what a pleasure *or* delight it is to travel by air

(c) *Litt* (*réussite*) **avec b.** felicitously; **texte écrit avec b.** felicitous text; **le salé et le sucré s'allient avec b.** savoury and sweet combine happily *or* are a happy combination

bonheur-du-jour, *pl* **bonheurs-du-jour** *nm* escritoire
bonhomie [bɔnɔmi] *nf* good-heartedness, good-naturedness, bonhomie; **avec b.** goodnaturedly
bonhomme, *pl* **bonshommes** [bɔnɔm, bɔ̃zɔm] *nm F* (*homme, type*) fellow, guy, *Br* chap, *Br* bloke; **un petit b.** a little fellow; **un vilain b.** a nasty piece of work; **c'est un sacré b.** he's a hell of a guy; **pourquoi pleures-tu, mon b.?** (*à un petit garçon*) what are you crying for, little fellow?; *Fig* **il va son petit b. de chemin** he's jogging along nicely; **dessiner des bonshommes** to draw little people
▶ **bonhomme**: **b. de neige** snowman; **faire un b. de neige** to make *or* build a snowman; **b. de** *ou* **en pain d'épice** gingerbread man; *Mec* **b. de verrouillage** plunger
boni [bɔni] *nm* (*bénéfice*) profit; (*excédent*) surplus, balance in hand
boniche [bɔniʃ] *nf Péj* (maid)servant, *Br* skivvy; **je ne suis pas ta b., fais-le tout seul!** I'm not your servant, do it yourself!; **faire la b. pour qn** to do sb's menial jobs for them, *Br* to skivvy for sb
bonification [bɔnifikasjɔ̃] *nf* (**a**) (*d'une terre, d'un vin*) improvement (**b**) *Com* bonus; **b. pour non sinistre** no claims bonus (**c**) *Sp* advantage
bonifié [bɔnifje] *adj* (*prêt*) at a reduced rate of interest
bonifier [bɔnifje] (*pr sub & impf* **n. bonifiions, v. bonifiiez**) **1** *vt* (**a**) (*terre, caractère etc*) to improve (**b**) *Com* (*pénurie etc*) to make up, to make good **2 se bonifier** *vpr* (*d'une personne, du vin etc*) to improve; **ses humeurs vont se b. avec le temps** his nature will improve with time
boniment [bɔnimɑ̃] *nm* (**a**) *Com* sales talk *or* pitch, patter; **faire du b. à qn** (*d'un vendeur*) to give sb the sales talk *or* the patter; **faire du b. à une femme** to chat a woman up; **faire du b. à qn pour qu'il fasse qch** to try to coax *or* talk sb into doing sth (**b**) *F* (*blague*) tall story; **tout ça c'est du b.** that's all eyewash *or* claptrap
bonimenter [bɔnimɑ̃te] *vi F* to dish out the sales talk *or* the patter
bonite [bɔnit] *nf* (*poisson*) bonito
bonjour [bɔ̃ʒur] *nm* (**a**) hello, *F* hi, *Fml* good day; (*le matin*) good morning; (*l'après-midi*) good afternoon; (*quand on est présenté à qn*) hello, how do you do?; **dis b. à la dame** (*à un enfant*) say hello to the lady; **(dis) b. à ta mère (de ma part)** (give) my regards *or* remember me to your mother, say hello to your mother for me; **c'est facile** *ou* **simple comme b.** it's as easy as pie, it's child's play

(**b**) *F Iron* **b. les dégâts!** what a mess!; (*ça va aller mal*) there'll be trouble!; **b. la soirée/l'odeur!** what an evening/smell!, *F* some bloody evening/smell!; **b. la propreté ici!** I don't think much of the way things are cleaned round here; **le périphérique le soir à six heures, b.!** the ring road at six o'clock at night, no way *or* forget it!
bon marché *adj inv* cheap; **acheter/vendre qch (à) b.** to buy/sell sth cheap(ly)
bonne [bɔn] *nf* (**a**) (*domestique*) maid, *Vieilli* maidservant; **b. à tout faire** general help, *Vieilli* maid of all work; **b. d'enfants** nurse, *Br* nanny (**b**) **en voilà une (bien) b.!** that's a good one!; **il en a de bonnes!** he must be joking *or* kidding!; **tu en as de bonnes!** you're having a laugh, aren't you?; **il m'en a raconté de bonnes sur toi!** he told me some interesting things about you!; **avoir qn à la b.** (*d'un employeur, d'un professeur*) to have a soft spot for sb; *F* **il t'a à la bonne** you're well in with him
Bonne-Espérance *n* **Cap de B.** Cape of Good Hope
bonne-maman, *pl* **bonnes-mamans** *nf Vieilli* grandmama
bonnement [bɔnmɑ̃] *adv* **tout b.** simply; **je lui ai dit tout b. que ...** I simply *or* just told him that ...
bonnet [bɔnɛ] *nm* (**a**) (*coiffure*) hat; (*de bébé*) bonnet; **b. de ski** ski cap; *Fig* **prendre qch sous son b.** (*faire de sa propre initiative*) to take it upon oneself to do sth, *F* to do sth off one's own bat; (*prendre la responsabilité*) to take on the responsibility for sth, to take sth on; **opiner du b.** to nod (one's) assent, to nod in agreement; *Fig* **avoir la tête près du b.** to have a short fuse; *Fig* **jeter son b. par dessus les moulins** to kick over the traces, to throw caution to the winds; **c'est b. blanc et blanc b.** it's six of one and half a dozen of the other; *Fig F* **gros b.** big shot, big noise, bigwig

(**b**) (*d'un soutien-gorge*) cup; **quelle profondeur de b.?** what size cup?

(**c**) *Zool* (*d'un ruminant*) second stomach, reticulum, honeycomb
▶ **bonnet**: **b. de bain** bathing *or* swimming cap; **b. de douche** shower cap; **b. d'évêque** bishop's mitre; **b. de nuit** nightcap; **être triste comme un b. de nuit** to be as cheerful as the grave; **b. phrygien** *ou* **rouge** Phrygian cap (*in French Revolution*); *Mil* **b. de police** forage cap
bonneterie [bɔnɛtri] *nf* (**a**) (*bas*) hosiery (**b**) (*commerce*) hosiery trade; (*magasin*) hosier's (shop)
bonnetier, -ière [bɔntje, -jɛr] *n* hosier
bonnette [bɔnɛt] *nf* (*objectif*) positive supplementary lens; (*de micro*) windshield; **b. anti-vent** (*d'un microphone*) windscreen, windshield
bonniche [bɔniʃ] *nf Péj* = **boniche**
bon-papa, *pl* **bons-papas** *nm Vieilli* grandpapa
bonsaï [bɔnzaj, bɔ̃zaj] *nm* (*arbre*) bonsai
bonsoir [bɔ̃swar] *nm* good evening; (*quand on se quitte tard, quand on se couche*) goodnight; **dire b.** *ou* **souhaiter le b. à qn** to say good evening/goodnight to sb
bonté [bɔ̃te] *nf* (**a**) (*qualité*) kindness, goodness, kindliness; **une femme d'une grande b.** a very kind *or* good woman; **sourire plein de b.** kind(ly) *or* benevolent smile; **ayez la b. de me dire ...** be so good as to tell me ..., please tell me ...; **auriez-vous la b. de ...?** would you be so good as to ...?; **faire qch par b. d'âme** to do sth out of the goodness *or* kindness of one's heart; *F* **b. divine** *ou* **du ciel!** good heavens!

(**b**) **bontés** kindnesses, acts of kindness, kind acts; **avoir des bontés pour qn** to show kindness towards sb; **remercier qn pour ses bontés** to thank sb for his/her kindness; **je ne m'attendais pas à tant de bontés** I didn't expect such kindness

(**c**) *Vieilli* (*de choses*) goodness, excellence
bonus [bɔnys] *nm* (*dans les assurances*) no-claims bonus
bon vivant 1 *adj* **il est b.** he enjoys life **2** *nm* man who enjoys life; **des bons vivants** people who enjoy life
bonze [bɔ̃z] *nm* (**a**) *Rel* Buddhist priest *or* monk, bonze (**b**) *Fig F* (*personnage important*) big shot, bigwig (**c**) *F* **vieux b.** bigheaded old fool
bonzerie [bɔ̃zri] *nf* Buddhist monastery
bonzesse [bɔ̃zɛs] *nf* Buddhist nun, bonze
boogie-woogie, *pl* **boogie-woogies** [bugiwugi] *nm Mus* boogie-woogie
book[1] [buk] *nm* **b. de contacts** contacts book
bookmaker [bukmɛkœr], *F* **book**[2] *nm* bookmaker, *F* bookie
booléen, -éenne [buleɛ̃, -eɛn] *adj Math, Ordinat* Boolean
boom [bum] *nm Com, Fin* boom
boomerang [bumrɑ̃g] *nm* boomerang; **avoir un effet b.** to have a boomerang effect; *F* **son projet a fait b.** his plan boomeranged *or* backfired
booster [bustœr] *nm* (*amplificateur*), *Astronaut* booster
booter [bute] *vi Ordinat* **b. (sur le lecteur B)** to boot (off the B drive)
boots [buts] *nfpl* ankle boots
boquer [bɔke] *vi Can* (*s'entêter*) to dig one's heels in
borate [bɔrat] *nm Ch* borate
borax [bɔraks] *nm Ch* borax
borborygme [bɔrbɔrigm] *nm* (*usu pl*) (*de l'estomac*) rumbling(s), gurgling(s); *Fig* **je ne comprenais pas ses borborygmes** I didn't understand his mumblings *or* mutterings; **borborygmes de la plomberie** gurgling noises in the plumbing
bord [bɔr] *nm* (**a**) *Naut* (*d'un navire*) side; **jeter qch/tomber** *ou* **passer par-dessus b.** to throw sth/to fall overboard; **moteur hors b.** outboard motor; **les hommes du b.** the ship's company, the crew; *Fig* **être du même b.** to be on the same side *or* of the same opinion; *Can* **se trouver du bon/mauvais b.** to be on the right/wrong side; **à b. d'un navire/d'un avion** on board *or* aboard a ship/a plane; **monter à b. (d'un bateau/d'un avion)** to go/come on board *or* aboard (a boat/a plane), to board (a boat/a plane); **prendre qn à son b.** to take sb on board *or* aboard; *Fig* **vous êtes (le) seul maître à b.** you're the one in charge

(**b**) *Naut* (*bordée*) tack; **courir** *ou* **tirer un b.** to tack, to make a tack

(**c**) (*d'une table, d'une assiette, d'un biscuit, des paupières*) edge; (*d'un vêtement*) border, hem; (*d'une falaise, d'un chemin*) edge, verge; (*d'un chapeau*) brim; (*d'un vase, d'une tasse*) rim, brim; (*d'une blessure*) lip; (*de l'œil*) rim; **b. du trottoir** kerb, *US* curb; **remplir un verre jusqu'au** *ou* **à ras b.** to fill a glass to the brim; **sur le** *ou* **au b. de la route** at *or* on the roadside, at *or* on the side of the road; *Can* **de l'autre b. de la rue** on the other side of the street; **auberge au b.** *ou* **sur le b. de la route** wayside *or* roadside inn; **hôtel au b. du lac** lakeside hotel; **se promener au b. du lac** to walk along the edge of the lake; **je l'ai trouvé au b. de la rivière** I found it on the river bank; **aller au b. de la mer** to go to the seaside; **se promener au b. de la mer** to walk by the sea; **maison au b. de la mer** house by the sea, seaside house; **maison sur le** *ou* **en b. de mer** house on the sea front *or* the (sea)shore; **vivre au b. de la mer** to live at the seaside *or* by the sea; **le b. de mer est très construit** there is a lot of development along the sea front; **b. à b.** edge to edge; *Can* **de b. en b.** from end to end; **chapeau à larges bords** broad- *or* wide-brimmed hat; *Fig* **au b. de la tombe** at death's door; **au b. des larmes** on the verge of tears; **au b. de la crise de nerfs/du désespoir/de la catastrophe** on the verge *or* brink of hysteria/of despair/of disaster; **un peu voleur/bête sur les bords** a bit light-fingered/stupid; **il est un peu menteur/provocateur sur les bords** he's a bit of a liar/an agitator

▶ **bord**: *Av* **b. d'attaque** (*d'une aile*) leading edge; **b. de fuite** (*d'une aile*) trailing edge; *Ordinat* **b. de reliure** inside margin

bordage [bɔrdaʒ] *nm* **(a)** *Couture* edging; **b. de pierres** stone kerb *or US* curb **(b)** *Can* **bordages** (*glace*) inshore ice **(c)** *Naut* (*d'un navire*) (*en bois*) planking; (*en fer*) plating

bordé [bɔrde] **1** *adj* edged, bordered **(de** with); **mouchoir b. de dentelle** lace-edged handkerchief; **boulevard b. d'arbres** tree-lined boulevard **2** *nm* **(a)** *Couture* edging, border **(b)** *Naut* (*d'un navire*) planking, planks; (*en fer*) plating

bordeaux [bɔrdo] **1** *nm* Bordeaux (wine); **b. rouge** claret **2** *adj inv* claret(-coloured), maroon

bordée [bɔrde] *nf* **(a)** *Naut* (*de coups de feu*) broadside; **lâcher une b.** to let fly a broadside; *Fig* **b. de jurons** *ou* **d'injures** torrent *or* hail of abuse **(b)** *Naut* (*distance*) tack; **courir une b.** to tack, to make a tack; **tirer des bordées** to tack; *F Fig* **tirer** *ou* **courir une b.** to go on a binge; *F* **être en b.** to be on a binge **(c)** *Naut* (*équipe*) watch; **b. de tribord/de bâbord** starboard/port watch **(d)** *Can* **b. (de neige)** heavy snowfall

bordel [bɔrdɛl] *nm très F* (*hôtel de passe*) brothel; *Arg* (*désordre*) mess; **quel b.!** what a mess!, what a shambles!; **tu as rangé ton b.?** have you cleared up your mess?; **mettre** *ou* **foutre le b. dans qch** to make a mess of sth, to mess sth up; (*dans une pièce*) to make a mess in sth; **tout le b.** the whole damn lot; **b.!** hell!; *Arg* **b. de merde!** shit!; *Vulg* **putain de b. de merde!** fucking hell!, fuck!

bordelais, -aise [bɔrdəlɛ, -ɛz] **1** *adj* of/from Bordeaux **2** *nm* **le B.** (*région*) the Bordeaux region **3** *nf* **bordelaise** (*futaille*) = cask of about 225 litres; (*bouteille*) = type of bottle for Bordeaux wine **4** *n* **B.** (*natif*) native of Bordeaux; (*habitant*) inhabitant of Bordeaux

bordélique [bɔrdelik] *adj F* (*pièce, bureau, organisation etc*) shambolic; **tu es très b.** you're a real slob

border [bɔrde] *vt* **(a)** (*garnir*) (*robe, manches etc*) to edge, to border **(de** with); **les peupliers qui bordent le chemin** the poplars lining the road; **les villes qui bordent la frontière** the towns that border the frontier; *Naut* **navire qui borde les côtes** ship skirting the coast; **b. le lit/les draps** to tuck in the bedclothes/the sheets; **b. qn (dans son lit)** to tuck sb in *or* up **(b)** *Naut* (*navire*) (*de bois*) to plank; (*de fer*) to plate **(c)** (*avirons*) to ship **(d)** (*voile*) to haul taut

bordereau, -eaux [bɔrdəro] *nm* (*formulaire*) form; *Com* statement; (*de marchandises*) invoice, account; (*dans un devis*) list, schedule; **b. de(s) prix** price list

▶ **bordereau**: **b. d'achat** inventory of purchases; *Compta* **b. de caisse** cash statement; *Com* **b. de chargement** cargo list; *Compta* **b. de codification** accounts coding sheet/form; *Compta* **b. de compte** statement of account; **b. de crédit** credit note; *Banque* **b. d'encaissement** pay-in slip; *Com* **b. d'escompte** list of bills for discount; **b. d'expédition** *ou* **d'envoi** dispatch note; *Compta* **b. d'imputation** accounting entry sheet/form; **b. de livraison** delivery note; **b. de paie** wage slip, salary advice; *Banque* **b. de remboursement** withdrawal slip; **b. de remise (d'espèces** *ou* **de chèques)** pay-in *or* paying-in slip; **b. de réservations** reservation sheet; *Compta* **b. de saisie** accounting input sheet/form, record form; **b. de salaire** wage slip, salary advice; (*liste des salaires payés*) wages sheet; **b. de versement** paying-in slip

bordure [bɔrdyr] *nf* **(a)** (*bord*) edge; (*d'un vêtement*) border, edge; (*d'un chapeau*) binding; (*de gant*) welt; *Tricot* band; **la b. du trottoir** the kerb, *US* the curb; **papier à b. noire** black-edged paper; **la banlieue se développe en b. de la ville** suburbs grow up around the edge of the town; **la maison est en b. de route** the house is by *or* at the roadside; **hôtel en b. de mer** seaside hotel, hotel by the sea **(b)** (*d'un miroir, d'un tableau etc*) frame, surround

bore [bɔr] *nm Ch* boron

boréal, -ale, -aux, -ales [bɔreal, -o] *adj* boreal, north(ern)

borgne [bɔrɲ] **1** *adj* **(a)** (*personne*) one-eyed, blind in one eye; *MecE* **trou b.** recessed hole; **mur b.** blind wall; **fenêtre b.** obstructed window **(b)** *Fig* (*maison, rue etc*) disreputable, shady **2** *n* one-eyed man/woman

borique [bɔrik] *adj Ch* (*acide*) boric, boracic

boriqué [bɔrike] *adj Pharm* **pommade boriquée** boracic ointment; **compresse en coton b.** boracic lint compress

bornage [bɔrnaʒ] *nm* (*des limites d'un terrain*) demarcation, marking out; **pierre de b.** boundary stone

borne [bɔrn] *nf* **(a)** (*limite*) boundary marker; (*pierre*) boundary stone; *F* (*kilomètre*) kilometre, *US* kilometer; **b. kilométrique** kilometre marker, ≈ milestone; *Fig* **il était planté là comme une b.** he stood there as if he had taken root; *F* **il y a 200 bornes entre les deux villes** the two towns are 200 kilometres apart; **bornes** (*d'un royaume, du savoir etc*) boundaries, limits, bounds; **dépasser toutes les bornes** to go too far; **sans bornes** boundless, limitless; **une joie sans bornes** boundless happiness; **il n'y a pas de b. à la vanité humaine** human vanity knows no bounds

(b) *Él* terminal; **b. de mise à la terre** *ou* **de masse** earth *or Am* ground terminal

▶ **borne**: *Naut* **b. d'amarrage** (*d'un quai*) bollard; **b. d'incendie** (fire) hydrant

borné [bɔrne] *adj* (*intelligence*) limited, restricted; (*esprit*) narrow; (*personne*) narrow-minded

borne-fontaine, *pl* **bornes-fontaines** *nf* **(a)** (*fontaine*) (public) drinking fountain **(b)** *Can* (*bouche d'incendie*) (fire) hydrant

borner [bɔrne] **1** *vt* (*terrain*) to mark out, to mark the boundary of, to demarcate; *Fig* (*vue, pouvoir, ambition, désirs, enquête etc*) to limit, to restrict **(à** to); **b. une route** to set up kilometre markers along a road; **le chemin qui borne la forêt** the path bordering the forest; **les pays qui bornent la France à l'est** the countries that border France in the east *or* that form France's eastern border

2 se borner *vpr* **(a)** (*d'une personne*) to restrict *or* limit oneself **(à** to); **je me borne au strict nécessaire** I restrict *or* limit myself to the absolute essentials; **se b. à faire qch** to limit *or* restrict oneself to doing sth

(b) (*des choses*) to be limited, to be restricted, to be confined **(à qch** to sth); **toute leur science se borne à cela** this is the (full) extent of their knowledge; **voici à quoi se borne son raisonnement** this is what his argument comes down to *or* boils down to; **ses visites se bornent à quelques jours** his visits are never any longer than a few days

borsalino [bɔrsalino] *nm* fedora

bortch [bɔrtʃ] *nm Culin* borsch(t), borshch

bosco [bɔsko] *nm Naut* bosun, boatswain

bosniaque [bɔsnjak, bɔznjak] **1** *adj* Bosnian **2** *n* **B.** Bosnian

Bosnie [bɔsni] *nf* Bosnia; **B-Herzégovine** Bosnia-Herzegovina

bosnien, -ienne [bɔsnjɛ̃, -jɛn] **1** *adj* Bosnian **2** *n* **B.** Bosnian

Bosphore (le) [ləbɔsfɔr] *nm* the Bosphorus

bosquet [bɔskɛ] *nm* copse, grove, thicket

boss [bɔs] *nm F* boss; *Fig* **c'est toi le b., après tout** you're the boss *or* you're in charge, after all

bossage [bɔsaʒ] *nm Archit* boss

bossa-nova, *pl* **bossas-novas** [bɔsanɔva] *nf Mus* bossa nova

bosse [bɔs] *nf* **(a)** (*d'un bossu, d'un chameau etc*) hump; *F* **il a roulé sa b. un peu partout** he's knocked about *or* been about a bit **(b)** (*sur la tête etc*) bump, lump, swelling; (*sur la surface du sol*) bump, unevenness; **se faire une b. en tombant** to fall and get a bump; **la route est pleine de bosses** the road is very bumpy *or* uneven; *Ski* **sauter dans les bosses** to jump moguls; *Fig* **avoir la b. du commerce/des maths** to have a good head for business/maths

bosselage [bɔslaʒ] *nm* embossing

bosseler [bɔsle] *vt* **(je bosselle, n. bosselons; je bossellerai)** **(a)** (*travailler*) to emboss **(b)** (*par accident*) to dent, to bash; **casserole toute bosselée** battered saucepan

bosselure [bɔslyr] *nf* **(a)** (*sur l'argenterie*) relief **(b)** (*de terrain, mur etc*) bumpiness, unevenness

bosser [bɔse] *F* **1** *vi* to work **2** *vt Scol* to bone up on, *Br* to swot up

bossette [bɔsɛt] *nf Aut* boss

bosseur, -euse [bɔsœr, -øz] *n F* hard worker, slogger

bossoir [bɔswar] *nm Naut* **(a)** (*pour l'ancre*) cathead; (*de navire*) bow **(b)** (*appareil de levage*) davit; **les bras de b.** the davit guys

bossu, -ue [bɔsy] **1** *adj* (*personne*) hunchbacked; (*animal*) humped; **tiens-toi droit, tu es complètement b.** straighten up, you're all bent; **tu deviens b.** you're getting a stoop **2** *n* hunchback; *F* **rire comme un b.** to laugh one's head off, to split one's sides (laughing)

bossué [bɔsɥe] *adj* (*bouilloire etc*) battered; (*front*) bony

bossuer [bɔsɥe] *vt* = **bosseler (b)**

boston [bɔstɔ̃] *nm* **(a)** *Cartes* boston **(b)** (*danse*) boston

bostonien, -ienne [bɔstɔnjɛ̃, -jɛn] **1** *adj* Bostonian **2** *n* **B.** Bostonian

bot [bo] *adj* **pied b.** club foot; (*personne*) clubfooted person; **main bote** club hand

botanique [bɔtanik] **1** *adj* botanical **2** *nf* botany

botaniste [bɔtanist] *n* botanist

botte¹ [bɔt] *nf* (*de fleurs*) bunch; (*de carottes, radis etc*) bunch, bundle; (*de foin, chanvre*) bale, bundle

botte² *nf* (*chaussure*) (high) boot; **une paire de bottes** a pair of boots; **des bottes en cuir** leather boots; *Fig* **sous la b. de l'envahisseur/l'ennemi** under the heel of the invader/the enemy; *Fig* **on entend le bruit des bottes** war is in the air; *Géog* **la b. de l'Italie** the boot of Italy; *F* **en avoir plein les bottes** to be fed up; *Fig F* **cirer** *ou* **lécher les bottes de qn** to lick sb's boots

▶ **botte**: **bottes de** *ou* **en caoutchouc** rubber boots, *Br* wellingtons, wellington boots, *F* wellies; **bottes de cavalier** *ou* **de cheval** riding boots; **bottes cuissardes** *ou* **d'égoutier** waders; **bottes de sept lieues** seven-league boots

botte[3] *nf Escrime* thrust, lunge, pass; **porter une b.** to thrust, to lunge; *Fig* **b. secrète** secret weapon

botte[4] *nf Scol F* = students who leave the École Polytechnique with the highest marks; **sortir dans la b.** to be among the best students in one's year

botté [bɔte] *nm Can* (*au football américain*) punt

botter [bɔte] **1** *vt* **(a) b. qn** (*le chausser*) to put sb's boots on; (*le fournir*) to supply sb with boots; **être bien botté** to be well shod; **botté de cuir** wearing leather boots; **le Chat botté** Puss in Boots **(b)** *F* **il lui a botté les fesses** *ou* **le derrière** he booted him up the backside *or* gave him a kick up the backside **(c)** *F* (*plaire à*) **ça me botte** I like that; **ça m'a vraiment botté de revoir ce film** I really enjoyed seeing that film again; **ça me botte de partir avec vous** I'm really glad *or Br F* chuffed I'm going with you **2** *vi Fb F* to kick the ball **3 se botter** *vpr* to put one's boots on

bottier [bɔtje] *nm* shoemaker, bootmaker

bottillon [bɔtijɔ̃] *nm* (*de femme*) ankle boot

bottin® [bɔtɛ̃] *nm* telephone directory, phone book; **être dans le b.** to be in the telephone directory *or* phone book; **b. mondain** ≈ Who's Who

bottine [bɔtin] *nf* (*de femme*) ankle boot; (*de bébé*) bootee

botulisme [bɔtylism] *nm Méd* botulism

boubou [bubu] *nm* bubu, boubou

bouc [buk] *nm* (billy) goat; (*barbe*) goatee (beard); **b. émissaire** scapegoat; *F* **puer comme un b., puer le b.** to stink (to high heaven), *Br* to pong

boucan [bukɑ̃] *nm Arg* row, din, racket; **un b. de tous les diables** the devil of a row; **faire un sacré** *ou* **du b.** to make *or* kick up a row *or* din

boucane [bukan] *nf Can* smoke

boucané [bukane] *adj* (*teint*) tanned, weatherbeaten

boucaner [bukane] *vt* (*viande, poisson etc*) to smoke, to cure; (*la peau de qn*) to tan

boucanier [bukanje] *nm* buccaneer

bouchage [buʃaʒ] *nm* (*d'une conduite etc*) blocking (up); (*d'une bouteille*) corking

bouche [buʃ] *nf* **(a)** (*de personne*) mouth; **avoir/parler la b. pleine** to have/to talk with one's mouth full; **une pipe à la b.** with a pipe in his mouth; **j'ai la b. sèche** my mouth is dry, I've got a dry mouth; **j'ai la b. pâteuse** my tongue is coated; **garder qch pour la bonne b.** to save sth until last; **cela fait venir l'eau à la b.** it makes your mouth water; *Fig* **faire la fine b.** to be fussy *or* choosy; **dire qch la b. en cœur** to say sth with a simper; **embrasser qn à pleine b.** to kiss sb passionately; **elle l'embrasse sur la b.** she kisses him on the mouth *or* lips; **manger à pleine b.** to eat greedily, to gobble one's food; **provisions de b.** food; **dépenses de b.** expenditure on food, money spent on food; **c'est une fine b.** he's a gourmet; **avoir une douzaine de bouches à nourrir** to have a dozen mouths to feed; **les bouches inutiles** unproductive people; **elle n'osait pas ouvrir la b.** she didn't dare open her mouth; **je l'ai appris de sa propre b.** I had it from his own lips; *Fig* **ôter** *ou* **enlever le pain de la b. de qn** to take the bread from sb's mouth; **son nom est dans toutes les bouches** everyone's talking about him, his name is on everyone's lips; **elle n'a que ce mot à la b.** that's all she ever says; **demeurer** *ou* **rester b. close** to remain silent, to hold one's tongue; **b. cousue!** not a word!, mum's the word!, don't breathe a word (of it)!; *Arg* **ta b.!** shut your mouth!, shut up!; *F* **il en avait la b. pleine** *ou* **plein la b.** he was full of it, he couldn't talk of anything else; **de b. à oreille** by word of mouth; (*officieusement*) off the record, unofficially; **la nouvelle est passée de b. en b.** the news went *or* did the rounds, the news went round *or* circulated

(b) (*de cheval, de poisson etc*) mouth; **cheval sans b.** *ou* **fort en b.** hard-mouthed horse; **cheval à la b. chatouilleuse** tender-mouthed horse

(c) (*d'une rivière, d'un cratère, d'un puits, d'un four etc*) mouth; (*d'un fusil, d'un canon*) muzzle

▶ **bouche**: *Constr etc* **b. d'accès** (*d'un égout*) manhole; **b. d'aération** air vent; **b. de chaleur** hot air vent; **b. d'eau** hydrant; **b. d'égout** manhole; **b. d'incendie** fire hydrant, *Am* fireplug; **b. de métro** underground *or Am* subway entrance

bouché [buʃe] *adj* **(a)** (*conduite etc*) blocked; **j'ai le nez b.** my nose is blocked, my nose is stuffed up; **j'ai les oreilles bouchées** my ears are blocked up; *Fig* **avoir l'esprit b., être b.** to be dense *or* thick; **être b. à l'émeri** to be a complete moron; **cette voie est bouchée** this is a dead-end job; **temps b.** cloudy *or* overcast weather **(b) cidre b.** bottled cider

bouche-à-bouche *nm inv* mouth-to-mouth resuscitation, *Br* kiss of life; **pratiquer** *ou* **faire le b. à un blessé** to give an injured person mouth-to-mouth resuscitation *or* the kiss of life

bouchée [buʃe] *nf* **(a)** (*quantité*) mouthful; **juste une b. pour goûter** just a mouthful to taste; *Fig* **acheter qch pour une b. de pain** to buy sth for a song *or* for next to nothing; **ne faire qu'une b. d'un mets** to polish off a dish quickly; *Fig* **ne faire qu'une b. de qn/qch** to make short work of sb/sth; *Fig* **mettre les bouchées doubles** to really get a move on, to really get going **(b)** *Culin* titbit; **b. (au chocolat)** chocolate; **b. à la reine** chicken vol-au-vent

boucher[1] [buʃe] **1** *vt* (*fente, trou*) to fill up *or* in, to stop (up); (*conduite, fenêtre etc*) to block (up); (*vue*) to block; (*bouteille*) to cork; *Fig* **cela servira à b. un trou** that will do as a stopgap, that will tide us/them/*etc* over; **j'ai l'impression d'être là uniquement pour b. un trou** I have the feeling I'm there just as a stopgap *or* a fill-in; **b. un creux** (*à l'estomac*) to fill a hole; **b. le passage à qn** to block sb's way, to stand in sb's way; **ta voiture bouche le passage** your car is in the way; **pousse-toi, tu me bouches la vue** move over, you're blocking my view; *F* **elle/ça m'en a bouché un coin** she/that shut me up, she/that took the wind out of my sails

2 se boucher *vpr* (*d'une conduite*) to get blocked (up) *or* clogged (up); **se b. le nez** to hold one's nose; **se b. les oreilles** to put one's fingers in one's ears; *Fig* to refuse to listen; **se b. les yeux** to put one's hands over one's eyes

boucher[2] *nm aussi Fig* butcher

bouchère [buʃɛr] *nf* (woman) butcher; (*épouse du boucher*) butcher's wife

boucherie [buʃri] *nf* (*boutique*) butcher's (shop); (*activité*) butchery; *Fig* (*massacre*) butchery, slaughter; **b. chevaline** horse butcher's (shop); **animaux de b.** animals for slaughter; *Fig* **ce fut une vraie b.** it was a real slaughter *or* bloodbath

bouche-trou, *pl* **bouche-trous** *nm F* stopgap, fill-in, stand-in; *Journ* filler; **servir de b.** to act as a stopgap *or* fill-in *or* stand-in

bouchon [buʃɔ̃] *nm* **(a)** (*d'une bouteille de limonade, d'un tube de colle etc*) cap, top; (*d'un tonneau*) stopper, plug, bung; **b. (de liège)** cork; **vin qui sent le b.** corked wine; **b. de verre** glass stopper; **b. à l'émeri** ground(glass) stopper **(b)** (*embouteillage*) (traffic) hold-up, traffic jam; **il y a un b. sur la Nationale 7** there's a hold-up *or* traffic jam on the N7; **trois kilomètres de b.** a three-kilometre tailback **(c)** *Pêche* (*d'une ligne*) float, bob **(d)** (*de paille*) wisp **(e)** *Région* (*petit restaurant*) **b. (lyonnais)** = small restaurant serving specialities of Lyons **(f) c'est plus fort que de jouer au b.** it's a bit much

▶ **bouchon**: **b. anti-vol** anti-theft cap; *Aut* **b. de pressurisation** pressure cap; *Aut* **b. de radiateur** radiator cap; *Aut* **b. de remplissage** filler plug *or* cap; *Aut* **b. de réservoir** fuel cap; *MecE* **b. de trop plein** *ou* **de vidange** drain(ing) plug

bouchonné [buʃɔne] *adj* corked

bouchonner [buʃɔne] **1** *vi Aut F* **ça risque de b. sur l'autoroute** there's a risk of hold-ups *or* congestion on the motorway; **ça bouchonne à partir d'Évreux** traffic is at a standstill from Évreux onwards **2** *vt* (*cheval*) to rub down

bouchot [buʃo] *nm* mussel bank *or* bed *or* farm

bouclage [buklaʒ] *nm* **(a)** *F* (*de prisonnier etc*) imprisonment, locking up **(b)** (*d'un quartier etc*) surrounding, sealing off, cordoning off **(c)** *Ordinat* looping; (*acoustique*) (audio) feedback, howl-round; **b. acoustique** acoustic feedback **(d)** *Typ* (*d'un journal*) putting to bed, edition time

boucle [bukl] *nf* **(a)** (*de ceinture, chaussure, harnais etc*) buckle

(b) (*de ruban, de ficelle, de cordage, d'une rivière, d'une route*), *Av* loop; **faire une b. pour retourner à ...** to loop back to ...; **b. à nœud coulant** running loop; **décrire de nombreuses boucles** (*d'une rivière*) to meander; **la Seine fait des boucles avant d'arriver à Rouen** the Seine twists and turns before it gets to Rouen

(c) (*anneau*) ring; **b. de rideau** curtain ring

(d) (*de cheveux*) curl, ringlet, lock

(e) *Sp* lap

(f) *TV, Cin* dialogue loop, film loop

(g) *Ordinat* **b. d'attente** wait loop; **b. de bande** tape loop; **b. sans fin** endless loop

▶ **boucle**: *TV, Cin* **b. de dialogue** dialogue *or* tape loop; **Boucles d'or** Goldilocks; **b. d'oreille** earring

bouclé [bukle] *adj* (*cheveux*) curly; (*personne*) curly-haired; *Ordinat* **système b.** looped system

boucler [bukle] **1** *vt* **(a)** (*ceinture etc*) to buckle, to fasten; (*chambre, maison etc*) to lock (up); **b. sa valise** to fasten one's suitcase; (*se préparer à partir*) to pack one's bags; *Aut* **b. sa ceinture** to put on *or* fasten one's belt, to belt up; *F* **b. une affaire** to finish off *or* settle a matter; *Bourse* **b. une position** to close (out) a position; **il a du mal à b. ses fins de mois** he finds it hard to make ends meet at the end of the month; *F* **boucle-la!** belt up!, shut up!; *Typ* **b. une édition de** *ou* **un journal** to put a newspaper to bed; *Journ* **b. un sujet** to file a story; **b. les comptes** to close the books

(b) b. la boucle *Av* to loop the loop; *Fig* to come full circle; **et voilà, la boucle est bouclée** and so we/they/*etc* come full circle

(c) *F* (*prisonnier etc*) to lock up, *F* to bang up

(d) (*quartier etc*) to surround, to seal off, to cordon off

(e) *Sp* (*adversaire*) to lap

2 *vi* (*des cheveux*) to curl, to be curly; **ses cheveux bouclent quand il pleut** her hair goes curly when it rains

3 se boucler *vpr F* **se la b.** to keep quiet

bouclette [buklɛt] **1** *nf* **(a)** (*de cheveux*) small curl, ringlet **(b)** (*de laine, moquette*) curl **2** *adj Tex* **laine b.** bouclé wool

bouclier [buklije] *nm* **(a)** (*arme défensive*), *Constr, Géol* shield; **il lui fit un b. de son corps** he shielded him with his body; *Fig* **on s'attend à une levée de boucliers** an outcry is expected **(b)** *Aut* bumper; **b. inférieur** undershield

▶ **bouclier**: **b. atomique** *ou* **nucléaire** nuclear shield; *Astronaut* **b. thermique** heat shield

Bouddha [buda] *nm* Buddha

bouddhique [budik] *adj* Buddhist

bouddhisme [budism] *nm* Buddhism

bouddhiste [budist] *adj, n* Buddhist

bouder [bude] **1** *vi* to sulk; **laisse-le b. dans son coin** leave him to sulk

2 *vt* **b. qn/qch** to refuse to have anything to do with sb/sth; **tu me boudes?** aren't you talking to me?; **b. son plaisir** to deny oneself; **il boude la peinture moderne** he's not interested in modern art, he doesn't like modern art; **en été les Parisiens boudent les salles de cinéma** Parisians stay away from *or* don't go to the cinema in summer; **le soleil boudera la plus grande partie du pays** most of the country won't have *or* see any sun

3 se bouder *vpr* not to talk to each other, to refuse to have anything to do with each other

bouderie [budri] *nf* (*état*) sulkiness; (*action*) sulk, fit of the sulks; **j'en ai marre de tes bouderies!** I'm fed up with your sulking!

boudeur, -euse [budœr, -øz] **1** *adj* sulky, sullen **2** *n* sulky person **3** *nf* **boudeuse** (*siège*) courting couch

boudin [budɛ̃] *nm* **(a)** *Culin* **b. (noir)** black pudding, *Am* blood sausage; **b. blanc** white pudding; *F* **s'en aller en eau de b.** (*d'un projet, d'une démarche etc*) to go to pot *or* down the drain *or* down the tubes **(b)** *F* **boudins** (*doigts*) fat *or* podgy fingers **(c)** *F* **faire du b.** to sulk **(d)** *Belg* (*traversin*) bolster **(e)** *Péj F* (*fille*) fat lump, lump of a girl **(f)** *Min etc* (*d'explosif*) sausage; (*de pâte à modeler, terre*) roll; *Naut* **b. gonflable** inflatable fender

boudiné [budine] *adj* **(a) b. dans un pantalon trop étroit** bursting *or* bulging out of a tight pair of trousers; **je suis complètement b. dans cette jupe** I'm bursting out all over in this skirt **(b)** (*doigts*) podgy, fat

boudiner [budine] **1** *vt* **(a)** *Tex* to rove, to slub **(b)** *Tech* (*fil de fer*) to coil **(c)** *F* **cette robe me boudine** this dress shows all my bulges, I'm bursting out of this dress **2 se boudiner** *vpr* **se b. dans ses vêtements** to squeeze into one's clothes

boudoir [budwar] *nm* **(a)** (*salon*) boudoir **(b)** (*biscuit*) sponge finger, *Am* ladyfinger

boue [bu] *nf* **(a)** (*terre détrempée*) mud; *Fig* **traîner qn dans la b.** to drag sb through the mud; *Fig* **couvrir qn de b.** to throw *or* sling mud at sb **(b)** *Constr* (*pisé*) (building) clay **(c)** (*vase*) sludge, sediment; (*dans une rivière etc*) silt; (*de l'océan*) ooze; **bain de b.** mud bath; **boues activées** radioactive mud; (*épuration des eaux*) activated sludge

bouée [bwe] *nf Naut* buoy; (*pour nager*) rubber ring; **b. sonore** sonobuoy; **b. à sifflet** whistling buoy; **b. à cloche** bell buoy; **b. d'amarrage** *ou* **de corps-mort** mooring buoy; **b. lumineuse** light buoy, floating light; **b. de sauvetage** lifebelt, lifebuoy; *Fig* lifeline; **elle se cramponne à cet espoir comme à une b.** she is clinging to this hope like a lifeline

boueux, -euse [buø, -øz] **1** *adj* (*route, bottes etc*) muddy; (*écriture, impression etc*) smudged, blurred **2** *nm F* dustman, *Am* garbage man *or* collector

bouffant [bufɑ̃] **1** *adj* (*manche*) puff(ed); (*jupe*) full; (*pantalon*) baggy; **cheveux bouffants** bouffant hair-do **2** *nm* (*d'une manche*) puff; (*des cheveux*) body

bouffarde [bufard] *nf F* (*pipe*) pipe

bouffe[1] [buf] *adj Mus* **opéra b.** opéra bouffe, comic opera

bouffe[2] *nf très F* (*aliments*) grub, *Br* nosh; **faire** *ou* **préparer la b.** to make the grub *or* nosh; **c'est l'heure de la b.!** grub('s) up!; **on pourrait se faire une petite b.** we could have a bite together

bouffée [bufe] *nf* **(a)** (*de fumée*) puff; (*de parfum*) whiff; (*d'air*) breath; **le souffle du printemps entrait dans la pièce par bouffées** spring air wafted into the room; **tirer une b. de sa pipe** to take a puff at one's pipe; **avoir une b. délirante** to be/become delirious; **b. de chaleur** blast of hot air; *Méd* hot flush, *Am* hot flash **(b)** (*d'éloquence, de colère etc*) (out)burst, fit; (*d'orgueil*) fit; **travailler par bouffées** to work by fits and starts

bouffer [bufe] **1** *vi* **(a)** (*d'une manche, d'un corsage etc*) to puff out, to balloon out; (*des cheveux*) to have body; **faire b. ses cheveux** to give body to one's hair

(b) *F* (*manger*) to eat; **j'ai bien bouffé** I've had a really good meal; **quand est-ce qu'on bouffe?** when's grub up?, when are we eating?

2 *vt* **(a)** *F* (*manger*) to eat, *Br* to nosh; **on n'a rien à b.** there's no grub, there's nothing to eat; *Fig* **il ne va pas te b.** he won't eat you; *Fig* **je l'aurais bouffé** I could have killed him; **ça me bouffe!** it really gets me!; **elle se laisse b. par ses enfants/son travail** she has no time for anything but her children/work, all her time is taken up by her children/work; **b. de l'essence** (*d'une voiture*) to be heavy on petrol, to be a gas guzzler; **b. des kilomètres** to drive around; *F* **b. du curé (à tous les repas)** to be very anti-clerical

(b) *F* (*argent, économies*) to blow, to run through

3 se bouffer *vpr F Fig* **elles se bouffent le nez constamment** they're always bickering, they're always having a go at each other

bouffetance [buftɑ̃s] *nf F* grub, *Br* nosh

bouffeur, -euse [bufœr, øz] *n F* guzzler; **un gros b. de viande** a great meat-eater; **c'est un b. de curé** he's very anti-clerical

bouffi [bufi] **1** *adj* (*yeux, visage*) puffy, puffed up, swollen; **b. d'orgueil** puffed up *or* swollen with pride; *Com* **hareng b.** bloater **2** *nm* bloater

bouffir [bufir] **1** *vt* to swell, to puff up **2** *vi* (*des yeux, du visage*) to become swollen, to puff up

bouffissure [bufisyr] *nf* **(a)** (*des yeux, du visage*) puffiness, swollenness **(b)** (*du style*) turgidity

bouffon, -onne [bufɔ̃, -ɔn] **1** *nm* buffoon, clown, fool; *Hist* jester **2** *adj* farcical, comical

bouffonner [bufɔne] *vi Vieilli* to play *or* act the buffoon

bouffonnerie [bufɔnri] *nf* (*caractère*) buffoonery; **faire des bouffonneries** to play *or* act the buffoon

bougainvillée [bugɛ̃vile] *nf*, **bougainvillier** [bugɛ̃vilje] *nm* bougainvillea

bouge [buʒ] *nm Péj* (*maison*) hovel, dump; (*bar*) low dive, sleazy bar

bougeoir [buʒwar] *nm* (*plat*) candleholder; (*haut*) candlestick

bougeotte [buʒɔt] *nf F* **avoir la b.** to be fidgety, to have the fidgets; (*voyager sans cesse*) to have itchy feet

bouger [buʒe] **(je bougeai(s), n. bougeons) 1** *vi* (*remuer, se déplacer*) to move; **rester sans b.** to keep still; **ne bougez pas!** don't move!, keep still!; **ne bouge pas (de là)** stay where you are!, don't move!; *Phot* **ne bougeons plus!** hold it!; **je ne bougerai pas de la terrasse** I won't move from the terrace, I'll stay on the terrace; **je n'ai pas bougé de chez moi pendant deux jours** I haven't been out *or* I've stayed in for two days; *Fig* **ce chemisier ne bouge pas au lavage** (*ne déteint pas*) this blouse doesn't run in the wash; (*ne rétrécit pas*) this blouse doesn't shrink in the wash; **les prix ne bougent pas** prices are (holding) steady; **les ouvriers/étudiants bougent** the workers/students are restless; *F* **ça bouge pas mal, dans cette ville** there's a lot going on *or* happening in this town

2 *vt F* to move, to shift; *Fig* **elle n'a pas bougé le petit doigt** she didn't lift a finger; **tu la connais, c'est difficile de la faire b.** you know what she's like, it's hard to get her to do anything

3 se bouger *vpr F* to move; **bouge-toi de là** shift yourself!; **il ne veut pas se b.** he won't shift himself; **bouge-toi un peu, fais quelque chose!** get up off your backside and do something!; **il faut te b. si tu veux avoir le poste** you'll have to get a move on if you want the job

bougie [buʒi] *nf* **(a)** (*en cire*) candle; **à la b., aux bougies** by candlelight; *F* **tu as mis de la b. partout sur la nappe!** you've got candle wax all over the tablecloth!; *Arch* **ampoule de 100 bougies** 100 watt bulb **(b)** *Aut* **b. (d'allumage)** spark plug, *Br* sparking plug **(c)** *Arg* (*visage*) mug, *Br* dial
bougnat [buɲa] *nm Vieilli* coal-merchant
bougnoul(e) [buɲul] *n Arg* (*terme injurieux*) Arab, *Br* wog
bougon, -onne [bugɔ̃, -ɔn] *F* **1** *n* grumbler, grouch **2** *adj* grumpy, grouchy
bougonnement [bugɔnmɑ̃] *nm F* grumbling, grousing
bougonner [bugɔne] *vi F* to grumble, to grouse
bougre [bugr] *nm F* **(a)** *Vieilli* (*type*) fellow, *Br* chap, *Br* bloke; **le pauvre b.** the poor devil; **ce n'est pas un mauvais b.** he's not a bad sort **(b) b. d'imbécile** damn(ed) fool, *Br* bloody idiot **(c)** *Arch* **b.!** blast!, damn it!; **b. que ça fait mal!** heck, that hurts! **(d)** *Vieilli* (*sodomite*) bugger
bougrement [bugrəmɑ̃] *adv* damn(ed); **il fait b. chaud** it's damn(ed) hot
boui-boui, *pl* **bouis-bouis** [bwibwi] *nm F* café, *Péj* dingy café
bouillabaisse [bujabɛs] *nf Culin* bouillabaisse (*Provençal fish soup*)
bouillant [bujɑ̃] *adj* **(a)** (*qui bout*) boiling; (*très chaud*) boiling hot; **il est b.** (*il a de la fièvre*) he's boiling hot **(b)** *Fig* (*ardent*) fiery, hot-headed, impetuous; **b. de colère** seething with anger; **b. d'impatience** bursting with impatience
bouille [buj] *nf* **(a)** *Arg* (*visage*) mug, face; **il a une bonne b.** he looks a good sort **(b)** (*pour la vendange*) grape tub
bouilleur [bujœr] *nm* **(a)** (*distillateur*) distiller; **b. de cru** home distiller **(b)** (*d'une chaudière*) water space
bouilli [buji] *Culin* **1** *adj* boiled **2** *nm* boiled meat, *Can* = beans, cabbage, potatoes, salt pork and ham cooked together for several hours; **b. de bœuf** boiled beef
bouillie [buji] *nf* **(a)** (*pour bébés*) baby food; (*à base de céréales*) baby cereal; **préparer la b. du bébé** to prepare the baby's food; **réduire en b.** (*légumes, fruits etc*) to mash, to pulp; **b. de légumes** mashed vegetables; **légumes en b.** mushy vegetables; *Fig* **les voitures ont été réduites en b.** the cars were completely smashed up; *F* **s'il me provoque je vais le mettre** *ou* **réduire en b.** if he provokes me I'll beat him to a pulp *or* I'll smash his head in! **(b)** (*pour le papier*) pulp **(c)** *Agr* **b. bordelaise** Bordeaux mixture
bouillir [bujir] (*prp* **bouillant**; *pp* **bouilli**; *pr ind* **je bous** [bu], **tu bous, il bout, n. bouillons, v. bouillez, ils bouillent**; *pr sub* **je bouille, n. bouillions**; *imp* **bous, bouillons, bouillez**; *impf* **je bouillais**; *p hist* **je bouillis**; *p sub* **je bouillisse**; *fu* **je bouillirai**) **1** *vi* to boil; **commencer à b.** to come to the boil; **cesser de b.** to go off the boil; **faire b.** to boil; **faire b. qch** to boil sth; **faire b. du linge** to boil laundry; *F* **cela fera b. la marmite** that will keep the pot boiling; *Fig* **b. de colère** to seethe with anger; **b. d'impatience** to burst with impatience; **cela me fait b.** that makes my blood boil

2 *vt F* (*lait, linge etc*) to boil
bouilloire [bujwar] *nf* kettle
bouillon [bujɔ̃] *nm* **(a)** (*d'un liquide en ébullition*) bubble; (*dans du verre*) (air) bubble; (*dans du métal*) blowhole; (*d'une étoffe*) puff; **bouillir à gros bouillons** to boil fast *or* hard; **au premier b.** as soon as it comes to the boil; **le sang sortait à gros bouillons** the blood was gushing out

(b) *Culin* (*liquide*) stock, bouillon; **b. gras/maigre** meat/clear stock; **b. de légumes** vegetable stock; **b. cube** stock cube; **boire un b.** (*en nageant*) to get a mouthful; *F* (*professionellement*) to come to grief, to suffer a heavy loss; **b. de culture** culture medium; *Fig* **b. d'onze heures** poisoned drink

(c) *Com* **bouillons** (*de livres, de journaux*) returns, unsold copies
bouillonnant [bujɔnɑ̃] *adj* bubbling; (*torrent*) foaming, seething; *Fig* **b. de vie/d'idées** bubbling over with life/ideas
bouillonnement [bujɔnmɑ̃] *nm* bubbling; (*de torrent*) foaming, seething; *Fig* **b. de la jeunesse** effervescence *or* impetuousness of youth
bouillonner [bujɔne] **1** *vi* **(a)** (*d'eau, de soupe, de bain*) to bubble; (*de torrent*) to foam, to seethe; *Fig* **toutes les idées qui bouillonnent dans sa tête** all the ideas seething in his head; **b. de colère** to seethe with anger; **b. d'impatience** to burst with impatience **(b)** *Com* (*d'un journal, d'un magazine*) to remain unsold **2** *vt Couture* **b. une manche** to gather a sleeve into a puff
bouillotte [bujɔt] *nf* hot-water bottle
bouillotter [bujɔte] *vi* to boil gently, to simmer
boul *abrév* **boulevard**
boulaie [bulɛ] *nf* birch plantation
boulange [bulɑ̃ʒ] *nf F* bakery trade
boulanger¹ [bulɑ̃ʒe] *nm* baker
boulanger² *vt* (**je boulangeai(s), n. boulangeons**) (*farine*) to work
boulangère [bulɑ̃ʒɛr] *nf* (woman) baker; (*épouse du boulanger*) baker's wife
boulangerie [bulɑ̃ʒri] *nf* **(a)** (*industrie*) bakery trade **(b)** (*lieu de fabrication*) bakery; (*magasin*) baker's (shop), bakery; **b.-pâtisserie** baker's and confectioner's (shop)
boule [bul] *nf* **(a)** (*sphère*) ball; *F* (*tête*) nut, head; **b. de poils** (*régurgité*) hairball; **quelle jolie petite b. de poils** (*chaton*) what a lovely fluffy little thing; **arbre en b.** bushy-topped tree; **se rouler** *ou* **se mettre en b.** (*d'un hérisson etc*) to roll *or* curl (itself) up into a ball; *F* **se mettre en b.** (*en colère*) to fly off the handle, to go up the wall; *F* **elle/ça me met en b.** she/it gets my back up *or* makes me see red; *F* **j'ai les nerfs en b.** I'm a bundle of nerves, my nerves are all on edge; **avoir une b. dans la gorge** to have a lump in one's throat; *F* **perdre la b.** to go off one's head, to go round the bend; *F* **tu perds la b. ou quoi?** are you off your head?; *Can* **sortir qch des boules à mites** to take sth out of mothballs, to dust sth off

(b) [①A10,d] (*pour jouer*) (*aux boules*) bowl; (*au billard, croquet, hockey*) ball; **jouer aux boules** to play bowls; **lancer la b.** to bowl; **la b.** (*au casino*) boule; *F* **avoir les boules** to be pissed off; (*avoir peur*) to be wetting oneself; **ça m'a foutu les boules** it pissed me off

(c) (*de machine à écrire*) golf ball; **imprimante à b.** golf-ball printer

▶ **boule**: **b. de billard** billiard ball; *Ordinat* **b. de commande** trackball; **b. de feu** fireball; **b. de naphtaline** mothball; **b. de neige** snowball; *Fig* **faire b. de neige** to snowball; **histoire qui fait b. de neige** story that snowballs; **b. de nerfs** bundle of nerves; *Ordinat* **b. de pointage** pointer; **b. puante** stink bomb; **b. Quiès®** earplug; **b. à thé** tea ball
bouleau, -eaux [bulo] *nm* (silver) birch (tree); (*bois*) birch (wood)
boule-de-neige, *pl* **boules-de-neige** *nf* (*fleur*) guelder rose, snowball tree
bouledogue [buldɔg] *nm* bulldog
bouler [bule] **1** *vi* to roll; *F* **envoyer b. qn** to send sb packing **2** *vt* **b. les cornes d'un taureau** to pad a bull's horns
boulet [bulɛ] *nm* **(a)** *Mil* **b. (de canon)** cannonball; *Fig* **tirer à boulet(s) rouge(s) sur qn** to go for sb hammer and tongs; **passer comme un b. (de canon)** to hurtle past *or* by **(b)** (*de bagnard*) ball and chain; *Fig* **c'est un b. qu'il traînera toute sa vie** it will be a millstone round his neck all his life **(c)** *Com* (*de charbon*) (coal) nut **(d)** (*de cheval*) fetlock (joint)
boulette [bulɛt] *nf* **(a)** (*de papier etc*) pellet, small ball **(b)** *Culin* meatball **(c)** *Vét* poison ball **(d)** *F* (*gaffe*) **faire une b.** to put one's foot in it, *Br* to drop a brick *or* a clanger
boulevard [bulvar] *nm* boulevard; **les grands boulevards** (*à Paris*) the main boulevards; **les boulevards extérieurs** (*à Paris*) the outer boulevards; **b. périphérique** orbital road, ring road; **théâtre de b.** light comedies; *Th* **c'est du bon b.** it's good light comedy
boulevardier, -ière [bulvardje, -jɛr] *adj* (*humour*) facile
bouleversant [bulvɛrsɑ̃] *adj* profoundly *or* deeply moving, shattering; (*pénible, effrayant*) deeply distressing; **c'était b. de vérité** it was a shattering experience; **elle est bouleversant dans le rôle de ...** she gives a profoundly *or* deeply moving performance as ...
bouleversé [bulvɛrse] *adj* shattered; **j'en suis encore tout b.** I still haven't got over it; **d'une voix bouleversée** in a voice full of emotion, in a very emotional voice; **le visage b. par l'émotion** his/her face twisted with emotion
bouleversement [bulvɛrsəmɑ̃] *nm* **(a)** (*de projets, de programmes, des habitudes etc*) disruption; **bouleversements politiques/économiques** political/economic upheavals **(b)** (*d'une personne*) emotion; **son b. était tel que ...** he was in such an emotional state that ..., he was so emotional that ...; **sa voix trahissait un b. bien plus profond que ...** her voice betrayed a far deeper emotion than ...
bouleverser [bulvɛrse] *vt* **(a)** (*projets, habitudes etc*) to disrupt; (*la vie de qn*) to turn upside down; (*paysage*) to change radically; **ce changement de majorité a bouleversé la vie du pays** this change of government threw the whole country into confusion

(b) (*émouvoir*) to shatter; **la nouvelle l'a complètement bouleversé** he was totally shattered by the news; **son accident l'a profondément bouleversé** his accident was something he found it hard to get over; **voir sur l'écran l'enfant qu'elle portait l'a profondément bouleversée** seeing the child she was carrying on the screen was a deeply *or* profoundly moving experience; **la voix de Piaf me bouleverse** I find listening to Piaf's voice a deeply *or* profoundly moving experience
boulier [bulje] *nm* **(a) b. (compteur)** abacus, counting frame **(b)** *Billard* scoring board

boulimie [bulimi] *nf Méd* bulimia; **faire de la b.** to eat compulsively; *Fig* **avoir une b. de connaissance** to have an unquenchable thirst for knowledge
boulimique [bulimik] *adj, n Méd* bulimic
boulingrin [bulɛ̃grɛ̃] *nm* lawn (*bordered by hedges etc*)
bouliste [bulist] **1** *n* bowls player **2** *adj* **club b.** bowling club
boulle [bul] *nm* boul(l)e, buhl; **cabinet de b.** buhl *or* boul(l)e cabinet
boulocher [bulɔʃe] *vi* (*d'un pull etc*) to pill
boulodrome [bulɔdrom] *nm* bowling alley
boulon [bulɔ̃] *nm* bolt; **b. à écrou** screw bolt; **b. à œil** eyebolt; **b. à oreilles** wing bolt; *Aut* **b. de roue** wheel bolt; **b. mécanique** machine bolt; *Rail* **b. d'attelage** coupling pin; *Fig* **le gouvernement doit à présent resserrer les boulons** the government must now tighten the screws
boulonnage [bulɔnaʒ] *nm* bolting
boulonner [bulɔne] **1** *vt MecE etc* to bolt **2** *vi F* to slog *or* slave (away)
boulonnerie [bulɔnri] *nf* **(a)** (*fabrique*) nut-and-bolt works; (*industrie*) nut-and-bolt trade **(b)** (*objets*) nuts and bolts
boulot[1], -otte [bulo, -ɔt] **1** *adj F* dumpy, plump, tubby **2** *n* dumpy *or* tubby person
boulot[2] [bulo] *F* **1** *nm* (*travail*) work; (*emploi*) job; **allez, au b.!** come on, (get) to work!; **refaire les peintures dans une maison, c'est du b.** to repaint a whole house is a lot of work *or* is quite a job; **aller au b.** to go to work; **rentrer du b.** to come back from work; *Fig* **c'est toujours moi qui fais le sale b.** it's always me that does the dirty work **2** *adj inv* **être b. b.** to be a workaholic, to be work-mad
boulotter [bulɔte] *F* **1** *vt* to eat; **il n'y a rien à b.** there's no grub, there's nothing to eat **2** *vi* to eat, *Br* to nosh
boum [bum] **1** *int* (*explosion*) bang!, boom!; (*chute*) bang!, crash!; *Enf* **bébé a fait b.** baby's had a tumble **2** *nm* **(a)** (*bruit*) bang; **on a entendu un grand b.** we heard a big bang **(b)** **en plein b.** in full swing **3** *nf* (*fête*) party (*for young people*)
boumer [bume] *vi Arg* **ça boume!** things are great!; **ça boume?** how's things?
bouquet[1] [bukɛ] *nm* **(a)** (*fleurs*) bunch of flowers, bouquet; (*petit*) posy; (*d'arbres*) clump; (*de plumes*) plume, tuft; **le b. de la mariée** the bride's bouquet **(b)** (*d'un vin*) bouquet, nose **(c)** (*d'un feu d'artifice*) final display; *F* **ça, c'est le b.!** that takes the biscuit *or Am* cake!, that's the last straw!
▶ **bouquet**: **b. final** final display; *Culin* **b. garni** bouquet garni, mixed herbs
bouquet[2] *nm* **(a)** (*lièvre*) hare; (*lapin mâle*) buck rabbit **(b)** (*crevette*) prawn
bouquetière [buktjɛr] *nf* flower seller
bouquetin [buktɛ̃] *nm* ibex
bouquin[1] [bukɛ̃] *nm F* (*livre*) book
bouquin[2] *nm* (*lièvre*) hare; (*lapin mâle*) buck rabbit
bouquiner [bukine] *vi F* (*lire*) to read
bouquiniste [bukinist] *n* second-hand bookseller
bourbe [burb] *nf* mud, mire
bourbeux, -euse [burbø, -øz] *adj* muddy, miry
bourbier [burbje] *nm* bog, quagmire; *Fig* mess; *Fig* **se tirer d'un b.** to get out of a mess
bourbillon [burbijɔ̃] *nm* (*d'un abcès, d'un furoncle etc*) core
bourbon [burbɔ̃] *nm* (*whisky*) bourbon
bourdaine [burdɛn] *nf* black alder
bourde [burd] *nf F* **(a)** (*balivernes*) tall story; **raconter des bourdes à qn** to have *or Am* to put sb on **(b)** (*faute*) blunder, *Br* boob, boo-boo; **faire une b.** to put one's foot in it, *Br* to drop a brick *or* a clanger
bourdon[1] [burdɔ̃] *nm* (*bâton*) pilgrim's staff
bourdon[2] *nm* **(a)** *Mus* (*de cornemuses*) drone; (*d'un orgue*) bourdon stop; (*note*) drone bass **(b)** (*cloche*) great bell **(c)** (*insecte*) bumblebee; **faux b.** drone; *Arg* **avoir le b.** to be down (in the dumps)
bourdon[3] *nm Typ* omission
bourdonnement [burdɔnmɑ̃] *nm* (*d'insectes*) buzz(ing), hum(ming); (*d'un moteur*) hum(ming); *Méd* **b. d'oreilles** buzzing *or* ringing in the ears; **avoir des bourdonnements d'oreilles** to have a buzzing *or* ringing in one's ears
bourdonner [burdɔne] *vi* (*d'insectes*) to buzz, to hum; (*d'une machine, d'un moteur*) to hum; (*des oreilles*) to buzz, to ring
bourg [bur] *nm* (*gros village*) small market town
bourgade [burgad] *nf* village, township
bourgeois, -oise [burʒwa, -waz] **1** *adj* **(a)** (*personne*) middle-class; **la classe bourgeoise** the middle class, the bourgeoisie; **quartier b.** middle-class area; **cuisine bourgeoise** simple *or* family *or* home cooking; **une belle maison bourgeoise** a grand house
(b) *Péj* (*conventionnel*) middle-class, bourgeois, conventional
2 *n* **(a)** middle-class person; **les grands b.** the upper middle class; **les petits b.** the lower middle class; **en b.** in plain *or* civilian clothes
(b) *Péj* (*béotien*) philistine; **chercher à épater le b.** to try to shock the establishment
(c) (*roturier*) commoner
(d) *Hist* (*citoyen*) burgess, burgher, citizen
3 *nf Arg* **la bourgeoise** (*épouse*) the wife, the missus, the old lady
bourgeoisement [burʒwazmɑ̃] *adv* conventionally; **vivre b.** to live comfortably *or* in a middle-class way; *Admin* **occuper b. un local** to occupy premises for residential purposes
bourgeoisie [burʒwazi] *nf* **(a)** middle class(es), bourgeoisie; **la haute/petite b.** the upper/lower middle class; **la moyenne b.** the middle class **(b)** *Hist* (*d'une ville*) burgesses, citizens, freemen
bourgeon [burʒɔ̃] *nm* **(a)** *Bot* bud; **en bourgeons** in bud **(b)** *F Vieilli* (*bouton*) spot, pimple **(c)** *Anat* **b. gustatif** taste bud, *Spéc* gustatory bud
bourgeonnement [burʒɔnmɑ̃] *nm* **(a)** *Bot* budding; (*saison*) budding time **(b)** *Méd* granulation
bourgeonner [burʒɔne] *vi* **(a)** *Bot* to bud **(b)** *F* (*avoir des boutons*) to come out in spots **(c)** *Méd* (*d'une blessure*) to granulate
bourgmestre [burgmɛstr] *nm* burgomaster
Bourgogne [burgɔɲ] **1** *nf* Burgundy **2** *nm* **(vin de) b.** burgundy (wine)
bourgot [burgo] *nm Can* moose caller
bourguignon, -onne [burgiɲɔ̃, -ɔn] **1** *adj* Burgundian; *Culin* **bœuf b.** bœuf bourguignon (*beef and vegetables cooked in red wine*) **2** *nm Culin* bœuf bourguignon **3** *n* **B.** Burgundian
bourlinguer [burlɛ̃ge] *vi* **(a)** *Naut* (*d'un navire*) to make heavy weather, to labour, *US* to labor, to toil **(b)** (*beaucoup naviguer*) to sail the seven seas; **il a bourlingué dans les mers de Chine** he has sailed the China Seas **(c)** *F* (*beaucoup voyager*) **b. de par le monde** to knock about the world; **il a beaucoup bourlingué** he's knocked about a lot
bourlingueur, -euse [burlɛ̃gœr, -øz] *F* **1** *adj* adventurous **2** *n* adventurer, rolling stone; **c'est un grand b.** he's knocked about a bit
bourrache [buraʃ] *nf* (*plante*) borage
bourrade [burad] *nf* push, shove; (*dans le dos etc*) thump, slap; (*dans les côtes*) dig, poke, prod
bourrage [buraʒ] *nm* **(a)** (*d'une chaise, d'un coussin etc*) stuffing, padding; (*d'un placard, d'un sac etc*) cramming, packing tight; (*d'une pipe avec du tabac*) filling; (*d'une mine, d'une arme à feu etc*) tamping; (*dans une imprimante*) jam; (*répété*) jamming; **b. de papier** paper jam, paper blockage **(b)** (*matériau*) stuffing, filling
▶ **bourrage**: **b. de crâne** *F* eyewash; *surtout Pol* (*propagande*) brainwashing
bourrasque [burask] *nf* squall, gust (of wind); **b. de neige** snow flurry; **le vent souffle en b.** the wind is gusting *or* squalling; *Fig* **une b. d'injures** a flurry of insults; *Fig* **elle est passée en b.** she paid a lightning visit; **arriver en b.** to arrive at top speed
bourratif, -ive [buratif, -iv] *adj F* (*aliment*) stodgy, filling
bourre[1] [bur] *nf* **(a)** (*pour rembourrer les chaises etc*) stuffing, padding, filling; (*de coton etc*) waste, fluff; *Bot* (*des bourgeons*) down, floss; *Tex etc* **b. de soie** floss silk, silk waste **(b)** (*d'arme à feu*) wad **(c)** *Arg* **de première b.** first-class, first-rate **(d)** *F* **à la b.** in a rush
bourre[2] *nm Arg* (*policier*) cop
bourré [bure] *adj* **(a)** (*plein*) packed, crammed (**de** with); **b. à craquer** full to bursting; **le coffre est b.** the boot is crammed full; **la tête bourrée de rêves** with his head full of dreams; **être b. de complexes** to be one big bundle *or* a mass of complexes; **il est b. d'antibiotiques** he's pumped full of antibiotics; **les kiwis sont bourrés de vitamines** kiwi fruits are packed *or* crammed with vitamins **(b)** *Arg* (*ivre*) plastered, smashed; **être complètement b.** to be smashed out of one's mind, to be legless
bourreau, -eaux [buro] *nm* **(a)** (*exécuteur*) executioner; (*qui pend*) hangman; (*tortionnaire*) torturer **(b)** *Fig* tormentor, torturer; **être le b. de qn** to torment *or* torture sb
▶ **bourreau**: **b. des cœurs** ladykiller; **b. d'enfants** child-beater; **b. de travail** workaholic
bourrée [bure] *nf* (*danse*) bourrée
bourrelé [burle] *adj* **b. de remords** stricken with remorse
bourrèlement [burɛlmɑ̃] *nm Litt* torment, anguish; (*de remords*) pangs
bourrelet [burlɛ] *n* **(a)** *F* **b. (de graisse)** (*au ventre*) spare tyre *or US* tire, roll of fat **(b)** (*contre les courants d'air*) weather strip, *Br* draught excluder **(c)** (*petit coussin*) pad, cushion
bourrelier [burəlje] *nm* saddler, harness maker
bourrellerie [burɛlri] *nf* saddlery

bourrer [bure] **1** *vt* **(a)** (*chaise, coussin etc*) to stuff, to pad; (*placard, sac etc*) to cram, to pack tight; (*pipe*) to fill; **b. une dissertation de références** to stuff *or* cram an essay with references; *F* **b. le crâne à qn** to stuff *or* fill sb's head with nonsense; (*d'un professeur*) to stuff *or* fill sb's head with facts; *Pol* to brainwash sb; **on nous bourre le crâne de publicités** we're brainwashed by advertising; *F* **b. le mou à qn** to pull the wool over sb's eyes; **b. qn de coups** to beat sb up

(b) (*de nourriture*) to fill up; **ne le bourre pas de biscuits** don't fill him up with biscuits

(c) *Mil, Min* (*chargement*) to ram home; (*trou d'explosion, mine*) to stem, to tamp

2 *vi* **aliment qui bourre** stodgy *or* filling food; **les bananes, ça bourre** bananas are filling

3 se bourrer *vpr* **(a)** (*de nourriture*) to stuff oneself, to fill oneself up (**de chocolat** with chocolate)

(b) *F* (*d'alcool*) to get plastered *or* smashed; **se b. la gueule** to get smashed out of one's mind, to get legless

bourriche [buriʃ] *nf* (*d'huîtres, de gibier etc*) basket, hamper

bourrichon [buriʃɔ̃] *nm F* **se monter le b.** to get worked up *or* excited, to work oneself up into a state; **monter le b. à qn contre qn** to stir sb up against sb, to set sb against sb

bourricot [buriko] *nm* (small) donkey

bourrin [burɛ̃] *nm Arg* (*cheval*) nag

bourrique [burik] *nf* (*ânesse*) she ass; *F* (*personne têtue*) pigheaded individual; **faire tourner qn en b.** to drive sb crazy *or* round the bend; **têtu comme une b.** as stubborn as a mule

bourru [bury] *adj* surly, gruff, rough

bourse [burs] *nf* **(a)** (*porte-monnaie*) purse, *Am* coin-purse; **c'est trop cher pour sa b.** it's beyond his means, he can't afford it; **b. bien garnie** well-lined purse; **la b. ou la vie!** your money or your life!; **tenir les cordons de la b.** to hold the purse-strings; **sans b. délier** without spending a penny; **faire b. à part** to have separate finances; **faire b. commune** to pool one's money, to share expenses

(b) *Anat* **bourses** scrotum; **b. séreuse** bursa

(c) *Scol, Univ* **b. (d'études)** grant; **b. de recherche** research grant

(d) *Fin* **la B. (des valeurs)** the Stock Exchange, the Stock Market; **la B. monte/est calme** the market is rising/is quiet; **en B.** on the Stock Exchange *or* Stock Market; **valeur côtée en B.** listed *or* quoted share; **jouer à la B.** to play the market, to speculate

▶ **bourse**: **b. de commerce** commodities exchange; *Fig* **b. coulisse** unlisted market; **b. de l'emploi** = employment exchange; *Com* **b. de fret** shipping exchange; **b. du travail** (*réunion*) = meeting of local trade unions for the purpose of reaching agreement on how best to defend their interests and provide community services; (*endroit*) = local trade union centre

boursicotage [bursikɔtaʒ] *nm Bourse* dabbling on the Stock Market

boursicoter [bursikɔte] *vi Bourse* to dabble on the Stock Market

boursicoteur, -euse [bursikɔtœr, -øz], **boursicotier, -ière** [bursikɔtje, -jɛr] *n Bourse* small-time speculator

boursier, -ière [bursje, -jɛr] **1** *adj* **(a)** *Bourse* **opérations boursières** Stock Exchange *or* Stock Market transactions **(b)** *Scol, Univ* **étudiant b.** grant holder **2** *n* **(a)** *Scol, Univ* grant holder **(b)** *Bourse* (Stock Exchange) operator

boursouflage [bursuflaʒ] *nm*, **boursouflement** [bursufləmɑ̃] *nm* (*de la chair, du visage etc*) puffiness; *Fig* (*du style*) turgidity

boursouflé [bursufle] *adj* (*visage, yeux*) swollen, puffy; (*peinture*) blistered; *Fig* (*style, discours*) turgid

boursoufler [bursufle] **1** *vt* (*visage*) to cause to swell, to puff up; (*peinture*) to blister **2 se boursoufler** *vpr* (*de la peinture*) to blister; (*du visage*) to swell, to puff up

boursouflure [bursuflyr] *nf* (*du visage etc*) swelling, puffiness; (*de peinture*) blister, bubbling; (*de pneu*) blister; *Fig* (*du style, d'un discours*) turgidity

bousculade [buskylad] *nf* (*agitation*) jostling, pushing and shoving, hustle; (*hâte*) rush; **une b. vers la porte** a rush for the door; **être pris dans la b.** to be caught up in the rush

bousculer [buskyle] **1** *vt* **(a)** (*faire tomber*) to knock over; *Fig* (*habitudes, journée*) to disrupt; **cela va b. vos idées** that'll liven up your ideas

(b) (*pousser*) **b. qn** to jostle sb, to bump *or* knock into sb, to knock against sb

(c) (*presser*) to rush; **je n'aime pas être bousculé** I don't like being rushed; **il est toujours bousculé** he's always in a rush

2 se bousculer *vpr* (*d'une foule etc*) to jostle, to push and shove; **les idées se bousculaient dans sa tête** his head was swimming *or* buzzing with ideas; **aux heures de pointe, les voyageurs se bousculent au portillon** in the rush hour the passengers jostle to get on; **les candidats ne se bousculent pas au portillon** applicants aren't exactly queuing up for the job; *Fig* **ça se bouscule au portillon** he can't get his words out

bouse [buz] *nf* dung; **b. de vache** cow dung; **une b.** a cowpat

bouseux [buzø] *nm F Péj* yokel, bumpkin, *Am* hick

bousier [buzje] *nm* (*insecte*) dung beetle

bousillage [buzijaʒ] *nm* **(a)** *F* (*d'un travail*) botching, bungling; (*résultat*) botch(-up), bungle **(b)** *Constr* cob, daub

bousiller [buzije] *F* **1** *vt* (*travail*) to botch (up), to bungle; (*voiture, vélo, appareil-photo etc*) to wreck; **b. qn** to bump sb off, to do sb in; **b. sa santé** to ruin one's health **2 se bousiller** *vpr* **se b. la santé** to ruin one's health

bousilleur, -euse [buzijœr, -øz] *n F* botcher, bungler

boussole [busɔl] *nf* compass; **b. de marine** mariner's compass; **b. de poche** pocket compass; *F* **perdre la b.** to go off one's head

boustifaille [bustifɑj] *nf Arg* grub, *Br* nosh

bout [bu] *nm* **(a)** (*extrémité*) end; **assembler deux planches b. à b.** to join two planks end to end *or* end on; **l'autre b.** (*de la rue, de la ville etc*) the other *or* far end; **de b. en b.** (*reprendre un travail etc*) from start to finish; *Naut* from stem to stern; **d'un b. à l'autre** (*dans l'espace*) from one end to the other; (*dans le temps*) from beginning to end; **lire un livre d'un b. à l'autre** to read a book from cover to cover *or* from start to finish; **d'un b. à l'autre de son œuvre** throughout his works, all through his works; **d'un b. de la semaine/de l'année à l'autre** from one end of the week/year to the next; *F* **il n'y a personne à l'autre b.** (*au téléphone*) there's nobody on the other end; *Fig* **je n'en vois pas le b.** I'm nowhere near the end of it; *Fig* **je n'arrive pas à joindre les deux bouts** I can't make ends meet; **au b. du compte** after all, at the end of the day, when all's said and done; **au b. de la rue** at the end/bottom/top of the street; **aller au b. du monde** to go to the ends of the earth; *F* **c'est le b. du monde** (*d'un lieu*) it's a godforsaken hole *or* a dump; **Roubaix, ce n'est tout de même pas le b. du monde!** it's not as though Roubaix is miles from anywhere; **au b. d'une heure/de quelques jours** after an hour/a few days; **au b. d'un moment** after a while; **c'est ce qu'elle répète à tout b. de champ** that's what she keeps saying all the time *or* at every opportunity; **nous ne sommes pas encore au b.** we're not through yet, we're not out of the wood(s) yet; **il n'est pas au b. de ses peines** his troubles aren't over yet; **jusqu'au b.** to the (very) end; **aller jusqu'au b.** to go the whole way *or F* hog; (*d'un projet etc*) to see it through; (*avoir des rapports sexuels*) to go the whole way; **aller jusqu'au b. de ses idées** to follow one's ideas through (to their logical conclusion); **il est au b. de sa carrière** he's reached *or* he's at the end of his career; **être à b.** to be exhausted; *F* to be all in; **pousser** *ou* **mettre qn à b.** to exasperate sb, *F* to drive sb round the bend; **à b. de patience** at the end of one's patience *or* tether; **être à b. de ressources** (*n'avoir plus rien à dire*) to have run out of ideas *or* suggestions; (*n'avoir plus d'argent*) to have run out of money *or* resources; **être à b. d'arguments** to have run out of arguments; **il est à b. de forces** he has no strength left (in him); **être au b. du rouleau** (*n'en pouvoir plus*) to be at the end of one's tether; (*n'avoir plus d'argent*) to have run out of money; **venir à b. de qch** (*achever*) to get through sth; **venir à b. de la résistance/l'opposition de qn** to break down *or* overcome sb's resistance/opposition; **venir à b. d'une épidémie** to stamp out an epidemic

(b) (*pointe*) tip, end; (*de tuyau de pipe*) mouthpiece; (*de fusil*) muzzle; (*d'une canne*) ferrule; **b. du doigt/du nez/de la langue** tip *or* end of the finger/nose/tongue; **avoir un mot sur le b. de la langue** to have a word on the tip of one's tongue; **b. du sein** (*de femme*) nipple; **à b. de bras** at arm's length; *Fig* **porter une entreprise à b. de bras** to carry a firm; **b. de pied, b. renforcé** toecap; **ciseaux à bouts ronds** round-ended scissors; **b. de l'archet** (*d'un violon*) point of the bow; **à b. portant** point-blank, at point-blank range; *Fig* **tenir le bon b.** to be well on the way to success; *F* **elle est diplomate jusqu'au b. des ongles** she's a diplomat to her fingertips; **on ne sait jamais par quel b. le prendre** you never know how to approach *or* tackle him; *Arg* **mettre les bouts** to skedaddle, *Br* to hop it

(c) (*morceau*) (*de ficelle, fromage, pain etc*) bit, piece; **b. de papier/tissu** scrap *or* piece *or* bit of paper/material; **b. de cigarette** cigarette end *or* butt *or* stub; **un b. de jardin/terrasse** a bit of garden/terrace; **un b. de ciel bleu** a patch of blue sky; **elle en connait un b. sur la question** she knows a thing or two about it; **un tout petit b. de femme** a tiny little (slip of a) woman; **un b. de temps** a little while, some while; **un bon b. de temps** quite a while; **nous avons fait un b. de chemin ensemble** we went part of the way together; *Fig (de deux amants)* we were together for a while; *(de deux étudiants)* we studied together for a while; **nous avons fait un bon b. de chemin** we've come/gone a long way; **pour aller à Paris, cela fait un b. de chemin** it's quite a (long) way to Paris

▸ **bout**: *Rel* **(messe du) b. de l'an** mass, memorial service *(held on the anniversary of sb's death)*; **b. de chou** small child; **quel adorable b. de chou!** what an adorable child!; *Cin, TV* **b. d'essai** screen test; **b. ferré** *(d'une canne)* ferrule; **b. filtre** *(d'une cigarette)* filter tip; *Él* **b. mort** *(d'une bobine)* dead end

boutade [butad] *nf* **(a)** *(trait d'esprit)* joke, jest **(b)** *(caprice)* whim, caprice

bout-dehors, *pl* **bouts-dehors** *nm Naut* boom; **b. de foc** jib boom

boute-en-train [butɑ̃trɛ̃] *nm inv* live wire; **c'est le b. de la soirée** he's the life and soul of the party; **c'est le b. de la classe** he's the bright spark of the class

bouteille [butɛj] *nf* bottle; *(contenu)* bottle(ful); **panier à bouteilles** bottle carrier; **nous allons boire une b.** we'll have a bottle (of wine) together; **c'est une bonne b.** it's a good drop (of wine); **mettre du vin en bouteilles** to bottle wine; **mise en bouteilles** bottling; *F* **aimer la b.** to like one's drink, to be fond of the bottle; **avoir dix ans de b.** *(d'un vin)* to be ten years old; *F* **prendre de la b.** to be getting on a bit, to be getting long in the tooth; **la b. de gaz est vide** the gas cylinder is empty; **acheter une b. de gaz/butane** to buy a cylinder of gas/butane

▸ **bouteille**: **b. isolante** vacuum flask, Thermos® (flask); *Él* **b. de Leyde** Leyden jar, electric jar; **b. d'oxygène** cylinder of oxygen; **b. thermos®** vacuum flask, Thermos (flask)

bouter [bute] *vt Arch* **b. l'ennemi hors de France** to drive the enemy out of France

bouteur [butœr] *nm Constr* bulldozer

boutiquage [butikaʒ] *nm* shop in shop

boutiquaire [butikɛr] *nm* shopping area

boutique [butik] *nf* shop, *surtout Am* store; *Fig Péj (lieu)* dump, hole; **b. de mode** clothes *or* fashion shop, boutique; **b. de vêtements/de produits diététiques** clothes/health food shop; **b. de cadeaux** gift shop; **b. de souvenirs** souvenir shop; **b. hors taxes** duty-free shop, tax-free shop; **tenir b.** to run a shop; **fermer b.** to shut up shop; **parler b.** to talk shop; *Fig* **être de la b.** to be in the same business; *F* **j'en ai assez de cette sale b.!** I'm sick of this rotten dump *or* hole!; *F* **il est temps que je change de b.** it's time I had a change of job; **robe b.** designer dress; **confection b.** boutique-styled

boutiquier, -ière [butikje, -jɛr] *n* shopkeeper, *Am* storekeeper

boutoir [butwar] *nm (d'un sanglier etc)* snout; *Fig* **coup de b.** attack **(contre** on)

bouton [butɔ̃] *nm* **(a)** *(de fleur)* bud; **b. de rose** rosebud; **en b.** in bud, budding

(b) *(sur un vêtement)* button; **b. à queue** shank button; **b. de plastron de chemise** stud; **b. de col** collar stud

(c) *(d'une porte, d'une radio etc)* knob; *Ordinat* button; *(qu'on pousse)* (push) button; *(d'un fleuret)* button; **b. (électrique)** switch; **appuyer sur le b.** to press the button; **b. de sonnerie** *ou* **de sonnette** *ou* **d'appel** bellpush

(d) *(sur le visage)* spot, pimple; *(à la suite d'une maladie)* spot; **b. d'acné** spot caused by acne; **avoir des boutons** to have spots, to be spotty; *Fig* **ça me donne des boutons** it brings me out in a rash

▸ **bouton**: **b. d'arrêt** off switch; **b. de contrôle de luminosité** brightness control button; **boutons de manchette** cufflinks; **b. de marche** on switch; *Ordinat* **b. radio** radio button; **b. de réglage du contraste** contrast control button; **b. de réglage (du volume)** volume control (knob); *Ordinat* **b. de réinitialisation** reset button; *Ordinat* **b. de souris** mouse button; *Ordinat* **b. de turbo** turbo button

bouton-d'or, *pl* **boutons-d'or** *nm (plante)* buttercup

boutonnage [butɔnaʒ] *nm* buttoning (up); **b. devant/dans le dos** front/back fastening; **b. à droite/gauche** right/left buttoning; **veste avec double b.** double-buttoning jacket

boutonner [butɔne] **1** *vt* **(a)** *(manteau etc)* to button (up), to fasten (up), to do up **(b)** *Escrime (adversaire)* to button **2 se boutonner** *vpr (d'un manteau etc)* to button (up); *F* **il a encore du mal à se b. tout seul** he still has difficulty doing up his buttons by himself; **la robe se boutonne par derrière** the dress buttons (up) at the back **3** *vi (d'une robe etc)* **b. par derrière** to button (up) at the back

boutonneux, -euse [butɔnø, -øz] *adj (adolescent, visage etc)* spotty, pimply

boutonnière [butɔnjɛr] *nf* **(a)** *(de vêtement)* buttonhole; **faire une b.** to make a buttonhole; **porter une fleur à la b.** to wear a buttonhole *or US* boutonniere; **porter une médaille à la b.** to wear a medal on one's lapel **(b)** *Chir* buttonhole; **faire une b. à qn** to make a buttonhole in sb; *Fig (avec une épée etc)* to pink sb

bouton-poussoir, *pl* **boutons-poussoir** *nm* push button

bouton-pression, *pl* **boutons-pression** *nm* press stud, *Am* snap fastener, *Br F* popper

bouturage [butyraʒ] *nm (de plantes)* propagation by cuttings

bouture [butyr] *nf* cutting; **faire des boutures** to take cuttings

bouturer [butyre] **1** *vi (des plantes)* to make suckers **2** *vt* to propagate by cuttings

bouvet [buvɛ] *nm* grooving plane

bouvier, -ière [buvje, -jɛr] **1** *n (pour les bœufs)* cowherd, cowhand; *(pour les troupeaux)* drover **2** *nm (chien)* sheepdog

bouvillon [buvijɔ̃] *nm* steer, young bullock

bouvreuil [buvrœj] *nm* bullfinch

bovidés [bɔvide] *nmpl Zool* bovids, *Spéc* Bovidae

bovin [bɔvɛ̃] **1** *adj (race, regard etc)* bovine; **un air b.** a bovine look **2** *nmpl* **bovins** bovines, cattle

bovinés [bɔvine] *nmpl Zool* bovines, cattle

bowling [buliŋ] *nm* **(a)** *(jeu)* (tenpin) bowling **(b)** *(endroit)* (tenpin) bowling alley

box[1], *pl* **boxes** [bɔks] *nm* **(a)** *(dans un dortoir)* cubicle; *Jur* **b. des accusés** dock **(b)** *Aut* lock-up (garage) **(c)** *(dans une étable)* stall, *Br* loose box

box[2], **box-calf** [bɔks(kalf)] *nm (cuir)* box calf

boxe [bɔks] *nf* boxing; **faire de la b.** to box; **gants/match de b.** boxing gloves/match; **b. anglaise** boxing; **b. française** kick boxing

boxer[1] [bɔkse] **1** *vi* to box; **b. contre qn** to box against *or* fight sb **2** *vt* to box against, to fight; *F (frapper)* to punch up

boxer[2] [bɔksɛr] *nm (chien)* boxer (dog)

boxer[3] [bɔksɛr] *nm (short)* shorts

boxer[4] [bɔksɛr] *nm (moteur)* boxer engine

boxeur [bɔksœr] *nm* boxer

box-office, *pl* **box-offices** [bɔksɔfis] *nm* box office; **une pièce/un film/un chanteur en tête du b.** a box-office hit

boxon [bɔksɔ̃] *nm F* brothel; *Fig* **quel b.!** what a mess!; **mettre le b. dans qch** to make a mess of sth

boy [bɔj] *nm (domestique)* boy

boyau, -aux [bwajo] *nm* **(a)** *(d'animal)* gut, bowel; **(corde de) b.** (cat)gut; **boisson à tordre les boyaux** *(fort)* drink that burns the throat; *(de mauvaise qualité)* rotgut **(b)** *(tuyau)* hose(pipe); *(de vélo)* tubular tyre *or US* tire **(c)** *(allée)* narrow alley(way); *Min* narrow gallery; *Mil* communication trench

boycott(age) [bɔjkɔt(aʒ)] *nm* boycott(ing)

boycotter [bɔjkɔte] *vt* to boycott

boycotteur, -euse [bɔjkɔtœr, -øz] *n* boycotter

boy-scout, *pl* **boy-scouts** [bɔjskut] *nm Vieilli* boy scout; *Fig* **mentalité de b.** boy-scout mentality

BP [bepe] **1** *nf (abrév* **boîte postale)** PO Box; **BP 5000** consumer information/protection body **2** *nm (abrév* **brevet professionnel)** vocational qualification; **BP de barman** vocational qualification in barwork; **BP de cuisinier** vocational qualification in catering

BPF [bepeɛf] *Fin (abrév* **bon pour francs)** *(sur chèque)* ≈ PAY

brabançon, -onne [brabɑ̃sɔ̃, -ɔn] **1** *adj* of/from Brabant **2** *n* **B.** *(natif)* native of Brabant; *(habitant)* inhabitant of Brabant **3** *nf* **la Brabançonne** the Belgian national anthem

Brabant [brabɑ̃] *nm* **(a)** *Géog* Brabant **(b)** *Agr* **b.** all-metal wheel plough; **charrue à double b.** two-furrow plough

bracelet [braslɛ] *nm* **(a)** bracelet; *(rigide)* bangle; *(de montre)* strap, bracelet, band; **b. de force** (leather) wrist-band **(b)** *(lien)* band

bracelet-montre, *pl* **bracelets-montres** *nm* wristwatch

brachial, -iale, -iaux, -iales [brakjal, -jo] *adj Anat (artère etc)* brachial

brachiopode [brakjɔpɔd] *nm (mollusque)* brachiopod

brachycéphale [brakisefal] *adj, n* brachycephalic

braconnage [brakɔnaʒ] *nm* poaching

braconner [brakɔne] *vi* to poach

braconnier [brakɔnje] *nm* poacher

bractée [brakte] *nf Bot* bract

bradé [brade] *adj* cut-price

brader [brade] *vt (marchandises)* to sell off; *(à prix réduits)* to sell dirt cheap *or* at knockdown prices

braderie [bradri] *nf (foire)* ≈ jumble sale, *Am* ≈ rummage sale; *(magasin)* cut-price *or* discount store; *(liquidation)* clearance sale

braguette [bragɛt] *nf (de pantalon)* flies, fly

brahmane [braman] *nm* Brahman, Brahmin

brahmanisme [bramanism] *nm* Brahmanism, Brahminism
brahmine [bramin] *nf* Brahmani
brai [brɛ] *nm* pitch, tar
braillard, -arde [brɑjar, -ard] **1** *adj F* (*foule etc*) yelling, noisy; (*enfant*) howling, bawling **2** *n* bawler; **petit b.** noisy brat
braille [brɑj] *nm* Braille; **lire en b.** to read Braille
braillement [brɑjmɑ̃] *nm* yelling; (*d'enfant*) howling, bawling; **pourquoi ces braillements?** (*d'un nourrisson*) what's all the howling about?
brailler [brɑje] **1** *vi* to yell; (*d'un enfant*) to howl, to bawl; **faire b. sa télévision** to have one's television blaring (out) **2** *vt* (*chanson*) to bawl (out); (*slogan*) to chant
brailleur, -euse [brɑjœr, -øz] *adj, n F* = **braillard**
braiment [brɛmɑ̃] *nm* (*d'un âne*) bray(ing)
brainstorming [brɛnstɔrmiŋ] *nm* brainstorming; **un b.** a brainstorming session
braintrust [brɛntrœst] *nm* brains trust
braire [brɛr] *vi* (*pr ind* **il brait, ils braient**; *fu* **il braira, ils brairont**; *cond* **il brairait, ils brairaient**) (**a**) (*d'un âne*) to bray (**b**) *F* = **brailler**
braise [brɛz] *nf* (**a**) (*charbons*) (glowing) embers; (*charbon de bois*) (live) charcoal; **cuire qch sur/sous la b.** to cook sth over/in the embers (of a fire); **des yeux de b.** glowing *or* burning eyes; *Fig* **être sur la b.** to be on tenterhooks (**b**) *Arg Vieilli* (*argent*) bread, dough
braiser [breze] *vt Culin* to braise
braisière [brezjɛr] *nf Culin* braising pan
bramement [brammɑ̃] *nm* (*hurlement*) howl(ing), wail(ing); (*de cerf*) bell(ing)
bramer [brame] *vi* (*hurler*) to howl, to wail; (*de cerf*) to bell
bran [brɑ̃] *nm* (*de son*) bran; **b. de scie** sawdust
brancard [brɑ̃kar] *nm* (**a**) (*bras*) (*d'une civière, d'une charrette etc*) shaft, pole; **ruer dans les brancards** (*d'un cheval*) to kick when between the shafts; *Fig* to kick over the traces, to rebel (**b**) (*civière*) stretcher
brancardier, -ière [brɑ̃kardje, -jɛr] *n* stretcher bearer
branchage [brɑ̃ʃaʒ] *nm* (*des arbres*) branches, boughs; **branchages** cut *or* lopped-off branches
branche [brɑ̃ʃ] *nf* (**a**) (*d'un arbre*) branch, bough; (*d'un nerf, d'une rivière etc*) branch; (*de l'industrie etc*) branch, sector; (*d'activité*) line of business; **b. d'activité** area of operations; **la maîtresse b.** the main branch; **céleris en branches** celery; **une b. de céléri** a stick of celery; *Arg* **vieille b.** old mate; *Fig* **avoir de la b.** to look distinguished; **notre b. de la famille** our branch of the family; **la b. maternelle** the mother's side, *Fml* the maternal line; **les branches de la physique** the branches of physics; **c'est une b. très littéraire** it is a very literary discipline; **branches des bois d'un cerf** tines of a stag's antlers
(**b**) (*d'un compas*) leg; (*d'une monture de lunettes*) side; (*d'une fourche*) prong; (*d'une hélice*) blade; (*d'une clé*) shank; (*d'un fer à cheval*) arm; **les branches d'un chandelier** the branches of a candelabra; **b. à coulisse** (*d'un trépied*) telescopic leg
branché [brɑ̃ʃe] *adj F* trendy, with-it; **être b. sur qch** to be really into sth; **il est b. tennis/techno** he's really into tennis/ techno music; **c'est très b. d'avoir des lunettes** wearing glasses is very trendy *or* is very with-it *or* is the in thing
branchement [brɑ̃ʃmɑ̃] *nm* (**a**) (*d'un appareil électrique, d'un téléphone*) connecting (up), connection; (*à une prise*) plugging in; (*de canalisations, de fils électriques*) branch(ing), junction; **(tube de) b.** branch pipe (**b**) *Rail* branch line; **b. de voie** junction, points (**c**) *Ordinat* branch
brancher [brɑ̃ʃe] **1** *vt* (**a**) (*appareil électrique, téléphone*) to connect (up); (*à une prise*) to plug in; *Tél* **b. qn** to put sb through, to connect sb; **b. une sonnerie sur le circuit de lumière** to connect a bell up to *or* run a bell off the light circuit; *Fig* **b. qn sur un sujet** to get sb onto *or* started on a subject; **il faut que je le branche sur cette affaire** I must get him interested in this business
(**b**) *F* (*plaire à*) **b. qn** to give sb a buzz; **la peinture, ça te branche?** are you into painting?; **on se fait un resto ce soir, ça te branche?** fancy a restaurant tonight?; **ta sœur a l'air de le b.** he seems to be interested in your sister
2 *vi* (*des oiseaux*) to perch, to roost (*on a branch*)
3 se brancher *vpr* (*des oiseaux*) to perch, to roost; (*d'un appareil électrique*) to plug in
branchette [brɑ̃ʃɛt] *nf* small branch, twig
branchial, -iale, -iaux, -iales [brɑ̃ʃjal, -jo] *adj Zool* branchial
branchie [brɑ̃ʃi] *nf* (*d'un poisson*) branchia, gill
branchu [brɑ̃ʃy] *adj* branchy, branching
brandade [brɑ̃dad] *nf Culin* **b. (de morue)** = salt cod pounded with garlic, oil and cream
brande [brɑ̃d] *nf* (**a**) (*bruyère*) heather (**b**) (*terrain*) heath(land)
Brandebourg [brɑ̃dbur] *nm* (**a**) Brandenburg (**b**) *Couture* **b.** frog; **brandebourgs** frogging; **à brandebourgs** frogged
brandir [brɑ̃dir] *vt* (*arme*) to brandish, to flourish; (*qch pour attirer l'attention*) to brandish, to wave; (*la menace de qch*) to hold up
brandon [brɑ̃dɔ̃] *nm* firebrand; (*flambeau de paille*) torch; *Fig* **c'est un b. de discorde** (*personne*) he's a firebrand; (*sujet, affaire*) it's a bone of contention
brandy [brɑ̃di] *nm* brandy
branlant [brɑ̃lɑ̃] *adj* shaky; (*dent*) loose; (*chaise, escalier*) rickety; (*immeuble*) ramshackle; *Fig* (*raison, réputation, vérité*) shaky
branle [brɑ̃l] *nm* (*mouvement*) swing; *Fig* impulse, impetus; **mettre une cloche en b.** to set a bell swinging *or* ringing; *Fig* **donner le b. à qch** to get sth going, to give an impetus to sth; **mettre qch en b.** to set sth in motion; **se mettre en b.** to get going
branle-bas *nm inv* (**a**) *Naut* **faire le b. de combat** to clear the decks for action; **b.!** action stations! (**b**) *Fig* commotion; **c'était le b. (de combat) dans la ville entière** the whole town was in turmoil; **dans le b. du départ** in the commotion of setting off; **que signifie tout ce b.?** what's all the commotion about?; **il met toute la maison en b.** he's turning the whole house upside down
branlée [brɑ̃le] *nf F* thrashing; **prendre** *ou* **recevoir une b.** to get a thrashing, to get thrashed
branlement [brɑ̃lmɑ̃] *nm* (*de la tête*) wagging, shaking
branler [brɑ̃le] **1** *vt* (**a**) (*tête*) to wag, to shake (**b**) *Vulg* (*masturber*) to jerk off, *Br* to wank off **2** *vi* to be shaky; (*de dent*) to be loose; (*de chaise, d'escalier*) to be rickety; (*de maison*) to be ramshackle; **b. dans le manche** (*d'un outil*) to have a loose handle; *Fig Arg* **mais qu'est-ce qu'il branle, il devrait être là!** what the hell's he up to, he should be here **3 se branler** *vpr Vulg* (*masturber*) to jerk off, *Br* to wank (off); *Fig* **franchement, je m'en branle** to be honest, I don't *or* couldn't give a fuck *or* a shit
branleur, -euse [brɑ̃lœr, -øz] *n Vulg* (*bon-à-rien etc*) nerd, *Br* wanker
braquage [brakaʒ] *nm* (**a**) *Aut* (*des roues*) turning; **(angle de) b.** (*d'une voiture*) steering lock; **rayon** *ou* **cercle de b.** turning circle; **b. (au) maximum** full lock (**b**) *Arg* (*vol*) hold-up; **faire un b.** to do a hold-up
braque [brak] **1** *nm* (*chien*) pointer **2** *adj F* nutty, crazy
braquer [brake] **1** *vt* (**a**) (*diriger, tourner*) to point; **b. un fusil sur qn/qch** to aim *or* point a gun at sb/sth; **b. une lunette sur qn/qch** to fix *or* train a telescope on sb/sth; **il a toujours l'œil braqué sur nous** he's got his eye on us all the time; **b. son attention sur qch** to fix one's attention on sth
(**b**) *Aut* (*voiture etc*) to turn
(**c**) (*monter*) (*qn*) to antagonize; **b. qn contre qn/qch** to turn sb against sb/sth; **il est braqué contre le projet** he's dead set against the plan
(**d**) *Arg* **b. une banque** to hold up a bank
2 se braquer *vpr* to dig one's heels in; **se b. contre qn** to set one's face against sb
3 *vi Aut* to turn the (steering) wheel; **b. (à fond)** to apply full lock; **b. à gauche** to turn the wheel hard over to the left; **b. au maximum** to apply full lock; **voiture qui braque mal** car that has a poor lock
braquet [brakɛ] *nm* gear ratio; **changer de b.** to change gear
bras [bra] *nm* (**a**) *Anat* arm; **b. droit/gauche** right/left arm; **allonger le b. vers qch** to reach (out) for sth, to stretch out one's arm for sth; **offrir/donner le b. à qn** to offer/give sb one's arm; **prendre le b. de qn** to take sb's arm; **avoir un panier au b.** to have a basket on one's arm; **au b. de qn** on sb's arm; **il est entré, un dossier sous le b.** he came in with a file under his arm; **b. dessus b. dessous** arm in arm; **les b. m'en tombent** I'm astounded, I'm flabbergasted; **cela m'a coupé b. et jambes** it stunned me; **assis, les b. croisés** sitting with one's arms folded *or* with folded arms; **rester les b. croisés** (*ne pas travailler*) to twiddle one's thumbs; (*être passif*) to stand idly by; *Fig* **avoir le b. long** to have a lot of influence *or F* clout; **accueillir qn les b. ouverts** to welcome sb with open arms; **avoir qn/qch sur les b.** to have sb/sth on one's hands; *Fig* **elle a la responsabilité de l'affaire sur les b.** she carries all the responsibility for the matter; **elle s'est retrouvée avec une famille sur les b.** she found herself with a family to look after *or* to take care of; *Litt Hum* **être dans les b. de Morphée** to be in the arms of Morpheus; **à b.** in one's arms; **voiture à b.** handcart; **tenir qch à b. tendus** *ou* **à bout de b.** to hold sth in one's outstretched arms; **en b. de chemise** in (one's) shirtsleeves; **il m'est tombé dessus à b. raccourcis** he pitched *or* laid into me; **une partie de b. de fer** an arm-wrestling match; **lancer qch/frapper à tour de b.** to throw sth/strike with all one's might; **faire un b. d'honneur**

(à qn) ≈ to stick two fingers up (to sb), *Br* to give (sb) the V-sign
(b) (*homme*) hand, worker; **manquer de b.** to be shorthanded; **elle c'est la tête, et moi les b.** she's the brains, I'm the brawn
(c) (*d'un fauteuil*) arm(rest); (*d'un levier, d'une ancre*) arm; (*d'une grue*) jib; (*d'une croix*) limb; (*d'une pompe*) handle; *Naut* (*de la vergue*) brace
(d) (*de fleuve*) arm
(e) (*pouvoir*) arm; **le b. séculier** the secular arm; **le b. de la justice** the arm of the law
(f) (*de mollusque*) tentacle
▶ **bras**: *Aut* **b. compensateur** compensator arm; *Aut* **b. de contrôle** control arm; *Aut* **b. de direction** steering arm; **b. droit: être le b. droit de qn** to be sb's right hand (man); **b. fisher** (*microphone*) fisher boom; **b. de lecture** pickup arm; **b. de manivelle** crank arm; *Aut* web; *Géog* **b. de mer** arm of the sea; **b. mort** backwater; *Aut* **b. oscillant** radius arm *or* rod; **b. pivotant** (*pour moniteur*) swivel arm; **b. porte-copies** (*pour claviste*) copy-holder; *Aut* **b. de suspension** suspension arm
brasage [brazaʒ] *nm Métal* brazing
braser [braze] *vt Métal* to braze
brasero [brazero] *nm* brazier
brasier [brazje] *nm* (*incendie*) blaze, inferno; **la voiture n'était plus qu'un b.** the car was a ball of flames; *Litt* **le b. du couchant** the fiery glow of the setting sun; **l'ardent b. des passions mortelles** the burning fire of human passion
brasiller [brazije] *vi* (*de la mer*) to glitter, to sparkle
bras-le-corps (à) *adv* **saisir qn à b.** to seize sb round the waist; **prendre un problème à b.** to get to grips with a problem, to tackle a problem head on
brassage [brasaʒ] *nm* **(a)** (*de la bière*) brewing **(b)** (*mélange*) mixing; *Aut* **b. des gaz** mixing; *Fig* **le b. de peuples/cultures** the (inter)mingling *or* (inter)mixing of races/cultures **(c)** *Naut* (*de la vergue*) bracing; *Av* (*d'une hélice*) swinging
brassard [brasar] *nm* armband; **b. de deuil** black armband
brasse [bras] *nf* **(a)** *Natation* **b. (coulée)** breaststroke; **nager la b.** to swim breaststroke; **b. papillon** butterfly (stroke); **en quelques brasses, tu es au bout de la piscine** in a few strokes you'll be at the end of the pool **(b)** (*ancienne mesure*) fathom
brassée [brase] *nf* armful; **par brassées** by the armful
brasser [brase] *vt* **(a)** (*bière etc*) to brew **(b)** (*mélanger*) to mix; **b. des affaires** to be doing good business; **b. les cartes** to shuffle the cards; **b. de l'argent** to handle large amounts of money; **b. de l'air *ou* du vent** to work without getting anything done **(c)** *Naut* (*vergue*) to brace; *Av* (*hélice*) to swing
brasserie [brasri] *nf* **(a)** (*fabrique*) brewery; (*industrie*) brewing, beer-making (industry) **(b)** (*restaurant*) restaurant (with bar), brasserie
brasseur, -euse [brasœr, -øz] *n* **(a)** (*fabricant de bière*) brewer **(b)** *Fig* **b. d'affaires** big businessman, tycoon **(c)** *Sp* breaststroke swimmer
brassière [brasjɛr] *nf* **(a)** (*de bébé*) (baby's) *Br* vest *or Am* undershirt **(b)** *Can* (*soutien-gorge*) bra, *Am* brassière **(c) b. de sauvetage** life jacket, life vest
brasure [brazyr] *nf* **(a)** (*résultat*) braze, (brazed) seam **(b)** (*opération*) brazing, hard-soldering **(c)** (*alliage*) hard solder
bravache [bravaʃ] **1** *nm* swaggerer, blusterer **2** *adj* swaggering, blustering; **d'un air b.** blusteringly
bravade [bravad] *nf* bravado; **par b.** out of bravado
brave [brav] **1** *adj* [①B10,D,3] **(a)** (*courageux*) brave, courageous **(b)** (*preceding the noun*) (*bon*) good; **ce sont de braves gens** they are good *or* decent people; **c'est un b. homme *ou F* type** he's a good *or* decent man *or* sort; **eh oui ma b. dame, c'est la vie** well, my dear lady, that's life I suppose **(c)** *Péj* **il est bien b.** (*pas futé*) he's nice enough, he's OK **2** *nm* **(a)** (*héros*) brave man **(b) mon b.** my good man **(c)** *Péj* **faire le b.** to bluster, to swagger
bravement [bravmɑ̃] *adv* **(a)** (*courageusement*) bravely, courageously **(b)** (*avec résolution*) boldly
braver [brave] *vt* **(a)** (*affronter*) (*la mort, le danger*) to brave, to face bravely; **toujours prêt à b. le danger** always ready to face danger **(b)** (*défier*) (*qn*) to defy, to stand up to; **b. les lois/le règlement** to defy *or* flout the law/the rules
bravo [bravo] **1** *int* bravo!; (*dans un débat*) hear, hear!; **un grand b. à toute l'équipe technique** a big hand *or* cheer for all the technical crew; **ah b.!** (*tu as encore fait une sottise!*) oh, well done! **2** *nmpl* **des bravos** applause, cheers
bravoure [bravur] *nf* **(a)** (*courage*) bravery, courage **(b)** *Mus* **chanter son air de b.** to sing one's bravura passage; *Littér* **morceau de b.** purple passage
break[1] [brɛk] *nm Aut* estate (car), *Am* station wagon
break[2] *nm Mus, Tennis, Fig* break; *Boxe* **b.!** break!; **balle de b.** break point
brebis [brəbi] *nf* **(a)** *Zool* ewe; **lait/fromage de b.** ewe's milk/ewe's-milk cheese **(b)** *Rel* sheep; **les b.** the flock
▶ **brebis**: **b. égarée** lost sheep; *Fig* **b. galeuse** black sheep
brèche [brɛʃ] *nf* (*dans un mur, une haie etc*) gap, opening; (*dans la coque d'un bateau*) hole; (*dans une lame*) notch; *Mil* breach; *Mil* **monter sur la b.** to stand in the breach; *Fig* **être toujours sur la b.** to be always on the go; **battre qch en b.** to demolish sth
bréchet [breʃɛ] *nm Orn* breastbone
bredouillage [brədujaʒ] *nm,* **bredouillement** [brədujmɑ̃] *nm* mumbling, muttering
bredouillant [brədujɑ̃] *adj* mumbling
bredouille [brəduj] *adj* empty-handed; **rentrer *ou* revenir b.** to come back empty-handed
bredouiller [brəduje] *vti* to mumble, to mutter
bredouilleur, -euse [brədujœr, -øz] **1** *adj* mumbling, muttering **2** *n* mumbler, mutterer
bref, brève [brɛf, brɛv] **1** *adj* brief, short; **soyez b.!** be brief!, make it short!; **répondre d'un ton b.** to answer curtly; *Ling* **voyelle brève** short vowel; **dans les plus brefs délais** as soon as possible
2 *adv* in short; **en b.** in brief; **raconter qch en b.** to relate sth in a few words *or* briefly; **b., il accepte** in short *or* in a word *or* to cut a long story short, he accepts; *F* **enfin b., elle n'est pas satisfaite** well, in short, she isn't satisfied; **une cousine ou une tante, enfin b., quelqu'un de sa famille** a cousin or an aunt, well anyway, one of his relatives
3 *nm Rel* (papal) brief
4 *nf* **brève** *Journ* spot news
bréhaigne [breɛɲ] *adj Vieilli* (*jument etc*) barren
brelan [brəlɑ̃] *nm Cartes* three of a kind, pair royal; **b. d'as** three aces
breloque [brəlɔk] *nf* **(a)** (*sur un bracelet etc*) charm; **bracelet à breloques** charm bracelet **(b)** *Mil* break-off; **battre la b.** to sound the dismiss; (*d'une montre*) to be on the blink; *Fig* (*intellectuellement*) to wander; **mon cœur bat la b.** (*bat vite*) my heart is racing; (*fonctionne mal*) my heart is playing me up
brème [brɛm] *nf* (*poisson*) bream
Brême [brɛm] *nf* Bremen
Brésil [brezil] *nm* Brazil
brésilien, -ienne [breziljɛ̃, -jɛn] **1** *adj* Brazilian; **maillot/slip b.** high-cut swimsuit/briefs **2** *n* **B.** Brazilian
brésiller [brezije] *Tech, Litt* **1** *vt* to break into small pieces; (*broyer*) to crumble, to pulverize **2** *vi* to crumble **3 se brésiller** *vpr* to crumble
Bretagne [brətaɲ] *nf* Brittany; **Basse-B.** Lower *or* Western Brittany
bretelle [brətɛl] *nf* **(a)** (*de soutien-gorge, robe etc*) (shoulder) strap; **(paire de) bretelles** (*de pantalon*) (pair of) braces *or Am* suspenders **(b)** (*lanière*) strap; **b. de fusil** rifle sling; **l'arme à la b.** with one's rifle slung over one's shoulder **(c)** (*route*) access road; *Rail* crossover; **b. d'autoroute** motorway link road, *Br* slip road, ramp; *Aut* **bretelle d'accès** spur, slip road; (*vers autoroute surélevée*) on-ramp; *Aut* **b. de sortie** exit; (*d'autoroute surélevée*) exit, off-ramp **(d)** *TV, Rad* (*magnétophone*) portable tape recorder
breton, -onne [brətɔ̃, -ɔn] **1** *adj* Breton **2** *nm Ling* Breton **3** *n* **B.** Breton
bretonnant [brətɔnɑ̃] *adj* **Breton b.** = Breton-speaking Breton who preserves local traditions; **la Bretagne bretonnante** = Breton-speaking Brittany where local traditions are preserved
brett(el)er [brɛtle, brete] *vt* **(je brettelle** [brɛtɛl]**, n. brettelons** [brɛtlɔ̃]**)** (*pierre etc*) to tool, to tooth; (*bijoux*) to hatch, to chase
bretzel [brɛdzɛl] *nm* pretzel
breuvage [brœvaʒ] *nm* **(a)** (*boisson*) beverage, drink **(b)** (*potion particulière*) potion; **b. magique** magic potion
brève [brɛv] **1** *adj voir* **bref 2** *nf* **(a)** *Journ* short (news) item **(b)** *Ling* (*syllabe*) short syllable; (*voyelle*) short vowel
brevet [brəvɛ] *nm* **(a)** (*titre*) diploma, certificate; *Naut* **passer son b. de capitaine** to obtain one's master's certificate, *F* to get one's ticket; *Jur* **(acte en) b.** contract delivered by a notary in the original **(b) b. (d'invention)** patent; **prendre un b.** to take out a patent **(c)** *Fig* (*d'honnêteté*) guarantee **(d)** *Hist* (*du roi*) (royal) warrant
▶ **brevet**: **b. d'apprentissage** indentures, articles; *Scol* **b. (des collèges)** *Br* ≈ GCSE; *Mil* **b. d'état-major** = staff college certificate; *Scol Arch* **b. d'études du premier cycle** *Br* ≈ GCSE, *Am* ≈ high school graduation; **b. d'études professionnelles** = vocational diploma; **b. de pilote** *Av* pilot's licence; *Mil* wings; **b. professionnel** vocational qualification; **b. de technicien** = vocational training certificate (for 16-year-olds), professional qualification in

hotel management; **b. de technicien supérieur** = vocational training certificate (for 18-year-olds)
brevetable [brəvtabl] *adj* patentable
breveté [brəvte] *adj* **(a)** *(invention)* patented; **inventeur b.** inventor holding letters patent **(b)** *(diplômé)* qualified; **officier b. (d'état-major)** = officer who has passed staff college
breveter [brəvte] *vt* **(je brevète, n. brevetons; je brevèterai)** *(invention)* to patent; **faire b. une invention** to take out a patent on an invention
bréviaire [brevjɛr] *nm Rel* breviary; *Fig* bible
brévité [brevite] *nf Ling (d'une voyelle etc)* shortness
bribes [brib] *nfpl* **b. de conversation** snatches *or* scraps of conversation; **des b. de finlandais** scraps *or* bits of Finnish; **les b. de sa fortune/du repas** the remnants of his fortune/ the leftovers of the meal; **apprendre qch par b.** to learn sth piecemeal *or* bit by bit
bric-à-brac [brikabrak] *nm inv* **(a)** *(vieux objets)* odds and ends, bric-à-brac, jumble; *Fig* jumble **(de** of**)**; **marchand de b.** second-hand dealer **(b)** **(boutique de) b.** second-hand shop, *F* junk shop
bric et de broc [brikedəbrɔk] *adv* **de b.** from one source and another, haphazardly; **maison meublée de b.** house furnished with bits and pieces
brick [brik] *nm* **(a)** *Naut* brig **(b)** *Culin* **b. à l'œuf** = egg enclosed in filo pastry and deep fried **(c)** *(carton)* carton; **b. de lait/de jus d'orange** carton of milk/orange juice; **lait vendu en b.** milk sold in cartons
bricolage [brikɔlaʒ] *nm* **(a)** *(travail)* do-it-yourself, *Br* DIY; **faire du b.** to do (some) do-it-yourself *or* DIY; **grande surface de b.** do-it-yourself centre, DIY superstore; **rayon b.** do-it-yourself department; **un mordu du b.** a do-it-yourself enthusiast, a do-it-yourselfer **(b)** *Péj (réparation)* botch-up; **c'est du b.!** it's a botch-up!
bricole [brikɔl] *nf* **(a)** *(babiole)* trifle, little thing; **bricoles** *(objets)* odds and ends; *(travaux)* odd jobs; **offrir une petite b. à qn** to give sb a little something; *F* **il va lui arriver des bricoles** he's going to get into a pickle; **s'occuper à des bricoles** to do odd jobs **(b)** *(pour tirer une charrette etc)* breast strap; *(de cheval)* breast harness
bricoler [brikɔle] **1** *vt* **b. une affaire** to arrange a piece of business *(often shady)*; **elle a bricolé une table** she's knocked together *or* knocked up a table; **il a bricolé le moteur** he's tinkered with the engine **2** *vi* to do do-it-yourself *or Br* DIY; **j'ai passé la matinée à b. dans la maison** I spent the morning doing odd jobs about the house
bricoleur, -euse [brikɔlœr, -øz] **1** *n* handyman, *f* handywoman, *F* do-it-yourselfer **2** *adj* **être b.** to be good with one's hands
bride [brid] *nf* **(a)** *(du harnais)* bridle; **lâcher la b. à un cheval/ à qn** to give free rein to a horse/to sb, to give a horse/sb his head; **laisser à un cheval/à qn la b. sur le cou** to give a horse his head/to give sb a free rein; *Fig* **lâcher la b. à un élève** to allow a pupil more freedom, to give a pupil his head; *Fig* **elle a la b. sur le cou** she has a free rein; **tenir un cheval en b., tenir la b. haute à un cheval** to curb *or* check a horse; *Fig* **tenir qn en b., tenir la b. haute à qn** to keep a tight rein on sb; **tenir ses passions en b.** to keep a tight rein on one's passions; **aller à b. abattue** *ou* **à toute b.** to ride at full speed, to ride full tilt, *F* to ride hell for leather; **partir à b. abattue** to set off at top speed; **fureur sans b.** unbridled fury
(b) *Couture (de boutonnière)* bar; *(pour un bouton)* loop; *(de bonnet)* string
(c) *Tech* strap, tie; *(d'un cylindre, d'un tuyau)* flange, collar; **b. de serrage** clamp, cramp; **tuyau à brides** flanged pipe
bridé [bride] *adj Aut* **moteur b.** governed engine; **yeux bridés** slant(ing) eyes, *Péj* slitty eyes
brider [bride] *vt* **(a)** *(cheval)* to bridle; *(qn, colère, passions, déception etc)* to restrain, to curb, to keep in check; **cette contrainte le bride** it's a restraint on him **(b)** *Culin (volaille)* to truss; *Naut (câble etc)* to lash **(c)** *Couture (boutonnière)* to bind **(d)** *(tuyaux)* to flange, to clamp
bridge [bridʒ] *nm* **(a)** *Cartes* bridge; **b. aux enchères** auction bridge; **b. contrat** contract bridge; **tournoi/club de b.** bridge tournament/club; **faire un b.** to have *or* play a game of bridge **(b)** *(prothèse dentaire)* bridge
bridger [bridʒe] *vi* **(je bridgeai(s); n. bridgeons)** to play bridge
bridgeur, -euse [bridʒœr, -øz] *n* bridge player
bridon [bridɔ̃] *nm* snaffle (bridle)
brie [bri] *nm* Brie
briefer [brife] *vt* to brief; **b. ses collègues sur une affaire** to brief one's colleagues on a matter
briefing [brifiŋ] *nm* briefing; **faire un b.** to hold a briefing
brièvement [briɛvmɑ̃] *adv* briefly
brièveté [briɛvte] *nf* brevity, briefness, shortness; *(de style, d'expression)* brevity
brigade [brigad] *nf* **(a)** *Mil* brigade **(b)** *(de policiers)* squad; *(d'ouvriers)* gang; **chef de b.** foreman
▶ **brigade**: *Av* **b. aérienne** group, *Am* wing; **b. anti-gang** organized crime squad; **b. de gendarmerie** squad of gendarmes; *Hist* **Brigades internationales** International Brigades; **b. de police** police squad; **b. des stupéfiants** *ou F* **des stups** drug squad
brigadier [brigadje] *nm* **(a)** *Mil* corporal; *(d'artillerie)* bombardier **(b)** **b. (de police)** (police) sergeant **(c)** *(d'un groupe d'ouvriers)* foreman **(d)** *Naut* bowman, bow oar(sman)
brigadier-chef, *pl* **brigadiers-chefs** *nm Mil* rank between corporal and sergeant, lance sergeant
brigand [brigɑ̃] *nm* *(pillard)* brigand, bandit; *(personne malhonnête)* crook; **le petit b.** the little scoundrel *or* rascal
brigandage [brigɑ̃daʒ] *nm* (armed) robbery, banditry; **des actes de b.** (armed) robbery
brigantin [brigɑ̃tɛ̃] *nm Hist, Naut* brigantine
brigantine [brigɑ̃tin] *nf Naut* spanker
brigue [brig] *nf Litt* intrigue
briguer [brige] *vt (faveur, amitié, poste etc)* to solicit; **b. des voix** to canvass (for votes)
brillamment [brijamɑ̃] *adv* brilliantly
brillance [brijɑ̃s] *nf (d'un bijou, du regard)* brilliance; *Opt* brilliancy; *TV (de l'image etc)* brightness; *Mus* brightness of tone
brillant [brijɑ̃] **1** *adj (carrière, élève, orateur etc)* brilliant; *(lumière, couleur)* bright, brilliant; *(pierre précieuse)* sparkling, glittering; *(cheveux, chaussures, cuir)* shiny, glossy; *(conversation)* sparkling; **spectacle b.** splendid sight; **elle avait les yeux brillants de fièvre/joie** her eyes were bright with fever/sparkling with joy; **la situation n'est pas brillante** the situation isn't brilliant; **il est promis à un b. avenir** he has a brilliant future ahead of him
2 *nm* **(a)** *(d'un métal)* brilliance, brightness; *(d'une pierre précieuse)* sparkle, glitter; *(d'un papier, d'un tissu)* shininess, glossiness, sheen; *(de chaussures)* shine, polish; *(de conversation)* sparkle; *(d'esprit, d'intelligence)* brilliance; **et vos cheveux retrouveront leur b. naturel** and your hair will regain its natural shine
(b) *(diamant)* brilliant; **monté/taillé en b.** mounted/cut as a brilliant
▶ **brillant**: **b. à lèvres** lip gloss
brillantine [brijɑ̃tin] *nf* brilliantine
briller [brije] *vi* **(a)** *(du soleil)* to shine; *(de l'acier)* to glint, to gleam; *(d'une bougie)* to glimmer; *(de l'eau)* to shimmer, to glisten; *(des étoiles)* to glitter, to twinkle; *(de la lune)* to gleam, to shine; *(du satin)* to shimmer, to shine; *(des phares)* to glare; *(des braises)* to glow; *(des yeux)* to shine, to gleam; *Prov* **tout ce qui brille n'est pas or** all that glitters is not gold; **faire b. ses chaussures** to shine *or* polish one's shoes; **des yeux qui brillent de colère/de joie** eyes shining *or* gleaming with anger/happiness; **la joie brillait sur son visage** his face shone with joy
(b) *Fig (exceller)* to shine, to excel, to do well; **il brille en société** he shines in company; **b. dans la conversation** to be a brilliant conversationalist; **b. par son savoir/son intelligence** to be extraordinarily knowledgeable/intelligent; **b. par ses dons d'orateur** to be an extraordinarily gifted speaker; **b. par son absence** to be conspicuous by one's absence; **elle ne brille pas par sa ponctualité** she's not noted for her punctuality
brimade [brimad] *nf (tour)* rag; *Scol, Mil* **brimades** ragging, *Am* hazing; *(plus grave)* bullying, victimization; **faire subir des brimades à qn** to rag *or Am* to haze sb; *(plus gravement)* to bully *or* victimize sb
brimbalement [brɛ̃balmɑ̃] *nm (de voiture, charrette etc)* shaking about; *(de bateau)* swaying, rocking
brimbaler [brɛ̃bale] *vti F* = **bringuebaler**
brimborion [brɛ̃bɔrjɔ̃] *nm* bauble, knick-knack
brimer [brime] *vt (recrue etc)* to rag, *Am* to haze; *(plus gravement)* to bully, to victimize; **il se croyait brimé** he felt he was being picked on *or* got at
brin [brɛ̃] **1** *nm* **(a)** *(d'herbe)* blade; *(de myrte, persil, romarin etc)* sprig; *(de mimosa, de muguet)* spray; *(de paille)* wisp; **un beau b. de fille** a fine-looking girl
(b) *F (petite quantité)* bit **(de** of**)**; **un b. d'air** a breath of air; **un b. d'ironie/de jalousie** a touch *or* hint of irony/ jealousy; **sa voix laissait transparaître un b. d'inquiétude** one could detect a note of concern in his voice; **faire un b. de toilette** to have a quick wash (and brush up); **faire un b. de causette** to have a little chat; **il lui a fait un b. de cour** he had a bit of a flirt with her

(c) (*de laine, corde, fil etc*) strand
(d) **brins d'une antenne** wires of an aerial
2 *adv* **un b.** a bit; **il est un b. ennuyeux** he's a bit of a bore

brindezingue [brɛ̃dzɛ̃g] *adj F* barmy, nutty

brindille [brɛ̃dij] *nf* twig

bringue[1] [brɛ̃g] *nf Arg* **grande b.** (*fille*) beanpole

bringue[2] *nf Arg* (*beuverie*) binge; **faire la b.** to go on a binge

bringuebaler [brɛ̃g(ə)bale], **brinquebaler** [brɛ̃kbale] **1** *vi F* (*d'une voiture, charrette etc*) to shake about; (*d'un bateau*) to sway, to rock; (*d'une chaîne*) to rattle **2** *vt Litt* to shake about

brio [brijo] *nm* **avec b.** with panache, brilliantly; *Mus* **con b.** con brio

brioche [brijɔʃ] *nf Culin* brioche; *F* **prendre de la b.** to develop a paunch *or* pot

brioché [brijɔʃe] *adj* **pain b.** = milk bread

brique [brik] **1** *nf* **(a)** (*de construction*) brick; **maison de** *ou* **en briques** brick(-built) house; **mur de briques** brick wall; *Arg* **bouffer des briques**, *F* **manger des briques à la sauce caillou** to have nothing to eat; **ne t'attends pas à ce que je mange des briques à la sauce caillou** you can't expect me to live on air **(b)** (*de savon*) bar, cake; (*de béton etc*) block, slab **(c)** *Arg* (*dix mille francs*) ten thousand francs, *F* ten grand **2** *adj inv* brick-red

▶ **brique**: **b. creuse** hollow brick; **b. pleine** solid brick; **b. tubulaire** hollow brick

briquer [brike] *vt* (*nettoyer*) to scrub down; *Naut* (*pont*) to holystone

briquet[1] [brikɛ] *nm* (*appareil*) (cigarette) lighter; *Arch* (*à amadou*) tinder box; **b.-tempête** pipe lighter, windproof lighter; **battre le b.** to strike a light

briquet[2] *nm* (*chien*) beagle

briquetage [brik(ə)taʒ] *nm* (*maçonnerie*) brickwork; (*trompe-l'œil*) imitation brickwork

briqueter [brik(ə)te] *vt* (**je briquette, n. briquetons; je briquetterai**) (*construire*) to brick; (*en trompe-l'œil*) to face with imitation brickwork

briqueterie [brikɛtri] *nf* brickworks, brickyard

briqueteur [brik(ə)tœr] *nm* bricklayer

briquetier [brik(ə)tje] *nm* brick manufacturer

briquette [brikɛt] *nf* briquette

bris [bri] *nm* **(a)** (*de verre, des scellés etc*) breaking **(b)** *Jur* **b. de prison** prison breakout; **b. de clôture** breaking and entering, *Spéc* breach of close

brisant [brizɑ̃] **1** *adj* **explosif b.** high explosive; **obus b.** high-explosive shell **2** *nm* **(a)** (*écueil*) reef, shoal; **brisants** (*vagues*) breakers **(b)** = **brise-lames**

brise [briz] *nf* breeze; *Naut* **forte b.** stiff breeze

brisé [brize] *adj* (*détruit*) broken; **ligne brisée** broken line; *Fig* **il est b.** he's a broken man; **b. de fatigue** exhausted, tired out; **b. de chagrin** crushed by grief, brokenhearted

brise-bise *nm inv* half curtain (*in lower half of window*)

brisées [brize] *nfpl* (*pour marquer la voie*) broken branches; (*d'un cerf etc*) track; *Fig* **suivre les b. de qn** to follow in sb's footsteps, to follow sb's lead *or* example; *Fig* **aller** *ou* **marcher sur les b. de qn** to poach on sb's territory

brise-fer *nm inv* clumsy person (who breaks everything)

brise-glace *nm inv* **(a)** (*navire*) ice breaker **(b)** (*d'une pile de pont*) ice breaker; (*d'un navire*) ice beam

brise-jet *nm inv* tap *or Am* faucet nozzle

brise-lames *nm inv* **(a)** (*digue*) breakwater, mole **(b)** (*le long d'une plage*) groyne

brisement [brizmɑ̃] *nm Fig* **b. de cœur** heartbreak

brise-mottes *nm inv Agr* brake harrow

briser [brize] **1** *vt* (*casser*) to break, to smash; (*mottes de terre, navire*) to break up; (*minerai*) to pound (up), to crush; (*opposition*) to crush, to break down; (*enthousiasme, espérances*) to crush; (*carrière, vie*) to ruin, to wreck; (*grève*) to break; *Vieilli* (*conversation*) to break off; **b. qn** (*d'une marche etc*) to exhaust sb, to wear *or* tire sb out; (*de difficultés, paroles pessimistes etc*) to wear sb down; **b. une porte** to break open *or* burst open a door; **b. qch en mille morceaux** to smash sth to smithereens *or* into a thousand pieces; **b. qch en éclats** to smash sth to bits *or* to pieces; **porter cette caisse m'a brisé les reins** carrying that box has done my back in; **brisé par la douleur** crushed by grief, heartbroken; **la voix brisée par l'émotion** his voice choked with emotion; **cela me brise le cœur** it breaks my heart; **c'est à vous b. le cœur** it's heartbreaking
2 *vi* **(a) b. avec qn** to break with sb; *Litt Vieilli* **brisons là!** not another word!, enough!
(b) (*des vagues*) to break
3 se briser *vpr* **(a)** (*des vagues, de la porcelaine, du verre etc*) to break; **se b. en mille morceaux** to break *or* smash into a thousand pieces; **cela se brise comme du verre** it's as fragile as glass
(b) *Fig* (*des espoirs*) to be shattered, to be dashed; (*des efforts*) to fail, to come to nothing

brise-tout *n inv* clumsy person (who breaks everything); **c'est un b.** he's like a bull in a china shop

briseur, -euse [brizœr, -øz] *n* **b. de grève** strike breaker; *F Péj* scab

brise-vent *nm inv* windbreak

bristol [bristɔl] *nm* Bristol board, thin cardboard; (*carte de visite*) visiting card

brisure [brizyr] *nf* **(a)** (*cassure*) break, crack **(b)** (*d'un gond*) break; (*d'un volet*) folding joint **(c) brisures** (*petits morceaux*) tiny pieces **(d)** *Hér* brisure

britannique [britanik] [①**A20**,d] **1** *adj* British; **les Îles Britanniques** the British Isles **2** *n* **B.** Briton, *Am* Britisher; **les Britanniques** the British

broc [bro] *nm* pitcher, (large) jug

brocante [brɔkɑ̃t] *nf* (*commerce*) dealing in secondhand goods; (*magasin*) secondhand shop; (*marché aux puces*) secondhand market

brocanter [brɔkɑ̃te] **1** *vi* to deal in secondhand goods **2** *vt* (*meubles anciens, objets d'occasion etc*) to deal in

brocanteur, -euse [brɔkɑ̃tœr, -øz] *n* secondhand dealer

brocarder [brɔkarde] *vt Vieilli Litt* (*qn*) to gibe at

brocart [brɔkar] *nm Tex* brocade; **rideaux de b.** brocade curtains

brochage [brɔʃaʒ] *nm* **(a)** (*de livre*) stitching, sewing **(b)** *Tex* brocading, figuring

broche [brɔʃ] *nf* **(a)** *Culin* spit; **faire cuire qch à la b.** to spit-roast sth; **poulet à la b.** chicken on the spit; **b. de boucher** meat skewer **(b)** (*bijou*) brooch **(c)** *Tech, Él* pin; **b. de charnière** hinge pin; **b. d'une serrure** gudgeon of a lock; *Él* **fiche à deux broches** two-pin plug; *Ordinat* **b. de sortie** pinout **(d)** *Tex* spindle **(e)** (*de dentiste*) broach; *Chir* pin

broché [brɔʃe] **1** *adj* **(a)** *Tex* brocaded **(b) livre b.** paperback (book) **2** *nm Tex* (*procédé*) brocading; (*tissu*) brocade

brocher [brɔʃe] *vt* **(a)** (*livre*) to stitch, to sew **(b)** *Tex* (*tissu*) to brocade, to figure; **tissu broché d'or** gold brocade

brochet [brɔʃɛ] *nm* [①**A12**,1,g] (*poisson*) pike

brochette [brɔʃɛt] *nf* **(a)** *Culin* (*broche*) skewer; (*plat*) kebab; **b. de fruits de mer** seafood kebab **(b)** (*de gens*) band, group; **b. de décorations** row of medals *or* decorations; *Iron* **vous faites une belle b.!** you're a fine lot!

brocheur, -euse [brɔʃœr, -øz] **1** *n* (*de livre*) bookbinder **2** *nf Typ* **brocheuse** stitching machine **3** *nm Tex* brocade loom

brochure [brɔʃyr] *nf* **(a)** (*prospectus etc*) brochure, pamphlet, booklet; **b. publicitaire/touristique** advertising/tourist brochure **(b)** (*de livres*) stitching, sewing **(c)** *Tex* brocaded pattern

brocoli [brɔkɔli] *nm* broccoli; **mange tes brocolis** eat your broccoli

brodequin [brɔdkɛ̃] *nm* laced boot; *Hist, Th* buskin; *Hist* **appliquer les brodequins à un supplicié** to put the boots on a torture victim

broder [brɔde] **1** *vt Couture* to embroider; *Fig* **b. une histoire** to embroider *or* embellish a story **2** *vi* **tu brodes** (*c'est inexact*) you're embroidering; **b. sur des faits** to embroider *or* embellish the facts; **b. sur un sujet** to elaborate on a subject

broderie [brɔdri] *nf* **(a)** (*ouvrage*) (piece of) embroidery; **broderies** embroidery **(b)** (*activité*) embroidery; **faire de la b.** to do embroidery, to embroider; **b. anglaise** broderie anglaise

brodeur, -euse [brɔdœr, øz] **1** *n* embroiderer **2** *nf* **brodeuse** (*machine*) embroidering machine

broiement [brwamɑ̃] *nm* = **broyage**

bromate [brɔmat] *nm Ch* bromate

brome [brom] *nm Ch* bromine

bromure [brɔmyr] *nm Ch* bromide; *Typ* **b. de page** page bromide

bronche [brɔ̃ʃ] *nf Anat* bronchus, *pl* bronchi; **elle est fragile des bronches** she has weak lungs *or* a weak chest; **affection des bronches** bronchial disorder

broncher [brɔ̃ʃe] *vi* **(a)** (*de cheval*) to stumble **(b)** (*réagir*) to react; **sans b.** without batting an eyelid, without turning a hair; **il n'a pas bronché** he didn't bat an eyelid; **le premier qui bronche aura des ennuis!** (*qui bouge*) the first one to move will get it!; (*qui se plaint*) the first one to complain will be in trouble!

bronchiole [brɔ̃ʃjɔl] *nf Anat* bronchiole

bronchique [brɔ̃ʃik] *adj Anat* bronchial

bronchite [brɔ̃ʃit] *nf Méd* bronchitis; **faire** *ou* **avoir une b.** to have bronchitis

bronchitique [brɔ̃ʃitik] *adj, n Méd* bronchitic

broncho-pneumonie [brɔ̃kopnømɔni], *pl* **broncho-pneumonies** *nf Méd* bronchopneumonia

bronchoscopie [brɔ̃kɔskɔpi] *nf Méd* bronchoscopy

brontosaure [brɔ̃tɔzɔr] *nm* brontosaurus
bronzage [brɔ̃zaʒ] *nm* **(a)** *(de la peau)* tanning; *(hâle)* (sun)tan; **b. intégral** all-over tan **(b)** *(d'une statue etc)* bronzing; *(d'un canon, de canons de fusil etc)* blueing
bronze [brɔ̃z] *nm (métal, objet d'art)* bronze; **b. à canon** gunmetal; *Fig* **un cœur de b.** a heart of stone; **c'est un homme de b.** he has a heart of stone
bronzé [brɔ̃ze] *adj* **(a)** *(visage etc)* (sun)tanned, bronzed **(b)** *(statue etc)* bronze(d)
bronzer [brɔ̃ze] **1** *vt* **(a)** *(peau etc)* to tan **(b)** *(statue etc)* to bronze; *(canon de fusil etc)* to blue **2** *vi* to tan, to get a tan; *(de la peau)* to tan; **il bronze vite** he tans quickly **3 se bronzer** *vpr* to sunbathe
bronzette [brɔ̃zɛt] *nf F* sunbathing; **faire (de la) b.** to do a bit of sunbathing, to sunbathe
bronzier [brɔ̃zje] *nm Beaux-Arts* maker of bronzes
brook [bruk] *nm Sp* water jump
broquette [brɔkɛt] *nf* (tin)tack
brossage [brɔsaʒ] *nm* brushing
brosse [brɔs] *nf* **(a)** *(ustensile)* brush; **b. métallique** wire brush; **b. de chiendent** scrubbing brush; **laver le sol à la b.** to give the floor a scrub, to scrub the floor; **donner un coup de b. à qch** to give sth a brush; **donner un coup de b. à qn** to give sb's hair a brush; **enlever la boue d'un coup de b.** to brush off the mud; **cheveux en b.** crew cut; **se faire couper les cheveux en b.** to have a crew cut; **il porte la b.** he has a crew cut; *Fig* **passer** *ou* **manier la b. (à reluire)** to crawl, to bow and scrape; *Can F* **partir sur une b.** *(biture)* to go on a pub crawl, *Am* to go bar-hopping
(b) *(pinceau large)* (paint)brush
(c) *(d'un renard)* brush
▸ **brosse**: **b. à cheveux** hairbrush; **b. à dents** toothbrush; **b. à habits** clothes brush; **b. à ongles** nailbrush
brosser [brɔse] **1** *vt* **(a)** *(tapis, manteau, cheveux etc)* to brush; *(sol)* to scrub; *(cheval)* to brush down; *Belg* **b. un cours** to skip *or* cut a lecture
(b) *(peindre)* to paint; **b. les décors d'une pièce** to paint the scenery for a play; **il nous a brossé un rapide tableau de la situation** he gave us a brief outline of the situation; **son article brosse un vaste tableau de la situation** his article paints a broad picture of the situation
(c) *Sp (balle, ballon)* to cut, to put spin on
2 se brosser *vpr (se nettoyer)* to brush oneself down, to brush one's clothes; **se b. les dents** to brush *or* clean one's teeth; **se b. les cheveux** to brush one's hair; *F* **tu peux te b.!** you can whistle for it!
brou [bru] *nm* **(a)** *(enveloppe des noix etc)* husk, hull, *Am* shuck **(b)** *(teinture)* **b. de noix** walnut stain
broue [bru] *nf Can Arg* froth; *Fig* **faire** *ou* **péter de la b.** to talk big, to show off
brouet [bruɛ] *nm* gruel, *Br* skilly, *Péj* slop
brouette [bruɛt] *nf* **(a)** *(de jardin)* wheelbarrow **(b)** *Hist (chaise fermée)* sedan chair *(on two wheels)*
brouettée [bruete] *nf* (wheel)barrowful, barrowload
brouetter [bruete] *vt* to carry in a wheelbarrow, to wheelbarrow
brouhaha [bruaa] *nm* hubbub, brouhaha
brouillage [brujaʒ] *nm Rad, Électron (accidentel)* interference; *(intentionnel)* jamming; *Télécom* scrambling; **b. sonore/visuel** sound/visual interference
brouillard [brujar] *nm* **(a)** *Météo* fog; **il y a du b.** it's foggy; **arrêté par le b., pris dans le b.** fogbound; *Fig* **je suis dans le b.** I'm in a fog; **b. givrant** freezing fog; **voir à travers un b., avoir un b. devant les yeux** to see things through a haze; *Fig* **foncer dans le b.** to push on regardless **(b)** *Com* day book; *Compta* **b. de caisse** cash book **(c)** *Phys* aerosol **(d)** *Aut* **b. carburé** fuel spray
brouillasse [brujas] *nf* = **bruine**
brouillasser [brujase] *v impers* = **bruiner**
brouille [bruj] *nf* quarrel, disagreement; **être en b. avec qn** to be on bad terms with sb, to have fallen out with sb; **c'est une petite b. qui ne durera pas** it's just a tiff, it won't last long
brouillé [bruje] *adj* **(a)** *(mélangé)* jumbled (up), mixed (up); *(contours etc)* blurred, fuzzy; *Tél* scrambled; **œufs brouillés** scrambled eggs; **teint b.** blotchy complexion **(b) être b. avec qn** to be on bad terms with sb, to have fallen out with sb; **ils sont brouillés** they're on bad terms *or* they've fallen out (with each other); **je suis brouillé avec les dates/la grammaire** I'm hopeless at dates/grammar
brouiller [bruje] **1** *vt* **(a)** *(mélanger) (idées)* to mix up, to jumble (up); **b. des œufs** to scramble eggs; **b. les cartes** to shuffle the cards; *Fig* to confuse the issue, to confuse things; **b. la combinaison d'un coffre** to scramble the combination of a safe; **b. la vue à qn** to blur sb's vision; **l'alcool brouille le teint** alcohol ruins your complexion; **b. les pistes** to cover one's tracks; **cela risquerait de me b. les idées** it might get me into a muddle; **cela a brouillé mes souvenirs** it's confused my memories
(b) *(amis etc)* to set against each other, to cause a disagreement between; **je ne voudrais pas vous b. avec elle** I wouldn't want to make you fall out with her
(c) *Rad, Électron (émission) (accidentellement)* to cause interference to; *(intentionnellement)* to jam; *Télécom* to scramble
2 se brouiller *vpr* **(a)** *(d'idées)* to get mixed up *or* jumbled (up); **tout s'est brouillé dans ma tête** I got all muddled up *or* mixed up; **le temps se brouille** it's clouding over
(b) *(de la vue, des yeux)* to get blurred; **yeux brouillés de larmes** eyes blurred with tears
(c) *(se disputer)* to quarrel, to fall out **(avec qn** with sb); *F* **elle s'est brouillée avec la physique** she's taken a dislike to physics
brouillerie [brujri] *nf F* tiff
brouilleur [brujœr] **1** *adj Rad, Électron* **émetteur b.** jamming station; **signal b.** jamming signal **2** *nm Rad, Électron* jammer, jamming transmitter; *Télécom* **(circuit) b.** scrambler
brouillon, -onne [brujɔ̃, -ɔn] **1** *adj* muddleheaded; *(au travail)* disorganized, unmethodical; **esprit b.** muddled mind; **travail b.** unmethodical work
2 *n* muddler
3 *nm (ébauche)* (rough) draft; *Scol (notes etc)* rough work; **(papier) b.** scrap *or Am* scratch paper; *Ordinat* **version b.** draft version; **prendre des notes au b.** to take rough notes; **faire un exercice au b.** to do an exercise in rough; **je ne vais pas lire ce b.!** I'm not going to read this scribble!; **(cahier de) b.** rough (note)book; *Fig* **cette présentation n'est qu'un b.** this is only a rough presentation
broum [brum] *int* brum, brum!
broussaille [brusaj] *nf (souvent pl)* scrub, brushwood; **cheveux en b.** tousled *or* unkempt hair; **sourcils en b.** shaggy *or* bushy eyebrows
broussailleux, -euse [brusajø, -øz] *adj (région)* scrubby, bushy; *(cheveux)* tousled, unkempt; *(sourcils)* bushy, shaggy; **terrain b.** scrubland
broussard [brusar] *nm* bushman
brousse¹ [brus] *nf* **la b.** the bush, *Austr* the outback; *F Fig* the back of beyond, the middle of nowhere; **feux de b.** bush *or* brush fires; *F* **son village est perdu en pleine b.** his village is at the back of beyond *or* in the middle of nowhere
brousse² *nf Région (fromage)* = cream cheese made from goats' or ewes' milk
broutage [brutaʒ], **broutement** [brutmɑ̃] *nm* **(a)** *(par les bêtes)* grazing, browsing **(b)** *MecE (des freins, de l'embrayage, d'un outil)* juddering, grabbing
brouter [brute] **1** *vt (herbe etc)* to graze, to feed on; *Fig F* **elle me les broute, celle-là!** she's a real pain!, she really gets on my nerves! **2** *vi* **(a)** *(des bêtes)* to graze **(b)** *(des freins, de l'embrayage, d'un outil)* to judder, to grab
broutille [brutij] *nf* trifle, trifling matter; **ils se sont disputés pour une b.** they argued over nothing
brownien [bronjɛ̃] *adj Phys* **mouvement b.** Brownian movement
browning [broniŋ] *nm* Browning
broyage [brwajaʒ] *nm (d'une pierre, des aliments par les dents etc)* crushing, grinding; *(du charbon)* pulverizing; *Tex (du chanvre etc)* braking
broyer [brwaje] *vt* **(je broie, n. broyons; je broierai)** *(pierre, aliments etc)* to crush, to grind; *(documents)* to shred; *(charbon)* to pulverize; *Tex (chanvre etc)* to brake; **b. des couleurs** to grind colours; **la machine lui a broyé la main** the machine crushed his hand; *Fig* **quand il te serre la main, il te la broie!** he has a crushing handshake!; *Fig* **b. du noir** to be down in the dumps
broyeur, -euse [brwajœr, -øz] **1** *adj (appareil etc)* crushing, grinding **2** *n (personne)* crusher, grinder; *Tex* hemp braker *or* dresser **3** *nm (machine)* crusher, grinder; *(de documents)* shredder; *(de charbon)* pulverizer
▸ **broyeur**: **b. d'évier** sink disposal unit; **b. d'ordures** waste *or Am* garbage disposal unit
brrr [br] *int F* brrr!
bru [bry] *nf Vieilli* daughter-in-law
bruant [bryɑ̃] *nm (oiseau)* bunting; **b. jaune** yellowhammer
brucelles [brysɛl] *nfpl* tweezers
brucellose [bryseloz] *nf Vét, Méd* brucellosis
bruche [bryʃ] *nm Ent* **b. des pois** pea beetle, weevil
brugnon [bryɲɔ̃] *nm (fruit)* nectarine
brugnonier [bryɲɔnje] *nm* nectarine (tree)
bruine [brɥin] *nf* drizzle
bruiner [brɥine] *v impers* to drizzle; **il bruine** it's drizzling
bruineux, -euse [brɥinø, -øz] *adj* drizzly

bruire [brɥir] *vi* (*prp* **bruissant**; *pr ind* **il bruit, ils bruissent**; *impf* **il bruissait**) (*des feuilles, d'une étoffe*) to rustle; (*d'une machine*) to hum; (*d'un ruisseau, du vent*) to murmur; (*des abeilles*) to buzz

bruissement [brɥismɑ̃] *nm* (*des feuilles, d'une étoffe*) rustle, rustling; (*d'une machine*) hum(ming); (*d'un ruisseau, du vent*) murmur(ing); (*des abeilles*) buzzing

bruit [brɥi] *nm* **(a)** (*son*) sound, noise; (*vacarme*) noise; (*tapage, scandale*) commotion, fuss; **on n'entend pas les bruits de la rue** you can't hear the noise from the street; **c'est très calme, il n'y a pas un b.** it's very quiet, there's not a sound; **quel b.!** what a row *or* din *or* racket!; **lutte contre le b.** noise abatement campaign; **b. métallique** clang; **b. de vaisselle** clatter of dishes; **b. de marteaux** (sound of) hammering; **b. de pas** (sound of) footsteps; **il y avait des bruits de voix** there was the sound of voices, voices could be heard; **b. sourd** thud; **c'est tombé avec un b. sourd** it fell with a thud; **faire du b.** (*d'un enfant, moteur etc*) to make a noise, to be noisy; **il fait du b. quand il mange** he's a noisy eater; **ça a fait un b. formidable** it made an incredible noise; **enlève tes chaussures, tu feras moins de b.** take off your shoes, you'll make less noise; **ne faites pas de b.!** (*soyez silencieux*) don't make a sound!; (*ne chahutez pas*) don't be noisy!; *Fig* **cette histoire a fait du b. à l'époque** the affair caused a sensation *or* scandal at the time; **beaucoup de b. pour rien** much ado about nothing; **faire grand b. de qch** to make a great to-do *or* a great fuss about sth; **sans b.** without a sound, silently; *Électron etc* **b. parasite** interference, noise
(b) *Méd* (*cardiaque, respiratoire*) murmur
(c) (*rumeur*) rumour, *US* rumor; **répandre** *ou* **faire courir un b.** to spread a rumour; **le b. court que ...** rumour has it that ...; **des bruits courent sur la démission du Premier Ministre** there are rumours that the Prime Minister is going to resign; **des bruits circulent** rumours are circulating *or* are going about *or* round; **faux b.** false rumour

▶ **bruit**: **b. d'ambiance** background noise; **b. blanc** white noise; **b. de fond** background noise; **b. du moteur** engine noise; **b. parasite** hiss; **b. de piste** (*d'un enregistrement*) hiss; **b. de roulement** road noise

bruitage [brɥitaʒ] *nm Th, Cin, TV* sound effects

bruiter [brɥite] *vt Th, Cin, TV* to add sound effects to

bruiteur [brɥitœr] *nm Th, Cin, TV* sound-effects man

brûlage [brylaʒ] *nm* **(a)** (*des mauvaises herbes, de l'herbe etc*) burning; (*de la peinture*) burning off; (*des cheveux*) singeing; **se faire faire un b.** to have one's hair singed **(b)** (*du café*) roasting

brûlant [brylɑ̃] *adj* (*très chaud*) burning (hot); (*café*) boiling (hot), scalding (hot); (*soleil*) burning, scorching, blazing; *Fig* (*paroles etc*) fiery, passionate; **il a les mains brûlantes** his hands are burning (hot); **désir b.** burning desire; **question brûlante** burning question; **le sujet est d'une actualité brûlante** it's one of the burning issues of the day

brûlé, -ée [bryle] **1** *adj* burnt; *Méd* **il est b. au premier/deuxième/troisième degré** he has first-/second-/third-degree burns; *Culin* **crème brûlée** crème brûlée; **vin b.** mulled wine; *F* **tête brûlée** hothead
2 *nm* **(a) odeur de b.** smell of burning, burnt smell; **goût de b.** burnt taste; **avoir un goût de b.** to taste burnt; **sentir le b.** (*être louche*) to look fishy; (*d'opinions*) to smack of heresy
(b) *Can* burnt-out woodland area
3 *n* (*accidenté*) burns victim; *Méd* **les grands brûlés** people with third-degree burns; **crier comme un b.** to scream like a madman

brûle-parfum(s) [brylparfœ̃] *nm inv* perfume burner

brûle-pourpoint (à) [abrylpurpwɛ̃] *adv* (*sans détour*) point-blank; *Arch* **tirer sur qn à b.** to fire at sb at point-blank range

brûler [bryle] **1** *vt* **(a)** (*papier, bois, objet, les morts etc*) to burn; (*détruire entièrement*) (*maison etc*) to burn down; (*métal*) to burn away; (*résistance électrique etc*) to burn out; (*peinture*) to burn off; (*blessure*) to cauterize; (*d'un acide*) to corrode; (*d'un consommateur*) (*électricité, combustible*) to use, to burn; (*bougie*) to burn; **elle fut brûlée vive** (*par accident*) she was burnt to death *or* burnt alive; (*par supplice*) she was burnt at the stake; **b. la cervelle à qn** to blow sb's brains out; *Agr* **b. le terrain** *ou* **la brousse** to burn the ground; **la chaudière brûle beaucoup de charbon** the boiler burns *or* uses a lot of coal; *Fig* **ils ont brûlé leurs dernières cartouches** they've shot their bolt
(b) (*pain, gâteau, rôti etc*) to burn; (*café*) to roast; (*cheveux*) to singe; (*linge*) to scorch; (*personne, peau, yeux etc*) to burn; **le lait est brûlé** the milk has caught; **l'argent lui brûle les doigts** money burns a hole in his pocket; **terre brûlée par le soleil** sun-scorched earth; **le soleil me brûle le dos** the sun is burning *or* scorching my back; *F* **b. la route** *ou* **le pavé** to scorch along *or* tear along the road; **la gelée a brûlé les bourgeons** the frost has nipped the buds; **la fumée me brûlait les yeux** the smoke made my eyes burn *or* sting *or* smart; *Fig* **b. les planches** to give an inspired performance
(c) *Aut* **b. un feu rouge** to jump the lights, to go through a red light; **b. un stop** to go straight through a stop sign, not to stop at a stop sign; **b. la politesse à qn** to leave sb abruptly, to leave without saying goodbye to sb; (*passer devant qn dans une queue*) to push in front of sb; *Sp* **b. un concurrent** to race past a competitor, to leave a competitor standing; **b. un signal** to overrun a signal
(d) *F* **b. un espion** to uncover a spy; **il est brûlé** his cover's blown
2 *vi* **(a)** (*flamber*) (*de bois, charbon etc*) to burn; (*de maison etc*) to burn, to be on fire, to be alight; (*être très chaud*) to be burning (hot); (*de l'eau*) to be boiling (hot), to be scalding (hot); *Méd* to be feverish; (*d'une blessure*) to smart; **j'ai la gorge qui brûle** my throat is burning; **j'ai les yeux qui brûlent** my eyes are burning *or* stinging *or* smarting; **b. lentement** *ou* **sans flamme** to smoulder; **laisser b. la lumière/l'électricité** to leave the light/the lights on *or* burning; **aïe, ça brûle!** ow, that's hot!; *F* **tu brûles** (*dans un jeu*) you're getting very warm; **b. de fièvre** to be burning (with fever)
(b) *Fig* **b. de curiosité** to be consumed with curiosity; **b. d'impatience de faire qch** to be burning (with impatience) *or* bursting (with impatience) to do sth; **b. (du désir) de faire qch** to be burning *or* dying to do sth; *F* **les mains lui brûlent** he is dying to be doing things; *F* **les pieds lui brûlent** he is itching to be off
(c) (*de la viande*) to burn; (*du lait*) to catch; **j'ai encore fait b. mon repas!** I've burnt my food again!
(d) *Litt, Vieilli* **b. (d'amour) pour qn** to languish for sb
3 se brûler *vpr* (*par accident*) to burn oneself (**avec** on); (*exprès*) to set fire to oneself; **se b. les doigts** to burn one's fingers; **se b. la langue** to burn *or* scald one's tongue; **se b. la cervelle** to blow one's brains out

brûleur [brylœr] *nm* **(a)** (*d'une cuisinière à gaz etc*) burner **(b) b. de café** coffee roaster

brûloir [brylwar] *nm* (*machine*) coffee roaster

brûlot [brylo] *nm* **(a)** (*écrit*) fierce attack **(b)** *Culin* (*au sucre*) burnt brandy **(c)** *Can* (*moustique*) gnat, midge **(d)** *Hist, Naut* fire ship

brûlure [brylyr] *nf* **(a)** (*blessure*) burn; *Méd* **b. au premier/deuxième/troisième degré** first-/second-/third-degree burn; **des traces de b. de cigarette sur un fauteuil** cigarette burns on an armchair **(b) (sensation de) b.** burning (sensation); **brûlures d'estomac** heartburn **(c)** *Agr* frost nip; (*par le soleil*) scorching; (*du maïs*) blight

brume [brym] *nf* mist, haze; **un banc de b.** a bank of mist; *Fig* **dans les brumes du sommeil** heavy with sleep; **englué dans les brumes de l'ivresse** in a drunken haze

▶ **brume**: **b. de beau temps** heat haze; **b. de chaleur** heat haze

brumeux, -euse [brymø, -øz] *adj* misty, hazy; *Fig* (*idées, explication etc*) hazy, vague, woolly

brumisateur [brymizatœr] *nm* atomizer, spray

brun, brune [brœ̃, bryn] **1** *adj* (*tissu, cheveux etc*) brown; (*peau, personne*) dark, swarthy, dusky; (*teint*) (*bronzé*) brown, tanned; **tabac b.** dark tobacco; **une bière brune** a brown ale; **il est b. de peau** he's dark-skinned; **elle est naturellement brune** she is a natural brunette **2** *n* (*personne*) **un b. /une brune** a dark(-haired) man/woman; **une belle brune** a lovely brunette **3** *nm* (*couleur*) brown; **b. foncé** dark brown **4 brune** *nf* **(a) à la brune** at dusk, at twilight **(b)** (*bière*) brown ale

brunante [brynɑ̃t] *nf Can* dusk, twilight

brunâtre [brynɑtr] *adj* brownish

brunch [brœntʃ] *nm* brunch

brunette [brynɛt] *nf* brunette

brunir [brynir] **1** *vi* (*de peau, personne*) to tan, to become tanned; (*de cheveux*) to darken, to go dark; (*de feuillages*) to turn brown; *Culin* (*de sucre*) to brown; **b. au soleil** to tan **2** *vt* (*peau*) to tan; (*cheveux*) to darken; *Tech* (*or, métal*) to burnish, to polish

brunissage [brynisaʒ] *nm Tech* burnishing, polishing

brunissement [brynismɑ̃] *nm* (*de la peau*) tanning; (*résultat*) tan

brunisseur, -euse [brynisœr, -øz] *n Tech* burnisher

brunissoir [bryniswar] *nm Tech* burnisher, polisher

brunissure [brynisyr] *nf* **(a)** (*des métaux*) burnish, polish **(b)** *Agr* (potato) blight *or* rot

brushing [brœʃiŋ] *nm* blow-dry; **se faire un b.** to blow-dry one's hair; **faire un b. à qn** to give sb a blow-dry, to blow-dry sb's hair; **coupe et b.** cut and blow-dry

brusque [brysk] *adj* **(a)** (*personne, manière, ton*) abrupt, curt, brusque; (*geste*) abrupt, brusque **(b)** (*arrêt, changement, départ etc*) sudden, abrupt; *Aut* **tournant b.** sharp bend

brusquement [bryskəmɑ̃] *adv* **(a)** (*soudainement*) suddenly, abruptly; **il a b. changé** he suddenly changed; **la route plonge b. /tourne b. à droite** the road dips sharply/turns sharply to the right **(b)** (*demander, dire etc sans ménagements*) abruptly, brusquely, curtly

brusquer [bryske] *vt* **(a) b. qn** (*être impoli envers*) to be abrupt *or* curt with sb; (*maltraiter*) to treat sb harshly **(b)** (*hâter*) (*décision*) to rush; **b. les choses** to rush things; **il ne faut rien b.** we mustn't rush things; **attaque brusquée** surprise attack; *F* **arrête de me b.** stop rushing me

brusquerie [bryskəri] *nf* abruptness, brusqueness; **avec b.** abruptly, brusquely

brut [bryt] **1** *adj* **(a)** (*pétrole*) crude; (*sucre*) unrefined; (*diamant*) rough, uncut; (*champagne*) extra-dry, brut; (*cidre*) dry; (*marbre, albâtre*) unpolished; (*bois, peau*) undressed; **toile brute** unbleached cloth; **produit b.** primary product; *Ordinat* **données brutes** raw data; **matières brutes** raw materials; **fonte brute** pig iron; **or b.** gold in nuggets; *Métal* **b. de fonte** *ou* **de coulée** rough cast; **à l'état b.** in its raw state; **il nous a exposé le projet à l'état b.** he gave us a general outline of the project; **faire de l'art b.** to produce primitive art; **faits bruts** bald *or* hard facts

(b) *Com* (*bénéfice, valeur, poids etc*) gross; **salaire b.** gross salary; **marge brute** gross profit margin; **montant b.** gross amount, gross

2 *nm* **(a)** (*pétrole*) crude (oil)

(b) (*champagne*) brut *or* extra-dry champagne

3 *adv* **le colis pèse b. 20 kilos** *ou* **20 kilos b.** the parcel weighs 20 kilos gross; **elle gagne b. 20 000 francs** *ou* **20 000 francs b.** she earns 20,000 francs gross, she grosses 20,000 francs

brutal, -ale, -aux, -ales [brytal, -o] *adj* (*violent*) (*personne, mort*) brutal, violent; (*impoli, brusque*) (*personne, paroles, révélation, franchise etc*) brutal; **force brutale** brute force; **coup b.** brutal *or* savage blow; **les faits brutaux** the hard *or* brutal facts; **vérité brutale** plain *or* unvarnished truth; **cette vérité était trop brutale pour elle** the truth was too shocking for her; **être b. avec qn** to treat sb roughly *or* harshly; **avec sa manière brutale de dire les choses** with his harsh way of saying things; **arrêt b.** sudden *or* abrupt stop; **frein/embrayage b.** fierce brake/clutch

brutalement [brytalmɑ̃] *adv* (*violemment*) brutally, violently; (*rudement*) harshly, roughly; (*sans ambages*) bluntly, plainly; (*soudainement*) abruptly, suddenly; **la route tourne b.** there is a sudden bend in the road, the road bends suddenly; **il a b. changé** he has suddenly changed

brutaliser [brytalize] *vt* (*femme, enfant, matériel etc*) to ill-treat, to maltreat; *F* **il ne faut pas me b.** (*laisse-moi réfléchir*) don't rush me

brutalité [brytalite] *nf* **(a)** (*de personne*) (*violence*) brutality, violence; (*grossièreté*) roughness; **il lui parle avec b.** he has such a rough tone when he speaks to him; **pas de b.!** no violence! **(b)** (*d'animal*) brutality, savagery **(c)** (*rapidité*) suddenness, abruptness **(d)** (*acte violent*) brutal act, brutality; **brutalités de la police** police brutality

brute [bryt] *nf* **(a)** (*personne violente*) brute, beast; (*personne grossière*) boor; **sale b.!** filthy beast!; **frapper qn comme une b.** to hit sb brutally *or* violently; **j'ai dû taper dessus comme une b. pour que ça entre** I had to bang at it like mad to get it to go in; **espèce de b. épaisse!** you great oaf!; **le gangster m'envoya une de ses brutes épaisses** the gangster sent one of his heavies to visit me **(b)** *Litt* (*animal*) brute beast

Bruxelles [brysɛl] *nf* Brussels

bruyamment [brɥijamɑ̃] *adv* (*parler, rire*) loudly; (*manger*) noisily

bruyant [brɥijɑ̃] *adj* (*rue, voisin*) noisy; (*succès*) resounding; (*rire, applaudissement*) loud; **un quartier peu b.** a quiet neighbourhood

bruyère [bryjɛr] *nf* **(a)** (*plante*) heather, heath; (*terre*) heath(land), moor(land) **(b) racine de b.** briar root; **pipe en** *ou* **de b.** briar pipe

bryone [brijɔn] *nf* (*plante*) bryony

BT [bete] *nm abrév* **brevet de technicien**

BTH [beteaʃ] *nm abrév* **brevet de technicien hôtelier**

BTS [beteɛs] *nm* (*abrév* **brevet de technicien supérieur**) **B. Action Commerciale** professional marketing qualification; **B. Force de Vente** professional sales qualification

buanderie [bɥɑ̃dri] *nf* laundry (room)

bubon [bybɔ̃] *nm Méd* bubo

bubonique [bybɔnik] *adj Méd* (*peste*) bubonic

Bucarest [bykarɛst] *nf* Bucharest

buccal, -ale, -aux, -ales [bykal, -o] *adj Anat* (*cavité etc*) buccal; *Méd* **vaccin b.** oral vaccine

buccodentaire [bykodɑ̃tɛr] *adj* (*hygiène*) oral

bucco-génital, -ale, -aux, -ales [bykoʒenital, -o] *adj* **rapports bucco-génitaux** oral sex

bûche [byʃ] *nf* (*morceau de bois*) log; *F* (*personne stupide*) blockhead; *F* **ramasser une b.** to come a cropper; *F* **ne reste pas là comme une b.!** don't just stand/sit there like a dummy!

▶ **bûche**: *Culin* **b. de Noël** Yule log

bûcher¹ [byʃe] *nm* **(a)** (*pour le bois*) woodshed **(b)** (*de supplice*) stake; **monter** *ou* **mourir sur le b.** to be burnt at the stake; **condamné au b.** sentenced to be burnt at the stake **(c)** (*funéraire*) (funeral) pyre

bûcher² *Scol F* **1** *vt* (*matière*) to bone up on, *Br* to swot up **2** *vi* to slog, to work hard; (*d'un élève, d'un étudiant*) to swot, *Am* to grind

bûcheron [byʃrɔ̃] *nm* woodcutter, woodman, lumberjack

bûchette [byʃɛt] *nf* (*de bois sec*) stick, twig; (*pour apprendre à compter*) stick

bûcheur, -euse [byʃœr, -øz] *F* **1** *n* slogger, hard worker; (*élève, étudiant*) swot, *Am* grind **2** *adj* (*étudiant etc*) hard-working

bucolique [bykɔlik] *Littér* **1** *adj* (*poème*) bucolic, pastoral **2** *nf* pastoral poem, bucolic

budget [bydʒɛ] *nm* budget; **b. de l'éducation** education budget; **b. de la marine/de la guerre** navy/army estimates; **inscrire** *ou* **porter qch au b.** to budget for sth; **boucler le b.** to balance the budget; **vacances/prix pour les petits budgets** budget holidays/prices

▶ **budget**: **b. des approvisionnements** purchase budget; **b. des charges** overhead budget, cost budget; **b. commercial** sales budget; **b. de fonctionnement** operating budget; *Compta* **b. des investissements** capital budget; **b. mensuel** monthly budget; **b. mercatique** marketing budget; **b. prévisionnel** provisional budget; **b. de production** production budget; *Mktg* **b. de prospection** market exploration budget; **b. publicitaire** advertising budget; *Compta* **b. de trésorerie** cashflow, cash budget; **b. des ventes** sales budget

budgétaire [bydʒetɛr] *adj* (*dépenses, contrôle*) budgetary; (*année*) financial; **comptabilité b.** budgeting; **contrainte b.** budget constraint; **déficit/excédent b.** budget deficit/surplus

budgétisation [bydʒetizasjɔ̃] *nf* inclusion in the budget

budgétiser [bydʒetize] *vt* to include in the budget, to budget for

buée [bɥe] *nf* (*sur les vitres etc*) condensation, steam; (*sur un miroir*) mist; **les vitres sont couvertes de b.** the windows are steamed up *or* covered with condensation; **faire de la b.** (*d'une cuisinière etc*) to make *or* produce steam

buffet [byfɛ] *nm* **(a)** (*meuble*) sideboard; **b. de cuisine** (kitchen) dresser **(b) b. (d'orgue)** organ chest **(c)** (*repas*) buffet (meal); **b. froid** cold buffet; **b. de salades** salad bar; **b. du petit déjeuner** breakfast buffet; **b. à volonté** unlimited buffet; **b. campagnard** = cold buffet made with country produce; **b. de gare** station buffet, refreshment room **(d)** *F* (*ventre*) belly; **je n'ai rien dans le b. depuis hier soir** I haven't had a bite to eat since yesterday evening; **se mettre quelque chose dans le b.** to get something inside one

buffetier, -ière [byftje, -jɛr] *n Vieilli* (*d'un buffet de gare etc*) buffet manager, *f* buffet manageress

buffle [byfl] *nm* [①**A12**,1,c; **A12**,1,g] buffalo; **cuir (de) b.** buffalo hide

bufflesse [byflɛs], **bufflonne** [byflɔn] *nf* cow buffalo

bug [bœg] *nm Ordinat* bug

bugle¹ [bygl] *nm Mus* (key) bugle, flugelhorn

bugle² *nf* (*plante*) bugle

building [bildiŋ] *nm* (*d'appartements, de bureaux*) tower block

buire [bɥir] *nf* ewer, flagon

buis [bɥi] *nm* (*arbre*) box (tree); (*bois*) box(wood); *Rel* **b. bénit** (blessed) palm

buisson [bɥisɔ̃] *nm* bush; (*plusieurs plantes*) thicket; **un b. de mûres** a bramble thicket

▶ **buisson**: *Bible* **b. ardent** burning bush; *Culin* **b. d'écrevisses** = crayfish served piled up on a dish

buissonneux, -euse [bɥisɔnø, -øz] *adj* (*terrain etc*) bushy; (*végétation*) scrubby

buissonnier, -ière [bɥisɔnje, -jɛr] *adj* **faire l'école buissonnière** to play truant *or Am* hook(e)y

bulbe [bylb] *nm* **(a)** *Bot* bulb, corm **(b)** *Anat* bulb; **b. (rachidien)** medulla oblongata **(c)** *Archit* onion dome

bulbeux, -euse [bylbø, -øz] *adj Bot* bulbous

bulgare [bylgar] **1** *adj* Bulgarian **2** *nm Ling* Bulgarian **3** *n* **B.** Bulgarian

Bulgarie [bylgari] *nf* Bulgaria

bulldozer [byldozœr] *nm* bulldozer; *Fig F* **c'est un b., sa sœur** his sister just bulldozes *or* steamrollers her way through things

bulle [byl] **1** *nf* **(a)** (*d'air etc*) bubble; *Méd* (*vésicule*) blister; (*enceinte stérile*) bubble; (*de bandes dessinées*) balloon; *Ordinat* **b. d'aide** help pop-up *Tech* **b. d'air** air-lock; **b. d'encre** (*d'une imprimante*) ink bubble; **b. de savon** soap bubble; **faire des bulles** to blow bubbles; *Méd* **enfant-/bébé-b.** = child/baby kept in sterile surroundings; *Fig F* **coincer la b.** to laze *or* lounge around **(b)** (*lettre du pape*) (papal) bull; **b. d'excommunication** bull of excommunication **2** *adj inv* **papier b.** Manila paper **3** *nm* (*papier*) Manila paper

bulletin [byltɛ̃] *nm* **(a)** (*communiqué*) bulletin; (*d'entreprise, etc*) news letter; *Scol* **b. (scolaire)** (school) report; *TV* **b. d'actualités** *ou* **d'informations** news bulletin *or* report, news sheet; **b. radiophonique** radio bulletin; *TV, Rad* **b. spécial** newsflash **(b)** (*papier, certificat*) **b. (d'enregistrement) de bagages** luggage ticket, *Am* baggage check; **b. de consigne** left-luggage *or Am* checkroom ticket

▶ **bulletin**: **b. d'annulation** cancellation form; **b. blanc** blank ballot paper; *Com* **b. de commande** order form; *Journ* **b. électronique** electronic news-sheet; **b. d'inscription** registration form; **b. météorologique** weather report; **b. de paie** pay (advice) slip, salary advice (note); **b. de participation** entry form; **b. de salaire** pay (advice) slip, salary advice (note); *Méd* **b. de santé** medical bulletin; **b. de souscription d'actions** share subscription form; *Scol* **b. trimestriel** end-of-term report; **b. de versement** paying-in slip *or* form; **b. de vote** ballot paper; **b. (de vote) nul** spoiled ballot paper

bulletin-réponse *nm* reply form *or* coupon; (*pour un concours*) entry form

bulleux, -euse [bylø, -øz] *adj Méd* covered with blisters; *Géol, Méd* (*pierre, fièvre*) vesicular

bull-terrier, *pl* **bull-terriers** [bulterje] *nm* bull terrier

bumping [bœmpiŋ] *nm Av* bumping

bungalow [bœ̃galo] *nm* bungalow

bunker [bunkɛr] *nm Mil* bunker; *Golf* bunker, *Am* sand trap

buraliste [byralist] *n* (*de bureau de poste*) clerk; (*d'impôts*) receiver of taxes; (*de bureau de tabac*) tobacconist

bure [byr] *nf Tex* frieze, rough homespun; (*habit religieux*) frock

bureau, -eaux [byro] *nm* **(a)** (*meuble*) desk; **ordinateur de b.** desk-top computer; *Pol* **déposer un projet de loi sur le b.** to table a bill

(b) (*lieu*) office; (*à la maison*) study; **ceci fera d'excellents bureaux** this will be very good office space; **je dois passer au b. à midi** I have to drop by the office at midday; **il y a une bonne ambiance au b.** there's a good atmosphere at *or* in the office; **fournitures de b.** office supplies; **b. central** (*de poste*) main post office; *Tél* exchange; **b. de police** police station; **b. de douane** customs house

(c) (*personnel*) office (staff)

(d) (*assemblée*) committee; **élire le b.** to elect the committee

(e) (*service d'une administration etc*) department, division, bureau; **Deuxième B.** Intelligence Branch *or* Service, *US* G2 (Division)

▶ **bureau**: *Com* **b. d'achat** buying *or* purchase office; **b. d'aide sociale** welfare office; **b. de change** bureau de change; **b. à cylindre** roll-top desk; *Com* **b. de départ** port of departure; *Com* **b. de destination** port of destination; **b. distributeur** (*des Postes*) main sorting post office; **b. de douane** customs office; *Ordinat* **b. électronique** electronic desktop; *Com* **b. d'enregistrement** registration office; *Com* **b. d'entrée** port of entry; **b. d'études** design *or* planning department *or* office; (*de recherche*) R&D department; *Com* **b. d'expédition** shipping office; **b. d'exportation** export office; **b. d'information** information office; **b. d'inscriptions** registration desk; **B. International du Travail** International Labour Office; **b. de location** box office; **b. des méthodes** organization and methods department, O&M department; **b. ministre** pedestal *or* kneehole desk; **b. d'ordonnancement** scheduling and planning department; *Com* **b. de passage** port of transit; **b. paysager** open-plan office; **b. de placement** employment agency *or* bureau; **b. de poste** post office; **b. de publicité** advertising agency; *Journ* **bureaux de rédaction** newspaper office; **b. de renseignements** enquiry *or* information desk; (*pièce*) information office; **bureau-satellite** branch office; *Can* **b. spécial de scrutin** advance poll; **b. de tabac** tobacconist's (shop); **b. de traduction** translation agency

bureaucrate [byrokrat] *n Péj* bureaucrat

bureaucratie [byrokrasi] *nf Péj* (*système*) bureaucracy; (*ensemble des fonctionnaires*) officialdom

bureaucratique [byrokratik] *adj Péj* bureaucratic

bureaucratisation [byrokratizasjɔ̃] *nf Péj* bureaucratization

bureaucratiser [byrokratize] *vt Péj* to bureaucratize

bureautique [byrotik] *nf* office automation

burette [byrɛt] *nf* (*pour l'huile*) oilcan, oiler; *Ch* burette; *Rel* cruet; *Vulg* **il me casse les burettes** he gets on my tits

burin [byrɛ̃] *nm* **(a)** (*de graveur*) graver, burin; (*gravure*) engraving, print **(b)** (*ciseau d'acier*) (cold) chisel

burinage [byrinaʒ] *nm Tech* chiselling, chipping

buriner [byrine] *vt* **(a)** (*avec un burin*) to engrave; **visage buriné** (*par le vent etc*) seamed face **(b)** *Tech* (*metal*) to chisel, to chip

burineur [byrinœr] *nm Tech* chipper, chiseller

Burkina [byrkina] *nm* Burkina-Faso

burkinabé [byrkinabe] **1** *adj* of/from Burkina-Faso **2** *n* **B.** (*natif*) native of Burkina-Faso; (*habitant*) inhabitant of Burkina-Faso

burlesque [byrlɛsk] **1** *adj* **(a)** (*air, situation, projet etc*) ludicrous, ridiculous **(b)** *Littér* (*poème, genre etc*) burlesque **2** *nm Littér* **le b.** the burlesque

burnous [byrnu(s)] *nm* (*d'Arabe*) burnous(e); (*de bébé*) hooded coat; *F* **faire suer le b.** to use sweated labour

bus [bys] *nm* **(a)** (*autobus*) bus **(b)** *Él* bus (bar) **(c)** *Ordinat* bus; **b. d'adresses** address bus; **b. de contrôle** control bus; **b. de données** data bus; **b. entrée/sortie** input/output bus; **b. d'interface** interface bus; **b. local** local bus; **b. rapide** high-speed bus; **b. système** system bus

busard [byzar] *nm* (*oiseau*) harrier

buse[1] [byz] *nf* **(a)** (*oiseau*) buzzard **(b)** *F* (*idiot*) fool

buse[2] *nf* (*tuyau*) pipe; *Métal* blast pipe; **b. d'injection** injector nozzle; *Aut* **b. de carburateur** carburettor choke tube; *Min* **b. d'aérage** air channel *or* pipe *or* shaft; **b. de ventilation** air vent

business [biznɛs] *nm F* (*affaire*) business; **mais qu'est-ce que c'est que ce b.?** what's going on?, what's all this?

businessman [biznɛsman], *pl* **businessmen** [biznɛsmen] *ou* **businessmans** *nm* businessman

businesswoman [biznɛswuman], *pl* **businesswomen** [biznɛswumen] *ou* **businesswomans** *nf* businesswoman

busqué [byske] *adj* (*nez*) hook(ed), aquiline, Roman

buste [byst] *nm* (*haut du corps*) chest; (*seins*) bust; *Beaux-Arts* **b. (en hermès)** bust; **peindre qn en b.** to paint a half-length portrait of sb

bustier [bystje] *nm* (*soutien-gorge*) long-line (strapless) bra; (*corsage*) bustier; **robe de bal/maillot à b.** strapless evening gown/swimming costume

but [by(t)] *nm* **(a)** (*objectif*) aim, purpose, object, goal; (*d'un voyage, d'une promenade etc*) destination, goal; **il faut avoir un b. dans la vie** you must have a goal *or* an aim *or* a purpose in life; **il l'a fait avec ce b. en tête** he did it with this aim *or* object in mind; **je vous ai blessé, ce n'était pas mon b.** I've hurt you, it wasn't my intention *or* I didn't mean to; **mesure ayant pour b. d'assurer …** measure intended to ensure …; **remplir un b.** to serve a purpose; **un b. personnel** a personal goal; **dans le b. de vous aider** with the object *or* aim *or* intention of helping you; **dans le b. de frauder** with intent to defraud; **dans ce b.** with this aim in view; **se fixer un b.** to set oneself a goal *or* target; **je suis encore loin du b.** I still have a long way to go; **nous sommes tout près du b.** we don't have far to go; **poursuivre son b.** to pursue one's goal *or* aim; **cette loi vise un double b.** this law has a two-fold objective; **il touche au b.** he has nearly reached his goal *or* achieved his aim; **aller droit au b.** to go straight to the point; **errer sans b.** to wander about aimlessly; **c'est le b. recherché** that's what we're aiming for; **c'est le b. de l'opération** that's the (whole) point of the operation; **un coup au b.** a direct hit; **association à b. non lucratif** non-profitmaking association, *Am* not-for-profit association

(b) *Fb etc* goal; **ligne de b.** goal line; **entrée du b.** goal mouth; **marquer un b.** to score a goal; **gagner/perdre (par) 3 buts à 1** to win/lose by 3 goals to 1; **être dans les buts, garder les buts** to be in goal

(c) tirer de b. en blanc to fire point-blank; **faire une offre/répondre de b. en blanc** to make an offer/answer on the spur of the moment; **elle me l'a dit de b. en blanc** she told me point-blank

butane [bytan] *nm Ch* butane; **gaz b.** butane (gas)

butanier [bytanje] *nm Naut* butane tanker

buté [byte] *adj* stubborn, obstinate; **visage b.** fixed *or* set *or* determined expression

butée [byte] *nf* **(a)** *Tech* thrust; **palier de b.** thrust block *or* bearing; **b. (d'arrêt)** stop **(b)** *Constr* abutment, buttress **(c)** *Aut* stop; **en b.** in full lock; **en b. à droite/gauche** in full right/left lock **(d)** *Typ* **texte en b. gauche/droite** left/right justified text

buter [byte] **1** *vi* **(a) b. contre qch** (*cogner*) to bump *or* bang into *or* against sth, to knock against sth; (*trébucher*) to stumble *or* trip over sth; **b. contre** *ou* **sur un problème/une difficulté** to come up against a problem/a difficulty **(b)** (*de poutres etc*) to abut, to rest **(contre** against) **2** *vt* **(a)** (*braquer*) **b. qn** to put sb's back up **(b)** (*mur*) to prop up, to buttress, to shore up **(c)** *Arg* (*tuer*) to bump off **3 se buter** *vpr* (*s'entêter*) to dig one's heels in, to get stubborn

buteur [bytœr] *nm Fb* goalscorer; *Rugby* kicker; **le meilleur b.** the top goalscorer

butin [bytɛ̃] *nm* booty; (*de pilleur*) spoils, plunder; (*de voleur*) loot; **le b. des recherches archéologiques** the finds from the archaeological dig

butiner [bytine] **1** *vi* (*des abeilles*) to gather pollen **2** *vt* (*renseignements etc*) to gather, to collect

butineur, -euse [bytinœr, -øz] *adj* pollen-gathering

butoir [bytwar] *nm Tech* stop, check; *Rail* buffer; **b. d'une porte** door stop(per); *Aut* **b. de pare-chocs** bumper guard, overrider

butor [bytɔr] *nm* **(a)** (*oiseau*) bittern **(b)** *F* (*lourdaud*) lout, *Br* yob

buttage [bytaʒ] *nm* (*de plantes*) earthing up

butte [byt] *nf* **(a)** (*colline*) hillock, knoll, mound; *Géol* **b. témoin** outlier **(b) b. (de tir)** butts; *Fig* **être en b. à qch** to be exposed *or* open to sth

butter [byte] *vt* **(a)** *Agr* (*sol*) to ridge; (*plantes, un rosier*) to earth up **(b)** *Arg* (*tuer*) **b. qn** to bump sb off

buvable [byvabl] *adj* **(a)** (*potable*) drinkable; **il est tout à fait b., ce petit vin!** it's a very drinkable little wine, this **(b)** *Méd* to be taken orally

buvard [byvar] **1** *adj* **papier b.** blotting paper **2** *nm* (*matière*) blotting paper; (*feuille*) piece *or* sheet of blotting paper; (*sous-main*) blotter

buvette [byvɛt] *nf* **(a)** (*dans une gare etc*) refreshment bar **(b)** (*dans une station thermale*) pump room

buveur, -euse [byvœr, -øz] *n* drinker; **c'est un grand** *ou* **gros b.** he's a heavy drinker; **une buveuse de bière** a beer-drinker

BVP [bevepe] *nm* (*abrév* **bureau de vérification de la publicité**) *Br* ≈ ASA, organization which monitors advertising

bye(-bye) [baj(baj)] *int* bye-bye

by-pass [bajpas] *nm inv Chir, Aut* bypass

byronien, -ienne [birɔnjɛ̃, -jɛn] *adj* Byronic

Byzance [bizɑ̃s] *n* Byzantium

byzantin, -ine [bizɑ̃tɛ̃, -in] **1** *adj* Byzantine; *Fig Péj* (*querelles etc*) byzantine **2** *n* **B.** Byzantine

C

C[1]**, c** [se] *nm* (*lettre*) C, c; **c cédille** c cedilla
C[2] (*abrév* **Celsius**) C
c' *voir* **ce**
CA [sea] *nm* **(a)** *Él* (*abrév* **courant alternatif**) AC **(b)** *Com* (*abrév* **chiffre d'affaires**) turnover
ça[1] [sa] **1** *pron dém* [①B14,3] **(a)** (*cela*) it, that; (*ceci*) it, this; **donne-moi ça** give it to me, give me that; **c'est dégoûtant ça** that's disgusting; **une petite femme haute comme ça** a little woman no taller than that *or* only so high; **je suis comme ça** I'm like that; *F* **alors comme ça, vous déménagez?** so you're moving, are you?; **allons, pas de ça!** hey! none of that!; **pas de ça chez nous** we don't want any of that here; **ce n'est pas si facile que ça** it isn't as easy as (all) that; **ça oui!** oh yes!, definitely!; **ça non!** oh no!, not on your life!; **il ne manquait plus que ça** that's all we/I/*etc* needed; **ça dépend** it *or* that depends; **à part ça, tout va bien** apart from that, everything's fine; **il y a un peu de ça, effectivement** yes, there's an element of *or* a bit of that; **ça me fait de la peine de le voir malade** it upsets me to see him ill; **elle n'était pas comme ça avant** she wasn't like that before; **ça va? – comme ça** how are you? – so-so; **... tout ça quoi** ... et cetera, et cetera; **qui/quand/où ça?** who/when/where('s that)?; **comment ça?** how's that?; **comment ça, elle est partie?** what do you mean 'she's gone'?; **c'est qui/quoi ça?** who's/what's that?; **ça alors!** goodness (me)!; **ça alors, c'est incroyable!** well I never! *or* blow me! that's incredible!; **ça y est!** that's it!; **c'est ça!** that's it!, that's right!
(b) *F* **ça bavarde là-bas dans le fond de la classe** there's talking going on at the back of the classroom; **regarde-moi ça!** just look at that!; **écoute-moi ça!**, just listen to this!; **c'est ça les hommes!** that's men for you!; **ça va, ça vient** (*les touristes etc*) they come and go; **ça arrive en retard et ça veut qu'on l'attende** he/she/*etc* arrives late, and then expects me/us/*etc* to wait for him/her/*etc*
(c) *F* (*le sexe*) it; **il ne pense qu'à ça** he's got a one-track mind, that's all he thinks about
2 *nm Psy* **le ça** the id
çà[2] [sa] **1** *adv* **çà et là** here and there **2** *int* **ah çà!** now then!; **ah çà! par exemple!** well, I'm blowed *or* damned!
cabale [kabal] *nf* **(a)** *Rel* cab(b)ala **(b)** (*complot*) cabal, plot; **monter une c. contre qn** to plot against sb **(c)** (*ligue*) cabal, faction
cabaliste [kabalist] *nm Rel* cab(b)alist
cabalistique [kabalistik] *adj* cab(b)alistic; *Fig* **des formules cabalistiques** arcane formulae
caban [kabɑ̃] *nm* car coat; *Naut* peajacket, reefer
cabane [kaban] *nf* **(a)** (*bicoque*) hut, *Péj* shack; (*en rondins*) (log) cabin; (*à outils etc*) shed, *Can* **c. à sucre** saphouse **(b)** *Arg* (*prison*) **en c.** in (the) clink, *Br* in the nick; **trente ans de c.** thirty years in (the) clink *or Br* in the nick; **faire de la c.** to do time, to be inside
▶ **cabane**: **c. à lapins** (rabbit) hutch; *Fig* **ils vivent dans des cabanes à lapins** they live in rabbit hutches *or* shoeboxes
cabanon [kabanɔ̃] *nm* **(a)** (*petite cabane*) hut, shed **(b)** (*en Provence*) (*maison de campagne*) (country) cottage **(c)** (*chalet de plage*) (beach) hut, cabin, chalet **(d)** (*cellule*) padded cell; *F* **il est bon pour le c.** he ought to be locked up
cabaret [kabarɛ] *nm* **(a)** (*boîte*) night club, cabaret **(b)** *Arch* (*auberge*) tavern, inn
cabaretier, -ière [kabartje, -jɛr] *n Arch* innkeeper, tavern keeper
cabas [kabɑ] *nm* **(a)** (*panier*) shopping basket; (*en tissu*) shopping bag **(b)** (*pour les fruits*) basket
cabestan [kabɛstɑ̃] *nm Naut* capstan; **c. horizontal** windlass; **grand c.** main capstan; **virez au c.!** heave!
cabillau(d) [kabijo] *nm* (fresh) cod
cabine [kabin] *nf* **(a)** (*de bateau, d'avion, vaisseau spatial etc*) cabin; *Naut* **c. de luxe** stateroom, de-luxe cabin **(b)** (*de piscine*) changing cubicle **(c)** (*de grue*) cab, house; (*de locomotive, camion*) cab; (*d'ascenseur*) cage, *Am* car; *Aut* **c. basculante** tilt cab **(d)** *TV etc* **c. du commentateur** commentary booth; **c. de montage** edit suite; **c. de présentation** announcer booth; **c. de régie** control room, control cubicle; **c. speak** presentation booth
▶ **cabine**: *Rail* **c. d'aiguillage** signal box; **c. de bain(s)** (*de plage*) beach hut; (*de piscine*) changing cubicle; **c. de douche** shower cubicle; **c. d'essayage** fitting room; *Av* **c. de pilotage** cockpit, flight deck; **c. téléphonique** (tele)phone *or* call box, telephone booth
cabinet [kabinɛ] *nm* **(a)** (*petite pièce*) small room; *F* **les cabinets** the toilet, *Br* the loo, *Am* the john
(b) (*lieu de consultation etc*) office; (*d'avocat*) chambers; (*de médecin*) consulting room, *Br* surgery, *Am* office; (*patients, clients etc*) practice; **c. conseil** consultancy; **c. d'experts-conseils** consultancy (firm); **c. d'audit** firm of auditors; *Mktg* **c. d'études** market research firm; **c. d'expertise comptable** accounting firm; **c. juridique** law firm; **c. de traduction** translation company
(c) *Pol Vieilli* cabinet; (*d'un ministre*) departmental staff; **question de c.** ministerial question; **homme de c.** adviser; **chef de c.** = principal private secretary
(d) (*meuble*) cabinet
(e) (*au musée*) **c. d'estampes** print room
▶ **cabinet**: *Hist* **c. de lecture** library, reading room; **c. noir** cubbyhole; **c. particulier** (*au restaurant*) private dining room; **c. de toilette** (small) bathroom *or Am* washroom
câblage [kɑblaʒ] *nm* **(a)** *Él* (*d'une maison, fils*) wiring, cabling; *Télécom* **c. en paire torsadée** twisted pair cabling **(b)** *Tex, Él* (*de fils etc*) twisting together **(c)** (*de message*) cabling **(d)** *TV* **le c. d'une ville** installing cable television in a town
câble [kɑbl] *nm* **(a)** *Él* cable, lead; *Télécom* cable; **poser un c.** to lay a cable; **la télévision par c., le c.** cable television **(b)** (*corde*) cable; **c. métallique** wire cable; (*à brins*) stranded wire **(c)** (*message*) cable, cablegram; **envoyer un c. à qn** to send sb a cable, to cable sb
▶ **câble**: **c. d'alimentation** supply *or* feed *or* power cable; *Naut* **c. d'amarrage** mooring cable; *Électron* **c. coaxial** coaxial cable; *Aut* **c. de démarrage** jump lead, *Am* jumper cable; **c. en fibre(s) de verre** glass fibre cable; *MecE* **c. de frein** brake cable; **c. hertzien** radio link; **c. d'imprimante** printer cable; **c. de masse** earth cable, *Am* ground cable; *Télécom* **c. en paire torsadée** twisted pair cable; *Ordinat* **c. parallèle** parallel cable; **c. de raccordement** connecting cable; **c. de remorque** towrope, towline; **c. de retour (à la masse)** return cable; *Ordinat* **c. série** serial cable; *Ordinat* **c. de souris** mouse cable
câblé [kɑble] *adj TV* cabled; *Ordinat, Télécom* hard-wired; **réseau c.** cable (TV) network
câbler [kɑble] *vt* **(a)** (*tordre ensemble*) (*fils*) to twist together **(b)** (*message*) to cable **(c)** *TV* (*ville, quartier*) to install cable television in
câbleur, -euse [kɑblœr, -øz] *n Tech* cable-layer
câblodiffuseur, *pl* **câblodiffuseurs** [kɑblodifyzœr] *nm* cable company
câblodistributeur [kɑblodistribytœr] *nm* cable company
câblodistribution [kɑblodistribysjɔ̃] *nf* cable television; *Am Admin* community antenna television
câblogramme [kɑblɔgram] *nm Arch* cablegram, cable
câblo-opérateur, *pl* **câblo-opérateurs** [kɑblɔɔperatœr] *nm* cable company
cabochard, -arde [kabɔʃar, -ard] *F* **1** *adj* pigheaded **2** *n* pigheaded person
caboche [kabɔʃ] *nf* **(a)** *F* (*tête*) nut; **mets-le toi dans la c.!** get that into your thick skull!; **avoir la c. dure** (*être bête*) to be thick; (*être têtu*) to be pigheaded, to be as stubborn as a mule **(b)** (*clou*) heavy-headed nail; (*de cordonnerie*) hobnail; (*pour les meubles*) stud (nail)
cabochon [kabɔʃɔ̃] *nm* **(a)** (*pierre précieuse*) cabochon **(b)** (*de carafe à liqueur*) (glass) stopper **(c)** (*pour les meubles*) stud (nail)
cabosser [kabɔse] *vt* (*métal, voiture etc*) to bash up; (*chapeau*) to bash in; **vieux chapeau cabossé** battered old hat; **voiture cabossée** bashed-up *or* beat-up car
cabot [kabo] *F* **1** *adj* = **cabotin 1**(*a*)= **2** *nm* **(a)** (*acteur*) =

cabotin 2(*a*) **(b)** *Péj* (*chien*) pooch, mutt **(c)** *Mil* corporal, corp
cabotage [kabɔtaʒ] *nm Naut* coasting, coastal trade, cabotage; *Av* cabotage; **grand/petit c.** offshore/inshore coastal traffic
caboter [kabɔte] *vi Naut* to coast
caboteur [kabɔtœr] *nm Naut* coaster
cabotin, -ine [kabɔtɛ̃, -in] *F Péj* **1** *adj* **(a)** (*acteur*) ham **(b)** (*personne*) histrionic; **il est c.** he's a show-off **2** *n* **(a)** (*mauvais acteur*) ham (actor, *f* actress), third-rate actor, *f* actress **(b)** (*vantard*) show-off
cabotinage [kabɔtinaʒ] *nm F Péj* **(a)** *Th* ham *or* third-rate acting **(b)** (*en politique etc*) histrionics; (*vantardise*) showing off
cabotiner [kabɔtine] *vi F Péj* to play to the gallery, to show off
caboulot [kabulo] *nm Arg* seedy pub, dive
cabrage [kabraʒ] *nm* (*de cheval*) rearing (up); *Av* (*du nez*) pulling up
cabré [kabre] *adj* (*cheval*) rearing
cabrer [kabre] **1** *vt* **(a)** (*cheval*) to rear up; (*avion*) to nose up **(b)** *Fig* **c. qn contre qn** to turn *or* set sb against sb **2** *vi Av* to nose up **3 se cabrer** *vpr* (*d'un cheval*) to rear (up); *Fig* **se c. contre qn/qch** to rebel against sb/sth
cabri [kabri] *nm Zool* kid; *Fig* **sauter comme un c.** to jump for joy
cabriole [kabrijɔl] *nf* (*saut, bond*) leap, caper; (*en danse*) cabriole; *Équitation* capriole, goat's leap; (*de gymnaste*) somersault; *Fig* clever manoeuvre *or US* maneuver; **faire des cabrioles** to caper about, to cavort about; **elle s'en est tirée par une c.** she cleverly manoeuvred *or US* maneuvred her way out of it
cabrioler [kabrijɔle] *vi* to caper *or* cavort about
cabriolet [kabrijɔlɛ] *nm* **(a)** *Aut* convertible **(b)** *Hist* (*voiture à cheval*) cabriolet
caca [kaka] *nm Enf, F* (*excrément*) pooh; **as-tu fait c.?** (*à un enfant*) have you done a pooh *or* a number two *or* a big job?; **jette ça, c'est (du) c.** throw that away, it's nasty *or* dirty; **c. d'oie** yellowish green
cacah(o)uète, cacahouette [kakawɛt] *nf* peanut; **beurre de c.** peanut butter
cacao [kakao] *nm* (*boisson, poudre*) cocoa; *Bot* cocoa bean, cacao bean
cacaoté [kakaɔte] *adj* cocoa-flavoured
cacaotier [kakaɔtje] *nm Bot* cacao (tree)
cacaoui [kakawi] *nm Can* long-tailed duck
cacaoyer [kakaɔje] *nm Bot* cacao (tree)
cacatoès [kakatɔɛs] *nm* cockatoo
cacatois [kakatwa] *nm Naut* royal (sail); **(mât de) c.** royal mast; **c. de perruche** mizzen royal
cachalot [kaʃalo] *nm* sperm whale, cachalot
cache [kaʃ] **1** *nf* hiding place, cache; **c. d'armes** arms cache, cache of arms **2** *nm* cover; *Phot* (*pour tirage*) mask; (*de caméra*) hood; (*pour corriger les bromures*) patch; (*volet*) vignette; *TV, Cin* **c. de caméra** camera matte; *TV, Cin* **c./contre c. (électronique)** (electronic) matte; *Ordinat* **c. disque physique** physical disk cache; *Ordinat* **c. du disque dur** hard disk cache; *Ordinat* **c. externe** external cache
caché [kaʃe] *adj* hidden; (*sentiment*) secret
cache-antivol *nm inv Aut etc* security cover
cache-cache *nm inv* hide-and-seek; **jouer à c.** to play hide-and-seek
cache-col *nm inv* scarf, muffler
cachectique [kaʃɛktik] *adj Méd* cachectic
cache-culbuteur *nm inv Aut* rocker cover
Cachemire [kaʃmir] *nm* Kashmir
cachemire [kaʃmir] *nm Tex* (*laine*) cashmere; (*motif*) paisley pattern; **chemise de c.** paisley(-pattern) shirt
cache-misère *nm inv* = coat or wrap hiding shabby appearance
cache-moyeu *nm inv Aut* hub cover
cache-nez *nm inv* scarf, muffler
cache-pot *nm inv* flowerpot holder
cache-poussière *nm inv* dust coat, *Am* duster
cacher[1] [kaʃe] **1** *vt* (*qn, qch*) to hide, to conceal; (*ses sentiments*) to hide, to conceal, to mask; **où a-t-il pu c. la clé?** where could he have hidden the key?; **le mur nous cache la vue** the wall blocks *or* hides our view; **c. qch à qn** to hide *or* conceal sth from sb; **c. son jeu** to keep one's cards hidden *or* close to one's chest; *Fig* **il a bien caché son jeu** he kept his cards close to his chest; **il n'y a rien de caché dans cette affaire** everything is open and aboveboard in this transaction; **je ne vous cache pas que je suis déçu** I won't hide *or* conceal from you that I'm disappointed, I won't hide *or* conceal my disappointment from you; **c. son âge** to keep one's age a secret; **pour ne rien te c.** to be completely open with you; **il ne cache pas que ...** he makes no secret of the fact that ...
2 se cacher *vpr* (*d'une personne*) to hide; (*d'une chose*) to be hidden; **les voleurs se cachent** the thieves are (in) hiding; **le soleil se cache** the sun isn't shining, the sun is behind a cloud; **elle ne se cache pas pour dire qu'elle est communiste** she doesn't hide the fact she's a communist; **se c. de qn** to hide from sb; **sa timidité se cache derrière une certaine rudesse** his shyness is hidden behind a bluff exterior; **je ne m'en cache pas** I make no secret of it; **en se cachant** secretly, *Péj* on the sly; **sans se c.** openly
cache-radiateur *nm inv* radiator cover
cachère [kaʃɛr] *adj Rel* kosher
cache-sexe *nm inv* G-string; (*d'indigène*) apron
cachet [kaʃɛ] *nm* **(a)** (*empreinte*) stamp; (*sceau*) seal; (*de fabricant*) (trade)mark; *Hist* **lettre de c.** = order under the King's private seal; *Fig* **le c. du génie** the stamp *or* hallmark of genius; **il a beaucoup de c.** he has a lot of style *or* a certain cachet; **manteau qui a du c.** stylish coat **(b)** (*d'artiste, avocat, conseiller etc*) fee; **courir le c.** (*d'un acteur*) to do any job that's going **(c)** *Pharm* tablet, pill; **un c. d'aspirine** an aspirin (tablet)
▶ **cachet**: **c. d'oblitération** postmark; **c. de la poste** postmark
cachetage [kaʃtaʒ] *nm* (*de lettres etc*) sealing
cache-tampon *nm inv* hunt-the-thimble *or* -slipper
cacheter [kaʃte] *vt* **(je cachette, n. cachetons; je cachetterai)** (*lettre, bouteille etc*) to seal; **cire à c.** sealing wax; **vin cacheté** vintage wine
cachette [kaʃɛt] *nf* (*pour chose*) hiding place; (*pour personne*) hiding place, hideaway; **en c.** secretly, *Péj* on the sly; **vendre en c.** to sell under the counter; **boire en c.** (*habituellement*) to be a secret drinker; **il boit en c. de sa famille** he hides his drinking from his family
cachexie [kaʃɛksi] *nf Méd* cachexia
cachot [kaʃo] *nm* **(a)** (*cellule*) dungeon **(b)** (*isolement*) solitary confinement
cachotterie [kaʃɔtri] *nf* mystery; **faire des cachotteries** to be secretive
cachottier, -ière [kaʃɔtje, -jɛr] **1** *adj* (*personne*) secretive **2** *n* secretive person; **petit c.!** you secretive little thing!
cachou [kaʃu] **1** *nm* **(a)** (*bonbon*) cachou **(b)** (*teinture*) catechu **2** *adj inv* reddish-brown
cacique [kasik] *nm* (*chef*) cacique; *F* (*personne importante*) bigwig, big shot; **les caciques du parti** the party bigwigs
cacochyme [kakɔʃim] *adj Hum* doddery
cacophonie [kakɔfɔni] *nf* cacophony
cacophonique [kakɔfɔnik] *adj* cacophonous
cactus [kaktys] *nm* [①**A13,8**] cactus
c-à-d. (*abrév* **c'est-à-dire**) i. e.
cadastral, -ale, -aux, -ales [kadastral, -o] *adj* (*registre, relevé*) cadastral
cadastre [kadastr] *nm Admin* (*registre*) cadastre; **employés du c.** survey staff
cadastrer [kadastre] *vt Admin* (*propriété*) to register in the cadastre
cadavéreux, -euse [kadaverø, -øz] *adj* (*teint*) deathly pale, *Litt* cadaverous
cadavérique [kadaverik] *adj* (*teint*) deathly pale; *Méd* cadaveric; **rigidité c.** rigor mortis; **la rigidité c. s'était déjà installée** rigor mortis had already set in
cadavre [kadɑvr] *nm* **(a)** (*de personne*) corpse, (dead) body, *Fml* cadaver; (*d'animal mort*) carcass, body; *F* **c'est un c. ambulant** he's a walking corpse **(b)** *Arg* (*bouteille*) empty (bottle), dead man
caddie [kadi] *nm* **(a)** *Golf* caddie **(b)** (*chariot*) trolley, *Am* cart
cadeau, -eaux [kado] *nm* **(a)** present, gift; **en c.** as a present, as a gift; **faire un c. à qn** to give sb a present *or* gift; **acheter un c. à** *ou* **pour qn** to buy sb a present *or* gift; **je n'en voudrais pas comme c.** I wouldn't have it as a gift; **j'aimerais mieux en faire c.** I'd rather give it away; *F* **il ne lui a pas fait de c.** (*il ne l'a pas épargnée*) he didn't spare her; *F* **ton frère, ce n'est pas un c.** your brother's a real pain; **partir avec eux, ce n'était pas un c.** going away with them was no picnic **(b)** *Mktg* free gift, freebie; **c. publicitaire** freebie, giveaway, free gift
▶ **cadeau**: **c. d'anniversaire** birthday present; **c. de Noël** Christmas present
cadenas [kadna] *nm* padlock; **fermer la porte au c.** to padlock the door
cadenasser [kadnase] **1** *vt* (*porte etc*) to padlock **2 se cadenasser** *vpr* **(a)** (*d'une personne*) to lock oneself away **(b)** (*d'une porte*) to padlock
cadence [kadɑ̃s] *nf* **(a)** (*d'un vers, mouvement*) cadence, rhythm; **en c.** rhythmically, in time; **taper dans ses mains en c.** to clap (one's hands) in time; **marcher en c.** to march,

to walk in time; **forcer la c.** to force the pace; **à la c. de ...** at the rate of ...; **c. de production** rate of production; *Mil etc* **c. du tir** rate of fire; **prendre la c.** to get in(to) step; **garder la c.** to keep in step **(b)** *Mus (accords)* cadence; *(de concerto)* cadenza

cadencé [kadɑ̃se] *adj* **(a)** rhythmic(al); **pas c., marche!** quick march!; **marcher au pas c.** to march, to walk in time; *(rapidement)* to march *or* walk in quick time **(b)** *Ordinat* **c. à** running at

cadencer [kadɑ̃se] *vt* **(je cadençai(s), n. cadençons)** *(son style etc)* to give rhythm to; **c. son pas** to walk in time

cadet, -ette [kadɛ, -ɛt] **1** *adj* **la sœur cadette** *(de deux)* the younger sister; *(de plus de deux)* the youngest sister; **avoir trois frères cadets** to have three younger brothers; **la branche cadette** the younger branch **2** *n* **(a)** *(de deux enfants)* younger (child *or* one); *(de plus de deux enfants)* youngest (child *or* one); **mon c.** my younger brother; **ma cadette** my younger sister; **il est mon c. de deux ans** he's two years younger than I am, he's two years my junior; **c'est le c. de mes soucis** that's the least of my worries **(b)** *Sp* junior; **épreuve des cadets** junior event **(c)** *Golf* caddie **(d)** *Hist, Mil* cadet

Cadix [kadis] *nf* Cadiz

cadmium [kadmjɔm] *nm Ch* cadmium

cadogan [kadɔgɑ̃] *nm* = **catogan**

cadrage [kadraʒ] *nm Cin, Phot etc (de l'image)* centring, *US* centering; *(plan)* frame; *(action)* framing; *Ordinat* positioning

cadran [kadrɑ̃] *nm* **(a)** *(d'horloge, de baromètre etc)* face, dial; *(d'instrument, de téléphone etc)* dial; *Can (réveil)* alarm-clock; **c. solaire** sundial; **faire le tour du c.** *(d'une personne)* to sleep (right) round the clock **(b)** *Naut* **c. de transmission d'ordres** engine-room telegraph; *Aut* **cadrans (de bord)** display panels

cadre [kadr] *nm* **(a)** *(de tableau, porte, miroir etc)* frame; *(de vélo etc)* frame(work); **une photo sous c.** a framed photo

(b) *(domaine)* limits, bounds; *(structure)* framework; **sortir du c. de ses fonctions** to exceed (the scope of) one's duties; **ne pas sortir du c. de la légalité** to remain within the bounds of the law; **l'analyse régionale ne rentre pas dans le c. de cet article** regional analysis is beyond the scope of this article; **s'inscrire dans le c. de** to come within the framework of; **dans le c. de ce programme/des réformes entreprises par le gouvernement** as part of this programme/the government's programme of reform

(c) *(décor)* setting; *(milieu)* environment; **c'est un c. splendide!** it's a splendid setting!; **le manoir et son c. de verdure** the manor and its leafy surroundings; **vivre dans le c. familial** to live in a family environment

(d) *Litt (de livre etc)* framework, outline

(e) *(dans un formulaire)* space, box; *Ordinat (pour graphique)* box; **c. réservé à l'administration** for official use only

(f) *Naut* berth

(g) *Rad* frame aerial, loop aerial

(h) *(caisse)* **c. d'emballage** packing case

(i) *(dans une entreprise)* executive, manager; **les cadres** the managerial staff, the management; *Mil* the (commissioned and non-commissioned) officers; *(d'unité réduite etc)* cadre, staff; **passer c.** *(dans une entreprise)* to become an executive, to be promoted to management; **une femme c.** a female executive *or* manager; **elle est c.** she's an executive, she's in management; **jeune c. dynamique** dynamic young executive, *F* whizz kid; **hors c.** seconded, on secondment; **être mis hors c.** to be seconded *or* detached; **rayé des cadres** dismissed; **c. en mercatique** marketing executive

▶ **cadre**: **c. moyen** middle manager; *Mil* **le C. Noir** = military riding school in Saumur; *Mil* **c. de réserve** reserve list; **c. supérieur** senior executive *or* manager; **c. de vie** environment; **cadres moyens** middle management; **cadres supérieurs** senior management

cadré [kadre] *adj TV, Cin* in-frame, on-frame

cadre-adresse, *pl* **cadres-adresses** *nm* address space

cadre-châssis, *pl* **cadres-châssis** *nm Aut* chassis frame

cadrer [kadre] **1** *vi* to tally **(avec** with) **2** *vt Cin, Phot* to centre, *US* to center; *(plan etc)* to frame; *Ordinat* to position

cadreur [kadrœr] *nm TV, Cin* cameraman, camera operator

caduc, -uque [kadyk] *adj* **(a)** *Bot (feuille etc)* deciduous **(b)** *Jur (legs)* null and void; *(accord)* lapsed; *(dette)* statute-barred

caducée [kadyse] *nm (symbole de la profession pharmaceutique)* caduceus

caducité [kadysite] *nf (d'un système etc)* outmoded nature

caecum [sekɔm] *nm Anat* caecum

CAF [seaɛf] **(a)** *Com (abrév* **coût, assurance, fret)** cif; **vente C.** sale on cif basis **(b)** *abrév* **Caisse d'allocations familiales**

cafard, -arde [kafar, -ard] **1** *nm* **(a)** *(insecte)* cockroach, *Am* roach **(b)** *F* **avoir le c.** to feel down *or* low, to be down in the dumps; **avoir un coup de c.** to feel a bit down *or* low **2** *n* **(a)** *F (rapporteur)* sneak, telltale **(b)** *Arch (faux dévot)* hypocrite **3** *adj* **air c.** hypocritical *or* sanctimonious air

cafardage [kafardaʒ] *nm F* sneaking, telling tales

cafarder [kafarde] *vi F* **(a)** *(rapporter)* to sneak, to tell tales **(b)** *(avoir le cafard)* to feel down *or* low, to be down in the dumps

cafardeur, -euse [kafardœr, -øz] *n F* sneak, telltale

cafardeux, -euse [kafardø, -øz] *adj F (endroit, soir)* miserable, depressing; **se sentir** *ou* **être c.** to feel down *or* low, to be down in the dumps

caf'conc' [kafkɔ̃s] *nm inv F abrév* **café-concert**

café [kafe] **1** *nm* **(a)** *(produit, boisson)* coffee; **c. vert/torréfié** unroasted/roasted coffee; **grain de c.** coffee bean; **c. en grains** whole coffee, coffee beans; **c. moulu** ground coffee; **c. en poudre** *ou* **instantané** instant coffee; **un c. (bien) serré** a (very) strong coffee; **un c. léger** a weak coffee; **deux cafés** two coffees; **glace au c.** coffee ice cream **(b)** *(lieu)* café *(also serving alcoholic drinks)*; **c. tabac** = cafe cum tobacconist's **(c)** *Hist, Littér* coffee-house **2** *adj inv* **c. (au lait)** coffee-coloured

▶ **café**: **c. complet** = Continental breakfast; **c. crème** white coffee, coffee with hot milk; **c. décaféiné** decaffeinated coffee; **c. au lait** white coffee, *Br* coffee with milk; **c. liégeois** = coffee ice cream topped with whipped cream, *Suisse* **c. nature** black coffee; **c. noir** black coffee; **c. turc** Turkish coffee

café-concert *nm* = cabaret (club)

caféier [kafeje] *nm* coffee tree

caféière [kafejɛr] *nf* coffee plantation

caféine [kafein] *nf* caffeine; **sans c.** decaffeinated, caffeine-free; **teneur en c.** caffeine content

cafet [kafɛt] *nf F abrév* **cafétéria**

cafetan [kaftɑ̃] *nm* kaftan, caftan

cafétéria [kafeterja] *nf* cafeteria

café-théâtre *nm Br* ≈ pub theatre

cafetier, -ière [kaftje, -jɛr] **1** *n* café owner **2** *nf* **cafetière (a)** *(récipient)* coffee pot; *(électrique)* coffee machine *or* maker; **cafetière automatique** *ou* **à pression** percolator **(b)** *F (tête)* nut, *Br* bonce

cafetier-limonadier, *pl* **cafetiers-limonadiers** *nm* café-owner

cafouillage [kafujaʒ] *nm F* muddle, shambles, mess; *(de moteur de voiture)* missing, misfiring

cafouiller [kafuje] *vi F* to get into a muddle; *(de projet)* to fall apart *or* to pieces; *(de moteur de voiture)* to miss, to misfire; *(de poste de télévision)* to be on the blink

cafouilleur, -euse [kafujœr, -øz] *F* **1** *adj (personne)* muddle-headed **2** *n* muddler

cafouillis [kafuji] *nm F* shambles, muddle; **c'est un énorme c.** it's a complete shambles; **le c. de ses explications** his muddled explanations; **dans le c. de ses explications j'ai perdu ma concentration** his explanations were so muddled I lost my concentration; **il y a beaucoup de c. dans la gestion de cette entreprise** the management of this company is really shambolic

caftan [kaftɑ̃] *nm* kaftan, caftan

cage [kaʒ] *nf* **(a)** *(pour animaux)* cage; *(pour poules)* coop; *(pour lapins)* hutch; *(de puits de mine)* cage; *(de maison)* shell, carcass, *Fb* goal; **mettre un oiseau en c.** to cage a bird, to put a bird in a cage; **c. à oiseau/aux lions** bird/lions' cage; *Fig F* **habiter une vraie c. à lapins** to live in a poky little place; *Fig* **être comme un lion en c.** to be like a caged animal; *Fig* **une c. dorée** a gilded cage; *Fb* **être dans les cages** to be in goal **(b)** *(de montre etc)* (protective) cover, case, casing

▶ **cage**: **c. d'ascenseur** lift *or Am* elevator shaft; *Ordinat* scroll box; *MecE* **c. à billes** ball race; **c. d' escalier** stairwell; *Él* **c. de Faraday** Faraday cage, electrostatic screen; *Anat* **c. thoracique** rib cage

cageot [kaʒo] *nm* **(a)** crate **(b)** *F Péj (fille très moche)* dog

cagibi [kaʒibi] *nm F* **(a)** *(remise)* shed, hut **(b)** *(débarras etc)* storage room, *Br* boxroom, lumber room

cagne [kaɲ] *nf Scol F* = second-year arts class preparing to compete for entrance to the École Normale Supérieure

cagneux, -euse [kaɲø, -øz] **1** *adj (personne)* knock-kneed; *(jambes)* crooked; **genoux c.** knock knees **2** *n* **(a)** *Scol F* = student in the cagne **(b)** *(personne qui a les genoux cagneux)* knock-kneed person

cagnotte [kaɲɔt] *nf (caisse commune)* kitty; *(de jeux)* pool, kitty, *surtout Am* pot; *F (économies)* nest egg

cagot, -ote [kago, -ɔt] *Péj* **1** *n* (sanctimonious) hypocrite **2** *adj* hypocritical, sanctimonious

cagoule [kagul] *nf* **(a)** (*de moine*) cowl **(b)** (*de pénitent, cambrioleur*) hood **(c)** (*passe-montagne*) balaclava (helmet)

cahier [kaje] *nm* **(a)** notebook; *Scol* exercise book **(b)** *Typ* signature, gathering, section **(c)** (*d'un journal*) section **(d)** (*revue*) review, journal

▶ **cahier**: **c. de bord** logbook; **c. de brouillon** rough (note)book; *Com, Ind* **c. des charges** (*d'un contrat*) specifications; (*d'une vente*) articles and conditions; *Hist, Fig* **c. de doléances** list of grievances; **c. d'enregistrement** (*de courrier*) mail book; (*d'appels reçus*) telephone log; **c. des prix** price manual; **c. de réclamations** complaints book; **c. de textes** homework book; **c. de travaux pratiques** special notebook for practical work

cahin-caha [kaɛ̃kaa] *adv F* **aller c.** (*de la santé*) to be so-so; (*d'une personne*) to struggle *or* limp along; **les affaires vont c.** business is slow *or* slack; **la vie continue c.** life goes on (as it must)

cahot [kao] *nm* (*de véhicule*) jolt; (*de route*) bump

cahotage [kaɔtaʒ] *nm* = **cahotement**

cahotant [kaɔtɑ̃] *adj* **(a)** (*voiture*) jolting, jolty **(b)** (*route*) bumpy, rough

cahotement [kaɔtmɑ̃] *nm* (*mouvement*) jolting, shaking, bumping; (*heurt*) jolt

cahoter [kaɔte] **1** *vt* to jolt, to shake; **vie cahotée** life full of ups and downs; **des enfants cahotés par le divorce** children shaken up by divorce **2** *vi* (*d'une voiture, d'une brouette etc*) to jolt along

cahoteux, -euse [kaɔtø, -øz] *adj* (*route*) bumpy, rough

cahute [kayt] *nf* shack, shanty, hut

caïd [kaid] *nm* **(a)** (*en Afrique du Nord*) kaid **(b)** *Arg* (*chef de bande*) gang leader; **un c. de la drogue** a drug(s) baron; **c'est le gros c. en maths** he's the maths expert; *F* **jouer les caïds** *ou* **au c. dans la cour de récréation** to be a playground bully; **il fait le c.** he's acting all high and mighty

caillage [kɑjaʒ] *nm* = **caillement**

caillasse [kajas] *nf* **(a)** *Géol* (gravelly) marl **(b)** *F* (*cailloux etc*) loose stones, scree; **marcher dans la c.** to walk on loose stones *or* scree

caille [kɑj] *nf* quail; **gras comme une c.** (as) plump as a partridge; **elle est chaude comme une c.** she's as snug as a bug in a rug; *F* **ma c.** my little dove

caillé [kɑje] *nm* curds

caillebotis [kɑjbɔti] *nm* **(a)** *Naut etc* grating **(b)** (*treillis, plancher*) duckboard(s)

caillebotte [kɑjbɔt] *nf* curds

caillebotter [kɑjbɔte] *vt Arch* (*lait*) to curdle

caillement [kɑjmɑ̃] *nm* (*du lait*) curdling; (*du sang*) clotting, coagulating, coagulation

cailler [kɑje] **1** *vt* (*lait*) to curdle; (*sang*) to clot, to coagulate **2** *vi* **(a)** (*du lait*) to curdle; (*du sang*) to clot, to coagulate; **faire c. du lait** to curdle milk **(b)** *F* **ça caille** it's freezing (cold), *Br* it's perishing **3 se cailler** *vpr F* **on se (les) caille** it's freezing (cold), *Br* it's perishing

caillette [kajɛt] *nf* (*des ruminants*) fourth stomach

caillot [kajo] *nm* (*de sang*) clot

caillou, -oux [kaju] *nm* **(a)** (*petite pierre*) stone; **cailloux d'empierrement** (loose) chippings, road metal; **avoir un c. dans sa chaussure** to have a stone in one's shoe; *Fig* **avoir le cœur dur comme un c.** to have a heart of stone **(b)** (*grosse pierre*) boulder, rock **(c)** *F* (*pierre précieuse*) stone **(d)** *Arg* (*tête*) nut, *Br* bonce; **il n'a plus un poil sur le c.** he's as bald as a coot

cailloutage [kajutaʒ] *nm* **(a)** (*action*) (*de route*) metalling; (*de voie ferrée*) ballasting **(b)** (*pierres*) (*de route*) road metal; (*de voie ferrée*) ballast

caillouter [kajute] *vt* (*route*) to metal; (*voie ferrée*) to ballast

caillouteux, -euse [kajutø, -øz] *adj* (*route etc*) stony; (*plage*) pebbly, shingly

cailloutis [kajuti] *nm* broken stones, chippings, gravel; (*de route*) road metal

caïman [kaimɑ̃] *nm* cayman, caiman

Caïn [kaɛ̃] *nm* Cain

Caire (le) [(lə)kɛr] *nm* Cairo

cairn [kɛrn] *nm* cairn

cairote [kerɔt] **1** *adj* of/from Cairo **2** *n* **C.** Cairene, person from Cairo

caisse [kɛs] *nf* **(a)** (*pour marchandises*) (packing) case; (*à outils, de rangement*) box, chest; (*à thé etc*) chest; (*de champagne, vin*) case; (*pour plantes*) tub; **c. à savon** soapbox; **c. de melons** crate of melons; **mettre des marchandises en c.** to case goods

(b) (*de piano, d'horloge*) case; (*de véhicule*) body(work), bodyshell; (*de poulie*) shell; *Aut* **c. de l'embrayage** clutch casing

(c) *Arg* (*voiture*) car, *Br* motor

(d) *Arg* (*poitrine*) chest; **il s'en va de la c.** his chest is giving out

(e) *Mus* drum; **c. claire** side *or* snare drum; **grosse c.** bass drum

(f) *Anat* **c. du tympan** middle ear

(g) *Com, Fin* (*coffre*) cash box; (*d'une caisse enregistreuse*) till; (*dans un magasin, un garage etc*) cash desk; (*dans un grand magasin*) cashpoint; (*dans un supermarché*) checkout; **c. (enregistreuse)** cash register; **les caisses de l'État** the coffers of the State; **payez à la c.** pay at the (cash) desk *or* at the till; **tenir la c.** to be in charge of the cash; (*dans un restaurant, un magasin etc*) to be the cashier; **passer à la c.** to go to the cash desk; (*dans un supermarché*) to go through the check-out; (*payer*) to pay; (*se faire payer*) to be paid; (*se faire licencier*) to be paid off

(h) (*argent*) cash (in hand); (*recette*) takings; **livre de c.** cashbook; **faire la** *ou* **sa c.** to balance (up) one's cash, to do the takings, *Br* to cash up; **avoir tant d'argent en c.** (*disponible*) to have so much money in hand; **elle est partie avec la c.** she made off with the cash *or* the takings; **'la c.!' hurla le malfaiteur** 'hand over the cash!' shouted the robber

(i) (*organisme*) fund; **c. de défense** (*d'une association etc*) fighting fund

▶ **caisse**: **c. d'allocations familiales** ≈ child benefit office; *Compta* **c. d'amortissement** sinking fund; **c. à claire-voie** crate; **c. comptable** cash register; **c. des dépôts et consignations** = administrative department of the French government in charge of investing and lending public money; *Naut* **c. à eau douce** freshwater tank; **c. électronique** electronic billing machine; **c. enregistreuse** cash register; **c. d'épargne** savings bank; **c. de garantie** credit guarantee institution; **c. à laser** laser checkout; *Pol* **c. noire** slush fund; *Can* **c. populaire** credit union; **C. Primaire d'Assurance Maladie** = French government department dealing with health insurance; **c. de retraite** ≈ pension fund

caissette [kɛsɛt] *nf* small box

caissier, -ière [kesje, -jɛr] *n* (*dans un restaurant, un magasin etc*) cashier; (*dans un supermarché*) checkout operator; *Banque* cashier, teller; **c. de nuit** (*dans un hôtel*) night auditor

caisson [kɛsɔ̃] *nm* **(a)** (*caisse*) box, case; *Mil* (*de munitions etc*) wagon, caisson, *Arg* **se faire sauter le c.** to blow one's brains out **(b)** locker, bin **(c)** *Archit* **plafond à caissons** panelled *or* coffered ceiling **(d)** (*pour travail sous-marin*) caisson; *Méd* **mal(adie) des caissons** caisson disease, decompression sickness; *F* the bends; **c. à air comprimé** decompression chamber **(e)** *Aut* bay

cajoler [kaʒɔle] *vt* **(a)** (*câliner*) to cuddle, to make a fuss of **(b)** *Vieilli* (*flatter*) to cajole, to coax, to wheedle

cajolerie [kaʒɔlri] *nf* (*câlin*) cuddle

cajoleur, -euse [kaʒɔlœr, -øz] **1** *adj* **(a)** (*câlin*) affectionate **(b)** *Vieilli* (*flatteur*) cajoling, wheedling, coaxing **2** *n Vieilli* (*flatteur*) cajoler, wheedler, coaxer

cajou [kaʒu] *nm* cashew (nut)

cake [kɛk] *nm* fruit cake; **mascara en c.** block mascara; *F* **être dans le c.** (*avoir la gueule de bois*) to be hung over, to have a hangover; (*être très fatigué*) to be all in

cal, *pl* **cals** [kal] *nm Bot, Méd* callus, callosity

calabrais, -aise [kalabrɛ, -ɛz] **1** *adj* Calabrian **2** *nm Ling* Calabrian dialect **3** *n* **C.** Calabrian

Calabre [kalabr] *nf* Calabria

calage [kalaʒ] *nm* **(a)** (*de pied de chaise etc*) wedging; (*de roue*) chocking **(b)** (*fait d'appuyer*) propping (up) **(c)** (*de manivelle à un axe etc*) wedging, keying; (*de roue à un axe etc*) fixing; (*de valve etc*) jamming, locking **(d)** *Aut* (*de moteur*) stalling **(e)** (*réglage*) adjustment; (*de valve, moteur*) tuning; *Aut* **c. d'allumage** ignition timing

calamar [kalamar] *nm* = **calmar**

calamine [kalamin] *nf* **(a)** *Minér* calamine **(b)** (*dépôt*) carbon deposits

calaminer (se) [səkalamine] *vpr* to get covered with carbon deposits

calamistré [kalamistre] *adj* **cheveux calamistrés** brilliantined hair

calamité [kalamite] *nf* (*désastre*) calamity, disaster; (*malheur*) (great) misfortune; **quelle c.!** what a disaster! *F* **ce mec, c'est une vraie c.!** this guy is a real *or* a walking disaster!

calamiteux, -euse [kalamitø -øz] *adj* disastrous, *Fml* calamitous

calandrage [kalɑ̃draʒ] *nm* (*dans la fabrication du papier*), *Tex* calendering; (*de pneu*) liner

calandre [kalɑ̃dr] *nf* **(a)** (*dans la fabrication du papier*), *Tex* calender **(b)** *Aut* radiator grille

calandrer [kalɑ̃dre] *vt Tex etc* to calender
calandreur, -euse [kalɑ̃drœr, -øz] *n* (*pour les papiers*), *Tex* calenderer
calanque [kalɑ̃k] *nf* (*en Méditerranée*) deep narrow creek
calcaire [kalkɛr] **1** *adj* (*sol, terrain*) chalky; (*roche*) calcareous; *Ch* **sel c.** calcium salt; **eau c.** hard water **2** *nm* **(a)** *Géol* limestone **(b)** (*dans les bouilloires*) fur
calcanéum [kalkaneɔm] *nm Anat* heel bone, *Spéc* calcaneum
calcédoine [kalsedwan] *nf Minér* chalcedony
calcification [kalsifikasjɔ̃] *nf Méd* calcification
calcination [kalsinasjɔ̃] *nf* calcination
calciner [kalsine] **1** *vt* (*brûler*) to char; *Ch, Ind* to calcine; **rôti calciné** joint burnt to a cinder; **désert calciné par le soleil** sun-baked desert **2 se calciner** *vpr* to burn
calcium [kalsjɔm] *nm Ch* calcium
calcul[1] [kalkyl] *nm* **(a)** (*compte*) calculation, reckoning, computation; **faire un c.** to make a calculation; **faux c., erreur de c.** miscalculation; *Ordinat* **calculs très rapides** number crunching
(b) *Scol* **le c.** arithmetic, sums; **faible en c.** bad at sums *or* arithmetic; **enseigner le c.** to teach arithmetic; **apprendre le c.** to learn (how) to count; **règle à c.** slide rule; **problème de c.** arithmetic problem
(c) (*prévision*) calculation; **agir par c.** to act from selfish *or* ulterior motives; **ça été un bon c. de notre part** it was a good move on our part, we did the right thing; **un mauvais c.** a miscalculation; **faire un bon c.** to calculate correctly; **faire un mauvais c.** to miscalculate; **selon nos calculs** according to our calculations
▶ **calcul**: *Math* **c. différentiel** differential calculus; *Math* **c. intégral** integral calculus; **c. mental** mental arithmetic; **c. des probabilités** theory of probability
calcul[2] *nm Méd* (*dans la vésicule*) stone, *Spéc* calculus; **avoir des calculs** to have stones in the bladder; (*aux reins*) to have kidney stones; **c. biliaire** gall stone; **c. rénal** kidney stone
calculable [kalkylabl] *adj* calculable
calculateur, -trice [kalkylatœr, -tris] **1** *n* (*personne*) **c'est un bon c.** he's good at *or* with figures **2** *nm* **(a)** *Ordinat* (desktop) calculator; **c. (électronique)** (electronic) computer **(b)** (*de poche*) (pocket) calculator **3** *nf* **calculatrice** (*machine*) (desktop) calculator; **c. de poche** pocket calculator **4** *adj* (*personne, politique*) calculating
calculé [kalkyle] *adj* (*insulte, risque*) calculated; (*méchanceté*) premeditated, calculated; (*insolence*) deliberate; **une bonté calculée** an act of kindness motivated by self-interest
calculer [kalkyle] **1** *vt* (*compter*) (*prix, surface d'un triangle etc*) to work out, to calculate; (*comportement, réflexions etc*) to plan, to calculate; (*conséquences*) to weigh (up); **c. qch de tête** to work sth out *or* calculate sth in one's head; **tout bien calculé** taking everything into account; **c. ses chances de réussite** to calculate *or* to weigh up one's chances of success; **c. ses dépenses au plus juste** to work out *or* calculate one's expenses to the nearest penny
2 *vi* to calculate; *Péj* (*économiser*) to count every penny; **c. vite et bien** to be quick and accurate at *or* with figures; **machine à c.** adding machine, (desk) calculator
calculette [kalkylɛt] *nf* (pocket) calculator
caldoche [kaldɔʃ] **1** *adj* = pertaining to the European community of New Caledonia **2** *n* **C.** = New Caledonian of European descent
cale[1] [kal] *nf Naut* **(a)** (*de navire*) hold; **eau de c.** bilge water; **fond de c.** bilge; **à fond de c.** down in the hold; *F Fig* **être à fond de c.** to be stony(-broke) *or Am* stone-broke **(b) mettre un navire sur c.** to lay down a ship
▶ **cale**: **c. à charbon** bunker; **c. de construction/de lancement** stocks/slip(way); **c. à eau** water tank; **c. de radoub** dry dock, graving dock; **c. sèche** dry dock
cale[2] *nf* **(a)** (*pour mettre un meuble d'aplomb etc*) wedge; (*pour bloquer une roue etc*) chock, block; *Aut* (*pour augmenter le jeu entre deux pièces*) shim, spacer; **c. de réglage** adjusting shim; **mettre une voiture sur cales** to put a car on blocks; *Av* **enlevez les cales!** chocks away! **(b)** (*support*) prop, strut; *MecE* (*d'arbre etc*) key
calé [kale] *adj F* (*problème, question, devoir etc*) difficult, tough; **être c. en qch** to be well up in sth, to know all about sth; **ça c'est c.!** that's cunning! that's clever!
calebasse [kalbas] *nf* (*fruit, récipient*) calabash, gourd
calèche [kalɛʃ] *nf* (*voiture*) barouche
calecif [kalsif] *nm F* boxer shorts
caleçon [kalsɔ̃] *nm* boxer shorts; (*de femme*) leggings, *Vieilli* **c. long** long underpants; *F* long johns; *Vieilli* **c. de bain** (swimming *or* bathing) trunks
calédonien, -ienne [kaledɔnjɛ̃, -jɛn] **1** *adj* Caledonian **2** *n* **C.** Caledonian
calembour [kalɑ̃bur] *nm* pun, play on words; **faire** *ou* **dire des calembours** to make puns, to pun, to play on words
calembredaine [kalɑ̃brədɛn] *nf souvent pl* nonsense
calendes [kalɑ̃d] *nfpl Antiq* calends; **renvoyer qn/qch aux c. grecques** to put sb/sth off indefinitely
calendos [kalɑ̃dos] *nm F* Camembert (cheese)
calendrier [kalɑ̃drije] *nm* **(a)** (*système, tableau*) calendar; **bloc c.** block calendar; **c. à effeuiller** tear-off calendar; **c. perpétuel** perpetual calendar; **c. Grégorien** Gregorian calendar **(b)** (*de voyage, travail etc*) timetable, programme, schedule
cale-pied *nm inv* toe clip
calepin [kalpɛ̃] *nm* notebook
caler[1] [kale] **1** *vt* **(a)** (*pied de chaise etc*) to wedge; (*roue*) to chock; **c. un chargement** to secure a load (firmly); **c. un malade avec des coussins** to prop up a patient on cushions
(b) (*manivelle à un axe etc*) to wedge, to key; (*roue sur un axe etc*) to fix; (*valve etc*) to jam, to lock
(c) *Aut* (*moteur*) to stall
(d) (*régler*) (*valve, moteur etc*) to adjust, to tune
(e) *F* (*remplir*) **ça vous cale (l'estomac)** it fills you up, it's really filling; **je suis calé** I'm full (up)
2 *vi* (*moteur*) to stall
3 se caler *vpr* **(a)** (*dans un fauteuil etc*) to settle (oneself) comfortably
(b) *F* **se c. les joues, se les c.** to stuff oneself, to have a good feed
caler[2] *vi Naut* **navire qui cale vingt pieds** ship that draws *or* whose draught is twenty feet (of water); **navire qui cale trop** ship that is too deep in the water
caler[3] **1** *vt Naut* (*mât*) to house; (*voile*) to strike **2** *vi* **(a)** *F* (*abandonner*) to give up **(b)** *Can* (*se dégarnir*) to have a receding hairline
caleter (se) [səkalte] *vpr Arg* = **(se) calter**
calfat [kalfa] *nm Naut* ca(u)lker
calfatage [kalfataʒ] *nm Naut* ca(u)lking
calfater [kalfate] *vt Naut* to ca(u)lk
calfeutrage [kalføtraʒ] *nm*, **calfeutrement** [kalføtrəmɑ̃] *nm* **(a)** (*de brèches*) blocking up, stopping (up), filling (in) **(b)** (*d'une pièce etc*) draught-proofing
calfeutrer [kalføtre] **1** *vt* **(a)** (*brèches*) to block up, to stop (up), to fill (in) **(b)** (*pièce etc*) to draught-proof, to make draught-proof **2 se calfeutrer** *vpr* (*pour avoir chaud*) to make oneself snug; (*pour être seul*) to shut oneself up *or* away
calibrage [kalibraʒ] *nm* **(a)** (*de pièce*) gauging, measuring; (*de thermomètre etc*) calibration; *Com* (*d'œufs, de fruits etc*) grading **(b)** *Phot* (*d'épreuve*) trimming **(c)** *Typ* (*de copie*) casting off
calibre [kalibr] *nm* **(a)** (*d'arme à feu, tuyau etc*) calibre, *US* caliber, bore; (*de balle etc*) calibre, size; (*d'œufs, de fruits etc*) grade; **fusil de c. 8 mm** *Mil* 8-mm calibre rifle; *Sp* 8-mm gauge gun; **canon de gros c.** heavy gun, large-bore gun; *Fig* **sa sœur est d'un autre c.** his sister is of quite a different calibre, *F* his sister is in a different league; **il n'est pas de ce c.-là** he's not a man of that calibre; **j'ai rarement vu une bêtise de ce c.!** I've rarely seen stupidity on such a scale!
(b) (*outil*) gauge, *US* gage; **c. d'épaisseur (à lames)** feeler gauge, set of feelers; **c. de profondeur** depth gauge
(c) (*pour la reproduction*) template
(d) (*de machine-outil*) jig, former
(e) *Arg* (*revolver*) shooter, *Am* rod; **un gros c.** a heavy pistol
calibrer [kalibre] *vt* **(a)** (*pièce*) to gauge, to measure; (*thermomètre etc*) to calibrate; *Com* (*œufs, fruits etc*) to grade; *Ordinat* (*couleurs*) to calibrate **(b)** *Phot* (*épreuve*) to trim **(c)** *Typ* (*copie*) to cast off
calibreur, -euse [kalibrœr, -øz] *n* calibrator; *Aut* **c. d'air** air bleed jet, air correction jet
calice[1] [kalis] **1** *nm Rel* chalice; *Fig* **boire le c. jusqu'à la lie** to drain the cup to the dregs **2** *int Can* hell!
calice[2] *nm Bot, Anat* calyx
calicot [kaliko] *nm* **(a)** *Tex Br* calico, *Am* unbleached muslin **(b)** (*portant une publicité etc*) banner **(c)** *Vieilli* (*personne*) draper's assistant
califat [kalifa] *nm* caliphate
calife [kalif] *nm* caliph; **vouloir être c. à la place du c.** to want to be top dog
Californie [kalifɔrni] *nf* California
californien, -ienne [kalifɔrnjɛ̃, -jɛn] **1** *adj* Californian **2** *n* **C.** Californian
californium [kalifɔrnjɔm] *nm Ch* californium
califourchon [kalifurʃɔ̃] **1** *adv* **à c.** astride; **se mettre à c. sur qch** to sit astride sth, to straddle sth; **monter à c. sur un**

cheval to ride a horse astride **2** *nm Can* bottom, backside, behind

câlin, -ine [kalɛ̃, -in] **1** *adj* (*enfant, regard, ton etc*) affectionate **2** *n* (*personne*) affectionate personne **3** *nm* cuddle; **faire un c. à qn** to give sb a cuddle

câliner [kaline] *vt* (*choyer*) (*enfant etc*) to make a fuss of; (*caresser*) to cuddle

câlinerie [kalinri] *nf* **(a)** (*tendresse*) fondness, tenderness **(b)** (*caresses etc*) caress; (*dans les bras*) cuddle; **faire des câlineries à qn** to cuddle sb

calisson [kalisɔ̃] *nm* = lozenge-shaped sweet made of marzipan

calleux, -euse [kalø, -øz] *adj* callous, horny

call-girl, *pl* **call-girls** [kolgœrl] *nf* call girl

calligramme [kaligram] *nm Littér* calligramme

calligraphe [kaligraf] *n* calligrapher, calligraphist

calligraphie [kaligrafi] *nf* calligraphy

calligraphier [kaligrafje] *vt* (*pr sub & impf* **n. calligraphiions, v. calligraphiiez**) (*lettre etc*) to write beautifully (and ornamentally); **nom calligraphié** beautifully (hand)written name

calligraphique [kaligrafik] *adj* calligraphic

callosité [kalozite] *nf* callus, callosity

calmant [kalmɑ̃] **1** *adj* (*mots etc*) calming, soothing; *Méd* (*pour les nerfs*) tranquillizing, sedative; (*pour la douleur*) painkilling **2** *nm Méd* (*pour les nerfs*) tranquillizer, sedative; (*pour la douleur*) painkiller

calmar [kalmar] *nm* squid

calme [kalm] **1** *nm* (*absence d'agitation*) calm, calmness; (*dans une situation difficile*) coolness, composure; (*de l'air, de la nuit*) stillness; (*du paysage*) peace and quiet, quiet(ness), peacefulness; **je cherche un peu de c.** I'm looking for some peace and quiet; **j'ai besoin d'être au c. pour écrire** I need (to have) peace and quiet in order to write; **moment de c.** lull; **je n'ai pas eu un moment de c. de toute la journée!** I haven't had a minute's peace all day!; **dans le c. de la nuit** in the still of the night; **du c.!** keep cool *or* calm!; **perdre son c.** to lose one's composure *or F* cool; **retrouver son c.** to regain one's composure, to calm down; **garder son c.** to keep one's composure, to keep calm *or* cool, *F* to keep one's cool; **il est toujours d'un c. incroyable** he is always incredibly calm *or* cool *or* composed; *Naut* **c. plat** dead calm; **les commerçants se plaignent que c'est le c. plat** traders are complaining that business is in the doldrums; **c'est le c. plat dans ma vie sentimentale** my love life is in the doldrums, there's nothing happening in my love life; **calmes équatoriaux** doldrums

2 *adj* (*nuit etc*) calm, still, quiet; (*personne, air*) calm, cool, composed; (*mer*) calm, smooth; (*ciel*) clear; *Com* (*marché*) quiet, flat, dull; **elle a des enfants très calmes** she has very placid children; **nos affaires sont calmes en août** business is quiet in August; **la Bourse a été c.** the Stock Market has been quiet *or* has had a quiet day

calmement [kalməmɑ̃] *adv* calmly

calmer [kalme] **1** *vt* (*personne*) (*rendre serein*) to calm (down); (*faire taire*) to quieten (down), *Am* to quiet down; (*foule etc*) to calm, to pacify; (*craintes*) to calm, to allay; (*douleur*) to soothe, to ease; (*conscience*) to ease; (*soif*) to quench; (*faim*) to appease; (*ardeur, passion*) to damp, to cool; (*fièvre*) to reduce, to bring down; *F* **je vais te le c. en moins de deux!** I'll soon shut him up *or* sort him out

2 se calmer *vpr* (*de personne*) (*devenir serein*) to calm down; (*se taire*) to quieten down, *Am* to quiet down; (*de tempête*) to abate, to die down, to blow over; (*de vent*) to drop, to subside; (*de mer*) to become calm; (*de pluie*) to ease off; **la douleur se calme** the pain is easing *or* subsiding

calomel [kalɔmɛl] *nm Pharm* calomel

calomniateur, -trice [kalɔmnjatœr, -tris] **1** *n* (*qui parle*) slanderer; (*qui écrit*) libeller **2** *adj* (*paroles*) slanderous; (*écrits*) libellous

calomnie [kalɔmni] *nf* (*parlée*) slander, *Fml* calumny; (*écrite, publiée*) libel; **répandre des calomnies sur qn** to cast aspersions on sb; **elle a été en butte à la c.** she has been a victim of slander/libel, she has been slandered/libelled

calomnier [kalɔmnje] *vt* to slander, to malign, *Fml* to calumniate; (*par écrit*) to libel

calomnieusement [kalɔmnjøzmɑ̃] *adv* slanderously; (*par écrit*) libellously

calomnieux, -ieuse [kalɔmnjø, -jøz] *adj* (*paroles*) slanderous; (*écrits*) libellous

caloporteur [kalopɔrtœr] **1** *adj* **fluide** *ou* **liquide c.** coolant **2** *nm* coolant

calorie [kalɔri] *nf* calorie; **régime basses calories** low-calorie diet; **l'avocat est riche en calories** avocados are high in calories; **ration de calories** calorie intake; **attention aux calories!** watch the calories!

calorifère [kalɔrifɛr] **1** *adj* heat-conveying **2** *nm* (slow-combustion) stove; *Can* radiator

calorifique [kalɔrifik] *adj Phys* calorific, thermal; **capacité c.** heat capacity

calorifuge [kalɔrifyʒ] **1** *adj* (heat-)insulating; (*vernis etc*) heat-proof; **le bois est c.** wood is a poor conductor of heat **2** *nm* heat insulator *or* insulation; (*pour chaudière, tuyau*) lagging

calorifugeage [kalɔrifyʒaʒ] *nm* (heat) insulation; (*de chaudière, tuyau*) lagging

calorifuger [kalɔrifyʒe] *vt* (**je calorifugeai(s), n. calorifugeons**) to insulate; (*chaudière, tuyau*) to lag

calorimètre [kalɔrimɛtr] *nm Phys* calorimeter

calorimétrie [kalɔrimetri] *nf Phys* calorimetry

calorimétrique [kalɔrimetrik] *adj Phys* (*unité etc*) calorimetric(al)

caloriporteur [kalɔripɔrtœr] *adj, nm* = **caloporteur**

calorique [kalɔrik] *adj* calorific; **ration c.** calorie intake

calorisation [kalɔrizasjɔ̃] *nf Tech* calorization, aluminium plating

calorstat [kalɔrsta] *nm Aut* thermostat

calot¹ [kalo] *nm* **(a)** (*grosse bille*) (large) marble **(b)** *Arg* (*œil*) peeper

calot² *nm Mil* forage cap, *Am* garrison cap

calotin [kalɔtɛ̃] *nm F Péj* **(a)** (*prêtre*) priest **(b)** (*bigot*) pious churchgoer

calotte [kalɔt] *nf* **(a)** (*chapeau rond*) skullcap; *Rel* calotte; (*de chapeau*) crown; *Arg Péj* **la c.** (*le clergé*) the priests; *Pol* the clerical party **(b)** *Litt* **la c. des cieux** the vault *or* canopy of heaven **(c)** *F* (*gifle*) cuff, clout; **flanquer une c. à qn** to give sb a clout, to box sb's ears

▶ **calotte**: *Anat* **c. du crâne, c. crânienne** top part of the skull, skullcap; *Géol* **c. glaciaire** ice cap; *Math* **c. sphérique** portion of a sphere

calotter [kalɔte] *vt F* (*personne*) to cuff, to clout

calquage [kalkaʒ] *nm* tracing

calque [kalk] *nm* **(a)** (*copie*) tracing; (*de poème, de portrait etc*) exact copy; **prendre un c. de qch** to make a tracing of sth, to trace sth; **(papier-)c.** tracing paper **(b)** *Ling* loan translation, calque

calquer [kalke] *vt* (*reproduire*) to trace, to make a tracing of; *Fig* to copy exactly, to imitate; **dessin calqué** tracing; **expression calquée sur l'anglais** expression copied from *or* modelled on the English; **c. sa conduite sur celle de qn que l'on admire** to model one's behaviour on that of sb one admires

calter (se) [səkalte] *vpr Arg* (*s'enfuir*) to scram, *Br* to scarper

calumet [kalymɛ] *nm* peace pipe, calumet; *Fig* **fumer le c. de la paix avec qn** to smoke the pipe of peace with sb

calva [kalva] *nm F abrév* **calvados**

calvados [kalvados] *nm* calvados, apple brandy

calvaire [kalvɛr] *nm* (*épreuve pénible*) agony, ordeal; *Rel* calvary; (*croix*) calvary, wayside cross; *Rel* **Le C.** (Mount) Calvary; **c'est un c. de devoir la supporter** it's agony having to put up with her; **sa vie fut un long c.** his life was one long ordeal

calvinisme [kalvinism] *nm* Calvinism

calviniste [kalvinist] **1** *adj* Calvinistic, Calvinist **2** *n* Calvinist

calvitie [kalvisi] *nf* baldness; **c. naissante** incipient baldness; **c. précoce** premature baldness

calypso [kalipso] *nm* (*danse*), *Mus* calypso

camaïeu, -eux [kamajø] *nm* (*peinture*) monochrome (painting); (*gravure*) tint drawing

camail [kamaj] *nm* **(a)** *Cathol* (*porté par-dessus le surplis*) cape **(b)** *Orn* (*du coq*) neck feathers, hackles

camarade [kamarad] *n* friend, *F* mate, pal; *Pol* (*terme d'adresse*) comrade, brother; **le c. Gorbatchev** comrade Gorbachov; **c. d'école** *ou* **de collège** school friend; **c. de classe** *ou* **de promotion** classmate; **c. de jeu** playmate; **c. de régiment** old army friend

camaraderie [kamaradri] *nf* camaraderie, comradeship

camard, -e [kamar, -ard] **1** *adj* (*nez*) flat; (*personne*) flat-nosed, with a flat nose **2** *nf F* **la camarde** the (Grim) Reaper

camarguais, -aise [kamargɛ, -ɛz] **1** *adj* of/from the Camargue **2** *n* **C.** (*natif*) native of the Camargue; (*habitant*) inhabitant of the Camargue

cambiste [kɑ̃bist] *Fin* **1** *nm* foreign exchange dealer **2** *adj* **marché c.** exchange market

Cambodge [kɑ̃bɔdʒ] *nm* Cambodia

cambodgien, -ienne [kɑ̃bɔdʒjɛ̃, -jɛn] **1** *adj* Cambodian **2** *n* **C.** Cambodian

cambouis [kɑ̃bwi] *nm* dirty oil, grease

cambrage [kɑ̃braʒ] *nm* bending; (*du pied, du dos*) arching; (*du bois etc*) cambering, curving

cambré [kɑ̃bre] *adj* bent; (*poutre*) cambered, arched; **pied**

très c. foot with a high instep; **taille cambrée** arched *or* curved back; **jambes cambrées** bow legs
cambrement [kɑ̃brəmɑ̃] *nm* = **cambrage**
cambrer [kɑ̃bre] **1** *vt* to bend; (*le dos, le pied*) to arch; (*bois etc*) to camber, to curve; **c. la taille** *ou* **les reins** to arch one's back **2 se cambrer** *vpr* to arch one's back
cambrien, -ienne [kɑ̃brijɛ̃, -jɛn] *adj, nm Géol* Cambrian
cambriolage [kɑ̃brijɔlaʒ] *nm* (*métier*) burglary, housebreaking; (*événement*) burglary, break-in
cambriole [kɑ̃brijɔl] *nf F* (*métier*) burglary, housebreaking
cambrioler [kɑ̃brijɔle] *vt* (*maison*) to break into, to burgle, *Am* to burglarize; **nous avons été cambriolés pendant les vacances** we were burgled *or* we had a burglary *or* break-in while we were on holiday
cambrioleur, -euse [kɑ̃brijɔlœr, -øz] *n* burglar, housebreaker
cambrous(s)e [kɑ̃brus, -us] *nf F* (*campagne*) country; **maison à la c.** *ou* **en pleine c.** house in the middle of nowhere *or* (out) in the sticks *or* at the back of beyond
cambrure [kɑ̃bryr] *nf* (*du bois etc*) camber, curve; (*du pied, du dos*) arch; **chaussures à forte c.** shoes with a high instep; **c. des reins** small of the back
cambuse [kɑ̃byz] *nf* **(a)** *Naut* storeroom **(b)** (*de chantier naval*) canteen **(c)** *Arg* (*chambre*) hole, place, room
cambusier [kɑ̃byzje] *nm* **(a)** (*à la cantine*) canteen keeper **(b)** (*de stocks*) storekeeper
came[1] [kam] *nf MecE* cam; **arbre à cames** camshaft; **moteur avec arbre à cames en tête** overhead camshaft engine; **à c. unique** single-cam; **c. de frein** expander
came[2] *nf Arg* **(a)** (*drogue*) dope, junk **(b)** (*diminutif de camelote*) (*objet de mauvaise qualité*) junk
camé, -ée [kame] *n Arg* junkie, druggie
camée [kame] *nm* cameo
caméléon [kameleɔ̃] *nm* (*reptile*), *Fig* chameleon
camélia [kamelja] *nm* camellia
camelot [kamlo] *nm* **(a)** *F* (*marchand dans la rue*) street vendor *or* seller **(b)** *Arch* (*vendeur de journaux*) newsvendor **(c)** *Hist Fr* **camelots du roi** royalists
camelote [kamlɔt] *nf F* **(a)** (*pacotille*) junk, trash, *Br* rubbish; **n'achète pas cette voiture, c'est de la c.!** don't buy that car, it's a pile of junk *or* an old junk heap! **(b)** (*toute marchandise*) stuff
camembert [kamɑ̃bɛr] *nm* **(a)** (*fromage*) Camembert (cheese) **(b)** (*diagramme*) pie-chart
camer (se) [səkame] *vpr Arg* to do drugs, to be on drugs; **il se came à l'héroïne** he's on heroin; **elle est complètement camée** she's as high as a kite
caméra [kamera] *nf Cin, TV* camera; **c. de télévision** television camera; **c. asservie** *ou* **esclave** slave camera; **c. banc-titre** rostrum camera; **c. d'animation** rostrum camera; **c. de reportage** hand-held camera; **c. en studio** studio (broadcast) camera; **c. grande vitesse** high speed camera; **c. isolée** isolated camera, ISO; **c. légère** lightweight camera, portable single camera; **c. portable** portable camera; **c. sans film** filmless camera; **c. vidéo** video camera; **c. à l'épaule** hand-held camera; *Mktg* **c. oculaire** eye (movement) camera
caméra-film, *pl* **caméras-film** *nf* film camera, motion picture camera, *esp Am* movie camera
cameraman [kameraman], *pl* **cameramen** *nm Cin, TV* cameraman
camérier [kamerje] *nm* (*du Pape, de cardinal*) chamberlain
camériste [kamerist] *nf Hist* lady-in-waiting
camerounais, -aise [kamrunɛ, -ɛz] **1** *adj* Cameroonian **2** *n* **C.** Cameroonian
Cameroun (le) [ləkamrun] *nm* Cameroon; *Hist* the Cameroons
caméscope [kamɛskɔp] *nm* camcorder
camion [kamjɔ̃] *nm* **(a)** *Aut* truck *Br* lorry; **c. de déménagement** removal van; **c. bâché** curtainsider; **c. de dépannage** breakdown truck, *Am* wrecker; **c. pour transport d'automobiles** (car) transporter; **c. réfrigéré** refrigerated lorry; **chauffeur de c.** lorry *or* truck driver **(b)** (*chariot*) dray, wag(g)on
camion-benne, *pl* **camions-bennes** *nm* dump(er) truck
camion-citerne, *pl* **camions-citernes** *nm* tanker, *Am* tank truck *or* trailer
camion-magasin, *pl* **camions-magasins** *nm* mobile shop
camionnage [kamjɔnaʒ] *nm* haulage, *Am* truckage; **régler le c.** to pay the haulage
camionner [kamjɔne] *vt* (*marchandises*) to transport by *Br* lorry *or* truck, *Am* to truck
camionnette [kamjɔnɛt] *nf* van, panel van, *Am* delivery truck; **c. de livraison** delivery van
camionneur [kamjɔnœr] *nm* **(a)** (*conducteur*) *Br* lorry driver, truck driver, *Am* trucker, teamster; (*de camionnette*) van driver **(b)** (*transporteur*) haulier, *Am* hauler, *Am* trucker
camisole [kamizɔl] *nf* **(a)** *Can* (*tricot de corps*) vest, *Am* undershirt **(b)** *Arch* (*chemise de nuit*) nightshirt **(c)** (*corsage*) camisole
▶ **camisole**: **c. de force** strait-jacket
camomille [kamɔmij] *nf* camomile; **tisane de c.** camomile tea; **prendre une c.** to have a cup of camomile tea
camouflage [kamuflaʒ] *nm* camouflage; (*de la vérité etc*) disguising, hiding; **le c. d'une rentrée d'argent** the concealment of a sum of money received; **le c. d'une faute** the covering up of a mistake
camoufler [kamufle] **1** *vt* to camouflage; (*vérité, intentions etc*) to disguise, to hide; (*faute*) to cover up; (*rentrée d'argent*) to conceal; **c. un bouton** to cover up *or* camouflage a spot; *Compta* **c. un bilan** to window-dress the accounts; **c. un meurtre en suicide** to make a murder look like suicide **2 se camoufler** *vpr* to camouflage oneself
camouflet [kamuflɛ] *nm* affront, snub; **essuyer un c.** to be snubbed
camp [kɑ̃] *nm* **(a)** (*campement*) camp; **établir un c.** to pitch camp; **lever le c.** to strike camp; **lit de c.** camp bed; **feu de c.** campfire; **partir faire un c., partir en c.** to go camping; *F* **ficher le c.** to clear off, to scram; *F* **fous-moi le c.!** clear off!, beat it! **(b)** (*parti*) camp; **changer de c.** to change sides; **le c. adverse** the opposing camp, the other side; **ils ne sont pas dans le même c.** they're on different sides **(c)** (*de jeux*) side; **tirer les camps** to pick sides; **faire deux camps** to form two teams
▶ **camp**: **c. (de vacances)** (children's) holiday camp, *Am* summer camp; **c. d'adolescents** holiday camp for teenagers, *Am* camp; **c. de concentration** concentration camp; **c. d'internement** internment camp; **c. de la mort** death camp; **c. de loisirs** holiday camp; **c. de prisonniers** prison camp; *Mil* **c. volant** temporary camp
campage-caravanage [kɑ̃paʒkaravanaʒ] *nm* camping-caravanning
campagnard, -arde [kɑ̃paɲar, -ard] **1** *adj* (*allure, accent etc*) country; (*simplicité*) rustic **2** *n* countryman, *f* countrywoman, *Péj* rustic
campagne [kɑ̃paɲ] *nf* **(a)** (*par opposition à la ville*) country(side); **à la c.** in the country; **en pleine c.** deep in the countryside; **vie à la c.** country life; **battre la c.** to scour *or* comb the countryside; *Fig* **son esprit bat la c.** his mind is wandering; **en rase c.** in (the) open country; **(maison de) c.** country house, place in the country

(b) *Mil* **en c.** in the field, on active service; **artillerie de c.** field artillery; **tenue de c.** field dress, combat dress; **entrer** *ou* **se mettre en c.** to begin operations, to take the field; *Fig* to set to work

(c) *Mil, Pol etc* campaign; *Mil* **faire c.** to fight a campaign; *Fig* **faire c.** *ou* **se mettre en c. pour qn/contre qch** to campaign on sb's behalf/against sth; **faire c. pour** *ou* **en faveur d'un candidat** to canvass *or* campaign for *or* on behalf of a candidate; *Pol* **entrer en c.** to start to campaign; **partir en c. contre le tabac** to launch an anti-smoking campaign; **c. publicitaire** *ou* **de publicité** advertising *or* publicity campaign, publicity drive; **c. commerciale/de vente** sales campaign; **c. de marketing/de promotion** marketing/promotional campaign; **c. télévisée** television campaign; **c. de presse** press campaign; **c. électorale** election campaign; **c. de calomnies** smear campaign; *Mil* **la c. d'Égypte** the Egyptian campaign
campagnol [kɑ̃paɲɔl] *nm* vole
campanile [kɑ̃panil] *nm Archit* campanile, bell tower
campanule [kɑ̃panyl] *nf* campanula
campé [kɑ̃pe] *adj* **bien c.** (*personne*) well built; **bien c. sur ses jambes** standing firmly on his feet; **portrait bien c.** well-sketched portrait; **récit bien c.** well-constructed story
campement [kɑ̃pmɑ̃] *nm* **(a)** (*action*) camping **(b)** (*installation*) camp, encampment; (*lieu*) camping ground *or* place; **établir un c.** to camp, to pitch camp; **replier le c.** to strike camp; **matériel de c.** camping equipment
camper [kɑ̃pe] **1** *vi* **(a)** (*faire du camping*) to camp; (*dans le jardin etc*) to camp out

(b) (*établir un campement*) to camp, to pitch camp, *Mil* to encamp; *Fig* (*dans un hôtel etc*) to camp out; *Fig* **ils campent ici depuis quinze jours** they've been camping out here for two weeks

2 *vt* (*troupes*) to encamp; (*planter*) (*histoire etc*) to put *or* place in context; **il a campé son chapeau sur sa tête** he stuck *or* planted his hat on his head; **un écrivain qui campe bien ses personnages** an author whose characters are well-rounded; *Th* **c. un personnage** to play a part effectively

3 se camper *vpr* **se c. devant qn** to plant oneself in front of sb
campeur, -euse [kɑ̃pœr, -øz] *n* camper
camphre [kɑ̃fr] *nm* camphor; **essence de c.** camphor oil

camphré [kɑ̃fre] *adj* (*huile etc*) camphorated
camphrier [kɑ̃frije] *nm* camphor tree
camping [kɑ̃piŋ] *nm* (**a**) (*activité*) camping; **faire du c.** to go camping; **c. libre** = non-site camping in suitable spots with permission if required; **c. à la ferme** farm camping; **c. sauvage** unauthorized camping (**b**) (*lieu*) camp(ing) site; **c. aménagé** camp site (with facilities)
camping-car, *pl* **camping-cars** *nm* camper, *Br* Dormobile®, *Am* motor-home, *Am* recreational vehicle
camping-caravaning *nm* camping-caravanning
camping-gaz *nm inv* camping stove
campos [kɑ̃po] *nm F* **donner c. à qn** to give sb a day/an afternoon/*etc* off
campus [kɑ̃pys] *nm* [①A13,8] campus; **vivre sur le c.** to live on campus
camus [kamy] *adj* (**a**) (*personne*) flat-nosed (**b**) (*nez*) flat
Canada [kanada] *nm* Canada; **être/aller au C.** to be in/to go to Canada
Canadair® [kanadɛr] *nm* fire-fighting plane
canadianisme [kanadjanism] *nm Ling* Canadianism
canadien, -ienne [kanadjɛ̃, -jɛn] **1** *adj* Canadian **2** *n* **C.** Canadian; **C. français(e)** French Canadian **3** *nf* **canadienne** (*veste*) sheepskin jacket; (*canoë*) Canadian canoe; (*tente*) ridge tent
canaille [kanɑj] **1** *nf* (*crapule*) scoundrel, rogue; **petite c.!** (*à un enfant*) you little devil *or* rascal!; *Vieilli* **la c.** the rabble, the riff-raff **2** *adj* (*action*) low, crooked; (*chanson, paroles*) vulgar, coarse; **il a un petit air c.** he has a roguish air about him
canaillerie [kanɑjri] *nf* (**a**) (*acte*) low(-down) *or* mean *or* dirty trick (**b**) (*d'une action*) lowness, crookedness; (*d'une chanson, d'une histoire etc*) vulgarity, coarseness
canal, -aux [kanal, -o] *nm* (**a**) *Constr* canal; **c. d'irrigation** irrigation canal; **c. maritime** *ou* **de navigation** ship canal; **c. de dérivation** diversion *or* bypass channel; **le C. de Mozambique** the Mozambique Channel; **le C. de Suez** the Suez Canal; **la Zone du C. (de Panama)** the Canal Zone
(**b**) (*de rivière*) channel
(**c**) (*conduite*) conduit, duct, pipe; **c. à air** *ou* **d'aérage** air passage *or* duct; **c. d'amenée** feeder; **c. de fuite** waste pipe; **c. de graissage** oil groove; **c. encreur** (*d'une imprimante*) ink channel
(**d**) *Anat, Bot* canal, duct; **c. alimentaire** alimentary canal; **c. biliaire** bile duct; **c. lymphatique** lymph vessel
(**e**) *Rad, TV, Ordinat* channel; *Can TV* (*chaîne*) channel; *Rad* **c. de fréquence à large bande** wide-band frequency channel; *TV* **c. mosaïque** multi-screen channel; *TV* **C. Plus** = French pay television channel; **c. de télévision** television channel; **c. vidéo** video channel
(**f**) *Fig* (*moyen*) channel; **par le c. de la poste** through the post
(**g**) *Écon, Mktg* channel; **c. de distribution** distribution channel; **c. de distribution court** one-level channel; **c. de distribution long** two/three-level marketing channel, conventional marketing channel; **c. de communication** promotional *or* communications channel; **c. de communication commerciale** marketing communications channel
canalisable [kanalizabl] *adj* **eau c.** water which can be channelled *or* canalized; *Fig* **une énergie difficilement c.** energy which is difficult to channel *or* direct
canalisation [kanalizasjɔ̃] *nf* (**a**) (*de rivière etc*) canalization (**b**) (*conduite*) conduit, pipe; (*conduites*) (system of) pipes, piping; *Él* wiring (**c**) (*pour pétrole etc*) pipeline (**d**) *Ordinat* **c. des commandes** command piping
canaliser [kanalize] *vt* (**a**) (*région, rivière etc*) to canalize (**b**) (*ressources*) to channel, to concentrate (**c**) (*trafic, foule etc*) to direct
cananéen, -enne [kananeɛ̃, -ɛn] *Bible* **1** *adj* Canaanite **2** *nm Ling* Canaanite **3** *n* **C.** Canaanite
canapé [kanape] *nm* (**a**) (*meuble*) sofa, couch, settee; **c. deux places** two-seater sofa, *Am* loveseat; **c. trois places** three-seater sofa; **c. convertible** sofa bed, bed settee (**b**) *Culin* canapé
canapé-lit, *pl* **canapés-lits** *nm* sofa bed, bed settee
canaque [kanak] **1** *adj* Kanak **2** *n* **C.** Kanak (*indigenous inhabitant of New Caledonia*)
canard [kanar] *nm* (**a**) [①A12,1,g] (*oiseau*) duck; (*mâle*) drake; **mare aux canards** duck pond; **chasse aux canards** duck shooting *or* hunting; *F* **mon petit c.** my pet, my darling; *F* **marcher comme un c.** to waddle; **marcher en c.** to walk with one's feet turned out (**b**) *F* (*fausse nouvelle*) false report, *Lit* canard (**c**) *F* (*journal*) rag (**d**) (*morceau de sucre*) = sugar lump dipped in coffee/brandy/*etc* (**e**) *Mus* false note (**f**) *Can* (*bouilloire*) kettle
► **canard**: **c. de Barbarie** Muscovy duck; *Culin* **c. laqué** Peking duck; *Culin* **c. à l'orange** duck à l'orange; **c. sauvage** wild duck; **c. siffleur** wi(d)geon
canardeau, -eaux [kanardo] *nm* duckling
canarder [kanarde] **1** *vi* (**a**) (*de navire*) to pitch (**b**) *Mus F* to play a false note; (*en chantant*) to sing a false note **2** *vt F* to snipe at, to take pot shots at; **se faire c. à coup de boules de neige** to be pelted with snowballs; *Fig* **il s'est fait c. de questions** he was bombarded with questions
canardière [kanardjɛr] *nf* (**a**) (*mare*) duck pond (**b**) (*lieu*) (*pour la chasse aux canards*) screen (**c**) (*fusil*) duck gun, punt gun
canari [kanari] **1** *nm* canary **2** *adj inv* (**jaune**) **c.** canary yellow
Canaries [kanari] *nfpl* **les (îles) C.** the Canary Islands, the Canaries
canasson [kanasɔ̃] *nm Arg* (*cheval*) nag
canasta [kanasta] *nf Cartes* canasta; **jouer à la c.** to play canasta
cancale [kɑ̃kal] *nf* Cancale oyster
cancan [kɑ̃kɑ̃] *nm* (**a**) *F* (*racontar*) (piece of) gossip; **cancans** tittle-tattle, gossip; **dire** *ou* **faire des cancans** to gossip, to tittle-tattle, to talk (**sur** about) (**b**) (*danse*) cancan; **danser le c.** to do *or* dance the cancan
cancaner [kɑ̃kane] *vi* (**a**) *F* (*médire*) to gossip, to tittle-tattle, to talk (**sur** about) (**b**) (*d'un canard*) to quack
cancanier, -ière [kɑ̃kanje, -jɛr] *F* **1** *adj* gossipy, fond of tittle-tattle **2** *n* gossip, scandalmonger
cancer [kɑ̃sɛr] *nm* (**a**) *Méd* cancer; **c. du poumon/du sein** lung/breast cancer, cancer of the lung/breast; **c. de la peau** skin cancer; **avoir un c.** to have cancer; **avoir un c. à** *ou* **de l'estomac/au** *ou* **du poumon** to have stomach/lung cancer; **mourir d'un c.** to die of cancer; *Fig* **le chômage est le c. du monde moderne** unemployment is the cancer of the modern world (**b**) *Astron, Astrol* **le C.** Cancer, the Crab; **être (du signe du) C.** to be (a) Cancer *or* Cancerian (**c**) *Géog* **le Tropique du C.** the Tropic of Cancer
cancéreux, -euse [kɑ̃serø, -øz] **1** *adj* (*tumeur etc*) cancerous **2** *n* cancer victim *or* sufferer; **les c. en phase terminale** terminal cancer patients, people with terminal cancer, people who are terminally ill with cancer
cancériforme [kɑ̃serifɔrm] *adj Méd* cancriform, cancroid
cancérigène [kɑ̃seriʒɛn] *adj* carcinogenic; **produit c.** carcinogen
cancérisation [kɑ̃serizasjɔ̃] *nf Méd* **cela aboutira à la c. de l'organe** that will result in the organ becoming cancerous
cancériser (se) [səkɑ̃serize] *vpr Méd* to become cancerous
cancérogène [kɑ̃serɔʒɛn] = **cancérigène**
cancérologie [kɑ̃serɔlɔʒi] *nf* cancerology
cancérologue [kɑ̃serɔlɔg] *n* cancer specialist
cancre [kɑ̃kr] *nm* (**a**) (*crustacé*) crab (**b**) *F* (*écolier*) dunce, duffer
cancrelat [kɑ̃krəla] *nm* cockroach, *Am* roach
cancroïde [kɑ̃krɔid] *nm Méd* cancroid
candélabre [kɑ̃delabr] *nm* (**a**) (*chandelier*) candelabra, candelabrum, *pl* candelabra (**b**) (*lampadaire*) lamp post
candeur [kɑ̃dœr] *nf* ingenuousness, guilelessness, artlessness; **un regard plein de c.** a guileless look
candi [kɑ̃di] *adj* candied; **fruits candis** crystallized fruit; **sucre c.** sugar candy, rock candy
candidat, -ate [kɑ̃dida, -at] *n* applicant, candidate (**à une place** for a job); (*à un examen*) candidate; **se porter c. aux élections** to stand *or* run for election
candidature [kɑ̃didatyr] *nf Pol* candidature, candidacy; (*à un poste*) application (**à** for); **poser sa c. à un poste** to apply for a post; **retirer sa c.** (*à un poste*) to withdraw one's application; *Pol* to stand down; **il a retiré sa c. à la présidence** he has stood down as a presidential candidate
► **candidature**: **c. spontanée** unsolicited application
candide [kɑ̃did] *adj* ingenuous, guileless, artless
candidement [kɑ̃didmɑ̃] *adv* ingenuously, guilelessly, artlessly
candidose [kɑ̃didoz] *nf Méd* candida
cane [kan] *nf* (female) duck (*as opposed to drake*)
cané [kane] *adj F* dead
caner [kane] *vi Arg* (*avoir peur*) to have the jitters; (*se dégonfler*) to chicken out, *Br* to bottle out; (*mourir*) to snuff it, to kick the bucket
caneton [kantɔ̃] *nm* (male) duckling
canette[1] [kanɛt] *nf* (*petite cane*) (female) duckling
canette[2] *nf* = **cannette**
canevas [kanvɑ] *nm* (**a**) *Tex* canvas; **broderie sur c.** tapestry (work) (**b**) *Beaux-Arts, Mus, Littér* (*de dessin, roman etc*) outline
caniche [kaniʃ] *nm* poodle
caniculaire [kanikylɛr] *adj* (*chaleur, journée etc*) scorching
canicule [kanikyl] *nf* heatwave; **quelle c.!** what a scorcher!; **la c.** the dog days; **pendant la c. du mois d'août** during the August heatwave
canif [kanif] *nm* penknife, pocket knife

canin, -ine [kanɛ̃, -in] **1** *adj* canine; **exposition canine** dog show **2** *nf* **canine** canine (tooth), eyetooth
caninette [kaninɛt] *nf* = motorized pooper-scooper (*motorbike used for cleaning dog dirt from the streets*)
canisse [kanis] *nf* = **cannisse**
caniveau, -eaux [kanivo] *nm* **(a)** (*le long des routes*) gutter **(b)** *Él* (*pour câble*) trough, conduit
cannabis [kanabis] *nm* cannabis
cannage [kanaʒ] *nm* **(a)** (*activité*) caning **(b)** (*résultat*) canework
canne [kan] *nf* **(a)** (*tige*) cane; **sucre de c.** cane sugar **(b)** (*pour s'appuyer*) (walking) stick, cane **(c)** (*de souffleur de verre*) blowpipe **(d)** *Can* (*de tomates etc*) can, *Br* tin **(e)** *Arg* (*jambe*) leg; **avoir de belles cannes** to have a nice pair of legs, to have great legs
▸ **canne**: *Méd* **c. anglaise** arthritic crutch; **c. blanche** white stick; *Fig* **les cannes blanches** the blind; **c. à pêche** fishing rod; **c. à sucre** sugar cane
canné [kane] *adj* **chaise cannée** cane(-seated) chair
canneberge [kanbɛrʒ] *nf* cranberry; **sauce aux canneberges** cranberry sauce
canne-épée, *pl* **cannes-épées** *nf* swordstick
cannelé [kanle] *adj* (*colonne etc*) fluted; (*pneu*) grooved; (*ongle*) ridged
canneler [kanle] *vt* **(je cannelle, n. cannelons; je cannellerai)** (*colonne*) to flute; (*pneu*) to groove
cannelier [kanəlje] *nm* cinnamon tree
cannelle[1] [kanɛl] *nf Culin* cinnamon; **bâton de c.** cinnamon stick; **à la c.** cinnamon(-flavoured)
cannelle[2] *nf* (*de tonneau*) spigot
cannellonis [kanɛlɔni] *nmpl* cannelloni
cannelure [kanlyr] *nf* **(a)** (*rainure*) groove; *Archit* (*de colonne*) fluting **(b)** (*de métal, carton*) corrugation **(c)** *Bot* **cannelures** striae **(d)** *Géol* fault fissure
canner [kane] *vt* (*chaise*) to cane
cannette [kanɛt] *nf* **(a)** (*petite bouteille*) (beer) bottle; **c. de bière** bottle of beer **(b)** *Tex* spool, cop
canneur, -euse [kanœr -øz] *n* cane worker
cannibale [kanibal] **1** *n* cannibal **2** *adj* (*pratiques etc*) cannibalistic; **tribu c.** tribe of cannibals
cannibalisation [kanibalizasjɔ̃] *nf* (*de machine*) cannibalization; *Com* **la c. d'un produit** the erosion of the market share of a product
cannibaliser [kanibalize] *vt* (*machine*) to cannibalize; *Com* (*produit*) to eat into the market share of
cannibalisme [kanibalism] *nm* cannibalism
cannisse [kanis] *nf Région* (*pour faire des clôtures etc*) split cane
canoë [kanɔe] *nm* canoe; **faire du c.** to canoe, to go canoeing; **remonter le fleuve en c.** to canoe up the river
canoéisme [kanɔeism] *nm* canoeing
canoéiste [kanɔeist] *n* canoeist
canoë-kayak *nm* canoeing
canon[1] [kanɔ̃] *nm* **(a)** (*pièce d'artillerie*) gun; *Hist* cannon; **c. de 105 mm/de 280 mm** 105 mm/280 mm gun; **poudre à c.** gunpowder; *F* **chair à c.** cannon fodder; **le c.** (*artillerie*) the guns; **le gros c.** the heavy guns **(b)** (*de carabine, montre, stylo*) barrel; (*de clé, serrure*) barrel, pipe; (*d'arrosoir*) spout; (*de seringue*) body; **fusil à deux canons** double-barrelled gun; **c. rayé** rifled barrel **(c)** *Arch* (*mesure*) = wine measure equivalent to 0.058 l. ; *F* **boire un c.** to have a glass of wine
▸ **canon[1]**: **c. à âme lisse** smooth-bore gun; **c. antiaérien** anti-aircraft gun; **c. antichar** anti-tank gun; **c. de bord** naval gun; **c. de char** tank gun; *Naut* **c. de chasse** bow chaser; **c. à électrons** electron gun; **c. lance-harpon** harpoon gun; **c. de marine** naval gun; **c. à neige** snow-blower; **c. paragrêle** cloud seeder; *Naut* **c. de retraite** sternchaser
canon[2] **1** *nm* **(a)** *Rel* (*d'un ordre, de la messe etc*) canon **(b)** (*règle*) canon; **selon les canons de la beauté** according to the canons of beauty **(c)** *Mus* canon; **c. à deux/trois voix** canon for two/three voices; **reprendre un chant en c.** to sing a round **(d)** *F* (*personne belle*) good-looker, stunner **2** *adj inv* **(a) droit c.** canon law **(b)** *F* (*beau*) gorgeous(-looking)
cañon [kanjɔn] *nm Géog* canyon, cañon
canonial, -ale, -iaux, -ales [kanɔnjal, -jo] *adj Rel* **(a)** (*heures etc*) canonical **(b)** (*du chanoine*) canonic(al)
canonique [kanɔnik] *adj* (*livre etc*) canonical; **âge c.** *Rel* (*de servante de prêtre*) canonical age; *F* venerable old age
canonisation [kanɔnizasjɔ̃] *nf Rel* canonization
canoniser [kanɔnize] *vt Rel* to canonize
canon-mitrailleuse, *pl* **canons-mitrailleuses** *nm Mil* pom-pom
canonnade [kanɔnad] *nf* gunfire; **une c.** a burst of gunfire
canonner [kanɔne] *vt* to shell, to bombard
canonnier [kanɔnje] *nm Mil* gunner
canonnière [kanɔnjɛr] *nf* **(a)** *Naut* gunboat **(b)** (*ouverture*) loophole
canot [kano] *nm Naut* **(a)** (*embarcation non pontée*) boat, dinghy; **grand c.** longboat, pinnace; **petit c.** jollyboat **(b)** *Can* (*canoë*) canoe
▸ **canot**: **c. automobile** motorboat, motor launch; **c. pneumatique** inflatable *or* rubber dinghy; **c. de sauvetage** lifeboat
canotage [kanɔtaʒ] *nm Naut* boating; (*à l'aviron*) rowing; (*à la voile*) sailing; *Can* (*en canoë*) canoeing; *Can* **faire du c.** to go canoeing
canoter [kanɔte] *vi Naut* to go boating; (*à l'aviron*) to go rowing; (*à la voile*) to go sailing; *Can* (*en canoë*) to go canoeing
canoteur [kanɔtœr] *nm* boater; (*à l'aviron*) rower; *Can* (*canoéiste*) canoeist
canotier [kanɔtje] *nm* **(a)** (*rameur*) rower, oarsman **(b)** (*chapeau*) boater, straw hat
cantal [kɑ̃tal] *nm* Cantal (cheese)
cantaloup [kɑ̃talu] *nm* (*fruit*) cantaloup (melon)
cantate [kɑ̃tat] *nf Mus* cantata
cantatrice [kɑ̃tatris] *nf* (*chanteuse d'opéra*) opera singer; (*de concert*) (concert) singer
cantharide [kɑ̃tarid] *nf* (*insecte*) cantharis, Spanish fly
cantilène [kɑ̃tilɛn] *nf Mus* cantilena
cantilever [kɑ̃tilevœr] *adj Constr* cantilever; **pont c.** cantilever bridge
cantine [kɑ̃tin] *nf* **(a)** (*réfectoire*) canteen; *Scol* dining hall; *Univ* refectory; *Scol* **déjeuner à la c.** to have school meals; *Scol* **la c. n'est pas bonne** the food at school is bad; **je les mets à la c. à la rentrée** they're going to start having shool meals next term **(b)** (*malle*) trunk; *Mil* uniform case, tin trunk; *Mil* **c. médicale** field medical chest
cantique [kɑ̃tik] *nm Rel* hymn; *Bible* **le c. des cantiques** the Song of Songs *or* of Solomon
canton [kɑ̃tɔ̃] *nm* **(a)** (*en France*) canton (= *administrative division of a department*); (*en Suisse*) canton; *Can* **les cantons de l'Est** the Eastern Townships **(b)** *Constr* (*de route, voie ferrée etc*) section
cantonade [kɑ̃tɔnad] *nf* **parler à la c.** not to speak to anyone in particular, to speak to all those present; *Th* to speak off; **elle l'a dit à la c.** she said it so that everyone could hear
cantonais, -aise [kɑ̃tɔnɛ, -ɛz] **1** *adj* Cantonese **2** *nm Ling* Cantonese **3** *n* **C.** Cantonese
cantonal, -ale, -aux, -ales [kɑ̃tɔnal, -o] *adj* canton, cantonal; **les (élections) cantonales** the cantonal elections
cantonnement [kɑ̃tɔnmɑ̃] *nm* **(a)** *Mil* (*des troupes*) quartering, billeting **(b)** (*de forêt*) section; (*avec droits de pêche*) stretch of river **(c)** *Mil* (*lieu*) quarters, billet
cantonner [kɑ̃tɔne] **1** *vt* (*isoler, limiter*) to confine **(dans qch** to sth); (*animaux, malades*) to isolate; *Mil* (*troupes*) to quarter, to billet; **c. les jeunes employés à des tâches dérisoires** to confine *or* restrict *or* limit junior employees to menial tasks **2** *vi* (*troupes*) to be billeted *or* quartered **3 se cantonner** *vpr* (*dans une pièce etc*) to shut oneself away; *Fig* (*se limiter*) to confine *or* limit oneself **(dans qch** to sth); **se c. à une tâche** to confine oneself to one task
cantonnier [kɑ̃tɔnje] *nm* (*sur les routes*) roadmender, roadman; *Rail* lineman
cantonnière [kɑ̃tɔnjɛr] *nf* (*de lit, de fenêtre*) valance
canular [kanylar] *nm F* hoax, *F* leg-pull; **monter un c.** to play a hoax
canule [kanyl] *nf Méd* cannula, canula; (*de seringue*) nozzle
canuler [kanyle] *vt* **(a)** *Arg* (*ennuyer*) **c. qn** to get on sb's nerves *or Br* wick **(b)** *Scol F* to play a practical joke on
canut, -use [kany, yz] *n* silk weaver (of Lyon)
canyon [kanjɔn] *nm* = **cañon**
CAO [seao] *nf Ordinat* (*abrév* **conception assistée par ordinateur)** CAD
caoua [kawa] *nm F* coffee
caoutchouc [kautʃu] *nm* **(a)** (*substance*) rubber; **c. synthétique** synthetic rubber; **c. mousse®** foam rubber, sponge rubber; **ballon en c.** rubber ball; *Bourse* **caoutchoucs** rubber shares, rubbers **(b)** *Vieilli* (*manteau*) waterproof (coat), raincoat, *Br* mackintosh; (*élastique*) rubber band, elastic band; **caoutchoucs** (*chaussures*) galoshes, overshoes, *Am* rubbers **(c)** *Bot* rubber plant
caoutchoutage [kautʃutaʒ] *nm* rubberizing, coating with rubber
caoutchouter [kautʃute] *vt* to rubberize, to coat with rubber
caoutchouteux, -euse [kautʃutø, -øz] *adj Péj* rubbery
CAP [seape] *nm* (*abrév* **Certificat d'aptitude professionnelle)** = vocational training certificate; **C. hébergement** certificate of vocational training in accommodation management
cap [kap] *nm* **(a)** *Géog* cape, headland; **le c. Horn** Cape Horn;

le C. Cape Town; *Hist* **la Colonie du c.** Cape Colony; **passer** *ou* **franchir** *ou* **doubler un c.** to round a cape; *Fig* to weather *or* overcome a difficulty; **quand on a franchi le c. de la quarantaine** when you've turned forty; **notre usine va passer le c. des mille employés** our factory will soon top the thousand-employee mark

(**b**) *Naut, Av* (*direction*) course, direction; **mettre le c. sur** ... to head for ..., to steer for ..., to set course for ...; **mettre le c. au large** to stand out to sea; **c. au vent/au large** head (on) to the wind/to sea; **changement de c.** change of course; **c. de collision** collision course; *Av* **conservateur de c.** directional gyro; **c. magnétique** magnetic course *or* heading

(**c**) **de pied en c.** from head to foot *or* toe, from top to toe

capable [kapabl] *adj* (**a**) **c. de qch** capable of sth; **être c. de faire qch** to be capable of doing sth, to be able to do sth; **je n'en suis pas c.** I can't do it; **il est c. de tout** he's capable of anything; **c. du meilleur comme du pire** capable of the best as well as the worst; **elle est bien c. d'oublier les clefs!** she's quite capable of forgetting the keys!; **cette maladie est c. de le tuer** this illness might well kill him *or* may be enough to kill him (**b**) (*compétent*) (*personne*) capable, able, competent; **élève très c.** very able pupil (**c**) *Jur* competent (**de faire** to do)

capacité [kapasite] *nf* (**a**) (*contenance*) (*de vase, accumulateur etc*) capacity; **c. d'accueil** (*d'un hôtel*) accommodation capacity, available beds; *Él* **c.** (**électrostatique**) capacitance

(**b**) (*aptitude*) ability, capability; **homme de grande** *ou* **de haute c.** very capable *or* able man, man of great ability; **je n'en ai pas les capacités** I don't have the ability *or* skills (to do it); **c. pour les affaires** business ability; **de grandes capacités intellectuelles** great intellectual abilities; **c. de concentration** attention span

(**c**) *Jur* capacity; **certificat de c. en droit** = certificate entitling holder to practise in some branches of the legal profession; **avoir c. pour faire qch** to be (legally) entitled *or* qualified to do sth; **c. de jouissance** legal right, legal entitlement

▶ **capacité**: **c. d'achat** purchasing power; *Ordinat* **c. d'adressage** address capability; **c. à emprunter** borrowing capacity; **c. d'endettement** borrowing capacity; *Com* **c. linéaire** shelf-space; *Ordinat* **c. de mémoire** memory capacity; **c. de production** production capacity; *Ordinat* **c. de stockage** storage capacity; *Méd* **c. vitale** vital capacity

caparaçon [kaparasɔ̃] *nm* caparison

caparaçonner [kaparasɔne] *vt* (*cheval*) to caparison

cape [kap] *nf* (**a**) (*vêtement*) cape; (*plus longue*) cloak; **film/roman de c. et d'épée** swashbuckling film/novel; *Fig* **sous c.** secretly, on the quiet; *Fig* **rire sous c.** to laugh up one's sleeve (**b**) *Naut* **être** *ou* **se tenir à la c.** to lie to, to be hove to; (**se**) **mettre à la c.** to heave to

capeline [kaplin] *nf* (*chapeau*) floppy hat

CAPES [kapɛs] *nm Univ* (*abrév* **Certificat d'aptitude au professorat de l'enseignement secondaire**) = postgraduate teaching certificate

capésien, -ienne [kapesjɛ̃, -jɛn] *n Scol F* ≈ graduate teacher

CAPET [kapɛt] *nm Univ* (*abrév* **Certificat d'aptitude au professorat de l'enseignement technique**) = postgraduate technical teaching certificate

Capharnaüm [kafarnaɔm] *nm Bible* Capernaum

capharnaüm [kafarnaɔm] *nm F* (*pièce en désordre*) tip, pigsty; (*désordre*) mess

cap-hornier, *pl* **cap-horniers** [kapɔrnje] *nm* sailing ship/sailor travelling round the Horn

capillaire [kapilɛr] **1** *adj* (**a**) (*tube, attraction*) capillary; *Anat* **les vaisseaux capillaires** the capillary blood vessels, the capillaries (**b**) **lotion c.** (*pour les cheveux*) hair lotion, hair tonic; **artiste c.** hair stylist **2** *nm* (**a**) *Bot* maidenhair (fern) (**b**) *Anat* **les capillaires** the capillaries

capillarité [kapilarite] *nf Phys* capillarity, capillary action

capilliculture [kapilikyltyr] *nf* hair care

capilotade [kapilɔtad] *nf F* **mettre qch en c.** to smash sth to pieces *or* to smithereens; **j'ai le dos en c.** my back's killing me

capitaine [kapitɛn] *nm* (**a**) *Mil, Naut* captain; *Naut F* skipper (**b**) (*de bande, gang etc*) leader, head; *Sp* captain, *F* skipper; *Mil* **un grand c.** a great (military) leader

▶ **capitaine**: *Mil, Av* **c.** (**d'aviation**) *Br* ≈ flight lieutenant, *Am* ≈ captain; *Naut* **c. de corvette** lieutenant commander; **c. de frégate** commander; **c. de gendarmerie** ≈ police superintendent; **c. d'industrie** captain of industry; **c. au long cours** master mariner; **c. de la marine marchande** captain *or* master (in the merchant navy); **c. des pompiers** ≈ fire chief; **c. de port** harbour *or US* harbor master; **c. de vaisseau** captain

capitainerie [kapitɛnri] *nf* harbour master's office

capital, -ale, -aux, -ales [kapital, -o] **1** *adj* (**a**) *Jur* (*crime etc*) capital; **la peine capitale** capital punishment, the death penalty

(**b**) (*essentiel*) essential; **le point c.** the essential *or* main point; **une décision capitale** a major decision; **c'est c.** it's essential; **il est c. qu'il soit présent à la réunion** it is essential for him to be at the meeting; **son défaut c.** his greatest fault; **d'une importance capitale** of capital *or* paramount importance, of the utmost importance; **les sept péchés capitaux** the seven deadly sins

(**c**) *Typ* **lettre capitale** capital (letter)

2 *nm* (**a**) *Fin* capital; **détenir 5% du c. d'une société** to have a 5% shareholding in *or* to hold 5% of the shares in a company; **c. et intérêt** principal and interest; **posséder un c.** to have some capital; **les capitaux qui circulent** the capital in circulation; **fuite des capitaux** flight of capital; **association c.-travail** profit-sharing scheme; *Fig* **le c. culturel d'un pays** the cultural wealth of a country; **ces jeunes diplômés représentent un véritable c. pour notre entreprise** these qualified young people are an asset to our company

(**b**) (*capitalistes*) **le c.** capital

3 *nf* **capitale** (**a**) (*ville*) capital (city)

(**b**) *Typ* capital (letter); (**écrire en**) **capitales d'imprimerie** (write in) block capitals *or* block letters

▶ **capital**: *Fin* **c. appelé** called-up capital; **c. de départ** start-up capital; **c. engagé** capital employed; **c. fixe** fixed capital; **c. flottant** floating capital; **c. improductif** idle capital, unproductive capital; **c. initial** start-up capital; **c.-investissement** investment capital; **c. nominal** nominal capital; **c. non appelé** uncalled capital; **c. réel** capital assets; **c. de réserve** reserve capital; **c. roulant** working capital; **c. de roulement** working capital; **c. social** (issued) share capital; **c. souscrit** subscribed capital; **c. souscrit et appelé** called-up subscribed capital; **c. souscrit et appelé, non versé** subscribed capital called and unpaid; **c. souscrit non appelé** uncalled subscribed capital; **capitaux fébriles** hot money; **capitaux permanents** long-term capital; **capitaux propres** equity, shareholders' equity *or* funds

capitalisable [kapitalizabl] *adj* (*intérêt etc*) capitalizable

capitalisation [kapitalizasjɔ̃] *nf* (*d'intérêt etc*) capitalization

capitaliser [kapitalize] **1** *vt* (*intérêt etc*) to capitalize **2** *vi* to save

capitalisme [kapitalism] *nm* capitalism

capitaliste [kapitalist] **1** *adj* capitalist, capitalistic **2** *n* capitalist

capital-risque *Fin nm sing* venture capital

capitation [kapitasjɔ̃] *nf Hist, Admin* capitation, poll tax

capiteux, -euse [kapitø, -øz] *adj* (*vin, parfum*) heady; (*charme*) sensuous; (*femme*) exciting, alluring

Capitole (le) [ləkapitɔl] *nm* (*de la Rome ancienne, de Toulouse, Washington*) the Capitol

capiton [kapitɔ̃] *nm* (*rembourrage*) padding, stuffing; (*entre les piqûres*) boss

capitonnage [kapitɔnaʒ] *nm* (*action, matière*) padding, stuffing

capitonner [kapitɔne] *vt* (*meubles*) to pad, to stuff

capitulaire [kapitylɛr] *adj Rel* **salle c.** chapter house

capitulation [kapitylasjɔ̃] *nf* capitulation, surrender; **c. sans conditions** unconditional surrender

capituler [kapityle] *vi* to capitulate, to surrender

capon, -onne [kapɔ̃, -ɔn] *F Vieilli* **1** *adj* cowardly, *F* yellow **2** *n* coward, *Br* funk

caporal, -aux [kapɔral, -o] *nm* (**a**) *Mil* lance corporal, *Am* private first class; **c. d'ordinaire** mess corporal; *Hist F* **le Petit C.** the Little Corporal, Napoleon (**b**) (*tabac*) caporal

caporal-chef, *pl* **caporaux-chefs** *nm Mil* corporal

caporaliser [kapɔralize] *vt* to militarize, to Prussianize

caporalisme [kapɔralism] *nm Mil* militarism; *Fig* authoritarianism

capot[1] [kapo] *nm* (**a**) *Aut* bonnet, *Am* hood; *Av* (*de moteur d'avion*) cowl(ing); *Naut* (*bâche*) tarpaulin; (*de lampe à arc etc*) cover, hood, casing; **c. antibruit** soundproof hood, acoustic hood; *Ordinat* **c. insonorisant** soundproof lid; **c. d'imprimante** printer hood; *Aut* **c. de ventilateur** cowl, cowling; *Aut* **c. moteur** bonnet, *Am* hood (**b**) *Naut* (*ouverture*) companion hatch

capot[2] *adj inv Cartes* **être c.** not to have taken a single trick

capotage [kapɔtaʒ] *nm* (*de bateau*) capsizing; *Aut, Av* overturning

capote [kapɔt] *nf* (**a**) *Aut* (*de décapotable*) top, *Br* hood, soft top; **baisser la c.** to put the top *or Br* hood down (**b**) *Mil* (*manteau*) greatcoat (**c**) (*de dame*) bonnet

▶ **capote**: *F* **c.** (**anglaise**) rubber, *Br* johnny

capoter[1] [kapɔte] *vt* (*véhicule*) (*garnir d'une capote*) to put a top *or Br* hood on; (*fermer la capote de*) to close the top *or Br* hood of

capoter² *vi* **(a)** *Naut* to capsize, to turn turtle; *Aut, Av* to overturn; *Fig* **notre projet a capoté** our plan fell through *or* came to nothing **(b)** *Can F* (*divaguer*) to talk drivel; **il est complètement capoté** he's completely off his head
cappucino [kaputʃino] *nm* cappuccino
câpre [kɑpr] *nf Bot, Culin* caper
caprice [kapris] *nm* **(a)** (*fantaisie*) whim, caprice, fancy; **faire qch par c.** to do sth on a whim *or* a sudden impulse; **on lui passe tous ses caprices** they indulge his every whim; **par un c. du destin** by a whim of fate; **les caprices de la mode** the vagaries of fashion **(b)** (*crise de colère*) tantrum; **faire un c./des caprices** to throw a tantrum/tantrums
capricieusement [kaprisjøzmɑ̃] *adv* capriciously
capricieux, -ieuse [kaprisjø, -jøz] **1** *adj* (*personne, courants, vent etc*) capricious; (*moteur*) temperamental; (*temps*) changeable; (*ruisseaux, etc*) meandering; **elle est capricieuse** she's always changing her mind; **le vol c. d'un papillon** the flitting of a butterfly **2** *n* capricious person; **un petit c.** a child who throws tantrums
capricorne [kaprikɔrn] *nm* **(a)** *Astron, Astrol* **le C.** Capricorn, the Goat; **être (du signe du) C.** to be (a) Capricorn; *Géog* **le Tropique du C.** the Tropic of Capricorn **(b)** (*insecte*) capricorn beetle
câprier [kɑprije] *nm* caper bush *or* plant
caprin, -ine [kaprɛ̃, -in] *adj Zool* goat, *Spéc* caprine; *Fig* goat-like
capsulage [kapsylaʒ] *nm* (*de bouteilles etc*) capping
capsule [kapsyl] *nf* **(a)** *Anat, Bot, Pharm* capsule **(b)** (*de bouteille*) cap, top **(c) c. (spatiale)** (space) capsule **(d)** (*d'armes*) (firing) cap, primer; **c. (fulminante)** (*de pistolet d'enfant*) cap **(e)** *Ch* **c. d'évaporation** evaporating dish **(f)** *Aut* **c. à dépression 'avance/retard'** vacuum advance/retard
capsuler [kapsyle] *vt* (*bouteille*) to seal, to cap, to put a cap on
captage [kaptaʒ] *nm* **(a)** (*des eaux*) collecting, impounding; *Él* (*du courant*) picking up; **c. d'une émission** picking up *or* reception of a broadcast **(b)** (*lieu*) water catchment
captateur, -trice [kaptatœr, -tris] *n Jur* inveigler; **c. de succession d'héritage** legacy hunter
captation [kaptasjɔ̃] *nf Jur* inveigling of an inheritance
captatoire [kaptatwar] *adj Jur* (*moyens d'obtenir un héritage*) inveigling
capter [kapte] *vt* **(a)** (*l'attention de qn*) to gain, to capture **(b)** (*courant électrique*) to pick up; (*eaux*) to catch, to impound **(c)** *Rad, Tél* (*messages*) to pick up; (*ligne*) to tap; **je n'arrive pas à c. France Inter** I can't pick up *or* get France Inter
capteur [kaptœr] *nm Phys* sensor; **c. solaire** solar panel; **c. de température** temperature sensor; *Ordinat* **c. photosensible** photosensitive *or* light-sensitive sensor; *Aut* **c. de charge** load sensor; **c. de choc/de collision** crash sensor; **c. de pollution** pollution sensor; **c. de vitesse** speed sensor
captieusement [kapsjøzmɑ̃] *adv* speciously
captieux, -ieuse [kapsjø, -jøz] *adj* (*argument etc*) specious
captif, -ive [kaptif, -iv] **1** *adj* **(a)** captive; *Fig, Litt* **être c. du plaisir** to be a slave to pleasure; **les citoyens captifs des ravisseurs** the members of the public held captive by the kidnappers **(b) ballon c.** captive balloon **2** *n* captive, prisoner
captivant [kaptivɑ̃] *adj* (*personne etc*) captivating; (*livre, film etc*) enthralling, gripping
captiver [kaptive] *vt* (*qn*) to captivate, to enthral; (*l'attention de qn*) to capture
captivité [kaptivite] *nf* captivity; **être en c.** to be in captivity
capture [kaptyr] *nf* **(a)** (*d'un voleur etc*) capture, catching; (*d'un navire*) capture, seizure **(b)** (*proie*) catch **(c)** *Ordinat* **c. vidéo** video capture
capturer [kaptyre] *vt* **(a)** (*voleur etc*) to capture, to catch; (*navire*) to capture, to seize **(b)** *Ordinat* to capture
capuche [kapyʃ] *nf* hood; (*de poche et en plastique*) rainhood
capuchon [kapyʃɔ̃] *nm* **(a)** (*de manteau etc*) hood; (*de moine*) cowl; (*pèlerine*) hooded cape; *Zool* **à c.** hooded **(b)** (*de stylo, tube de dentifrice etc*) cap, top; (*de chambre à air*) cap; (*de cheminée*) cowl; *Aut* **c. anti-poussière** dust cap
capucin [kapysɛ̃] *nm* **(a)** *Rel* Capuchin (friar) **(b)** *Zool* capuchin (monkey); *F* (*à la chasse*) hare
capucine [kapysin] *nf* **(a)** *Rel* Capuchin (nun) **(b)** *Bot* nasturtium
caque [kak] *nf* herring barrel; *Prov* **la c. sent toujours le hareng** what's bred in the bone will come out in the flesh
caquelon [kaklɔ̃] *nm* fondue dish
caquet [kakɛ] *nm* **(a)** (*de poules*) cackle, cackling **(b)** *F* (*bavardage*) cackle, prattle; **quel c. elle a!** she just prattles on and on!; **elle/ça lui a rabattu** *ou* **rabaissé le c.** she/that shut him up
caquetage [kaktaʒ], **caquètement** [kakɛtmɑ̃] *nm* **(a)** (*de poules*) cackle, cackling **(b)** *F* (*bavardage*) cackle, cackling, prattling
caqueter [kakte] *vi* (**je caquette, n. caquetons; je caquetterai**) **(a)** (*de poule*) to cackle **(b)** *F* (*bavarder*) to cackle, to prattle
caqueteur, -euse [kaktœr, -øz] *n F* cackler, prattler
car¹ [kar] **1** *conj* [①B55,A] for, because **2** *nm inv* **les si et les c.** the whys and wherefores
car² *nm* **(a)** bus, *Br* coach; **prendre le c.** to take the bus *or* coach, to go by bus *or* coach; **c. de ramassage scolaire** school bus; **c. de police** police van **(b)** *TV, Rad* **c. de reportage** outside broadcast van, OB van; **c. de radio-reportage** outside broadcast van, mobile broadcasting unit; **c. de transmission** transmitter van; **c. régie** outside broadcasting vehicle, OB unit **(c)** *TV* **c. monocaméra** single-camera unit; **c. multicaméra** multi-camera unit
carabe [karab] *nm* (*insecte*) ground beetle
carabin [karabɛ̃] *nm F* medical student, medic
carabine [karabin] *nf* rifle; **c. à air comprimé** air gun; **tir à la c.** rifle shooting
carabiné [karabine] *adj F* (*vent*) strong, stiff; (*orage*) violent, wild; **rhume c.** stinking *or* rotten cold; **fièvre carabinée** violent *or* raging fever; **j'ai une gueule de bois carabinée** I've got one hell of a hangover; **il m'a fait une scène carabinée** he made one hell of a scene
carabinier [karabinje] *nm* **(a)** (*en Espagne*) frontier guard **(b)** (*en Italie*) police officer, carabiniere **(c)** *Hist* carabineer
Carabosse [karabɔs] *nf* **la fée C.** the wicked fairy (Carabossa)
caraco [karako] *nm* camisole
caracole [karakɔl] *nf Équitation* caracole, half turn
caracoler [karakɔle] *vi Équitation* to caracole; *F* (*sautiller*) to prance about, to caper about; *Fig* **c. en tête** to be top dog, to be top of the league
caractère [karaktɛr] *nm* **(a)** (*personnalité*) character, nature, disposition; (*détermination*) character; **avoir (un) mauvais** *ou* **sale c.** to be bad-tempered *or Fml* ill-natured; **avoir (un) bon c.** to be good-tempered *or* good-natured; **avoir un c. gai/morose** to have a cheerful/morose character *or* nature, to be of a cheerful/morose disposition; *F* **quel fichu c.!** what a bad-tempered so-and-so!; *F* **elle a un c. de cochon** she's a bad-tempered so-and-so; **ce n'est pas dans son c. de se mettre en colère** it's not in his nature to get angry; **il est trop jeune de c. pour qu'on lui donne des responsabilités** he's too immature to be given any responsibilities; **avoir du c.** to have character; **manquer de c.** to lack (strength of) character, to have no backbone *or* spirit, to be spineless; **cette maison a beaucoup de c.** this house has a lot of character; **le c. français** the French character

(b) (*attribut*) characteristic, feature; (*aspect*) character, nature; **l'affaire a pris un c. grave** the matter has taken a serious turn; **publication de c. officiel** publication of an official nature; **ce village a un c. rural** this village has a rural character; *Biol* **c. héréditaire/acquis** hereditary/acquired characteristic *or* feature; **maladie sans c. de gravité** illness not considered to be serious

(c) (*signe*) character, letter; *Math etc* symbol; *Typ* **caractères** (*en métal*) type; **écrit en petits caractères** written in small print; **écrivez en caractères d'imprimerie** write in block letters *or* in (block) capitals, please print; *Typ* **en petits/gros caractères** in small/large type *or* print; *Typ* **c. accentué** accented *or* accent character; *Typ* **c. gras** bold character; **caractères gras** bold (type); **c. majuscule** upper-case character; **c. minuscule** lower-case character

(d) *Ordinat* character; **le choix** *ou* **la police de caractères d'une imprimante** the character set of a printer; **c. joker** wildcard; **c. d'effacement** delete character; **c. d'interruption** break character; **c. de changement de ligne** line feed character; **c. de changement de page** page break character; **c. de commande (d'impression)** (print) command character; **c. de contrôle** control character; **c. de fin de fichier** end of file character; **c. de fin de ligne** end of line character; **c. de retour arrière** backspace character; **c. en mode point** bit-mapped character, bitmap character; **c. flottant** floating character; **c. graphique** graphic character; **c. imprimable** printable character; **c. numérique** numeric(al) character; **c. à sept bits** seven-bit character
caractériel, -ielle [karakterjɛl] **1** *adj Psy* **trouble c.** emotional disturbance; **enfant c.** problem child, emotionally disturbed child **2** *n Psy* emotionally disturbed person; (*enfant*) problem child, emotionally disturbed child
caractérisation [karakterizasjɔ̃] *nf* characterization
caractérisé [karakterize] *adj* **une rougeole caractérisée** a typical *or* clear *or* unmistakable case of measles; **c'est de la méchanceté caractérisée** it's downright *or* sheer spite
caractériser [karakterize] **1** *vt* to characterize, to be characteristic of, to distinguish; **symptômes qui caractérisent une maladie** characteristic symptoms of an

illness; **la bonté qui la caractérise** her characteristic kindness **2 se caractériser** *vpr* to be characterized *or* distinguished (**par** by)
caractéristique [karakteristik] **1** *adj* characteristic, distinctive, typical; **c. de** characteristic of **2** *nf* **caractéristique** (*particularité*) characteristic, feature; **caractéristiques** (*d'une voitures, d'un avion etc*) specifications
caractérologie [karakterɔlɔʒi] *nf* characterology
carafe [karaf] *nf* (**a**) (*récipient*) (*pour le whisky etc*) decanter; (*pour le vin*) carafe (**b**) *F* **rester en c.** (*d'une personne*) to be (left) stranded; **une voiture restée en c. sur le bord de l'autoroute** a broken-down car on the side of the motorway; **tomber en c.** to break down (**c**) *F* (*tête*) nut, *Br* bonce
carafon [karafɔ̃] *nm* (*pour le whisky etc*) small decanter; (*pour le vin*) small carafe; *F* **mets-toi ça dans le c.** get that into your thick head *or* skull
caraïbe [karaib] **1** *adj* Caribbean **2** *nmpl* **Caraïbes** Caribs **3** *nfpl* **les Caraïbes** the Caribbean; **la mer des Caraïbes** the Caribbean (Sea)
carambolage [karɑ̃bɔlaʒ] *nm* (**a**) *Billard* cannon, *Am* carom (**b**) (*de voitures*) (multiple) pile-up
caramboler [karɑ̃bɔle] **1** *vi Billard* to cannon, *Am* to carom **2** *vt* **c. une voiture** to run into a car, to collide with a car **3 se caramboler** *vpr* **dix voitures se sont carambolées sur l'autoroute** there has been a ten car pile-up on the motorway
carambouillage [karɑ̃bujaʒ] *nm*, **carambouille** [karɑ̃buj] *nf F Vieilli* = fraudulent reselling of goods being paid for on credit
caramel [karamɛl] **1** *nm Culin* caramel; **bonbons au c., des caramels** (*mous*) caramels; (*durs*) toffees **2** *adj inv* caramel(-coloured)
caramélisation [karamelizasjɔ̃] *nf Culin* caramelization
caraméliser [karamelize] **1** *vt* (**a**) (*sucre*) to caramelize (**b**) (*moule*) to coat with caramel **2** *vi* to caramelize **3 se caraméliser** *vpr* (*rôti*) to brown (well); (*sucre*) to caramelize
carapace [karapas] *nf* (*de langouste etc*) shell, *Spéc* carapace; *Fig* shell; *Fig* **il est difficile de percer sa c.** it's difficult to get through to him; **la voiture était recouverte d'une c. de boue** the car was encrusted with mud
carapater (se) [səkarapate] *vpr F* to beat it, to scram, *Br* to scarper
carat [kara] *nm* (**a**) (*de métal, pierre*) carat; **or (à) dix-huit carats** eighteen-carat gold; *F* **je te donne jusqu'à trois heures, dernier c.** I'll give you till three o'clock at the latest (**b**) **c. métrique** carat (weight) (*0.2g*) (**c**) *F* (*année*) **il a dépassé les soixante carats** he's over sixty
Caravage (le) [ləkaravaʒ] *nm* Caravaggio
caravanage [karavanaʒ] *nm* = **caravaning**
caravane [karavan] *nf* (**a**) (*du désert*) caravan; *F* (*de touristes, d'écoliers etc*) conducted party, procession; **la c. du Tour de France** the caravan following the Tour de France cyclists (**b**) (*remorque*) caravan, *Am* trailer; **c. de tourisme** touring caravan
caravanier [karavanje] **1** *nm* (**a**) *Aut* caravanner (**b**) (*dans le désert*) caravaneer **2** *adj* **chemin c.** caravan route *or* track
caravaning [karavaniŋ] *nm* caravanning; **faire du c.** to go caravanning
caravansérail [karavɑ̃seraj] *nm* caravanserai
caravelle [karavɛl] *nf* (**a**) *Naut* car(a)vel (**b**) *Av* Caravelle®
carbochimie [karbɔʃimi] *nf Ch* organic chemistry
carbonade [karbɔnad] *nf* = **carbonnade**
carbonate [karbɔnat] *nm Ch* carbonate; **c. de soude** carbonate of soda, sodium carbonate; *Com* washing soda
carbone [karbɔn] *nm Ch* carbon; *Journ* black; **c. 14** carbon 14, radiocarbon; **datation au c. 14** radiocarbon dating; **(papier) c.** carbon (paper)
carbonifère [karbɔnifɛr] *adj, nm Géol* Carboniferous
carbonique [karbɔnik] *adj Ch* carbonic; **anhydride c., gaz c.** carbon dioxide; **acide c.** carbonic acid; **neige c.** dry ice
carbonisation [karbɔ̃nizasjɔ̃] *nf* carbonization
carbonisé [karbɔnize] *adj* (*forêt*) burnt to the ground; (*nourriture*) burnt to a cinder; (*corps*) horribly burnt, *F* burnt to a cinder
carboniser [karbɔnize] *vt* (*os, bois etc*) to carbonize; (*forêt*) to burn to the ground; (*viande*) to burn to a cinder
carbonnade [karbɔnad] *nf Culin* **bifteck à la c.** charcoal-grilled steak
carbonyle [karbɔnil] *nm Ch* carbonyl
carborundum [karbɔrɔ̃dɔm] *nm Ch* carborundum
carburant [karbyrɑ̃] **1** *nm* fuel; **c. liquide** liquid fuel; **c. volatil** light-fraction fuel **2** *adj* containing hydrocarbon; **mélange c.** mixture (of petrol *or Am* gas and air)
carburateur [karbyratœr] *nm Aut* carburettor, *US* carburetor; **c. double corps** twin choke carburettor; **c. à dépression constante** constant-depression carburettor; **c. à venturi variable** variable-venturi carburettor
carburation [karbyrasjɔ̃] *nf* (**a**) *Métal* carburization (**b**) (*de l'essence etc*) carburation
carbure [karbyr] *nm Ch* carbide; **c. de calcium** calcium carbide
carburé [karbyre] *adj* (**a**) *Métal* carburized (**b**) (*air*) carburetted
carburéacteur [karbyreaktœr] *nm Tech* aviation fuel
carburer [karbyre] **1** *vt Métal* to carburize **2** *vi* (**a**) **le moteur carbure mal** the mixture is wrong (**b**) *F* (*travailler*) **ça carbure ici** everyone here's working like mad; **qu'est-ce qu'on a carburé hier!** we worked like mad yesterday! (**c**) (*fonctionner à*) **il carbure au whisky** whisky keeps him going
carcajou [karkaʒu] *nm* wolverine, *Am* carcajou
carcan [karkɑ̃] *nm Hist* iron collar; *Fig* (*contrainte*) yoke, restraint; **le c. des horaires** scheduling constraints
carcasse [karkas] *nf* (**a**) (*pour la boucherie*) carcass; *F* (*de personne vivante*) body; *F* **promener sa c.** to walk (**b**) (*de parapluie, capote de voiture, abat-jour etc*) frame(work); (*de maison, bateau*) shell, skeleton; (*de moteur électrique*) carcass; (*de pneu*) casing, carcass, frame; (*caisse*) bodyshell; **c. diagonale** (*d'un pneu*) diagonal-ply carcass; **c. radiale** (*d'un pneu*) radial-ply carcass; **à c. radiale** (*pneu*) radial-ply
carcéral, -ale, -aux, -ales [karseral, -o] *adj* prison; **vie carcérale** prison life
carcinogène [karsinɔʒɛn] *adj Méd* carcinogenic
carcinologie [karsinɔlɔʒi] *nf Méd* oncology, study of cancer
carcinome [karsinom] *nm Méd* carcinoma
cardage [kardaʒ] *nm Tex* (**a**) (*de la laine etc*) carding, combing (**b**) (*de tissu*) teaselling
cardan [kardɑ̃] *nm Aut* **c., joint de C.** universal joint, Cardan joint
carde [kard] *nf* (**a**) *Culin* chard (**b**) *Tex* card, carding brush; (*tambour*) teasel
carder [karde] *vt Tex* (**a**) (*laine etc*) to card (**b**) (*tissu*) to teasel
cardeur, -euse [kardœr, -øz] *Tex* **1** *n* carder **2** *nf* **cardeuse** (*machine*) carding machine, carder
cardiaque [kardjak] **1** *adj* (*nerfs, murmure etc*) cardiac; **crise c.** heart attack; **être c.** to have heart trouble *or* a weak heart **2** *n* person with heart disease
cardigan [kardigɑ̃] *nm* cardigan
cardinal, -ale, -aux, -ales [kardinal, -o] **1** *adj* [①**A70**,16,1; **B56**,**A**] (*point, nombre, vertu*) cardinal **2** *nm* (**a**) *Cathol* cardinal (**b**) *Orn* cardinal (bird)
cardinalat [kardinala] *nm Cathol* cardinalship
cardinalice [kardinalis] *adj Cathol* of a cardinal; **revêtir la pourpre c.** to don the scarlet; **élever qn à la dignité c.** to make sb a cardinal
cardiogramme [kardjɔgram] *nm Méd* cardiogram
cardiographe [kardjɔgraf] *nm Méd* cardiograph
cardiographie [kardjɔgrafi] *nf Méd* cardiography
cardiologie [kardjɔlɔʒi] *nf Méd* cardiology
cardiologue [kardjɔlɔg] *n Méd* cardiologist, heart specialist; **chirurgien c.** heart surgeon
cardiorespiratoire [kardjɔrɛspiratwar] *adj Méd* cardiorespiratory
cardio-vasculaire [kardjɔvaskylɛr] *adj Anat, Méd* cardiovascular; *Méd* **accident c.** cardiovascular accident, *F* stroke
cardite [kardit] *nf Méd* carditis
cardon [kardɔ̃] *nm Bot, Culin* cardoon
carême [karɛm] *nm* (**a**) (*période*) Lent (**b**) (*jeûne*) (Lenten) fast(ing); **faire (son) c.** to keep Lent, to fast; *Fig* **face de c.** dismal face (**c**) *Litt* (*sermons*) (course of) Lenten sermons
carême-prenant, *pl* **carêmes-prenants** *nm Arch* Shrovetide
carénage [karenaʒ] *nm* (**a**) *Naut* (*de bateau*) careening, careenage; (*lieu*) careenage (**b**) *Av, Aut* streamlining
carence [karɑ̃s] *nf* (**a**) *Méd* deficiency (**de** in, of); **c. en vitamine E** deficiency in vitamin E, vitamin E deficiency; **maladie de** *ou* **par c.** deficiency disease; **c. alimentaire** nutritional deficiency; **c. affective** emotional deprivation; *Fig* **c. en personnel** staff shortage, shortage of staff (**b**) (*insuffisance*) shirking of one's obligations; **la c. du père** (*dans l'éducation de son enfant*) the father's non-participation (**c**) *Jur* insolvency
carencé [karɑ̃se] *adj Psy* emotionally deprived
carène [karɛn] *nf* (*de navire*) bottom, (underwater) hull; **abattre un navire en c.** to careen a ship
caréner [karene] *vt* (**je carène**; **je carénerai**) (**a**) *Naut* to careen (**b**) *Av, Aut* to streamline
carentiel, -ielle [karɑ̃sjɛl] *adj* **maladie carentielle** deficiency disease
caressant [karɛsɑ̃] *adj* (*regard, voix*) tender; (*vent*) soft, gentle; (*enfant*) affectionate; **d'une voix caressante** tenderly, affectionately

caresse [karɛs] *nf* **(a)** (*d'affection*) caress; **faire des caresses à** (*personne*) to caress; (*animal*) to stroke; *Litt* **la c. du soleil** the sun's caress **(b)** *Vieilli* (*flatterie*) flattery

caresser [karese] *vt* **(a)** (*par affection*) (*personne*) to caress; (*animal*) to stroke; **c. qn du regard** to look affectionately *or* tenderly at sb **(b)** (*espoir, rêve*) to cherish; (*idée*) to toy with; **c. un projet** to nurture a project **(c)** *Vieilli* (*flatter*) to flatter; **cette idée caresse son amour-propre** the idea flatters his self-esteem

car-ferry, *pl* **car-ferrys** *nm* car ferry

cargaison [kargɛzɔ̃] *nf* **(a)** [①A12,1,c,y] (*marchandises*) cargo, freight; **c. de charbon/de marchandises** cargo of coal/merchandise; **c. en vrac** bulk cargo; **c. flottante** cargo afloat; **c. mixte** mixed cargo **(b)** *F* (*de passagers, cadeaux etc*) load (**de** of); **toute une c. d'histoires belges** a whole load *or* repertoire of Belgian jokes; **j'avais préparé toute une c. d'excuses** I had all sorts of *or* a whole load of excuses prepared

cargo [kargo] *nm Naut* cargo boat, freighter; **c. mixte** cargo and passenger vessel

cargue [karg] *nf Naut* (*de voile*) brail

carguer [karge] *vt Naut* (*voile*) to take in, to brail (up)

cariant [karjɑ̃] *adj* **substance cariante** substance that causes tooth decay

cariatide [karjatid] *nf Archit* caryatid

caribou [karibu] *nm Zool* caribou

caricatural, -ale, -aux, -ales [karikatyral, -o] *adj* (*récit, description etc*) caricatured

caricature [karikatyr] *nf* (*dessin, description etc*) caricature; **le film est une c. de la vie ouvrière** the film is a caricature of working-class life; *F* **quelle c. que cette femme!** what a fright that woman is!

caricaturer [karikatyre] *vt* to caricature

caricaturiste [karikatyrist] *n* caricaturist

carie [kari] *nf* **(a)** *Méd* (*d'os*) caries, decay; **c. dentaire** tooth decay, *Spéc* dental caries; **avoir une c.** to have a tooth that needs filling **(b)** (*d'arbres*) blight; (*de céréales*) smut, bunt

carié [karje] *adj Méd* (*dent*) decayed, bad

carier [karje] *Méd* **1** *vt* to rot, to decay **2 se carier** *vpr* to rot, to decay

carillon [karijɔ̃] *nm* (*sonnerie*) chime(s), *Litt* carillon; (*ensemble de cloches*) peal of bells; (*de porte*) (door) chime(s); *Mus* tubular bells, chimes; **(horloge à) c.** chiming clock

carillonnement [karijɔnmɑ̃] *nm* (*de cloches*) chiming, ringing

carillonner [karijɔne] **1** *vi* (*faire sonner les cloches*) to ring the bells; (*des cloches*) to chime, to ring; **c. à la porte** to ring the (door) bell loudly **2** *vt* (*air*) to chime; (*fête religieuse*) to announce with a peal of bells; *Fig* **c. la nouvelle** to spread the news far and wide, to tell the news to all and sundry; **fête carillonnée** high festival

carillonneur [karijɔnœr] *nm* bellringer

cariste [karist] *n Tech* fork-lift truck driver

caritatif, -ive [karitatif, iv] *adj* charitable; **association caritative** charitable organization, charity

carlin [karlɛ̃] *nm* (*chien*) pug

carlingue [karlɛ̃g] *nf* **(a)** *Naut* ke(e)lson **(b)** *Av* cabin

carliste [karlist] *n Hist* Carlist

carmagnole [karmaɲɔl] *nf Hist* **(a)** (*veste*) jacket (*worn by Revolutionaries in 1793*) **(b)** *Mus* (*ronde*) carmagnole

carme [karm] *nm Rel* Carmelite (friar), White friar

Carmel [karmɛl] *nm* **(a)** *Rel* **le C.** the Carmelite order **(b)** (*couvent*) (*de carmes*) Carmelite monastery; (*de carmélites*) Carmelite convent

carmélite [karmelit] *nf Rel* Carmelite (nun)

carmin [karmɛ̃] **1** *adj inv* carmine, crimson **2** *nm* carmine

carminé [karmine] *adj* carmine, crimson

carnage [karnaʒ] *nm* carnage, slaughter; *Fig* **s'il n'arrête pas, je vais faire un c.** if he doesn't stop, I'll kill him

carnassier, -ière [karnasje, -jɛr] **1** *adj* (*animal*) carnivorous, flesh-eating; *Zool* (*dent*) carnassial; *Fig* (*cruel*) (*regard, sourire*) predatory **2** *nm* carnivore; **les carnassiers** carnivores, *Spéc* the Carnivora **3** *nf* **carnassière (a)** *Zool* carnassial (tooth) **(b)** (*sac*) game bag

carnation [karnasjɔ̃] *nf* **(a)** (*teint*) complexion; **c. de blonde** fair skin *or* complexion **(b)** *Beaux-Arts* flesh tint, *Spéc* carnation

carnaval, -als [karnaval] *nm* (*fête*) carnival; **un masque de c.** a carnival mask; **Sa Majesté C.** King Carnival

carnavalesque [karnavalɛsk] *adj* **tenue c.** carnival costume, *Péj* **un accoutrement c.** a ridiculous get-up

carne [karn] *nf* **(a)** *F* (*viande*) tough meat; (*vieux cheval*) old nag **(b)** *Arg* **quelle c.!** (*cet homme*) what a bastard!; (*cette femme*) what a bitch *or* cow!

carné [karne] *adj* **(a)** (*rose*) flesh-coloured *or US* -colored **(b)** **régime c.** meat diet

carneau, -eaux [karno] *nm Tech* flue

carnet [karnɛ] *nm* (*cahier*) notebook

▶ **carnet**: *Scol* **c. (de notes)** = (school) report; **c. d'adresses** address book; (*de publipostage*) address list; *Com* **c. ATA** ATA carnet; *Vieilli* **c. de bal** dance card; *Aut* **c. de bord** logbook, memorandum; **c. de chèques** cheque *or US* check book; *Com* **c. de commandes** order book; *Com* **c. communautaire** Community carnet; *Aut* **c. de constat amiable** = set of insurance documents to be completed at scene of accident; *Scol* **c. de correspondance** = school report book; *Aut* **c. d'entretien** (*d'une voiture*) servicing booklet; **c. d'épargne** savings book, passbook; *Journ* **c. mondain** society column; *Com* **c. de passage en douanes** carnet; **c. de route** logbook; **c. de santé** health record; **c. à souche(s)** counterfoil book; **c. de tickets** book of tickets; **c. de timbres** book of stamps; *Av* **c. de vol** log(book); **c. de voyage** travel documents

carnier [karnje] *nm* game bag

carnivore [karnivɔr] *Zool* **1** *adj* (*animal*) carnivorous, flesh-eating **2** *nm* carnivore; **les carnivores** carnivores, *Spéc* the Carnivora

carolingien, -ienne [karɔlɛ̃ʒjɛ̃, -jɛn] *Hist* **1** *adj* Carolingian, Carlovingian **2** *n* **C.** Carolingian, Carlovingian

Caron [karɔ̃] *nm Myth* Charon

caroncule [karɔ̃kyl] *nf Anat, Bot, Zool* caruncle; (*de dindon*) wattle

carotène [karɔtɛn] *nm* carotene

carotide [karɔtid] *adj* (*artère*) carotid

carottage [karɔtaʒ] *nm* **(a)** *F* (*vol*) pinching, *Br* nicking; (*escroquerie*) swindling, diddling **(b)** *Min* taking of cores

carotte [karɔt] **1** *nf* **(a)** (*plante*) carrot; *F* **la c. ou le bâton** the carrot and the stick; *F* **Poil de c.** Ginger; *F* **les carottes sont cuites** you've/he's/*etc* cooked your/his/*etc* goose, you're/he's/*etc* done for **(b)** *Min* core (sample); (*de tabac*) plug; *F* (*enseigne*) tobacconist's sign **(c)** *F* **tirer une c. à qn** to swindle *or* diddle sb **(d)** *Tennis F* drop shot **2** *adj inv* **cheveux (rouge) c.** ginger *or* red *or F* carroty hair

carotter [karɔte] *vt* **(a)** *F* (*voler*) (*qch*) to pinch, *Br* to nick; (*escroquer*) (*qn*) to swindle, to diddle, *Br* to do; **c. une permission/une signature** to wangle leave/a signature **(b)** *Min* to take a core (sample) of

carotteur, -euse[1] [karɔtœr, -øz], **carottier, -ière** [karɔtje, -jɛr] *n F* (*voleur*) thief; (*escroc*) swindler

carotteuse[2] *nf Min* core sampler

caroube [karub] *nf Bot* carob (bean)

caroubier [karubje] *nm Bot* carob (tree)

carpaccio [karpatʃio] *nm Culin* carpaccio

Carpates [karpat] *nfpl* **les C.** the Carpathian Mountains, the Carpathians

carpe[1] [karp] *nm Anat* carpus

carpe[2] *nf* (*poisson*) carp; **faire des yeux de c.** to make sheep's eyes; **être muet comme une c.** (*discret*) to be as silent as the grave; **tu restas muet comme une c. toute la soirée** you didn't open your mouth all evening; **bâiller comme une c.** to yawn one's head off

carpeau, -eaux [karpo] *nm* (*poisson*) young carp

carpette [karpɛt] *nf* (*tapis*) rug; *F Péj* **s'aplatir comme une c.** to behave like a doormat; *F Péj* **c'est une vraie c.** he's a doormat

carpiculture [karpikyltyr] *nf* carp farming

carpien, -ienne [karpjɛ̃, -jɛn] *adj Anat* (*os etc*) carpal

carquois [karkwa] *nm* quiver; *Litt* **il a vidé son c.** he has shot his bolt

carrare [karar] *nm* Carrara marble

carre [kar] *nf* (*de patin, ski*) edge; (*de livre etc*) corner; (*de planche etc*) cross section; *Ski* **lâcher les carres** to flatten *or* take the edge off the skis

carré, -ée [kare] **1** *adj* **(a)** (*figure, jardin etc*) square; (*épaules*) square, broad; *Math* **nombre c.** square number; **dix mètres carrés** ten square metres; **partie carrée** ≈wife-swapping party

(b) (*tranché*) (*réponse*) plain, straightforward, blunt; (*personne*) straightforward; **être c. en affaires** to be straightforward in one's business dealings

2 *nm* **(a)** square; *Can* (*place*) (public) square; **c. de papier** slip of paper; **c. de soie** silk square; **c. de choux** cabbage patch; *Naut* **c. (des officiers)** wardroom; *Mil* **former le c.** to get into square formation; *Cartes* **c. de valets** four jacks; **avoir une coupe au c.** *ou* **un c.** to have one's hair in a bob; *F* **s'il continue, je vais lui faire une tête au c.!** if he goes on like that, I'm going to punch his face in

(b) [①B56,C,4] *Math* (*d'un nombre*) square; **élever au c.** to square; *Math* **le c. de six, six au c.** six squared

(c) *Culin* **c. d'agneau** rack of lamb; **c. de l'Est** = type of soft cheese

(d) *(élève)* = second year student *(in certain Grandes Écoles)*

3 *nf* **carrée (a)** *Hist, Mus* breve

(b) *F (chambre)* room

▶ **carré**: *Rail* **c. Jeunes** = reduced-rate rail travel card for young people within France

carreau, -eaux [karo] *nm* **(a)** *(motif)* square; *(sur du tissu)* check; **tissu à carreaux** check(ed) material; *Beaux-Arts* **mettre un croquis au c.** to square up a sketch

(b) *(de céramique etc)* tile; *(dalle)* flag(stone)

(c) *(de fenêtre)* (window) pane; **laveur de carreaux** window cleaner *or Am* washer; **regarder aux carreaux** to look in at the window; **un c. cassé** a broken window

(d) *F* **carreaux** *(lunettes)* specs, glasses

(e) *(sol)* (tiled) floor; **laver le c.** to wash the floor; **coucher qn sur le c.** to lay sb out; **rester sur le c.** *(être tué)* to be killed on the spot; *(être blessé)* to be critically injured; *(être éliminé)* to be out of the running; *(d'un boxeur)* not to get up, to stay on the canvas *or* floor; **le c. des Halles** *(à Paris)* the (floor of the) market

(f) *Cartes* diamond; *Fig* **se tenir à c.** to keep a low profile

▶ **carreau**: *Min* **c. de mine** pit head

carrefour [karfur] *nm* **(a)** [ⓘA13,3,b] *(de route)* crossroads; **tête de c.** T-junction; **c. décalé** staggered junction; **c. ferroviaire** railway junction; *Fig* **être à un c.** to be at a crossroads; **un c. de nouvelles idées/de tendances** a place for the exchange of new ideas/trends **(b)** *(réunion)* forum, symposium

carrelage [karlaʒ] *nm* **(a)** *(action)* tiling **(b)** *(carreaux)* tiling, tiles; *(sol)* (tiled) floor; *(mur)* tiled wall

carreler [karle] *vt* **(je carrelle, n. carrelons; je carrellerai) (a)** *(mettre des carreaux sur) (sol, murs)* to tile **(b)** *(tracer des carreaux sur) (feuille de papier etc)* to draw squares on, to square

carrelet [karlɛ] *nm* **(a)** *(règle)* square ruler **(b)** *(aiguille)* large needle **(c)** *Pêche* square dipping net **(d)** *(poisson)* plaice

carreleur [karlœr] *nm* tiler, tile layer; *(d'une cour)* paver

carrément [karemɑ̃] *adv* **(a)** *Géom* square(ly); **pièce coupée c.** square-cut piece **(b)** *F* **il y est allé c.** he got straight to the point, he didn't beat about the bush, he didn't mess about; **je lui ai dit c. ce que je pensais** I told him straight (out) *or* bluntly *or* in no uncertain terms what I thought; **tu as c. tort** you're simply wrong, you're wrong and that's that

carrer [kare] **1** *vt (planche), Math (nombre etc)* to square **2 se carrer** *vpr* to settle (down) **(dans un fauteuil** in an armchair)

carrier [karje] *nm (ouvrier)* quarryman, quarrier; **(maître) c.** quarry master

carrière[1] [karjɛr] *nf* **(a)** *(professionnelle etc)* career; **faire c.** to make a career for oneself; **suivre une c.** *ou* **faire c. dans le commerce** to make a career in business; **en début/fin de c.** at the start/end of one's career; **c. politique/des armes** political/military career; **militaire de c.** regular (soldier); **diplomate de c.** professional *or* career diplomat; **elle est de la c.** she is in the diplomatic service

(b) donner c. à un cheval to give free rein to a horse; *Fig* **donner (libre) c. à son imagination** to give free rein *or* free play *or* full scope to one's imagination; **donner c. à ses sentiments, se donner c.** to let oneself go, to give free expression to one's feelings

carrière[2] *nf (lieu)* quarry; **c. à ciel ouvert** open quarry

carriérisme [karjerism] *nm Péj* careerism

carriériste [karjerist] *adj, n Péj* careerist

carriole [karjɔl] *nf* **(a)** *(petite charette)* light cart **(b)** *Can* sleigh, sled

carrossable [karɔsabl] *adj (chemin, route)* suitable for motor vehicles

carrossage [karɔsaʒ] *nm Aut* rake, camber

carrosse [karɔs] *nm* (horse-drawn) coach; **c. d'apparat** state coach; *F* **rouler c.** to live in great style; *Can* **c. de bébé** pram, *Am* baby carriage

carrosser [karɔse] *vt Aut (voiture etc)* to fit the body to; *Arg* **elle est bien carrossée** she's got curves in all the right places

carrosserie [karɔsri] *nf Aut* **(a)** *(construction)* coachbuilding **(b)** *(caisse) (de voiture etc)* body, coachwork, bodywork

carrossier [karɔsje] *nm Aut* coachbuilder

carroté [karɔte] *adj Can (chemise etc)* check(ed)

carrousel [karuzɛl] *nm* **(a)** *Hist (tournoi)* tournament; *(lieu)* tiltyard; *Equitation* carousel; *(manège de chevaux de bois)* roundabout, *Am* carousel **(b)** *Fig (succession rapide)* **le c. des ministres** the ministerial merry-go-round **(c)** *(d'une aérogare)* carousel; **c. de livraison des bagages** baggage carousel

carrure [karyr] *nf* **(a)** *(de personne)* build; *(de manteau)* width across the shoulders; **homme d'une belle c.** well-built man **(b)** *(de mâchoire etc)* broadness, squareness **(c)** *Fig* **elle est d'une grande c.** she's a very impressive woman; **il est d'une autre c. que ses concurrents** he is much more impressive than his competitors; **avoir la c. d'un cadre supérieur** to be senior management material

carry [kari] *nm* = **curry**

cartable [kartabl] *nm* school bag; *(à bretelles)* satchel

carte [kart] *nf* **(a)** *(géographique)* map; *Naut* chart; **dresser la c. d'une région** to map (out) an area

(b) *(feuille de carton)* card; *Com* business card; *Cartes* (playing) card; **jeu de (52) cartes** pack *or Am* deck of cards; **laisser sa c. chez qn** to leave one's card with sb; **avoir sa c. au parti** to be a card-carrying member of the party; **jouer aux cartes** to play cards; **une partie de cartes** a game of cards; **donner** *ou* **faire les cartes** to deal (the cards); *Fig* **donner c. blanche à qn** to give sb carte blanche *or* a free hand; **château de cartes** house of cards; **être balayé/s'écrouler comme un château de cartes** to be swept away/collapse like a house of cards; *Fig* **jouer cartes sur table** to put one's cards on the table; *Fig* **jouer la c. des libéraux** to play the liberal card *or* hand; *Fig* **jouer sa dernière c.** to play one's last card; **abattre ses cartes** to lay one's cards on the table; *Fig* **nous avons encores quelques bonnes cartes en main** we still have several cards up our sleeves; **c. maîtresse** *Cartes* master card; *Fig* trump card; *Fig* **c'était la c. forcée** it was Hobson's choice; *Fig* **connaître le dessous des cartes** to know the inside story; *Fig* **brouiller les cartes** to complicate matters, to confuse the issue; **femme en c.** registered prostitute

(c) c. (de restaurant) menu; **c. du jour** today's menu, menu for the day; **c. des vins** wine list; **manger à la c.** to eat à la carte; **horaires à la c.** flexitime; **nous vous proposons un vaste choix d'activités à la c.** choose from a vast range of activities

(d) *Ordinat* card; *(de clavier etc)* map

(e) *Com (de boutons etc)* card; **c. d'échantillons** sample card

▶ **carte**: **c. d'abonnement** *(pour la bibliothèque etc)* membership card *or* ticket; *(pour les transports, le théâtre etc)* season ticket; *Ordinat* **c. accélérateur graphique** graphics accelerator card; *Ordinat* **c. accélératrice** accelerator card; *Av* **c. d'accès à bord** boarding pass, embarkation card; **c. accréditive** charge card; **c. d'adhérent** membership card; **c. d'affaires** business card; *Ordinat* **c. d'affichage** display card; **c. d'alimentation** ration book; **c. American Express** American Express (card); **c. Amex** Amex (card); **c. d'animation d'images vidéo** video image animation card; **c. d'anniversaire** birthday card; *Ordinat* **c. audio** audio card; **c. bancaire** cash card, cheque card, banker's card; **c. bancaire à puce** banker's card; **c. Bleue** Visa® (card); *Ordinat* **c. de bus local** local bus card; **c. de chemin de fer** season ticket; **c. du ciel** astronomical map *or* chart; *Ordinat* **c. à circuit imprimé** *ou* **de circuits imprimés** printed circuit board, PCB; *Ordinat* **c. à circuit(s) intégré(s)** integrated circuit card, IC card; **c. de circulation** (rail/bus) pass; *Admin* **c. de commerce** trading licence; *Ordinat* **c. de communication** communication card; *Ordinat* **c. de connexion** connection card; *Ordinat* **c. de contrôle** control card; *Ordinat* **c. contrôleur de disque** disk controller card; **c. de crédit** credit card; **c. de débarquement** landing card; **c. d'électeur** voting card; *Av* **c. d'embarquement** boarding pass, embarkation card; *Ordinat* **c. d'E/S** I/O card; *Ordinat* **c. enfichable** slot-in card; **c. d'entrée** pass (card); **c. d'état-major** ≈ Ordnance Survey map, *Am* ≈ Geological Survey map; **c. d'étudiant** student card; **c. Eurocard Mastercard** Mastercard, Access; *Ordinat* **c. d'extension** expansion card *or* board; *Ordinat* **c. d'extension mémoire** memory expansion card *or* board; *Ordinat* **c. fille** daughterboard; *Rail* **c. famille nombreuse** reduced-rate card for families with three or more children; **c. fax** fax card; **c. de fidélité** frequent user card, valued customer card; *Biol* **c. du génome humain** map of the human genome; *Aut* **c. grise** ≈ (vehicle) registration document; **c. d'identité** identity card; *Ordinat* **c. d'interface** interface card; **c. internationale d'étudiant** International Student Identity Card; *Rail* **c. Inter-rail** Inter-Rail Card; **c. d'invitation** invitation (card); *Rail* **c. Jeunes** = reduced-rate rail travel card for young people within France; **c. à jouer** (playing) card; **c. de journaliste** press card; **c. de lecteur** library *or* reader's ticket; *Ordinat* **c. logique** logic card; **c. magnétique** magnetic card; **c. mécanographique** punch card; *Ordinat* **c. mémoire** memory card; *Ordinat* **c. mère** motherboard; *Ordinat* **c. à microcircuit** microcircuit card; *Ordinat* **c. modem** modem card; **c. à mémoire** smart card; **c. météorologique** meteorological *or* weather map *or* chart; **c. orange** *(à Paris)* = combined monthly pass for the underground, bus and suburban train; **c. de paiement** payment card; *Tél* **c. Pastel** phone card (*use of which is debited to one's own phone number*); *Mktg* **c. perceptuelle de marques** brand mapping; *Mktg* **c. perceptuelle de produits** product mapping; **c. perforée** punch card; *Ordinat* **c. à piste magnétique** magnetic stripe card; *Ordinat* **c. de polices de caractères** font card; **c. postale** (post)card; *Tél* **c. à prépaiement** phonecard (*with prepaid units*); **c. prépayée** prepaid card; **c. de presse** press card; *Ordinat* **c. principale** main board; *Ordinat* **c. processeur** processor card; **c. professionnelle** professional certificate; **c. à puce** smart card; **c. de réduction** discount card; **c. de représentant** sales representative's official identity card; *Ordinat* **c. réseau** network card; **c. routière** road map; *Ordinat* **c. SCSI** SCSI card; **c. de Sécurité Sociale** National Insurance Card; **c. de séjour** residence permit; *Ordinat* **c. son** *ou* **sonore** sound card; *Ordinat* **c. système** systems board; **c. T** reply-paid card; **c. de télécopie** fax card; **c. de téléphone** phonecard; **c. de train** railcard; (*abonnement, forfait*) rail pass; *Ordinat* **c. unité centrale** CPU board; *Rail* **c. Vermeil** ≈ Senior Citizen's railcard; *Aut* **c. verte** green card; *Ordinat* **c. vidéo** video card; **c. Visa**® Visa; **c. de visite** (visiting, *Am* calling) card; *Ordinat* **c. vocale** voice card; **c. de vœux** greetings card

carte-adaptateur, *pl* **cartes-adaptateurs** *nf Ordinat* **c. réseau** network adaptor card

carte-clé, *pl* **cartes-clés** *nf* key card; **c. électronique** electronic key card

carte-guide, *pl* **cartes-guides** *nf* (*pour séparer des fiches*) file separator *or* divider

cartel[1] [kartɛl] *nm* (*horloge*) wall clock

cartel[2] *nm* **(a)** *Écon* cartel, trust, combine; **c. de l'acier/de la drogue** steel/drug cartel; **c. de production** production cartel **(b)** *Pol* cartel, coalition

carte-lettre, *pl* **cartes-lettres** *nf* letter-card

cartellisation [kartelizasjɔ̃] *nf Écon* cartelization

carter [kartɛr] *nm* (*d'engrenages*) casing, housing; (*de mécanisme*) cover; *Aut* (*de vilebrequin*) crankcase; (*d'huile*) engine sump, oil sump; **fond de c.** sump

carte-réponse, *pl* **cartes-réponses** *nf* reply card *or* coupon

carterie [kartəri] *nf Com* card shop

cartésianisme [kartezjanism] *nm Phil* Cartesianism

cartésien, -ienne [kartezjɛ̃, -jɛn] *adj, n Phil, Math* Cartesian

carte-vue, *pl* **cartes-vues** [kart(ə)vy] *nf* picture postcard

carthaginois, -oise [kartaʒinwa, -waz] *Hist* **1** *adj* Carthaginian **2** *n* **C.** Carthaginian

cartilage [kartilaʒ] *nm Anat* cartilage; (*dans la viande*) gristle

cartilagineux, -euse [kartilaʒinø, -øz] *adj Anat* cartilaginous; (*viande*) gristly

cartographe [kartɔgraf] *n* cartographer

cartographie [kartɔgrafi] *nf* cartography; **c. des gènes** gene *or* genetic mapping

cartographique [kartɔgrafik] *adj* cartographic(al)

cartomancie [kartɔmɑ̃si] *nf* fortune telling (by cards), cartomancy

cartomancien, -ienne [kartɔmɑ̃sjɛ̃, -jɛn] *n* fortune teller (*who uses cards*)

carton [kartɔ̃] *nm* **(a)** (*matière*) cardboard; (*feuille, support*) piece of cardboard, (piece of) card; **poupée/masque de c.** cardboard doll/mask; *F* **maison de c.** jerry-built house; **envoyer un c.** to send (out) an invitation

(b) (*boîte*) (cardboard) box, carton; (*dossier*) (cardboard) file; **des cartons de déménagement** cardboard boxes for moving (house); **faire ses cartons** to pack (up) one's things in cardboard boxes; **le projet est resté dans les cartons** the project never got off the ground; **ça dort dans les cartons depuis des mois** it's been shelved for months

(c) *Beaux-Arts* cartoon, sketch

(d) faire un c. (*au tir*) to fill a target; **faire un bon c.** to make a good score; *Scol F* **se payer un c.** to get a bad *or F* rotten mark

(e) *Géog* inset (map)

▶ **carton**: *TV* **c. aide-mémoire** cue card; **c. bristol** Bristol board; **c. à chapeau(x)** hatbox; **c. de classement** file box; **c. à dessin** portfolio; **c. épais** millboard; *TV* **c. de générique** title card; **c. d'invitation** invitation (card); *Fb* **c. jaune** yellow card; **c. ondulé** corrugated cardboard; *TV* **cartons de promepteur** prompt cards; *Fb* **c. rouge** red card; **se prendre un c. rouge** to get a *or* the red card; *TV* **c. volant** flip card

cartonnage [kartɔnaʒ] *nm* **(a)** (*objets en carton*) cardboard articles; (*fabrication*) making of cardboard articles **(b)** (*reliure*) (*action*) binding in paper boards; (*couverture*) paper boards; **c. pleine toile** cloth boards; **c. souple** limp boards

cartonner [kartɔne] **1** *vt* (*livre*) to bind in boards, to case; **livre cartonné** hardback (book) **2** *vi Scol F* to do badly, to get bad *or F* rotten marks (**en** in)

cartonnerie [kartɔnri] *nf* **(a)** (*usine*) cardboard factory **(b)** (*commerce*) cardboard trade

cartonneux, -euse [kartɔnø, -øz] *adj* like cardboard; **neige cartonneuse** snow with a crust on top; **fromage c.** cheese that tastes like cardboard

cartonnier [kartɔnje] *nm* **(a)** (*fabricant*) cardboard manufacturer **(b)** (*meuble*) filing cabinet

carton-paille, *pl* **cartons-pailles** *nm* strawboard

carton-pâte, *pl* **cartons-pâtes** *nm* pasteboard; **décor de c.** cardboard scenery

cartoon [kartun] *nm* cartoon

cartouche [kartuʃ] **1** *nm Archit etc* cartouche; (*pour titre*) title **2** *nf* (*de fusil, d'explosif, de stylo*) cartridge; (*de machine à écrire*), *Phot* cartridge, cassette; *Mil etc* **cent cartouches** a hundred rounds (of ammunition)

▶ **cartouche**: **c. à blanc** blank cartridge; **c. de chasse** sporting cartridge; **c. de cigarettes** carton of cigarettes; **c. d'encre** (*d'une imprimante etc*) ink cartridge; **c. d'encre en poudre** (*d'une imprimante*) toner cartridge; *Ordinat* **c. de polices** font cartridge; **c. de rechange** (*de stylo*) refill; *Ordinat* **c. de stockage amovible** removable storage cartridge; **c. de toner** toner cartridge

cartoucherie [kartuʃri] *nf* (*fabrique*) cartridge *or* ammunition factory; (*dépôt*) cartridge *or* ammunition store

cartouchière [kartuʃjɛr] *nf* (*sac*) cartridge pouch; (*ceinture*) cartridge belt

carvi [karvi] *nm* (*plante*) caraway; **(graines de) c.** caraway seeds

caryatide [karjatid] *nf Archit* caryatid

caryotype [karjotip] *nm Biol* karyotype

cas [kɑ] *nm* **(a)** (*situation*) case, situation; (*événement*) occurrence; *Jur, Méd* case; **c. imprévu** unforeseen event; **c. général/particulier** general/particular case; **c. urgent** emergency *or* urgent case; **c'était un c. de légitime défense** it was self-defence; **c. litigieux** dispute; **dans le premier c.** in the first instance; **c'est le c. de le dire** you can say that again; **en pareil c.** in a similar situation, in similar circumstances; **que faire dans un c. de ce genre?** what can one do in a case *or* situation like this?; **c. de rougeole** case of measles; **ce malade est un c. désespéré** this patient is a hopeless case; *Fig* **c'est un c.!** he is a case!; **avez-vous envisagé tous les c.?** have you considered all possibilities *or* eventualities?; **il parle plusieurs langues étrangères mais ce n'est pas mon c.** he speaks several foreign languages but I don't; **dans son c., on peut faire une exception** an exception can be made in his case; **dans le c. qui nous occupe** in the case that we are concerned with; **si tel est votre c.** if that's your case

(b) faire (grand) c. de qn/qch to value sb/sth (highly), to have a high opinion of sb/sth, to set great store by sb/sth; **faire peu de c. de qch** to have a low opinion of sth, to set little store by sth; **je ne fais pas grand c. de votre ami** I don't think much of your friend; **ne faire aucun c. de qch** to take no notice of sth, to pay no attention to sth

(c) *Gram* case; **au c. nominatif** in the nominative (case)

(d) (*locutions*) **en** *ou* **dans ce c.** in that case, if that's the case, under those circumstances; **en aucun c.** under no circumstances, on no account, not on any account; **en tout c., dans tous les c.** in any case, anyway, in any event; **dans tous les c. il est trop tard** it's too late now anyway *or* anyhow; **dans ce c.-là, auquel c.** in that case; **le c. échéant** if necessary, if need be, should the need arise; **selon le c.** as the case may be; **en c. de nécessité** if need be, if necessary; **en c. de pluie/décès/d'absence** in the event of rain/death/absence; **en c. d'accident** in the event of an accident; **en c. d'urgence** in an emergency; **en c. de besoin tu peux m'appeler à n'importe quelle heure** if need be you can call me at any time; **j'ai pris un pull supplémentaire en c. de besoin** I took an extra sweater just in case; **au c. où** *ou* **dans le c. où il viendrait** in case he comes, if he should come; **au c. où ce serait exact** should it prove correct; *F* **je te le laisse au c. où** I'll leave it for you just in case

▶ **cas**: **c. de conscience** matter of conscience; **c. de divorce** divorce case; (*raisons*) grounds for divorce; **c. d'école** textbook case; **c. d'espèce** special case; **c. de figure** scenario; **c. limite** borderline case; **c. social** person with social problems

casanier, -ière [kazanje, -jɛr] **1** *adj* home-loving, *Péj* stay-at-home **2** *n* homebody, *Péj* stay-at-home

casaque [kazak] *nf* (*de jockey*) blouse, jacket; *Fig* **tourner c.** (*partir*) to turn tail, to flee; (*changer d'opinion*) to turn one's coat

casbah [kazba] *nf* casbah, kasbah

cascade [kaskad] *nf* **(a)** (*chute d'eau*) cascade, waterfall; *Fig* (*de boucles*) cascade; **c. de glace** ice fall; *Fig* **cascades de rires** peals of laughter; **ils ont connu des catastrophes en c.**

they experienced a whole string *or* chain of disasters; *Él* **montage en c.** connection in series; *Ordinat* **menus en c.** pull-down menus **(b)** *Cin* stunt

cascader [kaskade] *vi* **(a)** *Litt* (*tomber*) to cascade **(b)** *F Vieilli* (*faire la noce*) to lead a wild life

cascadeur, -euse [kaskadœr, -øz] **1** *adj F Vieilli* (*vie etc*) wild, loose **2** *n* **(a)** *Cin* stuntman, *f* stuntwoman; (*de cirque*) acrobat **(b)** *F Vieilli* (*noceur*) person of disorderly habits

cascher [kaʃɛr] = **kascher**

case [kɑz] *nf* **(a)** (*hutte*) hut, cabin

(b) (*de tiroir etc*) compartment, division; (*pour le courrier*) pigeonhole; (*de formulaire*) box; (*de grille de mots croisés, damier*) square; **cocher la bonne c.** tick the appropriate box; *F* **il lui manque une c., il a une c. vide** *ou* **une c. en moins** he's got a screw loose

(c) *Ordinat* button; (*en forme de boîte*) box; **c. 'annuler'** cancel button; **c. 'marche'** walk button; **c. d'aide** help button; **c. d'option** checkbox, option button; **c. de commande** command button; **c. de contrôle de taille** *ou* **de dimensionnement** size box; **c. de fermeture** close box; **c. de pointage** check box; **c. de saisie** input box; **c. zoom** zoom box

▶ **case**: **c. départ** (*dans les jeux*) start; *Fig* **retour à la c. départ** back to square one

caséeux, -euse [kazeø, -øz] *adj* caseous

caséine [kazein] *nf Ch* casein

casemate [kazmat] *nf Mil* blockhouse, pillbox

caser [kɑze] **1** *vt* **(a)** (*placer*) to put; **je ne sais pas où c. tous mes livres** I don't know where to put all my books; **j'ai réussi à tout c. dans ma chambre** I managed to find space for everything in *or* to get everything into my room; **c. des papiers** to file papers (away) **(b)** *F* (*établir dans une situation*) to fix up with a job, to find a job for; **elle est bien casée** she's got a good job **(c)** *F* (*marier*) **elle a trois filles à c.** she has three daughters to marry off *or* to find husbands for **2 se caser** *vpr F* (*se marier*) to (get married and) settle down; (*trouver un emploi*) to get oneself a job, to find a job

caserne [kazɛrn] *nf* [①A13,3,b] *Mil, Fig, F Péj* barracks; **quand j'étais à la c.** when I was in the army; **plaisanteries de c.** locker room jokes, coarse jokes; **c. de pompiers** fire station

casernement [kazɛrnəmɑ̃] *nm Mil* **(a)** (*de troupes*) quartering in barracks, barracking **(b)** (*lieu*) barrack block

caserner [kazɛrne] *vt Mil* (*troupes*) to quarter in barracks, to barrack

cash [kaʃ] *adv F* cash; **payer c.** to pay cash (down)

cash and carry [kaʃɛndkari] *Com* **1** *nm inv* cash-and-carry (store) **2** *adj inv* cash-and-carry

cash-flow [kaʃflo] *nm Com* cash flow

casier [kɑzje] *nm* **(a)** (*pour le courrier*) (*meuble*) (set of) pigeonholes; (*compartiment*) pigeonhole; (*pour ses vêtements etc*) locker; (*à tiroirs*) filing cabinet, *Am* file cabinet; **c. à bagages** luggage locker; **c. à clés et à courrier** key and mail rack; **c. à skis** ski rack; **c. à bouteilles** bottle rack; **c. à disques** record rack; **c. à musique** music cabinet **(b)** *Jur* **avoir un c.** to have a record **(c)** *Pêche* pot; **aller relever ses casiers** to go and lift one's pots

▶ **casier**: **c. judiciaire** police *or* criminal record; **avoir un c. judiciaire** to have a record; **avoir un c. judiciaire vierge** to have a clean record

casino [kazino] *nm* casino

casoar [kazɔar] *nm* **(a)** (*oiseau*) cassowary **(b)** (*plumet*) plume (*worn by cadets of Saint-Cyr*)

Caspienne [kaspjɛn] *nf* **la mer C.** the Caspian Sea

casque [kask] *nm* **(a)** (*de soldat, pompier etc*) helmet; (*de motocycliste*) (crash) helmet; **le port du c. est obligatoire** helmets must be worn **(b)** *Rad etc* headphones, headset, earphones; **écouter un disque au c.** to listen to a record on (one's) headphones **(c)** *Orn* casque; *Bot* helmet **(d)** (*de salon de coiffure*) (hair) drier

▶ **casque**: **c. colonial** pith helmet, topee; *Rad* **c. à écouteurs** headphones, headset, earphones; **c. intégral** crash helmet (*full-faced*); *TV, Rad* **c. interphone** headphone talkback; **Casques blancs** United Nations military observers; **Casques bleus** Blue Berets, United Nations peacekeeping force

casqué [kaske] *adj* helmeted

casquer [kaske] *vi Arg* (*payer*) to fork out, to shell out

casquette [kaskɛt] *nf* (*chapeau*) cap; *Fig* **avoir plusieurs casquettes** (*responsabilités*) to wear several hats; *Fig F* **avoir la c.** (**de plomb**) to be hung over, to have a hangover

cassable [kasabl] *adj* breakable

Cassandre [kasɑ̃dr] **1** *nf* Cassandra **2** *n Fig* prophet of doom, Cassandra; **jouer les C.** to be a Cassandra *or* a prophet of doom and gloom, to prophesy doom and gloom

cassant [kasɑ̃] *adj* **(a)** (*fragile*) fragile; (*cheveux*) brittle; **c. comme du verre** as fragile as glass **(b)** *Fig* (*brusque*) (*personne, ton etc*) abrupt, brusque **(c)** *Arg* (*fatigant*) **c'est pas trop c.** it's not (exactly) back-breaking work

cassate [kasat] *nf Culin* (*glace*) cassata

cassation [kasasjɔ̃] *nf* **(a)** *Jur* (*de jugement, testament etc*) annulment, *Spéc* cassation; **Cour de c.** Supreme Court of Appeal; **se pourvoir en c.** to take one's case to the Supreme Court of Appeal **(b)** *Mil* reduction to the ranks

casse[1] [kas] *nf Typ* (*boîte*) case; **bas/haut de c.** lower-/upper-case letter

casse[2] *nf* (*arbre*) cassia

casse[3] *nf* (*action*) breaking, breakage; (*ce qui est cassé*) damage, breakages; **il va y avoir de la c.** something will get broken; *F* (*des ennuis*) there'll be trouble; **est-ce qu'il y a eu de la c.?** was anything broken?, were there any breakages?; **payer la c.** to pay for the breakages *or* the damage; **vendre qch à la c.** to sell sth for scrap; **envoyer une voiture à la c.** to send a car to the scrapyard; **aller** *ou* **partir à la c.** (*d'une voiture etc*) to go for scrap

casse[4] *nm Arg* (*cambriolage*) break-in, burglary

cassé [kase] *adj* (*objet, jambe etc*) broken; (*vieillard*) bent, bowed; (*voix*) cracked; *F* (*ivre*) smashed, plastered; (*drogué*) stoned; **blanc c.** off-white

casse-cou **1** *nm inv* **(a)** (*passage*) danger *or* dangerous spot **(b)** **crier c. à qn** to warn sb (*of a danger*) **(c)** (*personne*) daredevil **2** *adj inv* (*endroit*) dangerous; (*personne*) reckless

casse-croûte *nm inv* **(a)** (*repas*) snack, bite **(b)** *Can* (*snack*) snack bar

casse-cul *F* **1** *adj inv* damned annoying **2** *n inv* (*personne*) pain (in the arse *or* backside)

casse-gueule *F* **1** *nm inv* (*endroit*) danger *or* dangerous spot; (*entreprise*) risky *or Br F* dodgy undertaking **2** *adj inv* (*endroit*) dangerous; (*entreprise*) risky, *Br F* dodgy

cassement [kasmɑ̃] *nm* **(a)** *Vieilli* **c. de tête** (*souci*) headache, worry; (*migraine*) splitting headache **(b)** *Arg, Vieilli* (*cambriolage*) break-in, burglary

casse-noisette(s) *nm inv* (pair of) nutcrackers, *Am* nutcracker

casse-noix *nm inv* **(a)** (pair of) nutcrackers, *Am* nutcracker **(b)** (*oiseau*) nutcracker

casse-pieds *F* **1** *adj inv* damned annoying; **ce qu'il est c.** what a pain in the neck (he is) **2** *n inv* (*personne*) pain (in the neck)

casse-pierre(s) *nm inv* (*masse*) stonebreaker's hammer; *Constr* (*machine*) stonebreaker, stone-crusher

casse-pipes *nm inv Arg* **aller au c.** *Mil* to go (off) to war *or* to the front; *Fig* to be heading for failure

casser [kase] **1** *vt* **(a)** (*briser*) (*assiette, jouet, jambe, bras etc*) to break; (*voiture*) to wreck; (*mur*) to break down, to pull down; (*brindille, ficelle*) to break, to snap; (*noix*) to crack; (*pierres*) to break, to crush; **j'ai dû c. le carreau** I had to smash the window; **c. du bois** to chop wood; *Av* to crash on landing

(b) (*moral*) to break; (*voix*) to strain; *F* (*qn*) to humiliate; (*billet, pièce*) (*dépenser*) to break; (*chaussures*) (*pour assouplir*) to break in; (*atmosphère*) to ruin; (*syndicats etc*) to break; **c. une grève** to break a strike; **c. les prix** to slash prices; **c. le marché** to break the market; **cette nouvelle m'a cassé le moral** the news depressed me; *Fig* **c. du sucre sur le dos de qn** to talk about sb behind his/her back; *Th F* **c. la baraque** to bring the house down; *F* **c. la baraque à qn** to ruin *or* spoil things for sb; *Fig* **c. la croûte** *ou* **la graine, c. une petite graine** to have a snack *or* a bite *or* something to eat; *F* **c. sa pipe** to kick the bucket, *Br* to snuff it; *Arg* **c. le morceau** (*avouer*) to spill the beans, to come clean; (*dénoncer*) to grass; *F* **ça ne casse rien, ça ne casse pas trois pattes à un canard, ça ne casse pas des briques** it's not up to much, it's nothing to write home about, it's no great shakes; **un spectacle à tout c.** a marvellous *or* fantastic *or* super show; **applaudir à tout c.** to bring the house down; **cela vaut 1 000 francs à tout c.** it's worth 1,000 francs at the very most *or* at the outside; **un homme cassé par l'adversité/la douleur/les échecs** a man broken by adversity/pain/failure

(c) (*locutions avec parties du corps*) *F* **c. les pieds à qn** to do sb's head in; *F* **elle me casse les pieds** (*m'ennuie*) she bores the pants of me; (*m'agace*) she gets on my nerves *or Br* wick; **ça fait deux mois qu'elle me casse les pieds pour que je t'en parle** she's been on at me for two months now to talk to you about it; *Vulg* **il nous casse les bonbons** *ou* **les couilles, il nous les casse** he gets on our tits; *F* **c. le cou** *ou* **la figure** *ou Arg* **la gueule à qn** to smash sb's face in; **c. la tête** *ou* **les oreilles à qn** to deafen sb; **c. les reins à qn** to ruin *or* break sb; **c. bras et jambes à qn** to knock sb for six

(d) (*dégrader*) (*officier*) to break, to reduce to the ranks; (*employé*) to demote

(e) *Jur* (*verdict*) to quash, to set aside; **c. un mariage** to annul *or* dissolve a marriage; **c. ses fiançailles** to break off one's engagement

(f) *très F* **c. de l'arabe** ≈ to go Paki-bashing; **c. du pédé** to go gay-bashing

2 *vi* to break; (*de brindille, ficelle*) to break, to snap; **attention, ça casse!** be careful, it's fragile!; **cela casse comme du verre** it's as fragile as glass; *Fig F* **ils ont cassé** (*se sont séparés*) they've broken up *or* split up

3 **se casser** *vpr* (a) (*se briser*) to break; (*de brindille, ficelle*) to break, to snap; **la poutre se cassa sous son poids** the beam broke under his weight; **elle s'est cassé la jambe** she's broken her leg; *F* **il ne s'est pas cassé pour m'aider** he didn't overstrain himself helping me; **le jour où je l'ai rencontré j'aurais mieux fait de me c. une jambe** I wish I'd never set eyes on him; *F* **se c. la figure** (*tomber*) to fall flat on one's face, to come a cropper; (*se blesser*) to smash oneself up; (*rater, faire faillite*) to come a cropper; **se c. la tête** to rack one's brains; *F* **ne te casse pas la tête!** don't worry about it!; *Iron* **dis donc, tu ne t'es pas cassé la tête!** well, you didn't exactly strain yourself, did you!; *Fig* **se c. le nez à la porte de qn** to find nobody in *or* at home; *Fig* **il s'est cassé le nez** he's failed, *F* he's come a cropper; **se c. les dents** to come a cropper; *Fig* **ne grimpe pas sur cet échafudage, tu vas te c. le cou!** don't climb up on that scaffolding, you'll break your neck!; *très F* **je me suis cassé le cul à lui trouver cette adresse** I really went out of my way *or Sl* bust a gut to find him that address

(b) *Arg* (*partir*) to split, to clear off; **tu viens? on se casse** we're out of here, are you coming?; **casse-toi!** get out of here! get lost!, beat it!; **elle s'est cassée de chez ses parents** she cleared out of her parents' place

casserole [kasrɔl] *nf* (a) (*de cuisine*) (sauce)pan; **veau à la** *ou* **en c.** braised veal; *Arg* **passer à la c.** (*subir des épreuves*) to go through it; (*sexuellement*) to be screwed *or* laid; (*être tué*) to get bumped off (b) *Arg* (*mauvais piano*) tinny piano; **chanter comme une c.** to screech, to sing appallingly (c) *Cin Arg* projector

casse-tête *nm inv* (a) (*massue*) club; (*matraque*) cosh (b) (*jeu*) puzzle, brainteaser; **c. chinois** Chinese puzzle; *Fig* **c'est un c. chinois** it's baffling (c) (*problème*) headache; **ça a été un c. pour placer tout le monde à table** it was a headache seating everyone at the table

cassette [kasɛt] *nf* (a) (*magnétique*) cassette, tape; **écouter/passer une c.** to listen to/to put on *or* play a cassette; **enregistrer qch sur c.** to record sth on (to) cassette; (*vidéo*) to make a video (recording) of sth (b) (*de bijoux*) casket; *Arch* **c. du roi** King's privy purse; **il ne veut jamais puiser dans sa c. personnelle** he never wants to pay for things out of his own pocket

▶ **cassette: c. d'alimentation** (*de copieuse*) paper tray; **c. audio** audio cassette; **c. audionumérique** digital audio tape; *Ordinat* **c. à bande magnétique** mag tape cassette; **c. compacte numérique** digital compact cassette, DCC; *Ordinat* **c. de fontes** font cassette; *TV etc* **c. prête à diffuser** *ou* **PAD** master tape; **c. de ruban** (*d'une imprimante*) ribbon cassette; **c. de toner** (*d'une imprimante*) toner cassette; **c. vidéo** video (cassette)

casseur, -euse [kasœr, -øz] 1 *n* (a) **c. de pierres** stonebreaker (b) (*manifestant*) rioter (c) (*ferrailleur*) scrap (metal) merchant, breaker; **dépôt de c.** breaker's yard; **c. de voitures** (car) breaker (d) *Arg* (*cambrioleur*) burglar 2 *adj* **il est c.** he's always breaking things

Cassin [kasɛ̃] *nm* **le mont C.** Monte Cassino

cassine [kasin] *nf Arch* (*petite maison*) small house

cassis[1] [kasis] *nm* (a) (*baie*) blackcurrant (b) (*arbuste*) blackcurrant bush (c) (*liqueur*) blackcurrant liqueur; **blanc c.** kir

cassis[2] [kɑsi(s)] *nm* (*creux en travers d'une route*) dip

cassis[3] [kasis] *nm Arg* (*tête*) nut, block

cassolette [kasɔlɛt] *nf* (a) (*pour parfums*) incense burner (b) *Culin* dish (for one person)

cassonade [kasɔnad] *nf* brown sugar

cassoulet [kasulɛ] *nm Culin* cassoulet (*stew of beans, pork, goose etc, a speciality of Languedoc*)

cassure [kasyr] *nf* break; (*dans du plâtre etc*) crack; *Fig* (*dans une amitié etc*) break, rupture; *Géol* fault; (*de tissu*) fold mark, crease; (*d'un pantalon*) crease

castagnette [kastaɲɛt] *nf* castanet; **jouer des castagnettes,** to play the castanets; *Fig F* **j'avais les dents qui jouaient des castagnettes** my teeth were chattering; **ses genoux jouaient des castagnettes** his knees were knocking

caste [kast] *nf* caste; **la c. des prêtres** the priest caste; **esprit de c.** class consciousness; **avoir l'esprit de c.** to be class conscious; **être hors c.** to be an outcast

castel [kastɛl] *nm* (*manoir*) manor (house), mansion; (*petit château*) small castle

castillan, -ane [kastijɑ̃, -an] 1 *adj* Castilian 2 *nm Ling* Castilian 3 *n* **C.** Castilian

Castille [kastij] *nf* Castile

casting [kastiŋ] *nm Cin, Th* casting

castor [kastɔr] *nm* (a) (*mammifère, fourrure*) beaver; **c. du Chili** (*mammifère*) coypu; (*fourrure*) nutria; **c. du Canada** (*mammifère*) muskrat; (*fourrure*) musquash (fur) (b) *Fig* (*association*) **(mouvement des) castors** = group of people building their own houses

castrat [kastra] *nm* eunuch; *Mus* castrato

castrateur, -trice [kastratœr, -tris] *adj Psy* castrating; *Fig* (*autoritaire*) repressive

castration [kastrasjɔ̃] *nf* castration; (*d'un étalon*) gelding; (*d'un chat, d'un chien*) neutering; (*d'une chatte, d'une chienne*) spaying; *Psy* **complexe de c.** castration complex

castrer [kastre] *vt* to castrate; (*étalon*) to geld; (*chat, chien*) to neuter; (*chatte, chienne*) to spay

castrisme [kastrism] *nm Pol* Castroism

castriste [kastrist] *adj, n Pol* Castroist

casuel, -elle [kazɥɛl] 1 *adj* (a) (*accidentel*) fortuitous (b) *Gram* **flexions casuelles** case endings 2 *nm* (*revenu variable*) perquisites

casuiste [kazɥist] *nm Rel, Fig Péj* casuist

casuistique [kazɥistik] *nf Rel, Fig Péj* casuistry

casus belli [kasysbɛli] *nm inv* casus belli

cataboliser [katabɔlize] *vt Biol* to catabolize

catabolisme [katabɔlism] *nm Biol* catabolism

catachrèse [katakrɛz] *nf Ling* catachresis

cataclysmal, -ale, -aux, -ales [kataklismal, -o] *adj* cataclysmal

cataclysme [kataklism] *nm Géol* cataclysm; *Fig* disaster, cataclysm

cataclysmique [kataklismik] *adj* cataclysmic, cataclysmal; *Fig* disastrous, cataclysmic

catacombes [katakɔ̃b] *nfpl* catacombs

catadioptre [katadiɔptr] *nm* (*de véhicule etc*) reflector; (*sur la route*) cat's eye

catafalque [katafalk] *nm* catafalque

cataire [katɛr] *nf* catmint, catnip

catalan, -ane [katalɑ̃, -an] 1 *adj* Catalan 2 *nm Ling* Catalan 3 *n* **C.** Catalan

catalepsie [katalɛpsi] *nf Méd* catalepsy; **tomber en c.** to have a cataleptic fit

cataleptique [katalɛptik] *adj, n Méd* cataleptic

catalogage [katalɔgaʒ] *nm* (*de livres etc*) cataloguing, *US* cataloging

Catalogne [katalɔɲ] *nf* (a) Catalonia (b) *Tex* rag rug

catalogue [katalɔg] *nm* catalogue, *US* catalog; **c. de vente par correspondance** mail-order catalogue; **je n'achète jamais rien sur c.** I never buy anything from a catalogue; **faire le c. de** to catalogue; **c. de films** film library; **c. méthodique** subject catalogue; **c. de normes** standards catalogue

cataloguer [katalɔge] *vt* (*livres*) to catalogue, *US* to catalog; *Fig Péj* (*étiqueter*) to label; **les médias l'ont cataloguée parmi les révolutionnaires** the media labelled her a revolutionary; **je l'ai catalogué tout de suite** I sized him up immediately

catalpa [katalpa] *nm Bot* catalpa

catalyse [kataliz] *nf Ch* catalysis; **four à c.** self-cleaning oven

catalyser [katalize] *vt Ch, Fig* to catalyse

catalyseur [katalizœr] *nm Ch, Fig* catalyst

catalytique [katalitik] *adj Ch* catalytic; *Aut* **pot c.** catalytic converter

catamaran [katamarɑ̃] *nm Naut* catamaran; *Av* (*d'un hydravion*) floats

cataphote® [katafɔt] *nm* = **catadioptre**

cataplasme [kataplasm] *nm Méd* poultice; **c. sinapisé** mustard poultice *or* plaster; *Fig* **c'est comme un c. sur une jambe de bois** it's worse than useless

catapultage [katapyltaʒ] *nm* catapulting; *Av* catapult launch(ing); *Fig* (*dans un poste etc*) catapulting; *Av* **crochet de c.** catapulting hook

catapulte [katapylt] *nf Av, Mil etc* catapult

catapulter [katapylte] *vt* to catapult; *Fig* (*qn*) to catapult (**dans un poste** into a post)

cataracte [katarakt] *nf* (a) (*d'eau*) cataract, falls; **des cataractes (de pluie)** torrents of rain (b) *Méd* cataract; **se faire opérer de la c.** to have a cataract operation

catarrhal, -ale, -aux, -ales [kataral, -o] *adj Méd* catarrhal

catarrhe [katar] *nm Méd* catarrh

catarrheux, -euse [katarø, -øz] *Méd* 1 *adj* (*personne*) catarrhal 2 *n* catarrhal person

catastrophe [katastrɔf] *nf* catastrophe, disaster; **c. ferroviaire/aérienne** rail/air disaster; **c. financière** crash;

c'est la c.! it's a disaster!; **ce n'est tout de même pas une c.!** it's not the end of the world!; **cet enfant/votre devoir est une c.** this child/your homework is a disaster; **c.!, il est déjà là!** panic stations! he's here already!; *Av* **atterrir en c.** to make a forced *or* emergency landing; **je suis passé au bureau en c.** I went to the office in a mad rush *or* a panic
catastrophé [katastrɔfe] *adj F* stunned; **il était c. de l'apprendre** he was stunned to learn it
catastropher [katastrɔfe] *vt F (qn)* to stun, to be a (great) blow to
catastrophique [katastrɔfik] *adj (événement, conséquence etc)* catastrophic, disastrous; *Fig (très mauvais)* disastrous, appalling
catastrophisme [katastrɔfism] *nm* catastrophism; *F* **sans vouloir faire du c.** without wishing to be pessimistic
catatonique [katatɔnik] *adj, n Méd* catatonic
catch [katʃ] *nm Sp* (all-in) wrestling; **faire du c.** to wrestle; **match** *ou* **rencontre de c.** wrestling match
catcher [katʃe] *vi Sp* to wrestle
catcheur, -euse [katʃœr, -øz] *n Sp* (all-in) wrestler
catéchèse [kateʃɛz] *nf Rel* catechism
catéchisation [kateʃizasjɔ̃] *nf Rel* catechization
catéchiser [kateʃize] *vt Rel* to catechize; *Fig (endoctriner)* to indoctrinate; *(sermonner)* to preach at, to lecture
catéchisme [kateʃism] *nm Rel (instruction, livre)* catechism; **aller au c.** to go to catechism class; *Fig* **ce livre est son c.** this book is his bible
catéchiste [kateʃist] *n Rel* catechist
catéchumène [katekymɛn] *n Rel* catechumen; *Fig* novice, tyro
catégorie [kategɔri] *nf* category; *(d'hôtel, de personnel)* grade; *(de légumes, fruits)* category, grade, class; *(de boxeur)* class; **légumes de première c.** grade one *or* class one *or* prime vegetables; **de dernière c.** of poor quality; **morceau de viande de première/deuxième c.** prime/second cut of meat; **il appartient à cette c. de gens qui ...** he belongs to that category *or* group of people who ...; **c. de produit** product category *or* class; **c. sociale** social category; **c. socio-professionnelle** socio-professional group, social stratum
catégoriel, -elle [kategɔrjɛl] *adj* **(a)** *Ind, Pol* **revendications catégorielles** differential claims **(b)** *Ling* **symbole c.** category symbol **(c)** *Phil* categorical
catégorique [kategɔrik] *adj (clair) (réponse etc)* categoric(al); *Phil (proposition etc)* categorical; **refus c.** categoric *or* flat refusal; **elle a été c. sur ce point** she was categorical *or* quite positive on this point; **il est c., il faut aller à l'hôpital** there's no question about it, you/*etc* will have to go to hospital; **je suis absolument c., c'est bien l'homme que j'ai vu** I'm absolutely positive that's the man I saw
catégoriquement [kategɔrikmɑ̃] *adv* categorically
catégorisation [kategɔrizasjɔ̃] *nf* categorization; *(de personnel)* grading
catégoriser [kategɔrize] *vt* to categorize; *(personnel)* to grade
caténaire [katenɛr] **1** *adj* **(a)** *Rail* **suspension c.** catenary **(b)** **réaction c.** chain reaction **2** *nf Rail* catenary
catgut [katgyt] *nm Chir* catgut
cathare [katar] *Hist Rel* **1** *adj* Cathar **2** *n* **C.** Cathar
catharsis [katarsis] *nf Psy, Littér* catharsis
cathartique [katartik] *adj Psy, Littér* cathartic
cathédrale [katedral] *nf* cathedral
cathèdre [katɛdr] *nf* cathedra
Catherine [katrin] *nf* **coiffer sainte C.** *(d'une femme)* to be 25 and still unmarried, to be left on the shelf
catherinette [katrinɛt] *nf* unmarried woman of 25 and over
cathéter [katetɛr] *nm Méd* catheter
cathétérisme [kateterism] *nm Méd* catheterization
catho [kato] *adj F* Catholic
cathode [katɔd] *nf Él* cathode
cathodique [katɔdik] *adj Él* cathodic; **rayons cathodiques** cathode rays; **tube à rayons cathodiques, tube c.** cathode-ray tube
catholicisme [katɔlisism] *nm* (Roman) Catholicism
catholicité [katɔlisite] *nf* **(a)** **la c.** *(catholiques)* the (Roman) Catholic Church **(b)** *(orthodoxie)* Catholicity
catholique [katɔlik] **1** *adj* **(a)** *Rel* (Roman) Catholic; *(universel)* catholic, universal **(b)** *F* **il/ce n'est pas (très) c.** he's/it's a bit fishy; *Hum* **cette façon de faire la soupe n'est pas très c.** this isn't a very orthodox way of making soup **2** *n* (Roman) Catholic
catilinaire [katilinɛr] *nf* lampoon
catimini (en) [ɑ̃katimini] *adv F* stealthily, on the sly *or* quiet; **entrer/sortir en c.** to steal *or F* sneak in/out; **je suis allé l'acheter en c.** I went to buy it on the quiet
catin [katɛ̃] *nf Arg, Vieilli (prostituée)* trollop, whore

cation [katjɔ̃] *nm Él* cation
catogan [katɔgɑ̃] *nm* hair ribbon *(for ponytail)*
Caton [katɔ̃] *nm* Cato
Caucase (le) [ləkokaz] *nm* the Caucasus
caucasien, -ienne [kokazjɛ̃, -jɛn] **1** *adj* Caucasian **2** *n* **C.** Caucasian
cauchemar [koʃmar] *nm aussi Fig* nightmare; **faire un c.** to have a nightmare; **vision de c.** nightmarish vision; **ça me donne des cauchemars rien que d'y penser** it gives me nightmares just thinking about it; **il me donne des cauchemars** I have nightmares about him; *Fig* **les réceptions officielles étaient son c.** official receptions were a nightmare to *or* for him
cauchemarder [koʃmarde] *vi* to have nightmares; *Fig* **cette idée me fait c.** the idea gives me nightmares
cauchemardesque [koʃmardɛsk], **cauchemardeux, -euse** [koʃmardø, -øz] *adj (vision etc)* nightmarish; **sommeil cauchemardeux** nightmare-filled sleep
caudal, -ale, -aux, -ales [kodal, -o] *adj Zool* caudal
cauri(s) [kori] *nm* cowrie (shell)
causal, -ale, -als *ou* **-aux, -ales** [kozal -o] *adj Gram, Phil* causal
causalité [kozalite] *nf Phil* causality; **rapport/principe de c.** causal relation/principle
causant [kozɑ̃] *adj F (personne)* chatty, talkative
cause [koz] *nf* **(a)** *(origine)* cause; **c. réelle/apparente** real/apparent cause; **c. de défiance** cause *or* reason for distrust; *Phil* **c. première/seconde** first/secondary cause; **quelle est la c. de son départ?** what caused him to leave?; **on ne connaît pas la c. de sa mort** the cause of death is unknown; **être (la) c. de qch** to be the cause of sth; **les enfants sont souvent c. de soucis** children are often a cause of worry; **c'est elle qui en est c.** it's her fault, she's to blame; **il s'est fâché, et non sans c.** he got angry, and with good reason; **il s'est mis en colère, et pour c.** he got angry, and for a very good reason; **absent pour c. de santé** absent for health reasons *or* on medical grounds; **fermé pour c. de décès/d'inventaire** closed owing to bereavement/for stocktaking; **à c. de** because of, on account of; **c'est à c. de moi qu'il a manqué le train** it was because of me (that) he missed the train, it was my fault he missed the train; **c'est à c. de toi!** it's all because of you!, it's all your fault!
(b) *Jur* case, (law)suit, action; **c. civile/criminelle** civil/criminal action *or* case; **plaider/gagner une c.** to argue/to win a case; **avocat sans causes** briefless barrister; **confier une c. à un avocat** to brief a barrister; **affaire en c.** case before the court; **entendre une c.** to hear a case; *Fig* **la c. est entendue** there's nothing more to be said; **être en c.** *(d'une personne, d'intérêts etc)* to be involved; **votre probité n'est pas en c.** your honesty is not in question *or* in doubt; **mettre en c. la probité de qn** to question sb's honesty; **mettre qn en c.** *Jur* to summon *or* sue sb; *(impliquer)* to implicate sb; **mettre qn hors de c.** to clear *or* exonerate sb; **il est maintenant hors de c.** he has now been cleared; **en tout état de c.** at all events, in any case; **en connaissance de c.** with full knowledge of the facts
(c) *(parti)* cause; **prendre fait et c. pour qn/qch** to take up sb's/sth's cause; **c'est une c. perdue (d'avance)** it's a lost cause; **faire c. commune avec qn** to side with sb, to join forces with sb
▶ **cause: c. célèbre** famous trial, cause célèbre
causer¹ [koze] *vt (qch)* to cause, to be the cause of; **c. un changement** to bring about a change; **son départ nous a causé beaucoup de chagrin** his departure distressed us greatly *or* caused us great distress; **c. des ennuis à qn** to cause sb problems, to give sb trouble
causer² *vi* **(a)** *(parler)* to chat, to talk **(de** about); **c. avec** *ou F* **à qn** to have a chat *or* a talk with sb; *F* **je ne lui cause plus!** *(je suis fâché avec elle)* I'm not talking to her!; **c. de** to talk about; **c. de la pluie et du beau temps, c. de choses et d'autres** to talk about this and that; **c. affaires/chiffons** to talk business/clothes; **cause toujours, tu m'intéresses!** how interesting!; **faire c. qn** to make sb talk, to get sb to talk **(b)** *(cancaner)* to talk, to gossip; **on commence à en c.** people are beginning to talk *or* gossip (about it)
causerie [kozri] *nf* **(a)** *(discussion)* chat, talk **(b)** *(conférence)* (informal) talk
causette [kozɛt] *nf F* little chat; **faire la c.** *ou* **un brin de c. avec qn** to have a little chat *or Br* a bit of a natter with sb
causeur, -euse [kozœr, -øz] **1** *n (personne)* chatterer **2** *nf* **causeuse** *(siège)* loveseat **3** *adj* chatty, talkative
causse [kos] *nm Géog* = limestone plateau in central and southern France
causticité [kostisite] *nf Ch* causticity; *Fig (d'une personne)* causticity; *(d'une remarque etc)* biting *or* caustic nature

caustique [kostik] **1** *adj Ch* caustic; *Fig (personne, esprit, humour)* caustic; *(remarque etc)* biting, caustic, cutting **2** *nm Ch* caustic **3** *nf Opt* caustic
caustiquement [kostikmɑ̃] *adv Fig* caustically, bitingly, cuttingly
cautèle [kotɛl] *nf Litt* wiliness, cunning
cauteleux, -euse [kotlø, -øz] *adj Litt* wily, cunning
cautère [kotɛr] *nm Méd* cautery; *F* **c'est un c. sur une jambe de bois** it's worse than useless, it won't do any good whatsoever
cautérisation [koterizasjɔ̃] *nf Méd* cauterization
cautériser [koterize] *vt Méd (blessure etc)* to cauterize
caution [kosjɔ̃] *nf* **(a)** *(gage), Com, Fin* security, guarantee; *Jur* bail; *Fig (appui)* support, backing; **c. de banque** bank guarantee; *Fin* **c. de bonne fin** performance bond; *Fin* **c. de soumission** bid bond; **il faut verser 1 000 F de c.** you/*etc* must pay a deposit of 1,000 francs; *Jur* **donner** *ou* **fournir c. pour qn** to go *or* stand bail for sb, to bail sb out; *Jur* **mettre qn en liberté sous c.** to release sb on bail; *Fig* **sujet à c.** *(nouvelles etc)* to be treated with caution, unreliable, unconfirmed; *Fig* **le gouvernement a donné sa c. au rachat** the takeover has the government's support *or* backing
(b) *(personne)* surety, security, guaranty; **se porter c. pour qn** *Jur* to go *or* stand bail for sb; *Com, Fin* to stand surety *or* security for sb
cautionnement [kosjɔnmɑ̃] *nm* **(a)** *(contrat)* surety bond **(b)** *(somme d'argent)* security, guarantee, guaranty; **c. électoral** deposit
cautionner [kosjɔne] *vt* **(a)** *(personne) Com, Fin* to stand surety for, to act as guarantor for; *Jur* to go *or* stand bail for, to bail out **(b)** *Fig (répondre de) (qch)* to answer for, to guarantee; **c. l'honnêteté de qn** to vouch for sb's honesty **(c)** *Fig (approuver) (idée, action, gouvernement etc)* to support, to back
cavalcade [kavalkad] *nf* **(a)** *(défilé)* cavalcade, procession **(b)** *Fig (bousculade)* swarm, stampede
cavalcader [kavalkade] *vi* **(a)** *(d'un groupe de gens etc)* to swarm (about) **(b)** *Arch* to ride *(in a cavalcade)*
cavale [kaval] *nf* **(a)** *Arg (évasion)* escape; **être en c.** to be on the run **(b)** *Litt (jument)* mare
cavaler [kavale] *Arg* **1** *vi* to rush around; *(fuir)* to take off, *Br* to scarper, *Br* to do a runner; **c. après qn** *(poursuivre de ses assiduités)* to chase after sb; **je n'ai pas envie de c. le jour de Noël** I don't want to be rushing around on Christmas Day **2** *vt* **c. qn** to get on sb's nerves, to plague *or* pester sb
cavalerie [kavalri] *nf* **(a)** *Mil* cavalry; **c. légère** light cavalry, light horse; **c. motorisée** motorized cavalry; **grosse c.** heavy *or* armoured cavalry; *Fig F* **Wagner et sa grosse c. de cuivres** Wagner and his heavy brass **(b)** *(ensemble de chevaux)* stable
cavaleur, -euse [kavalœr, -øz] *Arg* **1** *adj (homme)* womanizing; *(femme)* man-chasing **2** *n (homme)* skirt chaser, womanizer; *(femme)* man-chaser
cavalier, -ière [kavalje, -jɛr] **1** *n* **(a)** *(à cheval)* rider, horseman, *f* horsewoman; **habit de c.** riding costume; *Bible* **les (Quatre) Cavaliers de l'Apocalypse** the (four) Horsemen of the Apocalypse
(b) *(qui danse)* partner; *Fig* **faire c. seul** to go it alone, to act alone
2 *nm* **(a)** *Mil* trooper, cavalryman; *Échecs* knight; *Arch (gentilhomme)* gentleman; *Br Hist* **Cavaliers et Têtes rondes** Cavaliers and Roundheads
(b) *(accompagnateur de dame)* escort
(c) *Ordinat* jumper
(d) *Tech (clou)* staple; *(languette de fichier)* tab
3 *adj* **(a) allée** *ou* **piste cavalière** bridle path
(b) *(manière, personne)* cavalier, offhand
cavalièrement [kavaljɛrmɑ̃] *adv* in a cavalier manner, offhandedly
cave[1] [kav] *adj* **(a)** *(joues, yeux)* hollow, sunken **(b)** *Anat* **veine c.** vena cava
cave[2] *nf* **(a)** *(cellier, vins)* cellar; **c. à charbon** coal cellar; **c. à vin** wine cellar; **avoir une bonne c.** to have *or* keep a good cellar; *Fig* **de la c. au grenier** *(ranger, repeindre etc)* from top to bottom, thoroughly **(b)** *(cabaret)* nightclub **(c) c. à liqueurs** *(meuble)* drinks cabinet
cave[3] *nf Cartes* = stake
cave[4] **1** *nm Arg* **(a)** *(personne ne faisant pas partie du milieu)* outsider **(b)** *(dupe)* sucker, mug **2** *adj* **ce qu'il est c.!** what a sucker *or* mug (he is)!
caveau, -eaux [kavo] *nm* **(a)** *(petite cave)* small cellar **(b)** *(cabaret)* nightclub **(c)** *(funéraire)* burial vault
caver[1] [kave] **1** *vt Arch, Litt* to hollow (out), to dig (out), to excavate **2 se caver** *vpr (des yeux etc)* to become hollow *or* sunken
caver[2] *Cartes* **1** *vt Arch (miser)* to put up **2** *vi* to put up a stake **3 se caver** *vpr* **se c. de deux cents francs** to put up two hundred francs *(as a stake)*
caverne [kavɛrn] *nf* cave, cavern; *Anat (dans les poumons etc)* cavity; **homme des cavernes** caveman; **la c. d'Ali Baba** Ali Baba's cave; *Fig* **c'est une véritable c. d'Ali Baba** it's a real Aladdin's cave
caverneux, -euse [kavɛrnø, -øz] *adj* **(a)** *(rocher), Anat (tissu)* cavernous **(b)** *(voix, grognement)* sepulchral
caviar [kavjar] *nm* **(a)** caviar; **c. rouge** salmon roe **(b)** *Fig* **passer au c.** *(article de presse etc)* to censor
caviardage [kavjardaʒ] *nm* censoring
caviarder [kavjarde] *vt (article de presse etc)* to censor
caviste [kavist] *nm* cellarman
cavité [kavite] *nf* cavity, hollow; *Anat, Méd* cavity; **c. articulaire** *(d'un os)* socket; **c. buccale** oral cavity
Cayenne [kajɛn] *n (ville)* Cayenne; **poivre de C.** cayenne (pepper)
CC [sese] *nm Banque (abrév* **compte courant)** CA
cc [sese] *nm Él (abrév* **courant continu)** DC
C/C *abrév (nm* **compte (de) chèque)** C/A
CCB [sesebe] *nm (abrév* **compte de chèque bancaire)** C/A
CCI [sesei] *nf (abrév* **Chambre de commerce et de l'industrie)** Chamber of Commerce and Industry
CCP [sesepe] *nm (abrév* **compte courant postal, compte chèque postal)** = Giro account
CD [sede] *nm* **(a)** *(abrév* **corps diplomatique)** CD **(b)** *(abrév* **compact disc)** CD; **CD audio** audio CD; **CD photo** photo-CD; **CD vidéo** video CD
CDD [sedede] *nm (abrév* **contrat à durée déterminée)** fixed-term contract
CDI [sedei] *nm, abrév* **(a) (centre des impôts)** tax centre, tax office **(b) (contrat à durée indéterminée)** permanent contract
CD-I *(abrév* **compact disc-interactif)** CDI
CD-interactif *nm* interactive CD
CD-Rom *nm inv* CD-Rom; **C. interactif** interactive CD-Rom
CE [seə] **1** *nm (abrév* **Conseil de l'Europe)** Council of Europe **2** *nf (abrév* **Communauté Européenne)** EC
ce[1] [s(ə)] *pron dém* [①B14,A,2,b] **(c'** *before parts of* **être** *beginning with a vowel)* **(a)** [①B63,2] *(with adj or adv complement)* **c'est exact!** that's right!; **c'est tout à fait possible/fort probable** it's quite possible/highly probable; **ce doit être faux** it's probably untrue; **c'est sur votre bureau** it's on your desk; **le voilà, ce n'est pas trop tôt!** there he is, and about time too!; **est-ce** [ɛs] **assez?** is that enough?; **c'est facile** it's easy; **demain c'est dimanche** tomorrow is Sunday, it's Sunday tomorrow; **c'était inutile de sonner** you needn't have rung; **c'est assez qu'il veuille bien pardonner** it is enough that he is willing to forgive; **c'est à vous de vous en occuper** it's up to you to see to it; **c'est à toi, ce livre? – non, c'est à Paul** is this book yours? – no, it's Paul's
(b) [①B63,2] *(with noun or pron as complement; with a third person pl complement the verb should be in the plural but colloquial usage allows the singular)* **c'est moi/c'est nous/ce sont eux** *ou F* **c'est eux** it's me/us/them, *Fml* it is I/we/they; **c'est le médecin/c'est Monsieur Pierrot** *(à la porte, au téléphone etc)* it's the doctor/it's Mr Pierrot; **qui a dit ça? – c'est moi/lui/***etc* who said that? – me/him/*etc*, I/he/*etc* did; **est-ce vous, Jean?** is that you, Jean?; **qui est-ce?** who is it?, who's that?; **c'est un ami que j'avais quand j'étais étudiante** he was a friend of mine when I was a student; **c'est un bon soldat** he's a good soldier; **ce n'est pas un hôtel ici!** this is not a hotel!; **ce n'est pas là mon parapluie** that is not my umbrella; **est-ce que ce sont là vos enfants?** are those your children?; **ce ne sont pas mes chaussures** they *or* these *or* those aren't my shoes; *F* **c'est elles qui me l'ont dit** it was them who told me
(c) si ce n'est except; **personne si ce n'est vos parents** no one except (possibly) your parents
(d) *(representing a subject which has been isolated in order to stress it)* **Paris, c'est bien loin!, c'est bien loin, Paris!** it's a long way to Paris!, Paris is a long way away!; **le temps, c'est de l'argent** time is money; **c'est incroyable, ce vent** this wind is incredible
(e) *(used with* **que** *or* **qui** *to bring a word into prominence)* **c'est toi qui le dis!** that's what you say!, says you!; **c'est moi qui lui ai écrit** it was I *or F* me who wrote to him; **est-ce à moi que vous parlez?** are you speaking to me?; *Litt* **c'est un bon petit garçon que Jean!** what a fine little chap Jean is!; *Litt* **ce serait imprudence que d'y aller** it would be unwise to go (there)
(f) *(used with* **que** *to introduce a statement)* **c'est que maman est malade** mother's ill, you see, the point is

mother's ill; **c'est qu'il fait froid!** it's cold and no mistake!; **s'il chante, c'est qu'il est de bonne humeur** when *or* if he sings it means *or* it's because he's in a good mood; **ce n'est pas qu'il n'y tienne pas** it's not that he isn't keen on it, it isn't that he's not keen on it

(g) [①B61,1,b] (*used in* **est-ce-que** [ɛskə] *to introduce a question*) **est-ce que je peux entrer?** may I come in?; **est-ce qu'il est là?** is he there?

(h) (*locutions*) **pour ce faire** in order to do this; **ce faisant** in so doing, whilst doing so; **ce disant** saying which *or* this, so saying, with these words; **on l'a attaqué et ce** [sə] **en plein jour** he was attacked, and in broad daylight (too); **sur ce …** thereupon …, on that note …; **sur ce, il sortit son album de photos** whereupon he brought out his photo album; *Arch* **depuis ce …** since then …; **tenez-vous beaucoup à ce qu'il vienne?** are you very anxious for him to come?; **je ne m'attendais pas à ce qu'il soit là** I wasn't expecting him to be there; **tu te plains de ce que personne ne te téléphone** you're complaining that no one telephones you; **pour ce qui est de la qualité et du prix** with regard to *or* as regards quality and price; **pour ce qui est de cela** for that matter; **c'est te dire s'il était content** that shows you how happy he was; **c'est tout dire** that says it all; *Litt* **voilà, ce me semble, un avis excellent** that, to my mind, is excellent advice

(i) [①A31,d; A33,g; B16,g; B21,g] (*with a rel pron*) **ce qui, ce que** what; **je sais ce qui est arrivé** I know what has happened; **c'est ce qui est important** this is what's important; **voilà ce que j'ai répondu** this is what I answered; **je sais ce que c'est que la pauvreté** I know what poverty is; **si vous saviez ce que c'est que de vivre seul** if you knew what it meant *or* what it's like to live alone; **voilà ce que c'est que de mentir** that's what comes of telling lies; **c'est ce qu'il a dit** that's what he said, so he said; **voici ce dont il s'agit** this is the point, this is what it's all about; **ce qu'il y a de plus remarquable, c'est que …** what is most remarkable is that …, the most remarkable thing about it is …; **à ce qu'on dit** according to *or* from what they say; **voici ce à quoi** [səakwa] **j'avais pensé** this is what I had thought of

(j) [①A31,d; A33,g; B16,g; B21,g] (*referring back to a clause*) **ce qui, ce que** which; **ce qui compte, c'est que tu sois satisfait** what counts is that you're happy; **il faut avoir de l'argent, ce qu'elle n'a pas** you need to have money, which she doesn't have; **il l'a quittée, ce qui est dommage** he has left her, which is a pity; **il est déjà parti, ce que je ne savais pas** he has already gone, which I didn't know

(k) **tout ce qui, tout ce que** everything, all (that); **voici tout ce que j'ai d'argent** here's all the money I've got; **faites tout ce que vous voudrez** do whatever you like

(l) *F* **ce que …!** (*comme*) how…!; **(qu'est-)ce qu'elle a changé!** how she has changed!; **ce que tu as grandi!** how you've grown!, well, you have grown!; **ce qu'il peut être pénible!** he can be really tiresome!; **ce que j'ai faim!** I'm really hungry!

(m) (*with* **à** + *inf*) **c'est à mourir de rire** it's absolutely hilarious; **c'est à se demander s'il n'est pas fou** one may well wonder if he isn't mad; **c'est à voir** (*ça reste à prouver*) that remains to be seen, we'll have to (wait and) see; (*il faut le voir absolument*) you have to see it; **c'est à refaire** it will have to be done again

ce², cet, cette, ces [sə, sɛt, se *or* sɛ] *adj dém* (*the form* **cet** *is used before a n or adj beginning with a vowel or* **h** *mute*) **(a)** [①A30,9,a; B13,6,2,a] (*désigne quelque chose de proche dans l'espace ou dans le temps*) this, that, *pl* these, those; **un de ces jours** one of these days; **tu dois connaître cette histoire, tout le monde la connaît!** you must know this story, everyone does!; **il fera de l'orage cette nuit** there will be a storm tonight; **j'ai mal dormi cette nuit** I slept badly last night; **je l'ai vu/je le verrai ce matin/cet été/cette semaine** I saw him/I'll see him this morning/this summer/this week; **c'est une de ces femmes qui se plaignent tout le temps** she's one of those women who complain *or* she's the sort of woman who complains all the time

(b) (*par référence à une chose connue*) the; **j'ai encore cette impression que …** I still have the feeling that …; **rien de ce genre** nothing of the kind; **je n'ai jamais rien entendu/vu de ce genre** I've never heard/seen anything of the kind *or* anything like it

(c) **ce dernier** the latter

(d) **ces** the; **que prendront ces messieurs?** what will you take *or* have, gentlemen?; **ces dames sont au salon** the ladies are in the drawing room

(e) **ce …-ci** this; **ce…-là** that; **de ce côté-ci/de ce côté-là** on this/that side; **je ne connais pas ce livre-là** I don't know that book; **j'ai vu tous ces films, mais j'ai préféré ce film-ci à tous les autres** I've seen all these films, but I prefer this one to all the others; **prenez cette tasse-ci** take this cup; **je n'oublierai jamais ce jour-là** I'll never forget that day; **je la verrai ces jours-ci** I'll see her in a day or two; **il fait chaud ces jours-ci** it's been warm lately *or* the(se) last couple of days

(f) *F* (*en intensif*) **eh bien, et cette jambe?** well, how's that leg of yours *or* how's the leg?; **alors, cette lettre, tu me la fais lire?** so, do I get to read that letter of yours?; **et ce café, il arrive?** is that coffee on its way or what?; **et ce vent, qui ne tombe pas!** will that wind ever die down?; **mais laissez-la donc, cette enfant!** do leave that child alone!; **mais c'est qu'elle a grandi, cette petite!** that little girl has really grown!; **cette question!** what an absurd question!; **cette foule!** what a crowd!; **je lui ai écrit une de ces lettres!** I wrote him such a letter!; **j'ai une de ces faims!** I'm ravenous!; **elle a une de ces têtes!** (*elle est fatiguée, malade*) she looks awful!; (*elle est laide*) she's as ugly as sin!; **il a fait une de ces têtes quand je le lui ai montré** you should have seen his face when I showed it to him

céans [seɑ̃] *adv Arch* (here) within, in this house; *Hum* **le maître de c.** the master of the house

ceci [səsi] *pron dém inv* [①B14,3] this; **et tout c. pour rien, puisqu'il a fallu recommencer** and it was all for nothing, since we/*etc* had to start again; **c. étant dit, il faut quand même reconnaître qu'il a du talent** having said that, it must be admitted that he's talented; **écoutez bien c.** (now) listen to this; **le cas a c. de particulier que …** the case is peculiar in that …; **c. n'explique pas cela** one thing doesn't explain the other

cécité [sesite] *nf* blindness; **être frappé de c.** to be struck blind; **être atteint de c.** to be blind; **c. verbale** word blindness

cédant, -ante [sedɑ̃, -ɑ̃t] *Com, Jur* **1** *adj* (*partie*) granting, assigning **2** *n* grantor, assignor

céder [sede] **(je cède; je céderai) 1** *vt* (*donner*) (*qch*) to give up, to part with (**à** to); (*droit*) to give up, to surrender; *Jur* to transfer, to make over, to assign (**à** to); (*bail*) to dispose of, to sell; **c. sa place à qn** to give up one's seat to sb; **c. le pas à qn** to let sb go first, to give way to sb; **c. du terrain** to give *or* lose ground; *Fig* to back down; **'cédez le passage'** 'give way', *Am* 'yield'; **fonds de commerce à c.** business for sale; **'à c.'** 'for sale'; **je vous le céderai pour cent francs** I'll let you have it for a hundred francs; *Vieilli* **ne le c. en rien à qn** to be in no way inferior to sb; **pour l'intelligence elle ne (le) cède à personne** when it comes to intelligence she's second to none; **ces artistes russes ne le cédaient en rien à leurs contemporains français** these Russian artists were every bit as good as their French contemporaries

2 *vi* (*se soumettre*) (*d'une personne*) to yield, to give in (**à** to); (*s'écrouler*) (*d'une construction, corde etc*) to give way; **le terrain a cédé sous mes pieds** the ground gave way beneath me; **le câble a cédé sous l'effort** the rope gave way *or* parted under the strain; **c. sous le poids** to give way *or* break beneath the weight; **c. au sommeil** to succumb to sleep; **c. à la tentation** to give in *or* yield to temptation; *Fig* **leur argumentation cédera à la première analyse** their reasoning will fall apart at the first analysis; **il a cédé à nos revendications** he gave in to our demands; **c. devant les menaces/aux intimidations** to give in *or* yield to threats/to intimidation; **elle a fini par lui c.** (*d'une femme séduite par un homme*) she finally succumbed to *or* gave into him

cédétiste [sedetist] *Pol* **1** *adj* of *or* relating to the CFDT (*French trade union*) **2** *n* member of the CFDT

Cedex [sedɛks] *nm* (*abrév* **Courrier d'Entreprise à Distribution Exceptionnelle**) = special delivery service for business mail

cédille [sedij] *nf Gram* cedilla; **c c.** c cedilla

cédrat [sedra] *nm* (*arbre*) citron (tree); (*fruit*) citron; **confiture de cédrats** citron marmalade

cédratier [sedratje] *nm* citron (tree)

cèdre [sɛdr] *nm* (*arbre, bois*) cedar; **c. de Liban** cedar of Lebanon; **c. bleu** blue cedar; **table en c.** cedar table

CEE [seəə] *nf* (*abrév* **Communauté économique européenne**) EEC

CEG [seəʒe] *nm* (*abrév* **collège d'enseignement général**) = junior secondary school

cégep [seʒɛp] *nm Can* (*abrév* **collège d'enseignement général et professionnel**) = college of further education; **elle va au c. l'an prochain** she's going to CEGEP next year

cégétiste [seʒetist] *Pol* **1** *n* member of the CGT (*French trade union*) **2** *adj* **délégué c.** CGT delegate

CEI [seəi] *nm* (*abrév* **Communauté des états indépendants**) CIS

ceindre [sɛ̃dr] (*prp* **ceignant**; *pp* **ceint**; *pr ind* **je ceins, il**

ceint, n. ceignons; *impf* **je ceignais**; *p hist* **je ceignis**; *fu* **je ceindrai)** *Litt* **1** *vt* **(a)** to gird; **c. une épée** to gird on *or* buckle on a sword; **c. l'écharpe municipale** to put on *or* assume one's sash of office; **c. la couronne** (*d'un roi*) to put on *or* assume the crown

(b) c. ses reins to gird up one's loins; **c. ses reins d'une écharpe** to tie a sash round one's waist

(c) (*d'une couronne etc*) (*la tête de qn etc*) to encircle; **tête ceinte d'une couronne de lauriers** head wreathed with laurels

(d) c. une ville de murailles to encircle *or* surround a town with walls

2 se ceindre *vpr* **se c. les reins** to gird (up) one's loins

ceinture [sɛ̃tyr] *nf* **(a)** (*en cuir etc*) belt; (*d'une jupe, de pantalon*) waistband; (*du corps*) waist, middle; (*en lutte*) waist lock; **porter une c.** to wear a belt; **une c. de cuir** a leather belt; **élargir la c. d'une jupe** to let out the waistband of a skirt; **l'eau nous arrivait au niveau de la c.** we were up to our waists in water; **porter son écharpe en c.** to tie one's scarf round one's waist; **c. marron/noire** (*arts martiaux*) brown/black belt; **il est c. noire de judo** he's a black belt in judo; **coup au-dessous de la c.** blow beneath *or* below the belt; **desserrer sa c. après un bon repas** to loosen one's belt after a heavy meal; *Fig F* **se serrer** *ou* **se mettre la c.** to tighten one's belt; **faire c.** to go without; **il va tout le temps au restaurant, mais moi, c.!** he goes to restaurants all the time, but I have to go without

(b) (*marquant une délimitation*) enclosure; (*de murs*) circle; (*de collines*) belt

(c) *Rail* **chemin de fer de c.** (*autour d'une ville*) circle line; **la grande/la petite C.** (*à Paris*) the outer/inner circle railway

(d) *Archit* (*d'une colonne*) cincture

▶ **ceinture**: **c. de chasteté** chastity belt; **c. herniaire** (hernia) truss; *Méd* **c. orthopédique** surgical corset; *Anat* **c. pelvienne** pelvic girdle; **c. de sauvetage** lifebelt; *Anat* **c. scapulaire** pectoral *or* scapular arch *or* girdle; *Aut, Av* **c. de sécurité** seat belt, safety belt; **c. de sécurité à enrouleur** inertia reel seat belt; *Aut* **c. de sécurité statique** static seat belt; *Aut* **c. de sécurité trois points** lap and shoulder belt, three-point seatbelt; *Aut* **c. de sécurité ventrale** lap belt; **c. verte** green belt

ceinturer [sɛ̃tyre] *vt* **(a)** (*entourer*) to girdle, to surround; **ville ceinturée de murs** walled town **(b)** (*personne*) (*d'un lutteur*) to put a waist lock on; *Rugby, Fb* to to grab around the waist; **c. un homme dangereux** to collar a dangerous man

ceinturon [sɛ̃tyrɔ̃] *nm Mil etc* belt

cela [səla, sla] *pron dém* [①B14,3] **(a)** (*chose, fait etc*) that; **c., je ne pouvais pas le prévoir** I couldn't have foreseen that; **qu'est-ce que c'est que c.?** what's that?; **il me l'a expliqué très clairement, et c. sans s'énerver le moins du monde** he explained it to me very clearly, and without getting the least bit annoyed; **il y a deux ans de c.** that was two years ago; **c'est pour c. que je viens** that's what I've come for *or* why I've come; **ce n'est quand même pas pour c. que vous vous êtes disputés?** you didn't argue over a little thing like that, did you?; **sans c. je ne serais pas venu** but for that *or* otherwise I wouldn't have come; **à c. près** *ou* **à part c., nous sommes d'accord** we are agreed, with that one exception *or* except on that point; **s'il n'y a que c. de nouveau** if that's all that's new

(b) (**cela** *is the pron used as neut subject to all verbs other than* **être**, *and may be used with* **être** *as more emphatic than* **ce**) that, it; **c. ne vous regarde pas** that's *or* it's none of your business, that's *or* it's no business of yours; **c. m'est pénible de la voir si malheureuse** its very painful to me to see her *or* seeing her so unhappy

(c) (*dans locutions*) *F* **et pourquoi c.?** why is that?; **je trouve que tu exagères – et pourquoi c.?** I think you're exaggerating – why's that *or* how come?; **je l'ai vu – qui c.?/quand c.?/où c.?** I saw him – who (do you mean)?/when (was that)?/where (was that)?; **ce n'est plus c.** it's not what it was, it's not the same any more; **il n'y a que c. pour me tenir éveillé** that's the only thing that will keep me awake; **s'il n'y avait que c.** if that were the only problem; **ah, pour c., oui!** yes, indeed!, yes, of course!; **et avec c., madame?** (*dans un magasin*) anything else, madam?; **elle était très jolie, et avec c. toujours serviable** she was very pretty and moreover always willing to help

céladon [seladɔ̃] *adj inv* celadon

célébrant [selebrɑ̃] *Rel* **1** *adj* officiating **2** *n* celebrant

célébration [selebrasjɔ̃] *nf* celebration

célèbre [selɛbr] *adj* famous, celebrated (**par** for); **se rendre c. par un acte/une déclaration** to become famous because of something one did/said; **le cas si tristement c. de ...** the notorious case of ...

célébrer [selebre] *vt* (**je célèbre; je célébrerai**) **(a)** (*anniversaire, messe etc*) to celebrate; (*rite*) to solemnize, to perform; (*fête religieuse*) to observe, to keep; **c. des funérailles** to hold a funeral **(b)** (*qn*) to extol; **c. le courage de qn** to praise *or* pay tribute to sb's courage

célébrité [selebrite] *nf* (*notoriété*) fame, celebrity; (*personne*) celebrity

celer [səle] *vt* (**je cèle; je cèlerai**) *Arch, Litt* to conceal, to keep secret (**à** from)

céleri [sɛlri] *nm* celery; **pied de c.** head of celery; **morceau** *ou* **branche de c.** stick of celery; *Culin* **c. rémoulade** = celeriac in mayonnaise

céleri-rave, *pl* **céleris-raves** *nm* celeriac

célérité [selerite] *nf* speed, rapidity; **avec une étonnante c.** with astonishing speed, at an astonishing rate

célesta [selɛsta] *nm Mus* celesta, celeste

céleste [selɛst] *adj* celestial, heavenly; *Fig* (*divin*) divine; *Litt* **la voûte c.** the vault of heaven; **bleu c.** sky blue; *Fig* **la colère c.** divine wrath; **le C. Empire** the Celestial Empire

céliat [seliba] *nm* (*vie de célibataire*) single life; *Rel* (*chasteté*) celibacy; **vivre dans le c.** to remain single; **de plus en plus de femmes choisissent le c.** more and more women are choosing to remain single

célibataire [selibatɛr] **1** *adj* (*non marié*) unmarried, single; **mère c.** unmarried mother **2** *nm* bachelor; **un c. endurci** a confirmed bachelor **3** *nf* single woman; *Admin, Vieilli* spinster

celle, celle-ci, celle-là *pron voir* **celui**

cellérier, -ière [selerje, -jɛr] *n Rel* cellarer, *f* cellaress

cellier [selje] *nm* storeroom; (*cave*) cellar

cellophane® [selɔfan] *nm* cellophane; **fromage sous c.** cellophane-wrapped cheese

cellulaire [selylɛr] *adj* **(a)** *Biol* (*tissu etc*) cell; *Télécom* **téléphone c.** cellular phone, cellphone **(b) convoi c.** (*de la police*) police convoy; **voiture c.** police van; **prison** *ou* **régime c.** solitary confinement

cellule [selyl] *nf* **(a)** (*d'une prison, d'un couvent etc*) cell; *Fig* (*section politique*) cell, section; *Fig* (*élément*) unit; *Mil* **dix jours de c.** ten days in the cells *or F* the slammer; **les cellules du parti** the party cells; **réunion de c.** cell meeting; *Com* **c. d'achat** purchasing unit; *Aut* **c. de survie** passenger survival cell; **c. de télévente** telesales unit; *Fig* **la c. de la société** the social unit **(b)** *Biol* cell; **c. nerveuse** nerve cell; **différenciation des cellules** cell differentiation **(c)** *Av* airframe **(d)** *Phot etc* **c. photoélectrique** photoelectric cell, photocell; *TV* electric eye **(e)** (*de tourne-disque etc*) cartridge

cellulite [selylit] *nf Méd* cellulite; **avoir de la c.** to have cellulite; **traitement anti-c.** anti-cellulite treatment

cellulitique [selylitik] *adj Méd* **tissu c.** cellulite tissue

celluloïd [selylɔid] *nm* celluloid

cellulose [selyloz] *nf Ch, Com* cellulose

cellulosique [selylozik] *adj* (*vernis etc*) cellulose

celte [sɛlt] **1** *adj* Celtic **2** *n* Celt

celtique [sɛltik] **1** *adj* Celtic **2** *nm Ling* Celtic

celui, celle, *pl* **ceux, celles** [səlɥi, sɛl, sø, sɛl] *pron dém* [①A30,9,a; B13,6,2,a] **(a)** (*completed by an adj clause*) the one, *pl* those; **c. dont je t'ai parlé** the one *or* the man I told you about; **celle à qui j'ai écrit** the one *or* the woman I wrote to; **c. qui était parti le dernier** the one who started last; **c. que je t'avais recommandé** the one *or* the man I had recommended to you; **tous les plats sont sales, prends c. qui est dans le lave-vaisselle** all the dishes are dirty, take the one in the dishwasher

(b) (*quiconque*) he, she, *pl* those; **c. qui mange peu dort bien** he who eats little sleeps well

(c) (*followed by* **de**) **mes livres et ceux de Jean** my books and Jean's; **les hommes d'aujourd'hui et ceux d'autrefois** the men of today and those of former times; **le robinet de la cuisine fuit et c. de la salle de bain aussi** the tap in the kitchen's leaking and so is the one in the bathroom; **c. d'entre vous qui habite à Lyon** whichever one of you lives in Lyons; **ceux d'entre vous qui n'ont pas encore payé leur cotisation** those of you who haven't yet paid your subscription

(d) (*suivi d'un participe, d'un adjectif, d'un infinitif*) **tous ceux ayant la même idée** all those with the same idea; **toutes les maisons sont en bois sauf celles voisines de l'église** all the houses are built of wood except those near the church

(e) c.-ci, *pl* **ceux-ci** (*en indiquant du doigt*) this (one), *pl* these; (*en se référant à qn ou qch précédemment cité*) the latter; **c.-là,** *pl* **ceux-là** (*en indiquant du doigt*) that (one), *pl* those; (*en se référant à qn ou qch précédemment cité*) the former; **ceux-ci coûtent plus cher que ceux-là** these cost more than those do; **ah, c.-là! quel idiot!** he's such an idiot, that one!; **autre exemple, plus technique c.-là** another example, a more technical one this time

cément [semã] *nm* cement

cémentation [semãtasjɔ̃] *nf Métal* cementation, case hardening

cémenter [semãte] *vt Métal* (*acier*) to case-harden

CEN [seəɛn] *nf* (*abrév* **Comité européen de normalisation**) European standardization committee

cénacle [senakl] *nm* **(a)** (*côterie*) (literary) club, group, *Litt* coterie **(b)** *Antiq* cenacle; *surtout Bible* Cenacle, upper room of the Last Supper

cendre [sãdr] *nf* [①**A10**,f,i] **(a)** (*de matières brûlées*) ash(es), cinders; **c. de bois** wood ash; **cendres volcaniques** volcanic ash; *Tech* **cendres volantes** fly ash; **des cendres** *ou* **de la c. (de cigarette)** cigarette ash; **faire cuire des marrons sous la c.** to roast chestnuts in the ashes *or* embers; **mettre** *ou* **réduire une ville en cendres** to reduce a town to ashes; **maison réduite en cendres** house burnt to the ground; *Rel* **le mercredi des Cendres** Ash Wednesday; **visage couleur de c.** ashen face

(b) cendres (mortal) remains, ashes; **ses cendres seront transportées dans sa ville natale** his ashes will be taken to his home town; *Litt* **les cendres du passé** the embers of the past

cendré [sãdre] *adj* ash-grey, ashen, ashy; **blond c.** ash blond

cendrée [sãdre] *nf* **(a)** *Sp etc* (*piste*) cinder track, dirt track; (*mâchefer*) cinders **(b)** (*cartouche*) dust shot

cendrer [sãdre] *vt* (*chemin, piste*) to cinder

cendreux, -euse [sãdrø, -øz] *adj* **(a)** (*gris, terne*) ashen **(b)** (*qui contient de la cendre*) full of ashes, ashy, gritty

cendrier [sãdrije] *nm* (*pour fumeurs*) ashtray; (*d'un poêle*) ashpan; (*d'un fourneau*) ash pit *or* hole

Cendrillon [sãdrijɔ̃] *nf* **(a)** Cinderella **(b)** *Vieilli* **c.** (household) drudge, slavey

cène [sɛn] *nf* **(a)** *Bible, Beaux-Arts* **la (Sainte) C.** the Last Supper **(b)** *Rel* (*pour l'Église Protestante*) Holy Communion, Lord's Supper

cenelle [sənɛl] *nf* (*baie*) haw

cénobite [senɔbit] *nm* (*moine*) cenobite

cénotaphe [senɔtaf] *nm* cenotaph

cens [sãs] *nm* **(a)** *Hist* (*dans le système féodal*) (quit) rent; **c. électoral** = property qualification (*for the franchise*) **(b)** *Antiq* census

censé [sãse] *adj* supposed; **je ne veux pas qu'il sache que je suis là, je suis censée rester à la maison aujourd'hui** I don't want him to know I'm here, I was supposed to stay at home today; **je ne suis pas c. le savoir** (*cela est au-dessus de mes compétences*) I can't be expected to know that; (*c'est confidentiel*) I'm not supposed to know about it; **nul n'est c. ignorer la loi** ignorance of the law is no excuse

censément [sãsemã] *adv* supposedly

censeur [sãsœr] *nm* **(a)** (*de la presse etc*) censor **(b)** *Scol* (*d'un lycée*) (*homme*) vice-principal, deputy headmaster; (*femme*) vice-principal, deputy headmistress **(c)** (*juge*) critic, faultfinder; **c'est un c. juste/impartial** he's a fair/impartial critic **(d)** *Antiq* censor

censitaire [sãsitɛr] *Hist* **1** *adj* **électeur c.** elector qualified by his tax assessment; **suffrage** *ou* **système c.** voting system based on tax quota **2** *nm* eligible voter

censurable [sãsyrabl] *adj* open to censure, censurable

censure [sãsyr] *nf* **(a)** (*de la presse etc*) censorship; *Cin etc* (board of) censors; *Psy* censor; **c. de l'actualité** news blackout; **visa de c.** censor's certificate **(b)** *Pol* **voter une motion de c.** to pass a vote of censure *or* no-confidence **(c)** *Vieilli* censure, blame; **les censures de l'Église** the censure of the Church

censurer [sãsyre] *vt* **(a)** *Cin, Psy etc* to censor; *Cin* **c. une scène** to censor *or* cut a scene **(b)** (*critiquer*) (*qn, qch*) to find fault with, to censure

cent[1] [sã] [①**A12**,1,h,i; **B56**,A,c-d] **1** *adj* (*takes a plural* **s** *when multiplied by a preceding numeral but not when followed by another numeral; does not vary when used as an ordinal*) (a, one) hundred; **c. élèves** a hundred pupils, one hundred pupils; **deux cents hommes** two hundred men; **deux c. cinquante hommes** two hundred and fifty men; **page deux c.** page two hundred; **l'an trois c.** the year three hundred; **le numéro trois c. gagne** number three hundred is the winner, the winning number is three hundred; **avoir c. ans** to be a hundred (years old); **avoir c. deux ans** to be a hundred and two; **cent un** [sã œ̃] one hundred and one; **je te l'ai dit c. fois** (if I've told you once) I've told you a hundred times; **elle a eu c. fois l'occasion de le faire** she's had every chance to do it; **vous avez c. fois raison** you're absolutely right; **je préférerais c. fois lui dire tout de suite plutôt qu'attendre demain** I'd much rather tell him right away than wait until tomorrow; **habiter au c. de la rue Henri Martin** to live at number a hundred *or* to live at one hundred rue Henri Martin; **c. fois mieux** a hundred times better; **c'est la même maison, mais en c. fois plus grand** it's the same house, but a hundred times bigger; *F* **je ne vais pas t'attendre (pendant) c. sept ans** I'm not going to wait for you forever; **faire les c. pas** to pace up and down; *F* **être aux c. coups** to be frantic *or* in a panic; *F* **faire les quatre cents coups** to be up to all sorts of tricks; *F* **je vous le donne en c.** I'll give you three guesses!, guess!

2 *nm* a hundred; **je te parie à c. contre un que ...** I'll give you a hundred to one that ...; **sept pour c.** seven per cent; **une augmentation de deux cents pour c.** an increase of two hundred per cent, a two hundred per cent increase; *Ch* **solution à trente pour c.** thirty per cent solution; **c. pour c.** a hundred per cent; **il est c. pour c. Écossais, c'est un Écossais à c. pour c.** he's a hundred per cent Scottish; **je ne suis pas sûr à c. pour c.** I'm not a hundred per cent sure; *F* **elle gagne des mille et des cents** she earns a packet *or* a fortune; *Sp* **le c. mètres** the hundred metres; **courir le quatre cents mètres haies** to run the four hundred metre hurdles; *Com Vieilli* **un c. d'œufs** a hundred eggs

cent[2] [sɛnt] *nm surtout Can* (*pièce*) cent

centaine [sãtɛn] *nf* (about a) hundred; **une c. de francs** about a hundred francs, a hundred francs or so; **des centaines de livres** hundreds of books; **plusieurs centaines de personnes** several hundred people; **quelques centaines de francs** a few hundred francs; **atteindre la c.** (*d'éléments, de participants etc*) to be about a hundred; **les gens moururent par centaines/par centaines de mille** people died in (their) hundreds/hundreds of thousands *or* by the hundred/hundred thousand; **ils sont arrivés par centaines** they arrived in their hundreds; *Math* **la colonne/le chiffre des centaines** the hundreds column/figure

centaure [sãtɔr] *nm Myth* centaur

centaurée [sãtɔre] *nf* (*plante*) centaury

centenaire [sãtnɛr] **1** *adj* (*personne, arbre*) a hundred years old, hundred-year old; (*tradition etc*) age-old; **ma grand-mère est c.** (*elle a cent ans*) my grandmother is a hundred (years old); (*elle a plus de cent ans*) my grandmother is over a hundred (years old); **plusieurs fois c.** hundreds of years old; **toi, tu finiras c.!** you'll live to be a hundred!; **chêne c.** ancient oak **2** *n* centenarian **3** *nm* centenary, *Am* centennial

centésimal, -ale, -aux, -ales [sãtezimal, -o] *adj* (*fraction, échelle etc*) centesimal; *Méd* **dilution centésimale** dilution to one part per hundred

centiare [sãtjar] *nm* = one square metre

centième [sãtjɛm] **1** *adj* (*anniversaire etc*) hundredth **2** *n* hundredth **3** *nm* hundredth (part); **je n'ai pas compris le c. de ce qu'il disait** I didn't understand a fraction of what he was saying **4** *nf Th* hundredth performance

centigrade [sãtigrad] *nm* centigrade

centigramme [sãtigram] *nm* centigram(me)

centilitre [sãtilitr] *nm* centilitre, *US* centiliter

centime [sãtim] *nm* centime; **je ne lui donnerai pas un c.!** I won't give him a penny!; **ne pas avoir un c.** not to have a penny to one's name; *Admin* **centimes additionnels** special surtax

centimètre [sãtimɛtr] *nm* **(a)** (*unité de mesure*) centimetre, *US* centimeter; *Journ* **c. colonne** column centimetre **(b)** (*ruban*) tape measure

centrafricain, -aine [sãtrafrikɛ̃ -ɛn] **1** *adj* Central African; **République centrafricaine** Central African Republic **2** *n* **C.** Central African

Centrafrique [sãtrafrik] *nm* Central African Republic

centrage [sãtraʒ] *nm* centring, *US* centering; *Ordinat* **c. sur tabulation** centre tab

central, -ale, -aux, -ales [sãtral, -o] **1** *adj* central; (*point etc*) middle, central; (*principal*) central, main; **leur appartement occupe une position centrale dans la ville** their flat is located in the centre of the town *or* is centrally located; **quartier c. de la ville** central area of town, town centre; **Amérique/Asie centrale** Central America/Asia; **(prison) centrale** = county jail; **École centrale** = (university level) State school of engineering; **chauffage c.** central heating; **la maison a un chauffage c.** the house has central heating *or* is centrally heated

2 *nm* **(a) c. téléphonique** telephone exchange

(b) *Tennis* **le c.** the centre court

3 *nf* **centrale (a)** *Él* **centrale (électrique)** power station; **centrale thermique/nucléaire/hydraulique** thermal *or* coal-fired/nuclear/hydroelectric power station; **centrale surgénératrice** fast-breeder power station

(b) centrale (syndicale) group of affiliated trade unions

(c) *Scol F* **Centrale** = (university level) State school of engineering; **faire Centrale** to go to the École centrale

▶ **central**: *Com* **centrale d'achat** (central) purchasing *or* buying group; (*au sein d'une même entreprise*) central purchasing department; **centrale d'alerte** (*d'une voiture etc*) warning system; *Aut* **centrale de commande électronique** electronic control unit, ECU; **centrale de réservations** central reservations unit, central reservations office

centralien, -ienne [sɑ̃traljɛ̃, -jɛn] *n* student of the École centrale

centralisateur, -trice [sɑ̃tralizatœr, -tris] *adj* (*force etc*) centralizing

centralisation [sɑ̃tralizasjɔ̃] *nf* centralization, centralizing

centraliser [sɑ̃tralize] *vt* to centralize

centralisme [sɑ̃tralism] *nm Pol* centralism

centraliste [sɑ̃tralist] *nm Pol* centralist

centre [sɑ̃tr] *nm* **(a)** (*base etc*), *Pol* centre, *US* center; **c. d'un cercle** (*en géométrie*) centre of a circle; **cette question est au c. du débat** this question is at the centre of the debate; **il se croit** *ou* **se prend pour le c. du monde!** he thinks (that) the world revolves round him; **le c. de la ville** the town centre; **les grands centres urbains** the great urban centres; *Pol* **le c. droit/gauche** the centre right/left
(b) *Fb etc* (*passe*) **faire un c.** to make a cross
(c) *Rugby* centre; **premier/deuxième c.** inside/outside centre

▶ **centre**: **c. d'accueil** (*pour touristes*) visitor centre; (*pour toxicomanes etc*) centre; **c. d'affaires** business centre; (*dans aéroport, hôtel*) business lounge; *Compta* **c. d'analyse** cost centre; *Compta* **c. (d'analyse) auxiliaire/principal** secondary/main cost centre; *Compta* **c. d'analyse opérationnel** operational cost centre; *Compta* **c. d'analyse de structure** fixed cost centre; **c. d'art dramatique** drama centre; **c. d'artisanat** craft centre; *Phys* **c. d'attraction** centre of attraction; *Fig* centre *or* focus of attention; **c. de chèques postaux** PO cheque account centre; *Com* **c. commercial** shopping precinct, shopping centre *or* mall; **c. de conférences** conference centre; **c. culturel** arts centre; *Météo* **c. de dépression** storm centre; *TV, Rad* **c. de diffusion** broadcasting centre; *Aut* **c. d'essai** test centre; *Phys* **c. de gravitation** centre of attraction; **c. de gravité** centre of gravity; **c. d'hébergement** rescue centre; **c. hospitalier** hospital (complex); **c. hospitalier universitaire** university teaching hospital; **c. des impôts** tax centre *or* office; **c. industriel** industrial centre; **c. d'information** information centre; **c. d'intérêt** centre of interest; **c. d'intérêt touristique** tourist *or* visitor attraction; **c. de loisirs** leisure *or* recreation centre; **c. médical d'urgence** emergency medical service; **c. national de la recherche scientifique** = Science Research Council; **c. de recherche** research centre; **c. sportif** sports centre; **c. de tri** sorting office; *Rail* **c. de triage** shunting *or* marshalling yard; **c. universitaire** university; **c. de vacances** holiday centre

centrer [sɑ̃tre] *vt* to centre, *US* to center (**sur** on); (*roues, outils*) to adjust; *Fb etc* (*ballon*) to centre; *Tennis* **balle mal centrée** mishit; **la balle était bien centrée** the ball came right off the centre of his/her racket; **c. un texte sur une page** to centre a text on a page; **centré sur la production/les ventes** production-/sales-orientated *or* -oriented; **roman centré sur un personnage** novel centred *or* based on one character; **c. une discussion sur un sujet** to base *or* focus a discussion on a subject; **c. l'attention du lecteur sur qch** to focus the reader's attention on sth; **être trop centré sur soi-même** to be too self-centred

centre-répéteur, *pl* **centres-répéteurs** [sɑ̃trərepetœr] *nm TV, Rad* relay station

centre-ville [sɑ̃trəvil] *nm* town centre; (*d'une grande ville*) city centre, *Am* downtown area; **les boutiques du c.** the shops in the town centre, *Am* the downtown stores; **aller dans le c.** to go into the town centre, *Am* to go downtown

centrifugation [sɑ̃trifygasjɔ̃] *nf* centrifugation, centrifuging

centrifuge [sɑ̃trifyʒ] *adj* (*force etc*) centrifugal

centrifuger [sɑ̃trifyʒe] *vt* (*liquide*) to centrifuge

centrifugeur [sɑ̃trifyʒœr] *nm*, **centrifugeuse** [sɑ̃trifyʒøz] *nf* centrifuge; (*pour jus de fruits etc*) juice extractor

centripète [sɑ̃tripɛt] *adj* (*force etc*) centripetal

centrisme [sɑ̃trism] *nm Pol* centrism

centriste [sɑ̃trist] *Pol* **1** *adj* (of the) centre **2** *n* centrist; **les centristes** the centre

centuple [sɑ̃typl] **1** *adj* hundredfold; **mille est c. de dix** a thousand is a hundred times (as much as) ten **2** *nm* a hundred times; **je te le rendrai au c.** I'll repay you a hundred times over

centupler [sɑ̃typle] *vti* to increase a hundred times *or* a hundredfold

centurion [sɑ̃tyrjɔ̃] *nm Antiq* centurion

CEP [seəpe] *abrév* **certificat d'études primaires**

cep [sɛp] *nm* **(a) c. de vigne** [sɛdviɲ, sɛpdəviɲ] vinestock, vine plant **(b)** *Agr* (*d'une charrue*) sole

cépage [sepaʒ] *nm* (variety of) vine; **les cépages des vignobles bordelais** grapes from the Bordeaux vineyards

cèpe [sɛp] *nm* (*champignon*) cepe, boletus

cependant [s(ə)pɑ̃dɑ̃] **1** *conj* [①**A69**,b,iv; **B55**,A,1] however, yet, nevertheless, still, though; **c., je l'aime** but I still love him, I love him nevertheless; **le directeur, c., n'est pas d'accord** the manager, however, does not agree; **vous le saviez depuis longtemps, c., vous ne m'avez pas averti** you'd known about it for a long time but *or* and yet you didn't tell me **2** *adv Litt* meanwhile, in the meantime; **c. que** while, whilst

céphalée [sefale] *nf Méd* headache

céphalique [sefalik] *adj* cephalic

céphalopode [sefalɔpɔd] *nm* cephalopod, *pl* cephalopoda

céramique [seramik] **1** *adj* (*arts etc*) ceramic; **industries céramiques** pottery industry **2** *nf* (*art*) ceramics, (art of) pottery; (*matière*) ceramic, pottery; (*objet*) ceramic, piece of pottery; **dalles en c.** ceramic tiles

▶ **céramique**: *Méd* **c. dentaire** dental ceramics

céramiste [seramist] *n* ceramist, ceramicist

Cerbère [sɛrbɛr] *nm* **(a)** *Myth* Cerberus **(b)** *Fig* **c.** ill-tempered hall porter/janitor/concierge

cerceau, -eaux [sɛrso] *nm* **(a)** (*cercle*) hoop; **c. de jupon** crinoline hoop; **c. de baril** barrel hoop; **jouer au c.** to play with a hoop; **faire rouler un c.** to bowl a hoop **(b)** (*au-dessus d'un lit*) cradle

cerclage [sɛrklaʒ] *nm* (*de tonneaux*) hooping

cercle [sɛrkl] *nm* **(a)** *Math* circle; **le rayon du c.** the radius of the circle; **quart de c.** quadrant; **(arc de) grand c.** great circle; **entourer la bonne réponse d'un c.** to ring *or* put a circle round the correct answer; **former** *ou* **faire un c. (autour de qn/qch)** to form *or* make a circle (around sb/sth); **en c.** in a circle; **les avions décrivaient des cercles dans le ciel** the planes were circling
(b) (*d'amis etc*) circle, set; **le c. de la famille** the family circle; **il m'a introduit dans le c. de ses amis** he introduced me to his circle of friends
(c) (*association*) club; **c. littéraire** literary circle *or* society; **c. militaire** *ou* **des officiers** officers' club; **fonder un c.** to set up *or* start a society *or* club
(d) (*champ, domaine*) **c. d'activités** circle *or* sphere *or* range of activities; **le c. de ses occupations/responsabilités** the range *or* scope of his work/responsibilities
(e) (*objet circulaire*) hoop, ring; **c. d'une roue** (wheel) tyre; **c. d'arpenteur** protractor

▶ **cercle**: *Géog* **c. (polaire) arctique** Arctic Circle; *Com* **c. de qualité** quality circle; **c. vicieux** vicious circle; **se retrouver** *ou* **tomber dans un c. vicieux** to be caught in a vicious circle *or* in a catch 22 situation

cerclé [sɛrkle] *adj* **tonneau cerclé** hooped barrel; **lunettes cerclées d'écaille** horn-rimmed spectacles; **yeux cerclés de bistre** eyes with dark rings round them; **des doigts cerclés d'or** gold-ringed fingers

cercler [sɛrkle] *vt* (*tonneau*) to hoop; **une main de fer cercla son poignet** a steely grip enclosed *or* encircled his wrist

cercueil [sɛrkœj] *nm* coffin, *surtout Am* casket; **c. plombé** lead casket

céréale [sereal] *nf* cereal; **commerce des céréales** corn *or* grain trade; **culture des céréales** cereal-growing; **prendre des céréales au petit déjeuner** to have cereal for breakfast

céréalier, -ière [serealje, -jɛr] **1** *adj* (*production etc*) cereal **2** *n* cereal grower

cérébelleux, -euse [serebɛlø, -øz] *adj Anat* (*artère etc*) cerebellar

cérébral, -ale, -aux, -ales [serebral, -o] **1** *adj* (*artère etc*) cerebral; **hémorragie cérébrale** brain haemorrhage; **travail c.** intellectual work; **surmenage c.** mental exhaustion; **elle est trop cérébrale** she's too cerebral *or* intellectual **2** *n* intellectual, thinker

cérébro-spinal, -ale, -aux, -ales [serebrospinal, -o] *adj Anat, Méd* cerebro-spinal

cérémonial, -ale, -als *ou rare* **-aux, -ales** [seremɔnjal, -o] **1** *adj Arch* ceremonial **2** *nm* ceremonial; **c. de cour** court etiquette; **selon le c.** in accordance with protocol

cérémonie [seremɔni] *nf* ceremony; **c'était une c. de mariage très réussie** it was a very nice wedding ceremony; **faire une visite de c.** to make a ceremonial *or* formal visit (**à** to); **tenue** *ou* **habit de c.** dress suit; *Mil* **uniforme de c.** (full) dress uniform; **maître de c.** master of ceremonies, *Hum* **à toi de servir, puisque c'est toi le maître de c.** you can be mother and pour; *Fig* **sans cérémonies** (*réception, repas etc*) informal, casual; (*recevoir qn*) informally; (*renvoyer qn etc*) unceremoniously; **faire des cérémonies** to stand on ceremony; **voilà bien des cérémonies pour peu de choses!**

what a performance for such a little thing!; **sans plus de c.** without further ado

cérémonieusement [seremɔnjøzmɑ̃] *adv* ceremoniously, formally

cérémonieux, -ieuse [seremɔnjø, -jøz] *adj* ceremonious, formal

cerf [sɛr] *nm* [①A12,1,g] stag, *Litt* hart; *Culin* venison; **c. commun** (red) deer

cerfeuil [sɛrfœj] *nm Culin* chervil

cerf-volant, *pl* **cerfs-volants** *nm* **(a)** *(jeu)* kite; **lancer** *ou* **faire voler un c.** to fly a kite **(b)** *(insecte)* stag beetle

cerisaie [s(ə)rizɛ] *nf* cherry orchard

cerise [s(ə)riz] **1** *nf* *(fruit)* cherry; **clafoutis aux cerises** cherries baked in batter; **tarte aux cerises** cherry tart; **confiture de cerises** cherry jam; **rouge comme une c.** as red as a beetroot; *Fig* **la c. sur le gâteau** the icing on the cake **2** *adj inv* cherry(-red), cerise

cerisier [s(ə)rizje] *nm* *(arbre)* cherry tree; *(bois)* cherrywood

cérium [serjɔm] *nm Ch* cerium

CERN [sɛrn] *nm* *(abrév* **Conseil européen pour la recherche nucléaire**) CERN

cerne [sɛrn] *nm* **(a)** *(autour de la lune etc)* ring, circle; **avoir des cernes (sous les yeux)** to have (dark) shadows *or* circles under one's eyes **(b)** *(d'un arbre)* age ring

cerné [sɛrne] *adj* **avoir les yeux cernés** to have (dark) shadows *or* circles under one's eyes

cerneau, -eaux [sɛrno] *nm* *(fruit)* green walnut

cerner [sɛrne] *vt* **(a)** *(armée, ville etc)* to surround; **rendez-vous, vous êtes cernés!** give yourselves up, you're surrounded! *Fig* **je me sens cerné de toute part** I feel besieged **(b)** *(identifier)* *(question, vérité etc)* to grasp; **il commence à c. le problème** he's starting to see where the problem lies *or* to identify the problem; **une personne difficile à c.** a difficult person to figure out **(c)** *(noix)* to shell, to husk; *(arbre)* to ring **(d)** *(entourer)* to ring, to circle; **des silhouettes cernées d'ombre** shadowy figures

céroplastique [seroplastik] *nf* wax modelling

CERS [seəɛrɛs] *nf* *(abrév* **Commission européenne de recherche spatiale**) ESRO

certain, -aine [sɛrtɛ̃, -ɛn] **1** *adj* [①B10,D,3] **(a)** *(preuves, nouvelles etc)* certain, definite; **ils vont à un échec/une mort certain(e)** they're heading for certain failure/death; **s'il est bien une chose certaine** if one thing is sure *or* certain; **il est c. qu'elle viendra** it's certain *or* definite that she'll come, she'll definitely come; **il viendra, c'est c.** he'll definitely come; **il devrait venir, mais ce n'est pas c.** he should come, but it's not certain *or* definite; **il a été déçu, c'est c.** he was disappointed, of course *or* for sure; **tenir qch pour c.** *ou* **pour chose certaine** to look on sth as a certainty, to regard sth as definite; *F* **c'est sûr et c.** it's absolutely certain; *F* **j'en suis sûr et c.** I'm convinced of it; **il est c. de partir** he's sure *or* certain to leave; **j'en suis c.** I'm sure *or* certain of it; **moi, je n'en suis pas c.** I'm not so sure myself, I'm not entirely convinced

(b) [①A34,a,v; **B14**,B,1,c] *(avant le nom)* some, certain; **certaines gens affirment que ...** some (people) maintain that ...; **il a un c. charme, c'est indéniable** he has a certain charm, that's undeniable; **après un c. temps** after some *or* a certain time, after a while; **jusqu'à un c. point** up to a (certain) point; **dans un c. sens** in a sense, in a way; **je voudrais vous poser un c. nombre de questions** I'd like to ask you a number of *or* some questions; **on retrouve cette tradition dans certains pays** this tradition can be found in a number of *or* in certain countries; **dans certains cas, on ne peut pas le faire** in certain *or* some cases, it can't be done; **d'un c. âge** middle-aged; **il faut un c. courage pour le faire** you need a certain amount of courage to do it; **cela demande quand même un c. culot** it takes some nerve all the same; **c'est quand même à une c. distance d'ici!** it is quite a distance away; **si un c. M. Martin appelle, dites-lui que ...** if a (certain) Mr Martin calls, tell him ...; **une certaine Martine t'a appelé** there was someone called Martine on the phone for you

2 *pron* [①B15,B,2] **certains** some (people); **certains pensent le contraire** some people think the opposite *or* take the opposite view; **parmi ces gens, certains n'avaient jamais navigué** some of these people had never sailed; **certains d'entre nous/vous** some of us/you

certainement [sɛrtɛnmɑ̃] *adv* certainly, undoubtedly; **il réussira c.** he is sure to succeed; **vous l'avez c. lu** I'm sure you've read it; **tu dois c. le connaître** you must *or* you surely know him; **c.!** of course!, by all means!; **c. pas** certainly not

certes [sɛrt] *adv* **(a)** *(sans doute, bien sûr)* **je n'irais c. pas jusqu'à penser que ...** I certainly wouldn't go as far as believing that ...; **c., tout espoir n'est pas perdu ...** we/I/etc haven't given up hope of course, but ...; **il ne pouvait rien faire d'autre – c., mais il fallait qu'il nous en parle** he couldn't do anything else – granted, but he should have spoken to us about it **(b)** *Vieilli* most certainly; **oui c.!** yes indeed!

certificat [sɛrtifika] *nm* certificate; **montrer ses certificats** *(d'un couvrier etc)* to show one's references

▶ **certificat: c. d'aptitude au professorat de l'enseignement technique** = specialized teaching certificate for technical subjects; *Scol* **c. d'aptitude pédagogique à l'enseignement secondaire** = secondary school teaching certificate; **c. d'aptitude professionnelle** = vocational training certificate; **c. d'arrêt de travail** *(pour cause de maladie)* medical certificate; **c. d'assurance** insurance certificate; **c. de bonne vie et mœurs** character reference; **c. de capacité** *(d'employé)* certificate of proficiency; **c. de concubinage** = official document stating that two people are cohabiting; *Com* **c. de dépôt** *(de marchandises)* warehouse warrant; **c. d'entreposage** warehouse warrant; *Aut etc* **c. d'essai** test certificate; *Hist* **c. d'études (primaires)** = certificate given after an examination at the end of an elementary course of studies; *Scol, Hist* **c. d'études supérieures** *(unité de valeur)* = each of the four examinations for the licence; *(diplôme)* certificate so obtained; **c. de garantie** certificate of guarantee, guarantee certificate, warranty; **c. d'investissement** investment certificate; *Com* **c. de jaugeage** tonnage certificate; *Scol, Hist* **c. de licence** *(unité de valeur)* = each of the four examinations for the licence; *(diplôme)* certificate so obtained; *Méd* **c. médical** medical certificate; **c. de navigabilité** *Naut* certificate of seaworthiness; *Av* certificate of airworthiness; **c. de non-paiement** *(de chèque)* notification of unpaid cheque; *(de lettre de change)* certificate of dishonour; **c. d'origine** *Com* certificate of origin; *(d'un chien etc)* pedigree; *Fin* **c. provisoire** share certificate, (provisional) scrip; **c. de qualité** certificate of quality; **c. de résidence** certificate of residence; **c. sanitaire** health certificate; *Scol* **c. de scolarité** school attendance record; *Fin* **c. de titres** share certificate; **c. de travail** *(pour certifier qu'on est employé)* attestation of employment; *(pour certifier qu'on a été employé)* employer's reference; **c. de vaccination** vaccination certificate; **c. de valeur** certificate of value; *Aut* **c. de vérification du kilométrage** mileage verification certificate

certificateur [sɛrtifikatœr] *nm Jur* certifier, guarantor

certification [sɛrtifikasjɔ̃] *nf Jur, Com* certification, authentication; **c. d'une signature** witnessing of a signature

certifié, -ée [sɛrtifje] *Scol* **1** *adj* **professeur c.** = qualified (graduate) teacher **2** *n* qualified teacher

certifier [sɛrtifje] *vt* *(pr sub & impf* **n. certifiions, v. certifiiez**) *(document)* to certify; **c. une signature** to witness *or* authenticate a signature; *Jur* **copie certifiée conforme** certified true copy (of an original document); **c. une caution** to guarantee a surety; **c. qch à qn** to assure sb of sth; **il m'a certifié que la procédure était légale** he assured me the procedure was legal

certitude [sɛrtityd] *nf* certainty, certitude; **j'en ai la c.** I'm certain *or* sure of it; **dire qch avec c.** to speak with assurance

cérumen [serymɛn] *nm Physiol* earwax, *Spéc* cerumen

céruse [seryz] *nf* ceruse, white lead; **blanc de c.** white lead

cerveau, -eaux [sɛrvo] *nm Anat* brain; *(esprit)* mind, intellect, brains; *F* *(personne)* brain; *(d'un projet etc)* mastermind; **avoir une tumeur au c.** to have a brain tumour; **rhume de c.** cold in the head, head cold; **vin qui monte au c.** strong wine; **faire travailler son c.** to use one's brain; *F* **homme à c. étroit** *ou* **vide** man of limited intelligence, emptyheaded man; *F* **avoir le c. dérangé** *ou* **fêlé** to be mad *or* cracked *or* nuts; **c'est un c., elle pense à tout** she's a genius, she thinks of everything; **c. électronique** electronic brain

▶ **cerveau: c. antérieur** forebrain; **c. moyen** midbrain; **c. postérieur** hindbrain

cervelas [sɛrvəla] *nm Culin* saveloy

cervelet [sɛrvəlɛ] *nm Anat* cerebellum

cervelle [sɛrvɛl] *nf Anat* *(substance)* brain; *(esprit)* mind, intellect, brains; *Culin* **c. d'agneau** lamb's brains; **se brûler** *ou* **se faire sauter la c.** to blow one's brains out; **se creuser la c.** to rack one's brains; *F* **idée qui me trotte dans la c.** idea running through my head; **sans c.** brainless, dimwitted; **elle n'a rien** *ou* **elle n'a pas grand-chose dans la c.** she's got nothing between her ears; **avoir une c. de moineau** to be feather-brained *or* scatterbrained *or* empty-headed

cervical, -ale, -aux, -ales [sɛrvikal, -o] *adj Anat* cervical

cervidé [sɛrvide] *nm* cervid; **les cervidés** the deer family, *Spéc* Cervidae

Cervin [sɛrvɛ̃] *nm* **le (Mont) C.** the Matterhorn

cervoise [sɛrvwaz] *nf Hist* barley beer

CES [seəɛs] *nm Scol* (*abrév* **Collège d'Enseignement Secondaire**) ≈ secondary school, *Am* ≈ high school

ces *voir* **ce**

César [sezar] *nm* **(a)** *Hist* **Jules C.** Julius Caesar **(b)** *Cin* = French cinema award

césarien, -ienne [sezarjɛ̃, -jɛn] **1** *adj Hist* Caesarean **2** *nf Méd* **césarienne** Caesarean (section), *F* C section; **on lui a fait une césarienne** she had a Caesarean; **elle est née par césarienne** she was born by Caesarean, she was a Caesarean

césium [sezjɔm] *nm Ch* caesium

cessant, -ante [sɛsɑ̃, -ɑ̃t] *adj* **toute(s) affaire(s)** *ou* **chose(s) cessante(s)** immediately

cessation [sɛsasjɔ̃] *nf* cessation; **c. de paiements** suspension of payments; **cette entreprise est en c. de paiements** the company is unable to meet its financial obligations; **c. d'entreprise** ceasing of trading; **après la c. de l'entreprise** after the company ceased trading; **fermé pour cause de c. d'activité** business closed down; **c. des hostilités** ceasefire

cesse [sɛs] *nf* **(a) sans c.** constantly, continually, incessantly; **il est sans c. en train de travailler** he's constantly *or* continually working, he works incessantly; **il a plu sans c. pendant les vacances** it rained non-stop during the holidays; **il parle sans c.** he never stops talking, he talks non-stop **(b)** *Litt* **il n'aura (pas) de c. qu'il ne réussisse** he won't stop *or* rest until he has succeeded

cesser [sese] **1** *vi* to cease, to stop; **le vent a cessé** the wind has died down; **faire c. qch** to put a stop to sth; **la douleur devrait bientôt c.** the pain should go away *or* stop soon; **il faudra que ça cesse** this has to stop; **faire c. une rumeur** to scotch a rumour

2 *vt* **c. le travail** (*pour grève*) to walk out, to down tools; **c. les affaires** to close down; **c. toutes relations avec qn** to break off all relations with sb; **c. les paiements** to stop *or* suspend *or* discontinue payment(s); **cessez ces cris!** stop that shouting!; *Mil* **cessez le feu!** cease fire!; **c. de faire qch** to stop doing sth; **il n'a pas cessé de neiger pendant plusieurs jours** it hasn't stopped snowing for several days; **c. de fumer** to give up *or* stop smoking; **il n'a pas cessé de nous observer** he's been watching us all this time; **je n'ai jamais cessé de les voir** I've never stopped seeing them; *Litt* **ne c. de faire qch** to keep doing sth, to persist in doing sth; **il ne cesse de le dire et je pense qu'il a raison** he never stops saying so and I think he's right

cessez-le-feu [seselfø] *nm inv* ceasefire

cessible [sesibl] *adj Jur* transferable, assignable; (*pension etc*) negotiable

cession [sɛsjɔ̃] *nf Jur* transfer, assignment; **faire c. de qch à qn** to transfer *or* assign *or* surrender sth to sb; **acte de c.** certificate *or* deed of transfer; *Com* **c. de licence** licensing; **c. de licence de marque** corporate licensing; *Mktg* **c. de licence de nom** name licensing

cession-bail, *pl* **cessions-baux** *nf Fin* lease back

cessionnaire [sesjɔnɛr] *nm* **(a)** *Com* transferee, assignee; (*d'un effet de commerce, d'une créance*) holder; *Jur* assignee, cessionary **(b)** (*d'un chèque*) endorser

c'est-à-dire [sɛtadir] *conj* that is (to say), i. e.; **un parent, c. son oncle** a relative, that is to say, his uncle; **vous l'avez prévenu? – c. que non** did you let him know? – well, actually, I'm afraid I didn't; **c. que je n'étais pas au courant** the thing is that no one told me; **j'ai raté mon train, c. que je serai en retard** I missed my train so I'll be late; **elle m'en veut – c. qu'elle t'a attendue deux heures** she's annoyed with me – well, you did keep her waiting for two hours; **il m'agace! – c.?** he gets on my nerves – what do you mean by that?

césure [sezyr] *nf* caesura; *Ordinat* break, hyphenation; *Ordinat* **c. interactive** interactive *or* prompted hyphenation

CET [seəte] *nm Scol* (*abrév* **Collège d'Enseignement Technique**) ≈ technical college

cet *voir* **ce²**

cétacé [setase] *adj, nm Zool* cetacean

cétane [setan] *nm* cetane

C et F (*abrév* **coût et fret**) C&F

cette *voir* **ce²**

ceux *voir* **celui**

cévenol, -ole [sevnɔl] **1** *adj* (*habitant, natif*) of the Cévennes **2** *n* **C.** (*habitant*) inhabitant of the Cévennes; (*natif*) native of the Cévennes

Ceylan [selɑ̃] *nm* Ceylon

cf cf

CFA [seɛfa] (*abrév* **Communauté financière africaine**) **franc C.** CFA franc

CFAO [seɛfao] (*abrév* **Conception et fabrication assistée par ordinateur**) CADCAM

CFC [seɛfse] *nmpl Ch* (*abrév* **chlorofluorocarbures**) CFCs

CFDT [seɛfdete] *nf* (*abrév* **Confédération française démocratique du travail**) = French trade union

CFP [seɛfpe] *nm* (*abrév* **centre de formation professionnelle**) = training centre

CFTC [seɛftese] *nf* (*abrév* **Confédération française des travailleurs chrétiens**) = French trade union

CGC [seʒese] *nf* (*abrév* **Confédération générale des cadres**) = French trade union of managerial staff

CGI [seʒei] *nm* (*abrév* **Code général des impôts**) general tax code

CGT [seʒete] *nf* (*abrév* **Confédération générale du travail**) = French trade union

chabot [ʃabo] *nm* (*poisson*) (*de mer*) bullhead; (*d'eau douce*) chub

chacal, -als [ʃakal] *nm aussi Fig* jackal

cha-cha-cha [tʃatʃatʃa] *nm Mus* cha-cha(-cha)

chacon(n)e [ʃakɔn] *nf Mus* chaconne

chacun, -une [ʃakœ̃, -yn] *pron indéf* **(a)** [①A35-6,c] (*chaque personne d'un groupe*) each (one), every one; **chacune d'elles a refusé** each (one) *or* every one of them refused; **trois francs c.** three francs each; **ils ont pris c. son** *ou* **leur chapeau** each of them took their *or Fml* his hat, they each took their hat; **nous avons pris c. notre chapeau** each of us took our *or Fml* his hat, we each took our hat; **ils ont c. leurs qualités et leurs défauts** they each have their good and bad points; **ils sont partis c. de son** *ou* **de leur côté** they (each *or* all) went their separate ways

(b) (*tout le monde*) everybody, everyone; **c. pour soi** every man for himself; **c. ses goûts** everyone to their own taste; **c. son tour** each in turn; **on est passé c. son tour** everyone went past in turn; **c. son tour!** wait your turn!; *F* **tout un c.** all and sundry, every Tom, Dick and Harry; **c'est à la portée de tout un c.** it's within everyone's reach

chafouin, -ine [ʃafwɛ̃, -in] *adj* (*air*) foxy, sly; **personne à la mine chafouine** foxy- *or* sly-looking person

chagrin¹, -ine [ʃagrɛ̃, -in] **1** *adj Litt* chagrined; *Vieilli* sad, downcast; **esprits chagrins** malcontents **2** *nm* (*peine*) grief, sorrow, *Fml* affliction; *Vieilli* vexation, chagrin; **avoir du c.** to be sorrowful, to grieve; **il a un gros c.** (*d'un enfant*) he's very upset; **faire du c. à qn** to grieve *or* distress sb; **usé par le c.** careworn; **mourir de c.** to die of grief *or* of a broken heart; **un c. d'amour** an unhappy love affair

chagrin² *nm* (*cuir*) shagreen

chagrinant [ʃagrinɑ̃] *adj* distressing; *Vieilli* annoying, vexing

chagriner¹ [ʃagrine] **1** *vt* (*peiner*) to grieve, to distress; *Vieilli* to vex, to annoy; (*chiffonner*) to worry, to bother; **cela me chagrine lorsque je vois que ...** it grieves *or* pains me when I see that ...; **je ne voulais pas vous c. en vous le disant** I didn't want to upset you by telling you **2 se chagriner** *vpr* (*se désoler*) to grieve; (*s'inquiéter*) to fret

chagriner² *vt* (*cuir*) to shagreen, to grain

chah [ʃa] *nm* shah

chahut [ʃay] *nm F* racket, din; **faire du c.** to make a din, to kick up a din *or* a racket *or* a rumpus, to create an uproar; **les élèves ont fait un c. pour protester contre la décision** the pupils kicked up a racket to show their disapproval of the decision

chahuter [ʃayte] *F* **1** *vi* to make a din, to kick up a din *or* a racket *or* a rumpus, to create an uproar **2** *vt* (*maître d'école etc*) to bait; (*pièce de théâtre, orateur etc*) to boo; (*orateur*) to heckle, to barrack; **se faire c.** (*d'orateur*) to be *or* get heckled; **les filles se sont fait c. par les garçons** the boys gave the girls a hard time

chahuteur, -euse [ʃaytœr, -øz] *F* **1** *adj* (*étudiant etc*) rowdy, disorderly **2** *n* rowdy (person); (*dans un meeting politique*) heckler

chai [ʃɛ] *nm* wine and spirits store(house)

chaînage [ʃɛnaʒ] *nm* **(a)** (*arpentage*) chaining, chain measuring **(b)** *Constr* (*des murs*) tying, clamping; (*armature*) tie irons, (series of) clamps, ties **(c)** *Ordinat* chaining; (*de commandes*) piping

chaîne [ʃɛn] *nf* **(a)** (*d'acier, d'or etc*) chain; *Naut* cable; **la c. saute facilement** (*sur ma bicyclette*) the chain keeps coming off; **mettre un chien à la c.** to chain up a dog; **briser ses chaînes** to break free from one's chains; *Fig* to throw off one's chains *or* shackles; **faire la c.** (*pour faire passer des seaux etc*) to form a chain; *Ind* **travail/travailleur à la c.** assembly line *or* production line work/worker; **travailler à la c.** to work on the assembly *or* production line; *Naut* **le navire a cassé sa c.** the ship has parted her cable

(b) (*série*) (*d'hôtels, de magasins, de petits lacs*) chain; **une grande c. de supermarchés** a large supermarket chain; *Com* **c. intégrée** corporate-operated group; **c. volontaire** consortium; **c. volontaire de détaillants** voluntary retailer chain; **c. d'idées** train of thought; **réaction en c.** chain reaction

(**c**) (*par correspondance*) chain letter

(**d**) *Ch, Électron etc* chain

(**e**) *TV* channel; **c. de télévision** television channel; **changeons de c.** let's change channel; **qu'est-ce qu'il y a sur les autres chaînes?** what's on the other channels?; **c. publique/à péage** *ou* **payante** public *or* state-owned/subscription *or* pay channel; **c. commerciale** commercial channel; **c. d'information continue** news channel; **c. de cinéma** movie channel; **c. de jeux (interactifs)** (interactive) games channel; **c. de télé-achat** shopping channel; **c. généraliste** general-interest channel; **c. numérique** digital channel; **c. ouverte** public access channel; **c. spécialisée** specialized *or* specialist channel; **c. thématique** thematic *or* theme *or* specialist channel

(**f**) *Tex* warp

(**g**) *Ordinat* string; **c. de caractères** character string; **c. de recherche** search string; **c. à rechercher** search string

▶ **chaîne**: **c. alimentaire** food chain; **c. d'arpenteur** surveying chain, surveyor's chain; *Av* **c. de charters** back-to-back; *Aut* **c. de distribution** timing *or* camshaft chain; *Ind* **c. de fabrication** production line; *Ind* **c. du froid** cold chain; **c. (haute-fidélité)** hi-fi; *Ind* **c. de montage** assembly line; **c. de montagnes** range *or* chain of mountains; **c. de montre** watch chain; *Aut* **chaînes à neige** snow chains; *Ling* **c. parlée** speech chain; *Naut* **c. de port** harbour (chain) boom; **c. de solidarité** network of support; **c. de sûreté** door chain, safety chain; **c. de vélo** bicycle chain

chaîner [ʃɛne] *vt* (**a**) *Constr* (*murs etc*) to tie (**b**) (*Aut*) to put chains on (**c**) *Ordinat* (*fichiers*) to join; (*commandes*) to pipe

chaînette [ʃɛnɛt] *nf* (**a**) (*bijou, petite chaîne etc*) small chain; **c. antivol** chain lock (**b**) *Math* (**arc en**) **c.** catenary (curve) (**c**) *Couture* **point de c.** chain stitch

chaînon [ʃɛnɔ̃] *nm* (**a**) (*dans une chaîne*) link; *Fig* **le c. manquant** the missing link (**b**) *Géog* (*de montagnes*) secondary chain

chair [ʃɛr] **1** *nf* (**a**) (*chez l'homme et les animaux*) flesh; (*de pêche, de melon etc*) flesh, pulp; **en c. et en os** in the flesh, in person; **être (bien) en c.** (*d'un poulet*) to be nice and plump; (*d'une personne*) to be plump *or F* tubby; *Fig* **n'être ni c. ni poisson** to be neither fish nor fowl (nor good red herring); **une odeur de c. fraîche** a smell of fresh meat; *Fig* **il aime la c. fraîche** (*d'un séducteur*) he likes them young

(**b**) *Beaux-Arts* **chairs** flesh tints

(**c**) *Rel* body, *Péj* flesh; **la résurrection de la c.** the resurrection of the body; *Bible* **le Verbe s'est fait c.** the Word was made flesh; **c. de sa c.** his own flesh and blood; **souffrir dans sa c.** to suffer in the flesh; **la c. est faible** the flesh is weak; **péché de c.** sin of the flesh; **œuvre de c.** carnal knowledge

2 *adj inv* (**couleur**) **c.** flesh-coloured, *US* flesh-colored

▶ **chair**: **c. à canon** cannon fodder; **c. à pâté** sausagemeat; **c. de poule** gooseflesh, goose pimples, *Am* goose bumps; **cela vous donne** *ou* **on en a la c. de poule** it gives you goose pimples, it makes your flesh creep, *F* it gives you the creeps; **c. à saucisses** sausagemeat; *Fig F* **je vais en faire de la c. à saucisses** I'll make mincemeat of him

chaire [ʃɛr] *nf* (**a**) (*dans une église*) pulpit; **monter en c.** to go up into the pulpit (**b**) *Univ* (*fonction*) chair, professorship; (*tribune*) chair; **elle a été nommée à la c. d'anglais** she has been appointed to the chair of English; **être titulaire d'une c.** to hold a chair (**c**) (*trône*) chair, throne; **la c. de saint Pierre, la c. pontificale** the Chair of St Peter, the Holy See; **c. d'un évêque** bishop's throne

chaise [ʃɛz] *nf* (**a**) (*siège*) chair, seat; **c. de paille/cannée** straw/cane chair; **prenez donc une c.** have *or* take a seat; *Fig* **être assis** *ou très F* **avoir le cul entre deux chaises** to be in an awkward position; **porter qn en c., faire la c. à qn** to give sb a chair; **(jeu des) chaises musicales** (game of) musical chairs (**b**) *Naut etc* rope sling; **nœud de c.** bowline hitch

▶ **chaise**: **c. à bascule** rocking chair; *Can* **c. berçante** rocking chair; **c. de cuisine** kitchen chair; *Jur US* **c. électrique** electric chair; **passer à la c. électrique** to go to the (electric) chair; **c. d'enfant** (baby's) high chair; **c. haute** (baby's) high chair; **c. de jardin** garden chair; **c. longue** chaise longue; (*transatlantique*) deckchair; **faire de la c. longue** to have a rest, to put one's feet up; **c. percée** (night) commode; **c. pivotante** swivel chair; **c. à porteurs** sedan chair; **c. de poste** post chaise; **c. roulante** wheelchair

chaisier, -ière [ʃɛzje, -jɛr] **1** *n* chairmaker **2** *nf Vieilli* **chaisière** (*dans un jardin public etc*) chair attendant

chaland[1] [ʃalɑ̃] *nm Naut* barge, lighter; **transport par chalands** lighterage

chaland[2] (**-ande** [-ɑ̃d]) *n Vieilli* client; **attirer le c.** to attract customers *or* custom

chalandage [ʃalɑ̃daʒ] *nm Com* shopping

chaldaïque [kaldaik] **1** *adj* Chaldean **2** *n* **C.** Chaldean

Chaldée [kalde] *nf Hist, Géog* Chaldea

chaldéen, -enne [kaldeɛ̃, -ɛn] **1** *adj* Chaldean **2** *nm Ling* Chaldean **3** *n* **C.** Chaldean

châle [ʃɑl] *nm* shawl

chalet [ʃalɛ] *nm* (**a**) (*de montagne etc*) chalet (**b**) *Can* cottage (**c**) *Arch* **c. de nécessité** public convenience

chaleur [ʃalœr] *nf* (**a**) (*température*) heat, warmth; *Fig* warmth; (*d'un plaidoyer etc*) passion; **c. sèche/humide** dry/humid heat; **il fait une c. terrible dans ces dortoirs** it's terribly hot in these dormitories; **tu ne vas pas sortir par cette c.?** you're not going out in this heat, are you?; **vague de c.** heatwave; **il fait une c. lourde/accablante** it's very muggy/it's oppressively hot; **craint la c.** (*sur une étiquette*) store in a cool place; **c. spécifique/latente** specific/latent heat; *Méd* **éprouver des chaleurs, avoir des bouffées de c.** (*d'une femme ménopausée*) to have hot flushes; **sensation de c.** (*après un bain froid etc*) glow; **on a une impression de c. dès qu'on enfile ces gants** you feel warm as soon as you put these gloves on; *Méd* **coup de c.** heatstroke; **les chaleurs** the hot weather; **pendant les grandes chaleurs** during the hot season; **c. de coloris** warmth of colour; **rechercher la c. humaine** to look for human warmth; **parler avec c.** to speak warmly *or* enthusiastically; **il sera accueilli avec c.** he will receive a warm welcome

(**b**) (*des animaux*) heat, rut; **en c.** on heat, *surtout Am* in heat; *Fig Vulg* **il/elle est en c., celui-là/celle-là!** he/she's randy *or* horny *or* on heat, that one!

▶ **chaleur**: **c. animale** body heat; *Phys* **c. atomique d'un corps** atomic heat of a body

chaleureusement [ʃalørøzmɑ̃] *adv* warmly

chaleureux, -euse [ʃalørø, -øz] *adj* (*accueil etc*) warm, cordial, hearty; (*termes, paroles*) glowing; (*applaudissements etc*) enthusiastic; **remercier qn en termes c.** to thank sb warmly

châlit [ʃali] *nm* bedstead

challenge [ʃalɑ̃ʒ] *nm* (**a**) *Sp* challenge match, tournament (**b**) *Fig* (*défi*) challenge; **c'est un réel c. que de vouloir changer de travail à son âge** it's a real challenge to want to change jobs at his age

challenger [ʃalɑ̃ʒɛr] *nm Sp etc* challenger

chaloir [ʃalwar] *v impers Arch, Litt* (*used only in*) **peu me chaut, peu m'en chaut** I don't give a fig, I care not

chaloupe [ʃalup] *nf Naut* launch, longboat, tender; (*à rames*) rowing boat, *Am* rowboat; **c. de sauvetage** lifeboat; **c. à moteur** motor launch; **c. de pêche** fishing boat

chaloupé [ʃalupe] *adj* (*danse, démarche*) swaying

chalumeau, -eaux [ʃalymo] *nm* (**a**) *Tech* blowlamp, blowtorch; **faire une soudure au c.** to weld with a blowlamp; **c. oxyacétylénique** oxyacetylene torch (**b**) *Mus* pipe (**c**) *Vieilli* (*paille*) (drinking) straw; **c. de roseau** reed (**d**) *Can* spout (*for collecting sap of maple tree*)

chalut [ʃaly] *nm Pêche* trawl; **pêcher au c.** to trawl

chalutage [ʃalytaʒ] *nm Pêche* trawling

chalutier [ʃalytje] *nm* (*bateau*) trawler; (*pêcheur*) trawlerman

chamade [ʃamad] *nf* **mon cœur battait la c.** my heart was thumping *or* beating wildly

chamaillerie [ʃamajri] *nf F* (*dispute*) squabble, row

chamailler (se) [səʃamaje] *vpr F* to bicker, to squabble

chamailleur, -euse [ʃamajœr, -øz] **1** *adj* quarrelsome **2** *n* quarrelsome person, squabbler

chaman [ʃaman] *nm Rel* shaman

chamanisme [ʃamanism] *nm Rel* shamanism

chamarré [ʃamare] *adj* richly- *or* brightly-coloured *or US* -colored; **c. d'or** with gold brocade

chamarrer [ʃamare] *vt Litt* to bedeck, to adorn

chambard [ʃɑ̃bar] *nm F* (**a**) (*désordre*) disorder, shambles; (*bouleversement*) upset, upheaval (**b**) (*bruit*) din, racket; **faire du c.** to make *or* kick up a row; *Fig* **ça va faire du c., quand il l'apprendra!** there'll be an unholy row when he finds out *or* hell to pay when he finds out!

chambardement [ʃɑ̃bardəmɑ̃] *nm F* upset, upheaval; **un grand c. d'idées** a great shake-up of ideas

chambarder [ʃɑ̃barde] *vt F* (*mettre en désordre*) (*maison etc*) to turn upside down, to ransack; (*révolutionner*) (*un ordre établi, la société*) to turn upside down; **tout c.** to turn everything upside down; **c. les plans de qn** to upset sb's applecart

chambellan [ʃɑ̃bɛlɑ̃] *nm* chamberlain

chambouler [ʃɑ̃bule] *vt F* (*projets, maison etc*) to turn upside down; **il a fallu c. toutes nos vacances à cause de lui** he completely messed up our holiday plans; **tout est chamboulé** everything's all topsy-turvy *or* upside down

chambranle [ʃɑ̃brɑ̃l] *nm* (*d'une porte, d'une fenêtre*) frame; (*d'une cheminée*) mantelpiece

chambre [ʃɑ̃br] *nf* **(a)** (*pièce*) bedroom; (*d'un hôtel etc*) room; **c. à coucher** (*pièce*) bedroom; (*mobilier*) bedroom furniture; **c. d'amis** spare (bed)room, guest room; **c. d'enfants** children's room; (*pour bébé*) nursery; **c. meublée** furnished room; *Br* bed-sit(ter); **c. de bonne** maid's room; (*petit appartement*) attic room; **c. pour deux personnes** *ou* **double** double room; **c. à deux lits** room with twin beds, twin-bedded room; **c. pour une personne** *ou* **à un lit, c. individuelle** single room; **c. à lits jumeaux** twin(-bedded) room; **chambres attenantes** adjoining rooms; **chambres communicantes** connecting rooms; **c. avec petit-déjeuner** (*à la française*) continental plan; (*à l'anglaise*) Bermuda Plan; **vous auriez une c. (de) libre?** do you have any vacancies?; **faire c. à part** to sleep in separate rooms; **faire sa c.** to clean (out) *or* tidy (up) one's room; **garder la c.** to keep to one's room; **travailler en c.** to work at home; **ouvrier en c.** homeworker; **sportif/stratège en c.** armchair sportsman/strategist; **musique de c.** chamber music

(b) *Admin, Jur* chamber, house, division of a court of justice

(c) *Pol* **la C.** the House; **siéger à la C.** to sit in the House

(d) *Physiol* (*de l'œil*) chamber

(e) *Tech* (*d'un fusil, d'une serrure etc*) chamber; **pneu sans c.** tubeless tyre

▶ **chambre**: *Jur* **c. d'accusation** Court of criminal appeal; **c. d'agriculture** = farmers' association; **c. à air** (*d'un pneu*) inner tube; *Aut* **c. d'air** air *or* plenum chamber; *Aut* **c. d'alimentation** feed chamber; **c. ardente** ≈ Star Chamber; **C. basse** Lower House, Lower Chamber; **c. à bulles** *Phys* bubble chamber; *Aut* **c. de carburation** mixing chamber; *Naut* **c. des cartes** charthouse, chart room; **c. de chauffe** boiler room; *Naut* stokehold; **c. claire** camera lucida; *MecE* **c. de combustion** *ou* **d'explosion** combustion chamber; **C. de commerce (internationale)** (International) Chamber of Commerce; *Fin* **c. de compensation** clearing house; *Jur* **c. correctionnelle** District Court; **c. des députés** Chamber of Deputies; **c. d'écho** echo chamber; **c. forte** safety vault, strong room; **c. frigorifique** *ou* **froide** cold (storage) room, cold store; **c. à gaz** gas chamber; **C. haute** Upper House, Upper Chamber; **c. d'hôte** bed and breakfast; **c. d'ionisation** *Nucl* ionization chamber; **c. des machines** engine room; *Aut* **c. de mélange** mixing chamber; **c. des métiers** = guild chamber; **c. noire** *Phot* darkroom; *TV, Cin* loading room; *Jur* **c. des requêtes** appeal court; *Aut* **c. de résonance** resonating chamber; *Aut* **c. de turbulence** swirl chamber, turbulence combustion chamber; **c. de vapeur** steam room

chambrée [ʃɑ̃bre] *nf* **(a)** (*occupants d'une chambre*) room(ful) **(b)** *Mil* barrackroom

chambrer [ʃɑ̃bre] *vt* **(a) c. un vin** to bring wine to room temperature; **chambré** at room temperature **(b)** *F* **c. qn** to pull sb's leg **(c)** *Vieilli* **c. qn** to confine sb, to lock sb up, to keep sb locked up

chambrette [ʃɑ̃brɛt] *nf* little (bed)room

chambrière [ʃɑ̃brijɛr] *nf* **(a)** *Arch* chambermaid **(b)** (*fouet*) long whip, lunging whip

chameau, -eaux [ʃamo] **1** *nm Zool* camel; **en** *ou* **à dos de c.** on camel (back); **quel c.!** (*d'un homme*) what a bastard!; (*d'une femme*) what a cow *or* bitch! **2** *adj F* **ce qu'il/elle est c.!** what a bastard he is/bitch she is!; **ce qu'il peut être c. avec elle!** he can be such a bastard to her!

chamelier [ʃaməlje] *nm* camel-driver, cameleer

chamelle [ʃamɛl] *nf* she-camel

chamois [ʃamwa] **1** *nm* **(a)** *Zool* chamois; **(peau de) c.** chamois leather, shammy (leather) **(b)** *Sp* **c. d'or/d'argent/de bronze** = gold/silver/bronze skiing proficiency medal **2** *adj inv* buff

champ [ʃɑ̃] *nm* **(a)** *Agr* field; **c. de blé** field of wheat, wheatfield; **fleur des champs** wild flower; **courir les champs** to wander about the country; **aux champs** in the fields; **prendre** *ou* **couper à travers champs** to go *or* cut across country; **prendre la clef des champs** to run off, to decamp; **en plein(s) champ(s)** in the open (fields); **à tout bout de c.** repeatedly, at every possible opportunity; *Fig* **laisser le c. libre à qn** to leave the field free for sb, to give sb a free hand; **son assistante a le c. libre** his assistant has a free hand *or* rein; **donner le c. libre à qch** to give free rein to sth; *Fig* **le c. est libre** the coast's clear

(b) (*espace*) **prendre du c.** to give oneself (plenty of) room **(pour sauter** to jump); **donnez-moi du c.** give me (some) elbow room

(c) *Fig* (*domaine*) field; **ses lectures embrassent un c. très étendu** his reading covers a very wide field *or* a very wide range of subjects; **élargir le c. de son activité** to extend the scope *or* range of one's activities; **le c. de la connaissance** the field of (human) knowledge

(d) *Cin etc* shot, picture; *Opt* (*d'un télescope etc*) field; **c. optique** *ou* **visuel** *ou* **de vision** field of view *or* of vision; *Phot* **profondeur de c.** depth of focus; **hors c.** off camera; **en dehors du c.** out of shot *or* vision; **être dans le c.** to be in shot; **récit hors c.** voice over

(e) *Él, Électron, Rad* field

(f) *Ordinat* field; **c. calculé** calculated field; **c. de texte** text field; **c. mémo** memo field; **c. numérique** numeric field

(g) *Beaux-Arts* (*d'un tableau*) field, ground; *Hér* (*d'armoiries*) field

(h) *Chir* **c. opératoire** operative field

▶ **champ**: **c. d'aviation** airfield; *Mil* **c. de bataille** battlefield; *Hist* **c. clos** lists; **c. de courses** racecourse, *Am* racetrack; **c. de foire** fairground; **c. de glace** icefield; *Mil* **c. d'honneur** battlefield; **mort** *ou* **tombé au c. d'honneur** killed in action; *Phys* **c. magnétique** magnetic field; **c. de manœuvres** drill *or* exercise *or* parade ground; **c. de mines** minefield; **c. de neige** snowfield; *Ling* **c. sémantique** semantic field; **c. de tir** firing *or* shooting *or* rifle range; *Mil* practice ground; (*d'un fusil*) field of fire

Champagne [ʃɑ̃paɲ] **1** *nf* **(a)** (*région*) Champagne; **C. humide** wet Champagne; **C. pouilleuse** dry Champagne **(b)** (*eau-de-vie*) **fine c.** liqueur brandy **2** *nm* **(vin de) C.** champagne

champagnisation [ʃɑ̃paɲizasjɔ̃] *nf* champagnization

champagniser [ʃɑ̃paɲize] *vt* (*vin*) to champagnize

champenois, -oise [ʃɑ̃pənwa, -waz] **1** *adj* **(a)** (*de la région*) of Champagne **(b) méthode champenoise** (natural) champagnization method, champagne method **2** *n* **C.** (*natif*) native of Champagne; (*habitant*) inhabitant of Champagne

champêtre [ʃɑ̃pɛtr] *adj* rustic, rural; **vie c.** country life; *Admin* **garde c.** country *or* village policeman

champignon [ʃɑ̃piɲɔ̃] *nm* **(a)** *Bot* **c. (comestible)** mushroom; **c. vénéneux** poisonous mushroom, toadstool; *Fig* **pousser comme un c.** to (spring up like a) mushroom; *Fig* **ville c.** mushroom *or* boom town **(b)** [①A13,8] *Méd* fungus, fungoid growth **(c)** (*de modiste*) hatstand **(d)** *Aut F* accelerator (pedal); **appuyer sur le c.** to put one's foot down, *Am* to step on the gas

▶ **champignon**: **c. atomique** mushroom cloud; **c. de couche** button mushroom; **c. hallucinogène** hallucinogenic mushroom, *F* magic mushroom; *Culin* **c. noir** dried mushroom; **c. de Paris** button mushroom

champignonnière [ʃɑ̃piɲɔnjɛr] *nf* mushroom bed

champignonniste [ʃɑ̃piɲɔnist] *n* mushroom grower

champion, -ionne [ʃɑ̃pjɔ̃, -jɔn] **1** *n* **(a)** *Sp etc* champion; **le c. du monde d'escrime** the world fencing champion; **un c. de ski** a ski champion; **une championne de gym** a champion gymnast; *F* **c'est un c. du bricolage** he's a first-class handyman; **je suis vraiment le c. de la gaffe** I'm a great one for putting my foot in it

(b) (*d'une cause etc*) champion, defender; **se poser en** *ou* **se faire le c. de la protection des animaux** to champion the protection of animals

2 *adj* **(a)** *Sp* **l'équipe championne du monde** the world champions

(b) *F* great, *Br Dial* champion; **c'est c.!** it's first-rate!; **elle est championne, ta copine!** your girlfriend is terrific!; **pour les gaffes, il est c.!** he's a great one for putting his foot in it!

championnat [ʃɑ̃pjɔna] *nm* championship; **c. du monde de course à pied** world running championship

chançard, -arde [ʃɑ̃sar, -ard] *F* **1** *adj* (*personne*) lucky **2** *n* lucky person; **quel c.!** (he's a) lucky devil!

chance [ʃɑ̃s] *nf* **(a)** (*possibilité*) chance, likelihood; **vous avez toutes les chances d'être accusé, il y a toutes les chances (pour) que vous soyez accusé** there is every chance *or* likelihood that you will be accused; **il a compris qu'il fallait mettre toutes les chances de son côté** he realised he had to leave nothing to chance; **il a des chances d'être choisi** he stands a good chance of being chosen; **il a peu de chances de réussir** *ou* **de succès** he has little chance of succeeding, he's very unlikely to succeed; **elles ont des chances égales d'être nommées** they have an even chance of being appointed; **donner une** *ou* **sa c. à qn/qch** to give sb/sth a chance; **elle a une c. sur deux de gagner** she has a fifty-fifty chance of winning; **il y a une c. sur cent (pour) qu'elle le voie** there's a chance in a hundred that she'll see him; **il n'a aucune c. (de réussir)** he doesn't stand a chance *or* he has no chance (of succeeding); **calculer** *ou* **évaluer ses chances de succès** to work out one's chances of success; *F* **il y a une c.** *ou* **des chances** it's just possible; **il y a très peu de**

chances qu'elle puisse le faire à temps there's very little chance that she'll be able to do it on time; **il y a de grandes** *ou* **fortes chances pour qu'on le lui propose** there's every chance that he will be offered it

(**b**) (*sort*) (good) luck, fortune; **la c. lui sourit** fortune smiles on him; **tenter sa c.** to try one's luck, to chance it; **la c. peut tourner à tout moment** our/your/*etc* luck could change at any time; **souhaiter bonne c. à qn** to wish sb luck; **bonne c.!** good luck!; **quelle c.!** what a bit *or* stroke of luck!; **avec un peu de c., on pourra le faire** with a bit of luck, we'll be able to do it; **elle a eu la c. de le rencontrer de son vivant** she was lucky enough to meet him when he was still alive; **avoir de la c.** to be lucky *or* fortunate; **elle n'a pas eu de c.** she was unlucky; **il y a vraiment des gens qui n'ont pas de c.** some people really don't have any luck, *F* some people really get all the bad breaks; **porter c. à qn** to bring sb luck; **jour de c.** lucky day; **c'est bien ma c.!** just my luck!; **pas de c.!** hard luck!; **par c.** luckily, fortunately, by a stroke of luck; **la c. est avec nous** our luck's in

chancelant [ʃɑ̃slɑ̃] *adj* unsteady, wavering, shaky; (*courage, détermination*) wavering; (*mémoire*) shaky; **pas chancelants** staggering *or* tottering *or* unsteady footsteps; **une autorité chancelante** shaky *or* wavering authority; **le pouvoir est c.** the government is tottering *or* is on the brink of collapse; **santé chancelante** (*d'un vieillard etc*) delicate *or* poor health

chanceler [ʃɑ̃sle] *vi* (**je chancelle, n. chancelons**; **je chancellerai**) (*action*) to stagger, to totter; (*état*) to be unsteady (on one's legs); (*d'une chose*) to wobble; **avancer/reculer/entrer/sortir en chancelant** to stagger *or* totter forward/back/in/out; **l'uppercut le fit c.** the uppercut sent him reeling; **le régime chancelle** the government is tottering; **c. dans sa résolution** to waver *or* falter in one's resolution

chancelier [ʃɑ̃səlje] *nm* chancellor; *Admin* **c. de l'université** chancellor of the university; **Grand C.** (*en Grande-Bretagne*) Lord Chancellor; **c. de l'Échiquier** chancellor of the Exchequer

chancelière [ʃɑ̃səljɛr] *nf* (*pour les pieds*) footmuff

chancellerie [ʃɑ̃sɛlri] *nf Hist* (*d'une ambassade*) chancery

chanceux, -euse [ʃɑ̃sø, -øz] *adj* (*personne*) lucky, fortunate; **vous voilà bien c.!** you're lucky!, you're in luck!; *Can* **c.!** (you) lucky devil!

chanci [ʃɑ̃si] *adj Vieilli* mouldy, *US* moldy

chancre [ʃɑ̃kr] *nm Bot, Méd, Vét, Fig* canker; *Méd* **c. syphilitique** chancre; **c. mou** soft chancre; *Arg* **manger comme un c.** to eat like a horse, to make a pig of oneself

chandail [ʃɑ̃daj] *nm* sweater, jumper

Chandeleur (la) [laʃɑ̃dlœr] *nf Rel* Candlemas

chandelier [ʃɑ̃dəlje] *nm* (*à une branche*) candlestick; (*à plusieurs branches*) candelabra

chandelle [ʃɑ̃dɛl] *nf* (**a**) (*bougie en cire*) candle; (*de suif*) (tallow) candle; **s'éclairer à la c.** to use candlelight; **économies de bouts de c.** cheeseparing; **faire des économies de bouts de c.** to scrimp and save; **travailler/dîner à la c.** to work/dine by candlelight; **un dîner aux chandelles** a candlelit dinner; *Fig* **brûler la c. par les deux bouts** to burn the candle at both ends; (*dépenser trop d'argent*) to be extravagant (with money); *Fig* **le jeu n'en vaut pas la c.** the game is not worth the candle; *Fig* **tenir la c.** to play gooseberry, *Am* to feel like a fifth wheel; *Fig* **en voir trente-six chandelles** to see stars; *Fig* **je vous dois une fière c.** I owe you more than I can repay; **lancer qch en c.** to throw sth straight up in the air

(**b**) *F* (*de morve*) (*au bout du nez*) snot

(**c**) *Tennis* lob; *Fb* high ball; *Rugby* garryowen, up and under; *Gym* shoulder stand; **faire une c.** *Rugby* to do an up and under; *Tennis* to lob the ball; *Gym* **faire la c.** to do a shoulder stand

(**d**) *Av* (**montée en**) **c.** vertical climb; **monter en c.** (*d'un avion*) to climb vertically

(**e**) *Aut* chassis stand

chanfrein[1] [ʃɑ̃frɛ̃] *nm* (*de cheval*) nose, forehead

chanfrein[2] *nm Archit* chamfered edge, chamfer, bevelled edge

chanfreiner [ʃɑ̃frene] *vt MecE* to chamfer

change [ʃɑ̃ʒ] *nm* (**a**) *Fin* exchange; **le c. est avantageux** the exchange rate is good; **au c. du jour** at the current rate of exchange; *Fig* **gagner** *ou* **ne pas perdre au c.** to gain on *or* by the exchange, to lose nothing on the deal; *Fig* **je n'y perdais pas au c.** I came out (of it) ahead, I didn't lose by it; **lettre de c.** bill of exchange; **bureau de c.** bureau de change; **opérations de c.** (foreign) exchange transactions; **cours du c.** exchange rate, rate of exchange; **marché des changes** foreign exchange; **agent de c.** stockbroker; **contrôle des changes** exchange control

(**b**) (*chasse*) **donner le c. aux chiens** to put hounds on the wrong scent; *Fig* **donner le c. à qn** to put sb on a false scent *or* trail

(**c**) (*couche-culotte*) **c.** (**complet**) disposable nappy *or Am* diaper

changeable [ʃɑ̃ʒabl] *adj* changeable

changeant [ʃɑ̃ʒɑ̃] *adj* changeable, variable; **caractère c.** changeable *or* fickle disposition; **d'humeur changeante** moody; **temps c.** unsettled weather; **soie changeante** shot silk

changement [ʃɑ̃ʒmɑ̃] *nm* (**a**) (*d'air, de résidence, de condition etc*) change; *Scol* **c.** (**de section, de classe**) transfer; **il va y avoir du c.** there are going to be some changes, things are going to change; **ça va te faire un drôle de c. d'avoir un enfant** things will be very different for you when you've got a child; **il vous faudrait un c. d'air** *ou* **d'occupation** you need a change (of scenery); *Th* **c. de décor** scene shift *or* change; *Fig* **un c. de décor peut lui faire du bien** a change of scene *or* scenery may do him good; **il n'y a pas de c.** (*dans son état*) there's (been) no change; **la situation est restée longtemps sans c.** the situation stayed the same *or* remained unchanged for a long time; **son c. est radical, ce n'est plus le même!** he's changed completely, he isn't the same person any more!; **c. de programme** *TV, Cin* change in the (advertised) schedule; *Fig* (*de projets*) change of plan; **c. de programme, on ne va plus chez Paul** there's been a change of plan, we're not going to Paul's any more; **c. de prix** price change; *Mktg* **c. de marque** brand switching; **'c. de propriétaire'** 'under new ownership'; **c. de direction** under new management; **c. de régime** change of government; **c. climatique** *ou* **du climat** climate change, change in the climate; **c. de vent** shift of wind; *Rail* **il y a un c. à Valence** you have to change at Valence; **le voyage est sans c. jusqu'à Paris** the train *etc* goes straight through to Paris

(**b**) *Typ* **c. de page** page break; **c. de page obligatoire** hard page break; **c. conditionnel de page** soft page break; **c. de ligne facultatif** soft return; *Ordinat* **c. de ligne** line feed

▶ **changement**: **c. de focale** (*d'une caméra*) zooming; *Aut* **c. de rapports** gear shifting; **c. de vitesse** (*action*) change of gear, (manual) gear change; (*levier*) gear lever; *Th* **c. à vue** transformation scene

changer [ʃɑ̃ʒe] (**je changeai(s), n. changeons**) **1** *vt* (**a**) (*remplacer*), *Fin* to change, to exchange; **c. qch contre qch** to change *or* exchange sth for sth; **elle changerait bien sa place contre** *ou* **pour la tienne** (*situation professionnelle, familiale etc*) she'd happily swap places with you; **il doit c. sa voiture** he has to change his car, he has to get a new car; **c. les draps** to change the sheets; *Th* **c. le décor** to shift *or* change the scenery; **c.** (**la couche d'**)**un bébé** to change a baby('s nappy, *Am* diaper); **c. un malade** to put clean clothes on a sick person; **c. un billet de banque** to change a (bank)note; **c. des dollars contre des francs** to change dollars into francs; **c. de l'argent** to change money; **c. un métal en or** to turn *or* change a metal into gold; **la grenouille fut changée en prince** the frog was turned *or* changed into a prince

(**b**) (*modifier*) to change, to alter; (*divertir*) to be a change for; **ils partent vivre en Écosse, ça va les c.!** they're going to live in Scotland, that will be a change for them!; **cela te changera agréablement** *ou* **en bien** that will make a nice change for you; **une promenade me changera les idées** a walk will take my mind off things; **ça nous change du cinéma du coin** that makes a change from the local cinema; **c. sa façon de vivre** to change one's way of life; **ça ne change rien à rien** that doesn't change *or* alter anything, it makes absolutely no difference; **tu n'y changeras rien** there's nothing you can do about it; **elle ne changera pas une virgule au texte** she won't change *or* alter as much as a comma of the text; **cela ne change pas grand-chose** *ou* **rien au fait que...** that doesn't change *or* alter the fact that...; **mais cela ne change rien** *ou* **pas grand-chose à l'affaire** that makes no difference; **cette robe vous change** that dress makes you look different *or* changes you; **cette expérience l'a beaucoup changée** the experience has changed her a lot; **tu ne le changeras pas!** he'll never change!; *F* **ça vous change un homme!** it changes a man!; **voilà qui change les choses du tout au tout** that makes all the difference; **mais cela change tout!** that changes everything!; **c. un livre de place** to move a book; **c. les meubles de place** to change *or* move the furniture around; **c. un fonctionnaire de poste** to transfer a civil servant; **c. l'ordre des mots** to change the word order

2 *vi* (**a**) (*se modifier*) to (undergo a) change, to alter; **cette région a beaucoup changé** this region has changed a lot; **ça**

n'a pas changé, rien n'a changé nothing has changed; **le temps va c.** the weather's going to change; **il a changé en mal** *ou* **en pire/en bien** *ou* **en mieux** he's changed for the worse/the better; *Iron* **pour c.** (just) for a change; **et pour c., il était de mauvaise humeur** and just for a change, he was in a bad mood; **tu n'as pas changé** you haven't changed (a bit); *Rail etc* **où dois-je c.?** where do I change?; **je dois c. à Bordeaux** I have to change at Bordeaux; **ça ne pourra pas toujours durer comme ça, il faudra que ça change!** it can't go on like this, things will have to change

(b) **c. de** to change; **c. de position** to change position; **c. de secrétaire/de train/de travail** to change secretaries/trains/jobs; **c. de gouvernement** to have a change of government, to have a new government; **c. de main** to change hands, to use the other hand; *Fig* **c. de mains** to change hands; **c. de place avec qn** to change seats with sb; **c. d'amis** to change one's friends; **c. de vie** to change one's way of life; **c. de maison** to move (house); **la rue a changé de nom** the name of the street has been changed, the street has changed its name; **le magasin a changé de propriétaire** the shop is under new management; **c. de genre/de coiffure** to change one's style/hairstyle; **c. de vêtements** to change (one's clothes), to get changed; *F* **ton chapeau me va mieux, on peut c.?** (*échanger*) your hat suits me better, can we swap?; **c. de disque** to put another record on, to change the record; *Fig* **change de disque!** change the record!, give it a rest!; **c. de peau** (*de serpent*) to change *or* shed *or* slough its skin; **c. d'avis/d'opinion** to change one's mind/opinion; **c. de couleur** to change colour; **elle changea de visage** her expression changed *or* altered; **c. de sujet** to change the subject; **c. de route** to take another road; *Naut* **c. de route** *ou* **de cap** to alter course; *Aut* **c. de vitesse** to change gear; **la rivière a changé de cours** the river has shifted its course; **c. de ton** to change one's tune; **je te prie de c. de ton, ne me parle pas ainsi** please don't talk to me in that tone of voice, don't take that tone of voice with me; **ça change de l'ordinaire** it makes a change

3 se changer *vpr* **(a)** (*mettre d'autres vêtements*) to change (one's clothes)

(b) se c. les idées to change one's ideas

changeur, -euse [ʃɑ̃ʒœr, -øz] **1** *n* (*personne*) money changer **2** *nm* **(a)** *Rad* **c. de fréquence** frequency changer **(b) c. de disques** record changer; **c. de monnaie** change machine

Changhai [ʃɑ̃gaj] *nm* Shanghai

chanoine [ʃanwan] *nm Rel* canon; *F* **gras comme un c.** as round as a barrel; *F* **avoir une mine de c.** to be bursting with health; **vie de c.** easy life

chanson [ʃɑ̃sɔ̃] *nf* **(a)** *Mus* song; **c. d'amour** love song; **c. populaire** popular song; **la c. française** French songs; *F* **c'est toujours la même c.!** it's always the same old story; *F* **ça, c'est une autre c.!** that's quite another story!; *F* **on connaît la c.!** I've heard that one before!; *Vieilli* **chansons (que tout cela)!** nonsense! **(b)** *Littér* song, lay, verse chronicle; **la c. de Roland** the Song of Roland

▶ **chanson**: **c. à boire** drinking song; **c. de geste** chanson de geste, epic poem; **c. de marins** sea shanty; **c. réaliste** cabaret song, music hall song

chansonnette [ʃɑ̃sɔnɛt] *nf* little song, ditty

chansonnier [ʃɑ̃sɔnje] *nm* **(a)** (*artiste*) = person who sings in cabaret or in clubs **(b)** (*recueil*) song book

chant¹ [ʃɑ̃] *nm Mus* **(a)** (*d'une personne, d'un animal etc*) singing, song; **le c. du violon/de la mer/du vent** the sound of the violin/of the sea/of the wind; **le c. des oiseaux** the song of the birds, birdsong; **c. du grillon** chirping of the cricket; *Fig* **c'était son c. du cygne** it was his swan song **(b)** (*chanson*) song; (*mélodie*) melody, air; **c. de victoire** song of victory; **c. de guerre** battle *or* war song **(c)** (*art*) singing; **leçon/maître de c.** singing lesson/master; **apprendre le c.** to take singing lessons **(d)** *Littér* song, lyric; (*d'un poème*) canto

▶ **chant**: **c. choral** choral singing; **c. du coq** crowing of the cock; **au c. du coq** at cockcrow; **c. funèbre** dirge; *Rel* **c. grégorien** Gregorian chant; **c. de Noël** Christmas carol; **c. profane** secular song; **c. sacré** hymn; **c. des sirènes** siren song

chant² *nm* edge, side; **pierres (posées) de c.** *ou* **sur c.** stones set on edge *or* edgewise

chantage [ʃɑ̃taʒ] *nm* blackmail; **c. sentimental** *ou* **affectif** emotional blackmail; **faire du c.** to blackmail; **il lui fait du c. au suicide** he's using suicide threats to blackmail her

chantant [ʃɑ̃tɑ̃] *adj* melodious, tuneful; (*vers*) musical; (*accent, voix*) lilting, sing-song; **air c.** catchy tune

chantepleure [ʃɑ̃tplœr] *nf* (*de mur*) weephole; (*de gouttière*) spout

chanter [ʃɑ̃te] **1** *vt* (*chanson etc*) to sing; **c. victoire** to exult, *F* to crow; **c. les louanges/le courage de qn** to sing sb's praises/to praise sb's courage; **poète qui chante la grandeur d'un pays** poet who sings of the greatness of a country; *Rel* **c. la messe** to sing mass; **c. Noël** to celebrate Christmas in song; *Fig* **c. toujours la même chanson** to be always harping on about the same thing; *F* **qu'est-ce que vous me chantez là?** what are you talking about?; *F* **elle le chante sur tous les tons** she's always going on about it

2 *vi* (*d'une personne, d'un oiseau, de la bouilloire*) to sing; (*du coq*) to crow; **c. à pleins poumons** to sing at the top of one's voice; **c. juste/faux** to sing in tune/out of tune; *F* **c'est comme si je chantais** I'm wasting my breath; *Fig* **faire c. qn** to blackmail sb; *F* **est-ce que cela vous chante?** do you like the idea (of it)?, does that appeal to you?; **viens, si ça te chante** come along, if you fancy the idea; **il vient quand ça lui chante** he comes when he feels like it

chanterelle¹ [ʃɑ̃trɛl] *nf* **(a)** decoy (bird) **(b)** *Mus* (*d'un violon etc*) first *or* highest string; *F* **appuyer sur la c.** to hammer a point home, to rub it in

chanterelle² *nf* (*champignon*) chanterelle

chanteur, -euse [ʃɑ̃tœr, -øz] **1** *n* singer, vocalist; **c. des rues** street singer, busker; **c. de charme** crooner; **maître c.** (*qui fait du chantage*) blackmailer; *Mus, Hist* mastersinger, meistersinger **2** *adj* **oiseau c.** songbird

chantier [ʃɑ̃tje] *nm* **(a)** (*dépôt*) yard, depot; **c. de construction** builder's yard; **c. de bois** timberyard, lumberyard; *Rail* **c. de voies de garage et de triage** shunting yard

(b) (*lieu de construction*) (building) site; (*sur la route*) roadworks; **c. de construction** building site; **c. de démolition** demolition site; **chef de c.** site foreman; **travailler au c.** *ou* **sur le c.** to work on (the) site; **'c.'** 'men at work', 'road works'; **'fin de c.'** 'road clear'; **'c. interdit au public'** 'no admittance to the public'; *Min* **c. d'exploitation** working(s); *Naut* **c. naval** *ou* **de construction navale** shipyard; **c. de l'État** naval (dock)yard; **vaisseau sur le c.** vessel on the slips

(c) *Fig* **avoir une œuvre en c.** *ou* **sur le c.** to have a piece of work in the pipeline; **il a un film en c.** he's (in the process of) making a film; **il faudra mettre ce travail en c. demain** we must get started on this tomorrow; *Fig* **quel c.!** what a mess!, what a shambles!; *Fig* **la chambre est un vrai c.** *ou* **est en c.** the bedroom is a real tip; *F* **ils ont tout laissé en c.** they left the place in a complete mess *or* shambles; **je ne peux pas vous recevoir, la maison est en c.** (*il y a des travaux*) I can't invite you over, we've got workmen in

chantilly [ʃɑ̃tiji] *nf* **(crème) c.** Chantilly cream, sweetened whipped cream

chantonnement [ʃɑ̃tɔnmɑ̃] *nm* singing softly, crooning; (*fredonnement*) humming

chantonner [ʃɑ̃tɔne] *vti* to sing softly, to croon; (*fredonner*) to hum

chantoung [ʃɑ̃tuŋ] *nm Tex* shantung

chantourner [ʃɑ̃turne] *vt* to cut (using a fretsaw/jigsaw); **scie à c.** (*manuelle*) fretsaw; (*machine*) jigsaw, scroll saw

chantre [ʃɑ̃tr] *nm* **(a)** *Litt* (*poète*) poet, bard; **le c. des opprimés** (*qui célèbre leur cause*) the champion of the oppressed; **cet écrivain s'était fait le c. de la toute nouvelle république** this writer had championed the cause of the new republic; **les chantres des bois** the woodland chorus **(b)** *Rel* cantor; **grand c.** precentor

chanvre [ʃɑ̃vr] *nm* hemp; **cordage de** *ou* **en c.** hemp(en) rope; **c. indien** Indian hemp, hashish; *F* **cravate de c.** hangman's noose

chanvrier, -ière [ʃɑ̃vrije, -jɛr] **1** *adj* (*industrie etc*) hemp **2** *n* hemp grower/worker

chaos [kao] *nm* chaos; **tout est dans un c. épouvantable** everything is in a dreadful state of confusion, everything is dreadfully chaotic, chaos reigns

chaotique [kaɔtik] *adj* chaotic, confused

chapardage [ʃapardaʒ] *nm F* pinching, pilfering

chaparder [ʃaparde] *vt F* to pinch, to pilfer

chapardeur, -euse [ʃapardœr, -øz] *F* **1** *adj* pinching, pilfering **2** *n* thief, pilferer

chape [ʃap] *nf* **(a)** (*partie couvrante*) screed; *Aut* (*d'un pneu*) tread; (*d'un pont, d'une chaussée*) coping; **ils ont coulé une c. de béton sur la terrasse** they poured a concrete screed onto the terrace; *Fig* **ce ciel gris est une vraie c. de plomb** the grey sky is just like a lead weight; **s'enfermer dans une c. de silence** to retreat behind a wall of silence **(b)** *Rel* cope **(c)** *MecE* fork joint, yoke, clevis; (*de poulie*) shell; (*de bielle*) case; **c. de cardan** cardan fork

chapeau, -eaux [ʃapo] *nm* **(a)** (*coiffure*) hat; **carton** *ou* **boîte à c.** hatbox; **ruban de c.** hatband; **porter/mettre un c.** to wear/put on a hat; **saluer qn d'un coup de c.** to raise one's hat to sb; *Can* **donner un coup de c.** (*accepter les exigences de qn*) to give in; *Fig* **un coup de c. à** hats off to; **je vous donne un coup de c.** I take my hat off to you; **ça mérite un**

coup de c., c'est parfait that deserves to be praised, it's perfect; **tirer son c. à qn** to take off one's hat to sb; **c.!** bravo!, well done!; **chapeaux bas!** hats off!; **c. bas** hat in hand; **faire passer le c.** to pass the hat round; *F* **il travaille du c.** he's got a screw loose; *Fig* **c'est vous qui portez le c. dans cette affaire** you're carrying the can here

(b) *Bot (d'un champignon)* cap, *Spéc* pileus

(c) *Culin (de vol-au-vent, de bouchée à la reine)* lid, top; **c. de lampe** lampshade

(d) *Typ, Journ* introductory paragraph, lead-in

▶ **chapeau: c. de cardinal** cardinal's hat; **c. chinois** *Mus* crescent; *Zool* limpet; **c. cloche** cloche (hat); **c. à cornes** paper hat; **c. de gendarme** paper hat; **c. haut-de-forme** top hat; **c. melon** bowler hat; **c. mou** felt hat, trilby, *Am* fedora; **c. de paille** straw hat; **c. de pluie** rain hat; *Aut* **c. de roue** hub cap; *F* **prendre un virage sur les chapeaux de roues** to take a corner at top speed; *Fig* **la soirée/notre projet a démarré sur les chapeaux de roues** the evening/our plan got off to a great *or* cracking start; **c. de soleil** sun hat; **c. tyrolien** Tyrolean hat

chapeauter [ʃapote] *vt* **(a) elle était bien chapeautée** she was wearing a lovely hat **(b)** *Typ, Journ* to head **(c)** *Fig (contrôler)* to be in charge of, to head; **elle chapeaute les trois services** she's in charge of *or* heads (up) the three departments

chapelain [ʃaplɛ̃] *nm Rel* chaplain

chapelet [ʃaplɛ] *nm (de prière)* rosary; *Fig (d'invectives, d'insultes)* stream, string; *(de péniches, d'oignons etc)* string; **dire son c.** to say the rosary; **dire une dizaine de chapelet** to say a decade (of the rosary); *F* **débiter** *ou* **dévider** *ou* **défiler son c.** to have one's say, to speak one's mind; **c. de bombes** stick of bombs

chapelier, -ière [ʃapəlje, -jɛr] **1** *adj (commerce etc)* hat(-making) **2** *n* hatter

chapelle [ʃapɛl] *nf* **(a)** *(dans école, hôpital etc)* chapel; *(d'une église)* (side) chapel; *(d'une paroisse)* chapel of ease; **c. de la (Sainte) Vierge** Lady Chapel; **c. ardente** chapel of rest **(b)** *Mus Rel* choir and/or orchestra; **maître de c.** choir master **(c)** *Rel (objets pour la célébration de la messe)* ornaments and plate **(d)** *Littér, Beaux-Arts* clique, coterie; **esprit de c.** cliquishness, cliquiness

chapellerie [ʃapɛlri] *nf* **(a)** *Com* hat trade; *Ind* hat industry **(b)** *(magasin)* hatshop

chapelure [ʃaplyr] *nf Culin* breadcrumbs

chaperon [ʃaprɔ̃] *nm* **(a)** *(personne)* chaperon(e) **(b)** *(de faucon)* hood **(c)** *Littér* **le Petit C. rouge** Little Red Riding Hood **(d)** *Constr (d'un mur)* coping

chaperonner [ʃaprɔne] *vt* **(a)** *(jeune femme)* to chaperone **(b)** *Constr (mur)* to cope

chapiteau, -eaux [ʃapito] *nm* **(a)** *Archit (d'une colonne)* capital; *(d'une armoire etc)* cornice **(b)** *(d'un cirque)* big top; *(le cirque lui-même)* circus; **avoir lieu sous c.** to be held in a marquee **(c)** *(d'un alambic, d'une fusée)* head

chapitre [ʃapitr] *nm* **(a)** *(d'un livre), Fig* chapter; *(d'un budget etc)* heading, item; **inscrire une somme au c. des recettes/dépenses** to enter a sum under revenue/expenditure; *Fig* **nous aborderons demain ce c.** we will tackle this subject *or* matter tomorrow; **elle est sévère sur le c. de la discipline** she is strict as regards *or* in the matter of discipline; **en voilà assez sur ce c.** that's enough of that, let's drop the subject; **et maintenant, au c. des faits divers ...** and now for the news in brief ... **(b)** *Rel (assemblée)* chapter; **salle du c.** chapter house; *Fig* **avoir voix** *ou* **droit au c.** to have a say in the matter

chapitrer [ʃapitre] *vt* **c. qn** *(réprimander)* to tell sb off; *(faire la morale à)* to lecture sb

chapka [ʃapka] *nf* = fur hat worn in Russia

chaplinesque [ʃaplinɛsk] *adj (comique, personnage)* Chaplinesque

chapon [ʃapɔ̃] *nm Culin* capon

chaptalisation [ʃaptalizasjɔ̃] *nf* chaptalization

chaptaliser [ʃaptalize] *vt* to chaptalize

chaque [ʃak] **1** *adj* [①**A35-6**,c; **B14**,B,1,a] each, every; **c. femme doit pouvoir travailler et élever ses enfants** every woman *or* all women should be able to work as well as bring up their children; **c. chose à sa place** everything in its place; **c. chose en son temps** all in good time; **on fera c. chose en son temps** we'll do it all in good time; **c. fois qu'il vient** whenever *or* every time he comes; **j'y pense à c. instant** I think about it all the time **2** *pron F (= chacun)* **ces livres coûtent 100 francs c.** these books cost 100 francs each

char [ʃar] *nm* **(a)** *Mil* tank; **c. léger/moyen/lourd** light/medium/heavy tank; **régiment de chars** tank regiment *or* *Am* battalion **(b)** *(agricole)* cart, wagon **(c)** *Antiq* chariot; *Litt* **le c. de l'État** the Ship of State; *F* **arrête ton c.** stop exaggerating **(d)** *Can F (voiture)* car, *Am* automobile

▶ **char: c. d'assaut** tank; **c. à bancs** (horse-drawn) charabanc; **c. à bœufs** ox cart; **c. de carnaval** float; **c. de combat** tank; **c. funèbre** hearse; **c. de la mi-carême** float; **c. romain** Roman chariot; *Sp* **c. à voile** sand yacht; **faire du c. à voile** to go sand yachting

charabia [ʃarabja] *nm F* gibberish, gobbledegook

charade [ʃarad] *nf* charade

charançon [ʃarɑ̃sɔ̃] *nm (insecte)* weevil

charançonné [ʃarɑ̃sɔne] *adj* weevil(l)ed, weevil(l)y

charbon [ʃarbɔ̃] *nm* **(a)** *(combustible)* coal; *(poussière)* coal dust; **c. (de bois)** charcoal; **grillades au c. de bois** barbecued meat; **poisson grillé sur des charbons** barbecued fish; **marchand de c.** coal merchant, coalman; **soute à c.** coal bunker; **chauffage au c.** coal-fired heating; *Fig F* **aller au c.** *(au travail)* to go to work; *(s'y mettre)* to muck in, to get stuck in; **avoir un c. dans l'œil** to have a bit of grit in one's eye; *Fig* **être** *ou* **marcher sur des charbons ardents** to be on tenterhooks, to be like a cat on a hot tin roof

(b) *Beaux-Arts* charcoal; **dessin au c.** charcoal drawing

(c) *Ch* carbon; **balai de c.** carbon brush

(d) *Méd* charcoal; **c. actif** *ou* **activé** active *or* activated charcoal

(e) *(maladie) Agr, Bot* smut, black rust; *Méd, Vét* anthrax

charbonnage [ʃarbɔnaʒ] *nm* **(a)** *(exploitation)* coal mining **(b) charbonnages** collieries; **les Charbonnages de France** the (French) National Coal Board

charbonner [ʃarbɔne] **1** *vt* **(a)** *(noircir)* to (blacken with) charcoal **(b)** *Beaux-Arts (qch)* to make a charcoal sketch of **2 se charbonner** *vpr* **se c. le visage** to blacken one's face

charbonneux, -euse [ʃarbɔnø, -øz] *adj* **(a)** *(noir)* coal-black; *(yeux)* sooty; **dépôt c.** sooty deposit, carbon deposit **(b)** *Méd* anthracic, carbuncular; **mouches charbonneuses** anthrax-carrying flies

charbonnier, -ière [ʃarbɔnje, -jɛr] **1** *adj (industrie etc)* coal (mining); *(commerce etc)* charcoal; **navire c.** collier, coaler **2** *n* **(a)** *Com (marchand de charbon)* coal merchant, coalman; **noir comme un c.** as black as the ace of spades; *Prov* **c. est maître dans sa maison** *ou* **chez soi** an Englishman's home is his castle; **la foi du c.** simple faith **(b)** *Naut* coaler, collier **3** *nf* **charbonnière** charcoal kiln

charcuter [ʃarkyte] *F* **1** *vt (morceau de viande)* to hack up; **c. qn** to hack sb to pieces, to butcher sb; **ce médecin est réputé pour c. ses malades** this doctor has the reputation of being a butcher; **se faire c.** to get hacked to pieces *or* butchered **2 se charcuter** *vpr* to cut oneself to ribbons; **se c. le menton en se rasant** to nick one's chin shaving

charcuterie [ʃarkytri] *nf* **(a)** *Com (magasin)* ≈ delicatessen **(b)** *Ind* pork butchery, delicatessen trade **(c)** *Culin (produits)* **assiette de c.** plate of assorted cooked meats

charcutier, -ière [ʃarkytje, -jɛr] *n* **(a)** *(commerçant, fabricant)* pork butcher **(b)** *F Péj (chirurgien)* butcher

chardon [ʃardɔ̃] *nm* **(a)** *(plante)* thistle; *Culin* **c. à la liqueur** = coloured chocolate sweet with liqueur centre **(b) chardons** *(sur des grilles etc)* (clustered) spikes

chardonneret [ʃardɔnrɛ] *nm (oiseau)* goldfinch

charentais, -aise [ʃarɑ̃tɛ, -ɛz] **1** *adj* of Charente **2** *n* **C.** *(habitant)* inhabitant of Charente; *(natif)* native of Charente **3** *nf* **charentaise** slipper

charge [ʃarʒ] *nf* **(a)** *(poids)* load, burden; *(sur bateau)* cargo, freight; *(sur camion)* cargo, load; *(du moteur, sur les roues)* load; *(action) (de navire etc)* loading; **en c.** under load; **bête de c.** beast of burden; **je ne veux pas devenir une c. pour eux** I don't want to become a burden to them; *Fig* **la c. affective des paroles de qn** the emotional content of sb's words; **être à c. à qn** to be a burden to sb

(b) *(responsabilité)* responsibility; **prendre qn/qch en c.** to take charge of sb/sth, to assume *or* take responsibility for sb/sth; **se prendre en c.** to take care of oneself, to be responsible for oneself; **cela est à votre c.** that's your responsibility; **elle a la c. de réorganiser le service** she's got the job of reorganizing the department; **enfants confiés à ma c.** children entrusted to me *or* in my charge *or* in my care; **avoir c. d'âmes** *Rel* to have a cure of souls; *(d'un père)* to have children in one's care; *Vieilli* **femme de c.** housekeeper

(c) *(fonction)* **c. de notaire** notary's office; **c. d'avoué** solicitor's practice

(d) *(obligation financière)* charge, expense; **charges incompressibles** necessary expenses; **les réparations sont à la c. du locataire** the tenant is responsible for repairs; **être à la c. de qn** to be dependent on sb, to be supported by sb; *(appel etc)* to be chargeable to sb; **prendre un client en c.** *(de taxi)* to pick up a fare; **prise en c.** *(dans un taxi)* minimum fare; *(par la Sécurité Sociale)* agreement to pay medical expenses; **être pris en c. à cent pour cent par la Sécurité Sociale** to have one's medical expenses fully paid for by Social Security; **charges de famille** dependents; **deux enfants à c.** two dependent children; **charges locatives** maintenance charges; (*de locaux*) rental charges, rental expenses; (*de matériel*) lease charges; **loyer plus les charges** rent plus service charge (and maintenance costs)

(e) *Tech* load; *Av* **facteur de c.** load factor

(f) *Él* (*d'une batterie*) charge; (*d'un circuit etc*) load; **conducteur en c.** live conductor; **mettre une batterie en c.** to put a battery on charge

(g) *Phys* (*d'une particule électrique*) charge

(h) à c. de on (the) condition that, provided that; **j'accepte, mais à c. de revanche** I accept, but only on condition that you let me return the favour some time; **à c. pour vous de payer** on condition *or* provided that you pay

(i) *Mil* charge; **sonner la c.** to sound the charge; **c. de cavalerie** cavalry charge; *Fig* **revenir** *ou* **retourner à la c.** to come back *or* return to the attack

(j) *Jur* charge, indictment; **les charges contre lui sont très lourdes** the charges against him are very heavy; **quelles sont les charges contre elle?** what's she being charged with?; **témoin à c.** witness for the prosecution

(k) (*d'une histoire*) exaggeration; *Th* (*d'un rôle*) overacting; *Beaux-Arts Litt* (*d'un portrait, d'un personnage*) caricature; **jouer un rôle en c.** to overact a part

▶ **charge: c. admissible** safe load; *Compta* **c. constatée d'avance** prepayment; *Mil* **c. creuse** hollow(-shaped) charge; **c. d'explosif** (*de fusil etc*) explosive charge; *Compta* **c. fictive** fictitious cost; *Tech* **c. maximum (de rupture)** ultimate *or* breaking load; *Compta* **c. opérationnelle** overhead, operating cost; **c. à payer** sum payable; *Aut* **c. remorquable** towing weight, payload; *Tech* **c. de rupture** breaking *or* shearing stress; **c. de sécurité** safe load; **c. utile** carrying capacity; (*d'un véhicule*) capacity, payload; (*d'un missile*) payload; **c. à vide** empty weight; *Compta* **charges à payer** accrued expenses, accruals; *Compta* **charges courantes** current expenses; *Compta* **charges d'exploitation** operating costs, running costs; *Compta* **charges de structure** fixed costs; *Compta* **charges financières** interest and other finance charges; **charges fixes** fixed costs; *Compta* **charges incorporables** product expenses *or* charges; **charges nettes** net costs; *Compta* **charges patronales** employer contributions; **charges publiques** public expenditure; **charges sociales** national insurance contributions, *Am* social security charges (*paid by the employer*), welfare charges; *Compta* **charges sociales patronales** employer contributions; *Compta* **charges sociales salariales** employee contributions; **charges variables** variable costs

chargé, -ée [ʃarʒe] **1** *adj* **(a)** (*camion, navire etc*) loaded, laden; (*revolver, appareil-photo*) loaded; **bateau lourdement c.** heavily laden ship; **j'étais c. comme un bourricot** *ou* **un baudet** *ou* **un mulet!** I was loaded *or* weighed down, I felt like a packhorse!; *Fig* **avoir la conscience chargée** to have a guilty conscience; **avoir un passé c.** to have a past; **journée chargée** full *or* busy day; **nous avons un programme c.** we have a full programme; **regard c. de reconnaissance** look full of gratitude; **regard c. de sens** meaningful look; *Litt* **mourir c. d'ans** to die at a ripe old age; **personnage c. d'honneur** a person laden with honours; **le style est très c.** the style is very ornate; **temps c.** overcast weather; **avoir la langue chargée** to have a coated *or* furred tongue; **avoir l'estomac c.** to have an overloaded stomach; *Mil* **obus c.** live shell; *Phys* **particule chargée négativement/positivement** negatively/positively-charged particle

(b) lettre chargée = registered letter

(c) (*responsable*) responsible; **être c. de famille** to have family responsibilities; **être c. d'une mission** to be entrusted with a mission; **il est c. d'enquêter sur elle** he has been assigned to investigate her

2 *nm* **c. d'affaires** chargé d'affaires; *Mktg* **c. d'étude** marketing researcher; **c. d'études** project manager; **c. de mission** official representative; **c. de clientèle** account manager; **c. de compte** account manager; **c. de relations clients** customer relations manager

3 *n Univ* **c. de cours** = part-time university lecturer; *Can* lecturer

chargeable [ʃarʒabl] *adj Ordinat* loadable; **c. en résident** memory-loadable

chargement [ʃarʒəmɑ̃] *nm* **(a)** (*action*) (*d'un camion, d'un navire etc*) loading; *Naut* (*de marchandises*) shipping; **machine à laver à c. frontal** front-loading washing machine, *F* front-loader; *Rail* **voie de c.** goods siding **(b)** *Mil* (*d'une cartouche, d'une bombe, d'un obus etc, Phot d'un appareil-photo*) loading; *Él* (*d'une batterie*) charging; **appareil-photo à c. automatique** self-loading camera **(c)** (*marchandise*) load, cargo, freight; **le c. est arrivé à bon port** the cargo was brought safely to port *or* arrived intact; **c. bien arrimé** well-stowed cargo; **c. partiel** part load **(d)** (*d'une lettre*) registering

charger [ʃarʒe] **1** *vt* **(je chargeai(s), n. chargeons) (a)** (*camion, navire etc*) to load; **c. des marchandises** to load *or Naut* to ship goods; **navire chargé de blé** ship laden with wheat; **on charge les bagages dans la soute de l'avion** the luggage is loaded into the aeroplane's hold; *F* **c. un client** (*d'un chauffeur de taxi*) to pick up a fare

(b) (*alourdir, peser sur*) to overload, to weigh (down); **la voiture est trop chargée** the car is overloaded; **c. une étagère de livres** to overload a shelf with books; **chargé de paquets** weighed down with parcels

(c) (*remplir*) to fill; **c. son récit d'anecdotes** to pepper one's story with anecdotes; **table chargée de mets** table laden with food; **pièce chargée de décorations de mauvais goût** room cluttered with tasteless decorations; **mur chargé de tableaux** wall covered in paintings; **mets qui chargent l'estomac** food that lies heavy on the stomach; **le malade ne doit pas c. son estomac** the patient should not overload his stomach; **c. sa mémoire de dates inutiles** to clutter up one's mind with useless dates; **l'air est chargé du parfum des fleurs** the air is heavy with the scent of flowers

(d) (*fusil, appareil-photo etc*) to load; (*pipe*) to fill; *Él* (*batterie*) to charge; *Ordinat* to load (up)

(e) c. qn de faire qch to make sb responsible for doing sth, to give sb the responsibility for doing sth; **le patron l'a chargé d'écrire le rapport** the boss made him responsible for writing the report; **je te charge de lui transmettre l'information** I'm entrusting you to give him the information; **j'étais chargé de faire tout le courrier du service** I was in charge of *or* responsible for the department's mail; **être chargé de l'entretien** to be in charge of *or* responsible for maintenance

(f) (*portrait*) to turn into a caricature; (*qn*) to caricature; (*histoire*) to exaggerate, to embroider; *Th* (*rôle*) to overact; **c. une description** to overdo *or* exaggerate a description, *F* to lay it on thick

(g) (*attaquer*) to charge (at)

(h) *Jur* to charge, to accuse; **c. qn d'un crime** to charge sb with a crime; **on le charge de tous les péchés** he's charged with every sin in the book

(i) c. une lettre = to send valuables by post; (*l'affranchir*) to register a letter

2 *vi* **(a)** *Ordinat* to load up

(b) *Mil* to charge

3 se charger *vpr* **(a)** (*s'alourdir*) to weigh oneself down

(b) (*s'accuser*) to blame oneself

(c) se c. de (faire) qch to take care of sth, to look after sth, to take sth on; **je me charge de lui en parler** I'll talk to him about it; **je me charge des enfants de Marie quand elle travaille** I take care of *or* look after Marie's children when she's working; **je m'en chargerai** I'll see to it, I'll take care of it; **ne t'en fais pas, je me charge de lui** don't worry, I'll take care of him

(d) se c. automatiquement *Phot* to load automatically; *Ordinat* to load automatically, to autoload

chargeur [ʃarʒœr] *nm* **(a)** (*d'arme*) magazine, cartridge clip; *Phot* cartridge; *Él* (battery) charger; *Ordinat* loader; **c. automatique** self loader; **c. feuille à feuille** (*d'une imprimante*) single sheet feed **(b)** (*personne*) loader; (*expéditeur*) shipper

chargeuse [ʃarʒøz] *nf Tech* loader

charia [ʃarja] *nf Rel* sharia

chariot [ʃarjo] *nm* (*petite charrette*) wag(g)on, cart; (*caddie de supermarché*) trolley; (*pour diapositives*) cartridge; (*pour la manutention*) truck, trolley; (*d'hôpital*) trolley, *Am* gurney; *Cin* dolly; (*d'une machine à écrire*) carriage; **c. d'enfant** baby walker; **c. à bagages** luggage trolley; **le c. des desserts/à liqueurs** the dessert/drinks trolley; *Av* **c. d'atterrissage** landing gear, undercarriage; **c. à bras** handcart, barrow; **c. élévateur à fourche** fork-lift truck; *TV, Cin* **c. omnidirectionnel** crab(bing) dolly

▶ **chariot:** *Astron* **le Grand C.** the Great Bear, *Am* the (Big) Dipper; **le petit C.** the Little Bear, the Little Dipper

chariot-crabe, *pl* **chariots-crabes** *nm TV, Cin* crab(bing) dolly

charismatique [karismatik] *adj* charismatic

charisme [karism] *nm* charisma; **avoir du c.** to have charisma

charitable [ʃaritabl] *adj* charitable **(envers** to, towards); **œuvre** *ou* **fondation c.** charity; **vous êtes bien c.** it's very kind of you; **conseil c.** a friendly piece of advice

charitablement [ʃaritabləmɑ̃] *adv* charitably

charité [ʃarite] *nf* (**a**) (*amour*) charity, love; **faire qch par c.** to do sth out of charity; *Prov* **c. bien ordonnée commence par soi-même** charity begins at home; *Hist* **dame de c.** district visitor; *Rel* **les Filles** *ou* **les Sœurs de la C.** the Sisters of Charity; **faites-moi** *ou* **ayez la c. de venir/d'écouter mon histoire** please be kind enough to come/to listen to my story

(**b**) (*don*) act of charity; **faire la c. à qn** to give money *or* a donation to sb; **je ne tiens pas à ce qu'on me fasse la c.** I don't want charity; **vivre de charités** to live on charity; **demander la c.** to ask for charity; **la c., messieurs dames** (*dans la rue*) can you spare some change, please?

charivari [ʃarivari] *nm* din, row, racket; **un c. de rires et de pas** noisy laughter and footsteps

charlatan [ʃarlatɑ̃] *nm* (**a**) (*guérisseur*) charlatan; **remède de c.** quack remedy; **tous ces psys sont des charlatans** all these shrinks are quacks (**b**) (*qui exploite la crédulité publique*) conman, swindler

charlatanerie [ʃarlatanri] *nf* charlatanry, charlatanism

charlatanesque [ʃarlatanɛsk] *adj* (*remède etc*) quack

charlatanisme [ʃarlatanism] *nm* charlatanism

charleston [ʃarlɛstɔn] *nm* (*danse*) charleston

charlot [ʃarlo] *nm* (**a**) *F* (*personne peu sérieuse*) clown (**b**) *Cin* **C.** Charlie Chaplin

charlotte [ʃarlɔt] *nf Culin* charlotte; **c. au poire/au chocolat** pear/chocolate charlotte; **moule à c.** charlotte mould

charmant [ʃarmɑ̃] *adj* (*personne, chose*) charming, delightful; **une soirée charmante** a delightful evening; **ils se sont disputés devant nous, charmante soirée!** they argued right in front of us, what a delightful *or* charming evening!; **prince c.** Prince Charming; *Fig* **attendre son prince c.** to be waiting for Prince Charming *or* Mr Right to come along; *Iron* **et voilà qu'il pleut, ah, c'est c.!** now it's raining, marvellous!

charme[1] [ʃarm] *nm* (**a**) (*attrait*) charm, attraction; **elle a beaucoup de c.** she has great charm, she's very charming; **cela lui donne un certain c.** it gives him a certain charm; **c'est ce qui en fait le c.** that's what makes it so attractive, that's what makes it so charming, that's where its charm lies; **elle n'est pas belle, mais elle a du c.** she's not beautiful, but she is attractive; **faire du c.** to turn on the charm; **elle lui fait du c.** she's turning on the charm with him; **faire son numéro de c. à qn** to use one's charms on sb; **charmes** (*d'une femme*) (physical) attractions, charms; **vivre de ses charmes** to sell one's body for a living; **cette proposition ne manque pas de c.** the suggestion is not without a certain appeal; *Iron* **je suis peu sensible aux charmes des supermarchés** the appeal of supermarkets is lost on me; **chanteur de c.** crooner

(**b**) (*magie*) charm, spell; **être/tomber sous le c.** to be/fall under the spell; **tenir ses auditeurs sous le c.** to hold one's audience spellbound; **rompre le c.** to break the spell; *Fig* **se porter comme un c.** to be in the best of health, to be as fit as a fiddle

charme[2] *nm* (*arbre*) hornbeam

charmer [ʃarme] *vt* (**a**) (*plaire à*) to charm, to delight, to enchant; **elle n'a pas eu de mal à c. son auditoire** she had no difficulty winning over her audience; **être charmé de faire qch** to be delighted to do sth; **j'ai été charmé de vous rencontrer** it's been a pleasure to meet you; **elle est charmée du cadeau** she's delighted *or* enchanted with the gift (**b**) (*serpent etc*) to charm, to bewitch

charmeur, -euse [ʃarmœr, -øz] **1** *adj* (*regard etc*) charming, appealing; **un sourire c.** a charming *or* winning smile **2** *n* charmer

▶ **charmeur**: **c. de serpents** snake charmer

charmille [ʃarmij] *nf* (**a**) (*allée*) walk (bordered by hedges) (**b**) (*tonnelle*) bower, arbour

charnel, -elle [ʃarnɛl] *adj* (*désirs etc*) carnal; **acte c., union charnelle** carnal act

charnellement [ʃarnɛlmɑ̃] *adv Litt* carnally; **aimer qn c.** to love sb carnally *or* sexually; **connaître qn c.** to have carnal knowledge of sb

charnier [ʃarnje] *nm* (open) grave; *Arch, Litt* (*ossuaire*) charnel (house)

charnière [ʃarnjɛr] *nf* (*de porte etc*) hinge; *Mil* (*de deux armées etc*) (point of) junction; *F* **nom à c.** double-barrelled name; *Fig* **à la c. de deux grandes périodes** as one great era gives/gave way to another; *Fig* **être à un moment c. de sa vie** to be at a turning point in one's life; *Fig* **un domaine(-)c. (entre deux disciplines)** an area (inter)linking two disciplines; **époque/œuvre c.** transitional period/work

charnu [ʃarny] *adj* fleshy, plump; (*fruit*) pulpy; **des lèvres charnues** fleshy *or* full lips; *Hum* **la partie charnue de son anatomie** his behind *or* posterior

charognard [ʃarɔɲar] *nm* (**a**) *Zool* carrion-eater (**b**) *Arg* (*exploiteur*) shark, vulture

charogne [ʃarɔɲ] *nf* (**a**) (*d'animal*) carrion, decaying carcass (**b**) *Arg* (*salaud, crapule*) bastard; (*femme*) bitch

charpente [ʃarpɑ̃t] *nf* (*d'un bâtiment etc*) frame(work), skeleton; (*du corps*) frame; (*d'un roman etc*) framework, skeleton, structure; **bois de c.** timber; **avoir une solide c.** (*d'une personne*) to be solidly built

charpenté [ʃarpɑ̃te] *adj* built, constructed; **homme bien** *ou* **solidement c.** well-built man; **pièce de théâtre bien charpentée** well-constructed play

charpenter [ʃarpɑ̃te] *vt* (*roman etc*) to construct; **c. un discours** to construct *or* frame a speech

charpenterie [ʃarpɑ̃tri] *nf* (**a**) (*métier*) carpentry; **faire de la c.** to do carpentry (**b**) (*atelier*) carpenter's (work)shop; (*chantier*) timberyard

charpentier [ʃarpɑ̃tje] *nm* carpenter; **c. du bord** shipwright

charpie [ʃarpi] *nf* (**a**) **viande en c.** meat cooked to shreds; **mettre qch en c.** to tear sth to pieces *or* to shreds; **elle a déchiré son livre et en a fait de la c.** she tore her book to shreds; *F* **il vous mettra en c.** he'll make mincemeat out of you (**b**) (*pour faire de pansements*) lint

charretée [ʃarte] *nf* cartload, cartful; **nous avons eu droit à des charretées d'insultes** we were treated to a heap *or* a pile of insults

charretier, -ière [ʃartje, -jɛr] **1** *nm* carter, carrier; *Fig* **parler/jurer comme un c.** to talk like a fishwife/to swear like a trooper; **langage de c.** coarse language **2** *adj* **chemin c., voie charretière** cart track

charrette [ʃarɛt] *nf* cart; **qui va faire partie de la prochaine c. (de licenciements)?** who'll be included in the next round of redundancies?; *Vieilli* **être c.** to be working to a deadline; **faire une c.** to work round the clock; *Suisse F* **c. de Paul!** blinking Paul!

▶ **charrette**: *Hist* **c. anglaise** dogcart, trap; **c. des condamnés** tumbrel

charriage [ʃarjaʒ] *nm* (**a**) (*portage*) haulage, carriage (**b**) *Géol* thrusting, overthrust

charrier [ʃarje] (*impf & pr sub* **n. charriions, v. charriiez**) **1** *vt* (**a**) (*transporter*) to cart, to carry (**b**) (*entraîner*) to carry along, to wash down; **rivière qui charrie du sable** river that carries *or* brings down sand; **nuages charriés par le vent** wind-driven clouds (**c**) *Arg* (*se moquer de*) **c. qn** to wind sb up; **se faire c. par ses amis** to get the wind-up from one's friends **2** *vi Arg* (*exagérer*) to go too far *or* over the top; **il charrie vraiment!** he's really having you on!; *F* **(il ne) faut pas c.!** come off it!

charroi [ʃarwa] *nm* cartage, haulage, carriage

charron [ʃarɔ̃] *nm* cartwright, wheelwright

charroyer [ʃarwaje] *vt* (**je charroie**; **je charroierai**) to transport in a cart, to cart

charrue [ʃary] *nf* (**a**) *Agr* plough, *US* plow; **mener la c.** to drive the plough; *F* **mettre la c. avant les bœufs** to put the cart before the horse (**b**) *Can* snowplough, *US* snowplow

charte [ʃart] *nf* (**a**) (*convention*) charter; *Br Hist* **la Grande C.** Magna Carta; *Pol, Hist* **la C. de l'Atlantique** the Atlantic Charter; **la C. des Nations Unies** the United Nations Charter (**b**) (*document ancien*) (ancient) deed, title; **l'École des chartes** = the School of Palaeography and Librarianship (in Paris)

▶ **charte:** *Journ* **c. graphique** *ou* **rédactionelle** house-style book

charter [ʃartɛr] *nm* **(avion) c.** charter, chartered aircraft; **vol c.** charter flight; **voyager en c.** to take a charter; **c. partiel** partial charter

chartérisation [ʃarterizasjɔ̃] *nf* chartering

chartisme [ʃartism] *nm Br Hist* chartism

chartiste [ʃartist] *n* (**a**) *Univ* = student of the École des chartes (**b**) *Br Hist* chartist

chartreuse [ʃartrøz] *nf* (**a**) (*couvent*) Carthusian monastery, charterhouse (**b**) (*alcool*) Chartreuse; **c. jaune/verte** yellow/green Chartreuse

chartreux, -euse [ʃartrø, -øz] *n Rel* Carthusian (monk/nun)

Charybde [karibd] *nm* Charybdis; **tomber de C. en Scylla** to fall out of the frying pan into the fire

chas [ʃa] *nm* (*d'une aiguille*) eye

chasse [ʃas] *nf* (**a**) hunting; (*avec fusil*) shooting; (*événement*) hunt/shoot; **aller à la c.** to go hunting/shooting; **la c. est ouverte/fermée** the shooting season has begun/ended; **c. fermée** close season; **vivre de sa c.** to live off one's catch; **partager la c.** to share the bag; **faire bonne c.** to have good sport, to make a good bag; *Prov* **qui va à la c. perd sa place** if you leave your place someone will take it; **la c. vient de passer** (*les chasseurs*) the hunters have just gone by; (*à courre*) the hunt has just gone by; **fusil de c.** shotgun; **chien de c.** retriever; **couteau/habit de c.** hunting knife/coat

(**b**) (*réserve*) **c. gardée** private game preserve; *Fig* **ah non, c. gardée!** private property!, hands off!; **les chasses royales** the royal hunting grounds; **louer une c.** to rent a shoot (**c**) (*poursuite*) chase; **donner la c. à qch/qn, prendre qch/qn en c.** to chase *or* pursue *or* give chase to sth/sb; **se mettre en c. pour** to go on the hunt for; **faire la c. à qch** to hunt sth down *or* out; **faire la c. aux abus** to hunt *or* track down abuse; *F* **c. au mari** husband hunting; **faire la c. au mari** to be on the lookout for a husband

(**d**) *Mil, Av* **la c.** the fighter aircraft, the fighters; **pilote de c.** fighter pilot

(**e**) **c. (d'eau)** flush; **tirer la c. (d'eau)** to flush the toilet

(**f**) **être en c.** (*chienne, chatte*) to be on heat *or* in season

(**g**) (*épaisseur de la lettre*) width; (*d'une page*) overrun

(**h**) *Aut* caster

▶ **chasse: c. à la baleine** (*activité*) whaling; (*événement*) whale hunt; **c. à courre** hunting; **c. au chevreuil** deer hunting *or* stalking; **c. au faucon** falconry; **c. au furet** ferreting; **c. au gros gibier** big game hunting; **c. à l'homme** manhunt; **une c. à l'homme a été organisée à travers le pays** a national manhunt has been launched; **c. au lapin** rabbiting; (*avec un fusil*) rabbit shooting; **c. au lévrier** coursing; **c. aux papillons** butterfly catching; **c. aux rats** rat catching; **c. au renard** (*activité*) foxhunting; (*événement*) foxhunt; *Pol* **c. aux sorcières** witch hunt; **c. aux souris** mousing; **c. sous-marine** underwater fishing; **c. au trésor** treasure hunt

châsse [ʃɑs] *nf* (**a**) *Rel* reliquary, shrine (**b**) (*des lunettes*) mounting, frame

chassé [ʃase] *nm* (*danse*) chassé

chasse-clou(s), *pl* **chasse-clous** *nm* nail punch, nail set

chassé-croisé, *pl* **chassés-croisés** *nm* (**a**) (*du personnel etc*) rearrangement, reshuffling; **c. de conseillers** reshuffling of advisers; **le c. des vacanciers sur les routes** the busy flow of holidaymakers on the roads; **un c. d'intrigues** a mass of conflicting plots; **un c. de malentendus** a confusion of misunderstandings (**b**) (*danse*) set to partners

chasse-goupille, *pl* **chasse-goupilles** *nm* pin punch

chasse-marée *nm inv* (*bateau*) coasting lugger

chasse-mouches *nm inv* fly swatter

chasse-neige *nm inv* (**a**) (*engin*) snowplough, *US* snowplow (**b**) *Ski* snowplough, *US* snowplow; **virage (en) c.** snowplough turn; **descendre une piste en c.** to snowplough down a ski slope

chasser [ʃase] **1** *vt* (**a**) to chase, to hunt; **c. le renard/la perdrix** to go foxhunting/partridge shooting

(**b**) (*qn*) to drive away, to chase out *or* away; (*employé*) to dismiss, *F* to sack; (*brouillard etc*) to dispel; **c. qn du pays** to drive sb from the country; **il fut chassé de la classe** he was expelled from the class; **si tu ne paies pas ton loyer, les propriétaires vont te c.** if you don't pay your rent, the owners will evict you; **chasse le chat de la maison!** chase the cat out (of the house)!; **se faire c. de la maison par ses parents** to get thrown out by one's parents; **je ne veux pas vous c. mais il est tard** I'm not trying to get rid of you but it's getting late; **nous avons été chassés par les moustiques** we were chased *or* driven away by mosquitoes; **c. une mouche (du revers de la main)** to brush away a fly; **le vent chassait la pluie contre les vitres** the wind was driving the rain against the window panes; **le vent va c. les nuages** the wind will blow the clouds away; **c. une mauvaise odeur** to get rid of a bad smell; *Fig* **c. qn/qch de son esprit** to dismiss sb/sth from one's mind *or* thoughts

2 *vi* (**a**) to hunt, to go hunting; (*au fusil*) to shoot, to go shooting; **c. à courre** to hunt, to go hunting; **c. au furet** to ferret; *Fig* **c. sur les terres de qn** to poach on sb's preserve *or* territory

(**b**) (*venir*) to drive; **nuages qui chassent du nord** clouds driving from the north

(**c**) *Naut* (*d'une ancre*) to drag; **navire qui chasse sur ses ancres** ship dragging her anchors

(**d**) *Aut* to skid

(**e**) *Typ* (*d'un caractère*) to drive out; (*d'un texte*) to overrun

chasseresse [ʃasrɛs] *nf Littér* huntress; **Diane c.** Diana the Huntress

chasseur, -euse [ʃasœr, -øz] **1** *n* hunter, *f* huntress; (*surtout à courre*) huntsman; **c'est un bon c.** he's a good shot **2** *nm* (**a**) (*dans un hôtel etc*) pageboy, *Am* bellboy, bellhop (**b**) *Mil, Av* fighter; *Naut* **c. de sous-marins** submarine hunter (**c**) *Mil* rifleman, light infantryman, chasseur; **les chasseurs (à pied)** the light infantry; **les chasseurs alpins** the mountain light infantry

▶ **chasseur**: **c. d'autographes** autograph hunter; **c. de primes** bounty hunter; *aussi Fig* **c. de têtes** headhunter; *Fig* **elle a été recrutée par un c. de têtes** she was headhunted; **c. d'images** keen photographer; (*professionnel*) professional photographer

chasseur-bagagiste, *pl* **chasseurs-bagagistes** *nm* luggage porter, porter

chasseur-bombardier, *pl* **chasseurs-bombardiers** *nm* fighter-bomber

chassie [ʃasi] *nf* (*dans les yeux*) matter, rheum

chassieux, -euse [ʃasjø, -øz] *adj* (*yeux*) rheumy

châssis [ʃɑsi] *nm* (**a**) (*charpente*) frame; *Beaux-Arts* stretcher; **c. de porte/fenêtre** door/window frame; **c. mobile** sash; **c. dormant** sash (frame); **c. à guillotine** sash window (**b**) (*de jardin*) (cold) frame; **culture sous c.** forcing (**c**) *Aut* chassis; *Aut* **c. treillis** box section chassis; *Aut* **c. tubulaire** box section chassis, space frame chassis; *F* **quel beau c.!** (*d'une femme*) she's got a great figure, *Vieilli* what a chassis! (**d**) *Typ* chase

chaste [ʃast] *adj* chaste, pure; **un baiser c.** a chaste kiss; *Iron* **oreilles chastes** delicate ears

chastement [ʃastəmɑ̃] *adv* chastely, innocently

chasteté [ʃastəte] *nf* chastity, purity

chasuble [ʃazybl] *nf* (**a**) **robe c.** pinafore dress, *Am* jumper (**b**) *Rel* chasuble

chat, chatte [ʃa, ʃat] **1** *n* cat, *m* tom(cat); **le C. botté** Puss in Boots; **petit c.** kitten; *F* **mon petit c., ma petite chatte** my dear, my pet, my darling; *Fig* **il n'y avait pas un c. dans la rue** there wasn't a soul in the street; **langues de c.** langues de chat, finger biscuits; *Fig* **appeler un c. un c.** to call a spade a spade; **acheter c. en poche** to buy a pig in a poke; **avoir un c. dans la gorge** to have a frog in one's throat; **faire une toilette de c.** to give oneself a cat('s) lick *or* a lick and a promise; *Prov* **il ne faut pas réveiller le c. qui dort** let sleeping dogs lie; **à bon c. bon rat** tit for tat; **c. échaudé craint l'eau froide** once bitten twice shy; **quand le c. n'est pas là, les souris dansent** when the cat's away the mice will play; **jouer au c. et à la souris avec qn** to play cat and mouse with sb; **la nuit tous les chats sont gris** all cats are grey in the dark

2 *nm* (*jeu*) tag, tig; (*celui qui cherche*) it; **jouer à c.** to play tag *or* tig; **c. perché** off-ground tag *or* tig; **c'est toi le c.!** you're it!

▶ **chat**: **c. de gouttière** alley cat; **c. à neuf queues** cat-o'-nine-tails; **c. persan** Persian (cat); **c. sauvage** wildcat; **c. siamois** Siamese (cat)

châtaigne [ʃɑtɛɲ] *nf* (**a**) (*fruit*) (sweet) chestnut (**b**) *Arg* (*coup de poing*) smack, clout; **je vais lui flanquer une c.** I'm going to clobber him; **je me suis pris une c.** (*léger choc électrique*) I got a shock

▶ **châtaigne**: **c. d'eau** water chestnut

châtaigneraie [ʃɑtɛɲrɛ] *nf* chestnut grove, chestnut plantation

châtaignier [ʃɑtɛe] *nm* (*arbre, bois*) chestnut

châtain [ʃɑtɛ̃] **1** *adj* (*féminin rare*) (chestnut-)brown; **une femme c.** *ou* **aux cheveux châtains** a brunette; **cheveux c. (clair)** (light) brown hair **2** *nm* chestnut brown

château, -eaux [ʃɑto] *nm* (**a**) castle; (*manoir*) mansion, manor, hall; (*demeure de famille aristocratique*) stately home; *Hist* (royal) palace; **le c. de Versailles** the palace of Versailles; **les châteaux de la Loire** the Châteaux of the Loire; *Fig* **c'est la vie de c.** it's the life of Riley; *Fig* **elle mène la vie de c.** she leads a life of luxury; *Fig* **bâtir des châteaux en Espagne** to build castles in Spain *or* in the air (**b**) (*exploitation vinicole*) château; **vin mis en bouteille au c.** château-bottled wine; *Arg* **c.-la-Pompe** (drinking) water, Adam's ale

▶ **château**: *Naut* **c. d'arrière** afterdeck; *Naut* **c. d'avant** forecastle, fo'c'sle; **c. de cartes** house of cards; **c. d'eau** water tower; *Rail* tank; **c. fort** (fortified) castle; *Naut* **c. de poupe** afterdeck; *Naut* **c. de proue** forecastle, fo'c'sle

chateaubriand, châteaubriant [ʃatobrijɑ̃] *nm Culin* chateaubriand, porterhouse steak

châtelain [ʃɑtlɛ̃] *nm* (**a**) *Hist* lord of the manor (**b**) (*propriétaire d'un château*) owner of a château

châtelaine [ʃɑtlɛn] *nf* (**a**) *Hist* lady (of the manor) (**b**) (*propriétaire*) (woman) owner of a château; (*épouse du propriétaire*) wife of owner of a château (**c**) (*pour clés etc*) chatelaine

châtelet [ʃɑtlɛ] *nm Hist* small castle

chat-huant, *pl* **chats-huants** [ʃayɑ̃] *nm* tawny owl, brown owl

châtié [ʃɑtje] *adj* (*style*) polished; **en langage c.** in refined language

châtier [ʃɑtje] *vt* (*impf & pr sub* **n. châtiions, v. châtiiez**) (**a**) *Litt* (*enfant etc*) to chastise; **c. son corps** to mortify the flesh; **c. l'audace de qn** to punish sb for his impudence; *Prov* **qui aime bien châtie bien** spare the rod and spoil the child (**b**) (*style*) to polish

chatière [ʃatjɛr] *nf* (**a**) (*pour chat*) cat flap (**b**) (*pour aération*) ventilation hole (**c**) (*passage étroit*) narrow underground passage

châtiment [ʃɑtimɑ̃] *nm Litt* punishment, chastisement,

castigation; **c. corporel** corporal punishment; **il a reçu un c. sévère** he was severely punished

chatoiement [ʃatwamɑ̃] *nm* shimmer, iridescence, sheen

chaton[1] [ʃatɔ̃] *nm* **(a)** *(petit chat)* kitten **(b)** *Bot* catkin

chaton[2] *nm* **(a)** *(d'une bague)* bezel, setting **(b)** *(pierre)* stone

chatouille [ʃatuj] *nf F* **faire des chatouilles à qn** to tickle sb; **craindre la c.** *ou* **les chatouilles** to be ticklish

chatouillement [ʃatujmɑ̃] *nm* tickling; **éprouver** *ou* **avoir un c. dans la gorge** to have a tickle in one's throat

chatouiller [ʃatuje] **1** *vt* to tickle; **arrête de c. ta sœur!** stop tickling your sister!; *F* **c. les côtes à qn** to give sb a thrashing; **vin qui chatouille le palais** wine that pleases *or* titillates the palate; **de bonnes odeurs de cuisine nous chatouillaient les narines** delicious cooking smells were making our mouths water; **c. la curiosité** to excite *or* arouse curiosity; **c. l'amour-propre de qn** to flatter sb's vanity; **l'envie me chatouille d'aller voir ce qu'ils font** I'm itching to go and see what they're doing; **il ne faut pas le c. sur cette question, il risque de se mettre en colère** don't needle him on the subject, he might get angry

2 *vi* to tickle; **ah! ça chatouille!** oh! that tickles!

chatouilleux, -euse [ʃatujø, -øz] *adj* ticklish; *Fig* sensitive, touchy; **elle est très chatouilleuse** she's very ticklish; *Fig* **c. sur le point d'honneur** touchy where honour is concerned, touchy on a point of honour

chatouillis [ʃatuji] *nm F* gentle tickling, light tickling; **faire des c. à qn** to tickle sb gently

chatoyant [ʃatwajɑ̃] *adj* shimmering, iridescent; *(pierre, imagination etc)* sparkling; **soie chatoyante** shot silk

chatoyer [ʃatwaje] *vi* **(il chatoie; il chatoiera)** to shimmer; *(d'une pierre)* to sparkle; *Fig* **style qui chatoie** sparkling style

châtré [ʃɑtre] **1** *adj (homme) Péj* castrated; **taureau/étalon c.** steer, castrated bull/gelding, castrated stallion **2** *nm* eunuch; *F* **voix de c.** high-pitched *or* falsetto voice

châtrer [ʃɑtre] *vt* **(a)** to castrate, to emasculate; *(étalon)* to geld; *(chat)* to neuter **(b)** *(texte)* to censor, to expurgate

chatte [ʃat] *nf* **(a)** *voir* **chat (b)** *Vulg (sexe féminin)* pussy

chattemite [ʃatmit] **1** *nf* **faire la c.** to simper **2** *adj (manière)* smooth, ingratiating; *(air)* smooth

chatteries [ʃatri] *nfpl* **(a)** *(gestes de tendresse etc)* caresses; **se faire des c.** to caress each other **(b)** *(friandises)* delicacies, dainties

chatterton [ʃatɛrtɔn] *nm Él* (adhesive) insulating tape, *Am* friction tape

chat-tigre, *pl* **chats-tigres** *nm* tiger cat

chaud, chaude [ʃo, ʃod] **1** *adj* **(a)** *(modéré)* warm; *(intense)* hot; **un bon pull c.** a good warm jumper; **pendant la chaude saison** during the warm weather; **la soupe est toute chaude** the soup is steaming *or* piping hot; **repas c.** hot meal; **animal à sang c.** warm-blooded animal; *Culin* **à mettre dans un four c.** cook in a hot oven; **pleurer à chaudes larmes** to weep bitterly; **il est c., il a de la fièvre** he's very warm *or* hot, he's running a fever; **le soleil est déjà c.** the sun's already (quite) warm *or* hot; *Prov* **il faut battre le fer pendant qu'il est c.** strike while the iron is hot, make hay while the sun shines; *Fig* **avoir la tête chaude** to be hot-headed; **l'été va être c.** it'll be a hot summer; *Fig* there will be a lot of unrest this summer; **l'alerte fut chaude** it was a close *or* near thing; **les points chauds du Proche-Orient** the hot spots *or* flash points of the Middle East; **chaude discussion** heated discussion; *Fig* **elle n'est pas chaude pour le projet** she's not keen on *or* not over-enthusiastic about the project; **c'est un c. partisan/défenseur de …** he's a keen supporter/defender of …; **nouvelle toute chaude** hot news, hot gossip; **tout c. de …** straight from …, hotfoot from …; *Fig* **voix chaude** sultry voice; *Beaux-Arts* **tons chauds** warm tints

(b) *Fig* **avoir un tempérament c.** to be hot-tempered; **avoir le sang c.** to be hot-blooded; **être c.** to be hot stuff; **c'est un c. lapin** he's a randy devil

2 *adv* **j'aime manger c.** I like my food hot; **le malade doit manger c.** the patient must eat hot food; **il fait très c.** it's hot, it's very warm; **cela ne me fait ni c. ni froid** it makes no difference, it's all the same to me

3 *nm (intense)* heat; *(modéré)* warmth; **garder** *ou* **tenir qch au c.** to keep sth hot; **il doit rester au lit, gardez-le bien au c.** he must stay in bed, keep him warm; **je garde ton assiette au c.** I'll keep your plate warm; **chez soi, au c.** at home, in the warmth; **prendre un c. et froid** to catch a chill; **avoir c.** *(de personne)* to be *or* feel warm/hot; **tu as assez c.?** are you warm enough?; **tu n'as pas trop c.?** you're not too hot?; *F* **il a eu c.** he had a narrow escape; **je crève de c.!** I'm dying of heat!; **travailler un métal à c.** to hot-work a metal; **être opéré à c.** to have an emergency operation; **interroger les spectateurs à c.** to question the audience on the spot; *Fig* **souffler le c. et le froid** to blow hot and cold

chaudement [ʃodmɑ̃] *adv* warmly; **être vêtu c.** to be warmly dressed; **approuver c.** to approve heartily; **il a été c. défendu par elle** he was hotly defended by her

chaude-pisse [ʃodpis] *nf inv Arg* VD, clap

chaud-froid, *pl* **chauds-froids** *nm Culin* **c. de poulet/gibier** chaudfroid of chicken/game

chaudière [ʃodjɛr] *nf* **(a)** *(de chauffage)* boiler; **c. de chauffage central** central heating boiler; **c. à mazout/à gaz** oil-fired/gas boiler; **c. à vapeur** steam boiler *or* generator **(b)** *Arch (pour la lessive etc)* copper

chaudron [ʃodrɔ̃] *nm* cauldron, *US* caldron

chaudronnerie [ʃodrɔnri] *nf* **(a)** *Ind* boiler-making **(b)** *(objets)* boilers **(c)** *(atelier)* boiler works

chaudronnier, -ière [ʃodrɔnje, -jɛr] **1** *n (fabricant)* boiler maker **2** *adj* **industrie chaudronnière** boiler-making

chauffage [ʃofaʒ] *nm (d'une pièce etc)* heating; *(appareils etc)* heating system; *(dans une voiture)* (car) heater; **bois de c.** firewood; **appareil de c.** heater; **c. central** central heating; **c. urbain** district heating; **c. par le sol** underfloor heating; **c. à l'électricité/au gaz/au mazout** electric/gas/oil heating; **installer le c.** to put central heating in; **le c. est détraqué** the boiler *or* the heating is out of order; **mettre/arrêter le c.** to turn on/turn off the heating

chauffagiste [ʃofaʒist] *n Tech* heating engineer

chauffant [ʃofɑ̃] *adj* heating, warming; **couverture chauffante** electric blanket; **plaque chauffante** hot plate

chauffard [ʃofar] *nm F (mauvais conducteur)* roadhog, reckless driver

chauffe [ʃof] *nf Tech* firing, stoking; **surface de c.** heating surface; **chef de c.** head stoker; *Naut* **chambre de c.** stokehold; **bleu de c.** boiler suit

chauffe-assiettes *nm inv* plate warmer

chauffe-bain, *pl* **chauffe-bains** *nm* water heater

chauffe-biberon, *pl* **chauffe-biberons** *nm* bottle-warmer

chauffe-eau *nm inv* water heater; *(à réservoir)* immersion heater

chauffe-pieds *nm inv* footwarmer

chauffe-plats *nm inv* chafing dish, hot plate

chauffer [ʃofe] **1** *vt* **(a)** to heat (up), to warm (up); **c. une maison au gaz** to heat a house with gas, to have gas heating; **la chambre n'est pas chauffée** there's no heating in the bedroom, the bedroom's not heated; **c. le fer à blanc/au rouge** to make iron white-/red-hot; **chauffé à blanc/au rouge** white-/red-hot; *Aut* **c. le moteur** to warm up the engine; **c. une chaudière/une locomotive** to fire/stoke (up) a boiler/an engine

(b) *F* **c. qn** to cram *or* coach sb for an examination; **c. son public** to warm up one's audience; **il faut c. l'affaire** we're going to have to get things moving *or* hurry things along; **c. qn à blanc** to whip sb into a frenzy

2 *vi* **(a)** *(devenir chaud)* to get *or* become hot *or* warm; **ce radiateur chauffe bien/mal** this radiator gives out/doesn't give out a lot of heat; **la soupe chauffe** the soup's heating *or* warming up, the soup's on; **mets la soupe à c.** put the soup on (to heat); *F* **faites c. la colle!** that didn't sound very healthy!

(b) *F* **ça chauffe, ça va c.** things are beginning to heat up; **je te promets que ça va c. s'il est en retard!** I promise you there'll be trouble if he's late!; **ça chauffe, ce soir!** things are hotting up this evening!; **tu chauffes!** *(dans un jeu)* you're getting warmer!

(c) *(de roulement à billes etc)* to overheat, to run hot; **le moteur a tendance à c.** the engine tends to overheat *or* to get overheated

3 se chauffer *vpr* to warm oneself (**au soleil** in the sun); **se c. (les muscles)** to warm up, to limber up; **se c. au mazout** to have oil-fired (central) heating; **nous ne nous chauffions toujours pas** we still hadn't turned the heating on; *Fig* **je vais lui montrer de quel bois je me chauffe!** I'll show him what I'm made of!, I'll give him a (good) piece of my mind!

chaufferette [ʃofrɛt] *nf (pour les pieds)* footwarmer

chaufferie [ʃofri] *nf* boiler room

chauffeur, -euse[1] [ʃofœr, -øz] *n* **(a)** *(de voiture, bus, camion)* driver; *(employé)* chauffeur, driver; **c. de camion** truck *or Br* lorry driver; **c. routier** long-distance truck *or Br* lorry driver; **elle est chauffeuse de taxi** she's a taxi driver; **les chauffeurs du dimanche** Sunday drivers; **je n'ai pas l'intention de faire le c. toute la journée** I've no intention of chauffering people around all day **(b)** *(d'une locomotive à vapeur)* stoker

chauffeuse[2] [ʃoføz] *nf* low fireside chair

chaulage [ʃolaʒ] *nm (des murs etc)* whitewashing; *(du sol etc)* liming

chauler [ʃole] *vt* (*murs etc*) to whitewash; (*sol etc*) to treat with lime

chaume [ʃom] *nm* **(a)** (*paille*) thatch; **couvrir un toit de** *ou* **en c.** to thatch a roof; **toit de c.** thatched roof **(b)** (*ce qui reste des céréales*) stubble; (*champ*) stubble field

chaumer [ʃome] *vt Agr* **c. les champs** to clear fields (*of stubble*)

chaumière [ʃomjɛr] *nf* thatched cottage; *Fig* **roman à faire pleurer dans les chaumières** a tear-jerking novel; **on en parlera longtemps dans les chaumières** tongues will be wagging about this for a long time

chaussant [ʃosɑ̃] *adj* (*chaussure*) that fits well

chaussée [ʃose] *nf* **(a)** (*route*) roadway, *Am* pavement; **'c. glissante'** 'slippery (road) surface'; **'c. déformée'** 'temporary road surface' **(b)** (*digue*) dyke, embankment; (*dans un endroit marécageux*) causeway; **la C. des Géants** the Giant's Causeway **(c)** (*écueil*) reef, line of rocks

chausse-pied, *pl* **chausse-pieds** [ʃospje] *nm* shoehorn

chausser [ʃose] *vt* **1 (a)** (*chaussures, bottes etc*) to put on; **chaussé de pantoufles** wearing (his) slippers; **c. les étriers** to put one's feet into the stirrups; **c. ses lunettes** to put one's glasses on

(b) (*personne*) (*mettre des chaussures à*) to put shoes on; (*fournir en chaussures*) to supply with footwear, to make footwear for; **se faire c. chez Adrian** to buy *or* get one's shoes at Adrian's

(c) (*aller à*) to fit; **ce modèle te chausse mieux que l'autre** this style fits you better than the other one

(d) *Aut* (*voiture*) to put tyres on

(e) (*arbre*) to earth up

2 *vi* to fit; **souliers qui chaussent bien** shoes that fit well; **ce soulier chausse étroit** this shoe comes in a narrow fitting; **combien chaussez-vous?** what size do you take (in shoes)?; **elle chausse du 37** she takes a (size) four

3 se chausser *vpr* to put one's shoes on; **se c. tout seul** (*d'un enfant*) to put one's shoes on all by oneself; **se c. chez Simone** to buy one's shoes at Simone's

chausses [ʃos] *nfpl Hist* breeches; **coller aux c. de qn** to dog sb's footsteps

chausse-trap(p)e [ʃostrap] *nfpl Fig Litt* trap

chaussette [ʃosɛt] *nf* sock; **une paire de chaussettes** a pair of socks; **en chaussettes** in one's socks, in one's stockinged feet; **c. de ski/de sport/de tennis** ski/sports/tennis sock; *Arg* **un vrai jus de c.** watery coffee; **laisser tomber qn comme une vieille c.** to cast sb aside like an old rag

chausseur [ʃosœr] *nm* (*magasin*) shoe shop; (*fabricant*) shoe manufacturer

chausson [ʃosɔ̃] *nm* (*pantoufle*) slipper; (*de danse*) ballet shoe; (*de bébé*) (baby's) bootee; **se mettre en chaussons** to put one's slippers on

▶ **chausson**: *Culin* **c. aux pommes** apple turnover

chaussure [ʃosyr] *nf* **(a)** (*soulier*) shoe; **une paire de chaussures** a pair of shoes; **c. de ville/de sport/habillée** town/sports/dress shoe; **chaussures de marche** *ou* **de montagne** walking boots; **c. à talon** *ou* **haute** high-heeled shoe; **c. basse** flat shoe; **c. montante** ankle boot; **chaussures de ski** ski boots; *F* **trouver c. à son pied** to find the right woman/man **(b)** *Ind* (boot and) shoe industry *or* trade **(c)** (*sens large*) footwear

chauve [ʃov] **1** *adj* bald; *Fig* (*colline etc*) bare; *F* **c. comme un genou** *ou* **comme un œuf** *ou* **comme une bille** as bald as a coot **2** *n* bald(-headed) person

chauve-souris, *pl* **chauves-souris** *nf* bat

chauvin, -ine [ʃovɛ̃, -in] *Péj* **1** *n* chauvinist, jingoist **2** *adj* chauvinistic, jingoistic

chauvinisme [ʃovinism] *nm Péj* chauvinism, jingoism

chauviniste [ʃovinist] *adj, n Péj* = **chauvin 1, 2**

chaux [ʃo] *nf* lime; **c. vive** quicklime; **c. éteinte** slaked lime; **blanchir un mur à la c.** to whitewash a wall; **bâtir à c. et à sable** *ou* **à c. et à ciment** to build firmly *or* solidly; *Fig* **être bâti à c. et à sable** (*d'une personne*) to have an iron constitution

chavirer [ʃavire] **1** *vi* **(a)** (*de bateau etc*) to capsize, to overturn, *F* to turn turtle; *Fig* (*sombrer*) to collapse; **faire c.** to overturn, to cause to overturn; **les plus grands empires chavirent** even the greatest empires collapse *or* fall **(b)** (*tourner*) to reel, to spin (round); **tout chavire autour de moi** everything's spinning; **ses yeux chaviraient** he was showing the whites of his eyes **2** *vt* **(a)** (*bateau*) to capsize, to overturn **(b)** *F* (*retourner*) to overwhelm, to bowl over; **il en est tout chaviré** it's knocked him for six

chébran [ʃebrɑ̃] *adj inv F* (*branché*) trendy

chèche [ʃɛʃ] *nm* North African scarf

chéchia [ʃeʃja] *nf* fez

check-list, *pl* **check-lists** [tʃɛklist] *nf Av etc F* checklist

check-point [tʃɛkpɔint] *nm inv Mil* checkpoint

check-up [tʃɛkœp] *nm inv Méd* check-up; **faire un c. à qn** to give sb a check-up; **le médecin me conseille de faire un c.** the doctor is advising me to have a check-up

chef [ʃɛf] *nm* **(a)** (*de famille etc*) head; (*d'une tribu etc*) chief, chieftain; (*d'un parti politique etc*) leader; (*d'une entreprise*) head, manager; *F* (*patron*) boss; (*de jurés*) foreman; (*d'une école de pensée etc*) founder; **c.** (**cuisinier** *ou* **de cuisine**) (head) chef, chef de cuisine; **le plat du c.** the chef's special; **ingénieur en c.** chief engineer; **rédacteur en c.** chief editor; *Mil* **commandant en c.** commander-in-chief; **jouer au petit c.** to throw one's weight around; **il se débrouille comme un c.** he's getting on *or* doing very well; **bravo, tu es un c.** well done, you're a marvel!

(b) *Arch, Hum* head; *Litt* **faire qch de son (propre) c.** to do sth on one's own authority *or F* off one's own bat; **au premier c.** first and foremost

▶ **chef**: *Jur* **c. d'accusation** charge, count (of an indictment); **c. d'antenne** programme supervisor; *Ind* **c. d'atelier** (shop) foreman; **c. de bande** ringleader; **c. de bataillon** major; *Admin* **c. de bureau** office manager, *Vieilli* chief *or* senior clerk; *Parl* **c. de cabinet** = (minister's) principal private secretary; **c. chasseur** head porter, *Am* bell captain; **c. comptable** chief accountant; **c. de cuisine** head chef, chef de cuisine; **c. d'équipe** *Sport* captain; *Ind* foreman, charge hand; **c. d'état** head of state; **c. des exploitations** operations manager; **c. de fabrication** production manager, manufacturing manager; **c. de famille** head of the family; **c. de file** leader, lead manager; (*produit*) (market) leader; *Rail* **c. de gare** station manager; **c. du gouvernement** head of government; **c. de groupe** group supervisor *or* manager *or* leader; **c. de groupe de produits** group product manager; (*produit*) (product) (market) leader; **c. infirmier** charge nurse; **c. des informations** Public Relations *ou* PR manager; **c. de magasin** store manager; **c. de marque** brand manager; *TV, Cin* **c. montage** editor; **c. de musique** bandmaster; **c. de nage** stroke (oar); *TV, Cin* **c. opérateur** cinematographer, head of cameras; **c. opérateur cadreur** lighting-cameraman; **c. d'orchestre** conductor; **c. de partie boucher** larder chef; **c. de partie poissonnier** fish cook; **c. de partie** chef de partie; **c. pâtissier** chef patissier, pastry chef; **c. de publicité** advertising manager *or* executive; **c. de patrouille** patrol leader; **c. du personnel** personnel manager, head of personnel; **c. de petit déjeuner** breakfast chef; *TV* **c. de plateau** stage manager, floor boss; *TV etc* **c. de production** production head; *Com* **c. de produit** product manager; *Naut* **c. de quart** officer of the watch; **c. de rang** head waiter, chef de rang, station waiter, *Am* captain; **c. de rayon** (*dans un magasin*) head of department, department(al) manager, department head; (*dans un hôpital*) consultant; **c. de réception** (*dans un hôtel*) reception manager, front office manager; *Journ* **c. de rubriques** features editor; **c. serveur** waiting chef; **c. scout** scout leader; **c. de service** head of department, departmental manager; *TV etc* **c. de studio** studio supervisor; **c. de train** guard, *Am* conductor; **c. des traitements** Data Processing *ou* DP manager; **c. des ventes** sales manager; *Com* **c. de zone** area manager

chef-d'œuvre, *pl* **chefs-d'œuvre** [ʃɛdœvr] *nm* masterpiece, chef-d'œuvre; **c'est un c. de la littérature/de la peinture** it's a literary/artistic masterpiece

chef-lieu, *pl* **chefs-lieux** *nm* chief town (*of department*), ≈ county town, *Am* county seat

cheftaine [ʃɛftɛn] *nf* (*des Guides*) captain; (*des Jeannettes*) Brown Owl; (*des Louveteaux*) cubmistress

cheik(h) [ʃɛk] *nm* sheik(h)

chelem [ʃlɛm] *nm Cartes* slam; **grand c.** grand slam; **petit c.** little slam; **faire c. à qu** to make a slam against sb; **elle a fini par me faire c.** I ended up not winning a trick against her; *Tennis etc* **Grand C.** Grand Slam

chemin [ʃ(ə)mɛ̃] *nm* **(a)** (*route*) way, road; (*voie*) path, track; **le c. de la gare** the way to the station; **le c. de la gloire/réussite** the road to glory/success; **le plus court c. d'un point à un autre** the shortest distance between two points; *F* **prendre le c. des écoliers** to take a roundabout way *or* the long(est) way round; **demander son c.** to ask one's way; **c'est sur mon c.** it's on my way; *aussi Fig* **nous avons beaucoup de c. à faire** we've a long way to go; *Fig* **il a du c. à faire s'il veut vraiment devenir un concurrent important** he has a long way to go if he wants to become a serious contender; **il faut compter deux ou trois heures de c.** it will take two or three hours to get there; **faire la moitié du c.** to meet sb half way; **nous avons fait la moitié du c. ensemble/à pied** we went half the way together/on foot; **aller son c., aller son petit bonhomme de c.** to jog along;

s'arrêter en c. to stop on the way; *Fig* **maintenant que tu as fait le plus gros du travail, ce serait bête de t'arrêter en (si bon) c.** now that you've done most of the work, it would be silly to stop; **être en bon c.** to be getting on well; **nous ne pouvons pas nous arrêter en si bon c.** we can't give up now that we're doing so well; **leur affaire est en bon c.** their business is off to a good start; **elle n'en prend pas le c.** she's not going the right way about it; **c. faisant** on the way; **faire le c. à pied/en vélo/en voiture** to walk/cycle/drive all the way; **faire un bout de c. avec qn** to go part of the way with sb; *Fig* (*vivre*) to live with sb for a while; **ils ont fait un bout de c. ensemble** (*dans la vie professionnelle*) their careers followed similar paths for a while; **suivre le droit c.** to stay on the straight and narrow; *aussi Fig* **montrer le c.** to lead *or* show the way; *Fig* **il leur montre le c.** he's showing them the way; **à mi-c.** half-way; **pourquoi s'arrêter à mi-c.?** why stop half-way?; **se mettre en c.** to set out *or* off; **se mettre en c. pour** *ou* **prendre le c. de Paris** to set out *or* off for Paris; **être dans** *ou* **sur le c. de qn** to be *or* stand in sb's way; **ton vélo est sur le c., pousse-le** your bike is in the way, move it; **il a trouvé un certain nombre de difficultés sur son c.** he found a certain number of difficulties standing in his way; **se mettre dans le c. de qn** to stand in sb's way; **il n'a pas intérêt à se trouver sur mon c.** he'd better keep out of my way; *Fig* **trouver son c. de Damas** to see the light; **ne pas y aller par quatre chemins** *ou* **par trente-six chemins** to go straight to the point; *Fig* **elle fera son c.** she'll get on *or* make her way in life; **il est très ambitieux, il fera du c.** he's very ambitious, he'll go far *or* a long way *or* he'll go places; *Fig* **cette idée fait du c.** the idea is gaining ground; *Arch* **grand c.** highway, high road; **voleur de grand c.** highwayman; *F* **être toujours sur les chemins** to be always on the go

(**b**) *Ordinat* path

▶ **chemin**: *Ordinat* **c. d'accès** path; **c. creux** sunken road; **c. critique** critical path; **c. de fer** railway, *Am* railroad; *Ordinat* (*affichage*) thumbnail; *Journ* page allocation; **aller** *ou* **voyager en** *ou* **par c. de fer** to go *or* travel by rail *or* by train; **c. de fer omnibus/rapide** local/express service; **accident de c. de fer** rail(way) accident; **c. de fer français** French railways; **Chemins de fer nationaux du Canada** Canadian National Railways; **c. de halage** towpath; *Ordinat* **c. du papier** (*d'une imprimante*) paper path; **c. de randonnée** hiking trail; **c. piéton(nier)** footpath; **c. de ronde** covered way; *MecE* **c. de roulement pour billes** ball race; **c. de table** (table) runner; **c. de terre** dirt track; *Can Jur* **c. de tolérance** right of way; **c. de traverse** side road; **c. vicinal** by-road, minor road

chemineau, -eaux [ʃ(ə)mino] *nm* tramp, vagrant

cheminée [ʃ(ə)mine] *nf* (**a**) (*dans une maison*) fireplace; (**manteau de**) **c.** mantelpiece, chimneypiece; **il y a une c. dans chaque pièce** there's a fireplace in every room; **un feu dans la c.** a fire in the grate; **c'est sur la c.** it's on the mantelpiece; **c. en marbre** marble mantelpiece

(**b**) (*conduit*) chimney (stack); (*de bateau à vapeur*) funnel, smokestack; **c. d'usine** factory chimney; (**conduit de**) **c.** flue; **le Père Noël passe par la c.** Father Christmas comes down the chimney; **feu de c.** chimney fire; **c. d'aération** air shaft, ventilating shaft

(**c**) (*de lampe à huile*) chimney; **col c.** (*de pull etc*) cowl neck(line)

(**d**) *Géol* chimney; **faire une c.** (*d'un alpiniste*) to chimney

▶ **cheminée**: *Géol* **c. de fée** fairy chimney; *Géol* **c. volcanique** vent

cheminement [ʃ(ə)minmɑ̃] *nm* (**a**) (*progression*) progression, movement; **le c. des touristes devant les toiles célèbres** the filing past of the tourists in front of the famous paintings; **le c. des eaux** the advance of the water (**b**) *Mil* (*vers les positions ennemies*) advance (**c**) **c. de la pensée** advance *or* progress *or* development of thought; (*processus*) thought processes

cheminer [ʃ(ə)mine] *vi* (**a**) (*avancer*) to advance, to move along; **la caravane chemine dans le désert** the caravan makes its way through the desert; **les eaux cheminent dans des canaux souterrains** the water travels through the underground canals (**b**) *Mil* (*vers les positions ennemies*) to advance; *Fig* to gain ground; **laisser une idée c.** to let an idea gain ground

cheminot [ʃ(ə)mino] *nm* rail(way) worker, railwayman, *Am* railroader; (*employé*) rail(way) employee

chemisage [ʃ(ə)mizaʒ] *nm* (*d'une chaudière, d'un cylindre etc*) jacketing, casing; (*d'un fusil, d'un cylindre etc*) lining

chemise [ʃ(ə)miz] *nf* (**a**) (*vêtement*) shirt; **c. à manches longues/courtes** long-/short-sleeved shirt; **en (bras** *ou* **en manches de) c.** in one's shirtsleeves; *Fig* **il change d'avis comme de c.** he changes his mind as often as he changes his shirt; **se moquer de qch comme de sa première c.** not to give a damn *or* two hoots about sth; **il donnerait sa c. au premier venu** he'd give you the shirt off his back (**b**) (*classeur*) folder; **mettre un livre sous c.** to cover a book (**c**) (*de chaudière, de cylindre etc*) jacket(ing), casing, sheathing; (*de cylindre, de fourneau etc*) lining; (*de mur*) facing; *Aut* **c. flottante/humide/sèche** slip/wet/dry liner

▶ **chemise**: **c. américaine** (woman's) vest, *Am* undershirt; **c. de nuit** (woman's) nightdress; (*d'homme*) nightshirt; *Hist* **Chemises brunes** Brownshirts; *Hist* **Chemises noires** Blackshirts; *Hist* **Chemises rouges** Red Shirts

chemiser [ʃ(ə)mize] *vt* (*chaudière, cylindre etc*) to jacket, to case; (*fusil, cylindre etc*) to line

chemiserie [ʃ(ə)mizri] *nf Ind* shirt making; (*ensemble de vêtements*) shirts, underwear and ties; (*fabrique*) shirt factory; (*magasin*) gent's outfitters

chemisette [ʃ(ə)mizɛt] *nf* (*pour hommes*) short-sleeved shirt

chemisier [ʃ(ə)mizje] *nm* (**a**) (*fabricant*) shirt-maker; (*marchand*) men's outfitter (**b**) (*corsage*) blouse; **robe c.** shirt-waister

chênaie [ʃɛnɛ] *nf* oak grove *or* plantation

chenal, -aux [ʃ(ə)nal, -o] *nm* (**a**) (*d'une rivière, d'un port etc*) channel, fairway; **au milieu du c.** in mid channel (**b**) (*courant d'eau*) millrace

chenapan [ʃ(ə)napɑ̃] *nm Hum* rogue, scoundrel

chêne [ʃɛn] *nm* (*arbre*) oak; **c. vert** evergreen oak, holm oak, ilex; **table en c. (massif)** (solid) oak table; *Fig* **être fort comme un c.** to be as strong as an ox

chéneau, -eaux [ʃeno] *nm* (*d'un toit*) gutter

chêneau, -eaux [ʃɛno] *nm* oak sapling

chêne-liège, *pl* **chênes-lièges** *nm* cork oak

chenet [ʃ(ə)nɛ] *nm* firedog, andiron

chènevière [ʃɛnvjɛr] *nf* hemp field

chènevis [ʃɛnvi] *nm* hempseed

chenil [ʃ(ə)ni(l)] *nm* (**a**) (*pour chiens*) kennels (**b**) *Suisse* (*désordre*) mess, shambles

chenille [ʃ(ə)nij] *nf* (**a**) (*insecte*) caterpillar; (*d'une autochenille*) band; **c. processionnaire** processionary caterpillar; **véhicule à chenilles** tracked vehicle (**b**) *Tex* chenille

chenillé [ʃ(ə)nije] *adj* (*véhicule*) tracked

chenillette [ʃ(ə)nijɛt] *nf* small tracked vehicle; *Mil* carrier

chenu [ʃəny] *adj Litt* (*personne, tête*) hoary; **arbres chenus** old leafless trees

cheptel [ʃɛptɛl] *nm* (**a**) (*troupeaux*) livestock; **c. ovin d'une région** sheep population of a region (**b**) *Jur* **bail à c.** lease of livestock; **c. (vif)** livestock leased; **c. mort** farm equipment leased

chèque [ʃɛk] *nm* cheque, *US* check; **c. de 60 francs** cheque for 60 francs; **carnet de chèques** cheque book; **endosser un c.** to endorse a cheque; **faire** *ou* **remplir un c.** to write (out) *or* make out a cheque; **je peux vous faire un c.?** can I give you a cheque?; **à qui dois-je adresser le c.?** who should I make the cheque out to?; **payer qch par c.** to pay for sth by cheque; **toucher un c.** to cash a cheque; **encaisser un c.** (*en espèces*) to cash a cheque; (*le mettre sur son compte*) to pay in a cheque

▶ **chèque**: **c. bancaire** (bank) cheque; **c. de banque** banker's draft, *Am* cashier's check; **c. barré** crossed cheque; **c. en blanc** blank cheque; **c. bloqué** stopped cheque; *F* **c. en bois** rubber cheque; **c. certifié** certified cheque; **c. compensé** cleared cheque; **c. d'entreprise** company cheque; **c. nominatif** cheque made out to name; **c. non endossable** non-negotiable cheque; **c. à ordre** cheque to order; **c. au porteur** bearer cheque; **c. postal** post office cheque; **c. retourné** returned cheque; **c. sans provision** bad cheque, rubber cheque, cheque that bounces; **j'ai fait un c. sans provision** my cheque bounced; **c. stimulation-voyage** incentive travel cheque issued by companies; **c. de virement** transfer cheque; *Can* **c. visé** certified cheque; **c. de voyage** traveller's cheque

chèque-cadeau, *pl* **chèques-cadeaux** *nm* gift token *or* voucher; **un c. d'une valeur de 200 francs** a gift token to the value of 200 francs

chèque-livre, *pl* **chèques-livres** *nm* book token

chèque-repas, *pl* **chèques-repas** *nm*, **chèque-restaurant**, *pl* **chèques-restaurant** *nm* luncheon voucher

chéquier [ʃekje] *nm* cheque *or US* check book

cher, chère [ʃɛr] **1** *adj* [①B10,D,3] (**a**) (*aimé*) dear, beloved; **être c. à qn** to be dear to sb; **tout ce qui m'est c.** all that I hold dear; **ses espérances les plus chères** his most cherished hopes; **c'est mon vœu le plus c.** it's my dearest wish; **il a retrouvé sa chère maison/son c. bureau** he's back in his beloved house/office; **bien chers frères** dearly beloved brethren; **C. Monsieur** (*dans une lettre*) Dear Mr X; (*officiel*) Dear Sir; **chers amis de la nature** dear nature lovers; **bonjour, chère Madame** hello, my dear lady; *Iron* **écoutez, chère Madame, c'est tout ce que nous sommes en mesure**

de vous proposer I'm sorry Madam, but that's all we're able to offer you; **cette chère Marie!** dear old Marie!

(**b**) (*coûteux*) dear, expensive; **c'est trop c. pour moi** I can't afford it; **un petit restaurant pas c.** an inexpensive little restaurant; **la vie est chère en ville** it's expensive living in town, the cost of living is high in town(s); **ce n'est pas vendu assez cher** it's underpriced

2 *adv* **payer qch c./trop c.** to pay a high price/too much for sth; **c'est c. payer (sa liberté)** it's a high price to pay (for one's freedom); **il me le payera c.** I'll make him pay for it; **coûter c.** to cost a lot, to be expensive; **ça coûte trop c. pour moi** it's too expensive for me, I can't afford it; *Fig* **ça m'a coûté c. de dire ce que je pensais** speaking my mind cost me dearly; *Fig* **ça va vous coûter c.!** you'll pay dearly for this!; *F* **je donnerai c. pour savoir ce qu'il lui a dit** I'd give anything *or* a lot to know what he said to him; **je ne donne pas c. de son succès** I don't give much for his chances of success; **cela ne vaut pas c.** it's not worth much; *F* **je l'ai eu pour pas c.** I got it cheap

3 *n* **mon c.** my dear (fellow); **ma chère** my dear (girl); **ah ma chère! quel plaisir de vous voir!** (*avec préciosité*) how nice to see you, my dear!

chérant [ʃɛrɑ̃] *adj Can* pricey; **un plombier pas c.** a plumber who doesn't charge too much, an inexpensive plumber

chercher [ʃɛrʃe] **1** *vt* (**a**) (*essayer de trouver*) (*qch, qn*) to look for, to search for, *Fml* to seek; **je l'ai cherché partout** I searched *or* looked for it high and low, I hunted for it everywhere; **c. une maison à acheter** to look for a house to buy, to be house-hunting; **c. qn du regard** *ou* **des yeux** to look around for sb; **c. un mot dans un dictionnaire** to look up a word in a dictionary; **il cherchait des moyens de s'évader** he looked around for a means of escape; **c. un emploi** to look for a job; **c. son chemin** *ou* **sa voie/une solution** to try to find one's way/a solution; **c. ses mots** to search for words; **je cherche son nom** I'm trying to think of his name; *F* **où va-t-il donc c. tout cela?** where on earth does he get that from?; **mais qu'est-ce que tu vas c. là, pourquoi faut-il toujours que tu compliques les choses?** what on earth are you going on about, why do you always have to complicate matters?; **c. sa ruine** to court one's own ruin; **partir c. du secours** to go for help; *F* **il l'a bien cherché** he was asking for it

(**b**) **aller c. qn/qch** to (go and) fetch sb/sth; **envoyer c. qn/qch** to send for sb/sth; **je suis allé le c. à la gare** I went to meet him at the station; **viens me c. à 17 heures** come for me at 5 pm

(**c**) **c. à faire qch** to try to do sth; **c. à se faire connaître** to try to get oneself known, to try to make a name for oneself; **c. à se faire aimer** to try to make oneself popular; **c. à plaire** to aim to please; *Iron* **il ne faut pas c. à comprendre** don't even try to understand

(**d**) *F* (*atteindre*) to come to, to amount to; **cela va c. dans les 10 000 francs** it will cost about 10,000 francs, you're talking about something like 10,000 francs; **ça va c. dans les deux ans de prison** that will get you about two years in prison; **injures à magistrat, ça peut aller c. loin!** insulting a magistrate can get you into serious trouble!

(**e**) *F* (*provoquer*) to get at, to pick on; **tu me cherches?** are you looking for a fight?; **si tu me cherches tu vas me trouver** if you want a fight you'll get one

2 *vi* to look, to search; **qui cherche trouve** seek and ye shall find; **il faut c. plus** you'll have to look harder; **cherche!** (*à un chien*) fetch!

3 se chercher *vpr* to try to find oneself

chercheur, -euse [ʃɛrʃœr, -øz] **1** *adj* (**a**) (*spéculateur*) **esprit c.** enquiring mind (**b**) **tête chercheuse** (*d'un missile*) homing head **2** *n* (**a**) researcher, research worker (**b**) **c. d'or** gold digger **3** *nm* (**a**) *Opt* (*d'un télescope*) finger (**b**) **c. de fuites** gas leak detector

chère [ʃɛr] *nf* fare, food; **faire maigre c.** to eat frugally; **faire bonne c.** to have a good meal, to eat well; **aimer la bonne c.** to be a lover of good food

chèrement [ʃɛrmɑ̃] *adv* (**a**) (*affectueusement*) dearly, lovingly (**b**) (*à haut prix*) dearly, at a high price; **il a payé c. sa liberté** his freedom cost him dearly, he paid a high price for his freedom

chéri, -ie [ʃeri] **1** *adj* dear, beloved, darling; **mes enfants chéris** my dearest *or* beloved children; **à notre tante chérie** (*sur une tombe*) to our beloved aunt; **c. des dieux** beloved of the gods **2** *n* darling; **mon c., ma chérie** darling, dearest; **c'est le c. de tout le monde** he's everybody's darling *or* favourite

chérif [ʃerif] *nm* (Mohammedan) sherif

chérir [ʃerir] *vt* (*qn, liberté etc*) to cherish

chérot [ʃero] *adj m Arg* (*trop cher*) pricey; **ça lui avait coûté c.** it cost him an arm and a leg

cherra [ʃɛrra] *futur de* **choir**

cherry [ʃeri] *nm* cherry brandy

cherté [ʃɛrte] *nf* high price *or* cost; **c. de la vie** high cost of living

chérubin [ʃerybɛ̃] *nm* (*ange*), *F* cherub; **des chérubins** cherubs; *Rel Litt* cherubim; *F* **potelé et blond comme un c.** as chubby and blond as a cherub

chester [ʃɛstɛr] *nm* Cheshire cheese

chétif, -ive [ʃetif, -iv] *adj* (**a**) (*personne*) puny, sickly, scrawny; **arbuste c.** stunted *or* puny shrub (**b**) *Fig Litt* poor, miserable, wretched; **un repas fort c.** a meagre *or* skimpy *or* scanty meal

chétivement [ʃetivmɑ̃] *adv* (**a**) (*d'une façon malingre*) punily, weakly (**b**) (*médiocrement, mal*) poorly, miserably

chevaine [ʃəvɛn] *nm* (*poisson*) chub

cheval, -aux [ʃ(ə)val, -o] *nm* (**a**) *Zool* horse; **homme de c.** horse-lover, born horseman; **à c.** on horseback; **gendarme à c.** mounted policeman; **aller à c.** to ride; **monter sur son c.** to get on one's horse, to mount; **monter à c.** (*faire de l'équitation*) to ride, to go riding; **tu sais monter à c.?** can you ride?; **est-ce que tu montes à c.?** do you ride?; **se tenir bien/mal à c.** to have a good/poor seat, to sit a horse well/badly; **chute de c.** fall off a horse; **être à c. sur qch** to sit astride sth, to straddle sth; **le champ est à c. sur deux communes** the field straddles two villages; *Fig* **être à c. sur l'étiquette** to be a stickler for etiquette; **être à c. sur deux siècles** to straddle two centuries; *Fig* **monter sur ses grands chevaux** to get on one's high horse; **ça ne se trouve pas sous le sabot d'un c.** it doesn't grow on trees; *F* **travailler comme un c.** to work like a slave *or* a trojan; *F* **ce n'est pas un mauvais c.** he's not such a bad sort; *F* **c'est un vrai c., cette femme** she's a real carthorse that woman; *F* **il a mangé** *ou* **bouffé du c.!** he's full of beans!; *F* **remède de c.** drastic remedy; *F* **fièvre de c.** raging fever; *F* **avoir une santé de c.** to be as strong as a horse

(**b**) **petits chevaux** = type of board game

(**c**) *Tech, Aut* **une automobile de vingt chevaux,** *F* **une vingt chevaux** a twenty horsepower car

▶ **cheval**: *Gym* **c. d'arçons** (vaulting) horse; **c. d'attelage** carriage horse; **c. à bascule** rocking horse; **c. de bât** packhorse; **c. de bataille** warhorse, charger; *Fig* **c'est son c. de bataille** that's his hobby-horse, he rides the subject to death; **c. de bois** wooden horse; **c. de chasse** hunter; **c. de course** racehorse; **c. fiscal** (*pour taxer les automobiles*) horsepower; **c. de labour** plough horse; **c. de manège** school horse; **c. marin** seahorse; **c. pur sang** thoroughbred (horse); *F* **c. de retour** (*récidiviste*) repeat offender; **c. de selle** saddle horse; **c. de trait** carthorse, draughthorse; *Myth, Fig* **c. de Troie** Trojan Horse; **chevaux de bois** roundabout, merry-go-round

chevaler [ʃ(ə)vale] *vt Constr* (*mur etc*) to shore up

chevaleresque [ʃ(ə)valrɛsk] *adj* chivalrous, knightly

chevalerie [ʃ(ə)valri] *nf* (**a**) (*dignité*) knighthood (**b**) *Hist* (*institution*) chivalry; **roman de c.** tale of chivalry

chevalet [ʃ(ə)valɛ] *nm* (**a**) (*support*) stand, support, trestle; **c. de scieur** sawbench, sawhorse; **c. de peintre** easel (**b**) *Mus* (*de violon*) bridge (**c**) *Arch* **c. (de torture)** rack

chevalier [ʃ(ə)valje] *nm* (**a**) (*seigneur*) knight; **c. errant** knight errant; **armer** *ou* **faire qn c.** to knight sb, to make sb a knight (**b**) (*de la Légion d'Honneur etc*) Chevalier (**c**) (*oiseau*) sandpiper

▶ **chevalier**: *Bourse* **c. blanc** white knight; **c. d'industrie** swindler, crook; *Bourse* **c. noir** black knight; **C. de la Table Ronde** Knight of the Round Table; **c. servant** faithful admirer

chevalière [ʃ(ə)valjər] *nf* signet ring

chevalin, -ine [ʃ(ə)valɛ̃, -in] *adj* equine; **boucherie chevaline** horse-butcher's (shop); **figure chevaline** horsy face

cheval-vapeur, *pl* **chevaux-vapeur** *nm* (French) horsepower

chevauchant [ʃ(ə)voʃɑ̃] *adj* (*tuiles etc*) overlapping

chevauchée [ʃ(ə)voʃe] *nf* (**a**) (*course à cheval*) ride (**b**) (*personnes*) cavalcade

chevauchement [ʃ(ə)voʃmɑ̃] *nm* (*des tuiles etc*) overlap(ping); (*des fils électriques etc*) crossing; (*d'os fracturés*) (over)riding; *Typ* (*de caractères*) falling *or* dropping out of place; *Géol* (*de couches géologiques*) (over)thrust; *Géol* **faille de c.** overthrust fault; **le c. des horaires ne me permet pas d'assister à ces deux cours** I can't attend both classes because they overlap

chevaucher [ʃ(ə)voʃe] **1** *vi* (**a**) (*l'un sur l'autre*) to overlap; (*de fils électriques etc*) to cross; *Chir* (*d'os fracturés*) to (over)ride; *Géol* to overthrust; *Typ* (*de caractères*) to fall *or* drop out of place; *Menuis* **joint chevauché** lapped joint (**b**) *Littér* to ride (a horse) **2** *vt* (**a**) (*vide etc*) to span (**b**) (*mur etc*) to straddle, to be astride; *Littér* (*cheval etc*) to ride; *Vieilli* (*femme*) to ride; **c. un balai** (*d'une sorcière*) to ride a broomstick **3 se chevaucher** *vpr* to overlap

chevau-léger [ʃ(ə)voleʒe] *nm Hist* light horseman; **les chevau-légers** the light horse, the light cavalry

chevêche [ʃəvɛʃ] *nf* (*oiseau*) (sparrow) owl

chevelu, -ue [ʃəvly] **1** *adj* **(a)** (*personne*) long-haired **(b)** *Péj* hairy **(c)** *Astron* **comète chevelue** bearded comet **2** *n F Péj* **un c.** one of the long-haired brigade

chevelure [ʃəvlyr] *nf* **(a)** (head of) hair; **avoir une belle c.** to have beautiful hair *or* a beautiful head of hair; **femme à la c. rousse/blonde** red-haired/blonde woman; **c. emmêlée** tangled hair; *Fig* **la c. des saules** the verdure of the willows **(b)** *Astron* (*d'une comète*) tail

chevenne, chevesne [ʃəvɛn] *nm* (*poisson*) chub

chevet [ʃ(ə)vɛ] *nm* **(a)** (*tête de lit*) bedhead; **lampe de c.** bedside lamp; **table de c.** bedside table, *Am* night table, nightstand; **j'en ai fait mon livre de c.** I've made it my bedside reading *or* book; **rester au c. de qn** to stay at sb's bedside; **les ministres au c. de l'agriculture européenne** (*titre dans un journal*) ministers concerned about European agriculture **(b)** *Archit* (*d'une église*) apse

cheveu, -eux [ʃ(ə)vø] *nm* **(a)** (a single) hair; (*ensemble de la chevelure*) hair; **elle a le c. terne** she has dull hair; **avoir le c. rare** to be going thin *or* thinning on top; **un c. blanc** a grey hair; **il ne lui reste pas un c. sur le caillou** he hasn't a hair left on his head; **arriver comme un c. sur la soupe** to arrive at an awkward moment; **il s'en est fallu d'un c. que tout soit à refaire** we/*etc* came within a hair's breadth of having to do it all again; **à un c. près** by a hair's breadth; **à un c. près, je ratais mon train** I missed my train by a hair's breadth; **être à un c. de la ruine** to be within a hair's breadth of ruin; **si vous touchez à un seul c. de sa tête, vous vous en repentirez!** if you lay a finger on him *or* touch a hair on his head, you'll regret it

(b) cheveux hair; **avoir les cheveux longs/courts** to have long/short hair, to wear one's hair long/short; **des cheveux raides/frisés** straight/curly hair; **c. gris** grey hair; **j'ai commencé à avoir des cheveux blancs à l'âge de trente ans** I started to go grey when I was thirty; **se faire des cheveux (blancs)** to worry oneself sick; **en cheveux** without a hat (on), bare-headed; **perdre ses cheveux** to lose one's hair; *Fig* **s'arracher les cheveux** to tear one's hair out; *Fig* **couper les cheveux en quatre** to split hairs; **saisir un occasion par les cheveux** to jump at an opportunity; *F* **elles se sont prises aux cheveux, elles se sont empoignées par les cheveux** they had a set-to; **argument tiré par les cheveux** far-fetched argument; **cheveux d'ange** (*décorations de Noël*) angel hair; *Culin* angel-hair vermicelli

chevillard [ʃ(ə)vijar] *nm* wholesale butcher

cheville [ʃ(ə)vij] *nf* **(a)** *Anat* ankle; **jusqu'à la c.** ankle deep; **se fouler la c.** to sprain one's ankle; *Fig* **il ne vous arrive pas à la c.** he can't hold a candle to you; *F Péj* **tu as les chevilles qui enflent** you're getting too big for your boots *or Am* britches **(b)** (*pour accrocher*) peg, pin; (*pour boucher un trou*) peg, plug; **c. en bois** peg, dowel; **c. en fer** bolt; **c. maîtresse** kingpin; **c. ouvrière** (*d'un véhicule*) kingpin; *Fig* mainspring, kingpin; *Mus* **c. de violon** peg of a violin; *Com* **vente à la c.** wholesale butchery trade; *F* **être en c. avec qn** to be in cahoots with sb **(c)** *Littér* (*dans un vers*) padding

cheviller [ʃ(ə)vije] *vt* (*qch*) to pin, to bolt, to peg (together); *Fig* **avoir l'âme chevillée au corps** to be indestructible

cheviotte [ʃəvjɔt] *nf Tex* **c. écossaise** tweed

chèvre [ʃɛvr] **1** *nf* **(a)** goat; (*femelle*) she-goat, nanny goat; **fromage/lait de c.** goat's cheese/milk; **barbe de c.** goatee (beard); *F* **ménager la c. et le chou** to sit on the fence, *Lit, Prov* to run with the hare and hunt with the hounds; *Fig* **devenir c.** to go up the wall *or* round the bend; **il me rend c.!** he drives me up the wall *or* round the bend! **(b)** (*chevalet*) carpenter's sawhorse, trestle **2** *nm* goat('s) cheese

chevreau, -eaux [ʃəvro] *nm* kid; **gants de c.** kid gloves

chèvrefeuille [ʃɛvrəfœj] *nm* honeysuckle

chevrette [ʃəvrɛt] *nf* **(a)** (*chevreau*) kid, young (she-)goat **(b)** (*femelle du chevreuil*) (female) roe deer **(c)** (*trépied*) tripod

chevreuil [ʃəvrœj] *nm* roe deer, roebuck, *Can* deer; (*gibier*) venison; **peau de c.** buckskin, deerskin

chevrier, -ière [ʃɛvrije, -jɛr] **1** *n* goatherd, *f* goat girl **2** *nm* (small green) kidney bean

chevron [ʃəvrɔ̃] *nm* **(a)** *Constr* (*d'un toit*) rafter **(b)** *Mil etc* (service) stripe, chevron; *Hér* chevron; *Tex* (*motif*) **tissu à chevrons** herringbone pattern(ed) material

chevronné [ʃəvrɔne] *adj* (*qui a de l'expérience*) experienced, seasoned

chevrotain [ʃəvrɔtɛ̃] *nm* mouse deer, musk deer

chevrotant [ʃəvrɔtɑ̃] *adj* (*voix*) quavering, tremulous

chevrotement [ʃəvrɔtmɑ̃] *nm* (*de la voix*) quaver(ing), tremor; **avec des chevrotements dans la voix** with a quaver *or* a tremor in one's voice, in a quavering or trembling voice

chevroter [ʃəvrɔte] *vi* **(a)** (*de personne*) to sing *or* speak in a quavering voice, to quaver; **sa voix chevrote** his voice shakes *or* quavers **(b)** (*de chèvre*) to kid

chevrotine [ʃəvrɔtin] *nf* buckshot

chewing-gum, *pl* **chewing-gums** [ʃwiŋgɔm] *nm* chewing-gum

chez [ʃe] **1** *prép* [①B51] **(a)** (*dans la maison etc de*) **c. qn** at sb's house *or* home; **il n'est pas c. lui** he's not at home, he's not in; **elle est rentrée** *ou* **allée c. elle** she's gone home; **je l'ai reconduit c. lui** I took him home; **je vais c. moi** I'm going home; **je vais c. ma sœur/Nadine** I'm going to my sister's (house)/Nadine's (house); **C. Paul** (*restaurant, café etc*) Paul's; **venez c. nous** come to our house; **il vit c. nous** he lives with us; **vous vivez c. vos parents?** do you live with your parents?; **vous êtes ici c. vous, faites comme c. vous** treat the place as your own, make yourself at home; *Iron* **eh bien, mais faites comme c. vous** that's right, (you) just make yourself at home; **acheter qch c. l'épicier** to buy sth at the grocer's; **il est allé c. le dentiste/le pédicure** he's gone to the dentist('s)/the chiropodist('s); **chacun c. soi, et tout le monde s'en portera mieux** if people minded their own business, there wouldn't be any problems; (*pour des étrangers*) they should stay in their own countries, and then there wouldn't be any problems; **on dort mieux c. soi** you always sleep better in your own home; **je ne me sens pas c. moi, ici** I don't feel at home here; **chez ...** (*sur une lettre*) care of ..., c/o ...; **un bon vin bien de c. nous** one of our good local wines; **c. nous c'est mieux** it's better at home; **elle a été à l'école c. les sœurs** she went to a convent school; **derrière c. moi** behind my house; **il habite près de c. son ami** he lives near his friend

(b) (*en, dans*) with; **c'est devenu une habitude c. moi** it's become a habit with me; **ce que j'admire c. cet homme c'est ...** what I admire about *or* in the man is ...; **c'est quand même curieux, c. un homme de son âge** it is strange, for *or* in a man of his age; **c. Molière** in Molière

(c) (*au temps de*) during the time of; **c. les Vikings** during the Viking period

(d) (*parmi*) among; **cette expression est courante c. les jeunes** this expression is common among young people; **c. les Américains** among (the) Americans; **c. les animaux** in the animal kingdom, among animals

2 *nm inv* **son c.-soi** one's home, one's house

chiader [ʃjade] *Arg* **1** *vi* to swot **2** *vt* (*examen*) to swot (up) for; **système chiadé** elaborate system *or* plan

chialer [ʃjale] *vi Arg* to snivel, to blubber; *Can* to whine, to moan

chialeur, -euse [ʃjalœr, -øz] *n Arg* cry baby; *Can* whiner, moaner

chiant [ʃjɑ̃] *adj Vulg* bloody annoying *or* irritating; **qu'est-ce qu'elle est chiante, cette fille!** that girl's a pain in the arse!

chianti [kjɑ̃ti] *nm* chianti

chiard [ʃjar] *nm F* (*enfant*) brat, kid

chiasse [ʃjas] *nf Arg* **avoir la c.** (*la diarrhée*) to have the runs *or* the trots; (*avoir peur*) to have the wind up, to be shit-scared

chic [ʃik] **1** *nm* **(a)** (*savoir-faire*) skill, knack; **il a le c. des soirées réussies** he has the knack of *or* a knack for throwing successful parties; **elle a le c. pour me mettre au rage** she's really got the knack of making me angry, she really knows how to make me angry

(b) (*élégance*) smartness, stylishness; **il a du c.** he has style; **femme/chapeau qui a du c.** smart *or* stylish woman/hat

(c) *Beaux-Arts* **dessiner de c.** to draw without a model *or* from memory

2 *adj inv* **(a)** (*élégant etc*) smart, stylish, chic; **restaurant c.** fashionable *or* smart *or F* posh restaurant; **style c. et décontracté** elegant but relaxed style; **elle est c.** she's got style; **les gens c.** the smart set

(b) *F* **on a passé une c. soirée** we had a really good evening; **c'est un c. type** he's a good sort, *Am* he's a regular guy; **il a été très c. avec moi** he's been very decent *or* nice to me; **c'est c. de ta part** that's really good *or* decent of you

3 *int F* **c. (alors)!** great!

chicane [ʃikan] *nf* **(a)** (*querelle*) quibbling, wrangling; *Jur* chicanery, pettifoggery; **chercher c. à qn, faire des chicanes à qn** to try to pick a quarrel with sb; *Jur, Vieilli* **gens de chicane** pettifoggers **(b)** *Mil* zigzag trench; (*sur une route etc*) zigzag, chicane **(c)** *Aut* (*de silencieux*) baffle

chicaner [ʃikane] **1** *vi* to quibble (**sur** over, about); *Jur* to chicane, to pettifog; **c. sur les frais** to haggle *or* quibble over

the expense **2** *vt* **c. qn** to wrangle with sb (**sur** about); **c. qch** to haggle over sth **3 se chicaner** *vpr* to squabble (**avec** with)
chicanerie [ʃikanri] *nf esp Jur* quibbling, chicanery
chicaneur, -euse [ʃikanœr, -øz], **chicanier, -ière** [ʃikanje, -jɛr] **1** *n* quibbler, haggler **2** *adj* quibbling, haggling
chiche[1] [ʃiʃ] *adj* (*repas, récolte etc*) scanty, poor; (*personne*) mean, stingy; **être c. de louanges** to be sparing in one's praise; **il est plutôt c. de compliments** he's not very generous with his compliments; *F* **être c. de faire qch** to dare to do sth; **tu n'es pas c. d'y aller!** I bet you don't go!; **c. (que tu ne le feras pas)!** (I) bet you don't!; **c. (que je le fais)!** bet you I will!; **c.!** try it!, I dare you!
chiche[2] *adj* **pois c.** chick pea
chiche-kebab [ʃiʃkebab] *nm Culin* shish kebab
chichement [ʃiʃmɑ̃] *adv* stingily, meanly
chichi [ʃiʃi] *nm F* (*souvent pl*) **chichis** affected manners; **pas tant de c.!** don't make so much fuss!; **gens à c.** overpolite *or* gushing people; **faire des chichis** (*se donner des airs*) to put on airs; (*compliquer les choses*) to make a fuss; **repas sans c.** informal meal
chichiteux, -euse [ʃiʃitø, -øz] *adj F* fussy
chicorée [ʃikɔre] *nf* **(a)** (*plante*) **c. (frisée)** endive; **c. sauvage** chicory **(b)** (*en poudre*) (ground) chicory; **boire de la c.** to drink chicory (coffee)
chicot [ʃiko] *nm* (*d'un arbre, d'une dent*) stump
chiée [ʃje] *nf Vulg* loads, masses; **avoir une c. de livres** to have loads *or* masses of books; **elle a une c. de marmots** she has a swarm of brats *or* kids
chien, chienne [ʃjɛ̃, ʃjɛn] **1** *n* dog, *f* bitch; **jeune c.** puppy, pup; **'(attention) c. méchant'** 'beware of the dog'; *Natation* **nager à la c.** to dog(gy)-paddle; *Journ* **tenir** *ou* **s'occuper de la rubrique des chiens écrasés** to cover weddings and funerals; *Fig* **ils sont comme c. et chat** they fight like cat and dog; *Fig* **se regarder en chiens de faïence** to glare at one another; **un c. regarde bien un évêque** a cat may look at a king; **rompre les chiens** to call off the hounds; *Fig* (*dans une conversation*) to change the subject; *F* **ce n'est pas fait pour les chiens** it's there to be used; **garder à qn un c. de sa chienne** to have it in for sb; **je lui garde un c. de ma chienne** he won't get away with it; **entre c. et loup** at dusk *or* twilight; *Can* **avec cette femme, mon c. est mort** I don't have a chance with that woman any more; *Prov* **bon c. chasse de race** it runs in the family; **qui veut noyer son c. l'accuse de la rage** give a dog a bad name (and hang him); **c. qui aboie ne mord pas** his bark is worse than his bite; **il n'est pas bon à jeter aux chiens** hanging is too good for him; **métier de c.** drudgery; *F* **vie de c.** dog's life; *très F* **chienne de vie!** life's a bitch!; *F* **quel temps de c.!, quel c. de temps!** what awful *or* foul *or* filthy weather!; *Naut* **coup de c.** squall; *F* **je ne suis pas ton c.!** don't order me about!; **elle le traite comme un c.** she treats him like a dog; **mourir comme un c.** to die like a dog; *F* **nom d'un c.!** oh, hell!
2 *nm* **(a)** *F* (*style*) **avoir du c.** to have charm, to have a certain something
(b) être coiffée à la c. to wear a fringe
(c) *Tech* (*d'un fusil*) hammer; **se coucher en c. de fusil** to curl up in one's bed; **dormir en c. de fusil** to sleep curled up
3 *adj* **être c.** (*avare*) to be mean *or* stingy; (*méchant*) to be nasty
▶ **chien**: **c. d'appartement** lapdog; **c. d'arrêt** pointer; **c. d'aveugle** guide dog, *Am* seeing-eye dog; **c. bâtard** mongrel; **c. de berger** sheepdog; **c. de chasse** retriever, gundog; **c. couchant** setter; **faire le c. couchant auprès de qn** to fawn on *or* crawl to sb; **c. courant** hound; **c. de garde** guard dog, watchdog; **c. de manchon** lapdog; **c. de mer** dogfish; **c. policier** police dog; **c. de race** pedigree (dog); **c. de salon** lapdog; **c. savant** (*dans un cirque etc*) performing dog; (*enfant etc*) performing monkey; **c. de traîneau** husky
chien-chien, *pl* **chiens-chiens** *nm F* doggy
chiendent [ʃjɛ̃dɑ̃] *nm* **(a)** (*plante*) couch grass; **pousser comme du c.** to grow like a weed; *F* **voilà le c.!** that's the snag *or* the trouble **(b) brosse en** *ou* **de c.** scrubbing brush
chienlit [ʃjɑ̃li] *nf* **(a)** *F* (*pagaïe*) mess, shambles; **c'est la c.!** it's a shambles! **(b)** *Vieilli* (*carnaval*) masquerade; (*masque*) carnival mask
chien-loup, *pl* **chiens-loups** *nm* wolfhound
chiennerie [ʃjenri] *nf* (*avarice*) meanness, tightfistedness
chier [ʃje] *vi Vulg* to shit, to crap; **nul à c.** a load of crap; **ça va c. (des bulles)** there's going to be one hell of a row *or* stink!; **il n'y a pas à c.!** there are no two bloody *or Vulg* fucking ways about it!; **non mais tu chies dans la colle ou quoi?** what the fuck do you think you're doing?; **tu me fais c.** you're a pain in the arse; **elle me fait c.** she pisses me off; **ça me fait c. de voir qu'il ne prend pas de décision** it really pisses me off to see that he's not making a decision; **qu'est-ce qu'on se fait c. ici!** it's so bloody boring here!; **qu'est-ce que j'ai pu me faire c. à cette soirée** that party really bored the pants off me!; **je me suis fait c. à l'attendre pour rien** I got pissed off waiting for him and he never showed up; **il ne se fait pas c.** he can't be bothered
chiffe [ʃif] *nf* **(a)** *F* **mou comme une c.** like a wet rag; **c'est une c. (molle)** he's spineless, he's a drip *or* a weed **(b)** *Vieilli* rag
chiffon [ʃifɔ̃] *nm* **(a)** (*morceau de tissu*) rag; **c. (à épousseter** *ou* **à poussière)** duster; **c. non-pelucheux** lint-free rag; **passez un coup de c. sur l'étagère** give the shelf a dust; **on pourra en faire un c.** keep it for rags; **papier de c.** rag paper; *F* **parler chiffons** to talk (about) clothes **(b) mettre ses vêtements en c.** to leave one's clothes in a heap **(c)** *Péj* **c. de papier** scrap of paper; *F* **tu ne peux pas rendre ce c. à ton professeur!** you can't hand that rubbish in to your teacher!
chiffonnade [ʃifɔnad] *nf Culin* chiffonade
chiffonnage [ʃifɔnaʒ] *nm* (*de papier*) creasing, crumpling; (*de vêtement*) creasing, crumpling, rumpling
chiffonné [ʃifɔne] *adj* **(a)** (*vêtements*) creased, crumpled, rumpled; (*papier etc*) creased; **c'est tout c.** it's all creased **(b)** *Fig* (*visage etc*) tired(-looking), drawn; (*air*) worried, bothered
chiffonner [ʃifɔne] **1** *vt* **(a)** (*robe etc*) to rumple, to crease, to crumple; (*morceaux de papier etc*) to crumple **(b)** *F* (*ennuyer*) to worry, to bother; **quelque chose me chiffonne** something's bothering me **2** *vi* to do a bit of sewing **3 se chiffonner** *vpr* (*d'un tissu etc*) to crease, to crumple; **ça se chiffonne facilement** it creases easily, it's easily creased
chiffonnier, -ière [ʃifɔnje, -jɛr] **1** *n* ragman, rag-and-bone man, *Arch* rag picker; **se disputer comme des chiffonniers** to go at it hammer and tongs **2** *nm* (*meuble*) chiffonier
chiffrable [ʃifrabl] *adj* calculable; **le montant est facilement/difficilement c.** the sum is easy/difficult to calculate; **ce n'est pas c., les sommes sont colossales** it's impossible to calculate, the sums are colossal
chiffrage [ʃifraʒ] *nm* **(a)** (*d'une somme etc*) working out, calculating; (*estimation*) quantification **(b)** *Mus* (*de la basse*) figuring
chiffre [ʃifr] *nm* **(a)** figure, number, numeral; **chiffres arabes/romains** Arabic/Roman numerals; **nombre de trois chiffres** three-figure number; **inflation à deux chiffres** double digit inflation **(b)** (*total*) amount, total; **en chiffres** (*montant*) in figures; *F* **faire du c.** to make a fast turnover **(c)** (*code*) cipher, code; **(service du) c.** coding *or* cipher department; **officier du c.** cipher officer **(d)** (*d'un coffre-fort*) combination **(e)** (*monogramme*) monogram; **mouchoir brodé à son c.** handkerchief embroidered with one's monogram **(f)** *Mus* figure
▶ **chiffre**: **c. d'affaires (annuel)** (annual) sales figures, (annual) turnover; **faire un c. d'affaires de 4 millions de francs** to have a turnover of 4 million francs; **c. d'affaires critique** breakeven point; **c. d'affaires global** total sales; **c. d'affaires prévisionnel** projected turnover, projected sales revenue; *Ordinat* **c. ASCII** ASCII number; *Ordinat* **c. binaire** binary digit; **c. de vente** sales figures
chiffrement [ʃifrəmɑ̃] *nm* (*de message*) (en)coding, encryption; *Ordinat* **c. de données** data encryption
chiffrer [ʃifre] **1** *vt* **(a)** (*pages d'un livre etc*) to number
(b) (*somme etc*) to work out, to calculate; (*évaluer*) to quantify; **les dégâts ne sont pas encore totalement chiffrés** the extent of the damage has not yet been fully assessed; **détails chiffrés** (*d'un projet etc*) figures; **c. le coût de qch** to quantify the cost of sth
(c) (*qch*) to write in code, to code, to encode; **message chiffré** coded message, message in code
(d) (*linge etc*) to mark
(e) *Mus* (*basse*) to figure
2 *vi* to add up, to tally; **ça commence à c.** it's starting to add up
3 se chiffrer *vpr* **se c. à** to add up to, to amount to, to total; **à combien cela se chiffre-t-il?** how much does it work out at *or* add up to *or* come to *or* amount to?
chiffreur [ʃifrœr] *nm* **(a)** *Com* payments coding clerk **(b)** (*dans services secrets*) cipher clerk
chignole [ʃiɲɔl] *nf* **(a)** (*outil*) hand drill; (*électrique*) electric drill **(b)** *F* (*mauvaise voiture*) banger
chignon [ʃiɲɔ̃] *nm* chignon, bun; **se faire un c., coiffer ses cheveux en c.** to put one's hair in a bun; *Fig* **elles se sont crêpé le c.** they had a fight *or* a set-to
chihuahua [ʃiwawa] *nm* chihuahua
chiite [ʃiit] *adj, n Rel* Shiite
Chili [ʃili] *nm* Chile
chili (con carne) [ʃili(kɔnkarne)] *nm Culin* chili (con carne)

chilien, -ienne [ʃiljɛ̃, -jɛn] **1** *adj* Chilean **2** *n* **C.** Chilean
chimère [ʃimɛr] *nf* **(a)** *(monstre)* chimera **(b)** *Fig (rêve)* pipe dream, *Lit* chimera; **le pays des chimères** the land of fantasy *or* dreams; **se complaire dans des chimères** to live in a dream world; **ce ne sont que des chimères** they are only pipe dreams
chimérique [ʃimerik] *adj (esprit)* fanciful; **des monstres chimériques** mythical *or* fabled monsters; **rêve c.** pipe dream; **projet c.** unrealistic *or* fanciful plan; **elle s'est forgé un monde c.** she invented *or* created a dream world
chimie [ʃimi] *nf* chemistry; **cours de c.** chemistry course *or* class; **c. industrielle** chemical engineering; **c. minérale** inorganic chemistry; **c. nucléaire** nuclear chemistry; **c. organique** organic chemistry
chimiothérapie [ʃimjoterapi] *nf Méd* chemotherapy; **être en c.** to be having *or* undergoing chemo(therapy)
chimique [ʃimik] *adj* chemical; **réaction c.** chemical reaction; **symbole c. d'un corps** the chemical symbol of a body; **produit c.** chemical; **ces bonbons sont pleins de produits chimiques** these sweets are full of chemicals *or* additives; **société/raffinerie de produits chimiques** chemical company/refinery; *Phys* **rayons chimiques** actinic rays
chimiquement [ʃimikmɑ̃] *adv* chemically
chimiste [ʃimist] *n* chemist; **ingénieur c.** chemical engineer, industrial chemist
chimpanzé [ʃɛ̃pɑ̃ze] *nm* chimpanzee, *F* chimp
chinchilla [ʃɛ̃ʃila] *nm (mammifère, fourrure)* chinchilla; **veste en c.** chinchilla jacket
Chine [ʃin] *nf* China
chine [ʃin] **1** *nf* peddling; **vente à la c.** peddling, hawking **2** *n* (piece of) china **3** *nm* rice paper
chiner¹ [ʃine] *vt Tex (tissu)* to mottle; **laine chinée** mottled *or* chiné fabric
chiner² **1** *vt F* **c. qn** to make fun of sb, to pull sb's leg **2** *vi* to hunt for second-hand goods
chinetoque [ʃintɔk] *n Arg Vieilli (terme injurieux)* Chink(y)
chineur, -euse [ʃinœr, -øz] *n (brocanteur)* second-hand dealer; *(amateur)* antique-hunter
chinois, -oise [ʃinwa, -waz] **1** *adj* **(a)** *(de la Chine)* Chinese **(b)** *F (compliqué)* involved, complicated, over-elaborate **2** *nm* **(a)** *Ling* Chinese; *F* **c'est du c.** it's all double Dutch *or* Greek to me **(b)** *(orange)* = small green orange preserved in brandy **(c)** *Culin* chinois *(conical strainer)* **3** *n* **C.** Chinese (man), *f* Chinese (woman); **les C.** the Chinese
chinoiser [ʃinwaze] *vi* to quibble (**sur cent francs** over *or* about a hundred francs)
chinoiserie [ʃinwazri] *nf* **(a)** *(objet)* chinoiserie, Chinese curio **(b)** *F (complication)* unnecessary complication; **chinoiseries administratives** red tape
chintz [ʃints] *nm Tex* chintz; **des rideaux en c.** chintz curtains
chiot [ʃjo] *nm* pup(py)
chiottes [ʃjɔt] *nfpl Arg (toilettes)* bog, *Am* john; **aux chiottes, les impôts!** taxes are a load of crap!; **aux chiottes, l'arbitre/le président!** the referee's/president's an arsehole!
chiourme [ʃjurm] *nf Vieilli* galley slaves; *(bagnards)* convicts, prisonners
chiper [ʃipe] *vt F (voler) (qch)* to pinch, to swipe, to nick; **il s'est fait c. son stylo à l'école** he got his pen pinched *or* swiped *or* nicked at school
chipeur, -euse [ʃipœr, -øz] *F n* petty thief
chipie [ʃipi] *nf* bad-tempered woman; **vieille c.** old cow; **cette petite fille est une vraie c.** she's a real little madam
chipolata [ʃipɔlata] *nf* chipolata (sausage)
chipotage [ʃipɔtaʒ] *nm (fait de contester)* quibbling; *(marchandage)* haggling
chipoter [ʃipɔte] **1** *vi* **(a)** *(picorer)* to nibble, to pick at *or* play with one's food **(b)** *(contester)* to quibble (**sur** over, about); *(marchander)* to haggle (**sur** over, about) **2** *vt* **(a)** *(nourriture)* to play with, to pick at **(b)** *(prix)* to haggle over
chipoteur, -euse [ʃipɔtœr, -øz] **1** *adj* **(a)** *(avec la nourriture)* picky, fussy; **il est c.** he nibbles *or* picks at his food **(b)** *(ergoteur)* quibbling; **ils sont chipoteurs** they quibble over everything **(c)** *(marchandeur)* haggling, quibbling **2** *n* **(a)** *(avec la nourriture)* picky eater **(b)** *(ergoteur)* quibbler **(c)** *(marchandeur)* haggler, quibbler
chips [ʃips] *nfpl* **(pommes) c.** (potato) crisps, *Am* chips
chique¹ [ʃik] *nf* **(a)** *(de tabac)* quid; *Arg* **couper la c. à qn** to shut sb up; *Arg* **avaler sa c.** *(mourir)* to snuff it, to kick the bucket **(b)** *Belg* sweet
chique² *nf (insecte)* jigger
chiqué [ʃike] *nm F* sham; **c'est du c.** it's all put on *or* a put-up job *or* a fake; **faire du c.** to put on an act, to fake it
chiquement [ʃikmɑ̃] *adv F* **(a)** *(avec élégance)* smartly, stylishly **(b)** *(avec fair-play etc)* decently; **elle m'a c. invité** she was good *or* kind *or* decent enough to invite me
chiquenaude [ʃiknod] *nf* flick (of the finger); **donner une c. à qn** to flick sb with one's finger; **d'une c.** with a flick of the finger; **d'une c., il envoya la boulette de papier sur le bureau du prof** he flicked the pellet of paper onto the teacher's desk
chiquer [ʃike] **1** *vt (tabac)* to chew **2** *vi* to chew tobacco
chiqueur, -euse [ʃikœr, -øz] *n* tobacco chewer
chirographaire [kirɔgrafɛr] *adj Fin* unsecured
chirographie [kirɔgrafi] *nf,* **chiromancie** [kirɔmɑ̃si] *nf* palmistry, *Fml* chiromancy
chiromancien, -ienne [kirɔmɑ̃sjɛ̃, -jɛn] *n* palmist, *Fml* chiromancer
chiropracteur [kirɔpraktœr] *nm* chiropractor
chiropractie [kirɔprakti] *nf* chiropractic
chiropraticien, -ienne [kirɔopratisjɛ̃, -jɛn] *n* chiropractor
chiropraxie [kirɔpraksi] *nf* chiropractic
chiroptères [kirɔptɛr] *nmpl Spéc* Chiroptera
chirurgical, -ale, -aux, -ales [ʃiryrʒikal, -o] *adj* surgical
chirurgie [ʃiryrʒi] *nf* surgery; **c. plastique/esthétique/dentaire** plastic/cosmetic/dental surgery; **c. cardiaque** cardiac *or* heart surgery; **c. ambulatoire** day surgery
chirurgien [ʃiryrʒjɛ̃] *nm* surgeon; **c. esthétique** plastic surgeon; **c. dentiste** dental surgeon; **elle est c.** she's a surgeon
chistera [ʃistɛra] *nf* pelota racket, chistera
chiure [ʃjyr] *nf* flyspeck, insect dirt
ch-l. *abrév* **chef-lieu**
chlamydia, *pl* **chlamydiae** [klamidja, -dje] *nf Méd* chlamydia
chlâsse [ʃlɑs] *adj Arg* knackered; *(ivre)* legless, pissed
chleuh [ʃlø] *adj, nm Hist Arg Péj* Jerry
chlinguer [ʃlɛ̃ge] *vi F* to stink
chloral [klɔral], *pl* **chlorals** *nm Ch* chloral; *Pharm* **c. hydraté, hydrate de c.** chloral (hydrate)
chlorate [klɔrat] *nm Ch* chlorate
chlore [klɔr] *nm Ch* chlorine
chlorer [klɔre] *vt Ind* to chlorinate; **eau chlorée** chlorinated water
chlorhydrate [klɔridrat] *nm Ch* hydrochlorate
chlorhydrique [klɔridrik] *adj Ch (acide)* hydrochloric
chlorique [klɔrik] *adj (acide)* chloric
chlorofluorocarbure [klɔrɔflyɔrɔkarbyr] *nm Ch* chlorofluorocarbon
chloroforme [klɔrɔfɔrm] *nm* chloroform
chloroformer [klɔrɔfɔrme] *vt* to chloroform
chlorophylle [klɔrɔfil] *nf* chlorophyll
chlorophyllien, -ienne [klɔrɔfiljɛ̃, -jɛn] *adj* chlorophyllous
chloroquine [klɔrɔkin] *nf Pharm* chloroquine
chlorure [klɔryr] *nm Ch* chloride; **c. de chaux** chloride of lime, bleaching powder; **c. de calcium/sodium** calcium/sodium chloride
chlorurer [klɔryre] *vt* to chlorinate
choc [ʃɔk] *nm* **(a)** *(entre deux corps)* collision, impact, shock; **ça peut se casser au moindre c.** it can break at the slightest impact; **le c. des deux voitures** the collision of the two cars; **sous le c., sous la violence du c.** under the impact; **c. violent** violent collision; **c. arrière/latéral** rear/side impact; **c. frontal** head-on collision, frontal impact; **'résiste aux chocs'** 'shock-proof', 'shock-resistant'; **c. sourd** bump; **c. des verres** clink of glasses

(b) *(entre armées etc)* clash; **soutenir le c. de l'ennemi** to withstand the onslaught of the enemy; *Fig* **c. des opinions** clash *or* conflict of opinions

(c) *Med* shock

(d) *(émotion brutale)* shock; **ça a été un c. de l'apprendre** it was a shock to hear about it; **ça lui a fait un c. de le revoir** it gave her a shock to see him again; **être en état de c.** to be in a state of shock; **il est encore sous le c.** he's still in shock; **tenir le c.** to stand the shock

(e) de c. super-efficient; **troupes/commandos de c.** shock troops; **mesures de c.** shock measures; **personnalité de c.** high-powered *or* dynamic personality

▶ **choc**: **c. boursier** market crisis; **c. culturel** culture shock; **c. électrique** electric shock; **c. opératoire** post-operative shock; *Écon* **c. pétrolier** oil crisis; **c. en retour** *Él* return shock; *Fig* repercussion, backlash; **c. thermique** thermal shock
-choc [ʃɔk] *suff* drastic, shock; **images-/photos-c.** images/photos that shock; *Com, Fin* **prix-c.!** drastic reductions!; **programme-c.** crash programme
chochotte [ʃɔʃɔt] *F Péj* **1** *nf* lah-di-dah woman; *(homme)* pouf, fairy; **petite c., va!** you stuck-up so-and-so!; **tu n'oses pas sauter? c., va!** you don't dare jump? go on, you big wimp!; **faire sa c.** to put on airs, to be stuck up **2** *adj* lah-di-dah, affected, mannered; *(homme) (efféminé)* camp, affected; *(douillet)* oversensitive, squeamish
chocolat [ʃɔkɔla] **1** *nm* **(a)** chocolate; **c. aux noisettes/**

amandes hazelnut/almond chocolate; **tablette de c.** bar of chocolate; **éclair/gâteau/***etc* **au c.** chocolate éclair/cake/*etc* **(b)** (*boisson*) hot chocolate **(c)** (*confiserie*) chocolate; **une boîte de chocolats** a box of chocolates **2** *adj inv* chocolate-coloured; *F* **être c.** to have been let down

▶ **chocolat**: **c. blanc** white chocolate; **c. à croquer** plain *or* dark chocolate; **c. à cuire** cooking chocolate; **c. fondant** chocolate fondant; **c. au lait** milk chocolate; **c. noir** plain *or* dark chocolate

chocolaté [ʃɔkɔlate] *adj* (*boisson etc*) chocolate(-flavoured); **farine chocolatée** chocolate powder

chocolaterie [ʃɔkɔlatri] *nf* (*fabrique*) chocolate factory; (*magasin*) chocolate shop

chocolatier, -ière [ʃɔkɔlatje, -jɛr] **1** *adj* (*industrie etc*) chocolate **2** *n* (*confiseur*) chocolate-maker/-seller **3** *nf* **chocolatière** chocolate pot

chocottes [ʃɔkɔt] *nfpl F* **avoir les c.** to have the jitters; **ça m'a donné** *ou* **filé** *ou très F* **foutu les c.** it gave me the jitters

chœur [kœr] *nm* [①All,g,i; A13,8] choir; *Archit* choir, chancel; (*d'un chanteur de variétés, d'un opéra*), *Antiq* chorus; **les chœurs** (*d'un opéra, d'un spectacle*) the chorus; **elle est dans les chœurs** she's in the chorus, she's a member of the chorus; **chanter en c.** to sing in chorus; **enfant de c.** altar boy; (*qui chante*) choirboy; *F* **son air d'enfant de c.** his angelic *or* choirboy look; **le c. des contestataires** the body of protesters; **s'informer en c.** to enquire in chorus *or* unison; **en c.** together; **tous en c.!** all together!

choir [ʃwar] *vi* (*pp* **chu**; *pr ind* **je chois, il choit**; *p hist* **je chus**; *fu* **je choirai, je cherrai**, *the aux is* **être**) *Litt* **(a)** (*tomber*) **se laisser c. (dans un fauteuil)** to flop, to sink (into an armchair); *F* **laisser c. qn/qch** to drop sb/sth; **tu ne peux pas le laisser c., il faut aller au rendez-vous** you can't let him down, you'll have to keep the appointment **(b)** *Arch* to fall; … **et la bobinette cherra** … and the latch will drop

choisi [ʃwazi] *adj* **(a)** (*sélectionné*) selected; **morceaux choisis de …** selected passages *or* extracts from … **(b)** (*élégant*) select, choice; (*langage*) polished; **parler en termes choisis** to speak in carefully chosen terms, to choose one's words (carefully); **société choisie** select company

choisir [ʃwazir] **1** *vt* to choose, to pick, to select; **c. ses fréquentations/lectures** to choose *or* pick one's company/reading; **c. entre** *ou* **parmi plusieurs choses** to choose from (among) several things; **il faut c. si oui ou non tu l'achètes** you have to choose *or* decide whether or not to buy it; **à lui de c. quand il veut y aller** it's up to him to decide when he wants to go; **il a bien/mal choisi son moment!** he really picked *or* chose the right/wrong moment!; *Iron* **j'ai choisi mon jour pour aller me promener: il pleut** I really picked a good day to go for a walk: it's raining

2 *vi* to choose; **il faudra bien c.** you'll/we'll/*etc* have to choose *or* decide *or* make a choice; **c. de partir** to choose *or* decide to leave

choix [ʃwa] *nm* choice; **arrêter** *ou* **fixer son c. sur qch** to decide on sth, to choose sth; **mon c. est fait** I've made my choice; **faire le bon c.** to make the right choice; **l'embarras du c.** the difficulty in choosing; **avoir** *ou* **n'avoir que l'embarras du c.** to be spoiled for choice; **faites votre c.** take your pick; **vous avez le c.** the choice is yours, you have a choice; **je n'ai pas le c.** I don't have a choice; **je n'avais pas le c.** I had no choice; **je vous laisse le c.** you choose; **il nous laisse le c. de la date** he's letting us choose the date; **nous n'avons pas d'autre c. que de …** we have no option *or* choice but to …; **vous avez le c. entre … et …** you have the choice *or* you can choose between … and …; **viande** *ou* **poisson au c.** (*sur le menu*) choice of meat or fish; **on a droit à un dessert au c.** there is a choice of dessert; **les matières à option à l'université sont au c. de l'étudiant** optional subjects at university are chosen by the student; **de premier c.** (of the) best quality, first-class; **de second c.** of poor(er) quality; **morceaux de viande de c.** prime cuts; **un grand c. de sous-vêtements** a large *or* wide selection *or* a wide range of underwear; **c. de poésies** a selection of poems; *Admin* **être promu au c.** to be promoted by selection *or* on merit

choléra [kɔlera] *nm Méd* cholera; **avoir le c.** to have cholera

cholériforme [kɔlerifɔrm] *adj Méd* choleriform

cholérique [kɔlerik] *Méd* **1** *adj* choleraic **2** *n* cholera patient

cholestérol [kɔlɛsterɔl] *Méd nm* cholesterol; **taux de c.** cholesterol level; *F* **j'ai du c.** my cholesterol (level) is too high

cholestérolémie [kɔlɛsterɔlemi] *Méd nf* cholesterol level

chômable [ʃomabl] *adj* (*jour*) **jour c.** public holiday

chômage [ʃomaʒ] *nm* unemployment; **le c. touche une grande partie de la population** unemployment affects a high proportion of the population; **le c. des femmes/des jeunes** female/youth unemployment, unemployment among women/young people; **être au c.** to be unemployed *or* out of work *or F* jobless; **allocation** *ou* **indemnité de c.** unemployment benefit, *Br F* dole; **toucher le c.** to claim unemployment benefit, to be on unemployment *or Br F* on the dole; **s'inscrire au c.** to sign on; **c. d'une usine** closure of a factory

▶ **chômage**: **c. chronique** chronic unemployment; **c. conjoncturel** cyclical unemployment; **c. partiel** short-time (working); **être en c. partiel** to be on short time; **c. saisonnier** seasonal unemployment; **c. structurel** structural *or* long-term unemployment; **c. technique** lay-offs; **être en c. technique** to have been laid off

chômer [ʃome] **1** *vt* (*jour férié*) to keep; **jour chômé** public holiday, *Br* bank holiday **2** *vi* **(a)** (*ne pas travailler*) (*d'une usine*) to be *or* lie idle; (*d'un employé*) to be unemployed *or* out of work; *Fig* to do nothing; **vous n'avez pas chômé!** (*quel travail vous avez fait*) you've not been idle *or* twiddling your thumbs!; **l'an dernier je n'ai pas eu le temps de c.** I didn't have a spare moment all last year; **laisser c. une terre** to let land lie fallow **(b)** (*faire le pont*) **c. entre Noël et le jour de l'An** to take time off between Christmas and New Year

chômeur, -euse [ʃomœr, -øz] *n* unemployed person; **un million de chômeurs** a million unemployed; **les chômeurs** the unemployed; **les chômeurs de longue durée** the long-term unemployed

chope [ʃɔp] *nf* (*récipient*) beer mug, tankard; (*contenu*) mugful

choper [ʃɔpe] *vt Arg* **(a)** (*voler*) to pinch, to nick; **on m'a chopé mon portefeuille** I've had my wallet pinched *or* nicked, somebody's lifted my wallet **(b)** (*arrêter, prendre*) to catch, to nab; **se faire c.** to get caught *or* nabbed; **je l'ai chopé en train de fouiller dans mes affaires** I caught him rummaging through my things **(c)** (*attraper*) (*rhume*) to catch

chopine [ʃɔpin] *nf* **(a)** *F* (*contenant*) half-litre *or US* -liter bottle; **tu viens boire une c.?** (are you) coming for a drink? **(b)** *Can* (*mesure*) pint (0.568 l.)

choquant [ʃɔkɑ̃] *adj* (*attitude etc*) shocking; **un abus c.** a gross *or* shocking abuse

choquer [ʃɔke] **1** *vt* **(a)** (*qch contre qch*) to strike, to knock; **nous avons choqué nos verres** we clinked *or* chinked glasses

(b) (*contrarier, être désagréable à*) to shock, to offend; **ce qui choque le plus, dans ces images, c'est que …** the most shocking thing about these pictures is …; **être choqué de qch** to be scandalized *or* shocked at *or* by sth; **nous avons été choqués par son manque d'égard** we were shocked *or* appalled by his lack of consideration; **je suis tout à fait choqué par sa vulgarité** I am deeply shocked by his coarseness; **cela risque de c.** it might cause offence; **sons qui choquent l'oreille** sounds that grate on *or* offend the ear; **mot qui choque** offensive *or* rude word; **de telles paroles choquent dans la bouche d'une jeune fille** such language is shocking in the mouth of *or* coming from a young girl

(c) (*blesser moralement*) to shock; **j'ai été choqué de le voir tellement changé** I was shocked *or* it gave me a shock to see such a change in him; **la vue du sang l'a choqué** the sight of blood has shaken him

2 se choquer *vpr* **(a)** (*d'objets*) to knock against each other **(b)** to be shocked, to take offence (**de** at); **il n'y a pas de quoi se c.** there's nothing to be shocked at

choral, -ale, -als, -ales [kɔral] **1** *adj* choral; **chant c.** choral singing; **société chorale** choral society **2** *nm* choral(e) **3** *nf* [①All,g,i] **chorale** (*société*) choral society; (*chanteurs*) choir; **la c. de l'église** the church choir

chorée [kɔre] *nf Méd* chorea; *F* Saint Vitus' dance

chorégraphe [kɔregraf] *n* choreographer

chorégraphie [kɔregrafi] *nf* choreography; **faire la c. d'un spectacle** to choreograph *or* do the choreography for a show

chorégraphique [kɔregrafik] *adj* choreographic

choria [ʃɔrja] *nf Rel* (*Islam*) sharia

choriste [kɔrist] *n Mus* choir member; (*dans une église*) chorister; (*dans un opéra*) chorus singer; (*d'une comédie musicale*) chorus member; (*d'un chanteur*) backing singer

chorizo [tʃoriso] *nm Culin* chorizo

chorus [kɔrys] *nm* **(a)** **faire c.** to voice one's agreement; **ils ont fait c. avec lui** they voiced their agreement with him **(b)** (*jazz*) chorus; **reprendre un c.** to take up the chorus

chose [ʃoz] **1** *nf* **(a)** (*objet inanimé*) thing; **il aime les belles choses** he likes nice things; **les êtres et les choses** living creatures and objects *or* things; *Scol Vieilli* **leçon de choses** nature lesson; *Fig* **être la c. de qn** to belong to sb; **il la considère comme sa c.** he thinks he owns her

(b) (*abstrait*) thing; **j'ai appris une c. incroyable** I've heard something unbelievable; **une c. très grave vient de se passer** something very serious has just happened; **il se**

passe des choses au ministère there's something going on in the department; **quelque c. se prépare** something's brewing; **j'ai un tas de choses à faire** I've loads *or* masses of things to do; **c'est de deux choses l'une, soit il parle, soit ...** either he talks or ...; **chaque c. en son temps** everything in its own time; **on m'a dit des tas de choses à son sujet** I've been told heaps of things about him; **dites bien des choses de ma part à ...** remember me to ..., give my regards to ...; **il a dit des choses sur moi?** has he been saying things about me?; **elle dit de ces choses parfois!** the things she comes out with sometimes!; **j'ai bien des choses à vous raconter** I've a lot (of things) to tell you; **ce n'est pas c. aisée de ...** it's no easy matter to ...; **réaliser cela est une c., l'admettre en est une autre** being aware of it is one thing, admitting it is another; **la c. en question** the case in point; **je vais vous expliquer la c.** I'll explain it *or* the matter to you; **il a très bien pris la c.** he took it very well; **c'était vraiment la c. à éviter** that was the last thing to do; **cela n'est plus la même c.** that alters the case *or* things; **nous y sommes retournés, mais ce n'est plus la même c.** we went back (there), but it wasn't the same; *F* **être porté sur la c.** to be obsessed with sex, to have a one-track mind; **je vais te dire une (bonne) c.** I'm going to *or* let me tell you something; **c. curieuse, personne n'en savait rien** curiously enough, nobody knew anything about it; **avant toute c.** first of all, above all; **et, c. rare** for once; *Jur* **c. jugée** res judicata; *Pol* **la c. publique** the state, *Fml* res publica

(c) les choses things; **voici comment se sont passées les choses** here's how things happened; **il a bien/mal pris les choses** he took it well/badly; **prendre les choses à cœur** to take things to heart; **l'état des choses** the state of things; **dans l'état actuel des choses** as things are *or* stand at the moment; **les choses de ce monde** the things of this world; **par la force des choses** by *or* through force of circumstance; **il fait bien les choses** he does things in style; **il faut bien voir les choses en face** *ou* **telles qu'elles sont** you have to face up to things, you have to face facts; **les choses étant ce qu'elles sont** things being as *or* what they are; **ne pas faire les choses à demi** not to do things by halves; **ce documentaire sur l'alcoolisme va au fond des choses** this documentary on alcoholism gets to the heart of the matter *or* problem; **n'aie pas peur d'appeler les choses par leur nom** don't be afraid to call a spade a spade *or* to speak your mind

2 *nm F* (*truc*) whatsit, whatsitsname, thingummy; **passe-moi le c.** pass me the whatsit *or* the what-d'you-call-it; **Monsieur/Madame C.** Mr/Mrs what-d'you-call-him/her, what's-his-name/what's-her-name, Mr/Mrs thingummy; **le petit C.** little what's-his-name

3 *adj inv F* **être** *ou* **se sentir/avoir l'air tout c.** to feel/look funny *or* a bit peculiar

chosifier [ʃozifje] *vt Phil* to reify

chott [ʃɔt] *nm Géog* saline lake, shott

chou¹, -oux [ʃu] *nm* **(a)** (*plante*) cabbage; *F* **aller planter ses choux** to go and live in the country, to retire to the country; **faire ses choux gras de qch** (*s'enrichir*) to get rich on sth; **l'opposition a fait ses choux gras de ce scandale** the opposition had a field day with the scandal; **faire c. blanc** to draw a blank; **mon petit c.** darling, dear; **être dans les choux** to be in a fix *or* a mess; **rentrer dans le c. à qn** to attack *or* go for sb; **c'est bête comme c.** it's as easy as pie; *Fig* **feuille de c.** (*journal*) rag **(b)** (*ruban*) bow, rosette **(c)** *Culin* **pâte à choux** choux pastry

▶ **chou**: **c. de Bruxelles** Brussels sprout; **c. frisé** kale; *Culin* **c. à la crème** = cream bun; **c. de Milan** Savoy (cabbage); **c. pommé** round cabbage; **c. rouge** red cabbage

chou², -te [ʃu, ʃut] *adj inv au pl F* **elle est c.** *ou* **choute!** she's cute!; **c'est d'un c.!** it's so cute!

chouan [ʃwɑ̃] *nm Hist* chouan

chouannerie [ʃwanri] *nf Hist* the Chouan revolt

choucas [ʃuka] *nm* jackdaw

chouchou, -oute [ʃuʃu, -ut] *n F* pet, *m* blue-eyed boy; **le c. du prof** teacher's pet; **tu es sa chouchoute** you're his favourite *or* pet

chouchouter [ʃuʃute] *vt F* to pamper, to spoil; **il aime se faire c.** he enjoys being pampered

choucroute [ʃukrut] *nf Culin* sauerkraut; **c. garnie** sauerkraut with meat

chouette¹ [ʃwɛt] *nf* **(a)** (*oiseau*) **c. des clochers, c. effraie** screech owl, barn owl; **c. des bois** wood *or* brown owl; **c. hulotte** tawny owl **(b)** *F Péj* (*femme désagréable*) old shrew

chouette² *F* **1** *adj* terrific, marvellous, great; **c'est c.!** that's great *or* smashing!; **un type vraiment c.** a really great guy; **il a été très c. avec elle** he has been really good to her; *Iron* **tu as l'air c. avec ton chapeau!** you look (like) something else in that hat! **2** *int* **c. (alors)!** great!, fantastic!

chou-fleur, *pl* **choux-fleurs** *nm* cauliflower; **oreille en c.** cauliflower ear

chouïa [ʃuja] *adv F* **un c. (de)** a tiny bit, a smidgen; **tu devrais te reposer un c.** you should have a bit of a *or* a little rest

chou-navet, *pl* **choux-navets** *nm* swede, *Am* rutabaga

chou-palmiste, *pl* **choux-palmistes** *nm Bot* palm cabbage

chou-rave, *pl* **choux-raves** *nm* kohlrabi

chouraver [ʃurave] *vt F* to pinch, to nick; **on m'a chouravé mon vélo** I've had my bike pinched *or* nicked

chourer [ʃure] *vt* = **chouraver**

chow-chow, *pl* **chows-chows** [ʃuʃu, ʃawʃaw] *nm* chow (dog)

choyer [ʃwaje] *vt* **(je choie; je choierai)** to pamper, to coddle; **c. un espoir** to cherish a hope

chrême [krɛm] *nm Rel* chrism, holy oil

chrétien, -ienne [kretjɛ̃, -jɛn] **1** *adj* Christian **2** *n* Christian; **un bon c.** a good Christian

chrétiennement [kretjɛnmɑ̃] *adv* in a Christian manner, like a Christian; **mourir c.** to die a Christian death

chrétienté [kretjɛ̃te] *nf* Christendom

chris(-)craft® [kriskraft] *nm Naut* Chris Craft

Christ [krist] *nm* **(a) le C.** Christ; **Jésus-C.** [ʒezykri] Jesus Christ; **(b) c.** crucifix; **un c. d'ivoire/d'ébène** an ivory/ebony crucifix

christiania [kristjanja] *nm Ski* christiania, christie (turn)

christianisation [kristjanizasjɔ̃] *nf* christianization

christianiser [kristjanize] *vt* to christianize

christianisme [kristjanism] *nm* Christianity

chromage [kromaʒ] *nm* chromium plating

chromate [krɔmat] *nm Ch* chromate

chromatique [krɔmatik] *adj* **(a)** *Mus, Opt etc* chromatic **(b)** *Biol* chromosomal

chromatiquement [krɔmatikmɑ̃] *adv Mus* chromatically

chromatisme [krɔmatism] *nm Mus* chromaticism; *Beaux-Arts* range of colours

chrome [krom] *nm* **(a)** *Ch* chromium; (*sur auto etc*) chromium fitting; *F* **faire (briller) les chromes** (*de voitures, de bicyclettes etc*) to polish the chrome **(b)** *Ch* chrome; **jaune de c.** chrome yellow

chromé [krome] *adj* (*métal*) chromium-plated; **acier c.** chrome steel

chromer [krome] *vt* **(a)** (*métal*) to chromium-plate **(b)** (*acier*) to chrome

chromo [krɔmo] *nm F* chromo(lithograph), colour print

chromosome [krɔmozom] *nm Biol* chromosome; **c. somatique** autosome, somatic chromosome

chromosomique [krɔmozomik] *adj Biol* chromosomal; **maladie c.** chromosomal *or* genetic illness

chronicité [krɔnisite] *nf* (*d'une maladie, du chômage etc*) chronic nature, *Fml* chronicity

chronique¹ [krɔnik] *adj* (*maladie, chômage etc*) chronic; **mévente c.** slump in sales

chronique² *nf* **(a)** *Journ* (*financière etc*) news, report, column; **tenir la c. sportive** to write the sports column; *Fig* **défrayer la c.** to be the talk of the neighbourhood *or* town, to be the main topic of conversation **(b)** (*annale*) chronicle

chroniquement [krɔnikmɑ̃] *adv* chronically

chroniqueur, -euse [krɔnikœr, -øz] *n* **(a)** *Journ* columnist, editor; **c. judiciaire** court reporter **(b)** (*historien*) chronicler

chrono [krɔno] *nm F* stopwatch; **du 220 (km/h) (au) c.** recorded speed of 220 (km/h); **son temps était de 4 minutes 6 secondes, c. en main** his time by the clock was 4 minutes (and) 6 seconds

chronobiologie [krɔnobjɔlɔʒi] *nf Biol* chronobiology

chronogramme [krɔnogram] *nm* planner

chronographe [krɔnograf] *nm Tech* chronograph

chronologie [krɔnɔlɔʒi] *nf* chronology

chronologique [krɔnɔlɔʒik] *adj* chronological

chronologiquement [krɔnɔlɔʒikmɑ̃] *adv* chronologically

chronométrage [krɔnɔmetraʒ] *nm* time-keeping; (*d'une course*) timing

chronomètre [krɔnɔmɛtr] *nm* **(a)** (*pour le sport etc*) stopwatch **(b)** (*montre de précision*) chronometer; *Ordinat* timer

chronométrer [krɔnɔmetre] *vt* **(je chronomètre; je chronométrerai)** *Sp* to time

chronométreur [krɔnɔmetrœr] *nm* **(a)** *Sp* timekeeper **(b)** *Ind* time and motion (study) expert

chronométrique [krɔnɔmetrik] *adj* chronometric(al)

chrysalide [krizalid] *nf Ent* chrysalis, pupa; *Fig* **sortir de sa c.** to come out of one's shell

chrysanthème [krizɑ̃tɛm] *nm* chrysanthemum

chrysolithe [krizɔlit] *nf Minér* chrysolite, olivine

ch'timi [ʃtimi] *F* **1** *adj* from Northern France **2** *n* person from Northern France

CHU [seaʃy] *nm inv* (*abrév* **centre hospitalier universitaire**) ≈ teaching hospital

chuchotement [ʃyʃɔtmɑ̃] *nm* whisper; **chuchotements** whispering, whispers
chuchoter [ʃyʃɔte] **1** *vi* to whisper; **parler en chuchotant** to speak in a whisper **2** *vt* **c. qch à l'oreille de qn** to whisper sth in sb's ear
chuchoterie [ʃyʃɔtri] *nf* whispering, whispered conversation
chuchoteur, -euse [ʃyʃɔtœr, -øz] **1** *adj* whispering **2** *n* whisperer
chuintant, -ante [ʃɥɛ̃tɑ̃, -ɑ̃t] *Ling* **1** *adj* **sons chuintants** hushing sounds (*eg S, Z*); **consonne chuintante** palato-alveolar fricative **2** *nf* **chuintante** palato-alveolar fricative
chuintement [ʃɥɛ̃tmɑ̃] *nm* (**a**) *Ling* pronunciation of s as sh (**b**) (*sifflement*) hissing
chuinter [ʃɥɛ̃te] *vi* (**a**) (*de la chouette*) to hoot (**b**) *Ling* to pronounce s as sh (**c**) (*de la vapeur etc*) to hiss
chut [ʃyt] *int* hush!, sh!
chute [ʃyt] *nf* (**a**) (*fait de tomber*) fall; *Fig* (*d'un ministère etc*) fall, collapse; (*de pression, de température etc*) drop, fall; (*de ventes etc*) slump; **faire une c. (de cheval/moto)** to have a fall *or* a tumble *or* a spill (from one's horse/motorbike), to fall off (one's horse/motorbike); **une c. de 10 mètres** a 10 metre fall; **il a fait une c. de dix mètres** he fell ten metres; **'c. de pierres'** 'danger!, falling rocks'; **c. de pluie/neige** rainfall/snowfall; **c. du jour** nightfall; *Litt* **c. des feuilles** autumn, *Am* fall; **la c. des feuilles a eu lieu plus tôt que d'habitude cette année** the trees lost their leaves sooner than usual this year; **c. des cheveux** hair loss; **c. des prix** fall *or* drop in prices; **la c. de l'homme** the Fall; **il m'a entraîné dans sa c.** he has dragged me down with him; *Th* **c. d'une pièce** failure *or F* flop of a play; *Cartes* **avoir deux levées de c.** to be two tricks down; *Él* **c. de potentiel** voltage drop
(**b**) **c. d'eau** waterfall; **les Chutes Victoria** the Victoria Falls; **c. naturelle** natural waterfall; **hauteur de c.** (*d'eau*) fall, head
(**c**) (*du toit*) pitch; (*d'une robe*) hang; (*de la voix etc*) cadence; (*d'un poème, roman, d'une pièce etc*) end; (*d'histoire drôle*) punchline
(**d**) (*de bois*) off-cut; (*de tissu etc*) scraps, trimmings; (*de métal*) scrap
▶ **chute**: **c. libre** free fall; **descendre en c. libre** to (be in) free fall; *Fig* **ses résultats scolaires descendent en c. libre** his marks are plummeting *or* have taken a nose dive; **c. des reins** small of the back; *Th* **c. du rideau** fall of the curtain
chuter [ʃyte] *vi F* (*tomber*) to fall (down); *Fig* to come a cropper, to come to grief; *Th* (*d'une pièce de théâtre*) to be a failure, to flop; *Cartes* **c. de deux levées** to be two tricks down
chyme [ʃim] *nm Méd* chyme
Chypre [ʃipr] *nf* **(l'île de) C.** Cyprus
chypriote [ʃiprijɔt] **1** *adj* Cypriot **2** *n* **C.** Cypriot
ci[1] [si] *adv* here; **ce livre-ci** this book; **ces jours-ci** these days; **de-ci, de-là** here and there, on all sides; **par-ci, par-là** here and there; **ci-gît .../-gisent ...** here lies .../lie ...
ci[2] *pron dém inv F* **faire ci et ça** to do this and that; **comme ci, comme ça** so-so
ciao [tʃao] *int F* ciao
ci-après *adv* (*dans la suite du texte etc*) later, further on, below; *Jur* here(in)after
cibiche [sibiʃ] *nf F* fag, ciggie
cibiste [sibist] *n* user of citizen band radio, CB user
ciblage [siblaʒ] *nm Mktg* targeting; **c. stratégique** strategic targeting
cible [sibl] *nf* target, mark; (*en publicité*) target; **servir de c. aux railleries de qn** to be the butt *or* the target for sb's jokes; **déterminer/atteindre la c.** to define/to reach the target; **langue c.** target language; *Mktg* **marché c.** (*pour un produit*) target market; **c. commerciale/de communication** marketing/promotional target
ciblé [sible] *adj* (*campagne etc*) targeted (**sur** at)
cibler [sible] *vt Mktg* to target
ciboire [sibwar] *nm Rel* pyx, ciborium
ciboule [sibul] *nf Bot, Culin* spring onion, *Am* scallion
ciboulette [sibulɛt] *nf* (*plante*), *Culin* chive(s)
ciboulot [sibulo] *nm Arg* (*tête*) noddle, nut; **se creuser le c.** to rack one's brains; **en avoir dans le c.** to have a lot between one's ears; **elle en a dans le c., cette petite!** she's not just a pretty face, this girl!
cicatrice [sikatris] *nf* scar; *Fig* **cette séparation a laissé une c. profonde en lui** the separation scarred him deeply *or* left a deep scar on him
cicatriciel, -ielle [sikatrisjɛl] *adj* **tissu c.** scar tissue
cicatrisant [sikatrizɑ̃] **1** *adj* (*pommade etc*) healing, *Spéc* cicatrizing **2** *nm* healing lotion *or* cream
cicatrisation [sikatrizasjɔ̃] *nf* (*de blessure etc*) healing, closing (up), *Spéc* cicatrization
cicatriser [sikatrize] **1** *vt* (*blessure etc*) to heal; **le temps cicatrise toutes les blessures** time heals all wounds **2** *vi* (*d'une blessure etc*) to heal (up) **3 se cicatriser** *vpr* to heal up; *Fig* to heal
cicéro [sisero] *nm Typ* pica, twelve-point type
ciclosporine [siklɔspɔrin] *nf Ch* cyclosporin
ci-contre *adv* (**a**) (*en regard*) opposite; *Compta* **porté c.** as per contra (**b**) (*document etc*) attached
ci-dessous [sid(ə)su] *adv* below
ci-dessus [sid(ə)sy] *adv* above(-mentioned)
ci-devant [sid(ə)vɑ̃] **1** *adv* previously, formerly **2** *n inv Fr Hist* aristocrat
cidre [sidr] *nm* cider; **c. bouché** bottled cider; **c. doux/brut** sweet/dry cider
cidrerie [sidrəri] *nf* (*fabrique*) cider house
Cie (*abrév* **Compagnie**) Co
ciel [sjɛl], *pl* **ciels, cieux** [sjø] *nm* (**a**) (*espace*) sky; **être suspendu entre c. et terre** to hang in mid-air; **(couleur) bleu (de) c.** sky-blue; **trouée de c. (bleu)** patch of (blue) sky; **les ciels de l'Italie** the skies of Italy; *Beaux-Arts* **les ciels de Turner** Turner's skies; **carte du c.** map of the heavens; **à c. ouvert** in the open air, out of doors; **sous d'autres cieux** beneath other skies, in other climes; **lever les bras au c.** to raise one's arms to the sky *or* heavenwards; **lever les yeux au c.** to raise one's eyes to heaven; *F* **tomber du c.** to be thunderstruck; *Fig* **ça ne va pas te tomber du c.** it won't fall into your lap, you won't get it handed to you on a plate; *Fig* **remuer c. et terre** to move heaven and earth **(pour faire qch** to do sth); **être au septième c.** to be in seventh heaven; *Fig* **élever qn aux cieux** *ou* **jusqu'au c.** to laud sb to the skies
(**b**) (*paradis*) heaven; **il est monté au c.** he's gone to heaven; **notre Père qui es** *ou* **êtes aux cieux** our Father which *or* who art in Heaven; **le royaume des cieux** the Kingdom of Heaven; **le c. m'en est témoin** (as) Heaven is my witness; **(juste) c.!** (good) heavens!, heavens above!; **aide-toi, le c. t'aidera** God helps those who help themselves; **grâce au c.** thank heavens
(**c**) *pl* **ciels** *Rel* baldachin, canopy; (*de lit*) canopy; *Min* (*d'une carrière etc*) roof; **carrière/mine à c. ouvert** opencast quarry/mine
cierge [sjɛrʒ] *nm Rel* candle; **brûler un c. à un saint** to burn a candle to a saint
cigale [sigal] *nf* (*insecte*) cicada; *Fig F* (*dépensier*) spendthrift
cigare [sigar] *nm* (**a**) (*à fumer*) cigar (**b**) *Arg* (*tête*) nut, bonce; **avoir mal au c.** to have a headache; **mets-toi ça dans le c.** get that into your thick skull
cigarette [sigarɛt] *nf* cigarette
cigarillo [sigarijo] *nm* cigarillo
cigogne [sigɔɲ] *nf* (**a**) (*oiseau*) stork (**b**) (*levier*) crank lever
ciguë [sigy] *nf* (*plante*), *Méd* hemlock
ci-inclus [siɛ̃kly] **1** *adj* (*inv when it precedes the noun*) **la copie ci-incluse** the enclosed copy **2** *adv* **(vous trouverez) c. copie de votre lettre** please find enclosed a copy of your letter
CIJ [seiʒi] *nf* (*abrév* **Cour internationale de justice**) ICJ
ci-joint 1 *adj* (*inv when it precedes the noun*) attached, enclosed; **les pièces ci-jointes** the enclosed *or* attached documents **2** *adv* **vous trouverez c. quittance** please find receipt attached *or* enclosed
cil [sil] *nm* (**a**) (eye)lash; **battre des cils** to flutter one's eyelashes; **faux cils** false eyelashes (**b**) *Biol* cilium, hair, filament
cilice [silis] *nm* hair shirt
cillement [sijmɑ̃] *nm* blinking
ciller [sije] *vi* to blink; *Fig* **il n'a pas cillé** he didn't bat an eyelid
cimaise [simɛz] *nf* ogee moulding; (*à hauteur d'appui*) dado (rail)
cime [sim] *nf* (*d'une montagne etc*) summit; (*pic*) peak; (*d'un arbre, d'un mât etc*) top; *Fig* **être à la c. de la réussite** to be at the height *or* peak of one's success
ciment [simɑ̃] *nm* cement; **c. à prise rapide** quick-setting cement; **c. armé** reinforced concrete; **c. dentaire** amalgam
cimentation [simɑ̃tasjɔ̃] *nf* cementing
cimenter [simɑ̃te] *vt* to cement; *Fig* **c. une alliance/une amitié/une relation** to cement *or* consolidate an alliance/a friendship/a relationship
cimenterie [simɑ̃tri] *nf Ind* cement works
cimeterre [simtɛr] *nm* scimitar
cimetière [simtjɛr] *nm* cemetery, graveyard; (*d'église*) churchyard; **c. de voitures** scrapyard; **c. d'éléphants** elephants' graveyard
cimier[1] [simje] *nm* (*d'un casque*) crest
cimier[2] *nm* (*d'un cerf etc*) haunch; (*d'un bœuf*) rump
cinabre [sinabr] *nm* cinnabar

ciné [sine] *nm Br F* pictures, *Am* movies; **aller au c.** to go to the pictures
cinéaste [sineast] *n* film maker
ciné-club, *pl* **ciné-clubs** *nm* film club
cinéma [sinema] *nm* **(a)** (*art*) cinema, movies, *Am* motion pictures; **le c. de Pasolini** Pasolini's films; **l'invention du c.** the invention of cinema *or* motion pictures; **studio de c.** film studio; **faire du c.** (*d'un acteur*) to be a film *or* movie actor, to act in films; (*d'un metteur en scène, technicien etc*) to work in films; **acteur/actrice de c.** film *or* movie actor/actress; **critique de c.** cinema *or* film critic; **industrie du c.** film *or* movie industry, *Am* motion picture industry; *F* **c'est du c.** it's all an act, it's all put on; **elle a fait tout un c. pour ne pas y aller** she made a scene so that she didn't have to go; **arrête (un peu) ton c. et va te coucher!** stop making such a fuss and go to bed!
(b) (*salle*) cinema, *Am* movie theater, *Br F* pictures; **aller au c.** to go to the cinema; **ouvreuse de c.** usherette
▶ **cinéma**: **c. d'amateurs** amateur film-making, home movies; **c. d'animation** animation; **c. d'art et d'essai** (*genre*) art films, (*bâtiment*) art-house cinema; **c. muet** silent films; **c. multi-salle** multi-screen cinema, multiplex; **c. parlant** talking films; *F* talkies; **c. permanent** continuous performance; **c. en relief** three dimensional *or* 3-D films
cinémascope® [sinemaskɔp] *nm* cinemascope
cinémathèque [sinematɛk] *nf* film library *or* archives
cinématique [sinematik] **1** *adj* kinematic(al) **2** *nf* kinematics
cinématographe [sinematɔgraf] *nm* cinematograph
cinématographie [sinematɔgrafi] *nf* cinematography
cinématographier [sinematɔgrafje] *vt* to film
cinématographique [sinematɔgrafik] *adj* cinematographic; (*production etc*) cinema, film
cinématophotographie [sinematɔfɔtɔgrafi] *nf* camerawork
cinémomètre [sinemɔmɛtr] *nm Tech* speedometer, speed gauge
ciné-parc, *pl* **cinés-parcs** *nm Can* drive-in movie-theater
cinéphile [sinefil] **1** *adj* film- *or* movie-loving; **public c.** cinema-going public; **ils sont tous très cinéphiles dans cette famille** they're all great film-lovers *or* film *or* movie buffs in that family **2** *n* film *or* movie enthusiast *or* buff
cinéraire [sinerɛr] **1** *adj* (*urne etc*) cinerary **2** *nf* (*plante*) cineraria
Cinérama® [sinerama] *nm* Cinerama
ciné-roman, *pl* **ciné-romans** *nm* = picture book of a film; *Arch* (*film*) (film) serial
cinétique [sinetik] **1** *adj* (*énergie etc*) kinetic **2** *nf* kinetics
cing(h)alais, -aise [sɛ̃galɛ, -ɛz] **1** *adj* Sin(g)halese **2** *nm Ling* Sin(g)halese **3** *n* **C.** Sin(g)halese
cinglant [sɛ̃glɑ̃] *adj* (*pluie etc*) lashing; (*vent etc*) cutting, biting; (*froid*) bitter; (*remarque*) stinging, cutting, scathing
cinglé, -ée [sɛ̃gle] *F* **1** *adj* cracked, crazy; **il est complètement c.** he's off his rocker, he's round the twist **2** *n* loony, nutcase
cingler[1] [sɛ̃gle] *vi Naut* **un voilier qui cingle aux Canaries** a yacht making for *or* bound for the Canary Islands
cingler[2] *vt* (*visage*) (*du vent*) to sting; (*cheval etc*) to lash, to whip; (*qn*) to lash out at; **une branche m'a cinglé la figure** a branch whipped (against) my face; **la grêle lui cinglait le visage** the hail was stinging his face
cinoche [sinɔʃ] *nm F* cinema, *US* movie theater; **aller au c.** to go to the pictures *or* movies; **je me ferais bien un petit c. ce soir** I quite fancy going to the pictures tonight
cinoque [sinɔk] *Arg* **1** *adj* batty, crazy **2** *n* nutcase, headbanger
cinq [sɛ̃k] **1** *adj inv* five; **c. (petits) garçons** [sɛ̃(pti)garsɔ̃] five (little) boys; **c. hommes** [sɛ̃kɔm] five men; **j'en ai c.** [sɛ̃k] I've got five; **Henri C.** Henry the Fifth; **le c. mars** [sɛ̃(k)mars] the fifth of March, March the fifth; *Euph* **les c. lettres** ≈ a four-letter word; **je lui ai répondu en c. lettres** I told him where to go; **il était moins c.** it was a near thing *or* a close shave; **attends c. minutes** just give me a minute, *F* hang on a sec
2 *nm inv* **(a)** five; **le nombre c.** the number five; *Rad* **recevoir qn c. sur c.** to receive sb loud and clear; *Fig* **faire qch en c. sec** to do sth in five seconds flat; *Cartes* **un c. de pique** a five of spades; *Journ* **c. colonnes à la Une** a banner headline
(b) *Aut* **c. places** five-seater; **c. portes** five-door model
cinquantaine [sɛ̃kɑ̃tɛn] *nf* (about) fifty; **une c. de personnes** about *or* some fifty people, fifty or so people; **approcher la c.** to be getting on for fifty; **passer la c.** to be in one's fifties
cinquante [sɛ̃kɑ̃t] **1** *adj inv* fifty; **billet de c. francs** fifty-franc note; **page c.** page fifty; **demeurer au numéro c.** to live at number fifty; **les années c.** the fifties **2** *nm inv* fifty; **le numéro c.** the number fifty, 50; **c. pour cent ont refusé** fifty per cent refused
cinquantenaire [sɛ̃kɑ̃tnɛr] **1** *nm* fiftieth anniversary **2** *adj* fifty year(s) old
cinquantième [sɛ̃kɑ̃tjɛm] **1** *adj* fiftieth **2** *n* fiftieth; **être le c. dans un classement** to be placed *or* come fiftieth in a classification *or* grading **3** *nm* fiftieth (part)
cinquième [sɛ̃kjɛm] **1** *adj* fifth; **loger au c. étage** to live on the fifth *or Am* sixth floor; **être la c. roue de la charrette** *ou* **du carosse** to feel out of it, *Am* to feel like a fifth wheel **2** *n* fifth; **elle est arrivée la c.** she came (in) fifth, she came in in fifth place **3** *nm* fifth (part) **4** *nf* **(a)** *Scol* **(classe de) c.** ≈ second form *or* year (of secondary school), *Am* seventh grade **(b)** *Aut* fifth gear
cinquièmement [sɛ̃kjɛmmɑ̃] *adv* fifthly, in (the) fifth place
cintrage [sɛ̃traʒ] *nm* (*action*) bending; (*resultat*) bend
cintre [sɛ̃tr] *nm* **(a)** (*pour les vêtements*) coathanger, clothes hanger; **suspendre sa veste à un c.** to put one's jacket on a (clothes) hanger **(b)** (*courbure*) curve; **des épaules en c.** rounded shoulders **(c)** *Archit* (*d'un tunnel etc*) arch; (*d'une voûte*) soffit; **arc en plein c.** semicircular arch **(d)** *Th* **les cintres** the flies; **c. de lumière** lighting batten
cintré [sɛ̃tre] *adj* **(a)** (*fenêtre etc*) arched; (*poutre etc*) bent, curved; (*veste etc*) fitted; **taille cintrée** nipped-in waist **(b)** *F* crazy
cintrer [sɛ̃tre] *vt* **(a)** (*tuyau, rail etc*) to bend, to curve **(b)** (*fenêtre*) to arch **(c)** **c. une veste** to take in a jacket at the waist
CIO [seio] *nm* (*abrév* **Comité international olympique**) IOC
cipaye [sipaj] *nm* sepoy; *Hist* **la révolte des cipayes** the Indian Mutiny
cirage [siraʒ] *nm* **(a)** (*des sols etc*) waxing, polishing; (*des chaussures*) polishing **(b)** (*substance*) (shoe) polish; **c. de couleur/incolore** coloured/neutral polish; **c. pour cuir/parquet** leather/floor polish; *F* **être dans le c.** to be a bit fuzzy, to be confused, *Av* to be flying blind
circadien [sirkadjɛ̃] *adj Biol* **rythme c.** circadian rhythm
circlip [sirklip] *nm MecE* circlip
circoncire [sirkɔ̃sir] *vt* (*prp* **circoncisant**; *pp* **conconcis**; *pr ind* **je circoncis**; *pr sub* **je circoncise**; *p hist* **je circoncis**; *fu* **je circoncirai**) to circumcise
circoncis [sirkɔ̃si] *adj, n* circumcised (boy/man)
circoncision [sirkɔ̃sizjɔ̃] *nf* circumcision
circonférence [sirkɔ̃ferɑ̃s] *nf* **(a)** *Géom* circumference; (*d'un arbre*) circumference, girth; **avoir dix centimètres de c.** to have a circumference of ten centimetres, to be ten centimetres in circumference **(b)** (*d'une ville etc*) perimeter, boundaries
circonflexe [sirkɔ̃flɛks] *adj* (*accent*) circumflex
circonlocution [sirkɔ̃lɔkysjɔ̃] *nf* circumlocution; **parler par circonlocutions** to speak in a roundabout way; *F* to beat about the bush; **après de longues circonlocutions, il finit par nous déclarer que ...** after much beating about the bush, he eventually announced that ...
circonscription [sirkɔ̃skripsjɔ̃] *nf Admin etc* division, district, area; **c. électorale** (*au niveau municipal*) ward; (*au niveau national*) constituency, *Can* riding; **c. téléphonique** telephone code area
circonscrire [sirkɔ̃skrir] (*conj like* **écrire**) **1** *vt Math* to circumscribe, to draw a line round; (*espace, bloc de maisons*) to surround, to encircle (**par** with, by); (*limiter*) to limit; **c. son sujet** to define the scope of one's subject; **c. un incendie** to bring a fire under control, to contain a fire **2 se circonscrire** *vpr* to be bounded, to be limited; **le débat se circonscrit autour d'une seule idée** the whole debate centres on *or* is centred around one idea
circonspect [sirkɔ̃spɛ(kt)] *adj* circumspect, cautious, wary; **il était c. dans ses propos** he spoke cautiously; **il était c. dans le choix de ses fréquentations** he was careful in his choice of company
circonspection [sirkɔ̃spɛksjɔ̃] *nf* circumspection, caution, wariness; **avec c.** cautiously, warily
circonstance [sirkɔ̃stɑ̃s] *nf* **(a)** (*cas*) circumstance; **dans les circonstances actuelles, il faut se montrer prudent** given the circumstances *or* as things stand, we must tread carefully; **se retrouver dans des circonstances difficiles** to find oneself in difficult circumstances; **en pareille c.** under such circumstances, in such a case; **à la hauteur des circonstances** equal to the occasion; **eu égard aux** *ou* **étant donné les circonstances** all things considered, in *or* given the circumstances; **par un concours de circonstances** by a combination of circumstances; **profiter de la c.** to make the most of the opportunity; **vers de c.** occasional verse; **paroles de c.** words suited to the occasion, appropriate *or* suitable words; **ce ne serait pas de c.** it would not be appropriate
(b) *Jur* **circonstances et dépendances** appurtenances; **circonstances atténuantes** extenuating circumstances; **circonstances aggravantes** aggravating circumstances

circonstancié [sirkɔ̃stɑ̃sje] *adj (rapport)* detailed
circonstanciel, -ielle [sirkɔ̃stɑ̃sjɛl] *adj* **(a)** *Litt* circumstantial; **des mesures rigoureusement circonstancielles** measures dictated by exceptional circumstances; **déclaration/mesure circonstancielle** declaration/measure dictated by the circumstances **(b)** *Gram* **complément c. (de temps/de lieu)** adverbial complement (of time/place)
circonvenir [sirkɔ̃vnir] *vt (conj like* **venir***) (personne)* to take in
circonvolution [sirkɔ̃vɔlysjɔ̃] *nf Anat, Archit* convolution; *Archit (de volutes etc)* circumvolution
circuit [sirkɥi] *nm* **(a)** *Sp* round, lap; *(d'une course de motos etc)* circuit; **c. automobile** racing circuit; **c. de petites voitures** racing track
(b) c. (touristique) (organized) trip, tour; **c. en car** coach tour; **faire le c. des châteaux de la Loire** to tour the Loire châteaux
(c) *(chemin)* way; **refaire tout le c. à pied** to go all the way back on foot; **c. touristique** scenic *or* tourist route; **il faut faire un long c. pour passer d'un côté de l'île à l'autre** you have to make a long detour to get from one side of the island to the other
(d) *Él* circuit; **c. ouvert/fermé** open/closed circuit; **télévision à c. fermé** closed circuit television; **c. basse tension** low-tension circuit; **c. haute tension** high-tension circuit; **c. d'induction** inductive circuit; **c. intégré** integrated circuit; **c. de retour à la masse** earth return circuit; **mettre en c.** to connect, to switch on; **couper le c.** to switch off; **rétablir le c.** to switch on (again); **mettre une lampe hors c.** to disconnect a lamp; *Fig* **ils ont tendance à vivre en c. fermé** they tend to lead their own separate existence *or* to live in a closed world; *Fig* **ça fait longtemps que je ne suis plus dans le c.** I've been out of it for ages, I'm hopelessly out of touch; *Fig* **il est complètement hors c.** he's completely out of touch
(e) *Tech, Aut* **c. d'allumage** ignition system; **c. d'allumage par bobine** coil-ignition system; **c. de carburant étanche** sealed fuel system; **c. de charge** *(de batterie)* charging system; **c. de démarrage** starting circuit; **c. d'eau** water circuit; **c. de freinage** braking system; **c. de graissage** lubrication circuit; **c. hydraulique** hydraulic circuit; **c. d'injection d'essence** petrol injection system; **c. de lubrification** lubrication system; **c. oléopneumatique** air/hydraulic system; **c. de préchauffage** pre-heating system; **c. de refroidissement** cooling system
(f) *Ordinat* **c. de commande** command circuit; **c. de liaison** link circuit; **c. logique** logic circuit; **circuits de rafraîchissement** *ou* **de régénération** refresh circuitry
(g) *Econ* **c. de commercialisation** marketing network, trade *or* marketing channel; **c. de distribution** distribution channels *or* network; **circuits de vente** commercial channels
▶ **circuit**: **c. aventure** adventure holiday; *Électron* **c. imprimé** printed circuit
circulaire [sirkylɛr] **1** *adj* circular; **billet c.** excursion ticket; **scie c.** circular saw; *MecE* **mouvement c.** rotary motion **2** *nf* circular
circulairement [sirkylɛrmɑ̃] *adv* in a circle
circulation [sirkylasjɔ̃] *nf* **(a)** *(d'autos, d'avions)* traffic; **c. routière** road traffic; **c. aérienne** air traffic; **c. des trains** running of trains; **c. à sens unique/à deux sens** one-/two-way traffic; **c. interdite** no thoroughfare; **les embarras de la c.** traffic congestion; **route à grande c.** trunk road; **accident de la c.** road accident; **la c. est très difficile** the traffic is very heavy; **il y a beaucoup de c. sur les routes** there's a lot of traffic on the roads; *Fig* **disparaître de la c.** to drop out of circulation
(b) *(de l'air, du sang, de l'information, des marchandises etc)* circulation; *Méd* **problèmes de c.** circulation *or* circulatory problems; **mettre un livre en c.** to put a book into circulation; **mise en c. de qch** circulation of sth; **retirer un produit de la c.** to take a product off the market
(c) *Fin (des billets etc)* circulation; **c. des capitaux/des devises** circulation of capital/currency; **c. monétaire** circulation of money
(d) *Pol, Econ* **libre c. des travailleurs/des citoyens** free movement of workers/of citizens
circulatoire [sirkylatwar] *adj Anat* circulatory
circuler [sirkyle] *vi* **(a)** *(du sang, de l'air etc)* to circulate, to flow; *(d'une rumeur)* to circulate; **faire c. l'air** to circulate the air; *Fin* **les capitaux qui circulent** capital in circulation, circulating capital; **faire c. la bouteille** to pass *or* hand the bottle round; **faire c. une nouvelle** to spread a piece of news; **faire c. une pétition** to circulate a petition **(b)** *(en voiture)* to travel, to move about; **circulez, il n'y a rien à voir!** move along now, there's nothing to see!; **les autobus circulent jour et nuit** the buses run day and night; **on a du mal à c. en ville** it's not easy to drive in town; **on circule très mal à ce moment de la journée** it's very difficult to get anywhere at this time of day
circumnavigation [sirkɔmnavigasjɔ̃] *nf* circumnavigation
cire [sir] *nf* wax; *(encaustique)* (wax) polish; **bouchon de c.** *(dans l'oreille)* plug of earwax; **c. d'abeille** beeswax; **c. à cacheter** sealing wax; **personnage en c.** waxwork; **c. anti-corrosion** anti-corrosion wax
ciré [sire] **1** *adj* polished; **parquet c.** polished *or* waxed floor; **chaussures bien cirées** well-polished shoes; **toile cirée** oilcloth **2** *nm* oilskin
cirer [sire] *vt (sols, meubles etc)* to polish, to wax; *(corde etc)* to wax; **c. ses chaussures** to polish one's shoes; *F* **c. les bottes de qn** to lick sb's boots; *Arg* **il n'en a rien à c. (de tes histoires)** he doesn't give a damn (about your stories)
cireur, -euse [sirœr, -øz] **1** *n* **(a)** *(de chaussures)* shoeblack, *Am* shoeshine boy **(b)** *(de sols)* (floor) polisher **2** *nf* **cireuse** *(machine)* (electric) (floor) polisher
cireux, -euse [sirø, -øz] *adj* waxy
cirque [sirk] *nm* **(a)** circus; **c. forain** *ou* **ambulant** travelling circus; **aller au c.** to go to the circus; **gens du c.** circus people; **le c. Zavatta** Zavatta's circus **(b)** *F (chambard)* **quel c., ici!** it's like a zoo in here!; **quel c. pour obtenir ces renseignements!** what a performance *or* carry-on just to get this information!; **faire le c.** to rampage around; **faire tout un c.** to make a scene, to kick up a fuss; **arrête de faire ton c.!** stop your silly nonsense! **(c)** *Géol* cirque, corrie
cirrhose [siroz] *nf Méd* cirrhosis; **c. du foie** cirrhosis of the liver; **avoir une c. du foie** to have cirrhosis (of the liver)
cirro-cumulus [sirokymylys] *nm inv Météo* cirrocumulus
cirro-stratus [sirostratys] *nm inv Météo* cirrostratus
cirrus [sirys] *nm inv Météo* cirrus, *F* mare's tail
cisaille [sizɑj] *nf* **(a)** *(rognures en métal)* parings, cuttings **(b)** *(massicot)* guillotine **(c)** [①Al0,e] **cisailles** shears; *(pour câble)* wirecutters; **c. à haies** hedge clipper(s); **c. à bordures** edging shears
cisaillement [sizɑjmɑ̃] *nm* **(a)** *(du métal)* cutting, shearing; *(des branches)* pruning **(b)** *Tech (usure)* shearing, shear
cisailler [sizɑje] **1** *vt* **(a)** *(branches)* to prune **(b)** *(métal)* to cut, to shear **(c)** *(joue, main etc)* to slash **2 se cisailler** *vpr (d'un métal)* to shear (off)
cisalpin [sizalpɛ̃] *adj Antiq* on the Roman side of the Alps, Cisalpine; *Hist* **République cisalpine** Cisalpine Republic
ciseau, -eaux [sizo] *nm* **(a)** [①A10,e] **(paire de) ciseaux** (pair of) scissors; *(de jardin)* shears, clippers; **ciseaux à bouts ronds** blunt- *or* round-ended scissors; **ciseaux à ongles** nail scissors; **ciseaux de couturière** dressmaking scissors; *Couture* **ciseaux à denteler** pinking shears; **coup de ciseaux** snip (of the scissors); **donner des coups de ciseaux dans qch** to snip away at sth with a pair of scissors; *Fig* **donner des coups de ciseaux dans un texte** to prune *or* cut down a text **(b)** *Sp* **c., saut en ciseaux** scissors (jump); *Gym* **faire des ciseaux** to do the scissors **(c)** *Tech* chisel
ciselage [sizlaʒ] *nm* = **cisellement**
ciseler [sizle] *vt* **(je cisèle; je ciselerai)** *(or, argent)* to chase, to engrave; *(marbre)* to chisel; *Fig (poème etc)* to polish up, to work on; **c. un bijou** to engrave a design on a piece of jewellery; **visage délicatement ciselé** finely chiselled features
ciseleur [sizlœr] *nm* engraver
cisellement [sizɛlmɑ̃] *nm (de l'or, de l'argent)* chasing, engraving
ciselure [sizlyr] *nf (en or, en argent)* chasing, engraving; *(sur le bois)* chiselling, carving; *(sur un bijou, une pièce d'orfèvrerie)* (engraved) design
cistercien, -ienne [sistɛrsjɛ̃, -jɛn] *Rel* **1** *adj (moine, architecture)* Cistercian **2** *nm* Cistercian
citadelle [sitadɛl] *nf* citadel, stronghold; *Fig* **une c. du protestantisme** a Protestant stronghold, a stronghold of Protestantism
citadin, -ine [sitadɛ̃, -in] **1** *n* town-dweller, city-dweller **2** *adj* (belonging to a) town *or* city **3** *nf* **citadine** *Aut* supermini
citation [sitasjɔ̃] *nf* **(a)** *(extrait)* quotation; **la référence de la c.** the reference for the quotation, the quotation reference; **fin de c.** end of quotation; *(dans une dictée)* close quotation marks **(b)** *Jur* (writ of) summons; **c. des témoins** subpoena of witnesses; **notifier une c. à** *(accusé)* to serve a summons on; *(témoin)* to subpoena
▶ **citation**: *Mil* **c. (à l'ordre du jour)** ≈ mention in dispatches; *Jur* **c. à comparaître** *(accusé)* summons; *(témoin)* subpoena
cité [site] *nf* **(a)** *(ville)* city, (large) town; **droit de c.** freedom of the city; *Fig* **ce genre d'original n'a pas droit de c. dans notre entreprise** there is no room for eccentrics like him in our company, our company doesn't take kindly to eccentrics like him; *Fig* **gagner droit de c.** to be accepted **(b)** *(groupe d'immeubles)* (housing) estate
▶ **cité**: **c.-dortoir**, *pl* **cités-dortoirs** dormitory town; **c.-ghetto**,

pl **cités-ghettos** ghetto housing estate; **c.-jardin**, *pl* **cités-jardins** garden city; **c. ouvrière** (company-built) housing estate; **c. de transit** temporary settlement; **c. universitaire** = students' hall(s) of residence

Cîteaux [sito] *nm Rel* **l'ordre de C.** the Cistercian Order

citer [site] *vt* **(a)** (*rapporter*) to quote, to cite; **c. un auteur** to cite *or* quote (from) an author; **c. qn en exemple** to quote sb *or* hold sb up as an example; **c. les paroles de qn** to quote sb's words; **il a dit, je cite: ...** he said, and I quote, ... **(b)** (*énumérer*) to name, to list **(c)** *Jur* (*qn en justice*) to summon; (*témoin*) to subpoena **(d)** *Mil* **c. qn (à l'ordre du jour)** ≈ to mention sb in dispatches

citerne [sitɛrn] *nf* tank, cistern; **c. à mazout** oil tank

cithare [sitar] *nf Mus* **(a)** (*instrument moderne*) zither **(b)** *Antiq* cithara

citizen band [sitizənbɑ̃d] *nf* citizen's band, CB

citoyen, -enne [sitwajɛ̃, -ɛn] *n* citizen; **droits du c.** civic rights; **accomplir son devoir de c.** (*voter*) to do one's civic duty, to vote; **c. d'honneur** = freeman of a city; **elle se déclare citoyenne du monde** she claims that she's a citizen of the world; *F* **c'est un drôle de c.!** he's a queer customer!

citoyenneté [sitwajɛnte] *nf* citizenship; **la c. française** French citizenship; **c. d'honneur d'une ville** = freedom of a city

citrate [sitrat] *nm Ch* citrate

citrique [sitrik] *adj Ch* (*acide*) citric

citron [sitrɔ̃] **1** *nm* **(a)** (*fruit*) lemon; **jus de c.** lemon juice; **c. pressé** freshly squeezed lemon juice; **c. givré** lemon sorbet served inside the skin of a whole lemon; **essence de c.** lemon oil; **écorce de c.** lemon peel; **c. vert** lime **(b)** *Arg* (*tête*) nut **2** *adj inv* lemon-yellow, lemon; **jaune c.** lemon-yellow

citronnade [sitrɔnad] *nf* still lemonade, lemon squash

citronné [sitrɔne] *adj* (*par l'odeur*) lemon-scented; (*par le goût*) lemon-flavoured

citronnelle [sitrɔnɛl] *nf* **(a)** (*plante*) citronella **(b)** (*liqueur*) lemon liqueur

citronnier [sitrɔnje] *nm* (*arbre*) lemon tree

citrouille [sitruj] *nf* **(a)** (*plante*) pumpkin; **tarte à la c.** pumpkin pie; *F* **j'ai la tête comme une c.** my head is fit to burst **(b)** *Arg* (*tête*) nut

cive [siv] *nf Bot, Culin* chives

civet [sivɛ] *nm Culin* (*de gibier etc*) stew; **c. de lièvre** = jugged hare; *Culin* **un c. de lapin** (a) rabbit stew

civette[1] [sivɛt] *nf* **(a)** *Zool* civet (cat) **(b)** *Com* civet (perfume)

civette[2] *nf Bot, Culin* chives

civière [sivjɛr] *nf* (*brancard*) stretcher

civil, -ile [sivil] **1** *adj* **(a)** (*de l'État, du citoyen*) (*droits etc*) civil; **année civile** calendar year; **guerre civile** civil war; *Jur* **droit c.** civil law; *Jur* **se porter partie civile** = to sue for damages someone being tried in a criminal court; **le tribunal c.** civil court

(b) (*non ecclésiastique*) lay, secular; (*non militaire*) civilian; **mariage c.** civil marriage; **enterrement c.** non-religious burial; **dans la vie civile** in private *or* civilian life

(c) *Arch, Litt* polite, courteous

2 *nm* **(a)** (*personne*) **un c.** (*non ecclésiastique*) a layman; (*non militaire*) a civilian

(b) **dans le c.** in private *or* civilian life; **en c.** (*police*) in plain clothes; *Mil* in civilian clothes, in mufti, *F* in civvies

(c) *Jur* **poursuivre qn au c.** to sue sb in the civil courts, to bring a civil action against sb

civilement [sivilmɑ̃] *adv* **(a)** *Jur* **se marier c.** to be married at a registry office; **enterré c.** buried without religious ceremony; *Jur* **poursuivre qn c.** to bring a civil action against sb; **c. responsable** liable for damages **(b)** *Arch, Litt* politely, courteously, civilly

civilisable [sivilizabl] *adj* civilizable

civilisateur, -trice [sivilizatœr, -tris] **1** *adj* civilizing **2** *n* civilizer

civilisation [sivilizasjɔ̃] *nf* civilization; **la c. pré-colombienne** the pre-Colombian civilization; **les bienfaits de la c.** the benefits of civilization; **aire de c.** area *or* zone of influence of a civilization

civiliser [sivilize] **1** *vt* to civilize; *F* **c. qn** to make sb less uncouth *or* more refined **2** **se civiliser** *vpr* to become civilized; *F* **il commence à se c.** he's starting to become more civilized *or* refined

civilité [sivilite] *nf* **(a)** **civilités** courtesies, respects; **présenter ses civilités à qn** to pay one's respects to sb **(b)** *Litt, Vieilli* (*politesse*) civility, politeness, courtesy

civique [sivik] *adj* (*devoirs etc*) civic; (*droits*) civil; **avoir/développer le sens c.** to have/to foster a sense of civic responsibility; *Scol* **instruction c.** civics, *surtout Can* **bibliothèque c.** municipal *or* public library

civisme [sivism] *nm* good citizenship, public-spiritedness

clabaudage [klabodaʒ] *nm Litt* (*médisance*) (spiteful) gossip, backbiting

clabauder [klabode] *vi Litt* **(a)** (*d'un chien de chasse*) to bark (a lot) **(b)** *Fig* **c. sur** *ou* **contre qn** to say nasty things about sb

clabauderie [klabodri] *nf* = **clabaudage**

clabaudeur, -euse [klabodœr, -øz] **1** *adj* **(a)** (*chien*) barking **(b)** *Fig* gossiping, backbiting **2** *n Fig* gossip, scandalmonger

clac [klak] *int* click!; (*d'un fouet*) crack! (*d'un objet qui se casse*) snap!

clafoutis [klafuti] *nm Culin* **c. aux pommes/limousin** apples/(black) cherries baked in batter

claie [klɛ] *nf* **(a)** (*clôture*) fence **(b)** **c. à fruits** (wicker) fruit tray **(c)** (*crible*) screen, riddle

clair [klɛr] **1** *adj* **(a)** (*limpide, transparent*) (*eau etc*) clear; **teint c.** clear complexion; **ciel c.** clear *or* cloudless sky; **par temps c.** in clear weather, on a a clear day; **voix claire** clear voice; *Mus* **caisse claire** side *or* snare drum

(b) (*pièce etc*) bright, light; **il fait c.** (*jour*) it's (day)light; (*lumière*) there's plenty of light; **dans cette pièce, il fait plus c.** this room is brighter, there's more light in this room; **il ne fait pas très c. ici** there isn't much light here

(c) (*couleur*) light, pale; **robe bleu c.** pale blue dress

(d) (*sens etc*) clear, obvious, plain; **explication claire** clear *or* lucid explanation; **ce n'est pas très c., précisez** it's not very clear, be more precise; **il a été très c. là-dessus** he was very clear about it; **je vais être très c.** I'm going to make myself very clear; **il est c. qu'elle a tort** she is obviously *or* clearly wrong; **voilà qui est c.!** that's clear (enough)!; **c. comme le jour** *ou* **comme de l'eau de roche** crystal clear, as clear as daylight *or* crystal; **sa conduite n'est pas claire** his behaviour is suspicious *or F* fishy; **avoir l'esprit c.** *ou* **les idées claires** to be clear in one's mind *or* in one's ideas; **je n'avais pas les idées très claires ce jour-là** I wasn't thinking very clearly that day; **c'est c. et net** there are no two ways about it; **ils n'ont aucune intention de prolonger notre contrat, c'est c. et net** it's quite obvious that they have absolutely no intention of extending our contracts; **je veux une réponse claire et nette** I want a definite answer

(e) (*soupe*) thin; (*tissu*) light, thin

2 *adv* plainly, clearly; **voir c.** to see clearly; **il ne voit plus très c.** he can't see too clearly *or* well; **parler c.** to speak clearly; *Fig* **je commence à (y) voir c.** I'm beginning to see *or* understand; **son explication est très confuse, je n'y vois pas très c.** his explanation is very confused, I don't quite follow it

3 *nm* **(a)** (*lumière*) light; **c. de lune** moonlight; **au c. de (la) lune** in the moonlight; **les clairs d'une peinture** the (high)lights in a painting

(b) **en c.** in plain language; **message en c.** message in clear; *TV* **émission en c.** (*non crypté*) non-crypted broadcast

(c) **tirer du vin au c.** to decant wine; **sabre au c.** with drawn sword; *Fig* **tirer une affaire au c.** to clear a matter up; **mettre ses idées au c.** to get one's ideas straight; **mettre qch au c. avec qn** to sort sth out with sb, to get sth straight with sb

(d) **il passe le plus c. de son temps ...** he spends most *or* the better part of his time in ...

clairance [klɛrɑ̃s] *nf Méd* (*rénal*) clearance

claire [klɛr] *nf* oyster bed; **fines de c.** = particularly fine variety of fattened oysters, with a green tinge caused by algae

clairement [klɛrmɑ̃] *adv* clearly, plainly; **on le voit c. sur le tableau** it's clearly visible on the board; **expliquer c. qch à qn** to explain sth clearly to sb; **je te le dis c.** I'm telling you quite plainly

clairet, -ette [klɛrɛ, -ɛt] **1** *adj* **vin c.** light-red wine; **voix clairette** thin *or* high-pitched *or* reedy voice **2** *nf* **clairette** light sparkling wine **3** *nm* light-red wine

claire-voie, *pl* **claires-voies** *nf* **(a)** (*treillage*) open-work, lattice(-work); **porte à c.** (wicket) gate; **clôture à c.** fence, paling; **cloison à c.** grating; **caisse à c.** crate **(b)** *Archit* clerestory; *Naut* skylight, deadlight

clairière [klɛrjɛr] *nf* **(a)** (*dans forêt*) clearing, glade **(b)** *Tex* thin place

clair-obscur, *pl* **clairs-obscurs** *nm* **(a)** *Beaux-Arts* chiaroscuro, light and shade **(b)** (*lumière*) twilight

clairon [klɛrɔ̃] *nm* **(a)** (*trompette*) bugle; **jouer du c.** to play the bugle; **sonner le c.** to sound the bugle **(b)** (*joueur*) bugler

claironnant [klɛrɔnɑ̃] *adj* (*son*) loud, brassy; (*voix*) piercing, loud

claironner [klɛrɔne] **1** *vi* to sound the bugle; *Fig* (*crier*) to shout loudly **2** *vt* **c. une nouvelle** to broadcast *or* proclaim a piece of news; **il claironna que ...** he proclaimed that ...

clairsemé [klɛrsəme] *adj* (*population etc*) scattered, sparse; (*cheveux*) thin; (*maïs etc*) thinly sown; (*gazon*) sparse; (*arbres*) scattered

clairvoyance [klɛrvwajɑ̃s] *nf* perceptiveness, clearsightedness; (*paranormal*) clairvoyance; **il l'avait analysé avec c.** he had analysed it perceptively

clairvoyant [klɛrvwajɑ̃] **1** *adj* perceptive, clear-sighted; (*paranormal*) clairvoyant; **esprit c.** perceptive mind **2** *nm* clairvoyant

clam [klam] *nm* (*mollusque*) clam

clamecer [klamse] *vi Arg* (*mourir*) to snuff it, to kick the bucket

clamer [klame] *vt* to shout out, to proclaim; **c. son innocence** to proclaim *or* protest one's innocence; **c. son mécontentement** to proclaim one's displeasure

clameur [klamœr] *nf* clamour; (*du vent, de la tempête*) howling, roaring; **une c. de joie** a shout of joy; **on entendit une c. épouvantable lorsque le bateau coula** there were horrendous screams when the boat went down; **c. publique** hue and cry

clamser [klamse] *vi Arg* (*mourir*) to kick the bucket, to snuff it

clan [klɑ̃] *nm* **(a)** (*tribu*) clan; **c. irlandais/écossais** Irish/Scottish clan; **chef de c.** clan chief **(b)** (*groupe*) clan, clique

clandestinement [klɑ̃dɛstinmɑ̃] *adv* (*se réunir*) clandestinely, secretly; (*travailler, transporter, entrer dans un pays*) illegally; **voyager c.** to stow away

clandestin, -ine [klɑ̃dɛstɛ̃, -in] **1** *adj* (*réunion, atelier*) clandestine, secret; (*travailleur, pari*) illegal; **armée clandestine** underground forces; **mouvement c.** underground movement; **passager c.** stowaway **2** *n* (*voyageur*) stowaway; (*immigré*) illegal immigrant; (*travailleur*) illegal worker

clandestinité [klɑ̃dɛstinite] *nf* clandestineness; **dans la c.** in secret; **entrer dans/sortir de la c.** to go into/to come out of hiding; **passer dans la c.** to go underground

clap [klap] *nm Cin etc* clapper board, clapstick, slate; **c. de fin** tail slate

clapet [klapɛ] *nm* **(a)** *Tech* valve; (*de moteur*) poppet valve, mushroom valve; **c. d'admission/d'échappement** inlet/exhaust valve; **c. de dérivation** by-pass valve; **c. de limitation de pression** pressure limiting valve **(b)** *Él* rectifier **(c)** *Arg* (*bouche*) trap, *Br* gob; **ferme ton c.!** shut your trap!; **il a un de ces clapets!** he never stops (talking)!

clapier [klapje] *nm* **(a)** (*terriers*) rabbit warren **(b)** (*case*) **c. à lapins** rabbit hutch; **(lapin de) c.** tame rabbit; *F* **vivre dans un c. à lapins** to live in a rabbit warren **(c)** *Géol* (*dans les Alpes*) scree

clapir [klapir] **1** *vi* (*d'un lapin*) to squeal **2 se clapir** *vpr* (*d'un lapin*) to hide, to cower

clapotage [klapɔtaʒ] *nm,* **clapotement** [klapɔtmɑ̃] *nm* (*des vagues*) lapping

clapoter [klapɔte] *vi* (*des vagues*) to lap; **mer qui clapote** choppy sea

clapotis [klapɔti] *nm* (*des vagues*) lap(ping)

clappement [klapmɑ̃] *nm* (*de la langue*) click

clapper [klape] *vi* **c. de la langue** to click one's tongue

claquage [klakaʒ] *nm* **(a)** (*d'un muscle*) strain, pulling; **se faire un c.** to pull *or* strain a muscle **(b)** *Él* (electric) breakdown; **c. thermique** thermal breakdown

claquant [klakɑ̃] *adj Arg* (*fatigant*) killing, knackering

claque¹ [klak] *nf* **(a)** (*gifle*) slap, smack; **donner** *ou* **mettre** *ou très F* **tirer** *ou* **foutre une c. à qn** to give sb a slap *or* smack; **recevoir** *ou* **prendre une c.** to get a slap *or* a smack; *Fig* **se prendre une c.** to get a slap in the face; *Fig* **les centristes se sont pris une c. aux dernières élections** the last elections were a slap in the face for the centre party; **il mérite une bonne paire de claques** he deserves a good slap; *F* **c'est vraiment une tête à claques!** he's got a face you just want to slap!

(b) *Arg* **il (en) a sa c.** (*il est fatigué*) he's knackered *or* shattered; (*il en a assez*) he's fed up with it, he's had enough of it

(c) *Th* **la c.** hired clappers, claque **(d)** *Can* galoshes, *Am* rubbers

claque² **1** *adj, nm* **(chapeau) c.** opera hat, crush hat **2** *nm Arg* (*maison close*) whorehouse, *Br* knocking shop; (*tripot*) gambling den

claqué [klake] *adj F* knackered, shattered

claquement [klakmɑ̃] *nm* (*de porte*) slam(ming), bang(ing); (*de dents*) chattering; (*d'un fouet*) crack(ing); (*d'un drapeau*) flap(ping); (*des doigts*) snap(ping); (*des talons, de la langue*) click(ing); (*des sabots*) clatter(ing); (*dans un moteur*) slapping of pistons; **entendre un c. de porte** to hear a door bang, to hear the sound of a door banging; **des claquements de fouets** the cracking of whips

claquemurer [klakmyre] **1** *vt* **c. qn** to shut sb up **2 se claquemurer** *vpr* to shut oneself up; **se c. dans sa chambre** to shut oneself up in one's room, to stay cooped up in one's room

claquer [klake] **1** *vi* **(a)** (*d'une porte*) to slam, to bang; (*d'un drapeau*) to flap; (*des talons*) to click; (*des sabots*) to clatter; (*d'un piston*) to slap; **c. des mains** to clap, to applaud; **elle claque des dents** her teeth are chattering; **c. des doigts** to snap one's fingers; **faire c. sa langue** to click one's tongue; **faire c. la porte en sortant** to slam the door on the way out; *F* **c. du bec** to be hungry *or* starving

(b) *Arg* (*d'une personne*) to kick the bucket, to snuff it; (*d'un appareil*) to conk out; (*d'une ampoule électrique*) to go, to blow; *F* **l'affaire lui a claqué dans les doigts** *ou* **mains** the deal fell through; **il nous a claqué dans les mains avant que l'ambulance arrive** he died on us before the ambulance arrived

2 *vt* **(a)** (*porte*) to slam, to bang; (*ses doigts*) to snap; (*ses talons*) to click; **c. la langue** to click one's tongue

(b) (*gifler*) (*enfant etc*) to slap, to smack

(c) *F* (*fatiguer*) (*qn*) to tire *or* wear out

(d) *F* (*dépenser*) (*argent*) to squander, to blow; **il claque un fric monstre** he spends money like water; **il claque un fric monstre chez le coiffeur** he spends a fortune at the hairdresser's

3 se claquer *vpr* **(a)** *F* (*se fatiguer*) to tire *or* wear oneself out

(b) se c. un muscle/un ligament to pull a muscle/to tear a ligament

claquette [klakɛt] *nf* **(a)** *Cin* clapperboard **(b)** *Danse* **(danse à) claquettes** tap dancing, tap dance; **faire des claquettes** to do tap (dancing); **danseur de claquettes** tap dancer

claquoir [klakwar] *nm* clapper; *Cin* clapperboard

clarification [klarifikasjɔ̃] *nf* (*d'un liquide*) clarifying; *Fig* (*d'informations*) clarification

clarifier [klarifje] **1** *vt* to clarify; **c. la situation** to clarify the situation, to clear the matter up **2 se clarifier** *vpr* to (become) clear; **la situation se clarifie** the situation is becoming clear

clarine [klarin] *nf* cowbell

clarinette [klarinɛt] *nf* clarinet

clarinettiste [klarinɛtist] *n* clarinettist

clarisse [klaris] *nf Rel* **(sœur) c.** nun of the order of St Clare

clarté [klarte] *nf* **(a)** (*lumière etc*) light, brightness; **une douce/faible c.** a soft/dim light; **à la c. de la lune** by the light of the moon, by moonlight; **la c. de l'aurore** *ou* **de l'aube** the early morning light **(b)** (*transparence*) clearness, clarity; (*d'un verre etc*) transparency; (*du style etc*) clarity, lucidity; **la c. de son teint** the clearness of his complexion; **la c. de l'expression** clarity of expression; **parler avec c.** to speak clearly; **c. d'esprit** clear-headedness; **manquer de c.** (*d'une personne*) not to make oneself clear; (*d'un texte, un devoir, un argument*) to be unclear; *Litt* **avoir des clartés sur un sujet** to have some knowledge of a subject

clash [klaʃ] *nm F* clash, conflict; **je voudrais éviter tout c. avec elle** I want to avoid clashing with her

classable [klasabl] *adj* classifiable; **une personne difficilement c.** a person who is difficult to classify

classe [klas] **1** *nf* **(a)** (*catégorie*) class, division, category; *Admin etc* rank, grade; **c. d'âge** age group; *Av etc* **c. touriste/club** tourist/club class; **c. affaires** business class, club class, executive class; **c. économique** economy class; **voyager en c. affaires/club** to travel business/club class; *Rail* **billet de première/deuxième** *ou* **seconde c.** first-/second-class ticket; **différence de c. sociale** difference in *or* of social class; **les hautes classes (de la société)** the upper classes; **la c. moyenne/ouvrière** the middle/working class(es); **c. dirigeante/dominante** ruling/dominant class; **société sans c.** classless society; **conscience de c.** class consciousness

(b) (*qualité*) class; **elle n'est pas de la même c. que les autres** she's not in the same class as the others; **un biologiste/sportif de c. internationale** a biologist/sportsman of international rank, a world-class biologist/sportsman; **produits de première c.** top quality *or* first-class goods; **avoir de la c.** to have class *or* style; **cette robe a beaucoup de c.** that's a very classy *or* stylish dress, that dress has got a lot of class *or* style; **c'est la c.!** what class!

(c) [①All,g,i] *Scol* (*niveau*) class, form, *Am* grade; (*ensemble des élèves*) class; **c'est un cadeau offert par toute la c.** it's a present from the whole class; **il y a plusieurs classes de sixième au collège** there are several first-year classes at high school; **grandes classes, classes supérieures** upper forms, senior school; **c. de sixième/première/terminale** ≈ first year/lower sixth/upper sixth; **les petites classes** the junior school, the juniors; **il est dans quelle c.?** which *or* what class is he in?

(d) (*leçon*) class, lesson; **c. de français** French class; **aller en c.** to go to school; **être en c.** to be in *or* at school; **faire la c.** to teach; **livre de c.** schoolbook

(e) **(salle de) c.** classroom, schoolroom; **en sortant de c.** on coming out of school

(f) *Mil* (*de conscrits*) annual contingent; **la c. 1965** the 1965 class, the 1965 levy; **faire ses classes** to undergo basic training

(g) *Mil* (*rang*) **(soldat de) deuxième c.** private; *Mil, Av* aircraftman, *Am* airman (basic); **(soldat de) première c.** lance-corporal, *Am* private first class; *Mil, Av* leading *or* senior aircraftman, *Am* airman first class

(h) *Compta* group of accounts

2 *adj inv F* classy, stylish

▶ **classe**: *Scol* **c. de mer** school study trip to the seaside; *Scol* **c. de nature** nature study trip; *Scol* **c. de neige** school study trip to the mountains; **partir en c. de neige** = to go skiing with the school; **c. préparatoire** = preparatory class for the entrance examinations for the Grandes Écoles; **c. verte** school study trip to the countryside; *Scol* **partir en c. verte** = to spend time in the countryside with the school

classé [klase] *adj* **(a)** *Sp* ranked, graded; *Tennis* seeded **(b)** (*information*) classified; **cette information est classée** that information is classified **(c)** (*monument etc*) listed

classement [klasmɑ̃] *nm* **(a)** (*hiérarchie*) (*dans une classe, une course etc*) position, place; (*des plantes etc*) classification; **c. alphabétique/chronologique** alphabetical/chronological order; *Scol* **c. trimestriel** end of term results; *Scol* **ce trimestre je suis troisième au c.** I'm third in the class this term; **donner le c.** (*d'un concours*) to give the results; **avoir un bon/mauvais c.** to be well/badly placed; **c. hôtelier** hotel classification; **c. par étoiles** (*d'un hôtel etc*) star rating

(b) (*rangement*) (*de documents*) filing; (*d'articles*) sorting out, arranging; **faire du c.** to do some filing; **c. géographique** filing by geographical area; **c. horizontal** horizontal filing; **c. par ordre alphabétique** alphabetical filing

classer [klase] **1** *vt* **(a)** (*classifier*) to classify, to class; **les livres sont classés par ordre alphabétique d'auteurs** the books are arranged *or* classified in alphabetical order of author; **monument classé** listed monument; **classés par pays** classified according to country; **ce chanteur, que l'on classe parmi les meilleurs ténors ...** this singer, who is ranked among the best tenors ...; *Courses de chevaux* **non classés** also ran; *F* **je n'ai pas eu de mal à le c.** it didn't take me long to size him up *or* to work out what sort of a person he was

(b) (*documents*) to file; (*articles*) to sort out, to arrange; **c. une affaire** to consider a matter closed; **c'est une affaire classée** the matter's closed

2 se classer *vpr* to be classified, to rank; **ces faits se classent dans une autre catégorie** these facts fall into another category; **elle se classe parmi les meilleurs de son année** she's among the best in her year; *Sp etc* **se c. troisième** to be placed *or* to come in third; *Tennis etc* **il n'a pas réussi à se c.** he failed to get into the rankings

classeur [klasœr] *nm* (*meuble*) filing cabinet; (*d'écolier etc*) (looseleaf) binder, folder; *Ordinat* filer; **c. à anneaux** ring binder; **c. distributeur** index card box; **c. à levier** lever-arch file

classicisme [klasisism] *nm* classicism

classificateur, -trice [klasifikatœr, -tris] **1** *n* classifier **2** *adj* classifying

classification [klasifikasjɔ̃] *nf* classification; **c. socio-économique** socio-economic grouping

classifier [klasifje] *vt* (*impf, pr sub* **n. classifiions, v. classifiiez**) to classify

classique [klasik] **1** *adj* **(a)** *Scol* academic, for school use; **faire des études classiques** to study classics; **langues classiques** classical languages; **auteurs classiques** classical authors

(b) (*période, musique etc*) classical; (*beauté etc*) classic

(c) (*travail etc*) standard; (*exemple, plaisanterie, question etc*) classic; **vêtement/tenue c.** a classic garment/outfit; **aimer le style c.** to like the classic style; **guerre c.** conventional warfare; *F* **c'est le coup c.** it's the same old story; **ça, c'est c.** that's just typical (, that is)

2 *nm* **(a)** (*auteur*) classical author

(b) (*livre*) classic; **les classiques grecs/français** the Greek/French classics; **relire ses classiques** to reread the classics; **c'est un grand c. du jazz** it's a great jazz standard; **c'est un c. du genre** it's a classic of its kind *or* of the genre

(c) *Mus* classical music

classiquement [klasikmɑ̃] *adv* classically

claudication [klodikasjɔ̃] *nf Méd, Litt* limp(ing), *Spéc* claudication

claudiquer [klodike] *vi Litt* to limp

clause [kloz] *nf Jur etc* clause; **c. additionnelle** additional clause, rider; **c. pénale** penalty clause; **c. de style** formal clause; *Fin* **c. au porteur** pay to bearer clause; **c. d'annulation** cancellation clause; **c. d'arbitrage** arbitration clause; **c. compromissoire** arbitration clause; **c. contractuelle** clause of a/the contract; *Com* **c. d'exclusivité** exclusivity clause, exclusive rights clause; **c. d'exonération** exemption clause; *Fin* **c. d'indexation** cost escalation clause, indexation clause; **c. de franchise** excess clause; **c. de non-concurrence** non-competition clause; **c. de réserve de propriété** retention of title clause; **c. de résiliation** termination clause, cancellation clause; **c. de sauvegarde** safeguard clause; *Com* **c. ducroire** del credere clause; **c. dérogatoire** derogatory clause; *Fin* **c. à ordre**: to order; **c. de sortie** escape *or* get-out clause

clausé [kloze] *adj Com* (*connaissement*) dirty

claustra [klostra] *nm* stone railings

claustral, -ale, -aux, -ales [klostral, -o] *adj* monastic

claustration [klostrasjɔ̃] *nf* (*isolation*) confinement

claustrer [klostre] **1** *vt* (*isoler*) to confine, to shut up **2 se claustrer** *vpr* to shut oneself up; **se c. dans le silence** to retreat into silence

claustrophobe [klostrɔfɔb] *adj Méd* claustrophobic

claustrophobie [klostrɔfɔbi] *nf Méd* claustrophobia

claveau, -eaux [klavo] *nm Constr, Archit* archstone; **c. droit** keystone

clavecin [klavsɛ̃] *nm Mus* harpsichord

claveciniste [klavsinist] *n Mus* harpsichord player, harpsichordist

claveter [klavte] *vt* (**je clavette**; **je clavetterai**) *MecE* to key, to wedge, to cotter

clavette [klavɛt] *nf MecE* key (bolt), pin, cotter (pin)

clavicorde [klavikɔrd] *nm Mus* clavichord

clavicule [klavikyl] *nf Anat* collarbone, clavicle

clavier [klavje] *nm* **(a)** (*de piano, de machine à écrire etc*) keyboard; *Ordinat* **c. numérique** numerical *or* numeric keypad; **c. AZERTY** AZERTY keyboard; **c. QWERTY** QWERTY keyboard; **c. multi-fonction** multifunctional keyboard; **c. national** country keyboard; **c. par défaut** default keyboard (layout); **c. à infrarouge** infrared keyboard **(b)** *Fig* **le c. des émotions amoureuses** the range *or* gamut of love's emotions

claviste [klavist] *n* typesetter; *Ordinat* keyboarder

clayette [klɛjɛt] *nf* **(a)** (*petite claie*) wire tray *or* rack; (*dans un réfrigérateur*) (wire) shelf **(b)** (*cageot*) crate

clayon [klɛjɔ̃] *nm* (*pour les fromages*) wicker tray; (*pour les gâteaux*) cake rack

clé [kle] *nf* = **clef**

clean [klin] *adj inv F* straight, clean-living; **elle a un look c.** she has a clean-living *or* straight image

clearing [kliriŋ] *nm Écon* clearing; **accord de c.** clearing agreement

clébard [klebar] *nm*, **clebs** [klɛps] *nm Arg* (*chien*) pooch, mutt

clef [kle] *nf* **(a)** (*d'une porte, d'un code, d'un mystère*) key; **c. de maison** house key; **mes clefs de voiture** my car keys; **fausse c.** skeleton key; **trousseau de clefs** bunch of keys; **fermer une porte à c.** to lock a door; **donner un tour de c. à la porte** to lock the door; **tenir/mettre qch sous c.** to keep/put sth under lock and key; **on l'a mis sous c. depuis hier** he's been under lock and key since yesterday; **la c. est sur la porte** the key is in the lock; **louer une maison clefs en main** to rent a house with immediate *or* vacant possession; **usine clefs en main** turnkey factory *or Am* plant; **prix clefs en main** (*d'une voiture*) on-the-road price; (*d'une maison*) all-inclusive price; **les clefs de la ville** the keys to the city; **la philosophie, c. de la connaissance** philosophy, the key to (all) knowledge; **roman à c.** = novel introducing real characters under fictitious names; **mettre la c. sous la porte** to scarper, to do a runner; **prendre la c. des champs** (*d'un prisonnier etc*) to make a bid for freedom; **position-c.** key position; **industrie-c.** key industry; **un secteur(-)c. de la recherche** a key sector *or* area of research; *Fig* **enquête avec récompense à la c.** an investigation for the successful conclusion of which there is a reward; **il y a une forte somme d'argent à la c.** there is a large sum of money at stake *or* involved

(b) *Mus* clef; (*armature*) key signature; (*d'un instrument à cordes*) peg; (*d'un instrument à vent*) key; **c. de sol/de fa** treble/bass clef; **jouer avec des dièses à la c.** to play in sharp keys

(c) *Tech* wrench, spanner

(d) *Él* switch (key); *Télécom* **c. Morse** Morse key

(e) (*prise de lutte*) lock

(f) *Ordinat* key; (*du DOS*) switch; **c. d'index** index key; **c. de contrôle** control key; **c. gigogne** dongle

▶ **clef**: **c. allen** allen key; **c. anglaise** adjustable spanner, monkey wrench; **c. à bougie** (spark)plug spanner; **c. à cliquet** ratchet handle; *Aut* **c. de contact** ignition key; *Aut* **c.**

en croix wheelbrace, spider; **c. cruciforme** cruciform key; **c. à douille** box spanner; **c. dynamométrique** torque wrench; **c. mixte** combination spanner; **c. à molette** adjustable spanner, *surtout Am* monkey wrench; **c. à œil** ring spanner; **c. ouverte** open-ended spanner; **c. passe-partout** passkey, master key; **c. à pipe** box spanner; **c. plate** (open) end wrench; **c. à puce** computerized key; *Banque* **c. RIB** bank details; **c. des songes** (*livre*) = how to interpret your dreams; *Archit* **c. de voûte** (*d'une arche*) keystone, crown; *Fig* **c'est la c. de voûte de notre entreprise** he's the cornerstone of our firm

clématite [klematit] *nf* clematis

clémence [klemɑ̃s] *nf* **(a)** *Fig* (*de la température*) mildness; **si la c. du temps le permet** if the weather's mild enough **(b)** *Litt* clemency, mercy, leniency **(pour, envers** to(wards)

clément [klemɑ̃] *adj* **(a)** *Fig* (*température etc*) mild **(b)** *Litt* clement, merciful, lenient **(pour, envers** to, towards)

clémentine [klemɑ̃tin] *nf* (*fruit*) clementine

clenche [klɑ̃ʃ] *nf,* **clenchette** [klɑ̃ʃɛt] *nf* (*d'un loquet*) latch

Cléopâtre [kleɔpɑtr] *nf Antiq* Cleopatra

cleptomane [klɛptɔman] *n* kleptomaniac

cleptomanie [klɛptɔmani] *nf* kleptomania

clerc [klɛr] *nm* **(a)** (*dans un bureau*) clerk; **c. de notaire** ≈ solicitor's clerk; **petit c.** junior clerk **(b)** *Rel* cleric **(c)** *Arch* learned man, scholar **(d) il n'est pas besoin d'être grand c. pour ...** you don't have to be a genius in order to ...

clergé [klɛrʒe] *nm* [①All,f,ii] clergy

clérical, -ale, -aux, -ales [klerikal, -o] *adj, nm Rel* clerical

cléricalisme [klerikalism] *nm Rel* clericalism

clic [klik] **1** *nm* click, clicking; **entendre un c.** to hear a click *or* a clicking sound **2** *int* click

clic-clac *nm* (*d'un appareil-photo, d'une ceinture de sécurité*) click; (*des talons*) click-clack; (*des sabots*) clatter

cliché [kliʃe] *nm* **(a)** (*lieu commun*) cliché **(b)** *Phot* negative **(c)** *Typ* stereotype; (*de caractères*) plate; (*d'illustration*) block **(d)** *Ordinat* **c. de disque** disk dump; **c. mémoire** dump

clicheur [kliʃœr] *nm Ordinat* screen dump program

client, -ente [klijɑ̃, -ɑ̃t] *n* **(a)** *Com* client, customer; (*d'un médecin*) patient; (*d'un chauffeur de taxi*) fare; (*d'un hôtel*) guest; (*dans la publicité*) account; **c'est un bon c.** he's a good customer; **ici, le c. est roi** the customer is always right; **la France est un gros c. du Japon pour la robotique** France is one of Japan's big customers for robotics; **c. actuel** existing customer; **c. de passage** passing customer; **c. imprévu** chance customer; **c. potentiel** suspect, potential client, potential customer; **clients potentiels** potential clients, suspect pool; **c. régulier** regular customer; **c. sans réservation** (*dans un hôtel*) chance guest, walk-in; **clients de passage** passing trade; *Fig* **désolé, je ne suis pas c.** sorry, I'm not interested; *F* **c'est un drôle de c.** he's a queer customer

(b) *Compta* **c. douteux** doubtful debt, possible bad debt

clientèle [klijɑ̃tɛl] *nf* **(a)** (*d'un magasin*) customers, clientèle; (*d'une entreprise*) customer base; (*d'un médecin, d'un avocat*) practice; **c. actuelle** existing customers; **c. de passage** passing trade **(b)** (*fait d'acheter*) custom; **obtenir la c. d'un consommateur/d'un pays** to obtain a consumer's/country's custom *or* business; **accorder sa c. à** to give one's custom to, to patronize

clientélisme [klijɑ̃telism] *nm Péj* populism

clignement [kliɲmɑ̃] *nm* blink; **faire un c. d'œil** to wink

cligner [kliɲe] **1** *vt* **c. les yeux** to screw up one's eyes **2** *vi* **c. des yeux** to screw up one's eyes; **c. de l'œil à qn** to wink at sb

clignotant [kliɲɔtɑ̃] **1** *adj* (*yeux*) blinking; (*paupière*) twitching; (*étoile*) twinkling; (*lumière*) flickering, flashing; **feu** *ou* **signal c.** *Naut* intermittent signal; *Aut* flashing light **2** *nm* **(a)** *Aut* indicator, *Am* flasher; **mettre son c. (à droite/gauche)** to indicate (left/right) **(b)** *Écon* signal, indicator; **le c. de la hausse des prix/de la crise** the warning light *or* signal that prices are rising/that a recession is on the way

clignotement [kliɲɔtmɑ̃] *nm* (*des yeux*) blinking; (*des paupières*) twitching; (*d'une étoile*) twinkling; (*d'une lumière*) flickering, flashing

clignoter [kliɲɔte] *vi* **(a) c. des yeux** to blink **(b)** (*des paupières*) to twitch; (*d'une étoile*) to twinkle; (*d'une lumière*) to flicker, to flash; *Ordinat* (*d'un marqueur etc*) to flash, to blink

climat [klima] *nm aussi Fig* climate; **sous des climats plus ensoleillés** in sunnier climes; **c. de détente** relaxed atmosphere *or* climate; **travailler dans un c. d'hostilité** to work in a hostile atmosphere *or* in an atmosphere of hostility

climatique [klimatik] *adj* (*conditions etc*) climatic; **station c.** health resort

climatisation [klimatizasjɔ̃] *nf* air conditioning; **avoir la c. dans toutes les pièces** to have air conditioning in every room

climatiser [klimatize] *vt* to air-condition; **chambre climatisée** air-conditioned bedroom

climatiseur [klimatizœr] *nm* air conditioner; *Aut* climate control system

climatologie [klimatɔlɔʒi] *nf* climatology

climatologique [klimatɔlɔʒik] *adj* climatological

clin [klɛ̃] *nm Naut* **bordé à clin(s)** clinker built

clin d'œil [klɛ̃dœj] *nm* wink; **faire un c. à qn** to wink at sb; **en un c.** in the twinkling of an eye, in a flash; **dans ce film, le réalisateur fait un c. à Bergman** in this film, the director makes passing references to Bergman *or* nods at Bergman

clinicien [klinisjɛ̃] *adj, nm* **(médecin) c.** clinician

clinique [klinik] **1** *adj* (*médecine, essais etc*) clinical; **les signes cliniques d'une maladie** the clinical symptoms of an illness **2** *nf* **(a)** (*hôpital privé*) clinic; **chef de c.** senior registrar **(b)** (*observation des étudiants de médecine*) clinic; (*médecine*) clinical medicine

cliniquement [klinikmɑ̃] *adv* clinically

clinquant [klɛ̃kɑ̃] **1** *nm* tinsel; (*bijoux*) flashy jewellery; **c. du style** flashiness of style **2** *adj* flashy, showy; **un journaliste qui donne dans le c. et la vulgarité** a journalist who tends to be flashy and vulgar

clip [klip] *nm* **(a)** (*bijou*) clip **(b)** (*film*) clip; (*musical*) (music) video

clipart [klipart] *nm Ordinat* clip art

clipper [klipœr] *nm* **(a)** *Av* transport aircraft **(b)** *Naut* clipper

clique [klik] *nf* **(a)** (*gang*) clique, gang; *F* **et toute la c.** and the rest of the gang, and all the rest of them **(b)** *Mil* (*tambours et clairons*) band

cliquer [klike] *vi Ordinat* to click **(sur** on); **c. deux fois** to double-click

cliques [klik] *nfpl F* **prendre ses c. et ses claques** to pack up and leave, to pack one's bags and go

cliquet [klikɛ] *nm MecE etc* catch, pawl, ratchet

cliqueter [klikte] *vi* **(je cliquette; je cliquetterai)** (*de chaînettes etc*) to rattle; (*de fleurets, d'aiguilles à tricoter*) to click; (*de pièces de monnaie*) to clink, to chink; (*de clés etc*) to jingle, to jangle; *Aut* to knock, to pink

cliquetis [klikti] *nm* (*de chaînettes*) rattling; (*de pièces de monnaie, de breloques etc*) clink(ing), chinking; (*de clés etc*) jingling, jangling; (*de couverts*) clinking; (*de vaisselle*) clattering; (*de fleurets, d'aiguilles à tricoter*) clicking; (*d'une machine à écrire*) clack; *Aut* knocking, pinking; **j'entendis un léger c., on essayait de crocheter la serrure** I heard a slight scratching noise, somebody was trying to pick the lock

clisse [klis] *nf* (*pour bouteilles*) wicker covering; (*pour faire sécher des fromages*) wicker tray

clitoridien [klitɔridjɛ̃] *adj* clitoral

clitoris [klitɔris] *nm Anat* clitoris

clivage [klivaʒ] *nm* **(a)** (*dans la société*) divide; (*dans un parti politique*) split; **c. social** social divide; **c. idéologique** ideological rift **(b)** (*de roches etc*) cleavage **(c)** (*de diamants etc*) cleaving

cliver [klive] **1** *vt* (*diamants etc*) to cleave, to split **2 se cliver** *vpr* (*de roches etc*) to cleave, to split

cloaque [klɔak] *nm* **(a)** *aussi Fig* cesspool; **c. de vices** den of iniquity; **comment peut-il vivre dans ce c.?** how can he live in that pigsty *or* midden? **(b)** *Anat, Zool* cloaca **(c)** *Antiq* **le grand C.** the Cloaca Maxima

clochard, -arde [klɔʃar, -ard] *n F* tramp, *Am* hobo; **si tu continues comme ça, tu vas finir c.** if you carry on like that, you're going to end up destitute

clochardisation [klɔʃardizasjɔ̃] *nf* destitution

clochardiser [klɔʃardize] **1** *vt* to reduce to destitution; (*sans domicile*) to make homeless, to reduce to a state of vagrancy **2 se clochardiser** *vpr* to be reduced to destitution; (*sans domicile*) to be made homeless

cloche [klɔʃ] **1** *nf* **(a)** bell; **sonner les cloches** to ring the bells; *F* **sonner les cloches à qn** to give sb a good ticking off *or* a good rollicking; **se faire sonner les cloches** to get a good ticking off *or* a good rollicking; **fleurs en c.** bell-shaped flowers; *F* **déménager à la c. de bois** to do a moonlight flit; *Fig* **voilà un autre son de c.** that's quite a different version of events

(b) *Ch* bell jar; *Hort* cloche; *Culin* **c. (de métal)** metal dish cover

(c) (chapeau) c. cloche (hat)

(d) *F* **la c.** vagrancy; **être de la c.** to be a vagrant, to be of no fixed abode

(e) *Arg* **se taper la c.** to pig out, to stuff oneself

(f) *F* twit, idiot

2 *adj F* idiotic, stupid; **avoir l'air c.** to look stupid

▶ **cloche**: *Aut* **c. d'embrayage** clutch bell housing; **c. à fromage(s)** cheese dish cover; **c. à plongeur** diving bell

cloche-pied (à) *adv* **sauter à c.** to hop; **s'éloigner à c.** to hop away

clocher[1] [klɔʃe] *nm* **(a)** (*d'une église etc*) bell tower, steeple; **course au c.** point-to-point (race) **(b)** (*paroisse*) home town, home patch; **querelles** *ou* **disputes de c.** petty local quarrels, parish-pump quarrels; **esprit** *ou* **mentalité de c.** small-town mentality, parochialism

clocher[2] *vi* **(a)** *F* **il y a quelque chose qui cloche** there's something wrong somewhere; **il y a quelque chose qui cloche dans son histoire** there's something not right about his story; **je ne sais pas ce qu'il y a, mais ça cloche quelque part** I don't know what it is, but something's not right somewhere **(b)** *Arch* to limp, to hobble

clocheton [klɔʃtɔ̃] *nm Archit* (*d'une église*) (small) steeple; (*ornement*) pinnacle (turret)

clochette [klɔʃɛt] *nf* **(a)** (*petite cloche*) small bell, handbell **(b)** *Bot* bell-flower, bell-shaped flower

clodo [klodo] *F* **1** *nm* tramp, down-and-out, *Am* hobo **2** *adj* down-and-out

cloison [klwazɔ̃] *nf* **(a)** (*entre des pièces*) partition; **mur de c.** dividing wall; **percer une c.** to knock through a (dividing) wall; **coller l'oreille** *ou* **écouter à la c.** to listen through the wall **(b)** *Naut, Av* bulkhead; *Aut* partition, bulkhead; **c. étanche** *Naut* watertight bulkhead; *Av* pressure bulkhead; *Fig* watertight compartment; *Fig* **faire tomber les cloisons entre les classes** to bring down class barriers **(c)** *Biol* septum; *Anat* **c. nasale** nasal septum

cloisonnage [klwazɔnaʒ] *nm* partitioning

cloisonné [klwazɔne] *adj* **(a)** (*pièce*) partitioned (off); *Fig* **ces services sont très cloisonnés** these departments are highly compartmentalized **(b)** *Beaux-Arts* (*émaux*) cloisonné **(c)** *Biol* septate(d)

cloisonnement [klwazɔnmɑ̃] *nm* (*d'une pièce etc*) partitioning (off); *Fig* compartmentalization

cloisonner [klwazɔne] *vt* (*pièce etc*) to partition (off); *Fig* **c. la société** to put up class barriers

cloître [klwatr] *nm* **(a)** (*partie d'un monastère etc*) cloister(s) **(b)** (*monastère*) monastery, convent; **vie de c.** cloistered life

cloîtrer [klwatre] **1** *vt* (*qn*) to cloister; *Fig* to shut up *or* away; **nonne cloîtrée** enclosed nun **2 se cloîtrer** *vpr* (*de religieux*) to enter a convent *or* a monastery; *Fig* to shut oneself up *or* away, to live the life of a recluse

clonage [klonaʒ] *nm Biol, Ordinat* cloning

clone [klon] *nm Biol, Ordinat* clone

cloner [klone] *vt Biol, Ordinat* to clone

cloneur [klonœr] *nm Mktg* cloner

clope [klɔp] *Arg* **1** *nf, occ m* (*cigarette*) fag, ciggie, *Am* smoke; **la c. jaunit les doigts** cigarettes make your fingers go yellow; **des clopes!** nothing doing!, no way! **2** *nm* (*mégot*) (cigarette-)end *or* butt

clopin-clopant [klɔpɛ̃klɔpɑ̃] *adv F* **aller c.** to limp along, to hobble about; *Fig* **commerce qui va c.** business that struggles along

clopiner [klɔpine] *vi* to hobble

clopinettes [klɔpinɛt] *nfpl F* sweet FA, *surtout Am* zilch; **je ne vais quand même pas travailler pour des c.** I'm not going to work for peanuts

cloporte [klɔpɔrt] *nm* (*insecte*) woodlouse, *Am* sowbug

cloque [klɔk] *nf* **(a)** (*sur la peau, sur la peinture etc*) blister; **faire des cloques** to blister **(b)** *Agr* (*des arbres*) blight **(c)** *Arg* **être en c.** (*enceinte*) to be up the spout, to be knocked up, to be in the club

cloqué [klɔke] **1** *adj* (*peinture*) blistered; *Agr* (*feuille*) blighted, curled; *Tex* **tissu c.** seersucker **2** *nm Tex* seersucker

cloquer [klɔke] *vi* (*de la peinture*) to blister; (*de la peau*) to blister, to come up in a blister

clore [klɔr] (*pp* **clos**; *pr ind* **je clos, il clôt, ils closent**; *fu* **je clorai**) **1** *vt* (= **fermer** *which has taken its place in most uses*) **(a)** (*discussion etc*) to end; (*marché*) to conclude; (*compte*) to close; *Bourse* (*position*) to close out; **l'image qui clôt le livre** the image which ends the book, the image on which the book closes; **c. le débat** to close the meeting, to adjourn; *Ordinat* **c. une session** to log off, to log out **(b)** *Litt* (*passage, porte*) to close (off), to shut (up); (*terrain etc*) to enclose **2 se clore** *vpr* (*d'une réunion etc*) to (come to an) end

clos, -e [klo, -oz] **1** *adj* **(a)** (*fermé*) closed, shut; **volets c.** closed shutters; **trouver porte close** to find nobody in, to find nobody (at) home; **à la nuit close** after dark; *Jur* **à huis c.** in camera; **réunion à huis c.** closed session; **en vase c.** in isolation; **vivre en vase c.** to live in isolation, to live without any contact with the outside world **(b)** (*achevé*) finished, concluded; **la discussion est close** the discussion is closed; **l'incident est c.** the matter is closed; **les inscriptions seront closes le 5 mars** the closing date for applications is March 5th **(c)** (*entouré*) (*jardin, monde*) enclosed **2** *nm* enclosure; **c. (de vigne)** vineyard

close-combat [klozkɔ̃ba] *nm Sp* close combat

closerie [klozri] *nf* small park

clôture [klotyr] *nf* **(a)** (*enceinte*) enclosure, fence; (*en fer*) railing; *Can Sp* (*hockey sur glace*) rink; *Baseball* fence; **c. métallique** wire fence; **mur de c.** enclosing wall

(b) (*fermeture*) (*d'une réunion etc*) conclusion, end; (*d'un débat*) closure; **c. des inscriptions le 3 mars** closing date for applications: March 3rd; **discours de c.** closing speech; **prononcer la c. des débats** to pronounce closure; *Bourse* **cours en c.** closing price; **valeur du mark en c.** closing value of the mark, value of the mark at the close; **c. de la chasse** close of season

(c) *Ordinat* close; **c. de session** logging off

(d) *Com* (*d'un compte*) closing; *Bourse* (*d'une position*) closing (out); *Bourse* **c. par rachat** closure by repurchase; *Compta* **c. annuelle des livres** year-end closing of accounts; *Compta* **c. de l'exercice** end of the financial year

(e) *Rel* enclosure; **faire vœu de c.** to take a vow of enclosure

clôturer [klotyre] **1** *vt* **(a)** (*champ etc*) to enclose; (*avec barrière*) to fence in **(b)** (*session*) to close, to end, to conclude; *Pol* **c. les débats** to close the debate **(c)** *Com* (*comptes etc*) to close **2** *vi Bourse* to close; **le CAC 40 a clôturé en baisse/hausse de 9 points** the CAC 40 closed 9 points down/up; **c. à perte** to close at a loss

clou [klu] *nm* **(a)** nail; **souliers à gros clous** hobnail(ed) boots; **enfoncer un c. avec un marteau** to hammer in a nail; **ceinture à clous** studded belt; *F* **ça ne vaut pas un c.** it's not worth a penny *or Am* a red cent; *F* **des clous!** nothing doing!, no chance!, *esp Am* no way!; **pour des clous** for nothing; *F* **elle est maigre comme un c.** she is as thin as a rake; *F* **mettre qch au c.** to pawn sth

(b) (*d'un passage piéton*) stud; **traverser dans les clous** to cross at a pedestrian crossing *or Am* crosswalk

(c) *F* (*d'un spectacle etc*) star turn, chief attraction; **ça a été le c. de la soirée** it was the high point *or* highlight of the evening

(d) *Mil Arg* (*prison*) cooler, slammer

(e) *Méd* boil, carbuncle

(f) **(vieux) c.** (*voiture*) old banger; (*vélo*) old boneshaker

▶ **clou**: **c. cavalier** staple; **c. à crochet** hook; **c. doré** brass-headed nail, stud; **c. de girofle** clove; **c. sans tête** brad; **c. à souliers** shoe tack; **c. de tapissier** (upholstery *or* carpet) tack

clouer [klue] *vt* **(a)** to nail; **c. une caisse** to nail down a crate; *Fig F* **c. le bec à qn** to shut sb up **(b)** *Fig* (*qch, qn*) to pin down; **c. qn au sol** to pin sb down; **rester cloué sur place** to be rooted to the spot; **la neige a cloué tous les avions au sol** all planes were grounded due to snow; **être cloué au lit** to be confined to *or F* stuck in bed

clouté [klute] *adj* (*chaussures etc*) studded; **passage c.** pedestrian crossing, *Am* crosswalk

clouter [klute] *vt* (*chaussures etc*) to stud

clovisse [klɔvis] *nf* (*mollusque*) clam

clown [klun] *nm* clown; **numéro de clowns** clown act; *Fig* **ne fais pas le c.!** stop acting the fool *or* goat!, stop clowning around!; **c'est un vrai c.** he's a real comic *or* clown

clownerie [klunri] *nf* clowning; *Fig* clowning around, playing the fool

clownesque [klunɛsk] *adj* clownish

club [klœb] *nm* **(a)** (*association*) (*sportif, politique*) club; **c. de foot** football club; **c. sportif** *ou* **de sport** sports club; **c. de gymnastique** fitness centre, gym *Bourse* **c. des amis** fan club **(b)** (*de golf*) golf club **(c)** **(fauteuil) c.** club chair; **c. de vacances** holiday club, *Am* vacation center; **c. de compagnie aérienne** airline club

cluse [klyz] *nf Géog* cluse, transverse valley

clystère [klistɛr] *nm Méd Arch* clyster, enema

cm (*abrév* **centimètre**) cm

CNC [seɛnse] *nm abrév* **couple non cohabitant**

CNPF [seɛnpeɛf] *nm* (*abrév* **Conseil national du patronat français**) French employers' association, ≈ CBI

CNRS [seɛnɛrɛs] *nm* (*abrév* **Centre national de la recherche scientifique**) *Br* ≈ SRC (Science Research Council), *Can* ≈ Science Council of Canada

coaccusé, -ée [koakyze] *n Jur* co-defendant

coach [kotʃ] *nm* **(a)** *Aut* two-door car **(b)** (*entraîneur*) coach

coacquéreur [koakerœr] *nm* joint purchaser

coadjuteur, -trice [koadʒytœr, -tris] *n Rel* coadjutor

coadministrateur, -trice [koadministratœr, -tris] *n* co-director; *Jur* co-trustee

coagulable [kɔagylabl] *adj* capable of coagulating, coagulable

coagulant [kɔagylɑ̃] **1** *adj* coagulating, coagulative **2** *n* coagulant

coagulateur, -trice [kɔagylatœr, -tris] *adj* coagulative

coagulation [kɔagylasjɔ̃] *nf* coagulation, coagulating

coaguler [kɔagyle] **1** *vt (sang)* to coagulate; *(lait)* to curdle **2** *vi (du sang)* to coagulate, to clot; *(du lait)* to curdle **3 se coaguler** *vpr (du sang)* to coagulate, to clot; *(du lait)* to curdle

coalescence [kɔalɛsɑ̃s] *nf* coalescence

coalisé, -ée [kɔalize] **1** *adj* allied **2** *n* **les coalisés** the allies

coaliser [kɔalize] **1** *vt (partis)* to unite into a coalition **2 se coaliser** *vpr* to unite; *Pol* to form a coalition; *Fig* **ils se sont tous coalisés contre moi** they all ganged up on me *or* joined forces against me

coalition [kɔalisjɔ̃] *nf* **(a)** *(alliance)* coalition; **gouvernement de c.** coalition government **(b)** *Fig Péj* conspiracy; **former une c. contre qn/qch** to join forces against sb/sth

coaltar [koltar] *nm* coal tar; *F* **être dans le c.** to be completely out of it, to be in a daze

coassement [kɔasmɑ̃] *nm (de la grenouille)* croak; **des coassements** croaking, croaks

coasser [kɔase] *vi (d'une grenouille)* to croak

coassocié, -ée [koasɔsje] *n* copartner, joint partner

coassurance [koasyrɑ̃s] *nf* mutual assurance

coauteur [kootœr] *nm* **(a)** *(d'un livre etc)* joint author, co-author **(b)** *(d'un crime)* accomplice

coaxial, -ale, -aux, -ales [koaksjal, -jo] *adj* coaxial

COB [seobe] *nf Bourse (abrév* **Commission des opérations de Bourse**) = Stock Exchange watchdog, *US* ≈ SEC

cobalt [kɔbalt] *nm* cobalt; **bleu de c.** cobalt blue; **bombe au c.** cobalt bomb

cobaye [kɔbaj] *nm (mammifère), Fig* guinea pig; *Fig* **servir de c.** to act as a guinea pig

cobelligérant [kobeliʒerɑ̃] *adj, nm* cobelligerent

Coblence [kɔblɑ̃s] *nf* Koblenz

cobol [kɔbɔl] *nm Ordinat* COBOL

cobra [kɔbra] *nm* cobra

coca [kɔka] **1** *nm* **(a)** *F (boisson)* Coke®; **prendre un c.** to have a Coke **(b)** *Bot* coca **2** *nf Pharm* coca

cocagne [kɔkaɲ] *nf* **mât de c.** greasy pole; **pays de c.** land of milk and honey, land of plenty

cocaïne [kɔkain] *nf Pharm* cocaine

cocaïnomane [kɔkainɔman] *n* cocaine addict

cocarde [kɔkard] *nf* rosette; *Hist (sur un chapeau)* cockade; *Av* roundel, fuselage marking; *(dans un avion)* company crest; **la c. tricolore** = tricolour cockade, worn on 14 July

cocardier, -ière [kɔkardje, -jɛr] **1** *adj (chauviniste)* chauvinistic, jingoistic **2** *n* chauvinist, jingoist

cocasse [kɔkas] *adj F* comical, laughable

cocasserie [kɔkasri] *nf F* comical nature, ridiculousness

coccinelle [kɔksinɛl] *nf* **(a)** *(insecte)* ladybird, *Spéc* coccinella **(b)** *F* (Volkswagen®) beetle

coccyx [kɔksis] *nm Anat* coccyx

coche[1] [kɔʃ] *nm Arch* stagecoach; *Fig* **faire la mouche du c.** to buzz around self-importantly; *F* **rater** *ou* **louper** *ou* **manquer le c.** to miss the boat

coche[2] *nf* **(a)** *Vieilli* notch, nick; *(d'une flèche)* nock **(b)** *Ordinat* tick, *Am* checkmark

cochenille [kɔʃnij] *nf* cochineal

cocher[1] [kɔʃe] *nm* coachman, driver; *Arch* **c. de fiacre** cabman; *F* cabby

cocher[2] *vt* **(a)** *(nom etc)* to tick (off), *Am* to check; **c. la case appropriée** tick the appropriate box **(b)** *Vieilli (faire une entaille dans)* to nick, to notch

cochère [kɔʃɛr] *adj* **porte c.** carriage gateway *or* entrance

cochet [kɔʃɛ] *nm* cockerel

Cochinchine [kɔʃɛ̃ʃin] *nf Hist* Cochin-China

cochon, -onne [kɔʃɔ̃, -ɔn] **1** *nm* **(a)** *Zool* pig; *Fig* **copains comme cochons** as thick as thieves; *F* **tu es sale comme un c.** you're filthy; **petite cochonne!** you dirty little thing!; **quel c.!** *(qui ne nettoie pas après soi)* he leaves such a mess behind him; **gros** *ou* **gras comme un c.** as round as a barrel; **manger comme un c.** to eat like a pig; **tu écris comme un c.** your writing is appalling; **avoir des yeux de c.** to have piggy eyes; *Fig* **temps de c.** rotten *or* stinking weather; *Fig F* **eh ben mon c.!** you old rogue *or* devil!; **c'est une tête de c.** he's really pig-headed; *F* **un c. n'y retrouverait pas ses petits** what a pigsty!; *F Péj* **jouer un tour de c. à qn** to play a dirty *or* filthy trick on sb

(b) *F Péj (vicieux)* dirty old man; **tu es une petite cochonne!** you've got a filthy mind *or* a mind like a sewer!

(c) *Arg, Péj* dirty pig, swine; **jouer un tour de c. à qn** to play a dirty *or* rotten trick on sb; **c'est un c.** *(il raconte des histoires immondes)* he's got a filthy mind *or* a mind like a sewer; **quel vieux c.!** what a dirty old man!; **petite cochonne, va!** go away, you dirty thing!

2 *adj (histoire etc)* dirty, smutty, filthy; **film c.** dirty *or* porn *or* blue film; **dix mille francs, c'est pas c.** ten thousand francs? that's not bad; **c. qui s'en dédit** it's a deal

▶ **cochon**: **c. d'Amérique** peccary; **c. d'Inde** guinea pig; **c. de lait** suck(l)ing pig; **c. de mer** porpoise

cochonceté [kɔʃɔ̃ste] *nf F (propos)* filthy talk, foul language; *(vacherie)* dirty trick; **dire des cochoncetés** to use dirty language, to talk dirty

cochonnaille [kɔʃɔnaj] *nf F* foodstuffs made from pork

cochonner [kɔʃɔne] *vt F (travail etc)* to bungle, to botch, to muck up

cochonnerie [kɔʃɔnri] *nf Arg* **(a)** *(saleté)* mess; **faire des cochonneries** *(des saletés)* to make a mess; **dire des cochonneries** to say dirty *or* smutty things **(b)** *(chose sans valeur)* trash, rubbish; *(plat)* pigswill; **il ne mange que des cochonneries** he only eats junk food

cochonnet [kɔʃɔnɛ] *nm* **(a)** *(petit cochon)* piglet **(b)** *(aux boules)* jack

cocker [kɔkɛr] *nm* cocker spaniel

cockpit [kɔkpit] *nm (de voitures de courses), Naut, Av* cockpit

cocktail [kɔktɛl] *nm (boisson)* cocktail; *(soirée)* cocktail party; *Fig (mélange)* cocktail, mixture; **c. de fruits** fruit cocktail; **c. Molotov** Molotov cocktail

coco[1] [koko] *nm* **(a)** *(plante)* **noix de c.** coconut; **huile/beurre de c.** coconut oil/butter **(b)** *Arg (tête)* nut, bonce; *(estomac)* belly; **mets-toi ça dans le c.!** get that into your thick skull! **(c)** *(boisson)* = drink made from liquorice, lemon juice and water

coco[2] *nm* **(a)** *Enf* egg **(b)** *F (type)* fellow, bloke; **drôle de c.** odd bloke, strange guy; **toi mon c., je t'ai à l'oeil** just watch it, mate *or* chum **(c) mon petit c.** my darling, my pet

coco[3] *nf Arg (cocaïne)* coke, Charlie

coco[4] *adj, n F (communiste)* commie, red

cocon [kɔkɔ̃] *nm (du vers à soie etc)* cocoon; *Fig* **le c. familial** the family nest; **s'enfermer dans son c.** to retire into one's shell; **il faut sortir de ton c.** you must come out of your shell

cocontractant, -ante [kokɔ̃traktɑ̃, -ɑ̃t] *n Jur* contracting partner

cocooning [kɔkuniŋ] *nm* cocooning; **faire du c.** to cocoon

cocorico [kɔkɔriko] **1** *int* **(a)** *(du coq)* cock-a-doodle-doo! **(b)** *(des supporters etc)* three cheers for France! **2** *nm* **(a)** *(coq)* cock-a-doodle-do **(b)** *(cri)* = French victory cheer; *(victoire)* = French victory; **faire c.** to crow

cocoter [kɔkɔte] *vi F* to stink; **ça cocote ici** it stinks in here

cocotier [kɔkɔtje] *nm (arbre)* coconut palm; *Fig F* **secouer le c.** to get rid of the dead wood

cocotte [kɔkɔt] *nf* **(a)** *Enf* hen, chicken; *(en papier)* = bird made out of folded paper **(b)** *F* **ma c.** darling **(c)** *(prostituée)* tart **(d)** *Culin* (large) stewpan, casserole (dish) **(e)** *F* **hue, c.!** gee up!

cocotte-minute®, *pl* **cocottes-minute** *nf* pressure cooker

cocuage [kɔkɥaʒ] *nm Arg* cuckoldry

cocu, -e [kɔky] *F* **1** *n surtout m* deceived husband, *f* deceived wife; *(homme) Fml* cuckold; **faire c. son mari** to cheat on one's husband; **avoir une chance** *ou* **une veine de c.** to have the luck of the devil; **va donc, eh c.!** get lost, you sucker! **2** *adj* deceived, *Fml* cuckold(ed); **je suis c.** my wife is cheating on me

cocufier [kɔkyfje] *vt F* to be unfaithful to, to cheat on, *Fml* to cuckold

coda [kɔda] *nf Mus* coda

codage [kɔdaʒ] *nm* coding

code [kɔd] *nm* **(a)** *(symbole)* code; **ils communiquent par c.** they communicate in code; **écrire un message en c.** to write a message in code, to write a coded message; **déchiffrer un c.** to decipher *or* break *or* crack a code

(b) *Ordinat* code **les codes** the codes, the coding; **c. d'erreur** error code; **c. héxadécimal** hexa(decimal) code; **c. abrégé** shortcode; **c. machine** machine code; **c. couleurs** colour coding; **c. d'accès** access code; **c. d'arrêt** stop code; **c. d'autorisation d'accès** access authorization code; **c. d'identification** identification code; **c. d'imprimante** printer code; **c. d'instruction** instruction code; **c. de caractère** character code; **c. de commande** command code; **c. de contrôle** control code; **c. de contrôle de l'imprimante** printer control code; **c. de départ** start code; **c. inhibiteur** inhibit code; **c. natif** source code; **c. objet** object code; **c. source** source code; **c. ASCII** ASCII code

(c) *(ensemble de règles)* law; *(livre)* (copy of the) code; *Jur* statute book; *Aut* **passer le c.** to sit the written part of a driving test; **c. de la morale/de l'honneur** moral code/code of honour

(d) *Aut* **se mettre en code(s)** to dip *or Am* dim one's headlights; **rouler en code(s)** to drive with dipped headlights; **phares code(s)** dipped headlights

▶ **code**: **c. assujetti TVA** VAT registration number; **c. civil**

Civil Code, ≈ Common Law; **c. client** customer code, customer reference number; **c. de commerce** commercial law; **c. confidentiel** security code; (*d'une carte bancaire*) PIN; **c. général des impôts** general tax code; *Biol* **c. génétique** genetic code; *Banque* **code guichet** bank branch code; **c. de justice militaire** military law; **c. maritime** navigation laws; **c. pénal** penal code; *Banque* **c. porteur** PIN, personal identity number; **c. postal** postcode, postal code, *US* zip code; **C. de la route** Highway Code; **c. secret** secret code; **c. du travail** employment code, employment law, *Am* labor code, labor laws

codé [kɔde] *adj* coded; (*pour sécurité*) security-coded; (*image*) scrambled

code(-)barres, *pl* **codes(-)barres** *nm* bar code

codébiteur, -trice [kodebitœr, -tris] *n Jur* joint debtor

codéine [kɔdein] *nf Ch* codeine

codemandeur, -deresse [kodəmɑ̃dœr, -drɛs] *n Jur* joint plaintiff

coder [kɔde] *vt* (*message*) to code

codétenteur, -trice [kodetɑ̃tœr, -tris] *n Jur* joint holder

codétenu, -ue [kɔdetny] *n* fellow prisoner *or* inmate

codeur [kɔdœr] *nm Tech* coder

codex [kɔdɛks] *nm* pharmacopoeia

codicillaire [kɔdisilɛr] *adj Jur* codicillary

codicille [kɔdisil] *nm Jur* codicil

codification [kɔdifikasjɔ̃] *nf* (*des lois etc*) codification, classification; *Ordinat* **c. binaire** binary code; **c. décimale** decimal coding; **c. significative** coding by means of symbols, symbol coding

codifier [kɔdifje] *vt* (*lois etc*) to codify; (*mettre en système*) to systematize

codirecteur, -trice [kodirɛktœr, -tris] *n* joint manager, *f* joint manageress; (*d'un PDG etc*) co-director

coédition [koedisjɔ̃] *nf* (*procédé*) joint publishing; (*livre*) joint publication

coefficient [kɔefisjɑ̃] *nm* **(a)** *Math* coefficient; (*dans un concours ou examen*) coefficient, weighting factor; **on peut s'attendre à un c. d'erreur** a certain margin of error is to be expected; **c. d'occupation des sols** (*en urbanisme*) plot ratio

(b) *Compta* **c. d'exploitation** performance *or* operating ratio; **c. de liquidité** current ratio; **c. de rotation** stock turnover ratio; **c. de solvabilité** risk asset ratio

(c) *Tech* **c. de dilatation** coefficient of expansion; **c. d'écrasement/d'élasticité** modulus of compression/of elasticity; **c. de sécurité** safety factor; **le c. d'augmentation** the rate of increase; *Aut* **c. aérodynamique** *ou* **de pénétration dans l'air** drag coefficient; *Aut* **c. de traînée** drag coefficient, drag factor

cœlacanthe [selakɑ̃t] *nm Zool* coelacanth

cœliaque [seljak] *adj, n Méd* coeliac, *US* celiac

cœlioscopie [seljɔskɔpi] *nf Méd* coelioscopy

coentreprise [koɑ̃trəpriz] *nf* joint venture

coéquation [koekwasjɔ̃] *nf Admin* proportional assessment

coéquipier, -ière [koekipje, -jɛr] *n Sp etc* team mate

coercible [kɔɛrsibl] *adj* **(a)** *Phys* (*gaz etc*) coercible **(b) un bâillement difficilement c.** a yawn that is hard to suppress *or* stifle

coercitif, -ive [kɔɛrsitif, -iv] *adj* coercive; **le pouvoir c. de son discours** the persuasive power of his speech

coercition [kɔɛrsisjɔ̃] *nf* coercion

cœur [kœr] *nm* **(a)** *Anat* heart; **maladie de c.** heart disease; **greffe du c.** heart transplant; **c. droit/gauche** right/left side of the heart; **subir une opération à c. ouvert** to have open-heart surgery; **tué d'une balle en plein c** killed by a bullet in the heart; **en (forme de) c.** heart-shaped; *Fig* **faire la bouche en c.** to simper; **il est arrivé la bouche en c. pour me demander si …** he came simpering up to me to ask if …; *Fig* **joli comme un c.** as pretty as a picture; **serrer** *ou* **presser qn contre** *ou* **sur son c.** to hold sb close; *F* **faire le joli c.** to put on airs (and graces)

(b) (*ventre*) **avoir mal au c.** to feel sick *or Am* nauseous; **ça fait mal au c. de voir tout cet argent gaspillé** it makes you sick to see all that money wasted *or* go to waste; **cela soulève le c.** it's nauseating *or* sickening; *F* **avoir le c. solide** *ou* **bien accroché** to have a strong stomach

(c) (*siège des sentiments*) heart; **il a l'air dur, mais il a le c. sensible** he looks tough, but he has a tender heart; **avoir** *ou* **garder qch sur le c.** to have sth on one's mind; **tu ne peux pas garder ça sur le c., il faut que tu en parles** you can't keep that to yourself, you'll have to talk about it; **dire ce qu'on a sur le c.** to get it off one's chest; *Fig* **en avoir le c. net** to get to the bottom of it; *Fig* **ouvrir son c. à qn** to open one's heart to sb; **parler à c. ouvert** to speak freely; **avoir la rage au c.** to be seething with anger; **au fond du c.** in one's heart of hearts; **remercier qn de tout (son) c.** *ou* **du fond de son c.** to thank sb wholeheartedly *or* from the bottom of one's heart; **je l'espère de tout mon c.** I sincerely hope so; *Euph* **je sais qu'elle ne me porte pas dans son c.** I know she doesn't like me much *or* isn't very fond of me; **partir le c. léger** to set off with a light heart; **avoir le c. triste** *ou* **lourd** to be heavy-hearted; **avoir le c. gros** *ou* **serré** to have a heavy heart, to be sad at heart; **à c. joie** to one's heart's content; **de gaieté de c.** with a light heart; **ce n'était pas de gaieté de c. que je l'ai fait** I wasn't happy about doing it, I didn't enjoy doing it; **prendre** *ou* **avoir à c. de faire qch** to have one's heart set on doing sth; **la chose qui lui tient** *ou* **qu'il a** *ou* **prend à c. est de donner une éducation à sa fille** he has his heart set on giving his daughter an education; **ce projet lui tient à c.** this project is close to his heart; **ne pas avoir le c. de faire qch** not to have the heart to do sth; **elle n'a plus le c. à rien** she hasn't the heart for anything any more; **avoir le c. à rire** to be in the mood for laughing; **avoir le c. sur la main** to be very generous; **à votre bon c., m'sieurs dames** can you spare a few coins?; **femme de c.** warm-hearted woman; **je serai de c. avec vous** I'll be with you in spirit; **à vous briser** *ou* **fendre le c.** heartbreaking; **histoire d'une tristesse à vous fendre** *ou* **briser le c.** heartbreakingly sad story; **j'en avais le c. brisé** I was broken-hearted; **si le c. vous en dit** if you feel like it; **des gens selon mon c.** people after my own heart; **le c. a ses raisons** the heart has its reasons; **ta proposition lui est allée droit au c.** your offer went straight to his heart

(d) par c. by heart; **c'est du par c.** it's been learnt (off) by heart *or* parrot-fashion; **apprendre/savoir qch par c.** to learn/know sth by heart; *F* **je la connais par c.** I know her inside out

(e) (*courage*) courage, spirit; **avoir le c. de faire qch** to have the heart to do sth; **donner du c. à qn** to give sb courage; *F* **avoir du c. au ventre** to have plenty of guts; **faire contre mauvaise fortune bon c.** to make the best of a bad job, to put a good face on it

(f) (*énergie*) heart, will; **avoir** *ou* **mettre du c. à l'ouvrage** to put one's heart into one's work; **je n'ai pas le c. à l'ouvrage aujourd'hui** I haven't the heart for work today; **il était clair qu'il n'avait pas le c. à l'ouvrage** it was obvious that his heart wasn't in it; **faire qch de bon c.** *ou* **de grand c.** to do sth willingly *or* gladly; **rire de bon c.** to laugh heartily; **y aller de bon c.** to get down to it; **le c. n'y est pas** his/my/*etc* heart isn't in it

(g) (*amour*) **donner son c. à qn** to lose one's heart to sb; **aimer qn de tout son c.** to love sb with all one's heart; *Prov* **loin des yeux, loin du c.** out of sight, out of mind; **des histoires de c.** affairs of the heart; **une affaire de c.** an affair of the heart

(h) (*bonté*) **c'est un** *ou* **il a bon c.** he's kind-hearted, he's a kind-hearted soul; **avoir un c. d'or/de pierre** to have a heart of gold/of stone; **ne pas avoir de c.** to be heartless

(i) (*centre*) middle, core; *Fig* **le c. du problème** the heart of the matter; **au c. de la ville** in the centre of the town, in the heart of the city; **c. de palmier** heart of palm; **c. d'un chou/d'un artichaut** heart of a cabbage/artichoke heart; *F* **avoir un c. d'artichaut** to fall in love with every girl/man one meets, to be always falling in love; **fromage fait à c.** ripe cheese; **au c. de l'hiver/l'été** in the depths of winter/the height of summer

(j) *Cartes* heart(s); **dame de c.** queen of hearts; **avez-vous du c.?** have you any hearts?

(k) (*d'imprimante laser*) engine

coexistence [kɔɛgzistɑ̃s] *nf* coexistence (**avec** with); *Pol* **c. pacifique** peaceful coexistence

coexister [kɔɛgziste] *vi* to coexist (**avec** with)

COFACE [kɔfas] *nf* (*abrév* **Compagnie française d'assurance pour le commerce**) ≈ Export Credit Guarantee Department

coffrage [kɔfraʒ] *nm* **(a)** (*pour ouvrages en béton*) formwork, *Br* shuttering **(b)** *Min* (*pour galerie etc*) coffering, lining

coffre [kɔfr] *nm* **(a)** (*meuble*) chest; (*pour l'argent*) safe; (*à la banque*) safe(ty) deposit box; *Banque* **c. de nuit** night safe; **c. en bois** wooden chest; **c. à jouets** toy box; **c. à linge** linen chest; **percer** *ou* **ouvrir un c.** to break open *or* into a safe; **les coffres de l'État** the coffers of State **(b)** *Anat F* chest; **avoir du c.** (*avoir du souffle*) to have a sound chest, to have a lot of puff; (*avoir de la voix*) to have a powerful voice **(c)** *Aut* (*d'une voiture*) boot, *Am* trunk; *Aut* **c. de toit** car roof box, luggage box; **c. porte-skis** ski box; *Av* **c. à bagages** baggage compartment **(d)** (*d'une serrure, d'un piano etc*) case **(e)** *Naut* **c. d'amarrage** mooring buoy

coffre-fort, *pl* **coffres-forts** *nm* safe

coffrer [kɔfre] *vt F* **(a) c. qn** to put sb behind bars *or* inside *or* away; **faire c. qn** to have *or* get sb put inside *or* behind bars **(b)** *Min* (*galerie etc*) to coffer, to line

coffret [kɔfrɛ] *nm* **(a)** small box, casket; **c. à bijoux** jewellery box; **c. de disques** boxed set **(b)** *Ordinat* case; **modèle en c.** cased model
cogérance [koʒərɑ̃s] *nf* co-management, joint management
cogérant, -ante [koʒerɑ̃, -ɑ̃t] *n* joint manager, *f* joint manageress
cogérer [koʒere] *vt* **c. qch** to manage sth jointly
cogestion [koʒɛstjɔ̃] *nf* joint management, co-management
cogitation [kɔʒitasjɔ̃] *nf Iron, Vieilli* cogitation, reflection
cogiter [kɔʒite] *vi Vieilli* to cogitate, to think; **c. sur un problème** to ponder over a problem
cogito [kɔʒito] *nm Phil* cogito; **le c. de Descartes** the Cartesian cogito, Descartes' cogito
cognac [kɔɲak] **1** *nm* cognac **2** *adj inv* brandy(-coloured)
cognassier [kɔɲasje] *nm* quince (tree)
cogne [kɔɲ] *nm Arg* (*policier*) cop; (*bagarre*) punch-up; **il va y avoir de la c.!** there's going to be trouble *or* a punch-up!
cognée [kɔɲe] *nf* axe, *US* ax, hatchet; **jeter le manche après la c.** to throw in one's hand
cognement [kɔɲmɑ̃] *nm* (*bruit*) thumping, banging; (*d'un moteur etc*) knocking, combustion knock; **c. (du moteur) diesel** diesel knock
cogner [kɔɲe] **1** *vt* (*heurter*) to knock, to bump; *F* (*épouse, enfants etc*) to knock about; **c. qn en passant** to bump into sb (in passing); *F* **se faire c.** to get beaten up *or* knocked about; *F* **il cogne dur** he knows how to use his fists; **il l'a cogné dur** he hit him hard; *F* **son mari lui cogne dessus chaque fois qu'il est ivre** her husband knocks her about *or* gives her a thumping every time he gets drunk

2 *vi* **(a)** (*frapper, battre*) to bang (**sur** on); **il est tombé de la chaise et sa tête a cogné contre le bureau** he fell off his chair and bumped *or* banged his head on the desk; **c. du poing sur la table** to bang (one's fist) on the table, to thump the table; **c. à une porte** to bang *or* hammer on a door; **j'entends une volet c.** I can hear a shutter banging

(b) (*d'un moteur etc*) to knock

(c) *F* (*chauffer*) to be scorching; **ça cogne dur dehors** it's absolutely scorching outside, *très F* it's bloody hot outside

3 se cogner *vpr* to bump oneself; **se c. à** *ou* **contre qch** to knock against sth; *F* **ils se cognent dessus chaque fois qu'ils boivent** they bash each other about whenever they get drunk; *Fig* **se c. la tête contre les murs** to bang one's head against a brick wall
cogneur [kɔɲœr] *nm Boxe etc* hard hitter, bruiser
cogniticien, -ienne [kɔgnitisjɛ̃, -jɛn] *n Ordinat* knowledge engineer
cognitif, -ive [kɔgnitif, -iv] *adj Phil* cognitive; **thérapie cognitive** cognitive therapy
cognition [kɔgnisjɔ̃] *nf Phil* cognition
cohabitation [koabitasjɔ̃] *nf* cohabitation, living together; *Fr Pol* **sous le régime de la c.** during the period of cohabitation
cohabiter [koabite] *vi* to cohabit (**avec** with), to live together; **elle cohabite avec des amies** she lives with friends
cohérence [kɔerɑ̃s] *nf* (*d'une argumentation, d'un discours*) coherence; (*d'une argumentation, d'un comportement*) consistency; **cette explication/ce raisonnement/il manque de c.** that explanation/that line of argument/he is inconsistent; **parler sans aucune c.** to be totally incoherent
cohérent [kɔerɑ̃] *adj* (*argumentation*) coherent, consistent; (*comportement*) consistent; (*dans un discours*) coherent
cohéritier, -ière [kɔeritje, -jɛr] *n* coheir(ess), joint heir(ess)
cohésif, -ive [kɔezif, -iv] *adj* cohesive
cohésion [kɔezjɔ̃] *nf* cohesion, cohesiveness
cohorte [kɔɔrt] *nf* **(a)** *F* (*de gens*) horde, band **(b)** *Hist* cohort
cohue [kɔy] *nf* crowd, mob, throng
coi, coite [kwa, kwat] *adj* **se tenir c.** to keep quiet, to lie low; **en rester c.** to be (left) speechless
coiffage [kwafaʒ] *nm* **(a)** (*de cheveux*) hairdressing, doing sb's hair; (*de ses cheveux*) doing one's hair **(b)** (*pour recouvrir*) covering
coiffe [kwaf] *nf* **(a)** (*surtout de costume régional*) headdress **(b)** (*doublure de chapeau*) lining **(c)** (*pour recouvrir*) cover; *Mil* breech cover; **c. de fusée** fuse cap **(d)** (*du nouveau-né*) caul
coiffé [kwafe] *adj* **(a) être c. d'un chapeau** to be wearing a hat; **il est né c.** he was born with a caul; *Fig* he was born with a silver spoon in his mouth **(b) elle est bien coiffée ce soir** her hair is lovely this evening; **je ne suis pas encore coiffée** I haven't done my hair yet; **il est mal c.** his hair's a mess; **c. en arrière** with one's hair combed back; **il est c. en brosse** he has a crew cut
coiffer [kwafe] **1** *vt* **(a)** (*tête*) to cover; (*bouteille etc*) to cap; **c. un enfant d'un bonnet** to put a bonnet on a child('s head); **ce chapeau vous coiffe bien** that hat suits you; **il était coiffé d'un sombrero** he was wearing a sombrero; **montagne coiffée de neige** snow-capped mountain; **des nuages coiffent presque en permanence le Mont-Blanc** Mont-Blanc is almost permanently covered by clouds *or* has a near permanent cloud-cover; *Fig* **c. Sainte-Catherine** to be (left) on the shelf, to be 25 and still unmarried

(b) (*d'un coiffeur etc*) **c. qn** to do sb's hair; **il coiffe bien** he's a good hairdresser; **se faire c. (les cheveux)** to have one's hair done; **qui vous coiffe?** who does your hair, who's your hairdresser?; **sur ces photos, les mannequins sont coiffés par Maniatis** in these photos the models' hair-styling is by Maniatis; **se faire c. chez/par qn** to get one's hair done at sb's/by sb

(c) *Sp F* to overtake; *aussi Fig* **se faire c. (au poteau)** to be pipped at the post

(d) *F* (*organisation, service etc*) to head

2 se coiffer *vpr* **(a)** (*mettre*) **se c. d'une casquette** to put on a cap

(b) (*se peigner*) to do one's hair; **tu ne t'es pas coiffé aujourd'hui, tes cheveux sont emmêlés** you haven't done your hair today, it's all tangled
coiffeur, -euse [kwafœr, -øz] **1** *n* hairdresser, hair stylist; **c. pour hommes** barber **2** *nf* **coiffeuse** dressing table
coiffure [kwafyr] *nf* **(a)** (*de cheveux*) hairstyle; **changer de c.** to change one's hairstyle *or* hairdo **(b)** *Com* hairdressing; **salon de c.** hairdresser's, hairdressing salon; (*pour hommes*) barbershop, barber's **(c)** (*chapeau etc*) headgear; (*de costume régional etc*) headdress
coin [kwɛ̃] *nm* **(a)** (*angle*) (*de la bouche, de l'œil etc*) corner; **maison du** *ou* **qui fait le c.** corner house; **à tous les coins de rue** on every street corner; **l'épicier du c.** the grocer on the corner; (*du village etc*) the local *or* corner grocer; *F* **je ne voudrais pas le rencontrer au c. d'un bois** I wouldn't like to meet him down a dark alley *or* on a dark night; **mettre un enfant au c.** (*pour le punir*) to make a child stand in the corner; **regard en c.** sidelong glance; **lancer un regard en c. à qn** to look at sb sideways, to give sb a sidelong glance; **sourire en c.** half smile; **regarder qn du c. de l'œil** to look at sb out of the corner of one's eye; *Journ* **le c. du jardinier/santé** gardener's/health page; **ici, c'est le c. des enfants** this is the children's corner; **c. enfants** (*au restaurant*) children's area; *Rail* **c. fenêtre/couloir** window/aisle seat; **aux quatre coins du monde** in the four corners of the earth; **elle a visité les quatre coins du monde** she has travelled all over the world; **reliure avec coins** binding with leather corners

(b) (*endroit*) spot, place; **un petit c. pas cher** a cheap *or* inexpensive little place; **il habite dans le c.** he lives around here; **je ne suis pas du c.** I'm not local, I'm not from round here, I don't live round here; **les gens du c.** the locals; *F* **le petit c.** the smallest room (in the house), *Br* the loo; **coins et recoins** nooks and crannies; **il est resté dans son c. toute la journée** he's been very quiet all day; **c'est quelqu'un qui reste tout le temps dans son c.** he doesn't mix much, he stays in the background; **dans un c. de ma mémoire** in a corner of my memory, in the back of my mind; **mon stylo est introuvable, il a dû tomber dans un c.** I can't find my pen anywhere, it must have got lost somewhere; **j'ai dû le mettre dans un c.** I must have put it somewhere; **chercher qch dans tous les coins** to look everywhere *or* high and low for sth; *F* **connaître qch dans les coins** to know sth inside out; **au c. du feu** by the fireside

(c) (*parcelle*) patch; **c. des légumes** vegetable patch *or* plot; **c. de ciel bleu** patch of blue sky

(d) (*cale*) wedge; **en c.** wedge-shaped; **tranchant du c.** thin end of the wedge

(e) (*pour frapper les monnaies*) stamp, die; *Fig* **marqué au c. du génie** bearing the stamp *or* hallmark of genius
coinçage [kwɛ̃saʒ] *nm*, **coincement** [kwɛ̃smɑ̃] *nm* wedging, jamming
coincé [kwɛ̃se] **1** *adj* (*bloqué*) (*fermeture, porte, mécanisme*) jammed, stuck; *Aut* boxed in; *Psy F* uptight (about sex) **2** *n F* **c'est qui ces deux coincés?** who are those two uptight-looking characters?
coincer [kwɛ̃se] (**je coinçai(s), n. coinçons**) **1** *vt* **(a)** (*tiroir etc*) to jam, to stick; (*rails etc*) to wedge (up), to chock (up); **j'ai coincé mes cheveux dans ma fermeture éclair** I got my hair stuck *or* caught in my zip; **sa main était coincée derrière le radiateur** his hand was trapped *or* caught behind the radiator; **la voiture est coincée entre deux camions** (*en stationnement*) the car is boxed in by two lorries; **je ne peux pas doubler, je suis coincé entre deux camions** I can't overtake, I'm stuck between two lorries; **je suis resté coincé dans un embouteillage** I got snarled up in a traffic jam; **je suis coincé à Prague/dans l'ascenseur** I'm stuck in Prague/the lift; *Fig* **il est coincé tout le week-end** he's tied up all weekend

(b) (*acculer*) to corner; **il m'a coincé** (*je n'ai pas su* *répondre*) he had me cornered; *Fig* **il faut que je paie, je suis coincé** I'll have to pay, I'm stuck *or* I've no choice; **je vais me retrouver coincé avec deux mensualités à payer** I'll be stuck with two monthly instalments to pay

(**c**) *F* (*arrêter*) to run in, to nick; **il va finir par se faire c.** he'll end up getting nicked

2 *vi* to jam, to stick; *Fig* **notre proposition n'a pas été acceptée, ça coince au niveau de la direction** our proposal hasn't been accepted, there's a problem as far as management is concerned

3 se coincer *vpr* to jam, to stick; **se c. la tête dans des barreaux** to get one's head stuck in railings; **se c. le doigt dans la porte** to jam one's finger in the door; **évite de te c. le dos!** be careful not to hurt your back!; **il s'est coincé une vertèbre cervicale** he's got a trapped nerve

coïncidence [kɔɛ̃sidɑ̃s] *nf* coincidence; **par une étrange c.** by a strange coincidence

coïncident [kɔɛ̃sidɑ̃] *adj* coincident, coinciding

coïncider [kɔɛ̃side] *vi* to coincide (**avec** with); **leurs intérêts coïncident** they have similar interests; **tout coïncide! je connais le coupable** it all fits! I know who did it; **votre réponse ne coïncide pas avec la question posée** there is some discrepancy between your answer and the question that was asked; **tous les témoignages coïncident** the witnesses all bear each other out *or* tell the same story; **ces deux figures géométriques coïncident** the two shapes match each other perfectly

coin-coin 1 *nm inv* (*des canards*) quacking; **des c.** quacks, quacking **2** *int* quack! quack!

coin-cuisine, *pl* **coins-cuisine(s)** *nm* kitchen area, kitchenette

coïnculpé, -ée [koɛ̃kylpe] *n* co-defendent, co-accused

coing [kwɛ̃] *nm* (*fruit*) quince

coin-repas, *pl* **coins-repas** *nm* dining area *or* recess

coït [kɔit] *nm* coitus, coition

coke [kɔk] **1** *nm* (*combustible*) coke **2** *nf F* (*cocaïne*) coke

cokéfaction [kɔkefaksjɔ̃] *nf* coking

cokéfier [kɔkefje] *vt* to coke

cokerie [kɔkri] *nf* coking plant

col [kɔl] *nm* (**a**) (*d'une robe, d'une chemise etc*) collar; **faux c.** (*sur une chemise*) detachable collar; (*sur un verre de bière*) head; **c. de fourrure/de dentelle** fur/lace collar (**b**) (*d'une bouteille etc*) neck (**c**) *Géog* col (**d**) *Arch, Litt* (*de personne*) neck (**e**) *Anat* (*d'un os*) neck

▶ **col: c. blanc** white-collar worker; **c. bleu** blue-collar worker; **c. cassé** wing collar; **c. châle** shawl collar; **c. cheminée** turtleneck; **c. Claudine** Peter Pan collar; *Anat* **c. du fémur** neck of the femur; **c. marin** sailor's collar; **c. rond** round neck; **c. roulé** polo-neck (jumper); *Anat* **c. de l'utérus** cervix; **cancer du c. de l'utérus** cervical cancer; **c. en V** V-neck

cola [kɔla] *nm* (*plante*) cola, kola

colback [kɔlbak] *nm F* **attraper/prendre qn par le c.** to catch/grab sb by the scruff of the neck

col-bleu, *pl* **cols-bleus** *nm F* (*marin*) sailor, bluejacket

colchique [kɔlʃik] *nm* (*plante*) meadow saffron, autumn crocus, *Spéc* colchicum

cold-cream [koldkrim] *nm* cold cream

col-de-cygne, *pl* **cols-de-cygne** *nm Tech* swan neck

colégataire [kolegatɛr] *n Jur* co-legatee, joint legatee

coléoptère [kɔleɔptɛr] *nm* beetle; **les coléoptères** the Coleoptera

colère [kɔlɛr] **1** *nf* anger, *Lit* wrath; **il s'est mis** *ou* **il est entré dans une c. bleue** *ou* **noire** he flew into a towering rage; **piquer** *ou* **faire une c.** to fly into a rage, to throw a tantrum; **être blanc** *ou* **blême/rouge de c.** to be white/flushed with anger; **c. froide** cold fury; **être en c.** to be angry; **se mettre en c.** to get angry, to lose one's temper (**contre qn** with sb, *Am* at sb); **je suis en c. contre moi-même** I'm angry with myself; **mettre qn en c.** to make sb angry, to anger sb; **avec c.** angrily; **il avait des colères terribles** he was subject to terrible fits of anger; **pas la peine de passer ta c. sur moi** there's no point (in) taking your anger out *or* working your anger off on me; *Litt* **la c. de Dieu** the wrath of God

2 *adj* (*voix*) irate, angry; (*personne*) bad-tempered

coléreux, -euse [kɔlerø, -øz], **colérique** [kɔlerik] *adj* (*personne*) quick-tempered; (*disposition*) irritable

colibacille [kɔlibasil] *nm* colon bacillus

colibacillose [kɔlibasiloz] *nf Méd* colibacillosis

colibri [kɔlibri] *nm* hummingbird

colifichet [kɔlifiʃɛ] *nm* trinket, knick-knack

colimaçon [kɔlimasɔ̃] *nm* snail; **escalier en c.** spiral staircase

colin [kɔlɛ̃] *nm* [①**A12**,1,g] (*poisson*) hake, *Br* coley

colinéaire [kolineɛr] *adj Math* collinear

colin-maillard [kɔlɛ̃majar] *nm* (*jeu*) blind man's buff

colin-tampon *nm F Hum ou Vieilli* **se soucier de qch comme de c.** not to give two hoots about sth

colique [kɔlik] **1** *adj Anat* (*artère etc*) colic **2** *nf* severe stomach pains; (*surtout de bébé*) colic; *Méd* **c. néphrétique/hépatique** renal/biliary colic; **avoir la c.** (*douleur*) to have stomach ache; (*diarrhée*) to have diarrhoea; *Fig F* to have the wind up; *F* **cette idée suffit pour me donner la c.** the very idea puts the wind up me; *F* **quelle c.!** what a bore!, what a bind!

colis [kɔli] *nm* parcel, packet, package; **par c. postal** by parcel post; **c. chargé** registered and insured parcel

Colisée (le) [ləkɔlize] *nm* the Coliseum

colis-épargne *nm inv Com* saving stamps scheme

colistier [kolistje] *nm Pol* fellow candidate, *Am* running mate

colite [kɔlit] *nf Méd* colitis

collabo [kɔlabo] *n F* = **collaborateur (b)**

collaborateur, -trice [kɔlabɔratœr, -tris] *n* (**a**) (*associé*) fellow worker, associate, *Am* co-worker; *Journ* contributor; **collaborateurs d'une revue** contributors to a magazine (**b**) *Pol, Hist* collaborator, collaborationist

collaboration [kɔlabɔrasjɔ̃] *nf* (**a**) (*aide, soutien*) collaboration, co-operation (**avec** with); **travailler en étroite c.** to work closely together, to co-operate (**b**) *Pol* collaboration

collaborationniste [kɔlabɔrasjɔnist] *n Pol* collaborationist

collaborer [kɔlabɔre] *vi* (**a**) (*participer*) to collaborate, to co-operate (**avec** with); **c. à un journal** to contribute to a newspaper; **c. à un projet** to take part in a project; **les deux services collaborent étroitement** the two departments work closely together (**b**) *Pol, Hist* to collaborate

collage [kɔlaʒ] *nm* (**a**) (*d'affiches*) sticking up, putting up; (*de bois etc*) gluing, sticking; (*de papier etc*) pasting; *Beaux-Arts* collage; *Tech* sizing; (*de produits manufacturés*) bonding (**b**) (*du vin*) fining, clarifying

collagène [kɔlaʒɛn] *nm* collagen; **crème de beauté au c.** collagen(-based) cream

collant [kɔlɑ̃] **1** *adj* (**a**) (*adhésif*) sticky; (*peinture, vernis*) tacky; **papier c.** gummed paper (**b**) (*qui moule*) (*vêtement*) tight- *or* close-fitting; **pantalon c.** skintight trousers (**c**) *F* (*personne*) **qu'est-ce qu'il est c.!** you just can't shake him off *or* get rid of him!; **je m'en méfie, il est très c.** I'm wary of him, he's very clingy **2** *nm* [①**A10**,e] (pair of) tights, *Am* pantihose; **c. uni/fantaisie** self-coloured/patterned tights

collante [kɔlɑ̃t] *nf Scol F* = letter giving notice of the date and place of an examination

collapsus [kɔlapsys] *nm Méd* (*d'un malade*) collapse; **c. cardio-vasculaire** circulatory collapse

collatéral, -ale, -aux, -ales [kɔlateral, -o] **1** *adj* collateral; *Archit* **nef collatérale** side aisle; *Jur* **parents collatéraux** collaterals, relatives; **succession collatérale** collateral succession **2** *nm* (**a**) *Archit* side aisle (**b**) *Jur* **collatéraux** collaterals, relatives

collation [kɔlasjɔ̃] *nf* (**a**) (*repas*) light meal, snack (**b**) (*de documents etc*) collation (**c**) (*d'un titre etc*) granting, conferment

collationnement [kɔlasjɔnmɑ̃] *nm* (*de documents etc*) collating, collation

collationner [kɔlasjɔne] *vt* (*deux documents écrits*) to collate, to compare

colle [kɔl] *nf* (**a**) glue; (*pour papier peint*) (wallpaper) paste; **papier sans c.** unsized paper; *F* **c'est un vrai pot de c.** you just can't get rid of him, he sticks like a leech *or* like glue (**b**) *Scol etc F* (*question difficile*) difficult *or* sticky question, poser; (*examen oral*) oral exam; (*punition*) detention; **là, tu me poses une c., je ne sais pas** you've got me there, I don't know (**c**) *Arg* **vivre** *ou* **être à la c.** to be shacked up together

▶ **colle: c. blanche** paste; **c. à bois** wood glue; **c. de bureau** (paper) glue; **c. au caoutchouc** rubber solution; **c. forte** glue; **c. de poisson** isinglass; **c. en pot/stick/tube** a pot/stick/ tube of glue

collecte [kɔlɛkt] *nf* (**a**) (*ramassage*) collection; (*pour les pauvres etc*) collection; **la c. des ordures ménagères** the rubbish collection; **faire** *ou* **organiser une c.** to make *or* take a collection; **nous faisons une c. au profit des enfants malades** we're collecting for sick children *or* on behalf of sick children; **c. de données** data collection *or* gathering (**b**) *Rel* (*prière*) collect

collecter [kɔlɛkte] *vt* to collect

collecteur, -trice [kɔlɛktœr, -tris] **1** *n* collector; **c. d'impôts** tax collector **2** *nm Él* (*d'une dynamo etc*) ring, commutator; *Rad* **c. d'ondes** aerial; **c. d'échappement** exhaust manifold; *Aut* **c. d'admission** inlet manifold, throttle line; *Aut* **c. de sortie** (*turbine*) outlet manifold **3** *adj* **égout c.** main sewer

collectif, -ive [kɔlɛktif, -iv] **1** *adj* (*action, compte-rendu etc*) collective, joint; **billet (de train) c.** group (rail) ticket; **une vague de licenciements collectifs** a wave of mass redundancies; **ferme collective** collective (farm); **contrat c.**

collective agreement; **l'inconscient c.** the collective subconscious; **radiographie collective** mass radiography; *Can Jur* **recours c.** class action suit **2** *nm* **(a)** [①AII,g; B8,9] *Gram* collective noun **(b)** *Fin* **c. budgétaire** bill of supply **(c)** (*association*) co-operative

collection [kɔlɛksjɔ̃] *nf* **(a)** (*action*) collecting, gathering; **depuis l'âge de 10 ans il fait la c. des timbres** he's been collecting stamps since he was ten; **tu n'as jamais fait de c.?** have you never collected anything?

(b) (*de papillons etc*) collection; (*de livres*) series, collection; *Com* (*d'échantillons*) line; **sa c. de timbres** his stamp collection; **je possède la c. complète des Astérix** I own the complete set of Asterix stories; **pièce de c.** collector's item; **la c. d'hiver** the winter collection; **la nouvelle c. de chez Dior** Dior's new collection; *Beaux-Arts* **c. privée** private collection; *F* **j'en ai toute une c.** I've got a whole collection *or* set of them

collectionner [kɔlɛksjɔne] *vt* (*timbres etc*) to collect

collectionneur, -euse [kɔlɛksjɔnœr, -øz] *n* (*de timbres etc*) collector

collectivement [kɔlɛktivmɑ̃] *adv* collectively; **protester/agir c.** to protest/act as a group

collectivisation [kɔlɛktivizasjɔ̃] *nf Écon* collectivization

collectiviser [kɔlɛktivize] *vt Écon* to collectivize

collectivisme [kɔlɛktivism] *nm Écon* collectivism

collectiviste [kɔlɛktivist] *adj, n Écon* collectivist

collectivité [kɔlɛktivite] *nf* **(a)** (*groupe*) community; **le sens de la c.** community spirit; **vie en c.** community life *or* living; *Admin* **c. locale** local community; **la c. nationale** the nation, the country; **collectivités professionnelles** professional organizations; **c. publique** government organization **(b)** (*propriété en commun*) common ownership

collège [kɔlɛʒ] *nm* **(a)** [①A6,d,i] *Scol* school; **c. d'enseignement secondaire** ≈ secondary (modern) school, *Am* high school; **c. d'enseignement technique** technical college; **c. privé** private school; **le brevet des collèges** ≈ school leaving certificate; *Univ* **le C. de France** College de France (=*prestigious higher education institution*) **(b)** *Pol* **c. électoral** electoral body *or* constituency, *surtout US* electoral college **(c)** *Rel* college; **le Sacré C.** the College of Cardinals

collégial, -iale, -iaux, -iales [kɔleʒjal, -jo] **1** *adj* collegial, collegiate **2** *nf* **collégiale** collegiate church

collégialité [kɔleʒjalite] *nf* (*d'une société etc*) collegial structure

collégien, -ienne [kɔleʒjɛ̃, -jɛn] *n* **(a)** *Scol* schoolboy, schoolgirl **(b)** *Iron* innocent; **je n'aime pas être traité en c.** I don't like being treated like a child; **rougir comme un c.** to blush like a schoolboy; **je me suis fait avoir comme un c.** I fell for it like a fool, I should have known better

collègue [kɔlɛg] *n* **c. (de travail)** colleague, fellow worker, *surtout Am* co-worker

coller [kɔle] **1** *vt* **(a)** to stick; (*avec de la colle*) to stick, to glue, to paste (**à, sur** to, on); **c. le timbre sur l'enveloppe** to stick the stamp on the envelope; **la sueur avait collé ses cheveux** her hair was matted with sweat; **elle avait les paupières collées** her eyelids were stuck together; **c. son visage à** *ou* **contre la vitre** to press one's face to the window; **il est resté collé à la télé toute la soirée** he was glued to the TV all evening; **il est toujours le nez collé dans ses bouquins** he's always got his nose stuck in a book; **elle a toujours l'oreille collée aux portes** she's always listening at doors; *Fig* **c. qn au mur** to stick sb up against a wall (and shoot him)

(b) *F* (*mettre*) to stick, to put; **elle a collé le paquet dans un coin** she stuck the parcel in a corner; **ils ont collé le bébé chez la grand-mère** they've dumped the baby on the grandmother; **si tu continues je te colle en pension** carry on like that and I'll pack you off to boarding-school; **on m'a collé ce boulot sans que j'aie dit oui** I got stuck *or* saddled *or Br* lumbered with this job without any say in the matter; **c. une gifle à qn** to slap sb in the face; **si tu continues, je t'en colle une!** if you don't stop, I'll give you one!; **c. une punition à qn** to punish sb; **c. une contravention à qn** to slap a fine on sb

(c) **c. un élève** (*le retenir*) to keep a pupil in; (*lui poser une question difficile*) to catch a pupil out (with a difficult question); **c. un candidat** to fail a candidate

(d) *F* (*suivre*) to follow closely; **il me colle!** he sticks to me like glue!; **arrête de me c. au derrière** *ou très F* **au cul!** stop following me everywhere!

(e) *Ind* (*papier*) to size; (*produits manufacturés*) to bond; (*vin*) to clarify, to fine

(f) *Ordinat* to paste; *TV etc* (*bande etc*) to splice

2 *vi* **(a)** (*adhérer*) to stick (**à** to); **les pâtes ont collé à la casserole** the pasta has stuck to the pan; **robe qui colle au corps** clinging dress; *Fig* **il faut essayer de c. au style de l'auteur** you must try to stick to the author's style; **la peur qui lui collait à la peau** the fear that was ingrained in him *or* that was part of him

(b) *F* (*aller bien*) **ça ne colle pas entre eux** they don't hit it off; **ce qu'elle a dit ne colle pas** what she said doesn't make sense *or* doesn't add up; **leurs témoignages ne collent pas** their testimonies don't tally; **ça colle!** that's OK!; **ça ne va pas c. pour mercredi** it's no go for Wednesday

3 se coller *vpr* **(a)** (*adhérer*) to stick; **les feuilles se sont collées entre elles** the leaves were all stuck together; **elle se colla contre le mur** she flattened herself against the wall; **elle s'est collée contre lui** she clung to him; **c'est toi qui t'y colles** you're landed with it

(b) *Arg* **se c. avec qn** to shack up with sb

collerette [kɔlrɛt] *nf* **(a)** (*de vêtement*) collar; *Hist* (*fraise*) ruff **(b)** *Bot* (*de champignon*) annulus **(c)** *MecE* (*de tuyau*) flange

collet [kɔlɛ] *nm* **(a)** (*de manteau, robe etc*) collar; **saisir qn au c.** to collar sb, to seize sb by the scruff of the neck; **la police lui mit la main au c.** the police arrested him; **elle est très c. monté** she is very prim (and proper) *or* strait-laced **(b)** (*cape*) short cape **(c)** (*de dent, vis, violon etc*) neck; (*de raquette etc*) shoulder; *Bot* (*de champignon etc*) neck, collar; *Culin* **c. de mouton** neck *or* scrag of mutton **(d)** *MecE etc* (*de tuyau etc*) flange, collar, fillet **(e)** (*pour attraper de petits animaux*) snare, noose; **prendre des lapins au c.** to snare rabbits

colleter [kɔlte] (**je collette, n. colletons; je colletterai**) **1** *vt* to collar, to seize by the collar **2 se colleter** *vpr F* to tussle; **se c. avec qn** to tussle *or* grapple with sb; **se c. avec les difficultés** to struggle *or* grapple with problems

colleur, -euse [kɔlœr, -øz] **1** *n* **(a)** (*personne qui colle*) gluer, paster; **c. d'affiches** billsticker, billposter **(b)** *Scol F* examiner **2** *nf Cin* **colleuse** (film) splicer, splicing unit

collier [kɔlje] *nm* **(a)** (*bijou*) necklace, necklet; **c. de perles** pearl necklace, string of pearls; **c. de fleurs** garland of flowers

(b) (*de chien, d'esclave etc*) collar; **cheval de c.** draught horse; **cheval franc du c.** a willing *or* hard-working horse; *Fig* **elle a toujours été franche du c.** she's always been very frank and open; *Fig* **donner un coup de c.** to put one's back into it, to make a special effort; *Fig* **reprendre le c.** to get back into harness; **c. de barbe** narrow beard, fringe of beard

(c) *MecE* collar, ring; *Tech* (*de renfort*) clip; *Aut* clamp; **c. de serrage** clamping ring, clamp; **c. de fixation** bracket, clip; **c. de frein** brake band; **c. de palier** bearing collar

(d) *Zool* (*d'oiseau etc*) collar, ring; **pigeon à** *ou* **au c.** ringed *or* ring-necked pigeon

(e) *Culin* (*de bœuf, mouton*) neck

collimateur [kɔlimatœr] *nm Astron, Opt* collimator; *Fig* **attention, je vous ai dans mon** *ou* **le c.** careful, I've got my eye on you

colline [kɔlin] *nf* hill

collision [kɔlizjɔ̃] *nf* (*entre véhicules etc*) collision; **entrer en c. avec qch** to collide with *or* run into sth; **c. frontale** head-on collision, frontal collision; **c. latérale** side-on collision, side impact; **c. nucléaire** nuclear collision; *Fig* **c. des intérêts** clash of interests

collocation [kɔlɔkasjɔ̃] *nf* **(a)** *Jur* establishing the order of priority of creditors (*in bankruptcy*) **(b)** *Ling* collocation

collodion [kɔlɔdjɔ̃] *nm Ch etc* collodion

colloïdal, -ale, -aux, -ales [kɔlɔidal, -o] *adj Ch etc* colloidal

colloïde [kɔlɔid] *nm Ch* colloid

colloque [kɔlɔk] *nm* **(a)** (*conférence*) seminar **(b)** *F* (*conversation*) confab; **avoir un c. avec qn** to have a confab with sb; **être en c.** to be having a confab

collusion [kɔlyzjɔ̃] *nf Jur etc* collusion

collusoire [kɔlyzwar] *adj Jur* collusive

collutoire [kɔlytwar] *nm Pharm* mouth wash

collyre [kɔlir] *nm Pharm* eyewash, eye lotion

colmatage [kɔlmataʒ] *nm* **(a)** (*de trous dans la route etc*) filling in; (*de trou etc*) plugging (up); *Mil* (*de position*) consolidation **(b)** *Agr* (*de terrain*) warping

colmater [kɔlmate] *vt* (*trous dans la route etc*) to fill in; (*trou etc*) to plug (up); *Mil* (*position*) to consolidate

colo [kɔlo] *nf F abrév* **colonie de vacances**

colocataire [kolɔkatɛr] *n* flatmate, *Am* room mate; *Jur* joint tenant, co-tenant

Colomb [kɔlɔ̃] *nm* **Christophe C.** Christopher Columbus

colombage [kɔlɔ̃baʒ] *nm Constr* half-timbering; **maison à c.** half-timbered house

colombe [kɔlɔ̃b] *nf* (*oiseau*), *Pol Fig* dove; **c. biset** rock dove *or* pigeon; *F* **ma c.** my (little) dove

Colombie [kɔlɔ̃bi] *nf* (**a**) Colombia (**b**) **la C. britannique** British Columbia
colombien, -ienne [kɔlɔ̃bjɛ̃, -jɛn] **1** *adj* Colombian **2** *n* **C.** Colombian
colombier [kɔlɔ̃bje] *nm* (*pigeonnier*) dovecot(e), pigeon loft
colombin [kɔlɔ̃bɛ̃] *nm F* (*étron*) turd
Colombine [kɔlɔ̃bin] *nf Th* Columbine
colombophile [kɔlɔ̃bɔfil] **1** *adj* pigeon-fancying, pigeon-fanciers' **2** *n* pigeon fancier
colombophilie [kɔlɔ̃bɔfili] *nf* pigeon fancying
colon[1] [kɔlɔ̃] *nm* (**a**) (*pionnier*) settler, colonist (**b**) (*enfant dans une colonie de vacances*) child (at camp) (**c**) *Agr* farmer, smallholder
colon[2] *nm Mil Arg* colonel; **ben, mon c.!** well, I'm damned!
côlon [kolɔ̃] *nm Anat* colon; *Anat* **c. transverse** transverse colon
colonel [kɔlɔnɛl] *nm Mil* colonel; *Av* group captain, *US* colonel; *Mil* **oui mon c.** yes Colonel
colonelle [kɔlɔnɛl] *nf Mil* colonel's wife; *Av* group captain's wife, *US* colonel's wife
colonial, -iale, -iaux, -iales [kɔlɔnjal, -jo] **1** *adj* colonial **2** *nm* (*habitant*) colonial; (*soldat*) soldier of the colonial troops **3** *nf Hist, Mil* **la coloniale** the Colonial Army
colonialisme [kɔlɔnjalism] *nm Pol* colonialism
colonialiste [kɔlɔnjalist] *adj, n Pol* colonialist
colonie [kɔlɔni] *nf* (**a**) (*lieu*) colony, settlement; **vivre aux colonies** to live in the colonies; **administrations des colonies** administration *or* government of the colonies, colonial administration; **c. de vacances** (children's) holiday camp, *Am* summer camp; **envoyer ses enfants en c.** to send one's children to camp; **la c. anglaise de Paris** the English colony in Paris; **c. pénitentiaire** penal settlement *or* colony (**b**) (*d'animaux*) colony
colonisateur, -trice [kɔlɔnizatœr, -tris] **1** *adj* (*nation etc*) colonizing **2** *n* colonizer
colonisation [kɔlɔnizasjɔ̃] *nf* colonization, settlement; *Fig* invasion
coloniser [kɔlɔnize] *vt* (*région*) to colonize, to settle
colonnade [kɔlɔnad] *nf Archit* colonnade
colonnage [kɔlɔnaʒ] *nm* putting into columns
colonne [kɔlɔn] *nf* (**a**) *Archit* column, pillar; **lit à colonnes** four-poster bed
(**b**) (*file de personnes, soldats, choses*) column; **c. par deux/trois/quatre** column of twos/threes/fours; **c. de secours** relief column; **c. de véhicules en marche** column of moving vehicles; *Pol* **cinquième c.** fifth column
(**c**) (*d'un dictionnaire, journal*) column; **disposé en colonnes** tabular; *Journ* **écrire une c.** to write *or* have a column; *Journ* **cinq colonnes à la une** a front-page five-column spread; *Math* **dans la c. des dizaines** in the tens column; **des colonnes de chiffres/de noms** columns of figures/names
▶ **colonne** *Compta* **c. créditrice/débitrice** credit/debit column; *Aut* **c. de direction** steering column; **c. de fumée** column *or* plume of smoke; *Naut* **c. d'habitacle** binnacle; **c. de mercure** column of mercury; **c. montante** *Ind* rising main, riser (pipe); *Él* service cable, service conductor, riser; **c. Morris** = pillar used to advertise forthcoming events; *Anat* **c. vertébrale** spinal column, spine
colonnette [kɔlɔnɛt] *nf Archit* small column, colonnette
colopathie [kɔlɔpati] *nf Méd* colitis
colophane [kɔlɔfan] *nf* rosin, colophony
coloquinte [kɔlɔkɛ̃t] *nf* (**a**) (*plante*) colocynth, bitter apple (**b**) *Arg* (*tête*) nut, *Br* bonce
colorant [kɔlɔrɑ̃] **1** *adj* (*matière etc*) colouring, *US* coloring **2** *nm* (**a**) (*pour teindre*) colorant, dye (**b**) (*alimentaire*) colouring, *US* coloring; **sirop garanti sans c.** syrup guaranteed free from (artificial) colour(s)
coloration [kɔlɔrasjɔ̃] *nf* (**a**) (*fait de colorer*) colouring, *US* coloring; (*de daguerréotype etc*) tinting; **se faire faire une c.** to have one's hair tinted; *Fig Litt* **la tristesse donnait une c. inhabituelle à sa voix** sadness had altered his tone of voice; *Fig* **c. politique** politics, political colour (**b**) (*de la peau*) colour(ing), *US* color(ing)
coloré [kɔlɔre] *adj* coloured, *US* colored; **teint c.** florid *or* ruddy complexion; *Fig* **style c.** colourful *or US* colorful style
colorer [kɔlɔre] **1** *vt* to colour, *US* to color; **c. qch en vert** to colour sth green; *Fig* **c. un récit** to lend colour to a tale **2 se colorer** *vpr* (*de fruit*) to colour, *US* to color; (*de visage*) to become flushed; **sa voix s'est colorée de tendresse** a note of tenderness crept into his voice
coloriage [kɔlɔrjaʒ] *nm* (*action*) colouring, *US* coloring; (*dessin*) coloured *or US* colored drawing; **album** *ou* **livre de c.** colouring(-in) book
colorier [kɔlɔrje] *vt* (*impf, pr sub* **n. coloriions, v. coloriiez**) (*carte, dessin*) to colour *or US* color (in)
coloris [kɔlɔri] *nm* shade; (*de tableau, fruit etc*) colours, *US* colors; *Com* **carte de c.** shade card; **disponible en quatre c.** available in four shades *or* colours; (*combinaison de couleurs*) available in four colourways
colorisation [kɔlɔrizasjɔ̃] *nf Cin* colourization, *US* colorization
coloriser [kɔlɔrize] *vt Cin* to colourize *US* to colorize
coloriste [kɔlɔrist] *n* (**a**) *Beaux-Arts* colourist, *US* colorist (**b**) (*de cartes postales, jouets etc*) colourer, *US* colorer, painter (**c**) (*coiffeur*) colourist, *US* colorist
colossal, -ale, -aux, -ales [kɔlɔsal, -o] *adj* (*somme*) colossal, huge, gigantic; (*énergie*) colossal, enormous
colossalement [kɔlɔsalmɑ̃] *adv* colossally, hugely
colosse [kɔlɔs] *nm* (*statue*) colossus; (*homme, institution*) giant; **le c. de Rhôdes** the Colossus of Rhodes; *Fig* **un c. aux pieds d'argile** a giant with feet of clay
colostomie [kɔlɔstɔmi] *nf Chir* colostomy; **subir une c.** to have a colostomy
colostrum [kɔlɔstrɔm] *nm Physiol* colostrum
colportage [kɔlpɔrtaʒ] *nm* (*de marchandises*) hawking, peddling; **c. de fausses nouvelles** spreading of rumours
colporter [kɔlpɔrte] *vt* (*marchandises*) to hawk, to peddle; (*nouvelle, rumeurs*) to spread
colporteur, -euse [kɔlpɔrtœr, -øz] *n* hawker, pedlar; *Péj* **c. de ragots** gossipmonger
colposcopie [kɔlpɔskɔpi] *nf Méd* colposcopy
colt [kɔlt] *nm* Colt®
coltinage [kɔltinaʒ] *nm* (*d'une charge sur le dos*) porterage, carrying
coltiner [kɔltine] **1** *vt* (*charges*) to carry on one's back **2 se coltiner** *vpr F* **se c. qn/qch** to get stuck *or* landed *or Br* lumbered with sb/sth
coltineur [kɔltinœr] *nm* porter (*who carries heavy loads*); **c. de charbon** coal heaver
columbarium [kɔlɔ̃barjɔm] *nm* columbarium
col(-)vert, *pl* **cols(-)verts** *nm* (*oiseau*) mallard
colza [kɔlza] *nm* (*plante*) rape, colza; **huile de c.** rapeseed oil, colza oil
coma [kɔma] *nm Méd* coma; **être dans le c.** to be in a coma; **tomber dans le c.** to go *or* lapse into a coma; **il est dans un c. dépassé** he's brain-dead
comateux, -euse [kɔmatø, -øz] *Méd* **1** *adj* comatose **2** *n* patient in a coma
combat [kɔ̃ba] *nm* (**a**) *Mil* (*bataille*) fight, battle; (*activité*) combat; **c. corps à corps** hand-to-hand fight; (*activité*) hand-to-hand fighting; **c. aérien** dog fight; (*activité*) aerial combat; **c. naval** naval engagement *or* action; (*activité*) naval combat; **c. terrestre** land operation; (*activité*) land fighting; **tenue de c.** battledress; **gaz de c.** nerve gas; **c. de rue** street fight; **engager le c.** to go into action (**avec qn** against sb); **mettre hors de c.** to disable, to put out of action; **hors de c.** disabled, out of action; (*régiment*) out of action
(**b**) (*dispute*) fight; **c. de boxe** boxing match; **c. de coqs** cockfight
(**c**) *Fig* (*lutte*) fight; **c. contre la mort** fight against death; **le c. contre l'inflation** the battle *or* fight against inflation; **c'est un c. quotidien** it's a daily struggle; **même c.!** we're fighting for the same thing!; **continuons le c.!** the fight goes on!
combatif, -ive [kɔ̃batif, -iv] **1** *adj* combative, pugnacious; **esprit c.** fighting spirit; **il n'a rien de c.** he's no fighter **2** *n* fighter, battler
combativité [kɔ̃bativite] *nf* combativeness, pugnacity
combattant [kɔ̃batɑ̃] **1** *adj* fighting, combatant; *Mil* **unité combattante** combatant *or* fighting unit **2** *nm* (**a**) (*soldat*) combatant, fighter; **anciens combattants** ex-servicemen, *Am* veterans (**b**) (*dans une dispute*) fighter, brawler (**c**) (*oiseau*) ruff (**d**) *Mktg* **c. de front** front-line person
combattre [kɔ̃batr] (*conj like* **battre**) **1** *vt* (*ennemi*) to fight (against); (*maladie, théorie*) to fight; (*inflation etc*) to combat, to fight **2** *vi* to fight; **c. pour/contre qn/qch** to fight for/against sb/sth
combe [kɔ̃b] *nf Géog* coomb, anticlinal valley
combien [kɔ̃bjɛ̃] **1** *adv* (*conj when introducing a clause*) (**a**) (*comme*) how (much)!; **si tu savais c. je t'aime!** if you knew how (much) I love you!; **j'ai pu constater c. tu avais changé** I could see how much you'd changed; **c. crédules sont tous ces hommes!** how gullible all these men are!
(**b**) (*en nombre*) how many; **c. de** how many; **c. de fois?** how many times?, how often?; **c. sont-ils?** how many (of them) are there?; **je ne sais pas c. il y en a** I don't know how many (of them) there are; **et c. de gens furent tués dans cette guerre!** what a lot of people were killed in that war!
(**c**) (*en quantité*) how much; **c. de** how much; **c. vous dois-je?** how much do I owe you?; **(c'est) c.?**, **tu veux c.?**

(*d'argent*) how much do you want?; *F* **ça fait c.?** how much (is that)?, how much does that come to?; **depuis c. de temps est-il ici?** how long has he been here?; **il y en a pour c. de temps?** how long will it take?; **tu en as pour c. de temps?** how long will it take you?, how long will you be?; **c. de temps vous a-t-il fallu pour venir?** how long did it take you to come?; **c'est arrivé il y a je ne sais c. de temps** it happened such a long time ago; **c. y a-t-il d'ici à Londres?** how far is it (from here) to London?; **à c. sommes-nous de Paris?** how far are we from Paris?; **c'est à c. de kilomètres d'ici?** how many kilometres away is it? how far (away) is it?; **c. pèse-t-elle?** how much does she weigh?; **c. mesure-t-il?** how tall is he?; **elle est enceinte. — de c.?** she's pregnant. — how far gone is she?, how many months?; **il a fait c. au saut à la perche?** how high did he jump in the pole vault, what was his height in the pole vault?

2 *nm inv F* **le c. sommes-nous?/on est le c. aujourd'hui?** what's the date (today)?, what's today's date?; **il y a un car tous les c.?** how often is there a bus?; **tu chausses du c.?** what's your shoe size, what shoe size are you?, what shoe size do you take?

combientième [kɔ̃bjɛ̃tjɛm] *F* **1** *adj* **tu as été reçu c. à l'examen?** where did you come in the exam?; **tu es c. dans la liste?** where are you on the list?, what position are you in the list?; **c'est la c. fois que tu viens?** how often have you been now? **2** *n* **elle est arrivée la c.?** where did she come in?; **tu veux le c.?** which of them do you want?

combinaison [kɔ̃binɛzɔ̃] *nf* **(a)** (*de lettres, d'idées etc*), *Math, Ch* combination; (*de coffre-fort, cadenas*) combination; **c. financière** combine; **la c. gagnante** (*au tiercé*) the winning combination (of numbers); **une heureuse c. de couleurs** a pleasing combination of colours *or* colour scheme; *Ordinat* **c. de touches** key combination **(b)** (*solution*) scheme, plan **(c)** (*vêtement*) (*tenue de travail*) boiler suit; *Av* flying-suit; (*de femme*) slip; **c. de plongée** *ou* **de planche à voile** wetsuit

combinard, -arde [kɔ̃binar, -ard] *F* **1** *adj* scheming, devious; **il est c.** he's a real schemer **2** *n* schemer

combinateur [kɔ̃binatœr] *nm Él* controller, multiple-contact *ou* selector switch; *Rail* switchgroup

combinatoire [kɔ̃binatwar] *adj* combinative; *Math* combinatorial

combine [kɔ̃bin] *nf F* scheme, trick; **il a une c. pour entrer sans payer** he knows a way of getting in without paying; **il a trouvé la c. pour se faire embaucher** he's found a way of getting taken on; **il faut le mettre dans la c.** we'll have to let *or* bring him in on it

combiné [kɔ̃bine] **1** *adj* (*action etc*) combined, joint **2** *nm* **(a)** *Ch* compound **(b) c. (téléphonique)** receiver, handset **(c)** (*hi-fi*) radiogram; *Rad etc* **c. micro-casque** headset **(d)** *Ski* combined downhill and slalom competition **(e)** *Vieilli* (*sous-vêtement*) corselet

combiner [kɔ̃bine] **1** *vt* **(a)** (*forces, efforts etc*) to combine, to unite; (*nombres, idées etc*), *Ch* to combine **(b)** *F* (*plan*) to devise, to think out, to concoct; **qu'est-ce que tu as combiné?** what have you come up with?; **elle combine un sale coup** she's plotting something nasty, she's planning a dirty trick **2 se combiner** *vpr* to combine, to go together (**à, avec** with)

comble [kɔ̃bl] **1** *nm* **(a)** (*maximum*) (*du bonheur, de l'insolence*) height; (*du désespoir*) depth; (*de la gloire etc*) height, peak, summit; **le c. du ridicule serait de ...** it would be the height of absurdity to ...; **pour c. de malheur** to cap *or* crown it all; **ça c'est le** *ou* **un c.!** that's the limit *or* the last straw!; **elle était au c. de la joie** she was overjoyed, she was beside herself with joy

(b) *Archit* (*en bois*) roof timbers; (*en métal*) roof structure; **c. à deux pans** span roof; **c. brisé** curb roof; **loger sous les combles** to live in an attic; **combles aménageables** attic suitable for conversion; *Fig* **de fond en c.** from top to bottom; **modifier une organisation de fond en c.** to effect a major shake-up of an organization, to make sweeping changes in an organization

2 *adj* (*train, autobus, pièce etc*) (jam-)packed; (*mesure*) piled high; *Th* **on a fait salle c.** we had a full *or* capacity house; *Fig* **la mesure est c.** enough is enough, that's the limit

comblé [kɔ̃ble] *adj* (*personne*) happy, contented, satisfied; **il est c.** he has everything he could wish for

combler [kɔ̃ble] *vt* **(a)** (*puits, fossé, trou etc*) to fill in, to fill (up); (*une perte*) to make up, to make good; (*découvert*) to pay off; **c. une lacune** to fill a gap; **c. un besoin** to satisfy a need; **c. un retard** to make up for lost time **(b)** (*satisfaire*) (*personne*) to satisfy; **c. les vœux de qn** to fulfil *or* satisfy sb's desires; **vous me comblez** you are too kind, I'm overwhelmed; **c. qn de cadeaux** to shower sb with gifts; **elle a été comblée par la nature** she has been blessed by nature

comburant [kɔ̃byrɑ̃] *Ch etc* **1** *adj* combustive **2** *nm* combustive agent; *Astronaut* oxidant

combustibilité [kɔbystibilite] *nf* combustibility

combustible [kɔ̃bystibl] **1** *adj* combustible; **assemblage d'éléments combustibles** fuel assembly **2** *nm* fuel; (*de fusée*) propellant, fuel; **c. nucléaire** nuclear fuel; **c. liquide** liquid fuel

combustion [kɔ̃bystjɔ̃] *nf* combustion; **poêle à c. lente** slow-combustion stove; **c. vive** external combustion; **moteur à c. interne** internal combustion engine; **c. détonante** detonation, combustion knock

Côme [kom] *nf* Como; **le lac de C.** Lake Como

come-back [kɔmbak] *nm inv* (*d'une vedette*) come-back; **faire un c.** to make a come-back

comédie [kɔmedi] *nf* **(a)** *Th* (*pièce comique, genre*) comedy; **la c. et la tragédie** comedy and tragedy; **jouer la c.** to act; *Fig* to put on an act; **allons! pas de c.!** come on, stop acting!; **c'est une vraie c. quand il faut aller à l'école** it's a real fuss *or* palaver when it's time to go to school; **c'est toujours la même c.** it's the same old thing *or* story every time **(b)** *Arch* (*pièce de théâtre*) play

▶ **comédie: c. dramatique** drama; **c. musicale** musical; **c. de mœurs** comedy of manners

comédien, -ienne [kɔmedjɛ̃, -jɛn] **1** *n* (*acteur*) actor, *f* actress; (*acteur comique*) comic actor, *f* comedienne; *Fig* show-off; **comédiens ambulants** strolling players; *Fig* **c'est une comédienne** she is always putting on an act **2** *adj* **il est très c.** he's very theatrical *or* affected; **être plus c. que tragédien** to be more of a comic than a tragic actor

comédon [kɔmedɔ̃] *nm* blackhead

comestible [kɔmɛstibl] **1** *adj* edible; **denrées comestibles** food, foodstuffs, *Fml* comestibles **2** *nmpl* **comestibles** food, foodstuffs, *Fml* comestibles

comète [kɔmɛt] *nf* **(a)** *Astron* comet; (*feu d'artifice*) sky rocket; **l'année de la C.** the year of the comet (*1811, when Halley's Comet was seen for the first time*); *Fig* **tirer** *ou* **faire des plans sur la c.** to build castles in Spain, to indulge in pipe-dreams **(b)** (*tranchefile*) headband

comice [kɔmis] *nm* **(a) c. agricole** agricultural show; **comices agricoles** agricultural association **(b)** *Fr Hist* **comices** electoral meeting

comics [kɔmiks] *nmpl* comic strips, cartoon strips, *esp Am F* funnies

comique [kɔmik] **1** *adj* **(a)** *Th* (*acteur, auteur, rôle etc*) comic; **le genre c.** comedy **(b)** (*amusant*) (*histoire, visage etc*) comical, funny **2** *nm* **(a)** (*genre*) comedy; (*acteur*) comic actor; (*boute-en-train*) comic, comedian; **c. de répétition** comedy based on repetition; **c. de situation** situation comedy; **c. troupier** coarse *or* vulgar comedy **(b) le c. de l'histoire, c'est que ...** the funny part *or* the joke is that ...

comiquement [kɔmikmɑ̃] *adv* comically

comité [kɔmite] *nm* [ⓘAll,g,i] committee; **faire partie d'un c.** to sit on a committee; **cette décision sera prise en petit c.** the decision will be made by a select group; **ils se sont mariés en petit c.** they had a quiet wedding; **pour leur anniversaire ils seront en petit c.** they'll celebrate their anniversary with just a few friends (and relations); **un dîner en petit c.** a small dinner party

▶ **comité**: **c. consultatif** advisory committee *or* board; **c. de direction** executive *or* management committee; **c. d'enquête** board of enquiry; **c. d'entreprise** works council *or* committee; **c. d'hygiène et de sécurité** health and safety committee; **C. international olympique** International Olympic Committee; **c. de lecture** reading *or* selection committee; **c. secret** secret session; *Mktg* **c. synectique** idea committee; **c. d'usagers** users' committee

commandant, -ante [kɔmɑ̃dɑ̃, -ɑ̃t] **1** *nm* **(a)** (*officier*) (*d'unité etc*) commander, commanding officer; (*de camp, base etc*) commandant; *Naut* (*de bateau*) captain (*whatever his rank*); **c. en chef** commander-in-chief; *Naut* executive officer, first lieutenant; *Av* **c. de bord** captain **(b)** (*rang*), *Mil* major; *Mil, Av Br* squadron leader, *US* major; **c. en chef des forces aériennes** ≈ Marshal of the Royal Air Force, *US* ≈ General of the Air Force **2** *nf* **commandante** commanding officer's wife

commande [kɔmɑ̃d] *nf* **(a)** *Com* order; **faire** *ou* **passer une c.** to put in *or* place an order; **livrer une c.** to deliver an order; **fait sur c.** made to order; **ouvrage écrit sur la c. de l'éditeur** work commissioned by the publisher; **payable à la c.** payment with order; **c. export** export order; **c. ferme** firm order; **c. renouvelée** repeat order; *Fig* **sourire de c.** forced smile; **on ne peut pas rire sur c.** you can't laugh to order

(b) *MecE* (*action*) control, operation; (*dispositif*) control; (*mécanisme*) drive, driving (gear); **c. à distance** remote control; **c. manuelle/à pied** hand *or* manual/foot control;

c'est à c. manuelle it has hand *or* manual controls, it is manually controlled; **levier de c.** control lever; *Av* control column; **prendre les commandes** (*d'un avion etc*) to take over the controls; (*d'une société etc*) to take over, to take control; **avion à double c.** dual-control plane; *Él* **machine à c. électrique** electrically driven machine; *Aut* **c. d'allumage** ignition trigger; *Aut* **c. de démarreur** starter switch; *Aut* **c. de starter** choke control; *Aut* **c. de vitesse de croisière** cruise control; **c. par poignée** (*d'une moto etc*) twist grip; **c. tactile** (*des vitres d'une voiture etc*) one-touch operation; *Aut* **c. électronique du moteur** engine management system; *Aut* **commandes de conduite** driving controls

(c) *Ordinat* command; **c. DOS** DOS command; **c. d'annulation** undo command; **c. d'effacement** delete command; **c. d'insertion** insert command; **c. de copie** copy command; **c. écran précédent** screen up command; **c. écran suivant** screen down command; **c. erronée** bad command; **c. de formatage** formatting command; **c. imbriquée** embedded command; **c. de recherche** search *or* find command; **c. de recherche et remplacement** search and replace command, find and replace command; **c. de sauvegarde** save command; **c. de soulignage** underline command; **c. du système d'exploitation** operating system command; **à c. vocale** voice-activated

commandement [kɔmɑ̃dmɑ̃] *nm* **(a)** (*ordre*) command, order; *Jur* summons to pay before execution; **dès que je vous en donnerai le c., à mon c.** when I give the command *or* order, on my command; *Rel* **les Dix Commandements** the Ten Commandments **(b)** (*pouvoir*) command; **avoir/prendre le c.** to be in/to take command; **avoir le c. sur ...** to be in command of ..., to have command over ...; *Mil, Naut* **c. en chef** command-in-chief; **c. suprême, haut c.** high command

commander [kɔmɑ̃de] **1** *vt* **(a)** (*diriger*) to command, to be in command of; (*ordonner*) to command, to order; **il commande deux cents hommes** he has two hundred men under his command; **il n'aime pas qu'on le commande** he doesn't like being ordered about; *F* **sans vouloir vous c., est-ce que vous pourriez fermer la fenêtre?** I don't want to give orders, but could you close the window?

(b) (*marchandises, dîner etc*) to order; (*peinture, ouvrage*) to commission; **c. qch à qn** to order/commission sth from sb

(c) (*susciter*) to command; **c. le respect/l'attention** to command respect/attention

(d) (*dominer*) (*vallée etc*) to dominate, to command

(e) (*maîtriser*) (*sentiment, réaction etc*) to control

(f) *MecE* (*mouvement, valve etc*) to control; (*machine, arbre etc*) to drive

(g) *Ordinat* to drive; **commandé par menu** menu-driven; **commandé à la voix** voice-activated

2 *vi* **je lui ai commandé de se taire** I told *or* ordered him to be quiet; **qui est-ce qui commande ici?** who's in charge here?; **avez-vous déjà commandé?** (*au restaurant*) have you ordered yet?

3 se commander *vpr* **(a) ces choses-là ne se commandent pas** (*sont incontrôlables*) these things are beyond our control; **il faut apprendre à vous c.** you must learn to control yourself

(b) les pièces de cet appartement se commandent the rooms of this flat connect up *or* communicate with each other

commanderie [kɔmɑ̃dri] *nf* (*résidence*) commander's residence

commandeur [kɔmɑ̃dœr] *nm* commander

commanditaire [kɔmɑ̃ditɛr] *adj, nm Com* **(associé) c.** sleeping *or Am* silent partner; **nous ne savons pas qui sont les commanditaires de l'attentat** we don't know who is behind the attack

commandite [kɔmɑ̃dit] *nf Com* **(a) (société en) c.** mixed liability company, limited partnership **(b)** (*fonds*) interest of *or* capital invested by sleeping partner(s)

commandité [kɔmɑ̃dite] *adj, nm Com* **(associé) c.** active partner, general partner

commanditer [kɔmɑ̃dite] *vt* to finance; (*meurtre, attentat etc*) to be behind

commando [kɔmɑ̃do] *nm* (①**A12**,1,c) *Mil* commando (unit)

comme[1] [kɔm] *adv* **(a)** (*comparaison*) as; (*de la même manière*) like; **faites c. moi** do as I do; **se conduire c. un fou** to behave like a madman; **il n'est pas c. les autres** he isn't like the others; **tous furent appelés à participer à l'effort de guerre, les femmes c. les hommes** they were all called upon to join in the war effort, men and women alike; **sortir tous les jours, été c. hiver** to go out every day, summer and winter alike; **tout le monde fera la vaisselle, toi c. les autres** everyone will do the washing-up, and that includes *or* goes for you as well as the others; **tout c. un autre** (just) like anyone else; **nous étions c. un seul homme** we were as one man; **c. qui dirait** as one might say; **c. dit l'autre** as they say; **rusé comme un (vieux) renard** (as) sly *or* cunning as a fox; **doux c. un agneau** (as) gentle as a lamb; **haut c. trois pommes** knee-high to a grasshopper; **blanc c. neige** snow-white, white as snow; *F* **c. par hasard** as if by chance; **c. prévu** as planned; **il a été puni c. de juste** he's got his just deserts, he's been punished as he deserved; **quelque chose c. deux cents personnes** something like two hundred people; **P c. pomme** A as in apple; (*en apprenant l'alphabet*) A is for apple

(b) c. (si) (**si** *is expressed only before a finite verb*) as if, as though; **il travaille c. s'il avait vingt ans** he works as if *or* as though he were twenty, he works like a twenty-year-old; **ils faisaient c. si rien ne s'était passé** they acted as if *or* as though nothing had happened; **c. si de rien n'était** as if *or* as though nothing had happened; **c. si je ne le savais pas!** as if I didn't know!; **tu n'es pas content mais tu n'as qu'à faire c. si** you're not happy but you can act as if *or* as though you are; **il leva la main c. pour me frapper** he lifted his hand as if *or* as though to strike me; *F* **c'est tout c.** it comes *or* amounts to the same thing

(c) c. quoi je ne m'étais pas trompé! which only goes to show I was right!; *F* **voici un certificat c. quoi j'ai été malade** here's a certificate to say that I've been ill

(d) c. ça like that; *F* **c'est c. ça et c'est pas autrement** that's the way it is; **alors c. ça, on fait le mur?** so we're making a run for it, are we?; **(alors) c. ça vous venez de Paris?** so you come from Paris?; **elle est toujours c. ça?** is she always like that?; **puisque c'est comme ça, je m'en vais** if that's the way it is *or* things are, I'm going; **elle était grande comment ta truite?, – c. ça!** how big was your trout? – this big!; *F* **il me fait c. ça ...** he says to me just like that ...; **comment ça va? – c. ci, c. ça** how are you? – so, so

(e) drôle c. tout as funny as anything, incredibly funny; **c'est mignon c. tout** it's as cute as anything, it's so cute!; **c'est facile c. tout!** it's as easy as pie!, it's dead easy!

(f) (*tel que*) such as, like; **les bois durs c. le chêne et le noyer** hard woods such as *or* like oak and walnut; **avoir qn c. ami** to have sb as a friend

(g) (*immediately before finite verbs*) as; **faites c. il vous plaira** *ou* **vous voulez** do as you please; **insolent c. il est** insolent as he is; **belle c. elle est, elle n'aura pas de mal à trouver un mari** being as beautiful as she is, she won't have any trouble finding a husband; **c'est arrivé à peu près c. je l'avais prédit** it happened more or less as I predicted; **des montres c. on n'en fait plus maintenant** the kind of watches they don't make anymore

(h) (*en tant que*) as, in the way of; **qu'est-ce que vous avez c. légumes?** what have you got in the way of vegetables?, what (kinds of) vegetables do you have?; **je l'ai eue comme professeur** I had her as my *or* a teacher; **il a été vendu c. esclave** he was sold as a slave; **ce n'est pas mal c. film** it's not bad as films go

(i) *int* how!; **c. vous avez grandi!** how you've grown!; **c. elle est bête!** how stupid she is!; **c. je suis content de vous voir!** how glad I am to see you! am I glad to see you!; **c. tu as de grandes dents!** what big teeth you have!; **c. de bien entendu, il ne m'a pas appelé** as I might have known, he didn't call me; **c. c'est curieux, j'aurais juré l'avoir laissé là!** how odd!, I could have sworn I left it there!; *F* **c. tu y vas!** that's a bit much!

(j) *F* (= *comment*) how; **il y est arrivé Dieu sait c.** he managed it, God (only) knows how; **voilà c. elle est** that's just like her; **elle a fait les carreaux, faut voir c.!** you should see the way she's done the windows!

(k) *F* **elle a eu c. une hésitation avant de répondre** she seemed to hesitate before answering; **il était c. pantelant** he seemed to be gasping for breath; **à mon avis, on a c. un problème** I think we've got a bit of a problem (here); **j'ai c. l'impression qu'on s'est trompé de route** I have a feeling we're on the wrong road; **il y a là c. un hic!** there seems to be a bit of a catch!; **j'étais c. hypnotisé** it was as if *or* as though I was hypnotized

comme[2] *conj* [①**B55**,B] **(a)** (*puisque*) as, since, seeing that; **c. vous êtes mon ami, je vous dirai tout** as *or* since *or* seeing that you're my friend I'll tell you everything **(b)** (*alors que*) (just) as; **c. il allait frapper, on l'arrêta** (just) as he was about to strike he was arrested

commémoratif, -ive [kɔmemɔratif, -iv] *adj* commemorative **(de** of**)**; **service c.** memorial service; **monument c.** memorial

commémoration [kɔmemɔrasjɔ̃] *nf* commemoration; **en c. d'un événement/d'une personne** in commemoration of an event/a person

commémorer [kɔmemɔre] *vt* to commemorate

commençant, -ante [kɔmɑ̃sɑ̃, -ɑ̃t] **1** *adj* **une fièvre commençante** the beginnings of a fever; **se lever au jour c.** to get up at day break **2** *n* beginner; **manuel pour grands commençants** handbook for complete beginners

commencement [kɔmɑ̃smɑ̃] *nm* beginning, start; **commencements** beginnings, initial stage(s); **au c.** at the beginning *or* start *or* outset; *Bible* **au c. était le verbe** in the beginning was the word; **du c. jusqu'à la fin** from beginning to end, from start to finish; **il faut un c. à tout** you've got to start somewhere; *F* **c'est le c. de la fin** it's the beginning of the end

commencer [kɔmɑ̃se] **(je commençai(s), n. commençons) 1** *vt* **(a)** (*entreprendre*) to begin, to start (on), *Fml* to commence; **c. les hostilités** *ou* **la guerre** to commence hostilities, to start a war; **c. un traitement** to go on *or* start a course of treatment; **nous avons mal commencé l'année** we've made a bad start to the year; *Vieilli* **c. un élève en chimie** to give a pupil a grounding in chemistry

(b) (*être au début de*) to begin, to start (**par** with); **le mot qui commence la phrase** the word which starts the sentence

(c) *Typ* **c. en retrait** to indent

2 *vi* to begin, to start, *Fml* to commence; **c. à** *ou* **de faire qch** to begin *or* start to do sth, to begin *or* start doing sth; **l'année commence le 1er janvier** the year begins *or* starts on January 1st; **il commence à pleuvoir** it's beginning *or* starting to rain; **la pluie vient de c.** it's just started raining; **c. par faire qch** to begin *or* start by doing sth; **commençons par votre frère/le commencement** let's start *or* begin with your brother/at the beginning; **pour c., je dois vous dire …** to begin with *or* to start with *or* first of all, I must tell you …; **par où c.?** (*il y a tellement de choses à dire*) where to start?, where should *or* shall I begin?; **nous allions c. sans vous** we were going to start *or* begin without you; **à c. par …** beginning *or* starting with …; **je commence à en avoir assez!** I've had just about enough!; *F* **ça commence à bien faire** it's getting a bit too much, it's getting beyond a joke; *Iron* **ça commence bien!** that's a great start!; *F* **tu ne vas pas c.!, ne commence pas!** don't start!; *Enf* **c'est lui qui a commencé!** he started it!

commensal, -aux [kɔmɑ̃sal, -o] *n* **(a)** (*hôte*) table companion **(b)** *Biol* commensal

commensurable [kɔmɑ̃syrabl] *adj* commensurable (**avec** with, to)

comment [kɔmɑ̃] **1** *adv* **(a)** *interr* how; **c. allez vous?** how are you?; **c. (dites-vous)?** I beg your pardon?, what did you say?; **c. faire?** what can *or* should I/we/*etc* do?, what's to be done?; **c. s'appelle-t-il?** what's his name?, what's he called?; **c. dit-on 'soleil' en japonais?** how do you say 'sun' in Japanese?; **c. est-il, ce garçon?** what's this young man like?, what sort of young man is he?; **c. peut-il me dire des choses pareilles?** how can he talk to me like that *or* say such things to me?; **c. se fait-il que vous soyez toujours en retard?** how *or* why is it that you're always late?

(b) (*affirmation*) how, the way; **elle me dira c. faire** she'll tell me how (to do it); **il faut voir c. elle lui parle** you should see *or* hear the way *or* how she speaks to him; **faire qch n'importe c.** to do sth in a slapdash manner *or F* anyhow *or* any old how

(c) *int* what!; **c.! vous n'êtes pas encore parti!** what, haven't you gone yet!; **mais c. donc!** why of course!, by all means!; *F* **ça vous a plu? – et c.!** did you like it? – and how! *or* you bet!

2 *nm inv* **les pourquoi et les c.** the whys and wherefores

commentaire [kɔmɑ̃tɛr] *nm* **(a)** (*remarque*) comment, remark; **faire des commentaires** to make comments *or* remarks; **je te dispense de tes commentaires** I don't need *or* I can do without your comments; **un c. pertinent** a pertinent observation; *F* **cela se passe de c.** it speaks for itself, it's obvious; *F* **sans c.!, pas de c.!** no comment!; *F* **je ne veux pas de c.!** that's final!, don't argue!; *Péj* **les commentaires vont bon train** comment is rife **(b)** *Rad, TV* commentary; (*lecture d'un texte préparé*) narration; **c. sportif** sports commentary; **c. en direct** live commentary; **c. sur image** voice-over, voice-over narration

▶ **commentaire:** *Scol* **c. de texte** textual commentary

commentateur, -trice [kɔmɑ̃tatœr, -tris] **1** *n Rad, TV* commentator; **c. sportif** sports commentator **2** *nm Littér* commentator

commenter [kɔmɑ̃te] *vt* **(a)** (*expliquer*) (*texte*) to comment on; *Rad, TV* **c. une course** to do the commentary for *or* to give the commentary on a race; **c. l'actualité** *ou* **les événements** to comment on current events **(b)** (*donner son avis sur*) to comment on

commérage [kɔmeraʒ] *nm F* (piece of) gossip; **commérages** gossip, tittle-tattle

commerçant, -ante [kɔmɛrsɑ̃, -ɑ̃t] **1** *adj* commercial; **quartier c.** shopping area; **rue très commerçante** busy shopping street; **un sourire c.** a PR-type smile; **il n'est pas très c.** he doesn't look after his customers very well **2** *n* trader, merchant; (*qui tient un magasin*) shopkeeper; **c. en gros/en détail** wholesaler/retailer; **commerçants** traders, tradespeople; **petits commerçants** small traders *or* shopkeepers

commerce [kɔmɛrs] *nm* **(a) le c.** (*activité*) trade; (*secteur*) trade, commerce; (*affaires*) business, trade; **c. en** *ou* **de gros/détail** wholesale/retail trade; **le petit c.** shopkeepers, small traders; **c. intérieur/extérieur** home/foreign *or* overseas trade; **c. international** world trade, international trade; **il est dans le c.** he's in business; **ça se trouve dans le c.** you can buy it in the shops; **faire du c. avec le Japon** to do business with Japan, to have business dealings with Japan; **maison de c.** firm; **voyageur de c.** commercial traveller, sales rep(resentative); **école de c.** business school; **port de c.** commercial port; **faire du c.** to trade, to be in business; **cela fait marcher le c.** it's good for business *or* trade; **hors c.** not for (general) sale; **c. des chevaux** horse dealing; **c. associé** voluntary group, association of distributors; **c. d'exportation/ d'importation** export/import trade; **c. d'échange** countertrade

(b) (*magasin*) **(fonds de) c.** business; **commerces** highstreet shops; **ouvrir un c.** to open a business

(c) *Péj* (*trafic*) traffic, trade; **faire c. de son honneur/nom** to trade on one's honour/name; **faire c. de son corps** to sell one's body

(d) *Arch, Litt* (*relations*) intercourse, dealings; **avoir** *ou* **être en c. avec qn** to have dealings with sb; **être d'un c. agréable** to be easy to get on with *or* pleasant to deal with; **fuir le c. des hommes** to flee the company of men

commercer [kɔmɛrse] *vi* **(je commerçai(s); n. commerçons)** to trade, to deal (**avec** with)

commercial, -ale, -aux, -ales [kɔmɛrsjal, -jo] **1** *adj* (*rapports, pratiques etc*) business, commercial; (*embargo, tribunal*) trade; (*droit*) commercial; *Péj* **film c.** commercial film; **suivre une formation commerciale** to train in business studies **2** *nf Aut* **commerciale** (*voiture*) estate car, *Am* station wagon; (*camionnette*) small van **3** *n* salesman, representative; **c'est un c.** he's in sales

commercialement [kɔmɛrsjalmɑ̃] *adv* commercially

commercialisable [kɔmɛrsjalizabl] *adj* marketable

commercialisation [kɔmɛrsjalizasjɔ̃] *nf* marketing

commercialiser [kɔmɛrsjalize] *vt* (*produit*) to market; (*art*) to commercialize

commère [kɔmɛr] *nf* gossip

commettant [kɔmetɑ̃] *nm* **(a)** *Com, Jur* principal **(b)** *Pol* **commettants** constituents

commettre [kɔmɛtr] (*conj like* **mettre**) **1** *vt* **(a)** (*accomplir*) (*crime, péché, injustice*) to commit; **c. une erreur** to make a mistake; *Hum* **il a déjà commis deux pièces de théâtre** he's already to blame for *or* he's already perpetrated two plays

(b) *Jur* **c. qn à qch** to appoint sb to sth, to put sb in charge of sth; **c. un avocat d'office à qn** to assign a lawyer to sb

(c) *Arch* (*compromettre*) to expose; **c. sa réputation** to risk one's reputation

(d) *Arch* (*confier*) **c. qch à qn** to commit *or* entrust sth to sb *or* to sb's keeping, to entrust sb with sth

2 se commettre *vpr Litt* to compromise oneself; **se c. avec qn** to compromise oneself by associating with sb

comminatoire [kɔminatwar] *adj* **(a)** (*lettre*) threatening **(b)** *Jur* (*décret etc*) comminatory

commis [kɔmi] *nm* **(a)** (*employé*) clerk; (*dans un magasin*) (shop) assistant; *Culin* **commis chef** commis waiter; **c. de banque** bank clerk; **c. de cuisine** commis chef; **c. de rang** trainee chef de rang; **c. de salle** waiter; **c. principal** senior clerk; **c. aux écritures** book-keeper; **les grands c.** the senior civil servants **(b)** *Arch* **c. voyageur** commercial traveller

commisération [kɔmizerasjɔ̃] *nf* commiseration; **éprouver/avoir de la c.** to feel/have sympathy; **témoigner de la c. à qn** to show sb sympathy

commis-greffier, *pl* **commis-greffiers** *nm* assistant to the clerk of court

commissaire [kɔmisɛr] *nm* **(a)** *Sp* steward; *Sp* **c. des courses** race steward; **c. (de police)** ≈ (police) superintendent, *US* ≈ (police) captain; **c. principal** ≈ chief superintendent, *US* ≈ chief of police; *Naut* **c. de la Marine** = supply officer; *Naut* **c. du bord** purser; *Fin* **c. aux comptes** government auditor; **c. d'avaries** average adjuster; *Can* **c. d'école** school commissioner

(b) (*membre d'une commission*) commissioner, commission member; *CE* Commissioner, member of the Commission; **c. près du Conseil d'État** government representative on the

Council of State; **c. du gouvernment** government representative; **c. parlementaire** parliamentary commissioner

commissaire-priseur, *pl* **commissaires-priseurs** *nm* auctioneer

commissariat [kɔmisarja] *nm* **(a) c. (de police)** police station **(b)** *(fonction)* commissionership; **c. des comptes** auditorship; *Naut* **c. du bord** pursership **(c) c. de la marine** *ou* **maritime** = supply branch

commission [kɔmisjɔ̃] *nf* **(a)** *(course)* purchase; **il faut que j'aille faire les commissions** I have to go shopping

(b) *(comité)* commission, committee; *Parl* **renvoi d'un texte en c.** referral of a bill to a committee

(c) *(pourcentage)*, *Com* commission; *Fin* brokerage; **c. de deux pour cent** commission of two per cent; **3% de c.** 3% commission; **être payé à la c.** to be paid on a commission basis; *Com* **maison de c.** firm of commission agents, commission agency; **vente à c.** sale on commission

(d) *(charge)* commission; **avoir la c. de faire qch** to be commissioned *or* empowered to do sth

(e) *(service)* errand; **faire une c.** to run an errand; **on ne m'a pas fait la c.** I wasn't given the message

(f) *Enf* **la petite/grosse c.** number one/two

▶ **commission**: **c. d'acceptation** acceptance fee; **c. d'arbitrage** arbitration committee *or* board; **c. bancaire** bank commission *or* charge *or* fee; **c. de change** exchange commission; *Banque* **c. de compte** account fee; **c. de confirmation** confirmation fee *or* commission; *(pour crédit)* facility fee; **c. consultative** advisory committee; **c. d'encaissement** collection charge *or* fee; **c. d'enquête** board *or* committee of inquiry; **C. européenne** European Commission; **c. de garantie** guarantee commission; **C. des opérations de Bourse** = Stock Exchange watchdog, *US* ≈ Securities and Exchange Commission; **c. de paiement** collection charge, collection fee; **c. paritaire** joint commission *(with both sides equally represented)*; **c. parlementaire** parliamentary commission; **c. permanente** standing committee; **c. de tenue de compte** account handling fee; **c. de vente** sales commission

commissionnaire [kɔmisjɔnɛr] *nm* **(a)** *(messager)* messenger; *(à l'hôtel, au théâtre)* commissionaire **(b)** *Com* (commission) agent, broker; **c. exportateur/importateur** export/import agent; **c. de transport** *ou* **de roulage** forwarding agent, carrier; **c. en douane** customs agent *or* broker; **c. agréé en douane** authorized customs broker; **c. de transport** shipping agent; **c. ducroire** del credere agent; **c. à l'export** export agent

commissionner [kɔmisjɔne] *vt* to commission

commissure [kɔmisyr] *nf* *(de la bouche)* corner; *Anat, Bot etc* commissure

commode [kɔmɔd] **1** *adj* **(a)** *(pratique)* *(heure, lieu)* convenient, suitable; *(outil etc)* handy; *(maison etc)* convenient, comfortable; **c'est très c. pour ranger ses affaires** it's very handy for storing things in **(b)** *(facile)* easy; **ce que vous me demandez là n'est pas c.** what you are asking me isn't very easy **(c)** *(caractère etc)* easy-going, *Fml* accommodating; *F* **il n'est pas c.** he's a tough *or* an awkward customer **2** *nf* chest of drawers, commode

commodément [kɔmɔdemɑ̃] *adv* *(assis)* comfortably; *(situé)* conveniently

commodité [kɔmɔdite] *nf* **(a)** *(facilité)* convenience; **pour plus de c.** for greater convenience; **les commodités de la vie (moderne)** the comforts of (modern) life **(b) commodités** *(toilettes)* toilets, *Am* rest rooms

commodore [kɔmɔdɔr] *nm Mil* commodore

commotion [kɔmosjɔ̃] *nf* **(a) c. politique** political upheaval; *Méd* **c. cérébrale** concussion **(b)** *(émotion)* shock

commotionner [kɔmosjɔne] *vt* **(a)** *Méd* to concuss; **il a été fortement commotionné** he was severely concussed, he had severe concussion **(b)** *(choquer)* to shake (up), to shock; **cette nouvelle m'a commotionné** this news has given me a shock *or* has shaken me

commuable [kɔmɥabl] *adj Jur* *(peine)* commutable

commuer [kɔmɥe] *vt Jur* *(peine)* to commute **(en** to)

commun [kɔmœ̃] **1** *adj* **(a)** *(non exclusif)* common **(à** to); *(travail)* joint; *(ami)* mutual; *Math* **dénominateur c.** common denominator; **jardin c. à deux maisons** garden shared by two houses; **salle commune** common room; *(d'hôpital)* ward; **parties communes** communal areas; **maison commune** town hall; **avoir des intérêts communs** to have interests in common, to have common interests; **faire cause commune avec qn** to make common cause *or* join forces with sb; **il n'y a rien de c. entre eux** they've (got) nothing in common; **c'est sans commune mesure** there's no possible comparison; **vie commune** communal life; *(de couple)* conjugal life; **la vie commune n'est pas facile** living together isn't easy; **rechercher le bien c.** to seek the common good; **d'un c. accord** with one accord; **en c.** in common; **travailler en c.** to work together; **vivre en c.** to live communally; **mettre l'argent/les ressources en c.** to pool money/resources; **on s'est mis en c. pour lui acheter un cadeau** we all clubbed together to buy him a present

(b) *(courant)* *(coutume, opinion etc)* common, universal, general; *(événement etc)* common, usual, ordinary, everyday; **sens c.** common sense; [①A8,3,A,2] *Gram* **nom c.** common noun; **lieu c.** commonplace; **il est d'une force peu commune** he's unusually strong

(c) *(vulgaire)* common, vulgar

2 *nm* **(a)** *(de personnes etc)* common run, generality; **le c. (des mortels)** the ordinary *or* average man; **le c. des spectateurs n'a pas compris** the ordinary *or* average member of the audience didn't understand; **hors du c.** out of the ordinary

(b) communs outhouses, outbuildings

communal, -ale, -aux, -ales [kɔmynal, -o] **1** *adj* **(a)** *(conjoint)* *(terrain, propriété)* common, communal **(b)** *(de la commune)* *(propriété etc)* *Br* ≈ council; **école communale** ≈ local primary school **2** *nmpl* **communaux** common land **3** *nf* **communale** ≈ local primary school

communard, -arde [kɔmynar, -ard] **1** *adj Hist* of the Commune **2** *n* **(a)** *Hist* Communard **(b)** *Péj* *(communiste)* commie, red

communautaire [kɔmynotɛr] *adj* communal; *Pol* *(aide, politique)* community; *(surtout CE)* Community; **centre c.** community centre

communauté [kɔmynote] *nf* **(a)** *(collectivité)* community; *Rel* community, order; **c. de travail** working community; **c. urbaine** urban community; **C. urbaine de Montréal** Montreal Urban Community; **c. de hippies** hippie commune; **vivre en c.** to live communally; **elle est partie vivre en c.** she's gone off to live in a commune **(b)** *(d'intérêts, d'idées etc)* similarity, *Fml* community; *Jur* joint estate *(of husband and wife)*

▶ **communauté**: **C. Économique Européenne** European Economic Community

commune [kɔmyn] *nf* **(a)** *Admin Fr* commune *(smallest territorial division)* **(b)** *Hist Fr* *(ville autonome)* free town **(c)** *Pol* **la Chambre des Communes, les Communes** the (House of) Commons **(d)** *Hist Fr* **la C.** the Commune *(in 1789 and 1871)*

communément [kɔmynemɑ̃] *adv* commonly

communiant, -ante [kɔmynjɑ̃, -ɑ̃t] *n Rel* communicant; **premier c., première communiante** person taking his/her first communion

communicable [kɔmynikabl] *adj* *(impression, idée etc)* that can be communicated; *Jur* *(droit)* transferable; *(dossier etc)* that can be made available

communicant [kɔmynikɑ̃] *adj* *(chambres etc)* communicating, connecting

communicateur, -trice [kɔmynikatœr, -tris] *adj* *(fil etc)* connecting

communicatif, -ive [kɔmynikatif, -iv] *adj* **(a)** *(qui parle)* communicative, talkative; **peu c.** uncommunicative **(b)** *(rire etc)* infectious

communication [kɔmynikasjɔ̃] *nf* **(a)** communication; **avoir des problèmes de c.** to have problems *or* difficulties (in) communicating; **c. d'idées** interchange of ideas; **entrer** *ou* **se mettre en c. avec qn** to get in touch *or* in contact with sb; **mettre deux personnes en c.** to put two people in touch *or* in contact with each other; **je n'ai pas eu c. de ce message** the message wasn't passed on to me, I didn't get the message; **voies de c.** lines of communication, communication routes; **portes de c.** communicating doors; **toutes les communications sont coupées** all lines of communication are cut (off); **études de c.** media studies; **travailler dans la c.** to work in the media; *Ordinat* **progiciel de c.** communications *or F* comms package; *Mktg* **c. commerciale** marketing communications; **c. de données** data communications, datacomms; **c. de masse** mass communication

(b) *Tél, Télécom* **c. téléphonique** (telephone) call; **mettez-moi en c. avec M. Martin** put me through to Mr Martin; **je vous passe la c.** I'll put you through; **vous avez la c.** you're through; **la c. est mauvaise** the line is bad; **c. en P.C.V.** reverse charge *or* transferred charge call, *surtout Am* collect call; **c. hors circonscription** long-distance call; **c. interurbaine** long-distance call; **c. intra-circonscription** local call; **c. télématique** datacommunications, datacomms

(c) *Mktg* *(publicité)* promotion; **c. événementielle** event promotion; **c. institutionnelle** corporate promotion, corporate identity; **c. produit** product promotion; **c. sur le lieu de vente** point-of-sale promotion

(d) *(message)* communication, message; **transmettre une**

c. à qn to pass on a message to sb; **le président a une importante c. à nous faire** the president has an important message for us *or* has something important to communicate to us; **faire une c. dans un colloque** to read a paper to a conference; *Jur* **donner c. des pièces** to communicate documents

communier [kɔmynje] *vi* (*impf, pr sub* **n. communiions, v. communiiez**) *Rel* to receive (Holy) Communion

communion [kɔmynjɔ̃] *nf* **(a)** (*communauté*) communion; **être en c. de sentiments avec qn** to be in sympathy with sb; **être en c. avec la nature** to commune with nature **(b)** *Rel* Communion; **première c., c. privée** first Communion; **faire sa première c.** to make one's first Communion; **c. solennelle** solemn Communion

communiqué [kɔmynike] *nm* communiqué, official statement; **c. de presse** press release, press hand-out; **c. de sécurité routière** traffic news

communiquer [kɔmynike] **1** *vt* (*transmettre*) (*information, renseignements etc*) to communicate, to convey (**à qn** to sb); (*joie, peur etc*) to communicate (**à qn** to sb); (*maladie*) to pass on, to give (**à qn** to sb); **c. qch par écrit à qn** to communicate *or* convey sth in writing to sb; **c. ses impressions** to pass on *or* communicate one's impressions

2 *vi* **(a)** (*être en relation*) to communicate (**avec** with); **avoir du mal à c. avec qn** to find it hard *or* difficult to communicate with sb; **refus total de c.** total unwillingness to communicate

(b) (*d'une pièce*) to communicate (**avec** with); **toutes les chambres communiquent** all the bedrooms communicate with one another; **porte qui communique au** *ou* **avec le jardin** door that leads into the garden; **canal qui fait c. deux rivières** canal that connects two rivers

3 se communiquer *vpr* **(a)** (*se transmettre*) to spread; **l'incendie s'est communiqué aux maisons voisines** the fire has spread to the neighbouring houses

(b) *Vieilli* (*être communicatif*) to be communicative

communisant, -ante [kɔmynizɑ̃, -ɑ̃t] **1** *adj* (*personne, journal, parti etc*) with communist sympathies **2** *n* communist sympathizer, fellow traveller

communisme [kɔmynism] *nm* communism

communiste [kɔmynist] *adj, n* communist

commutable [kɔmytabl] *adj Télécom* switchable

commutateur [kɔmytatœr] *nm Él* **(a)** (*de dynamo etc*) commutator **(b)** (*bouton*) switch; **c. sélecteur** selector switch; **c. téléphonique** exchange; *Ordinat* **c. de données** data switch

commutatif, -ive [kɔmytatif, -iv] *adj Jur, Math* commutative

commutation [kɔmytasjɔ̃] *nf* **(a)** *Jur* (*de sentence*) commutation **(b)** (*changement*) substitution, *Fml* commutation; (*entre documents*) switching; *Gram* replacement, substitution; **le patron a décidé de la c. de deux employés** the boss decided to swap the duties of two employees **(c)** *Él* commutation, changeover; *TV etc* **c. de l'image** switching **(d)** *Ordinat* **c. d'interface/de circuits** interface/circuit switching; **c. de message/ de paquets** message/packet switching

commutatrice [kɔmytatris] *nf Él* rotary converter, transformer

commuté [kɔmyte] *adj* (*réseau*) switched

commuter [kɔmyte] **1** *vt* **(a)** *Jur* (*sentence*) to commute **(b)** *Él* (*courant*) to commutate, to switch over, to change over; **c. les fonctions** to swap duties **2** *vi* (*entre documents, écran*) to switch; **deux employés qui vont c.** two employees who are going to swap duties **3 se commuter** *vpr Ordinat* to switch

commuter[2] [kɔmytœr] *nm Av* commuter plane

Comores [kɔmɔr] *nf Géog* **les îles C.** the Comoro Islands

compacité [kɔ̃pasite] *nf* (*de la terre etc*) compactness; (*d'un métal*) density; (*de la foule*) denseness

compact [kɔ̃pakt] **1** *adj* **(a)** (*de petit format*) compact; **voiture compacte** small car, *Am* compact; **disque c.** compact disc **(b)** (*masse, formation etc*) compact, dense; (*foule*) dense; (*terre*) compact; (*métal*) dense; **majorité compacte** large *or* solid majority; **poudre compacte** pressed (face-)powder **2** *nm* compact disc

compact disc [kɔ̃paktdisk] *nm* compact disc

compacter [kɔ̃pakte] *vt* (*fichier, données*) to compress; (*base de données*) to pack

compacteur [kɔ̃paktœr] *nm Ordinat* **c. d'exécutables** execute file compressor; **compacteur de données** data compressor

compagne [kɔ̃paɲ] *nf* **(a)** (*camarade*) (female) companion; **mes compagnes de captivité** my fellow captives **(b)** (*concubine*) partner; (*épouse*) wife; (*d'un animal*) mate

compagnie [kɔ̃paɲi] *nf* **(a)** (*présence*) company, companionship; **n'avoir qu'un vieux chien pour toute c.** to have only an old dog for company; **tenir c. à qn** to keep sb company; **fausser c. à qn** to give sb the slip; **je vais vous fausser c.** this is where I leave you; **dame de c.** (lady's) companion; **être en c. d'amis proches** to be in the company of close friends, to be with close friends; **rechercher la c. de gens simples** to seek the company of simple people; **aller de c. avec …** to go hand in hand with …; **être de bonne/ mauvaise c.** to be good/poor company; **être de c. agréable** to be pleasant company; **je l'ai trouvé en joyeuse/galante c.** I found him in cheerful company/in the company of a lady; **ils ont voyagé de c.** they travelled together

(b) (*groupe*) company, party; **toute la c.** everybody, all of them/us

(c) *Com, Th etc* company; *Com* **la maison Thomas et C.** (the firm of) Thomas and Company

(d) *Mil* company; **c. de débarquement** landing party

(e) (*de perdrix*) covey

▶ **compagnie**: **c. aérienne** airline; **c. aérienne nationale** flag *or* national airline; **c. d'assurances** insurance company; **c. d'aviation civile** civil airline; *Rel* **la C. de Jésus** the Society of Jesus; **c. maritime** shipping line; **c. mère** parent company; **c. de navigation** shipping company; **c. pétrolière** oil company; **compagnies républicaines de sécurité** riot police; **c. de transports** carrier; **c. de transports nationale** flag carrier

compagnon [kɔ̃paɲɔ̃] *nm* **(a)** (*camarade*) companion; (*d'ouvrier*) mate; **c. d'études** fellow student; **c. de voyage** travelling companion; **c'était mon c. de jeu** I used to play with him; *Pol* **c. de route** fellow traveller; **c. d'infortune/de misère** companion in misfortune/in suffering **(b)** (*ouvrier*) journeyman **(c)** *F* (*plante*) **c. blanc/rouge** white/red campion **(d)** (*concubin*) partner; (*époux*) husband

comparable [kɔ̃parabl] *adj* comparable (**à** *ou* **avec qch/qn** to *or* with sth/sb); **ce n'est pas c.** there's no comparison

comparablement [kɔ̃parabləmɑ̃] *adv* comparatively

comparaison [kɔ̃parɛzɔ̃] *nf* **(a)** comparison; **c. des prix** price comparison; **faire la c. entre deux choses** to compare two things, to make a comparison between two things; **tu peux faire la c. toi-même** you can judge *or* see *or* make the comparison for yourself; **soutenir la c.** to bear *or* stand comparison; **il n'y a pas de c. possible** there's no possible comparison; **c'est sans c. avec …** it can't be compared with …; **il est sans c. le plus grand** he is by far *or* he is far and away the tallest; *Prov* **c. n'est pas raison** comparisons are odious; *Gram* **adverbe de c.** adverb of comparison, comparative adverb; **les degrés de c.** the degrees of comparison; **c. par paire** paired comparison

(b) (*locutions*) **en c. de …** compared with, in comparison with …; **par c.** by comparison; **par c. avec** *ou* **à** compared with

(c) *Littér* simile

comparaître [kɔ̃parɛtr] *vi* (*conj like* **paraître**) *Jur* **c. (en justice)** to appear (before a court); **c. en personne** to appear in person; **c. par avoué** to be represented by counsel; **c. comme témoin** to appear as a witness; **être appelé à c.** to be summoned to appear

comparant, -ante [kɔ̃parɑ̃, -ɑ̃t] *Jur* **1** *adj* appearing in court **2** *n* person appearing in court

comparateur [kɔ̃paratœr] *nm Aut etc* dial gauge

comparatif, -ive [kɔ̃paratif, -iv] **1** *adj* comparative; **publicité comparative** comparative advertising **2** [①A18-19,4; A22,c; B10-11,E; B12-13,F] *nm Gram* comparative; **adjectif au c.** comparative adjective; **c. d'infériorité** comparative of lesser degree

comparatiste [kɔ̃paratist] *n Ling* specialist in comparative linguistics; *Littér* specialist in comparative literature

comparativement [kɔ̃parativmɑ̃] *adv* comparatively; **il fait bien plus beau aujourd'hui, c. à hier** it's much nicer today compared with *or* to yesterday

comparé [kɔ̃pare] *adj* (*anatomie, histoire, littérature etc*) comparative; **c. à** compared with *or* to

comparer [kɔ̃pare] **1** *vt* to compare (**à** to; **avec** with); **il compare les étoiles filantes à des cheveux** he compares *or* likens shooting stars to strands of hair; **c. deux objets/ textes** to compare two objects/texts; **tu peux c., ma robe est plus large** you can see the difference, my dress is wider **2 se comparer** *vpr* **je ne peux pas me c. à toi** I can't compare myself with *or* to you; **Haendel ne peut pas se c. à Mozart** Handel can't be compared with *or* to Mozart; **ça ne se compare pas** there's no comparison

comparse [kɔ̃pars] *n Cin* extra; *Th* walk-on, super, *Fml* supernumerary; *Fig Péj* associate; *Th* **rôle de c.** walk-on part

compartiment [kɔ̃partimɑ̃] *nm* (*de wagon, boîte, tiroir etc*) compartment; (*d'échiquier, de damier*) square; *Rail* **c. de première classe** first-class compartment; **c. fumeurs** smoking compartment, smoker; **c. non-fumeurs** no-smoking compartment, non-smoker; **c. moteur** engine compartment; **c. à bagages** (*d'autocar*) luggage compartment

compartimentage [kɔ̃partimɑ̃taʒ] *nm* partitioning; (*d'une administration etc*) compartmentalization

compartimenter [kɔ̃partimɑ̃te] *vt* **(a)** (*diviser en espaces*) to partition, to divide into compartments **(b)** (*administration etc*) to compartmentalize

comparution [kɔ̃parysjɔ̃] *nf Jur* (*au tribunal*) appearance; **non-c.** non-appearance, default

compas [kɔ̃pa] *nm* **(a)** *Géom* (pair of) compasses; **c. à pointes sèches** dividers; **c. quart de cercle** wing compasses; *MecE etc* **c. d'épaisseur** callipers; *Fig F* **tout faire au c.** to do everything with precision; *Fig* **avoir le c. dans l'œil** to have an accurate eye **(b)** *Naut* **c. (de mer)** (mariner's) compass; **c. de route** steering compass; **c. gyroscopique** gyrocompass

compassé [kɔ̃pase] *adj* (*personne, manières, ton etc*) stiff, formal

compasser [kɔ̃pase] *vt* **(a)** (*distances sur la carte etc*) to measure with compasses; *Naut* (*carte*) to prick **(b)** *Litt* (*ses actes etc*) to control, to regulate

compassion [kɔ̃pasjɔ̃] *nf* compassion; **avec c.** compassionately

compatibilité [kɔ̃patibilite] *nf* compatibility

compatible [kɔ̃patibl] *adj* compatible (**avec** with); *Ordinat* **c. abc** abc-compatible; **ces deux fonctions ne sont pas compatibles** these two functions are incompatible *or* not compatible

compatir [kɔ̃patir] *vi* to sympathize; **c. au chagrin de qn** to sympathize with *or* feel for sb in his/her grief

compatissant [kɔ̃patisɑ̃] *adj* compassionate, sympathetic (**pour** to, towards)

compatriote [kɔ̃patriɔt] *n* compatriot, fellow countryman, *f* countrywoman

compensable [kɔ̃pɑ̃sabl] *adj* that can be compensated for; (*chèque*) clearable; *Fin* **c. à Paris** to be cleared at Paris

compensateur, -trice [kɔ̃pɑ̃satœr, -tris] **1** *adj* (*ressort, aimant etc*) compensating; *Él* (*courant*) equalizing; (*dynamo*) balancing; **indemnité compensatrice** compensatory payment, compensation; **pendule c.** compensation pendulum **2** *nm* (*de boussole etc*) compensator, balancer; *Av* trimming tab, trimmer; *Aut* **c. de frein** brake compensator

compensation [kɔ̃pɑ̃sasjɔ̃] *nf* **(a)** (*de perte*) compensation; **en c. de mes pertes** to compensate *or* as compensation for my losses; **en c. vous avez droit à deux jours de vacances** to compensate (for it) *or* to make up for it, you can have two days off; **il y a des compensations** there are compensations; *Jur* **c. des dépens** sharing of the costs; *Fin* **chambre de c.** clearing house

(b) *Él etc* (*de forces etc*) equalization, balancing; (*de son*) equalization; *Math* **loi de c.** law of large numbers

(c) *Naut* (*de boussole*) adjustment

(d) (*de chèque*) clearing; **caisse de c.** = equalization fund for payments such as child benefit, sickness benefit, pensions *etc*

(e) *Psy* compensation

compensatoire [kɔ̃pɑ̃satwar] *adj* compensatory; **droits compensatoires** countervailing duties

compenser [kɔ̃pɑ̃se] **1** *vt* **(a)** (*perte*) to compensate for, to make up for, to make good; (*défaut etc*) to compensate for, to make up for, to offset; *Jur etc* (*dettes*) to set off, to balance (out); (*chèque*) to clear; **talon** *ou* **semelle compensé(e)** built-up heel; **son efficacité compense son mauvais caractère** his efficiency compensates for *or* makes up for *or* offsets his bad temper; *Jur* **c. les dépens** to divide the costs **(b)** *Naut* (*boussole*) to adjust **2 se compenser** *vpr* to make up for each other, to offset each other

compère [kɔ̃pɛr] *nm* **(a)** (*de prestidigitateur etc*) accomplice, associate **(b)** *F Vieilli* (*camarade*) comrade, crony; **un bon c.** a pleasant companion

compère-loriot, *pl* **compères-loriots** *nm* **(a)** (*oiseau*) golden oriole **(b)** *Méd* (*sur la paupière*) stye

compétence [kɔ̃petɑ̃s] *nf* **(a)** (*capacité*) competence, ability, skill (**pour faire qch** to do sth); **avoir toutes les compétences requises pour faire qch** to have all the necessary skills to do sth; **c'est en dehors de mes compétences** it's beyond my capabilities; **faire qch avec beaucoup de c.** to do sth very competently **(b)** *Jur* (*de cour de justice etc*) competence, jurisdiction, powers; **cela ne rentre pas dans** *ou* **cela n'est pas de sa c.** that does not come within his province, that is outside his scope; **sortir de sa c.** to exceed one's powers

compétent [kɔ̃petɑ̃] *adj Jur etc* (*tribunal, autorité etc*) competent; **c. en matière de finance** conversant with finance; **je ne suis pas c. en la matière** I am not well up in the subject; **il est très c.** he's very competent; *Com* **adressez-vous au service c.** apply to the appropriate *or* relevant department, apply to the department concerned

compétiteur, -trice [kɔ̃petitœr, -tris] *n* competitor

compétitif, -ive [kɔ̃petitif, -iv] *adj Com* (*prix etc*) competitive

compétition [kɔ̃petisjɔ̃] *nf* **(a)** (*rivalité*) competition, rivalry; **être en c. avec qn** to be in competition with sb, to compete with sb; **c. entre partis politiques** rivalry between political parties; **esprit de c.** competitive spirit **(b)** *Sp* (*épreuve*) competition, event; **c. sportive** sports competition, sporting event; **faire de la c.** to go in for competitive sport; **du ski de c.** competitive *or* competition skiing

compétitivité [kɔ̃petitivite] *nf* competitiveness

compilateur, -trice [kɔ̃pilatœr, -tris] **1** *nm Ordinat* compiler; **c. croisé** cross-compiler **2** *n* **(a)** (*auteur*) compiler **(b)** *Péj* (*plagiaire*) plagiarist

compilation [kɔ̃pilasjɔ̃] *nf* **(a)** *Ordinat* compilation **(b)** (*enregistrement*) compilation **(c)** (*de documents*) compiling, compilation **(d)** *Péj* (*plagiat*) plagiarism

compiler [kɔ̃pile] *vt* **(a)** *Ordinat* to compile **(b)** (*réunir*) to compile **(c)** *Péj* (*plagier*) to plagiarize

complainte [kɔ̃plɛ̃t] *nf* **(a)** *Arch* (*plainte*) plaint **(b)** *Littér, Mus* lament

complaire [kɔ̃plɛr] (*conj like* **plaire**) **1** *vi Litt* **c. à qn** to please sb **2 se complaire** *vpr* to delight, to revel (**dans qch/à faire qch** in sth/in doing sth); **elle se complaît dans le malheur** she wallows in her misery

complaisamment [kɔ̃plɛzamɑ̃] *adv* **(a)** (*avec obligeance*) obligingly, kindly **(b)** (*avec vanité*) complacently, smugly

complaisance [kɔ̃plɛzɑ̃s] *nf* **(a)** (*bienveillance*) obligingness, kindness; **faire qch par c.** to do sth out of kindness; **faire qch par c. pour qn** to do sth to oblige sb; **auriez-vous la c. de le faire?** would you be so good *or* so kind as to do it?, would you oblige me by doing it?; **avoir des complaisances pour qn** to be indulgent towards sb; **sourire de c.** polite smile; **sourire d'un air de c.** to smile politely, to give a polite smile; *Com* **billet** *ou* **effet de c.** accommodation bill; **on a fini par lui délivrer un certificat de c.** he was finally issued with a medical certificate (*to which he was not entitled*)

(b) (*auto-satisfaction*) complacency, smugness, self-satisfaction; **il s'écoute avec c.** he likes the sound of his own voice; **ton plein de c.** self-satisfied *or* smug tone

complaisant [kɔ̃plɛzɑ̃] *adj* **(a)** (*bienveillant*) obliging, accommodating, kind (**envers, pour** towards); **prêter une oreille complaisante à qn** to lend sb a sympathetic *or* a willing ear **(b)** (*indulgent*) (*médecin*) indulgent; (*mari*) complaisant, indulgent **(c)** (*satisfait*) complacent, smug, self-satisfied

complément [kɔ̃plemɑ̃] *nm* (*reste*) rest, remainder; *Gram, Biol, Ch, Math* complement; **il faudra racheter cinq livres de lecture pour faire le c.** we'll have to buy five more readers to make up the numbers; **si on manque de dessert, on fera le c. avec des yaourts** if we're short of desserts, we'll use yoghurts instead; **demander un c. d'information** to ask for more *or* additional information; *Gram* **c. circonstanciel de temps** adverbial phrase of time; [①A73,b; B49-50,2-4] *Gram* **c. (d'objet)** object; *Gram* **c. d'objet direct/indirect** direct/indirect object

complémentaire [kɔ̃plemɑ̃tɛr] *adj* (*angle, couleur etc*) complementary; **pour tout renseignement c., s'adresser à …** for further *or* additional information apply to …

complémentarité [kɔ̃plemɑ̃tarite] *nf* complementarity

complet, -ète [kɔ̃plɛ, -ɛt] **1** *adj* **(a)** (*entier, intégral*) (*tenue, service etc*) complete, whole, entire; **rapport très c.** very full *or* comprehensive report; **se faire une idée complète de la situation** to get an overall *or* a complete picture *or* an overview of the situation; **deux jours complets** two full *or* whole days; **examen c.** full *or* thorough examination; **voyager dans le plus c. anonymat** to travel completely incognito; **votre devoir est loin d'être c.** your homework is a long way *or* far from being complete; **athlète c.** all-round athlete; **un c. abruti** a complete *or* total *or* absolute moron; **échec c.** complete *or* total *or* utter failure; **collection complète d'un auteur** complete works of an author, complete set of an author's works; **formation très complète** thorough training; *F* **c'est c.!** that's the last straw!, that's the limit!; **pain c.** wholemeal bread; **pâtes complètes** wholemeal pasta; **riz c.** brown rice

(b) (*rempli*) (*bus*), *Th* (*salle etc*) full; **'c.'** 'full (up)'; (*signe devant pension, hôtel etc*) 'no vacancies'

2 *nm* **(a) c. (-veston)** suit

(b) nous étions au grand c. we turned out in full force; **j'ai invité la famille au c. pour Noël** I've invited the whole family for Christmas; **j'attends que l'assistance soit au c. pour commencer** I'm waiting for everyone to arrive before I begin

complètement [kɔ̃plɛtmɑ̃] *adv* completely, totally, wholly; (*ruiné, perdu, idiot*) utterly, completely, totally; **c. nu** stark naked, completely naked; **finir c. un pot de crème** to finish off *or* polish off a pot of cream; **je n'ai pas pu le lire c.** I couldn't read all of it *or* the whole thing

compléter [kɔ̃plete] **(je complète, n. complétons; je compléterai) 1** *vt* (*collection, garde-robe, formation etc*) to complete; (*formulaire*) to complete, to fill in *or* out; **c. une somme** to make up a sum (of money); *Fig* **pour c. le tableau** ... to cap it all ... **2 se compléter** *vpr* to complement one another; **ils se complètent bien l'un l'autre** they're well-matched, they complement each other well

complétif, -ive [kɔ̃pletif, -iv] *adj, nf Gram* **(proposition) complétive** noun clause

complexe [kɔ̃plɛks] **1** *adj* (*caractère, question etc*) complex, complicated; *Gram* **sujet c.** compound subject; *Math* **nombre c.** complex number

2 *nm* **(a)** *Constr, Écon* complex; **vivre dans un grand c.** to live in a complex; **le c. industriel de la vallée du Rhône** the Rhone valley industrial complex; **c. commercial/sportif** shopping/sports centre *or* complex; **c. de loisirs** leisure complex; **c. hôtelier** hotel complex; **c. touristique** holiday *or* tourism complex

(b) *Psy* complex; **c. d'infériorité** inferiority complex; **c. d'Œdipe** Oedipus complex; *F* **ça me donne des complexes** it gives me a complex, it gives me hang-ups; *F* **avoir des complexes** to have a complex *or* a hang-up, to be hung up **(à cause de** about); *F* **être sans c.** to have no hang-ups; *F* **il est bourré de complexes** he's really hung up, he's full of complexes

complexé [kɔ̃plɛkse] *adj F* hung up, full of complexes **(par** about)

complexer [kɔ̃plɛkse] *vt F* **c. qn** to give sb a complex *or* a hang-up

complexifier [kɔ̃plɛksifje] **1** *vt* to make (more) complex **2 se complexifier** *vpr* to become (more) complex

complexion [kɔ̃plɛksjɔ̃] *nf* constitution; *Vieilli* temperament, disposition; **je suis gros de c.** I'm naturally fat, I'm predisposed to be fat

complexité [kɔ̃plɛksite] *nf* complexity

complication [kɔ̃plikasjɔ̃] *nf* **(a)** (*ennui*) complication; **faire des complications** to complicate the issue, to create *or* cause complications *or* problems **(b)** (*de situation etc*) complexity, intricacy **(c)** *Méd* **complications** complications

complice [kɔ̃plis] **1** *adj* **être c. de qch** to be party to sth; **des regards complices** knowing glances **2** *n* accomplice

complicité [kɔ̃plisite] *nf* complicity; *Jur* aiding and abetting; *Jur* **agir en c. avec qn** to act in collusion *or* complicity with sb; **accusé de c. de meurtre** accused of being an accessory to murder

complies [kɔ̃pli] *nfpl Rel* compline

compliment [kɔ̃plimɑ̃] *nm* **(a)** (*félicitation*) compliment; **avec les compliments de** with the compliments of; **avec les compliments de la maison** with the compliments of the house; **mes compliments au chef** my compliments to the chef; **faire des compliments à qn** to pay sb compliments, to compliment sb; **on lui a fait c. de sa jolie robe** she was complimented on her pretty dress; **(je vous fais) mes compliments** I congratulate you; *Iron* **mes compliments!** congratulations!; **faites-lui mes compliments** (please) give her my regards **(b)** (*discours*) speech of congratulation, congratulatory speech

complimenter [kɔ̃plimɑ̃te] *vt* to compliment, to congratulate **(de, sur** on); **il faut la c. pour son nouveau travail** we must congratulate her on her new job

complimenteur, -euse [kɔ̃plimɑ̃tœr, -øz] *Péj* **1** *adj* (*personne*) obsequious; **discours c.** flattering speech **2** *n* flatterer

compliqué, -ée [kɔ̃plike] **1** *adj* (*mécanisme, système etc*) complicated, intricate; (*style, texte, théorie etc*) complicated, involved; (*personne*) complicated; **je n'y arrive pas, c'est trop c.** I can't do it, it's too complicated; *F* **ce n'est pas c.!** it's quite simple! **2** *n F* complicated individual

compliquer [kɔ̃plike] **1** *vt* to complicate; **ça risque de c. les choses** that may *or* might well complicate matters **2 se compliquer** *vpr* (*d'une situation, de la vie, d'un problème*) to get complicated; *Littér, Th* (*d'une intrigue*) to thicken; **ça se complique!** things are getting a bit complicated; **il se complique l'existence** he's making life complicated *or* difficult for himself

complot [kɔ̃plo] *nm* plot, conspiracy; **tramer un c.** to hatch a plot; **mettre qn dans le c.** to let sb in on the plot

comploter [kɔ̃plɔte] **1** *vi* to plot, to conspire **(contre** against); **c. de faire qch** to plot *or* conspire to do sth **2** *vt* to plot; *F* **qu'est-ce que vous complotez là?** what are you cooking up *or* plotting now? **3 se comploter** *vpr* **je me demande ce qui se complote par ici** I wonder what's being hatched *or* plotted here

comploteur [kɔ̃plɔtœr] *nm* plotter, conspirator

compo [kɔ̃po] *nf Scol F* test; (*plus important*) exam

componction [kɔ̃pɔ̃ksjɔ̃] *nf* **(a)** *Rel* (*contrition*) compunction **(b)** *Iron* **avec c.** gravely, solemnly

comportement [kɔ̃pɔrtəmɑ̃] *nm* **(a)** behaviour, *US* behavior; **elle a un c. très bizarre avec les enfants** her behaviour towards children is very strange, she behaves very strangely towards children; **psychologie du c.** behaviourism, *US* behaviorism; **type de c.** behaviour pattern

(b) *Mktg* **c. d'achat** buying *or* purchase *or* purchasing behaviour *or US* behavior; **c. de l'acheteur** buyer *or* purchaser behaviour; **c. du consommateur** consumer behaviour; **c. post-achat** post-purchase behaviour

(c) *Aut* **c. en courbe** *ou* **en virage** cornering (ability); **c. routier** (road) handling; **c. sous-vireur** understeer; **c. survireur** oversteer

comportemental, -ale, -aux, -ales [kɔ̃pɔrtəmɑ̃tal, -o] *adj* behavioural, *US* behavioral

comporter [kɔ̃pɔrte] **1** *vt* **(a)** (*admettre*) to allow, *Fml* to allow of, *Fml* to admit of; **règle qui comporte des exceptions** rule that allows of *or* admits of exceptions

(b) (*comprendre*) to comprise; **la fusée comporte quatre étages** the rocket comprises *or* is made up of four stages; **les difficultés que cela comporterait** the difficulties this would involve *or* entail

2 se comporter *vpr* to behave **(vis-à-vis de, envers** towards); **mal se c.** to misbehave, to behave badly; **se c. en** *ou* **comme un lâche** to act *or* behave like a coward; **la voiture se comporte aussi bien sur neige que sur terrain sec** the car handles equally well on snow or dry ground

composant, -ante [kɔ̃pozɑ̃, -ɑ̃t] **1** *adj* (*partie*) component, constituent **2** *nm* component, constituent **3** *nf* **composante** (*de voltage, force, vitesse etc*) component; **c'est une des composantes de la vie de couple** it's one of the components of married life, it's one of the things that make up married life

composé, -ée [kɔ̃poze] [①**A14**,12; **B25-26**,C] **1** *adj* **(a)** (*salade*) mixed; (*intérêt, mot etc*) compound; *Ch* **corps c.** compound; *Gram* **temps c.** compound tense **(b)** *Bot* (*fleur*) composite **(c)** (*compassé*) (*attitude, comportement etc*) studied **2** *nm Ch, Gram etc* compound **3** *nfpl Bot* **composées** Compositae

composer [kɔ̃poze] **1** *vt* **(a)** (*créer*) (*poème, symphonie etc*) to compose, to write; (*bouquet*), *Pharm* (*ordonnance*) to make up

(b) *Typ* (*fonte*) to set, to compose, to typeset; **c. sur ordinateur** to computer typeset; *Tél* **c. un numéro** to dial a number

(c) (*faire partie de*) to make up; **quels sont les ingrédients qui composent ce plat?** which ingredients make up *or* go into this dish?; **les personnes qui composent notre famille** the people who make up our family, all the members of our family; **ce médicament est composé de nombreuses substances** this medicine is made up of *or* is composed of *or* consists of numerous substances

(d) c. son visage to compose one's features

2 *vi* **(a)** (*s'entendre*) to compromise **(avec** with)

(b) *Mus* to compose

(c) *Scol* to take *or* sit a test; **les élèves composeront en anglais demain** the pupils will take *or* sit an English test tomorrow

3 se composer *vpr* **(a) se c. de** to be made up of, to be composed of, to consist of

(b) se c. un visage de circonstance to put on a suitable expression

composeur [kɔ̃pozœr] *nm Tél* **c. de numéros** dialler

composeuse [kɔ̃pozøz] *nf Typ* photosetter, typesetting machine

composite [kɔ̃pozit] *adj* composite; **matériau c.** composite (material)

compositeur, -trice [kɔ̃pozitœr, -tris] *n* **(a)** *Mus* composer **(b)** *Typ* compositor, typesetter

composition [kɔ̃pozisjɔ̃] *nf* **(a)** (*de sonate, roman, poème etc*) composition, writing; (*d'une ordonnance etc*) making up; **un poème de ma c.** a poem I wrote (myself)

(b) (*éléments*), *Ch, Phys* (*de l'eau etc*) composition; **la c. d'un repas** the composition of a meal; **la c. des équipes n'est pas encore connue** the teams haven't been announced yet

(c) *Mus, Littér etc* (*œuvre*) composition

(d) *Scol* (*dissertation*) essay; (*examen*) test

(e) (*arrangement*) arrangement, compromise; **entrer en c. avec qn** to come to terms with sb

(f) être de bonne c. to be good-natured

(g) *Typ* typesetting, composition; *Typ* **c. (des caractères)** body setting; *Typ* **c. informatisée** computer typesetting; *Tél* **c. automatique de numéros** automatic dialling

compost [kɔ̃pɔst] *nm Agr* compost

compostage [kɔ̃pɔstaʒ] *nm* (*de billet*) (date) stamping; (*poinçonnage*) punching

composter¹ [kɔ̃pɔste] *vt Agr* (*terre*) to compost

composter² *vt* (*billet*) to (date) stamp; (*poinçonner*) to punch

composteur [kɔ̃pɔstœr] *nm* **(a)** (*machine*) date stamp; (*pour poinçonner*) ticket-punching machine **(b)** *Typ* composing stick

compote [kɔ̃pɔt] *nf Culin* compote, stewed fruit; **c. de pommes** apple compote, stewed apples; *F* **j'ai les jambes/la tête en c.** my legs feel like jelly/my brain's gone to mush; *F* **il lui a mis le visage en c.** he smashed his face to a pulp

compotier [kɔ̃pɔtje] *nm* fruit dish

compréhensibilité [kɔ̃preɑ̃sibilite] *nf* comprehensibility

compréhensible [kɔ̃preɑ̃sibl] *adj* **(a)** (*clair*) understandable, comprehensible; **c. du** *ou* **par le grand public** understandable by *or* comprehensible to the general public **(b)** (*justifié*) understandable; **c'est tout à fait c. de sa part** it's altogether understandable on his part

compréhensif, -ive [kɔ̃preɑ̃sif, -iv] *adj* **(a)** (*vaste*) comprehensive **(b)** (*personne*) understanding; **elle s'est montrée très compréhensive là-dessus** she was very understanding about it

compréhension [kɔ̃preɑ̃sjɔ̃] *nf* **(a)** (*fait de comprendre*) comprehension, understanding; **pour la bonne c. du texte** (in order) to fully understand the text; **cet élève a des problèmes de c.** this pupil has problems understanding *or* problems of comprehension **(b)** (*bienveillance*) understanding; **il est plein de c.** he is full of *or* very understanding

comprendre [kɔ̃prɑ̃dr] (*conj like* **prendre**) **1** *vt* **(a)** (*par l'esprit*) to understand, *Fml* to comprehend; **je ne comprends pas ce que vous voulez dire** I don't understand what you mean, *F* I don't get you; **difficile à c.** difficult *or* hard to understand; **c. une langue étrangère** to understand a foreign language; **je n'arrive pas à c. cette phrase** I can't make sense of this sentence; **c. la portée d'un acte** to realize *or* understand the consequences of an action; **je ne comprends pas comment/pourquoi il a fait ça** I don't understand *or* see how/why he did it; **ai-je bien compris?** have I understood correctly?; **dois-je c. que ...?** am I to understand *or* do you mean to say that ...?; **vous m'avez mal compris** you've misunderstood me; **on ne te comprend pas** (*tu parles trop vite*) nobody can understand *or* make out what you say; **je ne le comprends pas** (*il est étrange*) I can't understand him *or* fathom him out, I can't make him out; **il ne comprend rien à rien** he hasn't a clue about anything; **tu peux lui expliquer, il comprend les choses** you can explain to him, he understands about these things; **elle ne comprend pas la plaisanterie** she can't take a joke; **elle n'a pas compris la plaisanterie** she didn't get the joke; **tu comprends ce que je te dis?** do you understand what I'm saying; **je n'y comprends rien** I can't make head or tail of it, it makes no sense to me; **c'est à n'y rien c.** it's incomprehensible; **ne cherche pas, il n'y a rien à c.** don't even try to understand; **va y c. quelque chose** <u>you</u> try to make head or tail of it!, *Am* go figure!; **je lui ai fait c. que ... + *ind*** I gave him to understand that ...; (*avec autorité*) I made it clear to him that ...; **se faire c.** to make oneself understood; **me suis-je bien fait c.?** have I made myself clear?; **comment c. ce tableau/ce poème/l'art?** what is one to make of this picture/this poem/art?; **il faut la c.** you have to see things from her point of view, you have to put yourself in her shoes; **tu n'as pas encore compris qu'il n'en veut qu'à ton argent!** you still haven't realized *or* understood that he's only after your money!; **je n'ai toujours pas compris ce qui s'est passé** I still haven't quite realized *or* grasped *or* understood what has happened; *F* **j'ai compris ma douleur** I realized what I had let myself in for

(b) (*être composé entièrement de*) to comprise, to be made up of, to consist of; **cet organe comprend trois parties distinctes** this organ is made up of *or* comprises three separate parts

(c) (*inclure*) to include; **service non compris** service not included; **le prix comprend tous les frais d'hébergement** the price is fully inclusive of accommodation; **ils ont tous été punis, y compris le plus jeune** they were all punished, including the youngest *or* the youngest included

2 *vi* to understand; **ah! je comprends!** oh! I see!; **ça va, j'ai compris, ce n'est pas la peine de me faire un dessin!** OK, I understand, you don't need to spell it out to me!; **elle comprend vite** she's quick on the uptake, she catches on quickly; **tu comprends, on ne pouvait pas se le permettre** you see, we just couldn't afford it; **elle finira par c.** she'll understand eventually; **je comprends bien!** I understand!; *F* **elle est belle, n'est-ce pas? – je comprends!** she's lovely, isn't she? – you bet! *or* and how!

3 se comprendre *vpr* (*des gens*) to understand each other; **se c. soi-même** to know oneself; *F* **ça se comprend!** it's understandable!, it's not surprising!; **je me comprends!** <u>I</u> know what I'm talking about!

comprenette [kɔ̃prənɛt] *nf F* **il a la c. un peu dure** he's a bit slow on the uptake

compresse [kɔ̃prɛs] *nf* compress

compresser [kɔ̃prɛse] *vt* to compress

compresseur [kɔ̃prɛsœr] **1** *nm* **(a)** *MecE* (*à air, de gaz, de fluide*) compressor; (*de moteur*) supercharger, impeller, compressor; (*d'air conditionné*) blower, fan; *Aut* **c. Roots** Roots blower; *Aut* **c. centrifuge** centrifugal compressor; *Aut* **c. sur vilebrequin** crankshaft compressor; *Aut* **c. à palettes** vane compressor **(b)** *Ordinat* **c. de données** data compressor **2** *adj* compressing; *Constr* **rouleau c.** road roller, steamroller

compressibilité [kɔ̃prɛsibilite] *nf Phys* compressibility; (*de dépenses, peine de prison etc*) reducibility; **vous êtes assez optimiste quant à la c. des dépenses publiques** you're quite optimistic about the possibility of reducing *or* cutting government spending

compressible [kɔ̃prɛsibl] *adj* **(a)** (*comprimable*) compressible **(b)** (*dépenses, peine de prison etc*) reducible

compressif, -ive [kɔ̃prɛsif, -iv] *adj* (*bandage etc*) compressive

compression [kɔ̃mprɛsjɔ̃] *nf* **(a)** (*de gaz, vapeur etc*) compression; **temps de c.** compression stroke **(b)** (*réduction*) reduction, cutback; *Ordinat* (*de données*) compression; **c. des dépenses** spending cuts; **c. de crédit** credit squeeze; **c. du personnel** reduction of staff, cutback in staff; **mesure de c.** cutback, reduction

comprimable [kɔ̃primabl] *adj* compressible

comprimé [kɔ̃prime] **1** *adj* compressed; **air c.** compressed air; **outil à air c.** pneumatic tool **2** *nm Pharm* tablet; **un c. d'aspirine** an aspirin

comprimer [kɔ̃prime] *vt* **(a)** (*gaz, artère*), *Ordinat* (*fichier*) to compress; **c. la taille** to squeeze the waist in; **c. les dépenses** to cut down *or* reduce expenditure **(b)** (*sa colère, sa jalousie etc*) to curb, to repress, to restrain; (*larmes*) to repress, to hold back

compris [kɔ̃pri] *adj* **(a)** (*enregistré*) **bien c.** (fully) understood; **mal c.** misunderstood; **alors, c'est c.?** so, do you understand *or* have you understood?; **la leçon n'a pas été comprise** (the point of) the lesson wasn't understood; **tu fais tes devoirs immédiatement, c.!** you'll do your homework right now, (is that) understood *or* (do you) understand? **(b)** (*situé*) **la maison est comprise entre deux avancées de la mer** the house lies between *or* is bounded by two arms of the sea; **le passage c. entre les deux dialogues** the passage between the two dialogues

compromettant [kɔ̃prɔmɛtɑ̃] *adj* (*situation*) compromising; (*documents, photos*) incriminating, compromising

compromettre [kɔ̃prɔmɛtr] (*conj like* **mettre**) **1** *vt* **(a)** (*entacher*) (*qn, la réputation de qn etc*) to compromise; **être compromis dans un crime** to be implicated in a crime **(b)** (*mettre en péril*) (*vie, sécurité, vacances etc*) to jeopardize, to put in jeopardy **2 se compromettre** *vpr* to compromise oneself; (*s'engager*) to commit oneself; **il s'est compromis dans une affaire de fausses factures** he became implicated in a matter of forged invoices

compromis [kɔ̃prɔmi] *nm* **(a)** (*arrangement*) compromise, arrangement; **parvenir à un c.** to reach a compromise, to come to an arrangement; **cette robe est un c. entre l'élégance et la décontraction** this dress is neither too elegant nor too casual **(b)** *Jur* **mettre une affaire en c.** to submit an affair for arbitration; **c. de vente** provisional *or* preliminary sales agreement

compromission [kɔ̃prɔmisjɔ̃] *nf souvent Péj* **(a)** (*avec sa conscience*) compromising **(b)** (*résultat*) compromise

compta [kɔ̃ta] *nf F* accounting

comptabilisation [kɔ̃tabilizasjɔ̃] *nf Fin* posting, entering in *or* into the accounts; (*dénombrement*) counting; **la c. de l'actif d'une société** recording the assets of a company in the accounts *Bourse* **c. au prix de marché** marking to market

comptabiliser [kɔ̃tabilize] *vt Fin* to post, to enter in the accounts *Bourse* **c. au prix de marché** to mark to market

comptabilité [kɔ̃tabilite] *nf* **(a)** (*livres*) accounts; (*technique*) book-keeping, accounting, accountancy; **c. en partie simple/double** single-/double-entry book-keeping; **livre de c.** account book; **méthode de c.** book-keeping *or* accounting method; **tenir la c. d'une maison** to keep the books *or* the accounts of a firm; *Fin* **c. matières** stock record, stores accounts; **c. analytique** cost accounting; **c. bancaire** bank accounting; **c. commerciale** business accounting; **c. générale** general accounts; (*système*) financial accounting; **c. informatisée** computerized accounts; **c.-gestion financière** financial management accounting **(b)** (*service*) accounts department

comptable [kɔ̃tabl] **1** *adj* **(a)** *Com etc* (*travail etc*) bookkeeping, accounting; **pièce c.** voucher; **machine c.** accounting machine **(b)** (*responsable*) accountable; **être c. à qn de qch** to be accountable to sb for sth **2** *n* accountant; **c. agréé** chartered accountant, *US* certified public accountant; **expert c.** chartered accountant; (*vérificateur*) auditor

comptage [kɔ̃taʒ] *nm* counting

comptant [kɔ̃tɑ̃] **1** *adj* **argent c.** cash; *Fig F* **prendre qch pour argent c.** to take sth for gospel truth **2** *adv* **payer c.** to pay (in) cash **3** *nm* cash; **payer/acheter au c.** to pay (in)/buy for cash; *Com* **c. contre documents** cash against documents, CAD

compte [kɔ̃t] *nm* **(a)** *Fin, Banque* account; **tenir les comptes d'une maison** to keep the accounts *or* the books of a firm; **faire ses comptes** to make up *or* do one's accounts; **livre de comptes** account book; **la Cour des Comptes** ≈ the Audit Office; **versement à c.** payment on account; **régler son c.** to settle one's account; *Fig F* **régler son c. à qn** to settle sb's hash; **avoir un (petit) c. à régler avec qn** to have a bone to pick with sb, to have a score to settle with sb; **on réglera nos comptes plus tard** we'll settle up later; **règlement de c.** settling of accounts; *Fig F* settling of scores *or* accounts; **donner** *ou* **régler son c. à un employé** (*le renvoyer*) to dismiss an employee; **avoir un c. chez qn** to have an account with sb; **mettre un montant sur son c.** to pay a sum into one's account; **être/se mettre** *ou* **s'installer à son c.** to be/set up in business on one's own (account); **cela n'entre pas en ligne de c.** that has nothing to do with the matter, that doesn't come into it; **mettre un malheur sur le c. de qn** to lay a misfortune at sb's door, to blame sb for a misfortune; **apprendre qch sur le c. de qn** to learn sth about sb; **faire qch pour le c. de qn** to do sth on sb's behalf; **pour mon c., j'aimerais mieux rester ici** as far as I'm concerned, I'd prefer to stay here

(b) (*calcul*) reckoning, calculation; **faire le c. des dépenses** to add up *or* calculate the expenses; **le c. des morts** the death toll *or* tally; **le c. y est** (*somme*) it's the right amount; (*objets, personnes*) they're all here; **ça ne fait pas le c.** it doesn't come to the right amount; **c. rond** round sum; **acheter qch à bon c.** to buy sth cheap; **cela fait mon c.** it's just the thing for me, that suits me; **il y trouve son c.** he gets something out of it, there's something in it for him; **vous êtes loin du c.** you're wide of the mark; *Fig* **au bout du c., en fin de c.** in the end, at the end of the day; **tout c. fait** all things considered, taking everything into account; **à ce c.-là** in that case; **tenir c. de qch** to take sth into account *or* into consideration; **ne tenir aucun c. de qn/qch** to take no notice of sb/sth, to ignore *or* disregard sb/sth; **c. tenu de son assiduité** considering *or* bearing in mind *or* taking into account his regular attendance; **s'en tirer à bon c.** to get off lightly; *F* **il a son c.** (*il en a assez*) he's had enough; (*parce qu'il a bu*) he's had enough (to drink); *F* **son c. est bon** he's for it, he's had it

(c) (*explication*) **comptes** explanation; **demander des comptes à qn** to ask sb for an explanation, to call sb to account; **elle ne doit de comptes à personne** she is answerable to nobody; **rendre des comptes** to explain *or* justify oneself; **je n'ai de comptes à rendre à personne** I don't have to explain *or* justify myself to anyone; **rendre c. de qch** to account for sth; **se rendre c. de qch** to realize sth, to be aware of sth; **se rendre c. que ...** to realize that ...; **on lui a volé son portefeuille et elle ne s'est rendu c. de rien** someone stole his wallet and she didn't notice a thing; *F* **tu te rends c.!** would you believe it!; **c. rendu** report; (*littéraire*) (book) review; (*d'une réunion*) minutes; **faire le c. rendu** (*pendant la réunion*) to take the minutes; (*à la réunion suivante*) to read the minutes

(d) *Boxe* count; **rester sur le plancher pour le c.** to be counted out, to be out for the count

▶ **compte**: **c. accréditif** charge account; **c. d'actif** assets account; **comptes analytiques d'exploitation** operational cost accounts; **comptes annuels** annual accounts; **comptes approuvés** certified accounts; **c. d'attente** suspense account; **c. en banque** *ou* **bancaire** bank account; **c. bloqué** escrow *or* frozen *or* blocked account; **c. centralisateur** central account; **c. de charges** expense account; **c. chèque postal** = Giro account; **c. client** customer account; *Compta* account receivable, trade debtor; **c.-client** account; **responsable des comptes-clients** account executive; **c. des clients** (*d'un hôtel etc*) guest folio; **c. collectif** adjustment account, summary account; **c. de compensation** clearing account;
c. conjoint joint account; **c. de contrepartie** contra account; **c. de correspondant** correspondent bank account; **c. courant, c. chèques** current account, *Am* checking account; **c. à crédit** credit account; **c. créditeur** *Compta* account payable; (*à la banque*) account in credit, credit balance; **c. débiteur** *Compta* account receivable; (*à la banque*) account in debit, debit balance; **c. à découvert** overdrawn account; **c. de dépôt** deposit account; **c. en devises étrangères** foreign currency account; **c. divisionnaire** divisional account; **c. d'épargne** savings account, deposit account; **c. d'épargne- retraite** retirement savings account; **c. de l'exploitant** owner's capital account; **c. d'exploitation générale** trading account; **comptes de gestion** management accounts; **c. d'immobilisations** fixed asset account; **c. individuel** personal account; **c. joint** joint account; **c. livret** deposit account; **c. de passif** liabilities account; **c. permanent** = charge account, *Br* credit account; **c. de produits** income account, revenue account; **c. de régularisation** (*de l'actif*) prepayments and accrued income; (*du passif*) accruals and deferred income; **c. de réserve** reserve account; **c. de résultat** profit and loss account, *Am* income statement; **c. de résultat prévisionnel** interim profit-and-loss statement; **c. de stock** inventory account; **c. en souffrance** outstanding account, delinquent account; *Bourse* **c. à terme** forward account; **comptes de tiers** other debtors and creditors

compte à rebours *nm* countdown; **faire le c.** to count backwards; (*avant le lancement d'une fusée*) to count down

compte-clé, *pl* **comptes-clés** *nm Com* key-account

compte-gouttes *nm inv Pharm etc* dropper; **mesurer qch au c.** to dole sth out in driblets *or* sparingly; **il donne son argent au c.** he's very sparing with his money

compter [kɔ̃te] **1** *vt* **(a)** (*dénombrer*) to count; **je vous ai tous comptés?** have I counted you all?; **on ne compte plus les mécontents** we've lost count of the malcontents, we can't keep track of the malcontents; **c. dans ses rangs** to number among one's ranks; **on peut les c. (sur les doigts de la main)** you can count them on the fingers of one hand; **elle compte les jours** she's counting the days; **il y a de cela vingt ans bien comptés** a good twenty years have passed since then; *Fig* **c. les moutons** to count sheep; *Fig* **c. les points** *ou* **les coups** to keep score, to watch from the sidelines

(b) (*donner*) to pay; **c. cent francs à qn** to pay sb a hundred francs

(c) (*donner avec parcimonie*) to ration; **il leur compte leur argent de poche** he rations their pocket money; **marcher à pas comptés** to walk with measured tread; **ses jours sont comptés** his days are numbered

(d) (*inclure*) to include; **ils étaient vingt, sans c. le père et la mère** there were twenty of them, not counting the father and mother; **sans c. que ...** not to mention that ..., besides the fact that ...; **je le compte parmi mes meilleurs amis** I number *or* count *or* consider him among my best friends

(e) (*prévoir*) to allow, to reckon; **j'ai compté deux cents grammes par personne** I've allowed *or* reckoned two hundred grammes per person; **elle compte rentrer à dix heures** she expects *or* intends to be back at ten o'clock; **que comptes-tu faire?** what are you planning *or* intending to do?; **c'était sans c. les embouteillages** that was without allowing for traffic jams

(f) (*facturer*) to charge for; **c. qch à qn** to charge sb for sth; **il a compté 20 francs pour le déplacement** he charged 20 francs for the callout

2 *vi* **(a)** (*calculer*) to count; **c. de tête/sur ses doigts** to count in one's head/on one's fingers; **c. jusqu'à dix** to count up to ten; **mal c.** to miscount; **apprendre à c.** to learn (how) to count; **dépenser sans c.** to spend money freely *or* like water; **se dépenser sans c.** to give oneself freely; **avec un salaire en moins, ils sont obligés de c.** with one salary less they have to count the pennies *or* watch every penny; **il compte parmi les meilleurs** he's one of the best, he ranks among the best; *Admin* **à c. du 1er janvier** (with effect) from January 1st, as of January 1st

(b) (*être important*) to count, to matter; **ce qui compte, c'est le travail** work is what matters *or* counts; **ça ne compte pas** that doesn't count *or* matter; **il ne compte plus du tout pour elle** he doesn't mean anything to her any more; **elle ne compte pas,** *F* **elle compte pour du beurre** she doesn't count, she counts for nothing; **les heures supplémentaires comptent double** overtime counts double; **à table, il compte pour deux** he eats enough for two

(c) c. avec qn/qch to reckon with sb/sth; **c'est un adversaire avec lequel il faudra c.** he's an opponent who will have to be reckoned with; **il faut c. avec le vent** you have to allow for the wind

(d) c. sur qn/qch to count *or* rely *or* depend on sb/sth; **je ne compterais pas trop là-dessus** I wouldn't count on it too much, I wouldn't bank on it; **tu peux c. sur lui pour que tout soit fait à l'envers** you can rely *or* count on him to do everything all wrong; **j'y compte bien!** I should hope so!; **sans c. que** apart from the fact that; *F* **compte là-dessus et bois de l'eau!** you'll be lucky!, there's not much hope *or* chance of that!

(e) *Can Sp* to score

3 se c. *vpr* **comptez-vous** count yourselves, do a head-count; **ses échecs ne se comptent plus** he has had countless failures; **les maîtresses du roi se comptent par dizaines** the king has dozens of mistresses

compte-titres *pl* **comptes-titres** *nm Fin* share account

compte-tours [kɔ̃ttur] *nm inv* rev *or* revolution counter

compteur [kɔ̃tœr] *nm* meter; *Ordinat* counter; **c. d'électricité/à gaz/d'eau** electricity/gas/water meter; **le c. du taxi** the taximeter, the taxi's meter; **le c. marquait 47 francs** there was 47 francs on the meter; **relever le c.** to read the meter; *Aut* **c. de vitesse** speedometer; **c. kilométrique (totaliseur)** ≈ mil(e)ometer, *Am* odometer; *Aut* **c. journalier** trip recorder *or Am* odometer; *Nucl* **c. (de) Geiger** Geiger counter; *Mktg* **c. de circulation** traffic counter

comptine [kɔ̃tin] *nf* counting rhyme

comptoir [kɔ̃twar] *nm* **(a)** *Com* (*table*) counter; (*dans un bar*) bar; **garçon de c.** barman, bartender; **prendre une consommation au c.** to have a drink at the bar; **c. d'enregistrement** check-in desk; **c. d'information** information desk; **c. de réception** reception desk; **c. de vente** sales counter **(b)** (*cartel*) (marketing) syndicate **(c)** *Fin* bank; (*de banque*) branch; **c. d'escompte** discount house **(d)** (*dans un pays éloigné*) trading post

comptoir-caisse *pl* **comptoirs-caisses** *nm* cashier's desk

compulsation [kɔ̃pylsasjɔ̃] *nf* (*d'un ouvrage*) consultation

compulser [kɔ̃pylse] *vt* (*documents, livres etc*) to consult

compulsif, -ive [kɔ̃pylsif, -iv] *adj* (*buveur etc*) compulsive; **conduite compulsive** compulsive behaviour

compulsion [kɔ̃pylsjɔ̃] *nf* compulsion

computation [kɔ̃pytasjɔ̃] *nf* computation

comte [kɔ̃t] *nm* count; (*en Grande Bretagne*) earl

comté [kɔ̃te] *nm* **(a)** *Hist* earldom **(b)** *Admin* county **(c)** *Can Pol* riding **(d)** (*fromage*) = type of Gruyère cheese

comtesse [kɔ̃tɛs] *nf* countess

con, conne [kɔ̃, kɔn] **1** *très F adj* damn stupid, idiotic, *Br* bloody stupid; **elle est trop c.** *ou* **conne!** she's too damn stupid for words!; *F* **être c. comme la lune** *ou* **un balai** (*d'une personne*) to be as daft as a brush; **c. comme la lune** (*film etc*) damn stupid, *Br* bloody stupid; **c'est pas c.!** that's pretty clever! **2** *n très F* stupid bastard; **faire le c.** to fool *or* mess around; **pauvre c.!** poor bastard *or Br* sod!; **t'es vraiment le roi des cons** you really are an utter *or* a complete nerd; **quel c. ce mec!** what a stupid bastard that guy is!; **ce vélo à la c.!** this damn useless bike! **3** *nm Vulg* (*sexe*) cunt, twat

conard, -arde [kɔnar, -ard] *Vulg* **1** *adj* damn stupid, *Br* bloody stupid **2** *nm* damn fool, *Br* silly bugger

conasse [kɔnas] *nf Vulg* silly bitch, stupid cow

concassage [kɔ̃kasaʒ] *nm* (*de pierre etc*) crushing; (*de poivre*) grinding

concasser [kɔ̃kase] *vt* (*pierre etc*) to crush; (*poivre*) to grind

concasseur [kɔ̃kasœr] **1** *nm* crusher **2** *adj* **rouleau c.** crushing roller

concaténation [kɔ̃katenasjɔ̃] *nf* concatenation

concaténer [kɔ̃katene] *vt Ordinat* to concatenate

concave [kɔ̃kav] *adj* concave

concavité [kɔ̃kavite] *nf* **(a)** (*fait d'être concave*) concavity **(b)** (*creux*) hollow, cavity

concéder [kɔ̃sede] *vt* **(je concède, n. concédons; je concéderai)** **(a)** (*privilège, droit*) to concede, to grant; (*terrain, concession*) to grant **(b)** (*reconnaître*) **c. qu'on a tort** to admit that one is wrong; **il fait chaud, je (vous) le concède** it's warm, I grant you **(c)** *Sp* to give away, to concede; **c. un but** to give away *or* concede a goal

concélébrer [kɔ̃selebre] *vt Rel* to concelebrate

concentration [kɔ̃sɑ̃trasjɔ̃] *nf* **(a)** *Phys, Ch, Nucl* concentration; **grandes concentrations urbaines** conurbations, large urban agglomerations; *Fig* **une grande c. d'oiseaux** a large concentration *or* population of birds; **la c. des intellectuels dans la capitale** the concentration of intellectuals in the capital; **zone à haute c. de population** high-density area; *Typ* **impression à haute c.** high-density printing

(b) (*d'entreprises*) integration, merging; *Com* **c. horizontale/verticale** horizontal/vertical integration

(c) (*de l'esprit*) concentration; **manquer de c.** to lack concentration; **cela exige une très grande c.** it demands *or* requires great concentration

concentrationnaire [kɔ̃sɑ̃trasjɔnɛr] **1** *adj* of concentration camps; **la vie c.** life in a concentration camp **2** *n* concentration camp prisoner

concentré [kɔ̃sɑ̃tre] **1** *adj* **(a)** *Ch, Culin etc* concentrated; (*lait*) condensed **(b)** (*intellectuellement*) concentrating; **il était très c.** he was concentrating hard **2** *nm Ch, Culin etc* concentrate; **c. de tomates** tomato concentrate

concentrer [kɔ̃sɑ̃tre] **1** *vt* to concentrate; (*rayons du soleil*) to focus; **c. son espoir sur une chose** to concentrate *or* focus one's hopes on a thing **2 se concentrer** *vpr* **(a)** (*être attentif*) to concentrate **(sur** on); **taisez-vous, je me concentre** be quiet, I'm trying to concentrate **(b)** (*s'assembler*) (*d'une foule, d'élèves etc*) to gather; **la population se concentre de plus en plus dans les grandes villes** the population is concentrating more and more in the big cities

concentrique [kɔ̃sɑ̃trik] *adj Géom etc* concentric

concentriquement [kɔ̃sɑ̃trikmɑ̃] *adv* concentrically

concept [kɔ̃sɛpt] *nm* concept; **c. d'évocation** advertising concept

concepteur, -trice [kɔ̃sɛptœr, -tris] *n* ideas man, *f* woman; (*de logiciel*) writer, designer; **être c. dans une agence de publicité** to work as an ideas man *or* on the creative side in an advertising agency; **c. graphiste** graphics designer

concepteur-projecteur *pl* **concepteurs-projecteurs** *nm* ideas man and project manager

concepteur-rédacteur *pl* **concepteurs-rédacteurs** *nm* (*d'une agence de publicité*) copywriter

conception [kɔ̃sɛpsjɔ̃] *nf* **(a)** (*d'un enfant, d'une idée*) conception; *Rel* **l'Immaculée C.** the Immaculate Conception **(b)** (*vue*) concept, idea; **une toute nouvelle c. des mathématiques** a whole new way of looking at mathematics, a completely new approach to mathematics **(c)** (*création*) design, creation; **c. graphique** graphic design; **c. assistée par ordinateur** computer-aided *or* -assisted design

conceptualisation [kɔ̃sɛptɥalizasjɔ̃] *nf* conceptualization

conceptualiser [kɔ̃sɛptɥalize] *vt* to conceptualize

conceptuel, -uelle [kɔ̃sɛptɥɛl] *adj* conceptual

concernant [kɔ̃sɛrnɑ̃] *prép* concerning, with regard to, regarding; **c. votre départ, voici quelques informations** here's some information about your departure

concerner [kɔ̃sɛrne] *vt* to concern, to affect; **pour** *ou* **en ce qui concerne cette affaire** with regard to this matter, as far as this matter is concerned; **en ce qui me concerne** as far as I am concerned; **cela ne vous concerne en rien** that's none of your business, it's no concern of yours; (*vous n'êtes pas en cause*) it doesn't concern *or* affect you at all; **est-ce que cela vous concerne?** is it any business *or* concern of yours?; **ces problèmes vous concernent tous** these problems concern *or* affect you all; **ne pas se sentir concerné** not to feel affected; **prière de vous rendre au bureau pour affaire vous concernant** please come to the office to discuss a matter which concerns *or* involves you

concert [kɔ̃sɛr] *nm* **(a)** *Mus* concert; **salle de c.** concert hall; *Fig* **ce fut un c. d'approbations** there was a chorus of approval **(b)** (*accord*) **agir de c. avec qn** to act jointly *or* in conjunction *or Fml* in concert with sb, to take concerted action with sb; **nous sommes rentrés de c.** we came back together

concertant [kɔ̃sɛrtɑ̃] *adj Mus* concertante

concertation [kɔ̃sɛrtasjɔ̃] *nf* consultation; **travailler en c.** to work together; **la c. est de mise** we must work together *or* co-operate

concerté [kɔ̃sɛrte] *adj* (*action*) concerted, united

concerter [kɔ̃sɛrte] **1** *vt* (*plan etc*) to devise together **2 se concerter** *vpr* to consult (each other), to consult together; **ils se concertèrent sur les moyens d'action** they consulted each other as to how to act

concertina [kɔ̃sɛrtina] *nm Mus* concertina

concertiste [kɔ̃sɛrtist] *n* concert performer *or* artiste; (*dans un concerto*) soloist

concerto [kɔ̃sɛrto] *nm Mus* concerto

concessif, -ive [kɔ̃sɛsif, -iv] *adj Gram* concessive

concession [kɔ̃sɛsjɔ̃] *nf* **(a)** (*compromis*) concession; (*de terrain etc*) granting; (*d'un point dans une discussion etc*) yielding; **c. de franchise** grant of franchise; **c. de licence** licensing; **faire des concessions** to make concessions **(b)** (*terre etc*) concession; (*au cimetière*) plot; **c. à perpétuité** plot held in perpetuity **(c)** (*d'automobiles*) dealership; (*agence*) agency; (*contrat de franchisage*) franchise; **c. commerciale** agency

concessionnaire [kɔ̃sɛsjɔnɛr] **1** *adj* (*entreprise etc*) concessionary **2** *n Com* agent, dealer; (*de licence*) licensee; (*de brevet*) patentee; (*de contrat de franchisage*) franchisee; **votre c. Renault®** your Renault dealer; **c. export** export concessionaire

concevable [kɔ̃s(ə)vabl] *adj* conceivable

concevoir [kɔ̃s(ə)vwar] (*prp* **concevant**; *pp* **conçu**; *pr ind* **je conçois, n. concevons, ils conçoivent**; *impf* **je concevais**; *p hist* **je conçus**; *fu* **je concevrai**) **1** *vt* (**a**) (*enfant*) to conceive (**b**) (*comprendre*) (*concept etc*) to understand; **comment c. de semblables infortunes** it is difficult to imagine such misfortune; **je conçois fort bien que tu sois lasse de la vie à la campagne** I can quite understand that you are tired of living in the country

(**c**) (*imaginer*) (*plan*) to conceive, to devise, to think up; (*idée*) to conceive; **je ne conçois pas de ne jamais le revoir** I can't accept that I'll never see him again; **je ne conçois pas que ...** I find it hard to believe that ...

(**d**) (*éprouver*) **c. de l'amitié pour qn** to take a liking to sb; **elle en concut une profonde amertume** it made her very bitter

(**e**) (*uniquement au participe passé*) **télégramme/lettre ainsi conçu(e)** telegram/letter worded as follows *or* that reads as follows

(**f**) (*créer*) (*produit, maquette etc*) to design

2 se concevoir *vpr* **ça se conçoit** that's understandable; **cela se conçoit facilement** that is easy to understand *or* easily understood

conchyliculture [kɔ̃ʃilikyltyr] *nf* shellfish farming

concierge [kɔ̃sjɛrʒ] *n* (*d'immeuble, d'appartements*) caretaker, *Am* janitor, superintendent; (*dans un hôtel*) concierge, house *or* hall porter; *Scol* caretaker, *Am* janitor; *F* **c'est une vraie c.** he's/she's a terrible gossip

conciergerie [kɔ̃sjɛrʒəri] *nf* (**a**) (*loge*) caretaker's lodge (**b**) *Hist* **la C.** the Conciergerie (prison)

concile [kɔ̃sil] *nm Rel* council; **c. œcuménique** ecumenical council

conciliable [kɔ̃siljabl] *adj* reconcilable

conciliabule [kɔ̃siljabyl] *nm* (**a**) *F* (*conversation*) confab; **les enfants étaient en grand c.** the children were having a big confab (**b**) *Arch* (*réunion*) secret meeting, secret assembly

conciliaire [kɔ̃siljɛr] *adj* conciliar

conciliant [kɔ̃siljɑ̃] *adj* conciliatory

conciliateur, -trice [kɔ̃siljatœr, -tris] **1** *adj* conciliatory **2** *n* conciliator

conciliation [kɔ̃siljasjɔ̃] *nf* reconciliation, conciliation; **comité de c.** arbitration committee; **tentative de c.** attempt at reconciliation

conciliatoire [kɔ̃siljatwar] *adj* conciliatory

concilier [kɔ̃silje] (*impf, pr sub* **n. conciliions, v. conciliiez**) **1** *vt* (**a**) (*deux choses*) to reconcile; **c. sa vie professionnelle et ses enfants** to combine one's professional life with looking after one's children

(**b**) (*cœurs, estime etc*) to win, to gain; **sa droiture lui a concilié l'admiration de tous les employés** his uprightness won *or* gained him the admiration of all the employees

2 se concilier *vpr* (**a**) (*être compatible*) **se c. avec** to go with; **la prise de ces médicaments se concilie difficilement avec l'alcool** these drugs and alcohol don't go together *or* don't mix very well

(**b**) **se c. qn** *ou* **la faveur de qn** to win *or* gain sb's goodwill

concis [kɔ̃si] *adj* concise; **il a exposé la situation en termes c.** he described the situation concisely, he gave a concise description of the situation

concision [kɔ̃sizjɔ̃] *nf* concision, conciseness; **avec c.** concisely, with concision

concitoyen, -enne [kɔ̃sitwajɛ̃, -ɛn] *n* fellow citizen

conclave [kɔ̃klav] *nm Rel* conclave

concluant [kɔ̃klyɑ̃] *adj* conclusive; **peu c.** inconclusive

conclure [kɔ̃klyr] (*prp* **concluant**; *pp* **conclu**; *pr ind* **je conclus, n. concluons, ils concluent**; *impf* **je concluais**; *p hist* **je conclus**; *fu* **je conclurai**) **1** *vt* (**a**) (*terminer*) (*discours, réunion, repas, roman etc*) to conclude, to end (**par** with)

(**b**) (*signer*) (*accord, traité, contrat*) to enter into, to conclude; **c. une entente** to reach an understanding; **c. un marché** to conclude *or* strike *or F* clinch a bargain, to make a deal; **marché conclu!** it's a deal!, done!; *Com* **c'est une affaire conclue** it's a bargain, it's a deal; **c. une vente** to close a sale

(**c**) (*déduire*) to conclude; **nous avons conclu que ...** we came to the conclusion *or* concluded that ...; **que pouvons-nous c. de tout cela?** what conclusions can we draw from all this?; **j'en conclus que ...** I conclude that ...

2 *vi* (**a**) (*aboutir à la conclusion*) **on a conclu à sa bêtise** we concluded he was stupid; **le jury a conclu au suicide** the jury returned a verdict of suicide; **tout conclut en sa faveur** everything is in his favour

(**b**) (*achever*) **il faut savoir c.** you've got to know when to stop

conclusion [kɔ̃klyzjɔ̃] *nf* (**a**) (*fin*) (*de discours, réunion etc*) conclusion, end (**b**) (*action de mener à bien*) (*de traité, d'accord etc*) conclusion, concluding; **c. d'un contrat** signing of a contract (**c**) (*déduction*) conclusion; *Jur* finding, decision; *Jur* **conclusions** pleas, submissions; **les conclusions d'une enquête** the findings of an enquiry; **en c.** in conclusion; **tirer une c. de qch** to draw a conclusion from sth; *F* **c., l'échafaudage s'est écroulé** the result was that the scaffolding collapsed

concocter [kɔ̃kɔkte] *vt F* (*cocktail*) to concoct; (*histoire, excuse etc*) to concoct, to dream up; **qu'est-ce que tu nous as concocté là?** what's this you've concocted?, what kind of a concoction is this?

concombre [kɔ̃kɔ̃br] *nm* cucumber

concomitance [kɔ̃kɔmitɑ̃s] *nf* concomitance

concomitant [kɔ̃kɔmitɑ̃] *adj* (*circonstance, symptômes etc*) concomitant, accompanying

concordance [kɔ̃kɔrdɑ̃s] *nf* (**a**) (*de preuves, témoignages, dates etc*) agreement, *Fml* concordance; **la c. de leurs témoignages ne nous laisse pas de doutes quant à ...** the fact that their testimony agrees *or* tallies leaves us in no doubt as to ... (**b**) *Gram* **c. des temps** sequence of tenses (**c**) (*index*) concordance

concordant [kɔ̃kɔrdɑ̃] *adj* (*témoignages, déclarations*) in agreement

concordat [kɔ̃kɔrda] *nm* (**a**) *Rel* concordat (**b**) *Com* (*document*) (bankrupt's) certificate; (*accord*) composition

concorde [kɔ̃kɔrd] *nf* concord, harmony

concorder [kɔ̃kɔrde] *vi* (*de dates, preuves, témoignages etc*) to agree, to tally (**avec** with); **nos opinions ne concorderont jamais** we'll never be of the same opinion

concourant [kɔ̃kurɑ̃] *adj* (*lignes*) concurrent, converging; (*circonstances*) concurrent

concourir [kɔ̃kurir] *vi* (*conj like* **courir**) (**a**) (*de lignes*) to converge (**b**) (*concorder*) to combine, to unite; **c. à (faire) qch** to work towards (doing) sth; **tout a concouru à ma réussite** everything contributed to my success; **les témoignages concourent à prouver que ...** the evidence goes to prove that ... (**c**) *Sp etc* to compete; **c. (avec qn) pour un prix** to compete (with sb) for a prize

concours [kɔ̃kur] *nm* (**a**) (*aide*) aid, assistance, help; **prêter son c. à qn** to help *or* assist sb; **avec le c. de ...** with the participation of ...; **avec l'aimable c. de Sophie** assisted by Sophie; **c. financier** financial aid

(**b**) (*compétition*) competition, contest; *Scol etc* (*examen*) competitive examination; **se présenter à un c.** to go in for *or* enter a competition; *Scol etc* to sit a competitive examination; **recrutement par c.** competitive entry, recruitment by competition; **c. interne/externe** in-house *or* internal/open competition; **c. d'entrée** entrance examination; **c. de vente** sales contest

(**c**) (*d'événements*) coincidence; **par un c. de circonstances** by a combination of circumstances

(**d**) *Arch, Litt* (*de personnes*) concourse, gathering

(**e**) *Banque* loans outstanding, bank lending; **c. bancaire** bank lending

▶ **concours**: **c. agricole/hippique** agricultural/horse show; **c. de beauté** beauty contest; *Scol* **c. général** = competition between all the lycées at baccalauréat level

concret, -ète [kɔ̃krɛ, -ɛt] **1** *adj* (**a**) (*terme etc*) concrete; **cas c.** actual case, concrete example (**b**) **musique concrète** concrete music (**c**) (*réel*) concrete, tangible, real; **je veux des résultats concrets** I want concrete *or* tangible results **2** *nm* **le c.** (*par opposition à l'abstrait*) the concrete

concrètement [kɔ̃krɛtmɑ̃] *adv* in concrete terms; **c. qu'est-ce que ça a changé?** what has it changed in real terms?, what concrete changes has it led to?

concrétion [kɔ̃kresjɔ̃] *nf* concretion; *Méd* **concrétions calcaires** chalk stones

concrétiser [kɔ̃kretize] **1** *vt* (*idée, question*) to put in(to) concrete form; (*rêve*) to realize; (*projet, promesse*) to put into effect, to carry out; (*avantage*) to capitalize on; **c. qch en un accord** to firm sth up with an agreement; **ils n'ont pas réussi à c. leur domination** they were unable to capitalize on their domination **2 se concrétiser** *vpr* to materialize; **nos projets commencent à se c.** our plans are beginning to take shape

concubinage [kɔ̃kybinaʒ] *nm* cohabitation, *Fml* concubinage; **vivre** *ou* **être en c.** to live together (as man and wife), to cohabit

concubin, -ine [kɔ̃kybɛ̃, -in] *n Jur* concubine, common-law wife, *Péj* concubine

concupiscence [kɔ̃kypisɑ̃s] *nf* concupiscence

concupiscent [kɔ̃kypisɑ̃] *adj* concupiscent

concurremment [kɔ̃kyramɑ̃] *adv* (**a**) (*ensemble*) jointly; (*en même temps*) concurrently; **agir c. avec qn** to act jointly *or* in conjunction with sb (**b**) (*en concurrence*) competitively, in competition (**avec** with)

concurrence [kɔ̃kyrɑ̃s] *nf* (**a**) *Com, Écon etc* competition;

faire c. à qn/qch to compete with sb/sth; **la libre c.** free *or* open competition; **c. acharnée** cut-throat competition; **c. déloyale** unfair competition; **c. sauvage** unfair competition; (*acharnée*) cut-throat competition; **faire jouer la c.** to allow market forces to operate; **prix défiant toute c.** unbeatable price **(b) jusqu'à c. de ...** up to ..., not exceeding ..., to the amount of ... **(c)** *Vieilli* (*d'événements*) concurrence, coincidence

concurrencer [kɔ̃kyrɑ̃se] *vt* **(je concurrençai(s); n. concurrençons)** (*dans le commerce etc*) to compete with

concurrent, -ente [kɔ̃kyrɑ̃, -ɑ̃t] **1** *adj* **(a)** (*industries, produits etc*) competing, rival **(b)** *Vieilli* (*forces, actions etc*) combined **2** *n Com* competitor, rival; (*pour un prix etc*) competitor; (*pour un poste etc*) candidate; (*dans une émission de jeux etc*) contestant; *Com* **c. principal** major competitor; *Mktg* **c. tardif** late entrant

concurrentiel, -ielle [kɔ̃kyrɑ̃sjɛl] *adj* (*entreprises, prix etc*) competitive

concussion [kɔ̃kysjɔ̃] *nf* misappropriation of public funds

condamnable [kɔ̃danabl] *adj* reprehensible, blameworthy

condamnation [kɔ̃danasjɔ̃] *nf* **(a)** *Jur* (*jugement*) conviction **(pour** for); (*peine*) sentence; **il a déjà quatre condamnations à son actif** he already has four convictions; **c. à trois mois de prison** three-month prison sentence; **c. à mort** death sentence; **c. à perpétuité** life sentence; *Fig* **la c. d'un film par la critique** the slating *or* panning *or* condemnation of a film by the critics **(b)** (*reproche*) condemnation; **la c. de la société de consommation** the condemnation of the consumer society **(c)** (*fermeture*) (*d'une porte*) blocking *or* sealing up; *Aut* **c. automatique des portes** automatic door locking; *Aut* **c. centralisée des portes** central locking

condamné, -ée [kɔ̃dane] *n* prisoner; **un condamné à mort** a prisoner under sentence of death

condamner [kɔ̃dane] *vt* **(a)** *Jur* to sentence; **c. qn à mort/à trois mois de prison** to sentence sb to death/to three months' imprisonment; **c. qn à 10 000 francs d'amende** to fine sb 10,000 francs; *Fig* **tentative condamnée à l'insuccès** attempt doomed to failure; **le médecin l'a condamné** the doctor has given him up; **être condamné à la solitude** to be condemned to loneliness

(b) (*obliger à*) **cela me condamne à l'attendre** that means I have to wait for him; **pourquoi tant de gens sont-ils condamnés à mourir de faim?** why are so many people condemned to die of hunger?

(c) (*interdire*) to forbid; **la loi condamne la bigamie** bigamy is forbidden by law

(d) (*murer*) (*porte, pièce*) to block up, to seal up; *F* **as-tu condamné les portes de la voiture?** have you locked the (car) doors?; *Fig* **c. sa porte** to bar one's door to visitors

(e) (*blâmer*) (*qn*) to condemn, to blame; (*thèse, abus etc*) to condemn; **c. l'emploi d'un mot** to object to the use of a word

condé [kɔ̃de] *nm Arg* (*policier*) cop

condensateur [kɔ̃dɑ̃satœr] *nm Él* condenser, capacitor; *Opt* condenser

condensation [kɔ̃dɑ̃sasjɔ̃] *nf* condensation

condensé [kɔ̃dɑ̃se] **1** *adj* condensed; **lait c.** condensed milk; **texte c.** digest **2** *nm* digest

condenser [kɔ̃dɑ̃se] **1** *vt* (*gaz, cours etc*) to condense **(en** into); (*article, récit etc*) to condense, to cut down; *Ordinat* to condense; (*base de données*) to pack **2 se condenser** *vpr* to condense

condenseur [kɔ̃dɑ̃sœr] *nm Phys, Opt* condenser

condescendance [kɔ̃desɑ̃dɑ̃s] *nf* condescension; **parler avec c.** to speak with condescension *or* condescendingly

condescendant [kɔ̃desɑ̃dɑ̃] *adj* condescending

condescendre [kɔ̃desɑ̃dr] *vi* **c. à faire qch** to condescend to do sth

condiment [kɔ̃dimɑ̃] *nm Culin* condiment

condisciple [kɔ̃disipl] *n Univ* fellow student; *Scol* schoolmate

condition [kɔ̃disjɔ̃] *nf* **(a)** (*état*) condition; **les conditions de vie/travail** living/working conditions; **en bonne c.** in good condition; **cet athlète n'est pas en c. (pour courir)** this athlete isn't fit *or* isn't in shape (to run); **pour te mettre en c.** to get you into shape (mentally and physically); **mise en c. physique** getting fit *or* into shape; **les films de propagande mettaient les foules en c.** the propaganda films conditioned the crowds; **être en bonne/mauvaise c. physique** to be in good/bad (physical) condition *or* shape; **conditions atmosphériques** atmospheric conditions; **conditions du marché** market conditions; **voyager dans les meilleures conditions** to travel under the most favourable conditions; **attendre que des conditions plus favorables se présentent** to wait until conditions improve *or* are better; **dans ces conditions, je n'y vais pas** if that's the way it is, I'm not going; **faire une escalade dans de mauvaises conditions (météorologiques)** to climb in bad (weather) conditions; **les conditions n'étaient pas réunies** the conditions weren't quite right

(b) (*stipulation*) condition; **c. nécessaire et suffisante** necessary and sufficient condition; **une c. essentielle** an essential condition; **une c. sine qua non** a prerequisite, a sine qua non; **c'est la c. de votre réussite** that's what will determine your success; **conditions requises** requirements; faire ses conditions to name one's (own) terms; **mettre/imposer une c.** to lay down a condition; **il veut bien signer le contrat, mais il y met une c.** he's happy to sign the contract, but on one condition; **avez-vous posé vos conditions?** did you state your terms *or* conditions?; **offre sans c.** unconditional offer; **se rendre sans c.** to surrender unconditionally; **sous c.** conditionally; **acheter qch sous c.** to buy sth on approval; **d'accord, mais à une c.** OK, but on one condition; **tu peux partir quand tu veux, à c. de me prévenir** *ou* **à c. que tu me préviennes** you can leave when you like on condition that *or* provided *or* providing (that) you let me know; **tu peux y aller à la c. d'être rentrée à dix heures** you can go, provided *or* so long as *or* on condition that you're back by ten o'clock

(c) conditions (*d'une vente, d'un accord etc*) terms; **conditions d'un contrat** terms and conditions of a contract; **conditions de crédit** credit terms; **conditions de discompte** discount terms; **conditions d'entrée** entry requirements; **conditions de faveur** preferential terms; **conditions de livraison** delivery conditions; **conditions de paiement** terms of payment; **conditions de transport** conditions of carriage, conditions of transport; **conditions générales de vente** general (terms and) conditions of sale; **conditions particulières** (*d'un billet etc*) restrictions; **conditions particulières de vente** special conditions of sale

(d) (*sort*) condition; **la c. humaine** the human condition; *Jur* **la c. des étrangers** foreigners' (legal) status; **il faut transformer la c. des ouvriers** the workers' lot needs to be changed

(e) (*classe sociale*) station, status; **se marier avec qn de sa c.** to marry sb of the same social status; **se marier au-dessus/au-dessous de sa c.** to marry above/below one's station; *Arch* **personne de c.** person of rank

(f) *Arch* **être de** *ou* **en c. chez qn** to be in service with sb

conditionné [kɔ̃disjɔne] *adj* **(a) à air c.** air-conditioned; **il y a l'air c. dans toutes les pièces** there's air-conditioning in every room **(b)** *Com* **viande conditionnée** pre-packed meat **(c)** *Phil, Méd, Psy* (*proposition, réflexe*) conditioned

conditionnel, -elle [kɔ̃disjɔnɛl] **1** *adj* conditional **2** *nm* [①A50-1,13; B31-32,3] *Gram* conditional (mood)

conditionnellement [kɔ̃disjɔnɛlmɑ̃] *adv* conditionally

conditionnement [kɔ̃disjɔnmɑ̃] *nm* **(a)** (*d'air*) conditioning **(b)** *Com* (*fait d'emballer, emballage*) packaging; **c. d'expédition** shipping package **(c)** *Psy* conditioning

conditionner [kɔ̃disjɔne] *vt* **(a)** (*air*) to condition **(b)** (*être la condition de*) to govern; **la météo conditionne l'époque de la récolte** harvest time is determined by the weather conditions; **sa signature conditionne la validité du contrat** his signature is required for the contract to be valid **(c)** *Com* (*emballer*) to package **(d)** *Psy* (*qn*) to condition

conditionneur, -euse [kɔ̃disjɔnœr, -øz] **1** *nm* **c. d'air** air conditioner **2** *n Com* (*emballeur*) packer

condoléances [kɔ̃dɔleɑ̃s] *nfpl* condolences; **offrir** *ou* **présenter ses c.** to offer one's condolences *or* sympathy; **toutes mes c.** (please accept) my condolences *or* my deepest sympathy

condom [kɔ̃dɔm] *nm* condom

condominium [kɔ̃dɔminjɔm] *nm Pol* condominium

condor [kɔ̃dɔr] *nm* condor

conductance [kɔ̃dyktɑ̃s] *nf Él* conductance

conducteur, -trice [kɔ̃dyktœr, -tris] **1** *n Aut* driver; (*de machine*) operator; **c. ivre** drink-driver, drunk driver; **c. de bestiaux** drover; **c. d'autobus** bus driver; **c. de camions** truck *or Br* lorry driver; *Aut* **siège (du) c.** driver's seat; **c. de travaux** clerk of the works, (works) foreman; **c. d'hommes** leader of men **2** *nm* **(a)** *Él, Phys* (*de chaleur, d'électricité etc*) conductor **(b)** *Él* (*fil*) lead (wire), main **3** *adj Phys, Él* conductive, conducting

conductibilité [kɔ̃dyktibilite] *nf Phys, Él* conductivity

conductible [kɔ̃dyktibl] *adj Phys, Él* conductive

conduction [kɔ̃dyksjɔ̃] *nf Phys etc* conduction

conductivité [kɔ̃dyktivite] *nf Él* conductivity

conduire [kɔ̃dɥir] (*prp* **conduisant**; *pp* **conduit**; *pr ind* **je conduis, n. conduisons, ils conduisent**; *impf* **je conduisais**; *p hist* **je conduisis**; *fu* **je conduirai) 1** *vt* **(a)** (*emmener*) to take; (*en voiture*) to take, to drive; **j'ai dû le c. chez le dentiste de toute urgence** I had to rush him to the dentist; **c.**

qn à la gare to take *or* drive sb to the station; **on la conduisit à sa chambre** she was shown *or* taken to her room

(**b**) (*mener*) (*cheval, aveugle etc*) to lead; **c. qn à faire qch** to lead sb to do sth; **ses pas la conduisirent jusqu'à la chapelle** her footsteps led her to the chapel; **les traces de sang nous conduisirent jusqu'au lieu du crime** the bloodstains led us to the scene of the crime; **c. ses hommes au combat** to lead one's men into battle; **cela va nous c. à la catastrophe/ruine** it's going to lead us to disaster/ruin; **c. qn au désespoir/suicide** to drive sb to despair/suicide; **c'est l'appât du gain qui conduit tous ses actes** the thirst for wealth dictates his every action

(**c**) (*piloter*) (*voiture etc*) to drive; (*bateau*) to steer

(**d**) (*l'eau, le gaz etc*) to carry, to convey; **corps qui conduit bien l'électricité** good conductor of electricity

(**e**) (*diriger*) (*entreprise, affaire*) to manage, to run; **c. un orchestre** to conduct an orchestra

2 *vi* (**a**) *Aut* to drive; **elle conduit bien** she is a good driver

(**b**) (*mener*) to lead; **quel est le chemin qui conduit à la gare?** which is the way to the station?; **cette porte ne conduit nulle part** this door doesn't lead anywhere; **elle se laissa c. comme une enfant jusqu'à la cuisine** she let herself be led like a child into the kitchen

3 se conduire *vpr* (**a**) (*se diriger*) (*d'un engin*) **ça se conduit comment?** how do you drive it?

(**b**) (*se comporter*) to behave; **se c. mal** (*d'un enfant*) to behave badly, to misbehave; **se c. bien/mal avec qn** to behave well/badly towards sb

conduit [kɔ̃dɥi] *nm* (**a**) *Tech* conduit, pipe; *Constr, MecE* **c. d'aération** air duct; **c. de ventilation** ventilation shaft; *Naut* **c. de chaîne** hawse hole; *Aut* **c. d'aspiration** suction pipe; *Aut* **c. de carburant** fuel pipe; *Aut* **conduits d'échappement** exhaust manifold (**b**) *Anat* **c. auditif** auditory canal, *Spéc* meatus; **c. lacrymal** tear *or Spec* lachrymal duct; **c. urinaire** urinary canal

conduite [kɔ̃dɥit] *nf* (**a**) (*action d'accompagner*) **les chiens qui assurent la c. du troupeau** the dogs which drive the herd; *F* **faire un bout de c. à qn** to go part of the way with sb

(**b**) (*de voiture, charrette etc*) driving; (*de bateau, ballon*) steering; **c. à gauche/droite** (*d'une voiture*) left-/right-hand drive; (*d'un pays*) driving on the left/right; **ma voiture a la c. à gauche** my car is left-hand drive; **leçons de c.** driving lessons; **c. dangereuse** dangerous driving; **c. accompagnée** learning to drive accompanied by someone holding a full driving licence

(**c**) (*d'une entreprise, des affaires, opérations*) management, running; (*d'une armée, flotte etc*) command; (*d'une guerre*) conduct; **être sous la c. de qn** (*suivre des ordres*) to be under sb's leadership; (*suivre des conseils*) to be under sb's guidance; **c. des travaux** supervision of works

(**d**) (*comportement*) behaviour, *US* behavior, conduct; **je ne sais vraiment plus quelle c. adopter avec elle** I really don't know any more what line to take with her; **c'est ma seule ligne de c.** it's my guiding principle; **mauvaise c.** bad behaviour, misbehaviour, misconduct; **il a été relâché pour bonne c.** he was released for good behaviour; **adopter une c. différente** to start to behave differently; **un écart de c.** a misdemeanour; *Vieilli* **il manque de c.** he has no manners, he doesn't know how to behave; *Hum* **s'acheter une c.** to turn over a new leaf; *Scol* **zéro de c.** no marks for conduct

(**e**) *Tech* pipe, conduit, duct; **c. à air** *ou* **d'air** air duct; **c. d'eau** water pipe *or* main(s); **c. de gaz** gas pipe *or* main(s); **c. souple** hose, flexible pipe; **tuyau de c.** conduit pipe; *Aut* **c. d'arrivée du combustible** supply pipe

▶ **conduite**: **c. accompagnée** learning to drive accompanied by someone holding a full driving licence; *Psy* **c. d'échec** defeatist behaviour; **c. en état d'ivresse** drunk driving; *HydE etc* **c. forcée** (pressure) pipeline; *Aut* **c. fractionnée** stop-go driving; *Aut* **c. de frein** brake line; **c. intérieure** saloon (car), *Am* sedan; **c. montante** flow pipe, rising main; **c. normale** (*de boîte auto*) drive

condyle [kɔ̃dil] *nm Anat* condyle

cône [kon] *nm* (*objet, forme*) cone; **en forme de c.** cone-shaped; **c. de pin** pine cone; *Géol* **c. de déjection** alluvial cone; *Astron* **c. d'ombre** (*d'une planète etc*) umbra; *Naut* **c. de tempête** storm cone; **c. de signalisation** signal cone; **c. de chantier** traffic cone; *Aut* **c. d'embrayage** clutch cone; *Aut* **c. de friction** friction cone; *Aut* **c. de synchronisation** synchromesh cone, baulking cone

confection [kɔ̃fɛksjɔ̃] *nf* (**a**) (*d'un vêtement etc*) making; (*d'un repas*) preparation, making; **elle nous a offert des gâteaux de sa c.** she offered us some of her home-made cakes (**b**) (*industrie*) (ready-to-wear) clothing industry; **robe/vêtements de c.** ready-made *or* off-the-peg dress/clothes; **maison de c.** (ready-to-wear) clothes company; **travailler dans la c.** to work in the clothing industry *or F* rag trade

confectionner [kɔ̃fɛksjɔne] *vt* (*robe*) to make; (*plat*) to prepare, to make

confectionneur, -euse [kɔ̃fɛksjɔnœr, -øz] *n* clothes manufacturer

confédéral, -ale, -aux, -ales [kɔ̃federal, -o] *adj* confederal; **débat c.** debate within the confederation

confédération [kɔ̃federasjɔ̃] *nf* confederation, confederacy

confédéré [kɔ̃federe] **1** *adj* (*nations*) confederate; *Ind, Pol* **syndicat non c.** non-affiliated union **2** *n Hist* **les Confédérés** the Confederates

confédérer [kɔ̃federe] *vt* (**je confédère, n. confédérons; je confédérai**) to confederate

confer [kɔ̃fɛr] *vt* (*impératif*) cf, compare

conférence [kɔ̃ferɑ̃s] *nf* (**a**) (*congrès, colloque*) conference, meeting; **tenir c.** to hold a conference; **être en c.** to be in a meeting (**b**) *Univ etc* (*exposé*) lecture; **maître de conférences** lecturer; **salle de conférences** lecture room; **faire une c. sur l'alcoolisme** to lecture *or* to give a lecture on alcoholism

▶ **conférence**: **c. au sommet** summit (conference); *Com, Naut* **c. maritime** shipping conference; **c. de presse** press conference; *Journ* **c. de rédaction** (editors') conference

conférencier, -ière [kɔ̃ferɑ̃sje, -jɛr] *n* lecturer, speaker; *Univ* lecturer; **c. invité** guest speaker

conférer [kɔ̃fere] (**je confère, n. conférons; je conférerai**) **1** *vt* (**a**) (*privilèges etc*) to confer, to bestow (**à** on); **c. le grade de docteur à qn** to confer a doctor's degree on sb; **ils lui ont conféré tous les pouvoirs** they invested him with *or* granted him full authority; **par les pouvoirs qui me sont conférés** by the authority vested in me (**b**) (*textes*) to compare, to collate **2** *vi* to confer (**avec** with); **nous avons conféré de l'affaire** we talked the matter over, we conferred on the matter

confesse [kɔ̃fɛs] *nf* **aller/être à c.** to go to/to be at confession

confesser [kɔ̃fese] **1** *vt* (**a**) (*reconnaître*) to confess, to admit; **je confesse mon ignorance** I confess *or* admit my ignorance; **j'ai menti, je vous le confesse, mais ...** I admit *or* confess I lied, but ..., I lied, I admit it, but ...; **il confesse qu'il s'est trompé** he admits he was mistaken

(**b**) *Rel* (*ses péchés*) to confess; (*Dieu etc*) to declare one's belief in; (*sa foi*) to confess

(**c**) (*du prêtre*) (*pénitent*) to confess; *Fig F* **on trouvera les moyens de le c.** we'll find a way to make him talk

2 *vi* **ce prêtre ne confesse pas** this priest doesn't hear confessions

3 se confesser *vpr* to confess; *Rel* to confess (one's sins); *Rel* **se c. toutes les semaines** to go to confession every week

confesseur [kɔ̃fɛsœr] *nm* (**a**) *Rel, Fig* (father) confessor (**b**) *Hist* (*de sa religion, foi*) confessor

confession [kɔ̃fɛsjɔ̃] *nf* (**a**) (*aveu*) confession, admission; **faire la c. de qch** to confess to sth, to own up to sth; **je vais vous faire une c.** I've got a confession to make to you (**b**) *Rel* (*aveu*) confession; *F* **on te donnerait le bon Dieu sans c.** you look as though butter wouldn't melt in your mouth (**c**) *Rel* (*par un prêtre*) hearing of confession; **entendre qn en c.** to hear sb's confession (**d**) (*croyance*) denomination, faith, religion; **des élèves de toutes confessions** pupils of all denominations; **une école avec des élèves de toutes confessions** a multi-denominational school

confessional, -aux [kɔ̃fɛsjɔnal, -o] *nm Rel* confessional

confessionnel, -elle [kɔ̃fɛsjɔnɛl] *adj* (*querelles, affaires*) denominational

confetti [kɔ̃feti] *nm* [①A13,7] (piece of) confetti; **confettis** confetti; *F* **tu peux en faire des confettis!** you can chuck it out, you can throw it in the bin

confiance [kɔ̃fjɑ̃s] *nf* (**a**) (*foi*) trust, confidence, faith; **avoir c. en** *ou* **faire c. à qn/qch** to trust sb/sth, to have confidence *or* faith in sb/sth; **il n'a pas c. dans les médecins** he doesn't trust doctors, he has no confidence *or* faith in doctors; **elle a une c. aveugle en toi** she trusts you blindly *or* implicitly; **acheter qch en toute c.** to buy sth with complete confidence; **il me faut un homme de c.** I need a man I can trust *or* rely on; **c'est l'homme de c. du président** he's the one who has the president confidence; **comment regagner sa c.?** how can I/we/*etc* win back *or* regain his confidence *or* trust?; **abuser de la c. de qn** to abuse sb's trust; **digne de c.** trustworthy, reliable; **maison de c.** reliable firm; **c'est un poste** *ou* **emploi de c.** it's a position of trust; **avec c.** (*avec espoir*) confidently; **je vous parle en toute c.** I know I can trust you (with what I have to say); **tu sais que tu peux me faire c.** you know you can trust me; **faites-moi c.** trust me; *F* (*croyez-moi*) believe me; *Pol* **vote de c.** vote of confidence; **un climat de c. économique** a climate of economic confidence (**b**) (*assurance*) confidence; **manquer de c. en soi** to lack (self)-assurance *or* (self)-confidence

confiant [kɔ̃fjɑ̃] *adj* (**a**) (*qui fait confiance*) trusting, trustful (**b**) (*optimiste*) (*nature*) confident (**dans** in) (**c**) (*qui a confiance en soi*) (*manières etc*) (self-)confident, (self-) assured

confidence [kɔ̃fidɑ̃s] *nf* confidence; **faire une c. à qn** to confide something to sb, to tell sb a secret; **il ne me fait jamais de c.** he never confides in me; **faire c. de qch à qn** to confide sth to sb; **mettre qn dans la c.** to let sb into the secret; **dire qch en c.** to say sth in confidence *or* confidentially; **confidences sur l'oreiller** pillow talk

confident, -ente [kɔ̃fidɑ̃, -ɑ̃t] *n* confidant, *f* confidante

confidentialité [kɔ̃fidɑ̃sjalite] *nf* confidentiality; *Ordinat* **c. des données** data privacy

confidentiel, -ielle [kɔ̃fidɑ̃sjɛl] *adj* confidential; **à titre c.** confidentially, in confidence; (*non officiel*) off the record; **succès c.** modest *or* limited success

confidentiellement [kɔ̃fidɑ̃sjɛlmɑ̃] *adv* confidentially, in confidence

confier [kɔ̃fje] (*impf, pr sub* **n. confiions, v. confiiez**) **1** *vt* (**a**) (*laisser*) to entrust; **c. qch à qn** to entrust sb with sth, to entrust sth to sb; **c. qch à la garde de qn** to entrust sth to sb's care; **je leur ai confié les enfants** I left the children with them; **je n'oserais pas c. mes économies à cette banque** I wouldn't dare entrust my savings to this bank *or* entrust this bank with my savings

(**b**) (*dire*) to confide; **c. qch à qn** to confide sth to sb, to tell sb sth in confidence; **est-ce que je peux te c. un secret?** can I tell you a secret?, can I share a secret (with you)?

2 se confier *vpr* (**a**) *Fml* (*s'en remettre*) **se c. à qn/qch** to put one's trust in sb/sth

(**b**) (*s'épancher*) **se c. à qn** to confide in sb; **il ne se confie jamais** he never confides in anyone

configurable [kɔ̃figyrabl] *adj Ordinat* configurable

configuration [kɔ̃figyrasjɔ̃] *nf* (**a**) configuration; (*de bâtiment*) form, shape; (*du terrain*) lie (**b**) *Ordinat* configuration; **c. matérielle** hardware configuration

configurer [kɔ̃figyre] *vt Ordinat etc* to configure

confiné [kɔ̃fine] *adj* (**a**) (*atmosphère etc*) enclosed; (*air*) stale (**b**) (*enfermé*) shut away *or* up; **vivre c. chez soi** to live shut away *or* up indoors

confinement [kɔ̃finmɑ̃] *nm* confinement

confiner [kɔ̃fine] **1** *vi* **c. à** *ou* **avec un pays** (*d'un pays etc*) to border on *or* adjoin a country; *Fig* **courage qui confine à la témérité** courage verging *or* bordering on foolhardiness **2** *vt* to confine, to shut away *or* up **3 se confiner** *vpr* to confine oneself; **se c. chez soi** to shut oneself away *or* up indoors

confins [kɔ̃fɛ̃] *nmpl* (*de pays, d'état*) confines, borders; **aux c. de la science et de la métaphysique** on the border between science and metaphysics

confire [kɔ̃fir] *vt* (*prp* **confisant**; *pp* **confit**; *pr ind* **je confis, n. confisons, ils confisent**; *impf* **je confisais**; *p hist* **je confis**; *fu* **je confirai**) (*fruits etc*) to preserve; (*écorce, zeste etc*) to candy; **c. qch au sel/au vinaigre** to salt sth down/to pickle sth

confirmatif, -ive [kɔ̃firmatif, -iv] *adj* (*déclaration*) corroborative; (*jugement*) confirmative

confirmation [kɔ̃firmasjɔ̃] *nf* (**a**) (*de nouvelle etc*) confirmation, corroboration; **c. écrite** written confirmation; **c. de commande/de réservation** confirmation of an order/ reservation; **c. d'un jugement** confirmation of a sentence; **il m'en a donné c.** he gave me confirmation of it; **c'est la c. de ce que je pensais** that (just) confirms what I thought; **en c. de** in confirmation of (**b**) *Rel* confirmation; **donner la c. à qn** to confirm sb

confirmer [kɔ̃firme] **1** *vt* (**a**) (*nouvelle, jugement etc*) to confirm; **c. un traité** to ratify a treaty; **cela me confirme dans mon opinion** that confirms *or* strengthens me in my opinion; **elle n'a pas été confirmée dans ses fonctions** she was not given the job (which she had been doing temporarily); **l'exception confirme la règle** the exception proves the rule

(**b**) *Rel* (*qn*) to confirm

2 se confirmer *vpr* (*d'un rapport, de doutes etc*) to be confirmed; **le bruit ne s'est pas confirmé** the rumour proved false; **je pensais qu'il était bête et là, ça se confirme** I thought he was stupid and there's the proof of it *or* and I've been proved right

confiscation [kɔ̃fiskasjɔ̃] *nf* (*de propriété etc*) confiscation, seizure

confiserie [kɔ̃fizri] *nf* (**a**) (*de fruits etc*) preserving in sugar (**b**) (*magasin*) confectioner's (shop), *Br* sweetshop, *Am* candy store (**c**) (*bonbon*) *Br* sweet, *Am* candy; **des confiseries** confectionery, *Br* sweets, *Am* candy

confiseur, -euse [kɔ̃fizœr, -øz] *n* confectioner

confisquer [kɔ̃fiske] *vt* (*marchandises, propriété etc*) to confiscate, to seize; **le prof m'a confisqué ma balle** the teacher confiscated my ball; **le président veut c. le pouvoir** the president wants to seize power

confit [kɔ̃fi] **1** *adj* **fruits confits** crystallized *or* candied fruit; *Fig* **être c. en dévotion** to be steeped in piety **2** *nm Culin* **c. d'oie/de canard** conserve of goose/of duck

confiture [kɔ̃fityr] *nf Culin* jam; **c. de fraises** strawberry jam; **c. d'oranges** (orange) marmalade; *Fig* **ce serait donner de la c. aux cochons** that would be throwing *or* casting pearls before swine

confiturerie [kɔ̃fityrri] *nf* (**a**) (*commerce*) jam manufacture (**b**) (*fabrique*) jam factory

confiturier [kɔ̃fityrje] *nm* jam maker *or* manufacturer

conflagration [kɔ̃flagrasjɔ̃] *nf* cataclysm

conflictuel, -elle [kɔ̃fliktɥɛl] *adj* (*témoignages, intérêts etc*) conflicting; **situation conflictuelle** situation of conflict; **ils ont des rapports très conflictuels** they have a very adversarial relationship

conflit [kɔ̃fli] *nm* (**a**) (*divergence*) conflict; (*d'intérêts*) conflict, clash; **être en c.** to be at variance *or F* loggerheads (**avec** with); (*d'intérêts*) to conflict, to clash (**avec** with); **entrer en c. avec qn** to come into conflict with sb, to clash with sb; **le c. des générations** the generation gap; **arbitrage des conflits internationaux** arbitration of international disputes; **conflits sociaux** industrial disputes; **c. du travail** industrial dispute; **c. salarial** pay dispute; *Jur* **tribunal des conflits** = jurisdictional court which decides whether a matter should be dealt with by a civil or other court (**b**) (*lutte armée*) **c. (armé)** (armed) conflict, war

confluence [kɔ̃flyɑ̃s] *nf* confluence

confluent [kɔ̃flyɑ̃] *nm* (*de fleuves, veines etc*) confluence

confluer [kɔ̃flye] *vi* to meet, to join, to unite; **l'Oise conflue avec la Seine** the Oise flows into the Seine

confondant [kɔ̃fɔ̃dɑ̃] *adj* (*qui met en confusion*) confusing; (*qui trouble*) astounding

confondre [kɔ̃fɔ̃dr] **1** *vt* (**a**) (*réunir*) to merge, to mingle, to intermingle; **toutes tendances confondues, les électeurs ont voté en masse pour lui** voters of all political tendencies voted massively for him

(**b**) (*mélanger*) (*noms*) to confuse, to mix up; **je les confonds toujours** I always confuse them *or* mix them up, I always get them confused *or* mixed up

(**c**) (*sidérer*) (*qn*) to astound, to stagger; **son insolence me confond** I'm astounded by his insolence, his insolence astounds me

(**d**) (*démasquer*) (*criminel etc*) to find, to track down; **c. un menteur** to show up a liar

2 *vi* to be mistaken; **tu dois c., ce n'est pas ça** you must be mistaken, that's not it at all

3 se confondre *vpr* (**a**) (*de couleurs etc*) to merge, to blend (**en** into)

(**b**) (*de ruisseaux etc*) to merge, to flow into each other; (*d'intérêts etc*) to merge, to be identical; **se c. en excuses/ remerciements** to apologize profusely/to be profuse in one's thanks; **se c. en excuses/remerciements devant qn** to apologize profusely to sb/to thank sb profusely; **leurs voix se confondent au loin** their voices merge *or* mingle in the distance

confondu [kɔ̃fɔ̃dy] *adj* (**a**) (*décontenancé*) disconcerted; **je suis tout c. de votre bonté** I am overwhelmed by your kindness (**b**) (*sidéré*) astounded, dumbfounded (**de** at); **en rester confondu** to be (left) dumbfounded

conformation [kɔ̃fɔrmasjɔ̃] *nf* (*de collines, parties du corps etc*) conformation, structure

conforme [kɔ̃fɔrm] *adj* (**a**) (*identique*) **copie c. à l'original** exact copy; *Admin* **pour copie c.** certified true copy; *Fig* **elle est la copie c. de sa mère** she is the exact *or* very image of her mother (**b**) (*qui correspond à*) **il mène une vie c. à ses moyens** he lives according to his means; **la réalisation n'est pas c. à ce qui avait été prévu** it is not being carried out in keeping with *or* in accordance with what was agreed; **les sanitaires ne sont pas conformes** the sanitary installations are not standard; **non c.** (*pensée, idée*) unorthodox

conformé [kɔ̃fɔrme] *adj* **bien c.** (*enfant etc*) well-formed; **mal c.** (*membre etc*) misshapen

conformément [kɔ̃fɔrmemɑ̃] *adv* **c. à** in accordance with; **c. à la loi** according to *or* in accordance with the law; **c. à vos ordres** in accordance with your orders; **c. à ce qui a été prévu** according to *or* in accordance with what was planned; **tout se passe c. aux plans** everything's going according to plan

conformer [kɔ̃fɔrme] **1** *vt* to model (**à** on); **c. sa vie à certains principes** to shape one's life according to certain principles **2 se conformer** *vpr* **se c. à qch** to conform to sth, to comply with *or* abide by sth; **se c. à la règle** to conform to the rule; *Com* **se c. au modèle** to keep (to) the pattern

conformisme [kɔ̃fɔrmism] *nm (traditionalisme)* conformism, conventionalism; *Rel* conformism, conformity

conformiste [kɔ̃fɔrmist] **1** *n (traditionaliste)* conformist, conventionalist; *Rel (de l'Église anglicane)* conformist **2** *adj* conformist

conformité [kɔ̃fɔrmite] *nf (ressemblance)* similarity; *Rel* conformity; *(d'un produit aux normes)* compliance; **en c. avec** in accordance with; **être en c. de goûts avec qn** to have similar tastes to sb

confort [kɔ̃fɔr] *nm* comfort; **hôtel avec tout le c. moderne** hotel with every modern convenience *or F* with all mod cons; **manquer de c.** to be lacking in comfort, to be uncomfortable; **maison sans c.** a fairly primitive house; **elle aime bien son petit c.** she likes her creature comforts *or* her little comforts; **c. d'emploi** *(d'un ordinateur etc)* user-friendliness, ease of use; **c. visuel** *(d'un écran)* easiness on the eye; **médicament de c.** = medicine not considered essential and not reimbursed by Social Security

confortable [kɔ̃fɔrtabl] *adj (fauteuil, maison, chaussures etc) Fig* comfortable; *(financièrement)* comfortable, well off, comfortably off; **des appointements confortables** a comfortable *or* good salary; **une vie c.** a comfortable life(-style); *Fig* **il est plus c. de penser que tout va bien** it's easier *or* more comfortable to think that everything is going well

confortablement [kɔ̃fɔrtabləmɑ̃] *adv* comfortably; **installe-toi c.** make yourself comfortable; **être c. rémunéré** to be on a good salary, to be well paid

conforter [kɔfɔrte] *vt* to reinforce, to strengthen, to confirm; *(position, avance)* to consolidate; **cela me conforte dans mon opinion** that reinforces *or* strengthens *or* confirms my opinion

confraternel, -elle [kɔ̃fratɛrnɛl] *adj* fraternal, brotherly

confraternité [kɔ̃fratɛrnite] *nf* brotherliness

confrère [kɔ̃frɛr] *nm (de profession)* colleague; *(de société)* fellow member

confrérie [kɔ̃freri] *nf Rel* brotherhood, confraternity

confrontation [kɔ̃frɔ̃tasjɔ̃] *nf* **(a)** *Jur (d'un accusé avec un témoin)* confrontation, confronting; *Fig (d'opinions, d'idéaux etc)* clash, conflict **(b)** *(comparaison)* comparison **(à, avec** with); *(de textes)* comparison, collation

confronter [kɔ̃frɔ̃te] **1** *vt* **(a)** to confront; *(prisonnier)* to confront, to bring face to face **(avec, à** with); **être confronté à un problème** to be confronted with a problem **(b)** *(comparer)* to compare **(avec, à** with); *(textes)* to collate **2 se confronter** *vpr* **se c. à un adversaire** to confront an opponent; **nous nous sommes confrontés** we confronted each other **(au sujet de** about)

confucéen, -éenne [kɔ̃fyseɛ̃, -eɛn] *adj* Confucian

confucianisme [kɔ̃fysjanism] *nm* Confucianism

confus [kɔ̃fy] *adj* **(a)** *(mélangé) (masse etc)* confused, jumbled, chaotic; *(explication)* confused, muddled; *(bruit)* indistinct; *(vision)* dim, blurred; *(style, texte)* obscure, unclear; **une affaire pour le moins confuse** a confused *or* muddled business to say the least

(b) *(embarrassé)* embarrassed, abashed; **je suis c.** *(après un faux pas)* I'm so embarrassed, I don't know where to put myself; *(devant votre bonté)* I don't know what to say; **je suis c. de vous déranger** I'm so sorry to disturb you

confusément [kɔ̃fyzemɑ̃] *adv* confusedly, vaguely, indistinctly; **j'entrevoyais c. la solution du problème** I was slowly beginning to see a solution to the problem

confusion [kɔ̃fyzjɔ̃] *nf* **(a)** *(désordre)* confusion, disorder, disarray; **il a réussi à s'échapper, profitant de la c. générale** he managed to escape in the general confusion; **mettre la c. dans l'assemblée** to throw the audience into confusion; **jeter la c. dans les esprits** to confuse people; *Méd* **c. mentale** mental aberration; **un moment de c.** a moment of confusion, a moment's confusion

(b) *(erreur) (de noms, dates etc)* mix-up, confusion; **il y a eu c. entre deux personnes** they got two people mixed up *or* confused; **c'est une grossière c.** it's a stupid mix-up

(c) *(gêne)* embarrassment, confusion; **être rouge de c.** to blush with embarrassment, *Fml* to be covered in confusion

(d) *Jur* **avec c. des peines** the sentences to run concurrently

congé [kɔ̃ʒe] *nm* **(a)** *(vacances)* holiday, *Am* vacation; *Mil* leave; **il ne me reste plus de c. à prendre** I've used up all my holiday (entitlement); **en c.** on holiday, *Am* on vacation; *Mil* on leave; **un après-midi de c.** an afternoon off; **on a c. lundi** we've got Monday off, Monday's a holiday; **prendre c. de qn** to take (one's) leave of sb; **donner c. à qn** to dismiss sb

(b) *(avis de renvoi)* notice; **donner son c. à qn** to give sb his notice; **demander son c.** to hand in *or* give in one's notice, to give notice; **donner c. à un locataire** to give a tenant notice (to quit)

(c) *(autorisation)* authorization, permit; *(de vin en douane)* release; *Naut* **c. de navigation** clearance certificate

▶ **congé:** *Admin* **c. annuel** annual leave, annual holiday, *Am* vacation leave; **c. de longue durée** extended leave; **c. de maladie** sick leave; **c. de maternité** maternity leave; **c. parental d'éducation** = maternity/paternity leave; **c. payé** paid holiday *or* leave, *Am* paid vacation; **c. pour convenance personnelle** leave for personal reasons, compassionate leave; **c. sabbatique** sabbatical

congédiable [kɔ̃ʒedjabl] *adj* liable to be dismissed at any time; *Mil* due for discharge

congédier [kɔ̃ʒedje] *vt (impf, pr sub* **n. congédiions, v. congédiiez) (a)** *(employé)* to dismiss **(b)** *(visiteur)* to dismiss; *Mil, Naut (hommes)* to discharge

congelable [kɔ̃ʒlabl] *adj* suitable for freezing, freezable; **aliment non c.** foodstuff unsuitable for freezing

congélateur [kɔ̃ʒelatœr] *nm* freezer, deep-freeze

congélation [kɔ̃ʒelasjɔ̃] *nf (d'aliments)* (deep-)freezing; *(de l'eau etc)* freezing; *(de l'huile)* congealing; **point de c. de l'eau** freezing point of water; **sac (de) c.** freezer bag

congeler [kɔ̃ʒle] **(il congèle; il congèlera) 1** *vt (aliments)* to (deep-)freeze; *(eau etc)* to freeze; **viande congelée** frozen meat; **ne pas c.** do not freeze **2 se congeler** *vpr* to freeze

congénère [kɔ̃ʒenɛr] **1** *adj Biol* congeneric; *Anat (muscle)* congenerous **2** *nm Biol* congener; *F* **lui et ses congénères** him and his sort *or* his like

congénital, -ale, -aux, -ales [kɔ̃ʒenital, -o] *adj* congenital; *Méd* **malformation congénitale** congenital malformation; *F* **inconscience congénitale** innate *or* congenital thoughtlessness

congère [kɔ̃ʒɛr] *nf* snowdrift

congestif, -ive [kɔ̃ʒɛstif, -iv] *adj Méd* congestive

congestion [kɔ̃ʒɛstjɔ̃] *nf Méd* congestion; **c. cérébrale** stroke; **c. pulmonaire** congestion of the lungs

congestionné [kɔ̃ʒɛstjɔne] *adj (visage)* flushed, red; *(routes)* congested; **les routes sont très congestionnées** the roads are very congested, there's a lot of congestion on the roads

congestionner [kɔ̃ʒɛstjɔne] **1** *vt* **(a)** *Méd* to congest; *(visage)* to flush **(b)** *(boucher)* to block, to congest; **les voitures congestionnent la rue** the cars are blocking the street **2 se congestionner** *vpr* to become congested

conglomérat [kɔ̃glɔmera] *nm Écon, Géol* conglomerate

conglomération [kɔ̃glɔmerasjɔ̃] *nf* conglomeration

conglomérer [kɔ̃glɔmere] **(je conglomère, n. conglomérons; je conglomérerai) 1** *vt* to conglomerate **2 se conglomérer** *vpr* to conglomerate

Congo [kɔ̃go] *nm* **le C.** the Congo

congolais, -aise [kɔ̃gɔlɛ, -ɛz] **1** *adj* Congolese **2** *n* **C.** Congolese **3** *nm Culin* coconut cake

congratulations [kɔ̃gratylasjɔ̃] *nfpl* congratulations; **mes c. pour ta réussite** congratulations on your success

congratuler [kɔ̃gratyle] **1** *vt (qn)* to congratulate **(pour** on) **2 se congratuler** *vpr* to congratulate oneself, *F* to pat oneself on the back

congre [kɔ̃gr] *nm* conger (eel)

congrégation [kɔ̃gregasjɔ̃] *nf* **(a)** *Rel (communauté)* community *(group of monasteries)*; *(de cardinaux)* congregation **(b)** *Fig* assembly

congrès [kɔ̃grɛ] *nm* conference, convention; **C. des États-Unis** United States Congress; **membre du C.** congressman, *f* congresswoman; **palais des congrès** conference centre; **c. annuel** *(d'un parti politique)* annual conference

congressiste [kɔ̃grɛsist] *n* conference participant, *Am* conventioneer; *Pol* conference delegate

congru [kɔ̃gry] *adj* **(a) portion congrue** (income providing a) bare living; *Rel (de prêtre)* emolument; **réduire qn à la portion congrue** to put sb on short allowance **(b)** *Math* congruent **(c)** *Arch (adéquat)* sufficient, adequate

congruence [kɔ̃gryɑ̃s] *nf Math* congruence

congruent [kɔ̃gryɑ̃] *adj Math* congruent

conifère [kɔnifɛr] *nm Bot* conifer

conique [kɔnik, ko-] *adj* **(a)** *Géom* conical, cone-shaped; *Math* **section c.** conic section **(b)** *MecE etc (tige, goupille etc)* coned, tapering; **engrenage c.** bevel gearing

conjectural, -ale, -aux, -ales [kɔ̃ʒɛktyral, -o] *adj* conjectural

conjecture [kɔ̃ʒɛktyr] *nf* conjecture, surmise; **se perdre en conjectures** to get lost *or* lose oneself in conjecture(s); **ce n'est que pure c.** it's sheer conjecture

conjecturer [kɔ̃ʒɛktyre] **1** *vt* to conjecture about, to guess at **2** *vi* to conjecture, to hypothesize; **il conjecture sur ce qu'il ignore** he conjectures *or* makes guesses about things he knows nothing about

conjoint [kɔ̃ʒwɛ̃] **1** *adj* **(a)** joint, united; *Fin* **compte c.** joint account; *Jur* **legs c.** joint legacy; **légataires conjoints** colegatees **(b)** *Jur* (*marié*) married **2** *nm* spouse; **les conjoints** the husband and wife; **féliciter les conjoints** to congratulate the couple; **les conjoints n'ont pas été invités** partners weren't invited

conjointement [kɔ̃ʒwɛ̃tmɑ̃] *adv* jointly; *Jur* **c. et solidairement** jointly and severally

conjoncteur [kɔ̃ʒɔ̃ktœr] *nm Él* circuit closer

conjoncteur-disjoncteur, *pl* **conjoncteurs-disjoncteurs** *nm Aut* cut-out (valve), *Él* make-and-break (switch)

conjonctif, -ive [kɔ̃ʒɔ̃ktif, -iv] *adj* (*tissu etc*) connective, *Gram* **locution/proposition conjonctive** conjunctive phrase/clause

conjonction [kɔ̃ʒɔ̃ksjɔ̃] *nf* **(a)** (*réunion*) union; **la c. de nos efforts** our combined efforts **(b)** [①**A68-70; B55**] *Gram* conjunction; **c. de subordination/coordination** subordinating/coordinating conjunction

conjonctive [kɔ̃ʒɔ̃ktiv] *nf* (*de l'œil*) conjunctiva

conjonctivite [kɔ̃ʒɔ̃ktivit] *nf Méd* conjunctivitis; **faire** *ou* **avoir de la c.** to have conjunctivitis

conjoncture [kɔ̃ʒɔ̃ktyr] *nf* (*situation*) circumstances, situation; **dans la c. actuelle** at this (present) juncture, under the present circumstances, in the present situation; *Pol, Écon* **c. économique** overall economic situation; **étude de c.** study of the state of the economy

conjoncturel, -elle [kɔ̃ʒɔ̃ktyrɛl] *adj* relating to the current economic climate, economic; (*chômage*) cyclical; **crise conjoncturelle** economic crisis

conjoncturiste [kɔ̃ʒɔ̃ktyrist] *nm Écon* economic analyst

conjugable [kɔ̃ʒygabl] *adj Gram* conjugable

conjugaison [kɔ̃ʒygɛzɔ̃] *nf* [①**B22-23**] *Gram, Biol etc* (*de verbe, de cellules etc*) conjugation; *Fig Litt* **grâce à la c. de leurs efforts** thanks to their joint efforts

conjugal, -ale, -aux, -ales [kɔ̃ʒygal, -o] *adj* (*devoir*) marital, conjugal; **vie conjugale** married life; **le domicile c.** the marital *or* matrimonial home; **bonheur c.** wedded *or* married bliss; **le lit c.** the marriage bed

conjugalement [kɔ̃ʒygalmɑ̃] *adv* conjugally; **vivre c.** to live together as a married couple *or* as man and wife

conjugué [kɔ̃ʒyge] *adj* (*efforts etc*) joint, combined; *MecE* paired, twin; *Math, Opt* conjugate; *Bot* **feuilles conjuguées** conjugate leaves; **machines conjuguées** paired engines

conjuguer [kɔ̃ʒyge] **1** *vt* **(a)** *Gram* to conjugate **(b)** (*unir*) (*efforts*) to combine **2 se conjuguer** *vpr Gram* to be conjugated

conjuration [kɔ̃ʒyrasjɔ̃] *nf* **(a)** (*complot*) conspiracy, plot **(b)** (*charme*) exorcism, conjuration

conjuré, -ée [kɔ̃ʒyre] *n* conspirator

conjurer [kɔ̃ʒyre] **1** *vt* **(a)** (*implorer*) **c. qn de faire qch** to entreat *or* beg *or* beseech *or* implore sb to do sth; **je t'en conjure** I beg *or* beseech *or* implore you **(b)** (*écarter*) (*danger, mauvais sort etc*) to avert, to ward off **(c)** (*démon*) to cast out, to exorcise **(d)** *Arch* (*conspirer*) to plot **2 se conjurer** *vpr* to conspire (together) **(contre** against)

connaissable [kɔnɛsabl] *adj* knowable

connaissance [kɔnɛsɑ̃s] *nf* **(a)** (*savoir*) knowledge; **prendre c. de qch** to make oneself acquainted with sth, to study *or* examine sth; **avoir c. de qch** to be aware of sth; **donner c. de qch à qn, porter qch à la c. de qn** to inform sb of sth, to make sth known to sb; **il n'a jamais, à ma c., été malade** he has never, to my knowledge *or* as far as I know, had a day's illness; **en (toute) c. de cause** with full knowledge of the facts, advisedly; **je souhaite que vous preniez la décision en toute c. de cause** I hope you're making an informed decision; *Mktg* **c. de la marque** brand familiarity, brand awareness

(b) (*contact*) **faire c. avec qn, faire la c. de qn** to make sb's acquaintance, to meet sb; **quand je fis sa c.** when I first knew him; **lier c. avec qn** to strike up an acquaintance with sb; **une figure de c.** a familiar face; **en pays de c.** (*parmi des gens*) among familiar faces; *Fig* on familiar ground; **une personne de ma c.** someone I know, an acquaintance of mine

(c) (*personne*) acquaintance; **c'est une de mes connaissances** he is an acquaintance of mine; **je ne la connais pas, c'est une vague c.** I don't (really) know her, she's just an acquaintance; *F* **c'est une vieille c.** I've known him for ages, he's an old acquaintance; *F Vieilli* **je l'ai rencontré avec sa c.** I met him with his girlfriend

(d) (*maîtrise*) knowledge; *Jur* cognizance; *Phil* cognition; **la c. de soi** self-knowledge; **avoir la c. de plusieurs langues** to know several languages; **ma c. du russe/du droit** my knowledge of Russian/the law; **connaissances** knowledge; **avoir de grandes connaissances en mathématiques** to be very knowledgeable about *or* very well versed in mathematics; **elle a des connaissances en maths** she has some knowledge of maths; **avoir des connaissances sommaires sur qch** to have a basic *or* rudimentary knowledge of sth, to know the basics *or* rudiments of sth; **l'acquisition des connaissances** the acquisition of knowledge, the learning process

(e) (*conscience*) consciousness; **perdre c.** to lose consciousness; **avoir des pertes de c.** to have blackouts *or* fainting fits; **reprendre c.** to regain consciousness, to come round, to come to; **sans c.** unconscious; **il a toute sa c.** he's fully conscious

connaissement [kɔnɛsmɑ̃] *nm Naut, Com* bill of lading, waybill; **c. aérien** air waybill; **c. clausé** dirty bill; **c. de groupage** groupage bill; **c. de transbordement** transshipment bill of lading; **c. de transport combiné** combined transport bill of lading; **c. direct** through bill; **c. embarqué** shipped bill; **c. fluvial** inland waterway bill of lading; **c. maritime** marine bill of lading; **c. net** clean bill of lading; **c. périmé** stale bill

connaisseur, -euse [kɔnɛsœr, -øz] **1** *n* connoisseur, expert; **être bon c. en qch** to be an expert judge of sth **2** *adj* expert, knowledgeable; **je ne suis pas du tout c.** I'm by no means an expert; **regarder qch d'un œil c.** to look at sth with an expert eye

connaître [kɔnɛtr] (*prp* **connaissant**; *pp* **connu**; *pr ind* **je connais, il connaît, n. connaissons**; *impf* **je connaissais**; *p hist* **je connus**; *fu* **je connaîtrai**) **1** *vt* **(a)** (*détails*) to know, to be aware of, to be acquainted with; (*paroles d'une chanson*) to know; **c. les chemins** to be familiar with the roads; **tu connais la route?** do you know the way?; **je lui connaissais du talent** I knew he had talent; **faire c. qch** to bring sth to light, to make sth known; **faire c. ses intentions** to make one's intentions known; **je vous ferai c. mes intentions** I'll let you know what I intend to do; **il n'a jamais connu l'amour** he has never known *or* experienced love; **il a connu un destin tragique** his was a tragic fate; **elle n'a jamais connu la faim** she's never known hunger *or* what hunger means; **cette région connaît actuellement une famine** this region is now experiencing a famine; **je ne connais pas Milan** I don't know Milan, I'm not familiar with *or* acquainted with Milan; *F* **mais bien sûr, je ne connais que ça** it's something I'm totally familiar with, it's a subject I'm quite at home with it; **connaissez-vous la nouvelle?** have you heard the news?; **sa bonté ne connaît pas de limites** his goodness knows no bounds; **il est sorti, ni vu ni connu** he went out without anyone noticing; **elle ne connaît que son travail** she's only interested in her work, she lives for her work; *F* **elle en connaît un rayon sur la question** she knows a thing or two *or* quite a bit about the matter; **tu ne connais pas ta chance** you don't know how lucky you are, you don't know your luck; *F* **je connais la musique** *ou* **la chanson** I've heard it all before, it's the same old story

(b) (*personne*) to know, to be acquainted with; (*rencontrer*) to meet, to make the acquaintance of; **c. qn de nom/vue** to know sb by name/sight; **c. qn de réputation** to know sb by reputation, to have heard of sb; **c. son monde** to know the people one has to deal with; **méfie-toi, il connaît du monde** watch out, he knows people; **il est connu comme le loup blanc** everybody knows him *or* has heard of him; **il est connu ici** he's well known around here; **se faire c.** to introduce oneself; (*par le public etc*) to make a name for oneself, to become well-known; **je vous le ferai c.** I'll introduce him to you; *F* **j'en connais un qui ne va pas être content!** I know at least one person who's not going to be happy; *F* **je le connais par cœur/comme ma poche** I know him through and through/I can read him like a(n open) book; **ça c'est un diamant bleu ou je ne m'y connais pas!** that's a blue diamond, or I'm a Dutchman!, or I'm very much mistaken!; *F* **le foot, ça me connaît** I know all there is to know about football; *F* **si tu fais ça, je ne te connais plus** if you do that, I'll have nothing more to do with you *or* I'll disown you

(c) (*langue*) to know; (*science, art*) to know about, to be familiar with; **c. à fond** to have a thorough knowledge of, to be thoroughly conversant with; (*une langue*) to have a thorough command of; **elle connaît très bien le russe** she knows Russian very well, she has a very good command of Russian; **je ne connais pas cette théorie** I don't know *or* I'm not familiar with that theory; **il n'y connaît rien** he doesn't know anything about it

(d) (*reconnaître*) to know, to recognize; **c. le bien du mal** to know good from evil

(e) *Bible* (*femme*) to know

2 *vi Jur* **c. de qch** to take cognizance of sth

3 se connaître *vpr* **(a) se c. (soi-même)** to know oneself

(b) elle s'y connaît en hommes/en œnologie she knows all about men/wine; *F* **il s'y connaît** he's an expert (**c**) (*se rencontrer*) to meet; **ils se sont connus en 1970** they met in 1970

(**d**) **il ne se connaît plus** he has lost control of himself; **il ne se connaît plus de joie** he's beside himself with joy, he's walking on air

connard, -arde [kɔnar, -ard] *adj, n* = **conard**

connecter [kɔnεkte] **1** *vt Él, Électron* to connect; *Ordinat* **connecté** on line; **ne pas être connecté** not to be on line, to be off line; **connecté en anneau/bus/étoile** in a ring/bus/star configuration; **connecté en série** series-connected

2 se connecter *vpr Él, Électron* to be connected; *Ordinat* **se c. à un système** to log on to a system

connecteur [kɔnεktœr] *nm Él, Électron* connector; *Ordinat* **c. d'extension** expansion slot

connectivité [kɔnεktivite] *nf Ordinat* connectivity

connerie [kɔnri] *nf très F* damned *or Br* bloody stupidity; (*remarque, acte*) damned *or Br* bloody stupid thing; **c'est de la c., ne le crois pas!** it's bullshit *or* crap, don't believe it!; **tu as fait là une c. magistrale** that was bloody stupid of you; **dire** *ou* **raconter des conneries** to talk bullshit *or* crap; **ce sont des conneries** it's a load of crap *or Br* bollocks; **c'est bientôt fini, vos conneries?** will you stop pissing about!; **il a fait quelques conneries dans sa jeunesse** he did some pretty stupid things when he was young, he had a bit of a misspent youth

connétable [kɔnetabl] *nm Hist* constable

connexe [kɔnεks] *adj* connected, related

connexion [kɔnεksjɔ̃] *nf* (**a**) (*d'éléments, d'idées etc*) connection (**b**) *Él* connection

connivence [kɔnivɑ̃s] *nf* connivance, complicity; **agir/être de c. avec qn** to act/be in connivance *or* in collusion with sb, to connive with sb; **des regards de c.** conniving looks

connotation [kɔnɔtasjɔ̃] *nf* connotation

connoter [kɔnɔte] *vt* to imply, to connote; *Ling* to connote

connu [kɔny] **1** *adj* (*écrivain, chanteur etc*) well-known, famous; **c'est (un fait) bien c.!** that's a well-known fact!, everyone knows that!; **elle est bien connue, celle-là!** that's an old one!, that's an old joke! **2** *nm* **passer** *ou* **aller du c. à l'inconnu** to go from the known to the unknown

conque [kɔ̃k] *nf* (**a**) (*coquille*) conch (**b**) *Anat* external ear, *Spéc* concha

conquérant, -ante [kɔ̃kerɑ̃, -ɑ̃t] **1** *adj* (*nation etc*) conquering; *F* **air c.** swaggering air, swagger **2** *n* conqueror; **Guillaume le C.** William the Conqueror

conquérir [kɔ̃kerir] (*prp* **conquérant**; *pp* **conquis**; *pr ind* **je conquiers, n. conquérons, ils conquièrent**; *impf* **je conquérais**; *p hist* **je conquis**; *fu* **je conquerrai**) **1** *vt* (*pays, peuple*) to conquer; (*personne, animal*) to win over; **ils ont tout de suite été conquis par son charme** they were immediately won over by his charm; **se battre pour c. un marché** to fight (in order) to conquer *or* capture *or* win a market; **c. l'estime de qn** to win *or* gain sb's esteem **2 se conquérir** *vpr* to be (hard) won *or* earned

conquête [kɔ̃kεt] *nf* (**a**) (*action de conquérir*) conquest; **faire la c. d'un pays** to conquer a country; **faire la c. de qn** to make a conquest of sb; **vous avez fait sa c.** you've made a conquest!; **se lancer à la c. du pouvoir** to make a bid for power (**b**) (*territoire*) conquered territory (**c**) *F* (*personne*) conquest; **il nous a présenté sa dernière c.** he introduced us to his latest conquest

conquistador [kɔ̃kistadɔr] *nm* conquistador

consacré [kɔ̃sakre] *adj* (**a**) *Rel* (*vaisseau etc*) consecrated, sacred; (*terrain*) hallowed (**b**) (*coutume etc*) established; **selon l'expression consacrée** as the saying goes; **c. par l'usage** sanctioned by usage

consacrer [kɔ̃sakre] **1** *vt* (**a**) *Rel* (*autel, le pain et le vin etc*) to consecrate; **c. un évêque/un prêtre** to consecrate a bishop/to ordain a priest (**b**) (*sa vie à Dieu*) to dedicate (**à** to); (*son temps, énergie à qch*) to devote (**à** to); **c. sa vie à la lecture et à l'étude** to devote one's life to reading and study; **combien de temps pouvez-vous me c.?** how much time can you spare *or* give me? (**c**) (*souvenir, endroit etc*) to sanctify, to hallow (**d**) (*entériner*) to establish

2 se consacrer *vpr* **se c. à son travail/foyer** to devote oneself to one's work/family; **se c. à Dieu** to dedicate oneself to God

consanguin [kɔ̃sɑ̃gɛ̃] *adj* (**a**) **frère c. /sœur consanguine** half brother/sister (on the father's side); **mariage c.** marriage between blood relations, intermarriage (**b**) (*cheval etc*) inbred

consanguinité [kɔ̃sɑ̃g(ɥ)inite] *nf* (**a**) consanguinity (*through the father*) (**b**) (*de cheval etc*) inbreeding

consciemment [kɔ̃sjamɑ̃] *adv* consciously, knowingly, wittingly

conscience [kɔ̃sjɑ̃s] *nf* (**a**) *Physiol, Psy* consciousness; *Phil* (self-)consciousness; **perdre c.** to lose consciousness; **reprendre doucement c.** to slowly regain consciousness *or* come round; **à 80 ans elle a encore toute sa c.** at the age of 80 she is still very alert; **avoir c. de qch/d'avoir fait qch** to be aware *or* conscious of sth/of having done sth; **avoir c. de ses capacités** to be aware of one's abilities; **prendre c. de qch** to become aware of sth; **il finira par prendre c. de la gravité de la situation** he'll eventually wake up to the seriousness of the situation; **c'est la première fois que j'en ai pris c.** it's the first time that I have been aware of it; **prise de c.** sudden awareness

(**b**) (*morale*) conscience; **mauvaise c.** guilty *or* bad conscience; **j'ai bonne c.** my conscience is clear; **c'est un moyen pour se donner bonne c.** it's a way of easing one's conscience; **c. large** accommodating conscience; **écouter la voix de sa c.** to listen to (the voice of) one's conscience; *F* **il a la c. élastique** he is not over-scrupulous; **pour avoir la c. tranquille je vais vérifier que tout est bien fermé** to set my mind at rest, I'll just make sure everything's locked up; **faire qch par acquit de c.** to do sth for the sake of one's conscience; **dire qch en c.** to say sth in all consciousness; **manque de c.** unscrupulousness; **avoir qch sur la c.** to have sth on one's conscience; **ça m'est longtemps resté sur la c.** it was on my conscience *or* preyed on my mind for a long time; **liberté de c.** freedom of conscience

(**c**) (*dans son travail*) conscientiousness; **faire qch avec c.** to do sth conscientiously

▶ **conscience: c. de classe** class-consciousness; **c. collective** collective consciousness; **c. professionnelle** professional integrity; **c. de soi** self-awareness

consciencieusement [kɔ̃sjɑ̃sjøzmɑ̃] *adv* conscientiously

consciencieux, -ieuse [kɔ̃sjɑ̃sjø, -jøz] *adj* (*personne, travail*) conscientious

conscient [kɔ̃sjɑ̃] *adj* (**a**) (*lucide etc*) conscious; *Phil* (self-) conscious; **un être c.** a conscious being; **c'est un choix tout à fait c.** it's an entirely conscious choice; **être c. de qch** to be aware *or* conscious of sth; **être c. de ses devoirs** to be aware of one's duties, to know where one's duty lies; **es-tu c. que tu as failli tous nous tuer?** are you aware *or* do you realize that you nearly killed us all? (**b**) *Méd* conscious; **le malade n'est plus c.** the patient is no longer conscious *or* has lost consciousness

conscription [kɔ̃skripsjɔ̃] *nf Mil* conscription, *US* draft

conscrit [kɔ̃skri] *nm* (**a**) *Mil* (*qui a l'âge d'être inscrit*) person liable to conscription; (*qui fait son service*) conscript, recruit, *US* draftee (**b**) *Vieilli Fig* novice, greenhorn

consécration [kɔ̃sekrasjɔ̃] *nf* (**a**) (*d'église, d'évêque etc*) consecration; (*de prêtre*) ordination (**b**) (*du pain et du vin*) consecration (**c**) (*établissement*) (*de coutume, réputation*) establishing; **exposer dans cette galerie sera pour lui la c.** exhibiting in that gallery will establish his reputation

consécutif, -ive [kɔ̃sekytif, -iv] *adj* (**a**) (*qui se suivent*) consecutive; **pendant trois jours consécutifs** for three days running *or* in a row, for three consecutive days; *Gram* **proposition consécutive** consecutive clause (**b**) **c. à** following on; **fatigue consécutive à une longue marche** fatigue resulting from a long walk

consécutivement [kɔ̃sekytivmɑ̃] *adv* consecutively, in succession; **c. à** following

conseil [kɔ̃sεj] *nm* (**a**) (*recommandation*) (piece of) advice, *Fml* counsel; (*en marketing, promotion, finance etc*) consultancy; **c'est un homme de bon c.** he gives good *or* sound advice; **c'est un bon c.** that's a good piece of advice, that's good advice; **donner un c. à qn** to advise sb; **demander c. à qn** to ask sb's advice, to ask sb for advice; **j'ai besoin de tes conseils** *ou* **ton conseil** I need your advice; **suivre les conseils de qn** to follow *or* heed sb's advice; **j'écoutais les conseils de son expérience** I learned from his experience; **pouvez-vous me donner quelques conseils?** can you give me some hints *or* tips?; *prov* **la nuit porte c.** sleep on it

(**b**) (*assemblée*) council, committee; (*d'une entreprise*) board; (*réunion*) meeting; **les membres du c.** the members of the board, the board members; **tenir c.** to hold a meeting; *Fig* **tenir un c. de guerre** to hold a council of war; *Mil* **passer en c. de guerre** to be court-martialled

(**c**) (*conseiller*) *Arch* counsellor, counsel, adviser; (*en marketing, finance etc*) consultant; **avocat-c.** legal consultant; **ingénieur-c.** consulting engineer

(**d**) *Arch, Litt* (*résolution*) (firm) resolution; **ne savoir quel c. prendre** not to know what decision to make

▶ **conseil:** *Com* **c. d'administration** board of directors; *Scol* **c. de classe** = staff meeting, with possible participation of class representatives, to discuss individual pupils and their work, disciplinary matters etc; **c. en communication** media consultant; **C. constitutionnel** = independent body which may be appealed to pronounce on the constitutionality of Government decisions; *Scol etc* **c. de discipline** disciplinary committee; **passer en c. de discipline** to appear before the disciplinary committee; **c. économique** economic council; **c. d'entreprise** works committee; **C. d'État** Council of State; *Can* **c. exécutif** council of ministers, Cabinet; **c. de famille** *Jur* family council; *Hum* family conference; **c. fiscal** tax consultant; **C. général** regional council; *Jur* **c. judiciaire** = guardian, administrator, trustee (*of estate of mentally deficient young person*); **c. juridique** legal adviser; **C. de l'Europe** Council of Europe; **c. en mercatique** marketing consultancy; **le c. des ministres** the Cabinet; **c. municipal** local council; **c. en promotion** advertising consultancy; **c. des prud'hommes** = industrial tribunal, industrial court of arbitration; **c. en publicité** advertising consultant; **C. de sécurité** (*de l'O.N.U.*) Security Council; **c. de surveillance** supervisory board; **c. syndical** trade union council

conseiller [kɔ̃seje] *vt* **c. qn** to advise sb, to give advice to sb; (*d'un psychiatre etc*) to counsel sb; **c. qch à qn** to recommend sth to sb; **c. un jeune dans ses sorties/lectures/fréquentations** to advise a youngster as to where he should go/what he should read/the company he should keep; **je ne vous le conseille pas** I wouldn't if I were you, I wouldn't recommend it; **c. à qn de faire qch** to advise *or* recommend sb to do sth; **l'expérience me conseille d'attendre** experience tells me to wait; **nous avons été très mal conseillés** we were very badly advised, we were given very bad advice; **il est conseillé de ne pas fumer** it is advisable not to smoke

conseiller, -ère [kɔ̃seje, -jɛr] *n* (*qui donne son avis*) counsellor, adviser; (*spécialiste*) adviser, consultant; **la jalousie est mauvaise conseillère** do not be guided by jealousy; **c'est un très bon c.** he gives very good advice

▸ **conseiller**: **c. artistique** artistic adviser; **c. de clientèle** customer consultant; **c. commercial** marketing *or* sales consultant; **c. économique** economic adviser; **c. fiscal** tax consultant; **c. général** regional councillor; **c. en gestion (d'entreprise)** management consultant; **c. juridique** legal adviser; *Jur* **c. à la cour (d'appel)** appeal court judge; **c. en mercatique** marketing consultant; *Admin* **c. municipal** local councillor; *Scol* **c. d'orientation** careers adviser; **c. technique** technical adviser; **c. du travail** personnel consultant

conseilleur, -euse [kɔ̃sɛjœr, -øz] *n Péj* giver *or* dispenser of (unwanted) advice; *Prov* **les conseilleurs ne sont pas les payeurs** it's easy to give advice when you don't have to pay the price

consensuel, -elle [kɔsɑ̃sɥɛl] *adj* (*accord, décision*) reached by consensus

consensus [kɔ̃sɛ̃sys] *nm* consensus (of opinion)

consentant [kɔ̃sɑ̃tɑ̃] *adj* **(a)** *Jur* in agreement; (*partie*) consenting **(b) elle est consentante** she's willing

consentement [kɔ̃sɑ̃tmɑ̃] *nm* consent; **il lui faut le c. de ses parents** he needs his parents' consent; **donner son c. à qch** to give one's consent to sth, to consent to sth; **divorce par c. mutuel** divorce by mutual consent

consentir [kɔ̃sɑ̃tir] (*conj like* **sentir**) **1** *vi* to consent, to agree; **c. à qch/à faire qch** to consent *or* agree to sth/to do sth; **je consens (à ce) qu'il vienne** I consent *or* agree to his coming; **il a fini par c.** he finally agreed, *F* he came round in the end **2** *vt* **c. un prêt** to grant a loan; **c. une remise à qn** to allow sb a discount

conséquemment [kɔ̃sekamɑ̃] *adv* **(a) c. à** as a result of, *Fml* in consequence of **(b)** *Arch, Litt* consequentially

conséquence [kɔ̃sekɑ̃s] *nf* **(a)** (*résultat*) consequence, result; **il faut en subir les conséquences** we/you/*etc* must take the consequences; **tu traînes, tu traînes, c. on est encore en retard** you keep dawdling and as a result we're late again; **quelles en seront les conséquences?** what will be the consequences *or* outcome?; **cela ne tire pas à c.** it's of no consequence; **cet événement eut plus d'une heureuse c.** this event had several happy results; **cette erreur n'a pas eu de conséquences graves** this mistake didn't have any serious consequences *or* repercussions; **ton acte sera sans c. sur ton avenir** your action will have no effect on your future; **en c.** (*par conséquent*) consequently, as a result; **agir en c.** to take appropriate action; **en c. de** as a result of, *Fml* in consequence of; (*selon*) according to

(b) (*conclusion*) inference, conclusion

(c) (*importance*) importance, consequence; **personne sans c.** person of no importance *or Fml* consequence

conséquent [kɔ̃sekɑ̃] **1** *adj* **(a)** (*cohérent*) consistent; (*esprit*) rational; **il n'est pas c. dans ses actions** he's not consistent in his actions; **être c. avec soi-même** to be consistent **(b)** *Mus* **partie conséquente d'une fugue** answer of a fugue **(c)** *F* (*important*) (*somme*) tidy; (*affaire*) important **(d) par c.** consequently, accordingly, therefore **2** *nm Gram, Math* consequent

conservateur, -trice [kɔ̃sɛrvatœr, -tris] **1** *n* **(a)** (*gardien*) (*de musée*) curator, keeper; **c. de bibliothèque** librarian; **c. des hypothèques** registrar of mortgages; **c. des eaux et forêts** ≈ forestry commissioner **(b)** *Pol* conservative **2** *nm* (*alimentaire*) preservative; **sans c.** preservative-free, free of preservatives **3** *adj* **(a)** *Pol* conservative **(b)** (*procédé etc*) preserving, preservative

conservation [kɔ̃sɛrvasjɔ̃] *nf* **(a)** (*de fruits, viande etc*) preserving; **c. par le froid** refrigeration; (*congélation*) freezing **(b)** (*de bâtiments, santé etc*) preservation; *Biol* **instinct de c.** instinct of self-preservation; **des bâtiments en bon état de c.** well-preserved buildings; **c. des Eaux et Forêts** ≈ Forestry Commission **(c)** (*de droits, situation etc*) retention **(d)** (*d'archives*) keeping **(e)** (*d'hypothèques*) registration **(f)** (*état*) (state of) preservation; **des ossements en parfait état de conservation** perfectly preserved bones, bones in a perfect state of preservation

conservatisme [kɔ̃sɛrvatism] *nm Pol etc* conservatism

conservatoire [kɔ̃sɛrvatwar] **1** *adj Jur* (*acte etc*) conservatory; **mesures conservatoires** measures of conservation **2** *nm* **(a)** (*musée*) repository, museum; **C. des arts et métiers** museum and college of Arts and Crafts **(b)** (*de musique, d'art dramatique*) school, academy, conservatoire, *Am* conservatory; **le C. (de Paris)** the (Paris) Conservatoire

conserve [kɔ̃sɛrv] *nf* **(a)** (*alimentaire*) canned *or Br* tinned food; (*en bocal*) preserve; **boîte de c.** can, *Br* tin; **conserves au vinaigre** pickles; **petits pois en c.** canned *or* tinned peas; **mettre en c.** to can, *Br* to tin; **évitez de manger trop de conserves** try not to eat too much canned *or* tinned food, *F* try not to live out of cans *or* tins; *F* **tu ne vas pas en faire des conserves!** they're not museum pieces! **(b)** *Naut* **naviguer de c.** to sail together (**avec** with); *Fig* **de c.** together

conservé [kɔ̃sɛrve] *adj* **femme bien conservée** well-preserved woman

conserver [kɔ̃sɛrve] **1** *vt* **(a)** (*fruits, viande etc*) to preserve; **aliments conservés** (*dans des boîtes*) canned *or Br* tinned food; **c. des tomates en bocaux** to bottle tomatoes; **à c. à l'abri de la lumière** keep away from direct sunlight; **à c. à -6° C** store at -6° C

(b) (*bâtiments, meubles, vêtements etc*) to preserve; **cette vie de plein air l'a bien conservé** this outdoor life has kept him well preserved

(c) (*droits etc*) to retain, to keep, to maintain; (*emploi*) to keep; **il a conservé précieusement toutes ses lettres d'amour** he carefully kept *or* preserved all her love letters; **je n'en ai pas conservé un bon souvenir** I don't have good memories of it; **c. son sang-froid** *ou* **sa tête** to remain cool, to keep one's head; **elle a réussi à c. ses cheveux malgré le traitement** she has managed to keep *or* not to lose her hair in spite of the treatment; **c. l'allure** to keep up *or* maintain the speed; *Mil* **c. une position** to hold a position

2 se conserver *vpr* (*d'un aliment*) to keep; **articles qui ne se conservent pas** perishable goods

conserverie [kɔ̃sɛrvəri] *nf* **(a)** (*industrie*) canning industry **(b)** (*fabrique*) cannery, canning factory

considérable [kɔ̃siderabl] *adj* (*nombre, population*) considerable, substantial; (*propriété etc*) considerable, substantial, extensive; (*changement etc*) considerable, significant; **il lui reste un travail c. à faire** he has still got a considerable *or* substantial amount of work to do; **un changement d'une importance c.** a substantial change; **j'ai fait des dépenses considérables** I have been *or* have gone to considerable expense; **l'émotion fut c.** there was quite a stir

considérablement [kɔ̃siderabləmɑ̃] *adv* considerably, significantly

considérant [kɔ̃siderɑ̃] *nm Jur* preamble

considération [kɔ̃siderasjɔ̃] *nf* **(a)** (*examen attentif*) consideration, attention, thought; **sans c. de prix** without considering the price *or* thinking about the price; **cette offre mérite toute notre c.** this offer deserves our full attention *or* consideration; **après c. de votre demande** having considered *or* studied your application; **prendre en c.** to take into consideration *or* account; (*offre, demande d'emploi etc*) to consider; **en c. de** in consideration of

(b) (*constatation*) consideration, factor; **je ne peux pas entrer dans ces considérations** I can't go into that; **poussé par de nombreuses considérations** motivated by a variety of factors *or* considerations

(c) (*estime*) regard, esteem, respect; **agir avec/sans c.** to act considerately/inconsiderately; **n'avoir de c. pour personne** to have no consideration for anyone; **tu as agi**

sans aucune c. that was most inconsiderate of you; **jouir d'une grande c.** to be highly respected; **veuillez agréer, Monsieur, l'assurance de ma parfaite** *ou* **haute c.** (*dans une lettre*) yours truly; **agréez l'assurance de ma c. distinguée** yours faithfully, *Am* yours truly; **par c. pour** out of consideration *or* regard for

(d) considérations (*observations*) observations, reflections, thoughts (**sur** on)

considéré [kɔ̃sidere] *adj* (*personne*) highly regarded *or* respected

considérer [kɔ̃sidere] (**je considère, n. considérons; je considérerai**) **1** *vt* **(a)** (*étudier*) (*problème etc*) to consider, to weigh up; **tout bien considéré** taking everything into consideration *or* account, all things considered, on the whole; **c'est à c.** it's worth bearing in mind; (*à étudier*) it's worth considering; **considérant que …** considering that …

(b) (*regarder*) to consider, to gaze at, to contemplate

(c) (*estimer*) (*personne*) to respect; **on la considère beaucoup** she is highly thought of *or* respected, she is held in high regard; **je considère votre lettre comme frivole** I think your letter is flippant, I regard your letter as flippant; **je le considère comme mon meilleur ami** I regard him *or* consider him *or* look on him as my best friend; **je considère ce livre comme le meilleur de l'année** I consider this book (to be) the best of the year; **je considère que tu aurais pu te renseigner auparavant** I really think you could have found out beforehand

2 se considérer *vpr* to consider *or* regard oneself; **se c. comme responsable** to consider *or* hold oneself responsible

consignataire [kɔ̃siɲatɛr] *nm* **(a)** *Jur* depositary **(b)** *Com, Naut* consignee

consignation [kɔ̃siɲasjɔ̃] *nf* **(a)** (*d'argent*) deposit **(b)** *Com* (*de marchandises*) consignment; **marchandises en c.** goods on consignment **(c) un système pour la consignation des bouteilles** a money-back system for bottles

consigne [kɔ̃siɲ] *nf* **(a)** (*donnée à la sentinelle etc*) orders, instructions; **il a pour c. de ne laisser passer personne** his orders are to let nobody pass; **observer la c.** to obey orders; **c'est la c.** those are the orders; **consignes en cas d'incendie** fire notice, fire regulations **(b)** (*punition*), *Mil* confinement to barracks; *Scol* detention; **deux heures de c.** two hours' detention **(c)** *Rail* **c. (à bagages)** left-luggage office, *Am* checkroom; **c. automatique** lockers, *Br* left-luggage lockers **(d)** (*de bouteille etc*) deposit

consigner [kɔ̃siɲe] *vt* **(a)** (*argent etc*) to deposit; **bouteille consignée** returnable bottle; **c. l'emballage** to charge a refundable deposit on the packaging; **emballage non consigné** non-returnable packing **(b)** *Com* (*marchandises etc*) to consign (**à** to) **(c)** (*fait etc*) to record, to write down; **c. des impressions par écrit** to commit one's impressions to paper **(d)** *Mil* (*soldat*) to confine to barracks; *Scol* (*élève*) to keep in; **c. sa porte à qn** to bar one's door to sb **(e)** *Rail* **c. ses bagages** to put *or* deposit one's luggage in the left-luggage office *or Am* checkroom

consistance [kɔ̃sistɑ̃s] *nf* **(a)** (*d'un sirop, d'une crème etc*) consistency, consistence; **prendre c.** to thicken; *Fig* **ses projets semblent prendre (de la) c.** his plans seem to be taking shape; **tout cela n'était que rêve sans c.** it was all just a vague dream *or Fml* a dream without substance; **bruit sans c.** unfounded *or* groundless rumour; **donner de la c. à qch** to thicken sth; *Fig* **donner de la c. à un personnage** to flesh out *or* give substance to a character **(b)** (*de l'esprit, du caractère*) firmness, strength; **sans c.** spineless

consistant [kɔ̃sistɑ̃] *adj* (*substance*) firm, solid; (*sauce etc*) thick; (*repas*) substantial; (*argument*) well-founded, sound; (*méthode, raisonnement*) coherent, consistent

consister [kɔ̃siste] *vi* **c. en qch** to consist of sth; **le repas consiste en un sandwich et en une pomme** the meal consists of *or* comprises a sandwich and an apple; **en quoi consiste cette tâche?** what does the/this task consist of *or* involve *or* entail?; **c. dans qch** to consist in sth; **c. à faire qch** to consist in doing sth

consistoire [kɔ̃sistwar] *nm Rel* consistory

consœur [kɔ̃sœr] *nf* (female) colleague

consolable [kɔ̃sɔlabl] *adj* consolable

consolant [kɔ̃sɔlɑ̃] *adj* consoling, comforting; **ce qui est c., c'est que …** the comforting thing (about it) is that …

consolateur, -trice [kɔ̃sɔlatœr, -tris] **1** *n Litt* comforter, consoler **2** *adj* consoling, consolatory

consolation [kɔ̃sɔlasjɔ̃] *nf* (*soulagement*) consolation, solace, comfort; **chercher une c. dans qch** to seek consolation *or* solace *or* comfort in sth; **paroles de c.** words of comfort, comforting *or* consoling words; **lot** *ou* **prix de c.** consolation prize; **c'est ma seule c.** it's my only consolation

console [kɔ̃sɔl] *nf* **(a)** *Ordinat* console; *Ordinat* **c. opérateur** operator console; *Aut* **c. centrale** central console; *TV etc* **c. de mixage** sound mixer, mixing desk; *TV* **c. vidéo** video console, switcher **(b)** (*meuble*) console (table) **(c)** *Archit* console, corbel, bracket **(d)** *Mus* (*d'un orgue*) console; (*d'une harpe*) neck

consoler [kɔ̃sɔle] **1** *vt* to console, to comfort; **c. qn de sa peine** to comfort *or* console sb in his/her grief; **le temps console** time is a great healer; **si ça peut te c.** if that's any consolation *or* comfort to you; **ça me console de voir que ça t'est déjà arrivé** it consoles me *or* is a consolation that it's happened to you too

2 se consoler *vpr* to console oneself, to find comfort *or* consolation; **se c. en pensant que …** to console oneself with the thought that …; **se c. avec qn** to console oneself with sb; **se c. d'une perte/d'un échec/de la mort de qn** to get over a loss/a failure/sb's death; **elle s'en est vite consolée** she soon got over it; **je ne pourrai jamais m'en c.** I'll never get over it; **elles se sont consolées mutuellement** they consoled *or* comforted each other

consolidation [kɔ̃sɔlidasjɔ̃] *nf* **(a)** (*d'un édifice, d'un mur*) strengthening, reinforcement; (*d'une position, du pouvoir, d'une amitié etc*) consolidation, strengthening **(b)** *Méd* (*d'une blessure*) healing; (*d'une fracture*) knitting, setting **(c)** *Fin* (*d'une dette flottante*) funding; (*d'un bilan*) consolidation; *Mktg* **consolidation de ligne** line filling

consolidé [kɔ̃sɔlide] *Fin* **1** *adj* **dette consolidée** funded debt; **fonds consolidés** consols; **bilan c.** consolidated balance sheet **2** *nmpl* **consolidés** consols

consolider [kɔ̃sɔlide] **1** *vt* **(a)** (*édifice, mur, coutures*) to strengthen, to reinforce; (*position, régime, amitié etc*) to consolidate, to strengthen **(b)** *Méd* (*blessure*) to heal; (*fracture*) to knit, to set **(c)** *Fin* (*dette*) to fund; (*bilan*) to consolidate **2 se consolider** *vpr* **(a)** (*se renforcer*) (*d'un régime*) to consolidate its position; (*d'une amitié, de liens*) to become stronger **(b)** *Méd* (*d'une blessure*) to heal; (*d'une fracture*) to knit, to set

consommable [kɔ̃sɔmabl] *adj* (*solide*) edible; (*liquide*) drinkable; **ce produit n'est c. que cru/cuit** this product must be eaten raw/cooked before eating

consommateur, -trice [kɔ̃sɔmatœr, -tris] **1** *n* (*en général*) consumer; (*dans un restaurant, un café*) customer; **ce pays est un des premiers consommateurs de pétrole** this country is one of the biggest oil consumers; **mes grandparents sont de grands consommateurs de viandes fumées** my grandparents eat a lot of smoked meat; **défense des consommateurs** consumer protection; *Mktg* **c. final** end-user; **c. moyen** average user **2** *adj* **pays c.** consuming country

consommation [kɔ̃sɔmasjɔ̃] *nf* **(a)** (*d'électricité, de pétrole*) consumption, use; (*de nourriture*) consumption, eating; (*de boisson*) consumption, drinking; (*d'une voiture*) (petrol *or Am* gas) consumption; **cette viande est impropre à la c.** this meat is unfit for (human) consumption; **faire une grande c. de papier** to get through *or* go through *or* use (up) a lot of paper; **ils font une grande c. de viandes fumées** they get through *or* consume a lot of smoked meat; **c. quotidienne de vitamines** daily intake of vitamins; **c. des ménages** household consumption; **c. mondiale** world consumption; **biens de c.** consumer goods; **produits de grande c.** mass market products; **société de c.** consumer society; **crédit à la c.** consumer credit; *Aut* **c. d'huile** oil consumption; *Aut* **c. de carburant** fuel consumption; **c. de masse** mass consumption; *Aut* **c. en ville** urban fuel consumption; *Aut* **c. en vitesse de croisière** touring consumption; *Aut* **c. spécifique** specific fuel consumption, sfc; *Compta* **consommations de l'exercice** total annual expenses

(b) (*dans un café*) drink

(c) *Litt* (*d'un travail etc*) accomplishment; (*d'un crime*) perpetration; (*du mariage*) consummation; **jusqu'à la c. des siècles** until the end of time

consommé [kɔ̃sɔme] **1** *adj* (*habileté etc*) consummate; (*écrivain, diplomate etc*) consummate, accomplished **2** *nm Culin* consommé; **c. de poulet** chicken consommé

consommer [kɔ̃sɔme] **1** *vt* **(a)** (*électricité, pétrole etc*) to consume, to use; (*nourriture*) to consume, to eat; (*boisson*) to consume, to drink; **cette voiture consomme trop (d'essence)** this car is heavy on petrol *or Am* gas

(b) (*crime*) to perpetrate; (*mariage*) to consummate; *Litt* (*œuvre*) to accomplish, to achieve; **la rupture est consommée** they have broken up for good

2 *vi* to consume; (*dans un café*) to drink, to have a drink; **'à c. avant fin novembre'** 'best before end November'; **c. au bar** to (have a) drink at the bar; **c. sur place** to eat in

3 se consommer *vpr* (*de la nourriture, de boissons etc*) to be consumed; **ce plat se consomme froid** this dish is eaten cold

consomption [kɔ̃sɔ̃psjɔ̃] *nf* **(a)** *Méd* wasting, decline; *Arch* (*tuberculose*) consumption (**b**) *Arch, Litt* (*par le feu*) consuming

consonance [kɔ̃sɔnɑ̃s] *nf Mus, Ling* consonance; **mots aux consonances harmonieuses/bizarres** harmonious/odd-sounding words; **langue à c. germanique** German-sounding language

consonant [kɔ̃sɔnɑ̃] *adj Mus, Ling* consonant

consonantique [kɔ̃sɔnɑ̃tik] *adj Ling* consonant(al)

consonne [kɔ̃sɔn] *nf Ling* consonant; **c. occlusive/labiale/dentale** plosive/labial/dental (consonant)

consort [kɔ̃sɔr] **1** *adj* **prince c.** prince consort **2** *nm Péj* **et consorts** and company

consortial, -ale, -aux, -ales [kɔ̃sɔrsjal, -o] *adj Com, Fin* consortium, *Fml* consortial

consortium [kɔ̃sɔrsjɔm] *nm Com, Fin* consortium, syndicate; **c. de banques** banking consortium

conspirateur, -trice [kɔ̃spiratœr, -tris] **1** *n* conspirator; **ils se donnaient des airs de c.** they had a conspiratorial air about them **2** *adj* conspiratorial

conspiration [kɔ̃spirasjɔ̃] *nf* conspiracy, plot; *F* **mais c'est une c.** it's a conspiracy

conspirer [kɔ̃spire] *vi* (**a**) (*comploter*) to conspire, to plot (**contre** against) (**b**) (*contribuer*) to conspire; **tout conspire à me mettre en retard** everything's conspiring to make me late; **tout semble c. à son bonheur/la réussite du projet** everything seems to be conspiring to make him happy/to make the project a success

conspuer [kɔ̃spɥe] *vt* (*pièce de théâtre, orateur etc*) to boo, to shout down

constamment [kɔ̃stamɑ̃] *adv* constantly, continually, continuously

constance [kɔ̃stɑ̃s] *nf* (**a**) (*dans une tâche*) persistence, perseverance; (*en amour*) constancy; **manquer de c. en amour** to be fickle; **il a de la c. à t'attendre depuis cinq ans** he's patient to have waited for you for five years; **faire preuve d'une grande c. en amitié** to be unswerving in one's friendships; **travailler avec c.** to work steadily (**b**) (*de la température, d'un phénomène etc*) constancy, invariability

constant, -ante [kɔ̃stɑ̃, -ɑ̃t] **1** *adj* (**a**) (*cœur, préoccupation, souci*) constant; (*effort*) persistent; (*amitié, intérêt*) steady, unwavering; **être c. dans la recherche de qch** to be persistent in one's search for sth (**b**) *Rare* (*fait*) established (**c**) (*température*) constant; (*circulation*) continuous, uninterrupted; **à niveau c.** at a constant level (**d**) *Com* **en francs constants** in real terms **2** *nf Math, Phys etc* **constante** constant

constat [kɔ̃sta] *nm* (**a**) *Jur* certified *or* official statement *or* report; **dresser un c. d'accident** to write out an accident report; **c. amiable** (*formulaire*) = insurance form to be completed at scene of accident; **c. d'huissier** process server's affidavit; **c. de dommages** damages report (**b**) (*fait*) observation; **c. d'échec** acknowledgment *or* admission of failure; **faire un c. d'échec** to acknowledge *or* admit failure

constatation [kɔ̃statasjɔ̃] *nf* (**a**) (*d'un fait etc*) noting, noticing; **procéder aux constatations d'usage** to make the usual *or* routine investigations *or* inquiries (**b**) (*fait*) observation; **constatations d'une enquête** findings of an enquiry; **la première c. est la suivante** the first point to note is the following; **c'est une simple c.** it's a simple statement of fact (**c**) *Compta* **c. de stock** stock take

constater [kɔ̃state] *vt* (**a**) (*remarquer*) (*fait, amélioration etc*) to note, to notice, to observe; **c. une erreur** to discover *or* find a mistake; **je constate que ce que je propose n'est jamais retenu** I notice that what I suggest is never accepted; **vous pouvez c. vous-même qu'elle est partie** you can see for yourself that she's gone; **constate par toi-même!** see for yourself!; **je suis obligé de c. que je me suis trompé** I'm forced to the conclusion *or* to conclude that I've made a mistake

(**b**) (*enregistrer*) to record; **c. un décès** to certify a death; **les experts sont venus c. les dégâts** the experts came to assess the damage; *Com* **constaté d'avance** (*charge*) prepaid

constellation [kɔ̃stɛlasjɔ̃] *nf* constellation; **la constellation de la Croix du Sud** the Southern Cross; *Fig* **une c. de personnes célèbres** a constellation *or* galaxy of famous people

consteller [kɔ̃stɛle] **1** *vt* to spangle, to stud; **ciel constellé d'étoiles** star-spangled *or* star-studded sky; **robe constellée de pierreries** dress studded with jewels; **des taches de sang constellent sa chemise** his shirt is spattered with blood **2 se consteller** *vpr* **le ciel se constella d'étoiles** the stars came out in the sky; **le neige se mit à tomber, et le sol se constella de taches blanches** the snow began to fall and the ground was spotted with white

consternant [kɔ̃stɛrnɑ̃] *adj* (*nouvelles*) alarming, dismaying; **d'une bêtise consternante** alarmingly stupid

consternation [kɔ̃stɛrnasjɔ̃] *nf* consternation, dismay; **jeter la c. dans un groupe** to fill a group with consternation *or* dismay; **à la c. générale** to everyone's consternation *or* dismay

consterner [kɔ̃stɛrne] *vt* (*qn*) to dismay, to fill with consternation *or* dismay; **prendre un air consterné** to look dismayed

constipation [kɔ̃stipasjɔ̃] *nf Méd* constipation

constipé, -ée [kɔ̃stipe] **1** *adj Méd* constipated; *F* (*air, manière etc*) ill at ease, stiff, *F* constipated; **arrête de prendre cet air c.!** loosen up *or* relax a bit! **2** *n Méd* constipated person, sufferer from constipation; *Fig F* **quel c.!** what a stuffed shirt!

constiper [kɔ̃stipe] *Méd* **1** *vt* to constipate **2** *vi* **nourriture qui constipe** constipating food

constituant, -ante [kɔ̃stitɥɑ̃, -ɑ̃t] **1** *adj* (**a**) (*partie, élément*) constituent, component (**b**) *Hist* **l'Assemblée constituante** the Constituent Assembly (*of 1789*) **2** *nm* constituent part; *Hist* **les constituants** the members of the Constituent Assembly **3** *nf* **la Constituante** the Constituent Assembly (*of 1789*)

constitué [kɔ̃stitɥe] *adj* (**a**) (*autorité etc*) constituted, organized; **corps constitués** official bodies (**b**) *Anat* constituted, formed; **enfant bien c.** fine, healthy child; **enfant mal c.** child of poor constitution

constituer [kɔ̃stitɥe] **1** *vt* (**a**) (*faire partie de*) to form, to constitute, to make up; **parties qui constituent le tout** parts that form *or* constitute *or* (go to) make up the whole; **ce mobilier constitue tout mon bien** this furniture represents all my worldly goods, this furniture is all I own; **cet acte constitue un outrage aux bonnes mœurs** this action constitutes *or* represents an affront to public decency; **cela devrait c. un délit** that ought to constitute an offence; **être constitué de ...** to be made up of *or* consist of ...; **appartement constitué de six pièces** six-roomed flat

(**b**) (*créer*) (*comité, société commerciale, ministère, équipe etc*) to form, to set up; (*bibliothèque, fortune*) to build up

(**c**) *Jur etc* (*nommer*) to appoint; **c. qn président** to appoint sb president; **c. qn son héritier** to make sb one's heir; **c. une rente/une dot à qn** to settle an annuity/a dowry on sb

2 se constituer *vpr* (**a**) (*devenir*) **se c. prisonnier** to give oneself up; **se c. partie civile** to bring a civil suit for damages

(**b**) (*se réunir*) **ils se constituèrent en commission/en association** they formed a committee/an association

constitutif, -ive [kɔ̃stitytif, -iv] *adj* (**a**) (*composant*) constituent, component; **les éléments constitutifs de l'air** the constituent elements of air (**b**) *Jur* constitutive; **titre c.** (*d'une propriété*) title deed

constitution [kɔ̃stitysjɔ̃] *nf* (**a**) (*physique*), *Pol* constitution; **avoir une bonne c.** to have a sound constitution, to be fit; **loi conforme à la c.** law complying with the constitution (**b**) (*création*) (*de comité*) formation, setting up, constitution; (*de société commerciale*) formation, setting up; (*de ministère*) formation; (*de stocks*) constitution; (*de bibliothèque*) building up (**c**) *Jur* (*de rente, dot*) settlement; **c. de partie civile** institution of civil action; **c. d'avoué** briefing *or* instructing of a lawyer (**d**) (*de l'air, de l'eau*) composition

constitutionnaliser [kɔ̃stitysjɔnalize] *vt Jur* to constitutionalize

constitutionnel, -elle [kɔ̃stitysjɔnɛl] *adj* constitutional

constitutionnellement [kɔ̃stitysjɔnɛlmɑ̃] *adv* constitutionally

constricteur [kɔ̃striktœr] **1** *adj* (**a**) *Anat* **muscle c.** constrictor muscle (**b**) **boa c.** boa constrictor **2** *nm Anat* constrictor (muscle)

constriction [kɔ̃striksjɔ̃] *nf* (*des vaisseaux sanguins*) constriction

constrictor [kɔ̃striktɔr] *adj, nm* (**boa**) **c.** boa constrictor

constructeur, -trice [kɔ̃stryktœr, -tris] **1** *nm Constr* builder, constructor; **c. automobile** *ou* **d'automobiles** car *or* motor manufacturer; **c. naval** shipbuilder **2** *adj* (*esprit, démarche*) constructive; *Zool* **animaux constructeurs** home-building animals

constructible [kɔ̃stryktibl] *adj* **terrain c.** building land, land approved for development

constructif, -ive [kɔ̃stryktif, -iv] *adj* constructive

construction [kɔ̃stryksjɔ̃] *nf* (**a**) (*d'une maison, d'une route, d'un voilier etc*) construction, building, constructing; (*d'un roman, poème etc*) construction; (*d'une phrase*) structure, construction; **matériaux de c.** building *or* construction materials; **c. aéronautique** aircraft manufacturing; **c. mécanique** (mechanical) engineering; **c. navale** shipbuilding; **maison en c.** house under construction; **il y a plusieurs maisons en c. de l'autre côté de la rue** several houses are being built on the other side of the street; **appareil de c. japonaise** Japanese-built appliance, appliance of Japanese

manufacture; **jeu de c.** construction set; *Fig* **c'est une c. de l'esprit** it's purely hypothetical
(**b**) (*bâtiment*) building, construction, structure; **un grand nombre de nouvelles constructions** a large number of new buildings
(**c**) *Géom* figure, construction

construire [kɔ̃strɥir] (*prp* **construisant**; *pp* **construit**; *pr ind* **je construis, il construit, n. construisons**; *impf* **je construisais**; *p hist* **je construisis**; *fu* **je construirai**) **1** *vt* (**a**) (*maison, route, etc*) to build, to construct; **pendant qu'on construit la maison** while the house is being built; **région très construite** heavily built-up area; **c. l'Europe** to build a new Europe
(**b**) (*machine, bateau, avion etc*) to build, to construct; (*roman, poème etc*) to construct; (*théorie*) to construct, to put together; *Gram* **c. une phrase** to construct a sentence
2 se construire *vpr* (*d'une résidence etc*) to be built, to be constructed; **la région s'est beaucoup construite** there has been a lot of building in the area, the area has become very built-up; **il s'est construit beaucoup de maisons** a lot of houses have been built; *Gram* **après que se construit avec l'indicatif** après que takes the indicative

consubstantiation [kɔ̃sypstɑ̃sjasjɔ̃] *nf Rel* consubstantiation, real presence

consubstantiel, -ielle [kɔ̃sypstɑ̃sjɛl] *adj Rel* consubstantial, of one substance (**à avec** with)

consul [kɔ̃syl] *nm* consul; **le c. de France** the French consul; **c. général** consul general

consulaire [kɔ̃sylɛr] *adj* consular

consulat [kɔ̃syla] *nm* (*lieu*) consulate; (*charge*) consulship; *Hist Fr* **le C.** the Consulate (*1799*)

consultable [kɔ̃syltabl] *adj* (*livre etc*) available for consultation

consultant, -ante [kɔ̃syltɑ̃, -ɑ̃t] **1** *adj* consulting; **médecin c.** consultant **2** *n* consultant; **agence de consultants** consultancy; **c. en gestion** management consultant; **c. médias** media consultant

consultatif, -ive [kɔ̃syltatif, -iv] *adj* consultative, advisory; **à titre c.** in an advisory capacity; **assemblée consultative** consultative assembly

consultation [kɔ̃syltasjɔ̃] *nf* (**a**) (*conférence*) consultation, conference; **entrer en c. avec qn** to consult *or* confer with sb; **c. populaire** consultation of the people
(**b**) (*chez un avoué, médecin etc*) consultation; **le médecin est en c.** the doctor is with a patient *or* is seeing a patient; **cabinet de c.** *Méd* consulting room, *Br* surgery, *Am* office; *Jur* chambers; *Méd* **heures de c.** consulting *or* surgery hours; *Méd* **consultation externe** out-patients' department
(**c**) (*de livre*) consultation, consulting; **encourager la c. des dictionnaires** to encourage the use of dictionaries; **la c. de nos fichiers n'a rien donné** we couldn't find anything in our files; **je pourrai te le dire après c. de mon agenda** I'll be able to tell you after I've checked (in) my diary; **livre de c. facile** book that is easy to consult *or* use; *Ordinat* **c. de table** table look-up

consulter [kɔ̃sylte] **1** *vt* (*qn*) to consult; (*livre, plan etc*) to consult, to refer to; **c. qn du regard** to look questioningly at sb; **c. un médecin/un avocat** to consult a doctor/lawyer, to take medical/legal advice; **c. les horaires de départ** to check the departure times; **ouvrage à c.** reference work; **livre facile à c.** book that is easy to consult *or* use; **c. ses intérêts** to look after one's own interests
2 *vi* (*conférer*) to consult, to hold a consultation; *Méd* (*d'un docteur*) to see patients, *Br* to take surgery; (*d'un malade*) to go to the doctor('s)
3 se consulter *vpr* to consult each other, to confer; **ils se sont consultés avant de venir ici** they put their heads together *or* conferred before coming here; **se c. du regard** to look questioningly at one another

consumer [kɔ̃syme] **1** *vt* (**a**) (*brûler*) to consume; **consumé par le feu** consumed by fire, burnt up; *Fig* **consumé par l'ambition/le remords** consumed *or* eaten up with ambition/remorse; **les soucis/chagrins le consument** he is sick with worry/grief; **la jalousie le consume** he is consumed *or* eaten up with jealousy
(**b**) *Litt* (*fortune, énergie*) to waste
2 se consumer *vpr* (**a**) **les bûches se consumèrent lentement** the logs burned (away) slowly
(**b**) (*d'une personne*) to waste away, to pine away; **se c. en efforts inutiles** to wear oneself out in useless efforts; **elle se consume d'inquiétude/de chagrin** she's consumed *or* eaten up with worry/grief

consumérisme [kɔ̃symerism] *nm* consumerism

consumériste [kɔ̃symerist] *adj* consumer, consumerist

contact [kɔ̃takt] *nm* (**a**) (*relation, personne*) contact; **l'espion avoua que son c. travaillait à l'ambassade** the spy admitted that his contact worked at the embassy; **être en c. avec qn/qch** to be in contact with sb/sth; **entrer en c.** (*avec un virus etc*) to come into contact; (*contacter*) to get in contact; **garder/perdre le c. avec qn** to keep in touch/lose touch with sb; **mettre qn en c. avec qn** to put sb in contact *or* in touch with sb; **prendre c.** *ou* **se mettre en c. avec qn** to get in touch *or* in contact with sb, to contact sb; **prise de c.** first meeting; **j'ai su qu'il m'était hostile dès le premier c.** I knew that he was hostile towards me from the moment we met; **elle est d'un c. facile/difficile** she's easy/hard to get on with; **il va changer au c. de ces jeunes travailleurs** mixing with these young workers is going to change him; **elle s'est métamorphosée au c. de cette femme** she's completely changed since she met that woman
(**b**) (*toucher*) contact, touch; **au c. agréable** pleasant to the touch; **je n'ai jamais aimé son c.** I've never liked to be touched by him; **le c. de deux surfaces** the contact between *or* of two surfaces; **maladies transmises par c.** diseases transmitted by contact, contagious diseases; **au c. de l'eau** on contact with water
(**c**) *Tech* contact; *Él* contact, connection; **c. à la terre** contact to earth; **point de c.** contact point; **les fils sont en c.** the wires are in contact; **fiche** *ou* **cheville de c.** contact plug
(**d**) *Aut* contact, contact breaker point; **contacts** points; **c. coupé** ignition switched off; **c. mis** ignition switched on; **clef de c.** ignition key; **mettre/couper le c.** to switch on/off

contacter [kɔ̃takte] *vt* to contact, to get in touch *or* in contact with

contacteur [kɔ̃taktœr] *nm Él* contactor; (*du système d'allumage*) switch; **c. d'interdiction** inhibitor switch; **c. de coupure à inertie** inertia cut-off switch; **c. à solénoïde** solenoid switch

contagieux, -ieuse [kɔ̃taʒjø, -jøz] **1** *adj* (*maladie, virus etc*) contagious, infectious; (*personne*) contagious; (*rire, enthousiasme*) infectious **2** *n* contagious patient; **service des contagieux** isolation ward

contagion [kɔ̃taʒjɔ̃] *nf Méd* contagion; **pour prévenir tout risque de c.** to avoid any risk of contagion; **période de c.** contagious stage; *Fig* **la c. du rire** the infectiousness of laughter

contagiosité [kɔ̃taʒjosite] *nf Méd* contagiousness

container [kɔ̃tɛnɛr] *nm Ind* container

contaminateur, -trice [kɔ̃taminatœr, -tris] *Méd* **1** *adj* contaminating **2** *n* carrier

contamination [kɔ̃taminasjɔ̃] *nf* (*pollution*) contamination; *Méd* infection

contaminer [kɔ̃tamine] *vt* (*polluer*) (*eau etc*) to contaminate; *Méd* to infect; *Ordinat* **disque dur contaminé par un virus** virus-infected hard disk

conte [kɔ̃t] *nm* (**a**) (*histoire*) story, tale; **c. de fées** fairy tale *or* story; **elle vit dans un c. de fées** she's living in a dream world *or* in a world of her own; **elle vit un c. de fées** her life is a fairy tale; **contes de bonnes femmes** old wives' tales (**b**) *Vieilli, Litt* (*histoire invraisemblable*) (tall) story, yarn; **c. à dormir debout** cock-and-bull story

contemplateur, -trice [kɔ̃tɑ̃platœr, -tris] *n* contemplator

contemplatif, -ive [kɔ̃tɑ̃platif, -iv] **1** *adj* contemplative **2** *n* meditator; *Rel* contemplative

contemplation [kɔ̃tɑ̃plasjɔ̃] *nf* (**a**) (*d'un tableau etc*) contemplation; **être en c. devant la mer** to gaze (in contemplation) at the sea (**b**) (*méditation*) contemplation, meditation; **plongé dans la c.** lost in contemplation *or* meditation (**c**) *Rel* contemplation

contempler [kɔ̃tɑ̃ple] **1** *vt* (*nature, tableau etc*) to contemplate, to gaze at **2 se contempler** *vpr* (*dans un miroir*) to look at *or* contemplate oneself

contemporain, -aine [kɔ̃tɑ̃pɔrɛ̃, -ɛn] **1** *adj* (**a**) (*moderne*) contemporary (**b**) (*du même âge*) contemporary (**de** with); **être c. de qn** to be a contemporary of sb; **ils sont contemporains** they are contemporaries **2** *n* contemporary

contempteur [kɔ̃tɑ̃ptœr] *n* despiser

contenance [kɔ̃tnɑ̃s] *nf* (**a**) (*d'une bouteille etc*) capacity; (*d'un navire*) burden; **d'une c. de dix litres** capable of holding ten litres, with a capacity of ten litres (**b**) (*allure*) attitude, bearing; **avoir une c. modeste/fière** to have a modest/proud demeanour *or* bearing; **faire bonne c.** to put on a bold front; **perdre c.** to lose one's composure; **faire qch pour se donner (une) c.** to do sth to give oneself an air of assurance

contenant [kɔ̃tnɑ̃] *nm* (*par opposition à contenu*) container

conteneur [kɔ̃tnœr] *nm* (*pour le transport de marchandises*) container; **c. à bagages** baggage container

conteneur-avion, *pl* **conteneurs-avions** *nm* airfreight container

conteneurisation [kɔ̃tnœrizasjɔ̃] *nf Com* containerization

conteneuriser [kɔ̃tnœrize] *vt Com* to containerize

contenir [kɔ̃tnir] (*conj like* **tenir**) **1** *vt* (**a**) (*renfermer*) to contain; **le théâtre contient mille places** the theatre holds *or* seats a thousand; **le dictionnaire contient plus de cinquante mille articles** the dictionary contains *or* has more than fifty thousand entries; **cette bouteille a contenu du vin** this bottle has had wine in it, this bottle has contained wine; **lettre contenant chèque** letter enclosing cheque

(**b**) (*foule, sentiments etc*) to restrain, to keep *or* hold in check; (*colère*) to curb, to suppress; (*larmes*) to hold back; **c. l'ennemi** to contain the enemy, to keep the enemy in check

2 se contenir *vpr* to contain oneself, to control oneself; **apprendre à se c.** to learn self-control, to learn to control oneself

content [kɔ̃tɑ̃] **1** *adj* (*satisfait*) content, satisfied, pleased (**de** with); (*ravi*) glad; **être c. de son sort** to be content *or* satisfied with one's lot; **il est très c. ici** he's very happy here; **elle a l'air contente de sa nouvelle voiture** she seems pleased *or* happy with her new car; **tu n'as pas l'air c.** you don't look very happy *or* pleased; **je suis c. de vous/moi** I'm pleased with you/myself; **je suis très c. de vous voir** I'm very pleased to see you; **un air trop c. de soi** a smug manner; **tu peux être c. de toi, tu as vu ce que tu as fait!** I hope you're satisfied *or* happy – just look what you've done!; **non c. de mentir, il vole!** not content *or* satisfied with lying, he steals as well!; **votre père ne sera pas c.** your father won't be (very) pleased *or* happy, your father won't like it; **je suis fort c. que vous soyez venu** I'm so glad you've come; *F* **et si tu n'es pas c., c'est pareil** you can like it or lump it

2 *nm* **manger tout son c.** to eat one's fill; **s'amuser tout son c.** to enjoy oneself to one's heart's content; **avoir son c. de qch** to have one's fill of sth

contentement [kɔ̃tɑ̃tmɑ̃] *nm* (*état*) satisfaction, contentment (**de** at, with), *Litt* content; **c. de soi** self-satisfaction; **un sourire de c.** a satisfied *or* contented smile

contenter [kɔ̃tɑ̃te] **1** *vt* (*qn, curiosité*) to satisfy; (*caprice*) to satisfy, to gratify; **un rien le contente** the least thing makes him happy, he's very easily pleased *or* satisfied; **on ne peut pas c. tout le monde** you can't please everyone

2 se contenter *vpr* **se c. de (faire) qch** to be content *or* satisfied *or* happy with (doing) sth, to content oneself with (doing) sth; **il se contente de peu** he's easily satisfied; **il va falloir se contenter du strict nécessaire** we shall have to make do with the bare necessities; **je me contenterai de faire remarquer que ...** I will merely point out that ...; **il se contente d'un repas par jour** he only has *or* he is content with one meal a day; **pour tout repas, elle s'est contentée de sandwichs** by way of a meal, she just had sandwiches; **pour toute réponse, il s'est contenté de nous renvoyer la carte, signée** by way of reply, he merely returned the card to us, signed

contentieux, -ieuse [kɔ̃tɑ̃sjø, -jøz] **1** *adj* (*affaire*) contentious **2** *nm Admin* contentious business, matters in dispute; (*querelle grave*) bone of contention; *Jur* litigation; (*service*) legal department; **avoir un c. avec qn** to be in dispute with sb; **le c. franco-espagnol** the Franco-Spanish dispute; **chef du c.** (*d'une société*) head of legal department

contention[1] [kɔ̃tɑ̃sjɔ̃] *nf Litt* (*des facultés intellectuelles*) application, exertion; **c. d'esprit** intentness of mind

contention[2] *nf Méd* (*d'une fracture etc*) retention in place, setting; *Psy* (*au moyen d'une camisole etc*) restraint, restraining; **collant de c.** support stockings

contenu [kɔ̃tny] **1** *adj* (*passion, émotion*) restrained, suppressed, pent-up; (*style*) restrained **2** *nm* [①**A10**,f,i] (*d'un paquet, d'un sachet etc*) contents; (*de lettre, livre etc*) content; *Journ* **c. rédactionnel** editorial content; *Ling* **le c. d'un mot** the content *or* meaning of a word; *Psy* **c. latent/manifeste** latent/manifest content

conter [kɔ̃te] *vt* (*histoire etc*) to tell, to relate; *F* **allez c. ça ailleurs!** (go and) tell that to the marines!; **elle ne s'en laisse pas c.** you can't fool her, she's not easily taken in; **il m'en a conté de belles sur elle!** he told me some fine things about her!; *Hum* **c. fleurette à qn** to whisper *or* murmur sweet nothings to sb

contestable [kɔ̃tɛstabl] *adj* questionable, debatable

contestataire [kɔ̃tɛstatɛr] **1** *adj* anti-establishment **2** *n* protester; **c'est une c.** she's a rebel

contestation [kɔ̃tɛstasjɔ̃] *nf* (**a**) (*controverse*) dispute; **de graves contestations ont surgi au sein du parti** serious dissent has arisen within the party; **être en c. avec qn** to be at variance *or* issue with sb; **élever une c. sur qch** to raise an objection to sth; **il y a matière** *ou* **sujet à c.** there are grounds for dispute; **sans c. possible** beyond (all) question, beyond dispute (**b**) *Pol* protest

conteste [kɔ̃tɛst] *adv* **sans c.** indisputably, unquestionably, beyond question

contester [kɔ̃tɛste] **1** *vt* (*argument, droit*) to contest, to dispute, to challenge; (*document, information*) to question, to dispute; **point contesté** controversial point; **c. l'efficacité d'une méthode de travail** to question *or* dispute the effectiveness of a method of working; **je lui conteste le droit de ...** I contest *or* dispute *or* question his right to ...; **il est très contesté** he is very controversial; **je ne conteste pas qu'il ait eu beaucoup à faire** I don't dispute that he had a lot to do **2** *vi* to take issue (**sur** over); *Pol* to protest; **faire qch sans c.** to do sth without protest

conteur, -euse [kɔ̃tœr, -øz] *n* (**a**) (*narrateur*) narrator, storyteller (**b**) (*écrivain*) story-writer

contexte [kɔ̃tɛkst] *nm* context; **le c. permet de mieux comprendre certains mots** some words are more readily understood in context; **donner un c.** to give a context; **c. historique** (*d'un événement*) historical context; **il faut remettre cet événement dans son c.** we must put this event in its context; **dans le c. de l'économie européenne** (with)in the context of the European economy

contextuel, -elle [kɔ̃tɛkstyɛl] *adj Ling* contextual

contexture [kɔ̃tɛkstyr] *nf* (**a**) (*des os, des muscles etc*) (con)texture (**b**) *Vieilli* (*d'une histoire, d'un poème*) structure, framework

contigu, -uë [kɔ̃tigy] *adj* (*mur, maison etc*) adjoining, adjacent, *Fml* contiguous; (*idées, domaine, profession*) related; **c. à** *ou* **avec qch** next *or* adjacent *or Fml* contiguous to sth

contiguïté [kɔ̃tigɥite] *nf* (*d'une maison etc*) adjacency, proximity, *Fml* contiguity; *Fig* **c. des idées/des vues** closeness of ideas/opinions

continence [kɔ̃tinɑ̃s] *nf* continence

continent[1] [kɔtinɑ̃] *adj* continent

continent[2] *nm Géog* (**a**) (*étendue*) continent; **l'Ancien/le Nouveau C.** the Old/the New World (**b**) (*par rapport à une île*) mainland

continental, -ale, -aux, -ales [kɔ̃tinɑ̃tal, -o] **1** *adj* continental; **la France continentale** mainland France **2** *n* mainland inhabitant

contingence [kɔ̃tɛ̃ʒɑ̃s] *nf Phil* contingency; **les contingences de la vie quotidienne** everyday happenings *or* events; **ignorer les contingences** to ignore the incidentals

contingent [kɔ̃tɛ̃ʒɑ̃] **1** *adj Phil* contingent; (*peu important*) incidental **2** *nm* (**a**) *Mil* contingent; **le c. annuel d'une classe est de 250 000 hommes** the annual intake *or Br* call-up *or Am* draft totals 250,000 men; **les soldats du c.** the conscripted soldiers (**b**) (*quota*) quota; (*part*) share, contribution; (*de chambres d'hôtel*) block, allotment; **contingents d'importation** import quotas

contingentement [kɔ̃tɛ̃ʒɑ̃tmɑ̃] *nm Admin* fixing *or* introduction of quotas; **le c. des importations** the fixing of quotas on imports, the fixing of import quotas

contingenter [kɔ̃tɛ̃ʒɑ̃te] *vt Admin* (**a**) (*importations etc*) to fix quotas on; **des produits contingentés** fixed quota products (**b**) (*films etc*) to distribute according to a quota

continu [kɔ̃tiny] **1** *adj* (*ligne*) continuous, unbroken; (*discussion*) continuous; (*effort*) sustained, continuous; (*souffrance*) constant, endless; (*soin, attention*) constant; *Él* **courant c.** direct current; *Ordinat* **papier en c.** continuous paper **2** *nm Phil, Phys, Math* continuum

continuateur, -trice [kɔ̃tinɥatœr, -tris] *n* (*de qn*) successor; (*d'une politique*) upholder

continuation [kɔ̃tinɥasjɔ̃] *nf* continuation; **bonne c.!** all the best!

continuel, -elle [kɔ̃tinɥɛl] *adj* (*ininterrompu*) continuous; (*qui se répète*) constant, continual; **des plaintes continuelles** constant *or* unending *or* perpetual complaints; **c. devenir** (*de l'individu*) continual evolution *or* development

continuellement [kɔ̃tinɥɛlmɑ̃] *adv* (*de façon ininterrompue*) continuously; (*de façon répétitive*) constantly, continually

continuer [kɔ̃tinɥe] **1** *vt* (*poursuivre*) (*études, efforts, politique etc*) to continue (with), to carry on with, to go on with, to keep on with; **continue le repas/la discussion sans moi** go on *or* carry on with the meal/the discussion without me; **c. un trait** to continue *or* extend a line; **c. sa route** *ou* **son chemin** to continue on one's way

2 *vi* (**a**) (*dans le temps*) to go on; **c. à** *ou* **de faire qch** to go on *or* carry on doing sth, to continue doing sth *or* to do sth; **je continue à** *ou* **de me demander si ...** I keep wondering if ...; **continuez!** (*encouragement*) keep it up!, carry on!; (*après une interruption*) go on!, carry on!, continue!; **la guerre continue** the war is still going on; **la vie continue** life goes on; **si tu continues comme ça ...** if you go on *or* carry on like that ...

(**b**) (*dans l'espace*) to continue, to carry on; **jardin qui continue jusqu'à la rivière** garden that extends to the river

3 se continuer *vpr* (**a**) (*dans le temps*) to be continued, to be carried on; **une légende qui se continue à travers les siècles** a legend which endures through the centuries; **la fête se continua tard dans la nuit** the party went on late into the night

(**b**) (*dans l'espace*) to continue, to carry on

continuité [kɔ̃tinɥite] *nf* (*d'une action*) continuity; (*d'une tradition, d'une politique etc*) continuation; **assurer la c. d'une tradition** to carry on *or* perpetuate a tradition; *Fin* **c. d'exploitation** going-concern status

continûment [kɔ̃tinymɑ̃] *adv* continuously

continuum [kɔ̃tinɥɔm] *nm Math, Phys etc* continuum; **c. espace-temps** space-time continuum

contondant [kɔ̃tɔ̃dɑ̃] *adj* blunt; **objet/instrument c.** blunt object/instrument; **arme contondante** blunt instrument

contorsion [kɔ̃tɔrsjɔ̃] *nf* (*du corps, des membres*) contortion; **faire des contorsions** to contort oneself *or* one's body

contorsionner (se) [səkɔ̃tɔrsjɔne] *vpr* to contort one's body *or* oneself; **ses traits se contorsionnent sous la souffrance** his features are contorted *or* twisted with pain; **la sorcière que l'on brûlait se contorsionnait dans les flammes** the witch they were burning writhed in the flames

contorsionniste [kɔ̃tɔrsjɔnist] *n* contortionist

contour [kɔ̃tur] *nm* (**a**) (*silhouette*) outline, contour; **la route suit les contours de la montagne** the road follows the contours of the mountain (**b**) **contours** (*méandres*) twists and turns

contourné [kɔ̃turne] *adj* (*membre, arbre, forme*) twisted, contorted, crooked; (*meuble, pied de chaise etc*) (over)elaborate; *Péj* **style c.** tortuous *or* convoluted style

contournement [kɔ̃turnəmɑ̃] *nm* (*d'une montagne, d'un marais etc*) skirting; *Rail* **(voie de) c.** loop line

contourner [kɔ̃turne] *vt* (**a**) (*colline, forêt, île etc*) to go round, to skirt (round); (*ville*) to go round, to bypass, to skirt (round); (*obstacle*) to go *or* get round; **c. la loi/une difficulté** to get round *or* circumvent the law/a difficulty (**b**) *Vieilli* (*motif, vase etc*) to shape, to trace the outline of

contraceptif, -ive [kɔ̃traseptif, -iv] *Méd* **1** *adj* contraceptive; **la pilule contraceptive** the (contraceptive) pill **2** *nm* contraceptive; **c. local/oral** barrier/oral contraceptive

contraception [kɔ̃trasɛpsjɔ̃] *nf* contraception; **méthode de c.** method of contraception, contraceptive method; **changer de c.** to change one's method of contraception; **moyens de c.** contraceptive methods *or* techniques; **c. masculine/féminine** male/female contraception

contractant [kɔ̃traktɑ̃] *Jur* **1** *adj* (*partie*) contracting **2** *nm* contracting party

contracté [kɔ̃trakte] *adj* (**a**) (*muscles, visage etc*) tense, taut; *Fig* **il était très contracté** he was very tense (**b**) *Ling* contracted

contracter¹ [kɔ̃trakte] *vt* (**a**) (*alliance, mariage*) to contract, to enter into; (*dette, obligation*) to incur, to contract; **c. des obligations** to enter into commitments; **c. une assurance** to take out an insurance policy (**b**) (*habitude, goût, manie*) to acquire; (*maladie*) to contract, to catch

contracter² **1** *vt* (*muscles, visage, bouche*) to tense; **visage contracté par la douleur** face drawn with pain **2 se contracter** *vpr* (**a**) (*du cœur*) to contract; (*d'un muscle*) to tense (up), to contract; (*d'une personne*) to tense (up), to become tense (**b**) [①A63,23] *Ling* (*d'un mot, d'un article*) to contract, to be contracted

contractile [kɔ̃traktil] *adj Physiol* (*muscle etc*) contractile, contractible

contraction [kɔ̃traksjɔ̃] *nf* (**a**) (*d'un corps etc*) contraction; (*d'un muscle*) tensing, contraction; *Physiol* **sentir les premières contractions** (*d'une femme qui va accoucher*) to feel the first contractions (**b**) *Ling* contraction

▶ **contraction**: **c. de texte** précis, summary; **être bon en c. de texte** to be good at précis

contractuel, -elle [kɔ̃traktɥɛl] **1** *adj* (*obligations etc*) contractual; **agent c.** = contractor working for the (local) council **2** *n* (*auxiliaire de police*) = traffic warden, *Am* = traffic policeman/policewoman

contracture [kɔ̃traktyr] *nf Méd* spasm

contradicteur [kɔ̃tradiktœr] *nm* contradictor

contradiction [kɔ̃tradiksjɔ̃] *nf* (**a**) (*opposition*) contradiction; *Jur* opposition; **être en c. avec qn** to contradict; **porter la c. au sein d'un débat** to bring a dissenting voice into a debate; **esprit de c.** contrariness; **il ne supporte pas la c.** he can't stand being contradicted

(**b**) (*inconséquence*) contradiction, inconsistency; **être en c. avec qch** to contradict sth, to be at variance *or* inconsistent *or* incompatible with sth; **cette théorie est un tissu de contradictions** this theory is a web *or* tissue of contradictions *or* inconsistencies; **être en c. avec soi-même** to contradict oneself

contradictoire [kɔ̃tradiktwar] *adj* contradictory (**à** to), inconsistent (**à** with); (*rapports, idées etc*) contradictory, conflicting; *Jur* **jugement c.** judgment after hearing both parties; **débat c.** debate

contradictoirement [kɔ̃tradiktwarmɑ̃] *adv Jur* after hearing both parties

contraignant [kɔ̃trɛɲɑ̃] *adj* restricting

contraindre [kɔ̃trɛ̃dr] (*pp* **contraint**; *pr ind* **je contrains, n. contraignons, ils contraignent**; *impf* **je contraignais**; *p hist* **je contraignis**; *fu* **je contraindrai**) **1** *vt* (**a**) (*réprimer*) (*qn, sentiments, envie etc*) to restrain (**b**) (*obliger*) **c. qn à faire qch** to force *or* compel *or* oblige sb to do sth; **je fus contraint à** *ou* **de quitter mon pays** I was forced *or* compelled *or* obliged to leave my country; *Jur* **c. qn par voie de justice** to bring an action against sb **2 se contraindre** *vpr* (**a**) (*se retenir*) to restrain oneself (**b**) **se c. à faire qch** to force oneself to do sth, to make oneself do sth

contraint [kɔ̃trɛ̃] *adj* (*posture, style etc*) constrained, unnatural; (*sourire*) forced; (*attitude*) stiff, strained; **c. et forcé** under duress

contrainte [kɔ̃trɛ̃t] *nf* (**a**) (*retenue*) constraint, restraint; **parler sans c.** to speak freely *or* without inhibition; **rire sans c.** to laugh without inhibition

(**b**) (*obligation*) constraint; **obtenir qch par la c.** to get sth by force; **faire qch par c.** to be forced to do sth; **agir sous la c.** to act under pressure *or* duress; **c. sociale** social pressure *or* constraint(s); **contraintes du marché** market constraints; **il faut prendre en compte plusieurs contraintes** several constraints *or* limiting factors must be taken into account

(**c**) *Tech* **c. de cisaillement/de traction** shearing/tensile stress *or* strain; **c. en compression** compressive stress; **c. en flambage** bending stress; **c. en torsion** torsional stress

▶ **contrainte**: *Jur* **c. par corps** imprisonment for debt

contraire [kɔ̃trɛr] **1** *adj* (**a**) (*direction*) opposite; (*intérêt, avis etc*) conflicting; **en sens c.** in the opposite direction; **vent c.** adverse *or* contrary wind; **ils sont d'avis contraires** they have conflicting opinions; **sauf avis c.** unless I/you/*etc* hear to the contrary; **c. à la règle** *ou* **aux règlements** against the rules, contrary to the rules; **c. au contrat** contrary to the terms of the contract; **c. aux statuts** contrary to the articles of association

(**b**) (*défavorable*) **le sort lui est c.** fate is against him

2 *nm* opposite; **c'est le c.** it's the other way round; **tu connais sa sœur? c'est tout le c. (de lui)** you know his sister? she's the exact opposite (of him); **il ne vous dit pas le c.** he's not denying it; **(bien) au c.** on the contrary; **au c. de ses frères** unlike his brothers; **au c. de ses parents, il est plutôt à gauche** unlike *or* in contrast to his parents, he's a bit left-wing; **il dit toujours le c. de ce qu'on pourrait attendre de lui** he always says the opposite of what you might expect; **tu es en train de dire une chose et son c.** you're saying one thing and then the exact opposite

contrairement [kɔ̃trɛrmɑ̃] *adv* **c. à** contrary to; (*comparaison*) unlike; **c. à ce que nous avions décidé** contrary to what we had decided; **c. à son habitude, il sortit sans manteau** contrary to his habit, he went out without a coat, he went out without a coat, which was unusual for him; **c. à moi, elle aime l'opéra** unlike me, she likes opera

contralto [kɔ̃tralto] *nm Mus* contralto, *pl* contraltos

contrariant [kɔ̃trarjɑ̃] *adj* (*personne, esprit*) perverse, contrary; (*situation*) annoying, irritating, tiresome; **comme c'est c.!** how annoying!; **elle n'est pas contrariante** she's easy-going, *Péj* she's a bit of a yes-woman

contrarié [kɔ̃trarje] *adj* (*personne*) annoyed, bothered; (*projet*) thwarted; **se sentir c. (dans ses projets)** to feel thwarted (in one's plans); **un gaucher c.** a left-handed person forced to write with his/her right hand

contrarier [kɔ̃trarje] *vt* (*impf, pr sub* **n. contrariions, v. contrariiez**) (**a**) (*ennuyer*) to annoy, to irritate, to bother; **il cherche à la c.** he's trying to annoy her; **il y a quelque chose qui me contrarie** something's annoying *or* bothering me (**b**) (*contrecarrer*) (*projets, desseins*) to thwart, to frustrate; **c. les projets/desseins de qn** to interfere with *or* thwart sb's plans; **c. qn dans ses projets** to thwart sb in his/her plans (**c**) (*alterner*) (*lignes, formes, couleurs*) to alternate

contrariété [kɔ̃trarjete] *nf* (**a**) (*agacement etc*) annoyance, vexation; **éprouver une vive c.** to be extremely annoyed; **il a dû avoir une grosse/petite c.** something must have upset him a lot/a bit (**b**) (*d'intérêts, de goûts, de couleurs etc*) clash; **esprit de c.** contrariness

contrastant [kɔ̃trastɑ̃] *adj* contrasting
contraste [kɔ̃trast] *nm* contrast; **mettre une chose en c. avec une autre** to contrast one thing with another; **faire c. (avec)** to contrast (with); **en c. avec le rouge** in contrast to the red; **effet de c.** contrasting effect; *TV* **réglage du c.** contrast control *or* adjustment; **le goût du c.** a taste *or* liking for contrast(s); **le c. des idées** the contrast(ing) of ideas
contrasté [kɔ̃traste] *adj* **(a)** contrasted, contrasting; **photo bien/mal contrastée** photo with the right amount of/with not enough contrast **(b)** *Ordinat* highlighted
contraster [kɔ̃traste] **1** *vi* **c. avec qch** to contrast with sth; **couleurs qui contrastent** contrasting colours **2** *vt* to contrast; (*photo*) to add contrast to
contrat [kɔ̃tra] *nm* (*document, convention*) contract, agreement; **un c. de plusieurs milliards de dollars** a contract worth several billion dollars; **un c. de deux ans** a two-year contract; **rupture de c.** breach of contract; **passer un c. (avec qn)** to enter into an agreement (with sb); **décrocher un c.** to win a contract; **notre c. était que …** our agreement was that …; *Cartes* **réaliser son c.** to make one's contract
▶ **contrat**: **c. d'achat** purchase contract; **c. d'affacturage** factoring contract; **c. d'affrètement** contract of affreightment; **c. d'agence** agency contract; **c. d'apprentissage** training contract; **c. d'association** joint venture; **c. d'assurance** contract of insurance; **c. de bail** lease contract; **c. collectif** collective agreement; **c. de concession** licensing contract; *Fin* **c. couverture à terme** forward contract; **c. de crédit-bail** lease-purchase contract; **c. de distribution** distribution contract; **c. à durée déterminée** fixed-term contract; **c. à durée indéterminée** open-ended contract; **c. exclusif** sole contract; **c. de franchisage** franchise contract; **c. de gestion** management contract; **c. global** blanket contract; **c. hôtelier** contract between a hotel and a travel agent; *Aut* **c. de location** rental agreement; **c. de mariage** marriage contract; **c. de mission d'intérim** temporary contract; **c. notarié** notarized contract; **c. à plein temps** *ou* **à temps plein** full-time contract; **c. de prêt** loan agreement; *Com* **c. de représentation exclusive** sole agency contract; **c. de service** service contract; **c. social** social contract; *Com* **c. de système** systems contracting; **c. temporaire** temporary contract; **c. à temps partiel** part-time contract; *Fin* **c. à terme future**, futures contract; **c. de transport** contract of carriage; **c. de travail** contract of employment, *Am* labor contract; **c. de vente** bill of sale, sales contract
contravention [kɔ̃travɑ̃sjɔ̃] *nf Jur* (*envers un règlement etc*) contravention, infringement, violation; (*amende*) fine; (*pour stationnement non-autorisé*) (*amende*) (parking) fine; (*avis*) (parking) ticket; **être en c.** to be contravening the law; **donner une c. à qn** to book sb *or* to give sb a (parking) ticket
contre [kɔ̃tr] **1** *prép* [①A64; B52] **(a)** (*opposition*) against; **nager c. le courant** to swim against the current; **se battre c. qn** to fight against *or* with sb; **se fâcher c. qn** to get angry with sb; **c. son habitude** contrary to his usual practice; **ce serait aller c. sa nature** it would go *or* be against his nature; **l'Angleterre c. l'Irlande** England against *or* versus Ireland; **jouer c. l'Angleterre** to play against England; **la loi c. l'avortement** the anti-abortion law; **lutte c. l'alcoolisme/le cancer** fight against alcoholism/cancer; **je n'ai rien c. lui** I have nothing against him; **tout le monde est c. moi** everyone is against me

(b) (*protection*) **sirop c. la toux** cough mixture; **tu es assuré c. le vol?** are you insured against *or* for theft?; **bombe c. les acariens** spray against acarids

(c) (*échange*) (in exchange) for; **échanger une chose c. une autre** to exchange one thing for another; **il lui demande de l'argent c. son silence** he's asking him for money in exchange for his silence; **livraison c. remboursement** cash on delivery

(d) (*pour*) to; **parier à cinq c. un** to bet five to one; **le projet fut accepté, à dix voix c. deux** the plan was accepted by ten votes to two

(e) (*près*) against; **s'appuyer c. le mur** to lean against the wall; **lancer une balle c. un mur** to throw a ball against a wall; **sa maison est tout c. la mienne** his house is right next to mine *or* adjoins mine; **prendre un enfant c. son cœur** to hug a child; **danser joue c. joue** to dance cheek to cheek; **viens un peu c. moi** come and cuddle up to me a bit; **ils dorment l'un c. l'autre** they sleep cuddled up to each other

(f) (*en dépit de*) **faire c. mauvaise fortune bon cœur** to put a brave face on things; **c. toute apparence** despite appearances (to the contrary); **c. toute logique** against all logic; **c. toute attente** contrary to all expectation(s)

(g) (*comparaison*) compared to; **la livre est à 9 francs c. 8 francs le mois dernier** the pound stands at 9 francs compared to 8 francs *or* as against 8 francs last month

2 *adv* **(a)** (*opposition*) **parler/voter pour/c.** to speak/vote for/against; **je n'ai rien c., je ne suis pas c.** I have nothing against it; **beaucoup sont c.** a lot of people are against it; *F* **par c.** on the other hand

(b) (*proximité*) **le radiateur est allumé, mets-toi tout c.** the heater is on, stand right next to it

3 *nm* **(a)** **disputer le pour et le c.** to argue *or* dispute the pros and cons; **il y a toujours du pour et du c.** there are two sides to everything

(b) *Boxe, Escrime* counter

(c) *Billard* kiss

(d) *Cartes* double
contre-accusation, *pl* **contre-accusations** *nf* countercharge
contre-achat, *pl* **contre-achats** *nm* counterpurchase
contre-alizé, *pl* **contre-alizés** *nm Météo* anti-trade (wind)
contre-allée, *pl* **contre-allées** *nf* side road
contre-amiral, *pl* **contre-amiraux** *nm* rear admiral
contre-appel, *pl* **contre-appels** *nm Mil* check roll call, second call
contre-assurance, *pl* **contre-assurances** *nf* reinsurance
contre-attaque, *pl* **contre-attaques** *nf Mil, Fig* counter-attack
contre-attaquer *vi* to counter-attack
contrebalancer [kɔ̃trəbalɑ̃se] (**je contrebalançai(s); n. contrebalançons**) **1** *vt* (*poids*) to counterbalance; *Fig* to offset, to counterbalance **2 se contrebalancer** *vpr F* **se c. de qch** not to give a damn about sth; **il s'en contrebalance** he couldn't give a damn, he couldn't care less; **je me contrebalance de perdre mon boulot** I don't give a damn *or* I couldn't care less about losing my job
contrebande [kɔ̃trəbɑ̃d] *nf* **(a)** (*activité*) smuggling, contraband; **faire de la c.** to smuggle goods; **faire entrer des marchandises en c.** to smuggle in goods; **marchandises de c.** smuggled goods; **alcool de c.** bootleg alcohol **(b)** (*marchandises*) smuggled goods, contraband
contrebandier, -ière [kɔ̃trəbɑ̃dje, -jɛr] *n* smuggler
contrebas (en) [ɑ̃kɔ̃trəbɑ] *adv* lower down, (down) below, on a lower level; **le café est en c. de la rue** the café is below street level
contrebasse [kɔ̃trəbɑs] *nf Mus* (*instrument*) (double) bass; (*musicien*) (double) bass player
contrebassiste [kɔ̃trəbɑsist] *nm Mus* (double) bass player
contrebasson [kɔ̃trəbɑsɔ̃] *nm Mus* double bassoon, contrabassoon
contrebatterie [kɔ̃trəbatri] *nf Mil* counterbattery
contre-bord (à) [akɔ̃trəbɔr] *adv Naut* **courir à c.** to sail on opposite tacks *or* on parallel and opposite courses
contrebouter [kɔ̃trəbute], **contrebuter** [kɔ̃trəbyte] *vt Constr* to buttress, to shore up
contre-braquage [kɔ̃trəbrakaʒ], *pl* **contre-braquages** *nm Aut* opposite lock
contrebraquer [kɔ̃trəbrake] *vt Aut* to steer into the skid, to apply opposite lock
contrecarrer [kɔ̃trəkare] *vt* (*qn, projets*) to thwart
contrechamp [kɔ̃trəʃɑ̃] *nm Cin* reverse (angle) shot, reverse cut, reaction shot
contre-chant, *pl* **contre-chants** [kɔ̃trəʃɑ̃] *nm Mus* counterpoint
contrechâssis [kɔ̃trəʃɑsi] *nm inv* double (window) frame
contrecœur[1] [kɔ̃trəkœr] *adv* **à c.** reluctantly, unwillingly; (*donner*) grudgingly
contrecœur[2] *nm* **(a)** *Constr* (*d'une cheminée*) backplate, fireback **(b)** *Rail* (*au centre d'un croisement de voies ferrées*) guardrail, wingrail, checkrail
contrecoup [kɔ̃trəku] *nm* (*d'une balle*) ricochet; (*d'un coup*) jar; *Fig* (*d'une action, d'un désastre etc*) repercussions, after-effects; **les contrecoups de la guerre** the repercussions *or* after-effects of war
contre-courant, *pl* **contre-courants** [kɔ̃trəkurɑ̃] *nm* **(a)** countercurrent; **nager à c.** to swim against the current; *Fig* **aller à c. de qch** to go against the current *or* the tide of sth **(b)** *Aut* contra-flow
contredanse [kɔ̃trədɑ̃s] *nf* **(a)** (*danse, air*) quadrille, contredanse **(b)** *F* (*amende*) fine
contredire [kɔ̃trədir] (*pr ind* **je contredis, n. contredisons, v. contredisez**; *other tenses like* **dire**) **1** *vt* **(a)** (*qn*) to contradict **(b)** (*rapport etc*) to be inconsistent with, to be at variance with, to contradict; (*espérances*) to belie; **les événements contredisent ses prédictions** the events are at variance with his predictions **2 se contredire** *vpr* (*d'une personne*) to contradict oneself; (*de plusieurs personnes*) to contradict each other; **ces deux textes se contredisent** these two texts contradict each other *or* are at variance with each other

contredit [kɔ̃trədi] *adv* **sans c.** indisputably, unquestionably, undoubtedly

contrée [kɔ̃tre] *nf* (*région*) region; (*pays*) country, land; **ils sont partis vers des contrées lointaines** they went off to distant parts *or* lands

contre-écrou, *pl* **contre-écrous** *nm MecE* lock nut

contre-emploi, *pl* **contre-emplois** *nm Th, Cin etc* miscasting; **ce rôle est un c. pour lui** he's miscast in that role; **utiliser qn à c.** to miscast sb

contre-enquête, *pl* **contre-enquêtes** *nf Jur* counter-inquiry

contre-épreuve, *pl* **contre-épreuves** *nf* **(a)** (*épreuve*) counterproof **(b)** *Tech* (*vérification*) check test

contre-espionnage *nm* counter-espionage

contre-essai, *pl* **contre-essais** *nm* control *or* check test

contre-exemple, *pl* **contre-exemples** *nm* counter-example

contre-expertise, *pl* **contre-expertises** *nf* second expert valuation, counter-appraisal

contrefaçon [kɔ̃trəfasɔ̃] *nf* **(a)** (*pratique*) counterfeiting; (*de signature*) forging **(b)** (*produit*) fake, imitation; **méfiez-vous des contrefaçons** beware of imitations

contrefacteur [kɔ̃trəfaktœr] *nm* counterfeiter, forger; (*de signature*) forger

contrefaire [kɔ̃trəfɛr] *vt* (*conj like* **faire**) **(a)** (*calquer*) (*qn, la démarche de qn etc*) to imitate, to mimic; (*déguiser*) (*voix, écriture etc*) to disguise; *Vieilli* (*feindre*) to feign; **c. la folie** to feign madness **(b)** (*pièce, monnaie, produits de marque etc*) to counterfeit, to forge; (*signature*) to forge; (*vidéo, radio-cassette etc*) to pirate **(c)** (*déformer*) (*visage*) to distort, to deform

contrefait [kɔ̃trəfɛ] *adj* **(a)** (*argent etc*) counterfeit, forged; (*signature*) forged **(b)** (*déformé*) (*personne, visage*) deformed, misshapen

contre-feu, *pl* **contre-feux** [kɔ̃trəfø] *nm* **(a)** (*dans cheminée*) fireback **(b)** (*feu*) backfire

contre-fiche, *pl* **contre-fiches** [kɔ̃trəfiʃ] *nf Constr* brace, strut

contreficher (se) [səkɔ̃trəfiʃe] *vpr Arg* **je m'en fiche et m'en contrefiche** I don't give a damn, I couldn't care less; **il se contrefiche de ce que tu penses** he doesn't give a damn *or* couldn't care less about what you think

contre(-)fil, *pl* **contre(-)fils** [kɔ̃trəfil] *nm* (*dans un cours d'eau etc*) opposite direction; *Tech* **travailler le bois à c.** to work wood against the grain

contre-filet, *pl* **contre-filets** [kɔ̃trəfilɛ] *nm Culin* sirloin, tenderloin

contrefort [kɔ̃trəfɔr] *nm* **(a)** *Archit* buttress **(b)** *Géog* (*de montagne*) spur; **contreforts** foothills **(c)** (*de chaussure*) stiffener

contre-haut (en) [ɑ̃kɔ̃trəo] *adv* (up) above, higher up, on a higher level

contre-indication, *pl* **contre-indications** *nf Méd* contra-indication

contre-indiquer *vt Méd* to contra-indicate; *aussi Fig* **c'est contre-indiqué** it's inadvisable *or* unwise

contre-interrogatoire, *pl* **contre-interrogatoires** *nm Jur* cross-examination

contre-jour [kɔ̃trəʒur], *pl* **contre-jours** *nm* **(a)** (*éclairage défavorable*) (*pour un tableau etc*) light from behind; **tableau pendu à c.** picture hung against the light; **photo prise à c.** photograph taken against the light; **assis à c.** sitting with one's back to the light **(b)** *Beaux-Arts, Cin, Phot* backlight(ing); **un effet de c.** a backlit *or* contre-jour effect

contre-la-montre [kɔ̃trəlamɔ̃tr] *nm inv Sp* time-trial

contre-lettre, *pl* **contre-lettres** [kɔ̃trəlɛtr] *nm Jur* counter-letter, counter-deed

contremaître, -tresse [kɔ̃trəmɛtr, -trɛs] *n* foreman, *f* forewoman

contre-manifestant, -ante, *pl* **contre-manifestant(e)s** [kɔ̃trəmanifɛstɑ̃, -ɑ̃t] *n Pol* counter-demonstrator

contre-manifestation, *pl* **contre-manifestations** [kɔ̃trəmanifestasjɔ̃] *nf Pol* counter-demonstration

contremarche [kɔ̃trəmarʃ] *nf* **(a)** *Mil* countermarch **(b)** *Constr* (*d'un escalier*) riser

contremarketing [kɔ̃trəmarkətiŋ] *nm* countermarketing

contremarque [kɔ̃trəmark] *nf* **(a)** (*sur une pièce, une plaque d'or etc*) countermark **(b)** *Th* passout ticket

contremarquer [kɔtrəmarke] *vt* to countermark

contre-mesure, *pl* **contre-mesures** [kɔ̃trəm(ə)zyr] *nf* **(a)** (*mesure*) countermeasure; *Mil* **c. électronique** electronic countermeasure, jamming **(b)** *Mus* **jouer à c.** to play against the beat *or* out of time

contre-offensive, *pl* **contre-offensives** *nf Mil* counter-offensive

contre-offre, *pl* **contre-offres** *nf* counter-offer

contre-ordre, *pl* **contre-ordres** *nm* = **contrordre**

contrepartie [kɔ̃trəparti] *nf* **(a)** (*dans un débat etc*) opposite *or* opposing view; *Com, Fin* (*dans une transaction*) other party *or* side; *Bourse* **faire la c.** to operate against one's client **(b)** (*compensation*) compensation; **c. financière** financial compensation; **en c.** in return **(de** for) **(c)** (*en comptabilité*) (*d'une inscription*) counterpart; (*d'un registre*) duplicate; **en c.** per contra **(d)** *Mus* counterpart

contre-passation, *pl* **contre-passations** [kɔ̃trəpasasjɔ̃] *nf Compta* journal entry, contra- entry

contre(-)pente, *pl* **contre(-)pentes** [kɔ̃trəpɑ̃t] *nf* counterslope, opposite slope

contre-performance, *pl* **contre-performances** [kɔ̃trəpɛrfɔrmɑ̃s] *nf* (*d'athlète, d'homme politique etc*) substandard *or* poor performance

contrepèterie [kɔ̃trəpɛtri] *nf* spoonerism

contre-pied, *pl* **contre-pieds**,[kɔ̃trəpje] *nm* **(a)** (*inverse*) opposite; **prendre le c.** (*action*) to do the opposite **(de** from); (*opinion*) to take the opposite view **(de** to); **il prend toujours le c. de ce qu'on lui dit** he always does the opposite of what he's told/says the opposite of what people say **(b)** *Sp* **prendre son adversaire à c.** to wrong-foot one's opponent; **prendre la balle à c.** to take the ball on the wrong foot **(c)** (*à la chasse*) back scent

contre(-)placage, *pl* **contre-plaquages** [kɔ̃trəplakaʒ] *nm* (*action*) plywood construction; (*résultat*) plywood surface

contre(-)plaqué, *pl* **contre-plaqués** [kɔ̃trəplake] *nm* plywood

contre-plongée, *pl* **contre-plongées** [kɔ̃trəplɔ̃ʒe] *nf Cin, TV* low-angle shot; **vue en c.** low-angle view

contrepoids [kɔ̃trəpwɑ] *nm* **(a)** *Tech* counterweight, counterbalance; (*d'une horloge, d'un monte-charge*) balance weight; *Fig* counterbalance; *Fig* **faire c. à qch** to counterbalance sth, to balance sth out **(b)** (*d'un funambule*) balancing pole

contre-poil (à) [akɔ̃trəpwal] *adv* (*d'un tissu, d'un animal*) the wrong way; *F* **prendre qn à c.** to rub sb up the wrong way

contrepoint [kɔ̃trəpwɛ̃] *nm Mus, Fig* counterpoint; **se passer en c.** to happen concurrently

contrepoison [kɔ̃trəpwazɔ̃] *nm* antidote

contre-porte, *pl* **contre-portes** [kɔ̃trəpɔrt] *nf* inner door, *Am* screen door

contre-pouvoir, *pl* **contre-pouvoirs** [kɔ̃trəpuvwar] *nm* anti-establishment force

contre-pression, *pl* **contre-pressions** [kɔ̃trəprɛsjɔ̃] *nf Aut* back-pressure

contre(-)projet, *pl* **contre-projets** [kɔ̃trəprɔʒɛ] *nm* counterplan

contre-proposition, *pl* **contre-propositions** [kɔ̃trəprɔpozisjɔ̃] *nf* counterproposal

contre(-)publicité [kɔ̃trəpyblisite] *nf* adverse *or* bad publicity; *Fig* **cet article fait de la c. à son auteur** this article is a poor advertisement for its author

contrer [kɔ̃tre] *vt* **(a)** (*repousser*) to thwart; (*personne*) to block; **c. un argument** to counter *or* refute an argument; **se faire c.** to come a cropper **(b)** *Boxe* (*coup*) to counter **(c)** *Cartes* to double

contre-rail, *pl* **contre-rails** [kɔ̃trəraj] *nm Rail* guard *or* check rail

contre-réforme [kɔ̃trərefɔrm] *nf Hist Rel* Counter-Reformation

contre-révolution, *pl* **contre-révolutions** [kɔ̃trərevɔlysjɔ̃] *nf Pol* counter-revolution

contre-révolutionnaire, *pl* **contre-révolutionnaires** [kɔ̃trərevɔlysjɔnɛr] *adj, n* counter-revolutionary

contre-segmentation, *pl* **contre-segmentations** [kɔ̃trəsɛgmɑ̃tasjɔ̃] *nf Mktg* countersegmentation

contreseing [kɔ̃trəsɛ̃] *nm Jur* countersignature

contresens [kɔ̃trəsɑ̃s] *nm* **(a)** (*de mots etc*) misinterpretation; (*mauvaise traduction*) mistranslation; **comprendre qch à c.** to take sth the wrong way; **faire un c.** to misinterpret; **faire un c. dans une traduction** to make a mistake in a translation; **ce résumé de l'histoire est un c.** this summary of the story is a piece of nonsense **(b)** *Aut* **à c.** the wrong way, in the wrong direction; **prendre une rue à c.** to go the wrong way down a street; **voitures qui vont à c.** cars going in the opposite direction

contresignataire [kɔ̃trəsiɲatɛr] *adj, n Jur* countersignatory

contresigner [kɔ̃trəsiɲe] *vt* to countersign

contretemps [kɔ̃trətɑ̃] *nm* **(a)** (*ennui*) hitch, mishap, contretemps; **à moins d'un c.** unless there's a hitch; **voilà un c. bien fâcheux!** that's really made things awkward!; **arriver à c.** to arrive at the wrong moment **(b)** *Mus* offbeat; **jouer à c.** to play off the beat

contre-terrorisme [kɔ̃trətɛrɔrism] *nm* counterterrorism

contre-terroriste, *pl* **contre-terroristes** [kɔ̃trətɛrɔrist] *adj, n* counter-terrorist

contre-tirer [kɔ̃trətire] *vt* to run off counter-proofs from, to take a counter-proof of

contre-torpilleur, *pl* **contre-torpilleurs** [kɔ̃trətɔrpijœr] *nm Naut* destroyer
contre-transfert [kɔ̃trətrɑ̃sfɛr] *nm Psy* counter-transference
contretypage [kɔ̃trətipaʒ] *nm TV etc* duping
contretype [kɔ̃trətip] *nm TV etc* dupe, copy tape
contre-ut *nm Mus* top C
contre-valeur, *pl* **contre-valeurs** [kɔ̃trəvalœr] *nf Fin* exchange value
contrevenant, -ante [kɔ̃trəv(ə)nɑ̃, -ɑ̃t] **1** *adj* (*partie etc*) offending **2** *n* offender; (*à la loi*) contravener, infringer (**à** of)
contrevenir [kɔ̃trəv(ə)nir] *vi* (*conj like* **venir**) **c. à** to contravene, to infringe
contrevent [kɔ̃trəvɑ̃] *nm* (**a**) (*d'une fenêtre*) (outside) shutter (**b**) *Constr* brace, strut
contre(-)vérité, *pl* **contre(-)vérités** [kɔ̃trəverite] *nf* (**a**) (*affirmation fausse*) untruth, falsehood (**b**) *Vieilli* (*destinée à faire entendre le contraire*) ironical statement
contre-verrou, *pl* **contre-verrous** [kɔ̃trəvɛru] *nm Ordinat* lock inhibit
contre-visite, *pl* **contre-visites** [kɔ̃trəvizit] *nf* = for someone suspected of fraudulently claiming sickness benefit, visit to a specific doctor at Social Security's request; (*par médecin*) = house call made, at the request of an employer, by a doctor (approved by Social Security) to determine whether an employee is genuinely ill
contre-voie (à) [akɔ̃trəvwa] *adv Rail* **monter/descendre à c.** to get in/out on the wrong side of the train
contribuable [kɔ̃tribɥabl] *n* taxpayer; **c. à l'impôt foncier** = ratepayer
contribuer [kɔ̃tribɥe] *vi* to contribute; **c. à qch** to contribute to(wards) sth; **c. financièrement à qch** to contribute (money) to sth, to make a (financial) contribution to sth; **c. à faire qch** to help (to) do something; **nous y avons contribué pour une bonne part** we made a handsome contribution to it; **cela contribue pour beaucoup à la rendre heureuse** that goes a long way towards making her happy; **il a beaucoup contribué à ...** he has made a great contribution to ..., he has played a great part in ...
contributif, -ive [kɔ̃tribytif, -iv] *adj* contributory
contribution [kɔ̃tribysjɔ̃] *nf* (**a**) *Admin* (*impôt*) tax; **contributions** (*à l'État*) taxes; (*à la collectivité locale*) *Br* rates, *Am* local taxes; **(bureau des) contributions** tax office, *Br* Inland Revenue, *US* Internal Revenue; **lever** *ou* **percevoir une c.** to collect *or* levy a tax (**b**) (*part*) contribution, share; (*collaboration*) contribution (**à** to); **mettre qn à c.** to call on sb's services; **mettre qch à c.** to make use of sth
▶ **contribution**: **c. après remise** discounted contribution; **c. brute** gross contribution; **c. complémentaire** supplementary contribution; **contributions directes** direct taxation; **c. foncière** land tax; **contributions indirectes** indirect taxation; **c. nette** net contribution; **c. sociale généralisée** general social security contribution
contrit [kɔ̃tri] *adj* contrite, penitent
contrition [kɔ̃trisjɔ̃] *nf Rel, Litt* contrition, penitence
contrôlable [kɔ̃trolabl] *adj* (*vérifiable*) verifiable, that can be checked *or* verified; (*maîtrisable*) controllable; **des éléments difficilement contrôlables** elements that are hard to control
contrôle [kɔ̃trol] *nm* (**a**) (*vérification*) (*de l'information, de déclarations, de marchandises etc*) checking, verification; *Admin* (*des services*) inspection, supervision; *Com* (*des comptes*) auditing, checking; *Sp, Aut* check; (*des pneus*) checking; *Scol* test; *Th etc* **c. des billets** checking of tickets
(**b**) (*surveillance*) control; **exercer un c. sévère sur qn** to maintain strict control over sb, to keep sb under strict supervision; **échapper à tout c.** to get out of control; **(bureau de) c.** ticket office, booking office, *Am* reservation office; *Av* **tour de c.** control tower
(**c**) (*maîtrise*) (*d'un véhicule, d'une machine etc*) control; **avoir le c. de qch** to have control of sth, to be in control of sth; **perdre c. (de la situation)** to lose control (of the situation); **perdre le c. de son véhicule** to lose control of one's vehicle; **c. de soi-même** self-control; **perdre tout c. de soi** to lose all self-control
(**d**) (*marque*) hallmark; (*bureau*) assay office; **poinçon de c.** hallmark stamp
(**e**) *Mil etc* roll, list, register; **c. de service** duty roster; **rayer qn des contrôles de l'armée** to remove sb from the army list
(**f**) *Ordinat* **touche c.** control key
▶ **contrôle**: *Ordinat* **c. d'accès** access control; **c. de bagages** baggage check; *Compta* **c. du bilan** audit; **c. bancaire** banking controls; *Fin* **c. des changes** exchange control; **c. de comptes** audit; *Univ* **c. continu** continuous assessment; *Ordinat* **c. croisé** cross-check; **faire un c. croisé de** to cross-check; *Ordinat* **c. du curseur** cursor control; **c. à distance** remote control; **c. douanier** customs control; **c. d'efficacité mercatique** marketing efficiency study; **c. des émissions de moteur diesel** diesel emissions test; *Fin* **c. fiscal** tax inspection; **contrôles aux frontières** border controls; **c. d'identité** identity check; **c. de l'immigration** immigration control; **contrôles à l'importation** import controls; *Jur* **c. judiciaire** probation; **placé sous c. judiciaire** put on probation; **c. de luminosité** brightness control; **c. des naissances** birth control; **c. des passeports** passport control; **contrôles phytosanitaires** plant health checks; **c. des points de ventes** store audit; **c. de police** police check; (*lieu*) police checkpoint; **c. des prix** price control; **c. de qualité** quality control; *Com* **c. de la qualité totale** total quality control, TQC; *Aut* **c. radar** radar speed check; **contrôles sanitaires** health checks; *Ordinat* **c. de la souris** mouse control; **c. des stocks** inventory *or* stock control; *Aut* **c. technique** ≈ MOT test
contrôler [kɔ̃trole] **1** *vt* (**a**) (*vérifier*) (*travail*) to supervise, to check; (*comptes*) to check, to audit; (*billets*) to check; (*passeports*) to examine, to check, to inspect; (*information, fait etc*) to check, to verify
(**b**) (*surveiller*) to monitor; (*situation, presse*) to control; **c. les naissances** to control the birth-rate; **c. les prix** to control prices; **l'armée contrôle toute cette région** all of this region is under army control, this whole region is controlled by the army; **le parti ne contrôle plus ces éléments indisciplinés** the party can no longer control this unruly element; **contrôlé par ordinateur** computer-controlled
(**c**) (*maîtriser*) (*qn*) to control; **c. ses émotions/réactions** to control one's emotions/reactions
(**d**) (*argent, or*) to hallmark, to stamp
(**e**) *Ordinat* **contrôlé par le logiciel** software-controlled; **contrôlé par menu** menu-driven, menu-controlled
2 se contrôler *vpr* to control oneself
contrôleur, -euse [kɔ̃trolœr, -øz] **1** *n* (**a**) *Can* **Bureau du C. Général** Office of the Controller General; **c. des contributions** *ou* **impôts** tax inspector, inspector of taxes; **c. du crédit** credit controller; **c. financier** financial controller; **c. de gestion** management controller; **c. aux liquidations** controller in bankruptcy; *TV etc* **c. de réseau** network controller; **c. (de la) restauration** food and beverage manager
(**b**) (*du travail etc*) supervisor; (*dans un train, bus*) ticket inspector
(**c**) *Av* **c. de la circulation aérienne** *ou* **de trafic aérien** air traffic controller
2 *nm* (**a**) (*appareil*) regulator; *Rail* master controller; **c. d'atelier** time recorder, time-clock; *Aut* **c. de vigilance du conducteur** driver alertness monitor
(**b**) *Ordinat* **c. de disque** disk controller; **c. d'unité de disquette** floppy disk controller; **c. d'affichage** display *or* screen controller; **c. de bus** bus controller
contrordre [kɔ̃trɔrdr] *nm* counterorder, countermand; **il y a c.** the orders have been changed; **sauf c.** unless otherwise directed
controuvé [kɔ̃truve] *adj* false, fabricated, concocted
controversable [kɔ̃trɔvɛrsabl] *adj* controversial, debatable
controverse [kɔ̃trɔvɛrs] *nf* controversy, debate; **cela prête encore à c.** it is still a controversial topic, it is still surrounded by controversy, it is still a matter of controversy *or* for debate; **donner lieu à c.** to be controversial; **matière à c.** matter for debate
controverser [kɔ̃trɔvɛrse] *vt* (*question etc*) to debate; **question/idée controversée** controversial *or* much debated question/idea
contumace[1] [kɔ̃tymas] *nf Jur* non-appearance (in court); **condamné par c.** sentenced in absentia *or* in his absence
contumace[2] [kɔ̃tymas], **contumax** [kɔ̃tymaks] *adj Jur* contumacious, defaulting
contusion [kɔ̃tyzjɔ̃] *nf* contusion, bruise
contusionner [kɔ̃tyzjɔne] *vt* to contuse, to bruise
conurbation [kɔnyrbasjɔ̃] *nf* conurbation
convaincant [kɔ̃vɛ̃kɑ̃] *adj* convincing
convaincre [kɔ̃vɛ̃kr] *vt* (*conj like* **vaincre**) (**a**) (*persuader*) to convince (**de** of, **que** that); **c. qn de faire qch** to persuade *or Am* convince sb to do sth; **j'en suis convaincu** I'm convinced of it; **se laisser c.** to let oneself be persuaded *or* convinced *or* won over; **je l'ai finalement convaincu** I finally convinced him (**b**) (*prouver la culpabilité de*) **être convaincu de meurtre** to be convicted *or* found guilty of murder
convaincu [kɔ̃vɛ̃ky] **1** *adj* convinced; **parler d'un ton c.** to speak with conviction; **c'est un végétarien c.** he's a committed vegetarian **2** *n* **prêcher des convaincus** to preach to the converted
convalescence [kɔ̃valɛsɑ̃s] *nf* (**a**) *Méd* convalescence; **elle**

est en c. she's convalescing; **maison de c.** convalescent *or* nursing home **(b)** *Mil etc* sick leave

convalescent, -ente [kɔ̃valɛsɑ̃, -ɑ̃t] *adj, n* convalescent

convecteur [kɔ̃vɛktœr] *nm* convector (heater)

convection [kɔ̃vɛksjɔ̃] *nf Phys* convection

convenable [kɔ̃vnabl] *adj* **(a)** (*approprié*) appropriate, suitable, fitting; **juger c. de faire qch** to think it appropriate to do sth **(b)** (*décent*) (*comportement*) decent, respectable, acceptable; (*tenue*) decent, proper; **ce sont des gens très convenables** they are very decent *or* respectable people; **peu c.** unacceptable; **il n'est pas c. de faire du bruit en mangeant** it is not polite *or* nice *or* proper to make a noise when eating **(c)** (*acceptable*) (*salaire, restaurant, pantalon etc*) decent, adequate

convenablement [kɔ̃vnabləmɑ̃] *adv* **(a)** (*d'une façon appropriée*) appropriately, suitably, fittingly **(b)** (*avec décence*) correctly, properly, decently **(c)** (*de façon acceptable*) decently; **on peut manger très c. à la cantine** you can eat quite decently in the canteen

convenance [kɔ̃vnɑ̃s] *nf* **(a)** (*fait de convenir*) appropriateness, suitability, fitness; **pour (des raisons de) c. personnelle** for personal reasons; **mariage de c.** marriage of convenience; **trouver qch à sa c.** to find sth to one's liking *or* suitable; **il le fera à sa c.** he'll do it at his own convenience **(b)** *Litt* (*des goûts*) affinity **(c) les convenances** propriety, the proprieties, etiquette; **comportement contraire aux convenances** unseemly conduct, improper behaviour

convenir [kɔ̃vnir] (*conj like* **venir**) **1** *vi* **(a)** (*conj with* **avoir**) **c. à** (*aller, plaire*) to suit; **si cela vous convient** if that suits you, if that is convenient *or* all right (for you); **c'est exactement ce qui me convient** it's just what I need; **cet emploi lui convient parfaitement** that job suits him perfectly; **ce climat ne me convient pas** this climate doesn't suit me *or* agree with me; **il est difficile de trouver le mot qui convient** it's difficult to find the appropriate word; **robe qui convient à la circonstance** dress that suits the occasion, dress suitable for *or* befitting the occasion

(b) (*conj with* **avoir** *or Lit with* **être**) **c. de qch** (*être d'accord avec qch*) to agree on sth; (*le reconnaître*) to acknowledge *or* admit sth; **j'ai eu tort, j'en conviens** I was wrong, I admit it, I admit I was wrong; **il convient qu'il a eu tort** he admits that he was wrong

2 *v impers* (*conj with* **être**) **il convient de ...** (*il est souhaitable de*) it is advisable to ...; (*il est de bon ton de*) it is the done thing to ..., it is proper to ...; **ce qu'il convient de faire (c')est de ...** the right thing to do is to ...; **il convient que vous y alliez** you should *or* ought to go; **il fut convenu qu'ils le feraient venir** it was agreed that they would send for him; **comme convenu** as agreed

convention [kɔ̃vɑ̃sjɔ̃] *nf* **(a)** (*accord*) agreement; *Jur* (*d'un contrat etc*) article, clause; **c. écrite/verbale** written/verbal agreement; *Com* **c. d'exclusivité réciproque** mutual exclusivity agreement **(b) les conventions (sociales)** the (social) conventions; **de c.** conventional; *Péj* **amabilité/sourire de c.** superficial courtesy/smile; **par c. nous appelerons x la première inconnue de l'équation** the first unknown of the equation will be called x **(c)** *Pol* (*assemblée*) (extraordinary) assembly, *US* convention; *Hist Fr* **La C. (nationale)** the (National) Convention (*1792*)

▶ **convention**: *Com* **c. d'affrètement** contract of affreightment; **c. collective** collective agreement; *Pol* **c. internationale** international convention *or* agreement; **c. monétaire** monetary agreement

conventionné [kɔ̃vɑ̃sjɔne] *adj* **médecin c.** doctor attached to the health system, *Br* ≈ National Health Service doctor; **médecin non c.** ≈ private doctor; **clinique conventionnée** clinic attached to the health system

conventionnel, -elle [kɔ̃vɑ̃sjɔnɛl] **1** *adj* **(a)** (*valeur, symbole*), *Mil* (*armes etc*) conventional; *Ling* **langage c.** conventional language; **c'est quelqu'un de très c.** he's a very conventional person **(b)** *Jur* (*clause etc*) contractual **(c)** *Péj* (*peu sincère*) superficial; **affabilité conventionnelle** superficial affability **2** *nm Hist Fr* member of the National Convention

conventionnellement [kɔ̃vɑ̃sjɔnɛlmɑ̃] *adv* conventionally; *Jur* by agreement

conventionnement [kɔ̃vɑ̃sjɔnmɑ̃] *nm* (*d'une clinique, d'un médecin*) attachment to the health system

conventionner [kɔ̃vɑ̃sjɔne] *vt* (*clinique, médecin*) to attach to the health system

conventuel, -elle [kɔ̃vɑ̃tɥɛl] *adj Rel* (*maison*) conventual; (*vie*) monastic; **bâtiment c.** (*monastère*) monastery; (*couvent*) convent

convenu [kɔ̃vny] *adj* **(a)** (*prix, somme*) agreed, stipulated; (*date, moment*) agreed, appointed; **comme c.** as agreed **(b)** *Péj* (*langage, style, attitude etc*) conventional

convergence [kɔ̃vɛrʒɑ̃s] *nf* convergence; *Fig* **c. des idées** convergence of ideas, meeting of minds

convergent [kɔ̃vɛrʒɑ̃] *adj* (*lignes, idées, efforts etc*) convergent

converger [kɔ̃vɛrʒe] *vi* (**convergeant; ils convergeaient**) (*de routes, de lignes etc*) to converge; **toutes ces ruelles convergent vers le château** all these lanes meet at *or* converge on the castle; **nos efforts convergent vers le même but** all our efforts are focused on the same objective; **leurs opinions convergent** they are of like mind *or* one mind

convers, -erse [kɔ̃vɛr, -ɛrs] **1** *adj Rel* (*frère, sœur*) lay **2** *nf* **converse** converse

conversation [kɔ̃vɛrsasjɔ̃] *nf* conversation, talk; **être en grande c. (avec qn)** to be deep in conversation (with sb); **lier c.** *ou* **entrer en c.** *ou* **engager une c. avec qn** to get into conversation with sb, to strike up a conversation with sb; **avoir une longue c. avec qn** to have a long *or* lengthy conversation with sb; **faire la c. (à qn)** to chat (with sb); **voilà qui a arrêté net la c.** that stopped the conversation dead, that killed the conversation; **il a fait les frais de la c.** he was the main subject of conversation; **amener un sujet dans une c.** to introduce a topic into a conversation; **c. téléphonique** telephone conversation; **avoir de la c.** to be a good conversationalist; **elle n'a aucune c.** she is a poor conversationalist, she has no conversation; *Tél* **c. 'mains libres'** hands-free conversation

conversationnel, -elle [kɔ̃vɛrsasjɔnɛl] *adj Ordinat* **mode c.** conversational *or* interactive mode

converser [kɔ̃vɛrse] *vi* to converse, to talk (**avec** with)

conversion [kɔ̃vɛrsjɔ̃] *nf* **(a)** *Fin, Ordinat etc* (*changement*) conversion (**en** into); *Math* **c. des fractions** conversion of fractions; **c. d'entreprise** change in the line of business; **c. d'un emprunt** conversion of loan notes *or* stock; *Ordinat* **c. de fichier** file conversion; **c. de monnaies** currency conversion **(b)** *Ski* kick turn; *Mil etc* wheel(ing) **(c)** (*au catholicisme, au socialisme etc*) conversion (**à** to)

converti, -e [kɔ̃vɛrti] **1** *adj* (*pécheur etc*) converted **2** *n* convert

convertibilité [kɔ̃vɛrtibilite] *nf Fin* convertibility

convertible [kɔ̃vɛrtibl] **1** *adj* convertible (**en** into); **rente c.** convertible interest (*paid by the State on banks securing a national debt*); **obligations convertibles** convertible bonds; **canapé c.** sofa bed; **fauteuil c.** convertible armchair **2** *nm* **(a)** *Av* convertiplane **(b)** (*canapé*) sofa bed

convertir [kɔ̃vɛrtir] **1** *vt* **(a)** (*changer*) to convert (**en** into); **c. une pièce en bureau** to convert a room into an office; **c. des valeurs en espèces** to convert securities into cash; *Com, Fin* **c. des rentes** to convert stock; **c. un emprunt** to convert loan notes *or* stock **(b)** (*à une religion, un point de vue etc*) to convert (**à** to) **2 se convertir** *vpr* **(a)** (*à une religion etc*) to convert, to become converted (**à** to) **(b) se c. en** (*se transformer*) to change *or* turn into

convertissement [kɔ̃vɛrtismɑ̃] *nm Bourse, Fin* (*de valeurs en espèces*) conversion

convertisseur [kɔ̃vɛrtisœr] *nm* **(a)** *Métal* converter; *MecE, Aut* **c. de couple** torque converter; **c. catalytique à oxydation** oxidization catalytic converter; **c. de couple hydrodynamique** hydraulic (hydro-kinetic) fluid converter; **c. hydraulique** hydraulic converter; **c. multi-étagé** multi-stage converter **(b)** *Él, Électron* converter; *TV etc* **c. d'images** image converter; *TV etc* **c. numérique de graphiques** graphics digitizer; *Ordinat* **c. analogique numérique** digitizer

convexe [kɔ̃vɛks] *adj* convex

convexité [kɔ̃vɛksite] *nf* convexity

convict [kɔ̃vikt] *n Jur* convict

conviction [kɔ̃viksjɔ̃] *nf* **(a)** (*certitude*) conviction; **avoir la c. que ...** to be convinced that ...; **une c. personnelle** a personal conviction; **sans grande c.** without much conviction; **avec/sans c.** with/without conviction **(b)** *Jur* **pièce à c.** exhibit **(c) convictions** (*opinions*) convictions, beliefs

convier [kɔ̃vje] *vt* (*impf, pr sub* **n. conviions, v. conviiez**) **(a)** (*inviter*) to invite; **c. qn à un mariage** to invite sb to a wedding **(b) c. qn à faire qch** to urge *or* strongly advise sb to do sth

convive [kɔ̃viv] *n* (*à une table*) guest

convivial, -iale, -iaux, -iales [kɔ̃vivjal, -o] *adj* (*ambiance, soirée*) convivial; *Ordinat* user-friendly

convivialité [kɔ̃vivjalite] *nf* conviviality; *Ordinat* user-friendliness

convocation [kɔ̃vɔkasjɔ̃] *nf* **(a)** (*d'une assemblée etc*) calling together, convening; **recevoir une c.** to receive notice to attend; **c. à l'examen** notification of an examination **(b)** *Jur* summons

convoi [kɔ̃vwa] *nm* **(a) c. (funèbre)** funeral procession *or* cortège **(b)** *Mil* **c. (de troupes)** convoy of troops; **c. administratif** supply column; **c. de prisonniers** convoy of prisoners **(c)** *(de véhicules)* convoy; **'c. exceptionnel'** 'dangerous/wide load'; **c. automobile** motorcade; *Rail* **c. de marchandises** goods *or* freight train; *Rail* **c. postal** mail train **(d)** *Naut* convoy

convoiement [kɔ̃vwamɑ̃] *nm* convoying, escorting

convoiter [kɔ̃vwate] *vt* *(poste, richesse)* to covet, to be after; *(rôle)* to be after; *(femme)* to lust after; **c. des yeux** to look lustfully at

convoitise [kɔ̃vwatiz] *nf* covetousness; **regarder qch avec c.** to cast covetous glances *or* to look covetously at sth; **exciter les convoitises** to excite envy

convoler [kɔ̃vɔle] *vi Hum* **c. (en justes noces)** to marry; **c. en secondes noces** to remarry

convoluté [kɔ̃vɔlyte] *adj Bot* convolute(d), whorled

convoquer [kɔ̃vɔke] *vt* **(a)** *(assemblée)* to call together, to convene; **c. les actionnaires** to call the shareholders to a meeting; **c. une assemblée générale** to call a general meeting **(b)** *Admin etc* *(candidat)* to call in (for an interview); *(témoin)* to summon; **le directeur m'a convoqué (dans son bureau)** the manager called me in(to his office); **c. qn à un examen** to notify sb of an examination

convoyage [kɔ̃vwajaʒ] *nm* = **convoiement**; *Naut* **faire un c. entre deux ports** to escort ships between two ports

convoyer [kɔ̃vwaje] *vt* **(je convoie, n. convoyons, ils convoient, je convoierai)** *(bateau, troupes etc)* to convoy, to escort; *(des fonds)* to transport by armed guard

convoyeur [kɔ̃vwajœr] *nm* **(a)** *Mil, Naut* *(personne)* escort; *(navire)* convoy (ship), escort (ship) **(b)** *MecE, Ind* conveyor **(c) c. de fonds** security guard, armed security escort

convulser [kɔ̃vylse] **1** *vt* to convulse; **visage convulsé par la terreur** face convulsed by *or* with terror **2 se convulser** *vpr* to convulse, to be convulsed; **sa figure se convulsa** his face became contorted

convulsif, -ive [kɔ̃vylsif, -iv] *adj* convulsive; **rire c.** convulsive *or* uncontrollable laughter

convulsion [kɔ̃vylsjɔ̃] *nf* convulsion; **être pris de convulsions** to go into convulsions; **se tordre dans des convulsions** to double up *or* writhe in convulsions; *Fig* **c. politique** political upheaval

convulsionner [kɔ̃vylsjɔne] *vt Méd* to convulse

convulsivement [kɔ̃vylsivmɑ̃] *adv* convulsively

cooblígé, -ée [kɔɔbliʒe] *n Jur* joint obligor, co-obligor

cooccupant, -ante [kɔɔkypɑ̃, -ɑ̃t] *n* co-occupier

cool [kul] *adj F* cool; **il n'est pas très c., ton père** your father's a bit square *or* a bit of an old fogey; *Mus* **jazz c.** hip *or* cool jazz

coolie [kuli] *nm* coolie

coopérant [kɔɔperɑ̃] **1** *adj* co(-)operative **2** *n* *(à l'étranger)* aid worker; *(pendant le service militaire)* = Voluntary Service Overseas Worker *or* VSO Worker

coopérateur, -trice [kɔɔperatœr, -tris] **1** *n* **(a)** *(collègue)* co-worker, collaborator **(b)** *(dans une coopérative)* member of a co(-)operative **2** *adj* **agent c.** co(-)operating agent

coopératif, -ive [kɔɔperatif, -iv] **1** *adj* *(société, personne)* co(-)operative **2** *nf* **coopérative** *(association)* co(-)operative, co-op; *(magasin)* co(-)operative store, co-op; **c. de vente/production** sales/production co(-)operative; **c. d'achats** wholesale co-operative; **c. de crédit** credit union, co-operative credit society

coopération [kɔɔperasjɔ̃] *nf* **(a)** *(appui)* co(-)operation; **offrir sa c. à qn** to offer to co(-)operate with sb; **travailler en c. avec qn** to work in collaboration with sb **(b)** *Pol* ≈ Voluntary Service Overseas; **partir en c. en Afrique** to go off to do VSO in Africa **(c)** *Econ* co(-)operation; **société/mouvement de c.** co(-)operative society/movement

coopératisme [kɔɔperatism] *nm Écon* co(-)operation, co(-)operative system

coopérer [kɔɔpere] *vi* **(je coopère, n. coopérons; je coopérerai)** to co(-)operate **(à** in)

cooptation [kɔɔptasjɔ̃] *nf* co-option, co-opting, co-optation; **élu par c.** elected by co-option

coopter [kɔɔpte] *vt* to co-opt

coordinateur, -trice [kɔɔrdinatœr, -tris] *adj, n* = **coordonnateur**

coordination [kɔɔrdinasjɔ̃] *nf* *(du travail, d'un projet, des mouvements)* co(-)ordination; [①A68,1; B55,A] *Gram* **conjonction de c.** co(-)ordinating conjunction; *Gram* **avoir une fonction de c.** to act as a co(-)ordinating conjunction

coordonnateur, -trice [kɔɔrdɔnatœr, -tris] **1** *adj* co(-)ordinating **2** *n* *(personne)* co(-)ordinator; *Av* air-traffic controller

coordonné, -ée [kɔɔrdɔne] **1** *adj* *(mouvement, efforts etc)* co(-)ordinated; *(draps, serviettes etc)* matching; **écharpe et gants coordonnés** scarf and matching *or* co(-)ordinated gloves; *Gram* **proposition coordonnée** co(-)ordinate clause **2** *nfpl* **coordonnées (a)** *Math, Géog, Astron* co(-)ordinates **(b)** *F* **donnez-moi vos coordonnées** give me your address and phone number; **je ne connais pas ses coordonnées en ce moment** I don't know where *or* how to reach him at the moment

coordonner [kɔɔrdɔne] *vt* to co(-)ordinate **(à avec** with)

copain, copine [kɔpɛ̃, kɔpin] *F* **1** *n* pal, mate, *Am* buddy; **c. de classe** classmate; **c. de régiment** army mate; **sa nouvelle copine d'école** her new pal at school; **ma (petite) copine** my girlfriend; **mon (petit) c.** my boyfriend; **salut les copains!** *(en arrivant)* hi gang!; *(en partant)* see you gang!; **faire profiter les petits copains** to help out one's pals **2** *adj* pally; **ils sont très copains** they're great pals *or* mates *or Am* buddies; **ils sont très c-c.** they're very pally *or Am* buddy-buddy

copartageant, -ante [kopartaʒɑ̃, -ɑ̃t] *n Jur* coparcener, coheir, *f* coheiress

coparticipant, -ante [kopartisipɑ̃, -ɑ̃t] *n Jur* copartner

coparticipation [kopartisipasjɔ̃] *nf Jur* copartnership; **c. aux bénéfices** profit-sharing

copeau, -eaux [kɔpo] *nm* *(de bois, chocolat)* shaving; *(de métal)* cutting; **c. de tour** turnings

Copenhague [kɔpɛnag] *nf* Copenhagen

copiable [kɔpjabl] *adj* copiable

copiage [kɔpjaʒ] *nm* copying; *Scol* cribbing, copying

copie [kɔpi] *nf* **(a)** *(reproduction)* *(de document, lettre etc)* copy; *Journ, Typ* copy; **faire une c. de qch** to make a copy of sth; *Journ* **être en mal de c.** to be short of copy; *Admin, Jur* **pour c. conforme** certified accurate; **c. certifiée conforme** certified true copy; **c. au carbone** carbon copy; *Com* **c. authentique** certified copy; **c. de lettre** duplicate; **c. papier** paper copy; **c. stratégie (créative)** *(de publicité)* (creative) copy strategy; **c. de travail** working copy

(b) *Scol* *(d'examen)* paper; **rendre c. blanche** to hand in a blank paper; **c. simple/double** single/double sheet of paper

(c) *(d'un tableau, d'une statue etc)* copy, reproduction; *(d'un roman, d'un style etc)* imitation; **ce n'est qu'une pâle c. de l'original** it's only a pale imitation of the original

(d) *TV, Cin* copy, print; **c. de film** (film) print; **c. antenne** show copy, broadcast master, release print; **c. de montage** cutting copy, workprint; **c. exploitation** show copy; **c. positive** positive print; **c. standard** combined print

(e) *Ordinat* **c. sur papier** hard copy, printout; **c. de disquette** *(commande DOS)* diskcopy; **c. de sauvegarde** *ou* **de secours** backup (copy), security copy; **c. de sûreté** backup (copy)

copier [kɔpje] *(impf, pr sub* **n. copiions, v. copiiez)** **1** *vt* **(a)** *(texte, musique etc)* to copy; *(sons)* to dub off; **c. qch au propre** *ou* **au net** to make a fair copy of sth, to copy sth out (neatly); *Ordinat* **c. un document sur le disque dur** to back up *or* copy a document onto hard disk **(b)** *(statue, tableau etc)* to copy, to reproduce; *(qn, style etc)* to imitate; *Scol* to copy, to crib; **elle me copie en tout** she copies everything I do, she copies me in everything **2** *vi Scol* to copy, to crib; **il copie sur son voisin** he's copying *or* cribbing from *or* off the boy next to him

copier-coller *nm inv Ordinat* copy-and-paste

copieur, -ieuse [kɔpjœr, -øz] **1** *adj* copying, cribbing **2** *n Scol* copier, cribber **3** *nm* copying machine, (photo)copier **4** *nf* **copieuse** copier

copieusement [kɔpjøzmɑ̃] *adv* *(manger, boire)* copiously; **il s'est servi c.** he took a generous helping; **après un repas c. arrosé** after a meal washed down with a lot of wine; **je me suis fait c. insulter** I got well and truly insulted; **s'ennuyer c.** to be bored to tears

copieux, -ieuse [kɔpjø, -jøz] *adj* *(repas)* copious, hearty, square; *(portion, part, pourboire)* generous

copilote [kopilɔt] *nm Av* copilot

copinage [kɔpinaʒ] *nm F* cronyism; **dans ce milieu, tout ne marche que par c.** around here it's who you know that matters, what counts around here is who you're friendly with; **obtenir un poste par c.** to get a job *or* post through one's connections *or* through the people one knows

copine [kɔpin] *nf F voir* **copain**

copiner [kɔpine] *vi F* to be pals *or Am* buddies **(avec** with)

copinerie [kɔpinri] *nf F* = **copinage**

copiste [kɔpist] *n* **(a)** *(clerc etc)* copyist, transcriber; **faute de c.** clerical error **(b)** *(plagiaire)* copier, imitator

coposséder [kopɔsede] *vt* *(conj like* **posséder)** *Jur* to own jointly, to have joint ownership of

copossesseur [kopɔsɛsœr] *nm Jur* joint owner

copossession [kopɔsɛsjɔ̃] *nf Jur* joint ownership, co-ownership

copra(h) [kɔpra] *nm* copra; **huile de c.** coconut oil

coprésentateur, -trice [koprezɑ̃tatœr -tris] *n TV etc* co-presenter
coprésidence [koprezidɑ̃s] *nf* co-chairmanship, co-presidency
coprésident [koprezidɑ̃] *nm* co-chairman, co-president
coprocesseur [kɔprɔsesœr] *nm Ordinat* co-processor; **c. arithmétique** maths co-processor
coproducteur, -trice [koprodyktœr, -tris] *n TV etc* co-producer
coproduction [kɔprɔdyksjɔ̃] *nf* coproduction, joint production
coproduire [kɔprɔdɥir] *vt* to coproduce
copropriétaire [kɔprɔprijetɛr] *n Jur* co-owner, joint owner
copropriété [kɔprɔprijete] *nf Jur* co-ownership, joint ownership; (*propriétaires*) co-owners, joint owners; **acheter/posséder une maison en c.** to buy/own a house jointly; **c. différée** timeshare taken on a lease basis converting to ownership after a given period of time
copte [kɔpt] **1** *adj* Coptic **2** *nm Ling* Coptic **3** *n* **C.** Copt
copulation [kɔpylasjɔ̃] *nf* copulation
copuler [kɔpyle] *vi* (*des animaux, humains*) to copulate
copyright [kɔpirajt] *nm* copyright
coq[1] [kɔk] *nm* **(a)** (*oiseau*) cock, *Am* rooster; **jeune c.** cockerel; **le c. gaulois** the French cockerel; **au chant du c.** at cockcrow; **combat de coqs** cockfight(ing); **c. de combat** fighting cock; *F* **rouge comme un c.** as red as a beetroot; *F* **fier** *ou* **orgueilleux comme un c.** as proud as a peacock; *Fig* **mollets de c.** wiry *or* spindly legs; *Fig* **être comme un c. en pâte** to be in clover; *Fig* **le c. du village** the local Casanova; *Boxe* **poids c.** bantamweight **(b)** (*girouette*) weathercock
▶ **coq**: *Orn* **c. de bruyère** capercaillie, wood grouse; **c. faisan** cock pheasant; *Orn* **c. de roche** cock-of-the-rock; *Culin* **c. au vin** coq au vin
coq[2] *nm Naut* **(maître-)c.** (ship's) cook
coq-à-l'âne *nm inv* sudden change of subject; **passer du c., faire un c.** to jump from one subject to another
coquard, coquart [kɔkar] *nm F* black eye, shiner
coque [kɔk] *nf* **(a)** (*d'une noix, d'un fruit*) shell, husk; (*mollusque*) cockle; *Culin* **œuf à la c.** (soft-)boiled egg **(b)** (*d'un navire*) hull, bottom; (*d'un avion*) fuselage; (*d'une voiture*) body, shell, bodyshell; *Naut* **double c.** double bottom
coquelet [kɔklɛ] *nm Culin* cockerel
coquelicot [kɔkliko] **1** *nm Bot* (red) poppy **2** *adj inv* poppy-red
coqueluche [kɔklyʃ] *nf Méd* whooping-cough; **avoir la c.** to have whooping-cough; *Fig* **être la c. des adolescents** to be a teenage idol; *Fig* **être la c. du bureau** to be the darling of the office; *Fig* **il est devenu la c. de ces dames** he has become a heart-throb
coquelucheux, -euse [kɔklyʃø, -øz] *adj Méd* **une toux coquelucheuse** a whooping cough
coquerico [kɔk(ə)riko] *int, nm* = **cocorico**
coquet, -ette [kɔkɛ, -ɛt] **1** *adj* (*ville, jardin, intérieur etc*) charming; (*vêtements*) smart, stylish; *Vieilli* (*sourire*) coquettish, flirtatious; **elle est coquette** she likes smart clothes, she's very clothes-conscious; (*qui aime séduire*) she's very flirtatious; **il est trop c.** he's too conscious of his appearance; *F* **coquette somme** tidy sum, nice little sum **2** *nf Vieilli* **coquette** coquette, flirt
coquetier [kɔktje] *nm* egg-cup; *F* **gagner le c.** to hit the jackpot; *Iron* **ça y est, j'ai gagné le c.** that's it, I've really done it now!
coquettement [kɔkɛtmɑ̃] *adv* (*habillé*) smartly, stylishly; (*meublé*) stylishly, elegantly; (*sourire*) flirtatiously, coquettishly; *F* (*dédommager qn*) handsomely
coquetterie [kɔkɛtri] *nf* **(a)** (*vestimentaire*) consciousness of one's appearance; *Vieilli* (*désir de plaire*) coquetry, flirtatiousness; **faire des coquetteries** to put on an affected manner; **faire le fier par c.** to give oneself airs and graces; **avoir de la c. pour sa tenue** to be fastidious *or* particular about one's appearance; **avec c.** (*habiller, meubler*) stylishly, elegantly **(b)** *F* **avoir une c. dans l'œil** to have a cast in one's eye
coquillage [kɔkijaʒ] *nm* **(a)** (*mollusque*) shellfish; **manger des coquillages** to eat shellfish **(b)** (*coque vide*) shell
coquillard [kɔkijar] *nm* **(a)** *Hist* ruffian, rogue **(b)** *Arg* **je m'en tamponne le c.** I don't give a damn *or* a monkey's
coquille [kɔkij] *nf* **(a)** (*d'escargot, d'huître, d'œuf, de noix etc*) shell; *Fig* **sortir de sa c.** to come out of one's shell; *Fig* **rentrer dans sa c.** to go back *or* withdraw into one's shell **(b)** (*plat*) (scallop-shaped) dish **(c)** (*d'épée*) hand guard *or* shell **(d)** *Constr* (*d'un escalier en colimaçon*) soffit, underpart **(e)** *Métal* chill, chill mould; *Sp* box, shield; *Méd* **c. (plâtrée)** spinal plaster **(f)** *Typ* misprint, typo, literal
▶ **coquille**: **c. de beurre** (shell-shaped) pat of butter; **c. de noix** walnut shell; (*bateau*) cockleshell; **c. d'œuf** eggshell; **peinture c. d'œuf** eggshell paint; **c. Saint-Jacques** scallop; (*coquillage*) scallop shell
coquillettes [kɔkijɛt] *nf pl Culin* pasta shells
coquin, -ine [kɔkɛ̃, -in] **1** *n* **(a)** (*garnement*) rascal, scamp, rogue; **c. de sort!** (*en Provence*) hang it!, damn it!; **petit c. / petite coquine!** you little rascal! **(b)** (*canaille*) rogue, scoundrel **2** *nf Arch* **coquine** loose woman, hussy **3** *adj* (*sourire*) mischievous; (*sous-vêtement*) naughty; **un air c.** a flirtatious *or* coquettish look; **des histoires coquines** risqué stories
coquinement [kɔkinmɑ̃] *adv* (*d'une manière espiègle*) mischievously; (*coquettement*) coquettishly, flirtatiously; **avec un petit bibi c. posé sur l'oreille** with a little hat worn coquettishly over one ear
coquinerie [kɔkinri] *nf* mischievousness, roguishness; (*tour*) mischievous *or* roguish trick
cor [kɔr] *nm* **(a)** *Mus* horn; **cor (de chasse)** (hunting) horn; **sonner du c.** to sound *or* blow the horn; **les cors** (*dans un orchestre*) the horns; *Fig* **réclamer qch à c. et à cri** *Br* to clamour *or US* to clamor for sth **(b)** (*sur l'orteil, le pied*) corn; **avoir un c. au pied** to have a corn on one's foot **(c)** (*d'un andouiller*) tine; **un cerf (de) dix cors** a ten-pointer
▶ **cor**: **c. anglais** cor anglais, English horn; *Mus* **c. d'harmonie** French horn; **c. à piston** valve horn
corail[1], -aux [kɔraj, -o] *nm* **(a)** *Zool* coral; **récif de c.** coral reef; *Litt* **lèvres de c.** coral lips **(b)** *Rail* express (train)
corail[2] *adj inv* **(a)** (*couleur*) coral; **des lèvres rouge c.** coral-red lips **(b)** *Rail* **train c.** express (train)
corailleur, -euse [kɔrajœr, -øz] *n* (*pêcheur*) coral gatherer; (*artisan*) coral worker
corallien, -ienne [kɔraljɛ̃, -jɛn] *adj* coralline; **récif c.** coral reef
coranique [kɔranik] *adj* Koranic
Coran (le) [ləkɔrɑ̃] *nm* The Koran
corbeau, -eaux [kɔrbo] *nm* **(a)** (*oiseau*) crow; **grand c.** raven; **c. freux** rook; **noir comme un c.** raven- *or* crow-black **(b)** (*auteur de lettres anonymes*) writer of poison-pen letters **(c)** *Fig Péj* (*prêtre*) priest; *Vieilli* (*homme avide*) shark **(d)** *Archit* corbel, bracket
corbeille [kɔrbɛj] *nf* **(a)** (*panier*) basket **(b)** (*massif*) (round *or* oval) flower-bed **(c)** *Archit* (*d'un chapiteau corinthien*) bell, corbeil **(d)** *Bourse* ring, pit **(e)** *Th* dress circle **(f)** *Ordinat* wastebasket, *Am* trash
▶ **corbeille**: *Bot* **c. d'argent** sweet alyssum; **c. de fruits** fruit basket; **c. de mariage** wedding presents; *Bot* **c. d'or** rock alyssum; **c. à ouvrage** work basket; **c. à pain** bread basket; **c. à papier** wastepaper basket
corbillard [kɔrbijar] *nm* hearse
cordage [kɔrdaʒ] *nm* **(a)** (*action*) (*d'une raquette*) stringing **(b)** (*corde*) rope; **c. en chanvre** hemp rope; *Naut* **cordages** rigging; **le c.** (*d'une raquette*) the strings
corde [kɔrd] *nf* **(a)** (*lien*) rope; **danseur de c.** tightrope walker; **semelle/échelle de c.** rope sole/ladder; **sauter à la c.** to skip, *Am* to jump rope; *Gym* **grimper à la c.** to climb the rope; *Fig* **tirer sur la c.** to go too far, to push one's luck; *Fig F* **il pleut des cordes** it's raining cats and dogs, *Br* it's bucketing down

(b) (*d'instrument*) string; **c. (de boyau)** catgut; **c. de violon** violin string; **instrument à cordes** stringed instrument; **les cordes** (*dans un orchestre*) the strings; **orchestre à cordes** string orchestra; **double c.** double stopping; *Fig* **tu as touché** *ou* **fait vibrer la c. sensible** you've touched on a subject close to his/her heart; *Fig* **avoir plus d'une c. à son arc** to have more than one string to one's bow

(c) (*de pendu*) (hangman's) rope; *Fig F* **se mettre la c. au cou** to put one's head in the noose, to put a rope round one's own neck; *Arg* (*se marier*) to get spliced *or* hitched; **dire cela, c'était comme parler de c. dans la maison d'un pendu** that was a very tactless thing to say, you/he/*etc* really put your/his/*etc* foot in it; *Fig* **il ne mérite pas la c. pour le pendre** hanging's too good for him

(d) *Courses de chevaux* **la c.** the rails; **tenir la c.** (*de coureur*) to be on the inside; *Courses de chevaux* to hug the rails, to be on the inside; *Fig Vieilli* to have the advantage; *Aut* **prendre un virage à la c.** to hug the bend; *Boxe* **les cordes** the ropes; *Boxe, Fig* **être dans les cordes** to be on the ropes; **être renvoyé dans les cordes** to be thrown onto the ropes

(e) *Tex* thread; **drap/manteau usé jusqu'à la c.** *ou* **qui laisse voir la c.** threadbare cloth/coat; *Fig* **plaisanterie/histoire usée jusqu'à la c.** well-worn joke/story, old joke/story

(f) *Math* (*d'un arc*) chord

(g) *Fig* **ce n'est pas dans mes cordes** it's not in my line, it's not up my street, it's not my province
▶ **corde**: **c. cervicale** cervical nerve; **c. dorsale** spinal cord; **c. à linge** clothes *or* washing line; *Gym* **c. lisse** climbing rope; **c. à nœuds** knotted climbing rope; **c. raide** tightrope; *Fig*

être sur la c. raide to be walking a tightrope; **c. à sauter** skipping rope, *Am* jump-rope; *Anat* **cordes vocales** vocal cords
cordé [kɔrde] *adj Bot etc* cordate, heart-shaped
cordeau, -eaux [kɔrdo] *nm* **(a)** (*petite corde*) string, line; **un c. de jardinier** garden string *or* line; *Fig* **tiré au c.** perfectly straight, as straight as a die; *Fig* **lettres tracées au c.** perfectly regular letters **(b)** *Min, Mil* (*mèche*) fuse, match; **c. Bickford** Bickford *or* safety fuse **(c)** *Pêche* paternoster (line)
cordée [kɔrde] *nf* **(a)** *Com* **c. de bois** cord of wood **(b)** (*d'alpinistes*) rope, roped party; **premier de c.** leader, first on the rope **(c)** *Pêche* hook length
cordelette [kɔrdəlɛt] *nf* cord, string
cordelier, -ière [kɔrdəlje, -jɛr] **1** *n* **(a)** *Rel* (*religieux*) Franciscan friar, Cordelier; (*religieuse*) Franciscan nun **(b)** *Hist Fr* **le Club des Cordeliers** = a left-wing club of the Revolutionary period **2** *nf* **cordelière** (*de robe de chambre etc*) cord; *Archit* cable moulding
corder [kɔrde] *vt* **(a)** (*chanvre etc*) to twist into rope **(b)** (*malle etc*) to rope up **(c)** (*raquette*) to string **(d)** *Com* (*mesurer*) **c. du bois** to cord wood
cordial, -ale, -aux, -ales [kɔrdjal, -jo] **1** *adj* **(a)** (*accueil, atmosphère*) cordial, hearty, warm; (*paroles*) warm **(b)** (*haine, ennui, mépris etc*) deep(-seated) **(c)** *Pharm* (*médicament*) stimulating **2** *nm Pharm* tonic
cordialement [kɔrdjalmɑ̃] *adv* cordially, heartily, warmly; **c. vôtre** (*dans une lettre*) yours sincerely; **bien c.** best wishes; *Iron* **elle le déteste c.** she heartily detests him
cordialité [kɔrdjalite] *nf* cordiality, heartiness, warmth; **parler avec c.** to speak warmly
cordier [kɔrdje] *nm* **(a)** *Ind* ropemaker **(b)** *Mus* (*d'un violon etc*) tailpiece
cordillère [kɔrdijɛr] *nf Géog* cordillera
cordon [kɔrdɔ̃] *nm* **(a)** (*lien*) cord, string; (*d'un câble, d'une corde*) strand, twist; (*d'un ordre*) ribbon; *Électron, Él* lead; **corde à trois cordons** three-stranded rope; *Arch* **demander le c.** to ask the concierge to open the door; *Fig* **tenir les cordons de la bourse** to hold the purse-strings; *Fig F* **il faut couper le c.** you must get away from your mother's apron strings, you must branch out on your own **(b)** (*d'arbres etc*) row, line; (*de police, de troupes*) cordon; *Archit* (*dans un mur*) string course, cordon; (*d'une pièce de monnaie*) milled edge
▶ **cordon**: *Géog* **c. littoral** offshore bar; *Anat* **c. médullaire** spinal cord; *Anat* **c. ombilical** umbilical cord; *Él* **c. prolongateur** extension cable *or* lead; **c. sanitaire** cordon sanitaire; **c. de soie** silk cord; **c. de sonnette** bellpull
cordon-bleu, *pl* **cordons-bleus** *nm F* cordon bleu (cook)
cordonnerie [kɔrdɔnri] *nf* **(a)** (*métier*) shoe-repairing, shoemending; (*fabrication*) shoemaking **(b)** (*boutique*) shoe repairer's (shop), shoemender's (shop), cobbler's (shop)
cordonnet [kɔrdɔnɛ] *nm* braid, cord, twist
cordonnier, -ière [kɔrdɔnje, -jɛr] *n* **(a)** (*réparateur*) shoe repairer, shoe-mendor, cobbler **(b)** (*fabricant*) shoemaker; *Prov* **les cordonniers sont les plus mal chaussés** the shoemaker's wife is always the worst shod
Cordoue [kɔrdu] *nf* Cordoba
co-rédiger [koredize] *vt* to co-author
Corée [kɔre] *nf* Korea; **C. du Nord/du Sud** North/South Korea
coréen, -enne [kɔreɛ̃, -ɛn] **1** *adj* Korean **2** *n* **C.** Korean
coreligionnaire [kɔrəliʒjɔnɛr] *n* co-religionist
Corfou [kɔrfu] *nf* Corfu
coriace [kɔrjas] **1** *adj* **(a)** (*viande*) tough, leathery **(b)** (*personne, adversaire*) tough; **être c. en affaires** to be hard-headed in business **2** *n F* hard-headed *or* tough customer
coriandre [kɔrjɑ̃dr] *nf Bot, Culin* coriander
coricide [kɔrisid] *nm Pharm* corn remover
corindon [kɔrɛ̃dɔ̃] *nm Minér* corundum
Corinthe [kɔrɛ̃t] *nf* Corinth; *Culin* **raisins de C.** currants
corinthien, -ienne [kɔrɛ̃tjɛ̃, -jɛn] **1** *adj* Corinthian **2** *n* **C.** Corinthian
cormoran [kɔrmɔrɑ̃] *nm* (*oiseau*) cormorant
cornac [kɔrnak] *nm* elephant keeper, mahout
cornaline [kɔrnalin] *nf* cornelian
cornard [kɔrnar] *nm Arg* cuckold
corne [kɔrn] *nf* **(a)** (*d'animal, d'escargot*) horn; (*d'un insecte*) horn, antenna; **les cornes du diable** the devil's horns; **bêtes à cornes** horned animals; **vipère à cornes** horned viper; **donner un coup de c. à qn** (*d'un taureau*) to gore sb; (*d'un bélier, d'une chèvre*) to butt sb; *Fig F* **montrer** *ou* **faire les cornes à qn** to jeer at sb, to mock sb; *F* **ouh les cornes!** shame on you/him/*etc*!; *Fig F* **avoir** *ou* **porter des cornes** to be a cuckold; *Fig F* **faire (porter) des cornes à qn** to cuckold sb; *Fig* **prendre le taureau par les cornes** to take the bull by the horns
(b) (*matériau*) horn; **peigne de c.** horn comb
(c) (*cor*) horn
(d) *Naut* (*d'une voile aurique*) gaff
(e) (*d'un objet pointu*) tip; (*de la lune*) horn, cusp; (*d'une page*) dog-ear; (*d'un croissant*) end, tip; **chapeau à cornes** cocked hat; **faire une c. à une page** to turn down the corner of a page
(f) (*sur les pieds etc*) hard skin; **avoir de la c. au pied** to have hard skin *or* calluses on one's foot
▶ **corne**: **c. d'abondance** horn of plenty, cornucopia; **la corne de l'Afrique** the Horn of Africa; *Naut* **c. de brume** foghorn; **c. à chaussure** shoehorn; *Culin* **c. de gazelle** = horn-shaped cake
corné [kɔrne] *adj* **(a)** (*pied, main etc*) horny **(b)** **page cornée** dog-eared page
corned-beef [kɔrnbif] *nm* corned beef
cornée [kɔrne] *nf Anat* cornea
cornéen, -enne [kɔrneɛ̃, -ɛn] *adj Anat* corneal
corneille [kɔrnɛj] *nf* crow; **c. noire** carrion crow; **c. mantelée** *ou* **grise** *ou* **cendrée** hooded crow
cornélien, -ienne [kɔrneljɛ̃, -jɛn] *adj Littér* (*tragédie etc*) Cornelian; **situation cornélienne** = situation where there is a conflict between love and duty
cornemuse [kɔrnəmyz] *nf Mus* bagpipes; **joueur de c.** (bag)piper; **c. écossaise/bretonne** Scottish/Breton bagpipes
cornemuseur [kɔrnəmyzœr] *nm* (bag)piper
corner[1] [kɔrne] **1** *vt* **(a)** (*clamer*) to blare out; **c. les ordres à qn** to bawl out *or* yell out orders to sb; **c. qch aux oreilles de qn** to shout sth into sb's ear **(b)** (*page*) to turn down the corner of **2** *vi* **(a)** (*souffler dans une corne*) to sound a horn; *Aut Vieilli* to sound one's horn, to hoot, to honk **(b)** *F* **la télé nous cornait aux** *ou* **dans les oreilles** the telly was blaring; **les radios leur cornaient dans les oreilles que ...** radios were blaring out that ... **(c)** (*des oreilles*) to ring; **les oreilles lui cornent** his ears are ringing
corner[2] [kɔrnɛr] *nm Fb* corner; **tirer un c.** to take a corner
cornet [kɔrnɛ] *nm* **(a)** (*de papier*) cone; (*de bonbons, de dragées, de frites*) cornet; **c. de papier** paper cone; **il cria, les deux mains en c. pour mieux se faire entendre** he shouted, cupping his hands to his mouth to make himself heard better; *Arg* **se mettre quelque chose dans le c.** (*manger*) to get something inside one **(b)** *Mus* (*d'un orgue*) cornet stop **(c)** *Arch* small horn **(d)** *Anat* scroll *or* turbinate bone
▶ **cornet**: **c. (à pistons)** cornet; **c. acoustique** ear trumpet; **c. à dés** dice cup; **c. de glace** ice cream cone *or Br* cornet
cornette [kɔrnɛt] **1** *nf* **(a)** (*salade*) endive **(b)** (*coiffe religieuse*) cornet **(c)** *Mil, Arch* (*de la cavalerie*) pennant, standard **2** *nm Mil, Arch* (*officier*) cornet, ensign
cornettiste [kɔrnɛtist] *n Mus* cornetist, cornet player
corn-flakes [kɔrnflɛks] *nmpl* cornflakes
corniaud [kɔrnjo] *nm* **(a)** (*chien*) mongrel **(b)** *F* (*personne*) idiot, twit
corniche [kɔrniʃ] *nf* **(a)** *Archit* cornice **(b)** (*de rochers*) ledge; (*de glace, de neige*) cornice; **(route en) c.** corniche (road)
cornichon [kɔrniʃɔ̃] *nm* **(a)** gherkin **(b)** *F* (*personne*) idiot, nitwit
cornier, -ière [kɔrnje, -jɛr] **1** *adj* (at the) corner, angle; *Constr* **poteau c.** corner *or* angle post **2** *nf* **cornière** **(a)** *Constr* (*sous les combles*) valley **(b)** (*pièce en équerre*) angle (iron *or* bar)
cornique [kɔrnik] **1** *adj* Cornish **2** *nm Ling* Cornish
corniste [kɔrnist] *n Mus* horn player
cornouaillais, -aise [kɔrnwajɛ, -ɛz] **1** *adj* of *or* from Cornouaille **2** *nm Ling* Cornouaillais (dialect) **3** *n* **C.** (*natif*) native of Cornouaille; (*habitant*) inhabitant of Cornouaille
Cornouaille [kɔrnwaj] *nf* Cornouaille (*in Britanny*)
Cornouailles [kɔrnwaj] *nf* Cornwall
cornouille [kɔrnuj] *nf Bot* dogberry, cornel berry
cornouiller [kɔrnuje] *nm* **(a)** *Bot* corneltree **(b)** (*bois*) dogwood
cornu [kɔrny] *adj* (*animal, diable*) horned
cornue [kɔrny] *nf* **(a)** *Ch* retort; **charbon de c.** retort carbon **(b)** *Métal* steel converter
corollaire [kɔrɔlɛr] *nm* (*suite*) consequence, corollary; *Math* corollary
corolle [kɔrɔl] *nf Bot* corolla
coron [kɔrɔ̃] *nm* (*maison*) miner's cottage; (*quartier*) mining village
coronaire [kɔrɔnɛr] *adj Anat* coronary
coronarien, -ienne [kɔrɔnarjɛ̃, -jɛn] *adj Méd* coronary
corporatif, -ive [kɔrpɔratif, -iv] *adj* corporate, corporative
corporation [kɔrpɔrasjɔ̃] *nf* (*ordre*) corporate body; *Hist* (trade) guild; **la c. des pharmaciens** the guild of pharmacists, the pharmacists' guild; **c. de droit public** public corporation *or* body
corporatisme [kɔrpɔratism] *nm* corporatism

corporatiste [kɔrpɔratist] *adj* corporatist

corporel, -elle [kɔrpɔrɛl] *adj* (*être, nature*) corporeal; (*punition*) corporal; (*besoins, exercice*) bodily; (*hygiène*) personal; **expression corporelle** self-expression through movement; **odeur corporelle** body odour; *F* BO; *Psy* **schéma c.** body image

corporellement [kɔrpɔrɛlmɑ̃] *adv* corporeally, corporally, bodily

corps [kɔr] *nm* **(a)** *Anat* body; **un c. robuste/lourd** a strong *or* robust/heavy frame *or* body; **soigner son c.** to look after one's body, to take care of oneself; **elle a conservé un c. jeune** she still has a youthful body, she's well-preserved; **entrer dans l'eau à mi-c.** to go into the water up to one's waist; **un petit c. et de grandes jambes** a short body and long legs; **pleurer toutes les larmes de son c.** to cry one's heart out; **frémir/trembler de tout son c.** to quiver/tremble all over; **passer sur le c. de** *ou* **à qn** to run over sb; *Fig* to trample sb underfoot; *Fig* **il te passerait sur le c. pour obtenir ce qu'il veut** he'd sell his grandmother to get what he wants; *Fig* **il faudra d'abord qu'il me passe sur le c.!** he'll have to do it over my dead body!; *Fig* **je me demande ce qu'il a dans le c.** I wonder what makes him tick; **il n'a rien dans le c.** (*il n'a rien mangé*) he hasn't eaten anything; *Fig* he has no strength *or* energy; **ça va te tenir au c.** (*tu n'auras plus faim*) that'll fill you up, that'll stick to your ribs; **c'est une nourriture qui tient au c.** it's filling food; *F Vieilli* **c'est un drôle de c.** he's a strange character *or Br* bod; *Fig* **faire qch à son c. défendant** to do something reluctantly; *Fig* **se jeter à c. perdu dans un projet/son travail** to throw oneself heart and soul into a project/one's work; **se donner c. et âme à qn/à un travail** to give *or* devote oneself body and soul to sb/to a task; *Jur* **séparation de c.** legal *or* judicial separation; *Jur* **ils ont fait une séparation de c.** they are legally separated; **lutter c. à c.** to fight hand to hand; *Fig* **affronter la réalité c. à c.** to get to grips with reality

(b) (*cadavre*) body, corpse; **deux c. ont été retrouvés** two bodies have been recovered; **la levée du c. aura lieu à onze heures** the coffin will leave the house at eleven o'clock

(c) *Ch, Phys* body; **c. simple** simple body; **c. composé** compound (body)

(d) (*consistance*) (*de vin*) body; **avoir du c.** to have body; **vin qui a du c.** full-bodied wine, wine that has body; *Fig* **son projet manque de c.** his plan lacks substance; *Fig* **donner du c. à qch** to give substance to sth; *Fig* **prendre c.** (*d'un projet, d'une idée*) to take shape

(e) (*partie principale*) main part; (*d'un texte, d'un article etc*) body; (*d'une robe*) body, bodice; (*d'un cylindre, d'une pompe etc*) barrel; *Typ* (*de lettre*) body; **faire c. avec qch** to be an integral part of sth; *Naut* **perdu c. et biens** lost with all hands; *Typ* **force de c.** size of type body

(f) (*d'ancrage*) dolphin, moorings; **(bouée de) c. mort** (anchor) buoy

(g) (*groupe*) **le c. médical/enseignant** the medical/teaching profession; **les grands c. de l'État** = the highest sections of the French administration (*Conseil d'État, Cour des comptes etc*); **avoir l'esprit de c.** to have esprit de corps

(h) (*écrits*) corpus; **c. de lois** body of law(s)

▶ **corps**: *Mil* **c. d'armée** army corps; **c. de ballet** corps de ballet; *Constr* **c. de bâtiment** main (part of a) building; *Astron* **c. céleste** celestial *or* heavenly body; *Jur* **c. du délit** corpus delicti; **c. diplomatique** the diplomatic corps; **c. électoral** electorate; *Méd, Ch* **c. étranger** foreign body; **c. de garde** guardroom; **plaisanterie de c. de garde** barrackroom joke; *Physiol* **c. jaune** yellow body; *Constr* **c. de logis** main (part of a) building; **c. de la magistrature** magistrature; **c. de métier** trade; *Hist* corporation, g(u)ild; *Nucl* **c. noir** black body

corps-à-corps *nm* hand-to-hand fight, tussle; *Boxe* clinch

corpulence [kɔrpylɑ̃s] *nf* stoutness, corpulence; **être d'une forte c.** to be stoutly built *or* of stout build; **un homme d'une faible c.** a slightly built man; **ils n'ont pas la même c.** they are not of the same build

corpulent [kɔrpylɑ̃] *adj* stout, corpulent

corpus [kɔrpys] *nm Jur, Ling* corpus

corpusculaire [kɔrpyskylɛr] *adj* corpuscular

corpuscule [kɔrpyskyl] *nm* corpuscle

corral, -als [kɔral] *nm* corral, enclosure

correct [kɔrɛkt] *adj* **(a)** (*sans fautes*) (*langage, emploi etc*) correct; (*copie, plan etc*) accurate; **il serait plus c. d'employer le subjonctif** it would be more correct to use the subjunctive; *Can F* **il a dit oui? – c.!** did he agree? – correct! *or* right! **(b)** (*courtois*) (*personne*) correct, proper; **cela n'est pas c. de sa part** that's not right of him; **elle a été correcte avec moi** she behaved correctly towards me; **être c. en affaires** to behave correctly *or* honestly in one's business dealings **(c)** *F* (*acceptable*) (*repas, traduction etc*) acceptable, decent, reasonable; **son travail est c., sans plus** his work is all right, but nothing special

correctement [kɔrɛktəmɑ̃] *adv* **(a)** (*parler, employer*) correctly; **vous n'avez pas répondu c. à la question posée** you didn't answer the question correctly; (*sans faire d'erreur*) accurately **(b)** (*agir, être habillé*) correctly, properly; **veux-tu bien répondre c. quand on te parle!** will you talk properly when you're spoken to! **(c)** (*de façon acceptable*) reasonably; **elle gagne c. sa vie** she makes a decent *or* reasonable living

correcteur, -trice [kɔrɛktœr, -tris] **1** *n* (*personne*) corrector; *Scol* (*de copies d'examen*) examiner, marker; *Typ* proofreader; *Journ* copy reader; *Journ* **c. de mise en page** stone sub(-editor) **2** *nm Ordinat* checker; *Tech* corrector; **c. liquide** correcting fluid; *Ordinat* **c. d'orthographe** *ou* **orthographique** spellchecker; **c. de tonalité** tone control; *TV etc* **c. colorimétrique** colour corrector **3** *adj* (*verres etc*) correcting, corrective

correctif, -ive [kɔrɛktif, -iv] **1** *adj* corrective; *Méd* **gymnastique corrective** remedial exercises **2** *nm* **(a)** (*mise au point*) qualifying statement; **apporter des correctifs à une déclaration** to qualify a statement; *Com* **c. d'ajustement monétaire** currency adjustment factor **(b)** *Méd* corrective

correction [kɔrɛksjɔ̃] *nf* **(a)** (*d'une faute etc*) correction, correcting; *Scol* (*d'un exercice*) correcting, marking; *Typ* (*d'épreuves*) proofreading, correction, proofing; **faire des corrections à un texte** to make corrections to a text; **les corrections sont en rouge** the corrections are in red; **maison de c.** reformatory; **je crois, sauf c., qu'il vient demain** unless I'm mistaken, he's coming tomorrow; *Ordinat* **c. d'orthographe** spellcheck; *Av, Naut etc* **c. de compas** compass adjustment; *Aut* **c. d'avance** (*à l'allumage*) ignition advance adjustment

(b) (*pour punir*) beating, thrashing; **tu vas recevoir une bonne c.!** you'll get a good hiding!

(c) (*d'une robe, d'un discours, d'un style etc*) correctness; (*d'un comportement*) correctness, propriety; **il a été d'une parfaite c. avec moi** he behaved very correctly towards me; **c'est la plus élémentaire des corrections** it's basic good manners; **j'apprécie la c. en affaires** I appreciate honesty in business

correctionnel, -elle [kɔrɛksjɔnɛl] **1** *adj Jur* **peine correctionnelle** = penalty of more than five days' (but less than five years') imprisonment; **tribunal de police correctionnelle** court of summary jurisdiction **2** *nf F* **correctionnelle** criminal court; **passer en correctionnelle** to go before the criminal court

corrélatif, -ive [kɔrelatif, -iv] *adj, nm* correlative

corrélation [kɔrelasjɔ̃] *nf* correlation; **être en c. étroite** to be closely connected *or* related

corrélativement [kɔrelativmɑ̃] *adv* correlatively

correspondance [kɔrɛspɔ̃dɑ̃s] *nf* **(a)** (*échange de lettres*) correspondence; (*lettres*) letters, correspondence; **être en** *ou* **entretenir une c. avec qn** to correspond with sb, to be in correspondence with sb; **enseignement par c.** correspondence courses; **prendre des cours d'anglais par c.** to take a correspondence course in English; **c. commerciale** commercial *or* business correspondence; **publier la c. d'un auteur** to publish an author's correspondence *or* (collected) letters

(b) (*entre les trains*) connection; *Av* connecting flight; *Can* (*ticket*) transfer; **assurer la c. avec ...** (*d'un train, d'un bateau etc*) to connect with ...; **j'attends la c.** I'm waiting for my connection

(c) (*de goûts, entre deux choses etc*) correspondence; (*d'idées, de principes etc*) conformity

correspondant, -ante [kɔrɛspɔ̃dɑ̃, -ɑ̃t] **1** *adj* **(a)** (*page, illustration, Géom angle*) corresponding (**à** to)

(b) membre c. (*d'un institut etc*) corresponding member

2 *n* **(a)** *Journ* correspondent; **c. de guerre** war correspondent *or* reporter; **c. permanent** permanent *or* resident correspondent; **c. sur place** local correspondent; **c. à l'étranger** foreign correspondent

(b) (*au téléphone*) caller; (*ami à qui l'on écrit*) pen friend; *Tél* **le numéro de votre c. a changé** the number you have dialled has been changed; **votre c. est en ligne** your party is on the line

(c) (*agent de voyages*) **c. d'agréments** = travel agent (for rail and sea) who has not yet obtained qualifications; **c. de licence** travel agent (for airlines) who has not yet obtained qualifications; **c. local** (*pour les voyagistes*) resort representative

correspondre [kɔrɛspɔ̃dr] **1** *vi* **(a)** **c. à qch** to correspond to sth; **ce qu'il dit ne correspond pas à ses déclarations**

antérieures what he is saying doesn't tally with *or* square with his previous statements; **cela ne correspond pas à votre promesse** that wasn't what you promised; **la théorie ne correspond pas aux faits** the theory does not square with the facts; **son attitude correspond à ce qu'on m'en avait dit** his/her attitude fits in with *or* corresponds to what I was told; **j'ai les vis, mais pas les écrous qui correspondent** I have the screws but I don't have the nuts that go with them *or* the corresponding nuts

(b) (*communiquer*) (*de chambres etc*) to communicate; **ces deux pièces correspondent** these two rooms communicate with one another

(c) (*par lettres*) **c. avec qn** to correspond with *or* write to sb; **ils ont cessé de c.** they have stopped *or* are no longer writing (to each other)

2 se correspondre *vpr* (*être en relation*) to correspond; **leurs goûts se correspondent** they have similar *or* the same tastes; **ils se correspondent parfaitement** they are perfectly matched *or* suited

corrida [kɔrida] *nf* **(a)** (*de taureaux*) bullfight, corrida **(b)** *F* (*à l'aéroport, dans les magasins etc*) hassle, *Br* carry-on; (*dispute*) ding-dong argument; **quelle c.!** all hell broke loose!; **faire la c. dans sa chambre** to kick up a shindig *or* racket in one's bedroom

corridor [kɔridɔr] *nm* corridor, passage

corrigé [kɔriʒe] **1** *adj* corrected; (*press*) subbed; **données corrigées des variations saisonnières** seasonally adjusted figures; **en données corrigées des variations scisonnières** seasonally adjusted, adjusted for seasonal variations **2** *nm Scol* (*d'un exercice*) fair copy, correct version; (*ouvrage donnant les solutions*) key, *F* crib; **le professeur a donné un c. de l'exercice** the teacher gave a model answer to the exercise

corriger [kɔriʒe] (**je corrigeai(s), n. corrigeons**) **1** *vt* **(a)** (*erreur etc*) to correct, to put right, to rectify; (*mot mal orthographié, les défauts de qn, myopie*) to correct; *Scol* (*exercice etc*) to correct, to mark; *Typ* (*épreuves*) to (proof)read, to correct; *Journ* (*article*) to sub-edit, to sub; *Naut* (*compas*) to adjust; **je voudrais c. ce que vous avez dit** I'd like to correct what you've said; **c. le tir** *Mil* to adjust the fire; *Fig* to adjust one's position; **c. son jugement** to alter one's judgment; **c. qn d'une mauvaise habitude** to cure *or* break sb of a bad habit

(b) (*pour punir*) **c. qn** to give sb a beating *or* a thrashing; **se faire c.** to get a beating *or* a thrashing

2 se corriger *vpr* (*d'une personne*) to mend one's ways, to turn over a new leaf; **se c. de sa gourmandise** to cure oneself of one's greed; **elle ne s'est donc pas corrigée!** she hasn't mended her ways, then!

corrigible [kɔriʒibl] *adj* corrigible, rectifiable

corroboration [kɔrɔbɔrasjɔ̃] *nf* corroboration

corroborer [kɔrɔbɔre] *vt* to corroborate

corrodant [kɔrɔdɑ̃] *adj, nm* corrosive

corroder [kɔrɔde] *vt* (*métal, pierre*) to corrode, to eat away

corrompre [kɔrɔ̃pr] **1** *vt* **(a)** (*pervertir*) (*personne, jeunesse, mœurs, goût etc*) to corrupt; (*air*) to pollute; (*langage*) to debase **(b)** (*soudoyer*) to bribe **2 se corrompre** *vpr* (*de vin*) to go off; (*de goût*) to become corrupt(ed)

corrompu [kɔrɔ̃py] *adj* (*personne, mœurs, goût, texte, disquette*) corrupt; (*viande*) tainted, putrid; (*chairs*) putrid

corrosif, -ive [kɔrozif, -iv] **1** *adj* corrosive; *Fig* (*propos, humour, style*) caustic, scathing **2** *nm* corrosive

corrosion [kɔrozjɔ̃] *nf* (*d'un métal*) corrosion

corroyage [kɔrwajaʒ] *nm* (*du cuir*) currying; (*du métal*) welding

corroyer [kɔrwaje] *vt* (*pr ind* **je corroie, n. corroyons**; *fu* **je corroierai**) (*cuir*) to curry; (*métal*) to weld; (*bois*) to trim, to rough-plane

corroyeur [kɔrwajœr] *nm* currier

corrupteur, -trice [kɔryptœr, -tris] **1** *n* (*des mœurs*) corrupter; (*de témoins etc*) briber **2** *adj* (*influence, pouvoir etc*) corrupting

corruptible [kɔryptibl] *adj* (*juge, conscience*) corruptible; (*matériau*) corruptible, perishable

corruption [kɔrypsjɔ̃] *nf* corruption; (*de nourriture etc*) decomposition; (*fait de soudoyer*) bribery

corsage [kɔrsaʒ] *nm* **(a)** (*chemisier*) blouse **(b)** (*d'une robe*) bodice, body

corsaire [kɔrsɛr] **1** *nm* **(a)** *Hist* (*navire, homme*) corsair, privateer **(b)** (*pantalon*) breeches **2** *adj* **pantalon c.** breeches

Corse [kɔrs] *nf Géog* Corsica

corse [kɔrs] **1** *adj* Corsican **2** *nm Ling* Corsican **3** *n* **C.** (*personne*) Corsican

corsé [kɔrse] *adj* (*vin*) full-bodied; (*sauce, plat etc*) spicy; (*fromage*) strong, full-flavoured; **café (au goût) c.** full-flavoured coffee; *Fig* **histoire corsée** risqué *or* spicy story; **affaire corsée** tricky business

corselet [kɔrsəlɛ] *nm Ent, Mil etc* corselet

corser [kɔrse] **1** *vt* (*vin*) to strengthen, to fortify (*by adding spirits*); (*plat*) to spice up; (*café*) to strengthen; (*récit*) to liven up, to enliven; **c. l'action d'un drame** to intensify the action of a drama **2 se corser** *vpr* to intensify; **l'affaire se corse** (*d'une enquête etc*) the plot thickens; (*dans la vie*) things are getting serious; **ça se corse** things are getting difficult

corset [kɔrsɛ] *nm* corset; **c. orthopédique** *ou* **médical** (surgical) corset

corseter [kɔrsəte] *vt* (*pr ind* **je corsète, n. corsetons**; *fu* **je corsèterai**) to corset; *Fig* to restrict, to constrain

corsetier, -ière [kɔrsətje, -jɛr] *n* corset maker

corso [kɔrso] *nm* **c. (fleuri)** procession of floral floats

cortège [kɔrtɛʒ] *nm* **(a)** (*d'un souverain etc*) retinue, suite, train **(b)** (*défilé*) procession; **c. funèbre** funeral cortège; **c. nuptial** bridal procession; **défiler en c.** to go past in a procession, to process past; *Fig* **la vie de famille et son c. de problèmes** family life and its accompanying problems

cortex [kɔrtɛks] *nm Anat, Bot* cortex

cortical, -ale, -aux, -ales [kɔrtikal, -o] *adj Anat, Bot* cortical

corticoïde [kɔrtikɔid] *nm Méd* corticoid

corticosurrénal, -ale, -aux, -ales [kɔrtikɔsyrenal, -o] *adj Méd* adrenocortical

corticothérapie [kɔrtikɔterapi] *nf Méd* corticotherapy

cortisone [kɔrtizɔn] *nf Méd* cortisone

corvée [kɔrve] *nf* **(a)** (*obligation pénible*) chore; **les corvées ménagères** the household chores; **je suis de c. de vaisselle ce soir** I'm on washing-up duty tonight; **quelle c.!** what a drag *or* bind!; **c'est une c. que d'aller chez eux** going to see them is a real chore; *Can* **faire une c.** to pitch *or* muck in together (to get a job done) **(b)** *Mil* fatigue (duty); **(détachement de) c.** fatigue party; **être de c.** to be on fatigue (duty); **c. de cuisine(s)** cookhouse fatigue, *US* kitchen police; **c. de ravitaillement** supply duty **(c)** *Hist* corvée

corvette [kɔrvɛt] *nf Naut* corvette

coryphée [kɔrife] *nm* **(a)** (*dans un corps de ballet*) ballerina **(b)** (*d'une secte, d'un parti*) leader, chief

coryza [kɔriza] *nm Méd* head cold, *Spéc* coryza

cosaque [kɔzak] *nm* cossack

cosécante [kosekɑ̃t] *nf Math* cosecant

cosignataire [kosiɲatɛr] *adj, n* cosignatory

cosinus [kɔsinys] *nm Math* cosine

cosmétique [kɔsmetik] **1** *adj* cosmetic **2** *nm* **(a)** *Vieilli* hair cream **(b) les cosmétiques** cosmetics

cosmétologue [kɔsmetɔlɔg] *n* cosmetics expert, beautician

cosmique [kɔsmik] *adj* (*rayons etc*) cosmic

cosmogonie [kɔsmɔgɔni] *nf* cosmogony

cosmographie [kɔsmɔgrafi] *nf* cosmography

cosmologie [kɔsmɔlɔʒi] *nf* cosmology

cosmonaute [kɔsmɔnot] *n* cosmonaut

cosmopolite [kɔsmɔpɔlit] *adj* cosmopolitan

cosmopolitisme [kɔsmɔpɔlitism] *nm* cosmopolitanism

cosmos [kɔsmos] *nm Phil* cosmos; *Astronaut* outer space

cossard, -arde [kɔsar, -ard] *Arg* **1** *n* lazybones **2** *adj* lazy

cosse [kɔs] *nf* **(a)** (*de petits pois, fèves etc*) pod, husk, hull **(b)** *Naut* (*d'un cordage*) thimble, eyelet **(c)** *Él* (*d'un câble*) terminal **(d)** *Arg* **avoir la c.** to feel lazy

cossin [kɔsɛ̃] *nm Can F* (*truc*) whatsit, thingamabob, thingamajig, thingummy

cossu [kɔsy] *adj* (*personne*) well-to-do, well-off, wealthy; (*maison, intérieur etc*) opulent

costal, -ale, -aux, -ales [kɔstal, -o] *adj Anat* costal

costard [kɔstar] *nm Arg* suit

costaud, -aude [kɔsto, -od] **1** *adj* (*personne, valise etc*) sturdy; *F* (*alcool, épice*) strong **2** *nm* strong *or* sturdy man; *F* **tu peux avoir confiance, c'est du c.** trust me, it's sturdy stuff *or* it's sturdily made

costume [kɔstym] *nm* (*habit*) costume; (*complet*) suit; **c. trois-pièces** three-piece suit; **c. national** national costume *or* dress; **c. ecclésiastique** clerical dress; **c. de cérémonie** *ou* **d'apparat** ceremonial *or* formal dress; *F* **c. d'Adam** birthday suit; *F* **en c. d'Adam** in one's birthday suit, in the altogether; *Th* **répéter en c.** to have a dress rehearsal

costumé [kɔstyme] *adj* **bal c.** fancy-dress ball

costumer [kɔstyme] **1** *vt* **c. qn** to dress sb up; **il était costumé en Turc** he was dressed (up) as a Turk **2 se costumer** *vpr* to put on fancy dress, to dress up; **se c. en Turc** to dress up as a Turk

costumier, -ière [kɔstymje, -jɛr] *n* **(a)** *Com* costum(i)er, dealer in (fancy) costumes **(b)** *Th* wardrobe master, *f* wardrobe mistress; *Cin* costume supervisor

cosy [kɔzi] **1** *nm* corner divan (*with shelves*) **2** *adj F* cosy, *US* cozy, comfy

cotangente [kɔtɑ̃ʒɑ̃t] *nf Math* cotangent

cotation [kɔtasjɔ̃] *nf Bourse* quotation

cote [kɔt] *nf* **(a)** *Bourse, Com* quotation; (*liste*) list; **actions inscrites à la c.** listed shares; **retirer de la c.** (*société, action*) to delist; **marché hors c.** unlisted *or* over-the-counter *or* OTC market; *Courses de chevaux* **c. d'un cheval** odds on a horse; **c. d'une voiture à l'argus** listed price of a car in the car buyer's guide; *Pol* **pour faire monter sa c. de popularité** *ou* **d'amour** to increase his popularity (rating); *F* **avoir la c.** to be popular (**avec, auprès de** with); **alors, tu as la c.?** oh, you're popular!

(b) *Com, Jur* (*d'un document etc*) (classification) mark; (*d'un livre de bibliothèque*) classification *or* shelf mark, pressmark; *Jur* (*d'un navire*) character, classification

(c) (*de dépenses, d'impôts etc*) quota, share

(d) (*taille*) (indication of) dimensions; **c. d'origine** standard size

(e) *Géog* height; (*au-dessus de la mer*) elevation; (*d'un point dans un diagramme*) altitude; *Géog* **la c. 304** hill 304; **c. moins/plus 500** 500 below/above sea level

▶ **cote**: **c. d'alerte** *HydE* critical *or* flood level; *Fig* danger point; *Fin* **c. de clôture** closing price; **c. mal taillée** rough and ready settlement; *Admin* **c. mobilière** assessment on income; *Bourse* **c. officielle** official list; **c. des prix** *Bourse* sharelist; *Com* list of prices

côte [kot] *nf* **(a)** *Anat* rib; **c. à c.** side by side; *F* **se tenir les côtes** to split one's sides laughing; **on lui compterait les côtes, on lui voit les côtes** he's nothing but skin and bone; *Fig F* **avoir les côtes en long** to be bone-idle, to be lazy; *Culin* **plat de côtes** dish of spare ribs

(b) (*de melon, salade, feuille*) rib; **tissu à côtes** ribbed *or* corded material

(c) (*de colline*) slope; (*à monter, à descendre*) hill; *Constr* gradient; **vitesse en c.** speed uphill; *Aut* **démarrage en c.** hill start; **ma voiture a du mal à monter les côtes** my car has problems getting up hills; **à mi-c.** halfway up/down the hill

(d) (*rivage*) coast, coastline; **les côtes de (la) France** the coast of France, the French coast; **la C. (d'Azur)** the (French) Riviera; **faire c.** to beach, to run aground; *Naut* **jeter à la c.** to drive ashore, to strand; *Fig F* **être à la c.** to be on one's beam ends, to be hard up

▶ **côte**: **c. d'agneau** lamb chop *or* cutlet; **c. de bœuf** rib of beef; *Culin* **côtes découvertes** middle neck; *Anat* **côtes flottantes** floating ribs; *Géog* **la C. d'Ivoire** the Ivory Coast; **c. de porc** pork chop; *Culin* **c. première** loin chop

côté [kote] *nm* **(a)** (*du corps humain*) side; **il a le c. gauche entièrement paralysé** his left side is completely paralysed; **couché sur le c.** lying on one's side; **assis à mes côtés** sitting by my side; **aux côtés de qn** at sb's side; **avoir un point de c.** to have a stitch (in one's side)

(b) (*d'une montagne, d'une route, d'une table, d'une feuille etc*) side; **les côtés d'un rectangle** the sides of a rectangle; **les côtés de la médaille** the (two) sides of the medal; **une feuille de papier écrite des deux côtés** a sheet of paper written on on both sides; **de l'autre c. de** on the other side of; **passer de l'autre c. de la rue** to cross the street; *Th* **c. jardin** prompt side; **appartement c. jardin** flat *or Am* apartment overlooking the garden; **la tour penche d'un c.** the tower leans to one side *or* leans sideways; **ta jupe est plus longue d'un c. que de l'autre** your skirt is longer on one side than (on) the other; *Naut* **présenter le c. à qch** to be broadside on to sth; **navire sur le c.** ship on her beam ends; *Aut* **c. gauche** nearside; (*en GB*) offside

(c) (*aspect*) side, aspect; **le bon/le mauvais c. d'une affaire** the good/bad side *or* aspect of a matter; **le c. recherche m'intéresse plus que le c. enseignement** the research side interests me more than the teaching side; **il a un c. méchant** he has *or* there's a mean streak in him; **il a de bons côtés** he's got a good side to him, he's not all bad; **c'est son c. paternel qui ressort** it's the paternal streak in him coming out; **ça fait partie de ses mauvais côtés** it's one of his bad points; **le vent vient du bon c.** the wind is in the right quarter; **prendre la vie du bon c.** to look on the bright side of life; **voir le bon/mauvais c. des choses** to see the good/bad side of things

(d) (*endroit*) side, direction, way; **cerné de tous côtés** surrounded on all sides; **les gens affluaient de tous côtés** people streamed in from all directions; **se diriger du c. de Paris** to head towards *or* in the direction of Paris; **il habitait du c. de la rivière** he lived near the river; **on voit mieux de ce c.-là** you can see better from that side, you can see better from over there; **venez de ce c.** (*par ici*) come over here; (*à droite, à gauche*) come this side; **de ce c.-ci/-là** on this/that side; **ils s'en allèrent chacun de son c.** they went their separate ways; **vivre chacun de son c.** to live separately; **de quel c.?** (*direction*) in which direction?, which way?; (*position*) which side?; **se ranger du c. du plus fort** to side with the strongest; **il a toujours été du c. des opprimés** he's always been on the side of *or* sided with the oppressed; **mettre qn de son c.** to get sb on one's side; **je suis de ton c.** I'm on your side; **sa tante, du c. maternel** his aunt on his mother's side; *Fig* **être né du c. gauche** to be illegitimate; **d'un c. à l'autre** from side to side; **d'un c. ..., d'un autre c. ...** on the one hand ..., on the other hand ...; **de mon c., je pense que ...** for my part I think that ...; *F* **de ce c. il n'y a rien à craindre** there's nothing to worry about on that score

(e) *F* (*question*) **c. vitesse, cette voiture est remarquable** as far as speed is concerned *or* speedwise, this car is remarkable; **c. argent** moneywise, as far as money is concerned; **c. repos, ça aurait pu être mieux** on the relaxation side *or* front, it could have been better, it could have been more restful

(f) de c. (*sauter, se ranger etc*) to one side, aside; **faire un saut de c.** to leap to one side *or* aside, to jump sideways; **avoir une raie de c.** to have a side parting; **regard de c.** sidelong glance; *Fig* **mettre qch de c.** to put sth aside *or* to one side *or* on one side; *Fig* **mettre de l'argent de c.** to put money by *or* aside; *Fig* **j'ai 30 000 francs de c.** I've got 30,000 francs put by; *Fig* **laisser qn/qch de c.** to leave sb/sth out; *Fig* **laisser ses difficultés de c.** to put one's difficulties to one side

(g) à c. to one side; (*près*) nearby; **la maison est tout à c.** the house is quite near; **il habite à c.** he lives next door; **si vous voulez bien passer à c.** if you'd like to go that way; **les voisins d'à c.** the next-door neighbours; **les gens d'à c.** the people next door; **le salon est à c. de la cuisine** the drawing room is next to the kitchen; **à c. du lit** next to the bed; **il se tenait à c. de moi** he stood at *or* by my side, he stood next to me *or* beside me; **à c. l'un de l'autre** side by side; **tirer à c.** to miss the mark; **vous êtes à c. de la question** you're missing the point; **il est passé à c. de la question** *ou* **du sujet** he missed the point; *F* **tu es vraiment à c. de la plaque!** you're really not with it!; **passer à c. d'une difficulté** to avoid a difficulty; **passer à c. des choses importantes/de la vraie vie** to miss out on important things/on real life; **mes ennuis ne sont rien à c. des vôtres** my troubles are nothing compared with *or* beside yours; **il n'est rien à c. de vous** he's nothing compared to you

coteau, -eaux [kɔto] *nm* (*versant*) slope, hillside; (*colline*) hill

côtelé [kotle] *adj Tex* ribbed; **velours c.** corduroy

côtelette [kotlɛt, kɔ-] *nf Culin* chop, cutlet; **c. d'agneau/de porc** lamb/pork chop

coter [kɔte] *vt* **(a)** *Com, Bourse* (*prix, actions etc*) to quote; **des actions cotées en bourse** shares quoted on the Stock Exchange, listed *or* quoted shares; **être coté à 100 francs** to be trading at 100 francs; *F* **ma voiture est vieille, elle n'est plus cotée à l'argus** my car's old, it's not listed in the car buyer's guide any more; **très coté** *Courses de chevaux* well backed, well *or* highly fancied; *Fig* highly rated

(b) *MecE etc* (*dessins etc*) to mark the dimensions on; (*cartes*) to put references on; **point coté** (*de relevé*) reference point, landmark; (*sur une carte*) spot height

(c) *Com, Jur* (*documents etc*) to classify; **coté, daté et paraphé** numbered, dated and signed

coterie [kɔtri] *nf Péj* set, clique, coterie

côtier, -ière [kotje, -jɛr] **1** *adj* (*fleuve, défense etc*) coastal; (*pêche*) inshore; (*commerce*) coastwise; (*pilote*) coast(ing); **navigation côtière** coastal navigation, coasting **2** *nm* (*bateau*) coaster, coasting vessel

cotillon [kɔtijɔ̃] *nm* **(a) accessoires de c., cotillons** party novelties **(b)** *Arch* (*danse*) cotill(i)on **(c)** *Arch* petticoat; **courir le c.** to chase petticoats, to flirt with the ladies

cotisant, -ante [kɔtizɑ̃, -ɑ̃t] **1** *adj* (*membre*) paying (**de** to) **2** *n* (*à un club etc*) subscriber (**de** to); (*à une caisse*) contributor (**de** to)

cotisation [kɔtizasjɔ̃] *nf* **(a)** (*à une caisse etc*) contribution; **c. de Sécurité Sociale** ≈ National Insurance contribution; **c. chômage** unemployment contribution; **c. patronale** employer's contribution; **c. vieillesse** pension contribution; **cotisations ouvrières/salariales** employee contributions **(b)** (*à un club etc*) subscription

cotiser [kɔtize] **1** *vi* (*à un club*) to subscribe, to pay one's subscription (**à** to); (*à une caisse de retraite, mutuelle etc*) to contribute, to pay one's contributions (**à** to) **2 se cotiser** *vpr* (*pour acheter un cadeau etc*) to club together

côtoiement [kotwamɑ̃] *nm* contact (**de** with); **le c. des personnes célèbres lui monte à la tête** rubbing shoulders *or* mixing with celebrities is going to his head; **le c. quotidien de la mort** the daily contact with death

coton [kɔtɔ̃] **1** *nm* **(a)** (*plante, fil, tissu*) cotton; **fil de c.** sewing cotton; **chemise 100% c.** pure *or* 100% cotton shirt; *Fig F* **filer un mauvais c.** (*en parlant de la santé, des affaires*) to be in a bad way; (*avoir des fréquentations douteuses*) to be going off the rails

(b) c. (hydrophile) cotton wool, *Am* absorbent cotton; **un c.** a piece of cotton wool *or Am* absorbent cotton; *Fig F* **j'ai les jambes en c.** my legs feel like cotton wool *or* like jelly; *Fig F* **il a du c. dans les oreilles** he's cloth-eared *or* he's got cloth ears; *Fig* **élever un enfant dans du c.** to (molly)coddle a child

(c) (*des plantes*) down **2** *adj F* tough, tricky; **ça, c'est plutôt c.!** that's a bit tough *or* tricky!

▶ **coton**: **c. à broder** embroidery thread; **c. à repriser** darning thread *or* cotton

cotonnade [kɔtɔnad] *nf* cotton fabric; **s'habiller de cotonnades** to wear (clothes made of) cotton *or* cotton clothes

cotonner (se) [səkɔtɔne] *vpr* **(a)** (*d'un tissu*) to become fluffy, to fluff up **(b) fruit qui se cotonne** fruit that becomes woolly

cotonneux, -euse [kɔtɔnø, -øz] *adj* (*feuille, fruit*) downy; (*nuages*) fluffy, fleecy; (*son*) muffled; (*brouillard*) thick; **style c.** woolly style

cotonnier, -ière [kɔtɔnje, -jɛr] **1** *adj* (*industrie, articles etc*) cotton **2** *n* cotton worker, spinner **3** *nm Bot* cotton plant

coton-poudre, *pl* **cotons-poudre** *nm* guncotton, *US* nitrocotton

côtoyer [kotwaje] *vt* **(je côtoie, n. côtoyons; je côtoierai)** (*rivière, forêt etc*) to border on; (*personnes*) to mix with; *Fig* **cela côtoie le ridicule** it's verging *or* bordering on the ridiculous

cotre [kɔtr] *nm Naut* cutter

cottage [kɔtaʒ] *nm* (country) cottage

cotte [kɔt] *nf* **(a)** *F* (*bleu*) overalls; (*sans manches*) dungarees **(b)** *Mil* **c. d'armes** (*portée sur l'armure*) tunic; **c. de mailles** coat of mail **(c)** *Arch* (*jupon*) petticoat

cotutelle [kotytɛl] *nf Jur* joint guardianship

cotuteur, -trice [kotytœr, -tris] *n Jur* joint guardian

cotylédon [kɔtiledɔ̃] *nm Anat, Bot* cotyledon

cou [ku] *nm* (*de personne, d'animal, de bouteille etc*) neck; **une chaîne en or autour du c.** (with) a gold chain around his neck; **tendre le c.** to crane one's neck; **se jeter au c. de qn** to throw one's arms round sb's neck; **tordre le c. à une volaille** to wring a bird's neck; *Fig* **je vais lui tordre le c.!** I'll wring his neck (for him)!; *Fig F* **endetté jusqu'au c.** up to one's eyes in debt; *Fig* **prendre ses jambes à son c.** to take to one's heels, to show a clean pair of heels; **tu risques de te casser** *ou* **rompre le c.** watch *or* mind you don't break your neck

couac [kwak] *nm Mus* (*à la clarinette etc*) squeak, false note; (*de la voix*) false note; *Fig* discordant note; **faire un c.** to play a false note; (*d'un chanteur*) to sing a false note

couard, -arde [kwar] *Litt, Région* **1** *adj* cowardly **2** *n* coward

couardise [kwardiz] *nf Vieilli, Litt* cowardice

couchage [kuʃaʒ] *nm* **(a) (matériel de) c.** bedding; **sac de c.** sleeping-bag; **et pour le c., comment fait-on?** how about the sleeping arrangements? who's going to sleep where? **(b)** *Arg* (*rapports sexuels*) sleeping around, casual sex

couchant [kuʃɑ̃] **1** *adj* **(a) le soleil c.** the setting sun; **au soleil c.** at sunset, at sundown **(b) chien c.** setter; *Fig* **faire le chien c. auprès de qn** to fawn on sb **2** *nm* **(a)** sunset **(b)** (*ouest*) west; **dans la direction du c.** westward, in a westerly direction

couche [kuʃ] *nf* **(a)** (*de peinture*) coat; (*de beurre, crème solaire, poussière etc*) layer; *Géol* layer, stratum; **les couches de l'atmosphère** the layers *or* strata of the atmosphere; **la c. d'ozone** the ozone layer; **c. de glace** sheet of ice; **c. de fumier** (*au jardin*) hotbed; **champignons de c.** cultivated mushrooms; **couches sociales** social strata, levels of society; **c. d'apprêt** priming coat; **c. de fond** undercoat; **c. anticorrosion** underseal; **c. isolante** underlay; *Arg* **il a** *ou* **il en tient une c.!** he's really stupid *or Br* thick!, what an idiot!

(b) *Obst, Vieilli* **couches** confinement, labour, *US* labor; **femme en couches** woman in labour; **couches laborieuses** *ou* **pénibles** difficult (child)birth; **fausse c.** miscarriage; **faire une fausse c.** to have a miscarriage; **mourir en couches** to die in childbirth

(c) c. (de bébé) (baby's) nappy, *Am* (baby's) diaper; **mettre une couche au bébé** to put a nappy *or Am* diaper on the baby

(d) *MecE* **arbre de c.** engine shaft, main shaft, power shaft

(e) *Litt* bed

couché [kuʃe] *adj* **(a)** (*allongé*) lying (down); (*au lit*) in bed **(b)** (*incliné*) **écriture couchée** slanting *or* sloping writing; **blés couchés par le vent** wheat flattened by the wind **(c) papier c.** art paper

couche-culotte, *pl* **couches-culottes** *nf* disposable nappy *or Am* diaper

coucher[1] [kuʃe] *nm* **(a) l'heure du c.** bedtime **(b)** (*gîte*) accommodation; **cela va nous assurer le c.** we'll be sure of a bed for the night; **le c. et la nourriture** board and lodging **(c)** (*du soleil*) setting; **au c. du soleil** at sunset, at sundown; **un superbe c. de soleil** a magnificent sunset

coucher[2] **1** *vt* **(a)** (*mettre au lit*) to put to bed

(b) (*offrir un lit à*) to put up, to provide with a bed; **je ne peux pas vous c.** I can't put you up

(c) (*allonger, poser*) to lay down; **la pluie a couché les blés** the rain has flattened the wheat; **c. un navire** to throw a ship on her beam ends; **c. un fusil en joue** to aim a gun; **c. qn en joue** to (take) aim at sb; *Fig* **c. qn sur le carreau** to floor sb, to knock sb down

(d) (*écrire*) to set down, to put down, to inscribe; **c. qch par écrit** *ou* **sur le papier** to set *or* put sth down in writing; **c. qn sur son testament** to mention sb in one's will

2 *vi* **(a)** (*passer la nuit*) to sleep; **c. à l'hôtel/chez des amis** to spend the night *or* to sleep at a hotel/with friends; **c. à la belle étoile/sous la tente** to sleep in the open (air) *or* outside *or* under the stars/in a tent *or* under canvas; **je ne veux pas vous faire c. tard** I don't want to keep you up; *Fig* **c. sous les ponts** to sleep rough

(b) *F* **c. avec qn** to sleep with sb; **ils couchent ensemble** they're sleeping together; **elle ne couche pas** she doesn't sleep around

(c) (*à un chien*) **(allez) couché!** (lie) down!

3 se coucher *vpr* **(a)** (*au lit*) **(aller) se c.** to go to bed; **il est l'heure d'aller se c.** it's bedtime, it's time to go to bed; *F* **se c. comme** *ou* **avec les poules** to go to bed early; *F* **va te c.!** clear off!, leave me alone!; *Prov* **comme on fait son lit on se couche** as we make our bed, so must we lie in it

(b) (*s'allonger*) to lie down; **se c. à plat ventre** to lie flat on one's stomach; **ne te couche pas sur ton bureau! tiens-toi droit!** don't slouch over your desk, sit up straight!

(c) *Naut* **se c. sur le flanc** to heel over

(d) (*du soleil, de la lune*) to set, to go down

coucherie [kuʃri] *nf F* sleeping around, casual sex; **la c., ce n'est pas mon genre** I don't sleep around

couchette [kuʃɛt] *nf Naut* bunk; *Rail* couchette

coucheur [kuʃœr] *nm F* **c'est un mauvais c.** he's an awkward customer

couci-couça [kusikusa] *adv F* so-so

coucou [kuku] **1** *nm* **(a)** (*oiseau*) cuckoo **(b) (pendule à) c.** cuckoo clock **(c)** (*plante*) cowslip **(d)** *Av F* old crate **2** *int* **c.! (me voilà)** peek-a-boo!; **c.!** (*pour dire bonjour*) cooee!

coude [kud] *nm* **(a)** *Anat* elbow; **pull aux coudes usés** pullover with holes in the elbows; **mettre les coudes sur la table** to put one's elbows on the table; **coudes au corps** elbows in; **c. à c.** side by side, close together, shoulder to shoulder; **c. à c. fraternel** friendly jostling; **coup de c.** poke with the elbow; (*pour attirer l'attention*) nudge; **donner un coup de c. à qn** to jog sb with one's elbow; (*pour attirer l'attention*) to nudge sb, to give sb a nudge; *Fig* **se serrer les coudes** to stick together, to help one another; **jouer des coudes** (*à travers la foule*) to elbow one's way; *Fig* (*pour arriver à ses fins*) to manœuvre, *US* to maneuver; *Fig F* **lever le c.** to booze; **huile de c.** elbow grease; **mets-y de l'huile de c.** put some elbow grease into it, use a bit of elbow grease; *Fig* **garder qch sous le c.** to hold on to sth (without doing anything about it); *F* **se fourrer le doigt dans l'œil jusqu'au c.** to be barking up the wrong tree, to be completely mistaken

(b) (*d'une route, rivière etc*) (sharp) bend; *MecE* (*de barre, tuyau etc*) bend, elbow; (*d'arbre*) crank; **arbre à deux coudes** two-throw crankshaft

coudé [kude] *adj MecE* (*tuyau*) bent, angled, at an angle; (*arbre*) cranked

coudée [kude] *nf* **(a) avoir les coudées franches** to have plenty of elbow room **(b)** *Antiq* (*mesure*) cubit

cou-de-pied, *pl* **cous-de-pied** [kudpje] *nm Anat* instep

couder [kude] *vt MecE* (*tuyau etc*) to bend (at an angle), to angle; (*arbre*) to crank

coudoiement [kudwamɑ̃] *nm* contact, association **(de** with**)**

coudoyer [kudwaje] *vt* **(je coudoie, n. coudoyons; je coudoierai)** to come into contact with, to rub shoulders with, to mix with; *Fig* **un texte où la vanité de l'auteur coudoie le ridicule** a text in which the author's vanity borders on the ridiculous

coudre [kudr] (*prp* **cousant**; *pp* **cousu**; *pr ind* **je couds, il coud, n. cousons, ils cousent**; *impf* **je cousais**; *p hist* **je cousis**; *fu* **je coudrai) 1** *vt* (*ourlet etc*) to sew, to stitch; (*bouton*) to sew on, to stitch on; (*deux morceaux d'étoffe etc*) to sew *or* stitch together; **c. un bouton à une robe** to sew *or* stitch a button on a dress; **c. une jupe** to make (up) *or* sew (up) a skirt; **machine à c.** sewing machine; **c. une plaie** to sew up a wound **2** *vi* to sew

coudrier [kudrije] *nm* hazel (tree)

couenne [kwan] *nf* **(a)** (*de lard*) rind; *Fig Arg* **quelle c.!** what a twerp *or* nerd!, *Fig Arg* **se faire dorer la c.** to expose the body beautiful **(b)** *Méd* (diphtheric) membrane

couette[1] [kwɛt] *nf* **(a)** (*dans une housse*) duvet, continental quilt **(b)** *Région, Vieilli* (*lit de plumes*) feather bed **(c)** *MecE* bearing **(d)** *Naut* **couettes courantes** bilge ways

couette[2] *nf F* (*de cheveux*) bunch; **elle avait des couettes** she wore her hair in bunches; **se faire des couettes** to put *or* gather one's hair in bunches

couffe [kuf] *nf,* **couffin** [kufɛ̃] *nm* (straw) basket; (*pour bébé*) Moses basket

coug(o)uar [kug(w)ar] *nm* cougar, puma, mountain lion

couic [kwik] *int* eek!, squeak!, *Arg* **faire c.** to croak, *Br* to snuff it

couille [kuj] *nf Vulg* (*testicule*) ball, *Br* bollock; (*problème*) balls-up, *Am* ball-up; *Fig* **une c. molle** a drip; *Fig* **avoir des couilles (au cul)** to have balls *or* guts; **notre projet est parti en couilles** our plan has gone down the tubes

couillon [kujɔ̃] *nm Arg* cretin, dope

couillonner [kujɔne] *vt Arg* (*qn*) to con; **je me suis fait c.** I've been had *or* done *or* conned

couinement [kwinmɑ̃] *nm* (*d'animal*) squeak, squeal

couiner [kwine] *vi* (*d'un animal*) to squeak, to squeal; (*d'un enfant*) to whine

coulage [kulaʒ] *nm* **(a)** (*de statue etc*) casting; (*de métal fondu, de verre fondu, de savon etc*) pouring **(b)** *F* (*gaspillage*) waste; (*chapardage*) shrinkage; **c. de stocks** stock shrinkage

coulant [kulɑ̃] **1** *adj* (*liquide*) running, flowing; (*confiture, fromage etc*) runny; (*vin*) smooth; *Fig* (*personne*) easy-going; **nœud c.** slip *or* running knot; (*autour du cou*) noose; **style c.** easy *or* flowing style; **il est très c.** he's very easy to get on with *or* very easy-going **2** *nm* **(a)** (*anneau*) sliding ring; (*d'une ceinture*) loop **(b)** (*de plante*) runner

coule[1] [kul] *nf F* **être à la c.** to know the tricks of the trade, to know the ropes, to know what's what

coule[2] *nf* (*de religieux*) cowl

coulé [kule] **1** *adj* (*mouvement*) smooth **2** *nm* **(a)** *Mus* slur **(b)** (*pas de danse*) glide **(c)** *Billard* follow-through

coulée [kule] *nf* **(a)** (*de liquide*) flow; **c. de lave** lava flow; **c. de boue** mudslide **(b)** *Métal* (*de métal fondu*) casting; **trou de c.** tap(ping) hole, draw-hole **(c)** *Natation* glide, push-off

coulemelle [kulmɛl] *nf* parasol mushroom

couler [kule] **1** *vt* **(a)** (*liquide*) to pour, to run; (*métal fondu*) to cast; (*cire, ciment*) to pour; **c. une pièce/une statue** to cast a piece/a statue; **c. une bielle** to burn out a connecting rod

(b) (*navire*) to sink; *Fig* **c. qn** to bring sb down, to ruin sb, to discredit sb

(c) (*glisser*) **c. un sourire/regard à qn** to steal a smile/look at sb; **c. un mot à l'oreille de qn** to drop *or* whisper a word in sb's ear; *Mus* **c. un passage** to slur a passage

(d) c. des jours heureux to have some happy days; *F* **se la c. douce** to take things easy

2 *vi* **(a)** (*de liquide, rivière etc*) to run, to flow; (*sable*) to trickle; *Fig* (*de vers*) to flow; (*de fromage, maquillage*) to run; **faire c. l'eau** to turn the water on; **faire c. un bain** to run a bath; **la sueur coule sur son front** sweat is trickling *or* running down his/her forehead; **le sang a coulé** there was bloodshed; **ce scandale va faire c. de l'encre** this scandal is going to be much written about; *Fig* **ça coule de source** it's obvious; (*par voie de conséquence*) it follows naturally

(b) (*de navire*) to sink, to go down; (*entreprise*) to go under; **le nageur a coulé à pic** the swimmer sank like a stone

(c) *Litt* (*glisser*) to slide, to slip; **la martre coula le long du fossé** the marten slithered along the ditch

(d) (*de tonneau, stylo à plume*) to leak; (*de nez*) to run

3 se couler *vpr* (*se glisser*) to slip; **se c. entre les draps** to slip between the sheets, to slip into bed; **se c. dans la foule** to slip *or* disappear into the crowd; **se c. le long du mur** to hug the wall; **elle se laissa c. dans le fauteuil** she slid into the armchair

couleur [kulœr] *nf* **(a)** [①A7,d,ix; B10,D,1] colour, *US* color; **de quelle c. sont vos yeux?** what colour are your eyes?; **de quelle c. est sa voiture?** what colour car has he got?, what colour is his car?; **en quelle c. vas-tu repeindre la pièce?** what colour are you going to paint the room?; **c. paille/chair** straw-/flesh-coloured; **gens de c.** coloured people, coloureds; **des gens hauts en c.** colourful individuals; **la c., les couleurs** (*linge*) coloureds; **la lessive idéale pour vos couleurs** the ideal soap-powder for your coloureds; **photographie/télévision couleur** *ou* **en couleur(s)** colour photography/television; *Pol* **la c. d'un journal** the (political) colour *or* (political) complexion of a paper; *Fig* **suivant la c. du temps** it depends on which way the wind is blowing; *Fig* **sous c. de me rendre service** under the pretext *or* guise of doing me a service; *Fig* **style/personnalité sans c.** drab *or* colourless style/personality; *Fig* **immédiatement, ça a pris une autre c.** it immediately started to look different; *Fig F* **il en a vu de toutes les couleurs** he's had a hard time, he's been through the mill *or* through a lot; *Fig F* **elle nous en fait voir de toutes les couleurs** she gives us a hard time; *Fig F* **dépeindre qch sous des couleurs sombres** to paint a gloomy picture of sth, to present a gloomy view of sth; *Fig* **je n'en ai pas encore vu la c.** I've seen no sign of it yet; *Culin* **prendre c.** (*d'un rôti*) to brown

(b) (*de visage*) colour, *US* color; **perdre ses couleurs** to lose one's colour, to become pale; **sans c.** colourless, pale; *F* **quand il l'a su, il a changé de c.** he went pale *or* changed colour *or* blanched when he found out; **tu as repris des couleurs** you're getting your colour back, you're getting some colour (back) in your cheeks; **tu as pris des couleurs** you've caught the sun, you've got a touch of the sun; **tu as des couleurs aujourd'hui** you're looking well today; **le vin lui avait donné des couleurs** his face was flushed from the wine

(c) *Mil etc* **couleurs** (*drapeau*) colours, *US* colors, flag; **envoyer** *ou* **hisser les couleurs** to hoist the colours *or* the flag

(d) *Sp, Courses de chevaux* **couleurs** (*d'un club, d'une écurie*) colours, *US* colors; **défendre les couleurs de son club** to play for one's club

(e) (*peinture*) paint; **boîte de couleurs** box of paints, paintbox; **des crayons de c.** crayons, coloured pencils; **marchand de couleurs** *Br* ironmonger, hardware merchant

(f) *Cartes* suit; **jouer dans la c.** to follow suit; **annoncer la c.** to call (trumps); *aussi Fig F* to lay one's cards on the table

(g) (*en coiffure*) tint; **se faire faire une c.** to have one's hair tinted

▶ **couleur**: **couleurs complémentaires** complementary colours; **couleurs fondamentales** primary colours; *Fig* **c. locale** local colour; *Fig* **ça fait c. locale** it's really ethnic looking; **couleurs primaires** primary colours; **couleurs primitives** colours of the spectrum; **couleurs spectrales** colours of the spectrum

couleuvre [kulœvr] *nf* **(a)** (*serpent*) **c. (à collier)** grass snake; **c. lisse** smooth snake; **paresseux comme une c.** bone-idle; *Fig* **avaler des couleuvres** (*se faire humilier*) to eat humble pie; (*être naïf*) to believe *or* swallow anything **(b)** *Can* (*ver*) worm

coulis[1] [kuli] *adj* **vent c.** draught, *Am* draft

coulis[2] *nm* **(a)** *Constr* grout **(b)** *Métal* molten metal **(c)** *Culin* **c. de tomates/framboises** tomato/raspberry sauce *or Spéc* coulis

coulissant [kulisɑ̃] *adj* (*porte, panneau etc*) sliding

coulisse [kulis] *nf* **(a)** (*glissière*) runner; **fenêtre/porte à c.** sliding window/door; **trombone à c.** slide trombone; **regard en c.** sidelong glance **(b)** *Couture* hem (*through which to pass tape*) **(c)** *Th* (*rainure*) runner, groove; **les coulisses** the wings; **en coulisses** in the wings; *TV* behind-the-scenes; **avoir un laisser-passer pour aller dans les coulisses** to have a backstage pass; *Fig* **les coulisses de la politique** what goes on behind the scenes in politics; *Fig* **rester/être dans les** *ou* **en coulisses** to stay/be in the background **(d)** *Bourse* outside *or* unlisted market

coulissé [kulise] *adj* **jupe (à ceinture) coulissée** skirt with a drawstring waist

coulisseau, -eaux [kuliso] *nm* sliding block; (*de pièce de machine*) slide; (*de tiroir*) runner; *Aut etc* slider; *Aut* **c. de sélection** selector rod

coulisser [kulise] **1** *vi MecE etc* to slide **2** *vt* **(a)** (*tiroir*) to provide with runners **(b)** *Couture* (*bord*) to run up

coulissier [kulisje] *nm Bourse* outside broker

couloir [kulwar] *nm* **(a)** (*dans maison*) corridor, passage; (*d'un train*) corridor; *Sp* (*en athlétisme, natation*) lane; *Tennis* tramlines, *Am* alley; **bruits de c.** rumours, whispers **(b)** *Cin* **c. du film** film channel, track **(c)** *Géog* gully, gorge

▶ **couloir**: *Av* **c. aérien** air corridor; **c. d'autobus** bus lane; *Hist* **le c. de Dantzig** the Polish Corridor; *Pol etc* **c. humanitaire** aid corridor; *Naut* **c. de navigation** shipping lane

couloiriste [kulwarist] *nm Journ* lobby correspondent

coulpe [kulp] *nf* **battre sa c.** to beat one's breast

coup [ku] *nm* **(a)** (*choc*) blow, knock; (*à la porte*) knock, rap; **c. de bâton** blow (with a stick); **c. sur les doigts** rap over the knuckles; *Th* **les trois coups** = the three knocks given just before the curtain rises; **donner de grands coups dans la porte** to pound *or* bang on the door; **enfoncer un clou à coups de marteau** to hammer a nail in; **se donner un c. contre qch** to knock against sth; *Fig* **ça m'a fait un c.!** it gave me such a shock!; *Fig F* **tenir le c.** to hold out, to stick it out; *Fig* **il faut que je tienne le c.** I've got to keep going *or* stick it out; **rendre c. pour c.** to return blow for blow, to hit back, to strike back; *Fig* **faire les quatre cents coups** to sow one's wild oats; *Fig F* **donner un c. de canif dans le contrat** to have the occasional fling; **faire d'une pierre deux coups, faire c. double** to kill two birds with one stone; **corps couvert de coups** body covered with bruises; *Fig F* **faire une traduction à coups de dictionnaire** to do a translation using a dictionary; **c. manqué** miss; **fusil à deux coups** double-barrelled gun; **boire qch à petits coups** to sip sth; *F* **un c. de rouge** a glass of red wine; **allons boire un c.** let's go and have a drink; **saluer qn d'un c. de chapeau** to raise *or* tip one's hat to sb; **avoir un bon c. de fourchette** to be a hearty eater; **passer un c. d'éponge sur la table** to wipe over the table with a sponge, to give the table a wipe with a sponge; **donner un c. de frein** to brake; **éviter un obstacle par un c. de volant** to swerve to avoid an obstacle; **c. de cloche** stroke of the bell; **l'horloge sonna trois coups** the clock struck three; **sur le c. de midi** on the stroke of twelve; *F* **il va falloir en mettre un c.** we're going to have to pull out (all) the stops

(b) *Golf* stroke; *Fb* kick; *Boxe* blow, punch; *Échecs etc* move; *Cartes* **finir le c.** to finish the hand

(c) (*influence*) **agir sous le c. de la peur** to act through *or* out of fear; **j'ai répondu sous le c. de la colère** I answered in a fit of anger; **il est sous le c. d'une forte émotion** he's in a very emotional state; **tomber sous le c. de la loi** to come within the provisions of the law; **être sous le c. d'une condamnation** to have a current conviction

(d) (*essai*) attempt; **à tous les coups l'on gagne** you win every time; **tu as encore droit à un c.** you've still got another go; **d'un seul c.** at one go; **faire qch du premier c.** to do sth at the first attempt *or* shot; **j'ai deviné du premier c.** I guessed straight off *or* straight away; **marquer le c.** to mark *or* celebrate the occasion; **accuser le c.** to show that one has been affected; *F* **ça vaut le c.** it's worth it, it's worth while; **ça ne vaut pas le c.** it isn't worth it

(e) (*affaire*) business, job; **il prépare un mauvais c.** he's up to no good; **être sur un c.** to be on to something good *or* a good thing *or* a winner; *Journ* to have a lead; *F* **ça, c'est un sale c.!** what a dirty trick!; **c'est encore un c. de ton ami** it's another of your friend's tricks; **réussir un bon c.** to do well for oneself; **c'est le c. classique** it's the usual thing; *F* **il est dans le c.** (*dans le secret*) he knows what's going on; (*impliqué*) he's in on it; (*à la mode*) he's with it; **il faut la mettre dans le c.** we'll have to put her in the picture; (*l'impliquer*) we'll have to get *or* bring her in on it

(f) avoir le c. de main pour faire qch to have the knack of doing sth; **du (même) c.** (*en même temps*) at the same time; (*donc*) as a result, and so; **il fut tué sur le c.** he was killed outright; **sur le c., je n'ai pas compris** at the time, I didn't understand; **pour le c.** (*en conséquence*) as a result; (*cette fois*) this time; **après c.** after the event; **tout à c., tout d'un c.** suddenly, all of a sudden; **boire trois verres c. sur c.** to drink three glasses one after the other *or* in a row; **encore un c.** once again, once more; **à c. sûr** definitely

(g) *Arg* (*rapports sexuels*) screw, shag; **tirer un c.** to have a screw *or* shag; **c'est un bon c.** he's/she's a good screw *or* a good lay

► **coup**: **c. d'aile** stroke *or* flap of the wing; *Boxe* **c. bas** low punch, blow below the belt; *Fig F* **il m'a fait un c. bas** he played a lousy trick on me; **c. de bec** peck; *Jur* **coups et blessures** assault and battery; *F* **c. de bol** stroke of luck; **c. au but** direct hit; **c. de chance** stroke of luck; **c. de couteau/de poignard** stab (with a knife/dagger); **c. de crayon** pencil stroke; **il a un sacré c. de crayon** he's very good at drawing; **c. de dents** bite; *Tennis* **c. droit** forehand (stroke); **c. d'éclat** distinguished action, glorious deed, *Sp* **c. d'envoi** kickoff; **c. d'épée** (*sword*) thrust; **c. d'essai** trial shot; **il n'en est pas à son c. d'essai** it's not the first time he's done it; **c. d'État** coup (d'état); **c. de feu** shot; *Fig* (*dans un restaurant*) lunchtime rush; **c. de filet** cast; (*prise*) haul; *Sp* **c. franc** free kick; **c. de froid** *Météo* cold snap; *Méd* chill, cold; **c. de fusil** (gun)shot; **il fut tué d'un c. de fusil** he was shot dead; *F* **c. de gueule** shout; **c. de hache** blow *or* stroke (with an axe); *Fig* **faire un c. de Jarnac à qn** to deal sb a cruel and unexpected blow; **c. de grisou** firedamp explosion; **c. du lapin** rabbit punch; (*dans un accident de la circulation*) whiplash injury; **c. monté** put-up job; **l'accusé affirmait être victime d'un c. monté** the accused claimed it was a put-up job *or* claimed that he'd been framed; **c. de pied** kick; **c. de poing** punch; **il a reçu un c. de poing** he was punched; **c. de queue** flick of the tail; **c. de sifflet** blast of a whistle; **c. de soleil** sunburn; **c. de sonnette** ring of the bell; *Baseball* **c. sûr** strike; **c. de tabac** squall; **c. de téléphone** *ou F* **de fil** (tele)phone call; *Fb* **c. de tête** header; *Fig* impulsive act; *Fig* **faire qch sur un c. de tête** to do sth impulsively; *Rugby* **c. tombé** drop kick, drop; **c. de tonnerre** (*son*) clap *or* peal of thunder; **c. de vent** gust of wind; *Fig* **entrer dans une pièce en c. de vent** to burst into a room; *Fig* **partir en c. de vent** to rush off, dash off; *Fig* **je passe en c. de vent pour te dire ...** I've just dropped in to tell you ...; *F* **c. de veine** stroke of luck; *F* **c. de vieux: il a pris un c. de vieux** he's aged

coupable [kupabl] **1** *adj* (*personne*) guilty; **c. de vol** guilty of theft; **s'avouer c.** to admit one's guilt; **elle se sent c.** she feels guilty (about it); *Jur* **plaider c.** to plead guilty; **action c.** culpable act; **faiblesse c.** reprehensible weakness; **des pensées coupables** impure thoughts **2** *n* culprit, guilty party; *F* **qui est le c.? qui a cassé le vase?** own up *or* who's the guilty party? who broke the vase?

coupage [kupaʒ] *nm* **(a)** (*de vins*) blending, mixing **(b)** (*avec de l'eau*) diluting

coupant [kupɑ̃] *adj* sharp; **outils coupants** sharp(-edged) tools, edge tools; *Fig* **ton c.** sharp *or* cutting tone

coup-de-poing, *pl* **coups-de-poing** [kudpwɛ̃] *nm* **(a) c. (américain)** knuckle duster; *Fig* **opération c.** surprise *or* sudden raid; *Fig* **une opération c. contre l'alcool au volant** a crackdown on drunk driving; *Fig* **publicité c.** hard-hitting advertising, advertising that pulls no punches **(b)** (*silex taillé*) hand axe

coupe[1] [kup] *nf* **(a)** cup, bowl; **c. (à champagne)** (champagne) glass; **c. à fruits** fruit dish *or* bowl; **c. de glace** dish *or* bowl of ice cream; **j'ai bu quatre coupes** I drank four glasses *or* glassfuls; **boire la c. jusqu'à la lie** to drain the cup to the dregs; *Prov* **il y a loin de la c. aux lèvres** there's many a slip 'twixt cup and lip; *Fig* **la c. est pleine** that's the limit **(b)** *Sp* cup; **la c. de l'América** the America's Cup; *Fb* **la c. du monde** the World Cup; *Tennis* **la c. Davis** the Davis Cup; **jouer pour la c.** to play for the cup

coupe[2] *nf* **(a)** (*action*) (*du blé etc*) cutting; (*de tissu*) cutting (out); (*d'arbres*) cutting down, felling; **c. de cheveux** haircut; **une c. et un brushing** a cut and blow-dry; **acheter du fromage à la c.** to buy fresh cut cheese; **mettre un bois en c. réglée** to make periodical cuttings in a wood; *F* **mettre qn en c. réglée** to exploit sb systematically; **c. sombre** (*d'un secteur de forêt*) slight thinning; (*du personnel, des dépenses*) drastic cut

(b) (*pièce*) (*de tissu*) length; (*de bois*) piece

(c) (*forme*) (*d'un vêtement*) cut; **complet de bonne c.** well-cut suit

(d) *Archit* (*plan etc*) section; **c. longitudinale** *ou* **en long** longitudinal section; **c. transversale** *ou* **en travers** cross *or* transverse section; **la machine vue en c.** a section of the machine

(e) *Cartes* cut, cutting; **être sous la c. de qn** to lead after sb has cut; *Fig* to be under sb's thumb *or* power; *Fig* **tenir qn sous sa c.** to have sb under one's thumb *or* in one's power

(f) *Cin* cut; (*prise*) outtake

coupé [kupe] **1** *adj* **(a)** (*taillé*) cut; **costume mal c.** badly cut suit **(b) vin c. d'eau** wine and water **(c)** *Tennis* **balle coupée** cut, slice **(d)** (*interrompu*) cut off; **la route est coupée** the road is cut off *or* blocked; **être c. du monde** to be cut off from the outside world; **communication téléphonique coupée** cut-off telephone call **(e) cheval c.** gelding **2** *nm* **(a)** *Aut* coupé; *Am* two-door sedan; **c. cabriolet** drop-head coupé; **c. sport** sports coupé **(b)** (*pas de danse*) coupée

coupe-chou, *pl* **coupe-choux** *nm F* (cut-throat) razor

coupe-cigare(s), *pl* **coupe-cigares** *nm* cigar cutter

coupe-circuit *nm inv* *Él* cutout, circuit breaker

coupe-coupe *nm inv* machete

coupée [kupe] *nf* *Naut* (*ouverture*) gangway; **échelle de c.** accommodation ladder

coupe-faim *nm inv* appetite suppressant

coupe-feu *nm inv* firebreak; **porte c.** fire-door

coupe-file *nm inv* pass

coupe-frites *nm inv* chip-cutter *or* -slicer, *Am* French-fry-cutter *or* -slicer

coupe-gorge *nm inv* dangerous back alley *or* back street

coupe-jarret, *pl* **coupe-jarrets** *nm* *Vieilli* cut-throat

coupe-légumes *nm inv* vegetable-cutter *or* -slicer

coupelle [kupɛl] *nf* **(a)** (*petite coupe*) small dish **(b)** *Ch* cupel

coupe-ongles *nm inv* nail clippers

coupe-papier *nm inv* paper knife, letter opener

couper [kupe] **1** *vt* **(a)** (*trancher*) to cut; **c. de la viande en**

morceaux to cut up meat (into pieces); **c. une tomate en quartier** to cut a tomato into quarters, to quarter a tomato; **c. un arbre** to cut down *or* chop down *or* fell a tree; **c. du bois** to cut *or* chop wood; **c. les cheveux à qn** to cut sb's hair; **c. la tête** *ou* **le cou à qn** to cut off sb's head; **c. la gorge à qn** to slit *or* cut sb's throat; *Fig* **c. bras et jambes à qn** to stun sb; **c. les jambes à qn** (*fatiguer*) to do sb in, to wear sb out; **je vais lui c. les oreilles, à ce morveu** I'm going to tear *or* rip that brat's head off!; *Fig* **c. l'herbe sous le pied de qn** to cut the ground from under sb's feet, to pull the rug out from under sb's feet; **un brouillard/un silence/un accent à c. au couteau** a fog/a silence/an accent you could cut with a knife; *Fig* **c. les cheveux en quatre** to split hairs, to nitpick; **j'en donnerais ma tête à c., j'en mettrais ma main à c.** I'd stake my life on it, I'd bet my bottom dollar on it; *Fig* **c. l'aile** *ou* **les ailes à qn** to clip sb's wings; *Couture* **c. un vêtement** to cut out a garment; **c. un passage dans un roman** to cut a passage in a novel; *Sp* **c. une balle** to cut *or* slice a ball

(b) *Cartes* to cut; (*prendre avec l'atout*) to trump

(c) (*traverser*) to cut across, to cross; **sentier qui coupe la route** path that cuts across *or* crosses the road; **c. la route** *ou* **le chemin à qn** to cut in in front of sb; **c. la route d'un navire** to cut across the bows of a ship; **la droite AB coupe le plan** the straight line AB cuts the plane

(d) (*séparer*) to cut, to divide; **la rivière coupe le département en deux** the river divides *or* cuts the département in two; **la France est coupée est deux: il y a ceux qui votent à droite et les autres** France is divided: there are those who vote for the right and the rest; **la proue du navire coupait les vagues** the bow of the ship cut through the waves; **c. l'ennemi de ses bases** to cut off the enemy from its base; **c. la retraite à qn** to cut off sb's retreat

(e) (*interrompre*) to cut off; **ces chaussettes sont trop serrées, elles me coupent la circulation** these socks are too tight, they're cutting off my circulation; **c. le souffle à qn** to take sb's breath away; (*d'un coup de poing*) to wind sb; **c. ses effets à qn** to steal sb's thunder; (*le refroidir*) to take the wind out of sb's sails; **c. les vivres** to cut off supplies; **c. les vivres à qn** to stop sb's allowance; **c. l'appétit à qn** to spoil sb's appetite, to take sb's appetite away; **c. la parole à qn** to interrupt sb; *F* **ça te la coupe!** that's floored you!, that's taken the wind out of your sails!; *Arg* **c. le sifflet** *ou* **la musette à qn** (*égorger*) to slit sb's throat; *Fig F* **c. le sifflet** *ou* **la chique à qn** to shut sb up; **le rythme monotone de la vie quotidienne était coupé (par) de nombreuses fêtes religieuses** the monotony of daily life was broken *or* relieved by numerous religious festivals; *Tél* **c. la communication** to break off the call; **c. l'eau** to turn off the water; *Él* **c. le courant** *ou* **l'électricité** to switch off the current; (*de la compagnie d'électricité*) to cut off the power; *Aut* **c. l'allumage** *ou* **le contact** to switch off the ignition

(f) c. du vin (*en mélangeant*) to blend wine; (*avec de l'eau*) to water down *or* dilute wine

(g) (*du vent*) to sting, to lash, to whip

2 *vi* **(a)** (*trancher*) to cut; **le couteau coupe bien** the knife cuts well; **ce couteau coupe comme un rasoir** this knife is as sharp as a razor; **attention, ça coupe!** watch out *or* be careful, it's sharp!; *Fig* **c. dans le vif** to take drastic measures, to take strong *or* firm action

(b) *Tél* **ne coupez pas!** hold the line!; *Cin* **coupez!** cut!; **c. court à qch** to put a speedy end to sth

(c) *F* (*se dérober*) **c. à qch** to get out of doing sth; **c. à une corvée** to get out of *or* dodge *or* shirk a chore; **il n'y coupera pas** he won't get out of it

(d) *Cartes* to cut; **c'est à vous de c.** it's your turn to cut; **c. à carreau/à cœur** to trump with a diamond/heart

(e) c. à travers champs to cut across country; **c. par le plus court** to take a short cut

3 se couper *vpr* **(a) se c. les ongles/les cheveux/***etc* to cut one's nails/hair/*etc* **(b)** (*se blesser*) to cut oneself; **il s'est coupé le** *ou* **au doigt** he cut his finger; **elle s'est coupé les veines** she cut *or* slashed her wrists; *Fig* **il se couperait en quatre pour elle** he'd really put himself out for her, he'd bend over backwards for her

(c) (*de routes etc*) to intersect, to cross

(d) *F* (*se contredire*) to give oneself away

(e) se c. de qn to cut oneself off from sb, to sever links with sb

coupe-racines [kuprasin] *nm inv Agr* root-slicer *or* -cutter

couper-coller *nm inv Ordinat* cut and paste

couperet [kuprɛ] *nm* **(a)** (*pour la viande*) (meat) chopper, cleaver **(b)** (*de la guillotine*) blade, knife

couperose [kuproz] *nf* **(a)** (*du visage*) blotchiness, blotches, *Spéc* rosacea **(b)** *Ch Vieilli* **c. verte** green vitriol, ferrous sulphate; **c. bleue** blue vitriol, copper sulphate

couperosé [kuproze] *adj* (*teint*) blotchy, *Spéc* affected by rosacea

coupeur, -euse [kupœr, -øz] *n* (*de tissu, cuir etc*) cutter; *Fig* **c. de cheveux en quatre** hair-splitter, nitpicker; *Arch* **c. de bourses** pickpocket

coupe-vent *nm inv* **(a)** (*dispositif*) windbreak **(b)** (*blouson*) windcheater, *Am* windbreaker

couplage [kuplaʒ] *nm MecE* (*de roues etc*) coupling, connecting; (*de locomotives*), *Él, Électron* coupling; (*de publicité*) combination rate

couple [kupl] **1** *nm* **(a)** (*de gens*) couple; (*d'animaux, d'oiseaux*) pair; **c. bien assorti** well-matched couple; **ils font un joli c.** they make a lovely couple; **les invités sont tous venus en couples** the guests all came in couples, the guests all came with (their) partners; **vivre en c.** to live together (as a couple); **c. non cohabitant** = couple who pursue a relationship while maintaining separate living arrangements

(b) *Phys* couple; **c. moteur,** *MecE* **c. (de torsion)** torque; *Phys* **c. thermoélectrique** thermocouple; *Aut* **c. de démarrage** starting *or* cranking torque; *Aut* **c. de pont** final-drive gears; *Aut* **c. moteur** engine torque

(c) *Naut* frame, timber; **c. de construction** bulkhead

2 *nf* (*pour chiens etc*) leash

couplé [kuple] *nm Courses de chevaux* double; **c. placé** each-way double

coupler [kuple] *vt* **(a)** (*bateaux, wagons*) to couple, to attach together; *Él* (*prises*) to couple **(b)** (*chiens*) to leash together

couplet [kuplɛ] *nm* (*de chanson*) verse; *Fig F* tirade, little piece **(sur** about)

coupleur [kuplœr] *nm Électron* coupler; *Ordinat* **c. acoustique** acoustic coupler; *Aut* **c. hydraulique** fluid flywheel *or* coupling

coupoir [kupwar] *nm Tech* cutter

coupole [kupɔl] *nf* **(a)** *Archit* dome, cupola; *Fig* **être reçu sous la C.** to be made a member of the Académie Française **(b)** *Mil* cupola

coupon [kupɔ̃] *nm* **(a)** *Com* (*de tissu*) remnant **(b)** *Fin* **c. d'action** coupon; **c. attaché/détaché** *ou* **échu** cum/ex dividend **(c)** *Rail* **c. d'aller/de retour** outward/return half; **carnet de 10 coupons** book of 10 tickets; **c. de remboursement** redeemable coupon; **c. de vol** flight coupon

coupon-réponse, *pl* **coupons-réponse** *nm* reply coupon; **c. international** international reply coupon

coupure [kupyr] *nf* **(a)** (*au doigt etc*) cut; **se faire une c.** to cut oneself

(b) (*dans une pièce, un livre, un film*) cut; **c. de journal** *ou* **de presse** newspaper cutting *or* clipping, press cutting; **c. radio** radio blackout

(c) *Él* **c. (de courant)** power cut; **il y aura une c. de 5 heures à 7 heures** (*gaz/eau/électricité*) the gas/water/ electricity will be cut off between 5 and 7 o'clock

(d) *Fig* (*séparation*) split

(e) *Fin* denomination; **c. de 50 francs** 50-franc note; **50 000 francs en petites coupures** 50,000 francs in small notes *or* denominations; **en coupures usagées** in used notes *or Am* bills

(f) *Typ* **c. automatique de fin de ligne** automatic line break *or* wrap; **c. de mots** word splits; **c. de page** page break; **faire une c. de page** to do a page break

cour [kur] *nf* **(a)** (*de souverain*) court; **vivre à la c.** to live at court; **gens de c.** courtiers; **être bien/mal en c.** to be in/out of favour; **elle a une c. de prétendants** she has a circle of suitors

(b) (*faite à une femme*) courting, courtship; **faire la c. à une jeune fille/une femme** to court a girl/a woman; **faire la c. à qn** (*flatter*) to curry favour with sb

(c) *Jur* court; **messieurs, la C.!** ≈ all rise!; **Haute C.** High Court (*for impeachment of president or ministers*); **la C. suprême du Canada** the Supreme Court of Canada

(d) *Archit* courtyard, yard; **c. de ferme** farmyard; **c. d'honneur** main courtyard; **c. de récréation** *ou* **d'école** schoolyard, *Br* playground; **jouer dans la c.** (*de l'école*) to play in the playground; (*d'un groupe d'immeubles*) to play in the yard; **la c. des grands** playground for the older pupils; *Fig* **jouer dans la c. des grands** to be in the big league, to be in with the big boys; *Mil* **c. de quartier** barrack square; *Th* **côté c.** stage left; **appartement 3 côté c.** flat no 3 overlooking the yard

▶ **cour**: **la c. d'appel** the court of appeal; **c. d'Assises** Assize Court; **c. de justice** court of justice; **c. internationale de justice** International Court of Justice; **c. des comptes** =

Audit Office; **c. martiale** court martial; **passer devant la c. martiale, passer en c. martiale** to be court-martialled **(pour** for); *Hist* **c. des miracles** area frequented by beggars and criminals; *Fig* **c'était une vraie c. des miracles** it was a picture of every human misfortune under the sun

courage [kuraʒ] *nm* courage, bravery; **avoir du c.** to have courage, to be courageous; **perdre c.** to lose heart, to become discouraged; **prendre c.** to take heart; **donner du c. à qn** to give sb courage; **il lui a fallu un certain c. pour le faire** it took a certain amount of courage for him to do it; **se sentir le c. de faire qch** to feel up to doing sth; **prendre son c. à deux mains** to summon up all one's courage, to pluck up courage; **être plein de c.** to be full of energy; **(du) c.!** cheer up!, buck up!; (*pour continuer*) keep it up!, keep going!; **avoir le c. de ses opinions** to have the courage of one's convictions; **vous n'auriez pas le c. de les renvoyer!** you wouldn't have the heart to dismiss them!; **je n'ai pas le c. de faire la vaisselle ce soir** I'm not up to doing the dishes tonight; **se battre avec c.** to fight bravely *or* courageously; **bon c.!** good luck!, all the best!; *Iron* good luck!

courageusement [kuraʒøzmɑ̃] *adv* (*bravement*) courageously, bravely; (*résolument*) with a will

courageux, -euse [kuraʒø, -øz] *adj* **(a)** (*brave*) courageous, brave **(b)** (*énergique*) energetic; **il n'est pas très c. pour l'étude** he doesn't show much enthusiasm for studying

courailler [kuraje] *vi Can F* to chase after women

courailleur [kurajœr] *nm Can F* womanizer

couramment [kuramɑ̃] *adv* **(a)** (*facilement*) fluently; **parler c. une langue étrangère** to speak a foreign language fluently **(b)** (*généralement*) commonly; **ce mot s'emploie c.** this word is in current *or* common use; **on prend l'avion de plus en plus c.** it's becoming more and more common for people to go by plane

courant, -ante [kurɑ̃, -ɑ̃t] **1** *adj* (*eau*) running; (*compte etc*) current; **chien c.** hound; *Typ* **titre c.** running head(line); **dette courante** floating debt; **le mois c.** the current month; **le cinq c.** the fifth inst., the fifth of this month; **vie courante** everyday life; **mot d'usage c.** word in current *or* common *or* general use, everyday word; **monnaie courante** legal currency; *Fig* **c'est monnaie courante** it's quite usual *or* widespread, it's common practice; **prix c.** current price; (*liste*) price list; *Com* **marque courante** standard make; **de taille courante** of standard size

2 *nm* **(a)** (*dans une rivière etc*) current; **suivre/remonter le c.** to go with/against the current; *Fig* **suivre le c.** to swim *or* go with the tide; **c. d'air** draught, *US* draft; **c. sous-marin** undercurrent, undertow; **un c. ascendant** a thermal; *Fig* **c. de population** population movement; **c. de pensée** way of thinking; **c. politique/culturel** political/cultural trend; **écrire au c. de la plume** to write spontaneously *or* off the cuff

(b) *Él* **c. (électrique)** (electric) current, power; **c. continu/alternatif** direct/alternating current; **c. triphasé/biphasé** triphase/biphase current; **c. de repos** quiescent current; *Fig* **le c. ne passe pas entre eux** they're not on the same wavelength; *Fig* **le c. est tout de suite passé entre nous** we clicked right away; *Fig* **faire passer le c. avec son public** to get across to one's audience

(c) (*durée*) course; **dans le c. de l'année** in the course of the year; **dans le c. de la semaine** some day this week, in the course of the week

(d) au c. : il est au c. he knows (about it); **mettre qn au c. d'une décision** to tell *or* inform sb of a decision; **elle m'a mis au c.** she told me all about it, she put me in the picture; **je me suis mis très vite au c.** I got the hang of things very quickly; **le professeur est très au c. des nouvelles méthodes** the teacher is very up-to-date on *or* familiar with the new methods

3 *nf* **courante (a)** *Mus* (*danse*) courante

(b) *Arg* **la courante** (*diarrhée*) the runs, the trots

courbatu [kurbaty] *adj* (*personne*) aching *or* stiff (all over)

courbature [kurbatyr] *nf* ache, stiffness; **avoir des courbatures (partout), être plein de courbatures** to be aching *or* stiff (all over)

courbaturer [kurbatyre] *vt* (*qn*) to tire *or* wear out; **je me sens tout courbaturé** I'm aching *or* stiff all over

courbe [kurb] **1** *adj* curved, curving; **des lignes courbes** curves **2** *nf* curve; (*graphe*) graph; **la route fait une c.** the road curves *or* bends (round); *Math* **c. plane** plane curve; *Géog* **c. de niveau** contour (line); *Méd* **c. de température** temperature curve; **c. des prix/des salaires** price/salary curve; **c. de popularité** popularity curve; *Compta* **c. (d'évolution) des coûts** cost curve; **c. d'apprentissage** *ou* **d'assimilation** learning curve; *Mktg* **c. (d'évolution) de la demande** demand curve; *Mktg* **c. d'expérience** experience curve; *Mktg* **c. du cycle de vie (d'un produit)** (product) life-cycle curve

courber [kurbe] **1** *vt* to bend; **taille courbée par l'âge** figure bowed *or* stooped *or* bent with age; **c. la tête** to bow *or* bend one's head; *Fig* **c. l'échine** to submit; *Fig* **c. qn sous son autorité** to bend sb to one's will, to make sb submit to one's will **2** *vi* to bend; **c. sous le poids** to bend under the weight **3 se courber** *vpr* (*d'une personne*) to bend down, to stoop; **se c. devant qn** to bow to sb; *Fig* to submit to sb; **se c. en deux** to bend double; *Fig* **elle ne se courba jamais devant l'autorité** she never bowed (down) to authority

courbette [kurbɛt] *nf* (*salut*) bow; *Équitation* curvet; *Fig* **faire des courbettes à** *ou* **devant qn** to bow and scrape to sb

courbure [kurbyr] *nf* (*de ligne, surface etc*) curvature; (*d'un morceau de bois etc*) bend, curve; (*de poutre*) sagging; (*du dos*) curve; (*de la route*) camber; **c. double** *ou* **en S** S curve

courette [kurɛt] *nf* small (court)yard

coureur, -euse [kurœr, -øz] **1** *n* **(a)** *Sp etc* runner; **c. de fond/de demi-fond** long-distance/middle-distance runner; **c. de vitesse** sprinter; *Can Fig* **laisser la chance au c.** to give sb a chance; **les coureurs** (*oiseaux*) running birds, *Spéc* Ratitae, ratite birds **(b) c'est un c., une coureuse de bals/de cafés** he's/she's always at dances/in cafés **2** *nm* **c. (de jupons)** womanizer; **c. de dot** fortune-hunter **3** *nf* **coureuse** (*cavaleuse*) manhunter **4** *adj* (*homme*) womanizing; (*femme*) manhunting; **il est un peu c.** he's a bit of a womanizer; **elle est un peu coureuse** she's a bit of a manhunter

▶ **coureur: c. automobile** racing driver; *Can Hist* **c. de(s) bois** trapper; **c. cycliste** racing cyclist

courge [kurʒ] *nf* **(a)** (*plante*) marrow, *Am* squash **(b)** *F* (*imbécile*) wally, prat, *Br* berk

courgette [kurʒɛt] *nf* courgette, *Am* zucchini

courir [kurir] (*prp* **courant**; *pp* **couru**; *pr ind* **je cours, il court, n. courons, ils courent**; *pr sub* **je coure**; *p hist* **je courus**; *fu* **je courrai**, *the aux is* **avoir**) **1** *vi* **(a)** to run; (*de concurrents etc*) to race, to run (in a race); **monter/descendre la colline en courant** to run up/down the hill; **arriver en courant** to come running (up); *Fig* **faire qch en courant** to do sth in a hurry; *Fig* **cet acteur fait c. tout Paris** the whole of Paris is rushing to see this actor; **j'ai couru toute la journée à la recherche d'un cadeau original** I ran about *or* rushed about all day looking for an original present; **faire c. des chevaux** to race horses; **cours acheter du pain** run out *or Br* nip out and get some bread; **l'assassin court toujours** the murderer is still on the run; **c. après qn/qch** to run after sb/sth; **c. après les femmes** to run *or* chase after women; **cet homme me court après depuis plus de 5 ans** that man's been (running) after me *or* chasing me for more than five years; **c. après la gloire/les honneurs/l'argent** to chase after glory/honour/money; **c. après son argent** to chase up one's money; **j'ai couru le prévenir** I ran to warn him; **je cours l'appeler** I'll run and get him; **j'y cours** I'll go at once; **c. à sa perte** to be heading for disaster; **c. à la ruine** to be on the road to ruin; *Sp* **elle court dans l'équipe de France** she runs in the French team *or* is a member of the French running team; **ses doigts couraient sur les touches du piano** his fingers were running up and down the piano keys; **sa plume courait sur le papier** his pen was racing across the paper; **il laissait c. ses pensées** he let his mind wander; **c. sur ses 60 ans** to be pushing 60; **des frissons glacés couraient le long de son échine** icy shivers were running down his spine; **des nuages couraient dans le ciel** clouds were scurrying across the sky; *F* **tu peux toujours c.!** you haven't a hope!, you haven't a snowball's chance!; *Arg* **c. sur le haricot/sur le système à qn** to get up sb's nose *or* on sb's nerves *or Br* on sb's wick, to bug sb; **ça ne court pas les rues** you don't see something like that every day

(b) (*d'un navire*) to sail; **c. au large** to stand out to sea; **c. à terre** to stand in for the land; **c. devant le vent** to run *or* scud before the wind; **c. de l'avant** to forge ahead

(c) (*se propager*) (*d'un bruit*) to go round; **le bruit court que …** rumour has it that …, they say that …; **faire c. un bruit** to spread a rumour; **le lierre court le long du mur** the ivy crawls *or* runs along the wall; **les racines courent sous terre** the roots are spreading underground

(d) (*du sang, du vin*) to flow; (*de l'eau*) to rush, to run

(e) le mois qui court the current month; **par les temps qui courent** nowadays; *Fin* **les intérêts qui courent** the accruing interest; *F* **laisse c.!** forget it!, drop it!

(f) *Sp* (*participer à une course*) to run; **il courra chez Renault l'année prochaine** he'll be driving for Renault next year; **il court dans l'Équipe de France** he represents France

2 *vt* **(a) c. le cerf** to hunt the stag, to go staghunting; *Fig* **c. deux lièvres à la fois** to have two irons in the fire, to have a finger in more than one pie; **c. un risque** to run a risk; **vous courez un grave danger en restant ici** you're putting yourself in serious danger by staying here; **c. sa chance** to try one's luck

(b) c. une course to run a race

(c) c. le monde/la campagne to roam the world/the countryside; **c. les magasins** to go round the shops; **c. les théâtres** to go to all the theatres; **c. les filles** *ou* **le jupon** *ou Vieilli* **la prétentaine** *ou Can* **la galipote** to chase after women, to womanize; *Arch* **c. la gueuse** to go philandering

(d) *Naut* **c. un bord** to make a tack, to tack

3 se courir *vpr Sp* **la coupe se courra demain** the cup will be competed for tomorrow; **dans l'épreuve qui se courait aujourd'hui à Auteuil** in the race run at Auteuil today

4 *v impers* **il court des bruits sur lui** there are rumours going round about him

courlieu [kurljø] *nm*, **courlis** [kurli] *nm Orn* **c. (cendré), grand c.** curlew

couronne [kurɔn] *nf* **(a)** (*de fleurs, de lauriers etc*) wreath, crown; **c. funéraire** (funeral) wreath; **enterrement sans fleurs ni couronnes** simple burial (with neither flowers nor wreaths); **on a décidé de lui donner la c.** it was decided to declare him the winner *or* champion, it was decided to crown him champion

(b) (*de souverain*) crown; (*de noble*) coronet; **la c.** (*souveraineté*) the Crown; **aspirer** *ou* **prétendre à la c.** to lay claim to the throne; **la triple c.** the (pope's) tiara; *Sp* the Triple Crown

(c) (*pièce de monnaie*) crown; (*en reliure*) crown (size)

(d) (*anneau*) (*de nuages etc*) ring; (*pain*) ring-shaped loaf; *Bot, Archit* corona; *Anat* (*de dent*) crown; **se faire poser une c.** to have *or* get a tooth crowned; **en c.** in a ring *or* circle

(e) *MecE* (*de poulie, roue*) rim

▶ **couronne**: **c. dentée** (*d'un différentiel etc*) crown gear, crown wheel, ring gear; **c. d'embrayage** clutch ring; **c. d'épines** (*du Christ*) the crown of thorns; **c. de pont** crown wheel; *Astron* **c. solaire** solar corona

couronné [kurɔne] *adj* **(a)** (*de fleurs etc*) wreathed (**de** with); **lauréat c.** prizewinner; **roman c.** prizewinning novel **(b)** (*souverain*) crowned; **toutes les têtes couronnées de l'Europe y assistaient** all the crowned heads of Europe were present **(c)** *Vét* **cheval c.** broken-kneed horse

couronnement [kurɔnmɑ̃] *nm* **(a)** (*de souverain*) coronation, crowning **(b)** (*de jetée*) capping; (*de bâtiment, colonne*) top; (*de mur*) coping; (*de toit*) ridge **(c)** *Fig* (*réussite*) crowning achievement **(d)** (*sur le genou d'un cheval*) scar

couronner [kurɔne] **1** *vt* **(a)** (*auteur, élève etc*) to award a prize to; *Hist* (*vainqueur*) to crown with a wreath; **un diadème couronne sa tête** a diadem crowns his head; **des pics couronnés de neige** snow-capped peaks; **mes efforts furent couronnés de succès** my efforts were crowned with success; *F* **et pour c. le tout ...** and to cap *or* crown it all ...

(b) (*sacrer*) to crown; **c. qn roi** to crown sb king

(c) c. une dent to crown a tooth

(d) c. un cheval to let a horse down on its knees

2 se couronner *vpr* **(a)** to crown oneself

(b) se c. le genou to graze *or* skin one's knee

courre [kur] *vi Arch* = **courir** *still used in* **chasse à c.** hunting

courrier [kurje] *nm* **(a)** (*messager*) courier, messenger; **envoyer un document par c.** to send a document by courier

(b) (*lettres*) mail, letters, *Br* post; **par retour du c.** by return (of *Br* post *or Am* mail); **dépouiller son c.** to go through *or* open one's mail; **faire son c.** to write one's letters; **c. interne** internal mail; **c. personnalisé** personalized mail; **c. reçu** (*bac*) in-tray; **c. à expédier** (*bac*) out-tray; **c. électronique** electronic mail, e-mail

(c) (*bateau*) mail (boat); (*avion*) mail (plane); *Arch* (*voiture*) mail (coach); *Mil, Av* courier, liaison aircraft

(d) *Journ* (*titre*) = Mail; (*rubrique*) column; **c. des lecteurs** letters to the Editor, readers' letters; **c. du cœur** advice column, problem page, *F* agony column

courriériste [kurjerist] *n Journ* columnist

courroie [kurwa] *nf* **(a)** strap **(b)** *MecE* belt; **c. de transmission** driving belt; *Aut* **c. de ventilateur** fan belt; *Aut* **c. d'arbre à cames** cam *or* timing belt; *Aut* **c. d'entraînement** *ou* **de commande** drive belt

courroucé [kuruse] *adj Litt* (*personne*) incensed, angry

courroucer [kuruse] **(je courrouçai(s); n. courrouçons)** *Litt* **1** *vt* (*qn*) to incense, to anger **2 se courroucer** *vpr* to become incensed

courroux [kuru] *nm Litt* ire, wrath, anger

cours [kur] *nm* **(a)** (*de rivière*) course; (*du soleil, de la lune etc*) course, path; **descendre le c. de la Tamise** to go down the Thames; **le c. des siècles** the course of the centuries; **suivre le c. de ses idées** to follow one's train of thought; *Fig* **donner libre c. à son imagination/sa colère** to give free rein to one's imagination/anger; **la maladie suit son c.** the illness is running its course; **affaires en c.** business in hand; **travaux en c.** work in progress *or* in hand; **année en c.** current year; **en c. de route** during the journey, on the way; **en c. de production** in production; **au c. de la conversation** in the course of *or* during the conversation

(b) *Naut* **voyage au long c.** ocean voyage; **capitaine au long c.** captain of an ocean-going vessel

(c) (*d'argent*) currency; **avoir c.** (*d'une monnaie*) to be legal tender; (*d'une pratique*) to be current, to be in current use; **donner c. à un bruit** to spread a rumour

(d) *Fin, Bourse* price, quotation; (*de devises*) rate; **au c. (du jour)** at the current daily price; **quel est le c. du sucre?** what is the price *or* quotation for sugar?; **dans les c.** in the money; **hors des cours** out of the money

(e) (*leçon*), *Univ* lecture; *Scol* lesson; (*ensemble des leçons*) course; **faire un c. d'histoire** to give a history lecture/lesson/course; **elle ne veut plus aller en c.** she doesn't want to go to lectures/school any more; **il ne m'a pas rendu mes c.** he hasn't given me my notes back; **prendre** *ou* **suivre un c.** to take *or* do a course; **donner des c.** to give classes, to teach

(f) (*livre*) textbook, course book

(g) (*avenue*) walk, avenue

▶ **cours**: *Fin* **c. d'achat** *ou* **d'acheteur** bid price; *Fin* **c. des changes** exchange rates; *Fin* **c. de clôture** closing price; *Fin* **c. de compensation** clearing price, settlement price; **c. par correspondance** correspondence course; **c. de conduite** driving lesson; **c. d'eau** waterway; *Fin* **c. demandé** bid price; **c. élémentaire** primary classes; *Fin* **c. forcé** forced currency; **c. intensif** crash *or* intensive course; *Fin* **c. légal** legal tender; **c. magistral** lecture; *Fin* **c. du marché** market price; **c. moyen** intermediate classes; *Fin* **c. offert** bid price; **c. particulier** private lesson; **c. préparatoire** *Br* = first year infants' class, *Am* = nursery school; *Fin* **c. d'ouverture** opening price; *Fin* **c. réel de change** real exchange rate; **c. du soir** evening class, night class; *Fin* **c. spot** spot price; (*de devises*) spot rate; *Fin* **c. à terme** forward rate; *Fin* **c. vendeur** offer price; *Fin* **c. à vue** spot rate

course [kurs] *nf* **(a)** (*action de courir*) running; **au pas de c.** at a run; *Mil Br* at *or Am* on the double; **prendre sa c.** to set off; **arrêté en pleine c.** stopped in full flight; (*de qn qui parle*) stopped in mid-stream

(b) *Sp* (*épreuve*) race; (*discipline*) racing; (*à pied*) running; **champ** *ou* **terrain de courses** racecourse; **voiture de c.** racing car; *F* **être dans la c.** to be with it, to be in the know, to know what's what; **être encore dans la c.** to be still in the running; **la c. à la Maison Blanche** the race for the White House; *F* **ça va encore être la c. pour être à l'heure** it's going to be another mad rush to be on time

(c) (*excursion*) (*à pied*) hike; (*en montagne*) climb; (*de taxi*) journey; **payer (le prix de) la c.** (*en taxi*) to pay the fare

(d) (*achat*) **courses** shopping; **faire des courses** to do some shopping, to go shopping; **j'ai encore une c. /des courses à faire** I still have some shopping to do; **j'ai oublié mes courses au bureau** I've left my shopping at the office

(e) (*pour affaires*) errand; **faire une c.** to run an errand; **garçon de courses** errand boy

(f) (*de personne, navire, planète etc*) path, way, course; (*de projectile*) course, flight; **je poursuivis ma c.** I went on my way; *Fig F* **être à bout de c.** to be worn out *or* exhausted, to be done in

(g) *MecE, Aut* (*d'outil etc*) movement, travel; (*de piston*) stroke; **à bout de c.** at full stroke; **à mi-c.** at half stroke

(h) *Hist, Naut* privateering

▶ **course**: *MecE* **c. ascendante** upward stroke; *TV, Rad* **c. à l'audience** ratings war; *TV, Rad* **c. à l'audimat** ratings war; **c. automobile** motor *or* car race; (*discipline*) motor racing; **la c. aux armements** the arms race; **c. de chevaux** horse race; **les courses** the races; *MecE* **c. de compression** compression *or* bump stroke; *Sp; Fig* **c. contre la montre** race against the clock; **c. cycliste** cycle race; (*discipline*) cycling; *Sp* **c. d'élan** run-up; *Cyclisme* **c. à étapes** race in stages; **c. de fond** long-distance race; (*sport*) long-distance running; **la c. au nucléaire** the nuclear arms race; **c. d'obstacles** obstacle race; *Courses de chevaux* steeplechase; (*en athlétisme*) hurdle race; **c. à pied** race; (*discipline*) running; *Aut* **c. du piston** piston displacement *or* stroke; **c. de plat** flat race; **c. de relais** relay race; **c. en sac** sack race; **c. sur piste/route** track/road racing; **c. de taureaux** (*corrida*) bullfight; (*dans les rues*) bull-running; *MecE* **c. à vide** idle stroke; **c. de vitesse** sprint; (*discipline*) sprinting

courser [kurse] *vt F* to chase after, to run after

coursier, -ière [kursje, -jɛr] **1** *n* messenger, courier; (*à motocyclette*) biker **2** *nm* (*cheval*) steed

coursive [kursiv] *nf Naut* gangway

court[1] [kur] **1** *adj* short; **avoir les jambes courtes,** *F* **être c. sur pattes** to have short legs, to be short in the legs; **avoir la vue courte** to be shortsighted; *Fig* to lack forethought; **avoir l'intelligence c.** to be of limited intelligence; **avoir la respiration** *ou* **le souffle court(e)** to be short-winded, to be short of breath; *Naut* **vague courte** choppy sea; **le chemin le plus c.** the quickest *or* shortest way; *F* **il m'a donné 100 francs, c'est un peu c.** he gave me 100 francs, it might not be enough; *Bourse* **prendre une position courte** to go short; **c. intervalle** short *or* brief interval; **à c. terme** in the short term; **de courte durée** short-lived; (*contrat*) short-term; **avoir la mémoire courte** to have a short memory, to be forgetful; **pour faire c.** to cut a long story short

2 *adv* **(a)** short; **cheveux coupés c.** short hair, hair cut short; *Fig* **s'arrêter c.** to stop short *or* suddenly; **demeurer** *ou* **rester c.** to be at a loss; **tourner c.** (*d'une soirée, d'un concert etc*) to come to a sudden end; **couper c. à qch** to put a speedy end to sth

(b) tout c. : il est un peu bête—non, il est bête tout c. he's a bit stupid—no, he's stupid, full stop *or Am* period; **son prénom c'est Charles-Édouard, mais on l'appelle Charles tout c.** his first name is Charles-Édouard, but people just call him Charles *or* Charles for short

(c) prendre qn de c. (*en lui laissant peu de temps*) to give sb short notice; (*sans le prévenir*) to catch sb unawares

(d) à c. de short of; **à c. d'argent** short of money, hard up; **à c. de personnel** short-staffed; **il n'est jamais à c. d'arguments/d'idées** he's never at a loss for *or* short of an argument/ideas

court[2] *nm* **c. (de tennis)** (tennis)-court

courtage [kurtaʒ] *nm Com* (*profession*) brokerage, broking; (*commission*) brokerage, commission; **vendu par c.** sold on commission; **c. officiel** official brokerage

courtaud, -aude [kurto, -od] **1** *adj* **(a)** (*chien, cheval*) dock-tailed and crop-eared **(b)** (*personne*) dumpy, squat, stocky **2** *n* **(a)** (*chien*) dock-tailed and crop-eared dog; (*cheval*) dock-tailed and crop-eared horse **(b)** (*personne*) dumpy *or* squat *or* stocky person

court-bouillon, *pl* **courts-bouillons** *nm Culin* court-bouillon; **faire cuire qch au c.** to cook sth in a court-bouillon

court-circuit, *pl* **courts-circuits** *nm Él* short circuit

court-circuitage, *pl* **courts-circuitages** [kursikɥitaʒ] *nm Él* short-circuiting

court-circuiter [kursirkɥite] *vt Él* (*résistance etc*) to short-circuit; *Fig F* to bypass, to short-circuit; *Fig F* **c. la filière normale** to bypass the usual channels *or* procedures

court-courrier, *pl* **courts-courriers** *Av* **1** *adj* short-haul **2** *nm* short-haul plane

courtepointe [kurtəpwɛ̃t] *nf* (quilted) bedspread

courtier, -ière [kurtje, -jɛr] *n Com, Fin* broker, agent; **c. d'assurances** insurance broker; **c. maritime** ship broker; **c. en vins** wine broker; **c. d'affrètement** chartering broker; **c. de change** exchange broker; **c. de fret** freight broker; **c. de l'air** air broker

courtine [kurtin] *nf* curtain

courtisan [kurtizɑ̃] **1** *nm Hist* courtier; *Péj* (*flatteur*) sycophant **2** *adj* **manières courtisanes** obsequious *or* sycophantic manners

courtisane [kurtizan] *nf Hist, Litt* courtesan

courtiser [kurtize] *vt* **(a)** (*flatter*) to pay court to, *Péj* to fawn on **(b)** (*femme*) to court, to woo, to pay court to

court-jus, *pl* **courts-jus** *nm F* short, short circuit

courtoisement [kurtwazmɑ̃] *adv* courteously

courtoisie [kurtwazi] *nf* **(a)** (*politesse*) courtesy, courteousness **(envers** to, towards) **(b)** (*acte*) (act of) courtesy

courtois, -oise [kurtwa, -waz] *adj* (*poli*) courteous **(envers, avec, pour** to, towards); **dire non d'un ton très c.** to say no very courteously; *Littér* **la poésie courtoise** courtly poetry

court-vêtu *adj* (*femme*) short-skirted, in a short skirt

couru [kury] *adj* **(a)** (*recherché*) (*endroit, opéra etc*) popular **(b)** *F* **c'est c. (d'avance)** it's a sure thing *or Br* a (dead) cert; **c'était c.** it was bound to happen **(c)** *Courses de chevaux* **18 partants, tous courus** 18 starters, all ran

couscous [kuskus] *nm Culin* couscous

couscoussier [kuskusje] *nm* couscous steamer

couseuse [kuzøz] *nf* **(a)** (*couturière*) sewer, seamstress; (*de reliure*) stitcher **(b)** (*machine*) stitching machine

cousin[1], **-ine** [kuzɛ̃, -in] *n* cousin; **c. germain** first cousin; **cousins au second degré** *ou* **issus de germains** second cousins; *F* **c. à la mode de Bretagne** distant relation, sort of relation

cousin[2] *nm* (*insecte*) *F Br* daddy-longlegs

cousinage [kuzinaʒ] *nm Vieilli* **(a)** (*fait d'être cousin*) cousinship, cousinhood **(b)** (*famille*) **tout le c.** all the cousins

cousiner [kuzine] *vi* to be on friendly terms **(avec qn** with sb)

coussin [kusɛ̃] *nm* **(a)** (*de siège*) cushion; *Belg* (*oreiller*) pillow; (*de collier de cheval etc*) pad(ding); **c. d'air** air cushion **(b)** *Baseball Arg* base

coussinet [kusinɛ] *nm* **(a)** (*petit coussin*) small cushion **(b)** *MecE etc* bearing; **c. de tête de bielle** big end bearing; *MecE* **c. de palier** bearing bush; *Rail* **c. de rail** rail chair **(c)** *Archit* (*de colonne ionique etc*) coussinet, cushion

cousu [kuzy] *adj* sewn; **c. à la main,** *F* **c. main** hand-sewn; *Fig F* **c'est du c. main** it's first-rate; *Fig* **rester bouche cousue** to keep one's mouth shut, to keep mum; **bouche cousue!** not a word!, mum's the word!; **c. de fil blanc** obvious, blatant, patent; **mensonge c. de fil blanc** a blatant *or* obvious *or* patent lie; **être (tout) c. d'or** to be rolling in money

coût [ku] *nm* cost; **le c. de la vie** the cost of living; **c. de fonctionnement** operating *or* running cost; **le c. d'une erreur** the price *or* consequences of a mistake; **c. d'achat** purchase cost; (*sur bilan*) cost of goods purchased; **c. d'acquisition** acquisition cost; **coûts administratifs** administrative costs; **c. assurance fret** cost insurance freight; **c. complet unitaire** total unit cost; **coûts constatés** actual costs; **coûts cumulés** cumulative costs; **coûts de développement** development costs; **c. différentiel** differential cost; **c. (total) de distribution** (total) distribution costs; **c. de l'élaboration du produit** product development cost; **c. d'entretien** maintenance cost; **coûts d'exploitation** operational costs; **c. fixe (total)** (total) fixed cost; **coûts fonciers** landed costs; **c. de fret** freight cost; **c. et fret** cost and freight; **coûts hors-médias** below-the-line costs; **loyaux coûts** (*frais de contrat*) cost arising from the execution of a deed; **c. marginal** marginal cost; **c. moyen unitaire** average unit cost; **coûts opératoires** operating costs; **c. pour mille contacts** (*d'une publicité*) cost per thousand; **c. pour mille contacts utiles** (*d'une publicité*) cost per thousand of target audience; **c. préétabli** standard cost; **coûts prévisionnels** estimated costs; **c. de production** production cost; **c. réel d'exploitation** actual operating cost; **c. unitaire (de travail)** unit (labour) cost; **c. unitaire moyen pondéré** weighted average unit cost; **c. variable (unitaire)** (variable) unit cost

coûtant [kutɑ̃] *adj* **à prix c.** at cost price

couteau, -eaux [kuto] *nm* **(a)** [①A12,1,d] knife; **c. de cuisine** kitchen knife; **c. à pain** breadknife; **c. à fromage** cheese-knife; **c. à découper** carving knife; **c. éplucheur** *ou* **à éplucher** (potato)-peeler; **c. de poche** *ou* **pliant** pocket knife; **grand c. pliant** clasp knife; **c. à cran d'arrêt** flick knife, *Am* switchblade (knife); **c. à palette** *ou* **de peintre** palette knife; **c. à pierre** chisel, stonemason's knife; **c. de chasse** hunting *or Am* bowie knife; **recevoir un coup de c.** to be *or* get stabbed *or* knifed; **planter un c. dans le ventre de qn** to stab *or* knife sb in the stomach; **jouer du c.** to wield *or* brandish a knife; *Fig* **ils sont à couteaux tirés** they're at daggers drawn; *Fig* **mettre le c. sous** *ou* **sur la gorge à qn** to hold a gun to sb's head, to point a gun at sb's head; *Fig* **j'ai le c. sous la gorge** I've got a gun pointed at my head

(b) *Phys* (*de fléau de balance*) knife edge

(c) (*mollusque*) **(manche de) c.** razor shell, *Am* razor clam

(d) *Fig* **troisième c.** (*en politique, dans la Mafia, etc*) minion

couteau-scie, *pl* **couteaux-scies** *nm* **serrated knife**

coutelas [kutlɑ] *nm* **(a)** (*épée*) cutlass **(b)** (*de cuisine*) large (kitchen) knife

coutelier, -ière [kutəlje, -jɛr] *n* cutler

coutellerie [kutɛlri] *nf* **(a)** (*articles*) cutlery; **c. chirurgicale** surgical instruments **(b)** (*industrie*) cutlery industry; (*magasin*) cutlery shop; (*usine*) cutlery works

coûter [kute] **1** *vi* to cost; **c. cher/peu** to cost a lot/not to cost much, to be expensive/inexpensive; **cela vous coûtera cher** it'll cost you a lot; *Fig* you'll pay for that; **coûte que coûte** at all costs, whatever the cost, no matter what; *F* **l'argent ne lui coûte guère** money means nothing to him; **rien ne lui coûte** (*parce qu'il peut tout faire*) nothing is an effort to him, everything comes easy to him; (*il est très énergique*) he spares no effort

2 *v impers* **j'ai voulu l'aider, il m'en coûta** I tried to help him, to my cost; **il m'en coûte de le dire** it pains me to have to say this

3 *vt* to cost; **combien ça coûte?** how much does it cost?, how much is it?; **ça coûte cent francs** it costs a hundred francs, it's a hundred francs; **ça ne coûte rien** it's free, it doesn't cost anything; **cela coûte les yeux de la tête** it costs an arm and a leg, it costs the earth *or* a fortune; *F* **ça coûtera ce que ça coûtera!** never mind the cost!, hang the expense!; *F* **ça m'a coûté la peau des fesses** it cost me an arm and a leg, I had to pay through the nose for it; **cela lui a coûté la vie** it cost him his life; **le succès lui a coûté sa vie tranquille** success put an end to his quiet *or* peaceful life; **ça ne coûte rien d'essayer** there's no harm in trying; **ça me coûte de te quitter** it pains me to leave you; **lui dire tout ça m'a beaucoup coûté** telling him all that was very painful for me

coûteusement [kutøzmɑ̃] *adv* expensively

coûteux, -euse [kutø, -øz] *adj* costly, expensive, dear; **peu c.** inexpensive

coutil [kuti] *nm Tex* drill, twill; **c. pour matelas** ticking

co-utilisateur, *pl* **co-utilisateurs** [koytilizatœr] *nm* co-user

coutre [kutr] *nm* (*de charrue*) coulter

coutume [kutym] *nf* **(a)** (*tradition*) custom; **avoir c. de faire qch** to be in the habit of doing sth, to be accustomed to do sth; **plus aimable que de c.** nicer than usual; **comme de c.** as usual; **je me suis levé plus tard que de c.** I got up later than usual; **une fois n'est pas c.** it doesn't matter *or* it won't hurt for once **(b)** *Jur* (*recueil*) customary

coutumier, -ière [kutymje, -jɛr] **1** *adj* **(a)** (*habituel*) customary, usual; *Jur* **droit c.** customary law **(b)** *souvent Péj* **il est c. du fait** it's not the first time he's done that **2** *nm Jur* customary

couture [kutyr] **1** *nf* **(a)** (*activité*) sewing, needlework; **faire de la c.** to sew; **elle est dans la c.** she's in dressmaking; **haute c.** haute couture, high fashion; **maison de haute c.** fashion house **(b)** (*de vêtement*) seam; **sans c.** seamless; **c. rabattue/plate** run and fell/flat seam; **c. anglaise** French seam; **c. apparente** overstitching, topstitching; **faire une c. à grands points** to tack *or* baste a seam; *Fig* **battre qn à plate(s) couture(s)** to beat sb hollow; *Fig* **examiner qn/qch sur** *ou* **sous toutes les coutures** to examine sb/sth from every angle **2** *adj* **une veste c.** a designer jacket

couturé [kutyre] *adj* (*visage*) scarred

couturier, -ière [kutyrje, -jɛr] **1** *nm* **(a)** (*de haute couture*) couturier **(b)** *Anat* sartorius **2** *nf* **couturière (a)** (*femme*) dressmaker; (*ouvrière*) seamstress, needlewoman **(b)** *Th* = rehearsal preceding the final dress rehearsal **3** *adj Anat* **muscle c.** sartorial muscle, sartorius

couvage [kuvaʒ] *nm* = **couvaison**

couvain [kuvɛ̃] *nm* **(a)** (*amas*) nest of insect eggs **(b)** (*rayon*) brood comb

couvaison [kuvɛzɔ̃] *nf* **(a)** (*d'oiseau*) brooding *or* sitting time **(b)** (*d'œufs*) incubation, hatching

couvée [kuve] *nf* **(a)** (*d'œufs*) clutch **(b)** (*de poussins, F d'enfants*) brood

couvent [kuvɑ̃] *nm* (*de femmes*) convent; (*d'hommes*) monastery; (*école*) convent school; **entrer au c.** to go into a convent

couventine [kuvɑ̃tin] *nf* (*religieuse*) conventual; (*pensionnaire*) convent schoolgirl

couver [kuve] **1** *vt* **(a)** (*œufs*) (*d'une poule etc*) to sit on; (*d'un incubateur*) to hatch (out), to incubate; **c. quelque chose/une grippe** to be coming down with *or Br* sickening for something/flu; **c. qn des yeux** (*avec affection*) to look fondly at sb; **il est couvé par sa mère** he is mollycoddled by his mother

(b) (*tramer*) **c. des projets de vengeance** to meditate schemes of vengeance; **c. un complot** to hatch a plot

2 *vi* (*d'une poule etc*) to brood, to sit; (*du feu, de la passion*) to smoulder, *US* to smolder; (*d'une émeute*) to be brewing; **poule qui veut c.** broody hen; **la guerre civile couvait depuis longtemps** civil war had been brewing for a long time

couvercle [kuvɛrkl] *nm* (*de boîte, pot, casserole, bocal etc*) lid; (*qui se visse*) cap, top; *MecE* (*de piston*) cover; **c. vissé** screw cap *or* top; *Fig* **chaque pot a son c.** everyone will meet their ideal partner some day

couvert[1] [kuvɛr] *adj* **(a) c. de** covered with *or* in; **c. de boue/graffitis** covered with *or* in mud/graffiti **(b)** (*allée, marché etc*) covered; **piscine couverte** indoor swimming pool; *Fig* **parler à mots couverts** to speak in veiled terms; **ciel c.** overcast sky **(c)** (*avec un chapeau*) wearing a hat; **rester c.** to keep one's hat on **(d)** (*habillé*) covered up; **c. chaudement, bien c.** warmly dressed, well wrapped up **(e)** *Fig* (*protégé*) covered; (*emprunt*) secured; **je suis c. par mon assurance** I'm covered by my insurance; **avancer c. vers l'ennemi** to advance on the enemy under cover

couvert[2] *nm* **(a)** (*abri*) cover, shelter; **le gîte et le c.** board and lodging; **être à c.** to be undercover; *Com* (*pour un crédit*) to be covered; **se mettre à c.** to take cover; **se mettre à c. de la pluie** to shelter from the rain; **au c. de la nuit** under cover of darkness; **mettre ses intérêts à c.** to safeguard one's interests; **sous le c. de l'amitié** under the cover *or* cloak *or* pretence of friendship; **il a agi sous le c. de ses chefs** he acted with the authority of his superiors; **avancer à c. vers l'ennemi** to advance on the enemy undercover

(b) (*de cuisine*) knife, fork and spoon; **couverts** cutlery, *Am* flatware; **une ménagère 24 couverts** a canteen of 24 place settings; **c. à poisson** fish knife and fork

(c) (*à table*) place setting; **mettre le c.** to set *or Br* lay the table; **mettre trois couverts** to set *or Br* lay the table for three; *Fig* **vous trouverez toujours votre c. mis** you can come and have a meal with us anytime

(d) (*prix d'une place au restaurant*) cover charge

couverte [kuvɛrt] *nf Cér* glaze

couverture [kuvɛrtyr] *nf* **(a)** (*en tissu, laine etc*) covering, cover; **c.** (*sur un lit*) blanket; **c. chauffante** electric blanket; **c. de voyage** (travelling) rug; *Fig* **tirer la c. à soi** to take all the credit; **c. d'un livre** cover of a book; (*en papier*) dust cover *or* jacket of a book; **en c.** on the cover; *Fig* **sous c. d'amitié** under the cover *or* cloak of friendship; *Fig* **servir de c. à qn** to cover up for sb; *Mil* **troupes de c.** covering troops

(b) *Constr* roofing; **c. en tuiles** tiled roof

(c) *Agr* topping; **engrais en c.** surface *or* top dressing

(d) *Fin* cover; *Bourse* margin, hedge

(e) *Journ* **c. médiatique** media coverage *or* exposure; **c. d'un événement par un journaliste** coverage of an event by a journalist; **assurer la c. d'un événement** to cover an event, to give coverage to an event

▶ **couverture**: *Av* **c. aérienne** air cover; **c. d'assurance** insurance cover; **c. sociale** social security cover; **c. à terme** term insurance cover

couveuse [kuvøz] *nf* **(a)** (*poule*) brooder, sitter; **c. artificielle** (*pour œufs*) incubator **(b)** (*pour nouveaux-nés*) incubator; **il a dû être mis en c. à sa naissance** he had to be put in an incubator when he was born

couvrant [kuvrɑ̃] *adj* **(a)** (*qui protège*) covering **(b)** (*peinture etc*) that covers well

couvre-chef, *pl* **couvre-chefs** [kuvrəʃɛf] *nm F Hum* head-dress, headgear, hat

couvre-feu [kuvrəfø] *nm inv Mil* curfew

couvre-lit, *pl* **couvre-lits** [kuvrəli] *nm* bedspread, coverlet, counterpane; **c. piqué** quilt, *Am* comforter

couvre-livre, *pl* **couvre-livres** [kuvrəlivr] *nm* (dust) jacket *or* cover

couvre-nuque, *pl* **couvre-nuques** [kuvrənyk] *nm* (*de casquette*) flap (*to protect back of neck from sun*)

couvre-pied(s), *pl* **couvre-pieds** [kuvrəpje] *nm* quilt

couvre-plat, *pl* **couvre-plats** [kuvrəpla] *nm* dish cover

couvreur [kuvrœr] *nm* roofer; **c. en tuiles/ardoises** tiler/slater; **c. en chaume** thatcher

couvrir [kuvrir] (*prp* **couvrant**; *pp* **couvert**; *pr ind* **je couvre, il couvre, n. couvrons**; *pr sub* **je couvre**; *impf* **je couvrais**; *p hist* **je couvris**; *fu* **je couvrirai**) **1** *vt* **(a)** (*casserole, meuble, livre, Fin frais etc*) to cover (**de** with); (*emprunt*) to secure; **il faut c. cet enfant** that child needs to be covered up *or* wrapped up; **être couvert de poussière** to be covered with *or* in dust; **mur couvert de lierre** wall covered *or* overgrown with ivy, ivy-clad wall; **c. qn de cadeaux** to shower sb with gifts; **c. qn de son corps** to shield sb with one's body; **c. qn** (*contre les risques, avec une arme*) to cover sb; **lorsqu'il a agi, il était couvert par ses supérieurs** when he acted it was with the authority of his superiors; **c. la retraite de l'armée** to cover the army's retreat; **c. les risques** to insure against risks; **le bruit de la cascade couvre les voix** the noise of the waterfall drowns the sound of voices; *Cartes* **c. une carte** to cover a card; **c. cinquante kilomètres en une heure** to cover fifty kilometres in an hour; **c. un défaut/une faiblesse** to hide a fault/weakness; **prière de nous c. par chèque** kindly remit by cheque; **c. une enchère** to make a higher bid

(b) *Journ* **c. un événement** to cover an event

(c) *Constr* **c. un toit d'ardoises/de tuiles/de chaume** to slate/to tile/to thatch a roof

(d) *Zool* (*de mâle*) (*femelle*) to cover

(e) *Bourse* (*position*) to hedge

2 se couvrir *vpr* **(a)** (*pour sortir*) to wrap up, to put on warm clothes, to dress warmly; (*pour cacher sa nudité*) to cover oneself up; (*mettre son chapeau*) to put on one's hat; **se c. de gloire** to cover oneself with *or* in glory

(b) *Sp* to cover *or* protect oneself; *Escrime* to guard one's body; *Fig* (*se protéger*) to cover oneself; **se c. d'un alibi** to provide oneself with an alibi

(c) le temps *ou* **ça se couvre** it's clouding over, it's becoming overcast

(d) les arbres se couvrent de feuilles the trees are coming into leaf

cover-girl, *pl* **cover-girls** [kɔvœrgœrl] *nf F* cover girl

cow-boy, *pl* **cow-boys** [kobɔj] *nm* cowboy

coxal, -ale, -aux, -ales [kɔksal, -o] *adj Anat* coxal; **os c.** hip bone

coxalgie [kɔksalʒi] *nf Méd* coxalgia

coxarthrose [kɔksartroz] *nf Méd* arthritis of the hip

coyote [kɔjɔt] *nm* coyote, prairie wolf

CPAM [sepeaɛm] *nf Admin* (*abrév* **caisse primaire d'assurance maladie**) = French government department dealing with health insurance

cpp (*abrév* **caractères par pouce**) *Ordinat* cpi

cps (*abrév* **caractères par seconde**) *Ordinat* cps

CQFD [sekyɛfde] (*abrév* **ce qu'il fallait démontrer**) QED

crabe [krab] *nm* **(a)** (*crustacé*) crab; **marcher en c.** to walk sideways *or* crabwise **(b)** (*véhicule*) caterpillar-tracked vehicle

crabot [krabo] *nm Aut* dog clutch

crac [krak] **1** *int* (*de bois*) crack, snap; (*de tissu*) rip; *F* **et c.! il est tombé par terre** and bang! there he was on the floor **2** *nm* (*de bois*) crack, snap; (*de tissu*) rip

crac-crac *nm F* **faire c.** to do it

crachat [kraʃa] *nm* **(a)** (*salive*) spit, spittle; *Méd* sputum; **un c.** a gob of spit **(b)** *F* (*décoration*) gong

craché [kraʃe] *adj F* **c'est sa mère tout c., c'est le portrait c. de sa mère** he's the spitting image of his mother; **c'est lui tout c.!** that's just like him!, that's him all over!

crachement [kraʃmɑ̃] *nm* spitting; (*de haut-parleur*) crackling; **c. de sang** spitting of blood; **c. d'étincelles** shower of sparks; **c. de flammes** burst of flames

cracher [kraʃe] **1** *vi* (*de personne*) to spit; (*de stylo*) to splutter; (*de haut-parleur*) to crackle; *F* **il ne crache pas sur le champagne** he doesn't turn up his nose at champagne, he never says no to champagne; *Fig Péj* **c. sur qn** to spit at *or* on sb **2** *vt* (*salive etc*) to spit (out); (*d'une cheminée, d'un volcan etc*) (*fumée etc*) to belch out; **c. du sang** to spit blood; **il va finir par c. ses poumons** he's going to end up coughing his lungs up; **c. des injures** to hurl abuse; *F* **j'ai dû c. mille francs** I had to fork out *or* cough up a thousand francs

cracheur, -euse [kraʃœr, -øz] *n* **c. de feu** fire-eater

crachin [kraʃɛ̃] *nm* (fine) drizzle; **il tombe un petit c.** there's a light drizzle

crachiner [kraʃine] *v impers* to drizzle

crachoir [kraʃwar] *nm* spitoon, *Am* cuspidor; *Fig F* **tenir le c.** to monopolize the conversation; *Fig F* **tenir le c. à qn** to listen to sb rambling on and on

crachotement [kraʃɔtmɑ̃] *nm* (*de personne, feu, moteur*) spluttering, sputtering; *Rad* crackling

crachoter [kraʃɔte] *vi* (*d'une personne, d'un feu, d'un moteur*) to splutter, to sputter; *Rad* to crackle

crack [krak] *nm* **(a)** (*poulain*) crack *or* star horse; *F* (*personne*) genius, ace; **c'est un c. en anglais** he's a genius at English **(b)** (*drogue*) crack

cracker [krakœr] *nm Culin* cracker

cracking [krakiŋ] *nm Pétr* (*de pétrole brut*) cracking

Cracovie [krakɔvi] *nf* Cracow

cracra [krakra] *adj inv F* dirty

cradingue [kradɛ̃g], **crado** [krado], **crade** [krad] *adj F* filthy, *Br* grotty

craie [krɛ] *nf* chalk; **falaise de c.** chalk cliff; **c. de tailleur** tailor's *or* French chalk; **bâton de c.** stick of chalk; **inscrire qch à la c.** to chalk sth up

craindre [krɛ̃dr] (*prp* **craignant**; *pp* **craint**; *pr ind* **je crains, il craint, n. craignons, ils craignent**; *pr sub* **je craigne**; *impf* **je craignais**; *p hist* **je craignis**; *fu* **je craindrai**) **1** *vt* **(a)** (*redouter*) to fear, to be afraid of; **c. la mort** to fear *or* be afraid of death; **ne craignez rien!** (*n'ayez pas peur*) don't be frightened; (*ne vous inquiétez pas*) don't worry; **je crains de le laisser entrer** I am afraid to let him in; **je crains qu'il (ne) soit parti** I'm afraid he's left; **il est à c.** *ou* **il y a lieu de c. que … (ne) …** it is to be feared that …; **il n'y a pas à c. qu'il revienne** there is no fear of his coming back; **elle craint de le revoir** she's frightened *or* afraid of seeing him again; **c. pour qn** to fear for sb, to be anxious about sb

(b) (*ne pas supporter*) **ces plantes craignent le gel** these plants don't like *or* can't stand the frost; **je crains le froid** I can't stand *or* bear the cold; **craint l'humidité/le froid** keep in a dry/warm place, keep dry/warm

2 *vi F* **j'ai raté mon exam/mon train, ça craint** I've failed my exam/missed my train, what a pain; **du rose et du jaune, ça craint** pink and yellow together, that looks terrible; **pour mon voyage, ça craint** things don't look too good for my trip; **ça craint dans ce pays-là** things are in a real mess over there; **elle craint** she's really awful; **il commence à c., ton copain** that mate of yours is getting beyond a joke

crainte [krɛ̃t] *nf* fear; **dans la c. de tomber** for fear of falling; **de c. de se faire mal** for fear of hurting oneself, lest one should hurt oneself; **de c. que … (ne) +** *sub* **lest** lest; **il a parlé plus bas de c. qu'on ne l'entende** he spoke more quietly lest he (should) be overheard *or* for fear of being overheard; **il n'a rien dit par c. de ses parents** he said nothing for fear of his parents' reaction; **sans c.** (*employé comme adjectif*) fearless; (*employé comme adverbe*) fearlessly; **soyez sans c., n'ayez c.** have no fear; **la c. du gendarme** the fear of being caught; **un sujet de c.** a matter for concern, a worrying business; **avoir des craintes au sujet de qch** to have some fears *or* worries about sth; **je n'ai aucune c. quant à l'issue de ce projet** I've no fears *or* worries about how this project will turn out

craintif, -ive [krɛ̃tif, -iv] *adj* timid, timorous

craintivement [krɛ̃tivmɑ̃] *adv* timidly, timorously

cramer [krame] *F* **1** *vi* to burn; **tout a cramé** everything went up in flames *or* in smoke **2** *vt* to burn **3 se cramer** *vpr* to burn oneself; **se c. les doigts** to burn one's fingers

cramoisi [kramwazi] *adj* crimson; **devenir c.** (*de honte, de timidité etc*) to flush crimson; (*de colère*) to go purple in the face

crampe [krɑ̃p] *nf Méd* cramp; **avoir une c.** to have cramp; **j'ai une c. au pied** I've got (a) cramp in my foot; **c. de l'écrivain** writer's cramp; **crampes d'estomac** stomach cramps; *Vulg* **tirer sa c.** to get one's leg over

crampon [krɑ̃pɔ̃] **1** *nm* **(a)** *Constr etc* cramp (iron), staple, clamp, holdfast **(b) c. (à glace)** crampon **(c)** (*pour semelle de botte*) stud; (*de chaussure de course*) spike; (*de fer à cheval*) calk, cog **(d)** *Bot* tendril **(e)** *F* (*personne*) **quel c.!** what a leech! **2** *adj inv F* (*personne*) clinging

cramponnement [krɑ̃pɔnmɑ̃] *nm* clinging

cramponner [krɑ̃pɔne] **1** *vt* **(a)** *Constr* (*pierres etc*) to clamp, to cramp together **(b)** *F* **c. qn** (*s'accrocher à*) to cling to sb; (*importuner*) to pester sb **2 se cramponner** *vpr* to hold on, to hang on; **cramponne-toi!** hold on!; **se c. à qch/qn** to hold on to *or* to hang on to *or* to cling (on) to sth/sb; *Fig* **se c. à qn** to cling to sb; *Fig* **se c. à la vie/au pouvoir** to cling to *or* hang on to life/power; *Fig* **se c. à un espoir** to clutch at a hope; *Fig* **il se cramponne à cette idée** he clings to this idea

cran [krɑ̃] *nm* **(a)** (*entaille*) notch; (*roue à rochet*) tooth; (*de ceinture, lanière etc*) hole; *Fig* (*degré*) rung, step; **c. de l'armé** full cock notch; **c. de sûreté** *ou* **d'arrêt** safety catch; **le c. de sûreté est mis** the safety catch is on; **lâcher une courroie d'un cran** to let a strap out a hole; **resserrer sa ceinture d'un c.** to take one's belt in a notch; **avancer d'un c. dans la hiérarchie** to go up a rung *or* step in the hierarchy; *F* **être à c.** to be wound up; *F* **avoir du c.** to have guts **(b)** (*coiffure*) crimp; **le c. revient à la mode** crimping is coming back into fashion

crâne [krɑn] **1** *nm Anat* skull, *Spéc* cranium; **fracture du c.** fracture of the skull; **défoncer le c. à qn** to smash sb's skull *or* head in, to bash sb's brains in; *F* **avoir mal au c.** to have a headache; *F* **mets-toi ça dans le c.** get that into your head *or* thick skull **2** *adj Vieilli* (*air*) gallant

crânement [krɑnmɑ̃] *adv Vieilli* gallantly, bravely

crâner [krɑne] *vi F* to swagger, to show off

crâneur, -euse [krɑnœr, -øz] *F* **1** *n* show-off **2** *adj* swaggering, showy

crânien, -ienne [krɑnjɛ̃, -jɛn] *adj Anat* cranial; **la boîte crânienne** the cranium, the skull

craniologie [krɑnjɔlɔʒi] *nf* craniology

cranter [krɑ̃te] *vt* **(a)** (*roue etc*) to notch **(b)** (*cheveux*) to crimp

crapahuter [krapayte] *vi F* **(a)** (*d'un enfant etc*) to crawl about (all over the place) **(b)** *Mil* (*sur un terrain difficile*) to trudge along

crapaud [krapo] **1** *nm* **(a)** *Zool* toad; *F* (*gamin*) kid, child; *F* **c'est un vilain c.** he's an ugly little squirt *or* toad **(b) c. de mer** angler(-fish) **(c)** (*défaut*) flaw, blemish **(d)** (*fauteuil*) tub chair **(e)** (*piano*) baby grand (piano) **2** *adj* **(a) fauteuil c.** tub chair **(b) piano c.** baby grand (piano)

crapaudine [krapodin] *nf* **(a)** *Minér* toadstone **(b)** *Culin* **poulet à la c.** spatchcock (chicken) **(c)** *HydE* (*de tuyau d'arrivée d'eau*) grating, strainer **(d)** *MecE* pivot bearing *or* box *or* hole; (*de gond etc*) socket, gudgeon

crapette [krapɛt] *nf Cartes* Russian bank
crapule [krapyl] *nf F* (*canaille*) scoundrel, villain
crapuleusement [krapyløzmɑ̃] *adv* crookedly, dishonestly
crapuleux, -euse [krapylø, -øz] *adj* (**a**) sordid (**b**) *Arch* (*débauché*) debauched, dissolute
craquage [krakaʒ] *nm Tech* (*de pétrole brut*) cracking
craquelé [krakle] **1** *adj* cracked; *Cér* crackled **2** *nm Cér* (*faïence, porcelaine, verre*) crackle
craqueler [krakle] (**je craquelle, n. craquelons; je craquellerai**) **1** *vt* to crack; *Cér* to crackle **2 se craqueler** *vpr* to crack, to become cracked
craquelure [kraklyr] *nf* crack; *Cér* crackle; *Beaux-Arts* craquelure
craquement [krakmɑ̃] *nm* (*de bois qui casse*) crack, snap; (*d'escalier, de plancher etc*) creak(ing); (*de feuilles mortes*) crackling, crackle; (*de neige*) crunching; (*de chaussures*) squeak(ing), creak(ing); **des craquements effrayants** terrifying cracking/creaking noises
craquer [krake] **1** *vi* (**a**) (*faire un bruit sec*) (*de bois qui casse*) to crack, to snap; (*d'escalier, de plancher etc*) to creak; (*de feuilles mortes*) to crackle; (*de neige dure*) to crunch; (*de chaussures*) to squeak, to creak; **faire c. ses doigts** to crack one's fingers
(**b**) (*se déchirer*) to rip, to tear; **les coutures ont craqué** the seams have split; **plein à c.** full to bursting
(**c**) *F* (*échouer*) (*d'une amitié, d'une entente*) to be breaking down
(**d**) (*perdre le contrôle de soi*) to crack up; **elle craque nerveusement** she's cracking up; **j'étais sur le point de c.** I was at breaking point, I was about to crack up; **au bout d'une heure, j'ai craqué et je …** after an hour I just couldn't take any more and I …
(**e**) *F* (*être attiré*) **je craque** I can't resist it/them/*etc*; **elle craque toujours devant un éclair en chocolat** she can never say no to *or* resist a chocolate éclair; **ce mec me fait c.** that guy drives me wild; **j'ai fini par c.** I finally cracked *or* gave in *or* succumbed
2 *vt* (**a**) **c. une allumette** to strike a match
(**b**) *Tech* (*pétrole*) to crack
(**c**) (*déchirer*) to split, to rip
craqueter [krakte] *vi* (**il craquette**; **il craquettera**) to crackle; (*de grillon*) to chirp; (*de cigogne*) to call, to cry
crash [kraʃ] *nm Av* crash
crasse [kras] **1** *adj* (*ignorance etc*) crass, gross; **être d'une humeur c.** to be in a foul mood **2** *nf* (**a**) (*saleté*) filth, dirt; **vivre dans la c.** to live in squalor (**b**) *Métal* dross, scum, slag; (*résidus*) scale (**c**) *F* (*mauvais tour*) dirty trick; **faire une c. à qn** to play a dirty trick on sb, *Br* to do the dirty on sb
crasseux, -euse [krasø, -øz] *adj* (*mains, draps etc*) filthy, dirty; (*logement etc*) squalid
crassier [krasje] *nm* slag heap, *Scot* bing
cratère [kratɛr] *nm* (**a**) *Géog* (*de volcan*) crater (**b**) *Antiq* crater, (wine) bowl
cravache [kravaʃ] *nf* (riding) crop; *Fig* **à la c.** brutally
cravacher [kravaʃe] **1** *vt* (*cheval*) to use the crop on; (*personne*) to horsewhip **2** *vi F* (*pour finir qch*) to work like mad, *Br* to slog away
cravate [kravat] *nf* (**a**) (*d'homme*) tie, *Am* necktie; **c. blanche** (*sur carton d'invitation*) white tie, tails; **c. noire** (*sur carton d'invitation*) black tie, dinner jacket, *Am* tuxedo; **épingle de c.** tie-pin; *Mil* **c. d'un drapeau** bow and tassels of a colour stave; *Fig F* **c. de chanvre** hangman's rope; *F* **s'en jeter un derrière la c.** to knock back a drink (**b**) (*décoration*) insignia, ribbon (**c**) (*prise de lutte*) headlock (**d**) *Naut* sling
cravater [kravate] **1** *vt* (**a**) (*mettre une cravate à*) to put a tie on (**b**) (*attraper par le cou*) to grab round *or* by the neck; *Sp* to get in a headlock (**c**) *Arg* (*duper*) to take in, to take for a ride; (*arrêter*) to nick; **je me suis fait c.** (*dupé*) I got taken in *or* taken for a ride; (*arrêté*) I got nicked **2 se cravater** *vpr* to put a *or* one's tie on
crawl [krol] *nm Natation* crawl; **nager le c., faire du c.** to do the crawl
crawler [krole] *vi Natation* to do the crawl; **dos crawlé** backstroke, back crawl
crayeux, -euse [krɛjø, -øz] *adj* chalky; **d'un blanc c.** chalky-white; **teint c.** chalky *or* chalk-white complexion
crayon [krɛjɔ̃] *nm* (**a**) (*pour écrire*) pencil; **c. de plombagine** *ou* **à mine de plomb** lead pencil; **c. gras** soft lead pencil; *Spéc, TV etc* Chinagraph; **c. de couleur** coloured pencil, crayon; **c. feutre** felt(-tip) pen; **c. à bille** ballpoint pen; **c. lithographique** litho crayon, *Am* grease pencil; *Ordinat* **c. lumineux** *ou* **optique** light pen; **écrit au c.** written in pencil; **dessin au c.** pencil drawing (**b**) (*dessin*) pencil drawing *or* sketch (**c**) (*bâton*) stick; *Méd* pencil; **c. à lèvres** lip pencil; **c. noir** eye pencil, eyeliner; **c. à sourcils** eyebrow pencil
crayonnage [krɛjɔnaʒ] *nm* (**a**) (*action*) (*gribouillage*) doodling; (*dessin*) sketching; (*traits*) pencil marks (**b**) (*dessin*) pencil sketch
crayonner [krɛjɔne] *vt* (**a**) (*dessiner*) to draw *or* sketch in pencil, to make a pencil drawing *or* sketch of; (*gribouiller*) to doodle; *Typ* **crayonné** rough (**b**) (*noter*) to note down *or* write down (in pencil)
créance [kreɑ̃s] *nf* (**a**) (*foi*) credence, belief; **hors de c.** unbelievable, incredible; **trouver c.** to be believed; **ajouter c. à qch** to give credence to sth
(**b**) (*dette*) debt; *Jur* claim; **mauvaises créances** bad debts; **c. contestée** contested debt; **c. douteuse** doubtful debt, possible bad debt; **c. exigible** debt due; **c. garantie** secured debt; **c. hypothécaire** debt secured by a mortgage; **c. impayée** unpaid debt*or* unrecovered debt; **c. litigieuse** contested debt; **c. principale** principal debt; **c. privilégiée** preferred debt; **c. recouvrable** recoverable debt; **créances** receivables, accounts receivable; **créances clients** accounts receivable, trade debtors; **créances gelées** frozen credits
(**c**) *Arch* (*confiance*) trust; **lettres de c.** credentials
créancier, -ière [kreɑ̃sje, -jɛr] *n, adj* creditor; **c. hypothécaire** mortgagee; **c. nanti** secured creditor; **c. ordinaire** ordinary *or* unsecured creditor; **c. privilégié** preferred creditor
créateur, -trice [kreatœr, -tris] **1** *adj* (*pouvoir, génie*) creative; **une impulsion créatrice** a creative impulse *or* urge; **industrie créatrice d'emploi** job-creating industry **2** *n* creator; *Com* creator, designer; *Rel* **le C.** the Creator; **le c. exclusif d'un modèle** the sole *or* exclusive creator *or* designer of a model
créatif, -ive [kreatif, -iv] **1** *adj* creative **2** *n* designer
création [kreasjɔ̃] *nf* (**a**) (*fait de créer*) creation, creating; (*d'institution etc*) creation, founding, establishment; *Com* (*d'un nouveau produit*) creation, designing; *Th* (*d'une pièce*) first production; (*d'un rôle*) creation; **c. d'emplois** job creation; **la c.** (**du monde**) the creation (of the world); **je connais cette société depuis sa c.** I have known this firm since it was founded; **c. télévisuelle** television production
(**b**) (*chose créée*), *Com* new product; **les merveilles de la c.** the wonders of creation *or* of the universe; **une des plus belles créations humaines** one of the finest works of man; **sa robe était une c. de chez Jacques Fath** her dress was a creation by Jacques Fath; **la dernière c. d'un constructeur automobile** a car manufacturer's latest model; **la dernière c. d'un metteur en scène** a director's latest production
créativité [kreativite] *nf* creativity
créature [kreatyr] *nf* (**a**) (*être vivant*) creature; **c. humaine** human being (**b**) (*personne*) creature; *F* **une belle c.** a beautiful creature; **une pauvre c.** a poor *or* wretched creature (**c**) *Péj* (*protégé*) creature; (*prostituée*) trollop
crécelle [kresɛl] *nf* rattle; **quelle c.!** (*bavard*) what a chatterbox!; **voix de c.** rasping voice
crèche [krɛʃ] *nf* (**a**) (*garderie*) crèche, day nursery; **mettre ses enfants à la c.** to put one's children in the crèche (**b**) *Arg* (*chambre*) pad (**c**) (*de Noël*) crib, crèche; **c. vivante** = nativity play
crécher [kreʃe] *vi Arg* (*habiter*) to live; (*passer la nuit*) to crash
crédence [kredɑ̃s] *nf* credence (table), credenza
crédibilité [kredibilite] *nf* credibility
crédible [kredibl] *adj* credible
crédit [kredi] *nm* (**a**) *Fin, Com* credit; **lettre de c.** letter of credit; **carte de c.** credit card; **vendre/acheter qch à c.** to sell/buy sth on credit *or F* on tick; **faire c. à qn** to give sb credit; *Fig* to trust sb; **ouvrir un c. chez qn** to open a credit account with sb; **'la maison ne fait pas c. '** 'we do not give credit', 'no credit given', 'please do not ask for credit(, as a refusal often offends)'; **établissement** *ou* **société de c.** loan society, credit establishment; *Journ* **c. photographique** photographer's credit
(**b**) *Litt* (*influence*) credit, influence, repute; **être en c. auprès de qn** to have credit *or* influence with sb; **avoir du c. auprès de qn** to enjoy sb's confidence *or* trust; **il faut dire à son c. que …** it must be said to his credit that …
(**c**) (*du grand livre, bilan*) credit(or) side; **porter une somme au c. de qn** to credit sb with a sum, to place *or* carry a sum to sb's credit
(**d**) (*subvention*) **crédits** funds, allocation; **voter des crédits** to vote supplies
(**e**) *Can Scol* credit
▶ **crédit**: *Fin* **c. back to back** back to back credit; **c. bancaire** bank credit *or* loan; **c. en blanc** *ou* **à découvert** blank *or* open credit; **c. bloqué** frozen credit; **c. de campagne** stock financing loan; **c. à la consommation** *ou* **au consommateur** consumer credit; **c.** (**à**) **court terme** short-term credit;

Bourse **c. croisé** cross-currency swap; **crédits de développement** development loans; **c. documentaire** documentary credit, letter of credit; **c. documentaire révocable/irrévocable/renouvelable** revocable/irrevocable/revolving letter of credit; **c. dos à dos** back to back credit; **c. de droits** delay in payment of indirect taxes; **c. épargne-logement** home purchase loan; **c. foncier** = (government-controlled) building society; **c. gratuit** interest-free credit; **c. immobilier** home loan, mortgage; **c. d'impôt** (*abattement*) tax rebate; (*report*) tax credit; **c. (à) long terme** long-term credit; **c. (à) moyen terme** medium-term credit; **c. permanent** revolving credit; **c. 'red clause'** red clause credit; **c. à reporter** credit to be carried forward; **c. revolving** revolving credit; **c. à taux réduit** low-interest loan; **c. transférable** transferable letter of credit; **c. de TVA** VAT credit; **c. utilisable à vue** sight letter of credit

crédit-acheteur, *pl* **crédits-acheteurs** *nm* buyer credit

crédit-bail *nm* leasing

créditer [kredite] *vt* **(a)** *Fin* **c. qn d'une somme** to credit sb *or* sb's account with a sum, to place *or* carry a sum to sb's credit; **c. un compte** to credit an account **(b)** *Fig* **c. qn de qch** to give sb credit for sth, to credit sb with sth

créditeur, -trice [kreditœr, -tris] **1** *n* customer in credit **2** *adj* (*solde etc*) credit; (*qui concerne les créditeurs*) creditor; **être c.** to be in credit; **compte c.** account in credit; **solde c.** credit balance; **nation créditrice** creditor nation

crédit-fournisseur, *pl* **crédits-fournisseurs** *nm* supplier credit

crédit-relais, *pl* **crédits-relais** *nm* bridging loan

credo [kredo] *nm inv* credo, creed; *Rel* **le C.** the (Apostles') Creed; **c. politique** political credo *or* creed

crédule [kredyl] *adj* credulous

crédulité [kredylite] *nf* credulity, credulousness

créer [kree] **1** *vt* to create; **c. des emplois** to create jobs; **c. une chaire** to found *or* establish a chair; **c. une armée** to form an army; **c. l'événement** to be big news; **c. qch de toutes pièces** to create sth out of nothing; **c. une entreprise** to set up a business; **agence récemment créée** recently established agency; **c. une hypothèque** to create a mortgage; **le pouvoir de c.** the power of creation; **cette attitude va lui c. des problèmes** that attitude is going to cause him problems *or* create problems for him; **c. des difficultés à qn** to create *or* cause difficulties for sb; *Th* **c. un rôle** to create a part; **c. un spectacle/une pièce** to produce a show/a play (for the first time); **chemises créées par Dumaine** shirts created *or* designed *or* styled by Dumaine

2 se créer *vpr* **(a)** (*se former*) to be created **(b)** (*se faire*) **se c. une clientèle** to build up a clientele; **se c. des problèmes** to create problems for oneself

crémaillère [kremajɛr] *nf* **(a)** (*dans la cheminée*) trammel (hook); **pendre la c.** to have a housewarming (party) **(b)** *MecE* (toothed) rack; *Rail* rack rail; **c. (et pignon)** rack and pinion; **engrenage à c.** rack(-and-pinion) gearing; **chemin de fer à c.** rack *or* cog railway; *Aut* **c. de direction** steering rack

crémant [kremɑ̃] *adj, nm* (**champagne**) **c.** slightly sparkling champagne

crémation [kremasjɔ̃] *nf* cremation

crématoire [krematwar] **1** *adj* crematory; **four c.** *Br* cremator, *Am* cinerator **2** *nm Br* cremator, *Am* cinerator

crématorium [krematɔrjɔm] *nm* crematorium

crème [krɛm] **1** *nf* **(a)** *Culin* cream; (*sur le lait bouilli*) skin; **fromage à la c.** cream cheese; **fraises à la c.** strawberries and cream; **café c.** white coffee, coffee with milk; *Fig* **c'est la c. des hommes** he's the best of men, he's one of the best; *Fig F* **la c.** (*personne*) the cream

(b) c. pour chaussures shoe cream *or* polish

(c) (*liqueur*) **c. de menthe/de cassis** peppermint/blackcurrant liqueur

2 *nm F* **un grand c.** a large (cup of) white coffee

3 *adj inv Br* cream(-coloured), *US* cream(-colored)

▶ **crème**: **c. anglaise** (egg) custard; **c. anti-rides** anti-wrinkle cream; **c. de beauté** skin cream; **c. au beurre** butter cream; **c. brûlée** crème brûlée; **c. (au) caramel** caramel custard, crème caramel; **c. Chantilly** whipped cream; **c. fouettée** whipped cream; **c. fraîche** crème fraîche; **c. fraîche épaisse** double cream; **c. écran** barrier cream; **c. glacée,** *Can* **c. à la glace** ice cream; **c. hydratante** moisturizing cream; **c. de marrons** chestnut purée; **c. pâtissière** confectioner's custard; **c. à raser** shaving cream; **c. renversée** crème caramel (turned out of its mould); *Ch* **c. de tartre** cream of tartar

crémer[1] [kreme] *vt* (**je crème, n. crémons; je crémerai**) (*incinérer*) to cremate

crémer[2] *vi* (*du lait*) to cream

crémerie [krɛmri] *nf* (*magasin*) dairy, creamery; *F* **changer de c.** to go elsewhere

crémeux, -euse [kremø, -øz] *adj* creamy

crémier, -ière [kremje, -jɛr] *n* dairyman, *f* dairywoman

Crémone [kremɔn] *nf* Cremona

crémone [kremɔn] *nf* espagnolette

crénage [krenaʒ] *nm Typ* kerning

créneau, -eaux [kreno] *nm* **(a)** (*de rempart*) crenel, crenelle; (*meurtrière*) loophole, slit; **à créneaux** crenellated **(b)** *Aut* gap, space; **faire un c.** to reverse into a (parking) space; **stationnement en c.** parallel parking; **elle a raté son c.** she's parked badly *or* made a mess of parking **(c)** *Com* (market) niche, gap in the market, opening; **exploiter un nouveau c.** to fill a new gap *or* niche in the market **(d)** *Rad, TV* slot; **c. horaire** time slot

crénelage [krenlaʒ] *nm* **(a)** (*de rempart*) crenellation **(b)** (*de pièce de monnaie*) milling

crénelé [krenle] *adj* **(a)** (*rempart*) crenellated; (*muni de meurtrières*) loopholed **(b)** *Bot* (*feuille etc*) crenate(d) **(c)** (*pièce de monnaie*) milled; (*écrou*) castellated

créneler [krenle] *vt* (**je crénelle, n. crénelons; je crénellerai**) **(a)** (*mur etc*) (*munir de créneaux*) to crenellate; (*munir de meurtrières*) to cut loopholes in, to loophole **(b)** (*roue etc*) to notch, to tooth; (*pièce de monnaie*) to mill

crénelure [krenlyr] *nf* crenellation; *Bot* (*de feuille*) crenelling

créner [krene] *vt Typ* to kern

crénom [krenɔ̃] *int* **c. d'un pétard!, c. de nom!** for Pete's sake!

créole [kreɔl] **1** *adj* Creole; **boucles d'oreille créoles** hoop earrings **2** *n* **C.** Creole **3** *nm Ling* Creole **4** *nfpl* **créoles** (*boucles d'oreille*) hoop earrings

créosote [kreɔzɔt] *nf* creosote

créosoter [kreɔzɔte] *vt* to creosote

crêpage [krɛpaʒ] *nm* (*de cheveux*) backcombing; *F* **c. de chignons** dust-up, bust-up

crêpe [krɛp] **1** *nf Culin* pancake; **pâte à c.** pancake batter; **faire sauter des crêpes** to toss pancakes **2** *nm* **(a)** *Tex* crêpe, crape; (*pour le deuil*) black mourning crêpe; **c. de Chine** crêpe de Chine; **c. satin** satin crêpe; **voile de c.** mourning veil **(b)** (*caoutchouc*) crêpe (rubber); **semelles (de) c.** crêpe (-rubber) soles

crêpelé [krɛple] *adj* (*cheveux*) frizzy

crêper [krepe] **1** *vt* (*cheveux*) to backcomb; (*tissu*) to crimp **2 se crêper** *vpr Fig F* **se c. (le chignon)** to have a dust-up *or* bust-up

crêperie [krɛpri] *nf* creperie, pancake house

crépi [krepi] *adj, nm Constr* roughcast

crépier, -ière [krepje, -jɛr] **1** *n* (*personne*) pancake seller *or* maker **2** *nf* **crépière** pancake griddle

crépine [krepin] *nf* **(a)** (*de meubles capitonnés*) fringe **(b)** *Culin* caul **(c)** (*de pompe etc*) strainer, filter

crépir [krepir] *vt Constr* (*mur etc*) to roughcast

crépissage [krepisaʒ] *nm Constr* roughcasting

crépitation [krepitasjɔ̃] *nf* **(a)** (*du feu, d'étincelles etc*) crackling **(b)** *Méd* **c. osseuse** crepitation, crepitus; **c. pulmonaire** crepitations, crepitant rale

crépitement [krepitmɑ̃] *nm* (*de feu*) crackling; (*de la pluie*) pattering; (*de flamme de bougie*) sputtering, spluttering

crépiter [krepite] *vi* (*du feu*) to crackle; (*de la pluie*) to patter; (*d'une flamme de bougie, de beurre fondu etc*) to sputter, to splutter; **les applaudissements crépitèrent** there was a ripple of applause

crépon [krepɔ̃] *nm Tex* crepon; **papier c.** crêpe paper

crépu [krepy] *adj* (*cheveux*) frizzy, fuzzy, woolly

crépusculaire [krepyskylɛr] *adj* twilight; *Zool* crepuscular; **lumière c.** twilight, half light; **papillon c.** moth; **oiseau c.** night-bird

crépuscule [krepyskyl] *nm* twilight, dusk; *Fig* twilight; *Fig* **quand on arrive au c. de la vie** when one is in one's twilight years *or* in the twilight of one's life

crescendo [kreʃendo] *Mus* **1** *adv* crescendo; **aller c.** to grow louder and louder; *Fig* (*de besoin, plaintes etc*) to get more and more urgent **2** *nm inv* crescendo

cresson [krɛsɔ̃] *nm Bot* cress; **c. de fontaine** watercress

cressonnière [krɛsɔnjɛr] *nf* watercress bed *or* pond

Crésus [krezys] *nm Antiq* Croesus; **il est riche comme C.** he's as rich as Croesus

crésyl [krezil] *nm Ch* cresol, methyl phenol

crétacé [kretase] *adj, nm Géol* Cretaceous

Crète [krɛt] *nf* Crete

crête [krɛt] *nf* **(a)** (*d'oiseau*) crest; (*de coq*) comb; (*de crapaud*) horn; **c. de coq** cockscomb; *F* **baisser la c.** to look crestfallen **(b)** (*de montagne*) crest, ridge; (*de vague*) crest; *Constr* (*de toit*) crest, ridge; (*de parapet, mur*) crest, top; *Anat* (*d'os*) crest; (*de casque*) crest; *Géog* **(ligne de) c.** watershed **(c)** *Él* peak

crête-de-coq, *pl* **crêtes-de-coq** *nf Bot* cockscomb

crétinerie [kretinri] *nf* (*caractère*) imbecility, stupidity, idiocy; **des crétineries** stupid *or* idiotic things

crétin, -ine [kretɛ̃, -in] **1** *n Méd* cretin; *F* (*idiot etc*) cretin, moron, idiot **2** *adj F* cretinous, moronic, idiotic; **vous êtes encore plus c. que lui** you're even more of a cretin *or* a moron *or* an idiot than he is

crétinisant [kretinizɑ̃] *adj* mind-numbing

crétiniser [kretinize] *vt* to turn into a moron *or* an idiot

crétinisme [kretinism] *nm F* stupidity, idiocy; *Méd* cretinism

crétois, -oise [kretwa, -waz] **1** *adj* Cretan **2** *n* **C.** Cretan

cretonne [krətɔn] *nf Tex* cretonne

creusage [krøzaʒ] *nm*, **creusement** [krøzmɑ̃] *nm* (*d'un trou etc*) digging; (*d'un puits*) sinking, digging; (*d'un canal*) cutting, digging

creuser [krøze] **1** *vt* **(a)** (*trou, tranchée etc*) to dig; (*puits*) to sink, to dig; (*canal*) to cut, to dig; *Fig* (*un problème, une question etc*) to examine (closely), to look into (closely); **c. un chemin sous terre** to burrow one's way underground; *Fig* **c. un écart** to widen a gap; *Fig* **c. sa fosse** *ou* **sa tombe** to dig one's own grave; *Fig* **cela a creusé un abîme entre eux** it has created a gulf between them

(b) (*faire un trou dans*) to hollow (out); *Agr* (*sillon*) to plough; **c. la terre** to dig; **front creusé de rides** brow furrowed with wrinkles, deeply lined forehead; **la maladie lui avait creusé les joues** illness had hollowed his cheeks; *Fig* **travail qui creuse l'estomac** work that gives you an appetite

2 *vi* to dig; **c. dans le sable** to dig *or* burrow in the sand; **c. très profond** to dig down deep; *Fig* **plus on creuse, plus c'est intéressant** the more (deeply) you go in to it, the more interesting it becomes, the deeper you go, the more interesting it gets

3 se creuser *vpr* **(a)** (*de visage*) to grow hollow; **ses joues se creusent** his cheeks are falling in; **l'écart entre eux s'est creusé** the gap between them has widened *or* has got wider

(b) *Fig* **se c. (la tête)** to rack *or* cudgel one's brains **(pour faire** to do)

creuset [krøzɛ] *nm* **(a)** *Ch, Ind* crucible, melting pot; *Fig* melting pot **(b)** *Métal* (*de haut fourneau*) crucible **(c)** *Litt* (*épreuve de purification*) crucible; **au c. du malheur/de la souffrance** in the crucible of misfortune/suffering

creux, -euse [krø, -øz] **1** *adj* (*arbre, mur, dent*) hollow; (*voix*) hollow, deep; (*chemin*) sunken; **assiette creuse** soup plate; **yeux c.** sunken *or* deep-set eyes; **joues creuses** gaunt *or* hollow cheeks; *Fig* **avoir l'estomac** *ou* **le ventre c.** to be ravenous; **travailler le ventre c.** to work on an empty stomach; *Fig* **avoir la tête creuse** to be empty-headed; *Fig F* **avoir le nez c.** to be shrewd *or* far-sighted; **heures creuses** off-peak hours; **période creuse** (*dans l'industrie touristique*) slack season; **l'électricité coûte moins cher en période creuse** electricity costs less offpeak; *Péj* **paroles creuses** empty *or* meaningless words; **spéculations creuses** pointless speculation; *Couture* **pli c.** inverted *or* box pleat; *Fin* **marché c.** sagging market; *Naut* **mer creuse** rough sea

2 *adv* **sonner c.** to sound hollow; *Fig* to sound empty *or* false

3 *nm* (*de la main, de l'épaule etc*) hollow; (*d'arbre, dans un mur*) hole, cavity; (*dans le sol, une route*) hollow, dip; (*d'un rocher*) crevice, cavity; (*de l'estomac*) pit; (*d'une vague, une courbe*) trough; (*d'une voile*) belly; **tenir qch dans le c. de la main** to hold sth cupped in one's hand; **c'est si petit que ça tient dans le c. de la main** it's so small you can hold it in the palm of your hand; **succession de c. et de bosses** succession *or* series of bumps and hollows; **le c. des reins** the small of the back; **c. de l'aisselle** armpit; *Fig* **être au c. de la vague** (*d'une personne*) to be in the depths of despair, to have hit rock bottom; (*d'une entreprise*) to have hit rock bottom; *Litt* **dans le c. de, du c. de** in the depths of; *F* **avoir un c. dans l'estomac** to be ravenous; **j'ai un petit c.** I'm a bit peckish; **ce chanteur a du c.** *ou* **un bon c.** this singer has a fine bass voice; **une période de c.** a slack period

crevaison [krəvɛzɔ̃] *nf* (*d'un pneu*) puncture, flat

crevant [krəvɑ̃] *adj F* **(a)** (*travail, chaleur*) killing, exhausting, murderous; (*enfant*) exhausting **(b)** (*histoire etc*) hilarious, priceless, killing

crevard, -arde [krəvar, -ard] *F* **1** *adj* **(a)** (*malingre*) pitifully thin **(b)** (*affamé*) hungry, starving **2** *n* **(a)** (*personne, malingre*) pitifully thin person **(b)** (*personne affamé*) **c'est un c. celui-là** he's always hungry, he's a bottomless pit

crevasse [krəvas] *nf* (*dans la peau*) crack; (*dans un mur, le sol*) crack, crevice, fissure; (*dans un glacier*) crevasse; **avoir des crevasses aux mains** to have chapped hands

crevasser [krəvase] **1** *vt* (*mains*) to chap; (*terre, mur*) to crack, to make cracks *or* fissures in **2 se crevasser** *vpr* (*des mains*) to chap, to get chapped; (*de la terre*) to crack, to fissure

crevé [krəve] **1** *adj* burst; (*pneu*) punctured, flat; *F* (*mort*) dead; *F* (*fatigué*) worn out, fagged out, dead beat; **ça sent le rat c., ici** it smells as if something has died in here **2** *nm* (*dans une manche*) slash; **manches à crevés** slashed sleeves

crève [krɛv] *nf Arg* (*gros rhume*) stinker of a cold, stinking cold; **attraper la c.** to catch one's death of cold

crève-cœur *nm inv* (*peine profonde*) heartbreak, bitter disappointment; **c'est un vrai c. de devoir te quitter** it's heartbreaking *or* heartrending having to leave you

crève-la-faim *nm inv F* (*miséreux*) down-and-out

crever [krəve] **(je crève, n. crevons; je crèverai) 1** *vi* (*éclater*) to burst, to split; (*d'une bête, une plante, Arg d'une personne*) to snuff it, to kick the bucket; **mon pneu a** *ou F* **j'ai crevé** I've got a puncture *or* a flat; **c. de jalousie/d'orgueil** to be bursting with jealousy/pride; **il va en c. de jalousie** he's going to be madly jealous *or Br* as sick as a parrot; **c. d'envie de faire qch** to be dying to do sth; **j'en crève d'envie** I'm dying to; **c. de rire** to split one's sides laughing; *F* **c. de faim** (*mourir*) to starve to death; (*avoir faim*) to be starving *or* famished; *très F* **je crève la dalle** I'm dying of hunger, I'm absolutely starving; **c. d'ennui** to be bored to death; *F* **je crève de froid/de chaleur** I'm freezing/boiling *or* roasting; **il fait une chaleur à c.** it's stifling *or* boiling; *F* **qu'il crève!** he can go to hell!; *F* **plutôt c.!** I'd rather die!, I'll die first!

2 *vt* (*ballon, sac etc*) to burst; (*pneu*) to puncture; *Fig* **c. le cœur à qn** to break sb's heart; *Fig* **ça me crève le cœur de devoir abandonner cette maison** I'm heartbroken about *or* it's heartrending having to leave this house; **c. un œil à qn** to put out *or* gouge out sb's eye; (*accidentellement*) to blind sb in one eye; *Fig F* **ça crève les yeux** it stands out *or* sticks out a mile; *Cin Fig* **elle crève l'écran** she fills the screen with her presence; *Fig* **les réservations/inscriptions crèvent le plafond** the floor is sagging under the weight of reservations/registrations; **c. un cheval** to ride *or* work a horse to death

3 se crever *vpr* to knock oneself out

crevette [krəvɛt] *nf* (*crustacé*) **c. grise** shrimp; **c. (rose)** prawn; **aller à la pêche à la c.** to go shrimping; *F* **cette fille, c'est une vraie c.** she's a real Twiggy

crevettier [krəvɛtje] *nm* (*filet*) shrimping net; (*bateau*) shrimper, shrimp boat

CRF [seɛrɛf] *nf* (*abrév* **Croix-Rouge Française**) French Red Cross

cri [kri] *nm* cry, shout, call; (*perçant, aigu*) (*d'une personne*) scream; (*d'un animal, un oiseau*) cry; (*d'un criquet*) chirp; (*d'une souris*) squeak; **j'ai entendu des cris dans la rue** I heard shouts *or* shouting in the street; **je ne pouvais ignorer le c. de ma conscience** I couldn't ignore the voice of conscience, my conscience was troubling me; **c. d'angoisse/d'horreur** shriek *or* scream of anguish/horror; **pousser un c. aigu** to scream, to shriek; *F* **quand je lui ai dit ça, elle a poussé des cris** she screamed when I told her; **jeter** *ou* **pousser les hauts cris** to shout at the top of one's voice; *Fig* to protest (loudly), to give vent to one's indignation; **réclamer qch à grands cris** to clamour for sth; **appeler qn à grands cris** to shout to sb; (*qui est absent*) to call (loudly) for sb; *Fig F* **le dernier c.** the latest fashion *or* style; *Fig* **c'est le dernier c.** it's all the rage, it's the latest thing

▶ **cri**: **c. du cœur** cri de cœur; *Mil* **c. de guerre** war cry

criailler [kriaje] *vi* **(a)** (*d'un faisan, d'une pintade*) to cry; (*d'une oie*) to honk **(b)** (*crier*) to bawl, to shout **(c)** (*se plaindre*) to whine, to complain, *F* to grouse, to whinge, to moan

criailleries [kriajri] *nf pl* whining, complaining, *F* grousing, whinging, moaning

criailleur, -euse [kriajœr, -øz] *F* **1** *adj* whining, complaining; *F* whinging, moaning **2** *n* whiner, complainer, *F* grouser, moaner, whinger

criant [krijɑ̃] *adj* (*erreur*) glaring; (*contraste*) striking; (*abus*) flagrant; **injustice criante** flagrant *or* gross injustice; **c'est la preuve criante de sa mauvaise foi** it's clear proof of his bad faith; **je remarque des différences de traitement criantes** I see signs of glaringly different treatment; **être c. de vérité** (*témoignage, reportage*) to be clearly *or* obviously *or Fml* patently true, to ring true

criard [krijar] *adj* **(a)** (*enfant*) whining; **être c.** (*d'un enfant*) to be a whiner; *F* **femme criarde** scolding *or* nagging woman **(b)** *(aigu)* *(voix)* shrill, high-pitched, piercing; *Fig* **dettes criardes** pressing debts; **couleur criarde** loud *or* gaudy colour; **meublé avec un luxe c.** furnished ostentatiously

criblage [kriblaʒ] *nm (du grain etc)* sifting, riddling; *(du charbon, gravier etc)* screening; *(de fruit)* grading

crible [kribl] *nm* sieve, riddle; **c. à gravier/à sable** gravel/sand screen; **passer qch au c.** to sift *or* sieve *or* screen sth; *Fig* to go through sth with a fine-tooth comb

criblé [krible] *adj (de trous, balles etc)* riddled; **la peau criblée de cicatrices** skin covered in scars; *(d'acné, de vérole)* pock-marked skin; *Fig* **être c. de dettes** to be up to one's eyes in debt; **un ciel c. d'étoiles** a sky studded with stars, a star-studded sky

cribler [krible] *vt* **(a)** to sift, to riddle; *(gravier, charbon)* to screen; *(fruit)* to grade **(b)** *(trouer)* to pierce with holes; **c. qn/qch de balles** to riddle sb/sth with bullets; **c. qn de coups** to strike sb repeatedly; *Fig* **c. qn de reproches/d'injures/de sarcasme** to heap reproaches/abuse/sarcasm on sb; **c. qn de questions** to bombard sb with questions

cribleur, -euse [kriblœr, -øz] **1** *n* sifter, riddler, screener **2** *nf* **cribleuse** sifter, sifting machine

cric[1] [krik] *nm* (lifting) jack; **c. hydraulique** hydraulic jack; **c. rouleur** trolley jack; **soulever qch au c.** *ou* **à l'aide d'un c.** to jack sth up

cric[2] [krik] *int* crack!, snap!; **c.-crac!** *(d'une biscotte)* crunch; *(d'une clé tournant dans la serrure)* click

cricket [krikɛt] *nm Sp* cricket

cri(-)cri [krikri] *nm inv* **(a)** *(bruit)* *(de criquet)* chirping **(b)** *F* *(insecte)* cricket

criée [krije] *nf* **(vente à la) c.** (sale by) auction; **la c.** *(endroit)* the auction room; *Bourse* **à la c.** by open outcry

crier [krije] *(sub, p hist* **n. criions, v. criiez)** **1** *vi* **(a)** to cry, to call out, to shout; *(fort)* to scream, to shriek, to yell; **on ne peut pas parler avec lui, il se met tout de suite à c.** you can't talk to him, he just starts yelling *or* shouting; **ne criez pas!** don't shout!; **enfant qui crie** squalling child; **je lui ai crié de se dépêcher** I called out *or* shouted to him to hurry up; **c. de douleur** to cry out *or* scream *or* shriek with pain; **c. comme un sourd** *ou* **un putois** *ou* **un damné** *ou* **comme un cochon qu'on égorge** to shout one's head off; **c. contre** *ou* **après qn** to shout at sb; **c. au secours** to shout for help; **c. au scandale** to protest, to be up in arms; **ils crièrent au miracle** they described it as a miracle

(b) *(d'une souris etc)* to squeak; *(d'un criquet)* to chirp; *(d'un oiseau)* to call

(c) *(d'une porte, un essieu etc)* to squeak, to creak

(d) *(de couleurs)* to clash **(avec** with)

2 *vt* *(ordre)* to shout (out), to yell (out); **c. des injures à qn** to shout *or* yell abuse at sb; *Fig* **elle le crie sur tous les toits** she's shouting it from the rooftops; **c. la vérité** to proclaim the truth; **c. famine** to cry famine; **c. misère** to complain of hardship *or* distress; **c. vengeance** to call *or* cry out for vengeance; **c. son innocence** to protest one's innocence; **c. une vente** to put goods up for auction; **c. des légumes/des journaux** to sell *or* hawk vegetables/newspapers

crieur, -euse [krijœr, -øz] *n* **(a)** *(dans la rue)* (street) hawker; **c. de journaux** newspaper seller *or* vendor; *Hist* **c. public** towncrier **(b)** *Th* call-boy

crime [krim] *nm* **(a)** crime; *Jur* felony; **c. d'État, c. contre la sûreté de l'État** treason; **commettre un c.** to commit a crime; **être un c. de lèse-majesté** to be lèse-majesté; **le c. ne paie pas** crime doesn't pay; *Fig* **c'est un c. que d'avoir démoli cette maison** it's a crime *or* sin to have pulled down that house; **ce n'est pas un c.!** it's not a crime! **(b)** *(meurtre)* murder; **l'arme du c.** the murder weapon

▶ **crime**: **c. contre l'humanité** crime against humanity; **c. crapuleux** crime against property; **le c. organisé** organized crime; **crimes de guerre** war crimes

Crimée [krime] *nf* **la C.** the Crimea

criminaliser [kriminalize] *vt* **(a)** *Jur* *(affaire)* to refer to a criminal court **(b)** *(rendre criminel)* to criminalize

criminaliste [kriminalist] *n Jur* specialist in criminal law

criminalité [kriminalite] *nf* **(a)** *(d'un acte)* criminal nature **(b)** *(crimes)* crime, delinquency; **taux de c.** crime rate; **c. informatique** computer crime

criminel, -elle [kriminɛl] **1** *adj* **(a)** *Jur* *(acte, droit, législation, dessein)* criminal; *Litt* *(larmes, âme)* of a criminal; *(mains)* blood-stained; **la police pense que c'est un incendie c.** the police suspect arson **(b)** *F* **ce serait c. de la jeter** it would be criminal *or* a crime to throw it away **2** *n* *(malfaiteur)* criminal; *(assassin)* murderer; **c. de guerre** war criminal **3** *nm* **avocat au c.** criminal lawyer; **poursuivre qn au c.** to take criminal proceedings against sb

criminellement [kriminɛlmɑ̃] *adv* **(a)** *(de façon criminelle)* criminally **(b)** *Jur* before *or* in a court of law; **poursuivre qn c.** to take criminal proceedings against sb

criminologie [kriminɔlɔʒi] *nf* criminology

criminologiste [kriminɔlɔʒist] *n* criminologist

crin [krɛ̃] *nm* **le c.** *(d'un cheval)* the mane and tail; **matelas de c.** (horse)hair mattress; *Fig* **à tous crins** *(socialiste, féministe, révolutionnaire)* diehard, fanatical, out and out; *(conservateur)* dyed-in-the wool, diehard; *Vieilli* **être à c.** to be in a bad mood

crincrin [krɛ̃krɛ̃] *nm F* **(a)** *(mauvais violon)* squeaky violin, fiddle **(b)** *(bruit)* squeaking, scraping (sound)

crinière [krinjɛr] *nf* **(a)** *(d'un lion, un cheval)* mane; *(d'un casque)* (horsehair) plume **(b)** *F (d'une personne)* mop, mane

crinoline [krinɔlin] *nf Arch* crinoline; **robe à c.** crinoline (dress)

crinquer [krɛ̃ke] *vt Can* to wind up; **c. un mécanisme** to wind up a mechanism; *Fig* **il est crinqué** he's hopping mad

crique [krik] **(a)** *nf* creek, cove, bay **(b)** *nm F* *(croquemitaine)* **que le grand c. me croque si ...** I'll be damned if ...

criquet [krikɛ] *nm* *(insecte)* locust; **c. pèlerin** *ou* **migrateur** migratory locust

crise [kriz] *nf* **(a)** [①A14,10] *(marasme, période d'instabilité)* crisis; **c. ministérielle** cabinet crisis; **c. du pouvoir** leadership crisis; **c. de l'énergie** energy crisis; *Hist* **la c. de 1929** the Great Depression (of 1929); **vivre une période de c.** to be going through a crisis *or* *F* rough patch; **traverser une c.** to go through a crisis; **il est en pleine c. d'adolescence** he's being a typical teenager; **c. du logement** housing crisis *or* shortage

(b) *Méd* *(dans une maladie)* attack, crisis; **elle a été prise d'une c. d'appendicite** she was struck down with appendicitis, she went down with appendicitis; **c. cardiaque** heart attack; **avoir** *ou* **faire une c. cardiaque** to have a heart attack; **c. d'épilepsie** epileptic fit; **c. de foie** bilious attack; **c. de nerfs** attack of nerves, fit of hysterics

(c) *F* *(brusque accès)* **piquer une c.** *(de nerfs)* to have hysterics; *(de colère)* to fly *or* get into a rage; **c. de larmes** fit of crying, *F* crying jag; **être pris d'une c. de larmes** to burst into tears; **travailler par crises** to work in fits and starts; **c. de conscience** attack of conscience; *Rel* crisis of conscience; *F* **la c.!** what a hoot *or* scream!; **la c. aujourd'hui en classe!** it was a real hoot *or* scream in school today

crispant [krispɑ̃] *adj F* irritating, annoying; **c'est c., cette situation d'attente** it's irritating *or* annoying having to wait like this; **ce suspense est c.!** the suspense is killing me!; **elle est crispante** she's irritating, she gets on my nerves

crispation [krispasjɔ̃] *nf* *(des mains)* clenching; *(du visage)* tensing; *(de douleur)* wince; **donner des crispations à qn** to get on sb's nerves

crispé [krispe] *adj* *(personne)* on edge, tense; *(visage)* tense, strained; *(sourire, rire)* forced; **les deux mains crispées sur la serviette** clutching the briefcase with both hands; **c. par le rigor mortis** stiffened by rigor mortis; **visage c. par la douleur** face contorted *or* screwed up with pain

crisper [krispe] **1** *vt* **(a)** *(poings, mains)* to clench; *(muscles)* to contract, to tense; *(corps)* to tense; **c. le poing vers qn** to lift a clenched fist to sb

(b) *F* *(irriter)* to irritate, to annoy; **cela me crispe** it irritates me, it gets on my nerves

2 se crisper *vpr* to contract; **à cette nouvelle, son visage se crispa** his face tensed *or* froze on hearing the news; **ses mains se crispaient sur le volant** his hands were clutching the wheel; *Fig* **elle se crispe quand elle est en ma compagnie** she tenses up *or* gets all edgy when she's with me; **leur relations se sont crispées** relations between them have become strained

crispin [krispɛ̃] *nm* *(de gant)* gauntlet; **gants à c.** *(d'escrimeur, de motocycliste)* gauntlets

criss [kris] *nm* kris

crissement [krismɑ̃] *nm* *(de dents)* grating, grinding; *(de la craie sur le tableau)* squeak, squeaking; *(des freins)* squeal, screech, squealing, screeching; *(du gravier, de la neige)* crunch, crunching; **j'ai entendu le c. des pneus sur le gravier** I heard the tyres crunching on the gravel; **le c. des pneus** *(lorsqu'on freine trop brusquement)* the squeal of tyres

crisser [krise] *vi* *(des freins)* to squeal, to screech; *(de gravier, neige)* to crunch; *(de la craie)* to squeak; **c. des dents** to grind one's teeth

cristal, -aux [kristal, -o] *nm* **(a)** *Minér* crystal; **c. de roche** rock crystal **(b)** *(verre)* crystal; **cristaux** crystal(ware); **boule de c.** crystal ball; **regarder dans sa boule de c.** to look into one's crystal ball, to crystal gaze; **travail du c.** glass cutting and engraving; *Fig* **de c.** (*voix, eau*) crystal-clear; *Ordinat* **affichage à cristaux liquides** liquid crystal display **(c)** *Litt* (*eau*) pure water **(d) cristaux (de soude)** washing soda; **cristaux dessicatifs de silica-gel** silica-gel crystals

cristallerie [kristalri] *nf* (*verrerie*) crystal (glass) manufacture; (*fabrique*) (crystal) glassworks; (*collectif*) crystal(ware)

cristallin, -ine [kristalɛ̃, -in] **1** *adj* **(a)** (*roc etc*) crystalline; (*eau, voix etc*) crystal-clear; (*son, note*) ringing **(b)** *Phys* **réseau c.** crystal lattice **2** *nm Anat* (*de l'œil*) crystalline lens

cristallisation [kristalizasjɔ̃] *nf aussi Fig, Litt* crystallization; **la neige fait de belles cristallisations** snow produces beautiful crystal formations *or* structures

cristalliser [kristalize] **1** *vt aussi Fig, Litt* to crystallize **2** *vi* to crystallize; *Fig Litt* **son idéal a cristallisé autour de ce souvenir** his ideal took shape around that memory **3** *vpr* **se cristalliser** to crystallize; *Fig Litt* **son énergie s'est cristallisée dans ce projet** his energy became focused on the project

cristallographie [kristalɔgrafi] *nf* crystallography

critère [kritɛr] *nm* criterion; **son seul c. c'est l'avis de son père** his father's opinion is his only criterion; **critères de sélection** selection criteria; **quel sera votre c. déterminant** what will be the decisive factor *or F* what will swing it as far as you're concerned?; *F* **ce n'est pas un c.** (*on ne peut rien en conclure*) that's no criterion; *Ordinat* **c. de tri** sort criterion

critérium [kriterjɔm] *nm* **(a)** *Courses de chevaux* **c. des deux ans** = races to select the best two-year-old **(b)** *Sp* heat

critiquable [kritikabl] *adj* (*décision, choix, opinion etc*) open to criticism

critique¹ [kritik] *adj* (*qui décide, crucial*) critical, decisive, crucial; *Méd* **phase** *ou* **période c.** critical stage *or* period; *Pol etc* **c'est une phase c. dans les négociations** it's a critical *or* crucial stage in negotiations; **être** *ou* **se trouver dans une situation c.** to be *or* find oneself in a critical situation; *Méd* **il est dans un état c.** his condition is critical, *F* he is critical *or* on the danger list; **l'heure est c.** we are faced with a crisis, we have a crisis on our hands; **l'âge c.** the menopause; **le moment c.** the decisive moment; *Phys* **point c.** critical point; *Nucl, Fig* **masse c.** critical mass

critique² **1** *adj* (*esprit, personne*) critical; **examiner qch d'un œil c.** to examine sth critically *or* with a critical eye; **faire une analyse c.** to produce a critique *or* a critical analysis; **son attitude est trop c.** his attitude is too critical, he's too critical in his attitude

2 *nm* critic; **c. d'art/de cinéma** art/film critic; **c. de mode** fashion writer; **c. gastronomique** food critic

3 *nf* **(a)** (*jugement*) (art of) criticism; **c. des textes** textual criticism; **c. dramatique** dramatic criticism; **c. constructive** constructive criticism

(b) (*examen*) critical article *or* paper; *Th, Cin* review; **faire la c. d'une pièce** to review a play; **sa pièce a eu quelques bonnes critiques** his play got a few good reviews

(c) (*condamnation*) (*d'une politique, un régime etc*) criticism; **exercer une sévère c. sur soi-même** to be highly self-critical *or* a stern critic of oneself; **il ne supporte pas** *ou* **il n'accepte pas la c.** he can't take criticism; **ce n'est pas une c., mais ...** don't take this as a criticism, but ...; **formuler une** *ou* **des critique(s)** to express criticism, to make a criticism; **être l'objet des critiques du public** to be a target for public criticism

(d) la c. (*l'ensemble des critiques*) the critics; **la c. n'a pas aimé** the critics didn't like it

critiquer [kritike] **1** *vt* **(a)** (*examiner, juger*) **c. qch** to assess sth, to examine sth critically **(b)** (*condamner*) (*personne, attitude*) to criticize, to find fault with; **c. qn pour qch/pour ne pas avoir fait qch** to criticize sb for sth/for not doing sth; **ce n'est pas pour te c., mais ...** don't take this as a criticism, but ..., I don't mean to criticize (you), but ... **2** *vi* to criticize; **arrête de c.** stop criticizing

critiqueur, -euse [kritikœr, -øz] *n* captious *or* carping critic; **quelle critiqueuse celle-là!** she's so critical!

croassement [krɔasmɑ̃] *nm* (*de corneille*) caw(ing); (*de corbeau*) croak(ing); *Fig Litt* **les croassements odieux des vieillards** the spiteful comments of the old men

croasser [krɔase] *vi* (*de corneille*) to caw; (*de corbeau*) to croak

croate [krɔat] **1** *adj* Croatian **2** *nm Ling* Croat(ian) **3** *n* **C.** Croat(ian)

Croatie [krɔasi] *nf* Croatia

croc [kro] *nm* **(a)** (*crochet*) hook; **c. de boucherie** meat hook; **c. à fumier** muck rake; **c. de marinier** boat-hook **(b)** (*de loup, chien*) fang; **montrer ses crocs** to show one's teeth; **moustache en c.** handlebar moustache; *Arg* **avoir les crocs** to be famished, to be ravenous

croc-en-jambe, *pl* **crocs-en-jambe** *nm* (*pour faire tomber un adversaire*) trip; *Fig* dirty trick; **faire un c. à qn** to trip sb up; *Fig* to pull a fast one on sb

croche [krɔʃ] *nf Mus* quaver, *Am* eighth note; **double c.** semiquaver, *Am* sixteenth note

croche-pied, *pl* **croche-pieds** *nm* = **croc-en-jambe**

crocher [krɔʃe] **1** *vt* **(a)** *Naut* **c. qch** to hook (on to) sth, to seize sth with a hook; *Région* **c. sa veste** to hang up one's jacket **(b)** *F* (*se saisir de*) to grab hold of **2** *vi Naut* (*d'une ancre*) to grip, to bite, to hold

crochet [krɔʃɛ] *nm* **(a)** hook; **c. à vis** screw hook; **c. de boucherie** meat hook; **c. à boutons** buttonhook; **c. de bureau** spike file; *MecE* **c. d'arrêt** pawl, catch; **c. de sécurité** safety catch; *Fig* **vivre aux crochets de qn** to live off *or* sponge on sb

(b) (*pour l'ouvrage*) crochet hook; **(travail au) c.** crochet work; **faire du c.** to (do) crochet; **faire qch au c.** to crochet sth

(c) (*d'un serpent*) (poison) fang

(d) *Typ* square bracket

(e) (*détour*) **faire un c.** to make a detour; (*d'une route*) to take a sudden turn; (*d'une voiture, un cheval*) to swerve (*to avoid sth*)

(f) *Boxe* **c. du gauche/du droit** left/right hook

(g) *Mus* (*d'une croche*) hook

(h) *Rad* **c. radiophonique** talent contest (*on radio*)

crochetable [krɔʃtabl] *adj* (*serrure*) that can be picked, pickable

crochetage [krɔʃtaʒ] *nm* (*d'une serrure*) picking

crocheter [krɔʃte] *vt* (**je crochète, n. crochetons; je crochèterai**) **(a)** (*serrure*) to pick **(b)** (*piquer*) to hook, to pick up with a hook

crocheteur [krɔʃtœr] *nm* lockpicker, housebreaker

crochu [krɔʃy] *adj* (*fil de fer, nez etc*) hooked; (*doigts, mains*) claw-like; *Fig F* **avoir les doigts** *ou* **les mains crochu(e)s** to be mean *or* tight-fisted *or Am* a tightwad; *Hist, Phil* **atomes crochus** interlocking atoms; *Fig F* **nous nous sommes senti des atomes crochus** we hit it off; *Fig F* **je n'ai pas d'atomes crochus avec elle** I don't hit it off with her

croco [krɔko] *nm F* crocodile (skin); **sac en c.** crocodile(-skin) handbag

crocodile [krɔkɔdil] *nm* (*reptile*) crocodile; **sac à main en c.** crocodile(-skin) handbag; *Fig* **larmes de c.** crocodile tears

crocus [krɔkys] *nm* (*plante*) crocus

croire [krwar] (*prp* **croyant**; *pp* **cru**; *pr ind* **je crois, il croit, n. croyons, ils croient**; *impf* **je croyais**; *p hist* **je crus**; *fu* **je croirai**) **1** *vt* **(a)** to believe; **c. qch** to believe sth; **cela, je ne peux pas le c.** I can't believe that, I find that hard to believe; **vous ne sauriez c. combien je suis content** you can't think *or* imagine how glad I am; **j'aime à c. que ... +** *ind* I hope *or* trust that ...; **il est à c. que ... +** *ind* it would seem that ...; **tout porte à** *ou* **il faut c. que ...** there is every indication that ..., it would seem that ...; **je ne crois pas que cela suffise** I don't think that will be enough; **je crois que oui/non** I think *or* believe so/not; **n'en croyez rien!** don't believe (a word of) it!, *F* not a bit of it!; *F* **d'après ce que je crois ...** from what I've heard ...; **croyez-le ou non** believe it or not; **je vous croyais anglais/riche** I thought you were English/rich; **on croirait qu'il dort** you'd think he was asleep; **je ne suis pas celle que vous croyez** I'm not that kind of girl; **j'ai cru bien faire** I thought *or* believed I was doing the right thing; **j'ai cru devoir le prévenir** I thought I ought to warn him; **elle ne croyait pas si bien dire** she didn't know how right she was; **je n'aurais pas cru cela de lui** I wouldn't have *or* would never have thought it of him; **c. qn** to believe sb, to take sb's word for sth; **me croira qui voudra, mais ...** you may not believe this, but ...; *F Iron* **c'est ça, je te crois!** is that so?; **mais je te crois!** I believe you, I'll take your word for it; **croyez-moi, ce n'était pas facile** believe (you) me, it wasn't easy

(b) en c. qn to take sb's word for it; (*en suivant son conseil*) to take sb's advice; **vous pouvez m'en c.** (you can) take my word for it, you can take it from me; **s'il faut l'en c.** *ou* **à l'en c., ce n'est pas difficile** according to him *or* going by what he says it's not difficult; **je ne pouvais en c. mes yeux/mes oreilles** I couldn't believe my eyes/my ears

2 *vi* **(a)** (*concevoir etc*) to believe (**à** in); **personne ne croyait à la guerre** nobody thought war would break out, nobody thought there would be a war; **le médecin crut à une rougeole** the doctor thought it was measles; **franchement, je n'y crois pas** quite frankly, I don't believe it; **c'est à ne pas y c.** it's beyond belief, it's unbelievable; *F* **faut pas c.!** don't you believe it!; **vous**

croyez? do you really think so?; **j'ai cru nécessaire de …** I thought it necessary to …; **veuillez c.** *ou* **je vous prie de c. à l'expression de mes sentiments distingués** = yours sincerely

(**b**) (*adhérer, avoir foi*) to believe (in), to trust (in), to have faith in; **je ne crois pas à ses promesses** I don't believe *or* I have no faith in his promises; **c. en Dieu** to believe in God; **il ne croit plus** he has lost his faith (in God); **je ne peux pas c. sur commande, je dois comprendre** you can't just ask me to believe, I need to understand

3 se croire *vpr* (*avec attribut*) to think oneself; **il se croit intelligent** he thinks he's intelligent; **on se serait cru en octobre** it felt like October; **il se croit tout permis** he thinks he can do *or* get away with anything; *F* **qu'est-ce qu'il se croit?** who does he think he is?; *F* **il se croit sorti de la cuisse de Jupiter** he thinks a lot of himself, he thinks he's the bee's knees; **il s'y croit** he's getting above himself *or* too big for his boots *or Am* britches; **elle s'est toujours crue incapable de réussir** she never thought she would succeed

croisade [krwazad] *nf* (**a**) (*campagne*) crusade, campaign; **c. contre la drogue** anti-drugs campaign *or* crusade (**b**) *Hist* crusade; **partir en c.** to go on a crusade

croisé [krwaze] **1** *adj* (**a**) **feu** *ou* **tir c.** crossfire; **mots croisés** crossword; **rimes croisées** alternate rhymes; **race croisée** crossbreed; *Bourse* **participation croisée** cross-holding (**b**) (*manteau, veste*) double-breasted **2** *nm* (**a**) *Hist* crusader (**b**) *Tex* twill

croisée [krwaze] *nf* (**a**) (*rencontre*) crossing; **c. de chemins** crossroads; *Fig* **être à la c. des chemins** to stand at the crossroads, to be at a crossroads (**b**) (*châssis*) casement; (*fenêtre*) casement window

croisement [krwazmɑ̃] *nm* (**a**) (*de véhicules*) passing; (*de lignes, routes etc*) crossing, intersection; **c. de routes** *ou* **de rues** crossroads, junction; **c. dangereux** dangerous crossroads (**b**) (*des bras, jambes*) crossing (**c**) (*d'animaux*) crossing, crossbreeding; (*animal*) crossbreed, cross (**entre … et …** between … and …); **faire des croisements de races** to cross breeds; **c. consanguin** interbreeding

croiser [krwaze] **1** *vt* (**a**) (*d'une ligne, route*) to cross, to cut across, to intersect; **le pont croise l'autoroute** the bridge goes over *or* crosses the motorway; **c. un châle/une écharpe sur sa poitrine** to wear a shawl/a scarf; **elle a croisé un foulard sur son pull** she wore a scarf crossed over her sweater; **c. les jambes** to cross one's legs; **c. les bras** to fold one's arms; **c. le regard de qn** to meet sb's gaze *or* eyes; **je croise les doigts pour que tu réussisses** I've got my fingers crossed for you; **c. le fer avec qn** to have a sword fight with sb; *Fig* to cross swords with sb

(**b**) (*véhicule, personne*) to pass

(**c**) (*animaux, plantes*) to cross(breed)

2 *vi* (**a**) (*d'un vêtement*) **manteau qui ne croise pas assez** coat that does not have sufficient overlap

(**b**) *Naut* to cruise

3 se croiser *vpr* (**a**) (*de routes*) to cross, to intersect; (*de personnes*) to meet; **ces deux chemins se croisent** these two paths intersect; *Fig* **se c. les bras** to sit back, to sit with arms folded; **leurs vies n'ont fait que se c.** their paths barely crossed; **nous n'avons fait que nous c.** we saw each other only briefly *or* for a moment; **elles ne se sont jamais croisées bien qu'elles étaient dans la même université** their paths never crossed even though they went to the same university; **leurs regards se croisèrent** their eyes met; **nos lettres se sont croisées** our letters have crossed in the post

(**b**) *Hist* to go on a crusade

(**c**) (*s'accoupler*) to mate, to couple; **le cheval peut se c. avec l'âne** the horse can be crossed with the donkey

croiseur [krwazœr] *nm Naut* cruiser; **c. de bataille** battle cruiser; **c. lourd/léger** heavy/light cruiser

croisière [krwazjɛr] *nf Naut etc* (**a**) **vitesse/altitude de c.** cruising speed/altitude; **missile de c.** cruise missile; *Fig* **adopter l'allure de c.** to start ticking over normally; **atteindre le rythme de c.** to reach cruising speed; *Fig* to be working at a comfortable rate *or* tempo (**b**) (*voyage*) cruise; **faire une c.** (*d'une personne*) to go on *or* take a cruise; (*d'un navire*) to be cruising; **être en c.** to be on a cruise; **navire de c.** cruise ship; **c. fluviale/maritime** river-/sea-cruise

croisillon [krwazijɔ̃] *nm* (**a**) (*de croix, fenêtre*) crosspiece, crossbar; (*de chaise etc*) (cross)bar; *Archit* transept; **fenêtre à croisillons** lattice window (**b**) *Aut* trunnion block, spider

croissance [krwasɑ̃s] *nf* growth; (*d'une banlieue*) growth, spread; **en pleine c.** growing rapidly; **arrêté dans sa c.** (*arbre, enfant*) stunted; **enfant en pleine c.** growing child; **hormone de c.** (human) growth hormone; **finir sa c.** to stop growing; **c. économique** economic growth *or* development; **c. du marché** market growth; **c. par intégration** integrative growth; **c. zéro** zero growth

croissant¹ [krwasɑ̃] *adj* (*plante, tendance etc*) growing; (*richesse, angoisse etc*) growing, increasing; (*ordre*) ascending; (*chaleur, température*) increasing; *Math* (*nombre, fonction*) monotonic; **les jeunes diplômés arrivent en nombre c.** there's an increasing number of young graduates (on the market)

croissant² *nm* (**a**) crescent; **un c. de lune** a crescent moon; **le C. Rouge** the Red Crescent; **en c.** crescent-shaped (**b**) *Culin* croissant; **c. aux amandes** almond croissant

croître [krwɑtr] *vi* (*prp* **croissant**; *pp* **crû**, *f* **crue**; *pr ind* **je crois, il croît, n. croissons, ils croissent**; *p hist* **je crûs**; *fu* **je croîtrai**; *pr sub* **je croisse**; *p sub* **je crûsse**) to grow, to increase (in size); (*de plantes*) to grow; (*de la lune*) to wax; (*d'une rivière*) to rise, to swell; (*du vent*) to rise; **c. en volume/nombre** to increase in volume/number; **c. en beauté/sagesse** to grow in beauty/wisdom; **les jours croissent** the days are lengthening, the days are getting *or* growing longer; **aller croissant** (*de terreur*) to grow and grow; (*de suspense*) to get worse and worse; (*de bruit*) to get louder and louder; **l'inquiétude de la police va croissant** the police are increasingly anxious *or* concerned; **cela ne fait que c. et embellir** it's getting better and better; *Iron* it's getting worse and worse; **c. dans l'estime de qn** to rise in sb's esteem; *Prov* **mauvaise herbe croît toujours** ill weeds grow apace

croix [krwa] *nf* cross; **la sainte C.** the Holy Cross; **mettre en c.** to crucify; **le chemin de (la) C.** the Way of the Cross, the Via Dolorosa; (*les quatorze arrêts*) the stations of the Cross; **faire un chemin de c.** to do the stations of the cross; **le signe de (la) c.** the sign of the cross; **faire le signe de c.** to make the sign of the cross, to cross oneself; **porter une c. au cou** to wear a crucifix; **chacun porte sa c.** everyone has his cross to bear; **c. de bois c. de fer si je mens je vais en enfer** ≈ cross my heart (and hope to die); **c'est la c. et la bannière** it's the devil of a job; *Hist* **prendre la c.** to go on a crusade; **la c. (de la Légion d'honneur)** the Cross of the Legion of Honour; **en (forme de) c.** cross-shaped, in the shape of a cross; **mettre des bâtons en c.** to lay sticks crosswise; **mettre les bras en c.** to stretch one's arms out to the sides; **marquer qch d'une c.** to mark sth with a cross; *Fig* **ce jour est à marquer d'une c.** it's a red-letter day; **faire une c. en face d'un nom** to tick *or Am* to check off a name; **signer d'une c.** to make one's mark; *F* **faire une c. sur qch** to say goodbye to sth, to kiss sth goodbye; *Typ* **c. (mortuaire)** dagger

▸ **croix**: **c. gammée** swastika; **c. grecque** Greek cross; **c. de guerre** Military Cross; **c. latine** Latin cross; **c. de Lorraine** cross of Lorraine; **c. de Malte** Maltese cross; **la C-Rouge** the Red Cross (organization); **c. de Saint-André** St. Andrew's cross; *Astron* **la C. du Sud** the Southern Cross

cromlech [krɔmlɛk] *nm* cromlech

crooner [krunœr] *nm* (*chanteur*) crooner

croquant¹ [krɔkɑ̃] *adj* (*biscuit, pomme, feuilles de salade etc*) crisp, crunchy

croquant² *nm Péj* (*paysan*) (country) bumpkin, yokel

croque au sel (à la) [alakrɔksɛl] *adv Culin* = raw and seasoned only with salt

croque-madame [krɔkmadam] *nm inv Culin* = toasted cheese and ham sandwich topped with fried egg

croque(-)mitaine, *pl* **croque(-)mitaines** [krɔkmitɛn] *nm* bogeyman

croque-monsieur [krɔkməsjø] *nm inv Culin* = toasted cheese and ham sandwich

croque-mort, *pl* **croque-morts** [krɔkmɔr] *nm F* undertaker; **avoir une figure de c.** to have a long face, to look thoroughly miserable

croquenot [krɔkno] *nm F* clodhopper

croquer [krɔke] **1** *vi* **la salade croque sous la dent** lettuce is crisp *or* crunchy to eat; **c. dans** to bite into

2 *vt* (**a**) to crunch, to munch; *Fig* (*argent, fortune, héritage*) to squander; **chocolat à c.** plain chocolate; **à sucer ou à c.** may be sucked or chewed; *F* **il a croqué son sandwich en deux secondes** he wolfed down his sandwich in two seconds flat; *Fig* **c. la vie à belles dents** to make the most of life, to get the most out of life; **il est à c.** (*d'un enfant mignon*) he looks good enough to eat

(**b**) (*dessiner*) to sketch; *F* **elle est jolie** *ou* **mignonne à c.** she's as pretty as a picture

(**c**) *F* **c. le marmot** (*attendre*) to cool *or* kick one's heels

(**d**) *Fig* **c. une poulette** (*coucher avec*) to bed a young female

croquet [krɔkɛ] *nm* **(a)** *(jeu)* croquet; **faire une partie de c.** to have a game of croquet **(b)** *Couture* braid **(c)** *Culin* crisp almond biscuit
croquette [krɔkɛt] *nf Culin (de pomme de terre, poisson etc)* croquette; *(de chocolat)* chocolate drop; **croquettes** *(pour chien, chat)* biscuits, dry food
croqueuse [krɔkøz] *n F* **une c. de diamants** a gold-digger; **c. d'hommes** man-eater
croquignole [krɔkiɲɔl] *nf* = small crisp biscuit
croquignolet, -ette [krɔkiɲɔlɛ, -ɛt] *adj F* charming, delightful, *Am* cute
croquis [krɔki] *nm* sketch, rough drawing; *Journ* thumbnail; **faire un c. de qch** to make a (rough) sketch of sth, to sketch sth; *Fig* **faire un c. d'une situation** to sketch *or* outline a situation; *Fig* **il nous a fait un c. rapide de la situation** he gave us a quick rundown on the situation; *Tech* **c. coté** dimensional sketch
crosne [kron] *nm* Chinese artichoke *(similar to Jerusalem artichoke)*
cross [krɔs] *nm F,* **cross-country** [krɔskuntri] *nm Sp* cross-country running *or* racing; *(événement)* cross-country run *or* race
crosse [krɔs] *nf* **(a)** *(de fusil)* butt; *(de pistolet)* grip; *(de violon etc)* scroll; *Bot (de fougère)* croisier; *Culin* **c. de bœuf** knuckle of beef; *F* **lever** *ou* **mettre la c. en l'air** to surrender, to show the white flag, to lay down one's arms **(b)** *Sp (de hockey)* (hockey) stick; *(de golf)* (golf) club; *Fig F* **chercher des crosses à qn** to try to pick a fight with sb **(c)** *(d'évêque)* (bishop's) crook, crozier
crossman [krɔsman], *pl* **crossmen** [krɔsmen] *nm* cross-country runner
crotale [krɔtal] *nm (reptile)* rattlesnake, *Am F* rattler
crotte [krɔt] *nf* **(a)** *(de cheval, mouton, lapin etc)* dung, droppings; **des trottoirs couverts de crottes de chiens** pavements covered in dog dirt *or* droppings *or très F* shit; *Fig F* **c'est de la c. (de bique)** it's a load of rubbish *or* crap; *F* **elle ne se prend pas pourde la c. (de bique)** she thinks she's the bee's knees *or* the cat's pyjamas *or* the best thing since sliced bread; **une c. de** *ou* **en chocolat** a chocolate; *F* **ma petite c.** my dear, (my) darling; *F* **c.!** blast! *F* **c. de bique!** blow!, drat! **(b)** *Vieilli (boue)* mud
crotté [krɔte] *adj F* dirty, muddy, covered in mud
crotter [krɔte] **1** *vt (chaussures, manteau etc)* to cover in mud **2** *vi F (chien)* to do its business **3 se crotter** *vpr* to get dirty, to get covered in *or* with mud
crottin [krɔtɛ̃] *nm* **(a)** *(excrément) (de cheval)* dung, *Am F* road apples; *(de mouton)* droppings **(b)** *(fromage)* small goat's-milk cheese
croulant [krulɑ̃] **1** *adj (bâtiment)* crumbling, tumbledown, ramshackle; *Fig (empire)* crumbling, tottering, ramshackle; *F* **un vieux monsieur c.** a doddering old gent **2** *nm Arg* old fogey, old buffer; **les croulants** the crumblies; **un beau jour tu seras un vieux c.** you'll be a crumbly *or* an old dodderer yourself one of these days
crouler [krule] *vi (de bâtiment; Fig empire etc)* to crumble, to be on the point *or* verge of collapse; *(de la terre)* to give way, to crumble; **c. sous le poids de qch** to give way under the weight of sth; *Fig* **c. sous le poids des ans** *(d'une personne)* to be weighed down with age; *(d'une maison)* to be old and tumbledown; **il croule sous le travail depuis deux mois** he's been staggering under his workload for the last two months; **je croule de sommeil/de fatigue** I'm ready to drop, I'm asleep/dead on my feet; **se laisser c. dans un fauteuil** to slump into an armchair; **faire c. un projet** to ruin a plan; *Th* **faire c. la salle (sous les applaudissements)** to bring the house down
croup [krup] *nm Méd* croup; **avoir le c.** to have croup
croupade [krupad] *nf Équitation* curvet
croupe [krup] *nf* **(a)** *(de cheval)* rump, hindquarters; *F (de personne)* behind, rump, backside, *Am* butt; **monter en c.** to ride behind, *Arch* to ride pillion **(b)** *(de colline, coteau)* brow, crest, top; *(de dune)* top; *Archit (de toit)* hip
croupetons (à) [akruptɔ̃] *adv* squatting, crouching; **se tenir à c.** to squat (down); **marcher à c.** to walk crouched down
croupi [krupi] *adj (eau)* stagnant, foul
croupier [krupje] *nm (au casino)* croupier
croupière [krupjɛr] *nf (partie de harnais)* crupper; *Fig* **tailler des croupières à qn** *(attaquer)* to tear sb off a strip, to give sb a rocket; *(s'opposer à)* to spike sb's guns, to put a spoke in sb's wheel; *Fig* **se faire tailler des croupières** *(être attaqué)* to get torn off a strip; *(être opposé)* to be foiled *or* thwarted
croupion [krupjɔ̃] *nm (d'oiseau)* rump; *F (d'un poulet cuit, d'une volaille etc)* parson's *or US* pope's nose; *F (d'une personne)* backside, behind, *Am* butt; **se magner le c.** to get a move on
croupir [krupir] *vi* **(a)** *(d'une personne)* **c. dans** *(le vice, l'ignorance, l'oisiveté etc)* to wallow in; **c. en prison** to stagnate in prison **(b)** *(de l'eau)* to stagnate, to grow foul
croupissant [krupisɑ̃] *adj* stagnating; **eaux croupissantes** stagnant water
croustade [krustad] *nf Culin* croustade
croustillant [krustijɑ̃] *adj* **(a)** *(biscuit, pâté en croûte etc)* crisp; *(pain)* crusty **(b)** *F (histoire, détails etc)* spicy
croustiller [krustije] *vi (d'aliments)* to crunch; **pain qui croustille** crisp *or* crunchy bread
croûte [krut] *nf* **(a)** *(de pain, tarte etc)* crust; *(du fromage)* rind; *(d'une plaie)* scab; **la c. terrestre** the earth's crust; *Culin* **c. au fromage/à la tomate** = toasted cheese/tomato sandwich; **pâté en c.** = meat pie; *F* **casser la c.** to eat; **casser une c.** to have a snack, to have a bite to eat; *F* **à la c.!** let's eat!, grub's up!; *F* **gagner sa c.** to earn one's daily bread *or* one's bread and butter; **gratter la c.** to scratch the surface; **c. de rouille** layer of rust; *Méd* **croûtes de lait** cradle cap **(b)** *F (mauvaise peinture)* daub **(c)** *F (imbécile)* idiot, *Br* wally; **quelle c.!** what a wally!; **une vieille c.** an old fossil *or* buffer
croûter [krute] *vi F (manger)* to nosh
croûteux, -euse [krutø, -øz] *adj* scabby, covered with scabs
croûton [krutɔ̃] *nm* **(a)** *(de pain)* heel, end; **un c. de pain** the heel of a loaf **(b)** *Culin (dans la soupe, le potage)* croûton **(c)** *Arg* **(vieux) c.** old fossil, old stick-in-the-mud
croyable [krwajabl] *adj* believable, credible; **une histoire à peine c.** an unlikely story; **ce n'est pas c.** it's unbelievable *or* incredible
croyance [krwajɑ̃s] *nf (fait de croire)* belief; *(certitude)* belief, conviction; **c. en Dieu** belief in God; **croyances religieuses** religious beliefs
croyant, -ante [krwajɑ̃, -ɑ̃t] **1** *adj* believing; **il n'est pas c.** he's not a believer **2** *n* believer; **les croyants** *(de l'Islam)* the Faithful
CRS [seɛrɛs] *nm (abrév* **Compagnie républicaine de sécurité)** ≈ riot police, State security police; **un C.** a member of the State security police
cru[1] [kry] **1** *adj* **(a)** *(viande, poisson, légumes, Tex tissus, soie etc)* raw; *(lait)* unpasteurized; *(cuir)* untreated, raw; *(couleur, lumière)* crude, garish; *Fig (réponse, langage, personne)* blunt; **il mange sa viande crue** he eats his meat raw; *Fig* **dans le jour c.** in the full light of day

(b) *(licencieux)* crude, coarse; **cette plaisanterie est un peu crue** that's a rather coarse *or* crude joke

2 *adv* **je vous le dis tout c.** I'm not mincing my words, I'm telling you straight (out); **j'ai envie de l'avaler tout c.** I could eat *or* gobble him (all) up; *(je suis en colère)* I could strangle him; **manger c.** to eat raw food; **être chaussé à c.** to wear shoes without any socks; **monter à c.** to ride bareback
cru[2] *nm* vineyard; **les meilleurs crus** *(terroirs)* the best vineyards; *(vins)* the best wines; **un grand c.** a vintage wine; **vin du c.** local wine; **bouilleur de c.** home distiller; **les gens du c.** the locals; **la langue du c.** the local dialect; *Fig* **une histoire de son (propre) c.** a story of his own invention
cruauté [kryote] *nf* **(a)** *(dureté)* cruelty **(envers** to); *(de la vie)* cruelty, harshness; **faire preuve de c. mentale envers qn** to be guilty of mental cruelty to sb **(b)** *(acte)* (act of) cruelty; **les cruautés de son mari** her husband's cruelty
cruche [kryʃ] *nf* **(a)** *(récipient)* (earthenware) jug, pitcher; *(contenu)* jugful; *Prov* **tant va la c. à l'eau qu'à la fin elle se casse** the pitcher has gone to the well once too often **(b)** *F* idiot, ass, twit; **être c.** to be thick, to be an idiot; **avoir l'air c.** to look stupid *or* thick
cruchon [kryʃɔ̃] *nm (récipient)* small jug; *(contenu)* small jugful
crucial, -iale, -iaux, -iales [krysjal, -jo] *adj* **(a)** *(question, point)* crucial; **être d'une importance cruciale** to be crucially important, to be of crucial importance **(b)** *(incision etc)* cross-shaped
crucifère [krysifɛr] *adj* cruciferous
crucifiement [krysifimɑ̃] *nm (action)* crucifixion, crucifying; *(martyre)* crucifixion; **c. de la chair** mortifying *or* mortification of the flesh
crucifier [krysifje] *vt (pr sub, impf* **n. crucifiions, v. crucifiiez)** *(mettre en croix)* to crucify; *(torturer)* to torture; **c. la chair** to mortify the flesh
crucifix [krysifi] *nm inv* crucifix
crucifixion [krysifiksjɔ̃] *nf* crucifixion
cruciforme [krysifɔrm] *adj* cross-shaped, in the shape of a cross, *Fml* cruciform
cruciverbiste [krysivɛrbist] *n* crossword enthusiast *or* buff, crossword-puzzler

crudité [krydite] *nf* **(a)** *Culin* **crudités** raw vegetables **(b)** *(d'une couleur)* garishness; *(d'une lumière)* harshness **(c)** *(d'une expression)* *(caractère licencieux)* coarseness, crudeness; *(franchise)* bluntness

crue [kry] *nf* *(d'une rivière etc)* rising, swelling; *(niveau maximum)* flood; **rivière en c.** river in spate; **le Nil est un fleuve à c. périodique** the Nile floods periodically

cruel, -elle [kryɛl] *adj* *(personne)* cruel (**envers, avec** to); *(expérience, alternative, perte)* cruel, bitter; **une femme cruelle** *(en amour)* a cruel *or* hard-hearted woman

cruellement [kryɛlmɑ̃] *adv* cruelly; **c. déçu** bitterly disappointed; **c. éprouvé** sorely tried; **faire c. défaut** to be sorely lacking

cruiser [kruzœr] *nm* *(petit yacht)* cruiser

crûment [krymɑ̃] *adv* **(a)** *(durement)* *(parler)* *(sans détours)* bluntly; *(ouvertement)* openly, unabashedly **(b)** **éclairé c.** garishly lit

crustacé [krystase] *nm* **crustacés** shellfish, crustaceans, *Spéc* Crustacea; **la crevette est un c.** the prawn is a *or* prawns are shellfish; *Culin* **assiette de crustacés** seafood platter

cruzado [kruzado] *nm* crusado, cruzado

cryobiologie [krijobjɔlɔʒi] *nf* cryobiology

cryochirurgie [krijoʃiryrʒi] *nf* cryosurgery

cryoconservation [krijokɔ̃sɛrvasjɔ̃] *nf* cryoconservation

cryogène [krijoʒɛn] *adj* cryogenic; **mélange c.** freezing mixture

cryogénie [krijoʒeni] *nf* cryogenics

cryptage [kriptaʒ] *nm* encryption, encoding

crypte [kript] *nf Archit, Anat* crypt

crypté [kripte] **(a)** *adj TV* *(chaîne, film)* coded **(b)** *(message)* coded, in code

crypter [kripte] *vt* to encode; *Télécom* to encrypt, to scramble

cryptocommuniste [kriptokɔmynist] *adj, n* crypto-communist

cryptogénétique [kriptoʒenetik] *adj Méd* idiopathic

cryptogramme [kriptɔgram] *nm* cipher (message)

cryptographie [kriptɔgrafi] *nf* writing in cipher

cryptographique [kriptɔgrafik] *adj* cryptographic

CSG [seɛsʒe] *nf* *(abrév* **Contribution sociale généralisée***)* general social security contribution

cubage [kybaʒ] *nm* **(a)** *(action)* *(d'un tas de bois etc)* calculating the cubic content **(b)** *(volume)* *(d'un réservoir etc)* cubic capacity, volume

cubain, -aine [kybɛ̃, -ɛn] **1** *adj* Cuban **2** *n* **C.** Cuban

cube [kyb] **1** *nm* **(a)** *Géom, Math* cube; **élever un nombre au c.** to cube a number; **jeu de cubes** building blocks, (wooden) bricks **(b)** *Arg* student repeating a class for the second time **(c)** *Arg* **gros c.** *(moto)* large motor bike *(over 500 cc)*; **les gros cubes** heavy metal **2** *adj* *(mètre, centimètre etc)* cubic

cuber [kybe] **1** *vt Math* *(nombre etc)* to cube; *(évaluer)* to calculate the cubic capacity of **2** *vi* **(a)** *(contenir)* to have a cubic capacity of; **réservoir qui cube vingt litres** tank with a cubic capacity of twenty litres **(b)** *F* *(revenir cher)* to mount up, to work out expensive; **ça cube, ça finit par c.** it mounts up

cubique [kybik] **1** *adj* cubic; *Math* **racine c.** cube root **2** *nf* cubic (curve)

cubisme [kybism] *nm Beaux-Arts* cubism

cubiste [kybist] *adj, n Beaux-Arts* cubist

cubitainer [kybitenɛr] *nm* = large cubic plastic container *(for bulk purchase of wine etc)*

cubital, -ale, -aux, -ales [kybital, -o] *adj Anat* ulnar

cubitus [kybitys] *nm Anat* ulna

cucu(l) [kyky] *adj F* **c.** **(la praline)** *(personne, décoration)* twee; *(film, livre)* corny; **elle est gentille, mais un peu c.** she is nice and kind-hearted but she's not really clued up

cueillette [kœjɛt] *nf* *(action)* gathering, picking; *(fruits, noisettes, baies)* crop, harvest; **aller faire la c. de mûres** to go blackberry picking *or* blackberrying; **une tribu qui vit de la chasse et de la c.** a tribe of hunters and gatherers

cueilleur, -euse [kœjœr, -øz] *n* *(de fruit etc)* picker, gatherer

cueillir [kœjir] *vt* *(prp* **cueillant**; *pp* **cueilli**; *pr ind* **je cueille, il cueille, n. cueillons**; *impf* **je cueillais**; *p hist* **je cueillis**; *fu* **je cueillerai***)* *(fleurs, fruits etc)* to gather, to pick; **c. un baiser** to steal *or* snatch a kiss; *Fig* **c. des lauriers** to win laurels; *Fig Litt* **c. le jour, c. les roses de la vie** to make the most of life; *Fig Litt* **cueillez le jour** seize the day; *Fig Litt* **il faut c. les roses de la vie** gather ye rosebuds while ye may; *Fig* **le crochet de gauche l'a cueilli en plein estomac** the left hook got him right in the stomach; *Fig* **la mort l'a cueilli en pleine jeunesse** he was cut down in his prime; *F* **c. qn** *(passer le chercher)* to collect sb, to pick sb up; *(l'arrêter)* to pick sb up, to nab sb

cui-cui [kɥikɥi] **1** *nm* cheeping, chirping, chirruping **2** *int* cheep

cuiller, cuillère [kɥijɛr] *nf* **(a)** spoon; *(contenu)* spoon(ful); **c. à dessert** *ou* **à entremets** dessert spoon; **c. à soupe** soup spoon; **c. à café** teaspoon; *(plus petite)* coffee spoon; **petite c.** teaspoon; **c. à pot** ladle; **avaler une c. de sirop** to swallow a spoonful of medicine; **une c. pour papa, une c. pour maman** *(à un enfant)* one (spoonful) for Daddy, one (spoonful) for Mummy; **deux cuillers de sucre** two spoons *or* spoonfuls *or* spoonsful of sugar; *Fig F* **il n'y va pas avec le dos de la c.** he goes the whole hog, he doesn't go in for half measures, there are no half measures with him; *(il est franc)* he doesn't pull his punches *or* mince his words; *Fig F* **en deux** *ou* **trois** *ou* **cinq coups de c. à pot** in no time at all, in two shakes (of a lamb's tail); *Fig F* **être à ramasser à la petite c.** *(blessé)* to be badly hurt *or* smashed up; *(épuisé)* to be completely exhausted *or* all in; *(déprimé)* to be thoroughly depressed *or* down in the dumps; *Fig F* **on l'a ramassé à la petite c.** he was scraped off the pavement

(b) *Pêche* spoon (bait), trolling spoon; **pêcher la truite/***etc* **à la c.** to troll *or* spin for trout/*etc*

(c) *(d'une grenade)* safety catch

(d) *Constr* *(d'une drague)* scoop, bucket

(e) *Arg* *(main)* paw, mitt

cuillerée [kɥijere] *nf* spoonful; **une c. à soupe de sucre** a tablespoonful of sugar; **deux cuillerées à café de sel** two teaspoons *or* teaspoonfuls *or* teaspoonsful of salt; **une c. pour maman** *(à un enfant)* one (spoonful) for Mummy

cuilleron [kɥijrɔ̃] *nm* *(d'une cuillère)* bowl

cuir [kɥir] *nm* **(a)** *(tanné)* leather; *(veste)* leather jacket; **c. vert** *ou* **brut** rawhide; **c. en croûte** undressed leather; **c. verni** patent leather; **pantalon en** *ou* **de c.** leather trousers; **chaussures en c.** leather shoes; **c. à rasoir** razor strop; **cuirs de motocycliste** motorcycle leathers

(b) *(d'un éléphant, F d'une personne)* hide; **c. chevelu** scalp; **tanner le c. à qn** to tan sb's hide, to give sb a good hiding; *F* **je ne tiens pas à ce qu'on m'enfonce une aiguille dans le c.!** I don't fancy having a needle stuck in me!

(c) *F* *(mauvaise prononciation)* incorrect liaison *(intrusive t or z)*; **faire un c.** to make an incorrect *or* a false liaison *(par exemple* **cent idées** [sɑ̃zide]; **moi aussi** [mwazosi])

cuirasse [kɥiras] *nf* **(a)** *(protection)* cuirass, breastplate; *Fig* **trouver le défaut dans la c. de qn** to find sb's weak *or* vulnerable spot, to find a chink in sb's armour; *Fig* **une c. de froideur** an air of aloofness; *Fig* **entouré d'une c. d'une impénétrable froideur** surrounded by an impenetrable air of coldness; *Fig* **une c. d'égoïsme l'empêche de voir la souffrance morale de sa femme** he is so immured in selfishness that he is unable to see how much his wife is suffering **(b)** *(d'un navire de guerre, un blindé)* armour (plating); **plaque de c.** armour plate

cuirassé [kɥirase] **1** *adj* *(armé)* armour-plated, *US* armor-plated, armoured, *US* armored; *Naut* **croiseur c.** armour-plated cruiser; *Fig* **être c. contre les attaques** to be hardened to attack **2** *nm Mil, Naut* armoured ship; **c. (de ligne)** battleship

cuirassement [kɥirasmɑ̃] *nm* **(a)** *(d'un navire)* armouring **(b)** *(cuirasse)* armour-plating

cuirasser [kɥirase] **1** *vt* **(a)** *(navire)* to armour(-plate); *(machine)* to enclose, to protect **(b)** *Arch* *(soldat)* to put a cuirass *or* breastplate on **2 se cuirasser** *vpr Arch* to put on one's cuirass *or* breastplate; *Fig* **se c. contre qch** to arm *or* steel oneself against *or* harden oneself to sth

cuirassier [kɥirasje] *nm Mil* cuirassier

cuire [kɥir] *(prp* **cuisant**; *pp* **cuit**; *pr ind* **je cuis, il cuit, n. cuisons, ils cuisent**; *impf* **je cuisais**; *p hist* **je cuisis**; *fu* **je cuirai***)* **1** *vt* **(a)** *Culin* to cook; **c. à l'eau** to boil; **c. des légumes à la vapeur** to steam vegetables; **c. la viande sur le grill** to grill *or Am* broil the meat; **c. au four** to bake; **un four en terre cuit bien le pain** bread bakes well in a clay oven; *F* **va te faire c. un œuf!** go to hell!

(b) *(briques, poterie etc)* to fire, to bake

(c) *(détruire)* *(du soleil)* to bake; *(du gel)* to kill (off); **le gel a cuit les géraniums** the geraniums have suffered from frost-burn

2 *vi* **(a)** *(des aliments)* to cook; **le poulet a cuit trop longtemps** the chicken is overcooked; **pommes à c.** cooking apples; **chocolat à c.** cooking *or* baking chocolate; **c. à petit feu** *ou* **à feu doux** to cook slowly, to simmer; *Fig F* **au lieu de me laisser c. à petit feu!** instead of keeping me on tenterhooks; *Fig F* **c. (dans son jus)** *(avoir très chaud)* to be boiling; *Fig* **laisser c. qn dans son jus** to let sb stew (in their own juice); *Fig F* **on cuit dans cette salle** this room's like an oven (**b**) (*brûler*) (*des mains, joues*) to burn; (*des yeux*) to smart **3 se cuire** *vpr* **se c. au soleil/sur la plage** to bake *or* roast in the sun/on the beach

4 *v impers* **il vous en cuira** you'll be sorry (for it), you'll regret it

cuisant [kɥizɑ̃] *adj* (*douleur*) smarting, burning; (*froid*) biting; (*remarques*) caustic, biting, bitter; **déception cuisante** bitter disappointment; **un échec c.** a stinging defeat

cuiseur [kɥizœr] *nm* large cooking pot

cuisine [kɥizin] *nf* (**a**) (*pièce*) kitchen; *Naut* (cook's) galley; **éléments de c.** kitchen units; **ustensiles de c.** cooking utensils; **batterie de c.** (set of) pots and pans; *Mil* **c. roulante** field kitchen; *Ling* **latin de c.** dog Latin

(**b**) (*préparation*) (art of) cooking, cookery, cuisine; **faire la c.** to cook; **c'est lui qui fait la c.** he does the cooking; **il fait de la bonne c., il fait bien la c.** he's a good cook; **c. au beurre/à l'huile** cooking with butter/oil; **c. bourgeoise** plain *or* home cooking; **livre de c.** cookery *or* recipe book, cookbook

(**c**) *F* (*intrigue*) (dirty) tricks; **la c. parlementaire** parliamentary intrigue

(**d**) (*plats*) food; **restaurant renommé pour sa c.** restaurant famed for its food *or* cuisine; **la nouvelle c.** nouvelle cuisine

cuisiner [kɥizine] **1** *vi* to cook; **elle cuisine bien** she's a good cook **2** *vt* (**a**) (*dîner*) to make, to cook; **plats cuisinés** ready-cooked dishes, takeaway meals (**b**) *Fig F* **c. qn** to interrogate *or* grill sb

cuisinette [kɥizinɛt] *nf* kitchenette

cuisinier, -ière [kɥizinje, -jɛr] **1** *n* chef, cook; **c. en chef** executive chef **2** *nf* **cuisinière** cooker, stove; **c. électrique** electric cooker *or* stove

cuisinier-pâtissier, *pl* **cuisiniers-pâtissiers** *nm* pastry cook

cuissage [kɥisaʒ] *nm* **droit de c.** *Fig* sexual harassment (*by a superior*); *Hist* droit de seigneur

cuissard [kɥisar] *nm* (**a**) (*pour cycliste*) racing shorts (**b**) *Arch* (*partie de l'armure*) cuisse, thigh piece

cuissardes [kɥisard] *nfpl* (*bottes de femme*) thigh boots; (*de pêche*) waders

cuisse [kɥis] *nf Anat* thigh; *Culin* **c. de poulet** chicken leg; *F* drumstick; **cuisses de grenouilles** frogs' legs; *Fig* **avoir la c. légère** to sleep around, to be an easy lay; *F* **se croire sorti de la c. de Jupiter** to think a lot of oneself, to think one is the cat's whiskers

cuisseau, -eaux [kɥiso] *nm Culin* (*de veau*) leg

cuissettes [kɥisɛt] *nfpl* (*pour sportifs*) = short shorts

cuisson [kɥisɔ̃] *nf* (**a**) (*d'aliments*) cooking; **temps de c.** cooking time; **le porc demande une longue c.** pork has to be cooked for a long time; **plaque de c.** hob; **c. au grill** grilling; **c. en bain de friture** deep-fat frying; **c. à la vapeur** steaming (**b**) (*des briques, de la porcelaine*) burning, firing (**c**) (*sensation*) **une impression de c.** a burning sensation *or* feeling; **la c. de la fessée qu'elle avait reçue l'empêchait de s'asseoir** she was smarting so much after the spanking that she couldn't sit down; **la c. de son désir inassouvi le gardait éveillé** he lay awake burning with desire

cuissot [kɥiso] *nm Culin* (*de venaison*) haunch

cuistance [kɥistɑ̃s] *nf Arg* cooking; (*nourriture*) grub, nosh; **qui est-ce qui fait la c. ce soir?** who's cooking tonight?

cuistot [kɥisto] *nm F* cook

cuistre [kɥistr] *Péj* **1** *Litt nm* (**a**) (*vaniteux*) pedant (**b**) (*grossier personnage*) scoundrel **2** *adj* pedantic

cuistrerie [kɥistrəri] *nf Péj* (**a**) *Litt* pedantry (**b**) (*grossièreté*) scoundrelly behaviour

cuit [kɥi] *adj* (**a**) *Culin* cooked; **bien c.** well done; **c. à point** done to a turn; **trop c.** overdone, overcooked; **pas assez c.** underdone, undercooked; **c. au four** baked; **terre cuite** terracotta; **vin c.** = aperitif wine (**b**) *Fig F* **être c.** to be done for, to have had it; **c'est c.!** that's it!, we've had it!; **le cinéma, c'est c. pour ce soir** the cinema's out tonight; **c'est c. pour nos vacances** we've had it as far as a holiday is concerned; **c'est du tout c.** it's a cinch *or* a walkover *or* a doddle

cuite [kɥit] *nf* (**a**) (*de briques, poterie*) baking, firing (**b**) *F* (**se**) **prendre une** (**bonne**) **c.** to get plastered *or* tight, *Am* to tie one on

cuiter (se) [səkɥite] *vpr F* to get tight *or* plastered, *Am* to tie one on

cuivre [kɥivr] *nm* (**a**) (*métal*) **c.** (**rouge**) copper; **casserole en c.** copper saucepan; **doublé en c.** (*plaqué*) copper-plated; (*par le fond*) copper-bottomed; *Minér* **minerai de c.** copper ore; **c. jaune** brass; **les cuivres** copper(ware); (*jaunes*) brasses; **faire** (**briller**) **les cuivres** to polish the brassware, to do the brasses (**b**) *Mus* **les cuivres** the brass (section) (**c**) (*planche*) copperplate

cuivré [kɥivre] *adj* (**a**) (*hâlé*) (*peau, teint*) (*naturellement*) copper-coloured; (*par le soleil*) bronzed; **cheveux aux reflets cuivrés** auburn hair; **d'un rouge c.** coppery red (**b**) (*voix*) resonant, ringing; *Mus* **sons cuivrés** brassy tones

cuivrer [kɥivre] **1** *vt* (**a**) (*couvrir de cuivre*) to copper, to coat *or* sheath with copper (**b**) (*la peau, le teint*) to bronze **2 se cuivrer** *vpr* to turn the colour of copper, to turn coppery

cuivreux, -euse [kɥivrø, -øz] *adj Ch* (*oxyde*) cuprous

cul [ky] **1** *nm* (**a**) *Arg* (*d'une personne*) arse, *F* bum, *Am* ass, *F* fanny; **un beau c.** a great bum, a lovely arse; *Am* (*d'homme*) nice buns; *Vulg* **trou du c.** arsehole, *Am* asshole; **faux c.** bustle; *Fig* **c'est un faux c.** he's two-faced; **renverser qn c. par-dessus tête** to send sb flying *or* head over heels *or Vulg* arse over elbow; *Fig* **il en est tombé** *ou* **resté sur le c.** he was flabbergasted; **se taper le c. par terre** to roar with laughter, to split one's sides laughing; **des vacances? mon c.!** holidays? my arse!; **avoir le feu au c.** to be in a hell of a rush; (*sexuellement*) to be randy as hell; **être porté sur le c.** to be sex-mad; **un bouquin de c.** a dirty book; **revue de c.** porn magazine; **film de c.** blue *or* porn movie; **être comme c. et chemise** to be as thick as thieves; **ça vaut mieux qu'un coup de pied au c.** it's better than a kick in the pants; **avoir qn dans le c.** to hate sb's guts; **en avoir plein le c.** to be pissed off (**de qch** with sth), to have had a bellyful (**de qch** of sth); **ils l'ont dans le c.** they've had it, that's really screwed them up, that's them buggered; **on a les flics au c.** we've got the cops on our tail; *Mil Arg* **tirer au c.** to swing the lead, to shirk; **c'est un tire-au-c.** he's a shirker *or* skiver; *Can F* **n'avoir rien que le c. et les dents** to be at rock-bottom; *Arg* **quel c.!** what a bloody fool *or* prat *or* arsehole *or Am* asshole!

(**b**) *Arg* (*chance*) luck; **avoir du c.** to be lucky *or* jammy; **j'ai/elle a gagné le gros lot – quel c.!** I/she won the jackpot – you/the jammy devil!

(**c**) (*d'un animal*) haunches, rump

(**d**) (*d'un sac, un tonneau*) bottom; (*d'une bouteille*) bottom, base; **boire c. sec** to down one's drink in one go; **c. sec!** bottoms up!

(**e**) *Naut* (*d'un navire*) stern

2 *adj* silly; **elle est un peu c.** she's a bit of a twerp *or* twit *or* nerd

culasse [kylas] *nf* (**a**) *Mil* (*de fusil, pistolet*) breech; **c. mobile** (*de carabine*) bolt; **fusil se chargeant par la c.** breech loader; **bloc de c.** breech block (**b**) (*de moteur*) cylinder head; **joint de c.** cylinder head gasket; *Aut* **c. à flux opposés** cross-flow *or* hemispherical head; *Aut* **c. à flux transversal** cross-flow head

cul-blanc, *pl* **culs-blancs** *nm* (*oiseau*) wheatear

culbute [kylbyt] *nf* (**a**) (*cabriole*) somersault; **faire la c.** to turn a somersault (**b**) (*chute*) tumble, heavy fall; **faire une** *ou* **la c.** to fall; **le gamin chuta de son vélo et fit une c.** the kid came off his bike head over heels; *Fig F* **faire la c.** (*d'un gouvernement*) to fall; (*d'une entreprise*) to go bust; *Com* **les revendeurs font la c.** the dealers are making a killing *or* a huge profit

culbuter [kylbyte] **1** *vi* (**a**) (*se renverser*) (*d'un vase, un arbre, une statue etc*) to topple over; (*de qn*) to take a tumble; **la voiture a culbuté dans le fossé** the car overturned and landed in the ditch (**b**) *F* (*d'une entreprise*) to go bust *or Sl* belly up; (*d'un banquier, un homme d'affaires etc*) to come a cropper **2** *vt* (**a**) (*renverser*) to knock down *or* over; (*gouvernement*) to bring down (**b**) *Vieilli, Arg* (*femme*) to tumble

culbuterie [kylbytri] *nf Aut* rocker arms

culbuteur [kylbytœr] *nm* (**a**) (*jouet*) tumbler (**b**) (*de moteur*) rocker (arm) (**c**) *MecE* tripper device; (*de camion*) tipper

cul-de-basse-fosse, *pl* **culs-de-basse-fosse** [kydbɑsfos] *nm* dungeon

cul-de-jatte, *pl* **culs-de-jatte** [kydʒat] *nm* legless cripple

cul-de-lampe, *pl* **culs-de-lampe** [kydlɑ̃p] *nm* (**a**) *Archit* (*ornement*) bracket, corbel (**b**) *Typ* tailpiece

cul-de-poule [kydpul] *nm Arg* **faire la bouche en c.** to purse one's lips

cul-de-sac, *pl* **culs-de-sac** [kydsak] *nm* blind alley, cul-de-sac; *Fig* dead-end; **la rue se termine en c.** the street ends in a cul-de-sac *or* is a dead end; *Fig* **être dans un c.** to have reached a dead end

culée [kyle] *nf Archit* (*d'un contrefort*) pier; *Constr* (*d'un pont*) abutment (pier)

culinaire [kylinɛr] *adj* culinary; **l'art c.** the art of cooking, the culinary art; **les talents culinaires de son mari** her husband's talents as a cook; **recettes culinaires** recipes

culminant [kylminɑ̃] *adj* **point c.** (*d'une chaîne de montagnes*) highest point; (*du pouvoir*) zenith; (*de la renommée, gloire, d'une carrière*) height, peak

culminer [kylmine] *vi* (**a**) **le Mont-Blanc culmine à 4 807 mètres** Mont-Blanc is 4, 807 metres at its highest point (**b**) *Fig Bourse* (*de cours*) to reach its/their highest level, to peak; **sa carrière culmine** it's the crowning point *or* pinnacle of his career; **alors que sa carrière culminait** when his career was reaching its height *or* peak

culot [kylo] *nm* (**a**) *F* (*audace*) cheek, nerve; **tu ne manques pas de c.!, tu as du c.!** you've got a nerve *or* cheek!; **il a un sacré c.!** he's got a helluva nerve!; **il a tous les culots** he's got a lot of nerve, cheek is his middle name; **y aller au c.** to put a brave face on it, to brazen it out; **vas-y au c. et demande-lui son autographe** just breeze up and ask him for his autograph (**b**) (*de lampe, bouteille etc*) bottom, base; *Mil* (*de douille de cartouche, d'obus*) base; (*de cartouche*) head; *Él* (*d'ampoule*) base; *Aut* body of spark plug (**c**) (*dans une pipe*) dottle

culottage [kylɔtaʒ] *nm* (*d'une pipe*) colouring, seasoning

culotte [kylɔt] *nf* (**a**) (*pantalon*) **c. courte** short trousers; **c. de cheval** jodhpurs, riding breeches; *Fig F* jodhpur thighs; **c. de golf** plus fours; **c. de peau** lederhosen; *Fig F* **c'est la femme qui porte la c.** it's the wife who wears the trousers; *Can* **avoir des culottes** to have guts; *F* **user ses fonds de c. sur les bancs de l'école** to idle away one's time at school; *F* **faire dans sa c.** to be scared stiff, to have the jitters, *Sl* to wet *or* pee oneself

(**b**) [①A10,e] (*sous-vêtement*) (*de femme*) panties, knickers; (*d'enfant*) pants

(**c**) *F* **prendre une c.** (*aux cartes etc*) to lose heavily, *Am* to take a bath

(**d**) *Culin* (*de bœuf*) rump

culotté [kylɔte] *adj* (**a**) (*pipe*) seasoned; **un plafond c. par la fumée du tabac** a ceiling black with tobacco smoke (**b**) *F* (*audacieux*) full of cheek *or* nerve, cheeky; **il est c.** he's got one hell of a nerve (**de faire qch** doing sth)

culotter [kylɔte] *vt* (*pipe*) to colour, to season

culpabilisation [kylpabilizasjɔ̃] *nf Psy* (**a**) (*action*) making feel guilty (**b**) (*résultat*) (feeling of) guilt

culpabiliser [kylpabilize] *Psy* **1** *vt* **c. qn** to make sb feel guilty **2** *vi* to feel guilty

culpabilité [kylpabilite] *nf* guilt; **nier sa c.** to deny that one is guilty; *Jur* **verdict de c.** guilty verdict; **sa c. dans cette affaire a été établie** his guilt in the matter has been established; **sentiment de c.** feeling of guilt, guilty feeling

culte [kylt] *nm* (**a**) (*vénération*) worship; *Fig* cult; *Fig* **c. de la personnalité** personality cult, cult of the personality; **avoir le c. de l'argent** to worship money; *Fig* **avoir un c. pour qn, rendre** *ou* **vouer un c. à qn** to (hero) worship sb (**b**) (*religion*) form of worship, creed, religion; **liberté du c.** freedom of worship; **changer de c.** to change one's religion (**c**) (*service protestant*) (church) service

cul-terreux, *pl* **culs-terreux** *nm F Péj* country bumpkin, yokel, *Am* rube, *Am* redneck

cultivable [kyltivabl] *adj* suitable for cultivation

cultivateur, -trice [kyltivatœr, -tris] **1** *n* farmer; **petits cultivateurs** small farmers, smallholders **2** *nm* cultivator **3** *adj* agricultural, farming; **les peuples cultivateurs** agricultural people, farming communities

cultivé [kyltive] *adj* (**a**) *Agr* (*terre, champs*), *Biol* (*virus*) cultivated (**b**) (*personne*) cultivated, cultured; **gens cultivés** cultivated *or* educated people

cultiver [kyltive] **1** *vt* (**a**) (*sol*) to cultivate, to farm (**b**) *Agr* (*céréales, artichauts*) to raise, to grow, to cultivate; (*roses*) to raise, to grow; *Biol* (*virus*); *Fig* (*l'amitié de qn etc*) to cultivate; **c. son esprit** to cultivate *or* improve one's mind; **c. un goût** to cultivate *or* develop a taste; **il cultive la goujaterie** he makes a point of being boorish *or* he works hard at being boorish; *Fig* **il faut c. son jardin** = concentrate on things close to home and don't try to change the world **2** **se cultiver** *vpr* to improve one's mind

cultuel, -elle [kyltɥɛl] *adj* of *or* pertaining to worship; **édifice c.** place of worship

culture [kyltyr] *nf* (**a**) (*du sol*) cultivation; **c. fruitière** fruit farming; **c. sèche** dry farming; **cultures** land under cultivation

(**b**) (*de céréales, artichauts etc*) growing, raising; *Biol* **c. (microbienne/de tissus)** culture (of bacteria/of tissue); **bouillon de c.** culture medium

(**c**) (*intellectuelle*) culture, education; **c. scientifique** scientific knowledge *or* background; **question de c. générale** question of general knowledge; **avoir une solide c.** to have a sound education; **maison de la c.** = arts centre

(**d**) (*civilisation*) culture; **la c. gréco-romaine** Graeco-Roman culture *or* civilization; **c'est une autre c.** it's a different culture *or* way of life

▶ **culture**: **c. d'entreprise** corporate culture; **c. physique** physical training, *F* PT

culturel, -elle [kyltyrɛl] *adj* (*relations, milieu, attaché*) cultural; (*voyage*) educational; **centre c.** community arts centre; **choc c.** culture shock; **subir un choc c.** to suffer (from) culture shock

culturisme [kyltyrism] *nm* body building, *F* pumping iron

culturiste [kyltyrist] *n* body-builder

cumin [kymɛ̃] *nm* cumin; **c. des prés** caraway; **munster au c.** Munster (cheese) with caraway seeds

cumul [kymyl] *nm* **c. des fonctions, c. des mandats** plurality of offices, pluralism; **c. des traitements** drawing of more than one salary

cumulable [kymylabl] *adj* **des fonctions cumulables** offices which can be held simultaneously *or* concurrently; **des traitements cumulables** salaries which can be drawn concurrently *or* simultaneously; **ces deux réductions d'impôts ne sont pas cumulables** the two tax reductions may not be claimed at the same time

cumulard, -arde [kymylar, -ard] *nm F Péj* holder of several official positions (*for each of which a salary is drawn*)

cumulatif, -ive [kymylatif, -iv] *adj* cumulative

cumuler [kymyle] *vt* **c. des fonctions** to hold more than one office; **c. deux traitements** to draw two (separate) salaries; **il cumule plusieurs emplois** he has several jobs, *F* he's a moonlighter; **il cumulait la réputation de débauché, de joueur invétéré et de meurtrier** he combined the reputation of rake, inveterate gambler and murderer

cumulo-nimbus [kymylonɛ̃bys] *nm inv Météo* cumulo-nimbus

cumulo-stratus [kymylostratys] *nm inv Météo* strato-cumulus, cumulo-stratus

cumulus [kymylys] *nm inv Météo* cumulus

cunéiforme [kyneifɔrm] *adj* cuneiform

cupide [kypid] *adj* greedy, grasping, moneygrubbing

cupidement [kypidmɑ̃] *adv* greedily

cupidité [kypidite] *nf* cupidity, greed

Cupidon [kypidɔ̃] *nm Myth* Cupid

cuprifère [kyprifer] *adj* copper-bearing, *Spéc* cupriferous

cuprique [kyprik] *adj* cupric

curable [kyrabl] *adj* (*maladie etc*) curable; **la lèpre est c.** leprosy can be cured, leprosy is curable

curaçao [kyraso] *nm* curaçao (liqueur)

curage [kyraʒ] *nm* (*de canalisation, port*) clearing *or* cleaning out; (*de tuyau*) flushing

curare [kyrar] *nm* curare

curatelle [kyratɛl] *nf Jur* (*d'une succession*) trusteeship; (*d'un mineur, un aliéné*) guardianship

curateur, -trice [kyratœr, -tris] *n Jur* (*d'une succession etc*) trustee; (*d'un mineur, un aliéné*) guardian

curatif, -ive [kyratif, -iv] *adj* curative

cure [kyr] *nf* (**a**) *Méd* (course of) treatment; **c. thermale** hydrotherapy, course of treatment at a spa; **c. d'amaigrissement** diet; **faire une c. de lait/de repos** to go on a milk diet/rest cure; **elle a fait une c. à Vichy** she took the waters at Vichy; **c. de sommeil** sleep cure; **c. de sevrage** detoxification programme

(**b**) (*fonction de curé*) office of a parish priest; (*paroisse*) parish; (*presbytère*) presbytery; **obtenir une c.** to be appointed parish priest

(**c**) **n'avoir c. de qch** not to care about sth; **je n'en ai c. de toutes ses médailles** I don't care about all his medals; **tu peux toujours essayer de l'impressionner, elle n'en a c.** she won't take any notice of your attempts to impress her

curé [kyre] *nm Cathol* **parish priest;** *F* (*sans aucune distinction de rang*) **priest; monsieur le c. Father; il veut se faire c. he wants to become a priest** *or* **to enter the priesthood;** *Fig F* **bouffer** *ou* **manger du c. to be (violently) anti-clerical**

cure-dent(s), *pl* **cure-dents** *nm* toothpick

curée [kyre] *nf* parts of the stag given to the hounds; (*mise à mort*) kill; *Fig* **pays livré à la c. des mercenaires étrangers** country handed over to the tender mercies of foreign mercenaries; *Fig* **ce fut la c. entre les héritiers** the heirs started to fight over the spoils; *Fig* **les journalistes s'emparèrent de l'affaire et ce fut une véritable c.** the press acted like jackals once they got wind of the story

cure-ongles *nm inv* nail cleaner

cure-pipe, *pl* **cure-pipes** *nm* pipe-cleaner

curer [kyre] *vt* (*ses dents*) to pick; (*une canalisation, un port*) to clear *or* clean out; (*une rivière, un canal, un étang*) to dredge; (*pipe*) to scrape, to clean out; **se c. les ongles/les oreilles** to clean one's nails/to clean (out) one's ears

curetage [kyrtaʒ] *nm Chir* curetting, curettage

cureter [kyrte] *vt Chir* to curette

curette [kyrɛt] *nf Tech* scraper; *Chir* curette
curie¹ [kyri] *nf Antiq, Cathol* curia
curie² *nm Phys* curie
curieusement [kyrjøzmɑ̃] *adv* (*étrangement*) curiously, oddly; **les gens le regardaient c.** people looked at him curiously *or* gave him curious *or* funny looks
curieux, -ieuse [kyrjø, -jøz] **1** *adj* **(a)** (*intéressé*) curious, interested; (*esprit*) inquiring, curious; **être c. de tout/de la vie** to be curious about *or* interested in everything/life; **elle est curieuse d'archéologie** she's interested in archaeology; **je serai c. de voir cela** I'd be interested in seeing that
(b) (*indiscret*) curious, inquisitive, *F* nos(e)y
(c) (*étrange*) curious, odd, funny, peculiar; **par une curieuse coïncidence** by a strange coincidence; **chose assez curieuse** curiously *or* funnily enough; **ne me regarde pas comme une bête curieuse** don't look at me as if I had two heads
2 *n* inquisitive person, *F* nos(e)y parker, busybody; **méfie-toi, c'est un c.** watch out, he's nos(e)y; **un attroupement de c.** a crowd of onlookers *or* bystanders; **il était venu en c.** he came just to have a look
3 *nm* **le plus c. de l'affaire est que ...(+** *ind***)** the strangest *or* oddest part *or* thing about it is that ...
curiosité [kyrjozite] *nf* **(a)** (*intellectuelle*) curiosity, interest; **c. d'esprit** intellectual curiosity; **pour développer la c. de votre enfant** to arouse your child's sense of curiosity; **satisfaire sa c.** to satisfy one's curiosity; **regarder qn avec c.** to look at sb curiously *or* enquiringly
(b) (*indiscrétion*) curiosity, inquisitiveness, *F* nosiness; **par c.** out of curiosity; **par simple c., dites-moi ...** just out of curiosity, tell me ...; **la c. est un vilain défaut** = curiosity killed the cat
(c) (*monument*) interesting feature *or* sight; (*objet*) curio; **curiosités d'une ville** sights of a town
curiste [kyrist] *n* patient taking the waters (*at a spa*)
curling [kœrliŋ] *nm Sp* curling
curriculum vitae [kyrikylɔmvite] *nm* curriculum vitae, CV, *Am* résumé; **envoyer/établir son c.** to send (off)/draw up one's CV
curry [kyri] *nm Culin* curry; **poulet au c., c. de poulet** curried chicken, chicken curry
curseur [kyrsœr] *nm Ordinat* cursor; *Tech* (*de règle à calcul, compas*) cursor, slide, runner; *Ordinat* **position/déplacement du c.** cursor position/movement
cursif, -ive [kyrsif, -iv] *adj* **(a)** (*écriture*) cursive **(b)** (*rapide*) cursory
cursus [kyrsys] *nm Univ* programme, *US* program, course of study, curriculum; **établir son c.** to arrange one's course of study; **le c. médical** the medical degree course
curviligne [kyrviliɲ] *adj* curvilinear
cuspide [kyspid] *nf Anat, Bot* cusp
custode [kystɔd] *nf* **(a)** *Rel* (*pour hostie*) custodial **(b)** (*de voiture*) rear quarter panel; (*glace*) quarterlight
cutané [kytane] *adj* skin, *Spéc* cutaneous; **maladie cutanée** skin disease
cuti [kyti] *nf Méd F* skin test; **virer sa c.** to have a positive reaction to a skin test; *Fig* to have changed radically
cuticule [kytikyl] *nf Anat* epidermis, cuticle
cutiréaction [kytireaksjɔ̃] *nf Méd* = **cuti**
cutter [kœtœr, kytɛr] *nm* Stanley knife®
cuvage [kyvaʒ] *nm,* **cuvaison** [kyvɛzɔ̃] *nf* (*de vin, bière*) fermenting *or* fermentation in vats
cuve [kyv] *nf* (storage) tank, cistern; (*de machine à laver*) tub; (*pour la fermentation des alcools, du vin*) vat, tun; *Vieilli* **c. à lessive** laundry tub; *Phot* **c. à laver/à développement** washing/developing tank
cuvée [kyve] *nf* **(a)** (*quantité*) vatful, tunful **(b)** (*produit*) vintage; *Fig* batch; **vin de première c.** wine of the first growth *or* vintage; **c. de la maison** *ou* **du patron** house wine; *Fig* **être de la même c.** (*d'étudiants*) to be classmates, to be in the same year; *Fig* **la dernière c. du festival de Cannes** the latest batch of films from the Cannes festival
cuver [kyve] **1** *vi* **(a)** (*de vin, bière*) to ferment (*in the vats*) **(b)** *F* (*d'une personne*) to sleep it off **2** *vt F* **c. son vin** to sleep it off; **c. sa colère** to simmer down
cuvette [kyvɛt] *nf* **(a)** (wash)basin, (wash)bowl; **c. (de lavabo)** washbasin **(b)** (*de WC*) bowl, pan; (*de thermomètre*) bulb; *Phot* (developing) dish **(c)** (*dépression*), *Géog* basin, depression, *Br* punchbowl
CV [seve] *abrév* **1** *nmpl Aut* **(chevaux)** French administrative unit for car tax purposes **2** *nm* (*abrév* **curriculum vitae**) CV, *Am* résumé
cyan [sjan] *adj inv, nm* cyan
cyanhydrique [sjanidrik] *adj* **acide c.** prussic acid
cyanose [sjanoz] *nf Méd* cyanosis
cyanure [sjanyr] *nm Ch* cyanide; **empoisonnement au c.** cyanide poisoning
cyber [sibɛr] *nm* cyber
cyberespace [sibɛrɛspas] *nm* cyberspace
cybernéticien, -ienne [sibɛrnetisjɛ̃, -jɛn] *n* cybernetics expert, cyberneticist
cybernétique [sibɛrnetik] **1** *adj* cybernetic **2** *nf* cybernetics
cyberpunk [sibɛrpœnk] *nm* cyberpunk
cyclable [siklabl] *adj* **piste c.** cycle track
cyclamen [siklamɛn] *nm* cyclamen
cycle [sikl] *nm* **(a)** (*d'événements, de poèmes etc*), *Biol Ch* cycle; (*de conférences*) series; *Mktg* **c. commande-livraison-facturation** order-to-remittance cycle; *Mktg* **c. de commercialisation** trade cycle; *Mktg* **c. de la distribution** wheel of retailing; **c. économique** economic cycle; *Com* **c. d'exploitation** operating cycle; *Ordinat* **c. d'exécution** execute cycle; **c. menstruel** menstrual cycle; **c. solaire** solar cycle; *Mktg* **c. de vie** life-cycle; *Mktg* **c. de vie du produit** product life-cycle, PLC
(b) *Scol* **premier/second c.** junior/senior classes (*in secondary school*); **elle est prof dans le premier c.** she's a junior school teacher, *Am* she teaches junior school; **élèves du premier c.** junior pupils; **c. primaire/supérieur** primary/higher education
(c) *Aut* **c. d'allumage** ignition cycle; **c. à deux temps** two-stroke cycle; **c. à quatre temps** four-stroke cycle; **c. urbain** urban cycle
(d) (*véhicule*) cycle; **magasin/fabricant de cycles** cycle shop/manufacturer
cyclique [siklik] *adj* cyclical
cyclisme [siklism] *nm Sp* cycling
cycliste [siklist] *Sp* **1** *n* cyclist **2** *adj* (*course*) cycle; **coureur c.** racing cyclist
cyclo-cross [siklokrɔs] *nm Sp* cyclo-cross
cycloïdal, -ale, -aux, -ales [siklɔidal, -o] *adj Math* (*courbe etc*) cycloidal
cycloïde [siklɔid] *nf Math* cycloid
cyclomoteur [siklomɔtœr] *nm* moped
cyclomotoriste [siklomɔtɔrist] *n* moped rider
cyclonal, -ale, -aux, -ales [siklɔnal, -o] *adj Météo* cyclonic
cyclone [siklon] *nm Météo* (*tempête*) cyclone; (*zone de basse pression*) area of low pressure, depression, cyclone; **œil du c.** eye of the storm; *Fig* **elle est entrée comme un c.** she came in like a whirlwind
cyclonique [siklɔnik] *adj Météo* cyclonic
cyclope [siklɔp] *nm Myth* Cyclops; *Fig* **travail de c.** colossal undertaking, Herculean task
cyclopéen, -enne [siklɔpeɛ̃, -ɛn] *adj Fig* gigantic, colossal; **travail c.** Herculean task
cyclorama [siklorama] *nm TV, Cin* cyclorama, cyc
cyclothymie [siklotimi] *nf Psy* manic-depression
cyclothymique [siklotimik] *adj Psy* manic-depressive
cyclotourisme [sikloturism] *nm* bicycle touring, cycling holiday(s)
cyclotron [siklotrɔ̃] *nm Nucl* cyclotron
cygne [siɲ] *nm* swan; **jeune c.** cygnet; **c. mâle** cob; **c. femelle** pen; **duvet de c.** swansdown; **une robe d'une blancheur de c.** a pure *or* snowy white dress; *Fig* **c'est son chant du c.** it's his swansong; *Tech* **col de c.** swan neck
cylindrage [silɛ̃draʒ] *nm* (*de route, d'acier etc*) rolling; *Métal* **c. à froid** cold rolling
cylindre [silɛ̃dr] *nm* **(a)** *Math* cylinder **(b)** (*de moteur*) cylinder; (*de laminoir, essoreuse à rouleaux, calendre etc*) roller; *Aut* **c. de roue** wheel cylinder; **moteur à quatre cylindres** four-cylinder engine; *Aut* **une quatre cylindres** a four-cylinder (car); *Typ* **c. d'impression** printing cylinder, drum; **c. compresseur** road roller; **c. de friction** (*dans une imprimante*) friction cylinder
cylindrée [silɛ̃dre] *nf* (*de cylindre, moteur*) (cubic) capacity; **petite c.** (*voiture*) small car, *Am* compact; **grosse c.** large car, *F* tank
cylindrer [silɛ̃dre] *vt* (*route, pelouse, métal etc*) to roll
cylindrique [silɛ̃drik] *adj* cylindrical
cymbale [sɛ̃bal] *nf Mus* cymbal
cymbalier, -ière [sɛ̃balje, -jɛr] *nm* cymbal player, cymbalist
cynégétique [sineʒetik] **1** *nf* hunting **2** *adj* hunting; **les plaisirs cygénétiques** the pleasures of hunting
cynique [sinik] **1** *adj* **(a)** (*person, attitude etc*) cynical **(b)** *Phil* Cynic **2** *nm* **(a)** cynic **(b)** *Phil* Cynic
cyniquement [sinikmɑ̃] *adv* cynically
cynisme [sinism] *nm* **(a)** cynicism **(b)** *Phil* Cynicism
cynocéphale [sinosefal] *adj* dog-faced baboon
cynodrome [sinodrom] *nm* greyhound (racing) track, *F* dog track

cynophile [sinofil] *n* dog lover
cynor(r)hodon [sinorɔdɔ̃] *nm* (*fruit*) rosehip; **confiture/tisane de c.** rosehip jam/tea
cyprès [siprɛ] *nm* cypress (tree)
cypriote [siprijɔt] **1** *adj* Cypriot **2** *n* **C.** Cypriot
cyrillique [sirilik] *adj* (*alphabet etc*) Cyrillic
cystique [sistik] *adj Anat, Méd* (*conduit, bile, calcul etc*) cystic
cystite [sistit] *nf Méd* cystitis
cytise [sitiz] *nm* laburnum
cytologie [sitɔlɔʒi] *nf Biol* cytology
cytologique [sitɔlɔʒik] *adj* cytological
cytoplasme [sitɔplasm] *nm Biol* cytoplasm
cytoplasmique [sitɔplasmik] *adj Biol* cytoplasmic
czar [tsar] *nm* tsar, czar

D

D, d [de] *nm* (*lettre*) D, d; *Fig* **le système D** (= **débrouillardise**) resourcefulness; **c'est un champion du système D** he's extremely resourceful; **recourir au système D** to use one's wits; **comment tu as fait pour avoir toutes les places gratuitement? – système D!** how did you manage to get all the tickets for nothing? – I used my wits!

DAB [deabe] *nm Banque* (*abrév* **distributeur automatique de billets**) ATM

dab [dab] *nm Arg* (*père*) old man

dac, d'ac [dak] *int F* (*abrév* **d'accord**) OK; **si t'es pas d.** (*si tu ne veux pas*) if you don't want to; **c'est la mieux des trois, si t'es pas d., tu n'as qu'à ...** this is the best of the three, if you don't agree, then you should ...

dacron® [dakrɔ̃] *nm Tex* Terylene, *Am* Dacron®

dactyle [daktil] *nm* dactyl

dactylo [daktilo] **1** *n* (*abrév* **dactylographe**) typist **2** *nf* (*abrév* **dactylographie**) typing; **il est bon en d.** he's good at typing, he's a good typist; **j'ai besoin de la d. dans mon métier** I need typing *or* I need to be able to type in my job **3** *nm Can* (*machine à écrire*) typewriter

dactylo-facturière, *pl* **dactylos-facturières** *nf* typist invoice clerk

dactylographe [daktilograf] **1** *n Veilli* typist **2** *nm Can* (*machine à écrire*) typewriter

dactylographie [daktilografi] *nf* typing

dactylographier [daktilografje] *vt* to type

dactylographique [daktilografik] *adj* (*matériel etc*) typing

dactyloscopie [daktiloskɔpi] *nf* fingerprinting, *Spéc* dactyloscopy

dactyloscopique [daktiloskɔpik] *adj Spéc* dactyloscopic; **examen d.** fingerprint examination

dada [dada] **1** *nm* **(a)** *Enf* (*cheval*) gee-gee; **aller à d.** to play gee-gees **(b)** *F* (*sujet favori*) pet subject; **c'est son nouveau d.** it's his latest hobby-horse; **enfourcher son d.** to get on one's hobby-horse, to get on to one's pet subject **(c)** *Beaux-Arts, Littér* **le d.** Dadaism **2** *adj Beaux-Arts, Littér* Dadaist; **le mouvement d.** Dadaism

dadais [dadɛ] *nm F* gawk; **un grand d.** a great gawk

dadaïsme [dadaism] *nm Beaux-Arts, Littér* Dadaism

dadaïste [dadaist] *n, adj Beaux-Arts, Littér* Dadaist

DADS [deadeɛs] *nf Admin* (*abrév* **déclaration annuelle des données sociales**) PAYE and NIC return

dague [dag] *nf* (*épée*) dagger

daguerréotype [dagɛreotip] *nm Phot* daguerreotype

dahlia [dalja] *nm* dahlia

dahu [day] *nm* = imaginary animal figuring in stories told to the gullible

daigner [deɲe] *vt* to condescend, to deign; **le roi a daigné lui parler** the king condescended to speak to him; **elle n'a même pas daigné me voir** she wouldn't even (condescend to) see me

daim [dɛ̃] *nm* **(a)** (*animal*) (fallow) deer; (*mâle*) buck **(b)** (*peau*) suede; **gants/veste en d.** suede gloves/jacket

daine [dɛn] *nf* doe

dais [dɛ] *nm* canopy; **surmonté d'un d.** canopied; *Fig* **un d. de feuilles** a canopy of leaves

dakin [dakɛ̃] *nm Méd* (**solution de**) **d.** Dakin's solution

dal, dalle [dal] *nm Arg* **que d.** (*rien*) zilch, damn all; **j'y vois que d.** I can't see a bloody thing, I can see damn all; **j'ai pigé que d.** I didn't understand a bloody thing, I understood damn all

dalaï-lama [dalailama] *nm* Dalai Lama

dallage [dalaʒ] *nm* **(a)** (*action*) paving **(b)** (*revêtement*) flagstones

dalle [dal] *nf* **(a)** *Constr* flag(stone), paving stone; (*de marbre*) slab; **d. de moquette/linoléum** carpet/lino tile; **d. funéraire** gravestone, tombstone **(b)** *Arg* = **dal** **(c)** *Arg* **avoir** *ou* **crever la d.** to be starving; **j'ai une de ces dalles** I'm starving, I could eat a horse

daller [dale] *vt* (*avec dalles*) to flag, to pave

dalleur [dalœr] *nm* paver

dalmatien, -ienne [dalmasjɛ̃, -jɛn] *n* Dalmatian, *f* Dalmatian bitch

dalot [dalo] *nm Naut* scupper (hole)

daltonien, -ienne [daltɔnjɛ̃, -jɛn] **1** *adj* colour- *or US* color-blind **2** *n* colour-blind man/woman

daltonisme [daltɔnism] *nm* colour *or US* color blindness

dam [dam] *nm* **(a)** **au grand d. de qn** to the great displeasure of sb **(b)** *Rel* **peine du d.** eternal damnation

damage [damaʒ] *nm* (*de la terre*) ramming, tamping

damas [damas] *nm Tex* damask; **nappe en d.** damask tablecloth

damasquinage [damaskinaʒ] *nm* (*de lame*) damascening

damasquiner [damaskine] *vt* (*lame etc*) to inlay, to damascene

damassé [damase] **1** *adj* **(a)** *Tex* damask **(b)** *Métal* **acier d.** damask (steel), Damascus steel **2** *nm Tex* damask

damasser [damase] *vt Tex, Métal* to damask

dame¹ [dam] *nf* **(a)** (*femme*) lady, *pl* ladies; *F* (*épouse*) wife; *Arch* (noble) lady; **coiffeur/tailleur pour dames** ladies' hairdresser/tailor; **manteau/parapluie de d.** lady's coat/umbrella; **la première d. des États-Unis** the First Lady (of the United States); *F* **elle fait la grande d.** she puts on airs, she's all lah-di-dah; **dames** (*pour indiquer les toilettes*) ladies; **que prendront ces dames?** what will you take, ladies?; *F* **et pour vous, ma petite d.?** what can I get you, dear?; *F* **ma bonne d., si vous saviez!** my dear, if you only knew!; *F Vieilli* **vous pouvez venir avec votre d.** bring your good lady; *Jur* **la d. Simon** Mrs Simon; **les dames de France** the royal princesses of France

(b) [ⓘA10,d] (*pièce*) (*au jeu de dames*) = king; *Échecs, Cartes* queen; (*au trictrac*) piece; **jeu de dames** = (game of) draughts, *Am* checkers; **aller à d.** (*au jeu de dames*) to make a king; *Échecs* to queen (a pawn); *Cartes* **la d. de carreau/de trèfle** the queen of diamonds/clubs

(c) *Tech* (paving) beetle; (*pour tasser le sol*) (earth) rammer

▶ **dame**: **d. de compagnie** lady's companion; **d. d'honneur** lady-in-waiting, *Vieilli* maid of honour; *Naut* **d. de nage** rowlock, *Am* oarlock; **D. Nature** Mother Nature; *Bot* **d. d'onze heures** star of Bethlehem; *Hum, Péj* **d. patronnesse** Lady Bountiful; *F* **d. pipi** lavatory attendant

dame² *int* **d. oui!** well, yes!, why, yes!, rather!; **vous y allez? – d.!** are you going? – what else can I do?

dame-jeanne [damʒan], *pl* **dames-jeannes** *nf* demijohn

damer [dame] *vt* **(a)** (*au jeu de dames*) (*pièce*) to crown; *Fig F* **d. le pion à qn** to outdo sb **(b)** *Constr* (*terre*) to ram, to tamp

dameuse [damøz] *nf Ski* piste basher

damier [damje] *nm* draughtboard, *Am* checkerboard; **tissu à d.** checked material

damnable [danabl] *adj Rel* deserving of damnation; (*relations, idées*) to be condemned

damnation [danasjɔ̃] *nf* damnation; *F* **enfer et d.!** hell and damnation!, damn and blast!

damné, -ée [dane] **1** *adj* damned; *Fig* **c'est son âme damnée** he'd sell his soul for her **2** *n* damned soul; *Fig* **souffrir comme un d.** to suffer (sheer) torture

damner [dane] **1** *vt* to damn; *F* **faire d. qn** to drive sb crazy **2 se damner** *vpr* to incur damnation; *Fig* **il se damnerait pour elle** he would sell his soul to the devil for her

Damoclès [damoklɛs] *nm* **l'épée de D.** the sword of Damocles

damoiseau, -eaux [damwazo] *nm Hist* squire; *Hum* **alors, jeune d.** so, young man

damoiselle [damwazɛl] *nf Hist* damsel

damper [dampœr] *nm Aut* damper

dan [dã] *nm Sp* dan; **il est quatrième d.** he is a fourth dan

dancing [dãsiŋ] *nm* dance hall

dandinement [dãdinmã] *nm* (*de personne*) rolling gait, waddle; (*d'oie*) waddle

dandiner (se) [sədãdine] *vpr* (*d'une personne*) to have a rolling gait, to waddle; (*d'une oie*) to waddle; **se d. d'un pied sur l'autre** to shift from foot to foot; **marcher en se dandinant** to waddle

dandy [dãdi], *pl* **dandys** *nm* dandy

dandysme [dãdism] *nm* dandyism

Danemark [danmark] *nm* Denmark

danger [dãʒe] *nm* danger; (*cause de danger*) hazard; **il n'y a pas de d.** there's no danger, it's quite safe; **à l'abri du d.** out of danger; **être en d., courir un d.** to be in danger; **mettre en**

d. la vie de qn to endanger sb's life; **en d. de mort** in mortal danger; **hors de d.** out of danger; (*d'un malade*) out of danger, off the danger list; **ses jours ne sont plus en d.** (*d'un malade, d'un accidenté*) he's off the danger list *or* out of danger; **sans d.** (*employé adjectivement*) not dangerous, safe; (*employé adverbialement*) without danger, safely; **avec cette voiture, tu es un véritable d. public** you're a proper public menace with that car; *F* **pas de d.!** no fear!, not likely!; *F* **il n'y a pas de d. qu'il revienne** there's no danger of his coming back

dangereusement [dɑ̃ʒrøzmɑ̃] *adv* dangerously; **il est d. blessé** he is seriously injured; **vivre d.** to live dangerously

dangereux, -euse [dɑ̃ʒrø, -øz] *adj* dangerous (**pour** to, for); *Mil* **zone dangereuse** danger zone; **produit d.** dangerous *or* hazardous substance; **c'est d. pour la santé** it's bad for *or* harmful to your health; **il est d. de se pencher au dehors** it is dangerous to lean out

dangerosité [dɑ̃ʒrozite] *nf* dangerousness

danois, -oise [danwa, -waz] [①A20,d] **1** *adj* Danish **2** *nm Ling* Danish **3** *n* **(a) D.** Dane **(b) (grand) D.** (*chien*) Great Dane

dans [dɑ̃] *prép* [①A67] **(a)** (*à l'intérieur de*) in; **d. une boîte** in(side) a box; **il est d. sa chambre** he's in his room; **qu'est-ce que vous avez d. la main?** what have you got in your hand?; **il habite d. Paris même** he lives (right) in Paris; **lire qch d. un journal** to read sth in a newspaper; **tomber d. l'escalier** to fall down the stairs; **d. un rayon de dix kilomètres** within a radius of ten kilometres; **il pleut d. tout le pays** it's raining all over the country; **la main d. la main** hand in hand

(b) (*avec mouvement*) into; **mettre qch d. une boîte** to put sth in(to) a box; **il est entré d. leur chambre** he went into their room; **tomber d. l'oubli** to sink into oblivion; **glisser d. l'eau** to slide into the water; **il monta dans le train** he got into the train; **jette-le d. le vide-ordures** throw it down the chute

(c) (*pour faire sortir qch*) out of; **prendre qch d. qch** to take sth out of sth; **boire d. un verre** to drink out of a glass; **copier qch d. un livre** to copy sth out of *or* from a book; **découper un article d. le journal** to cut an article out of the paper; *Culin* **un morceau d. la poitrine** a cut off the breast

(d) (*de temps*) in; **d. vingt ans** in twenty years' (time); **d. l'après-midi** in *or* during the afternoon; **être d. sa vingt-cinquième année** to be in one's twenty-fifth year; *F* **d. le temps** long ago; **je faisais du vélo d. ma jeunesse** I used to cycle when I was young *or* in my youth; **payer d. les dix jours** to pay within ten days; **je serai prêt à partir d. cinq minutes** I'll be ready to leave in five minutes; **je dois le voir d. le mois/la semaine** I'll be seeing him sometime this month/week; **arriver d. l'heure qui suit** to arrive within the next hour

(e) (*environ*) about; **il a d. les quarante ans** he's about forty

(f) être d. le commerce/le bâtiment/l'informatique to be in trade/construction/computers; **être plongé d. sa réflexion** to be deep in thought; **faire les choses d. les règles** to do things according to the rules; **être d. le secret** to be in on the secret; **travailler d. le bruit/le calme** to work in noisy/calm surroundings; **je ne peux pas travailler dans le bruit/le calme** I can't work when it's noisy/quiet; **d. le doute, abstiens-toi** if in doubt, don't

(g) il est d. mes intentions de l'appeler I intend to call him, I have the intention of calling him; **d. son excitation/sa hâte/sa peur** in his excitement/hurry/fear; **d. ces circonstances** in *or* under the circumstances; **d. ce cas, faisons autre chose** in that case, let's do something else; **d. ce but** with this in mind, with this aim in view; **d. l'espoir de** in the hope of; **d. ces conditions, je refuse de signer** I refuse to sign under these conditions; **d. l'attente de votre réponse** awaiting your reply

dansable [dɑ̃sabl] *adj* **cet air n'est pas d.** it's not a tune you can dance to; **la musique que les jeunes écoutent maintenant n'est pas d.** you can't dance to the music that young people listen to nowadays

dansant [dɑ̃sɑ̃] *adj* **(a)** (*flamme*) dancing; (*reflet*) shimmering; (*lueur*) flickering **(b)** (*où l'on danse*) **thé d.** tea dance; **donner une soirée dansante** to give a dance **(c) une musique dansante** music you can dance to

danse [dɑ̃s] *nf* (*art*) dance; (*action*) dancing; (*musique*) dance tune; **elle aime la d.** she's fond of dancing; **le tango n'est plus une d. à la mode** the tango is no longer a fashionable dance; *Fig* **entrer dans la d.** to join in; *Vieilli F* **mettre une d. à qn** (*réprimander*) to tell sb off; (*frapper*) to beat sb

▶ **danse**: **d. classique** classical dancing, ballet; **d. folklorique** folk dance/dancing; *Méd* **d. de Saint-Guy** St Vitus's dance; **d. de salon** ballroom dance/dancing; **d. du ventre** belly dance/dancing

danser [dɑ̃se] **1** *vi* **(a)** to dance; **faire d. qn** to dance with sb; *Fig F* (*frapper*) to beat sb up; **le bouchon/le bateau danse sur l'eau** the cork/the boat is bobbing up and down on the water; *Fig* **d. devant le buffet** to go hungry; **vous dansez, mademoiselle?** would you like to dance?; *Fig* **je ne sais sur quel pied d.** (*à cause de ces instructions contradictoires*) I don't know if I'm coming or going **(b)** (*d'un cheval*) to prance **2** *vt* (*valse etc*) to dance **3 se danser** *vpr* (*d'une danse*) to be danced; **c'est un morceau qui se danse** it's a tune you can dance to

danseur, -euse [dɑ̃sœr, -øz] *n* dancer; **d. (classique** *ou* **de ballet)** ballet dancer, *f* ballerina; **d. étoile** lead dancer; **danseuse de cabaret** cabaret dancer; **danseuse étoile** prima ballerina; **d. de corde** tightrope walker; **d. mondain** (male) escort; *Péj* **entretenir une danseuse** (*avoir une maîtresse*) to keep a mistress; (*risquer de l'argent*) to take a gamble *or Am* flyer; **il est hors de question que notre entreprise entretienne une danseuse** the company can't afford not to play it safe; **se mettre en danseuse** to stand up on the pedals; **être en danseuse** to be standing on the pedals

dantesque [dɑ̃tɛsk] *adj* Dantean, Dantesque

Danube [danyb] *nm* Danube

danubien, -ienne [danybjɛ̃, -jɛn] *adj* of the Danube, Danubian

daphnie [dafni] *nf Zool* daphnia

dard [dar] *nm* **(a)** (*d'un insecte*) sting; (*d'un serpent*) forked tongue **(b)** *Pêche* spear, harpoon

darder [darde] *vt* (*lancer*) to hurl; *Fig* **il a dardé sur moi un regard chargé de haine** he shot *or* flashed a glance of hatred at me; **le soleil darde ses rayons sur la plage** the sun is beating *or* blazing down on the beach

dare-dare [dardar] *adv F* double-quick, on the double; **accourir d.** to come charging up, to come running

darne [darn] *nf Culin* (*de poisson*) steak

dartre [dartr] *nf Méd* scurf

dartreux, -euse [dartrø, -øz] *adj Méd* scabby

darwinien, -ienne [darwinjɛ̃, jɛn] *adj* Darwinian

darwinisme [darwinism] *nm* Darwinism

darwiniste [darwinist] *adj, n* Darwinist, Darwinian

DAS [das] *nf* (*abrév* **déclaration d'autorisation de sortie**) export licence

datable [databl] *adj* which can be dated; **ce parchemin est en trop mauvais état pour être d.** the parchment is not in good enough condition to be dated; **ces ossements sont parfaitement datables** it is quite possible to date the bones

datation [datasjɔ̃] *nf* dating

date [dat] *nf* [①A75-6,B-C; B58-9,B-C] date; **mettre la d. sur une lettre** to date a letter; **sans d.** (*lettre etc*) undated; **erreur de d.** mistake in the date; **la lettre porte la d. du 5 mai** the letter is dated (the) 5th May; **à quelle d. arrivent-ils?** what date do they arrive?, what date are they arriving on?; **à cette d.** at that time; **à cette d. j'étais déjà parti** I'd already left by then; **à d. fixe** on a fixed date; **à trente jours de d.** thirty days after date; *Fin* **emprunt à longue/à courte d.** long-/short-dated loan; **lettre en d. du 5 mai** letter dated (the) 5th May; *Com* **en d. du 15 courant** dated (the) 15th inst; **être le premier/dernier en d.** to come first/last; **prendre d. pour qch** to fix a date for sth; **faire d.** (*d'un événement*) to be memorable; **une fête qui a fait d.** a memorable *or* momentous party; **amitié de fraîche/de vieille** *ou* **de longue d.** recent/long-standing friendship; **je la connais de longue d.** I've known her (for) a long time; **d. d'achèvement** completion date, date of completion; **d.-butoir** deadline, cutoff date; **d. de clôture** closing date; **d. de départ** date of departure, departure date; **d. d'échéance** (*de dû*) maturity date; (*de terme*) expiry date; **d. d'émission** date of issue; **d. d'exigibilité** due date; **d. d'expiration** expiry date; **d. de facturation** date of invoice, invoice date; **d. limite** deadline; **d. limite de consommation/de vente/de fraîcheur** use-by/sell-by/best-before date; **d. limite de paiement** deadline for payment; **d. de naissance/de mariage** date of birth/marriage; **d. d'ouverture de l'exercice** first day of the financial year; **d. de parution** publication date; **d. de péremption** use-by date; **d. de retour** date of return; **d. de valeur** value date

dateline [dɛtlajn] *nf Journ* dateline

dater [date] **1** *vt* (*lettre etc*) to date; **lettre datée du 20** letter dated the 20th; **non daté** undated **2** *vi* to date (**de** from); **à d. de ce jour** from today; **à d. du 15** on and after the 15th; **de quand date votre dernier repas?** when did you last eat?; **événement qui date** memorable event; **robe qui date** old-fashioned dress; **cette mode commence à d.** this fashion is becoming dated *or* is beginning to date; **ça ne date pas d'hier** that's nothing new

dateur [datœr] **1** *adj* **tampon** *ou* **timbre d.** date stamp **2** *nm* date marker, date stamp; **d. automatique** automatic date stamping machine

datif [datif] *nm Gram* dative (case); **au d.** in the dative

dation [dasjɔ̃] *nf Jur* gift (*made to an heir in the course of one's lifetime to avoid inheritance tax*); **d. en paiement** payment in kind

datte [dat] *nf* date; **d. fourrée** stuffed date

dattier [datje] *nm* date palm, date tree

daube [dob] *nf Culin* = meat braised in wine and stock with vegetables; **bœuf en d.** braised beef

dauber [dobe] *vt* **(a)** *Culin* (*viande*) to braise **(b)** *Arch, Litt* (*personne*) to make fun of

daubière [dobjɛr] *nf Culin* = earthenware pot for braising

dauphin [dofɛ̃] *nm* **(a)** *Zool* dolphin **(b)** *Fr Hist* **D.** Dauphin **(c)** *Fig* (*à une position importante*) heir apparent

Dauphine [dofin] *nf Fr Hist* Dauphiness

dauphinois, -oise [dofinwa, -waz] **1** *adj* of/from the Dauphiné; *Culin* **gratin d.** = sliced potatoes baked with milk and browned on top **2** *n* **D.** (*natif*) native of the Dauphiné; (*habitant*) inhabitant of the Dauphiné

daurade [dɔrad] *nf* sea bream; **d. (royale)** gilthead (bream)

davantage [davɑ̃taʒ] *adv* more; **il m'en faut d.** I need more; **je n'en dis pas d.** I shall say no more; **je ne l'interrogerai pas d.** I won't question him any further; **vous êtes riche, mais il l'est (bien) d.** you're rich, but he's (much) richer; **elle est jolie, mais tu l'es bien d.** she's pretty but you're much prettier than she is; **nous ne resterons pas d.** we won't stay any longer; **se baisser d.** to stoop lower; **chaque jour d.** more and more every day; **encore** *ou* **même d.** even more; **veux-tu d. de pâtes?** do you want (some) more pasta?

davier [davje] *nm* **(a)** *Menuis* cramp **(b)** (*de dentiste*) forceps

DCA [desea] *nf Mil* (*abrév* **Défense contre avions**) anti-aircraft defence

DD *nm* (*abrév* **disque dur**) *Ordinat* HD

DDASS [das] *nf Admin* (*abrév* **Direction départementale de l'action sanitaire et sociale**) = local social work department, one of whose tasks is to deal with children who have been abandoned or ill-treated

DDT [dedete] *nm Ch* (*abrév* **Dichloro-Diphényl-Trichloréthane**) DDT

de [də] (*before vowels and h mute* **d'**; **de + le, les** *are contracted into* **du, des**) **1** *prép* **(a)** (*origine*) from; **il vient de Paris** he comes from Paris; **nous sommes de Montpellier** we are from Montpellier; **apprendre qch de source sûre** to hear sth from a reliable source; **l'idée est de vous** the idea is yours *or* comes from you; **je l'ai oublié? c'est bien de moi** did I forget it? that's just like me; **l'express d'Aberdeen** the Aberdeen express; **un vin d'Alsace** an Alsace wine; **sulfate de fer** iron sulphate; **du temps de nos pères** in our fathers' day; **sortir de table** to leave the table; **sortir de chez soi** to leave the house; **de pauvre, il devint riche** he went from rags to riches

(b) [①**A66-67**; **B52**] **de ... en ...** from ... to ...; **de jour en jour** from day to day; **errer de ville en ville** to wander from town to town

(c) de ... à ... from ... to ...; **du matin au soir** from morning till night; **de là à dire oui ...** as for saying yes ...; **de vous à moi ...** between ourselves ...; **de vingt à trente personnes** between twenty and thirty people; **serrurier de père en fils** locksmiths from father to son; **passer de la tristesse à la joie** to go from sadness to joy; **de temps à autre** from time to time; **il avait volé des sommes allant de 15 000 à 300 000 francs** he had stolen sums between 15,000 and 300,000 francs

(d) (*agent, moyen, instrument*) by; **accompagné de ses amis** accompanied by his friends; **il est détesté de tout le monde** everybody hates him; **apprécié des connaisseurs** appreciated by connoisseurs; **j'ai fait cela de ma propre main** it's all my own work; **armé de pierres** armed with stones; **les vautours se nourrissent de cadavres** vultures live on dead animals; **s'amuser d'un rien** to laugh over nothing

(e) (*manière*) **il m'a regardé d'un air amusé** he looked at me with an amused expression; **répondre d'une voix douce** to answer in a gentle voice; **d'un ton excédé** in an exasperated voice; **effleurer du doigt** to brush with one's finger

(f) (*cause*) **sauter de joie** to jump for joy; **ivre de joie** giddy with joy; **je tombe de fatigue** I'm so tired that I'm ready to drop; **faire qch de soi-même** to do sth of one's own accord; **de peur de la blesser** for fear of hurting her; **trépigner d'impatience** to stamp one's feet in *or* with impatience; **en rosir d'aise** to go pink with joy; **puni de sa gourmandise** punished for one's greed

(g) (*mesure*) **âgé de seize ans** sixteen years old; **un enfant de dix ans** a child of ten, a ten-year old child; **ma montre retarde de dix minutes** my watch is ten minutes slow; **il est plus grand que moi d'une tête** he's a head taller than I am; **une pièce de 20 centimes** a 20-centime piece; **la terrasse a vingt mètres de long** *ou* **est longue de vingt mètres** the terrace is twenty metres long; **un chèque de 100 francs** a cheque for 100 francs; **une hausse de 10%** a 10% increase; **vingt francs de l'heure** twenty francs an hour; **il a été condamné à deux ans de prison** he was sentenced to two years' imprisonment

(h) (*introduisant le complément de l'adj*) **digne d'éloges** worthy of praise, praiseworthy; **altéré de sang** thirsting for blood; **large de bassin** wide-hipped; **couvert de puces** covered in fleas; **calme de nature** calm by nature

(i) [①**B64**,7-8] (*propriété*) **le livre de Pierre** Peter's book; **le toit de la maison** the roof of the house; **le meilleur élève de la classe** the best pupil in the class; **les rues de Paris** the streets of Paris; **la chambre du second** the room on the second *or Am* third floor; **scène de rivière hollandaise** scene on a Dutch river; **la statue est de Rodin** the statue is by Rodin; **une aria de Bach** a Bach aria

(j) [①**B64**,7] (*matière*) **un pont de fer** an iron bridge; **une robe de soie** a silk dress

(k) (*pour différencier, préciser*) **le chien de berger** the sheepdog; **le chien du berger** the shepherd's dog; **la bataille de Culloden** the battle of Culloden; **Notre Dame de Lourdes** Our Lady of Lourdes; **un problème d'algèbre** an algebra problem; **la conférence de Berlin** the Berlin conference; **un hôtel de la rive gauche** a hotel on the left bank; **un conflit de générations** a clash of generations; **le journal d'hier** yesterday's paper; **le mois de mai** (the month of) May; **à quatre heures de l'après-midi** at four (o'clock) in the afternoon; **son devoir de père** his duties as a father; **un don de voyance** a gift of second sight; **la route de Paris** the Paris road; **le professeur de français** the French teacher; **une crème de beauté** a beauty cream; **un conseil d'ami** friendly advice

(l) (*partitif*) of; **un verre de vin** a glass of wine; **une livre de café** a pound of coffee; **quelque chose de bon** something good; **la moitié de ses économies** half of his savings; **je ne l'ai pas vu de la soirée** I haven't seen him all evening

(m) (*avec une préposition*) **près de la maison** near the house; **autour du jardin** round the garden; **à partir de ce jour-là** from that day (onward); **de par le roi** by royal decree

(n) (*pour introduire un complément d'objet*) **nous approchons de Paris** we're getting near *or* approaching Paris; **j'ai changé d'avis** I've changed my mind; **manquer de courage** to lack courage; **convenir d'une erreur** to admit an error

(o) [①**B31**,2,a; **B33**,b,iii; **B34**,c] (*pour introduire un infinitif*) **il est honteux de mentir** it is shameful to lie; **le mieux était de rire** it was best to laugh; **je crains de n'être en retard** I'm afraid I might be late; **j'aime mieux attendre que de me faire mouiller** I would rather wait than get wet

(p) (*introduisant une apposition ou un complément du prédicat*) **la ville de Paris** the city of Paris; **il est parti de nuit** he left by night; **je n'ai rien fait de tout le week-end** I haven't done anything all weekend; **on l'a traité de lâche** he was called a coward; **un drôle de type** a funny chap; *F* **il y a eu trois hommes de tués** three men were killed; *F* **c'est un grand pas de fait** that's a great step forward; *F* **la robe est d'un réussi!** the dress is perfect!

(q) (*dans titre d'ouvrage, de chapitre*) **de l'amour** (on) love; **des dangers du remords** (on) the dangers of remorse

(r) (*dans nom à particule*) **le Prince de Condé** the Prince of Condé

(s) *Litt* **la musique commença et les enfants de danser** the music began, and the children started to dance

2 *article partitif* [①**B4-5**,C] (*used also as pl of* **un, une**) **n'avez-vous pas d'amis?** haven't you got any friends?, don't you have any friends?; **sans faire de fautes** without making any mistakes; **je ne veux pas qu'on lui mette de collier** I won't have a collar put on him; **de grands artistes se trouvaient là** there were some distinguished artists there; **elle ne mange plus de viande** she no longer eats meat; **faire de la musique** to make music; **c'est du Bach, n'est-ce pas?** it's Bach, isn't it?; **je bois de l'eau** (*toujours*) I drink water; (*maintenant*) I am drinking water; **donnez-nous de vos nouvelles** let's hear from you; **avez-vous du pain?** have you any bread?; **donnez-moi de ce vin** give me some of that wine; **donnez-moi du bon vin** give me some good wine; **manger de tous les plats** to have something of everything; **ah ça, des problèmes, tu peux dire qu'elle en a!** she's got problems all right!; **mettre des heures à faire qch** to spend hours doing sth

dé[1] [de] *nm* **(a)** [①**A10**,d; **A13**,3,c] (*pour jouer*) die, *plus souvent* dice, *pl* dice; **un coup de dé** a throw of the dice; **jouer aux**

dés to play dice; **jeter les dés** to throw the dice; **les dés sont pipés** the dice are loaded; *Fig* **les dés sont jetés** the die is cast; *Culin* **couper en dés** (*légumes etc*) to dice **(b)** *Archit* (*de piédestal etc*) dado, die **(c)** *MecE* bearing (bush), brass
dé[2] *nm* **dé (à coudre)** thimble; *Fig* **un dé à coudre de whisky** a thimbleful of whisky
DEA [deəa] *nm* (*abrév* **diplôme d'études approfondies**) = post-graduate qualification which is a prerequisite for PhD candidates
dealer[1] [dilœr] *nm F* dealer
dealer[2] [dile] *vt F* to deal; **il deale de la coke** he deals coke
déambulateur [deɑ̃bylatœr] *nm* zimmer® (frame), walker
déambulatoire [deɑ̃bylatwar] *nm Archit* ambulatory
déambuler [deɑ̃byle] *vi* to stroll (about), to walk up and down, to saunter
débâcher [debɑʃe] *vt* (*terrain de tennis, piscine*) to take the covers off
débâcle [debɑkl] *nf* debacle; *Mil* debacle, rout; (*de glaces flottantes*) break(ing) up; *Fig* (*d'une affaire, une monnaie etc*) collapse; (*d'une grosse entreprise*) crash; (*d'une équipe de sport*) rout; *Fig* **rien ne laissait supposer une telle d. financière** (*d'une personne, petite entreprise*) financial ruin came quite without warning
débâillonner [debɑjɔne] *vt Fig* (*la presse*) to ungag, to unmuzzle
déballage [debalaʒ] *nm* **(a)** (*action*) unpacking **(b)** **(vente au) d.** pavement selling **(c)** *F* (*aveu*) confession, outpouring; (*révélations*) disclosure; **assister au d. public de sa vie privée** to see one's private life being discussed in public
déballer [debale] *vt* **(a)** (*produits, caisses*) to unpack **(b)** *F* (*un secret*) to give away, to disclose; (*sa vie privée*) to talk about, *F* to spill the beans about; (*la vérité*) to confess to; **je ne veux pas voir cette affaire déballée devant la presse** I don't want the press to get hold of this
déballonner (se) [sədebalɔne] *vpr F* to chicken out, *Br* to bottle out
débandade [debɑ̃dad] *nf* (*d'une armée, d'une équipe etc*) rout; **après le krach, ce fut la d. générale** there was general panic after the stock market crash; **c'est la d. dans cette entreprise** the company's in a shambles
débander[1] [debɑ̃de] **1** *vt* (*enlever le bandage de*) to remove a/the bandage from, to unbandage; **il faut lui d. les yeux** we'll have to take the blindfold off him **2** *vi Vulg* to lose one's erection; *Fig F* **travailler pendant des heures sans d.** to work non-stop for hours
débander[2] **(se)** *vpr* **(a)** (*d'une foule etc*) to disperse; *Mil etc* to scatter **(b)** (*de qch sous tension*) to relax; (*d'un arc*) to unbend
débaptiser [debatize] *vt* (*personne, rue etc*) to change the name of, to rename
débarbouillage [debarbujaʒ] *nm* face wash
débarbouiller [debarbuje] **1** *vt* **d. qn** to wash sb's face **2** **se débarbouiller** *vpr* to wash one's face
débarbouillette [debarbujɛt] *nf Can* (face) flannel, face cloth, *Am* washrag
débarcadère [debarkadɛr] *nm Naut* landing stage, jetty; (*de marchandises*) wharf
débardage [debardaʒ] *nm Naut* (*de bois etc*) unloading, unlading
débarder [debarde] *vt* **(a)** *Naut* (*bois etc*) to unload **(b)** *Rail* (*bois de charpente, pierres de carrière*) to convey to the railhead
débardeur [debardœr] *nm* **(a)** (*tricot*) tank top **(b)** (*personne*) docker, stevedore, *Am* longshoreman
débarqué, -ée [debarke] **1** *adj* landed **2** *n* **un nouveau d.** a new arrival
débarquement [debarkəmɑ̃] *nm* **(a)** (*de cargaison*) unloading; (*de passagers*) landing, disembarkation; **quai de d.** unloading bay **(b)** *Mil, Naut* landing; (*d'un train*) detraining; (*d'un bateau*) disembarkation; **troupes de d.** landing force; **d. sur plage** beach landing; *Hist* **le d.** the Normandy landings; *Fig* **quand toute la famille vient à la maison, c'est le d.** it's like the Normandy landings *or* like being invaded when all the family comes; **avec tous les cousins qui arrivent, ça va être un vrai d. ici** we're going to be overrun with all the cousins arriving **(c)** *Naut* (*d'un équipage*) paying off, discharge
débarquer [debarke] **1** *vt* **(a)** (*cargaison*) to unload; (*marchandises*) to offload; (*passagers d'un bateau*) to disembark, to land; (*passagers d'un bus*) to set down; (*pilote d'un navire*) to drop

(b) *Naut* (*équipage*) to pay off, to discharge; *F* **d. qn** to give sb the sack *or* push; *F* **se faire d., être débarqué** to get the sack *or* push

2 *vi* **(a)** (*d'un bateau, d'un avion*) to disembark; *surtout Can* (*d'un train, d'un bus*) to get off, to alight

(b) *Fig F* to turn up, to arrive; **j'ai débarqué dans cette ville hier** I arrived in town yesterday; **je débarque à peine** I've only just got here; **tu débarques!** where have you been?; **à chaque fois qu'on lui demande quelque chose, elle débarque complètement** whenever she's asked a question she's totally at sea *or* is totally lost; **ce type, il a toujours l'air de d.** that chap never seems to know what's going on
débarras [debara] *nm* **(a)** (*endroit*) boxroom, *Br F* glory hole **(b)** **bon d.!** good riddance!
débarrasser [debarase] **1** *vt* (*table etc*) to clear; **d. qn de qch** to relieve sb of sth; **je vais te d. de ce mauvais rhume/vilain bouton** I'll get rid of that rotten cold/nasty spot for you; **je vais te d. de cette manie de fumer** I'll cure you of the smoking habit; **d. qn de qn** to take sb off sb's hands; (*le tuer*) to get rid of sb for sb; *Fig F* **d. le plancher** to clear out **2** **se débarrasser** *vpr* **se d. de qch/qn** to get rid of sth/sb; **se d. d'une tâche difficile** to get out of a difficult job; **débarrassez-vous!** can I take your things?
débarrer [debare] *vt* (*porte etc*) to unbar
débat [deba] *nm* **(a)** (*organisé*) debate; **d. télévisé** discussion programme; (*politique*) televised debate; *Pol* **débats (parlementaires)** (parliamentary) debates, proceedings; **le film sera suivi d'un d. (portant) sur ...** the film will be followed by a discussion on ... **(b)** (*polémique*) argument, dispute; **trancher un d.** to settle an argument *or* a dispute; **un d. intérieur** an inner debate *or* conflict *or* struggle
débâtir [debɑtir] *vt* (*vêtement*) to remove the tacks from
débattement [debatmɑ̃] *nm Aut etc* clearance; **d. de roue** wheel deflection
débattre [debatr] (*conj like* **battre**) **1** *vt* (*discuter*) to debate, to discuss; **prix à d.** price by arrangement; **d. les conditions d'un contrat** to negotiate the conditions of a contract; **je n'ai pas débattu le prix** I didn't argue *or* haggle about the price; **d. d'une question** to discuss a matter **2** **se débattre** *vpr* to struggle; **se d. dans l'eau** to flounder, to splash (about) in the water; **se d. comme un forcené** *ou* **comme un beau diable** to struggle like a madman; **se d. contre des agresseurs** to defend oneself against attackers; **se d. contre une difficulté** to struggle with a problem
débauchage [deboʃaʒ] *nm* (*renvoi*) laying off; (*embauche*) head-hunting
débauche [deboʃ] *nf* debauchery; **il vit dans la d.** he lives a life of debauchery; **lieu de d.** den of vice; *Jur* **excitation des mineurs à la d.** incitement of minors to vice; *Fig* **le décor de cette pièce est une d. d'imagination** the set is extremely imaginative; **une d. de couleurs** a riot of colour
débauché, -ée [deboʃe] **1** *adj* debauched, profligate **2** *n* libertine, rake, *f* debauched woman
débaucher [deboʃe] **1** *vt* **(a)** (*inciter à la débauche*) to lead astray; **d. la jeunesse** to corrupt the young; *F* **est-ce que je peux te d. et t'inviter au cinéma/restaurant** can I tempt you with a film/dinner?; *F* **c'est lui qui m'a débauché hier soir** he led me astray last night

(b) **d. qn** (*l'inciter à la grève*) to induce sb to strike; (*le renvoyer*) to make sb redundant, to lay sb off; (*l'embaucher*) to head-hunt sb; **on a réussi à le d. de Toshiba avec un très beau salaire** they managed to lure *or* tempt him away from Toshiba with the promise of an excellent salary

2 **se débaucher** *vpr* to be corrupted; *F* **arrête de travailler et débauche-toi un peu** stop working for a bit and enjoy yourself
débecter [debɛkte] *vt Arg* **d. qn** to turn sb's stomach, to sicken sb
débet [debɛ] *nm Fin* balance due
débile [debil] **1** *adj* (*enfant*) sickly; (*corps*) weak, feeble; (*santé*) poor; *Péj* (*émission, film, livre etc*) stupid, idiotic; *Péj* **il est complètement d.** he's a complete idiot **2** *n* **un(e) d. mental(e)** a mental defective; *Péj* **c'est un d. mental, ce type!** the man's a complete idiot
débilitant [debilitɑ̃] *adj* debilitating, weakening; *Fig* demoralizing; **remède d.** debilitant; **des occupations débilitantes** tiring occupations
débilité [debilite] *nf* debility, weakness; *Péj* stupidity; **d. mentale** mental deficiency; *Péj* **les films que tu regardes sont d'une d.!** you watch such stupid *or* idiotic films!; **je ne supporte pas la d. du cinéma américain/de son nouveau copain** I can't stand American films/her new boyfriend — they are/he is so stupid
débiliter [debilite] *vt* to debilitate, to weaken
débinage [debinaʒ] *nm F* knocking, running down
débine [debin] *nf F* poverty; **être dans la d.** to be (stony) broke
débiner [debine] *F* **1** *vt* to knock, to run down **2** **se débiner** *vpr* to scram, to clear off
débineur, -euse [debinœr, -øz] *n F* knocker

débit¹ [debi] *nm* **(a)** (*ventes*) (retail) sale; **au d. de** to the debit of; **marchandises de bon d.** marketable *or* saleable goods; **la marchandise ne peut pas être fraîche ici, il n'y a aucun d.** the goods here can't be fresh, there's no turnover; **d. cumulé** cumulative debit; **d. de caisse** cash debit; *Ordinat* **d. de données** data throughput **(b) d. de tabac** tocacconist's (shop); **d. de boissons** bar **(c)** (*de bois*) cutting up **(d)** *Tech* (*de pompe etc*) discharge, delivery; *HydE* (*de rivière, de robinet etc*) flow; *Ind* output; *Él* power supplied; **d. d'air** (*dans un moteur*) air flow **(e)** (*d'un orateur*) delivery; **il a un de ces débits!** he really has the gift of the gab!

débit² *nm Fin* debit; **porter 1 000 francs au d. de qn** to debit sb with 1,000 francs

débitable¹ [debitabl] *adj* (*bois etc*) that can be cut up

débitable² *adj* (*compte*) that can be drawn on

débitant, -ante [debitɑ̃, -ɑ̃t] *n* **d. de tabac** tobacconist; **d. de boissons** pub owner, *Am* bar owner

débiter¹ [debite] *vt* **(a)** *Com* (*vendre*) to sell retail

(b) (*bois*) to cut up, to convert; (*viande*) to cut up

(c) *HydE* (*tant de litres par heure etc*) to discharge; *Ind* to produce; *Ordinat* to output; **les ascenseurs de la tour débitent 500 personnes par heure** the lifts in the tower handle 500 people per hour; **cette usine débite 250 voitures par jour** the output from the factory is 250 cars a day, the factory produces 250 cars a day

(d) (*texte, harangue*) to deliver; **l'acteur débite son texte de plus en plus vite** the actor's speaking his lines faster and faster; **ce n'est pas un acteur, il ne fait que d. le texte** he's no actor, he's merely reciting the text; *Péj* **d. des sottises** to talk rubbish; **il m'a débité toutes ces sottises sans s'arrêter** he trotted out all that nonsense to me non-stop; **d. des mensonges** to trot out one lie after another

débiter² *vt Com* (*inscrire au débit*) to debit; **d. une somme à qn, d. qn d'une somme** to debit sb with an amount; **d. un compte** to debit an account; **d. une somme d'un compte** to debit an account with an amount, to debit an amount to an account

débiteur¹, -euse [debitœr, -øz] *n* **(a)** *Péj Vieilli* person who holds forth *or* talks rubbish; **d. de calomnies** scandalmonger **(b)** *MecE* feeding device **(c)** shop assistant

débiteur², -trice [debitœr, -tris] **1** *n* debtor; *Fig* **je suis votre d.** I am indebted to you, I am in your debt **2** *adj* **(a)** *Com* **compte d.** debit account **(b)** *Cin* **bobine débitrice** top *or* delivery spool

▶ **débiteur**: **d. concordataire** bankrupt who has reached a settlement with his debtors; **d. insolvable** insolvent debtor; **d. principal** primary *or* principal debtor; **d. solidaire** joint and several debtor

débitmètre [debimɛtr] *nm Tech* flowmeter

déblai [deblɛ] *nm Constr, Rail etc* **(a)** excavation, cut(ting); **route en d.** sunken road **(b) déblais** spoil earth

déblaiement [deblɛmɑ̃] *nm* (*de terrain etc*) clearing

déblatérer [deblatere] **(je déblatère; je déblatérerai) 1** *vt* **d. des sottises** to talk nonsense; **d. des injures** to fling abuse **(contre** at); **il ne cesse de d. les pires insultes à ton égard** he's always extremely abusive about you **2** *vi* **d. contre** *ou* **sur qn/qch** to rail against sb/sth

déblayage [deblɛjaʒ] *nm* clearing; (*d'une chambre*) clearing out

déblayer [debleje] *vt* **(je déblaye, je déblaie) (a)** (*déblais etc*) to clear away, to remove; **d. la neige** to shovel away the snow **(b)** (*chambre*) to clear out; **d. un terrain** to clear a piece of ground; *Fig* **d. le terrain** (*pour des négociations etc*) to prepare *or* clear the ground *or* the way

déblocage [deblɔkaʒ] *nm* freeing, releasing; (*de machine*) unjamming; *Fin* (*des prix etc*) unfreezing; *Psy* **le d. d'inhibitions/de complexes** getting rid of inhibitions/complexes

débloquer [deblɔke] **1** *vt* **(a)** (*libérer, mettre en marche*) to free, to release; (*machine*) to unjam; *Fin* (*prix etc*) to unfreeze; **d. des fonds** to release funds, to make funds available **(b)** *Psy* **d. qn** (*ôter les complexes de*) to rid sb of his/her complexes; (*rendre moins timide*) to make sb less inhibited **2** *vi F* (*être fou*) to be off one's rocker; (*raconter n'importe quoi*) to talk nonsense; **son grand-père est vieux, il commence à d.** his grandfather is old and going gaga

débobiner [debɔbine] *vt* (*rouleau, fil etc*) to unwind

débogage [debɔgaʒ] *nm Ordinat* debugging

déboguer [debɔge] *vt Ordinat* to debug

débogueur [debɔgœr] *nm Ordinat* debugger

déboires [debwar] *nmpl* (*déceptions*) disappointments; (*ennuis*) problems, trouble; **essuyer bien des déboires** to suffer many disappointments *or* setbacks

déboisement [debwazmɑ̃] *nm* deforestation

déboiser [debwaze] *vt* (*région*) to deforest, to clear; *F* **se faire d. la colline** to have one's hair cropped

déboîtement [debwatmɑ̃] *nm* **(a)** (*d'un membre, d'une articulation*) dislocation **(b)** *Aut* pulling out

déboîter [debwate] **1** *vt* **(a)** *Tech* (*tuyau etc*) to disconnect, to uncouple **(b)** (*articulation, membre*) to dislocate **(c)** (*montre etc*) to remove from its case **2** *vi Aut* to pull out **3 se déboîter** *vpr* (*d'une cheville etc*) to become dislocated; **se d. l'épaule/le genou** to dislocate one's shoulder/knee, to put one's shoulder/knee out

débonder [debɔ̃de] **1** *vt* (*lavabo*) to unblock; (*fût*) to unbung; *Fig Vieilli* **d. son cœur** to pour out one's heart **2 se débonder** *vpr* (*d'un lavabo etc*) to unblock; (*d'un fût*) to become unbunged; *Fig Vieilli* (*d'une personne*) to pour out one's heart

débonnaire [debɔnɛr] *adj* goodnatured, easy-going; **répondre d'un ton d.** to answer goodnaturedly

débordant [debɔrdɑ̃] *adj* **(a)** (*expansif*) overflowing, brimming over **(de** with); **d. de santé** bursting with health; **avoir une imagination débordante** to be brimful of imagination; **faire preuve d'un enthousiasme/d'une activité débordant(e)** to be brimming *or* bubbling over with enthusiasm/brimful of energy **(b)** (*qui dépasse*) projecting, protruding; (*en se chevauchant*) overlapping

débordé [debɔrde] *adj* **(a)** (*de travail etc*) snowed under **(b) drap d.** (*pour préparer le lit*) turned-back sheet; (*défait*) untucked sheet; **mon lit est d.** my sheets have come untucked

débordement [debɔrdəmɑ̃] *nm* **(a)** (*d'une rivière etc*) overflowing; *Fig* (*d'enthousiasme, injures etc*) outburst, outpouring **(b) débordements** excesses, dissipation, dissolute living **(c)** *Mil* (*de l'ennemi*) outflanking

déborder [debɔrde] **1** *vi* **(a)** (*du contenu d'un verre etc*) to overflow, to brim over, to run over; **verre plein à d.** glass full to overflowing *or* to the brim; **la rivière a débordé** the river has overflowed its banks; **le lait a débordé de la casserole** the milk has boiled over; **les papiers débordent de la corbeille** the papers are spilling out of the wastepaper basket; **c'est la goutte d'eau qui fait d. le vase** it's the last straw; *TV, Rad etc* **d. sur le temps prévu** to overrun

(b) *Fig* **elle déborde de vie** she is bubbling over with *or* brimful of vitality; **d. d'imagination** to be brimful of imagination; **son cœur déborde de reconnaissance** his heart is brimming over with gratitude

2 *vt* **(a)** (*dépasser*) to project *or* extend beyond; *Mil* (*l'ennemi*) to outflank; **d. son adversaire** (*dans une course*) to overtake one's competitor; **cela déborde le cadre de mes responsabilités/de notre débat** that exceeds my responsibilities/the limits of our discussion

(b) d. (les couvertures d')un lit to untuck a bed; *Naut* **d. une embarcation** to shove off, to sheer off; **d. les avirons** to unship the oars

(c) (*enlever les bords de*) to remove the edging from; *Tech* **d. une tôle** to trim the edges of an iron plate

débotté [debɔte] *nm* **au d.** immediately, *Am* off the bat

débotter [debɔte] **1** *vt* **d. qn** to take off sb's boots **2 se débotter** *vpr* to take off one's boots

débouchage [debuʃaʒ] *nm* **(a)** (*d'un tuyau*) unblocking **(b)** (*d'une bouteille*) uncorking

débouché [debuʃe] *nm* **(a)** (*d'un passage etc*) opening; (*d'une vallée*) entrance **(b)** (*possibilité*) opening, opportunity; *Com Mktg* outlet, market; **cette formation n'offre aucun d.** the training does not lead to any career openings

déboucher [debuʃe] **1** *vt* **(a)** (*tuyau bouché etc*) to clear, to unblock

(b) (*bouteille*) to uncork, to remove the cork from

2 *vi* to emerge **(de** from), to come out **(de** of); **cet escalier débouche dans le grenier** the staircase leads to the attic; **cette rue débouche sur la place** this street runs into the square; **voilà sur quoi débouche la guerre** that's what war leads to; **ces études débouchent sur un métier intéressant** this course of study leads to a worthwhile career; **vos expériences ne débouchent sur aucun résultat** your experiments aren't leading anywhere, you're not getting any results with your experiments

3 se déboucher *vpr* (*de tuyau*) to clear, to become unblocked; **la bouteille se débouche facilement** the bottle opens easily, the cork is easily removed from the bottle

déboucheur [debuʃœr] *nm* drain clearer

débouchoir [debuʃwar] *nm* (*pour les sanitaires*) (rubber) plunger

déboucler [debukle] *vt* **(a)** (*ceinture etc*) to unbuckle **(b)** (*cheveux*) to take the curl out of

déboulé [debule] *nm* **tirer un lapin au d.** to shoot a rabbit as it bolts from cover

débouler [debule] **1** *vi* **(a)** *(tomber)* to fall head over heels **(b)** *F* *(arriver)* to turn up **(c)** *(du gibier)* to start, to bolt (from cover) **2** *vt F* **d. l'escalier** to run down the stairs

déboulonnage [debulɔnaʒ] *nm*, **déboulonnement** [debulɔnmɑ̃] *nm* **(a)** *Tech* unriveting, unbolting **(b)** *Fig (renvoi)* dismissal; **il procéda ensuite au d. systématique de ses anciens collègues** he then proceeded to systematically debunk his former colleagues

déboulonner [debulɔne] *vt* **(a)** *Tech* to unrivet, to unbolt **(b)** *Fig* to debunk; *(de son poste)* to get rid of, to kick out

débourber [deburbe] *vt* **(a)** *(étang, canal)* to clean out; **d. le vin** to draw off *or* decant wine **(b)** *(voiture etc)* to haul out of the mud

débourrer [debure] **1** *vt* **(a) d. un cheval** to break in a horse **(b) d. sa pipe** to scrape out one's pipe **2** *vi F (ne plus être saoul)* to sober up; **il n'a pas débourré depuis huit jours** he's been drunk for a week; **il ne débourre plus** he's never sober

débours [debur] *nm* expenses; *(pour services aux clients)* visitors paid out, VPO; **faire des d.** to lay out money

déboursement [debursəmɑ̃] *nm* paying out, *Fml* disbursement

débourser [deburse] *vt (argent)* to spend, to lay out, to pay, *Fml* to disburse; **sans rien d.** without spending a penny; **je suis toujours en train de d.** I'm always putting my hand in my pocket

déboussoler [debusɔle] *vt F* to disorientate, *surtout Am* to disorient; **je suis un peu déboussolée dans ce nouveau pays/dans mon nouvel appartement** I'm a bit disorientated *or* lost in this new country/my new apartment; **cette nouvelle l'a complètement déboussolé** the news completely threw him

debout [dəbu] **1** *adv* **(a)** *(chose)* upright, on end; *(personne)* standing; **mettre qch d.** to stand sth up *or* on end; **mettre les bouteilles d.** to stand the bottles up(right); **cent ans plus tard, la maison est encore d.** the house is still standing a hundred years later; **elle est d. toute la journée** she's on her feet all day; **rester d.** to stand; **places d. seulement** standing room only; **tenir d.** to be (standing) upright; **c'est si bas qu'on ne peut tenir d.** it's so low that you can't stand up straight; *Fig* **argument qui ne tient pas d.** argument that won't hold water *or* won't stand up; *Fig* **cette institution est** *ou* **tient encore d.** the institution is still in existence; **se tenir d.** to stand; **se tenir d. (sur ses pattes arrières)** *(d'un chien)* to stand on its hind legs; **se (re)mettre d.** to stand up; **conte** *ou* **histoire à dormir d.** silly *or* extravagant *or F* cock and bull story; **tous les matins je suis d. à six heures** I'm up *or* I get up at six o'clock every morning; **allons, d.!** *(hors du lit)* come on, get up!; **il va mieux, il est déjà d.** he's better, he's up *or* out of bed already

(b) *Naut* **d. à la mer** *ou* **à la lame/au vent** head on to the sea/to the wind

2 *adj* **(a)** *Jur* **magistrature d.** = public prosecutors

(b) *Naut* **vent d.** head wind

débouté [debute] *nm*, **déboutement** [debutmɑ̃] *nm Jur* nonsuit

débouter [debute] *vt Jur* to dismiss; **d. qn (de sa demande/de sa plainte)** to nonsuit sb

déboutonner [debutɔne] **1** *vt* to unbutton; *Vieilli* **rire à ventre déboutonné** to split one's sides laughing **2 se déboutonner** *vpr (d'une personne)* to undo one's buttons; *(d'une robe, d'une chemise etc)* to unbutton; *Fig (se confier)* to get it off one's chest

débraillé [debrɑje] **1** *adj (personne)* untidy, slovenly; *(tenue)* untidy, sloppy; **manières débraillées** bad manners **2** *nm* untidiness, slovenliness; **même au bureau, il est en d.** he's a sloppy dresser even at work

débrailler (se) [sədebrɑje] *vpr F* to loosen one's clothing; *Fig* **la conversation se débraille** the conversation is getting a bit out of hand

débranchement [debrɑ̃ʃmɑ̃] *nm Él* disconnection, unplugging

débrancher [debrɑ̃ʃe] *vt Él* to disconnect, to unplug

débrayage [debrɛjaʒ] *nm* **(a)** *Aut, MecE* declutching **(b)** *F (grève)* stoppage

débrayer [debrɛje] **(je débraye, je débraie) 1** *vt MecE* to throw out of gear **2** *vi* **(a)** *Aut* to release the clutch **(b)** *F (se mettre en grève)* to down tools; *(à la fin de la journée)* to down tools, to knock off

débridé [debride] *adj (passion)* unbridled; *(imagination)* vivid

débridement [debridmɑ̃] *nm* **(a)** *(d'un cheval)* unbridling **(b)** *Chir (d'une adhérence etc)* incision, slitting up; *(d'un furoncle)* lancing **(c)** *(déchaînement)* **le d. de son comportement/imagination** his unbridled behaviour/extremely vivid imagination

débrider [debride] **1** *vt* **(a)** *(cheval)* to unbridle **(b)** *Chir (adhérence etc)* to incise, to slit up; *(furoncle, plaie)* to lance **(c)** *Culin (volaille)* to untruss **2** *vi Fig* **travailler dix heures sans d.** to work ten hours at a stretch

débris [debri] *nmpl (d'un avion, une voiture)* remains, debris, wreckage; *(de verre, de bois)* splinters, fragments; **d. de métal** scrap (metal); **les d. d'une armée** the remnants of an army; **les d. de sa fortune** the remnants *or* remains of his fortune; *F* **ce n'est plus qu'un vieux d.** he's just an old wreck

débronzer [debrɔ̃ze] *vi* to lose one's tan

débrouillard, -arde [debrujar, -ard] *F* **1** *adj* resourceful, smart **2** *n* resourceful person; **c'est vraiment un d.** he's really resourceful

débrouillardise [debrujardiz] *nf* resourcefulness; **faire preuve de d.** to be resourceful

débrouiller [debruje] **1** *vt* **(a)** *(fil etc)* to unravel, to disentangle; **d. une affaire** to clear up *or* straighten out a situation; **d. une signature** to make out *or* decipher a signature

(b) *F* **d. qn** to wise sb up; **il faut le d. en anglais/en cuisine** he'll need to be taught some basic English/cooking

2 se débrouiller *vpr* to cope, to manage; *F* **qu'il se débrouille!** he'll have to manage!, he'll have to sort it out for himself!; **débrouillez-vous!** you'll just have to manage, you'll just have to sort it out for yourself; **il a un peu de mal à se d. avec son ordinateur** he's having some trouble coping with his computer; **je me débrouille en russe** I can get by in Russian; **elle s'est débrouillée pour rencontrer le directeur** she worked it so that she got to meet the director

débroussailler [debrusɑje] *vt* to clear of undergrowth; *Fig* **d. une question** to clarify a matter

débudgétisation [debydʒetizasjɔ̃] *nf* = transfer from one budget to another

débudgétiser [debydʒetize] *vt* = to transfer from one budget to another; **il faut d. l'État des dépenses de la sécurité sociale** the burden of social security should no longer be borne by the State

débusquer [debyske] *vt* to flush out (of cover)

début [deby] *nm* **(a)** *(commencement)* beginning, start; **au d.** at the start *or* beginning *or* outset; **au d. des hostilités** at the outbreak of hostilities; **au tout d., tout au d.** at the very start *or* beginning; **dès le d.** right at the start, from the outset **(de** of**)**; **je l'ai su dès le d.** I knew from the outset *or* (right) from the start *or* the beginning; **je le savais depuis le d.** I knew all along *or* from the start; **du d. à la fin** from start to finish; **appointements de d.** starting salary; **être en d. de carrière** to be at the start of one's career; *Hum* **il faut** *ou* **il y a un d. à tout** there's a first time for everything

(b) *(d'un acteur etc)* **débuts** first appearance, debut; **faire ses débuts** to make one's first appearance *or* one's début, *Am* to début; **faire ses débuts dans le monde** *(d'une jeune fille)* to come out; **société/entreprise à ses débuts** association/enterprise in its infancy

(c) *Ordinat* home; **aller au d.** *(commande)* go top

débutant, -ante [debytɑ̃, -ɑ̃t] **1** *adj* novice; **cours pour les skieurs débutants** skiing classes for beginners; **si vous êtes skieur d.** if you're learning (how) to ski; **conducteur d.** newly qualified driver **2** *n* **(a)** *(dans une matière, une discipline etc)* beginner; **cours pour grands débutants** classes for complete beginners **(b)** *Th* actor/actress making his/her début **3** *nf* **débutante** *(dans la haute société)* debutante, *F* deb

débuter [debyte] *vi* **(a)** *(commencer)* to begin, to start, to commence; **vous travaillerez ici pour d.** you'll work here to begin *or* start with; **le film débute par une séquence de meurtre** the film opens with a murder; **le concert a bien/mal débuté** the concert started well/badly, the concert got off to a good/bad start **(b)** *Cin, Th etc (de personne)* to make one's first appearance *or* one's début, *Am* to début; **mal/bien d. dans la vie** to get off to a bad/good start in life; **je débute dans le métier** I'm new to the business; **d. dans le monde** *(d'une jeune fille)* to come out; **faire d. une jeune fille dans le monde** to bring a girl out; **d. comme professeur** to start off as a teacher

déc [dek] *vi F voir* **déconner**

deçà [dəsa] **1** *prép* **en d. de qch** (on) this side of sth; **rester (très) en d. de la vérité** to be (very) short of the truth **2** *adv Arch* on this side; **d., delà** here and there, on all sides

déca [deka] *nm F (café)* decaf

décachetage [dekaʃtaʒ] *nm (d'une lettre)* unsealing, opening

décacheter [dekaʃte] *vt (conj like* **cacheter***) (lettre)* to unseal, to open

décade [dekad] *nf (période de dix jours)* period of ten days; *(période de dix ans)* decade

décadenasser [dekadnase] *vt* to unlock, to take the padlock off

décadence [dekadɑ̃s] *nf* decadence; **la d. d'une civilisation** *(processus)* the decline of a civilization; *(résultat)* the decadence of a civilization; **tomber en d.** to fall into decay; *(d'une personne)* to start to decline

décadent, -ente [dekadɑ̃, -ɑ̃t] **1** *adj* decadent **2** *n Littér, Beaux-Arts* Decadent
décadré [dekadre] *adj TV, Cin* out-of-frame
décaèdre [dekaɛdr] *Math* **1** *adj* decahedral **2** *nm* decahedron
décaféiné [dekafeine] *nm* decaffeinated (coffee); **j'achète toujours du d.** I always buy decaffeinated
décaféiner [dekafeine] *vt* to decaffeinate; **un café décaféiné** a (cup of) decaffeinated coffee
décagonal, -ale, -aux, -ales [dekagɔnal, -o] *adj Math* decagonal
décagone [dekagon] *nm Math* decagon
décaissable [dekɛsabl] *adj* (*charge*) payable
décaissement [dekɛsmɑ̃] *nm Com* (*d'une somme*) cash withdrawal *or* disbursement; **faire un d.** to make an outlay
décaisser [dekese] *vt* **(a)** (*marchandises etc*) to unpack **(b)** (*plante, arbuste*) to plant out **(c)** *Com* (*somme*) to pay (out); (*TVA*) to pay
décalage [dekalaʒ] *nm* **(a)** (*d'un instrument*) shifting the zero; (*quantité*) (amount of) shift; **le d. d'un meuble** the moving *or* shifting of a piece of furniture; **d. vers le haut** upward movement; **d. à droite/gauche** movement to the right/left **(b)** (*écart*) **le d. entre la réalité et les espoirs** the gap between reality and hopes; **d. d'opinions** difference of opinion **(c)** (*retard*) time lag; **un d. est prévu pour la date de la réunion** the meeting has been postponed
▸ **décalage**: **d. horaire** time difference; **souffrir du d. horaire** to have jet lag
décalaminage [dekalaminaʒ] *nm* (*de moteur*) decarbonizing, *F* decoking, decoke
décalaminer [dekalamine] *vt* (*moteur*) to decarbonize, *F* to decoke
décalcifiant [dekalsifjɑ̃] *adj Méd* decalcifying
décalcification [dekalsifikasjɔ̃] *nf Méd* decalcification
décalcifier [dekalsifje] *Méd* **1** *vt* to decalcify **2 se décalcifier** *vpr* to become decalcified
décalcomanie [dekalkɔmani] *nf Cér etc* (*procédé*) decal(comania); (*résultat*) decal(comania), transfer; **faire de la d.** to decal
décaler [dekale] **1** *vt* **(a)** (*meuble*) to move, to shift; (*instrument*) to shift the zero of; **d. l'heure** to alter the time, to change the time *or* the clock; **d. ses rendez-vous d'une heure** (*les avancer*) to bring one's meetings forward by an hour; (*les reculer*) to put one's meetings back by an hour; **(b)** *Tech* (*rivets*) to stagger **2 se décaler** *vpr* to move, to shift; **vous pourriez vous d. d'un rang/vers la gauche** you could move up a row/move to the left
décalitre [dekalitr] *nm* decalitre
décalogue [dekalɔg] *nm Rel* Decalogue
décalotter [dekalɔte] *vt* **(a)** *F* **d. une bouteille** to open *or* crack a bottle **(b)** *Méd* to pull back the foreskin of
décalquage [dekalkaʒ] *nm* (*de dessin*) tracing; (*par la chaleur etc*) transferring
décalque [dekalk] *nm* **(a)** (*de dessin*) tracing; (*par la chaleur etc*) transferring; **papier (à) d.** tracing paper **(b)** (*dessin*) tracing; (*image*) transfer; (*imitation*) copy
décalquer [dekalke] *vt* (*dessin*) to trace; (*par la chaleur*) (*plan, image en couleur*) to transfer
décamètre [dekamɛtr] *nm* decametre, *US* decameter
décamper [dekɑ̃pe] *vi F* to clear out *or* off; **décampez d'ici!** clear out *or* off!, get lost!; **tu vas d. et plus vite que ça!** clear off *or* clear out *or* get out! — on the double!
décan [dekɑ̃] *nm Astrol* decan
décanat [dekana] *nm* deanship
décanewton [dekanjutɔn] *nm* decanewton
décaniller [dekanije] *vi F* = **décamper**
décantation [dekɑ̃tasjɔ̃] *nf* decantation, decanting
décanter [dekɑ̃te] **1** *vt* (*vin*) to decant; *Fig* **d. ses projets** to mull over one's plans **2 se décanter** *vpr* (*de vin*) to settle; *Fig* (*de projets*) to become clearer; (*d'une situation*) to settle down, to become clearer; **laisser aux choses le temps de se d.** to give things time to settle down
décapage [dekapaʒ] *nm* (*d'un meuble etc*) stripping; (*au papier de verre*) sanding (down)
décapant [dekapɑ̃] **1** *adj* **(a) produit d.** stripper **(b)** *Fig* (*humour*) caustic, vitriolic **2** *nm* (*pour vernis, peinture*) remover, stripper
décaper [dekape] **1** *vt* **(a)** (*peinture, vernis*) to strip, to remove; *Tech* (*métal etc*) to scour, to clean; *Tech* (*objets métalliques*) to pickle, to dip; **d. un meuble au papier de verre** to sand down a piece of furniture; **d. une surface à peindre** to strip a surface for painting; **d. à la sableuse** to sand-blast **(b)** *Fig F* to shock **2** *vi Fig F* **des plaisanteries qui décapent** caustic *or* vitriolic jokes
décapeuse [dekapøz] *nf Tech* scraper
décapitation [dekapitasjɔ̃] *nf* decapitation, beheading
décapiter [dekapite] *vt* (*personne*) to decapitate, to behead; (*arbre*) to pollard; *Fig* **d. un complot/une association** to root out the ringleaders of a plot/the leaders of a society
décapode [dekapɔd] *nm* decapod
décapotable [dekapɔtabl] *Aut* **1** *adj* convertible, open-top; (*coupé*) drop-head **2** *nf* convertible, open-top
décapotage [dekapɔtaʒ] *nm* lowering the hood
décapoté [dekapɔte] *adj* open
décapoter [dekapɔte] *vt Aut* to lower the hood of
décapsulage [dekapsylaʒ] *nm* (*de bouteille*) opening
décapsuler [dekapsyle] *vt* (*bouteille*) to open, to take the top off
décapsuleur [dekapsylœr] *nm* bottle opener
décapuchonner [dekapyʃɔne] *vt* to take the top off
décarcasser (se) [sədekarkase] *vpr F* to bust a gut
décarreler [dekarle] *vt* (*surface, pièce*) to remove the tiles from
décarrer [dekare] *vi F* to get going, to hit the road
décartellisation [dekartelizasjɔ̃] *nf Écon, Hist* break-up of a cartel
décasyllabe [dekasilab] **1** *adj* decasyllabic **2** *nm* decasyllabic verse
décasyllabique [dekasilabik] *adj* decasyllabic
décathlon [dekatlɔ̃] *nm Sp* decathlon
décathlonien, -ienne [dekatlɔnjɛ̃, -jɛn] *n Sp* decathlete
décati [dekati] *adj* (*visage*) wrinkled, that has lost its freshness; (*immeuble*) shabby, rundown; **vieillard d.** decrepit old man
décatir [dekatir] **1** *vt Tex* (*étoffe*) to take the gloss *or* finish off **2 se décatir** *vpr* to lose one's freshness *or* one's beauty, to age
décauser [dekoze] *vt Belg* to malign
décavé [dekave] *adj* **(a)** *F* (*personne riche*) ruined; (*aux cartes*) cleaned out **(b)** (*visage*) drawn, pinched
décédé, -ée [desede] *adj, n surtout Admin* deceased
décéder [desede] *vi* (*conj like* **céder**, *aux* **être**) *surtout Admin* to die
décelable [deslabl] *adj* detectable
déceler [desle] *vt* (**je décèle**; **je décèlerai**) **(a)** (*découvrir*) to detect; **on a decelé des traces de pneu dans le jardin** tyre marks were found in the garden; **on décèle l'importance qu'a eue sa mère dans tous ses écrits** the importance of his mother can be detected in all his writings **(b)** (*indiquer*) to point to, to indicate; **sa voix décelait la peur** there was (a note of) fear in his voice
décélération [deselerasjɔ̃] *nf* deceleration
décélérer [deselere] *vi* to decelerate
décembre [desɑ̃br] *nm* [ⓘ**A75-6**,B-C; **B58-9**,B-C] December; **en d., au mois de d.** in (the month of) December; **le 25 d.** the 25th of December, December the 25th
décemment [desamɑ̃] *adv* **(a)** (*convenablement*) properly, *Fml* with decorum **(b)** (*correctement*) **elle parle anglais d.** her English is reasonable *or* quite good, she speaks quite decent English **(c)** (*raisonnablement*) reasonably; **d., je ne pouvais pas refuser** I could not reasonably refuse
décence [desɑ̃s] *nf* **(a)** (*bienséance*) (*de comportement*) propriety, decorum; (*d'habillement*) decency; **se tenir avec d.** to behave properly *or Fml* with decorum; **choquer la d.** to offend against decency; **des mots/un comportement qui choque(nt) la d.** offensive words/behaviour **(b)** (*tact*) decency; **il aurait dû avoir la d. de s'excuser** he ought to have had the decency to apologize **(c)** (*réserve*) decency; **parler avec d.** to speak in restrained terms
décennal, -ale, -aux, -ales [desenal, -o] *adj* decennial
décennie [deseni] *nf* decade
décent [desɑ̃] *adj* **(a)** decent; (*vêtements etc*) modest; (*comportement, attitude etc*) proper; **peu d.** indecent, unseemly **(b)** (*correct*) reasonable; **lire d'une manière décente** to read reasonably well
décentrage [desɑ̃traʒ] *nm* moving off centre
décentralisateur, -trice [desɑ̃tralizatœr, -tris] **1** *adj* decentralizing **2** *n Pol* advocate of decentralization, decentralizer
décentralisation [desɑ̃tralizasjɔ̃] *nf* decentralization; **la d. des grandes écoles est devenue nécessaire** it has become necessary to move the grandes écoles out of Paris
décentraliser [desɑ̃tralize] *vt* (*administration*) to decentralize; (*entreprise*) to move away from the capital
décentration [desɑ̃trasjɔ̃] *nf*, **décentrement** [desɑ̃trəmɑ̃] *nm Opt, Phot* decentring, throwing off centre
décentré [desɑ̃tre] *adj* off centre
décentrer [desɑ̃tre] **1** *vt* (*table, tableau*) to move off centre; *Opt, MecE etc* to put out of *or* off centre, to decentre **2 se décentrer** *vpr* to come *or* move off centre
déception [desɛpsjɔ̃] *nf* disappointment, *F* let-down; **éprouver une d.** to be disappointed; **d. sentimentale** unhappy love affair, disappointment in love

décérébrer [deserebre] *vt* to lobotomize
décernement [desɛrnəmɑ̃] *nm* (*d'un prix etc*) award
décerner [desɛrne] *vt* **(a)** (*prix etc*) to award; **d. un honneur à qn** to confer an honour on sb **(b)** *Jur* **d. un mandat d'arrêt contre qn** to issue a warrant for the arrest of sb
décès [desɛ] *nm surtout Admin* decease, (natural) death, demise; **acte de d.** death certificate; **fermé pour cause de d.** closed on account of bereavement
décevant [des(ə)vɑ̃] *adj* **(a)** (*résultat, livre, attitude etc*) disappointing **(b)** *Arch* (*mensonger*) (*apparence etc*) deceptive
décevoir [des(ə)vwar] *vt* (*conj like* **recevoir**) **(a)** to disappoint; **il m'a beaucoup déçu** I was very disappointed in him; **ce voyage m'a profondément déçu** I was very disappointed with the trip; **d. l'attente de qn** to disappoint sb, not to live up to sb's expectations **(b)** *Arch* (*tromper*) to deceive, to delude
déchaîné [deʃene] *adj* (*passion*) unrestrained, unbridled; (*spéculation*) wild; **craindre les éléments déchaînés** to fear the fury of the elements; **elle a dû faire face à une presse déchaînée** she had to face a press in full cry; **il est complètement déchaîné à l'idée de la fête** he's hyper *or* pretty worked up at the thought of the party; **être d. contre qn** to be furious with sb
déchaînement [deʃɛnmɑ̃] *nm* (*des éléments*) fury; (*des passions*) outburst; **d. de rage** outburst of fury, fit of rage; **pourquoi a-t-il fait preuve d'un tel d. contre moi?** why did he fly into a rage with me like that?; **le d. de la tempête** the breaking of the storm; **un d. de l'opinion** a great wave of public opinion
déchaîner [deʃene] **1** *vt* (*d'une personne*) (*passions, colère etc*) to arouse, to provoke; **d. l'hilarité** to provoke laughter **2 se déchaîner** *vpr* to break out; **la tempête s'est déchaînée** the storm broke; **se d. contre qn** to fly into a rage with sb
déchanter [deʃɑ̃te] *vi F* to become disillusioned
décharge [deʃarʒ] *nf* **(a)** (*tirs*) discharge, volley; **on lui a envoyé une d. de plombs pour le faire fuir** they fired a few rounds at him to scare him off; **de nombreuses décharges ont été entendues cette nuit** a lot of firing was heard last night; **d. (électrique)** electric shock; **d. d'adrénaline** rush of adrenalin

(b) *Jur* (*d'un accusé*) release, acquittal; (*d'une obligation*) discharge; **témoin à d.** witness for the defence; **dire qch à la d. de qn** to say sth in sb's defence

(c) *Fin* (tax) rebate; **porter une somme en d.** to mark a sum as paid; **d. de 50 pour cent** composition of 50p in the pound

(d) *Tech* (*sortie etc*) discharge, outlet; **tuyau de d.** wastepipe

(e) (*d'ordures*) dumping, tipping; **d. (publique)** rubbish dump, tip; **d. interdite** no dumping, tipping prohibited; **décharges sauvages** fly tipping, *Am* illegal dumping
déchargement [deʃarʒəmɑ̃] *nm* (*de bateau, cargaison etc*) unloading; (*de marchandises*) offloading, unloading
décharger [deʃarʒe] **(je déchargeai(s); n. déchargeons) 1** *vt* **(a)** (*vider*) (*comion bateau, cargaison etc*) to unload; (*marchandises*) to offload, to unload; (*d'un camion*) (*gravier*) to tip, to dump; (*réservoir etc*) to discharge, to empty; (*arme à feu*) to fire, to discharge; (*accumulateur*) to discharge; **d. son fusil sur** *ou* **contre qn** to fire one's gun at sb; *Fig* **d. sa conscience** to ease one's conscience **(de** of); **d. sa conscience auprès de qn** to unburden oneself to sb; **d. son cœur** to unburden one's heart; **d. sa colère sur qn** to vent one's anger on sb

(b) (*soulager*) (*cheval*) to relieve, to ease of part of its load; (*bateau*) to lighten; (*poutre*) to take the strain off; **d. qn d'une tâche/d'une responsabilité** to relieve sb of a task/a responsibility; *Jur* **d. qn d'une accusation** to acquit sb of a charge; **d. qn d'une dette** to discharge sb from a debt; **failli déchargé/non déchargé** discharged/undischarged bankrupt

2 *vi Typ* **encre qui décharge** ink that rubs off

3 se décharger *vpr* **(a)** (*d'une personne*) **se d. de qn/qch** to get rid of sb/sth; **se d. d'un fardeau** to put down *or* lay down a load; **se d. de qch sur qn** to shift the responsibility for sth onto sb; **se d. d'une tâche sur qn** to unload a task onto sb

(b) (*se vider*) (*d'une arme*) to go off; (*d'une pile*) to run down, to discharge; (*d'une colère*) to vent itself **(sur** on); **le fleuve se décharge dans un lac** the river flows into a lake
décharné [deʃarne] *adj* (*corps, membres etc*) emaciated; (*visage*) emaciated, gaunt; (*os*) stripped of flesh; *Fig* (*arbre*) bare; (*style*) bald
décharner [deʃarne] *vt* (*personne*) to emaciate; (*os*) to strip the flesh off
déchaussé [deʃose] *adj* **(a)** (*sans chaussures*) barefoot(ed) **(b) avoir les dents déchaussées** to have receding gums; **bâtisse aux murs déchaussés** building with unsound foundations
déchaussement [deʃosmɑ̃] *nm* (*de murs*) laying bare of foundations; **d. de dents** receding gums
déchausser [deʃose] **1** *vt* **(a)** (*enlever les chaussures à*) **d. qn** to take off sb's shoes; **d. ses skis** to take off one's skis **(b)** (*arbre*) to expose *or* (lay) bare the roots of; (*dent, fondations*) to expose **2 se déchausser** *vpr* **(a)** (*enlever ses chaussures*) to take off one's shoes **(b) ses dents se déchaussent** he has receding gums, his gums are receding
dèche [dɛʃ] *nf F* **être dans la d.** to be stony broke; **c'est la d.** I'm/we're/*etc* stony broke
déchéance [deʃeɑ̃s] *nf* **(a)** (*dégradation, chute*) (*physique*) deterioration, decline; (*morale*) downfall, ruin; **sa d. a été causée par l'alcool** drink was his downfall; **c'est la mort de son fils qui est à l'origine de sa d.** it was the death of his son which started him on the downward path **(b)** *Jur, Fin* (*de droits etc*) forfeiture; **action en d. de brevet** action for forfeiture of patent; **d. de l'autorité paternelle** loss of parental authority; **d. d'une police** expiry of a policy **(c)** *Compta* **tomber en d.** to lapse
déchet [deʃɛ] *nm* **(a) déchets** waste; **des déchets de tissu** scraps of fabric; **déchets radioactifs/industriels** radioactive/industrial waste; **déchets domestiques** household waste *or* rubbish; **déchets de métal** scrap (metal); **déchets de viande** scraps of meat **(b)** *Com* (*de poids, valeur*) loss, decrease; **il y a du d.** there is some wastage; **d. de route** loss in transit **(c)** *Péj* (*personne*) down-and-out; **un d. de la société** a social outcast
déchetterie [deʃɛtri] *nf* dump, *Br* rubbish dump, tip
déchiffonner [deʃifɔne] *vt* to smooth out the creases in
déchiffrable [deʃifrabl] *adj* (*inscription*) decipherable; (*écriture*) decipherable, legible; **code facilement d.** code that is easy to crack *or* break
déchiffrage [deʃifraʒ] *nm Mus* sight-reading
déchiffrement [deʃifrəmɑ̃] *nm* deciphering; *Ordinat* decryption; *Ordinat* **d. de données** data decryption
déchiffrer [deʃifre] **1** *vt* **(a)** (*inscription, écriture etc*) to decipher, to make out; (*message*) to decode; (*signaux*) to read, to interpret; **d. les sentiments d'une personne** to fathom *or* make out sb's feelings; **d. un mystère** to unravel a mystery **(b)** (*musique*) to read, to play at sight, to sight-read; **d. un morceau** to sight-read a piece; **je suis juste en train de d. ce morceau** I'm just learning this piece **2** *vi Mus* to sight-read
déchiffreur, -euse [deʃifrœr, -øz] *n* (*d'inscription*) decipherer; (*de message*) decoder; (*de message secret*) code-breaker; **d. de radar** radar scanner
déchiqueté [deʃikte] *adj* **(a)** (*bord*) jagged; (*littoral*) jagged, ragged; **papier à bords déchiquetés** deckle-edge paper **(b)** (*objet*) cut to bits *or* shreds; **une couverture déchiquetée** a tattered blanket
déchiqueter [deʃikte] *vt* **(je déchiquette; je déchiquetterai)** (*papier*) to cut/slash/tear into shreds; (*de machine*) to shred; (*chair*) to cut *or* tear to shreds; (*corps, poulet*) to hack to pieces
déchiqueteuse [deʃiktøz] *nf* shredder
déchiqueture [deʃiktyr] *nf* slash, long tear
déchirant [deʃirɑ̃] *adj* (*spectacle*) heartrending, harrowing; (*douleur*) agonizing; **des adieux déchirants** heartrending farewells
déchiré [deʃire] *adj* (*vêtement, couverture, Méd muscle, Fig nation etc*) torn; **être d. entre deux personnes** to be torn between two people
déchirement [deʃirmɑ̃] *nm* (*de tissu, vêtement etc*) tearing, *Fml* rending; *Méd* (*de muscle*) tearing; *Fig* (*peine*) heartbreak; **cette famille/ce parti connaît des déchirements terribles** the family/party is tearing itself apart
déchirer [deʃire] **1** *vt* **(a)** (*tissu, vêtement etc*) to tear, *Fml* to rend; (*papier*) to tear up; (*enveloppe*) to tear open; **d. qch en morceaux** to tear sth to pieces *or* bits *or* shreds

(b) *Fig* (*famille, pays*) to tear apart; **d. le cœur à qn** to break sb's heart; **des cris qui déchiraient le cœur** heartrending cries; **un cri aigu déchira le silence** a shrill scream pierced the silence; **des sons qui déchirent le tympan** ear-splitting sounds; **une toux qui déchire la poitrine** a hacking cough; **être déchiré de douleur/remords** to be racked with pain/remorse

2 se déchirer *vpr* **(a)** (*d'un tissu*) to tear; **il s'est déchiré un muscle** he's torn a muscle

(b) *Fig* **un couple qui se déchire** a couple who are tearing each other apart; **mon cœur s'est déchiré** I was heartbroken
déchirure [deʃiryr] *nf* (*dans un tissu*) tear, rent, slit, rip; (*blessure*) laceration; *Fig* (*peine, chagrin*) heartbreak; **le fait de quitter ses parents a été pour lui une véritable d.** it was

heartbreaking *or* heartrending leaving his parents; **une d. musculaire** a torn muscle

déchoir [deʃwar] *vi* (*pp* **déchu**; *pr ind* **je déchois, n. déchoyons, ils déchoient**; *p hist* **je déchus**; *fu* **je déchoirai**; *aux* **être** *or* **avoir**) **ce quartier a déchu** the area has gone down; **sa popularité déchoit** his popularity is declining; **la maison déchoit de son prestige** the firm is losing its prestige; **par ce mariage/à cause de cet emploi, il déchoit de son rang** he is marrying/the job is beneath him; **ce serait d. (que de s'abaisser à ces tâches vulgaires)** it would be demeaning (to stoop to such common tasks)

déchristianisation [dekristjanizasjɔ̃] *nf* dechristianization

déchristianiser [dekristjanize] **1** *vt* to dechristianize, to turn from Christianity **2 se déchristianiser** *vpr* to turn (away) from Christianity

déchu [deʃy] *adj* **ange d.** fallen angel; **roi d.** dethroned king; **police (d'assurance) déchue** expired (insurance) policy; **d. de la nationalité française** deprived *or* stripped of French nationality; **il est déchu de ses droits** he has been stripped of his rights

déci [desi] *nm Suisse* = decilitre of white wine

décibel [desibɛl] *nm Phys* decibel; **contrôler la puissance en décibels** to monitor the decibel level

décidé [deside] *adj* **(a)** (*fixé*) (*question etc*) settled **(b)** (*caractère, personne, manière*) determined; **d'un ton d.** in a decisive tone, decisively; **être d. à faire qch** to be determined *or* resolved to do sth, to be bent on doing sth; **elle y est bien décidée** she's quite determined *or* she has quite made up her mind to do it, she's quite bent on doing it; **elle est décidée à tout** she'll do anything

décidément [desidemɑ̃] *adv* **d. je n'ai pas de chance!** I really haven't any luck!; **d., elle est folle!** she must be mad!; **je n'ai d. pas envie de partir** I really have no desire to go, I have absolutely *or* positively no desire to go; **on ne peut d. rien faire sans que tu sois dans nos pattes** we can do absolutely nothing without you getting in our way; **je crois qu'il n'est d. bon à rien** in my opinion, he's a positive good-for-nothing

décider [deside] **1** *vt* **(a)** (*une question*) to decide, to settle; (*un voyage, une pause, la guerre etc*) to decide on; **voilà qui décide tout!** that settles it!; **d. un déménagement/une grève** to decide on a move/a strike, to decide to move/to strike; **c'est son manque de sérieux qui a décidé son renvoi** it was his casual attitude that settled the question of whether to sack him

(b) d. qn à faire qch to persuade *or* induce sb to do sth

(c) d. que + *ind* to decide that; **il fut décidé qu'on attendrait sa réponse** it was decided to wait for his reply, it was decided *or* settled that we/they/*etc* should wait for his reply

2 *vi* **(a)** (*prendre une décision*) to decide, to make *or* take a decision; **c'est moi qui décide ici** (*tu n'as rien à dire*) I'm the one who makes the decisions *or* who decides here; **je déciderai pour toi** (*si tu n'arrives pas à te décider*) I'll decide for you; *Jur* **d. en faveur du plaignant** to find for the plaintiff

(b) d. de qch to decide on sth; **c'est le patron qui doit d. de son renvoi** it's the boss who'll have to decide (on) whether or not to sack him; **un événement qui a décidé de sa carrière** an event that determined his career

(c) d. de faire qch to decide to do sth; **j'ai décidé de partir demain** I've decided to leave tomorrow

3 se décider *vpr* **(a)** (*prendre une décision*) to make up one's mind, to come to a decision; **elle n'arrive pas à se d.** she can't make up her mind; **allons, décidez-vous** come on, make up your mind; **se d. à qch** *ou* **à faire qch** to make up one's mind to do sth; **je ne peux pas me d. à le faire/le quitter** I can't bring myself to do it/to leave him; **je ne peux pas me d. au mariage/à la maternité** I can't make up my mind *or* come to a decision about getting married/having a baby, I can't decide whether to get married/have a baby; **se d. pour qn/qch** to decide on *or* in favour of sb/sth

(b) (*de problème, question*) to be decided *or* settled; **leur divorce s'est décidé très rapidement** their decision to get divorced came very quickly, they made their decision to get divorced very quickly

(c) *F* **cet engin ne se décide pas à marcher** this machine can't decide whether *or* make up its mind whether to start or not; **il ne se décide pas à faire beau** it can't decide *or* make up its mind whether to be fine or not

décideur, -euse [desidœr, -øz] *n* decision-maker

décigramme [desigram] *nm* tenth of a gram, decigramme

décilitre [desilitr] *nm* decilitre, *US* deciliter

décimal, -ale, -aux, -ales [desimal, -o] *adj* [①**A71**,2,b; **B56**,C,2] decimal

décimale [desimal] *nf* decimal

décimalisation [desimalizasjɔ̃] *nf* decimalization

décimaliser [desimalize] *vt* to decimalize

décimation [desimasjɔ̃] *nf* decimation

décimer [desime] *vt* to decimate

décimètre [desimɛtr] *nm* decimetre, *US* decimeter

décisif, -ive [desizif, -iv] *adj* **(a)** (*bataille, argument etc*) decisive; (*preuve*) conclusive; **au moment d.** at the critical *or* crucial moment; **prendre un tournant d.** to take a decisive turn **(b)** (*ton*) decisive

décision [desizjɔ̃] *nf* **(a)** (*choix*) decision; *Jur* ruling, award; **prendre/arriver à une d.** to make *or* take/to come to *or* reach a decision (**quant à, au sujet de** about); **elle a pris la d. de partir** she has decided to leave; **la d. ne m'appartient pas** it's not up to me to decide, it's not my decision; **forcer une d.** to bring matters to a head; **soumettre une question à la d. de qn** to submit a matter for sb's decision; *Sp* **faire la d.** (*d'un match*) to be the decider, to decide matters; **par d. judiciaire** by decision of the court; **d. arbitrale** arbitration ruling, decision by arbitration; **d. autonome** autonomous decision; **d. commune** joint decision; **d. d'achat** buying decision; *Jur* **d. de justice** court ruling

(b) (*détermination*) resolution, determination; **affirmer qch avec d.** to state sth decisively; **elle ne manque pas d'esprit de d.** she does not lack decisiveness

décisionnaire [desizjɔnɛr] *n* decision-maker

décisionnel, -elle [desizjɔnɛl] *adj* (*responsabilité*) decision-making; **avoir un poste d.** to have a job with decision-making responsibilities

déclamateur, -trice [deklamatœr, -tris] *n Péj* ranter, tub-thumper

déclamation [deklamasjɔ̃] *nf* **(a)** (*éloquence*) oratory, (art of) declamation; **il a une mauvaise d.** he declaims his lines badly **(b)** *Péj* (*emphase*) ranting, spouting; (*discours*) ranting *or* bombastic speech

déclamatoire [deklamatwar] *adj Péj* (*style*) declamatory, highflown; (*discours*) ranting, bombastic

déclamer [deklame] **1** *vt* **(a)** (*discours, vers*) to declaim **(b)** *Péj* **il déclame tout ce qu'il dit** he makes a performance out of everything he says **2** *vi Péj* to rant; *Litt* **d. contre qn** to rail against sb

déclarable [deklarabl] *adj* (*marchandises*) liable to duty; (*revenu*) declarable; **marchandise non d.** duty-free goods

déclarant, -ante [deklarɑ̃, -ɑ̃t] *n Jur, Admin* declarant; **d. de TVA** VAT-registered person

déclaration [deklarasjɔ̃] *nf* declaration, proclamation; (*de naissance, décès etc*) notification; *Compta* return; **d. de guerre** declaration of war; **d. de changement de domicile** notification of change of address; **d. d'accident/de vol/d'incendie** accident/theft/fire claim; **d. en douane** customs declaration; **faire une d. à la police** to make a statement to the police; **selon votre d. du …** according to your statement of the …; **le chef de l'État a une importante d. à faire** the President has an important announcement to make; **une d. de principe** a statement *or* declaration of principle; **d. d'amour** declaration of love; **il lui a fait une** *ou* **sa d.** he declared his love to her

▸ **déclaration**: **d. annuelle de résultats** annual statement of results; **d. annuelle des données sociales** PAYE and NIC return; *Ordinat* **d. de champ** field definition; **D. des droits de l'enfant** Declaration of the Rights of the Child; **D. des droits de l'homme** Declaration of Human Rights; **d. d'entrée** declaration *or* clearance inwards; **d. d'exportation** export declaration; **d. fiscale** tax return; **d. d'importation** import declaration; **d. d'impôts** tax return; *Hist* **D. d'indépendance** Declaration of Independence; *Compta* **d. de résultats** statement of results, financial statement; **d. de revenus** income tax return; **d. de sinistre** (*d'une assurance*) damage report; (*réclamation*) notice of claim, insurance claim; *Com* **d. de sortie** declaration outwards, clearance outwards; **d. sous serment** affidavit; *Com* **d. de transit** declaration of goods in transit; **d. de TVA** VAT return; *Admin* **d. d'utilité publique** = government decision that a large public works project is vital and should therefore go ahead despite public protest; **d. de valeur** declaration of value

déclaré [deklare] *adj* (*ennemi, intention etc*) declared, avowed; **un partisan d. de la peine de mort** an avowed supporter of the death penalty

déclarer [deklare] **1** *vt* (*ses intentions, désirs etc, à la douane*) to declare; (*revenus, Admin un décès, une naissance, un employé*) to register; *Ordinat* (*valeur etc*) to define; **d. son incompétence** to admit one's incompetence; *Cartes* **d. trèfle** to declare *or* call clubs; **elle a déclaré qu'elle n'en avait jamais eu connaissance** she declared that she had never known anything about it; **je déclare la séance levée** I declare the meeting closed; **d. qn roi** to declare sb king;

déclaré coupable found guilty; **déclaré coupable de vol** found guilty *or* convicted of theft; **d. la guerre à qn** to declare war on sb; **avez-vous quelque chose à d.?** have you anything to declare?; **rien à d.** nothing to declare

2 se déclarer *vpr* **(a)** *(se prononcer)* to speak one's mind; **se d. pour** *ou* **en faveur de/contre qch** to declare oneself in favour of/against sth

(b) *(faire une déclaration d'amour)* to declare one's love

(c) *(du feu, d'une maladie, d'une guerre)* to break out

(d) *(se dire)* **se d. l'auteur du méfait** to own up to the deed; **elle s'est déclarée satisfaite de l'accord passé** she declared herself satisfied with the agreement that was reached

déclassé [deklase] *adj* **(a)** *Sp (à une division inférieure etc)* relegated; *(hôtel)* downgraded **(b)** *Rail Vieilli* reclassed **(c)** *Péj (personne)* déclassé

déclassement [deklasmɑ̃] *nm* **(a)** *Sp (d'équipe de football)* relegation; *(d'hôtel)* downgrading **(b)** *(de personne)* loss of social position **(c)** *Rail Vieilli* reclassification

déclasser [deklase] *vt* **(a)** *Sp* to relegate; *(hôtel)* to downgrade **(b)** *Rail (passagers)* to transfer from one class to another **(c)** *(socialement)* to lower the social position of **(d)** *Mil (arme)* to declare obsolete; *Naut (navire de guerre)* to strike off the list **(e)** *Naut (marin)* to disrate **(f)** *(déranger) (papiers)* to put out of order

déclenchement [deklɑ̃ʃmɑ̃] *nm (d'un appareil)* starting (up), setting in motion; *(d'un mécanisme)* activation; *MecE (d'une pièce)* releasing, disengaging; *Phot* (shutter) release; **le d. de la sonnerie** the setting off of the alarm; *Fig* **le d. des protestations** the triggering (off) of protests

déclencher [deklɑ̃ʃe] *vt (appareil)* to start (up), to set in motion; *(mécanisme)* to activate, to trip; *(alarme)* to set off, to activate, to trip; *MecE (pièce)* to release, to disconnect, to disengage; *Fig (critiques, questions etc)* to trigger; *Mil* **d. une attaque** to launch an attack

déclencheur [deklɑ̃ʃœr] *nm Phot* shutter release; *MecE* trigger

déclic [deklik] *nm (mécanisme) (qui bloque)* pawl, catch; *(qui déclenche)* trigger; *(bruit)* click(ing sound); **chronomètre à d.** stopwatch; **la vue de cette photo a été pour lui un véritable d.** looking at the photo made something go click; **pour qu'il retrouve la mémoire, il suffirait d'un d.** all it would take for him to regain his memory is for something to go click

déclin [deklɛ̃] *nm (du talent, de la santé, de la vigueur, d'une civilisation, d'un art)* decline; *(de la beauté)* fading; *(du jour)* decline, close; *(de la lune)* waning; **être en d.** to be in decline, to decline; **le soleil/la lune est à** *ou* **sur son d.** the sun/moon is sinking *or* setting; **une civilisation à son d.** a civilization in decline; **au d. de sa vie** in his declining years

déclinable [deklinabl] *adj Gram* declinable

déclinaison [deklinɛzɔ̃] *nf* **(a)** *Astron (d'étoile)* declination; **d. magnétique** magnetic variation **(b)** *Gram* declension

déclinant [deklinɑ̃] *adj (lune)* waning; *(beauté, lumière)* fading; *(pouvoirs)* declining; **ses facultés déclinantes** his/her declining faculties

décliner [dekline] **1** *vi (de la lune)* to wane; *(d'une étoile, du talent, de la santé)* to decline; *(du jour)* to draw to a close; *(de la beauté)* to fade; *(de vivacité)* to decrease, to diminish; **une civilisation qui menace de d.** a civilization threatened with decline; **ses sentiments pour elle déclinent de jour en jour** his feelings for her are lessening day by day; **son intelligence décline** his/her mind is going

2 *vt* **(a)** *Fml (refuser) (offre, invitation)* to decline; *Com* **d. toute responsabilité** to accept no liability; **d. une juridiction** to refuse to acknowledge a jurisdiction

(b) *Gram* to decline

(c) *(réciter) (identité)* to state; **d. ses nom et prénoms** to state *or* give one's full name

(d) *Com* to produce; **cet imprimé est décliné dans tous les tons** the pattern is available in all shades

3 se décliner *vpr* **(a)** *Gram* to be declined

(b) *Com* to be available

déclive [dekliv] **1** *adj* sloping, inclined **2** *nf* **en d.** *(terrain, toit)* sloping

déclivité [deklivite] *nf* slope, incline, gradient, *Fml* declivity; **angle de d.** angle of gradient

décloisonnement [deklwazɔnmɑ̃] *nm* decompartmentalization

décloisonner [deklwazɔne] *vt* to decompartmentalize

déclouer [deklue] *vt* to take the nails out of

déco [deko] **1** *adj pl (abrév* **décoratifs)** **arts d.** art deco **2** *nf (abrév* **décoration)** decor, decoration; *(métier)* (interior) decorating, interior design; **j'aime beaucoup faire de la d.** I love decorating

décocher [dekɔʃe] *vt* **(a)** *(flèche)* to shoot, to let fly; **d. un coup/une ruade** to let fly with a punch/kick; **d. un coup/une ruade à qn** to hit out at/to kick sb **(b)** *Fig* **d. une remarque** to let fly with *or* fire off a comment; **d. une œillade à qn** to flash a glance at sb, to glance fleetingly at sb; **d. un sourire à qn** to flash a smile at sb

décoction [dekɔksjɔ̃] *nf* decoction

décodage [dekɔdaʒ] *nm* decoding; *(d'un code)* cracking

décoder [dekɔde] *vt* to decode; *(code)* to crack

décodeur [dekɔdœr] *nm TV, Ordinat* decoder; *Télécom* decoder, unscrambler

décoiffer [dekwafe] **1** *vt* **(a)** *(ôter le chapeau de)* **d. qn** to take off *or* remove sb's hat **(b)** *(ébouriffer)* **d. qn** to tousle sb's hair **2** *vi F Fig* **c'est un film qui décoiffe** it's an astonishing *or Sl* mind-blowing film; **ça décoiffe!** it's quite an experience, *Sl* it's mind-blowing; **je peux te dire que l'écouter parler, ça décoiffe!** listening to him talk is quite an experience, let me tell you **3 se décoiffer** *vpr* **(a)** *(se dépeigner)* to mess up one's hair **(b)** *(ôter son chapeau)* to remove one's hat

décoinçage [dekwɛ̃saʒ] *nm*, **décoincement** [dekwɛ̃smɑ̃] *nm (de pièce coincée)* loosening

décoincer [dekwɛ̃se] **(n. décoinçons; je décoinçai(s))** **1** *vt (pièce coincée)* to loosen; *F* **d. qn** to loosen sb up **2 se décoincer** *vpr F* to loosen up

décolérer [dekɔlere] *vi* **(je décolère; je décolérerai)** to calm down; **il ne décolérait pas** he was still fuming; **il n'a pas décoléré depuis huit jours** he's been angry for a week

décollage [dekɔlaʒ] *nm* **(a)** *(d'avion, de fusée, Fig d'industrie, d'économie)* takeoff **(b)** *(de timbre etc)* unsticking, ungluing

décollation [dekɔlasjɔ̃] *nm* decapitation, beheading

décollé [dekɔle] *adj* **il a les oreilles décollées** his ears stick out

décollement [dekɔlmɑ̃] *nm* **(a)** *Méd* **d. de la rétine** detachment of the retina; **d. de racines** body wave **(b)** *(de timbre etc)* unsticking, ungluing

décoller [dekɔle] **1** *vt (timbre, papier peint, affiche)* to remove; **d. une enveloppe à la vapeur** to steam open an envelope; *Fig F* **d. qn de la télé/du match de foot/de son livre** to prise *or* tear sb away from the TV/the football match/ their book

2 *vi* **(a)** *(d'un avion, une fusée, Fig un pays, une économie etc)* to take off

(b) *F (partir)* to leave, *F* to take off; **bon, on décolle?** shall we get moving?; **il ne décolle pas d'ici** he won't budge, he's staying put; **il ne décolle pas de la télé** he's glued to the TV; *Sp* **d. du peloton** to peel away from the pack

(c) *F (maigrir)* to fade away to nothing

3 se décoller *vpr (d'une enveloppe)* to come unstuck *or* undone; *Méd (de la rétine)* to become detached

décolletage [dekɔltaʒ] *nm (d'une robe) (action)* lowering of neckline; *(résultat)* neckline

décolleté [dekɔlte] **1** *adj* **robe décolletée** low-necked *or* low-cut dress; **femme décolletée** woman in a low-necked *or* low-cut dress; **tu ne trouves pas que c'est trop d.?** you don't think it's too low?; **robe décolletée dans le dos** dress cut low at the back; *Hum* **elle était décolletée jusqu'au nombril** *ou* **aux genoux** she was showing everything she'd got, she was showing a lot of cleavage

2 *nm* neck opening, neckline; **d. bateau** boat neck; **d. carré** square neck; **d. en pointe** *ou* **en V** V neck; **d. rond** round neck; **d. plongeant** plunging neckline; **en grand d.** *(en robe de soirée)* in full evening dress; **avoir un beau d.** to have a beautiful neck and shoulders; **il a jeté un œil dans mon d.** he looked down the front of my dress

décolleter [dekɔlte] **(je décollette** [dekɔlɛt]**)** **1** *vt (robe)* to cut out the neck of; **il faut te d. beaucoup plus que ça** you'll have to show much more than that; **pour son mariage, on va la d. un peu** for her wedding we'll give her a slightly lower neckline; **cette robe te décollette trop** the dress is too low(-cut) **2** se décolleter *vpr* to wear a low-necked dress

décolonisation [dekɔlɔnizasjɔ̃] *nf* decolonization

décoloniser [dekɔlɔnize] *vt* to decolonize

décolorant [dekɔlɔrɑ̃] **1** *adj* bleaching **2** *nm* bleaching agent, bleach

décoloration [dekɔlɔrasjɔ̃] *nf (d'un tissu)* discolouration, *US* discoloration, fading; *(des cheveux)* bleaching; **demander une d.** to ask for one's hair to be bleached

décolorer [dekɔlɔre] **1** *vt (tissu)* to discolour, *US* to discolor, to fade, to take the colour out of; *(cheveux)* to bleach **2 se décolorer** *vpr* to lose its colour, to fade, to bleach; **se d. les cheveux** to bleach one's hair

décombres [dekɔ̃br] *nmpl* ruins, debris

décommander [dekɔmɑ̃de] **1** *vt (réunion, dîner)* to cancel, to call off; *(invité)* to put off; *(marchandise)* to cancel (the order for) **2 se décommander** *vpr (chez le dentiste etc)* to cancel one's appointment; *(d'une invitation)* to cancel

décompacter [dekɔ̃pakte] *vt Ordinat* to uncrunch
décomplexer [dekɔ̃plɛkse] *vt F* to cure of hang-ups; **c'est le sport qui l'a décomplexé** it was sport that cured him of his hang-ups *or* that got rid of his complexes, sport made him feel better about himself
décomposable [dekɔ̃pozabl] *adj* (*texte*) that can be broken up, that can be divided into parts; (*composé*) that can be broken down
décomposé [dekɔ̃poze] *adj* (*viande, feuilles*) decomposed, rotten; *Fig* **il est arrivé complètement d.** (*par l'émotion*) he arrived quite distraught; (*par la peur*) he arrived quite terror-stricken
décomposer [dekɔ̃poze] **1** *vt* **(a)** *Phys, Ch etc* to decompose; **d. la lumière** to split light; **d. une fraction** to split up a fraction; **d. un pas de deux (en séquences)** to break down a pas de deux into separate sequences; **d. un problème** to break down a problem
(b) (*matière organique*) to decompose, to rot, to decay
(c) (*traits*) to contort, to distort; **la souffrance décomposait son visage** his/her face was drawn by suffering
2 se décomposer *vpr* **(a)** (*de corps*) to decompose, to decay; (*de viande*) to decompose, to rot; (*de feuilles*) to decompose, to rot, to decay
(b) (*du visage, des traits*) to become distorted with terror
décomposition [dekɔ̃pozisjɔ̃] *nf* **(a)** *Phys, Ch etc* decomposition; *Compta* **d. des résultats** breakdown of the results **(b)** (*de viande, feuilles*) decomposition, rotting; (*de corps*) decomposition, decay; *Fig* **la d. d'un empire** the decay of an empire **(c)** (*de traits*) distortion
décompresser [dekɔ̃prese] **1** *vt Tech* to decompress; *Ordinat* to decompress, to unbundle, to uncrunch **2** *vi Tech* to decompress; *Fig F* to unwind
décompresseur [dekɔ̃prɛsœr] *nm* decompressor
décompression [dekɔ̃prɛsjɔ̃] *nf* decompression; *Ordinat* decompression, unbundling; **avoir un accident de d.** (*d'un plongeur*) to get the bends; **robinet de d.** (*dans un moteur*) compression tap; (*dans une machine à vapeur*) petcock
décomprimer [dekɔ̃prime] *vt* to decompress
décompte [dekɔ̃t] *nm* **(a)** (*d'une somme à payer*) deduction; (*calcul*) calculation; **j'ai fait le d. de ce que vous m'avez payé et de ce que vous me devez** I've deducted what you've paid from what you owe me; *Fig Vieilli* **trouver du d.** to be disappointed **(à** in**)** **(b)** *Admin, Com* detailed account, breakdown
décompter [dekɔ̃te] **1** *vt* (*une somme d'un compte*) to deduct **2** *vi* (*d'une horloge*) to miscount (*on striking*)
déconcentration [dekɔ̃sɑ̃trasjɔ̃] *nf* **(a)** *Admin* devolution; (*d'une ville*) decongestion **(b)** *Ch* dilution
déconcentrer [dekɔ̃sɑ̃tre] **1** *vt* **(a)** *Admin* to devolve; **d. l'autorité gouvernementale** to decentralize government; **d. une ville** to decongest a city **(b) d. qn** to distract sb **2 se déconcentrer** *vpr* to lose concentration, to be distracted
déconcertant [dekɔ̃sɛrtɑ̃] *adj* disconcerting
déconcerté [dekɔ̃sɛrte] *adj* disconcerted, taken aback
déconcerter [dekɔ̃sɛrte] **1** *vt* **(a)** (*personne*) to disconcert; **il ne faut pas te laisser d. par ses questions** you mustn't let yourself be disconcerted *or F* thrown by his questions **(b)** *Litt* (*les plans de qn*) to upset, to confound, to frustrate **2 se déconcerter** *vpr* to be disconcerted, to lose one's self-assurance; **sans se d.** unabashed
déconditionnement [dekɔ̃disjɔnmɑ̃] *nm Psy* aversion therapy
déconditionner [dekɔ̃disjɔne] *vt Psy* to treat with aversion therapy; *Fig* **d. l'opinion publique** to shake up public opinion
déconfit [dekɔ̃fi] *adj* crestfallen, disheartened; **un air d.** a crestfallen look
déconfiture [dekɔ̃fityr] *nf F* (*aux élections, dans un combat etc*) defeat; (*d'une société*) collapse, failure, downfall, ruin; (*faillite*) bankruptcy, insolvency; **tomber en d.** to fail to meet one's liabilities, *F* to go under
décongélation [dekɔ̃ʒelasjɔ̃] *nf* defrosting, thawing
décongeler [dekɔ̃ʒle] *vt* **(je décongèle; je décongèlerai)** to defrost, to thaw
décongestif, -ive [dekɔ̃ʒɛstif, -iv] *adj, nm Méd* decongestant
décongestionner [dekɔ̃ʒɛstjɔne] *vt* **(a)** *Méd* (*poumons etc*) to relieve congestion in, to clear; **d. un malade** to relieve the congestion in *or* clear a patient's lungs **(b)** *Fig* (*rue*) to relieve congestion in; (*aéroport, université*) to relieve congestion at; (*administration*) to decentralize
déconnecter [dekɔnɛkte] *vt Él* (*fil etc*) to disconnect; *Fig* **les années qu'il a passées en Inde l'ont complètement déconnecté de la vie en Europe** the years he spent in India have put him completely out of touch with what is happening in Europe; **déconnecté de la réalité** out of touch with the real world
déconner [dekɔne] *vi F* (*en parlant*) to talk rubbish *or* drivel; (*en agissant*) to muck *or* fool around, to act the fool, *très F* to bugger around; (*d'une machine*) to act *or* play up; **tu déconnes complètement** you're talking a load of rubbish; **tu sais très bien qu'il a dit ça pour d.** you know very well he said it just as a leg-pull; **sans d.** *ou* **sans déc., c'était super** no fooling, it was great, it was great I kid you not; **sans d.!, sans déc!** (*en réponse*) you're joking!, no kidding!; **la télé déconne** the TV's acting *or* playing up, the TV's on the blink; **la voiture s'est mise à d.** the car's started to act *or* play up, the car's gone on the blink
déconneur, -euse [dekɔnœr, -øz] *n* (*en parlant*) person who talks rubbish *or* drivel; (*en agissant*) idiot, clown; **ce présentateur est un d.** that presenter talks a load of rubbish *or* drivel; **être (un) d. à l'école** to muck *or* fool around at school
déconseiller [dekɔ̃seje] *vt* to advise against; **d. qch à qn** to advise sb against sth; **d. à qn de faire qch** to advise sb against doing sth; **déconseillé à qn** (*d'un livre etc*) unsuitable for sb; **un livre à d. aux jeunes** an unsuitable book for young people; **c'est fortement déconseillé** it's extremely inadvisable *or* unwise; **il est déconseillé de laisser ce produit à la portée des enfants** this product should be kept out of children's reach
déconsidération [dekɔ̃siderasjɔ̃] *nf* disrepute, discredit; **tomber en d.** *ou* **dans la d.** to fall into disrepute
déconsidérer [dekɔ̃sidere] **(je déconsidère; je déconsidérerai) 1** *vt* to bring into disrepute **2 se déconsidérer** *vpr* (*d'une entreprise, d'une marque*) to fall into disrepute; (*d'une personne*) to lose respect; **elle s'est définitivement déconsidérée au sein de l'entreprise** she has lost all respect in the company
déconsignation [dekɔ̃siɲasjɔ̃] *nf Com* deconsignment
déconsigner [dekɔ̃siɲe] *vt* (*valise*) to collect from the left-luggage office; (*bouteille etc*) to return the deposit on
décontamination [dekɔ̃taminasjɔ̃] *nf* decontamination
décontaminer [dekɔ̃tamine] *vt* to decontaminate
décontenancé [dekɔ̃tnɑ̃se] *adj* disconcerted, confused
décontenancer [dekɔ̃tnɑ̃se] **(je décontenançai(s); n. décontenançons) 1** *vt* to disconcert, to confuse **2 se décontenancer** *vpr* to become disconcerted *or* confused
décontract [dekɔ̃trakt] *adj inv F* = **décontracté**; **en (tenue) d.** in casual dress, casually dressed
décontracté [dekɔ̃trakte] *adj* (*ambiance*) relaxed; (*attitude, individu*) relaxed, laid-back, casual; (*vêtement*) casual; **en tenue décontractée** in casual dress, casually dressed
décontracter [dekɔ̃trakte] **1** *vt* to relax **2 se décontracter** *vpr* to relax
décontraction [dekɔ̃traksjɔ̃] *nf* relaxation; **sa d. me sidère!** I'm amazed at how relaxed he is *or* laid back he is!; **amener un peu de d. dans les rapports avec ses employés** to make relations with one's employees a little more relaxed *or* less tense
déconvenue [dekɔ̃vny] *nf* mortification, disappointment; **quelle ne fut pas ma d. quand ...** I was mortified when ...; **quelle d.!** how mortifying!
décor [dekɔr] *nm* **(a)** (*d'une maison etc*) decor; **d. de table** table decoration, table centre **(b)** *Th, Cin, TV* set; **décors** sets, scenery; **en d. naturel** on location; *Aut F* **rentrer** *ou* **aller/envoyer qn dans le d.** to go/send sb off the road **(c)** (*environnement*) (*charmant, sordide*) surroundings; (*de montagnes, d'usines*) background, backdrop; *Fig* **il aurait besoin d'un changement** *ou* **de changer de d.** he needs a change (of scene)
décorateur, -trice [dekɔratœr, -tris] *n* **(a)** (*d'intérieur*) (interior) decorator **(b)** *Th* set *or* stage designer, scenic designer; (*peintre*) scene painter
décoratif, -ive [dekɔratif, -iv] *adj* decorative, ornamental; (*arbre*) ornamental; **arts décoratifs** decorative arts; *Péj* **n'avoir qu'un rôle d.** to have a purely decorative role
décoration [dekɔrasjɔ̃] *nf* **(a)** (*d'une maison, d'un appartement*) (interior) decoration, decor; (*d'une église*) ornamentation, embellishment; *TV etc* scenery design; **décorations de Noël** Christmas decorations; **d. florale** floral arrangement; **faire de la d. (d'intérieur)** to do interior decorating **(b)** (*médaille*) decoration, medal; **porter une d. à la boutonnière** to wear a decoration in one's buttonhole; **remise de décorations** investiture
décorer [dekɔre] *vt* **(a)** (*maison, appartement etc*) to decorate; **cette église est magnifiquement décorée de vitraux anciens** the church has some magnificent old stained glass **(b)** (*médailler*) to decorate **(de** with**)**
décorner [dekɔrne] *vt* **(a)** (*bovins etc*) to dehorn, to poll; *F* **un vent à d. les bœufs** a howling gale **(b)** (*page*) to smooth out
décorticage [dekɔrtikaʒ] *nm* (*de crevettes, noisettes*) shelling; (*de riz*) husking; (*d'orge*) hulling; *Fig* (*d'un texte, d'un auteur*) detailed analysis

décortication [dekɔrtikasjɔ̃] *nf (d'un arbre)* barking; *Méd (d'un organe)* decortication

décortiquer [dekɔrtike] *vt (crevettes, noisettes)* to shell; *(riz)* to husk; *(orge)* to hull; *(arbre)* to bark; *Méd (organe)* to decorticate; *Fig (texte)* to analyse in detail

décorum [dekɔrɔm] *nm* decorum, propriety; **observer le d.** to observe the proprieties

décote [dekɔt] *nf (de devises)* drop, fall (in value); *(d'impôts)* reduction; **d. de TVA** VAT rebate

découcher [dekuʃe] *vi (ne pas rentrer)* to stay out all night

découdre [dekudr] *(conj like* **coudre***)* **1** *vt (vêtement)* to unpick, to unstitch; *(ourlet)* to rip; *(bouton)* to take off, to remove **2** *vi* **en d.** to fight; **être toujours prêt à en d.** to be always ready for a fight **3 se découdre** *vpr (d'une poche, d'un ourlet)* to come unstitched *or* undone; *(d'un bouton)* to come off

découler [dekule] *vi* to follow (**de** from); **il en découle que ...** it follows that ...; **il découle de cette réunion que nous devrons ...** the outcome *or* upshot of the meeting is that we will have to ...; **ces licenciements découlent de la situation de crise** the layoffs are attributable to the crisis, the crisis is the reason for the layoffs

découpage [dekupaʒ] *nm* **(a)** *(de gâteau etc)* cutting up; *(de viande)* carving; *Couture (de patrons etc)* cutting out; *(d'une plaque de métal)* punching, stamping, cutting; *(du cuir etc)* punching, pinking; *Ordinat (de fichier, d'image)* splitting; *Pol* **d. électoral** division into constituencies; **matrices pour d.** cutting dies **(b)** *(résultat)* cutout; **cahier de découpages** scrap book; **faire du d.** *ou* **des découpages** to do some cutting out; **un enfant occupé à ses découpages** a child busy with his/her scraps **(c)** *Cin (scénario)* **d. (technique)** shooting script

découpe [dekup] *nf (dans un vêtement)* cut-out

découpé [dekupe] *adj* **(a)** *(sommet, montagne)* jagged; *(côte)* jagged, indented **(b)** *Bot* denticulate

découper [dekupe] **1** *vt (gâteau etc)* to cut up; *(viande)* to carve; *(plan, papier)* to cut out; *(métaux)* to stamp (out), to punch, to cut; *(cuir)* to punch, to pink; *Ordinat (fichier)* to split; *(disque dur)* to partition; **couteau à d.** carving knife; **scie à d.** fretsaw; **d. un article dans un journal** to cut an article out of a newspaper; **d. un texte en plusieurs parties** to divide a text into several parts; *Cin* **d. un scénario** to make a shooting script

2 se découper *vpr* to stand out, to show up (**sur** on, against); **son ombre se découpait sur le sol** his shadow stood out sharply *or* was etched on the ground; **sa silhouette se découpait dans le soleil** the sunlight threw his silhouette into sharp relief

découpeur, -euse [dekupœr, -øz] **1** *n (personne) (de viande)* carver; *Cin* cutter; **d. en cuir** leather cutter **2** *nf Tex* **découpeuse** *(machine)* shearing *or* cutting *or* pinking machine

découplé [dekuple] *adj* **bien d.** *(personne)* well built, muscular

découpler [dekuple] *vt (chiens de meute)* to slip, to uncouple; *(chevaux, wagons)* to uncouple

découpure [dekupyr] *nf* **(a)** *(action)* cutting out; *(avec poinçon)* punching, stamping (out); *(avec cisailles)* pinking; *(décoration)* fretwork **(b)** *(résultat) (par poinçonnage)* stamping **(c)** *(du littoral)* indentation; *Bot (dans une feuille)* denticulation

découragé [dekuraʒe] *adj* discouraged, disheartened

décourageant [dekuraʒɑ̃] *adj (nouvelle, situation, travail)* discouraging, disheartening; **vous êtes d.** *(vous n'y arriverez jamais)* you're hopeless; *(vous me découragez)* you're disheartening

découragement [dekuraʒmɑ̃] *nm* discouragement; **il n'éprouve plus que du d.** he feels totally discouraged *or* disheartened

décourager [dekuraʒe] **(je décourageai(s); n. décourageons)** **1** *vt* **(a)** *(démoraliser)* to discourage, to dishearten; **il est découragé au moindre échec** he loses heart *or* becomes discouraged at the slightest setback; **se laisser d.** to (let oneself) be discouraged *or* disheartened **(b)** *(dissuader)* to discourage, to deter; **d. qn de (faire) qch** to discourage *or* deter sb from (doing) sth, to put sb off (doing) sth; **un ton qui décourage tout humour** a tone that discourages any attempt at humour **2 se décourager** *vpr* to become discouraged *or* disheartened, to lose heart; **ne vous découragez pas!** don't get discouraged!, don't lose heart!; **il se décourage tout de suite** he gives up easily

découronner [dekurɔne] *vt (roi etc)* to dethrone, to depose; *Fig (héros etc)* to debunk; *(arbre)* to pollard

décours [dekur] *nm* **(a)** *(de la lune)* waning; **lune à son d.** moon on the wane **(b)** *Méd (de la fièvre)* abatement; *(d'une maladie)* decline

décousu [dekuzy] **1** *adj (ourlet etc)* undone, unstitched; *Fig (mots, idées etc)* disjointed, incoherent; *(remarques, conversation)* rambling, desultory; *(travail)* unmethodical **2** *nm (de mots, d'idées etc)* disjointedness; *(d'une conversation)* desultoriness

découvert [dekuvɛr] **1** *adj* uncovered; *(région etc)* open; *(ville etc)* exposed, unprotected; **une robe qui laisse les épaules découvertes** a dress that leaves the shoulders bare; **dormir d.** to sleep without any covers; **la tête découverte** bareheaded; **à visage d.** open, frankly; **coin de ciel d.** bit of blue sky

2 *nm* **(a)** *Fin* **d. (bancaire)** overdraft; **demander à bénéficier d'un d.** to apply for an overdraft; **avoir un d.** *ou* **être à d. de 2000 francs** *(autorisé)* to have a 2,000 franc overdraft; *(non autorisé)* to be overdrawn by 2,000 francs; *Fin* **être à d.** to be overdrawn; **compte à d.** overdrawn account; **mettre un compte à d.** to overdraw an account; **votre compte est à d. de 2000 francs** your account is overdrawn by 2,000 francs; **crédit à d.** unsecured credit; *Bourse* **vendre à d.** to go a bear, to sell short

(b) agir/parler à d. to act/speak openly; **mettre qch à d.** to expose sth to view; **s'avancer à d.** to move forward without cover

découverte [dekuvɛrt] *nf* **(a)** *(d'un pays etc)* discovery; *Mil* scouting, reconnoitring; **aller** *ou* **partir à la d.** to explore, to go exploring; **aller à la d. de qch** to go in search of sth; **faire la d. de qch** to discover sth **(b)** *(scientifique, d'une intrigue etc)* discovery; *Hum* **ce n'est pas une d.!** that's nothing new! **(c)** *TV, Cin etc* backdrop, backing; **d. photographique** photomural

découvreur, -euse [dekuvrœr, -øz] *n* discoverer

découvrir [dekuvrir] *(conj like* **couvrir***)* **1** *vt* **(a)** *(trouver, mettre à jour l'existence de) (virus, pénicilline, trésor, coupable etc)* to discover; *(erreur)* to discover, to detect; *(crime, intrigue)* to discover, to bring to light; *(secret, complot, intrigue)* to uncover; **il ne parvint pas à d. qui elle était** he couldn't find out who she was; **d. des qualités insoupçonnées en** *ou* **chez qn** to discover unsuspected qualities in sb; **de là-haut, on découvrait un paysage magnifique** from the top we had a magnificent view of the scenery

(b) *(apprendre à connaître) (la musique classique etc)* to discover; *(personne)* to get to know; **il découvrit alors l'enfer du goulag** he experienced the hell of the gulag camps

(c) *(enlever ce qui couvre)* to reveal; *(statue)* to uncover, to unveil; **il m'a découvert ses projets** he disclosed *or* revealed his plans to me; **la mer a découvert des kilomètres de sable blanc en se retirant** the ebbing tide uncovered *or* revealed *or* exposed miles of white sand; **d. un pot** to take the lid off a pot; **d. une maison** to take the roof off a house; **un décolleté qui découvre les épaules** a neck-line that leaves the shoulders bare; **sa chemise ouverte découvre sa poitrine velue** his open-necked shirt reveals *or* exposes his hairy chest; **d. ses dents** to bare *or* show one's teeth; **d. son cœur** to open one's heart, to bare one's soul; *Échecs* **d. une pièce** to uncover a piece; *Cartes* **d. son jeu** to show one's hand; *Mil* **d. la frontière/ses arrières** to leave the border/the rear exposed *or* open to attack

(d) *(apercevoir)* to perceive, to discern; *Naut (terre)* to sight; **craindre d'être découvert** to fear discovery *or* detection

2 *vi (d'un récif)* to uncover (at low tide)

3 se découvrir *vpr* **(a)** *(enlever son chapeau)* to take off one's hat; *(se déshabiller)* to take off some of one's clothing; **se d. la tête** to bare one's head; **le malade s'est découvert pendant la nuit** the patient's bedclothes fell off during the night; **en avril, ne te découvre pas d'un fil** ne'er cast a clout till May be out

(b) *Escrime, Mil* to expose oneself

(c) *(du ciel)* to clear

(d) *(apparaître)* to come into sight

(e) *(se révéler)* to come to light; **la vérité se découvre toujours** truth will out

(f) *(se trouver)* to discover; **se d. des parents éloignés** to discover some distant relatives; **il s'est découvert une passion pour le jardinage** he discovered (that) he had a passion for gardening

décrassage [dekrasaʒ] *nm*, **décrassement** [dekrasmɑ̃] *nm* cleaning, scouring; *Fig* **mon anglais aurait besoin d'un bon d.** my English needs brushing up

décrasser [dekrase] **1** *vt* to clean, to scour; *(chaudière)* to scale, to clean; *(canon d'une arme)* to remove the fouling from; *Fig F* **d. qn** to knock the corners *or* rough edges off sb **2 se décrasser** *vpr (se nettoyer)* to clean oneself up; *Fig (en courant etc)* to clean out the system; *Fig F (devenir plus sophistiqué)* to lose one's rough edges

décrédibiliser [dekredibilize] *vt* **toutes ces manœuvres l'ont complètement décrédibilisé auprès du public** he has lost all credibility with the public because of his manoeuvrings
décrément [dekremã] *nm Ordinat* decrement
décrêpage [dekrepaʒ] *nm* (*de cheveux*) straightening
décrêper [dekrepe] *vt* (*les cheveux*) to straighten
décrépir [dekrepir] **1** *vt* (*mur etc*) to strip the plaster *or* roughcast off **2 se décrépir** *vpr* (*de mur etc*) to flake
décrépit [dekrepi] *adj* (*maison, mur*) decrepit, dilapidated, tumbledown; (*personne*) decrepit
décrépitude [dekrepityd] *nf* decrepitude, decrepit condition
decrescendo [dekreʃɛndo] *Mus* **1** *adv* diminuendo, decrescendo; *Fig* **sa carrière va d.** his career's going downhill **2** *nm* diminuendo, decrescendo
décret [dekrɛ] *nm* decree, order; *Admin* **d. présidentiel** = Order in Council; *Fig* **c'est le d. de la mode** fashion decrees it
décréter [dekrete] *vt* (**je décrète**; **je décréterai**) (*état d'urgence, nomination*) to decree, to order; (*loi*) to enact; **d. de faire qch** to vow to do sth; **il a décrété qu'il n'irait plus jamais sur la Côte d'Azur** he has vowed that he will never go to the Cote d'Azur again; **quand elle décrète quelque chose** when she vows to do something; *Jur* **d. un moratoire** to declare a moratorium
décret-loi, *pl* **décrets-lois** *nm* = Order in Council
décrier [dekrije] *vt* to disparage, to run down; **il a été beaucoup décrié** a lot of people have disparaged him *or* run him down; **ce genre de pratique est assez décrié** a lot of people deplore this kind of thing
décrire [dekrir] *vt* (*conj like* **écrire**) **(a)** (*représenter*) to describe, to depict **(b)** *Math* (*courbe, cercle*) to describe, to draw; **la route décrit une courbe** the road bends; **les oiseaux décrivaient de grands cercles** the birds were circling
décrispation [dekrispasjɔ̃] *nf Pol* détente; **climat de d.** atmosphere of détente
décrisper [dekrispe] **1** *vt* (*personne*) to relax, to make less tense; **d. l'atmosphère** to lighten the atmosphere, to make the atmosphere less tense; **d. la situation** to ease the situation, to make the situation less tense; **la plaisanterie l'a décrispé** the joke made him relax *or* calmed him down **2 se décrisper** *vpr* to relax, *F* to lighten up
décrochage [dekrɔʃaʒ] *nm* (*de wagon*) uncoupling, disconnection; (*d'un tableau*) removal, taking down; *Rad, TV* (*d'émission*) blackout; **diffuser en d.** to broadcast its own programmes; *Rad, TV* **le d. a lieu à 19 h** regional programming begins at 7 pm
décrochement [dekrɔʃmã] *nm Géol* thrust
décrocher [dekrɔʃe] **1** *vt* **(a)** (*détacher*) (*manteau d'une patère, rideaux, tableau etc*) to take down; (*wagons etc*) to uncouple, to disconnect; (*fermoir*) to undo; *Tél* (*combiné*) to pick *or* lift up; **d. le téléphone** (*pour ne pas être dérangé*) to take the phone off the hook; (*pour répondre*) to pick up the phone; **décrochez** lift the receiver; **le téléphone est décroché** the phone's off the hook

(b) (*recevoir*) (*poste, prix, contrat etc*) to land; **d. la timbale** to hit the jackpot; **d. la croix** to receive a military decoration

2 *vi* **(a)** *Tél* to pick up the phone; (*pour ne pas être dérangé*) to take the phone off the hook

(b) *Mil* to beat a retreat, to withdraw

(c) *Fig F* (*ne plus se concentrer*) to switch off; **au bout de trois heures de réunion, je décroche** I tend to switch off after three hours in a meeting; **si cet élève décroche, il est perdu** if this pupil fails to keep up, he won't have a chance; **il commence souvent de nouvelles activités mais il décroche très vite** he often starts new activities but loses interest very quickly

(d) *F* (*arrêter de se droguer*) to kick the habit; **ça fait trois mois qu'il a décroché** he's been clean for three months

3 se décrocher *vpr* to come unhooked; **la médaille s'est décrochée** the medal has come unpinned; **se d. la mâchoire** to dislocate one's jaw; *F* **bâiller à se d. la mâchoire** to yawn one's head off
décrocheur, -euse [dekrɔʃœr, -øz] *n Can* dropout
décroisement [dekrwazmã] *nm* uncrossing
décroiser [dekrwaze] *vt* (*ses jambes etc*) to uncross
décroissance [dekrwasãs] *nf* (*de population*) decrease, decline
décroissant [dekrwasã] *adj* decreasing; **par ordre d.** in descending order
décroissement [dekrwasmã] *nm* (*de la lune*) waning; (*des jours*) shortening
décroît [dekrwa] *nm* **la lune est sur** *ou* **dans son d.** the moon is in its last quarter
décroître [dekrwatr] *vi* (*prp* **décroissant**; *pp* **décru**; *pr ind* **il décroît, ils décroissent**; *p hist* **il décrut**; *fu* **il décroîtra**) (*de force, population, nombre etc*) to decrease, to decline, to diminish; **les jours commencent à d.** the days are beginning to draw in *or* get shorter; **la lune décroît** the moon is on the wane; **l'intensité de son amour/de la lumière décroît** her love/the light is becoming less intense; **les eaux décroissent** the water level is dropping; **aller (en) décroissant** to be decreasing, to grow gradually less
décrottage [dekrɔtaʒ] *nm* (*de bottes etc*) cleaning
décrotter [dekrɔte] *vt* (*bottes etc*) to clean, to remove the mud from; (*semelles*) to scrape; *Fig F* **d. qn** to knock the rough edges off sb, to knock sb into shape; **il a vraiment fallu le d.** he had to have the rough edges knocked off, he had to be knocked into shape
décrottoir [dekrɔtwar] *nm* shoe scraper; **tapis d.** (wire) door mat
décrue [dekry] *nf* **(a)** (*de rivière etc*) fall, drop in level; **la d. des eaux** the drop in the water level **(b)** (*en nombre etc*) decrease, decline, fall
décryptage [dekriptaʒ] *nm* deciphering; (*de signaux*) decoding
décrypter [dekripte] *vt* to decipher
déçu [desy] *adj* disappointed; *Fig Iron* **elle ne va pas être déçue (du voyage)** she's got another think coming; *Fig Iron* **je ne suis pas d. du voyage!** a fine state of affairs!
déculottée [dekylɔte] *nf F* hammering
déculotter [dekylɔte] **1** *vt* **d. qn** (*enlever son slip*) to take sb's panties/underpants off; (*enlever son pantalon*) to take sb's trousers off, *F Vieilli* to debag sb **2 se déculotter** *vpr* (*enlever son slip*) to take one's panties/underpants off; (*enlever son pantalon*) to let down *or* to drop one's trousers; *Fig F* to grovel (**devant, pour** to)
déculpabilisation [dekylpabilizasjɔ̃] *nf* **la d. de l'avortement** removing the guilt surrounding abortion; **la d. des malades atteints du sida** removing the guilt feelings of AIDS victims
déculpabiliser [dekylpabilize] **1** *vt* **d. qn** to stop sb feeling guilty (**de qch** about sth); **d. la contraception** to take the guilt out of (using) contraception, to remove the aura of guilt surrounding contraception **2 se déculpabiliser** *vpr* to get rid of one's guilt feelings, to stop feeling guilty
déculturation [dekyltyrasjɔ̃] *nf* loss of culture
décuple [dekypl] **1** *adj* tenfold; **le prix de leur maison est d. de la nôtre** their house cost ten times as much as ours **2** *nm* tenfold increase
décuplement [dekypləmã] *nm* multiplication by ten; *Fig* quantum leap
décupler [dekyple] **1** *vt* to increase *or* multiply tenfold; *Fig* **la peur décuplait mon allure** fear quickened my pace (until I was almost running); **la douleur décupla ses forces** the pain gave him a surge of strength; **sa joie a été décuplée quand il a su que tu venais aussi** he was ecstatic when he found out you were coming too **2** *vi* to increase tenfold
dédaignable [dedɛɲabl] *adj* worthy of disdain; **cette somme n'est pas d.** this is a not inconsiderable sum; **cette offre n'est pas d.** it is not an offer to be sniffed at
dédaigner [dedeɲe] *vt* (*offre, proposition etc*) to turn up one's nose at, to sniff at, *Fml* to disdain, to scorn; (*injure, conseil*) to disregard; **d. qn** to treat sb with disdain *or* contempt, *Fml* to scorn sb; *Litt* **elle dédaigna de répondre** she disdained to reply; **cette proposition n'est pas à d.** it is not a proposal to be sniffed at; **il ne dédaigne pas un cigare de temps en temps** he is not averse to the occasional cigar, *F* he doesn't say no to the odd cigar
dédaigneusement [dedɛɲøzmã] *adv* disdainfully, contemptuously, scornfully
dédaigneux, -euse [dedɛɲø, -øz] *adj* disdainful, contemptuous, scornful (**de** of)
dédain [dedɛ̃] *nm* disdain, contempt, scorn (**de, pour** for); **avec d.** disdainfully, contemptuously, scornfully, with disdain *or* contempt; **témoigner du d. à qn** to show contempt for sb; **avoir le d. de** *ou* **pour qch** to despise sth; **elle n'a que du d. pour lui** she has nothing but contempt for him; **considérer qn avec d.** to look down on sb
Dédale [dedal] *nm Myth* Daedalus
dédale [dedal] *nm* (*de rues*) labyrinth, maze; **perdu dans le d. de ses réflexions** lost in the maze of one's thoughts
dedans [dədã] **1** *adv* inside; **la lettre est d.** the letter is inside; **une voiture nous est rentrée d., nous nous sommes fait rentrer d.** a car smashed into us; *F* **je vais lui rentrer d.** I'll smash his face in; *Fig F* **mettre** *ou* **ficher qn d.** (*le tromper*) to take sb for a ride; *Fig F* **donner d.** to fall into the trap; **marcher les pieds en d.** to be pigeon-toed; **en d.** (on the) inside, within; **il n'était pas si calme en d.** inwardly, he was not so calm; **en d. de** within; **de d.** from within; **il y a vraiment quelqu'un qui vit là-d.?** is somebody actually living there?; *F* **c'est un bon film mais il y a trop de violence d.** it's a good film but there's too much violence in it

2 *nm* (*d'une maison, d'une boîte*) inside, interior; (*d'une personne*) innermost heart; **agir du d.** to act on the *or* from inside; **au-d. et au-dehors** inside and out; **au-d.** (on the) inside, within; **au(-)d. de** inside, within; **elle le savait au(-)d. d'elle** inwardly, she knew it

dédicace [dedikas] *nf* **(a)** (*de livre etc*) dedication **(b)** *Rel* (*d'un édifice etc*) dedication, consecration

dédicacer [dedikase] *vt* (**je dédicaçai(s)**; **n. dédicaçons**) (*livre*) to write a dedication in; **d. son dernier livre** to sign copies of one's latest book; **livre dédicacé par l'auteur** signed copy of a book

dédicatoire [dedikatwar] *adj* dedicatory

dédié [dedje] *adj Ordinat* dedicated

dédier [dedje] *vt* **(a)** (*livre, film etc*) to dedicate **(b)** *Rel* (*édifice etc*) to dedicate, to consecrate

dédire (se) [sədedir] *vpr* (*conj like* **dire** *except pr ind* **v. v. dédisez**) **se d. de** (*déclaration*) to retract, to withdraw; (*accusation*) to withdraw; **se d. d'une promesse** to go back on one's word

dédit [dedi] *nm* (*de déclaration*) retraction, withdrawal; (*d'accusation*) withdrawal; (*de promesse*) breaking; (*pour rupture de contrat etc*) forfeit, penalty; **en cas de d., vous devrez payer 10% de la somme initiale** in the event of cancellation you will be required to pay 10% of the initial sum

dédommagement [dedɔmaʒmɑ̃] *nm* compensation; **50 000 francs de d.** 50,000 francs (in) compensation; **recevoir une somme en d. de qch** to receive a sum as *or* in compensation for sth; **en d. de la peine que je vous ai causée** to make up for the pain I caused you; **c'est un d. à** *ou* **pour votre patience** it's in recognition of your patience; **d. de non accès à bord** denied boarding compensation

dédommager [dedɔmaʒe] (**je dédommageai(s)**; **n. dédommageons**) *vt* to compensate, *Fml* to indemnify; **d. qn de qch** to compensate sb for sth; **comment pourrai-je te d.?** how can I ever repay you?; **d. qn d'une perte** to compensate sb for a loss, to make good sb's loss; **pour me d., il m'a invité au restaurant** he took me out to dinner to make up for it; **tiens, dédommage-toi avec ce billet** here, take it out of this

dédoré [dedɔre] *adj* tarnished, with the gilt rubbed off

dédorer [dedɔre] *vt* to remove the gilt from

dédouanage [dedwanaʒ] *nm* clearance (through customs)

dédouanement [dedwanmɑ̃] *nm* clearance through customs; *Fig* **le d. de la conscience** salving one's conscience

dédouaner [dedwane] **1** *vt* to clear (through customs), to take out of bond; **d. ses bagages** to clear one's luggage through customs; *Fig* **d. qn** to clear sb **2 se dédouaner** *vpr Fig* to clear one's name

dédoublage [dedublaʒ] *nm* **(a)** (*d'alcool*) diluting **(b)** (*de manteau etc*) removing the lining

dédoublement [dedubləmɑ̃] *nm* **(a)** (*d'une étoffe pliée etc*) opening out **(b)** *Psy* dividing *or* splitting into two; **d. de la personnalité** split personality **(c)** *Rail* **d. d'un train** running a relief train

dédoubler [deduble] **1** *vt* **(a)** (*étoffe pliée etc*) to open out; **d. les rangs** to form single file **(b)** (*partager*) to divide *or* split into two **(c) d. un train** to run a relief train **(d)** (*vêtement*) to remove the lining of **2 se dédoubler** *vpr* **(a)** (*d'une couverture*) to unfold **(b)** (*se diviser*) to divide, to split; (*cheveux, ongle*) to split; *Psy* to have a split personality; *F* **je ne peux pas me d.** I can't be in two places at once

dédramatisation [dedramatizasjɔ̃] *nf* making less alarming *or* dramatic

dédramatiser [dedramatize] *vt* to make less alarming *or* dramatic

déductibilité [dedyktibilite] *nf* deductibility

déductible [dedyktibl] *adj* deductible; **d. des impôts** tax deductible

déductif, -ive [dedyktif, -iv] *adj Phil* deductive

déduction [dedyksjɔ̃] *nf* **(a)** *Com etc* deduction, allowance; **faire d. des sommes payées d'avance** to deduct *or* allow for sums paid in advance; **d. fiscale** tax allowance; **d. forfaitaire** (*d'impôts*) standard allowance; **sous d. de 10%** less 10%; **sans d.** terms net cash; **d. faite des frais d'essence** after deduction of petrol costs **(b)** (*raisonnement*) deduction, inference

déduire [dedɥir] (*conj like* **conduire**) *vt* **(a)** (*enlever*) to deduct; **d. 5%** to take off *or* deduct 5%, to allow a deduction of 5% **(b)** (*conclure*) to deduce, to infer; **de là, on peut d. que …** from this it may be deduced that …

déesse [deɛs] *nf* goddess

défaillance [defajɑ̃s] *nf* **(a)** (*faiblesse*) (*morale*) failing, lapse; (*physique*) deficiency; **cet enfant a de sérieuses défaillances en lecture** the child has serious reading difficulties; **les défaillances des dirigeants de l'entreprise** management's failings; **sans d.** without flinching; **courage sans d.** unflagging *or* unfailing courage; **travailler sans d.** to work tirelessly; **d. de mémoire** memory lapse; **d. cardiaque** heart failure; **d. mécanique** mechanical failure; **la machine a eu une d.** the machine developed a fault; **d. d'entreprise** business failure **(b)** (*évanouissement*) fainting fit; **avoir une d.** (*s'évanouir*) to faint; (*faiblir*) to flag; **soudain, ce fut la d.** (*il faiblit*) all of a sudden, he flagged **(c)** *Jur* default(ing)

défaillant, -ante [defajɑ̃, -ɑ̃t] **1** *adj* **(a)** (*force, mémoire*) failing; (*santé*) declining; (*cœur*) weak; **d. de fatigue** exhausted **(b)** (*qui s'évanouit*) (*voix, personne*) faint; **il avançait d'un pas d.** he walked with a faltering step; **elle était défaillante de bonheur** she was giddy with delight **(c)** *Jur* defaulting **2** *n Jur* defaulter, absconder

défaillir [defajir] *vi* (*prp* **défaillant**; *pp* **défailli**; *pr ind* **il défaille, n. défaillons**; *impf* **je défaillais**; *p hist* **je défaillis**; *fu* **je défaillirai** *ou parfois* **je défaillerai**) **(a)** (*faiblir*) to become feeble; **sa mémoire/sa force commence à d.** his memory/strength is beginning to fail; **à cette nouvelle, son cœur défaillit** his heart sank at the news; **j'accomplirai le travail sans d.** I'll do the job without flinching **(b)** (*s'évanouir*) to faint; **d. de faim** to feel faint with hunger

défaire [defɛr] (*conj like* **faire**) **1** *vt* **(a)** (*nœud*) to undo, to untie; (*paquet*) to undo, to unwrap; (*valise*) to unpack; (*ourlet*) to unpick; (*robe etc*) to undo; (*fermeture éclair*) to unzip; **d. le lit** (*enlever les draps*) to strip the bed; (*pour se coucher*) to turn down the bed; (*le mettre en désordre*) to rumple the bedclothes; **d. ses cheveux** to let one's hair down

(b) (*détruire*) (*puzzle*) to take apart, to take to pieces; (*traité*) to cancel, to annul; (*alliance, mariage*) to break up; *F* **d. un marché** to cancel a deal

(c) *Litt* (*battre*) (*armée etc*) to defeat; (*personne*) to get the better of

(d) *Litt* **d. qn de qn/qch** to rid sb of sb/sth

(e) (*miner*) to devastate; **cette nouvelle l'a complètement défait** he was completely devastated by the news

2 se défaire *vpr* **(a)** (*de vêtements, d'un nœud*) to come undone; (*de cheveux*) to come down; (*de choses jointes les unes aux autres*) to come apart; (*de mariage*) to break up, to fall apart; (*de viande à la cuisson*) to fall apart

(b) se d. de qn/qch to get rid of sb/sth; **se d. de ses marchandises** to get rid of *or* sell off one's stock; **je ne veux pas m'en d.** I don't want to part with it; **se d. d'une mauvaise habitude** to get out of *or* break oneself of a bad habit

(c) (*s'altérer*) (*de personne, visage*) to become haggard *or* drawn

défait [defɛ] *adj* **(a)** (*traits, visage*) drawn, haggard; **la mine défaite** with a haggard expression; **il est arrivé à l'hôpital, complètement d.** he arrived at the hospital in a state of collapse; **elle était quelque peu défaite après l'échec de son livre** she was somewhat defeated after her book's lack of success **(b)** (*cheveux, apparence*) dishevelled **(c)** (*armée etc*) defeated

défaite [defɛt] *nf* defeat

défaitisme [defɛtism] *nm* defeatism

défaitiste [defɛtist] *adj, n* defeatist

défalcation [defalkasjɔ̃] *nf* deduction; **d. faite des frais** after deduction of expenses

défalquer [defalke] *vt* (*une somme d'un total*) to deduct

défatiguant [defatigɑ̃] **1** *adj* relaxing **2** *nm* muscle relaxant

défatiguer [defatige] **1** *vt* to relax; **un bon bain chaud va vous d.** a hot bath will relax you *or* help you (to) unwind **2 se défatiguer** *vpr* to unwind; **se d. les yeux** to rest one's eyes; **j'ai besoin de me d. la tête** I need to clear my mind

défaufiler [defofile] *vt Couture* to remove the tacks from

défausser[1] [defose] *vt* (*clé, tournevis etc*) to straighten (out)

défausser (se)[2] [sədefose] *vpr Cartes* to discard; **se d. à cœur** to discard one's hearts

défaut [defo] *nm* **(a)** (*imperfection*) (*d'une personne*) fault, shortcoming; (*de pierre précieuse, métal, verre, tissu*) flaw; (*d'une machine*) defect; **chacun a ses défauts** everyone has his faults; **la curiosité est un vilain d.** ≈ curiosity killed the cat; **c'est là son moindre d.** that's the least of his faults; **les défauts d'une explication/d'une théorie** the flaws in *or* shortcomings of an explanation/a theory; **avoir un d.** (*d'une machine*) to be defective; **il y a un d. de fonctionnement** it isn't working properly; **cette école n'a qu'un d.** the school has only one drawback; **sans d.** faultless, flawless; **mettre les chiens en d.** to throw the hounds off the scent; *Fig* **mettre qn en d.** to put sb on the spot; **prendre qn en d.** to catch sb napping; **être en d.** to be wrong; **d. de prononciation** speech impediment; **d. de fabrication** manufacturing fault *or* defects; *Com* **défauts apparents** visible defects; *Com* **défauts cachés** hidden defects

(b) (*manque*) lack; *Jur* default; **il y a, chez cet enfant, un d. de concentration** the child lacks concentration; **le temps me fait d.** I haven't got the time; **le courage lui a fait d.** his courage failed him; **les provisions font d.** there is a shortage of supplies, supplies are short; **les bonnes places font d.** there is a shortage of good jobs, good jobs are hard to come by; **la place fait d. chez moi** there is a shortage of space *or* space is in short supply at my place; **l'argent fait d. en ce moment** money is tight at the moment; **l'argent lui fait cruellement d.** he is very short of money; **le bon sens lui fait cruellement d.** he is sadly lacking in common sense; **sa** *ou* **la mémoire lui fait d.** he can't remember; **si ma mémoire ne me fait pas d.** if I'm not mistaken, if memory serves me right; **pécher par d.** to sin by omission, to commit a sin of omission; **ou à d., …** or, failing that, …; **à d. de qch** for lack of sth; **à d. de salaire intéressant, elle a au moins l'avantage de travailler près de chez elle** she might not have a very good salary but at least she works close to home; **le d. de l'épaule** the hollow of the shoulder; *Fig* **j'ai trouvé le d. de la cuirasse** *ou* **de l'armure** I've found the chink in his/*etc* armour; **frapper au d. de la cuirasse** *ou* **de l'armure** to aim for the chink in his/*etc* armour; *Jur* **faire d.** to fail to appear, to default; *Jur* **jugement par d.** judgment by default; **d. de paiement** failure to pay, non-payment, default on payment; **d. de livraison** default on delivery; *Banque* **chèque refusé pour cause de d. de provision** cheque refused by the bank because of insufficient funds; **'d. de provision'** (*tampon sur chèque*) ≈ refer to drawer

(c) *Math* **total approché par d.** total rounded down; *Ordinat* **lecteur/clavier par d.** default drive/keyboard

défaveur [defavœr] *nf* disfavour, *US* disfavor, discredit; **être en d.** to be in disfavour **(auprès de** with); **il faut vraiment être très désagréable pour s'attirer la d. de mon grand-père** you have to be really unpleasant for my grandfather to take against you

défavorable [defavɔrabl] *adj* unfavourable, *US* unfavorable **(à** to); **être d. à qn/qch** to be against sb/sth; **les conditions (nous) sont défavorables** conditions are against us

défavorablement [defavɔrabləmɑ̃] *adv* unfavourably, *US* unfavorably

défavorisé [defavɔrize] *adj* (*enfant, pays*) underprivileged; **candidat d.** candidate at a disadvantage; **les milieux les plus défavorisés** the underprivileged classes

défavoriser [defavɔrize] *vt* to put at a disadvantage, to disadvantage; **cette nouvelle loi défavorisera les couples non mariés** this new law will put unmarried couples at a disadvantage *or* will be unfair to unmarried couples; **d. les candidates** to favour male candidates over female ones; **le climat du désert défavorise les soldats occidentaux** Western soldiers are at a disadvantage in desert climates; **il est défavorisé par sa timidité** his shyness puts him at a disadvantage; **dans son testament, il a défavorisé sa femme par rapport à ses enfants** he favoured his children over his wife in his will

défécation [defekasjɔ̃] *nf Physiol* defecation

défectif, -ive [defɛktif, -iv] *adj* (*verbe etc*) defective

défection [defɛksjɔ̃] *nf Pol* defection; (*de partisan, soldat, allié*) defection, desertion; **je ne m'attendais pas à sa d.** I did not expect him to defect; **au moment de son divorce, il a assisté à la d. de tous ses amis** all his friends deserted him when he got divorced; **elle a été très déçue par les défections qui se sont produites la veille de la réception** she was very disappointed by the number of people who cancelled the day before the party; **à mon mariage, il n'y a eu qu'une seule d.** only one person didn't attend my wedding; **en cas de d.** in the event of cancellation; **faire d.** to desert, to defect, *F* to rat

défectueusement [defɛktɥøzmɑ̃] *adv* defectively

défectueux, -euse [defɛktɥø, -øz] *adj* defective, faulty

défectuosité [defɛktɥozite] *nf* **(a)** (*défaut*) defect, flaw **(b)** (*imperfection*) defectiveness

défendable [defɑ̃dabl] *adj* (*position, point de vue, théorie etc*) defensible; **ses théories ne sont absolument pas défendables** his theories are totally indefensible

défendeur, -deresse [defɑ̃dœr, -drɛs] *n Jur* defendant

défendre [defɑ̃dr] **1** *vt* **(a)** (*lutter pour ou contre, soutenir*) (*théorie, politique, la mémoire de qn, Jur accusé*) to defend; (*cause*) to defend, to champion; (*droit, opinion*) to defend, to uphold; (*ses amis, ses idées*) to defend, to stand up for **(contre** against); **il sait d. ses opinions** he can hold his own; **cette organisation défend les droits de l'homme** this organization defends *or* champions human rights; *Sp* **d. son titre de champion du monde/les couleurs de …** to defend one's world championship title/the colours of …

(b) (*protéger*) to defend, to guard **(contre** against, from); *Tennis* (*service*) to defend; **d. son pays contre l'envahisseur** to defend one's country against the invader; **la propriété est défendue par deux chiens** the estate is guarded by two dogs; **d. ses intérêts** to protect one's interests; **il a fait cela pour d. mes intérêts** he did it to defend *or* in defence of my interests; *Fig* **d. son bifteck** to look after number one; **de lourdes tentures défendaient la pièce contre les regards indiscrets** heavy curtains shielded the room from prying eyes; **l'isolation défend la pièce du froid** the insulation shields the room from cold; **les fourrures défendent les esquimaux du froid** fur clothing protects the Eskimos from the cold; *Fb* **Durant défendra les buts de l'équipe d'Aix** Durant will be the goalkeeper for Aix

(c) (*interdire*) to forbid, to prohibit; **fruit(s) défendu(s)** forbidden fruit; **d. qch à qn** to forbid sb sth; **son père lui a défendu l'entrée de sa maison** his father has forbidden him to set foot over the doorstep; **d. sa porte à qn** to close one's door to sb; **ce médicament est défendu aux enfants** this medicine must not be given to children; **il défend qu'on passe par là** he forbids anyone to go that way; **une herse de fer défendait l'entrée de la crypte** an iron portcullis barred the entrance to the crypt

(d) d. à qn de faire qch to forbid sb to do sth; **je te défends d'y aller** I forbid you to go; **son père lui défend de sortir le soir** his father does not allow him to go out at night; **il est défendu de fumer dans les classes** smoking is prohibited in the classrooms; **il m'est défendu de fumer** I'm not allowed *or* I'm forbidden to smoke; **il est défendu de parler au chauffeur** please do not speak to the driver

2 se défendre *vpr* **(a)** (*se protéger*) to defend oneself; **se d. de** *ou* **contre qch** to defend oneself against sth, to protect *or* shield oneself from *or* against sth; **se d. des agressions** to defend oneself against attack; **se d. avec un couteau** to defend oneself with a knife; **se d. de la pluie** to shelter from the rain; **se d. du froid** to protect oneself from the cold; **se d. contre la critique** to defend oneself against criticism; **se d. des tentations** to steer clear of temptation

(b) *F* (*se débrouiller*) **je me défends** I'm holding my own, I'm getting by *or* along; **je me défends en anglais/en tennis** I can hold my own *or* I can get by *or* along in English/at tennis; **il se défend bien en affaires** he's a good businessman; **il ne se défend pas mal avec son ordinateur** he's getting on quite well with his computer

(c) (*nier*) **se d. de faire/d'avoir fait qch** to deny doing sth

(d) (*se justifier*) **cette attitude peut se d.** this attitude is justifiable; **c'est une idée qui se défend** there is something to be said for the idea

(e) (*s'empêcher*) (*the pron is the indirect object*) **se d. de faire qch** to refrain from doing sth; **on ne peut se d. de l'aimer** you can't help liking him; **elle ne peut se d. d'un certain sentiment de culpabilité** she can't help feeling guilty; **se d. tout plaisir/toute gourmandise** to deny oneself all pleasure/sweet things

défenestration [defənɛstrasjɔ̃] *nf* defenestration

défenestrer [defənɛstre] *vt* to defenestrate

défense¹ [defɑ̃s] *nf* **(a)** (*soutien*) (*d'une politique, une théorie, une opinion etc*), *Jur* defence, *US* defense; **prendre la d. de qn** to defend sb; **sans d.** defenceless; **la meilleure d., c'est l'attaque** attack is the best form of defence; *Jur* **la parole est à la d.** the defence may now speak; *Jur* **assurer la d. de qn** to defend sb; **qu'avez-vous à dire pour votre d.?** what do you have to say in your defence?

(b) (*protection*), *Mil, Sp* defence, *US* defense; **combattre pour la d. de son pays** to fight in defence of one's country; **ligne de d.** line of defence; **moyen de d.** means of defence; **d. nationale** national defence; **d. côtière/aérienne** coastal/air defence; **d. contre avions** anti-aircraft defence; **d. passive** civil defence; *Physiol* **la d. de l'organisme** the organism's defence mechanisms; *Physiol* **défenses immunitaires** immune defences; **d. des consommateurs** consumer protection; *Mktg* **d. contre-offensive** counteroffensive defence; *Mktg* **d. mobile** mobile defence; *Mktg* **d. préventive** pre-emptive defence; *Jur* **légitime d.** self-defence

(c) (*interdiction*) **d. d'entrer/de fumer/de stationner** no entry *or* admittance/smoking/parking; **d. d'afficher** no bills; **c'est un secret, d. d'en parler à ton père!** it's a secret so don't go telling your father about it!; *Vieilli* **faire d. à qn de faire qch** to forbid sb to do sth

défense² *nf* (*d'éléphant, de sanglier etc*) tusk

défenseur [defɑ̃sœr] *nm* **(a)** (*d'un enfant, d'une ville etc*) protector, defender; (*d'une cause*) supporter, upholder; *Sp* defender **(b)** *Jur* counsel for the defence; **qui est son d.?** who's defending him?

défensif, -ive [defɑ̃sif, -iv] **1** *adj* defensive **2** *nf* **défensive** defensive; **être** *ou* **se tenir sur la défensive** to be on the defensive

défensivement [defɑ̃sivmɑ̃] *adv* defensively

déféquer [defeke] *vi* (**je défèque, n. déféquons; je déféquerai**) *Physiol* to defecate

déférence [deferɑ̃s] *nf* deference (**pour** for); **par d. pour …** in *or* out of deference to …

déférent [deferɑ̃] *adj* (*manière etc*) deferential

déférer [defere] (**je défère; je déférerai**) **1** *vt* (**a**) *Jur* (*une affaire devant un tribunal*) to submit, to refer; **d. qn à la justice** to hand sb over *or* give sb up to the police (**b**) *Arch* (*honneur*) to confer, to bestow (**à** on) **2** *vi* **d. à qn** to defer to sb; **d. aux ordres de qn** to comply with sb's orders; **d. à une demande** to accede to a request

déferlant, -ante [defɛrlɑ̃, -ɑ̃t] *adj, nf* (**vague**) **déferlante** breaker, beachcomber

déferlement [defɛrləmɑ̃] *nm* (*de vagues*) breaking; *Fig* (*d'enthousiasme, de violence, de racisme*) wave; **d. de colère** fit of anger; **d. de touristes/journalistes** invasion of tourists/reporters; **le d. des touristes sur la Côte d'Azur en juillet** the July invasion of the Côte d'Azur by tourists, the descent of tourists on the Côte d'Azur in July

déferler [defɛrle] **1** *vt* (*drapeau, Naut voile*) to unfurl **2** *vi* (*de vagues*) to break; **la foule déferle dans la rue** the crowd is surging down the street; **la joie/la colère/une rumeur déferlait dans toute la ville** joy/anger/a rumour spread through the entire city; **les vacanciers déferlent sur les routes** holiday-makers are taking to the roads in droves

défi [defi] *nm* (**a**) challenge; **lancer** *ou* **jeter un d. à qn** to challenge sb; **relever un d.** to take up a challenge; **la jeunesse a besoin de d.** young people need a challenge (**b**) (*provocation*) defiance; **mettre qn au d. de faire qch** to defy *or* dare sb to do sth; **avec un sourire de d.** with a smile of defiance, with a defiant smile; **d'un air de d.** defiantly, with a defiant air *or* an air of defiance; **son attitude est un d. à votre autorité** his attitude is a challenge to your authority; **son numéro est un d. aux lois de la pesanteur** his act defies the laws of gravity

défiance [defjɑ̃s] *nf* mistrust, distrust, suspicion, wariness; **inspirer** *ou* **éveiller la d.** to arouse suspicion; **mettre qn en d.** to make sb wary; *Pol* **motion de d.** motion of no confidence; **d. de soi-même** diffidence, lack of self-confidence

défiant [defjɑ̃] *adj* mistrustful, distrustful, cautious, wary

défibrillateur [defibrijatœr] *nm Méd* defibrillator

défibrillation [defibrijasjɔ̃] *nf Méd* defibrillation

déficeler [defisle] (*conj like* **ficeler**) **1** *vt* (*paquet etc*) to untie, to undo **2 se déficeler** *vpr* to come untied *or* undone

déficience [defisjɑ̃s] *nf* deficiency; **d. intellectuelle** mental deficiency; **d.** (**alimentaire**) malnutrition; **d. musculaire** muscle deficiency; **d. immunologique** immune deficiency; **d. en vitamine B** vitamin B deficiency

déficient, -iente [defisjɑ̃, -jɑ̃t] **1** *adj* deficient; (*muscle*) wasted, atrophied, deficient; (*raisonnement, théorie*) weak; **intelligence déficiente** (*insuffisance*) mental deficiency; **son intelligence déficiente, ses difficultés à se déplacer me faisaient de la peine** it upset me to see how he'd declined mentally and found it difficult to get about; **enfant d.** (*mentalement*) mentally deficient child; (*physiquement*) physically handicapped *or esp Am* challenged child **2** *n* **d. moteur** person with motor deficiency; **d. mental** person who is mentally deficient; **les déficients visuels** the visually impaired *or esp Am* challenged

déficit [defisit] *nm Fin* deficit; **d. budgétaire/commercial** budget/trade deficit; *Compta* **d. reportable** loss carry forward; **d. psychologique/mental** psychological/mental deficiency; **être en d.** to show a deficit; **combler un d.** to make good a deficit

déficitaire [defisitɛr] *adj* (*entreprise*) loss-making, unprofitable; (*compte*) showing a debit balance; (*budget etc*) showing a deficit; **être d.** (*d'un compte*) to be in debit; (*d'un budget, d'une entreprise*) to be in deficit; *Agr* **récolte d.** short crop

défier [defje] **1** *vt* (**a**) (*provoquer*) (*dans une lutte etc*) to challenge; **d. qn au combat/aux échecs** to challenge sb to a fight/to a game of chess

(**b**) (*inciter*) to defy; **je vous défie de faire mieux** I defy you to do better

(**c**) (*braver*) (*danger, mort, balles*) to brave, to face; (*la police*) to taunt; (*la presse*) to confront; **il ne craint pas de d. l'autorité paternelle** he's not afraid to stand up to his father

(**d**) (*résister à*) **d. l'imagination** to defy the imagination; **le spectacle défie toute description** the sight defies *or* is beyond description; **des prix qui défient toute concurrence** unbeatable prices

2 se défier *vpr Fml* **se d. de qn/qch** to mistrust *or* distrust sb/sth; **se d. de soi-même** to be diffident

défigurement [defigyrmɑ̃] *nm* (*d'une personne*) disfigurement; (*d'une statue*) defacement; (*de la vérité, du sens*) distortion

défigurer [defigyre] *vt* (*personne, paysage*) to disfigure; (*statue*) to deface; (*la vérité, sens*) to twist, to distort; (*la pensée, les intentions de qn*) to misrepresent; **l'acné la défigure** her acne disfigures her face; **d. un texte** (*d'un acteur*) to ruin a script

défilé [defile] *nm* (**a**) *Géog* defile, (mountain) pass (**b**) (*file*) parade, procession; *Mil* march past; *Av* flypast; (*de souvenirs, d'idées*) series; **un d. ininterrompu de touristes** an endless stream of tourists

▶ **défilé**: *Av* **d. aérien** flypast; **d. de mode** fashion show *or* parade

défilement [defil(ə)mɑ̃] *nm Ordinat* scrolling

défiler[1] [defile] **1** *vt* (*perles, collier*) to unstring, to unthread **2 se défiler** *vpr* (**a**) (*de perles etc*) to come unstrung (**b**) *Mil* **se d. du feu de l'adversaire** to take cover from enemy fire (**c**) *F* (*se dérober*) to slope off

défiler[2] *vi* (*passer en colonne*) to walk in procession; *Mil* to march past; **les manifestants défilent depuis ce matin** the demonstrators have been marching *or* trooping past since this morning; **des centaines de voitures défilent vers la côte** hundreds of cars are streaming towards the coast; **les images défilaient devant nos yeux** the pictures passed before our eyes; **les souvenirs défilaient dans sa mémoire** the memories came thick and fast; **le paysage défile à toute vitesse** the countryside is speeding past; *Mil* **d. en colonne par deux** to file off in twos; **faire d. une bande/une bobine de film** to run a tape/reel of film; *Ordinat* **faire d. un document** to scroll a document; *Ordinat* **d. vers le bas** to scroll down; *Ordinat* **d. vers le haut** to scroll up

défini [defini] *adj* (**a**) (*précis*) clearly defined; **mot bien/mal d.** well-/badly-defined word; **un travail bien d.** a clearly defined piece of work; *Ordinat* **d. par l'utilisateur** user-defined; *Ordinat* **pouvant être d. par l'utilisateur** user-definable (**b**) [①**A6-8; B3-4,2**] *Gram* definite; **passé d.** past definite, preterite, past historic

définir [definir] *vt* (*conditions, mot etc*) to define; **c'est difficile à d.** it's difficult to define; **il faut d. le poste** we'll have to define what the job entails, we'll have to draw up a job description; **comment vous définissez-vous?** how would you describe yourself?

définissable [definisabl] *adj* definable

définitif, -ive [definitif, -iv] *adj* (**a**) (*résolution, jugement, version etc*) final, definitive; (*argument*) definitive; **la biographie définitive de Proust** the definitive biography of Proust; **une séparation définitive** a permanent separation; **nommé à titre d.** permanently appointed; **ma décision est définitive** my decision is final; **veuillez noter la fermeture définitive du magasin** please note that the shop has closed down (**b**) **en définitive** when all is said and done

définition [definisjɔ̃] *nf* (**a**) (*d'un mot, de conditions etc*) definition; (*de mots croisés*) clue; **par d.** by definition; **d. de poste** job description (**b**) *TV* **télévision à haute d.** high definition television

définitivement [definitivmɑ̃] *adv* (*décider qch*) definitely; (*partir, s'installer*) for good; (*nommé*) permanently

défiscalisation [defiskalizasjɔ̃] *nf* removal *or* lifting of taxes

défiscaliser [defiskalize] *vt* to remove *or* lift the tax on

déflagration [deflagrasjɔ̃] *nf* combustion

déflagrer [deflagre] *vi* to combust

déflation [deflasjɔ̃] *nf Écon* deflation

déflationniste [deflasjɔnist] *Écon* **1** *adj* deflationary **2** *n* deflationist

déflecteur [deflɛktœr] *nm Aut etc* (*sur vitre*) deflector, quarterlight; **d. de faisceau** beam deflector; **d. de ventilateur** cowl, cowling

défleuraison [deflœrɛzɔ̃] *nf* falling of blossom

défleurir [deflœrir] **1** *vi* (*d'arbre etc*) to lose its blossom **2** *vt* (*plante*) to take the flowers off

déflexion [deflɛksjɔ̃] *nf* deflection

défloraison [deflɔrɛzɔ̃] *nf* = **défleuraison**

défloration [deflɔrasjɔ̃] *nf* (*d'une vierge*) deflowering

déflorer [deflɔre] *vt* (**a**) (*vierge*) to deflower (**b**) *Fig* (*révéler*) (*nouvelle*) to announce; (*secret*) to give away

défoliant [defɔljɑ̃] *nm Agr* defoliant

défoliation [defɔljasjɔ̃] *nf* defoliation

défonçage [defɔ̃saʒ] *nm* (*d'une boîte, une porte etc*) smashing in; (*d'un mur*) knocking down

défonce [defɔ̃s] *nf F* (*par la drogue*) trip; **être en pleine d.** to be on a trip

défoncé [defɔ̃se] *adj* (**a**) (*déterioré*) (*porte*) bashed in; (*fauteuil*) battered; **un matelas d.** a mattress with all the stuffing hanging out; **chemin d.** rough *or* bumpy road (**b**) *F* (*qui a pris de la drogue*) high, stoned

défoncement [defɔ̃smɑ̃] *nm* = **défonçage**
défoncer [defɔ̃se] **(je défonçai(s); n. défonçons) 1** *vt (boîte, porte etc)* to smash in, to bash in; *(mur etc)* to knock down; *(tonneau, bateau)* to stave in; *(route)* to break up, to cut up **2 se défoncer** *vpr F* **(a)** *(avec de la drogue)* to get high **(b)** *(faire un grand effort)* to sweat blood; **il s'est défoncé pour que tu aies ta voiture à temps** he sweated blood *or Sl* bust a gut so you would get your car back in time
déforestation [defɔrɛstasjɔ̃] *nf* deforestation
déformant [defɔrmɑ̃] *adj* distorting
déformation [defɔrmasjɔ̃] *nf (d'un membre)* deformation; *(d'un visage, de la vérité, Phot d'une image)* distortion; *(des faits, de la réalité)* distortion, misrepresentation; *(de la pensée)* misrepresentation; *(de vêtement, chaussure)* stretching out of shape; *(de métal)* buckling; *(de bois, Fig de l'esprit)* warping; **avoir une d. du pied** to have a deformed foot; **à cause de la d. de vos chaussures** because your shoes are all stretched out of shape; **il fume tellement qu'il souffre d'une d. du goût** he smokes so much that he's ruined his palate; **c'est son métier de psychanalyste qui conduit à cette d. de l'esprit chez lui** it's being a psychoanalyst that has warped his mind; **en tenant de tels propos, tu fais vraiment preuve d'une d. d'esprit inquiétante** you really must be warped to a disquieting extent to say things like that
▶ **déformation**: **d. professionnelle** = habits acquired through doing the type of work one does; **elle est professeur, c'est donc par d. professionnelle qu'elle répète tout tout le temps** it must be because she's a teacher that she repeats things all the time; **il fait de la d. professionnelle** he's like that because of his job
déformer [defɔrme] **1** *vt (membre)* to deform; *(vêtement, chaussure)* to stretch out of shape; *(métal)* to buckle; *(bois)* to warp; *(traits, vérité, Phot image)* to distort; *(réalité, faits)* to distort, to misrepresent; **visage/corps déformé par la douleur/la vieillesse** face/body distorted by *or* with pain/ with old age; **chaussée déformée** *(sur panneau)* uneven road surface; **d. la pensée de l'auteur** to misrepresent the author's thoughts; **je n'accepte pas que vous déformiez ce que j'ai dit** I won't have you twisting what I said; **il est déformé par son métier** his job has had an effect on him, he's like that because of what he does

2 se déformer *vpr* to get out of shape; *(de bois)* to warp; *(de métal)* to buckle; **ma vision des choses se déforme** I'm not seeing things straight
défoulement [defulmɑ̃] *nm Psy F* letting off steam; **avoir besoin de d.** to need to let off steam; **frapper les gens n'est pas un d.** hitting people is no way to let off steam; **laisser aux enfants des moments de d.** to give children time to let off steam; *F* **séance de d.** bitch session
défouler [defule] **1** *vt Psy* to liberate; **d. son agressivité sur qn** to vent one's aggressiveness on sb **2 se défouler** *vpr F* to let off steam; **tu n'as pas à te d. sur les enfants** you shouldn't take it out on the children; **elle se défoule dans son travail** she invests all her energies in her job **3** *vi F* **ça défoule** it helps you let off steam
défourner [defurne] *vt (poterie)* to remove from the kiln; *(pain)* to remove from the oven
défragmentation [defragmɑ̃tasjɔ̃] *nf Ordinat (de fichiers)* defragmentation
défragmenter [defragmɑ̃te] *vt Ordinat* to defragment
défragmenteur [defragmɑ̃tœr] *nm Ordinat* defragmenter
défraîchi [defrɛʃi] *adj (marchandises)* (shop)soiled; *(fleurs, beauté)* faded; *(vêtement)* shabby, past its best
défraîchir [defrɛʃir] **1** *vt (beauté, couleur, teint)* to fade **2 se défraîchir** *vpr (beauté, couleur, teint)* to fade
défraiement [defrɛmɑ̃] *nm* compensation; **je suis en droit d'attendre un d.** I'm entitled to compensation
défrayer [defreje] *vt* **(je défraie, je défraye; je défraierai, je défrayerai) (a) d. qn** to defray *or* pay sb's expenses; **être défrayé de tout** to have all expenses paid **(b) d. la conversation** *(la monopoliser)* to monopolize the conversation; *(en être le sujet)* to be the subject of conversation; **d. la chronique** to be in the news
défrichage [defriʃaʒ] *nm,* **défrichement** [defriʃmɑ̃] *nm (de terrain)* clearing
défricher [defriʃe] *vt (terrain pour la culture)* to clear, to reclaim; *(terrain en friche)* to bring into cultivation; *(terrain vierge)* to break; *Fig* **d. le terrain** to clear the ground; *Fig* **d. un sujet/un nouveau domaine scientifique** to do pioneer work in a subject/to pioneer a new field of science
défricheur, -euse [defriʃœr, -øz] *n Agr* land clearer, settler; *Fig (dans un domaine)* pioneer
défriper [defripe] *vt (vêtement chiffonné)* to smooth out
défriser [defrize] *vt (cheveux)* to uncurl, to straighten; *Fig F* **ça vous défrise?** does it bother you?; *Fig F* **ça me défrise de savoir que c'est lui qui a le poste** it really annoys me *or Br* it gets up my nose *or Sl* it pisses me off that he's got the job; *F* **qu'on puisse être aussi insolent, ça me défrise** cheek like that *Br* gets up my nose *or Am* tees me off
défroisser [defrwase] **1** *vt (vêtement)* to take the creases out of **2 se défroisser** *vpr* to lose its creases
défroque [defrɔk] *nf F (vieux habits)* rags
défroqué [defrɔke] **1** *adj (prêtre)* unfrocked **2** *nm* unfrocked priest
défroquer [defrɔke] **1** *vt* to unfrock **2** *vi* to leave the priesthood **3 se défroquer** *vpr* to leave the priesthood
défunt, -unte [defœ̃, -œ̃t] **1** *adj* deceased; **mon d. mari, mon mari d.** my late husband; *Litt* **des espoirs/amours défunts** lost hopes/loves **2** *n* deceased; **prier pour les défunts** to pray for the dead
dégagé [degaʒe] *adj (ton, manière)* free and easy; *(mouvements etc)* free; *(ciel, route)* clear; **allure dégagée** swinging stride; **vue dégagée** open view; **je voudrais une coupe avec la nuque très dégagée/les oreilles très dégagées** I'd like a style that's very short at the back/sides *or* that doesn't cover my neck/ears
dégagement [degaʒmɑ̃] *nm* **(a)** *(d'un gage)* redemption, taking out of pawn; *(d'une hypothèque)* redemption

(b) *(d'une route, des poumons etc)* clearing; *(du frein)* disengagement, release; *(de verrou)* loosening, slackening; *Pol, Mil* disengagement; *Fb* clearance; **escalier de d.** *(privé)* private staircase; *(de secours)* emergency stairs; **porte de d.** *(dans un cinéma etc)* (side) exit

(c) *(de vapeur, gaz etc)* escape, release; *(de chaleur)* emission, release; **tuyau de d.** waste pipe; *Fin* **d. de fonds** release of funds

(d) *(devant une maison etc)* open space, clearing; *Aut* clearance; **voie de d.** *Rail* siding; *Aut* slip road; *Aut* **itinéraire de d.** alternative route
dégager [degaʒe] **(je dégageai(s); n. dégageons) 1** *vt* **(a)** *(gage)* to redeem, to take out of pawn; *(hypothèque)* to redeem; **d. des titres** to release (pledged) securities; **d. des crédits** to release funds; **d. des profits** to show *or* yield a profit; **d. un bénéfice** to show *or* yield a profit; **d. sa parole** to go back on one's word; **d. qn d'une promesse** to release sb from a promise; **d. sa responsabilité d'une affaire** to disclaim responsibility in a matter; **être dégagé des obligations militaires** to have done one's national service

(b) *(libérer)* to free; *(route, pont etc)* to clear; *(verrou)* to loosen, to slacken; **d. le frein** to release the brake; **d. une ville** to relieve a town; **d. les blessés des décombres** to pull the injured clear of the wreckage; *Archit* **d. les vues** to open vistas; **robe qui dégage les épaules/le cou** dress that leaves the shoulders/the neck bare; *Fb* **d. le ballon en touche** to kick the ball over the touchline, to clear the ball; *F* **tu vas me d. toutes ces bricoles de tes étagères** I want you to clear all these odds and ends off your shelves

(c) *(laisser échapper) (vapeur, odeur)* to emit, to give off; *(chaleur)* to emit, to give out; **ce tableau dégage une grande sérénité** the painting gives off a feeling of great serenity

(d) *(isoler) (vérité)* to find out; *(impressions)* to get, to gain; *Pol* **d. une majorité** to secure a (working) majority; **d. l'idée principale d'un texte** to identify the main idea of a text; **qu'as-tu dégagé de ta mission?** what did you learn from your mission?; **quels sentiments dégages-tu de ton entretien avec le directeur?** what are your feelings now that you've spoken to the manager?

2 se dégager *vpr* **(a)** *(de ses menottes)* to free oneself **(de** from), to get free **(de** of); *(d'une voiture accidentée, d'une obligation)* to free oneself **(de** from); *(d'une situation difficile)* to extricate oneself **(de** from); **d'un effort violent, il s'est dégagé** he wrenched himself free; **se d. d'une promesse** to get out of a promise; **le ciel se dégage** the sky is clearing; **mon nez commence à se d.** my nose is starting to unblock

(b) *(du gaz, d'une odeur etc)* to be given off **(de** by); **il se dégage de l'oxygène** oxygen is given off; *Fig* **le calme qui se dégage de sa présence** the calm radiated by his presence; **le magnétisme qui se dégage d'elle** the magnetism she radiates

(c) *(ressortir)* to emerge, to come out; **la silhouette du navire s'est dégagée du brouillard** the ship loomed up out of the fog; **la vérité se dégage peu à peu** the truth is gradually coming out; **cette nécessité se dégage de l'étude de la situation** this need becomes apparent after studying the situation

3 *vi F* to clear off; **allez dégage!, je t'ai assez vu!** go on, clear off!, I've seen enough of you; **dégagez, s'il vous plaît** move along please, clear the way please
dégaine [degɛn] *nf F (démarche)* awkward gait; *(apparence)*

strange appearance; **il a vraiment une d. impossible quand il a bu** he walks in the funniest way when he's drunk!; **non mais tu as vu sa d. depuis qu'il fait de la moto!** have you seen how ridiculous he looks since he started riding a motorbike?
dégainer [degene] **1** *vt* (*épée*) to unsheathe, to draw; (*pistolet*) to draw **2** *vi* to draw
déganter (se) [sədegɑ̃te] *vpr* to take off one's gloves
dégarni [degarni] *adj* (*frigidaire, placard etc*) empty; **arbre d.** tree bare of leaves; **front d.** receding hairline; **mon portefeuille est d.** I'm rather low on funds
dégarnir [degarnir] **1** *vt* (*frigidaire, placard etc*) to empty; (*chambre, salle etc*) to empty, to clear; (*lit*) to strip; (*compte en banque*) to draw (heavily) on; *Mil* (*ville etc*) to withdraw troops from; (*robe*) to take the trimmings off; (*arbre*) to thin out **2 se dégarnir** *vpr* (*d'un arbre*) to lose its leaves; (*d'une tête*) to go bald; (*d'une salle etc*) to empty; **il commence à se d.** his hair is thinning, he's going bald; **les rayons se sont dégarnis en un rien de temps** the shelves were emptied *or* stripped bare in next to no time
dégât [dega] *nm* damage; **il y a eu du** *ou* **un sacré d.** there was a lot of damage; **les gelées ont fait des dégâts dans les vignobles** the frosts have caused a lot of damage in the vineyards; **limiter les dégâts** to limit the damage; *Fig* **il va falloir limiter les dégâts** we'll have to do some damage limitation; **l'alcool fait des dégâts terribles parmi la jeunesse** alcohol is wreaking havoc among young people; **dégâts matériels** material damage; **dégâts des eaux** water damage; **dégâts causés par le feu** fire damage; **dégâts causés par une tempête** storm damage
dégauchir [degoʃir] *vt* (*planche etc*) to surface, to rough plane; (*pierre*) to trim
dégauchissage [degoʃisaʒ] *nm*, **dégauchissement** [degoʃismɑ̃] *nm Tech* (*de planche*) surfacing, rough planing; (*de pierre*) trimming
dégauchisseuse [degoʃisøz] *nf* surfacing machine, surfacer
dégazage [degɑzaʒ] *nm* **(a)** *Ch* (*d'eau etc*) degassing; (*de circuit*) bleeding **(b)** (*de pétrolier*) cleaning out
dégazer [degɑze] *vt* **(a)** *Ch* (*eau etc*) to degas; (*freins, chauffage central*) to bleed **(b)** (*pétrolier*) to clean out
dégel [deʒɛl] *nm Météo, Pol* thaw; **le d. s'annonce** it's beginning to thaw
dégelée [deʒle] *nf F* thrashing, walloping; **il s'est pris une de ces dégelées** he got an awful thrashing *or* walloping
dégeler [deʒle] **(il dégèle; il dégèlera) 1** *vt* **(a)** (*lac, Fig personne*) to thaw (out); *Fig* **d. un auditoire** to warm up an audience; **d. l'atmosphère** to make the atmosphere less chilly; **d. les relations entre deux pays** to bring about a thaw in relations between two countries
(b) *Fin* (*avoir etc*) to unfreeze
2 *vi* (*d'un étang*) to thaw; (*de pieds*) to thaw out
3 *v impers* to thaw; **il** *ou* **ça dégèle** it's thawing
4 se dégeler *vpr* **(a)** (*d'un étang*) to thaw; (*de pieds*) to thaw out
(b) *Fig* (*de l'atmosphère*) to thaw out; **les relations entre ces deux pays se sont finalement dégelées** there has finally been a thaw in relations between the two countries
dégénératif [deʒeneratif] *adj* (*trouble, maladie*) degenerative
dégénéré, -ée [deʒenere] **1** *adj* **(a)** degenerate **(b)** *Psy* (*arriéré*) (mentally) defective **2** *n Psy* mental defective
dégénérer [deʒenere] *vi* **(je dégénère; je dégénérerai) (a)** (*s'abâtardir*) (*d'une race*) to degenerate (**de** from; **en** into); (*de qualité*) to deteriorate **(b)** (*mal tourner*) (*d'une conversation, un bal etc*) to degenerate (**en** into); **son rhume a dégénéré en bronchite** his cold developed into bronchitis; **à chaque fois qu'on se voit, ça finit toujours par d.** every time we see each other it ends up getting out of hand
dégénérescence [deʒenerɛsɑ̃s] *nf Méd* degeneration; *Fig* **on observe une nette d. de la moralité chez les jeunes** there has been a distinct decline in moral standards among young people
dégénérescent [deʒenerɛsɑ̃] *adj Méd* degenerating, degenerative
dégingandé [deʒɛ̃gɑ̃de] *adj F* gangling, lanky
dégivrage [deʒivraʒ] *nm Av, Aut* de-icing; (*d'un réfrigérateur*) defrosting; (*dispositif*) defroster
dégivrer [deʒivre] *vt Av, Aut* to de-ice; (*réfrigérateur*) to defrost
dégivreur [deʒivrœr] *nm Av, Aut* de-icer; (*de réfrigérateur*) defroster
déglaçage [deglasaʒ] *nm*, **déglacement** [deglasmɑ̃] *nm* (*d'une poêle à frire*) deglazing
déglacer [deglase] (*conj like* **glacer**) *vt Culin* (*poêle à frire*) to deglaze
déglinguer [deglɛ̃ge] *F* **1** *vt* (*appareil, meuble*) to smash up, to bust up; **ma moto est toute déglinguée** my motorbike is falling to pieces **2 se déglinguer** *vpr* (*d'une voiture, une moto etc*) to fall to pieces
déglutir [deglytir] *vt Physiol* to swallow
déglutition [deglytisjɔ̃] *nf Physiol* swallowing
dégobiller [degɔbije] *très F* **1** *vi* (*vomir*) to puke, to throw up **2** *vt* to puke up
dégoiser [degwaze] *F Péj* **1** *vt* (*discours etc*) to spout; **qu'est-ce qu'il dégoise?** what's he rattling *or* rabbiting *or* wittering on about? **2** *vi* to rattle *or* witter on
dégommage [degɔmaʒ] *nm F* (*renvoi*) sacking
dégommer [degɔme] *vt F* (*renvoyer*) to sack; (*vider*) to kick out; (*en gagnant*) to beat, to lick; **les militaires au pouvoir ont été dégommés** the military has been ousted from power *or F* has been kicked out
dégonflage [degɔ̃flaʒ] *nm F* chickening out *Br Sl* bottling out; **on a assisté à un d. généralisé** everybody chickened out; **dès qu'il a vu le patron, ça a été le d. total** as soon as he saw the boss he chickened out *or Br Sl* lost his bottle
dégonfle [degɔ̃fl] *nf F* = **dégonflage**
dégonflé, -ée [degɔ̃fle] **1** *adj* **(a)** (*pneu etc*) soft **(b)** *F* (*lâche*) chicken; **ce que tu peux être d.!** you really are chicken! **2** *n F* chicken; **vous n'êtes qu'une bande de dégonflés** you're all just chicken, *Br Sl* you've none of you any bottle
dégonflement [degɔ̃fləmɑ̃] *nm* (*de pneu*) deflating, deflation; *Com* cutback
dégonfler [degɔ̃fle] **1** *vt* **(a)** (*pneu, ballon etc*) to deflate, to let the air out of **(b)** (*gonflement*) to reduce, to bring down; **d. les prix** to bring prices down **(c)** (*héros*) to debunk; **d. la portée d'un événement** to play down *or* downplay the importance of an event **2 se dégonfler** *vpr* **(a)** (*de pneu, de ballon*) to deflate **(b)** (*de gonflement*) to go down **(c)** *F* (*de personne*) to chicken out, to get cold feet **3** *vi* (*de gonflement*) to go down
dégorgement [degɔrʒəmɑ̃] *nm* **(a)** (*d'un égout, d'un évier*) unblocking, clearing **(b)** (*de l'eau*) release; (*de la bile*) discharge
dégorger [degɔrʒe] **(je dégorgeai(s); n. dégorgeons) 1** *vt* **(a)** to discharge; **l'égout dégorge de l'eau sale** the drain is discharging dirty water; **la rue a dégorgé un flot de gens** a crowd of people surged from the street
(b) (*passage, tuyau*) to free, to clear, to unstop; **d. un évier bouché** to clear a blocked sink, to unblock a sink
(c) d. du vin = to remove sediment from wine prior to its final corking
2 *vi* **(a)** (*d'un égout, un étang*) to flow out, to discharge (**dans** into); (*d'une gouttière, une rivière*) to overflow
(b) *Culin* **faire d. des concombres/***etc* = to remove the water from cucumbers/*etc* by sprinkling them with salt
3 se dégorger *vpr* (*d'une rivière, d'un égout*) to empty (**dans** into)
dégot(t)er [degɔte] *vt F* to dig up
dégoulinade [degulinad] *nf* trickle
dégoulinement [degulinmɑ̃] *nm* trickling
dégouliner [deguline] *vi* to trickle; **la pluie me dégoulinait dans le cou** the rain was trickling down my neck; **je dégouline** I'm dripping, I'm soaking wet
dégoupiller [degupije] *vt* (*grenade*) to pull the pin out of
dégourdi, -ie [degurdi] **1** *adj* bright, sharp, smart; **il n'est pas très d.** he's not very bright, he's not really on the ball; **tu es d. comme un manche de pelle** you're not very smart, *Br F* you're as thick as two short planks **2** *n* **c'est un d./une dégourdie** he's/she's pretty bright, he's/she's got what it takes
dégourdir [degurdir] **1** *vt* (*membres*) to remove the stiffness *or* numbness from; *Vieilli* (*eau*) to take the chill off; **il faut que je dégourdisse ma jambe** I'll have to get the circulation going in my leg again; *Fig* **d. qn** to teach sb a thing or two, to smarten sb up **2 se dégourdir** *vpr* (*en marchant*) to restore the circulation; *Fig* to smarten up; **je vais me d. les jambes** I'm going to stretch my legs a bit
dégourdissement [degurdismɑ̃] *nm* removal of numbness; *Fig* **il a besoin d'un sacré d.** he really needs wising up
dégoût [degu] *nm* **(a)** (*répulsion*) disgust, distaste, loathing; **il a un véritable d. pour le beurre** he can't stand butter **(b)** (*aversion*) dislike; **avoir du d. pour qch** to dislike sth; **j'éprouve beaucoup de d. pour ce genre d'attitude** I really dislike that kind of attitude; **prendre qch en d.** to take a dislike to sth; **il a pris sa vie en d.** he grew weary of the life he was leading; **le d. de la vie** world-weariness; **le d. de soi** self-loathing
dégoûtant, -ante [degutɑ̃, -ɑ̃t] **1** *adj* (*vue, odeur, personne etc*) disgusting, revolting; **c'est d. de mentir/voler** it's disgusting to lie/steal; **elle gagne encore!, c'est d.!** she's won again!, it's disgusting! **2** *n* filthy character; **un vieux d.** a dirty old man

dégoûtation [degutasjɔ̃] *nf F* (a) (*dégoût*) disgust (b) (*saleté*) filth; **ta chambre est une vraie d.** your room is a pigsty *or Br* a tip; **je ne mettrai plus un pied dans ta chambre tant que cela restera une telle d.** I won't set foot inside your room until it's a bit less of a pigsty

dégoûté, -ée [degute] **1** *adj* (a) (*écœuré*) disgusted (**de** with), *F* sick (**de** of); **je suis d. de tes mensonges** I'm sick of your lies; **d. de la vie** weary of life; **je suis d. de la viande** I can't face eating meat (b) (*difficile*) fastidious, squeamish; *Iron* **vous n'êtes pas d.!** you're not fussy! **2** *n* **faire le/la dégoûté(e)** to turn up one's nose; **quand j'ai fait mon offre, il a fait le d.** when I told him my offer, he turned his nose up at it

dégoûter [degute] **1** *vt* to disgust; **la viande me dégoûte** meat turns my stomach; **tout cela me dégoûte** I'm sick of it all; **d. qn de qch** to put sb off sth; **c'est à vous d. de l'Espagne/des hommes!** it's enough to put you off Spain/men! **2 se dégoûter** *vpr* **se d. de qn/qch** to take a dislike to sb/sth; **il s'est dégoûté du chocolat** he's put himself right off chocolate

dégoutter [degute] *vi* to drip, to fall drop by drop (**de** from); **la pluie dégoutte de son chapeau** the rain is dripping from his hat; **un parapluie dégouttant d'eau** a dripping wet umbrella; **dégouttant de sueur** dripping with sweat

dégradant [degradɑ̃] *adj* (*travail*) degrading; (*remarque*) derogatory

dégradation [degradasjɔ̃] *nf* (a) (*détérioration*) (*de monument etc*) defacement; (*de matériel scolaire, l'environnement*) damage (**de** to); (*de données informatiques*) corruption; *Fig* (*de relations internationales*) deterioration; **cette maison est dans un état de d. pitoyable** the house is in a shocking state of repair; *Phys* **d. de l'énergie** dissipation of energy (b) (*en rang etc*) downgrading; **d. civique** loss of civil rights

dégradé [degrade] *nm* (*de couleurs*) gradation; *Phot* graduated shading; **cheveux coupés en d.** layered hair; **se faire faire un d.** to have a layer cut; *Ordinat* **d. de couleur** colour scale; *Ordinat* **d. de gris** grey scale; *Typ etc* **dégradés de gris** shades of grey

dégrader[1] [degrade] **1** *vt* (a) (*abîmer*) (*monument*) to deface; (*matériel, maison*) to damage; *Ordinat* (*données*) to corrupt

(b) *Fig* (*personne*) to degrade, to debase; **des conditions de vie qui dégradent la personne** degrading living conditions

(c) *Mil* to downgrade

2 se dégrader *vpr* (a) (*se détériorer*) (*de la santé, d'une situation*) to deteriorate; (*d'un bâtiment etc*) to fall into disrepair; **les bâtiments se sont beaucoup dégradés** the buildings have fallen into serious disrepair; **les relations internationales se dégradent** international relations are deteriorating

(b) (*s'abaisser*) to lower *or* demean oneself

(c) *Phys* (*d'énergie*) to dissipate

dégrader[2] *vt* (*couleurs, lumière*) to shade off, to gradate; *Phot* to vignette

dégrafer [degrafe] **1** *vt* (*robe etc*) to unhook, to unfasten, to undo; (*bracelet*) to unclasp, to unfasten **2 se dégrafer** *vpr* (a) (*d'un vêtement, un bracelet*) to come undone (b) (*d'une femme*) to undo one's dress

dégraissage [degrɛsaʒ] *nm* (a) *Culin* skimming; *Fig* **d. d'une entreprise** removing the fat from *or* downsizing a company; **ils ont fait de sérieux dégraissages dans l'ensemble du secteur** they have cut a substantial number of jobs in the sector (b) (*nettoyage*) dry cleaning

dégraisser [degrese] **1** *vt* (a) (*bouillon*) to skim the fat off; (*animal de boucherie*) to remove the fat from; *Fig* **d. une entreprise** to cut the fat from a company, to downsize a company; **d. les effectifs** to lay off staff (b) (*vêtements etc*) to dry-clean; **donner qch à d.** to hand sth into the dry-cleaner's **2** *vi Fig* (*d'une entreprise*) to cut the fat, to downsize

degré [dəgre] *nm* (a) (*unité*) (*de cercle, chaleur, gamme musicale*) degree; (*de boisson alcoolisée*) proof; **angle de 45 degrés** 45-degree angle; **dix degrés au-dessous de zéro** ten degrees below zero; **la température monte d'un d.** the temperature rises by one degree; **à combien de degrés est ce whisky?** what proof is this whisky?; **alcool à 90 degrés** 90 degree proof alcohol

(b) (*stade, niveau*) (*de parenté*) degree; **cousins au second d.** cousins once removed, second cousins; *Méd* **brûlure au troisième d.** third degree burn; *Math* **équation du second/du troisième d.** quadratic/cubic equation; *Scol* **éducation du premier/second d.** primary/secondary education; **les degrés de l'échelle sociale** the rungs of the social ladder; **le plus haut/bas d. de la société** the highest/lowest level of society; **atteindre le plus haut d. de la réussite** to reach the pinnacle of success; **elle est généreuse au plus haut d.** she is generous in the extreme; **je veux bien vous aider, mais seulement jusqu'à un certain d.** I'd be glad to help you, but only up to a point; **prendre une plaisanterie au premier d.** to take a joke seriously; **tu prends tout au premier d.** you take everything literally; **avec lui, il vaut mieux prendre les choses/la plaisanterie au deuxième d.** with him it's best not to take things/the joke at face value; **par degré(s)** by degrees, gradually; *Fig* **le d. zéro de l'informatique/de la civilisation** the beginnings of computer science/civilization, *Hum* **son bouquin, c'est le d. zéro de la littérature** his book hardly deserves to be classed as literature; **il en est resté au d. zéro de la lexicographie** he's absolutely hopeless as a lexicographer; **à un d. avancé de civilisation/recherches** at an advanced stage of civilization/research

(c) (*d'escalier*) step; (*d'échelle*) rung

▶ **degré: d. Celsius** degree Centigrade *or* Celsius; **d. Engler** degree Engler; **d. Fahrenheit** degree Fahrenheit; **d. Kelvin** degree Kelvin

dégréement [degremɑ̃] *nm Naut* (*d'un mât*) unrigging

dégréer [degree] *vt Naut* (*mât*) to unrig; (*grue*) to dismantle, to take down

dégressif, -ive [degresif, -iv] *adj Com* **tarif d.** tapering rate; **impôt d.** degressive taxation

dégressivité [degresivite] *nf* (*d'un impôt*) degressive nature

dégrèvement [degrɛvmɑ̃] *nm* (*d'impôt*) reduction, abatement; **d. fiscal** tax relief

dégrever [degrəve] *vt* (**je dégrève; je dégrèverai**) (*impôt*) to reduce, to diminish; (*contribuable*) to grant tax relief to; (*industrie*) to derate; (*édifice*) to reduce the assessment on; (*domaine*) to disencumber

dégriffé [degrife] **1** *adj* **manteau d.** = coat which has had its designer label removed and is sold at a reduced price **2** *nm* = item of clothing which has had its designer label removed and is sold at a reduced price

dégringolade [degrɛ̃gɔlad] *nf F* (*chute*) tumble; *Fig* (*d'un financier*) downfall; (*d'une firme etc*) collapse; **d. des prix** slump *or* collapse in prices

dégringoler [degrɛ̃gɔle] *F* **1** *vt* to rush *or* tear down, to come rushing *or* tearing down **2** *vi* (*d'une personne*) to tumble; *Fig* (*de prix*) to slump, to collapse; (*d'une entreprise*) to collapse; **d. dans la pente** to tumble down the slope

dégrippant [degripɑ̃] *nm* lubricating *or* penetrating oil

dégripper [degripe] *vt Tech* (*mécanisme*) to unseize, to free

dégrisement [degrizmɑ̃] *nm* sobering up; *Fig* disillusionment

dégriser [degrize] **1** *vt* to sober up; *Fig* to bring down to earth **2 se dégriser** *vpr* to sober up; *Fig* to become disillusioned (**au sujet de** about)

dégrossir [degrosir] *vt* (*bois*) to rough down, to trim; (*pierre*) to roughhew; *Fig* (*plan, travail etc*) to rough out; *F* **d. qn** to smooth out sb's rough edges; **il est un peu dégrossi depuis qu'il est à Paris** he's become a bit more polished since coming to Paris; **recrues mal dégrossies** raw recruits

dégrossissage [degrosisaʒ] *nm,* **dégrossissement** [degrosismɑ̃] *nm* (*de bois*) trimming

dégrouiller (se) [sədegruje] *vpr F* to get a move on; **allez! dégrouille!** come on, get a move on!; **tu pourrais te d. un peu?** could you get a bit of a move on?; **il n'arrive jamais à (se) d. assez pour être à l'heure** he never manages to get enough of a move on to be on time

dégroupage [degrupaʒ] *nm Com* deconsolidation

dégroupement [degrupmɑ̃] *nm* dividing into groups; **il va falloir procéder à un d. de la classe** the class will have to be divided into groups

dégrouper [degrupe] *vt* to divide into groups

déguenillé, -ée [degənije] **1** *adj* ragged, tattered, in rags, in tatters **2** *n* **un petit d.** a little ragamuffin

déguerpir [degɛrpir] *vi* to clear out *or* off; **d. en vitesse** to bolt; **faire d. l'ennemi** to scatter the enemy

dégueu [degø] *adj inv très F* = **dégueulasse**

dégueulasse [degœlas] **1** *adj très F* rotten; (*sale*) filthy; **un repas d.** a disgusting meal; **il fait un temps d.** it's rotten *or* filthy weather; **j'ai passé un week-end d.** I had a rotten weekend; **tu es d. d'avoir fait ça** that was rotten of you; **c'est pas d.** it's bloody good; **il est d. avec elle** he's rotten to her; **se balader en d.** to go around in sloppy old clothes **2** *n* **c'est un d.** he's a rotten bastard

dégueulasser [degœlase] *vt très F* to muck up, to mess up; **tu vas d. toute la maison** you're going to make the whole house filthy *or* get the whole house into a mess

dégueuler [degœle] *vi très F* to spew, to puke

dégueulis [degœli] *nm très F* puke, sick

déguisé [degize] *adj* (a) (*pour tromper*) disguised; (*pour s'amuser*) dressed up; **être d.** to be disguised *or* in disguise; **je me sens déguisée dans cette robe** I don't feel right in this dress, the dress isn't me **(b)** *Fig* (*voix, signature, égoïsme*) disguised; **avec une joie non déguisée** with unconcealed delight; *Culin* **fruits déguisés** = prunes, dates etc stuffed with almond paste

déguisement [degizmɑ̃] *nm* **(a)** (*pour tromper*) disguise, get-up; (*pour un bal masqué*) fancy dress, costume **(b)** *Fig* **sans d.** plainly, openly; **livrez-moi votre pensée sans d.** tell me frankly what you think

déguiser [degize] **1** *vt* **(a)** (*costumer*) to disguise; **d. un enfant en clown** to dress a child up as a clown **(b)** (*déformer*) (*sa voix, son écriture*) to disguise; (*la vérité*) to disguise, to conceal; **parler sans d. sa pensée** to speak plainly *or* openly **2 se déguiser** *vpr* (*pour ne pas être reconnu*) to disguise oneself; (*s'habiller*) to dress up; **se d. en pompier** to dress up as a fireman

dégurgiter [degyrʒite] *vt* to regurgitate; *Fig* **d. sa leçon** to regurgitate one's lesson

dégustateur, -trice [degystatœr, -tris] *n* wine taster

dégustation [degystasjɔ̃] *nf* tasting, sampling; **d. de vin** wine tasting; **ici, d. d'huîtres** oysters served here

déguster [degyste] **1** *vt* **(a)** (*tester*) (*vin etc*) to taste, to sample **(b)** (*savourer*) to savour, to eat/drink with relish; *Fig* (*livre etc*) to savour, to appreciate, to enjoy **(c)** *très F* **d. des coups** to get a good hiding; **qu'est-ce qu'on a dégusté!** we didn't half catch it! **2** *vi très F* to suffer; **toute sa vie, elle a dégusté** she's had a rough time of it all her life; **je te préviens, tu vas d.!** you're going to catch it, I can tell you!; **faire d. qn** to give sb a hard time

déhanché [deɑ̃ʃe] *adj* (*personne*) who walks with a sway of the hips; *Méd* slightly lopsided

déhanchement [deɑ̃ʃmɑ̃] *nm* swaying of the hips; (*quand on est immobile*) standing with all one's weight on one foot; *Méd* **je remarque un léger d.** I notice a slight lop-sidedness; **le d. de la statue** the curve of the statue's hip, the way the statue has all the weight on one foot

déhancher (se) [sədeɑ̃ʃe] *vpr* (*en marchant*) to sway one's hips; (*quand on est immobile*) to lean one's weight on one foot

déharnacher [dearnaʃe] *vt* to unharness

dehors [dəɔr] **1** *adv* outside; *Sp* out; **être d.** (*pas chez soi*) to be out; **coucher d.** to sleep out of doors *or* in the open; **dîner d.** (*en plein air*) to dine out of doors *or* in the open; (*au restaurant*) to dine out; **histoire à coucher d.** cock and bull story; *F* **mettre** *ou* **ficher** *ou* **foutre qn d.** to kick sb out; (*le renvoyer*) to sack sb; **mettre le nez** *ou* **le pied** *ou* **les pieds d.** to set foot outside (the door); **j'ai mis le nez d. vers 5 heures** I popped out at around 5 o'clock; *Naut* **toutes voiles d.** with every sail set; **de d.** from outside; **en d.** (on the) outside, outwards; **tourner la jambe en d.** to turn one's leg out; **en d. de la maison** outside the house; **en d. de sa compétence/de cela** apart from his competence/from that; **rester en d. d'une dispute** to keep out of an argument; **je te prie de rester en d. (de cette histoire)** please keep out of this; **en d. du sujet** beside the question; **cela s'est fait en d. de moi** (*sans que je le sache*) it was done without my knowledge; (*sans que j'y participe*) I had no part in it; *Boxe* **compter qn d.** to count sb out

2 *nm* **(a)** (*d'une maison etc*) outside, exterior; **au d.** on the outside; **ne pas se pencher au d.!** do not lean out of the window!; **agir du d.** to act from the outside

(b) les dehors (outward) appearance; **maison aux dehors imposants** house with an imposing exterior; **sous des dehors aimables** under a pleasant exterior

(c) (*en patinage*) outside edge

déhoussable [deusabl] *adj* (*canapé, siège*) with loose covers

déification [deifikasjɔ̃] *nf* deification

déifier [deifje] *vt* to deify, to make a god of

déisme [deism] *nm* deism

déiste [deist] *adj, n* deist

déité [deite] *nf* deity

déjà [deʒa] *adv* **(a)** (*dès maintenant*) already; (*si tôt*) yet; **faut-il que vous partiez d.?** must you go just yet?; **vous avez d. trop de travail** you have too much work as it is; **j'aurais dû le faire il y a d. trois jours** I should have done it three days ago as it is; **il est d. trois heures** it's already three o'clock; **tu as d. fini?** have you finished already?; **elle a d. 20 ans!** she's 20 already!; **c'est d. vieux** that's not exactly news; **tu crois qu'il en souffre encore? – ça m'étonnerait, c'est d. vieux** do you think he's still suffering? – I'd be surprised if he was, it was all so long ago

(b) (*auparavant*) before, previously; **je vous ai d. vu** I've seen you before; **j'avais d. lu ce livre** I'd read the book before, I'd already read the book; **d. en 1900** as early as 1900; **elle avait d. cet air bête quand elle était enfant** even as a child she looked stupid; **vous avez d. travaillé?** have you got work experience?

(c) (*intensif*) **10 jours de vacances, c'est d. ça!** *ou* **c'est d. quelque chose!** 10 days' holiday isn't bad at all!; **ce n'est d. pas si mal** that's not bad at all; *F* **c'est d. pas mal de gagner 9 000 francs** a salary of 9,000 francs isn't bad at all; *F* **une dinde de 4 kg, c'est d. la belle bête!** four kilos is not a bad weight at all for a turkey!; **il est d. assez gâté comme ça!** he's spoiled enough as it is; *F* **d. que je n'en ai pas beaucoup, si tu m'en prends la moitié ...** I haven't got much as it is, so if you take half ...

(d) *F* (*interrogatif*) **qu'est-ce que vous faites, d.?** what did you say your job was?; **qu'est-ce que tu m'as dit, d.?** what did you say?; **c'est quoi, d., son nom?** what was his name again?

déjanter [deʒɑ̃te] **1** *vt* (*pneu*) to remove from the rim **2** *vi très F* to be mad, to be off one's head *or* rocker; **tu déjantes complètement depuis que tu es avec cette fille** you haven't been right in the head since you started going with that girl; **il a complètement déjanté** he's gone right off his rocker **3 se déjanter** *vpr* (*d'un pneu*) to come off the rim

déjà-vu [deʒavy] *nm inv* **une impression de d.** a feeling of déjà vu; **leur spectacle n'a rien d'extraordinaire, c'est du d.** there's nothing very special about their show, it's all been done before

déjection [deʒɛksjɔ̃] *nf* **(a)** *Physiol* evacuation; **déjections** faeces **(b)** *Géol* ejecta

déjeté [deʒte] *adj* (*position, mur*) crooked, lopsided; **il est de plus en plus d.** his posture is getting worse and worse; **colonne vertébrale déjetée** deformed spinal column; **elle a la taille déjetée** she has one shoulder higher than the other; *Fig* **d. à cause de son travail** worn out by (his) work

déjeter [deʒte] **(il déjette; il déjettera) 1** *vt* to make lopsided; (*bois*) to warp; (*métal*) to buckle **2 se déjeter** *vpr* to grow lopsided; (*du bois*) to warp; (*du métal*) to buckle

déjeuner[1] [deʒœne] *nm* **(a)** [①**A6**,d,iii] (*repas de midi*) lunch, *Fml* luncheon; **prendre son d.** to lunch; **un d. d'affaires/de travail** a business/working lunch; **d. buffet** buffet lunch; **d. sur l'herbe** picnic (lunch); **je ne peux pas venir ce midi, j'ai un d.** I can't make it at noon, I'm already booked for lunch; **il y a des œufs pour le** *ou* **au** *ou* **à d.** it's eggs for lunch; **nous avons les Dupont à d. dimanche** the Duponts are coming for lunch on Sunday **(b)** *Suisse, Belg* (*petit-déjeuner*) breakfast **(c)** (*tasse et soucoupe*) breakfast cup and saucer **(d)** *Fig* **ça a été un d. de soleil** (*d'un tissu*) it soon faded; (*d'un sentiment, d'une résolution*) it soon faded, it didn't last long

déjeuner[2] *vi* **(a)** (*le matin*) to (have) breakfast **(b)** (*à midi*) to (have) lunch; **il est resté à d.** he stayed for lunch; **d. d'un sandwich** to have a sandwich for lunch; **tu as déjeuné de peu** you didn't have much for lunch; **d. à l'extérieur** to have lunch out

déjouer [deʒwe] *vt* (*complot, plans de qn*) to foil; **d. la surveillance du professeur** to evade the teacher's eye

déjuger (se) [sədeʒyʒe] *vpr* (*conj like* **juger**) to reverse one's judgment/decision/*etc*

DEL [deəɛl] *nf* (*abrév* **diode électroluminescente**) LED

delà [dəla] **1** *prép Arch, Litt* beyond; **par d. les mers/monts** beyond the seas/the mountains; **au d. de** beyond; **n'allez pas au d. de 300 francs** don't go above 300 francs; **elle est allée au d. de ses promesses** she was better than her word; **aller au d. de ses forces/moyens** to do more than one is capable of/to spend more than one can afford; **sa réussite va au d. de tout ce qu'il avait rêvé** he has succeeded beyond his wildest dreams; **par d. les âges** down through the ages; **il faut savoir juger les gens par d. les apparences** one shouldn't judge by appearances **2** *adv* **deçà, d.** here and there; **au(-)d.** beyond; **vous voyez ce sommet? au d., c'est l'Autriche** do you see that peak? Austria lies beyond that *or* on the other side; **avoir droit à 200 cigarettes, pas au d.** to be entitled to 200 cigarettes, no more; **son savoir ne va pas au d.** that's as much as *or* that's all he knows; **en d.** further away **3** *nm* **l'au-d.** the next world, the hereafter

délabré [delabre] *adj* (*maison, meubles*) dilapidated; **complètement d.** (*bâtiment*) ramshackle; **santé délabrée** ruined health

délabrement [delabrəmɑ̃] *nm* (*de maison, meubles*) dilapidated state; **depuis que sa femme est morte, son affaire va au d.** since his wife died, his business has been going under; **le d. de son entreprise** the ruin of his company

délabrer [delabre] **1** *vt* (*maison*) to dilapidate; (*santé*) to ruin; **la mort de sa femme lui a complètement délabré le moral** his wife's death has left him in a state of utter depression **2 se délabrer** *vpr* (*d'une maison etc*) to fall into disrepair, to become dilapidated; **sa santé se délabre** his health is deteriorating; **ses affaires se délabrent** his business is going to rack and ruin; **son moral se délabre** he's becoming more and more depressed

délacer [delase] **(je délaçai(s); n. délaçons) 1** *vt* (*chaussures etc*) to unlace, to undo **2 se délacer** *vpr* to come unlaced *or* undone

délai [delɛ] *nm* (*laps de temps*) time allowed, period; (*date limite*) deadline; **on vous accordera un d.** we will give you more time; **dans le d. prescrit** *ou* **fixé** within the required *or* allotted time; **d. d'un jour franc** one clear day, one whole day; **dans un d. de 10 jours** within 10 days; **il faut compter un d. de 10 jours** you must allow ten days; **livrer dans les délais** to deliver on time; **respecter** *ou* **tenir les délais** to meet the deadline; **dernier d.** (final) deadline; **vous devez me rendre votre dissertation lundi dernier d.** you must hand in your dissertation by Monday at the very latest *or* no later than Monday; **sans d.** without delay, immediately; **dans les plus brefs délais** as soon as possible; **livrable dans un d. de trois jours** can be delivered at three days' notice

▶ **délai**: **d. d'attente** waiting period; **d. de carence** waiting period; *Com* **d. de chargement** loading time; **d. de congé** term of notice; **d. de crédit** credit period; *Com* **d. d'embarquement** loading time; **d. d'exécution** deadline; (*de livraison, de production*) lead time; **d. garanti de livraison** guaranteed delivery period; **d. de garantie** guarantee period, term of guarantee; **d. de grâce** period of grace; **d. de livraison** delivery time *or* period, lead time; **d. de livraison: un mois** delivery within one month; *Com* **d. de paiement** (*fixé par contrat*) term of payment, payment period *or* term; **demander un d. de paiement** to request a postponement of payment; **d. de préavis = délai-congé; d. de production** production leadtime; **d. de réachat** repurchase period; **d. de récupération du capital investi** payback period; **d. de réflexion** time to think; *Com* cooling-off period; **d. de règlement** settlement period; **d. de rigueur** strict deadline; **avant le 20 février, d. de rigueur** by February 20th at the very latest; *Mil etc* **d. de route** travelling time; **d. de validité** period of validity

délai-congé, *pl* **délais-congés** *nm Jur, Com* (*à un employé ou employeur*) term of notice, notice period

délaissement [delɛsmɑ̃] *nm* **(a)** (*d'une femme, d'enfants etc*) (*abandon*) desertion, abandonment; (*négligence*) neglect; (*solitude*) loneliness; **être dans un grand d.** to be completely abandoned **(b)** (*d'un droit*) relinquishment, renunciation; (*à l'assureur*) abandonment

délaisser [delese] *vt* **(a)** (*abandonner*) to desert, to abandon, to forsake; (*négliger*) to neglect; **depuis qu'il est marié, il délaisse ses amis** he has dropped his friends since he got married; **cette profession est délaissée par la jeunesse** young people are turning their backs on the profession **(b)** *Jur* (*droit, succession*) to relinquish, to forgo; (*à l'assureur*) to abandon

délassant [delasɑ̃] *adj* (*bain etc*) relaxing; (*lecture*) light, entertaining

délassement [delasmɑ̃] *nm* relaxation, rest; **le sport est un d. pour elle** sport is a relaxation for her; **avoir besoin de d.** to need to relax; **nous nous sentions dans un état de d. total** we felt totally relaxed

délasser [delase] **1** *vt* to relax **2 se délasser** *vpr* to (take some) rest, to relax

délateur, -trice [delatœr, -tris] *n* informer, spy

délation [delasjɔ̃] *nf* denouncement

délavage [delavaʒ] *nm* (*de couleurs etc*) washing out

délavé [delave] *adj* **(a)** (*couleur etc*) washed out; **jean d.** (*volontairement*) faded *or* stone-washed jeans; (*à la lessive*) faded jeans **(b) terre délavée** sodden earth

délaver [delave] *vt* **(a)** (*tissu*) to fade **(b)** (*terre*) to soak (with water)

délayage [delɛjaʒ] *nm* (*de peinture etc*) thinning out; *Fig Péj* **ce devoir n'est que du d.** there's far too much padding in this work

délayer [deleje] *vt* **(je délaie, délaye; je délaierai, délayerai) (a)** (*poudre etc*) to add water to; (*peinture etc*) to thin **(dans** with); (*liquide*) to water down; **d. de la farine dans du lait** to mix flour with milk **(b)** *Fig* (*discours, texte, théorie*) to pad out

Delco® [dɛlko] *nm Aut* distributor

déléatur [deleatyr] *nm inv Typ* delete (mark), dele

délectable [delɛktabl] *adj* delicious, delightful

délectation [delɛktasjɔ̃] *nf* delight, *Fml, Hum* delectation

délecter [delɛkte] **1** *vt Litt* to delight **2 se délecter** *vpr* to enjoy oneself; **se d. à (faire) qch** to take delight in (doing) sth

délégant, -ante [delegɑ̃, -ɑ̃t] *n Jur* delegant

délégataire [delegatɛr] *n Jur* delegatee

délégateur, -trice [delegatœr, -tris] *n Jur* delegator

délégation [delegasjɔ̃] *nf* **(a)** (*action de déléguer*) (*de représentants*) delegation, deputing; (*de dette*) assignment, transfer; **agir en vertu d'une** *ou* **par d.** to act on the authority invested in one; **d. de pouvoir** delegation of authority; *Scol* **d. rectorale** (one-year) transfer **(b)** (*groupe*) delegation, body of delegates; **envoyer une d. auprès d'un ministre** to send a delegation to a minister; **venir en d.** to come in a delegation

délégué, -ée [delege] **1** *adj* **membre d.** delegate; **ministre d. à l'environnement** Minister for the Environment, Environment Minister **2** *n* (*à une réunion*) delegate; *Scol* representative (*at class meetings*)

▶ **délégué**: *Scol* **d. de classe** class representative (*at class meetings*); **d. commercial** sales rep(resentative); **d. des parents** parent representative (*at class meetings*); **d. du personnel** staff representative; (*syndiqué*) union representative; *Scol* **d. rectoral** = teacher on a one-year placement (*in a job other than the one to which he was originally assigned*); **d. syndical** union representative; (*d'usine*) shop steward

déléguer [delege] **(je délègue; je déléguerai) 1** *vt* **(a)** (*désigner*) **d. qn pour faire qch** to delegate sb to do sth **(b)** (*transmettre*) (*pouvoirs*) to delegate; **c'est un patron qui sait d. ses fonctions** he's a boss who knows how to delegate; **d. une créance** to assign a debt **2** *vi* to delegate

délestage [delɛstaʒ] *nm* (*d'un navire, d'un ballon*) unballasting; *Él* power cut; **pour assurer le d. des grandes artères** to relieve congestion on the main roads; **itinéraire de d.** alternative route

délester [delɛste] **1** *vt* (*navire, ballon*) to unballast; *Él* to cut off the power to; (*voie de communication*) to relieve congestion on; **d. qn d'un fardeau** to relieve sb of a burden; *F* **d. qn de son argent** to relieve sb of his/her money **2 se délester** *vpr* (*d'un navire, d'un ballon*) to jettison ballast; **se d. de ses paquets** to set down *or* relieve oneself of one's parcels

délétère [deletɛr] *adj* harmful, *Fml* deleterious; (*gaz*) noxious, poisonous; (*influence etc*) pernicious

délibérant [deliberɑ̃] *adj* (*assemblée*) deliberative

délibératif, -ive [deliberatif, -iv] *adj* (*fonction*) deliberative; **avoir voix délibérative** to be entitled to speak and vote

délibération [deliberasjɔ̃] *nf* **(a)** (*examen*) deliberation, debate, discussion; **pendant la d. du jury** during the jury's deliberations, *F* while the jury was out; **la question est en d.** the matter is under discussion *or* being deliberated **(b)** (*réflexion*) consideration, reflection, cogitation; **après mûre d.** after careful consideration **(c)** (*décision*) (*d'une assemblée*) resolution, decision, vote

délibéré [delibere] **1** *adj* **(a)** (*intentionnel*) deliberate, intentional; **agir de propos d.** to act deliberately *or* intentionally **(b)** (*résolu*) (*ton, manière*) deliberate, determined, resolute **2** *nm Jur* (*de juges*) consultation, private sitting; **mettre une affaire en d.** = to submit a matter for decision by the bench, *US* ≈ to take a matter under advisement

délibérément [deliberemɑ̃] *adv* deliberately

délibérer [delibere] *vi* **(a)** (*discuter*) to deliberate, to confer; **d. (avec qn) sur qch** to discuss a matter (with sb); **le jury s'est retiré pour d.** the jury retired to consider its verdict **(b)** (*réfléchir*) to deliberate, to reflect **(c)** (*décider*) **d. de qch** to decide sth; **le tribunal populaire délibérait de le condamner à mort** the people's tribunal was deciding whether to condemn him to death

délicat, -ate [delika -at] *adj* **(a)** (*fragile*) (*peau*) sensitive, tender; (*fleur etc*) delicate; (*santé*) delicate, frail, weak

(b) (*fin*) (*dentelle, ouvrage*) delicate; (*travail*) fine; (*plat*) fine, refined; **d'une facture très délicate** very delicately made

(c) (*raffiné*) (*goût, personne*) fine, refined, discerning, sensitive; (*geste*) graceful; (*comportement*) considerate; (*toucher*) delicate, gentle; **avoir les oreilles délicates** to dislike bad language; **avoir le palais d.** to have a discerning palate; **avoir des gestes délicats** to move gracefully; **il est toujours très d. avec les vieilles dames** he's always very considerate towards old ladies; **il a eu une attention délicate pour nous à l'occasion de notre mariage** he was very thoughtful *or* considerate when we got married; **quelle attention délicate!** how thoughtful!, how considerate!

(d) (*difficile*) (*situation, question, opération*) delicate, difficult, tricky; (*problème, travail*) difficult, tricky

(e) (*souvent avec négation*) (*scrupuleux*) (*personne*) scrupulous; (*conscience*) tender; **peu d.** not very scrupulous, rather unscrupulous

(f) (*exigeant*) **d. sur la nourriture** fussy about food; **qu'est-ce qu'il est d.!** isn't he fussy!; **faire la délicate** to put on airs (and graces)

délicatement [delikatmɑ̃] *adv* delicately; (*s'exprimer*) with delicacy; (*se comporter*) considerately, thoughtfully; **poser d. des verres sur un plateau** to put glasses down gently on a tray; **annoncer d. un décès à qn** to gently break the news of a death to sb; **d. brodé** finely embroidered; **plat d. préparé** dish prepared with great care

délicatesse [delikatɛs] *nf* (**a**) (*fragilité*) (*de la peau*) tenderness; (*d'une fleur, un tissu*) delicacy; (*d'un objet*) fragility; (*de la santé*) frailty

(**b**) (*finesse*) (*d'une dentelle, d'un ouvrage*) delicacy, fineness; (*d'un tableau*) fineness; (*d'une texture, d'un coloris*) fineness, softness; (*d'un plat*) refinement

(**c**) (*raffinement*) (*de goût*) refinement; (*d'un geste*) gracefulness; (*de toucher*) delicacy, gentleness; **d'un geste plein de d.** with an extremely graceful movement; **elle posa les verres sur la table avec d.** she gently put the glasses down on the table

(**d**) (*difficulté*) (*d'une situation*) delicacy, difficulty, awkwardness; (*d'une opération, d'une question, d'un problème, d'un travail*) difficulty; **ce que vous me demandez de lui dire est vraiment d'une d. incroyable** what you're asking me to tell him is extremely difficult *or* awkward; **il est en d. avec la police/le gouvernement** he has to watch his step with the police/the government; **nous sommes en d.** we've had words

(**e**) (*gentillesse*) considerateness, consideration; (*sensibilité*) tact; **agir avec d.** to behave considerately/tactfully; **elle avait des délicatesses pour moi** she treated me very considerately; **c'est une personne pleine de d.** he's/she's extremely thoughtful *or* considerate

délice [delis] *nm* delight, extreme pleasure; **cette tarte est un vrai d.** this tart is delicious; **quel d. de se plonger dans un bon bain chaud** what a delight it is to sink into a warm bath

délices [delis] *nfpl* delight(s), pleasure(s); **faire les d. de qn** to delight sb, to be the delight of sb; **faire ses d. de qch** to delight in sth; **c'est un lieu de d.** this place is heavenly

délicieusement [delisjøzmɑ̃] *adv* delightfully; (*en rapport avec le goût*) deliciously; **elle nous a reçus d.** she entertained us delightfully, she was a delightful hostess; **elle réussit d. la paëlla** she makes a delicious paella; **elle se laissa glisser d. dans l'eau** she slid into the water with delight

délicieux, -euse [delisjø, -øz] *adj* (*nourriture*) delicious; (*personne, robe etc*) delightful, charming

délictuel, -elle [deliktɥɛl] *adj Jur* = **délictueux**

délictueux, -euse [deliktɥø, -øz] *adj Jur* punishable; **acte d.** misdemeanour, offence, *US* offense

délié [delje] **1** *adj* slender, fine; (*doigts*) nimble, agile; **taille déliée** slim figure; **avoir la langue déliée** to be talkative; **un esprit d.** a sharp *or* astute mind **2** *nm Typ etc* thin stroke

délier [delje] **1** *vt* (**a**) (*défaire*) (*corde, rubans etc*) to untie, to undo; (*chaînes*) to undo, to loose; *Fig* **le vin lui a délié la langue** the wine loosened his tongue (**b**) (*libérer*) (*prisonnier*) to untie; **d. les mains à qn** to untie sb's hands; **d. qn d'une promesse/d'une responsabilité** to release sb from a promise/a responsibility **2 se délier** *vpr* (**a**) (*se défaire*) to come undone *or* untied, to come loose; *Fig* **sa langue s'est déliée** he began to talk, he found his tongue (**b**) **se d. d'un serment/d'une promesse** to free oneself from an oath/a promise

délimitation [delimitasjɔ̃] *nf* (*d'un territoire*) delimitation, demarcation; (*d'une responsabilité*) demarcation; (*d'un sujet*) definition; **poteau de d.** boundary post

délimiter [delimite] *vt* (*territoire*) to delimit, to demarcate; (*responsabilité, sujet etc*) to define, to set the limits of

délimiteur [delimitœr] *nm Ordinat* delimiter; **d. de bloc** block delimiter, block marker; **d. de champ** field delimiter

délinquance [delɛ̃kɑ̃s] *nf* delinquency; **d. juvénile** juvenile delinquency; **la petite d. des banlieues** petty crime in the suburbs

délinquant, -ante [delɛ̃kɑ̃, -ɑ̃t] *Jur* **1** *adj* delinquent; **jeunesse délinquante** juvenile delinquents **2** *n* offender; **d. juvénile** juvenile delinquent; **d. primaire** first offender

déliquescence [delikɛsɑ̃s] *nf* (**a**) *Ch* deliquescence (**b**) *Fig Péj* (*de civilisation, mœurs*) decay, decline; (*de relation, mariage etc*) deterioration; (*d'une personne*) decline; **tomber en d.** (*d'une civilisation*) to fall into decay *or* decline; (*d'un mariage*) to fall apart; (*d'une personne*) to decline

déliquescent [delikɛsɑ̃] *adj* (**a**) *Ch* deliquescent (**b**) *Fig Péj* (*civilisation*) in decay, decaying; (*personne*) declining; (*relation, mariage*) deteriorating; **mœurs** *ou* **habitudes déliquescentes** decadent ways

délirant [delirɑ̃] *adj Méd* (*malade, fièvre etc*) delirious; *F* **c'est d. de lui demander de tout payer!** it's madness to ask him to pay for everything!; **joie délirante** frenzied joy; **avoir une imagination délirante** to have a wild imagination; **une atmosphère complètement délirante** an atmosphere of total delirium

délire [delir] *nm* (**a**) *Méd* delirium; **d. alcoolique** alcoholic dementia; **d. de persécution** persecution mania; **d. de grandeur** delusions of grandeur; **d. hallucinatoire** hallucination; **être victime de délires hallucinatoires** to hallucinate; **d. collectif** mass hysteria; **avoir le d.** to be delirious, to wander (in one's mind); **crise** *ou* **accès de d.** attack of delirium; *Fig* **c'est du d.!** it's madness!; **c'est du d. de croire qu'il va divorcer pour toi** you must be off your head if you think that he's going to get a divorce for your sake

(**b**) (*frénésie*) frenzy; **foule en d.** delirious *or* ecstatic crowd; **son amour pour elle va jusqu'au d.** he is madly in love with her; **sa jalousie va jusqu'au d.** he is insanely jealous; *F* **cette soirée, c'est le d.!** it's a wild party!; **quand il arrive sur scène, c'est un vrai** *ou* **du d.** the audience goes wild when he appears on stage

délirer [delire] *vi* (*de malade*) to be delirious *or* lightheaded, to wander (in one's mind); (*dire n'importe quoi*) to rave; **d. de joie** to be delirious, to be mad with joy; **tu délires!** you're raving!

délirium tremens [delirjɔmtremɛ̃s] *nm* delirium tremens, *F* DTs; **avoir le d.** to have delirium tremens *or F* the DTs

délit [deli] *nm Jur* offence, misdemeanour; **en flagrant d.** red-handed; *Jur* in flagrante delicto; **prendre qn en flagrant d.** to catch sb red-handed *or* in the act; **pris en flagrant d. d'adultère** caught in flagrante delicto; *Fig* **pris en flagrant d. de gourmandise/de mensonge/d'ignorance** caught being greedy/lying/showing one's ignorance; **d. politique** political offence

▶ **délit**: **d. d'abus de biens sociaux** misappropriation of corporate funds; **d. civil** tort; **d. de fuite** failure to report an accident; **d. d'initié** insider dealing *or* trading; **d. d'opinion** = failure to toe the party line; **d. de presse** violation of the press laws

déliter (se) [sədelite] *vpr* (*se désintégrer*), *Fig* to fall apart

délivrance [delivrɑ̃s] *nf* (**a**) (*libération*) rescue, release

(**b**) (*soulagement*) relief; **c'est fini!, quelle d.!** it's over!, what a relief!; **son départ fut une vraie d.** it was a real relief when he left, his departure came as a real relief; **ses aveux lui furent une d.** it was a relief for him to confess; **il attendait la mort comme une d.** he was waiting for death as a release

(**c**) (*de marchandises*) delivery, handing over; (*de certificat, tickets*) issue

(**d**) (*accouchement*) delivery; (*du placenta*) delivery of the afterbirth; **la d. a été difficile** it was a difficult delivery

délivrer [delivre] **1** *vt* (**a**) (*libérer*) (*captif, otage etc*) to rescue; (*détenu*) to release, to set free; **d. qn de ses liens** to free sb from his bonds; *Fig* to set sb free (**de** from)

(**b**) (*soulager*) **d. qn d'un secret trop lourd** to share the burden of a secret with sb; **tu me délivres d'un grand poids** you've taken a weight off my shoulders

(**c**) (*remettre*) (*marchandises etc*) to deliver, to hand over; (*certificat, ticket*) to issue; (*licence*) to grant

(**d**) *Obst* **d. une femme** (*du placenta etc*) to deliver a woman of the afterbirth; (*l'accoucher*) to deliver a woman (of a child)

2 se délivrer *vpr* (*se libérer*) to free oneself; *Fig* **se d. de qn/qch** to get rid of sb/sth; **se d. de ses soucis** to shed one's worries

délocalisation [delɔkalizasjɔ̃] *nf Admin* relocation

délocaliser [delɔkalize] *vt Admin* to relocate, to shift

délogement [delɔʒmɑ̃] *nm* (*de locataire*) eviction; (*dans un hôtel*) room change

déloger [delɔʒe] (*conj like* **loger**) **1** *vi* to leave (home); **délogez de là!** get out of here! **2** *vt* to drive out; (*locataire*) to evict; (*l'ennemi, objet coincé*) to dislodge; **quand il est devant la télé, c'est vraiment difficile de le d.** you just can't shift him when he's in front of the telly

déloquer (se) [sədelɔke] *vpr Arg* to strip off, to get undressed

déloyal, -ale, -aux, -ales [delwajal, -o] *adj* (*ami etc*) disloyal, unfaithful; (*pratique*) unfair; **concurrence déloyale** unfair competition; *Sp* **jeu d.** foul play; **coup d.** foul

déloyalement [delwajalmɑ̃] *adv* (*agir*) (*d'un ami*) disloyally; (*d'un concurrent*) unfairly; (*jouer aux cartes*) dishonestly

déloyauté [delwajote] *nf* (*d'un ami*) disloyalty, treachery; (*d'un concurrent, une pratique*) unfairness

Delphes [dɛlf] *nfpl* Delphi

delta [dɛlta] *nm* (*lettre grecque*), *Géog* delta; *Av* **aile (en) d.** delta wing

deltaïque [dɛltaik] *adj Géog* delta, of a/the delta

deltaplane [dɛltaplan] *nm Sp* hang-glider; **faire du d.** to go hang-gliding

deltoïde [dɛltɔid] *adj, nm Anat* deltoid

déluge [delyʒ] *nm* deluge, flood; (*de pluie*) downpour; (*d'injures*) torrent; (*de larmes*) flood; **elle l'a noyé sous un d.**

de compliments she showered *or* overwhelmed him with compliments; *Rel* **le D.** the Flood; **après moi, le d.!** when I'm gone I don't care what happens!; **cela remonte au d.** it's as old as the hills

déluré [delyre] *adj* (*vif*) sharp, smart; *Péj* (*provocant*) forward

délurer [delyre] **1** *vt* (*dégourdir*) **d. qn** to teach sb a thing or two; *Péj* **ses années d'étudiante l'ont un peu trop délurée** she kicked over the traces a bit too much *or* she went a bit off the rails when she was a student **2 se délurer** *vpr* (*se dégourdir*) to learn a thing or two; *Péj* to run wild

délustrer [delystre] *vt Tex* (*étoffe*) to take the shine off

DEM (*abrév* **Deutsche Mark**) DM

démagnétisation [demaɲetizasjɔ̃] *nf Phys* demagnetization

démagnétiser [demaɲetize] *vt Phys* to demagnetize

démago [demago] **1** *adj, abrév* **démagogique 2** *n abrév* **démagogue**

démagogie [demagɔʒi] *nf* demagogy, demagoguery

démagogique [demagɔʒik] *adj* demagogic

démagogue [demagɔg] *nm* demagogue

demaillage [demajaʒ] *nm* laddering

démailler [demɑje] **1** *vt* (*tricot*) to unravel; **tes bas sont démaillés** your stockings are laddered, *Am* you have runs in your stockings **2 se démailler** *vpr* (*d'un collant*) to ladder, *Am* to run; **le filet se démaille** the net is torn

démailloter [demajɔte] *vt* **d. un bébé** to take off a baby's nappy *or Am* diaper

demain [dəmɛ̃] **1** *adv* tomorrow; **d. soir** tomorrow evening; **d. en huit** a week tomorrow, *Vieilli* tomorrow week; **à d.!** see you tomorrow!; **remettre un travail à d.** to postpone *or* put off a job till tomorrow; **d'ici d.** between now and tomorrow; **réponds-moi d'ici d.** give me an answer by tomorrow; **le journal de d.** tomorrow's paper; *F* **ce n'est pas pour d., ce n'est pas d. la veille** that won't happen for a long time yet; **d. il fera jour** tomorrow is another day; *F* **et d. on rase gratis!** pigs might fly!; **aujourd'hui ça ne va pas, mais d., on rase gratis!** things aren't going so well today but things'll be better tomorrow, I don't think; *Fig* **les parents de d.** tomorrow's parents

2 *nm* tomorrow; **tu as d. pour réfléchir** you've got tomorrow to think about it; *Fig* **des demains peu heureux** a not-too-rosy future

démanché [demɑ̃ʃe] **1** *adj* (*outil etc*) without a handle; (*épaule etc*) dislocated **2** *nm Mus* shift

démanchement [demɑ̃ʃmɑ̃] *nm* (*d'un outil etc*) removal of the handle; (*de l'épaule etc*) dislocation

démancher [demɑ̃ʃe] **1** *vt* (*outil etc*) to remove the handle of **2** *vi Mus* to shift **3 se démancher** *vpr* **(a)** (*d'un outil etc*) to lose its handle **(b)** (*se déboîter*) **se d. l'épaule/le bras** to put one's shoulder/arm out, to dislocate one's shoulder/arm; *F* **se d. pour obtenir qch** to move heaven and earth to get sth

demande [dəmɑ̃d] *nf* **(a)** (*requête*) request, application, query (**de** for); *Cartes* bid; **faire la d. de qch** to ask for sth; **faire qch à** *ou* **sur la d. de qn** to do sth at sb's request; **faire qch à la** *ou* **sur d.** to do sth on request; **d. (en mariage)** proposal (of marriage), *Vieilli* offer of marriage; **faire sa d. (en mariage)** to propose; **à la d. générale** by popular request; **il faut remplir une d.** you must fill in an application form; **adresser une d.** to apply in writing; **d. d'intervention** request for action; **d. de renseignements** enquiry, request for information

(b) *Écon* demand; **l'offre et la d.** supply and demand; **répondre à la d.** to meet demand; **répondre à la d. en qch** to meet the demand for sth; **la d. est en hausse/en baisse** demand is up/down; **d. des consommateurs** consumer demand; **d. du marché** market demand; **d. déclinante** declining *or* falling demand; **d. dérivée** derived demand; **d. élastique** elastic demand; **d. excédentaire** overdemand; **d. indésirable** unwholesome demand; **d. prévisionnelle** projected demand; **d. soutenue** full demand; **d. surabondante** overfull demand

(c) *Jur* **d. en divorce** divorce petition; **d. de dommages-intérêts** claim for damages; **d. principale** main claim; **d. accessoire** related claim; **d. subsidiaire** subsidiary claim; **d. en renvoi** request for referral to another court

(d) (*besoin*) (*de soins, d'affection*) need; **il est perpétuellement dans un état de d. affective** he's always looking for affection

(e) (*question*) question, inquiry, enquiry

▶ **demande**: **'demandes d'emploi'** (*rubrique*) 'situations wanted'; **d. d'emploi** job application; (*petite annonce*) job wanted advertisement; **faire une d. d'emploi** to apply for a job; **d. de rançon** ransom demand

demander [dəmɑ̃de] **1** *vt* **(a)** (*réclamer, vouloir*) (*une augmentation, l'addition, de l'argent, du travail, des preuves etc*) to ask for; **d. qch à qn** to ask sb for sth; **d. un renseignement à qn** to ask sb something, to ask sb for information; **d. à qn de faire qch** to ask sb to do sth; **on nous a demandé nos passeports** we were asked for our passports; **d. à qn son aide/sa protection/un conseil** to ask sb for help/protection/advice; **d. à qn son avis** to ask sb's opinion; **d. la permission/l'autorisation (de faire qch)** to ask (for) permission (to do sth); *Mil* **d. une permission** to ask for *or* apply for leave; **d. des dommages et intérêts** to claim damages; **d. le divorce** to apply for a divorce; **puis-je vous d. une faveur** *ou* **un service?** can I ask you a favour?; **d. l'ouverture d'une enquête** to call for an inquiry; **d. un rendez-vous** to request a meeting; (*chez le médecin*) to ask for an appointment; **d. audience** to request an audience; **d. la main de qn** to ask for sb's hand (in marriage); **il a fini par la d. en mariage** he eventually proposed (to her); **combien demandez-vous de l'heure?** how much do you charge an hour?; **combien en demande-t-elle?** how much is she asking for it?; **il ne demande que ça** he'd be only too pleased; *Hum* **que demande le peuple?** what more could I/he/*etc* ask (for)?; **je ne demande qu'une seule chose: qu'on me laisse tranquille** all I ask is to be left alone; **je ne demande qu'une seule chose: qu'il fasse beau** all I ask for is good weather; **il demande qu'on lui rende justice** he wants justice; **d. la parole** to ask to speak; **je demande la parole!** may I speak!

(b) (*nécessiter*) to need, to require; **la situation demande le plus grand tact** the situation needs *or* requires *or* calls for tactful handling; **ça demande de gros sacrifices** great sacrifices are called for; **cela demande mûre réflexion** that calls for careful consideration; **le voyage demande trois heures/une semaine** the journey takes three hours/a week; **ce travail demande toute votre attention** the work demands all your attention; **on demande un maçon** builder wanted; **article très demandé** article in great demand

(c) (*exiger*) to demand; **d. à qn plus qu'il n'en peut faire** to demand *or* expect from sb more than he can do; **c'est trop me d.** it's too much to ask of me, it's asking too much; **il ne faut pas lui en d. trop** you mustn't expect too much from him; **d. la lune** to ask for the moon; **d. l'impossible** to ask (for) the impossible

(d) (*s'enquérir de*) (*prix, cause, raison*) to ask, to enquire; **d. l'heure, d. l'heure qu'il est** to ask the time; **d. son nom à qn** to ask sb his/her name; **je n'ai pas compris ce qu'il m'a demandé** I didn't understand what he asked me; **d. son chemin à qn** to ask sb the way; **il m'a demandé de tes nouvelles** he asked me how you were; *F* **je ne t'ai rien demandé!** I didn't ask for your advice *or* opinion!; *F Hum* **je ne t'ai pas demandé l'heure qu'il est** mind your own business!; **je vous (le) demande, je vous demande un peu!** I ask you!

(e) (*appeler*) **on vous demande** you're wanted, somebody wants to see you; **on vous demande au téléphone** there is a call for you; **M. Dubois est demandé au téléphone** Mr Dubois is wanted on the telephone; (*annonce*) telephone for Mr Dubois; **un conseiller en peinture est demandé à la caisse no. 3** paint consultant to checkout 3 please; **qui demandez-vous?** who do you want to speak to?; **d. un médecin/un prêtre** to ask for a doctor/priest

2 *vi* **d. à faire qch** to ask (permission) to do sth; **il a demandé à sortir** he asked to leave the room; **je demande à parler** may I speak, please let me speak; **d. à manger/boire** to ask for something to eat/drink; **je ne demande qu'à rester ici** I would dearly love to stay here; **les suspects ne demandaient qu'à parler** the suspects were only too willing to speak; **je ne demande pas mieux que de vous aider** I'll be only too pleased to help you; **il demande à ce qu'on lui rende son argent** he's asking for *or* he wants his money back; **demande à ce qu'on vienne te chercher** ask someone to come and collect you; **ce vin demande à être bu frais** this wine requires to be drunk chilled; **tu vois, ce n'était pas difficile, il suffisait de d.!** see, it wasn't difficult, you only had to ask!; **il n'y a qu'à d.** you/he/*etc* only have/has to ask; **d. après qn** to ask after *or* for sb

3 se demander *vpr* to wonder, to ask oneself; **c'est ce que je me demande** that's what I'd like to know; **c'est à se d.** *ou* **on se demande** *ou* **on peut se d. s'il ne l'a pas fait exprès** it makes you wonder whether he didn't do it on purpose; **je me demande bien pourquoi/ce que/où ...** I really can't think why/what/where ...; **des choses comme ça, cela ne se demande pas!** you don't ask that sort of question

demandeur[1], -eresse [dəmɑ̃dœr, -rɛs] *n Jur* plaintiff; **d. en divorce** petitioner; **d. en appel** appellant

demandeur[2], -euse [dəmɑ̃dœr, -øz] *n* **(a) d. d'emploi** job seeker **(b)** *Com* customer, buyer; **si tu trouves la même robe en solde, je suis demandeuse** if you find the same dress in the sales I'll take it **(c)** *Tél* **d. (de la communication)** caller

démangeaison [demɑ̃ʒɛzɔ̃] *nf* itching; **j'ai une d.** I've got an itch, I'm itching; **j'ai des démangeaisons dans les jambes** my legs itch; *Fig F* **une d. de faire qch** a longing *or* an itching to do sth

démanger [demɑ̃ʒe] *vi* **(il démangea(it))** to itch; **l'épaule me démange** my shoulder's itching; *Fig* **la main lui** *ou* **le démangeait** he was itching *or* dying for a fight; **ça me démange de lui dire ce que je pense** I'm dying *or* itching to tell him what I think

démantèlement [demɑ̃tɛlmɑ̃] *nm* (*de fortifications*) demolition, demolishing; (*d'organisation, d'empire*) dismantling, breaking up

démanteler [demɑ̃tle] *vt* **(je démantèle; je démantèlerai)** (*fortifications etc*) to demolish, to destroy; (*organisation, empire etc*) to dismantle, to break up

démantibuler [demɑ̃tibyle] *F* **1** *vt* (*objet*) to break *or* smash up; **d. une machine** to smash a machine to pieces **2 se démantibuler** *vpr* to come to pieces

démaquillage [demakijaʒ] *nm* removal of make-up; **crème pour le d.** cleansing cream, make-up remover

démaquillant [demakijɑ̃] **1** *adj* **lotion/crème démaquillante** make-up removal *or* cleansing lotion/cream **2** *nm* make-up remover

démaquiller [demakije] **1** *vt* **d. qn** to remove sb's make-up **2 se démaquiller** *vpr* to remove one's make-up; **se d. les yeux** to remove one's eye make-up

démarcage [demarkaʒ] *nm* = **démarquage**

démarcatif, -ive [demarkatif, -iv] *adj* (*ligne*) of demarcation

démarcation [demarkasjɔ̃] *nf* demarcation; **ligne de d.** dividing line, boundary line, demarcation line; *Hist* demarcation line; **c'est sur ce problème que la d. entre les deux parties s'affirme** it is on this problem that the dividing line between the two parties is most evident; **on voit la d. de son fond de teint** you can see where her foundation stops, *F* she's got a tide mark

démarchage [demarʃaʒ] *nm Com* (*porte-à-porte*) door-to-door selling; (*prospection*) canvassing; **d. à distance** telephone prospecting and selling

démarche [demarʃ] *nf* **(a)** (*allure*) gait, step, walk; **d. majestueuse** majestic bearing; **reconnaître qn à sa d.** to recognize sb by his walk; **elle avait une d. digne** she moved with dignity **(b)** (*requête*) step; **faire une d. auprès de qn** to approach sb; **faire les démarches nécessaires pour s'inscrire** to take the necessary steps to enrol; **faire les premières démarches** to take the first steps **(c)** *Fig* (*cheminement*) process; **d. intellectuelle** thought process

démarcher [demarʃe] *Com* **1** *vi* (*faire du porte-à-porte*) to sell door-to-door; **d. pour des calendriers** to sell calendars door-to-door **2** *vt* (*prospecter*) (*clients*) to canvass for

démarcheur, -euse [demarʃœr, -øz] *n Com* **(a)** (*représentant*) door-to-door salesman/saleswoman **(b)** (*prospecteur*) canvasser; **d. en publicité** advertisement canvasser

démarketing [demarketiŋ] *nm* demarketing

démarquage [demarkaʒ] *nm* **(a)** (*de linge, de plat*) removal of the (identification) mark(s) **(b)** (*plagiat*) plagiarism **(c)** *Sp* breaking free from one's opponent

démarque [demark] *nf Com* marking down, markdown; **la d. inconnue** shrinkage

démarqué [demarke] *adj* **(a)** *Com* marked down **(b)** *Sp* unmarked

démarquer [demarke] **1** *vt* **(a)** (*linge, plat etc*) to remove the identification mark(s) from **(b)** *Com* (*marchandises*) to mark down **(c)** (*livre*) to plagiarize **(d)** *Sp* (*adversaire*) to leave unmarked **2 se démarquer** *vpr Sp* to break free from one's opponent; *Fig* **un élève qui se démarque des autres** a pupil who stands out *or* apart from the others

démarrage [demaraʒ] *nm* **(a)** (*de moteur etc*) start, starting; (*de voiture etc*) moving off; *Sp* (*soudain*) spurt; (*d'entreprise*) start-up; *Sp* **faire un d.** to put on a spurt; *Ordinat* **d. à chaud/froid** warm/cold start; **faire un d. en trombe** to shoot off; *Fig* **d. d'une affaire/d'une campagne publicitaire** start of a business/publicity campaign **(b)** (*d'un navire*) casting off

▶ **démarrage** *Aut*: **d. en côte** hill start; **d. à l'aide de câbles** jump start; **d. à l'embrayage** clutch start; **d. poussé** bump start

démarrer [demare] **1** *vi* **(a)** (*d'un train, d'une voiture etc*) to start, to move off; (*d'un conducteur*) to drive away *or* off; (*d'un coureur*) to put on a spurt; **d. en trombe** (*en voiture*) to shoot off; **d. en remorque** to tow-start; **d. à froid** to start from cold; **d. à l'aide des câbles** to jump start; *Fig* **son affaire commence à d.** his business is beginning to take off; *F* **j'ai toujours du mal à d. le matin** (*en voiture*) I always have trouble starting in the morning; *Fig* I always have trouble getting started *or* getting going in the morning

(b) (*de navire*) to cast off

2 *vt* **(a)** (*voiture, travaux etc*) to start; *Fig* (*affaire, campagne*) to start (up); (*caméras*) to roll; *Ordinat* to boot (up), to start up; **d. le moteur** (*sens mécanique*) to crank the engine

(b) (*navire*) to unmoor, to cast off

démarreur [demarœr] *nm Aut* starter (motor); *Ordinat* boot program

démasquer [demaske] **1** *vt* (*enlever le masque de*) to unmask; (*imposteur, espion*) to unmask, to expose; (*complot, mensonge*) to expose; *Fig* **d. ses batteries** to show one's hand **2 se démasquer** *vpr* to take off one's mask; *Fig* to drop the mask

dématage [demataʒ] *nm* dismasting

démâter [demate] *vt* to dismast

démêlage [demɛlaʒ] *nm* untangling

démêlant [demelɑ̃] **1** *adj* **produit d., crème démêlante** cream rinse **2** *nm* cream rinse

démêlé [demele] *nm* argument; **avoir un d. avec un collègue** to have an argument *or Fml* altercation with a colleague; **démêlés** (unpleasant) dealings; **avoir des démêlés avec la justice** to be in trouble with the law; **il a eu des démêlés avec la police** he's had a few run-ins with the police

démêler [demele] **1** *vt* (*fil, soie etc*) to disentangle, to unravel; (*cheveux*) to untangle, to comb out; *Fig* **d. un problème/un malentendu** to sort out a problem/clear up a misunderstanding; *Fig* **avoir qch à d. avec qn** to have sth to clear up *or* sort out with sb; *Fig* **on va d. ça ensemble** we'll sort it out together **2 se démêler** *vpr* **se d. de** to extricate oneself from

démêloir [demɛlwar] *nm* large-toothed comb

démembrement [demɑ̃brəmɑ̃] *nm* (*d'un empire etc*) breaking up, dismemberment; (*d'un poulet etc*) jointing; (*d'une propriété, d'un domaine*) dividing up, division

démembrer [demɑ̃bre] *vt* (*empire*) to break up, to dismember; (*poulet etc*) to cut up, to joint; (*royaume, domaine*) to divide (up)

déménagement [demenaʒmɑ̃] *nm* (*action*) moving (house); (*meubles*) furniture, things; **c'est pour quand le d.?** when are you/we/*etc* moving?; **entreprise de d.** removal firm; **camion de d.** furniture *or* removal van; **frais de d.** moving expenses *or* costs; **votre d. est arrivé** your furniture has arrived; **le d. de ta chambre dans la pièce du fond va prendre du temps** it's going to take some time to move you *or* your things into the back room; **le d. de l'entreprise ne s'est pas fait sans mal** the company's move did not go smoothly; **cette entreprise fait une moyenne de 6 déménagements par semaine** the company does an average of six removals a week; **en sept ans, j'ai fait sept déménagements** I've moved seven times in seven years; **tu veux bien m'aider à faire mon d.?** will you help me move?, will you help with my removal?

déménager [demenaʒe] **(je déménageai(s); n. déménageons) 1** *vt* to move; **qui est-ce qui vous déménage?** who's moving you?, which removal company are you using?; **d. ses meubles** to move house **2** *vi* **(a)** to move; (*d'une entreprise*) to move, to relocate; **où déménage-t-il?** where's he moving to?; *F* **d. à la cloche de bois** to do a moonlight flit; *Fig F* **il déménage!** he's off his head!, he's round the bend! *F* **allez! déménagez!** scram! buzz off! **(b)** *Fig F* **moutarde qui déménage** mustard that takes the top of your head off; **musique qui déménage** powerful music

déménageur [demenaʒœr] *nm* removal man, furniture remover *or Am* mover

démence [demɑ̃s] *nf* (*folie*) insanity, madness, lunacy; *Méd* dementia; **d. précoce** *Méd* dementia praecox, *F* premature senility; *F* **c'est de la pure d.!** it's sheer madness, it's insane!

démener (se) [sədemne] *vpr* (*conj like* **mener**) **(a)** (*s'agiter*) to thrash about, to throw oneself about, to struggle; **se d. comme un beau diable** (*pour échapper*) to struggle *or* fight like a madman; (*en dansant*) to thrash around; **se d. comme un beau diable pour faire qch** to break one's back to do *or* doing sth **(b)** (*se dépenser*) to exert oneself, to make a great effort; **ils se sont tellement déménés que ...** they exerted themselves to such an extent that ...; **ils avaient beau se d., l'incendie ne s'éteignait pas** despite their tremendous efforts, the fire continued to burn

dément, -ente [demɑ̃, -ɑ̃t] **1** *adj* (*fou*) mad, insane; *Méd* demented; *F* **quel monde! c'est d.!** what a crowd! it's unbelievable!; *F* **ce concert était d.** it was a great *or* terrific concert **2** *n* mad *or* insane person, lunatic; *Méd* demented person

démenti [demɑ̃ti] *nm* (flat) denial, contradiction; *Journ* disclaimer; **donner** *ou* **opposer un d. formel à une accusation** to deny an accusation; **publier** *ou* **faire paraître**

un **d.** to issue a denial; *Journ* to publish a disclaimer; **ses actions donnent un d. à ses paroles** his actions belie his words; **ces rumeurs restent sans d.** the rumours have not been denied

démentiel, -elle [demɑ̃sjɛl] *adj* mad, insane; *F* (*idée*) mad, insane, crazy; *F* (*tenue, prix*) wild, wicked

démentir [demɑ̃tir] (*conj like* **mentir**) **1** *vt* to deny; **je démens absolument avoir passé la nuit là-bas** I flatly deny spending the night there; **leur attitude dément complètement leur réputation** their attitude totally belies their reputation; *Litt* **il a démenti nos espérances** he has not come up to our expectations, he has disappointed us **2 se démentir** *vpr* (*cesser*) **politesse qui ne se dément jamais** unfailing courtesy; **il a fait preuve d'une attention qui ne s'est jamais démentie** he showed unfailing attention

démerdard, -arde [demɛrdar, -ard] *Arg* **1** *adj* resourceful; **il n'est vraiment pas d.** he's absolutely hopeless *or* useless **2** *n* resourceful person; **c'est un d.** he's pretty sharp, he's a smart cookie

démerder (se) [sədemɛrde] *vpr Arg* **(a)** (*s'en sortir*) to get out of the shit; **tu peux te d.?** can you cope *or* manage? **(b)** (*se débrouiller*) to cope, to manage, to get by; **elle est assez grande pour se d. seule** she's old enough to take care of *or* look after herself; **elle se démerde pas mal en cuisine/tennis** she's not a bad cook/tennis player; **elle se démerde pas mal en anglais** she gets by quite well in English; **la prochaine fois, tu te démerderas mieux et tu auras un billet à meilleur prix** if you manage things better next time you'll get a cheaper ticket; **se d. pour obtenir qch** to wangle sth

démerdeur, -euse [demɛrdœr, -øz] *adj, n Arg* = **démerdard**

démérite [demerit] *nm Litt* **je ne vois pas où est mon d.** I don't see how I'm at fault; **son d. vient du fait qu'elle n'a pas fait ce qu'elle avait promis** she's at fault because she didn't do what she promised; **faire à qn un d. de qch** to reproach sb for sth

démériter [demerite] *vi* to be at fault; **je ne vois pas en quoi il a démérité** I don't see how he is at fault; **d. auprès de qn** to come down in sb's estimation

démesure [deməzyr] *nf* disproportion, excessiveness

démesuré [deməzyre] *adj* (*mains, jardin*) huge, enormous; (*orgueil*) excessive, *Fml* inordinate; (*ambition*) excessive, *Fml* inordinate, unbounded; **il est d'une taille démesurée** he's enormously tall; **il a des mains démesurées par rapport à ses bras** his hands are out of proportion to his arms

démesurément [deməzyremɑ̃] *adv* (*haut*) enormously, *Fml* inordinately; (*augmenter ses prix*) excessively; **faire attendre qn d.** to keep sb waiting an inordinate length of time; **il a profité d. du nom de son père** he has taken excessive advantage of his father's name

démettre[1] [demɛtr] (*conj like* **mettre**) **1** *vt* (*articulation*) to dislocate **2 se démettre** *vpr* **se d. l'épaule/le genou** to dislocate one's shoulder/knee, to put one's shoulder/knee out

démettre[2] **1** *vt* **(a)** (*renvoyer*) **d. qn de ses fonctions** to deprive sb of (his/her) office, to remove sb from office *or* from his/her post **(b)** *Jur* (*débouter*) **d. qn de son appel** to dismiss sb's appeal **2 se démettre** *vpr* (*démissionner*) to resign; **se d. de ses fonctions** to resign office, to resign from one's job

demeurant (au) [odəmœrɑ̃] *adv* **il n'est pas très vif, mais bien gentil au d.!** he's not very bright but he's very nice all the same *or* for all that; **je ne vous donne pas mon avis, au d., je ne suis pas concerné** I'm not telling you what I think, after all it's none of my business

demeure [dəmœr] *nf* **(a)** (*résidence*) (place of) residence; **une belle d.** a beautiful home, *Fml, Litt* a fine residence; **dernière d.** last resting place **(b) il est ici à d.** he's here for good *or* to stay *or* permanently; *Jur* **meuble à d.** fixture **(c)** *Jur* **mettre qn en d. de payer** to give sb notice to pay; **mise en d.** formal notice, summons; *Fig* **je vous mets en d. de le faire immédiatement** I'm warning you that I want it done immediately **(d) il y a péril en la d.** you/I/he/*etc* must act immediately; **il n'y a pas péril en la d.** there's no great rush

demeuré, -ée [dəmœre] **1** *adj* mentally retarded, *Péj* halfwitted; *F* **il est complètement d., ce mec** the guy's a complete halfwit **2** *n* mentally retarded person, *Péj* halfwit

demeurer [dəmœre] *vi* **(a)** (*conj with* **être**) (*rester*) to remain; **je demeure convaincu que ...** I remain convinced that ...; **d. fidèle à qn** to stay faithful to sb; **l'affaire n'en demeurera pas là** the matter won't rest there; **demeurons-en là** let's leave it at that; **elle ne pouvait pas d. en place** she couldn't keep still; **elle demeurait assise à nous écouter** she sat listening to us; *Litt* **je suis demeuré des heures à t'attendre** I waited hours for you; *Litt* **il est demeuré des mois sans nouvelles** he had no news for months; *Fml* **l'affaire lui est demeurée de sa famille** he inherited the business from his family

(b) (*conj with* **avoir**) (*habiter*) to live, *Fml* to reside; **d. à la campagne** to live in the country; **il demeure rue de Rivoli** he lives in *or Am* on the rue de Rivoli

demi, -ie [dəmi] **1** *adj* **(a)** (*après un nom*) half; **deux heures et demie** (*durée*) two and a half hours; (*moment*) half past two; **un litre/kilo/centimètre et d.** a litre/kilo/centimetre and a half; **il gagne trois fois et demie ce que je gagne** he earns three and a half times as much as I do

(b) (*avant un nom ou un adjectif*) half; **un d-congé** a half-holiday; **une d-cuillère de sucre** half a teaspoon of sugar, a half-teaspoon of sugar; **d-cuit** half cooked

2 *nm* **(a)** (*moitié*) half; **deux plus un d.** two plus a half

(b) (*bière*) **un d.** = half a pint, a half

(c) *Fb* **les demis** the halfbacks; *Rugby* **d. de mêlée** scrum half; **d. d'ouverture** stand-off (half), fly half

3 *nf* **demie** half hour; **il est la demie** it's half past; **à la demie** at half past

4 *adv* half; **d. plein** half full; **à d.** half; **à d. mort** half dead; **à d. transparent** semi-transparent; **faire les choses à d.** to do things by halves; **croire qn à d.** to half believe sb; **ouvre la fenêtre à d.** open the window half way

NOTE *in all the following compounds* **demi** *is inv and the second component takes the plural*

demi-arbre *nm* halfshaft

demiard [dəmjar] *nm Can* half pint

demi-arrière *nm Fb* halfback

demi-bas *nm* knee-length sock; (*pour femmes*) knee-high

demi-botte *nf* half boot

demi-bouteille *nf* half bottle

demi-cercle *nm* semicircle, half circle; **en d.** in a semicircle

demi-circulaire *adj* semicircular

demi-clef *nf* half hitch

demi-deuil *nm* half mourning

demi-dieu *nm* demigod

demi-douzaine *nf* half dozen; **une d. d'œufs** half a dozen eggs, a half-dozen eggs; **une d. de fois** half a dozen times

demi-droite *nf Géom* semi-infinite line, half-line

demi-fin **1** *adj* **(a)** (*petits pois, haricots etc*) medium **(b)** (*or*) twelve carat **2** *nm* twelve-carat gold; **bracelet en d.** twelve carat bracelet

demi-finale *nf Sp* semifinal

demi-finaliste *n Sp* semifinalist

demi-fond *nm inv Sp* **(course de) d.** middle distance race

demi-frère *nm* half brother

demi-gros *nm* retail wholesale; **(commerce de) d.** cash and carry

demi-grossiste *n* cash-and-carry merchant

demi-heure [dəmijœr] *nf* **une d.** half an hour; **deux demi-heures** two half hours; **de d. en d., toutes les demi-heures** every half hour

demi-jour *nm* half light; (*crépuscule*) twilight, dusk

demi-journée *nf* half a day; (*de travail, de congé*) half day; **faire des demi-journées** to work half days; **j'ai pris ma d.** I took a half day

démilitarisation [demilitarizasjɔ̃] *nf* demilitarization

démilitariser [demilitarize] *vt* to demilitarize

demi-litre *nm* half litre *or US* liter; **un d. de vin** half a litre *or* a half litre of wine

demi-longueur *nf Sp* **une d.** half a length, a half length

demi-lune **1** *nf* half moon; (*fortification*) demi-lune **2** *adj inv* semicircular

demi-mal, *pl* **demi-maux** *nm* **il n'y a que** *ou* **ce n'est que d.** it could have been worse

demi-mesure *nf* **(a)** (*compromis*) half measure; **avec elle, il n'y a jamais de d.** there are never any half measures with her **(b)** (*pour chaussures etc*) half-size

demi-mondain, -aine **1** *adj* belonging to the demi-monde *or* fringes of society **2** *nf* **demi-mondaine** demi-mondaine

demi-monde *nm* demi-monde, fringes of society

demi-mort *adj* half-dead

demi-mot (à) [ad(ə)mimo] *adv* **comprendre à d.** to (know how to) take a hint; **il a compris à d.** he took the hint; **nous nous comprenons à d.** we don't have to spell everything out (to each other)

déminage [deminaʒ] *nm* mine clearance; *Naut* minesweeping

déminer [demine] *vt* to clear of mines

déminéralisation [demineralizasjɔ̃] *nf* demineralization

déminéraliser [demineralize] **1** *vt* to demineralize **2 se déminéraliser** *vpr* to become demineralized

démineur [deminœr] *nm* (*personne*) bomb disposal expert; (*navire*) minesweeper

demi-pause *nf Mus* minim rest, *Am* half-note rest
demi-pension *nf* (*à l'hôtel*) half board, *Am* American plan; **sept jours en d.** seven days half board; *Scol* **mon fils est en d.** my son is a day boarder
demi-pensionnaire *n Scol* day boarder
demi-place *nf* (*en voyage*) half fare; (*au théâtre etc*) half price
demi-pointe *nf* (*position*) demi-point; **(chausson de) d.** demi-point shoe
demi-portion *nf F Péj* weed; **eh toi, la d., viens ici!** come here titch!
demi-produit *nm Écon* semi-finished product
demi-quart *nm* **(a)** (*de compas*) half point **(b)** (*mesure*) = 2 ounces
demi-queue *adj, nm inv* **(piano) d.** baby grand (piano)
demi-reliure *nf* quarter binding; **d. à (petits) coins** half binding
démis [demi] *adj* (*épaule*) dislocated
demi-saison *nf* between season, mid season; **vêtements (de) d.** spring/autumn clothes
demi-sang *nm inv* halfbred (horse)
demi-sel **1** *adj inv* (*beurre etc*) slightly salted **2** *nm* **(a)** (*fromage*) (slightly salted) cream cheese **(b)** *F* petty crook
demi-sœur *nf* half sister
demi-solde **1** *nf Mil* half pay; **en d.** on half pay **2** *nm inv* half-pay officer
demi-sommeil *nm* drowsiness, somnolence
demi-soupir *nm Mus* quaver rest, *Am* eighth-note rest
démission [demisjɔ̃] *nf* **(a)** (*au travail*) resignation; **donner sa d.** to hand in *or Fml* tender one's resignation, to resign; *Fig* to give up **(b)** *Fig* (*abandon*) renunciation; **la d. du père** the father's abdication of his responsibilities
démissionnaire [demisjɔnɛr] *adj* who has resigned; *Fig* **père/mère d.** father/mother who has abdicated his/her responsibilities
démissionner [demisjɔne] **1** *vi* to resign (**de** from); *Fig* **je démissionne!** I give up! **2** *vt F Iron* to sack
demi-tarif *nm* half price; **billet d.** (*transports*) half fare (ticket); *Th, Cin* half-price ticket
demi-teinte *nf Beaux-Arts, Phot* halftone; *Fig* **il ne fait pas dans la d.** there are no half-measures with him
demi-ton *nm Mus* semitone
demi-tonneau *nm Av* half roll
demi-tour *nm* half-turn; *Mil* about-turn; *Aut* U-turn; *Aut* **d. en trois temps** three-point turn; **un d. de clé** a half-turn of the key; **faire d.** to turn and go back
démiurge [demjyrʒ] *nm* demiurge
demi-voix (à) [ad(ə)mivwa] *adv* in an undertone, under one's breath
demi-volée *nf Tennis* half volley
démo [demo] (*abrév* **démonstration**) *nf* demo
démobilisateur, trice [demɔbilizatœr, -tris] *adj* (*paroles, actions*) demotivating, discouraging
démobilisation [demɔbilizasjɔ̃] *nf* **(a)** (*de troupes*) demobilization, *F* demob **(b)** (*désintérêt*) apathy, lack of interest
démobiliser [demɔbilize] **1** *vt* **(a)** (*troupes*) to demobilize, *F* to demob **(b)** (*décourager*) to demotivate, to discourage; **cette campagne de presse a beaucoup contribué à d. les militants** the press campaign had a very demotivating effect on the militants **2 se démobiliser** *vpr* to become apathetic *or* discouraged
démocrate [demɔkrat] **1** *adj* democratic **2** *n* democrat
démocrate-chrétien, -ienne *adj, n Pol* Christian Democrat
démocratie [demɔkrasi] *nf* democracy; *F* **on est en d., après tout!** it's a free country!
démocratique [demɔkratik] *adj* democratic
démocratiquement [demɔkratikmɑ̃] *adv* democratically
démocratisation [demɔkratizasjɔ̃] *nf* democratization
démocratiser [demɔkratize] **1** *vt* to democratize **2 se démocratiser** *vpr* to become (more) democratic
démodé [demɔde] *adj* (*personne, manières*) old-fashioned; (*vêtement*) old-fashioned, out-of-date, out-of-fashion; (*équipement*) old-fashioned, out-of-date; (*idée, théorie*) old-fashioned, out-of-date, outmoded
démoder (se) [sədemɔde] *vpr* (*de vêtements etc*) to go out of fashion, to become old-fashioned
démodulation [demɔdylasjɔ̃] *nf* demodulation
démographe [demɔgraf] *n* demographer
démographie [demɔgrafi] *nf* demography
démographique [demɔgrafik] *adj* demographic; **statistiques démographiques** demographics; **poussée d.** population growth
demoiselle [dəmwazɛl] *nf* **(a)** (*femme célibataire*) single *or* unmarried woman, *Vieilli, Admin* spinster; **les demoiselles Dupin** the Misses Dupin; **c'est une vieille d.** she never married **(b)** (*jeune fille, employée*) young lady; **les demoiselles du téléphone** the young ladies on the switchboard **(c)** (*insecte*) dragonfly; **d. (de Numidie)** demoiselle (crane), Numidian crane **(d)** *Tech* paving beetle
▶ **demoiselle**: **d. de compagnie** lady's companion; **d. d'honneur** (*d'une souveraine*) lady-in-waiting, *Vieilli* maid of honour; (*d'une mariée*) bridesmaid
démolir [demɔlir] *vt* **(a)** (*maison, immeuble, quartier etc*) to demolish, to pull down; (*navire*) to break up; (*voiture, jouet etc*) to demolish, to wreck, to smash up; **d. une porte à coups de pied** to kick a door down
(b) *Fig* (*argument, théorie, adversaire, concurrent etc*) to demolish; (*réputation*) to ruin; (*gouvernement, autorité etc*) to undermine; (*auteur, cinéaste etc*) to slate; (*roman, film*) to demolish, to slate
(c) *F* (*battre*) to beat up, to bash about; (*fatiguer*) to tire; **je vais lui d. le portrait!** I'll smash his face in!; **il s'est fait d.** he got beaten up; **cette mauvaise grippe m'a démoli** that bad bout of flu laid me low *or* put me flat on my back; **tout ce travail l'a démolie** she's exhausted *or* shattered after all that work; **d. le foie de qn** (*de l'alcool*) to play havoc with *or* ruin sb's liver; **les piments m'ont démoli l'estomac** those chilis are playing havoc *or F* merry hell with my stomach
démolissage [demɔlisaʒ] *nm* (*d'un auteur etc*) severe criticism, *F* slating; (*d'une théorie, d'un argument*) demolition
démolisseur, -euse [demɔlisœr, -øz] *n* **(a)** (*de bâtiments*) demolition contractor; (*de bateaux*) shipbreaker **(b)** *Fig* (*d'un argument etc*) demolisher, destroyer
démolition [demɔlisjɔ̃] *nf* **(a)** (*d'une structure*) demolition, pulling down; **chantier de d.** demolition yard **(b)** *Fig* (*d'une théorie*) demolition **(c)** **démolitions** (*matériaux*) debris, rubble
démon [demɔ̃] *nm* **(a)** demon, devil, fiend; **le d.** the Devil; **cette femme est un d.** that woman's a (she-)devil; **cet enfant est un petit d.** that child is a little devil; **le d. de la jalousie** the demon of jealousy, the green-eyed monster; **le d. de midi** (*d'un homme*) the male menopause, mid-life crisis; (*d'une femme*) = midlife crisis **(b)** (*génie, esprit etc*) (good/evil) genius; *Myth* daemon
démonétisation [demɔnetizasjɔ̃] *nf* **(a)** (*d'argent*) demonetization, withdrawal from circulation **(b)** *Fig* (*d'une personne*) discrediting; **sa d. au sein de l'entreprise a été rapide** he quickly became discredited throughout the company; **pour accélérer sa d.** to speed up the process of discrediting him
démonétiser [demɔnetize] *vt* **(a)** *Fin* to demonetize, to withdraw from circulation **(b)** *Fig* (*personne*) to discredit
démoniaque [demɔnjak] **1** *adj* demonic, possessed by the devil; *Fig* (*personne, rire*) fiendish **2** *n* person possessed by the devil
démonstrateur, -trice [demɔ̃stratœr, -tris] *n* demonstrator
démonstratif, -ive [demɔ̃stratif, -iv] **1** *adj* **(a)** (*convaincant*) (logically) conclusive **(b)** (*personne*) demonstrative; **peu d.** undemonstrative **(c)** *Gram* demonstrative **2** *nm* [①A30,9; B13-14,A] *Gram* demonstrative
démonstration [demɔ̃strasjɔ̃] *nf* **(a)** (*preuve*) (*de théorème etc*) demonstration, proof; **d. par l'absurde** reductio ad absurdum; **faire la d. de qch** to demonstrate *or* prove sth **(b)** *Com* (*d'article*) demonstration; **je ne peux pas vous vendre cet appareil, il est en d.** I can't sell you this appliance, it's a demonstration model; **d. sur le lieu de vente** in-store demonstration; *Boxe* **assaut de d.** sparring match; *Mus* **cassette de d.** demo (tape); **appareil de d.** demonstration model; **est-ce que vous pouvez me faire la d. de cette machine à laver?** could you give me a demonstration of this washing machine? **(c)** (*manifestation*) (*de tendresse, joie etc*) demonstration; **faire de grandes démonstrations d'amitié** to make a great show of friendship; *Mil* **d. de force** display *or* show of force; **d. navale** naval display
démontable [demɔ̃tabl] *adj* (*machine, armoire etc*) that can be dismantled
démontage [demɔ̃taʒ] *nm* dismantling, taking to pieces, taking apart
démonté [demɔ̃te] *adj* **(a)** (*cavalier*) thrown; *Fig* (*déconcerté*) disconcerted, *F* thrown; (*troublé*) upset **(b)** (*mécanisme etc*) dismantled, taken to pieces, taken apart **(c)** (*mer*) stormy, raging
démonte-pneu, *pl* **démonte-pneus** [demɔ̃tpnø] *nm* tyre *or US* tire lever
démonter [demɔ̃te] **1** *vt* **(a)** (*appareil, moteur, armoire etc*) to dismantle, to take to pieces, to take apart; (*tente*) to dismantle, to take down; (*porte*) to remove from its hinges; (*pneu*) to remove; (*décor*) to strike

(**b**) (*cavalier*) to throw (off), to unseat
(**c**) (*déconcerter*) to disconcert, *F* to throw; (*troubler*) to upset; **la nouvelle m'a démonté** I was greatly upset *or* put out by the news; **ça me démonte de le voir dans un tel état** it upsets me to see him in such a state; **elle est complètement démontée depuis qu'elle sait qu'il va partir** she's been in a dreadful state since she found out that he was leaving; **se laisser d.** to get upset *or* flustered, to be thrown
2 se démonter *vpr* (**a**) (*d'un mécanisme*) to come apart, to dismantle
(**b**) *F* **elle ne se démonte pas pour si peu** she's not so easily put out *or* thrown

démontrable [demɔ̃trabl] *adj* demonstrable, provable

démontrer [demɔ̃tre] *vt* (*théorème, vérité*) to demonstrate; **d. qu'il est nécessaire de faire qch** to show *or* demonstrate *or* prove that it is necessary to do sth; *F* **d. qch par A + B** to prove sth conclusively

démoralisant [demɔralizɑ̃] *adj* demoralizing, disheartening

démoralisateur, -trice [demɔralizatœr, -tris] *adj* demoralizing, disheartening

démoralisation [demɔralizasjɔ̃] *nf* demoralization

démoraliser [demɔralize] **1** *vt* to demoralize, to dishearten **2 se démoraliser** *vpr* to become demoralized, to lose heart

démordre [demɔrdr] *vi* **ne pas d. de ses opinions** to stand by *or* stick to one's opinions; **elle ne veut pas en d.** she won't give up, she's sticking to her guns; **quand il a une idée, il n'en démord jamais** once he gets an idea in his head you can't shift him; **ça va être difficile de le faire d. de sa décision** it's going to be difficult to get him to change his mind

démotivation [demɔtivasjɔ̃] *nf* demotivation; **il ne faut pas laisser s'installer la d. au sein de l'équipe** we mustn't let the team become demotivated

démotiver [demɔtive] *vt* to demotivate; **ne te laisse pas d. par ses arguments stupides** don't let his stupid arguments put you off

démoulage [demulaʒ] *nm* (*d'un moulage*) removal from the mould *or US* mold; *Culin* turning out

démouler [demule] *vt* (*moulage*) to remove from the mould *or US* mold; *Culin* to turn out

démoustication [demustikasjɔ̃] *nf* clearing of mosquitoes; **il faut procéder à la d. de la région** the region must be cleared of mosquitoes

démoustiquer [demustike] *vt* to clear mosquitoes from

démultiplicateur, -trice [demyltiplikatœr, -tris] *MecE* **1** *adj* (*dispositif*) reducing, reduction **2** *nm* reduction system; **d. de vitesse** motor reduction unit

démultiplication [demyltiplikasjɔ̃] *nf MecE* (**a**) (*de voiture, machine*) gearing down, (gear) reduction (**b**) (*de vitesses*) reduction ratio

démultiplier [demyltiplije] *vt MecE* (*voiture, machine*) to gear down; (*de boîte de vitesses*) to reduce the gear ratio of

démuni [demyni] *adj* penniless; **d. de vêtements/papiers d'identité** without any clothes/identification; **d. d'argent** without any money, penniless; **d. de tout** destitute; **d. d'intérêt/d'intelligence/de talent** devoid of interest/ intelligence/talent; *Com* **être d. de qch** to be out of sth, to be sold out of sth

démunir [demynir] **1** *vt* to deprive **2 se démunir** *vpr* to leave oneself short; **se d. de qch** to part with sth

démuseler [demyzle] *vt* (**je démuselle**; **je démusellerai**) (*chien*) to unmuzzle; *Fig* **d. la presse** to ungag the press

démystifiant [demistifjɑ̃] *adj* (*histoire, étude etc*) which demystifies; **son film sur Mozart est tout à fait d.** his film enlightens us to the real Mozart

démystificateur, -trice [demistifikatœr, -tris] **1** *adj* (*histoire, étude etc*) which demystifies **2** *n* demystifier

démystification [demistifikasjɔ̃] *nf* demystification

démystifier [demistifje] *vt* (*impf & pr sub* **n. démystifiions, v. démystifiiez**) to demystify

démythification [demitifikasjɔ̃] *nf* demythologization; **on assiste à la d. de l'ordinateur** computers are no longer regarded with awe *or* are losing their mystique

démythifier [demitifje] *vt* to demythologize; (*ordinateur*) to remove the mystique surrounding

dénatalité [denatalite] *nf* fall in the birthrate

dénationalisation [denasjɔnalizasjɔ̃] *nf* denationalization

dénationaliser [denasjɔnalize] *vt* to denationalize

dénatter [denate] *vt* (*cheveux*) to unplait

dénaturalisation [denatyralizasjɔ̃] *nf* denaturalization

dénaturaliser [denatyralize] *vt* to denaturalize

dénaturant [denatyrɑ̃] *Ch* **1** *adj* denaturing **2** *nm* denaturant, denaturing agent

dénaturation [denatyrasjɔ̃] *nf Ch* denaturing

dénaturé [denatyre] *adj* (**a**) (*dépravé*) (*parents*) unnatural; (*goût*) unnatural, perverted (**b**) *Ch* (*transformé*) denatured

dénaturer [denatyre] *vt* (*mots*) to misrepresent, to distort; (*actions*) to misrepresent; *Ch* (*alcool etc*) to denature; **d. les faits** to distort the facts; **d. les paroles de qn** to misrepresent what sb has said

dénazification [denazifikasjɔ̃] *nf* denazification

dénazifier [denazifje] *vt* to denazify

dénégateur, -trice [denegatœr, -tris] *n* denier

dénégation [denegasjɔ̃] *nf* denial

déneigement [denɛʒmɑ̃] *nm* snow clearance *or* removal

déneiger [deneʒe] *vt* to clear (away) *or* remove snow from

dengue [dɛ̃g] *nf Méd* dengue fever

déni [deni] *nm Jur* denial, refusal; **d. de justice** denial of justice

déniaiser [denjeze] **1** *vt* (**a**) (*dégourdir*) **d. qn** to teach sb a thing or two, to smarten *or F* wise sb up (**b**) *F* (*faire perdre sa virginité à*) **c'est lui qui l'a déniaisée** he was her first **2 se déniaiser** *vpr* (*se dégourdir*) to smarten up, to get smart; *F* (*perdre sa virginité*) to lose one's virginity

dénicher [deniʃe] **1** *vt* (**a**) *F* (*trouver*) (*objet*) to find, to unearth; (*personne*) to find, to track down; **nous avons déniché une maison superbe** we've found a beautiful house; **on a déniché un restaurant très chouette** we've found *or F* sussed out a great restaurant; **elle est allée d. l'homme de sa vie au Canada** she went to Canada to find the man of her dreams (**b**) (*oiseau, œufs*) to take out of the nest (**c**) (*animal*) to drive out of hiding **2** *vi* (*d'un oiseau*) to leave the nest

dénicheur, -euse [deniʃœr, -øz] *n* (**a**) *Fig* (*d'objets*) searcher; **d. de curiosités/d'antiquités** curio/antique hunter; **c'est un d. de talents** he's good at spotting talent (**b**) (*d'oiseaux*) bird nester

dénicotinisation [denikɔtinizasjɔ̃] *nf* reduction of nicotine

dénicotiniser [denikɔtinize] *vt* to reduce the amount of nicotine in; **du tabac dénicotinisé** low nicotine tobacco

denier [dənje] *nm* (**a**) *Antiq* denarius; *Hist Fr* denier; **je l'ai payé de mes deniers** I paid for it with my own money; **payer jusqu'au dernier d.** to pay to the last farthing; **les deniers publics** public money *or* funds; *Cathol* **d. du culte** church offering (*given privately to parish priest*) (**b**) (*de bas*) denier; **bas de 30 deniers** 30 denier stockings

dénier [denje] *vt* (**a**) (*crime etc*) to deny; (*responsabilité*) to deny, to disclaim (**b**) **d. qch à qn** to refuse *or* deny sb sth; **d. à qn le droit de faire qch** to deny sb the right to do sth

dénigrant [denigrɑ̃] *adj* disparaging, denigrating

dénigrement [denigrəmɑ̃] *nm* disparagement, denigration

dénigrer [denigre] *vt* to disparage, to denigrate

dénivelé [denivle] **1** *adj* (*surface*) uneven **2** *nm* = **dénivelée**

dénivelée [denivle] *nf* difference *or* variation in level *or* height

déniveler [denivle] *vt* (*conj like* **niveler**) to make uneven

dénivellation [denivɛlasjɔ̃] *nf*, **dénivellement** [denivɛlmɑ̃] *nm* (**a**) (*écart*) difference in level *or* height; **d. d'une route** gradients *or* ups and downs of a road (**b**) (*action*) lowering/ lifting of level; (*d'une surface*) making uneven

dénombrable [denɔ̃brabl] *adj* [①**A9-11,3**] countable

dénombrement [denɔ̃brəmɑ̃] *nm* counting, enumeration; (*de la population*) census; *Méd* **d. des hématies** blood count

dénombrer [denɔ̃bre] *vt* to count, to enumerate; (*population*) to take a census of

dénominateur [denɔminatœr] *nm Math* denominator; **d. commun** common denominator; **plus petit d. commun** lowest common denominator

dénominatif, -ive [denɔminatif, -iv] *adj, nm Ling* denominative

dénomination [denɔminasjɔ̃] *nf* name, denomination, designation; **comment a été décidée la nouvelle d. de certaines régions?** how were the new names for certain regions decided on?; *Pharm* **d. commune** generic name; **d. commerciale** (*de produit*) trade name; **d. sociale** company name

dénommer [denɔme] *vt* to name; *parfois Péj* **un dénommé Charles** someone by the name of Charles; **est-ce que le dénommé Laurent va ...?** is that man/boy Laurent going to ...; **le dénommé Jacques Duval est prié de se rendre à la caisse no. 3** would Jacques Duval go to checkout 3; **ci-après dénommé** hereinafter referred to as

dénoncer [denɔ̃se] (**je dénonçai(s)**; **n. dénonçons**) **1** *vt* (**a**) (*à la police*) (*personne*) to denounce, to inform against; (*crime etc*) to expose; **d. qn à la police** to denounce sb to the police; **c'est elle qui a dénoncé son frère à ses parents** it was she who gave her brother away *or* told on her brother to her parents (**b**) (*protester contre*) (*traité, abus de pouvoir, la pollution etc*) to denounce; **d. un contrat** to terminate a contract, to cancel a contract (**c**) (*révéler*) to indicate, to

reveal; **son attitude dénonce sa méfiance des autres** his attitude betrays his mistrust of others **2 se dénoncer** *vpr* to give oneself up
dénonciateur, -trice [denɔ̃sjatœr, -tris] **1** *n* (*d'une personne*) informer; **il est le d. de ces crimes** he exposed the crimes **2** *adj* (*lettre*) of denunciation, accusing
dénonciation [denɔ̃sjasjɔ̃] *nf* denunciation
dénotation [denɔtasjɔ̃] *nf* denotation
dénoter [denɔte] *vt* to denote, to show, to indicate
dénouement [denumɑ̃] *nm* (*d'un événement*) result, outcome; (*d'une difficulté*) solution; (*d'une intrigue, une histoire*) ending; *Th* dénouement
dénouer [denwe] **1** *vt* (*nœud*) to untie, to undo, to loosen; **d. ses cheveux** to undo *or* let down one's hair; **d. une intrigue** to unravel a plot **2 se dénouer** *vpr* (*d'un nœud*) to come undone; (*de cheveux*) to come down; (*d'un mystère*) to be solved; (*d'une histoire, d'une enquête*) to end; **sa langue se dénoue** he's finding his tongue
dénoyautage [denwajotaʒ] *nm* (*d'un fruit*) stoning, *Am* pitting; *Fig Écon* removal of political appointees from the board
dénoyauter [denwajote] *vt* (*fruit*) to stone, *Am* to pit; *Fig Écon* **d. une entreprise** to remove political appointees from the board of a company
dénoyauteur [denwajotœr] *nm* (*machine*) stoner
denrée [dɑ̃re] *nf* (*pour l'homme*) foodstuff; (*pour le bétail*) feed; **denrées alimentaires** food products, foodstuffs; **denrées périssables** perishable goods; **denrées de consommation courante** staple foods, staples; *Fig* **la patience est une d. rare** patience is a rare commodity
dense [dɑ̃s] *adj* **(a)** *Phys* dense **(b)** (*foule*) dense; (*brouillard, forêt*) dense, thick; (*style*) concise, condensed, dense
densité [dɑ̃site] *nf* **(a)** *Phys* density; **d. moyenne** mean specific weight; **flacon à d.** specific gravity flask **(b)** (*de population etc*) density; *Ordinat* **à double d.** double-density; *Ordinat* **d. quadruple** quad density
dent [dɑ̃] *nf* **(a)** *Anat* tooth; **d. du fond/de devant/du haut/du bas** back/front/top/bottom tooth; **sans dents** toothless; **percer** *ou* **faire ses dents** (*d'un enfant*) to cut a tooth, to be teething; **se faire les dents sur qch** (*d'un chat, d'un enfant*) to cut one's teeth on sth; *Fig* **se faire les dents sur qn** to take it out on sb; **mal** *ou* **rage de dents** toothache; **coup de d.** bite; *Fig F* **avoir la d.** to be hungry; **manger/rire à belles dents** to eat hungrily *or* with relish/to laugh heartily; **manger du bout des dents** to pick at one's food; **rire du bout des dents** to force a laugh; **avoir les dents longues** (*être ambitieux*) to be ambitious, *F* to be hungry; **avoir la d. dure** to have a sharp tongue; **montrer les dents** to show one's teeth; *aussi Fig* **serrer les dents** to grit one's teeth; **ne pas desserrer les dents** not to open one's mouth; **avoir** *ou* **conserver** *ou* **garder une d. contre qn** to have a grudge against sb; **ils n'ont rien à se mettre sous la d.** they don't have a bite to eat; **parler entre ses dents** to mumble, to mutter; **être sur les dents** (*épuisé*) to be worn out; (*surmené*) to be overworked
(b) (*de peigne, scie*) tooth; (*de roue*) cog; (*de fourchette*) prong; (*de montagne*) (jagged) peak; (*de timbre*) perforation; **en dents de scie** serrated, jagged; *Fig* (*évolution, progrès*) uneven; **roue à dents** cogged wheel
▸ **dent**: **d. d'éléphant** elephant's tusk; **d. de lait** milk tooth, first tooth; **d. de sagesse** wisdom tooth
dentaire [dɑ̃tɛr] *adj Anat* (*hygiène, plaque, pulpe etc*) dental; **l'art d.** dentistry
dental, -ale, -aux, -ales [dɑ̃tal, -o] *Ling* **1** *adj* (*consonne*) dental **2** *nf* **dentale** dental consonant
dent-de-lion [dɑ̃d(ə)ljɔ̃], *pl* **dents-de-lion** *nf* dandelion
dent-de-loup [dɑ̃dlu], *pl* **dents-de-loup** *nf Aut* ratchet tooth, catch
denté [dɑ̃te] *adj Tech* (*couronne, anneau*) cogged, toothed; (*feuille*) jagged, *Spéc* dentate; **roue dentée** cogwheel
dentelé [dɑ̃tle] *adj* (*rivage*) jagged, indented; (*bord*) jagged; (*feuille*) serrated; (*timbre*) perforated
denteler [dɑ̃tle] *vt* (**je dentelle**; **je dentellerai**) to notch, to jag, to indent; (*timbre*) to perforate
dentelle [dɑ̃tɛl] *nf* **(a)** (*tissu*) lace; **d. aux fuseaux** pillow lace; **d. à l'aiguille** *ou* **au point** point lace; **robe de** *ou* **en d.** lace dress; **des dentelles de papier** paper doilies; *Culin* **crêpe d.** very thin pancake, crêpe; *Fig* **ne pas faire dans la d.** (*y aller carrément*) not to mince one's words; (*manquer de finesse*) to be clumsy; **ça n'est pas de la d.** it's nothing fancy **(b)** *Archit* = wrought ironwork that has the appearance of lace, ≈ *Am* gingerbread
dentellerie [dɑ̃tɛlri] *nf* lacemaking
dentellier, -ière [dɑ̃təlje, -jɛr] **1** *adj* (*industrie etc*) lace (-making) **2** *n* lacemaker **3** *nf* **dentellière** (*machine*) lacemaking machine
dentelure [dɑ̃tlyr] *nf* (*d'un rivage*) indentation; (*d'une montagne*) jagged summit; (*d'une feuille*) serration; (*d'un timbre*) perforation
dentier [dɑ̃tje] *nm* set of false teeth, dentures
dentifrice [dɑ̃tifris] **1** *nm* toothpaste, *Vieilli* toothpowder **2** *adj* **pâte d.** toothpaste; **eau d.** mouthwash; **poudre d.** toothpowder
dentine [dɑ̃tin] *nf Anat* dentine
dentiste [dɑ̃tist] *n* dentist
dentition [dɑ̃tisjɔ̃] *nf* **(a)** (*croissance*) cutting of teeth, teething; **d. définitive** *ou* **permanente** permanent teeth **(b)** (*arrangement*) arrangement of the teeth, *Spéc* dentition
denture [dɑ̃tyr] *nf* **(a)** (*dents*) set of teeth **(b)** (*dentier*) set of false teeth, denture **(c)** *MecE* teeth, cogs, gearing; (*du rotor*) rotor gear; **à d. hélicoïdale** spiral
dénucléarisation [denyklearizasjɔ̃] *nf* denuclearization
dénucléariser [denyklearize] *vt* to denuclearize
dénudation [denydasjɔ̃] *nf Fml* stripping, laying bare
dénudé [denyde] *adj* (*campagne, arbre*) bare; (*crâne*) bald; *Él* (*fil*) bare
dénuder [denyde] **1** *vt* (*colline*) to strip, to lay bare; (*arbre*) to strip; (*d'une robe*) to leave bare; **d. un arbre de son écorce** to strip a tree of its bark, to strip the bark off a tree **2 se dénuder** *vpr* **(a)** (*d'une colline*) to grow bare; (*d'un arbre*) to lose its leaves **(b)** (*se mettre à nu*) to strip (naked); **crâne qui se dénude** balding head
dénué [denɥe] *adj* **d. de** (*raison, intelligence, intérêt etc*) devoid of; **une famille dénuée de tout** a family with absolutely nothing, a destitute family; **d. de tout fondement** totally without foundation
dénuement [denymɑ̃] *nm* destitution, penury; **être dans le d.** to be destitute *or* poverty-stricken
dénuer (se) [sədenɥe] *vpr Litt* to deprive oneself (**de** of); **se d. de ses biens** to part with all one's possessions
dénutrition [denytrisjɔ̃] *nf Méd* malnutrition
déodorant [deɔdɔrɑ̃] *adj, nm* deodorant
déodoriser [deɔdɔrize] *vt* to deodorize
déontologie [deɔ̃tɔlɔʒi] *nf* professional ethics; **code de d.** professional code of ethics; (*écrit*) code of practice
déontologique [deɔ̃tɔlɔʒik] *adj* ethical; **règles déontologiques** rules of ethics
dépannage [depanaʒ] *nm* **(a)** (*d'un moteur, d'une voiture en panne etc*) (emergency) repairs; (*remorquage*) recovery; *Ordinat* trouble-shooting; **service de d.** breakdown service **(b)** (*pour rendre service*) helping out; **elle a eu besoin d'un petit d.** she needed a hand *or* a bit of help
dépanner [depane] *vt* **(a)** (*moteur, voiture en panne etc*) to repair, to do running repairs on; **il m'a dépanné** he got my car/TV/*etc* going again **(b)** *F* (*aider*) to help out; **peux-tu me d. de 100 francs?** could you help me out with 100 francs?
dépanneur [depanœr] *nm* **(a)** (*de voiture*) breakdown mechanic; (*de téléviseur*) (television) repairman **(b)** *Can* (*magasin*) corner shop, *Am* convenience store
dépanneuse [depanøz] *nf Aut* breakdown van *or* lorry, recovery vehicle, *US* wrecker
dépaquetage [depaktaʒ] *nm* unpacking
dépaqueter [depakte] *vt* (*conj like* **paqueter**) to unpack
déparasiter [deparazite] *vt* (*poste de radio*) to eliminate the interference in
dépareillé [depareje] *adj* (*gant*) odd; (*service de table*) incomplete; *Com* **articles dépareillés** oddments, job lot
dépareiller [depareje] *vt* (*paire d'objets*) to break up; (*paire de gants, chaussettes*) to lose one of; (*service, collection*) to make incomplete; **en cassant cette assiette, tu as dépareillé mon service de table** my dinner service is incomplete now that you've broken that plate
déparer [depare] *vt* to spoil, to mar; **d. le paysage** to be a blot on the landscape; **ce tableau ne dépare pas dans le salon** the painting looks very good in the living room
déparier [deparje] *vt* (*impf & pr sub* **n. dépariions, v. dépariiez**) to split up, to separate
départ [depar] *nm* **(a)** (*d'une personne, d'un véhicule etc*) departure; (*de bateau*) departure, sailing; **quel est le jour de ton d.?** when do you leave?; **dès son d., j'ai rangé sa chambre** I tidied his room as soon as he left; **mon d. de la maison a été douloureux** my leaving home was a painful experience; **le décès de sa mère l'a obligé à un d. précipité** his mother's death forced him to leave hurriedly; **les grands départs (en vacances)** the great holiday exodus; **pour moi, c'était le grand d.** it was the final departure; **le d. de la navette spatiale** the launch of the space shuttle; **le d. du courrier a été retardé** the post has been delayed; **être sur le d.** to be on the point of leaving *or* of departure; **produit de d.** original material; **excursions au d. de Nice** trips (leaving) from Nice; **le train au d. de la voie 9** the train standing at

platform 9; **le train à destination de Lille est au d. de la voie 9** the train to Lille will leave from platform 9; **d. anticipé** early departure; **d. différé** delayed departure; **d. matinal** early morning departure; *Com* **d. entrepôt** ex warehouse; *Com* **d. usine** ex works; *Com* **prix d. usine** price ex works; **d. volontaire** (*d'employé*) voluntary redundancy

(b) (*du travail*) departure; **exiger le d. d'un employé** to insist on the dismissal of an employee; **il accepte mal son d. en retraite/en préretraite** he's finding it difficult to come to terms with the prospect of retirement/early retirement

(c) (*début*) (*d'un projet, d'une entreprise etc*) start, beginning; **le d. d'une association** the foundation of an association; **point de d.** starting point, point of departure; **prendre qch comme point de d.** to take sth as one's starting point; **langue de d.** (*d'une traduction*) source language; **qui a eu l'idée de d.?** who had the original idea?; **prix de d.** (*à une vente aux enchères*) upset price; **salaire de d.** starting salary; **ça ne ressemble plus du tout au modèle de d.** it doesn't look anything like the original model now; **au d.** at first, to start *or* begin with; **si tu me l'avais dit au d.** if you had told me that at the start *or* the outset

(d) *Sp* (*d'une course etc*) start; **ligne de d.** starting line; *Golf* **(tertre de) d.** tee; **d. arrêté** standing start; **d. lancé** flying start; **faux d.** false start; **donner le d.** to start the race, *F* to give the off; *Sp, Fig* **prendre un bon/mauvais d.** to get off to a good/bad start

départager [departaʒe] *vt* (*conj like* **partager**) (*candidats, chansons etc*) to decide between; **d. les gagnants** to decide the winners; **d. les votes** to give the casting vote

département [departəmɑ̃] *nm Admin* **(a)** (*dans un ministère*) **d. (ministériel)** department; **le d. de la peinture moderne** (*dans un musée*) the modern art section **(b)** (*de la France*) = subdivision administered by a prefect

départemental, -ale, -aux, -ales [departəmɑ̃tal, -o] **1** *adj* departmental **2** *nf* **départementale** secondary *or Br* B road **3** *nm Journ* regional (paper)

départir [departir] (*conj like* **partir**, *occ like* **finir**) **1** *vt Litt* (*faveurs*) to distribute, to dispense, to deal out; (*tâches*) to distribute, to allocate **2 se départir** *vpr* **il ne se départ jamais de son calme** he never gets excited; **elle ne se départ jamais de sa bonne humeur** her good humour never deserts her, she is unfailingly good-humoured; **il est connu pour sa bonne humeur dont effectivement il ne se départ jamais** he is famous for his good humour, which never fails *or* deserts him

dépassé [depase] *adj* **(a)** (*démodé*) (*mode, technique, langage*) old-fashioned, out of date; **c'est d.** (*de faire ça*) it's medieval; **se marier à 20 ans, c'est complètement démodé** nobody gets married at 20 nowadays **(b)** (*perdu*) overwhelmed; **je suis d. (par les événements)** things are getting too much for me

dépassement [depasmɑ̃] *nm* **(a)** *Aut* overtaking, *Am* passing; **d. interdit** no overtaking **(b)** *Fin* **nous avons un d. de crédit à déplorer** we have failed to keep within our spending limit; **il y a un d. de crédit de plusieurs millions** the budget has been exceeded by several million francs; **pratiquer le d. d'honoraires** to charge more than will be reimbursed by Social Security; **d. budgétaire** failure to keep within the budget; *Compta* **d. de coût** cost overrun **(c) d. (de soi-même)** surpassing oneself

dépasser [depase] **1** *vt* **(a)** (*aller plus loin que*) (*personne, chose*) to pass, to go past *or* beyond; (*signal*) to overrun; **nous avons dépassé la boulangerie** we have passed *or* gone past the baker's; **cette maison dépasse l'alignement** the house projects beyond the building line; **d. le but** to overshoot the mark

(b) (*excéder*) to exceed; **d. la limite de vitesse** to exceed the speed limit; **d. la date limite** to miss the deadline; **ce produit a dépassé la date limite de vente** this product is past its sell-by date; **l'entretien ne dépassera pas un quart d'heure** the interview won't take *or* last more than a quarter of an hour; **d. la durée autorisée de 20 minutes** to take more than the 20 minutes allowed; *Fin* **d. un crédit** to exceed a credit limit; **toutes ces voitures dépassent nos moyens** all these cars are beyond our means; **ne pas d. la dose prescrite** do not exceed the stated dose; **il a dépassé la trentaine** he has turned thirty, he is over thirty

(c) (*à la course, en voiture*) to overtake, *Am* to pass;

(d) (*surpasser*) **d. qch en hauteur** to top sth, to be higher than sth; **d. qn de la tête** to stand a head taller than sb; **d. qn en intelligence/en beauté** to be more intelligent/beautiful than sb; **la beauté des lieux dépasse l'imagination** the scene is beautiful beyond all imagination; **les résultats ont largement dépassé nos espérances** the results far exceeded our expectations *or* were much better than we hoped for

(e) (*outrepasser*) **cela dépasse ma compétence** it lies beyond *or* outside my area of responsibility; **les mots ont dépassé ma pensée** I said it in the heat of the moment; **d. les bornes** to overstep the bounds *or* the mark, *Am* to be out of line; **cela dépasse mon entendement, cela me dépasse** (*d'un comportement*) it's beyond me; (*d'une discussion savante*) it's beyond me, it's over my head; **être dépassé par les événements** to be overtaken by events

2 se dépasser *vpr* to surpass oneself

3 *vi* **(a)** *Aut* to overtake, *Am* to pass; **il est interdit de d. sur ce pont** no overtaking on this bridge

(b) (*être trop long*) **votre jupon dépasse** your underskirt is showing; **son mouchoir dépasse de sa poche** his handkerchief is sticking out of his pocket

dépassionner [depasjɔne] *vt* (*débat, conversation*) to take the heat out of; **il faisait tout ce qu'il pouvait pour d. la conversation** he was doing everything he could to cool *or* calm things down

dépatouiller (se) [sədepatuje] *vpr F* to cope, to manage

dépaver [depave] *vt* (*cour, rue*) to take up the paving from

dépaysé [depeize] *adj* out of one's element; **je me sens d.** I feel like a fish out of water, I don't feel at home; **depuis qu'on l'a changé d'école, il se sent dépaysé** he feels totally lost since changing schools; *Iron* **il pleut autant que chez moi! – eh bien, comme ça tu ne seras pas d.!** it rains as much here as it does at home! – well at least you won't feel homesick!

dépaysement [depeizmɑ̃] *nm* (*négatif*) disorientation; (*positif*) change of scene; **c'est un grand d. pour lui d'être dans cette ville** he feels really lost in this town; **elle a besoin de d.** she needs a change of scene; **cela te ferait un d.** it would be a change of scene for you

dépayser [depeize] *vt* (*positivement*) to be a change of scene for; (*négativement*) to disorientate, *surtout Am* to disorient; **mes vacances m'ont beaucoup dépaysé** my holiday provided a great change of scene

dépeçage [depəsaʒ] *nm*, **dépècement** [depɛsmɑ̃] *nm* cutting up; *Fig* **le d. du pays fut achevé par les barbares** the barbarians completed the dismemberment of the country

dépecer [depəse] *vt* **(je dépèce, n. dépeçons; je dépècerai)** **(a)** (*carcasse, volaille*) to cut up; (*baleine*) to flense; **le lion dépèce sa proie** the lion tears its prey; **un corps dépecé** a dismembered body **(b)** *Fig* (*territoire*) to dismember

dépêche [depɛʃ] *nf* **(a)** (*lettre officielle*) (official) dispatch, message **(b) d. (télégraphique)** telegram, *F* wire; *Journ* **d. d'agence** agency copy; **nous avons appris par d. la démission du président** we have just heard over the wire that the president has resigned

dépêcher [depeʃe] **1** *vt* (*un courrier, un messager*) to dispatch **2 se dépêcher** *vpr* to hurry, to be quick; **dépêchez-vous!** hurry up!; **se d. de faire qch** to hurry to do sth; **dépêche-toi de finir ton travail** hurry up and finish your work; **se d. de rentrer** to hurry home

dépeigner [depeɲe] *vt* **d. qn** to ruffle sb's hair, to make sb's hair untidy; **elle est toute dépeignée** her hair's all dishevelled

dépeindre [depɛ̃dr] *vt* (*conj like* **peindre**) to depict, to picture, to describe

dépenaillé [dep(ə)naje] *adj* (*veste, pantalon etc*) ragged, tattered, in rags, in tatters; (*personne*) in rags, in tatters

dépénalisation [depenalizasjɔ̃] *nf* decriminalization

dépénaliser [depenalize] *vt* to decriminalize

dépendance [depɑ̃dɑ̃s] *nf* **(a)** (*solidarité*) dependence **(b)** (*d'un pays*) dependency; *Archit* **dépendances** outbuildings **(c)** (*asservissement*) dependence, *surtout US* dependency; **l'abus de somnifères peut créer une d.** excessive use of sleeping tablets can lead to dependence; **vivre dans la d. complète de qn** to be completely dependent on sb; **être sous la d. de qn** to be under sb's domination *or* control

dépendant [depɑ̃dɑ̃] *adj* dependent; **fonctions dépendantes l'une de l'autre** functions dependent on each other, interdependent functions; **être d. de qn** to be dependent on sb; **être d. de la drogue** to be dependent on drugs

dépendre[1] [depɑ̃dr] *vt* (*linge etc*) to take down

dépendre[2] *vi* to depend; **d. de qn/qch** to depend on sb/sth; **un pays qui dépend d'un autre** a country which is dependent on another; **tout dépend des circonstances** everything depends on the circumstances; **ces événements ne dépendent pas de nous** such events are beyond our control; **cela ne dépend que de toi** that depends on you alone; **il dépend de vous de le faire** it lies *or* rests with you to do it; **cela dépend,** *F* **cela dépend des fois** it depends; *F* **ça dépend s'il est marié** it depends whether he's married; **il dépend financièrement de ses parents** he is financially dependent on his parents; **je ne dépends pas de lui** I don't take orders from him; **ne d. que de soi(-même)** to be one's own boss; **l'étang dépend aussi de leur domaine** the pond is also part of their estate

dépens [depɑ̃] *nmpl* **(a) aux d. de** at the expense of; **faire qch aux d. d'autrui** to do sth at other people's expense; **vivre aux d. de qn** to live at sb's expense; **s'amuser aux d. de ses études** to enjoy oneself at the expense of one's studies; **il apprit à ses d. que …** he learnt to his cost that … **(b)** *Jur* costs; *Com* cost, expenses; *Jur* **être condamné aux d.** to be ordered to pay costs

dépense [depɑ̃s] *nf* **(a)** expenditure, expense, outlay; **dépenses** spending; **dépenses du ménage** household expenses; **dépenses courantes** current expenditure *or* expenses; **faire des dépenses** to spend money; **engager une d.** *ou* **des dépenses** to incur expenditure; **nous avons décidé d'engager les dépenses pour les travaux** we decided to go ahead and incur the expenditure of having the work done; **j'ai acheté une voiture mais je n'arriverai pas à couvrir la d.** I bought a car but I'll never be able to pay for it; **je n'arriverai pas à couvrir tes dépenses** I won't be able to pay for your extravagance; **je n'aurais pas dû faire cette d.** I shouldn't have spent that money; **pousser à la d.** to encourage people to spend; **c'est une grosse d.** it's a lot of money; **faire trop de d.** to spend too much (money); **on ne regardait pas à la d.** there was no stinting, they didn't mind the cost, they spared no expense; **faire de folles dépenses** to spend money extravagantly; **recettes et dépenses** income *or* receipts and expenditure

(b) *Tech* **d. à vide** wasted energy; *Fig* **d. de temps/d'énergie** expenditure of time/energy; **d. physique** physical exertion

(c) *(d'une communauté religieuse)* bursary

▶ **dépense**: *Écon* **d. nationale** national expenditure, *F* government spending; *Compta* **dépenses d'exploitation** operating costs; *Compta* **dépenses de caisse** cash expenditure; *Compta* **dépenses de création** above-the-line costs; *Compta* **dépenses de fonctionnement** operating costs; *Écon* **dépenses des consommateurs** consumer expenditure; *Écon* **dépenses des ménages** household expenditure; *Compta* **dépenses diverses** sundry expenses; **dépenses en capital** capital expenditure; **dépenses publiques** public spending, government spending

dépenser [depɑ̃se] **1** *vt* **(a)** *(de l'argent)* to spend; **il dépense peu en livres** he doesn't spend much on books

(b) *(temps)* to spend; *(énergie)* to use, to consume; **la voiture dépense très peu d'essence** the car uses *or* consumes very little petrol; **d. toute son énergie/ses forces (à faire qch)** to use up all one's energy/one's strength (in doing sth); **d. sa salive pour rien** *ou* **inutilement** to waste one's breath

2 *vi* to spend (money); **d. sans compter** to spend lavishly, to be free with one's money; **qu'est-ce que tu peux d. en un mois!** the amount you spend in a month!

3 se dépenser *vpr* to use up *or* consume energy; **j'ai besoin de me d.** I need some physical exercise; **se d. pour qn** to spare no trouble on sb's behalf; **il s'est dépensé sans compter pour obtenir ton passeport plus vite** he went to a great deal of trouble to get your passport faster; **se d. en démarches inutiles** to waste one's energies in useless activities

dépensier, -ière [depɑ̃sje, -jɛr] **1** *adj* extravagant **2** *n* **(a)** *(personne prodigue)* spendthrift **(b)** *(d'une communauté religieuse)* bursar

déperdition [depɛrdisjɔ̃] *nf* *(de tissu etc)* waste, wastage; *(de chaleur, d'énergie)* loss

dépérir [deperir] *vi* *(d'une personne)* to waste away; *(de la santé)* to decline; *(d'une fleur)* to wither; *(d'un arbre)* to decay; *(d'une affaire)* to go downhill

dépérissement [deperismɑ̃] *nm* *(d'une personne)* wasting away; *(d'une fleur)* withering; *(d'un arbre)* decay; *(d'une affaire, de la santé)* decline

dépersonnalisation [depɛrsɔnalizasjɔ̃] *nf* depersonalization

dépersonnaliser [depɛrsɔnalize] **1** *vt* to depersonalize **2 se dépersonnaliser** *vpr* to lose one's personality *or* character

dépêtrer [depetre] *F* **1** *vt* *(de la boue, Fig d'une situation difficile etc)* to extricate, to free; **d. qn d'une mauvaise affaire** to get sb out of a scrape **2 se dépêtrer** *vpr* *(de la boue, de racines etc)* to extricate *or* free oneself; *Fig* **se d. de qn** to get rid of sb, to shake sb off

dépeuplé [depœple] *adj* *(pays, région)* depopulated; *(étang)* empty; *(forêt)* cleared, thinned

dépeuplement [depœpləmɑ̃] *nm* *(d'un pays, d'une région)* depopulation; *(d'un étang)* unstocking; *(d'une forêt)* thinning, clearing

dépeupler [depœple] **1** *vt* *(pays, région)* to depopulate; *(étang)* to unstock; *(forêt)* to thin, to clear **2 se dépeupler** *vpr* *(d'un pays, d'une région)* to become depopulated; *(d'une salle)* to empty; *(d'un étang)* to become unstocked; *(d'une forêt)* to thin

déphasage [defazaʒ] *nm* **(a)** *Él* phase displacement; **d. en avant** (phase) lead; **d. en arrière** lag; **(b)** *Fig F* **il y a vraiment un d. entre les connaissances qu'on demande à un professeur et la réalité de l'enseignement** there's a big difference between the knowledge demanded of a teacher and the realities of teaching; **le d. est de plus en plus important entre le PDG et le conseil d'administration** the Chairman is increasingly out of step with the board

déphasé [defaze] *adj* **(a)** *Él* out of phase; **d. en arrière** lagging; **d. en avant** leading **(b)** *Fig F* *(personne)* *(désorienté)* disorientated, *surtout Am* disoriented

déphaser [defaze] *vt* **(a)** *Él* to dephase **(b)** *Fig F* *(personne)* to disorientate, *surtout Am* to disorient

dépiauter [depjote] *vt F* *(lapin etc)* to skin, to flay; *Fig* **d. un texte/un article** to pull a text/an article to pieces

dépigmentation [depigmɑ̃tasjɔ̃] *nf Méd* loss of pigmentation

dépilation [depilasjɔ̃] *nf* loss of hair

dépilatoire [depilatwar] *adj* depilatory; **crème d.** hair removing cream, depilatory

dépiler [depile] *vt Méd* to cause loss of hair from

dépiquer[1] [depike] *vt* *(pousses)* to transplant, to prick out

dépiquer[2] *vt Couture* to unstitch, to unpick

dépistage [depistaʒ] *nm* *(d'un criminel etc)* tracking down, detection; *(d'une maladie, d'un virus etc)* (early) detection; **d. obligatoire du sida** compulsory Aids screening

dépister [depiste] *vt* **(a)** *(gibier, criminel)* to track down; *(maladie)* to detect; **d. un traquenard** to spot a trap **(b)** *(chiens de chasse)* to put off the scent; *(poursuivant)* to throw off the scent; **il a dépisté la police** he threw the police off the scent, he gave the police the slip

dépit [depi] *nm* **(a)** *(ressentiment)* spite, resentment; **un accès de d.** a fit of pique; **par d.** out of spite; **elle s'est mariée avec lui par d. amoureux** she married him on the rebound; **il a agi par d. amoureux** he did it because he was disappointed in love; **pleurer de d.** to cry with vexation; **concevoir du d. de qch** to resent *or Br F* be choked about sth **(b) en d. de** in spite of, despite; **en d. du bon sens** *(illogiquement)* contrary to common sense

dépité [depite] *adj* annoyed; **être tout d.** to be thoroughly annoyed

dépiter [depite] *vt* to spite, to offend

déplacé [deplase] *adj* **(a)** *(pas à sa place)* out of (its) place; **avoir une vertèbre déplacée** to have a slipped disc; *Fig* **se sentir d.** to feel out of place **(b)** *(inconvenant)* *(observation, attitude etc)* unwarranted, uncalled-for **(c)** *Pol* **personne déplacée** displaced person

déplacement [deplasmɑ̃] *nm* **(a)** *(de meubles etc)* moving, shifting; *(de fonctionnaire, service)* transfer; *Méd* **d. de vertèbre** slipped disc; *Ordinat* **d. du curseur** cursor movement; *Ordinat* **d. entre fichiers** movement between files; **d. latéral** *(d'une caméra)* crabbing **(b)** *(voyage)* trip, journey; **déplacements** travel; **ces déplacements continuels** this constant travel *or* travelling; **les déplacements des cadres** executive travel; **être en d.** to be on a (business) trip; **frais de d.** travelling expenses **(c)** *Naut* *(d'un navire)* displacement; **d. en charge** displacement loaded, load displacement; **d. d'air** air displacement

déplacer [deplase] **(je déplaçai(s); n. déplaçons) 1** *vt* **(a)** *(changer de place)* *(objet)* to move, to shift; *(fonctionnaire, service)* to transfer; **il ne peut rien d., il a mal au dos** he can't carry anything, he has a bad back; *Fig* **d. la question** *ou* **le problème** to shift the focus of a problem; **vous déplacez le problème** you're dodging the issue; *Hum* **tout ce qu'il sait faire, c'est d. de l'air** he just runs around in circles

(b) ce navire déplace dix mille tonnes this ship has a displacement of ten thousand tons

2 se déplacer *vpr* **(a)** *(changer de place)* to change one's place, to move (around); **il est interdit de se d.** ≈ please remain seated; **avoir du mal à se d.** to have difficulty in moving *or* getting around; **se d. une vertèbre** to slip a disc

(b) *(voyager)* to move about, to travel; **son métier l'oblige à se d. souvent** he does a lot of travelling in his job

(c) *(bouger)* *(d'un bateau, un poisson etc)* to move

déplafonnement [deplafɔnmɑ̃] *nm* removal of the upper limit *or* ceiling

déplafonner [deplafɔne] *vt* *(prix)* to remove the upper limit *or* the ceiling on; *Fin* **d. un crédit** to raise the ceiling on a credit, to raise a credit limit

déplaire [deplɛr] *(conj like* **plaire)** **1** *vi* **d. à qn** *(irriter)* to displease *or* offend sb; *(ne pas plaire à)* to fail to please sb, to be displeasing to sb; **odeur qui déplaît** offensive *or* disagreeable smell; **tu lui déplais** he dislikes you; **il me déplaît de le faire** I dislike *or* don't like doing it; **il me déplaît d'avoir à vous le dire, mais ...** I hate *or* I don't like having to tell you this but ...; **il me déplairait vraiment d'avoir à vous faire d'autres remarques** I would be extremely displeased if I had to make any further comment; **cela ne me déplairait pas** I wouldn't mind (it); **il a tout fait pour nous déplaire** he has been utterly disagreeable; **cela m'a profondément déplu** I was greatly *or* most displeased by that; *Iron* **n'en déplaise à la compagnie** with all due respect to those present; **n'en déplaise à votre Altesse!** may it please your Highness!; **ne vous/leur en déplaise** whether you/they like it or not; **n'en déplaise à mes parents** whether my parents like it or not

2 se déplaire *vpr* to be displeased *or* dissatisfied; **il se déplaît à Paris** he doesn't like Paris; **il ne se déplaît pas à Paris** he quite likes Paris

déplaisant [deplɛzɑ̃] *adj* unpleasant, disagreeable

déplaisir [deplezir] *nm* displeasure, annoyance; **à son grand d.** to his great annoyance

déplantage [deplɑ̃taʒ] *nm* digging up, lifting

déplanter [deplɑ̃te] *vt* to take *or* dig up, to lift

déplantoir [deplɑ̃twar] *nm* hand fork

déplâtrage [deplɑtraʒ] *nm* **(a)** *(de mur etc)* stripping of plaster **(b)** *(d'un membre)* taking out of plaster

déplâtrer [deplɑtre] *vt* **(a)** *(mur etc)* to strip the plaster from **(b)** *(membre)* to take the plaster off; **on la déplâtre demain** she's having the plaster off tomorrow

dépliage [deplijaʒ] *nm* unfolding, opening out

dépliant [deplijɑ̃] **1** *adj (qui se déplie)* folding **2** *nm* leaflet; *(plus luxueux)* brochure; *(feuille pliée)* fold-out page; **d. promotionnel** promotional leaflet

dépliement [deplimɑ̃] *nm* = **dépliage**

déplier [deplije] *(pr sub & impf* **n. dépliions, v. dépliiez) 1** *vt (journal, carte)* to unfold, to open out, to spread out; *(mouchoir)* to unfold; *(canapé)* to open out; **d. les jambes** to stretch one's legs **2 se déplier** *vpr* to unfold, to open out

déplissage [deplisaʒ] *nm (d'un tissu etc)* taking the creases out, smoothing out

déplisser [deplise] **1** *vt (tissu etc)* to take the creases out of, to smooth out **2 se déplisser** *vpr (d'un tissu etc)* to lose its creases

déploiement [deplwamɑ̃] *nm* **(a)** *(d'ailes etc)* spreading out, unfolding; *(du drapeau)* unfurling; *(des troupes, navires etc)* deployment **(b)** *(de force, courage)* display; **un d. d'attentions** a display *or* show of attention

déplombage [deplɔ̃baʒ] *nm* **(a)** *(d'un compteur d'électricité, d'un paquet etc)* removal of seal **(b)** *(d'une dent)* removal of filling **(c)** *Ordinat* decoding, decrypting

déplomber [deplɔ̃be] *vt* **(a)** *(compteur d'électricité, paquet etc)* to remove the seal from **(b)** *(dent)* to remove the filling from **(c)** *Ordinat (logiciel)* to decode, to decrypt

déplorable [deplɔrabl] *adj (incident etc)* deplorable, regrettable; *(comportement, résultats etc)* deplorable, disgraceful

déplorablement [deplɔrabləmɑ̃] *adv* deplorably

déplorer [deplɔre] *vt* to deplore; **vous avez très mal agi et je le déplore** I think it is deplorable that you behaved so badly; **il est à d. que vous ayez eu cette conduite** it is deplorable that you behaved in such a way; **d. la mort de qn** to grieve over *or* mourn sb's death

déployer [deplwaje] **(je déploie, n. déployons; je déploierai) 1** *vt* **(a)** *(journal, carte)* to unfold, to open out; *(drapeau)* to unfurl; *(voiles, ailes)* to spread; *(troupes, police)* to deploy; **rire à gorge déployée** to roar with laughter **(b)** *(marchandises, patience etc)* to display, to show; **il a déployé un énorme effort** he made a tremendous effort; **il va falloir d. des trésors d'ingéniosité** we're/they're/*etc* going to have to be extremely ingenious **2 se déployer** *vpr (d'une voile, d'un drapeau)* to unfurl; *(de troupes, de police)* to deploy; *Mil* **se d. en éventail** to fan out

déplumé [deplyme] *adj* featherless; *F (chauve)* bald

déplumer (se) [sədeplyme] *vpr (d'un oiseau)* to moult; *F (d'une personne)* to go bald

dépoitraillé [depwatraje] *adj F Péj* with one's shirt/*etc* all undone (at the front)

dépolarisant [depɔlarizɑ̃] *Phys* **1** *adj* depolarizing **2** *nm* depolarizer

dépolarisation [depɔlarizasjɔ̃] *nf Phys* depolarization

dépolariser [depɔlarize] *vt Phys* to depolarize

dépoli [depɔli] *adj (verre)* frosted

dépolir [depɔlir] **1** *vt (surface)* to dull, to tarnish; *(verre)* to frost **2 se dépolir** *vpr* to become dull, to tarnish

dépolissage [depɔlisaʒ] *nm*, **dépolissement** [depɔlismɑ̃] *nm (de surface)* dulling, tarnishing; *(de verre)* frosting

dépolitisation [depɔlitizasjɔ̃] *nf* depoliticization

dépolitiser [depɔlitize] *vt* to depoliticize

dépolluer [depɔlɥe] *vt* to clean up

dépollution [depɔlysjɔ̃] *nf* cleaning up

déponent [depɔnɑ̃] *adj, nm Gram* deponent

dépopulation [depɔpylasjɔ̃] *nf* depopulation

déportation [depɔrtasjɔ̃] *nf* **(a)** *(d'un prisonnier)* transportation **(b)** *(en camp de concentration)* internment

déporté, -ée [depɔrte] *n* **(a)** *(exilé)* transported criminal **(b)** *(de camp de concentration)* internee, prisoner

déportement [depɔrtəmɑ̃] *nm* **(a)** *Aut* skidding, swerving **(b)** *Vieilli* **déportements** excesses, dissolute life

déporter[1] [depɔrte] *vt* **(a)** *(prisonnier)* to transport **(b)** *(en camp de concentration)* to send to a concentration camp

déporter[2] *vt (navire, avion)* to carry off course; **voiture déportée par la violence du vent** car blown off the road by the force of the wind

déposant, -ante [depozɑ̃, -ɑ̃t] *n* **(a)** *Fin* depositor **(b)** *Jur* deponent, witness

dépose [depoz] *nf (de tapis, moquette)* lifting, taking up; *(de moteur, radiateur)* removal

déposer[1] [depoze] *vt (enlever) (tapis, moquette)* to lift, to take up; *(rideaux)* to take down; *(moteur, radiateur)* to remove; **d. la clé à la réception** to leave the key at reception

déposer[2] **1** *vt* **(a)** *(valise, sac etc)* to put *or* set down; **d. une gerbe sur un tombeau** to lay a wreath on a grave; **ma voiture vous déposera à l'hôtel** my car will drop you at the hotel; **puis-je vous d. quelque part?** can I drop you somewhere?; **d. une lettre/un paquet chez qn** to drop off a letter/a parcel at sb's house; **défense de d. des ordures** no dumping, *Br* no tipping; **d. les armes** to lay down one's arms, to surrender; *Fml* **d. un baiser sur la joue/le front de qn** to kiss sb on the cheek/forehead; *Fml* **d. ses hommages aux pieds de qn** to pay homage to sb

(b) *(confier)* to deposit, to lodge in a safe place; *Com (marque, brevet)* to register; **d. une caution** to lodge *or* deposit security; **d. son argent à la banque** to deposit one's money at the bank; *Com* **marque déposée** registered trademark; *Jur* **d. une plainte contre qn** to prefer a charge *or* lodge a complaint against sb; *Com* **d. son bilan** to file one's petition (in bankruptcy); **d. un projet de loi** to table *or* bring in a bill

(c) *(monarque etc)* to depose

(d) *(d'un liquide) (dépôt)* to deposit

2 *vi* **(a) il faut laisser au liquide le temps de d.** the liquid must be given time to settle

(b) *Jur* **d. (en justice)** to give evidence **(contre** against)

3 se déposer *vpr (d'une substance)* to settle, to form a deposit

dépositaire [depozitɛr] *n* **(a)** *(de papiers confidentiels)* depositary; *Com* consignee; **d. de valeurs** holder of securities on trust; *Admin* **d. de l'autorité publique** = officer of the State; *Admin* **d. public** = government official with responsibility for the management of public funds **(b)** *Com (de produits)* agent; **d. agréé/exclusif** authorized/sole agent; **d. de journaux** newsagent

déposition [depozisjɔ̃] *nf* **(a)** *Jur* statement, deposition *(made by witness)*; **faire/recueillir une d.** to make/take a statement **(b)** *(d'un monarque)* deposing **(c)** *Beaux-Arts* **D. de croix** Deposition

dépositionner [depozisjɔne] *vt Mktg* to deposition

déposséder [depɔsede] *vt* **(je dépossède, n. dépossédons; je dépossèderai)** to dispossess, to deprive **(de** of); **d. qn de sa place** to deprive sb of *or* oust sb from his seat; **d. qn de sa charge** to remove sb from office, to deprive sb of his office; **se sentir dépossédé** to feel dispossessed

dépossession [depɔsɛsjɔ̃] *nf* dispossession

dépôt [depo] *nm* **(a)** *(action)* deposit, depositing; *(chose confiée)* deposit; **d. d'une gerbe** laying of a wreath; **le d. des manteaux au vestiaire est conseillé** customers are advised to leave their coats in the cloakroom; **faire un d.** *(d'argent)* to make a deposit; **banque de d.** deposit bank; **compte de d.** deposit account; *Com* **d. d'une marque de fabrique** registration of a trademark; *Pol* **d. d'un projet de loi** bringing in *or* tabling of a bill; **avoir** *ou* **détenir qch en d.** to hold sth in trust; **marchandises en d.** *(à la douane)* goods in bond; *Com* goods on sale or return

(b) *(entrepôt)* depot, depository, repository; *Rail* engine shed; *(prison)* prison, jail; **il a passé la nuit au d.** he spent the night in a detention cell; *Jur* **mandat de d.** warrant of committal *or* commitment (of prisoner)

(c) *(de précipité, boue etc) (action)* deposition, settling; *(résultat)* deposit, sediment; *(limon)* silt; *(dans une bouilloire)* fur; *(dans un chauffe-eau)* scale; **le d. d'un vin** the sediment in a wine; **il y a du d.** there is a sediment; *Géol*

d. calcaire/sédimentaire calcareous/sedimentary deposit
▶ **dépôt**: **d. bancaire** bank deposit; *Com* **d. de bilan** (filing of petition in) bankruptcy; **d. de bois** timber yard; **d. de bouteilles** bottle bank; **d. de distributeur** distribution depot; **d. d'espèces** cash deposit; **d. d'essence** petrol storage depot; **d. d'expédition** sending depot; **d. de fret** freight depot; **d. de garantie** security deposit; *Jur* **d. légal** registration of copyright; **d. de(s) marchandises** goods depot; (*entrepôt*) warehouse; *Mil* **d. de munitions** munitions depot; **d. d'ordures** rubbish dump *or Br* tip; **d. de pain** = bread shop (which does not make its own bread); **d. pour conteneurs** container depot; **d. de réception** receiving depot; **d. sacré** sacred trust; *Fin* **d. à terme** term deposit; **d. de verre** bottle bank; *Fin* **d. à vue** demand deposit, sight deposit

dépotage [depɔtaʒ] *nm*, **dépotement** [depɔtmɑ̃] *nm* **(a)** (*de liquide*) decanting **(b)** (*de plantes*) repotting; (*de semis*) planting out

dépoter [depɔte] *vt* **(a)** (*liquide*) to decant **(b)** (*plantes*) to repot; (*semis*) to plant out

dépotoir [depɔtwar] *nm* **(a)** (*dépôt d'ordures*) dump, *Br* rubbish tip; *Fig* **cette chambre est un vrai d.** this room is a real tip *or* dump **(b)** *Ind* sewage works

dépôt-vente, *pl* **dépôts-ventes** *nm* sales room

dépouille [depuj] *nf* **(a)** (*d'animal*) skin, hide; (*de serpent*) slough; **d. (mortelle)** (mortal) remains **(b)** **dépouilles** (*trésor de guerre*) spoils, booty

dépouillé [depuje] *adj* (*style*) bald; (*arbre*) bare; **vin d.** = wine that has lost its alcohol content; **d. de** lacking in; **ils vivent dans un décor très d.** they live in very Spartan surroundings

dépouillement [depujmɑ̃] *nm* **(a)** **d. volontaire de ses biens** relinquishment *or* renouncement of one's property; **ils vivent dans le d.** they live in utter poverty **(b)** (*examen*) **d. d'un rapport** examination *or* analysis of a report; **d. des votes** *ou* **du scrutin** counting of the votes; **d. du courrier** going *or* sorting through the mail **(c)** *TV etc* (*avant enregistrement*) breakdown

dépouiller [depuje] **1** *vt* **(a)** (*priver*) to deprive, to strip (**de** of); **d. qn de ses vêtements** to strip sb; **se faire d.** (*dans une affaire*) to lose all one's money; **se faire d. par des voleurs** to be robbed of all one's money; **d. un pays** to plunder a country; **d. un héritier** to rob an heir of his inheritance; **le décor est dépouillé de tout ornement** the surroundings are bare of all ornament; *Fig* **dans le film, le personnage est dépouillé de tout son charme** all the character's charm is lost in the film; *Litt* **la bise a dépouillé les bois** the wind has stripped all the trees bare

(b) (*examiner*) (*le courrier, numéros d'une revue*) to sort, to go through; **d. un inventaire** to examine *or* analyse an inventory; **d. le scrutin** to count the votes; **pour faire son mémoire, il a dépouillé tout Balzac** he analysed all of Balzac line by line for his thesis

(c) (*lapin etc*) to skin

2 se dépouiller *vpr* **(a)** (*d'un insecte, serpent*) to cast (off) its skin; (*d'un arbre*) to shed its leaves; (*du vin*) to lose its strength

(b) **se d. de qch** to deprive *or* divest *or* rid oneself of sth; **se d. de ses vêtements** to strip off one's clothes, *F* to strip; **les arbres se dépouillaient de leurs feuilles** the trees were dropping *or* shedding their leaves

dépourvu [depurvy] *adj* **(a)** **d. d'intelligence/d'intérêt** devoid of intelligence/interest; **pays d. d'arbres** treeless country; **être d. (d'argent)** to be penniless **(b)** **être pris au d.** to be caught off (one's) guard, to be taken by surprise

dépoussiérage [depusjeraʒ] *nm Ind* vacuum cleaning, dust removal

dépoussiérant [depusjerɑ̃] *nm* furniture polish

dépoussiérer [depusjere] *vt Ind* to vacuum-clean, to remove the dust from; *Fig* (*institution, traduction etc*) to modernize, to bring up to date; (*connaissances*) to brush up

dépravation [depravasjɔ̃] *nf* (moral) depravity

dépravé, -ée [deprave] **1** *adj* depraved **2** *n* degenerate, depraved person

dépraver [deprave] **1** *vt* to deprave **2 se dépraver** *vpr* to become depraved

dépréciateur, -trice [depresjatœr, -tris] *n* disparager, belittler

dépréciatif, -ive [depresjatif, -iv] *adj* (*expression, mot etc*) derogatory; **en termes dépréciatifs** in derogatory *or* disparaging terms

dépréciation [depresjasjɔ̃] *nf* **(a)** (*dévaluation*) depreciation, fall in value **(b)** (*mauvaise évaluation*) underrating, undervaluing; (*dénigrement*) disparagement; *Compta* **d. de créances** write-down of accounts receivable

déprécier [depresje] (*impf & pr sub* **n. dépréciions, v. dépréciiez**) **1** *vt* (*biens*) to undervalue; (*mérites, personne, livre*) to underrate **2 se déprécier** *vpr* **(a)** (*de valeurs*) to depreciate, to fall; (*de marchandises*) to depreciate, to fall in value **(b)** (*de personne*) to belittle oneself

déprédateur, -trice [depredatœr, -tris] **1** *n* **(a)** pillager **(b)** *Fin* embezzler **2** *adj* pillaging, *Fml* depredatory

déprédation [depredasjɔ̃] *nf* **(a)** (*pillage*) pillaging, *Fml* depredation **(b)** *Fin* (*de fonds etc*) misappropriation, embezzlement

déprendre (se) [sədeprɑ̃dr] *vpr* (*conj like* **prendre**) to detach oneself, to get free; **se d. d'une habitude/d'une personne** to get out of a habit/to get clear *or* free of a person

dépressif, -ive [depresif, -iv] *adj* depressive

dépression [depresjɔ̃] *nf* **(a)** (*affaissement*) depression; (*dans le sol*) hollow, dip; (*dans l'océan*) trough; *Astron* (*de l'horizon*) dip; *Mil* **angle de d.** (*d'une arme*) angle of depression **(b)** (*chute*) (*de valeur*) fall; **d. économique** economic depression, slump; *Météo* **d. (barométrique)** (barometric) depression, low, trough **(c)** *Psy* (mental) depression; **faire de la d.** to be in a state of depression; *Méd* **d. nerveuse** nervous breakdown

dépressionnaire [depresjɔnɛr] *adj Météo* **zone** *ou* **centre d.** trough, area of low pressure; **système d.** low-pressure system

dépressurisation [depresyrizasjɔ̃] *nf* depressurization

dépressuriser [depresyrize] *vt* (*avion, véhicule spatial*) to depressurize

déprimant [deprimɑ̃] *adj* depressing

déprime [deprim] *nf F* depression; **la d.** the blues; **c'est la d. dans tous les secteurs de l'économie** all sectors of the economy are depressed; **faire de la d.** to be in a state of depression; **avoir un (petit) coup de d.** to be (a bit) depressed

déprimé [deprime] *adj* **(a)** (*personne*) depressed **(b)** (*surface etc*) depressed, low, flat, flattened; **front d.** low forehead

déprimer [deprime] **1** *vt* **(a)** (*personne*) to depress **(b)** (*surface etc*) to depress, to lower **2** *vi F* to be depressed

déprogrammation [deprɔgramasjɔ̃] *nf* (*de rendez-vous, d'émission TV ou radio*) cancellation

déprogrammer [deprɔgrame] *vt* (*rendez-vous*) to cancel; *TV, Rad* (*émission*) to cancel, to take off the air; *Ordinat* to remove from a program

déprotection [deprɔtɛksjɔ̃] *nf Ordinat* unprotecting

DEPS [deəpeɛs] (*abrév* **dernier entré, premier sorti**) *Com* LIFO

dépucelage [depyslaʒ] *nm F* loss of one's virginity; **son d. a eu lieu l'été de ses 15 ans** she had sex for the first time the summer she was 15, the first time for her was the summer she was 15; **il a eu un d. difficile** his first sexual experience was a difficult one; **oublier son d.** to forget the first time one had sex

dépuceler [depysle] *vt F* to take the virginity of, to deflower; **se faire d.** to lose one's virginity, to have sex for the first time; **il faudrait qu'il se fasse d.** he needs to lose his virginity; **elle a été dépucelée très jeune** she first had sex at a very young age; **c'est lui qui l'a dépucelée** he was her first

depuis [dəpɥi] **1** *prép* [①**A67**; **B29**,**9**; **B52**] **(a)** (*temps*) since; **je ne suis pas sorti d. hier** I haven't been out since yesterday; **en vigueur d. le 1er avril** in force since April the first; **elle est handicapée d. l'âge de 5 ans** she has been handicapped since she was five *or* from the age of five; **ils ne se sont plus quittés d. leur rencontre** they haven't been apart since they first met; **d. ce temps-là, d. lors** since then, since that time; **d. ce jour, tout a changé** everything changed after that, since that day everything has changed; **je suis là d. le déjeuner** I've been here (ever) since lunch; **d. quand êtes-vous ici?** how long have you been here?; **d. quand est-il permis d'entrer sans frapper?** since when can you come in without knocking?

(b) (*durée*) for; **je suis ici d. trois jours** I've been here for three days; **d. combien de temps êtes-vous mariés?** how long have you been married (for)?; **il l'aime/vit ici d. toujours** he has always loved her/lived here; **d. le matin jusqu'au soir** from morning till night; **d. le temps que je te le dis** considering how often I've told you; *F* **comment vas-tu, d. le temps?** how have you been all this time?; **ça devait casser, d. le temps!** it had to break sometime!, it was bound to break sometime!; **arrivé d. peu** arrived a short while ago; **d. la nuit des temps** since the dawn of time; **d. des siècles** for centuries

(c) (*lieu etc*) from; **d. ma chambre, j'entends tout** I can hear everything from my room; **il ne m'a pas parlé d. Rouen** he hasn't spoken to me since (we left) Rouen; *Rad* **concert transmis d. Londres** concert broadcast from London; **un embouteillage d. La Rochelle** a traffic jam all the way from La Rochelle; **téléphoner d. chez soi** to ring from home

(d) (*ordre, quantité*) **chemises d. 30F (jusqu'à 150F)** shirts from 30 (to 150) francs; **des robes d. la taille 34** dresses from size 34 upwards

2 *adv* since (then), since that time; (*par la suite*) afterwards, later; **d. je comprends mieux son attitude** I've understood his attitude better since then *or* since that time; **je l'ai connu d.** I made his acquaintance later

3 *conj* **d. que** + *ind* since; **nous ne l'avons pas vu d. qu'il est marié** we haven't seen him since he got married; **d. qu'il sait qu'il va la voir, il ne tient plus en place** he hasn't been able to keep still since he found out he was going to see her; **d. qu'elle couche avec le patron, elle ne nous dit plus bonjour** she hasn't acknowledged us since she's been sleeping with the boss, now that she's sleeping with the boss she doesn't acknowledge us any more; **d. que le monde est monde** since the world began

dépuratif, -ive [depyratif, -iv] *adj, nm Méd* purgative

dépuration [depyrasjɔ̃] *nf* (*du sang*) cleansing

dépurer [depyre] *vt* (*sang*) to cleanse

députation [depytasjɔ̃] *nf* **(a)** (*action*) delegation, deputing, delegating; (*groupe*) deputation, delegation **(b)** *Pol* (*fonction de député*) membership of parliament; **la d. n'est pas une chose facile** it is not easy being a member of parliament; **candidat à la d.** parliamentary candidate; **se présenter à la d.** to stand for parliament

député [depyte] *nm* **(a)** (*représentant*) deputy, delegate **(b)** *Pol* ≈Member of Parliament **(de** for); **d. du parlement européen** Member of the European Parliament, MEP; **la Chambre des députés** ≈ the House of Commons; **elle a été élue d.** *ou* **députée** she was elected a Member of Parliament *or* to Parliament; **d.-maire** = MP and mayor

députer [depyte] *vt* to appoint as deputy *or* delegate, to depute; **on l'a député comme ambassadeur au Vatican** he has been appointed ambassador to the Vatican; **c'est lui qui a été député pour les négociations** he's been appointed *or* delegated to take charge of the negotiations

déqualification [dekalifikasjɔ̃] *nf* **la d. (professionnelle) est de plus en plus fréquente** more and more people are overqualified for their jobs *or* for the work they do; **les jeunes souffrent de la d.** young people are overqualified

déqualifier [dekalifje] *vt* (*de l'automatisation*) (*ouvrier*) to deskill; **on est souvent obligé de d. les gens qu'on embauche** it is frequently necessary to recruit people for jobs they are overqualified for

der [dɛr] *n F* (*abrév* **dernier**) **la d. des ders** the war to end all wars

déracinable [derasinabl] *adj* which can be uprooted; **le racisme n'est guère plus d. aujourd'hui qu'il y a un siècle** it is no easier to uproot *or* eradicate racism now than it was a century ago

déraciné, -ée [derasine] **1** *adj* uprooted **2** *n* person who has been uprooted

déracinement [derasinmɑ̃] *nm* (*d'une souche, Fig d'une personne*) uprooting; (*d'un défaut, d'un abus, d'une idée reçue etc*) eradication

déraciner [derasine] *vt* (*souche, arbre*) to uproot, to tear up by the roots; *Fig* (*personne*) to uproot; (*défaut, abus, idée reçue*) to eradicate; (*racisme, sexisme*) to uproot, to eradicate

déraidir [derɛdir] **1** *vt* (*membre, tissu etc*) to take the stiffness out of; *Fig* (*caractère de qn*) to soften **2 se déraidir** *vpr* (*d'un membre, tissu etc*) to lose its stiffness; (*d'une personne*) to unbend, to thaw

déraillement [derɑjmɑ̃] *nm Rail* derailment

dérailler [derɑje] *vi* **(a)** (*d'un train, d'un tram*) to become derailed, to leave the rails; (*d'une pointe de lecture*) to jump *or* leave the sound groove; **faire d. un train** to derail a train **(b)** *F* (*d'une machine etc*) to be on the blink; (*d'une personne*) (*dire une bêtise, se tromper*) to rave, to talk drivel; (*devenir gâteux*) to go ga-ga

dérailleur [derɑjœr] *nm* (*de bicyclette*) derailleur (gears)

déraison [derɛzɔ̃] *nf Litt* unreasonableness, folly

déraisonnable [derɛzɔnabl] *adj* foolish

déraisonnablement [derɛzɔnabləmɑ̃] *adv* foolishly

déraisonner [derɛzɔne] *vi Litt* to talk nonsense

dérangé [derɑ̃ʒe] *adj* (*esprit*) deranged, unbalanced; (*estomac*) upset; *F* **tu es complètement d.**! you're off your rocker!

dérangeant [derɑ̃ʒɑ̃] *adj* (*film, personnage*) disturbing

dérangement [derɑ̃ʒmɑ̃] *nm* **(a)** (*gêne*) disturbance, trouble; (*perturbation*) disturbed *or* unsettled state; **causer du d. à qn** to put sb to trouble *or* bother; **je ne veux pas te causer de d.** I don't want to put you to any trouble *or* bother; **excusez-moi pour le d.** I'm sorry to disturb *or* trouble you; **il faudrait le dédommager de son d.** we'll have to give him something for his trouble **(b)** (*désordre*) (*de livres, meubles etc*) disarrangement, disorder; *Él* (*dans la ligne etc*) fault; *Tél* **la ligne est en d.** the line is out of order, there's a fault on the line; **d. d'esprit** mental derangement; **d. de l'intestin** upset stomach

déranger [derɑ̃ʒe] **(je dérangeai(s); n. dérangeons) 1** *vt* **(a)** (*papiers, livres etc*) to disturb, to put out of order, to disarrange; (*chignon, mise*) to rumple; **il a dérangé ma chambre** he's made my room untidy

(b) (*gêner*) (*personne*) to disturb; **ne pas d.** (*sur panneau*) do not disturb; **je ne peux pas travailler, je suis sans arrêt dérangé** I can't work with all these interruptions; **cela vous dérange si j'ouvre la fenêtre?** would you mind if I opened the window?; **je vous dérange?** am I disturbing you?; *Iron* **je ne te dérange pas trop?** am I in your way?; **excusez-moi de vous d.** I'm sorry to disturb *or* trouble you; **si cela ne vous dérange pas** if it's no trouble to you, if that's all right by you, if you don't mind; **je ne voudrais pas vous d. pour rien** I wouldn't want to bring you out for nothing; *F Iron* **ça te dérangerait de me laisser tranquille?** would you mind very much leaving me alone?; *F* **et alors, ça te dérange?** what business is it of yours?, what's it to you?

(c) (*perturber*) (*personne, projets*) to upset; **d. l'esprit de qn** to affect the balance of sb's mind; **avoir le cerveau dérangé** to be deranged; **quelque chose lui a dérangé l'estomac** something has upset his stomach; *Tél* **la ligne est dérangée** the line is out of order; **le temps est complètement dérangé** the weather is all back to front

2 se déranger *vpr* **merci de vous être dérangé** thank you for putting yourself out *or* for the trouble you've gone to; **ne vous dérangez pas pour moi** please don't put yourself out *or* go to any trouble on my account; **nous pouvons nous d. à toute heure de la nuit** we can come out at any time of the night; **il ne se dérange jamais, c'est toujours nous qui devons y aller** he never comes to us, we always have to go to him

dérapage [derapaʒ] *nm* **(a)** *Aut* skid; *Av, Ski* sideslip; *Pol, Fig* bad mistake; *Fig* (*d'un budget, d'un horaire*) slippage; (*d'une conversation*) deterioration; *Aut* **d. contrôlé** controlled skid; *Fig* **le d. des prix** spiralling prices; **le d. inflationniste** the inflationary spiral; **il y a déjà eu plusieurs dérapages dans cette émission** there have already been several inappropriate outbursts in the programme; **il faudrait éviter tout d. dans les négociations de paix** there must be no hitches in the peace talks, the peace talks must not come unstuck *or* become derailed **(b)** *Naut* (*d'ancre*) dragging

déraper [derape] *vi* **(a)** *Aut* to skid; *Av, Ski* to sideslip; *Fig* (*des prix*) to be rising uncontrollably, to soar, to rise sharply; (*d'une conversation*) to deteriorate; *Fig* **le budget dérape** there's some slippage in the budget; *Fig* **il faut éviter que les négociations ne dérapent** the talks must not go wrong *or* come unstuck *or* become derailed; *Fig* **le débat a rapidement dérapé vers le duel** the discussion rapidly deteriorated into *or* turned into a fight; *Fig* **les commentaires ont dérapé vers une critique sévère** comment has turned into severe criticism **(b)** *Naut* (*d'un ancre*) to drag

dératé [derate] *nm F* **courir comme un d.** to run flat out

dératisation [deratizasjɔ̃] *nf* extermination of rats; (*pour éliminer cafards etc*) pest control

dératiser [deratize] *vt* to clear of rats

derby [dɛrbi] *nm* **(a)** *Courses de chevaux* derby; **le d. d'Epsom** the Derby **(b)** *Fb* local derby

derechef [dərəʃɛf] *adv Arch, Litt* a second time, yet again, once more

déréglé [deregle] *adj* **(a)** (*machine, horloge etc*) not working properly **(b)** (*estomac*) upset; (*esprit*) disordered; (*pouls*) irregular; (*temps*) unsettled **(c)** (*vie*) wild, dissolute; **il a des mœurs complètement déréglées** he is quite dissolute *or* debauched

dérèglement [derɛgləmɑ̃] *nm* **(a)** (*d'une machine, d'une horloge*) malfunctioning **(b)** (*du temps*) unsettled state; (*du pouls*) irregularity; **d. de l'esprit** mental derangement; **j'ai un d. de l'appétit** there is something wrong with my appetite; **d. hormonal** hormone disorder **(c)** (*de l'imagination*) disordered state; (*de la moralité*) dissoluteness; **il fait montre d'un d. de l'imagination** his imagination is getting out of control; *Vieilli, Hum* **dérèglements** dissolute behaviour

dérégler [deregle] **(je dérègle, n. déréglons; je déréglerai) 1** *vt* **(a)** (*horloge, machine etc*) to cause to malfunction; **tu as déréglé la pendule/le moteur à force de la/le démonter** you've dismantled the clock/the engine so many times that it's gone haywire **(b)** (*estomac*) to upset; (*personne, esprit, habitudes, temps*) to unsettle; **d. son sommeil** to disrupt one's sleeping pattern; **elle a complètement déréglé son appétit avec tous ses régimes** all these diets have completely disrupted her eating patterns **2 se dérégler** *vpr* (**a**) (*d'horloge, de machine etc*) to go wrong (**b**) (*de pouls*) to be irregular; (*d'estomac*) to be upset; **son esprit se dérègle** his mind is going; **elle s'est déréglé le système digestif** she's ruined her digestive system (**c**) (*de moralité*) to become dissolute; (*d'imagination*) to run wild, to get out of control

dérider [deride] **1** *vt* to cheer up, to brighten up; **c'est impossible de le d.** it's impossible to get a smile out of him **2 se dérider** *vpr* to cheer up, to brighten up

dérision [derizjɔ̃] *nf* derision, mockery; **dire qch par d.** to say sth derisively *or* mockingly; **geste de d.** derisive gesture; **tourner qch en d.** to deride sth; **c'est une d.!** (*chose insignifiante*) it's ridiculous *or* laughable!

dérisoire [derizwar] *adj* (*offre, salaire*) derisory, laughable; (*prix*) very low, rock-bottom; **vendre qch à un prix d.** to sell sth at a ridiculously *or* an absurdly low price; **cette objection me paraît d.** that seems an absurd objection to me

dérisoirement [derizwarmɑ̃] *adv* laughably, pathetically; **il est payé d.** he's paid a derisory *or* laughable *or* pathetic amount

dérivatif, -ive [derivatif, -iv] **1** *adj Ling* derivative **2** *nm* distraction (**à, de** from); **c'est un d. à sa douleur** it takes his mind off his grief; **le sport est un excellent d.** sport is an excellent way of taking your mind off things

dérivation [derivasjɔ̃] *nf* (**a**) *Aut* diversion; *HydE* (*d'un cours d'eau*) diversion, tapping; *Él* (*du courant*) shunt(ing), branching, tapping; *MecE* by-pass; **canal de d.** headrace, penstock; *Él* **monté en d.** shunt connected (**b**) *Ling, Math* derivation (**c**) *Naut, Av* drift

dérive [deriv] *nf Naut* drift, leeway; *Av* drift; **angle de d.** angle of drift, drift angle; **à la d., en d.** adrift; **navire en d.** drifting vessel; (**quille de**) **d.** *Naut* drop keel, centre board; *Av* fin; *Géog* **d. des continents** continental drift; *Fig* **tout va à la d.** everything has been left to drift; **un mariage/une entreprise qui part à la d.** a failing marriage/business; **des jeunes à la d. dans la grande ville** young people adrift in the big city

dérivé, -ée [derive] **1** *adj* (**a**) (*signification etc*) derived, secondary; *Math* (*fonction, courbe*) derived; **produit d.** *Ch* by-product; *Bourse* derivative (**b**) *Él* **courant d.** shunt current **2** *nm Ling* derivative; *Ch, Ind* derivative, by-product; **d. du sang** blood product **3** *nf Math* **dérivée** derivative

dériver[1] [derive] **1** *vt* (**a**) *HydE* (*cours d'eau*) to divert *or* tap the course of; *Él* (*courant*) to shunt, to branch (**b**) *Ling, Math* to derive **2** *vi Ling* to be derived (**de** from)

dériver[2] *vt Tech* to unrivet

dériver[3] *vi* (**a**) *Naut, Av* to drift; **d. à vau-l'eau** to drift downstream (**b**) *Fig* (*du sujet etc*) to drift away (**de** from)

dériveur [derivœr] *nm Naut* (**a**) (*bateau*) sailing dinghy (*with centreboard*) (**b**) (*voile*) storm sail

dérivomètre [derivɔmɛtr] *nm Av* drift meter

dermatite [dɛrmatit] *nf* dermatitis

dermato [dɛrmato] *n F* (*abrév* **dermatologue**) dermatologist

dermatologie [dɛrmatɔlɔʒi] *nf* dermatology

dermatologique [dɛrmatɔlɔʒik] *adj* dermatological

dermatologiste [dɛrmatɔlɔʒist], **dermatologue** [dɛrmatɔlɔg] *n* dermatologist

dermatose [dɛrmatoz] *nf Méd* dermatosis

derme [dɛrm] *nm Anat* derm

dermique [dɛrmik] *adj Anat* dermic, dermal

dermite [dɛrmit] *nf Méd* = **dermatite**

dernier, -ière [dɛrnje, -jɛr] **1** *adj* [①**B10**,D,3] (**a**) [①**A19**,g,ii] (*ultime*) last; (*marquant la fin*) final; **au d. moment** at the last (moment); **à la dernière minute** at the last minute; **des préparatifs de dernière minute** last minute preparations; **les derniers préparatifs** the final preparations; **faire un d. effort** to make a final *or* one last effort; **mettre la dernière main à qch** to give *or* put the finishing *or* final touches to sth; **j'ai dépensé jusqu'à mon d. sou** I've spent my last penny; **la dernière moitié du 16e siècle** the second half of the 16th century; **les derniers mètres de l'ascension** the final metres of the climb; **d. rappel** (*de facture*) final reminder; **d. paiement** final payment; **c'est mon d. prix** that's my final offer; *Bourse* **d. cours** closing price; *Journ* **dernière heure** copy deadline; *Journ* **dernière page** back page; *Journ* **dernière édition** final edition, late edition; **dernière proposition** final offer; **d. délai pour l'inscription** deadline for registration; **il faut libérer la chambre à 9h, d. délai** *ou F* **carat** the room has to be vacated by 9 o'clock at the very latest; **en d. recours** *ou* **ressort** as a last resort; **en dernière analyse** in the final analysis; **en d. lieu** last, lastly; **c'est la dernière personne à qui je demanderais un service** he's the last person I would ask a favour of; **pour la dernière fois** for the last time; **il veut toujours avoir le d. mot** he always has to have the last word; **je n'ai pas dit mon d. mot** I'm not done for yet, there's still fight left in me, you/they/*etc* haven't heard the last of me; **la peste n'a pas dit son d. mot** the plague is still with us, the plague has not been beaten; **c'est ma dernière chance** this is my last chance

(**b**) [①**A7**,d,vi; **A19**,9,ii] (*le ou la plus récent*(*e*)) last; **mardi d.** last Tuesday; **le mois d.** last month; **au cours des dernières années** over the past *or* last few years; **la dernière fois, il allait bien** he was well (the) last time I saw him; **je l'ai déjà fait la dernière fois** I did that the last time; **ces derniers temps, ces temps derniers** lately; **dernières nouvelles** latest news; **aux dernières nouvelles, il s'est marié** the last I heard, he had got married; **ce sont les dernières nouvelles que j'ai eues de lui** that's the last I've heard of him; **dernière édition** latest edition; **les derniers développements d'une affaire** the latest developments of an affair; **le d. roman de cet auteur** this author's latest novel; **la dernière mode, le d. cri** the latest fashion, the latest thing; **le d. modèle** the latest model; **mon dernier patron était anglais** my last boss was English

(**c**) (*dans l'espace*) last; **la dernière maison du village** the last house in the village; **le d. rang** the back *or* last row; **la dernière marche de l'escalier** (*en haut*) the top step; (*en bas*) the bottom step; **au d. étage** on the top floor; **le d. tiroir de la commode** the bottom drawer of the chest of drawers

(**d**) *Litt* (*extrême*) utmost; **vérité dernière** ultimate truth; **de la dernière importance** of the utmost *or* greatest importance; **au d. degré** to the utmost *or* highest degree; **le d. degré de la bêtise** the height of stupidity; **atteindre le d. degré de la bêtise** to be the height of *or* the last word in stupidity; **le d. degré de la misère** the depths of poverty; **dans la dernière misère** in utmost poverty; **être du d. bien avec qn** to be extremely friendly with sb, to be great friends with sb; **ils sont du d. bien** they're the best of friends *or* on the best of terms; **être de la dernière insolence avec qn** to be most insolent to *or* with sb; **se débattre avec la dernière énergie** to put up a fierce struggle; **jeter dans le d. désespoir** to cast into the depths of despair; **c'est du d. chic/ridicule** it's the height of elegance/ridiculousness

(**e**) (*le pire*) lowest, worst; **de d. ordre** very inferior; **être le d. élève de la classe** to be last in *or* bottom of the class; **il a été reçu d. au concours** he came in last in the competition; **un hôtel de dernière catégorie** a fourth-rate hotel; **une étoffe de la dernière qualité** *ou* **du d. choix** material of the poorest quality; **c'était la dernière chose à dire/faire** that's the last thing you/he/*etc* should have said/done; *Fml* **ils lui ont fait subir les derniers outrages** they subjected her to the worst outrages

(**f**) (*avec idée de mort*) last; **ils ont bien cru que leur dernière heure était venue** they really thought that their last hour had come; **je m'en souviendrai jusqu'à mon d. jour** *ou* **jusqu'à ma dernière heure** I shall remember it to my dying day; **nous sommes restés avec lui jusqu'à son d. souffle** we stayed with him until the last *or* the end; **rendre le d. soupir** to breathe one's last; **rendre les derniers devoirs à qn** to lay sb out; **recevoir les derniers sacrements** to receive the last rites; **ce sont ses dernières volontés** that was his dying wish; **les dernières dispositions du défunt** the dead man's last will and testament; **accompagner qn à sa dernière demeure** to accompany sb to his/her final resting place

2 *n* (**a**) (*dans classement*) last; *Sp* **il est arrivé le d.** *ou* **bon d.** he came in last; **le d. arrivé** the last to arrive; **il est le d. de sa promotion** he is bottom of his year; **dans les derniers** among the last; **les six derniers** the last six; **c'est le d. de mes soucis** that's the least of my worries; **elle est la dernière à qui je demanderais de l'aide** she's the last person I'd ask for help; **je les arrêterai tous jusqu'au d.** I'll stop each and every last one of them

(**b**) (*dans chronologie*) last, latest; **c'est notre petit d.** he's our youngest (child); **comment va la petite dernière?** how's the little one?; **ce d. répondit …** the latter answered …; **le d. en date** the most recent; **c'est toujours le d. à sortir** he's always last out

(**c**) *Péj* **on la traite comme la dernière des dernières** they treat her like dirt *or* the lowest of the low; **ton frère est vraiment le d. des crétins/des menteurs** your brother is the world's biggest fool/liar; *très F* **c'est vraiment la dernière des connes** she really is an utter prat

3 *nf* **dernière** (**a**) *Th* last night, final performance (**b**) (*nouveauté*) **tu as entendu la dernière de ton frère?** have you heard your brother's latest?

4 *adv* **en d.** last (of all); **cela vient en d.** that comes last; **il sort toujours en d.** he's always last out; **je mange toujours le meilleur en d.** I always keep the best till last

dernièrement [dɛrnjɛrmɑ̃] *adv* lately, of late, recently

dernier-né [dɛrnjene], *pl* **derniers-nés** *nm*, **dernière-née** [dɛrnjɛrne], *pl* **dernières-nées** *nf* youngest child

dérobade [derɔbad] *nf* **(a)** *(de qn, qch)* evasion, avoidance; **c'est le spécialiste de la d.** he's a past master at avoiding the issue; **il pratique beaucoup la d. pour ne pas payer ce qu'il lui doit** he gets out of paying what he owes her as much as he can **(b)** *(d'un cheval)* swerve, jib

dérobé [derɔbe] *adj* *(escalier, porte etc)* hidden, concealed, secret

dérobée (à la) [aladerɔbe] *adv* stealthily, secretly, on the sly; **regarder qn à la d.** to steal a glance at sb; **sortir à la d.** to steal out

dérober [derɔbe] **1** *vt* **(a)** *(voler)* to steal, to make away with; **d. qch à qn** to steal sth from sb; **d. un baiser** to steal a kiss

(b) *(cacher)* to hide, to conceal; **d. qch à qn** to hide sth from sb; **ce mur dérobe la vue** the wall hides the view; **d. qn au danger** to snatch sb from danger

2 se dérober *vpr* **(a)** *(s'échapper)* to escape, to steal away, to slip away (**à** from); **se d. aux regards** to escape observation, to avoid notice; **se d. à la curiosité de qn** to avoid sb's prying eyes; **se d. à son devoir** to evade *or* shirk one's duty; **je le lui ai demandé, mais il s'est dérobé** I asked him, but he avoided the issue

(b) *(manquer)* *(du sol, des genoux, des jambes)* to give way (**sous** beneath)

(c) *(de cheval)* to swerve, to jib

dérogation [derɔgasjɔ̃] *nf* *(pour passer un examen)* waiver, exemption; *Jur* waiver; *(à une loi)* derogation, impairment (**à** of); **d. à qch** departure from sth, exception to sth; **par** *ou* **en d. à cette règle** this rule notwithstanding, as an exception to this rule; **je n'admettrai aucune d.** I will allow no exceptions

dérogatoire [derɔgatwar] *adj Jur* **clause d.** waiver, *Spéc* derogatory clause

déroger [derɔʒe] *vi* **(je dérogeai(s); n. dérogeons) d. à l'usage/à la loi** to depart from custom/the law; **d. à un principe** to waive a principle; *Hist* **d. (à noblesse)** to lose rank; **d. à son rang** to lower *or* demean oneself

dérouillée [deruje] *nf très F* beating, belting

dérouiller [deruje] **1** *vt* **(a)** *(enlever la rouille de)* to take *or* get the rust off **(b)** *très F* *(battre)* to beat up **2** *vi très F* **(a)** *(être battu)* to get beaten up, to catch it; **qu'est-ce qu'il a dérouillé!** he really took a beating! **(b)** *(souffrir)* to suffer, to have a hard time; **depuis qu'il a cette otite, qu'est-ce qu'il dérouille** he's suffered agonies with that earache **3 se dérouiller** *vpr* **se d. les jambes** to stretch one's legs; **se d. la mémoire** to refresh one's memory

déroulement [derulmɑ̃] *nm* **(a)** *(d'une intrigue, des événements)* unfolding, development, progress; **nous avons besoin de connaître le d. de votre journée** we need to know how you spent the day; **le d. des travaux s'est passé normalement** the work went smoothly; **pendant tout le d. de la cérémonie** throughout the ceremony; **il a surveillé tout le d. des opérations** he monitored operations from start to finish **(b)** *(d'une bobine etc)* unwinding

dérouler [derule] **1** *vt* *(rouleau)* to unroll; *(store)* to let down; *(câble etc)* to unwind, to uncoil; **le serpent a déroulé ses anneaux** the snake uncoiled itself; *Ordinat* **d. un menu** to pull down a menu; *Fig Litt* **il a déroulé le fil de sa vie** he recounted *or* unfolded the story of his life

2 se dérouler *vpr* **(a)** *(d'un rouleau)* to come unrolled, to unroll; *(d'un store)* to come down; *(d'un câble etc)* to come unwound; *(d'un serpent)* to uncoil

(b) *Fig* to unfold; **le paysage se déroule devant nous** the landscape unfolds *or* stretches out before us; **les événements qui se déroulent à Paris** the events (that are) unfolding *or* taking place in Paris; **la manifestation s'est déroulée dans le calme** the demonstration went off peacefully *or* was peaceful; **son existence se déroule dans la plus grande monotonie** he leads the most monotonous of existences

dérouleur [derulœr] *nm Ordinat* tape drive, streamer; **d. de bandes** tape streamer

déroutage [derutaʒ] *nm* **d. de marchandises** rerouting of goods

déroutant [derutɑ̃] *adj* disconcerting

déroute [derut] *nf* *(débandade)* rout, disorderly retreat; **l'ennemi fut mis en d.** the enemy was put to flight *or* was routed

déroutement [derutmɑ̃] *nm Naut, Av* rerouting, diversion

dérouter [derute] *vt* **(a)** *(confondre)* to nonplus, *F* to throw **(b)** *(tromper)* to lead astray; **d. la police** to throw the police off the scent; **d. les soupçons** to divert suspicion **(c)** *(navire, avion etc)* to divert, to reroute

derrick [derik] *nm Pétr* derrick

derrière [dɛrjɛr] **1** *prép* **(a)** *(au dos de)* behind, *US* in back of; **il s'est caché d. le rideau** he hid behind the curtain; **les uns d. les autres** one behind the other; *aussi Fig* **les autres sont loin d. moi** the others are way behind me; **il faut toujours être d. elle** *ou* **son dos** you always have to be at her back; **il a laissé une femme et deux enfants d. lui** he left a wife and two children; **d. des abords chaleureux** behind a cordial facade; **faire qch d. (le dos de) qn** to do sth behind sb's back; **dire du mal d. (le dos de) qn** to say nasty things about sb behind his/her back; **c'est lui qui est d. tout ça** he's the one behind all this

(b) de d. from behind; **sortir de d. un buisson** to come out from behind a bush

(c) *Naut* *(bateau)* astern of; *(mât etc)* abaft

2 *adv* **(a)** *(en arrière)* behind, at the back, in the rear; **laisser qn d.** to leave sb behind; **regarder d.** to look back; **ton parapluie est d.** your umbrella is at the back; **enfiler un pull sens devant d.** to put on a pullover back to front; **ça se ferme d.** it fastens (up) at the back; *Aut* **aller** *ou* **monter d.** to sit in the back *or Am* in back; **taisez-vous, d.!** *(en voiture)* be quiet back there!; *(dans une pièce)* be quiet at the back!

(b) par d. from behind; **attaquer qn par d.** to attack sb from behind *or* from the rear; **cette robe s'attache par d.** the dress does up at the back; **il a dû passer par d.** he had to go round the back; *Fig* **elle le critique par d.** she criticizes him behind his back

(c) *Naut* astern; *(cabine)* aft

3 *nm* **(a)** *(d'édifice etc)* back, rear; **le d. de la tête** the back of the head; **porte de d.** back door; **pattes de d.** hind legs

(b) *(postérieur)* behind, backside, bottom, *Am* butt; *(d'un animal)* hindquarters; *Fig F* **il en est tombé sur le d.** it knocked him for six, he nearly fainted (with surprise); **recevoir des coups de pied dans le** *ou* **au d.** to get kicked in the behind *or* up the backside

déruralisation [deryralizasjɔ̃] *nf* rural depopulation

dérushage [derœʃaʒ] *nm TV, Cin* first view

derviche [dɛrviʃ] *nm* dervish; **d. tourneur** dancing *or* whirling dervish

des [de] *voir* **de**

dès [dɛ] *prép* [①B29-30,11] since, from, as early as, as long ago as; **d. sa jeunesse** from childhood; **d. l'abord** from the outset, from the (very) first; **d. maintenant,** *Fml* **d. à présent** from now on, *Fml* henceforth; **j'ai décidé de commencer le projet d. maintenant** I've decided to start on the project now *or* immediately; **d. 1840** as far back as 1840; **d. le matin** first thing in the morning; **d. son arrivée** the minute *or* the moment he arrives/arrived, as soon as he arrives/arrived; **d. mon retour** immediately on my return; **je te téléphonerai d. mon retour** I'll call you as soon as *or* immediately *or* the minute I get back; **d. sa première remarque, j'ai senti que ...** as soon as he spoke *or* from the moment he spoke I felt that ...; **d. les premiers froids** as soon as it starts to get cold; **elle est ivre d. le premier verre** she's tipsy after one drink, one drink and she's tipsy; **d. la porte il commença à crier** he had no sooner reached the door than he began to shout; **d. l'autoroute, on sentait la différence de température** as soon as we reached the motorway we could feel the difference in temperature; **d. Paris, la pluie tombait** it rained all the way from Paris; **d. que** + *ind* as soon as, the moment that; **d. lors** *(dans le temps)* then; *(par conséquent)* consequently, therefore; **ils vendirent leur maison et d. lors, partirent habiter à Paris** as soon as they sold their house they went off to live in Paris; **d. lors que vous refusez** seeing that *or* since you refuse

désabonnement [dezabɔnmɑ̃] *nm* cancellation (of subscription)

désabonner [dezabɔne] **1** *vt* **d. qn à une revue** to cancel sb's subscription to a magazine **2 se désabonner** *vpr* to stop subscribing, to cancel one's subscription (**à** to)

désabusé, -ée [dezabyze] *adj* disillusioned, disenchanted

désabusement [dezabyzmɑ̃] *nm* disillusionment, disenchantment

désabuser [dezabyze] *vt Litt* **d. qn** to disillusion sb, to open sb's eyes; **c'est un esprit désabusé** he's disillusioned

désacclimater [dezaklimate] *vt* **d. qn/qch** to remove sb/sth from their/its natural habitat

désaccord [dezakɔr] *nm* *(mésentente)* disagreement; *(d'intérêts etc)* clash; **les désaccords entre les États-Unis et Cuba** the disagreements *or* the dissension between the United States and Cuba; **c'est un de leurs désaccords** it's one of the things they disagree about; **être** *ou* **se trouver en d. avec qn sur qch** to disagree *or* be at odds with sb about sth; **sujet de d.** bone of contention; **d. entre la théorie et la pratique** discrepancy between theory and practice; **il y a d. entre ses paroles et sa conduite** his words are inconsistent *or* not in keeping with his conduct; **vivre en d. avec son époque** to be out of step with one's time

désaccordé [dezakɔrde] *adj Mus* out of tune

désaccorder [dezakɔrde] *Mus* **1** *vt* (*instrument*) to put out of tune **2 se désaccorder** *vpr* to go out of tune

désaccoupler [dezakuple] *vt* **(a)** *Tech* (*wagons*) to uncouple; *Él* to disconnect **(b)** (*chiens de meute*) to slip, to uncouple

désaccoutumance [dezakutymɑ̃s] *nf* **d. de** *ou* **à la drogue** breaking the habit of taking drugs; **la d. à la drogue est quelque chose de pénible** overcoming drug addiction is a painful process; *Fig* **j'étais tellement bien avec toi que la d. va être longue et douloureuse** being with you was so good that learning to live without you will be a long and painful process

désaccoutumer [dezakutyme] **1** *vt* **d. qn à (faire) qch** to get sb out of the habit of (doing) sth **2 se désaccoutumer** *vpr* to lose the habit; **se d. de (faire) qch** to get out of the habit of (doing) sth

désacralisation [desakralizasjɔ̃] *nf* (*de la famille etc*) desanctification

désacraliser [desakralize] *vt* (*famille etc*) to desanctify

désactivation [dezaktivasjɔ̃] *nf Phys Nucl* (*d'un site*) cleaning up; *Ordinat* deactivation

désactiver [dezaktive] *vt Phys Nucl* (*site*) to clean up; *Ordinat* to deactivate, to disable

désadaptation [dezadaptasjɔ̃] *nf* unsuitability; **il montre une d. au milieu scolaire** he shows signs of not being suited to school life

désadapter [dezadapte] *vt* **d. qn de qch** to wean sb away from sth; **le risque de les d. à** *ou* **de leur vie quotidienne** the danger of creating a gulf between them and their everyday life

désaffectation [dezafɛktasjɔ̃] *nf* (*d'un bâtiment public etc*) putting to another purpose; (*fermeture*) (*d'un bâtiment*) closing down; (*d'une église*) deconsecration

désaffecter [dezafɛkte] *vt* (*bâtiment public etc*) to put to another purpose; (*fermer*) (*bâtiment*) to close down; **église désaffectée** deconsecrated church

désaffection [dezafɛksjɔ̃] *nf* disaffection (**pour** with)

désagrafer [dezagrafe] **1** *vt* (*vêtement*) to unfasten, to undo **2 se désagrafer** *vpr* to unfasten *or* undo one's dress/*etc*

désagréable [dezagreabl] *adj* (*personne, remarque*) unpleasant, disagreeable (**à** to); (*odeur*) unpleasant, nasty; *Euph* **ce n'est pas d.** that's (a bit of) all right

désagréablement [dezagreabləmɑ̃] *adv* unpleasantly, disagreeably

désagrégation [dezagregasjɔ̃] *nf* disintegration, breaking up

désagréger [dezagreʒe] (**je désagrège, n. désagrégeons; je désagrégeai(s); je désagrégerai**) **1** *vt* to cause to disintegrate; **la bombe a complètement désagrégé l'immeuble** the bomb completely destroyed the building, *F* the bomb smashed the building to smithereens; **la météorite a désagrégé la navette spatiale** the space shuttle disintegrated when the meteorite hit it **2 se désagréger** *vpr* to disintegrate, to break up

désagrément [dezagremɑ̃] *nm* trouble; **causer à qn du d.** *ou* **des désagréments** (*d'une personne*) to cause unpleasantness for sb; **sa voiture lui cause beaucoup de désagréments** his car gives him lots of problems; **il a beaucoup de désagréments avec sa voiture** he's got a lot of problems with his car; **les désagréments de la situation** the unpleasantness of the situation; **l'éloignement et la solitude font partie des désagréments de la situation** distance and loneliness are two of the things that make this a difficult situation

désaimantation [dezɛmɑ̃tasjɔ̃] *nf* demagnetization

désaimanter [dezɛmɑ̃te] *vt* to demagnetize

désaligné [dezaliɲe] *adj* out of alignment, out of line

désaltérant [dezalterɑ̃] *adj* thirst-quenching

désaltérer [dezaltere] (**je désaltère, n. désaltérons; je désaltérerai**) **1** *vt* **d. qn** to quench sb's thirst **2** *vi* **le thé désaltère mieux qu'une boisson glacée** tea is more thirst-quenching than an ice-cold drink **3 se désaltérer** *vpr* to quench one's thirst

désambiguïsation [dezɑ̃bigɥizasjɔ̃] *nf* clarification

désambiguïser [dezɑ̃bigɥize] *vt* (*situation*) to clarify, to clear up; **il faut absolument d. ta situation avec lui vis-à-vis de ta famille** you really must make your relationship with him crystal-clear to your family; **un mot est souvent désambiguïsé par un contexte** a word in context is rarely ambiguous

désamorçage [dezamɔrsaʒ] *nm* (*d'une bombe, d'un obus etc, Fig d'un conflit*) defusing

désamorcer [dezamɔrse] (**je désamorçai(s); n. désamorçons**) *vt* (*bombe, obus etc, Fig conflit, querelle*) to defuse; *Fig* (*neutraliser*) (*complot*) to render harmless

désanamorphoser [dezanamɔrfoze] *vt* (*image*) to unsqueeze

désapparier [dezaparje] *vt* (*objets*) to remove one of a pair of, to spoil a pair of; (*couple d'oiseaux, d'animaux*) to separate; **j'ai un tas de gants désappariés** I've got piles of odd gloves

désappointement [dezapwɛ̃tmɑ̃] *nm Litt* disappointment

désappointer [dezapwɛ̃te] *vt Litt* to disappoint

désapprendre [dezaprɑ̃dr] *vt Fml* to forget (*exprès*) to unlearn

désapprobateur, -trice [dezaprɔbatœr, -tris] *adj* disapproving; **regard d.** disapproving look, look of disapproval

désapprobation [dezaprɔbasjɔ̃] *nf* disapproval (**de** of); **regard de d.** disapproving look, look of disapproval; **mumure de d.** murmur of disapproval

désapprouver [dezapruve] *vt* to disapprove of; **elle désapprouve mon projet** she disapproves *or* doesn't approve of my plan; **il désapprouve que je vienne** he disapproves of my coming; **je le désapprouve de ne pas avoir travaillé** I disapprove of the fact that he didn't work

désapprovisionné [dezaprɔvizjɔne] *adj* (*compte*) overdrawn

désarçonner [dezarsɔne] *vt* (*de cheval*) to unseat, to throw; *Fig* (*d'un adversaire, d'une question, d'une situation*) to floor, to throw

désargenté [dezarʒɑ̃te] *adj* **(a)** (*fourchette, cuillère etc*) tarnished **(b)** *F* (*personne*) broke

désarmant [dezarmɑ̃] *adj* (*sourire etc*) disarming

désarmé [dezarme] *adj* **(a)** (*personne*) (*qui n'a plus d'arme*) disarmed; (*qui n'a jamais eu d'arme*) unarmed, defenceless **(b)** (*arme*) unloaded **(c)** (*navire*) laid up, out of commission

désarmement [dezarməmɑ̃] *nm* **(a)** (*d'une personne*) disarming; *Mil, Pol* disarmament; *Mil, Pol* **d. progressif/multilateral/unilatéral** progressive/multilateral/unilateral disarmament **(b)** *Naut* (*de navire*) laying up

désarmer [dezarme] **1** *vt* **(a)** (*une personne, un pays*) to disarm; *Fig* **il montrait une franchise qui vous désarmait** he was disarmingly frank **(b)** (*arme*) (*enlever les balles de*) to unload; (*placer le cran de sûreté de*) to uncock **(c)** *Naut* (*navire*) to lay up **2** *vi* (*cesser*) (*always neg*) **haine/désir de vengeance qui ne désarme pas** unrelenting *or* relentless hatred/desire for vengeance; **sa colère ne désarme pas** he is still angry

désarrimage [dezarimaʒ] *nm Naut etc* (*d'une cargaison*) shifting

désarrimer [dezarime] *vt Naut etc* (*cargaison*) to shift

désarroi [dezarwa] *nm* disarray, confusion; **jeter qn dans le d.** to throw sb into disarray; **il est en plein** *ou* **dans un grand d.** he's in a state of utter disarray *or* confusion

désarticulation [dezartikylasjɔ̃] *nf Méd* dislocation

désarticuler [dezartikyle] **1** *vt Méd* to dislocate; *Fig* **d. un échafaudage** to dismantle scaffolding **2 se désarticuler** *vpr* to be double-jointed

désassemblage [dezasɑ̃blaʒ] *nm* dismantling

désassembler [dezasɑ̃ble] *vt* to dismantle, to take apart

désassembleur [dezasɑ̃blœr] *nm Ordinat* disassembler

désassortir [dezasɔrtir] *vt* (*conj like* **assortir**) **(a)** (*série, collection etc*) to spoil, to break up; **service de table désassorti** dinner service made up of odd pieces **(b)** (*magasin*) to clear (of stock)

désastre [dezastr] *nm* disaster, calamity; **d. financier** financial disaster, crash; **la soirée fut un vrai d.** the party was a disaster; **courir au d.** to court disaster

désastreusement [dezastrøzmɑ̃] *adv* disastrously

désastreux, -euse [dezastrø, -øz] *adj* disastrous; **un travail d.** a dreadful *or* an appalling piece of work

désatellisation [desatɛlizasjɔ̃] *nf* **l'évolution des mentalités a contribué à la d. de la Tchécoslovaquie** the fact that Czechoslovakia is no longer a satellite state is partly due to changes in thinking

désatomisation [dezatɔmizasjɔ̃] *nf* nuclear disarmament

désatomiser [dezatɔmize] *vt* to undertake the nuclear disarmament of

désavantage [dezavɑ̃taʒ] *nm* disadvantage, drawback; **avoir un d. sur qn** to be at a disadvantage compared with sb; **tourner au d. de qn** to go against sb; **cette solution a le d. d'être trop coûteuse** the drawback to *or* disadvantage of this solution is its expense; **c'est un d. de taille** it's a sizeable drawback; **il vous a été présenté à son d.** you saw him in a disadvantageous *or* an unfavourable light

désavantagé [dezavɑ̃taʒe] *adj* at a disadvantage, disadvantaged (**par** by)

désavantager [dezavɑ̃taʒe] *vt* (**je désavantageai(s); n. désavantageons**) to put at a disadvantage, to disadvantage; **être désavantagé par rapport à qn** to be at a disadvantage compared with sb; **être très désavantagé par sa taille** to be greatly handicapped by one's size, to be at a great disadvantage because of one's size; **il désavantage toujours son fils par rapport à sa fille** he always favours his daughter over his son

désavantageusement [dezavɑ̃taʒøzmɑ̃] *adv* disadvantageously, unfavourably, *US* unfavorably

désavantageux, -euse [dezavɑ̃taʒø, -øz] *adj* disadvantageous, unfavourable, *US* unfavorable

désaveu [dezavø] *nm* **(a)** (*reniement*) (*d'une action, d'une œuvre, d'une opinion*) disowning; (*d'une promesse, d'une parole*) retraction; *Jur* **d. de paternité** repudiation of paternity; **faire un d. public** to make a public retraction **(b)** (*condamnation*) disapproval; **encourir le d. de ses supérieurs** to incur the disapproval of one's superiors; **il a été l'objet du d. de toute la population** he was universally condemned

désavouer [dezavwe] **1** *vt* **(a)** (*renier*) (*action, œuvre, enfant, opinion etc*) to disown; (*promesse, parole*) to go back on, to retract; (*paternité*) to disclaim, to deny; **d. un mandataire** to withdraw recognition from an agent **(b)** (*condamner*) (*le comportement, les propos, l'attitude etc de qn*) to deplore **2 se désavouer** *vpr* to go back on one's word

désaxé, -ée [dezakse] **1** *adj* **(a)** *MecE* (*came etc*) eccentric; **roue désaxée** wheel out of true **(b)** (*esprit*) unbalanced **2** *n* unbalanced person

désaxer [dezakse] *vt* **(a)** *MecE* (*cylindre etc*) to set over; (*roue*) to put out of true **(b)** (*esprit*) to unbalance

descellement [desɛlmɑ̃] *nm* (*d'un cachet*) breaking; (*d'un document*) breaking the seal

desceller [desele] *vt* (*cachet*) to break; (*document*) to unseal, to break the seal of

descendance [desɑ̃dɑ̃s] *nf* **(a)** (*origine*) descent, *Fml* lineage **(b)** (*postérité*) descendants

descendant, -ante [desɑ̃dɑ̃, -ɑ̃t] **1** *adj* (*mouvement*) downward; **marée descendante** ebbing tide; *Mil* **garde descendante** old guard; **ligne descendante** (genealogical) line of descent; *Mus* **gamme descendante** descending scale **2** *n* descendant

descendeur, -euse [desɑ̃dœr, -øz] *nm Ski* downhill specialist *or* skier; *Cycling* downhill racer

descendre [desɑ̃dr] **1** *vi* (*the aux is* **être**, *occ* **avoir**) **(a)** (*allant vers le point de référence fixé*) to come down, *Fml* to descend; (*s'éloignant du point de référence fixé*) to go down, *Fml* to descend; **tu descends par l'escalier ou par l'ascenseur?** are you going to walk down or take the lift?; **d. d'un arbre/d'une échelle** to come *or* get down from a tree/a ladder; **d. d'une colline** to come down a hill; **peux-tu faire d. les enfants de cet arbre?** can you get the children down out of *or* down from that tree?; **peux-tu m'aider à d.?** can you help me down?; **d. en glissant/en courant/en boitant** to slide/run/limp down; *Av* **d. en vol plané** to glide down; **d. en parachute** to parachute down; **d. en rappel** to abseil down; **d. (de Paris) en province** to go to the provinces (from Paris); **d. (du nord) en voiture/en train** to travel down (from the north) by car/train; **d. dans le midi en voiture/en train** to travel to the south by car/train; **d. en ville** to go into town; **il faut d. par ce chemin** you have to go down by this path *or* take this path down; **on peut d. en une nuit?** can we do the journey down in one night?; *Fig* **d. dans la rue** to take to the streets; *Fig* **d. dans l'arène** to enter the fray; **d. du trône** to leave the throne; *Fig* **descends de ton nuage!** come down to earth!; **les scaphandriers sont descendus à 150 m de profondeur** the divers reached a depth of 150 m; **le premier nageur à d. en dessous des 23 secondes au 50 m nage libre** the first swimmer to break 23 seconds in the 50 m freestyle; *Sp* **d. en seconde division** to move down to the second division; *Fig* **d. plus avant** *ou* **plus à fond dans une question** to consider a question at a deeper level; *Fig* **d. en soi-même** to take a close look at oneself

(b) (*d'un escalier etc*) (*allant vers le point de référence fixé*) to come downstairs; (*s'éloignant du point de référence fixé*) to go downstairs; **tu peux d.? j'ai besoin de toi à la cuisine** can you come down(stairs)? I need you in the kitchen; **il est descendu à la cave** he's gone down(stairs) to the cellar; **il n'est pas encore descendu** he isn't down yet; **faites-le d.** (*en l'envoyant chercher*) send him down; (*en l'appelant*) call him down

(c) (*d'un véhicule*) to get off, *Fml* to alight; **je descends à Lille/à la prochaine** I'm getting off at Lille/at the next stop; **'aucun voyageur ne descend dans cette gare'** 'the train does not stop here'; **c'est ici que je descends** this is where I get off; **tout le monde descend!** (*au terminus*) all change!; **d. du train** to get off the train; **d. de cheval/de vélo/de moto** to dismount; **d. à terre** (*d'un bateau*) to go ashore, to land

(d) (*baisser*) (*de prix*) to come down, to fall; (*de température*) to drop, to fall; (*de marée*) to fall, to go out; **le baromètre descend** the glass is falling; **il faut faire d. la fièvre** we must bring his temperature down; **sa voix ne descend pas plus bas** his voice won't go any lower

(e) (*tomber*) (*de brouillard*) to come down; (*des ombres*) to fall; **le fleuve descend vers la mer** the river flows down to the sea; **le soleil descend sur l'horizon** the sun is sinking below the horizon; **la nuit/le soir va d.** it will soon be nightfall *or* dark; **le précipité descend au fond de l'éprouvette** the precipitate drops to the bottom of the test-tube; **une grande paix était descendue en lui** a great sense of peace came over him

(f) (*s'étendre*) to extend downwards; (*de route, rue*) to go downhill; **les cheveux lui descendent jusqu'à la taille** her hair comes down to her waist; **une robe qui descend jusqu'aux chevilles/genoux** an ankle-/knee-length dress, a dress that comes down to the ankles/knees; **ce chemin descend au village** this path goes down to the village; **la colline descend (en pente douce) jusqu'à la mer** the hill slopes (gently) down to the sea; **la route descend en lacets** the road winds down

(g) (*loger*) **d. chez des amis** to stay with friends; **d. à l'hôtel** to put up *or* stay at a hotel

(h) *F* **mon dîner ne descend pas** my dinner won't go down; **un petit verre pour faire d. mon repas** a drop of something to wash down my meal; **qu'est-ce qu'il descend dans les soirées!** he can really put it away at parties!

(i) *Fig* (*s'abaisser*) to lower oneself; **il est descendu bien bas** he has fallen very low; *Péj* **d. jusqu'au mensonge** to stoop to lying; **d. dans l'estime de qn** to go down in sb's estimation

(j) (*faire irruption*) **la police est descendue dans la boîte de nuit** the police raided the nightclub

(k) *Fig* (*venir de*) to be descended (**de** from); **ces gens-là descendent d'une ancienne famille** these people are descended from an ancient family

2 *vt* (*aux* **avoir**) **(a)** (*dévaler*) **d. les marches/la rue** to go down the steps/the street; **d. la rivière** to go downriver; **d. la rivière en nageant/en canoë/en radeau** to swim/canoe/raft downriver; **d. un escalier quatre à quatre** to race downstairs; *Mus* **d. la gamme** to run down the scale

(b) (*porter vers le bas*) (*allant vers le point de référence fixé*) to take down; (*s'éloignant du point de référence fixé*) to bring down; *F* (*déposer*) to drop, to put down; **d. la poubelle** to take the rubbish down; **peux-tu me d. mon pull?** will you bring me down my sweater?; **je vous descendrai à votre porte** I'll drop you at your door

(c) (*abaisser*) (*store, étagère*) to lower; **descends le tableau un peu plus vers la droite** move the picture down a bit on the right

(d) *F* (*repas, boisson*) to put away, to knock back, to sink; **il a descendu toutes les bières** he's guzzled all the beer

(e) *F* (*animal, homme, avion*) to bring down, to shoot down; **la police l'a descendu, il s'est fait d. par la police** he was shot down *or* shot dead by the police; *Fig* **d. qn en flammes** to shoot sb down in flames; *Fig* **ils l'ont descendu en beauté** they crucified him

descente [desɑ̃t] *nf* **(a)** (*action de descendre*) descent; *Ski* (*course*) downhill (race); *Ski* **faire de la d.** to do downhill (skiing); **j'ai faite une d. en rappel** I abseiled down; **la d. en rappel est dangereuse** abseiling is dangerous; *Cyclisme* **être bon en d.** to be good downhill *or* on the downhill sections; **c'était une d. difficile** (*en alpinisme*) it was a difficult descent; **d. de cheval** dismounting; *Av* **d. en vol plané** glide; **d. en parachute** parachute jump; **accueillir qn à la d. du train** to meet sb off the train; **d. interdite** (*sur panneau*) up only

(b) (*incursion*) raid; **d. de police** police raid; *Jur* **d. sur les lieux** visit to the scene (*of a crime etc*); *Fig* **faire une d. en boîte (de nuit)** to go to a nightclub; *Fb* **d. des avants** attack by the forwards

(c) *Méd* (*d'un organe*) prolapse

(d) (*pente*) slope, incline; **une d. rapide** a steep slope; **d. dangereuse** dangerous hill; **ralentir dans la d.** to slow down when going downhill

(e) (*tuyau*) downpipe, rainwater pipe

(f) *F* **il a une bonne d.** he can really put it away

▶ **descente**: *Beaux-Arts* **D. de croix** Deposition; **d. de lit** bedside rug

déscolarisation [deskɔlarizasjɔ̃] *nf* (*action*) removal from school; (*résultat*) lack of schooling *or* education; **les impératifs des travaux agricoles conduisent à la d. des enfants des milieux ruraux** children in rural areas are taken out of school because of the demands of farm work;

on assiste à une d. massive des jeunes gitans the level of school attendance among young gipsies is falling drastically
déscolariser [deskɔlarize] *vt* to remove from *or* take out of school
descripteur [dɛskriptœr] *nm Ordinat* descriptor
descriptible [dɛskriptibl] *adj* describable
descriptif, -ive [dɛskriptif, -iv] **1** *adj* descriptive **2** *nm* (*d'une maison*) description; (*d'une machine, d'un appareil*) instructions, explanatory leaflet; *Constr* specification; **un d. de vos souhaits** a list of what you would like, your wish list
description [dɛskripsjɔ̃] *nf* description; **d. orale/écrite** verbal/written description; **faire la d. de qn/qch** to give a description of sb/sth, to describe sb/sth; *Tech* **conforme à la d.** as described *or* represented; **d. commerciale** trade description; **d. de poste** job description
désectorisation [desɛktɔrizasjɔ̃] *nf* = freedom of choice (*by virtue of the fact that parents no longer need to send their children to the school designated for their area*); **la d. de l'école primaire se fera plus vite que celle de l'école secondaire** freedom of choice will come about in primary schools sooner than in secondary schools
désectoriser [desɛktɔrize] *vt* **d. le primaire/secondaire** = to allow parents to choose which primary/secondary school they send their children to, regardless of where they live
désembourber [dezɑ̃burbe] *vt* (*véhicule etc*) to extricate from the mud
désembourgeoiser [desɑ̃burʒwaze] **1** *vt* (*personne*) to make less conventional *or* less middle-class; (*profession, activité etc*) to make less middle-class, to remove the middle-class aura surrounding **2 se désembourgeoiser** *vpr* to become less conventional *or* less middle-class; **les facs de droit ont beaucoup de mal à se d.** law faculties are finding it very difficult to attract students from outside the middle classes
désembouteiller [dezɑ̃buteje] *vt* (*route*) to unblock; (*ligne téléphonique*) to unjam
désembrouiller [dezɑ̃bruje] *vt* (*signaux, données*) to unscramble
désembrouilleur [dezɑ̃brujœr] *nm* (*de signaux etc*) descrambler
désembuage [dezɑ̃bɥaʒ] *nm* demisting; **d. arrière** rear demister
désembuer [dezɑ̃bɥe] *vt* to demist
désembueur [dezɑ̃bɥœr] *nm* demister
désemparé [dezɑ̃pare] *adj* **(a)** (*personne*) at a loss; **il reste d.** he's quite at a loss; **très d.** very much at a loss **(b)** (*navire, avion*) disabled
désemparer [dezɑ̃pare] **1** *vt Naut* (*navire*) to disable **2** *vi* **sans d.** without stopping; **ils travaillent des heures sans d.** they work for hours on end
désemplir [dezɑ̃plir] **1** *vt* (*bouteille etc*) to partially empty **2** *vi* **son magasin ne désemplit pas** his shop is always full (of customers) **3 se désemplir** *vpr* to empty
désenchaîner [dezɑ̃ʃene] *vt* **d. qn** to unchain sb, to remove sb's chains
désenchantement [dezɑ̃ʃɑ̃tmɑ̃] *nm* **(a)** (*déception*) disillusion **(b)** *Vieilli* removal of a/the spell
désenchanter [dezɑ̃ʃɑ̃te] *vt* **(a)** (*décevoir*) to disillusion; **sourire désenchanté** wistful smile **(b)** *Vieilli* to remove a/the spell from
désenclavement [dezɑ̃klavmɑ̃] *nm* opening up
désenclaver [dezɑ̃klave] *vt* to open up
désencombrement [dezɑ̃kɔ̃brəmɑ̃] *nm* (*d'un passage etc*) clearing, freeing
désencombrer [dezɑ̃kɔ̃bre] *vt* (*passage etc*) to clear, to free (**de** of)
désencrasser [dezɑ̃krase] *vt* to clean
désencroûter [dezɑ̃krute] **1** *vt* **d. qn** to get sb out of his/her rut **2 se désencroûter** *vpr* to get out of the *or* one's rut; **j'ai besoin de me d.** I need to get out of this rut I'm in *or* out of my rut
désendettement [dezɑ̃dɛtmɑ̃] *nm* debt reduction, reduction in borrowings; **il faut aboutir au d. des ménages** household debt must be reduced; **le d. des pays de l'Est se fera progressivement** Eastern countries will gradually be relieved of their debt burden
désendetter (se) [sədezɑ̃dete] *vpr* to get out of debt, to clear one's debts
désenfiler [dezɑ̃file] **1** *vt* (*aiguille*) to unthread; (*perles etc*) to unstring **2 se désenfiler** *vpr* (*d'une aiguille*) to come unthreaded; (*de perles*) to come unstrung
désenflammer [dezɑ̃flame] *vt Méd* (*plaie etc*) to reduce the inflammation in
désenfler [dezɑ̃fle] **1** *vi* to become less swollen; **ma joue/cheville désenfle** the swelling in my cheek/ankle is going down, my cheek/ankle is less swollen **2 se désenfler** *vpr* = **1** *vi*
désenfumer [dezɑ̃fyme] *vt* to get rid of the smoke in
désengagement [dezɑ̃gaʒmɑ̃] *nm* disengagement
désengager [dezɑ̃gaʒe] (**je désengageai(s); n. désengageons**) **1** *vt* **d. qn** to release sb from an obligation; **d. sa parole** to go back on one's word **2 se désengager** *vpr* to free oneself of an obligation; **je ne peux pas me d.** I can't get out of it
désengorgement [dezɑ̃gɔrʒəmɑ̃] *nm* (*d'un tuyau etc*) unblocking
désengorger [dezɑ̃gɔrʒe] *vt* (**je désengorgeai(s); n. désengorgeons**) (*tuyau etc*) to unblock
désenivrer [dezɑ̃nivre] **1** *vt* **d. qn** to sober sb up **2** *vi* to sober up, to become sober; **il ne désenivre pas** he's never sober
désennuyer [dezɑ̃nɥije] (**je désennuie, n. désennuyons; je désennuierai**) **1** *vt* **d. qn** to keep sb amused **2 se désennuyer** *vpr* to amuse oneself, to keep oneself amused
désensabler [dezɑ̃sable] *vt* **(a)** (*bateau*) to get off the sand; (*voiture etc*) to dig out of the sand **(b)** (*chenal etc*) to dredge of sand
désensevelir [dezɑ̃səvlir] *vt* (*objet*) to dig up; (*cadavre*) to disinter, to exhume
désensibilisateur [desɑ̃sibilizatœr] *nm Phot* desensitizer
désensibilisation [desɑ̃sibilizasjɔ̃] *nf Méd, Phot* desensitization
désensibiliser [desɑ̃sibilize] *vt Méd, Phot* to desensitize; *Fig* **de telles images ont désensibilisé l'opinion** people have become hardened as a result of pictures such as these
désensorceler [dezɑ̃sɔrsəle] *vt* (**je désensorcelle, n. désensorcelons; je désensorcellerai**) to free from a/the magic spell
désensorcellement [dezɑ̃sɔrsɛlmɑ̃] *nm* removal of a/the spell
désentortiller [dezɑ̃tɔrtije] *vt* (*fil etc*) to untwist; (*laine etc*) to disentangle
désentraver [dezɑ̃trave] *vt* (*personne*) to unshackle; (*animal*) to unhobble
désenvaser [dezɑ̃vaze] *vt* **(a)** (*égout*) to clear out, to remove the sludge from; (*port*) to remove the silt from **(b)** (*voiture*) to get out of the mud, to extract from the mud
désenvoûtement [dezɑ̃vutmɑ̃] *nm* removal of a/the spell; **procéder au d. de qn** to remove a/the spell from sb
désenvoûter [dezɑ̃vute] *vt* to remove a/the spell from
désépaissir [dezepɛsir] *vt* (*sauce, cheveux*) to thin
déséquilibrant [dezekilibrɑ̃] *adj* (*effet*) unbalancing; **être d.** to have an unbalancing effect (**pour** on)
déséquilibre [dezekilibr] *nm* imbalance; **la chaise était en d.** the chair wasn't balanced properly; *Psy* **d. émotif** emotional maladjustment; *Méd* **d. nutritionnel** nutritional imbalance
déséquilibré, -ée [dezekilibre] **1** *adj* unbalanced **2** *n* unbalanced person
déséquilibrer [dezekilibre] *vt* (*personne*) (*mentalement, physiquement*) to unbalance; (*déconcerter*) to throw off balance; (*objet*) to unbalance, to throw out of balance
désert [dezɛr] **1** *adj* (*lieu*) deserted; (*pays, région*) uninhabited; **une île déserte** a desert island **2** *nm* desert; **d. de sable** sandy desert; **un d. de glace** an icy waste; *Fig* **prêcher dans le d.** to be a voice crying in the wilderness; *Fig* **entamer sa traversée du d.** to go into the wilderness; **après 5 années de traversée du d.** after 5 years in the wilderness
déserter [dezɛrte] **1** *vt* to desert; *Fig* (*cause*) to desert, to abandon; (*idéal*) to abandon; *Mil* **d. son poste** to desert one's post; **d. l'armée** to desert (from the army); **nos amis désertent notre maison depuis quelques temps** we've been deserted by our friends recently, our friends have been staying away recently **2** *vi* to desert
déserteur [dezɛrtœr] *nm* deserter
désertification [dezɛrtifikasjɔ̃] *nf Géog* desertification; *Fig* **la d. du Massif Central** the desertion of the Massif Central
désertion [dezɛrsjɔ̃] *nf* (*de l'armée, d'un parti*) desertion
désertique [dezɛrtik] *adj Géog* desert, of the desert; **région d.** desert region
désertisation [dezɛrtizasjɔ̃] *nf* = **désertification**
désescalade [dezɛskalad] *nf Pol, Mil* de-escalation
désespérance [dezɛsperɑ̃s] *nf Litt* loss of hope, despair
désespérant [dezɛsperɑ̃] *adj* **(a) c'est d.** it's enough to drive you to despair; **cet enfant est d.** that child will drive me to despair; **il fait un temps vraiment d.** the weather's really appalling; **tu es vraiment d'une stupidité désespérante** you really are incredibly stupid, you're so stupid you'll drive me to despair; **tu es vraiment d'une nullité désespérante** you really are absolutely hopeless **(b)** *Litt* (*image, vision*) heartbreaking
désespéré, -ée [dezɛspere] **1** *adj* (*sans espoir*) (*regard, discours*) desperate, of despair, despairing; (*situation*) desperate; (*extrême*) (*mesure, solution*) desperate; (*après décès, accident*) in despair, distressed; **être dans un état d.** to be in a hopeless *or* desperate state; **il est d. depuis la**

mort de sa femme he has been in despair since his wife died; **sa voix était désespérée** he sounded desperate **2** *n* **(a)** desperate person; **agir en d.** to act out of desperation, to commit an act of despair **(b)** (*suicidé*) suicide (victim)

désespérément [dezɛsperemɑ̃] *adv* (*avec désespoir*) despairingly, hopelessly; (*avec acharnement*) desperately

désespérer [dezɛspere] **(je désespère, n. désespérons; je désespérai) 1** *vi* to despair, to lose hope; **je ne désespère pas d'y arriver un jour** I still hope to get *or* I haven't given up hope of getting there one day; **d. de qn** to despair of sb; **il désespère de pouvoir rentrer chez lui** he despairs of ever getting home; **il désespère de sa situation** he's in despair about the situation he's in **2** *vt* to drive *or* reduce to despair; **il désespère sa femme par son attitude** he drives his wife to despair with his attitude **3 se désespérer** *vpr* to be in despair, to give way to despair

désespoir [dezɛspwar] *nm* **(a)** despair; **être au d.** to be in despair; **elle était au d. de ne pouvoir vous aider** she was distressed *or* extremely upset that she wasn't able to help you; **enfant qui fait** *ou* **est le d. de sa famille** child who is the despair of his family; **cette cuisine fait mon d.** this kitchen will drive me to despair; **réduire qn au d.** to drive sb to desperation *or* to despair; **en d. de cause** in desperation, when everything else fails **(b)** (*plante*) **d. des peintres** London pride

désétatisation [dezetatizasjɔ̃] *nf* denationalization

désétatiser [dezetatize] *vt Écon, Pol* (*industrie*) to denationalize

déshabillage [dezabijaʒ] *nm* undressing

déshabillé [dezabije] *nm* négligé(e); (*peignoir*) housecoat

déshabiller [dezabije] **1** *vt* to undress; **d. qn du regard** to undress sb with one's eyes, to mentally undress sb **2 se déshabiller** *vpr* to undress (oneself), to take off one's clothes; (*enlever son manteau etc*) to take off one's coat/*etc*

déshabituer [dezabitɥe] **1** *vt* **d. qn de (faire) qch** to get sb out of *or* break sb of the habit of (doing) sth **2 se déshabituer** *vpr* to get out of *or* lose the habit (**de** of)

désherbage [dezɛrbaʒ] *nm* weeding

désherbant [dezɛrbɑ̃] *nm* weedkiller

désherber [dezɛrbe] *vt* (*jardin, champ*) to weed

déshérence [dezerɑ̃s] *nf Jur* default of heirs, escheat; **tomber en d.** to escheat

déshérité [dezerite] **1** *adj* (*sans héritage*) disinherited; (*démuni*) deprived **2** *n* **les déshérités** the underprivileged

déshéritement [dezeritmɑ̃] *nm* disinheritance

déshériter [dezerite] *vt* to disinherit; *Fig Hum* **être déshérité par la nature** (*d'une personne inintelligente*) to be not very bright; (*d'une personne laide*) to be no oil painting

déshonnête [dezɔnɛt] *adj Arch* improper, immodest, unseemly

déshonnêtement [dezɔnɛtmɑ̃] *adv Arch* improperly, immodestly

déshonnêteté [dezɔnɛt(ə)te] *nf Arch, Litt* impropriety, immodesty, unseemliness

déshonneur [dezɔnœr] *nm* dishonour, *US* dishonor

déshonorant [dezɔnɔrɑ̃] *adj* (*comportement, métier*) dishonourable, *US* dishonorable; **des paroles déshonorantes pour notre famille/la profession** remarks that bring dishonour on *or* discredit the family/the profession

déshonorer [dezɔnɔre] **1** *vt* **(a)** (*discréditer*) to disgrace, to bring disgrace *or* dishonour *or US* dishonor on, to dishonour; **il se croirait déshonoré de serrer la main à des étrangers** he would feel it reflected on his honour *or* he would think it beneath him to shake hands with a foreigner; **être déshonoré par un jeune blanc-bec** to be put to shame by a complete beginner; *Vieilli* **d. une jeune fille/une femme** to seduce a girl/a woman **(b)** *Fig* (*abîmer*) (*paysage, édifice etc*) to disfigure, to spoil **2 se déshonorer** *vpr* to disgrace oneself

déshuiler [dezɥile] *vt* to extract *or* separate *or* remove oil from

déshumaniser [dezymanize] *vt* to dehumanize

déshumidification [dezymidifikasjɔ̃] *nf* dehumidification

déshydratation [dezidratasjɔ̃] *nf* dehydration

déshydrater [dezidrate] **1** *vt* to dehydrate; **je suis déshydraté** I'm dehydrated; **noix de coco déshydratée** desiccated coconut **2 se déshydrater** *vpr* to become dehydrated; **on se déshydrate beaucoup en avion** you get very dehydrated when you fly

déshydrateur [dezidratœr] *nm* dehydrator

déshydrogénation [dezidrɔʒenasjɔ̃] *nf Ch* dehydrogenation

déshydrogéner [dezidrɔʒene] *vt* **(je déshydrogène, n. déshydrogénons; je déshydrogènerai)** *Ch* to dehydrogenate

déshypothéquer [dezipɔteke] *vt* (*conj like* **hypothéquer**) (*domaine*) to disencumber

desiderata [deziderata] *nmpl* desiderata; **quels sont vos d.?** what can I do for you?

design [dizajŋ] **1** *nm* design; **ils sont entièrement meublés en d.** they have nothing but designer furniture; **société de d.** design company; **il fait du d. (industriel)** he's a(n industrial) designer, he's in (industrial) design **2** *adj* designer; **un intérieur très d.** a designer interior

désignation [deziɲasjɔ̃] *nf* **(a)** (*appellation*) designation; (*de marchandises etc*) description **(b)** (*choix*) appointment; **d. de qn pour un poste** appointment of sb to a position

designer [dizajnœr] *nm* designer; **d. graphiste** graphics designer; **d. presse** newspaper designer

désigner [deziɲe] **1** *vt* **(a)** (*signaler*) to point out, to indicate; **est-ce que tu peux le d.?** can you point him out?; **d. qch du doigt** to point sth out, to point at sth; **il a pris le siège qu'on lui avait désigné** he took the seat they pointed to *or* indicated; **d. qch à l'attention de qn** to call *or* draw sb's attention to sth; **je désigne à votre attention que ...** I would call *or* draw your attention to the fact that ...

(b) (*choisir*) to appoint; **d. un jour** to appoint *or* set *or* fix a day; **d. qn à** *ou* **pour un poste** to appoint sb to a position; **il est tout désigné pour le faire** he's just the man to do it, he's cut out for it; **sa compétence la désigne à cet emploi** her ability makes her the right person for the job; **il a été désigné pour nous représenter** he was chosen to represent us

(c) (*nommer*) to refer to; **d. qn par son nom** to refer to sb by name; **d. qn par un surnom** to call sb by a nickname; **on désigne, sous ce nom, tous les gaz de cette famille** this name is applied to all the gases in the family

2 se désigner *vpr* **se d. volontaire** to volunteer

désillusion [dezilyzjɔ̃] *nf* disillusion

désillusionnement [dezilyzjɔnmɑ̃] *nm* disillusionment

désillusionner [dezilyzjɔne] *vt* to disillusion

désincarcération [dezɛ̃karserasjɔ̃] *nf* (*des débris d'une voiture etc*) release, freeing

désincarcérer [dezɛ̃karsere] *vt* (*des débris d'une voiture etc*) to free

désincarné [dezɛ̃karne] *adj* disembodied; *souvent Iron* **il paraît totalement d.** he seems above it all

désincarner (se) [sədezɛ̃karne] *vpr* to become disembodied

désincrustant [dezɛ̃krystɑ̃] **1** *adj Tech* (*substance*) scaling; **masque d.** (*cosmétique*) face pack **2** *nm Tech* scale preventive

désincrustation [dezɛ̃krystasjɔ̃] *nf Tech* (*d'une chaudière etc*) scaling

désincruster [dezɛ̃kryste] *vt Tech* (*chaudière etc*) to scale; **un masque pour d. la peau** a mask for removing impurities from the skin

désindexation [dezɛ̃dɛksasjɔ̃] *nf* de-indexing

désindexer [dezɛ̃dɛkse] *vt* to de-index

désindustrialisation [dezɛ̃dystrijalizasjɔ̃] *nf* de-industrialization

désindustrialiser [dezɛ̃dystrijalize] *vt* to de-industrialize

désinence [dezinɑ̃s] *nf Gram* (flexional) ending

désinfectant [dezɛ̃fɛktɑ̃] *adj, nm* disinfectant

désinfecter [dezɛ̃fɛkte] *vt* to disinfect

désinfection [dezɛ̃fɛksjɔ̃] *nf* disinfection

désinflation [dezɛ̃flasjɔ̃] *nf Écon* disinflation

désinformation [dezɛ̃fɔrmasjɔ̃] *nf* disinformation

désinformer [dezɛ̃fɔrme] *vt* to disinform

désinsectisation [dezɛ̃sɛktizasjɔ̃] *nf* pest control

désinsectiser [dezɛ̃sɛktize] *vt* to clear of insects, to remove the insects from

désinstaller [dezɛ̃stale] *vt Ordinat* to de-install

désintégration [dezɛ̃tegrasjɔ̃] *nf* (*des roches*) weathering; *Nucl* (nuclear) disintegration; (*de l'atome*) splitting; *Fig* (*d'un groupe*) break-up; (*de la famille, de la société*) disintegration

désintégrer [dezɛ̃tegre] **(je désintègre, n. désintégrons; je désintégrerai) 1** *vt* (*roches*) to weather; *Nucl* (*matière*) to disintegrate; (*atome*) to split; *Fig* (*groupe, famille etc*) to break up **2 se désintégrer** *vpr* (*de roches*) to weather; *Nucl* (*de matière*) to disintegrate; (*d'atome*) to split; *Fig* (*d'un groupe, d'une famille*) to break up; (*d'un mariage*) to break up, to fall apart; (*de la société, de la famille*) to disintegrate

désintéressé [dezɛ̃terese] *adj* (*opinion, avis etc*) disinterested, impartial; (*motif*) disinterested, unselfish; (*personne*) disinterested, selfless; **il agit de manière tout à fait désintéressée** he is being quite impartial

désintéressement [dezɛ̃terɛsmɑ̃] *nm* **(a)** (*d'opinion, d'avis*) disinterestedness, impartiality; (*de motif*) disinterestedness, unselfishness; (*de personne*) disinterestedness, selflessness **(b)** *Com* (*de partenaire*) buying out; (*de créditeur*) paying off

désintéresser [dezɛ̃terese] **1** *vt Com* (*partenaire*) to buy out; (*créditeur*) to pay off **2 se désintéresser** *vpr* **se d. de qch/qn** to take no further interest in sth/sb

désintérêt [dezɛ̃terɛ] *nm* disinterest

désintermédiation [dezɛ̃tɛrmedjasjɔ̃] *nf* disintermediation
désintoxication [dezɛ̃tɔksikasjɔ̃] *nf Méd* detoxification; **faire une cure de d.** to undergo treatment for alcoholism/drug addiction, *US F* to be in detox
désintoxiquer [dezɛ̃tɔksike] *Méd* **1** *vt* to treat for alcoholism/drug addiction; *Fig* **il ne fait que regarder la télévision, il faut le d.!** all he does is watch television, we'll have to break him of the habit! **2 se désintoxiquer** *vpr* to come off alcohol/drugs; *Fig* **je cours tous les jours pour me d.** I run every day to clean out my system; *Fig* **aller à la campagne pour se d.** to go to the countryside to clean out one's system *or* to get the city air out of one's lungs
désinvestir [dezɛ̃vɛstir] *vt* **d. des capitaux** to divest
désinvestissement [dezɛ̃vɛstismɑ̃] *nm Fin* divestment
désinvolte [dezɛ̃vɔlt] *adj* (*manière*) casual, airy, unselfconscious; (*mouvements*) easy, free; **d. à l'égard de qn** casual *or* offhand with sb; **il a quand même été très d. en ne venant pas à mon anniversaire** it was very offhand of him not to come to my birthday party
désinvolture [dezɛ̃vɔltyr] *nf* (*naturel*) (*de manières*) unselfconsciousness; (*de mouvement*) ease; (*sans gêne*) casualness; **avec d.** casually; **sa d. devient insupportable** his casualness *or* his offhand *or* airy manner is becoming unbearable; **il travaille avec une d. qui commence à agacer au bureau** his casual approach to work is beginning to irritate people in the office
désir [dezir] *nm* **(a)** (*souhait*) desire; **avoir un d. de qch** to have a desire for something; **d. de plaire** desire to please; **d. ardent** craving, longing; **ardent d. de réussir** ardent desire to succeed; **selon le d. de son père** in accordance with his father's wishes; **éprouver le d. de faire qch** to want to do sth; **prendre ses désirs pour des réalités** to indulge in wishful thinking; **tes désirs sont des ordres** your wish is my command **(b) d. (sexuel)** (sexual) desire
désirable [dezirabl] *adj* desirable; **peu d.** undesirable
désirer [dezire] *vt* **(a)** (*souhaiter*) to want, to desire; **d. ardemment qch** to crave sth, to yearn *or* long for sth; **d. qch de qn** to want sth of *or* from sb; **je désire le voir** I want *or* wish to see him; **je désire qu'il vienne** I want him to come; **cela laisse à d.** it leaves a lot to be desired; **elle se fait d.** (*elle n'arrive pas*) she's keeping us waiting; **elle aime se faire d.** (*ce n'est pas une femme facile*) she plays hard to get; **je n'avais plus rien à d.** I had nothing left to wish for; **que désirez-vous?,** *F* **vous désirez?** (*dans un magasin*) can I help you?; (*qu'est-ce que je vous sers?*) what would you like? **(b)** (*sexuellement*) to desire; **je te désire** I want you
désireux, -euse [dezirø, øz] *adj* desirous (**de** of); **d. de plaire** anxious to please; **je serais très d. de la connaître** I would very much like to meet her
désistement [dezistəmɑ̃] *nm* **(a)** cancellation; *Jur* (*de réclamation*) waiver; (*de procès*) withdrawal **(b)** *Pol* withdrawal of one's candidature, standing down
désister (se) [sədeziste] *vpr* **(a)** *Jur* **se d. d'une poursuite** to withdraw an action; **se d. d'une demande** to waive a claim **(b)** *Pol* to withdraw (one's candidature), to stand down
desk [dɛsk] *nm Journ* desk
deskman [dɛskman] *nm Journ* deskman
désobéir [dezɔbeir] *vi* to be disobedient; **d. à qn/un ordre** to disobey sb/an order; **d. à une règle** to break a rule
désobéissance [dezɔbeisɑ̃s] *nf* disobedience (**à** of); **d. à une règle** disregard for *or* breaking of a rule
désobéissant [dezɔbeisɑ̃] *adj* disobedient (**à** of)
désobligeance [dezɔbliʒɑ̃s] *nf* disagreeableness (**envers** to)
désobligeant [dezɔbliʒɑ̃] *adj* (*personne, manière, mots etc*) disagreeable, ungracious (**envers** to)
désobliger [dezɔbliʒe] *vt* (**je désobligeai(s); n. désobligeons**) to offend
désobstruer [dezɔpstrye] *vt* (*tuyau, passage, tunnel etc*) to clear (of an obstruction)
désodé [desɔde] *adj* salt-free
désodorisant [dezɔdɔrizɑ̃] *adj, nm* deodorant
désodoriser [dezɔdɔrize] *vt* to deodorize
désœuvré [dezœvre] **1** *adj* unoccupied, idle; **me trouvant d.** finding myself with nothing to do, *F* being *or* finding myself at a loose end; **je ne supporte pas de rester d. plus de cinq minutes** I can't bear to be idle for more than five minutes **2** *n* **les désœuvrés** people with nothing to do
désœuvrement [dezœvrəmɑ̃] *nm* idleness; **par d.** to kill time, for want of something to do
désolant [dezɔlɑ̃] *adj* (*nouvelle etc*) distressing; **tu es vraiment d.** you drive me to despair; **ce temps est d.** this weather is very depressing
désolation [dezɔlasjɔ̃] *nf* **(a)** (*dévastation*) desolation, devastation, laying waste **(b)** (*affliction*) grief, sorrow; **être plongé dans la d.** to be grief-stricken; **sa fille ne fait plus de danse et c'est sa grande d.** she is heart-broken that her daughter has given up dancing
désolé [dezɔle] *adj* **(a)** (*région etc*) desolate, dreary **(b)** (*navré*) sorry; **je suis (terriblement) d. de vous avoir fait attendre** I'm (so *or* very) sorry to have kept you waiting; **d., je n'ai pas le temps** sorry, I haven't got the time; **je suis d. mais ce n'est pas la meilleure candidate** I'm sorry but she isn't the best candidate **(c)** (*affligé*) upset
désoler [dezɔle] **1** *vt* **(a)** (*affliger*) to distress, to grieve; **son échec à l'examen le désole** he's very upset about failing the exam **(b)** *Vieilli, Litt* (*pays etc*) to devastate, to ravage, to lay waste **2 se désoler** *vpr* to be distressed, to be upset
désolidariser (se) [sədesɔlidarize] *vpr* (*d'une personne*) to break away, to break ranks; **se d. de** *ou* **d'avec ses collègues** to break with one's colleagues; **se d. d'une cause** to withdraw one's support from a cause; **se d. d'un projet** to withdraw from a project
désopilant [dezɔpilɑ̃] *adj* screamingly funny, hilarious
désordonné [dezɔrdɔne] *adj* **(a)** (*chambre, bureau etc*) untidy; (*personne*) (*qui n'est pas organisé*) disorganized; (*qui ne range pas*) untidy; (*mouvements*) unco-ordinated; **une fuite désordonnée** a disorderly flight; **il a un esprit trop d.** he's too scatterbrained **(b)** *Litt* (*vie etc*) disorderly; (*dépenses*) reckless
désordre [dezɔrdr] *nm* **(a)** (*manque d'organisation*) disorder, confusion; (*manque d'ordre*) untidiness; **quel d.!** what a mess!; **il règne, dans leur maison, un d. incroyable** their house is incredibly untidy; **tu as mis du d. dans toute la maison, tu as mis toute la maison en d.** you've made the entire house untidy; **c'est un peu le d. dans ses papiers** his papers are not altogether in order; **c'est le d. dans sa dissertation** his thesis lacks organization *or* is not clearly thought out; **être en d.** (*d'une pièce etc*) to be untidy; **cheveux en d.** tangled *or* untidy hair; *Fig* **ça fait d.!** (*ça ne se fait pas*) it's just not done!; (*ce n'est pas sérieux*) that's a laugh!

(b) (*agitation*) **mettre le d. dans les rangs** to cause confusion in the ranks; **il arrive toujours à mettre un d. infernal dans la classe** he always manages to cause an uproar in the classroom; *F* **il a fait du d. dans la rue** he caused a disturbance in the street; **le d. qui règne à l'Assemblée nationale ces jours-ci** the present commotion in the National Assembly; **d. de la pensée** confused thinking

(c) désordres disturbances, riots; **de graves désordres ont éclaté** serious disturbances have broken out

(d) *Litt* (*licence*) licentiousness; **vivre dans le d.** to lead a life of licentiousness

(e) *Méd* disorder; **d. nerveux/fonctionnel/hormonal** nervous/functional/hormone disorder
désorganisation [dezɔrganizasjɔ̃] *nf* disorganization
désorganiser [dezɔrganize] **1** *vt* (*système etc*) to disrupt; (*plans etc*) to upset **2 se désorganiser** *vpr* to become disorganized
désorientation [dezɔrjɑ̃tasjɔ̃] *nf* disorientation; (*déconcertation*) confusion, bewilderment
désorienté [dezɔrjɑ̃te] *adj* (*perdu*) disorientated, *surtout Am* disoriented; (*déconcerté*) confused, bewildered; **après l'anesthésie, il était complètement d.** he was completely disorientated *or* totally confused after the anaesthetic
désorienter [dezɔrjɑ̃te] *vt* **(a)** (*égarer*) (*personne*) to disorientate, *surtout Am* to disorient; (*compas, instrument*) to throw out (of adjustment) **(b)** (*déconcerter*) to confuse, to bewilder; **l'anesthésie l'a désorienté** he is disorientated *or* confused because of the anaesthetic
désormais [dezɔrmɛ] *adv* from now on(wards), in future, *Litt* henceforth
désorption [dezɔrpsjɔ̃] *nf Ch* desorption
désossé [dezɔse] *adj* (*viande, poisson*) boned; *Fig* (*personne*) supple; *Péj* (*style etc*) flabby, flaccid
désossement [dezɔsmɑ̃] *nm* (*de viande, poisson*) boning
désosser [dezɔse] **1** *vt* (*viande, poisson*) to bone; *Fig* (*phrase, livre*) to dissect **2 se désosser** *vpr* to contort oneself
désoxydant [dezɔksidɑ̃] *Ch* **1** *adj* deoxidizing **2** *nm* deoxidizer
désoxyder [dezɔkside] *vt Ch, Métal* to deoxidize
desperado [dɛsperado] *nm* desperado
despote [dɛspɔt] **1** *nm* despot; *F* **sa fille est un d.!** her daughter is a regular tyrant! **2** *adj* **mari/femme d.** despotic husband/wife
despotique [dɛspɔtik] *adj* (*pouvoir etc*) despotic
despotiquement [dɛspɔtikmɑ̃] *adv* despotically
despotisme [dɛspɔtism] *nm* despotism
desquamation [dɛskwamasjɔ̃] *nf* peeling, *Spéc* exfoliation; *Méd* (*pathologique*) desquamation
desquamer [dɛskwame] **1** *vt* to exfoliate **2** *vi* to peel (off); *Méd* to desquamate **3 se desquamer** *vpr* to peel

desquels, desquelles [dekɛl] *voir* = **lequel**
dessaisir [desezir] **1** *vt Jur* **d. un tribunal d'une affaire** to remove a case from a court **2 se dessaisir** *vpr* **se d. de qch** to relinquish sth, to part with sth, to give sth up
dessaisissement [desezismɑ̃] *nm* **(a)** *Jur* **d. d'un tribunal d'une affaire** removal of a case from a court **(b)** (*abandon*) **d. de qch** relinquishment of sth
dessalage [desalaʒ] *nm* (*du poisson, de la viande etc*) soaking (*to remove salt*)
dessalaison [desalɛzɔ̃] *nf* **(a)** = **dessalage (b)** = **dessalement**
dessalé [desale] *adj* **(a)** (*viande, poisson etc*) soaked (*to remove salt*) **(b)** *F* (*personne*) wide awake, sharp
dessalement [desalmɑ̃] *nm* (*de l'eau de mer*) desalination
dessaler [desale] **1** *vt* **(a)** (*viande, poisson*) to remove the salt from (*by soaking*); (*eau de mer*) to desalinate **(b)** *F* **d. qn** to sharpen sb's wits **2** *vi Naut* to capsize **3 se dessaler** *vpr* **(a)** (*devenir moins salé*) to become less salty **(b)** *F* to learn a thing or two
dessangler [desɑ̃gle] *vt* (*horse*) to ungirth, to take the girths off
dessaouler [desule] *vti F* = **dessoûler**
desséchant [deseʃɑ̃] *adj* (*vent*) drying
desséché [deseʃe] *adj* (*étang, rivière*) dry, dried-up; (*sol, bouche*) dry, parched; (*peau*) dry; (*bois*) seasoned, dried; (*plante*) dry, withered; *Fig* (*personne*) (*maigre*) shrunken; (*insensible*) without feelings, without emotions, dried-up; **il est d.** (*insensible*) he's dead inside, he's got no feelings left
dessèchement [desɛʃmɑ̃] *nm* (*d'un étang, d'une rivière*) drying up; (*d'un sol*) drying; (*du bois*) seasoning, drying; (*d'une plante*) withering; *Vieilli Fig* (*du corps*) shrunkenness; *Fig* (*dureté*) (*d'une personne*) lack of feeling
dessécher [deseʃe] **(je dessèche, n. desséchons; je dessécherai) 1** *vt* (*sol, étang, rivière*) to dry up; (*bois*) to season; (*denrées alimentaires*) to dry; (*noix de coco*) to desiccate; (*du vent, de la chaleur etc*) (*plante*) to wither; (*peau*) to dry; (*bouche*) to dry, to parch; (*de maladie, l'âge etc*) (*corps*) to shrink; *Fig* **d. le cœur de qn** to harden sb's heart **2 se dessécher** *vpr* (*du sol*) to dry up, to become dry; (*d'un étang, d'une rivière etc*) to dry up, to go dry; (*d'une plante*) to wither; (*d'une personne*) (*maigrir*) to waste away; *Fig* (*devenir insensible*) to become insensitive
dessein [desɛ̃] *nm* intention, purpose, *Litt* design; **avoir le d. de faire qch** to intend to do sth; **former le d. de faire qch** to plan to do sth; **dans ce d.** with this intention, with this in mind; **à d.** on purpose, purposely, intentionally; **c'est à d. que je n'ai pas répondu** I deliberately didn't answer; **à d.** *ou* **dans le d. de vous revoir** in order to see you again
desseller [desele] *vt* (*cheval*) to unsaddle
desserrage [desɛraʒ] *nm* (*d'une vis*) loosening; (*d'une ceinture, d'un nœud*) slackening, loosening
desserrement [desɛrmɑ̃] *nm* loosening
desserrer [desere] **1** *vt* (*vis*) to loosen; (*ceinture, nœud*) to loosen, to slacken; (*poing, dents*) to unclench; (*frein à main*) to release, to take off; **d. son étreinte** to relax one's hold; **je n'ai pas desserré les dents** I didn't open my mouth, I didn't utter a word; **peux-tu d. les livres sur l'étagère?** can you move the books on the shelf so they're a bit less tightly packed? **2 se desserrer** *vpr* (*d'un vis*) to work loose; (*d'une ceinture, d'un nœud*) to come loose; (*d'étreinte*) to relax
dessert [desɛr] *nm* dessert, *Br* pudding, *Br* sweet; **venez pour le d.** come for dessert; **être privé de d.** to go without dessert; **qu'est-ce qu'il y a comme** *ou* **au d.?** what's for dessert?; **carte des desserts** dessert menu
desserte[1] [desɛrt] *nf* **(a)** (*service*) service; **d. d'un port par voie ferrée** rail service to a port; **chemin de d.** service road **(b)** *Rel* ministry
desserte[2] *nf* (*meuble*) sideboard; **d. (roulante)** trolley
dessertir [desɛrtir] *vt* (*pierre précieuse*) to remove from its setting
desservant [desɛrvɑ̃] *nm Rel* incumbent
desservir[1] [desɛrvir] *vt* (*conj like* **servir**) **(a)** (*de chemins de fer etc*) to serve; (*de porte*) to lead into; **ce train ne dessert pas toutes les gares** this train does not stop at every station; **ville bien desservie** town with efficient public transport **(b)** *Rel* (*paroisse etc*) to minister to
desservir[2] (*conj like* **servir**) **1** *vt* **(a)** (*table*) to clear **(b)** (*nuire à*) to do harm to; **desservir qn** to do sb a disservice; **cela risque de vous d.** that may be to your disadvantage; **cela desservirait mes intérêts** it would be detrimental to my interests; **son perfectionnisme la dessert** her perfectionism isn't doing her any good **2** *vi* to clear away **3 se desservir** *vpr* to do oneself a disservice; **il se dessert par sa malhonnêteté** he's not doing himself any good by being dishonest
dessiccatif, -ive [desikatif, -iv] *Méd* **1** *adj* (*produit*) drying **2** *nm* drying agent
dessiccation [desikasjɔ̃] *nf* dessication
dessiller [desije] **1** *vt* (*yeux*) to open; *Fig* **d. les yeux à** *ou* **de qn** to open sb's eyes (to the facts) **2 se dessiller** *vpr* (*des yeux*) to open; *Fig* **ses yeux se dessillèrent** his eyes were opened
dessin [desɛ̃] *nm* **(a)** (art of) drawing, sketching; (*croquis etc*) drawing; **être bon en d.** to be good at drawing, to be a good drawer; **d. à la plume** pen-and-ink sketch; **d. au trait** line drawing; **d. à main levée** free-hand drawing; **un d. d'enfant** a child's drawing; **les dessins de Degas** Degas' drawings; **faire du d. publicitaire** to be a commercial artist; *F* **faut-il que je te fasse un d.?** do I have to draw a picture *or* spell it out for you?; *Tech* **planche à d.** drawing board; **d. d'ensemble** general assembly drawing; **d. de profil** profile drawing **(b)** (*motif*) design, pattern; **tissu à d.** patterned fabric; **une robe avec de jolis dessins** a pretty patterned dress **(c)** (*contour*) (*d'un visage etc*) outline
▶ **dessin**: **d. assisté par ordinateur** computer assisted design; **d. humoristique** cartoon; **d. industriel** industrial drawing; **d. de mode** fashion design; *Cin* **dessin(s) animé(s)** cartoon(s)
dessinateur, -trice [desinatœr, -tris] *n* **(a)** (*artiste*) sketcher, drawer; **d. humoristique** cartoonist **(b)** (*de papier peint etc*) designer; (*de mode*) fashion artist **(c)** *Tech* draughtsman, *US* draftsman, -woman; **d. industriel** draughtsman; **d. cartographe** cartographer; **d. concepteur** (*de mobilier etc*) designer
dessiner [desine] **1** *vt* **(a)** to draw, to sketch; **d. qch d'après nature** to draw sth from nature; **d. à l'encre/à la craie** to draw in ink/chalk

(b) (*papier peint, tissu, plan etc*) to design

(c) *Fig* (*tracer*) to show, to outline; **les montagnes dessinent leur courbe sur le ciel** the line of the mountains stands out against the sky; **vêtement qui dessine bien la taille** garment that shows off the waist; **visage bien dessiné** finely chiselled face

2 se dessiner *vpr* **(a)** (*se voir*) to stand out, to be outlined; **les arbres se dessinent à l'horizon** the trees stand out *or* are outlined on the horizon; **parfois, un sourire se dessinait sur ses lèvres** a smile occasionally played *or* hovered on her lips

(b) (*se préciser*) to take shape; **nos projets de vacances se dessinent vaguement** our holiday plans are beginning to take shape; **on voit se d. un virage à gauche de l'opinion** we can see the beginnings of a shift to the left in public opinion
dessouder [desude] **1** *vt* to unsolder **2 se dessouder** *vpr* **le tuyau s'est dessoudé** the pipe has come unsoldered
dessoûler [desule] *F* **1** *vt* to sober up, to make sober **2** *vi* to become sober, to sober up; **il ne dessoûle pas depuis son mariage** he hasn't been sober since he got married
dessous [dəsu] **1** *adv* underneath; **passez (par-)d.** go underneath (it); **prendre/porter qch par (en) d.** to take hold of/carry sth from underneath; *Fig* **il fait des choses par (en) d.** he does things in an underhand way; **en d.** underneath; **l'appartement d'en d.** the downstairs flat, the flat downstairs; **regarder qn (par) en d.** to look at sb furtively *or* stealthily; **rire en d.** to laugh up one's sleeve; **agir en d.** to act in an underhand way; **ci-d.** below; **dans la note ci-d.** in the note below; **là-d.** under there; *Fig* **il y a quelque chose de bizarre là-d.** there's something funny about it; **au-d.** below; **son bureau est au-d.** his office is on the next floor down; **une maison avec un garage au-d.** a house with a garage underneath (it); *Fig* **pour vingt francs et au-d., vous ne trouverez rien de bien** you won't find anything decent for less than twenty francs; **il est bien au-d., il n'a pas ta valeur** he's not nearly as good as you

2 *prép* **(a) de d.** from under(neath) *or* beneath

(b) par-d. underneath

(c) au-d. de under; **au-d. de 500 francs, on ne trouve rien** you won't find anything under 500 francs; **un peu au-d. de Paris** slightly to the south of Paris; *Fig* **elle est bien au-d. de toi** she's not nearly as good as you; **il est au-d. de sa tâche** he's not up to the job; **être au-d. de tout** to be beneath contempt

(d) en d. de under(neath); **tu es très en d. de la vérité** you're not even close

3 *nm* **(a) les gens du d.** the people on the floor below (us), the downstairs neighbours; **d. d'une assiette** underside of a plate; **avoir le d.** to get the worst of it, to be defeated; **être dans le troisième** *ou* **trente-sixième d.** to be in the depths of despair; *Fig* **les d. de la politique** the shady side of politics; **je voudrais bien connaître le d. de toute cette histoire** I'd really like to know what they're not telling us (in this whole affair); *Fig* **connaître le d. des cartes** to be in the know, to know what's going on

(b) *mpl* (*sous-vêtements*) (ladies') underwear, *F* undies; (*raffiné*) lingerie

dessous de bouteille [d(ə)sudbutɛj] *nm inv* coaster

dessous-de-bras [d(ə)sudbra] *nm inv* dress shield

dessous-de-plat [d(ə)sudpla] *nm inv* table mat

dessous de robe *nm* slip, *Vieilli* petticoat

dessous-de-table [d(ə)sudtabl] *nm inv* backhander; *Fig* **verser un d. à qn** to pay sb a bribe, to give *or* slip sb a backhander

dessous de tasse [d(ə)sud(ə)tas] *nm inv* saucer

dessous-de-verre [d(ə)sudvɛr] *nm inv* coaster

dessus [dəsy] **1** *adv* (up)on (it/them); **il a marché d.** he trod on it; **mais il n'y a pas l'adresse d.** but the address isn't on it, but it doesn't have the address on (it); **avec du chocolat d.** with chocolate on top; **j'ai failli lui tirer d.** I nearly shot him; **vous avez mis le doigt d.** you've put your finger on it, you've hit the nail on the head; *Fig F* **il m'est tombé d. dans le métro** he buttonholed me *or* grabbed hold of me in the underground; **la police finira bien par lui mettre la main d.** the police will track him down eventually; **impossible de mettre la main d.!** (*d'une chose*) I just can't/couldn't lay my hands on it; **marcher bras d. bras dessous** to walk arm in arm; **au-d.** at the top, on top, above; **mettre les meilleures pommes (au-)d.** to put the best apples on top *or* at the top; **l'appartement au-d.** the flat upstairs, the upstairs flat; **avec de la crème au-d.** with cream on top; **vous ne trouverez rien au-d.** you'll find nothing better; **voir ci-d.** see above; **là-d.** up there; **il y a beaucoup à dire là-d.** a lot could be said on that score; *F* **ne compte pas là-d.!** don't count on it!; **là-d. elle partit** and with that, she left

2 *prép* **(a) de d.** from, off; **elle ne leva pas les yeux de d. son ouvrage** she didn't lift her eyes from *or* look up from *or* take her eyes off her work

(b) au-d. de above; **au-d. de 15 ans** over 15, more than 15 (years old); **au-d. de Lyon** (*au nord de*) north of Lyons; **nous volons au-d. de l'Alsace** we are flying over Alsace; *Fig* **il est bien au-d. de toi** he's much better than you are; **je suis au-d. de tout cela** I'm above all that; **au-d. de tout soupçon** above suspicion; **c'est au-d. de mes forces** I'm not strong enough (to do it); **c'est au-d. de mes capacités/moyens** I can't do/afford it; **rien n'est au-d. de sa foi** his faith can move mountains

(c) par-d. above, over; *F* **j'en ai par-d. la tête** I've had it up to here

3 *nm* (*de table etc*) top; **l'étage du d.** the top floor; *Th* **les d.** the flies; **avoir le d.** to have the upper hand, to be on top; **(re)prendre le d.** to get over it

dessus-de-lit [d(ə)sydli] *nm inv* coverlet, bedspread

déstabilisant [destabilizɑ̃], **déstabilisateur, -trice** [destabilizatœr, -tris] *adj* unsettling; *Pol, Fin* destabilizing; **cet incident a été très d. pour les élèves** the incident was very unsettling for *or* had a very unsettling effect on the pupils; **cela a été très d. pour le gouvernement** it has had an extremely destabilizing effect on the government

déstabilisation [destabilizasjɔ̃] *nf* unsettling; *Pol, Fin* destabilization

déstabiliser [destabilize] *vt* to unsettle; *Pol, Fin* to destabilize

déstalinisation [destalinizasjɔ̃] *nf Pol* destalinization

déstaliniser [destalinize] *vt Pol* to destalinize

destin [dɛstɛ̃] *nm* fate, destiny; **avoir un d. tragique** to be ill-fated; **qui aurait pu prévoir son d.?** who could have predicted his fate *or* what would become of him?; **le d. a voulu que …** fate decreed that …; **le d. nous a réunis** fate brought us together; **accepter son d.** to accept one's fate *or* destiny; **se mettre dans les mains du d.** to trust to fate; **nous nous souviendrons du d. tragique qui fut le sien** we shall remember his tragic fate

destinataire [dɛstinatɛr] *n* (*de lettre etc*) addressee, recipient; (*de marchandises*) consignee; (*de mandat postal*) payee

destination [dɛstinasjɔ̃] *nf* **(a)** (*direction*) destination; **quelle est votre d.?** where are you going to *or* heading *or* bound for?; **d. touristique** tourist destination; **trains/vols à d. de Paris** trains/flights to Paris; **articles à d. de la province et de l'étranger** goods for the provinces and for export; **arriver à d.** to arrive at one's destination **(b)** (*d'un édifice, d'une somme d'argent etc*) purpose

destinée [dɛstine] *nf* **(a)** (*vie*) destiny; **unir sa d. à celle de qn** to marry sb; *Litt* **il était promis à de si grandes destinées** he was destined for such great things **(b)** = **destin**

destiner [dɛstine] **1** *vt* **(a) d. qch à qn** to mean *or* intend sth for sb; **le sort qui nous est destiné** what fate holds in store for us; **cette remarque t'était personnellement destinée** the remark was meant for *or* aimed at you; **ce paquet vous est destiné** this parcel is meant for *or* addressed to you; **d. une somme d'argent à un achat** to allot *or* assign a sum of money to a purchase; **la recette du concert est destinée à la recherche contre le sida** the money from the concert will go to *or* is intended for Aids research; **il avait destiné son fils au barreau** he had intended his son for the bar; **on la destinait au fils du maire** they intended that she should marry the mayor's son; **cette salle est destinée aux répétitions** this room is used for rehearsals

(b) *Vieilli* (*prédestiner*) to destine; **nous étions destinés à nous rencontrer** we were destined *or* fated to meet

2 se destiner *vpr* **se d. à qch** to intend to take up sth (as a profession); **il se destine à la médecine** he intends to be a doctor

destituer [dɛstitɥe] *vt* (*renvoyer*) to dismiss, to discharge; *Mil* to discharge; (*fonctionnaire*) to remove from office; (*souverain*) to depose; **d. un général de son commandement** to relieve a general of his command

destitution [dɛstitysjɔ̃] *nf* dismissal; *Mil* discharge; (*d'un souverain*) deposition

déstockage [destɔkaʒ] *nm Com* destocking, reduction in stocks; *Compta* **d. de production** (*poste de bilan*) decrease in stocks

déstocker [destɔke] *vt Com* to destock, to reduce stocks of

destrier [dɛstrije] *nm Hist* charger, war horse

destroyer [dɛstrɔjœr, dɛstrwaje] *nm Naut, Mil* destroyer

destructeur, -trice [dɛstryktœr, -tris] **1** *adj* (*enfant, guerre etc*) destructive **2** *n* destroyer

destructible [dɛstryktibl] *adj* destructible

destructif, -ive [dɛstryktif, -iv] *adj* destructive

destruction [dɛstryksjɔ̃] *nf* (*de preuves, papiers, ville etc*) destruction; (*de rats etc, Fig d'une race*) extermination

destructuration [destryktyrasjɔ̃] *nf* deconstruction

destructuré [destryktyre] *adj* (*vêtement*) unstructured, deconstructed

destructurer [destryktyre] *vt* (*vêtement*) to deconstruct

désuet, -uète [desɥɛ, -ɥɛt] *adj* (*mot*) obsolete; (*théorie*) obsolete, antiquated, out-of-date; (*vêtement*) out-of-date, old-fashioned; (*charme*) old-fashioned

désuétude [desɥetyd] *nf* disuse; **tomber en d.** to fall into disuse; (*d'un mot*) to become obsolete; *Jur* (*d'un droit etc*) to lapse; (*d'une loi*) to fall into abeyance

désuni [dezyni] *adj* (*personnes*) divided, disunited; (*manœuvre*) unco-ordinated; **des amis désunis par la guerre** friends divided by war

désunion [dezynjɔ̃] *nf* (*de personnes*) lack of unity; (*dans la famille etc*) dissension

désunir [dezynir] **1** *vt* (*personnes, famille etc*) to divide; **questions qu'on ne peut pas d.** questions that cannot be treated separately (from each other), indissolubly linked questions; **des amants que le temps a désunis** lovers who grew apart with the passage of time **2 se désunir** *vpr* (*d'un athlète*) to lose one's stride

désynchronisé [desɛ̃krɔnize] *adj* out of synch

désyndicalisation [desɛ̃dikalizasjɔ̃] *nf* (*de la classe ouvrière*) decline in union membership **(de** among)

désyndicaliser [desɛ̃dikalize] *vt* (*entreprise*) to de-unionize

détachable [detaʃabl] *adj* detachable

détachage [detaʃaʒ] *nm* (*de vêtements etc*) stain *or* spot removal

détachant [detaʃɑ̃] **1** *adj* stain- *or* spot-removing **2** *nm* stain *or* spot remover

détaché [detaʃe] *adj* **(a)** loose, detached; (*animal*) untethered; **pièces détachées** spare parts **(b)** (*délégué*) seconded (*to another department*); *Mil* detached **(c)** *Fig* (*manière etc*) detached; **d. des biens de ce monde** detached from the world, unworldly

détachement [detaʃmɑ̃] *nm* **(a)** (*d'un employé*) secondment; **il est en d. à l'université de Cambridge** he has been seconded *or* is on secondment to the University of Cambridge **(b)** *Mil* (*de troupes*) detachment, draft, *US* detail; **d. de corvée** fatigue party **(c)** (*indifférence*) detachment **(de** from); **d. des biens de ce monde** detachment from the world, unworldliness

détacher[1] [detaʃe] **1** *vt* **(a)** (*défaire*) to detach; (*rideau*) to take down; (*chaîne*) to undo; (*animal*) to untether; *Rail* (*wagon à plate-forme*) to uncouple; **je ne peux pas en d. mes yeux** I can't take my eyes off it; **d. un chèque du carnet** to tear out a cheque; **d. les pétales d'une fleur** to pick *or* pluck the petals off a flower

(b) *Fig* **d. qn de qch** to turn sb away from sth; **son indiscrétion a détaché de lui tous ses amis** his lack of discretion cost him all his friends *or* caused all his friends to turn away from him; **ses parents ont réussi à le d. de ce chien** his parents managed to free him *or* get him away from the dog

(c) (*déléguer*) to attach, to second; *Mil* to detach; *Mil* **d. un officier auprès de qn** to detach an officer to serve with sb; **fonctionnaire détaché à un autre service** official temporarily attached *or* seconded to another department; **se faire d.** to be seconded; *Mil* to be detached

(d) (*découper*) **d. une figure dans un tableau** to make a figure stand out in a picture; **d. les syllabes d'un mot** to pronounce each syllable of a word separately; *Mus* **d. les notes** to detach the notes

2 se détacher *vpr* **(a)** (*de nœud etc*) to come undone; (*d'animal*) to break loose; (*de poignée*) to break *or* come off, to become detached; (*de bouton*) to come off; (*de pièces*) to come apart; (*de peinture*) to flake *or* come away *or* off; **l'écorce se détache** the bark is peeling off *or* coming away from the tree

(b) *Fig* **se d. de sa famille/qn** to separate *or* break away from one's family/sb; (*se désintéresser*) to grow apart from one's family/sb; **il s'est complètement détaché de toutes ces choses qui autrefois l'intéressaient** he has completely cut himself off from everything that used to interest him; **ils se sont beaucoup détachés l'un de l'autre** they've grown wide apart; **il s'est détaché peu à peu de la maison où il avait passé son enfance** he has gradually detached himself from his childhood home

(c) (*se séparer*) **un petit groupe de coureurs se détacha en avant** a small group *or* bunch of runners broke away (from the field) *or* pulled ahead (of the field)

(d) (*ressortir*) **se d. sur un fond/l'horizon** to stand out against a background/the horizon; **sa blondeur se détache beaucoup avec sa robe noire** her black dress emphasizes her blondness

détacher[2] *vt* (*nettoyer*) (*vêtements etc*) to remove stains *or* spots from

détacheur, -euse [detaʃœr, -øz] **1** *adj* **flacon d.** (bottle of) stain remover **2** *nm* stain remover

détail [detaj] *nm* **(a)** (*élément*) detail; **donner tous les détails** to enter *or* go into all the details, to give full details *or* particulars; **elle n'a pas donné de détails** she didn't go into detail, she didn't give any details; **raconter qch en d.** *ou* **dans les détails** to give a detailed account of sth; **décrire qch en d.** to describe sth in detail, to give a detailed description of sth; **elle va encore me faire le d. de ses vacances** she's going to give me yet another detailed account of her holiday; *Fig F* **ne pas faire de détails** not to make any exceptions; **sans faire de détails** without exception; **demander plus de détails** to ask for more details **(sur, à propos de** about, of); **nous n'avons pas encore de détails** there are no details as yet; **pour plus de détails** for more details; **c'est un d.** it's not important, it's a detail; **se perdre dans les détails** to get bogged down in detail; *Com* **le d. d'un compte** the items of an account; **le d. d'une facture** the breakdown of an invoice; **faire le d. de ses dépenses** to itemize one's expenses

(b) *Com* retail; **vendre au d.** to sell (goods) retail; **magasin de vente au d.** retail store; **marchand au d.** retailer; **prix de d.** retail price; **commerce de d.** retailing; **être dans le commerce de d.** to be in retailing

(c) *Admin, Mil* **service de d.** executive duties; **officier de d.** = quartermaster officer

détaillant, -ante [detajɑ̃, -ɑ̃t] *n Com* retailer; **d. indépendant** independent retailer; **d. spécialisé** specialist retailer

détaillé [detaje] *adj* **(a)** (*récit, description etc*) detailed **(b)** *Com* **état d. de compte** detailed *or* itemized statement of account

détailler [detaje] *vt* **(a)** *Com* (*marchandises*) to retail, to sell retail **(b)** (*énumérer*) (*raisons*) to list; *Com* (*facture*) to itemize **(c) d. qn (de la tête aux pieds)** to scrutinize sb, to look sb up and down

détaler [detale] *vi F* (*d'une personne*) to bolt, to take off; (*d'un cheval etc*) to bolt; **la souris détala vers son trou** the mouse bolted for *or* scuttled off to *or* scurried off to its hole

détartrage [detartraʒ] *nm* (*de chaudière*) descaling; (*de dents*) tartar removal, scaling

détartrant [detartrɑ̃] **1** *nm* (*pour chaudière*) scaler **2** *adj* **dentifrice d.** toothpaste for tartar removal

détartrer [detartre] *vt* (*chaudière*) to (de)scale; (*dents*) (*d'un dentiste*) to scale, to remove the tartar from; (*d'un dentifrice*) to remove the tartar from

détartreur [detartrœr] *nm* (*pour chaudière*) scaler

détaxation [detaksasjɔ̃] *nf* removal of tax

détaxe [detaks] *nf* tax refund *or* rebate

détaxer [detakse] *vt* to take the tax off, to remove the tax on; **marchandises détaxées** duty-free goods

détectable [detɛktabl] *adj* detectable

détecter [detɛkte] *vt* to detect

détecteur, -trice [detɛktœr, -tris] **1** *adj Tech* detecting, sensing; *Électron* **lampe détectrice** detector valve **2** *nm Tech* detector; *Électron* detector, sensor

▶ **détecteur**: *Aut* **d. d'anomalie** fault warning sensor; *Aut* **d. anti-pincement** anti-pinch sensor; *Aut* **d. de choc** crash sensor; *Aut* **d. de cognement** knock sensor; *Aut* **d. de collision** crash sensor; *Com* **d. de faux billets** forgery detector, detecting forged banknotes; **d. de fumée** smoke detector *or* alarm; **d. de mensonges** lie detector, *Spéc* polygraph; **d. de mines** mine detector; *Électron* **d. d'ondes** wave detector; *Électron* **d. de particules** particle detector; **d. de radar** radar detector; *TV etc* **d. transistorisé** solid-state sensor; *Ordinat* **d. de virus** virus detector

détection [detɛksjɔ̃] *nf* detection, location; **d. électromagnétique** radio location; **d. sous-marine** underwater detection; *Mil, Naut* **d. des mines** mine detection; **d. à ultrasons** ultrasound detection; *Ordinat* **d. d'erreurs** error detection; *Ordinat* **d. virale** virus detection

détective [detɛktiv] *nm* detective; **d. privé** private detective, *F* private eye; **d. d'hôtel** house detective, hotel detective

déteindre [detɛ̃dr] (*conj like* **teindre**) **1** *vt* to take the colour out of **2** *vi* (*d'un tissu*) to fade, to lose colour; **d. au lavage** to run in the wash; **le ruban a déteint sur ma robe** the colour of the ribbon has come off on my dress; *Fig* **cela déteint sur eux** it rubs off on them; *Fig* **j'espère que leur politesse déteindra sur elle** I hope some of their politeness rubs off on her

dételage [detlaʒ] *nm* **(a)** (*de chevaux*) unharnessing, unhitching **(b)** *Rail* (*de wagons*) uncoupling

dételer [detle] **(je dételle, n. dételons; je détellerai) 1** *vt* **(a)** (*chevaux*) to unharness, to unhitch; (*bœufs*) to unyoke **(b)** *Rail* (*wagons*) to uncouple **2** *vi F* to ease off, to stop working; **travailler dix heures sans d.** to work for ten hours without letting up, to work non-stop for ten hours; **on dételle à six heures** we stop (work) at six o'clock

détendeur [detɑ̃dœr] *nm Tech* pressure reducer, relief valve

détendre [detɑ̃dr] **1** *vt* (*cordage de raquette, cordes de guitare*) to slacken, to loosen; (*arc*) to unbend; **d. un ressort** to release a spring; **d. des relations/l'atmosphère** to make relations/the atmosphere less strained; **d. les nerfs** to steady the nerves **2 se détendre** *vpr* (*de tissu*) to stretch; (*de ressort*) to uncoil; (*de vapeur*) to be reduced in pressure; (*d'un gaz, de l'air chaud*) to expand; (*se relaxer*) to relax; **se d. pendant une heure** to relax for an hour; **son visage se détendit dans un sourire** his face relaxed into a smile; **la situation se détend** the situation is easing *or* is becoming less tense

détendu [detɑ̃dy] *adj* (*lâche*) slack; (*conversation etc*) relaxed

détenir [detnir] *vt* (*conj like* **tenir**) **(a)** (*passeport, titres etc*) to hold, to be in possession of; (*le pouvoir, Sp coupe, record du monde*) to hold; **d. un objet volé** to be in possession of a stolen object; **d. un secret** to have a secret **(b)** (*personne*) to detain, to keep *or* hold prisoner

détente [detɑ̃t] *nf* **(a)** (*relaxation*) recreation; **dans ses rares moments de d.** in the little time he has to relax; **j'ai besoin de quelques instants de d.** I need to relax for a few moments, I need a few moments' relaxation **(b)** (*de qch de tendu*) loosening, slackening; (*de relations etc*) easing; *Pol* détente; (*d'un athlète*) spring; **avoir une belle d.** to jump well, to be a good jumper; **d'une d. de la jambe droite, il prolongea le ballon dans le but anglais** stretching out his right leg, he sent the ball into the English goal; **travaillant tout en d., il parvint à sauter les 2 mètres** with a powerful spring, he managed to clear the two-metre mark **(c)** (*d'une arme*) trigger; *F* **dur à la d.** tight-fisted, stingy **(d)** *Tech* (*de la vapeur, des gaz*) expansion; (*dans un moteur*) explosion *or* power stroke; **soupape de d.** expansion valve

détenteur, -trice [detɑ̃tœr, -tris] *n* (*de droits d'auteur, titres, coupe etc*) holder; **d. de titres** stockholder, shareholder; **d. d'obligations** bondholder; **d. du record du monde** world record holder

détention [detɑ̃sjɔ̃] *nf* **(a)** (*de titres etc*) holding; (*d'armes à feu etc*) possession **(b)** (*captivité*) detention, imprisonment; **d. provisoire** detention pending trial

détenu, -ue [detny] *n* prisoner, inmate

détergence [detɛrʒɑ̃s] *nf* detergency

détergent [detɛrʒɑ̃] *adj, nm* detergent

déterger [detɛrʒe] *vt Tech* (*taches d'huile etc*) to clean, to remove

détérioration [deterjɔrasjɔ̃] *nf* deterioration

détériorer [deterjɔre] **1** *vt* (*matériel, santé*) to damage; (*marchandises*) to spoil; **la radio m'est revenue complètement détériorée** the radio came back absolutely ruined; **détérioré en cours de transport** damaged in transit **2 se détériorer** *vpr* to deteriorate

déterminable [determinabl] *adj* determinable, which can be determined

déterminant [determinɑ̃] **1** *adj* (*facteur, cause etc*) deciding, decisive; **sa présence a été déterminante pour la signature du contrat** his presence was the determining factor in the decision to sign the contract **2** *nm Ling* determiner; *Math* determinant

déterminatif, -ive [determinatif, -iv] [①A32,11,b] *Ling, Gram* **1** *adj* (*mot etc*) determinative, defining; **phrase déterminative** defining clause **2** *nm* determiner, determinative

détermination [determinasjɔ̃] *nf* **(a)** (*fermeté*) determination, resolution; **avec d.** with determination, determinedly, resolutely **(b)** (*résolution*) resolve, determination; **rien ne pourra faire flancher ma d.** nothing will make me any less determined, nothing will shake my resolve **(c)** (*d'une espèce, d'une date, d'une zone etc*) determination; (*du sang, d'une bactérie*) typing; **d. des prix** price setting

déterminé [determine] *adj* **(a)** (*domaine, objectif etc*) specific, particular; (*durée*) specific, set, definite; **dans un sens d.** in a given direction; **il faut arriver au but/à l'objectif d.** we have to achieve the goal/the objective that was set; **il l'a fait dans un but d.** he did it for a specific reason **(b)** (*personne, manière etc*) determined, resolute; **être d. à faire qch** to be determined to do sth

déterminer [determine] **1** *vt* **(a)** (*définir*) (*date, fait, nom, valeur etc*) to determine, to establish; (*espèce*) to determine; (*sang, bactérie*) to type; **d. un lieu de rendez-vous** to fix *or* decide on a meeting place **(b)** (*causer*) (*changement*) to cause, to give rise to; (*action, décision*) to determine, to dictate **(c)** (*décider*) **d. qn à faire qch** to induce *or* move *or* impel sb to do sth; **qu'est-ce qui vous a déterminé à partir?** what made you (decide to) leave? **(d)** *Gram* to determine **2 se déterminer** *vpr* to make up one's mind (**à faire qch** to do sth)

déterminisme [determinism] *nm Phil* determinism

déterministe [determinist] *Phil* **1** *n* determinist **2** *adj* determinist(ic)

déterré, -ée [detere] *n F* **il a un air** *ou* **une mine** *ou* **une tête de d.** he looks like death warmed up

déterrer [detere] *vt* (*trésor enfoui etc*) to dig up, to unearth; (*arbre*) to uproot; (*cadavre*) to exhume; *Fig* (*vieux livre etc*) to dig up

détersif, -ive [detersif, -iv] *adj, nm* detergent

détersion [detersjɔ̃] *nf* (*nettoyage*) cleaning with a detergent; *Méd* (*d'une plaie etc*) cleansing

détestable [detestabl] *adj* (*personne*) detestable, hateful; (*travail etc*) (*de mauvaise qualité*) awful, dreadful, very bad; (*inintéressant*) awful, ghastly; (*temps, humeur*) foul, ghastly

détestablement [detestabləmɑ̃] *adv* (*se conduire, chanter, parler*) extremely badly, appallingly; **faire la cuisine d.** to be an extremely bad *or* an appalling cook; **il parle anglais/travaille d.** his English/work is extremely bad *or* appalling

détester [deteste] *vt* to detest, to hate; **je déteste être dérangé** I hate to be *or* I hate *or* detest being disturbed; **elle ne déteste pas (de) courir** she's quite fond of running; **il ne déteste pas les bonbons** he rather likes sweets

déthéiné [deteine] *adj* (*thé*) decaffeinated

détonant [detɔnɑ̃] **1** *adj* (*substance*) explosive; **explosif d.** high explosive; *Tech, Fig* **mélange d.** explosive mixture **2** *nm* explosive

détonateur [detɔnatœr] *nm* detonator; *Fig* **être le d. de qch** to spark sth off

détonation [detɔnasjɔ̃] *nf* (*explosion*) detonation; (*bruit*) explosion; (*bruit d'arme à feu*) report, bang; *Aut* knocking, detonation

détoner [detɔne] *vi* (*de dynamite etc*) to detonate, to explode; (*de carburant*) to knock; **faire d. qch** to detonate sth

détonner [detɔne] *vi* (*d'un instrument*) to be out of tune; (*d'un chanteur*) to sing out of tune *or* off-key; (*d'un pianiste etc*) to play out of tune; (*de couleurs*) to clash; **ses bijoux détonnent dans ce milieu** her jewels are out of place *or* out of keeping in these circles; **il détonne dans cet entourage** he looks out of place in that circle; **la remarque détonne dans ce texte** the remark jumps out in this text *or* looks really out of place in this text

détordre [detɔrdr] **1** *vt* (*fil etc*) to untwist **2 se détordre** *vpr* (*de fil etc*) to come untwisted, to untwist

détortiller [detɔrtije] *vt* (*fil etc*) to untwist; (*cheveux etc*) to disentangle

détour [detur] *nm* **(a)** (*tracé*) (*d'une route, d'une rivière*) turn, curve, bend; **la route fait un brusque d.** the road makes a sharp turn *or* bends sharply; **je l'ai aperçue au d. du chemin** I spotted her as she was winding her way along the path; *Fig* **au d. de la conversation** in the course of the conversation

(b) (*dans un parcours*) detour; **faire un long d.** to make a long detour; **d. obligatoire de 5 km** (mandatory) 5 kilometre diversion; **ça vaut le d.** it's worth the trip; *Fig* **tu verrais son nouveau copain, il vaut le d.** her new boyfriend is really something

(c) *Fig* (*biais*) **user de détours pour arriver à un but** to achieve one's end in a roundabout way; **répondre sans d.** to give a plain *or* straightforward answer; **vous pouvez me parler sans d.** you can speak frankly to me

détourné [deturne] *adj* (*route, itinéraire*) indirect, roundabout; **chemin d.** by-road; *Fig* **par des voies détournées, de façon détournée** indirectly, in a roundabout way; **ce n'est pas la peine de prendre des chemins détournés pour me le dire** you might as well tell me straight out, why go all around the houses to tell me?

détournement [deturnəmɑ̃] *nm* (*d'une rivière etc*) diversion, diverting; (*du trafic*) diversion, rerouting

▶ **détournement**: *Fin* **d. d'actif** embezzlement of assets; **d. d'avion** hijacking; *Fin* **d. de fonds** misappropriation of funds, embezzlement; *Jur* **d. de mineur** corruption of a minor; **d. de pouvoir** take-over (of power)

détourner [deturne] **1** *vt* **(a)** (*trafic, rivière etc*) to divert; **d. un avion** to hijack a plane; **d. l'attention de qn** to divert *or* distract sb's attention; **d. qn de** (*son travail, mauvaises fréquentations*) to get sb away from; **d. qn de sa route** to take sb out of his way; **comment as-tu pu te laisser d. de ton devoir?** how could you have let yourself be distracted from your duty?; **d. qn du droit chemin** to lead sb astray; **il faut absolument le d. de ce projet** we really must get him to drop the idea; **d. la conversation** to change the subject; **d. les soupçons** to avert suspicion

(b) (*fonds*) to misappropriate, to embezzle (**à** from)

(c) d. la tête pour éviter de voir qn to look the other way *or* to turn one's head away so as not to see sb; **d. les yeux** to avert one's gaze, to look away, to turn one's eyes away

2 se détourner *vpr* to turn away *or* aside (**de** from); *Fig* **se d. de ses études/amis** to neglect one's studies/friends

détoxication [detɔksikasjɔ̃] *nf* detoxication

détoxiquer [detɔksike] *vt* to detoxicate

détracter [detrakte] *vt Litt* to denigrate, to disparage

détracteur, -trice [detraktœr, -tris] *n* detractor, disparager

détraqué, -ée [detrake] **1** *adj* (*appareil*) out of order; (*digestion, estomac*) upset; (*santé*) ruined; *F* (*personne*) (*psychologiquement*) unhinged; **ma radio est toute détraquée** there is something very wrong with my radio; **il a le cerveau d.** his mind is unhinged; **avoir les nerfs détraqués** to be a nervous wreck; **le temps est d.** the weather is unsettled **2** *n F* psycho

détraquement [detrakmɑ̃] *nm* (*d'un appareil, de la santé etc*) breakdown

détraquer [detrake] **1** *vt* (*appareil*) to put out of order; (*mécanisme*) to throw out of gear; *F* **cette déception lui a détraqué le cerveau** the disappointment has unhinged his mind; **ça va te d. l'estomac** that'll upset your stomach **2 se détraquer** *vpr* (*d'un appareil, de la santé etc*) to break down; (*de l'estomac*) to be upset; (*du temps*) to become unsettled; **se d. l'estomac/les nerfs** to upset one's stomach/to ruin one's nerves

détrempe[1] [detrɑ̃p] *nf* (*de mur*) distemper; *Beaux-Arts* tempera

détrempe[2] *nf* (*d'acier*) annealing

détremper[1] [detrɑ̃pe] *vt* (*gorger d'eau*) to soak; **champ/terre détrempé(e)** sodden *or* waterlogged field/earth

détremper[2] *vt* (*acier*) to anneal

détresse [detres] *nf* **(a)** (*angoisse*) distress, grief, anguish; **elle est dans une grande d.** she is extremely distressed *or* heartbroken **(b)** (*dénuement*) financial straits *or* difficulties; **être en d.** to be in financial difficulties, to have money problems **(c)** (*perdition*) **en d.** (*navire*) in distress; (*voiture, avion*) in difficulties; **signal de d.** distress signal, SOS; *Aut* **feux de d.** hazard warning lights, *F* hazards

détriment [detrimɑ̃] *nm* **au d. de qn/qch** to the detriment of sb/sth; **je l'ai appris à mon d.** I found it out to my cost

détritus [detritys] *nm* rubbish, refuse

détroit [detrwa] *nm Géog* strait(s), sound

détromper [detrɔ̃pe] **1** *vt* **d. qn** to put sb right **2 se détromper** *vpr* to realize that one was wrong; **il a fini par se d.** he finally realized his mistake *or* that he was wrong *or* mistaken; **je ne demande pas mieux que de me d.** I'll be quite happy to admit that I was mistaken; **détrompez-vous!** open your eyes!

détrôner [detrone] *vt* **(a)** (*monarque, Sp champion*) to dethrone **(b)** (*supplanter*) (*ancienne méthode etc*) to supersede

détrousser [detruse] *vt* **d. qn** *Hum* to relieve sb of his/her valuables; *Arch* to rob sb

détrousseur [detrusœr] *nm Arch* highwayman, footpad

détruire [detrɥir] (*prp* **détruisant**; *pp* **détruit**; *pr ind* **je détruis, n. détruisons**; *impf* **je détruisais**; *p hist* **je détruisis**; *fu* **je détruirai**) **1** *vt* **(a)** (*démolir*) (*édifice, ville etc*) to destroy; (*empire etc*) to destroy, to overthrow; (*bateau etc*) to break up, to scrap; (*voiture, avion etc*) to destroy, *F* to demolish, to write off

(b) (*anéantir*) (*maison, village*) to destroy; (*mariage*) to destroy, to wreck; (*moisson, alibi*) to ruin, to destroy; (*santé*) to ruin; **d. les espérances de qn** to destroy *or* dash sb's hopes; **il a détruit sa fortune au jeu** he spent all his money gambling

(c) (*tuer*) to kill; **l'épidémie va d. 200 000 personnes** the epidemic is likely to kill 200,000 people

2 se détruire *vpr* (*se suicider*) to kill oneself

dette [dɛt] *nf Fin, Fig* debt; **faire des dettes** to run into debt; **avoir des dettes** to be in debt, to have debts; **être criblé de dettes** to be crippled with debt; **avoir une d. de reconnaissance envers qn** to owe sb a debt of gratitude, to be under an obligation to sb; **être en d. envers qn** to be indebted to sb, to be under an obligation to sb; **payer sa d. à la justice** *ou* **à la société** to pay one's debt to society

▶ **dette: dettes actives** (*en comptabilité*) accounts receivable, assets; **d. consolidée** consolidated debt; **d. extérieure** foreign debt; **d. à court terme** *ou* **flottante** short-term *or* floating debt; **d. foncière** property charge; *Compta* **dettes fournisseurs** accounts payable; **d. d'honneur** debt of honour; (*hypothécaire*) mortgage debt; **d. de jeu** gambling debt *Compta* **dettes à long terme** long term liabilities; **dettes passives** (*en comptabilité*) accounts payable, liabilities; **d. privilégiée** preferred debt; **la d. publique** *ou* **de l'État** the National Debt; **d. véreuse** bad debt; *Compta* **dettes à court terme** current liabilities

DEUG [dœg] *nm* (*abrév* **Diplôme d'Études Universitaires Générales**) = degree (gained after a two-year course)

deuil [dœj] *nm* **(a)** (*perte*) bereavement; **fermé pour cause de d.** (*annonce*) closed owing to bereavement; **il y a eu plusieurs deuils dans leur famille** there have been several deaths in their family

(b) (*manifestation*) mourning; **porter le d., être en d.** to be in mourning; **porter le d. de qn** to be in mourning for sb; *Fig* **elle porte le deuil de sa jeunesse/de sa fortune** she is mourning the loss of her youth/fortune; **se mettre en d., prendre le d.** to go into mourning; **quitter le d.** to come out of mourning; *Fig* **la montagne est en d.** the mountain looks desolate; *Fig F* **il avait toujours les ongles en d.** his fingernails were always dirty; **grand d.** deep mourning; **semaine de d.** week of mourning; **décréter une journée de d. national** ≈ to order the flags to be flown at half mast *or Am* half-staff; *Vieilli* **conduire le d.** to be chief mourner; *F* **faire son d. de qch** to give sth up as *or* for lost

deutérium [døterjɔm] *nm Ch* deuterium

Deutéronome [døterɔnɔm] *nm Bible* Deuteronomy

deux [dø, *before a vowel sound in the same wordgroup* døz] **1** *adj inv* **(a)** two; **d. enfants** [døzɑ̃fɑ̃] two children; **j'en ai d.** [dø] I have two (of them); **d. ou trois** [døzutrwɑ] two or three; **d. fois** twice; **on a dû lui enlever les d. yeux** they had to remove both his eyes; **des d. côtés du fleuve** on either side *or* on both sides of the river; **tous (les) d.** both; **tous les d. jours** every other day, every two days, every second day; **nous/vous/eux d.** (*sujet*) we/you/these two, the two of *or* both of us/you/them; (*complément*) us/you/those two, the two of *or* both of us/you/them; **entre d. âges** middle-aged; **être pris entre d. feux** to be caught between two fires *or* in the middle; **d'un côté, j'écrasais le chat, de l'autre, je rentrais dans un mur, j'étais vraiment prise entre d. feux** I was in a real bind — I had to choose between running over the cat and crashing into a wall; **être assis** *ou* **avoir le derrière** *ou très F* **le cul entre d. chaises** to be in an awkward position; **vivre à d.** to live together; **à d. tranchants** (*lame*) double-edged; *Fig* two-edged; *Fig* **une économie/une Europe à d. vitesses** a two-speed economy/Europe; **faire d. poids d. mesures** to apply double standards; **de d. choses l'une, il viendra seul ou il ne viendra pas** he'll either come on his own or he won't come at all; **de d. choses l'une, soit tu pars en vacances avec nous, soit tu restes à la maison** either you come on holiday with us or you stay at home — take your pick *or* it's up to you; **en d. temps, trois mouvements** in two ticks, in no time at all, in next to no time; **les mathématiques/les ordinateurs et moi, ça fait d.** I just don't get on with mathematics/computers; **ma sœur et moi, ça fait d.** (*ne nous confondez pas*) my sister and I are two different people; (*nous sommes fâchés*) my sister and I just don't get along; *Vulg* **cette voiture de mes d.** that fucking car

(b) (*peu de*) **j'ai d. mots à lui dire** I've a bone to pick with him; **c'est à d. pas** *ou* **d. minutes d'ici** it's only a short distance away, it's two minutes away; **je reviens dans d. minutes** I'll be back in a minute *or F* a tick; **tu peux venir? – d. secondes!** can you come here? – just a minute!; **ça va te prendre d. secondes** it will only take you a minute; *F* **être à d. doigts de faire qch** to be on the verge of *or* within an inch of doing sth; **je suis à d. doigts de terminer** *ou* **d'avoir terminé** I've very nearly finished

(c) (*deuxième*) **Charles D.** Charles the Second; **chapitre d.** chapter two; *F* **il est arrivé d. ou troisième** he came in second or third; **il est numéro d. dans mes pensées** he takes second place *or* comes second in my thoughts; **c'est le numéro d. des fabricants de produits textiles** it's the second largest textile manufacturer

2 *nm inv* two; *Cartes* two, deuce; *Cartes* **le d. de cœur** the two of hearts; **la table de d.** the two times table; **d. fois d. font quatre** two times two *or* twice two is four; *Fig* **c'est clair comme d. et d. font quatre** it's as clear as day; **aujourd'hui nous sommes le d.** today is the second, it's the second today; **casser qch en d.** to break sth in two; **diviser** *ou* **couper une ligne en d.** to bisect a line; **marcher par d.** to walk in pairs *or* twos; (*dans une procession*) to march two abreast; **entrer d. par d.** to come in two by two *or* in twos; **à nous d.** (*entre amis*) let's get on with it (together); (*à un adversaire*) let's fight it out; *F* **il fera ça en moins de d.** he'll do it in two ticks *or* in no time at all *or* in next to no time; *F* **comme pas d.** as anything; **pas de d.** (*danse*) pas de deux; *Fig* **entre les d.** average, OK; **tu as froid ou chaud? – entre les d.** are you hot or cold? – I'm just right; **tu as réussi ton examen? – entre les d.** how did your exam go? – so-so; **alors, tu l'aimes ou tu ne l'aimes pas? – entre les d.** well, do you like it or not? – I'm not sure one way or the other; **tu as envie de venir? – je ne sais pas, entre les d.** do you want to come? – I don't know, I do and I don't; **jamais d. sans trois** it never rains but it pours; *F* **je n'ai fait ni une ni d.** I didn't think twice

deux-chevaux [døʃ(ə)vo] *nf inv Aut* deux-chevaux 2CV

deux-deux (à) *adj Mus* in two-two time

deux-huit (à) *adj Mus* in two-eight time

deuxième [døzjɛm] **1** *adj* second; **appartement au d. étage** second-floor flat, *Am* third-floor apartment; **le d. exportateur/annonceur du monde** the world's second largest exporter/advertiser; *Math* **équation du d. degré** quadratic equation; **d. classe** second class, standard class *Rugby* **d. temps** second phase **2** *n* second; **elle est née la d.** she is the second child; **3** *nm* (*étage*) **habiter au d.** to live on the second *or Am* third floor **4** *nf Journ* **deuxième de couverture** inside front cover, IFC

deuxièmement [døzjɛmmɑ̃] *adv* secondly, in the second place

deux-mâts [døma] *nm Naut* two-master

deux-pièces [døpjɛs] *nm inv* **(a)** (*maillot de bain*) two-piece (swimsuit); (*ensemble, tailleur*) two-piece **(b)** (*appartement*) two-roomed flat *or Am* apartment

deux-points [døpwɛ̃] *nm inv Typ* colon

deux-ponts [døpɔ̃] *nm inv Naut* two-decked ship; *Av* double-decker (aircraft)

deux-quatre *nm inv Mus* two-four time

deux-roues [døru] *nm inv* two-wheeled vehicle, two-wheeler; **je circule en d.** I get around on two wheels

deux-temps *nm inv* **(a)** *Mus* two-two time **(b)** (*moteur*) two-stroke (engine); **(mélange) d.** two-stroke mixture

deuzio [døzjo] *adv F* second(ly)

dévaler [devale] **1** *vi* to go down, to descend; (*de cours d'eau*) to rush down; **le jardin dévale jusqu'à la rivière** the garden slopes down *or* extends down to the river **2** *vt* **d. l'escalier** to rush down the stairs; **d. la rue à toute vitesse** to race down the street

dévaliser [devalize] *vt* (*banque*) to rob; (*maison*) to burgle; *F* (*frigo, placard etc*) to raid; *Fig* **j'ai dévalisé la boutique** I bought up the shop; **on a été dévalisé en manteaux rouges** all the red coats have been snatched up

dévalorisation [devalɔrizasjɔ̃] *nf* **(a)** (*action*) (*de la monnaie*) devaluation; *Com* (*de marchandises*) marking down; (*résultat*) (*de la monnaie*) fall in value, depreciation; *Com* (*de marchandises*) mark-down **(b)** *Fig* (*de qn, d'une politique*) discrediting

dévaloriser [devalɔrize] **1** *vt* (*monnaie*) to devalue; *Com* (*marchandises*) to mark down **2 se dévaloriser** *vpr* (*de monnaie*) to depreciate; *Com* (*de marchandises*) to lose value; (*d'une personne*) to put oneself down; **se d. dans l'esprit du public** to discredit oneself in the eyes of the public

dévaluation [devalɥasjɔ̃] *nf Écon* (*de la monnaie*) devaluation

dévaluer [devalɥe] **1** *vt* (*monnaie*) to devalue **2 se dévaluer** *vpr* to lose value

devancement [dəvɑ̃smɑ̃] *nm Mil* **d. d'appel** enlistment before call-up; *Fin* **d. d'une échéance** payment before the due date, pre-payment

devancer [dəvɑ̃se] *vt* (**je devançai(s)**; **n. devançons**) **(a)** (*dans un classement*) to come ahead of; **d. ses concurrents** to be ahead of the competition **(b)** (*distancer*) to leave behind, to out-distance, to outstrip; **je vous ai devancé** I got here before you **(c)** (*prévenir*) (*personne, critiques*) to forestall; (*demande, désirs de qn*) to anticipate; **d. son époque** to be ahead of one's time; *Mil* **d. l'appel** to enlist before call-up; *Fin* **d. une échéance** to settle an account early, to pay a bill before the due date

devancier, -ière [dəvɑ̃sje, -jɛr] *n* predecessor

devant [dəvɑ̃] **1** *prép* **(a)** (*en face de, en avant de*) in front of; **assis d. moi** sitting in front of me; **il est loin d. nous** he is a long way in front of *or* ahead of us; **marchez tout droit d. vous** carry straight on; **regardez d. vous** look where you're going; **je passe d. elle tous les jours** I pass her every day; **elle est passée d. moi dans la queue** she went in front of *or* ahead of me in the queue; **avoir du temps/de l'argent d. soi** to have time/money to spare; **tu as la vie d. toi** you've got your whole life ahead of you; **assis d. un verre de vin** sitting over a glass of wine; **navire d. Calais** ship off Calais

(b) (*en présence de*) in front of; **il l'a frappée d. les enfants** he hit her in front of the children; **éprouver de la gêne d. qn** to feel ill at ease with sb *or* in sb's presence; **je n'ai su que faire d. cette petite fille en pleurs** I didn't know what to do when faced *or* confronted with this little girl in tears; **s'incliner d. qn** to bow to sb; **paraître d. ses pairs** to appear before one's peers

(c) (*face à*) **être courageux d. le danger** to show courage in the face of danger; **égaux d. la loi** equal in the eyes of the law; **sa position d. ce problème** his position on the problem; **il ne sait quelle attitude adopter d. de tels problèmes/mon malheur** he doesn't know what attitude to adopt when faced with *or* in the face of such problems/my unhappiness; **d. cet état de choses/votre silence** in view of *or* given this state of affairs/your silence

2 *adv* **(a)** (*en face*) in front; **tu cherches la bibliothèque? tu es (juste) d.** you're looking for the library? you're right in front of it; **son magasin? je passe d. tous les jours** his shop? I pass *or* go past it every day; **il est passé d. et il ne l'a même pas vu** he went right past it and didn't even see it; **passer (par) d.** to come in the front way; **porter qch sens d. derrière** to wear sth back to front; **sa robe se ferme d.** her dress closes at the front *or Am* in front

(b) (*en avant*) **aller d.** to go in front, to lead the way; **marcher/courir d.** to walk on/run on ahead; **partir d. pour arriver le premier** to go on ahead so as to get there first; **envoyer qn d.** to send sb on (in front); **passe d.** go ahead *or* in front of me/us/*etc*; **s'asseoir d.** (*en voiture*) to sit in the front *or Am* in front; **ils sont d. sur la photo** they're at the front in the photograph; **tu n'as pas vu Martin? – je crois qu'il est d.** have you seen Martin? – he's up ahead I think; **les voleurs sont loin d. maintenant** the thieves are far ahead of us by now; **avoir des places d.** to have seats at the front; **vous pouvez passer des verres d.?** will you pass some glasses to the front?

(c) *Arch, Litt* **comme d.** as before

3 *nm* **(a)** front (part); **d. (de chemise)** (shirt) front; *Tricot* **d. gauche/droit** left/right front; **chambre sur le d.** front room; **dents de d.** front teeth; **pattes de d.** forelegs; *Com* **d. de caisse** checkout display; **prendre les devants** to go on ahead; *Fig* to make the first move; **gagner les devants** to take the lead

(b) aller au-d. de qn to meet sb on the way; **aller au-d. des vœux de qn** to anticipate sb's wishes; **courir au-d. du danger** to court danger, to go to meet danger; **tu vas au-d. de gros ennuis** you're looking for trouble

devanture [dəvɑ̃tyr] *nf* (*d'un édifice*) façade, front; **d. de magasin** (*façade*) shopfront; (*vitrine*) shop window

dévastateur, -trice [devastatœr, -tris] *adj* devastating

dévastation [devastasjɔ̃] *nf* devastation, destruction, havoc

dévaster [devaste] *vt* (*pays*) to devastate, to lay waste, *Fml* to ravage; (*cultures*) to devastate, to destroy, to ruin

déveine [devɛn] *nf F* (run of) bad luck; **être dans la d.** to be down on one's luck; **quelle d.!** (what) hard luck!

développé [devlɔpe] *nm* **(a)** *Sp* (*en haltérophilie*) press **(b)** (*en danse*) developpé

développement [devlɔpmɑ̃] *nm* **(a)** (*du corps*) development, growth; (*des muscles, des fleurs, des facultés etc*) development; **d. d'une entreprise** growth of a business; **d. durable** sustained development; **mon entreprise est en plein d.** my business is growing fast; **d. de produit** product development; **d. régional** regional development; *Écon* **un pays en voie de d.** a developing country; **personne n'aurait pu s'attendre à de tels développements** no-one could have expected such developments; **suivre les développements d'une affaire** to follow the developments of an affair; **un des développements possibles de l'affaire** one of the possible consequences of the scandal

(b) *Phot* developing, development

(c) (*des ailes*) spreading out, opening out; (*des branches d'un arbre etc*) spread; *Math* (*d'une expression contractée etc*) expansion, development

(d) *Cyclisme* = distance covered by a bicycle in one revolution of the pedals; **bicyclette avec un d. de … m** bicycle with a … inch gear *or* geared to … inches

(e) *Mus, Beaux-Arts* (*d'un thème, d'une dissertation*) development; *Fig* **se lancer dans de grands développements** to go into detailed explanations *or* great detail

développer [devlɔpe] **1** *vt* **(a)** (*muscles, facultés, commerce etc*) to develop

(b) (*ailes*) to spread out, to open out; *Math* (*expression contractée etc*) to expand, to develop

(c) *Phot* (*négatif*) to develop

(d) (*élargir*) (*sujet, idée, sa pensée*) to develop

(e) *Aut* (*chevaux*) to deliver; *Cyclisme* **bicyclette qui développe …** bicycle that has a gear of … *or* that is geared to …

2 se développer *vpr* **(a)** (*d'un enfant, d'un pays, de fleurs, de l'intelligence etc*) to develop; **l'affaire ne va pas tarder à se d. et se transformer en un véritable scandale** the affair will soon develop into a real scandal

(b) (*s'étendre*) to spread out, to expand, to extend; **la plaine se développe à perte de vue** the plain extends *or* stretches out as far as the eye can see

développeur [devlɔpœr] *nm* (*pour imprimante laser*) developer

développeuse [devlɔpøz] *nf* (*pour imprimante laser*) developer

devenir[1] [dəvnir] *nm* gradual change, development; **la langue est dans un perpétuel d.** language is in a constant state of flux

devenir[2] *vi* (*conj like* **venir**, *the aux is* **être**) to become; **il devint général** he became a general; **il était devenu (un) homme** he had grown into a man; **il devient vraiment indiscret** he's becoming *or* getting really indiscreet; **que devenez-vous ces temps-ci?** what are you up to these days?; **que devient votre cousin?** how is your cousin getting on?; **qu'est-il devenu?** what has become of him?; **que vais-je d. sans toi?** what will become of me without you?, what will I do without you?, where will I be without you?; **qu'est devenu mon livre?** what's happened to my book?; **d. grand** (*en taille*) to grow tall; (*en âge*) to grow up; **d. vieux** to grow old, to get old; **c'est à d. fou!** it's enough to drive you mad!; **d. tout rouge** to go all red, to blush; **quand je lui ai dit ça, il est devenu tout heureux/tout dépité** he was delighted/extremely annoyed when I told him

dévergondage [devɛrgɔ̃daʒ] *nm* **(a)** (*d'attitude, de personne*) shamelessness **(b)** (*de style, d'imagination*) extravagance

dévergondé, -ée [devɛrgɔ̃de] **1** *adj* **(a)** (*attitude, personne*) shameless **(b)** (*style, imagination*) extravagant **2** *n* shameless person; **cette petite dévergondée** the little hussy

dévergonder (se) [sədevɛrgɔ̃de] *vpr* to become (quite) shameless

dévernir [devɛrnir] *vt* (*meubles etc*) to take the varnish *or* the polish off

déverrouillage [devɛrujaʒ] *nm* (*de porte etc*) unbolting, unlocking; *Ordinat* unlocking; *Aut* **d. du capot par l'intérieur** internal bonnet release; *Aut* **d. du hayon par l'intérieur** internal hatchback release

déverrouiller [devɛruje] *vt* (*porte etc*) to unbolt, to unlock; (*arme*) to release the bolt of; *Ordinat* to unlock; (*majuscules*) to lock off; *Ordinat* **d. en écriture** (*fichier*) to unlock, to remove the read-only lock

dévers [devɛr] *nm* **(a)** (*d'un mur etc*) inclination, slope; (*d'une route dans un virage*) banking; *Rail* vertical slant, cant (*of outer rail at curve*) **(b)** (*dans le bois etc*) warp, twist

déversement [devɛrsəmɑ̃] *nm* (*liquide*) discharge, overflow; (*action*) pouring out

déverser[1] [devɛrse] **1** *vt* (*eau*) to pour; (*trop-plein d'un canal etc*) to discharge; (*détritus etc*) to tip, to dump; (*déchets*) to dump; **le train déversa des centaines de vacanciers sur le quai** the train deposited hundreds of holiday-makers on the platform; *Fig* **il a déversé des torrents d'injures sur sa femme** he showered his wife with abuse, he heaped abuse on his wife; **d. sa colère sur qn** to take one's anger out on sb **2 se déverser** *vpr* (*d'une rivière etc*) to empty, to flow **(dans** into)

déverser[2] **1** *vt* **(a)** (*mur etc*) to slope; (*route*) to bank; (*voie ferrée*) to raise the outer rail of **(b)** (*planche de bois*) to warp **2** *vi* **(a)** (*d'un mur etc*) to incline, to lean **(b)** (*du bois*) to warp

déversoir [devɛrswar] *nm* **(a)** (*de citerne, bassin etc*) overflow; *HydE* (*de barrage*) spillway **(b)** *Fig* (*exutoire*) outlet, safety-valve
dévêtir [devetir] (*conj like* **vêtir**) **1** *vt* to undress, to strip **2 se dévêtir** *vpr* (*complètement*) to undress, to strip, to take off one's clothes; (*partiellement*) to take off some of one's clothing
déviance [devjɑ̃s] *nf Psy* deviance
déviant [devjɑ̃] *adj Psy* deviant
déviation [devjasjɔ̃] *nf* deviation; *Aut* detour, *Br* diversion; (*d'un compas*) variation; (*de la colonne vertébrale*) curvature; (*de l'utérus*) displacement
déviationnisme [devjasjɔnism] *nm Pol* deviationism
déviationniste [devjasjɔnist] *adj, n Pol* deviationist
dévidage [devidaʒ] *nm Tex etc* (*de bobine*) unwinding; (*pour faire une bobine*) reeling, spooling
dévider [devide] *vt Tex etc* (*dérouler*) to unwind; (*pour faire une bobine*) to reel, to spool; **d. son rosaire** to reel off the rosary; *F* **il m'a dévidé son chapelet** he reeled off his whole story to me
dévideur [devidœr] *nm Ordinat* streamer
dévidoir [devidwar] *nm Tex* reeling machine, reel; (*pour tuyaux*) hose reel; (*pour câbles*) drum
dévier [devje] (*pr sub & impf* **n. déviions, v. déviiez**) **1** *vi* **(a)** to deviate, to swerve; *MecE* to run out of true; (*de la colonne vertébrale*) to be out of alignment, not to be straight; **faire d. une balle** to deflect a bullet; *Naut, Av* **d. de sa route** (*par accident*) to go *or* stray off course; (*volontairement*) to turn off *or* deviate from course; **clou qui a dévié lorsqu'on l'a enfoncé** nail which did not go in straight *or* which went in crooked

(b) *Fig* to deviate (**de** from); **elle ne dévie jamais de ses principes** she never deviates *or* never departs from her principles; **cette conversation dévie** this conversation is getting out of hand

2 *vt* (*coup, balle*) to turn aside, to deflect; *Phys* (*rayon*) to deflect; (*circulation*) to divert
devin, devineresse [dəvɛ̃, dəvinrɛs] *n* diviner; (*prophète*) soothsayer, *f* fortune teller; *F* **je ne suis pas d.** I can't tell *or* predict the future
devinable [dəvinabl] *adj* foreseeable
deviner [dəvine] *vt* (*énigme, secret etc*) to guess; (*futur*) to predict; (*la pensée de qn*) to read; **vous ne devinez pas?** can't you guess?; **devine qui j'ai vu/pourquoi il est là/comment il est venu** guess who I saw/why he's here/how he came; *F* **je ne pouvais pas d.!** how was I supposed to know!
devineresse *voir* **devin**
devinette [dəvinɛt] *nf* riddle, conundrum; (*jeu*) guessing game; **poser une d. à qn** to ask sb a riddle
devis [dəvi] *nm* (*descriptif*) estimate; *Tech* specification; **d. estimatif** estimate, quote; **ils m'ont fait un d. de 5 000 francs** they quoted me *or* they gave me a quote of 5,000 francs; **je voudrais qu'on me fasse un d.** I'd like an estimate *or* quote (**pour** for)
dévisager [devizaʒe] *vt* (**je dévisageai(s); n. dévisageons**) to stare *or* look hard at
devise [dəviz] *nf* **(a)** *Fin* currency; **devises étrangères** foreign currency; **d. internationale** international currency; **d. forte** strong *or* hard currency; **d. faible** soft *or* weak currency; **d. convertible** convertible currency; **d. non convertible** non-convertible currency; **marché des devises** currency market **(b)** [①**A12**,1,c] *Hér* device; (*d'une personne*) motto; *Fig* **telle est ma d.** that's my motto
deviser [dəvize] *vi* to converse
devise-titre, *pl* **devises-titres** *nf Fin* foreign security, exchange currency
dévissage [devisaʒ] *nm* **(a)** (*d'un écrou*) unscrewing **(b)** (*en montagne*) fall
dévisser [devise] **1** *vt* (*boulon, écrou etc*) to unscrew **2** *vi* (*d'alpiniste*) to fall **3 se dévisser** *vpr* to unscrew; (*par accident*) to come unscrewed; *Fig* **se d. la tête** *ou* **le cou** to screw one's head round
de visu [dəvizy] *adv* with my/his/*etc* own eyes; **je préfèrerais me rendre compte d.** I'd rather see it with my own eyes, I'd rather see for myself; **je veux m'assurer d. que tu as fait le travail** I want to see for myself that you've done the work
dévitalisation [devitalizasjɔ̃] *nf* (*d'une dent*) root canal treatment, *Spéc* devitalization; **subir plusieurs dévitalisations** to have root canal treatment on more than one tooth
dévitaliser [devitalize] *vt* (*dent*) to carry out root canal treatment on, *Spéc* to devitalize
dévitaminé [devitamine] *adj* lacking in vitamins
dévoiement [devwamɑ̃] *nm* (*d'un conduit etc*) canting, tilting
dévoilement [devwalmɑ̃] *nm* (*de visage, statue, plaque etc*) unveiling; *Fig* (*d'un nom, un secret etc*) disclosure, revelation; (*d'une conspiration*) unmasking; (*d'une fraude*) uncovering
dévoiler [devwale] **1** *vt* (*visage, statue, plaque etc*) to unveil; *Fig* (*nom, secret etc*) to reveal, to disclose; (*conspiration*) to unmask; (*fraude etc*) to uncover; **d. ses charmes** to show *or* reveal all **2 se dévoiler** *vpr* (*de secret etc*) to come to light
devoir[1] [dəvwar] *nm* **(a)** (*obligation morale ou sociale*) duty; **je l'ai fait par d.** I did it from a sense of duty; **avoir le sens** *ou* **le sentiment du d.** to have a sense of duty; **un homme/une femme de d.** a man/woman with a sense of duty; **manquer à son d.** to fail in one's duty; **faire** *ou* **remplir son d.** (**envers qn/la patrie**) to do one's duty (by sb/one's country); **se faire un d. de faire qch** to make a point of doing sth; **se mettre en d. de faire qch** to make it one's duty *or* responsibility to do sth; **il est de mon d. de vous le dire** it is my duty *or* my responsibility to tell you; **je sais ce qui est de mon d.** I know my duty, I know where my duty lies; **mes devoirs de citoyen/de père** my duties *or* obligations as a citizen/as a father; **avoir un d. de réserve** to be bound by professional secrecy

(b) *Scol* (*en classe*) test; (*à la maison*) homework; **un d. de latin** a Latin test; **faire ses devoirs** to do one's homework; **d. sur table** class test; **d. à rendre** take-home (exam); **devoirs de vacances** holiday homework

(c) *Vieilli* (*hommage*) **devoirs** respects; **rendre ses devoirs à qn** to pay one's respects to sb; **rendre à qn les derniers devoirs** to pay one's last respects to sb
devoir[2] (*prp* **devant**; *pp* **dû**, *f* **due**; *pr ind* **je dois, n. devons, ils doivent**; *pr sub* **je doive, n. devions, ils doivent**; *impf* **je devais**; *p hist* **je dus**; *fu* **je devrai**) **1** *vt* (*être redevable de*) **d. qch à qn** to owe sb sth, to owe sth to sb; **il me doit mille francs** he owes me a thousand francs; **il ne veut rien d. à personne** he doesn't want to owe anyone anything, he doesn't want to be indebted to anyone for anything; **d. du respect à son père** to owe respect to one's father; **je lui dois d'être en vie, je lui dois la vie** I owe my life to him, I owe him my life; **je lui dois bien cela** it's the least I can do for him, I owe him that at least; **il doit sa réussite à ses parents, sa réussite est due à ses parents** he owes his success to his parents; **je te dois une fière chandelle** I'm forever in your debt

2 *aux* [①**A58-9**,e-f; **B36-7**,k,1] **(a)** (*obligation*) **vous devez** *ou* **devrez vous trouver à votre poste à trois heures** you must *or* you have to be at your post at three o'clock; **elle a cru d. refuser** she thought it advisable to refuse; **tu dois honorer tes parents** you must honour your parents; **fais ce que dois, advienne que pourra** do your duty, come what may; **les commandes doivent être adressées à ...** orders should be sent to ...; **je ne savais pas ce que je devais faire** I didn't know what (I ought) to do; **il aurait dû m'avertir** he should have warned me, he ought to have warned me

(b) (*nécessité*) **tous les hommes doivent mourir** all men must die; **finalement, j'ai dû céder** I had to *or* I was obliged to give way in the end; **tu dois absolument lui en parler** you really must talk to him about it; **il ne devait plus les revoir** he was (destined) never to see them again; **cela devait arriver!** it was bound to *or* it had to happen!; **dût-il m'en coûter la vie** were I to die for it

(c) (*intention*) **je dois partir demain** I am (supposed) to *or* I have to leave tomorrow; **je devais la rencontrer à Paris** I was (supposed) to meet her in Paris; **je ne devais pas être là, mais j'ai changé d'avis** I hadn't planned on being there but I changed my mind; **le train doit arriver à midi** the train is due (to arrive) at twelve o'clock

(d) (*supposition*) **vous devez avoir faim** you must be hungry; **il doit être trois heures** it must be three o'clock; **il ne doit pas avoir plus de 40 ans** he can't be more than 40; **il a** *ou* **avait dû me prendre pour un autre** he must have taken me for someone else; **elle devait avoir cinq ans quand elle a eu son accident** she must have been five when she had the accident; **la pollution devrait s'accroître d'ici à la fin du siècle** pollution is expected to increase by the end of the century

3 se devoir *vpr* **(a)** (*être obligé de se consacrer à*) **je me dois à ma famille/mon travail** I must devote myself to my family/my work; **je me dois de le faire** it's my duty to do it

(b) comme il se doit as is (only) right and proper
dévoltage [devɔltaʒ] *nm* reduction of voltage
dévolter [devɔlte] *vt Él* (*courant*) to reduce the voltage of
dévolu [devɔly] **1** *adj Jur* (*héritage etc*) devolving (**à** to, upon); **part dévolue à la ligne paternelle** share that falls to the heirs on the father's side; **c'est le terrain qui lui a été d.** the land went to him; **être d. à qn de faire qch** to fall to sb's lot to do sth; **voilà la tâche qui vous a été dévolue** that is the task which has been assigned to you **2** *nm* **jeter son d. sur qch/qn** to set one's heart on sth/sb, to be determined to have sth/sb, *Hum Péj* to have designs on sth/sb

dévolution [devɔlysjɔ̃] *nf Jur* devolution; **d. d'un héritage à l'État** escheat

dévorant [devɔrɑ̃] *adj* **(a)** *(envie, besoin)* overwhelming; **avoir une faim dévorante** to be ravenous; **j'ai une envie dévorante de le voir** I've got a burning desire to see him **(b)** *(maladie)* wasting; *(passion)* devouring

dévorer [devɔre] *vt* **(a)** *(manger)* *(proie)* to devour; *(nourriture)* to devour, *F* to gobble up, to wolf down; **pour ne pas être dévoré par les moustiques** so as not to be eaten alive by mosquitos; **d. qn des yeux** *ou* **du regard/de baisers** to devour sb with one's eyes/with kisses; *Fig* **d. un livre** to devour *or* gobble up a book; *Fig* **d. la route** to tear along, to eat up the miles; **d. sa fortune** to squander one's fortune

(b) *(consumer)* *(de flammes)* to devour; *Fig* **l'ambition/la jalousie la dévore** she is consumed by *or* devoured by *or* eaten up with ambition/jealousy; **il ne faut pas que cela dévore tout votre temps** don't let it take up all your time; **l'angoisse le dévore** he's sick with worry; **dévoré de remords** eaten up *or* stricken with remorse

dévoreur, -euse [devɔrœr, -øz] *n* devourer; *Fig* **d. de livres** avid reader, bookworm; **d. de films** avid cinema-goer; **d. de pellicule** *Cin* avid *or* keen cinema-goer; *Phot* avid *or* keen photographer

dévot, -ote [devo, -ɔt] **1** *adj (fervent)* devout, religious, pious, *Péj* sanctimonious; *Rel* **être d. à un saint** to be a votary of a saint **2** *n* devout person, *Péj* bigot; *Arch* **faux d.** hypocrite

dévotement [devɔtmɑ̃] *adv* devoutly

dévotion [devosjɔ̃] *nf* **(a)** *(ferveur)* devoutness, piety; **faire ses dévotions** to make one's devotions, to say one's prayers; *Péj* **être confit en d.** to be sanctimonious; **fausse d.** hypocrisy **(b)** *(adoration)* devotion; **avoir une grande d. pour qn/qch** to be devoted *or* extremely attached to sb/sth; **avoir une grande d. pour un acteur/écrivain** to be a great admirer *or* a devotee of an actor/a writer; **être à la d. de qn** to be fanatically attached to sb

dévoué [devwe] *adj (ami etc)* devoted, staunch, loyal; **votre (tout) d.** *(dans une lettre)* ≈ yours sincerely; **être très/entièrement d. à qn** to be very attached/utterly devoted to sb

dévouement [devumɑ̃] *nm* **(a)** *(devoir)* self-sacrifice, devotion to duty; *(d'un scientifique etc)* dedication **(b)** *(amour)* devotion, devotedness; **soigner qn avec d.** to nurse *or* look after sb devotedly *or* with devotion

dévouer (se) [sədevwe] *vpr* **(a)** *(se consacrer)* to sacrifice oneself (**pour qn** for sb); **il faut que quelqu'un se dévoue** somebody has to do it **(b)** *Vieilli* **se d. à** to devote oneself to, to dedicate oneself to

dévoyé, -ée [devwaje] **1** *adj* astray **2** *n* delinquent

dévoyer [devwaje] **(je dévoie, n. dévoyons; je dévoierai)** **1** *vt Litt* to lead astray **2 se dévoyer** *vpr* to go astray, to leave the straight and narrow

dextérité [dɛksterite] *nf* dexterity, skill; **conduire ses affaires avec d.** to manage one's business cleverly *or* skilfully

dextre [dɛkstr] *nf Vieilli, Hum* right hand; **veux-tu t'asseoir à ma dextre?** will you sit on my right?

dextrine [dɛkstrin] *nf Ch, Ind* dextrin

DI [dei] *nf (abrév* **déclaration d'importation***)* import declaration

diabète [djabɛt] *nm Méd* diabetes; **d. sucré** (sugar) diabetes, *Spéc* diabetes mellitus; **avoir du d.** to have diabetes

diabétique [djabetik] *Méd* **1** *adj* diabetic; **être d.** to be (a) diabetic, to have diabetes **2** *n* diabetic; **chocolat/confiture pour diabétiques** diabetic chocolate/jam

diable [djɑbl] *nm* **(a)** devil; **le d.** the devil, Satan, *F* Old Nick; *F* **s'agiter** *ou* **se démener comme un beau d.** *ou* **comme un d. dans un bénitier** to struggle *or* fight like mad; *F* **il s'est défendu comme un beau d.** he put up quite a fight; **faire le d. (à quatre)** to kick up a row; **avoir le d. au corps** to be possessed; **tirer le d. par la queue** to be hard up; *Can* **parler au d.** to be psychic; **que le d. l'emporte!** the devil take him!; **(que) le d. m'emporte si j'y comprends quelque chose!** I'll be hanged *or* damned if I understand (it)!; **c'est le d. pour lui faire entendre raison** it's damned hard to make *or* it's the devil of a job making him see reason; **c'est bien le d. si ...** it would be surprising if ...; **ce n'est pas le d.** *(c'est facile)* it's not that difficult

(b) d.! (good) heavens!, goodness!; **où d. est-il allé?** where the devil has he gone?; **que d. cherche-t-il?** what the devil is he looking for?; **pourquoi d. m'a-t-il demandé cela?** why the devil did he ask me that?; **du d. si je peux te répondre!** I'm damned if I can tell you; **que d.!** for heaven's *or* goodness' sake!

(c) en d. extremely, *Fml* in the extreme; **têtu en d.** extremely obstinate, obstinate in the extreme; **il demeure au d.** he lives miles away; **au d. vauvert** a long way (away); **allez au d.!** go to hell!, *Vieilli* go to the devil!; **tu peux aller au d. avec tes belles promesses** you and your promises can go to hell; **envoyer qn au d.** to tell sb to go to hell; **au d. l'avarice/le régime!** to hell with the expense/the diet!; **à la d.** anyhow; *Culin* in a spicy sauce; **c'est fait à la d.** it's been done any old how; *Culin* **steak à la d.** devilled steak; **ce d. de parapluie** that wretched umbrella; **un d. de temps, un temps du d.** wretched *or* dreadful weather; **j'ai une faim du d.** *ou* **de tous les diables** I'm ravenous; **il fait un froid/une chaleur du d.** it's dreadfully cold/hot; **un bruit de tous les diables** a hell of a din

(d) un petit d. *(enfant)* a little devil; **pauvre d.!** poor devil *or* beggar!; **un drôle de petit d.** a funny little chap *or* beggar; **un grand d.** a big fellow; **c'est un bon d.** he's not a bad sort

(e) *(chariot)* (two-wheeled) trolley; *Rail* (railway porter's) barrow, luggage truck

(f) *(jouet)* jack-in-the-box

diable de mer *nm* angler (fish), frog fish

diablement [djɑbləmɑ̃] *adv F (fort, bon, amusant etc)* damn, damned, *Vieilli* devilish(ly); **il y a d. longtemps que je ne l'ai pas vu** I haven't seen him for a hell of a long time; **il faisait d. froid** it was hellish(ly) cold

diablerie [djɑbləri] *nf* **(a)** *F (espièglerie)* devilry, devilment **(b)** *Arch (sorcellerie)* devilry, sorcery **(c)** *(intrigue)* machination, intrigue

diablesse [djɑblɛs] *nf (diable femelle, méchante femme)* she-devil; *(jeune fille)* devil

diablotin [djɑblɔtɛ̃] *nf* **(a)** *(petit diable, enfant coquin)* little devil, imp **(b)** *(pétard)* (Christmas) cracker

diabolique [djabɔlik] *adj* diabolic(al), fiendish

diaboliquement [djabɔlikmɑ̃] *adv* diabolically, fiendishly

diabolo [djabɔlo] *nm* **(a)** *(jouet)* diabolo **(b)** *(boisson)* lemonade (drink) with syrup; **d. menthe** lemonade and mint (cordial)

diachronie [djakrɔni] *nf Ling* diachrony

diachronique [djakrɔnik] *adj Ling* diachronic

diaconesse [djakɔnɛs] *nf Rel* deaconess

diacre [djakr] *nm Rel* deacon

diacritique [djakritik] *adj Ling* diacritic(al); **signe d.** diacritic(al)

diadème [djadɛm] *nm* tiara

diagnostic [djagnɔstik] *nm Méd (de maladie)* diagnosis; **porter** *ou* **faire un d.** to make a diagnosis; **le d. de la maladie doit être porté le plus tôt possible** the disease must be diagnosed as soon as possible; **ce médecin a un d. très sûr** this doctor makes very reliable diagnoses; **quel est votre d.?** what's your diagnosis?; *Ordinat* **d. d'autotest** self-test diagnosis

diagnostique [djagnɔstik] *adj Méd (aptitude, signe etc)* diagnostic

diagnostiquer [djagnɔstike] *vt Méd, Fig* to diagnose; **on a diagnostiqué un diabète** the illness has been diagnosed as diabetes

diagnostiqueur [djagnɔstikœr] *nm Méd* diagnostician; **elle n'est pas bon d.** she's not a good diagnostician, diagnosis is not her strong point

diagonal, -ale, -aux, -ales [djagɔnal, -o] **1** *adj Math etc* diagonal **2** *nf* **diagonale** diagonal (line); **en diagonale** diagonally; *Fig* **lire qch en d.** to skim sth

diagonalement [djagɔnalmɑ̃] *adv* diagonally

diagramme [djagram] *nm* diagram; **d. circulaire** *ou* **à secteurs** pie chart; **d. en bâtons** *ou* **à barres** bar chart; **d. de relations fonctionnelles** functional relations diagram; **d. des flux** flowchart

dialectal, -ale, -aux, -ales [djalɛktal, -o] *adj Ling* dialectal

dialecte [djalɛkt] *nm* dialect; **en d.** in dialect

dialecticien, -ienne [djalɛktisjɛ̃, -jɛn] *n* dialectician

dialectique [djalɛktik] **1** *adj (argument)* dialectic(al) **2** *nf* dialectics

dialectiquement [djalɛktikmɑ̃] *adv* dialectically

dialogue [djalɔg] *nm* dialogue, *US* dialog; *Pol* dialogue, talks; **d. Nord-Sud** dialogue *or* talks between North and South; *Ordinat* **mode de d.** interactive mode; *Ordinat* **d. d'établissement de liaison** handshake, handshaking; **c'est un d. de sourds** it's a dialogue of the deaf

dialoguer [djalɔge] **1** *vi* to hold a dialogue *or US* dialog, to converse; *Ordinat* to communicate; **d. avec son ordinateur** to interact with one's computer **2** *vt Littér* to write in dialogue *or US* dialog form

dialoguiste [djalɔgist] *n Cin* dialogue writer

dialyse [djaliz] *nf Méd, Ch* dialysis; *Méd* **il faut qu'on lui fasse une d. tous les mois** he has to have dialysis once a month

dialyser [djalize] *vt Ch* to dialyse

dialyseur [djalizœr] *nm Méd* dialysis machine

diam [djam] *nm F (abrév* **diamant***)* sparkler, rock

diamant [djamɑ̃] *nm* diamond; **d. de première eau** diamond of the first water; **d. brut** rough diamond; **d. de vitrier** glass cutter, *Spéc* glazier's diamond, diamond point

diamantaire [djamɑ̃tɛr] **1** *adj Tech* (*pierre*) diamond-like, sparkling **2** *nm* (*tailleur*) diamond cutter; (*vendeur*) diamond merchant

diamantifère [djamɑ̃tifɛr] *adj Géol etc* (*région*) diamantiferous; (*gravier etc*) diamond-yielding *or* -bearing

diamétral, -ale, -aux, -ales [djametral, -o] *adj* diametric(al), diametral

diamétralement [djametralmɑ̃] *adv* diametrically; **opinions d. opposées** diametrically opposed views

diamètre [djamɛtr] *nm* diameter; **la roue a 60 cm de d.** the wheel is 60 cm in diameter *or* 60 cm across; *Aut* **d. de braquage hors tout** overall turning circle

diane [djan] *nf Mil, Arch, Litt* reveille; **battre** *ou* **sonner la d.** to sound reveille

diantre [djɑ̃tr] *int Arch, Litt* **que d. désirez-vous?** what the devil do you want?; **d., c'est cher!** it's devilishly expensive!

diapason [djapazɔ̃] *nm Mus* **(a)** (*ton*) pitch, diapason; *Fig* **se mettre au d. de la compagnie** to adapt oneself to the company, to fall in with the mood of the company **(b)** (*appareil*) tuning fork; (*à vent*) pitch pipe **(c)** (*registre*) compass, range

diaphane [djafan] *adj* diaphanous

diaphonie [djafɔni] *nf Rad etc* crosstalk

diaphragme [djafragm] *nm* **(a)** *Anat* diaphragm **(b)** *Tech* (*d'un télescope, d'une cellule électrique etc*) diaphragm; *Phot* (*d'un objectif*) diaphragm stop; *Mus* (*d'une enceinte*) soundbox; *Méd* (*contraceptif*) diaphragm, *F* (Dutch) cap; *Phot* **d. iris** iris diaphragm

diaphragmer [djafragme] *vti Phot* to stop down

diapo [djapo] *nf F* (*abrév* **diapositive**) slide, transparency

diaporama [djaporama] *nm* slide show

diapositive [djapozitiv] *nf Phot* slide, transparency; **d. en couleurs** colour slide

diapré [djapre] *adj* variegated, mottled, speckled

diaprer [djapre] *vt* to variegate, to mottle, to speckle

diaprure [djapryr] *nf Litt* iridescence; **elle portait une robe dont le satin faisait des diaprures** she wore a gown of iridescent *or* shimmering satin

diarrhée [djare] *nf Méd* diarrhoea; **avoir la d.** to have diarrhoea; **d. du voyageur** holiday tummy; *Fig Péj* **ce type fait de la d. verbale** the guy suffers from verbal diarrhoea

diarrhéique [djareik] **1** *adj Méd* diarrhoeic, diarrhoeal **2** *n* person subject to diarrhoea

diaspora [djaspɔra] *nf Rel, Pol* diaspora

diastole [djastɔl] *nf Physiol* diastole

diatomée [djatɔme] *nf* (*algue*) diatom

diatomique [djatɔmik] *adj Ch* diatomic

diatonique [djatɔnik] *adj Mus* (*échelle, intervalle*) diatonic

diatoniquement [djatɔnikmɑ̃] *adv Mus* diatonically

diatribe [djatrib] *nf* diatribe (**contre** against)

dichotomie [dikɔtɔmi] *nf* dichotomy

dichotomique [dikɔtɔmik] *adj* dichotomous; *Psy* **test d.** yes/no test, true/false test

dichromatique [dikrɔmatik] *adj* dichromatic

dico [diko] *nm F* (*abrév* **dictionnaire**) dictionary

dicotylédone [dikɔtiledɔn] *Bot* **1** *adj* dicotyledonous **2** *nf* dicotyledon

Dictaphone® [diktafɔn] *nm* Dictaphone®

dictateur [diktatœr] *nm* dictator; **ton de d.** dictatorial tone

dictatorial, -iale, -iaux, -iales [diktatɔrjal, -jo] *adj* dictatorial

dictatorialement [diktatɔrjalmɑ̃] *adv* dictatorially

dictature [diktatyr] *nf Pol, Fig* dictatorship; **d. militaire** military dictatorship; **d. du prolétariat** dictatorship of the proletariat; *Fig* **il fait de la d. intellectuelle** he tells people what to think

dictée [dikte] *nf* dictation; *Scol* dictation (exercise); **d. musicale** musical dictation; **prendre qch sous la d.** (*d'une secrétaire*) to take sth down in shorthand; **écrire qch sous la d. de qn** to write sth at sb's dictation; **agir sous la d. de son cœur/de sa conscience** to follow the dictates of one's heart/one's conscience

dicter [dikte] *vt* (*lettre etc*) to dictate; **d. ses conditions** to dictate *or* lay down one's conditions; **votre conscience vous dictera votre devoir** you must follow the dictates of your conscience; **d. sa volonté à qn** to impose one's will on sb; **je ne veux pas qu'on me dicte ma conduite!** I won't be dictated to!

diction [diksjɔ̃] *nf* diction; **professeur de d.** elocution teacher

dictionnaire [diksjɔnɛr] *nm* dictionary; **d. de langue** dictionary; **d. anglais-français** English-French dictionary; **le d. d'un enfant de 10 ans** the vocabulary of a 10-year-old child; **c'est un d. ambulant** he's a walking encyclopaedia; **elle parle comme un d.** she talks as if she'd swallowed a dictionary

▶ **dictionnaire**: **d. analogique** = thesaurus; **d. de césure** hyphenation dictionary; **d. électronique** electronic dictionary; **d. encyclopédique** encyclopaedic dictionary; **d. géographique** gazetteer; **d. de poche** pocket dictionary; **d. de synonymes** = thesaurus

dicton [diktɔ̃] *nm* (common) saying

didacticiel [didaktisjɛl] *nm Ordinat* tutorial (program); (*à l'école*) courseware, educational software

didactique [didaktik] **1** *adj* **(a)** (*ouvrage, voyage*) educational **(b)** (*mot, langage*) technical **2** *nf* didactics

didactiquement [didaktikmɑ̃] *adv* educationally

didactyle [didaktil] *adj Zool* didactyl(e)

dièdre [djɛdr] *Math* **1** *adj* (*angle*) dihedral **2** *nm* dihedron

diélectrique [dielɛktrik] *Él* **1** *adj* dielectric; (*milieu*) insulating, non-conducting **2** *nm* dielectric

diérèse [djerɛz] *nf Ling, Chir* diaeresis

dièse [djɛz] *Mus* **1** *nm* sharp; **double d.** double sharp **2** *adj* sharp; **fa d.** F sharp

diesel [djezɛl] **1** *nm* (*carburant*) diesel; **moteur d.** diesel engine **2** *nf* (*voiture*) diesel

diéséliste [djezelist] *n Tech* diesel fitter

diéser [djeze] *vt* (**je dièse, n. diésons; je diéserai**) *Mus* (*note*) to sharpen, *Am* to sharp

diète[1] [djɛt] *nf* diet; (*jeûne*) fast; **d. lactée** milk diet; **être à la d.** (*régime*) to be on a diet; (*jeûne*) to be fasting; **mettre qn à la d.** to put sb on a diet

diète[2] *nf Hist Pol* diet

diététicien, -ienne [djetetisjɛ̃, -jɛn] *n* dietitian, dietician

diététique [djetetik] *Méd* **1** *adj* (*menu, repas*) diet; (*supplément*) dietary; **magasin/restaurant d.** health food shop/restaurant **2** *nf* dietetics

dieu, -ieux [djø] **1** *nm* **(a)** god; **les dieux de l'Égypte ancienne** the gods of ancient Egypt; **beau comme un d. (grec)** like a Greek god; **il danse comme un d.** he's a wonderful dancer, *Vieilli* he dances divinely; **être aimé** *ou* **béni des dieux** to be blessed with good fortune, to be a favourite of the gods; **jurer ses grands dieux** to swear (by all that's holy)

(b) **D.** God; **D. le père** God the Father; *Fig* **ce n'est pas D. le père** he's not God Almighty; **la voix de D.** the voice of God; **croire en D.** to believe in God; **un homme de D.** a holy man; **s'il plaît à D., si D. (le) veut** please God, God willing; **D. merci!, D. soit loué** thank God!; **le bon D.** God; **recevoir le bon D.** to receive the Holy Sacrament; **on lui donnerait le bon D. sans confession** he looks as though butter wouldn't melt in his mouth; **mais qu'est-ce que j'ai fait au bon D. pour mériter ça/avoir un mari aussi stupide!** what in heaven's *or* God's name have I ever done to deserve this/to deserve such a stupid husband; *F* **y a pas de bon D.** there's no justice in the world; **pour l'amour de D.** for goodness' *or* God's sake; **devant D. et devant les hommes** ≈ by Almighty God; **D. vous bénisse** God bless you; **D. vous garde** God keep you; **D. m'en garde, à D. ne plaise** God forbid; **D. vous entende** may your prayers be answered; **D. sait si j'ai travaillé** goodness *or* heaven *or* God knows I've worked hard enough; **D. sait quoi** God knows what; **D. seul le sait** God only knows; *F* **il va y aller D. sait comment** he's going, God knows how (he'll get there); **D. m'est témoin que je n'ai pas dit cela** as God is my witness I never said that; **chaque jour** *ou* **tous les jours que D. fait** every day that God sends; *Vieilli* **à D. vat!** it's in God's hands now!

2 *int* **(a)** (*admis*) **mon D.!, grand D.!** God!, my God!, good God!; **grands dieux!** heavens!; **mon D. oui!** God, yes!; **mon D. je veux bien!** well, I don't mind!; **D. qu'elle est petite!** goodness *or* God she's small!; *F* **c'est pas D. possible!** it's just not possible, I refuse to believe it; **c'est pas D. possible d'être aussi bête!** it's just not heavenly possible to be that stupid!

(b) (*profane*) **bon D.!, D. de D.!, bon D. de bon D.!, (sacré) nom de D.!** for Christ's sake!, God almighty!, hell!

diffamant [difamɑ̃] *adj* (*paroles*) slanderous, defamatory; (*écrits*) libellous, defamatory

diffamateur, -trice [difamatœr, -tris] *n* (*en paroles*) slanderer; (*par écrit*) libeller

diffamation [difamasjɔ̃] *nf* defamation (of character); (*paroles*) slander; (*écrits*) libel; **une campagne de d.** a campaign of defamation; **poursuivre qn en d.** to sue sb for defamation of character; **procès en d.** slander/libel trial

diffamatoire [difamatwar] *adj* defamatory; (*paroles*) slanderous; (*écrits*) libellous

diffamer [difame] *vt* to defame; (*en paroles*) to slander; (*par écrit*) to libel

différé [difere] *adj* (*paiement, rente etc*) deferred; *Él* **coupe-circuit à action différée** time-lag cut-out; *Phot* **obturateur à**

action différée delayed action shutter; *Rad, TV* **émission en d.** (pre-)recorded broadcast; *Ordinat* **traitement d.** off-line processing

différemment [diferamɑ̃] *adv* differently

différence [diferɑ̃s] *nf* difference; **d. de goûts** differences of taste; **la d. de A à B** *ou* **entre A et B** the difference between A and B; **d. d'âges/d'opinions** age difference/difference of opinions; *Él* **d. de potentiel** potential difference, pd; **d. de prix** price difference; **quelle d. avec ...!** what a difference from ...!; **il n'y a pas de d. entre eux** there's nothing to choose between them; **cela ne fait pas de d.** it makes no difference *or* no odds; **il ne faut pas faire de d. entre ses enfants** you shouldn't treat your children differently, you should not discriminate between your children; **il y a trop de d. d'âge entre eux** there's too much of *or* too big an age gap *or* age difference between them; **faire la d. d'une chose avec une autre** *ou* **entre une chose et une autre** to distinguish *or* discriminate between two things; **c'est ça qui a fait la d.** that's what made the difference; **je vous dois la d.** I'll owe you the difference; **à la d. de ...** unlike ...; **à la d. que ...** except that ...

différenciateur, -trice [diferɑ̃sjatœr, -tris] **1** *adj* differentiating **2** *nm* **d. sémantique** semantic differential

différenciation [diferɑ̃sjasjɔ̃] *nf* differentiation; *Mktg* **d. de ligne** line featuring

différencier [diferɑ̃sje] (*impf & pr sub* **n. différenciions**) **1** *vt* to differentiate (**de, d'avec** from); *Math* (*équation etc*) to obtain the differential (coefficient) of; **rien ne les différencie** there's nothing to differentiate them **2 se différencier** *vpr* **(a)** (*de deux personnes*) to be different (from each other), to differ; **ils se différencient par leurs écharpes de couleurs différentes** you can tell them apart by their different coloured scarves **(b)** (*d'une personne*) **se d. de** to differentiate oneself from

différend [diferɑ̃] *nm* dispute, difference of opinion, disagreement (**entre** between); *Jur* dispute; **avoir un d. avec qn** to disagree *or* have a disagreement with sb (**sur** about); **ils ont un d. sur l'éducation des enfants** they disagree *or* differ on how the children should be educated; **il a un d. avec son voisin à propos de la clôture du jardin** he is at odds with his neighbour over the garden fence; **il a un d. avec son père qui empoisonne leurs relations depuis de nombreuses années** a long-standing difference of opinion between him and his father has poisoned their relationship

différent [diferɑ̃] *adj* **(a)** [①A66-7] (*distinct*) different (**de** *Br* from, *Am* than); **un avis d. du premier** a different opinion from the first, an opinion that differs from the first; **elle utilise une recette différente de la tienne** her recipe is different from yours **(b)** (*divers*) (*toujours au pl*) **différents** various; **différentes personnes l'ont vu** different *or* various *or* a number of people saw him; **à différentes reprises** at various times, off and on

différentiation [diferɑ̃sjasjɔ̃] *nf Math* differentiation

différentiel, -ielle [diferɑ̃sjɛl] **1** *adj* differential **2** *nm Aut etc* differential; *Com* **d. de prix** price differential; *Ling* **d. sémantique** semantic differential **3** *nf Math* **différentielle** differential

différer [difere] (**je diffère, n. différons; je différerai**) **1** *vt* (*retarder*) (*jugement*) to defer, to postpone; (*paiement*) to defer; (*décision, départ*) to postpone, to put off; *Fml* **d. de faire qch** to defer doing sth **2** *vi* (*être différent*) to differ; **nos origines diffèrent complètement** our backgrounds are completely different; **ils diffèrent de race et de langue** they differ in race and speech; **nous différons d'opinion** our opinions differ; **nous différons en tout** we differ on everything; **ils diffèrent par la taille** they differ in height, they are of different heights; **nous différons sur le choix de l'école des enfants** we differ *or* do not agree on which school the children should go to

difficile [difisil] **1** *adj* **(a)** (*ardu*) (*travail, situation etc*) difficult, hard; **d'accès d.** difficult to get to; **le plus d. est fait** the hardest *or* most difficult part is over; **il est très d. de le joindre** it is very difficult to contact him, he is very difficult to contact

(b) (*délicat*) difficult; **circonstances difficiles** difficult *or* trying circumstances; **les temps sont difficiles** times are hard; **il m'est d. d'accepter** it is difficult for me to accept, I can't very well accept; **les fins de mois sont difficiles** things are difficult at the end of the month

(c) (*personne*) difficult to get on with, hard to please; **enfant d.** difficult *or* problem child; **elle est d. à vivre** she is difficult to get on with; **il est d. sur la nourriture** he's difficult *or* fussy about his food; **elle est très d. sur la ponctualité/l'orthographe** she is very fussy about punctuality/spelling; **si la maison ne te plaît pas, c'est que tu es vraiment d.** you must be really hard to please *or* fussy if you don't like the house

2 *n* **faire le d.** to be hard to please; **ne faites pas le d.** don't be difficult, stop fussing

difficilement [difisilmɑ̃] *adv* with difficulty, not easily; **il apprend d.** he is a slow learner, he has learning difficulties; **on peut d. lui dire une chose pareille** you can hardly *or* you can't possibly tell him something like that; **c'est d. faisable** it's virtually impossible

difficulté [difikylte] *nf* difficulty; **être en d.** to be in difficulties *or* trouble; **cela ne présente aucune d.** that doesn't present any difficulty; **c'est sans d.** it's easy, it's not difficult; **aimer la d.** to like to make things difficult for oneself; **tourner la d.** to get round a difficulty; **faire** *ou* **soulever des difficultés** to create obstacles, to raise objections, to make difficulties; **cela ne fera pas de d., que je sache** there won't be any difficulty as far as I know; **se heurter à de graves difficultés** to come up against serious difficulties; **avoir de la d. à faire qch** to have difficulty doing sth, to find it hard *or* difficult to do sth; **avoir des difficultés matérielles** to be in financial difficulties; **créer des difficultés à qn** to put difficulties in sb's way, to make difficulties for sb; **difficultés de trésorerie** cashflow difficulties

difforme [difɔrm] *adj* (*personne*) deformed; (*membre*) malformed, misshapen, twisted; **troncs d'arbres difformes** gnarled treetrunks

difformité [difɔrmite] *nf* (*d'une personne*) deformity; (*d'un membre*) malformation; **la d. de son bras n'est pas irrémédiable** his malformed arm *or* the malformation in his arm is not incurable

diffracter [difrakte] *vt Opt* to diffract

diffraction [difraksjɔ̃] *nf Opt* diffraction

diffus [dify] *adj* (*lumière*) diffused; (*matière*) diffuse; (*pensée, idées*) vague; **éclairs d.** sheet lightning; **style d.** diffuse *or Fml* prolix style; **écrivain d.** verbose *or Fml* prolix writer

diffusément [difyzemɑ̃] *adv* (*penser*) vaguely; (*écrire*) in a diffuse style; **la musique/la conversation nous parvenait d.** we couldn't hear the music/the conversation very clearly

diffuser [difyze] **1** *vt* (*lumière, chaleur*) to diffuse, to spread; *Rad, TV* (*émission etc*) to broadcast, to air; (*idées, nouvelles*) to spread; (*livres, journaux*) to distribute **2 se diffuser** *vpr* (*d'idées, de nouvelles, de lumière, Phys des ondes*) to spread

diffuseur [difyzœr] *nm* **(a)** (*de lumière, de sèche-cheveux*) diffuser; (*dans un moteur*) mixer, diffuser; *TV, Rad* broadcaster; (*écran diffuseur*) scrim, diffuser; (*compresseur*) diffuser; (*d'un chauffage*) air vent; **d. de parfum** room scenter; *Aut* **à d. fixe** fixed-choke **(b)** (*de livres, journaux*) distributor

diffusion [difyzjɔ̃] *nf* **(a)** (*de lumière, chaleur*) diffusion **(b)** (*de nouvelles, d'idées*) spread, spreading; *Rad, TV* (*d'une émission*) broadcasting; (*de livres*) distribution; (*de journal*) circulation; *TV etc* **d. audio numérique** digital audio broadcasting; *TV etc* **d. de données par satellite** satellite data broadcasting; **d. de masse** (*d'un journal etc*) mass circulation; **d. directe par satellite** direct satellite broadcasting, DSB; **d. hertzienne** terrestrial broadcasting; **d. numérique** *Com* stock holding distribution; *TV etc* digital broadcasting; *TV, Rad* **d. terrestre** terrestrial broadcasting

digérer [diʒere] (**je digère, n. digérons; je digérerai**) **1** *vt* **(a)** (*nourriture*) to digest; **je ne digère pas le porc** pork does not agree with me, I find pork difficult to digest **(b)** *Fig* (*ce qu'on lit, ce qu'on apprend*) to digest, to take in, to assimilate; *F* (*accepter*) (*insultes etc*) to swallow; **je n'ai toujours pas digéré le coup qu'il m'a fait à Noël** I still haven't got over what he did to me at Christmas; **des vérités dures à d.** unpalatable truths **2** *vi* **je digère mal** my digestion is bad, I have bad digestion

digest [dajʒɛst, diʒɛst] *nm Journ* digest

digeste [diʒɛst] *adj F* (*aliment*) easily digestible; **ce livre est vraiment peu d.** the book is indigestible

digestibilité [diʒɛstibilite] *nf* digestibility

digestible [diʒɛstibl] *adj* digestible

digestif, -ive [diʒɛstif, -iv] **1** *adj* (*de la digestion*) digestive; (*substance*) which aids digestion; **le tube d.** the digestive tract; **avoir des troubles digestifs** to have digestive problems, to have problems with one's digestion **2** *nm* liqueur, after-dinner drink

digestion [diʒɛstjɔ̃] *nf* digestion; **elle a une d. difficile** she has problems with her digestion *or* digestive problems

digit [diʒit] *nm Ordinat* **(a)** (*chiffre*) digit **(b)** (*caractère*) character

digital[1], -ale, -aux, -ales [diʒital, -o] *adj Ordinat* digital; **code d.** digital code; **affichage d.** digital display; **horloge/montre à affichage d.** digital watch/clock

digital[2], -ale, -aux, -ales 1 *adj* (*nerf etc*) digital; **empreinte digitale** fingerprint; **prendre les empreintes digitales de qn**

to take sb's fingerprints, to fingerprint sb **2** *nf Bot, Méd* **digitale** digitalis; *Bot* **d. pourprée** foxglove

digitaline [diʒitalin] *nf Ch, Pharm* digitalin

digitaliser [diʒitalize] *vt Ordinat* to digitize

digitaliseur [diʒitalizœr] *nm Ordinat* digitizer

digne [diɲ] *adj* **(a)** (*méritant*) deserving, worthy (**de** of); **cela est d. de récompense** that deserves a reward; **d. d'éloges** praiseworthy; **d. de foi** reliable; **d. d'être remarqué** noteworthy; **il est d. d'être remercié** he deserves thanks *or* to be thanked; **il n'est pas d. d'être notre représentant** he does not deserve *or* he is not fit to be our representative; **il n'est pas d. de vivre** he is not fit to live; **ce film est d. d'être vu** it's a film worth seeing; **je ne suis pas d. de toi** I am not worthy of you, you're too good for me; **une mère d.** a fit mother

(b) (*à la hauteur*) **d. de** worthy of; **une attitude peu d. d'un chef d'État** an attitude that is hardly worthy of a head of state; **d. d'une mère** of a mother, motherly; **son attitude n'est pas d. d'une mère** her attitude is not motherly *or* not that of a mother; **il est d'une gentillesse avec toi d. d'une mère** he is almost motherly towards you; **d. de ce nom** worthy of the name; **prouver qu'on est une mère d. de ce nom** to prove that one is a fit mother; *Hum* **tu es bien le d. fils de ton père** you're your father's son all right; **un adversaire d. de soi** a worthy opponent; **un roman d. de la grande tradition française** a novel in the great French tradition; **tâchez de vous montrer d. de (représenter) la France** try to show that you're worthy to represent France

(c) (*honorable, décent*) (*air, personne etc*) dignified; **il est incapable de rester d. après trois verres de vin** after three glasses of wine, he is incapable of acting in a dignified fashion, he loses all dignity after three glasses of wine

dignement [diɲ(ə)mɑ̃] *adv* **(a)** (*avec dignité*) with dignity, in a dignified fashion; **il a réagi très d.** he reacted with great dignity **(b)** (*légitimement*) **être d. augmenté/récompensé** to be given a decent rise/reward

dignitaire [diɲitɛr] *nm* (*de l'Eglise*) dignitary

dignité [diɲite] *nf* **(a)** (*grandeur*) dignity; **elle manque de d.** she's undignified; **elle fit une entrée pleine de d.** she came in with great dignity; **toute personne a droit à la d.** everyone is entitled to their dignity **(b)** (*haute fonction*) high office *or* position, *Fml* dignity; **installer qn dans une d.** to install sb in an office

digramme [digram] *nm Ling* digraph

digraphie [digrafi] *nf Com* double-entry bookkeeping

digression [digrɛsjɔ̃] *nf* digression; **faire une d.** to digress, to stray *or* wander from the point

digue [dig] *nf HydE* dyke; (*d'une voie navigable etc*) embankment; (*en pierre*) breakwater; (*contre l'érosion*) sea wall; *Fig* (*aux passions etc*) barrier

diktat [diktat] *nm* diktat, dictate

dilapidateur, -trice [dilapidatœr, -tris] **1** *adj* spendthrift **2** *n* (*de fortune*) spendthrift, wastrel; (*de fonds publics, de biens*) embezzler

dilapidation [dilapidasjɔ̃] *nf* (*de fortune*) wasting, squandering; (*de fonds publics, de biens*) embezzlement, misappropriation

dilapider [dilapide] *vt* (*fortune*) to waste, to squander; (*fonds publics*) to misappropriate, to embezzle

dilatation [dilatasjɔ̃] *nf* (*des pupilles*) dilation; (*de l'estomac*) distension; (*des gaz*) expansion; *Constr* **joint de d.** expansion joint

dilater [dilate] **1** *vt* (*agrandir*) (*pupilles*) to dilate; (*estomac*) to distend; (*gaz*) to expand; **il a les pupilles dilatées** his pupils are dilated; *Fig* **d. le cœur** to cheer *or* gladden the heart **2 se dilater** *vpr* (*de pupilles*) to dilate; (*de l'estomac*) to become distended; (*d'un gaz*) to expand

dilatoire [dilatwar] *adj* (*tactique etc*) delaying; *Jur* dilatory; **faire des réponses dilatoires** to stall for time

dilemme [dilɛm] *nm* dilemma; **être dans un d.** to be in a dilemma; **être dans un profond d.** to be on the horns of a dilemma; *Mktg* **dilemmes** (*produits*) problem children, wildcats

dilettante [dilɛtɑ̃t] *n* dilettante, amateur; **faire des sciences en d.** to dabble in science

dilettantisme [dilɛtɑ̃tism] *nm* dilettantism, amateurism

diligemment [diliʒamɑ̃] *adv Litt* **(a)** (*avec soin*) diligently **(b)** (*avec rapidité*) promptly, quickly

diligence [diliʒɑ̃s] *nf* **(a)** *Litt* (*soin*) diligence, industry, application **(b)** *Litt* (*rapidité*) haste, dispatch; **faire d.** to hurry, to make haste **(c)** (*véhicule*) (stage)coach **(d)** *Jur* proceedings

diligent [diliʒɑ̃] *adj Litt* **(a)** (*appliqué*) diligent, industrious; **soins diligents** assiduous care **(b)** (*rapide*) speedy, prompt

diluant [dilɥɑ̃] *nm* thinner

diluer [dilɥe] *vt* (*boisson*) to dilute, to water down (**de** with); (*peinture*) to thin down (**de** with); (*pouvoir*) to weaken; (*discours, dissertation*) to pad

dilution [dilysjɔ̃] *nf* (*de peinture*) thinning down; (*de boisson*) dilution, watering down; (*de pouvoir*) weakening; (*de discours, dissertation*) padding; **d. de capital** dilution of capital

diluvien, -ienne [dilyvjɛ̃, -jɛn] *adj* **(a)** (*fossiles etc*) diluvian; (*dépôt, argile etc*) diluvial **(b)** *Fig* **pluie diluvienne** torrential rain, downpour

dimanche [dimɑ̃ʃ] *nm* [ⓘ**A75-6**,B-C; **B58-9**,B-C] Sunday; **d. des Rameaux/de Pâques** Palm/Easter Sunday; **ses habits du d.** one's Sunday clothes *or* best; *F* **un chauffeur du d.** a weekend *or* Sunday driver; **un peintre du d.** a weekend painter; **la promenade du d.** the (usual) Sunday stroll; **on passe tous les dimanches en famille** we spend every Sunday with the family; **je hais les dimanches** I hate Sundays

dîme [dim] *nf Hist* tithe; *Fig* **l'État prélève sa d. sur le tabac** the government takes its cut on tobacco

dimension [dimɑ̃sjɔ̃] *nf* **(a)** [ⓘ**B56-7**,D,1] (*grandeur*) dimension, size; **à deux/trois dimensions** two-/three-dimensional; **quelles sont les dimensions de la pièce?** how large is the room?, what is the size of the room?; **prendre les dimensions de qch** to take the measurements of sth, to measure sth; **taillé à la d.** cut to size; **coupé dans sa grande/petite d.** cut lengthways/crossways

(b) (*importance*) (*d'une faute*) magnitude, enormity; **te rends-tu compte de la d. de ta gaffe?** do you realize what an enormous blunder you made?; *Fig* **prendre les dimensions d'une expédition/d'une révolution** to take on the dimensions of an expedition/a revolution; **le suspens est une d. prépondérante de son œuvre** suspense is a significant feature of his work; **ce travail n'est pas à la d. de son talent** the work is not equal to his talent; **il n'a pas la d. d'un homme d'État** he is not the stuff that statesmen are made of; **cette découverte prend enfin ses vraies dimensions** people are finally realizing the true importance of this discovery

dimensionner [dimɑ̃sjɔne] *vt Ordinat* (*figure*) to size

diminué, -ée [diminɥe] *adj* **(a)** *Tex* (*tricot*) fully-fashioned; *Mus* (*intervalle*) diminished; *Archit* **colonne diminuée** tapering column **(b)** (*affaibli*) weakened, diminished; **c'est un homme d.** he is not the man he was; **il est très d. physiquement/mentalement** he is physically/mentally a lot weaker

diminuer [diminɥe] **1** *vt* (*prix*) to reduce, to lower; (*dépenses*) to reduce, to decrease, to cut down; (*salaire*) to reduce, to decrease, to cut; (*autorité, pouvoir, crédibilité etc*) to lessen, to diminish; (*son capital, l'importance de qch*) to diminish; **d. les chances de succès** to diminish *or* lessen *or* reduce the chances of success; **d. sa consommation d'alcool** to reduce *or* cut down one's alcohol consumption; **d. l'ardeur des foules** to decrease the crowds' fervour; **la maladie l'a considérablement diminuée** the illness has weakened her considerably; *Fig* **cela vous diminuerait aux yeux du public** it would lower *or* diminish you in the eyes of the public; **d. le son** to turn down the volume; **d. la semaine de travail** to reduce *or* cut the working week; **d. la longueur de qch** to make sth shorter, to shorten sth; **d. la hauteur de qch** to lower the height of sth; **d. la largeur de qch** to make sth narrower; *Tricot* **d. l'encolure de quatre mailles** to decrease four stitches at the neck

2 *vi* to diminish, to decrease, to lessen; (*de profits*) to decrease, to fall off, to decline; (*de prix*) to decrease, to fall; (*de fièvre*) to abate; (*de douleur*) to decrease, to diminish; **d. de vitesse** to slow down, to reduce speed; **les jours diminuent** the days are drawing in *or* are growing shorter; **ses forces ont diminué** his strength has declined; **sa toux a diminué** he is not coughing as much; *Naut* **d. de toile** to shorten sail

3 se diminuer *vpr* to lower *or* demean oneself

diminutif, -ive [diminytif, -iv] **1** *adj* diminutive **2** *nm* (*d'un nom commun*) diminutive; (*d'un nom propre*) pet name, nickname; **'jupette' est le d. de 'jupe'** 'jupette' is the diminutive (form) of 'jupe'

diminution [diminysjɔ̃] *nf* (*de nombre*) decrease, decline; (*de prix*) reduction, decrease, lowering; (*de dépenses*) cutting down; (*de salaire*) decrease; (*de vitesse*) slackening; (*du son*) fading; (*de fièvre*) abatement; (*de douleur*) decrease, lessening; *Tricot* **commencer les diminutions** to begin decreasing; *Tricot* **faire trois diminutions** decrease three stitches

dimorphe [dimɔrf] *adj Biol* dimorphic, dimorphous

dimorphisme [dimɔrfism] *nm Biol* dimorphism

dinanderie [dinɑ̃dri] *nf* brassware; (*de cuisine*) brass kitchen utensils

dinar [dinar] *nm* dinar
dînatoire [dinatwar] *adj Fml, Hum* (*apéritif, goûter*) copious, *Hum* mammoth
dinde [dɛ̃d] *nf* (**a**) (*volaille*) turkey hen; *Culin* turkey (**b**) *F* (*femme sotte*) stupid woman
dindon [dɛ̃dɔ̃] *nm* turkey (cock); *Fig* **être le d. de la farce** to be fooled *or* duped, to be made a fool of; **c'est le fisc qui est le d. de la farce** it's the tax man who's been conned
dindonneau, -eaux [dɛ̃dɔno] *nm* young turkey, turkey poult
dîner[1] [dine] *nm* [①**A6**,d,iii] (**a**) (*repas du soir*) dinner; **prendre son d.** to have one's dinner; **je donne un d. ce soir** I'm having a dinner party tonight; **je ne peux pas venir ce soir, j'ai un d.** I can't come this evening, I'm already booked for dinner; **il y a des pâtes pour le** *ou* **au** *ou* **à d.** it's pasta for dinner *or* supper; **nous avons les Dupont à d.** the Duponts are coming for dinner; **d. dansant** dinner-dance; **d-débat/-concert/-spectacle** dinner-debate/-concert/-show; **d. de gala** gala dinner; **d. de famille** family dinner (**b**) *Can, Belg* (*déjeuner*) lunch
dîner[2] *vi* (**a**) (*prendre le repas du soir*) to dine, to have dinner; **d. en ville** *or* **à l'extérieur** to dine out; **d. dehors** to eat out; **d. chez des amis** to dine *or* have dinner with friends; **à quelle heure dînez-vous?** what time do you have dinner?; **il est resté à d.** he stayed for dinner; **avoir/inviter qn à d.** to have/invite sb for *or* to dinner; **elle dîne de peu** she doesn't eat very much at dinner; **elle a dîné de peu** she didn't have much dinner, she didn't eat very much at dinner; **il dîna d'une tranche de jambon** he had a slice of ham for dinner; *Prov* **qui dort dîne** he who sleeps forgets his hunger

(**b**) *Can, Belg* (*déjeuner*) to (have) lunch; **elle est partie d.** she's gone to lunch
dînette [dinɛt] *nf F* (*service*) doll's teaset; (*repas*) dolls' tea party; **jouer à la d.** to have a dolls' tea party
dîneur, -euse [dinœr, -øz] *n* diner
ding [diŋ] *int* ting-a-ling
dingo[1] [dɛ̃go] *nm* (*animal*) dingo
dingo[2] *adj, n F* = **dingue**
dingue [dɛ̃g] *F* **1** *adj* (**a**) (*fou*) crazy, nuts (**de qn/qch** about sb/sth, **de faire qch** to do sth); **c'est complètement d. de croire qu'on va s'en sortir** it's absolutely crazy to think we're going to get out of this

(**b**) (*incroyable*) (*fête, fringues, bouquin*) great, terrific; **c'est d. ce que la ville a changé** it's incredible how much the town has changed; **c'est d. ce que la vie est chère** the cost of living is terrible; **c'est d., la pluie qui tombe ici** it's terrible how much it rains here, it rains a terrific lot here; **il a fait un orage d.** there was a terrific storm

2 *n* nutcase, crackpot, loony; **ce d. est arrivé chez moi sans prévenir** the nutcase turned up on my doorstep without warning; **envoyer qn chez les dingues** to send sb to the loony bin *or* funny farm; **c'est un d. de la moto** he's crazy *or* nuts about motorbikes; **d. d'informatique** computer freak
dinguer [dɛ̃ge] *vi F* **s'en aller d.** (*d'une personne*) to go flying; **sa voiture est allée d. contre un mur** his car went flying *or* headlong into a wall; **envoyer d. qn** (*le pousser*) to send sb flying (**contre** into); (*l'éconduire*) to send sb packing; **envoyer d. qch** to send sth flying; **je vais tout envoyer d.** I'm going to pack it all in
dinguerie [dɛ̃gri] *nf F* stupidity; **ce film est d'une d.!** it's an incredibly stupid film; **voilà sa dernière d.: s'acheter une moto!** you know what his latest mad *or* crazy idea is? – to buy a motorbike; **ils ne savent faire que les dingueries** they get up to all sorts of nonsense; **il est capable des pires dingueries** he's capable of doing the most idiotic things
dinosaure [dinɔzɔr] *nm* (*animal*), *Fig* dinosaur; *Fig* **dinosaures de la politique** political dinosaurs
diocésain, -aine [djɔsezɛ̃, -ɛn] *adj, n Rel* diocesan
diocèse [djɔsɛz] *nm Rel* diocese
diode [djɔd] *nf Rad* diode; *Ordinat* **d. électroluminescente** light-emitting diode
dionysiaque [djɔnizjak] **1** *adj* dionysiac **2** *nfpl* **les dionysiaques** the Dionysia
diorama [djɔrama] *nm* diorama
dioxine [diɔksin] *nf* dioxin
dioxyde [diɔksid] *nm Ch* dioxide
diphasé [difaze] *adj Él* (*système etc*) two-phase
diphtérie [difteri] *nf Méd* diphtheria; **avoir la d.** to have diphtheria
diphtérique [difterik] *adj Méd* diphther(it)ic, diphtherial
diphtongue [diftɔ̃g] *nf Ling* diphthong
diphtonguer [diftɔ̃ge] *vt Ling* to diphthongize
diplodocus [diplɔdɔkys] *nm* diplodocus
diplomate [diplɔmat] **1** *n* (*fonctionnaire, négociateur*) diplomat **2** *nm Culin* ≈ trifle **3** *adj* diplomatic
diplomatie [diplɔmasi] *nf* (*tact*), *Pol* diplomacy; **entrer dans la d.** to enter the diplomatic service; **user de d.** to be diplomatic
diplomatique [diplɔmatik] *adj* (**a**) (*service, corps, immunité etc*) diplomatic; **valise d.** diplomatic bag, *F* bag, *US* (diplomatic) pouch (**b**) (*habile*) diplomatic, tactful; **ce n'était pas très d. de sa part** that wasn't very diplomatic *or* tactful of him; **maladie d.** diplomatic flu
diplomatiquement [diplɔmatikmɑ̃] *adv* diplomatically
diplôme [diplom] *nm* (*d'enseignant, de docteur etc*) diploma; *Univ* degree; **elle a des diplômes** she has qualifications
▶ **diplôme**: **d. d'études approfondies** = university degree awarded after five-year course of study (*as a preliminary to a PhD*); **d. d'études supérieures spécialisées** = university degree awarded after five-year course of study; **d. d'études universitaires générales** = university degree awarded after two-year course of study; **d. d'études universitaires scientifiques et techniques** = university degree awarded after a two-year course of study in science and/or technical subjects; **d. universitaire de technologie** = qualification awarded after a two-year course of study in technology, ≈ HNC
diplômé, -ée [diplome] **1** *adj Univ* = graduate; (*architecte, infirmière*) qualified, certified; **un ingénieur d. de l'École Polytechnique** an engineering graduate of the Ecole Polytechnique **2** *n* holder of a diploma; *Univ* = graduate
diplômer [diplome] *vt* to confer a diploma on; *Univ* to confer a degree on, *Am* to graduate
diplopie [diplɔpi] *nf Méd* double vision, diplopia
dipode [dipɔd] *adj, n Zool* biped
dipsomane [dipsɔman], **dipsomaniaque** [dipsɔmanjak] *adj, n* dipsomaniac
dipsomanie [dipsɔmani] *nf* dipsomania
diptère[1] [diptɛr] *Ent* **1** *adj* two-winged, *Spéc* dipterous **2** *nm* dipter(an); **les diptères** the Diptera
diptyque [diptik] *nm* diptych; *Littér* two-part literary work
dirco [dirko] *nm* (*abrév* **directeur commercial**) marketing manager; (*en chef*) marketing director
dircom [dirkɔm] *nm* (*abrév* **directeur de la communication**) communications manager; (*en chef*) communications director
dire[1] [dir] *nm* statement, assertion; *Jur* allegation; **on ne peut pas se fier à leurs dires** you can't trust what they say; **au d. de l'expert** according to expert opinion *or* the experts; **selon son d., à son d., à ses dires** according to him, by his own account; **maintenir son d.** to stand by one's statement *or* what one said
dire[2] (*prp* **disant**; *pp* **dit**; *pr ind* **je dis, n. disons, vous dites, ils disent**; *impf* **je disais**; *p hist* **je dis**; *fu* **je dirai**) **1** *vt* (**a**) (*exprimer*) to say; **il ne savait plus quoi d.** he didn't know what to say; **dites 33** (*chez le médecin*) say "Ah"; **elle a dit 'amboule' au lieu d'ampoule'** she said 'amboule' instead of 'ampoule'; **c'est justement ce que j'allais d.!** that's just what I was about to say!; **alors, qu'est-ce qu'il t'a dit?** well, what did he say to you?; **vous ne m'en avez jamais rien dit** you never mentioned it *or* said a thing about it; **mettez que je n'ai rien dit** forget I said that; **il n'y a pas à d., c'est vraiment le meilleur** there's no two ways about it, it/he's really the best; **je ne sais que d. pour vous remercier** I don't know how to thank you; **je ne sais que d. pour vous consoler** I don't know what to say to comfort you; **elle n'a plus dit un mot** she didn't say another word; **ce ne sont pas des choses à d.** you don't say that kind of thing; **tu ne sais plus ce que tu dis!** (*tes mots dépassent ta pensée*) you don't know what you're saying; **arrête de d. n'importe quoi** stop talking nonsense; **j'ai un mot à te d.** (*pour mettre au courant*) I've got something to tell you; (*d'un ton menaçant*) I've something to say to you; **d. ce qu'on pense** to say what one thinks, to speak one's mind; **j'ai dit ce que j'avais à d.** I've said what I had to say; **ce disant ..., ceci dit ...** with these words ..., having said that ...; **un ami, que dis-je! un frère** a friend, no, a brother!; **c'est facile à d., c'est plus facile à d. qu'à faire** (it's) easier said than done; **d. bonjour à qn** to say hello to sb; **d. bonjour de la main** to wave hello; **d. bonsoir à qn** to say goodnight to sb, to wish sb goodnight; **comme on dit** as the saying goes, as they say; **comment dites-vous cela en français?** how do you say that in French?, what is the French for that?; **d. du mal de qn** to speak ill of sb; **je vous dis que non** no, I said; **je t'ai déjà dit que oui!** I've already said yes!; **là je ne dis pas non** I wouldn't say no; **sans mot d.** without (saying) a word; *Prov* **qui ne dit mot consent** silence is tantamount to consent; **pour ainsi d.** so to speak, as it were; *F* **on a comme qui dirait des ennuis** we have what you might call a few problems; **faire des stocks de sucre lorsqu'on habite à Moscou, je ne dis pas, mais à Paris!** stocking up on sugar

when you live in Moscow, that's fair enough *or* that's one thing, but in Paris!; **ou, pour mieux d.** ... or, to be more specific ...; **il est un peu lent, pour ne pas d. complètement idiot** he's a little slow or to put it bluntly he's a complete idiot; **autrement dit** in other words; **cela va sans d.** that goes without saying, of course, naturally; **il va sans d. que vous venez avec votre épouse** needless to say *or* naturally, your wife is invited as well, your wife is invited as well, of course; **comment dirais-je?** how shall I put it?; **je ne sais comment d.** I don't know how to put it; **qui dit mieux?** (*à une vente aux enchères*) any advance?; **dites toujours!** go on!, say it!, *F* fire away!; **il faut le d. vite!** it's easy to say!; **c'est vite dit** it's easier said than done; *Enf* **c'est celui qui dit, qui l'est!** it takes one to know one!

(b) (*informer*) to tell; **qui te l'a dit?** (*comment le sais-tu?*) who told you?; **elle m'a dit que tu étais à Paris** she told me (that) you were in Paris; **qui t'a dit ça?** (*ce n'est pas vrai*) who told you that?; **c'est Sophie qui me l'a dit** it was Sophie who told me; **elle a dit qu'elle arriverait en retard** she said she'd be late; **envoyer d. à qn que ...** to send word to sb that ...; **d. un secret** to tell a secret; **il faudra bien que tu le lui dises un jour** you'll have to tell him some day; **ne me dis rien, tu as gagné!** don't tell me *or* let me guess — you've won!; **ne me dis pas que tu as gagné!** don't tell me *or* don't say you've won!; **il dit dans sa lettre que ..., sa lettre dit que ...** he says in his letter that ...; **faire d. qch à qn** (*en le forçant*) to make sb say sth; (*pour prévenir*) to send word of sth to sb; **je lui ai fait d. de venir** I sent for him; **elle ne se le fit pas d. deux fois** she didn't wait to be told twice; *F* **je ne te le fais pas d.!** tell me something I don't know!; **faire d. qch par qn** to send word of sth through sb; **il a fait d. à son patron qu'il ne viendrait pas** he sent word to his boss that he wouldn't be coming in

(c) (*affirmer*) to tell; **moi, je vous dis qu'il ne viendra pas** I say he won't come; **je le dis et je le répète** let me make myself perfectly clear; **qui vous dit qu'elle est vraiment aveugle?** who says she's really blind?; **quand je vous le disais!, je vous l'avais bien dit!** I told you so!, didn't I say so?; **(puisque) je vous le dis!** take my word for it!; **il est vraiment parti avec elle? – (puisque) je vous le dis** has he really gone off with her? – you can take it from me (he has) *or* take my word for it; **je peux reprendre du gâteau? – (puisque) je vous le dis!** can I have some more cake? – of course you can!; *F* **c'est lui, je te dis** it's him, I tell you; **c'est moi qui vous le dis** let me tell you, believe me; **c'est toi qui le dis!**, *F* **que tu dis!** if you say so!; **je sais ce que je dis!** I know what I'm talking about!; *F* **à qui le dites-vous?** you're telling me!; **tu ne crois pas si bien d.!** you're telling me!, how right you are!, *Am* you've said a mouthful!; **on peut d. qu'il a eu de la chance** he was lucky, you might say; *F* **tu l'as dit (bouffi)!** you('ve) said it!; **c'est beaucoup d.** that's saying (quite) a lot, that's going rather far; **c'est peu d.** that's putting it mildly; **c'est peu d. de d. qu'il est petit!** he's small, and that's putting it mildly, he's small, to put it mildly, *Br* he isn't half small; *F* **je ne te dis pas la fête démente que c'était!** the party was so wild, it was unreal!; *F* **je ne te dis que ça** say no more, enough said; **vous m'en direz tant!** you don't say!; *Enf F* **on dit qu'on est des astronautes** let's be astronauts; **vous m'avez dit adorer la musique** you told me you loved music; **on le dit mort** they say he is dead, he is said *or* reported to be dead; **enfin, ça c'est ce qu'elle dit!** well, that's what she says!

(d) to say; *Enf* **je vais le d. à ma mère** I'm going to tell mum on you; **je vais le d.!** I'm going to tell!; *F* **je vais te dire** let me tell you; *F* **je te dis pas la surprise quand ils sont arrivés!** I can't tell you what a surprise it was when they arrived; **il a fait une tête quand il m'a vue, je te dis pas!** I can't describe the expression on his face when he saw me!; **à vrai d., à d. vrai** to tell the truth, to be truthful; **pour tout (vous) d.** to be honest (with you), to be truthful, to tell (you) the truth; **c'est (tout) d.** need I say more?; **c'est d. s'il t'aime** that shows how much he loves you; **à ce qu'elle dit** according to her; **entre nous soit dit, soit dit entre nous** between ourselves, between you and me, *F* between you, me and the gatepost; **soit dit en passant** *ou* **entre parenthèses** by the by, by the way, incidentally

(e) (*décider*) **aussitôt dit, aussitôt fait** no sooner said than done; **alors c'est dit, voilà qui est dit** (well then) that's settled, that's decided; **disons à quatre heures** let's say four o'clock, four o'clock, say; **ce qui est dit est dit** a promise is a promise; **tenez-vous cela pour dit** don't let me have to tell you again, that's my last word; **mais tout n'est pas dit** but that's not the last of it; **tant que tout n'est pas dit** while things are still up in the air, until things are definite one way or the other; **tant que tout n'est pas dit pour le mariage** until the wedding is definitely going to take place; **il est dit que je resterai célibataire** I'm destined to stay single

(f) (*penser*) to think (**de** of); **alors, qu'est-ce que tu en dis?** well, what do you think?; **qu'en dira-t-on?, qu'est-ce que les gens vont dire?** what will people say *or* think?; **qu'est-ce que tu dirais d'aller au cinéma?** how about going to see a film?; **on aurait dit qu'elle était hypnotisée/que c'était la fin du monde** you would have thought she was hypnotized/it was the end of the world; **avec sa canne, on aurait dit Charlot** he looked like Charlie Chaplin with his cane; **qui eût dit qu'elle se marierait?** who would have thought she'd get married?; **et d. qu'elle n'a que vingt ans!** and to think (that) she's only twenty!; **on dirait qu'il va pleuvoir** it looks like rain; **on dirait qu'il pleut** it looks as if it is raining; **on dirait du Mozart** it sounds like Mozart; **on dirait du gin** it tastes like gin

(g) (*ordonner*) **d. à qn de faire qch** to tell sb to do sth; **faites ce qu'on vous dit** do as you're told; **dites-lui d'entrer** tell *or* ask him to come in; **dites qu'on le fasse entrer** tell *or* ask them to show him in; **le prof a dit de lire le premier chapitre** the teacher said to read the first chapter; **taisez-vous, j'ai dit!** be quiet, I said!; **je ne le dirai pas deux fois!** I won't tell you twice *or* again!

(h) (*protester*) to say; **il est trop tard, je ne peux plus rien d.** it's too late, I can't say anything now; **j'ai eu une augmentation conséquente, je n'ai rien à d.** I got a decent rise, I can't complain; **tu as quelque chose à d. à ça?** have you got any objection?; **très bon travail, rien à d.** this is very good work, I have no complaints; **il y a beaucoup à d. sur ton travail** there's quite a lot I'd like to say about your work; **tu n'as rien à d.!** I don't want to hear a word out of you!; **je n'ai rien à d. contre lui** I have no objection to him; **il n'y a pas à d.** there's no denying it, there's no doubt about it; **il n'y a pas à d.** *ou* **on a beau d., c'est utile d'avoir un homme chez soi** there's no denying that it's useful to have a man about the house; **vous avez beau d. (le contraire)** you can say what you like; **tu as beau d. qu'elle ne ment pas** you can say she doesn't lie until you're blue in the face; **j'ai beau d. (tout ce que je veux), il ne m'écoute jamais** I can talk until I'm blue in the face, he never listens to me; **ce n'est pas pour d., mais** ... I hate to tell you this but ...; **ne pas avoir son mot à d.** not to have any say; **tu n'as pas ton mot à d. sur cette question** you don't have any say in the matter

(i) (*indiquer*) to show, to express; **horloge qui dit l'heure exacte** clock that tells the right time; **cela en dit long sur son courage** it speaks volumes for his courage; *Litt* **sa démarche/son visage disait son désespoir** his despair was evident in his gait/face; **qu'est-ce qui vous dit qu'il viendra?** how do you know he will come?; **ce nom/cette musique ne me dit rien** the name/the music means *or* conveys nothing to me; **quelque chose me dit que ...** something tells me that ...

(j) (*plaire*) to suit, to appeal to; **ça te dit?** what about it?, how about it?; **ça te dit de partir en vacances avec nous?** how about coming on holiday with us?; **si cela te dit, si le cœur t'en dit** if you feel like it; **cela ne me dit (trop) rien, cela ne me dit pas** I don't feel like it; **cela ne me dit trop rien de manger chinois ce soir** I don't feel like eating Chinese this evening; **en hiver, rien ne me dit** I don't feel like doing anything in winter; *F* **alors, ton tricot, qu'est-ce que ça dit?** how did your sweater turn out?; **pour l'instant, il ne dit pas grand chose** it doesn't look like much at the moment; **cela ne me disait rien de bon** *ou* **rien qui vaille** I didn't like the look of it; **le fait qu'il soit si hésitant ne me dit rien de bon** *ou* **rien qui vaille** I don't like the fact *or* I'm a bit concerned that he's hesitating so much

(k) (*réciter*) (*ses prières, la messe*) to say; **d. des vers** *ou* **de la poésie** to recite poetry; **d. son chapelet** to tell one's beads

(l) (*nommer*) **Jacques, dit Jacko** Jacques, also known as *or* alias *or F* aka Jacko; (*en le présentant*) Jacques, or Jacko to us

(m) (*signifier*) **vouloir d.** to mean; **je veux d. ...** that is to say ..., I mean ...; **que voulez-vous d. par là?** what do you mean by that?; **que veut d. ce mot?** what does this word mean?; *F* **ça dit bien ce que ça veut d.** it means what it says; **qu'est-ce à d.?** what does this mean?; **est-ce à d. qu'il ne viendra pas?** does this mean he won't come?; **qui dit bordeaux dit bon vin** Bordeaux is synonymous with good wine

(n) laisse-les d., ils sont stupides! let them talk, they're stupid!; **je me suis laissé d. que ...** I hear that ...

(o) dis donc, je viens de penser qu'on pourrait se voir ce

week-end by the way *or F* hey, I've just had a thought, we could see each other this weekend; **tu as grandi, dis donc!** goodness *or* my word you've grown!; **non mais dis donc, tu ne vas pas recommencer!** you're not going to start up again!; **dis donc, tu te fiches de moi!** you don't give a damn about me, do you!; **ben dis donc!** well I'm damned!; **tu m'emmènes, dis, sur ta moto?** take me for a ride on your motorbike, eh?, go on, give me a ride on your motorbike; **non mais, dis donc!** do you mind!

2 se dire *vpr* **(a)** *(réciproque)* **on se dit bonjour de temps en temps** we say hello from time to time

(b) *(penser)* **je me disais que tout était fini** I thought it was all over; **dis-toi bien que ça aurait pu être plus grave** tell yourself it could have been worse; **je me disais bien que je l'avais déjà vu quelque part** I knew I'd seen him before

(c) *(être correct)* **ça se dit en français?** can you say that in French?; **cela ne se dit pas** that isn't said; **des choses pareilles ne se disent pas** you don't say things like that; **cela se dit d'une personne mais certainement pas d'un objet** you can say that about *or* of a person but definitely not about a thing

(d) *(se croire)* **on se dirait en Suisse** you would think you were in Switzerland; **on se dirait en été** you would think it was summer

(e) *(se prétendre)* **elle se dit écossaise/à Londres** she says she is Scottish/in London

(f) comment ça se dit en français? how do you say that in French?

direct [dirɛkt] **1** *adj* **(a)** *(sans détour)* *(question, chemin)* direct, straight; *(personne)* direct, straightforward; **quel est le chemin le plus d. pour aller à la mairie?** what's the most direct way to get to the town hall; **d'ici, la route est directe** it's a straight road from here; **tu ne peux pas te tromper, c'est d.** you can't go wrong, it's a straight road; **il y a fait une allusion directe** he made a direct reference to it, he referred to it directly

(b) *(sans intermédiaire)* *(impôts, Tél ligne)* direct; **descendre de qn en ligne directe** to be a direct descendant of sb; [①B17-18,2; B49-50,2-3] *Gram* **complément d'objet d.** direct object; **mon supérieur d.** my immediate superior; **il y a des ventes directes au grand public dans leur entrepôt** they sell direct to the public from their warehouse; **être en rapport** *ou* **contact d.** *ou* **en relations directes avec qn** to be in direct contact with sb

(c) *(sans arrêt)* **train d.** through train, fast train; *Av* **vol d.** direct flight

2 *nm* **(a)** *Rad, TV* live broadcasting; **ce n'est jamais du d.** it's never broadcast live; **émission en d.** live broadcast; **vous allez entendre ce concert en d. de l'Opéra de Paris** you will hear this concert live from the Paris Opera House; **d. sur cassette** live-on-tape

(b) *Boxe* straight; **d. du droit/du gauche** straight right/left; **s'il continue de m'énerver, je lui mets un d. au menton** if he keeps on annoying me I'll punch him on the jaw

(c) *Rail* through *or* fast train **(pour** to)

(d) *Ordinat* **en d.** in direct mode

3 *adv F* directly; **je pars d. vers Grenoble** I'm going to Grenoble direct; **s'il recommence, je vais d. chez le proviseur** if he starts again, I'm going straight to the headmaster

directement [dirɛktəmɑ̃] *adv* **(a)** *(sans détour)* straight, directly; **en arrivant, je vais d. au lit** I'm going straight to bed when I arrive; **si tu prends ce chemin, tu arrives d. à la rivière** this road will take you straight to the river; **se précipiter d. sur un endroit/qch** to head straight for a place/sth; **elle est venue d. vers nous** she came straight towards us; **se diriger d. au nord** to go due north; **répondre d. à la question** to give a direct *or* straight answer to the question; **dis-moi d. combien tu veux** tell me straight out how much you want

(b) *(sans intermédiaire)* directly; **expédier des marchandises d. à qn** to send goods direct to sb; **d. du producteur au consommateur** direct *or* straight from the producer to the consumer

directeur, -trice [dirɛktœr, -tris] **1** *n Com* *(qui fait partie du conseil d'administration)* director; *(d'un magasin, d'un service)* manager; *Scol* headmaster, headmistress, *esp Am* principal; *Univ* *(d'une UER)* head; *(de prison)* governor; *(de journal)* editor; *(d'expédition etc)* leader; *Cin, Rad, TV* director **2** *adj* *(équipe, instances)* management, executive; *(force)* directing, managing, controlling; *(principe)* guiding; **comité d.** steering committee; **roue directrice** front wheel; **lignes directrices** guidelines; **l'idée directrice d'un livre** the central theme of a book

▶ **directeur**: **d. des achats** purchasing director/manager; **d. adjoint** deputy director/manager; **d. administratif et financier** administrative and financial manager; **d. administratif** executive director; **d. d'agence** branch manager; *TV, Rad* **d. d'antenne** controller, programme controller, network controller; **d. artistique** artistic director; *TV* production designer; *Journ* art editor, art director; **d. de banque** bank manager; *Pol* **d. de cabinet** *(d'un ministre)* ≈ principal private secretary; *TV, Cin etc* **d. de casting** casting director; *TV, Rad* **d. de chaîne** network controller; **d. de la clientèle** customer relations manager; **d. commercial** sales director/manager; **d. de la communication** communications director/manager; **d. des comptes-clients** accounts director/manager; *Rel* **d. de conscience** spiritual adviser; **d. de la création** creative director; **d. du crédit** credit manager; **d. de division** *(au siège)* divisional director; **d. d'exploitation** operations director/manager; **d. export** export director/manager; **d. financier** financial manager; *(en chef)* financial *or* finance director; **d. général** *(d'un ministère)* ≈ permanent under-secretary; *Com* chief executive officer, managing director; *(d'organisation internationale, EDF etc)* director general; **d. gérant** executive director; **d. (de l') informatique** computer manager; **d. intérimaire** temporary director/manager, interim manager, acting manager; *Journ* **d. de la fabrication** production director/manager; **d. de marché** market manager; **d. du marketing** marketing director/manager; **d. de marque** brand manager; **d. mercatique-vente** sales and marketing director/manager; **d. de la photographie** *Cin* director of photography, cinematographer; *Journ* picture editor; **d. de la publicité** advertising director/manager; **d. du personnel** personnel director/manager; **d. de production** production manager; **d. de produit** product manager, brand manager; **d. de** *ou* **des programmes** director of programmes, programmes director, programme controller; **d. de projet** project director/manager; **d. de recherche et développement** director of research and development, R&D director; **d. de recherche mercatique** marketing research director/manager; **d. de la rédaction** editorial director; **d. régional** regional director/manager, area director/manager, district manager; **d. régional des ventes** regional sales manager; **d. des relations publiques** public relations director/manager; **d. de service** head of department, unit manager; **d. des services techniques** technical director; *Rel* **d. spirituel** spiritual adviser; *TV, Rad* **d. de station** station manager; *TV, Rad* **d. de studio** studio manager; **d. de succursale** branch manager; **d. technique** technical manager; **d. de télévision** television director; *Univ* **d. de thèse** thesis director; **d. des ventes et du marketing** sales and marketing director/manager; **d. des ventes** sales director/manager

directif, -ive [dirɛktif, -iv] *adj Psy* *(entretien, questionnaire)* directive; *(question)* leading, directive; *Péj* *(personne, attitude)* managing; **ces instructions sont purement directives** these instructions are for guidance only; **c'est un chef très d.** he's the kind of manager who takes all the decisions himself; **il a des méthodes très directives** he's very managerial *or F* bossy

direction [dirɛksjɔ̃] *nf* **(a)** *(d'une affaire, d'une usine, d'un théâtre, d'une école)* management, running; *(d'un parti, d'un pays)* leadership; *(d'un procès, d'une enquête)* conduct; *(d'une équipe, de travaux, d'opérations)* management, supervision; **elle a été promue à la d. du journal/du lycée** she's been promoted to editor/headmistress; **orchestre (placé) sous la d. de Karajan** orchestra conducted by Karajan *or Am* under the baton of Karajan; **projet mené sous la d. du Pr. Lacroix** *(qui y a travaillé activement)* project carried out under the leadership of Prof. Lacroix; *(qui l'a supervisé)* project carried out under the supervision of Prof. Lacroix; **c'est lui qui a pris la d. des opérations** he was in charge of operations; **on lui a confié la d. d'une nouvelle équipe de recherches** he was put in charge of a new research team

(b) *(personnes)* *(d'une administration)* management; **une décision prise au niveau de la d.** a management decision; **j'irai me plaindre à la d.** I'll complain to the management

(c) *(lieux)* *(d'un conseil)* offices; *(d'une firme etc)* head office

(d) *Aut, Naut* *(mécanisme)* steering; *Aut* **la d. est un peu raide** the steering's a bit stiff

(e) *(orientation)* direction; *Naut* bearing, course; **changer de d.** to change direction; *Naut* to alter course; **toutes/autres directions** *(sur panneau)* all/all other directions; **ton devoir part dans toutes les directions** your homework goes off in all directions; **quelle d. ont-ils prise?** which way did they go?; **ce train va en d. de Paris** this train is going to

Paris; **ses recherches prennent une nouvelle d.** his research is taking a new direction; **chercher la solution dans une autre d.** to look elsewhere for the solution

▶ **direction**: *Aut* **d. assistée** power steering; **d. collégiale** collegiate management; **d. du contentieux** legal department; **d. des crédits** credit management; *Aut* **d. à crémaillère** rack and pinion steering; **D. départementale de l'action sanitaire et sociale** = office administering health and social services at regional level; **d. des entreprises** business management; **d. financière** financial management; (*service*) finance department; *Admin* **D. générale de la santé** = central administrative body for health and social services; **D. générale des Impôts** ≈ Inland Revenue, *US* IRS; **d. générale** general management, senior management; *Admin* **D. des hôpitaux** central government office for hospital administration; **d. de l'exploitation** operations management; (*service*) operations department; **d. de la production** production control; **d. de la rédaction** editorial department; **D. de la surveillance du territoire** = French secret service; *Aut* **d. mécanique** manual steering; **d. mercatique** marketing department; **d. du personnel** personnel management; (*service*) personnel department; **d. du trésor** finance department

directionnel, -elle [dirɛksjɔnɛl] *adj* (*antenne etc*) directional

directive [dirɛktiv] *nf* directive, order, instruction; *Pol* guideline

directoire [dirɛktwar] *nm* (**a**) *Hist Fr* **le D.** the Directoire (*1795*); **chaise D.** Directoire chair (**b**) executive board

directorial[1]**, -ale, -aux, -ales** [dirɛktɔrjal, -o] *adj Com etc* directorial, managerial

directorial[2]**, -ale, -aux, -ales** [dirɛktɔrjal, -o] *adj Hist Fr* (*constitution, gouvernement*) of the Directoire

directrice [dirɛktris] *nf voir* **directeur**

dirigé [diriʒe] *adj* controlled, managed; **économie dirigée** planned economy; *Scol* **activités dirigées** extra-curricular activities; *Univ* **travaux dirigés** classwork; (*en laboratoire*) lab work, practicals

dirigeable [diriʒabl] **1** *adj* dirigible **2** *nm Av* dirigible (balloon), airship

dirigeant, -ante [diriʒɑ̃, ɑ̃t] **1** *adj* (*principe, philosophie etc*) guiding; **classes dirigeantes** ruling classes; *Pol* **le rôle d. du parti Communiste** the leading role of the Communist Party **2** *n* (*d'un parti etc*) leader; (*d'un pays*) leader, ruler; **d. d'entreprise** company manager; **d. syndical** union leader

diriger [diriʒe] (**je dirigeai(s); n. dirigeons**) **1** *vt* (**a**) (*être à la tête de*) (*entreprise, affaire, usine, théâtre, école etc*) to manage, to run; (*pays*) to lead, to run; (*orchestre*) to conduct; (*journal*) to edit; (*expédition, débat*) to lead; (*procès, enquête, séance etc*) to conduct; (*travaux, une équipe*) to manage, to supervise; (*circulation*) to direct; **d. la production** to control production

(**b**) (*orienter*) (*fusil, arme, télescope*) to aim, to level, to point (**sur** at); (*personne*) to direct; (*navire*) to steer, to navigate; **d. un colis sur Paris** to send a parcel off to Paris; **d. ses pas vers …** to go *or* move towards …, to direct one's steps towards …; **peux-tu d. ta lampe vers le plafond?** can you move your lamp so it's pointing towards the ceiling?; **d. son regard vers** *ou* **sur qn/qch** to look at sb/sth; **d. son attention sur qch** to turn one's attention to sth; **d. ses accusations contre qn** to level *or* aim accusations at sb; **vers qui sont dirigées tes critiques?** who is your criticism aimed at?; **les filles sont souvent dirigées vers des études littéraires** girls are often steered towards arts subjects

2 se diriger *vpr* (**a**) (*aller*) **se d. vers un endroit** to make for *or* head for a place, to make one's way towards a place; **le navire se dirigea vers le port** the ship steered *or* headed for the harbour; **se d. vers qn** to go up to sb; **nous nous dirigeons vers une crise encore plus profonde** we are heading for an even greater crisis; **de plus en plus de femmes se dirigent vers l'informatique** more and more women are going into computers

(**b**) (*s'orienter*) **se d. à l'aide d'une boussole/du soleil** to use a compass/the sun to guide oneself; **je n'arrive jamais à me d. dans le noir** I can never find my way around in the dark

dirigisme [diriʒism] *nm Écon* state control, dirigisme

dirigiste [diriʒist] *Écon* **1** *adj* **système d.** state-controlled economy **2** *n* advocate of a state-controlled economy

discal, -ale, -aux, -ales [diskal, -o] *adj Méd* **hernie discale** slipped disc

discernable [disɛrnabl] *adj* discernible, visible

discernement [disɛrnəmɑ̃] *nm* (**a**) (*distinction*) discrimination (**de … et de …** between … and …) (**b**) (*jugement*) judgment, discernment; **agir sans d.** to act rashly

discerner [disɛrne] *vt* (**a**) (*distinguer*) to discern, to distinguish; **on discernait une maison dans le lointain** we could (just) see *or* make out a house in the distance (**b**) (*différencier*) **d. qch de qch** to distinguish sth from sth, to discriminate between sth and sth; **d. le bien du mal** to tell right from wrong (**c**) (*sentir*) to detect, to discern; **d. de la tristesse dans la voix de qn** to detect a note of sadness in sb's voice

disciple [disipl] *n* disciple, follower

disciplinable [disiplinabl] *adj* that can be disciplined

disciplinaire [disiplinɛr] *adj* (*mesure, sanction etc*) disciplinary

discipline [disiplin] *nf* (**a**) (*règlement*) discipline; **maintenir la d.** to maintain discipline *or* order; **un prof qui ne sait pas maintenir la d.** a teacher who cannot keep discipline (**b**) *Scol* (*matière*) subject, discipline, branch of learning; **quelles sont les disciplines enseignées ici?** what subjects are taught here? (**c**) (*fouet*) scourge

discipliné [disipline] *adj* disciplined

discipliner [disipline] **1** *vt* (*élèves*) to control, to maintain discipline over; **d. ses cheveux avec de la laque** to control one's hair with lacquer; *Fig* **d. ses instincts** to curb one's instincts **2 se discipliner** *vpr* to discipline oneself, to exercise self-control

disc-jockey, *pl* **disc-jockeys** [diskʒɔkɛ] *nm* disc-jockey

disco[1] [disko] *adj, nm inv* (**musique**) **d.** disco (music)

disco[2] *nf* (*abrév* **discothèque**) *F* disco

discobole [diskɔbɔl] *nm Sp* discus thrower

discographie [diskɔgrafi] *nf* discography

discographique [diskɔgrafik] *adj* (*rubrique, production*) record

discoïde [diskɔid], **discoïdal, -ale, -aux, -ales** [diskɔidal, -o] *adj* disc-shaped, *Spéc* discoid(al)

discompte [diskɔ̃t] *nm* discount

discontinu [diskɔ̃tiny] **1** *adj* discontinuous; (*ligne*) broken **2** *nm* discontinuity

discontinuer [diskɔ̃tinɥe] **1** *vi* to stop, to discontinue; **parler pendant des heures sans d.** to talk for hours on end without stopping *or* without a break **2** *vt Litt* to stop, to discontinue

discontinuité [diskɔ̃tinɥite] *nf* discontinuity

disconvenir [diskɔ̃vnir] *vi* (*conj like* **venir**, *the aux is* **avoir**) **d. de qch** not to agree with sth; **je n'en disconviens pas** I admit it, I don't deny it

discophile [diskɔfil] *n* record enthusiast

discordance [diskɔrdɑ̃s] *nf* (*de sons*) discordance, dissonance; (*d'opinions*) difference; (*de personnalités, couleurs*) clash

discordant [diskɔrdɑ̃] *adj* (*son*) discordant, dissonant; (*bruit*) grating, jarring; (*couleurs, personnalités*) clashing; (*preuves, opinions etc*) conflicting

discorde [diskɔrd] *nf* discord, dissension, strife; **semer la d.** to make trouble, to sow discord

discorder [diskɔrde] *vi* (*de couleurs, témoignages*) to clash (**avec** with); **sa voix discorde dans l'orchestre** her voice clashes with the orchestra

discothèque [diskɔtɛk] *nf* (**a**) (*organisme*) record library; (*collection*) record collection *or* library; (*meuble*) record cabinet (**b**) (*boîte de nuit*) discothèque, *F* disco

discount [diskunt] *nm* (**a**) (*rabais*) discount (**b**) (*magasin*) discount shop *or* store

discounter[1] [diskunte] *vt* to reduce the price of; **tout est discounté** there's a discount on everything, everything's reduced

discounter[2]**, discounteur** [diskuntœr] *nm* discount shop *or* store; (*personne*) discount trader

discoureur, -euse [diskurœr, -øz] *n Péj* speechifier

discourir [diskurir] *vi* (*conj like* **courir**) to discourse, *Péj* to air one's opinions (**sur** on)

discours [diskur] *nm* (**a**) (*allocution*) speech; **prononcer** *ou* **faire un d.** to make a speech; *Pol* **d-programme** policy statement; **d. d'ouverture** opening speech; **d. de clôture** closing speech; **d. du trône** Speech from the Throne (**b**) (*exposé*) discourse, dissertation, treatise; *Littér* **le D. de la méthode** the Discourse on Method (**c**) [ⓘ**A61**,21; **A73**,viii] (*langage*) speech; *Gram* **parties du d.**, parts of speech; **d. indirect/direct** indirect/direct *or* reported speech; **d. rapporté** reported speech (**d**) (*paroles*) talk; **tenir un d. à qn** to address sb at length; **se perdre en longs d.** to talk endlessly; **elle a** *ou* **tient un d. très clair** she speaks very clearly; **tous ces beaux d. ne nous avancent à rien** all this talk isn't getting us anywhere

discourtois [diskurtwa] *adj* discourteous

discourtoisement [diskurtwazmɑ̃] *adv* discourteously

discourtoisie [diskurtwazi] *nf Arch* discourtesy

discrédit [diskredi] *nm* discredit, loss of credit; **être en d. auprès de qn** to be in disfavour with sb; **jeter le d. sur qn** to bring discredit on sb

discréditer [diskredite] **1** *vt* (*théorie etc*) to discredit **2 se discréditer** *vpr* (*d'une idée, d'une théorie*) to become discredited (**auprès** *ou* **aux yeux de qn** in sb's eyes); (*d'une personne*) to discredit oneself (**auprès** *ou* **aux yeux de qn** with sb)

discret, -ète [diskrɛ, -ɛt] *adj* (**a**) (*plein de retenue*) (*personne, comportement etc*) discreet; **sous pli d.** under plain cover; **tu sauras rester d.?** you'll keep it to yourself, won't you?; *Iron* **il m'énerve avec ses allusions discrètes** those subtle hints of his are getting on my nerves; **sois d., il ne faut pas qu'elle l'apprenne** don't go repeating this, she mustn't find out (**b**) (*modeste*) (*personne*) quiet, unobtrusive, unassuming; (*vêtements*) sober, simple, plain; (*apparence*) inconspicuous; (*endroit*) quiet, secluded; **une discrète touche de bleu** a discreet touch of blue (**c**) *Math* (*quantité*) discrete; *Phys* (*fonction*) discontinuous

discrètement [diskrɛtmɑ̃] *adv* (**a**) (*avec retenue*) discreetly, with discretion; **il lui a parlé d.** he had a quiet word with him (**b**) (*modestement*) quietly, modestly, simply; **maquillé d.** discreetly made up

discrétion [diskresjɔ̃] *nf* (**a**) (*retenue*) discretion; **avoir de la d.** to be discreet; **d. assurée** discretion guaranteed; **la d. d'une intervention** the discreetness of an intervention; **user de qch avec d.** to use sth in moderation (**b**) (*sobriété*) **la d. avec laquelle elle se conduit** her unassuming behaviour; **s'habiller avec d.** to dress simply *or* plainly; **elle se maquille avec d.** she is always discreetly made up (**c**) **être à la d. de qn** to be in sb's hands; **pain à d.** unlimited bread, as much bread as one wants

discrétionnaire [diskresjɔnɛr] *adj* (*pouvoirs etc*) discretionary

discrètos [diskrɛtɔs] *adv F* on the quiet

discriminant [diskriminɑ̃] **1** *adj* discriminating **2** *nm Math* discriminant

discrimination [diskriminasjɔ̃] *nf* discrimination; **ils étaient victimes de d.** they were victims of discrimination, they were discriminated against; **d. raciale/sexuelle** racial/sexual discrimination; **sans d. de race ni de sexe** regardless of race or sex, without discrimination on the grounds of race or sex

discriminatoire [diskriminatwar] *adj* discriminatory, discriminating

discriminer [diskrimine] *vt Litt* to discriminate, to distinguish

disculpation [diskylpasjɔ̃] *nf* exoneration; **sa d. n'a pas été facile à obtenir** it was not easy to clear him *or* to prove him innocent

disculper [diskylpe] **1** *vt* **d. qn** to clear sb, to prove sb innocent, to exonerate sb (**de** of) **2 se discriminer** *vpr* to clear oneself, to prove oneself innocent (**de** of)

discursif, -ive [diskyrsif, -iv] *adj* discursive

discussion [diskysjɔ̃] *nf* discussion; (*plus passionnée*) argument; (*émission*) discussion programme; **avoir une d.** to have a discussion/an argument (**sur, à propos de** about); **la question est en d.** the question is under discussion; **sans d. possible** indisputably; **il s'exécuta sans d.** he complied without arguing (the point); **pas de d., au travail!** don't argue, get to work!

discutable [diskytabl] *adj* debatable, questionable; **tu as agi d'une manière qui est tout à fait d.** your behaviour was altogether questionable

discutailler [diskytaje] *vi F Péj* (*chicaner*) to quibble

discuté [diskyte] *adj* (*question*) disputed; (*livre, sujet*) much discussed; **être très d.** to be hotly disputed *or* the subject of much discussion

discuter [diskyte] **1** *vt* (*examiner*) to discuss, to debate; (*contester*) to question, to dispute; **d. un droit** to dispute a right; **d. un problème** to discuss a problem; **discutons la chose** let's discuss it, let's talk it over; *F* **d. le coup** *ou* **le bout de gras** to have a natter *or* a chat; **prix à d.** negotiable

2 *vi* (**a**) (*parler*) to discuss; (*débattre*) to debate; **d. avec qn sur qch** to debate sth with sb; **d. de politique** to discuss *or* talk politics, to argue about politics; **il faut qu'on en discute** we must discuss it; **d. du prix de qch** to haggle over the price of sth; **on ne peut pas d. avec toi** it's impossible to have a discussion with you; **on pourrait peut-être d. avant de se battre?** could we discuss it first before we start fighting?

(**b**) (*protester*) to argue (**avec** with); **ne discutez pas** no arguing, don't argue; **il n'y a pas à d.** I don't want any arguments *or* arguing; **suis-moi sans d.** follow me without any arguments, follow me and don't argue; **on ne discute pas avec la loi** the law's the law

3 se discuter *vpr* to be discussed *or* debated; **ça se discute** that's debatable

disert [dizɛr] *adj Litt* eloquent, fluent

disette [dizɛt] *nf* scarcity, *Fml* dearth; **d. d'eau** drought; **vivre dans la d.** to live in poverty

diseur, -euse [dizœr, -øz] *n* (**a**) **d./diseuse de bonne aventure** fortune teller (**b**) (*qui déclame*) orator

disgrâce [disgrɑs] *nf* disfavour, disgrace; **encourir la d. de qn** to incur sb's displeasure; **tomber en d.** (**auprès de qn**) to fall into disfavour (with sb)

disgracié [disgrasje] *adj* out of favour, in disgrace

disgracier [disgrasje] *vt* (*impf & pr sub* **n. disgraciions, v. disgraciiez**) (*ministre*) to dismiss

disgracieux, -ieuse [disgrasjø, -jøz] *adj* (*personne, mouvement, geste*) awkward, ungraceful; (*visage etc*) ugly

disjoindre [disʒwɛ̃dr] (*conj like* **joindre**) **1** *vt* to separate, to take apart; *Jur* **d. deux causes** to treat two cases separately **2 se disjoindre** *vpr* to come apart, to separate

disjoint [disʒwɛ̃] *adj* (*pièces*) separated; (*problèmes*) unconnected, separate

disjoncter [disʒɔ̃kte] *Él* **1** *vt* (*circuit*) to break **2** *vi* to fuse; *Aut* to cut out; *Fig F* to crack up

disjoncteur [disʒɔ̃ktœr] *nm Él* circuit breaker, cut-out

disjonctif, -ive [disʒɔ̃ktif, -iv] *adj* [ⓘ**B19,5**] disjunctive

disjonction [disʒɔ̃ksjɔ̃] *nf* (*de tuyaux, lames de parquet*) separation

dislocation [dislɔkasjɔ̃] *nf* (*d'une articulation*) dislocation; (*d'une machine etc*) taking to pieces, dismantling; (*d'un empire, d'un état etc*) dismemberment; *Géol* fault; *Mil etc* (*des troupes etc*) dispersal, breaking up

disloqué [dislɔke] *adj* (*épaule, genou*) dislocated; (*machine*) dismantled; (*empire, état etc*) dismembered, broken up

disloquer [dislɔke] **1** *vt* (*épaule, genou*) to dislocate; (*machine*) to take to pieces, to dismantle; (*troupes*) to break up, to disperse; (*empire, état*) to break up, to dismember **2 se disloquer** *vpr* (*d'un empire*) to break up, to fall to pieces; **son bras s'est disloqué** he's dislocated his arm

disparaître [disparɛtr] *vi* (*conj like* **paraître**) (**a**) (*s'en aller*) to disappear, to vanish; **elle a disparu sans laisser de traces** she has disappeared *or* vanished without trace; **la petite fille a disparu il y a une semaine** the little girl disappeared *or* went missing a week ago; *F* **disparais, je t'ai assez vu** clear off, I've had enough of you

(**b**) (*devenir invisible*) to disappear, to vanish; **d. dans la foule** to disappear *or* vanish into the crowd; *F* **d. de la circulation** to vanish from *or* drop out of circulation; **d. aux regards** to vanish from sight, to disappear from view

(**c**) (*mourir*) to die; **tous ses amis ont disparu** all his friends have died *or* are dead; *Naut* **disparu en mer** lost at sea; **faire d. qn** to get rid of sb

(**d**) (*finir*) (*d'un bouton*) to disappear, to vanish, to go away; (*d'une mode, d'une tradition*) to die out; **faire d. une tache/une difficulté** to get rid of *or* remove a stain/a difficulty; **faire d. la douleur** to make the pain disappear *or* go; **j'ai pris un cachet pour faire d. la douleur** I took a pill to relieve *or* get rid of the pain; **sa timidité disparaît peu à peu** his shyness is wearing off

disparate [disparat] *adj* (*différent*) dissimilar, *Fml* disparate; (*qui ne s'accorde pas*) ill-matched, ill-assorted; **couleurs disparates** clashing colours; **ils ont un mobilier très d.** no two pieces of their furniture are alike *or* the same

disparité [disparite] *nf* disparity

disparition [disparisjɔ̃] *nf* (**a**) (*départ, absence*) disappearance; **remarquer la d. de qch** to notice that sth has disappeared; **j'ai remarqué la d. de ma carte de crédit deux jours plus tard** I first missed my credit card two days later; **sa d. date de 6 mois** he disappeared or vanished six months ago, he has been missing for six months (**b**) (*mort*) death; **depuis la d. de son mari** since the death of her husband, since her husband died; **la d. des dinosaures ne s'est pas faite en un jour** dinosaurs did not disappear *or* vanish *or* die out overnight

disparu, -ue [dispary] **1** *adj* (**a**) *Mil* missing (in action); **être porté d.** to be reported missing; **marin d. en mer** sailor lost at sea (**b**) (*race, espèce etc*) extinct; (*monde, époque etc*) vanished, bygone (**c**) (*invisible*) **la cicatrice une fois disparue** once the scar has/had disappeared; **aussitôt le soleil d., elle rentra** she went home as soon as the sun had disappeared **2** *n* (**a**) (*défunt*) deceased; **nos chers disparus** our dear departed (**b**) *Mil* missing soldier (*believed dead*), *US* MIA (= missing in action)

dispatcher¹ [dispatʃœr, -ɛr] *nm* dispatcher

dispatcher² [dispatʃe] *vt* to dispatch

dispatching [dispatʃiŋ] *nm* dispatching; *Journ* assignment list

dispendieusement [dispɑ̃djøzmɑ̃] *adv Fml* expensively

dispendieux, -ieuse [dispɑ̃djø, -jøz] *adj* (*goûts, procédure etc*) expensive

dispensaire [dispɑ̃sɛr] *nm* free clinic, free health centre

dispensateur, -trice [dispɑ̃satœr, -tris] *n* (*de charité, justice etc*) dispenser

dispense [dispɑ̃s] *nf* **(a)** (*du service militaire etc*) exemption; *Rel* dispensation; **d. d'âge** age dispensation; **une d. d'âge peut être accordée dans les cas où ...** the age limit may be waived in cases where ... **(b)** (*certificat*) (certificate of) exemption

dispenser [dispɑ̃se] **1** *vt* **(a) d. qn de (faire) qch** to excuse *or* exempt sb from (doing) sth; **d. qn du service militaire** to exempt sb from military service; **dispensez-moi de ce voyage** spare me this journey; **se faire d. de sport** to be excused *or* let off sport, to get off sport; *Rel* **d. qn d'un vœu** to release sb from a vow; **je vous dispense de vos commentaires** you can keep your remarks to yourself **(b)** (*charité, faveurs etc*) to dispense, to distribute; *Méd* **d. des soins** to dispense care **2 se dispenser** *vpr* **se d. de (faire) qch** to get out of (doing) sth; **on peut s'en d.** we can do without it; *Hum* **il se dispense toujours de dire bonjour** he never says hello; **c'est un élève qui peut se d. de travailler en français** he can afford not to work at his French

dispersal [dispɛrsal] *nm Av* apron

dispersant [dispɛrsɑ̃] *nm Ch* dispersant, dispersal agent

dispersé [dispɛrse] *adj* (*feuilles, famille etc*) scattered, dispersed; (*travail etc*) lacking in order, disorganized

disperser [dispɛrse] **1** *vt* (*foule, famille*) to disperse, to scatter, to break up; (*feuilles*) to disperse, to scatter, to spread (far and wide); **d. une armée** to rout an army; *Fig* **d. son attention sur plusieurs choses** to divide one's attention among several things **2 se disperser** *vpr* (*de nuages*) to disperse, to break up; (*de foule, de famille*) to disperse, to scatter, to break up; *Fig* **tu as tendance à trop te d.** you tend to spread yourself too thin(ly)

dispersion [dispɛrsjɔ̃] *nf* **(a)** (*des gens, des feuilles*) scattering, dispersal; (*de la foule, des nuages*) dispersal, breaking up; (*de l'armée*) rout; *Fig* **la d. d'un esprit** an unfocused mind **(b)** *Opt* (*de la lumière*) dispersion, decomposition

disponibilité [dispɔnibilite] *nf* (*de personne, de sièges, de capital etc*) availability; **il a une grande d. d'esprit** he has a very receptive mind; *Mil* **la d.** the reserve; **mettre qn en d.** *Ind* (*en chômage*) to lay sb off; *Mil* to release sb temporarily from duty; **prendre une d.** to take a sabbatical, to take leave of absence; **demander une mise en d.** to ask for (a) leave of absence; *Com* **d. numérique** stock holding distribution; *Fin* **disponibilités** available funds, liquid assets

disponible [dispɔnibl] **1** *adj* available; (*actif*) liquid; **places disponibles** vacant *or* unoccupied seats; **il n'y avait plus un siège d.** there weren't any seats left, no seats were available; **êtes-vous d. ce soir?** are you free tonight?; *Mil* **officier d.** unattached officer, half-pay officer **2** *nm* **(a)** *Com* **marché du d.** spot market **(b)** *Fin* **le d.** liquid assets **(c)** *Mil* reservist

dispos [dispo] *adj* fit and well, in good form; **frais et d.** raring to go, *surtout Am* bright-eyed and bushy-tailed; **esprit d.** alert mind; **je n'ai pas l'esprit d. aujourd'hui** I don't feel very alert today

disposé [dispoze] *adj* **(a)** (*personne*) **être bien/mal d.** to be in a good/bad mood; **être bien d. pour** *ou* **envers qn** to be well disposed towards sb; **être** *ou* **se sentir d. à faire qch** to feel disposed *or* willing *or* in the mood to do sth; **je suis tout d. à pardonner** I am quite willing *or* fully prepared to forgive **(b)** (*arrangé*) arranged, set out; **fleurs disposées avec goût** tastefully arranged flowers

disposer [dispoze] **1** *vt* **(a)** (*objets*) to set out, to arrange; (*table*) to lay, to set; **il faudra d. le salon autrement** the living room will have to be re-arranged; **comment vas-tu d. les invités?** what are the seating arrangements for the guests?

(b) d. qn à (faire) qch to dispose *or* incline sb to (do) sth

2 *vi* **(a) d. de qn/qch** to have sb/sth at one's disposal; **disposez de moi** I am at your service; **toutes les heures dont je puis d.** every hour I can spare; **les renseignements dont je dispose** the information at my disposal; **vous pouvez en d.** you may use it; **d. de ses biens en faveur de qn** to dispose of *or* make over one's property to sb; **le droit des peuples à d. d'eux-mêmes** the right of people to self-determination

(b) *Fml* (*partir*) **vous pouvez d.** that will be all, you may go

(c) (*décider*) *Prov* **l'homme propose, Dieu dispose** man proposes, God disposes

3 se disposer *vpr* **se d. à qch/à faire qch** to get ready for sth/to do sth; **se d. à partir** to get ready to leave

dispositif [dispozitif] *nm* **(a)** *Tech* device; **d. de commande/de manœuvre** driving/controlling gear *or* mechanism; **d. de sûreté** safety device

(b) (*ensemble de moyens*) system, machinery; *Mil* plan of action; (*des troupes dans une bataille etc*) disposition, deployment; **d. d'attaque** attack force; **d. de défense** defence system

▶ **dispositif**: *Ordinat* **d. d'alimentation** power unit; (*pour papier*) sheet feed; **d. d'alimentation feuille à feuille** (*d'une imprimante*) cut sheet feed, stacker; **d. d'alimentation papier** (*d'une imprimante*) sheet feed, paper feed; *Aut* **d. antidémarrage** engine immobilizer; *Aut* **d. d'avance centrifuge** centrifugal advance mechanism; *TV etc* **d. de balayage** scanner; *TV etc* **d. de colorisation** colourizer; **d. de coupure** cut-out (device); **d. d'entraînement à traction** (*d'une imprimante*) tractor feed; *Ordinat* **d. de pointage à boule** trackball; *Aut* **d. de préchauffage** pre-heater; *Télécom* **d. de redirection d'appel** call-forwarding device; *Ordinat* **d. de sortie** output device; *Aut* **d. de verrouillage 'sécurité enfant'** child lock; *Ordinat* **d. de visualisation** display unit

disposition [dispozisjɔ̃] *nf* **(a)** (*arrangement*) (*d'une maison, d'un jardin etc*) layout; (*de texte, clavier*) layout; **réfléchir à la d. des sièges** to think about the seating plan; **d. du terrain** lie of the land; **comment est la d. des lieux?** what's the layout of the place?

(b) (*disponibilité*) disposal; **avoir la libre d. de son bien** to be free to dispose of one's property; **libre d. de soi-même** self-determination; **d. fiscale** tax provision; *Fin* **d. à vue** sight clause; **avoir qch à sa d.** to have sth at one's disposal; **mettre qch à la d. de qn** to put *or* place sth at sb's disposal, to make sth available to sb; **je suis à votre (entière) d.** I am at your disposal *or* (entirely) at your service

(c) (*humeur*) **être dans de bonnes/mauvaises dispositions** to be in a good/bad mood; **être dans de bonnes dispositions à l'égard de qn** to be favourably disposed towards sb; **choisis un jour où il sera dans les meilleures dispositions possibles pour t'écouter/te voir** choose a day when he'll be most likely to give you a favourable hearing/see you; **dans quelles dispositions est-il?** what kind of mood is he in?; **être en bonne d. pour faire qch** to be disposed *or* inclined *or* in the mood to do sth

(d) (*dons*) **avoir des dispositions pour qch** to have a natural ability *or* an aptitude for sth; **dispositions naturelles pour la musique** aptitude *or* natural bent for music; **cet enfant a des dispositions** he is a (naturally) gifted child

(e) (*tendance*) tendency, predisposition; **avoir une d. au rhumatisme** to have a tendency *or* to be predisposed to rheumatism; **d. à pleurer souvent** tendency to cry a lot

(f) dispositions (*préparatifs*) arrangements; **prendre des dispositions pour faire qch** to make the necessary arrangements to do sth; **prends tes dispositions pour être libre ce jour-là** make arrangements *or* arrange to be free that day; **vous n'avez qu'à prendre vos dispositions** you'll just have to make arrangements

(g) *Jur* **dispositions** (*d'un testament*) provisions, conditions; (*d'une loi*) clauses, provisions, conditions; **les dispositions contenues dans l'article 34** the provisions of article 34

disproportion [disprɔpɔrsjɔ̃] *nf* lack of proportion, disproportion **(entre** between)

disproportionné [disprɔpɔrsjɔne] *adj* out of proportion, disproportionate **(par rapport à, avec** to)

dispute [dispyt] *nf* **(a)** (*querelle*) dispute, quarrel, *Fml* altercation; **c'est un sujet de d. entre eux** it is a subject of dispute *or* bone of contention between them **(b)** *Arch* (*débat*) debate; **sujet en d.** subject under discussion

disputé [dispyte] *adj* **une question très disputée** a very controversial *or* hotly disputed matter; **un match très d.** a very hard-fought match; **ce poste sera très d.** there will be a lot of competition for the position; **c'est un héritage d. par tous les membres de la famille** the entire family is quarrelling over the inheritance

disputer [dispyte] **1** *vt* **(a)** (*contester*) **d. qch à qn** to contend with sb for sth; *Fml* **je ne peux imaginer palais qui puisse le d. en splendeur** I cannot imagine a palace to rival this one in splendour

(b) *Sp* **d. un match** to play a match; **d. une course (sur mille mètres)** to run a (thousand metre) race; *Fig* **d. le terrain** to fight every inch of the way

(c) *F* **d. qn** to tick *or* tell sb off; **il s'est fait d. par son père** he got ticked off *or* told off by his father, he got a ticking off *or* telling off from his father

2 *vi* **(a)** (*discuter*) to quarrel, to argue **(avec** with); **d. d'un sujet avec qn** to quarrel *or* argue with sb about *or* over a subject

(b) *Fml* (*rivaliser*) **d. de zèle/d'élégance avec qn** to vie with sb in zeal/elegance

3 se disputer *vpr* **(a)** (*se quereller*) to quarrel, to argue, to wrangle (**pour** over, about, **avec** with)
(b) (*se battre pour*) to fight for; **deux chiens qui se disputent un os** two dogs fighting over a bone; **ils se disputent à qui aura le plus gros morceau** they are arguing about who should get the biggest piece
(c) (*se jouer*) **le match se disputera à Wimbledon** the match will be played *or* will take place at Wimbledon; **la finale devrait se disputer entre les USA et l'Australie** the final is expected to be between the USA and Australia

disquaire [diskɛr] *n* record shop owner; **en vente chez tous les disquaires** on sale in all record shops

disqualification [diskalifikasjɔ̃] *nf Sp* disqualification

disqualifier [diskalifje] (*pr sub & impf* **n. disqualifiions, v. disqualifiiez**) **1** *vt* **(a)** *Sp* to disqualify **(b)** *Litt* (*discréditer*) to discredit **2 se disqualifier** *vpr* to disgrace oneself

disque [disk] *nm* **(a)** disc, *US* disk; *Rail* disc signal; *Aut* **frein à d.** disc brake; **appareil photo à disques** disc camera **(b)** *Mus* record; **mettre un d.** to play a record; *Fig F* **changer de d.** to change the record *or* subject **(c)** *Ordinat* disk; **station de travail sans d.** diskless workstation **(d)** *Sp* discus; **lanceur de d.** discus thrower; **arriver deuxième au lancer de d.** to come second in the discus

▶ **disque**: *Ordinat* **d. amovible** removable disk; **d. audionumérique** compact disc; *Ordinat* **d. cible** target disk; **d. compact** compact disc, CD; **d. compact vidéo** video compact disc; *Ordinat* **d. de démarrage** boot disk; *Ordinat* **d. de destination** target disk, destination disk; *Ordinat* **d. dur** hard disk; *Aut* **d. d'embrayage** clutch plate *or* disc; *Ordinat* **d. fixe** fixed disk; *Anat* **d. intervertébral** (intervertebral) disc; **d. laser** laser disc; **d. magnétique** magnetic disk; *Ordinat* **d. magnéto-optique** optical disk, optomagnetic disk; **d. maître** master disk; **d. microsillon** long-playing record, LP; *Ordinat* **d. optique** optical disk; *Ordinat* **d. souple** floppy disk; *Admin Aut* **d. de stationnement** parking disc; **d. de système** system disk; **d. en vinyle** vinyl disc

disquette [diskɛt] *nf Ordinat* diskette, disk, *F* floppy (disk); **sur d.** on diskette, on floppy; **d. de copie** copy disk; **d. de démarrage** boot disk, start-up disk; **d. de démonstration**, *F* **d. démo** demo disk; **d. de distribution** master disk; **d. haute densité** high-density disk; **d. d'installation** installation disk, installer; **d. optique** optical disk, floptical disk; **d. d'origine** source disk; **d. programme** program disk; **d. système** system disk, systems disk; **d. de travail** working disk, work disk; **d. vierge** blank unformatted disk

disruptif, -ive [disryptif, -iv] *adj* (*force, décharge électrique etc*) disruptive

dissection [disɛksjɔ̃] *nf* (*d'un corps, d'une œuvre littéraire etc*) dissection

dissemblable [disɑ̃blabl] *adj* dissimilar, unlike; **d. à qch** unlike sth, different from *or Am* than sth

dissemblance [disɑ̃blɑ̃s] *nf* dissimilarity, difference (**entre** between)

dissémination [diseminasjɔ̃] *nf* (*de graines, de peuple, d'amis etc*) scattering; (*de germes*) spreading; *Mil* (*de troupes*) deployment; (*d'idées*) spread, dissemination; (*de nouvelles*) spread; **la d. de notre famille date de deux siècles** our family has been scattered for two centuries; **depuis la d. de mon groupe d'amis** since my group of friends scattered *or* broke up; **le territoire est si étendu que cela favorise la d. des entreprises** the vastness of the area means that companies tend to be spread rather thinly

disséminer [disemine] **1** *vt* (*graines, groupe d'amis, peuple etc*) to scatter; (*germes*) to spread; *Mil* (*troupes*) to deploy; (*idées*) to spread, to disseminate; (*nouvelles*) to spread; **les écoles sont très disséminées** the schools are very thin on the ground **2 se disséminer** *vpr* to be scattered (**dans** about)

dissension [disɑ̃sjɔ̃] *nf* dissension, discord

dissentiment [disɑ̃timɑ̃] *nm* disagreement

disséquer [diseke] *vt* (**je dissèque**; **je disséquerai**) (*cadavre, œuvre littéraire etc*) to dissect

dissertation [disɛrtasjɔ̃] *nf* **(a)** *Scol* essay **(b)** *Vieilli* (*étude*) dissertation (**sur** (up)on)

disserter [disɛrte] *vi* **(a) d. sur un sujet** to discourse on a subject **(b)** *Péj* (*parler beaucoup*) to talk at length, *F* to hold forth; **d. pendant des heures** to hold forth for hours

dissidence [disidɑ̃s] *nf Rel, Pol* dissidence, dissent; **la d.** the dissidents, the dissident movement

dissident, -ente [disidɑ̃, -ɑ̃t] **1** *adj Pol* dissident; *Rel* dissenting **2** *n Pol* dissident; *Rel* dissenter, nonconformist

dissimilation [disimilasjɔ̃] *nf Ling* dissimilation

dissimilitude [disimilityd] *nf* dissimilarity

dissimulateur, -trice [disimylatœr, -tris] **1** *adj* dissembling **2** *n* dissembler, deceiver

dissimulation [disimylasjɔ̃] *nf* **(a)** (*hypocrisie*) dissembling, deceit; **agir avec d.** to act in an underhand way **(b)** (*de la vérité, de ses sentiments*) concealment; (*d'une faute*) covering up; *Jur* **d. d'actif** (fraudulent) concealment of assets

dissimulé [disimyle] *adj* **(a)** (*caché*) (*sentiments, défauts, rides etc*) hidden, concealed; **avec un plaisir non d.** with unconcealed delight **(b)** (*secret*) (*homme, caractère*) secretive

dissimuler [disimyle] **1** *vt* (*sentiments, vérité*) to hide, to conceal; (*faute*) to cover up; **d. qch à qn** to hide sth *or* keep sth (back) from sb; **il se dissimule la vérité** he's deceiving himself; **le rideau dissimule le siège des WC** the curtain screens off the lavatory; **d. ses revenus** to conceal one's income; **je ne (vous) dissimule pas que je souhaite partir** I cannot hide the fact that I want to leave **2 se dissimuler** *vpr* to be hidden, to hide; **sa jalousie ne peut se d.** he cannot hide his jealousy; **parmi tant de qualités se dissimule un défaut** a weakness lies hidden *or* lurks among so many qualities

dissipateur, -trice [disipatœr, -tris] **1** *n* spendthrift, squanderer, waster **2** *adj* (*personne*) spendthrift; (*gestion*) wasteful

dissipation [disipasjɔ̃] *nf* **(a)** (*d'argent*) squandering, wasting; (*de temps, d'énergie*) wasting; (*de nuages*) dispersal; (*de craintes, soupçons*) dispelling; (*de malentendu*) clearing up; **après d. des brouillards matinaux** after the morning mist lifts *or* clears; **d. calorique** heat dissipation **(b)** (*débauche*) dissipation, dissolute living; **une vie de d.** a dissolute life, a life of dissipation **(c)** (*à l'école*) inattentiveness, lack of attention

dissipé [disipe] *adj* **(a)** (*débauché*) dissipated, dissolute; **mener une vie dissipée** to lead a riotous life **(b)** *Scol* (*élève*) inattentive

dissiper [disipe] **1** *vt* **(a)** (*argent*) to squander, to waste; (*temps, énergie*) to waste; (*nuages*) to disperse, to scatter, to dispel; (*brouillard*) to disperse, to clear away, to dispel; (*malentendu*) to clear up; (*craintes, soupçons*) to dispel **(b)** (*distraire*) to distract; **il se laisse facilement d.** he is easily distracted **2 se dissiper** *vpr* **(a)** (*de soupçons, malentendu*) to vanish, to disappear; **le brouillard se dissipe** the fog is lifting *or* clearing (away); **ses doutes se sont dissipés** his doubts faded **(b)** (*se laisser distraire*) (*à l'école etc*) to be inattentive; **il se dissipe vite** his attention soon wanders

dissociable [disɔsjabl] *adj* separable

dissociation [disɔsjasjɔ̃] *nf* separation; *Ch* decomposition, dissociation; **la d. nécessaire entre la vie privée et la vie professionnelle** the need to keep one's private life separate from one's work

dissocier [disɔsje] **1** *vt* (*idées etc*) to separate; *Ch* (*composé*) to dissociate **2 se dissocier** *vpr* **se d. d'un groupe** to dissociate oneself from a group

dissolu [disɔly] *adj* (*personne, vie*) dissolute

dissolubilité [disɔlybilite] *nf* dissolubility

dissoluble [disɔlybl] *adj* **(a)** *Pol* (*assemblée etc*) which can be dissolved, dissoluble **(b)** *Arch* (*substance*) soluble

dissolution [disɔlysjɔ̃] *nf* **(a)** (*d'un parlement, d'un mariage*) dissolution **(b)** *Ch* (*d'une substance dans un liquide*) dissolving; (*colle*) rubber solution **(c)** (*d'un corps*) decomposition; (*d'une matière*) decomposition, breakdown **(d)** *Litt* (*débauche*) dissoluteness, licentiousness, profligacy

dissolvant [disɔlvɑ̃] **1** *adj* **(a)** (*qui dissout*) solvent **(b)** *Vieilli* (*climat*) debilitating; (*doctrine*) corrupt **2** *nm* solvent; (*pour ongles*) nail varnish remover

dissonance [disɔnɑ̃s] *nf Mus* discord; *Fig* clash

dissonant [disɔnɑ̃] *adj Mus* dissonant, discordant; *Fig* clashing

dissoudre [disudr] (*prp* **dissolvant**; *pp* **dissous,** *f* **dissoute**; *pr ind* **je dissous, il dissout, n. dissolvons**; *impf* **je dissolvais**; *p hist & p sub are lacking*; *fu* **je dissoudrai**) **1** *vt* **(a)** (*substance*) to dissolve **(b)** (*parlement, mariage*) to dissolve; (*association*) to dissolve, to break (up); (*entreprise*) to wind up **2 se dissoudre** *vpr* to dissolve; **se d. dans l'eau** to dissolve in water; *Fig* **colère qui se dissout en larmes** anger that dissolves into tears

dissuader [disɥade] *vt* **d. qn de faire qch** to dissuade sb from doing sth, to talk sb out of doing sth; **d. qn de partir** to persuade sb not to leave, to dissuade sb from leaving, to talk sb out of leaving

dissuasif, -ive [disɥazif, -iv] *adj* dissuasive; **ils pratiquent vraiment des prix dissuasifs** their prices are enough to put you off

dissuasion [disɥazjɔ̃] *nf* dissuasion (**de** from); *Mktg* demarketing; **d. nucléaire** nuclear deterrent; *Mil, Pol* **force de d.** deterrent

dissyllabe [disilab] **1** *adj* di(s)syllabic **2** *nm* di(s)syllable

dissyllabique [disilabik] *adj* di(s)syllabic

dissymétrie [disimetri] *nf* asymmetry

dissymétrique [disimetrik] *adj* asymmetric(al)

distance [distɑ̃s] *nf* [ⓘ**B57**,D,1,b] distance; **une faible d.** a short way *or* distance; **il y a une d. de 5 km entre ces deux points** there is a distance of 5 km between these two points, these two points are 5 km apart; **on ne voyait rien à cette d.** you couldn't see anything at that distance; **suivre qn à d./à peu de d.** to follow sb at a distance/at a short distance; **à quelle d. sommes-nous de la ville?** how far are we from the town?; **à une courte d.** a short distance away (**de** from), within easy reach (**de** of); **c'est à une grande d.** it's a long way away *or* off (**de** from); *Mil etc* **à petite** *ou* **faible d.** at short range; *Ordinat etc* **à d.** remote; *MecE* **commande à d.** remote control; **à d.** (*juger, influencer qn*) at *or* from a distance; **tenir qn à d.** to keep sb at a distance; **il me tient à d. de tous les projets intéressants** he keeps me away from all the interesting projects; **conserver** *ou* **garder ses distances, se tenir à d.** to keep at a distance, to remain aloof; *Fig* **il conserve** *ou* **garde ses distances par rapport à la gauche/aux intellectuels/à sa famille** he keeps at a distance *or* holds himself aloof from the left/intellectuals/his family; **se tenir à une d. respectueuse** to remain at a respectful distance; **je vous prie de vous tenir à une d. respectueuse de ma fille** please keep away from my daughter; **de d. en d.** at intervals; **prendre ses distances** *Mil* to dress; *Gym* to space out; *Fig* **prendre de la d.** to stand back (**par rapport à** from); *Sp, Fig* **tenir la d.** to go the distance, to stay *or* last the course

▶ **distance** *Aut* **d. d'arrêt** stopping distance; *Opt* **d. focale** focal length; **d. de freinage** braking distance; *Phot* **d. hyperfocale** hyperfocal distance; *Phot* **d. de mise au point minimale** minimum focusing distance, MFD; *Aut* **d. de sécurité** thinking distance; **d. tarifaire** (*dans un taxi*) chargeable distance

distancement [distɑ̃smɑ̃] *nm* (*de cheval*) disqualification

distancer [distɑ̃se] *vt* (**je distançai(s)**; **n. distançons**) **(a)** *Sp, Fig* (*devancer*) to outdistance, to outrun, to outstrip; **se laisser d.** to drop away, to fall *or* lag behind; **il se laisse d. par les autres** he is letting the others outdistance him *or* pull ahead; **le parti socialiste distance la droite de deux points** the socialists are two points ahead of the conservatives; **ce périodique distance tous les autres par sa qualité** this periodical surpasses all the others in quality **(b)** (*disqualifier*) (*cheval*) to disqualify

distant [distɑ̃] *adj* **(a)** (*éloigné*) distant; (*PC, modem*) remote; **nos deux maisons sont distantes d'un kilomètre l'une de l'autre** our two houses are a kilometre apart **(b)** *Fig* (*froid*) distant, standoffish, aloof; **elle est très distante avec moi** she's being very distant towards me

distendre [distɑ̃dr] **1** *vt* (*estomac*) to distend; (*muscle*) to strain, to pull; (*corde, fil etc*) to stretch to breaking point; *Fig* **le temps a distendu notre amitié** we've drifted apart with time **2 se distendre** *vpr* (*se relâcher*) (*d'une corde, d'un élastique, d'un vêtement, de la peau*) to stretch; (*de l'estomac*) to become distended, to swell; **il s'est distendu un muscle** he has pulled *or* strained a muscle; *Fig* **notre relation se distend** we're drifting apart

distension [distɑ̃sjɔ̃] *nf* (*de l'estomac*) distension; (*d'un muscle*) straining, pulling; (*d'une corde, d'un fil etc*) slackening, loosening; (*de la peau, d'un élastique*) stretching

distillat [distila] *nm Ch* distillate

distillateur [distilatœr] *nm* distiller

distillation [distilasjɔ̃] *nf* (*du whisky*), *Pétr* distillation, distilling; *Pétr* **d. fractionnée** fractional distillation

distiller [distile] **1** *vt* **(a)** (*alcool, pétrole etc*) to distil, *US* to distill; *Litt* (*ses pensées*) to refine; **eau distillée** distilled water **(b)** (*poison*) to distil, to exude; *Fig* (*colère, ennui etc*) to exude **2** *vi Ch* to distil, to exude (**de** from)

distillerie [distilri] *nf* (*lieu*) distillery; (*procédé*) distilling

distinct [distɛ̃(kt)] *adj* **(a)** (*séparé*) distinct, separate; **une organisation distincte de la nôtre** an organization that is distinct from ours, a different organization from ours; **mon poste est d. du sien en cela que je …** my job differs from his in that I … **(b)** (*clair*) (*silhouette, voix etc*) distinct, clear

distinctement [distɛ̃ktəmɑ̃] *adv* distinctly, clearly

distinctif, -ive [distɛ̃ktif, -iv] *adj* (*signe, trait etc*) distinctive, characteristic, distinguishing

distinction [distɛ̃ksjɔ̃] *nf* **(a)** (*différence*) distinction; **faire une d. entre deux choses** to make a distinction *or* to differentiate *or* distinguish between two things; **sans d.** without distinction, indiscriminately; **sans d. de race ou de couleur** irrespective *or* regardless of race or colour; **d. sociale** social *or* class distinction **(b)** (*dignité*) distinction, honour, *US* honor; (*décoration*) decoration **(c)** (*éminence*) distinction, eminence; **un personnage de haute d.** a highly distinguished person **(d)** (*élégance*) air of distinction, elegance; **avoir de la d.** to be distinguished

distinguable [distɛ̃gabl] *adj* distinguishable

distingué [distɛ̃ge] *adj* **(a)** (*remarqué*) (*écrivain, politicien etc*) distinguished, eminent, noted **(b)** (*élégant*) (*personne, maintien*) distinguished; (*goût*) refined; (*vêtement*) smart; **avoir un air d.** to look distinguished **(c) je vous prie d'agréer l'expression de mes sentiments distingués** (*dans une lettre*) yours truly

distinguer [distɛ̃ge] **1** *vt* **(a)** (*particulariser*) to distinguish, to mark, to characterize; **sa mise soignée le distinguait de la foule** his impeccable appearance made him stand out *or* set him apart from the crowd

(b) (*pour honorer*) to honour, *US* to honor; **il a été distingué pour son premier roman** he received an award for his first novel

(c) (*différencier*) to distinguish; **il a appris à d. les champignons** he has learnt how to tell the various kinds of mushroom apart *or* to distinguish between the various kinds of mushroom; **d. qch de qch** *ou* **d'avec qch** to distinguish *or* tell sth from sth; **on peut à peine les d. l'un de l'autre** you can hardly tell them apart; **à quoi les distingues-tu?** how do you tell them apart?

(d) (*discerner*) to discern, to perceive; **je ne peux pas d. ses traits** I cannot make out his features; **je l'ai distinguée dans la foule** I spotted her in the crowd; **d. une nuance d'amertume dans la voix de qn** to detect a trace of bitterness in sb's voice

2 se distinguer *vpr* **(a)** (*s'illustrer*) to distinguish oneself (**par** by); **il s'est surtout distingué par ses articles en neurobiologie** he was particularly noted for his articles on neurobiology; **on ne peut vraiment pas dire qu'il se distingue par son intelligence** he hardly stands out as being very intelligent; **il ne se distingue ni par son physique ni par ses qualités intellectuelles** neither his physical nor his intellectual qualities are anything out of the ordinary

(b) (*se différencier*) (*dans une foule etc*) to be noticeable *or* conspicuous, to stand out; **se d. des autres** to be distinguishable from others (**par** by); **il se distingue de son frère par son grand nez** you can tell him from his brother by his big nose; **leur maison se distingue des autres à cause de ses volets bleus** their house stands out from the others because of its blue shutters; **comment la reine se distingue-t-elle des autres abeilles?** in what way does the queen differ from the other bees?

(c) (*être perçu*) **au loin se distinguait la côte** the coastline could be seen in the distance

distinguo [distɛ̃go] *nm* difference; **il y a un d. à faire entre l'élégance et le raffinement** elegance and refinement are not quite the same thing *or* are not one and the same; **faire des distinguos entre les mots** to bring out the shades of meaning between words

distique [distik] *nm* **(a)** (*vers français*) couplet **(b)** *Antiq* distich

distordre [distɔrdr] *vt* (*traits, bouche*) to distort

distorsion [distɔrsjɔ̃] *nf* (*d'un visage, d'une image optique, d'une impulsion électrique etc*) distortion; (*entre deux facteurs, deux salaires*) imbalance; *Rad* **d. de phase** phase distortion; *Rad etc* **d. de crête** peak distortion; *Rad etc* **d. de fréquence** frequency distortion; *Rad etc* **d. harmonique** harmonic distortion; *TV etc* **d. de l'image** image distortion; *TV* **d. géométrique** geometric distortion

distraction [distraksjɔ̃] *nf* **(a)** (*inattention*) absent-mindedness, lack of attention, abstraction; **par d.** inadvertently, absent-mindedly; **avoir des moments de d.** to have moments of absent-mindedness; **c'est une d. que nous ne pouvons te pardonner** we cannot forgive such absent-mindedness on your part

(b) (*loisir*) amusement, recreation; **distractions** entertainment; **ce bled manque de d.** there's nothing to do in this place; **la lecture et le cinéma sont mes distractions préférées** reading and going to the cinema are my favourite forms of recreation *or* what I like doing best in my spare time; **depuis que ses enfants sont partis, elle n'a plus aucune d.** she's got nothing to occupy her mind now that her children have left home; **distractions en vol** in-flight entertainment

distraire [distrɛr] (*conj like* **traire**) **1** *vt* **(a)** (*l'attention de qn*) to distract, to divert; **d. qn de ses travaux** to distract sb from his work **(b)** (*divertir*) to divert, to entertain, to amuse; **j'aime bien que tu viennes me voir, ça me distrait** I like you to visit me, it gives me something else to think about **2 se distraire** *vpr* to amuse oneself; **elle a besoin de se d.** she needs to relax a bit *or* to enjoy herself

distrait [distrɛ] *adj* absent-minded; **air d.** absent-minded *or* abstracted *or* distracted look; **d'une oreille distraite** with only half an ear; **vous êtes d.** you're not paying attention; **élève d.** inattentive pupil

distraitement [distrɛtmɑ̃] *adv* absent-mindedly, abstractedly

distrayant [distrɛjɑ̃] *adj* (*livre, spectacle*) diverting, entertaining

distribanque [distribɑ̃k] *nf* cash dispenser

distribuer [distribɥe] *vt* **(a)** (*donner*) (*prix, bonbons etc*) to distribute, to hand out; (*provisions, vivres etc*) to distribute, to issue; (*ordres*) to hand out, to give out; (*cartes*) to deal; (*du facteur*) to deliver; **il a commencé à d. des coups** he started to lash out with his fists; **d. des sourires à tout le monde** to bestow smiles on everybody

(b) (*répartir*) **d. les fleurs en plusieurs classes** to classify flowers; *Th* **d. les rôles** to cast the parts (in a/the play), to cast a/the play; **d. un dividende** to pay a dividend; **appartement bien/mal distribué** well/badly laid out flat; **d. son temps de la façon la plus logique** to allocate *or* apportion one's time in the most logical fashion possible; **conduites qui distribuent l'eau dans la ville** pipes that supply water to the city; **expliquez de quelle manière le sang est distribué dans notre corps** explain how blood circulates through our body

(c) (*commercialiser*) (*produit, film, livres etc*) to distribute

distributaire [distribytɛr] *n Jur* distributee

distributeur, -trice [distribytœr, -tris] **1** *n Com* distributor, dealer **2** *nm* **(a)** *Cin* (film) distributor **(b)** *Tech, Aut* distributor

▶ **distributeur**: **d. agréé** authorized dealer, authorized distributor; **d. automatique** automatic vending machine, slot machine; **d. (automatique) de billets** cash dispenser, cash point, *Am* bank machine; *Rail etc* ticket machine; **d. (automatique) de boissons** drinks machine, drinks dispenser, drinks vending machine; **d. automatique de titres de transport** automatic ticket dispenser; **d. de cigarettes** cigarette machine; *Él* **d. de courant** distributor; **d. d'engrais** fertilizer spreader; **d. de presse** press distributor; *Tech* **d. de vapeur** steam distributor *or* regulator, steam valve

distributif, -ive [distribytif, -iv] *adj Gram* (*terme, pronom etc*) distributive

distribution [distribysjɔ̃] *nf* **(a)** (*don*) distribution; (*de fonctions, de tâches etc*) allocation, allotment; (*de rations, vivres*) issue; (*de lettres, marchandises*) delivery; *Scol* **d. des prix** prize giving, speech day; **il va y avoir une d. gratuite de saucissons au rayon charcuterie** sausages will be given away at the meat counter

(b) (*répartition*) (*d'une maison, d'un appartement*) layout; *Aut* distribution; *Bot* **d. des plantes** classification of plants; *Écon* **d. des richesses** distribution of wealth; *Th* **d. des rôles** (*action*) casting; (*liste*) cast; *Th, Cin* **d. par ordre d'entrée en scène** characters *or* cast in order of appearance; **d. des eaux** water supply; **d. d'une maladie selon les classes d'âge** incidence of a disease by age group; **d. d'un bénéfice** distribution of profits; **d. de dividende** payment of a dividend; **d. par câble** cable distribution

(c) *Com* distribution; **réseau de d.** distribution network; **droits de d.** distribution rights; **grande d.** large-scale distribution; **d. de masse** mass distribution; **d. exclusive** exclusive distribution; **d. numérique** stock holding distribution

distributionnel, -elle [distribysjɔnɛl] *adj Ling* (*analyse, linguistique*) distributive

distributivement [distribytivmɑ̃] *adv* distributively

distributivité [distribytivite] *nf Math* distributive law

district [distrikt] *nm* district, region

dit [di] **1** *adj* **(a)** (*décidé*) settled, fixed; **à l'heure dite** (*à l'heure convenue*) at the appointed *or* agreed time; (*à l'heure fixée*) at the time indicated; **au jour d.** on the appointed *or* agreed day **(b)** (*appelé*) called; **la zone dite tempérée** the temperate zone as it is called **2** *nm Arch, Littér* traditional story (*usually in verse*); **le d. des trois larrons** the story of the three thieves

dithyrambe [ditirɑ̃b] *nm* (*panégyrique*) eulogy; *Littér* dithyramb; **se lancer dans un d. sur qch** to go into raptures about sth

dithyrambique [ditirɑ̃bik] *adj* (*mots etc*) eulogistic; *Littér* dithyrambic

dito [dito] *adv* ditto

diurèse [djyrɛz] *nf Méd* diuresis

diurétique [djyretik] *adj, nm Méd* diuretic

diurne [djyrn] *adj Bot, Zool* diurnal

diva [diva] *nf Mus* diva

divagation [divagasjɔ̃] *nf* **(a)** (*dans un discours etc*) digression; **divagations d'un fou** ravings *or* ramblings of a madman **(b)** (*de rivière*) shifting from its course; *Jur* (*du bétail etc*) straying

divaguer [divage] *vi* **(a)** (*dans un discours*) to digress, to stray from the point; **malade qui divague** patient whose mind is wandering *or* who is rambling; **vous divaguez!** you're raving! **(b)** (*de rivière*) to shift its course; *Jur* (*de bétail etc*) to stray

divan [divɑ̃] *nm* **(a)** (*meuble*) divan, couch; **d-lit** divan (bed) **(b)** *Hist* divan

divergence [divɛrʒɑ̃s] *nf* (*de lignes, de rayons etc*) divergence; (*d'opinions*) difference

divergent [divɛrʒɑ̃] *adj* (*lignes*) divergent; (*opinions*) differing, different

diverger [divɛrʒe] *vi* (**il divergea(it)**; **n. divergeons**) (*de lignes, de rayons*) to diverge (**de** from); (*d'opinion*) to differ, to diverge (**de** from); **nos opinions divergent sur certains points** our opinions differ on certain points

divers [divɛr] *adj* **(a)** (*différent*) different, varied; (*rubrique*) miscellaneous; **le dessert consistait en fruits d.** there was a variety of fruit for dessert, there were various kinds of fruit for dessert; **à des heures diverses** at different times; **ils ont eu des fortunes diverses** they had varying fortunes; **des opinions très diverses** very varied opinions, a wide range of opinions; **une clientèle très diverse** a wide clientele, a wide range of customers; **frais d.** sundry expenses, sundries; *Journ* **faits d.** news items; **un fait d.** a minor incident

(b) (*always preceding the noun*) (*plusieurs*) various, a number of

(c) *Arch* (*nature etc*) changing, varying

diversement [divɛrsəmɑ̃] *adv* in various *or* different ways; **les participants ont d. compris la question** the contestants understood the question in different ways; **mes élèves ont d. réussi l'examen** my pupils had varying degrees of success in the exam

diversification [divɛrsifikasjɔ̃] *nf* diversification

diversifier [divɛrsifje] (*pr sub & impf* **n. diversifiions, v. diversifiiez**) **1** *vt* (*économie, cultures, produits, placements*) to diversify; (*activités, intérêts, couleurs etc*) to vary **2 se diversifier** *vpr* (*de compagnie*) to diversify

diversion [divɛrsjɔ̃] *nf* diversion; (*changement*) change, distraction; **faire d.** to create a diversion; **faire d. à la tristesse de qn** to cheer sb up; **cela fera une d. à tes ennuis** it will take your mind off your troubles

diversité [divɛrsite] *nf* (*variété*) variety, diversity; (*différence*) difference; **une grande d. de races/de milieux sociaux** a wide variety of races/classes; **étant donné la d. de leurs intérêts** given that they have such different *or* varying interests; **j'admire la d. de ses talents** I admire the variety of talents that he has **d. biologique** biological diversity, biodiversity

divertir [divɛrtir] **1** *vt* **(a)** (*amuser*) to entertain, to amuse **(b)** *Vieilli* (*coup etc*) to divert, to ward off; (*personne*) (*d'un projet, d'une intention etc*) to turn (away); (*attention*) to divert; (*somme d'argent*) to misappropriate **2 se divertir** *vpr* to enjoy oneself; **se d. de la stupidité/de la balourdise de qn** to laugh at sb's stupidity/clumsiness; **se d. l'esprit** to amuse *or* entertain oneself

divertissant [divɛrtisɑ̃] *adj* amusing, entertaining

divertissement [divɛrtismɑ̃] *nm* **(a)** (*amusement*) entertainment, amusement, diversion; **on manque de d. dans ce bled** there's nothing to do in this place; **il faut trouver des divertissements pour les enfants** we have to find something to amuse the children *or* for the children to do **(b)** *Mus* divertimento **(c)** *Jur* **d. de fonds** misappropriation of funds

dividende [dividɑ̃d] *nm Math, Fin* dividend; **d. brut** gross dividend; **d. cumulatif** cumulative dividend; **d. d'action** share dividend; **d. net** net dividend; **dividendes accrus** accrued dividends

divin [divɛ̃] **1** *adj* (*volonté etc*) divine; *F* (*musique, climat etc*) heavenly; **le d. Enfant** [divinɑ̃fɑ̃] the Holy Child **2** *nm* **le d.** the divine

divinateur, -trice [divinatœr, -tris] **1** *n Arch* diviner, soothsayer **2** *adj* (*don, pouvoir etc*) of prophecy

divination [divinasjɔ̃] *nf* **(a)** (*occultisme*) divination, soothsaying; **l'astrologie et autres méthodes de d.** astrology and other methods of telling the future **(b)** (*intuition*) intuition; **faire preuve d'un peu de d.** to do a bit of guesswork

divinatoire [divinatwar] *adj* (*science, art, don*) of divination; **baguette d.** divining rod, dowsing rod

divinement [divinmɑ̃] *adv* divinely

divinisation [divinizasjɔ̃] *nf* deification

diviniser [divinize] *vt* to deify

divinité [divinite] *nf* **(a)** (*nature de Dieu*) divinity, divine nature; (*du Christ*) godhead **(b)** (*dieu*) deity, god, divinity, *f* goddess

diviser [divize] **1** *vt* **(a)** (*partager*) to divide; (*travail, gains, héritage*) to divide, to share out (**entre** among); **divise le gâteau en trois** divide the cake in three; **ce pays est divisé**

en plusieurs provinces the country is divided into several provinces; **la semaine est divisée en jours** the week is divided *or* split up into days; **d. une question en plusieurs points** to break down a question into several points; *Math* **d. un nombre par un autre** to divide one number by another

(**b**) (*opposer*) to divide; **les questions déontologiques divisent les scientifiques** scientists are divided on questions of ethics; **l'opinion est divisée au sujet de cette affaire** opinion on the matter is divided; **d. pour (mieux) régner** divide and rule

(**c**) *Arch* (*délimiter*) **les Pyrénées divisent la France d'avec l'Espagne** the Pyrenees divide *or* separate France from Spain

2 se diviser *vpr* to divide (**en** into); **l'examen se divise en trois parties** the examination is divided into three parts; **l'équipe s'est divisée en deux** the team divided itself *or* split up into two groups; **le chemin se divise en deux** the road divides *or* forks

diviseur [divizœr] *nm* (**a**) *Math* divisor; **plus grand commun d.** highest common factor; **nombre/fraction d.** divisor number/fraction (**b**) *Tech* divider; *Él* **d. de courant** current divider

divisibilité [divizibilite] *nf* divisibility

divisible [divizibl] *adj* divisible

division [divizjɔ̃] *nf* (**a**) [①A71,7; B56,C,4] (*d'un tout en parties*), *Math* division (**en** into); **j'ai des divisions à faire** I've got some division to do; **je déteste les divisions** *ou* **faire des divisions** I hate division; **d. du marché** market division

(**b**) (*partie*) (*d'un tout*) part, portion, section; *Admin* division, department, branch; *Scol* group, section; *Mil, Naut* division; **les divisions d'un livre** the sections of a book; **d. de formation professionnelle** training division; **d. des exportations** export division; **d. internationale** international division

(**c**) (*désaccord*) discord, dissension, disagreement; **semer la d. au sein d'une famille** to cause dissent in a family; **depuis le dernier congrès, c'est la d. qui règne dans le parti** division has reigned in the party since the last congress

(**d**) *Typ* hyphen

▶ **division**: *Mil* **d. blindée** armoured division; *Mil, Biol* **d. cellulaire** cell division; **d. du travail** division of labour

divisionnaire [divizjɔnɛr] **1** *adj Mil* divisional; *Admin* **commissaire d.** ≈ (police) superintendent **2** *nm* (police) superintendent; *Mil* major general

divorce [divɔrs] *nm Jur* divorce; **les enfants sont ceux qui pâtissent le plus du d.** divorce is hardest on the children; **demander le d.** to ask for a divorce; *Jur* to sue for divorce, to file a petition for divorce; **obtenir le d.** to get a divorce; **être en instance de d.** to be getting a divorce, to have started divorce proceedings; **se solder par un d.** to end in divorce; *Fig* **le d. de la langue écrite (d')avec la langue parlée** the gulf between the written and the spoken language

▶ **divorce**: **d. à l'amiable** no-fault divorce; **d. par consentement mutuel** divorce by mutual consent

divorcé, -ée [divɔrse] **1** *adj* divorced **2** *n* divorced man/woman, divorcee

divorcer [divɔrse] *vi* (**je divorçai(s); n. divorçons**) **d. (d')avec qn** to divorce sb; **il veut d.** he wants a divorce; **ils ont divorcé l'année dernière** they got divorced *or* they got a divorce last year; **pourquoi est-ce que tu ne lui demandes pas de d.?** why don't you ask him for a divorce?; **un couple sur trois divorce** one marriage in three ends in divorce

divulgateur, -trice [divylgatœr, -tris] *n* (police) informer; (*de secrets*) betrayer

divulgation [divylgasjɔ̃] *nf* disclosure (**de** of)

divulguer [divylge] *vt* (*secret*) to divulge, to reveal, to disclose; (*nouvelle*) to reveal; **il a divulgué qu'il y aurait des licenciements** he revealed *or* disclosed that there would be layoffs

dix [dis] **1** *adj inv* (*at the end of the word group* [dis]; *before n or adj beginning with a vowel sound* [diz]; *before n or adj beginning with a consonant* [di]) (**a**) **il est d. heures** [dizœr] it's ten o'clock; **j'en ai d.** [dis] I have ten; **les d. commandements** the ten commandments; *Scol* **devoir noté sur d.** homework marked out of ten; **avoir d. sur d. à sa dictée** to get ten out of ten for dictation; **avoir d. sur d. à chaque œil** to have twenty-twenty vision

(**b**) (*ordinal uses etc*) **le d. mai** [lədimɛ] the tenth of May; **Charles D.** Charles the Tenth; **le numéro d.** number ten

2 *nm inv* (*souvent* [dis]) **d. et demi** [disedmi] ten and a half; **j'habite au d.** I live at Number 10; *Cartes* **le d. de trèfle** the ten of clubs; **le X est le signe du d. romain** X is ten in Roman numerals

dix-huit [dizɥi(t)] **1** *adj inv* eighteen; **le d. mai** the eighteenth of May **2** *nm inv* eighteen; **j'ai eu un d. en maths** ≈ I got 90% in maths

dix-huitième [dizɥitjɛm] *adj, n* eighteenth

dixième [dizjɛm] *adj, n* tenth

dixièmement [dizjɛmmɑ̃] *adv* tenthly, in tenth place

dixit [diksit] **il faut couper tous les arbres, Papa d.** all the trees have to be cut down Dad says *or* or so Dad says

dix-neuf [diznœf] **1** *adj inv* nineteen; **le d. mai** the nineteenth of May **2** *nm inv* nineteen

dix-neuvième [diznœvjɛm] *adj, n* nineteenth

dix-sept [dis(s)ɛt] **1** *adj inv* seventeen; **le d. mai** the seventeenth of May **2** *nm inv* seventeen

dix-septième [dis(s)ɛtjɛm] *adj, n* seventeenth

dizain [dizɛ̃] *nm Littér* ten-line stanza

dizaine [dizɛn] *nf* about ten; *Math* ten; *Math* **compter par dizaines** to count in tens; **une d. de personnes** ten or so people, about ten people; **il y a une d. d'années** about ten years ago, ten or so years ago

dizygote [dizigɔt] *Biol* **1** *adj* fraternal **2** *n* fraternal twin

DJ [didʒɛ] *nm Rad etc* DJ

djebel [dʒɛbɛl] *nm* jebel, mountain

djellaba [dʒɛlaba] *nf* djellaba

djihad [djiad] *nf* jihad

djinn [dʒin] *nm* djin(n), jinn

do [do] *nm Mus* (*note*) C; (*solfège*) doh

doc [dɔk] *nf* (*abrév* **documentation**)

docile [dɔsil] *adj* (*enfant, animal*) docile; (*cheveux*) manageable

docilement [dɔsilmɑ̃] *adv* docilely

docilité [dɔsilite] *nf* docility

dock [dɔk] *nm Naut* (**a**) (*bassin*) dock; **les docks** the dock(s), the dockyard; **d. de carénage/flottant** dry/floating dock (**b**) *Com* warehouses; **d. entrepôt** dock-warehouse; **d. frigorifique** cold storage dock

docker [dɔkɛr] *nm* docker, dock worker, *Am* longshoreman

docte [dɔkt] *adj Litt, Iron* (*when it precedes noun*) learned

doctement [dɔktəmɑ̃] *adv Litt, Iron* in a learned manner, learnedly

docteur [dɔktœr] *nm* (**a**) **d. (en médecine)** doctor (of medicine); **leur fille est d.** their daughter is a doctor; **le d. Thomas** Dr Thomas; **bonjour d.** good morning, doctor (**b**) *Univ* **d. ès lettres** = Doctor of Literature; **Mlle Laurent est d. ès sciences** Miss Laurent is a doctor of science; **d. en droit** doctor of law (**c**) *Rel* **les docteurs de l'Église** the Doctors of the Church

doctoral, -ale, -aux, -ales [dɔktɔral, -o] *adj Péj* (*air, ton*) pompous

doctoralement [dɔktɔralmɑ̃] *adv Péj* pompously

doctorat [dɔktɔra] *nm Univ* doctorate; **d. d'État** ≈ D. Litt. /D. Sc. /*etc*; **d. de 3e cycle** ≈ PhD

doctoresse [dɔktɔrɛs] *nf Vieilli* woman doctor

doctrinaire [dɔktrinɛr] *adj* doctrinaire

doctrinal, -ale, -aux, -ales [dɔktrinal, -o] *adj* doctrinal

doctrine [dɔktrin] *nf* doctrine, tenet

docudrame [dɔkydram] *nm TV* docudrama, dramatized documentary

document [dɔkymɑ̃] *nm* document

▶ **document**: *Com* **d. administratif unique** unique data folder; *Com* **documents contre acceptation** documents against acceptance; *TV, Cin* **d. d'archives** stock shot; *Aut* **documents de bord** vehicle documents; **d-canevas** (*de publipostage*) form document; *Com* **documents d'embarquement** shipping documents; *Typ* **d. d'exécution** artwork; *Com* **d. d'expédition** shipping document; **d. interne à l'entreprise** internal company document; **d. maître** master document; *Com* **documents maritimes** shipping documents; *Com* **d. d'offre** tender document; *Com* **documents contre paiement** documents against payment; **d. source** source document; *Compta* **d. de synthèse** financial statements; **d. transmissible** transferable document; *Com* **d. de transport combiné** combined transport document; **d. de travail** working document; **d.-type** (*de publipostage*) form document; **documents de voyage** travel documents

documentaire [dɔkymɑ̃tɛr] **1** *adj* (*intérêt, valeur etc*) documentary; **à titre d.** for (your) information; *Cin* **film d.** documentary **2** *nm* (**a**) *Cin* documentary (**b**) **d. touristique** travelogue

documentaliste [dɔkymɑ̃talist] *n* (**a**) (*d'archives*) documentalist, archivist; *Admin* keeper of records (**b**) *TV etc* researcher

documentariste [dɔkymɑ̃tarist] *n Cin* director of documentary films

documentation [dɔkymɑ̃tasjɔ̃] *nf* (*action*) research; (*documents*) documentation; **je cherche de la d. sur ...** I am looking for documentation on ...; **faire de la d.** to do research; **système de d. automatique** automated information service; **d. touristique** travel literature, tourist literature

documenter [dɔkymɑ̃te] **1** *vt* (*sujet*) to document; (*déclaration etc*) to support with documentary evidence; **d. qn sur une question** to brief sb on a question; **elle est bien documentée** she is well informed on the subject; **son étude n'était pas solidement documentée** his study was not well documented **2 se documenter** *vpr* to gather documentation *or* information *or* material

dodécaèdre [dɔdekaɛdr] *nm Math* dodecahedron

dodécagonal, -ale, -aux, -ales [dɔdekagɔnal, -o] *adj Math* twelve-sided, dodecagonal

dodécagone [dɔdekagon] *nm Math* dodecagon

dodécaphonique [dɔdekafɔnik] *adj Mus* twelve-tone, dodecaphonic

dodécaphonisme [dɔdekafɔnism] *nm Mus* twelve-tone system, dodecaphony

dodelinement [dɔdlinmɑ̃] *nm* (*de la tête*) nodding

dodeliner [dɔdline] *vi* **il dodelinait de la tête** his head kept falling forward *or* nodding

dodo[1] [dodo] *nm Enf* (*sommeil*) sleep, bye-byes; (*lit*) bed; **faire d.** to sleep; **aller au d.** to go to bed *or* to bye-byes; **qui c'est qui va faire un gros d.?** who's a sleepy boy/girl then?; **d.!** go to sleep!; **allez, au d.!** bed!

dodo[2] *nm* (*oiseau*) dodo

dodu [dɔdy] *adj F* plump, chubby

doge [dɔʒ] *nm Hist* doge

dogmatique [dɔgmatik] *adj* dogmatic

dogmatiquement [dɔgmatikmɑ̃] *adv* dogmatically

dogmatiser [dɔgmatize] *vi* to be dogmatic

dogmatisme [dɔgmatism] *nm* dogmatism

dogme [dɔgm] *nm* dogma

dogue [dɔg] *nm* mastiff; *Fig* **d'une humeur de d.** like a bear with a sore head

doigt [dwa] *nm* **(a)** finger; *Anat, Zool* digit; **d. de pied** toe; *Fig* **mettre les doigts de pied en éventail** to relax thoroughly, to do absolutely nothing; **le petit d.** the little finger; *F* **mon petit d. me l'a dit** a little bird told me; **lever le d.** (*en classe etc*) to put one's hand up; *Fig* **ne pas lever** *ou* **remuer le petit d.** not to lift a finger; **compter sur ses doigts** to count on one's fingers; **je peux compter mes amis sur les doigts de la main** I can count my friends on the fingers of one hand; **je ne sais rien faire de mes dix doigts** I'm not good with my hands; **porter une bague au d.** to wear a ring on one's finger; **promener ses doigts sur qch** to run one's fingers over sth; **elle a des doigts de fée** she's good with her hands; **il a les doigts verts** he has green fingers *or Am* a green thumb; **se faire taper sur les doigts** to be rapped over the knuckles, to get a rap over the knuckles; *Mus* **avoir un morceau dans les doigts** to have mastered a piece; **savoir qch sur le bout des doigts** to know sth inside out, to have sth at one's fingertips; **elle est élégante/spirituelle/méchante jusqu'au bout des doigts** she is elegant/witty/nasty through and through; **elle est française jusqu'au bout des doigts** she is French to her fingertips; **menacer qn du d.** to shake *or* wag one's finger at sb; **elle lui fit signe du d.** (**de venir**) she beckoned to him (to come over); **désigner** *ou* **montrer qn/qch du d.** to point at sb/sth; *Fig* **mettre le d. dans l'engrenage** to get involved; **il a mis le d. dans l'engrenage de la drogue** he got involved *or* mixed up in drugs; **vous avez mis le d. dessus** you've put your finger on it, you've hit the nail on the head; **je crois que je touche le problème du d.** I think I see what the problem is; **nous touchons le but/la vérité du d.** we're very close to *or* within an inch of our goal/the truth; *F* **se mettre** *ou* **se fourrer le d. dans l'œil (jusqu'au coude)** to be completely wrong; **fourrer ses doigts partout** to be into everything; **croiser les doigts** to cross one's fingers; **je croise les doigts** I've got my fingers crossed; **croisons les doigts pour que ça marche** let's cross our fingers that it works; *F* **mener qn au d. et à l'œil** to keep a tight rein on sb; **elle se laisse mener au d. et à l'œil par son mari** her husband only has to raise a finger and she jumps; **obéir au d. et à l'œil** to obey immediately; **filer** *ou* **glisser entre les doigts de qn** to slip through sb's fingers; **s'en mordre les doigts** to regret it; **j'ai voulu lui tenir tête et je m'en mords les doigts** I tried standing up to her and I regret it *or* I'm sorry I did; **ils sont ensemble comme les (deux) doigts de la main** they are very close; *F* **gagner les doigts dans le nez** to win hands down; **faire qch les doigts dans le nez** to do sth as easy as winking

(b) (*mesure*) finger's breadth; **la robe est trop courte d'un d.** the dress is a fraction too short; **un d. de cognac** a nip *or* drop *or* spot of brandy; **être à deux doigts de la mort** to be within an inch of death; **il s'en est fallu d'un d. pour que ça rate** it was a hair's breadth away from failing; **il s'en est fallu d'un d. pour qu'elle signe** she was a hair's breadth away from signing

(c) (*objet*) **doigts d'un gant** fingers of a glove; *Aut* **d. de distribution** rotor arm

doigté [dwate] *nm* **(a)** *Mus* (*d'un morceau de musique*) fingering; **exercises de d.** five-finger exercises **(b)** (*de dactylo*) touch; (*d'un chirurgien*) skill **(c)** *Fig* tact, diplomacy; **manquer de d.** to be tactless

doigter [dwate] **1** *vt* **(a)** (*d'un musicien*) to finger **(b)** (*d'un compositeur*) to mark with the proper fingering **2** *vi* to finger; **elle doigte bien/mal** her fingering is good/bad

doigtier [dwatje] *nm* fingerstall

doit [dwa] *nm Com* debit, liability; **d. et avoir** debits and credits; (*personnes*) debtors and creditors

dol [dɔl] *nm Jur* fraud, wilful misrepresentation

dolby® [dɔlbi] *nm* Dolby

doléances [dɔleɑ̃s] *nfpl* complaints; **faire ses d.** to air one's grievances

dolent [dɔlɑ̃] *adj* (*voix, personne etc*) doleful, plaintive

doline [dɔlin] *nf Géol* sink-hole, *Spéc* doline

dollar [dɔlar] *nm* dollar; **la zone d.** the dollar area; **d.-titre** dollar security; **dollars constants** dollars in real terms; **dollars courants** actual dollars

dolman [dɔlmɑ̃] *nm* dolman; (*de hussard*) short-skirted jacket

dolmen [dɔlmɛn] *nm* dolmen

dolomie [dɔlɔmi] *nf*, **dolomite** [dɔlɔmit] *nf Minér* dolomite; *Géog* **les Dolomites** the Dolomites

dolomitique [dɔlɔmitik] *adj Géol* dolomitic

dolosif, -ive [dɔlɔzif, -iv] *adj Jur* fraudulent

domaine [dɔmɛn] *nm* **(a)** (*propriété*) estate, property; *Jur* demesne; **il est interdit de chasser sur leur d.** hunting is forbidden on their land; **ils ont plusieurs domaines dans le vignoble bordelais** they own several pieces of land in the Bordeaux wine-growing area; **domaines de la Couronne** Crown lands; **D. (de l'État)** State(-administered) property; **d. public** public property; **cet ouvrage est tombé dans le d. public** this work is out of copyright *or* has come into the public domain, the copyright on this work has run out *or* lapsed; **le d. forestier** the national forests; **d. skiable** skiing area; **cette pièce est mon d.** this room is my domain

(b) (*rayon*) field; **d. d'une science** field *or* scope of a science; **d. des affaires** business domain; **d. de compétence** area of expertise, area of competence; **cela n'entre pas dans le d. de mes connaissances** that's not my field *or* domain; **ce n'est pas de mon d.** that's not my field *or* my line of country; **une intervention aussi délicate est du d. de la microchirurgie** such a delicate operation calls for microsurgery; **c'est du d. du possible** it is within the realm of possibility, it is not beyond the bounds of possibility; **il est bon dans tous les domaines** he is good in all fields *or* areas; **c'est son d. réservé** it's his private domain; *Mktg* **d. concurrentiel** competitive scope; *Mktg* **d. d'activité stratégique** strategic business area

domanial, -ale, -aux, -ales [dɔmanjal, -o] *adj* (*domaines, forêts etc*) national, (belonging to the) State

dôme [dom] *nm* **(a)** *Archit* dome, cupola **(b)** *Litt* (*du ciel, des arbres*) vault, canopy; *Géog* dome

domestication [dɔmɛstikasjɔ̃] *nf* domestication

domesticité [dɔmɛstisite] *nf* **(a)** (*service*) domestic service **(b)** (*personnel*) domestic staff, household **(c)** (*d'un animal*) domesticity; **la d. est impossible chez certaines races** some breeds are impossible to tame *or* domesticate

domestique [dɔmɛstik] **1** *adj* **(a)** (*vie, soucis*) domestic; (*occupations, tâches, déchets*) household; (*querelle*) family, domestic; **économie d.** home economics; **accidents domestiques** accidents in the home **(b) animal d.** domestic animal; (*qu'on a chez soi*) pet; **éléphant d.** tame *or* domesticated elephant **2** *n* servant, *Fml, Am* domestic

domestiquer [dɔmɛstike] *vt* (*animal*) to domesticate; (*personne*) to subjugate, to bring to a state of subjection; (*énergie atomique etc*) to harness

domicile [dɔmisil] *nm* (place of) residence, home, *Jur* domicile; **sans d. fixe** of no fixed abode *or* address; **élire d. au 3 rue Hoche** to take up residence at no 3, Rue Hoche; **dernier d. connu** last known address; **à d.** in one's home, at home; **travailler à d.** to work from home; **notre épicier livre à d.** our grocer has a (home) delivery service; **vous préférez être livré à d. ou au bureau?** do you want it delivered to your home or your office?; **franco à d.** carriage paid; *Jur* **d. conjugal** marital *or* matrimonial home; *Jur* **abandon du d. conjugal** desertion; **d. fiscal** tax domicile; *Sp* **match à d.** home game *or* match; **jouer à d.** to play *or* be at home; **P.S.G. joue à d. contre Lille** P.S.G. is at home to Lille

domiciliaire [dɔmisiljɛr] *adj* (*visite etc*) home

domiciliataire [dɔmisiljatɛr] *n* (*de chèque*) paying bank; (*d'effet*) paying agent

domiciliation [dɔmisiljasjɔ̃] *nf Com* domiciliation; **d. bancaire** paying bank

domicilié [dɔmisilje] *adj* resident, domiciled (**à** at); *Com* domiciled

domicilier [dɔmisilje] *vt* (*pr sub & impf* **n. domiciliions, v. domiciliiez**) *Com* to domicile

dominance [dɔminɑ̃s] *nf Biol* dominance

dominant, -ante [dɔminɑ̃, -ɑ̃t] **1** *adj* (*couleur, opinion etc*) predominating, prevailing; (*trait, idée etc*) dominant, outstanding; *Biol* **caractère d.** dominant (characteristic) **2** *nf* **dominante (a)** (*ce qui domine*) chief characteristic; **un ameublement avec une d. moderne** furniture which is predominantly *or* primarily modern; **la d. de son programme politique est la protection de l'environnement** environmental protection is the main plank of his platform; **elle avait une tenue très pâle, avec une d. rose** she was wearing a very pale outfit in which pink predominated *or* was the main colour **(b)** *Mus* dominant (note)

dominateur, -trice [dɔminatœr, -tris] **1** *n Litt* ruler **2** *adj* (*pays, caractère*) dominating; *Péj* (*personne, ton, attitude etc*) domineering, overbearing; **il exerce un pouvoir d. sur les gens qu'il dirige** he rules his staff with a rod of iron; **il a toujours des gestes dominateurs** he always acts in a domineering *or* overbearing fashion

domination [dɔminasjɔ̃] *nf* domination; **la d. de l'URSS sur les autres pays de l'Est** the USSR's domination of the other Eastern bloc countries; **d. morale** dominance, domination; **il exerce sur elle une telle d. morale que …** he dominates her so completely that …, *Fml* he has such sway over her that …; **d. de soi-même** self-control; **être sous la d. de qn** to be under sb's thumb

dominer [dɔmine] **1** *vt* **(a)** (*assujettir*) (*personne*) to dominate; (*empire*) to rule over; **l'ambition le domine** he is dominated by ambition; **se laisser d. par un collègue autoritaire** to let oneself be dominated by an authoritarian colleague; **d. une classe** (*d'un professeur*) to control a class

(b) (*surpasser*) (*adversaire, concurrent*) to surpass, *F* to be streets ahead of; **sa voix dominait toutes les autres** his voice rose *or* was heard above all the others; **dans son domaine, il domine absolument tous les savants** he stands head and shoulders above all the other scientists in his field

(c) (*prédominer dans*) (*travail, caractère, humeur*) to be the dominant feature of; **c'est la question du chômage qui domine les préoccupations du gouvernement** unemployment is predominant among the government's concerns; **le rouge domine toute sa garde-robe** red is the dominant colour in her wardrobe; **le sapin domine dans les forêts allemandes** fir is the predominant species of tree in German forests

(d) (*maîtriser*) (*timidité, passions*) to master, to overcome; (*larmes, Fig son sujet*) to master; (*paresse, envie de faire qch*) to overcome; *Fig* **d. la situation** to be master of the situation, to have the situation under control; *Sp* **d. la partie** to dominate the game

(e) (*surplomber*) to dominate; **le château domine la vallée** the castle dominates the valley; **il domine les enfants de son âge d'une tête au moins** he stands at least a head above other children of his age; **de sa terrasse, on domine la mer** you overlook the sea from his balcony

2 *vi* **(a)** (*l'emporter*) to dominate; **notre équipe a dominé tout le long du match** our team dominated the entire match *or* was in control throughout the match; **ce sont ses arguments qui dominent** his arguments carry the day; **ce pays commence à d. dangereusement** the country is beginning to be dangerously dominant; **leur entreprise domine dans le secteur du prêt-à-porter féminin** their company dominates the women's ready-to-wear sector; **notre entreprise domine largement dans ce secteur** our company is by far the largest in the sector; **elle domine de très loin sur ses collègues** she is *or* stands head and shoulders above her colleagues, she is far better than *or F* streets ahead of her colleagues; **il domine en taille sur les autres enfants de son âge** he is taller than the other children in his age group

(b) (*prédominer*) to be predominant; **c'est la couleur bleue qui domine** blue is the predominant *or* predominating colour; **les jeunes de moins de 15 ans dominent dans le club** young people under 15 are in the majority in the club; **chez lui, c'est l'égoïsme/la gentillesse qui domine** selfishness/kindness is his dominant characteristic; **parmi mes préoccupations, c'est l'avenir de mes enfants qui domine** my children's future is my main concern

3 se dominer *vpr* to be self-controlled, to control one's feelings; **il ne pouvait plus se d.** he couldn't control himself any longer; **dès qu'il boit deux verres, il n'arrive plus à se d.** two drinks and he loses all self-control

dominicain, -aine [dɔminikɛ̃, -ɛn] **1** *adj Rel* **(a)** (*moine, religieuse*) Dominican **(b)** *Géog* Dominican; (*natif, habitant*) of Santo Domingo; **la République Dominicaine** the Dominican Republic, Santo Domingo **2** *n* **(a)** *Rel* Dominican **(b)** *Géog* **D.** Dominican

dominical, -ale, -aux, -ales [dɔminikal, -o] *adj* **l'oraison dominicale** the Lord's prayer; **repos d.** day of rest; *Rel* Sabbath; **dans la religion chrétienne, le repos d. est une coutume** in Christianity, it is traditional for Sunday to be a day of rest; **ouverture d. des magasins** Sunday opening *or* shopping

dominion [dɔminjɔn] *nm Pol* dominion

domino [dɔmino] *nm* [①A10,d] domino; **jouer aux dominos** to play dominoes

dommage [dɔmaʒ] *nm* **(a)** (*préjudice*) damage, injury; **causer un d. à qn** to do sb harm *or* an injury; **il s'en est tiré sans d.** he came out of it unscathed

(b) (*dégâts matériels*) **dommages** damage; **aucun d. n'est à déplorer** no damage is reported; **les dommages causés par l'explosion sont énormes** the explosion caused tremendous damage

(c) **(quel) d.!** what a pity!, what a shame!; **c'est (bien) d. qu'elle ne soit pas venue** it's a (great) pity that she didn't come; **le plus d. c'est que tu ne l'aies jamais rencontré** it's a great pity that you never met him; **d. que tu n'aies pas le temps** it's a pity you haven't the time

▶ **dommage**: *Jur* **d. causé avec intention de nuire** malicious damage; **d. corporel** personal or physical injury; **dommages de guerre** war damages; **dommages et intérêts, dommages-intérêts** damages; **dommages-intérêts compensatoires** compensation; **d. matériel** damage to property; **d. moral** psychological damage; **dommages punitifs** punitive damages

dommageable [dɔmaʒabl] *adj* detrimental, injurious; *Jur* prejudicial; *Jur* **acte d.** tort

domotique [dɔmɔtik] *nf* home automation

domptable [dɔ̃(p)tabl] *adj* capable of being tamed *or* subdued, tamable

domptage [dɔ̃(p)taʒ] *nm* (*d'animal*) (*apprivoisement*) taming; (*dressage*) training; (*de cheval*) breaking in; (*de fleuve, de la nature*) taming; **le d. du criminel n'a pas été facile** it was not easy to subdue the criminal

dompter [dɔ̃(p)te] *vt* (*animal*) (*apprivoiser*) to tame; (*dresser*) to train; (*cheval*) to break in; (*ses sentiments, passions etc*) to subdue, to overcome; (*fleuve, la nature*) to tame; (*personne*) to subdue

dompteur, -euse [dɔ̃(p)tœr, -øz] *n* (*d'animaux*) tamer, trainer; **d. de chevaux** horse-breaker

DOM-TOM [dɔmtɔm] *nmpl* (*abrév* **Départements et Territoires d'Outre-mer**) = French Overseas Departments and Territories

DON [deoɛn] *Ordinat* (*abrév* **disque optique numérique**) CD-ROM

don [dɔ̃] *nm* **(a)** (*cadeau*) gift, present; (*à un musée, une œuvre*) donation; **d. de M. Roland** (*dans un musée*) gift of Mr Roland, donated by Mr Roland; **un d. en nature/espèces** a donation in kind/cash; **faire d. à qn de qch** to make a present *or* a donation of sth to sb; *Fig* **les dons de la terre** the fruits of the earth; **cet enfant est un d. du ciel** that child is a gift from heaven; **le d. de soi** self-sacrifice; **faire d. de sa vie à Dieu** to give one's life to God **(b)** (*aptitude*) gift, talent; **le d. des langues** a gift *or* talent for languages; *aussi Iron* **avoir le d. de faire qch** to have a gift *or* talent *or* a genius for doing sth

▶ **don**: **d. d'organes** organ donation; **d. du sang** blood donation; **d. de sperme** sperm donation

donataire [dɔnatɛr] *n Jur* donee

donateur, -trice [dɔnatœr, -tris] *n* donor

donation [dɔnasjɔ̃] *nf* donation, gift; *Jur* **d. entre vifs** gift (*made to avoid inheritance tax*)

donation-partage, *pl* **donations-partages** *nf Jur* = distribution of estate during one's lifetime to avoid inheritance tax

donc [dɔ̃k] **1** *conj* (*marque la conséquence*) so; **il répond exactement à mes besoins, j'en suis d. très satisfait** it's exactly what I need, so I'm very satisfied with it; **je pense, d. je suis** I think, therefore I am

2 *adv* **(a)** (*emphatique*) **vous voilà d. de retour** so you're back (again); **tu le savais d. depuis le début?** so you knew from the start?, you knew from the start then?; **que voulez-vous d.?** what(ever) do you want?; **mais taisez-vous d.!** do be quiet!, *F* do shut up!; **allons d.!** nonsense!, come on!, come now!; **comment d.?** how do you mean?; **pensez d.!** that's what you think!, that'll be the day!; **tu as d. oublié?** have you forgotten?; **où vas-tu d.?** [dɔ̃] where are you going?; **cela vous plaît d.?** you like it, then?, so you like it?

(b) (*après interruption ou digression*) **d. pour en revenir à notre sujet** so *or* well, to come back to our subject; **je disais d. que …** I was saying, then, that …, as I was saying …

dondon [dɔ̃dɔ̃] *nf F* fat woman/girl; **grosse d.** great lump of a woman/girl

donjon [dɔ̃ʒɔ̃] *nm* (*d'un château*) keep, donjon

don Juan [dɔ̃ʒɥɑ̃] *nm* Don Juan

donjuanesque [dɔ̃ʒɥanɛsk] *adj* Don Juan

donjuanisme [dɔ̃ʒɥanism] *nm* Don Juanism

donnant-donnant [dɔnɑ̃dɔnɑ̃] *adj* **c'est d., je te prête ma voiture et tu me prêtes ton aspirateur** it's only fair, I lend you my car and you lend me your vacuum cleaner; **avec elle, c'est toujours d.** she always expects something in return; **désormais, ce sera d.** from now on things are going to be a bit fairer around here, from now on it's going to be a two-way street around here

donne [dɔn] *nf Cartes* deal; **à vous la d.!** your deal!; **faire la d.** to deal; **fausse d.** misdeal; *Fig* **il y a fausse d.** there's been a mistake; *Fig* **nouvelle d.** new state of affairs; **il y a une nouvelle d. des pays de l'Est** the situation in the Eastern bloc has changed; **le partage du travail sera une nouvelle d. dans la situation économique** job-sharing will be a new factor in the economic situation

donné [dɔne] *adj* **(a)** given; **propriété donnée en dot** property given as a dowry; *F* **c'est d.** it's dirt cheap, it's a gift, I'm/he's/*etc* giving it away **(b)** (*défini*) given; **à un point d./une distance donnée** at a given *or* certain point/distance; **des quantités données** given quantities; **à un moment d.** then; **à un moment d. tu seras bien obligé de lui dire** you'll have to tell him some time *or* sooner or later **(c) étant d. deux triangles** given two triangles; **étant d. l'heure tardive** since it's so late; **étant d. qu'il était mineur** since *or* as he was a minor

donnée [dɔne] *nf* (*d'un problème etc*) given information; (*d'un roman etc*) fundamental idea *or* subject; [ⓘA9,b,i] **données** data; **si je n'ai pas toutes les données du problème** if I don't have all the data *or* information on the problem; **le traitement des données** data processing; **support de données** data carrier; **commutateur de données** data switch; **données nominatives** personal data; *Ordinat* **données numériques** digital data; *Ordinat* **données à sept bits** seven-bit data; *Ordinat* **banque/base de données** data bank/base

donner [dɔne] **1** *vt* **(a)** (*offrir*) (*quelque chose de concret, siège, livre, travail etc*) to give; **d. son sang** to give blood; **d. un cadeau à qn** to give a present to sb, to give sb a present; **il m'a donné 100 francs** he gave me 100 francs; **d. son corps à la science** to donate one's body to science; **d. sa place à une vieille dame** to give (up) one's seat to an old lady; **d. à boire à qn** to give sb something to drink; **c'est toi qui nous donnes à manger?** are you giving us lunch/*etc*?; **d. c'est d.** a gift is a gift

(b) (*faire don de*) (*temps, amour, hospitalité etc*) to give; **d. sa vie pour qn** to give one's life for sb; **d. son temps pour une cause** to give *or* donate one's time to a cause; **d. le jour** *ou* **la vie à un enfant** to give birth to a child; **d. la mort à qn** to kill sb

(c) (*céder, vendre*) to give; **je vous en donne dix francs** I'll give you ten francs for it; **je lui donne 40 francs de l'heure** I pay him 40 francs an hour; **je te donne mon pull contre ta jupe** I'll give you my sweater (in exchange) for your skirt, I'll swop my sweater for your skirt; **en d. à qn pour son argent** to give sb their money's worth; *Fig* **ah, il veut avoir plus de responsabilités, et bien, on va lui en d. pour son argent** if he wants more responsibility, we'll give him it and then some more *or* we'll give him as much as he wants and more; **elle donnerait n'importe quoi** *ou* **tout ce qu'elle a au monde pour que cela se réalise** she'd give anything for that to happen; **je donnerais beaucoup pour le savoir** I'd give a lot to know

(d) (*confier*) to give; **d. à qn qch à garder** to give sb sth to look after, *Fml* to entrust sb with sth; **d. ses chaussures à ressemeler** to leave one's shoes to be resoled; **d. un vêtement à nettoyer/au teinturier** to hand in a piece of clothing to be dry-cleaned; **d. ses enfants à garder** to leave one's children to be looked after

(e) (*dire, communiquer*) (*avis, détails, description, ordres, conseils etc*) to give; **d. l'heure** to tell the time; **vous pourriez me d. l'heure?** could you give me the time?; **le journal donne des nouvelles alarmantes sur la crise** the newspaper gives alarming news of the crisis; **tu lui donneras le bonjour de ma part** say hello to him for me; **tu pourrais d. des nouvelles de temps en temps!** you could let me/us/*etc* hear from you occasionally!; **je vous le donne en cent** *ou* **en mille** you'll never guess; **donnez-moi le jour et l'heure de votre arrivée** give me your date and time of arrival; *Péj* **il faudrait qu'on lui donne du 'Maître' pour qu'il soit satisfait** he won't be happy unless he's addressed as 'Maître'; **il lui a donné du 'Madame la Comtesse' toute la soirée** he 'Countess'd' her this and 'Countess'd' her that all evening

(f) (*octroyer*) (*sa parole, son accord, du temps, une chance, délai, occasion, pourboire etc*) to give; **j'y reviendrai plus tard, si l'occasion m'en est donnée** I'll go there again later if I get the chance; **d. sa fille en mariage à qn** to give one's daughter to sb in marriage; **d. sa confiance à qn** to put one's trust in sb

(g) (*causer*) (*de l'énergie, de l'appétit, des coliques etc*) to give; **cette odeur me donne mal à la tête** this smell is giving me a headache; **d. du souci à qn** to cause sb worry; **d. sujet** *ou* **matière à discussion** to be a subject for discussion *or* debate; **cela m'a donné l'idée de …** that gave me the idea to …; **son histoire donne plus à rire qu'à pleurer** his story is funny rather than sad, his story makes you want to laugh rather than cry; **toute cette histoire m'a donné à réfléchir/à rire** the entire business made me think/laugh; **d. envie de rire** to be laughable *or* comical; **ça me donne envie de rire** that makes me want to laugh; **d. faim/soif/sommeil/chaud/le vertige à qn** to make sb hungry/thirsty/sleepy/hot/dizzy; **cette fenêtre donne de la lumière dans la pièce** that window makes the room brighter; **je lui ai donné à entendre que …** I gave him to understand that …; **cela me donne à croire que …** it leads me to believe that …

(h) (*produire*) to give; (*de récoltes*) to yield; **arbre qui donne de beaux fruits** tree that gives *or* yields *or* bears fine fruit; **les arbres donnent de l'ombre** the trees give shade; **elle a donné trois beaux enfants à son mari** she gave *or* bore her husband three beautiful children; **d. le la avec un diapason** to give an A with a tuning fork; **d. de l'électricité** to produce electricity; **essai qui ne donne rien** fruitless *or* unsuccessful attempt; **une méthode qui ne donne rien** a method that doesn't work; *F* **ça n'a rien donné** nothing came of it, it didn't work out; **je me demande ce que cela va d.** I wonder what will come of it *or* what the result of it will be; *F* **qu'est-ce que ça donne?** how does it look?

(i) (*mettre*) to give; **d. un baiser/une caresse/une gifle/une fessée à qn** to give sb a kiss/a caress/a slap in the face/a spanking; **d. un coup de peigne à ses cheveux** to give one's hair a quick comb; **il faudrait d. une couche de peinture supplémentaire** we'll have to put on an extra coat of paint; **tu peux d. un coup de balai dans la cuisine?** can you give the kitchen a sweep?; *Fig* **tu donnes ta langue au chat?** do you give up *or* in?

(j) (*organiser*) (*bal, dîner, conférence etc*) to give; **d. une pièce de théâtre** to put on *or* perform a play; **qu'est-ce qu'on donne au cinéma aujourd'hui?** what's on at the cinema today?

(k) (*attribuer*) **on donne ses théories pour révolutionnaires** they say his theories are revolutionary, his theories are said to be revolutionary; **je lui donne vingt ans** I reckon he's about twenty; **les médecins lui donnent deux jours (à vivre)** the doctors give him two days (to live); **d. tort/raison à qn** to disagree/agree with sb

(l) (*conférer*) (*impression*) to give; (*poids, valeur*) to give, to lend; **d. un sens à sa vie** to give (a) meaning to one's life; **ta nouvelle coiffure te donne un air jeune** your new hairdo makes you look younger

(m) (*passer*) **tu peux me d. le livre qui est dans le tiroir/sur la table?** can you give me the book out of the drawer/off the table?; **il m'a donné son rhume** he gave me his cold, I caught his cold

(n) (*accorder*) **il n'est pas donné à tout le monde d'être (un) écrivain** not everybody can be a writer

(o) *Arg* (*vendre*) to grass on (**à** to)

2 *vi* **(a)** (*faire un don*) to give; **aimer d.** to like to give, to like giving

(b) (*cogner*) **le navire a donné sur les rochers** the ship ran onto *or* struck the rocks; **d. de la tête contre qch** to knock *or* strike *or* bump one's head against sth; *Fig F* **ne pas savoir où d. de la tête** not to know which way to turn; **sa tête alla d. dans le ventre de son adversaire** his head went straight into his opponent's stomach; **le soleil donne dans la pièce** the sun is streaming into the room

(c) (*tomber*) **d. dans le piège** *ou F* **le panneau** to fall into the trap; **d. dans** (*avoir un penchant pour*) to be given to; **il donne dans la bigoterie** he is rather bigoted; **il donne dans les petites minettes en ce moment** he really goes for young babes at the moment; **d. dans le genre théâtral** to lapse into the melodramatic

(d) (*produire*) **si les blés donnent cette année** if there is a good crop of wheat this year; *F* **s'ils se disputent, ça va d.** if they argue there'll be trouble; **leur chaîne/la musique a donné à fond toute la soirée** their stereo/the music was blaring all evening

(e) *(charger)* **faire d. un bataillon** to send a battalion into action

(f) *(déboucher)* **la fenêtre donne sur la cour** the window looks onto the yard; **cette porte donne sur** *ou* **dans le jardin** this door leads (out) into the garden

(g) *(s'allonger) (d'une corde, d'une jupe)* to stretch

(h) *Cartes* **mal d.** to misdeal; **c'est à qui de d.?** whose deal is it?

3 se donner *vpr* **(a)** *(se consacrer)* to devote oneself (**à** to); **elle s'est donnée entièrement** she gave fully of herself

(b) *(s'offrir)* **se d. en spectacle** to make an exhibition of oneself; **se d. des airs** to put on airs, to give oneself airs; **se d. un genre** to make out one is something one is not; **c'est un genre qu'elle se donne** it's just a front

(c) *(s'accorder)* **se d. toutes les chances de réussir** to give oneself every chance of succeeding; **se d. le temps de réflechir** to give oneself *or* take time to think; **s'en d. (à cœur joie)** to enjoy oneself (to the full), to have a good time, to have a field day; **se d. du bon temps** to have a good time, to enjoy oneself; **se d. bonne conscience** to salve one's conscience; **se d. pour tâche de ...** to set oneself the task of ...; **se d. pour mission** to make it one's mission to ...

(d) se d. un coup de peigne/brosse to give one's hair a quick comb/brush; **se d. un coup de marteau sur le pouce** to hit one's thumb with a hammer; **se d. du tourment** to torment oneself

(e) *(se prétendre)* **il se donne pour un grand musicien** he says he is *or* claims he is *or* claims to be a great musician

(f) *(sexuellement)* to give oneself

(g) *(choisir) (chef, président etc)* to choose, to select

(h) *(échanger)* **se d. des coups** to exchange blows, to hit each other; **se d. des baisers** to kiss each other; **se d. l'accolade** to embrace each other; **se d. une poignée de main** to shake hands

(i) *Cin* to be on, to be showing; **hier soir se donnait chez Maxim's la soirée d'adieu du Comte Orloff** Count Orloff's farewell party took place at Maxim's last night

4 *v impers* **c'est le spectacle le plus épouvantable qu'il m'a (jamais) été donné de voir** it was the most horrifying sight I'd ever been unfortunate enough to witness

donneur, -euse [dɔnœr, -øz] *n* **(a)** *Méd* donor; **d. de sang/sperme** blood/sperm donor; *Méd* **d. universel** universal donor; *Com* **d. d'ordre** principal; *Péj* **d. d'avis** *ou* **de conseils** know-all **(b)** *Cartes* dealer **(c)** *Arg (délateur)* grass

don-quichottisme [dɔ̃kiʃɔtism] *nm* quixotism

dont [dɔ̃] *pron rel* [ⓘA32-33; B21,e; B59,12,6] **(a)** *(exprimant le complément du verbe et indiquant la provenance)* **la pièce d. elle sort** the room she is coming out of; **la ville d. je viens** the town I come from; **la famille d. je descends** the family I am descended from *or* from which I am descended

(b) *(exprimant le complément du verbe et indiquant le moyen, la manière etc)* **la façon d. il me regardait/est habillé** the way (in which) he looked at me/is dressed

(c) *(au sujet de qui, de quoi)* **une fille d. on ne sait rien** a girl we know nothing about, *Fml* a girl about whom we know nothing; **un film d. on parle beaucoup** a film that is being talked about a lot; **un incident d. on se souviendra** an incident that will be remembered

(d) *(exprimant l'objet du verbe)* **le livre d. j'ai besoin** the book (that) I need; **voici ce d. il s'agit** this is what it's all about; **l'homme d. il s'agit** the man in question; **l'homme d. elle se moque** the man she's making fun of, *Fml* the man of whom she is making fun

(e) *(exprimant l'objet de l'adjectif)* **la femme d. il est amoureux** the woman he is in love with; **le groupe d'enfants d. vous êtes responsable** the group of children you are responsible for; **le souvenir d. elle est si honteuse** the memory she is so ashamed of

(f) *(exprimant le complément de nom et indiquant la possession, la qualité, la matière)* **la dame d. je connais le fils** the lady whose son I know; **la dame d. le fils vous connaît** the lady whose son knows you; **la chambre d. la porte est fermée** the room with the closed door; **cet objet d. le nom m'échappe** this object, the name of which escapes me

(g) *(exprimant le complément de nom et indiquant une partie d'un tout)* **quelques-uns étaient là, d. votre frère** there were a few people there, including your brother; **un rêve d. il ne me reste que cette image** a dream of which I remember nothing but this image, a dream I remember nothing about except this image; **un film d. voici le résumé** a film of which this is a summary; **la maison d. on voit le toit** the house whose roof can be seen; **le parti d. le chef vient de mourir** the party whose leader has just died

donzelle [dɔ̃zɛl] *nf F Péj* woman who puts on airs

dopage [dɔpaʒ] *nm* doping; *(athlétisme, cyclisme etc)* drug-taking; *Fig (de l'économie)* boosting

dopant [dɔpɑ̃] *nm Méd* dope; **produit dopant** drug

dope [dɔp] *nf F (drogue)* dope

doper [dɔpe] **1** *vt Sp etc* to dope; *Fig (économie, monnaie etc)* to boost, to give a boost *or* fillip to **2 se doper** *vpr* to take stimulants, to dope oneself

dope sheet [dɔpʃit] *nm TV* dope sheet

doping [dɔpiŋ] *nm* doping

doppler [dɔplɛr] **1** *adj Phys* **effet d.** Doppler effect **2** *nm Méd* = use of Doppler's method to determine speed at which the blood is circulating

dorade [dɔrad] *nf (poisson)* gilthead bream, sea bream

doré [dɔre] **1** *adj* **(a)** *(recouvert d'or)* gilded, gilt; **d. sur tranche** gilt-edged; **papier d.** gold-coloured paper **(b)** *(couleur d'or) (blé, lumière)* golden, honey-coloured; *(yeux)* golden (brown); *(peau)* golden (brown), honey-coloured; *Culin (gâteau passé au jaune d'œuf)* glazed; *(viande, pommes de terre, gâteau cuit)* browned, golden; **cheveux blond d.** golden hair **2** *nm Can (poisson)* wall-eyed pike, yellow pike

dorée [dɔre] *nf (poisson)* (John) Dory

dorénavant [dɔrenavɑ̃] *adv* from now on, *Fml* henceforth

dorer [dɔre] **1** *vt* **(a)** *(recouvrir d'or)* to gild; *Fig* **d. la pilule** to sugar the pill **(b)** *(donner une couleur dorée à) (peau)* to turn golden; *Culin (gâteau)* to glaze; *(viande, pommes de terre)* to brown; **le soleil dorait les cimes** the sun shed a golden light on the hilltops *or* turned the hilltops golden **2** *vi Culin* to brown **3 se dorer** *vpr* to turn a golden colour; **elle se dore** *ou F* **se dore la pilule au soleil** she's sunbathing, she's getting a suntan

doreur, -euse [dɔrœr, -øz] *n* gilder

dorique [dɔrik] *adj Archit* Doric

dorlotement [dɔrlɔtmɑ̃] *nm* coddling, pampering

dorloter [dɔlɔte] **1** *vt* to coddle, to pamper; **se laisser/se faire d.** to let oneself be/to be coddled *or* pampered **2 se dorloter** *vpr* to coddle *or* pamper oneself

dormant [dɔrmɑ̃] **1** *adj* **(a)** *(eau)* still, stagnant **(b)** *Tech* **serrure dormante** dead lock **(c)** *Fig Fml (passions, instincts, sensualité)* dormant **(d)** *Fin (capitaux, compte)* dormant **2** *nm (d'une porte, une fenêtre)* frame, casing

dormeur, -euse [dɔrmœr, -øz] **1** *adj* **poupée dormeuse** doll with eyes that close **2** *n (personne endormie)* sleeper; **ne réveille pas les dormeurs** don't waken the people who're sleeping; **un grand** *ou* **gros d.** a heavy sleeper; **en vacances je redeviens un gros d.** I sleep a lot when I'm on holiday; **je ne partirai plus en week-end avec ces dormeurs** I'm not going away with them for the weekend again, all they do is sleep **3** *nf* **dormeuse** *(boucle d'oreille)* sleeper **4** *nm (crustacé)* edible crab

dormir [dɔrmir] *vi* (*prp* **dormant**; *pp* **dormi**; *pr ind* **je dors, n. dormons**; *impf* **je dormais**; *p hist* **je dormis**) **(a)** to sleep; **il dort** he's sleeping, he's asleep; **d. profondément** *ou* **d'un profond sommeil** to be fast asleep, to be in a deep sleep; **bien/mal d.** to sleep well/badly; **elle dort d'un sommeil léger** she's a light sleeper; **d. du sommeil du juste** to sleep the sleep of the just; **je n'ai pas dormi de la nuit** I haven't slept a wink, I didn't sleep a wink *or* get a wink's sleep (all night), I didn't sleep all night; **il n'en dort pas** he can't (get to) sleep for thinking of it; **parler/pleurer/crier en dormant** to talk/cry/shout in one's sleep; **le café m'empêche de d.** coffee keeps me awake; *F* **ce n'est pas ça qui va m'empêcher de d.** I won't lose any sleep over it; **d. trop longtemps** to oversleep; **d. à poings fermés** *ou* **comme une souche** *ou* **comme un loir** *ou* **comme une marmotte** *ou* **comme une brute** *ou* **comme un sonneur** to sleep soundly *or* like a log; **ne d. que d'un œil** to sleep with one eye open; **vous pouvez d. tranquille** *ou* **sur les** *ou* **vos deux oreilles** you can rest easy; **avoir envie de d.** to be *or* feel sleepy *or* drowsy; **il dort debout** he's asleep on his feet, he can't keep his eyes open; **une histoire** *ou* **un conte à d. debout** a tall *or* cock-and-bull story; **il dort sur son travail** he's falling asleep over his work; *F* **ce n'est vraiment pas le moment de d.** there's no time for sleeping now

(b) *Fig (d'une ville, d'une forêt)* to be sleeping, to be asleep; **une espèce de génie dort en lui** he has a kind of latent genius; **elle a laissé ses projets d. trop longtemps** she waited too long to carry out her plans; **ce serait dommage de laisser d. tes talents de couturier** it would be a pity not to make use of your dressmaking talents *or* a pity to let your dressmaking talents go to waste; **un roman qui**

dort dans un tiroir a novel languishing in a drawer; **c'est idiot d'avoir des capitaux qui dorment** it's stupid to have capital lying idle, it's stupid not to make your capital work for you; **eau qui dort** stagnant *or* still water; *Prov* **il n'est pire eau que l'eau qui dort** still waters run deep

dormitif, -ive [dɔrmitif, -iv] *adj Méd* soporific

dorsal, -ale, -aux, -ales [dɔrsal, -o] **1** *adj* dorsal; **région dorsale de la main** back of the hand; *Av* **parachute d.** back-type parachute **2** *nf* **dorsale (a)** *Ling* dorsal consonant **(b)** *Géog* ridge; *Météo* **d. barométrique** ridge of high pressure

dortoir [dɔrtwar] *nm* dormitory; **ville-d., cité-d.** dormitory town

dorure [dɔryr] *nf* **(a)** *(couche d'or)* gilding **(b)** *Culin (d'un gâteau)* glazing (with egg yolk) **(c)** *(ornement doré)* gilt, gilding; **uniforme couvert de dorures** gold-braided uniform

doryphore [dɔrifɔr] *nm* Colorado beetle

DOS [dɔs] *nm Ordinat* DOS; **depuis le DOS, à partir du DOS** through (the) DOS

dos [do] *nm* **(a)** *Anat* back; **avoir le d. voûté** to be round-shouldered; *Fig* **il a bon d.** he's got a broad back *or* shoulders; **elle a bon d. la grève des postes, dis plutôt que tu n'as pas écrit** why don't you admit that you haven't written instead of blaming it on the postal strike?; *F* **j'en ai plein le d.** I'm sick of it, I'm fed up with it; **faire le gros d.** *(d'un chat)* to arch its back; *Fig (faire des difficultés)* to dig one's heels in, *Br F* to turn bolshie; **mon fils fait toujours le gros d. pour aller se coucher** my son always kicks up a fuss at bedtime; **tourner le d. à qn** to turn one's back on sb; *(quand on est debout/assis)* to stand/sit with one's back to sb; *Fig* **tous mes amis m'ont tourné le d.** all my friends have turned their back on me; **avoir le d. tourné à qch/qn** to have one's back to sth/sb; **dès qu'il a le d. tourné** the moment *or* as soon as his back is turned; **en d. d'âne** ridged, razor-backed; **pont en d. d'âne** humpbacked bridge; **attention, d. d'âne,** beware uneven road surface; **voyager à d. d'âne** to ride *or* travel on a donkey; **d. à d.** back to back; *Fig* **leur mère les a renvoyés d. à d.** their mother couldn't decide which of them was the guilty party; **je les renvoie d. à d.** I think they're equally guilty *or* as bad as each other; **on peut les renvoyer d. à d.** they're equally guilty; *F* **se mettre tout le monde à d.** to set everybody against you; **partir sac au d.** to set off with one's pack on one's back; **faire qch derrière** *ou* **dans le d. de qn** to do sth behind sb's back; **robe décolletée dans le d.** low-backed dress; **elle porte ses cheveux dans le d.** she wears her hair loose *or* down; **ça fait froid dans le d.** it's scary *or* creepy, it gives you the shivers; **j'en ai un frisson dans le d.** it sends a shiver down my spine; *Fig F* **la maison, on l'a dans le d.** we can kiss the house goodbye; *Fig F* **faire un enfant dans le d. à qn** to stab sb in the back; **je ne l'ai vu que de d.** I only saw him from the back, I only got a back view of him; **dormir sur le d.** to sleep on one's back; *Fig F* **depuis un mois, j'ai mon patron/le fisc sur le d.** I've had my boss/the tax man on my back for a month; *F* **il me tombe toujours sur le d.** *(il m'attaque)* he's always on my back; *(il arrive à l'improviste)* he's always just turning up; **le fisc va te tomber sur le d.** you're going to have the tax man on your back, you're going to bring the tax man down on you; **le repassage, c'est toujours sur son d. que ça tombe** he always gets landed with the ironing; **quand mes frères font des bêtises, c'est toujours sur mon d. que ça tombe** I always get the blame when my brothers do something stupid; **mettre qch sur le d. de qn** to saddle sb with sth; **quand il a été interrogé, il a tout mis sur mon d.** when he was questioned, he put all the blame on me; **il a tout mis sur le d. des petits copains et est parti tranquillement en vacances** he offloaded everything onto his friends and blithely went off on holiday; **il s'est mis une sale histoire sur le d.** he's landed himself in real trouble; **gagner de l'argent** *ou* **s'enrichir sur le d. de qn** to get rich off sb, to make money on sb's back; **je n'ai rien à me mettre sur le d.** I haven't a thing to wear; *F Vieilli* **faire la bête à deux d.** to have it off; *F Vieilli* **faire la bête à deux d. avec qn** to sleep with *or* have it off with sb

(b) *(d'une chaise, d'une page, d'un couteau etc)* back; *(du nez)* bridge; *(d'un livre)* spine; **signer au d. d'un chèque** to endorse a cheque; **voir au d.** (please) turn over, PTO; *Fin* **d. d'un effet** back of a bill

dosage [dozaʒ] *nm Ch etc (d'ingrédients)* proportioning; *Méd (de médicaments)* dosage; *Méd* **d. hormonal** test to determine hormone levels

dos-d'âne [dodan] *nm inv* bump; **pont en d.** hump-backed bridge

dose [doz] *nf Ch etc (d'un élément dans un mélange)* proportion, amount; *(de médicament)* dose; **d. mortelle** lethal dose; **ne pas dépasser la d. prescrite** do not exceed the stated dose; *Fig* **par** *ou* **à petites doses, à d. homéopathique** in small doses; **une légère d. d'ironie** a tinge of irony; *F* **il faut une sacrée d. de culot/d'humour pour faire cela** it takes a helluva nerve/a great sense of humour to do that; **forcer la d.** to overdo it; *F* **avoir sa d.** to have had more than enough; **avoir sa d. de lecture/de ménage/de cinéma américain** to have had one's fill of reading/housework/American films; *F* **en avoir sa d.** to have had one's fill, to have had more than enough; **la pluie, je t'assure que j'en ai ma d.** I've had my fill of rain *or* more than enough rain, let me tell you

doser [doze] *vt Ch etc (pour évaluer)* to determine the quantity of; *(pour constituer)* to proportion; *(médicament)* to measure out; **je n'arrive jamais à d. la farine dans mes gâteaux** I never manage to get the right amount of flour in my cakes; *Fig* **il faut savoir d. l'ironie** you have to get the amount of irony just right

doseur [dozœr] *nm* measure; **verre d.** *Culin* measuring jug; *(pour l'alcool)* measure

doseur-distributeur, *pl* **doseurs-distributeurs** *nm (de carburant)* fuel distributor

dossard [dosar] *nm Sp* number

dossier [dosje] *nm* **(a)** *(d'un siège)* back, backrest; **chaise à d. droit** straight-backed chair; **d. réglable** adjustable back; **d. rabattable** folding seatback; **d. repliable** folding seatback

(b) *(pièces, documents)* file, dossier; *(d'un prisonnier, un malade etc)* record; *(chemise)* folder, file; *Ordinat* file; **verser une pièce au d.** to file a document; **constituer un d. sur qn/qch** to build up a file on sb/sth; **d. d'appel d'offres** tender documents; **d. client** client file; **d. crédit** credit file; **d. 'divers'** miscellaneous file; **d. de domiciliation** domiciliation papers, domiciliation file; **d. de douane** customs papers *or* file; **d. d'information** information pack; **d. de lancement** *(d'un produit)* product launch file; **d. médical** medical record; *F* **d. offre** tender documents; **d. de presse** book of press cuttings, scrap book; **d. scolaire** school records; **d. suspendu** suspension file; *Ordinat* **d. système** system folder; **d. de voyage** travel documents;

(c) *(sujet)* question, matter; **le d. de la couche d'ozone est assez important** the ozone layer is a fairly important question *or* matter; **le dossier du GATT** the GATT question, GATT matters; **s'occuper du d. de l'environnement** to be responsible for environmental matters; **avoir un d. brûlant à traiter** to have a controversial issue to deal with; **je pense qu'il est temps de fermer le d. Staline** I think it's time to draw a line under the Stalin question

dot [dɔt] *nf* **(a)** *(pour un mariage)* dowry, marriage settlement; **il l'a épousée pour sa d.** he married her for her dowry; **coureur de d.** fortune hunter **(b)** *(pour une religieuse)* dowry

dotal, -ale, -aux, -ales [dɔtal, -o] *adj (propriété)* dotal; *Jur* **régime d.** (marriage) settlement in trust

dotation [dɔtasjɔ̃] *nf* **(a)** *(fonds) (d'hôpital, de collège etc)* endowment, foundation; *(à la famille royale, à un chef d'état)* allowance **(b)** *Can Admin* **agent de d.** staffing officer; **d. en effectifs** staff increase **(c)** *Compta* provision; **d. aux amortissements** depreciation provision, allowance for depreciation, charge to depreciation; **d. aux provisions** charge to provisions; **d. en capital** capital contribution

doter [dɔte] *vt (hôpital, collège etc)* to endow; *Vieilli (mariée)* to dower; **être doté de toutes les vertus** to be endowed with every virtue; **d. une usine d'un matériel neuf** to equip a factory with new plant; **la vie l'a dotée d'une intelligence remarquable** life has bestowed unparalleled intelligence on her *or* has endowed her with unparalleled intelligence; **d. une provision** to make a provision

douaire [dwɛr] *nm* dower

douairière [dwɛrjɛr] *adj, nf* dowager

douane [dwan] *nf Admin* customs; **passer à la d.** *ou* **au bureau de d.** to go through customs; **passer qch (en fraude) à la d.** to smuggle sth through customs; **formalités de d.** customs formalities; **à l'aéroport, les formalités de d. sont vraiment simplifiées** it's really easy to go through customs at the airport; **agent des douanes** customs officer; **marchandises en d.** bonded goods; **(droits de) d.** (customs) duty; **franc de d.** duty paid; **d. volante** mobile customs and excise unit

douanier, -ière [dwanje, -jɛr] **1** *adj* customs; **tarif d.** customs tariff; **union douanière** customs union; **barrières douanières** tariff barriers **2** *nm* customs officer

doublage [dublaʒ] *nm* **(a)** *(d'une feuille de papier, d'une couverture, d'un fil etc)* doubling, folding in half **(b)** *(d'une quantité, d'un salaire etc)* doubling **(c)** *(d'un manteau)* lining **(d)** *Cin (de voix)* dubbing; *(dans une scène)* doubling **(de for)**; **d. du film en anglais** English dubbing of the film; **d. du dialogue (en boucle)** dialogue looping **(e)** *Aut* **d. d'aile** wing valance

double [dubl] **1** *adj* **(a)** (*mesure, quantité, consonne, lit, chambre etc*) double; *Scol* **copie d.** double sheet of paper; **valise à d. fond** suitcase with a false bottom; **faire qch en d. exemplaire** to do sth in duplicate; **coup d.** (*au tir*) right and left; **mot qui fait d. emploi (avec un autre)** redundant word; **'vends micro-ondes, cause double emploi'** (*de petite annonce*) microwave for sale, duplicate item; **sa canne à pêche a une longueur d. de la mienne** his fishing rod is twice the length of *or* twice as long as mine; **fermer une porte à d. tour** to double-lock a door; **enfermer qn à d. tour** to lock sb in; **à d. effet** dual- *or* double-action; **outil à d. usage** dual-purpose tool; **à d. tranchant** (*couteau*) double-edged; *Fig* two-edged; **comptabilité en partie d.** double-entry bookkeeping; **d. allumage** (*de moteur*) dual ignition; **avoir une d. nationalité** to have dual nationality; **foyer à d. revenu** two-income household; **d. whisky** double *or* large whisky; *Mus* **d. croche** semi-quaver, *Am* sixteenth note; **d. mètre** rule (*which measures two metres*); **d. nœud** double knot; **doubles rideaux** curtains, *Am* drapes; *Fig* **faire coup d.** to kill two birds with one stone; **test en d. aveugle** double blind test; *Fig* **mettre les bouchées doubles** to work twice as hard; **d. vitrage** double glazing; **d. arbre à cames** twin cam, twin camshaft; **d. carburateur** twin carburettor; *Aut* **d. ligne blanche** double white line; *Journ* **d. colonne** double column; *Journ* **d. page** double-page spread; **l'article prend une d. page** it's a two-page spread; *Ordinat* **d. densité** double density; *Typ, TV, Cin* **d. prise** double-take; **d. interligne** double spacing; **en d. interligne** double-spaced; *Typ* **d. soulignement** double underlining; *Typ* **d. souligné** double underline

(b) (*ambigu*) **d. personnalité** dual personality; **mener une d. vie** to lead a double life; **mot à d. sens** ambiguous word; **agent d.** double agent; **jouer un d. jeu avec qn** to play a double game with sb; **je n'ai pas le don de d. vue** I'm not endowed with ESP, I'm not psychic, I don't have second sight

2 *adv* **voir d.** to see double

3 *nm* **(a)** (*quantité*) double; **j'ai le d. de votre âge** I'm twice your age; **ça m'a coûté le d.** it cost me twice as much *or* double; **mettre qch en d.** to double sth, to fold sth in two *or* half; *Tennis* **d. messieurs/dames/mixte** men's/ladies'/mixed doubles; **faire un d.** (*dans un jeu*) to throw a double

(b) (*exemplaire*) duplicate, copy; *Ordinat* backup; *Typ* carbon copy; **faire qch en d.** (*lettre, devoir, clé*) to make two copies of sth; **je dois tricoter le pull en d.** I'll have to make two pullovers of the same pattern; **avoir un d. des clefs** to have duplicate keys *or* a spare set of keys; **avoir un d. de tous les papiers importants** to have duplicates of all the important papers; **prends-le, je l'ai en d.** take it, I have two of them; **j'ai un timbre en d. dans ma collection** I have two copies of a stamp in my collection; **j'ai tous mes papiers en d. au cas où** I have duplicates *or* copies of all my papers just in case

(c) (*personne*) double

doublé [duble] **1** *adj* **(a)** doubled **(b)** (*veste, gants*) lined **(de** with) **(c)** *Cin* dubbed, re-voiced **2** *nm* **(a) d. (or)** gold plate, rolled gold; (*bijouterie*) gold-plated jewellery *or US* jewelry; **d. argent** silver plate; (*bijouterie*) silver-plated jewellery **(b)** (*à la chasse*), *Sp* double

double-bande, *pl* **doubles-bandes** [dubləbɑ̃d] *nf TV* double head

double-blanc, *pl* **doubles-blancs** [dubləblɑ̃] *nm* (*aux dominos*) double blank

double-clic, *pl* **doubles-clics** [dubləklik] *nm Ordinat* double-click; **faire un d.** to double-click

double-cliquer [dubləklike] *vi Ordinat* to double-click

double-commande, *pl* **doubles-commandes** [dubləkɔmɑ̃d] *nf Av, Aut* dual controls

double-corde, *pl* **doubles-cordes** [dubləkɔrd] *nf Mus* (*sur un violon etc*) double-stopping

double-crème, *pl* **doubles-crèmes** [dubləkrɛm] *nm* (type of) cream cheese

double-débrayage [dublədebrɛjaʒ] *nm Aut* double-declutching; **faire un d.** to double-declutch

double-décimètre, *pl* **doubles-décimètres** [dublədesimɛtr] *nm* = ruler, foot rule

double-fenêtre, *pl* **doubles-fenêtres** [dubləf(ə)nɛtr] *nf* sash window, double-hung window

doublement¹ [dubləmɑ̃] *adv* doubly

doublement² *nm* **(a)** (*d'un nombre, d'une somme, d'une lettre etc*) doubling; (*d'une feuille de papier*) folding in two *or* in half; (*d'une couverture, d'un fil*) folding in two *or* in half, doubling; *Ordinat* **d. de vitesse d'horloge** clock speed doubling **(b)** *Aut* overtaking, *Am* passing; **tenter un d.** to try to overtake; **d. interdit** no overtaking

doubler [duble] **1** *vt* **(a)** (*montant, taille etc*) to double; **d. le pas** to quicken one's pace

(b) (*feuille de papier*) to fold in two *or* in half; (*couverture, fil*) to fold in two *or* in half, to double; *Mus* **d. une partie** to double a part

(c) (*manteau, gant etc*) to line

(d) *Scol* **d. une classe** to repeat a year

(e) *Cin* (*film*) to dub; *Cin* (*acteur*) to stand in for; *Th* (*rôle, acteur*) to understudy; **d. une prise** to do a double-take

(f) (*passer*) **d. les gens dans une queue** to jump a queue, to sneak past the people in a queue; **d. une voiture** to overtake *or Am* pass a car; *Naut* **d. un cap** to double *or* make *or* weather a cape

(g) *F* (*trahir*) to double-cross; **on s'est fait d.** we've been double-crossed

2 *vi* **(a)** (*de population etc*) to double, to increase twofold

(b) *Aut* to overtake, *Am* to pass; **défense de d.** no overtaking, *Am* no passing

3 se doubler *vpr* **une haine qui se double de mépris** hatred coupled with contempt

doublet [dublɛ] *nm* (*pierre précieuse*), *Ling* doublet

doubleur [dublœr] *nm Ordinat* **d. de fréquence** clock speed doubler

doublon¹ [dublɔ̃] *nm Typ* double, word keyed twice

doublon² *nm Hist* (*monnaie*) doubloon

doublure [dublyr] *nf* **(a)** (*d'un vêtement, d'un sac de couchage etc*) lining **(b)** *Th* understudy; *Cin* stand-in; (*cascadeur*) stunt man/woman

douce [dus] *nf* **(a)** *F* (*petite amie*) girlfriend; **allez, viens ma d.** come on sweetheart **(b) en d.** discreetly, quietly, *F* on the Q.T.

douce-amère, *pl* **douces-amères** [dusamɛr] *nf* woody nightshade, bittersweet

douceâtre [dusɑtr] *adj* sweetish, *Péj* sickly sweet

doucement [dusmɑ̃] *adv* (*délicatement*) gently; (*bas*) softly; (*en faisant attention*) gently, carefully, slowly; **allez-y d.!** gently does it!, easy does it!; **les affaires vont d.** business is so-so; *F* **(allez-y) d. avec le vin** go easy on the wine, *Arg* **ça m'a fait d. rigoler** I had a good laugh over it; *F* **d. les basses!** take it easy!

doucereux, -euse [dusrø, -øz] *adj* **(a)** (*goût etc*) sweetish, *Péj* sickly (sweet) **(b)** (*personne*) smooth, smooth-tongued; (*voix, ton*) smooth, sugary

doucet, -ette [dusɛ, -ɛt] **1** *adj Arch* (*personne*) meek, mild **2** *nf* **doucette** (*plante*) corn salad, lamb's lettuce

douceur [dusœr] *nf* **(a)** (*d'un son, d'une matière etc*) softness; (*d'un climat*) mildness; (*d'une atmosphère*) pleasantness; **d. de vivre** easy *or* relaxed way of life; **les douceurs de l'amitié** the comforts *or* pleasures of friendship

(b) (*de caractère*) gentleness; (*d'un sourire*) sweetness; **traiter qn avec d.** to treat sb gently *or* with kindness; **employer la d. avec un enfant/un animal** to be gentle with a child/an animal; **en d.** gently; **la voiture a démarré en d.** the car started smoothly; **allez-y en d.!** gently does it!, easy does it!; **poser un avion en d.** to land an aircraft smoothly, to make a smooth landing

(c) (*sucreries*) **douceurs** sweets, sweet things; **aimer les douceurs** to have a sweet tooth; *Fig* **dire des douceurs à une femme** to say sweet nothings to a woman

(d) (*du miel, d'un parfum etc*) sweetness

douche [duʃ] *nf* **(a)** shower; (*installation*) shower (unit); **prendre une d.** to take a shower; **être sous la d.** to be in the shower; **préférer la d. au bain** to prefer a shower to a bath; **passer à la d.** to take a shower; **les douches** the shower room(s), the showers **(b)** *F* (*de pluie*) **on s'est pris une de ces douches!** we got soaked! **(c)** *Fig* disappointment; **plus jamais je ne voudrais me prendre une d. pareille** I don't want another disappointment like that ever again

▶ **douche**: **d. écossaise** (alternately) hot and cold shower; *Fig* **il a un caractère tellement changeant qu'avec lui, c'est toujours la d. écossaise** he is so unpredictable that you never know where you are with him; *Fig* **ça m'a fait l'effet d'une d. écossaise** it came as a bit of a shock; **d. froide** terrible disappointment, let-down

doucher [duʃe] **1** *vt* **(a)** (*pour laver*) **d. qn** to give sb a shower **(b)** *F* (*d'une averse*) to soak; **se faire d. par l'orage** to get soaked in the storm **(c)** *F* (*fustiger*) to tell off; (*décevoir*) to shock; **il s'est fait d. par le patron** he got a telling-off from the boss; **ça m'a vraiment douché** it came as a real shock

2 se doucher *vpr* to take a shower

douchette [duʃɛt] *nf* **(a)** (*pomme*) shower head **(b)** (*pour codes barres*) bar code reader

doudou [dudu] *nf Antilles* girl friend

doudoune¹ [dudun] *nf* (*anorak*) down jacket

doudounes² *nfpl F* (*seins*) boobs

doué [dwe] *adj* gifted, talented; **il n'est guère d. pour les langues** he has no gift for languages, he's no linguist; *Hum* **tu es vraiment d.!** that was really intelligent *or* clever!

douer [dwe] *vt* to endow (**de** with); **il est doué d'une bonne mémoire** he has a good memory

douille [duj] *nf* (*d'un outil etc*) socket; (*d'une ampoule électrique*) lamp socket; (*d'une cartouche etc*) case; *Culin* piping nozzle; **d. à (pas de) vis** screw lamp holder

douiller [duje] *vi F* (*coûter cher*) to cost an arm and a leg; **la prochaine facture de téléphone, ça va d.** the next phone bill is going to be sky-high; **c'est un restau qui douille** the prices are sky-high in that restaurant, it costs an arm and a leg to eat in that restaurant

douillet, -ette [dujɛ, -ɛt] **1** *adj* (**a**) (*coussin*) soft, downy; (*lit*) cosy (**b**) (*trop délicat*) **ne sois pas si d.!** don't be such a baby *or F* wimp! **2** *nf* **douillette** (*robe de chambre*) quilted housecoat *or Am* robe; (*de curé*) overcoat

douillettement [dujɛtmɑ̃] *adv* (*confortablement*) cosily; **quand il fait froid, je m'installe d. sous la couette** when it's cold, I snuggle down under the quilt; **j'étais d. enroulée dans mon châle** I was all snug and cosy *or* I was wrapped up warmly in my shawl; **élever un enfant d.** to coddle a child; **il a été élevé trop d.** he was coddled too much as a child; **sa mère le traite toujours d.** his mother still coddles him

douleur [dulœr] *nf* (**a**) (*physique*) pain; (*diffuse*) ache; **d. aiguë** sharp pain; **pousser un cri/des cris de d.** to cry out with *or* in pain; **j'ai une d. persistante dans le genou** I have a persistent ache in my knee; **se sentir des douleurs par** *ou* **dans tout le corps** to ache all over; **j'ai des douleurs dans le ventre** I've got pains in my stomach; **sans d.** (*accouchement*) painless (**b**) (*morale*) sorrow, grief; **il a eu la d. de perdre sa mère** he had the painful experience of losing his mother; **partager la d. de qn** to share sb's sorrow *or* grief, to feel for sb; **nous avons la d. de vous faire part du décès de ...** we regret to inform you of the death of ...

douloureusement [dulurøzmɑ̃] *adv* painfully; (*regarder qn*) sorrowfully; **il s'est cogné le genou d.** he gave himself a painful knock on the knee; **c'est une perte qu'elle ressent d.** she feels the loss deeply; **il a été d. atteint par la mort de sa grand-mère** his grandmother's death upset him very much *or* affected him deeply

douloureux, -euse [dulurø, -øz] **1** *adj* (**a**) (*coup, maladie, opération etc*) painful; (*au contact*) sore, tender; **mon dos est d. aujourd'hui** my back hurts *or* aches today, my back is hurting today (**b**) (*perte, événement etc*) sad, distressing; (*séparation*) painful; (*circonstances*) painful, distressing; (*regard*) pained, sorrowful; **des cris d.** heart-rending *or* mournful cries **2** *nf F* **la douloureuse** the bill; **apportez-moi la douloureuse** let's see what the damage is

doute [dut] *nm* (**a**) (*incertitude*) doubt, uncertainty; **être dans le d.** to be in doubt, to be doubtful (**au sujet de qch** about sth); **mettre qch en d.** to question sth, to cast doubt on sth; **mettre en d. la parole de qn** to doubt sb's word; **il n'y a pas de** *ou* **aucun d.** there's no doubt about it, it is beyond doubt *or* beyond (all) question; **laisser qn dans le d. est cruel** it's cruel to leave sb in doubt *or* in a state of uncertainty; **je ne lui ai laissé aucun d. quant à mes sentiments pour lui** I left him in no doubt about my feelings for him; **cela ne fait plus aucun d.** there is no longer any doubt about it; **nul d. qu'il (ne) soit mort** there is no doubt that he is dead; **sans d.** no doubt, probably; **sans aucun d.** without (any) doubt; **vous ne me reconnaissez pas, sans d.** I don't suppose you recognize me; **sans d. viendra-t-il, sans d. qu'il viendra** I expect he'll come, he'll probably come; *Prov* **dans le d., abstiens-toi** when in doubt, don't!

(**b**) (*soupçon*) doubt, misgiving, suspicion; **avoir des doutes sur** *ou* **au sujet de qn/qch** to have doubts *or* misgivings *or* suspicions about sb/sth; **avoir un d. (sur qch)** to have misgivings *or* doubts (about sth); **j'ai un d. sur la vérité de ce qu'il dit** I have doubts about whether he's telling the truth; **il y a quand même un d. sur son passé** there is still some doubt about his past

douter [dute] **1** *vi* to doubt; **il était à n'en point d. courageux** his courage was beyond all question; **d. de qn/qch** to doubt sb/sth; **je n'ai jamais douté de vos compétences** I have never doubted your ability; **je n'ai jamais douté de ta venue** I never doubted that you would come; **je n'ai jamais douté de te voir** I never doubted that I would see you; **d. du zèle de qn** to doubt *or* question *or* have doubts about sb's enthusiasm; **elle doute de vous avoir rencontré** she's not sure whether she's met you; **il ne doute de rien** he is full of self-confidence; **j'en doute** I doubt it, I have my doubts (about it); **j'en doute fort** I doubt it very much, I have very strong doubts

2 *vt* **je doute qu'il soit assez fort** I doubt whether he is strong enough; **je n'ai jamais douté que tu viennes** I never doubted that you would come; **je ne doute pas qu'il (ne) vous vienne en aide** I am confident that he will help you

3 se douter *vpr* **se d. de qch** to suspect sth; **il ne se doute de rien** he doesn't suspect anything; **je m'en doutais (bien)** I guessed *or* thought as much; **elle est surprise, je m'en doute** she is surprised, I'm sure *or* I dare say; **je ne me doutais pas qu'il fût là** I had no idea that he was there; **je me doute bien que c'est un peu difficile** I rather suspect *or* think it's going to be difficult; **j'étais loin de me d. que cela arriverait** I never thought for a moment that that would happen; *F* **on s'en serait douté!** I might have known *or* guessed!

douteux, -euse [dutø, -øz] *adj* (**a**) (*incertain*) doubtful; (*origine, authenticité*) doubtful, questionable; **il est d. qu'il vienne** it is doubtful whether he will come; **il n'est pas d. que ... (ne)** + *sub ou plus souvent* **que** + *ind* there is no doubt that ...; **créance douteuse** bad debt (**b**) (*honneur, compagnie, fraîcheur, mœurs etc*) dubious; **jour d.** dubious *or* uncertain light; **des vêtements d.** *ou* **d'une propreté douteuse** dubious clothes; **d'un blanc d.** of a dubious white; **d'un goût d.** (*plaisanteries, vêtements, pièce*) in dubious taste; **il a des petites copines d'un goût d.** he has some rather dubious girlfriends

douve [duv] *nf* (**a**) *Agr* trench, ditch; *Courses de chevaux* water jump; **douves** (*d'un château*) moat (**b**) (*planche*) stave

Douvres [duvr] *n* Dover

doux, douce [du, dus] **1** *adj* (**a**) (*au toucher*) smooth, soft; (*au goût*) mild; **eau douce** fresh water; (*non calcaire*) soft water; **poisson d'eau douce** freshwater fish; *F* **marin d'eau douce** landlubber; **peau douce** smooth *or* soft skin

(**b**) (*air, ton etc*) pleasant, agreeable; **d. souvenir** pleasant memory; **mener une vie douce** to lead a calm *or* peaceful life; *F* **se la couler douce** to take it easy; *F* **faire qch en d.** to do sth on the sly *or* the Q.T. ; **faire les yeux d. à qn** to make sheep's eyes at sb; *Iron* **douce perspective!** charming prospect!

(**c**) (*mouvement, voix, pente*) gentle; (*couleur, son*) soft, subdued; (*lumière*) mellow, soft, subdued; (*climat, hiver, tabac*) mild; (*moteur, suspension*) sweet; **chaleur douce** moderate heat; *Culin* **faire cuire à feu d.** to cook on a low heat *or* in a low oven; **lime douce** smooth file; **drogue douce** soft drug; **des médecines douces** alternative forms of medicine; **consonne douce** soft consonant

(**d**) (*nature, regard*) mild, gentle; **être d. avec les enfants** to be kind to children; (*d'un animal*) to be good *or* gentle with children; **être d. avec les animaux** to be kind to animals; **il est très d. avec son petit garçon** he's very gentle with his little boy; **d. comme un agneau** as gentle as a lamb

(**e**) *F* **c'est de la folie douce!** it's sheer madness!

2 *adv F* **filer d.** to tread warily, to watch one's step; **là, tout d.** steady, steady!

3 *nm* **préférer le sec au d.** to prefer dry (wine) to sweet

4 *n F* **c'est un d.** he's a gentle creature

douzain [duzɛ̃] *nm Littér* twelve-line poem

douzaine [duzɛn] *nf* [①A12,h,i; B57,E,2] dozen; **trois douzaines d'œufs** three dozen eggs; **une d. de personnes** about a dozen people, a dozen or so people; **il y a une d. d'années** about twelve years ago, a dozen or so years ago; **quand nous avions une d. d'années** when we were about twelve; **à la d.** by the dozen; *Fig* **il y en a à la d.** there are dozens *or* lots of them

douze [duz] **1** *adj inv* twelve; **le d. mai** the twelfth of May; **Louis D.** Louis the Twelfth; **d. heures** twelve o'clock (noon) **2** *nm inv* twelve

douzième [duzjɛm] *adj, n* twelfth

douzièmement [duzjɛmmɑ̃] *adv* twelfthly, in the twelfth place

doyen, -enne [dwajɛ̃, -ɛn] *n* (**a**) (*d'un chapitre, d'une faculté*) dean; (*d'un corps, d'une association etc*) doyen (**b**) (*personne la plus âgée*) senior; **elle est la doyenne de notre groupe** she's the oldest in *or* the oldest member of our group; **d. d'âge** oldest member

doyenné [dwajene] **1** *nm Rel* (*dignité, résidence*) deanery **2** *nf* **d. (du comice)** comice (pear)

drache [draʃ] *nf Région* downpour; **on s'est pris une de ces draches!** we got soaked *or* drenched!

dracher [draʃe] *vi Région* to pour

drachme [drakm] *nf* drachma

draconien, -ienne [drakɔnjɛ̃, -jɛn] *adj* (*règlement*) draconian; **régime d.** very strict diet

dragage [dragaʒ] *nm* (**a**) (*nettoyage*) (*d'une rivière, d'un port etc*) dredging (**b**) (*d'une rivière pour retrouver un corps etc*) dragging; **d. des mines** mine-sweeping

dragée [draʒe] *nf* (**a**) (*confiserie*) sugar(ed) almond; *Pharm* sugar-coated pill; **tenir la d. haute à qn** to make sb dance to one's tune (**b**) (*petit plomb*) small shot; *Arg* (*balle*) bullet

dragéifier [draʒeifje] *vt Pharm* (*pilule*) to coat with sugar, to sugar; **comprimé dragéifié** sugar-coated tablet

drageon [draʒɔ̃] *nm Bot* sucker

dragon [dragɔ̃] *nm* **(a)** *Myth, Fig* dragon; *Fig* **c'est un d. de vertu** she pretends to be such a paragon of virtue; **d. volant** (*reptile*) flying lizard **(b)** *Mil* dragoon; **dragons portés** ≈ motorized cavalry

dragonne [dragɔn] *nf* (*d'une épée, d'un sabre*) sword knot; (*d'un parapluie*) strap

drague [drag] *nf* **(a)** *HydE* dredger; (*grappin*) drag, grappling hook; *Pêche* dredge, dragnet; **d. suceuse** pump dredger; **d. à godets** bucket dredger **(b)** *F* (*pour séduire*) chatting up men/women; **alors la d., ça marche?** so, how's your love-life?; **il y a de la d. dans l'air** someone's getting the come-on; **un champion** *ou* **professionnel de la d.** an expert at chatting up women

draguer [drage] **1** *vt* **(a)** (*nettoyer*) (*rivière, port etc*) to dredge **(b)** (*pour retrouver qch*) (*étang etc*) to drag; (*bras de mer*) to sweep; *Pêche* (*huîtres etc*) to dredge for **(c)** *F* (*hommes, femmes*) to chat up, to try to pick up; **il m'a draguée** he tried to pick me up **2** *vi F* to chat up men/women; **ça drague sec** *ou* **dur ici** there's a lot of chatting up going on here

dragueur, -euse [dragœr, -øz] **1** *nm* **(a)** (*bateau*) dredger; **d. de mines** minesweeper **(b)** (*ouvrier*), *HydE* dredgerman; (*avec grappin*) dragman **2** *n F* chat-up merchant; **c'est une sacrée dragueuse** she's always chatting up the men

drain [drɛ̃] *nm* **(a)** (*conduit*) drain(pipe) **(b)** *Chir* drainage tube

drainage [drɛnaʒ] *nm* **(a)** (*d'un champ, d'une plaie etc*) drainage, draining **(b)** (*d'argent, de capital*) drain

drainer [drene] *vt* **(a)** (*sol, abcès*) to drain **(b)** (*commerce, capital, talent, ouvriers etc*) to draw, to attract

Dralon® [dralɔ̃] *nm* Dralon®

dramatique [dramatik] **1** *adj* dramatic; **l'art d.** drama; **école d'art d.** drama school; **auteur d.** playwright; *Fig* **il est arrivé quelque chose de d.** something dreadful *or* terrible has happened; **mais c'est d.!** that's dreadful *or* terrible!; **je ne considère pas son départ comme d.** I don't think his leaving is a tragedy; *F* **c'est pas d.** it's not a tragedy, it's not the end of the world **2** *nf* TV movie

dramatiquement [dramatikmɑ̃] *adv* dramatically

dramatisation [dramatizasjɔ̃] *nf* dramatization

dramatiser [dramatize] *vt* **(a)** (*événement etc*) to dramatize **(b)** (*roman*) to dramatize, to adapt for the stage

dramaturge [dramatyrʒ] *nm* dramatist, playwright

dramaturgie [dramatyrʒi] *nf* dramatic art

drame [dram] *nm* **(a)** (*genre littéraire*) drama; *Arch* (*pièce*) play; **d. lyrique** (*opéra*) opera; (*oratorio*) oratorio; **d. psychologique** psychological drama **(b)** *Fig* drama, tragedy; **la scène a tourné au d.** the scene took a tragic turn; **il ne faut pas en faire un d.** there's no need to make a drama out of it *or* to dramatize it; **ce n'est pas un d.** it's not the end of the world, it's nothing to get upset about; **il nous a fait tout un d. parce que son stylo avait disparu** he made quite a scene because his pen had disappeared; **d. reconstitué** drama documentary, dramadoc; **d. télévisé** television drama

drap [dra] *nm* **(a)** *Tex* cloth; **d. fin** broadcloth; **d. d'or/de soie** gold/silk brocade; *Hist* **le camp du D. d'or** the Field of the Cloth of Gold **(b) d. (de lit)** sheet; **d. de dessous/dessus** bottom/top sheet; **se mettre dans** *ou* **entre les draps** to go to bed; *Fig* **être dans de beaux** *ou* **mauvais** *ou* **vilains draps** to be in a fine mess *or* in a pickle *or* in a predicament **(c)** *Belg* (*serviette*) towel

▶ **drap**: **d. de bain** bath sheet; **d. mortuaire** pall; **d. de plage** beach towel

drapé [drape] **1** *adj* **(a)** (*couvert d'un drap*) covered with a sheet *or* a cloth **(b)** (*à plis*) draped; **robe drapée sur les épaules** dress draped at the shoulders **2** *nm* (*d'un vêtement*) drape

drapeau, -eaux [drapo] *nm* flag; *Mil* (regimental) colour; *Cin, TV* (*sur lumière*) flag, gobo; **arborer** *ou* **hisser un d.** to hoist a flag; *Mil* **présentation du d.** ≈ trooping the colour; *Fig* **être sous les drapeaux** to serve in the (armed) forces; **mourir pour le d.** to die for the flag *or* one's country; *Fig* **se ranger sous les drapeaux de la Serbie/des verts** to join the Serbian/greens' camp; *Arg* **planter un d.** to leave without paying (the bill); *Av* **mettre une hélice en d.** to feather a propeller; *Sp* **abaisser le d. à l'arrivée du premier concurrent** to flag in the winner

▶ **drapeau**: **d. blanc** white flag; **d. noir** black flag; **d. rouge** red flag

drapement [drapmɑ̃] *nm* (*de tissu*) draping

draper [drape] **1** *vt* **(a)** *Tex* (*laine*) to process **(b)** (*étoffe*) to drape **2 se draper** *vpr* to wrap oneself up, to drape oneself (**dans, de** in); *Fig* **se d. dans sa dignité** to stand on one's dignity

draperie [drapri] *nf* **(a)** (*usine*) cloth factory; (*commerce*) drapery (trade) **(b)** *Beaux-Arts* drapery **(c)** (*tenture*) curtains, *Am* drapes

drap-housse, *pl* **draps-housses** *nm* fitted sheet

drapier, -ière [drapje, -jɛr] **1** *n* (*marchand*) draper; (*fabriquant*) cloth manufacturer **2** *adj* (*industrie*) cloth(-making); (*ouvrier, marchand*) cloth

DRASS [dras] *nf Admin* (*abrév* **Direction Régionale des Affaires Sanitaires et Sociales**) = office administering health and social services at regional level

drastique [drastik] **1** *adj* drastic **2** *nm Méd* drastic purgative

drave [drav] *nf Can* (*de rondins*) drive

draver [drave] *vt Can* (*rondins*) to float, to drive

draveur [dravœr] *nm Can* driver, raftsman

draw-back [drobak], *pl* **draw-backs** *nm Com* drawback

dreadlocks [drɛdlɔks] *nfpl* dreadlocks

drelin [drəlɛ̃] *int Vieilli* ting-a-ling, tinkle

dressage [drɛsaʒ] *nm* **(a)** (*d'un mât, d'un monument, d'un échafaudage etc*) erection, raising; (*d'une tente*) pitching **(b)** *Tech* (*d'un morceau de bois etc*) trimming, dressing; (*d'une tige, d'une barre*) straightening **(c)** (*d'un animal*) training; *F* (*d'un enfant*) strict upbringing; *Équitation* **d. (élémentaire)** breaking in; *Équitation* **d. (supérieur)** dressage; **ce n'est pas une éducation qu'ils donnent à cet enfant, c'est un d.** that child isn't being brought up, he's being trained

dresser [drese] **1** *vt* **(a)** (*ériger*) (*mât, monument, échafaudage etc*) to erect, to put up, to raise; (*échelle, lit*) to put up; (*tente*) to pitch, to put up; (*bûcher*) to erect; **d. la tête** to hold up *or* lift one's head; (*pour regarder*) to look up; **d. les oreilles** to prick up *or* cock one's ears; *Fig* **d. l'oreille** to prick up one's ears; **une histoire à faire d. les poils** *ou* **les cheveux (sur la tête)** a hair-raising story, a story to make your hair stand on end

(b) *Tech* (*morceau de bois*) to trim, to dress; (*fil*) to straighten out

(c) (*établir*) (*plan, rapport, estimation etc*) to prepare, to draw up; (*liste, inventaire*) to prepare, to draw up, to make out; **d. un contrat** to draw up a contract; **d. une carte** to make a map; **pourriez-vous me d. la liste de ce dont vous avez besoin?** could you make a list for me of what you need?

(d) (*préparer*) (*piège*) to set; *Fig* **d. ses batteries** to draw up a battle plan *or* a plan of action *or Litt* one's batteries; **d. la table** *ou* **le couvert** to lay *or* set the table; **d. un plat** to put food on a plate, to arrange a dish

(e) (*animal, F enfant*) to train (**à faire qch** to do sth); (*cheval*) to break in; *Arch, Péj* (*recrue*) to train, to drill; *F* **ça le dressera!** that'll teach him, that'll put him in his place!; *Fig* **d. une personne contre une autre** to set one person against another

2 se dresser *vpr* **(a)** (*se lever*) to stand up, to rise; (*sur une chaise, dans un lit*) to sit up; (*se tenir droit*) to hold oneself erect *or* straight; (*d'un cheval*) to rear; (*d'un chien*) to stand up; **se d. sur la pointe des pieds** to stand on tiptoe; **ses cheveux se dressaient (sur sa tête)** his hair stood on end; *Fig* **quand je le vois, j'ai les poils qui se dressent** my hackles rise whenever I see him; **les obstacles qui se dressent sur notre chemin** the obstacles that stand *or* lie in our way; *Fig* **se d. contre qch** to rise up (in protest) against sth, to revolt against sth

(b) (*s'apprivoiser*) to be tamed; **les hérissons ne se dressent pas** hedgehogs can't be tamed

dresseur, -euse [drɛsœr, -øz] *n* (*d'animaux*) trainer; **d. de chevaux** horse-breaker; **d. de fauves** wild animal tamer

dressing(-room), *pl* **dressings** *ou* **dressing-rooms** [drɛsiŋ(rum)] *nm* dressing room

dressoir [drɛswar] *nm* dresser, sideboard

dreyfusard, -arde [drɛfyzar, -ard] *n Hist* supporter *or* defender of Dreyfus

dribble [dribl] *nm Fb etc* dribble

dribbler [drible] *Fb etc* **1** *vi* to dribble **2** *vt* (*ballon*) to dribble; **d. un joueur** to dribble round a player

dribbleur [driblœr] *nm Fb etc* dribbler

dribbling [dribliŋ] *nm Rugby* forward ruck

drill[1] [drij] *nm* (*singe*) drill

drill[2] [dril] *nm Mil etc* drill

drille[1] [drij] *nm F Vieilli* **c'est un bon** *ou* **joyeux d.** he's always good for a laugh

drille[2] *nf Tech* hand drill

driller [drije] *vt Tech* to drill, to bore

dring [driŋ] *int* ting-a-ling

drink [driŋk] *nm F* drink

drisse [dris] *nf Naut* halyard

drive [drajv] *nm Tennis, Golf* drive

drive-in [drajvin], *pl* **drive-ins** *nm* drive-in

driver[1] [drajvœr] *nm* **(a)** *Sp* (*dans les courses de trot*) driver **(b)** *Golf* (*club*) driver

driver² [drajve] **1** *vi Tennis, Golf* to drive **2** *vt* **(a)** *Tennis, Golf* (*balle*) to drive **(b)** (*dans les courses de trot*) to drive

drogman [drɔgmɑ̃] *nm Vieilli* dragoman

drogue [drɔg] *nf* **(a)** (*stupéfiant*) drug, narcotic; **d. dure/douce** hard/soft drug; **prendre de la d.** to take *or* be on drugs; **trafic de d.** drug trafficking; **l'argent de la d.** drug money; **il faut lutter contre la d. dans les lycées** we have to fight against drugs in high schools; *Hum* **moi, ma d., c'est le chocolat** chocolate is what I'm hooked on, I'm a chocaholic; *Fig* **la télévision est une d. pour beaucoup de gens** lots of people are television addicts *or* are hooked on television **(b)** *Vieilli* (*médicament*) remedy, medicine; *Péj* nostrum, quack remedy

drogué, -ée [drɔge] *n* drug addict; *Fig* **les drogués de l'information** information addicts; **les drogués de la cigarette** people hooked on cigarettes

droguer [drɔge] **1** *vt* **(a)** (*malade*) to dose (with medicine); **je déteste les médecins qui vous droguent** I hate doctors who force medicine on you **(b)** (*victime*) to drug; (*cheval de course etc*) to dope, *Arg* to nobble **2 se droguer** *vpr* **(a)** (*prendre des stupéfiants*) to take drugs; **il se drogue** he's taking drugs, he's on drugs; **il se drogue à l'héro** he's on heroin **(b)** *Pharm* to be always taking drugs; **elle est obligée de se d. pour dormir** she has to take drugs in order to be able to sleep

droguerie [drɔgri] *nf* (*magasin*) = hardware store, *Br* ironmonger's (*selling paint, cleaning materials etc*); (*commerce*) = hardware trade

droguet [drɔgɛ] *nm Tex Vieilli* drugget

droguiste [drɔgist] *nm* = hardware dealer, *Br* ironmonger (*dealing in paints, cleaning materials etc*); **épicier d.** grocer and general storekeeper

droit¹, droite [drwa, drwat] **1** *adj* **(a)** (*vertical*) straight; **se tenir d.** to hold oneself erect, to stand up straight; **d. comme un i** *ou* **un piquet** as straight *or* stiff as a poker; **col d.** stand-up collar; **jupe droite** straight skirt; **veste droite** boxy jacket; (*non croisée*) single-breasted jacket; *Math* **angle d.** right angle; **section droite** cross section

(b) (*non courbe*) (*route, ligne*) straight; **coup d.** *Escrime* straight thrust; *Tennis* forehand drive; **en ligne droite** in a straight line, as the crow flies; *Fig* **ces boucles d'oreille me viennent en droite ligne de ma grand-mère** I inherited these earrings from my grandmother; **ses idées viennent en droite ligne de celles de son père** he gets his ideas from his father; *Fig* **ne pas s'écarter du d. chemin** not to leave the straight and narrow; **ramener qn dans le d. chemin** to bring sb back to the straight and narrow; *Couture* **dans le d. fil** on the straight; *Fig* **son étude est dans le d. fil des conceptions freudiennes** his study is in line with Freudian concepts; *Naut* **mettre la barre droite** to right the helm; *Naut* **d. la barre!** helm amidships!

(c) (*honnête*) (*personne, conduite*) upright, honest

2 *adv* **c'est d. devant vous** *ou* **tout d.** it's straight ahead of you; **marcher d.** to walk straight *or* in a straight line; *Fig* to toe the line; **aller d. au fait** to get straight to the point; **aller** *ou* **courir d. à qch** to be heading straight for sth; **votre cadeau/proposition m'est allé(e) d. au cœur** I am deeply touched *or* moved by your gift/suggestion; **écrire d.** to write straight *or* in a straight line; *Naut* **d. devant, d. debout** right ahead

3 *nf* **droite** straight line; **tracer une d. reliant A à B** to draw a line connecting A and B

droit², droite 1 *adj* (*main, jambe, gant etc*) right; **être le bras d. de qn** to be sb's right-hand man; **du côté d.** on the right-hand side

2 *nf* **droite (a)** right (hand), right-hand side; **tourner à droite** to turn (to the) right; **rouler à droite** to drive on the right; **tenir** *ou* **garder sa droite** to keep to the right; **à ma droite, le château** to *or* on my right is the castle; **sur la droite, il y a un feu** on the right there is a traffic light; **reconnaître sa droite de sa gauche** to know one's left from one's right; **le placard de droite** the right-hand cupboard, the cupboard on the right; **à droite du placard** to *or* on the right of the cupboard; **regarder de droite à gauche** to look from right to left; **courir à d. et à gauche** to run about all over the place; **j'entends dire à droite et à gauche** *ou* **de d. et de gauche que ...** I hear from all quarters *or* on all sides that ...; *Naut* **(la barre) à droite!** starboard!

(b) *Pol* **la droite** the right (wing); **candidat/idées/journal de droite** right-wing candidate/ideas/newspaper; **voter à droite** to vote for the right

3 *nm Boxe* right; **crochet du d.** right hook; **direct du d.** straight right

droit³ *nm* **(a)** (*prérogative*) right; **d. de chasse/pêche** hunting/fishing rights; **le d. du plus fort** the law of the jungle; **avoir d. de vie et de mort sur qn** to have the power of life and death over sb; **avoir d. de regard sur qch** to have the right to approve sth, *F* to have a say on sth; **avoir le d. de savoir** to have the right to know; **tous droits réservés** all rights reserved; **faire valoir ses droits** to assert one's rights; **avoir d. à qch** to have a right to sth, to be entitled to sth; **il a d. à mes excuses** I owe him an apology; *F Iron* **il a eu d. aux inévitables recommandations** he was treated to the inevitable good advice; *F* **ce soir, on va encore y avoir d.** the same treat is in store for us again this evening; *F* **ils parlent de licencier 300 personnes, je sens que je vais y avoir d.** they're talking about laying off 300 people and I think that's going to include me; *F* **s'il pleut dans tout le pays, il n'y a pas de raison qu'on n'y ait pas d.** if it's raining all over the country there's no reason why here should be any exception *or* why we should escape; **ce coupon (vous) donne d. à ...** this coupon entitles you to ...; **avoir le** *ou* **être en d. de faire qch** to have a right to do sth, to be justified in doing sth, to be entitled to do sth; **je n'ai pas le d. de le faire** I'm not allowed to do it; **tu n'as pas le d. de me reprocher cela** you've no right to hold that against me; **avoir des droits sur qn/qch** to have rights over sb/sth; **tu n'as aucun d. sur les décisions de tes enfants** you have no say in your children's decisions; **à bon d.** (*d'une façon justifiée*) with good reason; (*selon la loi*) legitimately; **de d. et de fait** de facto and de jure; **à qui de d.** to whom it may concern; **s'adresser à qui de d.** to apply to the proper quarter *or* to an authorized person; **être dans son (bon) d.** to be within one's rights; **tu serais dans ton d. si tu lui demandais une compensation** you'd be within your rights asking for compensation; **de quel d. me critiques-tu?** by what right do you criticize me?, what gives you the right to criticize me?, what right have you to criticize me?; **de quel d. êtes-vous entré?** what right had you *or* what gave you the right to come in?; **faire d. à une demande** to comply with *or* accede to a request; **les droits de l'amitié** the claims of friendship; **Commission européenne des droits de l'homme** European Commission of Human Rights; **Convention relative aux droits de l'enfant** Convention on the Rights of the Child

(b) (*en argent*) fee, due; (*imposition*) duty; (*taxe*) tax; *Compta* **d. fixe** fixed rate of duty; **exempt de droits** duty-free; **allocation de fin de droits** = reduced amount of unemployment benefit (*paid to people whose benefit period has almost expired*); **(chômeur en) fin de droits** unemployed person whose benefit period is running out

(c) *Jur* law; **le d.** the law; **d. administratif** administrative law; **d. aérien** aviation law; **d. bancaire** banking law; *Jur* **d. de brevet** patent law; **d. civil** civil law; **d. commercial** commercial law; **d. communautaire** Community law; **d. de la consommation** consumer law; **d. constitutionnel** constitutional law; **d. coutumier** common law; **d. commun** common law; **d. des contrats** contract law; **d. criminel** criminal law; **d. douanier** customs legislation; **d. écrit** statute law; **d. fiscal** tax law; **d. hôtelier** hotel law; **d. international** international law; **d. de marque** trademark law; **d. des obligations** = law of contract; **d. pénal** criminal law; **d. public** public law; **d. privé** private law; **d. romain** Roman law; **d. des sociétés** corporate law; **d. du travail** labour laws; **faire son d.** to study *or* read law; **étudiant en d.** law student

▶ **droit**: **d. d'accès** right of access; **droits acquis** vested rights; *Com* **droits acquittés** duty paid; **d. d'admission** (*prérogative*) right of entry; (*imposition*) import duty; *Fin, Com* **droits ad valorem** ad valorem duty; **d. d'aînesse** birthright; *TV* **droits d'antenne** broadcasting rights; **d. d'asile** right of asylum; **droits d'auteur** royalties; **d. au bail** (*bien incorporel*) leasehold; (*comme bien incorporel*) right to a lease; *Av, Naut* **droits de cabotage** cabotage rights; **d. canon** canon law; **d. de cité** freedom of a city; *Fig* **il n'a pas d. de cité dans cette maison** he is not welcome in this house; **droits civils** civil rights; **droits du consommateur** consumer rights; *Com* **d. de courtage** brokerage (fee); **droits de diffusion** broadcasting rights; **d. divin: monarchie de d. divin** kingship by divine right; **droits de douane** (customs) duty; **d. d'entrée** (*coût*) admission fee; (*prérogative*) right of entry; (*imposition*) import duty; *Com* **droits exclusifs** sole rights; **droits d'exclusivité** exclusive rights; **droits d'exécution en public** performing rights; **droits d'exploitation d'un feuilleton** serial rights; **droits d'exploitation pour le monde entier** world(wide) rights; **droits d'exploitation à la télévision** TV rights; **droits d'exploitation vidéo** video rights; **d. de grève** right to strike; **droits d'inscription** registration fee; **droits internationaux** international rights; **droits d'interprète** performing rights; **d. de passage** right of way; **droits de** port harbour dues; *Jur* **d. de rachat** repurchase right, buyback right; *Journ* **d. de rectification** right of reply; *Journ* **d. de réponse** right of reply; **d. de reproduction** reproduction rights; **d. du sang: avoir le d. du sang** to have the nationality of one's parents; **d. du sol: avoir le d. du sol** to have the nationality of the country where one was born; *Fin, Com* **droits de sortie** export duty; **droits statutaires** statutory rights; **droits de succession** death duties; *Admin* **d. de timbre** stamp duty; *Fin* **droits de tirage** drawing rights; **droits de trafic** (*des compagnies aériennes*) traffic rights; **d. d'usage** right of use; **d. aux vacances** holiday entitlement; **droits de vote** voting rights

droitement [drwatmɑ̃] *adv* **faire son travail d.** to do an honest day's work; **il juge les gens d.** he judges people fairly

droitier, -ière [drwatje, -jɛr] **1** *adj* **(a)** right-handed **(b)** *Pol F* right-wing **2** *n* right-handed person

droiture [drwatyr] *nf* rectitude, honesty

drolatique [drolatik] *adj Litt* comic, humorous, droll

drôle [drol] **1** *adj* **(a)** (*amusant*) funny, amusing; **je ne trouve pas ça très d.** I don't think that's very funny; **ça ne va pas être d.** it's not going to be much fun; *F* **vous êtes d.! qu'auriez-vous fait à ma place?** you must be joking! what would you have done in my place?

(b) (*étrange*) funny, odd, queer, strange; **je l'ai trouvé d. hier** he was behaving rather oddly *or* strangely yesterday; **c'est d. que je ne t'aie pas reconnu tout de suite** it's funny *or* odd that I didn't recognise you immediately; **une d. d'odeur** a funny *or* queer *or* strange *or* peculiar *or* an odd smell; **quelle d. d'idée!** what a funny *or* queer *or* strange *or* peculiar *or* an odd idea!; **j'ai dû faire une d. de tête** I must have looked a bit taken aback; *F* **un d. de type** a queer fish, an odd sort; *F* **la d. de guerre** the phoney war (*1939*)

(c) *F* (*sacré*) **il faut une d. de patience** it needs an awful lot *or esp Am* a heck of a lot of patience; **il a une d. de force** he's awfully strong; **en voir de drôles** (*avoir des ennuis*) to have an awful time (of it); **ils en ont vu de drôles pendant leur voyage au Maroc** they had an incredible time on their trip to Morocco; **en faire voir de drôles à qn** to give sb an awful time (of it)

2 *adv F* **ça m'a fait tout d. de te voir là** it gave me a funny *or* queer *or* strange *or* peculiar *or* an odd feeling to see you there

3 *nm* **(a)** *Arch* (*mauvais sujet*) rascal, knave, scamp

(b) *Région* (*jeune garçon*) lad

drôlement [drolmɑ̃] *adv* **(a)** funnily, strangely, oddly **(b)** *F* (*sacrément*) awfully, awful; **les prix ont d. augmenté** prices have gone up an awful lot; **je me suis d. amusé** I had a great time, I had an awful(ly) good time *or* an awful lot of fun; **elle est d. bien** (*remarquable*) she's a terrific person; (*belle*) she's gorgeous, she's great-looking

drôlerie [drolri] *nf* (*caractère amusant*) funniness; (*action*) joke; (*parole*) joke, funny remark

drôlesse [drolɛs] *nf* **(a)** *Vieilli* (*femme effrontée*) bitch **(b)** *Région* (*jeune fille*) lass

dromadaire [drɔmadɛr] *nm* dromedary

drop (goal) [drɔp(gol)] *nm Rugby* drop goal

droppage [drɔpaʒ] *nm Av* (parachute) drop; **zone de d.** drop zone

drosophile [drɔzɔfil] *nf* fruit fly

drosser [drɔse] *vt Naut* (*du vent, courant*) to drive

dru [dry] **1** *adj* (*herbe, blé etc*) thick, dense; (*cheveux, barbe*) thick; (*pluie*) heavy **2** *adv* **tomber d.** to fall thick and fast; **pousser d.** (*de l'herbe etc*) to grow thickly

drugstore [drœgstɔr] *nm* drugstore

druide, druidesse [drɥid, drɥidɛs] *n* druid, druidess

druidique [drɥidik] *adj* druidic(al)

druidisme [drɥidism] *nm* druidism

drummer [drœmœr] *nm Mus* drummer

drupe [dryp] *n Bot* drupe

dry [draj] **1** *adj inv* dry; **champagne d.** dry champagne; **whisky d.** neat *or* straight whisky **2** *nm inv* dry martini

dryade [drijad] *nf* (*nymphe*) dryad, wood nymph

du [dy] *voir* = **de**

dû, due [dy] **1** *adj* **(a)** (*que l'on doit*) due, owing, owed; *Com* **en port dû** carriage forward **(b)** (*causé*) **ce retard est dû à …** this delay is due to …; **son licenciement est dû aux difficultés économiques de l'entreprise** he was made redundant because of *or* due to the company's economic difficulties; **sa maladresse est due à sa timidité** his clumsiness is caused by *or* is due to his shyness **(c)** (*approprié*) **en temps dû** in due course; **contrat rédigé en bonne et due forme** contract drawn up in due form, formal contract **2** *nm* due; **chacun sera rétribué selon son dû** everyone will be paid according to his due

dualisme [dɥalism] *nm* dualism

dualiste [dɥalist] **1** *adj* dualistic **2** *n* dualist

dualité [dɥalite] *nf* duality

dubitatif, -ive [dybitatif, -iv] *adj* doubtful, dubious

dubitativement [dybitativmɑ̃] *adv* doubtfully, dubiously

duc [dyk] *nm* **(a)** duke **(b)** (*oiseau*) horned owl; **grand d.** eagle owl

ducal, -ale, -aux, -ales [dykal, -o] *adj* ducal

duché [dyʃe] *nm* duchy, dukedom

duchesse [dyʃɛs] *nf* **(a)** duchess; *Péj* **elle fait la d.** she puts on airs **(b)** (*fruit*) **(poire) d.** duchess pear **(c)** *Culin* **pommes (de terre) d.** duchesse potatoes

ducroire [dykrwar] *nm Com* del credere; (*agent*) del credere agent

ductile [dyktil] *adj* ductile, tensile

ductilité [dyktilite] *nf* ductility

duègne [dɥɛɲ] *nf Arch* duenna, chaperon

duel[1] [dɥɛl] *nm* duel; **se battre en d.** to fight a duel; **provoquer qn en d.** to challenge sb to a duel; **d. oratoire** battle of words

duel[2] *nm Gram* dual (number)

duelliste [dɥelist] *nm* duellist

duettiste [dɥetist] *n Mus* duettist

duffel-coat, duffle-coat, *pl* **duffel-coats, duffle-coats** [dœfœlkot] *nm* duffel coat, duffle coat

dulcinée [dylsine] *nf Hum* love of one's life

dum-dum [dumdum], *pl* **dum-dums** *nf* dumdum bullet

dûment [dymɑ̃] *adv* duly, in due form

dumping [dœmpiŋ] *nm Com* dumping; **faire du d.** to dump; **être accusé de faire du d.** to be accused of dumping

dune [dyn] *nf* dune, sandhill

dunette [dynɛt] *nf Naut* poop (deck)

Dunkerque [dœ̃kɛrk] *nf* Dunkirk

duo [dɥo] *nm Mus* duet; *Th* duo; *F* **d. d'injures** slanging match

duodécimal, -ale, -aux, -ales [dɥodesimal, -o] *adj* duodecimal

duodénal, -ale, -aux, -ales [dɥɔdenal, -o] *adj Anat* duodenal

duodénite [dɥɔdenit] *nf Méd* duodenitis

duodénum [dɥɔdenɔm] *nm Anat* duodenum

duopole [dɥɔpɔl] *nm Com* duopoly

dupe [dyp] **1** *nf* dupe, *F* sucker; **prendre qn pour d.** to fool sb, to take sb in; **c'est un marché de dupes** I've/he's/*etc* been had *or* taken in *or* swindled **2** *adj* naive, gullible, easily deceived; **je ne suis pas d.** I'm not fooled *or* taken in; **il me ment, mais je n'en suis pas d.** I'm well aware that he's lying to me

duper [dype] **1** *vt* to dupe, to deceive, to fool, to take in **2 se duper** *vpr* to deceive oneself

duperie [dypri] *nf* (*tromperie*) deception; **victime d'une d.** victim of deception; **une vaste d.** one vast deception

dupeur, -euse [dypœr, -øz] *n Litt* trickster, deceiver

duplex [dyplɛks] **1** *adj inv Télécom* duplex; *TV, Rad* link-up **2** *nm inv* **(a)** *Rad, TV* **(émission en) d.** link-up **(b)** (*appartement*) maison(n)ette, *Am* duplex

duplexer [dyplɛkse] *vt Télécom* to duplex

duplicata [dyplikata] *nm inv* duplicate (copy)

duplicateur [dyplikatœr] *nm* duplicator, duplicating machine

duplication [dyplikasjɔ̃] *nf* **(a)** *Math* duplication; *Biol* doubling **(b)** *Télécom* duplexing; *Ordinat* **d. de logiciel** software copying

duplicité [dyplisite] *nf* duplicity, double dealing

dupliquer [dyplike] *vt Télécom* to duplex

dur [dyr] **1** *adj* **(a)** (*rigide*) (*substance*) hard; (*viande*) tough; **œuf d.** hard-boiled egg; **pain d.** stale bread; **être d. à cuire** (*de viande*) to take a lot of cooking; (*de personne*) to be a tough nut; **eau dure** hard water

(b) (*qui résiste à l'effort*) hard, difficult; **cette porte est dure (à ouvrir)** this door is stiff, this door is hard *or* difficult to open; *Aut etc* **commande dure** stiff control; **être d. à la peine** to be a tireless worker; **avoir l'oreille dure, être d. d'oreille** *ou F* **de la feuille** to be hard of hearing; **avoir la tête dure** to be obstinate *or* pig-headed; **avoir la vie dure** (*d'une personne, d'un animal*) to be hard to kill; *Fig* **les idées reçues ont la vie dure** preconceived ideas die hard; *F* **être d. à la détente** (*lent à comprendre*) to be slow on the uptake

(c) (*difficile*) (*travail etc*) hard, difficult; **c'est d. à croire** it's hard *or* difficult to believe; **enfant d.** difficult *or* problem child

(d) (*pénible*) hard, difficult; **hiver d.** hard *or* severe winter; **des scènes très dures** distressing *or* painful sights; **rendre la vie dure à qn** to make sb's life a misery; **la vie est dure** it's a hard life; **les temps sont durs** times are hard; **avoir un coup d.** to be dealt a severe blow; **une dure épreuve** a severe trial, a sore test; **être à dure école** to have a hard time of it

(e) (*sévère, cruel*) hard; **avoir le cœur d.** to be hard-hearted *or* callous; **être d. envers** *ou* **pour** *ou* **avec qn** to be hard *or* rough on sb; **c'est un tendre sous ses dehors très durs** he's quite soft-hearted under that tough exterior of his

2 *adv F (travailler, cogner)* hard; **le soleil tape d. ce matin** the sun is really beating down this morning; **croire qch d. comme fer** to be quite convinced of sth; **il croit d. comme fer que …** he is quite convinced *or* really believes that …; **d. d.!** (what a) bummer!; **d. d. la rentrée dans mon nouveau bahut!** what a bummer having to go to a new school next term!

3 *nm* **(a)** *Constr* **bâtiment en d.** permanent building

(b) *Arg (train)* train

4 *n F (personne)* **un d.** a tough guy, a hard nut; *Pol* a hard liner; **un d./une dure à cuire** a hard-boiled man/woman; **il aime bien jouer les durs** he likes to act tough

5 *nf* **coucher sur la dure** *(sur le sol)* to sleep on the floor; *(dehors)* to sleep rough; **vivre à la dure** to rough it; **il a été élevé à la dure** he's had a hard upbringing, he was brought up in the school of hard knocks; *F* **en dire de dures à qn** to tell sb where to get off; *F* **elle en a vu de dures** she's had a hard *or* tough time (of it)

durabilité [dyrabilite] *nf* durability

durable [dyrabl] *adj* durable, lasting, long-lasting

durablement [dyrabləmɑ̃] *adv* durably

duraille [dyraj] *adj F* hard; **il était d., le problème de maths** the maths question was a real pig; **se faire piquer son mec par sa meilleure copine, c'est plutôt d.** it's a bit of a bummer *or* downer when your best friend steals your man

duralumin® [dyralymɛ̃] *nm* Duralumin®

durant [dyrɑ̃] *prép* during; **d. toute sa vie, sa vie d.** during his whole life, throughout his life; **parler des heures d.** to talk for hours on end *or* for hours at a time; **d. quelques instants** for a few moments

durcir [dyrsir] **1** *vt* to harden, to make hard; *Fig* **d. la ligne du parti** to harden *or* stiffen the party line; **il a durci son opinion** his opinion has stiffened; **la France a decidé de d. ses positions au sujet de GATT** France has decided to take a tougher position *or* a harder *or* stiffer line on GATT **2** *vi (de pain, sol)* to harden, to become hard; *(du ciment etc)* to set, to harden **3 se durcir** *vpr* to harden; *Fig (d'opposition)* to stiffen; **ses traits se sont durcis** his features have hardened

durcissement [dyrsismɑ̃] *nm (de pain, du sol)* hardening; *(du ciment etc)* setting, hardening; *Fig (d'opposition, opinion)* stiffening; *(d'une attitude)* hardening

durée [dyre] *nf (d'un règne, de la guerre etc)* duration; *(d'un tissu, d'édifice etc)* lasting quality, wear; *(d'une ampoule)* life; *Mus (d'une note)* length, value; **bonheur de courte/longue d.** short-lived/lasting happiness; **d. d'un bail** duration *or* term of a lease; **contrat à d. illimitée** *ou* **indéterminée** permanent contract; **quelle est la d. de votre congé?** how long is your leave?, how long does your leave last?; **disque longue d.** long-playing record, *F* LP; *Cin* **d. de projection** running time; **d. de crédit** term of loan; **d. de séjour** length of stay; **d. de validité** period of validity; **d. de vie** lifespan; *(d'une pile etc)* life; *(d'une machine etc)* useful life; **d. de vol** flight time; **d. de voyage** journey time; **d. du travail** working hours; *Compta* **d. d'amortissement** depreciation period; *Rad* **d. d'écoute** listening time

durement [dyrmɑ̃] *adv* **(a)** *(avec vigueur) (se battre)* hard **(b)** *(péniblement)* **d. éprouvé** sorely tried **(c)** *(sévèrement, cruellement) (répondre, parler)* harshly, roughly; *(touché)* severely; **on l'a élevée d.** she had a harsh *or* hard upbringing; **très d. touché par qch** very hard hit by sth; **d. secoué dans un accident/par une nouvelle** severely *or* badly shaken up in an accident/by a piece of news

durer [dyre] *vi* **(a)** *(avoir une durée de) (d'un congé, d'une opération etc)* to last (for); **voilà trois ans que cela dure** it's been going on for three years; **votre congé dure combien de temps?** how long does your leave last *or* is your leave?

(b) *(continuer, perdurer)* to last; **cela ne durera pas** it can't *or* won't last; **pourvu que ça dure!** long may it last *or* continue!; **ça va d. longtemps, cette plaisanterie?** hasn't this gone on long enough?; **ça ne peut pas d.** this can't go on; *F* **ça durera ce que ça durera** it'll last as long as it's meant to last; **cette réparation n'est pas très solide mais ça durera ce que ça durera** it's not a brilliant repair job but it'll do for the moment *or* for the time being; **faire d. qch** *(une réunion, une conversation téléphonique, un repas)* to drag sth out; *(un manteau, un livre etc)* to make sth last; *Hum* **faire d. le plaisir** to prolong the agony; **tissu qui durera** material which will wear well; *Péj* **elle dure la mémé** the old woman is hanging on

(c) *F Région* **il ne peut pas d. en place** he can't stay put *or* keep still

dureté [dyrte] *nf* **(a)** *(d'une substance, de l'eau)* hardness; *(de la viande)* toughness **(b)** *(d'une personne, d'une voix)* harshness; *(d'un hiver, d'un climat)* severity; *(de traits)* hardness; **d. de cœur** hard-heartedness; **parler avec d.** to speak harshly

durillon [dyrijɔ̃] *nm (sur la main)* callus; *(sur le pied)* corn, callus

durit(e)® [dyrit] *nf Aut, Av etc* hose (connection), flexible pipe

duvet [dyvɛ] *nm* **(a)** *(sur le menton, un oisillon, une pêche etc)* down; **d. de l'eider/du cygne** eiderdown/swan's down **(b)** *(sac de couchage)* sleeping bag **(c)** *Suisse* duvet, continental quilt

duveté [dyvte] *adj* downy

duveter (se) [sədyvte] *vpr* to become downy

duveteux, -euse [dyvtø, -øz] *adj* downy

dwell [dwɛl] *nm Aut* dwell

dynamique [dinamik] **1** *adj* dynamic; *F* **c'est un type d.** he's lively *or* dynamic *or* go-ahead **2** *nf* dynamics; **la d. de groupe** group dynamics; **d. du marché** market dynamics

dynamiquement [dinamikmɑ̃] *adv* dynamically

dynamisant [dinamizɑ̃] *adj* motivating, stimulating

dynamisation [dinamizasjɔ̃] *nf* motivation, stimulation; **vous aurez en charge la d. de la classe** you'll be responsible for motivating *or* stimulating the class

dynamiser [dinamize] *vt* to motivate, to stimulate

dynamisme [dinamism] *nm* dynamism; *F (vitalité)* dynamism, vitality, drive

dynamiste [dinamist] *n Phil* dynamist

dynamitage [dinamitaʒ] *nm* dynamiting

dynamite [dinamit] *nf* dynamite

dynamiter [dinamite] *vt (édifice etc)* to dynamite, to blow up

dynamiteur, -euse [dinamitœr, -øz] *n* dynamiter

dynamo [dinamo] *nf Él* dynamo

dynamoélectrique [dinamoelɛktrik] *adj Él* dynamoelectric(al)

dynamogène [dinamɔʒɛn] *adj Physiol* energy-giving

dynastie [dinasti] *nf* dynasty

dynastique [dinastik] *adj* dynastic

dyne [din] *nf Phys* dyne

dysenterie [disɑ̃tri] *nf Méd* dysentery

dysentérique [disɑ̃terik] *adj Méd* dysenteric

dysfonctionnement [disfɔ̃ksjɔnmɑ̃] *nm (d'un organe)* dysfunction, malfunction; *(d'une institution, d'un service)* failure

dyslexie [dislɛksi] *nf Méd* dyslexia

dyslexique [dislɛksik] *adj* dyslexic

dysménorrhée [dismenɔre] *nf Méd* dysmenorrhoea, *US* dysmenorrhea

dyspepsie [dispɛpsi] *nf Méd* dyspepsia

dyspepsique [dispɛpsik], **dyspeptique** [dispɛptik] *adj, n Méd* dyspeptic

dysphasie [disfazi] *nf Méd* dysphasia

dystrophie [distrɔfi] *nf Méd* dystrophy; **d. musculaire progressive** muscular dystrophy

E

E, e [ə] *nm* (*lettre*) E, e
EAO [əao] *nm Ordinat* (*abrév* **enseignement assisté par ordinateur**) CAL
eau [o], *pl* **eaux** *nf* **(a)** (*liquide naturel*) water; **e. potable** drinking water; **e. non potable** water unfit for drinking; (*sur panneau*) not drinking water; **e. du robinet** tap water; **e. courante** running water; **faire mettre l'e. courante** to have water laid on; **e. en bouteille** bottled water; **laver le plancher à grande e.** to swab down the floor; **passer à l'e.** to rinse; **cuire à l'e.** to boil; **pommes de terre à l'e.** boiled potatoes; **whisky sans e.** neat whisky; **se mettre à l'e.** to go on the wagon; **service des eaux** water supply; **Société des Eaux** ≈ Water Board; **e. de la ville** main(s) water; **château d'e.** water tower; **conduite d'e.** water main(s); **il est tombé beaucoup d'e.** a lot of rain fell; **chaussures qui prennent l'e.** shoes that let in water; **faire de l'e.** (*d'une locomotive, d'un bateau*) to water, to take on water, *Vieilli* **être comme l'e. et le feu** to be as different as *or* to be like chalk and cheese; *F* **compte là-dessus et bois de l'e.!** don't count on it! *Fig* **mettre de l'e. dans son vin** to tone it down a bit; *F* **s'en aller en e. de boudin** to go down the tubes *or* up the spout; *F* **il y a de l'e. dans le gaz** there's trouble brewing; **il va y avoir de l'e. dans le gaz** there's going to be trouble; **pour éviter qu'il y ait de l'e. dans le gaz entre eux** to avoid any atmosphere between them; **il y a eu de l'e. dans le gaz tout le temps** there was always an atmosphere
(b) **ville d'eau(x)** spa; **prendre les** *ou* **aller aux eaux** to take *or* drink the waters
(c) (*étendue, masse*) water; **au bord de l'e.** by the water's side *or* edge; **restaurant au bord de l'e.** waterside restaurant; **sur l'e.** afloat; **tomber à l'e.** to fall into the water; *Fig* (*d'un plan*) to fall through; *Fig F* **mes vacances sont à l'e.** my holiday is up the spout *or* down the tubes; **mettre un navire à l'e.** to launch a ship; **se mettre à l'e.** to go in (for a swim); *Fig* **se lancer** *ou* **se jeter à l'e.** to take the plunge; *Fig* **apporter de l'e. au moulin de qn** to strengthen sb's case, to provide sb with ammunition; *Fig* **porter de l'e. à la rivière** *ou* **à la mer** to take coals to Newcastle; **il passera de l'e. sous les ponts avant que** *ou* **d'ici à ce que ...** it will be a long time before ...; **mais depuis, bien de l'e. est passée sous les ponts** a lot of water has flowed under the bridge since then, that was a long time ago; *Fig* **pêcher en e. trouble** to fish in troubled waters; *Fig* **nager** *ou* **naviguer en e. trouble** to sail close to the wind; **faire e.** (*d'un bateau*) to leak, to spring a leak; **cours d'e.** waterway; **jet d'e.** fountain; **pièce d'e.** (ornamental) lake; (*petite*) pond, pool, water feature; **eaux internationales/territoriales/françaises** international/territorial/French waters; **dimanche: grandes eaux à Versailles** the fountains will play at Versailles on Sunday; *Fig F* **c'était les grandes eaux** the waterworks started, he/she turned on the waterworks; *Fig F* **on va avoir droit aux grandes eaux** we'll be in for waterworks *or* floods of tears; *Fig* **dans ces eaux-là** or thereabouts; **mortes eaux** neap tides; **vives eaux** spring tides; **hautes/basses eaux** high/low water; *Fig* **nager entre deux eaux** (*ne pas s'engager*) to sit on the fence; **être dans les eaux d'un navire** to be in the wake of a ship; *Fig* **être** *ou* **naviguer dans les eaux de qn** (*rallier ses opinions*) to take the same line as sb; **il navigue dans les eaux de plusieurs peintres en vue** he hangs around several well known painters
(d) (*sécrétions du corps humain*) **être tout en e.** to be dripping with perspiration; **cela me fait venir** *ou* **me met l'e. à la bouche** it makes my mouth water; **j'ai l'e. à la bouche rien que d'y penser** my mouth is watering just thinking about it; **j'en ai l'e. à la bouche!** my mouth is watering (already)!; **cloque pleine d'e.** water blister; **poche des eaux** amniotic sac, bag of waters; **elle a perdu les eaux** her waters have broken
(e) (*d'un melon*) juice; **les concombres rendent beaucoup d'e.** cucumbers give off *or* out a lot of water
(f) (*pureté*) **de la plus belle e.** (*diamant, Fig charlatan etc*) of the first water; **ces deux-là sont de la même e.** they're two of a kind, they're tarred with the same brush
▶ **eau**: **e. bénite** holy water; **e. de Cologne** eau de Cologne; **e. déminéralisée** deionized water; **e. dentifrice** mouthwash; **e. distillée** distilled water; **e. douce** (*non salée*) fresh water; (*sans calcaire*) soft water; *F* **marin d'e. douce** landlubber; **e. dure** hard water; **e. de fleurs d'oranger** orange flower water; **e. gazeuse** carbonated *or* sparkling water; **e. grasse** washing-up water; **e. de Javel** bleach; **e. de lavande** lavender water; *Nucl* **e. lourde** heavy water; **e. de mélisse** = liqueur made from lemon balm; **e. minérale** (natural) mineral water; **e. oxygénée** hydrogen peroxide; **e. de parfum** eau de parfum; **e. plate** still water; **e. de pluie** rainwater; **e. de refroidissement** cooling water; **e. régale** aqua regia; **e. de roche** spring water; **e. de rose** rose water; *Fig* **roman/film à l'e. de rose** soppy *or* slushy novel/film; **e. rougie** = water with a drop of wine in it; **eaux de ruissellement** runoff; **e. de Seltz** soda water, Seltzer (water); **e. de source** spring water; **eaux territoriales** territorial waters; **eaux thermales** thermal *or* hot springs; **e. de toilette** toilet water, eau de toilette; **eaux usées** waste water; **traitement des eaux usées** waste water treatment; **e. de vaisselle** washing-up water
eau-de-vie, *pl* **eaux-de-vie** [odvi] *nf* (*de prune etc*) brandy
eau-forte, *pl* **eaux-fortes** *nf* **(a)** *Ch* aqua fortis, nitric acid **(b)** *Beaux-Arts* etching, etched engraving
eaux-vannes [ovan] *nfpl* sewage (water)
ébahi [ebai] *adj* astounded, *F* flabbergasted, staggered; **un regard é.** a look of blank astonishment
ébahir [ebair] **1** *vt* to astound, *F* to flabbergast, to stagger
2 s'ébahir *vpr* to be dumbfounded (**de** by)
ébahissement [ebaismɑ̃] *nm* astonishment
ébarbage [ebarbaʒ] *nm* (*d'un livre*) trimming the pages; (*d'une feuille de papier*) trimming the edges; (*d'une haie, pelouse etc*) clipping; (*d'une surface métallique*) removal of the burrs
ébarber [ebarbe] *vt* (*feuille de papier*) to trim (the edges of); (*livre*) to trim the pages of; (*haie, pelouse etc*) to clip; (*surface métallique*) to remove the burrs from
ébarbure [ebarbyr] *nf* (*de métal etc*) burr, paring; (*de papier*) trimming
ébats [eba] *nmpl* playing (about); **é. (amoureux)** lovemaking; **au milieu de leurs é. (amoureux)** in the middle of their lovemaking, while they were making love *or F* doing it
ébattre (s') [sebatr] *vpr* (*conj like* **battre**) to frolic, to play (about); (*des animaux*) to gambol
ébaubi [ebobi] *adj F* flabbergasted
ébauchage [eboʃaʒ] *nm* (*d'un tableau*) roughing out, sketching out; (*d'un roman etc*) roughing out, outlining
ébauche [eboʃ] *nf* (*d'un tableau*) rough sketch; (*d'un roman, poème etc*) outline, rough draft; (*d'une lettre, traduction*) draft; (*d'un projet*) outline; **faire l'é. de** (*roman, lettre, traduction*) to draft; (*tableau*) to make a rough sketch of, to sketch out; (*projet*) to outline; **ce projet n'est qu'à l'état d'é.** the plan is still sketchy; **l'architecte n'en est qu'à l'é. d'un plan** the architect is still only at the planning stage; **ils en sont à l'é. d'une amitié** there are the beginnings of a friendship between them; **il semble qu'il y ait une é. de réconciliation entre l'OLP et Israël** there seem to be the first tentative signs of a reconciliation between the PLO and Israel; **il n'y a qu'une é. de relations entre eux** relations between them are very tentative; **je n'ai réussi à avoir avec lui qu'une é. de conversation** I managed only a rather stilted conversation with him; **il a marmonné l'é. d'un remerciement** he grudgingly muttered a few words of thanks; **é. d'un sourire** suspicion *or* ghost of a smile; **é. d'un espoir** glimmer of hope
ébaucher [eboʃe] *vt* (*tableau, roman*) to rough out; (*projet, mise en scène*) to sketch out, to outline; (*lettre*) to draft, to make a draft of; (*réconciliation, amitié*) to take the first tentative steps towards; (*statue*) to rough-hew; **é. une traduction** to make a draft *or* rough translation, to draft a translation; **é. un sourire** to give a faint smile, to smile faintly; **é. un geste** to make a vague gesture; **les**

négociations de paix étaient à peine ébauchées et déjà ... peace talks had barely been mooted before ...; **é. des hypothèses** to put forward tentative hypotheses; **é. une conversation avec qn** to have a stilted conversation with sb

ébène [ebɛn] *nf* ebony; **(d'un noir) d'é., (noir) é.** jet black; *Hist* **(bois d')é.** slaves; **marchand d'é.** slave-trader

ébénier [ebenje] *nm* (*arbre*) ebony tree; **faux é.** laburnum

ébéniste [ebenist] *nm* cabinet maker

ébénisterie [ebenistəri] *nf* (*métier*) cabinet making; (*meuble*) cabinet work

éberlué [ebɛrlɥe] *adj F* flabbergasted

éblouir [ebluir] *vt aussi Fig* to dazzle; *Fig* **il a préparé ce plat pour vous é.** he prepared this dish to impress you

éblouissant [ebluisɑ̃] *adj* dazzling, blinding; *Fig* dazzling; **d'une beauté éblouissante** dazzlingly beautiful

éblouissement [ebluismɑ̃] *nm* dazzle, glare; *Fig* (*émerveillement*) amazement; *Fig* **quand on arrive chez eux, c'est un véritable é.** their place is dazzling; *Fig* **l'é. qu'il ressentit lorsqu'il la vit** his sense of dazzlement when he saw her; *Méd* **avoir des éblouissements** to have fits of dizziness

ébonite [ebɔnit] *nf* vulcanite, ebonite

éborgner [ebɔrɲe] *vt* **(a) é. qn** to blind sb in one eye, to put sb's eye out; **j'ai failli m'é.** I nearly put my eye out **(b)** (*arbre fruitier*) to disbud

éboueur [ebuœr] *nm* dustman, *Am* garbage man

ébouillanter [ebujɑ̃te] **1** *vt* to scald **2 s'ébouillanter** *vpr* to scald oneself

éboulement [ebulmɑ̃] *nm* **(a)** (*écroulement*) (*de falaise, côte, remblais*) collapse; **l'é. de la falaise/carrière a fait deux morts** two people were killed when the cliff collapsed/the quarry fell in; **il y a eu un é. dans la mine** there has been a cave-in at the mine; **si vous allez vers la carrière, méfiez-vous des éboulements** if you're going in the direction of the quarry, watch out for landslides **(b)** (*tas*) landslide, landslip

ébouler (s') [sebule] *vpr* (*d'une falaise, une côte*) to collapse, to slip; (*d'une mine*) to cave in; (*d'un remblais*) to collapse

éboulis [ebuli] *nm* mass of fallen earth; (*en montagne*) scree

ébourgeonnage [eburʒɔnaʒ] *nm,* **ébourgeonnement** [eburʒɔnmɑ̃] *nm* disbudding

ébourgeonner [eburʒɔne] *vt* (*arbre fruitier*) to disbud

ébouriffant [eburifɑ̃] *adj F* breathtaking, hair-raising

ébouriffé [eburife] *adj* **(a)** (*cheveux, personne*) dishevelled **(b)** *F* amazed

ébouriffer [eburife] *vt* **(a)** (*les cheveux de qn*) to ruffle, to tousle; **é. qn** to ruffle *or* tousle sb's hair **(b)** *F* **e. qn** (*époustoufler*) to take sb's breath away

ébranchage [ebrɑ̃ʃaʒ] *nm,* **ébranchement** [ebrɑ̃ʃmɑ̃] *nm* (*d'un arbre*) stripping *or* lopping the branches

ébrancher [ebrɑ̃ʃe] *vt* (*arbre*) to lop off *or* strip the branches from

ébranchoir [ebrɑ̃ʃwar] *nm* billhook

ébranlement [ebrɑ̃lmɑ̃] *nm* **(a)** (*tremblement*) (*de vitres, mur, édifice*) shaking; **l'é. des murs a été si violent qu'ils se sont lézardés** the walls shook so violently that they cracked; *Fig* **ce scandale a provoqué l'é. du gouvernement** the scandal caused the government to totter, the scandal rocked the government

(b) (*choc nerveux*) **é. de la raison** unhinging of the mind; **la mort de son ami a provoqué un véritable é. chez elle** she went to pieces after her friend's death

(c) (*départ, mise en route*) (*d'un train, une procession, un convoi etc*) departure

ébranler [ebrɑ̃le] **1** *vt* **(a)** (*édifice, mur*) to shake, to rock; (*vitres*) to shake **(b)** *Fig* (*personne*) to shake (up), to upset; (*confiance, nerfs, régime, dictature, économie*) to shake; **il ne faut pas te laisser é. par ses critiques** don't let his criticism get to you; **il a été très é. par l'annonce de cet accident** he was very shaken *or* upset by the news of the accident; **la nouvelle a ébranlé le pays tout entier** the entire country was rocked by the news **2 s'ébranler** *vpr* (*d'un train*) to start, to move off; (*d'une procession, un convoi, une caravane etc*) to move *or* set off

ébrécher [ebreʃe] *vt* **(j'ébrèche; j'ébrécherai)** (*assiette, tasse, verre, lame etc*) to chip; *Fig F* (*réputation*) to damage; *Fig F* (*son capital*) to make a hole in

ébréchure [ebreʃyr] *nf* chip

ébriété [ebriete] *nf* (state of) drunkenness *or* intoxication *or* inebriation; **en état d'é.** in a state of inebriation

ébrouement [ebrumɑ̃] *nm* **(a)** (*d'un cheval*) snorting, snort **(b)** (*d'ailes*) flap(ping); (*dans l'eau*) splashing about

ébrouer (s') [sebrue] *vpr* **(a)** (*d'un cheval*) to snort **(b)** (*d'ailes*) to flap; (*dans l'eau*) to splash about

ébruitement [ebrɥitmɑ̃] *nm* spreading

ébruiter [ebrɥite] **1** *vt* (*secret*) to give away; (*accord, pourparlers*) to leak; (*nouvelle*) to spread; **tu serais gentil de ne pas é. mon mariage** I'd be grateful if you didn't spread it around *or* if you didn't give it away that I'm getting married; **leur accord a été ébruité par des gens de l'intérieur** news of their agreement was leaked by people on the inside **2 s'ébruiter** *vpr* (*d'une nouvelle*) to spread, *F* to get (a)round

EBS [øbeɛs] *nf* (*abrév* **encéphalite bovine spongiforme**) BSE

ébullition [ebylisjɔ̃] *nf* boiling point; **l'é. de l'eau se fait à 90°** the boiling point of water is 90°, water boils at 90°; **arriver à é.** to come to the boil; **amener à é.** bring to the boil; **maintenir en é. pendant cinq minutes** boil for five minutes; *Fig* **en é.** (*village, maison*) in turmoil; (*personne*) very excited, worked up

écaillage [ekajaʒ] *nm* **(a)** (*d'un poisson*) scaling; (*des huîtres*) opening **(b)** (*de peinture*) flaking off, peeling off; (*d'émail*) scaling off, chipping

écaille [ekaj] *nf* (*d'un poisson*) scale; (*d'une tortue*) shell; (*de peinture*) flake; (*d'émail*) chip; *Litt Fig* **les écailles lui tombèrent des yeux** the scales fell from his eyes; **lunettes à monture d'é.** tortoiseshell-rimmed spectacles; **peigne en é.** tortoiseshell comb

écailler[1] [ekaje] **1** *vt* **(a)** (*poisson*) to scale; (*huître*) to open **(b)** (*chaudière*) to scale **2 s'écailler** *vpr* (*de l'émail*) to chip (off); (*de la peinture*) to peel (off), to flake (off)

écailler[2]**, -ère** [ekaje, -ɛr] **1** *n* (*marchand*) oyster seller; (*dans un bar, un restaurant*) oyster opener **2** *nf* **écaillère** oyster knife

écailleux, -euse [ekajø, -øz] *adj* (*poisson*) scaly; (*ardoise*) flaky

écale [ekal] *nf* (*d'une noix*) hull, husk; (*d'une châtaigne*) shuck

écaler [ekale] *vt* (*noix*) to hull, to husk; (*châtaignes*) to shuck

écarlate [ekarlat] **1** *adj* scarlet; **devenir é.** to blush, to go *or* turn scarlet **2** *nf* scarlet

écarquiller [ekarkije] *vt* **é. les yeux** to open one's eyes wide, to stare, *F* to goggle

écart[1] [ekar] *nm* **(a)** (*entre deux chiffres, deux températures*) difference **(de** in); *Compta* spread, variance; *Bourse* spread; *Mktg* gap; (*stratégie d'attaque*) bypass attack; **é. d'opinions/de points de vue** difference of opinions/points of view; **on constate de grands écarts dans ses résultats** his results are very uneven; **il y a des écarts de niveau trop importants dans cette classe** ability differs *or* varies too much in the class; **les écarts d'arrivée dans les commandes sont inquiétants** the differences in the arrival times of the orders are worrying; **il y a un é. important entre ma sœur et moi** there's a big (age) gap *or* a big difference in age between my sister and me; **il y a un é. de trois ans entre eux** there's a three-year gap *or* three years between them, they're three years apart; **l'é. entre les deux équipes s'est beaucoup réduit** the gap between the two teams has narrowed considerably; **é. de prix/de salaires** price/wage differential; **réduire l'é. entre deux salaires** to narrow the gap between two wages; *Com* **é. entre le prix de vente et le coût** margin between cost and selling price; *Bourse* **é. vertical** vertical spread; *Bourse* **écarts de cours** price spreads; *MecE* **é. admissible** tolerance

(b) (*distance*) (*entre étagères, tableaux etc*) distance, space; **l'é. entre chaque soldat doit être de ...** there must be (a distance of) ... between each soldier, soldiers must be ... apart; **faire le grand é.** to do the splits

(c) (*déviation*) *Tech* (*de l'aiguille d'une boussole*) deflection; **faire un é.** (*d'un piéton*) to step aside, to swerve; (*d'un cheval*) to shy; (*d'une voiture, un vélo*) to swerve; **il ne fait jamais d'écarts de régime** he never breaks his diet, he always keeps to *or F* sticks to his diet

(d) à. l'é.: j'ai mis mes verres en cristal à l'é. I've put my crystal glasses out of the way; **je préfère mettre cette éventualité à l'é.** I prefer not to think about that possibility; **je mets sa suggestion à l'é. pour l'instant** I'm putting *or* setting his suggestion aside for the moment; **se sentir à l'é.** to feel isolated *or* out of things; **se tenir à l'é.** to keep *or* stay in the background; (*du monde, de la foule etc*) to keep oneself apart, to hold oneself aloof; **se tenir à l'é. de la politique** to keep out of *or* away from politics; **mettre** *ou* **tenir qn à l'é.** to keep sb at a distance; **les autres enfants le mettent** *ou* **tiennent à l'é.** the other children don't let him join in; **tenir qn à l'é. (de qch)** to keep sb away (from sth); **il tient sa femme à l'é. de ses affaires** he keeps his wife out of his business, he doesn't involve his wife in his business; **un terrain à l'é. de la ville** a piece of land outside the town; **habiter à l'é.** to live in a remote *or* lonely spot

▶ **écart**[1]**: écarts de conduite** transgressions, misbehaviour; **ses écarts de conduite ont fini par lasser sa femme** his wife finally got tired of his behaviour *or F* carryings-on; **elle**

a cessé ses écarts de conduite she's stopped misbehaving, she's settled down; *Fin* **écarts de conversion** exchange adjustments; **écarts de jeunesse** youthful indiscretions; **écarts de langage** bad language; **faire des écarts de langage** to use bad language; *Compta* **é. net** net variance; **é. de prime** option spread; *Compta* **écarts de réévaluation** revaluation reserve; *Tech* **é. type** standard deviation

écart² *nm Cartes* **(a)** *(action)* discarding **(b)** *(carte)* discard

écarté¹ [ekarte] *adj* **(a)** *(maison, endroit)* isolated, lonely, remote **(b)** *(distant)* *(bras, pieds)* apart; *(yeux)* widely spaced; **avoir les dents écartées** to have gaps between one's teeth

écarté² *nm Cartes* (game of) écarté

écartelé [ekartəle] *adj Hér* quartered, quarterly

écarteler [ekartəle] *vt* **(j'écartèle; j'écartèlerai) (a)** *(criminel, Hér écu)* to quarter **(b)** *Fig* **se sentir é.** to be torn **(entre** between)

écartement [ekartəmɑ̃] *nm* **(a)** *(séparation)* separation; **l'é. des volets** the opening of the shutters; *Tech* **pièce d'é.** spacer **(b)** *(d'un obstacle)* setting aside; **depuis l'é. des gêneurs, la société va beaucoup mieux** things have been much better in the company since it got rid of the trouble-makers **(c)** *(distance)* *(entre des barres etc)* space, gap, clearance; *Rail* *(de la voie)* gauge; *Aut* **é. des essieux** wheelbase; *Aut* **é. des roues** track; *Aut* **é. des électrodes** spark *or* plug *or* electrode gap

écarter¹ [ekarte] **1** *vt* **(a)** *(séparer)* *(doigts)* to spread out; *(branches)* to part; *(rideaux)* to draw back, to open; *(ses bras)* to open; *(ses jambes)* to spread, to open; *(ses coudes)* to square; *(personnes, objets)* to move *or* push aside; **le service d'ordre devait é. les fans sur son passage** the marshals had to push a way for him through the crowd of fans; *Fig* **le temps nous écarte l'un de l'autre** we are drifting apart with time

(b) *(éliminer, exclure)* *(candidat, réclamation, solution, proposition)* to turn down; *(soupçon)* to divert; *(coup, danger)* to ward off, to avert; **é. les obstacles de son chemin** to brush aside the obstacles in one's path; **é. qn de son chemin** to push sb out of one's way; **ses interventions nous ont écartés de notre sujet** his interruptions caused us to stray *or* wander from the subject *or* to digress; **être écarté de son but** to be deflected from one's goal

2 s'écarter *vpr* **(a)** *(se séparer)* *(de personnes)* to move apart; *(de routes)* to diverge; **pour s'ouvrir, les portes de l'ascenseur s'écartent** the lift doors open by sliding apart; **plus on avance vers le nord, plus les maisons s'écartent les unes des autres** the further north you go, the further apart the houses become; **la foule s'est écartée sur le passage des pompiers** the crowd parted *or* drew aside to let the firemen through; *Fig* **nos chemins s'écartent de plus en plus** we are drifting further and further apart; *Fig* **nos aspirations/nos vies s'écartent de plus en plus** our aims in life/our lives are increasingly different

(b) *(s'éloigner)* *(de piéton)* to move *or* step aside; *(de voiture, de vélo)* to swerve; *(dévier)* to deviate, to stray **(de** from); **s'é. du sujet** to digress, to deviate *or* wander from the subject; **s'é. des règles** to depart from the rules; **ne vous écartez pas de la route** keep to the road; **s'é. du droit chemin** to stray from the straight and narrow

écarter² *vt Cartes* to discard

écarteur [ekartœr] *nm Aut* **é. de mâchoire** shoe expander

ecchymose [ekimoz] *nf* bruise, *Spéc* ecchymosis

Ecclésiaste (l') [leklezjast] *nm Bible* (the book of) Ecclesiastes

ecclésiastique [eklezjastik] **1** *adj* ecclesiastical **2** *nm* ecclesiastic, cleric, clergyman

écervelé, -ée [eservəle] **1** *adj* harebrained, scatterbrained **2** *n* scatterbrain

ECG [əseʒe] *nm Méd (abrév* **électrocardiogramme)** ECG

échafaud [eʃafo] *nm* **(a)** scaffold; **monter sur** *ou* **à l'é.** to go to the scaffold, to mount the scaffold; **finir sur l'é.** to die on the scaffold, *Hum* **tu vas finir sur l'é.** you'll end up in gaol **(b)** *Vieilli (estrade)* stand, platform

échafaudage [eʃafodaʒ] *nm* **(a)** *(passerelles etc)* scaffolding; *(d'objets)* pile; *Fig (d'une argumentation, théorie)* structure, fabric; **é. pour caméra** (camera) tower **(b)** *(procédé)* erection of scaffolding; *Fig* *(d'une fortune)* building up; *(d'une argumentation, théorie)* construction; **il perd son temps à des échafaudages de plans qui ne mènent jamais à rien** he wastes his time putting together *or* devising plans that never come to anything

échafauder [eʃafode] **1** *vi* to erect (a) scaffolding **2** *vt Fig* *(plan, système)* to put together, to devise; *(argumentation)* to put together, to construct

échalas [eʃala] *nm* *(pour soutenir une plante)* cane, stake; *Fig* **grand é.** beanpole; **il est sec comme un é.** he's a real beanpole

échal(l)ier [eʃalje] *nm* **(a)** *(clôture)* barrier, hurdle *(closing gap)* **(b)** *(échelle)* stile

échalote [eʃalɔt] *nf* *(plante)* shallot, *Can* scallion; *Can* **é. française** shallot

échancré [eʃɑ̃kre] *adj* low-cut; **robe échancrée dans le dos** dress cut low in the back, dress with a low back

échancrer [eʃɑ̃kre] *vt* *(robe etc)* to cut out the neckline of; *(planche)* to notch; **littoral échancré** indented coastline

échancrure [eʃɑ̃kryr] *nf* *(décolleté)* low neckline; *(découpe de veste)* vent, slit; *(d'une planche)* notch; *(d'un littoral)* indentation

échange [eʃɑ̃ʒ] *nm* **(a)** *(de prisonniers, d'idées, de coups etc)* exchange; **faire l'é. de qch pour** *ou* **contre qch** to exchange sth for sth; **recevoir/donner qch en é. (de qch)** to receive/give sth in exchange *or* in return (for sth); **est-il possible de faire l'é.?** is it possible to exchange it?, can it be exchanged?; *F* **on fait é.?** want to swop?; **é. d'appartement** flat swap; **de violents échanges entre la police et les manifestants** *(physique)* violent clashes between the police and demonstrators; *(verbal)* violent exchanges between the police and demonstrators; **échanges culturels** cultural exchanges; **c'est un é. de bons procédés** one good turn deserves another, I'm/he's/*etc* returning a favour; **nous faisons des échanges de bons procédés** we do favours for each other, we help each other out

(b) *Fin* exchange; *(commerce)* trade; **échanges commerciaux** trade; **échanges internationaux** international trade; **le volume des échanges** the volume of trade; **les échanges entre la France et l'Allemagne** trade between France and Germany

(c) *Bourse* **é. cambiste** treasury swap; **é. de créances** debt swap; **é. de créances contre actifs** debt equity swap; **é. de devises** currency swap; **é. financier** swap; **é. de taux d'intérêt** interest rate swap

(d) *Tennis* rally; **on va faire quelques échanges?** shall we knock a few balls about?

▸ **échange**: *Ordinat* **é. de données** data exchange *or* swap; *Ordinat* **é. de données dynamique** dynamic data exchange; *Ordinat* **é. de données informatisé** electronic data interchange; **é. linguistique** language exchange holiday; *Tech* **é. standard** standard replacement

échangeable [eʃɑ̃ʒabl] *adj* exchangeable

échanger [eʃɑ̃ʒe] *vt* **(j'échangeai(s); n. échangeons)** *(coups, idées, injures, lettres)* to exchange; *(objets, articles)* to exchange, to trade, *F* to swap, *Vieilli* to barter **(contre** for); **les articles soldés ne sont ni repris ni échangés** sales goods may not be returned or exchanged; **il m'a échangé un timbre espagnol contre un anglais** he traded *or F* swapped me a Spanish stamp for an English one; **é. des impressions** to exchange *or* compare impressions

échangeur [eʃɑ̃ʒœr] *nm* **(a)** *(sur une autoroute)* interchange; *(sur une route)* (clover leaf) intersection **(b)** *Phys* (heat) exchanger; *Aut* **é. air/air** air-to-air exchanger

échangisme [eʃɑ̃ʒism] *nm* partner swapping

échangiste [eʃɑ̃ʒist] **1** *n* partner swapper **2** *adj attrib* partner-swapping

échanson [eʃɑ̃sɔ̃] *nm Hist* cup-bearer

échantillon [eʃɑ̃tijɔ̃] *nm* **(a)** *(de tissu)* sample; *(d'un travail)* sample, specimen; *(pour un sondage)* population sample; *Méd* specimen; **prendre** *ou* **prélever des échantillons de qch** to take samples of sth, to sample sth; **catalogue d'échantillons** sample *or* pattern book; *Mktg* **non conforme à l'é.** not up to sample **(b)** *Vieilli* **brique/tuile d'é.** standard brick/tile

▸ **échantillon**: *Mktg* **é. aléatoire** random sample; **é. aréolaire** cluster (area) sample; **é. gratuit** free sample; **é. gratuit, ne peut être vendu** free sample, not for resale; **é. par quotas** quota sample; **é. probabiliste** probability sample

échantillonnage [eʃɑ̃tijɔnaʒ] *nm* **(a)** *(vérification)* sampling, testing; *(groupe de personnes)* sample; **l'é. se fait sur un produit sur cent** one product in a hundred is sampled *or* tested; **un é. est effectué systématiquement** sampling is done systematically **(b)** *Com* making up of samples; *(d'un tissu etc)* making up of patterns; **un é. de ce que je sais faire/de mes capacités** a sample of what I can do/of my ability; **voici un é. de sa bêtise** here's an example of how stupid he is

▸ **échantillonnage**: *Mktg* **é. aléatoire** random sampling; **é. empirique** purposive *or* non-random sampling; **é. non probabiliste** non-random *or* non-probability sampling; **é. par zone** area sampling

échantillonner [eʃɑ̃tijɔne] *vt* **(a)** *(vin)* to sample, to taste; *(population)* to sample **(b)** *Com* *(préparer des échantillons de)* to prepare samples of; *(tissues etc)* to prepare patterns of **(c)** *(étalonner)* *(articles)* to make according to sample

échantillonneur, -euse [eʃɑ̃tijɔnœr, -øz] *n Com* (*personne*) tester, sampler

échappatoire [eʃapatwar] **1** *nf* way out; **le sommeil est mon é.** sleep is my escape mechanism; **é. fiscale** tax loophole **2** *adj* **clause é.** escape clause

échappé [eʃape] *nm Sp* breakaway

échappée [eʃape] *nf* **(a)** *Sp* (*dans une course*) breakaway; **être dans l'é.** to be part of the breakaway group **(b)** (*espace libre*) space, gap, interval; **é. (de vue)** vista (**sur** over); **é. de lumière** shaft of light; **é. de ciel** patch of sky; **é. de soleil** burst of sunshine; **é. de beau temps** short spell of fine weather; *Fig* **faire qch par échappées** to do sth in fits and starts **(c)** (*pour véhicules*) turning space **(d)** (*d'un escalier*) headroom

échappement [eʃapmɑ̃] *nm* **(a)** (*de vapeur*) exhaust, release; *Aut* (*mouvement*) exhaust stroke; **(tuyau d')é.** waste-steam pipe; *Aut* exhaust (pipe); *Aut* **pot d'é.** silencer, *Am* muffler; *Aut* **(soupape d')é. libre** cut-out; **gaz d'é.** exhaust fumes; **clapet d'é.** exhaust cut-out **(b)** (*d'une montre*) escapement; **montre à é.** lever watch **(c)** *Ordinat* escape

échapper [eʃape] **1** *vi* **(a) é. à** (*qn*) to escape from; (*grippe, punition*) to escape *or F* dodge; (*corvées*) to get out of, to dodge; **é. à la mort** to escape death; **é. à un coup** to dodge a blow; **é. aux recherches** (*d'un criminel, un animal*) to evade capture; **cette édition a échappé à mes recherches** I missed this edition in my research; **é. à l'impôt** to avoid tax; **le prisonnier nous a échappé** the prisoner got away from us *or* escaped; **le vase m'a échappé des mains** the vase slipped out of my hands; **é. à tout contrôle** to be out of control; **cet enfant/ce chien échappe à notre contrôle** this child/dog has got out of hand *or* is beyond our control; **il n'y a pas moyen d'y é.** there is no escaping it *or* getting away from it; **je n'échapperai pas à une leçon de morale** I'm in for a sermon; **peux-tu é. quelques heures à ton patron?** can you get away from work for a few hours?; **on ne m'échappe pas comme ça** you don't get away *or* escape that easily; **é. à toute définition** to defy definition; **é. à la règle** to be an exception to the rule; **tu n'échappes pas à la règle** you're no exception to the rule; **leurs baisers n'ont pas échappé à mes regards** it did not escape my notice that they were kissing; **l'enfant a échappé à la vue de sa mère cinq minutes seulement** the child was out of his mother's sight for only five minutes; **ce fait a échappé à mon attention, ce fait m'a échappé** this fact escaped *or* slipped my attention, this fact escaped me; **rien ne lui échappe** he doesn't miss a thing; **son nom m'échappe** his name escapes *or* eludes me, his name has slipped my mind; *F* **vous l'avez échappé belle** you've had a narrow escape

(b) laisser é. (*qn, animal*) to let escape; (*de l'air d'un ballon*) to let out; (*vapeur*) to let off; (*larme*) to let fall; (*secret, soupir, cri, grossièreté*) to let out; (*faute d'orthographe, détail*) to overlook; **laisser é. son stylo** to let one's pen slip from one's fingers; **laisser é. l'occasion** to let the opportunity slip

(c) (*parole, cri etc*) **pas un mot ne lui a échappé** he didn't let anything slip, he didn't say a word; **je n'aurais pas dû le dire mais ça m'a échappé** I shouldn't have said it but it just slipped out; **un sanglot/une injure lui échappa** he let out a sob/an oath

2 s'échapper *vpr* (*s'évader*) to escape (**de** from); **s'é. de prison** to escape from prison, to break out of prison; **je n'arriverai jamais à m'é. de cette réunion de famille** I'll never manage to get out of this family reunion; *F* **il faut que je m'échappe pendant quelques minutes** I've got to go somewhere (else) for a few minutes, I must be off; **le gaz s'échappe** the gas is leaking; **un cri s'échappa de ses lèvres** a cry burst from his lips; **de hautes flammes s'échappaient de tous côtés** great flames were shooting from every side

3 *vt Can* (*laisser échapper*) to drop

écharde [eʃard] *nf* splinter

écharpe [eʃarp] *nf* [①**A12**,1,d] scarf; (*de cérémonie*) sash; (*au bras*) sling; **porter le bras en é.** to have one's arm in a sling; **en é.** diagonally, crosswise; **prendre une voiture en é.** to hit a car sideways on; **se prendre en é.** (*de voitures*) to collide at an angle; (*de trains*) to collide at the points

écharper [eʃarpe] *vt* (*membre, personne*) to slash; (*viande*) to hack (up); (*troupes*) to cut to pieces; **vous allez vous faire é.!** you'll get torn to pieces!

échasse [eʃas] *nf* **(a)** stilt; **être monté sur des échasses** to be on stilts; *F* (*avoir de longues jambes*) to have long legs, to be long in the leg **(b)** *Orn* stilt

échassier [eʃasje] *nm Orn* wader

échauder [eʃode] *vt* (*théière*) to warm; *Fig* **se faire é., être échaudé** to get one's fingers burnt, to burn one's fingers; **elle hésite à se remarier car son premier mariage l'a échaudée** she's reluctant to get married again because she got her fingers burnt the first time

échauffant [eʃofɑ̃] *adj Arch* (*aliment*) that causes constipation

échauffement [eʃofmɑ̃] *nm* **(a)** (*d'un sol, Tech*) heating; (*d'une pièce, d'un moteur, Fig Fin de l'économie*) overheating; (*d'une céréale, du foin*) fermenting; (*d'une corde*) chafing

(b) (*excitation*) overexcitement; **le débat a provoqué l'é. des esprits** the discussion got people worked up, people got rather worked up *or* tempers got rather heated during the discussion; **dans l'é. de la discussion** in the heat of the argument

(c) (*d'un athlète etc*) warm(ing)-up; **exercices d'é.** warm-up *or* limbering-up exercises

(d) *Arch* (*constipation*) constipation

échauffer [eʃofe] **1** *vt* **(a)** (*chauffer*) (*pièce, moteur*) to overheat; (*céréales, foin*) to cause fermentation in; **frottement qui échauffe les roues** friction that overheats the wheels **(b)** (*exciter*) **discussion qui échauffe les esprits** discussion that gets people worked up; *F* **é. la bile** *ou* **les oreilles** *ou* **les sangs de qn** to get up sb's nose, to get on sb's nerves **(c)** (*athlète*) to warm up **2 s'échauffer** *vpr* to become *or* get overheated; (*d'un athlète etc*) to warm *or* limber up; *Tech* to run hot, to heat; (*de céréales, du foin*) to ferment; **ne vous échauffez pas** don't get excited

échauffourée [eʃofure] *nf* scuffle, skirmish; (*entre bandes*) clash; *Mil* skirmish

échéance [eʃeɑ̃s] *nf* date of payment; (*terme d'un effet*) falling due, maturity; (*de contrat*) expiry date; **venir à é.** to fall due; **payable à l'é.** payable at maturity; **à trois mois d'é.** at three months' date; **billet à longue/courte é.** long-/short-dated bill; **politique à longue/courte é.** long-/short-term policy; **faire face à une é.** to meet a bill; **avoir de lourdes échéances** to have a lot of bills to pay each month, to have a lot of monthly payments to make

▶ **échéance**: *Fig* **l'é. électorale** election day, the elections; *Fin* **é. emprunt** loan maturity; *Compta* **échéances de fin de mois** end of month payments; *Bourse* **é. proche** short maturity, near month; **é. à vue** sight bill *or* maturity

échéancier [eʃeɑ̃sje] *nm* **(a)** *Fin* bill book; *Compta* due date file, aged debtor schedule; *Com* **é. de paiement** payment schedule **(b)** (*calendrier pour les travaux etc*) timetable, schedule

échéant [eʃeɑ̃] *adj* **(a)** *Fin* falling due **(b) le cas é.** if necessary, if need be

échec [eʃɛk] *nm* **(a)** (*défaite*) failure; (*revers*) check, setback; **l'é. des discussions** the failure *or* breakdown of the negotiations; **l'é. scolaire** doing badly at school, poor performance at school; **le milieu familial est très souvent à l'origine de l'é. scolaire** home life is frequently the reason why children do badly at school; **voué à l'é.** bound to fail, doomed to failure; **reconnaître son é.** to admit defeat *or* failure; **cela va se solder par un é.** it will end in failure; **subir un é.** to suffer a setback, *Can* **mettre en é.** (*au hockey*) to check; *Fig* **tenir l'ennemi en é.** to hold the enemy in check; **faire é. à** (*activités, agissements etc*) to put a stop to; **faire é. à qn/aux projets de qn** to foil *or* frustrate sb/sb's plans

(b) (*jeu*) **é.!** check!; **é. et mat** checkmate; **faire é. au roi** to check the king; **échecs** chess; **une partie d'échecs** a game of chess; **joueur d'échecs** chess player

échelle [eʃɛl] *nf* **(a)** ladder; **é. d'incendie** *ou* **de pompiers** fireman's ladder; **é. double** stepladder; **é. de corde** rope ladder; **é. coulissante** extension *or* extending ladder; **faire la courte é. à qn** to give sb a leg up *or Am* a boost; *F* **vous voulez me faire monter à l'é.** you're having *or Am* putting me on, you're pulling my leg *or Br* winding me up; **il faut tirer l'é., il n'y a plus qu'à tirer l'é.** there's no point in trying any further, we'd better give up

(b) *Fig* **l'é. sociale** the social ladder; **être en haut** *ou* **au sommet de l'é.** to be at the top of the tree *or* the ladder

(c) (*d'une carte, maquette etc*) scale; **l'é. est de 1/10 000** the scale is 1/10,000; **à quelle é. est fait ton train électrique?** what scale is your electric train?; **carte à petite/grande é.** small-/large-scale map; *Fig* **faire les choses sur une grande é.** to do things on a large scale; **à l'é. mondiale/nationale** on a world/national scale; **à l'é. de l'homme** on a human scale; *Ordinat* **intégration à grande/petite é.** large-/small-scale integration

(d) *Hist* **les échelles du Levant** the (commercial) ports of the Levant; **les échelles de Barbarie** the Barbary ports

(e) (*dans un collant*) ladder, *Am* run; **j'ai fait une é. à mon collant** I've laddered my tights, *Am* I have a run in my tights

(f) (*dans les cheveux*) **elle me fait des échelles** she cuts my hair in steps; **dommage qu'il y ait toutes ces échelles** it's a pity that it's all so uneven *or* all so up and down

▶ **échelle**: *Mktg* **é. d'attitudes** attitude scale; **é. de Beaufort** Beaufort scale; *Mktg* **é. de classement** rating scale; *Naut* **é. de commandement** *ou* **d'honneur** companion ladder; *Mus* **é. chromatique/diatonique/harmonique** chromatic/diatonic/harmonic scale; **é. des êtres** evolutionary ladder; **dans l'é. des êtres** on the evolutionary ladder; *Mktg* **é. d'importance** importance scale; *Rel* **é. de Jacob** Jacob's ladder; **é. de marée** tide gauge; **é. de meunier** open staircase; **é. mobile** (*des prix etc*) sliding scale; *Naut* **é. de revers** Jacob's ladder; **sur l'é. de Richter** on the Richter scale; **é. à saumons** fish ladder; *Mus* **é. des sons** scale; **à l'é. de temps humain** on a human time scale; *Naut* **é. de tirant d'eau** water *or* draught marks, *US* immersion scale; **é. des traitements** *ou* **des salaires** salary scale; **é. des valeurs** scale of values

échelon [eʃlɔ̃] *nm* **(a)** (*d'une échelle*) rung **(b)** (*degré d'une hiérarchie, organisation*) step, grade, *Fml, Hum* echelon; **monter par échelons** to rise by degrees *or* by successive stages; **les échelons de l'administration** the grades of the civil service; **le dernier/premier é.** the bottom/top grade *or* step; **il a gravi rapidement tous les échelons** he climbed the ladder rapidly; **j'en suis au dernier é.** I'm at *or* I've reached the top of my grade **(c)** (*niveau*) level; **à l'é. ministériel/directoriel** at ministerial/managerial level; **à l'é. régional/national** on a regional/national level; **à tous les échelons** at all levels, at every level; *Bourse* **é. de cotation** tick size

échelonnement [eʃ(ə)lɔnmɑ̃] *nm* **(a)** (*des paiements*) spreading out; (*des vacances*) staggering; **l'é. des travaux se fera sur plusieurs mois** the work will be spread out over several months; **le cours suit un é. bien précis** the course timetable is laid out very precisely **(b)** (*de poteaux, maisons*) row

échelonner [eʃ(ə)lɔne] **1** *vt* **(a)** (*objets*) to space out, to place at intervals; (*paiements*) to spread (out), to stagger; **congés échelonnés** staggered holidays **(b)** *Mil* (*troupes*) to dispose in echelon *or* in depth **2 s'échelonner** *vpr* (*d'objets*) to be spaced out; **les paiements s'échelonnent sur deux ans** the payments are spread (out) over two years; **les arbres s'échelonnent sur plusieurs kilomètres** the trees stretch for several kilometres; **la progression du cours s'échelonne sur dix niveaux** there are ten levels of difficulty in the course

écheniller [eʃ(ə)nije] *vt* (*arbres fruitiers etc*) to clear of caterpillars

écheveau, -eaux [eʃ(ə)vo] *nm* (*de fil etc*) hank, skein; *Fig* **é. de rues** maze of streets; **l'é. d'une intrigue** the intricacies *or* complexities of a plot; **un é. de mensonges/problèmes** a tissue of lies/a host of problems; **démêler l'é. d'une affaire compliquée** to untangle a complicated business

échevelé [eʃəvle] *adj* **(a)** (*personne*) dishevelled **(b)** *Fig* (*danse, fête*) wild; (*course*) mad

échevin [eʃ(ə)vɛ̃] *nm* **(a)** *Arch* municipal magistrate **(b)** *Belg* deputy mayor

échine [eʃin] *nf* **(a)** *Anat* spine, backbone; *Fig* **courber** *ou* **plier l'é.** to submit, to kowtow (**devant qn** to sb); *Fig* **avoir l'é. souple** *ou* **flexible** to bow and scrape **(b)** *Culin* loin (of pork); **une côte de porc dans l'é.** a pork loin chop

échiner (s') [seʃine] *vpr* (*se fatiguer*) to exhaust oneself, to tire oneself out (**à faire qch** doing sth); (*se donner du mal*) to go to great lengths, to make a great effort (**à faire qch** to do sth)

échiquier [eʃikje] *nm* **(a)** (*damier*) chessboard; **en é.** in a chequered *or Am* checkered pattern; *Fig Pol* **l'é. mondial/européen** the world/European stage *or* arena **(b)** *Br Pol* **l'É.** the Exchequer

écho [eko] *nm* **(a)** [ⓘA12,1,c] echo; **faire é.** to echo (back); **il y a de l'é.** there's an echo; *Fig* **se faire l'é. des opinions de qn** to echo *or* repeat sb's opinions; *Fig* **je n'ai eu aucun é. de leur discussion** I've heard nothing about their discussion; *Fig* **ma proposition/mon offre est restée sans é.** I got no feedback on my suggestion/offer, I never heard any more about my suggestion/offer; *Fig* **trouver un é.** to get a response **(b)** *Ordinat* echo; *Électron* **éliminateur** *ou* **suppresseur d'é.** echo suppressor; **échos parasites** clutter; **é. local** local echo **(c)** *TV* ghost(ing) **(d)** *Journ* **échos** news in brief; **échos mondains** gossip column

échographie [ekografi] *nf* (ultrasound) scan; **passer une é.** to have a scan

échoir [eʃwar] *vi* (*prp* **échéant**; *pp* **échu**; *pr ind* **il échoit, ils échoient**; *impf* **il échoyait**; *p hist* **il échut**; *fu* **il échoira**; *aux souvent* **être**) **(a) é. (en partage) à qn** to fall to sb; **le devoir m'échut de lui apprendre la nouvelle** it fell to me to break the news to him **(b)** *Fin* (*d'une dette etc*) to fall due; (*d'un investissement etc*) to mature; **abonnement échu** expired subscription; **billets échus** bills (over)due; **intérêts échus** outstanding interest, interest due; **intérêts à é.** accruing interest; **le terme échoit le 20 de ce mois** the date for payment is the 20th of this month; **le délai est échu** the deadline has expired

échoppe [eʃɔp] *nf Com* booth, stall; (*de cordonnier*) (cobbler's) small (work)shop

écho-sondeur, *pl* **écho-sondeurs** *nm Naut* echo sounder, sonic depth finder

échotier, -ière [ekɔtje, -jɛr] *n Journ* gossip columnist

échouage [eʃwaʒ], **échouement** [eʃumɑ̃] *nm* running aground; (*sur la plage*) beaching

échouer [eʃwe] **1** *vi* **(a)** *Naut* to run aground, to be stranded, to ground; (*d'une baleine*) to beach; **navire échoué** ship aground, stranded vessel *or* ship; **échoué à sec** high and dry; *Fig* **é. dans** (*pays hostile, bar mal famé etc*) to end *or* land up in **(b)** (*ne pas réussir*) (*d'un plan etc*) to fail, to come to nothing; (*d'une personne*) to fail; **é. à un examen** to fail an examination; **faire é.** (*projet*) to wreck; (*complot*) to foil **2** *vt Naut* (*bateau*) to beach, to run aground **3 s'échouer** *vpr Naut* to run aground, to be driven ashore; (*d'une baleine*) to beach

écimage [esimaʒ] *nm* (*d'un arbre*) topping, pollarding

écimer [esime] *vt* (*arbre*) to top, to pollard

éclaboussement [eklabusmɑ̃] *nm* splashing, spattering

éclabousser [eklabuse] *vt* (*avec un liquide*) to splash, to spatter (**de** with); *Fig* **é. qn** (*salir*) to damage sb's reputation, to sully sb's (good) name

éclaboussure [eklabusyr] *nf* (*de boue etc*) splash, spatter; *Fig* (*à la réputation*) blemish, blot, smirch; **le président n'a reçu aucune é. dans cette histoire** the president came out of the business with his reputation intact, none of the mud stuck to the president

éclair [eklɛr] **1** *nm* **(a)** *Météo* flash of lightning; **éclairs** lightning; **éclairs de chaleur** heat lightning; **il y a des éclairs** there's lightning; **rapide comme l'é.** quick as lightning *or* as a flash; *Fig* **en un é.** in a flash, quick as a flash; **la voiture passa comme un é.** the car flashed by; **la pensée traversa mon esprit comme un é.** the thought flashed through my mind **(b)** (*d'une arme etc, Fig de lucidité, génie*) flash; **lancer des éclairs** (*d'un diamant, des yeux etc*) to flash **(c)** *Culin* éclair **2** *adj inv* (*visite, attaque*) lightning; **guerre é.** blitzkrieg; **il a fait un passage é. au sein de la rédaction** he had a very brief spell on the editorial team

éclairage [eklɛraʒ] *nm* **(a)** (*fait d'éclairer*) lighting, illumination; *Cin, Th* lighting; (*par projecteurs*) floodlighting; **é. doux** soft lighting **(b)** *Fig* light; **sous cet é.** (seen) in this light; **montrer qch sous un autre é.** to show sth in a different light **(c)** *Mil, Naut* scouting

▶ **éclairage**: **é. d'ambiance** background light; **é. sur batterie** sungun; **é. clair-obscur** Rembrandt *or* chiaroscuro lighting; **é. de cyclorama** cyclorama light; **é. direct/indirect** direct/indirect lighting; **é. à l'électricité/au gaz** electric/gas lighting; *Aut* **é. intérieur automatique** courtesy light; **é. de plateau** stage lighting; **é. public** street lighting; **é. à la Rembrandt** Rembrandt lighting; *Aut* **é. de route** full-beam headlights; **é. de sécurité** emergency lighting; *Aut* **é. de ville** dipped headlights

éclairagiste [eklɛraʒist] *n Cin, Th* lighting technician *or* engineer

éclairant [eklɛrɑ̃] *adj* (*pouvoir etc*) lighting, illuminating; **fusée éclairante** flare; *Fig* **une explication éclairante** an enlightening *or* illuminating explanation

éclaircie [eklɛrsi] *nf* **(a)** (*dans les nuages etc*) break, opening, rift; *Météo* bright interval; *Fig* improvement **(b)** (*dans une forêt*) clearing, glade

éclaircir [eklɛrsir] **1** *vt* **(a)** (*rendre plus clair*) (*couleur, teinte, les cheveux etc*) to lighten; **é. le teint** to clear the complexion

(b) *Fig* (*élucider*) (*mystère*) to throw light on, to clear up; (*situation*) to clarify

(c) (*rendre moins épais*) (*forêt, sauce*) to thin; (*jeunes plants etc*) to thin out

2 s'éclaircir *vpr* **(a)** (*du temps*) to clear (up), to become bright(er); (*du ciel*) to clear, to brighten; (*du teint, de la voix*) to clear, to become clear(er); **s'é. la voix** to clear one's throat; *Fig* **l'avenir semble s'é.** the future seems to be getting brighter; **son visage s'éclaircit** his/her face brightened up *or* lit up; **mes idées se sont peu à peu éclaircies** my ideas gradually became clearer

(b) (*se dissiper*) (*d'un mystère, de doutes*) to be cleared up; (*de brouillard*) to clear (up)

(c) (*des cheveux*) to grow thin, to be thinning; **enfin les arbres s'éclaircirent** at length the trees thinned out

éclaircissage [eklɛrsisaʒ] *nm* **(a)** (*du verre*) polishing **(b)** (*de plantes*) thinning out

éclaircissant [eklɛrsisɑ̃] *adj* hair-lightening

éclaircissement [eklɛrsismɑ̃] *nm* (**a**) (*élucidation*) clarification, *Fml* elucidation; (*explication*) explanation; **l'é. de ce mystère a pris des mois** it was months before the mystery was cleared up; **demander des éclaircissements sur qch** to ask for an explanation of sth; **s'ils me demandent des éclaircissements sur mon rapport** if they ask me for clarification on my report (**b**) (*de cheveux*) lightening; **je me suis fait faire un é.** I had my hair lightened

éclairé [eklere] *adj* lit; *Fig* (*personne, esprit, public*) enlightened

éclairement [eklɛrmɑ̃] *nm* illumination, lighting

éclairer [eklere] **1** *vt* (**a**) (*pièce, vitrine etc*) to light, to illuminate; (*personne*) to light the way for; **é. un angle sombre** to light up a dark corner; **cafés éclairés au néon** cafés with neon lights, neon-lit cafés; **une pièce bien/mal éclairée** a well-lit/badly lit room; *Fig* **un sourire éclairait son visage** a smile lit up his/her face

(**b**) (*expliquer*) (*sujet*) to shed *or* throw light on; **é. qch d'un jour nouveau** to shed *or* throw new light on sth

(**c**) (*informer*) to enlighten; **éclairez-moi sur ce sujet** tell me what it's all about; *F* **si tu pouvais é. ma lanterne sur cette affaire** if you could put me in the picture about this matter

(**d**) *Mil* **é. le terrain** *ou* **la marche** to reconnoitre the ground, to scout

2 *vi* (*donner de la lumière*) **cette lampe éclaire mal** this lamp doesn't give a very good light

3 s'éclairer *vpr* (**a**) (*pour avoir de la lumière*) **il s'éclaire toujours au pétrole/gaz** he still has *or* uses oil lamps/gaslight; **s'é. à la bougie/avec une lampe de poche** (*pour voir le chemin*) to light one's way with a candle/torch, to use a candle/torch to see by

(**b**) (*devenir lumineux*) (*d'un bâtiment etc*) to light up; **son visage s'est éclairé** his/her face lit up *or* brightened

(**c**) *Fig* (*devenir compréhensible*) (*d'une situation etc*) to become clear(er); **tout s'éclaire**! things are *or* everything is becoming clear(er)!

éclaireur, -euse [eklɛrœr, -øz] **1** *nm* (**a**) *Mil* scout; *Naut* scouting vessel, scout; *Av* **avion é.** reconnaissance aircraft; *Mil, Fig* **partir en é.** to go off for a scout around; *Fig* **il est parti en é. pour voir s'il y avait de la place au restaurant** he's gone to check the seat situation in the restaurant; **il part un mois avant, en é.** he's leaving a month in advance to check things out (**b**) *Aut* **é. de coffre** boot *or Am* trunk light **2** *n* (boy) scout, *f* (girl) guide; **chef é.** scoutmaster, *f* guide captain

éclampsie [eklɑ̃psi] *nf Méd* eclampsia

éclat [ekla] *nm* (**a**) (*fragment*) (*de bois*) splinter; (*de pierre*) chip; (*de mica*) flake; **é. d'obus** piece of shrapnel; **éclats d'obus** shrapnel; **voler en éclats** to fly *or* burst into pieces; **un é. de verre** a fragment *or* splinter of glass; **éclats de verre** (*bris*) broken glass; (*projeté*) flying glass

(**b**) (*son*) (*de rire*) burst; **é. de colère** outburst of anger; **de grands éclats de voix** voices raised in anger; **partir d'un grand é. de rire** to burst out laughing; **rire aux éclats** to roar with laughter

(**c**) *Fig* (*scandale*) scandal, stir, fuss; **elle fait des éclats à chaque fois qu'elle sort** she causes commotion wherever she goes; **j'espère qu'il n'y aura pas d'é. pendant la réunion** I hope the meeting passes off quietly, I hope nobody makes a fuss at the meeting; **il adore provoquer des éclats dans les soirées mondaines** he loves creating a commotion at parties; **sans é.** quietly, without any fuss

(**d**) (*du soleil*) glare; (*d'un diamant*) glitter, lustre; (*du regard*) sparkle; (*de couleurs*) brilliance, vividness; **l'é. de ses yeux** the sparkle in his/her eyes; **l'é. de la jeunesse** the bloom *or* freshness of youth; **le soleil brille de son plus vif é.** the sun is (shining) at its brightest *or* most brilliant

(**e**) (*de style etc*) brilliance; (*d'une cérémonie, période, de la gloire etc*) splendour, *US* splendor; **action** *ou* **coup d'é.** brilliant feat; **il aime faire les choses avec é.** he likes to do things with style

éclatant [eklatɑ̃] *adj* (**a**) (*son, rire*) loud, ringing (**b**) (*lumière, couleur, succès*) dazzling, brilliant; (*bijoux*) sparkling, glittering; **teint é.** glowing *or* blooming complexion; **avoir des dons éclatants** to be brilliantly gifted; **être dans une forme éclatante** to be on brilliant *or* dazzling form; **éclatant de santé** glowing *or* blooming with health

éclaté [eklate] **1** *adj* (*groupe*) scattered, dispersed; (*programme, mesures*) fragmented, fragmentary; **paysage politique é.** fragmented political landscape; **avoir une vision éclatée des choses** to have a fragmented view of things **2** *nm* exploded view

éclatement [eklatmɑ̃] *nm* (*d'un obus*) bursting, explosion; (*d'une arme*) explosion; (*d'un pneu*) bursting, blow-out; (*d'un verre*) shattering; (*d'un convoi, un groupe etc*) dispersal; *Pol* **é. d'un parti** splitting (up) *or* fragmentation of a party; *Aut* **é. de l'étincelle** spark

éclater [eklate] **1** *vi* (**a**) (*d'un obus*) to burst, to explode; (*d'une arme*) to explode; (*d'une mine*) to blow up; (*d'un pneu, un ballon*) to burst; (*d'un verre*) to shatter; **faire é. qch** to burst/explode/shatter sth; **faire é. un pétard** to set off a firework; *Fig* **le groupe a fini par é.** the group finally split up

(**b**) (*de la guerre, un incendie, une épidémie, un conflit*) to break out; (*d'un orage, un scandale*) to break; (*de la colère*) to burst out; **quand la guerre éclata** at the outbreak of the war, when war broke out; **le tonnerre éclata** there was a clap of thunder; **l'hymne national éclata dans la salle** the people in the room broke into the national anthem

(**c**) *Fig* (*de personne*) **é. de rire** to burst out laughing; **é. en applaudissements** to burst into applause; **é. en sanglots** to burst into tears; **é. de colère** to fly into a rage

(**d**) (*être manifeste*) to be obvious *or* evident, to stand out; **les préjugés de l'auteur éclatent à chaque page** the author's prejudices stand out on every page; **l'indignation éclatait dans ses yeux** his eyes were blazing with indignation

2 s'éclater *vpr F* to have a wild *or* a really good time; **s'é. comme une bête** to freak out

3 *vt F* (*pneu*) to burst; *Fig F* **je vais l'é., je vais lui é. la tête** *ou* **la gueule** I'll smash his head in

éclateur [eklatœr] *nm Aut* spark gap

éclectique [eklɛktik] *adj, n* eclectic

éclectisme [eklɛktism] *nm* eclecticism

éclipse [eklips] *nf* (*de soleil, lune*) eclipse; *Fig* **é. totale de la raison/mémoire** total loss of reason/memory; *Fig* **après une longue é.** after a long absence

éclipser [eklipse] **1** *vt* (**a**) *Astron* (*soleil, lune*) to eclipse (**b**) *Fig* (*surpasser*) (*personne*) to eclipse, to outshine, to overshadow, *F* to put in the shade; (*événement, exploit etc*) to eclipse, to overshadow **2 s'éclipser** *vpr* (**a**) *F* (*s'esquiver*) to make off, to make oneself scarce (**b**) *Astron* to be eclipsed; (*être voilé*) to be obscured

écliptique [ekliptik] *adj, nm Astron* ecliptic

éclisse [eklis] *nf* (**a**) (*plaque de bois*) (wooden) wedge (**b**) (*éclat*) piece of split wood (**c**) *Méd* splint (**d**) *Rail* fishplate

éclisser [eklise] *vt Méd* (*membre*) to put in splints, to splint

éclopé, -ée [eklɔpe] **1** *adj* lame, limping **2** *nm Mil* temporarily disabled soldier **3** *n Hum* person with a limp

éclore [eklɔr] *vi* (*pp* **éclos**; *pr ind* **il éclôt, ils éclosent**; *impf* **il éclosait**; *no p hist*; *fu* **il éclora**; *aux souvent* **être**, *parfois* **avoir**) (**a**) (*d'œufs, de poussins*) to hatch (out), to be hatched; **faire é. un œuf** to hatch (out) an egg (**b**) (*de fleurs, bourgeons*) to open; *Fig* (*d'un talent*) to be born, to appear; **roses fraîches écloses** roses that have just opened; *Litt* **le jour est près d'é.** dawn is near; *Fig* **génie près d'é.** budding genius; *Fig* **faire é. un talent** to nurture *or* develop a talent

éclosion [eklozjɔ̃] *nf* (**a**) (*d'œufs, de poussins*) hatching (**b**) (*de fleurs*) opening, blooming; *Fig* (*d'un talent*) birth

écluse [eklyz] *nf* (**a**) (canal) lock; **droit d'é.** lock fee, lockage; **(porte d')é.** lock gate, sluice (gate); **é. de moulin** mill dam; *F Fig* **lâcher** *ou* **ouvrir les écluses** to turn on the waterworks (**b**) (*d'un dock*) tide gate

éclusée [eklyze] *nf HydE* lock water

écluser [eklyze] **1** *vt* (**a**) (*canal*) to equip with locks (**b**) (*péniche*) to pass through a lock (**c**) *F* (*boire*) to knock back **2** *vi F* **qu'est-ce qu'elle écluse!** she doesn't half knock it back!

éclusier, -ière [eklyzje, -jɛr] *n* lock keeper

éco- [ekɔ, eko] *préf* eco-

écœurant [ekœrɑ̃] **1** *adj* (**a**) (*dégoûtant*) (*nourriture*) nauseating, sickening; (*personne*) disgusting, sickening; **un peu é. si on en mange trop** a bit sickly if you eat too much of it; **il a une manière de manger vraiment écœurante** it's quite sickening *or* disgusting *or F* sick-making watching him eat, it really turns the stomach watching him eat

(**b**) (*décourageant*) disheartening, discouraging, demoralizing; **c'est é., elle a encore une augmentation!** it's sickening, she's got another rise!; **tu as une chance écœurante!** what disgusting luck!; **c'est é. ce que tu peux avoir de la chance** you're so lucky it makes me sick, *Can* **Steven est é. dans le rôle de Jake** Steven is unreal in the role of Jake

2 *nm Can* disgusting *or* loathsome man

écœuranterie [ekœrɑ̃tri] *nf Can F* (**a**) (*saleté*) filth (**b**) (*coup bas*) dirty trick; **elle m'a fait une é.** she played a dirty trick on me

écœurement [ekœrmɑ̃] *nm* (**a**) (*physique*) nausea; (*dégoût*) disgust, loathing; **manger du chocolat jusqu'à é.** to eat chocolate until you feel sick *or* to the point of nausea; *Fig* **j'ai jardiné jusqu'à é.** I've done so much gardening I'm sick (and tired) of it *or* I'm fed up; **sa cruauté a provoqué l'é. de tout**

le monde everyone was disgusted *or* nauseated by his cruelty, his cruelty turned everyone's stomach; **on ne peut le regarder agir sans é.** it's impossible to watch him at work without feeling disgust

(**b**) (*découragement*) discouragement, dejection; **maintenant c'est l'é.** now I've/he's/*etc* become discouraged *or* lost heart; **ça a été l'é. dans toute la classe** the entire class lost heart

écœurer [ekœre] *vt* (**a**) (*physiquement*) **e. qn** to nauseate sb, to make sb feel sick *or Am* nauseous; (*dégoûter*) to disgust sb, to make sb feel sick; (*révolter*) to disgust sb (**b**) (*décourager*) to dishearten, to discourage; **l'attitude de son patron l'écœure tellement que ...** he finds his boss's attitude so disheartening *or* discouraging that ...; *F* **elle est écœurée de son job** she is sick of *or* fed up with her job; **ça m'écœure que ...** it sickens me *or* makes me sick that ... (**c**) *Can F* (*donner envie*) **e. qn** to make sb green with envy

écoinçon [ekwɛ̃sɔ̃] *nm Constr* corner piece *or* stone

école [ekɔl] *nf* [①**A6**,d,i] (**a**) (*établissement*) school; **maîtresse/maître d'é.** (primary) school teacher; **reprendre l'é.** to go back to school; **les grandes écoles** = colleges of university level specializing in professional training

(**b**) (*enseignement*) school; **aller à l'é. jusqu'à 16 ans** to go to school until the age of 16; **faire l'é.** to teach; **faire l'é. buissonnière** to play truant *or Am F* hooky; **reprendre l'é.** to return to formal education, *Am* to go back to school; *F* **je n'ai pas é. aujourd'hui** I don't have any classes today; *Fig Hum* **tu peux retourner à l'é.** what did they teach you at school?; *Fig* **vous êtes à bonne é.** you're in good hands; *Fig* **à l'é. de la vie/misère** in the school of life/poverty

(**c**) (*mouvement*) (*de pensée, d'art, de littérature*) school; **faire é.** (*d'une théorie, d'un penseur etc*) to win a following

(**d**) *Mil* (*exercice*) drill, training; **é. du soldat** drill; **é. de tir** rifle drill, knotting and splicing; *Av* **appareil d'é.** training aircraft

▶ **école**: **é. de l'air** flying school; **É. des Arts et Métiers** = engineering college (*of university level*); **é. des Beaux-Arts** art school; **é. de commerce** business school; **é. de conduite** driving school; **é. confessionnelle** ≈ independent *or* private school; **é. de danse** dance *or* dancing school; **é. de dessin** art school; **é. d'équitation** riding school; **é. hôtelière** hotel school; **é. de journalisme** school of journalism; **é. libre** ≈ independent *or* private school; **é. maternelle** nursery school, kindergarten; **é. militaire** military academy; **é. de musique** music school; **É. nationale d'administration** = university level college that prepares students for senior posts in law and economics; **É. nationale supérieure d'ingénieurs** = university level college for the continuing education of qualified engineers; **é. normale** ≈ teacher training college; **É. normale supérieure** = university level college that prepares students for senior posts in teaching and other professions; **é. de police** police college *or US* academy; **é. primaire** primary school; **é. privée** ≈ independent *or* private school; **é. publique** state *or US* public school; **é. de secrétariat** secretarial college

écolier, -ière [ekɔlje, -jɛr] *n* (*du primaire*) (primary) schoolboy, *f* (primary) schoolgirl; **écoliers** schoolchildren; *Fig* **le chemin des écoliers** the longest way round; **papier é.** exercise paper

écolo [ekɔlo] *adj, n* (*abrév* **écologiste**) *F* green

écologie [ekɔlɔʒi] *nf* ecology

écologique [ekɔlɔʒik] *adj* ecological, environmental

écologisme [ekɔlɔʒism] *nm* concern for the environment, environmental awareness

écologiste [ekɔlɔʒist] *n* ecologist

écomusée [ekomyze] *nm* living museum (*showing man in his natural and social environment*)

éconduire [ekɔ̃dɥir] *vt* (*conj like* **conduire**) (**a**) (*congédier*) **é. qn** to get rid of sb, to show sb the door; **j'ai eu beaucoup de mal à les é.** I had a lot of trouble getting rid of them (**b**) (*refuser*) (*prétendant*) to reject, to turn down; (*suppliant, requérant*) (*en personne*) to turn away; (*par lettre*) to turn down

éconocroques [ekɔnɔkrɔk] *nfpl Arg* savings

économat [ekɔnɔma] *nm* (**a**) (*fonction*) stewardship, bursarship (**b**) (*bureau*) steward's *or* bursar's office (**c**) (*magasin*) staff (discount) store; *Com* (*coopérative*) multiple *or* chain store

économe [ekɔnɔm] **1** *n* (*d'un collège, d'une institution etc*) steward, bursar **2** *adj* economical, thrifty; **é. de paroles/de son temps/***etc* sparing with words/of one's time/*etc* **3** *nm* (**couteau**) **é.** potato peeler

économètre [ekɔnɔmɛtr] *n* econometrician, econometrist

économétrie [ekɔnɔmetri] *nf* econometrics

économétrique [ekɔnɔmetrik] *adj* econometric

économie [ekɔnɔmi] *nf* (**a**) (*système*) economy; **é. de troc** barter economy

(**b**) (*gain*) economy, saving; (*vertu*) economy, thrift; **avoir le sens de l'é.** to be thrifty, to be good with money; **elle n'a aucun sens de l'é.** she's no good at managing money, she's got no idea about money; **é. de temps** time saving; **faire une é. de temps/d'énergie/de vingt pour cent** to save time/energy/twenty per cent; **ça représentera une énorme é. de temps** it will be an enormous saving of time *or* an enormous time saver, it will save an enormous amount of time; **je vais faire l'é. d'un coup de fil** I'll save myself a phone call; **je pense qu'on ne pourra pas faire l'é. d'une réunion** I don't think we can do without a meeting, I think a meeting is essential; **ce mariage a vraiment été fait à l'é.** the wedding was really done on the cheap

(**c**) **économies** savings; **j'ai quelques économies** I have a few *or* some savings; **faire des économies** to save money; **je n'arrive pas à faire d'économies** I can't manage to save; **réaliser d'importantes économies** to save a lot of money, to make major savings; **faire des économies de chauffage** to save money *or* economize on heating; **prendre sur ses économies** to break into *or* draw on one's savings; **il n'y a pas de petites économies** every little helps

(**d**) (*organisation*) (*d'une œuvre littéraire, loi etc*) arrangement, structure

▶ **économie**: **é. dirigée** planned economy; **économies d'échelle** economies of scale; **é. d'entreprise** business management *or* studies; **é. libérale** open market economy; **é. de marché** market economy; **é. politique** political economy, economics; *F* **économies de bouts de chandelles** cheeseparing (economy)

économique [ekɔnɔmik] *adj* (**a**) (*problème, doctrine etc*) economic; **science économique** economics (**b**) (*bon marché, avantageux*) economical; **vitesse é.** (*d'une voiture etc*) economical speed; **cycle é.** (*d'un lave-vaisselle etc*) economy cycle; *Av* **classe é.** economy class; **bouteille/voiture é.** economy (size) bottle/economy car

économiquement [ekɔnɔmikmɑ̃] *adv* (*à peu de frais*), *Écon* economically; **les é. faibles** people on low incomes

économiser [ekɔnɔmize] **1** *vt* (*argent*) to economize, to save; (*temps, énergie*) to save; (*électricité etc*) to economize on, to save on; (*ressources etc*) to conserve, to husband; **économisez 100 F** 100 francs off, save 100 francs; **é. ses paroles** to be sparing of one's words; **é. ses forces** to conserve one's strength; **é. sa salive** to save one's breath **2** *vi* to economize, to save (**sur** on)

économiseur [ekɔnɔmizœr] *nm Aut* fuel-saving device, economizer; *Ordinat* **é. d'écran** screen saver

économiste [ekɔnɔmist] *n* economist

écope [ekɔp] *nf Naut* bailer, scoop

écoper [ekɔpe] **1** *vt* (**a**) (*barque*) to bail (out); **é. l'eau d'une embarcation** to bail out a boat *or* the water out of a boat (**b**) *F* (*recevoir comme punition*) **c'est encore moi qui ai écopé la punition** it was me that caught it again; **é. (de) cinq ans de prison** to cop *or* get five years' prison **2** *vi* to get the blame, to catch *or* cop it; **j'en ai marre d'é. pour les autres** I'm sick of getting the blame for what other people do

écorçage [ekɔrsaʒ] *nm* (*d'arbres*) barking; (*d'oranges*) peeling; (*de riz*) husking

écorce [ekɔrs] *nf* (**a**) (*d'un arbre*) bark; (*d'une orange*) rind, peel; (*de riz*) husk; (*de châtaigne*) skin (**b**) *Géog* **l'é. terrestre** the earth's crust (**c**) *Bot* cortex (**d**) *Fig* (*apparence*) outward appearance; **sous une é. de méchant, il cache un cœur d'ange** under that nasty exterior beats a heart of gold

écorcer [ekɔrse] *vt* (**j'écorçai(s); n. écorçons**) (*arbre*) to bark; (*orange*) to peel; (*riz*) to husk

écorché, -ée [ekɔrʃe] **1** *nm* (**a**) *Beaux-Arts* anatomical model, écorché (**b**) *Tech* sectional *or* cutaway view **2** *n Fig* **é. vif** tortured soul

écorchement [ekɔrʃəmɑ̃] *nm* (*d'un animal*), skinning

écorcher [ekɔrʃe] **1** *vt* (**a**) (*animal*) to skin; (*criminel*) to flay; *Fig F* **é. les clients** to fleece the customers (**b**) (*érafler*) (*jambe, peau etc*) to graze, to scrape; (*la gorge*) (*de l'alcool*) to burn, to rasp; (*d'un plat pimenté*) to burn; (*d'un bonbon*) to scratch; *Fig F* **é. une langue/un nom/***etc* to murder a language/name/*etc*; **son qui écorche l'oreille** sound that grates on the ear **2 s'écorcher** *vpr* to graze oneself; **s'é. le genou** to graze *or* scrape one's knee; **s'é. le tibia** to graze *or* bark one's shin

écorcheur, -euse [ekɔrʃœr, -øz] *n* (**a**) skinner (**b**) *Fig F* (*voleur*) extortionist; **ce sont de véritables écorcheurs** they rob you blind

écorchure [ekɔrʃyr] *nf* graze, scratch

écorner [ekɔrne] *vt* (**a**) (*meuble, statue etc*) to chip *or* damage the corner(s) of; **é. (les pages d')un livre** to dog-ear (the pages of) a book (**b**) *Fig* **é. son capital/ses économies** to break into one's capital/savings

écornifler [ekɔrnifle] *vt F Vieilli* (*repas, argent*) to cadge, to scrounge (**à qn** off sb)

écornifleur, -euse [ekɔrniflœr, -øz] *n F Vieilli* sponger, cadger, scrounger

écossais, -aise [ekɔsɛ, -ɛz] [①A21,d,ii] **1** *adj* (*paysage etc*) Scottish; (*whisky*) Scotch; (*personne*) Scottish, Scots; **tissu é.** tartan, plaid **2** *n* **É.** Scot, Scotsman, *f* Scotswoman **3** *nm* **(a)** (*tissu*) tartan, plaid **(b)** *Ling* Scots; (*langue celtique*) (Scots) Gaelic

Écosse [ekɔs] *nf* Scotland

écosser [ekɔse] *vt* (*pois*) to shell, to pod; (*haricots*) to shell

écosystème [ekosistɛm] *nm Biol* ecosystem

écot [eko] *nm* **payer son é.** to pay one's share

écotourisme [ekoturism] *nm* ecotourism

écoulement [ekulmɑ̃] *nm* **(a)** (*d'un liquide*) flow, discharge; *Constr* (*du toit etc*) run-off; **fossé d'é.** drain; **(tube d')é.** (*d'une baignoire*) waste pipe; **l'é. se fait mal** it's not flowing very well; **la boue qui est venue se mélanger à l'eau ne facilite pas l'é.** the water's not flowing very well because of the mud mixed in with it; *Av* **é. (des filets) d'air** air flow

(b) *Méd* discharge

(c) (*de la circulation*) flow; **l'é. de la foule dans le métro** the streams of people moving through the metro

(d) *Com* (*de marchandises*) sale; **marchandises d'é. facile** goods that sell easily *or* fast, goods with a ready sale; **l'é. de ces vieux parapluies sera plus facile** it will be easier to sell *or* dispose of these old umbrellas

(e) (*du temps*) passage, passing; **vous n'avez pas le droit de répondre après é. du temps** you must answer before the time is up

écouler [ekule] **1** *vt* (*marchandises*) to sell (off), to dispose of, to move; **é. des faux billets** to issue *or Jur* utter forged notes; *Com* **é. à perte** to sell at a loss **2 s'écouler** *vpr* **(a)** (*d'un liquide*) to flow out, to run out **(de** of); (*de la circulation*) to flow; **le public s'écoulait sagement du théâtre** the audience was leaving the theatre quietly; **faire s'é. l'eau** to run off *or* drain off the water; **son argent s'écoule à une vitesse!** his money is disappearing hand over fist! **(b)** (*de marchandises*) to sell, to move **(c)** (*du temps*) to pass, to elapse

écourter [ekurte] *vt* (*robe, texte, citation etc*) to shorten; (*visite, discours*) to curtail, to cut short; (*barbe, moustache*) to trim; (*queue de chien*) to dock

écoute[1] [ekut] *nf* **(a)** *Vieilli* **être** *ou* **se tenir aux écoutes** to listen, to eavesdrop; *Fig* to keep one's ears open; **être aux écoutes derrière la porte** to be listening at the door; *Mil* **poste d'é.** listening post

(b) *Tél, Rad* **é. de contrôle** monitoring; **se mettre** *ou* **se porter à l'é., prendre l'é.** to listen in, to tune in; *Mil, Rad* **être à l'é.** to be listening **(de** to); *Rad* **ne quittez pas l'é.!, restez à l'é.!** stay tuned (in)!, keep listening!; **heure de grande é.** *Rad* peak listening time; *TV* peak viewing time; **indice d'é.** ratings; **cette émission bénéficie d'une grande é.** the programme has a large audience *or* stands high in the ratings; **dès la première é. ...** (*d'un disque etc*) the first time you hear it ...; *Tél* **table d'é.** tapping equipment; **écoutes téléphoniques** telephone tapping; **elle est sur (table d')é.** her phone is being tapped

(c) être toujours à l'é. des autres to be always willing to lend a sympathetic ear to others; **avoir une bonne é.** *ou* **un bon pouvoir d'é.** to be a good listener; **tout le monde n'est pas capable d'é.** not everyone is a good listener *or* can listen

(d) (*d'un sanglier*) **écoutes** ears

écoute[2] *nf Naut* (*d'une voile*) sheet; **nœud d'é.** sheet bend; **point d'é.** clew

écouter [ekute] **1** *vt* **(a)** to listen to; *Rad* **vous écoutez France Inter** you are listening *or* tuned to France Inter; **savoir é.** to be a good listener; **je vais te faire é. un morceau** I'll play you some music; **é. qn jusqu'au bout** to hear sb out; **é. aux portes** to listen at doors, to eavesdrop; **écoutez!** listen!, look (here)!

(b) (*suivre*) (*qn, avis*) to listen to, to pay attention to; **ne les écoutez pas!** don't listen to them, don't pay them any attention!; **é. sa conscience** to listen to *or* be guided by one's conscience; **savoir se faire é.** to know how to command respect; **il faudrait quand même que tu te fasses é. par tes enfants/élèves** even so, your children/pupils ought to listen to you *or* obey *or* be obedient; **il est très écouté au sein du gouvernement** the government listens closely to him *or* to what he has to say, he has the ear of the government

2 s'écouter *vpr* **il s'écoute trop** he coddles himself; **elle a tendance à s'é. parler** she likes the sound of her own voice; **si je m'écoutais** if I did what I wanted

écouteur, -euse [ekutœr, -øz] *nm Tél* receiver; *Rad* **écouteurs** earphones, headphones; *TV, Rad* **é. auriculaire** earpiece

écoutille [ekutij] *nf Naut* hatchway

écouvillon [ekuvijɔ̃] *nm* (*pour bouteille, biberon*) (bottle) brush; *Méd* swab

écouvillonner [ekuvijɔne] *vt* (*bouteille*) to clean out; *Méd* (*cavité*) to swab

écrabouillage [ekrabujaʒ] *nm,* **écrabouillement** [ekrabujmɑ̃] *nm F* squashing, crushing

écrabouiller [ekrabuje] *vt F* to squash, to crush; **se faire é. par une voiture** to get flattened by a car

écran [ekrɑ̃] *nm* **(a)** (*pour protéger*) screen; **elle fit un é. de sa main** she shielded *or* shaded her eyes with her hand; **on ne peut pas voir le lac car les arbres font é.** you can't see the lake because it's screened by the trees; **elle se cachait derrière l'é. de ses cheveux** she was using her hair as a screen to hide behind; **il m'a fait é. de son corps pour me protéger** he shielded me with his body

(b) *TV* screen; *Cin, Phot* **é. (de projection)** screen; **porter une pièce à l'é.** to adapt a play for the screen; **la technique de l'é.** film technique; **Bourvil crève l'é. dans ce film** Bourvil gives a riveting performance in this film; **vedette de l'é.** film star; **prochainement sur vos écrans** coming to a cinema near you; **le petit é.** the small screen, television; **le grand é.** the big screen, cinema; **téléviseur à é. plat** flat-screen television

(c) *Ordinat* screen, display; **à l'é.** on screen

▶ **écran**: *Ordinat* **é. d'accueil** logo screen; *TV, Rad* **é. acoustique** acoustic screen; *Ordinat* **é. à affichage accéléré** accelerated display screen; *Ordinat* **é. d'aide** help screen; **é. antibruit** noise barrier; **é. antireflets** antiglare screen; **é. basse radiation** low radiation screen; **é. cathodique** cathode ray tube screen; **é. de cheminée** fire screen; **é. de cinéma** cinema *or* movie screen, motion picture screen; *TV* **é. de contrôle** control monitor; *TV* **é. de contrôle de l'image** picture monitor (screen); *TV* **é. de contrôle studio** studio monitor; **é. couleur** colour screen *or* display; *Ordinat* **é. à cristaux liquides** liquid crystal screen; *Ordinat* **é. de dialogue** dialog(ue) screen; *Ordinat* **é. à fenêtres** split screen; **é. de fumée** smoke screen; **é. haute résolution** high resolution screen; **é. à matrice active/passive** active/passive matrix screen; **é. monochrome** monochrome screen; *TV* **é.-mosaïque,** *pl* **écrans-mosaïques** multi-screen, multi-split screen; *Cin* **é. panoramique** wide screen; *Ordinat* **é. (à) plasma** (gas) plasma screen; *Ordinat* **é. pleine page** A4 screen; *Cin* **é. de projection** projection screen; *Ordinat* **é. protecteur** *ou* **de protection** shield; *Ordinat* **é. rétro-éclairé** back-lit screen; *Ordinat* **é. de saisie** input screen; **é. solaire** sun block; *Cin* **é. de sûreté** (*de projecteur*) cut-off; *Ordinat* **é. tactile** touch *or* touch-sensitive screen; *TV* **é. de télévision** TV screen; *TV* **é.-témoin,** *pl* **écrans-témoins** monitor; **é. total** sun block; *Ordinat* **é. de travail** working *or* work screen; *TV* **é. de vision** review screen; *TV* **é. de visualisation** display screen

écrasant [ekrazɑ̃] *adj* (*poids, défaite, impôts, responsabilité etc*) crushing; (*preuve, majorité, victoire*) overwhelming; (*travail*) back-breaking; (*chaleur*) overpowering

écrasé [ekraze] *adj* **nez é.** flat nose

écrasement [ekrazmɑ̃] *nm* (*d'un fruit*) crushing; (*accidentellement*) squashing; (*d'une personne, un animal*) (*par une voiture*) running over; *Fig* (*d'un peuple*) oppression; (*d'une armée, d'une équipe*) crushing defeat; *Ordinat* (*de données, d'un fichier*) zapping; *Av* **é. (au sol)** crash

écraser [ekraze] **1** *vt* **(a)** (*fruit*) to crush; (*accidentellement*) to squash; (*boîte, membre, ail*) to crush; (*carton*) to flatten; (*cafard*) to squash; (*mouche*) to swat; (*cigarette*) to stub out; (*piéton, chien etc*) to run over *or* down; **é. des œufs durs pour un plat** to mash up hard boiled eggs for a dish; **il s'est fait é. par une voiture** he was *or* got run down *or* over by a car; *F* **é. l'accélérateur** *ou* **le champignon** to step on the gas; **é. le frein** to jam on the brakes; *Fig F* **je compte sur toi pour é. le coup** I'm relying on you to keep quiet *or* not to say anything

(b) *Fig* (*assommer*) **é. d'impôts** to overburden with taxes; **écrasé d'impôts** crushed by taxation, staggering under the burden of taxation; **écrasé de travail** overwhelmed with *or F* snowed under with work; *F* **é. le marché** to glut *or* flood the market; **être écrasé de chaleur** to be dropping with the heat; **il écrase les gens de sa richesse** he uses his wealth to put other people down

(c) (*vaincre*) (*adversaire, troupes etc*) to crush; **il écrase tout le monde en latin** he is much better than everyone else at Latin

(d) *Ordinat* (*fichier*) to zap

(e) *Arg* **en é.** to sleep like a log

2 *vi Arg* **écrase!** shut up!, drop dead!, put a sock in it!

3 s'écraser *vpr* **s'é. au sol** (*d'une personne*) to crash to the ground; (*d'un avion*) to crash; **la neige s'écrasait sous nos**

pieds the snow crunched under our feet; *Fig* **on s'écrase devant le cinéma** there's a tremendous crush outside the cinema; *Fig F* **à sa place, je m'écraserais** if I were him I'd keep my head down *or* keep a low profile, *Arg* **écrase-toi!** shut it!, button it!

écraseur, -euse [ekrazœr, -øz] *n F* road hog

écrémage [ekremaʒ] *nm* **(a)** *(du lait)* creaming, skimming **(b)** *Fig* **ce lycée n'aurait pas de si bons résultats sans un sévère é. des élèves** the school wouldn't get such good results if it didn't choose only the very best pupils *or* if it didn't pick and choose its pupils; **le recrutement de leurs élèves passe par un sacré é.** they only take the crème de la crème; *Mktg* **é. du marché** market skimming

écrémer [ekreme] *vt* **(j'écrème; j'écrémerai)** *(lait)* to cream, to skim; *Mktg (marché)* to skim; *Fig* to take the best *or* the cream of, to cream off; **lait écrémé** skim(med) milk

écrémeuse [ekremøz] *nf* (cream) separator, creamer

écrêter [ekrete] *vt* **(a)** *(coq)* to remove the comb of **(b)** *Fig (revenus, prix etc)* to even out

écrevisse [ekrəvis] *nf (crustacé)* (fresh-water) crayfish; *F* **rouge comme une é.** as red as a lobster; *F* **marcher comme une é.** to walk backwards

écrier (s') [sekrije] *vpr* to cry (out), to exclaim

écrin [ekrɛ̃] *nm* (jewel) case

écrire [ekrir] *(prp* **écrivant**; *pp* **écrit**; *pr ind* **j'écris, n. écrivons, ils écrivent**; *p hist* **j'écrivis**; *fu* **j'écrirai) 1** *vt (letter, livre, chanson, ses mémoires etc)* to write; *(noter)* to write down; **é. qch à** *ou* **avec de l'encre** to write sth in ink; **machine à é.** typewriter; **écrit à la main** longhand, handwritten; **é. une lettre à la machine** to type a letter; **é. un mot à la hâte** to scribble a note; **é. un mot à qn** to drop sb a line; **é. à qn** to write to sb; **je lui ai écrit de venir** I've written asking him to come; *Ordinat* **é. qch sur un disque** to write sth to disk; **il est écrit que je ne peux pas y aller** I'm fated not to get there; **c'est écrit** it is bound to happen; **c'est écrit sur sa figure** you can tell from his/her face, it's written all over his/her face; **é. qch noir sur blanc** *ou* **en toutes lettres** to put sth in black and white; **tant que je ne verrai pas mon nom écrit noir sur blanc** until I see my name in black and white

2 *vi* to write; **il écrit bien** his (hand)writing is good, he has good handwriting; *(d'un écrivain)* he's a good writer, he writes well; **ce stylo écrit très bien** this pen writes very well; **é. dans les journaux** to write for the papers; **é. à l'encre** to use ink

3 s'écrire *vpr* **(a)** *(s'orthographier)* to be spelled; **comment ça s'écrit?** how do you spell it?

(b) *(correspondre)* **ils s'écrivent** they write to each other

écrit [ekri] *nm* **(a) consigner** *ou* **coucher qch par é.** to put *or* set sth down in writing; **convention par é.** written agreement **(b)** *(texte)* (written) document; **faire/signer un é.** to draw up/to sign a document; **les écrits de Bossuet** the writings *or* works of Bossuet; *Journ* **é. diffamatoire** libel **(c)** *Scol* **échouer à l'é.** to fail in the written examination

écriteau, -eaux [ekrito] *nm* notice

écritoire [ekritwar] *nf (coffret)* writing case

écriture [ekrityr] *nf* **(a)** *(système, caractères)* writing, script; *Ordinat* write

(b) *(main)* (hand)writing; **elle a une belle é.** her handwriting is good, she has good handwriting; **elle a une vilaine é.** *ou* **une é. de chat** her handwriting is dreadful

(c) *Compta* entry, item

(d) *Com* **écritures** accounts; **tenir les écritures** to keep the accounts; **employé aux écritures** accounts *or* ledger clerk

(e) *Rel* **l'É. sainte, les saintes Écritures** Holy Scripture, Holy Writ

(f) *Littér* writing; *TV, Cin* **é. de scénarios** scriptwriting, screenwriting

▶ **écriture**: **é. abrégée** speedwriting; **é. automatique** automatic writing; *Compta* **écritures comptables** accounting entries; *Compta* **é. de clôture** closing entry; *Typ* **é. grasse** bold typeface, boldface; *Compta* **é. d'inventaire** closing entries; *Compta* **écritures en partie double** double entry; **é. phonétique** phonetic script; *Compta* **é. de régularisation** adjusting entry; *Compta* **é. regroupement** consolidated entry

écrivailler [ekrivaje] *vi Péj* to be a hack (writer), to scribble

écrivailleur, -euse [ekrivajœr, -øz] *n*, **écrivaillon** [ekrivajɔ̃] *nm Péj* hack (writer), scribbler

écrivain [ekrivɛ̃] *nm* **(a)** author, writer; **femme é.** woman writer **(b)** *Arch* **é. public** (public) letter writer

écrivasser [ekrivase] *vi Péj* = **écrivailler**

écrivassier, -ière [ekrivasje, -jɛr] *n Péj* hack (writer), scribbler

écrou[1] [ekru] *nm Jur* committal (to prison); **sous é.** detained, in detention; **levée d'é.** release, discharge (from prison)

écrou[2] *nm Tech* nut; **é. à ailettes** *ou* **à oreilles** thumb *or* wing *or* butterfly nut; **é. crénelé** *ou* **à créneaux** *ou* **à encoches** castellated nut; **é. de réglage** adjusting *or* adjuster nut

écrouelles [ekruɛl] *nfpl Arch* scrofula, king's evil

écrouer [ekrue] *vt Jur* to imprison, to commit to prison

écroulement [ekrulmɑ̃] *nm (d'un édifice, un pont, une personne, de prix etc)* collapse; *(de terre, roche)* fall; *(d'un empire)* fall, collapse; **ce terrible mois a vu l'é. de ses espoirs** that dreadful month saw his hopes dashed

écrouler (s') [sekrule] *vpr* **(a)** *(d'un édifice, un pont, une personne, prix etc)* to collapse; *(d'espoirs)* to crumble away; **empire près de s'é.** empire on the verge of collapse **(b) s'é. sur une chaise** to drop *or* flop onto a chair; **s'é. de fatigue** to collapse *or* drop with exhaustion; **écroulé dans un fauteuil** slumped in an armchair; *F* **écroulé (de rire)** doubled up with laughter

écru [ekry] *adj (tissu)* unbleached, ecru, natural-coloured; **soie écrue** raw silk; **toile écrue** holland

ecstasy [ɛkstasi] *nf* ecstasy

ectoplasme [ɛktɔplasm] *nm Biol* ectoplasm

ECU [eky] *nm inv (abrév* **European Currency Unit)** ECU

écu [eky] *nm* **(a)** *(monnaie)* ECU; *Arch Fin* crown **(b)** *(bouclier)* shield; *Hér* escutcheon, coat of arms

écubier [ekybje] *nm Naut* hawsehole

écueil [ekœj] *nm Naut* reef, shelf; *Fig (danger)* pitfall; **donner sur les écueils** *(d'un bateau)* to strike the rocks; *Fig* **se heurter à un é.** to hit a snag; **il n'y avait pas d'harmonie dans l'entreprise: c'est là qu'était l'é.** this lack of harmony was the rock on which the company foundered

écuelle [ekɥɛl] *nf (assiette large)* bowl; **une é. de soupe** a bowl(ful) of soup; **é. du chien/chat** dog's/cat's bowl *or* dish

éculé [ekyle] *adj (chaussure)* down-at-heel; *Fig (tour, plaisanterie, argument etc)* well-worn, hackneyed

écumage [ekymaʒ] *nm (de la soupe, la confiture, du métal fondu)* skimming

écume [ekym] *nf (dans la bouche, sur la bière etc)* froth, foam; *(sur la mer)* foam; *(sur la soupe, la confiture, le métal fondu etc)* scum; **il avait l'é. à la bouche** he was foaming at the mouth; **cheval couvert d'é.** foam-covered horse; *Minér* **é. (de mer)** *(magnésite)* meerschaum

écumer [ekyme] **1** *vt* **(a)** *(soupe, confiture, métal fondu etc)* to skim **(b)** *(piller)* to scour, to pillage; **é. les mers** *(des pirates)* to scour the seas, to buccaneer; *Fig* **j'ai écumé tous les magasins pour le trouver** I scoured the shops looking for it **2** *vi (du vin, de la bouche etc)* to foam, to froth; *(de la mer)* to foam; *(de la soupe, la confiture, du métal fondu etc)* to form a scum; **cheval qui écume** foaming horse; **é. (de rage)** to foam (with rage)

écumeur [ekymœr] *nm* **é. (de mer)** buccaneer, pirate

écumeux, -euse [ekymø, -øz] *adj (mer, vagues)* foaming; *(bière)* foamy, frothy; *(confiture etc)* scummy

écumoire [ekymwar] *nf* skimmer, perforated spoon; **é. à friture** slotted spoon; *Fig* **troué comme une é.** riddled with holes

écureuil [ekyrœj] *nm* squirrel; **é. volant** flying squirrel

écurie [ekyri] *nf* stable; **é. (de courses)** *(de chevaux, voitures)* (racing) stable; **mettre les chevaux à** *ou* **dans l'é.** to stable the horses; *F* **quelle é.!** what a pigsty!; *Myth* **les écuries d'Augias** the Augean stables

écusson [ekysɔ̃] *nm* **(a)** *(de serrure)* key-plate, keyhole scutcheon **(b)** *Hér* escutcheon, shield, coat of arms **(c)** *(emblème d'étoffe)* badge; *Mil* tab, badge, (collar) patch

écuyer, -ère [ekɥije, -ɛr] **1** *nm* **(a)** *(instructeur)* riding master **(b)** *Arch (gentilhomme)* squire, armour-bearer; *(servant la famille royale)* equerry; *Hist* **grand é.** Master of the Horse **2** *n* rider, horseman, *f* horsewoman; **être bon é.** to ride well, to be a good rider; **é. de cirque** circus rider, equestrian, *f* equestrienne; **bottes à l'écuyère** riding boots

eczéma [egzema] *nm Méd* eczema; **avoir** *ou* **faire de l'é.** to have eczema

eczémateux, -euse [egzematø, -øz] *adj Méd* eczematous

edelweiss [edɛlvɛs, -vajs] *nf (plante)* edelweiss

Éden [edɛn] *nm Bible* **l'É., le jardin d'É.** Eden, the Garden of Eden; *Fig* **un é.** a paradise, a Garden of Eden

édénique [edenik] *adj Litt* idyllic

édenté [edɑ̃te] *adj (personne, peigne)* toothless; *(animal)* toothless, *Spéc* edentate

édenter [edɑ̃te] *vt (peigne, scie, lame etc)* to break the teeth of

EDF [ədeɛf, edeɛf] *nf (abrév* **Électricité de France)** (French) Electricity Board

EDI [ədei] *nm Ordinat (abrév* **échange de données informatisé)** EDI

édicter [edikte] *vt (loi)* to enact, to decree; *(peine)* to decree, to prescribe

édicule [edikyl] *nm* (*urinoir*) public convenience
édifiant [edifjɑ̃] *adj* edifying
édification [edifikasjɔ̃] *nf* **(a)** (*d'un monument etc*) erecting, erection, building; *Fig* (*d'un empire, d'une fortune etc*) building up **(b)** (*instruction morale*) edification, moral improvement; **pour votre é.** for your edification
édifice [edifis] *nm* building, *Fml* edifice; **édifices publics** public buildings; *Fig* **apporter sa pierre à l'é.** to make a contribution, to do one's bit; *Fig* **tout l'é. social** the whole fabric *or* structure of society
édifier [edifje] *vt* **(a)** (*bâtiment*) to build; *Fig* (*empire, fortune etc*) to build up; (*système*) to develop, to put together **(b)** (*d'un sermon etc*) to edify; *Iron* **ces dernières révélations nous ont tous édifiés** these latest revelations were an education for us all; **c'est sans doute pour nous é. qu'il a tenu ce discours** he probably made the speech for our edification
édile [edil] *nm* **(a)** (*dans l'ancienne Rome*) aedile **(b)** (*magistrat officiel*) municipal official, town councillor
Édimbourg [edɛ̃bur] *nm ou f* Edinburgh
édit [edi] *nm Hist* edict
éditer [edite] *vt* **(a)** (*publier*) (*livre etc*) to publish; (*disque*) to produce **(b)** (*commenter*) (*texte*) to edit **(c)** *Ordinat* to edit; **pouvant être édité** editable
éditeur, -trice [editœr, -tris] **1** *n* **(a)** (*d'une maison d'édition*) publisher **(b)** (*commentateur*) editor **2** *nm Ordinat* (*de programme*) editor
▶ **éditeur**: *Cin* **é. de film** film releasing company; *Ordinat* **é. d'icônes** icon editor; *Ordinat* **é. de liens** linker, link editor; *Ordinat* **é. orienté en lignes** line editor; **é. de logiciel** sofware company; **é. de presse** newspaper publisher; **é. de texte** text editor; **é. de vidéo** video publisher
édition [edisjɔ̃] *nf* **(a)** (*activité, métier*) publishing; **maison d'é.** publishing house *or* firm; **é. de disques** record production; **travailler dans l'é.** to work in publishing

(b) (*texte commenté*) edition; (*exemplaire*) edition, issue, impression; **é. scolaire** school edition; **é. originale** first edition; **é. (entièrement) revue et corrigée** major new edition, *Hum* **où est le sucre? – dans le placard, troisième é.!** where's the sugar? – for the third time, it's in the cupboard!

(c) *Journ* **dernière é.** final edition; **é. spéciale** special edition; **é. exceptionelle** extra; **é. locale** local edition

(d) (*action de commenter*) editing

(e) *Ordinat* editing; **é. de liens** linking; **é. pleine page** full page editing; **é. électronique** electronic publishing
éditique [editik] *nf Ordinat* desktop publishing
édito [edito] *nm Journ* (*abrév* **éditorial**) leading article, leader, editorial
éditorial, -iale, -iaux, -iales [editɔrjal, -jo] *Journ* **1** *adj* editorial **2** *nm* leading article, leader, editorial
éditorialiste [editɔrjalist] *n Journ* leader writer, editorialist, editorial writer
édouardien, -ienne [edwardjɛ̃, -jɛn] *adj Hist* Edwardian
édredon [edrədɔ̃] *nm* eiderdown, quilt
éducable [edykabl] *adj* teachable, *Fml* educable
éducateur, -trice [edykatœr, -tris] **1** *n* (*enseignant*) educator, instructor; (*spécialiste*) educationalist; **é. spécialisé** special education teacher **2** *adj* educational
éducatif, -ive [edykatif, -iv] *adj* educational
éducation [edykasjɔ̃] *nf* **(a)** (*enseignement*) education; **faire l'é. de qn** to educate sb; *Hum* **toute ton é. est à (re)faire!** your education has been sadly neglected!; **en rock toute mon é. est à faire** I know absolutely nothing *or* I'm totally ignorant about rock music; **l'é. politique de la jeunesse** the political education of young people **(b)** (*par les parents*) upbringing; **sans é.** ill-bred, uncouth; **avoir de l'é.** to be well-bred, to have good manners; **il manque d'é.** he has no manners, he is ill-mannered *or* ill-bred; **quel manque d'é.!** what manners! **(c)** *Fig* (*de la volonté, des réflexes, de l'esprit etc*) training
▶ **éducation**: **é. manuelle et technique** handicraft classes; **l'É. nationale** ≈ Department of Education; **é. permanente** continuing education; **é. physique** physical training *or* education; **é. professionnelle** vocational training; **é. religieuse** religious instruction; **é. sexuelle** sex education
édulcorant [edylkɔrɑ̃] **1** *adj* sweetening **2** *nm* sweetener; **é. de synthèse** artificial sweetener
édulcorer [edylkɔre] *vt* **(a)** (*médicament, boisson etc*) to sweeten **(b)** *Fig* (*théorie, compte rendu*) to water down; (*roman pornographique*) to tone down
éduquer [edyke] *vt* **(a)** (*donner un enseignement à*) (*enfant, peuple etc*) to educate **(b)** (*élever*) to bring up; **mal éduqué** ill-bred, ill-mannered **(c)** *Fig* (*volonté, esprit etc*) to train; **le goût est quelque chose qui s'éduque** taste has to be learnt

effaçable [efasabl] *adj* **(a)** (*encre, crayon, inscription*) erasable **(b)** *Ordinat* (*mémoire*) erasable
effaçage [efasaʒ] *nm* erasing
effacé [efase] *adj* (*personne, manières*) self-effacing, retiring; (*rôle*) small, insignificant; (*menton*) receding; **mener une vie très effacée** to live very quietly
effacement [efasmɑ̃] *nm* **(a)** (*d'un mot*) (*en gommant*) erasure; (*de message*) erasing; (*d'une bande magnétique*) blanking, erasing; *Ordinat* deletion; (*d'une tache*) removal; (*par le temps etc*) (*d'une inscription*) wearing away; (*des souvenirs*) fading; **ça a provoqué l'e. de la cassette vidéo** that erased (the contents of) the video *or* wiped the video clean **(b)** (*d'une personne*) self-effacement
effacer [efase] **(j'effaçai(s); n. effaçons) 1** *vt* **(a)** (*enlever*) (*mot*) to erase, to rub out; (*enregistrement, bande etc*) to wipe, to erase; *Ordinat* to erase, to delete, *F* to zap; **e. le tableau** to clean the blackboard; *Ordinat* **e. l'écran** to clear the screen; **e. une tache** to remove a stain; (*en lavant*) to wash out a stain; (*avec un chiffon*) to wipe off a stain; **e. des imperfections** to smooth out imperfections; **sculptures effacées par le temps** carvings worn away by time; **e. toutes traces de son passage** to remove *or* eliminate all traces of one's presence

(b) *Fig* **e. un mauvais souvenir** to erase *or* wipe out *or* blot out an unhappy memory; **le temps efface les douleurs** time heals all wounds; **comment dois-je faire pour e. ma faute?** what can I do to wipe out the memory of what I did?; **e. qch de sa mémoire** to blot sth out of *or* erase sth from one's memory; **il a réussi à e. toutes mes craintes** he made my fears vanish; *Fig* **on efface tout et on recommence** we'll wipe the slate clean and make a fresh start

(c) (*éclipser*) to put in the shade

(d) **e. le corps** to stand sideways; **e. les épaules** to throw back one's shoulders

2 s'effacer *vpr* **(a)** (*disparaître*) (*d'une inscription*) to wear away; *Fig* (*d'un sentiment, un souvenir*) to fade (away); **cela s'effacera à l'eau** it will wash off; **la tache ne s'est pas effacée au lavage** the stain didn't come out in the wash; **cette encre ne s'efface pas bien** anything written in this ink doesn't rub out very well; *Fig* **avec le temps, tout s'efface** everything fades with time; **ton chagrin s'effacera** you'll get over it

(b) (*s'écarter*) to stand *or* move aside, to move to one side; *Fig* **depuis quelque temps il s'était effacé** for some time he had kept in the background; **il s'est effacé devant moi pour me laisser passer** he stood aside to let me pass; **il a tendance à s'e. derrière elle** he tends to hide behind her
effaceur [efasœr] *nm* **e. (d'encre)** ink eraser
effarant [efarɑ̃] *adj* frightening, alarming; **ils pratiquent des prix effarants** their prices are frightening *or* shocking; **il y avait un monde e. sur les plages** there were an awful lot of people on the beach; **d'une naïveté effarante** alarmingly *or* shockingly naive
effaré [efare] *adj* alarmed
effarement [efarmɑ̃] *nm* alarm; **dans l'e.** alarmed
effarer [efare] *vt* to alarm, to scare; **son hypocrisie m'effare!** his/her hypocrisy astounds me!; **je suis effaré par les prix!** the prices are frightening *or* shocking!, I'm astounded at the prices!
effarouchement [efaruʃmɑ̃] *nm* startling, frightening (away)
effaroucher [efaruʃe] **1** *vt* **(a)** (*effrayer*) to scare, to alarm; (*faire reculer*) to scare away, to frighten away

(b) (*choquer*) to shock

2 s'effaroucher *vpr* **(a)** (*s'effrayer*) to be scared *or* alarmed **(de** by); **un chien qui s'effarouche peut être dangereux** a frightened dog can be dangerous; **elle s'effarouche pour un rien** she gets frightened at the least little thing, the least little thing frightens her; **il ne risque pas de s'e. pour si peu** he's unlikely to let a little thing like that frighten him

(b) (*s'offusquer*) to be shocked **(de** by, at)
effectif, -ive [efɛktif, -iv] **1** *adj* **(a)** (*efficace*) (*traitement etc*) effective, efficacious **(b)** (*réel*) (*travail, rendement etc*) effective, actual; *Fin* (*circulation*) active; (*valeur*) real **2** *nm* (*employés*) manpower, (number of) employees, staff; (*d'un club, bataillon etc*) strength, numbers; *Naut* complement; **à e. réduit** under *or* below strength; *Scol* **réduire l'e. des classes à 25** to reduce the size of classes *or* reduce class numbers to 25; **l'e. est au complet** we are at full strength *or* up to strength; *Mil* **les effectifs** the total strength; **crise d'effectifs** manpower crisis
effectivement [efɛktivmɑ̃] *adv* **(a)** (*réellement, de manière effective*) actually, in reality, really; **contribuer e. au processus de paix** to make a real contribution to the peace

process **(b)** *(en effet)* actually, in (actual) fact; **c'est pratique, hein? – e.!** it's practical, isn't it? – (yes) indeed! *or* indeed it is!; **e., on aurait pu prévoir un parapluie** we should have thought about bringing an umbrella, *F* we should have brought an umbrella right enough; **il a e. travaillé sur ce projet** he did actually work on the project

effectuer [efɛktɥe] **1** *vt (réforme, mesure etc)* to carry out, to bring into effect; *(mouvement, opération)* to execute; *(paiement)* to make, *Fml* to effect; *(voyage, calcul, Mil retraite)* to make; *(réconciliation)* to bring about; **e. des démarches** to take steps; *Com* **e. une commande** to place an order; **e. une réservation** to make a reservation **2 s'effectuer** *vpr (d'une réforme etc)* to be carried out, to be brought into effect; *(d'un mouvement, d'une opération)* to be executed; *(d'un paiement, voyage)* to be made; *(d'une réconciliation)* to be brought about

efféminé [efemine] *adj* effeminate

efféminer [efemine] *vt* to make effeminate; *Fig (effet)* to weaken, to diminish; *(pensée)* to emasculate

effervescence [efɛrvɛsɑ̃s] *nf (bouillonnement)* effervescence; *Fig (agitation)* agitation, turmoil; *(excitation)* excitement; **ville en e.** town seething with excitement *or* in (a) turmoil

effervescent [efɛrvɛsɑ̃] *adj (comprimé, aspirine etc)* effervescent; *Fig (tempérament)* excitable, exuberant; *(foule)* excited

effet [efɛ] *nm* **(a)** *(résultat, conséquence)* effect **(sur** on); **les mesures du gouvernement n'ont eu aucun e.** the government's measures have had no effect; **cela a eu pour e. de le mettre en colère** it had the effect of making him angry; **sa fréquentation a un e. désastreux sur ma fille** going out with him has had a disastrous effect on my daughter; **ce poison a pour e. de paralyser le système nerveux** this poison results in the paralysis of the nervous system; **faire de l'e.** to have an effect, to be effective; **son départ précipité a fait de l'e.** his hurried departure caused a stir; **faire de l'e. sur** to have an effect on; **ma remarque a fait son petit e.** my remark caused a stir; **faire e.** to take effect; **produire l'e. voulu** to produce the desired effect; **une relation de cause à e.** a cause and effect relationship; **à cet e.** with that in mind, *Fml* to that end, with this end in view; **cet appareil n'a pas été conçu à cet e.** the machine was not designed for that purpose; **sans e.** ineffective, ineffectual; **mes conseils sont restés** *ou* **demeurés sans e.** my advice had no effect *or* was ineffective; **sous l'e. de l'alcool/la drogue** under the influence of alcohol/drugs; **il t'a injurié sous l'e. de la colère** he wouldn't have insulted you if he hadn't been angry; **je suis encore sous l'e. de la colère** I'm still angry, I still haven't calmed down; **les feuilles sont tombées sous l'e. de la chaleur** the leaves dropped off with the heat; **ce n'est qu'un e. de sa timidité** it's only because he is shy; **à quel e.?** to what end?; **e. secondaire** side effect; **ce n'était qu'un e. du hasard** it was only by pure *or* sheer chance; **créer un e. de surprise** to cause a stir; **nous ne gagnerons cette bataille qu'en créant un e. de surprise** we won't win this battle unless we can take the enemy by surprise

(b) *(impression)* impression; **c'est l'e. que cela m'a fait** that's how it impressed *or* struck me; **quel e. ça te fait qu'elle revienne?** how do you feel about her coming back?; **les pleurs de sa femme ne lui firent aucun e.** his wife's tears had no effect on him; **elle me fait l'e. d'une fille plutôt équilibrée** she strikes me as being a fairly well-balanced girl; **sa réponse a fait l'e. d'une bombe** his answer came as *or* was a bombshell; *F* **et c'est tout l'e. que ça te fait?** is that all it means to you?; **à chaque fois qu'il me parle, ça me fait un drôle d'e.** I feel all funny inside whenever he talks to me; **ça m'a fait un drôle d'e.** it gave me a funny *or* strange feeling, it made me feel all funny *or* strange; **ça fait un drôle d'e. de penser que ...** it's funny *or* strange to think that ...; **il fit une pause pour mieux juger de l'e. de ses paroles** he paused to see what effect his words were having; **cela fait mauvais e. de le faire attendre** it looks bad to keep him waiting; **ça a fait bon e. que tu aies mis une jupe** your wearing a skirt made a good impression; **faire bon/mauvais e. à qn** to make a good/bad impression on sb; **faire de l'e.** to make a show, to attract attention; **dès que je l'ai vu, il m'a fait de l'e.** I fancied him the minute I saw him; **eh bien! elle te fait de l'e.!** she's got quite an effect on you, I see! *F* **ça m'a fait de l'e. de la voir si pâle** it gave me quite a turn to see her so pale

(c) *(but recherché, force artistique)* **manquer son e.** *(d'un discours)* not to have the desired effect; *(d'une plaisanterie)* to misfire, to fall flat; **il voulait faire une entrée triomphale mais il a manqué son e.** he wanted to make a triumphant entry but it fell flat; **soigner ses effets** to work hard to make the right impression; **rechercher les effets** to try to make an impression; **ménager ses effets** to have a sense of the dramatic; **un e. de contraste** contrasting effect; **e. de style** stylistic effect; **je n'ai jamais compris l'e. comique d'une chute** I've never understood what people find to laugh about when somebody falls, I've never understood what was so funny about somebody falling; *Litt* **phrases à e.** words used for effect; **un orateur qui fait des effets de voix** a speaker who makes striking use of his voice; **faire des effets de jambes** to show off one's legs, to draw attention to one's legs; *Beaux-Arts* **e. de lune** moonlight effect

(d) *(application)* effect; **mettre un projet à e.** to put a plan into action *or* into effect; **prendre e.** *(d'une loi etc)* to take effect, to come into effect *or* force; **e. rétroactif d'une loi/d'un accord** retroactive effect of a law/an argument; **augmentation avec e. rétroactif au 1er avril** rise retroactive *or* backdated to April 1st

(e) *Tennis* spin; **balle qui a de l'e.** ball that has spin; **donner de l'e. à sa balle** to put spin on one's ball; *Billard* **e. de côté** side (screw); **mettre trop d'e.** to put on too much spin

(f) *Tech* **e. utile** efficiency; **à simple e.** single-action, single-acting; **à double e.** double-action, double-acting; **e. Edison** Edison effect; **e. photoélectrique** photoelectric effect

(g) *Fin* bill; **e. bancaire** bill, draft; **e. de commerce** bill, draft; **e. de complaisance** accommodation bill; **e. à courte échéance** short, short-dated bill; **e. à date fixe** fixed-term bill; **e. domicilié** domiciled bill; **effets à l'encaissement** bills for collection; **e. endossé** endorsed bill; **e. escompté** discounted bill; **e. à l'encaissement** bill for collection; **e. libre** clean bill; **e. à longue échéance** long, long-dated bill; **e. à ordre** promissory note; **effets à payer** bills payable; **e. au porteur** bearer bill, bill made out to bearer; **effets publics** government stock *or* securities; **effets à recevoir** bills receivable; **e. à taux flottant** floating rate note, FRN; **e. à vue** sight bill *or* draft

(h) effets *(vêtements etc)* possessions, belongings; **effets personnels** personal effects; *Jur* goods and chattels

(i) en e. *(réellement)* actually, in (actual) fact; **oui, je m'en souviens, en e.** yes, I do remember; **j'ai dû partir, en e. j'étais pressé** I had to leave because I was in a hurry; **en e., c'est ce que je me suis dit** that's just what I thought; **mais c'est monstrueux! – en e.!** it's abominable! – isn't it just!

▶ **effet**: *Fin* **e. balançoire** see-saw effect; **e. boomerang** boomerang effect; **avoir un e. boomerang** to boomerang; **e. boule de neige** snowball effect; *Aut* **e. de chasse** caster action; **e. Doppler** Doppler effect; *Typ* **e. d'escalier** jagged appearance, jaggy; *TV, Rad* **e. Larsen** audio *or* acoustic feedback, howl-round; **e. d'optique** visual effect; *TV, Cin* **effets optiques** camera effects; **e. pervers** undesired effect; *Méd* side effect; **e. de serre** greenhouse effect; **des gaz à e. de serre** greenhouse gases; *Cin etc* **effets sonores** sound effects; *Cin etc* **effets spéciaux** special effects; *Ordinat, TV* **e. de transition** melt; *Phys* **e. tunnel** tunnel effect; **effets vidéo** video effects; *TV, Cin* **effets visuels** visual effects

effeuillage [efœjaʒ] *nm* **(a)** *(d'arbres fruitiers etc)* thinning out of leaves **(b)** *Hum F* striptease, strip

effeuillaison [efœjɛzɔ̃] *nf,* **effeuillement** [efœjmɑ̃] *nm* leaf fall

effeuiller [efœje] *vt (d'une personne) (arbre fruitier)* to thin out the leaves of; *(fleur)* to pluck the petals of; *(du vent) (arbre)* to blow off the leaves of; **e. la marguerite** to play 'he/she loves me, he/she loves me not'

effeuilleuse [efœjøz] *nf F* stripper, striptease artist

efficace [efikas] *adj (action, remède)* effective, *Fml* efficacious; *(machine)* efficient; *(personne)* efficient, capable; **prêter à qn un appui e.** to give sb useful *or* helpful support

efficacement [efikasmɑ̃] *adv* effectively; *(avec le minimum d'effort)* efficiently

efficacité [efikasite] *nf (d'un remède, d'une prière etc)* effectiveness, *Fml* efficacy; *(d'une machine etc)* efficiency

efficience [efisjɑ̃s] *nf* efficiency

efficient [efisjɑ̃] *adj* efficient

effigie [efiʒi] *nf* **(a)** *(portrait)* effigy; **pendre qn en e.** to hang sb in effigy **(b)** *(sur une pièce etc)* effigy, head

effilage [efilaʒ] *nm (d'un tissu)* fraying, ravelling out

effilé [efile] **1** *adj* **(a)** *(tissu)* frayed; **une frange effilée** a ragged fringe **(b)** *(allongé) (outil)* tapered, pointed; *(doigts)* tapering; *(silhouette)* rangy; **amandes effilées** slivered almonds **(c)** *(poulet)* dressed, drawn **2** *nm Tex* fringe

effilement [efilmɑ̃] *nm* **(a)** *(des doigts)* tapering **(b)** *(de tissu)* fraying

effiler [efile] **1** *vt* **(a)** *Tex* to fray **(b) e. les cheveux** to taper hair **2 s'effiler** *vpr* **(a)** *(d'un tissu)* to fray **(b)** *(d'un visage)* to taper, to come to a point

effilochage [efilɔʃaʒ] *nm Tex* (*en peignant*) teasing out
effiloche [efilɔʃ] *nf* (*de fils laissés libres*) fringe
effilocher [efilɔʃe] *Tex* **1** *vt* (*avec un peigne*) to tease out **2 s'effilocher** *vpr* (*d'un tissu*) to fray
efflanqué [eflɑ̃ke] *adj* (*animal*) lean, raw-boned; (*personne*) skinny, lanky
effleurement [eflœrmɑ̃] *nm* (*frôlement*) (light gentle) touch; (*de l'eau*) skimming; **touche à e.** touch-sensitive key
effleurer [eflœre] *vt* **(a)** (*frôler*) to touch lightly; (*accidentellement*) to brush (against); (*surface de l'eau*) to skim; *Fig* **e. un sujet** to touch on a topic; *Fig* **quelques soupçons l'avaient effleuré** some misgivings had crossed his mind; *Fig* **cette idée ne m'a jamais effleuré** the idea never crossed *or* entered my mind **(b)** (*égratigner*) (*peau*) to graze
efflorescence [eflɔrɛsɑ̃s] *nf* **(a)** *Ch* efflorescence **(b)** (*sur les fruits*) bloom **(c)** *Litt* **être en pleine e.** to be flourishing
efflorescent [eflɔrɛsɑ̃] *adj Ch* efflorescent
effluent [eflyɑ̃] **1** *adj* effluent **2** *nm* effluent; **e. urbain** (*no pl*) (sewage) effluent; **effluents radioactifs** radioactive waste
effluve [eflyv] *nm* (*émanation*) emanation; **de riches effluves** rich fragrance; *Fig Litt* **les effluves du passé** the ghosts of the past
effondré [efɔ̃dre] *adj* (*personne*) grief-stricken
effondrement [efɔ̃drəmɑ̃] *nm* (*d'un pont, un mur, un bâtiment etc*) collapse; (*d'un toit*) collapse, falling in; (*d'une mine*) caving in; *Géol* subsidence; *Fig* (*d'un plan*) falling through; (*d'une personne, une fortune, une monnaie*) collapse; (*d'un gouvernement, empire*) collapse, downfall; *Com* (*des prix, marchés*) slump (**de** in), collapse; **il est dans un état d'e. complet** he is in a state of total collapse
effondrer [efɔ̃dre] **1** *vt* (*briser*) (*toit*) to bring down; (*mur*) to break down **2 s'effondrer** *vpr* (*d'un pont, un mur, un bâtiment etc*) to collapse; (*d'un toit*) to collapse, to fall in, to cave in; (*d'une mine*) to cave in; *Fig* (*d'un plan*) to fall through; (*des prix*) to slump; (*d'une personne, d'un gouvernement, d'un empire*) to collapse; **toute son histoire s'effondre** his whole story is collapsing *or* falling to pieces; **s'e. en larmes** to break down and cry, to dissolve into tears; **s'e. dans un fauteuil** to collapse *or* sink *or* flop into an armchair
efforcer (s') [sefɔrse] *vpr* (**je m'efforçai(s)**; **n. n. efforçons**) to strive, to endeavour, *US* to endeavor; **s'e. de faire qch** to do one's utmost *or* one's best to do sth, to make every effort to do sth; **je m'y efforce** I'm doing my best *or* utmost; **s'e. vers un but** to strive towards a goal
effort [efɔr] *nm* **(a)** effort; **allons, encore un (petit) e.** come on, try again *or* a bit more effort; **son médecin lui a interdit tout e.** his doctor has forbidden any exertion; **cela va te demander un certain e.** you'll need to exert yourself a bit; **après bien des efforts** after a great deal of effort; *F* **après l'e., le réconfort** I/you/*etc* deserve this; *F* **appliquer la loi du moindre e.** to take the line of least resistance; *F* **il est partisan du moindre e.** he doesn't believe in exerting himself; **ce n'est pas en étant partisan du moindre e. que tu vas monter les échelons** you won't get ahead by just sitting back, you'll have to exert yourself if you want to get ahead; *Péj* **son travail sent l'e.** his work reeks of effort; **a progressé mais doit encore faire des efforts** has made progress but still needs to make an effort; **sans e.** effortlessly, without effort; **elle parle anglais sans e.** she speaks English effortlessly; **je suis prêt à faire un e. pour ton projet** I'm willing to help with your project; **faire un e. pour faire qch** to make an effort to do sth; **faire un violent e. pour se lever/s'en persuader** to make a great effort to get up/convince oneself; **faire un e. d'adaptation** to make an effort to adapt; **faire un e. d'imagination** to use one's imagination; **fais un petit e. d'imagination!** use a bit of imagination!; **cela demande un sacré e. d'imagination** it takes an awful lot of imagination, it puts quite a strain on the imagination; **faire un e. de mémoire** to rack one's brains; **faire un e. sur soi-même** to exercise self-control; **faire tous ses efforts pour réussir** to make every effort *or* do one's utmost to succeed; **faire l'e. de faire qch** to make the effort to do sth; **e. de volonté** effort of (the) will; **ce travail demande un e. intellectuel immense** this is a very demanding job intellectually
(b) *Méd Vieilli* strain, rick; **se donner** *ou* **attraper un e.** to rick one's back
(c) *MecE* strain, stress
▶ **effort**: *MecE* **e. de cisaillement** shearing stress; *Mktg* **e. de commercialisation** *ou* **de mercatique** marketing effort; **e. financier** financial outlay; **e. de guerre** war effort; *MecE* **e. de rupture** breaking strain; *MecE* **e. de tension** tensile stress; *MecE* **e. de torsion** torque; *Aut* **e. de traction** tractive effort, pull; *Aut* **efforts en virage** cornering force

effraction [efraksjɔ̃] *nf Jur* breaking and entering; **entrer par e.** to break in; **vol avec e.** burglary; **il n'y a pas eu e.** there was no sign of a burglary
effraie [efrɛ] *nf* (*oiseau*) barn owl, screech owl
effranger [efrɑ̃ʒe] (**j'effrangeai(s)**; **n. effrangeons**) **1** *vt* (*bords d'un tissu*) to fray **2 s'effranger** *vpr* to fray, to become frayed
effrayant [efrɛjɑ̃] *adj* frightening; *Fig* (*chaleur, appétit, charme*) tremendous; (*prix, bêtise, laideur*) frightening
effrayer [efreje] (**j'effraie, j'effraye, n. effrayons**; **j'effraierai, j'effrayerai**) **1** *vt* (*faire peur à*) to frighten, to scare; (*inquiéter*) to alarm; **l'énormité de la besogne nous effraie** the magnitude of the task appals *or* alarms us **2 s'effrayer** *vpr* to be frightened (**de** at); **elle s'effraie pour un rien** the least little thing frightens her, she takes fright at the least little thing; **je m'effraie de la lenteur avec laquelle elle travaille** I'm alarmed by how slowly she works; **d'après lui, il n'y a aucune raison de s'e.** according to him there's no need to be frightened *or* alarmed *or* there's no need for alarm
effréné [efrene] *adj* (*passion, curiosité etc*) unbridled, unrestrained; (*efforts*) frantic; (*galop*) frantic, mad
effritement [efritmɑ̃] *nm* (*du plâtre, d'un revêtement etc*) crumbling (into dust); (*de la roche*) weathering; *Fig* (*d'une autorité, une majorité, de fonds etc*) erosion
effriter [efrite] **1** *vt* to cause to crumble *or* disintegrate; (*du vent*) (*roche*) to weather **2 s'effriter** *vpr* (*de plâtre, d'un revêtement etc*) to crumble, to disintegrate; (*de la roche*) to weather; *Fig* (*d'une autorité, une majorité, de fonds etc*) to be eroded
effroi [efrwa] *nm Litt* terror, fear, dread; **je fus saisi d'e.** I was seized by terror, I was terror-stricken
effronté [efrɔ̃te] *adj* (*personne, manières etc*) impudent, insolent; (*mensonge, menteur*) barefaced, brazen
effrontément [efrɔ̃temɑ̃] *adv* impudently, insolently; (*mentir*) brazenly
effronterie [efrɔ̃tri] *nf* (*d'une personne, de manières etc*) effrontery, insolence, impudence; (*d'un mensonge*) brazenness
effroyable [efrwajabl] *adj* (*qui fait peur*) dreadful, appalling, horrifying; *F* (*énorme*) (*dépense, foule, erreur etc*) dreadful, terrible
effroyablement [efrwajabləmɑ̃] *adv F* dreadfully, terribly
effusion [efyzjɔ̃] *nf* **(a)** **e. de sang** bloodshed **(b)** (*exubérance*) effusiveness; **avec e.** effusively, gushingly; **une e. de tendresse** an outpouring of affection; **leurs effusions m'étouffent** I find their effusiveness stifling
égaiement [egemɑ̃] *nm* cheering up; **ils ont tous remarqué mon é. soudain** they all noticed that I was suddenly more cheerful *or* in a brighter *or* more cheerful mood
égailler (s') [segaje] *vpr* to disperse, to scatter
égal, -ale, -aux, -ales [egal, -o] **1** *adj* **(a)** (*équivalent*) (*part, poids etc*) equal; **être é. à** to be equal to, to equal; **toutes choses égales (d'ailleurs)** all (other) things being equal; **à travail é., salaire é.** equal pay for equal work; **la partie n'est pas égale** they/we/you are not evenly matched; **ils sont de force/d'intelligence égale** they are equally strong/intelligent; **à surface égale, je préfère mon appartement au sien** square foot for square foot, I prefer my flat to his
(b) (*constant*) (*respiration, son etc*) even, regular; (*allure, pouls*) steady; (*sol*) level, even; (*climat*) equable; **homme d'humeur égale** even-tempered man; **fournir un effort é.** to work steadily; **il reste é. à lui-même** he's still his same old self
(c) **cela m'est (bien) é.** it's all the same *or* all one to me; (*cela ne m'intéresse pas*) I don't care; **c'est é., elle aurait pu venir!** all the same, she could have come!
2 *n* equal; **s'associer avec ses égaux** to associate with one's equals; **elle est mon égale** she is my equal; **traiter qn d'é. à é., traiter qn en é.** to treat sb as an equal; **nous avons eu une discussion d'é. à é.** we had a discussion as equals *or* on equal terms *or* on an equal footing; **sans é.** unequalled, matchless; **à l'é. de** as much as; **il me chérit à l'é. d'un fils** he loves me like a son
égalable [egalabl] *adj* which can be equalled *or* matched; **son succès n'est pas é. par tout le monde** not everyone can match his success
également [egalmɑ̃] *adv* **(a)** (*de la même manière*) equally; **é. bon** equally good; **servir tout le monde é.** to give everyone an equal serving; **j'aime é. sa mère et son père** I like his mother as much as I do his father **(b)** (*aussi*) also, as well, too; **j'en veux é.** I want some too *or* as well
égaler [egale] *vt* **(a)** (*être égal à*) (*personne, score etc*) to equal, to match (up to) (**en** for); **deux et deux égalent quatre** two and two equal *or* make four; **é. un record** to equal a record; **rien n'égale sa beauté** her beauty is

unequalled **(b)** *Arch* (*rendre égal*) to make equal; **la douleur égale les hommes** grief makes all men equal; **peut-on é. Mozart à Bach?** can Mozart be considered the equal of Bach?

égalisateur, -trice [egalizatœr, -tris] *adj* (*système, effet etc*) equalizing, levelling; *Sp* **but/point é.** equalizer

égalisation [egalizasjɔ̃] *nf* **(a)** (*équilibrage*) equalization, equalizing; *Math* **é. à zéro** equating to zero; *Sp* **(but/point d')é.** equalizer; **réussir l'é.** to score the equalizer **(b)** (*nivellement*) (*du sol etc*) levelling, evening out

égaliser [egalize] **1** *vt* **(a)** (*salaires, pression etc*) to equalize, to make equal; **é. les cheveux de qn** to trim sb's hair; *Math* **é. une expression à zéro** to equate an expression to zero; *Sp* **é. la marque** to equalize, to draw level **(b)** (*sol*) to level, to even out **2** *vi Sp* to equalize

égaliseur [egalizœr] *nm Électron* equalizer; **é. graphique** graphic equalizer

égalitaire [egalitɛr] *adj, n* egalitarian

égalitarisme [egalitarism] *nm* egalitarianism

égalitariste [egalitarist] *adj, n* egalitarian

égalité [egalite] *nf* **(a)** (*équivalence*), *Pol* equality; *Tennis* deuce; **être sur un pied d'é. avec qn** to be on an equal footing *or* on equal terms with sb; **é. des chances** equal opportunities; **é. des salaires** equal pay; **à é. d'expérience** when there is *or* in the case of equal experience; *Sp* **à é.** (*équipes*) level; (*résultat*) drawn, tied; *Golf* all square; *Fig* **maintenant, nous sommes à é.** now we're even; *Sp* **course à é.** dead heat, tie; *Courses de chevaux* **parier à é. sur un cheval** to lay evens on a horse

(b) (*constance*) (*de la respiration, d'un son etc*) evenness, regularity; (*d'une allure, du pouls*) steadiness; (*du sol*) evenness; (*de l'esprit*) equanimity; **é. d'humeur** even-temperedness

égard [egar] *nm* **(a)** (*attention*) consideration; **avoir é. à qch** to take sth into consideration *or* into account, to make allowance(s) *or* to allow for sth; **eu é. aux circonstances** in view of *or* considering the circumstances; **eu é. à son âge** in view of *or* given his age; **sans é. à** regardless of, irrespective of

(b) à tous (les) égards in all respects, in every respect; **à certains égards** in some respects; **n'ayez aucune crainte à cet é.** don't worry about that, don't have any worries on that score; **être injuste à l'é. de qn** to be unjust to(wards) sb; **il a été très gentil à mon é.** he has been very kind to me

(c) (*respect*) consideration, respect, regard; **faire qch par é. pour qn** to do sth out of respect *or* consideration for sb; **être sans é.** *ou* **n'avoir aucun é. pour qn** to have no consideration for sb; **avoir des égards pour qn** to be considerate towards sb, to show sb consideration; **elle est toujours accueillie avec les égards dus à son rang** she is always greeted with the respect due to her rank; **il nous a reçus avec beaucoup d'égards** he received us very warmly

égaré [egare] *adj* **(a)** (*personne*) lost; (*animal*) stray, lost **(b)** (*hagard*) (*regard*) distraught; (*yeux*) wild

égarement [egarmɑ̃] *nm* **(a)** (*délire, distraction*) **é. (d'esprit)** (mental) aberration; **il a parfois des moments d'é.** sometimes what he says/does doesn't make much sense, *F* there are times when he's not all there **(b) égarements** (*dérèglements de conduite*) wild behaviour, wildness; **il est revenu de ses égarements** he has seen the error of his ways

égarer [egare] **1** *vt* (*perdre*) (*qn*) to lose; (*en donnant de mauvaises indications*) to mislead; (*objet*) to mislay, to lose; **il jouait à é. les nouveaux arrivants** it amused him to get the newcomers lost; *Fig* **égaré par tant de malheurs** distraught by so many misfortunes; **la douleur/colère vous égare** you don't know what you're saying because of the pain/because you're so angry; **il faut à tout prix é. ses soupçons** we have to avert his suspicions at all costs

2 s'égarer *vpr* **(a)** (*se perdre*) (*personne*) to lose one's way, to get lost; **colis qui s'est égaré** parcel that has got lost *or* gone astray

(b) (*dévier*) **s'é. du droit chemin** to wander from the straight and narrow

(c) (*sortir du sujet*) to stray *or* wander from the point; **son esprit s'égare** his mind is wandering

égayer [egeje] **(j'égaie, j'égaye, n. égayons; j'égaierai, j'égayerai) 1** *vt* (*malade, personne déprimée*) to cheer up; (*invités*) to amuse; (*conversation*) to liven up; (*pièce, robe, la vie de qn*) to brighten (up) **2 s'égayer** *vpr* (*s'amuser*) to have fun, to enjoy oneself; (*s'animer*) to cheer up; **s'é. aux dépens de qn** to have fun at sb's expense, to make fun of sb

Égée [eʒe] *adj* **la mer É.** the Aegean (Sea)

égéen, -éenne [eʒeɛ̃, -eɛn] *adj* Aegean

égérie [eʒeri] *nf* muse

égide [eʒid] *nf* aegis, shield; *Fig* **sous l'é. de** under the aegis *or* care of; *Fig* **se mettre sous l'é. des lois** to take refuge in the law

églantier [eglɑ̃tje] *nm* wild rose *or* dog rose (bush)

églantine [eglɑ̃tin] *nf* (*fleur*) wild *or* dog rose

églefin [egləfɛ̃] *nm* haddock

église [egliz] *nf* [①A6,d,i] **(a) l'É. (catholique romaine)** the (Roman) Catholic Church; **l'É. anglicane** the Church of England, the Anglican Church; **l'É. et l'État** Church and State; **gens d'É.** churchmen **(b)** (*bâtiment*) church; **l'é. Saint-Pierre** St. Peter's (church); **aller à l'é.** to go to church; **se marier à l'é.** to get married in (a) church, to have a church wedding

églogue [eglɔg] *nf Littér* eclogue

ego [ego] *nm inv* ego

égocentrique [egosɑ̃trik] **1** *adj* self-centred, egocentric **2** *n* self-centred *or* egocentric person

égocentrisme [egosɑ̃trism] *nm* egocentricity, self-centredness; *Psy* egocentrism

égoïne [egɔin] *nf* **(scie) é.** handsaw

égoïsme [egɔism] *nm* selfishness, egoism

égoïste [egɔist] **1** *n* egoist, selfish person **2** *adj* selfish, self-centred, egoistic

égoïstement [egɔistəmɑ̃] *adv* selfishly, egoistically

égorgement [egɔrʒəmɑ̃] *nm* (*d'un cochon, d'une personne etc*) cutting the throat

égorger [egɔrʒe] **(j'égorgeai(s); n. égorgeons) 1** *vt* **(a)** (*animal, personne*) to cut the throat of **(b)** *Vieilli* (*ruiner*) to bleed white *or* dry **2 s'égorger** *vpr Fig* to kill each other

égorgeur, -euse [egɔrʒœr, -øz] *n* (*assassin*) cut-throat

égosiller (s') [segozije] *vpr* (*en parlant*) to bawl, to shout (oneself hoarse); (*en chantant*) to sing at the top of one's voice, *F* to sing one's head off; **mais je m'égosille à vous le dire!** I've told you so till I'm blue in the face *or* I'm hoarse!

égotisme [egɔtism] *nm* egotism

égotiste [egɔtist] **1** *n* egotist **2** *adj* egotistic(al)

égout [egu] *nm* (*canalisation souterraine*) sewer; **eaux d'é.** sewage; **é. collecteur** main sewer; **bouche d'é.** manhole; **rat d'é.** sewer rat

égoutier [egutje] *nm* sewerman

égouttage [egutaʒ] *nm* (*de la vaisselle, d'un fromage frais etc*) draining

égouttement [egutmɑ̃] *nm* **(a)** (*de l'eau*) dripping **(b)** (*égouttage*) draining

égoutter [egute] **1** *vt* (*fromage frais, pâtes etc*) to drain **2 s'égoutter** *vpr* (*d'un fromage frais, de vaisselle etc*) to drain **3** *vi* to drain; **laisser é. la vaisselle** to leave the dishes to drain

égouttoir [egutwar] *nm* **(a)** (*dans l'évier*) draining board; (*mobile*) drainer, draining rack **(b)** (*passoire*) colander; **panier é.** (*d'une friteuse*) basket

égrappage [egrapaʒ] *nm* (*de raisins*) picking off

égrapper [egrape] *vt* (*raisins, baies*) to pick off from the bunch

égratigner [egratiɲe] **1** *vt* (*écorcher*) to scratch; *Fig* to have *or* take a dig at **2 s'égratigner** *vpr* to scratch oneself

égratignure [egratiɲyr] *nf* (*écorchure*) scratch; *Fig* dig, gibe; **je m'en suis sorti sans une é.** I escaped without a scratch

égrenage [egrənaʒ] *nm*, **égrènement** [egrɛnmɑ̃] *nm* (*de pois, maïs etc*) shelling; (*de raisins, baies*) picking off; *Fig* **égrènement de lumières** string of lights

égrener [egrəne] **(j'égrène, n. égrenons; j'égrènerai) 1** *vt* **(a)** (*maïs, pois etc*) to shell; (*raisins, baies*) to pick off **(b)** *Fig* **é. son chapelet** to tell one's beads; **la radio égrène les nouvelles** the radio keeps churning out the news; **é. ses souvenirs** to call up one's memories one by one **2 s'égrener** *vpr* **(a)** (*de raisins, baies*) to fall *or* drop from the bunch; (*du blé*) to seed **(b)** *Fig* (*d'un cortège*) to become strung out; **des lumières s'égrenaient le long du quai** a string of lights stretched along the quay

égrillard [egrijar] *adj* (*personne, chanson, histoire etc*) bawdy, ribald; **en société, il a des manières égrillardes** he tends to be bawdy in company

Égypte [eʒipt] *nf* Egypt

égyptien, -ienne [eʒipsjɛ̃, -jɛn] **1** *adj* Egyptian **2** *n* **É.** Egyptian **3** *nm Hist, Ling* Egyptian

égyptologie [eʒiptɔlɔʒi] *nf* Egyptology

égyptologue [eʒiptɔlɔg] *n* Egyptologist

eh [e] *int* hey!; **eh bien!** well!, now then!; **eh bien, comment ça va aujourd'hui?** so how are you today?; **eh bien, je ne sais pas** well I don't know; **eh bien, je vais m'en occuper** oh well, I'll deal with it; **eh oui!** that's right!; **eh! que voulez-vous que je fasse?** well what do you want me to do about it?

éhonté [eɔ̃te] *adj* (*mensonge, menteur etc*) shameless, barefaced, brazen

eider [ɛdɛr] *nm* (*oiseau*) eider (duck)

einsteinien, -ienne [ajnʃtɛnjɛ̃, -jɛn] *adj* of/typical of Einstein

éjaculation [eʒakylasjɔ̃] *nf Physiol* ejaculation; **é. précoce** premature ejaculation
éjaculer [eʒakyle] *vt Physiol* to ejaculate
éjectable [eʒɛktabl] *adj Av* **siège é.** ejector seat
éjecter [eʒɛkte] *vt* (*cartouche, pilote etc*) to eject; *F* (*expulser*) to throw *or* kick out (**de** of); **elle s'est fait é.** she was *or* got thrown *or* kicked out
éjection [eʒɛksjɔ̃] *nf* (*d'une cartouche, d'un pilote etc*) ejection; *F* (*expulsion*) throwing out, kicking out; **éjections volcaniques** ejecta
élaboration [elabɔrasjɔ̃] *nf* (*d'un plan, d'une idée*) working out, development; (*d'une constitution, une loi etc*) drawing up; **é. de concept** concept development; *Mktg* **é. de produit** product development
élaboré [elabɔre] *adj* (*technique, machine*) sophisticated; (*plan*) elaborate
élaborer [elabɔre] *vt* (*plan, idée*) to work out, to develop; (*constitution, loi etc*) to draw up; **é. le profil de qn** to profile sb
élagage [elagaʒ] *nm* (*d'un arbre, Fig d'un film, un roman etc*) pruning; *Mktg* **é. de la ligne** line pruning
élaguer [elage] *vt* (*arbre, Fig film, roman etc*) to prune
élagueur, -euse [elagœr, -øz] *n* pruner
élan[1] [elɑ̃] *nm* **(a)** *Sp etc* (*action de s'élancer*) (*avec les jambes*) run-up; (*avec les bras*) swing; *Sp* **prendre de l'é.** *ou* **son é.** to take a run(-up); **saut sans/avec é.** standing/running jump; **mal calculer son é.** to misjudge one's run-up; **d'un seul é.** (*en sautant*) at one bound; (*en courant*) in one burst; *Fig* **elle courut chez sa mère d'un seul é.** she ran all the way to her mother's without stopping

(b) *Fig* (*impulsion*) **donner de l'é. à l'industrie** to give a boost to industry

(c) (*vitesse*) momentum, impetus; **emporté par son é., il trébucha** carried away by his own momentum, he tripped; **emportée par son é. la voiture alla au fossé** gathering momentum, the car went into the ditch; **perdre de l'é.** to lose momentum; *Fig* **le général Dupont brisa l'é. des forces ennemies en Libye** General Dupont broke the momentum of the enemy forces in Libya; **impossible de les arrêter dans leur é.** it's impossible to stop them once they've got going *or* started

(d) (*transport*) (*d'enthousiasme*) burst, outburst; (*de tendresse, passion*) surge; **un é. créatif** a creative outburst; **dans un é. amoureux** in a surge of love; **il ne connaissait plus aucun des élans de sa jeunesse** he no longer felt the impulses of his youth; **éprouver un é. (naturel) vers qn** to feel (naturally) drawn to sb; **rien n'a jamais pu briser l'é. qui me portait vers elle** nothing could ever break the force which drew me towards her; **contenir** *ou* **maîtriser ses élans** to keep one's impulses in check

(e) (*ferveur*) fervour, *US* fervor; **parler avec é.** to speak with fervour *or* fervently

(f) (*accent*) **sa voix avait des élans lyriques** her voice had a lyrical ring; **le violon avait des élans plaintifs** the violin had plaintive tones

(g) *Phil* **é. vital** life force
élan[2] *nm* (*cerf*) (Scandinavian) elk; **é. du Canada** moose
élancé [elɑ̃se] *adj* (*silhouette, personne, arbre etc*) slim, slender; **aux formes élancées** (*bateau, voiture*) streamlined
élancement [elɑ̃smɑ̃] *nm* (*douleur*) shooting pain
élancer [elɑ̃se] **(j'élançai(s); n. élançons) 1** *vi* **ma jambe m'élance, ça m'élance dans la jambe** I've got shooting pains in my leg **2 s'élancer** *vpr* (*en courant*) to rush, to dash; *Sp* (*prendre son élan*) to take a run-up; **s'é. dans une course effrénée** to break into a mad dash; **s'é. sur qn** to rush *or* make a rush at sb; **le chat s'élança sur moi** the cat flew at me; **s'é. à l'assaut des vagues** (*d'un navire, un surfeur*) to take to the water, *Litt* to brave the seas; **s'é. à l'assaut d'un sommet** to attack *or* tackle a peak; **s'é. vers le ciel** to soar skywards **3** *vt* **la cathédrale élance ses flèches vers le ciel** the cathedral's spires soar skywards
élargir [elarʒir] **1** *vt* **(a)** (*route, rue etc*) to widen, to broaden; (*robe*) to let out; (*chaussures*) to stretch; (*tube*) to expand; (*trou*) to enlarge; (*propriété*) to enlarge, to extend, to add to; **robe qui élargit les épaules** dress which makes the shoulders look broader

(b) *Fig* (*groupe, gamme de produits*) to expand; (*connaissance, débat*) to broaden, to widen, to expand; (*horizon*) to broaden; **é. un marché** to broaden a market

(c) *Jur* (*prisonnier*) to release, to set free

2 *vi F* **il a élargi** he's got bigger

3 s'élargir *vpr* **(a)** (*d'une route, une rue etc*) to widen (out), to broaden (out); (*de chaussures, d'un jean etc*) to stretch

(b) *Fig* (*d'un groupe*) to expand; (*de son horizon*) to broaden; (*d'un débat*) to broaden, to widen; **ses idées se sont élargies au contact des jeunes** he became more broadminded through being in contact with young people
élargissement [elarʒismɑ̃] *nm* **(a)** (*d'une route, d'une rue etc*) widening, broadening; (*d'une robe*) letting out; (*de chaussures*) stretching; (*d'une propriété*) extension, enlargement **(b)** *Fig* (*d'un groupe, des connaissances*) expansion; (*de son horizon*) broadening; (*d'un débat*) broadening, widening, expansion; **l'é. de la CEE** the enlargement *or* expansion of the EEC; *Mktg* **é. du marché** market rollout **(c)** *Jur* (*d'un prisonnier*) release
élasticité [elastisite] *nf* (*d'un corps, d'une matière etc*) elasticity; (*d'un pas*) springiness (**de** of), spring (**de** in); *Fig* (*de principes etc*) flexibility; *Com* **é. de l'offre/de la demande** elasticity of supply/demand; *Com* **é. des prix** price elasticity
élastique [elastik] **1** *adj* **(a)** (*corps, matière etc*) elastic; **gomme é.** india rubber; **balle é.** rubber ball; **la viande est é.** the meat is rubbery; **d'un pas é.** with a springy *or* buoyant step **(b)** *Fig* (*règlement, principes etc*) flexible; **conscience é.** accommodating conscience **2** *nm* **(a)** *Couture etc* elastic; **en é.** elastic **(b)** (*de bureau*) elastic *or Br* rubber band; *Fig F* **les lâcher avec un é.** to have moths in one's wallet **(c)** (*jeu*) **jouer à l'é.** to play at elastics; **saut à l'é.** bungee jumping
élastiqué [elastike] *adj* elasticated
élastomère [elastɔmɛr] *nm Ch, Ind* elastomer
Elbe [ɛlb] **1** *nf* **(l'île d')E.** (the island of) Elba **2** *nm* (river) Elbe
électeur, -trice [elɛktœr, -tris] *n* **(a)** *Pol* elector, voter; **mes électeurs** the people who voted for me; **carte d'é.** voting *or* polling card **(b)** *Hist* **É.** Elector; **Électrice** Electress
électif, -ive [elɛktif, -iv] *adj* elective
élection [elɛksjɔ̃] *nf* **(a)** (*d'un député, un pape, une reine de beauté etc*) election; **é. partielle** by-election; **jour des élections** polling *or* election day; **annuler l'é. de qn** to unseat sb; **se présenter aux élections** to stand as a candidate (in the elections), to stand for election; **remporter les élections** to win the election **(b)** (*choix*) election, choice; **mon pays d'é.** the country of my choice; *Jur* **faire é. de domicile** to elect domicile; *Rel* **le peuple d'é.** the chosen people
▶ **élection**: **élections européennes** European elections; **élections législatives** (parliamentary) election(s), general election; **élections municipales** = local (council) elections; **é. présidentielle** presidential election
électoral, -ale, -aux, -ales [elɛktɔral, -o] *adj* (*campagne, comité, promesses*) election; **circonscription électorale** constituency, *Can* riding; **liste électorale** electoral register *or* roll; **corps é.** electorate
électoralisme [elɛktɔralism] *nm Péj* electioneering; **il ne fait que de l'é.** he's just electioneering, he's just out to get *or* catch votes
électoraliste [elɛktɔralist] **1** *adj* electioneering, vote-catching **2** *n* **tous ceux qui se sont présentés ne sont que des électoralistes** all of the candidates are just electioneering *or* are just out to get *or* catch votes
électorat [elɛktɔra] *nm* **(a)** *Pol* voters, electorate; **consulter l'é.** to go to the country; **l'é. communiste/féminin** the communist/female vote, communist/female voters **(b)** (*droit de vote*) franchise **(c)** *Hist* **É.** electorate
Électre [elɛktr] *nf* Electra
électricien, -ienne [elɛktrisjɛ̃, -jɛn] *n* electrician; **ingénieur é.** electrical engineer
électricité [elɛktrisite] *nf* electricity; **panne d'é.** power cut *or* failure; **faire poser** *ou* **installer l'é.** to have electricity put in *or* installed; **il faut refaire l'é. de la cuisine** we're going to have to rewire the kitchen; *Fig F* **il y a de l'é. dans l'air** the atmosphere is electric
▶ **électricité**: **é. atmosphérique** atmospherics; **é. statique** static (electricity)
électrification [elɛktrifikasjɔ̃] *nf* electrification
électrifier [elɛktrifje] *vt* (*chemin de fer etc*) to electrify; (*village etc*) to bring electricity to, to electrify
électrique [elɛktrik] *adj* **(a)** (*courant, train etc, Fig atmosphère*) electric **(b)** (*ingénierie*) electrical
électriquement [elɛktrikmɑ̃] *adv* electrically
électrisant [elɛktrizɑ̃] *adj Fig* electrifying
électrisation [elɛktrizasjɔ̃] *nf Él* electrification; **à é. positive** positively charged, charged with positive electricity; *Fig* **elle provoque l'é. des foules** she electrifies the crowds
électriser [elɛktrize] *vt Él, Fig* (*audience*) to electrify; *Él* **fil électrisé** live wire
électro- [elɛktro] *préf* electro-
électro-acousticien, -ienne, *pl* **électro-acousticien(ne)s** **1** *n* acoustoelectronics expert **2** *adj* acoustoelectronic
électro-aimant, *pl* **électro-aimants** *nm* electromagnet

électrocardiogramme [elɛktrokardjɔgram] *nm Méd* electrocardiogram
électrocardiographe [eletrokardjɔgraf] *nm Méd* electrocardiograph
électrocardiographie [elɛktrokardjɔgrafi] *nf Méd* electrocardiography
électrochimie [elɛktroʃimi] *nf* electrochemistry
électrochimique [elɛktroʃimik] *adj* electrochemical
électrochoc [elɛktroʃɔk] *nm Méd, Fig* electric shock; **traitement par électrochocs** electric shock treatment; **on lui a fait des électrochocs** he was given electric shock treatment
électrocuter [elɛktrɔkyte] *vt* to electrocute; **se faire é.** to be electrocuted
électrocution [elɛktrokysjɔ̃] *nf* electrocution
électrode [elɛktrɔd] *nf* electrode; **é. de masse** earth electrode
électrodynamique [elɛktrodinamik] **1** *adj* electrodynamic **2** *nf* electrodynamics
électro-encéphalogramme, *pl* **électro-encéphalogrammes** *nm Méd* electroencephalogram
électro-encéphalographie *nf Méd* electroencephalography
électrogène [elɛktrɔʒɛn] *adj Él* **groupe é.** generating unit; **appareil é.** (*d'un poisson*) electric organ
électroluminescent [elɛktrolyminesɑ̃] *adj* light-emitting
électrolyse [elɛktrɔliz] *nf* electrolysis
électrolyser [elɛktrɔlize] *vt* to electrolyse
électrolyte [elɛktrɔlit] *nm* electrolyte
électrolytique [elɛktrɔlitik] *adj* electrolytic
électromagnétique [elɛktromaɲetik] *adj* electromagnetic
électromagnétisme [elɛktromaɲetism] *nm* electromagnetism
électromécanicien, -ienne [elɛktromekanisjɛ̃, -jɛn] *n* electrical engineer
électromécanique [elɛktromekanik] **1** *adj* electromechanical **2** *nf* electromechanics
électroménager [elɛktromenaʒe] **1** *adj* **appareils électroménagers** household appliances *or US* electricals **2** *nm* household appliances *or US* electricals
électrométallurgie [elɛktrometalyrʒi] *nf* electrometallurgy
électrométallurgique [eletrometalyrʒik] *adj* electrometallurgical
électromètre [elɛktrɔmɛtr] *nm* electrometer
électromoteur, -trice [elɛktromɔtœr, -tris] **1** *adj* electromotive **2** *nm* electromotor
électron [elɛktrɔ̃] *nm Phys* electron
électronégatif, -ive [elɛktronegatif -iv] *adj* electronegative
électronicien, -ienne [elɛktrɔnisjɛ̃, -jɛn] *n* electronics specialist; **ingénieur é.** electronics engineer
électronique [elɛktrɔnik] **1** *adj* electronic; (*faisceau, flux, microscope, télescope*) electron **2** *nf* electronics; **é. aérospatiale** avionics
électroniquement [elɛktrɔnikmɑ̃] *adv* electronically
électronucléaire [elɛktronykleɛr] **1** *adj* (*industrie, centrale etc*) nuclear power; **énergie é.** nuclear power **2** *nm* nuclear power
électronvolt [elɛktrɔ̃vɔlt] *nm* electronvolt
électrophone [elɛktrɔfɔn] *nm* record player
électropositif, -ive [elɛktropozitif, -iv] *adj* electropositive
électroscope [elɛktrɔskɔp] *nm* electroscope
électrosensible [elɛktrosɑ̃sibl] *adj* electrosensitive
électrostatique [elɛktrostatik] **1** *adj* electrostatic **2** *nf* electrostatics
électrotechnique [elɛktrotɛknik] **1** *adj* electrotechnical **2** *nf* electrical engineering
électrothérapie [elɛktroterapi] *nf Méd* (*pratique*) electrotherapy; (*étude*) electrotherapeutics
électrovalve [elɛktrovalv] *nf Aut* solenoid; **é. de starter** starter solenoid
électrovanne [elɛktrovan] *nf* solenoid valve
élégamment [elegamɑ̃] *adv* (*vêtu*) elegantly, smartly; (*maquillée*) smartly; (*agir*) courteously; **coiffée é.** with an elegant *or* smart hairstyle
élégance [elegɑ̃s] *nf* elegance; (*d'un geste, d'un comportement*) courtesy; (*d'une méthode, d'une solution etc*) neatness; **l'é. du chat siamois** the elegance *or* grace of a Siamese cat; **habillé avec é.** elegantly *or* smartly dressed; **savoir perdre avec é.** to be a good loser; **elle a eu l'é. de ne pas protester** she had the courtesy not to protest
élégant, -ante [elegɑ̃] **1** *adj* (*vêtements, restaurant, style etc*) elegant; (*méthode, solution*) neat; (*geste, comportement*) courteous; **c'était une façon élégante de me dire que ...** it was a polite *or* diplomatic way of telling me that ...; **il use de procédés peu élégants** he uses rather callous measures **2** *nm Arch* **un é.** a man of fashion, a dandy **3** *nf* **une élégante** a well- *or* smartly *or* fashionably dressed woman
élégiaque [eleʒjak] *adj* elegiac
élégie [eleʒi] *nf* elegy
élément [elemɑ̃] *nm* **(a)** (*naturel*) element; **les quatre éléments** the four elements; *Fig* **être dans son é.** to be in one's element; *Fig* **je ne me sens pas dans mon é. ici** I'm not in my element here, I'm like a fish out of water here
(b) *Ch* element; *Phys* **é. radioactif** radioactive element
(c) (*partie*) (*d'une structure, un problème etc*) element, component, constituent; (*d'un médicament*) ingredient; **les éléments d'un ensemble** the elements *or* parts of a whole; *Tech* **é. chauffant** heating unit *or* element; *Aut* **é. filtrant en papier** paper filtering element; *Ordinat* **é. de menu** menu item; *MecE* **é. mobile** working part; *Électron* **é. de calculateur** *ou* **de calculatrice** *ou* **électronique** computer unit; **éléments préfabriqués** prefabricated *or* ready-made units; **mobilier formé d'éléments** modular furniture
(d) (*personne*) element; **les éléments indésirables de la population** the undesirable elements of the population; **l'é. féminin** the female element *or* contingent; **l'é. féminin est faiblement représenté dans cette société** there are few women in the company; **j'ai de bons éléments dans ma classe** I've got some good material in my class; **avec lui, nous avons perdu un très bon é.** we've lost a good man in him
(e) *Él* (*d'une batterie, d'un accumulateur*) cell; **batterie de cinq éléments** five-cell battery
(f) (*rudiment*) (*de science etc*) **éléments** elements, rudiments; **avoir quelques éléments en espagnol** to have elementary *or* rudimentary Spanish; **Éléments de chimie** Elementary Chemistry
(g) (*donnée*) **éléments** data, information; **l'é. décisif** the deciding factor; **aucun é. nouveau ne s'est produit** no new information has emerged
(h) *Mil* **éléments blindés/motorisés** armoured/motorized units
élémentaire [elemɑ̃tɛr] *adj* **(a)** *Ch, Phys* (*analyse chimique, particule d'atome etc*) elementary **(b)** (*de base*) (*connaissance*) elementary, rudimentary; (*cours, problème etc*) elementary; (*minimal*) (*habitation etc*) basic, rudimentary; *Scol* **cours é.** = second and third years of primary school; **cours é. de ski/danse** skiing/dance classes for beginners; **c'est é.!** (*évident*) it's elementary!, it's simple!; (*le minimum*) it's the least I/you/*etc* could do!; **cela fait partie de la politesse é.** it's only common courtesy
éléphant [elefɑ̃] *nm* elephant; **é. mâle/femelle** bull/cow elephant; **é. marin** *ou* **de mer** elephant seal, sea elephant; **é. d'Afrique/d'Asie** African/Indian elephant; **comme un é. dans un magasin de porcelaine** like a bull in a china shop
éléphanteau, -eaux [elefɑ̃to] *nm* elephant calf; (*très jeune*) baby elephant
éléphantesque [elefɑ̃tɛsk] *adj F* elephantine, gigantic, colossal; **elle est d'une bêtise é.** she is colossally stupid
éléphantiasis [elefɑ̃tjazis] *nf Méd* elephantiasis
élevage [elvaʒ] *nm* **(a)** (*de bovins, chevaux, moutons etc*) breeding, rearing; **l'é.** stock breeding; **é. intensif/en batterie** intensive/battery farming; **é. des animaux à fourrure** fur farming; **faire de l'é.** to breed *or* rear cattle, to be a stock breeder; **région d'é.** breeding area; **poulet d'é.** battery-reared chicken **(b)** (*ferme*) *Br* (stock) farm, *Am* ranch, *Austr* station
élévateur, -trice [elevatœr, -tris] **1** *adj* **chariot é. à fourche** fork-lift truck **2** *nm* **(a)** (*appareil*) elevator, lift, hoist; **é. à bascule** tip; **é. à augets** *ou* **à godets** bucket elevator; **é. (à fourche)** fork-lift truck **(b)** *Él* **é. de tension** step-up transformer
élévation [elevasjɔ̃] *nf* **(a)** (*action d'élever*) (*d'un mur, de la voix etc*) raising; (*de la température, des prix etc*) raising, increasing; (*d'une statue etc*) erection, setting up; *Rel* (*de l'hostie*) elevation; *Math* **é. d'un nombre au carré/à la puissance 10** raising a number to the square root/to the power of 10
(b) (*action de s'élever*) (*de température, prix etc*) rise, increase; **é. du niveau des eaux** rise in water level; **é. du pouls** quickening of the pulse
(c) *Fig* **lire Platon contribue à l'é. de l'esprit** reading Plato improves the mind; **é. des sentiments/du caractère** nobility of sentiments/character
(d) *Archit* (*projection*) elevation
(e) (*tertre*) rise (in the ground), mound
élévatoire [elevatwar] *adj* (*appareil*) lifting, hoisting
élevé [elve] *adj* **(a)** (*montagne, prix*) high; *Fig* (*style, esprit*) noble, elevated; (*rang, position*) high, exalted; **l'officier ayant le grade le plus é.** the senior *or* highest-ranking officer; **il occupe un rang é. dans ce parti** he ranks high in the party; **de rang é.** high-ranking; **pouls é.** rapid pulse **(b)** (*éduqué*) **bien é.** well brought up, well-bred, well-mannered;

mal é. badly brought up, ill-bred, ill-mannered; *F* **c'est très mal é. de parler la bouche pleine** it's very rude *or* very bad manners to speak with your mouth full; **c'est un mal é., ce garçon** he has bad manners, that boy

élève [elɛv] **1** *n Scol* pupil, student; (*d'un peintre, un musicien etc*) pupil **2** *nf* **(a)** (*animal*) young stock animal **(b)** (*plante*) seedling

▶ **élève: é. infirmière** student nurse; *Mil* **é. officier** cadet; **é. pilote** trainee *or* student pilot

élever [elve] **(j'élève, n. élevons; j'élèverai) 1** *vt* **(a)** (*faire monter*) (*niveau d'eau, voix etc*) to raise; (*prix, température etc*) to increase, to raise; (*charge*) to lift up, to raise; **é. un nombre au carré/au cube** to square/cube a number; **é. un nombre à la puissance 4** to raise a number to the power 4; **é. une perpendiculaire** to raise a perpendicular

(b) (*dresser*) (*monument, statue, mur etc*) to erect, to put up; (*les bras, le poing, les yeux*) to raise; *Fig* (*objection, difficultés*) to raise; *Fig* **quelqu'un a-t-il une critique à é.?** does anyone have any criticism to make?; *Fig* **é. des autels à qn** to praise sb to the skies

(c) (*rehausser*) (*immeuble, mur etc*) to raise, to make higher; (*plafond, plancher*) to raise; **é. un mur de 20 cm** to raise a wall by 20 cm, to make a wall 20 cm higher

(d) (*porter à un rang supérieur*) to promote **(au rang de** to)

(e) (*édifier*) (*esprit*) to improve; **é. le débat** to raise the tone of the proceedings

(f) (*éduquer*) (*enfant*) to bring up, to raise; **bébé élevé au sein/au biberon** breast-/bottle-fed baby; *F* **é. qn dans du coton** to raise sb in cotton wool, to coddle sb; *F* **j'ai été élevé à la dure** I was brought up the hard way

(g) (*faire l'élevage de*) (*bovins, chevaux etc*) to rear, to breed; (*lapins*) to breed; (*abeilles, volaille*) to keep

2 s'élever *vpr* **(a)** (*avec mouvement*) to rise (up); **l'hélicoptère s'élevait doucement dans les airs** the helicopter rose smoothly into the air; **un cri s'éleva** a shout went up

(b) (*sans mouvement*) to stand; **le château s'élève sur la colline** the castle stands on the hill; **la maison s'élevait dans le soleil couchant** the house stood silhouetted against the setting sun

(c) (*monter*) (*de la température, des prix etc*) to rise, to increase, to go up

(d) (*paraître*) (*de doutes, difficultés*) to arise

(e) (*protester*) **s'é. contre qch/qn** to rise up against sth/sb; **je m'élève contre la validité de ce testament** I contest the validity of this will

(f) *Fig* **s'é. à force de travail** to work one's way up; **s'é. socialement** to climb up the social ladder; **s'é. au-dessus des préjugés** to rise above prejudice; **ses pensées ne s'élèvent jamais au-delà de sa petite personne** his thoughts never rise above himself; **des lectures qui permettent à l'âme de s'élever** spiritually uplifting reading matter

(g) (*atteindre*) **s'é. à** to come to, to amount to

éleveur, -euse [elvœr, -øz] **1** *n* (*de bovins*) stock breeder, cattle farmer; **é. de chevaux/chiens** horse/dog breeder; **é. de moutons/poulets** sheep/poultry farmer **2** *nf* **éleveuse** (*pour poussins*) brooder

elfe [ɛlf] *nm* [①**A12**,1,d] elf

élider [elide] *Ling* **1** *vt* (*voyelle*) to elide **2 s'élider** *vpr* to be elided, to elide

éligibilité [eliʒibilite] *nf Pol* eligibility

éligible [eliʒibl] *adj Pol* eligible

élimé [elime] *adj* (*tissu, vêtement*) worn, threadbare

élimer [elime] **1** *vt* (*tissu, vêtement*) to wear thin **2 s'élimer** *vpr* to wear thin

élimination [eliminasjɔ̃] *nf aussi Physiol* elimination; **procéder par é.** to use a process of elimination; **en procédant par é.** by a process of elimination; *Sp etc* **concours sur le principe d'é.** knock-out competition; *Ind etc* **é. des déchets** waste disposal; *Rad* **é. des parasites** suppression of noise *or* interference

éliminatoire [eliminatwar] **1** *adj* (*examen*) qualifying; **5 est une note é.** five counts as a fail; **il a eu une note é.** he didn't get a pass mark; **épreuve é.** qualifying heat *or* round, qualifier **2** *nf* qualifying *or* eliminating heat *or* round, qualifier

éliminer [elimine] **1** *vt* (*candidat, suspect etc*) to eliminate; (*possibilité, théorie*) to rule out, to exclude; *Physiol* (*déchets*) to get rid of, to eliminate; **être éliminé** (*d'un candidat*) to be knocked out *or* eliminated; **ils ont tous été éliminés pour dopage** they were all disqualified for drug-taking **2** *vi Physiol* to get rid of *or* eliminate body wastes

élire [elir] *vt* (*conj like* **lire**) **(a)** (*candidat, représentant etc*) to elect; **é. un député** ≈ to elect *or* return a Member of Parliament; **é. qn président** to elect sb president, to vote sb in as president **(b) é. domicile** to take up residence **(à** in); *Jur* to elect domicile **(à** in)

élisabéthain, -aine [elizabetɛ̃, -ɛn] **1** *adj* Elizabethan **2** *n* **É.** Elizabethan

élision [elizjɔ̃] *nf* [①**B2**] *Ling* elision

élite [elit] *nf* élite, elite; **les élites** the élite; **l'é. de ...** the cream *or* élite of ...; **personnel d'é.** select *or* hand-picked personnel; **régiment/tireur d'é.** crack regiment/shot

élitisme [elitism] *nm* elitism

élitiste [elitist] *adj, n* elitist

élixir [eliksir] *nm* elixir; **l'é. de longue vie** the elixir of life; **é. parégorique** = medicine for treating diarrhoea, *Spéc* paregoric (elixir)

elle, *pl* **elles** [ɛl] *pron pers f* [①**A26**; **B17**; **B63**,2] **(a)** (*sujet*) (*personne*) she; (*chose*) it; (*bébé, animal, nation, voiture*) it, she; **elles** they; **e. chante** she sings; **elles dansent** they dance; **e. arrivée, la fête a pu commencer** once she had arrived the party was able to start; **e., dégoûtée, a fait la grimace** she grimaced in disgust; **e., e. n'aurait même pas levé le petit doigt** she wouldn't have raised a finger; **e., se marier? tu ne la connais pas!** her get married? you don't know her!; **qui a fait ça? – c'est e.** who did that? – she did *or* her; **ah!, e. est bien bonne, celle-là!** that's a good one!

(b) (*objet*) (*personne*) her; (*chose*) it; (*bébé, animal etc*) it, her; **elles** them; **et e., tu l'oublies?** and are you forgetting her?; **tu la connais, e.?** do you know her?; **tu les imagines, e. et lui, sur des skis!** imagine the pair of them on skis!

(c) (*avec qui, que*) **c'est e. qui est partie la première** she left first; **c'est e. que j'ai rencontrée dans la rue** it was her I met in the street; **son père est déjà là et e. qui n'arrive pas** her father's here already and she hasn't arrived yet; **c'est à e. qu'il veut avoir affaire** it's her he wants to talk to

(d) (*avec préposition*) **je suis content d'e./d'elles** I am pleased with her/them; **e. ne pense qu'à e.** she thinks only of herself; **dis-le-lui, à e.** tell her; **ce n'est pas à moi, c'est à e.** it's not mine, it's hers; **c'est à e. de dire si elle veut venir** it's up to her to say if she wants to come or not; **elle possède une entreprise à e.** she has her own company; **je l'ai entendu dire par une relation à e.** I heard it from a relation of hers; **un portrait d'e.** (*qu'elle a fait*) a portrait by her; (*où elle est représentée*) a portrait of her; **il aimait sa patrie et mourut pour e.** he loved his country and died for it

(e) (*dans comparaisons*) **il est mieux qu'e.** he is better than she is *or* than her; **il boit plus qu'e.** he drinks more than she does *or* than her; **je fais mon travail aussi bien qu'e.** I work as well as she does, my work is as good as hers; **je fais comme e.** I do what she does

(f) (*interrogatif, emphatique*) **viendra-t-e.?** will she come?; **ta directrice est-e. toujours en activité?** is your boss still working?; **la télévision est-e. toujours en panne?** is the television still not working?; **qu'e. est jolie, cette broche!** how pretty that brooch is!; **eh bien, ta cousine, e. n'est pas près de me revoir** well, your cousin isn't likely to see me again in a hurry

ellébore [ɛlebɔr] *nm* (*plante*) hellebore

elle-même [ɛlmɛm] *pron pers* (*d'une personne*) herself; (*d'une chose*) itself; (*d'un bébé, d'un animal, d'une nation*) itself, herself; **elles-mêmes** themselves; **mais e. n'est pas une modèle** but she's no paragon herself; **c'est e. qui me l'a dit** she told me so herself, she herself told me so

ellipse [elips] *nf* **(a)** *Gram* ellipsis **(b)** *Géom* ellipse

ellipsoïdal, -ale, -aux, -ales [elipsɔidal, -o] *adj Géom* ellipsoidal

ellipsoïde [elipsɔid] *Géom* **1** *adj* ellipsoidal **2** *nm* ellipsoid

elliptique [eliptik] *adj Gram, Géom* elliptical; **style e.** elliptical style

elliptiquement [eliptikmɑ̃] *adv Gram* elliptically

élocution [elɔkysjɔ̃] *nf* (*diction*) elocution; (*débit*) delivery; **avoir une é. trop rapide** to speak too quickly; **avoir une é. claire** to speak *or* enunciate clearly; **défaut d'é.** speech impediment *or* defect

éloge [elɔʒ] *nm* **(a)** (*discours*) eulogy; **é. funèbre** eulogy, funeral oration **(b)** (*louange*) praise; **faire l'é. de qn/qch** to speak very highly of *or* in praise of sb/sth; **faire son propre é.** to sing one's own praises, *Br* to blow one's own trumpet; **digne d'éloges** praiseworthy; **c'est tout à votre é. d'avoir accepté** it's to your credit that you accepted; **il fait du bénévolat et c'est tout à son é.** to his credit, he does volunteer work

élogieusement [elɔʒjøzmɑ̃] *adv* **parler é. de** to speak very highly of

élogieux, -ieuse [elɔʒjø, -jøz] *adj* (*discours, article etc*) of praise, *Fml* eulogistic, laudatory; **parler de qn/qch en**

termes é. to speak very highly of sb/sth; **les critiques ont été é. avec son dernier film** the critics praised his last film

éloigné [elwaɲe] *adj (endroit, passé, futur etc)* distant, remote; *(parent)* distant; **la ville est très éloignée** the town is a long way away *or* off, the town is very far away; **la ville est éloignée de cinq kilomètres** the town is five kilometres away; **ils sont éloignés d'un kilomètre** they are one kilometre apart, there is a kilometre between them; **maison éloignée de la gare** house a long way from the station; **notre mariage est encore à une date éloignée** our wedding is still a long way off; **la date en est trop éloignée pour que je puisse savoir si je serai libre** it's too far away for me to say whether I'll be free or not; **dans un avenir peu é.** in the near *or* not-too-distant future; **rien n'est plus é. de ma pensée** nothing is further from my thoughts; **se tenir é. de qch** to keep away from sth, to steer clear of sth; *Fig* **je ne suis plus é. de croire que ...** I'm coming round to believe that *or* to the belief that ...

éloignement [elwaɲ(ə)mɑ̃] *nm* **(a)** *(action) (d'une personne indésirable etc)* removal; **l'é. de sa famille est nécessaire à sa guérison** his family must be kept away if he is to recover **(b)** *(fait d'être éloigné)* absence; **je ne supporte plus notre é.** I can't bear us to be apart any longer; **plus l'é. dure, plus il renforce notre amour** the longer we are apart *or* the longer the separation lasts, the stronger our love grows; **l'é. est difficile à vivre** it is difficult to be apart *or* separated **(c)** *(distance) (dans l'espace)* distance, remoteness; *(dans le temps)* remoteness; **plus l'é. est grand, plus les objets paraissent petits** the greater the distance, the smaller objects seem; **l'é. de nos deux bureaux ne favorise pas la communication** the distance between our two offices does not help communication; **vivre dans l'é. des villes** to live far away from town; **vivre dans l'é. du monde** to live apart *or* withdrawn from the world

éloigner [elwaɲe] **1** *vt* **(a)** *(écarter dans l'espace) (personne, objet)* to move away, to take away, to remove; **é. qch de qch** to move sth away from sth; **é. qn du feu/de la voiture** to move sb away from the fire/car; **notre nouvelle maison nous éloigne du centre ville** our new house puts us at a distance from the centre of town; **é. les loups/les moustiques** to keep the wolves/mosquitoes away *or* at bay; **tes parents cherchent à m'é. de toi** your parents are trying to keep me away from you; **mon travail m'éloigne de toute vie sociale** my work makes it impossible to socialize **(b)** *(dans le temps)* **chaque jour m'éloigne un peu plus de cette époque** that time recedes with each day that passes **(c)** *(distraire, détourner)* **é. une crainte/une pensée/des soupçons** to banish a fear/dismiss a thought/avert suspicion; **é. qn de son travail** to keep sb away from his work **2 s'éloigner** *vpr* **(a)** *(s'écarter dans l'espace) (d'une personne)* to move away **(de** from); *(d'un objet)* to move away *or* off; **voudriez-vous vous é. un peu?** would you please stand further away *or* back, would you please move back *or* away a little; **ne vous éloignez pas!** don't go too far away!; **l'orage s'éloigne** the storm is passing; **les bêtes s'éloignent du camp grâce au feu** the animals keep away from the camp because of the fire; *Fig* **avec le temps, ce souvenir s'éloignera** the memory will fade with time **(b)** *(se distraire, se détourner)* **s'é. de la vérité** to stray *or* wander from the truth; **s'é. de son devoir** to neglect one's duty; **s'é. du sujet** to wander from the subject; **s'é. de tout le monde** to distance oneself from everybody; **je sens bien que tu t'éloignes (de moi)** I feel you're growing away from me; **le temps a fait qu'ils se sont éloignés l'un de l'autre** they drifted apart with time

élongation [elɔ̃gasjɔ̃] *nf Méd* pulled muscle; **se faire une é.** to pull a muscle

éloquemment [elɔkamɑ̃] *adv* eloquently

éloquence [elɔkɑ̃s] *nf* **(a)** *(loquacité) (d'une personne, Fig d'un tableau, de l'expression du visage)* eloquence **(b)** *(rhétorique)* oratory

éloquent [elɔkɑ̃] *adj (personne, discours)* eloquent; *Fig (silence, geste etc)* eloquent, expressive; **ces chiffres sont éloquents** the figures speak volumes *or* speak for themselves; **sa tête était assez éloquente pour qu'il n'ait pas eu besoin de parler** his face said it all, his face said it *or* spoke for him

élu, -ue [ely] **1** *adj Pol* elected; **président é.** president elect; *Bible* **le peuple é.** the chosen people **2** *n* **(a)** *Rel* **les élus** the elect **(b)** *Pol (député, conseiller)* elected representative; **les élus du peuple** the people's representatives **(c)** *Hum* **qui est l'heureuse élue?** who's the lucky girl *or* lady?; **l'é. de son cœur** the man of her choice

élucidation [elysidasjɔ̃] *nf* elucidation

élucider [elyside] *vt (mystère)* to clear up; *(question, problème)* to clarify

élucubrations [elykybrasjɔ̃] *nfpl Péj* flights of fancy, wild imaginings

élucubrer [elykybre] *vt Péj* to dream up

éluder [elyde] *vt* to evade, to elude

élusif, -ive [elyzif, -iv] *adj (réponse, attitude)* evasive

Élysée [elize] **1** *nm* **(a)** *Myth* **L'É.** Elysium **(b)** *Pol* **(le palais de) l'É.** the Élysée palace *(the residence of the President of the French Republic)* **2** *adj* **les Champs Élysées** *Myth* the Elysian Fields; *(à Paris)* the Champs Élysées

élyséen, -enne [elizeɛ̃, -ɛn] *adj* **(a)** *Myth* Elysian **(b)** *Pol* of the Élysée palace

em [ɛm] *nm Typ* em

émaciation [emasjasjɔ̃] *nf* emaciation

émacié [emasje] *adj (silhouette, visage etc)* emaciated

émacier (s') [semasje] *vpr* to become emaciated

émail, -aux [emaj, -o] *nm* enamel; *Cér* glaze; **en é.** *(casserole etc)* enamel(led)

émaillage [emajaʒ] *nm* **(a)** *(des métaux précieux etc)* enamelling **(b)** *Cér* glazing

émailler [emaje] *vt* **(a)** *(métal etc)* to enamel; **émaillé au four** stove-enamelled **(b)** *Cér (porcelaine)* to glaze **(c)** *Fig (des fleurs, étoiles etc) (champs, ciel etc)* to stud, to spangle; **style émaillé de métaphores** style studded with metaphors

émailleur, -euse [emajœr, -øz] *n* enameller

émaillure [emajyr] *nf* enamelling, enamel work

émanation [emanasjɔ̃] *nf* emanation; **é. fétide** foul odour; *Fig* **cet ordre, é. de sa volonté ...** this order, an expression *or* a product of his will ...

émancipateur, -trice [emɑ̃sipatœr, -tris] **1** *adj* liberating, emancipating **2** *n* emancipator

émancipation [emɑ̃sipasjɔ̃] *nf* emancipation; *Fig (de l'esprit, de la pensée etc)* liberation, freeing; *Fig* **il est nécessaire d'amener les adolescents à une certaine é. dans leur façon de penser** adolescents must be made to achieve a degree of independence in their thinking

émancipé [emɑ̃sipe] *adj (femme etc)* emancipated

émanciper [emɑ̃sipe] **1** *vt (peuple, esclave)* to emancipate; *(femme)* to emancipate, to liberate; *Fig (esprit, pensée etc)* to liberate, to free **2 s'émanciper** *vpr* to become emancipated; *Fig* to become liberated; *Fig* **elle n'a jamais réussi à s'é. de l'éducation stricte qu'elle a reçue** she never managed to break free from her strict upbringing; **elle s'est drôlement émancipée** she's too emancipated by half

émaner [emane] *vi* **é. de** *(de fumée etc, Fig d'un ordre, du pouvoir, du charme)* to emanate from

émargement [emarʒəmɑ̃] *nm* **(a)** *(initiales)* initialling (in the margin); *(signature)* signature; **feuille d'é.** *(de présence)* attendance sheet; *(de paie)* pay sheet; **é. du courrier** signing for the mail **(b)** *(annotation)* marginal note **(c)** *Typ (de pages)* trimming

émarger [emarʒe] **(j'émargeai(s); n. émargeons) 1** *vt* **(a)** *Admin (document, compte etc)* to initial (in the margin); *(signer)* to sign; *(courrier)* to sign for **(b)** *(annoter) (livre etc)* to make marginal notes in **(c)** *Typ (pages etc)* to cut down *or* trim the margins of **2** *vi* to draw one's salary; **il émarge aux fonds secrets** he's paid out of the secret funds

émasculation [emaskylasjɔ̃] *nf* emasculation

émasculer [emaskyle] *vt* to emasculate

embâcle [ɑ̃bɑkl] *nm (obstruction dans un cours d'eau)* blockage; *(par un bloc de glace)* ice block *or* jam

emballage [ɑ̃balaʒ] *nm* **(a)** *(action)* packing; *(dans du papier)* wrapping; **papier d'e.** wrapping paper **(b)** *(boîte etc)* packaging, packing (material); *(papier)* wrapping; **emballages vides** (returned) empties **(c)** *Cyclisme* (final) spurt

▶ **emballage**: **e. consigné** returnable *or* refundable packaging; **e. perdu** non-returnable *or* throwaway *or* disposable packaging; *Com* **e. récupérable** recoverable packaging; **e. sous vide** vacuum-packed

emballé [ɑ̃bale] *adj F* (mad) keen, enthusiastic; **e. pour qch** (mad) keen on sth

emballement [ɑ̃balmɑ̃] *nm* **(a)** *(de moteur)* racing; *(de cheval)* bolting; **l'e. du cheval a provoqué la mort du cavalier** the rider was killed when the horse bolted **(b)** *(enthousiasme soudain)* burst of enthusiasm; *(colère)* surge of anger; **prompt aux emballements** easily carried away; **pas d'e.** *(par enthousiasme)* let's not get carried away!; *(par colère)* let's not get worked up! **(c)** *Bourse* boom **(de** in); **cela aboutirait certainement à l'e. de l'économie** that would definitely lead to the economy spiralling out of control

emballer [ɑ̃bale] **1** *vt* **(a)** *(empaqueter)* to pack; *(dans du papier)* to wrap; *(marchandises)* to package; **emballé sous vide** vacuum-packed; *Arg* **e. qn** *(arrêter)* to nick sb; *Arg* **e. une fille** *(draguer)* to pull a bird (**b**) (*moteur*) to race, to rev

(**c**) *F* (*enthousiasmer*) to excite, to thrill; **ça ne m'emballe pas vraiment de les voir** I'm not exactly thrilled about seeing them *or* mad keen to see them; **être emballé par qn/qch** to be (mad) keen on sb/sth

2 s'emballer *vpr* (**a**) (*d'un moteur*) to race; (*d'un cheval*) to bolt, to run away

(**b**) *F* (*se laisser emporter*) (*par enthousiasme*) to get carried away, to get excited; (*par colère*) to get worked up

(**c**) *Bourse* (*des cours, d'une monnaie*) to spiral out of control

emballeur, -euse [ɑ̃balœr, -øz] *n* packer

embarbouiller [ɑ̃barbuje] **1** *vt* (*personne*) to muddle, to confuse **2 s'embarbouiller** *vpr* to get muddled up

embarcadère [ɑ̃barkadɛr] *nm* landing stage, jetty

embarcation [ɑ̃barkasjɔ̃] *nf* (small) boat, small craft

embardée [ɑ̃barde] *nf Aut* swerve; *Naut* yaw; **faire une e.** (*d'une voiture*) to swerve; (*d'un bateau*) to yaw

embargo [ɑ̃bargo] *nm* embargo; **mettre l'e. sur** to put an embargo on, to embargo; **lever l'e. sur** to raise *or* lift the embargo on

embarqué [ɑ̃barke] *adj Aut, Av etc* on-board

embarquement [ɑ̃barkəmɑ̃] *nm* (**a**) (*action d'embarquer*) *Naut* (*de passagers*) embarkation; (*de marchandises*) shipping; (*dans un train, avion, car*) (*de passagers*) boarding; (*de marchandises*) loading; *Rail, Mil* (*de troupes*) entrainment; *Rail* **quai d'e.** departure platform; (*de chargement*) loading platform

(**b**) (*action de s'embarquer*) *Naut* embarkation, boarding; *Rail, Av, Aut* boarding; **le vol 123 est prêt pour l'e.** flight 123 is ready for boarding *or* is now boarding; **e. immédiat porte 5** now boarding at gate 5; **carte d'e.** boarding card

embarquer [ɑ̃barke] **1** *vt* (**a**) *Naut* (*passagers*) to embark; (*marchandises*) to ship; (*dans un train, avion, car*) (*passagers*) to take on board; (*marchandises*) to load; *Rail, Mil* (*troupes*) to entrain

(**b**) *Naut* **e. de l'eau** to take in *or* ship water

(**c**) *F* (*emmener*) to take (with one); (*voler*) to pinch, to nick; (*arrêter*) to nick

(**d**) (*entraîner*) (*en week-end, au cinéma*) to take *or* carry off; *Fig* **son divorce l'a embarqué dans un procès sans fin** his divorce got him involved *or* embroiled in an endless lawsuit; **elle embarque toujours sa copine dans ses escapades** she always involves her friend in her escapades; **une entreprise mal embarquée** an undertaking that has got off to a bad start

2 *vi* (**a**) *Naut* (*partir*) to embark (**pour** for); **e.** (**sur un navire**) to go on board, to board (a ship); **e.** (**dans un train/un autobus**) to board *or* get on (a train/bus); **une personne supplémentaire peut e. dans ma voiture** there's room for one more in my car; **on embarque à 7h demain matin** we're leaving at 7 o'clock tomorrow morning

(**b**) *Naut* **le bateau embarque** the boat is taking in water

3 s'embarquer *vpr* (**a**) (*partir*) to embark (**pour** for); **s'e. sur un navire** to go on board *or* to board a ship

(**b**) *Fig* **s'e. dans** to get mixed up *or* involved in; (*une entreprise, une discussion*) to embark on; **dans quoi est-ce que je me suis embarqué?** what have I got myself into?

embarras [ɑ̃bara] *nm* (**a**) (*situation difficile*) difficulty, trouble; *F* fix; **tirer qn d'e.** to help sb out of trouble *or* a difficulty *or F* a fix; **n'avoir que l'e. du choix** to be spoiled for choice; **je suis dans l'e.** I'm in trouble *or F* in a fix *or* a bind

(**b**) (*difficulté financière*) **se trouver** *ou* **être dans l'e.** to be in (financial) difficulties

(**c**) (*gêne*) embarrassment; **répondre avec e.** to reply with embarrassment, to reply embarrassedly *or* in confusion; **plonger qn dans l'e.** to embarrass sb

(**d**) (*obstacle*) **je vous donne beaucoup d'e.** I'm putting you to a lot of bother *or* trouble; **faire des** *ou* **de l'e.** to make a fuss, to make a song and dance (**au sujet de** about); **être un e. pour les autres** to be a bother to other people

(**e**) *Aut* **e. de voitures, e. de la circulation** traffic hold-up

(**f**) *Méd* **e. gastrique** upset stomach

embarrassant [ɑ̃barasɑ̃] *adj* (**a**) (*qui encombre*) (*colis, valise etc*) cumbersome (**b**) (*qui gêne*) (*question, situation*) embarrassing, awkward

embarrassé [ɑ̃barase] *adj* (**a**) (*encombré*) (*table, pièce etc*) cluttered; **avoir les mains embarrassées** to have one's hands full

(**b**) (*confus*) (*gestes*) hampered; (*style*) awkward; **prononciation embarrassée** unclear *or* garbled pronunciation; **explications embarrassées** involved *or* confused explanations; **dès qu'il met un costume, ses gestes sont embarrassés** he feels hampered in a suit

(**c**) (*gêné*) (*personne, sourire, manière etc*) embarrassed; **je suis très e. de devoir lui dire** I am very embarrassed about having to tell him; **me voilà bien e.** I'm in a really awkward situation, I'm really embarrassed; **il n'est jamais e.** he's never at a loss

(**d**) *Méd* **avoir l'estomac e.** to have an upset stomach; **avoir la langue embarrassée** to have a coated *or* furred tongue

embarrasser [ɑ̃barase] **1** *vt* (**a**) (*encombrer*) (*personne*) to hamper; (*table, pièce etc*) to clutter up (**de** with); **est-ce que ma valise vous embarrasse?** is my case in your way?; **je peux poser mon manteau? il m'embarrasse** can I put my coat down? it's a bit of a nuisance

(**b**) (*gêner*) to embarrass; **tu m'embarrasses beaucoup en me demandant ce service** you really embarrass me *or* put me in a very awkward situation by asking me this favour

2 s'embarrasser *vpr* (**a**) (*s'encombrer*) to burden *or* hamper oneself (**de** with)

(**b**) (*s'inquiéter*) (*toujours négativement*) to trouble *or* bother oneself (**de** with), to be concerned (**de** about); **elle ne s'embarrasse pas de douceur** she doesn't worry about being gentle

(**c**) (*s'embrouiller*) **s'e. dans** (*vêtements, Fig mensonges etc*) to get tangled up in

embastiller [ɑ̃bastije] *vt* to put in jail; **tu vas finir par te faire e.** you'll end up in jail *or* behind bars

embauchage [ɑ̃boʃaʒ] *nm* (*de travailleurs etc*) taking on, hiring, engaging

embauche [ɑ̃boʃ] *nf* (**a**) (*action*) = **embauchage** (**b**) (*emploi*) employment; **chercher de l'e.** to look for a job *or* for employment; **il n'y a pas d'e.** there are no jobs *or* vacancies, *Am* we're/they're/*etc* not hiring at the moment

embaucher [ɑ̃boʃe] **1** *vt* (*travailleur etc*) to take on, to hire, to engage; **e. qn pour le poste de** *ou* **comme** to engage *or* recruit sb as; *F* **je me suis encore fait e. pour faire la vaisselle** I got hired again to do the washing-up **2** *vi* to recruit, to take on *or* hire *or* engage people **3 s'embaucher** *vpr* to get taken on *or* hired (**comme** as)

embaucheur, -euse [ɑ̃boʃœr, -øz] *n* employer; **les embaucheurs ne sont pas légion de nos jours** not many companies are recruiting people *or* taking people on these days

embauchoir [ɑ̃boʃwar] *nm* shoe tree; (*pour bottes*) boot tree

embaumement [ɑ̃bommɑ̃] *nm* (*de corps*) embalming

embaumer [ɑ̃bome] **1** *vt* (**a**) (*corps*) to embalm (**b**) (*parfumer*) to perfume, to scent; (*répandre une odeur de*) to be fragrant with; **air embaumé** fragrant *or* balmy air; **l'église embaume l'encens** the church is heavy with (the scent of) incense; **l'encens embaume l'église** the scent of incense fills the church **2** *vi* to be fragrant

embaumeur [ɑ̃bomœr] *nm* (*de corps*) embalmer

embéguiner (s') [sɑ̃begine] *vpr Vieilli* **s'e. de qn** to become infatuated with sb

embellie [ɑ̃beli] *nf* (*éclaircie*) bright spell; *Naut* calm spell, lull; *Fig* (*de l'économie, d'une situation etc*) improvement; **courte e.** bright interval

embellir [ɑ̃bɛlir] **1** *vt* (*pièce, parc etc*) to make (more) attractive; (*personne*) to make look (more) beautiful, to improve the looks of; *Fig* (*histoire, vérité etc*) to improve on, to embellish; **le mariage/la maternité l'embellit** married life/motherhood suits her **2** *vi* to grow (more) beautiful

embellissement [ɑ̃bɛlismɑ̃] *nm* (**a**) (*fait de rendre plus beau*) (*d'une pièce, d'un parc etc*) improvement; *Fig* (*d'une histoire, de la vérité etc*) embellishment; **e. de qn** improving sb's looks (**b**) (*décoration*) embellishment, embellishing touch; **il faudra apporter des embellissements à l'appartement** the flat needs improving *or* needs a few embellishing touches; **mettre des embellissements à sa voiture** to customize one's car

emberlificoter [ɑ̃bɛrlifikɔte] *F* **1** *vt* (**a**) (*empêtrer*) to tangle up, to entangle (**b**) (*duper*) to take in **2 s'emberlificoter** *vpr* **s'e. dans** (*vêtements, Fig mensonges etc*) to get tangled up in

embêtant [ɑ̃bɛtɑ̃] *adj F* (*personne, problème etc*) annoying; (*situation*) awkward; **c'est drôlement e.!** it's really annoying!

embêtement [ɑ̃bɛtmɑ̃] *nm F* (*agacement*) annoyance; (*souci*) worry, trouble; **faire des embêtements à qn** to cause *or* make trouble for sb

embêter [ɑ̃bete] *F* **1** *vt* (*agacer*) to annoy; (*ennuyer*) to bore; **ça m'embête d'y aller** (*ça m'ennuie*) I can't be bothered going *or* to go; (*ça me gêne*) I wish I didn't have to go; **ça m'embête d'arriver en retard** I don't like being late; **je suis drôlement embêté avec ma fille** I'm having a lot of trouble with my daughter **2 s'embêter** *vpr* to be/get bored (stiff); *Iron* **je vois que tu ne t'embêtes pas!** I see you don't do badly for yourself!; **s'e. avec** (*des histoires d'argent, des scrupules, sa belle-mère etc*) to bother oneself about *or* with

emblée (d') [ɑ̃ble] *adv* directly, right away, straight off; (*réussir*) at the first attempt

emblématique [ɑ̃blematik] *adj* emblematic(al); *Fig* symbolic

emblème [ɑ̃blɛm] *nm* (*insigne*) emblem, device; *Fig* (*symbole*) symbol; *Mktg* **e. de marque** brand mark

embobiner [ɑ̃bɔbine] *vt F* (*duper*) to take in; (*enjôler*) to get round; **ne vous laissez pas e.** don't let yourself be had *or* taken in

emboîtable [ɑ̃bwatabl] *adj* (*chaise*) stacking, stackable; (*boîte, table etc*) that fits into a nest

emboîtage [ɑ̃bwataʒ] *nm* **(a)** (*action d'emboîter*) = **emboîtement (b)** (*d'un livre*) casing; (*étui d'un livre*) slipcase

emboîtement [ɑ̃bwatmɑ̃] *nm* (*de chaises*) stacking; *Constr* (*de tuyaux, poutres etc*) jointing

emboîter [ɑ̃bwate] **1** *vt* **(a)** (*assembler*) (*morceaux, pièces etc*) to fit together *or* into each other; (*boîtes, tables etc*) to nest; (*chaises*) to stack; *Constr* (*tuyaux, poutres etc*) to joint; **e. le pas à qn** to follow close on sb's heels; *Fig* to follow suit, to follow sb's lead **(b)** (*envelopper*) **e. un livre** to case a book; **cette chaussure lui emboîte le pied** the shoe gives him good support **2 s'emboîter** *vpr* (*de pièces, morceaux etc*) to fit together *or* into each other; (*de boîtes, tables etc*) to nest; (*de chaises*) to stack

embolie [ɑ̃bɔli] *nf Méd* embolism; **e. gazeuse/pulmonaire** air/pulmonary embolism; **e. cérébrale** clot on the brain, *Spéc* cerebral embolism

embonpoint [ɑ̃bɔ̃pwɛ̃] *nm* stoutness, corpulence; **avoir de l'e.** to be stout *or* corpulent

embouché [ɑ̃buʃe] *adj F* **mal e.** foul-mouthed

emboucher [ɑ̃buʃe] *vt* **(a)** (*trompette etc*) to put to one's mouth; *Fig Vieilli* **e. la trompette** to trumpet the news **(b) e. un cheval** to put the bit in a horse's mouth

embouchure [ɑ̃buʃyr] *nf* **(a)** (*d'une trompette, sarbacane etc*) mouthpiece **(b)** (*d'un sac, vase etc*) opening, mouth **(c)** (*d'une rivière etc*) mouth

embourber (s') [sɑ̃burbe] *vpr* **(a)** (*d'une voiture etc*) to get stuck (in the mud) **(b)** *Fig Péj* to flounder, to get bogged down; **il s'est embourbé dans des explications compliquées** he got bogged down in complicated explanations

embourgeoisement [ɑ̃burʒwazmɑ̃] *nm* attainment of middle-class respectability; (*d'un quartier*) gentrification

embourgeoiser (s') [sɑ̃burʒwaze] *vpr* to become bourgeois *or* middle-class; (*d'un quartier*) to become gentrified

embout [ɑ̃bu] *nm* (*d'un parapluie, d'une canne etc*) ferrule, tip; (*d'un câble*) terminal; (*d'un tuyau*) nozzle; (*d'un tirant, fil etc*) connector

embouteillage [ɑ̃butɛjaʒ] *nm* **(a)** *Aut* (traffic) hold-up, traffic jam, *F* snarl-up; **tomber dans les embouteillages** to get caught in traffic **(b)** *Naut* (*de navires*) bottling up

embouteiller [ɑ̃buteje] *vt* **(a)** *Aut* (*rue, autoroute etc*) to block (up), to jam (up); (*circulation*) to tie up, to hold up, *F* to snarl up; **circulation embouteillée** congested traffic; **route embouteillée** road blocked with traffic **(b)** *Naut* (*navires*) to bottle up

emboutir [ɑ̃butir] *vt* **(a)** *Aut* to bash in; **tout l'arrière de ma voiture est embouti** the entire rear end of my car is bashed in; **je me suis fait e. par mon voisin** my neighbour crashed into me **(b)** (*métal*) to stamp, to press; **châssis en tôle emboutie** pressed steel frame **(c)** (*arrondir*) to emboss

emboutissage [ɑ̃butisaʒ] *nm* **(a)** *Aut* (*de voitures*) collision; **l'e. d'une voiture par un autobus** the collision between a bus and a car **(b)** (*de métaux*) stamping, pressing **(c)** (*fait d'arrondir*) embossing

embranchement [ɑ̃brɑ̃ʃmɑ̃] *nm* **(a)** (*croisement*) (*d'une route, d'un rail, d'une conduite etc*) junction; (*bifurcation*) (*sur une route*) fork **(b)** *Rail* branch line **(c)** *Biol* sub-kingdom, *Spéc* phylum

embrancher [ɑ̃brɑ̃ʃe] **1** *vt* (*route, conduite etc*) to connect up, to join up **(à** to) **2 s'embrancher** *vpr* to join (up) **(sur** with)

embrasement [ɑ̃brazmɑ̃] *nm* **(a)** *Arch* (*incendie*) conflagration **(b)** *Litt* **l'e. des cieux au soleil couchant** the blazing sunset **(c)** *Litt* (*agitation*) agitation, turmoil; **il faut éviter l'e. des esprits** we must avoid any flare-ups; **il ne pouvait pas lutter contre l'e. de son cœur** he could not fight against the love that flared up in his heart

embraser [ɑ̃braze] **1** *vt Litt* **(a)** (*maison, champs etc*) to set ablaze

(b) (*d'un coucher de soleil*) to set aglow

(c) *Fig* (*imagination*) to fire; (*foule*) to fire, to set alight, *Péj* to inflame

2 s'embraser *vpr* **(a)** (*prendre feu*) to blaze up

(b) (*rougeoyer*) to glow

(c) *Fig Litt* **dès que je l'ai vu, mon cœur s'est embrasé** the mere sight of him kindled a flame; **l'imagination des jeunes romantiques s'embrase trop vite** young romantics have an imagination that is too readily inflamed; **quand j'entendais des histoires sur l'Afrique, mon imagination s'embrasait** hearing stories about Africa fired my imagination; **les esprits s'embrasaient dans ces réunions** the meetings had an inflammatory effect on those present

embrassade [ɑ̃brasad] *nf* embrace, hug

embrasse [ɑ̃bras] *nf* (*d'un rideau*) tieback

embrasser [ɑ̃brase] **1** *vt* **(a)** (*donner un baiser à*) to kiss; **je t'embrasse de tout mon cœur** (*dans une lettre*) with fondest love; **e. qn sur la bouche/la joue** to kiss sb on the mouth/cheek

(b) *Vieilli* (*étreindre*) to embrace

(c) (*adopter*) (*croyance, religion, doctrine, théorie*) to embrace; (*carrière*) to take up; (*cause*) to embrace, to take up; **e. la carrière diplomatique** to enter the diplomatic service

(d) (*contenir*) (*sujet, période, cas de figure etc*) to embrace, to cover, to take in; **il faut e. tous les problèmes** we have to look at all the problems; **le cours embrassera l'ensemble du moyen âge** the course will cover the whole of the Middle Ages; **e. qch du regard** to take sth in at a glance; **il embrassa toute sa famille d'un regard satisfait** he cast a satisfied eye over his family

2 s'embrasser *vpr* to kiss (each other)

embrasure [ɑ̃brazyr] *nf* **(a)** *Constr* embrasure; **l'e. de la porte/fenêtre** the door/window recess **(b)** *Mil* (*dans un mur*) embrasure; *Naut* gun port

embrayage [ɑ̃brɛjaʒ] *nm* **(a)** (*action*) *Aut* letting in *or* engaging the clutch; *Tech* (*de pièces de moteur*) coupling, engaging **(b)** (*pièce*) *Aut* clutch; *Tech* coupling (gear); **pédale d'e.** clutch pedal

▶ **embrayage: e. à cônes** cone clutch; **e. à crabot** dog clutch; **e. à diaphragme** diaphragm spring *or* DS clutch; **e. électromagnétique** magnetic clutch; **e. à friction** friction clutch; **e. hydrodynamique** fluid clutch; **e. monodisque** single-plate *or* disc clutch; **e. multidisque** multi-disc clutch pack; **e. de prise directe** lock-up clutch

embrayer [ɑ̃breje] **(j'embraie, j'embraye, n. embrayons; j'embraierai, j'embrayerai) 1** *vt Tech* (*pièces de moteur*) to couple, to engage **2** *vi* **(a)** *Aut* to let in *or* engage the clutch **(b)** *F* (*commencer à parler de*) **e. sur** to get going *or* started on; **on pourrait peut-être e. sur un autre sujet** maybe we could change the subject

embrigadement [ɑ̃brigadmɑ̃] *nm* (*de supporters etc*) recruitment **(dans** to, into)

embrigader [ɑ̃brigade] *vt* (*supporter etc*) to recruit **(dans** to, into)

embringuer [ɑ̃brɛ̃ge] *F* **1** *vt* **e. qn dans qch** to get sb mixed up in sth; **il ne veut pas se laisser e. dans cette histoire** he doesn't want to get mixed up in it **2 s'embringuer** *vpr* to get mixed up **(dans** in)

embrocation [ɑ̃brɔkasjɔ̃] *nf Méd* embrocation

embrocher [ɑ̃brɔʃe] *vt* **(a)** *Culin* (*viande etc*) to put on a/the spit **(b)** *F* **e. qn** (*d'un coup d'épée*) to skewer sb

embrouillage [ɑ̃brujaʒ] *nm* = **embrouillement**

embrouillamini [ɑ̃brujamini] *nm F* confusion, muddle; **sa vie sentimentale est un tel e. que …** his love life is so complicated *or* involved that …; **comment veux-tu que je m'y retrouve dans cet e. de papiers?** how can I be expected to know what I'm doing when these papers are in such a muddle?

embrouillé [ɑ̃bruje] *adj* **(a)** (*fils*) tangled **(b)** *Fig* (*papiers, lettres etc*) mixed up, in a mess; (*situation, idées, arguments etc*) confused, muddled; (*style, affaire*) complicated, involved

embrouillement [ɑ̃brujmɑ̃] *nm* **(a)** (*de fils*) (*action*) tangling; (*état*) tangle **(b)** *Fig* (*d'une situation, d'idées etc*) (*action*) muddling, confusing; (*état*) muddle, confusion; **l'e. de la situation est tel que …** the situation is so confused that …; **cela a provoqué un tel e. dans son esprit que …** this confused him so much that …

embrouiller [ɑ̃bruje] **1** *vt* **(a)** (*fils*) to tangle (up)

(b) *Fig* (*personne, situation, idées etc*) to confuse, to muddle (up); **il a embrouillé la situation encore plus** he confused the situation even further, he made the situation even more confused; **il a réussi à m'e.** *ou* **à e. mes idées** he managed to confuse me; *F* **ni vu ni connu je t'embrouille** hey presto; *F* **… alors qu'il était avec une autre: ni vu ni connu je t'embrouille …** while all the time he was with another woman—talk about a con artist *or* about being conned!

2 s'embrouiller *vpr* (*d'une personne, d'une situation, d'idées etc*) to get muddled (up) *or* confused; **je me suis embrouillé dans mes rendez-vous** I got my appointments muddled, I got into a muddle with my appointments

embroussaillé [ɑ̃brusaje] *adj* (*sentier, jardin, dunes etc*) covered with *or* in bushes; **cheveux embroussaillés** tousled hair; **le jardin est complètement e.** the garden is completely overgrown

embrumé [ɑ̃bryme] *adj* (*temps*) misty; (*horizon*) hazy; *Fig* (*esprit*) (*par l'alcool*) fuddled, fogged; **il avait l'esprit e. par toutes ces paroles** all that talking had left him feeling less than clear-headed

embrumer [ɑ̃bryme] **1** *vt* (*paysage, ville etc*) to cover with mist *or* haze; *Fig* (*de l'alcool*) (*esprit*) to fuddle, to fog; **tous ces discours lui ont embrumé l'esprit** his mind is less than clear after all those speeches; **craintes qui embrument l'avenir** fears that darken the future **2 s'embrumer** *vpr* (*du ciel*) to become misty *or* hazy; (*du paysage, d'une ville, une île*) to become covered with mist *or* haze; *Fig* (*des idées*) to become foggy *or* cloudy; **avec chaque verre mon esprit s'embrumait un peu plus** with each glass, my brain became a little more fogged

embruns [ɑ̃brœ̃] *nmpl* spray, spindrift

embryologie [ɑ̃brijɔlɔʒi] *nf Biol* embryology

embryologique [ɑ̃brijɔlɔʒik] *adj Biol* embryologic(al)

embryologiste [ɑ̃brijɔlɔʒist] *n Biol* embryologist

embryon [ɑ̃brijɔ̃] *nm* embryo; *Fig* **un e. de roman/dissertation** an embryonic novel/dissertation; **je ne sais pas comment peut tourner ce magasin avec cet e. d'organisation** I don't know how the shop manages to operate when it's so lacking in organization

embryonnaire [ɑ̃brijɔnɛr] *adj Biol* embryonic; **sac e.** embryo sac; *Fig* **à l'état e.** in an embryonic state, in embryo; **le projet en est encore à un stade e.** the project is still at a very early stage *or* in its very early stages; *Fig* **étant donné l'état e. de son intelligence** given his limited intelligence

embryotomie [ɑ̃brijɔtɔmi] *nf Obst* embryotomy

embu [ɑ̃by] *Beaux-Arts* **1** *adj* (*couleur, tableau*) flat, dull **2** *nm* (*d'une couleur*) flatness, dullness

embûches [ɑ̃byʃ] *nfpl* traps; **tendre** *ou* **dresser des e. à qn** to set traps for sb; **sujet plein d'e.** tricky subject; **la vie est semée d'e.** life is full of pitfalls

embuer [ɑ̃bɥe] *vt* (*de la vapeur etc*) (*verre etc*) to mist up, to cloud; **yeux embués de larmes** eyes dimmed *or* clouded with tears; **pare-brise embué** misted(-up) windscreen

embuscade [ɑ̃byskad] *nf* ambush; **dresser** *ou* **tendre une e. à qn** to lay *or* set an ambush for sb; **attirer qn dans une e.** to ambush *or* waylay sb; **se tenir en e.** to lie in ambush *or* in wait; **tomber dans une e.** to be ambushed *or* waylaid

embusqué [ɑ̃byske] *nm* (**a**) *Mil* shirker, dodger (**b**) *Rugby* **les embusqués** the back row of forwards

embusquer [ɑ̃byske] *Mil* **1** *vt* (**a**) (*placer en embuscade*) to place in ambush (**b**) (*affecter loin du front*) to find a cushy posting for **2 s'embusquer** *vpr* (**a**) (*se mettre en embuscade*) to lie in ambush (**b**) (*se faire affecter loin du front*) to get a cushy posting

éméché [emeʃe] *adj F* slightly the worse for wear *or* drink, tipsy

émeraude [emrod] **1** *nf Minér* emerald **2** *nm* (*couleur*) emerald green **3** *adj inv* emerald green

émergence [emɛrʒɑ̃s] *nf* emergence; **c'est là que se trouve le point d'é. de la source** the spring emerges here; **leurs recherches ont abouti à l'é. d'une nouvelle hypothèse** a new hypothesis emerged from their research

émergent [emɛrʒɑ̃] *adj* emergent

émerger [emɛrʒe] *vi* (**j'émergeai(s); n. émergeons**) (**a**) to emerge (**de** from) (**b**) *Fig* (*de la vérité, d'un fait etc*) to emerge, to come to light; (*d'un nouvel écrivain etc*) to emerge; *F* (*d'une personne*) to come to; *F* **le dimanche, il n'émerge jamais avant midi** he never surfaces before noon on Sundays

émeri [emri] *nm* emery; **papier** *ou* **toile (d')é.** emery paper; **bouchon à l'é.** (ground glass) stopper; **bouché à l'é.** (*flasque*) stoppered; *F* (*personne*) bone-headed

émerillon [emrijɔ̃] *nm* (*oiseau*) merlin

émeriser [emrize] *vt* to coat with emery

émérite [emerit] *adj* (**a**) (*expérimenté*) (*artisan, ouvrier, médecin etc*) skilled, experienced (**b**) (*professeur*) emeritus

émerveillement [emɛrvɛjmɑ̃] *nm* (**a**) (*enchantement*) wonder, amazement (**b**) (*chose*) amazing *or* wonderful thing; **c'était un é.** it was amazing *or* wonderful; **un é. perpétuel** a constant source of amazement

émerveiller [emɛrveje] **1** *vt* (*enchanter*) to fill with wonder, to amaze; **être émerveillé par** to marvel at, to be filled with wonder by **2 s'émerveiller** *vpr* **s'é. de** *ou* **devant** (*s'étonner de*) to be amazed by; (*s'enchanter de*) to marvel at; **la jeunesse s'émerveille de pas grand-chose** it doesn't take much to amaze young people

émétique [emetik] *adj, n* emetic

émetteur, -trice [emɛtœr, -tris] **1** *adj* (**a**) *Fin* (*banque, organisme*) issuing; **é. de cartes** card issuer (**b**) *Rad* **poste é.** transmitter; **station émettrice** transmitting *or* broadcasting station **2** *n* (*de billets, d'actions etc*) issuer; (*d'un chèque*) drawer **3** *nm* (**a**) *TV, Rad* transmitter; **é. monophonique/stéréo** monoaural/stereo transmitter; **é. terrestre** ground transmitter (**b**) *Phys* (*de radiation, son etc*) emitter

émetteur-récepteur, *pl* **émetteurs-récepteurs** *nm Rad* transmitter-receiver, transceiver; **é. (portatif)** walkie-talkie

émettre [emɛtr] (*conj like* **mettre**) **1** *vt* (**a**) (*cri*) to give, to utter, to emit; (*rot, soupir*) to give; (*son*) to make, to emit; (*fumée*) to give off, to emit; (*chaleur*) to give out *or* off; (*lumière*) to give (out); **la seiche émet de l'encre** the cuttlefish ejects ink; **mon ordinateur émet un bruit bizarre** my computer is making a funny noise

(**b**) *Fig* (*opinion, avis*) to voice, to express; (*objection*) to voice, to raise, to put forward; (*idée*) to voice, to put forward

(**c**) *Rad, TV* to transmit, to broadcast

(**d**) *Fin* (*chèque, nouveau billet etc*) to issue; (*prêt*) to float; *Jur* (*fausse monnaie*) to utter; *Fin* **é. un emprunt** to issue loan stock, to make a bond issue; *Fin* **é. une lettre de crédit** to open a letter of credit

2 *vi Rad, TV* to transmit, to broadcast

émeu, -eus [emø] *nm* (*oiseau*) emu

émeute [emøt] *nf* riot, outbreak, disturbance; **tourner à l'é.** to turn into a riot; **de terribles émeutes dans tout le pays** dreadful riots *or* rioting throughout the country

émeutier, -ière [emøtje, -jɛr] *n* rioter

émietter [emjete] **1** *vt* (**a**) (*pain, fromage, roche etc*) to crumble (up) (**b**) *Fig* (*domaine, empire etc*) to break up; (*pouvoir*) to erode, to eat away at; (*fortune*) to fritter away, to squander; (*énergie, forces*) to waste **2 s'émietter** *vpr* (**a**) (*du pain, fromage, d'une roche etc*) to crumble (**b**) *Fig* (*d'un domaine, un empire, un pouvoir etc*) to crumble away; (*de l'énergie, des forces*) to drain away; **sa fortune s'émiettait au fil des années** his fortune disappeared little by little over the years

émigrant, -ante [emigrɑ̃, -ɑ̃t] **1** *adj* migrant **2** *n* emigrant

émigration [emigrasjɔ̃] *nf* (**a**) emigration; **pays à forte/faible é.** country with high/low emigration (**b**) *Zool* migration

émigré, -ée [emigre] *n Pol, Écon* migrant; *Hist* (political) exile, émigré; **travailleurs émigrés** migrant workers

émigrer [emigre] *vi* (**a**) to emigrate (**b**) *Zool* to migrate

émincé [emɛ̃se] *nm Culin* (*plat*) = thinly sliced meat or poultry in sauce; (*tranche*) thin slice (*of meat*)

émincer [emɛ̃se] *vt* (**j'émincai(s); n. émincons**) (*de la viande, des légumes etc*) to slice thinly

éminemment [eminamɑ̃] *adv* eminently

éminence [eminɑ̃s] *nf* (**a**) (*géographique*) hill, *Litt* eminence (**b**) *Anat* eminence; **l'é. du pouce** the ball of the thumb (**c**) *Rel* **son É. le Cardinal** his Eminence the Cardinal; *Fig* **l'É. grise** the power behind the throne, the éminence grise (**d**) *Arch* (*excellence*) eminence

éminent [eminɑ̃] *adj* (*personne*) eminent, distinguished; **il nous a rendu d'éminents services** he rendered us outstanding service

émir [emir] *nm* emir

émirat [emira] *nm* emirate; **les Émirats arabes unis** the United Arab Emirates

émissaire [emisɛr] **1** *adj* **bouc é.** scapegoat **2** *nm* (**a**) (*envoyé*) emissary (**b**) (*d'un lac*) outlet, drainage channel

émission [emisjɔ̃] *nf* (**a**) (*de son, fluide etc*) emission; (*de sons, cris etc*) utterance; (*de chaleur, lumière*) emission, giving out; **tuyau d'é.** discharge pipe

(**b**) *Rad, TV* (*action*) transmission, broadcasting; (*ce qui est émis*) programme, *US* program, broadcast, show; **poste d'é.** transmitter; **station d'é.** transmitting *or* broadcasting station; **une é. pour les enfants** a children's programme *or* broadcast

(**c**) *Électron* **é. électronique** electron emission; *Phys Nucl* **é. de particules** particle emission

(**d**) *Fin* (*de billets de banque, timbres-poste etc*) issue; *Bourse* **é. boursière** *ou* **d'actions** share issue; *Bourse* **é. d'actions gratuites** scrip issue; *Bourse* **é. obligataire** *ou* **d'obligations** bond issue

(**e**) *Jur* uttering

▶ **émission**: **é. de campagne (électorale) officielle** party political broadcast; **é. en différé** recorded broadcast; **é. en direct** live broadcast; **é. éducative** educational programme; **é. pour enfants d'âge pré-scolaire** pre-school programme; **é. d'expression directe** live debate programme; **é. d'expression directe (de formation politique)** party political broadcast; **é. en extérieur** outside broadcast, *Spéc* OB; **é. d'informations** news programme; **é. de jeux (télévisés)** (TV) game(s) show; **é. magazine** magazine programme; **é. payante** premium programme; **é. en public** audience show; **é. de radio** radio programme; **é. de reportage** feature programme; **émissions scolaires** schools broadcasting; **é. du service public** public service broadcast; **émissions du service public** public service broadcasting, PSB; **é. sportive** sports programme; **é. de télévision** television programme, telecast; **é. tout public** family programme; **é. de variétés** variety programme *or* show

emmagasinage [ɑ̃magazinaʒ] *nm* (*de marchandises*) storage, warehousing; (*d'électricité, de chaleur*) storing up, accumulation

emmagasiner [ɑ̃magazine] *vt* (*marchandises*) to store, to warehouse; (*électricité, chaleur*) to store up, to accumulate; *Fig* (*souvenirs, connaissances*) to store up

emmailloter [ɑ̃majɔte] *vt* **(a)** (*membre etc*) to wrap (up), to swathe; **l'infirmière m'a emmailloté la cheville dans un bandage** the nurse wrapped a bandage round my ankle; **bien emmailloté dans des couvertures** well wrapped up in blankets **(b)** *Arch* (*langer*) (*nourisson*) to swaddle

emmanchement [ɑ̃mɑ̃ʃmɑ̃] *nm* **(a)** fitting *or* fixing of a handle **(d'un outil** (on)to a tool) **(b)** (*d'une pièce à une autre*) fitting; **cela rendait l'e. des deux pièces impossible** it made it impossible to fit the two parts together

emmancher [ɑ̃mɑ̃ʃe] **1** *vt* **(a)** (*outil*) to fit *or* fix a handle to **(b)** (*tuyaux*) to fit together, to joint; (*pièce dans une autre*) to fit **(dans** to) **(c)** *Fig F* (*travail, affaire etc*) to get started on **2 s'emmancher** *vpr* (*de deux pièces*) to fit together; *Fig F* **bien/mal s'e.** to get off to a good/bad start

emmanchure [ɑ̃mɑ̃ʃyr] *nf* armhole; **la veste me serre aux emmanchures** the jacket's too tight at the armpits

emmêlement [ɑ̃mɛlmɑ̃] *nm* (*de fils, laine etc*) tangling; (*état*) tangle; *Fig* (*de faits, d'une histoire*) mixing up, muddling; (*état*) mix-up, muddle

emmêler [ɑ̃mɛle] **1** *vt* (*fil, cheveux etc*) to tangle; *Fig* (*faits, histoire*) to mix up, to muddle **2 s'emmêler** *vpr* (*de fils, cheveux etc*) to become tangled, to get in a tangle; *Fig* (*de faits, d'une histoire*) to become mixed up *or* muddled, to get into a muddle; *F* **s'e. les pédales** to get all mixed up *or* confused; *F* **s'e. les pédales dans ses dates** to get one's dates all mixed up

emménagement [ɑ̃menaʒmɑ̃] *nm* moving in; **nous avons dû remettre notre e. à plus tard** we had to put off moving in *or* we had to put our move off to later; **comment s'est passé ton e.?** how did the move go?

emménager [ɑ̃menaʒe] **(j'emménageai(s)) 1** *vi* to move in; **e. dans** to move into **2** *vt* (*meubles, personne*) to move in; **e. qn/qch dans** to move sb/sth into

emmener [ɑ̃mne] *vt* **(j'emmène; j'emmènerai) (a)** (*prendre avec soi*) (*enfant etc*) to take (with one); (*prisonnier etc*) to lead *or* take away; *F* (*objet*) to bring; **je vous emmène avec moi** I'm taking you with me; **je t'emmène passer le week-end à Florence** I'm taking you (off) to Florence for the weekend; **emmené en prison** taken off to prison; **cette année nous emmenons les enfants** we're taking the children away this year; **il m'a emmené à l'aéroport en voiture** he drove me to the airport; **e. promener qn** to take sb for a walk

(b) (*entraîner*) (*soldats, équipe de sport, peloton etc*) to lead; (*sprint*) to lead (in); **les coéquipiers se sont relayés pour e. leur leader** the other members of the team took turns acting as pacemaker for their leader

(c) (*transporter*) (*d'un bateau, d'un avion etc*) (*passagers*) to take, to carry

emmenthal [emɛ̃tal] *nm* (*fromage*) Emment(h)al (cheese)

emmerdant [ɑ̃mɛrdɑ̃] *adj Arg* (*qui contrarie*) damned *or Br* bloody annoying; (*qui ennuie*) damned *or Br* bloody boring; **ce que tu peux être e.!** you can be a real pain (in the bum *or* neck *or Am* butt)!

emmerde [ɑ̃mɛrd] *nf Arg* = **emmerdement**

emmerdement [ɑ̃mɛrd(ə)mɑ̃] *nm Arg* **emmerdements** (damned) bother, trouble; **depuis le début de l'année il ne lui arrive que des emmerdements** he's had a helluva time of it since the beginning of the year; **pour les emmerdements, j'ai été servi aujourd'hui!** I've had a bloody awful day!; **un e.** a damned *or Br* bloody nuisance; **j'ai encore eu un e. avec la bagnole/les flics** I had trouble with the car/the police again; **tu parles d'un e.!** what an absolute pain (in the neck *or* bum *or Am* butt)!

emmerder [ɑ̃mɛrde] **1** *vt Arg* **(a) e. qn** (*contrarier*) to get up sb's nose *or* on sb's nerves; (*ennuyer*) to bore sb stiff *or* silly *or* rigid; **ça m'emmerde mais il va vraiment falloir que j'y aille** it's a real pain (in the neck *or* bum *or Am* butt), but I'm going to have to go; **arrête d'e. ta sœur!** stop annoying your sister!

(b) (*comme défi*) **dis-lui que je l'emmerde!** tell him from me he can (go and) get stuffed!; **toi je t'emmerde!** get stuffed!, *Vulg* fuck you!; **moi les gens je les emmerde!** I don't give a shit *or Vulg* a fuck what people think!

2 s'emmerder *vpr Arg* to be bored stiff *or* silly *or* rigid; **qu'est-ce qu'on s'emmerde en colonie de vacances/avec eux** holiday camp is/they're bloody boring!; **je ne me suis pas emmerdée à faire le ménage pour que ...** I didn't go to all the bother *or* trouble of doing the housework just so that ...; **tu t'emmerdes bien** you're landing yourself right in it; *Iron* **tu ne t'emmerdes pas!** you're not doing badly for yourself!; (*tu as du culot*) you've got some *or* a helluva nerve!

emmerdeur, -euse [ɑ̃mɛrdœr, -øz] *n Arg* (*qui contrarie*) damned *or Br* bloody nuisance, pain (in the neck *or* bum *or Am* butt); (*qui ennuie*) helluva *or Br* bloody bore

emmitoufler [ɑ̃mitufle] **1** *vt* to wrap *or* muffle up **(dans, de** in) **2 s'emmitoufler** *vpr* to get muffled up **(dans, de** in); **tâche de bien t'e.** try to wrap up well

emmurer [ɑ̃myre] *vt* (*victime*) to immure, to wall in *or* up; (*d'une chute de pierres*) (*mineurs*) to trap

émoi [emwa] *nm* (*trouble*) emotion, agitation; (*plaisir*) excitement; (*anxiété*) anxiety; **être (tout) en é.** (*troublé*) to be all excited *or* all in a flutter; **toute la ville était en é.** the whole town was in a commotion; **non sans é.** in some agitation

émollient [emɔljɑ̃] *adj, nm* emollient

émoluments [emɔlymɑ̃] *nmpl* emoluments, remuneration

émondage [emɔ̃daʒ] *nm* **(a)** (*d'un arbre*) pruning, trimming **(b)** (*de graines*) cleaning

émonder [emɔ̃de] *vt* (*arbre, Fig livre, texte*) to prune, to trim

émondeur, -euse [emɔ̃dœr, -øz] *n* pruner

émondoir [emɔ̃dwar] *nm* pruning hook

émotif, -ive [emɔtif, -iv] **1** *adj* (*personne, réaction etc*) emotional **2** *n* emotional person

émotion [emosjɔ̃] *nf* emotion; *F* (*inquiétude*) fright, shock; **vive é.** strong emotion; (*exaltation*) excitement, thrill; **le meurtre de l'enfant a provoqué une vive é.** people were shocked by the child's murder; **l'atterrissage mouvementé a provoqué une vive é. parmi les passagers** the bumpy landing frightened the passengers; **ressentir une vive é.** (*attendrissement*) to be greatly moved; (*exaltation*) to be thrilled; (*peur*) to be very frightened; **parler avec é.** to speak emotionally; *F* **j'ai eu une é.** I've had a fright *or* shock; *F* **tu nous as vraiment donné des émotions** you gave us a real fright, you really frightened us

émotionnel, -elle [emosjɔnɛl] *adj Psy* (*réaction etc*) emotional

émotionner [emosjɔne] *vt F* to affect

émotivité [emotivite] *nf* emotionalism; **être d'une trop grande é.** to be too emotional

émoulu [emuly] *adj F* **jeune homme frais é. du collège/de son université** young man fresh from school/university

émoussé [emuse] *adj* (*pointe, lame etc*) blunt; *Fig* (*sentiment, qualité etc*) blunted, diminished; **une patience émoussée par le temps** patience diminished *or* worn thin by time; **il a l'appétit é. par la maladie** illness has blunted *or* taken the edge off his appetite

émousser [emuse] **1** *vt* (*lame, pointe, crayon, angle etc*) to blunt; *Fig* (*sens, passions etc*) to dull, to blunt; (*appétit*) to take the edge off; **le temps a émoussé sa résistance** time has lessened *or* worn away his resistance **2 s'émousser** *vpr* (*d'une lame, pointe etc*) to get blunt; *Fig* (*des sens, passions etc*) to become blunted *or* dulled; **mon appétit s'est émoussé depuis que je suis malade** I've not had much appetite *or* I haven't felt much like eating since I fell ill

émoustillant [emustijɑ̃] *adj* arousing, titillating

émoustiller [emustije] *vt* to arouse, to titillate

émouvant [emuvɑ̃] *adj* (*attendrissant*) moving, touching; (*bouleversant*) stirring, thrilling

émouvoir [emuvwar] (*pp* **ému**; *otherwise conj like* **mouvoir**) **1** *vt* (*toucher*) to move, to touch; (*inquiéter*) to upset; **é. qn (jusqu')aux larmes** to move sb to tears; **cela ne m'émeut pas le moins du monde** that doesn't upset me in the least; **encore tout ému de la rencontre** still very upset by the meeting; **facile à é.** emotional, easily moved

2 s'émouvoir *vpr* **(a)** (*s'enthousiasmer*) to get excited, to be roused; **le pays s'émeut** the country is in a state of excitement

(b) (*se troubler*) to be touched *or* moved; **rester sans s'é. à la vue de leur malheur** to remain unmoved by their plight; **ce qu'il me déclara sans s'é. le moins du monde** which he announced to me with perfect composure; *F* **pas de quoi s'é.** it's nothing to get worked up about

empaillage [ɑ̃pajaʒ] *nm* **(a)** (*d'animaux morts*) stuffing **(b)** (*de

plantes) mulching with straw **(c)** (*de chaises*) bottoming with straw
empaillé, -ée [ɑ̃paje] *adj* (*oiseau, renard etc*) stuffed; *F* **avoir l'air e.** to be self-conscious *or* awkward
empailler [ɑ̃paje] *vt* **(a)** (*animal mort*) to stuff **(b)** (*plantes*) to mulch with straw **(c)** (*chaise*) to bottom with straw
empailleur, -euse [ɑ̃pajœr, -øz] *n* (*d'animaux*) taxidermist
empalement [ɑ̃palmɑ̃] *nm* impalement
empaler [ɑ̃pale] **1** *vt* to impale **2 s'empaler** *vpr* to impale oneself
empanaché [ɑ̃panaʃe] *adj* plumed, decorated with plumes; *Fig* **style e.** pompous *or* flowery style
empannage [ɑ̃panaʒ] *nm Naut* gybe
empanner [ɑ̃pane] *vi Naut* to gybe
empaquetage [ɑ̃paktaʒ] *nm* packing (up)
empaqueter [ɑ̃pakte] *vt* **(j'empaquette; j'empaquetterai)** to pack up, to package
empaqueteur, -euse [ɑ̃paktœr, -øz] *n* packer
emparer (s') [sɑ̃pare] *vpr* **s'e. de** (*ville, otage, butin, pouvoir etc*) to seize; (*téléphone, porte-monnaie etc*) to grab (hold of), to seize; *Sp* (*ballon*) to take possession of, to get hold of; (*d'un doute, une obsession, de la jalousie etc*) (*personne*) to take hold of; **depuis que cette idée s'est emparée de mon esprit** since the idea took hold of me; **la presse s'est emparée de cette histoire** the press got hold of the story; **il s'est emparé de ce prétexte pour partir** he used it as a pretext to leave
empâté [ɑ̃pɑte] *adj* (*visage*) fleshy, bloated
empâtement [ɑ̃pɑtmɑ̃] *nm* **(a)** (*de la volaille*) fattening (up) **(b)** (*d'une personne, d'un visage*) bloating; (*d'un corps*) bloating, thickening; **on observe souvent un e. du visage chez les hommes à partir de 40 ans** men's features frequently coarsen after the age of 40 **(c)** *Beaux-Arts* impasto
empâter [ɑ̃pɑte] **1** *vt* **(a)** (*engraisser*) (*volaille*) to fatten (up) **(b)** (*épaissir*) (*corps*) to bloat, to thicken; (*visage*) to bloat, to coarsen; **la vie à la campagne l'a empâtée** she has put on weight in the country **(c)** (*couvrir d'une pâte*) (*langue*) to coat, to fur up; *Beaux-Arts* to impaste **2 s'empâter** *vpr* **(a)** (*d'une personne, d'un corps*) to become bloated; (*d'un visage*) to coarsen; **elle s'est empâtée depuis quelque temps** she has put on weight recently **(b)** (*de la langue*) to become coated, to fur up
empattement [ɑ̃patmɑ̃] *nm* **(a)** (*d'une voiture*) wheelbase **(b)** *Typ* serif **(c)** (*d'un mur*) footing
empatter [ɑ̃pate] *vt* (*mur*) to give footing to
empaumer [ɑ̃pome] *vt* **(a)** (*au jeu de paume*) (*attraper*) to catch in the palm of the hand; (*frapper*) to strike with the palm of the hand **(b)** *F Vieilli* **se laisser** *ou* **se faire e.** to be tricked *or* taken in **(c)** (*d'un magicien etc*) (*carte, pièce etc*) to palm
empêché [ɑ̃peʃe] *adj* (*retenu*) held up, detained
empêchement [ɑ̃pɛʃmɑ̃] *nm* **(a)** (*contretemps*) **j'ai eu un e.** I got held up *or* detained, something came up at the last minute; **en cas d'e., veuillez prévenir 24 heures à l'avance** please give us 24 hours notice if you cannot keep the appointment; **en cas d'e., nous remettrons la réunion à la semaine suivante** if anybody can't make the meeting, we'll postpone it to the following week **(b)** *Jur* **e. de mariage** impediment to marriage
empêcher [ɑ̃peʃe] **1** *vt* **(a)** (*action, événement etc*) to prevent; (*mouvement, progrès etc*) to obstruct, to impede; **empêché, il a envoyé ses excuses** he was unavoidably detained and sent his apologies; **ce vent empêchera la pluie** this wind will keep the rain off

(b) e. qn de faire qch to stop *or* prevent *or* keep sb from doing sth; **rien ne m'empêchera de te rejoindre** nothing will stop me (from) joining you; **il sera difficile de l'en e.** it will be difficult to stop *or* prevent him/her; **tu ne m'empêcheras pas de penser que j'ai raison** I still think I'm right, you won't convince me that I'm wrong; *F* **ce n'est pas ça qui m'empêchera de dormir** I won't lose any sleep over it; **la pluie empêche que nous (ne) sortions** the rain is preventing *or* stopping us from going out; **il n'y a rien qui t'empêche de lui téléphoner** there's nothing to stop you telephoning him; **je ne vous empêche pas de partir/dîner, au moins?** I hope I'm not keeping you from going/your dinner?

(c) il n'empêche que cela nous a coûté cher all the same *or* nevertheless it has cost us dear; **cela n'empêche pas qu'il aurait pu s'excuser** all the same *or* nevertheless, he could have apologized; *F* **n'empêche** all the same; *F* **qu'est-ce que ça empêche?** what does that matter?, what odds *or* difference does that make?; *F* **ça n'empêche rien!** that doesn't matter!, it makes no odds *or* difference!

2 s'empêcher *vpr* (*souvent nég*) **s'e. de faire qch** to stop oneself *or* prevent oneself *or* refrain from doing sth; **tu pourrais t'e. de fumer quand tu es chez elle** you could refrain from smoking when you're at her place; **je me suis empêché de me mettre en colère mais j'ai eu du mal** I managed not to get angry but it was difficult; **j'ai dû m'e. de tousser toute la nuit** I had to really make an effort not to cough all night; **je ne pouvais m'e. de rire** I couldn't help laughing, I had to laugh; **je ne peux pas m'e. de la taquiner** I can't help teasing her; **elle ne peut jamais s'e. de dire ce qu'il ne faut pas** she can never stop herself from saying what she shouldn't; **je ne peux pas m'en e.** I can't help it, I can't stop myself
empêcheur, -euse [ɑ̃pɛʃœr, -øz] *n F* **e. de danser** *ou* **de tourner en rond** spoilsport, wet blanket
empeigne [ɑ̃pɛɲ] *nf* (*de chaussure*) upper, vamp; *Arg* **gueule d'e.** ugly mug
empennage [ɑ̃pɛnaʒ] *nm* (*d'une flèche*) feathering, feathers; (*d'une bombe*) fins, vanes; (*d'une torpille*) fins; (*d'un avion*) empennage, tail
empenner [ɑ̃pɛne] *vt* (*flèche*) to feather
empereur [ɑ̃prœr] *nm* emperor
empesage [ɑ̃pəzaʒ] *nm* (*d'un col, d'une chemise etc*) starching
empesé [ɑ̃pəze] *adj* **(a)** (*col, chemise etc*) starched **(b)** *Fig* (*manière*) stiff, starchy, unbending; (*style*) stiff
empeser [ɑ̃pəze] *vt* **(j'empèse; j'empèserai)** (*col, chemise etc*) to starch
empester [ɑ̃pɛste] **1** *vt* **e. l'alcool/le parfum** to reek *or* stink of alcohol/perfume; **le frigo empeste le fromage** the fridge stinks of cheese; **le fromage empeste le frigo** the cheese is stinking out the fridge; **e. qn (avec sa fumée)** to stink sb out (with one's smoke) **2** *vi* to stink, to smell to high heaven
empêtrer (s') [sɑ̃petre] *vpr* to become entangled; **s'e. les pieds dans les broussailles** to get one's feet caught in the undergrowth; *Fig* **s'e. dans** (*explications, discours, mensonges*) to get tangled up in; *Fig* **s'e. dans une mauvaise affaire** to get involved *or* mixed up in a bad business; **s'e. de qn** to land oneself with sb
emphase [ɑ̃fɑz] *nf* pompousness, pomposity; **avec e.** pompously; **solennel mais sans e.** solemn but not pompous; **parler sans e.** to speak simply
emphatique [ɑ̃fatik] *adj* pompous
emphatiquement [ɑ̃fatikmɑ̃] *adv* pompously
emphysémateux, -euse [ɑ̃fizematø, -øz] *n Méd* emphysema sufferer
emphysème [ɑ̃fizɛm] *nm Méd* emphysema
empiècement [ɑ̃pjɛsmɑ̃] *nm* (*d'un vêtement*) yoke
empierrement [ɑ̃pjɛrmɑ̃] *nm* **(a)** (*action*) (*d'une route*) metalling, macadamization; *Rail* ballasting **(b)** (*couche de pierres etc*) (*d'une route*) macadam, (road) metal; *Rail* ballast
empierrer [ɑ̃pjere] *vt* (*route*) to metal, to macadamize; *Rail* to ballast
empiètement [ɑ̃pjɛtmɑ̃] *nm* encroachment **(sur** on); **c'est un e. sur ma vie privée** it's an encroachment on my private life; **cette barrière est un e. sur mon terrain** that fence encroaches on my land; **e. sur les droits de qn** infringement of sb's rights
empiéter [ɑ̃pjete] *vi* **(j'empiète; j'empiéterai) e. sur** (*le terrain, le temps, la vie privée de qn*) to encroach on; **cette affiche empiète sur l'autre** this poster overlaps the other; **son collègue essaie d'e. sur ses attributions** his colleague is trying to trespass on his territory; **e. sur les droits de qn** to infringe sb's rights
empiffrer (s') [sɑ̃pifre] *vpr F* to stuff *or* gorge oneself **(de** with)
empilable [ɑ̃pilabl] *adj* (*chaise, boîte etc*) stacking
empilage [ɑ̃pilaʒ] *nm*, **empilement** [ɑ̃pilmɑ̃] *nm* **(a)** (*action*) (*de livres, bois etc*) stacking, piling (up); **l'e. de tous ces voyageurs dans le wagon faisait peine à voir** it was painful to see all the passengers crammed into the carriage **(b)** (*pile*) pile, stack
empiler [ɑ̃pile] **1** *vt* **(a)** (*livres, bois etc*) to stack, to pile (up) **(b)** (*passagers dans un véhicule etc*) to cram **(c)** *F* (*duper*) to do; **se faire e.** to be done *or* had; **se faire e. par qn** to be done by sb **2 s'empiler** *vpr* **(a)** (*de livres, dossiers etc*) to pile up; (*former une pile*) to be piled up **(b)** (*de passagers*) **s'e. dans** to cram into
empire [ɑ̃pir] *nm* **(a)** (*domination*) authority, dominion; (*contrôle*) influence, control; **sous l'e. d'un tyran** ruled by a tyrant, under the rule *or Litt* sway of a tyrant; **avoir de l'e. sur qn** to have influence over sb; **user de** *ou* **exercer son e. sur qn** to use one's power over sb; **la religion exerce un véritable e. sur lui** religion has a real hold on him; **avoir de**

l'e. sur soi-même to be self-controlled; **avoir peu d'e. sur soi-même** to have little self-control; **avoir beaucoup d'e. sur soi-même** to be very self-controlled, to have a lot of self-control; **quand j'ai bu, je n'ai plus aucun e. sur moi-même** I lose all self-control when I drink; **faire qch sous l'e. de la boisson/de la colère** to do sth under the influence of drink/in a fit of anger; **elle s'est enfuie sous l'e. de la peur** she fled in fear

(b) *Hist, Pol* empire; *Hist* **le Saint-E. romain germanique** the Holy Roman Empire; *Hist Fr* **le premier E., l'E.** the First Empire; **le second E.** the Second Empire; **style/meubles E.** Empire style/furniture; **je ne changerais pas de travail pour un e.** I wouldn't change my job for all the tea in China *or* if you paid me

(c) (*groupe*) empire

▶ **empire**: **le Céleste E.** the Middle Kingdom, the Celestial Empire; **l'E. du Milieu** the Middle Kingdom, the Celestial Empire; **l'E. du Soleil-Levant** the Land of the Rising Sun

empirer [ɑ̃pire] **1** *vi* to worsen, to get *or* to grow worse, to deteriorate; **est-ce que les choses s'arrangent avec ton mari? – non, elles empirent** are things any better with your husband? – no, they're (getting) worse **2** *vt* to worsen, to make worse, to aggravate

empirique [ɑ̃pirik] *adj* empiric(al)

empirisme [ɑ̃pirism] *nm* empiricism

empiriste [ɑ̃pirist] *adj, n Phil* empiricist

emplacement [ɑ̃plasmɑ̃] *nm* **(a)** (*d'une tente, d'un édifice etc*) site, location; (*sur un marché, dans un parking*) space; **à l'e. d'un ancien tombeau** on the site of an old tomb; **e. publicitaire** (*sur un mur, dans un journal*) advertising space; *Naut* **e. de chargement** loading berth **(b)** *Ordinat* slot; **e. pour carte d'extension** expansion slot; **e. (pour) périphériques** extension slot; **e. d'évolutivité** upgrade slot; **e. pour carte** card slot

emplafonner [ɑ̃plafɔne] *vt F* to crash into; **elle s'est fait e. par mon voisin** my neighbour crashed into her

emplâtre [ɑ̃plɑtr] *nm* **(a)** *Pharm* (*pansement*) (sticking *or* adhesive) plaster; **e. contre** *ou* **pour les cors** corn plaster; *Fig* **c'est un e. sur une jambe de bois** it's (of) no earthly use; *F* **cette purée, quel e.!** this mashed potato is really stodgy **(b)** *F* (*personne*) wimp

emplette [ɑ̃plɛt] *nf* **(a)** (*achat*) purchase; **aller faire ses emplettes** to go shopping; **faire l'e. de qch** to buy *or* purchase sth **(b)** (*choses achetées*) **emplettes** shopping, purchases; **mes dernières emplettes** my latest purchases, the latest things I've bought

emplir [ɑ̃plir] **1** *vt* to fill (**de** with); **la foule emplissait les rues** the crowd filled the streets; **nouvelle qui m'emplit de joie** news that fills me with delight; **les enfants emplissaient la cour de rires** the playground was full of children's laughter **2 s'emplir** *vpr* to fill (up) (**de** with); **les verres s'emplissaient de vin** the glasses were being filled with wine

emploi [ɑ̃plwa] *nm* **(a)** (*utilisation*) use; **l'e. du béton est de plus en plus courant** concrete is being used increasingly; **ce mot est d'un e. rare** the word is rarely used; **je n'en aurais pas l'e.** I wouldn't have any use for it *or* get any use out of it; **quel e. vas-tu faire de tout cet argent/ce temps?** what are you going to do with all that money/time?; **je me demande quel e. il peut bien faire de ce vieux meuble?** I wonder what use he has for that old piece of furniture; **faire bon/mauvais e. de qch** to make good/bad use of sth, to put sth to good/bad use; **mode d'e.** directions *or* instructions for use; **prêt à l'e.** ready to use

(b) (*situation*) job; (*travail*) employment, work; **être sans e.** to be out of work *or* out of a job, to be unemployed; **chercher un e.** to be looking for work *or* a job; **avoir un e.** to have a job, to be in work; **la crise/situation de l'e.** the employment crisis/situation; **il faut faire quelque chose pour l'e.** something has to be done about employment; **agence nationale pour l'e.** (French state) employment agency, *Br* ≈Jobcentre®; *Journ* **demandes d'e.** situations wanted; **j'ai adressé plusieurs demandes d'e.** I sent off several job applications; *Journ* **offres d'e.** situations vacant; **création d'emplois** job creation; **sécurité de l'e.** job security; **partage de l'e.** job-sharing; *Écon, Pol* **plein e.** full employment; **les sans e.** the jobless

(c) *Th* **c'est elle qui tient l'e. de la fille de la star** she is cast as the star's daughter, she plays (the part of) the star's daughter; **on le cantonne dans des emplois de grand amoureux** he is typecast as the great lover; *Fig* **il a le physique** *ou* **la tête** *ou F* **la gueule de l'e.** he looks the part

▶ **emploi**: **emplois de proximité** = employment in the community (*as a way of reducing unemployment*) **e. saisonnier** seasonal employment; **e. du temps** timetable, schedule; **elle a un e. du temps très chargé** she has a very busy *or* full timetable *or* schedule; **e. vacant** vacancy

employé, -ée [ɑ̃plwaje] *n* employee; **e. (de bureau)** office worker; **e. de banque** bank clerk; **e. d'une administration** government employee, civil servant; **l'e. du gaz vient demain** the gas man's coming tomorrow; **e. aux écritures** accounts *or* ledger clerk; **e. des postes** post office clerk; **e. de mairie** town hall employee; **être e. des postes/de mairie** to work for the Post Office/at the town hall; **e. de chemin de fer** railway employee; **e. à l'enregistrement des bagages** check-in clerk; **être e. de maison** to do domestic work

employer [ɑ̃plwaje] (**j'emploie; j'emploierai**) **1** *vt* **(a)** (*utiliser*) (*outil, mot, technique, force etc*) to use; **e. toute son énergie à faire qch** to devote all one's energies to doing sth; **j'emploierai tous les moyens** I'll use whatever means I have to; **e. les grands moyens** to go to great lengths; **e. son temps à nettoyer/étudier** to spend one's time cleaning/studying; **il ne sait à quoi e. son temps** he doesn't know what to do with his time; **bien e. son temps** to use one's time well, to make good use of one's time, to put one's time to good use; **elle ne sait pas e. son argent** she doesn't know how to use her money; **à quoi vas-tu e. cette somme?** what are you going to spend the money on?; **cet ordinateur n'emploie que des disquettes de double densité** the computer only takes double density disks

(b) *Com* **e. une somme en recette** to put *or* enter an amount in the receipts

(c) (*faire travailler*) (*ouvrier, personnel etc*) to employ; **e. qn comme secrétaire** to employ sb as secretary; **e. qn à des corvées/des petits travaux** to employ sb to do the chores/odd jobs; **je suis employé par plusieurs sociétés** I am employed by *or* I work for several companies

2 s'employer *vpr* **(a)** (*d'une personne*) **s'e. à faire qch** to work on doing sth; **je m'y emploie** I'm working on it

(b) (*être utilisé*) to be used

(c) *Vieilli* **s'e. pour qn** to exert oneself on sb's behalf

employeur, -euse [ɑ̃plwajœr, -øz] *n* employer

emplumé [ɑ̃plyme] *adj* feathered

empocher [ɑ̃pɔʃe] *vt* **(a)** (*toucher*) (*argent, chèque etc*) to pocket, to receive **(b)** (*mettre dans sa poche*) to pocket

empoignade [ɑ̃pwaɲad] *nf F* brawl, punch-up

empoigne [ɑ̃pwaɲ] *nf F* **c'était la foire d'e. dans les magasins** it was bedlam in the shops, the shops were full of people pushing and shoving; **je n'ai jamais vu une vente aux enchères où c'était autant la foire d'e.** I've never seen such bedlam at an auction; **c'est la foire d'e. pour se faire servir** it's a real scrum getting served; **quelle foire d'e. ici!** what a scrum!; **la vie n'est qu'une foire d'e.** life's just a rat race *or* a free-for-all

empoigner [ɑ̃pwaɲe] **1** *vt* **(a)** (*attraper*) (*objet*) to grab (hold of), to grasp, to seize; (*personne*) to seize, to grab (hold of), *F* to collar **(b)** (*émouvoir*) (*lecteur, spectateur etc*) to grip, to thrill; **ce film m'a empoigné** I was gripped by the film **2 s'empoigner** *vpr* to brawl, to have a punch-up

empois [ɑ̃pwa] *nm* (laundry) starch; *Tex* dressing

empoisonnant [ɑ̃pwazɔnɑ̃] *adj F* (*irritant*) annoying, irritating; (*ennuyeux*) boring; **c'est vraiment e., ces retards continuels** these constant delays are an absolute pain

empoisonnement [ɑ̃pwazɔnmɑ̃] *nm* **(a)** (*intoxication*) (*d'une personne, de la nourriture*) poisoning **(b)** *F* (*souci, ennui*) problem; **je n'ai que des empoisonnements** I've got nothing but problems; **la vie avec lui est un e. continuel** life with him is just one thing after another; **quel e.!** what a pain (in the neck)!

empoisonner [ɑ̃pwazɔne] **1** *vt* **(a)** (*intoxiquer*) (*personne, nourriture, animal, flèche, étang*) to poison; *Fig* **empoisonné** (*trait, paroles*) poisonous, vicious; *Fig* **cette promotion est empoisonnée** this promotion is a pain in the neck; *Fig* **faire un cadeau empoisonné à qn** to give sb an unwelcome gift

(b) (*empester*) **du poisson pourri empoisonnait la pièce** there was a smell of rotten fish in the room, the room smelled of rotten fish; **des odeurs de cuisine empoisonnaient la pièce** the room was full of cooking smells; **odeur qui empoisonne l'air** smell that taints the air

(c) *Fig* (*altérer*) (*existence, mariage*) to poison; *F* (*irriter*) to annoy, to irritate; (*ennuyer*) to bore; **e. la vie de qn** to make sb's life a misery; **vraiment, ça m'empoisonne de devoir y aller** I'm really fed up about having to go; **il m'empoisonne à toujours me téléphoner** I'm fed up with his constant telephoning

2 s'empoisonner *vpr* **(a)** (*se tuer*) to poison oneself

(b) *Fig* (*s'ennuyer*) to be bored; **qu'est-ce qu'on s'empoisonne dans cette soirée!** this is a really boring party!; **s'e. l'existence** to make one's life a misery; **essaie de trouver ce livre mais ne t'empoisonne pas l'existence avec ça** try to find the book but don't go to too much trouble over it

empoisonneur, -euse [ɑ̃pwazɔnœr, -øz] *n* (**a**) (*criminel*) poisoner (**b**) *F* (*personne qui ennuie*) bore; (*personne qui irrite*) nuisance, pest

empoissonner [ɑ̃pwasɔne] *vt* to stock with fish

emporté, -ée [ɑ̃pɔrte] **1** *adj* (*personne*) irascible, quick-tempered; **avoir un caractère e.** to be irascible *or* quick-tempered, to be quick to lose one's temper; **d'un ton e.** irascibly **2** *n* irascible *or* quick-tempered person; **je ne veux plus travailler avec un e. pareil** I don't want to work with somebody who's so irascible *or* quick-tempered

emportement [ɑ̃pɔrtəmɑ̃] *nm* (**a**) (*colère*) (fit of) anger; **répondre avec e.** to reply angrily (**b**) *Litt, Vieilli* (*élan*) (*d'enthousiasme, d'excitation etc*) burst, surge; **dans l'e. de la discussion** in the heat of the debate

emporte-pièce [ɑ̃pɔrtəpjɛs] *nm inv Tech* punch; *Culin* pastry cutter; **découper qch à l'e.** to stamp *or* punch sth out; *Culin* to cut out (with a pastry cutter); *Fig* **style à l'e.** incisive style; *Fig* **mots à l'e.** biting *or* cutting words; *Fig* **répondre à l'e.** to reply incisively *or* trenchantly

emporter [ɑ̃pɔrte] **1** *vt* (**a**) (*partir et prendre avec soi*) to take (with one); (*enlever d'un lieu*) to take away; (*emmener*) to carry *or* take away; **e. un blessé sur un brancard** to carry off *or* take away a wounded man on a stretcher; **ils ont emporté de quoi manger** they took some food with them; **plats à e.** take-away food; *F* **il ne l'emportera pas au paradis** I'll get my own back on him sooner or later; **(que) le diable l'emporte!** to hell with him!; **le train qui m'emporte vers le nord** the train which is carrying *or* taking me northwards; **il a emporté son secret dans la tombe** he took his secret to the grave (with him)

(**b**) (*entraîner, arracher*) (*du courant, de la lave*) to sweep *or* carry away; **le choléra l'emporta** cholera carried him off; **il a eu une jambe emportée par un obus** a shell took *or* blew one of his legs off; **le vent emporta son chapeau** the wind blew his hat off *or* away; **la tempête a emporté le toit** the roof came off in the storm; *Fig* **autant en emporte le vent** promises are cheap, talk is easy; **cette moutarde vous emporte la bouche** *ou Arg* **la gueule** this mustard takes the roof off your mouth; *Fig* **se laisser e. par** (*la colère, l'enthousiasme, l'imagination, les sentiments*) to get *or* let oneself be carried away by

(**c**) (*conquérir*) (*fort, ville etc*) to take (by assault); **e. la victoire** to be victorious, to be the victor (**contre** over); **e. la décision** to win out, to carry the day; *F* **e. le morceau** to win one's case; **l'équipe nantaise l'a emporté par deux buts à zéro** the Nantes team won (by) two goals to nil; **le coureur hollandais l'emporte haut la main** the Dutch runner is winning hands down; **avec lui, c'est toujours l'amitié qui l'emporte** friendship is always the most important consideration *or* outweighs everything else as far as he's concerned; **considérations qui l'emportent sur toutes les autres** considerations that override *or* outweigh all others; **ce dossier/ce candidat/ce prototype l'emporte sur tous les autres** this file/candidate/prototype stands head and shoulders above the others *or* is streets ahead of the others; **en ce qui concerne le culot, elle l'emporte vraiment sur tout le monde** she's streets ahead of everybody when it comes to cheek; **ici, la pluie l'emporte sur le soleil** there's much more rain than sunshine here; **ici, le rugby l'emporte sur le foot** rugby is more important *or* popular than football here

2 s'emporter *vpr* (**a**) to lose one's temper, to fly into a rage (**contre qn** with sb)

(**b**) (*d'un cheval*) to bolt

empoté, -ée [ɑ̃pɔte] *F* **1** *adj* cack-handed **2** *n* cack-handed idiot

empoter [ɑ̃pɔte] *vt* (*plantes*) to pot

empourprer [ɑ̃purpre] **1** *vt* to tinge with crimson **2 s'empourprer** *vpr* (*d'un visage*) to flush, to go crimson; (*du ciel*) to turn crimson

empoussiéré [ɑ̃pusjere] *adj* covered with dust, dusty

empreindre [ɑ̃prɛ̃dr] (*prp* **empreignant**; *pp* **empreint**; *pr ind* **j'empreins, il empreint, n. empreignons, ils empreignent**; *impf* **j'empreignais**; *p hist* **j'empreignis**; *fu* **j'empreindrai**) **1** *vt* (*dans la cire*) to impress, to imprint, to stamp; *Fig* **visage empreint de mélancolie/de terreur** face marked *or* stamped with sadness/full of terror; *Fig* **c'est empreint dans mon esprit** it is stamped on my mind; *Fig* **article empreint d'un certain sérieux** article with serious overtones; *Fig* **des histoires empreintes de drame** stories tinged with drama **2 s'empreindre** *vpr* (*d'un visage, d'une expression etc*) to be marked *or* stamped (**de** with)

empreinte [ɑ̃prɛ̃t] *nf* (**a**) (*trace, impression*) impression, (im)print; *Typ* mould, *US* mold; (*de satellite*) footprint; **prendre l'e. de qch** to take an impression of sth; **les loups ont laissé des empreintes dans la neige** the wolves left tracks *or* footprints in the snow; **e. des roues** tyre tracks; **e. de pas** footprint; **e. de doigt** fingermark; **prendre** *ou* **relever les empreintes de qn** to take sb's fingerprints, to fingerprint sb; **relever les empreintes sur un revolver** to fingerprint a revolver

(**b**) *Fig* (*du génie, du passé, de l'éducation etc*) stamp, (hall)mark; **mettre son e. sur qch** to put one's stamp *or* mark on sth; **marquer qn/qch de son e.** to put one's stamp *or* mark on sb/sth; **être marqué de l'e. de qn** to bear sb's stamp *or* mark

▶ **empreinte**: **e. digitale** fingerprint; **e. génétique** genetic fingerprint; **avoir recours aux empreintes génétiques** to use genetic fingerprinting; **e. en plâtre** plaster cast; **e. vocale** voice print

empressé, -ée [ɑ̃prese] **1** *adj* (**a**) (*prévenant*) (*vendeur*) eager, willing; (*serviteur, docteur, admirateur etc*) attentive; **des soins empressés** assiduous attentions; **ils m'ont entouré de soins empressés** they gave me every care and consideration; **il lui fait une cour empressée** he is courting her assiduously (**b**) *Litt* (*pressé*) **il est e. à vous revoir** he is eager to see you again **2** *n Péj* **faire l'e. auprès de qn** to dance attendance on sb

empressement [ɑ̃prɛsmɑ̃] *nm* (**a**) (*prévenance*) (*d'un vendeur*) eagerness, willingness (**à faire qch** to do sth); (*d'un serviteur, docteur, admirateur etc*) attentiveness; **témoigner de l'e. auprès de qn** to pay marked attention(s) to sb; **son e. auprès des femmes est presque gênant** he is almost embarrassingly attentive to women

(**b**) (*hâte*) eagerness; **il montre peu d'e. à faire les travaux** he doesn't seem to be very eager *or* keen to do the work; **avec e.** eagerly; **tous les soirs il rentre chez lui avec e.** he hurries home every evening, he is eager to get home every evening; **mettre beaucoup d'e. à faire qch** to hasten to do sth

empresser (s') [sɑ̃prese] *vpr* (**a**) (*se dépêcher*) **s'e. de faire qch** to hurry to do sth; **il s'empressa de répondre à ma lettre** he lost no time in answering my letter (**b**) (*être prévenant*) **s'e. à faire qch** to do sth eagerly, to hasten to do sth; **s'e. auprès de qn** to pay marked attention(s) to sb; **s'e. autour d'un accidenté de la route** to be busy attending to the victim of a road accident; **tout le monde s'empresse autour d'elle** everyone crowds *or* flocks round her

emprise [ɑ̃priz] *nf* (**a**) (*domination*) hold; **avoir de l'e. sur qn** to have a hold over sb; **sous l'e. de l'alcool** under the influence of alcohol; **sous l'e. de son amour pour elle** swayed by his love for her; **c'est sous l'e. de la colère qu'il l'a mise à la porte** he fired her in a fit of anger (**b**) *Jur* (*de terres etc à des fins publiques*) expropriation, acquisition

emprisonnement [ɑ̃prizɔnmɑ̃] *nm* imprisonment; **e. à perpétuité** life imprisonment; **peine d'e.** prison sentence; **il a été condamné à une peine d'e. de cinq ans** he was sentenced to five years in prison *or Fml* to a five-year term of imprisonment, he was given a five-year prison sentence

emprisonner [ɑ̃prizɔne] *vt* (**a**) (*mettre en prison*) to imprison, to put in prison (**b**) *Fig* (*serrer*) (*esprit*) to imprison; **e. le buste dans un corset** to squeeze into a corset; **il ne supporte pas les cols roulés parce qu'il se sent emprisonné** he hates rollnecks because he feels constricted in them; **col qui emprisonne le cou** collar that is too tight

emprunt [ɑ̃prœ̃] *nm* (**a**) (*action*) borrowing; **faire l'e. de qch** to borrow sth; **donner qch à qn à titre d'e.** to give sth to sb as a loan *or* on loan; **ce n'est pas à moi, c'est un e.** it's not mine, it's borrowed; **nom d'e.** assumed name; **son nom de scène est un nom d'e.** he acts under an assumed name

(**b**) (*somme*) loan; **faire un e. à qn** to borrow (money) from sb; **faire un e.** (*auprès d'une banque etc*) to take out a loan; **e. public** public loan; **e. d'État** government loan; *Bourse* state bond; **e. à court/long terme** short-/long-term loan; **procéder à un nouvel e.** to make a new loan issue; **faire un e. de plusieurs millions à la banque** to borrow several million from the bank, to take out a bank loan of several million; **e. en devises** currency loan; **e. garanti** secured loan; **e. indexé** indexed loan; **e. obligataire** bond issue, loan stock; (*titre*) debenture bond; **e. obligataire convertible** convertible loan stock; **e. à terme** term loan

(**c**) *Ling* borrowing (**à l'anglais** from English)

emprunté [ɑ̃prœ̃te] *adj* (*manière, personne*) self-conscious, stiff, awkward; **il était tellement impressionné par elle qu'il en devenait e.** he was so impressed by her that it made him self-conscious; **dit-elle d'un ton e.** she said self-consciously *or* awkwardly

emprunter [ɑ̃prœ̃te] **1** *vt* (**a**) (*objet, argent*) to borrow (**à** from); **est-ce que je peux t'e. ton fiancé pour cette danse?** can I borrow your fiancé for this dance?; **elle a emprunté ses**

manières à sa mère she copies her mother's ways **(b)** *(route, chemin)* to take; **le cortège emprunta la rue de Rivoli** the procession took *or* went down the Rue de Rivoli **2** *vi* to take out a loan, to borrow; **e. sur** to borrow against

emprunteur, -euse [ɑ̃prœ̃tœr, -øz] *n* borrower

empuantir [ɑ̃pyɑ̃tir] *vt* to make stink; *(pièce)* to stink out, to make stink

ému [emy] *adj (touché)* moved, touched; *(passionné)* roused; **voix émue** voice filled with emotion; **garder un souvenir é. de qch** to retain a touching memory of sth; **j'en suis encore tout é.** I still haven't got over it; **être é. (jusqu')aux larmes par qch** to be moved to tears by sth; **il était trop é. pour s'asseoir/lui parler** he was too nervous to sit down/talk to her

émulateur [emylatœr] *nm Ordinat* emulator; **é. de terminal** terminal emulator; **é. graphique** graphics emulator

émulation [emylasjɔ̃] *nf* **(a)** *(concurrence)* competitiveness **(b)** *Ordinat* emulation; **é. de terminal** terminal emulation

émule [emyl] *n (imitateur)* emulator; *(concurrent)* competitor; **j'ai fait des émules** people followed my lead *or* example

émuler [emyle] *vt Ordinat* to emulate

émulseur [emylsœr] *nm (appareil)* emulsifier

émulsif, -ive [emylsif, -iv] *adj Pharm* emulsive; *Ch* emulsifying

émulsifiable [emylsifjabl] *adj Ch* emulsifiable

émulsifiant [emylsifjɑ̃] **1** *adj* emulsifying **2** *nm* emulsifier

émulsifier [emylsifje] *vt* to emulsify

émulsion [emylsjɔ̃] *nf* emulsion

émulsionner [emylsjɔne] *vt* to emulsify

EN [əɛn] *nf abrév* **École normale**

en[1] [ɑ̃] *prép* [①B53] **(a)** *(lieu)* in; *(avec mouvement)* to; **être/aller en ville/montagne** to be in/to go (in)to town/the mountains; **en province** in the country, in the provinces; **il est parti en mer** he's gone to sea; **une promenade en mer** a boat trip; **en tête/queue** at the head/in the rear; **la suite en page quatre** continued on page four; **aller en France/Amérique** to go to France/America; **être en Avignon/Arles** to be in Avignon/Arles; **être en Saône-et-Loire** to be in Saône-et-Loire; **regarder en l'air** to look up at the sky; **le mariage aura lieu en l'église Saint-Jean** the marriage will be celebrated *or* held at St. John's (Church); **c'était comment en classe aujourd'hui?** how was school today?; **le Christ en croix** Jesus on the cross; **garde ça en mémoire** keep that in mind; **de branche en branche** from branch to branch

(b) *(avec pron pers)* **il y a quelque chose en lui que j'admire** there is something I admire about him; **un homme en qui** *ou* **en lequel j'ai confiance** a man whom I trust; **c'est en nous-mêmes que nous devons chercher la réponse** we must look for the answer within ourselves; **en chaque être** in every being

(c) *(temps)* in; **en été/automne/hiver** in (the) summer/autumn/winter; **né en 1905** born in 1905; **en avril** in April; **aujourd'hui en huit** a week today; **on peut y aller en cinq heures** you can get there in five hours; **en l'an 1800** in (the year) 1800; **en ce temps-là** in those days, at that time; **d'année en année** from year to year, year by year; **son état s'aggravait de jour en jour** he was getting worse by the day; **fermé en semaine** closed weekdays; **il a été guéri en deux semaines** he was cured (with)in two weeks

(d) *(état)* in; **être en deuil/en loques/en tenue de sport** to be in mourning/in rags/in sports clothes; **lait en poudre** powdered milk; **en vers/prose** in verse/prose; **en direct** live; **laisser les choses en l'état** to leave everything as it is; **en l'absence du chef** in the absence of the boss; **en présence de mon avocat** in the presence of my lawyer; **arbres en fleur** trees in blossom *or* flower; **être en guerre** to be at war; **en vacances** on holiday

(e) *(composition)* made of; **montre en or** gold watch; **c'est en or** it's made of gold; **table en marbre** marble table; **évier en inox** stainless-steel sink; **pull en laine** woollen sweater

(f) *(description)* **escalier en spirale** spiral staircase; **chemin en pente** sloping road; **docteur en médecine** doctor of medicine; **peintre en bâtiment** house painter; **fort/faible en mathématiques** good/bad at mathematics; **parler en français/anglais** to speak in French/English; **marcher en silence** to walk in silence; **en votre honneur** in your honour

(g) *(annonce un changement)* into; **changé en serpent** changed into a serpent; **traduire une lettre en français** to translate a letter into French; **peindre qch en bleu** to paint sth blue; **de mal en pis** from bad to worse; **tomber en admiration devant** to be filled with admiration for

(h) *(indique une division)* **briser qch en morceaux** to break sth (in)to bits; **casser qch en deux** to break sth in two; **pièce en trois actes** play in three acts; **vendre en paquets/feuilles** to sell in packets/sheets

(i) *(manière)* **s'épuiser en d'inutiles efforts** to exhaust oneself in useless efforts; **venir en taxi/avion** to come by taxi/by plane *or* air; **en trois bonds** in three jumps

(j) *(comme)* **envoyer qch en cadeau** to send sth as a present; **donner qch à qn en compensation** to give sb sth by way of *or* as compensation; **il mourut en brave** he died like the brave man that he was; **agir en honnête homme** to act like an honest man; **prendre la chose en philosophe** to take it philosophically

(k) [①B35,1,c,ii] *(avec gérondif)* **il marchait en lisant son journal** he walked along reading his paper; **il répondit en riant** he answered with a laugh; **elle entra/sortit en dansant** she danced in/out; **on apprend en vieillissant** we learn as we grow older; **en faisant cela vous l'offenserez** you'll offend him by doing that; **en arrivant à Paris** on arriving in Paris; **en vous écrivant hier j'ai oublié de vous le dire** I forgot to mention it when writing to you yesterday; **en attendant** while waiting, in the meantime; **tout en tricotant elle nous racontait des histoires** as she knitted she told us stories; **s'enrhumer en marchant sous la pluie** to catch a cold (through *or* from) walking in the rain; **tout en étant riche, il vit très simplement** whilst (he is) rich, he leads a very simple life

en[2] *pron* [①B18,3] **(a)** *(de cet endroit)* from there; **il en revient** he's just come back from there; **où en étions-nous?** *(dans un livre, travail etc)* where were we?; **j'en sors à l'instant** I'm just leaving

(b) *(de ce fait)* **si vous étiez riche, en seriez-vous plus heureux?** if you were rich, would you be happier for it *or* any the happier?; **je n'en dors plus la nuit** it keeps me awake at night, I can't sleep at night for it; **j'en ris encore** I still laugh about it; **en tirer une conclusion** to draw a conclusion from it; **j'en suis encore toute retournée** I'm still all of a flutter

(c) *(remplaçant un nom régi par* **de)** **j'aime mieux n'en pas parler** *ou* **ne pas en parler** I would rather not speak about it; **combien en demande-t-il** *ou* **en veut-il?** how much does he want for it?; **qu'en pensez-vous?** what do you think of *or* about it?; **les rues en sont pleines** the streets are full of it/them; **il reçut une blessure et en mourut** he received a wound and died of *or* from it; **il en devint amoureux** he fell in love with her; **il faut en faire un film!** they should make a film of it *or* turn it into a film!; **que vais-je en faire, de cette table?** what am I going to do with this table?

(d) *(de choses, remplaçant le possessif)* **j'ai la valise mais je n'en ai pas la clef** I have the suitcase but I haven't (got) the key (for it); **prends la boîte mais n'en perds pas le couvercle** take the box, but don't lose the lid (to it); **je ne savais rien de cet endroit, je n'en connaissais que le nom** I didn't know anything about the place, I only knew the name

(e) *(remplaçant une proposition)* **il ne l'a pas fait, mais il en est capable** he didn't do it but he's (quite) capable of it

(f) *(nombre, quantité)* **j'en ai un/trois/plusieurs** I have one/three/several (of them); **combien en voulez-vous?** *(quantité)* how much do you want?; *(nombre)* how many do you want?; **elle en a déjà vu beaucoup pour son âge** she has already seen a lot for her age; **j'en ai** I have some; **je n'en ai pas** I don't have any, I have none; **en avez-vous?** do you have any, have you (got) any?; **parmi ses livres il y en a d'excellents** some of his books are excellent; **il en a mangé deux cuillerées** he ate two spoonfuls (of it)

(g) *(locutions)* **je n'en ai pas encore fini avec lui** I haven't done *or* finished with him yet; **si le cœur vous en dit** if you feel so inclined, if you feel like it; **en venir aux mains** to come to blows; **est-ce à ça que tu en es réduit?** have you been reduced to that?; **ne t'en fais pas!** don't worry!; **il en va de même pour toi** it's the same for you; **il en est ainsi** that's the way it is; **je n'en puis plus** I can't bear it any longer; **elle en aime un autre** she loves someone else; **à en croire les racontars** if we are able to believe the tales; **il y en a qui ...** some people ...

(h) *(après un impératif)* **prenez-en** take some; **prenez-en dix** take ten (of them); **va-t'en, allez-vous-en** go away; **va en chercher** go and get some; **donne-m'en!**, *F* **donne-moi-z-en!** give me some!; **souvenez-vous-en!** remember!

(i) *(après la forme pronominale de certains verbes)* **s'en aller** to go away; **il s'en est allé** he went away; **s'en retourner** to go back, to return

en[3] [ɛn] *nm Typ* en

ENA [ena] *nf abrév* **École nationale d'administration**

enamouré [ɑ̃namure], **énamouré** [enamure] *adj (regard, sourire etc)* amorous; **être e.** *ou* **é. de qn** to be enamoured *or US* enamored of sb

enamourer (s') [sɑ̃namure], **énamourer (s')** [senamure] *vpr* to become enamoured *or US* enamored **(de** of)

énarque [enark] *n* = graduate of the École nationale d'administration

en-arrière [ɑ̃narjɛr] *nm inv* (*au patinage*) backward glide

énarthrose [enartroz] *nf Anat* ball-and-socket joint, *Spéc* enarthrosis

en-avant [ɑ̃navɑ̃] *nm inv* (**a**) *Rugby* forward pass; (*dans les mains*) knock-on (**b**) (*au patinage*) forward glide

en-but [ɑ̃by(t)] *nm inv Rugby* in-goal

encabaner (s') [sɑ̃kabane] *vpr Can* to shut oneself up *or* away

encablure [ɑ̃kablyr] *nf Arch* (*mesure*) cable (length) (*approx 200 m*); *Hum* **je n'habite qu'à quelques encablures du bureau** I live a stone's throw from the office

encadré [ɑ̃kadre] **1** *nm* (*dans un texte*) box; (*presse écrite*) boxed article; (*petites annonces*) display advertisement; *Ordinat* **e. graphique** graphics box; *Ordinat* **e. texte** text box **2** *adj Typ* panelled-in, boxed

encadrement [ɑ̃kadrəmɑ̃] *nm* (**a**) (*d'un tableau, d'une fenêtre etc*) (*action*) framing; (*cadre*) frame; **dans l'e. de la porte** in the doorway; *Tech* **e. en caoutchouc** rubber seal

(**b**) *Admin, Ind, Sp etc* (*action d'encadrer*) (*du personnel, d'une équipe sportive*) management; (*d'un groupe d'enfants, de handicapés, d'étudiants*) supervision; *Mil* (*d'une unité*) officering; (*personnes qui encadrent*) (*du personnel, d'une équipe sportive*) management, managers; *Mil* officers; (*cadres*) executives; **fonctions d'e.** executive functions; **personnel d'e.** management, managerial staff; **e. d'une colonie de vacances** supervisory staff of a holiday camp

(**c**) *Écon* **e. du crédit** restriction on credit, credit restriction(s) *or* squeeze; **diminuer l'e. du crédit** to reduce credit restrictions, to loosen the credit squeeze; **e. des prix** price control(s)

encadrer [ɑ̃kadre] *vt* (**a**) (*tableau, photo, porte etc*) to frame

(**b**) (*entourer*) (*des mots, une phrase*) to circle; (*le visage*) to frame; **jardin encadré de haies** garden enclosed by hedges; **encadré par deux gendarmes** flanked by two policemen; **encadré de ses gardes du corps/de jolies filles** surrounded by his bodyguards/by pretty girls

(**c**) *Admin, Ind, Sp etc* (*personnel, équipe*) to manage; (*groupe d'enfants, de handicapés, d'étudiants*) to supervise; *Mil* (*unité*) to officer; **nous sommes bien encadrés** our management is good

(**d**) *F* (*supporter*) **je ne peux pas l'e.** I can't stand *or* abide him

(**e**) *Aut F* **il a encadré un arbre** he wrapped his vehicle round a tree

encadreur, -euse [ɑ̃kadrœr, -øz] *n* picture framer

encager [ɑ̃kaʒe] *vt* (**j'encageai(s); n. encageons**) (*oiseau, animal*) to cage; **tenir qn encagé** to keep sb caged up; **tenir un oiseau/un animal encagé** to keep a bird/an animal in a cage *or* caged up

encagoulé [ɑ̃kagule] *adj* hooded

encaissable [ɑ̃kɛsabl] *adj* cashable, *Br* encashable

encaisse [ɑ̃kɛs] *nf Com* cash (in hand); **e. de 1 000 francs** cash balance of 1,000 francs; **e. or et argent** *ou* **e. métallique d'un pays** gold and silver holding of a country; *Banque* **pas d'e.** no funds

encaissé [ɑ̃kese] *adj* (*vallée*) deep; (*rivière*) deeply embanked; (*route*) sunken

encaissement [ɑ̃kɛsmɑ̃] *nm* (**a**) (*d'un chèque*) cashing, paying in, *Br* encashment; (*d'argent*) receipt, collection; (*d'une traite*) collection; **donner un chèque à l'e.** to cash a cheque (**b**) (*d'une vallée*) depth; (*d'une rivière*) deep embankment; **dans l'e. de la route** in the deep cutting made by the road

encaisser [ɑ̃kese] **1** *vt* (**a**) (*chèque*) to cash, *Br* to encash; (*argent*) to receive, to collect; (*traite*) to collect; **e. de l'argent** (*sur son compte*) to pay in cash; *Bourse* **e. un premium** to receive a premium

(**b**) *F* (*supporter*) (*des coups, des remarques, des critiques*) to take; **je ne sais comment il fait pour e. les coups aussi bien** I don't know how he stands up to being hit; **je n'arrive plus à e. ma belle-mère** I can't take my mother-in-law any more; **je ne peux pas l'e.** I can't stand him

(**c**) (*resserrer*) (*de collines*) to hem in; *Tech* (*rivière etc*) to embank; **les montagnes encaissent la route/la rivière** the road/river is hemmed in by mountains on both sides

(**d**) *Com* **encaisser des marchandises** to pack goods

2 s'encaisser *vpr* (*d'une rivière, route etc*) to be hemmed in; **la route s'encaisse profondément entre les montagnes** mountains tower above the road on both sides

3 *vi F* **il sait e.** he can take it; **qu'est-ce qu'il a encaissé!** he took a lot of punishment; **elle a plutôt bien encaissé** she took it rather well; **e. sans broncher** to grin and bear it

encaisseur [ɑ̃kɛsœr] *nm* (*de loyer, dettes etc*) collector

encan [ɑ̃kɑ̃] *nm* **vendre qch à l'e.** to sell sth by *or* at auction; *aussi Fig* **mettre qch à l'e.** to put sth up for auction; *Fig* **la loi semble mettre la justice à l'e.** the law seems to put a low price on justice

encanaillement [ɑ̃kanajmɑ̃] *nm* slumming it; **l'e. des bourgeoises au XIXe siècle** middle class women's liking in the 19th century for the seamy side of life

encanailler (s') [sɑ̃kanaje] *vpr* to like slumming it, to hang around with doubtful characters; **il faudrait qu'elle s'encanaille un peu** she ought to break out *or* loosen up a bit and live

encapuchonner [ɑ̃kapyʃɔne] **1** *vt* (*qn, la tête de qn*) to put a hood on; (*machine*) to put a hood on, to cover (with a hood); (*stylo*) to put the top on; **encapuchonné** hooded **2 s'encapuchonner** *vpr* to put on a *or* one's hood

encart [ɑ̃kar] *nm Journ* slip sheet; (*attaché*) inset; (*mobile*) (loose) insert; **e. publicitaire** *Journ* advertising supplement; *TV, Rad* commercial break

encarter [ɑ̃karte] *vt* (**a**) *Typ* (*pages*) to inset; (*notice dans un livre*) to insert (**b**) (*épingles, boutons etc*) to card

en-cas [ɑ̃ka] *nm inv* snack (meal)

encaserner [ɑ̃kazɛrne] *vt Mil* to put in barracks; **être encaserné à** to be barracked at

encastrable [ɑ̃kastrabl] *adj* (*machine à laver, cuisinière etc*) that can be built in *or* fitted

encastré [ɑ̃kastre] *adj* (*machine à laver, cuisinière*) built-in, fitted; (*four, baignoire*) built-in; (*interrupteur*) flush-fitting, set-in

encastrement [ɑ̃kastrəmɑ̃] *nm* (**a**) (*action*) (*d'une machine à laver, cuisinière*) fitting, building in; (*d'un interrupteur*) flush-fitting, setting in (**b**) (*espace prévu*) recess

encastrer [ɑ̃kastre] **1** *vt* (*machine à laver, cuisinière*) to build in, to fit; (*four, baignoire*) to build in; (*interrupteur*) to flush fit, to set in **2 s'encastrer** *vpr* (*de deux éléments*) to fit together; **s'e. dans** (*d'une machine à laver, une cuisinière*) to fit into; **la voiture s'est encastrée sous un camion** the car embedded itself under a lorry

encaustiquage [ɑ̃kɔstikaʒ, ɑ̃ko-] *nm* (*d'un parquet, de meubles etc*) waxing, wax-polishing

encaustique [ɑ̃kɔstik, ɑ̃ko-] *nf* (*pour les meubles*) wax, polish

encaustiquer [ɑ̃kɔstike, ɑ̃ko-] *vt* (*parquet, meubles etc*) to wax, to polish

encavement [ɑ̃kavmɑ̃] *nm* (*du vin*) cellaring

encaver [ɑ̃kave] *vt* (*vin etc*) to cellar

enceindre [ɑ̃sɛ̃dr] *vt* (*conj like* **ceindre**) to surround (**de** with)

enceinte[1] [ɑ̃sɛ̃t] *nf* (**a**) (*mur*) (surrounding) wall; (*palissade*) fence (**b**) (*espace*) enclosure; (*d'église, de couvent etc*) precinct(s); *Courses de chevaux* ring; **dans l'e. du parc** within *or* inside (the confines of) the park; **il est interdit de pénétrer en voiture dans l'e. du parc** cars may not enter the park, cars are not allowed into the park; **dans l'e. de l'école** on school premises; **en dehors de l'e. de l'école** outside school (**c**) (*sonore*) **e.** (**acoustique**) speaker

enceinte[2] *adj* pregnant, *F* expecting, *Litt* with child; **femme e.** pregnant woman, expectant mother; **e. de cinq mois** five months pregnant; **être e. d'un petit garçon/de jumeaux** to be expecting a little boy/twins; **elle est e. de Paul** she's pregnant by Paul, she's expecting Paul's child; **mettre qn e.** to make *or* get sb pregnant

encens [ɑ̃sɑ̃] *nm* incense

encensement [ɑ̃sɑ̃smɑ̃] *nm* (**a**) *Rel* censing (**b**) *Fig* flattery, toadying

encenser [ɑ̃sɑ̃se] **1** *vt* (**a**) *Rel* to cense (**b**) *Fig* **e. qn** to flatter sb outrageously **2** *vi* (*d'un cheval*) to toss its head up and down

encenseur, -euse [ɑ̃sɑ̃sœr, -øz] *n* (**a**) *Rel* thurifer, censer bearer (**b**) *Fig Vieilli* sycophant

encensoir [ɑ̃sɑ̃swar] *nm Rel* censer; *Fig Péj* **donner des coups d'e.** to butter people up; **donner des coups d'e. à qui il faut** to butter up the right people

encéphalite [ɑ̃sefalit] *nf Méd* encephalitis; **e. léthargique** sleeping sickness; *Vét* **e. bovine spongiforme** bovine spongiform encephalopathy, BSE

encéphalogramme [ɑ̃sefalɔgram] *nm Méd* (electro)encephalogram

encéphalographie [ɑ̃sefalɔgrafi] *nf Méd* (electro)encephalography

encéphalomyélite [ɑ̃sefalɔmjelit] *nf Méd* encephalomyelitis

encerclement [ɑ̃sɛrkləmɑ̃] *nm* encircling, surrounding; **après l'e. de l'ennemi** after the enemy was surrounded *or* encircled

encercler [ɑ̃sɛrkle] *vt* (**a**) (*ennemi, manifestants etc*) to encircle, to surround (**b**) (*mot*) to circle, to ring

enchaîné [ɑ̃ʃene] *nm TV, Cin* dissolve, mix

enchaînement [ɑ̃ʃɛnmɑ̃] *nm* (**a**) (*série*) (*d'événements*) series, chain, train; (*d'idées, de mesures*) series (**b**) (*liaison*) (*d'idées, de séquences etc*) linking, connection; *TV, Cin* (*entre deux vues*) melt; **l'e. des paragraphes est très**

important the way in which the paragraphs follow on from each other *or* the paragraphs are linked is very important; **par un e. des idées** by connecting *or* linking up ideas **(c)** *Danse* sequence (of steps); *(en ballet)* enchaînement **(d)** *(dans un spectacle)* filler **(e)** *Ordinat* concatenation

enchaîner [ɑ̃ʃene] **1** *vt* **(a)** *(animal)* to chain up; *(prisonnier)* to chain up, to put in chains; *Fig (la presse, les passions)* to curb; **e. à un poteau** to chain (up) to a post

(b) *(lier) (idées, faits, mots etc)* to link (up), to connect; **il est incapable d'e. deux phrases** he can't string *or* put two sentences together; **ils enchaînaient les sujets très vite** they moved very quickly from one subject to another; **e. le tournage de plusieurs épisodes** to shoot several episodes one after the other; **pour la répétition de ce soir, on enchaîne toutes les scènes/chansons** at this evening's rehearsal we'll run through all the scenes/songs one after the other without a break

2 s'enchaîner *vpr (de faits, d'épisodes etc)* to be linked together; **on voit comme les choses s'enchaînent** you can see how things hang together *or* are linked together; **les événements se sont enchaînés si vite** things moved *or* happened so quickly

3 *vi* **(a)** *(continuer)* to move on, to go on, to carry on; **e. sur un sujet** to move on to a subject; **on enchaîne avec les nouvelles internationales** we'll move on to the international news

(b) *Cin* to dissolve, to fade *(into next scene)*; *Th* to carry straight on

enchanté [ɑ̃ʃɑ̃te] *adj* **(a)** *(magique etc) (personne, objet, endroit)* enchanted; **la Flûte enchantée** the Magic Flute **(b)** *(ravi)* enchanted, delighted; **être e. de qch** to be enchanted by *or* delighted with sth; **e. (de faire votre connaissance)** pleased to meet you, how do you do?

enchantement [ɑ̃ʃɑ̃tmɑ̃] *nm* **(a)** *(magie)* enchantment, magic; *(effet)* (magic) spell; **rompre un e.** to break a spell; **comme par e.** as if by magic; **c'est par e. qu'elle s'est transformé en princesse** she was magically turned into a princess **(b)** *(ravissement)* enchantment, delight; *(merveille)* delight; **être dans l'e.** to be enchanted *or* delighted **(de** by)

enchanter [ɑ̃ʃɑ̃te] *vt* **(a)** *(ensorceler)* to enchant, to bewitch, to cast a spell on **(b)** *(ravir, plaire à)* to enchant, to delight; **cette idée ne l'enchante pas** he's not taken with the idea *or* keen on the idea

enchanteur, -eresse [ɑ̃ʃɑ̃tœr, -rɛs] **1** *nm* **(a)** *(sorcier)* enchanter **(b)** *Fig (charmeur)* charmer **2** *nf* **enchanteresse** enchantress **3** *adj (sourire)* bewitching, captivating; *(discours, endroit etc)* enchanting, delightful, charming

enchâssement [ɑ̃ʃɑsmɑ̃] *nm (d'un bijou)* setting, mounting

enchâsser [ɑ̃ʃɑse] **1** *vt* **(a)** *Rel (relique)* to enshrine **(b)** *(bijou)* to set, to mount **(c)** *Fig (dans un texte)* to insert, to slot in **2 s'enchâsser** *vpr* to fit perfectly **(dans** into)

enchâssure [ɑ̃ʃɑsyr] *nf (support) (d'un bijou)* setting, mount

enchère [ɑ̃ʃɛr] *nf* bid; **les enchères, l'e.** the bidding; **commencer les enchères à 5 000 francs** to start the bidding at 5,000 francs; **faire** *ou* **porter une e.** to make a bid; **vente aux enchères** (sale by) auction; **couvrir une e.** to make a higher bid, to bid higher; **couvrir l'e. de qn** to bid higher than sb, to outbid sb; **pousser** *ou* **faire monter les enchères** to raise *or* push up the bidding; *Fig* to increase the stakes; **vendre/acheter qch aux enchères** to sell/buy sth at auction; **mettre qch aux enchères** to put sth up for auction, to auction sth (off); *Fig* **il l'a pour ainsi dire mise aux enchères** he auctioned her off *or* sold her to the highest bidder, so to speak; **il s'est mis aux enchères sur le marché de l'emploi** he sold himself to the highest bidder on the job market; *Cartes* **manille aux enchères** auction bridge; **système des enchères** *(au bridge)* bidding system

enchérir [ɑ̃ʃerir] *vi* **(a)** *(dépasser)* to make a higher bid; **e. de dix francs** to bid another ten francs; **e. sur qn** to outbid sb, to make a higher bid than sb; *Fig* to go one better than sb; **e. sur le prix des marchandises** to make a higher bid for the goods; **e. sur les idées de qn** to improve on sb's ideas **(b)** *Vieilli (devenir plus cher)* to rise *or* go up in price

enchérissement [ɑ̃ʃerismɑ̃] *nm Vieilli (de prix)* rise, increase

enchérisseur, -euse [ɑ̃ʃerisœr, -øz] *n* bidder; **au plus offrant et dernier e.** to the highest bidder

enchevaucher [ɑ̃ʃ(ə)voʃe] *vt (tuiles etc)* to fix *or* lay with an overlap

enchevêtré [ɑ̃ʃ(ə)vetre] *adj (écheveau, fils)* tangled, in a tangle; *(style, idées)* confused; *(affaires, revues)* in a mess; **un amas de branches enchevêtrées** a tangle of branches

enchevêtrement [ɑ̃ʃ(ə)vɛtrəmɑ̃] *nm (de fils, branches)* tangle; *(d'objets, d'idées)* confusion, muddle; **l'e. de ses idées est tel que ...** he is so confused that ...; **comment s'y retrouver dans cet e. d'événements?** how on earth are you supposed to make sense of these events when they're all so confused?

enchevêtrer [ɑ̃ʃ(ə)vetre] **1** *vt (fils, branches etc)* to tangle (up); *(situation)* to confuse, to muddle **2 s'enchevêtrer** *vpr (de fils, branches etc)* to get tangled *or* in a tangle; *(d'objets)* to get muddled (up) *or* mixed up; *(d'une situation)* to get confused *or* muddled

enchifrené [ɑ̃ʃifrəne] *adj Vieilli* **il est e.** his nose is blocked

enclave [ɑ̃klav] *nf (terrain), Fig* enclave; **l'escalier fait e. dans la pièce** the staircase leads directly from *or* into the room

enclaver [ɑ̃klave] *vt* **(a)** *(poutres etc)* to wedge in, to fit in **(b)** *(territoire)* to enclose, to make an enclave of; **domaine qui enclave deux petites terres** estate which encloses two small properties **(c)** *(une pièce dans une autre)* to fit **(dans** into); **e. deux anneaux l'un dans l'autre** to interlock two rings, to fit two rings together

enclenchement [ɑ̃klɑ̃ʃmɑ̃] *nm Tech (d'une vitesse, d'un mécanisme etc)* engaging; *(de pièces)* interlocking

enclencher [ɑ̃klɑ̃ʃe] **1** *vt (vitesse, mécanisme etc)* to engage; *(pièces)* to interlock; *Fig (entreprise, projet etc)* to set in motion, to get under way; *Fig* **maintenant que l'action est enclenchée** now that things have been set in motion *or* are under way **2 s'enclencher** *vpr (d'une vitesse, d'un mécanisme etc)* to engage; *(de pièces)* to interlock; *Fig* **bien/mal s'e.** to get off to a good/bad start

enclin [ɑ̃klɛ̃] *adj* inclined, disposed **(à faire qch** to do sth); **elle est encline à la paresse/à la panique** she is inclined *or* tends to be lazy/to panic; **il est e. à l'alcoolisme** he is inclined to drink, he has alcoholic tendencies

enclitique [ɑ̃klitik] *nm Ling* enclitic

enclore [ɑ̃klɔr] *vt (conj like* **clore)** to enclose; *(d'une palissade)* to fence in; *(d'un mur)* to wall in

enclos [ɑ̃klo] *nm* **(a)** *(espace)* enclosure; *(pour chevaux)* paddock **(b)** *(clôture)* enclosure; *(mur)* (enclosing) wall

enclume [ɑ̃klym] *nf* **(a)** anvil; **e. de cordonnier** (shoemender's) last; *Fig* **être entre le marteau et l'e.** to be between the devil and the deep (blue) sea **(b)** *Anat (de l'oreille interne)* anvil

encoche [ɑ̃kɔʃ] *nf (dans un morceau de bois)* notch **(à, sur** in); *(d'une flèche)* nock; *(pour répertoire à onglets)* notch; *Ordinat* **e. de protection contre l'écriture** write-protect notch; *Él* **armature à encoches** slotted armature

encochement [ɑ̃kɔʃmɑ̃] *nm* notching

encocher [ɑ̃kɔʃe] *vt (morceau de bois)* to notch; *(livre)* to thumb-index

encodage [ɑ̃kɔdaʒ] *nm Ling, Ordinat* encoding

encoder [ɑ̃kɔde] *vt Ling, Ordinat* to encode

encodeur [ɑ̃kɔdœr] *nm Ordinat* encoder

encoignure [ɑ̃kwaɲyr] *nf* **(a)** *(d'une pièce)* corner, angle **(b)** *(petit meuble)* corner cupboard

encollage [ɑ̃kɔlaʒ] *nm (à l'aide de colle) (de papier)* pasting; *(de bois)* glueing; *(à l'aide d'apprêt) (de papier, tissu, plâtre etc)* sizing; *Typ* perfect binding

encoller [ɑ̃kɔle] *vt (à l'aide de colle) (papier)* to paste; *(bois etc)* to glue, to apply glue to; *(à l'aide d'apprêt) (papier, tissu, plâtre etc)* to size

encolure [ɑ̃kɔlyr] *nf* **(a)** *(de chameau, d'autruche etc)* neck; *Courses de chevaux* **gagner d'une e.** to win by a neck **(b)** *(tour de cou)* neck size; **homme de forte e.** thickset *or* stocky man **(c)** *(échancrure) (d'un vêtement)* neck (opening); **e. carrée** square neck

encombrant [ɑ̃kɔ̃brɑ̃] **1** *adj (meuble, valise etc)* cumbersome, bulky; *(colis)* bulky; **ce canapé est e.** the sofa is too big, the sofa takes up too much space *or* is in the way; **c'est un personnage e.** he's always in the way; **un témoin e.** an unwanted witness **2** *nmpl Région* **les encombrants passent demain** the bulk refuse disposal people are coming tomorrow; **mettre qch aux encombrants** to put sth out for collection; **j'ai trouvé cette table aux encombrants** I found this table in among rubbish put out for collection

encombre [ɑ̃kɔ̃br] *nm* **sans e.** without mishap, safely; **il a obtenu son diplôme sans e.** he got his degree without any problem

encombrement [ɑ̃kɔ̃brəmɑ̃] *nm* **(a)** *(état) (du trafic etc)* congestion; *(des rues, de l'espace aérien)* overcrowding; *(de lignes téléphoniques)* jamming, blocking; *(de texte)* depth **(b)** *(amas)* clutter, litter; **il y a un tel e. de livres dans son bureau** his office is so cluttered up with books **(c)** *(espace, volume) (d'une voiture, d'un meuble etc)* (overall) dimensions **(d)** *Ordinat* footprint; **faible e. sur le disque dur** low use of hard disk space

encombrer [ɑ̃kɔ̃bre] **1** *vt (pièce)* to clutter (up); *(passage, route etc)* to obstruct, to block; *(lignes téléphoniques)* to jam, to block; **e. les rues** to congest the streets; **table encombrée**

de papiers table littered with papers; **sentier encombré de ronces** path overgrown with brambles; **les lignes téléphoniques sont vraiment encombrées** the telephone lines are really busy; **e. le marché** to glut *or* saturate the market; **j'ai les mains encombrées** my hands are full; **je ne veux pas de ce divan, il m'encombrerait** I don't want this sofa, it would just clutter my place up; **tu m'encombres, sors d'ici!** you're getting under my feet, get out!

2 s'encombrer *vpr* **s'e. de** (*colis, équipement etc*) to load oneself down with; *Fig* (*obligations, enfants etc*) to burden oneself *or* saddle oneself with

encontre (à l') [alãkɔ̃tr] *adv* in opposition; **je n'ai rien à dire à l'e.** I've nothing to say against it; **cela va à l'e. de la loi** that's against the law; **tu vas à l'e. de la loi** you're breaking the law; **tu n'as pas le droit d'aller à l'e. du projet** you have no right to try to stop *or* go against the project; **cela va à l'e. de ce qu'il proposait la semaine dernière** that's the opposite of *or* contradicts what he was saying last week; **ces nouvelles méthodes vont à l'e. de tout ce qu'on m'a toujours appris** these new methods go against *or* are contrary to *or* run counter to everything I've been taught

encorbellement [ãkɔrbɛlmã] *nm Archit* (*d'un mur etc*) corbelling; (*d'un étage supérieur*) overhang; **fenêtre en e.** oriel window

encorder (s') [sãkɔrde] *vpr* (*en alpinisme*) to rope up

encore [ãkɔr] *adv* **(a)** (*toujours*) still; **je cherche e. une explication** I am still looking for an explanation; **je ne suis e. qu'étudiant** I'm still only a student, I'm only a student as yet

(b) pas e. not yet; **elle n'est pas e. mariée** she isn't married yet, she's still not married; **elle n'est e. jamais** *ou* **e. pas venue me voir** she hasn't come to see me yet, she still hasn't come to see me; **un homme que je n'avais e. jamais vu** a man I'd never seen before

(c) (*davantage*) more; **e. un mot** (just) one word more; **en voulez-vous e.?** would you like some more?; **e. du vin, s'il vous plaît!** some more wine please!; **e. une tasse de café** another cup of coffee; **pendant trois mois e., pendant e. trois mois** for three months longer, for another three months; **il est e. plus beau que je ne le pensais** he's even better looking than I thought; **il y a e. moins de relief que dans mon pays** it's even flatter than where I come from; **réduire e. le prix** to reduce the price still *or* even further *or* more; **c'est e. pire** it's even worse, it's worse still

(d) (*de nouveau*) again; **voilà e. la pluie!** here's the rain again!; **nous l'avons e. vu hier** we saw him again yesterday; **qu'est-ce qu'il a fait e.** *ou* **e. fait?** now what's he done?, what's he done now *or* this time?; **il y a e. eu un meurtre d'enfant** another child has been murdered; **quoi e.?** now what?; **e. une fois** once more, once again; **e. autant** as much again; **e. vous!** (what) you again?

(e) (*en plus*) moreover, furthermore; **non seulement stupide, mais e. têtu** not only stupid, but also pigheaded *or F* but pigheaded to boot; **que faut-il que je prenne e.?** what else do I need to take?

(f) (*restrictif*) **e. s'il était reconnaissant!** if only he was at least grateful!; **si e. je savais où il se cache** if I only knew *or* if only I knew where he was hiding; **il aura peut-être une chance là-bas, et e.!** perhaps he'll have a chance over there, but only just *or* but not much of one!; **il vous donnera dix francs et e.!** he'll give you ten francs for it, if that!; *F* **il faudrait e. que je trouve une voiture!** now I have to find a car!; **(mais) e. faudrait-il qu'elle accepte!** she has to agree first!

(g) e. que + *sub* (al)though, even though; **e. qu'il ne me soit rien** (al)though he is nothing to me; **temps agréable e. qu'un peu froid** pleasant if *or* though rather cold weather

(h) il a dit qu'il avait bien aimé – mais e.? he said he liked it – but what exactly did he say?; **elle est sympa – mais e.?** she's nice – yes, go on!

(i) (*pas plus tard que*) **hier e. je lui ai parlé** I spoke to him only yesterday, I just spoke to him yesterday; **c'est ce que nous nous disions e. hier soir** *ou* **hier soir e.** that's what we were saying only *or* just last night

encorné [ãkɔrne] *adj* (*animal*) horned

encorner [ãkɔrne] *vt* (*d'un taureau*) to gore

encornet [ãkɔrnɛ] *nm* (*mollusque*) squid

encourageant [ãkuraʒã] *adj* (*personne*) encouraging; (*nouvelles, résultat, événement etc*) encouraging, heartening

encouragement [ãkuraʒmã] *nm* encouragement; **prime d'e.** incentive; **e. à la vertu/au crime** incentive to virtue/to crime; **recevoir peu d'encouragements à faire qch** to receive little encouragement *or* little inducement to do sth

encourager [ãkuraʒe] *vt* **(j'encourageai(s))** **(a)** (*personne*) to encourage; (*athlète, équipe*) to encourage, to cheer on; **ils m'ont beaucoup encouragé** they encouraged me a lot, they gave me a lot of encouragement; **être encouragé par qn** to be encouraged by sb, to receive *or* get encouragement from sb; **encouragé par les premiers résultats** encouraged *or* heartened by the first results; **elle l'a encouragé d'un sourire** she gave him an encouraging smile, she smiled at him encouragingly; **e. qn à faire qch** to encourage sb to do sth

(b) (*arts*) to encourage, to foster, to promote; (*plan*) to promote; **la presse encourage l'utilisation de certaines drogues** the press encourages the use of certain drugs; **l'oisiveté encourage le vice** idleness encourages *or* promotes vice

encourir [ãkurir] *vt* (*conj like* **courir**) (*dépense*) to incur; (*punition, reproches, sanctions*) to incur, to bring (up)on oneself; **e. des risques** to run risks; **il sait qu'il encourt une lourde punition** he knows he risks being severely punished

en(-)cours [ãkur] *nm inv* **(a)** *Banque* loans outstanding, exposure; **e. de crédit** exposure; **e. débiteur autorisé** authorized overdraft facility **(b)** *Compta* **e. de production de biens** work-in-progress

encrage [ãkraʒ] *nm Typ* inking (up)

encrassement [ãkrasmã] *nm* (*des vêtements, mains etc*) dirtying; *Aut* (*d'une bougie*) fouling, sooting (up); (*d'une machine etc*) clogging, choking

encrasser [ãkrase] **1** *vt* (*ses vêtements, mains etc*) to dirty; *Aut* (*bougie*) to soot up; (*machine etc*) to clog, to choke **2 s'encrasser** *vpr* to get dirty; *Aut* (*d'une bougie*) to soot up; (*d'une machine*) to get clogged *or* choked

encre [ãkr] *nf* **(a)** ink; **écrit à l'e.** written in ink; **cela a fait couler beaucoup d'e.** a lot has been written about it; **doigts couverts d'e.** inky fingers, fingers covered in ink; **noir comme de l'e.** inky black, black as ink; *Fig* **nuit d'e.** inky black night; *F* **c'est la bouteille à l'e.** it's got everyone scratching their head *or* stumped; *Psy* **test de la tache d'e.** inkblot *or* Rorschach test **(b)** *Zool* (*de seiche*) ink

▶ **encre**: **e. de Chine** Indian ink; **e. d'impression** printing ink; **e. en poudre** toner; **e. sympathique** invisible ink

encrer [ãkre] *vt Typ* to ink (up)

encreur [ãkrœr] *adj* **ruban e.** (typewriter) ribbon; *Typ* **rouleau e.** inker

encrier [ãkrije] *nm* inkwell, inkpot, inkstand

encroûté [ãkrute] *adj F* (*personne*) (stuck) in a rut, set in one's ways; **qu'est-ce que tu peux être e.!** what a stick-in-the-mud you are!; **vieux bonhomme e.** old fogey *or* stick-in-the-mud; **il mène une vie très encroûtée** he is very set in his ways

encroûtement [ãkrutmã] *nm* **(a)** (*d'une tuyauterie*) encrustation **(b)** *F* (*d'une personne*) sinking into a rut; **sortir** *ou* **tirer qn de son e.** to get sb out of his/her rut

encroûter [ãkrute] **1** *vt* **(a)** (*tuyauterie*) to encrust **(b)** *F* (*personne*) **la retraite l'a encroûté** retirement has made him set in his ways *or* got him into a rut **2 s'encroûter** *vpr* **(a)** (*d'une tuyauterie*) to become encrusted **(de** with) **(b)** *F* (*d'une personne*) to get into a *or* stuck in a rut, to become set in one's ways

enculé, -ée [ãkyle] *n Vulg* bugger, arsehole

enculer [ãkyle] *vt Vulg* to bugger; **va te faire e.!** bugger off!, sod off! *Fig* **e. les mouches** to nit-pick

encuver [ãkyve] *vt* (*peaux, raisins*) to vat

encyclique [ãsiklik] *nf Rel* encyclical

encyclopédie [ãsiklɔpedi] *nf* encyclop(a)edia; *F* **une e. vivante** a walking encyclop(a)edia

encyclopédique [ãsiklɔpedik] *adj* encyclop(a)edic

encyclopédiste [ãsiklɔpedist] *n* encyclop(a)edist

endémie [ãdemi] *nf* endemic (disease)

endémique [ãdemik] *adj Méd, Fig* endemic (**à** to)

endenter [ãdãte] *vt* **(a)** (*roue etc*) to tooth, to cog, to ratchet **(b)** (*assembler*) (*roues*) to mesh

endetté [ãdɛte] *adj* in debt; *Fig* in debt, indebted (**envers** to); **très e.** deep(ly) *or* heavily in debt

endettement [ãdɛtmã] *nm* (*action*) running *or* getting into debt; (*état*) debt; *Compta* indebtedness, gearing; **tu cours à l'e.** you'll run into debt; **l'e. des pays du Tiers Monde** the debt burden of Third World countries; **cela a provoqué l'e. du pays de l'Est** this caused the Eastern countries to get into debt; **ratio d'e.** debt ratio; **facilité d'e.** borrowing capacity

endetter [ãdɛte] **1** *vt* to get into debt **2 s'endetter** *vpr* to run *or* get into debt; **s'e. trop lourdement** to take on too many debts

endeuiller [ãdœje] *vt* (*famille, nation etc*) to plunge into mourning; (*événement*) to cast gloom over; **maison endeuillée** house in mourning

endèver [ãdeve] *vti Can F* **il m'endève, il me fait e.** he infuriates me

endiablé [ɑ̃djable] *adj (personne)* lively, full of life; *(musique, rythme etc)* wild, frenzied
endiguement [ɑ̃digmɑ̃] *nm* **(a)** *(action) (d'une rivière etc)* embanking, dyking (up) **(b)** *(digue)* embankment, dyke **(c)** *Fig (de l'inflation)* containment, holding in check; *(de la violence, la pauvreté, du chômage)* containment; **tenter l'e. de la violence/de la hausse des prix** to attempt to contain violence/price increases
endiguer [ɑ̃dige] *vt* **(a)** *(rivière etc)* to embank, to dyke (up) **(b)** *Fig (foule, colère, hausse des prix)* to hold back, to contain; *(inflation, pauvreté, chômage, violence)* to contain
endimanché [ɑ̃dimɑ̃ʃe] *adj* all dressed up, in one's Sunday best
endimancher (s') [sɑ̃dimɑ̃ʃe] *vpr* to put on one's best clothes *or* one's Sunday best, to get all dressed up
endive [ɑ̃div] *nf* endive; *(chicorée)* chicory; *F* **pâle comme une e.** as white *or* pale as a sheet
endocarde [ɑ̃dɔkard] *nm Anat* endocardium
endocardite [ɑ̃dɔkardit] *nf Méd* endocarditis
endocarpe [ɑ̃dɔkarp] *nm Bot* endocarp
endocrine [ɑ̃dɔkrin] *adj Physiol (glande)* endocrine
endocrinien, -ienne [ɑ̃dɔkrinjɛ̃, -jɛn] *adj Physiol (glandes etc)* endocrine, endocrinal
endocrinologie [ɑ̃dɔkrinɔlɔʒi] *nf* endocrinology
endoctrinement [ɑ̃dɔktrinmɑ̃] *nm* indoctrination
endoctriner [ɑ̃dɔktrine] *vt* to indoctrinate, *F* to brainwash
endogame [ɑ̃dɔgam] *adj* endogamous
endogamie [ɑ̃dɔgami] *nf* endogamy
endolori [ɑ̃dɔlɔri] *adj (bras etc)* sore, painful
endolorir [ɑ̃dɔlɔrir] **1** *vt (bras etc)* to make sore *or* painful **2 s'endolorir** *vpr* to become sore *or* painful
endolorissement [ɑ̃dɔlɔrismɑ̃] *nm Litt* pain, soreness
endommagement [ɑ̃dɔmaʒmɑ̃] *nm (action)* damaging **(de** of); *(résultat)* damage **(de** to)
endommager [ɑ̃dɔmaʒe] **(j'endommageai(s))** *vt* **(a)** to damage, to do damage to **(b)** *Ordinat* to corrupt; **fichier endommagé** damaged *or* corrupt file
endomorphine [ɑ̃dɔmɔrfin] *nf Physiol* endorphin
endormant [ɑ̃dɔrmɑ̃] *adj (ennuyeux) (discours, réunion etc)* boring, wearisome; *(tâche)* boring, humdrum
endormi, -ie [ɑ̃dɔrmi] **1** *adj* **(a)** *(personne)* asleep, sleeping; *(voix, village)* sleepy; **avoir l'air e.** to look sleepy; **j'ai la jambe endormie** my leg has gone to sleep *or* is numb **(b)** *F (inerte, lent) (personne)* inattentive, half-asleep **(c)** *Fig (passion, intérêt etc)* dormant **2** *n (personne inerte, lente)* slowcoach
endormir [ɑ̃dɔrmir] *(conj like* **dormir)** **1** *vt* **(a)** *(d'une drogue, un hypnotiseur etc)* to put *or* send to sleep; *(d'une mère etc) (bébé etc)* to send *or* lull to sleep **(b)** *(ennuyer)* to send *or* put to sleep **(c)** *(apaiser) (douleur)* to deaden; **e. les soupçons** to allay suspicion **2 s'endormir** *vpr* **(a)** to fall asleep, to go to sleep, *F* to drop off (to sleep) **(b)** *Fig (d'une douleur)* to die away; *(de soupçons)* to be allayed
endormissement [ɑ̃dɔrmismɑ̃] *nm* **(a)** falling asleep, *F* dropping off (to sleep) **(b)** *Ordinat* hibernation, sleep mode
endorphine [ɑ̃dɔrfin] *nf* = **endomorphine**
endos [ɑ̃do] *nm (sur chèque)* endorsement
endoscope [ɑ̃dɔskɔp] *nm Méd* endoscope
endoscopie [ɑ̃dɔskɔpi] *nf Méd* endoscopy
endossable [ɑ̃dosabl] *adj (chèque)* endorsable
endossataire [ɑ̃dosatɛr] *n* endorsee
endossement [ɑ̃dosmɑ̃] *nm (d'un chèque)* endorsement; **e. en blanc** blank endorsement
endosser [ɑ̃dose] *vt* **(a)** *(veste etc)* to put on **(b)** *(responsabilité)* to assume, to shoulder; **je ne vais pas encore e. tes erreurs** I'm not going to take the responsibility *or* shoulder the blame for your mistakes again **(c)** *(chèque)* to endorse; **e. en blanc** to blank endorse **(d)** *(en reliure) (livre)* to back
endosseur, -euse [ɑ̃dosœr, -øz] *n (d'un chèque)* endorser
endroit [ɑ̃drwa] *nm* **(a)** *(lieu)* place, spot; **c'est l'e. idéal pour un magasin** it's the ideal place *or* spot for a shop; **je ne sais plus à quel e. j'ai rangé mes lunettes** I don't know where I put my glasses; **avez-vous choisi l'e. de vos vacances?** have you decided where you're going on holiday?; **je me suis arrêté à cet e. du livre, j'ai arrêté ma lecture à cet e.** this is where I stopped reading, I stopped reading here; **ça me fait mal à cet e.** it hurts me (just) here; **c'est à cet endroit que ça vous fait mal?** is this where it hurts?; **par endroits** here and there, in places; **en plusieurs/certains endroits** in several/certain places; **rire au bon e.** to laugh in the right place; **le meilleur e. du film** the best bit *or* part of the film; *F* **le petit e.** *Br* the loo, *Am* the john
(b) *(bon sens)* right side; **ton pull n'est pas à l'e.** your sweater's on the wrong way round; *(les coutures ne sont pas à l'intérieur)* your sweater's on inside out; **remets ta poupée à l'e.** turn your doll the right way up; *Tricot* **maille à l'e.** plain stitch; **deux à l'e., deux à l'envers** knit two, purl two
enduire [ɑ̃dɥir] *(prp* **enduisant**; *pp* **enduit**; *pr ind* **j'enduis, il enduit**; *impf* **j'enduisais**; *p hist* **j'enduisis**; *fu* **j'enduirai)** **1** *vt* **e. de** *(peinture, ciment, colle etc)* to coat *or* cover with; *(crème, boue etc)* to smear with **2 s'enduire** *vpr* **s'e. de crème à bronzer** to smear *or* rub *or* cover oneself with suntan cream
enduit [ɑ̃dɥi] *nm* **(a)** *(de goudron, peinture etc)* coat, application **(b)** *Constr (plâtre)* plastering, coat of plaster; **e. de ciment** cement rendering; **e. imperméable** proofing **(c)** *Cér* glaze, glazing
endurable [ɑ̃dyrabl] *adj* endurable
endurance [ɑ̃dyrɑ̃s] *nf* **(a)** *(physique)* stamina, staying power, endurance **(b)** *(morale)* endurance, powers of resistance; **il n'a pas eu l'e. nécessaire pour résister à la pression** he wasn't tough enough to stand up to the pressure **(c)** *Aut etc* **épreuve/course d'e.** endurance trial/run
endurant [ɑ̃dyrɑ̃] *adj* **(a)** *(résistant)* tough; **elle n'était pas assez endurante** she wasn't tough enough *or* didn't have enough stamina **(b)** *Vieilli (patient)* enduring, long-suffering
endurci [ɑ̃dyrsi] *adj* **(a)** *(dur) (personne)* hard, callous; *(cœur)* hard **(b)** *(invétéré) (criminel)* hardened; *(célibataire)* confirmed; *(haine)* inveterate
endurcir [ɑ̃dyrsir] **1** *vt* **(a)** *(cuirasser) (qn, le cœur de qn)* to harden; **la vie va l'e.** life will toughen him up **(b)** *(rendre résistant)* to harden, to toughen (up); **être endurci à la fatigue** to be inured *or* hardened to fatigue **2 s'endurcir** *vpr* **(a)** *(moralement)* to become hard; **il s'est beaucoup endurci** he has become very hard **(b)** *(physiquement)* to toughen up, to become hardened
endurcissement [ɑ̃dyrsismɑ̃] *nm* **(a)** *(action) (moral) (de qn, du cœur de qn)* hardening; *(physique) (de qn)* hardening, toughening (up); **e. à la fatigue** inuring to fatigue **(b)** *(état) (moral)* hardness, callousness; *(physique)* hardness, toughness; **e. à la fatigue** being inured to fatigue
endurer [ɑ̃dyre] *vt (épreuve, mauvais traitement etc)* to endure, to bear; **je n'endure pas que tu partes** I can't bear the fact that you're leaving; **il fait trop chaud pour e. un manteau** it's too warm for a coat
enduro [ɑ̃dyro] *nm Sp* enduro
Énée [ene] *nm* Aeneas
Énéide (l') [leneid] *nf Littér* the Aeneid
énergétique [enɛrʒetik] **1** *adj* **(a)** *(médicament, nourriture etc)* energizing, energy-giving; **dépense é.** expenditure of energy **(b)** *Écon (ressources, besoins etc)* energy **2** *nf* energetics
énergie [enɛrʒi] *nf* **(a)** *(force)* energy; **apporter** *ou* **appliquer** *ou* **mettre toute son é. à une tâche/à faire qch** to devote *or* direct all one's energies to a task/to doing sth; **je n'ai pas assez d'énergie pour sortir ce soir** I haven't got the energy to go out this evening; **je ne me sens pas beaucoup d'é.** I'm not feeling very energetic; **avec é.** energetically; *(refuser, répondre)* forcefully, vigorously; **elle conduit avec é.** she's an aggressive driver; **il a fait face à la situation avec é.** he faced up to the situation with spirit; **l'é. d'un passage/d'un style** the vigour of a passage/style; **sans é.** *(adjectivement)* listless; *(adverbialement)* listlessly; **faire qch avec l'é. du désespoir** to do sth with the strength born of desperation
(b) *Ind* energy, power; **faire des économies d'é.** to save energy; **la crise de l'é.** the energy crisis
▶ **énergie**: **é. atomique** atomic energy, nuclear power; **é. cinétique** kinetic energy; **é. électrique** electrical power; **é. éolienne** wind power; **é. hydraulique** hydraulic power; **é. nucléaire** nuclear power; **é. potentielle** potential energy; **é. solaire** solar power *or* energy; **é. thermique** thermal power
énergique [enɛrʒik] *adj* **(a)** *(personne)* energetic, dynamic; *(vendeur)* aggressive; *(personnalité)* forceful; **une jeune femme é.** a young woman with plenty of spirit *or* drive; **un visage é.** a strong face **(b)** *(mesures)* strong, drastic; *(langage)* strong, forceful; *(geste)* emphatic, forceful; *(coup de pied, coup)* forceful; *(médicament, remède)* powerful
énergiquement [enɛrʒikmɑ̃] *adv (nier)* energetically, forcefully; *(agir, parler)* forcefully; *(refuser, répondre)* forcefully, vigorously; *(conduire)* aggressively; **s'y mettre é.** to put one's back into it
énergisant [enɛrʒizɑ̃] **1** *adj (médicament, nourriture etc)* energizing, energy-giving **2** *nm Méd* antidepressant
énergumène [enɛrgymɛn] *n F* maniac; **c'est un drôle d'é.** he's a queer fish
énervant [enɛrvɑ̃] *adj* **(a)** *(personne, habitude etc)* irritating; *(bruit)* nerve-racking **(b)** *Vieilli (climat)* enervating
énervé [enɛrve] *adj (agacé)* irritated; *(excité) (personne)* on

edge, edgy, agitated; (*rire*) nervous; **très é. à l'idée de …** all on edge at the idea of …

énervement [enɛrvəmɑ̃] *nm* (*agacement*) irritation; (*excitation*) edginess

énerver [enɛrve] **1** *vt* **(a) é. qn** (*agacer*) to get on sb's nerves, to irritate sb; (*exciter*) to get sb worked up, to agitate sb **(b)** *Vieilli* (*débiliter*) to enervate, to weaken **2 s'énerver** *vpr* to get excited *or* agitated *or* (all) worked up

enfaîteau, -eaux [ɑ̃fɛto] *nm Constr* ridge tile

enfaîtement [ɑ̃fɛtmɑ̃] *nm Constr* ridge tiling, ridging

enfaîter [ɑ̃fɛte] *vt Constr* (*toit*) to ridge

enfance [ɑ̃fɑ̃s] *nf* **(a)** (*jeunesse*) childhood; (*de garçon*) boyhood; (*de fille*) girlhood; **elle a eu une e. heureuse/difficile** she had a happy/difficult childhood; **dans mon e.** in my childhood, when I was a child; **depuis mon e.** ever since I was a child; **souvenir/camarade d'e.** childhood memory/friend; **petite e.** infancy, early childhood; **des souvenirs datant de la petite e.** memories of when one was very small, early childhood memories; **l'e. d'une civilisation** the dawn *or* beginning of a civilization; *F* **c'est l'e. de l'art** it's (mere) child's play; **industrie encore dans son e.** industry still in its infancy; **retomber en e.** to sink into one's second childhood *or* one's dotage

(b) (*enfants*) **l'e.** children

enfant [ɑ̃fɑ̃] *n* **(a)** (*jeune*) child, *pl* children; *Jur* (*mineur*) infant; **c'est une belle e.** she's a beautiful child; **e. en bas âge** infant; **éducation des enfants** children's education; **babil d'e.** childish prattle; **elle me parle comme à un e.** she talks to me as if I was a child; **les droits de l'e.** children's rights; **menu e.** children's menu; **l'e. qui est en chacun** the child in all of us; **je l'ai connu e.** I have known him since he was a child; *F* **c'est un jeu d'e.** it's child's play; *F* **il n'y a plus d'enfants** honestly, kids nowadays!; **se conduire en e., faire l'e.** to act *or* behave childishly *or* like a child, to be childish; **e. surdoué** exceptionally gifted child

(b) (*fils, fille*) child; **elle attend un e.** she's expecting a child *or* baby; *F* **il lui a fait un e.** she had a child by him; **être en mal d'e.** (*d'une femme*) to be broody; *F* **c'est son e.** (*création*) it's his baby *or* his brainchild; **couple sans e.** childless couple; **mourir sans enfants** to die childless *or Jur* without issue

(c) (*descendant*) **un e. du peuple** a child of the people; **un e. de Paris** a native of Paris

(d) (*terme d'affection*) *F* **salut, les enfants!** (*à des adultes*) hello people!, *Am* hi guys *or* gang!

▶ **enfant**: **e. de l'amour** love child; **e. de la balle** child who follows in his father's footsteps; **c'est un e. de la balle** he was born in a trunk; *Méd* **e. bleu** blue baby; **e. de chœur** *Rel* altar boy; *Fig* naive person; *Fig* **je ne suis pas un e. de chœur** (*moralement*) I'm no saint *or* no angel; (*du point de vue pratique*) I'm pretty hard-nosed; **e. gâté** spoilt child; **les enfants d'Israël** the children of Israel; *Rel* **l'E. Jésus** the Christ Child, *Enf* Baby Jesus; *Rel* **les enfants de Marie** the Legion of Mary; *Fig* **c'est une e. de Marie** she's an innocent; **cela fait bien longtemps que ce n'est plus une e. de Marie** it's a long time since she was as pure as the driven snow; **e. martyr** battered baby/child; **e. naturel** illegitimate child; *Jur* natural child; **e. prodige** child prodigy; *Rel, Fig* **e. prodigue** prodigal son; **e. terrible** dreadful child; *Fig* enfant terrible; **e. de troupe** army child *or F* brat; **e. trouvé** foundling; **e. unique** only child

enfantement [ɑ̃fɑ̃tmɑ̃] *nm* childbirth; *Fig* (*d'une œuvre littéraire*) production; **l'e. de son œuvre a pris des années** it was years before his book saw the light of day

enfanter [ɑ̃fɑ̃te] *vt* (*enfant*) to bear, to give birth to; *Fig* (*œuvre littéraire*) to produce, to give birth to; **la discorde enfante le crime** discord begets crime

enfantillage [ɑ̃fɑ̃tijaʒ] *nm* **enfantillage(s)** childishness, infantile behaviour; **de l'e. pur et simple** sheer childishness; **ne fais pas d'enfantillages!** don't be childish *or* infantile!

enfantin [ɑ̃fɑ̃tɛ̃] *adj* **(a)** (*voix*) child's; (*jeu, littérature*) children's; *Péj* (*remarque, action etc*) childish, infantile; **des voix enfantines** children's voices; **babil e.** childish prattle **(b)** (*élémentaire*) elementary; **c'est e.** it's child's play; **c'est d'une simplicité enfantine** it's childishly simple

enfariné [ɑ̃farine] *adj* (*visage, cheveux etc*) (*de farine*) covered with flour; (*de poudre*) smothered in powder; *F* **je suis arrivée, la gueule enfarinée, demander mon augmentation** I arrived in all innocence *or* quite unsuspecting to ask for my rise; **à chaque fois qu'il casse quelque chose, il vient la gueule enfarinée** whenever he breaks something he turns up looking all innocent *or* as if butter wouldn't melt in his mouth

enfer [ɑ̃fɛr] *nm* **(a)** *Rel etc* **l'e.** hell; **les enfers** the underworld; *Myth* Hades; **l'E. de Dante** Dante's Inferno; *Fig* **aller en e.** to go to hell; **il fait de ma vie un e.** he's making my life hell; **elle a vécu un véritable e.** she's been through sheer *or* a living hell; **c'est vraiment l'e. à la maison** it's sheer hell at home; **quelquefois c'est l'e. pour se garer ici** it can be hell trying to park here; **l'e. de la drogue/de la prostitution/du chômage** the living hell of drug addiction/of prostitution/of unemployment; **une vision d'e.** a vision of hell; **aller un train d'e.** to go at top speed *or F* hell for leather; **bruit d'e.** hellish noise; *F* **une soirée d'e.** (*génial*) a great *or* terrific party; **cette fille est d'e.!** she's a great *or* terrific girl

(b) (*dans une bibliothèque*) = library department containing books not available to the public

enfermement [ɑ̃fɛrməmɑ̃] *nm* imprisonment; **il menace sa fille d'e.** he's threatening to keep his daughter locked up; **je ferai tout pour faire cesser l'e. de mon mari** I'll do anything to free my husband

enfermer [ɑ̃fɛrme] **1** *vt* **(a)** (*qn, qch*) to shut up; **e. qch/qn (à clef)** to lock sth/sb up; **tenir qn enfermé** to keep sb shut up *or* locked up; **e. qn dehors** to shut *or* lock sb out; **j'ai été enfermé dans une pièce toute la journée** I've been shut up *or* cooped up in a room all day; **vivre trop enfermé** to stay at home too much; *F* **il est bon à e.** he ought to be locked up; *Fig* **e. un mot dans une définition trop étroite/qn dans un rôle inadéquat** to confine a word in an excessively narrow definition/sb in an inadequate role; **même les spectateurs l'ont enfermé dans le rôle du vampire** even the audiences have him typecast him as a vampire *or* don't expect to see him in anything but vampire parts; **e. qn dans ses contradictions** to trap sb in his own contradictions; **e. le savoir dans les bibliothèques** to lock away *or* shut away knowledge in libraries; **être enfermé dans ses pensées** to be wrapped up in one's thoughts

(b) (*entourer*) (*jardin, terrain, bâtiment*) to enclose, to surround; *Sp* (*concurrent*) to hem *or* box in

2 s'enfermer *vpr* to shut oneself up; (*à clef*) to lock oneself in; **s'e. dehors** to lock oneself out; *Fig* **s'e. dans le silence/un rôle** to retreat into silence/to confine oneself to a role; **depuis qu'il est prof, il s'est enfermé dans le rôle de M. je sais tout** he's turned into a real know-it-all since he became a teacher; **Johnny Weissmuller s'est enfermé dans le rôle de Tarzan** Johnny Weissmuller never tried to be anybody but Tarzan

enferrer (s') [sɑ̃fere] *vpr* to impale oneself (**sur** on); *Fig* (*dans une explication, ses mensonges etc*) to get tangled up *or* bogged down

enfichable [ɑ̃fiʃabl] *adj Él* that can be plugged in; *Ordinat* slot-in

enficher [ɑ̃fiʃe] *vt Él* to plug in

enfiévré [ɑ̃fjevre] *adj* (*front, Fig imagination*) fevered; *Fig* (*atmosphère*) feverish; (*foule*) in a fever (of excitement), at fever pitch

enfièvrement [ɑ̃fjɛvrəmɑ̃] *nm* fever (of excitement)

enfiévrer [ɑ̃fjevre] (**j'enfièvre; j'enfiéverai**) **1** *vt* **(a)** (*énerver*) (*qn, imagination de qn etc*) to excite, to fire, to stir **(b)** *Méd Vieilli* to make feverish **2 s'enfiévrer** *vpr* **(a)** (*se passionner*) to get excited *or* all worked up; **s'e. pour une cause** to become passionate about a cause **(b)** *Méd Vieilli* to grow feverish

enfilade [ɑ̃filad] *nf* **(a)** (*de portes, maisons, colonnes, couloirs etc*) succession, series; (*de pièces etc*) series, suite; **nos deux chambres sont en e.** we have adjoining rooms; **la cuisine et la buanderie sont en e.** the kitchen and the laundry room are next to *or* adjoin each other; **maisons en e.** row of houses; **je me suis perdue dans l'e. des couloirs** I got lost in the maze of corridors *or* the endless corridors **(b)** *Mil* enfilade; **tir d'e.** raking *or* enfilading fire

enfiler [ɑ̃file] **1** *vt* **(a)** (*aiguille*) to thread; (*perles*) to string

(b) (*rue, couloir etc*) to take, to go along

(c) (*vêtements*) to slip on, to pull on; (*pantalon, bas*) to pull on

(d) *Vulg* (*sexuellement*) to screw, to lay; **ce que je cherche, moi, le samedi soir, c'est e. une fille** I'm out to get laid on a Saturday night, I want to screw on a Saturday night

(e) (*troupes etc*) to enfilade, to rake

2 s'enfiler *vpr* **(a)** (*s'engager*) **s'e. dans un couloir/une rue** to go along a corridor/street

(b) *F* (*consommer*) (*boisson*) to down, to knock back; (*nourriture*) to put away, to guzzle; **s'e. un bon dîner** to have a slap-up meal; **je me suis enfilé un sandwich en vitesse** I grabbed a sandwich, I had a quick sandwich

(c) *F* (*avoir à supporter*) (*tâche*) to get stuck *or* landed with

(d) (*de gants, bottes*) to pull on, to go on; (*d'un étui*) to slide on

enfin [ɑ̃fɛ̃] *adv* **(a)** (*en dernier lieu*) last, finally, lastly; **e. et surtout** last but not least (**b**) (*plutôt*) **blonde, e. châtain clair** blond, well, light brown; **elle n'est pas mal, e. pour son âge** she's not bad – for her age, that is; **c'était une soirée géniale, e. je veux dire qu'on ne s'est pas ennuyé** it was a good party – we weren't bored, I mean

(**c**) (*finalement*) at last, finally, at length; **e. vous voilà!, vous voilà e.!** here you are at last!; **j'y suis e. arrivée** I finally managed, I managed it at last

(**d**) (*résignation*) that's that!; **e. c'est la vie** well, that's life!; **mais e., si elle est heureuse!** but as long as she's happy!; **mais e. bon, c'est son problème** oh well, that's his problem!; **e., n'en parlons plus!** let's forget it; **e.! ce qui est fait est fait** what's done is done

(**e**) (*exaspération*) **e. quoi, tu n'as plus 10 ans!** after all, you're not 10 any more!; **on est en République e., quoi!** it's a free country after all!; **mais e. je te l'avais déjà dit!** I'd already told you!; **mais e., c'est pas vrai!** I don't believe it!; **e., lâche-moi un peu!** give me some peace!, give it a rest!

(**f**) (*hésitation, pour résumer*) well; **e. je ne dis pas non, mais ...** well, I'm not saying no, but ...; **mais e., s'il acceptait!** but still, if he did accept!; **e. (bref) c'était la panique!** in short *or* in a word *or* to cut a long story short, it was panic!; **c'est un homme, e.!, il a sa dignité!** he's a man after all! he has his dignity!

enflammé [ɑ̃flame] *adj* (**a**) (*bois, brindille, torche*) burning, blazing; (*allumette*) burning; (*soleil, coucher de soleil*) fiery (**b**) (*joues*) (*de froid*) glowing; (*de fièvre, gêne, chaleur*) burning (**c**) *Méd* (*plaie, gorge etc*) inflamed (**d**) *Fig* (*discours, caractère etc*) fiery, passionate; **faire une déclaration enflammée à une femme** to make a passionate declaration to a woman

enflammer [ɑ̃flame] **1** *vt* (**a**) (*mettre en flammes*) to set light to, to set ablaze; **e. une allumette** to strike a match

(**b**) *Méd* (*plaie, gorge etc*) to inflame

(**c**) *Fig* (*qn, imagination de qn*) to excite, to fire, to stir up; **e. une dispute** to stir up a quarrel; **la colère enflamme son regard** his eyes are blazing with anger; **l'urgence de la situation enflamme ses talents d'orateur** the urgency of the situation is arousing his talents as a speaker

2 s'enflammer *vpr* (**a**) (*prendre feu*) to catch fire, to burst into flames, to blaze up

(**b**) (*d'une plaie, de la gorge etc*) to become inflamed

(**c**) (*d'une personne, de l'imagination etc*) to be stirred; **chaque jour, il s'enflamme pour une cause nouvelle/un auteur nouveau** he develops a passion for a new cause/a different author every day; **s'e. de colère** (*d'une personne*) to flare up; (*de joues*) to burn with anger

enflé [ɑ̃fle] **1** *adj* (*rivière, membre etc*) swollen; (*prix*) inflated; (*style*) inflated, turgid, bombastic **2** *nm F* **espèce d'e.!** you idiot!

enfléchure [ɑ̃fleʃyr] *nf Naut* ratline

enfler [ɑ̃fle] **1** *vt* (**a**) (*membre, rivière, paupières etc*) to swell, to cause to swell; (*prix*) to inflate; **e. les joues** to puff out *or* blow out one's cheeks; **e. les voiles** (*du vent*) to fill the sails; **e. la voix** to raise one's voice; **des paupières enflées** swollen eyelids; *Vieilli* **e. le nombre/la dépense** to swell *or* add to the number/the expense

(**b**) *Fig* (*exagérer*) (*histoire, son succès etc*) to exaggerate; **e. son style** to inflate one's style

2 *vi* (*d'un membre, des paupières, des joues etc*) to swell (up)

3 s'enfler *vpr* (**a**) (*d'un membre, des paupières, des joues etc*) to swell (up); (*d'une voix*) to rise

(**b**) (*d'une rivière etc*) to swell, to rise

(**c**) (*d'un style*) to become inflated *or* turgid

enflure [ɑ̃flyr] *nf* (**a**) (*d'un membre etc*) swelling (**b**) (*d'un style*) turgidity (**c**) *F* (*imbécile*) idiot

enfoiré, -ée [ɑ̃fware] *n Vulg* bugger, bastard

enfoncé [ɑ̃fɔ̃se] *adj* (*yeux*) deep-set; (*cavité, ravin etc*) sunken, deep; (*sol, village*) low-lying

enfoncement [ɑ̃fɔ̃smɑ̃] *nm* (**a**) (*action d'enfoncer*) (*d'un pieu, clou etc*) driving in; (*d'une aiguille etc*) sticking in, pushing in; (*d'une porte etc*) forcing, breaking open (**b**) (*action de s'enfoncer*) (*du sol*) giving way (**c**) (*creux*) (*dans le sol*) hollow, depression; (*dans le mur*) alcove, recess; *Naut* bay, bight; **dans l'e. de la porte** in the doorway

enfoncer [ɑ̃fɔ̃se] **(j'enfonçai(s)) 1** *vt* (**a**) (*pieu, clou etc*) to drive in; (*aiguille, épingle etc*) to stick in, to push in; **e. un clou dans une planche** to drive a nail into a plank; **e. un couteau dans** to thrust *or* plunge *or* stick a knife into; **e. au marteau** to hammer in; **e. la main dans sa poche** to thrust one's hand into one's pocket; **e. son chapeau sur sa tête** to jam *or* cram one's hat on one's head; **e. la clef dans la serrure** to insert the key in the lock; *Fig* **e. qn dans la misère** to plunge sb into poverty; *Fig F* **je ne peux pas lui e. cela dans la tête** I can't get it into his head; *Fig F* **vas-y, enfonce-moi, toi!** go on, rub it in!

(**b**) (*défoncer*) (*porte*) to break down *or* open; (*fût*) to stave in; (*voiture*) to smash into; **e. une porte à coups de pied** to kick a door in *or* down; *Fig* **e. une porte ouverte** to state the obvious

(**c**) *F* (*battre*) (*qn, équipe etc*) to hammer, to wipe the floor with

2 *vi* (*dans la boue, mer etc*) to sink; **le navire enfonçait** the ship was sinking; **nous y avons enfoncé jusqu'aux genoux** we sank into it up to our knees

3 s'enfoncer *vpr* (*d'un clou, couteau etc*) to sink *or* go in; (*d'un bateau*) to sink; (*du sol*) to subside, to give way; **la balle s'enfonça dans le mur** the bullet embedded itself in the wall; **s'e. dans son fauteuil** to sink into one's armchair; **s'e. dans l'ombre** to disappear in *or* be swallowed up by the darkness; **s'e. dans une rue/dans un bois** to go down a street/to plunge into a wood; **il s'est enfoncé trop loin dans la rue** he went too far along the street; **s'e. dans l'étude/dans la rêverie** to bury oneself in study/to sink into reverie; **s'e. dans le crime** to sink deep(er) into crime; **s'e. dans son opinion** to become entrenched in one's opinion

enfonceur, -euse [ɑ̃fɔ̃sœr, -øz] *n* **c'est un e. de portes ouvertes** he's got a gift for stating the obvious

enfonçure [ɑ̃fɔ̃syr] *nf* depression, hollow

enfouir [ɑ̃fwir] **1** *vt* to bury (**dans** in; **sous** beneath, under); *Agr* (*fumier*) to plough in; **les mains enfouies dans ses poches** with his hands buried in his pockets **2 s'enfouir** *vpr* **s'e. dans la campagne** to bury oneself in the country

enfouissement [ɑ̃fwismɑ̃] *nm* burying; *Agr* (*de fumier*) ploughing in

enfourcher [ɑ̃furʃe] *vt* (*cheval, vélo*) to get on, to mount; *Fig* **e. son dada** to get on one's hobbyhorse

enfourchure [ɑ̃furʃyr] *nf Vieilli* (*d'arbre, de jambes*) fork

enfournage [ɑ̃furnaʒ] *nm*, **enfournement** [ɑ̃furnəmɑ̃] *nm* (*de pain etc*) putting in the oven; (*de poteries, briques etc*) putting in the kiln

enfourner [ɑ̃furne] *vt* (*pain etc*) to put in the oven; (*poteries, briques etc*) to put in the kiln; *F* (*avaler*) to put away; **e. les passagers dans un autobus** to pack *or* cram passengers into a bus

enfourneur [ɑ̃furnœr] *nm* oven man; *Cér* kiln man

enfreindre [ɑ̃frɛ̃dr] *vt* (*prp* **enfreignant**; *pp* **enfreint**; *pr ind* **j'enfreins, il enfreint, ils enfreignent**; *impf* **j'enfreignais**; *p hist* **j'enfreignis**; *fu* **j'enfreindrai**) (*loi*) to infringe, to break; (*règlements*) to contravene, to act contrary to; (*ordres*) to disobey; (*vœu*) to break; **e. les dispositions d'un traité** to violate a treaty; **e. un contrat** to violate a contract

enfuir (s') [sɑ̃fɥir] *vpr* (*conj like* **fuir**) to run away, *Litt* to flee, to fly; (*d'un escroc*) to abscond; (*d'amoureux*) to elope; **s'e. de prison** to escape from prison; **à mesure que les jours s'enfuyaient** as the days flew by; *Litt* **mon bonheur menace de s'e.** my happiness is in danger of evaporating; **les côtes s'enfuyaient** the coastline receded

enfumé [ɑ̃fyme] *adj* (**a**) (*pièce, atmosphère*) smoky (**b**) (*murs etc*) smoke-blackened

enfumer [ɑ̃fyme] *vt* (**a**) (*pièce*) to fill with smoke (**b**) (*murs etc*) to blacken with smoke (**c**) (*personne, abeilles etc*) to smoke out

enfûtage [ɑ̃fytaʒ] *nm* (*d'un vin*) putting in barrels *or* casks

enfutailler [ɑ̃fytaje], **enfûter** [ɑ̃fyte] *vt* (*vin*) to put in barrels *or* casks

engagé [ɑ̃gaʒe] **1** *adj* (**a**) *Littér, Pol etc* (*littérature, artiste etc*) committed (**b**) *Archit* (*colonne etc*) engaged (**c**) **navire e.** ship on her beam-ends (**d**) *Mil* **soldat e.** volunteer **2** *nm Mil* **e. (volontaire)** volunteer; *Courses de chevaux, Cyclisme* **la liste des engagés** the list of starters

engageant [ɑ̃gaʒɑ̃] *adj* (*manière etc*) engaging, prepossessing; (*sourire*) winning, engaging; **il a écouté ma proposition d'un air e.** he listened to my suggestion sympathetically

engagement [ɑ̃gaʒmɑ̃] *nm* (**a**) (*promesse etc*) promise, undertaking, commitment; **faire honneur à** *ou* **tenir** *ou* **respecter ses engagements** to honour *or* meet *or* fulfil one's commitments; **e. écrit** written undertaking; *Fin* **e. à court terme** short-term undertaking; **contracter** *ou* **prendre un e.** to enter into an undertaking; **elle a pris l'e. de le faire** she undertook to do it; **sans e. (de votre part)** without obligation (on your part), without any commitment (on your part)

(**b**) *Fin* (*d'un capital*) tying up, locking up; (*de dépenses*) incurring

(**c**) (*mise en gage*) (*de bijoux etc*) pawning, pledging; (*d'un domaine*) mortgaging

(**d**) (*embauche*) (*d'un employé*) engagement, appointment, hiring; (*d'un pianiste etc*) booking; *Mil* (voluntary) enlistment; **se trouver sans e.** to be out of work; *Th* to be resting (**e**) *Sp* (*pour un événement sportif*) entering, entry

(**f**) (*commencement*) (*de conversation, négociations*) beginning, start, opening; (*d'entreprise, de projet etc*) setting in motion; *Jur* (*de poursuites*) institution; *Mil, Naut* (*bataille*) engagement, action; (*coup d'envoi*) *Fb* kick-off; (*au hockey*) bully-off; *Escrime* engagement; **l'e. des négociations ne pourra se faire avant le mois prochain** negotiations cannot begin *or* start before next month; **pour que l'e. du projet soit possible** in order to get the project under way *or* to set the project in motion

(**g**) (*à une cause etc*) commitment (**à** to)

(**h**) (*encouragement*) encouragement; **c'est un e. à poursuivre votre effort** it's an encouragement to continue your effort

(**i**) (*introduction*) (*du pied*) putting; (*d'une clé*) fitting, inserting; (*d'un véhicule*) driving (**dans** into)

(**j**) *Physiol* **e. du fœtus** engagement of the foetus

engager [ɑ̃gaʒe] (**j'engageai(s)**) **1** *vt* (**a**) (*lier par un obligation ou une promesse*) to commit, to bind; **e. sa parole** to pledge *or* give one's word; (*dans une affaire*) to commit oneself; **cette lettre ne vous engage pas** this letter does not bind *or* commit you; **cela vous engage à vie** it's a lifetime commitment; **cela ne vous engage à rien** it doesn't commit you to anything; **votre responsabilité est engagée dans cette affaire** you have certain responsibilities in this matter; **c'est ce que je crois, mais ça n'engage que moi** it's what I think, but it's just my way of looking at things

(**b**) *Fin* (*argent*) to lock up, to tie up; (*dépenses*) to incur; **e. sa fortune/des capitaux dans une affaire** to lock up *or* tie up one's fortune/capital in a deal

(**c**) (*mettre en gage*) (*au mont-de-piété*) to pawn; (*auprès de créanciers*) to pledge; (*propriété*) to mortgage

(**d**) (*embaucher*) (*employé*) to hire, to take on; (*pianiste etc*) to book; *Mil* (*recrue*) to enlist; (*mercenaire*) to hire

(**e**) (*commencer*) (*conversation, négociations*) to begin, to start, to open; (*entreprise, projet etc*) to get under way, to set in motion; *Jur* (*poursuites*) to institute, to start; **e. la partie** to begin the match *or* game; **la partie est maintenant bien engagée** the match is now well under way; **e. le jeu** *Fb* to kick off; (*au hockey*) to bully off; **e. le combat** to join battle, to engage; **e. les hostilités** to open hostilities; **e. des troupes** to bring troops into action, to engage troops

(**f**) (*entraîner*) to involve (**dans** in); **la nation tout entière se voit engagée dans ce conflit** the whole nation finds itself involved *or* caught up in this conflict; **e. qn dans une querelle** to involve sb in *or* draw sb into a quarrel

(**g**) (*inciter*) **e. qn à faire qch** (*d'une personne*) to urge *or* encourage sb to do sth; (*d'une situation, d'un événement*) to encourage sb to do sth; **je t'engage vivement à changer tes manières** I strongly advise you to change your ways

(**h**) (*introduire*) **e. le pied dans l'étrier** to put one's foot in the stirrup; **e. la clef dans la serrure** to fit *or* insert the key in the lock; **e. un véhicule dans une allée** to drive a vehicle into a lane

(**i**) *Sp* (*inscrire sur liste des concurrents*) to enter; **cet entraîneur a deux chevaux engagés dans cette course** this trainer has two horses entered in the race

(**j**) (*entraver*) (*corde etc*) to catch, to foul, to entangle; (*machinerie*) to jam; **e. une ancre** to foul an anchor; **e. un aviron** to catch a crab; **e. un vaisseau** to run a ship aground

(**k**) *Tech* (*engrenage*) to engage, to put into gear; *Aut* **e. la première** to change into first (gear)

2 s'engager *vpr* (**a**) (*promettre*) **s'e. à faire qch** to promise to do sth, to commit oneself to do sth, *Fml* to undertake to do sth; **s'e. par traité à faire qch** to contract to do sth; **je m'engage à vous payer dans le 30 jours** I promise to pay you within 30 days; **je me suis trop engagé pour reculer** I have gone too far *or* I'm too far in to pull out now; **s'e. vis-à-vis de qn** to commit oneself to sb; **je ne veux pas m'engager** (*sentimentalement*) I don't want to get involved

(**b**) (*prendre position*) (*écrivain, intellectuel*) to commit oneself

(**c**) (*se lancer*) **s'e. dans une aventure/un combat/une affaire** to get involved in an adventure/a fight/a deal

(**d**) (*se faire embaucher*) **s'e. chez qn** to be *or* get taken on by sb; **s'e. comme cuisinier** to get (oneself) a job as *or* get taken on as a cook

(**e**) *Mil* to enlist, to join up

(**f**) (*se loger*) to fit; **un tube s'engage dans l'ouverture** a pipe fits into the opening

(**g**) (*pénétrer*) **s'e. dans une rue/forêt** to turn into a street/ to enter a forest; **il s'engagea dans le passage pour piétons sans regarder à droite ni à gauche** he stepped out onto the pedestrian crossing without looking left or right; **la voiture s'engagea dans le rond-point** the car pulled out onto the roundabout; **nous nous engageâmes dans un étroit boyau** we moved into a narrow passageway; *Fig* **s'e. dans les ornières d'un pragmatisme aveugle** to be stuck in a rut of blind pragmatism

(**h**) (*commencer*) (*d'une bataille, conversation etc*) to begin

(**i**) *Sp* **s'e. pour une course** to enter for a race

(**j**) (*d'une corde, hélice etc*) to foul, to become fouled; (*d'une machine*) to jam

engazonnement [ɑ̃gazɔnmɑ̃] *nm* (*fait de semer*) sowing with grass seed

engazonner [ɑ̃gazɔne] *vt* (*semer*) to sow with grass seed

engeance [ɑ̃ʒɑ̃s] *nf F* **quelle e.!** what a crew!

engelure [ɑ̃ʒlyr] *nf* chilblain

engendrement [ɑ̃ʒɑ̃drəmɑ̃] *nm* (**a**) (*d'enfant*) fathering, *Bible* begetting (**b**) (*de chaleur etc*) generation; (*de maladie, pauvreté*) breeding

engendrer [ɑ̃ʒɑ̃dre] *vt* (**a**) (*enfant*) to father, *Bible* to beget; (*d'un étalon etc*) to sire (**b**) *Fig* (*conflit*) to engender, to give rise to; (*maladie, pauvreté*) to breed; (*chaleur etc*) to generate, to develop

engin [ɑ̃ʒɛ̃] *nm* (*machine*) machine; (*outil*) device, contrivance; *Mil* (*missile*) missile; *F* (*objet*) thing; **engins de pêche** fishing tackle; **passage d'engins** heavy plant crossing; **engins de guerre** engines of war; **e. amphibie** amphibious craft *or* vehicle; **e. blindé** armoured vehicle; **e. blindé de reconnaissance** armoured car; **e. de mort** deadly weapon; **e. prohibé** illegal hunting/fishing device; **e. spatial** spacecraft; **e. de terrassement** earthmoving machine; **e. de manutention** machine for handling goods

engineering [ɛndʒiniriŋ] *nm* engineering

englober [ɑ̃glɔbe] *vt* (**a**) (*inclure*) to include (**dans** in); **e. les innocents parmi les coupables** to include the innocent with the guilty (**b**) (*annexer*) to merge (**dans** into); **ces États furent englobés dans l'Empire** these states were merged into the Empire

engloutir [ɑ̃glutir] **1** *vt* (**a**) (*avaler*) (*boisson*) to gulp down; (*nourriture*) to wolf down (**b**) (*submerger*) (*bateau, village etc*) to engulf, to swallow up (**c**) (*son capital etc*) (*d'une entreprise, projet etc*) to swallow up; (*d'une personne*) to sink (**dans** in) **2 s'engloutir** *vpr* (*d'un bateau*) to sink

engloutissement [ɑ̃glutismɑ̃] *nm* (**a**) (*d'une boisson*) gulping down; (*de la nourriture*) wolfing down (**b**) (*d'un village etc*) engulfing, swallowing up; (*d'un bateau*) sinking (**c**) (*d'une fortune etc*) swallowing up

engluage [ɑ̃glyaʒ] *nm*, **engluement** [ɑ̃glymɑ̃] *nm* (**a**) (*de brindilles, d'un oiseau*) liming (**b**) (*enduit*) (bird)lime

engluer [ɑ̃glye] **1** *vt* (*brindilles, oiseau*) to lime **2 s'engluer** *vpr* (*d'un oiseau*) to get caught in lime; **s'e. les doigts** to get sticky fingers; *Fig* **s'e. dans une situation difficile/des problèmes/des dettes** to get bogged down in a difficult situation/problems/debts

engoncer [ɑ̃gɔ̃se] *vt* (*d'un manteau etc*) **e. qn** to make sb look hunched up; **être engoncé dans sa veste** to be hunched up in one's jacket

engorgement [ɑ̃gɔrʒəmɑ̃] *nm* (**a**) (*action*) (*d'un passage, tuyau etc*) choking, blocking, clogging; **e. des marchés** glutting of the markets (**b**) (*bouchon*) obstruction, stoppage; *Méd* engorgement, congestion

engorger [ɑ̃gɔrʒe] (**j'engorgeai(s)**) **1** *vt* (**a**) (*passage, tuyau etc*) to choke (up), to block, to clog (**b**) (*marché*) to glut (**c**) *Méd* (*organe*) to engorge, congest **2 s'engorger** *vpr* (**a**) (*d'un tuyau etc*) to become choked (up) *or* blocked (up) *or* clogged (**b**) *Méd* (*d'un organe*) to become engorged *or* congested

engouement [ɑ̃gumɑ̃] *nm* (**a**) (*admiration*) infatuation, craze (**pour qn/qch** for sb/sth) (**b**) *Méd* (*d'une hernie*) obstruction

engouer (s') [sɑ̃gwe] *vpr* (**a**) *Méd* (*d'une hernie*) to become obstructed (**b**) **s'e. de qn/qch** to become infatuated with *or* go crazy over sb/sth

engouffrement [ɑ̃gufrəmɑ̃] *nm* (*d'un vaisseau par la mer etc*) engulfment, engulfing, swallowing up

engouffrer [ɑ̃gufre] **1** *vt* (*bateau etc*) to engulf, to swallow up; **e. une fortune** to swallow up a fortune; *F* **e. sa nourriture** to devour *or* gulp down *or* wolf down one's food; *F* **qu'est-ce que j'ai engouffré!** I really wolfed *or* gulped it down! **2 s'engouffrer** *vpr* (*d'un bateau etc*) to be engulfed *or* swallowed up; **il s'engouffra dans la gare** he plunged *or* dived into the station; **le vent s'engouffra par la porte** the wind swept in through the door

engoulevent [ɑ̃gulvɑ̃] *nm* (*oiseau*) nightjar

engourdi [ɑ̃gurdi] *adj* (**a**) (*membre, corps etc*) numb; **j'ai le pied e.** my foot has gone to sleep *or* is numb (**b**) *Fig* (*esprit*) dull, sluggish

engourdir [ɑ̃gurdir] **1** *vt* (**a**) (*membre, corps etc*) to numb (**b**) (*endormir*) (*esprit, douleur*) to dull **2 s'engourdir** *vpr* (**a**) (*d'un membre etc*) to grow numb, to go to sleep (**b**) *Fig* (*de*

l'esprit) to become dull *or* sluggish **(c)** (*d'un animal qui hiberne*) to become dormant
engourdissement [ɑ̃gurdismɑ̃] *nm* **(a)** (*état*) (*d'un membre etc*) numbness; (*de l'esprit*) dullness, sluggishness; (*d'un animal qui hiberne*) torpor **(b)** (*action*) (*d'un membre etc*) numbing; (*de l'esprit, d'une douleur*) dulling
engrais [ɑ̃grɛ] *nm* **(a)** (*pour l'élevage*) **mettre des bœufs à l'e.** to put cattle to fatten **(b)** (*fertilisant*) fertilizer; **e. (animal)** manure; **e. chimiques** chemical fertilizers; **e. verts** green fertilizers
engraissage [ɑ̃grɛsaʒ] *nm*, **engraissement** [ɑ̃grɛsmɑ̃] *nm* (*des animaux*) fattening
engraisser [ɑ̃grese] **1** *vt* **(a)** (*animaux*) to fatten **(b)** (*personne*) to make fat **(c)** (*terre*) to fertilize **2** *vi* (*d'une personne, d'un animal*) to get fat **3 s'engraisser** *vpr* (*s'enrichir*) to grow fat; **l'État s'engraisse sur le dos des travailleurs** the State grows fat at the workers' expense
engrangement [ɑ̃grɑ̃ʒmɑ̃] *nm* (*des céréales*) getting in, *Litt* garnering
engranger [ɑ̃grɑ̃ʒe] *vt* **(j'engrangeai(s); n. engrangeons)** (*céréales*) to get in, *Litt* to garner
engrenage [ɑ̃grənaʒ] *nm* **(a)** *Tech* (*roues dentées*) gears; (*disposition du système*) gearing; **e. hélicoïdal** helical *or* screw gear; **système** *ou* **jeu d'engrenages** train *or* set of gears; *Aut* **e. de démarrage** starter gear; **e. à train planétaire** planetary gearing; **engrenage(s) de transmission** driving gear; **e. en prise constante** constant-mesh gear; **e. à variations progressives** gradually variable gear; **e. à vis sans fin** worm gears
(b) *Fig* (*des événements*) chain, mesh, web; **être pris dans l'e.** to be *or* get caught (up) in the system; **l'e. de la violence/de l'agressivité** the spiral of violence/aggression; **mettre le doigt dans l'e.** to get caught up in it
engrènement [ɑ̃grɛnmɑ̃] *nm* **(a)** *Agr* (*d'un moulin etc*) feeding with grain **(b)** *Tech* engaging, meshing
engrener [ɑ̃grəne] **(j'engrène; j'engrènerai) 1** *vt* **(a)** *Agr* (*moulin, batteuse*) to feed grain into **(b)** *Tech* (*pignons*) to engage, to mesh; **e. dans** to engage into, to mesh with; *F* **e. une affaire** to set a thing going **2 s'engrener** *vpr Tech* to engage **(dans** into), to mesh **(dans** with)
engrenure [ɑ̃grənyr] *nf Tech* (*disposition de roues*) gearing
engrosser [ɑ̃grose] *vt Arg* (*femme*) to make pregnant, *Br* to put in the club; **se faire e.** to get (oneself) made pregnant **(par** by)
engueulade [ɑ̃gœlad] *nf F* (*réprimande*) bawling out; (*querelle*) row, *Br* slanging match; **passer une e. à qn** to give sb a bawling out, to bawl sb out; **recevoir une e.** to get a bawling out
engueuler [ɑ̃gœle] *F* **1** *vt* **e. qn** (*réprimander*) to give sb hell, to give sb a roasting; **se faire e.** to be given a roasting; **e. qn comme du poisson pourri** to call sb every name under the sun **2 s'engueuler** *vpr* to have a row *or Br* slanging match
enguirlander [ɑ̃girlɑ̃de] *vt* **(a)** (*décorer*) to garland **(de** with) **(b)** *F* = **engueuler 1**
enhardir [ɑ̃ardir] **1** *vt* to embolden, to put courage into, to give courage to **2 s'enhardir** *vpr* to become bold(er); **s'e. à faire qch** to pluck up the courage to do sth
enharmonie [ɑ̃narmɔni] *nf Mus* enharmonic change
enharmonique [ɑ̃narmɔnik] *adj Mus* enharmonic
enharnacher [ɑ̃arnaʃe] *vt* (*cheval*) to harness
énième [enjɛm] **1** *adj* nth; **pour la é. fois** for the nth *or* umpteenth time **2** *n* nth
énigmatique [enigmatik] *adj* enigmatic
énigmatiquement [enigmatikmɑ̃] *adv* enigmatically
énigme [enigm] *nf* (*problème, mystère*) enigma, riddle; (*devinette*) riddle; **proposer une é. à qn** to ask sb a riddle; **trouver le mot** *ou* **la clé de l'é.** to find the answer to the riddle, to guess *or* solve the riddle; **parler par énigmes** to speak in riddles; **ce garçon est une é. pour moi** I can't make the boy out; **ça, c'est une é. pour moi** it's a mystery to me
enivrant [ɑ̃nivrɑ̃] *adj* (*parfum*) intoxicating, heady; (*vitesse*) exhilarating, dizzying; **vivre dans un luxe e.** to live in fabulous luxury
enivrement [ɑ̃nivrəmɑ̃] *nm* **(a)** (*par l'alcool*) intoxication, inebriation **(b)** *Fig* exhilaration; **dans l'e. de** intoxicated *or* exhilarated by
enivrer [ɑ̃nivre] **1** *vt* **(a)** (*avec de l'alcool*) to intoxicate, to inebriate, to make drunk **(b)** *Fig* (*exalter*) to intoxicate, to exhilarate; **enivré par le succès** intoxicated *or* exhilarated by success **2 s'enivrer** *vpr* **(a)** (*devenir ivre*) to become intoxicated *or* inebriated **(de** with), to get drunk **(de** on) **(b)** *Fig* **s'e. de mots** to get drunk on words
enjambée [ɑ̃ʒɑ̃be] *nf* stride; **marcher à grandes enjambées** to stride along
enjambement [ɑ̃ʒɑ̃bmɑ̃] *nm Littér* enjamb(e)ment
enjamber [ɑ̃ʒɑ̃be] *vt* (*obstacle, fossé etc*) to step over *or* across; (*d'un pont*) (*rivière etc*) to span
enjeu [ɑ̃ʒø] *nm* **(a)** (*au jeu*) stake **(b)** *Mil, Pol etc* stakes; **quel est l'e.?** what is at stake?, what are the stakes?
enjoindre [ɑ̃ʒwɛ̃dr] *vt* (*conj like* **joindre**) *Litt* **e. à qn de faire qch** to enjoin *or* call upon *or* charge sb to do sth
enjôlement [ɑ̃ʒolmɑ̃] *nm* **(a)** (*action*) cajoling, wheedling, coaxing **(b)** (*paroles etc*) cajolery, blandishment
enjôler [ɑ̃ʒole] *vt* to cajole, to wheedle, to coax
enjôleur, -euse [ɑ̃ʒolœr, -øz] **1** *n* coaxer, cajoler, wheedler **2** *adj* coaxing, cajoling, wheedling
enjolivement [ɑ̃ʒɔlivmɑ̃] *nm* (*ornement*) embellishment, ornament; (*dans un récit*) embellishment
enjoliver [ɑ̃ʒɔlive] *vt* (*pièce, robe etc*) to embellish, to ornament; (*faits, histoire etc*) to embellish, to embroider
enjoliveur, -euse [ɑ̃ʒɔlivœr, -øz] **1** *n* **c'est un e.** he likes to embellish *or* embroider his stories **2** *nm Aut* hubcap, wheel trim; **e. de phare** headlamp rim
enjolivure [ɑ̃ʒɔlivyr] *nf* (*ornement*), *Fig* embellishment
enjoué [ɑ̃ʒwe] *adj* vivacious, lively, playful
enjouement [ɑ̃ʒumɑ̃] *nm* vivaciousness, liveliness, playfulness
enkystement [ɑ̃kistəmɑ̃] *nm Méd* encystation, encystment
enkyster (s') [sɑ̃kiste] *vpr Méd* (*d'une tumeur*) to become encysted, to encyst
enlacement [ɑ̃lasmɑ̃] *nm* **(a)** (*de rubans, branches*) intertwining, interlacing **(b)** (*en entourant*) enlacing, entwining
enlacer [ɑ̃lase] **(j'enlaçais) 1** *vt* **(a)** (*rubans, branches*) to intertwine, to interlace; (*entourer*) to entwine, to enlace, to twine round; (*papiers*) to tie up **(b)** (*étreindre*) to clasp in one's arms, to hug, to embrace **2 s'enlacer** *vpr* **(a)** (*s'étreindre*) to hug, to embrace (each other); **amants enlacés** lovers (clasped) in an embrace **(b)** (*s'entrelacer*) to intertwine, to interlace
enlaidir [ɑ̃ledir] **1** *vt* (*personne*) to make ugly, to disfigure; (*paysage, ville etc*) to disfigure; **cette robe l'enlaidit** that dress makes her look ugly **2** *vi* to grow ugly *or* plain **3 s'enlaidir** *vpr* to make oneself look ugly *or* plain
enlaidissement [ɑ̃lɛdismɑ̃] *nm* (*de personne*) (*par accident*) disfigurement; (*naturel*) growing ugly *or* plain, loss of good looks; (*de paysage, ville etc*) disfigurement
enlevage [ɑ̃lvaʒ] *nm* (*dans une course d'aviron*) spurt
enlevé [ɑ̃lve] *adj* (*représentation, style etc*) lively, spirited; (*danse, sonate etc*) performed in a lively *or* spirited fashion
enlèvement [ɑ̃lɛvmɑ̃] *nm* **(a)** (*de meubles, d'une étiquette, d'une tache, de peinture*) removal, removing; (*des bagages, ordures*) collection; **e. des ordures** garbage disposal; *Com* **e. et livraison** collection and delivery **(b)** (*kidnapping*) kidnapping, abduction; *Jur* **e. de mineur** abduction of a minor; **e. d'enfant** baby-snatching **(c)** *Mil* (*d'une position*) taking, storming, carrying
▶ **enlèvement**: *Hist* **l'e. des Sabines** the rape of the Sabine women
enlever [ɑ̃lve] **(j'enlève; j'enlèverai) 1** *vt* **(a)** (*vêtements, étiquette, bouton, couvercle etc*) to remove, to take off; (*meubles etc*) to remove, to take away; (*tapis*) to take up; (*rideaux*) to take down; (*pelure, peinture etc*) to peel off, to remove; (*tache*) to remove, to take out; **e. le couvert** to clear away, to clear the table; *F* **il a fallu lui e. les végétations** he had to have his adenoids removed *or* taken out; *Litt* **enlevé par la mer** carried away *or* washed away by the sea; **la mort l'enleva à vingt ans** death carried him off at twenty; **e. qch à qn** to take sth away from sb; **enlève-lui ces allumettes des mains** take those matches off him; **enlève-toi de là!** get off there!; **une bombe lui a enlevé les jambes** a bomb took off *or* blew off his legs; **il m'a enlevé mes cors** he removed my corns; **cette erreur n'enlève rien à votre valeur** this mistake takes nothing away from *or* in no way detracts from your merit; **cela m'a enlevé tout mon courage/toute ma bonne humeur** it has drained me of all courage/of my good humour; **e. à qn la garde d'un enfant** to remove *or* take a child from sb's care *or* custody; **e. à qn le goût de qch** to take away sb's taste for sth
(b) (*kidnapper*) to kidnap, to abduct; **se faire e. par son amant** to elope (with one's lover)
(c) (*remporter*) *Mil* (*position*) to take, to carry, to storm; *Sp etc* (*course, victoire, prix*) to win; (*commande, contrat*) to win, to secure; **e. la décision** to win *or* carry the day, to win through; **e. les suffrages** *Pol* to win *or* capture votes; *Fig* to be liked by everyone, to be universally liked
(d) (*soulever*) (*poids, couvercle*) to raise, to lift (up); (*ballon*) to send up; **le vent enlève la poussière** the wind raises the dust; **e. son cheval** (*le faire bondir*) to lift one's horse; (*le faire partir*) to set one's horse at full gallop; *Fig* **la foule fut enlevée par ces paroles** the crowd was carried away by these words

(**e**) **e. un morceau** (**de musique**) to play a piece (of music) in a lively *or* spirited fashion

2 s'enlever *vpr* (**a**) (*d'un couvercle*) to come off; (*de la peinture, peau etc*) to come *or* peel off; (*d'une tache*) to come out

(**b**) (*de marchandises*) to sell quickly, to be snapped up; **ça s'enlève comme des petits pains** it's selling like hot cakes

(**c**) (*d'un ballon etc*) to rise

(**d**) (*d'un cheval*) to take off

enlisement [ɑ̃lizmɑ̃] *nm* (*dans les sables mouvants etc*) sinking

enliser [ɑ̃lize] **1** *vt* (*voiture, roue etc*) (*dans la boue, le sable etc*) to get stuck **2 s'enliser** *vpr* (*d'une personne*) (*dans un marécage etc*) to sink, to be sucked down; (*d'une voiture etc*) (*dans la boue, le sable etc*) to sink, to get stuck; *Fig* **s'e. dans ses explications/habitudes** to get bogged down in one's explanations/habits

enluminer [ɑ̃lymine] *vt* (**a**) (*illustrer*) (*manuscrit, livre etc*) to illuminate (**b**) (*colorer*) (*gravure, carte etc*) to colour, *US* to color (**c**) *Fig* **visage enluminé** flushed *or* glowing face

enlumineur, -euse [ɑ̃lyminœr, -øz] *n* (*artiste*) illuminator

enluminure [ɑ̃lyminyr] *nf* (**a**) (*action d'illustrer*) (*d'un manuscrit etc*) illumination, illuminating (**b**) (*action de colorer*) (*de gravures etc*) colouring, *US* coloring (**c**) *Fig* (*d'un visage*) colour, *US* color (**d**) (*lettre, dessin*) illumination

enneigé [ɑ̃neʒe] *adj* (*montagne, champ etc*) snow-covered; (*route, village etc*) snowbound, snowed-up

enneigement [ɑ̃nɛʒmɑ̃] *nm* (*action*) snowing up; (*état*) snow cover; **bulletin d'e.** snow report

ennemi, -ie [ɛnmi] **1** *n* [①A11,g,i] enemy; **se faire un e. de qn** to make an enemy of sb, to turn sb against one; **passer à l'e.** to go over to the enemy; **e. public numéro un** public enemy number one; **les ennemis de la liberté** the enemies of freedom; *Prov* **le mieux est l'e. du bien** leave well alone; **je suis e. de la bouffonnerie** I hate *or* won't have buffoonery **2** *adj* enemy; **le camp e.** the enemy('s) camp; **en pays e.** in enemy country

ennoblir [ɑ̃nɔblir] *vt* (**a**) (*esprit etc*) to ennoble, to elevate (**b**) *Tex* (*tissu etc*) to improve (the quality of)

ennui [ɑ̃nɥi] *nm* (**a**) (*souci*) worry, anxiety; (*problème*) problem; **avoir des ennuis** (*soucis*) to be worried *or* anxious; (*problèmes*) to have problems; **avoir des ennuis de santé/d'argent/de voiture** to have health/money/car problems; **avoir des ennuis avec la police** to be in trouble with the police; **avoir des ennuis avec ses voisins** to have trouble *or* problems with one's neighbours; **si tu continues, tu vas avoir des ennuis** if you carry on, you'll be in trouble; **petits ennuis** minor worries, *Péj* petty worries; **créer** *ou* **susciter** *ou* **faire des ennuis à qn** to make trouble for sb, to create problems for sb; **je ne voudrais pas vous attirer d'ennuis** I wouldn't want to get you into trouble; **quel e.!** what a nuisance *or* bother *or F* bind!; **l'e., c'est que je ne lui ai rien expliqué** the trouble is that I haven't explained anything to him

(**b**) (*lassitude*) boredom, *Litt* ennui; **ils me font mourir d'e.** they bore me to death *or* stiff; **sa conversation est d'un e.!** his conversation is so boring!

ennuyé [ɑ̃nɥije] *adj* (**a**) (*contrarié*) annoyed, bothered (**de** about) (**b**) (*las*) bored (**de** with)

ennuyer [ɑ̃nɥije] (**j'ennuie; j'ennuierai**) **1** *vt* (**a**) (*contrarier*) to annoy, to bother; **cela vous ennuierait-il d'attendre?** would you mind waiting?; **je ne voudrais pas vous e.** I don't want to bother you; **cela m'ennuie de ne pouvoir le lui expliquer** it annoys me that I can't explain it to him; **je suis très ennuyé de la savoir fâchée** it bothers *or* upsets me a lot to know that she is angry

(**b**) (*agacer*) to annoy, to irritate; **qu'est-ce qu'elle m'ennuie avec ses chichis!** I'm really getting tired of the fuss she makes!

(**c**) (*lasser*) to bore; **il m'ennuie à mourir** he bores me to death

2 s'ennuyer *vpr* to be/get bored; **je m'ennuie à ne rien faire** (*maintenant*) I'm bored *or F* fed up with doing nothing; (*en général*) I get bored if I have nothing to do; **s'e. de faire qch** to get tired of doing sth

ennuyeux, -euse [ɑ̃nɥijø, -øz] *adj* (**a**) (*contrariant*) annoying, irritating; **comme c'est e.!** what a nuisance! (**b**) (*lassant*) boring, tedious, dull; **mortellement e.** deadly boring *or* dull

énoncé [enɔ̃se] *nm* (**a**) (*des faits*) statement; (*d'un problème, Jur d'une sentence*) terms; (*d'un contrat, d'une loi etc*) text, wording; (*d'une question*) wording (**b**) *Ling* utterance

énoncer [enɔ̃se] (**j'énonçai(s)**) **1** *vt* (*opinion, fait, conditions etc*) to state **2 s'énoncer** *vpr* (*d'une opinion*) to be stated

énonciation [enɔ̃sjasjɔ̃] *nf* (*d'un fait etc*) stating, statement

enorgueillir [ɑ̃nɔrgœjir] **1** *vt* to make proud **2 s'enorgueillir** *vpr* **s'e. de qch/d'avoir fait qch** to be proud of *or* pride oneself on sth/having done sth

énorme [enɔrm] *adj* (*personne, édifice, succès, quantité, perte etc*) enormous, huge; **il a été élu à une é. majorité** he was elected by a huge *or* overwhelming majority; **mensonge é.** whopping lie, whopper; **raconter des choses énormes** to say outrageous things; **il n'est pas mort, c'est déjà é.** he's still alive, which is incredible

énormément [enɔrmemɑ̃] *adv* enormously, hugely, tremendously; **je le regrette é.** I'm extremely *or F* awfully sorry; **elle a é. changé** she has changed enormously *or* a great deal; **é. de bien/d'argent** an enormous amount *or* a great deal of good/money; **é. de gens** a great many *or F* lots of people

énormité [enɔrmite] *nf* (**a**) (*d'une demande, d'un péché, d'un crime etc*) enormity, outrageousness (**b**) (*taille démesurée*) (*d'une personne, d'un édifice*) enormousness, hugeness; **l'é. du gaspillage** the huge *or* enormous amount wasted (**c**) (*bévue*) (dreadful) blunder; **commettre une é.** to put one's foot right in it, to make a (dreadful) blunder; **ce traité est plein d'énormités** this treaty is full of (written) mistakes *or F* howlers (**d**) **dire des énormités** to say the most outrageous things

enquérir (s') [sɑ̃kerir] *vpr* (*conj like* **acquérir**) to inquire, to make inquiries (**de** about); **s'e. du prix** to ask the price; **il s'est enquis de vous/de votre santé** he inquired *or* asked after *or* about you/your health

enquête [ɑ̃kɛt] *nf Jur, Parl etc* inquiry; (*policière*) investigation(s), inquiries; (*sondage*) survey, opinion poll; *Mktg* market probe; **l'inspecteur mène l'e.** the inspector is leading the investigation(s) *or* inquiries; **ouvrir une e.** to set up *or* open an inquiry; **faire** *ou* **procéder à une e. sur qch** *Jur etc* to hold *or* conduct an inquiry into sth; (*de la police*) to carry out *or* conduct an investigation into sth; **commission d'e.** court of inquiry; *Br Parl* select committee; **elle a décidé de faire sa petite e.** she decided to investigate; *Com* **e. sur les prix** price survey

▶ **enquête**: *Jur* **e. administrative** public inquiry; **e. omnibus** omnibus survey; **e. postale** postal survey; **e. par questionnaire** questionnaire survey; **e. scientifique** scientific investigation; **e. sociologique** sociological survey; **e. par sondage** sample survey; **e. téléphonique** telephone interviewing *or* survey

enquête-pilote, *pl* **enquêtes-pilotes** *nf Mktg* pilot survey

enquêter [ɑ̃kete] *vi Jur* to hold an inquiry; (*de la police*) to make investigations; (*faire un sondage*) to conduct a survey (**sur** into); **e. sur une affaire** to inquire into a matter, to investigate a matter

enquêteur, -euse [ɑ̃kɛtœr, -øz] **1** *adj Jur* **commissaire e.** investigating commissioner **2** *n* investigator; (*qui fait un sondage*) researcher; *Journ* interviewer; *Mktg* pollster

enquêtrice [ɑ̃kɛtris] *nf* investigator; (*qui fait un sondage*) researcher; *Journ* interviewer; *Mktg* pollster

enquiquinant [ɑ̃kikinɑ̃] *adj F* (*agaçant*) irritating, annoying; (*lassant*) boring

enquiquinement [ɑ̃kikinmɑ̃] *nm F* (*souci, problème*) nuisance; **enquiquinements** trouble; **mon patron me fait des enquiquinements** my boss is giving me trouble; **je n'ai que des enquiquinements avec ma voiture** I have nothing but trouble with my car, my car gives me nothing but trouble

enquiquiner [ɑ̃kikine] *vt F* (*agacer*) to irritate, to annoy; (*lasser*) to bore (stiff)

enquiquineur, -euse [ɑ̃kikinœr, -øz] *n F* nuisance, pest; (*raseur*) (crashing) bore

enraciné [ɑ̃rasine] *adj* (*habitude, haine etc*) deep-rooted, deep-seated; **elle est enracinée dans cette région/ses habitudes** she is firmly rooted in this region/her habits

enracinement [ɑ̃rasinmɑ̃] *nm* (**a**) (*action d'enraciner*) (*d'un jeune arbre*) digging in (**b**) (*action de s'enraciner*) (*d'un arbre, Fig d'une idée etc*) taking root; (*d'une personne*) putting down of roots

enraciner [ɑ̃rasine] **1** *vt* (**a**) (*arbre etc*) to dig in, to root (**b**) *Fig* (*principes etc*) to establish, to implant **2 s'enraciner** *vpr* (*d'un arbre*) to take root; *Fig* (*d'une personne*) to put down roots; *Fig* (*de sentiments, d'habitudes, d'une coutume etc*) to take root, to become established *or* deeply rooted

enrageant [ɑ̃raʒɑ̃] *adj* infuriating, maddening

enragé, -ée [ɑ̃raʒe] **1** *adj* (**a**) (*chien etc*) rabid (**b**) *F* (*partisan etc*) rabid, out-and-out; (*sportif etc*) keen **2** *n F* fanatic; **un e. de golf** a golf fanatic *or* enthusiast, a keen golfer

enrager [ɑ̃raʒe] *vi* (**j'enrageai(s); n. enrageons**) to be furious; **elle enrage de ne pas pouvoir le faire** she's furious at not being able to do it; **faire e. qn** to infuriate *or* madden sb; (*taquiner*) to tease sb

enrayage [ɑ̃rɛjaʒ] *nm* (**a**) (*blocage*) (*d'une roue*) locking; (*d'un *mécanisme, d'une arme etc)* jamming **(b)** *(montage des rayons) (d'une roue)* spoking

enrayer 1 *vt* **(a)** *(bloquer) (arme à feu, machine etc)* to jam; *(roue)* to lock; *Fig* **e. une maladie/un fléau** to arrest *or* check a disease/scourge **(b)** *(équiper de rayons) (roue)* to spoke **2 s'enrayer** *vpr* **(a)** *(d'une arme à feu, machine etc)* to jam **(b)** *(d'une épidémie)* to abate

enrayure [ɑ̃rɛjyr] *nf (rayons) (d'une roue)* spokes

enrégimenter [ɑ̃reʒimɑ̃te] *vt* **(a)** *(dans un parti, une organisation etc)* to enrol **(b)** *Mil* to form into regiments

enregistrable [ɑ̃r(ə)ʒistrabl] *adj (musique, émission etc)* recordable

enregistrement [ɑ̃r(ə)ʒistrəmɑ̃] *nm* **(a)** *(action d'inscrire) (de faits etc)* recording; *Jur (de la naissance, d'un acte etc)* registration; *(d'une commande)* booking, entering (up); *(de bagages)* check-in; **guichet d'e.** *(à l'aéroport etc)* check-in (desk); **e. anticipé** advanced check-in; **e. d'une compagnie** incorporation of a company; *Admin* **droit d'e.** stamp duty

(b) *Tech (action, disque etc)* recording; *Ordinat (de données)* logging, recording; **e. comptable** accounting entry; *Ordinat* **e. de transactions** transaction logging; **e. vidéo** video recording; **e. sur bande/cassette** tape/cassette recording; **studio d'e.** recording studio; *TV, Rad* **e. son** *ou* **sonore** audio *or* sound recording; **e. vocal** voice recording; *TV* **camion d'e. (du son)** sound van; **passer un e.** to play a recording

(c) *Ordinat (article de base de données)* record

enregistrer [ɑ̃r(ə)ʒistre] **1** *vt* **(a)** *(inscrire) (faits etc)* to record; *Jur (naissance, acte etc)* to register; *(commande)* to book, to enter (up); *(bagages)* to check in; **société enregistrée** incorporated company; **les meilleures ventes enregistrées depuis des mois** the best recorded sales for months; **e. le courrier** to log the mail

(b) *F (mémoriser)* to note, to memorize

(c) *Tech (musique, émission etc)* to record, to tape; *(données)* to store; **e. un disque** to make a record; **e. sur bande** to tape, to record on tape; **e. au magnétoscope** to video, to record on video; **musique enregistrée** recorded music; *Ordinat* **programme enregistré** stored programme

2 s'enregistrer *vpr (d'une cassette etc)* to record

enregistreur, -euse [ɑ̃r(ə)ʒistrœr, -øz] **1** *adj (appareil, mécanisme)* recording; **caisse enregistreuse** cash register **2** *nm (appareil)* recorder

▶ **enregistreur**: **e. à bande** (strip) chart recorder; **e. de pression** pressure recorder; **e. de son** *ou* **sonore** sound recorder; **e. à tambour** drum recorder; *Ind* **e. de temps** time clock *or* recorder; *Av* **e. de vol** flight recorder, *F* black box

enrhumer [ɑ̃ryme] **1** *vt* **e. qn** to give sb a cold; **être enrhumé** to have a cold **2 s'enrhumer** *vpr* to catch a cold

enrichi, -ie [ɑ̃riʃi] *adj* **(a)** *(personne)* wealthy, *Péj* nouveau riche; *Fig* **il est sorti e. de ses voyages** his travelling has enriched his mind; **céréales enrichies en vitamines** cereals with added vitamins, vitamin-enriched cereals; **liquide vaisselle e. en lanoline** washing-up liquid with added lanolin *or* enriched with lanolin **(b)** *Typ (texte)* enhanced **(c)** *Phys (uranium)* enriched

enrichir [ɑ̃riʃir] **1** *vt* **(a)** *(qn, pays)* to enrich, to make rich(er) **(b)** *Fig (art, collection, esprit etc)* to enrich; **e. la langue française** to enrich the French language **(c)** *Phys (uranium etc)* to enrich; **e. la terre** to enrich the soil **(d)** *Typ (texte)* to enhance **2 s'enrichir** *vpr* **(a)** *(d'une personne, d'un pays)* to grow rich(er) **(b)** *Fig (d'une langue etc)* to grow *or* become richer **(de** with; **en** in); **s'e. à force de lectures/de voyages** to enrich one's mind through reading/travel

enrichissant [ɑ̃riʃisɑ̃] *adj (expérience etc)* enriching

enrichissement [ɑ̃riʃismɑ̃] *nm* **(a)** *(de l'esprit, d'une collection etc)* enriching, enrichment; *(d'entreprise)* increase in capital; **e. personnel** personal enrichment **(b)** *Phys (de l'uranium etc)* enrichment **(c)** *Typ (attribut)* enhancement, special typographical feature **(d)** *TV, Rad* **e. audio** audio sweetening

enrobage [ɑ̃rɔbaʒ] *nm*, **enrobement** [ɑ̃rɔbmɑ̃] *nm (action, enveloppe)* coating; **e. de sucre/chocolat** sugar/chocolate coating

enrober [ɑ̃rɔbe] *vt (bonbon, pilule etc)* to coat **(de** with); *Fig* **e. une nouvelle peu agréable dans un flot de paroles** to wrap up a piece of unpleasant news in a mass of words; *Hum* **il est un peu enrobé** he's a bit chubby *or* plump

enrôlé [ɑ̃role] *nm Mil* enlisted man

enrôlement [ɑ̃rolmɑ̃] *nm* enrolment; *Mil* enlistment

enrôler [ɑ̃role] **1** *vt (membres, travailleurs)* to enrol, to recruit; *Mil* to enlist; *Hist* **e. de force** to press-gang, to impress **2 s'enrôler** *vpr* to enrol; *Mil* to enlist

enroué [ɑ̃rwe] *adj (personne, voix)* hoarse, husky

enrouement [ɑ̃rumɑ̃] *nm* hoarseness, huskiness

enrouer [ɑ̃rwe] **1** *vt (voix, personne)* to make hoarse *or* husky **2 s'enrouer** *vpr* to get hoarse; **s'e. à force de crier** to shout oneself hoarse

enroulable [ɑ̃rulabl] *adj* winding; *Aut* **ceinture de sécurité e.** inertia-reel seat belt

enroulement [ɑ̃rulmɑ̃] *nm* **(a)** *(de tissu, tapis etc)* rolling up; *(de câble, ruban etc)* winding up **(b)** *Él (fil)* coil, winding; **e. du champ d'excitation** field winding; **e. en série** series winding **(c)** *(ornement)* scroll, volute

enrouler [ɑ̃rule] **1** *vt* **(a)** *(rouler) (carte, tapis etc)* to roll up; *(câble, ruban etc)* to wind up **(b)** *(envelopper)* to wrap up **(dans** in) **2 s'enrouler** *vpr (d'un serpent etc)* to coil (up); *(d'un film, fil etc)* to wind; **s'e. dans une couverture** to wrap oneself up in a blanket

enrouleur [ɑ̃rulœr] *nm Aut* **e. (de ceinture de sécurité)** inertia reel, safety belt retractor; **ceinture de sécurité à e.** inertia-reel seat belt

enrubanner [ɑ̃rybane] *vt* to decorate with a ribbon/ribbons

ENS [əɛnɛs] *nf abrév* **École normale supérieure**

ensablement [ɑ̃sabləmɑ̃] *nm* **(a)** *(d'un bateau)* running aground, stranding **(b)** *(d'un port)* silting up; *(de tuyaux)* choking up (with sand) **(c)** *(dépôt) (amené par l'eau)* sandbank, sand bar; *(amené par le vent)* sand dune

ensabler [ɑ̃sable] **1** *vt* **(a)** *(sur le sable) (bateau)* to strand, to run aground; *(véhicule)* to get stuck in the sand **(b)** *(d'une inondation) (terre)* to cover with sand; *(port, rivière)* to silt up, to sand up **2 s'ensabler** *vpr* **(a)** *(d'un bateau, véhicule, poisson)* to get stuck in the sand **(b)** *(d'un port, d'une rivière)* to silt up; *(de tuyaux)* to get choked up (with sand)

ensachage [ɑ̃saʃaʒ] *nm (de bonbons etc)* bagging; *(de céréales etc)* sacking

ensacher [ɑ̃saʃe] *vt (bonbons etc)* to put into bags, to bag; *(céréales etc)* to put into sacks, to sack

ensanglanter [ɑ̃sɑ̃glɑ̃te] *vt (chemise, corps etc)* to stain with blood; **e. une nation** to plunge a nation into a bloodbath; **mains ensanglantées** bloodstained *or* bloody hands; **événement ensanglanté par un attentat** event marred by the bloody violence of an assassination attempt

enseignant, -ante [ɑ̃sɛɲɑ̃, -ɑ̃t] **1** *adj* teaching; **corps e.** teaching profession **2** *n* teacher

enseigne [ɑ̃sɛɲ] **1** *nf* **(a)** *(panonceau) (d'un magasin, cinéma etc)* sign; **e. au néon** neon sign; **à l'e. du Lion d'or** at the (sign of the) Golden Lion; **e. bancaire** big bank; *Fig F* **nous sommes tous logés à la même e.** we are all in the same boat; *Prov* **à bon vin point d'e.** good wine needs no bush **(b)** *Litt* **à telle e. que ...** so much so that ... **(c)** *Hist, Mil (drapeau etc)* ensign **2** *nm* **(a)** *Hist, Mil (soldat)* standard-bearer, ensign **(b)** *Naut* **e. (de vaisseau)** *Br* sub-lieutenant, *US* ensign

enseignement [ɑ̃sɛɲmɑ̃] *nm* **(a)** *(instruction)* teaching; **l'e. de l'anglais** the teaching of English; **méthode d'e.** teaching method; **il est dans l'e.** he is a teacher, he teaches **(b)** *(éducation, formation)* education; **e. des** *ou* **pour adultes** adult education; **e. du premier/second degré, e. primaire/secondaire** primary/secondary education; **e. supérieur** higher education **(c)** *(leçon tirée de l'expérience)* lesson; **tirer un e. de qch** to learn a lesson from sth

▶ **enseignement**: **e. assisté par ordinateur** computer-aided *or* -assisted learning; **e. à distance** distance learning; **e. en groupe** group teaching; **e. libre** private education; **e. mixte** coeducation; **e. par correspondance** teaching by correspondence courses; **e. technique** technical education

enseigner [ɑ̃sɛɲe] **1** *vt* **(a)** *(apprendre)* to teach; **e. la grammaire à qn** to teach sb grammar; **e. à qn à faire qch** to teach sb (how) to do sth; **e. l'anglais** to teach English; **l'expérience nous enseigne que ...** experience teaches *or* shows us that ... **(b)** *Vieilli (indiquer)* to show, to point out; **e. à qn son devoir** to point out his/her duty to sb **2** *vi* **il enseigne** he's a teacher, he teaches

ensemble [ɑ̃sɑ̃bl] **1** *adv* together; **vivre e.** to live together; **ils se marièrent e.** they married (each other); **aller (bien) e.** *(de personnes)* to be well-matched; *(de choses)* to go together; **ils vont mal e.** *(de personnes)* they're ill-matched; **on pourrait partir tous e.** we could all go together *or* in a group; **ne répondez pas tous e.** don't all answer at once *or* at the same time; **vendre tous ses meubles e.** to sell all one's furniture at once

2 *nm* **(a)** *(totalité)* whole, entirety; **l'e. du travail est bon** the work as a whole is good; **l'e. d'un tableau** the general effect of a picture; **vue d'e.** comprehensive *or* general view, overall picture; **idée d'e.** *(d'un sujet)* broad *or* general idea; **dans l'e.** on the whole, taken all round, by and large; **la classe, prise dans son e., a un bon niveau** the class, (taken) as a whole, is of a good standard

(b) *(unité)* cohesion, unity; **mouvement d'e.** combined movement; **l'exécution manque d'e.** the execution lacks cohesion *or* is ragged; **avec e.** all together, in unison, as one

(c) (*groupe*) (*de gens*) group; (*d'objets, de faits, de conditions*) set; (*de meubles*) suite; (*de services etc*) package; **e. vocal** (small) choir; **e. de couleurs** harmonious (group of) colours; **e. de données** set of data; *Mktg* **e. de besoins** need set; *Mktg* **e. de considérations** consideration *or* product (choice) set

(d) (*vêtements*) ensemble, outfit; **e. pantalon** *Br* trouser suit, *Am* pant suit

(e) (*d'habitations*) block; **grand e.** residential estate

(f) *Math* set; **e. vide** empty set

(g) *Aut* **e. moteur-boîte** power unit

ensemblier [ɑ̃sɑ̃blije] *nm* interior decorator; *Cin, TV* assistant set designer

ensemencement [ɑ̃s(ə)mɑ̃smɑ̃] *nm* **(a)** *Agr* sowing **(b)** *Biol* seeding

ensemencer [ɑ̃s(ə)mɑ̃se] *vt* **(j'ensemençai(s))** **(a)** *Agr* (*champ*) to sow **(b)** *Biol* (*milieu de culture*) to seed

enserrer [ɑ̃sere] *vt* (*objet, partie du corps*) to encircle tightly; **e. qn dans ses bras** to clasp sb in one's arms, to embrace *or* hug sb

ensevelir [ɑ̃səvlir] **1** *vt* **(a)** *Litt* (*enterrer*) (*corps*) to bury, to entomb; *Fig* (*secret*) to hide away; **l'avalanche a enseveli le village sous la neige** the avalanche buried the village in snow; *Fig* **il a été enseveli sous des tonnes de lettres** he was snowed under with letters **(b)** (*mettre dans un linceul*) (*corps*) to shroud **2 s'ensevelir** *vpr* (*dans un livre, à la campagne etc*) to bury oneself

ensevelissement [ɑ̃səvlismɑ̃] *nm* (*de mort*) burial; (*dans un linceul*) shrouding; (*sous la neige, des décombres etc*) burying; *Fig* (*de secret*) hiding away

ensilage [ɑ̃silaʒ] *nm* (*de récoltes*) ensilage

ensiler [ɑ̃sile] *vt* (*récoltes*) to ensile

ensoleillé [ɑ̃sɔleje] *adj* (*lieu, jour etc*) sunny

ensoleillement [ɑ̃sɔlɛjmɑ̃] *nm* **(a)** (*état*) sunniness **(b)** (*période*) sunny period; **cinq journées d'e.** five days of sun(shine)

ensoleiller [ɑ̃sɔleje] *vt* **(a)** (*pièce, mur etc*) to bathe in sunlight **(b)** *Fig* (*la vie de qn etc*) to brighten (up), to light up

ensommeillé [ɑ̃sɔmeje] *adj* (*personne*) sleepy, drowsy; (*yeux, visage*) sleepy

ensorcelant [ɑ̃sɔrsəlɑ̃] *adj* (*sourire etc*) bewitching

ensorcelé [ɑ̃sɔrsəle] *adj* bewitched, under a spell

ensorceler [ɑ̃sɔrsəle] *vt* **(j'ensorcelle; j'ensorcellerai)** **(a)** (*envoûter*) to bewitch, to cast *or* put a spell (up) on **(b)** *Fig* (*qn*) to bewitch, to captivate

ensorceleur, -euse [ɑ̃sɔrsəlœr, -øz] **1** *adj* bewitching **2** *nm* sorcerer; *Fig* charmer **3** *nf* **ensorceleuse** sorceress; *Fig* enchantress

ensorcellement [ɑ̃sɔrsɛlmɑ̃] *nm* **(a)** (*action*) bewitching; (*état*) bewitchment; (*sorcellerie*) sorcery **(b)** *Fig* (*charme*) charm, spell

ensuite [ɑ̃sɥit] *adv* (*plus tard*) after(wards), later; (*puis*) then, next, after that; **et e.?** what then?, what next?; *F* **e. de quoi/de cela, il s'est mis en colère** after which/after that he lost his temper; **les pompiers marchaient en tête, e. venait la musique** the firemen led the procession, next came the band; **d'abord, c'est très cher, et e. ça ne te va pas du tout** for one thing it's very expensive and for another it doesn't at all suit you

ensuivre (s') [sɑ̃sɥivr] *vpr* (*conj like* **suivre**) to follow, to ensue, to result; **jusqu'à ce que mort s'ensuive** (*battre qn etc*) to death; **les résultats qui s'ensuivent** the results which ensue *or* follow; **il s'ensuit qu'il est sans emploi** the consequence is he's out of a job; *F* **et tout ce qui s'ensuit** and all the rest of it, and all that goes with it, *Litt* **vos erreurs s'ensuivront de graves sanctions** your errors will result in grave punishment

ensuqué [ɑ̃syke] *adj Région, F* dazed, in a daze

entablement [ɑ̃tabləmɑ̃] *nm Archit* (*au-dessus d'une colonnade*) entablature; *Constr* (*support de toit*) coping

entacher [ɑ̃taʃe] *vt* **(a)** (*l'honneur de qn*) to sully, to besmirch, to cast a slur on **(b)** *Jur* (*contrat etc*) to vitiate; **entaché de nullité** voidable

entaille [ɑ̃taj] *nf* **(a)** (*dans un morceau de bois etc*) notch; (*longue*) groove; **à entailles** notched; (*longues*) grooved **(b)** (*blessure*) gash, cut; (*superficielle*) nick, cut; **se faire une e. au menton** to cut one's chin

entailler [ɑ̃taje] **1** *vt* **(a)** (*morceau de bois etc*) to notch; (*d'une longue encoche*) to groove **(b)** (*blesser*) to gash, to cut; (*superficiellement*) to nick, to cut **2 s'entailler** *vpr* **s'e. le doigt** to cut one's finger

entame [ɑ̃tam] *nf* **(a)** (*de pain, jambon etc*) first slice **(b)** *Cartes* (*d'une couleur*) opening (card)

entamer [ɑ̃tame] *vt* **(a)** (*pain, jambon etc*) to start on, to cut into; (*fût*) to broach; (*bouteille, pot de confiture etc*) to start on, to open; (*défense*) to penetrate, to breach; (*chair*) to cut into; **e. la peau** to break the skin; **doutes qui entament la foi/les convictions de qn** doubts that undermine *or* shake sb's faith/convictions; **e. l'honneur de qn** to damage sb's honour; **e. son capital** to break into one's capital

(b) (*commencer à entreprendre*) (*travail, recherche etc*) to begin, to commence, to start (on); (*négociations*) to start, to open; **e. une conversation** to strike up a conversation; **e. des démarches** to begin to take steps, to initiate steps; **e. des relations avec qn** to enter into relations with sb; *Jur* **e. des poursuites contre qn** to initiate *or* institute proceedings against sb; **e. un sujet** to broach a subject; *Com* **e. une vente** to open a sale

(c) *Cartes* **e. trèfle** to open clubs

entartrage [ɑ̃tartraʒ] *nm* (*d'une chaudière etc*) furring (up), scaling

entartrer [ɑ̃tartre] **1** *vt* (*chaudière etc*) to fur (up), to scale **2 s'entartrer** *vpr* (*d'une chaudière*) to fur (up), to become furred; (*des dents*) to scale up

entassement [ɑ̃tasmɑ̃] *nm* **(a)** (*de pierres etc*) piling (up), heaping (up); (*de caisses etc*) stacking **(b)** (*de passagers, bétail etc*) crowding *or* packing together

entasser [ɑ̃tase] **1** *vt* **(a)** (*pierres, livres, vêtements etc*) to pile (up), to heap (up); (*caisses etc*) to stack (up); (*argent*) to amass, to pile up **(b)** (*serrer*) (*passagers, bétail etc*) to pack *or* crowd *or* cram together **2 s'entasser** *vpr* **(a)** (*d'objets*) to pile up **(b)** (*de personnes*) to crowd *or* huddle together

ente [ɑ̃t] *nf* **(a)** *Agr etc* (*greffe*) scion, graft; (*porte-greffe*) stock **(b)** (*de pinceau*) handle

entendement [ɑ̃tɑ̃dmɑ̃] *nm* understanding; **dépasser l'e.** to be beyond all understanding

entendeur [ɑ̃tɑ̃dœr] *nm* **à bon e. salut!** a word to the wise (is enough)

entendre [ɑ̃tɑ̃dr] **1** *vt* **(a)** [①A40,C,1,a; B33,2,b,i] (*ouïr*) to hear; **j'entendis un cri** I heard a cry; **je n'entends rien (de ce que tu dis)** I can't hear a thing (you're saying); **on l'entend à peine** you can hardly hear him/it, he/it is scarcely audible; **je pouvais à peine me faire e.** I could hardly make myself heard; **parlez plus fort, je ne vous entends pas bien** speak up, I can't hear you very well; **je l'entendis rire** I heard him laugh *or* laughing; **tu n'as pas entendu quelque chose?** didn't you hear anything?; **on n'entend que toi, ici! c'est lassant à la fin!** yours is the only voice we can hear, it's so annoying!; **e. qch de ses propres oreilles** to hear sth with one's own ears; **je ne veux plus e. parler de lui** I don't want to hear him mentioned again *or* to hear another word about him; **e. dire que ...** to hear (it said) that ...; **on a entendu dire que sa femme l'a quitté** it is rumoured *or* said that his wife has left him; **je le sais parce que je l'ai entendu dire** I know it by *or* from hearsay; **e. qn dire qch** to hear sb say sth; **e. parler de** (*connaître l'existence de*) to hear of; (*être au courant de*) to hear about; **je ne veux pas en e. parler!** I don't want to hear (a word) about it!; **celui-là, il va e. parler de moi** *ou* **du pays!** he'll get a piece of my mind *or* a good ear-bashing!; **celui-là, il va m'e.!** he'll hear me!; **je ne veux pas en e. plus!** I don't want to hear any more *or* another word about it!; **il répétait, à qui voulait l'e., que ...** he'd tell anyone who would listen that ...; **je l'entends d'avance** *ou* **d'ici!** I can hear it already!; **e. des voix** to hear voices; *F* **ce qu'il ne faut pas e.!** I've heard it all now! *F* **qu'entends-je, qu'ouïs-je, qu'acoustiqué-je?** *ou* **qu'entends-je, qu'ouïs-je, rêvé-je ou dors-je?** ≈ I can't believe my ears!

(b) (*écouter*) (*suppliant etc*) to hear, to listen to; **on le congédia sans l'e.** he was dismissed without a hearing *or* without being heard; **e. la messe** to hear a mass; **e. qn en confession** to hear sb's confession; **aller e. un concert** to go to a concert; **à vous e., il a eu tort** judging from *or* going by what you say, he was in the wrong; **refuser d'e. une requête** to turn a deaf ear to a request; **e. raison** to listen to reason; **il n'a rien voulu e.** he would not listen; *Jur* **l'affaire sera entendue demain** the case will be heard *or* comes up (for hearing) tomorrow; **le juge a entendu les témoins** the judge heard the witnesses; **que Dieu entende nos prières** may our prayers be answered

(c) (*comprendre*) (*langue, passage d'un texte etc*) to understand; **ce n'est pas ainsi qu'il l'entend** he doesn't see it that way *or* like that; **donner à e. à qn que ...** (*faire croire*) to lead sb to believe that ...; (*faire comprendre*) to give sb to understand that ...; **laisser e. qch** to insinuate *or* imply sth; **il n'entend pas la plaisanterie** he can't take a joke; **je n'y entends rien** I don't know the first thing about it

(d) (*vouloir dire*) to mean; **qu'entendez-vous par là?** what do you mean by that?

(**e**) (*vouloir*) **e. faire qch** to intend *or* mean to do sth; **il n'y entend pas malice** he means *or* intends no harm; **faites comme vous l'entendez** do as you think best, do as you please; **j'entends que vous veniez** I expect you to come; **je n'entends pas qu'on le vende** I won't hear of it being sold; **elle voulait trouver du travail, mais lui ne l'entendait pas ainsi** she wanted to get a job, but he wouldn't hear of it

2 *vi* (*par l'ouïe*) to hear; **il entend mal** he is hard of hearing; **il est impossible de se faire e. ici!** it's impossible to make youself heard here!; **un bruit se fit e.** a noise was heard; **attends, j'ai mal entendu!** hold on, I don't think I heard you right!; **tu entends!** (*menace*) do you hear (me)!

3 s'entendre *vpr* (**a**) (*sympathiser*) to get on; **ils s'entendent bien** they get on (well); **je ne m'entends pas du tout avec elle** I don't get on at all with her; **je crois que nous sommes faits pour nous e.** I think we were made to get on well together; **nous n'étions pas faits pour nous e.** we weren't suited to each other; **ils s'entendent comme larrons en foire** they are as thick as thieves

(**b**) (*se mettre d'accord*) to agree; **s'e. directement avec qn** to come to a direct understanding with sb; **s'e. pour commettre un crime** to conspire to commit a crime; **il faudrait vous e., il est venu ou il n'est pas venu?** get your story straight, did he come or not?; **entendons-nous bien!** (*mettons les choses au clair*) let's get things straight!

(**c**) (*être perçu par l'ouïe*) to be heard; **sa voix ne s'entend guère** his voice is hardly audible *or* can hardly be heard; **on ne s'entend plus ici** you can't hear yourself speak *or* think here

(**d**) (*être compris*) to be understood; **cela s'entend** of course, that goes without saying

(**e**) **s'e. à, s'y e. à** (*être habile à*) (*chevaux, voitures etc*) to know (all) about, to understand; **s'e. aux affaires** to have a good head for business; **elle s'y entend à mettre de l'huile sur le feu** she has a knack for adding fuel to the fire

entendu, -ue [ɑ̃tɑ̃dy] **1** *adj* (**a**) (*complice, informé*) (*regard, sourire*) knowing; **d'un air e.** knowingly; **intérêt bien e.** enlightened self-interest (**b**) (*décidé*) **très bien, (c'est) e.** fine, agreed *or* all right!; **c'est une affaire entendue** that's agreed *or* settled; **et bien e., vous toucherez la moitié du bénéfice** and of course, you'll get half the profit **2** *n Vieilli* **faire l'e.** to pretend to know all about it

enténébrer [ɑ̃tenebre] *vt* (**il enténèbre**; **il enténébrera**) *Litt* to envelop *or* plunge in darkness *or* gloom

entente [ɑ̃tɑ̃t] *nf* (**a**) (*entre personnes*) (*accord*) agreement, understanding (**entre** between); (*relation*) harmony; **arriver à une e.** to reach an agreement *or* understanding; **terrain d'e.** common ground; **après e. avec les autorités** after consultation with the authorities; **il faut vivre en bonne e. avec ses voisins** one must live in harmony with one's neighbours; **la bonne/mauvaise e. qui règne dans la famille** the good/bad feeling that prevails in the family (**b**) (*compréhension*) **mot à double e.** word with a double meaning

▶ **entente**: *Hist* **E. Cordiale** Entente Cordiale; **e. industrielle** (*cartel*) combine

enter [ɑ̃te] *vt* (*arbre*) to graft

entérinement [ɑ̃terinmɑ̃] *nm Jur* ratification, confirmation; *Fig* endorsement

entériner [ɑ̃terine] *vt Jur* to ratify, to confirm; *Fig* (*approuver*) (*action, nouveau mot etc*) to endorse

entérique [ɑ̃terik] *adj Méd* enteric, intestinal

entérite [ɑ̃terit] *nf Méd* enteritis

enterrement [ɑ̃tɛrmɑ̃] *nm* (**a**) (*sous la terre*) burial, *Fml* interment; *Fig* **c'est l'e. de tous mes projets/espoirs** that has killed off all my plans/hopes; *Hum* **c'était vraiment un e. de première classe** it really got the thumbs down; *Hum* **faire un e. de première classe à un projet** to give a plan the thumbs down, to shelve a plan for good (**b**) (*cérémonie*) funeral; *F* **figure** *ou* **tête d'e.** long face; **faire une tête d'e.** to look sombre (**c**) (*cortège*) funeral procession

enterrer [ɑ̃tere] **1** *vt* (**a**) (*enfouir*) (*qch*) to bury, to put in the earth; (*bulbes*) to plant (**b**) (*inhumer*) (*corps*) to bury, *Fml* to inter; *F* **il nous enterrera tous** he will outlive us all; *Fig* **e. un projet** to scrap a plan; *Fig* **e. un désaccord/une querelle** to bury a disagreement/a quarrel; *Fig* **elle désire e. toute cette affaire** she wants the whole thing buried and forgotten; *Fig* **e. sa vie de garçon** to have a stag party *or* night **2 s'enterrer** *vpr Fig* **il s'est enterré au fin fond de la campagne normande** he buried himself in the depths of the Normandy countryside

entêtant [ɑ̃tɛtɑ̃] *adj* (*vin, parfum, musique etc*) heady

en-tête, *pl* **en-têtes** [ɑ̃tɛt] *nm* (*d'une lettre, d'un document*) heading; *Com* letterhead; *Typ* (*d'une page etc*) headline; *Ordinat* header; **e. de facture** billhead; *Journ* **e. de colonne** column header; **papier à e.** headed paper

entêté, -ée [ɑ̃tete] **1** *adj* obstinate, stubborn **2** *n* obstinate *or* stubborn person

entêtement [ɑ̃tɛtmɑ̃] *nm* obstinacy, stubbornness; **e. à faire qch** persistence in doing sth

entêter [ɑ̃tete] **1** *vt* **e. qn** (*d'un vin, d'une odeur, de la musique etc*) to go to sb's head, to make sb giddy **2 s'entêter** *vpr* to persist, to be persistent; **s'e. dans une opinion** to persist in an opinion; **s'e. à faire qch** to persist in doing sth

enthousiasmant [ɑ̃tuzjasmɑ̃] *adj* (*plan, idée etc*) exciting

enthousiasme [ɑ̃tuzjasm] *nm* enthusiasm (**pour** for); **avec e.** enthusiastically, with enthusiasm; **faire qch sans e.** to do sth half-heartedly *or* without enthusiasm

enthousiasmer [ɑ̃tuzjasme] **1** *vt* (*personne*) to fire *or* fill with enthusiasm; **il est revenu enthousiasmé** he came back full of *or* fired with enthusiasm **2 s'enthousiasmer** *vpr* to be/become enthusiastic, to enthuse (**pour** about)

enthousiaste [ɑ̃tuzjast] **1** *n* enthusiast **2** *adj* enthusiastic

entiché [ɑ̃tiʃe] *adj* infatuated (**de** with), *F* crazy (**de** about)

enticher (s') [sɑ̃tiʃe] *vpr* **s'e. de qn/qch** to become infatuated with *or F* crazy about sb/sth

entier, -ière [ɑ̃tje, -jɛr] **1** *adj* (**a**) (*sans division, sans diminution*) (*ville, boîte, quantité etc*) whole, entire; (*pas cassé, pas entamé*) (*assiette, gâteau etc*) intact, whole; (*boîte, bouteille etc*) full; **lait e.** whole milk, *Br* full-cream milk; **la France entière** the whole of France; **il a mangé le gâteau tout e.** he ate the whole (of the) cake; **pendant des heures entières** for hours on end; **conserver sa réputation entière** to keep one's reputation intact; **le problème reste e.** the problem is no nearer solution *or* remains unsolved; *Math* **nombre e.** integer, whole number; **cheval e.** stallion; **payer place entière** *Rail* to pay full fare; *Th* to pay full price

(**b**) (*absolu*) (*autorité, confiance etc*) complete, full; **l'entière direction de qch** the entire *or* sole management of sth; **se donner tout e. à son travail** to devote oneself entirely to one's work; **elle est tout(e) entière à ce qu'elle fait** she is engrossed in *or* intent on what she is doing; **jouir d'une entière liberté** to enjoy complete *or* total freedom; **donner entière satisfaction** to give complete *or* total satisfaction

(**c**) (*sans compromis*) (*personne*) unyielding, uncompromising

2 *nm* (**a**) (*totalité*) entirety; **raconter une histoire dans son e.** to relate a story in its entirety; **en e.** wholly, entirely, totally; **il a lu le livre en e.** he read the whole (of the) book *or* the entire book; **il a fait ses devoirs en e.** he has done all (of) his homework; **nom en e.** name in full, full name

(**b**) *Math* (*nombre*) integer, whole number

entièrement [ɑ̃tjɛrmɑ̃] *adv* entirely, wholly, completely; **il n'est pas e. mauvais** he's not all bad

entièreté [ɑ̃tjɛrte] *nf* entirety

entité [ɑ̃tite] *nf* entity; *Compta* item

entoilage [ɑ̃twalaʒ] *nm* (**a**) (*action*) (*de carte etc*) mounting on canvas; *Couture* stiffening with canvas (**b**) (*toile*) canvas mount

entoiler [ɑ̃twale] *vt* (*carte etc*) to mount on canvas; *Couture* to stiffen with canvas; **carte entoilée** canvas-mounted map

entôler [ɑ̃tole] *vt Arg* (*en particulier d'une prostituée*) (*client etc*) to fleece, to rob

entomologie [ɑ̃tɔmɔlɔʒi] *nf* entomology

entomologique [ɑ̃tɔmɔlɔʒik] *adj* entomological

entomologiste [ɑ̃tɔmɔlɔʒist] *n* entomologist

entonner[1] [ɑ̃tɔne] *vt* (*vin etc*) to barrel, to cask

entonner[2] *vt* (*commencer à chanter*) (*chanson*) to strike up, to start; *Vieilli* **e. les louanges de qn** to sing sb's praises

entonnoir [ɑ̃tɔnwar] *nm* (**a**) (*ustensile*) funnel; **en (forme d')e.** funnel-shaped (**b**) (*cavité*) funnel; (*produit par une bombe etc*) crater

entorse [ɑ̃tɔrs] *nf* (**a**) *Méd* sprain, wrench; **se faire une e. à la cheville/au poignet** to sprain *or* twist *or* wrench one's ankle/wrist (**b**) *Fig* **faire une e. à la loi/au règlement** to bend *or* stretch the law/the rules; **faire une e. à la vérité** to twist *or* distort the truth; **faire une e. à son régime** to break one's diet; **tu peux bien faire une petite e. à tes habitudes** you can surely make an exception

entortillement [ɑ̃tɔrtijmɑ̃] *nm* (**a**) (*action*) (*d'un fil, papier etc*) twisting, wrapping; (*d'un serpent, du lierre etc*) twisting, twining, coiling (**b**) (*état*) entwinement

entortiller [ɑ̃tɔrtije] **1** *vt* (**a**) (*envelopper*) (*bonbon etc*) to wrap (up) (**dans** in); (*enrouler*) (*fil, papier etc*) to twist, to wrap (**autour de** round)

(**b**) (*circonvenir*) (*personne*) to get round

(**c**) (*embrouiller*) (*phrases, réponses etc*) to make convoluted; **e. une demande dans des explications fumeuses** to wrap up a request in woolly explanations

2 s'entortiller *vpr* (**a**) (*d'un serpent, du lierre etc*) to twist, to twine, to coil (**autour de** round)

(b) (*s'empêtrer*) to get entangled, to get tangled (up) **(dans** in); **il s'est entortillé les pieds dans le tapis** he got his feet entangled *or* tangled (up) in the carpet; *Fig* **elle s'entortillait dans des explications compliquées** she tied herself in knots with complicated explanations

(c) (*s'enrouler*) (*dans une couette etc*) to wrap oneself up **(dans** in)

entour [ɑ̃tur] *nm* **à l'e. de** (*ville etc*) round (about); *Litt* **les entours de** the environs *or* surroundings of

entourage [ɑ̃turaʒ] *nm* **(a)** (*bordure*) (*d'une ouverture, d'un parterre de fleurs etc*) border; (*d'un bijou*) setting; **miniature avec un e. de perles** miniature set in pearls **(b)** (*amis, relations*) circle (of friends/acquaintances); (*collègues*) associates; (*de ministre etc*) attendants; (*de souverain*) entourage, suite; **dans son e. proche** in his close circle

entourer [ɑ̃ture] **1** *vt* **(a)** (*border, enceindre*) to surround **(de** with); **e. un champ d'une clôture** to fence in a field; **veuillez e. la bonne réponse en rouge** please circle *or* ring the correct answer in red; **e. qn de ses bras** to put one's arms round sb, to hold *or* take sb in one's arms; **cheminée entourée de marbre** fireplace enclosed in marble

(b) (*être autour de*) to surround; (*armée*) to encircle, to surround; **les gens qui vous entourent** the people around *or* about you; **le monde qui nous entoure** the world around us; **entouré d'amis** surrounded by friends; **un rang de perles entourait son cou** a string of pearls encircled her neck, she had a string of pearls round her neck; **entouré de mystère** wrapped *or* shrouded in mystery

(c) (*s'occuper de*) (*personne*) to rally round; **il est très entouré (d'amis)** he is surrounded by friends; **e. qn de soins/respect** to lavish attention on sb/to show respect to sb; **au moment de son divorce, sa famille l'a beaucoup entouré** his family rallied round *or* supported him at the time of his divorce

2 s'entourer *vpr* **s'e. d'amis/de belles choses** to surround oneself with friends/fine things

entourloupe [ɑ̃turlup] *nf*, **entourloupette** [ɑ̃turlupɛt] *nf F* dirty trick; **faire une e. à qn** to play a dirty trick on sb

entournure [ɑ̃turnyr] *nf* (*de vêtement*) armhole; *F* **être gêné aux entournures** (*mal à l'aise*) to feel awkward *or* ill at ease; (*financièrement*) to feel the pinch

entracte [ɑ̃trakt] *nm* **(a)** *Th, Cin* (*intervalle*) *Br* interval, intermission; **à l'e.** in the *Br* interval *or* intermission **(b)** *Th* (*pièce*) entr'acte, interlude

entraide [ɑ̃trɛd] *nf* mutual aid

entraider (s') [sɑ̃trede] *vpr* to help one another *or* each other

entrailles [ɑ̃trɑj] *nfpl* (*du corps*) entrails, intestines, bowels; *Litt* (*de la mère*) womb; *Fig* **les e. de la terre** the bowels of the earth; *Fig* **ce reportage m'a remué les e.** this report made a deep and painful impression on me; *Fig* **ne pas avoir d'e.** to be heartless

entrain [ɑ̃trɛ̃] *nm* (*d'une fête, musique, conversation etc*) liveliness, spirit; (*d'une personne*) high spirits, spirit, liveliness; **être plein d'e., avoir de l'e.** (*d'une personne*) to be full of life *or* of go; **musique pleine d'e.** lively music; **manger avec e.** to eat with gusto; **travailler avec e.** to work with a will; **donner plus d'e. à la conversation** to liven up the conversation; **ça manque d'e., tout ça** that's all a bit half-hearted; **faire qch sans e.** to do sth half-heartedly

entraînant [ɑ̃trɛnɑ̃] *adj* (*air, rythme, style*) lively; (*éloquence*) stirring

entraînement [ɑ̃trɛnmɑ̃] *nm* **(a)** (*d'un élève etc*), *Sp, Courses de chevaux* training; **un e.** a training session, a work-out; **suivre un e.** to follow a training programme; **à l'e.** in training; **il s'est blessé à l'e.** he hurt himself training; **il a marqué un but comme à l'e.** he scored a text-book goal; **match d'e.** practice game; **terrain d'e.** training *or* practice ground; **avoir de l'e.** to be well trained; *Fig F* **toi qui as de l'e., fais-le** you've had a lot of practice at this type of thing, you do it; **manquer d'e.** to be out of training

(b) *Tech* drive; **arbre d'e.** drive shaft; *Aut* **e. par chaîne** chain drive; **e. à friction** (*d'une imprimante*) friction feed; **e. à picots** *ou* **à traction** (*d'une imprimante*) tractor drive *or* feed

(c) *Litt* (*des passions*) force; **céder à des entraînements** to get carried away

entraîner [ɑ̃trene] **1** *vt* **(a)** (*d'une rivière etc*) to sweep along, to carry away; (*d'une locomotive etc*) to pull, to draw (along); **e. qn quelque part** to drag *or* take sb off somewhere; **il m'a entraîné chez lui** he took me along to his house; **il vous entraînera dans sa chute** he will drag you down with him

(b) *Tech* (*partie de machine etc*) to drive; *MecE* **entraîné par courroie** belt-driven

(c) (*exercer une influence sur*) **e. qn à faire qch** to lead *or* induce sb to do sth; **être entraîné dans un piège** to be lured *or* led into a trap; **cela nous entraînera dans des problèmes** that will lead *or* get us into problems; **entraîné par l'éloquence de l'orateur** carried away by the speaker's eloquence; **se faire e.** to be *or* get led astray; **se laisser e.** to allow oneself to be led astray; **se laisser e. à faire qch** to be drawn into doing sth

(d) (*causer*) (*accident, malheur etc*) to result in, to bring about; (*problème, dépense etc*) to entail, to involve; **cela entraînera un retard** it will involve *or* lead to delay; **décision qui peut e. des inconvénients** decision that may give rise to difficulties

(e) (*former*) (*élève etc*) to train; *Sp* (*athlète, équipe*) to coach, to train; (*cheval de course etc*) to train; (*cycliste*) to pace; **e. qn à faire qch** to train sb to do sth

2 s'entraîner *vpr* (*d'un élève etc*) to train oneself; *Sp* to train; **s'e. à faire qch** to train oneself to do sth

entraîneur [ɑ̃trɛnœr] *nm* **(a)** *Sp* (*d'un athlète, d'une équipe*) coach, trainer; (*d'un cheval etc*) trainer; (*d'un cycliste*) pacemaker, pacer **(b)** (*chef*) **e. d'hommes** leader of men

entraîneuse [ɑ̃trɛnøz] *nf* **(a)** (*dans une boîte de nuit etc*) hostess **(b)** *Sp* (*d'une athlète, d'une équipe*) coach, trainer; (*d'un cheval etc*) trainer

entrant [ɑ̃trɑ̃] **1** *adj* (*fonctionnaire*) newly appointed; (*représentant parlementaire*) newly elected; **les élèves entrants** the new pupils **2** *n* **les entrants et les sortants** those entering and those leaving

entrapercevoir [ɑ̃trapɛrsəvwar] *vt* (*conj like* **apercevoir**) to catch a fleeting glimpse of

entrave [ɑ̃trav] *nf* **(a)** (*d'un cheval etc*) hobble; **entraves** (*d'un forçat etc*) fetters, shackles **(b)** *Fig* hindrance, impediment **(à** to); **e. à la circulation** hindrance to traffic; **e. à la liberté/à la bonne marche de la justice** interference with freedom/with the due process of the law

entravé [ɑ̃trave] *adj* **jupe entravée** hobble skirt

entraver [ɑ̃trave] *vt* **(a)** (*cheval etc*) to hobble; (*forçat etc*) to put in fetters *or* shackles **(b)** *Fig* (*action, carrière etc*) to hinder, to hamper, to impede; **e. la circulation** to hold up *or* block the traffic **(c)** *F* (*comprendre*) to get; **je n'y entrave rien** *ou* **que dalle** I don't get it (at all)

entre [ɑ̃tr] *prép* [ⓘ**A65; B53**] **(a)** (*deux choses, personnes, dates etc*) between; **choisir e. deux choses** to choose between two things; **distance de 10 kilomètres e. deux villes** distance of 10 kilometres between two towns; **e. deux et trois (heures)** between two and three (o'clock); *Fig* **e. les deux** (*ni l'un ni l'autre*) between the two; (*comme ci comme ça*) so-so; **être e. la vie et la mort** to be between life and death; **être e. deux âges** to be middle-aged; *Fig* **voir qn/faire qch e. deux portes** to see sb/to do sth for a brief moment

(b) (*parmi*) among(st); **un homme dangereux e. tous** a most dangerous man; **un homme qu'il admirait entre tous** a man he admired above all others; **un jour e. mille** a day in a thousand; **il y avait e. autres, un Dürer et un Rembrandt** there were, among(st) other things *or* others, a Dürer and a Rembrandt; **ce jour e. tous** this day of all days; **d'e.** (from) among; **plusieurs d'e. nous** several of us; **l'un d'e. vous** one of you; **hésiter e. plusieurs solutions/routes/robes** to hesitate between several solutions/roads/dresses; **elle l'a choisi e. tous les hommes présents** she chose him from among all the men present

(c) (*dans*) **tomber e. les mains de l'ennemi** to fall into the enemy's hands; **tenir qch e. les mains** to hold sth in one's hands; **serrer qn e. ses bras** to clasp sb in one's arms, to hug sb; **parler e. ses dents** to mumble, to mutter; **e. ces murs** within these walls

(d) (*rapport réciproque*) (*deux personnes*) between; (*plus de deux personnes*) among(st); **ils se sont mis d'accord e. eux** they agreed among(st) themselves; **qu'est-ce qu'il y a de semblable e. lui et moi?** what similarities are there between him and me?; **mais qu'y a-t-il e. eux, exactement?** but what's (going on) between them exactly?; **soit dit e. nous** between ourselves; **nous dînerons e. nous** we'll have dinner alone *or* by ourselves; **nous sommes e. amis** we are among(st) friends; **se marier e. cousins** to intermarry with cousins; **discuter e. connaisseurs** to talk as one expert to another; *F* **il faut que je te parle e. quat'z'yeux** I've got to talk to you in private

(e) (*à travers*) through; **se faufiler e. les arbres** to thread one's way through *or* between *or* among(st) the trees; **passer e. les mailles** to slip through the net; **lire e. les lignes** to read between the lines

entrebâillement [ɑ̃trəbɑjmɑ̃] *nm* **l'e. de la porte/fenêtre** the half-open door/window

entrebâiller [ɑ̃trəbaje] *vt* (*porte, fenêtre*) to half-open; **la porte était entrebâillée** the door was ajar *or* half-open

entrebâilleur [ɑ̃trəbɑjœr] *nm* door chain

entrechat [ɑ̃trəʃa] *nm* **(a)** (*saut de danse*) entrechat **(b)**

(*gambade*) leap; **faire des entrechats** to prance (about), to cavort

entrechoquer [ɑ̃trəʃɔke] **1** *vt* to knock *or* bang together; **e. des verres** to chink glasses **2 s'entrechoquer** *vpr* to knock *or* bang against one another; (*de verres*) to chink; *Fig* (*de personnalités, d'idées etc*) to clash; **elle parle tellement vite que les mots s'entrechoquent** the words come tumbling out when she speaks

entrecôte [ɑ̃trəkot] *nf Culin* rib steak, entrecôte

entrecoupé [ɑ̃trəkupe] *adj* (*discours, sommeil, voyage etc*) interrupted, broken; (*représentation, lecture etc*) interrupted; **d'une voix entrecoupée** with a catch in one's voice

entrecouper [ɑ̃trəkupe] *vt* (*discours, voyage, représentation etc*) to interrupt (**de** with)

entrecroisement [ɑ̃trəkrwazmɑ̃] *nm* (*de lignes etc*) intersection, crisscross; (*de fils etc*) interlacing

entrecroiser [ɑ̃trəkrwaze] **1** *vt* (*lignes etc*) to intersect, to (criss)cross; (*fils etc*) to interlace **2 s'entrecroiser** *vpr* (*de lignes, routes etc*) to intersect, to (criss)cross; (*de fils etc*) to interlace

entre-déchirer (s') [sɑ̃trədeʃire] *vpr* to tear each other to pieces

entre-deux [ɑ̃trədø] *nm inv* **(a) il est arrivé dans l'e.** he arrived in the intervening period **(b)** *Couture* (*bande*) insertion

entre-deux-guerres [ɑ̃trədøgɛr] *nm inv* inter-war years (*1918-1939*)

entre-dévorer (s') [sɑ̃trədevɔre] *vpr* to devour one another *or* each other

entrée [ɑ̃tre] *nf* **(a)** (*action d'entrer*) entry, entrance; **e. (en scène) d'un acteur** an actor's entrance (on to the stage); **à leur e., tous se levèrent** as they entered, everybody stood up; **faire son e.** to make one's entrance; **faire une e. triomphale/discrète** to make a triumphant/discreet entrance; **faire son e. dans le monde** (*d'une fille*) to come out (into society); **l'e. en gare du train** the entry of the train into the station; **l'e. du Japon dans la deuxième guerre mondiale** the entry of Japan into the Second World War; **depuis l'e. en guerre du pays** since the country entered the war; **mon e. dans cette société date de six mois** I joined this company six months ago; **e. en fonction** assumption *or* taking up of one's duties; **l'e. en fonction du nouveau directeur est prévue pour ...** the new director is scheduled to take up his post on ...; **e. en fusion** beginning to melt; **e. en ébullition** coming to the boil; *Fig* **à l'e. de l'hiver** at the beginning of winter; *Fig* **d'e. (de jeu)** from the outset, from the very beginning

(b) (*accès*) admission, admittance (**dans un** *ou* **d'un lieu** to a place); **se voir refuser l'e. d'un lieu** to find oneself refused admission *or* entry to a place; **avoir ses entrées dans un lieu** to have the run of a place; **avoir ses entrées chez** *ou* **auprès de qn** to have free access to sb; **e. interdite** no admittance, no entry; **e. interdite au public/aux moins de 12 ans** public/under 12s not admitted, no admittance to the public/to under 12s; **e. interdite à tout véhicule** vehicles prohibited; **payer son entrée** to pay one's admission fee *or* entrance fee; **prendre une e. au musée/théâtre** to buy a museum/theatre ticket; **film qui fait des records d'e.** film that breaks box-office records; **on a fait 1 000 entrées le premier soir** a thousand people came on the first night; **e. à l'hôpital** admission into hospital

(c) (*action de devenir membre*) **e. dans l'armée/le club/le parti** joining the army/club/party; **e. dans l'enseignement/la finance** going into *or* taking up teaching/finance; **e. à l'université** going to university; **e. au couvent** going into a convent, taking the veil; **l'e. de la Norvège dans la CEE** Norway's entry into the EEC; **mon e. dans cette famille ne s'est pas vraiment bien passée** I didn't fit into the family very well

(d) *Com* entry; (*de marchandises importées*) importation; **droit d'e.** import duty; **e. en douane** inward customs clearance

(e) (*voie d'accès*) way in, entrance, entry (**de** to); (*d'un tunnel, port etc*) entrance, mouth; (*vestibule*) entrance hall; **e. réservée au personnel** staff entrance; **e. des fournisseurs** tradesmen's entrance; **e. principale** main entrance

(f) (*ouverture*) **e. de clef** keyhole; **e. d'air** air intake; *Rad* **e. de poste** lead-in

(g) *Ordinat* (*processus*) input, entry; (*information*) entry; (*touche*) enter (key); (*de caractère etc*) entering; **données d'e.** input (data); **e. (par le) clavier** keyboard input; **e. (à partir du) scanneur** scanned input; **e. de données à distance** remote data entry; **e. de gamme** entry level; **e. de papier** paper input; **e. opérateur** operator input; **e./sortie** input/output; **e./sortie parallèles** parallel input/output

(h) *Culin* starter

(i) (*de dictionnaire, livre de comptes etc*) entry

(j) *Compta* **e. d'argent** cash received

▶ **entrée: e. des artistes** stage door; **e. libre** (*dans un musée*) admission free, free admission; (*dans une boutique*) no obligation to buy; **e. en matière: après cette e. en matière** after this introduction; **e. de service** service entrance; **e. en vigueur** coming into force *or* effect *or* operation

entre-égorger (s') [sɑ̃tregɔrʒe] *vpr* to cut one another's *or* each other's throats

entrefaites [ɑ̃trəfɛt] *nfpl* **sur ces e.** at that moment

entrefilet [ɑ̃trəfilɛ] *nm Journ* paragraph, short item

entregent [ɑ̃trəʒɑ̃] *nm* social sense, savoir-faire; **elle a de l'e.** she knows how to get on with people

entrejambe [ɑ̃trəʒɑ̃b] *nm Couture* crotch, crutch; **hauteur de l'e.** inside leg measurement

entrelacement [ɑ̃trəlasmɑ̃] *nm* (*de rubans, fils, branches*) intertwining, interlacing, interweaving

entrelacer [ɑ̃trəlase] (*conj like* **lacer**) **1** *vt* (*rubans, fils, branches*) to intertwine, to interlace, to interweave; **les mains entrelacées** with one's/their/*etc* fingers entwined; *Ordinat* **écran entrelacé** interlaced screen **2 s'entrelacer** *vpr* to intertwine, to interlace, to interweave

entrelacs [ɑ̃trəla] *nm* interlaced design, tracery

entrelarder [ɑ̃trəlarde] *vt Culin* (*viande*) to lard; *Fig* **e. un discours de citations** to interlard a speech with quotations

entremêlement [ɑ̃trəmɛlmɑ̃] *nm* **(a)** (*action*) (inter)mingling **(b)** (*résultat*) (inter)mixture

entremêler [ɑ̃trəmele] **1** *vt* to (inter)mix, to (inter)mingle; **e. des couleurs** to mix *or* blend colours; **ordres entremêlés de jurons** orders interspersed with oaths **2 s'entremêler** *vpr* to (inter)mix, to (inter)mingle

entremets [ɑ̃trəmɛ] *nm Culin* dessert, *Br* sweet

entremetteur, -euse [ɑ̃trəmɛtœr, -øz] *n* (*dans une querelle*) intermediary, mediator; (*dans une liaison amoureuse*) go-between

entremettre (s') [sɑ̃trəmɛtr] *vpr* (*conj like* **mettre**) (*dans une querelle*) to intervene, to mediate; (*dans une liaison amoureuse*) to act as go-between

entremise [ɑ̃trəmiz] *nf* intervention, mediation; **par l'e. de qn** through sb

entrepont [ɑ̃trəpɔ̃] *nm Naut* 'tween decks; **passager d'e.** steerage passenger

entreposage [ɑ̃trəpozaʒ] *nm* storing; (*en douane*) bonding

entreposer [ɑ̃trəpoze] *vt* to store; (*en douane*) to bond; **e. des marchandises** to warehouse goods, to put goods in a warehouse

entrepositaire [ɑ̃trəpozitɛr] *nm* (*employé*) warehouseman

entrepôt [ɑ̃trəpo] *nm* warehouse, store; **e. (de la douane)** bonded warehouse; **e. frigorifique** cold store; **e. de stockage** warehouse; **marchandises en e.** goods in store; (*en douane*) goods in bond; **e. privé/public** private/public bonded warehouse

entreprenant [ɑ̃trəprənɑ̃] *adj* enterprising, go-ahead; (*auprès des femmes*) forward

entreprendre [ɑ̃trəprɑ̃dr] *vt* (*conj like* **prendre**) **(a)** (*commencer*) (*tâche, étude, voyage etc*) to undertake; **e. des démarches** to take steps; **e. de faire qch** to undertake to do sth **(b) e. une femme** to make advances to(wards) a woman **(c)** (*entretenir*) **elle m'a entrepris sur son sujet favori** she engaged me in conversation about *or* started talking to me about her favourite subject

entrepreneur, -euse [ɑ̃trəprənœr, -øz] *n* **(a)** *Constr* contractor; **e. (en bâtiment)** building contractor; **e. de transports** carrier, *Br* haulier, *Am* hauler; **e. de pompes funèbres** undertaker, funeral director, *Am* mortician **(b)** (*patron*) businessman

entreprise [ɑ̃trəpriz] *nf* **(a)** (*action, initiative*) enterprise, undertaking, venture; *Écon* **la libre e.** free enterprise; **l'e. privée** private enterprise

(b) (*firme*) company, firm, enterprise; **chef d'e.** company head; **e. commerciale** business enterprise *or* operation; *Mktg* **e. dauphin** runner-up company; *Mktg* **e. dominante/défendable/à la traîne** dominant/tenable/trailing firm; **e. exportatrice** export company; **e. familiale** family business; **e. industrielle** manufacturing concern *or* company; *Mktg* **e. innovatrice** innovator, market pioneer company; **e. multinationale** multinational (company); **e. en participation** joint venture; **e. de pompes funèbres** undertaker's, funeral director's; **e. prestataire de services** service company; **e. privée** private company; **e. publique** public corporation; **e. de transports** haulage *or* carrying company; **e. unipersonnelle** one-man business, sole trader; **e. unipersonnelle à responsabilité limitée** sole trader with limited liability

(c) *Jur* (*louage*) contracting; **travail à l'e.** contract work, work by *or* on contract; **mettre qch à l'e.** to put sth out to contract

(d) *Vieilli* **entreprises** (*tentatives de séduction*) advances

entrer [ɑ̃tre] **1** *vi* (*aux* **être**) **(a)** (*aller*) to go in, to enter; (*venir*) to come in, to enter; (*réussir à pénétrer*) to get in; **e. dans une salle** to enter *or* go into/come into a room; **entrez!** come/go in!; **entre dans la voiture/l'ascenseur** get into the car/lift; **défense d'e.** no admittance, private; **il a réussi à e. sans payer** he managed to get in without paying; **je n'aime pas les gens qui entrent sans frapper** I don't like people who come in *or* enter without knocking; **faire e. qn** (*en l'appelant*) to call sb in; **faites e.** send *or* show him/her/them in, have him/her/them come in; **fais-le e.!** (*chez soi*) let him in; (*au bureau*) send *or* show him in; **laisser e. qn/qch** to let sb/sth in; **e. en passant** to drop in, to look in (**chez qn** on sb); **je n'ai fait qu'e. et sortir** I just dropped in for a moment; **empêcher qn d'e.** to keep sb out, to stop sb entering *or* getting in; **le voleur est entré par la fenêtre** the thief got in through the window; **il n'a pas pu e.** he couldn't get in; **le train entre en gare** the train is pulling into the station; **le navire entre au port** the ship is coming into harbour; **e. en courant/en dansant** to run/dance in; **e. furtivement** to sneak in, to steal in; **e. dans un pays** to enter a country; *Th* **Hamlet entre (en scène)** enter Hamlet; **vous qui entrez ici, abandonnez toute espérance** abandon hope, all ye who enter here

(b) (*devenir membre*) **e. dans l'armée/la police** to join the army/the police; *Mil* **e. dans la carrière** to become an officer; **e. en religion** to take (holy) orders; **il est entré à l'hôpital comme infirmier** he joined *or* started working at the hospital as a nurse; **e. aux PTT** to start working for the Post Office; **e. au service de qn** to enter sb's service; **e. dans la Communauté européenne** to join the European Community

(c) (*être admis*) **e. à l'université** to go to university; **j'entre à l'hôpital demain** I'm going into hospital *or Am* the hospital tomorrow; **e. en maternelle** to start nursery school

(d) (*pénétrer, s'infiltrer*) (*de l'eau, de l'air etc*) to go/come in; **le clou est entré dans le mur** the nail went into the wall; **nous constatons que la balle est entrée dans le crâne et l'a traversé de part en part** we can see that the bullet entered the skull and came through the other side; **la clef n'entre pas dans la serrure** the key won't *or* doesn't go *or* fit in the lock; **les liens étaient tellement serrés qu'ils lui sont entré dans les chairs** the straps were so tight that they cut into his flesh; **une pareille idée ne lui serait jamais entrée dans la tête** such an idea never entered his head; **faire e. une idée dans la tête de qn** to put an idea in sb's head; *Fig* **le doute/la peur entra dans son esprit** his mind filled with doubts/fear

(e) (*tenir*) **on n'entrera jamais à vingt dans cette petite pièce** we'll never get twenty people into that small room; **la télévision n'entre pas dans le carton** the television won't *or* doesn't go *or* fit in the box; *F* **ça ne veut pas e.** it won't go in; **faire e. qch dans qch** to insert *or* put sth in sth; **je ne peux pas faire e. toutes mes affaires dans une seule valise** I can't get *or* fit all my things in one suitcase

(f) *Ordinat* to log in *or* on

(g) *Com* (*de marchandises importées*) to enter, to be imported; **ces marchandises sont entrées en fraude sur le territoire** these goods were smuggled into the country

(h) (*marque le début de*) **e. dans une colère terrible** to get extremely angry; **la Roumanie entre en démocratie** Romania is embracing democracy; **elle entre tout juste en convalescence** she's just beginning to convalesce; **e. en ébullition** to begin to boil, to come to the boil; **e. en effervescence** to begin to effervesce; **e. en fonction** to take up one's duties; **e. dans la vie active** to start one's working life; **e. en vigueur** to come into force *or* effect *or* operation; **e. dans sa vingtième année** to turn nineteen; **e. dans une ère nouvelle** to enter a new era; *Mil* **e. en campagne** to take the field; *Mil* **e. en guerre** to enter the war; **e. en méditation** to begin to meditate; **on entre en hiver** Winter is just beginning; *Com* **e. en liquidation** to go into liquidation

(i) (*faire partie de*) **e. dans une catégorie** to fall into a category; **cela ne peut pas e. en ligne de compte** that cannot be taken into account *or* consideration; **cela entre dans ses projets** that is part of his plans; **il est entré dans ma vie tout d'un coup** he came into my life all of a sudden; **dans tout ceci l'imagination entre pour beaucoup** in all this imagination plays a large part; **e. dans la légende** to become a legend; **e. dans l'histoire** to go down in history; **aucun produit chimique n'entre dans la composition de ce dessert** no chemical product goes into the making of this dessert; *Com* **e. dans un marché** to enter a market

(j) **e. dans** (*danse, débat etc*) to join in; (*les idées, les vues, les sentiments de qn etc*) to share, to go along with sb; **e. dans les détails/de longues explications** to go into the details *or* into detail/long explanations; *TV, Cin* **e. dans le champ** to come into shot

(k) **e. dans** (*heurter*) (*arbre, mur etc*) to go into, to run into; *F* **on est entré dans le décor** we went off the road

2 *vt* (*aux* **avoir**) **(a)** (*introduire*) to bring in; (*vu de l'extérieur*) to take in; **e. des marchandises en fraude** to smuggle in goods

(b) (*enfoncer*) **elle a failli m'e. son parapluie dans l'œil** she nearly poked me in the eye with her umbrella; **il m'a entré ses dents/ongles dans le cou** he sank his teeth/nails into my neck

(c) *Ordinat* (*données*) to enter, to input; (*au clavier aussi*) to key up *or* in

3 *v impers* **il entre beaucoup de calculs dans sa générosité** there's a lot of calculation behind his generosity; **il n'entre pas dans mes projets de me marier tout de suite** getting married right away is not part of my plans

entre-rail, *pl* **entre-rails** [ɑ̃trərɑj] *nm Rail* (*d'une voie*) gauge

entresol [ɑ̃trəsɔl] *nm* entresol, mezzanine (floor)

entre-temps [ɑ̃trətɑ̃] **1** *adv* meanwhile, in the meantime **2** *nm inv Arch* **dans l'e.** in the meanwhile

entretenir [ɑ̃trət(ə)nir] (*conj like* **tenir**) **1** *vt* **(a)** (*soigner*) (*maison, jardin, routes etc*) to maintain, to keep up; (*machine*) to maintain; (*d'un fournisseur*) (*appareil*) to service; **e. qch en bon état** to keep sth in good condition *or* repair; **une moquette facile à e.** a carpet which is easily looked after; **j'entretiens la voiture moi-même** I look after the car myself; **e. sa santé/sa beauté** to look after *or* take care of one's health/beauty; **e. sa forme** to keep fit; **e. son français** to keep up one's French; **e. le feu** to keep the fire going

(b) (*pourvoir à la subsistance de*) (*famille, maîtresse, flotte etc*) to maintain, to support, to keep; **je ne veux pas me faire e.** I don't want to be a kept man/woman

(c) (*nourrir*) **e. des soupçons/des craintes** to entertain *or* harbour suspicions/fears; **e. une correspondance avec qn** to keep up a correspondence with sb; **e. l'espoir de qn** to keep sb's hopes alive; **e. qn dans l'ignorance** to keep sb in ignorance; **e. qn dans l'erreur** to allow sb to continue to labour under a misapprehension; **il faut e. l'idée que la paix va revenir** we must keep alive the idea that peace will return; **e. de bonnes relations avec** (*personne*) to remain on good terms with; (*pays*) to maintain good relations with

(d) (*parler à*) **e. qn de qch** to converse *or* talk with sb about sth, to discuss sth with sb

(e) *Compta* (*comptes*) to keep in order

2 s'entretenir *vpr* **(a) s'e. avec qn (de qch)** to converse *or* talk with sb (about sth)

(b) (*se maintenir en forme*) to keep fit

entretenu [ɑ̃trətny] *adj* **(a) femme entretenue** kept woman **(b) bien/mal e.** (*maison, jardin etc*) well-kept/badly kept **(c)** *Rad* (*oscillations*) sustained; (*ondes*) undamped, continuous

entretien [ɑ̃trətjɛ̃] *nm* **(a)** (*soins*) (*d'une maison, d'un jardin, des routes etc*) upkeep, maintenance; (*d'une machine*) maintenance; (*par le fournisseur*) (*d'un appareil*) servicing, service; **facile/difficile d'e., d'e. facile/difficile** easy/difficult to maintain; **cher à l'e.** expensive to maintain; **e. des chambres** (*d'hôtel*) room servicing; **personnel d'e.** maintenance staff; **manuel d'e.** service manual; **produits d'e.** (household) cleaning materials

(b) (*subsistance*) (*d'une famille, armée etc*) support, maintenance

(c) (*conversation*) conversation, talk; (*audience*) interview; **j'ai eu un e. avec lui** I had a talk *or* conversation with him; **j'ai réussi à décrocher un e.** (*pour une embauche*) I managed to get myself an interview; **e. téléphonique** telephone conversation; **avoir des entretiens avec le patronat** to hold talks *or* discussions with the employers

(d) *Mktg* **e. assisté par ordinateur** computer-assisted interviewing; **e. centré** structured interview; **e. de groupe** group interview; (*activité*) group interviewing; **e. libre** *ou* **non structuré** unstructured interview; **e. organisé** arranged interview; **e. spontané** intercept interview; **e. structuré** structured interview; **e. par téléphone** telephone interview; (*activité*) telephone interviewing

entretoile [ɑ̃trətwal] *nf Couture* (lace) insertion

entretoise [ɑ̃trətwaz] *nf Aut* spacer; (*étai*) strut; **e. de réglage** distance piece

entre-tuer (s') [sɑ̃trətɥe] *vpr* to kill one another *or* each other

entre-voie, *pl* **entre-voies** [ɑ̃trəvwa] *nf Rail* space between tracks

entrevoir [ɑ̃trəvwar] *vt* (*conj like* **voir**) to catch sight *or* a glimpse of; (*indistinctement*) to make out; **je n'ai fait que l'e.** I caught only a glimpse of him; **il entrevoyait la vérité** he had an inkling of the truth; **j'entrevois des difficultés** I foresee difficulties

entrevue [ɑ̃trəvy] *nf* interview; (*entre hommes politiques,* *hommes d'affaires etc*) meeting; **avoir/fixer une e. avec qn** to have/arrange an interview *or* a meeting with sb

entrisme [ɑ̃trism] *nm Pol* entryism

entriste [ɑ̃trist] *n, adj Pol* entryist

entropie [ɑ̃trɔpi] *nf Phys* entropy

entrouvert [ɑ̃truvɛr] *adj* (*fenêtre, fleur etc*) half-open; (*gouffre*) gaping, yawning; **laissez la porte entrouverte** leave the door ajar; **la bouche entrouverte** with one's mouth half-open

entrouvrir [ɑ̃truvrir] (*conj like* **ouvrir**) **1** *vt* (*porte, yeux, bouche etc*) to half-open **2 s'entrouvrir** *vpr* to half-open; (*d'un gouffre*) to open up, to gape, to yawn

entuber [ɑ̃tybe] *vt F* (*duper*) to con, to have; **il s'est fait e.** he was conned *or* had

enturbanné [ɑ̃tyrbane] *adj* turbaned, wearing a turban

énucléation [enykleasjɔ̃] *nf Chir* enucleation

énucléer [enyklee] *vt Chir* (*tumeur, œil*) to enucleate

énumératif, -ive [enymeratif, -iv] *adj* enumerative

énumération [enymerasjɔ̃] *nf* enumeration, listing

énumérer [enymere] *vt* **(j'énumère, n. énumérons; j'énumérerai)** to enumerate, to list

énurésie [enyrezi] *nf Méd* enuresis

énurétique [enyretik] *n, adj Méd* enuretic

envahir [ɑ̃vair] *vt* (*pays etc*) to invade, to overrun; *Com* **e. le marché** to flood the market; **envahi par les mauvaises herbes** overgrown with weeds; **envahi par l'eau** flooded; **quand le doute/le sommeil nous envahit** when we are overcome with doubt/sleep; **la politique envahit tout** politics gets into everything; *Fig F* **je ne voulais pas les e.** (*déranger*) I didn't want to intrude (upon them)

envahissant [ɑ̃vaisɑ̃] *adj* (*voisins*) intrusive; (*plantes*) invasive; *Fig* (*désir, soupçon, odeur etc*) overwhelming

envahissement [ɑ̃vaismɑ̃] *nm* invasion

envahisseur [ɑ̃vaisœr] *nm* invader

envasement [ɑ̃vazmɑ̃] *nm* (*d'un port etc*) silting up

envaser [ɑ̃vaze] **1** *vt* (*port etc*) to silt up; (*bateau*) to run on the mud **2 s'envaser** *vpr* (*d'un port etc*) to silt up; (*d'un bateau, d'une personne*) to get stuck in the mud

enveloppant [ɑ̃vlɔpɑ̃] *adj* **(a)** (*couvrant*) **ce manteau est bien e.** this coat covers well; **regard e.** look that takes everything in; *Aut* **pare-chocs e.** wrapround bumper **(b)** *Fig* (*séduisant*) (*personne, mots, manières etc*) captivating

enveloppe [ɑ̃vlɔp] *nf* **(a)** (*d'un colis etc*) wrapper, wrapping

(b) (*pour lettre*) envelope; **envoyer qch sous e.** to send sth under cover; **e. timbrée** stamped envelope; **e. timbrée avec nom et adresse** stamped addressed envelope, SAE

(c) (*apparence*) **un bon cœur sous une rude e.** a rough diamond; *Litt* **l'e. mortelle** *ou* **charnelle** ≈ this mortal coil

(d) (*somme d'argent*) **l'e. de la recherche** the research budget; **de combien est l'e. du service/du projet?** how high is the departmental budget/the budget for the project?; **e. budgétaire** (allotted) budget, budget allocation; *F* **recevoir une e.** (*pot-de-vin*) to receive a bribe

(e) (*revêtement*) (*d'une chaudière*) sheathing, casing, jacket; *Aut* (*d'un pneu*) outer cover, casing

(f) (*des graines etc*) husk, hull

▶ **enveloppe**: **e. autocollante** self-seal envelope; **e. calorifuge** lagging; **e. à fenêtre** window envelope; **e. matelassée** padded envelope, Jiffy bag®; *Philat* **e. premier jour** first-day cover; **e. T** ≈ business reply *or* reply-paid envelope

enveloppé [ɑ̃vlɔpe] *adj F* **bien e.** (*personne*) well-padded, plump

enveloppement [ɑ̃vlɔpmɑ̃] *nm* **(a)** (*action*) (*d'un colis etc*) wrapping (up); *Mil* **manœuvre d'e.** pincer movement, envelopment **(b)** *Méd* (*linges*) pack; **e. froid** cold pack

envelopper [ɑ̃vlɔpe] **1** *vt* **(a)** (*marchandises, bébé etc*) to wrap (up); **e. un paquet** to wrap up *or* do up a parcel; **enveloppé de bandages** swathed in bandages; **e. des remarques désagréables dans des phrases gentilles** to wrap up unpleasant remarks in kind words

(b) (*entourer*) (*personne*) to surround, to encircle, to close in on; **la nuit nous enveloppa** darkness closed in on us; **enveloppé de mystère/brume** shrouded in mystery/in mist; **e. qch du regard** to take sth in with one's gaze

2 s'envelopper *vpr* **s'e. dans une couverture** to wrap oneself up in a blanket; *Fig* **s'e. dans son silence** to immure oneself in silence

enveloppe-retour, *pl* **enveloppes-retour** *nf* reply-paid envelope

envenimé [ɑ̃v(ə)nime] *adj* (*plaie*) poisoned, septic; *Fig* **discussion envenimée** acrimonious discussion

envenimement [ɑ̃v(ə)nimmɑ̃] *nm* (*d'une plaie*) poisoning; *Fig* (*d'une querelle, discussion*) embittering; (*d'une situation*) aggravation

envenimer [ɑ̃v(ə)nime] **1** *vt* (*plaie*) to poison, to make septic; *Fig* (*querelle, discussion*) to envenom, to embitter; (*situation*) to aggravate **2 s'envenimer** *vpr* (*d'une plaie*) to fester, to turn septic; *Fig* (*d'une querelle, discussion*) to grow acrimonious; (*d'une situation*) to become aggravated

envergure [ɑ̃vɛrgyr] *nf* **(a)** (*d'un oiseau, avion*) wingspread, wingspan **(b)** *Fig* (*ampleur*) scope; **de grande e., d'e.** (*réforme, rapport, question*) far-reaching, wide-ranging; (*opération, firme*) large-scale; **esprit de grande e.** wide-ranging mind; **leur affaire commence à prendre de l'e.** their business is beginning to expand *or* grow **(c)** (*de personne*) calibre, *US* caliber; **homme d'e./de cette e.** man of calibre/of this calibre; **cet homme manque d'e.** this man is of a low calibre

envers[1] [ɑ̃vɛr] *nm* (*d'un document, d'une assiette etc*) reverse, back; (*d'une médaille, pièce*) reverse; **l'endroit et l'e. d'un tissu** the right and the wrong side of a material; **l'e. de la vie** the seamy side of life; *Fig* **l'e. du décor** the other side of the picture; **à l'e.** (*du mauvais côté*) inside out; (*avec le haut en bas*) the wrong way up, upside down; (*dans le mauvais sens*) the wrong way round, back to front; (*en désordre*) upside down; **le monde à l'e.** the world turned upside down; *Hum* **il travaille? c'est le monde à l'e!.** he's working? wonders will never cease!; **j'ai la tête à l'e.** my brain is in a whirl; *Tricot* **une maille à l'endroit, une maille à l'e.** knit one, purl one

envers[2] *prép* toward(s); **juste e. tous** just to(wards) *or* with everyone; **leur devoir e. leur patrie** their duty to(wards) their country; **avoir une dette e. qn** to be indebted to sb; **e. et contre tous** in spite of everyone, in the face of all opposition

enviable [ɑ̃vjabl] *adj* enviable

envi (à l') [alɑ̃vi] *adv* **faire qch à l'e.** to vie with one another in doing sth, to try to outdo each other doing sth

envie [ɑ̃vi] *nf* **(a)** (*désir*) desire (**de qch** for sth; **de faire** to do); **avoir e. de qch/de faire qch** to want sth/to do sth; **j'ai des envies de fraises** I have cravings for strawberries; *F* **j'ai une de ces envies de champagne!** I've got a real craving for champagne!, I could really do with some champagne!; **ce gâteau plein de crème me fait e.** I like the look of *or Br* I fancy that cake filled with cream; **j'avais e. de dormir/boire/manger** I felt sleepy/thirsty/hungry; **avoir e. de rire/de vomir** to feel like laughing/being sick, to want to laugh/be sick; **être pris d'une terrible e. de rire** to have a terrible urge to laugh; *F* **ça m'a pris comme une e. de pisser** it was a sudden urge; **avoir bien** *ou* **très e. de faire qch** to really want to do sth; **brûler d'e. de faire qch** to be burning *or* dying to do sth; **donner à qn l'e. de faire qch** to make sb want to do sth; **il a e. que je fasse cela** he wants me to do that; **je n'ai pas e. que ça se sache** I don't want it to be known; **c'est une e. qui te passera** you'll get over your craving; *F* **ça va lui passer son e.** it'll be just what he wants; **je vais lui ôter l'e. de s'amuser** I'll stop his messing around; **avoir e. de qn** (*sexuellement*) to want sb; *F* **avoir e.** (*avoir besoin d'uriner*) to want *or* have to go; (*de sexe*) to want it

(b) (*jalousie*) envy; **être dévoré d'e.** to be consumed *or* green with envy; **faire e. à qn** to make sb envious; **regarder qch avec e.** to look enviously at sth; **cette situation confortable, ça fait e.** a good job like that makes people envious; **porter e. à qn** to envy sb

(c) (*au doigt*) hangnail; (*sur la peau*) birthmark

envier [ɑ̃vje] *vt* (*impf, pr sub* **n. enviions**) to envy, to be envious of; **e. qch à qn** to envy sb sth; **je t'envie de ne jamais avoir faim!** I envy your never being hungry!; **elle n'a rien à e. à personne** she has no cause to be envious of anyone

envieux, -ieuse [ɑ̃vjø, -jøz] **1** *adj* envious (**de** of) **2** *n* envious person; **faire des e.** to make people envious

environ [ɑ̃virɔ̃] **1** *adv* [①A64] (*à peu près*) about, around; **il a e. quarante ans** he is about *or* around forty **2** *nmpl* **environs** (*d'une ville etc*) surroundings, surrounding area; **habiter aux** *ou* **dans les environs de Paris** to live in the vicinity of *or* near Paris; **aux environs de Pâques/cinq heures** around Easter/five o'clock; **aux environs de cent francs** in the region *or* vicinity of a hundred francs, about *or* around a hundred francs

environnant [ɑ̃virɔnɑ̃] *adj* (*campagne etc*) surrounding

environnement [ɑ̃virɔnmɑ̃] *nm* **(a)** (*naturel, personnel*) environment; **protection de l'e.** environmental protection, protection of the environment; **qui ne nuit pas à l'e.** environment-friendly; **e. commercial** business environment; **e. du marché** market environment; *Com* **e. institutionnel/mercatique** corporate/marketing environment **(b)** *Ordinat* environment; **e. partagé** shared environment

environnemental, -ale, -aux, -ales [ɑ̃virɔnmɑ̃tal, -o] *adj* environmental

environnementaliste [ɑ̃virɔnmɑ̃talist] *n* environmentalist

environner [ɑ̃virɔne] **1** *vt* to surround; **environné de** surrounded by **2 s'environner** *vpr* **s'e. d'intellectuels** to surround oneself with intellectuals

envisageable [ɑ̃vizaʒabl] *adj* conceivable, imaginable; **ce n'est pas e.** it's inconceivable *or* unimaginable

envisager [ɑ̃vizaʒe] *vt* **(j'envisageai(s))** (*considérer*) (*question, situation, remède etc*) to consider; (*imaginer comme possible, projeter*) (*conséquence, événement etc*) to envisage; **e. l'avenir** to look to the future; **le cas que nous envisageons** the case under consideration; **cas non envisagé** unforeseen case; **comment envisagez-vous la question?** what are your views on *or* how do you see the matter?; **il n'envisageait pas de partir** he wasn't thinking of leaving, he wasn't considering leaving; **e. un chiffre d'affaires** to forecast turnover

envoi [ɑ̃vwa] *nm* **(a)** (*action*) (*d'un représentant, de troupes etc*) sending; (*d'une lettre, d'un colis etc*) sending, dispatch(ing); (*d'argent, de fonds*) sending, remittance; (*de marchandises*) sending, dispatch(ing), forwarding; **e. par mer** shipment; **faire un e. tous les mois** to send *or* dispatch goods every month; **e. exprès** express delivery; **e. groupé** grouped consignment; **e. postal** postal delivery; **e. recommandé** recorded delivery; **faire un e. de fonds à qn** to send *or* remit funds to sb; **e. contre paiement** cash with order

(b) coup d'e. *Fb* kickoff; (*d'un événement, festival, projet etc*) start, *F* kickoff

(c) (*ce qui est envoyé*) (*colis*) parcel; (*lettre*) letter; (*marchandises*) consignment **(de** of); **e. de l'auteur** presentation copy

(d) *Littér* (*d'un poème*) envoi

envol [ɑ̃vɔl] *nm* (*d'oiseaux*) taking flight *or* wing; (*d'un avion*) takeoff; **piste d'e.** (takeoff) runway; *Naut* **pont d'e.** flight deck

envolée [ɑ̃vɔle] *nf* **(a)** (*action*) (*d'oiseaux*) flight **(b)** *Fig* **e. lyrique/oratoire** flight of lyricism/oratory **(c)** *Fin* (*hausse rapide*) **l'e. du dollar** the rapid rise in the dollar

envoler (s') [sɑ̃vɔle] *vpr* **(a)** (*d'un oiseau*) to fly away, to fly off; (*d'un avion*) to take off; **faire s'e. des oiseaux** to put birds to flight; **mon avion s'envole** *ou* **je m'envole dans une heure** my plane takes off *or* my flight leaves in an hour **(b)** *Fig* **le franc français s'envole** the French franc is rising rapidly; **s'e. dans les sondages** to rise rapidly in the opinion polls **(c)** (*emporté par le vent*) (*d'un chapeau etc*) to blow off; (*de papiers etc*) to blow away; **le temps s'envole** time flies **(d)** *F* (*disparaître soudainement*) (*d'une personne, d'un sac à main etc*) to vanish, to disappear

envoûtant [ɑ̃vutɑ̃] *adj* (*fascinant*) bewitching, captivating

envoûtement [ɑ̃vutmɑ̃] *nm* **(a)** (*maléfice*) bewitchment **(b)** *Fig* (*fascination*) bewitchment, captivation; **cette région me fait l'effet d'un e.** this region has a bewitching *or* captivating effect on me

envoûter [ɑ̃vute] *vt* (*en employant la magie*) to bewitch; *Fig* (*fasciner*) to bewitch, to captivate

envoûteur, -euse [ɑ̃vutœr, -øz] *n* sorcerer, *f* sorceress

envoyé, -ée [ɑ̃vwaje] **1** *adj* **bien e.** (*Sp balle, Fig F remarque*) well-aimed; *F* **c'est e.!** (*bien dit*) well said!; (*bien exécuté*) well done! **2** *n* (*messager*) messenger; (*d'un parti etc*) representative; (*d'un gouvernement*) envoy; *Journ* **e. spécial** special correspondent; *Journ* **e. de la rédaction** staff correspondent

envoyer [ɑ̃vwaje] **(j'envoie, n. envoyons; j'enverrai) 1** *vt* (*qn*) to send; (*lettre, colis etc*) to send, to dispatch; (*argent*) to send, to remit; (*marchandises*) to send, to dispatch, to ship; (*ses excuses, condoléances etc*) to send; **e. par courrier** to mail, *Br* to post; **e. qn à Paris** to send sb to Paris; **e. une lettre à qn** to send sb a letter, to send a letter to sb; **e. un publipostage à** to mailshot; **je lui ai envoyé mes félicitations** I sent him my congratulations; **envoyez-moi un petit mot** drop me a line; **e. sa démission** to send in *or Fml* to tender one's resignation; **elle lui a envoyé un regard noir/une gifle** she gave him a black look/slap (in the face); **e. un baiser à qn** to blow sb a kiss; **e. chercher qn** to send for sb; **j'ai envoyé (qn) prendre de ses nouvelles** I sent sb to ask after him; *F* **je ne le lui ai pas envoyé dire** I told him straight *or* to his face; *F* **e. promener** *ou* **balader** *ou* **paître qn, e. qn sur les roses** to send sb packing; *F* **j'en ai assez, je vais tout e. promener** *ou* **valser** *ou* **dinguer** I've had enough, I'm going to chuck it all in *or* throw in the towel; *Naut* **e. les couleurs/une vergue** to hoist the colours/send up a yard

2 *vi Naut* **envoyez!** about ship!

3 s'envoyer *vpr* **(a)** (*par courrier etc*) **ils s'envoient des cartes postales régulièrement** they regularly send postcards to each other

(b) *F* **s'e. un verre de vin** to knock back a glass of wine; *F* **s'e. une corvée** to get landed *or* stuck with a tedious job; *Arg* **il ne pense qu'à s'e. en l'air** all he thinks about is having sex *or Br* having it off *or* away; *Arg* **s'e. une fille/un mec** to have sex *or Br* have it off *or* away with a girl/guy

envoyeur, -euse [ɑ̃vwajœr, -øz] *n* sender; **retour à l'e.** return to sender

enzyme [ɑ̃zim] *n* enzyme; **produit de lavage aux enzymes** cleaning product with biological action

éocène [eɔsɛn] *Géol* **1** *adj* (*période*) Eocene **2** *nm* Eocene

éolien, -ienne [eɔljɛ̃, -jɛn] **1** *adj* **harpe éolienne** aeolian harp; **érosion éolienne** wind erosion; **énergie éolienne** wind energy; **moteur é.** wind-powered engine **2** *nf* **éolienne** wind turbine

épagneul, -eule [epaɲœl] *n* spaniel; **é. breton** Brittany spaniel

épais, -aisse [epɛ, -ɛs] **1** *adj* (*cheveux, doigt, mur, tranche, sauce etc*) thick; (*feuillage, brouillard*) dense, thick; (*foule, buisson*) dense; (*livre*) thick, fat; (*ombre, nuit*) deep, dark; (*silence*) deep; **é. de deux mètres** two metres thick; **avoir la taille épaisse** to be thickset; *F* **avoir l'esprit é.** to be dense *or* thick; **peu é.** thin **2** *adv* **(a)** (*pousser, semer*) thick(ly) **(b)** *F* (*beaucoup*) **il n'y en a pas é.** there's not much of it **3** *nm* **couper dans l'é.** to cut into the thick part; **au plus é. de la foule/forêt** in the heart of the crowd/forest

épaisseur [epɛsœr] *nf* **(a)** (*de cheveux, d'un mur, d'une sauce etc*) thickness; (*d'un feuillage, du brouillard*) density, thickness; (*d'une foule*) density; (*d'une ombre, de la nuit*) darkness; **le mur a deux pieds d'é.** the wall is two feet thick; **courroie en trois épaisseurs** three-ply belt; **une é. de tissu** a layer of material; **le peu d'é. d'une planche** the thinness of a board **(b)** (*d'un esprit*) dullness **(c)** (*profondeur*) (*d'une personne, d'un personnage de roman etc*) depth

épaissir [epesir] **1** *vt* (*sauce, peinture etc*) to thicken; (*ombre, mystère*) to deepen **2** *vi* (*d'une sauce etc*) to thicken, to get thick(er); (*d'une personne*) to fill out **3 s'épaissir** *vpr* (*de cheveux, du brouillard, d'une sauce etc*) to thicken, to get thick(er); (*d'une personne*) to fill out; (*d'une ombre, d'un mystère*) to deepen

épaississant [epɛsisɑ̃] *nm* (*substance*) thickener

épaississement [epɛsismɑ̃] *nm* (*du brouillard, d'une sauce etc*) thickening; (*d'une personne*) filling out

épanchement [epɑ̃ʃmɑ̃] *nm* **(a)** *Arch, Litt* (*d'un liquide*) pouring out, discharge; *Méd* **é. de synovie** synovial extravasation **(b)** *Fig* (*de sentiments*) outpouring, *Litt* effusion; (*de pensées*) outpouring

épancher [epɑ̃ʃe] **1** *vt* **(a)** *Arch, Litt* (*liquide*) to pour out, to discharge; *Fig* **é. sa bile** to vent one's spleen **(b)** *Fig* (*son amour, ses soucis etc*) to pour out; **é. son cœur** to pour out one's heart, to unbosom oneself **2 s'épancher** *vpr* **(a)** *Arch, Litt* (*d'un liquide*) to pour out; *Méd* (*du sang etc*) to extravasate **(b)** *Fig* (*d'une personne*) to pour out one's heart, to unbosom oneself

épandage [epɑ̃daʒ] *nm* (*de fumier etc*) spreading; **champs d'é.** sewage farm

épandeur, -euse [epɑ̃dœr, -øz] *n* (*machine*) (*de fumier, d'asphalte etc*) spreader

épandre [epɑ̃dr] **1** *vt* (*fumier etc*) to spread **2 s'épandre** *vpr Litt* to spread **(sur** over)

épanoui [epanwi] *adj* (*fleur*) in full bloom, full-blown; (*visage, sourire*) beaming; **une jeune femme épanouie** a young woman in full bloom

épanouir [epanwir] **1** *vt* (*fleur, pétales*) to open out; (*voiles, plumes*) to spread; **un large sourire lui épanouit le visage** his face broadened into a grin **2 s'épanouir** *vpr* **(a)** (*d'une fleur*) to open out, to bloom **(b)** (*d'un visage*) to beam, to light up; (*d'une personne heureuse*) to beam **(c)** (*d'une jeune fille, personnalité, civilisation etc*) to blossom

épanouissant [epanwisɑ̃] *adj* (*travail, vie etc*) fulfilling

épanouissement [epanwismɑ̃] *nm* **(a)** (*action*) (*d'une fleur*) opening out, blooming; (*d'un visage*) lighting up; (*d'une jeune fille, personnalité, civilisation etc*) blossoming **(b)** (*plénitude*) (full) bloom; **elle a trouvé l'é. physique et moral** she is at her physical and mental peak

épargnant, -ante [eparɲɑ̃, -ɑ̃t] *n* saver, investor; **les petits épargnants** small savers *or* investors

épargne [eparɲ] *nf* **(a)** (*action, vertu*) saving, economy; *Fig* (*de temps, forces*) saving; **caisse d'é.** savings bank; **plan d'é.-logement** *Br* ≈ building society (savings) account, *Am* ≈ savings and loan association account; **plan d'é.-retraite** personal pension scheme *or* plan; **é. salariale** save as you earn, SAYE **(b)** (*sommes*) savings **(c)** (*épargnants*) **la petite é.** small savers *or* investors; **l'é. privée** private investors

épargner [eparɲe] **1** *vt* **(a)** (*argent, provisions*) to save (up), to put by; (*beurre, sel etc*) to be sparing with **(b)** (*énergie,* *temps*) to save; **é. ses forces** to save one's strength; **épargne-moi tes explications/tes jérémiades/les détails!** spare me your explanations/your complaining/the details!; **é. à qn la peine de faire qch** to save sb the trouble of doing sth **(c)** (*prisonnier etc*) to spare, to have mercy on; **elle a toujours tenté d'é. ses enfants** she has always tried to shield her children; **l'incendie a épargné notre village** the fire spared our village **2** *vi* to save (**sur qch** on sth)

éparpillement [eparpijmɑ̃] *nm* **(a)** (*action*) (*d'objets, de foin etc*) scattering; (*d'une foule, de troupes etc*) scattering, dispersal; *Fig* (*des efforts, de l'attention etc*) dissipation **(b)** (*état*) scattered state

éparpiller [eparpije] **1** *vt* (*objets, foin etc*) to scatter, to strew about; (*foule, troupes etc*) to scatter, to disperse; *Fig* (*efforts, attention etc*) to dissipate **2 s'éparpiller** *vpr* (*d'objets etc*) to scatter; (*d'une foule, de troupes etc*) to scatter, to disperse; *Fig* (*d'une personne*) to dissipate one's energies

épars [epar] *adj* (*maisons, moutons etc*) scattered; (*végétation, population, informations*) sparse; (*cheveux*) thin

éparvin [eparvɛ̃] *nm Vét* (*d'un cheval*) spavin

épatant [epatɑ̃] *adj F* splendid, wonderful

épate [epat] *nf F* swank, swagger; **faire de l'é.** to show off, to swank; **on l'a fait à l'é.** it was done to show off

épaté [epate] *adj* **(a)** (*table etc*) splay-footed; (*nez*) flat **(b)** *F* (*étonné*) dumbfounded, flabbergasted

épatement [epatmɑ̃] *nm* **(a)** (*d'un nez*) flatness **(b)** *F* (*étonnement*) astonishment, amazement

épater [epate] *vt* **(a)** (*rendre plat*) to flatten out the base of **(b)** *F* (*étonner*) to astound, to amaze; **rien ne l'épate, il ne se laisse pas é.** nothing surprises him, he isn't easily impressed

épaulard [epolar] *nm* killer whale, grampus, orc

épaule [epol] *nf* shoulder; **large d'épaules** broad-shouldered; **hausser les épaules** to shrug (one's shoulders); *Culin* **é. d'agneau** shoulder of lamb; **donner un coup d'é. à qn** to shoulder sb; *Fig* to give sb a push in the right direction; **charger un fardeau sur son é.** to shoulder a burden; *Mil* **l'arme sur l'é.** with rifle at the slope; **rouler les épaules** (*en marchant*) to swagger

épaulé-jeté, *pl* **épaulés-jetés** [epoleʒ(ə)te] *nm* (*en haltérophilie*) clean-and-jerk

épaulement [epolmɑ̃] *nm* **(a)** (*mur*) revetment, retaining wall **(b)** (*rempart*) breastwork **(c)** (*d'une colline*) shoulder

épauler [epole] **1** *vt* **(a)** (*fusil*) to bring to one's shoulder **(b)** **é. qn** (*aider*) to back sb up **(c)** (*mur*) to retain, to support **(d)** *Couture* to attach shoulder pads to **2** *vi* to take aim

épaulette [epolɛt] *nf* **(a)** (*bretelle*) (*d'une combinaison*) shoulder-strap **(b)** *Mil* epaulette **(c)** (*rembourrage*) shoulder pad

épave [epav] *nf* (*navire, voiture*) wreck; *Fig* (*loque humaine*) (human) wreck; *Fig* **les épaves de la société** the flotsam of society; **épaves flottantes** flotsam; **épaves rejetées** jetsam

épeautre [epotr] *nm* spelt

épée [epe] *nf* sword; *Escrime* épée; **coup d'é.** swordthrust; *Fig* **coup d'é. dans l'eau** wasted effort; **Marc est une bonne é.** Marc is a good swordsman; *Fig* **é. de Damoclès** Sword of Damocles

épeiche [epɛʃ] *nf Orn* great spotted woodpecker

épeichette [epɛʃɛt] *nf Orn* lesser spotted woodpecker

épéiste [epeist] *n Escrime* épéeist

épeler [eple] **(j'épelle; j'épellerai) 1** *vt* **(a)** (*mot, nom etc*) to spell; **mot mal épelé** misspelt word **(b)** (*lire avec difficulté*) (*texte*) to spell out **2** *vi* to spell

épépiner [epepine] *vt* (*raisins, tomates etc*) to remove the seeds *or* pips from, to deseed; (*pommes*) to core

éperdu [epɛrdy] *adj* (*regard*) distraught, frantic; (*amour, besoin etc*) violent; (*résistance*) desperate; **é. de joie/douleur** frantic with joy/grief

éperdument [epɛrdymɑ̃] *adv* (*aimer*) madly, to distraction; (*travailler*) desperately, frantically; **é. amoureux** head over heels in love, madly in love; *F* **je m'en fiche é.** I couldn't care less, I don't give a damn

éperlan [epɛrlɑ̃] *nm* (*poisson*) smelt, sparling

éperon [eprɔ̃] *nm* **(a)** (*d'un cavalier*) spur; **donner de l'é. à son cheval, piquer de l'é.** to spur (on) one's horse; **gagner ses éperons** to win one's spurs **(b)** (*d'une violette, d'une montagne, d'un coq*) spur **(c)** *Hist* (*d'un vaisseau de guerre*) ram **(d)** (*d'un pont*) cutwater

éperonner [eprɔne] *vt* **(a)** (*cheval*) to spur (on), to put spurs to; *Fig* **é. qn** to spur *or* urge sb on **(b)** *Hist* (*vaisseau ennemi*) to ram **(c)** (*bottes etc*) to spur, to put spurs on

épervier [epɛrvje] *nm* **(a)** (*oiseau*) sparrowhawk; *Pol Fig* hawk **(b)** *Pêche* castnet

éphèbe [efɛb] *nm Iron* (*beau jeune homme*) Adonis, Apollo

éphélide [efelid] *nf* freckle

éphémère [efemɛr] **1** *adj* (*bonheur etc*) ephemeral, short-lived, fleeting; **ce chanteur n'a connu qu'un succès é.** this singer enjoyed only a short-lived *or* brief success **2** *nm Ent* mayfly, ephemera

éphéméride [efemerid] *nf* **(a)** (*calendrier*) tear-off *or* block calendar **(b)** *Astron* (*publication annuelle*) ephemeris; **éphémérides** (*tables*) ephemerides

Éphèse [efɛz] *n* Ephesus

épi [epi] *nm* **(a)** (*de grain*) ear; (*de fleur*) spike; **blés en é.** wheat in the ear; **monter en é.** (*de céréales*) to ear; **é. de maïs** *Agr* corncob; *Culin* corn on the cob **(b)** (*mèche de cheveux*) tuft of hair; **ses cheveux font des épis** his hair sticks up in tufts **(c)** (*jetée*) spur, groyne; *Rail* (*de voie*) spur; *Aut* **stationnement en é.** angle parking; *Constr* **appareil en é.** herringbone bond

▶ **épi**: *Archit* **é. de faîtage** finial

épicarpe [epikarp] *nm Bot* epicarp

épice [epis] *nf* spice; **pain d'é.** ≈ gingerbread; **quatre épices** allspice

épicé [epise] *adj* (*nourriture, plat etc*) highly spiced, spicy, hot; (*assaisonnement*) spicy, hot; *F* **conte é.** spicy story

épicéa [episea] *nm* (*arbre*) spruce

épicentre [episɑ̃tr] *nm* (*d'un tremblement de terre*) epicentre

épicer [epise] *vt* **(j'épiçai(s))** (*nourriture, plat etc*) to spice; *F* (*histoire etc*) to spice up, to add a bit of spice to

épicerie [episri] *nf* **(a)** (*produits*) groceries; **é. fine** delicatessen; **être dans l'é.** to be in the grocery business **(b)** (*magasin*) grocer's (shop) **(c)** *Can Fig* **liste d'é.** (*de griefs etc*) shopping list

épicier, -ière [episje, -jɛr] *n* grocer; *Fig Péj* **d'é.** (*idées, littérature etc*) common-or-garden; (*encre, savon etc*) cheap, ordinary; *Fig Péj* **mentalité d'é.** small-town mentality

épicurien, -ienne [epikyrjɛ̃, -jɛn] **1** *adj* epicurean; *Phil* Epicurean **2** *n* epicure; *Phil* Epicurean

épicurisme [epikyrism] *nm* **(a)** *Phil* Epicureanism **(b)** (*recherche du plaisir*) epicur(ean)ism

épicycloïdal, -ale, -aux, -ales [episiklɔidal] *adj MecE* (*engrenage*) epicyclic

épidémie [epidemi] *nf Méd, Fig* epidemic

épidémiologie [epidemjɔlɔʒi] *nf* epidemiology

épidémiologique [epidemjɔlɔʒik] *adj* epidemiological

épidémique [epidemik] *adj Méd* epidemic; *Fig* contagious

épiderme [epidɛrm] *nm Anat, Bot* epidermis, skin; *Fig* **avoir l'é. sensible** *ou* **délicat** to be thin-skinned *or* touchy

épidermique [epidɛrmik] *adj* (*tissu etc*) epidermal, epidermic; *Fig* **une réaction é.** a kneejerk reaction

épier [epje] *vt* (*impf, pr sub* **n. épiions, v. épiiez**) (*espionner*) (*qn, les activités de qn etc*) to spy on, to keep a watch on; (*observer pour découvrir*) (*signe, occasion etc*) to watch out for; (*la réaction de qn*) to watch for

épigastre [epigastr] *nm Anat* epigastrium

épigastrique [epigastrik] *adj Anat* epigastric

épiglotte [epiglɔt] *nf Anat* epiglottis

épigone [epigon] *nm Litt* (*successeur*) epigone

épigramme [epigram] *nf* epigram

épigraphe [epigraf] *nf* epigraph

épigraphie [epigrafi] *nf* epigraphy

épilation [epilasjɔ̃] *nf* removal of unwanted hair (**de** from); (*des sourcils*) plucking

épilatoire [epilatwar] *adj* (*crème etc*) hair-removing, depilatory

épilepsie [epilɛpsi] *nf Méd* epilepsy; **crise d'é.** epileptic fit

épileptique [epilɛptik] *adj, n Méd* epileptic

épiler [epile] **1** *vt* to remove unwanted hair from; (*sourcils*) to pluck **2 s'épiler** *vpr* **s'é. les jambes à la cire** to wax one's legs

épilogue [epilɔg] *nm* epilogue; *Fig* **j'attends l'é. de cette histoire** I'm waiting for the rest of the story

épiloguer [epilɔge] **1** *vt Arch* to pass censure on **2** *vi* to go on (and on), to hold forth (**sur** about)

épinard [epinar] *nm* (*plante*) spinach; *Culin* **épinards** spinach; **épinards en branches** leaf spinach; **un pull vert é.** a spinach-green sweater

épine [epin] *nf* **(a)** (*arbre*) thornbush **(b)** (*piquant*) *Bot* thorn, prickle; *Zool* spine, prickle; **tirer une é. du pied à qn** (*tirer d'embarras*) to get sb out of a mess; (*soulager*) to relieve sb's mind

▶ **épine**: **é. blanche** hawthorn; *Anat* **é. dorsale** backbone; **é. noire** blackthorn; **é. de rat** butcher's broom

épinette [epinɛt] *nf* **(a)** *Can Bot* spruce **(b)** *Mus* spinet **(c)** (*cage*) hen coop

épinettière [epinɛtjɛr] *nf Can* spruce grove

épineux, -euse [epinø, -øz] **1** *adj* **(a)** (*arbuste, tige*) thorny, prickly, spiky; (*poisson*) spiny; *Fig* (*question, problème*) thorny, tricky; *Fig* **être dans une situation épineuse** to be in a tricky *or* ticklish situation **(b)** *Anat* (*excroissance*) spinous **2** *nm* thornbush

épinglage [epɛ̃glaʒ] *nm* pinning

épingle [epɛ̃gl] *nf* pin; **attacher avec des épingles** (*cheveux, poster*) to pin up; (*morceau de tissu, feuilles*) to pin together; *Fig* **tiré à quatre épingles** dressed up to the nines; *Fig* **tirer son é. du jeu** to extricate oneself; *Fig* **chercher une é. dans une botte de foin** to look for a needle in a haystack; *Fig* **monter qch en é.** (*exagérer*) to make too much of sth

▶ **épingle**: **é. à chapeau** hatpin; **é. à cheveux** hairpin; **virage en é. à cheveux** hairpin *Br* bend *or Am* turn; **é. de cravate** tiepin; **é. à linge** clothes *Br* peg *or Am* pin; **e. de nourrice** safety pin; **é. de signalisation** (*d'une fiche*) marker tag; **e. de sûreté** safety pin

épingler [epɛ̃gle] *vt* **(a)** (*attacher*) to pin, to fasten with a pin/pins (**à** to; **sur** on); **é. ses cheveux** to pin up one's hair **(b)** *F* (*arrêter*) to nab, to collar

épinière [epinjɛr] *adj Anat* **moelle é.** spinal cord

épinoche [epinɔʃ] *nf* stickleback

Épiphanie [epifani] *nf Rel* Epiphany

épiphénomène [epifenɔmɛn] *nm* epiphenomenon

épiphyse [epifiz] *nf Anat* epiphysis

épique [epik] *adj* epic; **poème é.** epic (poem)

épiscopal, -ale, -aux, -ales [episkɔpal, -o] *adj Rel* episcopal

épiscopat [episkɔpa] *nm* (*fonction, ensemble des évêques*) episcopate

épiscope [episkɔp] *nm* episcope

épisiotomie [epizjɔtɔmi] *nf Chir* episiotomy

épisode [epizɔd] *nm* episode; **feuilleton** *ou* **film à épisodes** serial; **la suite au prochain é.** tune in again to find out what happens next; *Fig* I'll let you know what happens; *Fig* **ce n'est qu'un é. malheureux** it's just an unfortunate episode

épisodique [epizɔdik] *adj* (*intermittent*) episodic; (*accessoire*) minor

épisodiquement [epizɔdikmɑ̃] *adv* occasionally, now and again

épisser [epise] *vt* (*corde, câble*) to splice

épissure [episyr] *nf* splice

épistémologie [epistemɔlɔʒi] *nf* epistemology

épistémologique [epistemɔlɔʒik] *adj* epistemological

épistolaire [epistɔlɛr] *adj* epistolary; **être en relation é. avec qn** to correspond with sb; **nous n'avons que des relations épistolaires** our only contact is by letter

épistolier, -ière [epistɔlje, -jɛr] *n* letter writer

épitaphe [epitaf] *nf* epitaph

épithélium [epiteljɔm] *nm Biol* epithelium

épithète [epitɛt] *nf* [①**A17**] epithet; *Gram* attribute

épitoge [epitɔʒ] *nf* **(a)** *Univ* (*bande d'étoffe*) ≈ (graduate's) hood **(b)** *Antiq* (*vêtement*) cloak

épitomé [epitɔme] *nm* (*abrégé d'un ouvrage*) epitome

épître [epitr] *nf* epistle; (*partie de la messe*) Epistle; **côté de l'é.** (*de l'autel*) Epistle side

éploré, -ée [eplɔre] *adj* (*personne*) tearful, weeping; (*expression, voix*) tearful

épluchage [eplyʃaʒ] *nm* (*de fruits, pommes de terre etc*) peeling; (*d'une salade*) cleaning; (*de crevettes*) peeling, shelling; (*de noisettes, pois*) shelling; *Fig* (*d'un texte, journal etc*) detailed examination

épluche-légumes [eplyʃlegym] *nm inv* vegetable *or* potato peeler

éplucher [eplyʃe] *vt* (*fruits, pommes de terre etc*) to peel; (*salade*) to clean; (*crevettes*) to peel, to shell; (*noisettes, pois*) to shell; *Fig* (*texte, journal, publicités etc*) to go through *or* examine in detail; *Fig* **ma mère épluche mon emploi du temps** my mother checks up on how I spend my time

épluchette [eplyʃɛt] *nf Can* **é. de blé d'Inde** corn-husking party

éplucheur, -euse [eplyʃœr, -øz] *n* (*instrument, personne*) peeler; **é. de pommes de terre** potato peeler

épluchure [eplyʃyr] *nf* (*pelure*) peeling

épointage [epwɛ̃taʒ] *nm* (*en cassant*) (*d'un crayon*) breaking the point; (*en usant*) (*d'une aiguille, d'un crayon, d'un outil etc*) blunting

épointé [epwɛ̃te] *adj* (*aiguille, crayon, outil etc*) blunt

épointer [epwɛ̃te] *vt* (*en cassant*) (*crayon*) to break the point of; (*en usant*) (*aiguille, crayon, outil etc*) to blunt

éponge [epɔ̃ʒ] *nf* **(a)** (*naturelle*) sponge **(b)** *Com* sponge; **donner un coup d'é. à qch** to wipe sth with a sponge; **effacer une tache d'un coup d'é.** to sponge out a stain; *Fig* **passons l'é.** let's forget it; *Boxe* **jeter l'é.** to throw in the sponge *or* towel; *Fig* **l'industrie française jette l'é. dans le domaine de la construction automobile** French industry is throwing in the sponge *or* towel as regards the building of cars; *Tex* **tissu é.** (terry) towelling; **serviette é.** terry towel; *F* **il boit comme une é., c'est une véritable é.** he drinks like a fish

▶ **éponge**: **é. métallique** (pan) scourer, scouring pad; **é. végétale** vegetable sponge, loofah

épongeage [epɔ̃ʒaʒ] *nm* (*d'un liquide*) sponging up, mopping up; (*d'une surface*) sponging (down)

éponger [epɔ̃ʒe] (**j'épongeai(s); n. épongeons**) **1** *vt* **(a)** (*liquide*) to sponge up, to mop up **(b)** (*surface*) to sponge (down), to mop; (*cheval, voiture etc*) to sponge down; (*le front de qn*) to mop **(c)** *Fin* (*déficit etc*) to mop up, to absorb **2 s'éponger** *vpr* **s'é. le front** to mop one's brow

épontille [epɔ̃tij] *nf Naut* shore, prop

épontiller [epɔ̃tije] *vt Naut* to prop, to shore (up)

épopée [epɔpe] *nf Littér, Fig* epic

époque [epɔk] *nf* **(a)** (*historique*) epoch, era, age; *Géol* age, period; **l'é. glaciaire** the ice age; **la Belle é.** ≈ the Edwardian era; **quelle é. (nous vivons)!** what times we live in!; **il n'est plus de son é.** he's out of step *or* tune with the times; **meubles d'é.** period furniture, (genuine) antique furniture; **à l'é., elle était très reconnue** at the time she was highly regarded; **faire é.** (*d'une invention, déclaration etc*) to leave its mark on history; **découverte qui fait é.** epoch-making discovery

(b) (*moment précis*) time; **à l'é. de sa naissance** at the time of his birth; **à cette é. de l'année** at this time of year; **à l'é., je faisais le grand écart** I was doing the splits at the time

épouillage [epujaʒ] *nm* delousing

épouiller [epuje] *vt* to delouse

époumoner (s') [sepumɔne] *vpr* (*en criant*) to shout oneself hoarse; (*en chantant*) to sing oneself hoarse; **c'est ce que je m'époumone à te dire!** I've told you so until I'm hoarse

épousailles [epuzɑj] *nfpl Arch* nuptials, wedding

épouse [epuz] *nf* [①**A12**,1,d] wife; *Admin* spouse

épousée [epuze] *nf Vieilli* bride

épouser [epuze] *vt* **(a)** to marry, *Vieilli* to wed; **é. une grosse dot** to marry (into) money **(b)** *Fig* (*cause, doctrine etc*) to espouse, to take up, to adopt; **les Français ont épousé le golf** the French have taken to golf; **é. la forme de qch** to take on the exact shape of sth; **sa robe épousait les courbes de son corps** her dress hugged the curves of her body; **la route épouse la colline** the road follows the hill round

époussetage [epustaʒ] *nm* (*de meubles etc*) dusting

épousseter [epuste] *vt* (*conj like* **jeter**) (*meubles etc*) to dust; (*vêtements etc*) to brush (the dust from); (*cheval*) to rub down

époustouflant [epustuflɑ̃] *adj F* amazing, astounding

époustoufler [epustufle] *vt F* to amaze, to astound

épouvantable [epuvɑ̃tabl] *adj* dreadful, appalling

épouvantablement [epuvɑ̃tabləmɑ̃] *adv* dreadfully, appallingly

épouvantail [epuvɑ̃taj] *nm* (*dans un jardin*) scarecrow; *Péj* (*personne laide ou bizarrement habillée*) fright; (*personne terrifiante*) bogey; (*chose terrifiante*) bugbear, bogey

épouvante [epuvɑ̃t] *nf* terror, fright; **jeter** *ou* **porter l'é. dans un pays** to spread terror in a country; **saisi d'é.** terror-stricken, frightened to death; **film d'é.** horror film; **elle pense à cette rencontre avec é.** she is dreading the meeting

épouvanté [epuvɑ̃te] *adj* terror-stricken

épouvanter [epuvɑ̃te] **1** *vt* to terrify, to scare **2 s'épouvanter** *vpr* to take fright (**de** at)

époux [epu] *nm* husband; *Admin* spouse; **les é.** the married couple, the husband and wife; **les é. Thomas** Mr and Mrs Thomas

éprendre (s') [seprɑ̃dr] *vpr* (*conj like* **prendre**) **s'é. de** (*qn*) to fall in love with; (*son travail, une idée etc*) to become passionate about

épreuve [eprœv] *nf* **(a)** (*essai*) test, trial; **faire l'é. de qch** to test sth; **mettre qch/qn à l'é.** to put sth/sb to the test; **à l'é. du feu/de l'eau** fireproof/waterproof; **à l'é. des balles** bulletproof; **l'é. de vérité pour ...** the critical test for ...; **mécanisme à toute é.** foolproof mechanism; **bonté/courage à toute é.** unfailing kindness/courage; **être mis à rude é.** (*d'une personne, de la patience, de l'honneur etc*) to be severely tested; (*de jouets etc*) to be roughly treated *or* handled; **les bateaux/arbres ont été mis à rude é. par la tempête** the boats/trees took a battering from the storm

(b) *Scol, Univ* (*écrite*) (examination) paper; (*orale*) test

(c) *Sp* (*d'une rencontre d'athlétisme*) event

(d) (*adversité*) trial, ordeal; **dans l'é.** in adversity; **passer par de rudes épreuves** to go through a bad *or* hard time

(e) *Typ* proof; **les épreuves d'un livre** the proofs of a book; **première é.** galley (proof); **dernière é., é. finale** final proof

(f) *Phot* print; *Cin* **épreuves (de tournage)** rushes

▶ **épreuve**: *Typ* **é. bonne à filmer** camera-ready copy, CRC; *Typ* **é. de calage** machine proof; *Sp* **é. contre la montre** time trial; *Sp* **é. éliminatoire** (preliminary) heat; *Sp* **é. d'endurance** endurance test; *Hist* **é. du feu** ordeal by fire; *Sp* **é. finale** final; **é. de force** trial of strength, showdown;

Typ **épreuves d'imprimerie** printer's proofs; **épreuves d'initiation** initiation rites; **é. d'outrance** resistance test; *Typ* **é. ozalide** ozalid; *Typ* **é. de page** page proof; *Sp* **é.-phare** major event; *Sp* **épreuves sur piste** track events; **é. de résistance** resistance test

épris [epri] *adj* **(a)** **é. de qn** in love with sb **(b)** **é. de qch** passionate about sth

éprouvant [epruvɑ̃] *adj (pénible)* trying, tiring

éprouvé [epruve] *adj* **(a)** *(testé) (remède)* proven, well-tried; *(spécialiste, loyauté etc)* proven; *(allié)* trusty, staunch; *(matériaux)* tested **(b)** *(famille)* stricken; *(région)* hard-hit; **troupes très éprouvées** troops that have suffered a great deal

éprouver [epruve] *vt* **(a)** *(tester) (machine, matériaux, méthode etc)* to test; *(personne, courage etc)* to put to the test, to test **(b)** *(ressentir) (sensation, douleur etc)* to feel, to experience; **les sentiments qu'il éprouve pour moi** the feelings that he has for me **(c)** *(subir) (perte)* to sustain, to suffer; *(difficultés)* to meet with

éprouvette [epruvɛt] **1** *nf* test tube **2** *adj* **bébé é.** test-tube baby

epsilon [ɛpsilɔn] *nm (lettre grecque)* epsilon

épucer [epyse] *vt* **(j'épuçai(s); n. épuçons)** *(chien etc)* to rid of fleas

épuisant [epɥizɑ̃] *adj* exhausting

épuisé [epɥize] *adj* **(a)** *(très fatigué)* exhausted, tired out, worn out **(b)** *(sol, mine)* exhausted, worked out; *Él* **pile épuisée** dead battery; *Phys Nucl* **uranium é.** depleted *or* impoverished uranium **(c)** *Com (livre, édition)* out of print; *(marchandises)* sold out, out of stock; **tous nos stocks sont épuisés** all our stocks are exhausted

épuisement [epɥizmɑ̃] *nm* **(a)** *(fatigue)* exhaustion; **danser/marcher jusqu'à é.** to dance/walk till one drops; **rouler/nager jusqu'à é.** to drive/swim until one is exhausted; **mort d'é.** dead with exhaustion **(b)** *(de provisions, de munitions, d'une mine, d'un sol, d'un stock etc)* exhaustion; *(de ressources)* depletion; *(d'une citerne)* draining, emptying; *Phys Nucl (de l'uranium)* depletion, impoverishment; *Com* **jusqu'à. é. des stocks** while stocks last

épuiser [epɥize] **1** *vt* **(a)** *(fatiguer)* to exhaust, to wear *or* tire out

(b) *(provisions, munitions etc)* to use up, to exhaust; *(mine, sol)* to exhaust, to work out; *(ressources)* to deplete; *(citerne)* to drain, to empty; *(stock)* to exhaust, to run low on; *(marchandises)* to sell out; **é. un sujet** to exhaust a subject; **cette marche a épuisé toute mon énergie** that walking has used up all my energy

(c) *(lettre de crédit)* to use up

2 s'épuiser *vpr* **(a)** *(se fatiguer)* to exhaust oneself, to tire *or* wear oneself out; **je m'épuise à vous le dire** I've told you so until I'm blue in the face

(b) *(d'une source etc)* to dry up, to run dry; *(d'un stock, de l'argent, de provisions etc)* to run out, to give out

épuisette [epɥizɛt] *nf* **(a)** *Pêche* landing net **(b)** *Naut (pelle)* scoop, bailer

épurateur [epyratœr] *nm Tech* purifier; **é. de gaz** gas purifier, (gas) scrubber

épuration [epyrasjɔ̃] *nf (de l'eau)* purification; *(du gaz)* purification, scrubbing; *(du pétrole, d'un minerai)* refining; *Fig (d'une langue, d'un style)* refining; *Pol* purge, purging

épure [epyr] *nf* working drawing; *(dessin fini) (d'un édifice, moteur etc)* finished plan

épurer [epyre] *vt (eau)* to purify; *(gaz)* to purify, to scrub; *(pétrole, minerai)* to refine; *Fig (langue, style)* to refine; *Pol (parti, personnel etc)* to purge

équarrir [ekarir] *vt* **(a)** *(bois, pierre)* to square **(b)** *(animal)* to quarter, to cut up

équarrissage [ekarisaʒ] *nm* **(a)** *(du bois, de la pierre)* squaring **(b)** *(de carcasses d'animaux)* quartering, cutting up; **chantier d'é.** knacker's yard

équarrisseur [ekarisœr] *nm* knacker

équarrissoir [ekariswar] *nm* **(a)** *(couteau)* knacker's knife **(b)** *(abattoir)* knacker's yard

Équateur [ekwatœr] *nm* Ecuador

équateur [ekwatœr] *nm* equator; **sous l'é.** at *or* on the equator; **é. magnétique** magnetic equator; *Astron* **é. céleste** celestial equator

équation [ekwasjɔ̃] *nf* equation; *Math* **é. du premier/du deuxième degré** simple/quadratic equation; *Compta* **é. de bénéfice** profit equation; *Compta* **é. de coût** cost equation; *Mktg* **é. de la demande** demand equation; *Mktg* **é. de réponse de marché** sales-response function; *Mktg* **é. de vente** sales equation

équatorial, -iale, -iaux, -iales [ekwatɔrjal, -jo] **1** *adj* equatorial **2** *nm Astron* equatorial (telescope)

équatorien, -ienne [ekwatɔrjɛ̃, -jɛn] **1** *adj* Ecuadorian **2** *n* **É.** Ecuadorian

équerre [ekɛr] *nf* **(a)** *(instrument)* **é. (à dessin)** set square; **é. à coulisse** (sliding) calliper gauge; **fausse é.** bevel square; **é. à onglet** mitre square; **é. d'arpenteur** cross-staff **(b)** **en é., à l'é.** at right angles; **d'é.** square, straight; **mettre qch d'é.** to square sth **(c)** *(pièce métallique)* corner plate

équestre [ekɛstr] *adj (statue, sports etc)* equestrian; *(exercices etc)* (horse)riding

équeuter [ekøte] *vt (fruit)* to remove the stalk(s) from

équiangle [ekɥiɑ̃gl] *adj Géom* equiangular

équidés [ek(ɥ)ide] *nmpl Zool* Equidae

équidistance [ekɥidistɑ̃s] *nf* equidistance

équidistant [ekɥidistɑ̃] *adj* equidistant (**de** from)

équilatéral, -ale, -aux, -ales [ekɥilateral, -o] *adj Géom* equilateral

équilibrage [ekilibraʒ] *nm* balancing

équilibrant [ekilibrɑ̃] *adj (élément)* balancing; **poids é.** counterweight; *Psy* **c'est un facteur é. dans la vie d'un enfant** it's a stabilizing factor in a child's life

équilibre [ekilibr] *nm* **(a)** *(d'un corps, objet)* balance, equilibrium; *(d'un avion)* stability; **avoir le sens de l'é.** to have a sense of balance; **mettre qch en é.** to balance sth; **tenir qch en é. sur son nez** to balance sth on one's nose; **perdre l'é.** to lose one's balance; **faire perdre l'é. à qn** to throw sb off (his/her) balance; **cet acrobate fait de l'é.** *ou* **des tours d'é.** this acrobat does balancing tricks; **la chaise est en é. instable** the chair is precariously balanced

(b) *(mental)* (mental) balance *or* equilibrium; **elle manque d'é.** she is unbalanced

(c) *Pol* **budget en é.** balanced budget; **é. budgétaire** balanced budget; **é. européen** balance of power in Europe; **l'é. des rapports/des forces** *(entre deux pays)* the balance of relations/power; **l'é. de la terreur** the balance of terror

(d) *(des éléments d'un ensemble)* balance, harmony; *TV, Cin* **é. des couleurs** colour balance

équilibré [ekilibre] *adj (chargement, repas etc)* balanced; *(personne)* well-balanced, stable; *(vie)* regular, stable; **mal é., non é.** unbalanced; **vie peu équilibrée** irregular *or* unstable life

équilibrer [ekilibre] **1** *vt (charge, éléments d'une composition etc)* to balance; *(bateau, avion)* to trim; **é. qch par un contrepoids** to counterbalance sth; **é. un budget** to balance a budget, to break even; *Aut* **é. les roues** to balance the wheels; **cette expérience dans le monde du travail l'a équilibré** this work experience has stabilized him **2 s'équilibrer** *vpr* to balance each other (out); *(budget)* to balance

équilibreur [ekilibrœr] *nm Av* stabilizer

équilibriste [ekilibrist] *n (acrobate)* equilibrist; *(funambule)* tightrope walker

équille [ekij] *nf (poisson)* launce, sand eel

équin [ekɛ̃] *adj* equine; **pied é.** club foot

équinisme [ekinism] *nm Méd (difformité)* club foot

équinoxe [ekinɔks] *nm* equinox; **é. de printemps/d'automne** spring/autumn(al) equinox; **vent d'é.** equinoctial gale

équinoxial, -iale, -iaux, -iales [ekinɔksjal, -jo] *adj* equinoctial

équipage [ekipaʒ] *nm* **(a)** [①**A11**,g,iii] *(d'un navire, avion)* crew; *Naut* **maître d'é.** boatswain; *Naut* **les hommes d'é.** the crew; **les membres de l'é.** the crew **(b)** *(suite)* equipage, retinue; **arriver en grand é.** to arrive in state **(c)** *Hist (voiture, chevaux etc)* equipage **(d)** *Vieilli (tenue)* attire **(e)** *(équipement) Mil* train, equipment; *Tech* equipment, gear; **é. de construction** builder's *or* building equipment *or* gear

équipe [ekip] *nf* [①**A11**,g,i] **(a)** *Sp* team; *(d'un canot à rames)* crew; **sport d'é.** team sport

(b) *(personnes qui travaillent ensemble) (de chercheurs, médecins etc)* team; *(d'ouvriers)* gang; *Mil* working party; **travailler par équipes** to work in shifts; **chef d'é.** (gang) foreman; **encourager le travail d'é.** to encourage teamwork; **esprit d'é.** team spirit; **faire é. avec qn** to team up with sb; *F* **nous étions une é. de joyeux lurons** we were a cheerful crew *or* lot; *F* **en voilà une fine é.!** what a crew!

(c) *Mktg* **é. commando** venture team; **é. commerciale** marketing team

▶ **équipe**: *Cin* **é. caméra** camera crew; *Sp* **é. de cricket** cricket team *or* eleven; *Rail* **é. de conduite** *ou* **de locomotive** engine crew; **é. de création** creative team; **é. de dactylos** typing pool; *Com* **é. dirigeante** management team; *Journ* **é. d'investigation** investigative team; **é. de jour** day shift; **é. de nuit** night shift; *Journ* back-bench; *TV, Cin* **é. de prise de vue** camera crew; *TV, Cin* **é. de production** production team; **é. de secours** rescue team; *Journ* **é. de soutien** back-bench; **é. de télévision** television crew; *Com* **é. de vente** sales team *or* force

équipée [ekipe] *nf* (*frasque*) escapade, lark; (*promenade, voyage*) jaunt

équipement [ekipmɑ̃] *nm* **(a)** (*action*) (*d'un atelier, d'une cuisine*) equipping, equipment, fitting out (**de** with); **é. en hommes** manning; **plan d'é. national** national development plan **(b)** (*matériel*) equipment; (*d'un soldat*) kit; (*de camping, ski etc*) gear, equipment **(c)** (*installations*) facilities

▶ **équipement**: **é. automobile** car accessories; **équipements collectifs** public facilities *or* amenities; **é. électrique** electrical fittings; **é. industriel** industrial plant; *Ordinat* **é. informatique** computer equipment; *Aut* **é. intérieur** internal fittings; **é. routier** road signs; *Aut* **équipements spéciaux** (*chaînes*) chains; (*pneus cloutés*) studded tyres; **e. de survie** survival kit

équipementier [ekipmɑ̃tje] *nm Aut* parts manufacturer

équiper [ekipe] **1** *vt* (*atelier, cuisine etc*) to equip, to fit out (**de** with); (*sportif, armée etc*) to equip, *Br* to kit out (**de** with); **é. un navire** (*d'appareils etc*) to equip *or* fit out a ship; (*en hommes*) to man a ship; **é. une voiture pour la neige** to equip a car for the snow; **é. une ville en terrains de sport** to provide a town with sports grounds; **appartement avec cuisine équipée** flat with cooking facilities; *F* **comme vous voilà équipé!** what a get-up! **2 s'équiper** *vpr* to equip oneself

équipier, -ière [ekipje, -jɛr] *n Sp* team member; *Naut* crew member; *Naut* **mené par 14équipiers** manned by a crew of 14, with a 14-man crew

équitable [ekitabl] *adj* **(a)** (*marché, partage etc*) equitable, fair, just **(b)** (*personne*) impartial, fair-minded, fair

équitablement [ekitabləmɑ̃] *adv* equitably, fairly

équitation [ekitasjɔ̃] *nf* (horse)riding, *Fml* equitation; **faire de l'é.** to go riding; **école d'é.** riding school

équité [ekite] *nf* equity, equitableness, fairness

équivalence [ekivalɑ̃s] *nf* equivalence; *Univ* **avoir/obtenir une é.** to have/get an equivalent diploma; **ce diplôme est une é. du bac** this diploma is the equivalent of the baccalauréat

équivalent [ekivalɑ̃] **1** *adj* equivalent (**à** to) **2** *nm* equivalent; **sans é.** without equal, unequalled

équivaloir [ekivalwar] *vi* (*conj like* **valoir**) to be equivalent *or* equal (**à** to); **cela équivaut à un refus** that amounts to a refusal

équivoque [ekivɔk] **1** *adj* **(a)** (*ambigu*) (*mots, faits, attitude etc*) equivocal, ambiguous **(b)** (*douteux*) (*conduite, honnêteté, passé etc*) questionable, doubtful, dubious **2** *nf* **(a)** (*ambiguïté*) ambiguity; **sans é.** (*adj*) unequivocal; (*adv*) unequivocally **(b)** (*malentendu*) misunderstanding (**sur** about)

érable [erabl] *nm* (*arbre, bois*) maple; **é. à sucre** sugar maple; **sirop/sucre d'é.** maple syrup/sugar

érablière [erablijɛr] *nf Can* maple grove

éradication [eradikasjɔ̃] *nf* eradication

éradiquer [eradike] *vt* to eradicate

érafler [erafle] **1** *vt* (*genou etc*) to scratch, to graze; (*cuir etc*) to scuff; (*bois, meuble*) to scratch **2 s'érafler** *vpr* **s'é. le coude** to graze *or* scrape one's elbow

éraflure [eraflyr] *nf* (*au genou etc*) scratch, graze; (*sur cuir etc*) scuff (mark); (*sur bois, meuble*) scratch (mark)

éraillé [eraje] *adj* **(a)** (*tissu*) frayed; (*surface*) scratched; (*corde*) fretted **(b) yeux éraillés** bloodshot eyes **(c)** (*voix*) hoarse

éraillement [erajmɑ̃] *nm* **(a)** (*d'un tissu*) fraying; (*d'une corde*) fretting; (*d'une surface*) scratching **(b)** (*éraflure*) scratch **(c)** (*de voix*) hoarseness

érailler [eraje] **1** *vt* **(a)** (*tissu*) to fray; (*ourlet etc*) to unravel; (*corde*) to fret **(b)** (*peau, surface etc*) to scratch **(c)** (*voix*) to make hoarse **2 s'érailler** *vpr* **(a)** (*d'un ourlet etc*) to unravel, to come unravelled; (*d'un tissu*) to fray; (*d'une corde*) to fret **(b)** (*d'une voix*) to become hoarse

éraillure [erajyr] *nf* (*marque*) scratch

erbium [ɛrbjɔm] *nm Ch* erbium

ère [ɛr] *nf* era; **en l'an 1150 de notre è.** in (the year) 1150 AD; **avant notre è.** BC; **è. de prospérité** period of prosperity

érecteur, -trice [erɛktœr, -tris] *adj Physiol* erector

érectile [erɛktil] *adj* erectile

érection [erɛksjɔ̃] *nf* **(a)** (*d'une statue, d'un mât etc*) erection, setting up, raising **(b)** *Physiol* erection; **être en é.** to have an erection

éreintage [erɛ̃taʒ] *nm* = **éreintement (b)**

éreintant [erɛ̃tɑ̃] *adj F* (*travail etc*) backbreaking, exhausting

éreinté [erɛ̃te] *adj F* exhausted, worn out

éreintement [erɛ̃tmɑ̃] *nm* **(a)** (*fatigue*) exhaustion **(b)** (*critique sévère*) savage criticism, *Br* slating

éreinter [erɛ̃te] **1** *vt* **(a)** (*fatiguer*) (*personne, animal*) to exhaust, to wear *or* tire out **(b)** (*critiquer*) (*livre, représentation, auteur etc*) to criticize savagely, *Br* to slate **2 s'éreinter** *vpr* to exhaust oneself, to wear *or* tire oneself out (**à faire** doing)

éreinteur, -euse [erɛ̃tœr, øz] *n* savage critic

erg[1] [ɛrg] *nm Phys* (*unité*) erg

erg[2] *nm Géog* erg

ergol [ɛrgɔl] *nm Astronaut* propellant

ergonomie [ɛrgɔnɔmi] *nf* ergonomics

ergonomique [ɛrgɔnɔmik] *adj* ergonomic

ergot [ɛrgo] *nm* **(a)** (*d'un coq etc*) spur; *F* **monter** *ou* **se dresser sur ses ergots** (*se montrer menaçant*) to show one's teeth **(b)** (*d'un chien etc*) dewclaw **(c)** *Agr, Pharm* ergot **(d)** *Tech* lug; **e. d'arrêt** stop lug; **e. de tracteur** (*d'imprimante*) tractor pin

ergotage [ɛrgɔtaʒ] *nm* quibbling, cavilling

ergoté [ɛrgɔte] *adj* **(a)** (*oiseau*) spurred; (*chien*) dewclawed **(b)** *Agr* (*seigle, blé*) affected with ergot

ergoter [ɛrgɔte] *vi* to quibble, to cavil (**sur** about)

ergoteur, -euse [ɛrgɔtœr, -øz] **1** *adj* cavilling, quibbling **2** *n* quibbler, caviller

ergothérapeute [ɛrgoterapøt] *n* occupational therapist

ergothérapie [ɛrgoterapi] *nf* occupational therapy

Érié [erje] *nm* **le Lac É.** Lake Erie

ériger [eriʒe] (**j'érigeai(s)**) **1** *vt* **(a)** (*dresser*) (*statue, temple, mât etc*) to erect, to set up, to raise **(b)** (*créer*) (*bureau, tribunal etc*) to establish, to set up **(c)** *Fig* **é. qn en** to set sb up as, to elevate sb to the status of; **é. qch en** to elevate sth to the status of, to present sth as; **é. une église en cathédrale** to raise a church to (the dignity of) a cathedral **2 s'ériger** *vpr* **s'é. en spécialiste** to set oneself up as a specialist

ermitage [ɛrmitaʒ] *nm* hermitage

ermite [ɛrmit] *nm* hermit; **vivre en e.** to live the life of a recluse

éroder [erɔde] *vt* (*côte, rochers etc*) to erode, to wear away; (*métaux etc*) to corrode, to eat away

érogène [erɔʒɛn] *adj* erogenous

éros [eros] *nm* **(a)** *Psy* **l'é.** Eros **(b)** *Myth* **É.** Eros

érosif, -ive [erozif, -iv] *adj* erosive

érosion [erozjɔ̃] *nf* erosion, wearing away; *Fig* erosion; **é. dentaire** dental erosion; *Fig* **é. monétaire** depreciation of money

érotique [erɔtik] *adj* erotic

érotiquement [erɔtikmɑ̃] *adv* erotically

érotisation [erɔtizasjɔ̃] *nf* eroticization

erotiser [erɔtize] *vt* to eroticize

érotisme [erɔtism] *nm* (*caractère érotique*) eroticism; (*goût pour le plaisir sexuel*) erotism

érotologue [erɔtɔlɔg] *n* sexologist

érotomane [erɔtɔman] *n* erotomaniac

errance [ɛrɑ̃s] *nf Litt* roving, wandering; **vie d'e.** roving *or* wandering life

errant [ɛrɑ̃] *adj* (*personne, vie etc*) roving, wandering; **chevalier e.** knight errant; **le Juif e.** the Wandering Jew; **chien e.** stray dog; **pensées errantes** wandering thoughts

errata [ɛrata] *nm inv Typ* errata; **feuille d'e.** errata slip

erratique [ɛratik] *adj* erratic

erratum [ɛratɔm], *pl* **errata** *nm Typ* erratum, *pl* errata

erre [ɛr] *nf* **(a)** *Naut* (*lancée*) way; **e. pour gouverner** steerage way; **avoir de l'e.** to have way on; **perdre de l'e.** *ou* **son e.** to lose way **(b) erres** (*d'un cerf etc*) track, spoor, slot; *Fig* **suivre les erres de qn** to follow in sb's footsteps

errement [ɛrmɑ̃] **1** *nm Fin* **é. du marché** market fluctuation **2** *nmpl* **errements** erring *or* bad ways; **retomber dans** *ou* **revenir à ses anciens errements** to fall back into one's bad old ways

errer [ɛre] *vi* **(a)** (*d'un marcheur etc*) to wander (about), to roam, to rove; **e. par les rues** to wander about *or* roam the streets; **e. comme une âme en peine** to wander about like a lost soul; **laisser e. ses pensées** to let one's thoughts wander *or* stray **(b)** *Litt* (*se tromper*) to err, to be mistaken

erreur [ɛrœr] *nf* **(a)** (*faute, inexactitude*) error, mistake; **e. de plume** slip of the pen; **e. de date** mistake in the date; **e. de jugement** error of judgment; **e. de sens** wrong meaning; **faire** *ou* **commettre une e.** to make a mistake; **faire e.** to be mistaken; **par e.** by mistake; **sauf e.** if I am not mistaken; **sauf e. ou omission** errors and omissions excepted; **il y a e. sur la personne** you've/they've/*etc* got the wrong person; **il n'y a pas d'e. (possible)** there's no doubt about it; *F* **c'est un malin, pas d'e.** he's a smart one and no mistake; **e.!** wrong!, not so!

(b) (*opinion fausse*) error; **être dans l'e.** to be under a misapprehension, to be mistaken; **induire qn en e.** to mislead sb

(c) (*action regrettable ou blâmable*) error; **revenir de ses erreurs** to turn over a new leaf

(d) *Ordinat* error; **message d'e.** error message; **correction des erreurs** error correction

▶ **erreur:** *Ordinat* **e. d'analyse (syntaxique)** parse error; *Ordinat* **e. d'arrondi** rounding error; **e. de calcul** miscalculation; **e. d'échantillonnage** sampling error; *Ordinat* **e. d'écriture** write error; *Ordinat* **e. d'entrée** input error; *Ordinat* **e. disque** disk error; **e. de jeunesse** youthful error; **e. judiciaire** miscarriage of justice; *Ordinat* **e. de lecture** read error; *Ordinat* **e. de logiciel** software *or* system error; *Ordinat* **e. de parité** parity error; *Ordinat* **e. de programmation** program *or* programming error; *Ordinat* **e. de saisie** keyboarding error; *Ordinat* **e. de syntaxe** syntax error; **e. typographique** printing error; (*coquille*) misprint

erroné [erɔne] *adj* (*déclaration etc*) erroneous

erronément [erɔnemɑ̃] *adv* erroneously

ersatz [ɛrzats] *nm inv* ersatz, substitute; **e. de café/littérature** ersatz coffee/literature

erse[1] [ɛrs] *adj, nm Ling* Erse

erse[2] *nf Naut* grummet, grommet

éructation [eryktasjɔ̃] *nf* belch

éructer [erykte] **1** *vi* to belch **2** *vt Fig* **é. des injures** to hurl abuse

érudit, -ite [erydi, -it] **1** *adj* erudite, scholarly, learned **2** *n* scholar

érudition [erydisjɔ̃] *nf* erudition, learning, scholarship; **discourir avec é.** to talk learnedly

éruptif, -ive [eryptif, -iv] *adj* (*maladie, roche etc*) eruptive

éruption [erypsjɔ̃] *nf* **(a)** (*d'un volcan*) eruption; **faire é., entrer en é.** to erupt **(b) é. dentaire** *ou* **des dents** cutting of teeth **(c)** *Méd* rash, eruption **(d)** *Fig* (*de colère, joie etc*) eruption, outburst

érysipèle [erizipɛl] *nm Méd* erysipelas

érythème [eritɛm] *nm Méd* rash, *Spéc* erythema; **é. fessier** nappy *or Am* diaper rash; **é. solaire** sunburn

Érythrée [eritre] *nf* Eritrea

E/S *abrév Ordinat* **(entrée/sortie)** I/O

ès [ɛs] *prép* (= **en les**) **docteur ès lettres/sciences** ≈ PhD, DPhil; **licencié(e) ès lettres/sciences** ≈ Bachelor of Arts/ Science, BA/BSc; *Admin, Jur* **ès qualités** ex officio

esbroufe [ɛzbruf] *nf F* bluff(ing); **faire de l'e., y aller à l'e.** to bluff; **avoir qn à l'e.** to bluff sb

esbroufer [ɛzbrufe] *vt F* to bluff

esbroufeur, -euse [ɛzbrufœr, -øz] *n F* bluffer

escabeau, -eaux [ɛskabo] *nm* **(a)** (*tabouret*) (wooden) stool **(b)** (*marchepied*) stepladder, *Br* (pair of) steps; **e. de bibliothèque** library steps

escadre [ɛskadr] *nf Naut* squadron; *Av* **e. aérienne** wing; **chef d'e.** *Naut* squadron commander; *Av* wing commander

escadrille [ɛskadrij] *nf* **(a)** *Naut* flotilla **(b)** *Av* (*unité*) flight

escadron [ɛskadrɔ̃] *nm* **(a)** *Mil* squadron; **e. de chars** armoured squadron; **chef d'escadron(s)** major **(b)** *Av* squadron; **e. de chasse/bombardement** fighter/bomber squadron **(c)** *Fig* (*groupe*) (*de touristes, journalistes etc*) troop, band

escalade [ɛskalad] *nf* **(a)** (*action*) (*d'un mur, d'une falaise etc*) climbing, scaling; *Sp* (rock)climbing; **faire de l'e.** to go (rock)climbing **(b)** (*parcours*) climb **(c)** (*d'une guerre, des prix, de la violence etc*) escalation; **les charges locatives n'ont pas cessé leur e.** service charges are still escalating; **on a remarqué son e. verbale** it was noted that he got more and more carried away as he spoke

▶ **escalade**: *Sp* **e. libre** free climbing

escalader [ɛskalade] *vt* to climb, to scale; *Hist, Mil* (*forteresse*) to escalade

escalator [ɛskalatɔr] *nm* escalator

escale [ɛskal] *nf* **(a)** (*temps d'arrêt*) *Naut* call; *Av* stop(over), layover; **faire e.** *Naut* to put into port; *Av* to touch down; **faire e. à Londres** *Naut* to put in *or* call at London; *Av* to stop over at London; *Av* **escales prévues** scheduled stops; **vol sans e.** nonstop flight; **une e. de quatre heures** *Naut* a four-hour call; *Av* a four-hour stop(over) **(b)** (*lieu*) *Naut* port *or* place of call; *Av* stop(over)

escalier [ɛskalje] *nm* **(a)** [①**A10**,f,i] (*marches*) (flight of) stairs; (*cage*) staircase; **rencontrer qn dans l'e.** *ou* **dans les escaliers** to meet sb on the stairs; *Fig* **j'ai l'esprit de l'e.** I always think of an answer when it's too late; *Ski* **monter en e.** to sidestep; *Fig F* **avoir des escaliers dans les cheveux** to have unevenly cut hair **(b)** *MecE* step; **en e.** stepped **(c)** *Typ* (*de titres*) step effect; **courbe en e.** jaggy

▶ **escalier**: *Naut* **e. des cabines** companionway; **e. en colimaçon** spiral staircase; **e. d'honneur** main *or* grand staircase; **e. mécanique** escalator, *Can* **e. mobile** escalator; **e. roulant** escalator; **e. de secours** fire escape; **e. de service** backstairs; **e. à vis** spiral staircase

escalope [ɛskalɔp] *nf Culin* escalope

escamotable [ɛskamɔtabl] *adj* (*antenne, Av train d'atterrissage*) retractable; (*meuble*) foldaway, collapsible; *Aut* (*phares*) retractable

escamotage [ɛskamɔtaʒ] *nm* **(a)** (*par un illusionniste*) conjuring away, vanishing; **tour d'é.** vanishing trick **(b)** *Fig* (*d'une tâche*) skipping; (*d'un problème, d'une question*) dodging **(c)** *Av* (*d'un train d'atterrissage*) retraction **(d)** (*vol*) stealing

escamoter [ɛskamɔte] *vt* **(a)** (*d'un illusionniste*) to conjure away, to make vanish **(b)** *Fig* (*éviter*) (*tâche*) to skip; (*problème, question*) to dodge **(c)** *Av* (*train d'atterrissage*) to retract **(d)** (*voler*) to sneak off with, to steal; **on m'a escamoté ma montre** someone's sneaked off with *or* stolen my watch

escamoteur, -euse [ɛskamɔtœr, -øz] *n* **(a)** (*illusionniste*) conjuror **(b)** (*voleur*) sneak thief

escampette [ɛskɑ̃pɛt] *nf F* **prendre la poudre d'e.** (*s'enfuir*) to make off, *Br* to do a bunk

escapade [ɛskapad] *nf* (*excursion*) jaunt; (*fugue*) running off *or* away; **faire une e.** to run off *or* away

escarbille [ɛskarbij] *nf* cinder

escarboucle [ɛskarbukl] *nf* (*pierre précieuse*) carbuncle

escarcelle [ɛskarsɛl] *nf* **tomber dans l'e. de qn** (*de l'argent, d'une collection de tableaux etc*) to come sb's way; (*de la direction d'une entreprise etc*) to end up *or* wind up in sb's hands; **tout le département est tombé dans l'e. des socialistes** the whole department ended up *or* wound up in the hands of the socialists

escargot [ɛskargo] *nm* snail; **allure d'e.** snail's pace; *F* **il marche comme un e.** he's walking at a snail's pace; **nous avancions à la vitesse d'un e.** we were moving at a snail's pace; *Fig* **opération e.** slowing down of the traffic (*by protesting truck drivers*)

escargotière [ɛskargɔtjer] *nf* **(a)** (*parc*) snailery **(b)** (*plat*) snail dish

escarmouche [ɛskarmuʃ] *nf* skirmish

escarpé [ɛskarpe] *adj* (*route, montagne, pente*) steep; (*falaise*) sheer

escarpement [ɛskarpəmɑ̃] *nm* (*versant*) steep slope; *Géog* escarpment; *Géog* **e. de faille** fault scarp

escarpin [ɛskarpɛ̃] *nm* pump, *Br* court shoe; (*pour danser*) pump

escarpolette [ɛskarpɔlɛt] *nf Vieilli* (*balançoire*) swing

escarre, eschare [ɛskar] *nf Méd* scab; (*dû aux draps etc*) bedsore

Escaut (l') [lɛsko] *nm* the Scheldt

eschatologie [ɛskatɔlɔʒi] *nf* eschatology

Éschyle [eʃil] *nm* Aeschylus

escient [ɛsjɑ̃] *nm* **à bon e.** wisely, judiciously; **à mauvais e.** unwisely

esclaffer (s') [sɛsklafe] *vpr* to burst out laughing, to roar with laughter, to guffaw

esclandre [ɛsklɑ̃dr] *nm* (*scandale, tapage*) (noisy) scene; **faire** *ou* **causer un e., faire de l'e.** to make a scene

esclavage [ɛsklavaʒ] *nm* (*état*) slavery; (*action*) enslavement; **réduire qn en e.** to enslave sb, to reduce sb to slavery; *Fig* **l'e. du bureau** the drudgery of the office; *F* **mais c'est de l'e.!** (*exploitation*) but it's slave labour!

esclavagisme [ɛsklavaʒism] *nm* slavery; (*doctrine*) pro-slavery

esclavagiste [ɛsklavaʒist] **1** *n* pro-slaver **2** *adj* **état e.** slave state

esclave [ɛsklav] **1** *n* slave; **marchand d'esclaves** slave trader; **il fut vendu comme e.** he was sold into slavery; *Fig* **elle est l'e. de sa famille** she is a slave to her family; *Fig* **être l'e. de la mode/de son travail** to be a slave to fashion/one's work **2** *adj* **être e. de ses habitudes** to be a slave to *or* the slave of one's habits

escogriffe [ɛskɔgrif] *nm* **(grand) e.** (*homme grand*) beanpole

escomptable [ɛskɔ̃tabl] *adj Compta* discountable

escompte [ɛskɔ̃t] *nm* **(a)** *Com* discount; **accorder** *ou* **faire un e. sur les prix** to allow *or* give a discount on the prices; **maison d'e.** cut-price *or* discount store; **à e.** at a discount; *Can* **50% d'e. sur toute la marchandise** 50% discount on all goods; **e. professionnel** (*au détaillant*) trade discount; **e. sur les achats en gros** *ou* **en quantité** volume purchase discount, quantity *or* bulk discount; **e. à forfait** forfaiting

(b) *Fin* **e. (de banque)** discount; **e. officiel, taux d'e.** (bank) discount rate; **e. de caisse** *ou* **au comptant** cash discount; **e. commercial** trade discount; **e. de règlement** discount for early payment, settlement discount; **prendre à l'e. un effet de commerce** to discount a bill of exchange

escompter [ɛskɔ̃te] *vt* **(a)** *Fin* (*traite*) to discount **(b)** (*s'attendre à*) to expect, to anticipate (**que** that); **e. une hausse** to anticipate an increase; **e. faire** to expect to do, to anticipate doing; **le succès escompté** the expected *or* anticipated success

escorte [ɛskɔrt] *nf Mil, Naut etc* escort; **faire e. à qn** to escort sb; **sous (bonne) e.** under escort; **conduire un prisonnier sous (bonne) e.** to escort a prisoner; *Naut* **sous l'e. d'une corvette** convoyed *or* escorted by a corvette

escorter [ɛskɔrte] *vt* to escort; *Naut* to convoy, to escort

escorteur [ɛskɔrtœr] *nm Naut* escort (vessel)

escouade [ɛskwad] *nf* **(a)** (*d'ouvriers*) squad, gang; (*de touristes, jeunes gens etc*) group **(b)** *Hist, Mil* squad

escrime [ɛskrim] *nf Sp* fencing; **faire de l'e.** to fence

escrimer (s') [sɛskrime] *vpr* to fight; **s'e. à faire qch** to do all one can to do sth, to try very hard to do sth

escrimeur, -euse [ɛskrimœr, -øz] *n Sp* fencer

escroc [ɛskro] *nm* swindler, crook

escroquer [ɛskrɔke] *vt* (*qn*) to swindle, to cheat, to trick; **e. qch à qn, e. qn de qch** to swindle *or* to cheat *or* to trick sb out of sth

escroquerie [ɛskrɔkri] *nf* (*action*) swindling; (*résultat*) swindle; *Jur* (*délit*) fraud; **mais c'est de l'e.!** it's a swindle, *Br* it's daylight robbery!

escudo [ɛskydo] *nm* (*monnaie*) escudo

esgourde [ɛsgurd] *nf Arg* ear, *Br* lughole

eskimo [ɛskimo] **1** *adj inv* Eskimo, *Am* Inuit; **les coutumes eskimos** Eskimo customs **2** *nm Ling* Eskimo **3** *n* **E.** Eskimo

Ésope [ezɔp] *nm* Aesop

ésotérique [ezɔterik] *adj* esoteric

ésotérisme [ezɔterism] *nm* esotericism

espace [ɛspas] **1** *nm* **(a)** (*étendue, distance*) space; **laisser de l'e.** to leave space *or* room; **un e. de dix mètres entre deux choses** a distance *or* space *or* gap of ten metres between two things; **laisser un e. entre deux mots** to leave a space between two words; **l'e. parcouru** the distance covered

(b) (*durée*) **pendant le même e. de temps** in the same space of time; **en l'e. d'une semaine** within a week

(c) (*vide*), *Astron* space; **regarder dans l'e.** to stare into space; **e. extra-atmosphérique** outer space; **vol** *ou* **voyage dans l'e.** space flight

(d) *Géom* space; **e. à trois/quatre dimensions** three-/four-dimensional space

(e) *Ordinat* **e. disque** disk space; **e. insécable** hard space; **e. mémoire** memory space; **e. ressort** soft space; **e. de stockage** storage space

(f) *Mktg* **e. d'exposition** display area; **e. de PLV** in-store advertising space

2 *nf Typ* space; **e. fine/moyenne/forte** hair/middle/thick space

▶ **espace**: **e. aérien** airspace; *Typ* **e. blanc** space; *Com* **e. cargo** cargo space; *TV, Cin* **e. filmique** filmic space; *Admin* **e. judiciaire européen** common European legal framework; **e. mort** dead space; *Aut* clearance volume; **e. publicitaire** advertising space; **e. de rangement** storage space; **e. de rayonnage** shelf space; **e. social européen** common European social legislation; **e. vital** living space; **espaces verts** green spaces

espacement [ɛspasmɑ̃] *nm* **(a)** (*action*) spacing out; (*résultat*) spacing; (*distance*) space, distance; *Ordinat* **e. arrière** backspace; *Aut* **e. des sièges** seat pitch; **barre d'e.** (*d'une machine à écrire etc*) space bar **(b)** *Typ* spacing; **e. des caractères/lignes** character/line spacing; **e. fixe/proportionnel** fixed/proportional spacing

espacer [ɛspase] **(j'espaçai(s)) 1** *vt* (*objets, lignes, paiements, visites etc*) to space out; **e. des choses d'un mètre** to space things out a metre apart; **il faut e. nos rencontres** we must meet less often **2 s'espacer** *vpr* **(a)** (*de visites, lettres, cris etc*) to become less frequent **(b)** (*de personnes*) **espacez-vous** space yourselves out

espace-temps *nm inv Math, Phys* space-time (continuum)

espadon [ɛspadɔ̃] *nm* swordfish

espadrille [ɛspadrij] *nf* espadrille, rope-soled sandal

Espagne [ɛspaɲ] *nf* Spain

espagnol, -ole [ɛspaɲɔl] [①A20,d] **1** *adj* Spanish **2** *nm Ling* Spanish **3** *n* **E.** Spaniard; **les Espagnols** the Spanish, the Spaniards

espagnolette [ɛspaɲɔlɛt] *nf* (window) fastener (*long vertical bar with pivoting central catch*)

espalier [ɛspalje] *nm* **(a)** (*mur*) wall (*for espaliers*); **(arbre en) e.** espalier **(b)** *Gym* wall bars

espar [ɛspar] *nm Naut* spar

espèce [ɛspɛs] *nf* **(a)** (*sorte*) kind, sort; **gens/livres de toute e.** people/books of all kinds *or* of every description; **il portait une e. de chemise à fleurs** he wore a kind *or* a sort of flowery shirt; **cela n'a aucune e. d'importance** that's of no importance whatsoever, that's not at all important; *F* **cette e. d'idiot** that stupid idiot, that silly fool; *F* **e. d'idiot!** you idiot!; *F* **une e. de mec bizarre** a strange sort of guy; *Péj* **l'e. de blonde qui lui sert de femme** that blonde he calls his wife; **des gens de son e.** people like him, people of his kind *or* sort; **un escroc/menteur/avare de la pire e.** a crook/liar/miser of the worst sort *or* kind, the worst sort *or* kind of crook/liar/miser

(b) *Jur* **cas d'e.** specific case; **loi applicable en l'e.** law applicable to the case in point; *Fig F* **je suis un cas d'e.** I'm a special case

(c) espèces (*argent*) cash; *Hist* (*monnaie métallique*) coin; **payer en espèces** to pay in cash; **espèces sonnantes et trébuchantes** hard cash; *Compta* **espèces en caisse** cash in hand

(d) [①A13,3,b] *Bot, Zool* species; **l'e. humaine** the human race, mankind; **e. en voie de disparition** endangered species

(e) *Rel* (Eucharistic) species

espérance [ɛsperɑ̃s] *nf* hope; **vivre dans l'e.** to live in hope; **dans l'e. de faire** in the hope of doing; **dans l'e. que** in the hope that; **contre toute e.** against *or* contrary to all expectation; **au-delà de nos espérances** beyond our expectations, beyond expectation; **fonder son e. sur qn/qch** to found one's hopes on sb/sth; **mettre ses espérances en qch** to pin one's hopes on sth; **l'affaire n'a pas répondu à nos espérances** the business did not come up *or* live up to our expectations; **cet enfant donne de grandes espérances** this child shows great promise *or* is very promising; *Hum* **avoir des espérances** to have expectations (*of an inheritance*); **tu es toute mon e.** you are my only hope

▶ **espérance**: **e. de vie** life expectancy

espérantiste [ɛsperɑ̃tist] *Ling* **1** *n* Esperantist **2** *adj* (*société etc*) Esperanto

espéranto [ɛsperɑ̃to] *nm Ling* Esperanto

espérer [ɛspere] **(j'espère; j'espérerai) 1** *vt* (*qch*) to hope for; (*s'attendre à*) (*qn, qch*) to expect; **j'espère vous revoir** I hope to see *or* I'll see you again; **j'espère qu'il viendra** I hope that he comes *or* will come; **je n'espère pas qu'il vienne** I don't expect him to come; **je ne vous espérais plus** I had given you up, I wasn't expecting you to come any more **2** *vi* **(a) e. en Dieu** to trust in God **(b) j'espère bien** I hope so; **espérons!** let's hope so!

esperluète, esperluette [ɛspɛrlɥɛt] *nf* ampersand

espiègle [ɛspjɛgl] **1** *adj* (*enfant, réponse etc*) mischievous **2** *n* (*enfant*) imp; **petit(e) e.** little monkey

espièglerie [ɛspjɛgləri] *nf* **(a)** (*caractère*) mischievousness; **par pure e.** out of pure mischief **(b)** (*tour*) prank

espion, -ionne [ɛspjɔ̃, -jɔn] *n* (*d'une puissance étrangère*) spy, secret agent; (*de police*), *Fig* spy; **avion-/satellite-e.** spy plane/satellite

espionnage [ɛspjɔnaʒ] *nm* espionage, spying; **faire de l'e.** to spy; **réseau/roman d'e.** spy network/novel; **l'e. industriel** industrial espionage

espionner [ɛspjɔne] **1** *vt* (*qn, les mouvements de qn etc*) to spy on **2** *vi* to spy

espionnite [ɛspjɔnit] *nf F Hum* spy fever

esplanade [ɛsplanad] *nf* esplanade

espoir [ɛspwar] *nm* **(a)** (*espérance*) hope; **avoir l'e. de faire qch** to have hopes of *or* to be hopeful of doing sth; **avoir de l'e.** to have hope(s); **dans l'e. de vous revoir** in the hope of seeing you again; **avoir bon e.** to be full of hope; **reprendre e.** to be *or* become hopeful again; **mettre son e. en qch/qn** to put one's hopes in *or* to pin one's hopes on sth/sb; **nourrir l'e. de faire qch** to live in hope of doing sth; **c'est sans e.** it's hopeless; **il n'y a plus d'e.** there's no hope any more, all hope is gone *or* lost; **tous les espoirs sont permis** things look hopeful; *Prov Iron* **l'e. fait vivre** hope springs eternal

(b) (*personne, chose*) hope; **vous êtes/ce plan est leur seul e.** you are/this plan is their only hope; **un e. du tennis français/de la chanson française** one of the most promising French tennis players/French singers; **ce sont les espoirs du patinage artistique** they are the most promising figure skaters around

esprit [ɛspri] *nm* **(a)** (*intellectuel*) mind; **d'e. lent** slow-witted; **d'e. vif** quick-witted; **avoir l'e. large/étroit** to be broad-/narrow-minded; **avoir l'e. tranquille** to be easy in one's mind; **avoir l'e. libre** to have a clear mind; **avoir l'e. mal tourné** to have a dirty mind; **perdre l'e.** to go out of one's mind; **elle avait l'e. ailleurs** her thoughts were *or* her mind was elsewhere; **où aviez-vous l'e.?** what were you thinking of?; **c'est une vue de l'e.** that's theoretical *or* all theory; **présence d'e.** presence of mind; **ça m'est sorti de l'e.** it slipped my mind, it went clean out of my head; **qu'avez-vous à l'e.?** what are you thinking of?; **elle n'avait pas l'e. à ce qu'elle faisait** her mind wasn't on *or* she didn't have her mind on what she was doing; **je n'ai pas l'e. à plaisanter ce matin** I'm not in the mood for joking *or* in a joking mood this morning; *Hum* **l'e. est fort mais la chair est faible** the spirit is willing but the flesh is weak; **une pareille idée ne me serait jamais venue à l'e.** such an idea would never have occurred to me *or* crossed my mind *or* entered my head; **dans mon e., ça ne veut pas dire la même chose** to my mind that doesn't mean the same thing; **dans mon e., ils arrivaient demain** I thought they were coming tomorrow; **avoir l'e. de se taire** to have the (good) sense to be silent; **perdre/reprendre ses esprits** to lose/regain consciousness

(b) (*attitude, qualité*) spirit; **e. de compétition** competitive spirit; **e. d'entreprise** enterprise spirit, spirit of enterprise; **avoir bon e.** to be good-natured; **faire du mauvais e.** to be negative; **je n'ai pas l'e. de sacrifice** I'm not the sort to make sacrifices; **avoir l'e. d'analyse/scientifique** to have an analytical/a scientific (turn of) mind

(c) (*humour*) wit; **avoir de l'e.** to be witty; **mots** *ou* **traits d'e.** witticisms, witty remarks; **faire de l'e.** to display one's wit

(d) (*personne*) person; **un e. dangereux** a dangerous person *or* man/woman; **un e. fort** a freethinker; **les grands esprits de notre siècle** the great minds of our century; *Prov* **les grands esprits se rencontrent** great minds think alike

(e) (*sens*) spirit; **s'attacher à l'e. de la loi plutôt qu'à la lettre** to go by the spirit of the law rather than the letter; **c'est dans cet e. qu'a été conçue cette organisation** it is in this spirit that the organization was conceived

(f) (*désincarné*) spirit; (*fantôme*) spirit (of the dead), ghost; **le Saint-E., l'E. saint** the Holy Ghost, the Holy Spirit; *Hum* **je ne suis pas un pur e., il faut bien que je mange** I'm flesh and blood, I do have to eat; **l'e. malin** the Evil One; **e., es-tu là?** (*dans une séance de spiritisme*) is there anybody there?

(g) *Ch etc* (volatile) spirit

(h) *Méd Arch* **esprits animaux** animal spirits

▶ **esprit**: **e.-de-bois** wood alcohol; **e. brut** raw spirits; **e. de caste** class consciousness; **e. de chapelle** cliquishness; **e. de clan** clannishness; **e. de clocher** parochialism; **e. de corps** esprit de corps; **e. d'équipe** team spirit; **e. de famille** family feeling; **e. frappeur** spirit-rapper; **e.-de-sel** spirits of salt; **e.-de-vin** spirits of wine

esquif [ɛskif] *nm Litt* (*embarcation*) skiff; **frêle e.** frail barque *or* vessel

esquille [ɛskij] *nf* splinter (of bone)

esquimau, -aude, -aux [ɛskimo, -od, -o] **1** *adj* (*occ inv in feminine*) Eskimo, *Can* Inuit, *Can Péj* Eskimo; **chien e.** husky **2** *n* **E.** Eskimo, *Can* Inuit, *Can Péj* Eskimo **3** *nm* **(a)** (*glace*) **e.** ® ≈ choc-ice (*on a stick*), *Am* ≈ ice-cream bar, Eskimo Pie® **(b)** *Ling* Eskimo, *Can* Inuit, *Can Péj* Eskimo

esquimautage [ɛskimotaʒ] *nm Sp* (canoe) roll

esquintant [ɛskɛ̃tɑ̃] *adj F* (*travail, voyage etc*) exhausting, tiring; (*personne*) tiresome

esquinter [ɛskɛ̃te] *F* **1** *vt* **(a)** (*fatiguer*) to do in, to wear out **(b)** (*abîmer*) (*montre, outil etc*) to do in, to ruin; (*voiture etc*) to bash up, *Br* to prang; (*blesser*) to do in; **il a eu le bras esquinté dans sa chute** he did his arm in when he fell **(c)** (*critiquer*) (*auteur, film etc*) to slam, *Br* to slate **2 s'esquinter** *vpr* **(a)** (*se fatiguer*) to do oneself in, to wear oneself out (**à faire** doing) **(b)** (*s'abîmer*) **s'e. la santé/les yeux** to ruin one's health/eyes (**à faire** doing); **je me suis esquinté la jambe en tombant** I did my leg in when I fell

esquisse [ɛskis] *nf Beaux-Arts* (rough) sketch; *Typ* (*de page*) rough layout; *Fig* (*d'un projet, d'un roman etc*) sketch, outline; *Fig* **l'e. d'un sourire** the ghost *or* suggestion of a smile; *Fig* **l'e. d'une aide de la part du gouvernement** the tiniest amount of aid from the government

esquisser [ɛskise] **1** *vt* (*portrait etc*) to sketch; *Fig* (*plan, roman, personnage etc*) to sketch, to outline; *Fig* **e. un sourire** to give a slight smile; *Fig* **e. un geste** to make a slight gesture; *Fig* **e. un geste de la main** to give a slight wave, to sketch a wave **2 s'esquisser** *vpr* **un sourire s'esquissa sur son visage** he gave a slight smile; *Fig* **un plan commençait à s'e. dans mon esprit** a plan started to take shape in my mind

esquive [ɛskiv] *nf Sp etc* (*mouvement*) dodge; *Fig* (*d'une question, d'un problème etc*) dodging, evasion; *Boxe etc* **e. de la tête** dodge

esquiver [ɛskive] **1** *vt* (*coup, Fig question, problème, devoir, créancier etc*) to avoid, to dodge, to evade **2** *vi* **e. (de la tête)** to dodge **3 s'esquiver** *vpr* to slip away *or* off, to make oneself scarce

essai [esɛ] *nm* **(a)** (*test, épreuve*) (*d'un produit, d'une machine, d'une voiture etc*) test, trial; *Com* **à l'e.** on a trial basis; **faire l'e. de qch** to test sth, to try sth out; **faites un e. avant de vous décider** try it out before you decide; **mettre qn/qch à l'e.** to put sb/sth to the test; **prendre qch/qn à l'e.** to take sth/sb on trial, to take sth on approval/sb on probation; **pilote d'e.** test pilot; *Cin* **bout d'e.** screen test

(b) (*tentative*) attempt, try; **faire un e.** to have a try, to make an attempt; **elle fait des essais de jardinage plutôt infructueux** she makes rather fruitless attempts at gardening; **au premier e.** at the first attempt *or* try; **coup d'e.** trial go *or* attempt

(c) *Littér* essay

(d) *Métal* (*de l'or, de l'argent*) assay(ing); **fourneau d'e.** assay furnace

(e) *Rugby* try; **marquer un e.** to score a try; **transformer un e. (en but)** to convert a try

▶ **essai**: *Ordinat* **e. approfondi** beta test; *TV, Cin* **e. (de) caméra** camera test; **e. à banc** bench test; *Aut* **e. de chute** drop test; *Aut* **e. de collision frontale CE** EC frontal impact test; *MecE* **e. en endurance** endurance test; *Mktg* **e. gratuit** free trial; *TV, Cin* **e. image** test shot; **e. nucléaire** nuclear test; *Ordinat* **e. de performance** benchmark; *Ordinat* **e. préliminaire** alphatest; **essais de produit** product testing; *Aut* **e. routier** *ou* **sur route** road test; *TV, Rad* **e. de voix** voice test; *Av* **essais en vol** test flights

essaim [esɛ̃] *nm* (*d'abeilles, d'étudiants etc*) swarm; (*de filles*) bevy

essaimage [esɛmaʒ] *nm* **(a)** (*d'abeilles*) swarming; *Fig* (*de la population, d'une famille*) spreading; *Fig* **l'e. de notre entreprise** the expansion of our firm's branch network **(b)** (*époque*) swarming time

essaimer [eseme] **1** *vi* (*des abeilles*) to swarm; *Fig* (*d'une population, d'une famille*) to spread; (*d'une firme*) to expand **2** *vt* (*d'une firme*) (*usines, filiales etc*) spread

essayage [esɛjaʒ] *nm* (*de vêtements, chaussures etc*) trying on, fitting; **on fera les rectifications après le deuxième e.** adjustments will be made after the second fitting; **cabine** *ou* **salon d'e.** fitting room

essayer [eseje] (**j'essaie, j'essaye, n. essayons; j'essaierai, j'essayerai**) **1** *vt* **(a)** (*tester*) (*machine, produit etc*) to test, to try out; (*pour la première fois, avant d'acheter etc*) (*nouveau gadget, restaurant, coiffeur etc*) to try (out); (*voiture*) to test-drive, to try out; (*vin, plat etc*) to try, to taste; (*vêtements, chaussures etc*) to try on; (*utiliser*) (*remède, politesse, sa force etc*) to try

(b) [ⓘ**A43**,b,ii] (*tenter*) **e. de faire qch** to try *or* attempt to do sth; **n'essaie pas de me mentir** don't try lying *or* to lie to me; **essayez de l'attraper** try to *or* and catch it; **laissez-moi e.** let me (have a) try; **sois courageux! – on va e.!** be brave! – I'll try!; **e. les maths/les agences matrimoniales** to try maths/the marriage bureaux

(c) *Métal* (*minerai*) to assay

2 s'essayer *vpr* **s'e. à qch/à faire qch** to try one's hand *or* one's skill at sth/at doing sth

essayeur, -euse [esɛjœr, -øz] *n* **(a)** (*de vêtements*) fitter **(b)** (*d'une machine, d'un produit etc*) tester **(c)** (*d'or, d'argent*) assayer

essayiste [esejist] *n* essayist

esse [ɛs] *nf* **(a)** (*crochet*) S-hook **(b)** (*cheville d'essieu*) linchpin **(c)** (*de violon etc*) f-hole, sound hole

essence [esɑ̃s] *nf* **(a)** *Aut* petrol, *Am* gas, gasoline; **à essence** petrol-powered; **poste d'e.** filling station, petrol *or Am* gas station; *F* **faire de l'e.** to fill up **(b)** (*extrait*) (*de plante, café, viande etc*) essence; **e. de citron** lemon oil; **e. de roses** rose oil, attar of roses **(c)** (*caractère fondamental*), *Phil* essence; **par e.** essentially **(d)** (*espèce*) (*d'arbre*) species; **essences résineuses** resinous trees, conifers

▶ **essence**: **e. à faible indice d'octane** low-octane petrol; **e. à indice d'octane élevé** high-octane petrol; **e. ordinaire** two-star petrol, *Am* regular gas; **e. sans plomb** unleaded (petrol *or Am* gas), lead-free petrol *or* gas; **e. de térébenthine** oil *or* spirits of turpentine

essentiel, -ielle [esɑ̃sjɛl] **1** *adj* **(a)** (*fondamental*) (*vérité, caractère etc*) essential; (*raison*) basic, main

(b) (*nécessaire*) essential, necessary (**à, pour** for); **il est e. d'avoir compris ce point** it is essential *or* necessary to have understood this point

(c) (*très important*) essential; **il est e. d'avoir lu ce livre** it is essential to have read this book

2 *nm* **l'e.** (*le point central*) the main point; (*les points centraux*) the main points; (*la majeure partie*) the main *or* greater part (**de** of); **l'e. des effectifs est resté à la base** the greater part *or* most of the men stayed at base; **n'apportez que l'e.** bring only the (bare) essentials *or* the basics; **l'e. est d'agir/que tu lui parles** the main *or* important thing is to act/that you talk to him; **vous avez la santé, c'est l'e.** you're healthy, that's the main *or* important thing

essentiellement [esɑ̃sjɛlmɑ̃] *adv* **(a)** (*par nature*) essentially, fundamentally **(b)** (*principalement*) essentially, mainly; (*avant tout*) above all

esseulé [esœle] *adj* (*abandonné*) alone; (*solitaire*) lonely

essieu, -ieux [esjø] *nm* axle; (*de chariot*) axle tree; **e. avant/arrière** front/rear axle; **e. fixe** dead axle

essor [esɔr] *nm* (**a**) (*d'un oiseau*) flight; **prendre son e.** to fly off *or* away (**b**) *Fig* (*d'une industrie, d'une économie, d'un pays etc*) (rapid) growth, expansion; **e. économique** economic expansion; **prendre son e.** to take off; **prendre un grand e.** to grow *or* expand very rapidly; **industrie en plein e.** booming *or* fast-growing industry; **donner un nouvel e. à qch** to give a lift *or* boost to sth; **l'économie connaît un nouvel e.** the economy is experiencing a new boom *or* is expanding rapidly again

essorage [esɔraʒ] *nm* (*de linge*) spin-drying; (*à la main, avec une essoreuse à rouleaux*) wringing

essorer [esɔre] *vt* (*vêtements*) to spin(-dry); (*à la main, avec une essoreuse à rouleaux*) to wring; (*salade*) to spin

essoreuse [esɔrøz] *nf* spin-dryer; **e. à rouleau** wringer, mangle; **e. à salade** salad spinner

essoufflé [esufle] *adj* out of breath, short of breath, winded

essoufflement [esufləmɑ̃] *nm* shortness of breath, breathlessness; *Fig* **en raison de l'e. de l'économie** because the economy is running out of steam

essouffler [esufle] **1** *vt* (*qn, cheval*) to wind, to make out of breath **2 s'essouffler** *vpr* to get out of breath *or F* puff; *Fig* (*d'un roman, d'une personne créative, de l'économie etc*) to run out of steam; *Fig* **s'e. à faire qch** to struggle to do sth

essuie-glace, *pl* **essuie-glaces** [esɥiglas] *nm Aut* windscreen *or Am* windshield wiper; **e. arrière** rear wiper; **e. deux vitesses** two-speed wiper; **e. intermittent à plusieurs vitesses** variable speed intermittent wiper

essuie-main(s) [esɥimɛ̃] *nm inv* hand towel

essuie-meubles [esɥimœbl] *nm inv* duster

essuie-phare, *pl* **essuie-phares** [ɛsɥifar] *nm* headlamp wiper

essuie-pieds [esɥipje] *nm inv* doormat

essuie-tout [esɥitu] *nm inv* kitchen paper

essuie-verres [esɥivɛr] *nm inv* glass cloth

essuie-vitre, *pl* **essuie-vitres** [ɛsɥivitr] *nm* windscreen *or Am* windshield wiper

essuyage [esɥijaʒ] *nm* (*de vaisselle*) wiping, drying; (*d'une surface mouillée*) wiping (down); (*d'eau etc*) wiping up, mopping up; (*nettoyage*) wiping (clean); (*époussetage*) dusting

essuyer [esɥije] **(j'essuie; j'essuierai) 1** *vt* (**a**) (*sécher*) (*assiettes etc*) to wipe, to dry; (*surface*) to wipe (down); (*nettoyer*) to wipe (clean); (*épousseter*) to dust; (*éponger*) (*liquide*) to wipe up, to mop up; (*larmes*) to wipe away; **e. la vaisselle** to dry the dishes, to dry up; **e. ses pieds avant d'entrer** to wipe one's feet before going/coming in

(**b**) (*subir*) (*défaite, perte*) to suffer; (*insultes, reproches etc*) to suffer, to endure, to be subjected to; **e. un refus** to meet with a refusal; **e. le feu de l'ennemi** to come under enemy fire; **e. une tempête** to weather a storm

2 s'essuyer *vpr* to wipe oneself, to dry oneself; **s'e. les pieds/la bouche/les yeux** to wipe one's feet/mouth/eyes

est[1] [ɛ] *voir* **être**[2]

est[2] [ɛst] **1** *nm* east; **un vent d'e.** an easterly wind; **le vent d'e.** the east wind; **à l'e. de Suez** (to the) east of Suez; **vers l'e.** eastward, towards the east; *Géog, Pol* **l'E.** the East; *Pol* **le bloc de l'E.** the Eastern bloc; *Pol* **les pays de l'E.** the countries of the Eastern bloc; **l'Allemagne de l'E.** East Germany **2** *adj inv* (*côte, pente, régions etc*) eastern; (*direction*) easterly, eastward

establishment [establiʃmɛnt] *nm Pol* establishment

estacade [ɛstakad] *nf Naut* (*pieux*) stockade; (*jetée*) pier (on piles)

estafette [ɛstafɛt] *nf* (**a**) *Hist* (*courrier*) courier (**b**) *Mil* (*agent de liaison*) liaison officer

estafilade [ɛstafilad] *nf* (*d'un rasoir, d'une épée*) gash

est-allemand, -ande [ɛstalmɑ̃, -ɑ̃d] **1** *adj* East German **2** *n* **E.-A.** East German

estaminet [ɛstaminɛ] *nm* (small) café, bar (*esp in N France and Belgium*)

estampage [ɛstɑ̃paʒ] *nm* (**a**) *Tech* (*d'un métal, d'une pièce, du cuir etc*) stamping (**b**) *F* (*action d'escroquer*) swindling, fleecing; (*résultat*) swindle

estampe [ɛstɑ̃p] *nf* (**a**) (*image*) print; **cabinet des estampes** (*d'une bibliothèque*) print room; *Hum* **tu es allée voir ses estampes japonaises?** did he show you his etchings? (**b**) (*outil*) stamp

estamper [ɛstɑ̃pe] *vt* (**a**) *Tech* (*métal, pièce, cuir etc*) to stamp (**b**) *F* (*escroquer*) to swindle, to fleece

estampeur, -euse [ɛstɑ̃pœr, -øz] *n* (**a**) *Tech* (*personne, outil*) stamper (**b**) *F* (*escroc*) swindler

estampillage [ɛstɑ̃pijaʒ] *nm* (*d'un document etc*) stamping; (*de marchandises*) marking

estampille [ɛstɑ̃pij] *nf* (*sur un document etc*) stamp; (*sur un produit*) mark

estampiller [ɛstɑ̃pije] *vt* (*document etc*) to stamp; (*marchandises*) to mark

este [ɛst] **1** *adj* Estonian **2** *nm Ling* Estonian **3** *n* **E.** Estonian

ester [ɛstɛr] *nm Ch* ester

esthète [ɛstɛt] *n* aesthete, *US* esthete

esthéticien, -ienne [ɛstetisjɛ̃, -jɛn] *n* (**a**) (*spécialiste des soins de beauté*) beautician, beauty specialist (**b**) (*artiste, poète etc*) aesthetician, *US* esthetician

esthétique [ɛstetik] **1** *adj* aesthetic, *US* esthetic; (*beau*) aesthetically *or US* esthetically pleasing; **chirurgie e.** plastic surgery **2** *nf* (*science*) aesthetics, *US* esthetics; (*beauté*) aesthetic *or US* esthetic quality; **ça manque d'e.** it's not very aesthetically *or US* esthetically pleasing

esthétiquement [ɛstetikmɑ̃] *adv* aesthetically, *US* esthetically

esthétisme [ɛstetism] *nm* aestheticism, *US* estheticism

estimable [ɛstimabl] *adj* (**a**) (*honorable*) (*personne, qualité*) estimable (**b**) (*assez bon*) (*travail, artiste etc*) fairly good (**c**) (*calculable*) (*frais, perte*) assessable

estimatif, -ive [ɛstimatif, -iv] *adj* (*coût etc*) estimated; **devis e.** estimate, quotation

estimation [ɛstimasjɔ̃] *nf* (**a**) (*détermination de la valeur*) (*d'un prix, d'une distance, d'un poids etc*) estimation; (*de marchandises*) valuation, appraising; (*de dommages, besoins*) assessment, estimation; **faire une e.** to give an estimation/a valuation/an assessment; **e. approximative** rough estimate; *Mktg* **e. des besoins** needs assessment; *Compta* **e. des frais** estimate of costs (**b**) (*valeur, quantité estimée*) estimate

estime [ɛstim] *nf* (**a**) (*respect*) esteem, regard; **avoir de l'e. pour qn/qch** to esteem sb/sth; **avoir beaucoup d'e. pour qn/qch** to have great regard for sb/sth, to hold sb/sth in high regard; **tu as baissé dans mon e.** you have gone down in my estimation; **tenir qn en grande/en médiocre e.** to think highly/little of sb, to hold sb in high/low regard; **avoir un succès d'e.** to be a critical (though not a popular) success (**b**) *Naut* reckoning; **à l'e.** by dead reckoning; *Fig* by guesswork; **navigation à l'e.** dead reckoning

estimer [ɛstime] **1** *vt* (**a**) (*déterminer la valeur de*) (*prix, distance, poids etc*) to estimate; (*marchandises*) to value, to appraise; (*dommages*) to assess; *Naut* to reckon; **faire e. une maison** to have a house valued; **les experts estiment que les pertes s'élèvent à plusieurs milliards** the experts estimate the losses at *or* that the losses total several hundred million; *Naut* **longitude estimée** longitude by dead reckoning

(**b**) (*considérer*) to consider, to think (**que** that); **j'estime qu'il est de mon devoir de parler** I consider *or* think it (is) my duty *or* that it is my duty to speak; **je n'estime pas que vous ayez besoin d'y aller** I don't consider *or* think it (is) necessary for you to go, I don't think you need to go; **il n'a pas estimé nécessaire de me prévenir** he didn't consider *or* think it (was) necessary to warn me

(**c**) (*respecter*) (*qn*) to have a high opinion of, to think highly of, to esteem; (*les qualités de qn, la musique etc*) to value, to have a high opinion of; **elle est estimée de tous** she is highly thought of *or* is esteemed by everyone; **j'estime son dévouement à sa juste valeur** I value his dedication at its true worth

2 s'estimer *vpr* **s'e. satisfait/heureux** to consider oneself satisfied/lucky

estivage [ɛstivaʒ] *nm Agr* (*du bétail etc*) summering on mountain pastures

estival, -ale, -aux, -ales [ɛstival, -o] *adj* (*résidence, vêtements, travail etc*) summer; **station estivale** summer resort

estivant, -ante [ɛstivɑ̃, -ɑ̃t] *n* (summer) holiday-maker *or Am* vacationer

estiver [ɛstive] *vt Agr* (*bétail etc*) to summer on mountain pastures

estoc [ɛstɔk] *nm* **frapper d'e. et de taille** to cut and thrust

estocade [ɛstɔkad] *nf* (*en tauromachie*) deathblow; **donner l'e. à** (*taureau, Fig adversaire*) to deal the deathblow to

estomac [ɛstɔma] *nm* stomach; **avoir l'e. vide** *ou* **creux/plein** to have an empty stomach/be full (up); **creux de l'e.** pit of the stomach; **mal d'e.** stomach ache; **avoir un e. d'autruche** to have a cast-iron stomach; **avoir l'e. dans les talons** to be ravenous *or* starving; *Fig F* **avoir de l'e.** (*courage*) to have plenty of guts; (*culot*) to have plenty of cheek; *Fig F* **la faire à l'e.** to try it on (**à qn** with sb)

estomaqué [ɛstɔmake] *adj F* staggered, astounded, flabbergasted

estomaquer [ɛstɔmake] *vt F* to stagger, to astound, to flabbergast

estompage [ɛstɔ̃paʒ] *nm Beaux-Arts* stumping, shading off (with a stump)

estompe [ɛstɔ̃p] *nf Beaux-Arts* stump; **dessin à l'e.** stump drawing

estompé [ɛstɔ̃pe] *adj* (*contour, image, couleurs etc*) indistinct, blurred; (*souvenirs*) blurred, dim; *Ordinat* dimmed
estomper [ɛstɔ̃pe] **1** *vt Beaux-Arts* (*dessin*) to stump, to shade off (with a stump); *Fig* (*paysage, contour, souvenir etc*) to blur, to dim; (*contraste*) to tone down; (*rides*) to smooth out; **le temps estompera la douleur** time will ease the pain **2 s'estomper** *vpr* (*d'un souvenir*) to become blurred; (*de la douleur*) to ease; (*des rides*) to be smoothed out; (*des couleurs*) to fade; (*des contours*) to fade, to blur
Estonie [ɛstɔni] *nf* Estonia
estonien, -ienne [ɛstɔnjɛ̃, jɛn] **1** *adj* Estonian **2** *nm Ling* Estonian **3** *n* **E.** Estonian
estoquer [ɛstɔke] *vt* (*d'un matador*) (*taureau*) to kill
estourbir [ɛsturbir] *vt F* **(a)** (*tuer*) to do in **(b)** (*étonner*) to astound, to knock sideways; **je suis encore tout estourbi de la chance que j'ai eue** I'm still quite astounded how lucky I was
estrade [ɛstrad] *nf* dais, rostrum, platform; **e. réservée à la presse** press box
estragon [ɛstragɔ̃] *nm Bot, Culin* tarragon
estrapade [ɛstrapad] *nf Hist* (*supplice*) strappado; *Naut* dipping from the yard arm
estrogène [ɛstrɔʒɛn] *nm Physiol* oestrogen, *US* estrogen
estropié, -ée [ɛstrɔpje] **1** *adj* crippled, maimed **2** *n* cripple
estropier [ɛstrɔpje] *vt* (*impf, pr sub* **n. estropiions**) **(a)** (*personne*) to cripple, to maim **(b)** *Fig* (*valse, langue étrangère etc*) to murder; (*mot, nom*) to mispronounce; (*texte*) to mutilate
estuaire [ɛstɥɛr] *nm* estuary
estudiantin [ɛstydjɑ̃tɛ̃] *adj* (*vie, univers etc*) student
esturgeon [ɛstyrʒɔ̃] *nm* sturgeon
et [e] **1** *conj* (*note there is no liaison with* **et: j'ai écrit et écrit** [ʒeekrieekri]) **(a)** and; **toi et moi partirons demain** you and I will leave tomorrow; **c'est un homme de grande énergie, et qui arrivera** he is a man of great energy, who will succeed; **et son frère et sa sœur** both his brother and his sister; **je ne peux pas et répondre au téléphone et ouvrir la porte** I can't answer the phone and open the door; **et d'un, il pleut et de deux, je n'ai pas envie d'y aller** first(ly) it's raining, and second(ly) I don't want to go; **j'aime le café, et vous?** I like coffee, do you?; **et les dix francs que je vous ai prêtés?** and (what about) the ten francs I lent you?; **et le garçon de se sauver** at this the boy ran off; **et elle de rire!** and she burst out laughing!

(b) (*dans les nombres etc*) **vingt/trente/***etc* **et un** twenty/thirty/*etc*-one; **soixante et onze** seventy-one; **il est quatre heures et demie** it's half past four

2 *nm* **(a) et commercial** ampersand

(b) *Ordinat* **ET** AND; **circuit ET** AND gate
étable [etabl] *nf* cowshed
établi[1] [etabli] *nm* (work)bench
établi[2] *adj* (*gouvernement, réputation etc*) established; **l'Église établie** the Established Church; **considérer qch comme chose établie** to take sth for granted; **l'ordre é.** the established order
établir [etablir] **1** *vt* **(a)** (*créer*) (*forme de gouvernement, affaire, paix, relations, contact etc*) to establish; (*agence*) to set up; (*édifice*) to put up, to erect; (*barrage, voie ferrée*) to construct; (*lieu de résidence*) to settle, to fix; (*machinerie*) to install; (*voile*) to set; (*camp*) to pitch; (*prix*) to fix, to set; (*taxe, tribunal etc*) to institute, to create; (*plan, proposition etc*) to draw up; (*règlement*) to prescribe, to lay down; (*principe*) to lay down; (*devis, facture, bilan, budget*) to draw up; **é. un chèque** to make out *or* write a cheque; **é. un chèque à l'ordre de** to make a cheque payable to; **é. une balance** to strike a balance; **é. une moyenne** to work out an average; **é. un record** to set a record

(b) (*démontrer*) (*fait, l'innocence de qn*) to establish, to prove; **é. une accusation** to establish *or* substantiate a charge; **é. un parallèle entre** to establish *or* draw a parallel between

(c) (*asseoir*) (*autorité, droits, réputation etc*) to establish; (*fortune*) to establish, to build up (**sur** on); **é. le silence** to establish silence; **é. une démonstration sur des arguments solides** to base a proof on sound arguments

(d) (*pourvoir d'une situation*) to set up (**dans** in; **comme** as); **il a établi tous ses enfants** he has settled all his children, he has set all his children up in life; *Vieilli* **il lui reste une fille à é.** (*à marier*) he still has a daughter at home

2 s'établir *vpr* **(a)** (*dans une ville, un pays etc*) to settle (**à, dans, en** in)

(b) (*pour exercer un métier*) **s'é. épicier** to set (oneself) up as a grocer; **elle s'est établie à son compte** she set up (in) business on her own

(c) (*se poser en*) **s'é. chef/juge** to set oneself up as a leader/judge

(d) (*d'une coutume, d'une idée, de rapports etc*) to become established; **le silence s'est enfin établi** silence was established at last
établissement [etablismɑ̃] *nm* **(a)** (*création*) (*de forme de gouvernement, affaire, paix etc*) establishment; (*d'agence*) setting up; (*d'édifice*) putting up, erection; (*d'un lieu de résidence*) settling, fixing; (*de machinerie*) installation; (*de voile*) setting; (*de camp*) pitching; (*de prix*) fixing; (*de taxe, tribunal*) institution, creation; (*de plan, proposition etc*) drawing up; (*de règlement*) prescribing, laying down; (*de principe*) laying down; *Télécom* **é. d'appel** call connection; *Fin* **é. d'un compte** opening an account, setting up an account; **é. des menus** (*dans un restaurant*) menu planning; *Com* **é. des prix** pricing

(b) (*démonstration*) (*de fait, innocence de qn*) establishment, proving

(c) (*d'autorité, de droits, réputation etc*) establishment

(d) (*de ses enfants*) settling

(e) (*institution*) establishment, institution; **é. thermal** hydropathic establishment, spa; **é. hospitalier** hospital; **é. scolaire** educational establishment; **é. pénitentiaire** prison, penal establishment; **é. bancaire** bank; **é. de crédit** credit institution; *Compta* **é. déclarant** company making the return; **é. financier** financial institution; *Fin* **é. payeur** paying bank

(f) *Hist* **établissements** (*colonies*) settlements, colonies

(g) *Com* business, firm; **les établissements Martin** Martin & Co; **é. principal** main branch *or* office; **é. industriel** factory
étage [etaʒ] *nm* **(a)** (*d'un bâtiment*) floor, storey, *US* story; **à deux étages** two-storeyed, *US* two-storied; **au troisième é.** on the third floor, *Am* on the fourth floor; **monter à l'é.** to go upstairs; **dévaler les étages** to race down the stairs; **elle est dans les étages** she's somewhere upstairs

(b) (*d'une construction, d'un terrain*) level; (*d'un jardin*) terrace; (*d'un gâteau*) tier; **gâteau à quatre étages** four-tiered cake

(c) *Géol* stage, formation

(d) *Tech* stage; **compression par étages** compression by stages; **fusée à trois étages** three-stage rocket

(e) *Péj* **de bas é.** (*esprit, histoire etc*) mediocre, second-rate; **individu de bas é.** worthless individual

(f) *Can Sp* **le deuxième é.** the (club) management
étagement [etaʒmɑ̃] *nm* (*de plantations, vignes*) terracing
étager [etaʒe] (**j'étageai(s)**) **1** *vt* **(a)** (*sièges, livres, groupe de personnes etc*) to arrange in tiers; **jardin étagé** terraced garden; **vignes étagées** vines arranged in terraces; **poulie étagée** cone pulley **(b)** *Tech* **compression étagée** compression by stages, staged compression **2 s'étager** *vpr* (*des maisons, vignes etc*) to rise in tiers
étagère [etaʒɛr] *nf* [①A12,d] (*meuble*) (set of) shelves; (*planche*) shelf
étai[1] [etɛ] *nm Naut* (*cordage*) stay; **voile d'é.** staysail
étai[2] *nm Constr etc* stay, prop, strut; **é. de mine** pit prop
étaiement [etɛmɑ̃] *nm Constr etc* shoring (up), propping (up)
étain [etɛ̃] *nm* **(a)** (*métal*) tin; **é. battu, é. en feuilles** thin sheet tin; **papier d'é.** tinfoil, silver paper **(b)** (*pour la vaisselle, les bijoux*) pewter; **vaisselle d'é.** pewter (plate); **une très belle collection d'étains** a very fine collection of pewter (pieces)
étal, -als [etal] *nm* **(a)** (*de boucher*) (butcher's) stall, meat stall **(b)** (*au marché*) (market) stall
étalage [etalaʒ] *nm* **(a)** *Com* (*des marchandises*) display, show; (*vitrine*) (display) window; **faire l'é.** to set out one's goods; (*vitrine*) to dress the window(s); **mettre qch à l'é.** to display sth for sale; **article qui a fait l'é.** *Br* shopsoiled *or Am* shopworn article

(b) *Fig* (*de richesse, des connaissances etc*) display, show, parading; **faire é. de ses bijoux/son savoir/sa richesse** to show off *or* parade one's jewels/knowledge/wealth; **faire é. de sa force** to show one's strength; **elle fait é. de sa vie privée** she flaunts her private life
étalager [etalaʒe] *vt* (**j'étalageai(s)**) *Com* (*marchandises*) to display for sale
étalagiste [etalaʒist] *n* window dresser
étale [etal] *Naut* **1** *adj* (*mer, marée*) slack; (*brise*) steady **2** *nm ou f* **é. du flot** slack water
étalement [etalmɑ̃] *nm* **(a)** (*du linge à sécher, de papiers sur la table etc*) spreading out; (*d'une nappe, du beurre etc*) spreading; (*de la peinture etc*) application; (*des marchandises*) displaying **(b)** (*des vacances, paiements etc*) staggering (**sur** over); (*des travaux, d'un cours etc*) spreading (out) (**sur** over); (*de paiements*) spreading
étaler [etale] **1** *vt* **(a)** (*étendre*) (*linge à sécher, papiers etc*) to spread out, to lay out; (*nappe, beurre etc*) to spread; (*peinture, onguent*) to apply (**sur** to); (*marchandises*) to display (for sale); (*ses cartes*) to lay down

(**b**) *Fig* (*montrer*) (*sa richesse, ses connaissances*) to display, to show off, to parade; (*ses malheurs*) to parade, to draw attention to; **é. sa vie** to tell one's life story; **é. une affaire au grand jour** to make a matter public; *Hum* **la culture, c'est comme la confiture: moins on en a, plus on l'étale** = people who don't have much culture have to make the most of it

(**c**) (*échelonner*) (*vacances, paiements, envoi du courrier etc*) to stagger (**sur** over); (*travaux, cours, opération etc*) to spread (**sur** over); **é. les remboursements sur plusieurs exercices** to spread (out) the repayments over several financial years

(**d**) *Naut* (*courant, vent*) to stem

(**e**) *F* (*faire tomber*) (*personne*) to lay out, to floor

2 s'étaler *vpr* (**a**) (*d'un village, parc etc*) to spread out; **arbre à cime étalée** large-crowned tree; **cette peinture s'étale mal** this paint goes on badly

(**b**) (*parader*) (*des gens riches etc*) to flaunt oneself; **son succès s'étale à la une des journaux** his success is splashed across the front pages

(**c**) (*se vautrer*) to sprawl

(**d**) *F* (*tomber*) **s'é. par terre** to fall flat on the ground; **s'é. de tout son long** to go *or* measure one's length

(**e**) (*des vacances, paiements etc*) to be spread (**sur** over)

étalon[1] [etalɔ̃] *nm* (*cheval*) stallion

étalon[2] *nm* (*modèle de mesure*) standard; *Fig* (*modèle*) standard, yardstick; **mètre é.** standard metre; *Écon* **l'é.-or** the gold standard; **é. monétaire** monetary standard

étalonnage [etalɔnaʒ] *nm*, **étalonnement** [etalɔnmɑ̃] *nm* (**a**) (*action de vérifier*) (*d'un poids, d'une mesure*) standardization; (*d'un instrument*) gauging, testing (**b**) (*action de graduer*) (*d'un thermomètre etc*) calibration (**c**) *Psy* (*d'un test*) standardization

étalonner [etalɔne] *vt* (**a**) (*vérifier*) (*poids, mesure*) to standardize; (*instrument*) to gauge, to test (**b**) (*graduer*) (*thermomètre, baromètre etc*) to calibrate (**c**) *Psy* (*test*) to standardize

étamage [etamaʒ] *nm* (**a**) (*de cuivre etc*) tinning; (*d'une tôle de fer*) tinplating (**b**) (*d'un miroir*) silvering

étambot [etɑ̃bo] *nm Naut* sternpost

étamer [etame] *vt* (**a**) (*cuivre etc*) to tin; (*tôle de fer*) to tinplate (**b**) (*miroir*) to silver

étameur [etamœr] *nm* tinner, tinsmith

étamine[1] [etamin] *nf Tex* muslin; (*pour filtrer, cribler*) butter muslin, cheesecloth; **passer à l'é.** (*liquide*) to filter; (*farine etc*) to sift

étamine[2] *nf Bot* stamen

étanche [etɑ̃ʃ] *adj* (*bateau, toit etc*) watertight; (*montre, bottes etc*) waterproof; **é. à l'eau/à l'air/à la poussière** watertight/airtight/dustproof; **cloison é.** *Naut* watertight bulkhead; *Fig* (*entre services, disciplines etc*) impenetrable barrier, *esp Am F* Great Wall of China

étanchéité [etɑ̃ʃeite] *nf* (*d'un bateau, toit etc*) watertightness; (*d'une montre, de bottes etc*) waterproofness; **é. à l'eau/à l'air** watertightness/airtightness; **vérifier l'é.** to check for leaks (**de** in)

étancher [etɑ̃ʃe] *vt* (**a**) (*liquide*) to check the flow of; (*sang*) to staunch; (*les larmes de qn*) to dry; *Naut* **é. une voie d'eau** to stop a leak (**b**) (*sa soif*) to quench, to slake (**c**) (*rendre étanche*) to make watertight

étançon [etɑ̃sɔ̃] *nm Constr, Naut* (*étai*) shore, stanchion

étançonnement [etɑ̃sɔnmɑ̃] *nm* shoring up

étançonner [etɑ̃sɔne] *vt* to shore up

étang [etɑ̃] *nm* pond, pool

étant [etɑ̃] *voir* **être[2]**

étape [etap] *nf* (**a**) (*lieu*) stop(over), stopping place; **faire é.** to stop; **nous avons fait é. à Bordeaux** we stopped over(night) at Bordeaux; **brûler une é.** (*d'un train, un autobus*) to go past *or* miss a stop, to fail to stop (at a scheduled stop); **comme nous étions pressés, nous avons brûlé l'é. de Strasbourg** since we were in a hurry, we missed out Strasbourg *or* we didn't stop in Strasbourg; **brûlons la prochaine é. et continuons jusqu'à Lyon** let's press on to Lyons without stopping; *Fig* **brûler les étapes** (*dans une entreprise, un métier*) to move up the ladder very quickly; (*dans une tâche*) to cut corners

(**b**) (*distance à parcourir*) (*d'un voyage, d'une course etc*) stage, leg; **à** *ou* **par petites étapes** by *or* in easy stages; **nous avons fait hier une é. de 500 kilomètres** we covered *or* did 500 kilometres yesterday

(**c**) *Fig* (*phase*) (*d'une vie, d'un processus etc*) stage; **une procédure en deux étapes** a two-stage *or* -step procedure; **l'é. suivante consiste à …** the next step is to …; **é. par é.** stage by stage, step by step, one stage *or* step at a time; **par étapes** by *or* in stages *or* steps

état [eta] *nm* (**a**) (*façon d'être*) state, condition; *Phys* state; **à l'é. solide/liquide/naturel** in its solid/liquid/naturel state; **é. du ciel** weather conditions; **é. de la mer** conditions at sea; **l'é. des routes** road conditions; **é. du marché** state of the market; **à l'é. neuf** (*dans une petite annonce*) as new; **à l'é. pur** (*métal*) unalloyed; *Fig* **c'est de la bêtise/de l'incompétence à l'é. pur** it is sheer *or* downright stupidity/incompetence; **retourner à l'é. sauvage** to revert to the wild; **une plante qui pousse à l'é. sauvage** a plant which grows in the wild; **dans l'é. actuel des choses** given the current state of affairs; **dans l'é. actuel de nos connaissances** given what we know at the moment; **être dans un triste/piteux é.** to be in a sorry/pitiful state; *Hum* **elle est dans un é. intéressant** (*enceinte*) she's in the family way; **tu ne devrais pas porter cette valise dans ton é.** you shouldn't be carrying that case in your condition; *F* **être dans tous ses états** to be in a real *or* terrible *or* dreadful state; **il n'y a pas de quoi se mettre dans un é. pareil!** there's no point getting into such a state (about it)!; **te voilà dans un bel é.!** that's some state you're in!; **tu as vu dans quel é. tu t'es mis?** have you seen the state you've got yourself into?; **on a retrouvé des ossements en parfait é. de conservation** we found some perfectly preserved bones; **en (bon) é.** (*machine, voiture, maison etc*) in good condition *or* repair; **navire en bon é. (de navigabilité)** seaworthy ship; **en mauvais é.** in bad condition; **en é. de rouler** (*voiture*) roadworthy; **en é. de voler** (*avion*) airworthy; **être en é. de marche** to be in working order; *Aut* to be roadworthy, to be in a roadworthy condition; *Méd* **être en é. de manque** to have withdrawal symptoms; *Psy* **en é. de veille** in a waking state; **remettre en é.** (*maison etc*) to renovate, to repair; (*moteur*) to overhaul, to recondition; **tenir qch en é.** to look after sth, to keep sth in good repair; **laisser les choses en l'é.** to leave things as they are *or* stand; **vendre qch en l'é.** to sell sth as it is; **être/se sentir en é. de faire qch** to be/feel up to doing sth; **elle n'est plus en é. de travailler** she's not up to working any more; **tu n'es pas en é. de conduire** you're in no condition *or* in no fit state to drive; **le blessé n'est pas encore en é. de parler** the injured man is still not in a condition to talk; **je ne suis pas en é. de vous répondre** I am not in a position to give you an answer; **êtes-vous en é. de le recevoir?** (*décemment habillé*) are you presentable?, are you fit to be seen?; (*assez bien portant*) do you feel up to seeing him?, are you up to seeing him?; **nous sommes maintenant en é. d'affirmer que les otages ont tous été libérés** we are now in a position to confirm that the hostages have all been released; **être hors d'é.** to have broken down; **il faut mettre ces terroristes hors d'é. de nuire** these terrorists must be prevented from doing harm; (*mettre en lieu sûr*) these terrorists must be put out of harm's way

(**b**) **faire é. de** to refer to, to mention

(**c**) (*profession*) **militaire/épicier de son é.** soldier by profession/grocer by trade

(**d**) *Fr Hist* (*groupe social*) **le Tiers É.** the Third Estate

(**e**) (*autorité centrale*) **l'É.** the state *or* State; **coup d'É.** coup (d'état); **le budget de l'É.** the state budget; **homme/femme d'É.** statesman/stateswoman; **pour des raisons d'É.** for reasons of state; **un É. dans l'É.** a state within a state; **É. membre** member state

(**f**) (*nation, territoire aux États-Unis*) state; **servir d'é. tampon** to serve as a buffer state

(**g**) (*rapport*) (*imprimé*) form; (*des dépenses, ventes*) statement, list; (*des paiements, marchandises*) schedule, list; **rayer qn des états** to strike sb off the rolls

(**h**) *Ordinat* **en é. de veille** in standby mode; **é. d'attente** wait state; **sans é. d'attente** with zero wait states

▶ **état**: **é. d'alerte** state of alert; **être en é. d'alerte** to be on the alert; *Mil* to be in a state of alert; **états d'âmes: avoir des états d'âme** to engage in soul-searching; **je n'ai pas eu d'états d'âme avant de le virer** I didn't engage in too much soul-searching before I fired him; **tu nous embêtes avec tes états d'âme** you're getting on our nerves with your constant soul-searching; *Compta* **é. de caisse** cash statement; **é. de choc: en é. de choc** in a state of shock; **é. de choses** state of affairs, situation; *Admin* **é. civil** (*à la mairie*) register *or Br* registry office; **actes de l'é. civil** = birth, marriage and death certificates; **informer l'é. civil d'un décès** to register a death; *Compta* **états comptables** accounting records; *Compta* **états comptables et commerciaux** internal company records; **é. de compte** *Can* bank statement, statement of account; *Compta* position on an account; **é. d'ébriété: en é. d'ébriété** in a state of intoxication; **é. d'esprit** state *or* frame of mind; **é. de fait: c'est un é. de fait** it's an undeniable *or* established fact; *Jur* **é. de frais** bill of costs; **les États généraux** the States General; **é. de guerre** state of war; **l'é. de guerre a été déclaré** a state of war has been declared; **é. d'impression** report form; *Fin* **é. imprimé** printed statement *or* form; **é. d'ivresse: en é. d'ivresse** in a state of intoxication; **é. des lieux** inventory of fixtures (*in rented premises*); **le propriétaire est tenu de faire l'é. des lieux avec son locataire** the landlord is obliged to agree an inventory of fixtures with the tenant; **é. néant** nil return; **é. nominatif** list of names, (nominal) roll; **é. providence** welfare state; *Compta* **é. de rapprochement** reconciliation statement; *Compta* **é. récapitulatif** final assessment, adjustment account; **é. de santé** state of health; **é. second** (state of) trance; *Admin, Mil* **états de service** service record; **é. de situation** status *or* state-of-play report; *Compta* **é. TVA** VAT statement *or* return

étatique [etatik] *adj Pol* (of the) state; **l'appareil é.** the machinery of state

étatisation [etatizasjõ] *nf* (*action*) establishment of state control (**de** over); (*doctrine*) state control

étatisé [etatize] *adj* state-controlled, state-run

étatiser [etatize] *vt* (*firme etc*) to bring under state control

étatisme [etatism] *nm* state control

étatiste [etatist] **1** *adj* **système é.** system of state control **2** *n* partisan of state control

état-major, *pl* **états-majors** *nm* **(a)** *Mil* (*officiers*) (general) staff; **officier d'é.** staff officer; **carte d'é.** *Br* ≈ Ordnance Survey map, *US* ≈ Geological Survey map **(b)** (*lieu*) headquarters **(c)** (*d'une firme*) senior staff, management; (*d'un parti politique*) leadership

États-Unis [etazyni] *nmpl* [①A11,g,ii] **les É. (d'Amérique)** the United States (of America), *F* the States

étau, -aux [eto] *nm* **(a)** *Tech* vice, *US* vise; **é. d'établi** bench vice **(b)** *Fig* (*restrictions*) stranglehold; **les kidnappeurs sentaient l'é. se resserrer autour d'eux** the kidnappers could feel the net closing around them; **je suis prise là-dedans comme dans un é.** I can't get out of it, they've/he's/ *etc* got me in a stranglehold

étayage [etɛjaʒ] *nm Constr etc* shoring, propping (up)

étayer [eteje] **(j'étaie, j'étaye; j'étaierai, j'étayerai) 1** *vt* **(a)** *Constr etc* (*mur etc*) to prop (up), to shore (up) **(b)** *Fig* (*argumentation*) to buttress; (*déclaration, théorie etc*) to support, to back up; **pour é. ses allégations** in support of his allegations **2 s'étayer** *vpr* **s'e. sur** (*d'une théorie, de la défense etc*) to be based *or* founded on

etc [ɛtsetera] *adv* etc

et c(a)etera [ɛtsetera] *adv* etcetera

été[1] [ete] *nm* [①A6,d,v] summer; **é. comme hiver j'habite la campagne** I live in the country winter and summer alike; **en é.** in (the) summer *or* summertime; **pendant l'é. 1989** in the summer of 1989; **l'é. prochain** next summer; **un jour d'é.** a summer('s) day; **heure d'é.** summer time, *Am* daylight (saving) time; **temps/vêtements d'é.** summer weather/ clothes

▶ **été**[1]: **é. indien** Indian summer; **é. de la Saint-Martin** Indian summer

été[2] *voir* **être**[2]

éteignoir [etɛɲwar] *nm* (candle) snuffer; **en é.** conical

éteindre [etɛ̃dr] (*conj like* **teindre**) **1** *vt* **(a)** (*incendie, bougie, cigarette etc*) to extinguish, to put out; (*gaz*) to turn off; (*lumière, radio, radiateur etc*) to switch off, to turn off; *F* (*pièce*) to switch off (the lights) in

(b) *Tech* (*chaux*) to slake, to slack; (*fer chauffé au rouge etc*) to quench

(c) *Fig* (*mettre fin à*) (*dette*) to pay off; (*querelle*) to put an end to; **é. le feu de l'ennemi** to silence the enemy's guns

(d) *Fig* (*affaiblir*) (*couleur*) to fade, to soften; **les couleurs ont été éteintes par le temps** the colours have faded with time; **le temps éteint les passions** passions fade with time

2 s'éteindre *vpr* **(a)** (*d'un incendie, d'une cigarette, d'une lampe etc*) to go out

(b) *Fig* (*s'affaiblir*) (*d'une couleur, une passion*) to fade; (*d'un son, de rires*) to die away, to subside; (*d'une voix*) to die away; **le jour s'éteint** daylight is failing *or* fading

(c) *Fig* (*disparaître*) (*d'une personne*) to pass away, to die; (*d'une race, famille*) to become extinct, to die out

3 *vi* **(a)** to switch off (the lights) **(dans** in)

(b) laisser é. le feu to let the fire go out

éteint [etɛ̃] *adj* **(a) être é.** (*d'un incendie, d'une cigarette, d'une lampe etc*) to be out; (*de l'électricité, d'une radio etc*) to be off; *Aut* **rouler tous feux éteints** to drive without (any) lights **(b)** (*race, famille, volcan*) extinct **(c)** *Fig* (*couleur*) dull; (*yeux*) dull, lacklustre; (*voix*) faint, lifeless; **depuis qu'elle l'a laissé, il a l'air tout é.** all the life seems to have gone out of him *or* all of the stuffing seems to have been knocked out of him since she left him; **je l'ai trouvée éteinte hier soir** I found her rather subdued last night

étendard [etɑ̃dar] *nm* **(a)** *Mil* (*drapeau*) standard **(b)** *Fig* (*symbole*) banner; **lever l'é. de la révolte** to raise the standard of revolt; **se ranger sous l'é. de qn** to join sb's camp

étendoir [etɑ̃dwar] *nm* **(a)** (*cordes*) clotheslines **(b)** (*cour*) drying yard; (*salle*) drying room

étendre [etɑ̃dr] **1** *vt* **(a)** (*déployer*) (*carte, nappe etc*) to spread (out); (*linge*) to hang up; (*beurre, onguent, fumier etc*) to spread; (*peinture*) to apply **(sur** to), to spread **(sur** on, over); **é. qn** to stretch sb out; **é. le bras** to stretch out *or* reach out (one's arm); **é. les bras** to open one's arms wide, to spread out one's arms; **é. ses ailes** to spread its wings; **é. qn (par terre) d'un coup de poing** to knock sb down *or F* flat, *F* to deck sb; *Boxe etc* **se faire é.** to go down, *F* to be decked; *F* **se faire é. à un examen** to fail an exam

(b) (*développer*) (*influence, pouvoir, connaissances etc*) to extend, to widen, to expand; (*limites, propriété*) to extend; **é. une peau** to stretch a skin; **é. la pâte** to roll out the dough; **é. les termes d'une loi** to widen *or* broaden the terms of a law; **é. sa connaissance des langues étrangères au chinois et au japonais** to expand *or* extend one's knowledge of foreign languages to include Chinese and Japanese

(c) (*diluer*) (*vin, lait etc*) to dilute; **é. d'eau une boisson** to water down a drink

(d) *Ordinat* (*mémoire*) to upgrade

2 s'étendre *vpr* **(a)** (*s'allonger*) to lie down, to stretch out; *Fig* **s'é. sur un sujet** to dwell on a subject; *Fig* **il ne s'est pas étendu sur les raisons de son absence** he didn't enlarge *or* expand on the reasons for his absence

(b) (*aller*) to stretch, to extend; **la ligne s'étend depuis Ivry jusqu'à Charenton** the line stretches *or* extends *or* runs from Ivry to Charenton; **aussi loin que le regard peut s'é.** as far as the eye can see; **notre parc s'étend sur plusieurs hectares** our grounds spread over several acres; **son combat contre l'alcoolisme ne s'étend pas jusque chez lui** his anti-drinking campaign does not extend to his own home

(c) (*se développer*) (*d'un incendie, d'une épidémie, d'une grève etc*) to spread; (*d'une fortune, d'une affaire, d'un empire etc*) to expand, to grow larger; (*d'un pouvoir*) to widen, to increase; (*d'une influence*) to spread, to widen, to increase; (*des connaissances, du vocabulaire*) to widen, to broaden

étendu, -ue [etɑ̃dy] **1** *adj* **(a)** (*plaine, forêt, Fig connaissances, vocabulaire*) wide, extensive; *Fig* (*influence*) far-reaching, widespread

(b) (*bras, jambes*) outstretched; **é. sur un divan** stretched out *or* lying on a couch

(c) (*dilué*) diluted **(de** with)

2 *nf* **étendue** (*d'un champ, d'une région etc*) area, extent; (*d'une calamité, grève, épidémie*) scale, extent; (*d'eau, de sable etc*) expanse, stretch; (*de terre etc*) expanse, tract; (*d'une voix, d'un instrument*) range, compass; (*des connaissances, du vocabulaire, du pouvoir de qn etc*) extent, scope; **sur une grande étendue** over a wide area; **sur toute l'étendue du champ** over the entire field; **te rends-tu compte de l'étendue de ton erreur?** do you realize the extent *or* the magnitude of your error?

éternel, -elle [etɛrnɛl] **1** *adj* **(a)** (*être, Dieu etc*) eternal; **le père é.** the everlasting Father

(b) (*vie, joie etc*) eternal, everlasting; **neiges éternelles** eternal snow

(c) *Fig* (*regrets*) eternal, endless; (*amour*) eternal, undying; (*discussion, recommendations, bavardages*) endless, never-ending; **vous aurez droit à ma reconnaissance éternelle** I shall be eternally grateful to you; **un é. causeur** an inveterate chatterer; **tu es un é. mécontent** you're never satisfied; **fumant son éternelle cigarette** smoking the inevitable cigarette

2 *nm* **(a) l'É.** (*Dieu*) the Eternal; *Hum* **c'est un grand fumeur/grand paresseux devant l'É.** he's an incurable smoker/incurably lazy

(b) l'é. féminin the archetypal female

éternellement [etɛrnɛlmɑ̃] *adv* **(a)** (*durer, attendre, rester etc*) for ever; **é. reconnaissant** eternally grateful **(b)** (*continuellement*) constantly, for ever; **il est é. mécontent** he's never satisfied; **elle a é. raison** she's always right; **il est é. en retard** he's constantly *or* always late

éterniser [etɛrnize] **1** *vt* **(a)** *Litt* **é. le nom/la mémoire de qn** to immortalize sb's name/memory; **si nous pouvions é. cette heure** if only we could make this hour last for ever **(b)** (*prolonger*) (*discussion, crise, procès etc*) to drag out (for ever) **2 s'éterniser** *vpr* (*d'une discussion, d'une crise, d'un procès etc*) to drag on (for ever); **j'ai horreur que les adieux s'éternisent** I hate long drawn-out goodbyes; **s'é. chez qn** to outstay one's welcome

éternité [etɛrnite] *nf* eternity; **de toute é.** from time immemorial; **il y a une é.** *ou* **des éternités que je ne vous ai vu** it's ages since I saw you, I haven't seen you for ages; **j'aimerais autant que notre visite ne dure pas une é.** I really don't want to stay longer than necessary; **j'ai attendu pendant une é.** I waited an eternity, I waited for ages
éternuement [etɛrnymɑ̃] *nm* sneeze
éternuer [etɛrnɥe] *vi* to sneeze
êtes [ɛt] *voir* **être**[2]
étêtage [etɛtaʒ] *nm*, **étêtement** [etɛtmɑ̃] *nm* (*d'un arbre*) pollarding, topping
étêter [etete] *vt* (*poisson, clou etc*) to remove the head from; (*arbre*) to pollard, to top
éthane [etan] *nm Ch* ethane
éthanol [etanɔl] *nm* ethanol
éther [etɛr] *nm* ether; *Litt* (*air, ciel*) ether
éthéré [etere] *adj* (*région, Ch sel*) ethereal
éthéromane [eterɔman] *n* ether addict
Éthiopie [etjɔpi] *nf* Ethiopia
éthiopien, -ienne [etjɔpjɛ̃, -jɛn] **1** *adj* Ethiopian **2** *n* **É.** Ethiopian
éthique [etik] **1** *adj* **(a)** (*problème etc*) ethical **(b)** *Gram* **datif é.** ethical dative **2** *nf* (*science, règles de conduite*) ethics; **l'é. puritaine** the Puritan ethic
ethnie [ɛtni] *nf* ethnic group
ethnique [ɛtnik] *adj* (*groupe etc*) ethnic
ethnocentrisme [ɛtnosɑ̃trism] *nm* ethnocentrism
ethnographe [ɛtnɔgraf] *n* ethnographer
ethnographie [ɛtnɔgrafi] *nf* ethnography
ethnographique [ɛtnɔgrafik] *adj* ethnographic(al)
ethnolinguistique [ɛtnolɛ̃gɥistik] *nf* ethnolinguistics
ethnologie [ɛtnɔlɔʒi] *nf* ethnology
ethnologique [ɛtnɔlɔʒik] *adj* ethnological
ethnologue [ɛtnɔlɔg] *n* ethnologist
éthologie [etɔlɔʒi] *nf* ethology
éthologique [etɔlɔʒik] *adj* ethological
éthologiste [etɔlɔʒist] *n* ethologist
éthyle [etil] *nm Ch* ethyl
éthylène [etilɛn] *nm Ch* ethylene
éthylène-glycol *nm inv* ethylene glycol
éthylique [etilik] **1** *adj Ch* ethylic; **alcool é.** ethyl alcohol **2** *n Méd* alcoholic
éthylisme [etilism] *nm Méd* alcoholism
éthylomètre [etilɔmɛtr], **éthylotest** [etilotɛst] *nm* Breathalyzer®
étiage [etjaʒ] *nm* (*baisse d'eaux*) low water; (*niveau le plus bas*) lowest water level; **échelle d'é.** water gauge
étincelage [etɛ̃slaʒ] *nm* **(a)** *Tech* **soudure par é.** flash welding **(b)** *Méd* electrotherapy
étincelant [etɛ̃slɑ̃] *adj* (*diamant, métal, lac etc*) sparkling, glittering; (*étoile*) twinkling, glittering; (*yeux, Fig esprit, conversation, livre etc*) sparkling; **un diamant plus é. que celui-là** a diamond that sparkles more than that one; **le lac était é. sous le soleil** the lake sparkled in the sunlight; **elle avait les yeux étincelants de colère/de convoitise/de joie** her eyes glinted *or* flashed with anger/gleamed with envy/ sparkled with joy
étinceler [etɛ̃sle] *vi* **(il étincelle; il étincelait; il étincellera)** (*d'un diamant, métal, lac etc*) to sparkle, to glitter; (*d'une étoile*) to twinkle, to glitter; (*des yeux, Fig de l'esprit, la conversation, un livre etc*) to sparkle; **ses yeux étincelaient de joie/de colère/de convoitise** his eyes sparkled with joy/ glinted *or* flashed with anger/gleamed with envy; **é. de propreté** to be sparkling clean
étincelle [etɛ̃sɛl] *nf* **(a)** (*du feu, d'allumage etc*) spark; **lancer des étincelles** to throw out sparks; (*d'un diamant, des yeux*) to sparkle, to flash; *Fig* **elle a fait des étincelles à ses derniers examens** she was brilliant *or* she shone in her last exams; *Fig F* **ça va faire des étincelles, il va y avoir des étincelles** sparks will fly; *Fig F* **j'ai peur de faire des étincelles** I'm afraid of causing trouble **(b)** *Fig* (*de vie, génie*) spark; (*de bon sens*) spark, glimmer; **il a eu une é. de génie** he had a stroke of genius, he had a brilliant idea; **une é. de courage** a fleeting moment of courage
étincellement [etɛ̃sɛlmɑ̃] *nm* (*d'un diamant, métal, lac etc*) sparkle, glitter; (*d'une étoile*) twinkle, glitter; (*des yeux*) sparkle
étiolement [etjɔlmɑ̃] *nm* **(a)** (*d'une plante*) legginess, stragginess; *Agr* (*intentionnel*) blanching; **pour empêcher l'é. de vos plantes** to stop your plants going leggy *or* straggly **(b)** *Méd* etiolation **(c)** *Fig* (*de l'esprit, la mémoire etc*) deterioration
étioler [etjɔle] **1** *vt* **(a)** (*plante*) to make leggy; *Agr* (*intentionnellement*) to blanch; **une plante étiolée** a leggy *or* straggly plant **(b)** **e. qn** (*du manque d'air*) to weaken sb, to make sb sickly; (*de la maladie*) to leave sb in a weakened condition *or* sickly; **une intelligence étiolée** an intellect in decline **2 s'étioler** *vpr* **(a)** (*d'une plante*) to go leggy **(b)** (*d'une personne*) to grow sickly, to go into a decline **(c)** (*de l'esprit, de la mémoire etc*) to deteriorate
étiologie [etjɔlɔʒi] *nf Méd* (*étude, causes*) aetiology, *US* etiology
étique [etik] *adj* emaciated
étiquetage [etiktaʒ] *nm* (*de bagages, colis etc*) labelling; (*de marchandises*) labelling, ticketing; **é. de l'apport nutritionnel** nutritional labelling; **é. de la composition** ingredient labelling; **é. des pourcentages** (*des principaux ingrédients*) percentage labelling; **é. du prix** price marking
étiqueter [etikte] *vt* **(j'étiquète; j'étiquèterai)** **(a)** (*bagage, colis etc*) to label; (*marchandises*) to label, to ticket **(b)** *Fig* (*personne*) to label **(comme** as)
étiqueteur, -euse [etiktœr, -øz] **1** *n* (*personne*) labeller **2** *nf* **étiqueteuse** (*machine*) labelling machine, labeller
étiquette [etikɛt] *nf* **(a)** (*d'une valise, d'un colis etc*) label; (*indiquant le prix*) (price) label, ticket; **coller une é. sur un paquet** to label a parcel, to stick a label on a parcel **(b)** *Fig* (*désignation*) (*d'une personne*) label; **coller une é. à qn** to stick a label on sb, to label sb; **é. politique** political affiliation; **quelle est son é. politique?** what are his politics? **(c)** (*protocole*) etiquette; **l'é. de la cour** Court etiquette *or* ceremonial
▶ **étiquette**: **é. d'adresse** address label; **é. autocollante** self-adhesive *or* sticky label; *Com* **é. de calibrage** (*d'un produit*) grade label; *Com* **é. descriptive** descriptive label; **é. 'fabriqué en'** 'made-in' label; **é. gommée** sticky label; **é. d'identification** (*d'un produit*) identification label; *Com* **é. magnétique** security tag; *Com* **é. porte-prix** price label; *Com* **é. d'un produit** product label; *Com* **é. promotionnelle** promotional label
étirable [etirabl] *adj* **film é.** cling film
étirage [etiraʒ] *nm* (*d'un métal, du verre etc*) drawing (out); **é. à chaud/froid** hot/cold drawing; **é. du fil** wire drawing
étirer [etire] **1** *vt* (*métal, verre etc*) to draw (out); (*fil, textiles*) to draw **2 s'étirer** *vpr* **(a)** (*se détendre*) (*d'une personne*) to stretch; **s'é. les jambes/les bras** to stretch one's legs/arms **(b)** (*s'allonger*) (*d'un tissu, vêtement*) to stretch **(c)** (*se prolonger*) (*d'une journée, d'une réunion etc*) to drag on (for ever); **la semaine s'étire en longueur** the week is dragging
étoffe [etɔf] *nf* **(a)** *Tex* material, fabric; **étoffes de soie** silk fabrics **(b)** *Fig* **avoir l'é. d'un chef d'état/d'un écrivain/d'un héros** to have the makings of a statesman/writer/hero; **elle a de l'é.** she's got character, there's a lot to her; **manquer d'é.** (*d'un film, un roman*) to lack substance, to be thin *or* insubstantial
étoffé [etɔfe] *adj* (*voix*) rich, full; **homme é.** stout *or* thickset man; **discours é.** pithy speech
étoffer [etɔfe] **1** *vt Fig* (*discours, livre, caractère*) to flesh out **2 s'étoffer** *vpr* (*d'une personne*) to fill out
étoile [etwal] *nf* **(a)** *Astron* star; **à la clarté des étoiles** in the starlight; **un ciel sans étoiles** a starless sky; **un ciel (par)semé d'étoiles** a starry *or* star-studded sky; **coucher** *ou* **dormir à la belle é.** to sleep in the open *or* out of doors; **né sous une bonne/mauvaise é.** born under a lucky/an unlucky star; **croire** *ou* **avoir foi en son é.** to believe in *or* trust to luck; *F* **voir des étoiles (en plein midi)** to see stars
(b) (*ornement, objet etc*) star; *Typ* asterisk, star; **é. à cinq branches** five-pointed star; **les graviers ont fait des étoiles sur le pare-brise** the gravel starred the windscreen; **hôtel cinq étoiles** five-star hotel; **c'est un deux étoiles** it has a two-star rating
(c) *Aut* roundabout, *Am* traffic circle
(d) *Cin, Th* (*vedette*) star; **une grande é. de la chanson** a big singing star; **é. montante** rising star
(e) *Ordinat* **connecté en é.** in a star configuration
▶ **étoile**: *Astron* **é. du berger** the evening star; **é. de David** Star of David; *Astron* **é. filante** shooting star; *Zool* **é. de mer** starfish; *Astron* **é. polaire** Pole Star; *Astron* **é. triple** triple star
étoilé [etwale] *adj* **(a)** (*ciel*) starry, star-studded; (*nuit*) starry, starlit; **la Bannière étoilée** the Star-Spangled Banner, the Stars and Stripes **(b)** (*fêlé*) (*pare-brise*) starred
étoiler [etwale] **1** *vt* **(a)** (*parsemer d'étoiles*) to stud with stars; *Fig* (*parsemer*) to stud **(de** with); **la nuit étoile le ciel** the night sky is studded with stars **(b)** (*pare-brise, verre etc*) to star, to make a star-shaped crack in **2 s'étoiler** *vpr* (*du ciel*) to fill with stars
étole [etɔl] *nf* (*fourrure*), *Rel* stole
étonnamment [etɔnamɑ̃] *adv* astonishingly, amazingly, surprisingly
étonnant [etɔnɑ̃] **1** *adj* astonishing, amazing; **rien d'é. à cela**

that's not surprising, no wonder; **ce n'est pas é. qu'il soit malade** it's not surprising *or* it's no wonder that he's ill; **comme c'est é., il m'avait dit le contraire** how strange *or* odd, he had told me the opposite; **c'est é. mais personne n'a été blessé** it's amazing *or* astonishing that no-one was hurt; **chose étonnante, il est arrivé** astonishingly *or* amazingly *or* surprisingly (enough), he arrived; **vous êtes é.!** you amaze me sometimes!

2 *nm* **l'é. est qu'il soit venu** the astonishing *or* amazing *or* surprising thing is that he came

étonné [etɔne] *adj* surprised; (*plus fort*) astonished, amazed (**de qch** at sth; **de voir** to see); **un regard é.** a surprised look; (*plus fort*) a look of astonishment *or* amazement, an astonished look; **je suis très é. qu'on ne m'ait rien dit** I'm amazed *or* astonished *or* extremely surprised that nobody said anything to me

étonnement [etɔnmɑ̃] *nm* astonishment, amazement, surprise; **frappé** *ou* **saisi d'é.** taken aback; **à mon grand é.** to my great surprise, much to my surprise, to my amazement; **imaginez (quel a été) mon é. quand ...** imagine my surprise *or* astonishment when ...; **faire l'é. de tout le monde** to astonish *or* surprise everybody

étonner [etɔne] **1** *vt* to astonish, to amaze, to surprise; **cela ne m'étonnerait pas** it wouldn't surprise me, I wouldn't be the least bit surprised; **ça ne m'étonne pas du tout** it doesn't surprise me in the least, I'm not the least bit surprised; **ce qui m'étonne, c'est qu'il a menti** what surprises *or* astonishes me is that he lied; **cela m'étonne qu'elle soit venue** I'm surprised *or* astonished *or* amazed that she came; **il n'est pas venu? ça m'étonne** *ou* **voilà qui m'étonne** he didn't come? that's surprising; *F* **alors ça, ça m'étonnerait** that'll be the day; **ça m'étonne de toi, tu m'étonnes** I'm surprised at you; *F* **tu m'étonnes!** you don't say!, tell me something I don't know!; **tu m'étonneras toujours!** you never cease to astonish me!

2 s'étonner *vpr* to be astonished, to be surprised, to wonder (**de** at); **je m'étonne de vous voir** I'm astonished *or* surprised to see you; **je m'étonne qu'il ne voie pas le danger** it amazes me *or* I am astonished that he does not see the danger; **comment s'é. qu'il ait refusé?** can you wonder *or* is it any wonder that he refused?; **je ne m'étonne plus de rien** nothing surprises me any more; **essaie, tu pourrais t'é. toi-même** try, you might surprise yourself

étouffant [etufɑ̃] *adj* (*air, chaleur, Fig atmosphère*) stifling, suffocating; (*temps*) oppressive, sultry; **une journée étouffante** a stifling hot day

étouffe-chrétien [etufkretjɛ̃] *nm inv, adj inv F* **sa tarte est un é., c'est de l'é. sa tarte** her tart is pure stodge; **c'est un peu é.** it's a bit stodgy

étouffée [etufe] *nf Culin* **cuire à l'é.** to braise

étouffement [etufmɑ̃] *nm* **(a)** (*asphyxie*) suffocation; **sensation d'é.** feeling of breathlessness, stifling feeling; **la victime a été tuée par é.** the victim was suffocated (to death); **mourir d'é.** to die of *or* from suffocation **(b)** *Fig* (*d'un scandale*) hushing up; (*de rumeurs, d'un complot, d'une révolte*) suppression

étouffer [etufe] **1** *vt* **(a)** (*personne*) (*avec un oreiller etc*) to suffocate, to smother; (*en serrant*) to suffocate, to choke; (*de plantes*) to choke; **la chaleur m'étouffe** the heat is stifling (me); *Iron* **ce ne sont pas les scrupules qui l'étouffent** he's not overscrupulous; **ça t'étoufferait de dire merci?** would it choke you to say thank you?; **ça t'étoufferait d'être poli?** it wouldn't kill you to be polite!

(b) *Fig* (*cri, passion, créativité*) to stifle; (*bâillement, rire*) to stifle, to smother, to suppress; (*feu*) to smother; (*révolte*) to quell, to suppress; (*scandale, affaire*) to hush up; (*son*) to muffle; *Mus* to damp; *Él* (*étincelle*) to quench; **é. un sanglot** to stifle a sob, to choke back a sob; **é. un scandale dans l'œuf** to nip a scandal in the bud

2 *vi* to suffocate; **é. de rire/colère** to choke with laughter/anger; *Fig* **dans cette ville, j'étouffais** I was suffocating in that town; **on étouffe ici** it's stifling here

3 s'étouffer *vpr* to suffocate; (*en mangeant*) to choke; **je me suis étouffé avec une bouchée de pain** I choked on a piece of bread; **plantes qui s'étouffent** plants that choke one another

étouffoir [etufwar] *nm* (*d'un piano*) damper

étourderie [eturdəri] *nf* **(a)** (*caractère*) carelessness, thoughtlessness, *F* scattiness; **faute d'é.** foolish mistake; **par é.** inadvertently, in an unthinking moment; **il est d'une é. incroyable** he is incredibly scatterbrained *or F* scatty **(b)** (*action*) foolish mistake

étourdi, -ie [eturdi] **1** *adj* (*irréfléchi*) thoughtless, careless; (*écervelé*) (*personne*) scatterbrained, featherbrained, *F* scatty **2** *n* (*écervelé*) scatterbrain, featherbrain **3** *nf Arch* **à l'étourdie** thoughtlessly, heedlessly

étourdiment [eturdimɑ̃] *adv* without thinking

étourdir [eturdir] **1** *vt* (*personne*) (*d'un coup, choc etc*) to stun, to daze; *Fig* (*d'un vin, d'éloges etc*) to make dizzy *or* giddy; **bruit qui étourdit les oreilles** deafening noise; *Fig* **je suis toute étourdie** my head's spinning **2 s'étourdir** *vpr* to let one's hair down, to live it up; **s'é. dans la boisson** to drown one's sorrows (in drink)

étourdissant [eturdisɑ̃] *adj* **(a)** (*bruit*) deafening, ear-splitting **(b)** (*nouvelles, succès etc*) staggering, stunning, astounding; **e. de beauté** astoundingly *or* staggeringly *or* stunningly beautiful, stunning; **e. de bêtise** astoundingly *or* staggeringly stupid

étourdissement [eturdismɑ̃] *nm* **(a)** (*vertige*) giddiness, dizziness; **avoir un é.** to feel giddy *or* dizzy; **cela me donne des étourdissements** it makes me feel giddy *or* dizzy, it makes my head spin *or* swim **(b)** *Litt* (*griserie*) (feeling of) euphoria; **vivre dans l'é.** to be euphoric

étourneau, -eaux [eturno] *nm* **(a)** (*oiseau*) starling **(b)** *F* (*personne*) scatterbrain

étrange [etrɑ̃ʒ] *adj* strange, peculiar, odd; **chose é., il est revenu** strange to say *or* strangely enough *or* oddly enough, he came back

étrangement [etrɑ̃ʒmɑ̃] *adv* strangely, oddly, peculiarly; **cela ressemble é. à la rougeole** it looks suspiciously like measles

étranger, -ère [etrɑ̃ʒe, -ɛr] **1** *adj* **(a)** (*d'un autre pays*) foreign; **Ministère des affaires étrangères** *Br* ≈ Foreign (and Commonwealth) Office, *US* ≈ State Department

(b) (*inconnu*) strange, unfamiliar (**à** to); **sa voix ne m'est pas étrangère** his voice is not unfamiliar; **la haine lui est étrangère** he doesn't know what hatred is; **la musique lui est étrangère** he has no knowledge of music, *F* music is a closed book to him

(c) (*extérieur*) foreign (**à** to); *Méd, Fig* **corps é.** foreign body; **entrée interdite à toute personne étrangère** no entry to unauthorized personnel; **des éléments étrangers se sont introduits dans l'enceinte de l'école** outsiders entered the school premises; **elle est étrangère à cette firme/au projet** she isn't a member of this firm/involved in the plan; **il est é. à tout ce qui s'est passé ici** he doesn't have anything to do with what happened here

2 *n* **(a)** (*d'un autre pays*) foreigner; *Admin* alien

(b) (*d'un autre groupe*) stranger, outsider; **ce club est fermé aux étrangers** the club is for members only; **je suis un é. ici** I'm a stranger here, *F* I'm a foreigner in these parts

3 *nm* **l'é.** (*pays étrangers*) foreign countries *or* parts; **aller/vivre à l'é.** to go/live abroad; **correspondant à l'é.** foreign correspondent; **voyages à l'é.** foreign travel; **investissement à l'é.** foreign *or* outward investment

étrangeté [etrɑ̃ʒte] *nf* (*d'une conduite, d'une robe etc*) strangeness, oddness, peculiarity

étranglé [etrɑ̃gle] *adj* (*passage, vallée etc*) narrow; (*taille*) nipped-in; (*voix*) strangled, choked, choking; *Méd* (*hernie*) strangulated

étranglement [etrɑ̃gləmɑ̃] *nm* **(a)** (*d'une personne*) strangling, strangulation; *Lutte* stranglehold; *Fig* (*de la liberté, la presse*) stifling; **il est mort par é.** he died of strangulation, he was strangled; **ce n'est pas l'é. qui a provoqué la mort** strangulation was not the cause of death; *Fig* **ces mesures représentent un véritable é. pour les petits épargnants** these measures have small savers in a stranglehold

(b) (*action de resserrer*) (*de la taille*) narrowing; (*d'un tube etc*) constriction, narrowing; *Aut, Tech* throttling; **soupape d'é.** throttle valve; *Méd* **é. herniaire** strangulated hernia

(c) (*partie resserrée*) (*d'une rivière*) narrow part, narrows; (*d'une route*) bottleneck; **la route présente un é.** the road bottlenecks *or* forms a bottleneck

étrangler [etrɑ̃gle] **1** *vt* **(a)** (*qn*) to strangle, to throttle; *Fig* (*liberté, la presse*) to stifle; **sa cravate l'étrangle** his tie is choking *or* strangling him; **la colère l'étrangle** he is choking with rage; *Fig* **les impôts m'étranglent** taxes are killing me

(b) (*resserrer*) (*taille, tube etc*) to constrict; *Tech* (*vapeur etc*) to throttle; *Méd* (*vaisseau sanguin*) to strangulate; *Aut* **é. le moteur** to throttle (down) the engine

2 s'étrangler *vpr* **(a)** (*en mangeant*) to choke (**avec** on); **s'é. (de colère/d'indignation/de rire)** to choke (with anger/indignation/laughter)

(b) (de voix) to choke; (*de paroles*) to stick in one's throat; **j'entendis un sanglot s'é.** I heard a choked sob; **mais les mots se sont étranglés** but the words died on his lips, but he couldn't get the words out

(c) (*se resserrer*) (*d'une rivière*) to narrow; (*d'une rue*) to narrow, to (form a) bottleneck

étrangleur, -euse [etrɑ̃glœr, -øz] **1** *n* (*personne*) strangler **2** *nm Aut, Tech* throttle

étrave [etrav] *nf Naut* stem; **de l'é. à l'étambot** from stem to stern; **lame d'é.** bow wave

être[1] [ɛtr] *nm* **(a)** *Phil* (*existence*) being; **l'ê. et le néant** being and nothingness

(b) (*âme*) being; **tout mon ê. se révolte à cette idée** my entire being rebels at the idea; **du fond de son ê.** from the depths of his being

(c) (*personne*) being; *Biol, Litt* being, creature; **je ne veux partager ce secret qu'avec un ê. cher** I want to share this secret only with someone close to me; **elle pensait aux êtres chers qui étaient si loin** she thought of her loved ones so far away; **l'ê. aimé** the beloved; **pauvres petits êtres!** poor little things!; **c'est un ê. hors du commun** he/she is someone out of the ordinary *or* is no common mortal; **c'est un ê. méprisable** he's a despicable creature; **un ê. supérieur** a higher *or* superior being; **nul ê. au monde ne t'a aimé plus que moi** no one in the world loved you more than I; **ê. fantastique/mythique/surnaturel** fantastic/mythical/ supernatural creature; *Litt* **un ê. de feu/lumière/ténèbres** a creature of fire/light/darkness

▶ **être**[1]: **ê. humain** human being; **l'Ê. suprême** the Supreme Being; **ê. vivant** living creature; **on n'a trouvé aucun ê. vivant sur cette planète** we found no living creature on the planet

être[2] *vi* (*prp* **étant**; *pp* **été**; *pr ind* **je suis, tu es, il est, n. sommes, v. êtes, ils sont**; *pr sub* **je sois, tu sois, il soit, n. soyons, v. soyez, ils soient**; *imp* **sois, soyons, soyez**; *impf* **j'étais**; *p hist* **je fus, tu fus, il fut, n. fûmes, v. fûtes, ils furent**; *p sub* **je fusse**; *fu* **je serai**) **(a)** (*exister*) to be; **je pense, donc je suis** I think, therefore I am; *Rel* **je suis celui qui est** I am that I am; **ce temps n'est plus où ...** the days are gone when ...; **l'ancien projet n'est plus** the old plan is a thing of the past; *Fml* **elle n'est plus** she is no longer with us; **quand on pense que tout cela aurait pu ne pas ê.** to think that all that may never have happened; **si cela était** if that were the case; **(et) quand cela serait** even if it were the case; **cela étant** that being so *or* the case; **la plus belle voiture qui soit** the finest car there is; **eh bien, soit!** very well then!; **ainsi soit-il** so be it, amen; *Rel* amen; **maudit soit-il!** damn him to hell! *Prov* **on ne peut pas ê. et avoir été** you can't stay young for ever; **nous sommes le dix** it's the tenth (today); **la vérité est entre ces extrêmes** the truth lies between these extremes

(b) (*copule*) to be; **c'est ma mère** this is my mother; (*au téléphone*) it's my mother; **c'est le chef le gare** he's the stationmaster; **c'est un** *ou* **il est chef de gare** he's a stationmaster; **soit AB la base d'un triangle** let AB be the base of a triangle; **soit un triangle ABC** given a triangle ABC; **l'homme est mortel** man is mortal; **nous étions deux/ plusieurs** there were two/several of us; **vous êtes tout pour moi** you mean everything to me; **c'est quelqu'un!** he/she's somebody!; *F* **est-il drôle!** he's so funny!

(c) (+ *adv*) to be; **vous êtes ici chez vous** treat this place like your own; **elle est très mal/beaucoup mieux** she is very ill/much better; **ê. bien avec qn** to be on good terms with sb

(d) (*locutions avec 'à' + nom*) **ê. au travail/à son bureau** to be at work/at one's desk; **ê. à l'agonie** to be dying; **vous n'êtes pas à ce que je dis** you're not paying attention to what I'm saying; **il est tout à son travail** he is entirely engrossed in his work; **il est à Paris** he is in Paris; **le temps est au beau** the weather's set fair; **le temps est à l'orage** there's a storm brewing; **les prix sont à la baisse** prices are on the decrease, prices are coming down

(e) (*locutions avec 'de' + nom*) **ce tableau est de Gauguin** this picture is by Gauguin; **il est de Londres** he is from London; **il était de la CIA** he was a member of the CIA; **il n'est pas des nôtres** he isn't one of us, he isn't with us; **serez-vous des nôtres, ce soir?** will you be joining us this evening?; **il est de mes amis** he's a friend of mine, he's one of my friends; **ê. de service** to be on duty; **ils sont de la même promotion** they're in the same year *or Am* class; **cet enfant est d'un caractère étrange** this child has a strange character *or* nature; **l'enfant est-il de lui?** is the child his?; **c'était d'un simple!** it was so simple!; **je suis de noce samedi prochain** I've got a wedding next Saturday

(f) (+ *à* + *inf*) **j'étais là à l'attendre** I was there waiting for him; **la maison est à louer** the house is to let; **elle est tout le temps à se plaindre** she's always *or* forever complaining; **elles étaient encore à médire** they were running people down again; **c'était à prévoir** it was to be expected; **c'est à craindre** I fear so

(g) (+ *à* + *inf avec idée d'obligation*) **cette idée est à creuser** this idea will have to be thoroughly looked into; **c'est à prendre ou à laisser** take it or leave it; **lui seul est à blâmer** he alone is to blame

(h) [①B61,3,b,i] (*avec 'ce'*) **je sais ce qui est arrivé** I know what happened; **savez-vous ce que c'est?** do you know what it is?; **est-ce vrai?** is it true?; **serait-ce vrai?** can it be *or* could it (possibly) be true?; **ce n'est pas qu'il soit ingrat, mais ...** it's not that he's ungrateful, but ...; **ne fût-ce que, ne serait-ce que** if only; **vous venez, n'est-ce pas?** you're coming, aren't you?; **vous ne venez pas, n'est-ce pas?** you're not coming, are you?; **n'est-ce pas qu'il a de la chance?** isn't he lucky?; *Litt* **je le ferais (si ce) n'était que je dois partir** I would do it if I didn't have to leave; **n'était mon rhumatisme** if it weren't *or* wasn't for my rheumatism; **il l'aurait bien épousée, n'eût été qu'il la trouvait trop orgueilleuse** he would gladly have married her, were it not for the fact that he found her too proud

(i) [①B27,E,2,b] (*impers*) **il est midi** it is twelve o'clock; **il est temps de partir** it is time to go; **il est de mon devoir de rester** it is my duty to stay; *Litt* **il n'est que de comparer les deux pour se rendre compte de leur différence** one need only compare the two to become aware of the difference between them; **il n'est point d'amours sans larmes** there is no love without tears; **comme si de rien n'était** as if nothing had happened; **soit dit sans offense** if you don't mind my saying so; **il était une fois une fée** once upon a time there was a fairy; **un héros, s'il en fut (jamais)** a hero, if ever there was one; **il est à craindre/prévoir que ...** it's feared/ expected that ...; **il est à croire/espérer que ...** it's to be believed/hoped that ...; **il fut un temps où ...** there was a time when ...; **il m'est très douloureux de vous annoncer ...** it is with great sorrow that I inform you ...; **il m'est impossible de vous répondre** it's impossible for me to give you an answer; **il est probable qu'ils sont déjà mariés** they're probably already married

(j) (*avec 'en' indéterminé*) **où en sommes-nous?** how far have we got?, where are we?; **où en êtes-vous de vos travaux?** how far have you got with you work?; **l'affaire en est là** that is how things stand; **j'en étais là de mes suppositions quand ...** I'd reached that point *or* I'd got that far in my assumptions when ...; **si vous m'aviez écouté, on n'en serait pas là** if you had listened to me, we wouldn't be where we are now; **vous n'en êtes pas encore là!** you haven't come to that (point *or* stage) yet!; **il n'en est pas à son coup d'essai** this is not his first attempt; **je ne sais plus où j'en suis** I don't know where I am *or* what I'm doing; **j'en suis à me demander si ...** I'm beginning to wonder whether ...; **nous n'en sommes pas à le renvoyer** we haven't reached the point of sacking him yet; **on n'en est pas à un franc près** we're not going to quibble over a franc; **j'en suis pour mon argent** I've spent my money to no purpose, I've thrown my money away; **j'en suis pour mille francs** I'm a thousand francs the poorer; **c'en est trop!** it's too much!, this is past bearing!; **c'en est assez!** enough!; **il en est de l'homme comme de la nature** it's the same with man as with nature; **puisqu'il en est ainsi** since that's how things are; **il n'en est rien!** nothing of the kind!; **comment pourrait-il en ê. autrement?** how could it be any other way?, how could things be any different?; **il en est** (*d'un complot, d'une société secrète etc*) he's one of them; (*est homosexuel*) he's one of them, he's the other way inclined; **nous allons faire une partie de golf, vous en êtes?** we're going to have a round of golf, can we count you in? *or* are you game? *or* are you up for it?

(k) (*avec 'y' indéterminé*) **il y est pour quelque chose** he's got something to do with it; **j'y suis pour un tiers** I'm in for a third share; **ça y est!** that's it!; **ça y est? tu as fini?** is that it? have you finished?; **vous y êtes?** (*vous comprenez?*) are you with me?, have you got it?; (*vous avez trouvé?*) have you got it?

(l) (*appartenir*) **ê. à qn** to belong to sb; **à qui sont ces livres?** whose books are these?, who do these books belong to?; **la victoire est à nous** victory is ours; **je suis à vous dans un moment** I'll be with you in a moment; **sois à moi!** be mine!; **c'est à vous de jouer** it's your turn to play; **c'est à vous de veiller sur l'enfant** it's your job *or* it's up to you to look after the child

(m) [①B25-26,C; B36,I,2,c,ii] (*avec* **aller, rester, tomber** *etc aux temps composés*) **il est déjà arrivé** he has already arrived; **il est arrivé hier** he arrived yesterday; **elle est née en 1950** she was born in 1950

(n) [①B36,I,2,c,ii] (*avec vpr aux temps composés*) **nous nous sommes trompés** we (have) made a mistake; **ils se sont aimés** they loved each other; **elle s'est fait mal** she (has) hurt herself

(o) [①A53,16; B36,J] (*pour indiquer le passif*) to be; **il fut puni par son père** he was punished by his father; **il est aimé de tout le monde** he is loved by everyone; **j'entends ê. obéi** I mean to be obeyed (**p**) *F* (= *aller aux temps composés et au passé simple*) **j'avais été à Paris** I had been to Paris; **j'ai été voir Martin** I've been *or* I went to see Martin; **vous avez été trop loin** you went too far, you've gone too far; **ça a été** (*ça a marché*) it went OK

(**q**) (= *s'en aller au passé simple*) **il s'en fut ouvrir la porte** he went off to open the door

(**r**) **quand il fut pour partir** just as he was about to leave

étreindre [etrɛ̃dr] *vt* (*prp* **étreignant**; *pp* **étreint**; *pr ind* **j'étreins, il étreint, n. étreignons**; *impf* **j'étreignais**; *p hist* **j'étreignis**; *fu* **j'étreindrai**) (*qn*) to embrace, to clasp in one's arms; **spectacle qui vous étreint le cœur** sight that wrings one's heart, heart-rending sight; **la peur/la douleur l'étreignait** fear/pain gripped him; **la douleur l'étreignait trop fort** the pain had too strong a grip *or* hold (on him); *Prov* **qui trop embrasse mal étreint** = that's what comes of trying to do too much at once

étreinte [etrɛ̃t] *nf* (**a**) (*entre personnes*) embrace; **ils ne pouvaient cesser leurs étreintes** they couldn't stop embracing *or* hugging (**b**) *Lutte* lock (**c**) *Fig* (*pression*) grip; **tu ne peux imaginer ce qu'est l'é. de la misère** you cannot imagine what it's like to be in the grip of poverty; **l'é. de la douleur se faisait sentir de plus en plus** the pain was strengthening its grip *or* hold

étrenne [etrɛn] *nf* (**a**) (*cadeau*) **étrennes** New Year's gift; **les étrennes du facteur/de l'éboueur** ≈ the postman's/dustman's Christmas box (**b**) (*premier usage*) **avoir l'é. de qch** to have the first use of sth, to be the first person to use sth, *F* to christen sth; **pour une fois, tu auras l'é. d'un manteau** you'll have a new coat for once

étrenner [etrene] **1** *vt* (*objet*) to use for the first time, *F* to christen; (*vêtement*) to wear for the first time; **c'est moi qui vais é. les nouveaux bureaux** I'll be the first person to use the new offices **2** *vi Arg* **tu vas é.!** (*être puni*) you're going to catch *or* get it!

êtres [ɛtr] *nmpl Arch* **connaître les ê. d'une maison** to know one's way about a house

étrier [etrije] *nm* (**a**) *Équitation* stirrup; **vider les étriers** to be thrown; *Fig* to be thrown *or* disconcerted; *Fig* **avoir le pied à l'é.** to be on the point of leaving; (*être en bonne voie pour réussir*) to be off to a good start; *Fig* **il a eu du mal à mettre le pied à l'é.** he had trouble getting started *or* getting off the ground; *Fig* **mettre le pied à l'é. à qn** to give sb a helping hand; **boire** *ou* **prendre le coup de l'é.** to have one for the road

(**b**) *Méd* **é. (de soutien)** stirrup, leg rest; **é. (de traction** *ou* **de réduction)** calliper

(**c**) *Anat* (*de l'oreille*) stirrup bone

(**d**) *Aut* stirrup, shackle; (*de frein*) caliper

étrille [etrij] *nf* (**a**) (*brosse*) currycomb (**b**) *Zool* small edible crab

étriller [etrije] *vt* (**a**) (*cheval*) to curry (**b**) *F* (*réprimander*) **é. qn** to give sb a dressing-down *or* a telling-off (**c**) *F* (*faire payer trop cher*) to fleece, to sting

étripage [etripaʒ] *nm* (*d'un poisson, d'un lièvre*) gutting; (*d'un poulet etc*) drawing; *F* (*tuerie*) bloodbath, slaughter

étriper [etripe] **1** *vt* (*poisson, lièvre*) to gut; (*poulet etc*) to draw; *Fig F* **je vais l'é.** I'll murder *or* slaughter him, I'll have his guts for garters **2 s'étriper** *vpr F* (*se battre*) to make mincemeat of each other

étriqué [etrike] *adj* (**a**) (*vêtement*) skimpy, tight (**b**) *Fig* (*perspective, vie*) narrow; (*avenir*) limited

étriquer [etrike] *vt Couture* (*vêtement*) to make too tight; **cette robe vous étrique** that dress is too tight on you

étriver [etrive] *Can* **1** *vt* to irritate, to annoy **2** *vi* **faire é.** to drive mad

étrivière [etrivjɛr] *nf* stirrup leather

étroit [etrwa] *adj* (**a**) (*peu large*) (*ruban, sentier, épaules, Fig esprit, vue*) narrow; (*espace, pièce etc*) narrow, confined, cramped; *Fig* (*idées*) hidebound; *Fig* **la voie étroite** the straight and narrow; *Fig* **avoir l'esprit é.** to be narrow-minded

(**b**) (*serré*) (*nœud*) tight; (*manteau etc*) tight(-fitting); *Fig* (*amitié, lien etc*) close; **je suis en rapport é. avec sa sœur** I am in close contact *or* touch with his sister; **être en étroite collaboration avec** to work closely *or* in close co-operation with; **règlements étroits** strict rules; **sous étroite surveillance** under close surveillance; **le sens é. d'un mot** the strict meaning of a word

(**c**) **être à l'é.** (*dans son logement etc*) to be cramped for room; (*financièrement*) to be in straitened circumstances

étroitement [etrwatmɑ̃] *adv* (**a**) (*nouer, tenir*) tightly; *Fig* (*lier, collaborer*) closely (**b**) (*observer une règle*) strictly; **surveiller qn é.** to watch sb closely, to keep a close watch on sb

étroitesse [etrwatɛs] *nf* (*d'un ruban, d'un sentier, des épaules etc*) narrowness; *Fig* **é. d'esprit** narrow-mindedness; **l'é. de ce bureau** the lack of space in this office

étron [etrɔ̃] *nm* piece of excrement, *Vulg* turd

étrusque [etrysk] **1** *adj* Etruscan **2** *n* **É.** Etruscan

Ets *Com* (*abrév* **établissements**) **Ets Legrand** Legrand

étude [etyd] *nf* (**a**) *Scol, Univ etc* (*action*) (*d'un sujet, texte, auteur etc*) study, survey; **voyage d'études** educational *or* study tour; **aimer l'é.** to like studying; **faire des études de français/de droit** to study *or Br* read French/law; **il a fait ses études à Eton/Oxford** he was educated at Eton/he went to *or* studied at Oxford; **payer les études de qn** to pay for sb's education; **faire de brillantes études** to do extremely well at university; **j'ai arrêté mes études à 16 ans** I left school when I was 16; **négliger ses études** to neglect one's studies; **achever ses études** to finish one's studies *or* education; *Péj* **cela sent l'é.** it reeks of effort

(**b**) *Scol* (*heure*) (private) study period, *Br* prep; (**salle d'**)**é.** (private) study room, *Br* prep room; **je laisse mes enfants à l'é. jusque 5 heures** = I leave the children in homework class until 5 o'clock

(**c**) (*action de considérer*) (*d'une question, d'un plan etc*) study, investigation, survey; *Constr* survey; **bureau d'études** research department; **ingénieur d'études** design engineer; **voyage d'études** study *or* field trip; **procéder à l'é. d'une question, mettre une question à l'é.** to study *or* investigate *or* go into a question

(**d**) (*texte, musique, peinture etc*) study; *Mus* **é. pour violon** violin study; *Beaux-Arts* **é. de tête** study of a head

(**e**) (*bureau*) office; (*d'un avocat*) office, *Br* chambers; (*charge*) (*d'un juriste*) practice

▶ **étude**: *Mktg, Com* **é. AIO** AIO research; **é. d'audience** audience research; **é. des besoins** needs study *or* analysis; **é. de cas** case study; **é. commerciale** marketing study; **études commerciales** *Mktg* marketing research; (*dans école de commerce etc*) business studies; **é. de communication** communications study; **é. comparative** comparative study; **é. du comportement** behavioural study *or* analysis; **é. du comportement du consommateur** consumer behaviour study; **é. auprès des consommateurs** consumer *or* customer survey; **é. auprès des consommateurs finaux** end-user survey; **é. documentaire** desk research; **é. de faisabilité** feasibility study; **é. du lectorat** readership survey; **é. de marché** market research; **une é. de marché** a market study; **faire une é. de marché** to do market research; **ce cabinet est spécialisé dans les études de marché** the company specializes in market research; **é. de marché standard** omnibus survey; **é. mercatique** marketing study; **études qualitatives** qualitative research; **études quantitatives** quantitative research; **é. de satisfaction de la clientèle** customer satisfaction survey; **é. sur le terrain** field study; **études sur le terrain** field research; **études sur les ventes** sales research

étudiant, -ante [etydjɑ̃, -ɑ̃t] **1** *n* student; **é. en médecine/en droit/en lettres** medical/law/arts student; **é. de première/seconde année** first/second-year student, *US* freshman/sophomore **2** *adj* (*vie, mouvement etc*) student

étudié [etydje] *adj* (**a**) (*soigneusement préparé*) (*effet, discours etc*) carefully prepared; **prix très étudiés** very fair prices (**b**) *Péj* (*affecté*) (*politesse, geste*) affected, studied; (*manières, sourires*) affected

étudier [etydje] (*impf, pr sub* **n. étudiions**) **1** *vt* (**a**) *Scol, Univ etc* (*sujet, texte, auteur etc*) to study; *Scol* (*leçon*) to prepare; *Mus, Th* (*instrument, rôle etc*) to study; **é. une matière en vue d'un examen** to read up a subject for an examination

(**b**) *Péj* (*son apparence etc*) to study; **elle étudie ses poses** she strikes poses

(**c**) (*considérer*) (*question, plan, théorie etc*) to study, to examine; **sa demande mérite d'être étudiée** his application merits examination

(**d**) (*observer*) (*société, personne, visage etc*) to study

2 *vi* to study

3 s'étudier *vpr* (**a**) (*se regarder, s'analyser*) to study *or* examine oneself, to take stock of oneself; *Péj* (*manquer de naturel*) to be affected

(**b**) (*s'observer l'un l'autre*) to study each other, to take stock of each other; **ils se sont longuement étudiés** they took careful stock of each other

(**c**) *Arch* **s'é. à faire qch** to take pains to do sth, to make a point of doing sth; **il s'étudiait à m'éviter** he studiously avoided me

étui [etɥi] *nm* case; **é. (de revolver)** holster; **é. de cartouche** cartridge case; **é. à lunettes** glasses case; *Naut* **é. de voile** sail cover

étuvage [etyvaʒ] *nm Ch, Ind* (*séchage*) drying; (*stérilisation*) sterilization

étuve [etyv] *nf* **(a)** (*aux thermes*) steam room; **é. sèche** hot-air steam cabinet; **é. humide** steam *or* vapour bath **(b)** *Ch, Ind etc* (*pour sécher*) drying oven; (*pour stériliser*) sterilizer; **é. à incubation** *ou* **à cultures** incubator **(c)** *F* (*lieu où il fait trop chaud*) oven

étuvée [etyve] *nf Culin* **à l'é.** braised

étuver [etyve] *vt* **(a)** (*sécher*) (*fruit etc*) to dry; (*stériliser*) (*vêtements contaminés etc*) to sterilize **(b)** *Culin* to braise

étymologie [etimɔlɔʒi] *nf* (*science, origine*) etymology

étymologique [etimɔlɔʒik] *adj* etymological

étymologiquement [etimɔlɔʒikmɑ̃] *adv* etymologically

étymologiste [etimɔlɔʒist] *n* etymologist

étymon [etimɔ̃] *nm* etymon

eu [y] *voir* **avoir**[1]

eucalyptus [økaliptys] *nm* eucalyptus; **essence d'e.** eucalyptus oil

Eucharistie (l') [løkaristi] *nf Rel* the Eucharist

eucharistique [økaristik] *adj Rel* Eucharistic(al)

Euclide [øklid] *nm* Euclid

euclidien, -ienne [øklidjɛ̃, -jɛn] *adj Math* Euclidean

eugénique [øʒenik] *nf,* **eugénisme** [øʒenism] *nm* eugenics

euh [ø] *int* er

eunuque [ønyk] *nm* eunuch

euphémique [øfemik] *adj* euphemistic

euphémiquement [øfemikmɑ̃] *adv* euphemistically

euphémisme [øfemism] *nm* euphemism

euphonie [øfɔni] *nf* euphony

euphonique [øfɔnik] *adj* euphonious, euphonic

euphorbe [øfɔrb] *nf Bot* euphorbia

euphorie [øfɔri] *nf* euphoria

euphorique [øfɔrik] *adj* euphoric

euphorisant [øfɔrizɑ̃] **1** *adj* (*effet, atmosphère etc*) exhilarating; *Méd* (*drogue*) anti-depressant, *Spéc* euphoriant **2** *nm* anti-depressant drug, *Spéc* euphoriant

Euphrate [øfrat] *nm* **l'E.** the Euphrates

eurafricain, -aine [ørafrikɛ̃, -ɛn] **1** *adj* Eurafrican **2** *n* **E.** Eurafrican

Eurasie [ørazi] *nf* Eurasia

eurasien, -ienne [ørazjɛ̃, -jɛn] **1** *adj* Eurasian **2** *n* **E.** Eurasian

eurêka [øreka] *int* eureka

eurent [yr] *voir* **avoir**[1]

Euripide [øripid] *nm* Euripides

EURL [əyɛrɛl] *nf Com* (*abrév* **entreprise unipersonnelle à responsabilité limitée**) trader with limited liability

euro- [øro] *préf* Euro-

eurobanque [ørobɑ̃k] *nf* Eurobank

eurobudget [ørobydʒɛ] *nm* Eurobudget

eurochèque [øroʃɛk] *nm* Eurocheque

eurocommunisme [ørokɔmynism] *nm* Eurocommunism

eurocrate [ørokrat] *n* Eurocrat

eurocrédit [ørokredi] *nm* Euroloan

eurodevise [ørodəviz] *nf Fin* Eurocurrency

eurodollar [ørodɔlar] *nm Fin* Eurodollar

eurofranc [ørofrɑ̃] *nm* eurofranc

euromarché [øromarʃe] *nm Fin* Euromarket

euromissile [øromisil] *nm* Euromissile

euromonnaie [øromɔnɛ] *nf Fin* Eurocurrency

euro-obligation *nf Fin* Eurobond

Europe [ørɔp] *nf* Europe; **l'E. verte** (European) Community agriculture *or* farming; **l'E. des douze** the Europe of the Twelve

européanisation [øropeanizasjɔ̃] *nf* Europeanization

européaniser [øropeanize] **1** *vt* to Europeanize **2 s'européaniser** *vpr* to become Europeanized

européen, -enne [øropeɛ̃, -ɛn] **1** *adj* European **2** *n* **E.** European

eurosceptique [ørosɛptik] *n Pol* Eurosceptic

eurostratégique [ørostrateʒik] *adj Mil* Eurostrategic

Eurotunnel [ørotynɛl] *nm* Channel tunnel, Chunnel

Eurovision [ørovizjɔ̃] *nf* Eurovision

eut [y] *voir* **avoir**[1]

euthanasie [øtanazi] *nf* euthanasia

eutrophe [øtrɔf], **eutrophique** [øtrɔfik] *adj* eutrophic

eutrophisation [øtrɔfizasjɔ̃] *f* eutrophication

eux [ø] *voir* **lui**[2]

évacuateur, -trice [evakɥatør, -tris] *adj* (*tuyau etc*) drainage

évacuation [evakɥasjɔ̃] *nf* **(a)** (*de matières du corps*) evacuation, voiding, discharge; (*d'eau, de pus etc*) draining (off); **course d'é.** (*d'un moteur*) exhaust stroke **(b)** (*de population, troupes, blessés etc*) evacuation; (*d'une salle etc*) evacuation, clearing; *Naut* (*d'un bateau*) abandoning; *Mil* **hôpital d'é.** clearing hospital

évacué, -ée [evakɥe] *n* evacuee

évacuer [evakɥe] *vt* **(a)** (*matières du corps*) to evacuate, to discharge, to void; (*vapeur*) to vent; (*eau, pus etc*) to drain (off) **(b)** (*faire partir*) to evacuate; **faire é. tous les habitants** to evacuate all the inhabitants **(c)** (*quitter*) (*forteresse, ville etc*) to evacuate, to vacate; **faire é. une salle** to evacuate *or* clear a hall; *Naut* **é. le bâtiment** to abandon ship **(d)** *Fig* (*problème*) to get rid of, to solve; **c'est une question que je préfèrerai é. le plus vite possible** it's a matter I'd like to dispose of as soon as possible

évadé, -ée [evade] *n* escaped prisoner, fugitive

évader (s') [sevade] *vpr* (*de prison, de la réalité etc*) to escape (**de** from)

évaluateur, -trice [evalɥatœr, -tris] *n Can* valuer, appraiser

évaluation [evalɥasjɔ̃] *nf* **(a)** (*action*) (*d'une propriété, d'un bien etc*) valuation, appraisal; (*des dommages*) assessment; (*d'un poids, d'un nombre, des risques etc*) estimation; *Com* **é. du coût** cost assessment; **é. des coûts** cost analysis **(b)** (*quantité, valeur*) (*d'une propriété, d'un bien etc*) valuation; (*des dommages*) assessment; (*d'un poids, d'un nombre, des risques etc*) estimate

évaluer [evalɥe] *vt* to evaluate; (*propriété, bien etc*) to value, to appraise; (*dommages*) to assess (**à** at); (*poids, nombre, risques etc*) to estimate; *Fin* **é. le(s) coût(s) de** to cost

évanescent [evanesɑ̃] *adj* evanescent

évangélique [evɑ̃ʒelik] *adj Rel* evangelical

évangélisateur, -trice [evɑ̃ʒelizatœr, -tris] **1** *adj* evangelistic **2** *n* evangelist

évangélisation [evɑ̃ʒelizasjɔ̃] *nf* evangelization

évangéliser [evɑ̃ʒelize] *vt* to evangelize

évangélisme [evɑ̃ʒelism] *nm* evangelism

évangéliste [evɑ̃ʒelist] *nm* evangelist; (*auteur de l'un des Évangiles*) Evangelist

évangile [evɑ̃ʒil] *nm* **(a)** *Rel* **l'É.** the Gospel; **l'É. selon saint Jean** the Gospel according to St. John; **l'é. du jour** the gospel for the day; *Fig* **prendre qch pour parole d'é.** to take sth for gospel (truth); *Fig* **ce n'est pas l'é.** it's not Holy Writ **(b)** *Fig* (*livre important*) bible

évanoui [evanwi] *adj* unconscious; **tomber é.** to fall down in a faint; **on l'a trouvé é.** he was found unconscious *or* in a (dead) faint

évanouir (s') [sevanwir] *vpr* **(a)** (*disparaître*) (*d'une silhouette, apparition, ombre*) to vanish, to disappear; (*d'un souvenir, rêve*) to fade (away); (*d'un son*) to die away, to fade away **(b)** (*perdre conscience*) to faint

évanouissement [evanwismɑ̃] *nm* **(a)** (*disparition*) (*d'un fantôme, d'une personne etc*) vanishing, disappearance; (*d'un souvenir, rêve*) fading; (*d'un son*) dying away, fading away **(b)** (*syncope*) faint(ing fit); **avoir un é.** to faint **(c)** *Aut* (*de freins*) fade

évaporation [evapɔrasjɔ̃] *nf* evaporation

évaporé, -ée [evapɔre] *Péj* **1** *adj* featherbrained, scatterbrained **2** *n* featherbrain, scatterbrain

évaporer [evapɔre] **1** *vi* **faire é. un liquide** to evaporate a liquid **2** *vt Arch* **é. un liquide** to evaporate a liquid **3 s'évaporer** *vpr* **(a)** (*d'un liquide, parfum etc*) to evaporate **(b)** *F* (*disparaître*) to vanish (into thin air)

évasé [evaze] *adj* (*vase, tuyau etc*) wide-mouthed; (*vêtement*) flared

évasement [evazmɑ̃] *nm* (*d'un vase, tuyau etc*) wide mouth; (*d'un vêtement*) flare

évaser [evaze] **1** *vt* (*vase, verre etc*) to widen (out) the opening of; (*tuyau, conduite etc*) to open out; (*ouverture*) to widen; *Couture* (*vêtement*) to flare **2 s'évaser** *vpr* to widen, to open out; *Couture* to flare

évasif, -ive [evazif, -iv] *adj* evasive

évasion [evazjɔ̃] *nf* **(a)** (*de prison etc*) escape (**de** from); **réussir son é.** to succeed in escaping; **le roi de l'é.** the master escaper **(b)** *Fig* (*distraction*) escape; (*hors de la réalité*) escapism; **avoir besoin d'é.** to need to escape; **littérature d'é.** escapist literature

▶ **évasion**: **é. de capitaux** flight *or* exodus of capital; **é. fiscale** tax evasion

évasivement [evazivmɑ̃] *adv* evasively

Ève [ɛv] *nf* Eve; *F* **je ne le connais ni d'È. ni d'Adam** I don't know him from Adam

évêché [eveʃe] *nm* (*diocèse*) bishopric, see; (*palais*) bishop's palace; (*dignité*) bishopric

éveil [evɛj] *nm* **(a)** (*action*) (*de la nature, la curiosité, la nation etc*) awakening; **être en é.** (*d'une personne*) to be on the alert; (*de l'esprit*) to be alert **(b)** (*alerte*) **donner l'é.** to raise the alarm; **donner l'é. à qn** to alert sb, to put sb on his/her guard

éveillé [eveje] *adj* **(a)** (*non endormi*) awake; **rêve é.** waking dream; **tenir qn é.** to keep sb awake; **é. ou endormi** waking or sleeping **(b)** (*vif*) (*personne*) wide-awake, alert, bright; **garçon (à l'esprit) é.** bright boy

éveiller [eveje] **1** *vt Litt* (*qn*) to awake(n); *Fig* (*curiosité, soupçons, jalousie etc*) to arouse, to awaken; (*intelligence,* *imagination etc*) to bring out, to develop **2 s'éveiller** *vpr* (*d'une personne*) to awake(n); *Fig* (*de la curiosité, des soupçons etc*) to be aroused; (*de l'intelligence, de l'imagination etc*) to show itself, to develop; *Litt* **elle s'éveille à l'amour** she is awakening to love

événement [evɛnmɑ̃] *nm* event, occurrence; *Fig* (*livre, spectacle etc important*) event; **attendre la suite des événements** to await the course of events; **créer l'é.** to make big news; **semaine fertile en événements** eventful week; **é. médiatique** media event; **les événements (de mai 68)** the events of '68 (*student unrest etc*); *Hum* **quand il fait la vaisselle, c'est (tout) un é.** when he does the dishes it's a cause for celebration *or* it's a red letter day

événementiel, -elle [evɛnmɑ̃sjɛl] *adj* (*information, histoire, programme télévisé etc*) factual

évent [evɑ̃] *nm* **(a)** (*de la nourriture, d'un vin, d'un parfum*) mustiness; (*de la bière*) flatness, staleness **(b)** (*d'une baleine*) blowhole, spout **(c)** *Tech* vent(hole)

éventail [evɑ̃taj] *nm* **(a)** (*instrument*) fan; **en é.** fan-shaped; *Fig F* **elle est restée les doigts de pied en é. toute la matinée** she lazed around all morning; **voûte en é.** fan vaulting **(b)** (*choix*) (*de marchandises, salaires, possibilités etc*) range, mix, set; **é. de produits** product *or* sales mix

éventaire [evɑ̃tɛr] *nm* **(a)** (*d'un marchand ambulant etc*) tray **(b)** (*étal*) (street) stall

éventé [evɑ̃te] *adj* (*nourriture, vin, parfum etc*) musty; (*bière*) flat, stale; *Fig* (*secret*) well-known

éventer [evɑ̃te] **1** *vt* **(a)** (*vêtements*) to air; (*grain*) to expose to the air; (*mine, mèche*) to ventilate **(b)** (*avec un éventail etc*) to fan **(c)** *Fig* (*découvrir*) (*secret, complot*) to find out, to discover; **é. la mèche** to discover *or* find out the secret; **le secret est éventé** the secret is out **2 s'éventer** *vpr* **(a)** (*de la nourriture, d'un vin, d'un parfum*) to go musty; (*de la bière*) to go flat *or* stale **(b)** (*avec un éventail etc*) to fan oneself

éventration [evɑ̃trasjɔ̃] *nf Méd* rupture, hernia

éventrer [evɑ̃tre] *vt* (*personne, animal*) to disembowel, to eviscerate; (*poisson*) to gut; (*volaille*) to draw; (*colis*) to rip *or* tear open; (*fût, boîte*) to break *or* smash open; (*porte*) to burst open; (*sac, matelas*) to slit open

éventreur [evɑ̃trœr] *nm* disemboweller; **Jack l'É.** Jack the Ripper

éventualité [evɑ̃tɥalite] *nf* **(a)** (*circonstance*) eventuality, contingency, possibility; **parer à toute é.** to provide for all eventualities *or* contingencies; **dans l'é. d'un changement de date** in the event of a change of date; **dans cette é.** if that happens *or* should happen **(b)** (*possibilité*) (*de guerre etc*) possibility

éventuel, -elle [evɑ̃tɥɛl] *adj* (*successeur, profits, guerre etc*) possible, potential; **client é.** potential *or* prospective customer

éventuellement [evɑ̃tɥɛlmɑ̃] *adv* possibly; **il viendra avec sa cousine et é. avec sa tante** he'll come with his cousin and possibly with his aunt; **faites cet exercice en vous servant é. d'un dictionnaire** do this exercise using a dictionary if necessary; **j'aurais é. besoin de votre concours** I may need your help (later); **tu veux venir avec nous? – é.!** do you want to come with us? – possibly!

évêque [evɛk] *nm Rel* bishop, *Prov* **un chien regarde bien un é.** a cat may look at a king; **bonnet d'é.** bishop's mitre; *F* (*d'une volaille*) parson's nose

évertuer (s') [sevɛrtɥe] *vpr* **s'é. à faire qch** to do one's utmost *or* make every effort to do sth; **je m'évertue à lui répéter que c'est impossible** I'm tired of telling him that it's impossible; **s'é. sur qch** to struggle with sth

éviction [eviksjɔ̃] *nf* (*d'un rival, d'une tête de parti etc*) ousting, supplanting; (*d'un locataire*) eviction; **depuis son é. du parti** since his ousting *or* since being ousted from the party

évidage [evidaʒ] *nm* (*d'une pierre, du bois etc*) hollowing out, scooping out

évidement [evidmɑ̃] *nm* (*action*) (*d'une pierre, du bois etc*) hollowing out, scooping out; *Chir* scraping out

évidemment [evidamɑ̃] *adv* **(a)** (*bien sûr*) of course **(b)** *Arch* (*incontestablement*) obviously, clearly

évidence [evidɑ̃s] *nf* **(a)** (*d'un fait, de la vérité etc*) obviousness, clearness; **se rendre à l'é.** to yield to *or* face the facts; **nier** *ou* **refuser l'é.** to deny the obvious *or* what is obvious; **de toute é., à l'é.** clearly, obviously; **mais c'est une é.!, mais c'est l'é. même** but it's obvious *or* self-evident! **(b) être en é.** (*d'un objet*) to be in a prominent position, to be conspicuous; **mettre en é.** (*marchandises*) to display prominently; (*idée*) to give prominence to, to underline; **je vais les laisser bien en é. sur la table** I'll leave them in a prominent position on the table; **se mettre en é.** to try to get oneself noticed

évident [evidɑ̃] *adj* (*erreur, vérité, preuve, raisonnement*) obvious, clear, plain; **il est é. qu'elle se trompe** it is obvious *or* clear that she is mistaken; **il était d'une évidente mauvaise foi** he was obviously *or* clearly insincere; **tu crois qu'on va réussir? – c'est é.!** do you think we'll succeed? – of course (we will)!; *F* **c'est pas é.!** (*pas facile*) it's not so easy

évider [evide] *vt* (*pierre, bois etc*) to hollow out, to scoop out; *Culin* (*tomate, pomme etc*) to scoop out

évier [evje] *nm* sink

évincer [evɛ̃se] *vt* (**j'évinçai(s)**) (*rival, tête de parti etc*) to oust (**de** from), to supplant; (*locataire*) to evict

éviscération [eviserasjɔ̃] *nf Chir* evisceration

éviscérer [evisere] *vt* (**j'éviscère, n. éviscérons**) to eviscerate

évitable [evitabl] *adj* avoidable

évitage [evitaʒ] *nm Naut* **(a)** (*mouvement*) (*d'un bateau*) swinging; **bassin d'é.** turning basin **(b)** (*espace*) room to swing, sea room

évitement [evitmɑ̃] *nm* **(a)** (*action d'éviter*) avoidance; **faire une manœuvre d'é.** to take evasive action; *Biol* **réaction d'é.** avoiding reaction **(b)** *Rail* **voie** *ou* **gare d'é.** siding; **ligne d'é.** loop line

éviter [evite] **1** *vt* **(a)** (*ne pas heurter*) to avoid, to miss; (*ne pas subir*) to avoid, to steer clear of; (*ne pas rencontrer*) (*qn*) to avoid, to keep clear of; (*regard*) to avoid; **é. l'alcool/le sucre** to avoid *or* keep off alcohol/sugar; **é. un coup** to avoid *or* dodge a blow; **é. la question** to avoid *or* dodge the issue; **é. de faire qch** to avoid doing sth; **évite de recommencer!** don't start again!; **j'essaie d'é. qu'il ne le découvre** I'm trying to avoid his discovering it; **é. que le vent n'entre dans la maison** to prevent the wind getting into the house, to keep the wind out of the house; **évite que ça se sache** don't let it get out, prevent it getting out

(b) (*épargner*) **é. des ennuis/une corvée à qn** to save *or* spare sb trouble/a chore; **ça m'évitera d'avoir à le faire** it will save me having to do it

2 *vi Naut* **é. sur l'ancre** to swing at anchor; **évité au vent** riding the wind

3 s'éviter *vpr* **(a) s'é. qch** to avoid sth

(b) (*se fuir*) to avoid each other

évocable [evɔkabl] *adj Jur* **cause é.** case that may be transferred to a higher court

évocateur, -trice [evɔkatœr, -tris] *adj* evocative, suggestive (**de** of)

évocation [evɔkasjɔ̃] *nf* **(a)** (*par la magie*) (*d'un esprit etc*) evocation, calling forth, conjuring up **(b)** (*d'un souvenir, du passé etc*) evocation, conjuring up, recalling; **à l'é. de son premier amour** when she recalled her first love; (*mentionné par un tiers*) when reference was made to her first love; **le pouvoir d'é. d'un lieu/mot** the evocative power of a place/word

évolué [evɔlɥe] *adj* (*race, pays, société*) (highly) developed, advanced; (*personne*) mature, broadminded; *Ordinat* (*langage*) high-level

évoluer [evɔlɥe] *vi* **(a)** (*se déplacer*) (*d'un bateau, de troupes etc*) to manœuvre, *US* to maneuver; (*d'un danseur, d'un cerf-volant, d'un poisson etc*) to move around; *Fig* (*dans la haute société etc*) to move; **j'ignore dans quel milieu elle évolue maintenant** I don't know what circles she moves in now **(b)** (*se développer*) (*d'une théorie, d'une science, d'une ville, d'une entreprise etc*) to evolve, to develop; (*d'une personne, d'une maladie*) to develop **(c)** *Ordinat* **faire é.** to upgrade

évolutif, -ive [evɔlytif, -iv] *adj* evolutionary; *Méd* (*maladie*) progressive; *Ordinat* upgradeable; **méthode évolutive, ski é.** short-ski method; **poste é.** position with promotion prospects

évolution [evɔlysjɔ̃] *nf* **(a)** (*déplacement*) (*d'un bateau, de troupes etc*) **évolutions** manœuvres, *Am* maneuvers; (*d'un danseur, d'un patineur etc*) movements **(b)** (*développement*) (*d'une théorie, d'une science, d'un peuple, d'un conflit etc*) evolution, development; (*d'une personne, d'une maladie*) development; *Biol* evolution; **être contre toute é.** to be against any development; **suivre une lente é.** to evolve *or* develop slowly

évolutionnisme [evɔlysjɔnism] *nm Biol* evolutionism

évolutionniste [evɔlysjɔnist] *Biol* **1** *adj* evolutionist(ic) **2** *n* evolutionist

évolutivité [evɔlytivite] *nf Ordinat* upgradeability

évoquer [evɔke] *vt* **(a)** (*se remémorer*) (*souvenir, passé etc*) to recall, to conjure up, to evoke **(b)** (*faire penser à*) to be reminiscent of; **qu'est-ce que cela vous évoque?** what does that remind you of *or* conjure up for you?; **son nom/ce visage ne m'évoque rien** his name/this face means nothing to me *or* doesn't ring a bell with me **(c)** (*aborder*) to touch on, to mention; **nous n'avons fait qu'é. le sujet** we've only touched on the subject **(d)** (*par la magie*) (*esprit, démon, mort etc*) to evoke, to call forth, to conjure up

ex [eks] *n F* ex; **un de mes ex** one of my exes
ex- [ɛks] *préf* ex-; **ex-femme/-champion** ex-wife/-champion
ex abrupto [exsabrypto] *adv* straight off
exacerbation [ɛgzasɛrbasjɔ̃] *nf* exacerbation
exacerber [ɛgzasɛrbe] **1** *vt* (*douleur, irritation etc*) to exacerbate, to aggravate; **susceptibilité exacerbée** exaggerated sensitivity; **nationalisme exacerbé** extreme nationalism **2 s'exacerber** *vpr* to become acute
exact [ɛgza(kt)] *adj* **(a)** (*précis*) (*quantité, poids, nombre, calcul etc*) exact, precise; (*fidèle*) (*rapport, description, copie etc*) exact, accurate; (*juste*) (*solution, mot, réponse etc*) right, correct; **l'heure/la date exacte** the right *or* correct *or* exact time/date; **une montre exacte** a precise *or* accurate watch; **e. à un millimètre près** correct *or* accurate to within a millimetre; **c'est e.** (*vrai*) it's quite true, it's a fact; **il est e. que j'ai dit cela** it's quite true that I said that; **vous vous appelez bien Martin? – e.!** your name is Martin? – correct!
(b) (*ponctuel*) punctual, on time; **il est e. à payer son loyer** he is punctual in paying his rent, he pays his rent on time; **je n'ai pu être e. au rendez-vous** I couldn't be on time for the appointment
(c) *Litt* (*strict*) (*discipline, obéissance etc*) strict, rigorous
exactement [ɛgzaktəmɑ̃] *adv* (*précisément*) (*calculer, placer etc*) exactly, precisely; (*fidèlement*) (*rapporter, reproduire etc*) exactly, accurately; (*avec justesse*) (*répondre, raisonner etc*) correctly; **il est e. deux heures** it is exactly *or* precisely two o'clock; **c'est très e. ce que je veux dire** that's exactly *or* precisely what I mean; **e. le même** exactly the same; **je sais e. combien** I know exactly *or* precisely how much; **un effet e. contraire** a directly opposite effect
exaction [ɛgzaksjɔ̃] *nf* **(a)** (*d'impôt etc*) exaction; (*vol*) extortion **(b) exactions** (*actes cruels*) atrocities
exactitude [ɛgzaktityd] *nf* **(a)** (*précision*) (*d'une quantité, d'un calcul etc*) exactness, precision; (*fidélité*) (*d'un rapport, d'une copie etc*) exactness, accuracy; (*justesse*) (*d'une solution, réponse etc*) correctness; **calculer/mesurer avec e.** to calculate/measure exactly *or* precisely **(b)** (*ponctualité*) punctuality; **avec e.** punctually; *Prov* **l'e. est la politesse des rois** punctuality is the politeness of kings
ex æquo [ɛgzeko] **1** *adv Scol, Sp etc* **être (classés) e.** to tie, to be equally placed; **être troisième e.** to tie for third place, to be placed equal third; **être e. avec qn** to tie with sb, to be placed equal with sb **2** *n inv* **il y avait trois e. pour la première place** three people tied for first place; **départager les e.** to break the tie
exagération [ɛgzaʒerasjɔ̃] *nf* exaggeration; **sans e.** (*faire un récit*) without exaggerating; (*boire, aimer le chocolat etc*) in moderation; **on peut dire sans e. que ...** it is no exaggeration to say *or* one can say without exaggeration that ...; **se montrer ferme sans e.** to be firm without overdoing it *or* going to extremes
exagéré [ɛgzaʒere] *adj* (*commentaire, récit, geste*) exaggerated; (*prix, salaire*) exorbitant, excessive; (*pessimisme, nationalisme*) excessive; **confiance exagérée** overconfidence; **il n'est pas e. de dire que ...** it is no exaggeration to say that ...; **dire qu'il est bête, c'est un peu e.** it's a bit much *or* a bit excessive to say that he's stupid
exagérément [ɛgzaʒeremɑ̃] *adv* excessively; **il lui fait e. confiance** he trusts him/her far too much; **elle a e. tardé avant de répondre** she delayed for far too long before replying
exagérer [ɛgzaʒere] **1** *vt* (*faits, vérité, danger, qualités de qn etc*) to exaggerate, to overstate; (*forme, proportions etc*) to exaggerate; **il ne faut rien e., n'exagérons rien** things should be kept in proportion, let's not exaggerate **2** *vi* (*en parlant*) to exaggerate; (*abuser*) to go too far, to overstep the mark; **il faut toujours que tu exagères!** you always exaggerate!; **il ne faut pas e.!** that's a bit excessive *or* much!; *F* **faut pas e. mon vieux** don't exaggerate!; **sans e., il y en avait bien soixante** without exaggeration there were sixty of them **3 s'exagérer** *vpr* **s'e. qch** to overestimate sth
exaltant [ɛgzaltɑ̃] *adj* (*discours, musique, expérience etc*) exciting
exaltation [ɛgzaltasjɔ̃] *nf* **(a)** (*excitation*) (great) excitement; *Méd* overexcitement; **e. mystique** exaltation; **il a préparé son départ dans l'e.** he got ready to leave in (a state of) great excitement **(b)** (*action de louer*) (*de la vertu, d'une personne etc*) exalting, extolling **(c)** *Rel* **E. de la Sainte Croix** Exaltation of the Cross
exalté, -ée [ɛgzalte] **1** *adj Péj* (*discours, sentiment*) wild, impassioned; (*imagination, esprit*) wild; (*personne*) fanatical, hot-headed **2** *n Péj* fanatic, hothead
exalter [ɛgzalte] **1** *vt* **(a)** (*exciter*) (*imagination, esprit*) to stir, to fire; (*ressentiment, orgueil etc*) to intensify; **ses voyages/lectures/expériences l'ont exalté** his travels/reading/experiences fired his imagination **(b)** (*louer*) (*qn, les qualités de qn*) to exalt, to extol, to glorify **2 s'exalter** *vpr* to get excited
exam [ɛgzam] *nm F* exam
examen [ɛgzamɛ̃] *nm* **(a)** (*observation, analyse*) (*d'un document, d'un spécimen, de faits etc*) examination; (*des comptes*) inspection; **après un e. attentif de la situation/du problème** after a careful examination of the situation/problem; **cette assertion ne supporte pas l'e.** this assertion will not bear examination; **mettre une question à l'e.** to examine *or* look into *or* go into a matter; **après e., e. fait** (up)on examination
(b) *Méd* **e. (médical)** (medical) examination, medical, checkup; **e. de la vue** sight *or* eye test; **e. médical complet** complete checkup
(c) *Scol, Univ etc* exam, examination; **passer un e.** to sit *or* take an exam; **faire passer un e. à qn** to examine sb; **être reçu/refusé à un e.** to pass/fail an exam; **jury d'e.** examining body, examiners
▶ **examen**: **e. blanc** mock exam; **e. de conscience** soul-searching; *Jur* **e. contradictoire** examination made in the presence of both parties to a contract; **e. d'entrée** entrance exam; **e. partiel** (*année*) half-year exam; (*semestre, trimestre*) half-term exam; **e. de passage** end-of-year exam, *Am* final exam; **e. prénuptial** premarital checkup
examinateur, -trice [ɛgzaminatœr, -tris] *n* examiner
examiner [ɛgzamine] **1** *vt* **(a)** (*étudier, analyser*) (*document, spécimen, faits etc*) to examine; (*comptes*) to inspect, to go through; (*machinerie*) to check; **e. une question** to examine *or* look into *or* go into a matter; **e. une demande** to consider a request; **e. les lieux** to inspect the premises
(b) (*regarder, observer*) **e. l'horizon** to scan *or* survey the horizon; *Fig* **elle m'a examiné de la tête aux pieds** she eyed me from head to toe *or* up and down
(c) *Méd* (*patient*) to examine; **se faire e. par un médecin** to have oneself *or* be examined by a doctor
(d) *Scol, Univ etc Arch* to examine; **e. qn en algèbre** to examine sb in algebra
2 s'examiner *vpr* **(a)** (*dans une glace etc*) to examine oneself
(b) (*de plusieurs personnes*) (*s'observer*) to examine each other
exanthème [ɛgzɑ̃tɛm] *nm Méd* exanthema
exaspérant [ɛgzasperɑ̃] *adj* exasperating, irritating, aggravating
exaspération [ɛgzasperasjɔ̃] *nf* **(a)** (*énervement*) exasperation, irritation, aggravation **(b)** *Vieilli* (*d'une douleur, d'un sentiment*) aggravation
exaspérer [ɛgzaspere] **(j'exaspère; j'exaspérerai) 1** *vt* **(a)** (*énerver*) (*qn*) to exasperate, to irritate, to aggravate **(b)** (*douleur, sentiment*) to aggravate **2 s'exaspérer** *vpr* (*d'une douleur, d'un sentiment*) to become acute
exaucement [ɛgzosmɑ̃] *nm* (*d'un souhait, désir*) granting, fulfilment
exaucer [ɛgzose] *vt* **(j'exauçai(s), n. exauçons) (a)** (*souhait, désir*) to grant, to fulfil; **exauce ma prière!** hear my prayer! **(b) e. qn** to grant sb's wish, to hear *or* answer sb's prayer; **te voilà exaucé** your prayer is answered
ex cathedra [ɛkskatedra] *adv Rel, Fig* ex cathedra
excavateur, -trice [ɛkskavatœr, -tris] *n Constr* excavator, (mechanical) digger
excavation [ɛkskavasjɔ̃] *nf* **(a)** (*trou*) excavation; (*creusée par une bombe*) crater **(b)** (*action*) excavation, excavating
excaver [ɛkskave] *vt* to excavate
excédant [ɛksedɑ̃] *adj* exasperating, tiresome
excédent [ɛksedɑ̃] *nm* (*de nourriture, de sucre dans le sang etc*) surplus, excess; (*d'un budget, d'une balance*) surplus; **somme en e.** sum in excess; **budget en e.** surplus budget; **e. budgétaire** budget(ary) surplus; **vous garderez l'e.** you will keep what is left over; **e. de poids** excess weight; **e. de dépenses** deficit; **e. de bagages** excess luggage *or* baggage; **e. de blé** wheat surplus; **la balance commerciale est en e.** the trade balance shows a surplus, there is a trade surplus; *Compta* **e. de caisse** cash overs
excédentaire [ɛksedɑ̃tɛr] *adj* (*production*) excess, surplus; (*poids*) excess; (*budget*) surplus; **balance commerciale e.** trade surplus
excéder [ɛksede] *vt* **(j'excède, n. excédons; j'excéderai) (a)** (*dépasser*) (*quantité, somme, période, Fig limite etc*) to exceed; **e. les moyens de qn** to be beyond sb's means **(b)** (*outrepasser*) (*forces, compétences*) to be beyond; **e. ses pouvoirs** to exceed *or* overstep one's powers **(c)** (*irriter*) to exasperate; **j'étais excédé** I was exasperated, I had lost all patience **(d)** *Vieilli* (*épuiser*) to tire *or* wear out; **excédé de fatigue** worn out, tired out
excellemment [ɛksɛlamɑ̃] *adv Litt* excellently

excellence [ɛksɛlɑ̃s] *nf* **(a)** excellence; *Scol* **prix d'e.** class prize (*for all-round standard*); **c'est le chercheur/l'homme à femmes par e.** he's the researcher/ladies' man par excellence; **c'est un têtu/paresseux par e.** he's stubbornness/laziness itself **(b)** (*titre*) **Son/Votre E.** His/Her/ Your Excellency

excellent [ɛksɛlɑ̃] *adj* excellent, first-rate (**en** at, in); **en excellente santé** in the best of health, in excellent health

exceller [ɛksele] *vi* to excel (**en** at, in; **à faire qch** in doing sth)

excentré [ɛksɑ̃tre] *adj* **(a)** (*quartier, maison etc*) far from the centre, remote **(b)** *Tech* off centre

excentricité [ɛksɑ̃trisite] *nf* **(a)** (*caractère, acte bizarre*) eccentricity **(b)** (*d'un quartier, d'une maison etc*) remoteness **(c)** *Math etc* (*d'un cercle, d'une orbite etc*) eccentricity

excentrique [ɛksɑ̃trik] **1** *adj* **(a)** (*bizarre*) (*personne, comportement, idée etc*) eccentric, odd **(b)** (*loin du centre*) (*faubourg, quartier etc*) remote, far from the centre **(c)** *Math etc* (*cercle, orbite etc*) eccentric **2** *n* (*personne*) eccentric **3** *nm* (*mécanisme*) eccentric

excentriquement [ɛksɑ̃trikmɑ̃] *adv* eccentrically

excepté [ɛksɛpte] **1** *prép* except, apart from, with the exception of; **tous les jours e. quand il pleut** every day except *or* apart from *or* with the exception of when it rains; **la maison nous convient e. qu'il n'y a pas de garage** the house suits us except (for the fact) that there's no garage **2** *adj* **les femmes exceptées** except for *or* apart from the women; **j'aime tous leurs meubles, le bahut e.** I like all their furniture except for *or* apart from the sideboard

excepter [ɛksɛpte] *vt* to exclude, to except (**de** from), to make an exception of; **si l'on excepte une seule rue** with the exception of *or* apart from one street; **sans e. les enfants** without excluding the children, including the children

exception [ɛksɛpsjɔ̃] *nf* **(a)** exception (**à** to); **faire une e.** to make an exception (**pour** for); **faire une e. à une règle** to make an exception to a rule; **faire e. à une règle** to be an exception to a rule; **c'est l'e. qui confirme la règle** it's the exception that proves the rule; **à quelques exceptions près** with a few exceptions; **à quelques rares exceptions près** with very few exceptions; **à une e. près** with one exception; **sans e.** without exception; **tous, à l'e. du docteur** *ou* **e. faite du docteur** all, except (for) *or* with the exception of the doctor; **c'est un être d'e.** he's an exceptional person **(b)** *Jur* objection, plea (*by the defence*)

exceptionnel, -elle [ɛksɛpsjɔnɛl] *adj* **(a)** (*qui fait exception*) (*circonstances, situation etc*) exceptional; **congé e.** special leave **(b)** (*remarquable*) exceptional, outstanding; **sa femme/sa voiture/son livre n'a rien d'e.** his wife/his car/his book is nothing special

exceptionnellement [ɛksɛpsjɔnɛlmɑ̃] *adv* exceptionally; **e. tu peux partir maintenant** just this once you can leave now; **nous ouvrirons e. le soir de Noël** we will open specially on Christmas Eve

excès [ɛksɛ] *nm* **(a)** (*excédent, démesure*) excess; **e. de l'offre sur la demande** excess of supply over demand; **pécher par e. de zèle, faire de l'e. de zèle** to be overzealous; **l'e. de ses prétentions** his excessive claims, the excessive nature of his claims; **c'est un peu un e. de précautions** these are rather excessive precautions; **avec e.** (*boire, fumer, travailler etc*) excessively, to excess; **manger avec e.** to overeat, to eat excessively *or* to excess; **dépenser avec e.** to overspend; **réagir avec e.** to overreact (**à qch** to sth); **sans e.** (*manger, utiliser etc*) in moderation; **(jusqu')à l'e.** to excess, excessively; **se dépenser à l'e.** to overexert oneself; **gentil/ scrupuleux à l'e.** kind/scrupulous to a fault, overkind/ overscrupulous; **tomber dans l'e.** to overdo it, *F* to go over the top; **tomber dans l'e. inverse** to go to the other extreme

(b) (*abus*) excess; **commettre** *ou* **se laisser aller à des e.** to overdo things, to go too far; **des e. (de table)** overeating, overindulgence; **faire des e. (de table)** to overeat, to overindulge; **évitez tout e.** avoid overdoing things; (*alimentaire*) avoid overeating

▶ **excès**: **des e. de conduite** loose living; **des e. de langage** immoderate language; *Jur* **e. de pouvoir** action ultra vires; *Aut* **e. de vitesse** speeding, exceeding the speed limit; **faire un e. de vitesse** to speed, to exceed the speed limit

excessif, -ive [ɛksɛsif, -iv] *adj* (*longueur, chaleur, quantité etc*) excessive; (*opinion, idée*) extreme; (*optimisme, idéalisme*) excessive, unwarranted; (*prix*) exorbitant, excessive; (*langage*) immoderate; (*orgueil*) inordinate; **des mois de travail e. l'a rendu malade** he has become ill through months of overwork; **il est e.** he goes to extremes; **il fait un vent e. pour sortir le bébé** it's far too windy to take the baby out

excessivement [ɛksɛsivmɑ̃] *adv* **(a)** (*trop*) excessively; **manger e.** to overeat, to eat excessively *or* to excess; **il avait bu e.** he had been drinking to excess **(b)** (*extrêmement*) extremely

exciper [ɛksipe] *vi Jur* to put in a plea, *Litt* **e. de son ignorance/sa bonne foi** to plead ignorance/one's good faith

excipient [ɛksipjɑ̃] *nm Pharm* excipient

exciser [ɛksize] *vt Chir* to excise, to cut out

excision [ɛksizjɔ̃] *nf Chir* excision

excitabilité [ɛksitabilite] *nf* excitability

excitable [ɛksitabl] *adj* excitable

excitant [ɛksitɑ̃] **1** *adj* (*nouvelles, débat, film, perspective, sexuellement etc*) exciting; (*effet*) stimulating **2** *nm* stimulant

excitation [ɛksitasjɔ̃] *nf* **(a)** (*action*) (*à la violence, au racisme etc*) incitement (**à** to); **e. à la révolte** incitement to rebellion **(b)** (*résultat*) excitement; **e. (sexuelle)** (sexual) arousal *or* excitement; **dans l'e. du moment** in the excitement of the moment **(c)** *Él, Physiol* excitation

▶ **excitation**: *Jur* **e. des mineurs à la débauche** incitement of minors to commit immoral acts

excité, -ée [ɛksite] **1** *adj* **(a)** (*énervé*) worked-up; (*plein d'anticipation*) excited **(b)** (*sexuellement*) excited **2** *n* (*personne*) hothead

exciter [ɛksite] **1** *vt* **(a)** (*attiser*) (*curiosité, jalousie etc*) to excite, to arouse; (*pitié*) to arouse; (*appétit*) to whet; (*rire*) to provoke; **e. l'envie de tout le monde** to make everybody envious; **e. la pitié de qn** to move sb to pity, to arouse sb's pity

(b) (*encourager*) to urge on; **e. qn à la révolte** *ou* **à se révolter** to incite sb to revolt; **e. qn contre qn** to set sb against sb; **e. la meute contre le gibier** to urge on the pack to hunt their quarry

(c) (*énerver*) (*intellectuellement*) to excite, to thrill; (*physiquement*) to excite; (*sexuellement*) to arouse, to excite; **excité à l'idée de partir en vacances** excited *or* thrilled at the idea of going on holiday; **trop e. qn** to overexcite sb; **le café/le tabac excite** coffee/tobacco acts as a stimulant

(d) *F* (*irriter*) to irritate, to annoy

(e) *Physiol* (*nerf, muscle*) to excite, to stimulate; *Él* (*dynamo*) to excite

2 s'exciter *vpr* to get excited, to get worked up; (*sexuellement*) to get aroused *or* excited

exclamatif, -ive [ɛksklamatif, -iv] *adj* exclamatory; *Gram* **proposition exclamative** exclamation, interjection

exclamation [ɛksklamasjɔ̃] *nf* exclamation; **pousser des exclamations** to exclaim

exclamer (s') [sɛksklame] *vpr* (*de joie, de surprise, d'admiration*) to exclaim, to shout out; (*de douleur, colère*) to cry out, to shout out (**de** in, with); **'toi ici!' s'exclama-t-il** 'you here!' he exclaimed; **s'e. sur la montée du chômage/ de la violence** to make a lot of noise about rising unemployment/violence

exclu, -ue [ɛkskly] **1** *adj* **(a)** (*non compris*) **le prix des travaux, TVA exclue** the cost of the work, excluding VAT; **le mois d'août jusqu'au 31 e.** the month of August excluding the 31st **(b)** (*impensable*) out of the question, impossible; **il est e. que** + *sub* it's out of the question *or* impossible that; **il est e. qu'il vienne avec nous** it's out of the question for him to come with us, *F* there's no way he's coming with us; **il n'est pas e. que ...** it's not out of the question that ... **2** *n* outcast; **les exclus de la société** social outcasts, the outcasts of society; **les exclus du progrès** those whom progress has ignored *or* passed by

exclure [ɛksklyr] (*prp* **excluant**; *pp* **exclu**; *pr ind* **j'exclus, n. excluons**; *impf* **j'excluais**; *p hist* **j'exclus**; *fu* **j'exclurai**) **1** *vt* **(a)** (*expulser*) (*d'un parti, d'une école etc*) to expel; (*d'une fonction publique*) to remove; (*d'une salle, réunion*) to eject (**de** from)

(b) (*ne pas permettre ou admettre*) to exclude (**de** from); **e. le pain de son régime** to exclude *or* cut out bread from one's diet; **e. l'alcool de sa table** not to allow alcohol in the house; **elle a exclu le rouge dans ses vêtements** she doesn't wear anything with red in it; **e. la TVA de la somme** to exclude the VAT from *or* leave the VAT out of the sum; **l'alcool est exclu de la vente le dimanche** alcohol is not allowed to be sold on Sundays

(c) (*ne pas considérer*) to rule out; **e. la possibilité d'un accord** to rule out the possibility of an agreement; **cette hypothèse est à e.** this possibility is out of the question; **cela n'exclut pas que vous puissiez enseigner** that doesn't rule out the possibility of your teaching

2 s'exclure *vpr* (*de théories etc*) to be mutually exclusive

exclusif, -ive [ɛksklyzif, -iv] **1** *adj* **(a)** (*non partagé*) (*occupation, intérêt etc*) exclusive; (*but, mission*) sole; *Com* (*droit, agent etc*) exclusive, sole; (*article, modèle, reportage, interview etc*) exclusive; **une interview exclusive** an exclusive (interview); **il a un intérêt e. pour les papillons** he is solely interested in butterflies; **pendant les vacances, son occupation exclusive a été de courir** during the holidays, running was his sole activity

(b) (*sélectif*) (*dans ses opinions*) self-opinionated; (*dans ses goûts*) selective; **elle est très exclusive dans ses amitiés** she is very selective in her choice of friends; **il est e. en amour** he's a one-woman man

2 *nf* **exclusive** (*mesure d'exclusion*) bar; **prononcer l'exclusive contre, frapper d'exclusive** to bar, to debar; **sans exclusive** without exception

exclusion [ɛksklyzjɔ̃] *nf* **(a)** (*expulsion*) (*d'un parti, d'une école etc*) expulsion; (*d'une fonction publique*) removal; (*d'une salle, réunion*) ejection (**de** from); **e. temporaire** suspension **(b) e. sociale** exclusion, exclusion from society **(c) à l'e. de** to the exclusion of; (*à l'exception de*) with the exception of

exclusivement [ɛksklyzivmɑ̃] *adv* exclusively, solely; **parking e. réservé aux clients de l'hôtel** customer parking only; **il aime e. les opéras de Verdi** he likes Verdi's operas to the exclusion of all others; **de lundi jusqu'à vendredi e.** from Monday to Friday exclusive

exclusivisme [ɛksklyzivism] *nm* exclusivism

exclusiviste [ɛksklyzivist] *n* exclusivist

exclusivité [ɛksklyzivite] *nf* **(a)** *Com* (*droit*) sole *or* exclusive rights (**de** in); *TV, Cin* (*de film*) first run; **en e.** exclusively; **avoir un contrat d'e.** to have an exclusive contract (**chez** with); **ce modèle se trouve en e. chez ...** this model is exclusive to *or* can only be found at ...; **c'est notre journal qui a eu l'e. de son interview** our paper had an exclusive with him; **en e. dans le Figaro** a Figaro exclusive; **film en e.** exclusive film; **film en première e.** first showing; *Fig* **ne pas avoir l'e. de l'intelligence/de la beauté** not to have a monopoly on intelligence/beauty

(b) *Com* (*article*) exclusive article; (*film*) exclusive film; *Journ* (*article*) exclusive, scoop; **c'est une e. Mercedes** it's exclusive to Mercedes

(c) (*des sentiments*) selectiveness

excommunication [ɛkskɔmynikasjɔ̃] *nf* excommunication

excommunier [ɛkskɔmynje] *vt* (*impf, pr sub* **n. excommuniions**) to excommunicate

excoriation [ɛkskɔrjasjɔ̃] *nf* (*éraflure*) graze, *Spéc* excoriation

excorier [ɛkskɔrje] *vt* (*peau*) to graze, *Spéc* to excoriate

excrément [ɛkskremɑ̃] *nm often pl* **excrément(s)** excrement

excrémentiel, -elle [ɛkskremɑ̃sjɛl] *adj* excremental

excréter [ɛkskrete] *vt* (**j'excrète; j'excréterai**) to excrete

excréteur, -trice [ɛkskretœr, -tris] *adj* excretory

excrétion [ɛkskresjɔ̃] *nf* **(a)** (*action*) excretion, excreting **(b)** (*déchet*) **excrétions** excreta

excrétoire [ekskretwar] *adj* excretory

excroissance [ɛkskrwasɑ̃s] *nf* excrescence

excursion [ɛkskyrsjɔ̃] *nf* (*en car, voiture etc*) excursion, trip; (*d'une journée*) day trip, day tour; (*de plusieurs jours*) tour; (*lors d'une escale*) shore excursion, trip ashore; (*à pied*) hike, long walk; **faire une e., partir en e.** to go on an excursion *or* a trip/a tour/a hike *or* a walk; **e. en car** coach trip

excursionner [ɛkskyrsjɔne] *vi Vieilli* (*en car, voiture etc*) to go on excursions *or* trips; (*pendant plusieurs jours*) to go touring; (*à pied*) to go hiking *or* walking

excursionniste [ɛkskyrsjɔnist] *n* (*en car, voiture etc*) tourist, excursionist, *Br* tripper; (*à pied*) hiker, walker

excusable [ɛkskyzabl] *adj* excusable, forgivable; **ce n'est absolument pas e.** it's absolutely inexcusable *or* unforgivable

excuse [ɛkskyz] *nf* **(a)** (*raison*) excuse; **une bonne e.** a good excuse; **ce n'est pas une e.!** that's no excuse!; **trouver une e. à qch/pour faire qch** to find an excuse for sth/for doing sth; **je prends mon travail comme e. pour ne pas partir** I'm making my work the excuse for not going; **tu lui trouves toujours des excuses** you're always finding excuses for him; **tu n'as aucune e. de ne pas avoir prévenu** you have no excuse for not letting us know; **c'est sans e.** it's inexcusable *or* unforgivable

(b) excuses (*regrets*) apology; **faire** *ou* **présenter ses excuses à qn** to make one's apologies *or* to apologize to sb; **je vous fais mes plus plates excuses** *ou* **mes excuses les plus plates** you have my humble apologies; **il exige des excuses** he is demanding an apology; **je vous dois des excuses** I owe you an apology; **lettre d'excuses** letter of apology

(c) *F* **faites e.!** sorry!

(d) (*au tarot*) excuse

excuser [ɛkskyze] **1** *vt* **(a)** (*justifier*) (*qn, action*) to excuse, to make excuses for, to apologize for; **e. qn auprès de qn** to apologize for sb to sb; **l'ignorance n'excuse rien** ignorance is no excuse

(b) (*pardonner*) (*qn, erreur, colère etc*) to excuse; **excusez-moi, veuillez m'e.** excuse me, pardon me, I'm sorry; **excuse-moi de te déranger** I'm sorry to disturb you, excuse me for disturbing you; **excuse-moi de ne pas t'avoir téléphoné** I'm sorry I didn't phone you; **excusez-moi de vous le faire remarquer** excuse me for saying so, I hope you don't mind my mentioning it; *Fml* **je vous prie de m'e.** I do beg your pardon; **excusez ma curiosité mais ...** excuse *or* forgive my curiosity but ...; **tu es tout excusé** there's no need to apologize, that's quite all right; *Hum* **excusez du peu!** would you believe!, if you please!

(c) (*dispenser*) to excuse; **se faire e.** to ask to be excused; **peux-tu m'e. auprès de lui?** can you ask him to excuse me?; **liste des présents, absents, excusés** list of those present, those absent and those from whom apologies have been received; **e. un juré** to excuse a juror (from attendance)

2 s'excuser *vpr* to apologize; *Iron* **surtout ne t'excuse pas!** an apology wouldn't go amiss!; **s'e. auprès de qn** to apologize to sb; **s'e. de qch/de faire qch** to apologize for sth/doing sth; *F* **je m'excuse!** sorry!, excuse me!; *Prov* **qui s'excuse s'accuse** he who excuses himself accuses himself

exécrable [ɛgzekrabl] *adj* atrocious, abominable, execrable

exécrablement [ɛgzekrabləmɑ̃] *adv* atrociously, abominably, execrably

exécration [ɛgzekrasjɔ̃] *nf Litt* (*du crime etc*) execration, detestation; **avoir qn/qch en e.** to loathe sb/sth

exécrer [ɛgzekre] *vt* (**j'exècre; j'exécrerai**) *Litt* to execrate, to loathe, to detest

exécutable [ɛgzekytabl] *adj* feasible; *Ordinat* (*programme*) executable

exécutant, -ante [ɛgzekytɑ̃, -ɑ̃t] *n Mus* performer, executant; **il n'a été qu'un simple e.** he was just doing what he was told *or* carrying out orders

exécuter [ɛgzekyte] **1** *vt* **(a)** (*effectuer*) (*travail, plan*) to execute, to carry out; (*ordres, décision*) to carry out, to act upon; (*promesse*) to carry out, to fulfil; (*danse, morceau de musique, contrat*) to perform, to execute

(b) (*confectionner*) (*peinture, décor etc*) to produce, to execute

(c) *Ordinat* (*programme*) to execute, to run; (*commande*) to execute, to carry out

(d) *Jur* (*débiteur*) to distrain upon; (*décret, loi etc*) to enforce, to give effect to

(e) (*mettre à mort*) (*criminel etc*) to execute, to put to death; *Sp F* (*battre*) (*adversaire*) to slaughter; *F* (*critiquer*) (*travail, auteur etc*) to savage; **à chaque fois qu'il ouvrait la bouche, il était exécuté** every time he opened his mouth, he was torn to pieces

2 s'exécuter *vpr* to comply; **il faudra bien vous e.** you'll have to bring yourself to do it

exécuteur, -trice [ɛgzekytœr, -tris] **1** *n* **(a)** *Jur* **e. testamentaire** executor; **exécutrice testamentaire** executrix **(b)** *Arch* (*d'un plan, d'une tâche*) executant **2** *nm* (*bourreau*) **e. (des hautes œuvres)** executioner

exécutif, -ive [ɛgzekytif, -iv] *Pol* **1** *adj* (*pouvoir etc*) executive **2** *nm* **l'e.** the executive

exécution [ɛgzekysjɔ̃] *nf* **(a)** (*d'un plan, travail*) execution, carrying out; (*d'ordres, d'une décision*) carrying out; (*d'une promesse*) fulfilment; (*d'une danse, d'un morceau de musique*) performance, execution; (*d'une peinture, d'un roman etc*) execution; *Mil, Hum* **e.!** jump to it! at the double!; **droit d'e.** performing rights; **difficultés d'e. d'un morceau de musique** difficulties in the execution of a piece of music; **mettre un projet à e.** to put a plan into execution *or* operation, to carry out a plan; **travaux en voie d'e.** work in progress

(b) *Ordinat* running, execution

(c) *Jur* (*d'un débiteur*) distraint (**de** upon); (*d'une loi, d'un décret etc*) enforcement

(d) (*mise à mort*) **e. (capitale)** execution; **ordre d'e.** death warrant; *Mil* **peloton d'e.** firing squad *or* party

(e) *Bourse* **e. au prix du marché** execution at market

exécutoire [ɛgzekytwar] *adj Jur* **(a) jugement (de force) e.** enforceable decision (*of the court*) **(b)** (*formule*) executory

exégèse [ɛgzeʒɛz] *nf* exegesis

exégète [ɛgzeʒɛt] *n* exegete

exemplaire[1] [ɛgzɑ̃plɛr] *adj* **(a)** (*comportement, courage*) exemplary **(b) c'était une punition e.** the punishment was intended as an example

exemplaire[2] *nm* **(a)** (*livre, gravure etc*) copy; **en deux/trois exemplaires** in duplicate/triplicate; **photocopier un texte en 20 exemplaires** to make 20 photocopies of a text; **édition tirée à dix mille exemplaires** edition of ten thousand copies

(b) (*spécimen*) (*de plante, d'animal etc*) example

exemplairement [ɛgzɑ̃plɛrmɑ̃] *adv* exemplarily; **elle a vécu e.** she led an exemplary life; **il a été puni e.** he was punished as an example to others

exemple [ɛgzɑ̃pl] *nm* **(a)** (*modèle*) example, model (**pour** for); **donner l'e.** to set an example (**à** to); **suivre l'e. de qn,**

prendre e. sur qn to follow sb's example; **suivre le mauvais e. de qn** to follow sb's bad example; **prendre qn pour** *ou* **comme e.** to take sb as one's model, to model oneself on sb; **citer qn/qch en e.** to quote sb/sth as an example; **prêcher d'e.** to practise what one preaches; **faire un e.** (*en punissant qn*) to set an example; **servir d'e. à qn** (*d'une réussite etc*) to be an example to sb; (*d'une punition etc*) to be a lesson *or* a warning to sb; **infliger une punition à qn pour l'e.** to punish sb as an example *or* a warning to others

(b) (*cas*) example, instance; (*mot, phrase*) example; **il est l'e. même du type qui ne sait pas ce qu'il veut** he's the perfect example of someone who doesn't know what he wants; **sans e.** without parallel, unparalleled; **être d'une gentillesse/d'un égoïsme sans e.** to be of unparalleled kindness/egoism; **j'en connais plein: e., ma mère** I know lots: my mother, for example *or* for instance

(c) **par e.** for example, for instance; **un de ces jours, par e. dimanche** one of these days, say *or* for example *or* for instance on Sunday; *F* **par e.!** (*étonnement*) well really!; *F* **ah ça par e.!** (*stupeur*) oh no!; **ah non, par e.!** I should think not!

exemplification [ɛgzɑ̃plifikasjɔ̃] *nf* exemplification

exemplifier [ɛgzɑ̃plifje] *vt* to exemplify

exempt, -te [ɛgzɑ̃, -ɑ̃t] **1** *adj* **e. de** (*service militaire etc*) exempt from; (*anxiété, danger, maladie etc*) free from; **e. de soucis** free from care, carefree; **e. de droits (de douane)** free of duty, duty-free, non-dutiable; **e. d'impôts** tax exempt, exempt from tax; **e. de TVA** zero-rated; **e. de port** carriage free; **elle a eu une vie dont tout souci était e.** she has had a life free from all care; **sa remarque n'était pas exempte d'une certaine amertume** his remark was not without a trace of bitterness **2** *n* (*personne*) exempt (**de** from)

exempter [ɛgzɑ̃te] **1** *vt* (*d'impôt, de service militaire etc*) to exempt (**de** from); (*d'anxiété, de risques etc*) to safeguard (**de** against); **e. qn de faire qch** to exempt *or* excuse sb from doing sth **2 s'exempter** *vpr* **s'e. de qch/de faire qch** to get out of sth/doing sth

exemption [ɛgzɑ̃psjɔ̃] *nf* exemption (**de** from); **liste d'exemptions** (*de la douane*) free list; **e. d'impôts** tax exemption

exerçable [ɛgzɛrsabl] *adj Bourse* exerciseable

exercé [ɛgzɛrse] *adj* (*œil, oreille*) trained; (*main*) practised; **avoir l'œil/l'oreille exercé(e) pour** *ou* **à faire qch** to have a trained eye/ear for doing sth; **c'est une tricoteuse exercée** she's a good knitter

exercer [ɛgzɛrse] **(j'exerçai(s)) 1** *vt* **(a)** (*former*) (*son corps, esprit*) to exercise; (*mémoire*) to train; *Mil* (*soldats*) to drill; **e. qn à qch/à faire qch** to train sb in sth/to do sth; **e. son esprit à l'art de la rhétorique** to train one's mind in the art of rhetoric

(b) (*user de*) (*autorité, talent etc*) to exercise; **e. son influence sur qn** to exert *or* exercise one's influence on sb, to bring one's influence to bear on sb; **e. une pression sur qch/qn** to exert pressure on sth/sb; **e. ses droits** to exercise one's rights; **e. un contrôle sur** to exercise control over

(c) (*profession*) to practise; **e. des fonctions** to carry out duties; **j'exerce le métier de journaliste** I'm a journalist by profession

(d) *Bourse* (*option*) to exercise; **e. par anticipation** to exercise in advance

2 *vi* (*d'un médecin, juriste etc*) to practise, to be in practice

3 s'exercer *vpr* **(a)** (*d'un chanteur, sportif etc*) to practise; **s'e. à qch/à faire qch** to practise sth/doing sth; **s'e. au piano** to practise the piano

(b) (*se manifester*) (*autorité, pouvoir*) to make itself felt; **sa mauvaise foi s'exerce aussi contre ses proches** his close relations also feel the effects of his dishonesty

exercice [ɛgzɛrsis] *nm* **(a)** (*physique*) exercise; **faire des exercises** to do (some) exercises; **prendre** *ou* **faire de l'e.** to (take) exercise; **manquer d'e.** to lack exercise; **e. physique** physical exercise

(b) *Mil* drill(ing); **être à l'e.** to be on parade; **faire l'e.** to drill

(c) *Sp, Mus, Scol etc* (*mouvement, tâche*) exercise; **exercices de grammaire** grammar exercises; **faire ses exercices** to do one's exercises; **faire des exercices au piano** to do (some) piano exercises; **e. d'évacuation en cas d'incendie** fire drill

(d) (*du pouvoir, d'un droit*) exercise; (*d'une profession*) practice; **dans l'e. de ses fonctions** in the exercise *or* discharge of one's duties; **être en e.** (*d'un avocat etc*) to be in practice, to be practising; **avocat en e.** practising barrister; **le président en e.** the president in office; **être condamné pour e. illégal de la médecine** to be sentenced for the illegal practice of medicine *or* for practising medicine illegally

(e) *Rel* **l'e. du culte** public worship

(f) (*en comptabilité*) financial year, *Am* fiscal year; **bilan en fin d'e.** end-of-year balance sheet; **e. bénéficiaire** profitable year

▶ **exercice**: *Compta* **e. budgétaire** budgetary *or* financial *or Am* fiscal year; **e. comptable** financial *or* accounting *or Am* fiscal year; **e. en cours** current financial year, *Am* current fiscal year; **e. écoulé** last financial year; **e. financier** financial *or Am* fiscal year; **e. fiscal** tax year

exerciseur [ɛgzɛrsizœr] *nm* (*appareil de gymnastique*) exerciser; (*pour poitrine*) chest expander

exergue [ɛgzɛrg] *nm* (*d'une médaille*) inscription, *Spéc* exergue; (*d'une illustration*) inscription; (*d'un texte*) epigraph; *Fig* **mettre une idée en e.** to highlight an idea, to point up an idea

exfoliant [ɛksfɔljɑ̃] **1** *adj* exfoliating **2** *nm* face/body scrub, *Spéc* exfoliant

exfoliation [ɛksfɔljasjɔ̃] *nf* exfoliation

exfolier (s') [sɛksfɔlje] *vpr* to exfoliate, to scale off

exhalaison [ɛgzalɛzɔ̃] *nf* (*odeur, vapeur*) exhalation

exhalation [ɛgzalasjɔ̃] *nf* (*action*) exhalation, exhaling

exhaler [ɛgzale] **1** *vt* (*odeur, vapeur etc*) to give off; (*soupir*) to breathe; *Fig* (*joie, colère etc*) to give vent to, to vent; *Fig* **cette maison exhale la tristesse** sadness pervades this house **2 s'exhaler** *vpr* (*d'une odeur, de la vapeur etc*) to be given off

exhaussement [ɛgzosmɑ̃] *nm* (*d'un mur, édifice etc*) increase in the height

exhausser [ɛgzose] *vt* (*mur, édifice etc*) to heighten, to increase the height of; **e. une maison d'un étage** to add a storey to a house

exhaustif, -ive [ɛgzostif, -iv] *adj* exhaustive

exhaustivement [ɛgzostivmɑ̃] *adv* exhaustively

exhaustivité [ɛgzostivite] *nf* exhaustiveness

exhiber [ɛgzibe] **1** *vt* **(a)** (*documents etc*) to produce; (*passeport, carte d'identité etc*) to present, to show **(b)** (*animaux*) to exhibit, to show **(c)** *Péj* (*ses connaissances, richesses, vêtements*) to show off, to flaunt; (*photos etc*) to show off; **e. ses muscles** to show off *or* display one's muscles **2 s'exhiber** *vpr* to flaunt oneself

exhibition [ɛgzibisjɔ̃] *nf* **(a)** *Jur* (*de documents*) production **(b)** (*présentation*) (*d'animaux*) show **(c)** *Péj* (*étalage*) (*de connaissances, richesses*) flaunting, showing off; (*de muscles*) display; **pourquoi ces exhibitions?** why are you flaunting yourself/is he flaunting himself/*etc*?

exhibitionnisme [ɛgzibisjɔnism] *nm* exhibitionism

exhibitionniste [ɛgzibisjɔnist] *n* exhibitionist

exhortation [ɛgzɔrtasjɔ̃] *nf* exhortation (**à qch** to sth; **à faire qch** to do sth)

exhorter [ɛgzɔrte] *vt* to exhort (**à qch** to sth; **à faire qch** to do sth), to urge (**à faire qch** to do sth)

exhumation [ɛgzymasjɔ̃] *nf* (*d'un corps*) exhumation; (*d'un trésor, des vestiges d'une ville etc*) digging up, excavation; *Fig* (*de vieux documents etc*) unearthing; (*de vieilles rancunes, souvenirs etc*) digging up; (*d'une ancienne loi, coutume etc*) exhumation

exhumer [ɛgzyme] *vt* (*corps*) to exhume; (*trésor, vestiges d'une ville etc*) to dig up, to excavate; *Fig* (*vieux documents etc*) to unearth; (*vieilles rancunes, souvenirs etc*) to dig up; (*ancienne loi, coutume etc*) to exhume

exigeant [ɛgziʒɑ̃] *adj* (*personne, travail etc*) demanding, exacting; **être trop e.** (*d'une personne*) to expect too much, to be too demanding; *Iron* **je ne suis pas e. : je demande juste la fortune et la célébrité!** I don't want much: just fame and fortune!

exigence [ɛgziʒɑ̃s] *nf* **(a)** (*caractère*) **elle est d'une e. insupportable** she's intolerably demanding **(b)** (*condition*) (*d'un client etc*) demand, requirement; (*d'un métier, milieu*) demand; **l'e.** *ou* **les exigences de l'étiquette** the demands *or* requirements of etiquette

exiger [ɛgziʒe] *vt* **(j'exigeai(s)) (a)** (*demander en insistant*) (*action, paiement, silence etc*) to demand, to require, to insist on (**de** from); (*rançon*) to demand; **trop e. des forces de qn** to overtax sb's strength; **e. qu'une chose soit faite** to insist on a thing being done, to demand that a thing be done; **j'exige des excuses/que vous vous excusiez** I demand an apology/that you apologize; **j'exige réparation** I demand redress; **j'exige d'être payé immédiatement** I demand to be paid *or* I insist on being paid immediately, I demand *or* insist on immediate payment; **le port de la cravate est exigé** ties must be worn

(b) (*nécessiter*) (*soin, action etc*) to require, to necessitate, to call for; **prendre les mesures qu'exigent les circonstances** to take the necessary measures; **ces plantes**

exigent des engrais particuliers these plants require *or* need special fertilizer; **aucune qualification particulière n'est exigée pour ce poste** no special qualification is required *or* needed for this post
exigibilité [ɛgziʒibilite] *nf Fin* **date d'e.** due date; **e. de taxe** tax liability; **e. immédiate** immediately due
exigible [ɛgziʒibl] *adj (dette, impôt)* payable, due (for payment); **le paiement est e. dès réception de la facture** payment is due upon receipt of the invoice
exiguïté [ɛgzigɥite] *nf (d'un lieu)* crampedness, tininess; *Vieilli (d'une somme)* meagreness
exigu, -uë [ɛgzigy] *adj (lieu)* cramped, tiny; *Vieilli (somme)* meagre, slender
exil [ɛgzil] *nm (expulsion)* exile; **envoyer qn en e.** to send sb into exile, to exile sb; **vivre en e.** to live in exile; **se sentir en e.** to feel like an exile
exilé, -ée [ɛgzile] *n (personne)* exile
exiler [ɛgzile] **1** *vt (d'un pays)* to exile (**de** from); *(d'une ville, de la cour etc)* to banish (**de** from); *Fig* **on l'a exilé à l'autre bout de la classe** he was banished *or* exiled to the other end of the classroom **2 s'exiler** *vpr Pol* to go into (voluntary) exile; *Fig* to cut oneself off *or* withdraw (from the world); **il s'est exilé à la campagne pour terminer son livre** he withdrew to the country to finish his book; **s'e. à l'autre bout du monde** to go into self-imposed exile on the other side of the world; **s'e. de la ville** to cut oneself off from the town
existant [ɛgzistɑ̃] **1** *adj* existing; **lois existantes** existing laws, laws in force **2** *nm Com* **e. en caisse/en magasin** cash/stock in hand
existence [ɛgzistɑ̃s] *nf* **(a)** *Phil (être)* existence, (state of) being **(b)** *(vie)* existence, life; **changer d'e.** to change one's (way of) life; **mener une e. tranquille** to lead a quiet existence *or* life; **dans l'e.** in life **(c)** *(présence, réalité)* existence (**de** of) **(d)** *(durée) (d'une institution etc)* life; **il est improbable que ce gouvernement puisse dépasser un an d'e.** it's unlikely that this government can stay in existence for longer than a year **(e)** *Compta* **existences en caisse** cash on hand
existentialisme [ɛgzistɑ̃sjalism] *nm Phil* existentialism
existentialiste [ɛgzistɑ̃sjalist] *adj, n Phil* existentialist
existentiel, -elle [ɛgzistɑ̃sjɛl] *adj* existential
exister [ɛgziste] *vi (vivre, être réel, se trouver)* to exist; *Com* to be available; **il existe** *(il y a)* there is, *pl* there are; **existe-t-il une vie sur Mars?** does life exist on Mars?, is there life on Mars?; **la maison existe toujours** the house still exists *or* is still standing; *Com* the firm still exists *or* is still in existence; **je n'arrive pas à croire qu'un autre monde puisse e.** I just can't believe that there is another world *or* that another world exists; **les roses noires, ça n'existe pas** there is no such thing as a black rose, black roses don't exist; **rien n'existe pour lui que l'art** nothing but art matters to him; **pour elle, l'amour/le bonheur/le danger n'existe pas** love/happiness/danger doesn't exist for her; **et l'amitié, cela existe, non?** there is such a thing as friendship, isn't there?; **je ne veux pas vous déranger, faites comme si je n'existais pas** I don't want to disturb you, pretend I'm not here *or* I don't exist; *Hum* **si ta sœur/le vélo n'existait pas, il faudrait l'inventer** if your sister/the bicycle didn't exist, we would have to invent her/it
exit [ɛgzit] *adv Th* exit; **e. les gardes** exit *or esp Fml* exeunt the guards; *Fig F* **e. le ministre des affaires étrangères** out goes *or* exit the foreign minister
ex-libris [ɛkslibris] *nm (vignette)* bookplate, ex-libris
ex navire [ɛksnavir] *adj, adv Com* ex ship
ex nihilo [ɛksniilo] *adv, adj inv* out of *or* from nothing, ex nihilo
exocet [ɛgzɔsɛ(t)] *nm* **(a)** *(poisson)* flying fish **(b) E.** ® *(missile)* Exocet
exocrine [ɛgzɔkrin] *adj Physiol* exocrine
exode [ɛgzɔd] *nm* **(a)** *(émigration)* exodus; *Hist Fr* **l'e.** the exodus *(of the French civilian population in 1940)* **(b)** *Bible* **l'E.** *(livre)* Exodus; *(émigration des Hébreux)* the Exodus
▸ **exode**: **e. des capitaux** flight of capital; **l'e. des cerveaux** the brain drain; **e. rural** rural depopulation
exogame [ɛgzɔgam] *adj (tribu etc)* exogamous
exogamie [ɛgzɔgami] *nf* exogamy
exonération [ɛgzɔnerasjɔ̃] *nf* exemption; **e. d'impôts** *or* **fiscale** tax exemption; **e. de TVA** exemption from VAT; **e. de responsabilité** exemption from liability
exonérer [ɛgzɔnere] *vt* **(j'exonère; j'exonérerai)** *(qn)* to exempt; *(marchandises)* to exempt from import duty; **être exonéré d'impôts** to be exempt from tax; **exonéré de TVA** VAT-exempt, zero-rated
exophtalmie [ɛgzɔftalmi] *nf Méd* exophthalmus, exophthalmos
exophtalmique [ɛgzɔftalmik] *adj Méd (goitre)* exophthalmic
exorbitant [ɛgzɔrbitɑ̃] *adj (prix, demande etc)* exorbitant
exorbité [ɛgzɔrbite] *adj (yeux)* protruding; *Fig* **ils regardaient, les yeux exorbités** they were watching with their eyes bulging (out of their heads)
exorciser [ɛgzɔrsize] *vt (démon, possédé)* to exorcize; *(démon)* to cast out; *(fantôme)* to lay; *Fig (ses peurs, les démons de sa jeunesse etc)* to exorcize
exorcisme [ɛgzɔrsism] *nm* exorcism
exorciste [ɛgzɔrsist] *n* exorcist
exorde [ɛgzɔrd] *nm* exordium
exosmose [ɛgzɔsmoz] *nf Phys* exosmosis
exotique [ɛgzɔtik] *adj* exotic; **une collection d'objets exotiques** a collection of exotica; **poisson e.** tropical fish
exotisme [ɛgzɔtism] *nm* exoticism
expansé [ɛkspɑ̃se] *adj (polystyrène)* expanded
expansibilité [ɛkspɑ̃sibilite] *nf (d'un gaz, de l'eau)* expansibility
expansible [ɛkspɑ̃sibl] *adj (gaz, eau)* expansible
expansif, -ive [ɛkspɑ̃sif, -iv] *adj* **(a)** *(exubérant) (personne)* expansive, outgoing **(b)** *Phys (force etc)* expansive
expansion [ɛkspɑ̃sjɔ̃] *nf* **(a)** *Phys (des gaz, de l'univers etc)* expansion; **l'univers en e.** the expanding universe **(b)** *(développement) (d'une ville, industrie etc)* expansion; *(d'idées, d'une culture etc)* spread(ing); **e. coloniale** colonial expansion; **taux d'e. économique** economic growth rate; **être en pleine e.** *(d'une économie, entreprise)* to be booming **(c)** *(exubérance)* expansiveness; **avec e.** expansively **(d)** *Ordinat* **carte d'e.** expansion card
expansionnisme [ɛkspɑ̃sjɔnism] *nm* expansionism
expansionniste [ɛkspɑ̃sjɔnist] *adj, n* expansionist
expansivité [ɛkspɑ̃sivite] *nf* expansiveness
expatriation [ɛkspatrijasjɔ̃] *nf* expatriation; *Fin* **e. de capitaux** movement of capital abroad
expatrié, -ée [ɛkspatrije] **1** *adj* expatriate, *F* expat; *(réseau de vente etc)* overseas **2** *n* expatriate, *F* expat
expatrier [ɛkspatrije] *(impf, pr sub* **n. expatriions) 1** *vt (qn)* to expatriate; *(capitaux)* to move abroad **2 s'expatrier** *vpr* to settle abroad
expectative [ɛkspɛktativ] *nf (attente)* expectation (**de** of); **nous vivons dans l'e.** we are living in hope; **rester dans l'e.** to wait and see
expectorant [ɛkspɛktɔrɑ̃] *adj, nm Méd* expectorant
expectoration [ɛkspɛktɔrasjɔ̃] *nf (action, crachat)* expectoration
expectorer [ɛkspɛktɔre] *vt* to expectorate
expédient [ɛkspedjɑ̃] **1** *adj Fml* expedient **2** *nm* expedient, makeshift; **vivre d'expédients** to live by one's wits; **user d'expédients** to resort to evasion
expédier [ɛkspedje] *vt (impf, pr sub* **n. expédiions) (a)** *(envoyer)* to dispatch, to send off; *Com* to dispatch, to ship; **e. des marchandises par navire** to send goods by sea, to ship goods; **e. un colis par chemin de fer** to dispatch *or* send *or* ship a parcel by rail; **e. par fret aérien** to airfreight; *F* **expédiez-le-moi!** *(personne)* send him along (to me)!; *F* **e. qn dans l'autre monde** *ou* **au cimetière** to dispatch sb to the next world

(b) *(se débarrasser de)* to get rid of, to dispose of; **elle a expédié ses enfants chez sa belle-mère/en colonie de vacances/au lit** she sent *or* packed her children off to her mother-in-law's/to camp/to bed; **il a tendance à e. ses patients un peu vite** *(d'un médecin)* he tends to pack his patients out of the surgery rather quickly

(c) *(faire rapidement) (tâche etc)* to deal promptly with; *(ses devoirs, sa dissertation)* to dash off; **e. son déjeuner** to make short work of one's lunch; **e. les affaires courantes** to deal with *or* get rid of the day-to-day matters

(d) *Jur (contrat, acte etc)* to draw up
expéditeur, -trice [ɛkspeditœr, -tris] **1** *n* **(a)** *(d'une lettre, d'un colis etc)* sender; **e./expéditrice J. Martin** from *or* sender J. Martin **(b)** *Com (de marchandises)* shipper, consigner; *(par bateau)* shipper **2** *adj (bureau, compagnie, gare etc)* shipping, dispatching
expéditif, -ive [ɛkspeditif, -iv] *adj* speedy, expeditious; **il est toujours très e. avec ses patients** he spends very little time with his patients; **je n'aime pas beaucoup ces méthodes expéditives** I don't appreciate this hasty way of doing things
expédition [ɛkspedisjɔ̃] *nf* **(a)** *(envoi)* dispatch, sending; *Com* shipping, shipment; **e. par mer** shipping, shipment; **bulletin d'e.** waybill; *Com* **e. de détail** retail shipment; **e. exclusive** exclusive shipment; **e. maritime** maritime shipment; **e. par avion** airfreighting; **e. par bateau** shipping; **e. par chemin de fer** sending by rail, railfreighting; **e. par courrier** mailing; **e. par la poste** mailing; *Com* **e. partielle** part shipment *or* consignment; *Com* **e. port à port** port to port shipment; *Com* **expéditions** *(service)* dispatch (department), shipping (department)

(b) *(marchandises)* consignment, shipment

(c) *(voyage, opération militaire)*, *Fig* expedition; **partir en e.** to go (off) on an expedition; *Fig* **dis donc, pour venir chez toi, quelle e.!** it's quite an expedition *or* a trek getting to your place!

(d) *Admin* **il est chargé de l'e. des affaires courantes** he is in charge of day-to-day matters; **je préfère m'occuper d'abord de l'e. des affaires courantes** I prefer to deal with *or* get rid of the day-to-day matters first

(e) *Jur* *(d'un contrat etc)* (authentic) copy

expéditionnaire [ɛkspedisjɔnɛr] **1** *adj Mil* expeditionary **2** *n Com* shipping clerk

expérience [ɛksperjɑ̃s] *nf* **(a)** *(pratique)* experience; **avec l'e., tu sauras que ...** you'll find out with experience that ...; **il a de l'e.** he's got experience, he's experienced; **elle a deux ans d'e.** she has two years' experience; **il nous faut quelqu'un qui a de l'e.** we need someone with experience; **avoir l'e. de qch** to have experience of sth, to be experienced in sth; **il a l'e. des enfants/de ce genre de voitures** he is used to children/this kind of car; **savoir qch par e.** to know sth from experience; **sans e.** inexperienced **(de** in), with no experience **(de** of); **il est sans e. de la vie** he has no experience of life

(b) *(essai)* experiment; **faire l'e. de** *(mauvaise humeur, douleur)* to experience; *(la vie à deux)* to experience, to try; *(machine)* to try out; **j'ai fait l'e. de la douleur** I've experienced pain, I've had experience of pain; **j'en ai malheureusement fait l'e.** that has been my experience unfortunately, as I've discovered to my cost; **nous avons décidé de tenter l'e.** we've decided to give it a try *or* a go; **tu pourrais tenter l'e. des clubs de rencontre** you could give dating agencies a try

(c) *(test scientifique)* experiment; **e. en laboratoire** laboratory experiment; **e. sur le terrain** field experiment; **faire une e.** to carry out *or* do an experiment **(sur** on)

expérimental, -ale, -aux, -ales [ɛksperimɑ̃tal, -o] *adj* experimental

expérimentalement [ɛksperimɑ̃talmɑ̃] *adv* experimentally

expérimentateur, -trice [ɛksperimɑ̃tatœr, -tris] *n* experimenter; *(scientifique)* (scientific) research worker

expérimentation [ɛksperimɑ̃tasjɔ̃] *nf* experimentation; **l'e. de ce produit n'a pas encore été faite** the product has not yet been tested; **e. sur l'homme** *(d'un vaccin etc)* human experiments, tests on humans

expérimenté [ɛksperimɑ̃te] *adj* experienced; **elle a un œil e. pour repérer les bonnes affaires** she's got a good eye for a bargain

expérimenter [ɛksperimɑ̃te] **1** *vt* *(tester)* *(remède, modèle, vaccin etc)* to test, to try out **(sur** on); **cette machine a été longuement expérimentée** the machine has been thoroughly tested **2** *vi* to experiment, to carry out experiments

expert [ɛkspɛr] **1** *adj* expert, skilled **(en, dans** in; **à faire qch** in doing sth); **elle est experte à vous faire douter de vous-même** she is an expert at making you doubt yourself; **être e. en la matière** to be an expert in the matter **2** *nm* expert; *(d'assurance, d'objets d'art)* valuer, appraiser; *Naut* surveyor; **e. financier/fiscal** financial/tax expert

expert-comptable, *pl* **experts-comptables** *nm Br* ≈ chartered accountant, *Am* ≈ certified public accountant

expertise [ɛkspɛrtiz] *nf* **(a)** *(évaluation)* *(d'une œuvre d'art etc)* (expert) valuation, appraisal; *Assurances* *(de dommages)* (expert) assessment; *Jur* expert opinion *or* testimony; *Assurances* **rapport d'e.** assessor's report, claims adjuster's report; *Naut* **e. d'avarie** damage survey; **e. médico-légale** forensic examination; *Jur* **e. contradictoire** valuation made in the presence of both parties to a contract **(b)** *(rapport)* expert's report **(c)** *(compétence)* expertise

expertiser [ɛkspɛrtize] *vt* *(œuvre d'art etc)* to value, to appraise; *(dommages)* to assess

expert-répétiteur, *pl* **experts-répétiteurs** *nm Fin* loss *or* average adjuster

expiable [ɛkspjabl] *adj* which can be atoned for; **tu as commis une faute, certes, mais elle est e.** yes, you made a mistake but you can make up for it *or* make atonement

expiation [ɛkspjasjɔ̃] *nf* atonement **(de** for), expiation **(de** of)

expiatoire [ɛkspjatwar] *adj* expiatory

expier [ɛkspje] *vt* *(impf, pr sub* **n. expiions)** *(péché, crime)* to atone for, to pay the penalty for, *Fml* to expiate; *(erreur)* to atone for, to make up for

expirant [ɛkspirɑ̃] *adj Litt* *(personne)* dying; *(flamme)* dying, guttering; **voix expirante** faint *or* barely audible voice

expiration [ɛkspirasjɔ̃] *nf* **(a)** *(respiration)* breathing out, exhalation, *Spéc* expiration; **pendant** *ou* **sur l'e.** on exhalation, as you/he/*etc* exhale(s) *or* breathes out **(b)** *(d'un contrat, un bail etc)* *Br* expiry, *Am* expiration; **venir** *ou* **arriver à e.** to expire, to run out

expirer [ɛkspire] **1** *vi* **(a)** *Litt* *(mourir)* to die, *Fml* to expire; *Fig* *(d'une flamme, d'une vague)* to die; *(d'un feu)* to go out; *(d'un son)* to die *or* fade away **(b)** *(d'un contrat, un bail etc)* to expire, to run out; **mon congé est expiré** my leave is up *or* has expired **(c)** *(respirer)* to breathe out, to exhale, *Spéc* to expire **2** *vt* *(air)* to breathe out, to exhale, *Spéc* to expire

explétif, -ive [ɛkspletif, -iv] *adj, nm Gram* expletive

explicable [ɛksplikabl] *adj* explicable, explainable; **ces phénomènes ne sont explicables que par le paranormal** such phenomena can only be explained *or* accounted for in terms of the paranormal; **sa conduite est difficilement e.** his behaviour is difficult to explain, it is difficult to account for his behaviour

explicatif, -ive [ɛksplikatif, -iv] *adj* explanatory; *Com* **notice explicative** directions for use; *Gram* **proposition relative explicative** non-defining relative clause

explication [ɛksplikasjɔ̃] *nf* explanation **(à** for); **je ne comprends pas les explications de la machine** I don't understand the instructions for the machine; **il a quitté la réunion sans aucune e.** he left the meeting without (giving) any explanation; **donner l'e. de qch** to account for *or* explain sth; **j'exige des explications!** I demand an explanation!; **avoir une e. avec qn** *(discuter)* to talk things over with sb; *(se disputer)* to have it out with sb; **je crois qu'il va falloir que nous ayons une petite e. tous les deux** I think we're going to have to have a little talk, you and I; **il y a eu une violente e. entre les deux équipes** there was a violent altercation between the two teams

▶ **explication**: *Scol, Univ* **e. de textes** literary appreciation

explicite [ɛksplisit] *adj* explicit **(sur** about)

explicitement [ɛksplisitmɑ̃] *adv* explicitly; **formuler e. une demande** to make an explicit request

expliciter [ɛksplisite] *vt* *(texte, pensées, clause d'un contrat etc)* to clarify; **il n'a pas voulu e. ses intentions** he did not want to be explicit about what he meant to do

expliquer [ɛksplike] **1** *vt* **(a)** *(communiquer)* *(ses idées, plans etc)* to explain **(à qn** to sb); **ce serait trop long à e.** it would take too long to explain

(b) *(élucider)* *(doctrine, théorème etc)* to explain, to expound, to elucidate; *(mystère, signification)* to explain

(c) *(indiquer la raison de)* *(action, fait, attitude etc)* to explain, to account for

2 s'expliquer *vpr* **(a)** *(communiquer ses idées)* to explain oneself; *(se justifier)* to justify one's behaviour, to explain oneself; **me serais-je mal expliqué?** perhaps I didn't make myself clear *or* wasn't plain enough; **je m'explique** this is what I mean, let me explain; **elle s'est expliquée sur différents reproches qu'on lui faisait** she justified herself with regard to the things they reproached her with

(b) *(comprendre)* **je ne m'explique pas pourquoi** I can't understand why

(c) *(être explicable)* **cela s'explique facilement** that's easily understandable *or* explainable; **il y a des choses qui ne s'expliquent pas** some things can't be explained; **c'est bizarre mais ça s'explique** it's strange but it can be explained *or* there's an explanation for it; **sa mort ne s'explique que par un suicide** his death can only be put down to suicide, suicide is the only explanation for his death; **le mauvais temps s'explique par la présence d'une dépression** the presence of a depression explains the bad weather; **et bien voilà, tout s'explique!** so you see, there's a reason for everything!

(d) *(de plusieurs personnes)* to talk things over; **s'e. avec qn** *(discuter)* to talk things over with sb; *(se disputer)* to have it out with sb; **expliquez-vous une bonne fois pour toutes** get it sorted out once and for all; **viens un peu, on va s'e. dehors** come on, we'll settle this outside; **ils se sont expliqués au couteau** they settled it with knives

exploit [ɛksplwa] *nm* **(a)** *(sportif, oratoire etc)* feat, achievement; *(militaire, amoureux)* exploit; **il est arrivé à l'heure, tu te rends compte d'un e.!** he arrived on time, which was quite an achievement for him! **(b)** *Jur* **e. (d'huissier)** writ

exploitable [ɛksplwatabl] *adj* *(terre)* farmable; *(mine, forêt)* workable; *(ressources naturelles)*, *Fig, Péj* exploitable; **tes documents ne sont pas exploitables dans l'optique de mes recherches** I can't make use of your documentation for my research; **e. par ordinateur** machine readable; **corpus e. par ordinateur** computerized corpus; *Fig Péj* **elles sont facilement exploitables** they are easily exploited *or* easy to exploit

exploitant [ɛksplwatɑ̃] *n* **(a)** *Com, Ind* *(de mine)* operator; **les exploitants de l'entreprise** the people running the company; **e. (agricole)** farmer; **petits exploitants** small farmers **(b)** *Cin* exhibitor

exploitation [ɛksplwatasjɔ̃] *nf* (**a**) (*action*) (*d'une mine, forêt etc*) working; (*d'une ligne de chemin de fer, ligne aérienne, ferme etc*) running, operation; (*d'une terre*) farming; (*des ressources naturelles*), *Fig, Péj* exploitation; *Com* (*d'un brevet*) commercialization; *Ordinat* **système d'e.** operating system; **société d'e.** development company; **mettre une terre en e.** to bring a piece of land into cultivation; **faire l'e. industrielle de qch** to produce sth on an industrial scale; **e. capitaliste** capitalist exploitation; **l'e. de l'homme par l'homme** the exploitation of man by man; *Fig Péj* **c'est de l'e.!** it's exploitation!
(**b**) (*entreprise*) concern; **e. agricole** farm; **petite e. agricole** small farm, smallholding; **e. forestière** forestry concern *or* operation; **e. minière** mine; **e. à ciel ouvert** open cast mine; **e. industrielle** industrial concern; **e. commerciale** business (concern); **e. familiale** family business

exploiter [ɛksplwate] *vt* (**a**) (*mine*) to work; (*forêt*) to work, to exploit; (*ressources naturelles, brevet*) to exploit; (*invention*) to use; (*chemin de fer, ferme, journal etc*) to run, to operate; (*terre*) to farm; *Fig* (*situation, talent, idée etc*) to exploit, to make the most of, to capitalize on (**b**) *Péj* (*abuser de*) (*qn, l'ignorance de qn etc*) to exploit, to take (unfair) advantage of

exploiteur, -euse [ɛksplwatœr, -øz] *n* (*de main-d'œuvre, de l'ignorance de qn etc*) exploiter

explorateur, -trice [ɛksplɔratœr, -tris] *n* (*personne*) explorer

exploration [ɛksplɔrasjɔ̃] *nf* (**a**) (*d'un pays, d'une maison, Fig d'un sujet etc*) exploration; **voyage d'e.** voyage of discovery; **partir en e.** to go off exploring *or* on an exploration (**b**) *Méd* exploration

exploratoire [ɛksplɔratwar] *adj* exploratory

explorer [ɛksplɔre] *vt* (**a**) (*pays, maison, Fig sujet, possibilité etc*) to explore (**b**) *Méd* (*blessure, cavité*) to explore, to probe

exploser [ɛksploze] *vi* (**a**) (*d'une bombe*) to explode, to go off; (*d'un avion, d'une chaudière etc*) to explode, to blow up; (*d'un gaz*) to explode; **faire e. une bombe** to explode a bomb (**b**) *Fig* (*se mettre en colère*) to explode, *F* to blow one's top; **sa colère explosa** his anger erupted *or* exploded

explosible [ɛksplozibl] *adj* (*gaz etc*) explosive

explosif, -ive [ɛksplozif, -iv] **1** *adj* (*obus, force etc, Fig situation, question, tempérament etc*) explosive; *Ling* (*consonne*) plosive; **il est d'un tempérament e.** he tends to explode *or* erupt *or F* blow his top **2** *nm* explosive

explosion [ɛksplozjɔ̃] *nf aussi Fig* explosion; **e. atomique** atomic explosion; **e. volcanique** volcanic explosion *or* eruption; **faire e.** to explode; **e. de fureur/rires** explosion *or* (out)burst of fury/laughter; **e. démographique** population explosion; **e. des naissances** baby boom

expo [ɛkspo] *nf F* (= **exposition**) exhibition

exponentiel, -ielle [ɛkspɔnɑ̃sjɛl] *adj, n Math* exponential

export [ɛkspɔr] *nm* = exportation; **l'e., le service e.** the export branch; *Ordinat* **e. de données** data export

exportable [ɛkspɔrtabl] *adj* exportable

exportateur, -trice [ɛkspɔrtatœr, -tris] **1** *n* exporter **2** *adj* exporting; **pays e. de vin** wine-exporting country

exportation [ɛkspɔrtasjɔ̃] *nf* (*action*) export(ation), exporting; (*produit*) export; *Ordinat* (*d'un fichier*) exporting; *Ordinat* (*données exportées*) exported data; **le montant des exportations a augmenté de 10% cette année** exports have risen by 10% this year; **ce produit marche très fort à l'e.** this product is doing very well on the export market, we export a lot of this product; **l'e. de nos produits a rencontré un vif succès** our products have been very successful on the export market; **réservé à l'e.** reserved for export, for export only; **articles d'e.** exports; **faire de l'e.** to export; **exportations visibles/invisibles** visible/invisible exports; **commerce d'e.** export trade; **e. kangourou** piggybacking

exporter [ɛkspɔrte] *vt Com, Ordinat* to export (**vers** to); **ces articles s'exportent mal** these items are difficult to export; *Fig* **ce genre de coutume s'exporte mal** this type of custom does not export *or* travel well; **cette mode a été** *ou* **s'est exportée dans le monde entier** the fashion has spread throughout the world

exposant, -ante [ɛkspozɑ̃, -ɑ̃t] **1** *n* (*artiste, firme etc*) exhibitor **2** *nm* (**a**) *Math* exponent, (power) index (**b**) *Typ* (*chiffre, lettre*) superscript, superior; **3 en exposant** superscript 3

exposé [ɛkspoze] *nm* (**a**) (*de faits, d'une situation etc*) statement, account, report; *Scol, Univ* presentation; **faire un e. des faits** to give an account of the facts; **après avoir fait un bref e. de la situation** after outlining the situation; **faire l'e. d'un projet** to sketch out a plan; **e. verbal (de mission)** briefing; *Compta* **e. de la situation de l'entreprise** statement of the company's position (**b**) (*discours*) (short) talk; **faire un e.** to give a (short) talk (**c**) *Jur* **e. des motifs** (*d'un projet de loi*) preamble

exposer [ɛkspoze] **1** *vt* (**a**) (*montrer*) (*marchandises, œuvres d'art etc*) to exhibit, to show, to display; **objet exposé** exhibit; **ça fait très longtemps qu'il n'a pas exposé** he hasn't exhibited anything for a very long time; **être exposé (sur un lit de parade)** to lie in state; **e. des marchandises en vitrine** to display goods for sale
(**b**) (*expliquer*) (*plans, raisons, problème etc*) to set out, to unfold, to expound; (*ses griefs, problèmes, son point de vue*) to air; **je leur ai exposé ma situation** I explained my situation to them
(**c**) (*présenter*) (*à la chaleur, lumière etc*) to expose (**à** to); (*à la critique, un danger etc*) to expose, to lay open (**à** to); *Hist* (*nouveau-né*) to expose; **il faut e. cette plante à la lumière le plus possible** the plant must receive *or* get as much light as possible; **parce que la plante n'était pas du tout exposée** because the plant wasn't getting any light at all; **exposé à tous les vents** exposed *or* open to the four winds; **maison exposée au nord** house facing north; *Phot* **e. un film à la lumière** to expose a film
(**d**) (*risquer*) (*sa vie, son honneur etc*) to risk, to take chances with; **e. qn** to put sb in danger
(**e**) *Mus* to introduce; *Littér* to set out
2 s'exposer *vpr* to put oneself in danger; **s'e. à des critiques** to lay oneself open *or* expose oneself to criticism; **il s'expose à des poursuites** he is laying himself open to prosecution; **s'e. au soleil** to expose oneself to the sun; **si tu t'exposes trop longtemps** if you stay in the sun too long

exposition [ɛkspozisjɔ̃] *nf* (**a**) (*action de montrer*) (*de marchandises, d'œuvres d'art, de fleurs etc*) display; (*d'un corps*) lying in state
(**b**) (*dans un musée, une galerie*) exhibition
(**c**) (*salon, foire*) exhibition, show; **salle d'e.** exhibition room, *Can* showroom; **e. interprofessionnelle** trade exhibition *or* show; **e. commerciale** trade exhibition; **E. universelle** world fair; *Mktg* **e. sur le lieu de vente** point of sale display; *Mktg* **e. sur le marché** market exposure
(**d**) (*de faits, raisons etc*) exposition
(**e**) (*au froid, danger etc*) exposure (**à** to); (*d'une maison*) aspect, exposure; *Phot* exposure; **e. solaire** exposure to the sun; **il lui faut au minimum une heure d'e. (à la lumière) par jour** it needs at least an hour of light a day; *Fin* **e. aux risques** exposure
(**f**) *Littér, Mus* exposition, introduction; *Mus* **d'e.** introductory, expository; *Littér* **scène d'e.** prologue

exposition-vente, *pl* **expositions-ventes** *nf Com* show, exhibition (*where the items are for sale*)

exprès[1], -esse [ɛksprɛs] **1** *adj* (*explicite*) (*ordre, mise en garde etc*) express, distinct, explicit; **vous avez l'interdiction expresse de jouer dans la rue** you are expressly forbidden to play in the street; **défense expresse de fumer** smoking strictly prohibited **2** *adj inv, nm Arch* **(lettre/paquet) e.** special delivery *or Br* express letter/parcel; **par** *ou* **en e.** (by) special *or Br* express delivery

exprès[2] [ɛksprɛ] *adv* (*à dessein*) on purpose, intentionally, deliberately; (*spécialement*) specially, especially; **elle est sortie e. pour l'acheter** she went out specially *or* expressly to buy it; **je ne l'ai pas fait e.** I didn't mean to do it, I didn't do it on purpose *or* intentionally *or* deliberately; **je n'ai pas fait e. d'être méchante avec elle** I didn't mean to *or* set out to be nasty to her, I wasn't nasty to her on purpose; **j'ai déclenché l'alarme sans le faire e.** I set off the alarm without meaning to; **il fait e. de vous contredire** he makes a point of contradicting you; **j'aurais voulu le faire e., je n'y serais pas arrivé** I couldn't have done it if I'd tried *or* if I'd wanted to; **c'est fait e.** it's (quite) intentional *or* deliberate; **c'est fait e. pour ranger des crayons** it's designed *or* meant for holding pencils; **elle est trop grande, ta robe – c'est fait e.** your dress is too big for you – it's meant to be (that way *or* like that); **on dirait un fait e.** you'd think it was done on purpose *or* was intentional; *Iron* **comme (par) un fait e., il pleuvait** and of course *or* wouldn't you know it, it was raining

express [ɛksprɛs] **1** *adj* (**a**) (*train*) fast, express (**b**) (*coffee*) espresso **2** *nm* (**a**) (*train*) fast train (**b**) (*café*) espresso (coffee)

expressément [ɛksprɛsemɑ̃] *adv* (**a**) (*catégoriquement*) expressly (**b**) (*spécialement*) expressly, specially

expressif, -ive [ɛksprɛsif, -iv] *adj* (*langage, musique, regard, visage etc*) expressive

expression [ɛksprɛsjɔ̃] *nf* (**a**) (*d'un sentiment, d'une pensée, d'une opinion, d'une douleur etc*) expression; (*du visage*) expression, look; **il faudrait que tu soignes l'e.** you'll have to express yourself better; **l'e. de nos idées doit se faire par le biais d'un journal** we must express our ideas in a newspaper; **au-delà de toute e.** (*employé comme adjectif*) inexpressible; (*employé comme adverbe*) inexpressibly; **veuillez recevoir l'e. de mes sentiments distingués** (*en fin* de lettre) (quand le destinataire n'est pas nommé dans l'introduction) yours faithfully; (quand le destinataire est nommé) yours sincerely; **l'e. de son visage ne changea pas** his expression didn't change; **un visage plein d'e.** a very expressive face, a face full of expression; **auteur d'e. anglaise** author writing in English; **sans e.** expressionless; *Mus* **jouer avec e.** to play with expression *or* feeling

(b) *(locution)* expression, phrase; **e. familière** colloquialism, colloquial expression; **e. figée, e. toute faite** set *or* fixed expression

(c) *Math* expression; *Fig* **la famille, réduite à sa plus simple e.** the family, reduced to its simplest expression; *Hum* **une jupe réduite à sa plus simple e.** a skirt that leaves little to the imagination, an itsy-bitsy skirt; *Fig* **un meublé dont le mobilier était réduit à sa plus simple e.** a furnished room that hardly merited the term

▶ **expression**: **e. algébrique** algebraic expression; **e. corporelle** self-expression, music and movement; *Ordinat* **e. logique** logical expression; *Ordinat* **e. de sélection** selection command; *Ordinat* **e. de tri** sort command

expressionnisme [ɛkspresjɔnism] *nm Beaux-Arts* expressionism

expressionniste [ɛkspresjɔnist] *adj, n Beaux-Arts* expressionist

expressivement [ɛkspresivmɑ̃] *adv* expressively

expressivité [ɛkspresivite] *nf* expressiveness

exprimable [ɛksprimabl] *adj* which can be expressed, expressible; **sa douleur/joie n'était pas e.** his pain/happiness was inexpressible

exprimer [ɛksprime] **1** *vt* **(a)** *(par des mots) (sentiment, pensée, opinion, douleur etc)* to express (**à qn** to sb); *(d'un regard, geste etc) (douleur, plaisir etc)* to express, to show **(b)** *Math (quantité, valeur etc)* to express **(c)** *(extraire en pressant) (jus)* to squeeze out (**de** from) **2 s'exprimer** *vpr (en parlant, en agissant etc)* to express oneself; **si l'on peut s'e. ainsi** if one may put it this way *or* like this; **le président ne s'est pas encore exprimé sur ce sujet** the president has yet to voice an opinion on the matter; **s'e. par gestes** to use sign language

expropriation [ɛksprɔprijasjɔ̃] *nf Jur (de propriété, propriétaire)* expropriation

exproprier [ɛksprɔprije] *vt (impf, pr sub* **n. expropriions)** *Jur* to expropriate

expulser [ɛkspylse] *vt* **(a)** *(étranger)* to deport, to expel; *(locataire)* to evict; *(perturbateur etc)* to eject; *(élève, étudiant, membre de parti etc)* to expel (**de** from); *Sp (joueur)* to send off **(b)** *Physiol* to expel

expulsif, -ive [ɛkspylsif, -iv] *adj Méd* expulsive

expulsion [ɛkspylsjɔ̃] *nf* **(a)** *(d'un étranger)* deportation; *(d'un locataire)* eviction; *(d'un perturbateur etc)* ejection; *(d'un élève, d'un membre de parti etc)* expulsion; *Sp (d'un joueur)* sending off **(b)** *Physiol* expulsion

expurgation [ɛkspyrgasjɔ̃] *nf (d'un livre etc)* expurgation

expurger [ɛkspyrʒe] *vt* **(j'expurgeai(s))** *(livre etc)* to expurgate; **un récit très expurgé de cette histoire** an expurgated *or* sanitized version of the matter

exquis [ɛkski] *adj* **(a)** *(beauté, manières, goût, nourriture etc)* exquisite; *(personne, sourire, temps)* delightful **(b)** *(douleur)* exquisite

exsangue [ɛksɑ̃g, ɛgzɑ̃g] *adj (patient, organe, visage etc)* anaemic, *US* anemic; *Fig (œuvre d'art etc)* anaemic, bloodless; *(pays)* bled white; *(entreprise, région)* on its knees; *Fig* **elle est devenue e.** she turned deathly pale, the blood drained from her face; *Fig* **il est sorti e. de cette épreuve** he was drained by the ordeal

exsanguino-transfusion, *pl* **exsanguino-transfusions** [ɛksɑ̃g(ɥ)inotrɑ̃sfyzjɔ̃] *nf Méd* exchange transfusion

exsudation [ɛksydasjɔ̃] *nf* exudation

exsuder [ɛksyde] *vti* to exude

extase [ɛkstɑz] *nf* **(a)** *Rel, Psy* ecstasy, trance **(b)** *(admiration)* rapture, ecstasy; **être en e. devant qch/qn** to be in raptures *or* ecstasies over sth/sb, to be rapturous about sth/sb; **tomber en e. devant qn/qch** to go into raptures over sb/sth

extasié [ɛkstɑzje] *adj (personne, regard)* ecstatic, enraptured

extasier (s') [sɛkstɑzje] *vpr (impf, pr sub* **n. n. extasiions)** to be in *or* go into ecstasies *or* raptures (**sur** about; **devant** over); **elle s'est longuement extasiée sur ses enfants/devant mes géraniums** she went into great raptures about her children/my geraniums

extatique [ɛkstatik] *adj (personne, regard)* ecstatic, enraptured; *(état, vision)* ecstatic

extenseur [ɛkstɑ̃sœr] **1** *adj Anat (muscle)* extensor **2** *nm* **(a)** *Gym* (chest) expander **(b)** *Anat* extensor

extensibilité [ɛkstɑ̃sibilite] *nf (de fibres)* ability to stretch, stretchability; *(d'un métal)* tensile nature

extensible [ɛkstɑ̃sibl] *adj* **(a)** *(métal)* tensile; *(vêtement, tissu)* stretch; *Fig (idée, définition etc)* flexible; *Fig* **ma fortune n'est malheureusement pas e.** unfortunately my funds are not limitless *or F* I'm not made of money **(b)** *Ordinat* upgradeable; *(mémoire)* expandable, upgradeable

extensif, -ive [ɛkstɑ̃sif, -iv] *adj* **(a)** *Agr* **culture extensive** extensive farming **(b) sens e.** *(d'un mot)* extended meaning

extension [ɛkstɑ̃sjɔ̃] *nf* **(a)** *(d'un muscle, bras, ressort etc)* stretching, extension; **être en e.** *(d'un ressort)* to be released; *(d'un gymnaste etc)* to be stretched out

(b) *Fig (d'un territoire, d'une firme etc)* enlargement, expansion; *(d'un contrat)* extension; *(d'une maladie, d'une langue, d'un incendie etc)* spread; **leur but est l'e. du territoire** territorial expansion is their aim; **il veut l'e. de ses pouvoirs** he wants to extend his powers; **il faut éviter l'e. de l'épidémie/de l'incendie** the epidemic/fire must be prevented from spreading; **cette langue a forcément une e. restreinte** the language is necessarily restricted to a fairly small area; **donner de l'e. à une loi** to extend a law; *Com* **e. du commerce** business expansion; **prendre de l'e.** *(d'une entreprise etc)* to expand, to grow; *(d'une maladie, d'un incendie)* to spread; **e. de nom de fichier** file name extension

(c) *(d'un mot)* extended meaning; **par e.** by extension

(d) *Ordinat* expansion; **e. mémoire** memory expansion *or* upgrade; **carte d'e.** expansion board

(e) *Mktg* **e. de la gamme** range stretching; **e. de la marque** brand extension; **e. de ligne** line extension; **e. de marché** market expansion

exténuant [ɛkstenɥɑ̃] *adj* exhausting

exténuation [ɛkstenɥasjɔ̃] *nf (du corps, de l'esprit)* exhaustion

exténuer [ɛkstenɥe] **1** *vt* to exhaust; **être exténué (de fatigue)** to be exhausted *or* worn out **2 s'exténuer** *vpr* to exhaust oneself, to tire oneself out (**à faire** doing); **je m'exténue à lui dire de ne pas y aller** I'm tired of telling him not to go

extérieur [ɛksterjœr] **1** *adj* **(a)** *(surface, partie etc)* exterior, outer, external; *(escalier, éclairage, poche, intérêts etc)* outside; *(port, boulevards)* outer; *(signe, apparence etc)* outward, external; *(facteur, cause)* external; *Péj (gentillesse, pitié etc)* superficial; *(fragilité, assurance)* outward; **il habite dans un quartier e. à la ville** he lives outside the city; **pour des raisons qui te sont complètement extérieures** for reasons that have absolutely nothing to do with you; **elle est extérieure à cette entreprise/ce service** she doesn't work for this company/this department; **avoir des activités extérieures** to have outside interests; *Péj* **sa fragilité est toute extérieure** her fragility is all on the surface; **le côté e. de qch** the outer side *or* outside of sth; **le monde e.** the outside world; **fonds extérieurs** external financing; **sans aide extérieure** without outside help, *F* under one's own steam

(b) *(étranger) (commerce, politique etc)* external, foreign

2 *nm* **(a)** *(d'un bâtiment, d'une boîte etc)* exterior, outside; **vu de l'e.** seen from the outside; **vue de l'e., cette entreprise a l'air de bien marcher** judging by appearances, the company seems to be doing well; **à l'e.** *(d'un bâtiment)* outside; *(d'une boîte etc)* on the outside; **à l'intérieur et à l'e.** inside and out; **juger de l'e.** to judge by appearances; *Sp* **match à l'e.** away match; **à l'e. de la gare/ville** outside the station/town; **cette peinture est prévue pour l'e.** the paint is intended for outside use

(b) l'e. *(pays étrangers)* foreign countries; **à l'e.** abroad; **de l'e.** from abroad; **les relations avec l'e.** foreign relations

(c) *Cin* location shot; **il tourne en e.** he's on location

extérieurement [ɛksterjœrmɑ̃] *adv* **(a)** *(dehors)* externally, on the outside **(b)** *(en apparence)* on the surface

extériorisation [ɛksterjɔrizasjɔ̃] *nf (d'un sentiment)* manifestation, display; *Psy* exteriorization, externalization

extérioriser [ɛksterjɔrize] **1** *vt (sentiment)* to show, to express; *Psy* to exteriorize, to externalize **2 s'extérioriser** *vpr (d'un sentiment)* to show *or* manifest itself; *(d'une personne)* to express oneself, to externalize; **il s'extériorise tellement peu** he shows so little of what he's feeling

extériorité [ɛksterjɔrite] *nf* exteriority

exterminateur, -trice [ɛkstɛrminatœr, -tris] **1** *adj (rage)* destructive **2** *n* exterminator, destroyer

extermination [ɛkstɛrminasjɔ̃] *nf (d'une race, d'une armée etc)* extermination, destruction

exterminer [ɛkstɛrmine] *vt (race, armée etc)* to exterminate, to destroy, to wipe out

externat [ɛkstɛrna] *nm* **(a)** *(école)* day school **(b)** *(élèves)* day pupils **(c)** *Méd* non-resident (medical) studentship

externe [ɛkstɛrn] **1** *adj* **(a)** *(surface, partie etc)* external, outside, outer; *(cause)* external; **côté e.** outside; **angle e.**

exterior angle; *Ordinat* **dispositif e.** external device; *Pharm* **à usage e.** for external use only **(b) élève e.** day pupil **2** *n* **(a)** (*élève*) day pupil **(b)** *Méd* **e. (des hôpitaux)** non-resident (medical) student, *Am* extern

exterritorialité [ɛksteritɔrjalite] *nf* ex(tra)territoriality

extincteur, -trice [ɛkstɛ̃ktœr, -tris] **1** *adj* (*matériel etc*) extinguishing **2** *nm* fire extinguisher

extinction [ɛkstɛ̃ksjɔ̃] *nf* **(a)** (*d'un incendie etc*) extinguishing, putting out; *Mil* **e. des feux** lights out; **l'e. des feux** *ou* **des lumières se fait à 22h** lights out is at 10 pm; *Aut* **e. retardée** (*d'une lumière*) delayed cut-off **(b)** *Jur* (*d'un droit etc*) extinguishment; *Compta* **e. d'une dette** discharge of a debt **(c)** (*d'une race, espèce*) extinction; **espèce menacée** *ou* **en voie d'e.** endangered species; **depuis l'e. des dinosaures** since dinosaurs became extinct **(d) e. de voix** loss of one's voice; **avoir une e. de voix** to have lost one's voice

extirpateur [ɛkstirpatœr] *nm Agr* (*instrument*) weeder

extirpation [ɛkstirpasjɔ̃] *nf* (*d'une plante, de mauvaises herbes*) uprooting; *Chir* (*d'une tumeur etc*) extirpation

extirper [ɛkstirpe] **1** *vt* (*plante*) to root out *or* up; *Fig* (*vices*) to eradicate, to root out; *F* **e. qn de son lit** to drag sb out of bed; **e. qn d'une situation impossible/un piège** to extricate sb from an impossible situation/a trap; **je n'ai pas réussi à lui e. un mot** I couldn't drag *or* get a word out of him **2 s'extirper** *vpr* **s'e. de son lit/de dessous la couette** to drag oneself out of bed/from beneath the quilt; **s'e. de son pull/d'un enchevêtrement de racines** to extricate oneself from one's pullover/a tangle of roots

extorquer [ɛkstɔrke] *vt* (*argent, promesse etc*) to extort, to wring (**à qn** from sb)

extorqueur, -euse [ekstɔrkœr, -øz] *n* extortioner

extorsion [ɛkstɔrsjɔ̃] *nf* extortion; **e. de fonds** extortion of funds

extra [ɛkstra] **1** *nm inv* **(a)** *aussi Culin* (special) treat; **faire/s'offrir un e.** to do/treat oneself to something special; **on s'est fait un petit e. en achetant du homard** we gave ourselves a bit of a treat by buying lobster

(b) (*serviteur*) extra help *or* hand; **faire des e. chez qn** to do occasional work for sb; **pour la soirée, on prendra deux extras** we'll take on two extra people for the party

2 *adj inv* (*de qualité supérieure*) (*vin, repas, vêtement etc*) first-class, first-rate; *F* (*remarquable*) (*personne, roman, vacances etc*) terrific, fantastic, fabulous; **tu viens passer le week-end avec nous? c'est e.!** you're spending the weekend with us? (that's) fantastic *or* terrific!

extra- [ɛkstra] *préf* extra-

extra-comptable *adj Compta* (*ajustement*) off-balance sheet

extraconjugal, -ale, -aux, -ales [ɛkstrakɔ̃ʒygal, -o] *adj* extramarital

extracteur [ɛkstraktœr] *nm* (*appareil, instrument*) extractor

extractible [ɛkstraktibl] *adj* (*autoradio*) removable

extractif, -ive [ɛkstraktif, -iv] *adj* extractive

extraction [ɛkstraksjɔ̃] *nf* **(a)** (*de dents*) extraction, *F* pulling; (*de charbon, minerai*) extraction, mining; (*de pierres*) quarrying; (*de pétrole, de gaz etc*) extraction; *Chir* (*d'une balle etc*) removal **(b)** *Math* (*d'une racine carrée ou cubique*) extraction **(c)** *Fig* **de haute/basse e.** of noble/humble extraction *or* birth

extrader [ɛkstrade] *vt* to extradite

extradition [ɛkstradisjɔ̃] *nf* extradition

extra-dry *adj* (*boisson alcoolisée*) extra dry

extra-fin *adj* **(a)** (*petit, fin*) (*pois, aiguille etc*) extra-fine **(b)** *Com* (*de qualité supérieure*) (*chocolat*) superfine, top-quality; (*beurre*) top quality

extra-fort 1 *adj* extra-strong **2** *nm Couture* bias binding

extra(-)galactique *adj Astron* extragalactic

extraire [ɛkstrɛr] (*conj like* **traire**) **1** *vt* (*épingle, clou etc*) to pull out, to draw out; (*dent*) to extract, to take out, to pull (out); (*charbon, minerai*) to extract, to mine; (*pierre*) to quarry; (*pétrole, gaz, jus etc*) to extract; (*citation, passage etc*) to extract, to excerpt; (*balle, qch de son portefeuille etc*) to take out, to remove; (*blessés, corps*) (*d'une voiture, des décombres*) to free; **cette citation est extraite du Roman de la rose** this quotation is taken from the Roman de la rose; **e. des plants** to lift seedlings; *Math* **e. une racine** to extract a root

2 s'extraire *vpr* **s'e. de sa voiture** to free oneself from *or* wriggle out of *or* squeeze out of one's car

extrait [ɛkstrɛ] *nm* **(a)** (*produit*) extract, essence; **e. de viande** meat extract; **e. de lavande** lavender essence; **e. de café** coffee extract **(b)** (*d'un livre, discours, auteur etc*) extract, excerpt; (*de film*) extract, clip; *Jur, Fin* (*d'un acte, compte rendu*) abstract; **e. de presse** press cutting; *TV* **extraits pré-enregistrés** recorded highlights

▶ **extrait**: **e. de baptême** certificate of baptism, baptismal certificate; **e. de casier judiciaire** = documentary evidence that one does not have a criminal record; **e. de compte** *Compta* statement of account; *Banque* bank statement; **e. de film** film clip; **e. de naissance** birth certificate

extrajudiciaire [ɛkstraʒydisjɛr] *adj* extrajudicial

extra-légal, -ale, -aux, -ales *adj* bordering on the illegal; **ils ont employé des méthodes extra-légales** they used methods that bordered on the illegal *or F* that were legally a bit iffy; **les procédés extra-légaux ne lui font pas peur** he's not bothered about sailing a bit close to the wind *or* doing things that are not altogether above board

extra-lucide, *pl* **extra-lucides** *adj, n* (**voyante**) **e.** clairvoyant

extra-muros [ɛkstramyros] **1** *adj inv* (*quartier*) suburban, outside town **2** *adv* (*habiter*) outside town, in the suburbs; **se promener e.** to go for a stroll in the suburbs

extraordinaire [ɛkstraɔrdinɛr] *adj* **(a)** (*spécial*) (*réunion, mesures etc*) extraordinary, special; (*messager, mission*) special; **assemblée générale e.** extraordinary general meeting; **frais** *ou* **dépenses extraordinaires** (*non prévues*) extras; (*uniques*) non-recurring expenditure

(b) (*étonnant*) (*nouvelles, événement etc*) extraordinary, astonishing; **cela n'a rien d'e.** that's nothing out of the ordinary; **cela n'a rien d'e. après ce que tu lui as dit** that's not surprising given what you said to him

(c) (*remarquable*) (*personne, beauté, succès*) extraordinary, outstanding; (*chaleur, prix*) extraordinary; *F* (*très bon*) (*livre, vin etc*) really good; **elle est vraiment e. dans cette robe** she looks quite extraordinary in that dress; **elle a fait un travail e.** she did outstanding work; **par e.** by a *or* some remote chance; **si par e. tu la voyais** if by some remote chance you should see her; **quand par e. nous nous rencontrons** when we meet, which we rarely do

extraordinairement [ɛkstraɔrdinɛrmɑ̃] *adv* extraordinarily

extra-parlementaire *adj* extra-parliamentary

extraplat [ɛkstrapla] *adj* (*montre, calculette etc*) slimline

extrapolation [ɛkstrapɔlasjɔ̃] *nf* extrapolation

extrapoler [ɛkstrapɔle] *vi* to extrapolate (**à partir de** from)

extrascolaire [ɛkstraskɔlɛr] *adj* (*activités etc*) extra-curricular

extrasensible [ɛkstrasɑ̃sibl] *adj* (*phénomène*) extrasensory

extra(-)sensoriel, -ielle *adj Psy* (*perception etc*) extrasensory

extrasystole [ɛkstrasistɔl] *nf Physiol* extrasystole

extra(-)terrestre, *pl* **extra(-)terrestres** *adj, n* extraterrestrial

extraterritorial, -ale, -aux, -ales [ɛkstratɛritɔrjal, -o] *adj* extraterritorial

extraterritorialité [ɛkstratɛritɔrjalite] *nf* extraterritoriality

extra-utérin *adj Méd* **grossesse extra-utérine** ectopic pregnancy

extravagance [ɛkstravagɑ̃s] *nf* **(a)** (*d'une idée, d'un comportement, de vêtements etc*) extravagance; (*d'une personne*) eccentricity; (*de dépenses*) exorbitance; (*d'un désir*) immoderateness; **des idées d'une telle e.** such extravagant ideas **(b)** (*action, remarque*) piece of nonsense; **il a dit un tas d'extravagances** he talked a lot of nonsense

extravagant, -ante [ɛkstravagɑ̃, -ɑ̃t] **1** *adj* (*idée, comportement, vêtements etc*) extravagant; (*personne*) eccentric; (*prix, demande*) exorbitant; (*désir*) immoderate **2** *n* eccentric (person)

extraversion [ɛkstravɛrsjɔ̃] *nf Psy* extroversion

extraverti, -ie [ɛkstravɛrti] *adj, n Psy* extrovert

extrême [ɛkstrɛm] **1** *adj* **(a)** (*point, limite etc*) far, extreme, farthest; (*jeunesse, vieillesse*) extreme; (*froid, plaisir etc*) extreme, intense; **à l'e. limite, j'accepterai d'attendre une semaine de plus** I'll agree to wait another week at the most *or* at the outside; **il pousse la pingrerie jusqu'à son point e.** he takes meanness to extremes; **tu ne m'appelles qu'en cas d'e. urgence** only call me in cases of extreme urgency *or* if it's extremely urgent; **d'une maigreur e.** extremely thin; **j'ai l'e. regret de vous annoncer que ...** I am extremely sorry to tell you that ...; *Pol* **e. droite/gauche** far *or* extreme right/left

(b) (*excessif*) (*mesure, solution*) extreme, drastic, severe; (*cas, situation, opinion*) extreme; **elle est e. en tout** she is extreme in everything; **être e. dans ses opinions** to hold extreme opinions

2 *nm* extreme; **les extrêmes** (*de chaleur et froid, Math d'une proportion*) the extremes; **il passe d'un e. à l'autre** he goes from one extreme to the other; **prudent à l'e.** cautious in the extreme *or* to a fault; **pousser les choses à l'e.** to take *or* carry matters to extremes; **elle a réagi à l'e.** her reaction was rather extreme; **il la déteste à l'e.** he cordially detests her; **les extrêmes se touchent** extremes meet

extrêmement [ɛkstrɛmmɑ̃] *adv* extremely, exceedingly

extrême-onction *nf Rel* extreme unction

extrême-oriental, -ale, -aux, -ales 1 *adj* Far East, Far Eastern **2** *n* **E. Oriental**

Extrême-Orient (l') *nm* the Far East

extrémisme [ɛkstremism] *nm* extremism

extrémiste [ɛkstremist] *adj, n* extremist
extrémité [ɛkstremite] *nf* **(a)** (*bout*) (*d'un lac, d'une route, d'une jambe, d'une corde etc*) end; (*d'un doigt, d'une aile etc*) tip; (*d'une aiguille, une épée etc*) point; **les extrémités** (*pieds et mains*) the extremities, the hands and feet; **j'ai les extrémités glacées** my hands and feet are frozen
(b) (*excès*) **extrémité(s)** extremes; **pousser qch à l'e.** to carry *or* take sth to extremes; **pousser qn à une e.** *ou* **à des extrémités** to drive sb to extremes; **en venir à des extrémités** to resort to extreme measures; (*à la violence*) to resort to violence
(c) (*situation désespérée*) extremity; **dans cette e.** in this extremity; **réduit à l'e.** in dire distress *or* straits, reduced to extremity; **être à la dernière** *ou* **à toute e.** to be at the point of death, to be close to death
extrinsèque [ɛkstrɛ̃sɛk] *adj* extrinsic; **valeur e.** (*de monnaie*) face value
extroversion [ɛkstrɔvɛrsjɔ̃] *nf Psy* extroversion, extraversion
extroverti, -ie [ɛkstrɔvɛrti] *adj, n Psy* extrovert, extravert
extrusion [ɛkstryzjɔ̃] *nf Tech* extrusion
exubérance [ɛgzyberɑ̃s] *nf* (*d'une personne, de la végétation, d'un style etc*) exuberance; **avec e.** with exuberance, exuberantly
exubérant [ɛgzyberɑ̃] *adj* (*personne, végétation, joie, style etc*) exuberant
exultation [ɛgzyltasjɔ̃] *nf* exultation
exulter [ɛgzylte] *vi* to exult, to rejoice (**de faire** in doing)
exutoire [ɛgzytwar] *nm* outlet (**à sa colère** for one's anger)
ex-voto [ɛksvɔto] *nm inv Rel* ex-voto, votive offering
eye-liner [ajlajnœr], *pl* **eye-liners** *nm* eyeliner

F

F, f [ɛf] *nm inv* (*lettre*) F f; **un F2/3/***etc* (*appartement*) a two-/ three-/*etc* roomed flat *or Am* apartment
F (**a**) (*abrév* **franc(s)**) F, fr (**b**) (*abrév* **Fahrenheit**) F
f (*abrév* **féminin**) f
fa [fa] *nm inv Mus* (*note*) F; (*quand on chante la gamme*) fa; **clef de fa** bass clef, F clef
FAB [ɛfabe] *Com* (*abrév* **franco à bord**) FOB
fable [fɑbl] *nf* (**a**) (*légende*) fable; **célèbre dans la f.** famous in fable (**b**) (*invention*) story, tale; **c'est pure f.** it's pure invention; **être la f. de la ville** to be the laughing stock of the whole town
fabliau, -aux [fɑblijo] *nm Littér* fabliau
fablier [fɑblije] *nm* book of fables
fabricant, -ante [fabrikɑ̃, -ɑ̃t] *n* maker, manufacturer; **f. de chapeaux** hat maker *or* manufacturer; **f. d'automobiles** car maker *or* manufacturer; **gros/petit f.** large/small manufacturer
fabricateur, -trice [fabrikatœr, -tris] *n* **f. de fausse monnaie** counterfeiter, forger; **f. de faux papiers** forger of documents; **f. de fausses nouvelles** scandalmonger
fabrication [fabrikasjɔ̃] *nf* (**a**) (*à la main*) making; *Ind* manufacture, manufacturing; **f. artisanale** production by craftsmen; **produits de f. artisanale** handmade products; **f. industrielle** industrial manufacture; **f. assistée par ordinateur** computer-aided manufacture; **f. sous contrat** contract manufacturing; **défaut de f.** manufacturing defect; **secret de f.** trade secret; **f. en série** mass production; **elle a amené une tarte de sa f.** she brought along a tart she had made herself; **n'employer que la meilleure f.** to employ only the best workmanship; **article de f. française** article made in France

(**b**) (*de fausses nouvelles*) fabrication; (*de document, fausse monnaie*) forging

(**c**) *Typ* layout

fabrique [fabrik] *nf* (**a**) (*fabrication*) manufacture; **prix de f.** manufacturer's *or* factory price; **marque de f.** trademark (**b**) (*établissement*) factory; **f. de papier** paper mill (**c**) *Rel* **(conseil de) f.** = (parochial) church council, vestry
fabriquer [fabrike] *vt* (**a**) *Ind* (*étoffes, bicyclettes etc*) to manufacture; **f. des véhicules en série** to mass-produce vehicles; **fabriqué en série** mass-produced

(**b**) (*artisanalement*) to make; **nous fabriquons nos produits à la main** we make our products by hand; *Fig* **l'entraîneur qui a fabriqué le champion de ski** the coach who created *or* made the ski champion; **cela a contribué à f. son personnage médiatique** that helped to turn him into a media figure *or* to make a media figure out of him

(**c**) (*pour tromper*) (*mensonge, histoire*) to make up, to fabricate; (*faux papiers*) to forge; **f. de la fausse monnaie** to counterfeit *or* forge money; **histoire fabriquée de toutes pièces** completely made-up *or* fabricated story

(**d**) *F* (*faire*) to do; **qu'est-ce qu'il fabrique?** what's he up to?, what's he doing?; **qu'est-ce que j'ai pu f. avec mon briquet?** what can I have done with my lighter?; **je me suis tout à coup demandé ce que je fabriquais là** I suddenly wondered what I was doing there

fabulateur, -trice [fabylatœr, -tris] **1** *adj aussi Psy* fantasizing **2** *n* compulsive liar
fabulation [fabylasjɔ̃] *nf* fantasizing; (*pathologique*) compulsive lying
fabuler [fabyle] *vi* to fantasize; (*pathologique*) to make things up, to fabricate
fabuleusement [fabyløzmɑ̃] *adv* fabulously
fabuleux, -euse [fabylø, -øz] *adj* (**a**) (*qui appartient à la légende*) (*bête*) fabulous, mythical; (*caractère, exploits*) mythical, legendary (**b**) *Fig* (*incroyable*) (*aventure, temps, somme d'argent, film etc*) fabulous, fantastic
fabuliste [fabylist] *nm* fabulist
FAC [ɛfase] *nm Admin abrév* **fonds d'aide et de coopération**
fac [fak] *nf F* university; **f. de droit/de lettres** faculty of law/ arts; **à la f., en f.** at university
façade [fasad] *nf* (**a**) (*de bâtiment*) façade; **hôtel en f. sur la place** hotel facing the square (**b**) (*apparence*) pretence, façade, show (**de** of); **elle a l'air méprisant – non, ce n'est qu'une f.** she looks scornful – no, it's just a pretence *or* a front; **ne faire qch que pour la f.** to do sth just for show; **générosité/patriotisme de f.** sham generosity/patriotism (**c**) *F* (*visage*) **se ravaler la f.** (*se maquiller*) to put on *or* do one's face; **démolir la f. à qn** to smash sb's face in (**d**) (*d'un modem etc*) front panel
face [fas] *nf* (**a**) (*visage*) face; **jeter des accusations à la f. de qn** to throw accusations in sb's face; **elle n'a pas hésité à lui jeter à la f. qu'il était hypocrite** she told him straight to his face that he was a hypocrite; **les blessés de la f.** those with facial injuries; **sauver la f.** to save (one's) face; **perdre la f.** to lose face; **tomber f. contre terre** to fall flat on one's face; **f. de carême** long face; *Péj* **f. de rat** ratface; *Fig* **la f. du monde** the face of the world; **crier à la f. du monde** to shout to the whole world

(**b**) *Litt* (*surface*) **la f. des eaux/de la terre** the face of the waters/of the earth

(**c**) (*côté*) (*d'une lame d'épée*) flat; (*d'une lentille, d'un disque*) side; (*d'une médaille*) obverse; (*d'une pièce*) head (side); **f.!** (*en jouant à pile ou face*) heads!; **f. avant** front; **f. arrière** back; **polyèdre à douze faces** twelve-sided polyhedron; **à deux faces** (*disquette*) double-sided; **tissu (à) double f.** reversible fabric; **ruban adhésif à double f.** double-sided adhesive tape; **la f. cachée de la lune** the hidden side of the moon; **considérer qch sous toutes ses faces** to consider sth from all sides *or* from every angle; **c'est une des nombreuses faces du problème** it's one of the many aspects of the problem; **change le disque de f.!** turn the record over!; **dans son nouveau disque, je préfère la f. A à la face B** on his new record I prefer the A side to the B side *or* I prefer side A to side B

(**d**) **faire f. à** to face, to be facing *or* opposite; *Fig* (*responsabilités, dépenses, besoins*) to meet; (*situation, difficultés*) to face up to; **faire f. à ses créanciers** to face up to one's creditors; **les deux maisons se font f.** the two houses face *or* are facing *or* are opposite each other

(**e**) **portrait de f.** full-face portrait; **vue de f.** front view; *Th* **place de f.** front-facing seat; **se présenter de f.** to be face on; **il l'a attaquée de f.** he attacked her from the front; *Fig* he attacked her openly; **la maison (d')en f.** the house opposite; **regarder qn (bien) en f.** to look sb (full *or* straight) in the face; **si elle l'apprend, je n'oserais plus la regarder en f.** if she found out, I wouldn't be able to look her in the face again; **il n'ose pas le lui dire en f.** he daren't tell him to his face; **regarder les choses/la mort en f.** to face facts/death; **en f. de** opposite, facing; **les maisons en f. de l'école** the houses opposite *or* facing the school; **en f. l'un de l'autre, l'un en f. de l'autre** opposite each other, facing each other; **si tu les mets l'un en f. de l'autre** if you put them face to face *or* opposite each other; **en f. du professeur, il change d'attitude** in front of the teacher his attitude changes; **on est en f. d'un problème difficile** we are faced with a difficult problem

(**f**) **f. à** facing; **la chambre f. à la mienne** the room facing mine; **f. à cette situation, on n'avait pas le choix** faced with that situation we had no choice; **f. à f.** face to face (**avec** with); **mettre deux témoins f. à f.** to bring two witnesses face to face; **on s'est retrouvé f. à f.** we found ourselves face to face

face-à-face *nm inv* face-to-face encounter/debate
face-à-main, *pl* **faces-à-main** *nm* lorgnette
face-texte, *pl* **faces-textes** *nm Journ* facing matter
facétie [fasesi] *nf* joke; **dire des facéties** to crack jokes; **faire des facéties** to play jokes *or* pranks
facétieux, -ieuse [fasesjø, -jøz] *adj* (*petit garçon, regard*) mischievous
facette [fasɛt] *nf* (*d'un diamant, de l'œil d'un insecte, Fig d'une personnalité, d'un problème etc*) facet; **(taillé) à facettes** (cut) in facets, facetted; **une personnalité/une histoire/une réalité à facettes** a multi- *or* many-facetted

personality/story/reality; **examiner un problème sous toutes ses facettes** to examine a problem from every angle

facetter [fasete] *vt* to facet

fâché [fɑʃe] *adj* **(a)** (*mécontent*) angry, annoyed; **être f. contre qn** to be angry *or* annoyed with sb; **être f. avec qn** to have fallen out with sb; **ils sont fâchés** they've fallen out *or* they're on bad terms (with each other); **tu n'es pas f., au moins?** you're not angry, are you?; **elle est fâchée avec les maths** she can't get on with maths, she has problems *or* trouble with maths; *Hum* **tu es f. avec l'ordre/ton rasoir?** being tidy/shaving doesn't come naturally to you, does it?

(b) (*désolé*) sorry; **être f. de qch/pour qn** to be sorry about sth/for sb; *Iron* **je ne suis pas f. que ça soit terminé** I'm not exactly sorry *or* sad that it has finished; **je ne suis pas f. de m'asseoir** I'm glad to get the weight off my feet

fâcher [fɑʃe] **1** *vt* **(a)** (*rendre mécontent*) to annoy, to make angry, to anger; **ton attitude me fâche beaucoup** your attitude annoys me a lot *or* makes me very angry **(b)** (*affliger*) to grieve **2** *vpr* **se fâcher (a)** (*se mettre en colère*) to get angry *or* annoyed, to lose one's temper; **attention! je vais me f.!** be careful or I'll get angry!; **se f. contre qn** to get annoyed *or* angry with sb; *F* **se f. tout rouge** to blow one's top, to go up the wall **(b)** (*se brouiller*) to fall out, to quarrel (**avec qn** with sb)

fâcherie [fɑʃri] *nf* quarrel, disagreement

fâcheusement [fɑʃøzmɑ̃] *adv* **(a)** (*malheureusement*) unfortunately **(b)** (*surpris*) unpleasantly; (*impressionné*) unfavourably, *US* unfavorably

fâcheux, -euse [fɑʃø, -øz] **1** *adj* (*événement, question, complication, changement etc*) unfortunate, annoying; (*position, situation*) awkward, unfortunate; (*nouvelles*) annoying; (*exemple*) unfortunate; **j'ai eu la fâcheuse idée de lui en parler** I had the unfortunate idea of talking to him about it; **il serait f. que tu arrives en retard** it would be a pity if you arrived late; **c'est f.!** what a nuisance!, how annoying! **2** *n* (*importun*) nuisance

facho [faʃo] *adj, n F Péj* fascist

facial, -ale, -iaux, -ales [fasjal, -jo] *adj* (*muscle, angle etc*) facial; **massage f.** facial *or* face massage

faciès [fasjɛs] *nm* **(a)** (*aspect du visage*) features; *Méd* facies **(b)** *Bot, Géol* facies

facile [fasil] **1** *adj* **(a)** (*travail, problème, vie etc*) easy; **c'est f. à faire** it's easy to do *or* easily done; **c'est f. à dire** that's easily said; **c'est plus f. à dire qu'à faire** it's easier said than done; **avoir la vie f.** to have an easy life; **c'est f. comme bonjour** it's as easy as pie, it's child's play; **il lui est f. de le faire** it's easy for him (to do it); **f. d'emploi** easy to use; **d'une mise en place f., f. à installer** easily installed; **besognes faciles** light *or* easy tasks

(b) (*caractère*) easy-going; **homme f. à vivre** man easy to get along with *or* to get on with; **il n'a pas l'air f. en affaires** he doesn't seem an easy man to do business with; **f. à émouvoir** easily moved; **cet enfant est f.** this child is no problem; *Péj* **femme f.** woman of easy virtue, loose woman

(c) (*superficiel*) (*plaisanterie, littérature, style etc*) facile

(d) (*qui vient facilement*) **il n'a pas la parole f.** words don't come easily to him; **il n'a pas l'argent f.** he's a bit tight-fisted; **un milieu où l'argent est f.** an environment where there's plenty of money around; **elle a les larmes faciles** she is easily moved to tears; **avoir la gâchette f.** to be trigger-happy; **elle a la plume f.** she is a fluent writer, writing comes easily to her

2 *adv* (*au moins*) easily, at least; **on met trois jours f. pour traverser l'île** it takes easily *or* at least three days to cross the island; **en trois jours, j'aurai lu f. deux livres** I'll easily read two books in three days

facilement [fasilmɑ̃] *adv* easily; **il rit f.** it's easy to make him laugh; **je mettrai f. deux jours pour le faire** it'll take me easily *or* at least two days to do it

facilité [fasilite] *nf* **(a)** (*d'une tâche, d'un problème etc*) easiness; (*à faire qch*) ease; **avec f.** easily, with ease; **les enfants comprennent l'informatique avec une f. déconcertante** children understand computers with disconcerting ease; *Péj* **elle choisit toujours la f.** she always chooses the easy option *or* the easy way out; **c'est une solution de f.** it's the easy solution *or* way out

(b) (*moyen, occasion*) **avoir toutes facilités pour faire qch** to have every opportunity of doing sth

(c) (*aptitude*) aptitude, talent (**pour qch** for sth); **écrire avec f.** to write fluently *or* with ease; **f. à faire qch** aptitude for doing sth; **f. de parole** fluency; **elle a beaucoup de facilités pour les/en maths** she has great aptitude for maths

▶ **facilité**: **f. d'accès pour fauteuils roulants** wheelchair access; **f. d'accès pour personnes handicapées** disabled access; *Banque* **f. de caisse** overdraft *or* cash facility; *Banque* **facilités de crédit** credit facilities; **f. d'écoulement** (*d'un produit*) saleability; **f. d'emploi** (*d'un ordinateur etc*) user-friendliness, ease of use; **facilités de paiement** credit *or* payment facilities; *Com* **f. de reprise** trade-in facility; **facilités de transport** transport facilities

faciliter [fasilite] *vt* to make easier; **f. qch à qn** to make sth easier for sb; **cela ne va pas f. les choses** it won't make things (any) easier

façon [fasɔ̃] *nf* **(a)** (*manière de faire qch*) way, manner; **ils vivent encore à la f. de leurs ancêtres** they still live in the manner of their ancestors *or* as their ancestors did; **il n'y a pour toi qu'une seule f. de t'en sortir** there's only one way for you to come through all right; **il n'y a pas trente-six façons de le faire** there are no two ways of doing it; **avoir une f. à soi de faire qch** to have one's own way of doing sth; **je le ferai à ma f.** I shall do it (in) my own way; **ce n'est qu'une f. de parler** it's just a manner of speaking; **ce n'est pas une f. de parler à son père** that's no way to speak to one's father; **ce n'est pas une f. de parler pour un petit garçon** that's no way for a little boy to speak; **je ne tolèrerai pas ces façons de parler** I won't tolerate that sort of language; **tu pars en vacances? – oui, f. de parler, je vais garder mes neveux** are you going on holiday? – yes, I suppose you could say that *or* in a manner of speaking *or* sort of, I'm looking after my nephews; **ce n'est pas ma f. de faire** it's not my way of doing things; **ils agissent tous de la même f.** they all act alike *or* in the same way; **elle a une curieuse f. de voir les choses** she has a strange way of looking at things; **de la bonne f.** properly, in the right way; **la f. dont l'anglais est enseigné** the way (in which) English is taught

(b) de cette f. (in) this way, *Fml* thus; **venez avec nous, de cette f. cela ne vous coûtera rien** come with us, that way it won't cost you anything; **d'une** *ou* **de f. générale, on peut dire que …** generally speaking, one can say that …; **d'une f. ou d'une autre** one way or another, somehow or other; **de toute f. j'irai** anyhow *or* anyway *or* in any case I shall go; **en aucune f.!** not at all!, by no means!; **cela ne me dérange en aucune f.** it doesn't disturb me in any way

(c) [①B31,f] **de f. à** so as to; **parlez de f. à vous faire comprendre** speak so that you can be understood; **elle parle de f. à ce que tout le monde l'entende** she speaks so that *or* in such a way that everyone can hear her

(d) [①B31,f] **de (telle) f. que** so that; **parlez de f. qu'on vous comprenne** speak so that you can be understood; **il pleuvait de telle f. que je fus obligé de rentrer** it was raining so hard that I had to go home; *Vieilli* **il pleuvait, de f. que je fus obligé de rentrer** it was raining, (and) so I had to go home

(e) façons (*comportement*) manners, behaviour; **en voilà des façons!** what a way to behave!; **ce ne sont pas des façons!** that's no way to behave!

(f) sans façon(s) (*personne*) unaffected, straightforward; **traiter qn sans f.** to treat sb in an offhand manner; **un repas sans f.** an unpretentious *or* a simple meal; **non merci, sans f.** no thanks, really (not); **sans plus de façons** without further *or* any more ado; **faire des façons** to make a fuss; **on est entre nous, on ne va pas faire de façons** we're all friends here, we won't stand on ceremony

(g) (*exécution*) making, fashioning; (*style*) style; **f. d'un manteau** making (up) of a coat; (*coupe*) cut of a coat; **matière et f.** material and labour; **compter cinquante francs de f.** to charge fifty francs for labour; **on travaille à f.** (*dans une annonce*) customers' own materials made up; **un poème de sa f.** a poem of his own composition; **robe qui a bonne f.** well-cut dress; *Agr* **donner une f. à la terre** to cultivate the soil; **cuir f. porc** imitation pigskin; **sac f. cuir** imitation leather bag

faconde [fakɔ̃d] *nf* (*de l'élocution*) fluency, volubility, *Péj* garrulousness; **avoir de la f.** to be fluent *or* voluble, *Péj* to be garrulous; **quelle f.!** he/she talks so much!, *F* what a bletherer!

façonnage [fasɔnaʒ] *nm* **(a)** (*action de travailler*) (*du bois*) working, shaping; (*sur un tour*) turning; (*de l'argile*) fashioning **(b)** (*fabrication*) (*à la main*) making, fashioning; *Couture* making (up); *Ind* manufacturing **(c)** *Fig* (*d'une personne*) shaping

façonné [fasɔne] *adj Tex* (*tissu*) figured

façonnement [fasɔnmɑ̃] *nm* = **façonnage**

façonner [fasɔne] *vt* **(a)** (*travailler*) (*bois, métal, pierre etc*) to work, to shape; (*sur un tour*) to turn; (*argile*) to fashion; *Agr* **f. la terre** to work the soil **(b)** (*fabriquer*) (*à la main*) to make, to fashion; *Couture* to make (up); *Ind* to manufacture **(c)** *Fig* (*personne, caractère*) to mould, *US* to mold, to shape; **f. qn à son image** to mould sb in one's own image

façonnier, -ière [fasɔnje, -jɛr] **1** *adj* (*personne*) affected, mannered **2** *nm Ordinat* computer bureau

fac-similé, *pl* **fac-similés** [faksimile] *nm* facsimile

factage [faktaʒ] *nm* **(a)** (*de marchandises*) carriage (and delivery); **payer le f.** to pay the carriage **(b)** (*de lettres etc*) delivery

facteur [faktœr] *nm* **(a)** (*de la poste*) postman, *Am* mailman **(b)** (*élément*) factor; **le f. chance/humain/temps** the chance/human/time factor; **f. coût** cost factor; *Méd* **f. de risque** risk factor; *Mktg* **f. de situation** situational factor; **f. déterminant** determining factor, determinant; *Méd* **f. rhésus** rhesus factor **(c)** *Math* factor; **f. premier/commun** prime/common factor; **mettre un nombre en facteurs** to factorize a number **(d)** *Mus* (*fabricant*) maker; **f. d'orgues** organ builder; **f. de pianos** piano maker

factice [faktis] *adj* **(a)** (*objet*) false, artificial; (*articles en vitrine*) dummy; (*moustache, barbe*) false; **cuir/diamant f.** imitation leather/diamond; **les bouteilles de parfum en vitrine sont factices** the bottles of perfume in the window are dummies **(b)** *Fig* (*joie, pitié etc*) false, feigned; (*sourire*) forced; (*beauté*) artificial

factieux, -ieuse [faksjø, -jøz] **1** *adj* factious, seditious **2** *n* agitator, troublemaker

faction [faksjɔ̃] *nf* **(a)** *Mil* sentry duty, guard; **être de** *ou* **en f.** to be on guard *or* on sentry duty; **mettre qn en f.** to put sb on guard; *Fig* **j'ai dû me mettre en f. devant sa porte** I had to wait around outside his door **(b)** (*groupe*) faction

factionnaire [faksjɔnɛr] *nm* (*sentinelle*) sentry, guard; **poser/relever un f.** to post/relieve a sentry *or* guard

factitif, -ive [faktitif, -iv] *adj Gram* causative, factitive

factoriel, -ielle [faktɔrjɛl] *adj, nf Math* factorial

factoring [faktɔriŋ] *nm Com* factoring

factorisation [faktɔrizasjɔ̃] *nf Math* factorization

factotum [faktɔtɔm] *nm* factotum

factrice [faktris] *nf* postwoman, *Am* mailwoman

factuel, -elle [faktɥɛl] *adj* factual

facturation [faktyrasjɔ̃] *nf* invoicing, billing; **(service de) f.** invoice department

facture[1] [faktyr] *nf* **(a)** (*style*) (*d'un morceau de musique, d'un poème, d'un tableau etc*) construction; (*d'un artiste etc*) style, technique **(b)** *Mus* (*fabrication*) making; (*d'orgues*) building

facture[2] *nf Com* invoice, bill (of sale); **faire** *ou* **dresser** *ou* **établir une f.** to make out an invoice; **f. d'électricité/de gaz** electricity/gas bill; **selon** *ou* **suivant f.** as per invoice; *Écon* **la f. pétrolière de la France** France's oil bill

▶ **facture**: **f. d'achat** purchase invoice; **f. d'avoir** credit note; **f. certifiée** certified invoice; **f. client** guest bill; **f. commerciale** commercial invoice; **f. de confirmation** confirmation invoice; **f. consulaire** consular invoice; **f. de débit** debit note; **f. détaillée** itemized invoice; **f. de doit** debit note; **f. douanière** customs invoice; **f. à l'exportation** export invoice; **f. pro forma** pro forma invoice; **f. provisoire** pro forma invoice; **f. rectificative** amended invoice; **f. de transitaire** forwarding agent's invoice; **f. de vente** sales invoice

facturer [faktyre] *vt* (*marchandises*) to invoice; **le papier nous a été facturé cent francs** we were invoiced a hundred francs for the paper

facturette [faktyrɛt] *nf* credit card sales slip

facturier, -ière [faktyrje, -jɛr] **1** *nm* (*livre*) sales book; **f. d'entrée** purchase ledger; **f. de sortie** sales ledger **2** *n* (*employé*) invoice clerk; **f. d'entrée** purchase ledger clerk; **f. de sortie** sales ledger clerk

facultatif, -ive [fakyltatif, -iv] *adj* optional; **arrêt f.** request stop

facultativement [fakyltativmɑ̃] *adv* optionally

faculté [fakylte] *nf* **(a)** (*don, capacité*) faculty, ability, power; **facultés de l'esprit** *ou* **intellectuelles** intellectual faculties; **ne pas avoir la f. de marcher** to be unable to walk; **jouir de toutes ses facultés** to be in possession of all one's faculties; **elle n'a plus toutes ses facultés** she no longer has all her faculties; **homme doué de grandes facultés** man of great abilities

(b) (*droit*) right; (*possibilité*) option; **avoir la f. de faire qch** (*droit*) to have the right to do sth; (*possibilité*) to have the option of doing sth; **f. de rachat** buy-back option

(c) *Vieilli* **facultés** (*ressources*) resources, means; **elle dépense au-dessus de ses facultés** she spends beyond her means

(d) *Univ* faculty; **professeur de f.** = (university) professor; *Vieilli* **la F.** the Faculty of Medicine; (*les médecins*) the medical profession; *Hum* **la F. m'interdit de boire** I'm forbidden to drink — doctor's orders; **à la f., en f.** at university; **entrer en f.** to go to university

▶ **faculté:** *Com* **facultés assurées** insured cargo

fada [fada] *F* **1** *adj* (*fou*) screwy, crazy **2** *n* crackpot

fadaise [fadɛz] *nf* silly remark; (*chose insignifiante*) trifle; **débiter des fadaises** to talk nonsense *or* twaddle

fadasse [fadas] *adj F* (*goût, boisson, nourriture etc*) insipid, bland; (*couleur*) pale, washed-out; (*livre, style etc*) dreary, dull

fade [fad] *adj* (*plat, boisson, goût etc*) insipid, bland; (*plaisanterie*) tame; (*compliments*) banal, bland; (*couleur*) drab, washed-out; (*odeur*) stale; (*livre, conversation, style etc*) dull, dreary; (*beauté*) insipid

fadé [fade] *adj F* **être f.** (*remarquable*) to beat them all, to take the cake *or* the biscuit

fadeur [fadœr] *nf* **(a)** (*d'un plat, d'une boisson, de goût etc*) insipidness, blandness; (*d'une plaisanterie*) tameness; (*de compliments*) banality; (*d'une couleur*) drabness; (*d'une odeur*) staleness; (*d'un livre, style etc*) dullness, dreariness; (*d'une beauté*) insipidness **(b)** **fadeurs** (*compliments*) banal *or* bland compliments; **dire des fadeurs à qn** to pay sb banal *or* bland compliments

fading [fadiŋ] *nm Rad* fading; *Aut* (brake) fade

faf [faf] *n F* fascist

fafiot [fafjo] *nm Arg* banknote, *Am* bankbill

fagot [fago] *nm* bundle of firewood; *Fig* **sentir le f.** to savour of heresy; *Fig* **bouteille de vin de derrière les fagots** bottle of wine from the hidden store *or* kept for special occasions; *Fig* **un repas de derrière les fagots** an extra-special meal; **une idée de derrière les fagots** a remarkable idea

fagotage [fagɔtaʒ] *nm* **(a)** (*du bois*) tying up in bundles **(b)** *Péj* (*accoutrement*) ridiculous get-up *or* rig-out

fagoter [fagɔte] **1** *vt* **(a)** (*bois*) to tie up in bundles **(b)** *Péj* (*accoutrer*) to rig *or* deck out; **mal/bizarrement fagoté** badly/oddly dressed **2 se fagoter** *vpr Péj* to rig *or* deck oneself out

faiblard [fɛblar] *adj F* (a bit) weak, weakish

faible [fɛbl] **1** *adj* **(a)** (*physiquement*) (*personne, membres etc*) weak, feeble; (*cœur, yeux, constitution*) weak; (*arche, branche etc*) weak, unstable; (*pays, armée etc*) weak; **être f. des jambes/du cœur/***etc* to have weak legs/a weak heart/*etc*; **avoir la vue f.** to have weak *or* poor eyesight; **le sexe f.** the weaker sex; **une f. femme** a helpless woman

(b) (*intellectuellement*) (*personne, idée, style, film etc*) weak, poor; (*intelligence*) low; **élève f. en chimie** pupil weak *or* poor in *or* at chemistry; **f. d'esprit** feeble-minded; **côté/point f.** weak side/point; **et le terme est f.!** and that's putting it mildly!

(c) (*moralement*) (*personne*) weak, soft; (*caractère*) weak; **être f. avec qn** to be weak *or* soft with sb; **f. de caractère** weak-willed

(d) (*léger*) (*café, vin etc*) weak; (*son, voix*) faint, quiet; (*odeur*) faint, slight; (*lumière*) faint, dim; (*vent*) light; *Mus* **temps f.** weak *or* unaccented beat; **boisson f. en alcool** low-alcohol drink; **f. en calories** low-calorie

(e) (*petit*) (*quantité, majorité etc*) small; (*avantage, différence, réaction, chance, espoir*) slight; (*prix, revenu, loyer etc*) low; (*récolte, rendement*) poor; (*vitesse*) low, slow; **à une f. hauteur/profondeur** not very high up/deep down; **cela ne vous en donne qu'une f. idée** that gives you only a vague idea of it; *Naut* **f. tirant d'eau** shallow draught; **à f. émission** low-emission

(f) *Gram* (*verbe, conjugaison*) weak

2 *n* (*personne sans force morale*) weakling, weak person; **les faibles** the weak; **les faibles d'esprit** the feeble-minded; **défendre le f. et l'opprimé** to defend the weak and oppressed

3 *nm* **(a)** (*défaut*) weak point, weakness; **le f. chez moi, c'est ...** my weak point *or* weakness is ...

(b) (*penchant*) weakness; **avoir un f. pour qch/qn** to have a weakness for sth/a soft spot for sb; **prendre qn par son f.** to take advantage of sb's weakness

faiblement [fɛbləmɑ̃] *adv* (*résister, insister, protester*) weakly, feebly; (*éclairer*) faintly, dimly; (*parler, crier*) quietly, faintly; (*entendre*) faintly; **f. attiré/parfumé** slightly attracted/flavoured

faiblesse [fɛblɛs] *nf* **(a)** (*physique*) (*d'une personne, des membres etc*) weakness, feebleness; (*du cœur, de la vue, d'une constitution etc*) weakness; (*d'une arche, d'une branche, d'un gouvernement, d'une armée etc*) weakness; (*syncope*) (sudden) faintness; **elle eut une f.** she (suddenly) felt faint; **je tombais de f.** I was ready to drop (with exhaustion); **donner des signes de f.** (*d'une machine*) to be showing signs of wear and tear; *Vieilli* **tomber en f.** to swoon, to faint

(b) (*intellectuelle*) (*d'un élève, argument, style etc*) weakness, poorness; **f. d'esprit** feeble-mindedness

(c) (*morale*) weakness (**envers qn** towards sb); **f. de caractère** weakness of character; **la f. humaine** human weakness *or* frailty; **la f. d'une mère** a mother's indulgence; **avoir la f. de faire qch** to be weak enough to do sth; **dans un moment de f. je lui ai dit oui** in a moment of weakness I said yes to him; **avoir des faiblesses pour qn** to have a soft spot for sb

(d) (*manque d'intensité*) (*d'un son, d'une odeur, d'une lumière*) faintness; (*du vent*) lightness

(e) (*petitesse*) (*d'une quantité, majorité etc*) smallness; (*d'une différence, réaction etc*) slightness; **la f. de leurs revenus** their low income

(f) (*défaut*) (*d'une personne*) weakness, failing; (*d'une œuvre d'art, d'une théorie etc*) weakness

faiblir [fɛblir] *vi* to weaken; (*de la vue, du cœur, de la lumière*) to fail; (*de la voix*) to lose its strength, to fail; (*du vent*) to abate, to drop; (*du courage*) to fail, to flag; **sa force faiblit** he's not as strong as he was; **le film faiblit vers la fin** the film falls off *or* tails off towards the end

faïence [fajɑ̃s] *nf* **(a)** (*matière*) earthenware **(b)** (*objet*) piece of earthenware; **faïences** crockery, earthenware

faïencerie [fajɑ̃sri] *nf* **(a)** (*articles*) crockery, earthenware **(b)** (*fabrique*) pottery (works) **(c)** (*commerce*) pottery (trade)

faïencier, -ière [fajɑ̃sje, -jɛr] *n* (*fabricant*) crockery *or* earthenware maker; (*marchand*) crockery *or* earthenware dealer

faignant, -ante [fɛɲɑ̃, -ɑ̃t] *adj, n F* = **fainéant**

faille [faj] *nf* **(a)** *Géol* fault; **ligne de f.** fault line **(b)** *Fig* (*dans un argument*) flaw; (*dans une amitié*) rift, breach; **sans f.** (*raisonnement*) flawless; (*dévotion*) unfailing; (*fidélité*) unwavering; **faire preuve d'une volonté sans f.** to be iron-willed, to have a will of iron

faillibilité [fajibilite] *nf* fallibility

faillible [fajibl] *adj* fallible; **tout le monde est f.** anybody can make a mistake

failli, -ie [faji] *adj, n Jur* bankrupt; **f. concordataire** bankrupt who has reached a settlement with his debtors; **f. réhabilité** discharged bankrupt

faillir [fajir] *vi* (*prp* **faillant**; *pp* **failli**; *pr ind* **je faux, il faut, n. faillons**; *p hist* **je faillis**; *fu* **je faillirai**; *used mostly in inf, p hist and compound tenses*) **(a)** (*manquer*) **f. à son devoir** to fail in *or* fall short of one's duty; **f. à une promesse/sa parole** to fail to keep a promise/one's word; **sans f.** unfailingly; **dont la loyauté n'avait jamais failli** whose loyalty had never wavered or faltered; **ne pas f. à sa réputation** to live up to one's reputation; **la mémoire me faut** my memory fails me

(b) j'ai failli manquer le train/le croire I nearly or almost missed the train/believed him; **il faillit être écrasé** he narrowly missed being run over; **j'ai bien failli me noyer** I (was) very nearly drowned; **j'ai failli lui en parler** I nearly spoke to him about it; *Iron* **j'ai failli attendre so**, decided to show up, did you?

faillite [fajit] *nf* **(a)** *Com* bankruptcy, insolvency; **être en (état de) f.** to be bankrupt *or* insolvent; **f. simple** bankruptcy; **f. frauduleuse** fraudulent bankruptcy; **faire f.** to go bankrupt; **déclarer** *ou* **mettre qn en f.** to declare sb bankrupt **(b)** (*échec*) (*d'un projet, d'espoirs etc*) failure; **la mort de l'acteur principal, c'était la f. du film** the death of the main actor meant the collapse of the film

faim [fɛ̃] *nf* hunger; **avoir f.** to be *or* feel hungry; **avoir très** *ou* **grand f. , avoir une grosse f.** to be *or* feel very hungry; **avoir un peu f.** *ou F* **une petite f.** to be *or* feel a bit hungry; **je n'ai plus f. du tout** I'm not at all hungry any more; **avoir une f. de loup** to be ravenous; **mourir de f.** to die of hunger *or* starvation, to starve to death; (*avoir très faim*) to be starving; **j'ai une de ces faims,** *F* **je crève de f.** I'm starving; **manger à sa f.** to eat one's fill; **rester sur sa f.** to remain hungry; *Fig* to be left unsatisfied; **tromper sa f.** to take the edge off one's appetite; *Fig* **avoir f. de gloire/d'absolus** to hunger *or* thirst after glory/absolutes

faîne [fɛn] *nf* beechnut

fainéant, -ante [fɛneɑ̃, -ɑ̃t] **1** *adj* lazy, idle **2** *n* lazybones, idler

fainéanter [fɛneɑ̃te] *vi* to idle about, to loaf about; **f. au lit** to laze in bed

fainéantise [fɛneɑ̃tiz] *nf* laziness, idleness

faire[1] [fɛr] *nm* **(a) il y a loin du dire au f.** saying is one thing, doing another **(b)** *Beaux-Arts, Littér* technique

faire[2] (*prp* **faisant** [fəzɑ̃]; *pp* **fait** [fɛ]; *pr ind* **je fais, il fait, n. faisons** [fəzɔ̃], **v. faites** [fɛt], **ils font**; *pr sub* **je fasse**; *imp* **fais, faisons, faites**; *p hist* **je fis**; *fu* **je ferai**) **1** *vt* **(a)** (*façonner*) to make; **f. un gâteau/du cidre** to make a cake/cider; **statue faite en** *ou* **de marbre** statue made (out) of marble; **vêtements tout faits** ready-made clothes; **expressions toutes faites** ready-made *or* set phrases; **f. un poème/un tableau** to write a poem/paint a picture; **f. un chèque de 100 francs** to make out *or* write (out) a cheque for 100 francs; **je vais lui f. un chèque** I'll make him out *or* write him (out) a cheque; **f. la guerre** to wage war; **faites l'amour pas la guerre** make love not war; **f. des provisions** to lay in provisions; **f. de l'eau/du charbon** to take in water/coal; **f. un miracle** to work *or* perform a miracle; **ferme où on fait de la betterave** farm that grows beet

(b) (*créer*) to make; **Dieu a fait l'homme à son image** God made *or* created man in his own image; **ils ne veulent pas f. d'enfants** they don't want to have (any) children; *F* **f. un enfant à qn** to make *or* get sb pregnant; **ma femme m'a fait deux merveilleuses petites filles** my wife has given me two wonderful little girls; **f. ses petits** (*d'une chienne, chatte*) to have her litter, to have her pups/kittens; **les vieilles gens sont ainsi faits** old people are like that, that's how old people are; **comment est-il fait?** (*à quoi ressemble-t-il?*) what does he look like?; **il n'est pas fait pour cela** he is not the man *or* is not cut out for that; **jambe bien faite** shapely leg

(c) f. un geste to make a gesture; **elle lui fit un signe de la main** she waved to him; *F* **f. de l'œil à qn** to make eyes at sb, to give sb the eye

(d) *Arg* **tu es fait, mon vieux!** you've had it, chum!; **on m'a fait ma montre** (*volé*) someone's pinched my watch

(e) (*se livrer à une activité*) to do; **qu'est-ce que vous faites?** what are you doing?; **qu'est-ce que vous faites toute seule dans votre grande maison?** what do you do all alone in your big house?; **qu'est-ce qu'il y a à f.?** what is there to do?; **il n'y a rien à f.** (*pour résoudre le problème*) there is nothing to be done, there's no help for it; **je n'ai rien à f.** I've nothing to do; **je n'ai rien à f. avec eux** I have nothing to do with them; **il n'a rien à f. ici** he has no business here; **que f.?** what is/was to be done?, what can/could he/we/*etc* do?; **je ne sais que f.** I don't know what to do; **qu'allez-vous f. de votre fils?** what are you going to do with your son?; **qu'avez-vous fait de mon parapluie?** what have you done with my umbrella?; **n'avoir que f. de qch** to have no need of sth; **autant que f. se peut** as far as (is) possible; **c'est la dernière chose à f.** it's the last thing that ought to be done; **je le regardais f.** I watched him doing it; **est-ce que je peux ouvrir la fenêtre? – faites donc!** may I open the window? – do!, by all means!; **faites vite!** be quick about it!, look sharp!; **nous avons fort à f. avec nos quatre garçons** we've got our work cut out *or* our hands full with our four boys; **il n'a pas le temps de vous voir aujourd'hui, il a fort à f.** he doesn't have time to see you today, he's extremely busy; **homme à tout f.** odd-job man; **grand bien vous fasse!** much good may it do you!; **c'est bien fait (pour toi)!** it serves you right!; **c'est toujours ça de fait** it's something done (at least); *F* **traverser la Manche à la nage, faut le f.!** swimming the Channel is no easy matter, not everybody can swim the Channel; *F* **mettre du sel à la place du sucre, faut le f. quand même!** putting salt in instead of sugar, how stupid can you get!, you really have to be stupid to put salt in instead of sugar!; **voilà qui est fait** that's done

(f) (*dire*) to say; **'vous partez demain!' fit-il** 'you leave tomorrow!' he said *or* exclaimed; **il fit un petit 'oh' de surprise** he gave a little 'oh' of surprise

(g) (*accomplir*) **f. son devoir** to do one's duty; **f. la ronde** to go *or* do one's rounds; *F* **f. ses besoins** to relieve oneself; (*d'un chien, d'un chat*) to do its business

(h) f. un métier to practise a trade; **f. les cuirs/la laine** to deal in leather/wool; **nous ne faisons que le gros** we are wholesalers only; **quel article faites-vous?** what's your line?; **nous ne faisons plus les pulls en laine** we don't do *or* stock woollen sweaters any more

(i) (*pratiquer, étudier*) **f. du sport** to do sport; **f. de la politique** to be involved in politics; **on ne va pas f. de politique, mais c'est quand même un problème grave, non?** we don't want to bring politics into it, but it's a serious problem all the same, isn't it?; **j'ai fait de l'anglais à l'école** I did English at school; **il fait sa médecine/son droit** he is reading *or* studying medicine/law; *F* **elle veut f. Polytechnique** she wants to go to *or* study at the Polytechnique; *F* **il veut f. médecin/pompier** he wants to be a doctor/fireman; **f. son apprentissage** to serve *or* do one's apprenticeship

(j) *F* (*maladie*) to have; **il doit f. une crise de foie** he must have liver trouble; **tu ne vas quand même pas en f. une maladie!** there's no need to get so upset about it *or* to take it that way!; *F* **tu ne vas pas nous f. une crise!** you're not going to have one of your tantrums!

(k) (*déplacement*) **f. quelques pas sur le trottoir/dans la**

rue to go *or* take a few steps along the pavement/along the street; **f. les magasins** to go round *or* do the shops; **f. une promenade** to go for a walk; **ce représentant fait la province** this representative does *or* covers the provinces; *F* **on a fait l'Inde l'année dernière** we did India last year; *F* **f. du cent à l'heure** to go *or* do a hundred kilometres an hour

(l) (*causer*) to cause; **f. pitié/peur** to arouse pity/fear; **ça fait peur!** it's frightening!; **f. peur à qn** to frighten sb, to scare sb; **cela me fait de la peine que tu partes** it makes me sad *or* upsets me that you're going

(m) (*mesure*) to amount to, to come to; **combien cela fait-il?, ça fait combien?** how much does that come to?, what does that make?; **deux fois deux font quatre** two twos are four, twice two is four; **je vous fais les deux cadres pour 200 francs** I can let you have both frames for 200 francs; **ça fait trois jours qu'il est parti** it's three days since he left; **ça fait bien deux ans (que je ne l'ai pas revu)** it's a good two years (since I last saw him); **ce poulet fait trois kilos** this chicken weighs three kilos; **combien faites-vous la livre de chocolat?** how much do you charge for a pound of chocolate?

(n) 'cheval' fait 'chevaux' au pluriel 'cheval' becomes 'chevaux' in the plural

(o) (*être*) to be; **f. l'admiration de tous** to be admired by everyone; **cela fera mon affaire** that will suit me; **quel taquin vous faites!** what a tease you are!

(p) (*importer*) **qu'est-ce que ça fait?** what does it matter?, who cares?; **ça fait qu'on va le déranger encore une fois** it means we'll have to disturb him again; **qu'est-ce que cela vous fait?** what's that to you?; **si cela ne vous fait rien** if you don't mind; **cela ne fait rien** never mind, it doesn't matter; *F* **qu'est-ce que ça peut bien te f.?** what has that got to do with you?; *F* **ça me fait que je dois encore t'attendre** it means I have to wait for you again

(q) (*remplaçant le verbe qui précède*) **pourquoi agir comme vous le faites?** why do you act as you do?; **il m'a traité comme il aurait fait d'un** *ou* **pour un animal** he treated me as he would an animal

(r) (*former*) **je ferai de toi un homme** I'll make a man of you; **cette solution a fait beaucoup d'heureux** this solution made a lot of people happy; **elle en a fait un paresseux** she's made him lazy; **elle en a fait un vaurien** she's turned him into a good-for-nothing; **f. des chaussures à son pied** to break in a pair of shoes; *Prov* **l'habit ne fait pas le moine** appearances are deceptive

(s) (*arranger*) **f. la chambre/ses chaussures** to clean *or* do the room/one's shoes; **f. le ménage/la vaisselle** to do the housework/the washing-up; **f. les vitres** to do *or* clean the windows; **f. la poussière** to do the dusting; **f. du rangement dans ses affaires** to put one's things in order, to tidy up one's things; **f. sa valise** to pack one's (suit)case; **f. ses ongles** to do one's nails; *Cartes* **à qui de f.?** whose call is it?

(t) *F* **ça fait riche** it looks expensive; *F* **ça fait jeune** it makes you look young; **vases qui font bien sur la cheminée** vases that look good on the mantelpiece; **ça fera très bien avec ton tailleur vert** that'll go very well with your green suit; **il ne fait pas quarante ans** he doesn't look forty; **ça fait bizarre de savoir qu'elle ne vit plus ici** it's funny to think she doesn't live here any more

(u) *Th, Cin* (*jouer le rôle de*) to play; **moi je fais le gendarme et toi le voleur** I'll be the cop and you can be the robber; **f. celui qui sait tout** to be a know-all; **un des invités faisait le croupier** one of the guests acted as croupier; **elle ne va pas f. la reine ici** she isn't going to queen it here; **f. le mort** to pretend to be dead; *Fig* to play dead; (*au bridge etc*) to be dummy; **f. l'imbécile, f. l'idiot** to play *or* act the fool

(v) (*locutions avec 'en'*) **ne t'en fais pas** don't worry; **il n'en fait qu'à sa tête** he does what he likes; **n'en faites rien** don't do any such thing; **c'en est fait de lui** it's all over for him, he's done for

(w) (*locutions avec 'y'*) **rien n'y fit** it was no use; **que voulez-vous que j'y fasse?** what do you expect me to do about it?; **il sait y f.** he knows how to go about things; **il sait y f. avec les enfants** he's good with children, he knows how to handle children

(x) *F* (*faire croire*) **la f. à qn** to take sb in; **on ne me la fait pas!** nothing doing!, I'm not going to be had!

2 *vi F* (*faire ses besoins*) to relieve oneself; **un chien a fait sur la pelouse** a dog has made a mess *or* done its business on the lawn

3 *v impers* [①**B27**,E,2,a; **B63**,3] **(a) il fait beau (temps)** it's fine (weather); **il fait froid/chaud** it's cold/hot; **il fait du soleil/de la neige** it's sunny/snowing; **par le froid qu'il fait** in this cold weather

(b) il fait bon près de la cheminée it's nice by the fireside; **il fait mauvais voyager par ces routes** it is hard travelling on these roads; **il fait bon parler à ses amis** it's nice *or* good to talk to one's friends; **il faisait mauvais paraître avec ces gens-là** it was bad to be seen with people like that

4 *v aux* **(a)** (*avec 'que'*) **il ne fait que lire toute la journée** he does nothing but read all day; **je n'ai fait que le toucher** I only touched it; **je ne fais que d'arriver** I have only just arrived; **je n'ai que f. de vos problèmes** your problems are of no concern to me; **c'est ce qui fait que je suis venu si vite** that is why *or* this is how it happens that I came so quickly; **les événements qui font que les choses sont comme elles sont** the events that make things what they are; **faites qu'il vienne demain** see to it *or* make sure that he comes tomorrow

(b) [①**A55**,b,iv; **B34**,d] (*le nom ou le pronom objet est sujet de l'infinitif*) **le soleil fait fondre la neige** the sun makes the snow melt *or* melts the snow; **nous l'avons fait sortir par la porte de derrière** we made him leave by the back door; **on le fit chanter** he was made to sing; **il nous a fait venir** he sent for us; **faites-le entrer** show him in; **f. attendre qn** to keep sb waiting

(c) [①**A55**,b,iv; **B34**,d] (*avec verbe pronominal*) **faire asseoir qn** to make sb sit down; **f. coucher un enfant** to put a child to bed; **je le fis s'arrêter** I made him stop

(d) [①**A55**,b,iv; **B34**,d] (*le nom ou le pronom est objet de l'infinitif*) **f. bâtir une maison** to have *or* get a house built; **f. f. deux exemplaires** to have *or* get two copies made; **faites-le réparer** get *or* have it mended

(e) [①**A40**,B,1,a] **f. f. qch à qn** to get sb to do sth, to have sb do sth; **il lui a fait f. son repassage** he got her to do his ironing, he had her do his ironing; **il fit lâcher prise à son adversaire** he made his opponent let go, he got his opponent to let go; **faites-lui lire cette lettre** get him to read *or* make him read this letter; **je lui ai fait observer qu'il se faisait tard** I pointed out to him that it was getting late; **faites-lui comprendre qu'il n'est pas le bienvenu** make him understand that he is not welcome; **je le ferai examiner par un médecin** I shall have *or* get him examined by a doctor

5 se faire *vpr* **(a)** (*devenir meilleur*) (*fromage*) to ripen; (*vin*) to mature; **il s'est fait seul** he's a self-made man

(b) (*devenir*) to become; **se f. vieux** to become *or* grow *or* get old; **si ça continue, je vais me f. bonne sœur** I'm going to become a nun if things go on like this

(c) (*s'adapter*) **se f. à qch** to get used *or* accustomed to sth; **se f. à la fatigue** to become resistant *or* inured to tiredness; **tes chaussures vont finir par se f.** your shoes will eventually get worn in; **permettre aux engrenages de se f.** to run in the gears

(d) se f. des amis/relations to make friends/contacts; **cette couleur de vernis ne se fait plus** they've stopped making that shade of varnish, that shade of varnish has been discontinued; **ces choses-là ne se font pas** these things are not done; **cela se fait beaucoup dans cette partie du monde** it's very common in this part of the world; **les robes en lamé se font beaucoup cette année** lamé dresses are very popular *or* are in this year; **se f. une opinion/une idée sur qch** to form an opinion/get some idea about sth; *F* **se f. tant par mois** to make *or* earn so much a month; **(ne) t'en fais pas** don't worry

(e) (*impers*) **il se fait tard** it's getting late; **il se fit un long silence** a long silence followed, there was a long silence; **comment se fait-il que vous soyez en retard?** how is it that you're late?

(f) (*s'accomplir*) to happen; **il pourrait bien se f. que je ne revienne pas** I might very well not come back; **le miracle s'est fait tout seul** the miracle came about *or* happened by itself; **le mariage ne se fera pas** the marriage will not take place *or* will not happen

(g) [①**A53**,16; **B36**,J,2,d] (+ *inf*) **se f. photografier** to have *or* get oneself photographed, to have one's photograph taken; **un bruit se fit entendre** a noise was heard; **ne vous faites pas tant prier** don't take so much asking; **elle adore se f. attendre** she loves making people wait for her; **il ne se le fit pas dire deux fois** he didn't need to be told twice; **il s'est fait punir** he's got himself punished; *Vulg* **il peut aller se f. foutre** he can fuck off

(h) il se fait plus pauvre qu'il ne l'est he makes himself out to be poorer than he is

(i) *Vulg* (*sexuellement*) **il va se la f.** he's going to screw *or* lay her; *Fig* **il faut se la f. quand elle est de mauvaise humeur** she's a real pain in the backside when she's in a bad mood

faire-part *nm inv* (*d'un mariage, d'une naissance, d'un décès etc*) announcement; **le présent avis tiendra lieu de f.** friends please accept this intimation

faire-valoir *nm inv* **(a)** *Agr* farming; **exploitation en f. direct** farm run by the owner **(b)** (*personne*) foil; (*de comique*) stooge

fair-play [fɛrplɛ] **1** *adj inv* **être f.** to be fair, to play fair **2** *nm inv* fair play; **faire preuve de f.** to play fair

faisabilité [fəzabilite] *nf* feasibility; **étude de f.** feasibility study

faisable [fəzabl] *adj* feasible

faisan [fəzɑ̃] *nm* **(a)** [①**A12**,1,g] **(coq) f.** (cock) pheasant; **f. doré** golden pheasant **(b)** *Arg* (*escroc*) crook

faisandage [fəzɑ̃daʒ] *nm Culin* (*du gibier*) hanging

faisandé [fəzɑ̃de] *adj* **(a)** *Culin* (*viande*) high, gamy **(b)** *F* (*corrompu*) (*littérature, personne, société etc*) decadent; (*milieu politique*) corrupt

faisandeau, -eaux [fəzɑ̃do] *nm* young pheasant

faisander [fəzɑ̃de] *vt Culin* (*gibier*) to hang

faisanderie [fəzɑ̃dri] *nf* pheasantry

faisane [fəzan] *nf* **(poule) f.** hen pheasant

faisceau, -eaux [fɛso] *nm* **(a)** (*rayons*) beam; **f. lumineux** *ou* **de lumière** beam of light, *Spéc* pencil of rays; **f. laser** laser beam; **f. de particules** particle beam

(b) *Électron* **f. d'électrons** *ou* **électronique** electron beam; **f. hertzien** electromagnetic wave; *TV* **f. cathodique explorateur** scanning electron beam; **f. radar** radar beam; *Aut* **f. convergent** converging beam; *Aut* **f. divergent** diverging beam; *Aut* **f. parallèle** parallel beam

(c) (*de branches etc*) bundle; *Anat* (*de fibres*) fasciculus, fascicle; (*d'ampoules électriques*) cluster; *Rail* (*de voies de garage*) group; *Aut* **f. du radiateur** radiator core; *Fig* **un f. d'habitudes/de preuves** a body of customs/proof; **un f. d'amitiés** a network of friendships; *Antiq* **les faisceaux** the fasces; *Archit* **colonne en f.** clustered column; *Mil* **former/rompre les faisceaux** to pile/unpile arms

faiseur, -euse [fəzœr, -øz] *n* **(a)** (*qui fabrique qch*) maker; *Prov* **les grands diseurs ne sont pas les grands faiseurs** the greatest talkers are the least doers; **f. de dentelles** lacemaker; **f. de ponts** bridge builder; *Vieilli* **costume du meilleur f.** suit from the best tailor; **f. de miracles** miracle worker; **f. de tours** conjurer; **f. d'embarras** fusspot, *Am* fussbudget; **f. de projets** schemer; *TV, Rad* **f. d'audimat** = television/radio personality guaranteed to boost the ratings; **f. de mariages** matchmaker; **faiseuse d'anges** backstreet abortionist **(b)** *Péj* (*poseur*) pushy type

faisselle [fɛsɛl] *nf* (*fromage*) type of fromage frais; (*récipient*) = basket/pot for draining cheese

fait[1] [fɛ] *adj* **(a)** (*mûr*) (*fromage*) ripe; **fromage f. à cœur** fully ripe cheese; **une expression toute faite** a cliché; **j'ai fait la vaisselle, vite f., bien f.** that's the washing up done; **être bien f. de sa personne** to be good-looking; *Culin* **f. maison** home-made

(b) avoir les ongles/yeux faits to have nail polish/eye makeup on

(c) être f. pour qch/qn to be made for sth/sb; **cette voiture est faite pour la ville** this car is made *or* designed for town driving; **ils sont faits l'un pour l'autre** they're made for each other; **il est f. pour faire du cinéma/pour être avocat** he's cut out to act in films/to be a lawyer; *F* **on peut mettre un chapeau dans cette boîte – oui, c'est f. pour** you can put a hat in this box – yes, that's what it's for; **ça fait joli – c'est f. pour** that looks pretty – it's supposed *or* meant to; **sers-toi, c'est f. pour** help yourself, that's what it's there for

fait[2] *nm* **(a)** (*acte*) act; **le f. de boire** (the act of) drinking; **observer les (moindres) faits et gestes de qn** to watch sb's every move; **rendre compte de ses faits et gestes** to give an account of oneself; (*surtout à la police*) to give an account of one's movements; **f. d'armes** feat of arms; **f. de guerre** feat; **cela est du f. de Martin** this is Martin's doing; **prendre qn sur le f.** to catch sb in the act *or* red-handed; **quels sont les faits?** (*dans un procès*) what are the facts?; **quels sont les faits reprochés à mon client?** what is my client being accused of *or* charged with?; **où étiez-vous au moment des faits?** where were you at the time in question?; **se livrer à des voies de f.** to resort to force *or* to violence; **parler n'était pas son f.** he was no talker; **dire son f. à qn** to tell sb what one thinks, to give sb a piece of one's mind

(b) (*réalité*) fact; **f. accompli** fait accompli; **prendre f. et cause pour qn** to stand up for sb; **ceci est un f.** this is a (matter of) fact; **roi de nom plutôt que de f.** king in name rather than in fact; **possession de f.** actual possession; **il est de f. que c'était un traître** it is a fact that he was a traitor; **aller droit au f.** to go *or* get straight to the point; **en venir au f.** to come to the point; **être au f. de la question** to be acquainted with the facts of the matter; **mettre qn au f.** to acquaint sb *or* make sb acquainted with the facts; **être le f. de** to be characteristic of; **c'est le f. de tous les incapables que de se chercher des excuses** incompetents always try to find excuses for themselves; **la renaissance du judo français est le f. de quelques champions** the renaissance of judo in France is entirely due *or* attributable to a few champions; **être au f. (de la question)** to be au fait; **je suis au f.** I know all about it; **être sûr de son f.** to be sure of one's facts; **au f.!** get to the point!; **au f., que venez-vous faire ici?** by the way, what have you come here for?; **en f., de f.** as a matter of fact, in point of fact, in actual fact, actually; **de f., cela est un refus** that is in effect a refusal; **de ce f.** for that reason, on that account; **du f.** *ou* **par le f. qu'il boite** owing to the fact that *or* because he limps; **par le seul f. d'y être** by the mere fact of *or* simply by being there; **expert en f. de vins** expert as regards wine *or* when it comes to wine; **en f. de soupe, c'était du bouillon clair** it wasn't so much soup as stock

(c) (*événement*) occurrence, event; **un f. nouveau s'est produit** there was a new development; *Journ* **'faits divers'** 'news in brief' (*dealing with local and human interest stories*); **f. divers** news item; **tenir la rubrique des faits divers** = to cover weddings and funerals

faîtage [fɛtaʒ] *nm Constr* **(a)** (*poutre*) rooftree, ridgepole **(b)** (*couverture*) ridge sheathing; (*tuiles*) ridge tiling

faîte [fɛt] *nm* **(a)** *Constr* (*d'un toit*) ridge **(b)** *Géog* **ligne de f.** watershed, crest line **(c)** (*d'une maison, d'un arbre etc*) top; **le f. de la gloire** the height *or* pinnacle of glory

faîtière [fɛtjɛr] *adj, nf Constr* **(tuile) f.** ridge tile; **(lucarne) f.** skylight

faitout *nm*, **fait-tout** *nm inv* [fɛtu] stewpot

faix [fɛ] *nm* **(a)** (*poids*) burden, load; **le f. des années** the weight of years; **le f. des impôts** the burden of taxation **(b)** *Obst* foetus and placenta

fakir [fakir] *nm* fakir

falaise [falɛz] *nf* cliff

falbalas [falbala] *nmpl Couture* furbelows, flounces; *Fig* (*de l'architecture, la poésie baroque*) frills and furbelows, extravagances

fallacieusement [falasjøzmɑ̃] *adv* fallaciously; (*promettre*) misleadingly

fallacieux, -ieuse [falasjø, -jøz] *adj* (*argument, raisonnement etc*) specious; (*espoir*) false; (*promesse, apparence*) misleading; **sous un f. prétexte** on false pretexts

falloir [falwar] (*no prp*; *pp* **fallu**; *pr ind* **il faut**; *pr sub* **il faille**; *impf* **il fallait**; *p hist* **il fallut**; *fu* **il faudra**) **1** *v impers* [①**A58**,e; **B28**,f,ii; **B37**,K,5] **(a)** (*être nécessaire*) **il lui faut un nouveau pardessus** he needs a new overcoat; **avez-vous tout ce qu'il (vous) faut?** have you got all you want *or* require *or* need?; **faut-il tout cela?** is all that necessary?; **c'est juste ce qu'il (me) faut** that's the very thing (I want), that's just the (right) thing; **nous en avions plus qu'il ne nous en fallait** we had more than enough *or* than we needed; **il m'a fallu trois jours pour le faire** it took me three days to do it; **il faut compter deux heures pour y aller** you'll have to allow two hours to get there; **il va bien f. que tu le lui dises** you're going to have to tell him; **je l'ai fait parce qu'il le fallait** I did it because I had to; **elle fera ce qu'il faut** she will do what is necessary *or* what needs *or* has to be done; **il a tout ce qu'il faut pour réussir** he has everything he needs *or F* he's got what it takes to succeed; **je lui ai tout donné, qu'est-ce qu'il lui faut de plus!** I've given him everything, what more does he want!; *F* **il faut ce qu'il faut!** you might as well do things in style!; **il me faudrait une livre de beurre** I need a pound of butter

(b) comme il faut properly; **se conduire comme il faut** to behave properly *or* in a civilized manner *or* in the right way; **il/elle est très comme il faut** he's very gentlemanly/she's very ladylike; **ce sont des gens très comme il faut** they're very decent *or* respectable people; **votre toilette est tout à fait comme il faut** your dress is just right

(c) (*devoir*) **il faut partir** I/we/you/*etc* must go *or* have to go; **il faut dire qu'il s'est bien comporté** it must be said *or* I am bound to say he behaved well; **il nous faut le voir, il faut que nous le voyions** we must see him, we have to see him; **il lui faut se dépêcher** he must hurry; **il faudra marcher plus vite** we shall have to walk faster; **il fallait porter plainte** you should have *or* ought to have made a complaint; **il fallait le dire!** you should have said so!, why didn't you say so?; **il n'aurait pas fallu attendre** you shouldn't have *or* ought not to have waited; **comme il fallait s'y attendre** as was (only) to be expected; **il faut qu'il ait été fâché pour dire cela** he must have been angry to have said that; **c'est ce qu'il faudra voir!** we must see about that!; **la police a arrêté l'homme qu'il ne fallait pas** the police have arrested the wrong man; **elle fera mieux la prochaine fois – oui, faut voir** she'll do better next time – well, we'll see (about that); **elle est habillée/lui a répondu, faut voir comment!** you wouldn't believe the way she's dressed/she answered him; *F* **tu vas le lui dire? – faut bien!** are you going to tell him? – I've got to, I've got no choice!; **je vous en prie, il ne fallait pas!** you shouldn't have!; **c'est simple, mais il fallait y penser** it's simple once you've thought of it; **il a fallu qu'elle apprenne cet accident!** of course, she would have to hear about the accident!; **encore faut-il que ce soit vrai** even so, it still must be true; **il ne faudrait pas que je les rencontre** it would never do for me to meet them; **il ne faudrait pas qu'il le dise deux fois** he'd better not say it again; **il ne faudrait pas que je vous mette en retard** I'd better not make you late; **il ne faut pas y aller** you mustn't go there

(d) (*with le = noun clause*) **il viendra s'il le faut** he will come if need be *or* if necessary *or* if he has to; **vous êtes revenu à pied? – il l'a** *ou* **il a bien fallu** you walked back? – there was nothing else for it, I had no choice

2 s'en falloir *vpr* **il s'en faut de deux francs** it is two francs short; **je ne suis pas satisfait, il s'en faut de beaucoup** *ou* **tant s'en faut** I am not satisfied, far from it *or* not by a long way; **il s'en faut de beaucoup que l'autobus (ne) soit plein** the bus is far from being full; **il s'en est fallu de peu** *ou* **peu s'en est fallu qu'il ne mourût** he very nearly died, it was touch and go whether he died; **cinq livres ou peu s'en faut** the best part of five pounds, very nearly five pounds; **il s'en est fallu de rien qu'il (ne) fût écrasé** he was within an ace *or* an inch *or* a hair's breadth of being run over; **il s'en faut de peu qu'il accepte** he is more than half inclined to accept; **il s'en faudrait de peu pour que le projet démarre** it wouldn't take much for the plan to get off the ground; **vous êtes satisfait? – peu s'en faut!** are you satisfied? – not at all!

falot[1] [falo] *nm* **(a)** (*lanterne*) (hand) lantern **(b)** *Mil F* court martial

falot[2]**, -ote** [falo, -ɔt] *adj* (*terne*) (*personne*) dreary, drab

falsificateur, -trice [falsifikatœr, -tris] *n* (*de documents, de comptes*) falsifier; (*d'une signature*) forger; (*de la nourriture, d'un vin etc*) adulterator

falsification [falsifikasjɔ̃] *nf* (*de documents, de comptes etc*) falsification; (*d'une signature*) forging; (*de la nourriture, d'un vin etc*) adulteration; *Fig* (*de la pensée de qn, de la vérité*) misrepresentation

falsifier [falsifje] *vt* (*impf, pr sub* **n. falsifiions, v. falsifiiez**) (*document*) to falsify; (*signature*) to forge; (*nourriture, vin etc*) to adulterate; (*élections*) to rig; **f. les comptes** *ou* **écritures** to falsify *or* doctor the accounts; **f. la pensée de l'auteur** to misrepresent the author's thinking

falzar [falzar] *nm très F* (pair of) trousers, *Am* (pair of) pants

famé [fame] *adj* **mal f.** disreputable, seedy, *Fml* of ill repute

famélique [famelik] *adj* (*personne, chien*) half-starved; **les ventres faméliques de l'Afrique** the starving of Africa

fameusement [famøzmɑ̃] *adv F* (*très*) incredibly, really; **on s'est f. bien amusé** we had a whale of a time; **il a f. réussi son coup** he really pulled it off

fameux, -euse [famø, -øz] *adj* **(a)** (*ayant bonne réputation*) famous; (*ayant mauvaise réputation*) notorious **(par, pour** for); **c'est un f. coquin, celui-là** he's quite a lad!; **c'est donc ça ton f. régime miracle!** so this is your famous miracle diet! **(b)** *F* (*très bon*) splendid, marvellous, tremendous; (*très mauvais*) terrible, awful; **vous commettez une fameuse erreur** you're making a terrible *or* an awful *or* a (mighty) big mistake; **ce n'est pas f. ton boulot/son dernier roman** your job/his latest novel isn't up to much *or* isn't anything special; **c'est pas f.** it's not brilliant

familial, -iale, -iaux, -iales [familjal, -jo] **1** *adj* (*vie, conflits etc*) family; (*pension, hôtel*) family-run, owner-managed; *Com* (*paquet, pot etc*) family-size; **entreprise familiale** family firm; **l'ambiance est familiale** there is a family atmosphere; **allocations familiales** child benefit, *Am* dependent's allowance **2** *nf Aut* **familiale** (family) estate car, *Am* station wagon

familiarisation [familjarizasjɔ̃] *nf* familiarization

familiariser [familjarize] **1** *vt* **f. qn avec qch** to familiarize sb with sth, to get sb used to sth; **je ne suis pas encore familiarisé avec les lieux** I don't know my way around yet **2 se familiariser** *vpr* **se f. avec qch** (*en le pratiquant*) to familiarize oneself with sth, to get to know sth; (*en s'y habituant*) to get accustomed *or* used to sth; **se f. avec un lieu** to get to know a place, to get to know one's way around; **peu familiarisé avec** unfamiliar *or* unacquainted with; **il n'est pas encore très familiarisé avec cet ordinateur/avec les animaux** he hasn't really got used to this computer/to animals yet

familiarité [familjarite] *nf* **(a)** (*intimité*) familiarity; **être d'une grande f. avec qn** to be on very familiar terms with sb; **être d'une trop grande f. avec qn** to be too familiar *or* overfamiliar with sb **(b)** (*comportement amical*) informality, friendliness; **se permettre trop de familiarités avec qn** to be too familiar *or* to take liberties with sb; **pas de f., je vous prie** please don't be familiar

familier, -ière [familje, -jɛr] **1** *adj* **(a)** (*avec qn*) familiar; (*amical*) friendly; **être f. avec qn** to be on familiar terms with sb; **il s'est montré trop f.** he was too familiar, he was overfamiliar; **expression familière** colloquial *or* familiar expression, colloquialism; **le langage f.** colloquial *or* familiar language; **animal f.** pet

(b) (*habituel*) familiar; **visage qui lui est f.** face which is familiar *or* well-known to him; **ta voix ne lui est pas familière** he doesn't know *or* recognize your voice; **mon cadre f.** my usual surroundings; **cette question lui est familière** he is familiar with the subject; **le mensonge lui est f.** he is a habitual liar

(c) (*de la maison*) **dieux familiers** household gods

2 *n* (*d'un café, club etc*) regular visitor **(de** to), regular **(de** of); (*d'une sorcière*) familiar; **un f. de la maison** a regular visitor to the house, an intimate friend of the household

familièrement [familjɛrmɑ̃] *adv* familiarly; (*amicalement*) informally; **ces insectes que l'on nomme f. ...** these insects, which are commonly *or* familiarly known as ...; **il lui donna f. une petite tape sur la joue** he gave her a friendly little pat on the cheek

familistère [familistɛr] *nm* workers' co-operative association

famille [famij] *nf* **(a)** [①A11,g,i] (*mère, père, enfants*) family; (*ensemble des parents*) family, relatives, relations; **il faut que je vous présente à ma f.** (*parents*) I must introduce you to my parents; (*conjoint, enfants*) I must introduce you to my family; **f. nombreuse** large family; **réduction f. nombreuse** family reduction *or* discount; **f. monoparentale** one-parent *or* single-parent family; **f. patchwork, f. tuyau de poêle** patchwork family (*consisting of children, parents etc of divorced parent's new spouse*); **charges de famille** dependants; **chef de f.** head of the family; *Admin* householder, head of the household; **soutien de f.** (main) wage earner, breadwinner; **fils de f.** young man of good social standing; **il a épousé une jeune fille de bonne f.** he married a girl from a good family *or* a well-bred girl; **avoir l'esprit de f.** to have family feeling; **dîner/passer le week-end en f.** to dine/spend the weekend at home with one's family; **avec eux je me sens en f.** I feel quite at home with them; **nous réglons toujours nos problèmes en f.** we always settle our problems within the family; **c'est de f.** it runs in the family; **pension de f.** (small) boarding house; *Jur* **prévenir la f.** to inform the next of kin; *Cartes* **le jeu des sept familles** happy families; *F* **on va se faire un repas des familles** we'll make ourselves a nice little meal; **on s'est fait une petite soirée des familles** we had a cosy little *or* nice little evening together; *Fig* **ils appartiennent à la même f. politique/littéraire** they belong to the same political/literary grouping; **f. de produits** product family

(b) *Ling, Bot, Zool* family

famine [famin] *nf* famine; **crier f.** to plead poverty, to complain of hard times; **salaire de f.** starvation wages; **prendre une ville par la f.** to starve a city into submission

Famtour [famtur] *nm* (*tourisme*) familiarization tour, fam trip

fan [fan] *nm F* (*admirateur*) fan

fana [fana] *F* **1** *adj* (*enthousiaste*) dead keen **(de** on), mad **(de** about, on) **2** *n* **f. du football/de la moto** football/motorbike fanatic *or* freak

fanage [fanaʒ] *nm* (*du foin*) tedding, tossing

fanal, -aux [fanal, -o] *nm* lantern; *Rail* (*de locomotive*) headlight; *Naut* (*sur les côtes*) beacon, lantern; (*sur un bateau*) (ship's) lantern

fanatique [fanatik] **1** *adj* fanatical; **être f. de qn/qch** to be mad about *or* on sb/sth **2** *n* (*enthousiaste*) fanatic; *Pol, Rel* fanatic, zealot; **f. du football** football fanatic; **fanatiques de Pavarotti** Pavarotti fans; **je ne suis pas un f. du poisson** I'm not mad *or* crazy about fish

fanatiquement [fanatikmɑ̃] *adv* fanatically

fanatisation [fanatizasjɔ̃] *nf* fanaticization; **la f. des foules était due à une propagande très bien menée** extremely skilful propaganda turned the crowds into fanatics *or* made the crowds fanatical

fanatiser [fanatize] *vt* to turn into fanatics, to make fanatical; **des religieux fanatisés** religious fanatics

fanatisme [fanatism] *nm* (*enthousiasme*) fanaticism **(pour** for); *Pol, Rel* fanaticism, zealotry

fanchon [fɑ̃ʃɔ̃] *nf* kerchief, headscarf

fandango [fɑ̃dɑ̃go] *nm* fandango

faner [fane] **1** *vt* **(a)** (*foin*) to ted, to toss **(b)** (*couleur, étoffe etc*) to fade; (*fleur, plante*) to fade, to wither, to wilt **2** *vpr* **se faner** (*d'une fleur, plante*) to fade, to wither, to wilt; (*d'une couleur,*

étoffe, Fig de la beauté, la santé, un souvenir etc) to fade; **une odeur de parfum fané** a smell of stale perfume
fanes [fan] *nfpl* (*de carottes*) tops; (*de radis*) stalks
faneur, -euse [fanœr, -øz] *Agr* **1** *n* (*ouvrier*) haymaker **2** *nf* **faneuse** (*machine*) tedder, tedding machine
fanfare [fɑ̃far] *nf* **(a)** (*air*) (*de cuivres*) flourish, fanfare; *Fig* **réveil en f.** brutal awakening **(b)** (*orchestre*) brass band; *Mil* military band; **la f. du village** the village band
fanfaron, -onne [fɑ̃farɔ̃, -ɔn] **1** *adj* boastful **2** *n* braggart, boaster; **faire le f.** to brag, to boast; **alors, on ne fait plus le f. maintenant, hein?** we're not so high and mighty now, are we!
fanfaronnade [fɑ̃farɔnad] *nf* **(a)** (*caractère*) bragging, boasting **(b) fanfaronnades** (*actes, propos*) bragging, boasting
fanfaronner [fɑ̃farɔne] *vi* to brag, to boast
fanfreluche [fɑ̃frəlyʃ] *nf* (*sur une robe, un rideau etc*) trimming, *Péj* frill
fange [fɑ̃ʒ] *nf Litt* mire, mud; *Fig* **élevé dans la f.** brought up in the gutter; *Fig* **croupir dans la f.** to be living surrounded by filth; *Fig* **par le scandale, elle a été traînée dans la f.** in the scandal she *or* her name was dragged through the mud *or* mire
fangeux, -euse [fɑ̃ʒø, -øz] *adj Litt* miry, muddy; *Fig* murky
fanion [fanjɔ̃] *nm* (*de club, bateau, corps d'armée etc*) pennant, pennon; *Ski* (*de balisage*) flag
fanon [fanɔ̃] *nm* **(a)** (*de baleine*) whalebone, baleen **(b)** (*de bœuf*) dewlap; (*d'oiseau*) wattle; (*de cheval*) fetlock **(c)** *Rel* (*de mitre*) lappet
fantaisie [fɑ̃tezi] *nf* **(a)** (*envie*) **il a eu** *ou* **il lui a pris la f. de se baigner** he took it into his head to go swimming, he had a sudden idea *or* notion to go swimming; **chacun s'amusait à sa f.** everyone amused themselves as the fancy took them *or* as they pleased; **qu'est-ce que c'est que cette f.?** what's come over you?; **il lui passe toutes ses fantaisies** he gives in to her every whim; **nous ne pouvons nous permettre aucune f.** we can't afford to indulge ourselves
(b) articles (de) f. fancy goods; **pain (de) f.** fancy bread (*not sold by weight*); **bijoux (de) f.** costume *or* novelty *or* fancy jewellery; **du rhum f.** = inexpensive rum of less than usual strength and quality
(c) (*imagination*) imagination; **sa vie manque de f.** his life is very dull *or* unexciting; **donner un peu de f. à sa vie** to add a bit of excitement to one's life; **elle était d'une f. rafraîchissante** she was refreshingly imaginative
(d) (*œuvre*), *Mus* fantasia; *Littér* fantasy
fantaisiste [fɑ̃tezist] **1** *adj* **(a)** (*original, peu orthodoxe*) (*personne*) unconventional, unorthodox, different; (*procédés*) unorthodox; **elle a des horaires fantaisistes** she keeps strange *or* odd hours; **je ne veux pas d'employé f.** I don't want any oddballs working for me **(b)** (*inventé, sans fondement*) (*interprétation, histoire etc*) fanciful, far-fetched; **les déclarations fantaisistes que vous avez faites à la presse** your extremely fanciful statements to the press **2** *n* **(a)** (*original*) eccentric; (*qui manque de sérieux*) unreliable person **(b)** *Th* variety artist
fantasmagorie [fɑ̃tasmagɔri] *nf* phantasmagoria; **des histoires pleines de fantasmagories** fantasies
fantasmagorique [fɑ̃tasmagɔrik] *adj* phantasmagoric(al)
fantasme [fɑ̃tasm] *nm* (*situation imaginée*) fantasy; **tu vis dans tes fantasmes** you're living in a fantasy world
fantasmer [fɑ̃tasme] *vi* to fantasize (**sur** about)
fantasque [fɑ̃task] *adj* (*personne, manières etc*) whimsical; (*histoire, forme etc*) odd, weird
fantassin [fɑ̃tasɛ̃] *nm* foot soldier, infantryman
fantastique [fɑ̃tastik] **1** *adj* **(a)** (*imaginaire*) (*être, animal etc*) imaginary **(b)** (*surnaturel*) (*lumière, atmosphère etc*) weird, eerie **(c)** (*incroyable*) (*idée, histoire etc*) fantastic **(d)** (*formidable*) (*succès, plan, somme etc*) fantastic; **paysage d'une beauté f.** fantastically beautiful scenery **(e)** *Beaux-Arts, Cin, Littér* fantastic **2** *nm* **le f.** the fantastic; (*art*) fantasy art; (*littérature*) fantasy literature
fantastiquement [fɑ̃tastikmɑ̃] *adv* fantastically; (*d'une manière surnaturelle*) weirdly, eerily
fantoche [fɑ̃tɔʃ] **1** *nm* (*marionnette, Fig personne*) puppet **2** *adj* **gouvernement f.** puppet government
fantomatique [fɑ̃tɔmatik] *adj* ghostly
fantôme [fɑ̃tom] *nm* ghost, phantom; **train f.** ghost train; *Mus* **le Vaisseau F.** the Flying Dutchman; **ville f.** ghost town; **membre(-)f.** phantom limb; *Fig* **ce n'est plus qu'un f.** (*très maigre*) he's just a skeleton, he's nothing but skin and bone; *Pol* **gouvernement/cabinet f.** shadow government/cabinet
fanzine [fɑ̃zin] *nm* fanzine
faon [fɑ̃] *nm* fawn, calf
faquin [fakɛ̃] *nm Arch, Pej* varlet
FAR [far] *nf Mil* (*abrév* **force d'action rapide**) = (French) strike force, *US* ≈ RDF
far [far] *nm* **f. breton** custard flan (with prunes)
farad [farad] *nm Él* (*unité*) farad
faramineux, -euse [faraminø, -øz] *adj F* phenomenal, staggering; **il lui a fait des compliments pour le moins f.** his compliments were slightly over the top
farandole [farɑ̃dɔl] *nf* farandole
faraud, -aude [faro, -od] *F Vieilli* **1** *adj* swanky, swaggering **2** *n* swaggerer; **faire le f.** to swagger
farce [fars] **1** *nf* **(a)** *Culin* stuffing **(b)** (*tour*) (practical) joke, prank, trick; **faire des farces à qn** to play tricks *or* (practical) jokes on sb; *Com* **farces et attrapes** tricks and jokes; **magasin de farces et attrapes** joke shop **(c)** *Th, Fig* farce; **la situation va tourner à la f.** the situation is becoming farcical *or* is turning into a farce **2** *adj F Vieilli* funny, comical
farceur, -euse [farsœr, -øz] **1** *adj* (*rire, œil*) roguish, mischievous **2** *n* **(a)** (*qui fait des tours*) (practical) joker, prankster; **je me demande qui est le petit f. qui m'a fait ça** I wonder who the joker is that I have to blame for this **(b)** (*blagueur*) joker, wag; **c'est un f. qui vous aura dit cela** somebody's been pulling your leg
farcir [farsir] **1** *vt* **(a)** *Culin* (*volaille, légume etc*) to stuff
(b) *Fig* (*bourrer*) to cram, to stuff (**de** with); **arrête de lui f. le crâne avec tes histoires** stop filling his head with your nonsense; *F* **j'ai la tête farcie** my head's fit to burst
2 se farcir *vpr* **(a) se f. la tête d'idées romantiques** to fill one's head with romantic ideas
(b) *F* (*travail, lessive etc*) to get landed *or* stuck *or Br* lumbered with; **on va encore devoir se f. ta mère tout le week-end** we're going to have to put up with your mother again all weekend; **je ne l'aime pas moi non plus, il faut se le f.** I don't like him either, he's impossible *or* really hard to get on with; **tu as lu son livre? il faut se le f.** have you read his book? it's really hard going
fard [far] *nm* makeup; **f. à joues** blusher; **f. à paupières** eye shadow; **la vérité sans f.** the plain unvarnished truth; **parler sans f.** to speak candidly *or* openly; *F* **piquer un f.** to go red, to blush
fardage [fardaʒ] *nm Com* (*de marchandises inférieures*) camouflaging
fardeau, -eaux [fardo] *nm* burden, load; *Fig* burden; **le f. des impôts** the burden of taxation; *Fig* **c'est un lourd f. qu'il traîne** it's a millstone round his neck
farder [farde] **1** *vt* **(a)** (*maquiller*) (*qn, son visage*) to make up; **trop fardé** over made-up; **f. la vérité/les faits** to gloss over *or* disguise the truth/facts; **le film présente une version fardée de cet événement** the film presents a dressed-up *or* cosmetic version of the event **(b)** *Com* (*marchandises inférieures*) to camouflage **2** *vpr* **se farder** to make up one's face, to put on one's make-up; **se f. les yeux** to put eye shadow on
farfadet [farfadɛ] *nm* (hob)goblin, sprite
farfelu, -ue [farfəly] *F* **1** *adj* (*personne, idée etc*) weird, way-out **2** *n* weirdo
farfouiller [farfuje] *vi F* to rummage (about)
faribole [faribɔl] *nf* (*propos*) piece of nonsense; **dire des fariboles** to talk nonsense
farinacé [farinase] *adj* farinaceous
farine [farin] *nf* **(a)** flour; **folle f.** flour dust, mill dust; **f. d'avoine** oatmeal; **f. de maïs** cornflour, *Am* cornstarch; **f. de moutarde** mustard powder; **f. de poisson** fish meal; *F* **de la même f.** of the same kind; **ce sont gens de (la) même f.** they are birds of a feather; *F* **rouler qn dans la f.** to take sb for a ride **(b)** *Tech* **f. de forage** bore dust
fariner [farine] *vt Culin* to coat with flour, to flour
farineux, -euse [farinø, -øz] **1** *adj* **(a)** (*qui est recouvert de farine*) floury, covered with flour; *Péj* (*au goût*) floury **(b)** (*contenant de la fécule*) (*nourriture*) starchy, *Spéc* farinaceous **2** *nmpl* starchy food, *Spéc* farinaceous food
farlouse [farluz] *nf Orn* meadow pipit
farniente [farnjɛnte] *nm* (pleasurable) idleness, dolce farniente
farouche [faruʃ] *adj* **(a)** (*pas apprivoisé*) (*animal, oiseau*) timid, shy; **leurs chats ne sont pas farouches** their cats are quite tame **(b)** (*timide*) (*personne*) shy **(c)** (*acharné, violent*) (*ennemi, résistance, regard etc*) fierce; **volonté f.** iron *or* unshakeable will **(d)** (*peu civilisé*) (*gens, pays etc*) wild, uncivilized
farouchement [faruʃmɑ̃] *adv* fiercely
fart [far(t)] *nm* (ski) wax
fartage [fartaʒ] *nm* (*de skis*) waxing
farter [farte] *vt* (*skis*) to wax
fascicule [fasikyl] *nm* **(a)** (*d'une publication*) instalment, part, section; (*brochure*) brochure, leaflet; **publier un livre par fascicules** to publish a book in parts *or* instalments **(b)** *Mil* **f. de mobilisation** call-up instructions

fasciculé [fasikyle] *adj Bot* fascicular, fasciculate
fascinant [fasinɑ̃] *adj (personne)* fascinating; *(beauté, yeux, sourire etc)* captivating, bewitching
fascinateur, -trice [fasinatœr, -tris] *adj Litt* captivating, bewitching
fascination [fasinasjɔ̃] *nf* fascination
fascine [fasin] *nf (de brindilles)* faggot; *Constr* fascine
fasciner[1] [fasine] *vt* **(a)** *(d'un serpent) (proie)* to fascinate, to hypnotize **(b)** *(attirer l'attention de)* to fascinate; *(charmer)* to captivate, to bewitch; **cette volonté me fascine** this wish has me in its grip *or* in its power; **elle se laisse f. par l'argent** she lets herself be blinded *or* dazzled by money
fasciner[2] *vt Constr (rive etc)* to line with fascines; **route fascinée** corduroy road
fascisant [faʃizɑ̃] *adj Pol* fascistic
fasciser [faʃize] *vt Pol* to make fascist
fascisme [faʃism] *nm Pol* fascism
fasciste [faʃist] *adj, n Pol* fascist
faste[1] [fast] *nm (no pl) (d'une cérémonie)* pomp, splendour, *US* splendor; *(d'une demeure)* sumptuousness, splendour; **mariage sans f.** quiet wedding; **la cérémonie aura lieu sans f.** the ceremony will be a simple affair
faste[2] *adj* **jour f.** *Antiq* lawful day; *(jour favorable)* lucky day; **période f.** good period; **je paie la note, je suis dans une période faste!** I'll pay the bill, I'm in the money, I'm flush
fast-food, *pl* **fast-foods** [fastfud] *nm* **(a)** *(restauration)* fast food **(b)** *(lieu)* fast-food restaurant, fast-food bar
fastidieusement [fastidjøzmɑ̃] *adv* tiresomely, tediously
fastidieux, -ieuse [fastidjø, -jøz] *adj* dull, tiresome, tedious; **besognes fastidieuses** drudgery
fastoche [fastɔʃ] *adj F* dead easy
fastueusement [fastɥøzmɑ̃] *adv* sumptuously, lavishly
fastueux, -euse [fastɥø, -øz] *adj (personne, vie)* lavish; *(ameublement, dîner etc)* sumptuous
Fat [fat] *nf Ordinat* FAT
fat [fa(t)] **1** *adj (personne)* conceited, self-satisfied **2** *nm* conceited *or* self-satisfied person
fatal, -als [fatal] *adj* **(a)** *(mortel) (accident, résultat etc)* fatal; **heure fatale** fatal hour, hour of death; **coup f.** deadly *or* fatal blow; **le choc lui a été f.** the shock killed him **(b)** *(nuisible) (beauté, oubli)* fatal; **f. à qn** fatal *or* disastrous for sb; **erreur fatale** fatal mistake; *Ordinat* fatal error; **femme fatale** femme fatale **(c)** *(inévitable)* inevitable; **c'est f.** it's bound *or* sure to happen, it's inevitable; **on ne peut pas échapper au cours f. des choses** you can't avoid the inevitable
fatalement [fatalmɑ̃] *adv* inevitably; **ils devaient f. se fâcher** they were bound to fall out
fatalisme [fatalism] *nm* fatalism
fataliste [fatalist] **1** *n* fatalist **2** *adj* fatalistic
fatalité [fatalite] *nf* **(a)** *(destin)* fate; **poursuivi par la f.** pursued by fate; **c'est la f.!** it's just bad luck!; **c'est (comme) une f.** it's an awful coincidence **(b)** *(malédiction)* misfortune **(c)** *(inévitabilité)* inevitability
fatidique [fatidik] *adj* fateful
fatigabilité [fatigabilite] *nf* tendency to get tired; **il est d'une grande f.** he gets tired very easily
fatigable [fatigabl] *adj* easily tired
fatigant [fatigɑ̃] *adj* **(a)** *(épuisant)* tiring, exhausting; **c'est f. pour le cœur** it strains the heart; **c'est f. pour les yeux** it's tiring on the eyes, it's a strain on the eyes **(b)** *(lassant)* annoying, tiresome, wearisome; **c'est f. de ne jamais réussir** it's annoying *or* tiresome *or* wearisome never to be successful
fatigue [fatig] *nf* **(a)** *(d'une personne, des membres etc)* tiredness, weariness, fatigue; **tomber** *ou* **être mort de f.** to be dead tired, to be ready to drop; **ressentir une grande/légère f.** to feel very/a bit tired *or* weary; **f. nerveuse** nervous exhaustion; **f. intellectuelle** mental strain; **f. oculaire** eyestrain; **état de f. générale** general fatigue **(b)** *Tech (d'un métal, d'une pièce etc)* fatigue **(c)** *(effort pénible)* strain, effort; **épargner** *ou* **éviter à qn la f. de qch/de faire qch** to save sb the strain *or* effort of sth/of doing sth
fatigué [fatige] *adj* **(a)** *(épuisé) (personne, membres etc)* tired (out), weary; *(traits, regard, voix etc)* tired; *(yeux, cœur)* strained; *(cerveau)* tired, overworked; **f. par le voyage** travel-worn, travel-weary **(b)** *Fig* **f. de qch/qn** tired *or* weary of sth/sb; **f. de faire qch** tired *or* weary of doing sth **(c)** *Méd (dérangé) (estomac, foie etc)* upset **(d)** *(usé) (vêtements, chaussures etc)* worn (out), shabby; *(moteur)* worn out
fatiguer [fatige] **1** *vt* **(a)** *(épuiser) (personne)* to tire (out), to make tired *or* weary; *(cheval)* to tire; *(surmener)* to overwork; **f. le cœur/les yeux** to strain the heart/the eyes; *Iron* **si ça ne te fatigue pas trop évidemment** not if it's too tiring for you *or* it's not too much of an effort of course

(b) *(soumettre à un long usage etc) (machine, moteur, solive etc)* to strain; *(vêtements, chaussures etc)* to wear out; *(champ, sol)* to exhaust, to impoverish; **f. un livre** to give a book a lot of hard wear

(c) *(remuer) (salade)* to mix, to toss; *(sol)* to turn over

(d) *(importuner)* to annoy, to irritate; *(lasser)* to weary, to wear down

2 *vi (d'une personne)* to tire, to get tired (out); *(d'un bateau, moteur)* to labour, *US* to labor; *(d'une solive etc)* to show strain; **je commence à f. sérieusement** I'm beginning to get really tired

3 se fatiguer *vpr (d'une personne)* to get tired (out), to tire; *(en travaillant beaucoup)* to tire oneself out **(à faire qch** doing sth); **se f. les yeux/le cœur** to strain one's eyes/heart; *Iron* **il ne s'est pas (trop) fatigué** he didn't exactly exert himself; **ne te fatigue pas, je m'en occupe** don't bother, I'll see to it; **c'était bien la peine que je me fatigue à préparer le repas** a fat lot of use it was me wearing myself out getting the meal ready; **ne vous fatiguez pas, je suis au courant** don't waste your breath, I know all about it; **se f. de qch/qn** to get tired *or* to tire of sth/sb; **se f. de faire qch** to get tired *or* to tire of doing sth
fatras [fatra] *nm (d'idées, de papiers etc)* jumble, muddle, hotchpotch
fatuité [fatɥite] *nf* (self-)conceit, self-satisfaction
fauber(t) [fobɛr] *nm Naut* (deck) swab, mop
faubourg [fobur] *nm* **(a)** *(quartier périphérique)* suburb; **accent des faubourgs** (Parisian) working-class accent **(b)** *(quartier de grande ville)* district
faubourien, -ienne [foburjɛ̃, -jɛn] **1** *adj (accent etc)* (Parisian) working-class **2** *n* working-class Parisian
fauchage [foʃaʒ] *nm* **(a)** *(du blé, d'un champ de blé etc)* reaping; *(de l'herbe, d'une prairie etc)* mowing, cutting **(b)** *Mil (de troupes)* mowing down; *(procédé de tir)* sweeping of the ground (with machine-gun fire)
fauchaison [foʃɛzɔ̃] *nf* **(a)** *(saison)* reaping time; *(où l'on fauche l'herbe)* mowing time **(b)** *(action)* = **fauchage (a)**
fauchard [foʃar] *nm Agr* double-edged slasher
fauche [foʃ] *nf F* **(a)** *(vol)* pinching, thieving; **méfie-toi, il y a de la f. au lycée** watch out, there's a lot of thieving going on at school **(b)** *(manque d'argent)* pennilessness; **c'est vraiment la f. en ce moment** I'm really broke just now
fauché [foʃe] *adj F* **f. (comme les blés)** (flat) broke, stony-broke, *Am* stone-broke
faucher [foʃe] **1** *vt* **(a)** *(blé, champ de blé etc)* to reap; *(herbe, prairie etc)* to mow, to cut; *F* **f. l'herbe sous le pied de qn** to cut the ground from under sb's feet **(b)** *(abattre) (d'une voiture, une mitraillette) (piétons, troupes etc)* to mow down; *(d'une guerre, une maladie)* to wipe out; *Rugby, Fb etc* **f. son homme** to bring down one's man **(c)** *F (voler)* to swipe, to pinch; **elle m'a fauché ma montre/mon mari** she has swiped *or* pinched my watch/husband **2** *vi* **(a)** *F* **ça fauche par ici** things get swiped *or* nicked round here **(b)** *Mil* to sweep the ground (with machine-gun fire)
faucheur, -euse [foʃœr, -øz] **1** *n (personne)* reaper; *(qui fauche les herbes)* mower **2** *nm (insecte)* harvestman, *Am* daddy-long-legs **3** *nf* **faucheuse** *(machine)* reaper; *(pour herbes)* mower; **la Faucheuse** *(la Mort)* the Grim Reaper
faucheux [foʃø] *nm (insecte)* harvestman, *Am* daddy-long-legs
faucille [fosij] *nf* sickle, (reaping) hook; **la f. et le marteau** the hammer and sickle
faucon [fokɔ̃] *nm* **(a)** *(oiseau)* falcon, hawk; **f. mâle** tercel, tiercel; **f. pèlerin** peregrine falcon; **chasser au f.** to hawk; **chasse au f.** hawking, falconry **(b)** *Pol* hawk
fauconneau, -eaux [fokɔno] *nm Orn* young falcon
fauconnerie [fokɔnri] *nf* **(a)** *(lieu)* hawk house, falcon house **(b)** *(chasse)* falconry, hawking
fauconnier [fokɔnje] *nm* falconer
faufil [fofil] *nm Couture* basting *or Br* tacking thread
faufilage [fofilaʒ] *nm Couture* basting, *Br* tacking
faufiler [fofile] **1** *vt Couture* to baste, *Br* to tack **2** *vpr* **se faufiler** *(se glisser)* to thread one's way **(dans, entre, parmi** through); *(entrer)* to slip in, to sneak in; **il s'est faufilé jusqu'au premier rang** he worked his way to the front; **il s'était faufilé parmi les invités** he had slipped in *or* sneaked in with the guests; **se f. entre les voitures** to nip in and out of the traffic, to thread one's way through the traffic
faufilure [fofilyr] *nf Couture* **(a)** *(résultat)* basted *or Br* tacked seam **(b)** *(action)* basting, *Br* tacking
faune[1] [fon] *nm Myth* faun
faune[2] *nf (animaux)* fauna, animal life; *Fig Péj* **la f. des boîtes de nuit** the nightclub set; **il fréquente une f. bizarre** he associates with a funny crowd
faunesque [fonɛsk] *adj* faun-like
faussaire [fosɛr] *n* forger
fausse [fos] *adj voir* **faux[1]**

faussement [fosmɑ̃] *adv* wrongly, falsely; **un sourire f. aimable** a deceptively pleasant smile
fausser [fose] **1** *vt* **(a)** *(sens, réalité, résultat, faits etc)* to distort; *(informations, chiffres)* to distort, to skew; *(l'esprit, le jugement de qn)* to warp **(b)** *(clé, serrure, axe etc)* to buckle, to bend, to twist **(c) f. compagnie à qn** to give sb the slip **2 se fausser** *vpr* **(a)** *(d'une voix)* to become forced *or* strained **(b)** *(d'une clé, d'une serrure, d'un axe etc)* to buckle, to bend
fausset[1] [fosɛ] *nm Mus* falsetto; **chanter f.** to sing falsetto; *Fig* **voix de f.** falsetto *or* high-pitched voice
fausset[2] *nm (d'un tonneau)* spigot, vent peg; **trou de f.** vent hole
fausseté [foste] *nf* **(a)** *(d'une déclaration, idée etc)* falseness, falsity **(b)** *(de caractère)* duplicity
faut [fo] *voir* **falloir**
faute [fot] *nf* **(a)** *(erreur)* mistake, error; **f. d'étourderie** *ou* **d'inattention** careless *or* thoughtless mistake; **f. de français** = grammatical mistake *or* error; *Ordinat* **f. de frappe** miskey, keying error, typo; **f. d'impression** misprint; **f. de jugement** error of judgment; **f. d'orthographe** spelling mistake; **faire une f.** to make a mistake *or* an error
(b) *(responsabilité)* fault; **être en f.** to be at fault; **trouver** *ou* **prendre qn en f.** to catch sb out; **c'est la f. de** *ou F* **à Pierre** it's Pierre's fault, Pierre's to blame; *F* **ce n'est quand même pas ma f. s'il pleut!** it's hardly my fault if it rains!, you can hardly blame me if it rains!; *F* **ce n'est pas (de) ma f.** it's not my fault, I'm not to blame; **à qui la f.?** whose fault is it?, who's to blame?; **c'est un peu (de) ma f.** I'm partly to blame; **il a été puni par ma f.** it's my fault he was punished; *F* **c'est la f. de personne** it's nobody's fault, nobody's to blame; **c'est la f. à pas de chance** it's just bad luck
(c) *(manque)* **le courage lui a fait f.** his courage failed him; **la main-d'œuvre nous fait f.** we're short of labour; **votre jovialité nous a fait f.** we missed your joviality; **et pourtant ce n'est pas l'envie qui lui faisait f.** and yet it's not because he didn't want to; **ne se faire f. de rien** to deny oneself nothing; **nous ne nous faisons jamais f. de lui écrire** we never fail to write to him; **il ne s'est pas fait f. de le lui dire devant tout le monde** he made sure he told him in front of everybody; **sans f.** without fail; **f. d'argent/de temps** for lack *or* want of money/time; **f. d'essayer** for want of trying; **f. de preuves** *(relâcher qn)* for lack of evidence; **f. d'ordres précis** in the absence of definite instructions; **f. de paiement** for non-payment; *Compta* **faute de provision** for lack of funds; **f. de quoi** failing which, otherwise; **f. de réponse satisfaisante** failing a satisfactory reply
(d) *(délit)* offence, *US* offense; *(mauvaise action)* misdemeanour, *US* misdemeanor; *(péché)* sin, transgression; *(mauvaise conduite)* misconduct; **f. professionnelle** professional misconduct
(e) *Fb* foul; *Tennis* fault; *Fb* **commettre une f. sur qn** to foul sb; *Tennis* **double f.** double fault; **f. de pied** foot fault; **faire une double f. /une f. de pied** to double-fault/foot-fault; *Fb* **f. de main** hand ball; **faire une f. de main** to handle the ball
fauter [fote] *vi F Vieilli (d'une femme)* to go astray
fauteuil [fotœj] *nm* **(a)** armchair, easy chair; **f. à oreillettes** wing chair; **f. à bascule** rocking chair; **f. pliant** folding chair; **f. de dentiste** dentist's chair; **f. roulant** wheelchair; *Th* **f. d'orchestre** seat in the stalls *or Am* orchestra; *Th* **f. de (premier) balcon** dress-circle seat, *Am* balcony seat; *Fig* **arriver dans un f.** *(sans peine)* to win hands down, *Br* to walk it; **il a remporté la course/les élections dans un f.** he won the race/election hands down; **l'épreuve de maths est très simple, tu vas la remporter dans un f.** the maths test is very simple, you'll pass it with flying colours *or Br* you'll walk it
(b) *(d'une assemblée)* chair; **occuper le f.** to be in the chair; **le f. de président** the chairmanship
(c) f. (d'académicien) seat (in the French Academy)
fauteur [fotœr] *nm* **f. de troubles** *ou* **de désordre** agitator, troublemaker; **f. de guerre** warmonger
fautif, -ive [fotif, -iv] **1** *adj* **(a)** *(incorrect)* faulty, incorrect; **calcul f.** miscalculation; **mémoire fautive** defective memory **(b)** *(coupable)* at fault, in the wrong **2** *n* person at fault *or* in the wrong; **va savoir qui est le f. dans cette histoire!** who knows who's at fault *or* to blame in this business!
fautivement [fotivmɑ̃] *adv* incorrectly; **j'avais f. éteint mes phares** I had switched off my headlights by mistake
fauve [fov] **1** *adj* **(a)** *(couleur)* fawn, tawny **(b) bête f.** *(grand félin)* big cat; *Arch (cerf, daim)* deer **(c) odeur f.** musky smell **(d)** *Beaux-Arts* Fauve, Fauvist **2** *nm* **(a)** *(grand félin)* big cat; **chasse aux (grands) fauves** big-game hunting; **cette chambre sent le f.** it smells sweaty *or* of sweat in this room; **tu sens le f.** you smell sweaty *or* of sweat **(b)** *(couleur)* fawn **(c)** *Beaux-Arts* Fauve, Fauvist
fauverie [fovri] *nf (dans un zoo)* big-cat house
fauvette [fovɛt] *nf Orn* warbler; **f. d'hiver** *ou* **des haies** hedge sparrow, dunnock; **f. des roseaux** reed warbler
fauvisme [fovism] *nm Beaux-Arts* Fauvism
faux[1], fausse [fo, fos] **1** *adj* **(a)** *(qui n'est pas vrai)* false, untrue; **il est f. qu'elle soit ...** it's false *or* untrue that she is ...; **fausse nouvelle** false report; **f. témoin** perjurer; **f. témoignage** false evidence; *(délit)* perjury; **faire un f. témoignage** to give false evidence, to commit perjury; **donner de f. espoirs à qn** to give sb false hope
(b) *(qui n'est pas d'origine)* *(cheveux, dents, cils etc)* false; *(bijoux etc)* imitation, fake; *(docteur)* bogus; **fausse monnaie** fake *or* counterfeit money; **fabriquer de la fausse monnaie** to counterfeit money; **f. seins** *F* falsies; **j'ai eu une fausse joie** I got excited about nothing; **elle m'a fait une fausse joie en me le faisant croire** she built up my hopes by making me believe it; **fausse clef** skeleton key; **fausse cartouche** dummy cartridge; **f. plafond** false ceiling; **fausse fenêtre** blind window; *Ling* **f. ami** false friend; **faire un f. sens** to give an inaccurate translation/definition; **un f. Monet** a forged *or* fake Monet; *Anat* **fausses côtes** floating ribs; *Typ* **f. titre** half title; **fausse sortie** *Mil* feint sortie; *Th* fake *or* sham exit; *Fig* **il a fait une fausse sortie** he pretended to leave
(c) *Péj (hypocrite) (personne)* false, deceitful; *(honte, pudeur, modestie)* false; **c'est un f.** *F* **jeton** *ou très F* **cul** he's a hypocrite *or F* a phoney; **un f. frère** a false friend
(d) *(incorrect)* wrong; **fausse date** wrong date; **vous avez fait un f. numéro** you've got *or* dialled the wrong number; **raisonnement f.** unsound *or* faulty reasoning; **présenter qch sous un f. jour** to present sth in a false light, to misrepresent sth; **situation fausse** awkward situation; **balance fausse** inaccurate scales; *Aut* **f. alignement** misalignment; **f. poids** false weight; **faire un f. mouvement** to make an awkward movement; **f. pas** slip, stumble; *Fig* faux pas, (social) blunder; **faire un f. pas** *(en marchant)* to stumble, to trip; *Fig* to put one's foot in it, to make a faux pas; *(faire un écart de conduite)* to make a faux pas; **un f. pas en montagne peut vous coûter la vie** one false step in the mountains can cost you your life; *Méd* **fausse couche** miscarriage; **faire fausse route** to take the wrong road; *Fig* to be on the wrong track; **f. calcul** miscalculation; **faire un f. calcul** to miscalculate; *Mus* **fausse note** wrong note; *Fig* false note; *Fig* **il n'y a eu aucune fausse note** there were no hitches, everything went smoothly
2 *adv* **(a) chanter f.** to sing out of tune, to sing off key; **cela sonne f.** that doesn't sound right; **ses paroles sonnent f.** his words have a hollow ring (to them); **rire qui sonne f.** hollow laugh(ter)
(b) poser le pied à f. to miss one's footing; **accuser qn à f.** to wrongly *or* falsely accuse sb; **porter à f.** to be out of true
3 *nm* **(a)** *(ce qui n'est pas vrai)* **le f.** the false; **distinguer le vrai du f.** to distinguish truth from falsehood
(b) *(imitation) (œuvre d'art)* forgery, fake; **(bijouterie en) f.** costume *or* imitation jewellery
(c) *(contrefaçon)* forgery; *Jur* **usage de f.** use of forgeries; **inculpé pour f. et usage de f.** charged with forgery and use of forgeries; **s'inscrire en f. contre qch** to dispute the validity of sth; *Compta* **f. en écritures** forgery
faux[2] *nf* **(a)** *Agr* scythe **(b)** *Anat* falx
faux-bourdon, *pl* **faux-bourdons** *nm* **(a)** *Mus* fauxbourdon **(b)** *Ent* drone
faux-filet, *pl* **faux-filets** *nm Culin* sirloin, tenderloin
faux-fuyant, *pl* **faux-fuyants** *nm* **(a)** *(prétexte)* subterfuge, evasion, dodge; **chercher des faux-fuyants** to hedge, to prevaricate; **une réponse claire et nette, sans f.** a straight answer with no hedging *or* without any ifs and buts **(b)** *Arch (sentier)* bypath
faux-monnayeur, *pl* **faux-monnayeurs** *nm* forger, counterfeiter
faux-rond, *pl* **faux-ronds** *nm Aut* run-out
faux-semblant, *pl* **faux-semblants** *nm* pretence, sham
faveur [favœr] *nf* **(a)** *(aide, considération)* favour, *US* favor; **gagner** *ou* **obtenir la f. de qn** to gain sb's favour; **recevoir des marques de f. de qn** to receive signs of favour from sb; **avoir la f. de qn** to be in favour with sb; **être en (grande) f. auprès de qn** to be in (high) favour with sb; **perdre la f. de qn** to fall out of favour with sb; **prix/traitement de f.** preferential *or* special price/treatment; **billet de f.** complimentary ticket; *Jur, Fin* **en f. de** in favour of
(b) *(bienfait)* favour, *US* favor; **faire une f. à qn** to do sb a favour; **nous feriez-nous la f. de venir dîner chez nous** would you do us the favour of coming to have dinner with us; **par f. spéciale** as a special favour; **elle lui accorde ses faveurs** she bestows her favours on him
(c) plaider en f. de qn to plead in sb's favour *or US* favor;

Vieilli **on lui fit grâce en f. de sa jeunesse** he was let off in consideration of his youth; **quête en f. de qn/qch** collection in aid of sb/sth
(d) **à la f. de qch** with the help of sth; **à la f. de la nuit** under cover of darkness
(e) (*ruban*) ribbon

favorable [favɔrabl] *adj* (a) (*bienveillant*) (*opinion*) favourable, *US* favorable (**à** to); **il est f. à cette idée** he is in favour of this idea; **elle vous est f.** she is favourably disposed towards you; **elle a présenté les choses sous un jour f.** she presented things in a favourable light *or* favourably
(b) (*convenable*) favourable, *US* favorable; (*situation, occasion, circonstances*) auspicious; (*vent*) favourable, fair; **le moment était f. pour lui parler** it was a good moment to speak to him; **recevoir un accueil f.** to be given a favourable reception; **peu f.** unfavourable, *US* unfavorable

favorablement [favɔrabləmɑ̃] *adv* favourably, *US* favorably

favori, -ite [favɔri, -it] **1** *adj* (*personne, objet, cheval de course etc*) favourite, *US* favorite **2** *n* (*personne*) favourite, *US* favorite **3** *nf* **favorite** (*maîtresse du roi*) favourite *or US* favorite (mistress) **4** *nm Courses de chevaux* favourite, *US* favorite; **le grand f.** the odds-on *or* clear favourite

favoris [favɔri] *nmpl* sideburns, (side) whiskers

favoriser [favɔrize] *vt* (a) (*avantager*) (*qn*) to favour, *US* to favor; **le fait qu'elle soit une femme peut la f.** the fact that she's a woman may work in her favour; **les événements l'ont/ne l'ont pas favorisé** events were in his favour *or* on his side/not in his favour *or* against him; **favorisé par le destin** blessed by fate (b) (*encourager*) (*commerce, arts, crime, maladie, croissance etc*) to encourage, to promote (c) (*faciliter*) (*entreprise, fuite etc*) to assist, to further

favorite [favɔrit] *adj, nf voir* **favori**

favoritisme [favɔritism] *nm* favouritism, *US* favoritism; **essayez de ne pas faire de f.** try not to show favouritism

fax [faks] *nm* (*appareil*) fax (machine); (*message*) fax; **envoyer qch par f.** to send sth by fax, to fax sth; **numéro de f.** fax number; *Ordinat* **f. modem** fax modem; **f. sur papier ordinaire** plain paper fax

faxer [fakse] *vt* to fax

fayot, -ote [fajo] *Arg* **1** *nm* (*haricot sec*) bean **2** *n Péj* crawler, creep

fayotage [fajotaʒ] *nm Arg Péj* crawling

fayoter [fajote] *vi Arg Péj* to crawl, to creep

FB *nm abrév* **franc belge**

fco *adv Com abrév* **franco**

FCP [ɛfsepe] *nm Fin* (*abrév* **fonds commun de placement**) investment trust, mutual fund

f. c(t). (*abrév* **fin courant**) at the end of this month

FDM (*abrév* **fin de mois**) end of month

féal, -ale, -aux, -ales [feal, -o] *adj Arch* (*vassal etc*) feal, faithful, trusty

fébrifuge [febrifyʒ] *adj, nm Méd* febrifuge; *Pharm* antifebrile, antipyretic

fébrile [febril] *adj* (*pouls, patient etc*) feverish, febrile; *Fig* (*activité, conversation etc*) feverish; **tout le village était f.** the entire village was in a state of excitement

fébrilement [febrilmɑ̃] *adv* feverishly; (*parler, préparer qch*) excitedly, hurriedly

fébrilité [febrilite] *nf* feverishness

fécal, -ale, -aux, -ales [fekal, -o] *adj* faecal, *US* fecal; **matières fécales** faeces, *US* feces

fèces [fɛs] *nfpl* (a) faeces, *US* feces (b) *Ch* sediment, precipitate

fécond [fekɔ̃] *adj* (*femme, animal, œuf, esprit*) fertile; (*terre*) fruitful; (*travail, idée*) fruitful, productive; (*sol, imagination*) fertile, rich; (*auteur, peintre, sculpteur etc*) prolific, productive; **ses films sont féconds en ...** his films are full of ...

fécondabilité [fekɔ̃dabilite] *nf Physiol* fertilizability; **taux de f.** fertility rate

fécondable [fekɔ̃dabl] *adj* fertilizable

fécondateur, -trice [fekɔ̃datœr, -tris] *adj* fertilizing

fécondation [fekɔ̃dasjɔ̃] *nf Biol* (*d'un œuf, ovule*) fertilization; (*d'une femme, d'un animal femelle*) impregnation; (*d'une fleur, plante*) pollination; **f. in vitro** in vitro fertilization; **f. artificielle** (*d'une femme*) artificial insemination; (*d'une fleur, plante*) artificial pollination

féconder [fekɔ̃de] *vt Biol* (*œuf, ovule*) to fertilize; (*femme, animal femelle*) to impregnate; (*fleur, plante*) to pollinate

fécondité [fekɔ̃dite] *nf* (a) *Physiol* fertility, *Fml* fecundity; **taux de f.** reproduction rate (b) *Fig* (*d'un sol, de l'imagination etc*) fertility; (*d'une idée*) fruitfulness, productiveness; (*d'un écrivain*) productiveness

fécule [fekyl] *nf* starch; *Culin* **f. de pommes de terre** potato starch *or* flour

féculent [fekylɑ̃] **1** *adj* (*aliment*) starchy **2** *nm* starchy food; **tu manges trop de féculents** you eat too much starchy food *or* starch

FED [ɛfəde] *nm* (*abrév* **Fonds européen de développement**) EDF

FEDER [fedɛr] *nm* (*abrév* **Fonds européen de développement régional**) ERDF

fédéral, -ale, -aux, -ales [federal, -o] **1** *adj* federal **2** *nm Hist US* Federal; **les fédéraux** (*le FBI*) the Feds

fédéraliser [federalize] *vt* to federalize

fédéralisme [federalism] *nm* federalism

fédéraliste [federalist] *adj, n* federalist

fédérateur, -trice [federatœr, -tris] **1** *adj* federative **2** *n* unifier

fédératif, -ive [federatif, -iv] *adj* federative

fédération [federasjɔ̃] *nf* (*d'états*) federation; **f. de syndicats (ouvriers)** amalgamated (trade) unions; **f. sportive** sports federation

fédéré [federe] **1** *adj* (*états*) federate **2** *nm Hist* federate

fédérer [federe] (**je fédère; je fédérai**) **1** *vt* (*états*) to federate, to federalize **2 se fédérer** *vpr* to federate

fée [fe] *nf* fairy; **pays des fées** fairyland; *Fig* **doigts de f.** nimble fingers; **une f. du logis** an ideal homemaker

feed-back [fidbak] *nm inv Électron, Physiol etc* feedback

feeder [fidœr] *nm* (a) *Él* feeder (cable) (b) (*de gaz*) (gas) pipeline

feeling [filiŋ] *nm* (*sensibilité*) feeling; **avoir un bon f. pour qch** to have a good feeling about sth; **faire qch au f.** to do sth by feel

féerie [fe(e)ri] *nf* (a) *Th, Cin* fantasy, extravaganza (b) (*spectacle merveilleux*) enchantment; **une f. de lumières** an enchanting display of lights (c) *Vieilli* (*pouvoir des fées*) (power of) enchantment; (*monde des fées*) fairyland

féerique [fe(e)rik] *adj* (a) (*château, monde etc*) fairy, magic (b) *Fig* (*d'une beauté irréelle*) (*vue, paysage etc*) magical, enchanting

feignant, -ante [fɛɲɑ̃, -ɑ̃t] *Arg* **1** *adj* (bone) idle, lazy **2** *n* loafer, idler

feindre [fɛ̃dr] (*prp* **feignant**; *pp* **feint**; *pr ind* **je feins, n. feignons**; *pr sub* **je feigne**; *impf* **je feignais**; *p hist* **je feignis**; *fu* **je feindrai**) **1** *vt* (*maladie, surprise etc*) to feign, to simulate, to sham; **f. de faire qch** to pretend to do sth, to make a pretence of doing sth **2** *vi Litt* to dissemble; **inutile de f.** it's no use pretending

feint [fɛ̃] *adj* (a) (*simulé*) (*maladie, joie etc*) feigned, assumed, sham (b) *Archit* (*porte, fenêtre*) blind, dummy

feinte [fɛ̃t] *nf* (a) *Boxe, Escrime, Mil* feint; *Fb, Rugby etc* **faire une f. (de passe)** to (sell a) dummy (b) (*ruse*) ruse, trick, dodge; *Vieilli* (*dissimulation*) sham, pretence, *US* pretense; **sans f.** frankly, without pretence

feinter [fɛ̃te] **1** *vi Boxe, Escrime* to feint, to make a feint; *Fb, Rugby etc* to (sell a) dummy **2** *vt F* (*duper*) to take in

feldspath [fɛldspat] *nm Minér* fel(d)spar

fêlé, -ée [fele] **1** *adj* (a) (*verre, voix etc*) cracked (b) *Fig F* **il a le cerveau f.** *ou* **la tête fêlée, il est f.** he's a bit cracked *or* crazy; **tu es complètement f. de le lui avoir dit!** you're absolutely crazy to have told him! **2** *n F* maniac; **f. du jazz/des chocolats** jazz/chocolate freak

fêler [fele] **1** *vt* (*verre, porcelaine etc*) to crack **2 se fêler** *vpr* (*du verre, de la porcelaine, de la voix etc*) to crack

félicitations [felisitasjɔ̃] *nfpl* congratulations; **adresser des f. à qn** to congratulate sb (**pour qch** on sth); **(toutes mes) f.!** (many) congratulations!; **il a eu les f. du jury** he was congratulated by the jury, he received the jury's congratulations

félicité [felisite] *nf* bliss, felicity, happiness

féliciter [felisite] **1** *vt* to congratulate; **f. qn pour** *ou* **sur qch/d'avoir fait qch** to congratulate sb on sth/on having done sth; **je ne vous félicite pas!** you'll get no praise from me! **2 se féliciter** *vpr* (*être content*) to be pleased *or* satisfied (**de qch** with sth); (*se louer*) to congratulate oneself (**de qch** on sth; **d'avoir fait qch** on having done sth); **félicitons-nous de ce que nous avons la vie sauve** let us be thankful we came out alive

félidés [felide] *nmpl Zool* **les f.** the cat family, *Spéc* the Felidae

félin, -ine [felɛ̃, -in] **1** *adj* (*race*) feline; *Fig* (*grâce, souplesse etc*) feline, cat-like **2** *nm* feline; **les grands félins** the big cats; *Spéc* the great felines

fellah [fella] *nm* fellah, Arab peasant

fellation [felasjɔ̃] *nf* fellatio

félon, -onne [felɔ̃, -ɔn] *Hist, Litt* **1** *adj* treacherous, disloyal **2** *n* traitor

félonie [felɔni] *nf Hist, Litt* (*déloyauté*) treachery, disloyalty; (*acte*) act of treachery

felouque [fəluk] *nf (bateau)* felucca

fêlure [felyr] *nf* crack; **f. du crâne** fracture of the skull; *Fig* **une f. dans notre amitié/leur couple** a rift between us/them

femelle [fəmɛl] **1** *adj* **(a)** *(sexe)* female; *(animal)* she-, female; *(éléphant, baleine)* cow; *(oiseau)* hen **(b)** *Tech (vis)* female; *Él* **prise f.** socket **(c)** *Bot* female, *Spéc* pistillate **2** *nf (animal)* female; *très F Péj (femme)* female

féminin, -ine [feminɛ̃, -in] **1** *adj (personne, charme etc)* feminine; *(hormone, population)* female; *(équipe, groupe, magazine, mode etc)* women's; **le sexe f.** the female sex; **vêtements féminins** women's clothes, clothes for women; **les conquêtes féminines d'un homme** a man's female conquests **2** *nm* [①**A16**,E; **B6-7**,A-B] *Gram* feminine; **ce mot est du f.** this word is feminine; **au f.** in the feminine

féminisant [feminizɑ̃] *adj (gène)* feminizing

féminiser [feminize] **1** *vt* **(a)** *(donner le caractère féminin à)* to make feminine; *(rendre efféminé)* to make effeminate; **si tu te teins les cheveux en blond, ça va te f. un peu trop** if you dye your hair blond you'll look a bit too feminine; **f. une profession** to bring *or* introduce more women into a profession; **profession très féminisée** largely female profession, female-dominated profession

(b) *Biol (animal mâle)* to feminize

(c) *Gram (mot)* to make feminine

2 se féminiser *vpr* **(a)** *(d'une femme)* to become more feminine; *(devenir efféminé)* to become effeminate; **la profession se féminise** the profession is attracting more and more women

(b) *Biol (d'un animal mâle)* to feminize

féminisme [feminism] *nm* feminism

féministe [feminist] *adj, n* feminist

féminité [feminite] *nf* femininity

femme [fam] *nf* **(a)** [①**A14**,12,c] *(personne)* woman, *pl* women; **les femmes, la f.** *(le sexe féminin)* women, womankind; **l'émancipation de la f.** the emancipation of women; **cherchez la f.** there's got to be a woman behind it; **elle est très f.** she's very feminine; **la f. de ma vie** the woman of my dreams, the only woman for me; **être très f. du monde** to be a wonderful hostess; **f. auteur** woman author, authoress; **f. ministre** female minister; **f. metteur en scène** woman *or* female director; **f. de tête** woman with a good head on her shoulders; **f. médecin** woman *or* lady doctor; **parapluie de f.** lady's umbrella; **elle n'est pas f. à se plaindre** she's not the sort (of woman) to complain; **une bonne f.** a simple *or* good-natured woman; *F (femme)* a woman; **sa bonne f. de mère** his old mother; *F Péj* **ma bonne f.** *(épouse)* my *or* the missus, my old woman; *Péj* **une vieille bonne f.** a little old woman; **contes/remèdes de bonne f.** old wives' tales/remedies

(b) [①**A12**,1,d] *(épouse)* wife; *Vieilli* **chercher f.** to look for a wife; **prendre f.** to take a wife; **il l'a prise pour f.** he took her as his wife; *Jur* **la f. Dupont** the wife of Dupont

▶ **femme**: **f. de chambre** housemaid; *(dans un hôtel)* maid, *Br* chambermaid, room attendant; **f. de charge** housekeeper; **une f. fatale** a femme fatale; **f. au foyer** housewife, *Am* home-maker; **f. d'intérieur** houseproud housewife; **je ne suis vraiment pas une f. d'intérieur** I'm not really keen on housework, I'm not houseproud; **f. de ménage** cleaning lady, domestic help; **une f. du monde** a society woman, a woman who moves in the best social circles; **une f.-objet** a sex object; **f. de service** cleaner, *Br* charwoman; **f. soldat,** *pl* **femmes-soldats** woman soldier

femmelette [famlɛt] *nf Péj (femme)* weak woman, weakling; *(homme)* weakling

fémoral, -ale, -aux, -ales [femɔral, -o] *adj Anat* femoral

fémur [femyr] *nm Anat* femur, thighbone

FEN [fɛn] *nf abrév* **Fédération de l'Éducation Nationale**

fenaison [fənɛzɔ̃] *nf* **(a)** *(action)* haymaking, hay harvest **(b)** *(saison)* haymaking season

fendage [fɑ̃daʒ] *nm Tech (d'ardoises, du bois)* splitting, cleaving

fendant [fɑ̃dɑ̃] *Arg* **1** *adj* hysterically funny **2** *nm (pantalon)* trousers, *Am* pants

fendeur [fɑ̃dœr] *nm Tech (d'ardoises, de bois etc)* splitter

fendillé [fɑ̃dije] *adj (pierre, bois, peau, peinture etc)* cracked; *(vernis, porcelaine)* crazed

fendillement [fɑ̃dijmɑ̃] *nm (du bois, de la peau, de la peinture etc)* cracking; *(du vernis, de la porcelaine)* crazing

fendiller [fɑ̃dije] **1** *vt (pierre, bois, peau, peinture etc)* to crack; *(vernis, porcelaine)* to craze **2 se fendiller** *vpr (du bois, de la peau, de la peinture etc)* to crack; *(du vernis, de la porcelaine)* to craze

fendre [fɑ̃dr] **1** *vt (bois, ardoise, diamant etc)* to split, to cleave; *(sol, mur, plâtre etc)* to crack, to fissure; **f. le crâne/la lèvre à qn** to split (open) sb's skull/lip; **f. les eaux** to plough through the waters; **f. l'air** to cleave the air; *(d'un son)* to rend the air; **f. la foule** to force *or* push one's way through the crowd; **il gèle à pierre f.** it's freezing hard, there's a hard frost; **c'était à f. l'âme** *ou* **le cœur** it was heartbreaking *or* heartrending; **la vue de cet enfant abandonné lui fendit le cœur** the sight of the abandoned child broke his heart *or* made his heart bleed; **bruit à f. la tête** *ou* **à vous f. les oreilles** ear-splitting noise

2 se fendre *vpr* **(a)** *(du bois)* to split, to crack; **se f. le crâne/la lèvre** to split (open) one's skull/lip; *F* **se f. la pipe** *ou* **la gueule** *ou* **la poire** *(rire)* to split one's sides (laughing); *(s'amuser)* to have a good laugh

(b) *Escrime* to lunge

(c) *Arg* **se f. de 200 francs** to fork out *or* shell out 200 francs; **il s'est fendu d'un bouquet de fleurs** he forked out *or* shelled out for a bunch of flowers; **tu ne t'es pas fendu** it didn't break you *or* the bank; *(pas fatigué)* you didn't bust a gut

fendu [fɑ̃dy] *adj (jupe)* slit; *(crâne, lèvre)* split; *(assiette)* cracked; *(sabot)* cloven; **né avec le palais f.** born with a cleft palate; **sourire f. jusqu'aux oreilles** broad grin, grin like a Cheshire cat; **yeux bien fendus** large *or* wide-open eyes; **des yeux fendus en amandes** almond-shaped eyes; **vis à tête fendue** slotted screw

fenestrage [fənɛstraʒ] *nm,* **fenêtrage** [fənɛtraʒ] *nm (d'un bâtiment)* windows, *Spéc* fenestration; *Ordinat* windowing

fenêtre [f(ə)nɛtr] *nf* **(a)** *Archit* window; **f. à guillotine** sash window; **f. croisée** *ou* **à battants** casement window; **f. à coulisse** sliding window; **f. en saillie** bay window; *(courbe)* bow window; *Rail, Av* **siège côté f.** window seat; *TV* **f. d'observation** observation window; **regarder par la f.** to look out of the window; *Fig* **une f. sur le monde/l'actualité** a window on the world/on current events

(b) *(dans un document)* blank, space; *(dans une enveloppe)* window; **enveloppe à f.** window envelope

(c) *Astronaut* **f. de lancement** (launch) window

(d) *Ordinat* window; **f. d'aide** help window; **f. d'édition** editing *or* edit window; **f. de dialogue** dialog(ue) window; **f. déroulante** pull-down window; **f. graphique** graphics window; **f. activée** active window

fenêtrer [fənetre] *vt (bâtiment)* to put windows in; *(bandage)* to fenestrate

fenil [fəni(l)] *nm* hayloft

fennec [fenɛk] *nm Zool* fennec

fenouil [fənuj] *nm Bot, Culin* fennel

fente [fɑ̃t] *nf* **(a)** *(fissure) (dans le bois)* split, crack; *(dans le sol, un mur etc)* crack **(b)** *(ouverture) (d'une tirelire, boîte aux lettres etc)* slot, slit; *(dans un volet)* slit, gap; *(dans un mur)* crack; *(dans une tête de vis)* slot, groove; *(de jupe, manche, poche)* slit; *(de veste)* vent **(c)** *Escrime* lunge

féodal, -ale, -aux, -ales [feɔdal, -o] *adj* feudal

féodalisme [feɔdalism] *nm* feudalism

féodalité [feɔdalite] *nf Hist* feudalism, feudal system

fer [fɛr] *nm* **(a)** *(métal)* iron; **minerai de f.** iron ore; **f. coulé** *ou* **de fonte** cast iron; **f. en saumon** *ou* **en gueuse** pig iron; **f. forgé** wrought iron; **fil de f.** wire; *Fig* **discipline de f.** iron discipline; **homme de f.** man of iron *or* steel; **dur comme (le) f.** as hard as iron; **j'y crois dur comme f.** I believe in it very firmly; **une santé de f.** an iron constitution; **avoir une volonté de f.** to have an iron will *or* a will of iron

(b) *(partie métallique) (d'une hache, flèche)* head; *(d'une pelle)* blade; *(d'un lacet)* tag; **f. de lance** spearhead; *Fig* **le f. de lance du libéralisme** the spearhead of liberalism; **le f. de lance de l'industrie française** the flagship of French industry

(c) *(arme)* sword; **croiser** *ou* **engager** *ou* **battre le f. avec qn** to cross swords with sb; **par le f. et par le feu** by force of arms

(d) *(instrument)* **f. (à repasser)** *(pour le linge)* iron; **f. électrique/à vapeur** electric/steam iron; **donner un coup de f. à qch** to iron *or* press sth; **f. à friser** curling tongs *or* iron; *Obst Vieilli* **fers** forceps; **f. à souder** soldering iron; **marquer au f. rouge** to brand

(e) *Golf* iron; **grand f.** driving iron; **f. droit** putter; **un f. 6** a (number) 6 iron

(f) fers *(chaînes)* irons, chains, fetters; **être aux fers** to be in irons *or* chains; *Fig* **mettre aux fers** to fetter; *Fig* **briser les fers** to throw off one's chains

(g) f. (à cheval) horseshoe; **en f. à cheval** horseshoe-shaped; **tables disposées en f. à cheval** tables arranged in a horseshoe pattern; **mettre un f. à un cheval** to shoe a horse; **perdre un f.** to cast a shoe; *F* **tomber les quatre fers en l'air** *(d'une personne)* to fall flat on one's back

(h) *Méd* **(sels de) f.** iron

fer-blanc, *pl* **fers-blancs** *nm* tin(plate); **boîte en f.** tin can; **articles en f.** tinware

ferblanterie [fɛrblɑ̃tri] *nf* **(a)** *(industrie)* tinplate industry;

(*commerce*) tinplate trade (**b**) (*boutique*) hardware store, *Br* ironmonger's (shop) (**c**) (*articles en fer-blanc*) tinware; (*quincaillerie*) hardware, *Br* ironmongery

ferblantier [fɛrblɑ̃tje] *nm* (**a**) (*ouvrier*) tinsmith (**b**) (*marchand*) hardware dealer, *Br* ironmonger

féria [ferja] *nf* (annual) festival (*in Spain and Southern France*)

férié [ferje] *adj* **jour f.** (public) holiday, *Br* bank holiday, *Am* legal holiday; **lundi prochain est f.** next Monday is a (public) holiday

férir [ferir] *vt* **sans coup f.** without any difficulty

ferler [fɛrle] *vt* (*voile*) to furl

fermage [fɛrmaʒ] *nm* (**a**) (*mode d'exploitation*) (tenant) farming (**b**) (*loyer*) (farm) rent

fermail, -aux [fɛrmaj, -o] *nm Arch* (ornamental) clasp

ferme[1] [fɛrm] **1** *adj* (**a**) (*chair, fruit, beurre etc*) firm; (*pâte*) stiff; (*terre*) firm, solid; *Fig* (*personne, action, décision etc*) firm; (*écriture*) firm, steady; **poutre f.** firm *or* rigid beam; **la terre f.** dry land, terra firma; **fromage à pâte f.** hard cheese; **le malade n'est pas encore f. sur ses jambes** the patient is not yet steady on his legs; **il répondit d'une voix f.** he replied in a firm *or* steady voice; **d'un pas f.** with a firm step; **le marché reste très f.** the market continues very steady; **il faut être f. avec elle** you must be firm with her; **j'ai la f. intention de le lui dire** I firmly intend telling him; **être f. dans ses desseins/sa décision** to be firm *or* steadfast in one's intentions/decision; **attendre qn/qch de pied f.** to be more than ready for sb/sth

(**b**) (*date*) firm, definite; (*prix*) firm; **prendre un engagement f.** to enter into a firm undertaking; **vente/offre f.** firm *or* definite sale/offer

2 *adv* (*frapper, pousser etc*) hard; (*parler etc*) firmly; (*travailler, boire*) hard; (*discuter*) keenly; **s'ennuyer f.** to be bored stiff *or* rigid; **batailler f.** to fight hard; **tenir f.** (*d'une personne*) to stand fast *or* firm, to hold one's own (**contre** against); (*d'un clou etc*) to hold fast; **j'y travaille f.** I'm working hard on it; **croire fort et f. aux esprits** to be a firm believer in spirits; **vendre f.** to make a firm sale; **acheter f.** to make a firm purchase

ferme[2] *nf* (**a**) (*exploitation agricole*) farm; (*maison*) farmhouse; (*bâtiments*) farm buildings; **petite f.** small farm, *Br* smallholding; **f. d'élevage** cattle farm; **produits de la f.** farm produce (**b**) (*mode d'exploitation*) **bail à f.** farming lease; **prendre une terre à f.** to take a lease of *or* to lease a piece of land; **donner une terre à f.** to farm out *or* lease out a piece of land (**c**) *Hist Admin* (*de taxes*) farming (out) (**d**) *Constr* (*d'un toit, pont*) truss (**e**) *Th* flat

fermé [fɛrme] *adj* (**a**) (*magasin, boîte, etc*) closed, shut; (*route*) closed; (*vêtement*) fastened, done up; (*mer*) landlocked; **bout f.** (*d'un tuyau*) dead end; **c'est f. à clé** it's locked; **dormir à poings fermés** to sleep soundly *or* like a log; **je pouvais y aller les yeux fermés** I could go there blindfold *or* with my eyes closed *or* shut; **être f. à qch** (*d'une personne*) to have no feeling for *or* no appreciation of sth; **il a l'esprit f. aux mathématiques** mathematics is a closed book to him; **il a une attitude plutôt fermée face aux jeunes** he is an old fogey; *Ling* **voyelle fermée** closed vowel; *Tech* **position fermée** off position

(**b**) (*impénétrable*) (*expression, visage*) impassive, inscrutable

(**c**) (*sélect*) (*société, club, milieu*) exclusive, select

(**d**) *Él* (*circuit*) closed

fermement [fɛrməmɑ̃] *adv* firmly

ferment [fɛrmɑ̃] *nm* (*de vin, Fig de mécontentement*) ferment; **f. lactique** bacillus used in yoghurt-making

fermentation [fɛrmɑ̃tasjɔ̃] *nf* (*du vin*) fermentation; *Fig* agitation, unrest, ferment

fermenter [fɛrmɑ̃te] *vi* (**a**) (*du vin, de la bière*) to ferment, to work; (*de la pâte*) to rise (**b**) *Fig* (*de l'esprit, de passions*) to be in a ferment

fermer [fɛrme] **1** *vt* (**a**) (*porte, fenêtre, boîte, parapluie, livre etc*) to close, to shut; (*vêtement*) to fasten, to do up; *Ordinat* (*fichier, fenêtre*) to close; (*commande*) to end; **f. violemment la porte** to slam *or* bang the door (shut); **f. sa porte à qn** to close one's door to sb; *Fig* **f. la porte à qch** to close the door on sth; **f. la porte à clef/au verrou** to lock/bolt the door; **f. les rideaux** to draw *or* close the curtains; **f. une maison** to shut up a house; **f. boutique** to shut up shop; **f. une liste/un débat** to close a list/a debate; **fermez la parenthèse** close brackets; *Fig* **fermons la parenthèse et revenons à notre sujet** let's leave that now and get back to the subject; **f. la frontière** to close (off) the frontier; **f. une carrière à qn** to close a career to sb; **f. un robinet/l'eau/le gaz** to turn off a tap/the water/the gas; **f. l'électricité/la radio** to turn off *or* switch off the light/the radio; *Él* **f. un circuit** to close a circuit; *TV, Cin* **f. par un volet** to wipe off; *Fin* **f. un compte** to close an account; *Rail* **f. la voie** to close (off) the line; **f. les yeux** to close *or* shut one's eyes; **manger la bouche fermée** to eat with one's mouth closed *or* shut; *F* **je n'ai pas pu f. l'œil de la nuit** I couldn't sleep a wink all night; *Fig* **il faut f. les yeux sur ses erreurs** one has to turn a blind eye *or* close *or* shut one's eyes to his mistakes; *très F* **ferme ta gueule!, ferme-la!, la ferme!** shut up!, shut it!, shut your mouth *or* trap!

(**b**) **f. la marche** to bring up the rear

2 *vi* (*d'une porte, boîte, d'un magasin etc*) to close, to shut; (*d'un vêtement*) to fasten, to do up; **le couvercle ferme mal** the lid doesn't shut *or* close properly; **on ferme le lundi** we close *or* shut on Mondays, we are closed *or* shut on Mondays; **on ferme!** we're closing!, it's closing time!

3 se fermer *vpr* (*d'une porte, boîte, des yeux etc*) to close, to shut; (*d'un vêtement*) to fasten, to do up; (*d'une plaie*) to heal, to close up; **à cette demande son visage se ferma** at this request his face froze; **tu te fermes toujours quand on te parle de tes parents** you always clam up when people talk to you about your parents; *TV, Cin* **se f. en fondu** to fade out

fermeté [fɛrməte] *nf* (**a**) (*de la chair, d'un fruit, du sol, de l'écriture etc*) firmness; (*d'une pâte*) stiffness; *Bourse* **f. des cours** steadiness of prices (**b**) (*résolution*) firmness; (*dans l'adversité*) steadfastness; **f. d'esprit/de caractère** strength of mind/of character; **agir avec f.** to act firmly; **faire preuve de f. envers qn** to be firm with sb

fermette [fɛrmɛt] *nf* (*petite ferme*) small farm; (*maison de campagne*) (small) farmhouse

fermeture [fɛrmətyr] *nf* (**a**) (*action*) (*des grilles, d'une porte etc*) closing, shutting; (*d'une route, frontière, liste, d'un débat*) closing; *Ordinat* (*de fichier, fenêtre*) closing; (*de commande*) ending; *TV, Cin* fade; *TV, Cin* **f. en fondu** fade out; *TV, Cin* **f. au noir** fade out, fade-to-black; **f. automatique des portières** (*annonce*) doors close *or* shut automatically; *Aut* remote control locking; *Aut* **f. centralisée** central locking; **f. à clef** locking; **f. des ateliers** (*définitive*) closing down of the workshops; **heure de f.** (*d'un magasin*) closing time; (*d'une usine, d'un bureau*) finishing time; **il venait me chercher à la f. du bureau** he came for me after work; **f. de la pêche/chasse** close of the fishing/hunting season; **f. d'un compte** closing of an account; *Él* **f. du circuit** closing of the circuit

(**b**) **f. d'esprit** narrow-mindedness

(**c**) (*dispositif*) (*de vêtement, sac etc*) fastener; **f. éclair**®, **f. à glissière** zip (fastener), *Am* zipper; **f. à rouleau** (*d'un magasin*) revolving shutter

fermier, -ière [fɛrmje, -jɛr] **1** *nm* (**a**) *Agr* farmer; (*locataire*) (tenant) farmer (**b**) *Hist, Admin* **f. général** farmer general **2** *nf* **fermière** (woman) farmer; (*épouse*) farmer's wife **3** *adj* **beurre f.** dairy butter; **poulet f.** farm *or* free-range chicken

fermoir [fɛrmwar] *nm* (*agrafe*) (*d'un bracelet, sac, livre etc*) clasp; (*bouton-pression*) (snap) fastener

féroce [ferɔs] *adj* (*animal, personne*) ferocious, savage, fierce; (*regard, attaque, critique*) fierce, ferocious; (*joie, moquerie etc*) savage, cruel; (*appétit*) ravenous; (*désir*) raging, wild; **bête f.** wild animal *or* beast

férocement [ferɔsmɑ̃] *adv* ferociously, savagely, fiercely

férocité [ferɔsite] *nf* ferocity, ferociousness; **avec f.** fiercely

Féroé [ferɔe] *nm* **les îles F.** the Faroe Islands, the Faroes

ferrage [fɛraʒ] *nm* (*d'un cheval*) shoeing; (*d'une roue*) rimming (in metal)

ferraillage [fɛrɑjaʒ] *nm Constr* (*d'un bâtiment en béton armé*) (steel) framework

ferraille [fɛrɑj] *nf* (**a**) (*métaux*) old iron, scrap (iron); **tas de f.** scrap heap; *F* (*vieille auto*) heap of scrap iron; **mettre qch à la f.** to put sth on the scrap heap; **faire un bruit de f.** to rattle, to clank; **marchand de f.** scrap merchant (**b**) *F* (*petite monnaie*) loose *or* small change

ferraillement [fɛrɑjmɑ̃] *nm* (**a**) *Péj* (*combat à l'épée*) sword rattling (**b**) (*bruit*) (*d'une voiture etc*) rattling, clanking

ferrailler [fɛrɑje] *vi* (**a**) *Péj* (*se battre à l'épée*) to clash swords; *Fig* **f. avec qn** to cross swords with sb, to clash with sb; **j'ai longtemps ferraillé avec l'ordinateur avant de comprendre comment il marchait** I had a long battle with the computer before I understood how it worked (**b**) (*faire un bruit de ferraille*) to clank, to rattle

ferrailleur [fɛrɑjœr] *nm* (**a**) *Péj* (*bretteur*) sword rattler (**b**) (*revendeur*) scrap merchant

ferrate [fɛrat] *nm Ch* ferrate

ferré [fɛre] *adj* (**a**) (*canne*) metal-tipped; (*chaussure*) hobnailed; (*roue*) metal-rimmed; (*cheval*) shod; (*lacet*) tagged; **cheval f. à glace** roughshod horse; *Rail* **voie ferrée** (*rails*) track; (*route*) railway *or* *Am* railroad (line); **les utilisateurs de la voie ferrée** railway *or* *Am* railroad users;

par voie ferrée by rail; *Rail* **réseau f.** railway *or Am* railroad system *or* network **(b)** *F* (*calé*) **être f. sur** (*sujet, chimie etc*) to be well up in *or* on

ferrer [fere] *vt* **(a)** (*canne*) to tip with metal; (*chaussure*) to nail; (*roue*) to rim with metal; (*cheval*) to shoe; (*lacet*) to tag **(b)** *Pêche* (*poisson*) to strike

ferret [ferɛ] *nm* (*de lacet*) tag

ferreur [ferœr] *nm* **f. de chevaux** shoeing smith, *Br* farrier

ferreux, -euse [ferø, -øz] *adj Ch, Minér* ferrous; **alliages f.** iron alloys, ferro-alloys

ferricyanure [ferisjanyr] *nm Ch* ferricyanide

ferrique [ferik] *adj Ch* (*sel etc*) ferric

ferrite [ferit] *nf* ferrite; *Ordinat* **mémoire à f.** ferrite core memory

ferro- [ferɔ] *préf* ferro-

ferrochrome [ferɔkrom] *nm Métal* ferrochrome, ferrochromium

ferrocyanure [ferɔsjanyr] *nm Ch* ferrocyanide

ferroélectricité [ferɔelɛktrisite] *nf* ferroelectricity

ferroélectrique [ferɔelɛktrik] *adj* ferroelectric

ferromagnétique [ferɔmaɲetik] *adj* ferromagnetic

ferromagnétisme [ferɔmaɲetism] *nm* ferromagnetism

ferronnerie [ferɔnri] *nf* **(a)** (*objets*) **f. (d'art)** (decorative) ironwork, wrought ironwork; **grille en f.** wrought-iron gate **(b)** (*métier*) ironwork **(c)** (*atelier*) ironworks

ferronnier, -ière [ferɔnje, -jɛr] *n* **(a)** (*artisan*) **f. (d'art)** worker in wrought iron **(b)** (*commerçant*) ironware dealer

ferrotypie [ferɔtipi] *nf Phot* ferrotype

ferroviaire [ferɔvjɛr] *adj* (*réseau, compagnie, trafic etc*) railway, *Am* railroad; **transports ferroviaires** rail transport; **les grandes lignes ferroviaires** the main railway *or Am* railroad lines

ferrugineux, -euse [feryʒinø, -øz] *adj* ferruginous; **source ferrugineuse** chalybeate spring

ferrure [feryr] *nf* **(a)** (*garniture*) (iron) fitting; **ferrures de porte** door fittings; **ferrures en cuivre** brass fittings **(b)** (*d'un cheval*) shoeing

ferry [feri], *pl* **ferries** *nm* ferry; **f. roulier** roll-on roll-off ferry; **f. trans-Manche** cross-Channel ferry

ferry-boat, *pl* **ferry-boats** [feribot] *nm* (*pour voitures*) (car) ferry; (*pour trains*) (train) ferry

fertile [fertil] *adj* (*sol, champ etc*) fertile; *Fig* (*esprit, imagination*) fertile, inventive; (*compositeur, écrivain etc*) inventive; **semaine f. en événements** eventful week; **la semaine fut f. en discussions** the week was packed with discussions

fertilisable [fertilizabl] *adj* fertilizable

fertilisant [fertilizɑ̃] **1** *adj* fertilizing **2** *nm* fertilizer

fertilisation [fertilizasjɔ̃] *nf* fertilization

fertiliser [fertilize] *vt* to fertilize

fertilité [fertilite] *nf* (*du sol, de l'imagination etc*) fertility

féru [fery] *adj* **f. d'un sujet** passionately interested in a subject; **être f. d'une idée** to be set on an idea; *Arch* **f. de qn** smitten with sb

férule [feryl] *nf Hist Scol* ferule (*ruler for punishment on the hands*); *Fig* **être sous la f. de qn** to be under sb's sway *or* domination *or* rule

fervent, -ente [fervɑ̃, -ɑ̃t] **1** *adj* (*dévotion, admirateur, chrétien etc*) fervent, ardent, keen; (*amour*) ardent; (*prière*) fervent; (*approbation*) enthusiastic **2** *n* devotee (**de** of)

ferveur [fervœr] *nf* fervour, *US* fervor; **avec f.** (*prier*) fervently, earnestly; (*travailler*) with enthusiasm; (*aimer*) ardently; (*écouter*) eagerly

fesse [fes] *nf* **(a)** *Anat* buttock; **fesses** buttocks, behind, bottom; *F* **donner à qn un coup de pied aux fesses** to give sb a kick in the pants *or* up the backside; *très F* **poser ses fesses** *ou* **une f.** (*s'asseoir*) to park one's backside; *très F* **attraper qn par la peau des fesses** to grab hold of sb just in time; *très F* **serrer les fesses** (*avoir peur*) to have the wind up, to have the jitters; (*être courageux*) to sit tight; *très F* **occupe-toi de tes fesses!** mind your own damn business!; *très F* **avoir qn aux fesses** to have sb on one's tail; *très F* **coller aux fesses de qn** to stick to sb like glue; (*d'un camion etc*) to sit on sb's tail; *très F* **film/revue de fesses** porn *or* dirty film/magazine, tit and bum magazine; *très F* **histoire de fesses** dirty story; (*aventure*) purely sexual affair

(b) (*de navire*) tuck

fessée [fese] *nf* **(a)** (*coups*) spanking; **donner une f. à qn** to give sb a spanking, to spank sb **(b)** *Fig* (*défaite*) drubbing

fesse-mathieu, *pl* **fesse-mathieux** [fesmatjø] *nm Vieilli* skinflint, Scrooge

fesser [fese] *vt* **f. qn** to spank sb, to smack sb's bottom

fessier, -ière [fesje, -jɛr] **1** *adj Anat* (*muscle etc*) buttock, *Spéc* gluteal; **poche fessière** (*de pantalon etc*) hip pocket **2** *nm* **(a)** *Anat* gluteal muscle **(b)** *F* (*fesses*) backside, behind

festif, -ive [festif, -iv] *adj* festive

festin [festɛ̃] *nm* feast, banquet; **quel f.!** what a feast!, what a spread!; **faire (un) f.** to feast

festival, -als [festival] *nm* festival; **f. du film** film festival; **f. culturel** arts festival

festivalier, -ière [festivalje, -jɛr] **1** *adj* festival **2** *n* (*participant*) festival participant; (*visiteur*) festival-goer

festivités [festivite] *nfpl* festivities, celebrations

feston [festɔ̃] *nm* **(a)** (*de fleurs*) festoon **(b)** *Couture* scallop; **à festons** scalloped; **point de f.** buttonhole stitch

festonner [festɔne] *vt* **(a)** (*de guirlandes*) to festoon **(b)** *Couture* to scallop

festoyer [festwaje] *vi* (**je festoie; je festoierai**) to feast

fêtard, -arde [fetar, -ard] *n F* reveller

fête [fet] *nf* **(a)** (*de village*) fete, fête, fair; (*de ville*) festival; **f. champêtre** *ou* **de village** village fete *or* fair; **f. de la bière** beer festival

(b) (*soirée*) party; **donner une f.** to give a party; **faire une f.** to have a party; **une petite f.** a party

(c) (*gaieté*) **air de f.** festive air; **le village était en f.** the village was in a festive mood; **faire la f.** to have a wild time, to live it up; **faire f. à qn** to welcome sb with open arms; **mon chien me fait f. quand je rentre le soir** my dog is all over me when I come back in the evening; **être de la f.** to be one of the party; **se faire une f. de (faire) qch** to look forward to (doing) sth; **il ne s'était jamais vu à pareille f.** he had never had such a good time; *Iron* **il n'était pas à la f.** it wasn't much fun for him

(d) (*du saint dont on porte le nom*) saint's *or* name day; **souhaiter une bonne f. à qn** to wish sb a happy saint's day; *Iron* **ça va être ta f.!** you're in for it!; **on va lui faire sa f.!** he'll get what's coming to him!

(e) (*célébration*), *Rel* feast, festival; (*civile*) holiday; **jour de f.** *Rel* feast day; (*jour férié*) public holiday; **les fêtes (de fin d'année)** the Christmas and New Year holidays; **c'est f. demain** tomorrow is a holiday; *Fig* **ce n'est pas tous les jours f.** Christmas comes but once a year; *F* **elle est de bonne humeur?, c'est la f.!** she's in a good mood?, put the flags out!

▶ **fête: f. foraine** fun fair; *Beaux-Arts* **f. galante** fête galante; **f. légale** bank holiday, *Am* legal holiday; **f. des mères** Mother's Day; **f. mobile** mov(e)able feast; **la f. des Morts** All Souls' Day; **f. nationale** national holiday; **la f. nationale du 14 juillet** Bastille Day; **la f. nationale de la victoire** *Br* ≈ Armistice Day, *US* ≈ Veterans Day; **f. des pères** Father's Day; **f. du travail** Labour Day

Fête-Dieu, *pl* **Fêtes-Dieu** *nf Rel* Corpus Christi

fêter [fete] *vt* **(a)** (*victoire, événement, Noël etc*) to celebrate; **f. la naissance de qn** to celebrate sb's birthday; **f. ses soixante ans** to celebrate one's sixtieth birthday; **f. un saint** to keep a saint's day; **le projet est fini? il faut f. cela!** the project's finished? let's celebrate! *or* that calls for a celebration! **(b)** (*accueillir chaleureusement*) to fete

fétiche [fetiʃ] *nm* (*objet de culte*) fetish; (*mascotte*) mascot; **couleur/nombre f.** lucky colour/number

fétichisme [fetiʃism] *nm* fetishism

fétichiste [fetiʃist] **1** *adj* fetishistic **2** *n* fetishist

fétide [fetid] *adj* fetid, rank, stinking, foul

fétidité [fetidite] *nf* fetidness

fétu [fety] *nm* **f. (de paille)** (wisp of) straw; **être emporté comme un f.** to be blown along like a straw in the wind

fétuque [fetyk] *nf Bot* fescue (grass)

feu[1] [fø], *pl* **feux** **1** *nm* **(a)** (*élément, flammes, incendie*) fire; **le f. et l'eau** fire and water; **mettre (le) f. à qch** to set fire to sth, to set sth on fire; *F* **flanquer** *ou très F* **foutre le f. à qn** to put a match to sth; **mettre une ville à f. et à sang** to put a town to fire and sword; **prendre f.** to catch fire; **faire du f.** to make a fire; **allumer/faire un f.** to light/make a fire; *Fig* **jouer avec le f.** to play with fire; **faire f. des quatre fers** (*d'un cheval*) to make the sparks fly; *Fig* (*d'une personne*) to go all out; **il fait f. de tout bois** he makes the most of his opportunities, he turns everything to account; *F* **avoir le f. au derrière** *ou très F* **au cul** to be in a tearing hurry; **enlever de la peinture au f.** to burn paint off; **en f.** on fire; **joues en f.** burning cheeks; **visage en f.** flushed face; **j'avais la gorge en f.** my throat was burning *or* on fire; **soleil de f.** fiery sun; **f. de forêt** forest fire; **il y a le f. à la grange!** the barn's on fire!; **au f.!** fire!; *Fig* **faire la part du f.** to cut one's losses; *F* **il n'y a pas le f. (au lac)** there's no particular hurry; **il n'y a pas de quoi crier au f.** there's nothing to get excited about; **jeter f. et flamme (contre qn)** to be in a rage (with sb), to rage (at sb); **est-ce que vous avez du f.?** have you got a light?

(b) (*passion*) ardour, *US* ardor, passion; *Arch* (*amour*) love; **tout f. tout flamme** burning with enthusiasm; **parler avec f.** to speak passionately; **dans le f. de la discussion/l'action** in the heat of the debate/the action; **avoir le f. sacré** to burn with enthusiasm; **il a un tempérament de f.** he has a fiery temperament

(**c**) (*matières allumées*) fire; **f. nu** open fire; **garniture de f.** fire irons; **au coin du f.** by the fire(side)

(**d**) **mettre une chaudière en f.** to fire up a boiler

(**e**) (*supplice*) **condamner qn au f.** to condemn sb to be burnt at the stake; **j'en mettrais la main au f.** I would swear to it; **épreuve du f.** ordeal by fire; **faire mourir qn à petit f.** to kill sb slowly, to make sb die a lingering death; *Fig* to keep sb on tenterhooks

(**f**) *Culin* (*de cuisinière*) burner; **faire cuire à f. doux** *ou* **à petit f.** to cook gently *or* over a low heat; (*au four*) to cook in a slow oven; **à grand f., à f. vif** over a high heat; (*au four*) in a hot oven; **ustensiles qui vont au f.** fireproof utensils; **cuisinière à quatre feux** four-burner cooker; **j'ai du lait sur le f.** I've got some milk on the stove; **coup de f.** (slight) burning; *Fig* busiest time; **nous sommes arrivés en plein coup de f.** we arrived right at the busiest time

(**g**) (*maison*) **hameau de 50 feux** hamlet of 50 houses; **n'avoir ni f. ni lieu** to be homeless, to have neither hearth nor home

(**h**) *Mil etc* (*tir*) fire; (*combat*) action; **arme à f.** firearm; **bouche à f.** piece of ordnance *or* artillery; **faire f. (sur qn)** to fire *or* shoot (at sb); **commencer** *ou* **déclencher** *ou* **ouvrir le f.** to open fire; **f.!** fire!; **sous le f.** under fire; **faire long f.** (*d'un pistolet, Fig d'un plan etc*) to hang fire; *Fig* **leur amitié ne fera pas long f.** their friendship won't last long; **aller au f.** to go into action; **coup de f.** (gun)shot; **tirer des coups de f.** to fire shots; **nous avons reçu des coups de f.** we were fired on *or* shot at; **il n'a jamais vu le f.** he has never seen action; *Fig* **être entre deux feux** to be caught in the middle, to be in the crossfire

(**i**) *Naut* (*lumière*) light; **feux (d'entrée) de port** harbour lights; **droits de feux** light dues; **f. à occultations** *ou* **à éclipses** occulting light; **feux de route** navigation lights; **feux de mouillage** (*d'un navire*) anchor lights; **f. de tribord** starboard light

(**j**) *Av* (*lumière*) light; **feux de balisage** boundary lights; **feux de piste** runway lights; **feux de bord** *ou* **de navigation** navigation lights

(**k**) *Aut* (*de signalisation*) light; **f. rouge** (*lumière*) red light; (*objet*) (traffic) lights, *Am* traffic light; **f. orange/vert** amber/green light; **feux tricolores** traffic lights; **feux (de signalisation)** (traffic) lights; **attendre au(x) feu(x)** to wait at the lights; *Fig* **donner le f. vert** to give the green light *or* the go-ahead (**à** to)

(**l**) *Aut* (*de véhicule*) light; **tous feux éteints** without lights; **f. de brouillard** *ou* **antibrouillard** fog lamp; **feux de croisement** dipped headlights, *Am* low beams; **feux de détresse** hazard (warning) lights, *F* hazards; **feux de position** sidelights; **feux de recul** reversing lights; **feux de route** driving lights, headlights on full beam *or Am* high beam; **en feux de route** on full beam; **feux arrière** rear lamps, tail lights; **feux blancs** driving lights, headlights and side lights; **feux de freinage** brake lights; **feux de stationnement** parking lights; **f. de gabarit** side lamp; **f. de plaque** number plate light; **f. de stop** brake light

(**m**) *Rail* **f. d'avant** (*d'une locomotive*) headlight; **f. d'arrière** (*d'un train*) tail *or* rear light

(**n**) **feux d'un diamant** fire *or* sparkle of a diamond; **une pierre qui brille de mille feux** a stone that sparkles brilliantly; **yeux pleins de f.** flashing eyes; **être sous les feux des projecteurs** to be in the glare of the spotlights; *Fig* to be in the limelight; **il est sous les feux de l'actualité** he is very much in the news at the moment

(**o**) **mettre une fusée à f.** to fire a rocket; **mise à f.** blastoff, launch

2 *adj inv* **rouge f.** flame-coloured; **chien noir et f.** black-and-tan dog

▶ **feu**: **f. d'artifice** fireworks; (*spectacle*) firework display; **ça a été un véritable f. d'artifice, ce débat** there were real fireworks at the debate; **f. de Bengale** Bengal light; **f. de camp** campfire; **f. de cheminée** fire in the hearth; **f. de joie** bonfire; **f. roulant** running fire, drumfire; *Fig* **un f. roulant de questions** a barrage of questions

feu² *adj* (*inv if preceding article or poss adj*) late; **la feue reine, f. la reine** the late queen; **f. mon père** my late father; **fils de feue Berthe Dupont** son of the late Berthe Dupont, son of Berthe Dupont deceased

feudataire [fødatɛr] *nm Hist* feudatory

feuillage [fœjaʒ] *nm* leaves, foliage

feuillaison [fœjɛzɔ̃] *nf* leafing, coming into leaf

feuille [fœj] *nf* (**a**) [①**A12**,1,d] (*de plante, d'arbre*) leaf; **f. morte** dead leaf; *Av* **descente en f. morte** dead-leaf dive; *F* **il est dur de la f.** he's hard of hearing (**b**) **f. de métal** sheet of metal; **fer en feuilles** sheet iron; **f. d'or** gold leaf; **f. d'étain** tinfoil; **f. de bois** thin board (**c**) (*de papier*) sheet; **f. volante** *ou* **mobile** loose sheet; **feuilles d'un livre** leaves of a book; **bonnes feuilles** advance proofs (**d**) (*journal*) paper

▶ **feuille**: **f. d'accompagnement** covering document; **f. des arrivées et des départs** (*d'un hôtel etc*) arrival and departure list, A&D list; *Compta* **f. d'avancement** flow sheet; *Ordinat* **f. de calcul** spreadsheet; **f. de chou** cabbage leaf; *F Péj* (*journal*) rag; **oreilles en f. de chou** cauliflower ears; *TV etc* **f. de conducteur** cue sheet; *TV, Cin* **f. d'exposition** exposure sheet; **f. de garde** (*d'un livre*) fly leaf; **f. d'impôt** tax return; *Compta* **f. de liquidation** settlement note; **f. de maladie** = form given by doctor to patient for claiming reimbursement from Social Security, sick note; *TV etc* **f. de mixage** cue sheet; **f. des mouvements** (*d'un hôtel etc*) arrival and departure list, A&D list; **f. d'occupation journalière** (*d'un hôtel*) daily density chart, daily forecast chart; *TV, Rad* **f. d'ordre de passage à l'antenne** rundown sheet; **f. de paie** *ou* **paye** payslip; **f. de présence** attendance sheet; (*d'un employé*) time sheet; **f. de réservation** reservation form, booking form; **f. des réveils** (*d'un hôtel etc*) call sheet; **f. de route** *Com* waybill; *Mil* travel warrant; **f. de service** (duty) roster; **f. de soins** medical expense claim form; **f. de style** style sheet; **f. de température** temperature chart; **f. de travail** worksheet; **f. de versement** paying-in slip; **f. de vigne** (*sur sculpture*) vine leaf, fig leaf; *Culin* stuffed vine leaf; *Av* **f. de vol** flight plan

feuillée [fœje] **1** *nf Litt* greenery, branches **2** *Mil* **feuillées** (*dans un camp*) latrines

feuille-morte *adj inv, nm inv* (*couleur*) russet

feuilleret [fœjrɛ] *nm Tech* rabbet plane, grooving plane

feuillet [fœjɛ] *nm* (**a**) (*d'un livre*) leaf; **à feuillets rechargeables** loose-leaf (**b**) (*de bois*) thin sheet

feuilletage [fœjtaʒ] *nm Culin* (**a**) (*action*) (*d'une pâte*) rolling and folding (**b**) (*de la pâte*) flakiness (**c**) (*pâte*) flaky pastry

feuilleté [fœjte] **1** *adj* (*roche*) foliated, laminated, lamellar; (*verre*) laminated; **pare-brise (en verre) f.** laminated windscreen *or Am* windshield; *Culin* **pâte feuilletée** flaky pastry, puff pastry, *Am* puff paste **2** *nm Culin* **un f.** a pastry (*made from flaky pastry*); **un f. au jambon/au fromage** a ham/cheese pastry

feuilleter [fœjte] *vt* (**je feuillette**; **je feuilletterai**) (**a**) *Culin* (*pâte*) to roll and fold (**b**) **f. un livre** to turn over the pages of a book; (*sommairement*) to leaf through *or* flip through a book (**c**) *Ordinat* to scroll; **f. en arrière** to page up, to scroll up; **f. en avant** to page down, to scroll down

feuilleton [fœjtɔ̃] *nm* (**a**) *Journ* (*chronique*) (regular) feature (**b**) *Journ, Rad, TV* (*histoire*) serial, serial drama; (*populaire*) soap (opera); **publier un roman en feuilletons** to serialize a novel

feuilletoniste [fœjtɔnist] *n Journ* (*auteur de romans-feuilletons*) serial writer; (*chroniqueur*) feature writer

feuillu [fœjy] **1** *adj* (*ayant beaucoup de feuilles*) leafy; (*à feuilles*) broad-leaved **2** *nm* broad-leaved tree

feuillure [fœjyr] *nf Menuis* rabbet, groove

feulement [følmɑ̃] *nm* (*de tigre*) snarl, growl; (*de chat*) growl

feuler [føle] *vi* (*d'un tigre*) to snarl, to growl; (*d'un chat*) to growl

feutrage [føtraʒ] *nm* (**a**) *Tech* (*du poil, de la laine, d'un tissu*) felting (**b**) (*d'une surface, d'un objet*) felting, covering with felt (**c**) (*d'un vêtement de laine*) matting, felting

feutre [føtr] *nm* (**a**) *Tex* felt; **chaussons de f.** felt slippers (**b**) (*chapeau*) felt hat, fedora (**c**) (**crayon**) **f.** felt(-tip) pen, felt-tip; **stylo f.** felt-tip (pen)

feutré [føtre] *adj* (**a**) (*garni de feutre*) felt(-covered); **porte feutrée** baize door (**b**) (*son*) muffled; **à pas feutrés** silently; **s'éloigner à pas feutrés** to steal away, to slip quietly away; **traverser la pièce à pas feutrés** to pad across the room (**c**) (*après le lavage*) (*lainage*) matted

feutrer [føtre] **1** *vt* (**a**) *Tech* (*poil, laine*) to felt, to make into felt (**b**) (*garnir de feutre*) to cover with felt, to felt (**c**) *Fig* (*son*) to muffle **2** *vi* (*d'un vêtement en laine*) to become matted, to felt **3 se feutrer** *vpr* (*d'un vêtement en laine*) to become matted, to felt

feutrine [føtrin] *nf* felt; (*sur table de billard*) baize

fève [fɛv] *nf* (**a**) (*plante, graine*) broad bean; (*dans la galette des Rois*) charm (**b**) *Can* (*haricot*) bean; **f. verte** string bean; **f. jaune** wax bean (**c**) **f. de cacao** cocoa bean

février [fevrije] *nm* [①**A75-6**,B-C; **B58-9**,B-C] February **en f.** in February; **au mois de f.** in (the month of) February; **le sept f.** (on) the seventh of February, (on) February the seventh, *Am* (on) February seventh

fez [fɛz] *nm* fez

FF *nm abrév* **franc(s) français**

FFI [ɛfɛfi] *nfpl Hist* (*abrév* **Forces françaises de l'intérieur**) = French Resistance forces in France during World War Two

FFL [ɛfɛfɛl] *nfpl Hist* (*abrév* **Forces françaises libres**) Free French Army
fi [fi] *int Vieilli, Hum* **(a)** fie!, for shame! **(b) faire fi de qch** to scorn sth; **je fais fi de toutes vos remarques** I don't give a fig for what you have to say
fiabilité [fjabilite] *nf* reliability, dependability
fiable [fjabl] *adj* reliable, dependable
fiacre [fjakr] *nm* (*voiture à cheval*) hackney (carriage *or* cab)
fiançailles [fjɑ̃sɑj] *nfpl* engagement; **pendant leurs f.** while they were engaged, during their engagement
fiancé, -ée [fjɑ̃se] **1** *adj* engaged (**à** *ou* **avec qn** to sb) **2** *nm* fiancé; **les fiancés** (*couple*) the engaged couple **3** *nf* **fiancée** fiancée
fiancer [fjɑ̃se] **1** *vt Vieilli* to betroth (**à** *ou* **avec qn** to sb) **2 se fiancer** *vpr* to become *or* get engaged (**à** *ou* **avec qn** to sb)
fiasco [fjasko] *nm* fiasco; (*spectacle*) flop; **faire f.** (*d'un projet*) to come to nothing; (*d'un spectacle*) to be a flop, to flop
fiasque [fjask] *nf* (Italian) flask
fibranne [fibran] *nm Tex* staple fibre *or US* fiber
fibre [fibr] *nf* **(a)** fibre, *US* fiber; **riche en fibres (alimentaires)** rich in (dietary) fibre; **panneau de fibres agglomérées** fibreboard, *US* fiberboard; **coton à fibres longues** long-staple cotton; **fibres synthétiques** synthetic fibres; **la f. optique** fibre optics; **fibres optiques** optical fibres; **câble en fibres optiques** fibre optic cable; **f. de verre** glass fibre, fibreglass, *US* fiberglass; **f. de carbone** carbon fibre
(b) *Fig* **faire jouer la f. paternelle/patriotique** to play on paternal/patriotic feelings; **elle n'a pas la f. maternelle** she's not the maternal sort
fibreux, -euse [fibrø, -øz] *adj* (*tissu*) fibrous; (*viande*) stringy
fibrillation [fibrijasjɔ̃] *nf Méd* fibrillation
fibrille [fibrij] *nf* small fibre *or US* fiber; *Physiol, Bot* fibril(la)
fibrine [fibrin] *nf Physiol* fibrin
fibrineux, -euse [fibrinø, -øz] *adj Physiol* fibrinous
fibrinogène [fibrinɔʒɛn] *nm Physiol* fibrinogen
fibrociment® [fibrosimɑ̃] *nm* fibrocement
fibromateux, -euse [fibrɔmatø, -øz] *adj Méd* fibromatous
fibrome [fibrom] *nm Méd* fibroma, fibroid
fibroscope [fibrɔskɔp] *nm Méd* fibrescope, *US* fiberscope
fibroscopie [fibrɔskɔpi] *nf Méd* fibreoptic endoscopy
fibule [fibyl] *nf* (*agrafe*) fibula
ficaire [fikɛr] *nf Bot* lesser celandine, pilewort
ficelage [fis(ə)laʒ] *nm* **(a)** (*action*) tying up **(b)** (*liens*) string(s)
ficelé [fis(ə)le] *adj* **(a)** (*lié*) (*colis, prisonnier etc*) tied up **(b)** *F* (*habillé*) got up; **être f. comme l'as de pique** to be dressed like a scarecrow **(c)** *F* **c'est bien/mal f.** (*d'un texte, d'une histoire, d'un film*) it hangs/doesn't hang together well; **un scénario bien f.** a well-crafted screenplay
ficeler [fis(ə)le] *vt* (**je ficelle; je ficellerai**) (*colis, prisonnier*) to tie up
ficelle [fisɛl] **1** *nf* **(a)** (*mince corde*) string; **les ficelles de la marionnette** the puppet's strings **(b)** *Fig* **c'est lui qui tire les ficelles** he's the one who pulls the strings; **les ficelles du métier** the tricks of the trade; **connaître les ficelles (du métier)** to know the ropes, to know the tricks of the trade; **la f. est un peu grosse** that won't fool anybody **(c)** (*pain*) small French stick **2** *adj Vieilli* crafty, wily
fiche [fiʃ] *nf* **(a)** *Él* (*prise*) plug; (*broche*) pin; *Tél* (patch) plug; (*électrique*) jack plug
(b) (*morceau de papier*) slip (of paper); (*formulaire*) form; (*dépliant*) leaflet; **faire des fiches de lecture** to write a book report; **fiches-cuisine/-tricot/-santé** (*dans un magazine*) cookery/knitting/health cards
(c) (*carte*) (index) card; **jeu de fiches** card index; **mettre des informations en** *ou* **sur fiche(s)** to card-index data
(d) (*cheville*) (*en fer, bois etc*) peg, pin
▸ **fiche¹**: **f. d'accueil** registration form; *Admin* **f. anthropométrique** = (criminal) dossier; **f. d'appréciation** customer satisfaction questionnaire; **f. d'arrivée** registration form; **f. de blocage** (*d'un hôtel etc*) block card, reservation rack card, room rack card; **f. cartonnée** index card; **f. client** customer record; (*d'un hôtel etc*) room rack card; (*sur ordinateur*) guest folio, guest file; **f. de compte** accounts card; **f.-contact** contacts file; *Ind* **f. de contrôle** checking form, *Br* docket; **f. courrier** mail checklist *or* file; **f. dentaire** dental chart; **f. d'entretien** service record; *Ordinat* **f. d'état** report form; **f. d'état civil** = record of civil status (*birth details and marital status*); **f. explicative** information sheet; **f. de facture** account card; **f. fournisseur** supplier file; *Ordinat* **f. gigogne** dongle; **f. d'hôtel** (*clé*) key card; *Compta* **f. d'imputation** data entry form; **f. d'inscription** registration form; **f. Kardex** (*d'un hôtel etc*) guest history card; **f. médicale** medical record (card); **f.-message** message form; **f. d'observations** (*questionnaire d'évaluation*) comment card; **f. d'occupation** (*d'un hôtel etc*) room rack card; **f. de paie** payslip; **f. à perforations marginales** edge punched card; **f. perforée** perforated card; *Com* **f. de pointage** clocking-in card; **f. de police** registration card to be filled in by hotel guests from non-EU countries; (*au débarquement*) landing card; **f. de poste** (*descriptif des tâches à accomplir*) task sheet; **f. de présence** (*de salarié*) attendance sheet; **f.-prospect** potential-customer file; **f. signalétique** personal details card; **f. de stock** stock sheet; **f. en T** T-card; **f. technique** specifications sheet; **f. téléphonique** telephone jack plug; (*broche*) telephone jack; (*pour message*) telephone memo; **f. verticale suspendue** vertical suspension file; **f. à visibilité** visible card record; **f. voyageur** (*d'un hôtel etc*) registration card for foreign guests; **f. Whitney** (*d'un hôtel etc*) Whitney card
fiche² *vt, vpr F* = **ficher²**
ficher¹ [fiʃe] **1** *vt* **(a)** (*enfoncer*) (*clou, pieu etc*) to drive in; (*lame*) to plunge; (*épingle*) to stick in; **f. une épingle dans qch** to stick a pin into sth **(b)** (*mettre sur fiche*) (*informations*) to file (away), to put on file; (*personne*) to put on file; **il est fiché aux stups** the drugs squad have got him on their files **2 se ficher** *vpr* to stick (**dans** in); **la flèche se ficha en plein milieu de la cible** the arrow hit the middle of the target; **la balle se ficha dans le mur** the bullet became embedded in the wall
ficher² (*inf souvent* **fiche**; *pp* **fichu**) *F* **1** *vt* **(a)** (*mettre*) to stick, to shove, *Br* to bung; **f. par terre** (*chapeau etc*) to chuck on the ground; *Fig* (*gouvernement*) to bring down, to overthrow; (*projet*) to mess up, to put paid to; **t'as tout fichu par terre** you've messed everything up; *aussi Fig* **f. qn à la porte** to chuck sb out; **f. qn dedans** to land *or* drop sb in it
(b) (*faire*) to do; **il n'a rien fichu de la journée** he's done damn all all day, he hasn't done a thing all day
(c) (*donner*) **f. une gifle à qn** to give sb a slap in the face; **fiche-moi la paix!** leave me alone!, clear off!; **je t'en fiche!** no way!, you must be joking!; **je t'en ficherai, tiens, moi, des petits copains à ton âge!** boyfriends at your age – what are you thinking of!; **ça la fiche mal** (*fait mauvais effet*) it looks really bad (**de faire** to do)
(d) f. le camp to shove off, to clear off; **fiche-moi le camp!** shove off!, clear off!; **va te faire fiche!** get lost!, go to hell!
2 se ficher *vpr* **(a)** (*se mettre*) **se f. par terre** (*tomber*) to fall flat; **se f. dedans** (*se tromper*) to make a boo-boo *or* a blunder; **soyons attentifs pour ne pas nous f. dedans cette fois** let's take care we don't land ourselves in it this time
(b) se f. de qn/qch (*tourner en ridicule*) to make fun of sb/sth; (*mépriser*) not to give a damn about sb/sth; **vous vous fichez de moi!** what do you take me for?; **ça, c'est se f. du monde!** well, what a damned cheek!, that's just not taking things seriously!; **je m'en fiche (pas mal)** I don't give a damn, I couldn't care less; **elle s'en fiche que son père ne soit pas d'accord** she doesn't give a damn *or* couldn't care less if her father doesn't agree
fichet [fiʃɛ] *nm* (*utilisé au trictrac*) peg
fichette [fiʃɛt] *nf* **f. client** (*d'un hôtel etc*) reservation card; **f. d'arrivée** arrival form
fichier [fiʃje] *nm* **(a)** (*ensemble de fiches*) card index, card-index system; **(b)** (*boîte*) card-index box; (*meuble*) card-index cabinet; (*à tiroirs*) card-index filing cabinet **(c)** *Ordinat* file; **volume du f.** file size
▸ **fichier**: **f. à accès aléatoire** random access file; **f. actif** active file; **f. d'adresses** address file; **f. d'application** application file; **f. ASCII** ASCII file; **f. de base de données** database file; **f. BAT** batch file; **f. (des) clients** client *or* customer file; **f. de commande** command file; *Journ* **f. de coupures** cuttings file; **f. en cours** current file; **f. de destination** target file; **f. document** document file; **f. d'entrée** input file; **f. exécutable** executable *or* execute file; **f. historique** history file; **f. à imprimer** print(er) file; **f. indexé** indexed file; **f. d'intendance** control file; **f. journal** logging file; **f. Kardex** (*d'un hôtel etc*) guest history file; **f. en lecture seule** read-only file; **f. maître** master file; **f. non structuré** flat file; **f. par points** bitmap file; **f. rotatif** rotating card index, rotary (card) file; **f. des salariés** personnel files; **f. de sauvegarde** backup file; **f. de secours** backup file; **f. séquentiel** batch *or* sequential file; **f. de sortie** output file; **f. source** source file; **f. système** system file; **f. (de) texte** text file; **f. de travail** working *or* work file; **f. de tri temporaire** temporary sort file
fichtre [fiʃtr] *int Vieilli, F* **(a)** (*étonnement*) golly!, good gracious! **(b)** (*admiration*) my!, *Br* I say! **(c)** (*contrariété*) blow!, blast! **(d)** (*intensif*) **f. oui!** I should say so!, rather!; **f. non!** not likely!, no fear!
fichtrement [fiʃtrəmɑ̃] *adv Vieilli F* (*extrêmement*) awfully, frightfully; **je n'en sais f. rien!** how the heck should I know?
fichu¹ [fiʃy] *adj F* **(a)** (*maudit*) rotten, awful; **quel f. pays!** what a godforsaken country!; **quel f. temps!** what filthy *or* awful weather!; **tu as vraiment un f. caractère!** nobody can

say a word to you; **cette fichue machine** this damn *or* bloody machine

(b) (*en mauvais état, perdu*) **il est f.** he's done for, it's all up with him, he's had it; **c'est f.!** (*sans espoir*) (we can) forget it!; **c'est f. pour dimanche** Sunday's out, we can forget Sunday; **ma robe/voiture est fichue** my dress/car has had it

(c) (*habillé*) **être bien/mal f.** to be well/badly turned out *or* dressed

(d) (*bâti, conçu*) **elle est vraiment bien fichue, cette fille** that girl's got a great body on her; **c'est bien/mal f.** it's well/ badly designed

(e) **être mal f.** (*un peu malade*) to be out of sorts, *Br* to be off colour

(f) (*capable*) **elle serait fichue d'oublier le rendez-vous** she'd be quite capable of forgetting the appointment, I wouldn't put it past her to forget the appointment; **il n'est pas fichu de faire cuire des pâtes** he's not even capable of cooking pasta, even cooking pasta is beyond him

fichu[2] *nm* headscarf; (*couvrant les épaules*) fichu, (small) shawl

fictif, -ive [fiktif, -iv] *adj* **(a)** (*imaginaire*) fictitious, imaginary **(b)** (*faux*) (*promesse*) false; (*nom, adresse etc*) false, fictitious; (*lutte*) sham **(c)** *Fin* **valeur fictive** (*de billets*) face value

fiction [fiksjɔ̃] *nf* (*fait imaginé*), *Littér* fiction; **film de f.** fictional film; **livre de f.** work of fiction; **la réalité dépasse la f.** truth is stranger than fiction; **la politique-f.** political pie in the sky; **roman de politique-f.** political novel

fictivement [fiktivmɑ̃] *adv* **(a)** (*par la pensée*) in one's imagination *or* mind **(b)** *Littér* fictitiously

ficus [fikys] *nm Bot* ficus

fidéicommis [fideikɔmi] *nm Jur* trust

fidéicommissaire [fideikɔmisɛr] *nm Jur* trustee

fidèle [fidɛl] **1** *adj* **(a)** (*loyal*) (*ami, supporter, serviteur etc*) faithful, loyal; (*époux, chien*) faithful; **lecteur/client f.** regular *or* loyal reader/customer; **rester f. à une promesse** to stand by *or* keep a promise; **rester f. à la mémoire de qn** to remain true *or* faithful to sb's memory; **être f. à ses engagements** to stand by one's commitments; **rester f. à ses idées** to remain true to one's ideas; **peu f.** unfaithful; *Iron* **f. à lui-même, il a oublié mon anniversaire** true to character *or* true to form, he forgot my birthday; **comment l'as-tu trouvé? – f. à lui-même** how did you find him? – his usual self; **elle est toujours f. au poste** she never misses a day; *Mktg* **f. à la marque** brand-loyal

(b) (*exact*) (*copie, traduction, récit etc*) faithful, accurate; (*traducteur, historien, témoin*) accurate; (*mémoire, souvenir*) reliable; **la traduction n'est pas f. au texte** the translation is not faithful to the original; **le document est peu f. aux événements** the document is not a faithful *or* an accurate account of what happened

2 *n* (*partisan*) (loyal) supporter; *Com* regular *or* loyal customer; (*lecteur de journal*) regular *or* loyal reader; *TV* regular *or* loyal viewer; **je suis un f. de votre émission** I always watch *or* I never miss your programme; *Rel* **les fidèles** the faithful; (*à l'église*) the congregation

fidèlement [fidɛlmɑ̃] *adv* **(a)** (*servir*) faithfully, loyally; *Com* loyally **(b)** (*traduire, reproduire etc*) accurately, faithfully

fidélisation [fidelizasjɔ̃] *nf* **f. de la clientèle** building of customer loyalty; **f. à la marque** creation of brand loyalty

fidéliser [fidelize] *vt* (*clients, lecteurs, spectateurs etc*) to win the loyalty of; **f. la clientèle** to create customer loyalty; **f. une équipe** to keep a team together

fidélité [fidelite] *nf* **(a)** (*loyauté*) (*d'un ami, chien etc*) faithfulness; (*d'un époux*) faithfulness, fidelity; *Com* (*d'un client, lecteur, spectateur etc*) loyalty; **serment de f.** oath of allegiance; **f. conjugale** marital fidelity; **f. à ses engagements** standing by one's commitments; *Mktg* **f. du consommateur** consumer loyalty; *Mktg* **f. à la marque** brand loyalty; **f. à** *ou* **de la couleur** colour fidelity **(b)** (*exactitude*) (*d'une traduction, copie etc*) faithfulness, accuracy; (*de la mémoire*) reliability; **haute f.** high fidelity, hi-fi

Fidji [fidʒi] *nfpl* **les îles F.** Fiji, the Fiji Islands

fidjien, -ienne [fidʒjɛ̃, -jɛn] **1** *adj* Fijian **2** *nm Ling* Fijian **3** *n* **F.** Fijian

fiduciaire [fidysjɛr] **1** *adj* (*prêt, devise etc*) fiduciary; **monnaie f.** paper money; **société f.** trust company; *Jur* **en dépôt f.** in trust **2** *nm Jur* fiduciary, trustee

fiduciairement [fidysjɛrmɑ̃] *adv Jur* in trust

fief [fjɛf] *nm* **(a)** *Hist* fief **(b)** *Fig* (*spécialité*) domain **(c)** **f. électoral** loyal constituency; **un f. socialiste** a socialist stronghold

fieffé [fjefe] *adj* (*menteur, ivrogne*) inveterate

fiel [fjɛl] *nm* **(a)** (*de bœuf, volaille etc*) gall **(b)** *Fig* (*venin*) bitterness, venom, malice; **plein de f.** venomous; **épancher son f.** to vent one's spleen

fielleux, -euse [fjɛlø, -øz] *adj* bitter

fiente [fjɑ̃t] *nf* (*d'oiseaux*) droppings

fienter [fjɑ̃te] *vi* (*d'un oiseau*) to leave droppings

fier[1], **-ère** [fjɛr] **1** *adj* **(a)** (*digne*) proud; **courage f.** noble courage; **être trop f. pour mendier** to be too proud to beg; **être f. de ses enfants** to be proud of one's children; **je n'étais pas f. de moi** I wasn't proud of myself; **être f. de qch/d'avoir fait qch** to be proud of sth/of having done sth; **il n'y a pas de quoi être f.** that's nothing to boast about *or* to be proud of; **f. comme Artaban** as proud as a peacock

(b) (*hautain*) proud, haughty; **alors, on est moins f., n'est-ce pas?** not quite so high and mighty now, are we?; *F* **c'est une fille pas fière** she's not a stuck-up girl; *F* **il n'est pas f. pour deux sous** he's not at all stuck-up

(c) (*extrême*) **f. imbécile** first-rate *or* real idiot; **tu m'as fait une fière peur** you gave me a fine *or* real fright; **vous avez eu une fière idée** you've had a great idea

2 *n* **faire le f.** to show off; **il fait le f. avec sa nouvelle voiture** he's showing off with his new car; **inutile de faire le f., ça sera pareil pour toi** it's no good giving yourself airs (and graces), it'll be the same for you

fier[2] **(se)** [səfje] *vpr* (*impf & pr sub* **n. n. fiions) se f. à qn/qch** (*avoir confiance en*) to trust sb/sth; (*compter sur*) to rely on *or* count on sb/sth; **fiez-vous à moi** (*action*) leave it to me; (*renseignement*) take my word for it; **ne te fie pas aux apparences** don't trust *or* go by *or* go on appearances; **se f. à la parole de qn** to take sb's word for it, to believe sb; **ne vous y fiez pas** beware!; (*n'y croyez pas*) don't count on it

fier-à-bras, *pl* **fiers-à-bras** *nm* swaggerer, braggart

fièrement [fjɛrmɑ̃] *adv* **(a)** (*dignement*) proudly **(b)** *Arch* (*d'une manière hautaine*) haughtily **(c)** *Vieilli F* (*extrêmement*) famously

fiérot, -ote [fjero, -ɔt] *F* **1** *adj* (*personne*) cocky **2** *n* **faire le f.** to swagger (around)

fierté [fjɛrte] *nf* **(a)** (*satisfaction*) pride; **tirer f. de qch** to take pride in sth; **ma fille/maison est ma f.** my daughter/house is my pride and joy; **la réussite de l'entreprise est notre f.** we pride ourselves on the success of the venture; **c'est avec f. que je vous présente ...** I take pride in presenting to you ..., I proudly present to you ... **(b)** (*arrogance*) pride, haughtiness **(c)** (*amour-propre*) pride, self-respect

fiesta [fjɛsta] *nf F* (*fête*) binge, fling; **faire une** *ou* **la f.** to live it up, to have a wild time; **c'est la f.!** it's party time!

fièvre [fjɛvr] *nf* **(a)** *Méd* (*maladie*) fever; (*température*) temperature; **elle a 40 de f.** her temperature's at 40, she has a temperature of 40 degrees; **avoir beaucoup de f.** to have a high temperature; **avoir (de) la f.** to be feverish, to have a (high) temperature; *F* **avoir une f. de cheval** to have a raging fever

(b) (*excitation*) excitement, frenzy; **sans f.** calmly; **dans la f. de la campagne électorale** in the heat *or* excitement of the electoral campaign; **dans la f. de l'action/des débats** in the heat of the action/debates; **travailler avec f.** to work feverishly; **elle en parle avec f.** she speaks of it excitedly

(c) (*désir*) passion **(de qch** for sth); (*rage*) urge **(de faire qch** to do sth)

▶ **fièvre**: **f. amarile** *ou* **jaune** yellow fever; **f. de Malte** Malta fever; **f. paludéenne** malaria; **f. quarte** quartan fever; **f. typhoïde** typhoid (fever)

fiévreusement [fjevrøzmɑ̃] *adv* feverishly, frantically

fiévreux, -euse [fjevrø, -øz] *adj* **(a)** *Méd* (*pouls, personne etc*) feverish **(b)** *Fig* (*activité, préparations etc*) feverish, frantic; (*imagination*) feverish; (*attente*) anxious

fifille [fifij] *nf F* little girl, daughter; **f. à son papa** daddy's little girl

fifre [fifr] *nm* **(a)** (*instrument*) fife **(b)** (*joueur*) fife (player)

fifrelin [fifrəlɛ̃] *nm Vieilli* **ce ne vaut pas un f.** it's not worth a penny

fifty-fifty [fiftififti] *adv* **faire f., partager f.** to go halves *or* fifty-fifty; **partager qch f.** to share sth fifty-fifty *or* half and half

figé [fiʒe] *adj* (*sauce, huile*) congealed; (*sourire*) fixed; (*style*) stilted; (*société*) fossilized; **locution figée** set phrase; **elle est figée dans cette situation** she is stuck in this situation

figer [fiʒe] **(figeant; il figeait) 1** *vt* (*sang*) to coagulate, to congeal; (*huile, sauce*) to congeal; **des cris à vous f. le sang** bloodcurdling cries; **ce spectacle lui a figé le sang** the sight made his blood run cold; **figé sur place** rooted to the spot

2 se figer *vpr* (*du sang*) to coagulate, to congeal; (*de l'huile, d'une sauce*) to congeal; *Fig* (*d'un regard, de traits*) to freeze; **elle se fige si on lui en parle** she justs stares past you if you talk to her about it; **se f. dans une attitude/un point de vue** to persist in an attitude/a point of view; **son sang se figea (dans ses veines)** his blood ran cold; **son**

sourire se figea quand il entendit la nouvelle his smile froze when he heard the news

fignolage [fiɲɔlaʒ] *nm F* (*d'un travail, dessin etc*) touching up

fignoler [fiɲɔle] *F* **1** *vt* (*travail, dessin etc*) to put the finishing touches to, to touch up **2** *vi* to be meticulous

fignoleur, -euse [fiɲɔlœr, -øz] **1** *adj* meticulous **2** *n* perfectionist, meticulous worker

figue [fig] *nf* (*fruit*) fig; **f. de Barbarie** prickly pear

figuier [figje] *nm* fig (tree); **f. de Barbarie** prickly pear

figurant, -ante [figyrɑ̃, -ɑ̃t] *n Th* walk-on, supernumerary, *F* super; *Cin* extra; **rôle de f.** *Th* walk-on (part), bit part; *Cin* bit part; *Fig* **avoir un rôle de f. dans qch, n'être qu'un f. dans qch** to take no active part *or* be just an onlooker in sth

figuratif, -ive [figyratif, -iv] **1** *adj* (*plan*) figurative; (*art, artiste*) figurative, representational **2** *n* figurative *or* representational artist

figuration [figyrasjɔ̃] *nf* **(a)** (*représentation*) figuration, representation **(b)** *Th* (*acteurs*) walk-on actors, *F* supers; (*rôle*) walk-on (part), bit part; **faire de la f.** to do walk-on parts, to play bit parts **(c)** *Cin* (*acteurs*) extras; (*rôle*) bit part; **faire de la f.** to play bit parts

figurativement [figyrativmɑ̃] *adv* figuratively

figure [figyr] *nf* **(a)** (*visage*) face; **jeter qch à la f. de qn** to throw sth in sb's face; *F* **casser la f. à qn** to smash sb's face in; *F* **se casser la f.** to fall flat on one's face; *Fig* (*échouer*) to come a cropper; **je me suis cassé la f. en vélo/dans les escaliers** I fell off my bike/down the stairs

(b) (*mine*) face, *Fml* countenance; **faire bonne f. à qn** to act pleasantly towards sb; **faire bonne f.** to make a good impression; **faire une drôle de f.** to pull a face, to give a funny look; **faire triste f.** to pull a long face; **ne plus avoir f. humaine** to be totally disfigured; *Hum* **mes vieilles chaussures n'ont plus f. humaine** my old shoes are falling to pieces

(c) (*représentation, image*) figure; **figures de cire** waxworks, waxwork figures; *Cartes* **les figures** *Br* the court cards, the face cards; **figures géométriques** geometrical figures; **livre avec figures dans le texte** book with figures *or* diagrams in the text; **prendre f.** to take shape; **faire f. de riche** to give an impression of wealth; **elle fait f. d'intellectuelle dans ce milieu** she gives the impression of *or* has the appearance of an intellectual amongst these people; **faire pauvre** *ou* **piètre f.** to cut a sorry figure

(d) (*personnage*) figure; **les grandes figures de la Guerre** the great figures of the War

(e) (*de danseur, patineur etc*) figure; **figures libres** freestyle; **figures imposées** compulsory figures

(f) *Ling* figure; **f. de mots** *ou* **de rhétorique** figure of speech; **f. de style** stylistic device

figure de proue *nf* (*d'un bateau, Fig d'un parti politique etc*) figurehead

figuré [figyre] **1** *adj* **(a)** (*plan*) diagrammatic **(b)** *Ling* **sens f.** figurative meaning **2** *nm Ling* **au f.** in the figurative sense, figuratively; **au propre comme au f.** literally and figuratively

figurément [figyremɑ̃] *adv* figuratively

figurer [figyre] **1** *vt* to represent; **une croix figure une église sur le plan** a cross stands for *or* represents *or* indicates a church on the map; **la scène figure le camp des brigands** the scene shows *or* represents the brigands' camp

2 *vi* **(a)** (*se trouver*) to appear, to figure; **je ne veux pas que mon nom figure dans l'affaire/le livre** I don't want my name to appear *or* figure in the matter/the book; **f. dans un catalogue/une bibliographie** to be listed *or* appear in a catalogue/a bibliography; **voici les chevaux qui figurent à l'arrivée** here are the names of the winning horses

(b) *Th* to have a walk-on (part); *Cin* to have a bit part

3 se figurer *vpr* to imagine (**que** that); **se f. qch** to imagine sth; **figurez-vous la situation** imagine the situation, picture the situation (to yourself); **ne vous figurez pas que je sois satisfait** don't get the idea that I'm satisfied; **si tu te figures que je vais te pardonner, tu te trompes** if you imagine I'm going to forgive you, you're mistaken; **je suis à sec, figure-toi** believe it or not, I'm broke; **figure-toi que nous aussi on a loué une maison dans ce village** would you believe it, we've rented a house in that village as well

figurine [figyrin] *nf* figurine, statuette

fil [fil] *nm* **(a)** *Tex* (*brin*) thread, yarn; (*de toile d'araignée*) thread; (*tissu*) linen; **f. de coton/nylon** cotton/nylon thread *or* yarn; **f. de lin** linen yarn *or* thread; **des draps pur f.** (pure) linen sheets; **gants de f.** cotton gloves; **laine trois/quatre fils** three-/four-ply wool; *Fig* **astuce cousue de f. blanc** obvious *or* blatant trick; *Fig* **c'est cousu de f. blanc** you can see right through it, it won't fool anybody; *Fig* **de f. en aiguille** little by little, bit by bit, gradually; **démêler les fils d'une intrigue** to unravel the threads of a plot; *Fig* **trouver le f. d'Ariane** *ou* **le f. conducteur** to find the clue (to the mystery); **il n'y a pas de f. conducteur dans ce roman** there's no unifying thread in this novel; **mince comme un f.** as thin as a rake

(b) (*de câble, corde etc*) strand; (*de marionnette*) string; *Fig* **c'est lui qui tient les fils** he's the one who holds (all) the strings; *Fig* **être dans le droit f. de qch** to be in line with sth; **le droit f. du parti n'a pas changé depuis dix ans** the party line hasn't changed in ten years; *Fig* **sa vie ne tenait qu'à un f.** his life hung by a thread; **il ne tenait qu'à un f. qu'il soit renvoyé** it was touch and go whether he would be dismissed; *F* **avoir un f. à la patte** (*être tenu par un engagement*) to be tied down; *F* **se mettre un f. à la patte** to tie oneself down; *Sp* **être coiffé sur le f.** to be pipped at the post, to be beaten at the wire

(c) (*métallique*) wire; *F* **donner du f. à retordre à qn** to give sb trouble

(d) *Él* **f. (électrique)** (electric) wire; **f. (souple)** lead, cord, *Br* flex; **f. téléphonique** telephone wire; *Tél* **donner** *ou* **passer un coup de f. à qn** to give sb a call, to call sb (up), *Br* to give sb a ring, *Br* to ring sb (up); **recevoir** *ou* **avoir un coup de f. de qn** to get a (phone) call from sb; **être au bout du f.** to be on the line *or* phone; **je viens d'avoir Martin au bout du f.** I've just had Martin on the line *or* phone; **télégraphie/téléphonie sans f.** wireless telegraphy/telephony; **téléphone sans f.** cordless telephone

(e) (*de bois, viande*) grain; **les haricots verts ont des fils** *ou* **sont pleins de fils** the green beans are stringy; **haricots sans fils** stringless beans; **contre le f., à contre-f.** against *or* across the grain; **dans le sens du f.** with the grain; **couper dans le droit f.** (*bois*) to cut along the grain; (*tissu*) to cut on the straight

(f) *Fig* (*cours*) **au f. de l'eau** with the current, downstream; **se laisser aller au f. de l'eau** to let oneself drift (with the current); **au f. des jours/semaines/heures** as the days/weeks/hours go by, with the passing days/weeks/hours; **le f. des événements** the chain of events; **perdre/reprendre le f. de la conversation** to lose/pick up the thread of the conversation; **j'ai perdu le f., je ne sais plus où j'en suis** I've lost the thread, I don't know where I am any more; **suivre le f. des idées de qn** to follow the thread of sb's ideas

(g) (*d'un couteau, d'une épée etc*) edge; **donner le f. à un rasoir** to put an edge on a razor; *Fig* **le président est sur le f. du rasoir** the president is on a knife edge; *Litt* **passer des prisonniers au f. de l'épée** to put prisoners to the sword

▶ **fil**: **f. à bâtir** basting thread; **f. de bougie** (spark) plug lead; **f. à coudre** (sewing) thread, cotton; **f. à couper le beurre** cheesewire; *Fig* **il n'a pas inventé le f. à couper le beurre** he'll never set the Thames on fire; **f. dentaire** dental floss; **f. d'Écosse** lisle thread; **chaussettes en f. d'Écosse** lisle socks; **f. de fer** wire; **fil(s) de fer barbelé(s)** barbed wire; **f. de masse** *ou* **de terre** earth (wire), *Am* ground (wire); **f. de la vierge** gossamer

filage [filaʒ] *nm Tex* spinning

filament [filamɑ̃] *nm* **(a)** (*de viande*) fibre, *US* fiber; (*de lampe électrique*) filament; **ça a trop de filaments pour être mangé** it's too stringy to eat **(b)** *Biol* filament

filamenteux, -euse [filamɑ̃tø, -øz] *adj* filamentous

filandière [filɑ̃djɛr] *nf Arch Tex* (hand-)spinner

filandreux, -euse [filɑ̃drø, -øz] *adj* **(a)** (*viande, légumes*) stringy **(b)** *Fig Péj* (*explication, phrase etc*) involved, confused

filant [filɑ̃] *adj* **(a)** (*qui coule*) fluid **(b)** **étoile filante** shooting star, falling star

filasse [filas] **1** *nf* (*matière*) tow; **f. de chanvre** hemp **2** *adj inv* **cheveux (blond) f.** tow-coloured hair; **aux cheveux (blond) f.** tow-headed, tow-haired

filateur [filatœr] *nm* (spinning) mill owner

filature [filatyr] *nf* **(a)** *Tex* (*action*) spinning **(b)** (*fabrique*) (spinning) mill; **f. de coton** cotton mill **(c)** (*par un détective etc*) shadowing, tailing; **il a été pris en f.** he was shadowed *or* tailed

fil-de-fériste, *pl* **fil-de-féristes** [fildəferist] *n* high-wire artist

file [fil] *nf* **(a)** (*de gens, voitures etc*) line; **f. (d'attente)** queue, *Am* line; *Av* stacking; **se mettre** *ou* **se ranger en f.** to line up; **prendre la f., se mettre à la f.** to join the queue *or Am* line; *Ordinat* **f. d'attente** print queue *or* list; **mettre en f. d'attente** to spool; **marcher à la f.** *ou* **en f.** to walk in single file *or* one behind another; **à la** *ou* **en f. indienne** in single *or* Indian file; **entrer/sortir en f.** *ou* **à la f.** to file in/out; **cinq bières à la f.** five beers in a row *or* in succession *or* one after another; **trois jours à la f.** *ou* **de f.** three days in a row *or* in succession; *Aut* **stationner en double f.** to double-park

(b) *Aut* (*couloir*) lane; **ne changez pas de f.** keep in lane; **rouler dans** *ou* **sur la f. de droite** to drive in the right-hand lane

filé [file] **1** *adj* **(a)** (*bas, collant*) with a run, *Br* laddered **(b)** **verre f.** spun glass **2** *nm Tex, Tech* thread; **f. d'or** gold thread

filer [file] **1** *vt* **(a)** (*coton, verre etc*) to spin; *Fig* **f. des jours heureux** to live very happily; *F* **ils filent le parfait amour** they are living love's dream

(b) *Naut* (*câble*) to pay out, to run out; (*amarres*) to slip

(c) (*métaphore*) to spin out, to draw out; *Mus* (*note*) to draw out, to sustain; (*huile*) to pour out in a trickle; *Cartes* **f. les cartes** to lay the cards down slowly; **il m'a filé entre les doigts** he slipped between my fingers

(d) (*d'un détective etc*) (*suspect*) to shadow, to tail

(e) *F* (*donner*) **f. qch à qn** to give sb sth; **je lui ai filé ma voiture/un conseil** I gave him my car/a piece of advice; **f. un coup de pied/une gifle à qn** to give sb a kick/a slap; **f. de l'aide** *ou* **un coup de main à qn** to give sb a hand

(f) (*démailler*) (*bas, collant*) to put a run in, *Br* to ladder

2 *vi* **(a)** (*passer très vite*) **le temps file** time flies; **laisser f. un câble** to pay out a cable; **l'argent lui file entre les mains** *ou* **les doigts** money runs through his hands *or* fingers like water; **train qui file à toute vitesse** train rushing along at full speed; **les voitures filaient sur la route** cars were speeding along the road; *Naut* **f. (à) vingt nœuds** to proceed at twenty knots

(b) *F* (*partir en vitesse*) to dash *or* rush off; **f. (en douce)** to slip away *or* off; **allez, filez!** clear off!, scram!; (*dépêchez-vous*) off you go!; **f. à l'anglaise** to leave; (*sans se faire remarquer*) to slip away; (*pour éviter qn* (*qch*)) to do a runner

(c) *F* **f. doux** to toe the line, to behave oneself

(d) (*de bas, collant*) to run, *Br* to ladder; **j'ai un bas qui file** I've got a run *or Br* ladder

(e) la lampe file the lamp is smoking

(f) (*de l'huile etc*) to run

filet[1] [filɛ] *nm* **(a)** (*de lumière*) thin streak; (*d'air*) thin stream; (*d'eau, de bave*) trickle, dribble; (*de sang*) trickle; (*de fumée etc*) thread, wisp; **f. de voix** thin *or* weak voice; *Culin* **ajoutez-y un f. de citron/vinaigre** add a dash of lemon/vinegar; **f. d'une vis** thread *or Spéc* worm of a screw **(b)** *Anat* (*de la langue*) frenum, string **(c)** *Bot* (*d'étamine*) filament **(d)** (*de reliure*), *Archit* filet **(e)** *Typ* rule **(f)** *Culin* (*de poisson, bœuf etc*) fillet; **f. mignon** filet mignon (*small fillet steak*) **(g)** (*de harnais*) snaffle

filet[2] *nm* **(a)** (*ouvrage à mailles*) net; (*au cirque*) (safety) net; **f. de pêche** fishing net; **f. à papillons** butterfly net; **être pris au f.** to be caught with a net; *Fig* **faire tomber** *ou* **attirer qn dans ses filets** to ensnare sb; **un beau coup de f. pour la police** a good haul for the police; **travailler sans f.** (*d'un trapéziste*) to work without a net; *Fig* to go out on a limb, to take risks; **f. à provisions** string *or* net bag; **f. pour cheveux** hairnet; *Rail* **f. à bagages** luggage rack **(b)** *Tennis, Fb etc* net; *Tennis* **monter au f.** to go up to the net; **balle de f.** let (ball); **juge de f.** net-cord judge

filetage [filtaʒ] *nm Tech* **(a)** (*action*) threading, screw cutting **(b)** (*filets*) (*de vis*) thread, *Spéc* worm; *MecE* **f. Acmé** Acme thread; **f. Whitworth** Whitworth thread

fileter [filte] *vt* **(je filète; je filèterai)** *Tech* **(a)** (*métal*) to wiredraw; (*fil*) to draw **(b)** (*boulon, tige etc*) to thread, to screw

fileur, -euse [filœr, -øz] *n Tex* (*de métier à tisser*) spinner

filial, -ale, -aux, -ales [filjal] **1** *adj* filial **2** *nf Com* **filiale** subsidiary (company); **filiale consolidée** consolidated subsidiary; **filiale de distribution** marketing subsidiary; **filiale de vente** sales subsidiary

filialement [filjalmɑ̃] *adv* filially

filiation [filjasjɔ̃] *nf* **(a)** (*lien de parenté*) filiation; **en f. directe** in direct line; **un descendant en f. directe** a direct descendant **(b)** *Litt* (*famille*) descendants **(c)** *Fig* (*de mots, d'événements etc*) relationship (**de** between); **des théories en f. directe avec ce texte** theories directly related to this text

filière [filjɛr] *nf* **(a)** *Admin* channels; **la f. administrative** the (usual) official channels; **passer par** *ou* **suivre la f.** (*pour obtenir qch*) to go through official channels; (*comme employé*) to work one's way up; **choisir la f. nucléaire** to go down the nuclear road, to choose the nuclear path; *Scol* **suivre une f. scientifique/commerciale** to study scientific/business subjects

(b) (*de trafiquants, terroristes etc*) network; **remonter la f.** to go back along the network (to the person at the top); **démanteler une f.** to break up a ring

(c) *Tech* (*pour fileter une vis*) screw plate; (*pour étirer*) draw(ing) plate; **travailler un métal à la f.** to draw a metal

(d) *Zool* (*d'une araignée, d'un ver à soie*) spinneret

(e) *Fin* **f. électronique** electronic transfer

filiforme [filifɔrm] *adj* **(a)** *Zool* filiform, threadlike **(b)** *F* (*très mince*) (*personne, jambes etc*) spindly

filigrane [filigran] *nm* **(a)** (*ouvrage d'orfèvrerie*) filigree; **broche en f.** filigree brooch **(b)** (*de papier, billet de banque etc*) watermark; *Fig* **lire en f.** to read between the lines; **apparaître en f. dans qch** to be implicit in sth

filigrané [filigrane] *adj* **(a)** (*broche*) filigreed **(b)** (*papier*) watermarked

filin [filɛ̃] *nm* rope

fille [fij] *nf* **(a)** (*descendante directe*) daughter; *Fig* **la superstition est (la) f. de l'ignorance** superstition is born of ignorance

(b) (*enfant*) girl; **petite f.** little girl; **jeune f.** girl, young woman; **faire la jeune f. de la maison** (*à un cocktail*) to pass *or* hand round the snacks; **ma pauvre f.!** my poor child *or* dear!; **nom de jeune f.** maiden name; **école de filles** girls' school; *Fig* **jouer la f. de l'air** to escape, to get out

(c) (*femme*) woman; **vieille f.** old maid, spinster; **habitudes de vieille f.** old-maidish habits; *Vieilli* **rester f.** to remain single *or* unmarried

(d) *Rel* **les filles de Port-Royal** the sisters *or* nuns of Port-Royal

▶ **fille**: **f. de cuisine** kitchenmaid; **f. de ferme** farm girl; **f. d'honneur** maid of honour; *surtout Vieilli* **f. de joie** fille de joie, prostitute; **f. à matelots** prostitute (*whose customers are primarily sailors*); **f. publique** prostitute; **f. des rues** streetwalker; **f. de salle** (*dans un hôtel*) waitress; (*dans un hôpital*) nursing auxiliary; **f. de service** maidservant; *Vieilli* **f. à soldats** prostitute (*whose customers are primarily soldiers*)

fille-mère, *pl* **filles-mères** *nf Péj, Vieilli* unmarried mother

fillette [fijɛt] *nf* **(a)** (*petite fille*) little girl **(b)** *Arg* (*bouteille*) (*de vin*) half-bottle

filleul, -eule [fijœl] **1** *nm* godson, godchild; **f. de guerre** = soldier in action 'adopted' by a woman, who sends letters, parcels etc **2** *nf* **filleule** goddaughter, godchild

film [film] *nm* **(a)** *Phot* film

(b) *Cin* (*pellicule*) film; (*œuvre*) film, picture, movie, *Am* motion picture; **le f.** (*art*) film, cinema; **tourner un f.** to make a film; *F* **il n'a rien compris au f.** he hasn't taken anything in

(c) *Fig* (*déroulement*) (*d'événements*) sequence; **revoir le f. de sa vie** to look back over one's life

(d) (*couche*) film; **f. alimentaire** cling film; **f. dentaire** (dental) plaque; **sous f. plastique** shrink-wrapped; **f. transparent** transparency; **recouvert d'un f. protecteur** covered with a protective film

▶ **film**: **f. d'action** action film, action movie; **f. d'actualité** newsreel, news film; **f. d'animation** animated film, cartoon; **f. d'archives** library film; **f. d'aventures** adventure film; **f. catastrophe** disaster film; **f. documentaire** documentary film; **f. dramatique** drama; **f. d'entreprise** corporate film, corporate video; **f. d'espionnage** spy film; **f. d'épouvante** horror film or movie, thriller; **f. à faible budget** low-budget movie; **film fantastique** science fiction film; **f. de genre** genre film; **f. à gros succès** blockbuster movie; **f. de guerre** war film; **f. d'horreur** horror film *or* movie, **f. institutionnel** corporate video; **f. long métrage** feature film; **f. muet** silent film, silent movie; **f. noir** film noir; **f. parlant** talkie; **f. plat** two-dimensional film; **f. policier** detective film; **f. porno(graphique)** pornographic film, blue movie; **f. publicitaire** promotional film; **f. en relief** stereoscopic film; **f. de science-fiction** science fiction film; **f. semi-documentaire** semi-documentary; **f. sonore** sound film; **f. à succès** box-office hit; **f. de suspense** thriller; **f. télévisé** television film; **f. en 3D** 3D film; **f. vidéo** video film

filmage [filmaʒ] *nm Cin* filming

filmer [filme] **1** *vt* **(a)** *Tech* (*enduire*) to cover with a film **(b)** *Cin* to film; (*scène*) to film, to shoot **2** *vi Cin* to film

filmique [filmik] *adj* cinematic, filmic

filmographie [filmɔgrafi] *nf Cin* filmography

filmologie [filmɔlɔʒi] *nf* film studies

filmothèque [filmɔtɛk] *nf* microfilm library

filoguidé [filogide] *adj* wire-guided

filon [filɔ̃] *nm* **(a)** *Min* vein, seam, lode **(b)** *F* (*situation lucrative*) cushy job; **il tient le f., il a déniché** *ou* **trouvé le (bon) f.** he's struck it rich; *Fig* **trouver un f.** to find a goldmine; **j'ai un bon f. pour avoir des vidéos gratuites** I know where I can get free videos easily

filou [filu] *nm* **(a)** (*escroc*) rogue, swindler, crook **(b)** (*enfant*) rascal, rogue

filoutage [filutaʒ] *nm* swindling, cheating

filouter [filute] *vt* **(a)** *Vieilli* **f. qch à qn** to steal sth from sb **(b) f. qn** to swindle *or* cheat sb

filouterie [filutri] *nf* **(a)** (*action*) swindling, cheating **(b)** (*manœuvre*) swindle, fraud

fils [fis] *nm* son; **elle et ses deux f.** she and her two boys *or* sons; **c'est bien le f. de son père** he's a chip off the old block; **être le f. de ses œuvres** to be a self-made man; **c'est le f.**

spirituel de René Char he's the spiritual son of René Char; **M. Duval f.** Mr Duval junior; **le f. Duval** young Duval; *Rel* **le F. de Dieu/de l'homme** the Son of God/of Man

▶ **fils**: **f. de famille** young man of good social standing; *Péj* **f. à papa** daddy's boy; *Vulg* **f. de pute** son of a bitch

filtrage [filtraʒ] *nm* **(a)** (*d'un liquide, gaz, son etc*) filtering **(b)** *Fig* (*contrôle*) (*des informations, visiteurs etc*) screening

filtrant [filtrɑ̃] *adj* filtering; **verre f.** filter glass; **lunettes à verres filtrants** glasses with filter lenses

filtration [filtrasjɔ̃] *nf* filtration, filtering

filtre [filtr] *nm Tech, Phot, Él etc* filter; **(bout) f.** filter (tip); **je fume des (cigarettes) f.** I smoke filter-tipped cigarettes *or* filter tips; **(café) f.** filter coffee; **papier f.** filter paper

▶ **filtre**: **f. à air** air filter; *Rad, TV* **f. anti-parasites** interference filter *or* suppressor; **f. audio** audio filter; **f. à brouillard** (*pour une caméra*) fog filter; **f. à café** coffee filter; **f. à carburant** fuel filter; **f. au charbon** carbon filter; **f. à combustible** fuel filter; **f. correcteur** corrective filter; **f. couleur** colour medium; *Phot* **f. de couleur** *ou* **coloré** colour filter; *Ordinat* **f. écran** screen filter; **f. à essence** petrol filter; **f. à huile** oil filter; *Ordinat* **f. d'importation/exportation** import/export filter; **f. à particules** dust filter; **f. à pollen** pollen filter; *TV, Cin* **f. pour objectif de caméra** camera lens filter

filtrer [filtre] **1** *vt* **(a)** (*eau, café, gaz, son, lumière etc*) to filter **(b)** *Fig* (*contrôler*) (*informations, visiteurs etc*) to screen **2** *vi* (*d'un liquide*) to filter, to percolate, to seep **(à travers** through); (*d'une nouvelle*) to leak out, to filter out; **la lumière filtrait à travers** *ou* **par les branches** the light filtered through the branches; **ils n'ont rien laissé f. de ses déclarations** they have said nothing about his statement, *F* they're keeping a very tight lid on what he said

fin¹ [fɛ̃] *nf* **(a)** (*dernier moment*) (*de film, réunion, travail etc*) end, conclusion; (*de contrat, de bail etc*) expiry, expiration; (*d'empire, de régime etc*) end, fall; (*d'un espoir, de malheurs etc*) end; (*mort*) end, death; *Cin* **'f.'** 'The End'; **le cinquième en partant de la f.** the fifth from the end, the last but four; **f. du jour** close of day; **f. du mois** end of the month; *Com* **f. de mois** monthly statement; **de f. de mois** end-of-month; **assurer ses fins de mois** to make sure one has enough money at the end of the month; **avoir des fins de mois difficiles** to be always short of money at the end of the month; **f. de l'exercice** end of the financial year; **de f. d'exercice** year-end; **en f. d'exercice** at the end of the financial year; **payable f. courant/prochain** payable at the end of this/next month; **on se reverra f. mars** *ou* **à la f. de mars** we'll meet again at the end of March; **en f. de soirée** towards the end of the evening; **il a faibli en f. de trimestre** his work fell off towards the end of the term; **il est venu vers la f. de l'après-midi** he came late in *or* towards the end of the afternoon; **en f. d'année** at the end of the year; **jusqu'à la f. des temps** *ou* **des siècles** till the end of time; **le vocabulaire est à la f. du livre** the vocabulary is at the back of the book; **à la f. de la liste, en f. de liste** at the bottom *or* end of the list; **sans f.** (*emploi adjectival*) endless; (*plaintes, interrogatoire*) endless, never-ending; (*emploi adverbial*) endlessly; **vis sans f.** endless screw; **il parle sans f.** he never stops talking, he talks endlessly; **f. prématurée** untimely death *or* end; **il a eu une belle f. /une f. affreuse** he had a good/terrible end *or* death; **on sent bien que la f. n'est pas loin** we've a feeling the end is not far away *or* it can't be long now; **vers la f., il n'était plus le même** he wasn't the same towards the end; **le lave-vaisselle est sur sa f.** the dishwasher is on its last legs; **toucher** *ou* **tirer à sa f.** (*d'un projet, d'une union*) to come *or* draw to an end *or* a close; **l'année touche** *ou* **tire à sa f.** the year is drawing to an end *or* a close; **votre participation touche à sa f.** your participation will soon be over *or* at an end; **le contrat touche à sa f.** the contract will expire soon; **être en f. de course** (*d'une vis*) to be screwed fully home; (*d'un piston*) to have reached the end of its stroke; *Fig* (*d'une personne*) to have come to the end of the road; **chômeur en f. de droits** unemployed person who is coming to the end of his benefit; **mettre f. à qch** to put an end *or* a stop to sth; **mettre f. à sa vie** *ou* **ses jours** to put an end to one's life; **elle se marie pour faire une f.** she's getting married in order to settle down; **prendre f., avoir une f.** to come to an end; **mener une affaire à bonne f.** to bring a matter to a successful conclusion, to deal successfully with a matter; **c'est la f.** this is the end; **la f. du monde** the end of the world; **ce n'est pas la f. du monde** it's not the end of the world; *F* **c'est la f. de tout** that's the (absolute) end; **c'est Patrick qui a dit** *ou* **eu le mot de la f.** it was Patrick who had the last *or* final word; **à la f. il répondit** in the end *or* finally *or* at last he answered; *F* **tu es stupide à la f.** you really are very stupid; **tu m'ennuies à la f.!** you're really annoying me!; **en f. de compte** (*après tout*) in the end, after all; (*tout bien considéré*) all things considered, taking everything into account; (*pour conclure*) finally, to conclude; *F* **à la f. des fins** when all's said and done, at the end of the day

(b) (*but*) end, aim, purpose; **la f. justifie les moyens** the end justifies the means; **arriver** *ou* **parvenir** *ou* **en venir à ses fins** to achieve one's ends *or* aims *or* purpose, to get what one wants; **une f. en soi** an end in itself; **à cette f. il faut avoir beaucoup de patience** to this end *or* in order to achieve this one must have a lot of patience; **à quelle f.?** for what purpose?, to what end?, with what end in view?; **je vous le fais parvenir à toutes fins utiles** I'm sending it to you should you need it; **aux fins de faire qch** with a view to doing sth; **à seule(s) fin(s) de l'aider** for the sole purpose of helping him; *Jur* **aux fins de débauche** for immoral purposes

(c) *Jur* **renvoyé des fins de la plainte** discharged, acquitted

▶ **fin**: *Ordinat* **f. de ligne** line end; *Ordinat* **f. de page** pagebreak; *Ordinat* **f. de page obligatoire** hard page break; *Ordinat* **f. de paragraphe** paragraph break; **f. de race:** *adj inv* **comportement f. de race** degenerate behaviour; *Com* **f. de série** discontinued line; *Ordinat* **f. de session enregistrée à ...** logoff timed at ...; **f. de siècle:** *adj inv* **style/mœurs f. de siècle** fin de siècle *or* decadent style/morals

fin², fine¹ [fɛ̃, fin] **1** *adj* **(a)** (*mince*) (*papier, tranche*) thin; (*étoffe*) fine, thin; (*cheveux, pluie, grains, sable, aiguille, pointe*) fine; (*traits*) fine, delicate; (*silhouette*) slender; (*cheville*) neat

(b) (*de première qualité*) fine, first-class; **vins fins** choice *or* fine wines; **or f.** pure *or* fine gold; **lingerie fine** fine lingerie; **des souliers fins** elegant shoes; **un repas f.** a choice *or* exquisite meal; **fines herbes** mixed herbs, fines herbes; **épicerie fine** delicatessen

(c) (*expert*) fine; **f. connaisseur de vins** fine judge of wine; **f. tireur** crack shot; **fine lame** fine swordsman; **f. stratège** fine *or* expert strategist; **fine cuisinière** gourmet cook; **avoir l'ouïe fine** to have sharp ears *or* an acute ear *or* a keen ear; **avoir le nez f.** to have a keen sense of smell; *Fig* **elle a le nez f.** she's sharp

(d) (*subtil*) subtle; **une fine mouche** a sharp customer; **fine ironie** subtle irony; **il est trop f. pour vous** he's too clever for you; **elle n'est pas très fine, cette jeune femme** that young woman isn't very bright; **bien f. qui le prendra** it would take a smart man to catch him; *Iron* **qu'est-ce que c'est f.!** oh, very funny!

(e) dans le f. fond du hangar/du panier right at the back of the shed/the bottom of the basket; **au f. fond de la Sibérie** in deepest Siberia; **au f. fond de moi** in my heart of hearts; **le f. mot de l'histoire** the truth of the matter

2 *nm* **(a) le f. du f.** the ultimate, the nec plus ultra

(b) jouer au (plus) f. to have a battle of wits

3 *adv* **(a) tout était f. prêt** everything was absolutely ready; **être f. soûl** to be blind drunk

(b) (*finement*) finely; **café moulu f.** finely ground coffee; **des crayons taillés f.** sharp-pointed pencils

final, -ale, -als, -ales [final] *adj* **(a)** final; *Sp* **les épreuves finales** the finals; **point f.** full stop, *Am* period; *Fig* **mettre un point f. à une affaire** to put a stop *or* an end to a matter; **va te coucher, point f.!** bed time! and that's final! **(b)** *Phil, Gram* (*cause, proposition*) final

finale [final] **1** *nf* **(a)** *Sp* final; **f. de coupe** cup final; **aller/être en f.** to go *or* get through to/to be in the finals **(b)** (*de mot*) final *or* end syllable **2** *nm Mus* (*d'opéra etc*) finale

finalement [finalmɑ̃] *adv* in the end, finally

finaliser [finalize] *vt* to finalize

finaliste [finalist] *adj, n* finalist

finalité [finalite] *nf* (*objectif*) aim, objective; *Phil* finality; *Biol* adaptation

finance [finɑ̃s] *nf* **(a)** finance; **monde de la f.** financial world, world of finance; **la haute f.** high finance; (*le milieu*) the financiers, the bankers; **être dans la f.** to be in finance; *F* **faire qch moyennant f.** to do sth for a consideration *or* for a fee **(b) finances** finances; **nos finances sont mal en point** our finances are in bad shape; **lois de finances** financial laws; **ministre des Finances** minister of Finance, *Br* ≈ Chancellor of the Exchequer, *US* ≈ Secretary of the Treasury; **le Ministère des Finances** the Treasury

financement [finɑ̃smɑ̃] *nm* financing, funding; (*surtout d'un mécène*) (financial) backing; **f. à court terme** short-term financing; **f. par endettement** debt financing; **f. à long terme** long-term financing; **f. à moyen terme** medium-term financing

financer [finɑ̃se] *vt* **(je finançai(s), n. finançons)** to finance, to fund; (*surtout d'un mécène*) to back, to put up the money for

financier, -ière [finɑ̃sje, -jɛr] **1** *adj* financial; **avoir des problèmes financiers** to be in financial *or Fml* pecuniary difficulties; **crise financière** financial crisis; **le marché f.** the money market; *Culin* **sauce financière** = white sauce containing small pieces of sweetbread, dumplings and mushrooms **2** *nm* financier

financièrement [finɑ̃sjɛrmɑ̃] *adv* financially

finasser [finase] *vi* to resort to trickery

finasserie [finasri] *nf* trick

finasseur, -euse [finasœr, -øz], **finassier, -ière** [finasje, -jɛr] *n Vieilli* trickster

finaud, -aude [fino, -od] **1** *adj* wily, cunning **2** *n* crafty devil

finauderie [finodri] *nf* trickery

fine[2] [fin] *nf* liqueur brandy; **une f. à l'eau** = a brandy and soda

finement [finmɑ̃] *adv* **(a)** (*délicatement*) finely, delicately **(b)** (*subtilement*) (*analyser, apprécier*) subtly; **elle avait f. prévu ce coup-là** she had shrewdly *or* cleverly foreseen that that would happen

finesse [finɛs] *nf* **(a)** (*d'un tissu*) fineness; (*d'exécution*) delicacy; (*du sable*) fineness; (*de taille*) slenderness, slimness **(b)** (*subtilité*) subtlety; **f. d'ouïe/de l'odorat** keenness *or* acuteness of hearing/of smell; **f. de goût** good taste; **f. d'esprit** shrewdness; **discours plein de f.** speech full of subtlety *or* finesse; **elle a beaucoup de finesse** she's very shrewd; **parodie pleine de f.** clever *or* subtle parody; **finesses d'un métier** niceties *or* subtleties *or* fine points of a craft; **il connaît toutes les finesses du métier** he knows all the tricks of the trade **(c)** (*d'une pointe, d'une image optique etc*) sharpness; (*d'une lame*) keenness

finette [finɛt] *nf Tex* brushed cotton

fini [fini] **1** *adj* **(a)** (*terminé*) finished, over; **c'est f. (tout cela), tout est f.** that's all over (and done with); **c'est f. entre nous** we're finished, it's all over between us; **(c'est) f. de rire** the fun's over; **c'est un homme f.** he's finished, he's done for **(b)** (*ouvrage*) well finished; **cette robe est mal finie** this dress is badly finished; *Péj* **un idiot f.** a complete idiot; **un alcoolo/voleur f.** an out-and-out drunkard/thief **(c)** (*espace, temps, nombre*) finite **2** *nm* **(a)** (*d'un produit manufacturé*) finish **(b) le f. et l'infini** the finite and the infinite

finir [finir] **1** *vt* (*tâche, études, conversation etc*) to finish; (*vie*) to end; **f. un tableau/une sculpture** to finish (off) a picture/sculpture; **tu as fini ton assiette?** have you finished what's on your plate?; **ils ont fini la soirée au poste** the evening ended with them in the police station; **je vais f. ces chaussures** I'll wear these shoes out

2 *vi* to end, to finish; **quand est-ce que ça finit?** when does it end *or* finish?; **comment est-ce que ça a fini?** how did it end?; **à quelle heure tu finis?** what time do you finish?; **f. en pointe** to end *or* terminate in a point; **une histoire qui finit bien/mal** a story with a happy/sad ending; **tout est bien qui finit bien** all's well that ends well; **il finira mal** he'll come to a bad end; **ça va mal f. tout ça!** no good will come of all that!, it will all end in disaster!; **l'histoire ne finit pas là** that's not the end of the story; **f. à l'hôpital/dans un fossé** to end up *or* finish up in hospital/a ditch; **en f. avec qn/qch** to be *or* have done with sb/sth; **il faut en f. avec ces idées reçues** we must break with *or* shake off these preconceived ideas; **je voudrais en f.** I want to get it over (with); **il voulait en f. (avec la vie)** he wanted to put an end to it all *or* to end it all; **vous n'avez pas encore fini tous les deux!** are you two still at it!; *F* **c'est pas bientôt fini, ce bordel?** is this racket going to stop soon?; **cela n'en finit pas** there's no end to it; **il n'en finit plus de se préparer dans la salle de bain** he takes ages in the bathroom getting ready; **pour f.** to cut a long story short; **histoires/ennuis à n'en plus f.** endless *or* interminable stories/problems; **et pour f., voici le dessert** and to finish (with), here's dessert; **cette route n'en finit pas** this road seems to go on (and on) for ever; **elle a des jambes à n'en plus f.** she has incredibly long legs; **f. de faire qch** to finish doing sth; **f. par faire qch** to end up (by) doing sth; **tu vas f. par le faire pleurer** you'll end up (by) making him cry; **elle finira par t'oublier/s'y habituer** she'll forget you/get used to it in the end *or* eventually; **la justice finit par triompher** justice triumphs in the end *or* in the long run *or* eventually; **tout finit toujours par arriver** everything comes to those who wait

finish [finiʃ] *nm Sp* (*fin*) finish; (*impulsion finale*) finish, final burst; **il a un bon f.** he has a strong finish; *Fig* **on l'a eu au f.** we got him in the end

finissage [finisaʒ] *nm Ind* finishing (off)

finissant [finisɑ̃] *adj* finishing; (*société*) in decline; **le jour f.** dusk, twilight

finisseur, -euse [finisœr, -øz] *n Ind, Sp* finisher

finition [finisjɔ̃] *nf* finishing; (*résultat*) finish; **les finitions** the finishing touches; *Couture* **les finitions sont très soignées** it's very well finished; *Tricot* **je déteste faire les finitions** I hate the sewing up

finlandais, -aise [fɛ̃lɑ̃dɛ, -ɛz] [ⓘ**A20**,d] **1** *adj* Finnish **2** *n* **F.** Finn

Finlande [fɛ̃lɑ̃d] *nf* Finland

finnois [finwa] [ⓘ**A20**,d] **1** *adj* Finnish **2** *nm Ling* Finnish

finno-ougrien, -ienne [finougrijɛ̃ -jɛn] *adj, nm Ling* Finno-Ugric

fiole [fjɔl] *nf* **(a)** (*flacon*) phial, flask **(b)** *Arg* (*tête*) nut, *Br* bonce; (*visage*) mug; **se payer la f. de qn** to make a fool of sb

fion [fjɔ̃] *nm Arg Vulg* arse, *Am* ass

fiord [fjɔr] *nm Géog* fjord, fiord

fioriture [fjɔrityr] *nf* (*d'une écriture*) flourish; (*du style*) embellishment; *Mus* fioritura, ornament, embellishment; **une lettre pleine de fioritures** a flowery letter

fioul [fjul] *nm* fuel oil

FIP [fip] (*abrév* **France Inter Paris**) = French radio station broadcasting mainly light music

firmament [firmamɑ̃] *nm Litt* firmament

firme [firm] *nf* [ⓘ**A11**,g,i] firm

FIS [fis] *nm* (*abrév* **Front islamique du salut**) **le F.** the FIS, the Islamique Salvation Front

fisc [fisc] *nm Admin* tax department ≈ Inland Revenue, *US* ≈ Internal Revenue; **avoir des ennuis avec le f.** to have problems with the taxman

fiscal, -ale, -aux, -ales [fiskal, -o] *adj* fiscal; **l'administration fiscale** the tax(ation) authorities; **timbre f.** revenue stamp; **fraude/évasion fiscale** tax evasion/avoidance; **paradis f.** tax haven; **abri f.** tax shelter

fiscalement [fiskalmɑ̃] *adv* from a tax point of view, fiscally

fiscalisation [fiskalizasjɔ̃] *nf* taxing, taxation

fiscaliser [fiskalize] *vt* to tax

fiscaliste [fiskalist] *n* tax specialist

fiscalité [fiskalite] *nf* tax system; **f. des entreprises** corporate taxation; **optimiser la f. de qch** to improve the tax efficiency of sth, to make sth more tax efficient

fissa [fisa] *adv F* **faire f.** to get a move on, to get one's skates on

fissible [fisibl] *adj Phys* fissionable, fissile

fissile [fisil] *adj* **(a)** = **fissible (b)** (*roche*) fissile, tending to split

fission [fisjɔ̃] *nf Nucl* fission; **f. de l'atome** atomic fission, splitting of the atom

fissuration [fisyrasjɔ̃] *nf* cracking, fissuring

fissure [fisyr] *nf* crack, fissure; *Fig* (*entre amis*) split; **les fissures du mur** the cracks in the wall; **cette dispute provoqua une f. dans notre amitié** this quarrel caused a rift in our friendship

fissurer [fisyre] **1** *vt* to crack, to fissure; *Fig* to split (up) **2 se fissurer** *vpr* to crack, to fissure; *Fig* to split (up)

fiston [fistɔ̃] *nm F* son, lad; **allons (mon) f.!** now then, young fellow *or* my lad *or* sonny!

fistule [fistyl] *nf Méd* fistula

fistuleux, -euse [fistylø, -øz] *adj Méd* fistulous

FIV [ɛfive] *nf Biol* (*abrév* **fécondation in vitro**) IVF

fivète [fivɛt] *nf Biol* in vitro fertilization

fixage [fiksaʒ] *nm* fixing; *Phot* **bain de f.** fixing bath

fixateur, -trice [fiksatœr, -tris] **1** *nm* (*de teintures*) fixer; *Phot* fixer, fixing solution *or* bath; *Biol* fixative; (*pour cheveux*) hair spray, lacquer **2** *adj* **bactéries fixatrices d'azote** nitrogen-fixing bacteria

fixatif [fiksatif] *nm* (*pour dessins*) fixative

fixation [fiksasjɔ̃] *nf* **(a)** (*de date*) fixing; **f. de prix** price setting *ou* fixing, pricing; **f. d'un prix d'appel** loss-leader pricing; **f. d'un prix de soumission** sealed-bid pricing; **f. de l'impôt** tax assessment; **f. du prix en fonction du coût** cost-plus pricing; **f. du prix en fonction du taux de rentabilité souhaité** target-return pricing; **f. du prix optimal** optimal pricing; **f. du prix unitaire** unit pricing

(b) (*d'étagère etc*) fixing; (*de sables mouvants, Ch d'azote*) fixation; **f. par bride** *ou* **par collier** clamping; **vis de f.** fixing screw, set screw; **patte de f.** anchor(ing) clip

(c) *MecE* attachment, anchor; *Ski* (ski) binding

(d) *Psy* fixation (**à qn** on sb); **faire une f. sur qch/qn** to become obsessed with *or* fixated on sth/sb

fixe [fiks] **1** *adj* **(a)** (*immobile*) fixed; **idée f.** obsession, idée fixe; **regard f.** fixed *or* steady gaze; **grue f.** fixed *or* stationary crane; **essieu f.** dead axle; *Mil* **f.!** attention! **(b)** (*arrêté*) fixed; **prix f.** fixed *or* set price; **à prix f.** at fixed prices; **frais fixes** fixed costs; **traitement f.** fixed salary; **adresse f.** permanent address; **sans domicile f.** of no fixed abode; **prendre ses repas à heure f.** to eat at fixed *or* set times; *Ordinat* **disque f.** fixed disk; **beau (temps) f.** set fair (weather); **arrêt f.** compulsory stop **2** *nm* fixed salary

fixé [fikse] *adj* **(a)** (*date, heure, jour*) agreed, appointed; **à la date fixée** on the agreed *or* appointed day **(b) être f. sur qch** to have made up one's mind about sth; **je ne suis pas fixé** I haven't made my mind up yet; **eh bien, maintenant, tu es f.** well, now you know

fixe-chaussettes [fiks(ə)ʃosɛt] *nm inv* suspender, *Am* garter

fixement [fiksəmɑ̃] *adv* fixedly; **regarder f. qch** to stare at sth

fixer [fikse] **1** *vt* **(a)** (*immobiliser*) to fix; **les vis qui fixent la serrure** the screws that hold the lock; *Fig* **f. qch dans sa mémoire** to implant sth in one's memory; **f. l'attention de qn** to hold *or* engage sb's attention; **f. son attention sur qch** to fix *or* focus one's attention on sth; **f. les yeux sur qch/qn** to fix one's eyes on sth/sb, to gaze *or* stare at sth/sb; (*scruter*) to look hard *or* intently at sth/sb; **f. qn (du regard)** to stare at sb; **ça va le f.** that will make him settle down

(b) *Ch, Phot* to fix

(c) (*déterminer*) (*date, heure, jour*) to fix, to set, to arrange; (*rendez-vous*) to fix, to arrange; (*dommages, taxes*) to fix, to set; (*conditions, règlements*) to fix, to lay down; **f. un salaire** to fix a salary; **f. le prix de** to price; **f. un prix** to set a price, to fix a price

(d) f. qn sur qch to put sb in the picture about sth

2 se fixer *vpr* **(a)** (*s'installer*) to settle down

(b) (*s'arrêter*) to become fixed; **l'orthographe du mot se fixe au XVIII siècle** the spelling of the word became fixed in the 18th century; **se f. un objectif** to set oneself a target; **elle s'est fixée sur cette idée** she's got the idea in her head (and nothing will shift it); **il s'est fixé sur ce type d'écran** he has gone for *or* decided on this type of screen

fixisme [fiksism] *nm Biol* creationism

fixité [fiksite] *nf* (*du regard*) fixity, steadiness

fjord [fjɔr(d)] *nm Géog* fjord, fiord

flac [flak] *nm, int* plop; **faire f.** to plop

flaccidité [flaksidite] *nf* flabbiness, flaccidity

flacon [flakɔ̃] *nm* small (stoppered) bottle; (*de laboratoire*) flask; **f. à parfum** perfume bottle; **f. à liqueur** liqueur decanter

fla-fla [flafla] *nm F* show, ostentation; **faire du f.** to show off

flagada [flagada] *adj inv F* washed out, all in, dead beat

flagellation [flaʒɛlasjɔ̃] *nf* flogging, whipping; (*sur soi-même*) flagellation

flagelle [flaʒɛl] *nm Biol* flagellum

flagellé [flaʒele] *adj, nm Biol* flagellate

flageller [flaʒele] **1** *vt* to flog, to whip **2 se flageller** *vpr* to scourge oneself

flageolant [flaʒɔlɑ̃] *adj* shaking, trembling; **j'ai les jambes flageolantes** my legs are shaking *or* trembling

flageoler [flaʒɔle] *vi* (*des jambes*) to shake, to tremble; **elle flageole sur ses jambes** (*de peur*) she is shaking at the knees; (*de fatigue*) she's dead on her feet

flageolet[1] [flaʒɔlɛ] *nm Mus* flageolet

flageolet[2] *nm Bot, Culin* flageolet (bean)

flagorner [flagɔrne] *vt Péj* to fawn on, to toady to

flagornerie [flagɔrnəri] *nf Péj* fawning, toadying

flagorneur, -euse [flagɔrnœr, -øz] *n Péj* toady, sycophant

flagrant [flagrɑ̃] *adj* (*injustice, mensonge etc*) flagrant, blatant; **pris en f. délit** caught in the act, caught red-handed; **pris en f. délit de mensonge** caught (out) lying; *F* **c'est f.!** it's (glaringly) obvious!

flair [flɛr] *nm* **(a)** (*des chiens*) scent, (sense of) smell, nose **(b)** (*d'une personne*) intuition; **avoir du f.** to have good intuition

flairer [flere] *vt* **(a)** (*d'un chien*) (*gibier*) to scent, to smell (out), to nose out; *Fig* **f. le danger** to scent *or* smell *or* sense danger; **f. le mensonge** to detect a lie; **f. que** to sense that **(b)** (*sentir*) to smell

flamand, -ande [flamɑ̃, -ɑ̃d] **1** *adj* Flemish **2** *nm Ling* Flemish **3** *n* F. Fleming

flamant [flamɑ̃] *nm* [①A12,1,c] flamingo; **f. rose** pink flamingo

flambage [flɑ̃baʒ] *nm* **(a)** (*des cheveux, d'un poulet etc*) singeing; (*d'une aiguille*) sterilization; (*d'un bûcher*) charring **(b)** (*d'une plaque de métal*) buckling, collapse

flambant [flɑ̃bɑ̃] **1** *adv* **f. neuf** brand new **2** *adj* **(a)** (*bûche, soleil*) blazing, flaming **(b) houille flambante** bituminous *or* soft coal **3** *nm* bituminous *or* soft coal

flambard [flɑ̃bar] *nm F* **faire le f.** to show off

flambé [flɑ̃be] *adj* **(a)** *Culin* flambé(ed) **(b)** *F* **il est f.** he's done for, his goose is cooked

flambeau, -eaux [flɑ̃bo] *nm* **(a)** (*torche*) torch; **descente/retraite aux flambeaux** torch-lit descent/procession; **à la lueur des flambeaux, aux flambeaux** by torchlight; *Fig* **reprendre le f.** to take up the torch; *Fig* **passer le f. aux futures générations** to hand on the torch to future generations **(b)** (*chandelier*) candlestick

flambée [flɑ̃be] *nf* **(a)** (*feu*) blaze, blazing fire; **faire une f. dans la cheminée** to light a fire in the hearth **(b)** *Fig* (*de violence*) flare-up, outbreak; (*des prix*) upsurge, escalation; (*de colère*) outburst

flambement [flɑ̃bmɑ̃] *nm* (*d'une plaque de métal*) buckling, collapse

flamber [flɑ̃be] **1** *vi* **(a)** (*brûler*) to blaze; **f. comme une allumette** to burn like matchwood **(b)** (*prix*) to escalate **(c)** (*d'une barre de métal etc*) to buckle, to collapse **2** *vt* (*cheveux, volaille etc*) to singe; *Culin* to flambé; **f. une aiguille** to sterilize a needle (in a flame); *Fig* **elle a flambé l'argent du ménage au jeu** she gambled away *or* blew the housekeeping money; **c'est fou ce qu'elle flambe comme argent** it's crazy the amount of money she throws away!

flambeur [flɑ̃bœr] *nm Arg* big-time gambler

flamboiement [flɑ̃bwamɑ̃] *nm* blazing, blaze

flamboyant [flɑ̃bwajɑ̃] *adj* **(a)** (*feu*) blazing; (*yeux*) blazing, flashing **(b)** *Archit* flamboyant

flamboyer [flɑ̃bwaje] *vi* **(il flamboie)** (*du feu*) to blaze; **f. de colère** (*des yeux*) to blaze *or* flash with anger

flamingant, -ante [flamɛ̃gɑ̃, -ɑ̃t] **1** *adj* (*ville, personne*) Flemish-speaking **2** *n Pol* Flemish nationalist

flamme [flam] *nf* **(a)** (*de feu*) flame; **en flammes** on fire, ablaze; **dévoré par les flammes** consumed by flames; **retour de f.** (*d'une arme*) back flash; *Tech* backfire, backfiring; *Fig* backlash; **passer à la f.** to singe **(b)** *Litt* (*amour*) passion, love; **déclarer sa f. à une femme** to declare one's love for a woman **(c)** (*enthousiasme*) fire, enthusiasm; **discours plein de f.** fiery speech **(d)** (*drapeau*) pennant, streamer **(e)** (*sur lettre*) (*marque postale*) slogan

flammèche [flamɛʃ] *nf* spark

flan [flɑ̃] *nm* **(a)** *Culin* (baked) custard; (*tarte*) custard pie; **f. chimique** *ou* **en poudre** custard powder **(b)** (*d'une pièce, d'un disque etc*) blank **(c)** *Typ* mould, *US* mold **(d)** *Fig* **en rester** *ou* **en être comme deux ronds de f.** to be flabbergasted; *F* **c'est du f.** it's rubbish!; *F* **j'ai dit ça au f.** I said it just for the sake of it *or* just for something to say; *F* **y aller au f.** to try it on, to bluff

flanc [flɑ̃] *nm* (*d'un animal*) side, flank; (*d'une personne*) side; (*d'un pneu*) wall, profile, side wall; **route à f. de coteau** road following the hillside; **être sur le f.** (*malade*) to be laid up; (*épuisé*) to be quite worn out; **ces difficultés l'ont mise sur le f.** these problems really took it out of her; **battre des flancs** (*d'un cheval*) to heave, to pant; *Mil* **par le f. droit!** by the right!; **attaquer de f.** to attack on the flank; **le navire se présentait de f.** the ship was broadside on; **prêter le f. à la critique** to lay oneself open to criticism; *F* **tirer au f.** to shirk, *Br* to skive

flancher [flɑ̃ʃe] *vi F* (*faiblir*) to give in, to weaken; **ce n'est pas le moment de f.!** don't give in now!; **son cœur a flanché** his heart gave out; **sans f.** without flinching

flanchet [flɑ̃ʃɛ] *nm Culin* flank

Flandre [flɑ̃dr] *nf* Flanders

flandrin [flɑ̃drɛ̃] *nm Arch F* **grand f.** gangling *or* gangly fellow

flanelle [flanɛl] *nf Tex* flannel; **f. (de) coton** flannelette; **pantalon de f. grise** grey flannels; *F* **il devrait mettre sa f.** he ought to wear his jacket

flâner [flɑne, flane] *vi* **(a)** (*se promener*) to stroll, to saunter **(b)** (*perdre son temps*) to hang about; **perdre son temps à f.** to idle away one's time

flânerie [flɑnri, flanri] *nf* (*balade*) strolling; (*oisiveté*) idling

flâneur, -euse [flɑnœr, flanœr, -øz] *n* **(a)** (*promeneur*) stroller **(b)** (*oisif*) idler, loafer

flanquer[1] [flɑ̃ke] *vt* (*bâtiment, Mil colonne, ennemi*) to flank; **flanqué de deux agents** flanked by two policemen

flanquer[2] *F* **1** *vt* (*jeter*) to chuck, to fling, to throw; **f. une gifle/un coup de pied à qn** to give sb a slap/kick; **f. qn à la porte** *ou* **dehors** to throw sb out; (*licencier*) to fire sb, *Br* to sack sb; **f. la trouille** *ou* **les jetons à qn** to give sb the jitters, to put the wind up sb **2 se flanquer** *vpr* **se f. par terre** to come a cropper, to take a tumble; **elle s'est flanquée dans le ravin** she plunged into the ravine

flapi [flapi] *adj F* dead beat, fagged out

flaque [flak] *nf* puddle; **f. de sang** pool of blood

flash, *pl* **flashes** [flaʃ] *nm* **(a)** *Phot* flash(light) **(b)** *Cin* flash; **f. publicitaire** commercial **(c)** *TV, Rad* newsflash; **f. d'information** newsflash; *TV, Rad* **f. spécial** (special) newsflash

flashant [flaʃɑ̃] *adj F* flashy

flash-back [flaʃbak] *nm inv* flashback; **faire un f.** to flash back

flasher [flaʃe] *vi F* **f. sur qch/qn** to really fall for sth/sb

flasque[1] [flask] *adj* (*chair*) flabby, flaccid; (*style*) limp; (*chapeau*) floppy

flasque[2] *nf* flask

flasque[3] *nm Mil* (*d'un affût de canon*) cheek; *Aut* hubcap, wheel disc; (*d'une roue*) flange

flatter [flate] **1** *vt* **(a)** (*complimenter*) to flatter; **f. qn sur son bel esprit** to flatter sb on his wit; **je suis flatté de votre proposition** I am flattered by your proposal

(b) (*avantager*) **cette coupe ne la flatte pas** that style doesn't flatter her; **peintre qui flatte ses modèles** painter who flatters his sitters (**c**) (*plaire*) (*l'oreille*) to delight, to be pleasing to, to please; **spectacle qui flatte les yeux** sight that is pleasing to the eye; **plat/vin qui flatte le palais** dish/wine that delights the taste buds *or* the palate; **f. les caprices de qn** to pander to *or* humour *or* indulge sb's whims

(**d**) (*tromper*) to delude; **f. qn de l'espoir de qch** to hold out false hopes of sth to sb

(**e**) (*animal*) to stroke, to caress; **f. un cheval** to pat a horse

2 se flatter *vpr* to flatter oneself, to delude oneself; **elle se flattait de réussir** she flattered herself *or* felt sure that she would succeed; **il se flatte qu'on a** *ou* **ait besoin de lui** he flatters himself that he is indispensable; **se f. de son habileté** to congratulate oneself on one's cleverness; **se f. d'avoir fait qch** to pride oneself on having done sth; **à ta place, je ne m'en flatterais pas** if I was in your place it's not something I'd be proud of

flatterie [flatri] *nf* flattery; **ce ne sont que de viles flatteries** it's just base flattery

flatteur, -euse [flatœr, -øz] **1** *adj* (*remarque, portrait, couleur*) flattering; (*personne*) full of flattery; **peu f.** unflattering; **il a fait un tableau f. de la situation** he painted a rosy picture of the situation **2** *n* flatterer

flatulence [flatylɑ̃s] *nf Méd* flatulence; **avoir des flatulences** to suffer from flatulence

flatulent [flatylɑ̃] *adj Méd* flatulent

flatuosité [flatɥozite] *nf* wind; *Méd* flatus

FLE [flə] *nm* (*abrév* **français langue étrangère**) French as a foreign language

fléau, -aux [fleo] *nm* (**a**) (*calamité*) scourge, curse; *Fig* plague, pest, bane; *F* **c'est un vrai f.!** he's/it's a real pain! (**b**) (*à céréales*) flail (**c**) (*d'une balance*) beam, arm

fléchage [fleʃaʒ] *nm* (*de direction*) signposting

flèche[1] [flɛʃ] *nf* (**a**) (*projectile*) arrow; **pistolet à flèches** dart gun; **fer de f.** arrowhead; **faire f. de tout bois** to use all available means, to use all means at one's disposal; **partir en** *ou* **comme une f.** (*d'une personne*) to shoot off; **monter en f.** (*d'un avion*) to shoot (straight) up; (*des prix*) to shoot up, to rocket; *Fig* **elle lui a décoché des flèches méchantes** she let fly a few barbed remarks in his direction; **je ne supporte plus ses petites flèches** I can't stand his digs at me any longer

(**b**) (*de direction*) arrow; **suivre les flèches** to follow the arrows; **f. lumineuse** pointer; (*de sortie de secours etc*) luminous arrow; *Aut* **f. de direction** trafficator

(**c**) **chevaux attelés en f.** horses driven tandem; **cheval de f.** leader, leading horse

(**d**) (*d'une église*) spire

(**e**) (*d'une grue*) jib, boom

(**f**) *Naut* (*d'un mât*) pole; (*d'un cutter*) topsail

(**g**) *Archit* (*d'une arche*) rise; *Av* (*d'un plan à profil d'aile*) camber

(**h**) (*d'un câble*) sag, dip

(**i**) *Ordinat* **f. de défilement** scroll arrow; **f. vers la droite** right arrow; **f. vers la gauche** left arrow; **f. vers le bas** down arrow; **f. vers le haut** up arrow; **flèches verticales** up and down arrow keys

flèche[2] *nf* (*de lard*) flitch

flécher [fleʃe] *vt* (*route, direction*) to arrow; **itinéraire fléché** arrowed *or* signposted route

fléchette [fleʃɛt] *nf* [①**A10**,d] dart; **jouer aux fléchettes** to play darts

fléchi [fleʃi] *adj Ling* **forme fléchie** inflected form

fléchir [fleʃir] **1** *vt* (**a**) (*bras, jambe*) to bend, to flex; **f. le genou devant qn** to bend *or* bow the knee to sb (**b**) (*émouvoir*) to sway; **se laisser f.** to let oneself be swayed **2** *vi* (**a**) (*se ployer*) to bend; (*des jambes, troupes etc*) to give way; (*d'un câble, d'une poutre*) to sag (**b**) (*diminuer*) (*de prix*) to fall; **les prix fléchissent** prices are falling, prices are coming down; **le dollar fléchit** the dollar is weakening *or* falling; **son autorité fléchit** his authority is weakening; **elle n'a pas fléchi** she didn't give in *or* yield

fléchissement [fleʃismɑ̃] *nm* (**a**) (*du genou etc*) bending; (*d'une poutre etc*) yielding, bending; (*d'un câble etc*) sagging (**b**) (*des prix*) falling, drop; (*des devises*) weakening; *Bourse* **f. des cours** fall *or* drop in share prices

fléchisseur [fleʃisœr] *adj, nm Anat* (**muscle**) **f.** flexor

flegmatique [flɛgmatik] *adj* phlegmatic, imperturbable

flegmatiquement [flɛgmatikmɑ̃] *adv* phlegmatically, imperturbably

flegme [flɛgm] *nm* (**a**) (*imperturbabilité*) phlegm, imperturbability; **faire perdre son f. à qn** to make sb lose their composure *or F* cool; **le f. britannique** British phlegm (**b**) *Méd* phlegm

flémingite [flemɛ̃ʒit] *nf F* total laziness; **il fait de la f. aiguë** he's being bone idle

flemmard, -arde [flɛmar, -rd] *n F* lazy sod *or* so-and-so

flemmarder [flemarde] *vi F* to lounge about; **f. au lit** to laze in bed

flemmardise [flemardiz] *nf F* laziness, idleness

flemme [flɛm] *nf F* laziness, idleness, slacking; **j'ai la f. de le faire** I can't be bothered to do it; **tirer sa f.** to lounge about

flet [flɛ] *nm* flounder

flétan [fletɑ̃] *nm* halibut

flétri [fletri] *adj* withered

flétrir[1] [fletrir] **1** *vt* (*peau*) to wither; (*couleurs etc*) to fade; (*plantes*) to wither (up), to wilt **2 se flétrir** *vpr* (*des plantes*) to wither, to wilt; (*de la peau*) to wither

flétrir[2] *vt* (**a**) (*crime*) to stigmatize; *Hist* (*criminel*) to brand (**b**) (*la réputation de qn*) to blacken, to sully, to stain

flétrissure[1] [fletrisyr] *nf* withering

flétrissure[2] *nf* (*déshonneur*) stain, blemish

fleur [flœr] *nf* (**a**) *Bot* flower; (*d'arbre*) blossom, bloom; **arbre en fleur(s)** tree in blossom *or* in flower *or* in bloom; **fleurs des champs** wild flowers; **fleurs en pot** flowering pot plant; **ni fleurs, ni couronnes** ≈ no flowers by request; **envoyer des fleurs à qn** to send sb flowers; *Fig* to pat sb on the back; **f. artificielle/en papier** artificial/paper flower; **tissu à fleurs** flowered *or* flowery material; *Fig* **faire une f. à qn** to do sb a favour; *Fig* **elle le couvre de fleurs** she heaps praise (up)on him; **être f. bleue** to be (naively) romantic; *F* **elle y est arrivée comme une f.** she managed it without a hitch *or* a problem

(**b**) *Fig Litt* **dans** *ou* **à la f. de l'âge** in the prime of life; **dans la première f. de la jeunesse** in the first flush *or* flower of youth; **la fine f. de la société** the cream of society

(**c**) (*d'antimoine, de vin etc*) **fleurs** flowers

(**d**) **à f. de** on the surface of; **à f. d'eau** just above (the surface of) the water; **voler à f. d'eau** to skim the water; **émotions à f. de peau** skin-deep emotions; **avoir les nerfs à f. de peau** to be all on edge

(**e**) (*d'une peau*) hair side, grain side

(**f**) **f. de farine** top-quality flour

fleurage [flœraʒ] *nm* (*sur un tissu, tapis*) floral pattern

fleurdelisé [flœrdəlize] **1** *adj* decorated with fleurs-de-lis; *Hér* fleury **2** *nm Can* (*drapeau du Québec*) flag of Quebec

fleurer [flœre] *vt Litt* to smell of; **f. la violette** to smell of violets; *Fig* **ça fleure l'intrigue/les pots-de-vin** it smacks of a plot/of bribery, I/he/*etc* can smell a plot/bribery

fleuret [flœrɛ] *nm* (*épée*) foil; *Min* borer

fleurette [flœrɛt] *nf* (**a**) **conter f. à qn** to whisper sweet nothings to sb (**b**) **crème f.** ≈ single cream

fleuri [flœri] *adj* (**a**) (*en fleurs*) in bloom, in flower, in blossom; (*orné de fleurs*) (*tissu, robe*) flowered, flowery; (*vaisselle*) flower-patterned; **village f.** ≈ village taking part in a flower competition; **avoir la boutonnière fleurie** to have a flower in one's buttonhole; (*décoré*) to wear a decoration (**b**) (*sentier etc*) flowery; (*teint*) florid; (*style*) flowery, florid

fleurir [flœrir] (*prp* **fleurissant,** *Litt* **florissant**; *impf* **il fleurissait,** *Litt* **il florissait**) **1** *vi* (**a**) (*des plantes*) to flower, to bloom, to blossom (**b**) (*de l'art, du commerce etc*) (*usu* **florissant, florissait**) to blossom, to flourish, to prosper **2** *vt* (*table*) to decorate with flowers; (*boutonnière*) to put a flower in; (*tombe*) to lay flowers on

fleuriste [flœrist] *n* (**a**) (*commerçant*) florist, flower seller (**b**) (*horticulteur*) flower grower (**c**) (*de fleurs artificielles*) artificial flower maker

fleuron [flœrɔ̃] *nm* (**a**) (*ornement*) flower, fleuron; *Archit* finial; **c'est le plus beau f. de notre collection** it's the jewel in our collection (**b**) *Bot* floret

fleuve [flœv] **1** *nm* river (*as opposed to tributary*); **f.** (**côtier**) short coastal river; *Fig* **un f. de sang/de larmes** a river of blood/a flood of tears; **des fleuves de boue** rivers of mud **2** *adj inv* **roman-f.** saga; **discours-f.** lengthy speech

flexibilité [flɛksibilite] *nf* flexibility; (*de matériaux*) pliability; (*du corps*) flexibility, suppleness, litheness

flexible [flɛksibl] **1** *adj* (**a**) (*souple*) flexible, supple; (*matériaux*) pliable; **tuyau f.** hose(pipe) (**b**) (*adaptable*) (*personne*) flexible; (*disposition*) accommodating; (*malléable*) pliable, pliant; **avoir des horaires flexibles** to work flexible hours, to be on flexitime **2** *nm* (*tuyau*) hose(pipe); *Él* flexible lead, *Br* flex; *Aut* **f. de frein** brake hose

flexion [flɛksjɔ̃] *nf* (**a**) (*fléchissement*) flexion, bending; *Gym* **f. du corps** trunk exercise; *MecE* **effort de f.** bending stress (**b**) (*d'une tige*) buckling, collapse (**c**) *Ling* (*de mot*) inflexion; **langue à flexions** inflected language

flexionnel, -elle [flɛksjɔnɛl] *adj Ling* inflected; **langue flexionnelle** inflected language

flibuste [flibyst] *nf Hist* (*piraterie*) buccaneering, freebooting; (*pirates*) buccaneers, freebooters

flibustier [flibystje] *nm* (**a**) *Hist* buccaneer, freebooter (**b**) *Arch F* (*escroc*) cheat, crook

flic [flik] *nm F* (*policier*) cop, copper; **voilà les flics!** it's the cops!

flicage [flikaʒ] *nm F* (*par la police*) heavy policing; *Fig* heavy-handed supervision

flicaille [flikɑj] *nf F* **la f.** the pigs

flic flac *nm* splish splash; (*d'un fouet*) crack

flingue [flɛ̃g] *nm F* (*arme*) shooter, piece

flinguer [flɛ̃ge] *F* **1** *vt* to gun down **2 se flinguer** *vpr* to blow one's brains out; **il n'y a pas de quoi se f.** it's not the end of the world; **c'est à se f.!** it's enough to make you chuck yourself under a train!

flip-flap, *pl* **flips-flaps** [flipflap] *nm Gym* back(ward) flip

flippant [flipɑ̃] *adj F* (*déprimant*) grim; (*effrayant*) creepy

flipper¹ [flipœr] *nm* (*appareil*) pinball (machine); (*jeu*) pinball; **jouer au f.** to play pinball

flipper² [flipe] *vi F* **(a)** (*d'un drogué*) to be spaced out **(b)** (*s'angoisser*) to freak out; **ça me fait f.** that freaks me out; **elle flippe à cause de son travail** her work is freaking her out

fliquer [flike] *vt F* to police heavily; **fliqué** overrun with cops; *Fig* **au bureau, on a vraiment l'impression d'être fliqués** in the office we really feel we're being watched like criminals

flirt [flœrt] *nm* **(a)** (*amourette*) flirtation, flirting; **ce n'est qu'un f.** I/he/*etc* was only flirting **(b)** *Vieilli* **mon f.** my boyfriend/girlfriend; **un de mes anciens flirts** an old flame of mine

flirter [flœrte] *vi* to flirt; *F* **f. avec le danger** to flirt with danger; *Fig* **il flirte avec la police/l'opposition** he's flirting with the police/the opposition

FLN [ɛfɛlɛn] *nm Hist* (*abrév* **Front de Libération Nationale**) = national liberation front in Algeria

FLNC [ɛfɛlɛnse] *nm* (*abrév* **Front de Libération National de la Corse**) = Corsican liberation front

FLNKS [ɛfɛlɛnkaɛs] *nm* (*abrév* **Front de libération nationale kanak et socialiste**) Kanak national liberation front in New Caledonia

floc [flɔk] *int, nm* splash

flocage [flɔkaʒ] *nm Tex* flocking

floche [flɔʃ] *adj* flossy; **soie f.** floss silk

flocon [flɔkɔ̃] *nm* **(a)** (*de neige, céréale*) flake; **flocons d'avoine** oat flakes; *Can* **flocons de maïs** cornflakes; **purée en flocons** instant mashed potato **(b)** (*de laine, coton*) tuft, flock

floconneux, -euse [flɔkɔnø, -øz] *adj* fleecy, fluffy

floculation [flɔkylasjɔ̃] *nf Ch* flocculation

flonflons [flɔ̃flɔ̃] *nmpl* tiddly-om-pom-pom

flop [flɔp] *nm F* flop; **faire un f.** to be a flop

flopée [flɔpe] *nf F* **une f., des flopées** (*d'enfants, de gens*) loads, masses

floquer [flɔke] *vt Tex* to flock

floraison [flɔrɛzɔ̃] *nf* **(a)** (*d'arbre*) flowering, blossoming; **l'arbre est en pleine f.** the tree is in full flower *or* blossom **(b)** *Fig* upsurge (**de** in)

floral, -ale, -aux, -ales [flɔral, -o] *adj* floral; **exposition florale** flower show

floralies [flɔrali] *nfpl* flower show

flore [flɔr] *nf Bot* flora; *Physiol* **f. intestinale** intestinal flora

floréal [flɔreal] *nm Hist* eighth month of the French Republican calendar (*April-May*)

florès [flɔrɛs] *nm Litt Vieilli* **faire f.** to prosper

Floride [flɔrid] *nf* Florida

florifère [flɔrifɛr] *adj* flower-bearing, *Spéc* floriferous; **plante très f.** prolific flowerer

florilège [flɔrilɛʒ] *nm* anthology

florin [flɔrɛ̃] *nm* florin

florissant [flɔrisɑ̃] *adj* (*affaire, pays, peuple*) flourishing, prosperous; (*santé, mine*) blooming; **d'une santé florissante** in the best of health

flot [flo] *nm* **(a)** (*marée*) flood (tide); *Litt* **les flots bleus** the ocean blue; **elle s'endormit, bercée par le bruit des flots** she fell asleep, lulled by the sound of the waves

(b) (*de larmes*) flood; (*de sang, d'injures*) torrent, stream; (*de gens, voitures*) stream; **un f. de paroles** a torrent *or* flood of words; **entrer à flots** (*de gens, du soleil*) to flood in, to stream in; **f. de dentelle/rubans** cascade of lace/ribbons; **couler à flots** to pour out

(c) être à f. (*d'un bateau*) to be afloat; *Fig* (*d'une personne*) to have one's head above water; **mettre un navire à f.** to launch a ship; **remettre un navire à f.** to refloat a ship; **mon compte en banque est à f.** my bank account is in the black *or* in credit; **remettre qn à f.** to put sb back in the black; **ce cours vous permettra de vous remettre à f. en russe** this course will get you going in Russian again *or* will bring your Russian back up to scratch again

flottabilité [flɔtabilite] *nf* buoyancy; **caisson** *ou* **réservoir de f.** buoyancy tank

flottable [flɔtabl] *adj* **(a)** (*d'un cours d'eau*) floatable (*for rafts of wood*) **(b)** (*du bois*) floatable, buoyant

flottage [flɔtaʒ] *nm* (*de bois*) floating; **bois de f.** raft wood; **train de f.** timber raft

flottaison [flɔtɛzɔ̃] *nf* floating; *Naut* **(ligne de) f.** waterline; **f. en charge** load line; **f. lège** light waterline

flottant [flɔtɑ̃] *adj* **(a)** (*dette, moteur etc*) floating; (*chiffre*) fluctuating; *Ordinat* **virgule flottante** floating point **(b)** (*toge, cheveux*) flowing, loose; **filet f.** drift net **(c)** (*électorat, opinion*) undecided, wavering; **électeur f.** floating voter

flotte [flɔt] *nf* **(a)** (*bateaux*) fleet; **f. de ligne** *ou* **de combat** battle fleet; **f. de commerce** merchant fleet; **être dans la f.** to be in the navy; **f. aérienne** air fleet; **f. marchande** merchant marine **(b)** *F* (*pluie*) rain; (*eau*) water; **il tombe de la f.** it's pouring with rain; **c'est de la f., ce café!** this coffee's like water!

flottement [flɔtmɑ̃] *nm* **(a)** (*d'une ligne de troupes etc*) wavering, swaying; (*d'un drapeau*) flapping, fluttering; (*d'une chaîne, roue*) wobble; (*d'une devise*) fluctuation **(b)** (*hésitation*) wavering, hesitation; **il y eut un moment de f.** there was a moment's hesitation; **il y a toujours des flottements dans ses exposés** there are always some uneven patches in his talks

flotter [flɔte] **1** *vi* **(a)** (*sur l'eau*) to float **(b)** (*au vent*) to float, to stream; (*des cheveux*) to stream **(c)** (*hésiter*) to waver, to hesitate; (*des pensées*) to wander; **un sourire flottait sur ses lèvres** a smile played *or* hovered on his lips **(d)** (*des devises*) to fluctuate; **faire f.** to float **(e)** (*des vêtements*) to hang loosely; **il flotte dans ses vêtements** his clothes are far too big for him, *F* his clothes drown him **2** *vt* **f. du bois** to float timber (*down a stream*); **bois flotté** driftwood **3** *v impers F* **il flotte** it's raining

flotteur [flɔtœr] *nm* **(a)** (*ouvrier*) raftsman (*in charge of timber raft*) **(b)** (*d'une canne à pêche, d'un hydravion, carburateur etc*) float **(c)** (*d'un robinet*) ball; **robinet à f.** ballcock

flottille [flɔtij] *nf* (*de bateaux*) flotilla; (*d'avions*) squadron; **f. de pêche** fishing fleet

flou [flu] **1** *adj* (*contour, peinture*) blurred; (*image*) blurred, fuzzy, out of focus; (*son*) muffled, indistinct; (*horizon*) hazy; (*idée*) hazy, vague; (*cheveux*) soft, fluffy; (*robe*) loose(-fitting)

2 *nm* (*d'un contour, d'une image*) blur, fuzziness; (*d'un son*) indistinctness; (*de l'horizon*) haziness; (*d'une idée*) haziness, vagueness; (*des cheveux*) softness, fluffiness; (*d'une robe*) looseness; **le f. revient à la mode** loose-fitting clothes are back in fashion; **f. artistique** *Phot* soft-focus effect; *Fig* deliberate vagueness; **elle a préféré rester dans un f. artistique** she preferred to remain deliberately vague

flouer [flue] *vt F* to swindle; **se faire f.** to be swindled, to be done

flouse, flouze [fluz] *nm Arg* (*argent*) bread, dough, cash

FLQ [ɛfɛlky] (*abrév* **franco long du quai**) FAS

fluctuant [flyktɥɑ̃] *adj* fluctuating; **un esprit f.** a weathercock; **elle est fluctuante dans ses projets** her plans are liable to change

fluctuation [flyktɥasjɔ̃] *nf* fluctuation; **f. des prix** price fluctuation; **f. saisonnière** seasonal fluctuation; **fluctuations de tension** voltage fluctuations

fluctuer [flyktɥe] *vi* to fluctuate

fluent [flyɑ̃] *adj* (*sol*) flowing, loose; *Méd* **hémorroïdes fluentes** bleeding piles

fluet, -ette [flyɛ, -ɛt] *adj* (*personne*) thin, slender; (*voix*) thin, reedy

fluide [flyid] **1** *adj* (*huile, situation*) fluid; (*style, pensée*) fluid, flowing; **la circulation était f.** the traffic was flowing steadily; **les accords fluides de la sonate** the fluid chords of the sonata; *Phys* **la mécanique des fluides** fluid mechanics **2** *nm* **(a)** fluid; **f. de nettoyage** cleaning fluid; *Aut* **f. de frein** brake fluid; **f. aéré** aerated fluid; **f. d'embrayage** clutch fluid; **f. de refroidissement** coolant; **f. moteur** engine fluid **(b) avoir du f.** (*d'un médium*) to have strange powers

fluidifier [flyidifje] *vt* to thin, to fluidify

fluidité [flyidite] *nf* fluidity; **f. de la circulation** steady flow of traffic

fluo [flyo] *adj inv F* fluorescent

fluor [flyɔr] *nm Ch* fluorine; **dentifrice au f.** fluoride toothpaste; *Minér* **spath f.** fluorspar

fluoration [flyɔrasjɔ̃] *nf* (*de l'eau*) fluoridation

fluoré [flyɔre] *adj* **dentifrice f.** fluoride toothpaste

fluorescence [flyɔresɑ̃s] *nf* fluorescence

fluorescent [flyɔresɑ̃] *adj* fluorescent; **rose/vert f.** fluorescent pink/green

fluorine [flyɔrin] *nf Minér* fluorspar

fluorure [flyɔryr] *nm Ch* fluoride

flûte [flyt] **1** *nf* **(a)** (*instrument*) flute; **f. à bec** recorder; **f. de Pan** panpipes; **f. traversière, grande f.** concert flute; **petite f.**

piccolo **(b)** (*musicien*) flautist, flute (player), *US* flutist **(c)** (*pain*) small French stick **(d)** (*verre*) flute; **f. à champagne** champagne flute **(e)** *F* **flûtes** (*jambes*) pins; **jouer** *ou* **se tirer des flûtes** to show a clean pair of heels **2** *int F* blow!, drat!; **f. alors, il est déjà parti!** blow it *or* drat it, he's gone already!

flûté [flyte] *adj* **voix flûtée** flute-like *or* piping voice

flûtiau, -aux [flytjo] *nm* penny whistle

flûtiste [flytist] *n* flautist, flute player, *US* flutist

fluvial, -iale, -iaux, -iales [flyvjal, -jo] *adj* river *attrib* fluvial; **police fluviale** river police; **pêche fluviale** river fishing, angling; **alluvions fluviales** fluvial deposits; **port f.** river port

fluviatile [flyvjatil] *adj* **mollusques fluviatiles** river *or* freshwater molluscs

flux [fly] *nm* **(a)** (*de mots*) flow, stream **(b)** (*marée montante*) flow, flood; **le f. et le reflux** the ebb and flow; *Pol F* the swing of the pendulum; *Fig* **le f. et le reflux des visiteurs** the coming and going of visitors; **f. de fonds** flow of funds; **f. de trésorerie** cashflow; **f. monétaire** cashflow **(c)** *Méd* flow, flux; **f. menstruel** menstrual flow **(d)** *Ch, Métal* flux **(e)** *Phys, Él* **f. magnétique** magnetic flux; **f. lumineux** luminous *or* light flux; **f. électronique** electron flow *or* stream

fluxion [flyksjɔ̃] *nf Méd* inflammation; **f. à la joue** swollen cheek; **f. de la gencive** gumboil; **f. de poitrine** pneumonia

FM [ɛfɛm] *nf* (*abrév* **modulation de fréquence**) FM

FMI [ɛfɛmi] *nm* (*abrév* **Fonds monétaire international**) IMF

FN [ɛfɛn] *nm* (*abrév* **Front National**) French extreme right-wing party

FNAC [fnak] *nf* (*abrév* **Fédération nationale d'achat des cadres**) chain of stores selling cut-price books, hi-fis, photographic equipment etc

FNGS [ɛfɛnʒeɛs] *nm* (*abrév* **Fonds national de garantie des salaires**) national guarantee fund for the payment of salaries

FNI [ɛfɛni] *nfpl Mil* (*abrév* **forces nucléaires intermédiaires**) INF

FNSEA [ɛfɛnɛsəa] *nf* (*abrév* **Fédération nationale des syndicats d'exploitants agricoles**) farmers' union, = *Br* NFU

FO [ɛfo] *nf* (*abrév* **Force ouvrière**) = French trade union

FOB [ɛfɔbe], **fob** *adj inv, adv* FOB; **vente f.** FOB sale

foc [fɔk] *nm Naut* jib; **grand f.** main *or* outer jib; **petit f.** fore staysail; **f. d'artimon** mizzen-topmast staysail

focal, -ale, -aux, -ales [fɔkal, -o] *adj Math, Opt* focal

focalisation [fɔkalizasjɔ̃] *nf Opt, Électron* focusing; *Mktg* targeting; *Mktg* **f. stratégique** strategic targeting

focaliser [fɔkalize] **1** *vt Opt, Électron* to focus; *Fig* **f. son attention/l'attention de qn sur qch** to focus one's/sb's attention on sth **2 se focaliser** *vpr* to focus (**sur** on)

foehn [føn] *nm* **(a)** (*vent*) foehn **(b)** *Suisse* (*sèche-cheveux*) hair-dryer

fœtal, -ale, -aux, -ales [fetal, -o] *adj* f(o)etal

fœtus [fetys] *nm* f(o)etus

fofolle [fɔfɔl] *F* **1** *adj f* nutty, daft **2** *nf* nutty *or* daft woman

foi [fwa] *nf* **(a) bonne f.** sincerity, honesty; **mauvaise f.** insincerity, dishonesty; *Phil* bad faith; **il est de bonne/mauvaise f.** he is sincere/insincere; **je le lui ai dit en toute bonne f.** I told him that in good faith; **témoin de bonne/mauvaise f.** truthful/untruthful witness; **témoin digne de f.** trustworthy *or* reliable *or* credible witness; **ma f., oui!** yes indeed!; **c'est ma f. vrai** that is certainly *or* definitely true; *Arch* **f. d'honnête homme** on my word as a gentleman; **sur la f. de sa lettre** on the strength of his letter

(b) (*confiance*) belief, trust, confidence; **avoir f. en qn/qch** to have faith in *or* to believe in sb/sth; **avoir f. en l'avenir** to have confidence in the future; **ajouter** *ou* **attacher f. à une nouvelle** to give credence to *or* to credit *or* to believe (in) a piece of news; **texte qui fait f.** authentic text; **la lettre doit partir avant le 29, le cachet de la poste faisant f.** the letter must be postmarked no later than the 28th; *Jur* **en f. de quoi** in witness whereof; **ligne de f.** *Opt* zero alignment; *Naut, Av* lubber line

(c) *Rel* faith, belief; **avoir la f.** to have faith; *Fig* **il faut vraiment avoir la f.** you have to be really dedicated; *Iron* **il n'y a que la f. qui sauve** faith is a wonderful thing; **acte/article de f.** act/article of faith; **profession de f.** profession of faith; *Cathol* confirmation; *Pol* (*d'un candidat*) mission statement; **répandre la f.** to spread the Word; **la f. démocratique** faith *or* belief in democracy; **il n'a ni f. ni loi, il est sans f. ni loi** he fears neither God nor man

foie [fwa] *nm* liver; *Culin* **f. de veau/volaille** calf's/chicken liver; **huile de f. de morue** cod-liver oil; *Fig F* **se ronger** *ou* **se manger les foies** to be climbing the walls, to go beserk; *très F* **avoir les foies** to be scared out of one's wits; **ça m'a foutu les foies** it scared me out of my wits

▶ **foie: f. gras** foie gras

foin [fwɛ̃] *nm* **(a)** (*fourrage*) hay; **faire les foins** to make hay; **tas de f.** haycock; **meule de f.** haystack; **rhume des foins** hay fever; *F* **faire du f.** (*scandale*) to kick up *or* make a fuss; (*bruit*) to kick up *or* make a din; **ce scandale a fait du foin dans le milieu politique local** this scandal made waves in local political circles **(b)** (*d'artichaut*) choke **(c)** *Arch* **f. de ...** the devil take ...

foire [fwar] *nf* fair; **f. commerciale** trade show; **f. internationale** international (trade) fair; **f. professionnelle** trade fair; **f. commerciale de Marseille** Marseilles trade fair; **champ de f.** fairground; *F* **c'est la f. ici** (*désordre*) it's chaos in here; (*bruit*) it's bedlam in here; **faire la f.** to have a good time, to have fun

foire-exposition, *F* **foire-expo** *pl* **foires-expositions, foires-expos** *nf* trade fair *or* exhibition

foirer [fware] *très F* **1** *vi* (*rater*) **la mission/le plan/la soirée a complètement foiré** the mission/the plan/the evening was a complete balls-up *or Am* ballup *or* cockup; **ses prévisions ont complètement foiré** his predictions were a mile out; **il a tout fait f.** he cocked everything up; *Mil* **fusée qui foire** shell that doesn't go off **2** *vt* to cock up, to mess up

foireux, -euse [fwarø, -øz] *adj* **(a)** *très F* (*qui échoue*) hopeless; **c'est un plan f.** that plan is going to be a cock up **(b)** *F* (*lâche*) chicken, yellow **(c)** *Vulg* (*qui a la diarrhée*) suffering from the runs *or* the trots

fois [fwa] *nf* **(a)** (*occasion*) time; **une f.** once; *Belg* **venez une f. voir** (*donc*) just come and see; **une f. et une seule** just the once, once and once only; **il était une f. un roi** once upon a time there was a king; **deux f.** twice; **par deux f.** not once but twice; **combien de f.?** how many times?, how often?; **trois f. quatre font douze** three times four is twelve; **trois f. plus grand** three times as big; **je l'ai acheté pour trois f. rien** I bought it for next to nothing; **il faut du beurre? – oui, mais trois f. rien** do you need some butter? – yes, but the smallest amount *or* but hardly any; **tu t'es fait mal? – non, c'est trois f. rien** have you hurt yourself? – no, it's nothing at all; **encore une f.** once more, once again; **y regarder à deux f.** (**pour faire qch**) to think twice (before doing sth); **une (bonne) f. pour toutes** once and for all; **la première/deuxième f.** the first/second time; **c'est la première f. que j'en fais** it's my first time, it's the first time I've done it; **une dernière f., arrête!** for the last time, stop it!; **cette f.** this time; **pour cette f.** this once; **une autre f.** another time, on another occasion; **d'autres f.** at other times; **bien des f.** many times, often; **deux f. par jour** twice daily *or* a day; **il faut le boire en une f.** you must drink it at *or* in one go *or F* in a oner; **toutes les f.** *ou* **chaque f. que j'y pense** every time that *or* whenever I think about it; **pour une f. tu as raison** you're right for once; **pour une f. que je peux y aller, il faut qu'il vienne aussi!** it's the one time I can go *or* for once I can go and he has to come as well!; **c'est la seule f. où j'ai regretté** that's the only time when *or* that I had regrets; **il y a des f. où je me demande à quoi tu penses** there are times when I wonder what you're thinking about; **une f. que vous aurez des informations** once you have *or* as soon as you have some information; **à la f.** at the same time, at once; **à la f. utile et pas cher** both useful and inexpensive; **pas trop vite, une chose à la f.** slow down, one thing at a time; **pas tous à la f.!** one at a time!, not all at once!, not all at the same time!; **je n'arrive pas à écouter de la musique et lire à la f.** I can't listen to music and read at the same time; *Fig* **tu ne peux pas courir deux lièvres à la f.** you can't do two things at once *or* at the same time

(b) *F* **des f.** (*parfois*) sometimes; **vous n'auriez pas un câble de remorque, des fois?** you haven't by any chance got a towrope?; **des f. qu'il viendrait** in case he should come; **non, mais des f.!** really now!

foison [fwazɔ̃] *nf* **(a)** *Arch* abundance, plenty **(b) à f.** in abundance; **il y en a à f.** there are plenty of them, they are abundant; **des pommes à f.** apples in abundance, apples galore

foisonnant [fwazɔnɑ̃] *adj* abundant, plentiful

foisonnement [fwazɔnmɑ̃] *nf* **(a)** (*prolifération*) abundance, proliferation **(b)** (*multiplication*) multiplying **(c)** (*augmentation de volume*) swelling, expansion

foisonner [fwazɔne] *vi* **(a)** to abound (**de, en** in, with); **le gibier foisonne ici** game is plentiful here; **il foisonne de bonnes idées** he's bursting with good ideas; **une école d'art où les jeunes talents foisonnent** an art school bursting with young talent **(b)** (*d'animaux*) to multiply **(c)** (*augmenter de volume*) to swell, to expand

fol [fɔl] *adj voir* **fou**

folâtre [fɔlatr] *adj* (*personne*) playful, lively; (*agneau, poulain*) frisky

folâtrer [fɔlɑtre] *vi* (*d'une personne*) to romp, to frolic; (*d'un agneau etc*) to gambol, to frisk about
folâtrerie [fɔlɑtrəri] *nf Arch* **(a)** (*d'un agneau*) friskiness; (*d'un chaton*) playfulness **(b)** (*blague*) frolic, romp
foldingue [fɔldɛ̃g] *F* **1** *adj* crazy, nutty **2** *n* nutter
foliacé [fɔljase] *adj Bot* foliaceous
foliaire [fɔljɛr] *adj Bot* foliar
foliation [fɔljasjɔ̃] *nf Bot* foliation
folichon, -onne [fɔliʃɔ̃, -ɔn] *adj* playful, lighthearted; *F* **ce n'est pas f.** it's not much fun
folichonner [fɔliʃɔne] *vi Arch* to play *or* romp about
folie [fɔli] *nf* **(a)** *Méd* madness, lunacy; **accès de f.** fit of madness; **être pris de f.** to go mad; **avoir un grain de f.** to be a bit touched; **aimer qn à la f.** to be madly in love with sb, to love sb to distraction; **aimer qch à la f.** to be mad on sth, to be crazy about sth; *F* **c'est de la f., tout ce monde!** all these people, it's crazy *or* madness!
(b) (*inconscience*) folly; **c'est de la f.!** it's madness!, it's crazy!; **c'est de la f. douce** it's sheer madness!, it's absolutely crazy!; **il a eu la f. de céder** he was mad enough to give in; **dire des folies** to talk wildly, to say crazy things; **faire des folies** to do crazy things; (*faire des achats extravagants*) to go mad; *Hum* **faire des folies de son corps** to put oneself about
(c) *Archit* folly
▶ **folie**: **f. furieuse** raving madness; **f. des grandeurs** delusions of grandeur, megalomania
folio [fɔljo] *nm* folio
foliole [fɔljɔl] *nf Bot* leaflet
folioter [fɔljɔte] *vt* to folio; (*par page*) to paginate
folk [fɔlk] *adj, nm Mus* folk
folklo [fɔlklo] *adj F* (*bizarre*) weird; **il est f.** he's a weirdo *or* an oddball
folklore [fɔlklɔr] *nm* folklore; *F* **c'est du f., ce n'est pas sérieux** it's a bit daft, you can't take it seriously
folklorique [fɔlklɔrik] *adj* (*costume*) traditional; **danses folkloriques** folk *or* country dances; *F* **c'était f.** it was off-the-wall
folkloriste [fɔlklɔrist] *n* folklorist, specialist in folklore
folle [fɔl] *adj voir* **fou**
follement [fɔlmɑ̃] *adv* **(a)** (*avec excès*) madly, foolishly, rashly; **être f. amoureux** to be madly in love **(b)** (*au plus haut point*) madly, wildly; **s'amuser f.** to have a wonderful time
follet, -ette [fɔlɛ, -ɛt] *adj* **(a)** *Arch* **esprit f.** elfish spirit, sprite, (hob)goblin; **feu f.** will-o'-the-wisp, Jack-o'-lantern; *Fig* **c'est un vrai feu f.** he's here today and gone tomorrow **(b) poil f.** (*d'un oiseau, visage*) down; **cheveux follets** stray lock(s)
follicule [fɔlikyl] *nm Bot, Anat* follicle
folliculine [fɔlikylin] *nf Anat* folliculin
fomentateur, -trice [fɔmɑ̃tatœr, -tris] *n* agitator, troublemaker
fomentation [fɔmɑ̃tasjɔ̃] *nf* fomentation
fomenter [fɔmɑ̃te] *vt* to stir up, *Fml* to foment
fonçage [fɔ̃saʒ] *nm* **(a)** (*de tonneau*) bottoming, heading **(b)** (*de puits*) boring, sinking
foncé [fɔ̃se] *adj* (*couleur*) dark; **bleu f.** dark blue
foncer [fɔ̃se] **(je fonçai(s), n. fonçons) 1** *vt* **(a)** (*teinte*) to darken
(b) *Culin* (*moule*) to line
(c) (*tonneau*) to bottom, to head
(d) (*pieu*) to sink, to drive (in); (*puits*) to sink, to bore
2 *vi* **(a) f. sur qn** to rush at *or* swoop (down) on sb; (*d'un taureau, joueur de football*) to charge (at) sb
(b) *F* (*se déplacer très vite*) to speed along; (*se hâter*) to get a move on; **la voiture a foncé dans la foule** the car ploughed into the crowd; *F* **f. dans le tas** to charge in with fists flying; *Fig F* **ne te pose pas de questions, fonce!** don't ask any questions, just do it!
(c) (*s'assombrir*) to darken
fonceur, -euse [fɔ̃sœr, -øz] *F* **1** *n* dynamic *or* go-ahead type **2** *adj* dynamic, go-ahead
foncier, -ière [fɔ̃sje, -jɛr] **1** *adj* **(a)** of land; **propriété foncière** landed property; **le propriétaire f.** the landowner; **rente foncière** ground rent; **impôt f.** land tax; **crédit f.** land bank **(b)** *Fig* (*fondamental*) (*honnêteté*) fundamental, basic **2** *nm* land tax
foncièrement [fɔ̃sjɛrmɑ̃] *adv* fundamentally, basically
fonction [fɔ̃ksjɔ̃] *nf* **(a)** (*poste*) office; **la f. publique** the public *or* civil service; **entrer en fonction(s), prendre ses fonctions** to take up one's duties; **être en f.** to be in office; **cela ne fait pas partie de mes fonctions** that's not part of my duties, that doesn't come within my remit; **voiture/appartement de f.** company car/flat; (*de fonctionnaire*) car/flat that goes with the job
(b) (*rôle*) function; **faire f. de gérant** to act as manager; **cette table fait f. de table à café** this table acts *or* serves as a coffee table; **adjectif qui fait f. d'adverbe** adjective that is used *or* functions as an adverb; *Anat* **fonctions de l'estomac/du cœur** functions of the stomach/heart; **c'est la f. qui crée l'organe** necessity is the mother of invention
(c) *Math* function; **f. inverse** inverse function; **être f. de** to be a function of; *Mktg* **f. de la demande** demand function, market demand function
(d) en f. de (*résultats etc*) according to; **exprimer une quantité en f. d'une autre** to express one quantity in terms of *or* as a function of another; **les prix varient en f. de la demande** prices vary in accordance with *or* according to demand
(e) *Ordinat* **f. booléenne** Boolean function; **f. de comptage de mots** word count facility; **f. de contrôle** control function; **f. 'couper-coller'** cut-and-paste facility; **f. d'éditeur de texte** text editing feature; **f. multimédia** multimedia facility; **f. multitâche** multitasking facility; **f. recherche et remplacement** search and replace function; **f. de recopie** copy function; **f. de sauvegarde** save function; **f. de vérité** truth function
fonctionnaire [fɔ̃ksjɔnɛr] *n* official, civil servant; **haut/petit f.** high-/low-ranking official *or* civil servant; *Péj* **mentalité de f.** bureaucratic mentality
fonctionnalisme [fɔ̃ksjɔnalism] *nm* functionalism
fonctionnaliste [fɔ̃ksjɔnalist] *adj* functionalist
fonctionnalité [fɔ̃ksjɔnalite] *nf* functionality
fonctionnariser [fɔ̃ksjɔnarize] *vt* (*employés, profession*) to make part of the public *or* civil service
fonctionnarisme [fɔ̃ksjɔnarism] *nm Péj* officialdom, bureaucracy, *F* red tape
fonctionnel, -elle [fɔ̃ksjɔnɛl] *adj* functional
fonctionnellement [fɔ̃ksjɔnɛlmɑ̃] *adv* functionally
fonctionnement [fɔ̃ksjɔnmɑ̃] *nm* **(a)** (*du gouvernement, d'un plan etc*) functioning, working **(b)** (*d'une machine etc*) functioning, operation, running, working; **en (bon) état de f.** in (good) working order; **mauvais f.** malfunction, fault; **panne due à un mauvais f. du carburateur** breakdown due to a malfunction in the *or* a malfunctioning carburettor; **cycle de f.** operating cycle; *Ordinat* **f. en réseau** networking
fonctionner [fɔ̃ksjɔne] *vi* (*d'une machine, d'un mécanisme*) to function, to work; (*d'une personne*) to function, to operate; *Ordinat* to run; **les trains ne fonctionnent plus** the trains are no longer running; **les freins n'ont pas fonctionné** the brakes failed, the brakes didn't work; **faire f. une machine** to operate *or* work a machine; *Él* **f. sur courant continu** to operate *or* run on direct current; **f. sur piles** to run on batteries, to be battery-operated; **dans cette atmosphère mon cerveau ne peut pas f.** my brain can't function in this atmosphere
fond [fɔ̃] *nm* **(a)** (*partie la plus profonde*) bottom; (*de chapeau*) crown; (*de chaise, de pantalon*) seat; (*de tonneau*) bottom, head; (*de la gorge*) back; **abîme sans f.** bottomless chasm; **boîte à double f.** box with a false bottom; **bateau à f. plat** flat-bottomed boat; **f. de cylindre/chaudière** cylinder/boiler head; **f. de bouteille** dregs; **il n'en reste qu'un f.** there's only a drop left; **râcler ses fonds de tiroir** to scrape around (*for money*); **du f. du cœur** from the bottom of one's heart; **tu connais le f. de ma pensée** you know what my thoughts *or* feelings really are; *Fig* **au f., dans le f.** basically; **dans le f. elle n'est pas méchante** she's not a bad sort at heart *or* deep down *or* she's basically not a bad sort; **au f., c'est ce qu'il voulait** (deep down) that's what he really wanted; **au f. il était très flatté** in his heart of hearts he was extremely flattered; **aller au f. d'une affaire/d'un problème** to get to the bottom *or* root of a matter/problem; **à f.** (*étudier*) thoroughly; **enfoncer un clou à f.** to hammer a nail home, to drive a nail all the way in; **respire à f.** breathe deeply; **on a fait le ménage à f. dans la cuisine** we cleaned the kitchen thoroughly; **se consacrer** *ou* **se donner à f. à qch** to devote oneself totally to sth; **il s'est engagé à f. dans le combat écologique** he committed himself wholeheartedly *or* body and soul to the struggle for the environment; **connaître un sujet à f.** to have a thorough knowledge of a subject; **à f. (de train)** (at) full tilt; *Fig* **elle a touché le f.** she's hit rock bottom
(b) (*de l'océan*) bottom, bed; **il n'y a pas assez de f. pour plonger/jeter l'ancre** the water isn't deep enough for diving/for dropping anchor; **f. de sable** sandy bottom; **prendre f.** (*d'une ancre*) to bite, to grip; **envoyer un navire par le f.** to send a ship to the bottom; **grands fonds** ocean depths *or* deeps; **courant de f.** undertow; **lame de f.** groundswell
(c) (*fondement*) **rebâtir une maison de f. en comble** to rebuild a house from top to bottom; *Fig* **il a un bon f.** he's good at heart *or* basically good; **faire f. sur qn/qch** to rely *or*

depend on sb/sth; **le f. et la forme** the form and the content *or* substance; **le f. de cette politique** the essential features of this policy; **question de f.** fundamental question; *Journ* **article de f.** feature (article); *Mus* **jeu de f.** (*d'un orgue*) pipe stop; **f. sonore** *ou* **musical** background music *or* sound

(d) (*partie la plus éloigne*) (*d'une peinture*) background; (*d'un espace clos*) far end; **la salle du f.** the room at the end, the far room; *F* **fonds de boutique** oddments, old stock; **au (fin) f. du désert/de l'Australie** in the heart of the desert/Australia; **au fin f. de la campagne** in the depths of the country; *Th* **toile de f.** backdrop, backcloth; *Fig* **avec la guerre en toile de f.** against a backdrop of war; *Tennis* **ligne de f.** baseline; **bruit de f.** background noise; **sur un f. de musique tzigane** with gipsy music in the background

(e) *Sp* **le f.** long-distance running; **course de (grand) f.** long-distance race; *Ski* cross-country race; **coureur de f.** long-distance runner; **ski de f.** cross-country skiing, langlauf; **cheval qui a du f.** horse with staying power

▶ **fond**: **f. d'artichaut** artichoke heart; **f. de cale** bilge; **tous les mutins furent enfermés à f. de cale** the mutineers were all locked away in the bottom of the hold; **f. musical** background music *Méd* **f. d'œil** examination of the retina; **f. de robe** (full-length) slip; **f. scénique** scenic background; **f. sonore** background music; **f. de teint** foundation (cream)

fondamental, -ale, -aux, -ales [fɔ̃damɑ̃tal, -o] *adj* (*principe, postulat, différence, erreur, contradiction*) basic, fundamental; **il est f. que tout soit prêt à temps** it is (absolutely) essential that everything is ready in time; **le vocabulaire f. d'une langue** the basic *or* base vocabulary of a language; **pierre fondamentale** foundation stone; **couleurs fondamentales** primary colours; *Mus* **son f.** (*d'une corde*) root, generator; *Univ* **recherche fondamentale** basic research

fondamentalement [fɔ̃damɑ̃talmɑ̃] *adv* fundamentally, basically

fondamentalisme [fɔ̃damɑ̃talism] *nm Rel* fundamentalism

fondamentaliste [fɔ̃damɑ̃talist] *n* **(a)** (*scientifique*) scientist engaged in basic research **(b)** *Rel* fundamentalist

fondant [fɔ̃dɑ̃] **1** *adj* melting; **poire fondante** pear that melts in the mouth; **un chocolat f.** a fondant chocolate; **viande fondante** very tender meat; **tons fondants** blended shades (of colour) **2** *nm* **(a)** (*bonbon*) fondant; **un f. au chocolat** a chocolate fondant **(b)** *Tech* flux

fondateur, -trice [fɔ̃datœr, -tris] **1** *n* (*d'une ville, société etc*) founder **2** *adj* **membre f.** founder *or* founding member; **les mythes fondateurs d'une culture** the underlying myths of a culture

fondation [fɔ̃dasjɔ̃] *nf* **(a)** (*d'une ville, d'un hôpital etc*) founding, foundation; **f. d'une entreprise** setting up of a business **(b)** (*fonds*) endowment (fund), foundation **(c)** (*établissement*) foundation **(d)** *Constr* **fondations** foundations

fondé [fɔ̃de] **1** *adj* (*doutes, peurs*) well-founded, justified; **vos craintes ne sont pas fondées** your fears are groundless *or* unfounded *or* unjustified; **mal f.** (*soupçons*) groundless, ill-founded; **établissement f. en 1850** established 1850; **être f. à croire** to have good reason(s) to believe; **qu'est-ce qu'il y a de f. dans ces bruits?** is there any justification for anything in these reports?, is anything in these reports justified? **2** *nm Jur* **f. de pouvoir** agent (*holding power of attorney*); (*mandant*) proxy; (*directeur de banque*) manager with signing authority

fondement [fɔ̃dmɑ̃] *nm* **(a)** (*base*) foundation, base; **soupçons sans f.** groundless *or* unfounded suspicions **(b)** *F* (*derrière*) behind, backside; (*anus*) back passage

fonder [fɔ̃de] **1** *vt* (*ville*) to found; (*société, journal*) to start, to set up; **f. une famille** to start a family; **f. un hôpital** (*en donnant un legs*) to found a hospital; **f. ses espérances sur qch** to base *or* build one's hopes on sth; **document fondé sur des témoignages réels** document based on authentic accounts; **théorie fondée sur des textes scientifiques** theory based on scientific texts

2 se fonder *vpr* **se f. sur qch** (*d'une personne*) to go by sth, to base oneself on sth; (*d'une remarque, théorie*) to be based on sth; **sur quoi se fonde-t-il pour le nier?** what are his grounds for denying it?; **un espoir qui se fondait sur une information fausse** a hope that was based on misinformation

fonderie [fɔ̃dri] *nf* **(a)** (*extraction*) (*de minerai*) smelting; (*fusion*) (*de métaux*) founding, casting **(b)** (*usine*) (*d'extraction*) smelting works; (*de fusion*) foundry

fondeur[1] [fɔ̃dœr] *nm* (*maître de forges*) ironmaster; (*ouvrier*) (*d'extraction*) smelter; (*de fusion*) (metal) founder; **f. en cuivre** brass founder; **f. en caractères, f. typographe** type founder

fondeur[2]**, -euse** [fɔ̃dœr, -øz] *n Ski* cross-country skier

fondre [fɔ̃dr] **1** *vt* **(a)** (*liquéfier*) (*minerai*) to smelt; (*métal*) to melt down; (*sucre*) to dissolve; (*neige, cire etc*) to melt; **f. deux fils ensemble** to fuse two wires together

(b) (*fabriquer*) (*cloche, arme etc*) to cast, to found

(c) *TV etc* to fade; **f. des teintes** to blend colours

(d) *Com* (*compagnies*) to amalgamate, to merge

2 *vi* **(a)** (*se liquéfier*) to melt; (*de la neige*) to melt, to thaw; (*du sucre*) to dissolve; **le beurre fond au soleil** butter melts in the sun; **faire fondre le beurre dans une casserole** melt the butter in a saucepan; *Él* **faire f. un fusible** to blow a fuse; *Fig* **mon cœur fondit (de pitié)** my heart melted (with pity); **je fonds** my heart melts; **f. en larmes** to dissolve in(to) tears; **l'argent lui fond entre les doigts** money runs through his fingers; **il fond à vue d'œil** he's visibly wasting away

(b) fondre sur sa proie to pounce upon *or* to swoop (down) upon one's prey

3 se fondre *vpr* to merge; (*de compagnies*) to amalgamate, to merge; **se f. dans la brume** to disappear into the mist; **se f. dans la foule** to merge *or* blend into the crowd; **leur maison se fond dans le paysage** their house merges into the landscape; **se f. dans l'anonymat** to hide under the cloak of anonymity

fondrière [fɔ̃drijɛr] *nf* pothole (*full of water*); **une fondrière marécageuse** a bog; *Can* **f. de mousse** muskeg

fonds [fɔ̃] *nm* [①**A10**,f,i] **(a)** *pl* (*argent*) fund

(b) (*organisme*) fund; **F. monétaire international** International Monetary Fund; **F. national de garantie des salaires** national guarantee fund for the payment of salaries; **F. européen de développement** European Development Fund; **F. européen de développement régional** European Regional Development Fund; **F. social européen** European Social Fund

(c) *pl* (*ressources*) funds; **réunir des f.** to raise funds; **je n'ai pas les f. suffisants pour ouvrir un magasin** I don't have the (necessary) funds *or* capital to open a shop; **mise de f.** paid-in capital; **mouvement de f.** flow of capital; **rentrer dans ses f.** to recoup one's losses; **être en f.** to be in funds; **appel de f.** call upon shareholders; **ne pas toucher à ses f.** not to touch one's capital; **placer son argent à f. perdus** to purchase an annuity; **je l'ai aidé, mais je savais que c'était à f. perdus** I helped him, but I knew I wouldn't get my money back; **prêt à f. perdus** loan without security

(d) (*dans un musée*) collection; *Fig* **c'est un f. inestimable pour les chercheurs** it is an invaluable resource for researchers; **le f. commun de toutes les langues indoeuropéennes** the common stock of all Indo-European languages

(e) *Bourse pl* stocks, securities; **f. d'État, f. publics** Government stock(s)

▶ **fonds**: **f. de caisse** float; **f. de chômage** unemployment fund; **f. de clientèle** customer base; **f. de commerce** business; **f. de commerce à vendre** business for sale (as a going concern); **f. commercial** goodwill; **f. commun** common fund, pool; **f. commun de placement** investment trust, mutual fund; **f. d'épargne-retraite** retirement savings fund; **f. de garantie** guarantee fund; **f. de grève** strike fund; **f. d'investissement** investment fund; **f. de prévoyance** contingency fund; **f. propres** equity; **f. publics** government funds; (*valeurs*) government stocks; **f. de réserve** reserve funds; **f. de roulement** working capital; **f. de secours** emergency fund; **f. de terre** (piece of) land

fondu, -ue [fɔ̃dy] **1** *adj* (*beurre*) melted; (*plomb, lave*) molten; **neige fondue** (*qui tombe*) sleet; (*par terre*) slush

2 *nm* **(a)** (*de couleurs*) blending

(b) *Cin* dissolve, fade; **faire un f.** to fade; **faire un f. au noir** to fade to black; **s'ouvrir en f.** to fade in; **ouverture en f.** fade-in; **fermeture en f.** fade-out; **f. enchaîné** mix, lap dissolve, dissolve; **faire un f. enchaîné** to fade in-fade out; **f. par ondulation** ripple dissolve; **f. par passage au flou** defocus dissolve

3 *nf Culin* **fondue (savoyarde)** (cheese) fondue; **fondue bourguignonne** fondue bourguignonne, beef fondue

fongible [fɔ̃ʒibl] *adj* fungible

fongicide [fɔ̃ʒisid] **1** *adj* fungicidal **2** *nm* fungicide

fongueux, -euse [fɔ̃gø, -øz] *adj Méd* fungous

fontaine [fɔ̃tɛn] *nf* **(a)** (*source*) spring; **Fontaine de Jouvence** Fountain of Youth; *Prov* **il ne faut pas dire 'f., je ne boirai pas de ton eau'** never say never **(b)** (*construite*) fountain **(c)** (*petit réservoir*) cistern; **f. filtrante** *ou* **de ménage** (household) filter

fontainier [fɔ̃tenje] *nm* **(a)** water engineer **(b)** (*qui cherche de l'eau*) well borer *or* sinker

fontanelle [fɔ̃tanɛl] *nf Anat* fontanel(le)

fonte[1] [fɔ̃t] *nf* **(a)** (*de neige*) melting, thawing; (*d'or, d'argent etc*) melting down; (*de minerai*) smelting; *Métal* casting, founding; **pièces de f.** castings; **(fer de) f., f. de fer** cast iron; **f. d'acier** cast steel; **poêle en f.** cast-iron stove; *Méd* **f. musculaire** wasting of muscle **(b)** *Typ* font; **f. bitmap** bitmap font; **f. de caractère** character font; **f. écran** screen font; **f.**

imprimante printer font; **f. reconnue optiquement** OCR-font; **f. vectorielle** outline font

fonte[2] *nf* (*d'une selle*) holster

fonts [fɔ̃] *nmpl* **f. baptismaux** (baptismal) font; **tenir un enfant sur les f. baptismaux** to be godfather/godmother to a child

foot [fut] *nm F* football, soccer; **jouer au f.** to play football *or* soccer

football [futbol] *nm Br* football, soccer, *Am* soccer

footballeur, -euse [futbolœr, -øz] *n* football *or* soccer player, footballer

footeux [futø] *nm F* (*joueur*) football *or* soccer player; (*supporter*) football *or* soccer fan

footing [futiŋ] *nm* jogging; **faire son f.** to go jogging, to jog

for [fɔr] *nm* **le f. intérieur** the conscience; **dans** *ou* **en son f. intérieur** in one's heart of hearts, deep (down) inside

forage [fɔraʒ] *nm* **(a)** (*action*) (*de puits*) drilling, boring, sinking; **f. pétrolier** drilling oil-wells **(b)** (*trou*) borehole, drill hole

forain, -aine [fɔrɛ̃, -ɛn] **1** *adj* **(a)** (*itinérant*) itinerant; **spectacle f.** travelling show; **hercule f.** strongman (*at a fair*); **baraque foraine** fairground stall; **fête foraine** funfair; **marchand f.** stallholder **(b)** *Naut* **mouillage f.** open berth **2** *n* fair stallholder

forban [fɔrbɑ̃] *nm* pirate, buccaneer; *Fig* rogue, crook

forçage [fɔrsaʒ] *nm* **(a)** (*de plantes*) forcing **(b)** = **forcement (c)** *MecE* **introduction d'air par f.** ram air induction

forçat [fɔrsa] *nm* (*prisonnier*) convict; (*galérien*) galley slave; *Fig* **mener une vie de f.** to slave away, to work like a slave; **la maçonnerie est un métier de f.** building work is really backbreaking; **je ne supporte plus cette vie de f.** I can't stand this slavery any more

force [fɔrs] **1** *nf* **(a)** (*vigueur*) strength; **être à bout de force(s)** to have no strength left; **je n'ai pas beaucoup de f.** I've not got much strength, I'm not very strong; **donner des forces** to give strength; **(re)prendre des forces** to (re)gain strength; **ménager ses forces** to save *or* conserve *or Fml* husband one's strength; **la maladie le laissa sans f.** the illness left him (feeling) weak, the illness sapped his strength; **ne pas sentir sa f.** not to know one's own strength; **cette épreuve est au-dessus de ses forces** this test is beyond him *or* is too much for him; **lui parler fut au-dessus de mes forces** it was too much for me to speak to him; **il le frappa avec f.** he hit him hard *or* forcefully; **mon doute revint avec f.** my doubts returned with renewed force; **de toutes ses forces** (*pousser, frapper etc*) with all one's strength *or* might; **j'essaie de toutes mes forces de le convaincre** I'm trying as hard as I can to convince him; **elle le veut de toutes ses forces** she wants it with all her heart; **vouloir à toute f. faire qch** to be determined to do sth, to want to do sth at all costs; **il veut à toute f. qu'on soit rentré à minuit** he wants us to be back at midnight at all costs; **elle n'avait plus la f. de répondre** she didn't have the strength (left) to answer, she had no strength left to answer; **je ne me sens pas/ne suis pas de f. à faire cela** I don't feel/I'm not up to *or* equal to doing it; **elle ne se sentait pas la f. de lui en parler** she didn't feel up to talking to him about it; **de f. égale, de même f.** equally matched, well matched; **ce qui fait votre f., c'est ...** your strength is ...; **être bâti en f.** to be stocky, to be strongly built; **dans la f. de l'âge** in the prime of life

(b) (*courage*) **f. d'âme** moral strength, fortitude; **elle a une sacrée f. de caractère** she has incredible strength of character

(c) tour de f. tour de force; *Constr* **(jambe de) f.** force piece, strut; **f. de résistance à la tension** tensile strength

(d) (*violence*) force; **faire appel à** *ou* **avoir recours à la f.** to resort to force; **céder à la f.** to give in *or* yield to force; **faire qch de vive f.** to do sth by sheer force; **entrer** *ou* **pénétrer de f. dans une maison** to force one's way into a house; **faire entrer qch de f. dans qch** to force sth into sth; **f. lui fut d'obéir** he was obliged to obey, he had no option but to obey; *Jur* **un cas de f. majeure** (*en assurance*) a case of absolute necessity, an act of God; **c'était un cas de f. majeur** there was no other option, circumstances were beyond my/our/your/*etc* control; *Naut* **faire f. de voiles** to crowd on (all) sail; **faire f. de rames** to row *or* pull hard; *Prov* **la f. prime le droit, f. passe droit** might is right; **il devra le faire, de gré ou de f.** he'll have to do it whether he wants to or not, he'll have to do it willy-nilly

(e) (*d'un coup, du vent, d'un argument*) force; **vent de f. 8** force 8 gale; **les forces de la nature** the forces of nature; **f. vitale** life force; **c'est une f. de la nature** he's a mighty force; **par la f. des choses** through force of circumstance; **la f. de l'habitude** force of habit; **dans toute la f. du mot** in the strongest sense of the word, in every sense of the word

(f) à f. de by (dint of); **à f. d'y penser** by (dint of) thinking about it; **à f. de travailler** by (dint of) hard work; **à f. d'explications** by (dint of) explanation; **à f. de volonté** by sheer force of will; **à f. de répéter** by constant repetition; **il s'est enroué à f. de crier** he shouted himself hoarse; **à f. de jouer dehors le soir, tu vas t'enrhumer** by playing outside in the evening you'll end up with a cold; **il va se lasser, à f.** he'll get tired of it in the long run

(g) *Phys* **f. motrice** motive power; *Fig* driving force; **f. d'inertie** inertia; **f. vive** kinetic energy, momentum; *Él* **f. (électrique)** (electric) power; **prise de f.** power point; **f. centrifuge** centrifugal force; **f. centripète** centripetal force; **f. de traction** traction *or* tractive force; **forces d'inertie** inertia forces; **forces de cisaillement** shear forces; *Aut* **forces en virage** cornering force

(h) les forces armées the armed forces, the services; **f. tactique** *ou* **d'intervention** task force; **la f. publique, les forces de police** *ou* **de l'ordre** the police (force), the forces of law and order; **les forces vives du pays** the country's resources; **nous étions là en force(s)** we were there in (full) force; **ils sont arrivés en f.** they arrived in force; *Écon* **les forces du marché** market forces; *Mktg* **forces, faiblesses, opportunités et menaces** strengths, weaknesses, opportunities and threats, SWOT; **f. de travail** workforce; **f. de vente** sales force; **forces nucléaires intermédiaires** intermediate-range nuclear forces

2 *adj inv Arch, Litt* **f. gens/anecdotes** a great number of *or* (very) many people/anecdotes; **f. bière** copious amounts of beer

forcé [fɔrse] *adj* **(a)** (*obligé*) forced; *Av* **atterrissage f.** forced *or* emergency landing; *Jur* **travaux forcés** hard labour; *F* **mariage f.** shotgun wedding, forced marriage; **la comparaison est un peu forcée** the comparison is a bit forced; **exemple f.** far-fetched example **(b)** (*affecté*) **rire/sourire f.** forced laugh/smile **(c)** (*involontaire*) **prendre un bain f.** to fall in (the water) **(d)** *F* **c'est f.!** it's inevitable!

forcement [fɔrsəmɑ̃] *nm* forcing (open); **f. de blocus** blockade running

forcément [fɔrsemɑ̃] *adv* inevitably; **nous étions f. en retard** inevitably *or* of course, we were late; **elle le sait f. déjà** she's bound to *or* she must know already; **elle sera f. déçue** she's bound to be disappointed; **f.!** of course; **pas f.** not necessarily; **l'herbe est verte, f., il a plu tous les jours** the grass is green but it's not surprising, it has been raining every day

forcené, -ée [fɔrsəne] **1** *adj* **(a)** *Arch* (*personne*) lunatic, mad **(b)** (*extrême*) (*marche, imagination*) frenzied; (*amateur de bons vins etc*) passionate; (*individualisme*) fanatical, rabid; **un goût f. du travail** a fanatical liking for work **2** *n* maniac, madman, *f* madwoman; **crier comme un f.** to scream like a madman/madwoman

forceps [fɔrsɛps] *nm Obst* forceps; **accouchement au f.** forceps delivery

forcer [fɔrse] **(je forçai(s)) 1** *vt* **(a)** (*obliger*) to force, to compel; **f. qn à faire qch** to force *or* compel sb to do sth, to make sb do sth; **sans vouloir te f. il faudrait faire la vaisselle** I don't want to force you, but the washing-up has to be done; **personne ne t'y force** no one is forcing you; **f. la main à qn** to force sb's hand; **f. le respect/l'admiration (de qn)** to command sb's respect/admiration; **être forcé de faire qch** to be forced to do sth; **f. une femme** to violate *or* rape a woman; *Mil* **f. un poste** to take a post by storm *or* by force; **f. une serrure/un coffre** to force (open) a lock/a safe; **f. la caisse** to force open the till, to break into the till; **f. une porte** to force (open) *or* break open a door; **f. la porte de qn** to force one's way into sb's place; **f. le destin** to force the hand of destiny

(b) (*voix*) to force; (*mât*) to strain; (*plaque*) to buckle; *F* **f. la note** to overdo it; **f. l'allure** *ou* **le pas** to force the pace; **f. le sens** to strain *or* distort the meaning; **f. un cheval** to override a horse; **f. des fleurs** to force flowers; **f. un cerf** to run down a stag, to bring a stag to bay; **f. la dose d'un médicament** to take/give too large a dose of a medicine

(c) *Ordinat* (*justification, coupure de page*) to force

2 *vi* **f. de voiles** to crowd on sail; **f. sur les avirons** to strain at the oars; **le vent force** the wind is rising; *Cartes* **f. sur l'annonce de qn** to overcall *or* overbid sb; **tu y arriveras sans f.** you'll get there without straining yourself *or* without too much effort; **essayez de garder les jambes raides, mais ne forcez pas** try to keep your legs straight, but don't strain yourself; **ne force pas, ça doit se fermer tout seul!** don't force it, it has to close by itself!; *F* **f. sur la bouteille** to overdo the drinking; **je crains d'avoir forcé sur le poivre** I'm afraid I've overdone (it with) the pepper

3 se forcer *vpr* (*s'obliger*) to force oneself; **se f. à faire qch** to force oneself to do sth

forcing [fɔrsiŋ] *nm Sp* sustained pressure; *Fig F* **il a fallu faire le f. pour qu'il accepte** we had to put on a lot of pressure to get him to accept; **avoir qn au f.** to pressurize sb, to put pressure on sb

forcir [fɔrsir] *vi* (**a**) (*d'une personne*) to fill out, to get bigger (**b**) (*des éléments*) **le vent/la tempête forcit** the wind is picking up/the storm is getting stronger

forclore [fɔrklɔr] *vt Jur* to debar

forclusion [fɔrklyzjɔ̃] *nf Jur* debarment; *Fin* foreclosure

forer [fɔre] *vt* (*roche*) to drill, to bore; (*puits*) to drill, to bore, to sink

forestier, -ière [fɔrɛstje, -jɛr] **1** *adj* (*zone*) forest(ed); **chemin f.** forest road; **essences forestières** forest trees; **une exploitation forestière** a forestry development; **garde f.** forester, forest warden, *US* ranger **2** *nm* forester

foret [fɔrɛ] *nm* (**a**) (*vrille*) drill (**b**) **f. à bois** gimlet; **f. de charpentier** auger (**c**) (*vilebrequin*) (brace) bit

forêt [fɔrɛ] *nf* forest; **f. vierge** virgin forest; **région couverte de forêts** forest(ed) region; *Admin* **le service des Eaux et Forêts** *Br* ≈ the Forestry Commission, *US* the Forest Service; *Fig* **une f. de mâts** a forest of masts; *Prov* **les arbres vous cachent la f.** you can't see the wood *or Am* forest for the trees; *Culin* **F. noire** Black Forest gateau

foreur [fɔrœr] *nm* borer, driller; *Pétr* **f. d'exploration** oil prospector, *US F* wildcatter

foreuse [fɔrøz] *nf* (*outil*) drill; *Min etc* rock drill; **f. à main** hand drill

forfaire [fɔrfɛr] *vi* (*conj like* **faire**) *Arch, Litt* **f. à son devoir** to fail in one's duty; **f. à l'honneur** to forfeit one's honour; **f. à sa parole** to break one's word

forfait[1] [fɔrfɛ] *nm* (*crime*) heinous crime

forfait[2] *nm* (*contrat*) fixed-price contract; *Fin* lump sum; **le f. comprend les frais de location et d'entretien du matériel** the set *or* fixed price includes the cost of hire and maintenance of the equipment; **f. (-voyage)** package (deal); **travail à f.** fixed-price work; **travailler au f.** to do fixed-price work; **prix à f.** all-in price; **et pour un f. de 500 francs** and for an all-in price of 500 francs, and for 500 francs all in; **vente à f.** outright sale; **f. avion + location de voiture** fly drive; **f. de remontées mécaniques** ski *or* lift pass; **f. de ski** ski pass; **f.-vacances** holiday package; **f. week-end** weekend package; *Com* **f. de port** carriage forward

forfait[3] *nm Courses de chevaux* fine, forfeit (*paid for scratching a horse*); **déclarer f. pour un cheval** to scratch a horse; **déclarer f.** (*d'un athlète, concurrent*) to scratch; *Fig* to throw in the towel; **l'équipe a déclaré f.** the team withdrew

forfaitage [fɔrfɛtaʒ] *nm* forfaiting

forfaitaire [fɔrfɛtɛr] *adj* **marché f.** fixed-price contract; **paiement f.** lump sum; **indemnités forfaitaires** basic allocation; **prix f.** all-in price; **voyage à prix f.** package tour

forfaitairement [fɔrfɛtɛrmɑ̃] *adv Fin* in a lump sum; (*facturer*) in a lump sum, in one amount

forfaiture [fɔrfɛtyr] *nf* (*abus de pouvoir*) abuse of authority; **f. au devoir/à l'honneur** breach of duty/honour

forfanterie [fɔrfɑ̃tri] *nf* bragging, boasting

forge [fɔrʒ] *nf* forge; **f. (de maréchal-ferrant)** smithy; **mener un cheval à la f.** to take a horse to the blacksmith's; **f. de serrurier** locksmith's workshop; **maître de forges** ironmaster; **pièce de f.** forging

forgeable [fɔrʒabl] *adj* (*métal*) forgeable

forgeage [fɔrʒaʒ] *nm* forging

forger [fɔrʒe] (**je forgeai(s)**) **1** *vt* (**a**) (*métal*) to forge; **fer forgé** wrought iron; **cela forge le caractère** it forms *or* moulds the character, it is character-forming; **f. un homme** to form a man's character; *Prov* **c'est en forgeant qu'on devient forgeron** practice makes perfect

(**b**) (*inventer*) (*histoire, excuse*) to fabricate, to make up; (*mot*) to coin; (*accusation*) to trump up; (*vision*) to conjure up; **histoire forgée de toutes pièces** completely fabricated *or* made-up story

2 se forger *vpr* **se f. une réputation** to carve out a reputation for oneself; **se f. un idéal de vie** to create an ideal lifestyle for oneself

forgeron [fɔrʒərɔ̃] *nm* (black)smith

forgeur, -euse [fɔrʒœr, -øz] **1** *n* (*de nouvelles, mensonges*) inventor, fabricator; (*de mots*) coiner **2** *nm Litt* (*forgeron*) metal worker

formage [fɔrmaʒ] *nm Tech* forming

formaldéhyde [fɔrmaldeid] *nm* (*parfois f*) *Ch* formaldehyde

formalisation [fɔrmalizasjɔ̃] *nf* formalization

formaliser [fɔrmalize] **1** *vt* to formalize; **logique formalisée** formal logic **2 se formaliser** *vpr* to take offence (**de** at), to take exception (**de** to)

formalisme [fɔrmalism] *nm* (**a**) formality; **f. administratif** bureaucracy, *F* red tape; **f. intransigeant** rigid obsession with formalities (**b**) *Beaux-Arts* formalism

formaliste [fɔrmalist] **1** *adj* (**a**) formalistic (**b**) *Beaux-Arts* formalist **2** *n* formalist

formalité [fɔrmalite] *nf* (**a**) (*procédure*) formality; **c'est une pure f., ce n'est qu'une f.** it's just a formality; **formalités douanières** customs formalities; **formalités d'entrée** entry requirements; **sans autre f.** without further ado (**b**) (*cérémonie*) formality; **sans formalité(s)** informal

format [fɔrma] *nm* (*de livre*), *Ordinat* format; (*de papier*), *Phot* size, format; **f. de poche** pocket size; *Typ* **f. paysage** landscape format; *Typ* **f. portrait** portrait format; **f. tabloïd** tabloid format; **f. de page** page format *or* layout; *Ordinat* **f. ASCII** ASCII format; **f. carte de crédit** credit card format; **f. d'impression** print format; **f. d'écran** screen format; **f. de fichier** file format; **f. de papier** paper format; *TV etc* **f. de présentation** show format

formatage [fɔrmataʒ] *nm Ordinat* formatting; **f. de bas niveau** low-level format(ting); **f. de haut niveau** high-level format(ting); **f. logiciel** soft sectoring

formater [fɔrmate] *vt Ordinat* to format

formateur, -trice [fɔrmatœr, -tris] **1** *adj* formative; **expérience formatrice** formative experience **2** *n* trainer

formation [fɔrmasjɔ̃] *nf* (**a**) (*constitution*) formation; (*de caractère*) forming, development; **la f. du goût/de la personnalité** the development of taste/the personality; **volcan en voie** *ou* **en cours de f.** volcano in the process of formation; **mot de f. savante** word of learned origin; **la f. du pluriel en anglais** the formation of the plural in English

(**b**) (*éducation*) training; **avoir une excellente f.** to have an excellent training; **elle a reçu une f. littéraire/scientifique** she received a literary education/a scientific training; **il lui faut une f.** he needs (some) training; **il est technicien de f.** he trained as a technician; **f. continue** *ou* **permanente** continuing education, continuous training; **f. professionnelle** vocational training; **f. courte** *ou* **accélérée** intensive training; **être en f.** to be undergoing training; **stage de f.** training course; **f. sur le tas** *ou* **par la pratique** on-the-job training

(**c**) (*de roche*) formation; *Mil* **f. serrée** close formation

(**d**) (*groupe*), *Mil* unit; *Mus* group; **une petite f. de jazz** a small jazz band; **f. aérienne** aerial unit; **f. politique** political group

forme [fɔrm] *nf* (**a**) (*configuration*) form, shape; **formes** (*d'un bateau*) lines; (*d'une personne*) figure; (*d'une femme*) curves; **les formes d'un tableau/paysage** the lines of a picture/shapes of a landscape; **vêtement qui épouse les formes** close-fitting *or* figure-hugging garment; **en f. d'œuf** egg-shaped; **gomme en f. de voiture** eraser in the shape *or* form of a car, car-shaped eraser; **yeux en f. de billes** eyes like marbles; **sous la f. d'une nymphe** in the form *or* shape of a nymph; **c'est une différente f. d'esprit** it is a different way of thinking; **l'histoire racontée sous une nouvelle f.** history told in a new way; **présenter les choses sous une autre f.** to present things in a different *or* in another way; **statistiques sous f. de tableau** statistics in tabular form; **le produit existe aussi sous f. de bombe aérosol** the product also comes as an aerosol spray; **sous toutes ses formes** in all its forms *or* guises; **sans f.** shapeless; **prendre f.** to take shape; **mettre en f.** (*texte*) to format

(**b**) (*procédure*) form; **arrêt cassé pour vice de f.** judgment quashed on a technical point; **renvoyer qn sans autre f. de procès** to dismiss sb without further ado; **avertir qn dans les formes** to give sb formal *or* due warning; **il faut y mettre les formes** it must be done tactfully; **faire qch dans les formes** to do sth in the accepted way; **de pure f.** purely formal; **vérification de pure f.** routine check; **pour la f.** as a matter of form

(**c**) **être en f.** to be on form *or* in good form; **être très en f.** *ou* **en pleine f.** *ou* **en grande f.**, *F* **tenir** *ou* **péter la f.** to be in great form, *F* to be in cracking form; **ne pas être en f., être en mauvaise f.**, *F* **ne pas avoir la f.** not to be on form, to be in poor form; **c'est bon pour la f.** it's good for you, it'll do you good; *F* **alors, c'est la f.?** how are you doing?

(**d**) *Ind* former, forming block; (*pour fromage etc*) mould, *US* mold; (*de cordonnier*) last; (*pour élargir*) shoe tree; (*de chapelier*) block; **chapeau haut de f.** top hat

(**e**) *Naut* dock

(**f**) *Typ* forme, *US* form

(**g**) *Com* **f. sociale** type of company

formé [fɔrme] *adj* fully formed, fully developed; **jeune fille formée** fully-developed girl; **un personnel bien f.** well-trained staff

formel, -elle [fɔrmɛl] *adj* (**a**) (*ordre*) express; (*démenti*) flat, categorical; (*veto*) absolute; **défense formelle** strict prohibition; **il a été tout à fait f. sur ce point** he was quite adamant *or* definite on this point; **je suis f.** I'm (absolutely) positive **(b)** (*de principe*) (*distinction, attitude*) formal **(c)** *Phil* (*cause*) formal

formellement [fɔrmɛlmɑ̃] *adv* **(a)** (*interdit*) strictly; **promettre f.** to promise faithfully; **s'engager f. à régler ses dettes** to vow to pay off one's debts; **accuser f. qn** to specifically accuse sb; **l'homme a été f. reconnu** the man was positively identified **(b)** (*en considérant la forme*) formally; **une argumentation f. inattaquable** an argument that cannot be attacked on formal grounds

former [fɔrme] **1** *vt* **(a)** (*créer*) (*gouvernement, collection etc*) to form; *Rail* (*train*) to make up; **f. un projet/des idées** to form a plan/ideas; **les murs forment un carré** the walls form a square; **ils forment une famille unie** they are a united family; **ils forment une bonne équipe/un beau couple** they make a good team/a lovely couple

(b) (*pilote, cheval etc*) to train; (*caractère*) to form, to mould, *US* to mold; **f. son esprit/son goût** to develop one's mind/taste; **f. l'oreille/l'œil** to train the ear/eye; **cela forme le caractère** it forms *or* moulds the character, it is character-forming; **cette université a formé des hommes remarquables** this university has turned out *or* produced some remarkable men; *MecE* **f. par roulage** to roll

(c) nous avons formé des vœux pour sa réussite we wished him every success

2 se former *vpr* **(a)** (*se développer*) to form, to develop; (*apparaître*) (*d'un fruit*) to form; (*d'un plan*) to take shape; **des cristaux se forment dans la roche** crystals form in rock; **une jeune fille qui se forme** a girl who is developing; **se f. en cortège/en carré** to form (into) a procession/(into) a square

(b) (*apprendre son métier*) to train oneself; (*s'instruire*) to educate oneself; **se f. aux affaires** to acquire a business training; **se f. sur le tas** to learn on the job

formica® [fɔrmika] *nm* formica; **en f.** formica

formidable [fɔrmidabl] *adj* **(a)** (*extraordinaire*) tremendous **(b)** (*bon*) great, fantastic; *Iron F* **tu es/c'est f.!** you're/it's incredible! **(c)** *Vieilli* (*effrayant*) fearsome, formidable

formidablement [fɔrmidabləmɑ̃] *adv* **(a)** (*énormément*) tremendously, fantastically; **nous avons été f. accueillis** we were given a tremendous *or* fantastic welcome **(b)** *Arch* (*de manière effrayante*) formidably, fearsomely

formique [fɔrmik] *adj Ch* (*acide*) formic

formol [fɔrmɔl] *nm Ch* formalin, formol

formulable [fɔrmylabl] *adj* **une opinion difficilement f.** an opinion that is difficult to formulate; **une théorie f. en termes clairs** a theory that can be clearly formulated

formulaire [fɔrmylɛr] *nm* **(a)** (*imprimé*) form; **remplir un f.** to fill in *or* out a form; **f. E111** form E111; **f. d'appréciation** customer satisfaction questionnaire; **f. d'assurance** insurance form; **f. de détaxe** tax free shopping form; *Ordinat* **f. de saisie** input form **(b)** (*recueil*) formulary; (*de pharmaciens*) formulary, pharmacopoeia

formulation [fɔrmylasjɔ̃] *nf* formulation, wording

formule [fɔrmyl] *nf* **(a)** [①A13,6] *Math, Ch etc* formula

(b) (*paroles*) expression, phrase; **f. magique** magic formula; **f. de début** (*d'une lettre*) opening; **f. de politesse** (*au début d'une lettre*) standard opening; (*à la fin*) standard closure; **f. finale** *ou* **de politesse** letter ending, closure; **selon la f. consacrée** as the expression goes; **trouver la f. juste** to find the right phrase

(c) (*méthode*) formula; **c'est la f. idéale pour les vacances en famille** it's the ideal formula for a family holiday; **nous vous proposons différentes formules de crédit/de remboursement** we offer you various credit/repayment options *or* methods *or* formulae; **nous avons aussi une f. à 1 000 francs** we also have a one-thousand-franc option

(d) *Aut* **f. un/deux** Formula One/Two

(e) *Admin* (*formulaire*) form; **f. de demande de crédit** credit application form; **f. de réponse** reply form; *Com* **f. de soumission** tender form; **f. de télégramme** telegram form

formule-hôtel, *pl* **formules-hôtel** *nf* hotel package

formuler [fɔrmyle] *vt* (*doctrine*) to formulate; (*document*) to draw up; (*souhait*) to express; (*proposition*) to formulate, to put into words; (*plainte*) to lodge; (*règlement*) to formulate, to lay down

fornication [fɔrnikasjɔ̃] *nf* fornication

forniquer [fɔrnike] *vi* to fornicate

fors [fɔr] *prép Litt* except, save; **tout est perdu f. l'honneur** all is lost save honour

forsythia [forsisja] *nm Bot* forsythia

fort [fɔr] **1** *adj* **(a)** (*vigoureux*) strong; **f. comme un Turc** *ou* **un bœuf** as strong as an ox; **utiliser la manière forte** to use strong-arm tactics, to use force; **trouver plus f. que soi** to meet one's match; **s'attaquer à plus f. que soi** to take on more than one can handle; **courage, il faut être f.** cheer up! you/we/*etc* must be strong; **f. de son expérience** with a wealth of experience behind one; **f. de son récent succès** bolstered by one's recent success; **f. de ses certitudes** secure in the strength of one's convictions; **f. de son bon droit** in the knowledge that right is on one's side; **c'est une forte tête** he's very strong-minded; **un esprit f.** a freethinker; **avoir affaire à forte partie** to be up against a strong opponent; **être f. en mathématiques/en ski/aux échecs** to be good at mathematics/skiing/chess; **elle est forte sur la question** she is well up in *or* knowledgeable about the matter; **il est f. pour critiquer, mais quand il faut travailler ...** he's good at criticizing, but when it comes to working ...

(b) (*corde, boisson, sauce, haleine etc*) strong; (*fièvre, vent*) high; (*chaleur*) intense, great; (*lumière*) strong, bright, intense; (*pluie, mer*) heavy; (*voix*) loud; **moutarde forte** strong mustard; *Fig* **elle a fait (une) forte impression** she made a strong impression; **avoir une forte odeur** to have a strong smell; **c'est plus f. que moi!** I can't help it!; **j'avais une forte envie de rire/de lui casser la figure** I was very tempted to laugh/to smash his face in; *F* **c'est trop f.!, c'est un peu f. (de café)!** that's a bit much!; **ce qu'il y a de plus f., c'est qu'on n'y peut rien** the worst of it is that nothing can be done about it; **à plus forte raison** all the more so **(que** since)

(c) place/ville forte fortress/fortified town

(d) se faire f. de faire qch to be sure *or* convinced one can do sth; **elles se font f. de le retrouver** they are sure *or* convinced they can find it

(e) (*gros*) (*personne*) large, stout; (*lèvres*) thick, full; (*poitrine*) large; **homme à la forte charpente** solidly built man; **elle est forte des hanches** she's big round the hips, she has large hips; **forte somme** large sum of money; **forte différence** big *or* great difference; **forte baisse** (*de prix*) slump; **forte hausse des prix** sharp *or* big rise in prices; **forte pente** steep slope; **armée forte de cinq mille hommes** five-thousand-strong army, army five thousand strong; *Com* **prix f.** full price; **acheter qch au prix f.** to buy sth at *or* for the full price, to pay (the) full price for sth

2 *adv* **(a)** (*parler, crier, chanter*) loudly, loud; (*tirer*) hard; **frapper f.** to strike *or* hit hard; *F* **y aller f.** to overdo it, to go over the top; **sentir f.** to smell strong; *F* **faire (très) f.** to do brilliantly, to do really well

(b) (*très*) very, extremely; **il a été f. mécontent** he was very *or* extremely annoyed; **j'en suis f. aise** I'm very pleased; **c'est f. dommage** it's a great *or* real pity; **f. bien** very well; **f. heureusement, il était là** he was there, which was very fortunate

(c) (*beaucoup*) **j'ai f. à faire** I have a great deal *or* a lot to do; **nous avons eu f. à faire avec cette jeune fille/ce radiateur électrique** we had our work cut out with that girl/that electric heater; **j'en doute f.** I very much doubt it

3 *nm* **(a)** (*spécialité*) strong point, forte; **la politesse n'est pas son f.** politeness is not his strong point *or* his forte; **le f. et le faible de l'affaire** the strong and weak points of the matter; **le f. d'un bois** the heart of a wood; **au plus f. de l'hiver** in the depths of winter; **au f. de l'été/de l'épidémie** at the height of summer/of the epidemic; **au (plus) f. du combat** in the thick of the fight; **le plus f., c'est que je lui avais déjà dit** the best of it is, I'd already told him; *Prov* **la raison du plus f. est toujours la meilleure** might is right

(b) (*citadelle*) fort, stronghold

▶ **fort**: *F* **f. en gueule** loud-mouthed; **c'est un f. en gueule** he's a loudmouth; *Péj* **f. en thème** swot, *Am* grind; **forts des Halles** market porters

fortement [fɔrtəmɑ̃] *adv* (*désirer, souhaiter, influencé*) strongly, greatly; (*tirer, pousser*) hard; (*impressionner*) greatly; **insister f. sur qch** to insist firmly *or* strongly on sth; **j'espère f. qu'il viendra** I very much *or* I sincerely hope he'll come; **f. épicé** highly spiced; **f. critiqué** strongly *or* highly criticized; **f. irrité** greatly *or* extremely irritated; **c'est f. conseillé** it's strongly advised; **f. charpenté** solidly built

forteresse [fɔrtərɛs] *nf* fortress, stronghold; **f. volante** flying fortress

fortiche [fɔrtiʃ] *F* **1** *adj* clever, smart **2** *n* **(a)** clever *or* smart cookie; **c'est un f. en chimie** he's really good at chemistry **(b)** *Vieilli* (*personne robuste*) brawny person

fortifiant [fɔrtifjɑ̃] **1** *adj* (*nourriture, boisson*) fortifying; (*air*) bracing, invigorating **2** *nm Méd* tonic

fortification [fɔrtifikasjɔ̃] *nf* (*action, ouvrages*) fortification

fortifier [fɔrtifje] (*impf & pr sub* **n. fortifiions**) **1** *vt* **(a)** (*ville*) to fortify; (*mur, corps*) to fortify, to strengthen; (*muscles*) to tone up, to strengthen **(b)** (*sentiment, impression*) to strengthen; **cela m'a fortifié dans ma décision** that strengthened me in my decision **2 se fortifier** *vpr* **(a)** (*devenir plus fort*) to get *or* become stronger; **il faut qu'il se fortifie le dos** he has to strengthen his back **(b)** *Mil* to raise a line of defences; (*en creusant des tranchées*) to dig oneself in

fortin [fɔrtɛ̃] *nm* small fort

Fortran [fɔrtrɑ̃] *nm Ordinat* FORTRAN

fortuit [fɔrtɥi] *adj* (*rencontre, événement*) chance, fortuitous; **dans cette affaire, rien n'est f.** nothing is fortuitous *or* nothing can be put down to chance in this matter; **toute ressemblance avec des personnes existantes ou ayant existé serait purement fortuite** any resemblance to persons living or dead is entirely coincidental; *Jur* **cas f.** act of God

fortuitement [fɔrtɥitmɑ̃] *adv* by chance, fortuitously

fortune [fɔrtyn] *nf* **(a)** (*chance*) fortune, chance, luck; **chercher f.** to try one's luck; **revers de f.** reversal of fortune, setback in one's fortunes; **mauvaise f.** misfortune; **avoir la bonne/la mauvaise f. de rencontrer qn** to have the good fortune/misfortune to meet sb, to be fortunate/unfortunate enough to meet sb; **faire contre mauvaise f. bon cœur** to make the best of a bad job; **connaître des fortunes diverses** to have varying (degrees of) success; **la f. d'une théorie/d'une œuvre d'art** the fortunes of a theory/a work of art; **dîner à la f. du pot** to take pot luck; **inviter qn à la f. du pot** to invite sb to come and take pot luck; *Prov* **la f. sourit aux audacieux** fortune favours the brave; **installation de f.** temporary *or* makeshift installation; **lit de f.** makeshift bed; **réparations de f.** makeshift *or* emergency repairs; **moyens de f.** makeshift means; *Naut* **mât de f.** jury mast; **(voile de) f.** cross-jack (foresail); **f. de mer** perils of the sea

(b) (*richesse*) fortune, wealth; **faire f.** to make one's fortune *or* a fortune; **avoir de la f.** to be well off; **sa f. est importante** he has a considerable fortune, he has considerable wealth; **c'est une grosse f.** he's a very wealthy man; **être l'artisan de sa f.** to be a self-made man; **valoir une f.** to be worth a fortune; **voilà toute ma f.** that's all I've got

fortuné [fɔrtyne] *adj* **(a)** (*riche*) rich, wealthy, well-off **(b)** *Arch, Litt* (*chanceux*) fortunate, happy

forum [fɔrɔm] *nm* forum; **f. sur l'éducation** forum *or* symposium on education; *Rad etc* **f. populaire** vox pop

fosse [fos] *nf* **(a)** (*creux*) pit, hole; (*abyssale*) trough; *Sp* (sand) pit; *Anat* fossa; *Min* pit; **les animaux des grandes fosses** animals living on the ocean bed **(b)** (*tombe*) grave; **f. commune** common grave; *F* **avoir un pied dans la f.** to have one foot in the grave; **creuser sa f. avec ses dents** to eat oneself into an early grave

▶ **fosse**: **f. d'aisances** cesspool; **f. aux lions** lions' den; *Th* **f. d'orchestre** orchestra pit; **f. à purin** liquid manure pit; *Aut* **f. (de réparation)** inspection pit; **f. septique** septic tank

fossé [fose] *nm* **(a)** (*tranchée, au bord de la route*) ditch; (*douve*) moat; *Géol* trough **(b)** *Fig* (*entre personnes*) gulf; **le f. ne cesse de se creuser entre eux** there is an ever-widening gulf between them; **le f. des générations** the generation gap

▶ **fossé** *Géol* **f. d'effondrement** rift valley; *Aut* **f. d'inspection** inspection pit

fossette [fosɛt] *nf* dimple

fossile [fosil] **1** *nm* fossil; *F* **un vieux f.** an old fossil **2** *adj attrib* fossil

fossilifère [fosilifɛr] *adj* fossiliferous

fossilisation [fosilizasjɔ̃] *nf* fossilization

fossiliser [fosilize] **1** *vt* to fossilize **2 se fossiliser** *vpr* to fossilize, to become fossilized; *Fig* **les mentalités se sont fossilisées** attitudes have become fossilized

fossoyeur [foswajœr] *nm* gravedigger; *Fig* destroyer

fou [fu], **fol, folle** [fɔl] (*the form* **fol** *is used in the masculine before a vowel or h mute*) **1** *adj* **(a)** (*dément*) mad, insane; **devenir f.** to go mad *or* insane; **f. à lier** raving mad, out of one's mind; **cette musique/situation me rend f.** the music/situation is driving me mad; **il y a de quoi devenir f.** it's enough to drive you mad; **f. de joie/de terreur/de rage/d'inquiétude** beside oneself with joy/fear/rage/worry; **être f. de qn** to be mad *or* crazy about sb; **être f. d'amour pour qn, être f. amoureux de qn** to be madly in love with sb; **entre eux, c'est l'amour f.** they're madly in love, they're crazy about each other; **vivre l'amour f.** to be madly in love; **f. de peinture/ski** mad *or* crazy about painting/skiing, dead keen on painting/skiing; **des diamants? mais tu es f.!** diamonds? you're mad *or* crazy!; **tu serais f. de ne pas accepter** you'd be mad *or* crazy not to accept; *F* **pas folle, la guêpe!** there are no flies on her!, she's not stupid!; **il n'est pas f.** he's no fool

(b) folles illusions wild delusions; *Bible* **les vierges folles** the foolish virgins; **les années folles** the Roaring Twenties; **un fol espoir** a foolish *or* mad hope

(c) (*énorme*) tremendous; **succès f.** tremendous *or* wild success; **mettre un temps f. à faire qch** to take absolutely ages to do sth; **il gagne un argent f.** he makes pots of money, he rakes it in; **à une allure folle** at breakneck speed; **il y avait un monde f.** there was an enormous *or* a tremendous crowd; **un prix f.** an exorbitant price; *F* **c'est f. ce que c'est grand!** it's incredible how big it is!; **d'une gaieté folle** wildly happy

(d) (*incontrôlé*) (*mèche de cheveux*) stray, loose; (*camion*) runaway; (*boussole, aiguille*) crazy; (*roue*) idle, free; (*poulie*) loose; **f. rire** (uncontrollable) giggling; **avoir un f. rire** to have (a fit of) the giggles; *F* **avoir une patte folle** to have a gammy *or Am* gimpy leg; **herbes folles** rank weeds; *Bot* **folle avoine** wild oats

2 *n* lunatic, madman, *f* madwoman; **f. furieux** raving lunatic, maniac; **espèce de vieille folle!** crazy old woman!; *F* **il travaille comme un f.** he works like mad; **c'est une histoire de fous** I can't make head (n)or tail of it; *F* **maison de fous** madhouse; **f. du volant** reckless driver; *Litt* **la folle du logis** (wild *or* fevered) imagination; **faire le f.** to play *or* act the fool; **plus on est de fous plus on rit** the more the merrier

3 *nm* **(a)** *Échecs* bishop

(b) *Hist* (*bouffon*) jester, fool

(c) *Orn* **f. de Bassan** gannet

4 *nf Péj F* **folle** (*homosexuel*) queen; **grande folle** raving queen

fouace [fwas] *nf Culin* = **fougasse**

foucade [fukad] *nf Litt* caprice, passing whim

foudre[1] [fudr] **1** *nf* lightning, *surtout Bible* thunderbolt; **la f. est tombée sur la maison** the house was struck by lightning; **maison frappée par la f.** house struck by lightning; *Fig* **coup de f.** love at first sight; **j'ai eu le coup de f. pour cette maison** I fell in love with this house at first sight **2** *nmpl* **foudres** (*colère*) wrath **3** *nm* **un f. de guerre** a great warrior; *Fig* **ce n'est pas un f. de guerre** he wouldn't say boo to a goose; **f. d'éloquence** powerful orator

foudre[2] *nm* (*tonneau*) tun, large cask

foudroyant [fudrwajɑ̃] *adj* (*attaque, nouvelles*) devastating; (*regard*) withering; (*succès*) stunning, staggering; **progrès foudroyants** lightning progress; **une mort foudroyante** a sudden death; **poison f.** devastatingly lethal poison

foudroyer [fudrwaje] *vt* (**je foudroie; je foudroierai**) to strike; **être foudroyé** to be struck by lightning; **arbre foudroyé** tree struck by lightning; *Fig* **l'apoplexie l'a foudroyé** he was struck down by apoplexy; **la mort l'a foudroyé alors qu'il n'avait que 30 ans** he was struck down when he was only 30; **elle le foudroya du regard** she gave him a withering look; **cette nouvelle m'a foudroyé** I was thunderstruck *or* devastated by the news; **la division fut foudroyée par la puissance de feu de l'ennemi** the division was decimated by enemy fire power

fouet [fwɛ] *nm* **(a)** whip; **donner le f. à qn** to whip *or* flog sb; **faire claquer son f.** to crack one's whip; **coup de f.** lash, stroke; *Fig* fillip, stimulus; **l'air de la mer lui a donné un coup de f.** the sea air has perked him up *or* given him a lift; **donner un coup de f. à l'économie** to give a fillip to the economy, to stimulate *or* boost the economy; **être frappé de plein f.** (*d'une cible*) to receive a direct hit; **frapper la balle de plein f.** to connect well with the ball; **il a reçu le ballon de plein f.** the ball came straight at him; **collision de plein f.** head-on collision

(b) (*de cuisine*) whisk

(c) (*de l'aile d'un oiseau, de la queue d'un chien*) tip; *Naut* (*d'une poulie*) tail

fouettement [fwɛtmɑ̃] *nm* (*d'une voile*) flapping; (*d'une corde, de la pluie etc*) lashing

fouetter [fwete] **1** *vt* **(a)** (*personne*) to whip, to flog; (*cheval*) to whip; (*œufs*) to beat, to whisk; (*crème*) to whip; **ils l'ont fouetté jusqu'au sang** they whipped *or* flogged him until he bled; **la pluie fouette les vitres** the rain is lashing (against) the panes; *F* **il n'y a pas de quoi f. un chat** there's nothing to make a fuss about; *F* **avoir d'autres chats à f.** to have other fish to fry

(b) *Fig* (*exciter*) to excite, to stimulate; **vent qui fouette le sang** wind that makes the blood tingle; **le sang fouetté par le désir** spurred on *or* stimulated by desire

2 *vi* **(a)** (*d'un câble*) to lash, to whip; (*d'une voile*) to flap; **la pluie fouette contre les vitres** the rain is lashing (against) the panes

(b) *F* (*puer*) to stink, to pong

(c) *Arg* (*avoir peur*) to be scared stiff

foufou [fufu] *F* **1** *adj m* nutty, daft **2** *nm* nutter

foufoune [fufun], **foufounette** [fufunɛt] *nf Vulg* (*sexe de femme*) pussy, *Br* fanny

fougasse [fugas] *nf Culin* flat bread (*sometimes stuffed with anchovies, olives etc*)

fougeraie [fuʒrɛ] *nf* patch of ferns

fougère [fuʒɛr] *nf* fern; **f. aigle** bracken; **f. arborescente** tree fern

fougue [fug] *nf* fire, spirit, passion; **la f. de la jeunesse** youthful high spirits; **cheval plein de f.** spirited horse

fougueusement [fugøzmɑ̃] *adv* fierily; (*embrasser*) passionately

fougueux, -euse [fugø, -øz] *adj* (*personne*) fiery, ardent, spirited; (*cheval*) spirited; **tempérament f.** fiery temperament

fouille [fuj] *nf* **(a)** (*fosse*) excavation, pit; **f. à ciel ouvert** open pit **(b)** *Archéol* **fouilles** dig, excavations; **faire des fouilles** to carry out excavations *or* a dig **(c)** (*d'un suspect, voyageur*) search(ing), frisking; (*d'un lieu*) search(ing); **passer à la f.** to be searched *or* frisked; **la police a fait une f. complète de ses bureaux** the police made a thorough search of his offices **(d)** *très F* (*poche*) pocket; *Fig* **se remplir les fouilles, s'en mettre plein les fouilles** to line one's pockets

fouillé [fuje] *adj* detailed

fouille-merde, *pl* **fouille-merdes** *n très F* muckraker

fouiller [fuje] **1** *vt* (*maison*) to search; (*personne*) to search, to frisk; (*tiroir*) to search (through), to go through; (*valise*) to go through; (*bois*) to scour, to comb; (*terre*) to dig; *Archéol* (*emplacement d'un ancien site*) to excavate; **f. toutes ses poches** to go through *or* look in all one's pockets; **ses yeux fouillaient la salle** his eyes *or* he scanned the room; **f. un problème** to go thoroughly into a problem, to explore a problem thoroughly

2 *vi* **(a)** (*d'un lapin*) to burrow; (*d'un cochon*) to root

(b) f. dans une armoire/sa poche to search *or* rummage in a cupboard/in one's pocket; **j'ai fouillé dans toutes les poches sans rien trouver** I've gone through *or* searched all the pockets without finding anything; **f. dans les papiers de qn** to search through *or* go through sb's papers; **f. dans les librairies pour trouver un livre** to search around in bookshops for a book; **quand je n'ai rien à faire, je vais f. dans les librairies** when I've nothing to do, I go and rummage around *or* poke around in bookshops; **f. dans le passé** to delve into the past; **f. dans sa mémoire** to search one's memory

3 se fouiller *vpr* to go through one's pockets; *Arg* **tu peux te f.!** nothing doing!; **il peut se f. s'il croit qu'on lui en donnera!** if he thinks we're going to give him some, he's got another think coming!

fouilleur, -euse [fujœr, -øz] **1** *n* **(a)** *Archéol* excavator, digger **(b)** (*à la douane*) officer who carries out body-searches **(c)** (*fouineur*) rummager, searcher; **f. de brocantes/de bibliothèques** an avid frequenter of second-hand shops/libraries **2** *nf Agr* **fouilleuse** subsoil plough *or US* plow

fouillis [fuji] *nm* (*de papiers, jouets etc*) jumble, muddle; (*de lianes*) tangle; **range ton f.** put away your mess; **c'est le f. ici** it's a mess in here

fouinard, -arde [fwinar, -ard] *F* **1** *adj* nosy, prying, inquisitive **2** *n* nosy parker, pryer

fouine [fwin] *nf Zool* stone marten; *F* **à tête de f.** weasel-faced, ferret-faced

fouiner [fwine] *vi F* to ferret about, to nose about; **f. dans les affaires d'autrui** to poke one's nose into other people's business

fouineur, -euse [fwinœr, -øz] *adj, n F* = **fouinard**

fouir [fwir] *vt* to dig; (*d'animaux*) to burrow, to dig

fouisseur, -euse [fwisœr, -øz] **1** *adj* (*animal*) burrowing **2** *n* burrower

foulage [fulaʒ] *nm* **(a)** (*de raisins*) pressing, crushing **(b)** (*du cuir*) tanning; (*de tissu*) fulling **(c)** *Typ* impression

foulant [fulɑ̃] *adj* pressing, crushing; **pompe foulante** force pump; *F* **ce n'est pas bien f.** it won't kill you/her/*etc*

foulard [fular] *nm* **(a)** scarf **(b)** *Tex* foulard

foule [ful] *nf* **(a)** [①All,g,i] (*de gens*) crowd, *Litt* throng; (*d'idées, de souvenirs*) host; **j'ai une f. de choses à te raconter/à faire** I've got lots of things to tell you/to do; **il y a f.** there are crowds of people (there); **il n'y a pas f.** there's hardly anyone around; **psychologie des foules** crowd psychology; **mouvement de foule(s)** movement in the crowd; **entrer en f.** to crowd in; **les réfugiés arrivent en f. à la frontière** the refugees are flocking to the border; **faire f. autour de qn** to crowd round sb, to mob sb; **fuir la f.** to flee the crowds; **quelle f. dans les rues!** how crowded the streets are!; *Vieilli* **on en trouve en f.** there are loads of them

(b) *Can* (*du caribou*) migration

foulée [fule] *nf* **(a)** *Sp, Équitation* stride; **parcourir les champs à longues foulées** to stride over the fields; **courir à petites foulées** to trot along; *Sp* **courir** *ou* **rester dans la f. d'un concurrent** to follow close behind a competitor, to slip-stream; **avoir une bonne f.** to have a good stride; *Fig* **dans la f., j'ai aussi vérifié les comptes** while I was at it, I also checked the accounts **(b) foulées** (*d'animaux sauvages*) track(s), spoor

fouler [fule] **1** *vt* **(a)** (*herbe*) to trample (down), to tread down; (*raisins*) to press, to crush; **f. qch aux pieds** to trample sth underfoot; *Fig* **les droits de l'homme sont foulés aux pieds!** human rights have been trampled underfoot!; **nous foulions pour la première fois le sol de Grèce** we were setting foot for the first time on Greek soil

(b) *Tex* (*tissu*) to full; (*cuir*) to tan

2 se fouler *vpr* **(a) se f. la cheville** to sprain *or* twist one's ankle

(b) *F* **se f. (la rate)** to strain oneself, to overexert oneself; **tu ne t'es pas foulé!** you didn't (exactly) strain *or* overexert yourself!

fouleur, -euse [fulœr, -øz] *n* **(a)** (*de raisins*) (*personne*) winepresser **(b)** *Tex* (*personne*) (*de tissu*) fuller; (*de cuir*) tanner

fouloir [fulwar] *nm* (*pour le raisin*) wine press

foulon [fulɔ̃] *nm Tex* (*de tissu*) fuller; **chardon à f.** fuller's teasel; **terre à f.** fuller's earth; **(moulin à) f.** fulling mill

foulonnier [fulɔnje] *nm* = **fouleur (b)**

foulque [fulk] *nf Orn* coot

foultitude [fultityd] *nf F* **une f.** loads, masses (**de** of)

foulure [fulyr] *nf* sprain; **f. du poignet/de la cheville** sprained wrist/ankle

four [fur] *nm* **(a)** (*de cuisine*) oven; **f. à gaz** gas oven; **f. électrique** electric oven; **f. de boulanger** baker's oven; **f. à micro-ondes** microwave (oven); **faire cuire au f.** (*pain*) to bake; (*viande*) to roast; **il fait noir comme dans un f.** it's pitch black; **vaisselle allant au f.** ovenware; **plat allant au f.** ovenproof dish; *F* **ouvrir une bouche (grande) comme un f.** to open one's mouth really wide; **on ne peut être à la fois au f. et au moulin** you can't be in two places at the same time; *Culin* **petits fours** petits fours

(b) *Ind* kiln; (*avec combustion du contenu*) furnace; **f. à chaux** lime kiln; **f. à briques** brick kiln; **f. à émaux** enamelling kiln; **f. solaire** solar furnace

(c) *F* (*fiasco*) flop; **la pièce/l'exposition a fait un f.** the play/exhibition was a flop; **il a fait un f. avec son discours** his speech was a flop

fourbe [furb] **1** *adj* cheating, double-dealing, two-faced **2** *n* cheat, rogue, double-dealer

fourberie [furbəri] *nf* **(a)** (*hypocrisie*) deceit, cheating, double-dealing **(b)** (*action*) underhand trick

fourbi [furbi] *nm F* **(a)** (*attirail*) gear, tackle, *Br* clobber; (*de soldat*) kit; **tout le f.** the whole (kit and) caboodle; *Fig* **quel f., je ne retrouve rien!** what a muddle *or* mess, I can't find anything! **(b)** (*truc*) thingummy, thingy

fourbir [furbir] *vt* (*métal*) to polish up, to shine up, to furbish; *Fig* **f. ses armes** to prepare for battle

fourbissage [furbisaʒ] *nm* (*du métal*) polishing, furbishing

fourbu [furby] *adj* exhausted, tired out

fourche [furʃ] *nf* **(a)** *Agr* fork; **f. à foin** hayfork, pitchfork; **remuer le sol à la f.** to fork the ground; **chariot (élévateur) à f.** forklift (truck); *Aut* **f. d'attelage** trailer hitch **(b)** (*de bicyclette, d'arbre, de route, de rivière*) fork; (*de pantalon*) crotch, *Br* crutch; *Aut* Y junction; **mes cheveux ont des fourches** my hair has split ends; **en forme de f.** forked; **la route fait une f.** the road forks **(c)** *Hist* **les Fourches Caudines** the Caudine Forks; *Fig* **passer sous les fourches caudines** to suffer torments

fourchée [furʃe] *nf* (*de foin*) pitchforkful

fourcher [furʃe] **1** *vi* **(a) sa langue a fourché** he made a slip of the tongue **(b)** *Arch* to fork, to divide **2** *vt* (*sol*) to fork

fourchet [furʃɛ] *nm Vét* foot rot

fourchette [furʃɛt] *nf* **(a)** (*ustensile*) fork; **f. à poisson/à dessert** fish/dessert fork; *F* **il a un joli** *ou* **bon coup de f., c'est une bonne f.** he's a hearty eater, he has a healthy *or* hearty appetite; **manger avec la f. du père Adam** to eat with one's fingers **(b)** *Mil, Fin* bracket; **prendre une cible en f.** *ou* **à la f.** to bracket a target; **f. de salaire** wage bracket; **f. de prix** price bracket *or* range **(c)** *Cartes* tenace **(d)** (*d'un volatile*) wishbone; (*d'un sabot de cheval*) frog **(e)** (*de balance*) beam support **(f)** *MecE* belt guide, shifter; **f. de débrayage** clutch throw-out fork; **f. d'embrayage** clutch fork

fourchu [furʃy] *adj* forked; (*bâton, menton*) cleft; **pied f.** cloven hoof; **avoir les cheveux fourchus** to have split ends; **avoir la langue fourchue** to speak with a forked tongue

fourgon¹ [furgɔ̃] *nm* (*de cheminée*) poker; (*de four*) (fire) rake

fourgon² *nm* **(a)** *Aut* van; **f. automobile** (motor) van; **f. blindé** armoured van **(b)** *Rail* **f. de queue** rear (brake) van, guard's van, *Am* caboose

▶ **fourgon: f. à bagages** luggage van, *Am* baggage car; **f. à bétail** cattle truck; **f. cellulaire** police van *or Am* wagon; **f. funèbre, f. funéraire, f. mortuaire** hearse

fourgonner [furgɔne] **1** *vt* (*feu*) to poke, to rake **2** *vi* to poke the fire; *F* **f. dans un tiroir** to poke about *or* rummage about in a drawer

fourgonnette [furgɔnɛt] *nf* (small *or* light) van

fourguer [furge] *vt F* (*vendre*) to flog; (*donner*) to unload; **f. qch à qn** (*vendre*) to flog sb sth; (*donner*) to unload sth onto sb

fourmi [furmi] *nf* ant; *Fig* **c'est une vraie f.** he's/she's a busy bee, he's/she's always beavering away (at something); **avoir des fourmis dans les jambes** to have pins and needles in one's legs

fourmilier [furmilje] *nm* anteater

fourmilière [furmiljɛr] *nf* anthill, ants' nest; *Fig* **cette banlieue est une véritable f. (humaine)** this suburb is swarming *or* teeming with people

fourmi-lion, *pl* **fourmis-lions** *nm Ent* ant-lion

fourmillement [furmijmɑ̃] *nm* **(a)** (*d'insectes*) swarming; **un f. de détails/d'idées** a welter of details/ideas **(b)** (*dans les membres*) pins and needles

fourmiller [furmije] *vi* to swarm, to teem; **les vers fourmillaient dans ce fromage** the cheese was alive with maggots; *Fig* **la ville fourmille d'ingénieurs** the town is swarming *or* teeming with engineers; **ouvrage qui fourmille de fautes** work teeming *or* riddled with mistakes; **f. d'idées** to be bursting with ideas; **f. d'impressions** to be full of impressions

fournaise [furnɛz] *nf* **cette chambre est une (vraie) f.** this room's like an oven

fourneau, -eaux [furno] *nm* **(a)** (*de chaudière*) furnace; **f. d'une pipe** bowl of a pipe **(b) f. de cuisine** (kitchen) range; **f. à gaz** gas stove *or Br* cooker; **c'est David qui est aux fourneaux ce soir** David is the chef this evening **(c)** *Métal* furnace; **haut f.** blast furnace **(d)** *Min* **f. de mine** mine chamber, blast hole

fournée [furne] *nf* (*de pains*) batch; *Fig F* batch, contingent

fourni [furni] *adj* **(a)** (*magasin, bibliothèque etc*) **(bien) f.** well-stocked **(b)** (*cheveux*) thick; (*barbe*) bushy, thick; **barbe peu fournie** sparse *or* thin beard

fournil [furni] *nm* bakehouse

fourniment [furnimɑ̃] *nm F* gear, *Br* clobber

fournir [furnir] **1** *vt* **(a)** (*approvisionner*) to supply; **f. qch à qn, f. qn en qch** to supply sb with sth; **qui fournit la famille royale?** who is the Royal Family's supplier?, who supplies the Royal Family?

(b) (*produire*) to supply, to provide; (*documents*) to produce, to furnish; (*idées*) to provide; **f. une caution** to give a guarantee, to provide security; **vignoble qui fournit un bon vin** vineyard that yields *or* produces a good wine; **l'ENA fournit de futurs hauts fonctionnaires** the ENA produces *or* turns out the senior civil servants of the future; **f. un effort considérable** to make a considerable effort; **f. des renseignements à qn** to supply *or* provide *or* furnish sb with information; **vous devez f. votre carte d'identité** you must present *or* show your identity card; **il pourra peut-être te f. du travail** he might be able to give you some work; **f. le gîte et le couvert** to provide board and lodging; **cela te fournira l'occasion de le rencontrer** it will provide you with *or* give you the opportunity of meeting him; **f. une bonne raison à qn** to provide sb with *or* give sb a good reason; **pièces à f.** required documents; *Cartes* **f. du trèfle** to follow a club lead; *Sp* **f. un jeu remarquable** to play an outstanding game

2 *vi Vieilli* **f. aux dépenses** to defray the expenses; **f. aux besoins de qn** to supply sb's wants

3 se fournir *vpr* **(a) se f. en qch** to get in supplies of sth; **ils se fournissent (en vin) chez ce négociant** they get their supplies (of wine) from this merchant

(b) (*d'une barbe etc*) to grow thick

fournissement [furnismɑ̃] *nm Fin* contribution (*in shares*)

fournisseur, -euse [furnisœr, -øz] **1** *n Com* supplier; **l'entrée des fournisseurs** the tradesman's entrance; **f. de navires** *ou* **de la marine** ships' chandler; **le plus grand f. français en meubles** the biggest French supplier of furniture; **f. attitré** approved *or* official supplier; (*habituel*) regular supplier; **f. principal** prime supplier; **f. secondaire** secondary supplier **2** *adj* **les pays fournisseurs de la France** the countries that supply France (with goods), France's suppliers

fourniture [furnityr] *nf* **(a)** (*approvisionnement*) supplying, provision **(b) fournitures** supplies; **façon et fournitures** making-up and materials; **fournitures et services** supplies and services

▶ **fourniture**: **fournitures de bureau** office supplies; **fournitures de navires** ships' chandlery; **fournitures scolaires** educational stationery

fourrage [furaʒ] *nm* fodder, forage; **f. sec/vert** hay/silage; **rentrer du f.** to harvest forage

fourrager[1] [furaʒe] **(n. fourrageons; je fourrageai(s)) 1** *vi* (*pour s'alimenter*) to forage; *F* (*fouiller*) to rummage, to forage **2** *vt* **(a)** *F* (*papiers*) to rummage through **(b)** *Arch* (*pays*) to pillage, to ravage

fourrager[2], -ère [furaʒe, -ɛr] **1** *adj* **plantes fourragères** fodder crops; **betterave fourragère** mangel-wurzel **2** *nf* **fourragère (a)** (*champ*) field sown with fodder crop **(b)** *Mil* fourragère, shoulder braid

fourré [fure] **1** *adj* **(a)** (*manteau, gants etc*) (fur-)lined; (*bois*) thick, dense; **chocolats fourrés à la crème** chocolate creams; **bonbon f.** sweet with a soft centre, *Am* candy with a soft center **(b)** *Escrime* **coup f.** exchanged hit, double hit; *Fig* **méfie-toi, c'est un coup f.** look out, it's a trap; **faire un coup f. à qn** to trick sb; *Vieilli* **paix fourrée** hollow *or* mock peace **2** *nm* thicket; (*à la chasse*) cover

fourreau, -eaux [furo] **1** *nm* (*d'épée*) sheath, scabbard; (*de parapluie*) cover; (*robe*) sheath dress; **remettre l'épée au f.** to sheathe one's sword; *MecE* **soupapes à fourreaux** sleeve valves **2** *adj* **jupe/robe f.** pencil skirt/sheath dress

fourrer [fure] **1** *vt* **(a)** *F* (*mettre*) to stick; **je les avais fourrés dans le coin** I'd stuck them in the corner; **f. ses mains dans ses poches** to stick *or* stuff *or* shove one's hands in one's pockets; **mais où ai-je bien pu f. ça?** where on earth have I stuck it?; **f. son nez partout** to poke *or* stick one's nose into everything; **f. qn au trou** to stick *or* chuck sb in jail; **il est toujours fourré dans mes pattes** he's always under my feet; **il est toujours fourré au bistrot** he's always stuck in the pub

(b) (*avec de la fourrure*) to line (with fur)

(c) *MecE* (*jointure*) to pack

(d) f. un chocolat/une crêpe de liqueur to fill a chocolate/a pancake with liqueur; **f. une dinde de marrons** to stuff a turkey with chestnuts

2 se fourrer *vpr F* **il s'est fourré dans le coin/sous le lit** he got into the corner/under the bed; **où est-il allé se f.?** wherever has he got to? wherever has he hidden himself?; **je ne savais plus où me f.** I didn't know where to put myself; **se f. dans une sale affaire** to get involved in a nasty business; *F* **il se fourre les doigts dans le nez** he picks his nose; *Fig F* **si tu crois que je vais l'attendre, tu te fourres le doigt dans l'œil** if you think I'm going to wait for him, you've got another think coming

fourre-tout [furtu] **1** *nm inv* **(a)** (*pièce*) junk room; (*placard*) junk cupboard **(b)** (*sac*) *Br* holdall, carryall; *Aut* storage pocket **2** *adj inv* **sac f.** *Br* holdall, carryall; **placard f.** junk cupboard; *Péj* **une loi f.** a mishmash *or* ragbag of a law

fourreur [furœr] *nm* furrier

fourrier [furje] *nm Mil* quartermaster sergeant

fourrière [furjɛr] *nf* (*pour animaux, voitures*) pound; **mettre un chien/une voiture en f.** *ou* **à la f.** to impound a dog/a car

fourrure [furyr] *nf* **(a)** (*peau préparée, vêtement*) fur; **manteau de f.** fur coat **(b)** (*pelage*) fur, coat **(c)** (*de jointure*) packing; *Aut* **f. de frein** brake lining

fourvoiement [furvwamɑ̃] *nm Litt* going astray

fourvoyer [furvwaje] **(je fourvoie; je fourvoierai)** *Litt* **1** *vt* to mislead, to lead astray **2 se fourvoyer** *vpr* to lose one's way; *Fig* to make a mistake, to go astray

foutaise [futɛz] *nf très F* bullshit, crap; **c'est de la f.!** that's (a load of) bullshit *or* crap!

foutoir [futwar] *nm très F* dump, tip

foutre[1] [futr] (*pp* **foutu**; *pr ind* **je fous, n. foutons)** *très F* **1** *vt* **(a)** (*mettre*) **je me demande où elle a pu le f.** where the hell has she put it?; **f. qch par terre** to chuck *or* fling sth on the ground; **f. qn à la porte** to chuck sb out; **f. le bordel** to create havoc *or* chaos; **f. qn en rogne** *ou* **en pétard** to make sb hopping mad; **ça la fout mal** that won't look too good; **ça a tout foutu en l'air** that screwed *or Vulg* fucked everything up

(b) (*faire*) to do; **il ne fout rien** he does damn all *or Br* bugger all; **il n'a pas l'air de f. grand-chose** he doesn't seem to do much at all; **qu'est-ce que tu fous dans mon bureau?** what the hell are you doing in my office?; **ça fait deux heures que je t'attends, qu'est-ce que tu fous?** I've been waiting for you for two hours, what (the hell) are you playing at?; **je ne sais pas quoi f. de lui/de cette vieille table** I don't know what the hell to do with him/this old table; **je n'en ai rien à f.** I couldn't give a damn, I couldn't care less; **qu'est-ce que ça peut f.?** so what?, what the hell does it matter?; **qu'est-ce que ça peut f. qu'on soit en retard?** so what if we're late, what the hell does it matter if we're late?; **qu'est-ce que ça peut te/lui f.?** what the hell is it to you/him?, what the hell does it matter to you/him?; **f. le camp** to piss off, *Br* to bugger off; **qu'il aille se faire f.** he can piss off *or Vulg* fuck off *or Br* get stuffed; **va te faire f.!** piss off!, *Vulg* fuck off!, *Br* get stuffed!

(c) (*donner*) **je vais lui f. une bonne raclée** I'll give him a good hiding; **elle m'a foutu la honte** (*d'elle*) I was ashamed of her; (*de moi*) she made me ashamed of myself; **f. la trouille à qn** to put the wind up sb, to scare sb stiff; **ça nous a foutu un coup** it gave us a nasty shock; **qu'est-ce qui m'a foutu un empoté pareil!** what an absolute oaf you are!; **je t'en fous!** some chance!, you'll be lucky!; **je t'en foutrais, du champagne!** champagne, you'll be lucky! *or* I should coco!

(d) *Vieilli, Vulg* (*posséder sexuellement*) to fuck

2 se foutre *vpr* **(a)** (*se mettre*) **il s'est encore foutu dans une affaire louche** he's got (himself) mixed up in some shady business again; **se f. par terre** to fall flat on one's face; **se f. sur la gueule** to beat the living daylights out of each other; **se f. en l'air** to top oneself; **il se fout dedans!** he's damn well wrong!

(b) se f. de qn/qch (*se moquer de*) to make fun of sb/sth, to take the piss *or Br* the mickey out of sb/sth; (*être indifférent à*) not to give a damn about sb/sth; **se f. de la gueule de qn** to take the piss *or Br* the mickey out of sb; **tu te fous du monde ou quoi?** who the hell do you think you are?; **c'est vraiment se f. (de la gueule) du monde!** he/they/*etc* must think we're absolute idiots!; **elle se fout complètement de ce que j'en pense** she doesn't give a damn (about) what I think of it; **je m'en fous** I don't give a damn

foutre[2] *nm Vulg* (*sperme*) come, *Br* spunk

foutre[3] *adv F Vieilli* damned; **je n'en sais f. rien** I know damn all about it

foutrement [futrəmɑ̃] *adv F* damn, *Br* bloody; **f. bien** damn well, *Br* bloody well; **je n'en sais f. rien** I know damn all *or Br* bugger all about it

foutriquet [futrikɛ] *nm Péj Vieilli* little runt *or* squirt

foutu [futy] *adj Vulg* **(a)** (*maudit*) damn (awful), *Br* bloody (awful)

(b) (*en mauvais état, perdu*) ruined; **il est f.** he's had it, he's done for; **ma bagnole/robe est foutue** my car/dress has had it; **c'est f.!** forget it!; **pour la fête de demain, c'est f.** you can forget the party tomorrow; **c'est f. pour mon augmentation** I can forget *or* it's goodbye to my pay rise

(c) (*bâti, conçu*) **elle est plutôt bien foutue** she's got a great body; **c'est bien/mal f.** it's well/badly designed

(d) (*malade*) **je suis mal f.** I feel really *or Br* bloody awful

(e) (*capable*) **elle n'est même pas foutue de le faire** she's not up to doing it; **elle serait foutue de le lui dire** she's quite likely to tell him

fox(-terrier), *pl* **fox(-terriers)** [fɔks(terje)] *nm* fox terrier

fox-trot [fɔkstrɔt] *nm inv* foxtrot

foyer [fwaje] *nm* **(a)** (*domicile*) home, household; *surtout Mktg* household unit; **le f. familial** the (family) home; **le f. conjugal** the marital home; **rentrer dans ses foyers** to return home; **mère** *ou* **femme au f.** housewife; **homme au f.** househusband; **fonder un f.** to start a family; *Fin* **f. fiscal** household (*as a tax unit*)

(b) f. d'étudiants student residence; **f. de jeunes travailleurs** young workers' hostel; **f. d'accueil et d'hébergement** (*pour les gens à la rue*) hostel for the homeless

(c) *Scol* common room; *Th* foyer; **f. des artistes** green room

(d) (*de chaleur, d'infection*) source; (*d'incendie, d'érudition, de conflits*) seat, centre, *US* center; **f. d'intrigue** hotbed of intrigue

(e) (*âtre*) fireplace, hearth; (*de locomotive*) firebox; **f. de chaudière** boiler furnace

(f) (*de lentille, courbe etc*) focus; **verres à double f.** bifocal lenses, bifocals

frac [frak] *nm* tail coat, tails

fracas [fraka] *nm* (*de verre cassé, du tonnerre*) crash; (*de l'orage*) din; (*des armes*) clash; (*vacarme*) racket, din; **faire du f.** (*d'un événement*) to create a sensation; **à grand f.** with a lot of fuss, with a great to-do; **elle sortit avec f.** she stormed out

fracassant [frakasɑ̃] *adj* (*bruit*) deafening; *Fig* **c'est une nouvelle/révélation fracassante** it's a shattering *or* staggering piece of news/revelation; **succès f.** resounding success

fracasser [frakase] **1** *vt* to smash (to pieces), to shatter; **il aurait eu la tête fracassée** he would have smashed his head in **2 se fracasser** *vpr* to crash, to smash; **tu vas te f. la tête!** you'll smash your head in!

fractal, -ale, -aux, -ales [fraktal] **1** *adj* fractal **2** *nm* fractal

fraction [fraksjɔ̃] *nf* **(a)** [ⓘ**A70**,16,2; **B56**,C,1] *Math* fraction; **f. ordinaire** vulgar fraction; **f. décimale** decimal fraction; **f. périodique** recurring decimal **(b)** (*partie*) part, portion; *Pol* splinter group; **ça a duré une f. de seconde** it lasted a fraction of a second *or* a split second; *Compta* **f. d'intérêt** interest accrued **(c)** *Rel* (*du pain*) breaking

fractionnaire [fraksjɔnɛr] *adj* fractional; **nombre f.** improper fraction

fractionnel, -elle [fraksjɔnɛl] *adj* (*tactique*) divisive

fractionnement [fraksjɔnmɑ̃] *nm* **(a)** (*d'une propriété, d'un groupe*) dividing up, splitting up **(b)** *Ch* fractional distillation; (*d'huiles minérales*) cracking **(c)** *Com* breaking bulk

fractionner [fraksjɔne] **1** *vt* **(a)** (*diviser*) to divide up, to split up; *Math* to fractionize; **f. le paiement** to pay in instalments; **nous allons devoir f. l'opération en plusieurs phases** we'll have to break down *or* split the operation into several stages **(b)** *Ch* (*distillation*) to fractionate; (*huiles minérales*) to crack **2 se fractionner** *vpr* (*de gens, d'objets*) to split up, to divide up; **le groupe se fractionne en deux** the group splits *or* divides in two

fractionnisme [fraksjɔnism] *nm Pol* (*tactique*) divisive tactics; (*caractère*) factionalism

fractionniste [fraksjɔnist] *n Pol* factionalist

fracture [fraktyr] *nf* **(a)** (*d'une serrure, porte*) breaking open, forcing **(b)** *Méd, Géol* fracture; **f. du crâne** fractured skull; **f. simple** simple *or* closed fracture; **f. multiple** multiple fracture; **f. ouverte** open fracture

fracturer [fraktyre] **1** *vt* **(a)** (*serrure, porte, coffre-fort*) to break open, to force **(b)** (*os*) to fracture **2 se fracturer** *vpr* to fracture, to break; **se f. le tibia** to fracture one's tibia

fragile [fraʒil] *adj* (*construction*) fragile, flimsy; (*verre*) brittle; (*personne, santé*) fragile, frail, delicate; (*estomac*) weak, delicate; (*autorité*) weak, unstable; (*bonheur*) precarious, fragile; (*équilibre*) delicate; (*hypothèse*) shaky; **elle est f. des poumons/de la gorge** she has delicate lungs/a delicate throat; **ne la brutalise pas, elle est encore f.** (*psychologiquement*) don't treat her roughly, she's still (feeling) fragile

fragilisation [fraʒilizasjɔ̃] *nf* weakening

fragiliser [fraʒilize] *vt* to weaken

fragilité [fraʒilite] *nf* (*d'une construction*) fragility; (*du verre*) brittleness; (*d'une personne*) frailty, weakness, fragility; (*d'une hypothèse*) shakiness; (*d'un équilibre*) delicacy

fragment [fragmɑ̃] *nm* (*de pierre*) fragment, piece; (*d'os*) fragment, splinter; (*de chanson, conversation*) fragment, snatch; (*d'un livre*) extract

fragmentaire [fragmɑ̃tɛr] *adj* fragmentary; (*connaissances*) sketchy, patchy, fragmentary

fragmentation [fragmɑ̃tasjɔ̃] *nf* fragmentation

fragmenter [fragmɑ̃te] *vt* to fragment, to split up; (*travail*) to divide up, to split up; **f. la publication d'un ouvrage** to publish a work in parts

frai [frɛ] *nm* **(a)** (*action, période*) spawning (*of fish*) **(b)** (*œufs*) spawn; (*poissons*) fry **(c)** (*de pièces de monnaie*) abrasion, wear

fraîche [frɛʃ] *adj voir* **frais[1]**

fraîchement [frɛʃmɑ̃] *adv* **(a)** (*recevoir*) coolly; **accueillir qn f.** to give sb a cool reception; *F* **ça va f. ce matin** it's a bit chilly this morning **(b)** (*récemment*) **f. marié/divorcé/arrivé** newly *or* recently married/divorced/arrived; **fleurs f. cueillies** freshly picked flowers

fraîcheur [frɛʃœr] *nf* **(a)** (*température*) freshness, coolness; **dans la f. du soir** in the cool of the evening; **une sensation de f.** a feeling of freshness; **rechercher un peu de f.** to seek out a cool spot **(b)** (*de fleurs, nourriture, couleurs, d'idées, de film etc*) freshness; (*de la jeunesse*) freshness, bloom; **elle a perdu sa f. d'esprit** she has lost her freshness of mind

fraîchir [frɛʃir] *vi Météo* **(a)** (*devenir frais*) to freshen, to grow colder *or* cooler **(b)** (*du vent*) to freshen

frais[1], fraîche [frɛ, frɛʃ] **1** *adj* **(a)** (*froid*) (*vent*) fresh, cool; *Fig* (*réception*) cool; (*rafraîchi*) chilled; **un accueil plutôt f.** a rather cool welcome

(b) (*récent*) (*pain, fruits, fleurs, traces*) fresh; (*souvenir*) recent, fresh; **air f.** fresh air; **œufs f.** fresh *or* new-laid eggs; **les croissants sont tout f. de ce matin** the croissants are fresh this morning; **de fraîche date** not long ago, recently; **amis de fraîche date** recent friends; **l'encre est encore fraîche** the ink is still wet; **peinture fraîche** wet paint

(c) teint f. fresh complexion; **avoir l'haleine fraîche** to have fresh breath; **cette robe n'est plus très fraîche, mais elle fera l'affaire** this dress isn't very fresh any more, but it will do; **f. et dispos** hale and hearty; **être f. comme un gardon** to be bright-eyed and bushy-tailed; **être fraîche comme une rose** to be as fresh as a daisy; *F* **me voilà f.!** I'm in a nice mess *or* a pretty fix!

(d) avoir de l'argent f. to have new money

2 *adv* **il fait f.** it's cool *or* fresh; **servir/boire f.** serve/drink chilled *or* cool; **roses toutes fraîches** *ou* **f. cueillies** freshly picked roses; **herbe f.** *ou* **fraîche coupée** freshly *or* newly cut grass; **il est f. débarqué de sa province** he is fresh from the country; **f. émoulu de l'université** fresh out of *or* from university; **rasé de f.** freshly shaven; **peint de f.** freshly painted

3 *nm* **prendre le f.** to take some *or* a breath of (fresh) air; **à**

mettre *ou* **à conserver au f.** to be kept cool *or* in a cool place; **mettre le vin au f.** to put the wine to cool; *Fig F* **ils l'ont mis au f.** they've put him in the cooler, they've locked him up *or* put him inside; *Météo, Naut* **avis de grand f.** gale warning

4 *nf* **à la fraîche** in the cool part of the day

frais[2] *nmpl* expenses, costs; **f. d'un procès** costs of a lawsuit; **j'ai eu beaucoup de f. ce mois-ci** I've had a lot of expense(s) this month; **faire de gros f.** to go to great expense; **faux f.** incidental expenses; **note de f.** expense account; **tous f. payés** all expenses paid; *Jur* **être condamné aux f.** to be ordered to pay costs; **rentrer dans ses f.** to cover one's expenses; *Fig* **j'ai fait les f. de la plaisanterie** the joke was at my expense; *Fig* **faire les f. de la conversation** to keep the conversation going; (*à ses dépens*) to be the subject of the conversation; **faire les f. d'une politique** to pay the price for a policy; **faire qch à ses f.** to do sth at one's own expense; **à grands/à peu de f.** at great/little cost; **se mettre en f.** to go to great expense, *F* to put oneself out of pocket; **se mettre en f. de politesse** to go out of one's way to be polite; **j'en suis pour mes f.** it's been a lot of trouble for nothing, I've been wasting my time; **exempt de f., sans f.** free of charge; (*sur une lettre de change*) no expenses; *F* **aux f. de la princesse** at the expense of the government/the firm/*etc*; **f. accessoires** incidental costs *or* expenses; **f. d'achat** purchase costs; **f. d'adhésion** membership charge; **f. administratifs** administrative costs; **f. d'administration** administrative costs; (*en échange d'un service*) handling charge; **f. d'administration générale** general overheads, general administration costs, *Am* general overhead; **f. d'agence** agency fee; **f. d'annulation** cancellation charge; **f. de banque** bank charges; **f. de camionnage** haulage; **f. de constitution** (*de société*) startup costs; (*de compte*) set-up fee; **f. consulaires** consular fees; **f. de déplacement** travelling *or* travel expenses; **f. de douane** customs duties; **f. d'entrée** (*d'une sicav*) front-end *or* front-load fees; **f. d'envoi** carriage costs; **f. d'établissement** startup costs; **f. d'exploitation** operating costs, operational costs; **f. financiers** interest charges, financial costs; **f. fixes** fixed charges; *Com* **f. généraux** overheads, *Am* overhead; **f. de gestion** administration costs; **f. inclus** inclusive of costs; **f. d'inscription** membership fee; **f. de manutention** handling charges; **f. de pilotage** pilotage; **f. de port** carriage; **f. portuaires** port charges; **f. de représentation** expense account, entertainment allowance *or* expenses; **f. de réservation** booking fee, reservation charge; **f. de scolarité** school fees; **f. de tenue de compte** account charges; (*de compte bancaire*) bank charges; **f. variables** variable costs

fraisage [frɛzaʒ] *nm* **(a)** *Métal* (*de surface*) milling; (*de trou*) reaming; (*de trou de vis*) countersinking **(b)** (*par le dentiste*) drilling

fraise[1] [frɛz] **1** *nf* **(a)** (*fruit*) strawberry; **f. des bois** wild *or Am* field strawberry; **tarte aux fraises** strawberry tart; **confiture de fraises** strawberry jam; **sirop de f.** strawberry cordial; *Fig* **sucrer les fraises** to have the shakes; *Arg* **un coup en pleine f.** a punch in the kisser; *Arg* **amène ta f.!** get yourself *or très F* your arse over here!; *Arg* **il est tout le temps à ramener sa f.** he's always sticking his oar in **(b)** *Méd* strawberry (mark) **2** *adj inv* (*couleur*) strawberry-pink; **f. écrasée** crushed strawberry; **écharpe f.** strawberry-pink scarf

fraise[2] *nf* **(a)** *Culin* (*de veau, d'agneau*) caul **(b)** *Arch* (*col*) ruff **(c)** (*de dinde*) wattle **(d)** *MecE* milling cutter, mill; **f. (conique)** countersink **(e)** (*de dentiste*) drill

fraiser [freze] *vt* **(a)** (*dent*) to drill **(b)** *MecE* (*surface*) to mill; (*trou*) to ream; (*trou de vis*) to countersink

fraiseraie [frɛzrɛ] *nf* strawberry field

fraiseuse [frɛzøz] *nf MecE* milling machine

fraisier [frezje] *nm* **(a)** *Bot* strawberry plant **(b)** *Culin* strawberry cream cake

fraisil [frezi(l)] *nm* coal cinders

fraisure [frezyr] *nf* countersink, countersunk hole

framboise [frɑ̃bwaz] **1** *nf* (*fruit*) raspberry; (*liqueur*) raspberry liqueur; **tarte aux framboises** raspberry tart **2** *adj inv* raspberry

framboisé [frɑ̃bwaze] *adj* raspberry-flavoured, *US* raspberry-flavored

framboisier [frɑ̃bwazje] *nm* **(a)** *Bot* raspberry bush *or* cane **(b)** *Culin* raspberry cream cake

franc[1] [frɑ̃] *nm* (*monnaie*) franc; **f. suisse/belge** Swiss/Belgian franc; **f. or** gold value of the franc; **ancien/nouveau f.** old/new franc; **f. constant** inflation-adjusted franc, franc in real terms; **francs courants** actual francs; **je l'ai eu pour trois francs six sous** I got it for next to nothing; **f. symbolique** nominal sum; **un f. symbolique de dommages et intérêts** token damages

franc[2], **franche** [frɑ̃, frɑ̃ʃ] **1** *adj* **(a)** (*sincère*) (*personne*) frank, open, candid; (*réponse, conversation*) frank, candid; **je serai f. (avec vous)** I'll be frank *or* candid *or* honest (with you); **pour être f.** to be frank *or* candid; **sa réponse a au moins le mérite d'être franche** at least he answered frankly *or* candidly; **un regard f.** an open look; **un oui f. et massif** a clear and overwhelming yes; **être f. comme l'or** to be totally frank; **être f. du collier** to be completely open; (*serviable*) to be compliant

(b) (*libre*) free; **f. de tout droit** duty-free; **f. d'avarie particulière** free of particular average; **f. d'impôts** tax free, free of tax; **f. de casse** free of breakage; **f. de toute avarie** free of average; **zone/ville franche** free zone/city; **port f.** free port; *Fb* **coup f.** free kick; *Mil* **corps f.** commando (unit)

(c) (*net*) (*couleur, vin*) pure; (*rupture*) clean; (*escroc*) downright, out-and-out; **situation franche** clear *or* unequivocal position; **c'est un f. Breton** he's a true Breton; **vin f. de goût** wine clean to the taste; **terre franche** loam; **ça a été une franche rigolade** it was an absolute scream; **huit jours francs** eight clear days

2 *adv* **pour parler f.** frankly *or* candidly speaking; **parlons f.** let's be frank (with each other)

franc[3], **franque** [frɑ̃, frɑ̃k] *Hist* **1** *adj* Frankish **2** *n* **F.** Frank

français, -aise [frɑ̃sɛ, -ɛz] **1** *adj* French; **impossible n'est pas f.** impossible? there's no such word (in the language); **c'est bien f. cette attitude** that's a typically French attitude

2 *adv* **acheter f.** to buy French; **rouler/boire/manger f.** to drive French cars/drink French wine/eat French food; **imprimer à la française** to print portrait

3 *nm Ling* French; **parler f.** to speak French; (*correctement*) to speak properly; *F* **tu ne comprends pas le f.?** ≈ don't you understand (plain) English?

4 *n* **F.** Frenchman, *f* Frenchwoman

franc-bord, *pl* **francs-bords** *nm Naut* freeboard; **bordé à f.** carvel built

franc-bourgeois, *pl* **francs-bourgeois** *nm Hist* freeman

France [frɑ̃s] *nf* France; **vivre/aller en F.** to live in/go to France; **les vins de F.** French wines; **F. 2/3** = French second/third TV channel (*state-owned*); **F. Info** = news radio station (*state-owned*); **F. Inter** = French radio station (*state-owned*)

Francfort [frɑ̃kfɔr] *n* Frankfurt; **saucisse de F.** frankfurter

franchement [frɑ̃ʃmɑ̃] *adv* **(a)** (*ouvertement*) frankly, candidly, openly; **(très) f., je ne sais pas quoi dire à ça** (quite) frankly, I don't know what to say to that; **je vais te parler f.** I'll be frank with you; **il me l'a dit f.** he told me openly; **y aller f.** to go right ahead with it; **vas-y f., appuie sur la manette** go on, push the joystick hard

(b) (*tout à fait, vraiment*) really; **c'était f. stupide/mauvais** it was really *or* downright stupid/bad; **j'en suis f. dégoûté** I'm absolutely sick of it; **f., tu comprends ça, toi?** honestly (now), do you understand that?; **non, mais f.!** no, honestly *or* really!; **tu as de ces idées, f.!** the ideas you have, honestly *or* really!

franchir [frɑ̃ʃir] *vt* (*obstacle, difficulté*) to get over, to clear; (*fossé*) to jump (over), to clear; (*rapides*) to shoot; (*limite*) to exceed; (*porte*) to pass *or* walk through; (*rivière, frontière*) to cross; **la panthère franchit le mur d'un seul bond** the panther cleared *or* jumped over the wall in one bound; **f. la ligne d'arrivée** to cross the finishing line; **f. le Rubicon** to cross the Rubicon; **f. le pas** to take the plunge; **f. le seuil** to step over *or* to cross the threshold; **f. le mur du son** to break (through) the sound barrier; **si l'on franchit un certain cap** if a certain point is passed; **f. la barre des 3 millions** to pass the 3 million mark

franchisage [frɑ̃ʃizaʒ] *nm Com* franchising

franchise [frɑ̃ʃiz] *nf* **(a)** (*sincérité*) frankness, openness, candour, *US* candor; (*franc-parler*) plain speaking, outspokenness; **en toute f.** quite frankly; **parler avec f.** to speak frankly *or* candidly **(b)** (*exonération*) exemption; **faire entrer qch en f.** to import sth duty-free; **entrée en f.** free import; **bagages en f.** baggage allowance **(c)** (*d'assurance*) excess, *Am* deductible **(d)** *Hist* **charte de f.** charter (of freedom) (*of city*) **(e)** *Com* franchise

▶ **franchise**: **f. (de) bagages** baggage allowance; **f. douanière** exemption from customs duties; **f. fiscale** tax exemption; **f. postale** = official paid; **f. de TVA** VAT exemption, zero-rating; **en f. de TVA** VAT-exempt, zero-rated

franchisé, -ée [frɑ̃ʃize] **1** *n Com* franchisee **2** *adj* **magasin f.** franchise

franchiser [frɑ̃ʃize] *vt* to franchise

franchiseur, -euse [frɑ̃ʃizœr, -øz] *n Com* franchisor

franchissable [frɑ̃ʃisabl] *adj* (*route*) passable; (*col de montagne*) negotiable; (*obstacle*) surmountable

franchissement [frɑ̃ʃismɑ̃] *nm* (*d'obstacle*) clearing; (*de fossé*) jumping; (*de rivière*) crossing

franchouillard, -arde [frɑ̃ʃujar, -ard] *F Péj* **1** *adj* archetypally French **2** *n* archetypal Frenchman/Frenchwoman
francisation [frɑ̃sizasjɔ̃] *nf* **(a)** *(d'un mot étranger)* gallicizing, *F* Frenchifying **(b)** *Naut* registry as a French ship
franciscain, -aine [frɑ̃siskɛ̃, -ɛn] *adj, n Rel* Franciscan
franciser [frɑ̃size] *vt* **(a)** *(mot étranger)* to gallicize, *F* to Frenchify **(b)** *Naut (bateau)* to register as French
francisque [frɑ̃sisk] *nf* = emblem of the Vichy government
francité [frɑ̃site] *nf* Frenchness
franc-maçon, *pl* **francs-maçons** *nm* freemason
franc-maçonnerie *nf* freemasonry
franc-maçonnique *adj* masonic
franco [frɑ̃ko] *adv* **(a)** *Com* **f. (de port)** post(age) paid, carriage free, carriage paid; **f. de port et d'emballage** post(age) and packing paid; **f. d'emballage** free of packing charges; **livré f.** delivered free *or* post(age) paid; **f. (à) bord** free on board, FOB; **f. de douane** free of customs duty; **f. frontière** free at frontier; **f. gare de réception** free on rail; **f. le long du navire** free alongside ship; **f. long du bord** free alongside ship; **f. long du quai** free alongside ship; **f. rendu** free at; **f. transporteur** free carrier; **f. wagon** free on rail **(b)** *F* **vas-y f.!** go right ahead!
franco-allemand *adj* Franco-German
franco-américain *adj* Franco-American
franco-canadien, -ienne 1 *adj* French Canadian **2** *nm Ling* Canadian French
francophile [frɑ̃kɔfil] *adj, n* francophile
francophilie [frɑ̃kɔfili] *nf* love of all things French
francophobe [frɑ̃kɔfɔb] **1** *n* francophobe **2** *adj* francophobe, francophobic
francophobie [frɑ̃kɔfɔbi] *nf* francophobia
francophone [frɑ̃kɔfɔn] **1** *adj* French-speaking **2** *n* French speaker
francophonie [frɑ̃kɔfɔni] *nf* French-speaking world
franc-parler *nm* plain speaking, outspokenness; **avoir son f.** to speak one's mind, to be outspoken, not to mince one's words
franc-tireur *pl* **francs-tireurs** *nm Mil* franc-tireur, irregular (soldier); *Fig* maverick
frange [frɑ̃ʒ] *nf (de carpette, cheveux etc), Fig* fringe
franger [frɑ̃ʒe] *vt* **(je frangeai(s))** to fringe, to border
frangin [frɑ̃ʒɛ̃] *nm F* brother
frangine [frɑ̃ʒin] *nf F* sister
frangipane [frɑ̃ʒipan] *nf Culin* almond paste, frangipane
frangipanier [frɑ̃ʒipanje] *nm Bot* frangipani (tree)
franglais [frɑ̃glɛ] *nm F* Franglais
franquette [frɑ̃kɛt] *nf* **à la bonne f.** simply, without ceremony; **on mangera à la bonne f.** we will eat simply; **un repas à la bonne f.** a simple meal; **c'est à la bonne f. chez eux** they don't stand on ceremony at home
franquisme [frɑ̃kism] *nm* Francoism
franquiste [frɑ̃kist] **1** *adj* pro-Franco **2** *n* supporter of Franco
frappant [frapɑ̃] *adj (image, ressemblance etc)* striking
frappe [frap] *nf* **(a)** *(dactylographie)* typing; *Ordinat* keying; **elle a une f. rapide** she can type/key fast; **la lettre est à la f.** the letter is being typed/keyed; **faute de f.** typing/keying error; **vitesse de f.** typing/keying speed; *Ordinat* **f. au kilomètre** continuous input; *Ordinat* **f. en continu** type-ahead **(b)** *(de pièces de monnaie)* striking, minting **(c)** *Baseball* hit; *Boxe* punch; *Fb* strike, kick **(d)** *Mil* **force de f.** strike force **(e)** *Arg* **petite f.** hoodlum
frappé [frape] *adj* **(a)** iced, well chilled; **café f.** iced coffee; **champagne f.** chilled champagne, champagne frappé **(b)** *F (fou)* crazy
frappement [frapmɑ̃] *nm* striking; *(bruit)* knocking
frapper [frape] **1** *vt* **(a)** to hit, to strike; **f. légèrement** to tap; **être frappé à mort** to be fatally *or* mortally wounded; **la balle l'a frappé en plein cœur** the bullet hit him right in the heart; **f. des marchandises d'une taxe** to impose a duty on goods; **être frappé par une maladie** to be struck down by a disease; **être frappé par un deuil** to be suffering from bereavement; **être frappé de mutisme** to be struck dumb; **f. qn d'étonnement** to strike sb with amazement; **cela a frappé son imagination** that caught his imagination; **ce qui m'a frappé le plus, c'était son sang-froid** what struck *or* impressed me most was his coolness; **je fus frappé par leur ressemblance** I was struck by their resemblance; **je suis frappé de le retrouver dans cette situation** I'm surprised to find him in this situation; **ça vous frappe** it really hits *or* strikes you; *Th* **f. les trois coups** to give the three knocks *(at the start of a play)*; *Fig* **f. un grand coup** to strike a decisive blow; *Fig* **f. à la tête** to strike at the top

(b) *(médaille)* to strike; *(pièces de monnaie)* to strike, to mint; *(papier peint)* to emboss; *(motif)* to punch (out), to cut out; *(cuir)* to block

(c) *(lettre)* to type; *Ordinat* to key; *Ordinat* **f. au kilomètre** to input continuously

(d) *(refroidir)* to ice; *(boisson)* to chill; **f. le champagne** to put the champagne on ice

2 *vi* **(a)** to strike, to hit; **f. du poing sur la table** to bang (on) the table; **f. à la porte** to knock on *or* at the door; **f. doucement à la porte** to tap on *or* at the door; **la prochaine fois vous pourrez entrer sans f.** next time you can come in without knocking; **entrez sans f.** *(notice)* come *or* go straight in; **on frappe** there's someone (knocking) at the door; *Fig* **vous frappez à la bonne/mauvaise porte** you've come to the right/wrong place; **il va falloir f. à toutes les portes** we will have to ask for help from all quarters

(b) f. des mains *ou* **dans ses mains** to clap (one's hands); **f. du pied** to stamp (one's foot)

(c) *F (agir)* to strike; **le gang a encore frappé** the gang has struck again; **la grippe va f. durement** the flu will hit everyone hard

3 se frapper *vpr* **(a) se f. les cuisses** to slap one's thighs; **se f. le front** to slap one's forehead; **se f. la poitrine** to beat one's chest

(b) *F* to get oneself worked up, to get oneself into a flap *or* panic; **ne vous frappez pas** don't panic, don't flap
frappeur, -euse [frapœr, -øz] **1** *n Métal* striker; *(de papier peint)* embosser **2** *adj* **esprit f.** spirit-rapper
frasque [frask] *nf* escapade, prank; **frasques** carryings-on, misbehaviour; **faire des frasques** to get up to mischief *or* to no good; **ses frasques de jeunesse** his youthful indiscretions
fraternel, -elle [fratɛrnɛl] *adj* fraternal, brotherly; **geste f.** friendly gesture
fraternellement [fratɛrnɛlmɑ̃] *adv* fraternally, in a fraternal manner; **nous nous embrassâmes f.** we kissed like brothers
fraternisation [fratɛrnizasjɔ̃] *nf* fraternization
fraterniser [fratɛrnize] *vi* to fraternize
fraternité [fratɛrnite] *nf* fraternity, brotherhood; **on trouve une certaine f. d'esprit entre eux** you can see a certain kinship of spirit between them
fratricide [fratrisid] **1** *adj* fratricidal **2** *nm (crime)* fratricide **3** *n (personne)* fratricide
fraude [frod] *nf* fraud; *(à un examen)* cheating; **f. électorale** electoral fraud, vote rigging; **f. fiscale** tax evasion; **en f.** fraudulently, unlawfully; **passer qch en f.** to smuggle sth in/out; **il entra en f. dans le pays** he entered the country illegally *or* unlawfully
frauder [frode] **1** *vt* to defraud, to cheat, to swindle; **f. le fisc** to evade tax; **f. la douane** to defraud customs, to smuggle; **vin fraudé** adulterated wine **2** *vi* to cheat **(sur** on); **f. sur la marchandise** to cheat the customer; **il a l'habitude de f. dans le métro** he always avoids buying a ticket for the underground, he's a fare-dodger
fraudeur, -euse [frodœr, -øz] *n* defrauder, cheat; *(trafiquant)* smuggler; **le nombre de fraudeurs dans les transports en commun a diminué** the number of fare-dodgers on public transport has decreased
frauduleusement [frodyløzmɑ̃] *adv* fraudulently; **je le vis se glisser f. dans le cinéma** I saw him slipping into the cinema without paying
frauduleux, -euse [frodylø, -øz] *adj* fraudulent; **édition frauduleuse** pirated edition
frayer [freje] **(je fraye** *ou* **fraie, n. frayons; je frayerai** *ou* **fraierai) 1** *vt* **(a) f. un chemin** to clear a path; *Fig* to blaze a trail; **f. la voie à qn** to pave the way for sb

(b) *(d'un cerf)* to scrape, to rub; *Vét (d'un cheval)* to gall

2 *vi* **(a)** *(d'un poisson)* to spawn

(b) *Fig* **f. avec qn** to mix *or* associate with sb; **je ne fraye pas avec des gens de cette espèce** I don't mix with that sort of people; **elle fraye peu** she doesn't mix much, she's not much of a mixer

3 se frayer *vpr* **se f. un passage** to clear a way (for oneself); **se f. un chemin à travers la foule** to force *or* push *or* elbow one's way through the crowd; *Fig* **se f. un chemin dans ...** to make one's way in ...
frayeur [frɛjœr] *nf* fright **(de** of); **tu m'as fait une de ces frayeurs!** you really frightened me!, you gave me such a fright!; **j'ai eu une f., j'ai cru que j'avais oublié mes clés** I had *or* got a fright, I thought I had forgotten my keys; **vous me donnez des frayeurs** you're getting me worried; **se remettre de ses frayeurs** to recover from one's fright
fredaine [frədɛn] *nf* prank, escapade; **faire des fredaines** to get into *or* up to mischief; *(amoureuses)* to carry on
fredonnement [frədɔnmɑ̃] *nm (d'un air)* humming
fredonner [frədɔne] *vti* to hum
free-jazz [fridjaz] *nm Mus* free jazz, free-form jazz
free-lance [frilɑ̃s] **1** *adj inv* freelance **2** *nm* **travailler en f.,**

faire du f. to work freelance, to do freelance work, to freelance **3** *n inv* freelance, freelancer

freesia [frezja] *nm Bot* freesia

freeware [friweʀ] *nm Ordinat* freeware; **freewares** freeware programs

freezer [frizœr] *nm* freezer compartment

frégate [fregat] *nf* **(a)** *Naut* frigate; **capitaine de f.** commander **(b)** *Orn* frigate bird

frein [frɛ̃] *nm* **(a)** *Aut* brake; **il a fallu donner un coup de f. très rapide** we had to brake very suddenly; *Fig* **donner un coup de f. à une entreprise** to put a brake on an undertaking; **un coup de f. à la création d'entreprises** a check to reduce the number of new firms; **mettre un f. à qch** to curb *or* check sth; **mettre un f. aux désirs de qn** to curb *or* bridle sb's desires; **mettre un f. à la montée de la colère** to stem *or* curb *or* check the rising tide of anger; **curiosité/imagination sans f.** unbridled curiosity/imagination; **f. à l'expansion** brake on growth

(b) (*mors*) bit; **ronger son f.** (*d'un cheval, Fig d'une personne*) to champ at the bit

(c) *Anat* (*de la langue*) fr(a)enum

▶ **frein**: **f. à air (comprimé)** airbrake; **freins arrière** rear brakes; **freins assistés** power brakes; **freins avant** front brakes; **freins à bande** band brakes; *Can* **f. à bras** handbrake, *Am* parking brake; **f. à disque** disc brake; **f. sur échappement** exhaust brake; **f. d'embrayage** clutch stop; **f. à main** handbrake, *Am* parking brake; **f. moteur** engine brake; **utilisez votre f. moteur** (*sur panneau*) engage low gear; **f. à pédale** foot brake; **f. au pied** foot brake; **f. secondaire** emergency brake; **f. de stationnement** handbrake, *Am* parking brake; **f. à tambour** drum brake; **f. sur transmission** transmission brake; **f. à vide** vacuum brake

freinage [frɛnaʒ] *nm* **(a)** (*action*) braking; *Fig* slowing (down); **distance de f.** braking distance; **traces de f.** skid marks; *Av* **parachute de f.** brake parachute **(b)** (*système*) brake system, brakes

freiner [frene, frɛne] **1** *vt* **(a)** (*véhicule*) to brake

(b) (*ralentir*) to slow down; **des arbres ont freiné sa chute** trees broke his fall

(c) (*inflation, production etc*) to curb, to check; **f. qn** to keep sb in check, to restrain sb

2 *vi* to brake; **f. à bloc** to jam on *or* slam on the brakes; *Fig* **ce sont les patrons qui freinent** it's the bosses who are back-pedalling; **il voudrait moderniser l'usine mais son père freine des quatre fers** he'd like to modernize the factory, but his father is putting a brake on that idea

3 se freiner *vpr Fig* to keep oneself in check, to restrain oneself

freinte [frɛ̃t] *nf Com* wastage, loss in volume/weight (*during transit or manufacture*)

frelatage [frəlataʒ] *nm* (*du vin, de la nourriture etc*) adulteration

frelater [frəlate] *vt* (*vin, nourriture*) to adulterate; **une vie frelatée** a corrupt life

frêle [frɛl] *adj* (*personne, enfant, voix*) frail, weak; (*silhouette*) frail; (*embarcation, cabane*) flimsy, frail

frelon [frəlɔ̃] *nm* hornet

freluquet [frəlykɛ] *nm F* (young) whippersnapper

frémir [fremir] *vi* **(a)** (*vibrer*) to quiver; (*des vitres*) to shake, to rattle; (*des feuilles*) to rustle; (*du vent*) to sigh; (*de l'eau chaude*) to simmer; **l'air frémissait encore des échos d'une flûte lointaine** the air was still vibrating to the echoes of a distant flute **(b)** (*d'une personne*) (*de peur*) to shake, to tremble, to shudder, to quake; (*de froid*) to shiver, to shudder; (*de plaisir, joie, d'impatience*) to tremble, to quiver; (*de colère, d'inquiétude*) to shake, to tremble, to quiver (**de** with); **il m'a fait si peur, j'en frémis encore** he scared me so much I'm still shaking *or* trembling

frémissant [fremisɑ̃] *adj* (*eau*) simmering; (*voix*) trembling, shaky; (*feuillage, chair*) quivering, trembling; **sensibilité frémissante** quivering sensitivity

frémissement [fremismɑ̃] *nm* **(a)** (*des feuilles*) rustle; (*de l'eau chaude*) simmering; (*du vent*) sighing; **le f. des champs de blé sous la brise** the wheatfields quivering in the breeze

(b) (*frisson*) (*de peur*) shudder; **f. de plaisir/joie** thrill of pleasure/joy; **un f. de colère/d'impatience/d'inquiétude** a quiver of anger/impatience/anxiety; **avec un f. de crainte** shaking *or* quaking with fear; **avec un f. dans la voix** with a trembling *or* shaky voice; **des frémissements parcouraient son corps** he was shaking *or* trembling all over; **un léger f. parcourut tous les auditeurs** a slight shudder went through the audience

frênaie [frɛnɛ] *nf* ash plantation

french-cancan [frɛnʃkɑ̃kɑ̃] *nm* cancan

frêne [frɛn] *nm* (*arbre*) ash (tree); (*bois*) ash

frénésie [frenezi] *nf* frenzy; **applaudir avec f.** to applaud frantically; **travailler/parler avec f.** to work/talk frenziedly; **f. d'achat** buying spree

frénétique [frenetik] *adj* frenzied, frantic; (*enthousiasme*) wild

frénétiquement [frenetikmɑ̃] *adv* frenziedly, frenetically

fréquemment [frekamɑ̃] *adv* frequently

fréquence [frekɑ̃s] *nf* **(a)** (*occurrence*) frequency; **la f. d'un mot dans un texte** the frequency of a word in a text; **f. du pouls** pulse rate; **f. d'achat** purchase frequency

(b) *Phys, Rad etc* frequency; (*de son*) tone; **basse/haute f.** low/high frequency; **très haute f.** very high frequency; **bande de fréquences** frequency band; **modulation de f.** frequency modulation; **f. absolue** absolute frequency; **f. cumulée** cumulative frequency; *Ordinat* **f. d'horloge** clock speed *or* frequency; **f. d'horloge du microprocesseur** microprocessor clock frequency; **f. porteuse** carrier; **f. radio** radio frequency; **f. de rafraîchissement** refresh rate; **f. réglée** adjusted frequency; **f. relative** relative frequency; **f. sonore** audio frequency

fréquent [frekɑ̃] *adj* frequent; **il est f. de voir des jeunes couples divorcer** you frequently *or* often see young couples getting divorced; **il est peu f. que ...** it is not very often that ...

fréquentable [frekɑ̃tabl] *adj* **des gens peu fréquentables** people you wouldn't want to associate with; **il redeviendra peut-être f. s'il paye des dettes** people will perhaps want to know him again if he pays his debts; *Hum* **tôt le matin, il n'est pas f.** he's not in the best of moods *or* he's not nice to know early in the morning

fréquentatif, -ive [frekɑ̃tatif, -iv] *adj Gram* frequentative

fréquentation [frekɑ̃tasjɔ̃] *nf* **(a)** (*fait d'aller à*) frequenting (**de** of); **f. des théâtres** theatre-going; **la f. des cinémas a baissé** cinema-going has decreased; **cela demande une f. assidue** it requires regular attendance; **f. des grands auteurs** acquaintance with the great writers **(b) fréquentations** company; **mauvaises fréquentations** bad company; **elle a de mauvaises fréquentations** she keeps bad company; **surveillez ses fréquentations** keep a watch on the company he keeps; **ce ne sont pas des fréquentations pour une jeune fille** these are not the sort of people a young girl should be associating with

fréquenté [frekɑ̃te] *adj* (*endroit, route*) busy; **bar f. par les étudiants** bar frequented by students, student bar; **hôtel bien f.** hotel with a good clientele; **endroit mal f.** place with a bad reputation

fréquenter [frekɑ̃te] **1** *vt* **(a)** (*endroit*) to frequent

(b) f. qn to see sb regularly; (*comme petite amie, petit ami*) to go out with sb; **nous ne nous fréquentons plus beaucoup** we don't see much of each other any more; **je fréquente peu ce genre de personnes** I don't associate much with that type of person; **quels gens fréquente-t-il?** who does he go around with?, what company does he keep?; **je t'interdis de f. les voisins** I forbid you to speak to the neighbours; **parmi tous ceux que je fréquente** amongst all my acquaintances

2 se fréquenter *vpr* to see each other regularly; (*d'un petit ami et d'une petite amie*) to go out with each other

frère [frɛr] *nm* **(a)** brother; **ils s'aiment comme des frères** they love each other like brothers; **on va partager en frères** we'll share it amicably; *F* **tu es un f. (pour moi)** you're a real friend; **faux f.** false friend; **alors, vieux f., quoi de neuf?** well, old chum *or* pal, what's new?; **les hommes sont tous frères** all men are brothers; **pays/peuples frères** sister countries/nations **(b)** [①A13,4] *Rel* friar; **mes bien chers frères** dearly beloved brethren; **j'ai fait mes études chez les frères** I studied with the brothers

▶ **frère**: **f. lai** lay brother; **f. de lait** foster brother; *F* **f. trois-points** freemason; **frères d'armes** brothers-in-arms

frérot [frero] *nm F* kid *or* little brother

fresque [frɛsk] *nf* fresco; **peinture à f.** painting in fresco; **ce roman est une f. historique** this novel is a historical epic; **le film est une f. sociale sur l'Italie des années 50** the film is a social portrait of Italy in the 50s

fresquiste [frɛskist] *adj, n* (**peintre**) **f.** fresco painter

fressure [fresyr] *nf* (*d'un veau, mouton etc*) pluck; *Culin* fry

fret [frɛ(t)] *nm* **(a)** (*prix*) (*de navire etc*) freight, freightage; **payer le f.** to pay the freight **(b)** (*louage*) chartering; **prendre un navire à f.** to charter a ship; **donner un navire à f.** to freight (out) a ship; **avion de f.** charter aircraft **(c)** (*cargaison*) (*d'un bateau, avion*) cargo, freight; (*d'un camion*) load, freight; **f. aérien** air freight; **expédier par f. aérien** to airfreight; **f. express** express freight; **f. intérieur** inland freight; **f. maritime** sea *or* ocean freight; **f. par conteneur** containerized freight; **f. à forfait** through freight

fréter [frete] *vt* (**je frète**; **je fréterai**) (*donner en location*) (*bateau*) to freight (out), to charter; (*avion*) to charter; (*prendre en location*) (*voiture*) to hire

fréteur [fretœr] *nm* ship charterer, freight forwarder; (*armateur*) shipowner; **f. et affréteur** owner and charterer

frétillant [fretijɑ̃] *adj* (*poisson*) wriggling, wriggly; *Fig* (*personne*) lively; **elle était toute frétillante à l'idée de le revoir** she couldn't keep still at the thought of seeing him again

frétillement [fretijmɑ̃] *nm* (*d'un poisson*) wriggling; (*d'une queue*) wagging; *Fig* fidgeting

frétiller [fretije] *vi* (*d'un poisson*) to wriggle; **le chien frétille de la queue** the dog is wagging its tail; **l'enfant frétille d'impatience** the child is fidgeting with impatience; **f. de joie** to quiver with joy

fretin [frətɛ̃] *nm Pêche, Fig* (**menu**) **f.** small fry

frette[1] [frɛt] *nf Tech* (binding) hoop, collar, ferrule; (*d'axe*) band; **f. de moyeu** (*de roue*) nave ring

frette[2] *nf Archit, Hér* fret

freudien, -ienne [frødjɛ̃, -jɛn] *adj Psy* Freudian

freudisme [frødism] *nm Psy* Freudianism

freux [frø] *nm* rook; **colonie de f.** rookery

friabilité [frijabilite] *nf* crumbliness, *Spéc* friability

friable [frijabl] *adj* crumbly, *Spéc* friable

friand [frijɑ̃] **1** *adj* fond of delicacies; **être f. de qch** to be fond of sth; **être f. de sucreries** to have a sweet tooth; *Fig* **f. de louanges** fond of praise **2** *nm Culin* (*feuilleté*) small savoury pastry; (*gâteau*) small almond cake

friandise [frijɑ̃diz] *nf* titbit, delicacy

Fribourg [fribur] *n* (*en Allemagne*) Freiburg; (*en Suisse*) Fribourg

fric [frik] *nm F* (*argent*) dough, *Br* dosh; **j'ai plus de f.!** I'm out of dough!, I'm skint!

fricassée [frikase] *nf Culin* fricassee; *Belg* bacon omelette; *F* **f. de museaux** hugging and kissing

fricasser [frikase] *vt Culin* to fricassee

fricatif, -ive [frikatif, -iv] *adj, nf Ling* fricative

fric-frac, *pl* **fric-frac(s)** *nm Arg* burglary, break-in

friche [friʃ] *nf* fallow land; **f. industrielle** industrial wasteland; **rester** *ou* **être en f.** to lie fallow, to remain uncultivated; *Fig* **une idée/un projet qui est** *ou* **reste en friche** an idea/a plan which has not yet been taken up; **elle laisse son talent/son génie en f.** she's letting her talent/genius go to waste

frichti [friʃti] *nm F* grub, *Br* nosh

fricot [friko] *nm F* grub; **faire le f.** to do the cooking

fricotage [frikɔtaʒ] *nm F* fiddling

fricoter [frikɔte] *F* **1** *vt Culin* to cook; *Fig* (*manigancer*) to scheme, to plot; **je me demande ce qu'il fricote** I wonder what he's up to *or* what he's cooking up **2** *vi* (**a**) (*trafiquer*) to be on the fiddle (**b**) (*avoir des relations sexuelles*) **ils fricotent ensemble** they're sleeping together

fricoteur, -euse [frikɔtœr, -øz] *n F* (*trafiquant*) wide boy

friction [friksjɔ̃] *nf* (**a**) (*massage*) rubdown; (*du cuir chevelu*) scalp massage (**b**) *Phys, MecE* friction; **embrayage à f.** friction clutch; **réduire les frictions** to reduce friction; **entraînement par f.** (*d'une imprimante*) friction feed (**c**) *Fig* (*heurt*) friction; **cause de f.** cause of friction; **cela reste un point de f.** that remains a bone of contention

frictionnel [friksjɔnɛl] *adj* (*chômage*) temporary

frictionner [friksjɔne] **1** *vt* (*membre*) to rub; **f. qn** to rub sb down, to give sb a rubdown; **f. la tête de qn** to massage sb's scalp, to give sb a scalp massage **2 se frictionner** *vpr* to rub oneself down

fridolin [fridɔlɛ̃] *nm F* (*terme injurieux*) Kraut, Fritz; **les fridolins** Jerry

frigidaire® [friʒidɛr] *nm* refrigerator, fridge; *F* **mettre un projet au f.** to put a plan into cold storage *or* on ice

frigide [friʒid] *adj* (*femme*) frigid; *Litt* (*cœur, caractère*) cold, icy

frigidité [friʒidite] *nf* frigidity, frigidness

frigo [frigo] *nm F* fridge, refrigerator; *F* **mettre un projet au f.** to put a plan into cold storage *or* on ice

frigorification [frigɔrifikasjɔ̃] *nf* (*de viande*) refrigerating, refrigeration

frigorifié [frigɔrifje] *adj* frozen; *F* **être f.** (*d'une personne*) to be frozen stiff

frigorifier [frigɔrifje] *vt* (*viande*) to refrigerate

frigorifique [frigɔrifik] *adj* refrigerating, *Am* frigorific; **appareil f.** refrigerator; **mélange f.** freezing mixture; **wagon f.** refrigerator van; **entrepôt f.** cold store

frigoriste [frigɔrist] *nm* refrigerating engineer

frileusement [friløzmɑ̃] *adv* with a shiver

frileux, -euse [frilø -øz] *adj* (*personne*) sensitive to the cold; **je suis très f.** I really feel the cold, I'm very sensitive to cold, I'm a chilly sort of person; **une attitude/réponse frileuse** a timid attitude/answer

frilosité [frilozite] *nf Litt* sensitivity to the cold; *Fig* nervousness, hesitancy

frimaire [frimɛr] *nm Hist* third month of the French Republican calendar (*Nov-Dec*)

frimas [frimɑ] *nm Litt* (hoar)frost, rime

frime [frim] *nf F* show, pretence; **tout ça, c'est de la f.** that's all show *or* all put on; **il le fait pour la f.** he does it for show

frimer [frime] *vi F* to show off

frimeur, -euse [frimœr, -øz] *n F* show-off

frimousse [frimus] *nf F* sweet *or* pretty little face

fringale [frɛ̃gal] *nf F* hunger; **avoir la f.** to be ravenous *or* starving *or* famished; *Fig* **une f. de qch** a craving for sth; **avoir une f. de voyage** to have itchy feet, to have an urge to travel

fringant [frɛ̃gɑ̃] *adj* (*cheval*) spirited, lively, frisky; (*personne*) dashing

fringuer [frɛ̃ge] **1** *vt F* to dress; **bien fringué** well turned out, well dressed **2** *vi Arch* to prance about, to skip about **3 se fringuer** *vpr* to get dressed; **il ne sait pas se f.** (*il n'a aucun goût*) he's got no dress sense

fringues [frɛ̃g] *nfpl F* (*vêtements*) gear, togs, clothes; **elle est folle de f.** she's clothes-mad, she's mad about clothes

friper [fripe] **1** *vt* (*vêtement*) to crumple, to crush; **visage fripé** crumpled face **2 se friper** *vpr* (*d'un vêtement*) to get crushed *or* crumpled

friperie [fripri] *nf* (*magasin*) second-hand clothes shop; (*vêtements*) second-hand clothes

fripes [frip] *nfpl* second-hand clothes

fripier, -ière [fripje, -jɛr] *n* second-hand clothes dealer

fripon, -onne [fripɔ̃, -ɔn] *F* **1** *n Vieilli* rogue, knave; *Fig* **petit f. /petite friponne!** you little rascal *or* devil! **2** *adj* (*sourire, regard, air*) mischievous, roguish

friponnerie [fripɔnri] *nf Vieilli* (*caractère*) roguery, knavery; (*action*) mischievous prank

fripouille [fripuj] *nf* (**a**) *F* rogue, scoundrel (**b**) *Arch* (*racaille*) rabble, riff-raff

friqué [frike] *adj F* loaded, rolling in it

friquet [frikɛ] *nm* tree sparrow

frire [frir] (*pp* **frit**; *pr ind* **je fris, tu fris, il frit**; *no pl*; *fu* **je frirai**; *for the vt the parts wanting are supplied by* **faire f.**) **1** *vt* to fry; **je fris du poisson** I'm frying fish **2** *vi* to fry; **le poisson frit** the fish is frying

frisant [frizɑ̃] *adj* **lumière frisante** oblique light

Frise [friz] *nf* Friesland

frise [friz] *nf Archit* frieze; *Th* **frises** border

frisé, -ée [frize] **1** *adj* (*cheveux*) curly; (*personne*) curly-haired; **salade frisée** curly lettuce; **velours f.** uncut velvet, terry; **elle est frisée comme un mouton** she's got frizzy hair **2** *nf* **frisée** (*chicorée*) curly endive **3** *n F* (**a**) (*enfant*) curly-haired child (**b**) *F* (*terme injurieux*) Kraut, Fritz, *Br* Jerry

friselis [frizli] *nm Litt* (*des feuilles*) rustling

friser [frize] **1** *vi* (*d'une personne*) to have curly hair **2** *vt* (**a**) (*cheveux*) to curl; **f. (les cheveux de) qn** to curl sb's hair; **fer à f.** curling tongs (**b**) (*approcher*) **f. l'accident** to have a narrow escape; **on a frisé la catastrophe** we came within a hair's-breadth *or* an inch of disaster; **on frise la dispute** we're close to arguing *or* to an argument; **cela frise l'impertinence** it's verging on the impertinent; **il frisait la soixantaine** he was close on sixty

frisette [frizɛt] *nf* (*de cheveux*) ringlet, small curl

frison[1] [frizɔ̃] *nm* (*de cheveux*) curl; (*de bois, papier etc*) shaving

frison[2], **-onne** [frizɔ̃, -ɔn] **1** *adj* Friesian; **vache frisonne** Friesian cow **2** *nm Ling* Friesian **3** *n* **F.** Friesian

frisotter [frizɔte] **1** *vt* **f. (les cheveux de) qn** to crimp *or* frizz sb's hair **2** *vi* to curl, to be frizzy

frisquet, -ette [friskɛ, -ɛt] *adj F* (*vent*) chill(y); **il fait f.** it's a bit chilly *or Br F* parky

frisson [frisɔ̃] *nm* (*de froid, peur*) shiver, shudder; (*de plaisir*) thrill; **avoir des frissons** to shiver, *F* to have the shivers; **j'en ai des frissons** it makes me shudder; **ça me donne des frissons rien que d'y penser** it makes me shudder just thinking of it; *Fig* **le f. de l'eau/des arbres** the rippling of the water/quivering of the trees

frissonnement [frisɔnmɑ̃] *nm* (*action*) shivering, shuddering; (*tremblement*) shudder, shiver; **un f. de plaisir** a thrill of pleasure

frissonner [frisɔne] *vi* (**a**) (*de froid, de peur*) to shiver, to shudder; **f. de joie** to be thrilled (**b**) (*du feuillage*) to quiver; (*de l'eau*) to ripple

frisure [frizyr] *nf* (*des cheveux*) curliness; **frisures** curls, curly hair; **se faire faire des frisures** to have one's hair curled

frit, frite [fri, frit] **1** *adj* (**a**) *Culin* fried; **pommes de terre frites** *Br* chips, French fried potatoes, (French) fries (**b**) *Arg* **il est f.** he's had it **2** *nf* (**a**) *Culin* **frites** *Br* chips, (French) fries; **un steak frites, s'il vous plaît!** steak and chips, please **(b)** *F* **avoir la frite** to be on form; **ça va te donner la frite** that'll perk you up

friterie [fritri] *nf* chip stall

friteuse [fritøz] *nf* deep fryer, *Br* chip pan; **f. électrique** electric fryer

fritillaire [fritilɛr] *nf Bot* fritillary

fritter [frite] *vt* (*métal*) to sinter

friture [frityr] *nf* **(a)** (*action*) (*de la nourriture*) frying; (*huile*) (deep) fat, oil (*for frying*); (*aliments*) fried food; **f. (de poissons)** fried fish **(b)** *Rad, Tél* **(bruits de) f.** crackling (noise), interference **(c)** *Belg* (*friterie*) chip stall

Fritz [frits] *nm inv F* (*terme injurieux*) Fritz, *Br* Jerry

frivole [frivɔl] *adj* frivolous

frivolement [frivɔlmɑ̃] *adv* frivolously

frivolité [frivɔlite] *nf* **(a)** (*caractère*) frivolity, frivolousness; (*vétille*) trifle **(b)** *Couture* **frivolités** (fancy) trimmings

froc [frɔk] *nm* **(a)** (*de moine*) habit, frock, gown; **prendre le f.** to become a monk; **jeter le f. aux orties** to leave the priesthood **(b)** *F* (*pantalon*) trousers, *Am* pants; *très F* **faire dans son f.** to shit oneself

froid [frwa] **1** *adj* **(a)** (*vent, temps, bain, radiateur etc*) cold; **à table!, ça va être f.!** come and eat, it's getting cold!; **repas f.** cold meal; **buffet f.** cold buffet; **viandes froides** cold meat(s)

(b) *Fig* (*personne*) cold; (*manière, accueil*) cold, chilly; (*style*) cold, unemotional; **se montrer** *ou* **être f. avec** *ou* **envers qn** to be cold towards sb, to treat sb coldly *or* coolly; **garder la tête froide** to remain cool (and collected), to keep one's composure; **cela me laisse f.** it leaves me cold; **colère froide** controlled *or* suppressed anger; **la guerre froide** the cold war

2 *adv* **soluble à f.** soluble when cold; *Aut* **démarrer à f.** to start from cold; **parler à f. d'une catastrophe** to speak calmly *or* unemotionally about a catastrophe; *Méd* **opérer à f.** to perform non-emergency surgery; **prendre** *ou* **cueillir un adversaire à f.** to catch an opponent unawares *or* off guard *or Br* on the hop

3 *nm* **(a)** cold; **il fait f.** it's cold; *F* **il fait un f. de canard** *ou* **de loup** it's freezing (cold); *Météo* **coup de f.** cold snap; **prendre (un coup de) f.** to catch a chill *or* a cold; **les grands froids** the coldest part of the winter; **une vague de f.** a cold spell; **avoir f.** to be *or* feel cold; **j'ai f. aux mains** my hands are cold, I've got cold hands; *Fig* **cela m'a fait** *ou* **donné f. (dans le dos)** it sent (cold) shivers down my spine; *Fig* **elle n'a pas f. aux yeux** she's very determined, she's got plenty of nerve; **battre f. à qn** to cold-shoulder sb

(b) *Fig* coolness; **ils sont en f.** there's a coolness between them; **je suis en f. avec lui** there's a coolness between me and him; **jeter un f.** to cast a chill

(c) l'industrie du f. the refrigerating industry; **le f. industriel** refrigeration; **la chaîne du f.** the refrigeration chain

froidement [frwadmɑ̃] *adv* **(a)** (*avec réserve*) coldly, coolly; **être f. accueilli** to be given a cold welcome *or* cool reception; **il les a abattus f.** he shot them in cold blood *or* cold-bloodedly **(b)** (*calmement*) calmly; **il faut étudier f. le problème** we must consider the problem calmly

froideur [frwadœr] *nf* **(a)** (*de manière*) coldness, chilliness; **sa f. me met mal à l'aise** his coldness makes me ill at ease; **il est toujours d'une très grande f. avec moi** he is always very cold towards me; **avec f.** coldly **(b)** (*indifférence*) coldness, indifference; **contempler le spectacle avec f.** to look coldly on; **analysons le problème avec f.** let us analyse the problem calmly **(c)** (*manque de sensualité*) coldness, iciness

froidure [frwadyr] *nf* cold; **par ces temps de f.** in this cold weather

froissant [frwasɑ̃] *adj* hurtful, wounding

froissement [frwasmɑ̃] *nm* **(a)** (*action*) (*de muscle*) bruising; (*de papier, tissu etc*) crumpling, creasing **(b)** (*bruit*) (*du papier, de la soie etc*) rustle, rustling **(c)** *Fig Vieilli* (*d'intérêts*) conflict, clash **(d)** (*vexation*) **un f. d'amour-propre** a blow to one's pride; **éviter tous froissements** to avoid ruffling any feathers *or* hurting anyone's feelings; **il risque d'y avoir des froissements entre elles** there's a chance of some hurt feelings between them

froisser [frwase] **1** *vt* **(a)** (*muscle*) to bruise; (*tissu, papier*) to crumple, to crease **(b) f. qn** to offend sb, to give offence to sb, to hurt *or* wound sb's feelings **2 se froisser** *vpr* **(a)** (*d'un tissu*) to crease, to crumple **(b)** (*d'une personne*) to take offence *or* umbrage **(de** at), to take exception **(de** to)

frôlement [frolmɑ̃] *nm* (*contact*) brushing **(contre** against); (*son*) rustle

frôler [frole] **1** *vt* (*effleurer*) to brush, to touch lightly; **l'avion a frôlé la cime des arbres** the plane skimmed the treetops; **f. les murs** to hug the walls; **il a frôlé la mort** he came close to death *or* had a brush with death; **on a frôlé la catastrophe/la dispute** we came close to disaster/to arguing; **ton attitude frôle le ridicule** your attitude verges on *or* borders on the ridiculous **2 se frôler** *vpr* to touch one another lightly, to brush each other; **les deux voitures se sont frôlées** the two cars brushed past each other

fromage [frɔmaʒ] *nm* cheese; **f. bien fait** ripe cheese; **omelette/soufflé au f.** cheese omelette/soufflé; *Fig F* **pas la peine d'en faire un f.** it's not worth making a fuss about; *F* **un gentil petit f.** a nice little earner

▶ **fromage**: **f. blanc** fromage frais; **f. fermenté** fermented cheese; **f. fondu** cheese spread; **f. frais** fromage frais; **f. à pâte molle/dure** soft/hard cheese; **f. à pâte persillée** blue(-veined) cheese; *Culin* **f. de tête** brawn, *Am* headcheese

fromager, -ère [frɔmaʒe, -ɛr] **1** *adj* cheese; **industrie fromagère** cheese industry **2** *n* (*commerçant*) cheese merchant, *Br* cheesemonger; (*fabricant*) cheesemaker

fromagerie [frɔmaʒri] *nf* (*lieu de fabrication*) cheese dairy; (*magasin*) cheese shop

froment [frɔmɑ̃] *nm* wheat; **pain de f.** wheaten bread; **farine de f.** wheat flour

fronce [frɔ̃s] *nf Couture* gather; **jupe à fronces** gathered skirt

froncement [frɔ̃smɑ̃] *nm* wrinkling, puckering; **f. de(s) sourcils** frown

froncer [frɔ̃se] *vt* **(je fronçai(s))** **(a)** (*plisser*) to wrinkle, to pucker; **f. les sourcils** to frown, *Litt* to knit one's brows **(b)** *Couture* to gather

frondaison [frɔ̃dɛzɔ̃] *nf* (*apparition des feuilles*) foliation; (*feuillage*) foliage

fronde[1] [frɔ̃d] *nf Bot* frond

fronde[2] *nf* **(a)** (*arme*) sling; (*jouet*) catapult, *Am* slingshot **(b)** *Hist* **la F.** the Fronde; *Fig* **esprit de f.** spirit of revolt *or* rebellion

fronder [frɔ̃de] **1** *vt Vieilli* (*critiquer*) to lampoon **2** *vi* **(a)** *Hist* to belong to the Fronde; *Fig* to rebel **(b)** *Arch* to use one's sling

frondeur, -euse [frɔ̃dœr, -øz] **1** *n* **(a)** *Hist* member of the Fronde **(b)** (*rebelle*) rebel **2** *adj* rebellious, anti-authority

front [frɔ̃] *nm* **(a)** (*de personne*) forehead, *surtout Litt* brow; **marcher le f. haut** to walk with one's head (held) high; **relever le f.** to hold one's head high; **courber** *ou* **baisser le f.** to submit; **faire f. à qn/qch** to face up to *or* stand up to sb/sth; **faire f.** to face up to things; **et vous avez le f. de me dire cela!** you have the nerve to tell me that!

(b) (*de bâtiment*) front, face; (*de colline*) brow; *Pol* front; **f. de bataille** battle front; *Mil* **le f.** the front (line); **partir sur le** *ou* **au f.** to go (up) to the front; **nouvelles du f.** news from the front; *Météo* **f. chaud/froid** warm/cold front; *Pol* **f. commun** united *or* common front; **faire f. commun contre qn/qch** to join forces against sb/sth

(c) de f. (*côte à côte*) side by side, one next to the other; **marcher à trois de f.** to walk three abreast; **mener plusieurs choses de f.** to have several things on the go at once; *Mil* **marche de f.** march in line; *Naut* **en ligne de f.** line abreast

(d) vue de f. front view; **attaque de f.** frontal attack; **attaquer qn de f.** to attack sb from the front; *Fig* to attack sb head-on; **aborder un problème de f.** to tackle a problem head-on; **heurter qn/qch de f.** to run head-on into sb/sth

▶ **front**: **f. de mer** (sea)front; **le F. populaire** = French left-wing coalition in power 1936-38; *Min* **f. de taille** working face, coal face

frontal, -ale, -aux, -ales [frɔ̃tal] **1** *adj* frontal; (*collision*) head-on; *Ordinat* front-end; **ordinateur f.** front end; **os f.** frontal bone; **chargement f.** front loading; *Min* **lampe frontale** cap lamp **2** *nm Anat* frontal bone; *Com* facing; **f. de rayonnage** shelf facing **3** *nf Com* **frontale** shelf facing

frontalier, -ière [frɔ̃talje, -jɛr] **1** *adj* **régions frontalières** frontier *or* border regions **2** *n* inhabitant of the frontier zone; (*travailleur*) cross-border commuter

fronteau, -eaux [frɔ̃to] *nm* **(a)** *Archit* small pediment **(b)** *Rel* (*de nonne*) frontlet

frontière [frɔ̃tjɛr] **1** *nf Pol* frontier, border; *Fig* boundary; **f. naturelle** natural frontier; **f. linguistique** linguistic boundary; **incident de f.** border incident; *Fig* **ma liberté ne connaît pas de f.** my freedom knows no bounds; **faire reculer les frontières du savoir** to roll back the frontiers of knowledge; **aux frontières de la vie et de la mort** between life and death; **se situer à la f. du possible** to stretch the bounds of what is possible; **dépasser les frontières du possible** to go beyond the bounds of what is possible **2** *adj* (*ville*) frontier, border; **poste f.** border *or* frontier post

frontispice [frɔ̃tispis] *nm* frontispiece

front-office [frɔ̃tɔfis] *nm Banque* front office

fronton [frɔ̃tɔ̃] *nm Archit* pediment; (*à la pelote basque*) fronton

frottage [frɔtaʒ] *nm* (*d'un membre etc*) rubbing, chafing; (*des sols etc*) polishing

frottée [frɔte] *nf Vieilli* **(a)** (*volée*) beating, thrashing **(b) f. (d'ail)** garlic bread

frottement [frɔtmɑ̃] *nm* **(a)** (*friction*) rubbing; *Méd* **f. pleural** pleural rub; *Phot* **marques de f.** stress marks; *Fig* **il y a quelques frottements entre eux** there is some friction between them **(b)** *MecE* friction; (*de freins*) binding; **f. de glissement** sliding friction; **usure par f.** abrasion

frotter [frɔte] **1** *vt* (*membre*) to rub; (*sol*) to rub; (*avec une brosse*) to brush; (*cuivre*) to polish; **je vais te f. le dos pour te réchauffer** I'll rub your back to warm you up; **si je t'y reprends, je te frotterai les oreilles!** if I catch you at it again, I'll give you what for!; **f. une allumette** to strike a match; *Vieilli* **être frotté de latin** to have a smattering of Latin

2 *vi* to rub; **la roue frotte (contre le frein)** the wheel is rubbing (against the brake)

3 se frotter *vpr* **(a) se f. les mains** to rub one's hands (together); *Fig* to rub one's hands; **se f. les yeux** to rub one's eyes; **se f. contre qch/qn** to rub (up) against sth/sb

(b) *Fig* **se f. aux artistes** to rub shoulders with artists; **se f. au monde professionnel** to be in contact with the professional world; **des gens auxquels il vaut mieux ne pas se f.** people it's best to keep away from *or* not to get involved with; **ne vous y frottez pas!** don't get involved!, don't meddle!; *Fig* **qui s'y frotte s'y pique** if you meddle, you'll get your fingers burnt

frotteur, -euse [frɔtœr, -øz] **1** *n* (*personne*) floor polisher **2** *nm* (*de train électrique*) sliding contact, (collecting) shoe; *Aut* slipper

frotti-frotta [frɔtifrɔta] *nm F* **faire du f.** to rub up against each other

frottis [frɔti] *nm* **(a)** *Beaux-Arts* scumble **(b)** *Biol* (*pour examen au microscope*) smear; **f. vaginal** cervical smear

frottoir [frɔtwar] *nm* (*ustensile*) rubber; (*brosse*) scrubbing brush; (*de boîte d'allumettes*) friction strip; (*de dynamo*) brush

frou-frou, froufrou, *pl* **frou(-)frous** [frufru] *nm* (*bruit*) (*d'une robe en soie, de feuilles*) rustle, rustling; (*vêtement féminin*) frill

froufroutant [frufrutɑ̃] *adj* frilly

froufrouter [frufrute] *vi* to rustle

froussard, -arde [frusar, -ard] *F* **1** *adj* yellow, chicken **2** *n* chicken, coward

frousse [frus] *nf F* fear, fright; **avoir la f.** to be scared, to have the wind up; **avoir la f. de faire qch** to be scared to do *or* of doing sth; **ça m'a donné** *ou* **foutu la f.** that scared me to death *or* put the wind up me

fructidor [fryktidɔr] *nm Hist* twelfth month of the French Republican calendar (*August-September*)

fructifère [fryktifɛr] *adj* fruitbearing

fructification [fryktifikasjɔ̃] *nf* (*d'un arbre*) fruition, fructification; (*d'un investissement*) yield; *Fig* (*d'une idée, d'un projet*) fruition

fructifier [fryktifje] *vi* (*d'arbres*) to bear fruit, *Spéc* to fructify; *Fig* **ses placements commencent à f.** his investments are beginning to show *or* yield a profit; **il sait faire f. son argent** he knows how to get a return on his money

fructose [fryktoz] *nm* fructose

fructueusement [fryktɥøzmɑ̃] *adv* fruitfully, profitably

fructueux, -euse [fryktɥø, -øz] *adj* fruitful, profitable

frugal, -ale, -aux, -ales [frygal, -o] *adj* (*personne, repas*) frugal

frugalement [frygalmɑ̃] *adv* frugally

frugalité [frygalite] *nf* frugality

frugivore [fryʒivɔr] **1** *adj* (*animal*) fruit-eating **2** *n* fruit-eater

fruit[1] [frɥi] *nm* fruit; **manger des fruits** to eat (some) fruit; **manger un fruit** to eat some fruit *or* a piece of fruit; **producteur de fruits** fruit grower; **f. vert** unripe fruit; **le f. d'un mariage** the offspring of a marriage; **le f. de plusieurs années de travail** the fruit of several years' work; **porter des fruits** (*d'un arbre*) to bear fruit; *Fig* **porter ses fruits** (*d'une action, d'un investissement etc*) to bear fruit; **avec f.** to good purpose

▶ **fruit**: **fruits des bois** fruits of the forest; **fruits confits** crystallized fruit; *Culin, Rel* **f. défendu** forbidden fruit; **fruits déguisés** = dates, prunes etc stuffed with almond paste; **fruits de mer** seafood; **f. de la passion** passion fruit; **fruits rafraîchis** fruit salad soaked in alcohol; **fruits rouges** red berries and currants; *Fig* **f. sec** failure; **fruits secs** dried fruit

fruit[2] *nm Constr* (*d'un mur, contrefort etc*) batter

fruité [frɥite] *adj* fruity

fruiterie [frɥitri] *nf* (*magasin*) fruiterer's *or* greengrocer's shop, *Am* fruit store; (*local*) fruit storeroom

fruiticulteur, -trice [frɥitikyltœr, -tris] *n* fruit grower

fruitier, -ière[1] [frɥitje, -jɛr] **1** *adj* **arbre f.** fruit tree **2** *n* fruit dealer, *Br* fruiterer, greengrocer **3** *nm* **(a)** (*local*) fruit storeroom; (*étagère*) stand of fruit trays **(b)** (*verger*) orchard

fruitière[2] *nf Suisse* cheese dairy

frusques [frysk] *nfpl F* (*vêtements*) gear, togs, *Br* clobber

fruste [fryst] *adj* (*style, personne*) rough, unpolished; (*pièce, statue*) worn

frustrant [frystrɑ̃] *adj* frustrating

frustration [frystrasjɔ̃] **(a)** *Psy* frustration **(b)** (*d'un légataire*) cheating, defrauding

frustré, -ée [frystre] **1** *adj* frustrated **2** *n* frustrated person; **c'est un f.** he's so frustrated

frustrer [frystre] *vt* **(a)** *Psy* to frustrate **(b)** (*priver*) **f. qn de qch** to deprive sb of sth; **vous l'avez frustré de sa victoire/réussite** you robbed *or* deprived him of his victory/success; **on m'a frustré de mes biens** I have been cheated out of *or* defrauded of my property

FS [ɛfɛs] *abrév* **franc suisse**

fuchsia [fyʃja] **1** *nm Bot* fuchsia **2** *adj inv* fuchsia

fucus [fykys] *nm* fucus, sea wrack

fuel [fjul] *nm* fuel oil

fugace [fygas] *adj* fleeting, transient; **impression f.** fleeting impression

fugacité [fygasite] *nf Litt* fleetingness, transience

fugitif, -ive [fyʒitif, -iv] **1** *adj* **(a)** (*personne*) fugitive, runaway **(b)** (*fugace*) (*désir, émotion*) transitory, fleeting, ephemeral, short-lived; **ombre fugitive** fleeting shadow **2** *n* fugitive, runaway

fugitivement [fyʒitivmɑ̃] *adv* fleetingly

fugue [fyg] *nf* **(a)** *Mus* fugue **(b) faire une f.** to run away

fuguer [fyge] *vi F* to run away

fugueur, -euse [fygœr, -øz] **1** *adj* who runs away a lot **2** *n* runaway

fuir [fɥir] (*prp* **fuyant**; *pp* **fui**; *pr ind* **je fuis, n. fuyons, ils fuient**) **1** *vi* **(a)** (*s'enfuir*) to run away, to flee **(devant** from); **f. de son pays** to flee one's country; **faire f.** to put to flight; **bête à faire f.** as stupid as can be; **le temps fuit** time flies, time is slipping by; **f. devant les responsabilités** to shirk one's responsibilities; *Naut* **f. devant le vent** to scud *or* run before the wind; **il a le regard qui fuit** he has shifty eyes; **f. à toutes jambes** to run off at top speed *or* as fast as one can

(b) (*de l'horizon*) to recede

(c) (*d'un robinet, tonneau etc*) to leak; (*de gaz, d'eau*) to leak, to escape

2 *vt* **(a)** (*éviter*) (*responsabilité, amis, journalistes*) to shun, to avoid; (*question*) to evade, to avoid; **f. sa famille** to shun one's family; *Litt* **f. le monde** to flee society; **le sommeil me fuit** I cannot sleep

(b) (*abandonner*) to flee, to run away from; **f. son pays** to flee one's country

3 se fuir *vpr* **arrête de te f. et fais face à tes responsabilités!** stop running away from yourself and face up to your responsibilities!

fuite [fɥit] *nf* **(a)** flight **(devant** from); **prendre la f.** to take flight; **être en f.** to be on the run; **mettre l'ennemi en f.** to put the enemy to flight; *F* **la f. des cerveaux** the brain drain; **la f. des capitaux** the flight of capital; **renversé par une voiture qui a pris la f.** run over by a hit-and-run driver; *Fig* **la f. en avant de la consommation** the headlong rush of consumerism; **la course aux armements est une f. en avant** the arms race is being blindly pursued by all governments; **à partir de là, c'était la f. en avant** from then on there was no turning back; **la seule solution possible était la f. en avant** the only possible solution was to keep on going, the only way out was forward

(b) (*de liquide, gaz, d'information*) leak; **f. de gaz** gas leak; **il y a eu des fuites en histoire** some of the history questions leaked out

(c) (*devant des difficultés, des problèmes*) evasion, avoidance

(d) la f. du temps the passage *or* passing of time

(e) *Beaux-Arts* **point de f.** vanishing point

fulgurant [fylgyrɑ̃] *adj* (*lumière*) flashing; (*attaque, changement*) lightning; *Méd* (*douleurs*) stabbing, searing; **une découverte fulgurante** a dazzling discovery; **une idée fulgurante** a sudden and brilliant idea; **lancer un regard f. à qn** to look daggers at sb; **elle a connu un succès f.** she was brilliantly successful; **une explication d'une clarté fulgurante** a brilliantly clear explanation

fulguration [fylgyrasjɔ̃] *nf* lightning; *Méd* fulguration

fulgurer [fylgyre] *vi* to flash

fuligineux, -euse [fyliʒinø, -øz] *adj* (*couleur*) smoky, sooty; (*ciel*) murky

fulmicoton [fylmikɔtɔ̃] *nm* guncotton

fulminant [fylminɑ̃] *adj* (*ton*) exceedingly angry, furious; (*poudre*) fulminating; *Spéc* (*douleur*) fulminant

fulminer [fylmine] **1** *vt* (*accusations*) to thunder, to roar **2** *vi* **f. contre qn/qch** to fulminate *or* inveigh against sb/sth

fumage[1] [fymaʒ] *nm*, **fumaison** [fymɛzɔ̃] *nf* (*d'une terre*) manuring, dressing, dunging

fumage[2] *nm*, **fumaison** *nf* (*de poisson, viande*) smoking, smoke-curing

fumant [fymɑ̃] *adj* **(a)** (*âtre, cendres*) smoking **(b)** (*soupe, cheval etc*) steaming; *F* **f. de colère** fuming **(c)** *F* (*remarquable*) terrific, sensational; **faire un coup f.** to pull off a masterstroke

fumasse [fymas] *adj F* fuming

fumé [fyme] *adj* **(a)** (*poisson, viande etc*) smoked, smoke-cured **(b) verre f.** smoked glass; **verres fumés** dark lenses; (*lunettes*) dark glasses, sunglasses

fume-cigare [fymsigar] *nm inv* cigar holder

fume-cigarette [fymsigarɛt] *nm inv* cigarette holder

fumée [fyme] *nf* **(a)** (*de feu, cigarette etc*) smoke; **rideau de f.** smokescreen; **noir de f.** lampblack; **la f. (du tabac) vous gêne-t-elle?** do you mind my smoking?; *Fig* **partir** *ou* **s'en aller en f.** to go up in smoke; *Prov* **il n'y a pas de f. sans feu** there's no smoke without fire **(b)** (*de la soupe etc*) steam; (*du charbon de bois*) fumes; (*d'alcool*) vapours, *US* vapors

fumer[1] [fyme] *vt* (*terre*) to manure, to dress, to dung

fumer[2] **1** *vi* **(a)** (*d'un âtre, d'une lampe, d'un moteur*) to smoke **(b)** (*d'un fumeur*) to smoke; **défense de f.** no smoking; **f. comme un pompier** *ou* **un sapeur** to smoke like a chimney; **f. tranquillement** to have a quiet smoke; **il est allé en f. une dans la cour** he went for a smoke *or* to have a smoke in the yard **(c)** (*de la soupe etc*) to steam **(d)** *F* (*de colère*) to fume **2** *vt* **(a)** (*poisson, viande*) to smoke(-cure) **(b)** (*pipe, tabac etc*) to smoke **il fumait Rothman sur Rothman** he was chainsmoking Rothmans

fumerie [fymri] *nf* **f. d'opium** opium den

fumerolle [fymrɔl] *nf* (*de volcan*) smoke and gas

fumet [fymɛ] *nm* **(a)** (*de la nourriture qui cuit*) aroma, (pleasant) smell; (*du vin*) bouquet **(b)** (*à la chasse*) scent

fumeterre [fymtɛr] *nf Bot* fumitory

fumeur, -euse [fymœr, -øz] *n* smoker; **f. de pipe/cigares** pipe/cigar smoker; **f. d'opium** opium smoker; *Rail* **compartiment fumeurs/non fumeurs** smoking/non-smoking compartment, *F* smoker/non-smoker

fumeux, -euse [fymø, -øz] *adj* (*lampe*) smoky, smoking; (*ciel, idées, explications, projets*) hazy; **quel esprit f.!** what a woolly mind!

fumier [fymje] *nm* **(a)** (*engrais*) manure, dung; **fosse à f.** slurry pit **(b)** (*tas*) dunghill, manure heap **(c)** *Vulg* (*salaud*) bastard; **espèce de f.!** you bastard!; **le f.!, il m'a menti!** he lied to me, the bastard!

fumigation [fymigasjɔ̃] *nf* fumigation; *Méd* inhalation

fumigène [fymiʒɛn] **1** *nm* (*en horticulture*), *Mil* smoke-producing device **2** *adj Mil* **grenade f.** smoke grenade

fumiger [fymiʒe] *vt* **(je fumigeai(s))** to fumigate

fumiste [fymist] **1** *nm* **(a)** *F* (*sur qui on ne peut compter*) clown, joker **(b)** (*installateur*) heating engineer **(c)** *Vieilli* (*farceur*) practical joker **2** *adj F* unreliable, irresponsible

fumisterie [fymistəri] *nf* **(a)** (*métier*) heating engineering **(b)** *F* (*farce*) con, farce; **c'est une vaste f.** it's a huge con, it's an absolute farce

fumivore [fymivɔr] *adj* smoke-absorbing

fumoir [fymwar] *nm* smoking room; (*pour la viande, le poisson etc*) smokehouse

fumure [fymyr] *nf* (*de champ*) manuring, dressing, dunging

funambule [fynɑ̃byl] *n* tightrope walker, *Spéc* funambulist

funambulesque [fynɑ̃bylɛsk] *adj* **(a) l'art f.** the art of tightrope walking; **acrobatie f.** high-wire acrobatics **(b)** *Fig* (*idées, projet etc*) (*original*) fantastic, bizarre; (*casse-cou*) reckless

funboard [fœnbɔrd] *nm* funboard

funèbre [fynɛbr] *adj* **(a)** (*cérémonie*) funeral; **hymne** *ou* **chant f.** dirge; **marche f.** funeral *or* dead march **(b)** (*lugubre*) funereal, gloomy

funérailles [fyneraj] *nfpl* funeral; **f. nationales** state funeral

funéraire [fynerɛr] *adj* (*dépenses*) funeral; (*urne*) funeral, funerary; **pierre f.** tombstone, gravestone; **drap f.** pall

funeste [fynɛst] *adj* **(a)** *Litt* (*accident*) deadly, fatal **(b)** (*erreur, conséquences*) fatal, disastrous, catastrophic; **influence f.** disastrous influence; **être f. à qch** to be fatal to sth **(c)** *Arch* (*triste*) funereal, gloomy

funiculaire [fynikylɛr] **1** *adj* funicular **2** *nm* funicular (railway)

funk [fœnk] *adj inv, nm Mus* funk

funky [fœnki] *Mus* **1** *adj inv* funky **2** *nm* funky music

fur [fyr] *nm* **au f. et à mesure** as one goes along, bit by bit; **au f. et à mesure, j'ai compris comment ça fonctionnait** I understood how it worked as I went along *or* bit by bit; **au f. et à mesure des besoins** as and when required, as needed; **au f. et à mesure de la progression des travaux** as work progresses; **au f. et à mesure de ses recherches** as he progressed with his research; **au f. et à mesure que tu en as besoin** as and when you need it; **je repasse mon linge au f. et à mesure que je le lave** I iron my clothes as soon as I've washed them

furax [fyraks] *adj F* livid, *Am* fit to be tied

furet [fyrɛ] *nm* **(a)** (*animal*) ferret; **chasse au f.** ferreting; **chasser au f.** to go ferreting; **jeu du f.** ≈ hunt-the-slipper **(b)** *Fig Arch* nosy parker

furetage [fyrtaʒ] *nm* **(a)** (*pour lapins*) ferreting **(b)** *Fig* prying, nosing around; (*dans l'armoire*) rummaging (about), ferreting (about)

fureter [fyrte] *vi* **(je furette; je furetterai) (a)** (*chasser*) to ferret, to go ferreting **(b)** (*chercher*) to pry, to nose around; **f. dans les armoires** to ferret (about) *or* rummage (about) in the cupboards

fureteur, -euse [fyrtœr, -øz] **1** *n* **(a)** (*chasseur*) ferreter **(b)** *F Péj* nosy parker **2** *adj* prying, *F* nosy; **regard f.** inquisitive look

fureur [fyrœr] *nf* **(a)** (*colère*) fury, rage; **être en f.** to be in a rage *or* fury, to be furious; **tu vas le mettre en f.** you'll infuriate *or* enrage him, you'll make him furious; **se mettre dans une f. (noire)** to fly into a (towering) rage; **la f. des combats dans le Golfe** the battle raging in the Gulf; **la f. des flots** the fury of the waves **(b)** (*passion*) passion; **aimer qn/qch avec f.** to be passionately fond of sb/sth; **avoir la f. de bâtir** to be mad on building; **la f. du jeu** a passion for gambling; **faire f.** to be all the rage

furia [fyrja] *nf F* (*d'une foule*) frenzy; **ils n'ont pas pu résister à la f. bordelaise** they had no answer to the Bordeaux team's furious onslaught

furibard [fyribar] *adj F* livid, *Am* fit to be tied

furibond [fyribɔ̃] *adj* furious; **elle lui a lancé un regard f.** she glared at him

furie [fyri] *nf* **(a)** (*passion*) fury; **critiquer qn/se battre avec f.** to criticize sb/fight furiously; **applaudir/crier avec f.** to applaud/shout frantically; **la f. du jeu** a passion for gambling; **en f.** infuriated, enraged; **se mettre en f.** to fly into a rage **(b)** *Myth* **les Furies** the Furies; *Fig* **c'est une f.** she's a shrew; **comme une f.** like a wild thing

furieusement [fyrjøzmɑ̃] *adv* **(a)** furiously **(b)** *Vieilli, Hum* (*très*) extremely, really; **on s'est f. amusé** we had a great time

furieux, -ieuse [fyrjø, -jøz] **1** *adj* **(a)** (*en colère*) furious; **être f. contre qn** to be furious with sb; **elle est furieuse qu'on ne l'ait pas prévenue** she's furious that nobody told her; **il est f. contre lui-même** he's furious with himself; **être f. de qch** to be furious with *or* at sth; **je suis f. de constater que vous n'avez fait aucun effort** I'm furious to see that you've made no effort at all; **rendre qn f.** to enrage *or* infuriate sb; **taureau f.** mad *or* raging bull; **tempête furieuse** raging *or* howling storm; **il a un f. appétit** he has a tremendous appetite; **un f. désir de vivre** a tremendous desire to live; **pousser des cris f.** to shout furiously

(b) (*forcené*) mad; **c'est un fou f.** he's a raving lunatic

2 *n* **c'est un f.** he's a raving lunatic

furoncle [fyrɔ̃kl] *nm Méd* boil, *Spéc* furuncle

furonculose [fyrɔ̃kyloz] *nf Méd* furunculosis

furtif, -ive [fyrtif, -iv] *adj* furtive, stealthy

furtivement [fyrtivmɑ̃] *adv* furtively, stealthily; **entrer/sortir f.** to steal in/out, to enter/leave furtively

fusain [fyzɛ̃] *nm* **(a)** (*arbre*) spindle tree **(b)** *Beaux-Arts* (*crayon*) charcoal (pencil); (*dessin*) charcoal (drawing)

fusant [fyzɑ̃] *adj* fusing; **obus f.** time shell

fuseau, -eaux [fyzo] *nm* **(a)** *Tex* spindle; (*pour dentelle*) bobbin; **f. de quenouille** distaff; **en f.** tapered, tapering; **jambes en f.** slender legs **(b) f. horaire** time zone **(c)** *F* **fuseaux** (*pantalon*) ski pants; **la mode du f.** *ou* **des fuseaux revient** ski pants are coming back into fashion

fusée [fyze] *nf* **(a)** (*projectile*) rocket; **lancer une f.** to launch a rocket; **avion-f.** rocket-propelled aircraft; **il est parti comme une f.** he shot off like a rocket **(b)** (*de bombe etc*) fuse, *US* fuze **(c)** (*d'arbre, d'axe*) spindle; *Aut* stub axle, hub carrier

▶ **fusée**: **f. air-air** air-to-air missile; **f. d'appoint** booster; **f. de détresse** distress rocket; **f. de direction** stub axle; **f. éclairante** flare; **f.-engin** missile; **f. à étages** multistage rocket; **f. à un étage** one-stage rocket; *Astronaut* **f. interplanétaire** space rocket; **f. percutante** percussion fuse; **f. à pétard** maroon; *Naut* **f. porte-amarre** life(-saving) rocket; **f. porteuse** carrier rocket; **d. de signalisation** signal rocket; **f. sonde** probe; **f. à temps** time fuse; **f. volante** sky rocket

fuselage [fyzlaʒ] *nm Av* fuselage

fuselé [fyzle] *adj* (*colonne, doigts*) tapering; *Aut* streamlined

fuseler [fyzle] *vt* **(je fuselle; je fusellerai)** to taper; *Aut* to streamline

fuser [fyze] *vi* **(a)** *(de cire chaude)* to run, to melt; *Fig* **des rires fusèrent de toutes parts** there were bursts of laughter from all sides, laughter erupted from all sides; **des cris/des remarques fusèrent de toutes parts** cries/comments were suddenly heard from all sides **(b)** *Ch (de sel)* to crackle **(c)** *(de fusible)* to burn slowly

fusibilité [fyzibilite] *nf* fusibility

fusible [fyzibl] **1** *adj* fusible **2** *nm Él* fuse, *US* fuze; *(fil métallique)* fuse wire; **f. de sûreté** safety fuse, cut-out

fusiforme [fyzifɔrm] *adj* spindle-shaped

fusil [fyzi] *nm* **(a)** *(arme)* gun, rifle; *Fig* **changer son f. d'épaule** to change (one's) tack; **entendre un coup de f.** to hear a shot; **c'est un de nos meilleurs fusils** he's one of our best shots; **coup de f.** gunshot, rifle shot; *F (dans un hôtel)* overcharging, fleecing; *F* **c'est le coup de f., dans ce restaurant** the prices in this restaurant are extortionate; *F* **quel coup de f.!** what a rip-off! **(b)** *(d'un briquet à amadou)* steel; *(pour aiguiser)* (sharpening) steel

▶ **fusil**: **f. à air comprimé** air gun; **f. automatique** automatic gun *or* rifle; **f. à chargeur** magazine rifle; **f. de chasse** shotgun, sporting gun; **f. à deux coups** double-barrelled gun; **f. harpon** harpoon gun; **f. rayé** rifle

fusilier [fyzilje] *n* fusilier; **f. marin** marine

fusillade [fyzijad] *nf (tir)* fusillade, rifle fire

fusiller [fyzije] *vt* **(a)** *(par un peloton d'exécution)* to shoot; *Fig* **f. qn du regard** to look daggers at sb **(b)** *F Vieilli (abîmer)* to wreck, to ruin

fusil-mitrailleur, *pl* **fusils-mitrailleurs** *nm* light machinegun

fusion [fyzjɔ̃] *nf* **(a)** *(par la chaleur)* melting, *Spéc* fusion; *Métal* smelting; **point de f.** melting point; **fer en f.** molten iron **(b)** *Nucl* fusion **(c)** *Fig (d'idées, de philosophies etc)* merging, combining **(d)** *(de compagnies, partis politiques etc)* merger; **fusions-rachats** mergers and acquisitions; *Ordinat* **f. de fichiers** file merge

fusionnement [fyzjɔnmɑ̃] *nm Com (de compagnies)* merger, amalgamation

fusionner [fyzjɔne] **1** *vi (de sociétés, communes, partis politiques)* to merge, to amalgamate **2** *vt (sociétés, communes, partis politiques)* to merge, to amalgamate; *Ordinat* to merge

fustigation [fystigasjɔ̃] *nf Litt* castigation

fustiger [fystiʒe] *vt* **(je fustigeai(s))** *Arch (battre)* to thrash, to beat; *Fig Litt (critiquer)* to castigate

fût [fy] *nm* **(a)** *(de fusil)* stock; *(de scie, de raquette etc)* handle **(b)** *(de colonne, cheminée)* shaft; *(de candélabre)* stem; *(de rivet)* shank; *(d'arbre)* bole **(c)** *(baril)* cask, barrel; *(pour l'huile)* drum; **tirer de la bière du f.** to draw beer from the wood *or* cask *or* barrel

futaie [fytɛ] *nf* forest *(producing timber from full-grown trees)*; **arbre de haute f.** full-grown tree

futaille [fytɑj] *nf (baril)* cask, barrel

futaine [fytɛn] *nf Tex* fustian

futal [fytal] *nm*, **fute** [fyt] *nm F* trousers, *Am* pants

futé, -ée [fyte] **1** *adj* cunning, wily, crafty **2** *n* **c'est un petit f.** he's a cunning *or* crafty devil

futile [fytil] *adj (argument, occupation)* trivial, trifling; *(prétexte)* idle; *(personne)* frivolous

futilement [fytilmɑ̃] *adv* frivolously

futilité [fytilite] *nf* triviality; **s'occuper à des futilités** to fritter away one's time; **une conversation pleine de futilités** a conversation full of trivialities

futur, -ure [fytyr] **1** *adj* future; **la vie future** the life to come; **les générations futures** future *or* coming generations; **f. acheteur** prospective buyer; **un f. artiste** a budding artist; **f. client** prospective client; **mon f. emploi/appartement** my next job/flat; **mon f. mari** my future husband, my husband-to-be

2 *n Hum* **mon f. /ma future** my fiancé/fiancée, my intended

3 *nm* **(a)** *(avenir)* future; **le f. m'inquiète** I am worried about the future; **quel f. pour l'Europe?** what will Europe's future be?

(b) [①**A49-50; B29,** 6-7] *Gram* future (tense); **au f.** in the future (tense)

futurisme [fytyrism] *nm Beaux-Arts, Archit* futurism; **le f. de cet avion étonne tous les visiteurs** all the visitors are stunned by how futuristic the plane is

futuriste [fytyrist] *Beaux-Arts, Archit* **1** *adj* futuristic **2** *n* futurist

fuyant [fɥijɑ̃] *adj* **(a)** *(ligne, menton)* receding; *Beaux-Arts* **lignes fuyantes** perspective lines **(b)** *(personne, attitude)* evasive; *(yeux)* shifty

fuyard, -arde [fɥijar, -ard] **1** *adj Arch* shy, timid **2** *n* fugitive, runaway

FV *nf (abrév* **fréquence vocale***)* voice frequency

G

G, g [ʒe] *nm* (*lettre*) G, g; **une force égale à plusieurs G** a force of several G
g. *abrév* **(a)** **gauche (b) gramme(s)**
gabardine [gabardin] *nf* **(a)** *Tex* gabardine **(b)** (*imperméable*) gabardine (raincoat)
gabare [gabar] *nf* **(a)** *Naut* sailing barge; (*pour charger, décharger un navire*) lighter; (*chaland*) transport vessel, store ship, scow **(b)** *Pêche* dragnet
gabarit [gabari] *nm* **(a)** *Naut* (*d'un bateau*) model; (*d'une pièce de bateau*) mould, *US* mold; *Constr* (*d'un bâtiment*) outline **(b)** *Tech* template, templet; *Ordinat* template; **g. d'assemblage** assembly jig, assembling gauge; **tour à g.** copying lathe **(c)** *Rail* (*sous un pont*) clearance; **g. de chargement** loading gauge; **g. d'écartement (des voies)** rail *or* track gauge **(d)** *F* **un grand/petit g.** a huge/tiny man/woman; **des gens de son g.** people of his calibre
gabegie [gabʒi] *nf* (*mauvaise gestion*) mismanagement; (*désordre*) muddle, chaos
gabelle [gabɛl] *nf Hist* salt tax
gabelou [gablu] *nm Péj* customs officer
gabier [gabje] *nm Naut* topman; **g. breveté** able(-bodied) seaman
gable [gabl], **gâble** [gɑbl] *nm Archit* gable; (*charpente*) (triangular) window canopy
gabonais, -aise [gabɔnɛ, -ɛz] **1** *adj* Gabonese **2** *n* **G.** Gabonese
Gabon (le) [ləgabɔ̃] *nm* Gabon
gâchage [gɑʃaʒ] *nm* **(a)** (*du mortier, du plâtre*) mixing **(b)** (*gaspillage*) waste, wasting **(c)** **g. des prix** price undercutting
gâche¹ [gɑʃ] *nf* **(a)** (*pour le plâtre*) trowel **(b)** (*de pâtissier*) spatula
gâche² *nf* **(a)** (*d'une serrure*) (box) staple, keeper; (*d'une fenêtre*) (latch) catch; (*d'un pêne*) striking box *or* plate, strike box; *Aut* **g. de porte** striker plate **(b)** *MecE* (*pour cliquet*) notch
gâchée [gɑʃe] *nf Constr* (*de ciment etc*) batch
gâcher [gɑʃe] *vt* **(a)** (*gâter*) to spoil; (*bâcler*) (*travail*) to bungle, to botch, to mess up; (*gaspiller*) (*nourriture, pellicule etc*) to waste; (*fortune*) to waste, to squander; **il a gâché notre plaisir/la soirée** he spoiled our pleasure/the evening; **tu as tout gâché en lui racontant ça** you've spoilt *or* ruined everything by telling him that; **g. ses chances de succès** to spoil one's chances; **g. sa vie** to waste one's life; **g. le métier** to spoil it for others (*by undercutting them*); **g. le marché** to spoil the trade **(b)** (*mélanger*) (*mortier, plâtre*) to mix; **g. la chaux** to slack lime
gâchette [gɑʃɛt, gaʃɛt] *nf* **(a)** (*d'une arme*) trigger; *F* **avoir la g. facile** to be trigger-happy **(b)** (*d'une serrure*) spring catch **(c)** *MecE* pawl **(d)** *Électron* gate
gâcheur, -euse [gɑʃœr, -øz] **1** *adj* wasteful **2** *n* waster **3** *nm Constr* plasterer's mate
gâchis [gɑʃi] *nm* **(a)** (*mortier*) wet mortar **(b)** (*désordre*) mess; (*gaspillage*) waste; **vous avez fait un beau g. dans la cuisine!** you've made a right mess in the kitchen!; **je ne supporte pas le g.** I can't stand waste *or* wastefulness; **quel g.!** what a waste!
gadelle [gadɛl] *nf Can Bot* redcurrant
gadget [gadʒɛt] *nm* gadget, *F* gizmo; **des mesures-gadgets** gimmicky measures
gadgétisation [gadʒetizasjɔ̃] *nf* **la g. des voitures/ordinateurs** the adding of gadgets to cars/computers; **la g. de la société** the increasing use of gadgets in society
gadgétiser [gadʒetize] *vt* to add gadgets to; **g. la société** to increase the use of gadgets in society
gadgétomanie [gadzetɔmani] *nf F* mania for gadgets
gadin [gadɛ̃] *nm F* **prendre** *ou* **ramasser un g.** to come a cropper
gaditan, -ane [gaditɑ̃, -an] **1** *adj* of *or* from Cadiz **2** *n* **G.** (*natif*) native of Cadiz; (*habitant*) inhabitant of Cadiz
gadoue [gadu] *nf* (*boue*) mud, slush; (*engrais*) sewage sludge
Gaël [gaɛl] *nm* Gael
gaélique [gaelik] *adj, nm Ling* Gaelic
gaffe [gaf] *nf* **(a)** *F* (*maladresse*) blunder, booboo; **faire une g.** to put one's foot in it, to make a blunder **(b)** (*perche*) boathook; *Pêche* gaff; *Arg* **avaler sa g.** to die, to kick the bucket **(c)** *F* **faire g.** to pay attention; **fais g.!** look out!, watch it! **(d)** *Arg* prison warder, screw
gaffer¹ [gafe] **1** *vt* **(a)** (*objet flottant etc*) to hook; *Pêche* (*saumon etc*) to gaff **(b)** *F* **gaffe un peu la nana!** get a look at that chick! **2** *vi F* **(a)** (*commettre une bévue*) to put one's foot in it, to make a blunder **(b)** *F* (*regarder*) to look; **gaffe un peu!** have a look!
gaffer² [gafœr] *nm TV, Cin* gaffer
gaffeur¹, -euse [gafœr, -øz] *n F* blunderer, blundering fool; **c'est un g.** he's always putting his foot in it
gaffeur² *TV etc nm* **g. grip** gator clip
gag [gag] *nm Th, Cin etc* gag; **tu es renvoyé – c'est un g.?** you're fired – you're kidding *or* joking; **son pantalon a craqué au milieu de la réunion, le g.!** his trousers split during the meeting, what a scream!
gaga [gaga] *F* **1** *n* old dodderer **2** *adj* gaga
gage [gaʒ] *nm* **(a)** *Com, Jur* security; (*chez le prêteur sur gages*) pledge; *Fig* (*garantie*) guarantee; **laisser qch en g.** to leave sth as security; **mettre qch en g.** to pawn sth; **mise en g.** pawning; **prêteur sur gages** pawnbroker; **ma montre est en g.** my watch is in pawn; **lettre de g.** debenture bond; (*pour hypothèque*) mortgage bond; *Jur* **g. mobilier** mortgage over assets, mortgage over property; **rester en g.** to remain as surety; **votre parole sera le meilleur des gages** your word will be the best guarantee

(b) (*preuve*) token; **les ambassadeurs nous ont apporté des gages de bonne volonté** the ambassadors brought us tokens of goodwill *or* goodwill tokens; **g. d'amour** token of love, love token; **je t'offre ce livre en g. de notre amitié** I offer you this book as a token of our friendship

(c) (*aux jeux*) forfeit

(d) (*salaire*) **gages** wages, pay; *Péj* **être aux gages de qn** to be in the pay of sb; **tueur à gages** hired assassin *or* killer

gagé [gaʒe] *adj* (*montre, bijoux etc*) pawned; *Jur* pledged; (*emprunt*) secured; **meubles gagés** furniture under distraint; **recettes non gagées** unassigned *or* unpledged revenue
gager [gaʒe] *vt* (**je gageai(s); n. gageons**) **(a)** *Litt* **je gagerais que ...** I would wager *or* bet that ... **(b)** (*emprunt*) to guarantee, to secure; **g. qch** to deposit sth as security, to pledge sth as security
gageur [gaʒœr] *Jur nm* pledgor
gageure [gaʒyr] *nf* **(a)** (*action difficile*) difficult undertaking, challenge; **réussir la g. de faire qch** to succeed in the difficult task of doing sth **(b)** (*pari*) *Litt* wager, *Can* bet
gagiste [gaʒist] *nm Jur* pledgee
gagnant, -ante [gaɲɑ̃, -ɑ̃t] **1** *adj* (*billet, numéro, combinaison etc*) winning; **jouer un cheval g.** to back a winner *or* a winning horse **2** *n* winner; **partir g.** (*à une course*) to start favourite; *Fig* to be bound to succeed; **il joue g.** he can't lose
gagne-pain [gaɲpɛ̃] *nm inv* livelihood; **trouver un g.** to find a job; **il n'aime pas ce qu'il fait, c'est juste un g.** he doesn't like what he does, it's just a way of earning a living *or* of making his bread and butter
gagne-petit [gaɲpəti] *nm inv* low wage earner; *Péj* (*personne qui n'a aucune ambition*) small-timer
gagner [gaɲe] **1** *vt* **(a)** (*comme rémunération*) to earn; **g. douze mille francs par mois** to earn twelve thousand francs a month; **g. gros** to earn *or* make big money; (*d'une société*) to make large profits; **g. sa vie** to earn one's living; **g. bien/mal sa vie** to earn *or* make/not to earn *or* make a good living; **g. de quoi vivre** to earn a living, to earn enough to live on; *F* **g. sa croûte** *ou* **son bifteck** to earn one's crust; *F* **g. des mille et des cents** to earn *or* make a fortune *or* a packet; **ce que je gagne suffit à nos besoins** I earn enough to keep us; *F* **il l'a bien gagné** he's earned it; *F* **j'ai gagné ma journée!** it's just not my day!

(b) (*obtenir*) (*réputation, fortune, avantages*) to gain; (*se concilier*) (*partisan, mari*) to win over; (*profiter*) to gain (**à** by); **g. du temps** to save time; (*sur un délai serré*) to gain time; **g. des parts de marché** to gain share; **chercher à g. du temps** to play for time; **g. de l'espace** to save space; **j'ai gagné trois places dans la queue** I've moved up three places in the queue; **c'est autant de gagné, c'est toujours ça de gagné** that's something, anyway; **nous ne gagnerons rien à attendre** there is nothing to be gained *or* we'll gain nothing by waiting; **nous n'y avons gagné que des problèmes** all it brought us was problems; **et moi, qu'est-ce que j'y gagne?** and what do I get out of it?, what's in this for me?, and where do I come in?; **tu as tout à g.** you've everything to gain; **il n'y a rien à y g.** there's nothing to be gained by it, it won't get you anywhere

(**c**) (*victoire*) to win, to gain; (*bataille, guerre*) to win; *Fig* **la partie n'est pas gagnée** we haven't won yet; **je vais essayer de faire le travail que vous me demandez mais ce n'est pas gagné!** I'll try to do the work you want me to do, but I can't promise anything!; **si elle dit oui, c'est gagné** if she says yes, then everything's OK *or* all right

(**d**) (*jeu, course, prix, somme*) to win; **g. qn à une cause** to win sb over to a cause; **g. qn à une idée** to sell sb an idea; **g. la confiance/l'estime/l'amitié de qn** to win *or* gain sb's confidence/respect/friendship

(**e**) (*atteindre*) (*ville, sortie, porte*) to reach, to get to; **g. le haut** to reach *or* get to the top; *Naut* **g. le port** to reach port, *Spéc* to fetch into port

(**f**) (*de maladie, d'infection*) to spread to; **l'enflure a gagné la gorge** the swelling has spread to the throat; **le rire gagna l'assemblée tout entière** the laughter spread through the whole audience

(**g**) (*rattraper*) **g. un navire** to gain on *or* overhaul a ship; **g. le devant** to forge ahead, to take the lead; **la nuit nous gagna** darkness overtook us; **le feu/l'épidémie gagne** the fire/the epidemic is spreading; **g. du terrain** to gain ground; (*sur la mer etc*) to reclaim land; **la mer gagne du terrain** the sea is encroaching on the land; **la faim nous gagnait** we were getting hungry; **le doute/la peur/la joie les gagne** doubt/fear/joy overcomes them *or* sweeps over them; **gagné par le sommeil/la peur/les larmes** overcome by sleep/by fear/with tears; *Naut* **g. le vent** to make *or* fetch to windward; **g. le vent d'une pointe** to weather a headland; **g. de l'avant** to forge ahead

2 *vi* (**a**) (*être vainqueur*) to win; **g. dans un fauteuil** to walk it, to win by a walkover; **g. haut la main** to win hands down

(**b**) (*profiter*) **g. à qch/à faire qch** to benefit from sth/from doing sth; **tu gagnerais à partir** it would be in your (best) interest *or* to your advantage to leave; **il ne gagne pas à se montrer trop empressé envers elle** it isn't to his advantage to be too attentive to her, he won't get anything out of being too attentive to her; **g. à être connu** to improve with acquaintance; **j'ai gagné au change** I got the best of the bargain *or* deal

(**c**) (*croître*) to increase; **g. en intensité** to increase *or* gain in intensity; **g. en profondeur/beauté** to increase in depth/beauty, to become deeper/more beautiful; **g. en vigueur** to become stronger; **le mécontentement gagne en force** there is increasing discontent

(**d**) *Naut* **g. au vent** to make *or* fetch to windward

gagneur, -euse [gaɲœr, -øz] **1** *n* winner; **avoir un tempérament** *ou* **un caractère de g.** to be a winner **2** *nf Arg* **gagneuse** (*prostituée*) pro

gai [gɛ, ge] *adj* (*chanson*) cheerful, merry, lively; (*personne*) cheerful, merry, lively, in good spirits; (*voix*) cheerful, cheery; (*chambre, couleur etc*) bright, cheerful; **g. comme un pinson** happy as a lark *or* a sandboy; **avoir un naturel g.** to be of a cheerful disposition; *F* **être un peu g.** (*ivre*) to be tipsy *or* tight; **avoir le vin g.** to get merry when one drinks; *Iron* **ça va être g.!** that will be nice!; *Iron* **il vérifie en permanence ce que je fais, c'est g.** he's continually checking what I'm doing, it's charming *or* really nice; **tout cela n'est pas très g.** it's all a bit depressing

gaiement [gemɑ̃, gemɑ̃] *adv* cheerfully, merrily, gaily; *Iron* **allons-y g.!** let's get on with it!

gaieté [gete] *nf* cheerfulness, gaiety; **vous n'êtes pas/cela n'est pas d'une g. folle!** you're/it's hardly a bundle of fun *or* laughs!; **déborder de g.** to be bubbling over with high spirits; **retrouver sa g.** to recover one's spirits, to perk up, to buck up; **je ne le fais pas de g. de cœur** I don't enjoy doing it, it's not something I do willingly

gaillard, -arde [gajar, -ard] **1** *adj* (**a**) (*vigoureux*) (*personne*) strong, vigorous; **un petit vent g.** a good stiff breeze, a lively breeze; **frais et g.** hale and hearty; **il se sentait g.** he felt in good form; **mon grand-père est encore très g. pour son âge** my grandfather is still very sprightly for his age

(**b**) *Vieilli* (*jovial*) (*humeur*) merry, lively, cheerful; (*grivois*) (*histoire, commentaire*) bawdy, off-colour, *US* off-color

2 *n* (*homme*) hearty *or* vigorous type; **un grand et solide g.** a great strapping man; **tu ne vas pas pleurer, un grand g. comme toi!** you're not going to cry, a big guy like you!; **toi mon g., tu ne perds rien pour attendre!** just you wait, chum *or Br* mate *or Am* fella; **c'est un sacré g.!** (*vigueur sexuelle*) he's quite a lad *or* stud!; **une grande gaillarde** a strapping woman; (*légère*) a bit of a girl; *Arch* **un vert g.** a rip

3 *nm Naut* **g. d'avant** forecastle; **g. d'arrière** poop; **haut de g.** deep-waisted

4 *nf* **gaillarde** (*danse*) galliard

gaillardement [gajardəmɑ̃] *adv* (**a**) (*gaiement*) cheerfully, good-humouredly (**b**) (*sans faiblir*) boldly, bravely, gallantly

gaillardise [gajardiz] *nf* **conter des gaillardises** to tell risqué *or* off-colour stories *or* jokes

gaillette [gajɛt] *nf* (*de charbon*) lump

gaîment [gemɑ̃, gemɑ̃] *adv* = **gaiement**

gain [gɛ̃] *nm* (**a**) (*d'une compétition, d'une guerre etc*) winning; *Jur* **avoir** *ou* **obtenir g. de cause** to win one's case; **donner g. de cause à qn** to decide in favour of sb; **il y a chances égales de g. et de perte** it's an even chance, there's a fifty-fifty chance

(**b**) (*profit*) gain, profit; (*salaire*) earnings; (*au jeu*) winnings; **g. d'argent** financial gain; **avoir l'amour du g.** to love making money; **un g. de temps/place** a saving of time/space; **ça nous fait un sacré g. de temps/de place** that saves us an awful lot of time/space; **g. retiré d'une lecture/d'une expérience** benefit *or* profit acquired from reading/from an experience

(**c**) *Él etc* gain; **g. en courant** current gain; **g. en tension** voltage magnification; *Électron* **g. d'étage** stage gain; *Phys Nucl* **g. de régénération** breeding gain

▶ **gain**: *Compta* **g. latent** unrealized gain; *TV etc* **g. vidéo** video gain

gainage [gɛnaʒ] *nm MecE, Constr etc* casing, sheathing, sleeving; *Nucl* (*du combustible etc*) canning, casing, cladding

gaine [gɛn] *nf* (**a**) (*cache*) case, casing; **g. en cuir** leather case; **g. métallique** metallic sheath *or* sleeve; **câble sous g.** sheathed cable; **g. souple** flexible sheath; *Phys Nucl* **g. d'électrons/d'ions** electron/ion sheath (**b**) *Anat, Bot* sheath (**c**) (*sous-vêtement*) girdle, corset, foundation (garment) (**d**) *Géol* gangue, matrix (**e**) *Constr, Min etc* shaft, duct

▶ **gaine**: **g. d'aération** ventilation shaft

gaine-combinaison, *pl* **gaines-combinaisons** *nf* corselet

gaine-culotte, *pl* **gaines-culottes** *nf* panty girdle

gainer [gene] *vt* (*de cuir, de soie, de nylon etc*) to sheath, to cover (**de** in)

Gal *n Mil* (*abrév* **Général**) Gen

gal [gal] *nm Phys* gal

gala [gala] *nm* gala; **en habit** *ou* **tenue de g.** in gala dress, in full dress; *Fig* in one's best clothes, in one's Sunday best; **inutile de mettre ton habit de g.** don't bother putting on your best clothes *or* getting dressed up; **dîner en grand g.** to dine in state, to dine with great ceremony; **g. de bienfaisance** *ou* **de charité** charity gala

Galaad *nm Littér* Galahad

galactique [galaktik] *adj* galactic

galactogène [galaktɔʒɛn] *adj, nm Physiol* galactagogue

galamment [galamɑ̃] *adv* (*avec politesse*) politely, courteously; (*d'un homme*) gallantly, like a gentleman; *Litt* (*noblement*) honourably, *US* honorably; **se tirer g. d'une affaire** to come out of an affair with honour *or US* honor

galandage [galɑ̃daʒ] *nm Constr* brick partition

galant[1] [galɑ̃] **1** *adj* (*homme*) gallant, chivalrous, gentlemanly; *Arch* (*élégant*) gay, elegant; **homme g.** ladies' man; **vers galants** love poems; **femme galante** woman of loose morals; *Hum* **être en galante compagnie** to be in the company of the opposite sex; **rendez-vous g.** romantic rendezvous; **g. homme** gentleman, man of honour; **se conduire en g. homme** to behave like a gentleman **2** *nm Vieilli, Litt* gallant; (*coureur de jupons*) philanderer; **faire le g. auprès d'une dame** to court *or* pay court to a lady; (*flirter*) to flirt with a lady

galanterie [galɑ̃tri] *nf* (**a**) (*envers les femmes*) gallantry, chivalry, courteousness; **dire des galanteries à qn** to pay sb compliments (**b**) (*intrigue*) love affair, intrigue

galantine [galɑ̃tin] *nf Culin* galantine

Galatée [galate] *nf Myth* Galatea

Galatie [galasi] *nf* Galatia

galaxie [galaksi] *nf Astron* galaxy

galbe [galb] *nm* (*d'un meuble, d'un balustre etc*) curve; (*des jambes, hanches etc*) curve(s), contour; (*d'une voiture*) sweep, lines

galbé [galbe] *adj* (*jambe etc*) shapely

galber [galbe] *vt* (*vase, commode etc*) to give curves to; *Tech* (*feuille de métal*) to curve, to bend (lightly)

gale [gal] *nf* **(a)** *Méd* scabies; *Méd* **g. bédouine** prickly heat; *Fig* **je n'ai pas la g.**! I haven't got the plague! **(b)** *F* (*personne*) nasty person; *F* **être mauvais comme la g.** to be a nasty character *or Br* piece of work **(c)** *Vét* (*de mouton*) scab; (*de chien, chat*) mange **(d)** *Bot* scab

galée [gale] *nf Typ* composing galley

galéjade [galeʒad] *nf Région* tall story; **débiter** *ou* **dire des galéjades à qn** to pull sb's leg

galéjer [galeʒe] *vi Région* to tell tall stories

galène [galɛn] *nf Minér* galena, sulphide of lead

galéopithèque [galeɔpitɛk] *nm Zool* flying lemur

galère [galɛr] **1** *nf* **(a)** *Hist* (*navire*) galley; *Naut* **avirons en g.**! rest on your oars!; **condamné aux galères** sentenced to penal servitude

(b) (*locutions*) *F Litt* **après plusieurs mois de g.** after several months of hassle; *Litt* **je me suis mis dans une g. pas possible** I got myself into an incredible mess *or* pickle; **c'est une vraie g.** it's a real pain *or* drag; **c'est la g. pour se garer le samedi** it's a (real) hassle *or* pain to find a parking space on Saturdays; **et vogue la g.**! let's see what happens!; *Hum* **mais que diable allait-il faire dans cette g.?** but what the hell was he doing mixed up in that?;

2 *adj F* (*plans*) crazy, madcap; (*vacances*) hassle-filled; **c'est g. de trouver une cabine téléphonique dans cette ville** it's a (real) hassle to find a phone box in this town

galérer [galere] *vi F* to have a hard time (of it)

galerie [galri] *nf* **(a)** (*passage, salle*) gallery; *Can* (*véranda*) porch **(b)** *Th* balcony, gallery; **première g.** dress circle; **seconde g.** upper circle; **la troisième g.** the gallery, *F* the gods; **tout ce qu'il fait, c'est pour (épater) la g.** everything he does is just showing off *or* playing to the gallery **(c)** *Min* gallery, level, drift; **g. d'avancement** heading **(d)** *Aut* (*sur toit*) roof rack, roof rail **(e)** (*sur meuble*) cornice **(f)** (*d'une digue*) run

▶ **galerie**: **g. d'art** art gallery; *Él* **g. des câbles** cable tunnel; **g. marchande** shopping arcade; **g. de portraits** portrait gallery

galérien [galerjɛ̃] *nm* galley slave; **travailler comme un g.** to work like a (galley) slave; *F* **mener une vie de g.** to lead a dog's life

galeriste [galrist] *n* gallery owner

galet [galɛ] *nm* **(a)** (*caillou*) pebble; **galets** shingle, pebbles; **plage de galets** shingly *or* shingle beach **(b)** *MecE* roller, runner, wheel; **g. de roulement** travelling *or* running wheel; *Aut* **g. de direction** roller **(c)** *Pêche* (*d'un filet*) float **(d)** *Ordinat* (*dans souris*) roller

galetas [galta] *nm* (*sous les toits*) garret, attic; *Péj* (*taudis*) hovel

galetouse [galtuz] *nf Arg* mess tin, dixie

galette [galɛt] *nf* **(a)** (*crèpe de blé noir*) buckwheat pancake **(b)** (*biscuit rond sablé*) butter biscuit; *Naut* (ship's) biscuit; *F* **plat comme une g.** flat as a pancake **(c)** *Arg* (*argent*) dough, bread; **il a de la g.** he's loaded, he's rolling in it

▶ **galette**: **g. des Rois** Twelfth Night cake

galetteux, -euse [galɛtø, -øz] *adj Vieilli F* loaded, rolling in it

galeux, -euse [galø, -øz] *adj* (*chien*) mangy; (*arbre*) scabby; (*pelouse*) patchy; *Méd* **plaie galeuse** sore caused by scabies; **murs galeux** peeling *or* flaking walls; *Fig* **des mauvais garçons g.** some evil-looking types

galgal, -als [galgal] *nm Archéol* cairn, barrow

galibot [galibo] *nm Min* pit boy

Galice [galis] *nf* (*en Espagne*) Galicia

Galicie [galisi] *nf* (*en Pologne*) Galicia

galicien, -ienne [galisjɛ̃, -jɛn] **1** *adj* Galician (*in Spain or Poland*) **2** *n* **G.** Galician (*in Spain or in Poland*)

Galien [galjɛ̃] *nm* Galen

Galilée[1] [galile] *nf Bible* Galilee

Galilée[2] *nm Hist* Galileo

galiléen, -enne [galileɛ̃, -ɛn] **1** *adj* Galilean **2** *n* **G.** Galilean

galimatias [galimatja] *nm* gibberish

galion [galjɔ̃] *nm Naut* galleon

galipette [galipɛt] *nf F* somersault; **faire des galipettes** to do somersaults; (*ébats amoureux*) to have it off, to bonk

galipot [galipo] *nm* **(a)** *Com* (*résine*) galipot, white resin **(b)** *Can* **courir le g.** to chase women

galle [gal] *nf Bot* gall; **g. de chêne** oak apple

Galles [gal] *nf* **le pays de G.** Wales; **Prince de G.** Prince of Wales; *Tex* Prince of Wales check

gallican, -ane [galikɑ̃, -an] *adj, n Rel* Gallican

gallicanisme [galikanism] *nm Rel* Gallicanism

gallicisme [galisism] *nm* Gallicism

gallinacé [galinase] *Orn* **1** *adj* gallinaceous **2** *nmpl* **gallinacés** Gallinaceae

gallique[1] [galik] *adj Hist* Gallic

gallique[2] *adj Ch* (*acide*) gallic

gallium [galjɔm] *nm Ch* gallium

gallois, -oise [galwa, -waz] **1** *adj* Welsh **2** *nm Ling* Welsh **3** *n* **G.** Welshman, *f* Welshwoman; **les G.** the Welsh

gallomanie [galɔmani] *nf* Gallomania

gallon [galɔ̃] *nm* gallon

gallo-romain, *pl* **gallo-romains** [galorɔmɛ̃] *adj* Gallo-Roman

gallup [galœp] *n* **sondage g.** Gallup poll

galoche [galɔʃ] *nf* clog (*with leather upper*); *F* **menton en g.** jutting chin

galon [galɔ̃] *nm* **(a)** *Couture* braid; **g. de finition** upholstery binding **(b)** *Mil* **galons** (*de sous-officier*) stripes; (*d'officier*) bands, gold braid; *Naut* (*d'officier*) stripes; (*dans la marine marchande*) bands; **priver qn de ses galons** to reduce sb to the ranks; **gagner ses galons** to win *or* get *or* earn one's stripes; *F* **prendre du g.** to be promoted; *F* **arroser ses galons** to celebrate one's promotion

galonné [galɔne] *nm Arg* (*officier*) officer; (*sous-officier*) NCO

galonner [galɔne] *vt Couture* to (trim with) braid; **habit galonné d'or** gold-trimmed coat

galop [galo] *nm Équitation* gallop; **prendre le g.** to break into a gallop; **au g.** at a gallop; **grand g., triple g.** full gallop; **g. de manège** hand gallop; **petit g.** canter; **partir au (grand** *ou* **triple) g.** to gallop away; *Fig* **arriver au (grand** *ou* **triple) g.** to come like a shot; *Fig* **faire qch au g.** to do sth double-quick *or* at top speed; **allez, au travail! et au g.**! come on, to work!, and be quick about it! *or* and make it snappy! *Scol* **g. d'essai** mock exam; *Fig* **ce séminaire ne constitue qu'un g. d'essai** this seminar is just a trial run

galopade [galɔpad] *nf* **(a)** *Équitation* gallop; **le bruit d'une g.** the sound of galloping **(b)** (*bruit*) stampede

galopant [galɔpɑ̃] *adj* (*chevaux etc*) galloping; (*inflation etc*) galloping, runaway; **démographie galopante** rapid population growth; **phtisie galopante** galloping consumption; **le flot g. des vagues** the rushing waves

galoper [galɔpe] **1** *vi* **(a)** *Équitation* to gallop; **se mettre à g.** to break into a gallop **(b)** *Fig* (*courir*) to charge along; (*çà et là*) to gallop *or* rush around; **g. après qn/qch** to run after sb/sth; **il galopa jusqu'au bourg** he charged off to the village; **les enfants galopaient dans le salon** the children were charging around in the living room **2** *vt Rare* (*cheval*) to gallop

galopeur, -euse [galɔpœr, -øz] *n* (*cheval*) galloper

galopin [galɔpɛ̃] *nm F* urchin, ragamuffin; **espèce de petit g.**! you little rascal *or* devil!

galure [galyr] *nm*, **galurin** [galyrɛ̃] *nm F* hat, *Br F* titfer

galvanique [galvanik] *adj* (*cellule etc*) galvanic; **plaqué g.** electroplate; **dorure g.** electrogilding

galvanisation [galvanizasjɔ̃] *nf* (*métallisation*) galvanization, galvanizing; *Él* galvanism

galvaniser [galvanize] *vt* **(a)** (*entreprise*) to give new life to, to inject new life into; (*foule, corps, organe*) to galvanize **(b)** *Métal* to galvanize; (*de zinc*) to zinc; *Él* to (electro)plate; **tôle galvanisée** galvanized (sheet) iron

galvanisme [galvanism] *nm Méd* galvanism

galvano [galvano] *nm Typ F* electro

galvanomètre [galvanɔmɛtr] *nm Él* galvanometer

galvanoplastie [galvanoplasti] *nf* galvanoplasty, electrodeposition; *Ind* electroplating; *Typ* electrotyping

galvanoplastique [galvanɔplastik] *adj* galvanoplastic

galvanoscope [galvanɔskɔp] *nm* galvanoscope; *Télécom* (linesman's) detector

galvanotype [galvanotip] *nm Typ* electrotype

galvanotypie [galvanotipi] *nf Typ* electrotyping

galvaudage [galvodaʒ] *nm* (*de talent, capacités*) prostituting

galvauder [galvode] **1** *vt* (*nom, réputation*) to bring into disrepute; (*talents, dons*) to prostitute; **g. un mot** to overuse a word **2 se galvauder** *vpr* to damage one's reputation

gambade [gɑ̃bad] *nf* leap, gambol, caper; *Équitation* gambade; **gambades** capers; **faire des gambades** to leap *or* frisk about, to gambol, to caper

gambader [gɑ̃bade] *vi* to leap *or* frisk about, to gambol, to caper

gambas [gɑ̃bas] *nfpl* large prawns

gamberge [gɑ̃bɛrʒ] *nf Arg* **ton plan manque de g.** your plan shows a lack of thought; **il va falloir une bonne g. pour s'en sortir** we'll need to have a good think to get out of this one; **être en pleine g.** to be deep in thought; (*rêver*) to be daydreaming

gamberger [gɑ̃bɛrʒe] *F* **1** *vi* to think deeply; **tu gamberges trop pour être heureux** you spend too much time thinking to be happy; **tu ne vas pas te mettre à g. pour si peu** you're not going to start brooding over such a small thing **2** *vt* to work out, to figure out; *F* **c'est lui qui a gambergé le coup de la banque** he's the one who masterminded the bank job

gambette[1] [gɑ̃bɛt] *nm* (*oiseau*) redshank

gambette[2] *nf Arg* (*jambe*) pin, leg; **jouer** *ou* **tricoter des gambettes** to beat it, to leg it

Gambie [gɑ̃bi] *nf* the Gambia

gambiller [gɑ̃bije] *vi Arg, Vieilli* (*danser*) to jig about

gambit [gɑ̃bi] *nm Échecs* gambit; (**pion de**) **g.** gambit pawn

gamelle [gamɛl] *nf* (*de soldat*) dixie, mess tin; (*d'ouvrier*) billy(can); *Hum* (*assiette*) plate; **préparer la g. du chien** to prepare the dog's food; *F* (**se**) **ramasser** *ou* (**se**) **prendre une g.** to come a cropper, to fall flat on one's face

gamète [gamɛt] *nm Biol* gamete

gamétocide [gametɔsid] *nm Méd* gametocide

gamétogénèse [gametoʒenɛz] *nf Biol* gametogenesis

gamin, -ine [gamɛ̃, -in] **1** *n* (*enfant*) kid, child; **une gamine de dix ans** a girl of ten; **ce n'est qu'un grand g.** (*d'un adulte*) he's just a big kid **2** *adj* (**a**) (*espiègle*) lively, mischievous (**b**) **elle est encore gamine** she's still just a child (**c**) (*puéril*) childish

gaminerie [gaminri] *nf* (*acte*) childish prank *or* trick; (*comportement*) childishness, childish behaviour; **il a passé l'âge de ces gamineries** he's too old to behave so childishly *or* in such a childish way

gamma [gama] *nm* (*lettre*), *Phot* gamma; *Phys, Nucl* **rayons g.** gamma rays

gammaglobuline [gamaglɔbylin] *nf Biol* gamma globulin

gamme [gam] *nf* (**a**) (*de couleurs, de services, d'articles etc*) range; **une vaste g. de produits** a vast range of products; **g. de prix** price range; **toute la g. des sensations** the whole gamut *or* range of sensations; **produit bas/haut de g.** bottom-of-the-range *or* down-market/top-of-the-range *or* up-market product (**b**) *Mus* scale; **g. montante/descendante** rising/falling scale; **faire des gammes** to do *or* practise scales; *Fig* **faire ses gammes** to learn the ropes

▶ **gamme**: *Aut* **g. moyenne** mid-range; *Aut* **g. de transmission** driving range

gammée [game] *adj* **croix g.** swastika

gamopétale [gamopetal] *adj Bot* gamopetalous

ganache [ganaʃ] *nf* (**a**) *Culin* = filling for cakes made from chocolate, butter and cream (**b**) *F* (*imbécile*) fool, idiot; **vieille g.** old codger, *Br* old buffer (**c**) (*d'un cheval*) lower jaw, jowl

Gand [gɑ̃] *nm* Ghent

gang [gɑ̃g] *nm* [ⓘAll,g,i] gang; **guerre des gangs** gang warfare

ganga [gɑ̃ga] *nm* pintailed (sand) grouse

Gange (le) [ləgɑ̃ʒ] *nm* the Ganges

ganglion [gɑ̃glijɔ̃] *nm* (**a**) *Anat* ganglion; **g. nerveux** ganglion cell; **ganglions lymphatiques** lymph nodes *or* glands; **j'ai des ganglions** my glands are swollen, I have swollen glands; (**b**) *Vét* spavin

ganglionnaire [gɑ̃glijɔnɛr] *adj Anat* ganglionic; **fièvre g.** glandular fever

gangrené [gɑ̃grəne] *adj* (**a**) *Méd* gangrenous, gangrened (**b**) *Fig* corrupt

gangrène [gɑ̃grɛn] *nf* (**a**) *Méd* gangrene; **avoir la g.** to have gangrene; **g. gazeuse** gas gangrene; **g. des os** necrosis (**b**) *Fig* canker

gangrener [gɑ̃grəne] (**il gangrène**; **il gangrènera**) **1** *vt* (**a**) *Méd* to gangrene (**b**) *Fig* to corrupt **2 se gangrener** *vpr* (**a**) *Méd* to become *or* go gangrenous (**b**) *Fig* to become corrupt

gangreneux, -euse [gɑ̃grənø, -øz] *adj Méd* gangrenous

gangster [gɑ̃gstɛr] *nm* gangster

gangstérisme [gɑ̃gsterism] *nm* gangsterism

gangue [gɑ̃g] *nf* (*de pierre précieuse, de minerai*) gang(ue), matrix; *Fig* (*couche*) (*de boue, de glace etc*) layer; *Fig* **il n'a jamais pu sortir de la g. de son éducation/de la religion** he was never able to free himself from the straitjacket of his education/of religion

ganse [gɑ̃s] *nf* (*cordon*) braid, (plaited) cord, edging, piping

gansé [gɑ̃se] *adj* (*vêtement*) braided

ganser [gɑ̃se] *vt* (*vêtement*) to braid, to trim

gant [gɑ̃] *nm* glove; (*armure*) gauntlet; **mettre ses gants** to put one's gloves on; **gants en daim/tissu** suede/fabric gloves; **gants fourrés** lined gloves; **gants de caoutchouc** rubber gloves; *Fig* **cela vous va comme un g.** (*de vêtement*) it fits you like a glove; (*de couleur*) it suits you down to the ground *or* to a T; **ce métier lui va comme un g.** the job suits her down to the ground, the job is tailor-made for her; *Fig* **il faut prendre** *ou* **mettre des gants pour l'approcher** *ou* **avec lui** you have to handle him with kid gloves (on); **tu as intérêt à prendre** *ou* **mettre des gants pour le lui dire** you'd do well to tell him gently; **jeter le g. à qn** to throw down the gauntlet to sb; **relever le g.** to take up the gauntlet, to accept the challenge; *Fig* **souple comme un g.** easygoing

▶ **gant**: **g. de boxe** boxing glove; **g. de crin** massage glove; **g. de Neptune** glove sponge; **g. de toilette** ≈ facecloth, (face) flannel, *Am* washcloth

ganteIé [gɑ̃tle] *adj* gauntleted; **la main gantelée** the mailed fist

gantelet [gɑ̃tlɛ] *nm* gauntlet

ganter [gɑ̃te] **1** *vt* to glove **2** *vi* **g. du sept** to take a (size) seven in gloves **3 se ganter** *vpr* to put one's gloves on

ganterie [gɑ̃tri] *nf* (**a**) (*industrie*) glove-making; (*commerce*) glove trade (**b**) (*fabrique*) glove factory; (*magasin*) glove shop; (*rayon*) glove counter *or* department

gantier, -ière [gɑ̃tje, -jɛr] *n* glover

gantois, -oise [gɑ̃twa, -waz] **1** *adj* of/from Ghent **2** *n* **G.** (*natif*) native of Ghent; (*habitant*) inhabitant of Ghent

garage [garaʒ] *nm* (**a**) (*de voiture*) garage; **g. à plusieurs étages** multi-storey car park, *US* tiered parking lot; **g. de** *ou* **à bicyclettes** bicycle *or* bike shed; **g. de canots** boathouse, boat shed; **g. d'autobus** bus depot; **g. d'avions** (aircraft) hangar; *Rail* **g. de machines** engine shed; **j'ai mis la voiture au g.** I've put the car in the garage; *Can* **vente de g.** garage sale (**b**) (*atelier*) garage; **ma voiture est au g. jusqu'à la semaine prochaine** my car is at the garage until next week (**c**) *Rail* shunting, sidetracking

garagiste [garaʒist] *nm Aut* (*propriétaire*) garage owner; (*mécanicien*) garage mechanic; **j'emmène la voiture chez le g.** I'm taking the car to the garage

garance [garɑ̃s] **1** *nf* (**a**) *Bot* madder(wort); *F* **petite g., g. de chien** squinancy wort (**b**) (*teinture*) madder (dye) **2** *adj inv* madder

garant, -ante [garɑ̃, -ɑ̃t] *n* guarantor; **se rendre** *ou* **se porter g. de qn** to answer for sb; (*devant la justice*) to go bail for sb; (*à la banque*) to stand guarantor for sb; **g. solidaire** joint and several guarantor; **tout sera fini en temps voulu, je m'en porte g.** everything will be finished on time, I can vouch for *or* guarantee it; **ça va marcher, j'en suis garante** it will work, I give you my word; **être g. de ses faits** to be answerable *or* accountable for one's actions; **les pays seront garants du respect de l'accord** the countries will be guarantors of the agreement

garantie [garɑ̃ti] *nf* (**a**) (*précaution*) guarantee, safeguard (**contre** against); (*gage*) guarantee; **prendre des garanties contre le vol/les risques d'incendie** to take precautions against theft/fire risk

(**b**) (*de l'exécution d'un contrat*) guarantee, pledge; (*d'un paiement*) security, guaranty; **fonds déposés** *ou* **détenus en g.** funds lodged *or* held as security for sb; **elle m'a donné toutes les garanties que ...** she gave me every guarantee that ...

(**c**) *Com* (*de qualité etc*) guarantee, warranty; **vendu avec g.** sold with a guarantee; **la voiture est encore sous g.** the car is still under guarantee; **il va essayer, mais c'est sans g.** he'll try, but there's no guarantee (that he'll succeed); **lettre de g. d'indemnité** letter of indemnity

(**d**) *Fin* underwriting; **syndicat de g.** underwriters' syndicate

▶ **garantie**: **g. accessoire** collateral security; **g. bancaire** bank guarantee; **g. de bonne exécution** *ou* **de bonne fin** performance bond; **g. contractuelle** contractual guarantee; **g. conventionnelle** contractual cover; **g. de crédit acheteur** buyer credit guarantee; **g. de crédit à l'exportation** export credit guarantee; **g. d'exécution** contract bond; *Com* **g. limitée** limited warranty; *Com* **g. légale** legal guarantee; *Fin* **g. offre** bid bond; *Jur* **g. parlementaire** (*d'un député*) parliamentary privilege; *Com* **g. pièces et main d'œuvre** parts and labour warranty; *Com* **g. prolongée** extended warranty; *Com* **g. totale** full warranty

garantir [garɑ̃tir] **1** *vt* (**a**) (*dette, montre etc*) to guarantee; **créance garantie** secured debt; **pendule garantie** (**pour**) **deux ans** clock guaranteed for two years; **g. un fait** to vouch for a fact; **je vous en garantis le succès** I guarantee (you) success, I guarantee that you'll be successful; **je vous garantis qu'il viendra** I guarantee that he'll come; **je te garantis que je l'ai aperçu dans la foule** I can vouch for the fact that I spotted him in the crowd; **je peux te g. qu'il ne reviendra pas** I can guarantee you he won't come back, he won't come back, I warrant you; **elle m'a garanti qu'elle serait à l'heure** she gave me a guarantee that she'd be on time; **je te le garantis** I can vouch for it

(**b**) *Fin* (*émission d'actions etc*) to underwrite; **g. un emprunt** to secure a loan

(**c**) (*protéger*) to protect (**de** against, from); **ce double vitrage va vous g. du froid** this double-glazing will protect *or* shield you from the cold

(**d**) *Jur* **g. qn contre qch** to indemnify sb from *or* against sth

2 se garantir *vpr* **se g. contre le froid/le vent** to protect oneself from the cold/the wind

garce [gars] *nf* (**a**) *F Péj* bitch, cow; **g. de vie!** what a bitch of a life!, what a damn awful life! (**b**) *Vieilli* (*prostituée*) whore, tart

garçon [garsɔ̃] *nm* (**a**) (*enfant mâle*) boy; **école de garçons**

boys' school; **petit g.** small *or* little boy; **se sentir un petit g. à côté de qn** to feel like a child beside sb, to feel dwarfed by sb; **tu es un grand g. maintenant** you're a big boy now

(b) (*fils*) boy, son

(c) (*jeune homme*) young man; **un g. d'une vingtaine d'années** a young man of about twenty; **un bon** *ou* **brave g.** a good lad; **un beau** *ou* **joli g.** a handsome young man; **il est assez beau g.** he's quite a good-looking *or* handsome young man; **un mauvais g.** a bad sort

(d) (*serveur*) waiter

(e) *Vieilli* (*célibataire*) bachelor; **il est encore g.** he's still single *or* still a bachelor; **vieux g.** confirmed bachelor; **des habitudes de vieux g.** bachelor habits *or* ways

▶ **garçon**: **g. d'ascenseur** liftboy, lift attendant, *Am* elevator operator; **g. boucher** butcher's boy; **g. de bureau** office boy; *Naut* **g. de cabine** (cabin) steward; **g. de café** *ou* **de restaurant** waiter; **g. coiffeur** hairdresser's assistant; **g. de courses** errand *or* message boy; **g. d'écurie** groom; **g. d'étage** floor waiter; **g. de ferme** farm hand; **g. d'honneur** best man; **g. manqué** tomboy; **g. de pont** deck steward; **g. de recette** bank messenger

garçonne [garsɔn] *nf* **(a) être coiffé à la g.** (*d'une femme*) to have an urchin cut; **style/vêtements à la g.** boyish style/ clothes **(b)** *Vieilli* bachelor girl

garçonnet [garsɔnɛ] *nm* (*petit garçon*) little boy; *Com* **taille g.** small boy's size

garçonnier, -ière [garsɔnje, -jɛr] *adj* boyish

garçonnière [garsɔnjɛr] *nf Vieilli* bachelor flat *or Am* apartment

garde¹ [gard] *nf* **(a)** (*protection*) (*d'une personne, chose*) care; **confier qch/qn à la g. de qn, confier la g. de qch/qn à qn** to entrust sb with (the care of) sth/sb; **c'est son oncle qui en a la g.** he's in the care of his uncle; **être sous bonne g.** to be in safekeeping; **avoir qch en g.** to have charge of sth; **que Dieu nous ait en g.** may God protect us; **je vous laisse les enfants en g.** I'm leaving the children in your care *or* safekeeping *or* charge; **droit de g.** (right of) custody

(b) (*surveillance*) (*d'une frontière, d'une machine etc*) guarding; **soldat de g. à la porte** soldier on guard at the door; **être de g.** to be on guard *or Naut* on duty; **monter la g.** to mount guard; **la police assurera la g. du tribunal** the police will guard the court, the court will be under police guard; **à la g.!** guard turn out!; **assurer la g. de nuit** to be on night call *or* duty; *Mil* **poste de g.** guardroom; **chien de g.** guard dog, watchdog; **sentinelle de g.** duty sentry; **médecin de g.** doctor on duty; **pharmacie de g.** emergency *or* duty chemist

(c) (*méfiance*) **mettre qn en g. contre qch/qn** to put sb on his guard against sth/sb, to warn sb against sth/sb; **être** *ou* **se tenir sur ses gardes** to be on one's guard; **prendre g. à qn/qch** to watch out for sb/sth, to beware of sb/sth; **prenez g. aux orties!** mind *or* watch the nettles!; **prenez g.!** watch out!, look out!, take care!; (*menace*) watch out!

(d) (*attention*) **prendre g. à qch/qn** to attend to *or* pay attention to sth/sb; **un fait auquel on n'a pas pris g.** a fact that has been left out of consideration; **faire qch sans y prendre g.** to do sth without realizing it; **je n'y ai pas pris g.** I didn't notice anything; **prendre g. que ... (ne)** + *sub* to be careful *or* to take care that ...; **prenez g. qu'il (ne) vous voie** be careful *or* take care (that) he doesn't see you; **prendre g. à** *ou* **de ne pas faire qch** to be careful *or* take care not to do sth; **prenez g. à** *ou* **de ne pas vous perdre** mind you don't get lost; be careful *or* take care not to get lost; *Vieilli* **prendre g. de faire qch** to be careful *or* take care to do sth; **prenez g. de tomber** mind you don't fall

(e) (*groupe de soldats*) **le corps de g., la g.** the guard; **relever la g.** to change the guard; **la g. à cheval** the Horseguards; **la g. à pied** the Footguards

(f) *Boxe, Escrime* (*position d'attente*) guard; **se mettre en g.** to take one's guard, to square up; *Escrime* **en g.!** en garde!

(g) *Aut* **g. au sol** ground clearance

(h) *Tech* (*partie d'une épée*) hilt; **gardes** (*d'une serrure*) wards

(i) *Cartes* covering card; **avoir une g. à cœur** to have a covering card in hearts

▶ **garde**: *Fin* **g. en dépôt de titres** safe custody; *Mil* **g. descendante** old guard; *Mil* **g. du drapeau** colour *or Am* color guard; **g. d'enfants** child-minding; *Jur* **g. des enfants** (*après un divorce*) custody of the children; **g. d'honneur** guard of honour *or Am* honor; *Hist* **la G. impériale** the Imperial Guard (*of Napoleon*); **la G. mobile** = the security police; *Mil* **g. montante** new *or* relieving guard; **g. de nuit** (*pour un malade*) night nurse (*privately employed*); **la G. républicaine** - the Republican Guard (*of Paris*); *Jur* **g. à vue** police custody; **il a été mis/est resté en g. à vue** he was put/was kept in police custody

garde² **1** *nm* **(a)** (*sentinelle*) guard **(b)** (*soldat d'une garde*) guardsman **2** *nf* (*pour les malades*) nurse; (*pour les enfants*) nanny

▶ **garde**: **G. des Archives** *Br* ≈ Master of the Rolls; **g. champêtre** rural policeman; **g. du corps** bodyguard; *Mil* **gardes du corps** lifeguards; **g. forestier** forester, forest warden, *Am* ranger; **g. mobile** = member of the security police; **g. de nuit** (*pour un malade*) night nurse (*privately employed*); *Mil* night watchman; *Hist, Admin* **G. des Sceaux** = Minister of Justice

gardé [garde] *adj* **(a)** *Cartes* **roi g.** guarded king; **dame gardée** guarded queen **(b) toute(s) proportion(s) gardée(s)** all things considered, making all due allowance

garde-à-vous *nm inv Mil* (position of) attention; **se mettre** *ou* **être** *ou* **se tenir au g.** to stand to attention; **au g.** at attention; **g.!** attention!

garde-barrière, *pl* **gardes-barrière(s)** [gard(ə)barjɛr] *n* level-crossing *or Am* grade-crossing keeper

garde-boue [gard(ə)bu] *nm inv* (*d'une bicyclette etc*) mudguard

garde-chasse, *pl* **gardes-chasse(s)** [gard(ə)ʃas] *nm* gamekeeper

garde-chiourme, *pl* **garde(s)-chiourme(s)** [gard(ə)ʃjurm] *nm Hist* (*de galériens*) warder; *Fig* (*personne autoritaire et brutale*) martinet, tyrant

garde-corps [gard(ə)kɔr] *nm inv* (*mur*) parapet, balustrade; *Naut* (*corde*) guard rope; *Naut* **g. arrière** stern rail

garde-côte, *pl* **garde-côte(s)** [gard(ə)kot] *nm* (*bateau*) coastguard vessel; *Vieilli* (*soldat*) coastguard

garde-feu [gard(ə)fø] *nm inv* fireguard

garde-fou, *pl* **garde-fous** [gard(ə)fu] *nm* (*mur*) parapet, balustrade; (*en fer*) (*d'un pont etc*) railing, guardrail; *Fig* safeguard

garde-frein, *pl* **gardes-frein(s)** [gard(ə)frɛ̃] *nm Rail* brakesman, *US* brakeman

garde-frontière, *pl* **gardes-frontière(s)** [gard(ə)frɔ̃tjɛr] *nf* frontier guard

garde-ligne, *pl* **gardes-ligne(s)** [gard(ə)liɲ] *nm Rail* track watchman

garde-magasin, *pl* **gardes-magasin(s)** *nm* warehouseman; *Mil* quartermaster

garde-malade, *pl* **gardes-malade(s)** [gard(ə)malad] *n* nurse

garde-manger *nm inv* meat safe

garde-meuble, *pl* **garde-meuble(s)** [gard(ə)mœbl] *nm* furniture repository, warehouse; **mettre une table au g.** to put a table into storage *or* store

gardénal® [gardenal] *nm Méd* ≈ Luminal®

gardénia [gardenja] *nm* gardenia

garde-pêche¹, *pl* **gardes-pêche** [gard(ə)pɛʃ] *nm* (*personne*) water bailiff, *Am* fish warden

garde-pêche² *nm inv* (*bateau*) fisheries protection vessel

garde-place, *pl* **garde-place(s)** [gard(ə)plas] *nm Rail* reservation ticket holder; (*ticket*) reservation ticket

garde-port, *pl* **gardes-port(s)** [gard(ə)pɔr] *nm* wharfmaster (*on river*)

garder [garde] **1** *vt* **(a)** (*surveiller*) (*maison, boutique, sac, enfants*) to look after, to mind; (*prisonnier*) to guard, to watch over; **g. un troupeau** to tend a flock; *F* **nous n'avons pas gardé les cochons ensemble!** don't take liberties!; **comment peut-il me parler ainsi, nous n'avons pas gardé les cochons ensemble!** how can he talk to me like that, what a liberty!; *Jur* **g. qn à vue** to keep *or* hold sb in custody

(b) (*protéger*) to protect (**de** from); **si au moins cela pouvait te g. de faire des bêtises** if that could at least stop you (from) acting stupidly; **que Dieu nous garde de la souffrance!** may God protect *or* save *or* deliver us from suffering!

(c) (*conserver*) to keep; **g. un vêtement (sur soi)** to keep a garment on; **g. qn à dîner/pour le week-end** to get sb to stay for dinner/for the weekend; **g. qn en otage** to keep *or* hold sb hostage; **par cette chaleur il vaut mieux g. le lait au réfrigérateur** it's better to keep the milk in the fridge in this heat; **g. une pièce intacte** to keep a room as it was left *or* in its original state; *Journ* **g. la Une** to hold the front page

(d) (*continuer d'avoir*) to keep; (*somme d'argent*) to keep, to put by; **g. ses illusions/son innocence** to keep one's illusions/innocence; **g. son sang-froid** to keep cool (and collected); **g. rancune à qn** to harbour *or US* to harbor resentment against sb, to bear a grudge against sb; **g. les yeux fermés** to keep one's eyes closed; **g. le sourire** to keep (on) smiling; **g. son sérieux** to keep a straight face; **g. la ligne** to keep *or* maintain one's figure; **je garde un bon/ mauvais souvenir de mon séjour en Italie** I have (kept) a good/bad memory of my stay in Italy (**e**) (*rester dans*) **g. la chambre** to keep to *or* stay in one's room; **être obligé de g. le lit** to have to stay in bed, to be laid up

(**f**) (*réserver*) to keep, to save; **garde-moi une place à côté de toi!** save *or* keep me a place next to you!; **je vous ai gardé du café** I've kept *or* saved you some coffee; *Fig* **g. une dent contre qn, g. un chien de sa chienne à qn** to hold a grudge against sb, to have it in for sb; *Fig* **g. une poire pour la soif** to keep something for a rainy day; *Fig* **g. qch pour la bonne bouche** to save sth up as a treat; **g. le meilleur pour la fin** to save *or* keep the best till last

(**g**) (*respecter*) **g. ses distances/son rang** to keep one's distance/one's rank; **g. un secret** to keep a secret; **garde ça pour toi** (*je ne veux pas qu'on l'apprenne*) keep that to yourself

2 se garder *vpr* (**a**) (*se méfier de*) **se g. de qn/qch** to beware of sb/sth

(**b**) (*s'abstenir de*) **se g. de faire qch** to take care *or* be careful not to do sth; **gardez-vous (bien) de le perdre** mind you don't lose it!, take care *or* be careful not to lose it!; **je m'en garderai bien!** there's no chance of me doing that!, I'll do no such thing!, *F* no fear!

(**c**) *Cartes* **se g. à trèfle** to keep a covering card in clubs

(**d**) *F* (*conserver*) **tes réflexions, tu peux te les garder!** you can keep your opinion(s) *or* thoughts *or* comments to yourself!; **ses amis/ses soirées, elle peut se les g.!** she can keep *or* stick her friends/parties!

(**e**) (*se conserver*) (*denrées*) to keep; **viande qui ne se garde pas bien** meat that does not keep well

garderie [gard(ə)ri] *nf* (**a**) (*pour enfants en bas âge*) *Br* day nursery, *Am* daycare center; (*dans magasin, université etc*) *Br* crèche, *Am* baby-sitting service; (*le soir, après l'école*) child-minding service (**b**) (*de garde forestier*) beat, domain

garde-rivière, *pl* **gardes-rivière(s)** [gard(ə)rivjɛr] *nm* river policeman

garde-robe, *pl* **garde-robes** [gard(ə)rɔb] *nf* wardrobe; **renouveler sa g.** to renew *or* replenish one's wardrobe

gardeur, -euse [gardœr, -øz] *n* (*d'animaux*) keeper; **g. de cochons** pig keeper, *Vieilli* swineherd; **g. de vaches** cowherd; **g. de moutons** shepherd

garde-voie, *pl* **gardes-voie** [gard(ə)vwa] *nm Rail* track watchman

gardian [gardjɑ̃] *nm* (*en Camargue*) herdsman

gardien, -ienne [gardjɛ̃, -jɛn] *n* (*concierge*) caretaker, *Am* janitor; (*de musée, de parking*) attendant; *Fig* (*de libertés, traditions etc*) guardian; **g. des intérêts publics** guardian *or* protector of the public interest; **se poser en g. de l'ordre** to set oneself up as a guardian *or* an upholder of public order

▶ **gardien**: *Sp* **g. (de but)** goalkeeper; **g. d'immeuble** caretaker, porter, *Am* janitor; **g. de nuit** night watchman; **g. de la paix** policeman; **g. de phare** lighthouse keeper; **g. de prison** prison warder *or Am* guard

gardiennage [gardjɛnaʒ] *nm* (*de ponts*) guarding; (*d'un bâtiment*) caretaking; (*d'un port*) security; **société de g.** security firm

gardon [gardɔ̃] *nm* roach; *Fig* **frais comme un g.** fresh as a daisy, bright-eyed and bushy-tailed

gare[1] [gar] *nf Rail* (railway *or Am* railroad) station, train station; **(colis à prendre) en g.** (parcel) to be (left till) called for; **chef de g.** stationmaster, station manager; **g. d'arrivée/de départ** station of arrival/departure; **quelle est la g. d'arrivée à Londres?** what station does the train arrive at in London?; **entrer** *ou* **arriver en g.** (*d'un train*) to arrive in *or* come into the station; **quai numéro 3, le train entre en g.** the train is now approaching platform 3; **café/hôtel de la g.** station café/hotel

▶ **gare**: **g. aérienne** air terminal; *Naut* **g. (fluviale)** dock; **g. de marchandises** goods *or* freight station; **g. maritime** harbour *or US* harbor station; **g. routière** bus *or* coach station, bus depot; **g. routière (de marchandises)** road haulage depot; **g. de triage** marshalling yard; **g. de voyageurs** passenger station

gare[2] *int* (**a**) (*menace*) **g. à toi si on l'apprend** woe betide you if anyone finds out; *F* **si je te reprends à voler du gâteau, g. à tes fesses!** if I catch you stealing cake again, you've had it *or Br* you're for it! (**b**) (*attention*) **g. à la casse!** mind you don't break it!; **g. à la peinture!** mind the paint!; *Vieilli* **g. les coups de fusil des chasseurs!** watch out *or* mind out for the hunters and their guns; **sans crier g.** without warning

garenne [garɛn] *nf* (**a**) (rabbit) warren; **lapin de g.** wild rabbit (**b**) (*réserve*) fishing preserve

garer [gare] **1** *vt* (*voiture*) to park; (*train*) to shunt on to a siding; (*bateau*) to dock; **g. un avion** to park a plane; (*mettre à l'abri*) to put a plane in the hangar **2 se garer** *vpr* (**a**) *Aut* to park; **la voiture s'est garée le long du trottoir** the car parked beside *or* drew in beside the pavement; **j'ai eu de la peine à me g.** I had trouble parking; **se g. facilement** to have no trouble parking; **tu trouveras à te g. dans le quartier** you'll find somewhere to park in the area (**b**) **se g. de qch/qn** to avoid *or* steer clear of sth/sb

Gargantua [gargɑ̃tɥa] *nm F* glutton, guzzler

gargantuesque [gargɑ̃tɥɛsk] *adj* gargantuan; **un appétit/repas g.** a gargantuan appetite/meal

gargariser (se) [səgargarize] *vpr* to gargle; *F Péj* **se g. de formules pédantes** to delight *or* revel in pedantic expressions

gargarisme [gargarism] *nm* (*produit*) gargle; (*action de se gargariser*) gargling; **il doit (se) faire un g. par jour** he has to gargle once a day

gargote [gargɔt] *nf Péj* cheap restaurant

gargotier, -ière [gargɔtje, -jɛr] *n Péj* (**a**) (*patron d'une gargote*) owner of a cheap restaurant; **je vais aller dire deux mots au g.** I'm going to give the guy who runs this cheap place a piece of my mind (**b**) (*mauvais cuisinier*) poor cook

gargouille [garguj] *nf* (**a**) *Archit* gargoyle (**b**) (*d'un gouttière, d'une pompe*) (water)spout

gargouillement [gargujmɑ̃] *nm* (**a**) (*de l'eau*) gurgling (**b**) (*de l'estomac*) rumbling, gurgling; **j'ai eu des gargouillements pendant toute la réunion** my stomach rumbled *or* gurgled all through the meeting

gargouiller [garguje] *vi* (**a**) (*de l'eau*) to gurgle (**b**) (*de l'estomac*) to rumble, to gurgle (**c**) **sol qui gargouille sous les pas** squelchy *or* squishy ground

gargouillis [garguji] *nm* = **gargouillement**

garnement [garnəmɑ̃] *nm* (*enfant*) scamp, rascal, imp

garni [garni] **1** *adj* (**a**) **bien g.** (*bourse*) well-lined; (*magasin*) well-stocked; (*maison*) well-appointed; **panier g.** food hamper, hamper of food (**b**) *Culin* garnished; (*plat, viande*) with vegetables; **choucroute garnie** sauerkraut with sausages (**c**) *Vieilli* (*meublé*) (*chambre*) furnished **2** *nm Vieilli* (*meublé*) furnished room(s)

garnir [garnir] **1** *vt* (**a**) (*munir de ce qui protège, renforce etc*) to fit out (**de** with); (*commode, tiroir*) to line; (*fauteuil*) to stuff; **garni de feutre** felt-lined; **g. un mur de plaques de polystyrène** to cover *or* line a wall with polystyrene tiles

(**b**) (*embellir, compléter*) (*robe, chapeau etc*) to trim (**de** with); **une robe garnie de dentelle** a dress trimmed with lace, a lace-trimmed dress; **la passementerie qui garnit cette veste est très colorée** the braid trimming on that jacket is very colourful

(**c**) *Culin* (*plat*) to garnish; **une entrecôte garnie de pommes frites et de salade** a rib steak (served) with chips and salad; *Can* **une pizza tout garni** one pizza all dressed

(**d**) (*remplir*) to fill; (*cave*) to stock; **g. une étagère de disques** to fill a shelf with records

2 se garnir *vpr* **la salle se garnit** the hall *or Th* the house is beginning to fill up *or* is filling up

garnison [garnizɔ̃] *nf Mil* garrison; **mettre une g. dans une ville** to garrison a town; **ville de g.** garrison town; **être en g.** *ou* **tenir g. dans une ville** to be garrisoned *or* stationed in a town

garnissage [garnisaʒ] *nm* (**a**) (*remplissage*) (*d'un coussin, d'une couette etc*) stuffing; (*décoration*) (*d'un manteau*) trimming; *Aut* **g. de plafond** headliner, headlining; *Aut* **g. de siège** seat trim (**b**) *Tech* (*d'un piston*) packing; (*d'une chaudière*) lagging (**c**) (*matériau*) packing, stuffing; *Métal* (*d'un fourneau*) lining (**d**) *Tex* (*d'un tissu*) napping, raising

garniture [garnityr] *nf* (**a**) (*d'un fusil*) mountings; (*d'un navire*) rigging; (*d'une commode*) (metal) furnishings; **garnitures d'une serrure** wards of a lock; **g. d'une pompe à incendie** hose of a fire engine; **g. intérieure d'une voiture** upholstery *or* interior trim of a car

(**b**) (*ornement*) (*d'un chapeau, d'une robe etc*) trimming, decoration

(**c**) *Culin* (*d'un plat*) garnish; (*légumes*) vegetables; (*d'un vol-au-vent*) filling; **pour la g., vous avez le choix entre des haricots verts ou des frites** to go with it, you have a choice of green beans or chips

(**d**) *Tech* (*de joint*) packing; (*de piston*) stuffing (piece); (*de chaudière*) lagging; *Typ* furniture

▶ **garniture**: **g. de bureau** desk set; **g. de cheminée** mantelpiece ornaments; **g. d'embrayage** clutch lining; **g. de feu** *ou* **de foyer** (set of) fire irons; *Aut etc* **g. de frein** brake lining; (*de disque de frein*) brake pad; **g. de lit** bedding; **g. de toilette** toilet set

garrigue [garig] *nf Géog* garrigue

garrocher [garɔʃe] *vt Can Arg* (*pierres etc*) to throw

garrot[1] [garo] *nm* (**a**) *Méd* tourniquet; **appliquer un g. (à qn)** to put a tourniquet on (sb) (**b**) *Hist* **(supplice du) g.** gar(r)otting, gar(r)otte

garrot² *nm Zool* (*de cheval, de vache etc*) withers
garrottage [garɔtaʒ] *nm* **g. d'une blessure** putting a tourniquet on a wound
garrotte [garɔt] *nf Hist* gar(r)otte, gar(r)otting
garrotter [garɔte] *vt* (*prisonnier etc*) to tie up; *Fig* **g. les opposants au régime/l'opinion publique** to muzzle *or* silence the régime's opponents/public opinion
gars [gɑ] *nm F* (*jeune homme*) lad, young man; (*homme*) guy, *Br* bloke; **un petit g.** a little boy; **un beau g.** a good-looking *or* handsome young man; **un brave g.** a good lad; **un drôle de g.** an odd guy *or Br* bloke; **allons-y, les g.!** come on, lads *or* boys!; **bonjour, mon petit g.!** (*à un enfant*) hello, young man!
Gascogne [gaskɔɲ] *nf* Gascony; **le golfe de G.** the Bay of Biscay
gascon, -onne [gaskɔ̃, -ɔn] **1** *adj* Gascon **2** *nm Ling* Gascon **3** *n* **G.** Gascon; **offre** *ou* **promesse de G.** hollow *or* empty promise
gasconnade [gaskɔnad] *nf* boasting, bragging
gas(-)oil [gazɔjl, gazwal] *nm* diesel oil *or* fuel, *US* gas oil, Derv
gaspard [gaspar] *nm Arg* rat
gaspillage [gaspijaʒ] *nm* (*d'argent*) wasting, squandering; (*de nourriture, temps*) wasting; **je n'admets pas le g. de nourriture** I won't allow food to be wasted; **c'est du g.** it's a waste, it's wasteful; **pas de g.!** don't be wasteful!; **quel g.!** what a waste!; **c'est un vrai g. de temps/d'argent** it's a real waste of time/money
gaspiller [gaspije] *vt* (*argent, son talent, ses dons*) to waste, to squander; (*eau, papier, son énergie*) to waste, to waste, to squander; **g. son temps (à faire qch)** to waste one's time (doing sth)
gaspilleur, -euse [gaspijœr, -øz] **1** *n* spendthrift **2** *adj* wasteful
gastéropode [gasterɔpɔd] *nm Zool* gast(e)ropod
gastralgie [gastralʒi] *nf Méd* stomach pains, *Spéc* gastralgia
gastralgique [gastralʒik] *adj Méd* gastralgic
gastrectomie [gastrɛktɔmi] *nf Chir* gastrectomy
gastrique [gastrik] *adj* gastric; **embarras g.** stomach upset, upset stomach
gastrite [gastrit] *nf Méd* gastritis
gastro-entérite, *pl* **gastro-entérites** [gastroɑ̃terit] *nf Méd* gastroenteritis
gastro-entérologie [gastroɑ̃terɔlɔʒi] *nf Méd* gastroenterology
gastro-entérologue, *pl* **gastro-entérologues** [gastroɑ̃terɔlɔg] *n Méd* gastroenterologist
gastro-intestinal, -ale, -aux, -ales [gastroɛ̃testinal, -o] *adj Méd* gastrointestinal
gastronome [gastrɔnɔm] *nm* gastronome, gourmet
gastronomie [gastrɔnɔmi] *nf* gastronomy
gastronomique [gastrɔnɔmik] *adj* gastronomic(al)
gastropode [gastrɔpɔd] *nm Zool* gast(e)ropod
gâté [gɑte] *adj* **(a)** (*pourri*) (*fruit*) damaged, spoilt; (*dents*) rotten, decayed; **viande gâtée** meat that has gone off *or* is bad, bad meat **(b)** *Fig* **enfant g.** spoilt *or* pampered child; **l'enfant g. de la famille/de la littérature russe** the blue-eyed boy of the family/of Russian literature
gâteau [gɑto], *pl* **gâteaux 1** *nm* **(a)** cake; **faire un g.** to make *or* bake a cake; **g. d'anniversaire** birthday cake; *F* **c'est du g.** it's a piece of cake, it's child's play; *F* **ce n'est pas du g. de la convaincre** it's no easy matter convincing her; *F* **avoir sa part du g.** to have one's slice *or* share of the cake; *F* **se partager le g.** to share out the cake **(b)** (*masse compacte, plate*) cake; (*de fulmicoton etc*) disc **2** *adj inv F* **papa g.** (*qui cède tout à ses enfants*) indulgent father; **c'est un vrai papa g.** he's a real soft touch with his children; *F* **marraine g.** fairy godmother
▶ **gâteau**: **g. de cire** honeycomb; **g. marbré** marble cake; **g. de miel** honeycomb; **g. de riz** ≈ rice pudding; **g. sec** biscuit, *Am* cookie; **g. de semoule** ≈ semolina pudding
gâter [gɑte] **1** *vt* **(a)** (*paysage, plaisir*) to spoil, to ruin; **la grêle gâte le blé** hail damages wheat; **les mouches gâtent la viande** flies infect meat; **ce qui ne gâte rien** which is no bad thing
(b) (*choyer*) (*enfant, mari*) to spoil, to pamper, to overindulge; **il a été très gâté à Noël,** he was really spoilt at Christmas; **on n'est (vraiment) pas gâtés: de la pluie, du vent, le froid!** marvellous, isn't it: rain, wind, cold!; **la vie ne les avait pas gâtés** life hadn't treated them kindly; **il n'est pas gâté par la nature** nature hasn't been very kind to him
2 se gâter *vpr* (*affaires, temps*) to take a turn for the worse, to deteriorate; **le poisson se gâte facilement** fish easily goes bad *or* off
gâterie [gɑtri] *nf* **(a)** (*petit cadeau*) treat, small present **(b)** (*friandise*) (*pour enfants*) treat, goody **(c)** *Euph* **faire une petite g. à qn** to go down on sb
gâte-sauce [gɑtsos] *nm* kitchen boy; *Péj Vieilli* (*cuisinier*) bad cook
gâteux, -euse [gɑtø, -øz] *F* **1** *n* doddering old man/woman, old dodderer **2** *adj* (*sénile*) senile; *F* gaga; **avec leurs petits-enfants, ils sont complètement g.** they're totally besotted with their grandchildren, they absolutely dote on their grandchildren
gâtifier [gɑtifje] *vi F* to go gaga; **il commence à g. sérieusement, le grand-père** grandad's going gaga *or* soft in the head
gâtisme [gɑtism] *nm Méd* senility, senile decay; *Fig* **leurs épanchements sentimentaux ne sont rien moins que du gâtisme** the way they bill and coo you'd think they were going soft in the head
GATT [gat] *nm Écon* (*abrév* **General Agreement on Tariffs and Trade**) GATT
gauche [goʃ] **1** *adj* **(a)** (*maladroit*) (*personne, attitude, démarche, style etc*) awkward, clumsy; (*tentative*) clumsy, bungling; **attraper un objet d'un geste g.** to catch an object awkwardly *or* clumsily
(b) *Tech* (*déformé*) (*surface etc*) warped, crooked, out of true
(c) (*par opposition à droit*) left; **main g.** left hand; *Fig* **mariage de la main g.** living together; *Fig* **se lever du pied g.** to get out of bed on the wrong side; **rive g.** left bank; **côté g.** *Aut* (*quand on conduit à gauche*) nearside; (*quand on conduit à droite*) offside; *Équitation* nearside
2 *nf* **(a)** (*côté*) left; **assis à ma g.** seated on my left; **mon voisin de g.** my left-hand neighbour; **le tiroir de g.** the left-hand drawer; **le magasin de g.** the shop on the left; **à g.** on the left(-hand side), to the left; **tournez à g.** turn left; **la première rue à g.** the first street on the left; **sur votre g., vous pouvez voir la tour Eiffel** on your left(-hand side) you can see the Eiffel Tower; **à g. de la porte d'entrée/de Marie** on *or* to the left of the entrance/of Marie; **en France, on double à g.** in France, you overtake on the left; **conduire à g.** to drive on the left; **lire de g. à droite** to read from left to right; *F* **mettre de l'argent à g.** to put some money aside *or* away; **heureusement, elle avait de l'argent à g.** fortunately she had some money put aside *or* tucked away; *F* **passer l'arme à g.** to kick the bucket; **vis/hélice à pas de g.** left-handed screw/left-hand propeller; *F* **jusqu'à la g.** to the end, to the last; **ils nous ont eus jusqu'à la g.** they cheated us left, right and centre
(b) *Pol* **la g.** the left; **politique/gouvernement/***etc* **de g.** left-wing politics/government/*etc*; **homme de g.** man of the left; **l'extrême g.** the far *or* extreme left; **être à g.** to be on the left, to be left-wing; **voter à g.** to vote for the left
3 *nm Boxe etc* (*poing gauche*) left; **feinter du g.** to feint with the left; **un crochet du g.** a left hook
gauchement [goʃmɑ̃] *adv* awkwardly, clumsily
gaucher, -ère [goʃe, -ɛr] **1** *adj* left-handed **2** *n* left-hander; *Boxe* southpaw; **g. contrarié** = natural left-hander brought up to be right-handed
gaucherie [goʃri] *nf* awkwardness, clumsiness
gauchi [goʃi] *adj Tech* = **gauche 1 (b)**
gauchir [goʃir] **1** *vi* (*du bois etc*) to warp; (*du fer*) to buckle **2** *vt* **(a)** (*déformer*) to warp; (*fer*) to buckle **(b)** *Av* **g. l'aileron** to bank **(c)** *Fig* (*idée, événement, témoignage, réalité*) to distort, to misrepresent **3 se gauchir** *vpr* (*de bois*) to warp; (*de fer*) to buckle
gauchisant, -ante [goʃizɑ̃, -ɑ̃t] **1** *adj* **écrivain g.** writer with left-wing tendencies **2** *n* **c'est un g.** he has left-wing tendencies, *F* he's a bit of a lefty
gauchisme [goʃism] *nm Pol* leftism
gauchissement [goʃismɑ̃] *nm* **(a)** (*de bois etc*) warping; (*de fer*) buckling **(b)** *Av* banking
gauchiste [goʃist] **1** *adj Pol* left-wing, leftist **2** *n* left-winger, leftist, *F* lefty
gaudriole [godrijɔl] *nf F Vieilli* **(a)** (*plaisanterie grivoise*) dirty *or* saucy *or* broad joke **(b) il/elle ne pense qu'à la g.** he's/she's only interested in one thing, he's/she's got a one-track mind
gaufrage [gofraʒ] *nm* (*du cuir, papier*) embossing; (*du lin*) goffering, fluting; (*d'une couverture*) blocking
gaufre [gofr] *nf* **(a)** *Culin* waffle; **moule à gaufres** waffle iron **(b) g. de miel** honeycomb
gaufrer [gofre] *vt* (*cuir, velours, papier*) to emboss, to figure; (*lin*) to goffer, to flute; (*fer*) to corrugate; (*couverture*) to block
gaufrette [gofrɛt] *nf* wafer (biscuit)
gaufrier [gofrije] *nm* waffle iron
gaufrure [gofryr] *nf* (*sur cuir*) stamped design; (*sur lin*) goffering
Gaule [gol] *nf Antiq* Gaul

gaule [gol] *nf* pole; *Pêche* fishing rod
gauler [gole] *vt* **(a)** (*arbre fruitier, noyer*) to beat, to thrash; (*fruits, noix*) to bring down (*using a pole*) **(b)** *F* (*attraper*) **se faire g.** to get caught
gaullien, -ienne [goljɛ̃, -jɛn] *adj* de Gaulle-like
gaullisme [golism] *nm Pol* Gaullism
gaulliste [golist] *adj, n Pol* Gaullist
gaulois, -oise [golwa, -waz] **1** *adj* Gallic; **esprit g.** (broad) Gallic humour; **contes g.** saucy *or* spicy stories **2** *nm Ling* Gaulish **3** *n* **les G.** the Gauls **4** *nf* **Gauloise®** Gauloise (*popular brand of cigarette*)
gauloiserie [golwazri] *nf* (*plaisanterie*) broad *or* saucy joke; (*caractère*) sauciness
gausser (se) [səgose] *vpr Litt* **se g. de qn** to laugh at *or* make fun of *or* sneer at sb; **vous vous gaussez!** you jest!
gavage [gavaʒ] *nm* (*engraissement*) (*de la volaille*) force-feeding, cramming; *Méd* tube-feeding
gave [gav] *nm Géog* (mountain) torrent (*in the Pyrenees*)
gaver [gave] **1** *vt* (*engraisser*) (*volaille*) to force-feed, to cram; (*personne*) (*de nourriture*) to fill up, to stuff (**de** with); *Méd* to force-feed; *Fig* **g. qn de qch** to cram *or* stuff sb with sth; **j'ai été gavée de littérature classique** I had classical literature crammed into me; **la télévision gave les enfants de dessins animés** television feeds children a constant diet of cartoons **2 se gaver** *vpr F* (*de chocolat, cacahuètes etc*) to gorge oneself (**de** on), to stuff oneself (**de** with); *Fig* **se g. de romans policiers/jeux vidéo** to read detective novels/play video games till they're coming out of one's ears
gavotte [gavɔt] *nf Mus* gavotte
gay [gɛ(e)] *adj, nm F* (*homosexuel*) gay
gaz [gaz] *nm* **(a)** gas; **gisement de g.** gas field; **faire la cuisine au g.** to cook by gas; **cuisinière à g.** gas cooker; *Culin* **sur le g.** on the gas; **allumer/couper le g.** to light/turn off the gas; **réchaud à g.** gas stove (*for camping*); **usine à g.** gasworks; **chambre à g.** gas chamber; *F* **il y a de l'eau dans le g.** things aren't going too well, things are looking bad **(b)** *Aut F* **mettre les g.** to put one's foot down, *Am* to step on the gas; *Av* to open up the throttle; **à pleins g.** (*rouler*) flat out; (*partir*) with the throttle full open **(c)** *Méd* **avoir des g.** to have wind; **lâcher un g.** to break wind
▶ **gaz**: **g. ammoniac** ammonia gas; **g. asphyxiant** poison gas; **g. carbonique** carbon dioxide; **g. comprimé** compressed gas; **g. domestique** domestic gas; **g. d'échappement** exhaust fumes *ou* gas; **g. d'éclairage** town gas; **g. hilarant** laughing gas; **g. inerte** inert gas; **g. lacrymogène** tear gas; **g. des marais** marsh gas; **g. naturel** natural gas; **g. de pétrole liquéfié** liquefied petroleum gas; **g. rare** rare gas; **g. toxique** poison gas; **g. de ville** town gas; **la cuisinière est-elle branchée sur le g. de ville?** is the kitchen connected to the mains gas?
gazage [gɑzaʒ] *nm Mil* gassing
gaze [gaz] *nf* **(a)** gauze; *Méd* **g. oxygénée** antiseptic *or* sterilized gauze **(b)** *Vieilli* (*voile*) thin veil
gazé, -ée [gɑze] **1** *adj* gassed; **soldats gazés** soldiers killed by (poison) gas **2** *n* (poison) gas victim
gazéification [gazeifikasjɔ̃] *nf Ch* gasification; (*des boissons*) carbonation
gazéifier [gazeifje] *vt* (*pr sub, impf* **n. gazéifiions, v. gazéifiiez**) *Ch* to gasify; (*boissons*) to carbonate
gazelle [gazɛl] *nf* gazelle
gazer [gɑze] **1** *vt Mil* (*troupes*) to gas **2** *vi F* (*aller vite*) to zoom along; **ça gaze!** everything's OK *or* fine!; **ça gaze?** all right?, everything OK?; **ça ne gaze pas très fort pour lui** things aren't going too well for him
gazetier [gaztje] *nm Arch* journalist
gazette [gazɛt] *nf Vieilli* (*journal*) gazette, newspaper; *F* **c'est une vraie g.** he/she knows all the local gossip; *F* **cette femme est la g. de l'immeuble** that woman can tell you *or* knows everything that goes on in the building
gazeux, -euse [gazø, -øz] *adj* **(a)** *Ch* gaseous **(b)** (*eau*) carbonated, fizzy; (*boisson*) fizzy, sparkling
gazier, -ière [gɑzje, -jɛr] **1** *adj* **l'industrie gazière** the gas industry **2** *nm* **(a)** (*dans une usine à gaz*) gas works employee; (*chargé des installations dans les immeubles etc*) gas fitter, gasman **(b)** *Arg* (*individu*) guy, *Br* bloke
gazinière [gɑzinjɛr] *nf* gas cooker
gazoduc [gɑzɔdyk, gaz-] *nm* gas pipeline, gas main
gazogène [gɑzɔʒɛn, gaz-] *nm* gas producer, gas generator; **gaz de g.** producer gas
gazole [gazɔl] *nm* = **gas(-) oil**
gazoline [gazɔlin] *nf* gasoline, gasolene
gazomètre [gɑzɔmɛtr] *nm* gasometer, gas holder
gazon [gɑzɔ̃] *nm* **(a)** (*herbe*) grass, turf **(b)** (*surface*) lawn; **défense de marcher sur le g.** keep off the grass **(c)** (*motte de terre*) turf, sod **(d)** *Bot* **g. mousse** mossy saxifrage
gazonnage [gɑzɔnaʒ] *nm* turfing, planting with turf
gazonné [gɑzɔne] *adj* grass-covered, turfed
gazonnement [gɑzɔnmɑ̃] *nm* = **gazonnage**
gazonner [gɑzɔne] **1** *vt* to cover with turf, to turf **2** *vi* (*d'un terrain*) to become covered with grass
gazouillant [gazujɑ̃] *adj* (*oiseau*) twittering, warbling, chirping; (*bébé*) babbling, gurgling; (*enfant*) prattling; **ruisseau g.** babbling brook
gazouillement [gazujmɑ̃] *nm* (*des oiseaux*) twittering, warbling, chirping; (*d'un bébé*) babbling, gurgling; (*des enfants*) prattle, prattling; (*de l'eau qui coule*) babbling, murmuring
gazouiller [gazuje] *vi* (*d'un oiseau*) to twitter, to warble, to chirp; (*d'un bébé*) to babble, to gurgle; (*d'un enfant*) to prattle; (*d'eau*) to babble, to murmur
gazouilleur, -euse [gazujœr, -øz] *adj* (*oiseau*) twittering, warbling, chirping; (*bébé*) babbling, gurgling; (*enfant*) prattling; **ruisseau g.** babbling brook
gazouillis [gazuji] *nm* = **gazouillement**
GB [ʒebe] *nf* (*abrév* **Grande-Bretagne**) GB
G-C [ʒese] *abrév* **grand-croix**
GDF [ʒedeɛf] *nm abrév* **Gaz de France**
geai [ʒɛ] *nm Orn* jay
géant, -ante [ʒeɑ̃, -ɑ̃t] **1** *n* **(a)** *Myth* giant, *f* giantess **(b)** (*personne anormalement grande*) giant; *Gym* **pas de g.** giant stride; *Fig* **avancer** *ou* **aller à pas de g.** to make great strides, to make spectacular progress; **la Chaussée des Géants** the Giant's Causeway **(c)** (*personne exceptionnelle*) giant; **les géants de la politique** the giants of politics, the political giants; **les géants de l'art** the great masters; **les géants du football** the football(ing) greats **2** *adj* **(a)** (*arbre, écran etc*) giant, gigantic; *Com* **carton g.** giant(-size) packet **(b)** *F* (*super*) **c'est g.** fantastic!, *Arg* wicked!
gecko [ʒeko] *nm* gecko
géhenne [ʒeɛn] *nf Bible* Gehenna, Hell
geignard, -arde [ʒɛɲar, -ard] *F* **1** *adj* (*personne, voix*) whining, *Br* whingeing **2** *n* whiner
geignement [ʒɛɲmɑ̃] *nm* (*action*) whining; (*résultat*) whine
geindre [ʒɛ̃dr] *vi* (*prp* **geignant**; *pp* **geint**; *pr ind* **je geins, il geint, n. geignons, ils geignent**; *impf* **je geignais**; *p hist* **je geignis**; *fu* **je geindrai**) **(a)** (*gémir*) to moan, to groan; **g. de douleur** to moan *or* groan with pain **(b)** *F* (*se plaindre constamment*) to whine, *Br* to whinge
gel [ʒɛl] *nm* **(a)** *Météo* frost; *Fig* **g. des négociations** suspension of negotiations; **g. des subventions** freezing of subsidies; **g. des armements/des crédits** the arms/credit freeze **(b)** (*dans les produits cosmétiques*) (*pour les cheveux*) gel; **dentrifrice en g.** gel toothpaste; **se mettre du g.** to put gel on one's hair **(c)** *Ch* gel
▶ **gel**: **g. douche** shower gel; *CE* **g. des terres** set-aside
gélatine [ʒelatin] *nf* gelatin(e); *Culin* **feuille de g.** sheet of gelatine
gélatiné [ʒelatine] *adj* gelatinized
gélatineux, -euse [ʒelatinø, -øz] *adj* gelatinous
gelé [ʒ(ə)le] *adj* (*lac, rivière*) frozen; (*nez, main etc*) frostbitten; (*plante*) frost-nipped; *Fig* (*assistance*) cold, indifferent; *Fin* (*bloqué*) (*fonds*) frozen; **mourir g.** to freeze to death; *F* **je suis complètement g.** I'm absolutely frozen *or* freezing; *F* **être g. jusqu'aux os** to be chilled to the marrow *or* bone; **ils ont eu les pieds gelés** they had frostbite in their feet
gelée [ʒ(ə)le] *nf* **(a)** (*gel*) frost; **forte g.** hard frost **(b)** *Culin* jelly; (*à base de fruits*) jelly, *Am* jello; **g. de veau/poulet** veal/chicken jelly; **œufs en g.** eggs in jelly; **g. de cassis** blackcurrant jelly *or Am* jello
▶ **gelée**: **g. blanche** hoar (frost), white frost; **g. royale** royal jelly
geler [ʒ(ə)le] (**je gèle, n. gelons; je gèlerai**) **1** *vt* **(a)** to freeze; (*lac, rivière*) to freeze (over); (*route*) to make icy; **froid qui gèle les conduites d'eau** cold that freezes the water pipes; **fleurs gelées par le froid** flowers nipped by the frost

(b) *Fin* (*bloquer*) (*crédits, capital*) to freeze

2 *vi* (*d'un lac, d'une rivière*) to freeze (over); **l'étang a gelé d'un bout à l'autre** the pond has *or* is completely frozen over; **plantes qui gèlent facilement** plants easily damaged by frost; **on gèle dans cette salle** it's freezing in this room; **tu ne gèles pas, toi?** aren't you freezing *or* frozen?

3 *v impers* **il gèle** it is freezing; **il gèle à pierre fendre** it's freezing hard; **il a gelé blanc cette nuit** there was a white frost last night

4 se geler *vpr* (*personne*) to freeze; *très F* **on se les gèle aujourd'hui** it's damned cold, *Br* it's brass monkey weather
gélifiant [ʒelifjɑ̃] *nm* gelling agent
gélifier [ʒelifje] *Ch* **1** *vt* (*transformer en gel*) to gel **2 se gélifier** *vpr* to gel
gélinotte [ʒelinɔt] *nf* **g. (des bois)** hazel grouse; **g. des prairies** prairie chicken

gélose [ʒeloz] *nf Ch* agar-agar
gélule [ʒelyl] *nf Pharm* capsule
gelure [ʒ(ə)lyr] *nf* frostbite
Gémeaux (les) [leʒemo] *nmpl Astron, Astrol* Gemini; **être (du signe des) Gémeaux** to be (a) Gemini
gémellaire [ʒemelɛr] *adj* twin
gémellité [ʒemelite] *nf* **taux de g.** incidence of twin births
gémination [ʒeminasjɔ̃] *nf Biol etc* gemination
géminé [ʒemine] *adj* **(a)** *Biol* (*feuilles*) geminate, twin; *Ch* geminate; *Archit* **colonnes géminées** twin columns **(b)** *Ling* **consonnes géminées** doubled *or* geminate consonants
gémir [ʒemir] *vi* **(a)** (*d'une personne*) to groan, to moan; (*d'une porte*) to creak; (*du vent*) to moan; **g. de douleur** to groan *or* moan with pain; **g. sous le joug de la tyrannie** to groan under the yoke of tyranny **(b)** (*d'une colombe, tourterelle*) to coo
gémissant [ʒemisɑ̃] *adj* (*personne*) moaning, groaning; **voix gémissante** wailing voice; **essieu g.** creaking axle
gémissement [ʒemismɑ̃] *nm* **(a)** (*d'une personne*) groan, moan; (*de porte*) creaking; (*de vent*) moaning; **je ne supporte plus tes gémissements** I can't bear your moaning *or* groaning any longer **(b)** (*d'une colombe etc*) cooing
gemmage [ʒɛmaʒ] *nm* tapping (*of trees for resin*)
gemme [ʒɛm] **1** *nf* **(a)** *Minér* gem (stone), precious stone **(b)** (*sève*) pine resin **(c)** *Bot Arch* (leaf) bud **2** *adj* **pierre g.** gem stone; **sel g.** rock salt
gemmé [ʒeme, ʒɛ-] *adj Litt* gemmed, jewelled
gemmer [ʒeme, ʒɛ-] *vt* to tap
gemmeur [ʒɛmœr] *nm* tapper
gémonies [ʒemɔni] *nfpl Litt* **traîner** *ou* **vouer qn aux g.** to hold sb up to public obloquy
gênant [ʒɛnɑ̃] *adj* **(a)** (*embarrassant*) (*personne*) embarrassing; (*situation, silence*) embarrassing, awkward; (*témoin*) awkward; **j'ai trouvé extrêmement g. que tu abordes ce sujet** it was extremely embarrassing of you to mention the subject **(b)** (*encombrant*) (*objet*) cumbersome; **votre fils n'est pas g.** your son is no trouble *or* no bother; **il peut être très g. quand il nous interrompt** he can be a real nuisance when he interrupts us; **les jupes longues sont gênantes** long skirts are awkward *or* are a nuisance
gencive [ʒɑ̃siv] *nf* **(a)** *Anat* gum; **abcès à la g.** abscess on the gum, gumboil **(b)** *F* **un coup dans les gencives** a punch on the jaw; *Fig* **prends ça dans les gencives!** take that!; **elle lui a envoyé dans les gencives tout ce qu'elle avait contre lui** she told him to his face everything she didn't like about him
gendarme [ʒɑ̃darm] *nm* **(a)** gendarme, = policeman, *Br* ≈ police constable; **gendarmes à cheval** mounted police; **gendarmes motocyclistes** motorcycle police; **sa mère est un vrai g.** his mother is a real battle-axe; **jouer aux gendarmes et aux voleurs** to play (at) cops and robbers; *F* **faire le g.** to boss people about; *F* **la peur du g.** the fear of being caught; **chapeau de g.** paper hat **(b)** (*d'une pierre précieuse*) flaw **(c)** *Géol* rock pinnacle, gendarme **(d)** *Culin F* (*hareng saur*) red herring; (*saucisson*) = flat, dry sausage
▶ **gendarme**: *Aut F* **g. couché** sleeping policeman
gendarmerie [ʒɑ̃darməri] *nf* **(a)** (*corps*) (*en France*) gendarmerie, = police force; **g. nationale** = national police force, gendarmerie; **la G. royale du Canada** the Royal Canadian Mounted Police **(b)** (*lieu*) gendarmes' headquarters
gendarmer (se) [səʒɑ̃darme] *vpr* (*contre qn, une proposition etc*) to kick up *or* create a fuss (**contre** about); **il n'y a pas de quoi se g.** there's nothing to get worked up about
gendre [ʒɑ̃dr] *nm* son-in-law
gène [ʒɛn] *nm Biol* gene; **structure du g.** gene structure; **banque/famille de gènes** gene bank/family
gêne [ʒɛn] *nf* **(a)** (*confusion*) embarrassment; **éprouver une certaine g. à parler en public** to feel rather ill at ease *or* embarrassed when speaking in public; **ressentir de la g. en présence de qn** to feel ill at ease *or* embarrassed in sb's presence; **elle a ressenti une certaine g. à le lui demander** she felt rather embarrassed *or* awkward about asking him; **je n'aurais aucune g. à le faire** I wouldn't be at all embarrassed about doing it; **où (il) y a de la g., (il n')y a pas de plaisir** there's no point in standing on ceremony

(b) (*dérangement*) inconvenience; **nous prions nos clients de bien vouloir excuser la g. occasionnée par les travaux** we apologize to customers for the inconvenience caused by the work; **vous ne me causerez aucune g.** you won't inconvenience me in the least, you won't cause me any inconvenience

(c) (*difficulté physique*) discomfort; **sentir une g. respiratoire** *ou* **pour respirer** to have difficulty (in) breathing; **elle éprouve une g. intense à avaler** she has great difficulty swallowing

(d) (*manque d'argent*) **être dans la g.** to be short of money, to be in financial difficulties

(e) *Arch* (*physique, morale*) torture
gêné [ʒene] *adj* **(a)** (*embarrassé*) embarrassed, ill at ease; **je suis tellement gênée de tous ces cadeaux que vous me faites** I'm so embarrassed by all these presents you're giving me; *F* **il n'est pas g., lui!** he's got a nerve!; **elle avait l'air g. d'arriver si tard** she seemed embarrassed at arriving so late; **je serais trop g. de le lui dire** I'd be too embarrassed to tell him; **silence g.** embarrassed *or* awkward *or* uneasy silence; *F* **être g. aux entournures** to be ill at ease; **être g. par un vêtement** to be hampered by a garment

(b) (*qui manque d'argent*) short of money, in financial difficulties; *F* **être g. aux entournures** to be short of money
généalogie [ʒenealɔʒi] *nf* **(a)** (*ascendance*) genealogy, descent; (*d'un cheval, d'un chien etc*) pedigree **(b)** (*science*) genealogy
généalogique [ʒenealɔʒik] *adj* genealogical; **livre g.** (*de chevaux*) stud book; (*du bétail*) herd book
généalogiquement [ʒenealɔʒikmɑ̃] *adv* genealogically
généalogiste [ʒenealɔʒist] *n* genealogist
gêner [ʒene] **1** *vt* **(a)** (*perturber, empêcher*) (*activité*) to interfere with; **g. la circulation** to hold up *or* block the traffic; **g. le passage** to be in the way; **g. la vue** to obstruct *or* block the view; **ma valise vous gêne-t-elle?** is my case in your way?; **pousse-toi, tu vois bien que tu gênes!** move along, you can see you're in the way!; **je veux bien venir avec vous mais je ne veux pas vous g.** I'd love to come with you but I don't want to be in the *or* your way; **les enfants me gênent quand je dois me concentrer** the children disturb *or* bother me when I have to concentrate; **ça me gêne dans mon travail** it disturbs me when I'm trying to work; **une bonne nous gênerait dans notre intimité** a maid would intrude on our privacy; **ce point de côté me gêne pour marcher** this stitch in my side makes it difficult for me to walk; **recule-toi, tu me gênes pour passer** move back, you're in my way *or* you're stopping me from getting past; **si tu pouvais te pousser, tu me gênes pour passer les vitesses** could you move over, I can't change gear with you there; **j'ai été gêné par le manque de temps/ma méconnaissance du milieu** I was hindered *or* hampered by the lack of time/my ignorance of the milieu; **j'ai été gêné par le bruit/la lumière/le monde** I was disturbed by the noise/ the light/the people; **ça te gêne si je mets la musique plus fort?** do you mind if I turn up the music?; **cela vous gênerait-il que je revienne demain?** would it disturb you *or* bother you *or* put you out if I come back tomorrow?; **cela ne te gênerait pas de me prêter ta voiture?** would you mind lending me your car?; **ce qui me gêne, c'est que …** what bothers me is that …; **le froid ne me gêne pas** I don't mind the cold; **la fumée vous gêne-t-elle?** do you mind my smoking?

(b) (*serrer*) **mes souliers me gênent** my shoes pinch *or* are too tight; **cette ceinture/ce col me gêne** this belt/this collar is too tight; **cette jupe trop étroite me gêne pour marcher** I find it hard to walk in this tight skirt

(c) (*mettre mal à l'aise*) to embarrass; **cela me gênerait de le rencontrer** it would be awkward for me to meet him, I would feel uncomfortable meeting him; **sa présence me gêne** I feel awkward *or* embarrassed in his presence, his presence makes me feel ill at ease; **ça me gêne qu'il écoute** I feel uneasy with him listening; *F* **et alors, ça te gêne?** what's it to you?, any objections?

2 se gêner *vpr* **(a) je ne me suis pas gêné pour le lui dire** I didn't hesitate to tell him so, I made no bones about telling him so; **ne te gêne pas pour le lui faire remarquer** go right ahead and point it out to him; **il trouve que le café ne vient pas assez vite? qu'il ne se gêne surtout pas pour le faire!** he thinks the coffee's taking too long? he can always make it himself!; **il ne se gêne pas avec nous** he doesn't stand on ceremony with us; **elle aurait tort de se g.** she has no need to feel embarrassed; *Iron* **il ne se gêne pas!** he's not backward in coming forward! *Iron* **ne vous gênez pas!** make yourself at home! *Iron* **faut pas se g.!** don't mind me!

(b) (*dans un lieu*) to be in each other's way; **il y a beaucoup de place, nous ne nous gênerons pas** there's a lot of room, we won't be in each other's way
général, -ale, -aux, -ales [ʒeneral, -o] **1** *adj* general; **assemblée/amnistie générale** general assembly/amnesty; **appeler à une grève générale** to call a general strike; **dans l'intérêt g.** in the general interest; **à la surprise générale** to everyone's surprise; **à la demande générale, nous allons rechanter la dernière chanson** by popular request we are going to sing the last song again; **satisfaire à la demande générale** to satisfy popular *or* general demand; *Th*

répétition générale dress rehearsal; **état g.** general *or* overall condition; **médecine générale** general medicine; **inspecteur g.** inspector general; **quartier g.** headquarters; *Hist Fr* **états généraux** States General; **officier g.** *Mil etc* general officer; *Naut* flag officer; **le consentement g.** common consent; **d'une façon générale** generally speaking; **en règle générale** as a general rule, generally; **en g.** (*globalement*) in general; (*habituellement*) as a rule, generally; **la nature humaine en g.** human nature in general; **en g., elle se couche tôt** she goes to bed early as a rule, she generally goes to bed early

2 *nm* **(a)** (*ce qui est universel*) **le g.** the general; **passer du g. au particulier** to go from the general to the particular

(b) *Mil* general

3 *nf* **générale (a)** *Th* dress rehearsal

(b) *Mil* (*alerte*) alarm call; **battre la générale** to call to arms, to sound the alarm; *Naut* to beat to quarters

(c) bonjour, madame la générale (*qui s'appelle Leclerc*) hello, Mrs Leclerc

▶ **général**: **g. d'armée** (army) general; **g. d'armée aérienne** air chief marshal, *Am* major general; **g. de brigade** brigadier, *Am* brigadier general; **g. de brigade aérienne** air commodore, *Am* brigadier general; **g. de corps d'armée** lieutenant general; **g. de corps d'armée aérienne** air marshal, *Am* lieutenant general; **g. de division** major general; **g. de division aérienne** air vice-marshal, *Am* major general

généralement [ʒeneralmɑ̃] *adv* generally; **il y a g. une trentaine d'élèves par classe** there are generally *or* usually about thirty pupils in a class

généralisable [ʒeneralizabl] *adj* that can be generalized

généralisateur, -trice [ʒeneralizatœr, -tris] *adj* (*esprit, méthode*) generalizing

généralisation [ʒeneralizasjɔ̃] *nf* **(a)** (*extension*) generalization; **craindre la g. d'un conflit** to fear that a conflict will spread; *Méd* **g. d'un cancer** spread of a cancer **(b)** (*de propos*) generalization; **une g. hâtive** a sweeping generalization; **faire des généralisations** to make generalizations, to generalize; **tomber dans les généralisations** to lapse into generalization(s)

généraliser [ʒeneralize] **1** *vt* to generalize; **g. une loi** to extend a law; **il a tendance à tout g.** he tends to generalize; *Méd* **un cancer généralisé** a generalized cancer **2** *vi* to generalize; **on ne peut pas g.** you can't generalize **3 se généraliser** *vpr* (*d'une utilisation*) to become widespread; (*d'un usage, un conflit, une grève*) to spread; **la crise économique s'est généralisée** the economic crisis has spread

généralissime [ʒeneralisim] *nm* generalissimo, commander-in-chief

généraliste [ʒeneralist] **1** *n Méd* general practitioner, GP **2** *adj* **médecin g.** general practitioner, GP; **radio/télévision g.** general-interest radio/television

généralité [ʒeneralite] *nf* **(a)** (*majorité*) **dans la g. des cas** in the majority *or* generality of cases, in most cases **(b)** (*notion générale*) generality; **s'en tenir à des généralités** to confine oneself to generalities *or* to general remarks; **exposer quelques généralités dans un cours d'introduction** to present some general ideas in an introductory course

générateur, -trice [ʒeneratœr, -tris] **1** *adj* (*machine etc*) generating; (*force, organe*) generative; **g. de** productive of; **un colorant alimentaire g. de troubles gastriques** a food colouring which causes gastric problems; *Fig* **une situation génératrice de conflits/d'idées** a situation that generates *or* produces conflict/ideas; **une situation peu génératrice d'emplois** a situation that generates *or* produces few jobs; **son discours a été g. de nombreuses questions** his speech threw up *or* raised a great many questions; *Él* **station** *ou* **usine génératrice** generating station *or* plant; **chaudière génératrice** steam boiler

2 *nm* generator

3 *nf* **génératrice** generator, generating set; *Phys, Nucl* **génératrice nucléaire** nuclear power reactor

▶ **générateur**: *Ordinat* **g. de caractères** character generator; *TV aussi* caption generator; *TV, Cin* **g. de couleur** colour synthesizer; *Ordinat* **g. d'écrans** screen generator; **g. d'effets numériques** digital effects generator; **g. d'effets spéciaux** (special) effects generator, SEG; *Él* **g. d'électricité** electricity generator; *Ordinat* **g. d'états** report generator; **g. graphique** graphics generator; *Électron* **g. d'impulsions** pulse generator; *Ordinat* **g. de menus** menu builder; **g. de signaux** *Électron* signal(ling) generator; *TV* colour coder; *Ordinat* **g. de son** sound generator; *TV etc* **g. de synchro** synchronizing generator, sync pulse generator, SPG; *TV, Cin* **g. de titres graphiques** graphic titler; **g. de vapeur** (steam) boiler, steam generator

génératif, -ive [ʒeneratif, -iv] *adj* generative

génération [ʒenerasjɔ̃] *nf* **(a)** [①All,g,i] (*classe d'âge, degrés de filiation*) generation; **la g. actuelle** the present generation; **la jeune g.** the younger generation; **ils ne sont pas de la même g.** they are not (of) the same generation; **les gens de ma g.** the people of my generation; **de g. en g.** from generation to generation, through the generations; **immigrés de la deuxième g.** second-generation immigrants; **la g. pub/vidéo/***etc* the advertising/video/*etc* generation; **la nouvelle g. d'ordinateurs/de machines à laver** the new generation of computers/washing machines

(b) (*action de générer, produire*) generation; (*de vapeur etc*) generation, production; (*de métaux*) formation

▶ **génération**: *Ordinat* **g. automatique de textes** automatic generation of texts; *Ordinat* **g. d'écrans** screen generation; *Biol* **g. spontanée** spontaneous generation

générer [ʒenere] *vt* **(je génère, n. générons; je générerai) (a)** (*faire naître*) (*idées, images, formes*) to generate **(b)** (*produire*) (*électricité, vapeur etc*) to generate, to produce

généreusement [ʒenerøzmɑ̃] *adv* generously; **il nous a servi g. à manger** he gave us a generous meal; **il nous a g. versé à boire** he gave us a generous amount to drink

généreux, -euse [ʒenerø, -øz] **1** *adj* (*charitable*) generous; *Vieilli* (*noble*) (*âme*) noble, generous; **il est très g. avec les enfants** he is very generous with (the) children; **un don g.** a generous gift; **terre généreuse** fertile soil; **vin g.** generous wine, wine with a fine bouquet; **elle a des formes généreuses** she has generous curves, she is a buxom woman **2** *n* generous person

générique [ʒenerik] **1** *adj* generic; **produit g.** no-name *or* generic product **2** *nm Cin, TV* credits, titles; **faire le g.** to do the captions; **son nom ne figure pas au g.** his name doesn't appear in the credits, he doesn't get a credit; **g. de fin** end titles; *TV, Cin* **g. sur déroulant** crawl

générosité [ʒenerozite] *nf* (*libéralité*) generosity; **avec g.** generously; **g. de cœur** kindness of heart; **dans un élan de g.** in a sudden fit of generosity; **n'abuse pas de ma g.** don't abuse my generosity; **générosités** acts of generosity

Gênes [ʒɛn] *nf* Genoa

genèse [ʒənɛz] *nf* genesis; *Bible* **la G.** (the Book of) Genesis

genet [ʒ(ə)nɛ] *nm* jennet

genêt [ʒ(ə)nɛ] *nm Bot* broom

généticien, -ienne [ʒenetisjɛ̃, -jɛn] *n* geneticist

génétique [ʒenetik] **1** *adj* genetic; **code/empreinte/manipulation g.** genetic code/fingerprint/engineering; **fond g. commun** gene pool **2** *nf* genetics

génétiquement [ʒenetikmɑ̃] *adv* genetically

genette [ʒ(ə)nɛt] *nf* genet

gêneur, -euse [ʒɛnœr, -øz] *n* nuisance

Genève [ʒ(ə)nɛv] *nf* Geneva

genevois, -oise [ʒənvwa, -waz] **1** *adj* Genevan **2** *n* **G.** Genevan

genévrier [ʒənevrije] *nm* juniper

génial, -ale, -aux, -ales [ʒenjal, -o] *adj* **(a)** (*inspiré par le génie*) (*invention, livre, tableau etc*) brilliant; **œuvre géniale** work of genius, brilliant work; **compositeur g.** composer of genius, brilliant composer **(b)** *F* (*extraordinaire*) (*idée, film, soirée etc*) brilliant, great; **c'est g.!** that's brilliant *or* great!; **un mec g.** a great guy; **tu es g.!** you're a genius!, you're brilliant!

génialement [ʒenjalmɑ̃] *adv* brilliantly

génie[1] [ʒeni] *nm* **(a)** [①A13,8,y] (*qualité, personne*) genius; **homme de g.** man of genius; **une idée/invention de g.** a brilliant idea/invention; **un trait de g.** a stroke of genius; **avoir le g. de qch/pour faire qch** to have a genius *or* gift for sth/for doing sth; *Iron* **tu as vraiment le g. pour te faire des ennemis** you have a real genius *or* a real gift for making enemies **(b)** (*allégorie*) spirit; **g. d'une langue** genius *or* spirit of a language **(c)** (*être mythique*) genie; **son mauvais g.** his evil genius; **le petit g. de la forêt** the forest sprite; **les génies des contes arabes** the genies *or* the jinn of the Arabian Nights

génie[2] *nm Tech* engineering; *Mil* **le (Corps du) G.** *Br* ≈ the Royal Engineers, the Engineers, *US* ≈ the Corps of Engineers, the Engineer Corps; *Mil* **officier du g.** engineer officer; *Mil* **soldat du g.** engineer, *Br* sapper

▶ **génie**: **g. aéroporté** airborne engineers; **g. de l'air** aviation engineers; **g. atomique** atomic *or* nuclear engineering; (*corps*) atomic *or* nuclear engineers; **g. civil** civil engineering; (*corps*) civil engineers; *Méd* **g. génétique** genetic engineering; *Tech* **g. maritime** marine *or* naval architecture; (*corps*) marine *or* naval architects

genièvre [ʒənjɛvr] *nm* **(a)** (*fruit*) juniper berry; (*arbre*) juniper (tree); *Pharm* **essence de g.** juniper oil **(b)** (*alcool*) gin

génique [ʒenik] *adj Méd* **thérapie g.** gene therapy

génisse [ʒenis] *nf* heifer

génital, -ale, -aux, -ales [ʒenital, -o] *adj* genital; **les organes génitaux** the genitals, the genital organs; **appareil g.** genitalia

géniteur, -trice [ʒenitœr, -tris] **1** *nm Zool* sire **2** *n Hum* father, *f* mother; **nos géniteurs** our parents

génitif [ʒenitif] *nm* [①A15-16,D] *Gram* genitive (case); **au g.** in the genitive

génito-urinaire, *pl* **génito-urinaires** [ʒenitoyrinɛr] *adj Anat* genito-urinary

génocide [ʒenɔsid] *nm* genocide

génoise[2] *nf* sponge cake

génois, -oise[1] [ʒenwa, -waz] **1** *adj* Genoese **2** *n* **G.** Genoese

génome [ʒenom] *nm* genome

génotype [ʒenɔtip] *nm* genotype

genou, *pl* **-oux** [ʒ(ə)nu] *nm* **(a)** *Anat* knee; **sa robe lui arrivait au-dessus du g. /aux genoux** her dress came down to just above the knee/to her knees; **enfoncé jusqu'aux genoux dans la boue** knee-deep in mud, up to one's knees in mud; **avoir les genoux en dedans** to be knock-kneed; **à genoux** kneeling, on one's knees; **se mettre à genoux** to kneel (down), to go down on one's knees; *Fig* **être à genoux devant qn** to worship sb; *Fig* **se mettre à genoux devant qn** to go down on one's knees to sb; *Fig* **demander qch à genoux** to ask for sth on bended knee; **plier** *ou* **ployer** *ou* **fléchir le g. devant qn** to bend the knee to sb; *Fig* **être sur les genoux** to be on one's last legs, to be about to drop; **ce projet m'a mis sur les genoux** this project has worn *or* tired me out; **tenir un enfant sur ses genoux** to hold a child on one's knee *or* in one's lap; **sur les genoux des dieux** in the lap of the gods; **faire du g. à qn** to play footsie with sb

(b) *MecE* **joint à g.** ball-and-socket joint

genouillère [ʒ(ə)nujɛr] *nf* **(a)** (*protection du genou*) kneepad, knee guard; *Méd* knee bandage **(b)** *MecE* **articulation à g.** toggle joint

genre [ʒɑ̃r] *nm* **(a)** [①A13,3,a] (*sorte*) kind, sort, type; **quel g. de voitures/de livres?** what kind *or* sort *or* type of cars/books?; **quel g. de vie mène-t-il?** what kind *or* sort of (a) life does he lead?; **toutes les tentatives de ce g. ont échoué** all attempts of this kind *or* sort have failed; **c'est plus dans son g.** that's more in his line; **dans son g., c'est un artiste** he is an artist in his way; **très bon dans son g.** very good of its kind; **décorations en tout g.** *ou* **en tous genres** decorations of all kinds; **c'est ce qu'on fait de mieux dans le g.** it's the best of its kind; **c'est dans le g. de …** it's like …; **un peu dans le g. de …** rather *or* a bit like …; **elle est unique en son g.** she is one of a kind; **un voyage vraiment unique en son g.** a journey unique of its kind; **ce n'est pas mon g.** it's not my style; **coucher à droite et à gauche, ce n'est pas mon g.** I'm not into sleeping around, sleeping around's not my thing; **c'est tout à fait mon g.** (*cette robe*) it's just my style; (*ce mec*) he's just my type; **c'est tout à fait son g. d'arriver en retard** it's just like her to be late; **ce n'est pas son g.** that's not like him; **ce n'est pas le g. (de femme) à se plaindre** she's not the sort (of woman) to complain; **sa nouvelle copine est du genre pot de colle** his new girlfriend's the clinging sort *or* kind; **tu vois le g.?** you know the sort?; **vin blanc g. sauternes** white wine of the Sauternes type; **étui g. maroquin** case in imitation morocco

(b) *Beaux-Arts, Littér* genre; **le roman policier est un g. littéraire très populaire** the detective novel is a very popular literary genre; **le g. comique** comedy; **le g. tragique** tragedy; **peinture de g.** genre painting; **tableau de g.** genre painting *or* picture

(c) (*race*) race; *Bot, Zool etc* genus, *pl* genera; **le g. humain** the human race, mankind

(d) (*goût*) **c'est bon/mauvais g.** it is good/bad form *or* in good/bad taste; *Péj* **bon chic, bon g.** ≈ preppy

(e) [①B5-6,3,A] *Gram* gender; **s'accorder en g. et en nombre** to agree in gender and number

gens [ʒɑ̃] *nmpl* **(a)** (*individus*) people; **il y avait peu de g. dans la salle** there were not many people in the hall; *Th* there was a poor house; **de braves g.** good people; **de petites g.** people of modest means; **des g. sans histoires** nice, ordinary people; **beaucoup de g.** *ou* **bien des g. l'ont vu** lots of *or* many people have seen it; **que vont dire les g.?** what will people say?; *F* **un tas de g. pense(nt) que …** loads of people think that …; **qui sont ces g.-là?** who are these people?; **il y a des g. qui …** there are (some) people who …, some people …

(b) (*individus de même profession, état etc*) **les g. du pays** *ou F* **du coin** the locals, the local people; **jeunes g.** (*garçons et filles*) young people; (*jeunes hommes*) young men

(c) (*nation*) **le droit des g.** the law of nations

(d) *Vieilli* (*domestiques*) servants, domestics; (*de roi etc*) retinue

▶ **gens**: **g. d'affaires** business people, *Vieilli* **g. d'Église** clergy; **g. de lettres** men of letters; **g. de maison** domestic servants; **g. du monde** society people; **g. de théâtre** theatre *or* theatrical people; **g. du voyage** travelling people

gent [ʒɑ̃] *nf Arch, Hum* race, tribe; **la g. moutonnière** the ovine race; **la g. masculine** the male sex

gentiane [ʒɑ̃sjan] *nf* **(a)** *Bot* gentian **(b)** (*liqueur*) gentian bitters

gentil[1]**, -ille** [ʒɑ̃ti, -ij] *adj* **(a)** (*aimable*) kind, nice; **tu es bien g. de m'aider** it's very nice *or* kind *or* good of you to help me; **elle a été très gentille pour** *ou* **avec moi** she was very nice *or* kind to me; *Iron* **elle est bien gentille** she's harmless enough; **c'est g. de votre part (de m'écrire)** it is kind *or* good of you (to write to me); **dire un mot g. à qn** to say a kind word to sb; **sois gentil(le)** (*à un enfant*) be a good boy/girl; (*à un adulte*) be an angel, be a dear; **tu veux bien être g. et aller me chercher des cigarettes** would you be an angel *or* a dear and fetch me some cigarettes; **tu n'as pas été g., tu n'auras pas de bonbon** you haven't been good *or* you've been naughty, you won't get a sweet

(b) (*agréable*) nice; **un g. petit village** a nice *or* pretty little village; **c'est g. chez eux** it's nice at their place, they've got a nice place

(c) (*considérable*) **une gentille somme** a nice little sum

gentil[2] *nm Hist, Rel* Gentile

gentilhomme [ʒɑ̃tijɔm], *pl* **gentilshommes** [ʒɑ̃tizɔm] *nm* gentleman; *Hist* **g. de la Chambre du Roi** gentleman of the Privy Chamber

gentilhommière [ʒɑ̃tijɔmjɛr] *nf* **(a)** country seat, manor house **(b)** (*en Belgique*) boarding house for men

gentilité [ʒɑ̃tilite] *nf Hist, Rel* Gentiles

gentillesse [ʒɑ̃tijɛs] *nf* (*bonté*) kindness; **elle a fait cela par g.** she did that out of kindness; **auriez-vous la g. de …** would you be so kind as to …; **elle a eu la g. de venir elle-même** she was kind enough to come herself; **dire des gentillesses à qn** to say nice *or* kind things to sb

gentillet, -ette [ʒɑ̃tijɛ, -ɛt] *adj* rather *or* quite nice; **roman g.** silly or *F* soppy novel

gentiment [ʒɑ̃timɑ̃] *adv* (*aimablement*) kindly; (*sagement*) nicely; **elle m'a g. proposé de venir avec moi** she kindly offered to come with me; **elle m'a g. tenu compagnie** she was kind enough to keep me company, she kindly kept me company

gentleman, *pl* **gentlemen** [dʒɛntləman] *nm* gentleman; *Courses de chevaux* amateur jockey

gentleman-farmer, *pl* **gentlemen-farmers** [dʒɛntləmanfarmœr] *nm* gentleman farmer

génuflexion [ʒenyflɛksjɔ̃] *nf* genuflexion; **faire une g.** to genuflect

géo [ʒeo] *nf Scol F* geography, geog

géocentrique [ʒeosɑ̃trik] *adj Astron* geocentric

géocentrisme [ʒeosɑ̃trism] *nm* geocentrism

géochimie [ʒeoʃimi] *nf* geochemistry

géode [ʒeɔd] *nf* geode

géodésie [ʒeɔdezi] *nf* geodesy, geodetics

géodésique [ʒeɔdezik] *adj* geodesic, geodetic; **point g.** triangulation point

géodynamique [ʒeodinamik] **1** *adj* geodynamic **2** *nf* geodynamics

géographe [ʒeɔgraf] *n* geographer

géographie [ʒeɔgrafi] *nf* **(a)** (*science*) geography; **g. économique** economic geography; **g. humaine** human geography **(b)** (*livre*) geography book

géographique [ʒeɔgrafik] *adj* geographic(al); **carte g.** map; **dictionnaire g.** gazetteer; **Institut G. National** *Br* ≈ Royal Geographical Society

géographiquement [ʒeɔgrafikmɑ̃] *adv* geographically

geôle [ʒol] *nf Litt* jail, *Br* gaol

geôlier, -ière [ʒolje, -jɛr] *n Litt* jailer, *Br* gaoler

géologie [ʒeɔlɔʒi] *nf* geology

géologique [ʒeɔlɔʒik] *adj* geological

géologiquement [ʒeɔlɔʒikmɑ̃] *adv* geologically

géologue [ʒeɔlɔg] *n* geologist

géomagnétique [ʒeomaɲetik] *adj* geomagnetic

géomagnétisme [ʒeomaɲetism] *nm* geomagnetism

géomancie [ʒeɔmɑ̃si] *nf* geomancy

géométral, -ale, -aux, -ales [ʒeɔmetral, -o] **1** *adj* (*projection, élévation*) flat (*as opposed to perspective view*) **2** *nm* flat projection

géomètre [ʒeɔmɛtr] *nm* **(a)** geometer, geometrician; **(arpenteur) g.** (land) surveyor **(b)** *Ent* geometer (moth)

géométrie [ʒeɔmetri] *nf* geometry; **g. plane** plane geometry; **g. analytique** analytical *or* co-ordinate geometry; **g. dans l'espace** *ou* **à trois dimensions** solid *or* three-dimensional geometry; *Av* **avion à g. fixe/variable** fixed-/variable-geometry *or* fixed-/swing-wing aircraft; *Fig* **à g. variable** that varies according to circumstances

géométrique [ʒeɔmetrik] *adj* geometric(al); **progression g.** geometrical progression; **esprit g.** orderly mind

géométriquement [ʒeɔmetrikmɑ̃] *adv* geometrically

géomorphologie [ʒeomɔrfɔlɔʒi] *nf* geomorphology

géophone [ʒeɔfɔn] *nm* geophone, sound detector

géophysicien, -ienne [ʒeofizisjɛ̃, -jɛn] *n* geophysicist

géophysique [ʒeofizik] **1** *adj* geophysical **2** *nf* geophysics

géophyte [ʒeɔfit] *nm Bot* geophyte

géopolitique [ʒeopɔlitik] *nf* geopolitics

georgette [ʒɔrʒɛt] *nf Tex* **crêpe g.** georgette (crepe)

Géorgie [ʒeɔrʒi] *nf* Georgia; **G. du Sud** South Georgia

géorgien, -ienne [ʒeɔrʒjɛ̃, -jɛn] **1** *adj* Georgian **2** *n* **G.** Georgian

Géorgiques (les) [leʒeɔrʒik] *nfpl Littér* (*de Virgile*) the Georgics

géostationnaire [ʒeostasjɔnɛr] *adj Astronaut* **satellite g.** geostationary satellite

géosynchrone [ʒeosɛ̃krɔn, ʒeosɛ̃kron] *adj* geosynchronous

géosynclinal, -aux [ʒeosɛ̃klinal, -o] *Géol nm* geosyncline

géothermie [ʒeotɛrmi] *nf* geothermics

géothermique [ʒeotɛrmik] *adj* geothermal

gérance [ʒerɑ̃s] *nf* (*action*) (*d'une entreprise*) management; (*fonction*) managership; **mettre un commerce en g.** to appoint a manager for a business; **prendre un commerce en g.** to take over the management of a business; **une g. de cinq ans** a five-year managership; **g. libre** tenant management; (*entreprise*) rented business

géranium [ʒeranjɔm] *nm* (*sauvage*) geranium, crane's bill; (*plante d'ornement*) pelargonium, *F* geranium

gérant, -ante [ʒerɑ̃, -ɑ̃t] *n* manager, *f* manageress; **g. d'un journal** managing editor of a newspaper; **g. d'affaires** business manager; **g. majoritaire** manager with a controlling interest; **g. minoritaire** manager with a minority interest; **g. non associé** salaried manager, manager with no holding in a business

gerbage [ʒɛrbaʒ] *nm* **(a)** (*des céréales*) binding, sheaving **(b)** (*action d'empiler*) (*de tonneaux, de ballots*) stacking, piling

gerbe [ʒɛrb] *nf* **(a)** [①A12,1,d,y] (*de blé*) sheaf; **mettre le blé en gerbes** to bind the wheat into sheaves, to sheave *or* sheaf the wheat; **g. de fleurs** spray of flowers; **g. d'étincelles** shower of sparks; **g. de feu** burst of flame; **g. d'eau** spray *or* shower of water **(b)** *Mil* cone of fire **(c)** *Vulg* **avoir la g.** (*avoir envie de vomir*) to feel like throwing up *or* puking; (*vomir*) to throw up, to puke

gerber [ʒɛrbe] *vt* **(a)** (*mettre en gerbes*) (*céréales*) to bind, to sheave, to sheaf **(b)** *Tech* (*empiler*) (*tonneaux, cageots, caisses*) to stack, to pile **(c)** *Vulg* (*vomir*) to throw up, to puke, *Am* to upchuck; **ça me fait g. de voir que ...** it makes me puke to see that ...

gerbera [ʒɛrbera] *nm Bot* gerbera

gerbeuse [ʒɛrbøz] *nf* (*pour tonneaux etc*) stacker, stacking machine

gerbier [ʒɛrbje] *nm* (*de céréales*) stack

gerbille [ʒɛrbij] *nf* gerbil

gerboise [ʒɛrbwaz] *nf* jerboa

gerce [ʒɛrs] *nf* **(a)** (*fente*) (*dans le bois*) crack, fissure **(b)** *Ent* clothes moth

gercé [ʒɛrse] *adj* cracked; (*mains, lèvres*) chapped

gercer [ʒɛrse] **(il gerçait; il gerça) 1** *vt* (*mains, lèvres*) to chap; (*bois, terre*) to crack **2** *vi* (*des lèvres, mains*) to chap **3 se gercer** *vpr* (*des lèvres, mains*) to chap

gerçure [ʒɛrsyr] *nf* (*sur la peau*) chap; (*dans le sol*) crack, fissure; *Tech* (*dans le bois*) shake, flaw; (*dans le métal*) hair crack, hairline; **avoir des gerçures aux mains/lèvres** to have chapped hands/lips; **pour éviter d'avoir des gerçures** to avoid chapped hands/lips

gérer [ʒere] **(je gère, n. gérons; je gérerai)** *vt* (*journal, hôtel etc*) to manage, to run; (*région, état etc*) to manage, to administer; (*finances, conflit, situation difficile*) to manage; (*temps*) to organize, to manage; **mal g. ses finances** to mismanage one's finances; **g. la crise** to see the crisis through, to manage the crisis; **g. une affaire** to handle a matter

gerfaut [ʒɛrfo] *nm* gyrfalcon, gerfalcon

gériatre [ʒerjatr] *nmf Méd* geriatrician

gériatrie [ʒerjatri] *nf Méd* geriatrics

gériatrique [ʒerjatrik] *adj Méd* geriatric

germain[1], -aine [ʒɛrmɛ̃, -ɛn] *Hist* **1** *adj* Germanic, Teutonic **2** *n* **G.** German, Teuton

germain[2] *adj Jur* **frère g.** full brother; **sœur germaine** full sister; **cousin g.** first cousin; **cousins issus de germains** second cousins

germandrée [ʒɛrmɑ̃dre] *nf Bot* germander

germanique [ʒɛrmanik] **1** *adj* **(a)** *Hist* (*relatif aux Germains*) Germanic, Teutonic **(b)** (*relatif aux Allemands et à l'Allemagne*) German **2** *nm Ling* Germanic

germanisant, -ante [ʒɛrmanizɑ̃, -ɑ̃t] *n* Germanophile

germanisation [ʒɛrmanizasjɔ̃] *nf* Germanization

germaniser [ʒɛrmanize] *vt* to Germanize

germanisme [ʒɛrmanism] *nm* Germanism

germaniste [ʒɛrmanist] *n Ling* Germanist, student of German

germanium [ʒɛrmanjɔm] *nm Ch* germanium

germanophile [ʒɛrmanɔfil] *adj, n* Germanophile

germanophobe [ʒɛrmanɔfɔb] **1** *adj* Germanophobic **2** *n* Germanophobe

germanophobie [ʒɛrmanɔfɔbi] *nf* Germanophobia

germanophone [ʒɛrmanɔfɔn] **1** *adj* German-speaking **2** *n* German speaker

germe [ʒɛrm] *nm* **(a)** (*embryon, plantule etc*), *Biol* germ; (*de pomme de terre*) eye; **germes de soja** bean sprouts **(b)** (*virus*) germ; **germes pathogènes** pathogenic bacteria; *Fig* **les germes d'une révolution/de la corruption** the seeds of a revolution/of corruption; **contenir qch en g.** to contain the seeds of sth

germer [ʒɛrme] *vi* (*d'une plante*) to germinate; (*des pommes de terre*) to sprout; *Fig* (*d'une idée, d'un plan*) to germinate

germicide [ʒɛrmisid] **1** *nm* germicide **2** *adj* germicidal

germinal, -aux, -ale, -aux, -ales [ʒɛrminal, -o] **1** *adj Biol* germinal **2** *nm Hist* the seventh month of the French Republican calendar (*March-April*)

germinateur, -trice [ʒɛrminatœr, -tris] *adj* germinative

germinatif, -ive [ʒɛrminatif, -iv] *adj Biol* germinative, germinal; **plasma g.** germ plasm

germination [ʒɛrminasjɔ̃] *nf Biol* germination

germoir [ʒɛrmwar] *nm* **(a)** (*pour les plantes*) seed tray **(b)** (*d'une brasserie*) malt house, malting

gérondif [ʒerɔ̃dif] *nm Gram* **(a)** [①A42-44] gerund **(b)** (*cas latin*) gerundive; **au g.** in the gerundive

gérontocratie [ʒerɔ̃tɔkrasi] *nf Pol* gerontocracy

gérontologie [ʒerɔ̃tɔlɔʒi] *nf Méd* gerontology

gérontologue [ʒerɔ̃tɔlɔg] *n Méd* gerontologist

gérontophile [ʒerɔ̃tɔfil] *n* gerontophile

gérontophilie [ʒerɔ̃tɔfili] *nf* gerontophilia

gésier [ʒezje] *nm Orn* gizzard; *Arg* (*estomac*) guts

gésir [ʒezir] *vi* (*used only in the following forms: prp* **gisant**; *pr ind* **il gît, n. gisons, vous gisez, ils gisent**; *impf* **je gisais** *etc*) *Litt* to lie; **il gisait dans son sang** he was lying *or* weltering in his blood; **ci-gît/-gisent ...** (*sur une tombe*) here lies/lie ...; **des papiers froissés gisaient çà et là** crumpled papers were lying here and there; *Fig* **c'est là que gît le lièvre** that's the crux of the matter

gesse [ʒɛs] *nf Bot* vetch, everlasting pea; **g. odorante** sweet pea

gestapo [gɛstapo] *nf Hist* Gestapo; **un officier de la g.** a Gestapo officer

gestation [ʒɛstasjɔ̃] *nf Physiol* gestation; *Fig* **projet/livre/***etc* **en g.** plan/book/*etc* in preparation

geste[1] [ʒɛst] *nm* **(a)** (*mouvement*) gesture; **faire un g.** to make a gesture; **pas un g. ou je tire** one move and I'll shoot; **le moindre g., et toute la classe est punie!** one move out of any of you and the entire class will be punished; **d'un g., il nous a fait entrer** he waved us in, he gestured to us to go/come in; **saluer qn d'un g.** to wave to sb; **il lui montra la porte d'un g.** he gestured him towards the door; **il me le fit comprendre d'un g.** he indicated it to me with a gesture; **d'un g., elle m'indiqua où se trouvait le coffre-fort** she gestured to where the safe was; **d'un g. de la main** with a wave of the hand; **je te l'indiquerai d'un g. de la main** I'll indicate it to you; **faire un g. (de la main)** (*pour dire au revoir*) to give a wave (of one's hand), to wave; **sans faire un g.** without moving; **écarter qn d'un g.** to wave sb aside; **g. de résignation** shrug of resignation; **joindre le g. à la parole** to suit the action to the word

(b) (*action*) gesture; **un beau g.** a fine *or* handsome gesture; **un g. de générosité** a generous gesture; **faire un g.** to make a gesture; **tu pourrais faire un g. pour les aider** you could do something to help them; **faire un g. pour les sans-abri** to do something for the homeless, to do something to help the homeless; **elle n'a pas fait un g. (pour l'aider)** she didn't do a thing *or* lift a finger (to help him); **avoir le g. large** to be generous

geste[2] *nf Littér* **(chanson de) g.** chanson de geste (*mediaeval verse chronicle of heroic exploits*)

gesticulation [ʒɛstikylasjɔ̃] *nf* gesticulation, gesticulating

gesticuler [ʒɛstikyle] *vi* to gesticulate

gestion [ʒɛstjɔ̃] *nf Fin* (*d'une entreprise, de travaux, des comptes etc*) management; (*d'affaires*) conduct; **mauvaise g.** bad management, mismanagement

▶ **gestion**: **g. administrative** administration; **g. de bases de**

données database management; *Ordinat* **g. des césures** hyphenation control; **g. de la communication** communications management; **g. de comptes-clés** key-account management; **g. par consensus** consensus management; *Ordinat* **g. des couleurs** colour management; *Ordinat* **g. des disquettes** disk management; **g. de la distribution physique** physical distribution management; **g. d'entreprise** business management; *Ordinat* **g. de fichiers** file management; **g. financière** financial management; **g. hôtelière** hotel administration *or* management, hospitality management; *Com* **g. logistique** logistics management; **g. de marque** brand management; *Com* **g. des matières** materials management; *Ordinat* **g. de mémoire** memory management; **g. mercatique** marketing management; *Ordinat* **g. multifeuille** (*de tableur*) multi-spreadsheet handling; **g. par objectifs** management by objectives; *Ordinat* **g. du papier** paper handling; *Ordinat* **g. de parc réseau** network management; *Ind* **g. de la production** production control; **g. de produits** product management; **g. qualité** quality control, quality management; **g. de la qualité totale** total quality management, TQM; **g. des ressources humaines** human resources management; **g. des sociétés** business management; *Ordinat* **g. sonore** sound handling, sound management; **g. de stocks** inventory management; **g. des stocks** inventory *or* stock control; **g. stratégique** strategic management

gestionnaire [ʒɛstjɔnɛr] **1** *adj* administrative **2** *n* **(a)** administrator; (*d'un service*) manager **(b)** *Ordinat* manager, driver; **g. de fichiers** file manager; **g. de fichiers et de répertoires** filer; **g. de la souris** mouse driver; **g. de mémoire** memory manager; **g. de projets** project management package; **g. de périphérique** device driver; **g. de réseau** network manager

gestuel, -elle [ʒɛstɥɛl] **1** *adj* gestural **2** *nf* **gestuelle** body language

Gethsémani [ʒɛtsemani] *n Bible* Gethsemane

geyser [ʒɛzɛr] *nm* geyser

Ghana [gana] *nm* Ghana

ghanéen, -éenne [ganeɛ̃, -eɛn] **1** *adj* Ghanaian **2** *n* **G.** Ghanaian

ghetto [gɛto] *nm* ghetto

gibbeux, -euse [ʒibø, -øz] *adj* gibbous

gibbon [ʒibɔ̃] *nm* gibbon

gibbosité [ʒibozite] *nf* hump

gibecière [ʒibsjɛr] *nf* (*de chasseur*) game bag

gibelotte [ʒiblɔt] *nf Culin* **g. (de lapin)** fricassee of rabbit cooked in white wine

giberne [ʒibɛrn] *nf Hist* cartridge pouch; *Prov* **tout soldat a un bâton de maréchal dans sa g.** every private has the makings of a general

gibet [ʒibɛ] *nm* gibbet, gallows

gibier [ʒibje] *nm* game; **menu g.** small game; **gros g.** big game; *Fig* big game, big fish; **manger du g.** to eat game; *Fig* **beau g.** attractive women

▶ **gibier**: **g. d'eau** waterfowl; **g. à plumes** game birds; **g. à poil** game animals; *Fig* **g. de potence** gallows bird

giboulée [ʒibule] *nf* sudden shower *or* downpour; **giboulées de mars** ≈ April showers

giboyeux, -euse [ʒibwajø, -øz] *adj* abounding in game, well stocked with game

gibus [ʒibys] *nm* opera hat, crush hat

giclée [ʒikle] *nf* (*d'eau, de sang*) spurt

giclement [ʒikləmɑ̃] *nm* (*de boue*) splashing up; (*de sang*) spurting

gicler [ʒikle] *vi* (*du sang*) to spurt; (*de l'eau*) to spurt out, to squirt out; (*de la boue*) to splash up; **faire g. de l'eau avec un pistolet à eau** to squirt water out of a water pistol; **et ça m'a giclé à la figure** and it splashed into my face

gicleur [ʒiklœr] *nm Aut* jet; **g. de ralenti** idling jet

gifle [ʒifl] *nf* slap (in the face); *Fig* slap in the face; **donner** *ou F* **flanquer une g. à qn** to slap sb (in the face), to give sb a slap (in the face); **prendre** *ou* **recevoir une g.** to get a slap (in the face)

gifler [ʒifle] *vt* **g. qn** to slap sb (in the face), to give sb a slap (in the face); **visage giflé par le vent** face lashed by the wind; *Fig* **mots qui giflent** stinging words

GIG [ʒig or ʒeiʒe] *nm abrév* **grand invalide de guerre**

GIGN [ʒeiʒeɛn] *nm abrév* (**groupe d'intervention de la gendarmerie nationale**) special task force of the gendarmerie

giga [ʒiga] *adj inv F* mega

gigahertz [ʒigaɛrts] *nm Phys* gigahertz

gigantesque [ʒigɑ̃tɛsk] *adj* gigantic; **d'une taille g.** gigantic, of a gigantic size

gigantesquement [ʒigɑ̃tɛskəmɑ̃] *adv* gigantically

gigantisme [ʒigɑ̃tism] *nm Méd* gi(g)antism; *Fig* **le g. des villes** the gigantic size of the cities

gigaoctet [ʒigaɔktɛ] *nm Ordinat* gigabyte

gigogne [ʒigɔɲ] *adj* **la mère G.** ≈ the Old Woman who lived in a shoe; **une mère G.** = the mother of a large and ever-increasing family; **tables gigognes** nest of tables; **lits gigognes** beds that fit one inside the other; **poupées gigognes** nest of (Russian) dolls; *Mil* **fusées gigognes** multistage rocket

gigolette [ʒigɔlɛt] *nf Culin* leg of turkey

gigolo [ʒigɔlo] *nm F* gigolo

gigot [ʒigo] *nm* **(a)** *Culin* (*d'agneau, de mouton*) leg **(b)** (*d'un cheval*) hind leg; *F Hum* (*d'une personne*) leg, thigh

gigoter [ʒigɔte] *vi* **(a)** *F* (*se trémousser*) to wriggle, to fidget **(b)** (*d'un animal à l'agonie*) to give a convulsive jerk

gigue[1] [ʒig] *nf* (*danse*) jig

gigue[2] *nf* **(a)** *Culin* (*de chevreuil*) haunch **(b)** *Arch F* **gigues** (*jambes*) stumps, pins **(c)** *F* **une grande g.** (*fille grande et maigre*) a beanpole (of a girl)

gilde [gild] *nf Hist* guild

gilet [ʒilɛ] *nm* (*sans manches*) waistcoat, *Am* vest; (*veste en laine*) cardigan; *Fig F* **venir pleurer dans le g. de qn** to come crying to sb

▶ **gilet**: **g. d'armes** fencing jacket; **g. pare-balles** bulletproof jacket; **g. de sauvetage** life jacket

gin [dʒin] *nm* gin; **g. tonic** gin and tonic, G and T

gindre [ʒɛ̃dr] *nm* baker's assistant

gingembre [ʒɛ̃ʒɑ̃br] *nm* ginger; **racine de g.** root ginger, fresh ginger; **biscuits au g.** ginger biscuits

gingival, -ale, -aux, -ales [ʒɛ̃ʒival, -o] *adj Anat* gingival

gingivite [ʒɛ̃ʒivit] *nf Méd* gingivitis

ginseng [ʒɛsɑ̃, ʒinsɑ̃g] *nm Bot* ginseng

girafe [ʒiraf] *nf* **(a)** [①A12,1,g,y] (*animal*) giraffe; *Fig* (*personne*) beanpole; *F* **peigner la g.** to waste one's time; (*ne rien faire*) to do damn all; *Fig* **avoir un cou de g.** to have a long neck **(b)** *Cin Arg* (*de micro*) boom; **g. avec plate-forme d'opérateur** perambulator

girafeau, -eaux [ʒirafo], **girafon** [ʒirafɔ̃] *nm* baby giraffe

girandole [ʒirɑ̃dɔl] *nf* **(a)** (*chandelier*) girandole, candelabra; (*feux d'artifice*) girandole **(b)** (*grappe*) (*de fleurs*) cluster; (*de bijoux*) girandole

girasol [ʒirasɔl] *nm Minér* fire opal, girasol

giration [ʒirasjɔ̃] *nf* gyration; *Naut* **cercle de g.** turning circle

giratoire [ʒiratwar] *adj* (*mouvement*) gyratory; **sens g.** roundabout, *Am* traffic circle

giravion [ʒiravjɔ̃] *nm Av* rotary wing aircraft, rotorcraft

girelle [ʒirɛl] *nf Zool* rainbow wrasse

girl [gœrl] *nf* chorus girl, showgirl

girofle [ʒirɔfl] *nm Bot* clove; **un clou de g.** a clove; **huile de g.** oil of cloves

giroflée [ʒirɔfle] *nf Bot* stock; **g. jaune** *ou* **des murailles** wallflower; *Fig F* **une g. (à cinq feuilles)** a slap in the face

giroflier [ʒirɔflije] *nm Bot* clove tree

girolle [ʒirɔl] *nf* chanterelle (mushroom)

giron [ʒirɔ̃] *nm* **(a)** (*partie du corps*) lap; **tenir un enfant dans son g.** to hold a child in *or* on one's lap; *Fig* **garder un enfant dans son g.** to wrap a child in cotton wool, to mollycoddle a child; **se réfugier dans le g. familial** to take refuge in the bosom of one's family; **le g. de l'Église** the bosom of the Church **(b)** *Constr* (*d'une marche*) tread

girond [ʒirɔ̃] *adj F* (*souvent au sujet d'une femme*) curvy; *Pej* on the plump side

girondin, -ine [ʒirɔ̃dɛ̃] **1** *adj* **(a)** *Hist* Girondist **(b)** **le vignoble g.** the vineyards of the Gironde **2** *n* **G.** (*natif*) native of the Gironde; (*habitant*) inhabitant of the Gironde **3** *nm Hist* Girondist

girouette [ʒirwɛt] *nf* weathercock, (weather)vane; *Fig* (*personne*) weathercock

gisant [ʒizɑ̃] **1** *adj Litt* (*personne*) lifeless **2** *nm Beaux-Arts* (*sur une tombe*) recumbent figure

gisement [ʒizmɑ̃] *nm* **(a)** *Minér* deposit; *Min* lode, vein; **g. pétrolifère** oilfield; **gisements houillers** coal deposits **(b)** *Av Naut* bearing; **g. à la boussole** compass bearing

▶ **gisement**: *Com* **g. de clientèle** pool of customers, potential customers, *Archéol* **g. préhistorique** prehistoric site

gitan, -ane [ʒitɑ̃, -an] **1** *adj* gipsy; **la culture gitane** gipsy *or* Romany culture **2** *n* gipsy **3** *nf* **Gitane**® Gitane® (*popular brand of cigarette*)

gîte[1] [ʒit] *nm* **(a)** (*logement*) lodging, resting place; (*d'un cerf*) lair; (*d'un lièvre*) form; **ne pas avoir de g.** to be homeless; **revenir au g.** to return to one's home; **offrir le g. et le couvert à qn** to offer sb board and lodging; **trouver un lièvre au g.** to find a hare sitting **(b)** *Min* stratum, bed, deposit; **gîtes houillers** coal deposits

▶ **gîte**: **g. 'camping-caravaning' à la ferme** campsite in close proximity to a farm; **g. 'chambre d'hôte'** bed and breakfast; *Culin* **g. de derrière** shank; *Culin* **g. de devant** shin, *Am* shank; **g. d'enfants** holiday placements for children with a rural family; **g. équestre** rural gîte with horses for hire; **g. d'étape** transit accommodation for hikers, cyclists etc; *Culin* **g. à la noix** silverside; **g. rural** gîte, self-catering holiday cottage/apartment; **g. rural communal** gîte communally owned by a village or group of villages

gîte² *nf Naut* list(ing); **avoir** *ou* **prendre de la g.** to list, to heel; **donner de la g. sur tribord** to list to starboard

gîter [ʒite] *vi* **(a)** *Naut* to list, to heel **(b)** *Vieilli* (*loger*) to lodge; (*d'un animal*) to find shelter; (*d'un oiseau*) to perch

giton [ʒitɔ̃] *nm* catamite

givrage [ʒivraʒ] *nm Av* icing

givre [ʒivr] *nm* **(a)** *Météo* frost, hoar frost, rime **(b)** (*dans un réfrigérateur, sur un pare-brise etc*) frost

givré [ʒivre] *adj* **(a)** (*couvert de givre*) (*arbre, gazon*) covered with frost; *Av* iced up **(b)** *Culin* **orange givrée** = orange sorbet served in an orange skin; **un verre givré avec du sucre** a glass frosted with sugar **(c)** *F* (*fou*) nuts, batty; **il est complètement g.** he's completely off his rocker

givrer [ʒivre] **1** *vt Météo* to cover with frost **2** *vi Av* to ice up **3 se givrer** *vpr Av* to ice up

givreux, -euse [ʒivrø, -øz] *adj* (*diamants*) with icy flecks

givrure [ʒivryr] *nf* (*sur un diamant*) icy fleck

glabre [glɑbr] *adj Biol* glabrous, smooth; **visage g.** (*rasé*) clean-shaven face; (*imberbe*) hairless face

glaçage [glasaʒ] *nm* **(a)** *Culin* (*d'un gâteau*) icing, *Am* frosting; (*de la pâte à tarte*) glazing **(b)** *Tech* glazing

glaçant [glasɑ̃] *adj Fig* (*manière, accueil*) frosty, icy; *Vieilli* (*froideur, vent*) icy

glace [glas] *nf* **(a)** (*eau à l'état solide*) ice; **patiner sur la g.** to skate on the ice; **cube de g.** ice cube; *Can* **sur g.** (*boisson*) on the rocks; **vous voulez de la g.?** do you want ice (in it)?; **avec g. ou sans g.?** with or without ice?; **g. pilée** crushed ice; **un pain de g.** a block of ice; **glaces de fond** bottom ice, anchor ice; **g. flottante** floating ice, drift ice; **navire retenu** *ou* **pris par les glaces** icebound ship; *Fig* **rester de g.** to remain impassive; *Fig* **un accueil de g.** a frosty *or* icy reception; *Fig* **rompre la g.** to break the ice

(b) (*vitre*) (pane of) glass; (*miroir*) mirror; **se regarder dans la g.** to look at oneself in the mirror; *Fig* **il ne peut plus se regarder dans la g.** he can't look himself in the face; **Galerie des Glaces** (*à Versailles*) Hall of Mirrors

(c) (*crème congelée*) ice cream; **une glace** an ice cream, *Br* an ice; **g. à la vanille/à la fraise** vanilla/strawberry ice cream; **g. à l'italienne** soft ice cream; **un cornet de g.** a(n ice-cream) cone *or Br* cornet; **marchand de glaces** ice-cream man *or* seller

(d) *Culin* (*sur gâteau*) icing, *Am* frosting; (*sur pâte à tarte*) glaze

(e) (*défaut*) (*d'un diamant*) flaw

▶ **glace**: *Aut* **g. de custode** quarterlight, quarterwindow; **g. à main** hand mirror; **g. sans tain** two-way mirror

glacé [glase] *adj* **(a)** (*rivière, lac*) frozen; (*pièce*) freezing (cold), icy (cold); (*avec des glaçons*) (*café*) iced; **l'eau est glacée** the water is icy cold *or* freezing (cold); **j'ai les pieds glacés** my feet are freezing *or* frozen, my feet are (as) cold as ice; **g. jusqu'aux os** chilled to the bone *or* marrow; *Fig* **accueil/politesse glacé(e)** frosty *or* icy reception/politeness; **regard g.** cold stare **(b)** (*brillant*) (*papier, Phot épreuve*) glossy; **gants glacés** glacé kid gloves; **soie glacée** watered silk, glazed thread; *Culin* **cerises glacées** glacé cherries

glacer [glase] **(je glaçai(s); n. glaçons) 1** *vt* **(a)** (*congeler*) to freeze; (*refroidir*) to chill; *Fig* **cela me glace (le sang)** it makes my blood run cold; **des hurlements/des propos à vous g. le sang** spine-chilling words *or* blood-curdling screams; **il me glace** he gives me the creeps; **g. qn d'effroi/de terreur** to paralyse *or* freeze sb with fear/terror **(b)** *Culin* (*gâteau*) to ice, *Am* to frost; (*pâte à tarte*) to glaze **(c)** *Tech* to glaze **2 se glacer** *vpr* (*de l'eau*) to freeze; **son sang se glaça** his blood ran cold

glacerie [glasri] *nf* (*fabrique*) glass works; (*commerce*) glass trade

glaceur [glasœr] *nm* glazer

glaceux, -euse [glasø, -øz] *adj* (*diamant*) flawed

glaciaire [glasjɛr] **1** *adj Géol* (*vallée*) glacial; **période g.** ice age **2** *nm* ice age

glacial, -ale, -als *or* **-aux, -ales** [glasjal, -o] *adj* (*pl rarely used*) **(a)** (*température, froid, temps, air*) freezing, icy; **vent g.** icy *or* cutting *or* bitter wind; **zone glaciale** arctic region **(b)** *Fig* (*ton, manière, accueil, ambiance, politesse*) frosty, icy; (*sourire*) frosty; **elle est vraiment glaciale, cette femme** that woman is a real cold fish

glacialement [glasjalmɑ̃] *adv* frostily, icily

glaciation [glasjasjɔ̃] *nf* glaciation

glacier¹ [glasje] *nm Géol* glacier

glacier² *nm* (*fabricant*) ice-cream maker; (*vendeur*) ice-cream seller; **pâtissier-g., g-confiseur** confectioner and ice-cream seller

glacière [glasjɛr] *nf* **(a)** (*de pique-nique*) cool bag *or* box, *Austr F* Esky® **(b)** *F* (*de frigidaire*) freezer compartment, icebox; **cette chambre est une vraie g.!** this room's like an icebox! **(c)** *Arch* (*local*) ice room

glacis [glasi] *nm* **(a)** *Mil, Géol* glacis **(b)** *Constr* ramp **(c)** *Beaux-Arts* glaze

glaçon [glasɔ̃] *nm* (*pendant*) icicle; (*pour rafraîchir une boisson*) ice cube; (*sur une rivière*) **glaçons** drift *or* broken ice; **vous prendrez votre whisky avec ou sans glaçons?** would you like ice in your whisky?; **avec ou sans glaçons?** with or without ice?; **un whisky avec des glaçons** a whisky on the rocks; *Fig F* **c'est un g.!** he's a cold fish!; **j'ai les pieds comme des glaçons** my feet are like blocks of ice

glaçure [glasyr] *nf Cér* glaze

gladiateur [gladjatœr] *nm* gladiator; **combat de gladiateurs** gladiatorial combat

glaïeul [glajœl] *nm* gladiolus, *pl* gladioli; **g. des marais** (sword) flag

glaire [glɛr] *nf* **(a)** *Vieilli* (*d'œuf*) white **(b)** *Méd* mucus, phlegm; **g. cervicale** cervical mucus

glaireux, -euse [glɛrø, -øz] *adj* glairy, glaireous

glaise [glɛz] *nf* **(terre) g.** clay

glaiser [gleze] *vt* **(a)** (*amender avec de la glaise*) (*sol*) to clay, to dress with clay **(b)** (*enduire de glaise*) to line with clay

glaiseux, -euse [glɛzø, -øz] *adj* clayey

glaisière [glɛzjɛr] *nf* clay pit

glaive [glɛv] *nm Arch, Litt* blade, sword; *Fig Litt* **le g. de la justice** the sword of justice

glanage [glanaʒ] *nm* gleaning

gland [glɑ̃] *nm* **(a)** (*passementerie*) tassel **(b)** *Bot* acorn; **glands** (*pour les cochons*) mast **(c)** *Anat* glans; *Fig très F* **tu es un vrai g.** you're a stupid prick

glande [glɑ̃d] *nf Anat, Bot* gland; **g. surréanale** suprarenal gland; **glandes sexuelles** sexual glands; *Vulg* **foutre les glandes à qn** (*énerver*) to piss off; (*mettre mal à l'aise*) to put the wind up sb; *Vulg* **avoir les glandes** (*être énervé*) to be pissed off; (*être mal à l'aise*) to have the wind up

glander [glɑ̃de] *vi très F* (*ne rien faire*) to loaf around; (*attendre*) to hang around; **mais qu'est-ce qu'il glande, il devait arriver à trois heures** where the hell is he, he was supposed to be here at three; **ça fait deux ans qu'il glande** that's two years now he's been loafing around *or* doing sweet FA; **je me demande ce qu'il glande toute la journée** I wonder what the hell he gets up to all day; **j'en ai rien à g.** I don't give a shit

glandeur, -euse [glɑ̃dœr, -øz] *n très F* layabout; **c'est un vrai g., ce mec-là** the guy does sweet FA

glandouiller [glɑ̃duje] *vi très F* (*ne rien faire*) to loaf around; **arrête de g. et fais quelque chose d'utile** (*ne rien faire*) get off your backside and do something useful; (*ne rien faire d'utile*) stop mucking around and do something useful

glandulaire [glɑ̃dylɛr], **glanduleux, -euse** [glɑ̃dylø, -øz] *adj* glandular; **infection glanduleuse** glandular infection

glane [glan] *nf Agr* **(a)** (*action*) gleaning; **glanes** gleanings **(b)** (*d'oignons*) string, rope

glaner [glane] *vt Agr* to glean; *Fig* **g. des renseignements** to glean information

glaneur, -euse [glanœr, -øz] *n Agr* gleaner

glapir [glapir] **1** *vi* (*d'un chien*) to yelp, to yap; (*d'un renard*) to bark; (*d'une personne, d'une radio, d'un saxophone*) to shriek **2** *vt* to shriek

glapissant [glapisɑ̃] *adj* (*chien*) yapping, yelping; **voix glapissante** shrill voice

glapissement [glapismɑ̃] *nm* (*de chiots*) yapping, yelping; (*de renards*) barking; (*de personne, tempête, vent*) shrieking; **on entendait les glapissements de la concierge dans l'escalier** the concierge could be heard shrieking on the stairs

glas [glɑ] *nm* knell; **sonner le g.** to toll the knell; *Fig* **sonner le g. de qch** to sound the death knell for sth

glasnost [glasnɔst] *nf* glasnost

glaucome [glokom] *nm Méd* glaucoma

glauque [glok] *adj* **(a)** (*couleur*) blue-green, *Litt* glaucous **(b)** (*trouble*) (*eau*) murky; *F* (*film, plaisanteries*) tasteless, in bad taste; **je suis partie très vite, l'ambiance était g.** I left very quickly since the atmosphere was pretty heavy; **il est un peu g., son copain** his friend's a bit creepy

glaviot [glavjo] *nm très F* gob of spit

glavioter [glavjɔte] *vi très F* to spit, *Br* to gob

glèbe [glɛb] *nf* **(a)** *Arch* (*motte de terre*) clod; (*terre lourde et grasse*) heavy soil **(b)** *Arch, Litt* (*sol cultivé*) glebe, soil, land

glène¹ [glɛn] *nf Anat* socket

glène² *nf Naut* coil of rope

glissade [glisad] *nf* sliding; (*pas de danse*) glissade; **faire une g.** *ou* **des glissades** to slide; *Av* **g. sur l'aile** side slip; *Av* **g. sur la queue** tail slide

glissage [glisaʒ] *nm* sliding down (*of cut timber in the mountains*)

glissant [glisɑ̃] *adj* **(a)** (*anguille, trottoir etc*) slippery; *Fig* **c'est un terrain g.** it's a delicate *or* tricky subject; **elle est sur un terrain g.** she is on dangerous ground **(b)** *MecE* **joint g.** sliding joint, slip joint

glisse [glis] *nf* **(a)** *Ski* (*aptitude à glisser*) glide **(b)** **sports de g.** = sports involving sliding motion, e. g. skiing, surfing, windsurfing

glissé [glise] *adj, nm* (*de danseur*) **(pas) g.** glissé

glissement [glismɑ̃] *nm* (*action*) sliding; *Av* sideslipping; *Pol* **g. à gauche** *ou* **vers la gauche** swing to the left

▶ **glissement**: *Électron* **g. de fréquence** frequency variation; *Ling* **g. de sens** shift in meaning; *Géol* **g. de terrain** landslide; (*moins important*) landslip

glisser[1] [glise] **1** *vi* **(a)** (*par accident*) to slip; (*d'une roue*) to skid; **le couteau lui a glissé des mains** the knife slipped from his hands; **son pied a glissé** his foot slipped; *Fig* **g. entre les mains** *ou* **les doigts de qn** to slip through sb's fingers; *Av* **g. sur l'aile** to sideslip

(b) (*volontairement*) (*sur la glace, la neige etc*) to slide; **faire g.** (*pièce d'une machine*) to slide; **se laisser g. le long d'une corde** to slide down a rope; *Ordinat* **faire g.** (*pointeur etc*) to drag; **g.-lâcher** to drag and drop

(c) (*avancer comme en glissant*) (*sur l'eau*) to glide; *Fig* **un sourire ironique glissa sur ses lèvres** an ironic smile stole over his face

(d) **g. sur** (*sujet*) to touch lightly on, to skip over; **l'épée lui glissa sur les côtes** the sword glanced off his ribs; *Fig* **mes reproches ont glissé sur lui comme l'eau sur les plumes d'un canard** I took him to task but it was like water off a duck's back; **rien ne l'émeut, tout glisse sur lui** nothing bothers him, it's all water off a duck's back; **glissons (là-dessus)** let's not dwell on that, let's skip over that

(e) (*avoir une surface glissante*) to be slippery; **fais attention, ça glisse ce matin** watch out, it's slippery this morning; **la chaussée glisse beaucoup** the road is very slippery

2 *vt* (*introduire, passer etc*) to slip; **g. une lettre sous la porte** to slip a letter under the door; **g. qch dans la poche de qn** to slip sth into sb's pocket; **essaie de g. quelques citations dans ta dissertation** try to slip a few quotations into your essay; **g. un mot à l'oreille de qn** to drop a word in sb's ear; **g. un mot à qn** to have a quick word with sb; **j'ai glissé votre nom pendant le débat** I dropped your name into the debate

3 se glisser *vpr* to slip **(dans** into); **il s'est glissé discrètement dans la salle de conférence** he slipped discreetly into the lecture theatre; **se g. dans son lit** to slip *or* creep into bed; **retrouvez les erreurs qui se sont glissées dans le texte** locate the errors that have crept *or* slipped into the text

glisser[2] *Ordinat nm* **g. d'icônes** icon drag

glisser-lâcher, *pl* **glissers-lâchers** *Ordinat nm* drag and drop; **g. d'icônes** icon drag and drop

glissière [glisjɛr] *nf* **(a)** *MecE* runner, slide; *Com* shelf strip; **à g.** sliding; **fermeture à g.** zip (fastener), *Am* zipper; **porte à glissières** sliding door; **banc à glissières** (*en aviron*) sliding seat **(b)** **g. (de sécurité)** crash barrier **(c)** *Ind* (*pour le charbon*) chute

glissoir [gliswar] *nm* **(a)** (*d'une machine*) slide, sliding block **(b)** (*pour le bois*) timber slide *or* chute

glissoire [gliswar] *nf* slide (*on ice or snow*)

global, -ale, -aux, -ales [glɔbal, -o] *adj* (*somme*) total, inclusive, global; (*paiement*) lump; **une vision globale des problèmes** an overall *or* a global view of the problems; *Scol* **méthode globale** word recognition method

globalement [glɔbalmɑ̃] *adv* overall, all in all; **on peut g. s'estimer gagnant** overall *or* all in all we've come out on top

globalisation [glɔbalizasjɔ̃] *nf* globalization

globaliser [glɔbalize] *vt* (*problèmes*) to lump together; **essayez de g. vos réponses** try to give a general answer

globalité [glɔbalite] *nf* **prendre un problème dans sa g.** to tackle a problem as a whole; **répondre à la g. des questions** to give an answer to cover all questions

globe [glɔb] *nm* **(a)** (*sphère*) globe, sphere **(b)** (*terre*) globe; (*des insignes royaux*) orb; **la surface du g.** the surface of the globe; **une partie inhabitée du g.** an uninhibited part of the globe; **faire le tour du g.** to go round the world; **le g. du soleil** the orb of the sun **(c)** (*en verre*) (*d'une pendule*) glass dome *or* cover; **g. électrique** electric light globe; **statuette sous g.** statuette under glass; **c'est à conserver sous g.** it ought to be kept under glass; *Fig* **conserver qn/qch sous g.** to keep sb/sth under wraps **(d)** *Météo* **g. de feu** fireball, globe lightning

▶ **globe**: **g. oculaire** *ou* **de l'œil** eyeball; **g. terrestre** (*la terre*) earth; (*objet*) globe

globe-trotter [glɔbtrɔtœr], *pl* **globe-trotters** *nm* globetrotter

globine [glɔbin] *nf Biol* globin

globulaire [glɔbylɛr] *adj* globular; *Méd* **numération g.** blood count

globule [glɔbyl] *nm* (*d'air, d'eau*) globule; *Physiol* (blood) corpuscle, blood cell; *Pharm* small pill; **globules blancs/rouges** white/red corpuscles *or* blood cells

globuleux, -euse [glɔbylø, -øz] *adj* globular; **yeux g.** protruding eyes

globuline [glɔbylin] *nf Biol, Ch* globulin

glockenspiel [glɔkɛnʃpil] *nm Mus* glockenspiel

gloire [glwar] *nf* **(a)** (*renom*) glory, fame; **se couvrir de g.** to cover oneself in glory; **être au sommet de la g.** to be at the height of one's fame; **elle a eu son heure de g.** she has had her hour of glory; **il est mort en pleine g.** he died at the height of his fame; **se faire** *ou* **tirer g. de qch** to glory in sth, to pride oneself on sth; **travailler pour la g.** to work for the glory (of it) *or* for nothing; **ce n'est pas la g.** it's not exactly brilliant

(b) (*personne célèbre*) celebrity; **une g. oubliée** a forgotten celebrity; **il est la g. de notre école** he is the pride of our school

(c) (*splendeur*) **la g. de Dieu** the glory of God; **la famille royale dans toute sa g.** the royal family in all its splendour

(d) (*manifestation de respect*) glory, praise; **rendre g. à Dieu/qn** to glorify God/sb; **g. à Dieu!** glory (be) to God!; **g. aux soldats morts pour la France!** glory to the soldiers who died for France!; **à la gloire de qn** in praise of sb

(e) *Beaux-Arts* (*auréole*) glory, nimbus

glomérule [glɔmeryl] *nm Anat* glomerulus

gloria [glɔrja] *nm* **(a)** *Rel* Gloria **(b)** *F Arch* (*café*) = coffee served with spirits

glorieusement [glɔrjøzmɑ̃] *adv* gloriously

glorieux, -euse [glɔrjø, -øz] **1** *adj* **(a)** (*mémorable*) glorious; **ce n'est pas très g.** it's not exactly brilliant **(b)** (*illustre*) glorious; **porter un nom g.** to have an illustrious name; **il est promis à un avenir g.** he has a glorious future ahead of him; **un soldat g.** a renowned soldier **(c)** *Arch, Litt* (*fier*) proud **(de** of); *Péj* **g. de qch** vain *or* conceited about sth **2** *nmpl* **les g.** the saints in glory

glorification [glɔrifikasjɔ̃] *nf* glorification

glorifier [glɔrifje] (*impf, pr sub* **n. glorifiions, v. glorifiiez) 1** *vt* to glorify, to praise **2 se glorifier** *vpr* to boast; **se g. de (faire) qch** to glory in (doing) sth, to boast of (doing) sth

gloriole [glɔrjɔl] *nf F* **pour la g.** for the kudos of it; **faire qch par g.** to do sth in order to show off; **c'est une attitude de g.** he's just showing off

glose [gloz] *nf* (*explication*) gloss, *Péj* **gloses** gossip; **g. marginale** marginal note; **dire la vérité sans g.** to speak the plain *or* unvarnished truth

gloser [gloze] **1** *vt* (*expliquer*) (*texte*) to gloss, to expound **2** *vi* to comment **(sur** on), *Péj* to gossip **(sur** about), *Vieilli* **g. sur qch/qn** (*critiquer*) to find fault with sth/sb

glossaire [glɔsɛr] *nm* **(a)** (*pour termes spécifiques*) glossary **(b)** (*d'une langue*) vocabulary

glossine [glɔsin] *nf* tsetse fly

glossolalie [glɔsɔlali] *nf* glossolalia

glottal, -ale, -aux, -ales [glɔtal, -o] *adj Ling, Anat* glottal

glotte [glɔt] *nf Anat* glottis; *Ling* **coup de g.** glottal stop

glouglou [gluglu] *nm* **(a)** (*bruit d'un liquide*) glug-glug, gurgle; **faire g.** to gurgle **(b)** (*cri de la dinde*) gobble

glouglouter [gluglute] *vi* (*de la dinde*) to gobble

gloussement [glusmɑ̃] *nm* (*de la poule*) clucking, cluck; (*de la dinde*) gobbling, gobble; *F* (*d'une personne*) chuckling, chuckle, chortle

glousser [gluse] *vi* (*d'une poule*) to cluck; (*d'une dinde*) to gobble; *F* (*d'une personne*) to chuckle, to chortle

glouteron [glutrɔ̃] *nm Bot* burdock, burr

gloutonnement [glutɔnmɑ̃] *adv* gluttonously, greedily

gloutonnerie [glutɔnri] *nf* gluttony, greed

glouton, -onne [glutɔ̃, -ɔn] **1** *adj* greedy, gluttonous **2** *n* glutton **3** *nm Zool* wolverine

glu [gly] *nf* (*pour prendre les oiseaux*) bird lime; (*colle*) glue; **prendre des oiseaux à la g.** to lime birds; *Fig F* **c'est une vraie g., ce type!** the guy clings like a limpet *or* sticks like glue

gluant [glyɑ̃] *adj* (*collant*) sticky; (*paroi, limace*) slimy

gluau, -aux [glyo] *nm* lime twig (*for catching birds*)

glucide [glysid] *nm Biol, Ch* carbohydrate; **riche en glucides** (*aliment*) high *or* rich in carbohydrates

glucose [glykoz] *nm* glucose; **g. sanguin** blood sugar
glucosé [glykoze] *adj* containing glucose; **une solution glucosée** a glucose solution
glutamate [glytamat] *nm* glutamate
gluten [glytɛn] *nm* gluten; **sans g.** gluten-free
glutineux, -euse [glytinø, -øz] *adj* glutinous
glycémie [glisemi] *nf Méd* glycaemia
glycérine [gliserin] *nf Ch* glycerin(e), glycerol
glycériner [gliserine] *vt* to put glycerin(e) on
glycérol [gliserɔl] *nm Ch* glycerol, glycerin(e)
glycine[1] [glisin] *nf* wisteria, wistaria
glycine[2] *nf Biol, Ch* glycine
glycogène [glikɔʒɛn] *nm Ch* glycogen
glycol [glikɔl] *nm Ch* glycol
glyphe [glif] *nm Archéol* glyph, groove, channel
glyptique [gliptik] *nf* glyptics
GM [ʒeɛm] *nm* (*abrév* **gentil membre**) holiday maker (at the Club Méd)
GMS [ʒeɛmɛs] *nfpl* (*abrév* **grandes et moyennes surfaces**) large and medium commercial outlets
gnangnan [ɲɑ̃ɲɑ̃] *F* **1** *adj inv* drippy; (*livre*) soppy; **elle est g.** she's a real drip **2** *n* drip
gnaule [ɲol] *nf F* rotgut
gneiss [gnɛs] *nm Géol* gneiss
gniole [ɲol] *nf F* rotgut
gnocchi [ɲɔki] *nmpl Culin* gnocchi
gnognote, gnognotte [ɲɔɲɔt] *nf F* **c'est de la g.** (*mauvaise qualité*) it's a load of rubbish; **c'est pas de la g., cette voiture** that car is quite something
gnole, gnôle [ɲol] *nf F* rotgut
gnome [gnom] *nm* gnome; *Fig Péj* (*homme*) dwarf, midget
gnomique [gnomik] *adj* gnomic
gnon [ɲɔ̃] *nm F* (*coup de poing*) thump, wallop; **se prendre un g.** to get thumped *or* walloped; **on lui a filé un g. dans le pif** he got a thump *or* he got thumped on the nose
gnose [gnoz] *nf* **(a)** *Hist Rel* gnosticism **(b)** *Vieilli* gnosis
gnosticisme [gnɔstisism] *nm Hist Rel* gnosticism
gnostique [gnɔstik] *adj, n Rel* gnostic
gnou [gnu] *nm* gnu, wildebeest
gnouf [ɲuf] *nm Mil Arg Br* glasshouse
go (tout de) [tud(ə)go] *adv F* **tout de go** straight away; **répondre tout de go** to answer straight off *or* straight out
GO 1 *nfpl Rad* (*abrév* **grandes ondes**) LW **2** [ʒeo] *nm* (*abrév* **gentil organisateur**) activity organizer (at the Club Méd)
Go *nm Ordinat* (**gigaoctet**) GB
goal [gol] *nm Sp* goalkeeper, *F* goalie
gobelet [gɔblɛ] *nm* (*en argent, étain, cristal*) tumbler; **(verre) g.** tumbler; **g. en plastique/carton** plastic/paper cup; **tour de g.** conjuring trick (*with tumblers*); *Vieilli Fig* trick
gobeletier [gɔblətje] *nm* (*fabricant*) glassware manufacturer; (*vendeur*) glassware dealer
gobe-mouches [gɔbmuʃ] *nm inv* **(a)** *Orn* flycatcher **(b)** *Bot* **dionée g.** Venus's fly trap, Venus flytrap **(c)** *F* (*personne*) simpleton, dope
gober [gɔbe] **1** *vt* (*nourriture*) to gulp down; *Fig* **g. le morceau** *ou* **l'hameçon** to swallow *or* rise to the bait; *F* **g. des mouches** to stand gaping; *Fig* **il gobe tout ce qu'on lui dit** he believes everything he's told, he'll swallow anything; *F* **je ne peux pas la g.** I can't stand her **2 se gober** *vpr F* to think a lot of oneself, to fancy oneself
goberger (se) [səgɔbɛrʒe] *vpr* **(je me gobergeai(s); n. n. gobergeons)** *F* (*prendre ses aises*) to take things easy, to look after oneself; (*faire bombance*) to live it up, to have a ball
gobeur, -euse [gɔbœr, -øz] *n* gulper, swallower; *Fig F* **c'est un g.** he's very gullible, he'll swallow anything
gobie [gɔbi] *nm* goby
godailler [gɔdaje] *vi* = **goder**
godasse [gɔdas] *nf F* shoe
godelureau, -eaux [gɔdlyro] *nm Péj Vieilli* popinjay
godemiché [gɔdmiʃe] *nm* dildo
goder [gɔde] *vi* (*d'un vêtement*) to pucker (up), to ruck (up); **g. aux genoux** to bag at the knees
godet [gɔdɛ] *nm* **(a)** (*récipient*) pot; **g. à couleur** saucer for mixing watercolours; **g. à huile** (*d'une machine*) waste oil cup; **g. d'une pipe** bowl of a pipe; *F* **viens boire un g.** come and have a jar **(b)** (*de noria*) scoop; (*d'un dragueur, d'un excavateur, d'une roue à eau*) bucket; *MecE* (*au pied d'une machine*) socket; *Min* skip; **roue à godets** overshot wheel **(c)** *Couture* (*ondulation*) flare; (*lé*) gore; **à godets** flared; (*à lés*) gored
godiche [gɔdiʃ] *F* **1** *adj* (*empoté*) clumsy, hamfisted **2** *nf* **quelle g., cette fille!** what a lump (of a girl)!
godille [gɔdij] *nf* **(a)** *Naut* scull; **aller à la g.** to (single-)scull **(b)** *Ski* wedeln; **faire de la g.** to wedeln
godiller [gɔdije] *vi* **(a)** *Naut* to (single-)scull **(b)** *Ski* to wedeln
godilleur [gɔdijœr] *nm Naut* sculler
godillot [gɔdijo] *nm Mil* boot; *F* (*gros soulier*) clodhopper
goéland [gɔelɑ̃] *nm* gull; **g. argenté** herring gull
goélette [gɔelɛt] *nf Naut* (*navire*) schooner; **(voile) g.** trysail
goémon [gɔemɔ̃] *nm* wrack
goglu [gɔgly] *nm Can* (*oiseau*) bobolink
gogo (à)[1] [agogo] *adv F* galore; **avoir de l'argent à g.** to have money galore *or* to burn
gogo[2] *nm F* sucker, mug
goguenard [gɔgnar] *adj* mocking
goguenardise [gɔgnardiz] *nf* mockery
goguenot [gɔgno] *nm Arg* **(a)** *Vieilli* (*pot de chambre*) po, jerry **(b) goguenots** bog, *Am* john
gogues [gɔg] *nmpl Arg* = **goguenots**
goguette [gɔgɛt] *nf F* **être en g.** to be (a bit) tight *or* merry; (*faire la noce*) to be out for a good time
goï, *pl* **goïm** [gɔj, gɔim] *nm Rel juive* goy, *pl* goyim
goinfre [gwɛ̃fr] *F* **1** *n* greedyguts, pig **2** *adj* greedy, piggish
goinfrerie [gwɛ̃frəri] *nf* gluttony, guzzling
goinfrer (se) [səgwɛ̃fre] *vpr F* to guzzle, to gorge oneself; **se g. de qch** to gorge oneself on sth, to guzzle sth
goitre [gwatr] *nm Méd Br* goitre, *US* goiter
goitreux, -euse [gwatrø, -øz] *Méd* **1** *adj* (*cou, gonflement, personne*) goitrous **2** *n* goitrous person
golden [gɔldɛn] *nf inv* Golden Delicious (apple)
golem [gɔlɛm] *nm* (*dans le folklore juif*) golem
golf [gɔlf] *nm Sp* golf; **on fait un g. demain?** how about a game of golf tomorrow?; **(terrain de) g.** golf course; **g. miniature** miniature golf; **jouer au g.** to play golf; **pantalon de g.** plus fours
golfe [gɔlf] *nm* gulf, bay; **le G. Persique** the Persian Gulf; **les États** *ou* **les pays du G.** the Gulf States; **la guerre du Golfe** the Gulf War
golfeur, -euse [gɔlfœr, -øz] *n* golfer
gomina® [gɔmina] *nf* hair cream, brilliantine
gominer (se) [səgɔmine] *vpr* to plaster down one's hair (*with brilliantine etc*); **cheveux gominés** plastered-down hair
gommage [gɔmaʒ] *nm* **(a)** (*action d'enduire de gomme*) gumming **(b)** *Tech* (*des valves, des pistons*) sticking, gumming **(c)** (*pour effacer*) erasing, *Br* rubbing out **(d)** (*produit de beauté*) face scrub; **se faire un g.** to give oneself a face scrub; **g. pour le corps** body scrub
gommant [gɔmɑ̃] *adj* **crème gommante, soin g.** face scrub
gomme [gɔm] *nf* **(a)** (*substance*) gum; **boule de g.** gum **(b)** (*pour effacer*) eraser, *Br* rubber; *F* **histoire à la g.** pointless story; **idée/soirée à la g.** pathetic idea/party; **individu à la g.** useless individual **(c)** *F* **mettre (toute) la g.** to get a move on, to get one's skates on; *Aut* to put one's foot down
▶ **gomme**: **g. arabique** gum arabic; **g. à crayon** eraser, *Br* rubber; **g. à encre** ink eraser; **g. laque** shellac; **g. à mâcher** chewing gum; **g. pour machine à écrire** typewriter eraser *or Br* rubber
gomme-gutte, *pl* **gommes-guttes** [gɔmgyt] *nf* gamboge
gomme-laque, *pl* **gommes-laques** *nf* shellac, lac
gommer [gɔme] *vt* **(a)** (*enduire de gomme*) to gum **(b)** (*effacer*) to erase, *Br* to rub out; *Fig* **g. une partie de son passé/un souvenir pénible** to erase part of one's past/a painful memory **(c) g. les cellules mortes de la peau** to remove dead skin **(d)** *Tech* to stick, to gum; **piston gommé** gummed piston
gomme-résine, *pl* **gommes-résines** *nf* gum resin
gommette [gɔmɛt] *nf* coloured *or US* colored sticker
gommeux, -euse [gɔmø, -øz] **1** *adj* gummy, sticky; **plante gommeuse** gum-yielding plant **2** *nm F Vieilli* dandy, fop, *Am* dude
gommier [gɔmje] *nm* gum tree
gonade [gɔnad] *nf Biol* gonad
gond [gɔ̃] *nm* (*de porte*) hinge; **mettre une porte dans ses gonds** to hang a door; **sortir de ses gonds** (*d'une porte*) to come off its hinges; *Fig F* to fly off the handle, to lose one's temper
gondolage [gɔ̃dɔlaʒ] *nm* (*du bois*) warping; (*du papier*) curling; (*d'une plaque de fer*) buckling
gondolant [gɔ̃dɔlɑ̃] *adj F* (*histoire*) side-splitting, hilarious
gondole [gɔ̃dɔl] *nf* **(a)** (*barque*) gondola **(b)** (*présentoir*) island, gondola
gondolement [gɔ̃dɔlmɑ̃] *nm* = **gondolage**
gondoler [gɔ̃dɔle] **1** *vi* (*du bois*) to warp; (*du papier*) to curl; (*d'une plaque de fer*) to buckle **2 se gondoler** *vpr* **(a)** = **1** *vi*; **mon disque s'est gondolé à la chaleur** my record's warped in the sun, the sun's warped my record **(b)** *F* (*rire*) to fall about laughing, to split one's sides laughing
gondolier, -ière [gɔ̃dɔlje, -jɛr] *n* gondolier
gonfalon [gɔ̃falɔ̃] *nm,* **gonfanon** [gɔ̃fanɔ̃] *nm Hist* gonfalon, gonfanon

gonflable [gɔ̃flabl] *adj* inflatable

gonflage [gɔ̃flaʒ] *nm* inflation; **vérifier le g. (des pneus)** to check the tyre *or US* tire pressure

gonflant [gɔ̃flɑ̃] **1** *adj* **(a)** *(coiffure)* bouffant **(b)** *très F (énervant)* maddening, irritating **2** *nm (d'une coiffure)* bouffant; **mousse qui donne du g. à vos cheveux** mousse that gives body to your hair

gonflé [gɔ̃fle] *adj* **(a)** *(boursouflé) (yeux)* swollen, puffy; *(visage)* bloated, swollen, puffy; *(estomac)* bloated, swollen; *(pieds, chevilles)* swollen; *Fig* **g. d'orgueil** puffed up with pride; **avoir le cœur g. de chagrin** to be heart-broken; **elle avait les yeux gonflés de larmes** her eyes were swollen with tears **(b)** *Naut (voile)* full **(c)** *F* **tu es g.** *(culotté)* you've got a nerve; **c'est g. ce qu'il a fait là** what he did took some nerve; **g. à bloc** keyed up; *(en pleine forme physique)* full of beans; *(sûr de soi)* sure of oneself; *Aut F* **moteur g.** hotted-up *or* souped-up engine **(d)** *(exagéré)* **prix gonflés** excessive prices

gonflement [gɔ̃fləmɑ̃] *nm* **(a)** *(des pneus, d'un ballon)* inflating, inflation; *(de l'estomac)* swelling **(b)** *(exagération) (de prix)* excessive increase; *(de résultats, statistiques)* exaggeration

gonfler [gɔ̃fle] **1** *vt* **(a)** *(pneu)* to blow up, to pump up, to inflate; *(ses joues)* to puff out, to blow out; **g. un ballon/un matelas pneumatique** to inflate *or* blow up a balloon/an airbed; **le vent gonfle les voiles** the wind fills the sails; **les bons résultats de son fils la gonflent d'orgueil** her son's good results make her as proud as a peacock; **cette bonne nouvelle gonfla son cœur de joie** the good news filled his heart with joy

(b) *(faire augmenter de volume)* to swell; **torrent gonflé par les pluies** torrent swollen by the rains

(c) *Fig (grossir) (résultats, conséquences)* to exaggerate; **g. les chiffres d'un sondage** to inflate *or* exaggerate the figures from a poll; **g. l'importance de qch/qn** to exaggerate *or* overstress the importance of sth/sb; **le prof a gonflé les notes** the teacher bumped up the marks; **g. un événement** to hype an event

(d) *Aut F (un moteur)* to hot up, to soup up

(e) *très F (énerver)* **g. qn** to get on sb's nerves, to irritate sb; **il nous les gonfle avec ses matchs de foot** he really gets on our nerves *or* he's a real pain in the neck with his football matches

2 *vi* to swell; **le bois a gonflé** the wood has swollen; **laisser g. les haricots toute une nuit** to leave the beans to soak all night; **laisser de la pâte g.** to let dough rise

3 se gonfler *vpr* = **2** *vi*; **les poumons se gonflent** the lungs fill; *Fig* **se g. d'orgueil** to swell up with pride; **se g. de colère** to be bursting with rage; **mon cœur s'est gonflé de joie à cette nouvelle** my heart filled with joy at the news

gonflette [gɔ̃flɛt] *nf F Péj* pumping iron; **faire de la g.** to pump iron

gonfleur [gɔ̃flœr] *nm* (air) pump

gong [gɔ̃(g)] *nm* **(a)** *Mus* gong **(b)** *Boxe* bell; *Fig* **sauvé par le g.** saved by the bell

goniomètre [gɔnjɔmɛtr] *nm Rad* goniometer, position finder, direction finder; *Mil* dial sight

goniométrie [gɔnjɔmetri] *nf* goniometry, position finding, direction finding

gonococcie [gɔnɔkɔksi] *nf Méd* gonorrhoea, *US* gonorrhea

gonocoque [gɔnɔkɔk] *nm Méd* gonococcus

gonze [gɔ̃z] *nm Arg Vieilli (homme)* guy, *Br* bloke

gonzesse [gɔ̃zɛs] *nf très F (femme)* chick, *Br* bird, *Am* broad

gordien [gɔrdjɛ̃] *adj Fig* **trancher le nœud g.** to cut the Gordian knot

goret [gɔrɛ] *nm* piglet; *F (enfant malpropre)* little pig; **manger comme un g.** to eat like a pig

goretex® [gɔrtɛks] *nm Tex* Gore-Tex

gorge [gɔrʒ] *nf* **(a)** *(gosier, cou)* throat; **avoir mal à la g., avoir un mal de g.** to have a sore throat; **un serrement de g.** a lump in one's throat; **avoir la g. serrée** to have a lump in one's throat; **parler avec la g. serrée par la peine/l'angoisse** to speak in a voice trembling with sorrow/anguish; **crier à pleine g.** *ou* **à g. déployée** to shout at the top of one's voice; **rire à pleine g.** *ou* **à g. déployée** to roar with laughter; *Fig* **faire des gorges chaudes de qch/qn** to laugh sth/sb to scorn; **trancher la g. à qn** to cut sb's throat; *Fig* **s'il le devine, il va me trancher la g.** if he guesses, he'll kill me; **le chien lui a sauté à la g.** the dog leapt at his throat; **ce n'est pas une raison pour me sauter à la g.** that's no reason to jump down my throat; *Fig* **avoir le couteau sous la g.** to have a gun at one's head; *Fig* **je le tiens à la g.** I've got him by the throat, I've got a stranglehold on him; *Fig* **prendre qn à la g.** to get sb in a stranglehold; **nous étions pris à la g., nous ne pouvions rien faire d'autre** we were in a stranglehold *or* we had a gun at our heads, we couldn't do anything else; **pris à la g. par ses créanciers, il ...** with his creditors holding a gun to his head, he ...; **faire rentrer à qn ses mots dans la g.** to make sb eat his/her words; *Fig* **cela m'est resté en travers de la g.** that stuck in my throat *or* gullet; *Fig* **rendre g.** to make restitution; **je lui ferai rendre g.** I'll make him pay it back

(b) *(poitrine) (d'une femme)* bosom, breast; *(d'un pigeon)* breast

(c) *Géog* gorge

(d) *Tech* groove; *Archit* quirk, gorge; *(d'un écrou)* furrow; *(d'un pistolet, d'un étui à cartouches)* neck; *(d'un verrou)* tumbler; *Archit* **moulure à g.** grooved moulding

gorgé [gɔrʒe] *adj* **une éponge gorgée d'eau** a sponge full of water; **sol g. d'eau** sodden soil; **champs gorgés d'eau** waterlogged fields; **des fruits gorgés de soleil** sun-kissed fruit; **g. de sang** gorged with blood

gorge-de-pigeon *adj inv* dove-coloured, *US* dove-colored

gorgée [gɔrʒe] *nf (de vin)* mouthful; **petite g.** sip; **boire qch à petites gorgées** to sip sth; **avaler qch/finir son verre d'une g.** to swallow sth/finish one's glass in one (gulp)

gorger [gɔrʒe] **(je gorgeai(s), n. gorgeons) 1** *vt (oies)* to cram **2 se gorger** *vpr* to stuff oneself **(de** with), to gorge oneself **(de** on, with); **la terre se gorgea d'eau** the ground became waterlogged; *Fig* **elle semblait se g. de sa présence** it seemed as if she couldn't see enough of him

Gorgone [gɔrgɔn] *nf Myth* Gorgon

gorgonzola [gɔrgɔ̃zɔla] *nm* Gorgonzola (cheese)

gorille [gɔrij] *nm* **(a)** *(mammifère)* gorilla **(b)** *Fig F* gorilla, bodyguard

gosier [gozje] *nm (pharynx)* throat, gullet; **avoir une arête dans le g.** to have a fishbone stuck in one's throat; *F* **avoir le g. sec** to be dry *or* thirsty; **rire à plein g.** to laugh loudly *or* heartily; *F* **avoir le g. en pente** to have a permanent thirst, to like one's drink

gospel [gɔspɛl] *nm* gospel (music)

gosse [gɔs] *n* **(a)** *(enfant) F* kid; **c'est encore une g.** she's just a kid; **elle est venue avec ses deux gosses** she came along with her two kids **(b)** *F (jeune homme, jeune fille)* **c'est une belle g.** she's a smashing girl; **il est plutôt beau g.** he's quite good-looking **(c)** *Can Arg* **gosses** balls

▶ **gosse**: **g. de riches** spoilt rich kid

gosser [gɔse] *vt Can F* to whittle

Goth [gɔt] *n Hist* Goth

gotha [gɔta] *nm* **le g. du show-business/de la finance** the show-business/financial elite; **le G.** *(almanach)* ≈ Burke's Peerage

gothique [gɔtik] **1** *adj* Gothic **2** *nm Archit, Ling* Gothic **3** *nf Typ* Gothic, *Br* black letter; **écrire en g.** to write in Gothic script

gotique [gɔtik] *nm Ling* Gothic

gouache [gwaʃ] *nf Beaux-Arts* gouache; **peindre à la g.** to paint in gouache

gouailler [gwaje] *vi Vieilli* to joke

gouailleur, -euse [gwajœr, -øz] *Vieilli* **1** *adj (ton)* joking, mocking, bantering **2** *n* joker

goualante [gwalɑ̃t] *nf F Vieilli* popular song

gouape [gwap] *nf Arg* lout

gouda [guda] *nm Culin* Gouda

goudron [gudrɔ̃] *nm* tar; **g. (de gaz** *ou* **de houille)** coal tar; **g. de bois** wood tar; **g. minéral** asphalt, bitumen

goudronnage [gudrɔnaʒ] *nm* tarring

goudronner [gudrɔne] *vt* to tar; **route goudronnée** tarred road; **toile goudronnée** tarpaulin; **papier goudronné** tar-lined paper

goudronneur [gudrɔnœr] *nm* tar sprayer *or* spreader

goudronneuse [gudrɔnøz] *nf (machine)* tar sprayer; *(pour l'asphalte)* asphalt spreader

goudronneux, -euse [gudrɔnø, -øz] *adj* tarry; *(huile)* gummy

gouffre [gufr] *nm* gulf, abyss, chasm; *(tourbillon)* whirlpool, vortex; *Géol* sinkhole, *Br* swallow hole; **g. béant** yawning gulf *or* chasm; **g. sous-marin** oceanic abyss; *Fig Litt* **le g. de l'oubli/du désespoir** the depths of oblivion/despair; *Fig* **être au bord du g.** to be on the edge of the abyss; *Fig* **c'est un g. d'ignorance** the depths of his ignorance are unfathomable; *Fig* **cette voiture est un g.** this car just swallows up money, with this car it's like pouring money into a bottomless pit; *Mktg* **g. financier** *(produit)* financial disaster, dog

gouge [guʒ] *nf Tech* gouge, hollow chisel

gougère [guʒɛr] *nf Culin* gougère *(choux pastry with cheese)*

gougnafier [guɲafje] *nm F* nerd

gouine [gwin] *nf Arg (lesbienne)* dyke, les

goujat [guʒa] *nm* boor, churl

goujaterie [guʒatri] *nf* boorishness, churlishness

goujon[1] [guʒɔ̃] *nm* gudgeon; *F* **taquiner le g.** to do a bit of fishing

goujon² *nm Constr (en maçonnerie)* gudgeon; *Menuis* tenon; *MecE* bolt, stud; *Menuis* **g. perdu, g. prisonnier** dowel (pin); *MecE* **g. de jonction** assembling pin, bolt; **g. de charnière** hinge pin; **g. d'arbre** shaft gudgeon
goujonner [guʒɔne] *vt Menuis* to dowel; *Constr* to joggle; *MecE* to pin, to bolt
goulache, goulasch [gulaʃ] *nf ou m Culin* goulash
goulag [gulag] *nm* Gulag
goulée [gule] *nf F* big mouthful, gulp; **j'ai besoin d'une bonne g. d'air pur** I need a good lungful of fresh air; **il tira sur son havane, et aspira une grosse g.** he drew deeply on his cigar
goulet [gulɛ] *nm* (a) *Géog (défilé)* gully; **g. d'étranglement** bottleneck (b) *Naut (chenal) (d'un port)* gut, bottleneck, narrows; **le G. de Brest** the Brest Channel
gouleyant [gulɛjɑ̃] *adj (vin)* pleasant, easy-drinking
goulot [gulo] *nm (d'une bouteille)* neck; **boire au g.** to drink (straight) from the bottle; *Fig* **g. d'étranglement** bottleneck; *Fig Vulg* **refouler du g.** to have foul breath
goulotte [gulɔt] *nf Tech* chute; *(d'un wagonnet à charbon)* spout
goulu, -ue [guly] **1** *adj* (a) *(glouton)* greedy, gluttonous; *(regards)* hungry, greedy (b) **pois g.** sugar pea **2** *n (personne)* glutton
goulûment [gulymɑ̃] *adv* greedily, voraciously; *(regarder)* hungrily, greedily
goupil [gupi] *nm Arch* fox
goupille [gupij] *nf Tech* pin; **g. fendue** split pin, cotter; **g. d'arrêt** stop bolt
goupiller [gupije] **1** *vt* (a) *Tech* to pin; *(boulon)* to cotter (b) *F (arranger)* to fix (up); **bien/mal goupillé** well/badly organized; **je me demande ce qu'il est en train de g.** I wonder what he's up to **2 se goupiller** *vpr F (d'une montre, un mécanisme)* to work; *Fig* **ça s'est bien goupillé** it worked out well; **ça s'est mal goupillé** it didn't work out
goupillon [gupijɔ̃] *nm* (a) *Rel (pour eau bénite)* sprinkler, aspergillum (b) *(pour biberons, bouteilles)* bottle brush
gourance [gurɑ̃s] *nf F* boob, bloomer, *Am* goof; **faire une g.** to (make a) boob, to make a bloomer, *Am* to goof
gourbi [gurbi] *nm* (a) *(cabane)* hut, shack (b) *F (taudis)* hovel
gourd [gur] *adj* numb (with cold); **avoir les doigts gourds** to have numb fingers
gourde [gurd] **1** *nf* (a) *Bot* gourd (b) *(récipient pour boissons)* flask; *(coloquinte)* gourd (c) *F (personne stupide)* dope, dimwit **2** *adj F* dopey, dimwitted
gourdin [gurdɛ̃] *nm* club, cudgel, bludgeon
gourer (se) [səgure] *vpr F* to boob, to make a boob *or* bloomer, *Am* to goof; **se g. de route** to lose one's way; **se g. d'adresse** to get the wrong address
gourgandine [gurgɑ̃din] *nf Vieilli* loose woman
gourmand, -ande [gurmɑ̃, -ɑ̃d] **1** *adj (personne)* greedy; **être g. de** *(sucreries)* to be fond of; *Fig* to be greedy for; **ma voiture est vraiment gourmande en essence** my car really gobbles up the *Br* petrol *or Am* gas; **cet appareil est très g. d'électricité** this appliance gobbles up *or* consumes a lot of electricity; **pois g.** sugar pea, mangetout, *Am* snowpea **2** *n (personne)* gourmand **3** *nm (branche parasite)* sucker
gourmander [gurmɑ̃de] *vt Litt* to rebuke, to chide
gourmandise [gurmɑ̃diz] *nf* (a) greediness; **avec g.** greedily (b) **gourmandises** delicacies, *F* goodies
gourme [gurm] *nf* (a) *Méd Vieilli* impetigo (b) *Vét* strangles (c) *Fig Vieilli* **jeter sa g.** to sow one's wild oats
gourmé [gurme] *adj Litt Péj* stiff, starchy, affected
gourmet [gurmɛ] *nm* gourmet; *Fig (connaisseur)* connoisseur; **un fin g.** a discerning gourmet
gourmette [gurmɛt] *nf* (a) *(d'une montre)* chain; *(bracelet)* chain (bracelet) (b) *(pour les chevaux)* curb (chain)
gourou [guru] *nm Rel Hindu, Fig* guru
gousse [gus] *nf (de légumineuses)* pod; **g. d'ail** clove of garlic; **g. de vanille** vanilla pod
gousset [gusɛ] *nm* (a) *(poche)* fob (pocket); **il a le g. bien garni** his pockets are well lined; **montre de g.** fob watch (b) *MecE* (shoulder) bracket, stay plate, gusset (plate)
goût [gu] *nm* (a) *(sens)* taste; *F* **faire passer le g. du pain à qn** *(le tuer)* to do away with sb; *(ôter l'envie de recommencer)* to put a stop to sb's little games

(b) *(saveur)* taste, flavour, *US* flavor; *(du vin)* bouquet; **g. amer/épicé** bitter/spicy taste; **avoir un g. de terroir** *(de pain)* to have a taste of the country; *(d'un accent)* to have a rural twang; **cela a le g. de la banane/du gin** it tastes like banana/gin; **donner du g. à un mets** to give a dish flavour; **manquer de g., ne pas avoir de g.** *(d'un plat)* to be tasteless, to have no taste; **sans g.** *adj* tasteless; *adv* tastelessly

(c) *(préférence)*, *Culin* **ajouter du sucre et du citron selon son g.** add sugar and lemon to taste; **chacun ses goûts, des goûts et des couleurs on ne discute pas, tous les goûts sont dans la nature** everyone to his (own) taste, there's no accounting for taste; **affaire de g.** matter of taste

(d) *(prédilection, convenance)* taste, liking; **avoir des goûts de luxe** to have expensive tastes; **il a des goûts bizarres** he has strange tastes; **une maison/un homme à mon g.** a house/a man to my taste *or* liking; **elle n'est pas à mon g.** I don't care for her, she's not to my taste *or* liking; **trouver qch/qn à son g.** to find sth/sb to one's taste *or* liking; **le g. des affaires** a taste *or* liking for business; **g. passager** passing fancy; **avoir du g. pour** *ou* **le g. de qch** to have a taste *or* liking for sth; **faire qch par g.** to do sth from inclination, to do sth because one likes to; **je n'habite pas ici par g.** I don't live here from choice; **je le fais par g. du travail bien fait** I do it because I like to see work well done; **prendre g. à qch** to acquire a taste *or* develop a liking for sth; **avec le temps elle y a pris g.** it grew on her, she developed a liking for it; **elle n'a plus (de) g. à rien** she no longer wants to do anything; **reprendre g. à la lecture/à la musique** to regain one's taste for reading/music; **reprendre g. à la vie** to regain one's zest for living, to find life worth living again

(e) *(discernement, jugement)* taste; **g. parfait** perfect taste; **il a du g.** he has (good) taste; **une femme de g.** a woman of taste; **remarque d'un g. douteux** remark in doubtful taste; **une plaisanterie/image de mauvais g.** a joke/picture in bad taste; **une robe de mauvais g.** a tasteless dress; **décoration de bon g.** tasteful decoration; **elle s'habille avec g.** she has (a) good dress sense, she has good taste in clothes

(f) *Litt (style)* style, manner; **peint dans le g. de Watteau** painted in the style *or* manner of Watteau; **quelque chose dans ce g.-là** something like that, something of that sort
goûter¹ [gute] *nm* snack; *(à quatre heures)* (afternoon) tea; **l'heure du g.** teatime; **elle est invitée pour le g.** *ou* **à un g.** she has been invited to tea
goûter² **1** *vt* (a) *(savourer) (nourriture)* to taste; *(pour la première fois) (nourriture, boisson)* to taste, to try (b) *Fig (aimer, apprécier) (la musique, la beauté de la nature etc)* to enjoy, to appreciate; **g. le silence de la nuit** to savour *or* relish the silence of night **2** *vi* (a) **g. à quatre heures** to have tea *or* a snack at four o'clock (b) **g. de qch** to taste sth; *Fig* **elle a goûté de tous les petits boulots** she's had a go at all sorts of jobs; **g. à qch** to taste sth, to try sth
goûteur, -euse [gutœr, -øz] *n* taster
goutte [gut] **1** *nf* (a) *(d'un liquide)* drop; **g. à g.** drop by drop; **tomber g. à g.** *(d'un liquide)* to drip; *Fig* **c'est la g. d'eau qui fait déborder le vase** it's the last straw, it's the straw that breaks/broke the camel's back; **se ressembler comme deux gouttes d'eau** to be as like as two peas in a pod; *Fig* **c'est une g. d'eau dans la mer** it's a drop in the ocean; **il suait à grosses gouttes** the sweat was pouring off him; **il n'y a pas eu une g. de pluie depuis trois mois** there hasn't been a drop of rain for three months; **il tombait quelques gouttes** it was spitting with rain; *F* **avoir la g. au nez** to have a runny *or* dripping nose; **g. d'eau** drop of water; *(bijou)* drop

(b) *(petite quantité)* drop; **g. de cognac** *(dans une sauce)* dash *or* drop of brandy; **boire une goutte de cognac après le repas** to have a drop *or* nip of brandy after one's meal; **encore une g. de café?** a drop more coffee?; *F* **boire la g.** to have a nip

(c) *Pharm* **gouttes** drops; **prendre des gouttes** to take drops; **gouttes pour le nez** nose *or* nasal drops; **gouttes auriculaires** ear drops

(d) *Méd* gout; **avoir la g.** to suffer from *or* have gout, to be gouty

2 *adv Arch, Hum* **je n'entends g. à ce que vous dites** I don't understand a word of what you're saying; *Litt* **je n'y vois g.** I can't see a thing
goutte-à-goutte *nm inv Méd* drip; **g. intraveineux** intravenous drip; **on lui fait un g.** he's on an drip; **on a dû lui faire** *ou* **mettre un g.** he had to be put on a drip
gouttelette [gutlɛt] *nf* droplet, tiny drop
goutter [gute] *vi* to drip
goutteux, -euse [gutø, -øz] *Méd* **1** *adj (personne)* gouty **2** *n* gout sufferer
gouttière [gutjɛr] *nf* (a) *(le long du toit)* gutter, guttering (b) *(le long du mur)* drainpipe, downpipe, *Am* downspout (c) *Anat (d'un os)* groove (d) *Méd* cradle, (cradle-like) splint (e) *Typ (de page)* gutter
gouvernable [guvɛrnabl] *adj (bateau, entreprise, équipe)* manageable; *(pays)* governable; **peu g.** *(entreprise, équipe)* unmanageable; *(pays)* ungovernable
gouvernail [guvɛrnaj] *nm Naut* rudder; **roue du g.** (steering) wheel; **tenir le g.** to be at the wheel *or* at the helm, to steer; *Fig* **tenir le g. de l'État/d'une affaire** to be at the helm of the state/a business
▶ **gouvernail**: **g. de direction** *Av* rudder; *Naut* **g. de plongée**

(*d'un sous-marin*) horizontal rudder; **g. de profondeur** *Naut* diving rudder, plane, hydroplane; *Av* elevator

gouvernant, -ante[1] [guvɛrnɑ̃, -ɑ̃t] **1** *adj* (*classe, parti*) governing, ruling **2** *nmpl* **les gouvernants** those in power

gouvernante[2] [guvɛrnɑ̃t] *nf* (*qui garde les enfants*) governess; (*qui s'occupe d'une personne, d'un hôtel*) housekeeper; **g. d'étage** (*d'un hôtel*) floor housekeeper; **g. du soir** (*d'un hôtel*) turndown housekeeper; **g. générale** (*d'un hôtel*) executive *or* head housekeeper

gouverne [guvɛrn] *nf* **(a)** *Naut* steering; *Fig* **pour votre g.** for your guidance **(b)** *Av* **gouvernes** control surfaces; **g. compensée** balanced surface; **g. de direction** rudder; **g. de profondeur** elevator

gouvernement [guvɛrnəmɑ̃] *nm* [①**A11**,g,i] *Pol* government; **le g. français/britannique** the French/British government; **g. monarchique/républicain/parlementaire** monarchic(al)/ republican/parliamentary government; **g. de cohabitation** = government in which the President and the parliamentary majority are from different parties; **sous le g. Giscard** during Giscard's term of office, during Giscard's administration; **le chef du g.** the head of (the) government; **former un nouveau g.** to form a new government

gouvernemental, -ale, -aux, -ales [guvɛrnəmɑ̃tal, -o] *adj* governmental; **politique gouvernementale** government(al) policy; **le parti g.** the governing *or* ruling party, the party in government; **un journal g.** a government newspaper

gouverner [guvɛrne] **1** *vt* **(a)** (*diriger*) (*un pays*) to govern, to rule; (*dominer*) to control; **Dieu gouverne l'univers** God is the ruler of the universe; **g. ses passions/sa colère/sa jalousie** to control *or* govern one's passions/anger/jealousy; *Tech* **mouvement gouverné par un pendule** movement regulated *or* governed *or* controlled by a pendulum

(b) *Naut* (*bateau*) to steer; **faire g.** to con; **g. sur un port** to steer *or* stand *or* head for a port, to bear in with a port; **g. à la lame** to steer by the sea; **gouvernez droit!** steady!

(c) *Gram* **verbe qui gouverne l'accusatif** verb that governs *or* takes the accusative

(d) *Vieilli* to manage, to administer; **bien g. ses ressources** to husband one's resources

2 *vi* **(a)** *Pol* to govern; **un parti qui gouverne depuis des années** a party which has governed *or* has been in government for years

(b) *Naut* **navire qui ne gouverne plus** ship that no longer answers to her helm; **bateau qui gouverne bien** boat that steers well

3 se gouverner *vpr* **(a)** *Pol* to govern oneself, to be self-governing; **droit des peuples à se g. eux-mêmes** right of peoples to self-government **(b)** (*se maîtriser*) to control oneself

gouverneur [guvɛrnœr] *nm* (*d'une province, d'une banque etc, d'un État des États-Unis*) governor; *Mil* (*d'une position fortifiée*) commanding officer, *Can* **G. Général** Governor General; *Can* **Lieutenant-G.** Lieutenant-Governor

goy, goyim [gɔj, gɔim] *nm Jewish Rel* goy, *pl* goyim

goyave [gɔjav] *nf* guava

goyavier [gɔjavje] *nm Bot* guava (tree)

GPAO [ʒepeao] *nf Ordinat* (*abrév* **gestion de production assistée par ordinateur**) computer-aided production

GPO [ʒepeo] *nf* (*abrév* **gestion par objectifs**) MBO

GQG [ʒekyʒe] *nm Mil* (*abrév* **grand quartier général**) GHQ

GR [ʒeɛr] *nm* (*abrév* **(sentier de) grande randonnée**) official hiking trail, long-distance footpath

gr *abrév* **(gramme(s))** gr

Graal (le) [lәgral] *nm Littér* the (Holy) Grail; **la quête du G.** the quest for the (Holy) Grail

grabat [graba] *nm* (*de paille, de chiffons*) pallet

grabataire [grabatɛr] **1** *adj* bedridden **2** *n* bedridden invalid

grabuge [grabyʒ] *nm F* rumpus; **il y aura du g.** there'll be a rumpus *or Br* ructions; **ça va faire du g. s'il l'apprend!** there's going to be a stink if he finds out!

Grâce [grɑs] *nf Myth* **les trois Grâces** the three Graces

grâce [grɑs] *nf* **(a)** (*charme*) grace, gracefulness, charm; **avoir de la g.** to be graceful; **avec g.** gracefully; **se déplacer avec g.** to move gracefully; **il fait des grâces devant le miroir** he's preening himself in front of the mirror

(b) (*bienveillance, faveur*) favour, *US* favor; **obtenir/ accorder une g.** to obtain/to grant a favour; **faire une g. à qn** to do sb a favour *or* a kindness; **faites-moi la g. d'oublier cette histoire** do me the favour *or* kindness of forgetting this matter; **c'est trop de grâces que vous me faites!** you really are too kind!; **demander une g. à qn** to ask a favour of sb; **trouver g. devant qn** *ou* **auprès de qn** *ou* **aux yeux de qn** to find favour in sb's eyes; **se mettre dans** *ou* **entrer dans** *ou* **obtenir les bonnes grâces de qn** to obtain the good graces of sb, *F* to get into sb's good books; **de g.!** for pity's sake!; **les grâces de Dieu** God's blessings; *Com* **jours** *ou* **terme de g.** days of grace; *Rel* **en état de g.** in a state of grace; *Fig* **le président a joui d'une période d'état de g. après son élection** the president could do no wrong after he was elected, the president enjoyed a honeymoon with the voters after he was elected; *Fig* **être en g. auprès de qn** to be in sb's good books; **l'an de g. 1802** the year of grace 1802; **coup de g.** coup de grâce; **donner le coup de g. à un animal** to put an animal out of its misery *or* pain

(c) (*volonté*) **de bonne g.** willingly, readily; **de mauvaise g.** unwillingly, grudgingly; **il aurait mauvaise g. à nous laisser ici** (*après ce que nous avons fait pour lui*) it would be ungracious of him to leave us here

(d) g. à qn/qch (*avec l'aide de*) thanks to sb/sth; **g. à votre aide** thanks to your help; **g. à Dieu** with God's help, by God's grace

(e) (*remerciements*) **rendre g. à Dieu** to give thanks to God; **(rendons) g. à Dieu!** thanks be to God!; **action de grâce(s)** thanksgiving; *Can* **Jour de l'action de g.** Thanksgiving Day

(f) *Jur* pardon; **lettre(s) de g.** reprieve; **demander** *ou* **crier g.** to beg *or* plead for mercy; **g.!** mercy!; **droit de g.** right of reprieve; **accorder sa g. à qn** to pardon sb; **je vous fais g. cette fois-ci** I'll let you off this time; **je vous fais g. du reste** I'll spare you the rest; (*ne m'en dites ou n'en faites pas plus*) you needn't do *or* say any more; **je vous fais g. des détails** I'll spare you the details; **je vous fais g. des 50 francs qui manquaient** I'll let you off *or* overlook the missing fifty francs

(g) (*titre honorifique*) **sa G. le duc** His Grace the Duke

▶ **grâce**: **g. présidentielle** presidential pardon

gracier [grasje] *vt* (*impf, pr sub* **n. graciions, v. graciiez**) to reprieve

gracieusement [grasjøzmɑ̃] *adv* **(a)** (*avec grâce*) gracefully; **se déplacer g.** to move gracefully **(b)** (*aimablement*) graciously, kindly **(c)** (*gratuitement*) free of charge, gratis; **la maison est heureuse de vous remettre g. ce stylo** the company is pleased to offer you this pen with its compliments

gracieuseté [grasjøzte] *nf* graciousness, kindness; **faire une g. à qn** to do sb a kindness *or* a favour *or US* a favor

gracieux, -euse [grasjø, -øz] *adj* **(a)** (*qui a de la grâce, du charme*) (*figure, style etc*) graceful **(b)** (*aimable*) charming **(c)** (*gratuit*) free (of charge); **à titre g.** gratis, free of charge; **exemplaire envoyé à titre g.** complimentary *or* presentation copy **(d)** (*pour exprimer le respect*) **notre g. souverain** our gracious Sovereign

gracile [grasil] *adj* (*tige, cou*) slender; (*personne*) slim, slender

gracilité [grasilite] *nf* slenderness, slimness

Gracques (les) [legrak] *nmpl Antiq* the Gracchi

gradation [gradasjɔ̃] *nf* gradation

grade [grad] *nm* **(a)** *Mil, Admin* rank; **avoir le g. de caporal/ sergent** to have the rank of corporal/sergeant; **monter en g.** to be promoted; **ça va le faire monter en g.** that will get him promoted; *F* **en prendre pour son g.** to be hauled over the coals, to be given a ticking off **(b)** *Univ* **g. universitaire** (university) degree **(c)** *Math* grade **(d)** *Tech* (*de l'huile de voiture*) grade

gradé [grade] *nm* **(a)** *Mil* non-commissioned officer, NCO; **tous les gradés** all ranks (*commissioned and non-commissioned*) **(b)** *Naut* **les gradés** the petty officers

gradient [gradjɑ̃] *nm* gradient

gradin [gradɛ̃] *nm* **(a)** (*d'amphithéâtre, de stade*) row *or* tier of seats; *Sp* **être assis dans les gradins** *Br Fb* to be sitting on the terraces; *Am Baseball* to be sitting in the bleachers **(b)** *Tech* **poulie à gradins** cone pulley, stepped pulley; *Él* **disposer les balais en gradins** to stagger the brushes (*of a dynamo*)

graduation [gradɥasjɔ̃] *nf* **(a)** (*d'une échelle*) graduation **(b)** (*ensemble des divisions*) graduation, scale

gradué [gradɥe] *adj* **(a)** (*qui porte une graduation*) graduated; **verre g.** measuring glass **(b)** (*progressif*) (*exercices, problèmes etc*) graded, progressive

graduel, -elle [gradɥɛl] *adj* gradual

graduellement [gradɥɛlmɑ̃] *adv* gradually

graduer [gradɥe] *vt* **(a)** (*thermomètre, verre etc*) to graduate **(b)** (*doses*) to increase gradually

graffiter [grafite] *vt* to cover with graffiti

graffiteur, -euse [grafitœr -øz] *n* graffiti artist, graffitist

graffiti [grafiti] *nmpl* [①**A10**,f,i] graffiti; **un g.** a piece of graffiti

graillé [graje] *adj Can* (*pour faire qch*) well-equipped; *F* (*bien monté*) well-hung

grailler [grɑje] *vi* **(a)** (*parler*) to speak hoarsely *or* huskily; (*d'une corneille*) to caw **(b)** *Arg* (*manger*) to eat, *Br* to nosh

graillon [grɑjɔ̃] *nm* **sentir le g.** to smell of burnt fat; **avoir un goût de g.** to taste greasy

graillonner [grajɔne] *vi* (*parler*) to speak hoarsely *or* huskily

grain[1] [grɛ̃] *nm* **(a)** (*graine, fruit de petite taille*) grain; **poivre en grains** peppercorns

(b) (*céréales, pour volaille*) grain; **entrepôt de g.** granary; **alcool de g.** grain alcohol; **poulet de g.** corn-fed chicken

(c) (*granule*) (*de sable, de poudre*) grain; (*de poussière*) speck; **g. de chapelet** rosary bead; *Fig* **g. de coquetterie/d'originalité** touch *or* hint of coquetry/originality; **un g. de folie** a touch of madness; **pas un g. de bon sens/de vérité** not a grain *or* not an ounce of common sense/of truth; *Fig F* **il a un g.** he's not quite right in the head, he's not all there

(d) *Tex* (*d'un tissu*) grain, texture; (*d'une peau*) rough side; **côté g. du cuir** grain side of leather; **contre le g.** against the grain; **à gros grains** coarse-grained; **à grains fins/serrés** fine-/close-grained; **ruban gros g.** petersham

(e) *Pharm* pellet

(f) *Phot* grain

▶ **grain**: **g. de beauté** beauty spot, mole; **g. de blé** grain of wheat; **g. de café** coffee bean; **g. de grenade** pomegranate seed; **g. de moutarde** mustard seed; **g. d'orge** barleycorn, grain of barley; **g. de poivre** peppercorn; **g. de raisin** grape; **g. de sel: mettre son g. de sel** to put *or* stick one's oar in, *Am* to put in one's ten cents' worth

grain[2] *nm Naut* squall; **essuyer un g.** to meet with a squall; **veiller au g.** to look out for squalls; *Fig* to keep a weather eye open

graine [grɛn] *nf Bot* seed; **monter en g.** (*d'une plante*) to run *or* bolt to seed; *Fig* (*d'une femme*) to be (left) on the shelf; (*d'une personne*) to shoot up; *F* **regarde un peu ce qu'a fait ton cousin, et prends-en de la g.!** just look at what your cousin's done and take a leaf out of his book!; **c'est une mauvaise g.** he's a bad lot, *Péj* **g. de voyou/voleur!** you little lout/thief!; *F* **casser la g.** to have a bite to eat, to have a snack

▶ **graine**: **g. d'anis** aniseed; **g. de lin** linseed; **g. de moutarde** mustard seed; **g. d'orge** barleycorn, grain of barley; *Menuis* barleycorn

grainer [grene] *vt* (*poudre à canon*) to granulate; (*cire*) to shred; (*sel*) to grain

graineterie [grɛntri] *nf* (*commerce*) seed trade; (*boutique*) seed shop

grainetier, -ière [grɛntje, -jɛr] *n* corn chandler

graissage [grɛsaʒ] *nm* **(a)** *Tech* greasing, oiling, lubrication; **huile de g.** lubricating oil; **circuit de g.** lubrication system; **faire faire un g.** to have one's car lubricated **(b)** *Typ* emboldening

graisse [grɛs] *nf* **(a)** (*d'animal, de personne*) fat; *Tech* grease; **g. animale/végétale** animal/vegetable fat; **pistolet** *ou* **pompe** *ou* **injecteur à g.** grease gun **(b)** *Typ* thickness of type; (*de caractère*) weight **(c)** (*altération*) **tourner à la g.** (*d'un vin*) to become ropy

▶ **graisse**: **g. de baleine** blubber; **g. pour engrenages** gear lubricant; **g. pour essieux** axle grease; **g. lubrifiante** lubricant; *Tech* **g. minérale** crude paraffin, mineral jelly; **g. de phoque** seal blubber; **g. de porc** lard; **g. au silicone** silicone grease

graisser [grese] **1** *vt* **(a)** (*enduire de graisse*), *Tech* to grease, to oil, to lubricate; (*bottes*) to oil, *Br* to dubbin; **g. ses vêtements** (*par accident*) to get grease on one's clothes, to make one's clothes greasy; **g. la patte à qn** to grease sb's palm, to bribe sb **(b)** *Typ* to embolden **2** *vi* **(a)** (*d'un vin*) to become ropy **(b)** **onguent qui ne graisse pas** non-greasy ointment

graisseur, -euse [grɛsœr, -øz] *MecE* **1** *adj* **godet g.** grease box; **pistolet g.** grease gun **2** *n* (*ouvrier*) greaser, oiler **3** *nm* (*appareil*) greaser, lubricator; (*point de graissage*) grease *or* lubrication nipple, nipple

graisseux, -euse [grɛsø, -øz] *adj* **(a)** (*taché de graisse*) greasy **(b)** (*tumeur, tissu*) fatty; **bourrelet g.** roll of fat **(c)** (*altéré*) (*vin*) ropy

graminacées [graminase] *nfpl Bot* Graminaceae

graminé [gramine] *Bot* **1** *adj* graminaceous **2** *nfpl* **graminées** grasses, *Spéc* Gramineae

grammage [gramaʒ] *nm* (*du papier*) grammage, gms

grammaire [gramɛr] *nf* **(a)** (*science, règles*) grammar; **faute/règle de g.** grammatical error/rule **(b)** (*livre*) grammar (book)

grammairien, -ienne [gramɛrjɛ̃, -jɛn] *n* grammarian

grammatical, -ale, -aux, -ales [gramatikal, -o] *adj* grammatical

grammaticalement [gramatikalmɑ̃] *adv* grammatically

gramme [gram] *nm* gram(me) (= 0.0353 oz); **ne pas/perdre prendre un g.** not to lose/not to put on an ounce; *Fig F* **il n'a pas un g. de fantaisie/bon sens** he hasn't an ounce of imagination/common sense

gramophone [ɡramɔfɔn] *nm* gramophone

grand, grande [grɑ̃, grɑ̃d] **1** *adj* [①B10,D,3] **(a)** (*de taille*) big, large; **grande ville/maison** large *or* big town/house; **grands bras/grandes jambes** long arms/legs; **grande distance** great distance; **c'est à une grande distance d'ici** it's a long way away from here; **plus g. que nature** larger than life; **un g. lit** a big *or* large bed; (*à deux personnes*) a double bed; **la grande échelle** (*des pompiers*) the (firemen's) tall *or* long ladder; **faire de grands pas** to take big *or* large strides; *Fig* **marcher à grands pas vers la gloire/la sagesse** to stride towards glory/wisdom; **la démocratie avance à grands pas** democracy is making great strides, democracy is advancing by leaps and bounds; **avancer à grands pas vers la paix/la réussite** to make great strides towards peace/success; **avancer à grands pas vers la catastrophe/la guerre** to advance rapidly towards disaster/war; *Opt* **(objectif) g. angle** wide-angle lens; **un g. A** a capital A; **le G. Montréal** Greater Montreal; **une grande société** a big *or* large company; **les grandes sociétés pétrolières** the big *or* large *or* major oil companies

(b) (*en hauteur*) tall; **homme g.** tall man; **un g. homme blond** a tall fair man; **un g. palmier** a tall palm tree; **cet enfant est très g. pour son âge** that child is very tall for his age; **pas plus g. que ça** only so high

(c) (*principal*) chief, main; **la grand-rue** the high street, *Am* the main street; **la grand-messe** high mass; **le g. salon** the main drawing room; **grande ligne** inter-city line

(d) (*qui n'est plus enfant*) **quand tu seras g.** when you're big *or* grown up, when you're old enough; **elle n'est pas assez grande pour comprendre** she's not old enough to understand; **je suis assez g. pour me débrouiller tout seul** I'm big *or* old enough to fend for myself; **un g. garçon** a big boy; **son g. frère** his big brother

(e) (*en quantité, intense*) **g. bruit** loud noise; **g. froid** severe *or* intense cold; **g. vent** high wind; **g. désordre** great disorder; **g. buveur** big *or* heavy *or* hard drinker; **grandes pluies** heavy rain; **laver** *ou* **nettoyer à grande eau** (*sol, cour etc*) to wash down (with large quantities of water); **le g. air leur fera du bien** the fresh air will do them good; **vivre au g. air** to live in the open air; **il fait g. jour** it's broad daylight; **étaler sa vie privée au g. jour** to expose one's private life to the public gaze; **sa malhonnêteté/le scandale est apparu(e) au g. jour** his dishonesty/the scandal has been exposed

(f) (*pour insister*) **une grande heure/journée** a full *or* good hour/day; **il est g. temps que tu le lui dises** it's high time you told him; **avec le plus g. plaisir** with the greatest (of) pleasure; **ils sont grands amis** they are great friends

(g) (*important, puissant*) great; **une grande découverte** a great discovery; **un g. nombre** a large number; **le g. nombre n'apprécierait pas ce genre de films** the majority (of people) wouldn't appreciate this type of film; **grande diffusion** (*de journaux etc*) mass circulation; **grande distribution** mass distribution; **dans le plus g. détail** in the greatest *or* fullest detail; **en grande partie** largely, to a great extent; **un g. jour** a big *or* great day; **grandes dates de l'histoire** great dates in history; **g. changement** big *or* major *or* great change; **un g. amour** a great love; **le g. amour** true love; **nous étions au g. complet** we were all there; **l'équipe/la famille au g. complet** the whole team/family; **un acteur sans g. talent** an actor with little talent, an undistinguished actor; **un homme de g. talent** a very talented man, a man with great talent; **grands vins** great *or* vintage wines; **un g. cru de bordeaux** a great Bordeaux vintage; **un g. savant/écrivain** a great scientist/writer; **une grande dame** a great lady, a grand lady; **une grande dame de la littérature** a great literary lady; **grands hommes** great men; **un g. seigneur** a nobleman; **se donner des grands airs** to give oneself airs (and graces)

(h) (*fastueux, ambitieux*) **un g. projet** a great *or* grand plan; **un g. mariage** a big wedding

(i) (*dans un titre, un grade*) **g. officier de la légion d'honneur** Grand Officer of the Legion of Honour

2 *adv* **faire g.** to do things in a big way *or* on a large *or* grand scale; **voir g.** (*avoir de vastes projets*) to have big ideas, to think big; **ils avaient vu g. pour le banquet** they didn't do things by halves for the banquet; **ouvrir la fenêtre tout g.** to open the window wide; **faire les choses en g.** to do things in a big way *or* on a large *or* grand scale; **ils voient toujours tout en g.** they always see everything on a grand scale; **statue en g.** life-size statue; **reproduction en g.** enlarged copy; **je veux la même photo en g.** I want the same photo but enlarged; **le même poupée, mais en g.** the same doll, but bigger *or* larger; **yeux grand(s) ouverts** wide open eyes; **il était assis là, la bouche grande ouverte** he was sitting there with his mouth wide open; **ouvrir toutes**

les fenêtres en g. to open all the windows wide; **il n'y avait pas g. monde** there weren't many people there; **il n'y a pas g. vent** there's not much wind, it's not very windy

3 *n* (*personne de grande taille, adulte*) **grands et petits** (*en taille*) big and small; (*en âge*) old and young, grown-ups and children; *Scol* **les grands** the senior boys (and girls), the seniors; **mon g.** my friend; **ma grande** my dear; *Scol* **la cour des grands** the older children's playground; *Fig* **jouer dans la cour des grands** to be like the big boys

4 *nm* (*homme, état puissant*) **g. (d'Espagne)** grandee; **les grands** the great men; **les grands de ce monde** those in high places; **Alexandre le G.** Alexander the Great; *Pol* **les Grands** the Great Powers; **les Quatre Grands** the Big Four; **les grands du pétrole** the oil giants

▶ **grand**: **g. blessé** seriously wounded person; **les grands blessés** the seriously wounded; **la grande bourgeoisie** the upper middle class; **g. brûlé** seriously burned person; (*d'un point de vue médical*) serious burns case; **g. écran** wide screen; (*au cinéma*) big screen; *Scol* **les grandes classes** *Br* the upper forms, *Am* the higher grades; **les grands départs** the holiday rush; **grande école** = prestigious university-level institute with competitive entrance examination; **g. ensemble**, *pl* **grands ensembles** housing estate; **vivre dans un g. ensemble** to live on a housing estate; *Journ* **g. format** broadsheet; **g. livre des achats** purchase ledger; **g. livre des comptes** accounts ledger; **g. livre général** nominal ledger, general ledger; **g. livre de paie** wages ledger; **g. livre des ventes** sales ledger; **grandes marées** spring tides; *Naut* **le g. mât** the mainmast; **le g. monde** (high) society; **le g. Nord** the far North; *Rad* **grandes ondes** long wave; *Ordinat* **g. ordinateur** mainframe; **grande personne** grown-up; **le g. public** the general public, the public at large; **un film pour le g. public** a film for everybody; **les grandes puissances** the great *or* major powers; *Mil* **g. quartier général** general headquarters; **g. reporter** senior reporter, chief reporter; *Ordinat* **g. réseau** wide area network; **grande surface** superstore; **les grandes vacances** the summer holidays *or Am* vacation; *Univ* the long vacation

grand-angle [grɑ̃tɑ̃gl], *pl* **grands-angles,** [grɑ̃zɑ̃gl] **grand-angulaire** [grɑ̃tɑ̃gylɛr], *pl* **grands-angulaires** [grɑ̃zɑ̃gylɛr] *Opt* **1** *adj* wide-angle **2** *nm* wide-angle lens

grand-chose 1 *pron indéf* (*souvent employé avec pas*) (*peu de choses*) **pas g.** not much; **elle ne fait pas g.** she doesn't do much; **il n'y a pas g. qui le fasse rire** there's not much that makes him laugh; **il ne sera** *ou* **ne fera jamais g.** he'll never amount to much; **cela ne fait pas g.** it's of no great importance, it doesn't matter much; **il prend des médicaments mais ça ne fait pas g.** he takes medicine, but it doesn't help much; **la mort de son chien ne lui a pas fait g.** his dog's death didn't bother him much; **cela ne vaut pas g.** it's not worth much; **ça n'a pas servi à g.** it wasn't much use; **ce ne sont que quelques fleurs, ce n'est pas g.** it's just a few flowers, nothing much

2 *n F* (*personne*) **un/une pas g.** a dead loss

grand-croix, *pl* **grands-croix 1** *nf inv* Grand Cross (*of the Legion of Honour*) **2** *nm* Knight Grand Cross

grand-duc, *pl* **grands-ducs** *nm* **(a)** (*noble*) grand duke; *F* **faire la tournée des grands-ducs** to go out on the town **(b)** (*oiseau*) great horned owl, eagle owl

grand-ducal, -ale, -aux, -ales *adj* grand-ducal

grand-duché, *pl* **grands-duchés** *nm* grand duchy

Grande-Bretagne [grɑ̃dbrətaɲ] *nf* Great Britain

grande-duchesse, *pl* **grandes-duchesses** *nf* grand duchess

grandelet, -ette [grɑ̃dlɛ, -ɛt] *adj F Vieilli* tallish

grandement [grɑ̃dmɑ̃] *adv* **(a)** (*noblement*) grandly, nobly **(b)** (*généreusement*) **faire les choses g.** to do things lavishly *or* on a lavish *or* grand scale **(c)** (*largement*) greatly; **se tromper g.** to be greatly mistaken; **avoir g. raison/tort** to be completely *or* absolutely right/wrong; **avoir g. le temps** to have ample time; **il est g. temps de/que …** it is high time to/that …; **avoir g. de quoi vivre** to have plenty to live on

grandeur [grɑ̃dœr] *nf* **(a)** (*taille*) size; (*d'un arbre*) height, size; **échelle de grandeurs** scale of sizes; **g. nature** full-size(d), life-size(d); **une poupée de la g. d'un enfant de deux ans** a doll the size of *or* as big as a two-year-old child; **deux vases de la même g.** two vases (of) the same size; **nous sommes de la même g.** we are the same height *or* size; *Fig* **regarder qn du haut de sa g.** to look down on sb

(b) (*importance, ampleur*) importance; (*d'un amour, d'un sentiment, d'une folie*) greatness; (*d'une conception*) grandeur; *Math* magnitude; *Astron* **étoile de première g.** star of the first magnitude

(c) (*importance dans la société*) **se donner des airs de g.** to give oneself airs (and graces); **avoir la folie des grandeurs** to have delusions of grandeur

(d) (*gloire*) greatness, grandeur; **une chanteuse d'opéra très admirée au temps de sa g.** an opera singer greatly admired when she was at her peak; **g. et décadence d'un empire** rise and fall of an empire; **la g. de Rome** the grandeur *or* greatness of Rome

(e) (*dignité, noblesse*) nobility; **g. d'âme** magnanimity, nobility of soul

(f) (*titre honorifique*) **sa G. l'archevêque** His Grace the Archbishop; **votre G.** (*à un duc, une duchesse, un archevêque*) Your Grace

grand-guignol *nm inv Péj* **c'est du g.** it's all blood and thunder

grand-guignolesque [grɑ̃giɲɔlɛsk] *adj Péj* (*personne*) blood-and-thunder; (*pièce de théâtre, film etc*) gruesome

grandiloquence [grɑ̃dilɔkɑ̃s] *nf* grandiloquence

grandiloquent [grɑ̃dilɔkɑ̃] *adj* grandiloquent

grandiose [grɑ̃djoz] *adj* (*cérémonie, proportions*) imposing, grandiose; (*spectacle, vue*) imposing, awe-inspiring; **sa gaffe a quand même été g.** his blunder was a real beauty

grandir [grɑ̃dir] **1** *vi* (*en taille*) to grow; (*en âge*) to grow up; **elle a grandi** she has grown, she is taller; **il a grandi en un rien de temps** he shot up really quickly; **un arbre qui grandit vite** a tree which grows quickly, a fast-growing tree; **il comprendra en grandissant** he'll understand as he grows up *or* grows older; *Fig* **g. en sagesse/beauté** to increase *or* grow in wisdom/beauty; **son influence/son importance/sa compréhension grandit** his influence/importance/understanding is increasing *or* growing; **sa faim allait grandissant** he grew more and more hungry

2 *vt* **g. l'importance de qch** to exaggerate *or* overstate the importance of sth; **ses talons la grandissent** her heels make her look taller; *Fig* **ses malheurs l'ont grandi** his misfortunes have made him stronger; (*aux yeux des autres*) his misfortunes have increased his stature; **il est sorti grandi de ce conflit/de cette épreuve** he came out of this conflict/the ordeal a stronger person; **cela ne la grandit pas à mes yeux** that does not improve her standing in my eyes

3 se grandir *vpr* **se g. en se haussant sur la pointe des pieds** to make oneself taller by standing on tiptoe

grandissant [grɑ̃disɑ̃] *adj* (*influence, peur, torpeur etc*) growing, increasing

grandissement [grɑ̃dismɑ̃] *nm* **(a)** *Opt* magnification **(b)** *Vieilli* growth, increase

grandissime [grɑ̃disim] *adj F* marvellous, tremendous; **g. favori** firm favourite

grand(-)livre, *pl* **grands(-)livres** *nm Com* ledger

grand-maman, *pl* **grand(s)-mamans** *nf* grandma, granny

grand-mère, *pl* **grand(s)-mères** *nf* grandmother; *F* (*vieille femme*) old granny

grand-messe, *pl* **grand(s)-messes** *nf Rel* high mass; *Fig* ritual; (*de parti politique*) jamboree

grand-oncle [grɑ̃tɔ̃kl], *pl* **grands-oncles** [grɑ̃zɔ̃kl] *nm* great-uncle

grand-papa, *pl* **grands-papas** *nm* grandpa, grandad

grand-peine (à) *adv* with great difficulty

grand-père, *pl* **grands-pères** *nm* grandfather; *F* (*vieil homme*) grandad, grandpa

grand-prêtre, *pl* **grands-prêtres** *nm* high priest

grand-route, *pl* **grand-routes** *nf* main road

grand-rue, *pl* **grand-rues** *nf* high street, main street

grands-parents *nmpl* grandparents

grand-tante, *pl* **grand(s)-tantes** *nf* great aunt

grand-vergue, *pl* **grand(s)-vergues** *nf Naut* main yard

grand-voile, *pl* **grand(s)-voiles** *nf Naut* mainsail

grange [grɑ̃ʒ] *nf* barn

granit(e) [granit] *nm* granite; *Fig Litt* **cœur de g.** heart of stone

granité, -ée [granite] **1** *adj* granite-like **2** *nm* **(a)** *Tex* pebble weave **(b)** *Culin* (*glace*) = water ice

graniteux, -euse [granitø, -øz] *adj Minér* granitic

granitique [granitik] *adj* granitic

granivore [granivɔr] **1** *adj* granivorous **2** *n* granivore

granulaire [granylɛr] *adj* granular

granulation [granylasjɔ̃] *nf Tech* granulation

granule [granyl] *nm* granule; *Pharm* small pill

granulé [granyle] **1** *adj* granulated **2** *nm Pharm* granule

granuler [granyle] *vt* to granulate

granuleux, -euse [granylø, -øz] *adj* granular; *Biol* **cellule granuleuse** granule cell

grape(-)fruit, *pl* **grape(-)fruits** [grɛpfrut] *nm* grapefruit

graphe [graf] *nm* graph

grapheur [grafœr] *nm Ordinat* graphics package

graphie [grafi] *nf Ling* written form

graphique [grafik] **1** *adj* (*signe, méthode etc*) graphic; **arts graphiques** graphic arts; *Ordinat* **palette g.** graphics palette

2 *nm* diagram; (*sur un axe*) graph; *Ordinat* graphic; *Ordinat* **g. de gestion** management chart; **g. de type camembert** pie chart; **g. de type lignes** line chart; **g. financier** financial chart; **g. à secteurs** pie chart; **g. à tuyaux d'orgue** bar chart; **g. à** *ou* **en barres** bar chart

graphiquement [grafikmɑ̃] *adv* graphically

graphisme [grafism] *nm* **(a)** (*écriture*) hand(writing) **(b)** *Beaux-Arts* **le g. élégant de Degas** Degas's elegant style of drawing *or* handling of line; *Ordinat* **graphismes** graphics

graphiste [grafist] *n* graphic designer, graphic(s) artist

graphitage [grafitaʒ] *nm Tech* graphitization

graphite [grafit] *nm* graphite

graphité [grafite] *adj* **huile graphitée** graphite oil

graphiteux, -euse [grafitø, -øz], **graphitique** [grafitik] *adj* graphitic

graphologie [grafɔlɔʒi] *nf* graphology

graphologique [grafɔlɔʒik] *adj* graphological

graphologue [grafɔlɔg] *n* graphologist

grappe [grap] *nf* **(a)** (*de raisin*) bunch; (*de lilas, de glycine*) cluster; *Fig* (*de gens*) cluster, group; *Vulg* **lâche-moi la g.** piss off **(b)** *Bot* raceme

grappillage [grapijaʒ] *nm* **(a)** (*de raisin*) gleaning **(b)** *Fig* (*d'argent*) making something on the side; (*petits vols*) pilfering

grappiller [grapije] **1** *vi* (*dans un vignoble*) to glean **2** *vt* **(a)** *Fig* (*recueillir au hasard*) to pick up; **g. des renseignements** to glean information **(b)** *Fig* (*détourner*) to make on the side; (*piquer, voler*) to pilfer

grappin [grapɛ̃] *nm* **(a)** *Naut* grapnel, grappling (hook *or* iron); *Fig F* **mettre le g. sur qch/qn** to get one's hands on *or* get hold of sth/sb **(b)** (*benne*) (*d'un dragueur*) grab; (*d'une grue*) clutch

gras, grasse [grɑ, grɑs] **1** *adj* **(a)** (*viande, nourriture, tissu*) fatty; **matières grasses** fats; **yaourt à 0% de matière grasse** fat-free yoghurt; *Ch* **acide g.** fatty acid; **mardi g.** Shrove Tuesday

(b) (*gros*) (*personne, animal*) fat; (*poulet*) plump; **g. comme un porc** *ou* **un cochon** as fat as a pig; *très F* **être g. du bide** to be flabby round the stomach; *Fig* **tuer le veau g.** to kill the fatted calf; **plante grasse** succulent (plant)

(c) (*graisseux*) (*chiffon, cheveux etc*) greasy; **eaux grasses** swill

(d) (*épais*) (*terre*) heavy, clayey; (*boue*) thick, slimy; **crayon g.** soft lead pencil; **crème pour peaux grasses** cream for greasy skin; **vin g.** ropy wine; **toux grasse** loose *or* phlegmy cough; **voix grasse** throaty voice; **rire g.** throaty laugh

(e) *Typ* bold; **caractères g.** bold(-faced) type

(f) *Fig* **offrir une grasse récompense** to offer a handsome reward; **faire la grasse matinée** to have a lie-in

(g) (*graveleux*) (*histoire*) dirty, smutty

2 *adv* **(a) faire g., manger g.** to eat meat (*esp on a fast day*); *Arg* **il n'y en a pas g.** (*non comptable*) there's not much of it; (*comptable*) there aren't many of them; **des gens comme lui, il n'y en a pas g.!** there aren't many people like him!

(b) rire g. to laugh coarsely

3 *nm* **(a)** *Anat* **le g. de la jambe/du bras/du ventre** the fleshy part of the leg/arm/stomach

(b) (*du jambon, de la viande*) fat

(c) *Typ* bold; **en g.** in bold, in bold(-faced) type

gras-double, *pl* **gras-doubles** *nm Culin* tripe

grassement [grɑsmɑ̃] *adv* **(a)** (*confortablement*) **vivre g.** to live off the fat of the land **(b)** (*d'une façon peu élégante*) **rire g.** to laugh coarsely **(c)** (*largement*) **récompenser qn g.** to reward sb handsomely *or* generously; **g. payé, g. rétribué** very well paid

grasseyement [grasɛjmɑ̃] *nm* pronunciation of one's r's from the back of the throat

grasseyer [graseje] *vi* to pronounce one's r's from the back of the throat

grassouillet, -ette [grɑsujɛ, -ɛt] *adj* (*personne*) plump, chubby

grateron [gratrɔ̃] *nm Bot* goose-grass, cleavers

gratifiant [gratifjɑ̃] *adj* rewarding, gratifying

gratification [gratifikasjɔ̃] *nf* **(a)** (*prime*) bonus; **g. de fin d'année** end of year bonus **(b)** *Psy* gratification

gratifier [gratifje] *vt* (*impf, pr sub* **n. gratifiions, v. gratifiiez**) **(a) g. qn de qch** to present sb with sth; **il a été gratifié d'une grosse récompense** he was presented with a large reward; *Iron* **être gratifié d'une amende** to be landed with a fine; **et je fus gratifié d'une paire de gifles** and my reward was a slap in the face **(b)** *Psy* (*personne*) to gratify

gratin [gratɛ̃] *nm* **(a)** *Culin* gratin; **un g. de pâtes/de poisson** a pasta/fish gratin; **au g.** au gratin, (cooked) with (breadcrumbs and) grated cheese; **chou-fleur au g.** = cauliflower cheese **(b)** *Fig F* **le g.** (*le beau monde*) the upper crust

▶ **gratin**: **g. dauphinois** = sliced potatoes baked with milk and browned on top

gratiné, -ée [gratine] **1** *adj* **(a)** *Culin* sprinkled with (breadcrumbs and) cheese, au gratin **(b)** *Fig F* **une addition gratinée** an enormous bill; **c'est g.!** that's a bit much!; **une histoire gratinée** an incredible story; **il était g., l'exam de ce matin!** this morning's exam was a real killer *or* was really stiff!; **son mari, il est g.** her husband's a prize idiot **2** *nf Culin* **gratinée** onion soup au gratin

gratiner [gratine] **1** *vt* to cook au gratin **2** *vi* **un plat qui gratine au four** a dish browning in the oven

gratis [gratis] **1** *adv* gratis, for nothing, free of charge **2** *adj* (*billet*) free

gratitude [gratityd] *nf* gratitude

grattage [grataʒ] *nm* **(a)** (*d'un mur*) scraping; *Chir* (*d'un os*) scraping **(b)** *Tex* teaseling, napping, raising

gratte [grat] *nf* **(a)** *F* (*profits illicites*) pickings, profits on the side; **faire de la g.** to make a bit on the side **(b)** *F* (*guitare*) guitar; **jouer de la g.** to play the guitar **(c)** *Can* snowplough, *US* snowplow

gratte-ciel *nm inv* skyscraper

gratte-cul, *pl* **gratte-culs** *nm* rosehip

gratte-dos *nm inv* backscratcher

grattement [gratmɑ̃] *nm* scratching

gratte-papier *nm inv Péj* pen-pusher

gratte-pieds *nm inv* (metal) doormat

gratter [grate] **1** *vt* **(a)** (*avec les ongles*) to scratch; (*avec qch de dur*) to scrape; (*effacer*) (*mot, inscription*) to scratch out; (*tache*) to scrape off; **g. (la terre) du pied** (*d'un cheval*) to paw the ground; **g. le dos de qn** to scratch sb's back; *F* **ça me gratte terriblement** it makes me itch like mad; **poil à g.** itching powder; **vin qui gratte le gosier** wine that is harsh *or* rough on the throat; *Fig* **g. les fonds de tiroir** to scrape around for money; **c'est une affaire où il n'y a pas grand-chose à g.** you can't make much out of that

(b) *F* (*dépasser*) (*un coureur, une autre voiture*) to overtake, to pass; *Fig* to overtake

(c) *Tex* **laine grattée** brushed wool

2 *vi* **(a) pull qui gratte** scratchy pullover; **g. à la porte** to tap at the door; *Fig* **il a l'air très cultivé, mais si tu grattes un peu ...** he has a very cultured air, but if you scratch away his veneer a bit ...; **pas besoin de g. beaucoup pour s'apercevoir qu'il est bête** it soon becomes pretty obvious that he's stupid

(b) g. du violon/de la guitare to scrape away on the fiddle/to strum away on the guitar

(c) (*ne pas glisser*) **plume qui gratte** scratchy nib

(d) *F* **j'ai gratté toute la nuit** (*travaillé*) I slaved away all night; (*écrit*) I scribbled away all night

3 se gratter *vpr* **(a)** to scratch oneself; **se g. jusqu'au sang** to scratch oneself raw; **se g. la tête/l'oreille** to scratch one's head/ear

(b) *très F* **tu peux toujours te g.!** you can whistle for it!, nothing doing!

gratteron [gratrɔ̃] *nm Bot* goose grass, cleavers

grattoir [gratwar] *nm* scraper; *Typ* slice; **g. de bureau** erasing knife, scraper eraser

grattons [gratɔ̃] *nmpl* pork scratchings

grat(t)ouiller [gratuje] *vt F* **(a)** (*démanger*) **ça me grattouille** it makes me itch **(b)** (*guitare*) to strum away on

gratuit [gratɥi] *adj* **(a)** free (of charge); **à titre g.** gratis, free of charge; **prêt à titre g.** free loan **(b)** *Fig* (*acte, insulte, violence etc*) gratuitous

gratuité [gratɥite] *nf* **(a) la g. de l'enseignement/des soins hospitaliers** free education/hospital care **(b)** *Fig* (*d'une insulte, de la violence etc*) gratuitousness

gratuitement [gratɥitmɑ̃] *adv* **(a)** for nothing, free (of charge) **(b)** *Fig* (*sans motif*) gratuitously, without provocation

gravats [gravɑ] *nmpl* **(a)** (*après criblage de plâtre*) (*du plâtre*) screenings **(b)** (*après démolition*) rubble

grave [grav] **1** *adj* **(a)** (*digne, solennel*) (*visage*) grave, serious; (*ton*) grave, solemn; (*expression*) sober, solemn; (*très important*) (*affaires*) important, weighty; (*qui a des conséquences fâcheuses*) (*blessure*) serious; **elle ne s'absente de son travail que pour raison g.** she never stays away from work except for serious reasons; **faire** *ou* **commettre une g. erreur** to make a serious mistake; **subir une g. opération** to undergo a serious operation; **accident qui a fait un mort et deux blessés graves** accident in which one person died and two were seriously injured; **hélas!, il y avait plus g.** alas! there was worse to come

(b) *Mus* (*note, voix*) low, deep; **sons graves** bass tones (**c**) *Gram* **accent g.** grave (accent)

(**d**) *Arch* (*lourd*) heavy; *Phys* **corps g.** heavy body

2 *nm Mus* **sa voix n'est belle que dans le g.** *ou* **les graves** his voice is attractive only in the low registers

gravé [grave] *adj* **pierre gravée** engraved stone; **image gravée** graven image

graveleux, -euse [gravlø, -øz] *adj* (**a**) (*terre*) gravelly (**b**) (*histoire, chanson*) smutty, dirty

gravelle [gravɛl] *nf Méd Arch* gravel

gravement [gravmɑ̃] *adv* (**a**) (*avec dignité*) gravely, solemnly (**b**) (*d'une manière importante, dangereuse*) **g. malade/blessé** seriously ill/injured; **il s'est g. trompé** he was seriously *or* greatly mistaken; **il est g. menacé** he faces a serious threat

graver [grave] *vt* (*matériau, motif*) to engrave; *Mus* **g. un disque** to make *or* cut a record; **g. à l'eau-forte** to etch; *Fig* **cela reste gravé dans ma mémoire** *ou* **en moi** it is engraved on my memory; *Fig* **ce n'est pas gravé sur son front** you can't tell from looking at him

graveur [gravœr] **1** *nm* engraver; **g. à l'eau-forte** etcher; **g. sur bois** wood engraver **2** *adj* **bain g.** etching bath

gravide [gravid] *adj Méd* gravid

gravier [gravje] *nm* gravel; **couvrir un chemin de g.** to cover a path with gravel, to gravel a path

gravillon [gravijɔ̃] *nm* (fine) gravel, grit; **gravillons** *Br* loose chippings, *Am* gravel

gravillonnage [gravijɔnaʒ] *nm* (fine-)gravelling

gravillonner [gravijɔne] *vt* to (fine-)gravel

gravimétrie [gravimetri] *nf Phys* gravimetry

gravimétrique [gravimetrik] *adj Phys* gravimetric

gravir [gravir] *vt* (*montagne, escalier*) to climb; (*échelle*) to climb, to mount; *Fig* **g. les échelons** to climb the ladder

gravissime [gravisim] *adj* extremely serious

gravitation [gravitasjɔ̃] *nf Phys* gravitation

gravitationnel [gravitasjɔnɛl] *adj Phys* gravitational; **force gravitationnelle** force of gravity

gravité [gravite] *nf* (**a**) *Phys* gravity; **g. spécifique** specific gravity; **centre de g.** centre of gravity; **alimentation par g.** gravity feed (**b**) (*réserve, sérieux*) gravity, seriousness (**c**) (*danger*) (*d'une maladie, d'une opération*) seriousness; **blessure sans g.** slight *or* minor wound; **accident/chute sans g.** minor accident/fall (**d**) (*importance*) (*d'un problème*) gravity, seriousness

graviter [gravite] *vi* (**a**) to revolve (**autour de** round); **g. autour de la terre** to orbit the earth; *Fig* **g. autour de qn** to hover around sb; **les flatteurs qui gravitent dans les hautes sphères du pouvoir** the flatterers who move in the higher echelons of power (**b**) *Vieilli* to gravitate (**vers** towards)

gravois [gravwa] *nmpl Vieilli* = **gravats**

gravure [gravyr] *nf* (**a**) (*action*) engraving; **g. à l'eau-forte** etching; **g. en creux** intaglio engraving; **g. en taille-douce** copperplate engraving; **g. sur bois** woodcutting, wood engraving (**b**) (*ouvrage*) engraving; **g. à l'eau-forte** etching; **g. en taille-douce, g. sur cuivre** copperplate (engraving); **g. sur bois** woodcut, wood engraving; **g. en couleurs** colour print; **g. hors texte** full-page plate; **g. avant la lettre** proof before letters; **g. de mode** fashion plate; *Fig* **cette fille est une g. de mode** that girl's a real fashion plate

grayé [greje] *adj Can* (*pour faire qch*) well-equipped; *F* (*bien monté*) well-hung

gré [gre] *nm* (**a**) (*goût*) **à mon g., selon mon g.** to my liking, to my taste; (*à ma guise*) as I please *or* like; **elle va et vient à son (bon) g.** she comes and goes as she pleases *or* likes; **je m'habille à mon g.** I dress to please myself; **trouver qch à son g.** to find sth to one's liking; **une chambre à mon g.** a room that I like *or* that suits me, a room to my liking

(**b**) (*volonté*) **se marier contre le g. de son père** to get married against one's father's wishes; **elle a dû accepter contre son g.** she had to accept against her will; **bail renouvelable au g. du locataire** lease renewable at the option of the tenant; **de mon propre g., de mon plein g.** of my own free will, of my own accord; **de bon g.** willingly, gladly; **de mauvais g.** reluctantly; **bon g. mal g.** whether we/you/*etc* like it or not, willy-nilly; **il faut qu'il vienne de g. ou de force** he has to come whether he wants to or not, he has to come willy-nilly; **au g. des flots** at the mercy of the waves; **de g. à g.** by (mutual) agreement; *Fig* **au g. des événements/circonstances** (*agir, changer d'avis etc*) according to how events turn out/to circumstances

(**c**) *Fml* (*gratitude*) **savoir g. à qn de (faire) qch** to be grateful to sb for (doing) sth; **nous vous saurions g. de bien vouloir ...** we would be grateful if you would kindly ...; *Vieilli* **savoir mauvais g. à qn de qch** to be annoyed with sb about sth

grèbe [grɛb] *nm* grebe

grébiche [grebiʃ], **grébige** [grebiʒ] *nf* (**a**) *Typ* (*d'un manuscrit etc*) file number (**b**) (*classeur*) loose-leaf binder

grec, grecque [grɛk] **1** *adj* Greek; **les orateurs grecs** the Greek orators; **tragédie grecque** Greek tragedy; **profil g.** Grecian profile **2** *nm Ling* Greek; **g. ancien/moderne** Ancient/Modern Greek **3** *n* **G.** Greek **4** *nf* **grecque** (**a**) *Culin* **à la g.** stewed with olive oil and herbs (**b**) *Archit, Beaux-Arts* Greek key pattern, Greek border

Grèce [grɛs] *nf* Greece

gréciser [gresize] *vt* to Hellenize; **g. un mot** to give a Greek form to a word

gréco-latin, -ine [grekolatɛ̃, -in], *pl* **gréco-latin(e)s** *adj Ling* Gr(a)eco-Latin

gréco-romain, -aine, *pl* **gréco-romain(e)s** [grekorɔmɛ̃, -ɛn] *adj* Gr(a)eco-Roman

gredin, -ine [grədɛ̃, -in] *n F Vieilli* (*vaurien*) rascal, wretch; *F* **petit g.!** you little rascal *or* horror!

gredinerie [grədinri] *nf Vieilli* (*acte*) mean *or* underhand action; (*conduite*) mean *or* underhand behaviour

gréement [gremɑ̃] *nm Naut* (**a**) (*ensemble des voiles*) rigging; (*équipement*) gear (**b**) (*disposition des mâts et des voiles*) (*d'un bateau*) rig; **g. Marconi** Bermuda rig

gréer [gree] *vt Naut* (*mât, bateau etc*) to rig; (*hamac, filets etc*) to sling; **gréé en carré** square-rigged; **g. une vergue** to send up a yard

gréeur [greœr] *nm Naut* rigger

greffage [grɛfaʒ] *nm Chir, Bot* grafting

greffe¹ [grɛf] *nf* (**a**) *Chir* (*de peau, de tissu*) graft; (*d'organe*) transplant; *Bot* graft, slip; **g. du cœur/du rein** heart/kidney transplant; **g. hépatique** liver transplant (**b**) *Bot* (*action*) **g. par œil détaché** budding; **g. en écusson** shield grafting *or* budding

greffe² *nm* (**a**) *Jur* clerk of the court's office (**b**) *Fin* (*de société par actions*) registry

greffé, -ée [grɛfe] *n Méd* **g. cardiaque** *ou* **du cœur** heart transplant patient

greffer [grefe] *vt Chir, Bot* (*peau, tissu, bouture*) to graft; *Chir* (*organe*) to transplant

greffeur [grefœr] *nm Bot* grafter, budder

greffier [grefje] *nm* (**a**) *Jur* clerk (of the court) (**b**) *Admin, Fin* registrar (**c**) *Arg* (*chat*), pussy(cat), moggy

greffoir [grɛfwar] *nm* grafting knife

greffon [grɛfɔ̃] *nm Chir* (*de tissu, de peau*) graft; (*d'organe*) transplant; *Bot* graft, slip

grégaire [gregɛr] *adj* gregarious; **l'instinct g.** the herd instinct

grégarisme [gregarism] *nm* gregariousness

grège [grɛʒ] *adj* (**a**) **soie g.** raw silk (**b**) (*couleur*) whitish-beige

grégeois [greʒwa] *adj Hist, Mil* **feu g.** Greek fire

grégorien, -ienne [gregɔrjɛ̃, -jɛn] **1** *adj* (*rite, réforme*) Gregorian; **chant g.** Gregorian chant **2** *nm* Gregorian chant

grêle¹ [grɛl] *adj* (*jambe, membres, main*) skinny; (*tige, silhouette*) slender; (*voix, son*) shrill; *Anat* **intestin g.** small intestine

grêle² *nf* hail; **orage de g.** hailstorm; *Fig* **g. de coups/balles** hail *or* shower of blows/bullets

grêlé [grele] *adj* (*peau*) pockmarked

grêler [grele] **1** *v impers* **il grêle** it's hailing **2** *vt* (*cultures etc*) to damage by hail; **la région a été complètement grêlée** the whole region has been hit by hail

grelin [grəlɛ̃] *nm Naut* hawser

grêlon [grɛlɔ̃] *nm* hailstone

grelot [grəlo] *nm* (small) bell; (*de traîneau*) sleigh bell; *Arg* **avoir les grelots** (*avoir peur*) to have the wind up

grelottement [grəlɔtmɑ̃] *nm* (**a**) (*tremblement*) shivering (**b**) (*tintement*) jingling, tinkling

grelotter [grəlɔte] *vi* (**a**) (*trembler*) **g. de froid/de peur** to shiver *or* tremble *or* shake with cold/fear (**b**) (*tinter*) to jingle, to tinkle

greluche [grəlyʃ] *nf Péj très F* chick, *Br* bird

Grenade [grənad] *nf* (**a**) (*en Espagne*) Granada (**b**) (*aux îles du Vent*) Grenada

grenade [grənad] *nf* (**a**) (*projectile*), *Mil* grenade; **g. à main** hand grenade; **g. fumigène** smoke grenade; **g. lacrymogène** tear-gas grenade; *Naut* **g. sous-marine** depth charge (**b**) (*fruit*) pomegranate

grenadier¹ [grənadje] *nm* (*arbre*) pomegranate (tree)

grenadier² *nm Mil* grenadier; *Fig* tall and masculine woman; **boire comme un g.** to drink like a fish

grenadière [grənadjɛr] *nf Mil* (*d'un fusil*) band

grenadine [grənadin] *nf* (**a**) *Culin* grenadine (**b**) *Tex* grenadine

grenaillage [grənɑjaʒ] *nm Tech* shot blasting

grenaille [grənɑj] *nf* (**a**) (*en métal*) shot; **g. de plomb** lead shot (**b**) (*pour la volaille*) refuse grain, tailings (**c**) *Belg* **grenailles errantes** (*sur panneau*) loose chippings, *Am* gravel

grenailler [grənɑje] *vt* (*métal*) to granulate

grenat [grəna] **1** *nm* garnet **2** *adj inv* garnet-red
grené [grəne] **1** *adj* (*dessin*) stippled; (*cuir*) grainy **2** *nm* (*de dessin*) stipple; (*de cuir*) grain
greneler [grənle] *vt* (**je grenelle, n. grenelons; je grenellerai**) (*papier, cuir*) to grain
grener [grəne] (**je grène, n. grenons; je grènerai**) **1** *vi* (*des céréales etc*) to seed **2** *vt* **(a)** (*réduire en grains*) (*poudre à canon*) to granulate; (*cire*) to shred; (*sel*) to grain **(b)** (*donner un aspect grené à*) (*papier, cuir*) to grain
grènetis [grɛnti] *nm* (*d'une pièce*) milled edge
grenier [grənje] *nm* **(a)** (*pour grain, fourrage*) granary; **g. à foin** hayloft; **g. à blé** corn loft, *Am* wheat loft; *Fig* **l'Égypte était le g. du monde ancien** Egypt was the granary of the ancient world **(b)** (*sous les combles*) attic, garret; **chercher qch de la cave au g.** to hunt high and low for sth, to search the house from top to bottom for sth; **ranger la maison de la cave au g.** to tidy up the house from top to bottom
grenouillage [grənujaʒ] *nm F Péj* shady dealing, scheming
grenouille [grənuj] *nf* **(a)** (*animal*) frog **(b)** *F* (*tirelire*) ≈ piggy bank; **manger la g.** to make off with the cash
▶ **grenouille**: *Fig* **g. de bénitier** Holy Joe; **g. taureau** *ou* **mugissante** bullfrog
grenouiller [grənuje] *vi F Péj* to go in for shady dealing, to scheme
grenouillère [grənujɛr] *nf* **(a)** (*marécage*) frog-pond **(b)** (*pour bébé*) sleepsuit
grenu [grəny] **1** *adj* **(a)** (*blé etc*) grainy, full of grain **(b)** (*cuir, peau etc*) grained; (*sel*) coarse-grained, crystalline **2** *nm* graininess, granularity
grenure [grənyr] *nf* **(a)** *Beaux-Arts* stippling, stipple **(b)** (*du cuir*) grain(ing)
grès [grɛ] *nm* **(a)** *Géol* sandstone **(b)** (*céramique*) **poterie de g., g. cérame** stoneware; **cruche en g.** stoneware jug
gréseux, -euse [grezø, -øz] *adj* gritty, sandy; **roches gréseuses** sandstone rocks, sandstones
grésil [grezi(l)] *nm* fine hail
grésillement [grezijmɑ̃] *nm* (*du feu*) crackling; (*de la flamme*) sputtering; (*d'une poêle à frire*) sizzling
grésiller[1] [grezije] *v impers* to hail
grésiller[2] *vi* (*du feu*) to crackle; (*de la flamme*) to sputter; (*d'une poêle à frire*) to sizzle
gressin [grɛsɛ̃] *nm Culin* bread stick
grève [grɛv] *nf* **(a)** (*arrêt du travail*) strike; **se mettre en g.** to go on *or* come out on strike, to strike, to take strike action *or* industrial action; **être en g., faire g.** to be on strike; **g. des trains/de la poste** train/postal strike; **briseur de g.** strike breaker; **piquet de g.** (strike) picket; **droit de g.** right to strike; **lancer un ordre de g.** to issue a strike order **(b)** (*le long de la mer*) (sea)shore, *Litt* strand; (*d'un fleuve*) (river) bank, *Litt* strand; **les grèves de la Loire** the sandbanks of the Loire; *Hist* **la (place de) G.** = open space on the banks of the Seine where dissatisfied workmen used to assemble
▶ **grève**: **g. de la faim** hunger strike; **faire une g. de la faim** to be/go on hunger strike; **g. générale** general strike; **g. partielle** partial strike; **g. perlée** go-slow (strike), *Am* slowdown; **g. de protestation** protest strike; **g. sauvage** wildcat strike; **g. de solidarité** sympathy strike; **g. sur le tas** sit-down strike; **g. surprise** lightning strike; **g. tournante** staggered strike; **g. du zèle** work-to-rule, go-slow
grever [grəve] *vt* (**je grève, n. grevons; je grèverai**) **(a)** (*alourdir*) (*succession*) to burden, to encumber; (*pouvoir d'achat*) to restrict; **grevé d'impôts** weighed down *or* burdened with tax; **ce week-end aux sports d'hiver a grevé notre budget** this winter sports weekend has put a strain on our budget **(b)** *Jur* (*propriété*) to mortgage
gréviste [grevist] **1** *n* striker; **g. de la faim** hunger striker **2** *adj* **mouvement g.** strike movement
gribiche [gribiʃ] *nf* loose-leaf binder
gribouillage [gribujaʒ] *nm* (*écriture*) scrawl, scribble; (*dessin*) doodle
gribouille [gribuj] *nm Vieilli* simpleton, nitwit, *Br* clot
gribouiller [gribuje] *vti* (*écrire*) to scribble, to scrawl; (*dessiner*) to doodle
gribouilleur, -euse [gribujœr, -øz] *n* scribbler
gribouillis [gribuji] *nm* = **gribouillage**
grief [grijɛf] *nm* grievance, ground for complaint; **faire g. à qn de qch** to hold sth against sb; **on lui a fait g. de ne pas se mêler aux autres** it was held against him that he didn't mix with the others
grièvement [grijɛvmɑ̃] *adv* seriously, severely, badly
griffe [grif] *nf* **(a)** (*d'animal*) claw; (*d'un faucon*) claw, talon; **faire ses griffes** (*d'un chat*) to sharpen its claws; *Fig* to cut one's teeth; **coup de g.** scratch; **donner un coup de g. à qn** to claw *or* scratch sb; *Fig* to have a dig at sb; *Fig* **montrer les griffes** to show one's claws; *Fig* **arracher qn des griffes de qn** to snatch sb out of sb's clutches; *Fig* **tomber/être sous** *ou* **entre les griffes de qn** to fall into/be in sb's clutches
(b) *MecE etc* claw, clip, clamp; (*outil*) dog; (*sur un bijou*) claw; **accouplement/embrayage à griffes** claw coupling/clutch; **griffes de monteur** climbing irons
(c) *Bot* (*de la vigne*) tendril; (*d'asperge*) crown
(d) (*empreinte*) stamped signature; (*ce qui sert à faire cette empreinte*) (signature) stamp; (*sur vêtements*) label; *Fig* stamp; **g. de grande marque** designer label; **g. de réception** received stamp; **on reconnaît la g. de Zola dans ce roman** the novel bears Zola's stamp; **on reconnaît la g. de Saint-Laurent** you can recognize the Saint-Laurent style
griffé [grife] *adj* designer; **foulard g.** designer scarf
griffer [grife] *vt* **(a)** (*d'un animal*) to scratch, to claw **(b)** (*signer*) (*vêtement*) to put one's label on; **Chanel a griffé cette veste** this jacket bears the Chanel label
griffon [grifɔ̃] *nm* **(a)** *Myth* griffon, gryphon, griffin **(b)** (*chien*) griffon (terrier) **(c)** (*oiseau*) griffon (vulture)
griffonnage [grifɔnaʒ] *nm* (*écriture*) scrawl, scribble; (*dessin*) quick sketch
griffonnement [grifɔnmɑ̃] *nm Beaux-Arts* (*en cire*) wax model; (*en terre*) clay model
griffonner [grifɔne] *vt* (*écrire*) to scrawl, to scribble; (*dessiner*) to sketch quickly
griffu [grify] *adj* **patte griffue** clawed foot; **main griffue** claw-like hand
griffure [grifyr] *nf* scratch
grigner [griɲe] *vi Tex* to pucker, to crinkle up
grignotage [griɲɔtaʒ] *nm* nibbling; *Fig* (*de libertés*) erosion
grignotement [griɲɔtmɑ̃] *nm* nibbling
grignoter [griɲɔte] **1** *vt* to nibble (at); *Fig* (*libertés*) to erode; *Fig* **g. son capital/ses économies** to eat into one's capital/one's savings; **les zones industrielles grignotent nos campagnes** industrial estates are gradually disfiguring our countryside **2** *vi* to nibble
grignoteur, -euse [griɲɔtœr, -øz] *n* nibbler
grigou [grigu] *nm F* skinflint, miser
gri-gri [grigri] *nm* amulet; (*porte-bonheur*) charm
gril [gril] *nm* **(a)** (*de cuisine*) grill, *Am* broiler; **faire cuire qch sur le g.** to grill sth, *Am* to broil sth; *Fig F* **être/mettre qn sur le g.** to be/keep sb on tenterhooks **(b)** *Tech* grating (*protecting sluice gate*); *Rail, Naut* gridiron; *Th* grid, gridiron **(c)** *Anat* **g. costal** rib cage
grill [gril] *nm* **(a)** *TV etc* (*pour l'éclairage*) pipe grid **(b)** *Culin* steakhouse, grill
grillade [grijad] *nf Culin* grilled *or Am* broiled meat, grilled *or Am* broiled chop *or* cutlet; (*assortiment*) mixed grill; **on va faire des grillades** we're having a barbecue
grillage[1] [grijaʒ] *nm* **(a)** (*de noix, de café etc*) roasting **(b)** *Métal* (*de minerais*) calcining, roasting **(c)** *Tex* singeing
grillage[2] *nm* **(a)** (metal) grating, grill(e); **g. en fil de fer** wire netting; **poser un g. électrifié** to put up an electrified fence **(b)** *Él* (*de plaque d'accumulateur*) grid, frame
grillager [grijaʒe] *vt* (**je grillageai(s); n. grillageons**) **(a)** (*garnir d'un grillage*) to fit a grill(e) to; **fenêtre grillagée** window covered with wire mesh; **verre grillagé** wired glass **(b)** (*entourer d'un grillage*) to surround with wire netting
grille [grij] *nf* **(a)** (*à l'entrée d'un parc, jardin etc*) (entrance) gate; (*clôture basse*) (*autour d'un monument etc*) railings; **séparé de la rue par une g.** separated from the road by railings **(b)** (*pour l'écoulement*) (*d'un évier, d'un égout etc*) grating, grate **(c)** (*à mailles fines*) screen, netting; (*du parloir d'un couvent*) grill(e) **(d)** *Él* (*d'un accumulateur, d'un tube à électrons*) grid; **courant de g.** grid current **(e)** (*tableau quadrillé*) (*de mots croisés*) grid
▶ **grille**: **g. d'analyse par fonction** functional analysis chart; **g. d'avancement** career structure; **g. d'entrée d'air** air vent; *Aut* **g.-calandres**, *pl* **grilles-calandres** grille; **g. d'horaires** timetable, schedule; *Compta* **g. d'imputation** table of account codes; **g. indiciaire** salary structure *or* scale; **g. produit/marché** product/market grid; *Rad, TV* **g. des programmes** programme schedule *or* grid; *Aut* **g. de radiateur** radiator grille; **g. de réchauffeur** heater matrix; *Ordinat* **g. de saisie** input grid; **g. des salaires** salary scale
grille-calandre, *pl* **grilles-calandres** *nf Aut* grille
grille-pain *nm inv* toaster
griller[1] [grije] **1** *vt* **(a)** (*rôtir, passer au gril*) (*viande*) to grill, *Am* to broil; (*pain*) to toast; (*café, marrons*) to roast
(b) *Métal* (*minerai*) to roast, to calcine
(c) *Tex* to singe
(d) (*brûler*) to scorch, to burn; *Él F* (*ampoule, fusible, moteur etc*) to burn out; **végétation grillée par le soleil** vegetation scorched by the sun; *F* **g. une cigarette** to smoke *or* have a cigarette, *Arg* **il est grillé** (*dévoilé*) his game's up; (*rayé*) he's had it; **g. un concurrent** to leave a competitor

standing; *Aut F* **g. un feu rouge** to jump the lights; *F* **g. les étapes** (*dans sa carrière*) to shoot up the ladder; (*dans un travail*) to cut corners

2 *vi* **(a)** *Culin* (*d'un morceau de viande*) to grill, *Am* to broil; (*d'un morceau de pain*) to toast; (*de marrons*) to roast; *Fig* **g. d'impatience** to be burning with impatience; **g. d'impatience à faire qch** to be burning to do sth; *Fig* **g. d'envie de faire qch** to be bursting *or* itching to do sth

(b) *Él* (*sauter*) to burn out

3 se griller *vpr* **se g. au soleil** to roast in the sun; *F* **se g. auprès de qn** to blot one's copybook with sb

griller[2] *vt* (*fenêtre*) to cover with wire mesh

grilloir [grijwar] *nm* grill

grillon [grijɔ̃] *nm* cricket

grill(-room), *pl* **grill-rooms** [grilrum] *nm* grill (room)

grimaçant [grimasɑ̃] *adj* grimacing

grimace [grimas] *nf* grimace; **faire une g.** to make *or* pull a face, to grimace; **arrête de faire des grimaces au professeur** stop making faces at the teacher; **faire la g.** (*avec dégoût*) to pull a long face; **faire une g. de douleur** to wince; **faire des grimaces** (*être maniéré*) to put on airs; *Prov* **on n'apprend pas à un vieux singe à faire des grimaces** ≈ don't teach your grandmother how to suck eggs

grimacer [grimase] **(je grimaçai(s), n. grimaçons) 1** *vi* to grimace, to make *or* pull a face; **g. de douleur** to grimace *or* wince with pain **2** *vt* **g. un sourire** to force a smile, to give a wry smile

grimacier, -ière [grimasje, -jɛr] *adj* grimacing; *Vieilli* (*maniéré*) affected

grimage [grimaʒ] *nm Th* (*action*) making up; (*résultat*) make-up

grimer [grime] **1** *vt Th* (*un acteur, son visage*) to make up **2 se grimer** *vpr Th* (*d'un acteur*) to make up

grimoire [grimwar] *nm* **(a)** (*de sorcier*) book of spells **(b)** (*ouvrage confus et illisible*) piece of gibberish *or* mumbo-jumbo

grimpant [grɛ̃pɑ̃] **1** *adj* (*animal*) climbing; **plante grimpante** climbing plant, climber; **rosier g.** climbing rose **2** *nm Arg* (*pantalon*) trousers, *Am* pants

grimpe [grɛ̃p] *nf* rock-climbing; **faire de la g.** to go rock-climbing

grimpée [grɛ̃pe] *nf* (stiff) climb

grimper [grɛ̃pe] **1** *vi* **(a)** (*monter*) to climb (up); (*faire de l'escalade*) to climb; **il a** *ou* **est grimpé sur la muraille** he climbed (up) on to the wall; **la route grimpe jusqu'au col** the road climbs (up) to the pass; **ça grimpe** it's steep; *Fig* **g. au pouvoir** to climb to power **(b)** (*de plantes*) to climb **(c)** *Fig* (*des prix*) to climb **2** *vt F* (*montagne, échelons*) to climb (up); **g. l'escalier** to climb (up) *or* go up the stairs

grimpette [grɛ̃pɛt] *nf F* (*chemin*) short, steep climb

grimpeur, -euse [grɛ̃pœr, -øz] **1** *adj* (*oiseau*) climbing **2** *nm* climber; (*de rocher*) rock-climber; (*en cyclisme*) hill climber; **c'est un bon/mauvais g.** (*d'un cycliste*) he's good/bad on hills

grinçant [grɛ̃sɑ̃] *adj* **(a)** (*qui grince*) creaking **(b)** (*caustique*) (*remarque*) caustic; **elle a un humour g.** she has a caustic wit

grincement [grɛ̃smɑ̃] *nm* (*d'une porte, de roues etc*) creaking; **g. de dents** grinding *or* gnashing of teeth; *Fig* **il y a eu des grincements de dents** there was much gnashing of teeth

grincer [grɛ̃se] *vi* **(je grinçai(s); n. grinçons)** (*d'une porte, de roues etc*) to creak; (*d'une chauve-souris*) to squeak; **g. des dents** to grind *or* gnash one's teeth; **cela fait g. des dents** it sets your teeth on edge; **porte qui grince sur ses gonds** creaking door

grincheux, -euse [grɛ̃ʃø, -øz] **1** *adj* grumpy, bad-tempered **2** *n* grump, grumpy *or* bad-tempered person

gringalet [grɛ̃galɛ] **1** *nm* (*homme, garçon*) (little) shrimp, weakling **2** *adj m* puny

gringue [grɛ̃g] *nm F* **faire du g. à qn** to chat sb up, *Am* to sweet-talk sb

griotte [grijɔt] *nf* **(a)** *Bot* morello (cherry); **chocolats aux griottes** cherry liqueur chocolates **(b)** *Minér* griotte (marble)

grippage [gripaʒ], **grippement** [gripmɑ̃] *nm Tech* (*d'un palier, d'un piston etc*) seizing, jamming, binding

grippal, -ale, -aux, -ales [gripal, -o] *adj Méd* flu; **soulage les états grippaux** relieves flu symptoms; **virus g.** flu virus

grippe [grip] *nf* **(a)** *Méd* flu, *Fml* influenza; **se faire vacciner contre la g.** to be vaccinated against flu; **attraper/avoir la g.** to catch *or* get/have (the) flu; **g. intestinale** gastric flu **(b) prendre qn/qch en g.** to take a dislike to sb/sth

grippé [gripe] *adj* **(a)** *Méd* **être g.** to have (the) flu **(b)** *Tech* (*moteur, mécanisme etc*) seized(-up) **(c)** *Méd* (*visage*) pinched, drawn

gripper [gripe] **1** *vt MecE* (*mécanisme*) to seize up, to jam **2** *vi* **(a)** (*d'une étoffe*) to crinkle (up), to wrinkle, to pucker **(b)** (*de paliers*) to seize (up), to bind, to jam **3 se gripper** *vpr* = **2** *vi*

grippe-sou, *pl* **grippe-sou(s)** *nm* skinflint, miser, Scrooge

gris [gri] **1** *adj* **(a)** (*couleur*) grey, *US* gray; (*temps*) cloudy, dull, overcast; **il fait g. ce matin** it's cloudy *or* dull *or* overcast this morning, it's a grey *or* dull morning; **g. de poussière** grey with dust; **robe g. clair** light grey dress; **aux cheveux g.** grey-haired; *Anat* **substance grise** grey matter; *F* **faire fonctionner sa matière grise** to get one's grey matter working; **vin g.** rosé wine; **faire grise mine** to look anything but pleased; **faire grise mine à qn** to give sb a cool welcome

(b) (*ivre*) tipsy

2 *nm* **(a)** (*couleur*) grey, *US* gray; *Ordinat* **tons de g.** shades of grey; **s'habiller en g.** to dress in *or* wear grey

(b) (*cheval*) grey, *US* gray

(c) (*tabac gris*) = shag

▶ **gris**: **g. acier** steel grey; **g. anthracite** charcoal grey; **g. ardoise** slate grey; **g.-bleu** blue-grey; **g. perle** pearl grey; **g. pommelé** (*cheval*) dapple-grey; **g. souris** soft grey; **g.-vert** greenish-grey

grisaille [grizɑj] *nf* **(a)** (*caractère morne*) greyness, dreariness, *Am* grayness **(b)** *Beaux-Arts* grisaille; **peindre en g.** to paint in grisaille

grisailler [grizɑje] **1** *vt Beaux-Arts* **g. qch** to paint sth in grisaille **2** *vi* to turn *or* go grey *or US* gray

grisant [grizɑ̃] *adj Fig* (*succès, atmosphère*) intoxicating, exhilarating, heady; (*aventure, soirée*) exhilarating; **à une vitesse grisante** at (an) exhilarating speed

grisâtre [grizɑtr] *adj* greyish, *US* grayish

grisbi [grizbi] *nm Arg* (*argent*) dosh, *Br* lolly

grisé [grize] *Ordinat nm* grey *or US* gray tone; **en g.** (*article*) dimmed

griser [grize] **1** *vt* **(a)** (*rendre gris*) to make grey *or US* gray; *Ordinat* to shade **(b)** (*enivrer*) to make drunk *or* tipsy; *Fig* **grisé par le succès** carried away *or* intoxicated by *or* with success **2 se griser** *vpr* **se g. d'air pur** to get drunk on fresh air; **se g. des paroles de qn/de musique** to get carried away by sb's words/by music

griserie [grizri] *nf* **(a)** (*ivresse*) tipsiness **(b)** *Fig* (*exaltation*) exhilaration, excitement

grisette [grizɛt] *nf Arch* = young dressmaker/milliner/florist/*etc* (*usu of easy virtue*)

gris-gris *nm* amulet; (*porte-bonheur*) lucky charm

grisonnant [grizɔnɑ̃] *adj* (*cheveux*) greying, *US* graying, touched with grey *or US* gray; **avoir les tempes grisonnantes** to be greying at the temples; **un cinquantenaire g.** a greying fifty-year-old

grisonner [grizɔne] *vi* (*de cheveux, personne*) to go grey *or US* gray

grisou [grizu] *nm Min* firedamp; **coup de g.** firedamp explosion

grive [griv] *nf* (*oiseau*) thrush; **soûl comme une g.** drunk as a lord; *Prov* **faute de grives on mange des merles** beggars can't be choosers, half a loaf is better than none

grivelé [grivle] *adj* (*plumage*) speckled

grivèlerie [grivɛlri] *nf Jur* = (offence consisting of) ordering a meal in a restaurant without having the money to pay for it

grivoiserie [grivwazri] *nf* (*plaisanterie*) risqué *or* saucy joke; (*histoire*) risqué *or* saucy story; (*acte*) rude gesture

grivois, -oise [grivwa, -waz] *adj* (*histoire, chanson, plaisanterie*) risqué, saucy, bawdy

grizzli, grizzly [grizli] *nm* grizzly (bear)

Groenland [grɔɛnlɑ̃(d)] *nm* Greenland

groenlandais, -aise [grɔɛnlɑ̃dɛ, -ɛz] **1** *adj* of *or* from Greenland **2** *nm Ling* Greenlandic **3** *n* **G.** Greenlander

grog [grɔg] *nm* grog, toddy

groggy [grɔgi] *adj inv F* groggy

grognard [grɔɲar, -ard] **1** *nm Hist* = soldier of Napoleon's Old Guard **2** *n Vieilli* grumbler

grognasse [grɔɲas] *nf Vulg Péj* old bag, old cow

grognasser [grɔɲase] *vi F* to grumble, to grouse, *Br* to whinge

grogne [grɔɲ] *nf F* grumbling; **c'est la g. chez les ouvriers/dans le milieu étudiant** the workers/the students are grumbling

grognement [grɔɲmɑ̃] *nm* **(a)** (*d'un cochon*) grunt(ing); (*d'un chien, ours*) growl(ing); **pousser des grognements** (*d'un cochon*) to grunt **(b)** (*d'une personne*) growl; **pousser un g.** to growl

grogner [grɔɲe] **1** *vi* **(a)** (*d'un cochon*) to grunt; (*d'un chien*) to growl **(b)** (*d'une personne*) to grumble, to grouse, to moan; **g. contre qn** to grumble *or* complain about sb **2** *vt* **g. un refus/une réponse** to growl out a refusal/an answer

grognon [grɔɲɔ̃] **1** *n* grumbler, grouser, moaner **2** *adj* (*f* **grognon** *or* **grognonne**) grumpy, grumbling; **c'est une femme g.** *ou* **grognonne** she's always grumbling *or* moaning, she's a grumpy woman; **qu'est-ce que tu peux être g.!** what a grumbler *or* grouser *or* moaner you are!

grognonner [grɔɲɔne] *vi F* to grouse, to grumble, to moan

groin [grwɛ̃] *nm* (*d'un cochon*) snout; *Fig Péj* (*de personne*) ugly face

grole, grolle [grɔl] *nf très F* (*chaussure*) shoe

grommeler [grɔmle] (**je grommelle, n. grommelons; je grommellerai**) **1** *vi* to mutter; (*d'un sanglier*) to snort, to grunt **2** *vt* **g. un juron** to mutter an oath

grommellement [grɔmɛlmɑ̃] *nm* muttering

grondement [grɔ̃dmɑ̃] *nm* (**a**) (*d'un chien*) growl(ing), snarl(ing) (**b**) (*du tonnerre*) rumble, rumbling; (*d'un torrent de montagne, des vagues, d'un moteur*) roar(ing); (*des canons*) booming

gronder [grɔ̃de] **1** *vi* (**a**) (*d'un chien*) to growl, to snarl (**b**) (*du tonnerre*) to rumble; (*des canons*) to boom; (*des vagues*) to roar; **la révolte/le mécontentement gronde** there are rumblings of rebellion/discontent **2** *vt* (*réprimander*) to scold, to tell off; **attention, tu vas te faire g.!** watch out, or you'll get into trouble!; **g. qn d'avoir fait qch** to scold sb *or* tell sb off for having done sth

gronderie [grɔ̃dri] *nf* scolding

grondeur, -euse [grɔ̃dœr, -øz] *adj* (**a**) (*voix*) scolding, nagging; (*humeur, tempérament*) peevish (**b**) (*orage, torrent etc*) rumbling

grondin [grɔ̃dɛ̃] *nm* gurnard, gurnet

groom [grum] *nm* (**a**) (*dans un hôtel*) page, *Am* bellhop (**b**) *Équitation Arch* groom

gros, grosse[1] [gro, gros] **1** *adj* (**a**) (*grand*) big, large; **g. morceau** big *or* large piece, lump; *Fig* **l'examen de statistiques, voilà le g. morceau** the statistics exam is the big one; **grosse corde** thick *or* stout rope; **g. pullover** thick *or* heavy *or* chunky sweater; **g. souliers** strong *or* stout shoes; **grosses chaussettes** thick *or* heavy socks; **g. moteur** high-powered engine; **g. doigt de pied** big toe; **de grosses lèvres** thick lips; **avoir un g. ventre** (*être bien en chair*) to have a paunch, to have a pot(belly); **avoir une grosse tête** to have a large head; *Fig* **avoir la grosse tête** to be big-headed, to be swollen-headed; **prendre** *ou* **attraper la grosse tête** to get big-headed; **une orange grosse comme le poing** an orange the size of *or* as big as your fist; *Fig* **un mensonge g. comme une maison** *ou* **comme ça** a whopping lie, a whopper of a lie; *Fig* **faire les g. yeux** to glare, to glower; **yeux g. de larmes** eyes swollen with tears; **avoir le cœur g.** to have a heavy heart, to be sad at heart; **je suis parti le cœur g.** I left with a heavy heart; *Fig* **elle a un cœur g. comme ça** she's so big-hearted; *Péj* **g. nigaud** *ou* **bêta!** you big *or* great ninny *or Br* twit!; **écrire qch en g. caractères** to write sth in big *or* large letters; **g. utilisateur** heavy user; **g. mangeur** big *or* hearty eater; **g. buveur** heavy *or* big drinker; **g. appétit** big *or* hearty appetite; **g. rhume** heavy cold; **grosse fièvre** high fever; **un g. kilo** a good kilo; **avoir un g. chagrin** to be very upset; **une grosse récolte** a bumper harvest; *Naut* **grosse mer** heavy *or* rough sea; **g. temps** stormy *or* rough weather; **grosse averse/pluie** heavy shower/rain; **g. vent** high wind; **grosse cavalerie** heavy cavalry

(**b**) (*corpulent*) big, fat, stout; **un g. bébé** a big *or* fat baby; **un g. bonhomme** a fat gentleman

(**c**) (*pas fin*) **grosse toile** coarse linen; **grosse voix** gruff voice; **faire la grosse besogne** to do the heavy work

(**d**) (*grossier*) **un peu g.** not very subtle, a bit too obvious; **c'est un peu g.!** that's a bit much!; **g. rire** coarse laugh; **grosse indélicatesse** gross impropriety

(**e**) (*important*) **grosse somme** large sum (of money); **ce n'est pas une grosse affaire** (*entreprise*) it's not a big company; (*préoccupation*) it's no big deal; **grosse commande** bulk order; **la plus grosse partie de nos affaires/notre personnel** the bulk of our business/our staff; **grosse faute** serious *or* gross mistake; **g. propriétaire (terrien)** big landowner; **grosse héritière** wealthy heiress

(**f**) **être g. de conséquences/menaces/***etc* to be heavy with consequences/threats/*etc*

2 *adv* (*beaucoup*) **gagner g.** to earn a lot, to make big money; **ça peut rapporter g.** it can bring in a lot; **je donnerais g. pour savoir qui a fait ça** I'd give a lot to know who did that; **il y a g. à parier qu'il ne viendra pas** a hundred to one he won't come!; **il risque g.** he's taking a big risk, he's risking a lot; **jouer g.** *Cartes* to play for high stakes; *Fig* to take a big risk, to risk a lot

3 *n* (*personne corpulente*) large *or* fat man/woman; **eh bien, mon g.!** well, old boy *or Br* old man!; (*à un enfant*) well, my boy!, well, son!; **se faire manger par les g.** to be gobbled up by the big boys

4 *nm* (**a**) (*partie la plus importante*) bulk; **le g. de la cargaison/du personnel** the bulk of the cargo/the staff; **le g. de l'armée** the main body *or* the bulk of the army; **le g. du peuple** the mass *or* bulk of the people; **le g. d'une mission** the main part of a mission; **le plus g. est fait** the biggest part of the job is done; **le plus gros du courrier** the bulk of the mail; **le g. de l'été/l'hiver** the height of summer/depths of winter; **g. d'un mât** thick end of a mast

(**b**) *Com* wholesale (trade); **marchand de g.** wholesaler; **vente de g.** wholesale; **ils ne vendent/font que du g.** they only sell/deal wholesale; **commerce de g.** wholesale business; **boucher de g.** wholesale butcher

(**c**) **écrire en g.** to write in big *or* large letters; **raconter ce qui s'est passé en g.** to tell roughly what happened; **il y avait en g. quinze personnes** there were roughly *or* about fifteen people there; **acheter en g.** to buy wholesale; (*en grosse quantité*) to buy in bulk; **vendre en g.** to sell wholesale

▶ **gros**: *F* **g. bonnet** big shot, bigwig; *Typ* **g. corps** headings type, headline type; **g. gibier** big game; *F* **grosse légume** big shot, bigwig; **g. mot** swearword; *TV, Cin* **g. plan** tight shot; *TV, Cin* **en g. plan** in close-up; *TV, Cin* **en très g. plan** very close up; *TV, Cin* **g. plan d'objet/de tête** insert/head shot; **g. porteur polyvalent** multi-purpose large-capacity jet; **g. rouge** rough red wine; **g. sel** cooking salt; *Typ* **g. tirage** best-seller; *Journ* **g. titre de deuxième ordre** second lead, half lead

gros-bec, *pl* **gros-becs** *nm* hawfinch, grosbeak

gros-cul, *pl* **gros-culs** *nm F* lorry, *Am* truck

groseille [grozɛj] *nf* **g. (rouge)** redcurrant; **g. (blanche)** white currant; **g. à maquereau** gooseberry; **gelée de groseille(s)** redcurrant jelly

groseillier [grozeje] *nm* (red)currant bush; **g. à maquereau** gooseberry bush

gros-grain, *pl* **gros-grains** *nm Tex* grosgrain

Gros-jean [groʒɑ̃] *nm Prov* **se retrouver G. comme devant** to be back where one started

grosse[2] [gros] *nf* (**a**) *Com* gross (**b**) *Jur* engrossment (**c**) *Arch* (*écriture*) roundhand (writing)

grossesse [grosɛs] *nf* pregnancy; **interruption volontaire de g.** termination of pregnancy; **robe de g.** maternity dress; **pendant sa g.** during her pregnancy, while *or* when she was pregnant

▶ **grossesse**: **g. extra-utérine** *or* **ectopique** ectopic pregnancy; **g. gémellaire** twin pregnancy; **g. nerveuse** false *or* phantom pregnancy; **g. à risque** high-risk pregnancy

grosseur [grosœr] *nf* (**a**) (*taille, volume*) size; (*des lèvres*) thickness; **un objet de la g. d'un œuf** an object the size of an egg (**b**) *Méd* lump, growth

grossier, -ière [grosje, -jɛr] *adj* (**a**) (*impoli*) (*personne*) rude (**envers** to); (*vulgaire*) (*personne, air*) uncouth, coarse; (*langage, plaisanterie*) coarse, crude; **un g. personnage** an uncouth individual; **il a été on ne peut plus g.** he was extremely rude; **parler d'un ton g.** to speak coarsely *or* crudely

(**b**) (*commun, rudimentaire*) (*nourriture, tissu, vaisselle etc*) coarse, rough; (*méthode*) crude; (*dessin*) crude, rough; (*goûts, traits du visage*) unrefined, coarse; **c'est un esprit g.** he's ignorant, he's a Philistine

(**c**) (*de taille*) **stupidité grossière** crass stupidity; **ignorance grossière** gross *or* crass ignorance; **faute grossière** gross mistake, blunder; **une ruse grossière** a very obvious trick

grossièrement [grosjɛrmɑ̃] *adv* (**a**) (*imparfaitement*) roughly, crudely; **table g. façonnée** roughly *or* crudely made table (**b**) (*approximativement*) roughly; **calculer g. un prix/le nombre de personnes** to roughly calculate a price/the number of people (**c**) (*de façon importante*) **se tromper g.** to be grossly mistaken (**d**) (*de façon impolie*) (*parler, répondre*) rudely

grossièreté [grosjɛrte] *nf* (**a**) (*caractère rudimentaire*) (*d'un objet fabriqué*) coarseness, roughness (**b**) (*incorrection*) (*de manières, personne*) coarseness (**c**) (*parole grossière*) **dire des grossièretés à qn** to say crude *or* coarse things to sb

grossir [grosir] **1** *vt* **objet grossi trois fois** object magnified three times; **torrent grossi par les pluies** torrent swollen by the rain; **ce pantalon le grossit** those trousers make him look fatter; **g. les rangs des mécontents** to swell the ranks of the discontented; **g. sa voix** to raise one's voice; *Fig* **g. les faits/une histoire/une affaire** to exaggerate the facts/a story/a matter; **g. l'importance de qch/le rôle de qn dans une action** to exaggerate the importance of sth/sb's part in an action

2 *vi* (*d'animaux, de fruits*) to get bigger *or* larger; (*de personne*) to put on weight, to get fatter; (*de mer*) to get rough, to rise; (*de rivière*) to swell; **elle a grossi de deux kilos** she has put on two kilos; **elle a beaucoup grossi** she has put on a lot of weight *or* has got fatter

grossissant [grosisɑ̃] *adj* **(a)** (*qui devient plus gros*) (*foule, bruit*) growing, swelling **(b)** (*qui rend plus gros*) enlarging; **verre g.** magnifying glass

grossissement [grosismɑ̃] *nm* **(a)** (*augmentation de taille*) increase in size **(b)** (*action de rendre plus gros*) (*d'un objet à travers un verre*) magnification, enlargement **(c)** (*capacité d'un instrument d'optique*) (*d'un verre*) magnification, magnifying power

grossiste [grosist] *n* wholesaler, wholesale dealer; **g. généraliste** general wholesaler; **g. importateur** import wholesaler

grosso modo [grosomɔdo] *adv* roughly; **il y avait g. cinquante personnes** there were roughly fifty people; **g. c'est une comédie** roughly speaking *or* broadly speaking it's a comedy; **raconter l'affaire g.** to give a general account of the matter

grossoyer [groswaje] *vt* **(je grossoie, n. grossoyons; je grossoierai)** *Jur* (*document*) to engross

grotesque [grɔtɛsk] **1** *adj* (*personne, allure, idée*) ludicrous, ridiculous; *Beaux-Arts* (*personnage*) grotesque **2** *nm Littér, Beaux-Arts* **le g.** the grotesque; **cet homme/cette situation est d'un g.!** the man's/the situation's ludicrous *or* ridiculous! **3 grotesques** *nfpl Beaux-Arts* grotesques

grotesquement [grɔtɛskəmɑ̃] *adv* ludicrously, ridiculously

grotte [grɔt] *nf* cave; **g. naturelle/préhistorique** natural/prehistoric cave; **g. artificielle** grotto

grouillant [grujɑ̃] *adj* swarming, crawling, alive **(de** with); **rue grouillante de monde** street swarming with people; **foule grouillante** teeming crowd

grouillement [grujmɑ̃] *nm* swarming; **le g. des asticots dans la viande avariée** the maggots swarming around in the rotten meat; **son esprit torturé n'était plus qu'un g. sans nom de pensées incohérentes** his tortured mind was nothing but a teeming mass of incoherent thoughts

grouiller [gruje] **1** *vi* **(a)** *Vieilli* (*bouger*) to move **(b)** (*de touristes, clients etc*) to swarm around; **la foule grouillait dans la rue** the street was teeming *or* swarming with people; **g. de** to swarm *or* crawl with; **fromage qui grouille de vers** cheese swarming *or* crawling *or* alive with maggots; **ce bouquin grouille de bonnes idées** this book is teeming with good ideas **2 se grouiller** *vpr Arg* to get a move on, to get one's skates on; **grouille(-toi)!** get cracking!, get a move on!, get your skates on!

grouillot [grujo] *nm Bourse* messenger (boy); *TV, Cin* runner, best boy, gopher

groupage [grupaʒ] *nm Com* groupage, consolidation; (*de paquets*) bulking

groupe [grup] *nm* **(a)** [①**A11**,g,i] (*de gens, choses*) group; (*d'arbres*) group, clump; (*musiciens*) group, band; (*d'étoiles*) group, cluster; **marcher en g.** to walk in a group; **un g. de touristes descendit du car** a party *or* group of tourists got out of the coach; **travailler/acheter qch en g.** to work/buy sth as *or* in a group; **se mettre en groupes de trois** to get into *or* form groups of three; **ils arrivaient par groupes de deux ou trois** they arrived in twos and threes; **faire partie d'un g. de rock** to be in a rock group *or* band

(b) *Ling* **g. verbal/nominal/de mots** verbal/nominal/word group; **g. consonantique** consonant cluster

(c) *Mil* **g. de combat** squad; **demi-g.** section, *US* half squad; **g. d'artillerie** battery, *US* battalion; **g. d'intervention** task force; **g. d'aviation** squadron (*of transport aircraft*)

▶ **groupe**: *Pol, Écon* **G. des 7** Group of Seven; **g. d'âge** age group; *Mktg* **g.-cible**, *pl* **groupes-cibles** target group; **g. de consommateurs** consumer group, customer group; *Pol* **g. de contact** contact group; *Él* **g. électrogène** generating set, generator; **g. ethnique** ethnic group; **g. d'étude** study group; **g. financier** financial group; **g. hospitalier** hospital complex; **g. hôtelier** hotel group; **g. industriel** industrial group; **g. d'intérêt** interest group; **g. d'intérêt commun** common-interest group; **g. d'intervention de la gendarmerie nationale** special task force of the gendarmerie; **g. linguistique** language group; *Aut* **g. moto-propulseur** powerplant; **g. multimédia** communications conglomerate, multimedia; *Pol* **g. parlementaire** parliamentary group; **g. de presse** press group, newspaper company, newspaper group; *Pol* **g. de pression** pressure group; **g. de prix** price bracket; *Mktg* **g. de prospects** prospect pool; **g. de protection de l'environnement** environmental protection group; *Méd* **g. à risque** risk group; *Méd* **g. sanguin** blood group; **quel est votre g. sanguin?** what's your blood group?, what blood group are you?; **g. scolaire** (*bâtiments*) school complex; (*élèves*) school party; **g. socio-économique** socio-economic group; **g. stratégique** strategic group; *Mktg* **g. suivi** (*panel*) control group; **g. test de consommateurs** consumer group focus; **g. de travail** working party, work group; *Com* **g. volontaire** voluntary group

groupé *adj Com* consolidated

groupement [grupmɑ̃] *nm* **(a)** (*action*) grouping; *Ind, Com* (*d'intérêts*) pooling; **g. des enfants d'après l'âge** classification of children by age groups **(b)** (*association*) group; **g. de consommateurs** consumer(s') group; **g. de détaillants** retailers' group **(c)** *Mil* group, formation; **g. d'infanterie** brigade group, *US* battle group; **g. tactique** task force

▶ **groupement**: **g. d'achat** purchasing cooperative, purchasing group; *Com* **g. à l'export** consolidation for export; **g. d'intérêt économique** economic interest group, intercompany partnership; **g. professionnel** trade association

grouper [grupe] **1** *vt* to group (together); (*moyens, ressources*) to pool; *Com* to consolidate, to group; (*paquets*) to bulk; **si nous groupons nos informations, nous aurons plus vite un résultat** if we pool our information, we'll get a result more quickly **2 se grouper** *vpr* (*dans une association*) to join together, to form a group; (*dans un lieu*) to gather; **se g. autour du feu** to gather round the fire; **se g. autour d'un chef** to gather *or* rally round a leader; **essayons de rester groupés** let's try to stay in a group

groupeur [grupœr] *nm Com* consolidator; **g. de fret aérien** air freight consolidator; **g. maritime** maritime freight consolidator; **g. routier** road haulage consolidator

groupie [grupi] *nf F* groupie

groupuscule [grupyskyl] *nm Pol Péj* small group; **des groupuscules néo-nazis** small neo-Nazi groups

grouse [gruz] *nf Zool* grouse

gruau [gryo] *nm* **(a) (farine de) g.** (fine) wheat flour; **pain de g.** fine wheaten bread **(b) g. (d'avoine)** groats

grue [gry] *nf* **(a)** (*oiseau*) crane; *F* **faire le pied de g. (en attendant qn)** to hang about (waiting for sb), to kick *or* cool one's heels (waiting for sb); **cou de g.** long scraggy neck **(b)** *MecE* crane; *TV, Cin* cherry picker; **g. à volée** *ou* **à flèche** jib crane; **g. à pivot** revolving crane; **g. à flotteur** pontoon crane; *Rail* **g. d'alimentation** (water) crane; *TV, Cin* **g. de prise de vue** camera crane; **g. hydraulique** *TV, Cin* simon crane **(c)** *Arg* (*prostituée*) tart

gruger [gryʒe] *vt* **(je grugeai(s); n. grugeons) (a)** to swindle; **se faire g.** to be swindled **(b)** *Can* **g. l'avance de qn** (*dans un sondage etc*) to eat into sb's lead

grume [grym] *nf* **(a)** (*écorce*) bark; **bois en g.** rough timber, undressed timber **(b)** (*bûche*) log

grumeau, -eaux [grymo] *nm* **(a)** (*dans une sauce etc*) lump; **pâte à crêpes pleine de grumeaux** lumpy pancake mixture **(b) grumeaux de sel** specks of salt

grumeler (se) [səgrymle] *vpr* **(il se grumelle; il se grumellera) (a)** (*d'une sauce*) to go lumpy **(b)** (*du lait*) to curdle, to clot

grumeleux, -euse [grymlø, -øz] *adj* **(a)** (*sauce*) lumpy **(b)** (*lait*) curdled **(c)** (*d'aspect granuleux*) (*poire*) gritty

grutier [grytje] *nm* crane driver *or* operator

gruyère [gryjɛr] *nm* Gruyère (cheese); **crème de g.** = processed Gruyère (cheese)

GSS [ʒeɛsɛs] *nf* (*abrév* **grande surface spécialisée**) specialist superstore

Guadeloupe [gwadlup] *nf* Guadeloupe

guano [gwano] *nm* guano

Guatemala [gwatemala] *nm* Guatemala

guatémaltèque [gwatemaltɛk] **1** *adj* Guatemalan **2** *n* **G.** Guatemalan

gué [ge] *nm* ford; **passer une rivière à g.** to ford a river

guéable [geabl] *adj* (*rivière*) fordable

guède [gɛd] *nf Bot* woad, pastel

guéer [gee] *vt* (*cours d'eau*) to ford

guéguerre [gegɛr] *nf F* squabble; **c'est la g. entre les différents chefs de service** the different heads of department are squabbling (amongst themselves)

guelfe [gɛlf] *nm Hist* Guelph

guelte [gɛlt] *nf Com Vieilli* commission, percentage (*on sales*)

guenille [gənij] *nf* **(a)** (old) rag; **en guenilles** in rags (and tatters) **(b)** (*chose sans intérêt*) worthless object

guenon [gənɔ̃] *nf* **(a)** *Zool* female monkey **(b)** *F* (*femme*) ugly woman, fright

guépard [gepar] *nm* cheetah

guêpe [gɛp] *nf* **(a)** (*insecte*) wasp; **nid de guêpes** wasps' nest; **piqûre de g.** wasp sting; *Fig* **taille de g.** wasp waist **(b)** (*femme rusée*) **une fine g.** an artful *or* crafty woman; *F* **pas folle, la g.!** she's nobody's fool!

guêpier [gepje] *nm* **(a)** (*nid*) wasps' nest; *Fig* (*situation*) sticky *or* tricky situation; **se fourrer** *ou* **tomber dans un g.** to get oneself into a sticky *or* tricky situation **(b)** (*oiseau*) bee eater

guêpière [gɛpjɛr] *nf* basque

guère [gɛr] *adv* [①**B60**,B] (*always with neg expressed or* *understood*) hardly (any), not much, not many, very little, very few; **je ne l'aime g.** I don't care much for him; **je n'ai g. dormi** I didn't get much sleep, I hardly slept, I didn't sleep much; **cette histoire n'a g. eu de conséquences** this business had hardly any *or* very few consequences; **il n'a g. d'argent/temps** he hasn't much money/time, he has hardly any money/time; **vous n'en avez g. non plus** (*non comptable*) you haven't much either; (*comptable*) you haven't many either; **je n'en sais g. plus** I hardly know anything more about it, I don't know much more about it; **il ne nous en parle g.** he hardly *or* scarcely talks to us about it; **je ne suis g. invitée à ces soirées** I'm hardly ever *or* scarcely ever invited to these parties; **il n'est g. plus grand que toi** he's hardly *or* scarcely taller than you; **il ne tardera g. à venir** he'll not be long in coming, he'll be here before long; **on ne tarda g. à entendre parler de lui dans les journaux** it wasn't long before he was mentioned in the newspapers; **tout cela n'a g. duré longtemps** all that didn't last very long; **il n'y a g. qu'elle qui soit au courant** she's about the only one (who's) in the picture; **il ne mange g. que du pain** he eats hardly anything but bread; **cela ne se dit plus g.** you don't hear that much now, hardly anybody says that now; **je n'y tiens plus g.** I'm not as keen (on it) as I used to be; **il n'en reste plus g.** (*non comptable*) there's hardly any left; (*comptable*) there are hardly any left; **il n'y a g. plus de six ans** it's barely more than six years ago; **la voyez-vous? – g.!** do you see her? – hardly ever!; **et celui-là, comment le trouvez-vous? – g. mieux!** and that one, what do you think of it? – hardly better *or* not much better!; **tu as mieux dormi qu'hier? – oh, g. mieux!** did you sleep better than yesterday? – hardly!

guéret [gerɛ] *nm* fallow land

guéri [geri] *adj* cured; (*rétabli*) better, recovered; *Fig* **être g. d'une peur/d'un préjugé** to be cured of a fear/a prejudice; **je ne pense plus à lui, je suis guérie** I don't think of him any more, I've got over him

guéridon [geridɔ̃] *nm* pedestal table, gueridon, dumb waiter

guérilla [gerija] *nf* **(a)** (*guerre*) guer(r)illa warfare **(b)** *Vieilli* (*groupe*) band *or* troop of guer(r)illas

guérillero [gerijero] *nm* guer(r)illa

guérir [gerir] **1** *vt* (*qn, une maladie*) to cure; (*une blessure*) to heal; *Fig* **g. qn d'une habitude** to cure *or* break sb of a habit **2** *vi* (*d'une personne*) to get better, to be cured, to recover; (*d'une blessure*) to heal; (*d'une maladie*) to get better, to be cured; **il n'en guérira pas** *Méd* he won't recover from it; *Fig* he won't get over it; *Fig* **un chagrin qui ne guérit pas** an incurable grief, a grief that cannot be cured **3 se guérir** *vpr* to get better, to be cured; **se g. de sa timidité** to get over *or* overcome one's shyness; *Fig* **se g. de ses préjugés** to overcome one's prejudices, to cure oneself of one's prejudices

guérison [gerizɔ̃] *nf* **(a)** (*rétablissement*) recovery; **en voie de g.** on the way *or* road to recovery; **attends la g. complète avant de sortir** wait until you are completely recovered before going out **(b)** (*action de guérir*) (*d'une maladie*) cure; (*d'une blessure*) healing; *Fig* **la g. d'une peine** the healing of a sorrow

guérissable [gerisabl] *adj* curable; (*blessure*) that can be healed

guérisseur, -euse [gerisœr, -øz] **1** *n* healer, *Péj* quack (doctor) **2** *nm* (*d'une tribu*) medicine man

guérite [gerit] *nf* **(a)** *Mil* sentry box **(b)** (*petit abri*) (*pour gardien*) cabin, shelter

guerre [gɛr] *nf* **(a)** (*conflit armé*) war; (*technique*) warfare; **la g. a éclaté entre …** war has broken out between …; **déclarer la g. à un pays** to declare war on a country; **pays en g.** country at war; **se mettre en g.** to go to war; **en temps de g.** in wartime, in time of war; **état de g.** state of war; **crime/criminel de g.** war crime/criminal; *Mil, Fig* **ruses de g.** tactics; **invalide de g.** war invalid, disabled ex-serviceman; **nom de g.** nom de guerre; *Fig* pseudonym, nom de guerre; **on entre dans une logique de g.** war is the only logical outcome; **faire la g. à** *ou* **contre un pays** to wage war on *or* against a country; **nous avons fait la g. ensemble contre la Prusse** we fought *or* served together against Prussia; *Arch* **le Ministère de la G.,** *F* **la G.** the Ministry of War, the War Department; *Hist* **la Grande G.** the Great War; **la première/la deuxième g. mondiale** the First/Second World War, World War One/Two

(b) *Fig* **partir en g. contre la drogue/l'injustice** to declare war on drugs/injustice; **elle fait la g. à son fils pour qu'il ne fume pas** she's fighting a running battle with her son about smoking; **faire la g. aux inégalités/concurrents** to wage war on inequality/competitors; **entre Jean et lui, c'est la petite g.** Jean and he are always trying to score off each other; **c'est la g. entre elle et son mari** it's war between her and her husband; **être en g. ouverte avec** *ou* **contre qn** to be openly at war with sb; **de g. lasse j'y consentis** I gave in for the sake of peace and quiet; **il est sur le pied de g. depuis 8 heures ce matin** he's been on the go since 8 o'clock this morning; **à la g. comme à la g.** we'll/you'll/*etc* have to do the best we/you/*etc* can, we'll/you'll/*etc* have to make the best of what we've/you've/*etc* got; (*tous les moyens sont justifiés*) if that's the way he/*etc* wants it (that's the way he'll/*etc* get it); **c'est de bonne g.** it's fair enough, all's fair in love and war

▶ **guerre**: **g. de 70** Franco-Prussian War; **g. aérienne** air war; **g. atomique** atomic war; (*technique*) atomic warfare; **g. bactériologique** germ warfare; **g. de Cent Ans** Hundred Years' War; **g. chimique** chemical warfare; **g. civile** civil war; **g. conventionnelle** conventional warfare; *Eng* **g. des Deux-Roses** War of the Roses; **g. éclair** blitzkrieg; **g. économique** economic warfare; **g. d'embuscade** guerilla warfare; **g. des étoiles** star wars; **g. froide** cold war; **g. idéologique** ideological war; **g. de libération** war of liberation; **g. des nerfs** war of nerves; **g. planétaire** global war; **g. de positions** static warfare; *Com* **g. des prix** *ou* **des tarifs** price war; **guerres de religion** wars of religion; **g. sainte** holy war; **g. terrestre** land war; **g. totale** total war; **g. de tranchées** trench warfare; **g. de Trente Ans** Thirty Years' War; **g. d'usure** war of attrition

guerrier, -ière [gɛrje, -jɛr] **1** *adj* warlike, martial; **danse guerrière** war dance; **il est d'humeur guerrière** he is in a belligerent mood **2** *nm* warrior

guerroyer [gɛrwaje] *vi* **(je guerroie, n. guerroyons; je guerroierai)** to war, to wage war (**contre** against); *Fig* **g. contre l'inégalité/l'hypocrisie** to struggle against *or* wage war on inequality/hypocrisy

guet [gɛ] *nm* **(a)** (*action*) watch; *Mil* **poste de g.** lookout post; **faire le g.** to be on watch *or* on the lookout **(b)** *Hist* (*patrouille*) watch

guet-apens [gɛtapɑ̃], *pl* **guets-apens** *nm* (*piège*) ambush, trap; *Fig* trap; **attirer qn dans un g.** to ambush sb; **tomber dans un g.** to fall into an ambush *or* a trap, to be ambushed

guêtre [gɛtr] *nf* gaiter

guetter [gete] *vt* (*une occasion*) to watch out for; **le guépard guettait sa proie** the cheetah was lying in wait for its prey; **g. l'arrivée/la sortie/le passage de qn** to watch out for sb arriving/leaving/going past; **je guette les petites annonces** I keep an eye on the small ads; **le surmenage/la dépression le guette** overwork/depression will get him in the end; **ce qui te guette, toi, c'est une bonne indigestion** you're heading for a nasty attack of indigestion

guetteur [gɛtœr] *nm Mil, Naut* lookout (man); **poste de guetteurs** lookout post

gueulante [gœlɑ̃t] *nf Arg* uproar, din; **elle a poussé une g.** she raised the roof, she kicked up a stink

gueulard¹, -arde [gœlar, -ard] **1** *adj* **(a)** *très F* (*qui crie*) loudmouthed **(b)** *F* (*gourmand*) greedy **2** *n* **(a)** *très F* (*personne qui crie*) loudmouth **(b)** *F* (*gourmand*) greedy guts

gueulard² *nm* **(a)** *Métal* (*d'un four*) mouth **(b)** *Naut* loudhailer

gueule [gœl] *nf* **(a)** (*d'un animal, d'un poisson*) mouth; *Fig* **se jeter dans la g. du loup** to put one's head in the lion's mouth

(b) *très F* (*bouche*) mouth; *Vulg* **il pue de la g.** his breath stinks; **ça emporte** *ou* **arrache la g.** it takes the roof of your mouth off; **c'est un fort en g.** *ou* **une grande g.** he's a loudmouth; **avec sa grande g., il fallait qu'il parle** he's such a blabbermouth *or* he's got such a big mouth it's no wonder he gave the game away; **coups de g.** shouting session; **(ferme) ta g.!** shut your mouth *or* face!, shut it!; **s'en mettre plein la g.** to stuff oneself; **se bourrer la g.** to get plastered *or* sloshed; **une fine g.** a gourmet; **crever la g. ouverte** to die like a dog

(c) *très F* (*visage*) mug, face; **il est arrivé, la g. enfarinée, pour …** he turned up, innocence itself, to …; **se fendre la g.** to laugh one's head off, to split one's sides laughing; **avoir une sale g.** (*être moche*) to have an ugly mug; (*avoir mauvaise mine*) to look rotten; (*avoir l'air déprimé*) to look down in the mouth; **faire une sale g.** to pull a long face; **faire une drôle de g.** to pull *or* make a strange face; **il a été arrêté pour délit de sale g.** he was arrested because they didn't like the look of his face; **il/ce fromage a une bonne g.** I like the look of him/this cheese; **avoir une belle g.** to have a pretty face; **faire la g.** to sulk; **faire la g. à qn** to be in a huff *or* a bad mood with sb; **faire une g. d'enterrement** to look thoroughly depressed; **casser la g. à qn** to smash sb's face in; **se casser la g.** to fall flat on one's face, to come a cropper; *Fig* (*d'une entreprise*) to come a cropper; **se foutre de** *ou* **se payer la g. de qn** to take the piss out of sb; **(s')en prendre plein la g.** to get a right mouthful (of abuse); **sa g. ne me revient pas** I don't like the look of him (**d**) *F* (*allure*) **elle a de la g. cette fille** she's quite a girl, that girl's really got something (about her); **ce tableau a de la g.** that's some picture; **ce chapeau a une drôle de g.** that hat looks odd

(**e**) (*ouverture*) (*d'un sac, d'un puits, d'un tunnel etc*) mouth; (*d'un fusil*) muzzle

▶ **gueule**: **g. de bois** hangover; **se réveiller avec/avoir la g. de bois** to wake up with/have a hangover; *Hist Mil* **gueules cassées** = soldiers with serious facial injuries; **g. noire** coal-miner

gueule-de-loup, *pl* **gueules-de-loup** *nf* (**a**) *Bot* snap-dragon (**b**) *Constr* (chimney) cowl, chimney jack (**c**) (*de machine*) (exhaust) muffler

gueulement [gœlmɑ̃] *nm F* (*cri*) yell; (*cris*) yelling, yells; **pousser des gueulements** to yell

gueuler [gœle] *très F* **1** *vi* to yell, to bawl; **si je suis en retard, ça va g. à la maison** if I'm late I'll get bawled out at home; **faire g. la radio/sa télévision** to turn the radio/one's television up full blast **2** *vt* (*chanson, ordres etc*) to bawl out, to yell out

gueules [gœl] *nm Hér* gules

gueuleton [gœltɔ̃] *nm F* blowout; **faire un bon petit g. entre amis** to have a good blowout with some friends

gueuletonner [gœltɔne] *vi F* to have a blowout

gueuse[1] [gøz] *nf* **g. (de fonte), fer en g.** pig

gueuserie [gøzri] *nf* (**a**) *Arch, Litt* (*condition*) beggary (**b**) *Vieilli* (*action*) foul deed

gueux, gueuse[2] [gø, gøz] *n* (**a**) *F* **courir la gueuse** to chase women; (*de façon générale*) to be a woman-chaser (**b**) *Arch, Litt* (*mendiant*) beggar (**c**) *Vieilli* (*fripon*) rascal, rogue

gueuze, gueuse[3] [gøz] *nf* (*bière*) = type of Belgian beer

gugusse [gygys] *nm* clown; *F* **faire le g.** to clown *or* fool around, to act the fool; *F* **quel g., ce type!** what a clown this guy is!

gui[1] [gi] *nm Bot* mistletoe; **boules de g.** clumps of mistletoe

gui[2] *nm Naut* (**a**) (*espar*) boom (**b**) (*corde*) guy(rope)

guibol(l)e [gibɔl] *nf F* (*jambe*) pin, leg; **j'en ai plein les guiboles** my legs have had it; *Vieilli* **jouer des guibolles** to stir one's stumps

guiches [giʃ] *nfpl* kiss curls

guichet [giʃɛ] *nm* (**a**) ticket desk, ticket office; *Banque* position, window, *Am* wicket; *Th* box office; **g. automatique** (*pour billets*) automatic ticket machine; *Banque* **g. automatique (de banque)** cash dispenser, *Am* ATM, *Am* automatic teller machine; **g. fermé** (*sur panneau*) position closed; *Th etc* **on joue à guichets fermés** the performance is sold out (**b**) (*dans une porte*) grille, grating; (*dans une prison etc*) wicket (gate) (**c**) *Cr* wicket; **gardien de g.** wicketkeeper

guichetier [giʃtje] *nm* (*de banque*) (counter) clerk, assistant, teller

guidage [gidaʒ] *nm* (**a**) *Électron* (*d'un avion*) guidance; **tête de g.** homing head; *Av* **g. par radio-maillage** *ou* **par radio-mailles** grid guidance (**b**) *MecE* (*d'une pièce mobile*) guiding; (*sur un tour de forage*) centring, *US* centering; *Aut* steering

guide [gid] **1** *nm* (**a**) (*personne*) guide; **g. dans un musée** museum guide; **g. local** local guide; **n'oubliez pas le g.** don't forget the guide; **la loyauté a toujours été son g.** loyalty has always guided him

(**b**) (*manuel*) guide (book); **g. touristique/des rues de Londres** tourist/London street guide; **g. gastronomique** restaurant guide, good food guide; **g. de conversation** phrase book; **g. de voyages** travel directory

(**c**) *Tech* **g. de courroie** belt guide; *Aut* **g. chaîne** chain guide; **g.-classement** file divider; *Électron* **g. d'ondes** wave guide; **g.-papier** (*d'une imprimante*) paper guide; **g.-ruban** (*d'une imprimante*) ribbon guide; **g.-sortie** (*d'une fiche*) file extraction marker

(**d**) *Typ* **g. de caractères** type book; **g. du style maison** house-style book

2 *nf* (**a**) *Équitation* rein; *Fig* **mener la vie à grandes guides** to live in lavish style

(**b**) (*fille faisant du scoutisme*) (girl) guide, *Am* girl scout; **g. aînée** ranger

▶ **guide**: **g.-conférencier**, *pl* **guide-conférenciers** guide; **g. de haute montagne** mountain guide; **g.-interprète**, *pl* **guide-interprètes** bilingual tour guide

guide-âne, *pl* **guide-âne(s)** *nm Vieilli* beginner's handbook

guide-fil *nm inv* thread guide

guider [gide] *vt* (*qn, cheval*) to guide; *Tech* **guidé par radio** radio-controlled; **g. un enfant dans le choix d'une carrière** to guide a child in the choice of a career; **se laisser g. par son intuition** to be guided by one's intuition

guidon [gidɔ̃] *nm* (**a**) (*de vélo*) handlebars; *Fig F* **moustaches en g. de bicyclette** handlebar moustache (**b**) *Mil* (*étendard*) guidon, pennant; *Naut* (*pavillon*) burgee (**c**) (*viseur*) (*d'une arme à feu*) foresight, bead

guignard, -arde [giɲar, -ard] **1** *n F Vieilli* (*malchanceux*) unlucky person **2** *nm* (*oiseau*) **pluvier g.** dotterel

guigne[1] [giɲ] *nf Bot* heart cherry; *F* **se soucier de qch/qn comme d'une g.** not to give *or* care a damn *or* a fig about sth/sb

guigne[2] *nf F* (*malchance*) bad luck; **porter la g. à qn** to bring sb bad luck; **avoir la g.** to be out of luck

guigner [giɲe] *vt* (*qn, qch*) to sneak a look at, to give a surreptitious *or* sidelong glance at; *Fig* (*avoir des vues sur*) to have one's eye on; *Cartes* **g. le jeu du voisin** to sneak a look at one's opponent's hand

guignol [giɲɔl] *nm* (**a**) (*personnage*) ≈ Punch; *F Péj* (*personne*) clown, joker; *F* **faire le g.** to clown around, to play *or* act the fool (**b**) (*spectacle*) ≈ Punch and Judy show; **aller au g.** ≈ to go to see the Punch and Judy show; *Fig F* **c'est du g.!** it's a farce *or* joke!

guignolet [giɲɔlɛ] *nm* cherry brandy; **un g. kirsch** a cherry brandy with kirsch

guignon [giɲɔ̃] *nm F Vieilli* bad luck

guilde [gild] *nf* (**a**) (*club*) (*pour disques, livres etc*) club (**b**) *Hist* guild; **g. de commerçants** merchant guild

guili-guili [giligili] *nm inv F* tickle; **faire g. à qn** to tickle sb

Guillaume [gijom] *nm* William; **G. le Conquérant** William the Conqueror

guillaume [gijom] *nm Menuis* rabbet(ing) plane; **g. à onglet** mitre plane, *US* miter plane

guilledou [gijdu] *nm F Vieilli* **courir le g.** to chase after women; (*d'une façon générale*) to be a woman-chaser

guillemets [gijmɛ] *nmpl* inverted commas, quotation marks, *F* quotes; **mot entre g.** word in inverted commas *or* quotation marks; **mettez ce mot entre guillemets** put this word in inverted commas *or* quotation marks; **ouvrez/fermez les g.** (*en dictant*) quote/unquote, open/close inverted commas *or* quotation marks; **c'est un artiste entre guillemets** he's an artist, in inverted commas *or* quote unquote; *Typ* **g. fermants** closing quote marks; *Typ* **g. ouvrants** opening quote marks; *Typ* **g. simples** single quotes

guillemot [gijmo] *nm* guillemot

guilleret, -ette [gijrɛ, -ɛt] *adj* (**a**) (*gai*) (*personne, ton, pas*) jaunty, lively (**b**) (*léger*) (*plaisanterie*) risqué

guillotine [gijɔtin] *nf* guillotine; **fenêtre à g.** sash window; **cisailles à g.** guillotine shears; **aller à la g.** to go to the guillotine

guillotiner [gijɔtine] *vt* to guillotine

guimauve [gimov] *nf Bot* marsh mallow; *Culin* **(pâte de) g.** marshmallow; *Bot* **g. rose** hollyhock; *Fig Péj* **c'est de la g.** it's pure sentimentality, *F* it's soppy *or* slushy; **des romans à la g.** sentimental *or F* soppy *or* slushy novels

guimbarde [gɛ̃bard] *nf* (**a**) *Mus* Jew's harp (**b**) *F* (*vieille voiture*) (old) jalopy, *Br* old banger (**c**) (*outil*) router plane, grooving plane

guimpe [gɛ̃p] *nf* (**a**) (*de religieuse*) wimple (**b**) (*chemisette*) chemisette

guincher [gɛ̃ʃe] *vi F* to dance

guindage [gɛ̃daʒ] *nm* hoisting

guindé [gɛ̃de] *adj* (*personne, air*) stiff, starchy; (*atmosphère*) strained; (*langage*) affected; (*style*) stilted, stiff; (*réception*) posh

guindeau, -eaux [gɛ̃do] *nm Naut* windlass

guinder [gɛ̃de] **1** *vt Tech* to hoist, to windlass; *Naut* (*mât*) to send up, to sway up **2** *se guinder* *vpr* (*d'une personne, d'une ambiance*) to become stiff; (*d'un style*) to become stilted *or* stiff; (*d'une ambiance*) to become strained

Guinée [gine] *nf* Guinea

guinée [gine] *nf Arch* (*monnaie*) guinea

guinéen, -enne [gineɛ̃, -ɛn] **1** *adj* Guinean **2** *n* **G.** Guinean

guingois [gɛ̃gwa] *adv* **de g.** askew, lopsided; **il se tenait un peu de g.** he was standing a bit lopsided; *Fig* **tout va de g.** everything's going wrong

guinguette [gɛ̃gɛt] *nf* café (*with music and dancing, often in the open*)

guipure [gipyr] *nf* guipure (lace)

guirlande [girlɑ̃d] *nf* (*de fleurs etc*) garland; **g. de Noël** piece of tinsel; **g. de papier** paper chain; **g. de perles** string of pearls; **g. lumineuse** string of lights; *Ordinat* **connecté en g.** in a token ring configuration

guise [giz] *nf* **faire qch à sa g.** to do sth as one pleases *or* likes; **faire** *ou* **agir à sa g.** to do as one pleases *or* likes; **il n'en fait qu'à sa g.** he just does as he pleases *or* likes; **à ta g.!** as you please *or* like!; **en g. de** by way of

guitare [gitar] *nf* guitar; **g. électrique** electric guitar; **g. hawaïenne** Hawaiian guitar; **g. sèche** acoustic guitar; **g. classique** classical guitar

guitariste [gitarist] *n* guitarist, guitar player
guitoune [gitun] *nf* **(a)** *F* (*tente*) tent **(b)** *Mil Arg* dugout, shelter
guppy [gypi] *nm* guppy
guru [guru] *nm Rel Hindu, Fig* guru
gus [gys] *nm F* guy
gustatif, -ive [gystatif, -iv] *adj* gustative, gustatory; **papilles gustatives** taste buds
gustation [gystasjɔ̃] *nf* tasting, *Spéc* gustation
gutta-percha [gytapɛrka], *pl* **guttas-perchas** *nf* gutta-percha
guttural, -ale, -aux, -ales [gytyral, -o] **1** *adj* (*son*) guttural; (*voix*) throaty, guttural; *Anat* **artère gutturale** carotid artery **2** *nf Ling* **gutturale** guttural
guyanais, -aise [gɥijanɛ, -ɛz] **1** *adj* Guianese, Guianan **2** *n* **G.** Guianese, Guianan
Guyane [gɥijan] Guiana; **G. française** French Guiana; *Hist* **G. britannique** British Guiana
guyot [gɥijo] *nf* guyot (pear)
gym [ʒim] *nf F* gym; **faire de la g.** to do gym; **un cours de g.** a gym class
gymkhana [ʒimkana] *nm Sp* rally
gymnase [ʒimnɑz] *nm Sp* gymnasium
gymnaste [ʒimnast] *n* gymnast
gymnastique [ʒimnastik] **1** *adj* gymnastic; **partir au pas g.** to set off at a jog trot **2** *nf* gymnastics; *Fig* **g. de l'esprit** mental gymnastics; *Fig* **il faut faire toute une g. pour sortir de cette auto** you have to be a contortionist to get out of this car
▸ **gymnastique**: **g. corrective** remedial gymnastics; **g. matinale** morning exercises; **g. respiratoire** breathing exercises; **g. rythmique** eurhythmics
gymnote [ʒimnɔt] *nm* electric eel
gynécée [ʒinese] *nm Antiq, Bot* gynaeceum
gynécologie [ʒinekɔlɔʒi] *nf* gynaecology, *US* gynecology
gynécologique [ʒinekɔlɔʒik] *adj* (*examen*) gynaecological, *US* gynecological
gynécologue [ʒinekɔlɔg] *n* gynaecologist, *US* gynecologist
gypaète [ʒipaɛt] *nm* bearded vulture, lammergeyer
gypse [ʒips] *nm Minér* gypsum, plasterstone
gypseux, -euse [ʒipsø, -øz] *adj Minér* gypseous
gypsophile [ʒipsɔfil] *nf Bot* gypsophila
gyrocompas [ʒirokɔ̃pɑ] *nm Naut* gyrocompass
gyromètre [ʒirɔmɛtr] *nm Av* gyrometer
gyrophare [ʒirofar] *nm* flashing *or* rotating light
gyropilote [ʒiropilɔt] *nm Av* gyropilot, automatic pilot
gyroscope [ʒirɔskɔp] *nm* gyroscope; *Av* **g. directionnel** directional gyroscope
gyroscopique [ʒirɔskɔpik] *adj* gyroscopic; **compas g.** gyrocompass
gyrostat [ʒirɔsta] *nm* gyrostat

H *Words beginning with an aspirate* **h** *are shown by an asterisk*

H, h [aʃ] **1** *nm* [①A4,2,A,a; B3] *(lettre)* H, h; **h muet** mute h; **h. aspiré** aspirate h; *Mil etc* **l'heure H** zero hour; **bombe H** H bomb **2** *nm F* **H** *(haschisch)* hash; **trois grammes de H** three grams of hash

***ha** [ɑ] *int* ah!; **ha, ha!** *(rire)* ha!, ha!

***habanera** [abanera] *nf* habanera

habeas corpus [abeaskɔrpys] *nm Jur* habeas corpus

habile [abil] *adj* **(a)** clever, skilful; *(rusé)* cunning; *(film, roman)* clever; **il faut être h. pour faire cette réparation** it takes skill to do this kind of repair; **elle n'est pas h. de ses mains** she's not good with her hands; **mains habiles** skilled hands; **façonner qch d'une main h.** to make sth skilfully; **h. à faire qch** clever at doing sth; **il est h. en affaires** he's a good businessman; **ce n'était pas très h. de ta part** that wasn't very clever *or* bright of you **(b)** *Jur* **h. à succéder** able *or* competent to inherit

habilement [abilmɑ̃] *adv (avec adresse)* cleverly, skilfully, *US* skillfully; *(avec ruse)* cunningly

habileté [abilte] *nf* **(a)** *(adresse)* ability, skill **(b)** *(intelligence)* cleverness; **texte commenté avec h.** cleverly analysed text **(c)** *Jur* = **habilité**

habilitation [abilitasjɔ̃] *nf Jur* **h. de qn à faire qch** enabling (of) sb to do sth

habilité [abilite] *nf Jur* ability, title; **avoir h. à hériter** to be entitled to succeed

habiliter [abilite] *vt Jur* **h. qn à faire qch** to enable *or* entitle sb to do sth; **habilité à signer** *(employé de banque)* authorized to sign

habillage [abijaʒ] *nm* **(a)** *(d'un enfant etc)* dressing; **l'h. des petits prend beaucoup de temps** dressing the children takes ages **(b)** *Culin (de la viande, du gibier à plumes)* dressing; *(de la volaille)* drawing and trussing; *(d'un poisson)* cleaning **(c)** *(des arbres)* pruning, trimming **(d)** *(d'une montre etc)* assembly, putting together **(e)** *Tech (d'une chaudière etc)* lagging **(f)** *Com (de marchandises)* packaging **(g)** *Aut* **h. intérieur** trim **(h)** *(de page)* design, presentation **(i)** *TV, Rad* **h. chaîne** station identification *(including on-air promos, transitions and titles)* **(j)** *Compta* **h. de bilan** window-dressing of a balance-sheet

habillé [abije] *adj* **(a)** dressed; **être bien/mal h.** to be well/badly dressed; **h. en femme/cosmonaute** dressed up as a woman/spaceman; **h. de bleu/d'un complet** dressed in blue/in a suit; **h. chaudement** warmly clad *or* dressed; **h. légèrement** lightly clad *or* dressed; **s'endormir tout h.** to go to sleep with one's clothes on **(b)** *(élégant)* smart; **soirée habillée** reception, formal *or F* dressy occasion; **trop h.** *(robe)* too dressy; *(personne)* over-dressed; **cette robe est très h.** this dress is very smart; **ce n'est pas très h.** it isn't very dressy

habillement [abijmɑ̃] *nm* **(a)** *(action)* clothing, dressing **(b)** *(vêtements)* clothes, dress **(c)** *(industrie)* clothing industry

habiller [abije] **1** *vt* **(a)** *(de vêtements)* to dress; **h. un enfant en soldat** to dress a child up as a soldier; *Fig Vieilli* **h. qn pour l'hiver** to tell sb off

(b) *Culin (viande, gibier à plumes)* to dress; *(volaille)* to draw and truss; *(poisson)* to clean

(c) *(arbre)* to prune, to trim

(d) *(montre etc)* to put *or* piece together; *(pièces)* to assemble; *Typ* **h. une gravure** to run type round a block

(e) *(fournir en vêtements)* to clothe; **elle se fait h. par Lacroix** she has clothes made for her by Lacroix, she buys *or* gets her clothes at Lacroix; **qui habille la princesse?** who makes the princess's clothes?, where does the princess get her clothes?; **ma mère nous habillait** my mother made all our clothes

(f) *(garnir)* to cover (up), to wrap up; *(chaudière etc)* to lag; *Com (marchandises)* to label, to package; **h. une pièce** to decorate a room; **tableau de bord habillé de cuir** leather-padded dash(board); **h. des meubles de housses** to put loose covers on furniture; *TV etc* **h. le décor** to dress set

(g) *(aller)* to suit; **un rien t'habille** you look good in anything; **il suffit d'un rien pour l'h.** she looks good in anything, she can wear anything; **ce tissu l'habille bien/mal** this material suits/does not suit him *or* flatters/does not flatter him

2 s'habiller *vpr* **(a)** to dress (oneself), to get dressed; *(d'un prêtre etc)* to robe; **il ne sait pas encore s'h. tout seul** he can't get dressed by himself yet, he can't dress himself yet; **elle s'habille n'importe comment** she wears any old thing; **elle ne sait pas s'h.** she has no dress sense; **comment vous habillez-vous pour la soirée?** what are you wearing to the party?; **s'h. chaudement/légèrement** to dress warmly/lightly; **s'h. long/court/jeune** to wear long/short/young clothes; **s'h. en femme** to dress up as a woman

(b) s'h. sur mesure to have one's clothes made to measure; **elle s'habille chez Dior** she buys her clothes from Dior; **s'h. de neuf** to put on one's new clothes *or* one's new outfit

(c) *(pour le dîner etc)* to dress; **faut-il s'h.?** do we have to get dressed up?

habilleur, -euse [abijœr, -øz] *n Th* dresser; *TV etc* **habilleuse** wardrobe mistress

habit [abi] *nm* **(a)** dress, costume; **habits** clothes; **mettre ses habits** to put on one's clothes; **il faut l'aider à mettre ses habits/enlever ses habits** he has to be helped on/off with his clothes; *Vieilli* **marchand d'habits** *(fripier)* dealer in second-hand clothes; **h. de travail** working clothes; **le costume et la cravate, ce sont mes habits de travail** I wear a suit and tie to work

(b) h. (de soirée) evening dress, tails; **l'h. est de rigueur** formal *or* evening dress must be worn

(c) *(d'une sœur, d'un moine)* habit; **prendre l'h.** *(d'un homme)* to become a monk *or* priest, to take holy orders; *(d'une femme)* to become a nun; *Prov* **l'h. ne fait pas le moine** appearances can be deceptive

▶ **habit: h. de cheval** riding habit *or* clothes; **h. de cour** court dress; **h. du dimanche** Sunday best; **ils arrivèrent en habits du dimanche** they came in their Sunday best; **h. ecclésiastique: en h. ecclésiastique** in clerical attire *or* garb; **h. vert** *green coat worn by member of the Académie française*; **il rêvait à l'h. vert** he dreamed of becoming a member of the Académie

habitabilité [abitabilite] *nf* **(a)** *(d'une maison)* habitability, fitness for habitation **(b)** *(capacité)* capacity; **une h. de 5 personnes** space for 5 people

habitable [abitabl] *adj* (in)habitable, fit for habitation; **l'appartement est immédiatement h./n'est pas h.** the apartment is ready to move into/is uninhabitable

habitacle [abitakl] *Av* cockpit; *Naut* binnacle; *Aut* passenger compartment, cabin

habitant, -ante [abitɑ̃, -ɑ̃t] **1** *n* **(a)** *(d'une ville)* inhabitant, resident; *(d'une maison)* occupier, occupant; **ville de 10 000 habitants** town of 10,000 inhabitants; **nombre d'habitants au kilomètre carré** number of inhabitants per square kilometre; **loger chez l'h.** *Mil* to be billeted with the locals; *(en voyage)* to rent a room in sb's house **(b)** *Litt* **les habitants des bois** the inhabitants *or* creatures of the woods **(c)** *Can (fermier)* small-scale farmer, *Can* habitant [abitɑ̃] **2** *adj Can Péj* **il est un peu h.** he's a bit of a country bumpkin

habitat [abita] *nm* **(a)** *(action) (d'un animal, d'une plante)* habitat **(b)** *(de personnes)* accommodation; **h. rural/urbain** rural/urban housing; **h. nomade/sédentaire** nomadic/sedentary settlement; **dans cette région l'h. est groupé/dispersé** in this area the houses are grouped/scattered

habitation [abitasjɔ̃] *nf* **(a)** habitation; **impropre à l'h.** unsuitable *or* unfit for human habitation; **locaux à usage d'h.** premises for residential use **(b)** *(lieu)* dwelling (place), residence, abode; **une h. bien aménagée/située/chauffée** a well-equipped/well-situated/well-heated house; **changer d'h.** to change one's residence; **groupe d'h.** *(lotissement)* housing estate

▶ **habitation: h. à loyer modéré** *Br* ≈ council flat/house, *US* public housing unit

habiter [abite] **1** *vt* (*maison, lieu*) to live in; **la région n'est pas habitée** the area is uninhabited; **c'est très peu habité par ici** very few people live around here; **cette pièce n'a jamais été habitée** this room has never been used; **Vénus est-elle habitée?** is there life on Venus?; **une planète habitée** an inhabited planet; **vaisseau spatial habité** manned spacecraft; *Fig* **la certitude qui m'habite** my personal conviction; **le calme qui l'habite depuis peu** the inner calm which he has recently acquired; **elle est habitée par la haine** she is full of hatred

2 *vi* to live (**à** in, at); **h. (à) Paris/la campagne** to live in Paris/in the country; **j'habite au 3, place des Cardeurs** I live at number 3, place des Cardeurs; **h. en Italie** to live in Italy; **vous habitez chez vos parents?** do you live with your parents?; **elle habite avec son frère/cet homme** she lives with her brother/this man

habitude [abityd] *nf* **(a)** habit, custom; **bonne/mauvaise h.** good/bad habit; **faire qch par h.** to do sth from *or* out of habit, to do sth from force of habit; **prendre l'h. de faire qch** to get into the habit of doing sth; **se faire une h. d'arriver en retard** to have a habit of being late; **avoir l'h.** *ou* **avoir pour h. de faire qch** to be in the habit of doing sth; **ça ne la gênera pas, elle a l'h.** that won't bother her *or* she won't mind, she's used to it; **je n'ai pas l'h. de mentir** I'm not in the habit of lying; **prendre de mauvaises habitudes** to get into bad habits, to pick up bad habits; **c'est une question d'h.** it's a question of habit; **avoir une longue h. du travail en commun** to have long experience of working together; **nous avons une longue h. de l'édition** we have long experience in the field of publishing; **ce n'est pas une h. chez moi, ce n'est pas dans mes habitudes** I don't make a habit of it; **à** *ou* **selon** *ou* **suivant son h.** as he usually does/did, as is/was his custom *or Fml* wont; **se défaire d'une h., perdre une h.** to get out of a habit, to break a habit; **faire perdre une h. à qn** to break sb of a habit; **d'h.** usually, ordinarily, normally; **meilleur que d'h.** better than usual; **comme d'h.** as usual; **plus tôt que d'h.** earlier than usual; **habitudes d'achat** shopping habits, buying habits; **habitudes d'écoute** listening habits; *TV* viewing habits

(b) (*dextérité*) knack; **je n'en ai plus l'h.** I'm out of practice

(c) habitudes ways, customs; **les habitudes du pays** the customs of the country

habitué, -ée [abitɥe] *n* (*d'une maison*) frequent *or* regular visitor; (*d'un restaurant, d'un magasin*) regular customer, regular; **c'est un h. de la maison** (*client*) he's a regular (customer)

habituel, -elle [abitɥɛl] *adj* usual, customary, regular; **cette attitude ne lui est pas habituelle** this is not his usual attitude, he doesn't usually take this attitude; **c'est le problème h. avec elle** it's the usual problem with her; *F* **c'est le coup h.** it's the same old story, it's par for the course; **elle nous a fait le coup h.** she's played the usual *or* the same old trick on us

habituellement [abitɥɛlmɑ̃] *adv* usually, habitually, regularly; **elle arrive h. vers 18 heures 30** she usually arrives around half past six

habituer [abitɥe] **1** *vt* to accustom, *Fml* to habituate; **h. qn à qch** to get sb used to sth, to accustom sb to sth; **il faut h. les enfants au rythme de l'école** you have to get the children used *or* accustomed to the pace of school; **h. des enfants à la politesse** to get children into the habit of being polite; **h. qn à la fatigue** to accustom sb to fatigue; **il faut h. son esprit à la concentration** you have to get used to concentrating; **maintenant j'y suis habitué** I'm used to it now; **je ne m'y suis toujours pas habitué** I still haven't got used to it; **elle est habituée à rester seule** she's used to being alone; **h. qn à faire qch** to get sb into the habit of doing sth, to get sb used to doing sth; **il faut les h. à manger peu de sucre** you must get them into the habit of *or* get them used to not eating much sugar

2 s'habituer *vpr* to get used, to get *or* grow accustomed (**à** to); **tu verras, tu vas t'y h.** you'll get used to it, you'll see; **s'h. à travailler très tôt le matin** to get used to working very early in the morning; **je n'arrive pas à m'y h.** I just can't get used to it; **je ne m'habituerai jamais à …** I'll never get used to …; **s'h. à une idée** to get used to an idea

***hâblerie** [ɑbləri] *nf* **(a)** (*attitude*) bragging, boasting **(b)** (*propos*) boast

***hâbleur, -euse** [ɑblœr, -øz] **1** *adj* bragging, boasting, boastful **2** *n* boaster, braggart

***Habsbourg** [apsbur] *nm Hist* **la maison de H.** the House of Hapsburg

***hachage** [aʃaʒ] *nm* (*de viande etc*) chopping (up), mincing; (*de la paille etc*) cutting

***hache** [aʃ] *nf* axe, *US* ax; **h. à main** hatchet; **fait** *ou* **taillé à coups de h.** rough-hewn, hacked out; **visage taillé à coups de h.** angular face; **exécuter qn à la h.** to chop sb's head off; *Vieilli* **porter la h. dans les dépenses publiques** to axe *or* cut public spending

▶ **hache**: *Arch* **h. d'abordage** scuttling axe; *Arch* **h. d'armes** battleaxe; **h. de guerre** tomahawk; *Fig* **enterrer la h. de guerre** to bury the hatchet

***haché** [aʃe] **1** *adj* **(a)** minced, chopped; **bifteck h.** minced beef, mince, *Am* ground beef; **steak h.** steak mince **(b)** (*style etc*) staccato, jerky; **un film h. par des publicités** a film interspersed with adverts **(c)** (*dessin*) (cross)hatched; (*carte*) hachured **2** *nm* = **hachis**

***hache-légumes** *nm inv Culin* vegetable cutter

***hachement** [aʃmɑ̃] *nm* = **hachage**

***hache-paille** *nm inv Agr* chaffcutter

***hacher** [aʃe] *vt* **(a)** to chop (up); (*viande*) to mince, *Am* to grind; **la grêle a haché les récoltes** the crops have been cut to shreds by the hail; **h. menu** to mince finely, to chop up small; *Fig* **h. qn menu comme chair à pâté** to make mincemeat of sb; *Fig* **se faire h.** (*se faire battre*) to be cut to pieces; **elle est prête à se faire h. pour lui** she'd do anything for him; **si tu reviens à cette heure, tu vas te faire h. menu** if you come home at this hour, you'll have your head in your hands!; *Fig* **plutôt me faire h. (menu) que de dire oui** I'd rather die than say yes

(b) = **hachurer**

***hachette** [aʃɛt] *nf* hatchet

***hache-viande** *nm inv Culin* mincer

***hachis** [aʃi] *nm Culin* (*à la viande*) minced *or Am* ground meat, mince; (*au poisson*) chopped fish; **h. de veau** minced veal; **h. Parmentier** (*au boeuf*) ≈ cottage pie; (*avec viande blanche*) = dish similar to cottage pie, made with white meat; (*au mouton*) ≈ shepherd's pie; **h. d'herbes** chopped herbs

***hachisch** [aʃiʃ] *nm* hashish; **fumer du h.** to smoke hash

***hachoir** [aʃwar] *nm Culin* **(a)** (*couteau*) chopper **(b)** (*planche*) chopping board **(c)** (*électrique*) mincing machine, mincer

***hachurage** [aʃyraʒ] *nm Ordinat* hatching

***hachure** [aʃyr] *nf* (cross)hatching; (*sur une carte*) hachures; **carte en hachures** hachured map

***hachurer** [aʃyre] *vt* to (cross)hatch; (*carte*) to hachure

***hacienda** [asjɛnda] *nf* hacienda

***haddock** [adɔk] *nm Culin* smoked haddock

Hadrien [adrijɛ̃] *nm* Hadrian; **le mur d'H.** Hadrian's wall

***Haendel** [ɛndɛl] *nm* Handel

***hagard** [agar] *adj* (*visage*) haggard, drawn; (*expression, regard, yeux*) wild, distraught

hagiographe [aʒjɔgraf] *n* hagiographer

hagiographie [aʒjɔgrafi] *nf* hagiography

hagiographique [aʒjɔgrafik] *adj* hagiographic(al)

***haie** [ɛ] *nf* **(a)** (*clôture*) hedge(row) **(b)** *Sp* hurdle; *Équitation* fence; *Sp* **course de haies** hurdle race, *F* hurdles; **400 mètres haies** 400 metre hurdles **(c)** (*d'arbres, de pieux, de curieux etc*) line, row; **faire** *ou* **former la h.** to line up

▶ **haie**: **h. d'honneur** guard of honour *or US* honor; **h. vive** quickset hedge

***haïku** [aiku] *nm* haiku

***haillon** [ɑjɔ̃] *nm* (*vêtements*) rag; **être en haillons** to be in rags (and tatters); **des enfants en haillons** children dressed in rags (and tatters)

***haine** [ɛn] *nf* hatred (**pour** of, for), hate; **avoir de la h. pour qch/qn** to hate *or* detest sth/sb; **éprouver de la h. pour qn/qch** to feel hatred for sb/sth; **prendre qch/qn en h.** to take a strong aversion to sth/sb; **en h.** *ou* **par h. de qch** out of hatred of *or* for sth; *très F* **j'ai la h.!** I'm bloody furious; *très F* **les jeumes de la cité ont la h.** young people on the estate are full of rage

***haineusement** [ɛnøzmɑ̃] *adv* with (bitter) hatred

***haineux, -euse** [ɛnø, -øz] *adj* full of hatred *or* hate; **regard h.** a look full of hatred; **d'un ton h.** with hate in his/her/*etc* voice; **une femme haineuse** a woman full of hatred

***haïr** [air] (**je hais** [ɛ], **tu hais, il hait, n. haïssons**; *imp* **hais**; *otherwise regular*) **1** *vt* to hate, to detest, to loathe; **c'est ce que je hais le plus au monde** I hate *or* detest *or* loathe that more than anything else in the world; **h. qn d'avoir fait qch** to hate sb for doing *or* having done sth; *Can F* **h. qn à s'en confesser** to hate sb's guts **2 se haïr** *vpr* (*soi-même*) to hate oneself; (*de deux personnes*) to hate each other; *Hum* **elles se haïssent cordialement** they cordially detest each other; **je me hais de lui avoir menti** I feel really bad about lying to him, I hate myself *or* I can't forgive myself for lying to him

***haire** [ɛr] *nf* (*chemise*) hairshirt

***haïssable** [aisabl] *adj* hateful, detestable

***Haïti** [aiti] *nf* Haiti

***haïtien, -ienne** [aisjɛ̃, -jɛn] **1** *adj* Haitian **2** *n* **H.** Haitian

***halage** [alaʒ] *nm* **(a)** (*d'un navire*) warping, hauling **(b)** (*remorquage*) towing; **chemin de h.** towpath; **corde de h.** towing line

***halal** [alal] *adj inv* (*viande*) halal, slaughtered according to Muslim law
***hâle** [ɑl] *nm* (sun)tan, sunburn
***hâlé** [ɑle] *adj* (sun)tanned, sunburnt
haleine [alɛn] *nf* breath; **avoir l'h. fraîche** to have fresh breath; **avoir mauvaise h., avoir l'h. forte** to have bad breath; **à son h., j'ai compris qu'il avait bu** I could tell from his breath that he'd been drinking; **retenir son h.** to hold one's breath; **(tout) d'une h.** all in one breath, in the same breath; **reprendre h.** to get *or* catch one's breath, to get one's breath back; **sans avoir le temps de reprendre h.** without having time to get one's breath back; **perdre h.** to get out of breath, to lose one's breath; **courir à perdre h.** to run until one is out of breath; **discuter à perdre h.** to argue nonstop *or F* hammer and tongs; **hors d'h.** out of breath, breathless; **travail de longue h.** long and exacting task; **tenir qn en h.** to keep sb in suspense
***haler** [ale] **1** *vt* **(a)** (*navire*) to warp **(b)** (*péniche etc*) to tow **(c) h. une embarcation au sec** to haul up a boat (onto the beach) **(d)** *Naut* (*cordage etc*) to pull, to haul in, to heave **2** *vi Naut* **h. sur une manœuvre** to haul *or* pull on a rope, to heave at a rope
***hâler** [ɑle] *vt* (*du soleil etc*) to tan, to brown; **pour h. votre teint pâle** to tan your pale skin
***haletant** [al(ə)tɑ̃] *adj* (*coureur*) panting, gasping, breathless, out of breath; (*malade*) panting, gasping; **respiration haletante** panting, gasping; **voix haletante** breathless *or* gasping voice; *Fig* **elle est haletante d'impatience** she is consumed with impatience
***halètement** [alɛtmɑ̃] *nm* (*d'un coureur*) panting, gasping (for breath), puffing (and blowing); (*d'un malade*) panting, gasping; (*d'une locomotive*) puffing
***haleter** [al(ə)te] *vi* **(je halète; je halèterai)** (*d'un coureur*) to pant, to gasp (for breath), to puff (and blow); (*d'un malade*) to pant, to gasp; *Fig Litt* (*d'une locomotive*) to puff; *Fig* **le cinéaste fait h. son public** the film-maker keeps his audience on the edge of their seats
***haleur, -euse** [alœr, -øz] *n* (*de bateaux*) hauler, tower
***half-track** [aftrak] *nm Mil* half-track
***hall** [ol] *nm* entrance hall; (*d'un hôtel*) foyer, lobby; (*d'un aéroport*) lounge; **h. d'accueil** reception, lobby; **h. d'aéroport** airport lounge; **h. d'entrée** entrance hall; **h. d'entrée d'hôtel** hotel lobby; **h. d'exposition** exhibition hall; **h. de réception** foyer, lobby; **h. de gare** station concourse; **c'est un vrai h. de gare ici!** it's like Piccadilly Circus here!; **h. des départs** departure lounge
***hallage** [alaʒ] *nm Com* market trader's dues
***hallali** [alali] *nm* mort; **sonner l'h.** to blow the mort
***halle** [al] *nf* (covered) market; (*grande salle*) hall; **h. aux poissons** fish market; **h. au blé** corn exchange; **les Halles (centrales)** the Halles (*the central market in Paris*)
***hallebarde** [albard] *nf Arch* halberd, halbert; *F* **il pleut** *ou* **tombe des hallebardes** it's raining cats and dogs
***hallebardier** [albardje] *nm Arch* halberdier
***hallier** [alje] *nm* **(a)** thicket, copse **(b) halliers** brushwood
Halloween [alɔwin] *nf* Halloween
hallucinant [alysinɑ̃] *adj* (*drogue etc*) hallucinatory; (*pensée*) haunting; (*ressemblance etc*) striking; **paysage h. de beauté** strikingly beautiful scenery; **c'est h.!** it's incredible!, I don't believe it!
hallucination [alysinasjɔ̃] *nf* hallucination, delusion; **avoir des hallucinations** (*d'un malade, d'un ivrogne*) to have hallucinations; *Fig* (*se tromper*) to imagine *or* see things; **une h. collective** a collective *or* mass hallucination
hallucinatoire [alysinatwar] *adj* hallucinatory
halluciné, -ée [alysine] **1** *adj* hallucinating; *Fig F* mad **2** *n* person who suffers from hallucinations; *Fig F* madman, *f* madwoman; **il me regardait de son air d'h.** he looked at me like a madman *or* with that wild staring look in the eyes
halluciner [alysine] *vt Rare* to make hallucinate, to cause to hallucinate
hallucinogène [alysinɔʒɛn] *Pharm* **1** *nm* hallucinogen **2** *adj* hallucinogenic
***halo** [alo] *nm* **(a)** *Météo etc* halo; *Fig* **un h. de gloire** a cloud of glory; **s'entourer d'un h. de mystère** to shroud oneself in mystery **(b)** *Opt* blurring **(c)** *Phot* fogging, *Spéc* halation
halogène [alɔʒɛn] **1** *adj* halogenous **2** *nm* halogen; **lampe à h.** halogen lamp; **h. à quartz** quartz-halogen
***halte** [alt] *nf* **(a)** (*arrêt*) stop, halt; **faire h.** to (make a) halt, to stop; **h.(-là)!** stop!, halt!; *Fig* **h.-là, je ne suis pas d'accord!** hold on *or* not so fast, I don't agree!; **h. à l'armement!** stop the arms build-up!; **dire h. à l'inflation** to put a stop *or* an end to inflation **(b)** (*lieu*) stopping place, resting place; *Rail* halt
***halte-garderie** [alt(ə)gardəri], *pl* **haltes-garderies** *nf* crèche
haltère [altɛr] *nm* dumb-bell; **des haltères de 3 kilos** 3-kilo dumb-bells; **faire des haltères** to do weightlifting *or* weight training
haltérophile [alterɔfil] *n* weightlifter
haltérophilie [alterɔfili] *nf* weightlifting; **elle fait de l'h.** she does weightlifting *or* weight training
***halva** [alva] *nm* halva
***hamac** [amak] *nm* **(a)** hammock; **accrocher/décrocher un h.** to sling/unsling a hammock **(b)** (*fiche*) suspension file
hamadryade [amadrijad] *nf Myth* hamadryad, dryad, wood nymph
hamamélis [amamelis] *nm Bot* witch hazel, *Spéc* hamamelis
***Hambourg** [ɑ̃bur] *nm* Hamburg
***hambourgeois, -oise** [ɑ̃burʒwa, -waz] **1** *adj* of Hamburg **2** *n* **H.** Hamburger
***hamburger** [ɑ̃burgœr] *nm Culin* hamburger
***hameau, -eaux** [amo] *nm* hamlet
hameçon [amsɔ̃] *nm* (fish-)hook; **h. sans œillet** blind hook; *Fig* **mordre à l'h.** to swallow *or* rise to the bait
hameçonner [amsɔne] *vt* **(a)** (*poisson*) to hook **(b)** (*ligne de pêche*) to put hooks on
***hammam** [amam] *nm* Turkish baths
***hammerless** [amɛrlɛs] *nm* hammerless sporting gun
***hampe[1]** [ɑ̃p] *nf* **(a)** (*d'un drapeau etc*) staff, pole; (*d'une lance etc*) stave, shaft; (*d'un harpon*) shank; *Typ* (*qui dépasse vers le haut*) ascender; **la h. du p** the stem of the p; *Typ* **h. montante** ascender **(b)** *Bot* flower spike
***hampe[2]** *nf Culin* (*de bœuf*) = cut taken between the flank and the sirloin; (*de la venaison*) breast
***hamster** [amstɛr] *nm Zool* hamster; **h. doré** golden hamster
***han** [ɑ̃] *int* oof!; **pousser un h. à chaque coup** to (give a) grunt at every stroke
***hanap** [anap] *nm Arch* goblet, tankard
***hanche** [ɑ̃ʃ] *nf* **(a)** *Anat* hip; **déformation congénitale de la h.** congenital hip deformity; **les poings sur les hanches** (with his/her/*etc*) hands on (his/her/*etc*) hips, (with) arms akimbo; **il refusait d'avancer, les mains sur les hanches** hands on hips, he refused to go any further; **rouler les hanches** to swing one's hips; **être large des hanches** to have broad hips, *F* to be broad in the beam; **tour de hanches** hip measurement; **perdre quelques centimètres de tour de hanches** to lose a few centimetres from one's hips **(b)** (*d'un cheval*) haunch; **hanches** hindquarters **(c)** *Naut* (*d'un navire*) quarter; **par la h.** on the quarter
***hand-ball** [ɑ̃dbal] *nm Sp* handball; **jouer au h.** to play handball; **ballon de h.** handball
***handballeur, -euse** [ɑ̃dbalœr, -øz] *n Sp* handball player
***handicap** [ɑ̃dikap] *nm aussi Fig* handicap; *Fig* **la Pologne part avec un h.** Poland is handicapped from the outset; **elle partait dans la vie avec un sérieux h.** she started out in life with a serious handicap *or* seriously disadvantaged
handicapant [ɑ̃dikapɑ̃] *adj* (*maladie*) disabling; *F* **ça peut être très h.** that can be a great handicap; *F* **ne pas avoir de voiture en ville est h.** being without a car in town is a handicap
handicapé, -ée [ɑ̃dikape] **1** *adj* handicapped; (*physiquement*) handicapped, disabled; **h. mental** mentally handicapped; **h. physique** physically handicapped, (physically) disabled **2** *n* handicapped person; (*physique*) handicapped *or* disabled person; **h. moteur** person with motor impairment; **les handicapés mentaux** the mentally handicapped; **les handicapés (physiques)** the disabled, the physically handicapped
***handicaper** [ɑ̃dikape] *vt* to handicap
***handicapeur** [ɑ̃dikapœr] *nm Courses de chevaux* handicapper
handisport [adispɔr] *adj Sp* **tennis/équipement h.** tennis/sports equipment for the disabled *or* handicapped; **jeux handisports** games for the handicapped *or* disabled
***hangar** [ɑ̃gar] *nm* **(a)** shed, shelter; (*grand*) warehouse; (*pour les trains, bus etc*) depot; **h. à bateaux** boathouse **(b)** *Av* hangar
***hanneton** [an(ə)tɔ̃] *nm* cockchafer, maybug, *Am* June beetle *or* bug; *F* **une dispute/un examen pas piqué(e) des hannetons** a stinker of an argument/ exam; *F* **une réponse pas piquée des hannetons** an astounding answer; *F* **je vous ai amené un petit vin pas piqué des hannetons** I've brought you an unbelievable little wine
***Hanovre** [anɔvr] *nm* Hanover
***hanovrien, -enne** [anɔvrijɛ̃, -ɛn] *Hist* **1** *adj* Hanoverian **2** *n* **H.** Hanoverian
***hanse** [ɑ̃s] *nf Hist* Hanse, Hansa; **la H.** the Hanseatic league
***hanséatique** [ɑ̃seatik] *adj Hist* Hanseatic
***hanté** [ɑ̃te] *adj* haunted; **maison hantée** haunted house; **être hanté par un souvenir/une impression** to be haunted by a memory/a feeling
***hanter** [ɑ̃te] *vt* (*d'un fantôme*) (*maison etc*) to haunt; **cette idée le hante** he is obsessed *or* haunted by the idea; **ce souvenir me hante** the memory haunts me; *Fig* **il passait**

ses nuits à h. les bistrots he spent every night in the pub, he went on a pub-crawl every night

***hantise** [ɑ̃tiz] *nf* haunting memory *or* thought; **j'ai la h. de ce genre de réunion** I dread this kind of meeting

***happe** [ap] *nf* **(a)** *Menuis* cramp *or* clamp iron **(b)** *(anneau)* staple; **anneau à h.** ring and staple

***happement** [apmɑ̃] *nm* snapping (up), snatching, seizing

***happening** [apniŋ] *nm* happening

***happer** [ape] *vt (des oiseaux etc) (insectes etc)* to snap up, to catch; **la voiture a été happée par un train** the car was hit by a train; **la machine a happé sa main** his hand got caught in the machine; *Fig* **h. qn** to buttonhole sb

happy end, happy ending [apiɛnd(iŋ)] *nf* happy ending; **j'aime les happy ends** I love happy endings

***haquenée** [akne] *nf Arch* palfrey

hara-kiri [arakiri], *pl* **hara-kiris** *nm* hara-kiri; **(se) faire h.** to commit hara-kiri

***harangue** [arɑ̃g] *nf* harangue; *F* **nous avons eu droit à une de ses harangues** we were treated to one of his harangues *or* lectures

***haranguer** [arɑ̃ge] *vt* to harangue, to lecture

***haras** [ara] *nm* stud farm

***harassant** [arasɑ̃] *adj* exhausting

***harassé** [arase] *adj* worn out, exhausted; **h. de travail** overwhelmed with work

***harassement** [arasmɑ̃] *nm* fatigue, exhaustion

***harasser** [arase] *vt* to tire out, to exhaust

***harcelant** [arsəlɑ̃] *adj* harassing *or* pestering

***harcèlement** [arsɛlmɑ̃] *nm* harassment, harassing; **le h. sexual** sexual harassment

***harceler** [arsəle] *vt* **(je harcèle; je harcèlerai)** *(personne)* to harass; *Mil* to harry, to harass; *(animal)* to bait; **h. qn de ses questions** to badger *or* pester *or* plague sb with one's questions; **h. qn pour obtenir qch** to pester sb for sth; **elle est harcelée de soucis** she's plagued by worries; **les remords/regrets le harcèlent** he's tormented *or* plagued by remorse/regrets

***harceleur, -euse** [arsəlœr, -øz] *n* tormentor, pesterer

***hard** [ard] **1** *F adj* **la scène était un peu h.** the scene was a little risqué; **porno h.** hard *or* hard-core porn **2** *nm Mus* hard rock; *Ordinat* hardware; *(porno)* hardware

***harde[1]** [ard] *nf (de cerfs)* herd, bevy

***harde[2]** *nf (pour la meute)* leash

***hardes** [ard] *nfpl* rags

***hardi** [ardi] **1** *adj (audacieux)* bold, daring; *(téméraire)* rash; *(osé)* impudent, brazen; **écriture hardie** bold hand(writing); **faire un commentaire h.** to make a bold comment; **jugement h.** rash judgement; **mensonge h.** barefaced lie; **un décolleté h.** a daring neckline; **une interprétation hardie** a bold interpretation **2** *int* go on!, go to it!; **h. les gars!** come on lads!

***hardiesse** [ardjɛs] *nf (audace)* boldness, daring; *(effronterie)* impudence, effrontery; *(originalité)* boldness; **avoir la h. de faire qch** to be so bold as to do sth; **il a eu la h. de m'écrire** he had the audacity to write to me; **remarque la h. du style de ce peintre** note the boldness of this painter's style; **hardiesses** liberties; **se permettre des hardiesses envers qn** to take liberties with sb

***hardiment** [ardimɑ̃] *adv (avec audace)* boldly, audaciously, daringly; *(avec effronterie)* impudently; *(à la légère)* rashly; **vous avez agi bien h.** you acted very rashly

***hard-top** [ardtɔp], *pl* **hard-tops** *nm Aut* hard top

***hardware** [ardwɛr] *nm Ordinat* hardware

***harem** [arɛm] *nm* harem

***hareng** [arɑ̃] *nm* [①A12,1,g] herring; **h. (salé et) fumé** kipper; **h. saur** red *or* smoked herring; **h. bouffi** bloater; *F* **être sec comme un h.** to be as skinny *or* thin as a rake; *F* **on était serré comme des harengs dans le bus** we were packed together like sardines in the bus

***harengère** [arɑ̃ʒɛr] *nf* fishwife

***harenguier** [arɑ̃gje] *nm* herring boat

***hargne** [arɲ] *nf* bad temper, surly disposition; **parler/répondre/s'exprimer avec h.** to speak/answer/express oneself bad-temperedly *or* aggressively; **... dit-il avec h.** ... he snapped; **propos pleins de h.** aggressive remarks

***hargneusement** [arɲøzmɑ̃] *adv* bad-temperedly; aggressively

***hargneux, -euse** [arɲø, -øz] *adj (personne)* bad-tempered, cantankerous, aggressive; *(femme)* nagging; *(chien)* snarling, vicious, fierce; **ton h.** aggressive tone

***haricot** [ariko] *nm* **(a)** bean; **haricots en grains** dried beans; *F* **des haricots!** not a sausage *or* bean!; *F* **c'est la fin des haricots** we've had it now; *très F* **courir sur le h. à qn** to tee sb off, *Br* to get on sb's wick *or* up sb's nose **(b)** *Culin* **h. de mouton** = Irish stew **(c)** *(bol)* kidney dish

▶ **haricot**: **h. beurre** butter bean; **h. blanc** haricot bean; **h. d'Espagne** scarlet runner; **h. mange-tout** mange-tout; **h. à rames** runner bean; **h. rouge** (red) kidney bean; **h. vert** French *or Am* string bean

***haridelle** [aridɛl] *nf* old horse, nag

***harissa** [arisa] *nf Culin* harissa

***harki** [arki] *nm Mil* harki *(Algerian soldier who fought on French side during the War of Independence; also his descendants)*

***harle** [arl] *nm Orn* merganser

harmonica [armɔnika] *nm Mus* harmonica, mouth organ; **jouer de l'h.** to play the mouth organ *or* harmonica

harmonie [armɔni] *nf* **(a)** *Mus* harmony; **table d'h.** *(d'un piano)* sounding board **(b)** *(accord)* harmony; **être en h. avec qch** to be in keeping *or* in harmony with sth, to fit in with sth; **vivre en h.** to live in harmony *or* harmoniously; **l'h. qui règne dans cette famille** the harmony which reigns within this family **(c)** *(de l'orchestre)* wind section

harmonieusement [armɔnjøzmɑ̃] *adv* harmoniously; **des couleurs qui s'unissent h.** colours which go well together

harmonieux, -euse [armɔnjø, -øz] *adj (son)* harmonious, melodious, tuneful; *(arrangement etc)* harmonious; **couleurs harmonieuses** harmonious colours

harmonique [armɔnik] *adj, nm Mus* harmonic

harmoniquement [armɔnikmɑ̃] *adv* harmonically

harmonisation [armɔnizasjɔ̃] *nf* harmonization, harmonizing; *Ling* **h. vocalique** vowel harmony

harmoniser [armɔnize] **1** *vt* **(a)** *Mus (mélodie etc)* to harmonize **(b)** *(mettre en accord)* to harmonize; *(couleurs)* to match **2 s'harmoniser** *vpr* to be in keeping *or* in harmony, to harmonize, to agree **(avec** with**)**; **ces couleurs s'harmonisent très bien** these colours go very well together; **s'h. avec qch** *(de couleurs)* to match *or* go well with sth

harmoniseur [armɔnizœr] *nm Rad etc* harmonizer

harmonium [armɔnjɔm] *nm* harmonium

***harnaché** [arnaʃe] *adj (d'un cheval)* harnessed; *F* **il part à la pêche tout h.** he goes off fishing all kitted out; *F* **curieusement h.** wearing the strangest gear *or* get-up

***harnachement** [arnaʃmɑ̃] *nm* **(a)** *(action)* harnessing **(b)** *(harnais)* harness; *(selles etc)* saddlery; *F (vêtements)* (absurd) rig-out, get-up; **sortir dans un curieux h.** to go out wearing the strangest rig-out *or* get-up *or* gear

***harnacher** [arnaʃe] **1** *vt (cheval etc)* to harness; *F* **h. qn** to dress sb up, to rig sb out; **il fallait voir comment elle était harnachée** you should have seen the ridiculous outfit she was wearing **2 se harnacher** *vpr* to rig oneself out; **il faut toujours s'h. pour aller en montagne** you must always get properly kitted out for the mountains

***harnais** [arnɛ] *nm* **(a)** *(sellerie)* harness; *Fig* **reprendre le h.** to get back into harness, to go back to work again; **blanchir sous le h.** to spend one's life in the same occupation, to grow grey in service; *Aut* **h. de sécurité** safety harness **(b)** *Arch (armure)* armour **(c)** *MecE* **h. d'engrenage** train of gear wheels, gearing

***harnois** [arnwa] *nm Arch* = **harnais (b)**

***haro** [aro] *nm* **(clameur de) h.** outcry, hue and cry; **crier h.** to raise a hue and cry **(sur** about**)**; **crier h. sur le baudet** to scream for blood

harpagon [arpagɔ̃] *nm* miser, skinflint, scrooge; **c'est un h.** he's a real miser

***harpe** [arp] *nf Mus* harp; **jouer** *ou* **pincer de la h.** to play the harp; **h. éolienne** Aeolian harp

***harpie** [arpi] *nf* **(a)** *Myth* harpy; *Fig* harpy, shrew; **j'ai vu la concierge, cette h.** I've seen the caretaker, the old battleaxe **(b)** *Orn* harpy eagle

***harpiste** [arpist] *n Mus* harpist

***harpon** [arpɔ̃] *nm Pêche* harpoon; **pêche** *ou* **chasse (sous-marine) au h.** (underwater) spear fishing

***harponnage** [arpɔnaʒ], **harponnement** [arpɔnmɑ̃] *nm* harpooning

***harponner** [arpɔne] *vt* **(a)** *Pêche* to harpoon **(b)** *très F (de la police) (personne)* to nab, to collar; *(coincer) (personne)* to stop, to corner, to grab; **se faire h. par qn** to get cornered *or* nabbed by sb

***harponneur** [arpɔnœr] *nm Pêche* harpooner

***hasard** [azar] *nm* **(a)** chance, luck; **coup de h.** stroke of luck, fluke; **c'est vraiment un coup de h., je ne m'y attendais pas du tout** it's a real stroke of luck, I wasn't expecting it at all; **par un coup de h.** by mere chance, by coincidence; **un heureux h. a fait qu'il a été muté dans la même région que moi** by a stroke of luck he was transferred to the same area as me; **par un heureux h.** by a happy coincidence; **ne rien laisser au h.** to leave nothing to chance; **le h. a voulu** *ou* **fait que je ...** as luck would have it I ...; **le h. fit que** + *ind*, **le h. voulut que** + *sub* (as) luck would have it; **le h. fait bien les choses!** what a stroke of luck!; **au h.** at random, *Péj* haphazardly; **j'en ai pris un au h.** I took one at random; **marcher au h.** to walk aimlessly; **au h. de ses voyages** in the course of his travels, as he travelled from one place to another; **au h. de mes lectures** in the course of my reading; **par h.** by accident, by chance; **par pur h.** quite by chance, entirely by accident; **par le plus grand des hasards** by the merest chance; **si par h. vous le voyez** if you (should) happen to see him; **sauriez-vous son adresse par h.?** do you happen to know his address?, do you know his address by any chance?; **et comme par h., il est tombé malade** and as if by chance, he fell ill; **à tout h.** on the off chance, just in case; **je te le dis à tout h.** I'm telling you on the off chance that *or* just in case you're interested; **à tout h., je vais lui demander** I'll ask him just in case *or* on the off-chance

(b) (*danger*) risk, danger, hazard; **les hasards de la guerre** the hazards of war

***hasardé** [azarde] *adj* (*entreprise etc*) hazardous, risky, foolhardy; (*paroles etc*) rash

***hasarder** [azarde] **1** *vt* (*sa vie etc*) to risk, to venture, to hazard; **h. une opinion** to hazard *or* venture an opinion; **h. 500 francs** to gamble 500 francs **2 se hasarder** *vpr* to take risks; **se h. à faire qch** to venture to do sth, to risk doing sth; **se h. dans la jungle** to venture (out) into the jungle

***hasardeux, -euse** [azardø, -øz] *adj* hazardous, perilous, risky; **entreprise hasardeuse** risky business; **paroles hasardeuses** rash words

***hasch** [aʃ] *nm F* (*drogue*) hash, pot

***haschisch** [aʃiʃ] *nm* hashish; **fumer du h.** to smoke hashish

***hase** [az] *nf Zool* (*d'un lièvre, d'un lapin de garenne*) doe

***hassidisme** [asidism] *nm Rel* Chassidism, Hassidism

hast [ast] *nm Arch* shaft; **arme d'h.** shafted weapon

***hâte** [at] *nf* haste, hurry; **avoir h. de faire qch** to be in a hurry to do sth; (*avoir envie*) to be eager *or* to long to do sth, to look forward to doing sth; **j'ai h. de trouver un nouvel appartement** I can't wait to find a new flat; **j'ai h. de te revoir** I'm looking forward to seeing you again; **mettre trop de h. à faire qch** to be in too great a hurry *or* too much of a hurry to do sth; **il n'a qu'une h.: que tout soit fini** all he wants is to get it over with; **à la h.** in a hurry, in haste, hastily, hurriedly; **travail fait à la h.** slapdash work; **déjeuner à la h.** to hurry over one's lunch, *F* to bolt one's lunch; **en h.** hastily, in haste, hurriedly; **ils sont venus en h.** they came hurriedly *or* without delay; **en toute h.** posthaste, as quickly as possible; **sans h.** without haste, in a leisurely way

***hâter** [ate] **1** *vt* (*événement*) to hasten, to hurry along; (*fruit etc*) to force; **h. les choses** to hurry things up *or* along; **h. le pas** to quicken one's pace *or* step; **h. le mouvement** to hurry things up *or* along **2 se hâter** *vpr* to hurry, to hasten; **se h. de faire qch** to hurry to do sth, to lose *or* waste no time in doing sth; **je vais me h. de prendre rendez-vous** I'm going to waste no time in making an appointment; **hâtez-vous lentement** more haste, less speed

***hâtif, -ive** [atif, -iv] *adj* **(a)** (*printemps, fruit etc*) early **(b)** (*mesure, décision etc*) hasty, hurried, ill-considered, premature

***hâtivement** [ativmɑ̃] *adv* hastily, in a hurry, hurriedly; **se diriger h. vers ...** to hurry towards ...

***hauban** [obɑ̃] *nm Naut* (*cordes*) shrouds, rigging; (*corde, câble*) guy, stays

***haubaner** [obane] *vt Naut* to guy, to stay, to brace

***haubert** [obɛr] *nm Arch* coat of mail

***hausse** [os] *nf* **(a)** (*de prix, de la température*) rise, increase; **h. de prix** price rise *or* increase *or* hike; **la h. des matières premières** the rise *or* increase in the price of raw materials; **baromètre en h.** rising barometer; *Com, Fin* **marché à la h.** rising *or* bull market; **h. de 4%** 4% rise; *Bourse* **h. des cours** stock market rise; **l'immobilier est en h.** house prices are going up; **le blé a subi une h. considérable** wheat has gone up considerably (in price); **h. à la pompe** rise in the price of petrol; *Bourse* **jouer à la h.** to speculate on a rising market, to bull the market; *Bourse* **spéculateur à la h.** bull **(b)** *Tech* prop, block, stand **(c)** *Mil* (*de fusil*) (back)sight, sighting gear

***haussement** [osmɑ̃] *nm* **h. d'épaules** shrug (of the shoulders); **il accueillit la nouvelle par un h. d'épaules/avec un h. de sourcil** he welcomed the news with a shrug (of his shoulders)/with raised eyebrow(s)

***hausser** [ose] **1** *vt* (*lever*) to raise, to lift; (*élever*) to raise, to make higher, to heighten; (*augmenter*) (*prix*) to put up, to increase, to raise; **h. la voix** to raise one's voice; **h. les épaules** to shrug (one's shoulders); **h. les sourcils** to raise one's eyebrows **2** *vi Naut* (*d'un terrain, d'un phare*) to rise (over the horizon) **3 se hausser** *vpr* to raise oneself (up); **se h. sur la pointe des pieds** to stand on tiptoe *or* one's toes; **se h. jusqu'à qn** to raise oneself to sb's level; **je me suis haussé jusqu'à la fenêtre** I hauled myself up to the window; **se h. jusqu'au poste de P-DG** to climb to the position of Chairman, to rise to be Chairman

***haussier** [osje] *nm Bourse F* bull

***haut, haute** [o, ot] **1** *adj* **(a)** high; (*herbe*) tall, long; (*édifice etc*) tall, high, lofty; **femme de haute taille** tall woman; **mur h. de six mètres** wall six metres high; **h. comme trois pommes** knee high to a grasshopper; **pièce haute de plafond** room with a high ceiling; **les pièces sont hautes de plafond** the rooms have high ceilings; **des talons hauts** high heels; **un front h.** a high forehead; **marcher la tête haute** *or* **le front h.** to hold one's head up; *Fig* to walk with one's head held high *or* one's head up; **h. sur pattes** long-legged; **la lune/Vénus était haute dans le ciel** the moon/Venus was high up in the sky; **les hautes latitudes** the high latitudes; **en haute montagne** high in the mountains; **les hauts plateaux** the high plateaus *or* plateaux; **hautes terres** highlands, uplands; **les Hautes Terres (de l'Écosse)** the Highlands (of Scotland); **haute mer** open sea, high sea; **hautes eaux** high water; **à marée haute** at high tide, at high water; **la mer était haute** the tide was in *or* high; **je ne la tiens pas en haute estime** I don't hold her in very high regard *or* esteem; **avoir une haute idée de soi-même** to have a high opinion of oneself; *Fig* **avoir/garder la main haute sur ses affaires** to be in/to retain control of one's affairs

(b) (*supérieur*) upper, higher; **les hautes branches** the upper branches, the top branches; **l'étage le plus h.** the top floor; **la plus haute branche** the topmost *or* uppermost branch; **ville haute** upper part of the town; **les hautes classes** (*de la société*) the upper classes; **les hautes mathématiques** higher mathematics; **le H.-Rhin** (*département*) the Haut-Rhin; **le h. Rhin** (*fleuve*) the upper Rhine; *Naut* **les hautes voiles** the upper sails

(c) (*éminent*) exalted, important, great; **de la plus haute importance** of the greatest *or* utmost importance; **de h. rang** of high rank, high-ranking; **les plus hautes instances policières** the highest-ranking *or* most senior police authorities; **h. comique** high comedy

(d) (*note de musique*) high; **voix haute** loud voice; (*aiguë*) high(-pitched) voice; **lire à haute voix** to read aloud; **elle parlait à haute voix** she spoke aloud *or* out loud; **pousser les hauts cris** to shout out loud; **elle n'a jamais une parole plus haute que l'autre** she never raises her voice; **avoir le verbe h.** to be high and mighty

(e) (*ancien*) **la haute antiquité** remote *or* earliest antiquity; **le h. Moyen Age** the Early Middle Ages

(f) (*extrême*) **mécanisme de haute précision** precision device; **h. en couleurs** (*personnage, récit*) colourful; **haute pression** high pressure; **mécanisme de** *ou* **à haute sécurité** high security device; *Rad* **haute fréquence** high frequency; **à haute valeur ajoutée** high value added

2 *adv* **(a)** high (up), above, up; **h. les mains!** hands up!; **h. les cœurs** cheer up!; **parler h.** to speak loudly; **parlez plus h.!** speak up!; **parle moins h.!** keep your voice down!; **une voix h. perchée** a high-pitched voice; **parler** *ou* **penser tout h.** to talk *or* think aloud *or* out loud; **dire tout h. ce que tout le monde pense tout bas** to say out loud what everyone else is thinking; **parler h. et clair** to speak one's mind; **je l'ai déjà dit h. et clair** I've already said it quite openly; **femme h. placée** woman in a high position; **des gens h. placés** highly placed people, people in high office; **viser h.** to aim *or* set one's sights high; **il la place très h. dans son estime** he has a very high opinion of her, he holds her in very high regard *or* esteem; *Naut* **l'ancre est h.** the anchor is up; **gagner h. la main** to win hands down; **ils ont remporté la course h. la main** they won the race hands down

(b) (*en arrière*) back; **remonter plus h. (dans le temps)** to go further back; **comme il est dit plus h.** as indicated above *or* earlier; **ainsi que nous l'avons déjà vu plus h.** as we have already seen (above)

3 *nm* **(a)** height; **le mur a six mètres de h.** the wall is six metres high; *Fig* **regarder qn du h. de sa grandeur** to look down one's nose at sb; **tomber de (son) h.** to fall flat on the ground, to fall headlong; (*être surpris ou déçu*) to fall flat on one's back, to be floored *or* flabbergasted

(b) (*partie supérieure*) top, upper part; *Mktg* (*du marché*) high end, top end; **h.!** (*sur caisse*) this side up!; **la poste se trouve dans le h. du village** the Post Office is at the top end of the village; **le h. de la robe est en dentelle** the top of the dress is made of lace; **du h. de l'escalier** from the top of the stairs; **elle est tombée du h. de l'escalier** she fell all the way down the stairs; **les hauts et les bas** (*de la vie etc*) the ups and downs; **avoir** *ou* **connaître des hauts et des bas** to have one's ups and downs; **h. de l'eau** high water; **les hauts (d'un navire)** the topsides (of a ship); **l'étage du h.** the top floor; **le**

monsieur du h. the gentleman upstairs; **arriver en h. de la côte** to reach the top of the hill; **une fois en h. de la côte, je me suis rendu compte que ...** once I was at the top of the hill, I realized ...; **dévaler du h. de la côte** to hurtle down the hillside; **vers le h.** upwards; **lever les bras vers le h.** to raise *or* lift one's arms; **pousser vers le h.** to push upwards; **gloire à Dieu au plus h. des cieux** Glory to God in the Highest; **de** *ou* **du h. en bas** downwards, from top to bottom; **regarder qn de h. en bas** to look sb up and down; **regarder qn de h.** to look down on sb; **traiter qn de h.** to patronize sb; **prendre les choses de h.** to be very aloof *or* detached; **il a pris sa remarque de h.** he took his remark very scornfully *or* disdainfully; **en h.** above, at the top; *Naut* aloft; (*étage supérieur*) upstairs; **lancer qch en h.** to throw sth (up)/in(to) the air; **en h. du placard** at the top of the cupboard; **tout en h.** at the very top, right at the top; *Naut* **en h. tout le monde!** all hands on deck!; **en h. de l'échelle** at the top of the ladder; **d'en h.** from above, from on high; (*vu de l'étage inférieur*) from upstairs; **les gens/l'appartement d'en h.** the people (from) upstairs/the flat upstairs; *Fig* **la décision vient d'en h.** the decision comes from the top

4 *nf F* **haute** upper crust; **un gars de la h.** a toff; **elle ne fréquente que la h.** *ou* **les gens de la h.** she only associates with the upper crust

▶ **haut**: **le h. allemand** High German; *Compta* **h. de bilan** (*fonds propres*) shareholders' funds; *Géog* **le h. Canada** Upper Canada; *Typ* **h. de casse** upper case, *F* caps; **haute Cour de justice** high court of justice; **haute couture** haute couture; **défilé de haute couture** designer fashion show; **haute cuisine** haute cuisine; **je vous préviens, ce n'est pas de la haute cuisine** I warn you, it's nothing fancy; *Ordinat* **haute densité** *adj, n* high density; *Com* **haute direction** senior management; **h. fait** act of bravery; *Mil* deed of valour; *Iron* infamous deed; **haute finance** high finance; **h. fonctionnaire** high-ranking official; **h. de gamme** *adj, n* top of the range; **h. lieu: un h. lieu touristique** a tourist Mecca; **en h. lieu** in high places; **je dois en parler en h. lieu** I must go to the top about it; **la haute magistrature** the superior judiciary; **le h. du panier** the top of the heap, the pick of the bunch; **ils ne fréquentent que le h. du panier** they mix only with the cream of society; **haute performance** *adj* high-performance; **haute résolution** high resolution; **haute saison** high season; **haute société** high society; **les gens de la haute société** members of *or* people in high society; **haute technologie** high technology, high tech, hitech; **haute trahison** high treason

***hautain** [otɛ̃] *adj* haughty, lofty

***hautainement** [otɛnmɑ̃] *adv* haughtily, loftily

***hautbois** [obwa] *nm Mus* oboe

***hautboïste** [oboist] *n Mus* oboe player, oboist

***haut-de-chausse(s)** [od(ə)ʃos], *pl* **hauts-de-chausse(s)** *nm Arch* breeches

***haut-de-forme** [od(ə)fɔrm], *pl* **hauts-de-forme** *nm* top hat

***haute-contre** [otkɔ̃tr], *pl* **hautes-contres** *Mus* **1** *nf* (*voix*) counter tenor **2** *adj, nm* counter tenor

***haute-fidélité** [otfidelite] *adj* hi-fi, high fidelity; **chaîne h.** hi-fi

***hautement** [otmɑ̃] *adv* (*à un haut degré*) highly; *Vieilli* (*ouvertement*) openly

hauteur [otœr] *nf* height, elevation; (*d'une étoile, d'un triangle etc*) altitude; *Mus* (*d'une note de musique*) pitch; (*des idées etc*) loftiness; **l'immeuble a une h. de 400 mètres** the building is 400 metres high; **sa h. est telle qu'on s'en sert comme d'un point de repère dans la ville** it is so high that it serves as a landmark in the town; **prendre de la h.** (*d'un avion etc*) to climb, to gain height; **pour résoudre ce problème, il convient de prendre de la h.** in order to solve this problem, we must rise above it; **le peu de h. du plafond** the lowness of the ceiling; **le pont manque de h. pour laisser passer les camions** there isn't enough clearance for lorries under the bridge; **tomber de (toute) sa h.** to fall flat on one's face *or* headlong; **à la h. de qch** abreast of *or* level with sth; **l'eau nous arrivait à la h. des épaules** the water came up to our shoulders; **arriver à la h. de qn/qch** to draw level with sb/sth; **être** *ou* **se montrer à la h. d'une tâche** to be *or* to prove equal to *or* up to a task, *F* to be up to a job; **être à la h. de la situation** to be equal to *or* up to the situation; *F* **être à la h.** to be up to it; *Fig Litt* **la h. de vues d'un fonctionnaire** the loftiness *or* lofty attitude of a civil servant; **avoir une grande h. de vues** to be lofty-minded; *Naut* **à la h. du cap Horn** off *or* abreast of Cape Horn; **à la h. de Grenoble, il faudra commencer à penser à mettre les chaînes** when you get to Grenoble, you will have to start thinking about putting the snow chains on; **il y a un embouteillage à la h. du Mans** there is a traffic jam near Le Mans; **ils habitent à la h. de l'église** they live up by the church; *Sp* **saut en h.** high jump; **faire du saut en h.** to do the high jump; **à h. de** (*s'engager*) up to; *Bourse* **M. Martin, actionnaire de Perrier® à h. de 5%** Mr Martin, a shareholder in Perrier® with *or* holding 5% of the shares; **il participe à h. de 30 pour cent** he is contributing up to 30 per cent

▶ **hauteur**: **h. d'appui: à h. d'appui** at elbow height; *Couture* **h. du dos** = length of back; **h. libre** (*d'un pont etc*) headroom; *Ordinat* **h. de ligne** line height; *Typ* **h. de page** page depth; **h. de passage** (*d'un pont etc*) headroom; *Aut* **h. au plafond** headroom; **h. sous plafond** ceiling height; **quelle est la h. sous plafond?** what is the height of *or* how high is the ceiling?

Haute-Volta [hotvɔlta] *nf* Upper Volta

***haut-fond**, *pl* **hauts-fonds** *nm* (*dans la mer, dans une rivière*) shoal, shallow; **contourner le h.** to negotiate the shallow waters

***haut(-)fourneau** [ofurno], *pl* **hauts(-)fourneaux** *nm Métal* blast furnace

***haut-le-cœur** [ol(ə)kœr] *nm inv* (*de l'estomac*) heave; **avoir un/des h.** to retch, to heave; **j'ai eu un h. de dégoût** my stomach heaved in disgust; **cette vision me donna un h.** the sight of it made me feel sick

***haut-le-corps** [ol(ə)kɔr] *nm inv* (sudden) start, jump; **faire un h.** (*d'un cheval*) to start; **avoir un h.** (*d'une personne*) to give a start, to jump

***haut-mal** *nm inv Méd Arch* falling sickness

***haut-parleur**, *pl* **haut-parleurs** *nm* loudspeaker, Tannoy®; *Rad, TV etc* (loud-)speaker; **h. d'interphone** intercom loudspeaker; **h. d'ordres** intercom loudspeaker

***haut-relief**, *pl* **hauts-reliefs** *nm Beaux-Arts* high relief, alto-relievo

***hauturier, -ière** [otyrje, -jɛr] *adj Naut* of the high seas; **navigation hauturière** ocean navigation; **pilote h.** deep-sea pilot; **pêche hauturière** deep-sea fishing

***havage** [avaʒ] *nm Min* cutting

***havanais, -aise** [avanɛ, -ɛz] **1** *adj* of/from Havana **2** *n* **H.** (*natif*) native of Havana; (*habitant*) inhabitant of Havana

***Havane** [avan] **1** *nf* Havana **2** *nm* **h.** Havana (cigar) **3** *adj inv* **cuir h.** (light) brown *or* tan leather

***hâve** [ɑv] *adj* (*visage*) haggard, emaciated, gaunt; (*joues*) sunken; (*peau*) pale, pallid

***haveuse** [avøz] *nf Min* (*machine*) coalcutter

***havrais, -aise** [ɑvrɛ, -ɛz] **1** *adj* of/from Le Havre **2** *n* **H.** (*natif*) native of Le Havre; (*habitant*) inhabitant of Le Havre

***havre** [ɑvr] *nm Litt* haven, harbour, *US* harbor; *Vieilli* (*port*) port; **un h. de paix** a haven of peace

***havresac** [avrəsak] *nm* haversack; *Mil* knapsack, pack

Hawaï [awai] *n* Hawaii; **les îles H.** Hawaii, the Hawaiian Islands

hawaïen, -ïenne [awajɛ̃, -jɛn] **1** *adj* Hawaiian; **guitare hawaïenne** Hawaiian guitar **2** *n* **H.** Hawaiian

***Haye (la)** [laɛ] *nf* the Hague

***hayon** [ajɔ̃] *nm* (*d'une voiture*) hatchback, tailgate; (*d'un camion*) tailgate; (*d'une charrette*) tailboard

HD *Ordinat* (*abrév* **haute densité**) HD

HDL-cholestérol [aʃdeɛlkɔlɛsterɔl] *nm Méd* HDL cholesterol, high-density lipoproteins

***hé** [e] *int* **(a)** (*pour interpeller*) hey (there)!; **(b)** (*pour renforcer*) **hé! hé!** well, well!; **hé oui!** yes indeed!

***heaume** [om] *nm* helm(et)

***heavy metal** [ɛvimetal] *nm Mus* **h.** heavy metal; **écouter du h.** to listen to heavy metal

hebdo [ɛbdo] *nm* weekly; **h. télé** TV magazine

hebdomadaire [ɛbdɔmadɛr] *adj, nm* weekly

hebdomadairement [ɛbdɔmadɛrmɑ̃] *adv* weekly, once a week

hébergement [ebɛrʒ(ə)mɑ̃] *nm* (*logement*) accommodation, *Am* accommodations; (*fait d'héberger*) putting up, taking in; **h. de courte durée** short-stay accommodation; **h. de transit** transit accommodation; **h. de vacances** holiday accommodation; **h. en pension complète** board and lodging

héberger [ebɛrʒe] *vt* (**j'hébergeai(s); n. hébergeons**) (*hôte payant*) to accommodate, to put up; (*ami*) to put up; (*sans-abri, réfugié*) to take in; (*fugitif*) to harbour, *US* to harbor

hébété [ebete] *adj* (*expression etc*) dazed, bewildered; **h. de douleur** numb with grief; **h. par l'alcool** in a drunken stupor

hébétement [ebɛtmɑ̃] *nm* stupefaction, bewilderment

hébéter [ebete] *vt* (**j'hébète; j'hébéterai**) (*sens etc*) to dull, to stupefy; (*personne*) to daze

hébétude [ebetyd] *nf* stupor

hébraïque [ebraik] *adj* Hebraic, Hebrew

hébraïsant, -ante [ebraizɑ̃, -ɑ̃t] *n (érudit, étudiant)* Hebraist
hébraïser [ebraize] *vt* to hebraize
hébraïsme [ebraism] *nm* Hebraism
hébraïste [ebraist] *n* Hebraist, Hebrew scholar
hébreu, -eux [ebrø] **1** *adj* (**hébraïque** *is used for the feminine*) Hebrew **2** *nm Ling* Hebrew; *F* **c'est de l'h. pour moi** it's double Dutch *or* all Greek to me **3** *n* **H.** Hebrew
Hébrides (les) [lezebrid] *nfpl* the Hebrides
HEC [aʃəse] *nf (abrév* **Hautes Études Commerciales**) *(à Paris, à Montréal)* = prestigious business school; **faire H.** to study at the HEC; **les anciens élèves de H.** the former students of the HEC
hécatombe [ekatɔ̃b] *nf* slaughter, massacre, *Lit* hecatomb; *Fig F* **ça a été une h. cette année au bac!** the bac results were disastrous this year!
hectare [ɛktar] *nm* hectare (= 2.47 acres)
hectique [ɛktik] *adj Méd (fièvre)* hectic
hecto [ɛkto] *nm (hectogramme)* hectogram(me); *(hectolitre)* hectolitre, *US* hectoliter
hectogramme [ɛktɔgram] *nm* hectogram(me)
hectolitre [ɛktɔlitr] *nm* hectolitre, *US* hectoliter
hectomètre [ɛktɔmɛtr] *nm* hectometre, *US* hectometer
hectométrique [ɛktɔmetrik] *adj* hectometric
hectopascal, -als [ɛktɔpaskal] *nm Météo* millibar
hectowatt [ɛktɔwat] *nm Él* hectowatt
hédonisme [edɔnism] *nm* hedonism
hédoniste [edɔnist] **1** *n* hedonist **2** *adj* hedonist(ic)
hégélianisme [egeljanism] *nm Phil* Hegelianism
hégélien, -ienne [egeljɛ̃, -jɛn] *adj, n Phil* Hegelian
hégémonie [eʒemɔni] *nf* hegemony; **l'h. des USA sur le monde** the USA's position of hegemony in the world
hégire [eʒir] *nf Rel* Hegira
***hein** [ɛ̃] *int F* eh?, what?; **h., que dis-tu?** what did you say?; **il fait beau aujourd'hui, h.?** fine *or* nice day, isn't it?; **et qu'est-ce que tu lui diras, h.?** so, what are you going to tell him now, eh?; **qu'est-ce que tu veux, h., que j'arrête de travailler?** you want me to stop working, is that it?; **ne refais jamais ça, h.!** don't ever do that again, OK?; **h. qu'il fait bien la cuisine!** he does cook well, doesn't he?
hélas [elɑs] *int* alas!; **mais h., c'était trop tard** but sadly *or Fml* alas it was too late; **h., trois fois h.!** alas and alack!
Hélène [elɛn] *nf* **H. de Troie** Helen of Troy
***héler** [ele] *vt* (**je hèle**; **je hélerai**) *(personne, taxi, navire)* to hail
hélianthe [eljɑ̃t] *nm Bot* helianthus
hélianthine [heljɑ̃tin] *nf Ch* helianthin(e), methyl orange
héliaque [eljak] *adj Astron* heliac(al)
hélice [elis] *nf* **(a)** *Math, Archit* helix; **escalier en h.** spiral staircase; *Biol* **double h.** double helix **(b)** *Av* propeller; *Naut* propeller, screw; *(d'un appareil ménager)* screw
hélico [eliko] *nm F* 'copter, chopper
hélicoïdal, -ale, -aux, -ales [elikɔidal, -o] *adj* helicoid(al), helical; **mèche hélicoïdale** twist drill
hélicoïde [elikɔid] *adj, nm Math* helicoid
hélicon [elikɔ̃] *nm Mus* helicon
hélicoptère [elikɔptɛr] *nm Av* helicopter; *Mil* **h. de combat** helicopter gunship
héligare [eligar] *nf* heliport
héliocentrique [eljɔsɑ̃trik] *adj Astron* heliocentric
héliographe [eljɔgraf] *nm* heliograph
héliographie [eljɔgrafi] *nf* heliography
héliograveur [eljɔgravœr] *nm* photogravure worker
héliogravure [eljɔgravyr] *nf* photogravure
héliomarin [eljɔmarɛ̃] *adj Méd* **cure héliomarine** = course of treatment based on sun and sea air; **centre h.** = seaside convalescent home where heliotherapy is used
héliothérapie [eljɔterapi] *nf Méd* heliotherapy; **h. artificielle** sunray treatment
héliotrope [eljɔtrɔp] *nm Bot* heliotrope
héliport [elipɔr] *nm* heliport
héliportage [elipɔrtaʒ] *nm* transport by helicopter
héliporté [elipɔrte] *adj* **(a)** *(transporté par hélicoptère)* transported by helicopter; **troupes héliportées** airborne troops **(b)** *(effectué par hélicoptère)* **mission héliportée** helicopter mission
hélisurface [elisyrfas] *nf Naut, Pétr* helideck; *(sur un immeuble)* helipad
hélitreuiller [elitrøje] *vt* to winch into a helicopter
hélium [eljɔm] *nm Ch* helium
hélix [eliks] *nm Anat, Zool* helix
hellébore [elebɔr] *nm Bot* hellebore
hellène [elɛn] **1** *adj* Greek; *Hist* Hellenic **2** *n* **H.** Hellene
hellénique [elenik] *adj* Greek; *Hist* Hellenic; **la politique h. à l'égard de la communauté Européenne** Greek policy in relation to the European Community
hellénisant, -ante [elenizɑ̃, -ɑ̃t] **1** *adj* Hellenistic **2** *n* Hellenist
hellénisation [elenizasjɔ̃] *nf* Hellenization
helléniser [elenize] *vt* to Hellenize
hellénisme [elenism] *nm* Hellenism
helléniste [elenist] *n* Hellenist
hellénistique [elenistik] *adj Hist* Hellenic
***hello** [ɛllo] *int F* hello
helvète [ɛlvɛt] *adj, n Hist (suisse)* Helvetian
Helvétie [ɛlvesi] *nf Hist* Helvetia
helvétique [ɛlvetik] *adj* Helvetic, Swiss; **le gouvernement h.** the Swiss government; **la Confédération h.** the Swiss Federal Republic
helvétisme [ɛlvetism] *nm Ling* Swiss French expression
***hem** [ɛm] *int (pour attirer l'attention, se racler la gorge)* ahem!; *(question)* eh?, what?; *(exprimant le doute, la gêne etc)* h'm; **enfin, h., je ne peux pas te le dire comme ça ...** well, h'm, you see, I can't really tell you just like that ...
hématie [emasi] *nf Physiol* red blood corpuscle
hématologie [ematɔlɔʒi] *nf Méd* haematology, *US* hematology
hématologique [ematɔlɔʒik] *adj Méd* haematological, *US* hematological
hématologiste [ematɔlɔʒist], **hématologue** [ematɔlɔg] *n Méd* haematologist, *US* hematologist
hématome [ematom] *nm Méd* haematoma, *US* hematoma; **se faire un h.** to bruise oneself; **contre les hématomes** for bruises
hémicycle [emisikl] *nm Archit* hemicycle; **en h.** *(voûte etc)* semicircular; *Pol* **les députés présents dans l'h.** *(à l'Assemblée nationale)* the MPs present in the chamber
hémiplégie [emipleʒi] *nf Méd* hemiplegia
hémiplégique [emipleʒik] *adj, n Méd* hemiplegic
hémiptère [emiptɛr] **1** *adj* hemipterous, hemipteran **2** *nm* hemipteran
hémisphère [emisfɛr] *nm* hemisphere; *Anat* **h. cérébral** cerebral hemisphere; *Géog* **l'h. nord/sud** the northern/ southern hemisphere
hémisphérique [emisferik] *adj* hemispheric(al)
hémistiche [emistiʃ] *nm* hemistich
hémoculture [emɔkyltyr] *nf* haemoculture, *US* hemoculture, blood culture
hémodialyse [emɔdjaliz] *nf Méd* haemodialysis, *US* hemodialysis
hémoglobine [emɔglɔbin] *nf* haemoglobin, *US* hemoglobin; **des flots d'h.** *(dans un film etc)* blood and gore
hémophile [emɔfil] *Méd* **1** *adj* haemophilic, *US* hemophilic **2** *n* haemophiliac, *US* hemophiliac
hémophilie [emɔfili] *nf Méd* haemophilia, *US* hemophilia; **atteint d'h.** suffering from haemophilia, haemophiliac
hémoptysie [emɔptizi] *nf Méd (des voies respiratoires)* haemoptysis, *US* hemoptysis, spitting of blood
hémorragie [emɔraʒi] *nf Méd* haemorrhage, *US* hemorrhage, bleeding; **h. interne** internal bleeding; *Fig* **il faut arrêter cette h. humaine** we must stop this squandering of human life; **h. des capitaux** drain of capital; **l'h. des réserves d'or** the heavy drain on the gold reserve; **l'h. des cerveaux** the brain drain
hémorragique [emɔraʒik] *adj Méd* haemorrhagic, *US* hemorrhagic
hémorroïdaire [emɔrɔidɛr] *adj, n Méd* (**personne**) **h.** person suffering from haemorrhoids *or US* hemorrhoids
hémorroïdal, -ale, -aux, -ales [emɔrɔidal, -o] *adj Méd* haemorrhoidal, *US* hemorrhoidal
hémorroïdes [emɔrɔid] *nfpl Méd* haemorrhoids, *US* hemorrhoids, piles; **traitement anti-h.** treatment for haemorrhoids *or* piles; **avoir des h.** to have haemorrhoids *or* piles
hémostatique [emɔstatik] *Méd* **1** *adj* haemostatic, *US* hemostatic **2** *nm* haemostat(ic), *US* hemostat(ic)
hendécagone [ɛ̃dekagɔn] *nm* hendecagon
hendécasyllabe [ɛ̃dekasilab] **1** *adj* hendecasyllabic **2** *nm* hendecasyllable
***henné** [ene] *nm Bot* henna; **se faire un h.** to henna one's hair, to give one's hair a henna rinse; **les cheveux teints au h.** hennaed hair; **feuilles de h.** henna leaves; **h. naturel** natural henna
hennin [enɛ̃] *nm Hist* hennin
***hennir** [enir] *vi* to whinny, to neigh; *(d'une personne)* to bray
***hennissement** [enismɑ̃] *nm (action)* whinnying, neighing; *(d'une personne)* braying; *(cri)* whinny, neigh; *(d'une personne)* bray
***henry** [ɑ̃ri], *pl* **henrys** *nm Él* henry
***hep** [ɛp] *int* hey (there)!
héparine [eparin] *nf Pharm* heparin
hépatique [epatik] **1** *adj* hepatic **2** *n* person suffering from a liver complaint **3** *nf Bot* hepatic, liverwort

hépatisme [epatism] *nm Méd* liver ailments
hépatite [epatit] *nf Méd* hepatitis; **h. A/B/C** hepatitis A/B/C
hépatologie [epatɔlɔʒi] *nf Méd* hepatology
heptacorde [ɛptakɔrd] *Mus* **1** *adj* seven-stringed **2** *nm* heptachord (instrument/scale)
heptaèdre [ɛptaɛdr] *nm* heptahedron
heptagonal, -ale, -aux, -ales [ɛptagɔnal, -o] *adj* heptagonal
heptagone [ɛptagɔn] *nm* heptagon
heptamètre [ɛptamɛtr] *nm* heptameter
heptasyllabe [ɛptasilab] *adj* heptasyllabic
Heptateuque (l') [lɛptatøk] *nm Bible* the Heptateuch
héraldique [eraldik] **1** *adj* heraldic **2** *nf* heraldry
héraldiste [eraldist] *n* heraldry expert
***héraut** [ero] *nm* **(a)** *Hist* **h. (d'armes)** herald **(b)** *Litt* (*du printemps etc*) herald, harbinger
herbacé [ɛrbase] *adj Bot* herbaceous
herbage [ɛrbaʒ] *nm* (*prairie*) pasture; (*herbe*) grass, pasture; **emmener les vaches dans les herbages** to put the cows out to grass *or* to pasture *or* to graze
herbager[1] [ɛrbaʒe] *vt* **(j'herbageai(s); n. herbageons)** *Agr* **h. les bœufs** to put cattle out to grass *or* to pasture *or* to graze
herbager[2], **-ère** [-ɛr] *n Agr* grazier
herbe [ɛrb] *nf* **(a)** (*de gazon etc*) grass; **brin d'h.** blade of grass; **touffe d'h.** tuft of grass; **faire de l'h.** (*pour les lapins etc*) to cut grass; **couper l'h.** to cut the grass; *Fig* **couper l'h. sous le pied de qn** to cut the ground from under sb's feet; **déjeuner sur l'h.** to picnic, to have a picnic (lunch); *Golf* **être dans l'h. longue** to be in the rough
(b) (*plante*) herb; *F* (*drogue*) grass; *Culin* **fines herbes** mixed herbs; **omelette aux fines herbes** omelette with herbs; **herbes marines** seaweed; **herbes médicinales** medicinal herbs; **mauvaise h.** weed; *Fig* **le garçon a grandi comme une mauvaise h.** the boy has shot up *or* really sprouted
(c) en h. (*blé etc*) green, unripe; *Fig* (*poète, pianiste etc*) budding; *Fig* **manger son blé en h.** to eat one's seed corn
▶ **herbe: h. au cœur** lungwort; **h. aux chats** catmint, *Am* catnip; **h. aux écus** moneywort; **h. à éternuer** sneezewort; **h. aux poumons** lungwort; *Can* **h. à la puce** poison ivy; **h. aux puces** fleawort; **h. sacrée** wild vervain; **h. à tous les maux** wild vervain
herbeux, -euse [ɛrbø, -øz] *adj* grassy
herbicide [ɛrbisid] **1** *adj* (*weed-killing*) herbicidal; **produit h.** weedkiller, herbicide **2** *nm* weedkiller
herbier [ɛrbje] *nm* (*collection*) herbarium; **faire un h.** to build up a collection of dried plants
herbivore [ɛrbivɔr] *Zool* **1** *adj* herbivorous **2** *nm* herbivore
herborisation [ɛrbɔrizasjɔ̃] *nf* botanizing, gathering of plants
herboriser [ɛrbɔrize] *vi* to botanize, to gather plants; **les enfants herborisent** the children are gathering plants
herboriste [ɛrbɔrist] *n* herbalist
herboristerie [ɛrbɔristəri] *nf* (*boutique*) herbalist's (shop); (*commerce*) herb trade
herbu [ɛrby] *adj* grassy
***hercher** [ɛrʃe] *vi Min* (*charbon, minerai*) to haul
Herculanum [ɛrkylanɔm] *nm* Herculaneum
Hercule [ɛrkyl] *nm* Hercules; **travail d'H.** Herculean task; **il est bâti en h.** he's built like a tank; **c'est un h.** he's a real Hercules; **h. de foire** (professional) strong man
herculéen, -enne [ɛrkyleɛ̃, -ɛn] *adj* Herculean
hercynien, -ienne [ɛrsinjɛ̃, -jɛn] *adj Géol* Hercynian
***hère** [ɛr] *nm* **pauvre h.** poor creature *or* devil *or Br* blighter
héréditaire [erediter] *adj* (*titre etc*) hereditary; (*maladie*) hereditary, that runs in the family; **haine h.** inherited hatred; **c'est h.!** it runs in the family!, it's in the blood!
héréditairement [ereditermɑ̃] *adv* hereditarily
hérédité [eredite] *nf* **(a)** *Biol* heredity; **avoir une h. chargée** *ou* **une lourde h.** to come from a family with a history of mental/physical illness; **h. de la couronne** royal succession by birth **(b)** *Jur* (*droit*) right of inheritance
hérésiarque [erezjark] *nm* heresiarch
hérésie [erezi] *nf* heresy; **considéré comme une h.** considered sacrilegious; *Fig* **c'est une h.!** that's sacrilege!; **boire ce vin avec ce repas, c'est une h.** it's absolute sacrilege to drink a wine like this with this meal
hérétique [eretik] **1** *adj* heretical **2** *n* heretic
***hérissé** [erise] *adj* **(a)** (*garni*) bristling (**de** with); **planche hérissée de pointes** plank covered in *or* bristling with spikes; **mur h. de tessons de bouteilles** wall with broken glass all along the top **(b)** (*cheveux*) (standing) on end, spiky; (*moustache*) bristly; (*tige, fruit*) prickly; **les cheveux hérissés sur la tête** hair standing on end
***hérissement** [erismɑ̃] *nm* bristling
***hérisser** [erise] **1** *vt* **(a)** (*d'un animal*) to bristle (up); **h. ses plumes** (*d'un oiseau*) to ruffle up its feathers
(b) (*poil, cheveux*) to make stand on end; **les rochers hérissent la côte** the coastline is bristling with rock; **parcours hérissé d'obstacles** course scattered with obstacles; *Fig* **l'épreuve était hérissée de pièges** the test was full of pitfalls, the test had one pitfall after another; *Fig* **il a été hérissé par cette remarque** the remark got his back up *or* made him bristle; **ta remarque l'a profondément hérissé** your comment really got his back up; *Fig* **h. sa conversation de citations** to lard *or* pepper one's conversation with quotes
2 se hérisser *vpr* to bristle (up); (*des poils, des cheveux*) to stand on end; *Fig* (*d'une personne*) to get one's back up, to bristle; **mes cheveux se sont hérissés d'horreur** my hair stood on end with horror
***hérisson** [erisɔ̃] *nm* **(a)** hedgehog; *Fig* bristly person; **h. de mer** sea urchin; (*poisson*) porcupine fish **(b)** (*pour bouteilles*) bottlebrush; (*de cheminée*) (sweep's) flue brush **(c)** *Agr* toothed cylinder *or* roller
héritage [eritaʒ] *nm* inheritance, heritage; *Fig* (*spirituel, intellectuel*) inheritance; **part d'h.** portion; **faire** *ou* **recueillir un h.** to receive a legacy; (*argent*) to come into money; **il l'a eu par h.** he inherited it, it was handed down to him; *Fig* **h. de honte** legacy of shame
hériter [erite] **1** *vi* **h. d'une fortune** to inherit *or* succeed to *or* come into a fortune; **j'ai hérité de ce service de table** I inherited this table linen, this table linen was handed down to me; **elle a hérité de l'intelligence de son père** she inherited her intelligence from her father; **h. de qn** to receive an inheritance from sb; *Hum* **tu t'achètes encore une moto, tu as hérité ou quoi?** you're buying another motorbike, have you won the pools? *or* have you come into a fortune?; **et c'est moi qui ai hérité de tous ses problèmes d'argent** and I'm the one who's been landed with all his money problems
2 *vt* **h. une fortune de son grand-père** to inherit a fortune from one's grandfather; *Fig* **h. une tradition** to inherit a tradition
héritier, -ière [eritje, -jɛr] *n* heir, *f* heiress; **lui donnera-t-elle un h.?** will she give him an heir?; **h. de qch/qn** heir to sth/sb; **les héritiers d'une longue tradition** the heirs to a long tradition; **h. présomptif** *Jur* next of kin; (*du trône*) heir apparent; **h. légitime** *ou* **naturel** rightful heir, *Spéc* heir-at-law
hermaphrodisme [ɛrmafrɔdism] *nm Biol* hermaphroditism
Hermaphrodite [ɛrmafrɔdit] *nm Myth* Hermaphroditus
hermaphrodite [ɛrmafrɔdit] **1** *nm Biol* hermaphrodite **2** *adj* hermaphrodite, hermaphroditic
herméneutique [ɛrmenøtik] **1** *adj* hermeneutic **2** *nf* hermeneutics
Hermès [ɛrmɛs] *nm Myth* Hermes
hermès [ɛrmɛs] *nm* **(buste en) h.** bust where the shoulders, chest and arms have been cut away at an angle
hermétique [ɛrmetik] *adj* **(a)** (*philosphie, alchimie*) hermetic; *Fig* (*texte etc*) abstruse, obscure; **un poète h.** an abstruse poet **(b)** (*visage*) impenetrable; **je suis absolument h. à ce genre d'humour** that kind of humour goes straight over the top of my head **(c)** (*sceau*) tight (closed), hermetically sealed, hermetic; **joint h.** airtight *or* watertight joint
hermétiquement [ɛrmetikmɑ̃] *adv* (*scellé etc*) hermetically; (*fermé*) tightly
hermétisme [ɛrmetism] *nm Littér* hermetism; (*d'un texte etc*) abstruseness, obscurity
hermine [ɛrmin] *nf Zool* stoat, ermine; *Com* (*fourrure*) ermine; **manteau d'h.** ermine coat
herminette [ɛrminɛt] *nf* adze
***herniaire** [ɛrnjɛr] *adj* (*tumeur etc*) hernial; **bandage h.** truss
***hernie** [ɛrni] *nf Méd* hernia, rupture; *Aut* (*dans un pneu*) bulge, swelling; **h. étranglée** strangulated hernia; **h. discale** slipped disc
***hernié** [ɛrnje] *adj Méd* (*intestin etc*) herniated
Hérode [erɔd] *nm* Herod
Hérodote [erɔdɔt] *nm* Herodotus
héroï-comique [erɔikɔmik], *pl* **héroï-comiques** *adj* mock-heroic
héroïne[1] [erɔin] *nf* (*de roman*) heroine
héroïne[2] *nf Ch* heroin; **prendre de l'h.** to take heroin
héroïnomane [erɔinɔman] *n* heroin addict
héroïnomanie [erɔinɔmani] *nf* heroin addiction
héroïque [erɔik] *adj* heroic; **les temps héroïques de l'aviation** the pioneering days of aviation
héroïquement [erɔikmɑ̃] *adv* heroically
héroïsme [erɔism] *nm* heroism; **faire preuve d'h.** to be heroic, to show heroism
***héron** [erɔ̃] *nm* heron; **h. cendré** (grey *or* common) heron
***héros** [ero] *nm* [ⓘA12,1,c] hero; **un h. de la guerre/de la Révolution Française** a war hero/a hero of the French

Revolution; **le h. de la fête** the guest of honour; **le h. national** the national hero; **le h. du jour** the hero of the day *or* hour; **mourir en h.** to die like a hero, to die a hero's death
herpès [ɛrpɛs] *nm Méd* herpes; (*buccal*) cold sore
herpétique [ɛrpetik] *adj Méd* herpetic
herpétologie [ɛrpetɔlɔʒi] *nf* herpetology
***hersage** [ɛrsaʒ] *nm Agr* harrowing
***herscher** [ɛrʃe] *vi* = **hercher**
***herse** [ɛrs] *nf* **(a)** *Agr* harrow **(b)** *Hist* (*de forteresse*) portcullis **(c)** *Th* batten
***herser** [ɛrse] *vt Agr* to harrow
***herseur** [ɛrsœr] *nm Agr* harrower
***herseuse** [ɛrsøz] *nf Agr* harrow
hertz [ɛrts] *nm Él* hertz
hertzien, -ienne [ɛrtsjɛ̃, -jɛn] *adj Él* hertzian; *Rad* **réseau h.** radio relay system; *TV, Rad* **par voie hertzienne** terrestrially broadcast
hésitant, -ante [ezitɑ̃, -ɑ̃t] **1** *adj* hesitant, wavering, undecided; (*voix, pas etc*) faltering **2** *n* **il faut convaincre les hésitants** we must convince the waverers
hésitation [ezitasjɔ̃] *nf* hesitation, hesitancy, wavering; **parler avec h.** to speak hesitatingly; **après bien des hésitations** after much hesitation; **sans h.** unhesitatingly, without hesitation; **sans h., je choisirai celui-ci** I have no hesitation in choosing this one
hésiter [ezite] *vi* **(a)** (*être dans l'incertitude*) to hesitate, to waver; **h. sur qch/entre deux choses** to hesitate over sth/between two things; **h. sur ce que l'on fera** to hesitate as to what one will do; **j'hésite sur la démarche à suivre** I'm hesitating as to *or* dithering over what to do; **je ne sais pas, j'hésite** I don't know, I can't make up my mind *or* I'm undecided; **elle hésitait à t'en parler** she didn't like *or* she wasn't sure whether to talk to you about it; **il n'hésita pas une seconde à se jeter à l'eau** without a moment's hesitation, he jumped into the water; *Fig* without a moment's hesitation he took the plunge; **il n'y a pas à h.** there's no room *or* time for hesitation; **il n'y a pas à h., c'est le premier qu'il faut choisir** there are no two ways about it, you have to choose the first one

(b) (*en parlant*) to hesitate, to falter; **elle hésite trop dans ses réponses** she is too hesitant in her answers; **h. devant l'obstacle** (*d'un cheval*) to refuse a fence
Hespérides (les) [lezɛsperid] *nfpl Myth* **le Jardin des H.** the garden of the Hesperides
hétaïre [etair] *nf Antiq* hetaera
hétéro [etero] *F* **1** *adj* straight, hetero **2** *n* straight, hetero
hétéroclite [eterɔklit] *adj* (*collection*) heterogeneous, ill-assorted; (*bizarre*) unusual, strange, odd, eccentric; **mélange h.** odd assortment
hétérodoxe [eterɔdɔks] *adj* heterodox
hétérodoxie [eterɔdɔksi] *nf* heterodoxy
hétérodyne [eterɔdin] *adj, nf Rad* heterodyne (receiver)
hétérogène [eterɔʒɛn] *adj* (*différent*) heterogeneous; (*collection etc*) incongruous; (*assemblée*) mixed
hétérogénéité [eterɔʒeneite] *nf* heterogeneousness, heterogeneity
hétéroplastie [eterɔplasti] *nf Chir* heteroplasty
hétérosexualité [eterɔseksɥalite] *nf* heterosexuality
hétérosexuel, -elle [eterɔseksɥɛl] *adj, n* heterosexual
***hêtraie** [ɛtrɛ] *nf* beech grove *or* plantation
***hêtre** [ɛtr] *nm* (*bois, arbre*) beech; **h. rouge** *ou* **pourpre** copper beech
***heu** [ø] *int* (*pour exprimer le doute*) h'm!; (*en hésitant*) er…
heur [œr] *nm Iron, Litt* **je n'ai pas l'h. de la connaître** I have not the pleasure of her acquaintance; **je n'ai pas eu l'h. de lui plaire** I did not have the good fortune to win his favour
heure [œr] *nf* **(a)** (*soixante minutes*) hour; *Scol* **h. de cours** period; **elle a dix heures de cours par semaine** she has ten periods *or* ten hours of lessons a week; **une h. de cours, ça peut être trop long pour les enfants** one-hour lessons can be too long for children; **j'ai attendu une bonne h.** I waited a full *or* good *or* solid hour; **on met une bonne h./deux bonnes heures pour y aller** it takes a good hour/a good two hours to get there; **cent kilomètres à l'h.** a hundred kilometres an hour; **faire du cent kilomètres h.** to do 100 kilometres an hour; **être payé à l'h.** to be paid by the hour; **travailler à l'h.** to work by the hour; **toucher 30 francs l'h.** *ou* **de l'h.** to get 30 francs an hour; **semaine de 40 heures** 40-hour week

(b) [①**A75**,**A**; **B58**,**A**] (*de la journée*) **à toutes heures du jour** at all hours of the day; **à toute h.** at any time, at all hours of the day, round the clock; **ouvert à toute h.** open 24 hours (a day); **repas chauds à toute h.** hot meals 24 hours a day; **un médecin de garde peut être appelé à toute h. du jour ou de la nuit** a doctor is on call round the clock *or* at all times; **disponible/à votre service à toute h. du jour ou de la nuit** available/at your service round the clock; **tout à l'h.** (*dans le passé*) just now, a few minutes ago; (*dans le futur*) soon, presently, in a few minutes; **on repartira tout à l'h.** we'll be leaving again in a few minutes; **je l'ai vu tout à l'h.** I saw him just a few minutes ago; **à tout à l'h.!** (*dans un futur proche*) so long!, see you soon *or* later!; **de bonne h.** early, in good time; (*dans l'histoire*) at an early period; **il est de trop bonne h. pour rentrer** it's too early to go home; **d'h. en h.** hour by hour, hourly; **la situation s'aggrave d'h. en h.** the situation is getting worse by the hour *or Fml* deteriorating hourly; *Fig* **la situation peut s'inverser à toute h.** the situation can *or* could change at any time; **tout peut exploser à toute h.** everything could blow up at any moment *or* at any time; *Journ* **nouvelles de dernière h.** latest news, stop-press (news); **quelle h. est-il?** what time is it?, what's the time?; **quelle h. avez-vous?** what time do you make it?; **est-ce que vous avez l'h. exacte** *ou* **juste?** do you have the right time?; **demande-lui l'h.** ask him the time *or* ask him what time it is; **il est deux heures** it's two o'clock; **cinq heures moins dix** ten (minutes) to *or US* of five; **dix-huit heures** eighteen hundred (hours); **vingt heures quarante** eight forty pm; **le train de neuf heures** the nine o'clock train; **où serai-je demain à cette h.-ci?** where will I be this time tomorrow?; **que fais-tu debout à cette h.-ci?** what are you doing up at this time?; **à cette h.-ci je devrais déjà être parti** I should have left by now; **à une h. avancée (de la journée)** late in the day; **à une h. avancée (de la nuit)** late on (in the night); **à cinq heures juste(s)** *ou* **sonnant(es)** *ou* **tapant(es)** at five (o'clock) on the dot, at five o'clock sharp, (right *or* exactly) on the stroke of five; **mettre sa montre à l'h.** to set one's watch; **ma montre n'est pas à l'h.** my watch is wrong; **les trains partent à l'h.** the trains leave on the hour; (*sans retard*) the trains leave on time; *Rel* **livre d'heures** Book of Hours

(c) *Fig* **le parti communiste est à l'h. de la Russie** the Communist party is under Russian influence; **vivre à l'h. espagnole** to adopt a Spanish lifestyle, to go Spanish; **les Britanniques vont devoir se mettre à l'h. européenne** the British are going to have to come into line with the rest of Europe; **mettre l'administration à l'h. de l'informatique** to bring (the) administration into the computer age

(d) (*moment précis*) **l'h. du dîner/déjeuner** dinner/lunch time; **c'est l'h. du goûter/de la toilette** it's time for a snack/time to get washed and ready; **c'est l'h. des mamans** (*à la maternelle*) it's home time; **l'h. d'aller se coucher** bedtime; **son h. est venue** his time has come; **il va arriver, c'est son h.** he'll be here soon, it's his usual time; **à l'h. dite** at the appointed *or* agreed time; **être à l'h.** to be punctual *or* on time; **arriver à l'h. exacte** to arrive dead on time; **arriver/avoir fini avant l'h.** to arrive/have finished ahead of time; **il est** *ou* **c'est l'h.** it's time; **c'est l'h. de partir** it's time to go; *Journ* **h. d'imprimer** press time; **h. d'arrivée** arrival time; **h. d'arrivée prévue** estimated time of arrival, ETA; **h. de départ** (*d'un hôtel*) check-out time, departure time; **h. de départ prévue** estimated time of departure, ETD; **h. du vol** flight time; **cette mode a eu son h.** this fashion has had its day; **j'attends mon h.** I'm biding my time; **un partisan de la première h.** a supporter from the word 'go'; **un partisan de la dernière h.** a late convert to the cause, *F* a Johnny-come-lately

(e) (*moment présent*) **pour l'h.** for the present, for the time being; **l'h. est grave** these are difficult times; **la question de l'h.** the question of the moment, the current question; **à l'h. qu'il est** by this time, by now; (*maintenant*) nowadays, now; **nous n'en savons pas plus à l'h. qu'il est** that's all we know for the time being, we don't know anything more at the moment; **faire qch sur l'h.** to do sth at once *or* right away

(f) *Fig* **à ses heures, il était charmant** he could be charming when he liked *or* when he felt like it *or* when he was in the mood

(g) **à la bonne h.!** well done!, good (for you)!

▶ **heure**: **heures d'affluence** rush hour, peak period; **h. astronomique** sidereal time; *Can* **h. avancée** *Br* Summer Time, *Am* daylight(-saving) time; **heures de bureau** office hours; **heures creuses** off-peak hours, slack period; *Journ* **h. de l'édition** edition time; **h. d'été** *Br* Summer Time, *Am* daylight(-saving) time; *TV etc* **h. de grande écoute** prime time, peak viewing time; **h. de gloire: il a eu son h. de gloire** he has had his hour *or* his moment of glory; **l'h. de Greenwich** Greenwich mean time; **h. légale** official *or* standard time; **h. limite** deadline; **h. limite d'enregistrement** check-in time; **h. machine** machine-hour; **heures d'ouverture** opening hours; **heures de pointe** rush hour, peak period; **heures supplémentaires** overtime; **faire**

des heures supplémentaires to do overtime; **les heures supplémentaires ne sont pas payées** overtime is unpaid

heureusement [œrøzmɑ̃] *adv* **(a)** (*par bonheur*) luckily, fortunately, *Fml* happily; **h. que j'étais là** it's a good thing I was there, fortunately I was there **(b)** (*avec succès*) successfully; **commencer h.** to begin auspiciously, to get off to a good start; **h. exprimé** well expressed; **vivre h.** to live happily; **il a décrit très h. leur vie ensemble** he gave a good description of their life together

heureux, -euse [œrø, -øz] **1** *adj* **(a)** happy; **qu'est-ce que tu as, tu n'es pas h.?** what's wrong, are you unhappy?; **être h. en ménage** to be happily married; **ils furent h. et eurent beaucoup d'enfants** ≈ they lived happily ever after; **h. comme un poisson dans l'eau** as happy as a sandboy; **vivre h.** to live happily; **je suis très h. de ce cadeau** I'm very happy *or* pleased with this gift; **je suis très h. de vous faire savoir que …** I'm very happy *or* pleased to inform you that …; **nous sommes très h. de vous annoncer le mariage de …** we are very happy *or* pleased to announce the marriage of …; **nous serions h. que vous acceptiez** we would be glad if you accepted; **je serais très heureuse si …** I would be very happy *or* pleased if …; **époque heureuse** happy times; **heureuse année!** Happy New Year!; **heureuse jeunesse!** the joys of youth!

(b) (*favorable*) successful; (*formulation etc*) apt, *Litt* happy, felicitous; **avoir une heureuse façon de s'exprimer** to express oneself well; **la formulation n'est pas toujours très heureuse dans ce texte** this text is not always very well worded; **h. mariage** joyful wedding (ceremony); **mariage h.** happy marriage; **un h. mariage de couleurs** a successful blend of colours; **l'issue heureuse des négociations** the successful outcome of the negotiations; **une solution heureuse** a happy solution; **un choix h.** a good choice; *Fig* **début h.** auspicious beginning; **le résultat n'est pas très h.** it wasn't very successful, it didn't work out

(c) (*favorisé*) fortunate, favoured, *US* favored; **h. au jeu/en amour** lucky at cards/in love; **il peut s'estimer h.** he can think *or* consider himself lucky; **estime-toi h. d'avoir été sélectionné** think *or* consider yourself lucky to have been chosen; *Bible* **h. sont les pauvres en esprit** blessed are the poor in spirit

(d) (*chanceux*) lucky, fortunate; **c'est fort h. pour vous** that's very lucky for you; **c'est h. que vous soyez libre** it's a good thing *or* a good job that you're free; *F* **encore h. qu'il ait gardé le ticket de caisse!** it's just as well that he held on to the receipt!; *F* **elle m'avait prévenu, encore h.!** it's a good thing she warned me!; **par un h. hasard** by a happy coincidence

2 *n* **vous avez fait un h.** you have made one man very happy; **si tu le lui donnes, tu vas faire un h.** if you give it to him, you will make him a happy man

▶ **heureux**: **h. événement** happy event

heuristique [œristik] **1** *adj* heuristic **2** *nf* heuristics

***heurt** [œr] *nm* (*des intérêts, des couleurs etc*) clash; (*des véhicules*) collision; **leur collaboration ne va pas sans heurts** their collaboration has its ups and downs *or* its rough patches; **tout s'est fait sans h.** everything went smoothly *or* without a hitch

***heurté** [œrte] *adj* (*style*) abrupt, halting; (*ton*) abrupt; *Beaux-Arts* (*couleurs*) contrasting; **exécution** *ou* **jeu heurté(e) au piano** jerky style of playing the piano

***heurter** [œrte] **1** *vt* **(a)** (*personne, chose*) to knock (against), to run into, to bump into; (*personne*) to collide with; *Naut* (*rocher*) to hit, to strike; **h. qch de la tête** to knock *or* bump one's head against sth

(b) (*sentiments etc*) to shock, to offend; **ces théories vont h. de front un bon nombre d'idées reçues** these theories will clash head-on with a good number of received ideas; **h. toutes les idées reçues** to go against *or* run counter to convention

2 *vi* **h. à la porte** to knock at *or* on the door; **sa tête a heurté contre le pare-brise** he hit his head against the windscreen, his head struck the windscreen

3 se heurter *vpr* **(a)** (*se cogner*) to collide (with each other); **se h. à** *ou* **contre qn/qch** to run (slap) into *or* collide with *or* bang into *or* bump into sb/sth; **les deux voitures se sont heurtées à 120 km/h** the two cars crashed into each other at 120 kph; **je me suis heurtée contre un mur** I crashed into a wall; **se h. la tête à** *ou* **contre qch** to knock *or* bump one's head against sth; *Fig* **se h. à l'indifférence générale** to come up against general apathy *or* indifference; **se h. à une difficulté** to come up against a difficulty; **se h. aux idées reçues** to come into conflict with *or* to clash with received opinion

(b) (*de couleur, intérêt etc*) to clash; **des couleurs/goûts qui se heurtent** clashing colours/tastes, colours/tastes which clash; *Fig* **au cours de la réunion, ils se sont heurtés violemment** during the meeting they clashed violently; **il est très fréquent qu'ils se heurtent** they're always clashing (with each other) *or* crossing swords

***heurtoir** [œrtwar] *nm* (*de porte*) (door) knocker; (*amortisseur*) catch, stop; *Rail* buffer

hévéa [evea] *nm Bot* hevea

hexacorde [ɛgzakɔrd] *nm Mus* hexachord

hexadécimal, -ale, -aux, -ales [ɛgzadesimal, -o] *adj Ordinat* hex, hexadecimal

hexaèdre [ɛgzaɛdr] **1** *adj* hexahedral **2** *nm* hexahedron

hexagonal, -ale, -aux, -ales [ɛgzagɔnal, -o] *adj* hexagonal; *Fig* French

hexagone [ɛgzagɔn] *nm* hexagon; **l'H.** France

hexamètre [ɛgzamɛtr] **1** *adj* hexametric(al) **2** *nm* hexameter

HF *Rad etc* (*abrév* **haute fréquence**); HF

hi [i] *int* (*en riant*) ha ha; (*en pleurant*) boo-hoo

hiatal, -ale, -aux, -ales [jatal, -o] *adj Méd* hiatal; **hernie hiatale** hiatus hernia

***hiatus** [jatys] *nm* (*dans une narration etc*) gap, break, hiatus; *Ling, Anat* hiatus; *Fig* **le h. entre la production et les besoins** the gap *or* discrepancy between production and needs

hibernal, -ale, -aux, -ales [ibɛrnal, -o] *adj* (*germination, sommeil etc*) winter, *Spéc* hibernal

hibernant [ibɛrnɑ̃] *adj* (*animal*) hibernating

hibernation [ibɛrnasjɔ̃] *nf* hibernation; *Fig* **être dans un état d'h. intellectuelle** to be in a state of intellectual hibernation; **la gauche sort de son h.** the left is coming in from the cold; **il est temps qu'il sorte de son h.** it's (about) time he started taking an interest in things again; **mettre un dossier en h.** to shelve a document; **h. artificielle** suspended animation, *Spéc* cryogenic suspension

hiberner [ibɛrne] *vi* to hibernate

hibiscus [ibiskys] *nm Bot* hibiscus

***hibou, -oux** [ibu] *nm* owl; **jeune h.** owlet; **des yeux de h.** eyes like saucers; *Péj* **quel vieux h.!** he is a real recluse!

***hic** [ik] *nm F* **voilà le h.!** that's the snag *or* the trouble!; **le h., c'est que …** the trouble *or* snag is that …

***hickory** [ikɔri] *nm Bot* hickory

hidalgo [idalgo] *nm F* Latin hunk

***hideur** [idœr] *nf* (*qualité*) hideousness

***hideusement** [idøzmɑ̃] *adv* hideously

***hideux, -euse** [idø, -øz] *adj* hideous; **h. à voir** hideous-looking; **un crime h.** a hideous *or* heinous crime; **des vices/pensées hideuses** evil vices/thoughts

hiémal, -ale, -aux, -ales [jemal] *adj Litt* winter

hier [jɛr] **1** *adv* yesterday; **h. matin, h. dans la matinée** yesterday morning; **h. (au) soir** yesterday evening, last night; **on s'en souvient comme si c'était h.** I/we/*etc* can remember it as if it were (only) yesterday; **le journal d'h.** yesterday's paper; *Fig* **cela ne date pas d'h.** that's nothing new; *F* **je ne suis pas né d'h.** I wasn't born yesterday **2** *nm* **tu avais tout h.** *ou* **toute la journée d'h. pour te décider** you had all (day) yesterday to make up your mind

***hiérarchie** [jerarʃi] *nf* hierarchy; **h. des valeurs sociales** scale of social values; **être en haut/bas de la h.** to be at the top/bottom of the hierarchy

***hiérarchique** [jerarʃik] *adj* hierarchical; **il est mon supérieur h.** he is senior (in rank) to me; **par (la) voie h.** through (the) official channels

***hiérarchiquement** [jerarʃikmɑ̃] *adv* hierarchically; **il lui est h. supérieur** he is superior (in rank) to him

hiérarchisation [jerarʃizasjɔ̃] *nf* **h. des fonctions** grading of jobs

hiérarchisé [jerarʃize] *adj* (*système*) hierarchical

***hiérarchiser** [jerarʃize] *vt* (*organiser*) to form into a hierarchy; (*régler*) (*état etc*) to structure *or* to classify according to a hierarchical system; **pour fonctionner, il est nécessaire qu'une société soit hiérarchisée** a society must have a hierarchy in order to function; **h. les emplois** to grade jobs

hiératique [jeratik] *adj* **(a)** (*sacré*) hieratic **(b)** (*geste*) solemn; **port de tête h.** regal carriage

***hiéroglyphe** [jerɔglif] *nm* hieroglyph(ic)

***hiéroglyphique** [jerɔglifik] *adj* hieroglyphic(al)

***hi-fi** [ifi] *adj, nf Rad etc F* hi-fi; **chaîne h.** hi-fi; **magasin de h.** hi-fi shop

***hi-han** [iɑ̃], *pl* **hi-hans** *int, nm* (d'âne) hee-haw

hi hi [ii, hihi] *int* (*rire nerveux*) hee-hee!; (*pleurs*) boo-hoo!

hilarant [ilarɑ̃] *adj* hilarious; *Ch* **gaz h.** laughing gas

hilare [ilar] *adj* (*visage*) beaming, grinning; **il était h.** he was beaming *or* grinning all over his face

hilarité [ilarite] *nf* hilarity, mirth; **provoquer l'h. générale** to cause general hilarity

***hile** [il] *nm Anat, Bot* hilum

himalayen, -enne [imalajɛ̃, -ɛn] *adj* Himalayan; **la chaîne himalayenne** the Himalayan (mountain) range; *Fig* **les sommets himalayens de la bêtise** the (absolute) height of stupidity

***hindi** [indi] *adj nm Ling* Hindi

hindouisme [ɛ̃duism] *nm* Hinduism

hindouiste [ɛ̃duist] *adj, n* Hindu

hindou, -oue [ɛ̃du] **1** *adj* Hindu **2** *n* **H.** Hindu

Hindoustan [ɛ̃dustɑ̃] *nm Géog* Hindustan

hindoustani [ɛ̃dustani] *nm Ling* Hindustani

hinterland [intɛrlɑ̃d] *nm* hinterland

***hippie** [ipi] *adj, n* hippie

hippique [ipik] *adj* relating to horses, equine; **concours h.** horse show

hippisme [ipism] *nm* horse riding; (*courses*) horse racing

hippocampe [ipɔkɑ̃p] *nm Myth* hippocampus; (*poisson*) sea horse

Hippocrate [ipɔkrat] *nm Antiq* Hippocrates; **le serment d'H.** the Hippocratic oath

hippocratique [ipɔkratik] *adj* Hippocratic

hippodrome [ipɔdrom] *nm* racecourse; *Antiq* hippodrome, circus

hippomobile [ipɔmɔbil] *adj* horse-drawn

hippophagique [ipɔfaʒik] *adj* **boucherie h.** horsemeat butcher

hippopotame [ipɔpɔtam] *nm* [①A13,8] hippopotamus, *F* hippo; **il avait une carrure d'h.** he was built like an ox

hippopotamesque [ipɔpɔtamɛsk] *adj F Hum* hippopotamus-like, of a hippopotamus; **une lourdeur/grâce h.** the weight/grace of a hippo

hippotechnie [ipɔtɛkni] *nf* (technique of) horse breeding and training

***hippy** [ipi] *adj, n* hippie

hirondelle [irɔ̃dɛl] *nf* **(a)** (*oiseau*) swallow; *Prov* **une h. ne fait pas le printemps** one swallow doesn't make a summer; *Culin* **nid d'h.** bird's nest **(b)** *F Vieilli* (*agent de police*) cycle cop

▶ **hirondelle**: **h. de cheminée** swallow tern; **h. de fenêtre** house martin; **h. de mer** tern; **h. de rivage** sand martin

***hirsute** [irsyt] *adj* (*personne*) hairy, *Spéc* hirsute; (*barbe, ours*) shaggy

hispanique [ispanik] *adj* Hispanic, Spanish

hispanisant, -ante [ispanizɑ̃, -ɑ̃t] *n* student of/expert on Spanish

hispanisme [ispanism] *nm Ling* Hispanicism

hispano-américain, -aine [ispanɔamerikɛ̃, -ɛn], *pl* **hispano-américain(e)s 1** *adj* Hispano-American, Spanish-American **2** *n* **H.** Hispano-American, *F* Hispanic

hispano-arabe [ispanɔarab], **hispano-moresque** [ispanɔmɔrɛsk], *pl* **hispano-arabes, -moresques** *adj* Hispano-Moorish, Hispano-Moresque

hispanophone [ispanɔfɔn] **1** *adj* Spanish-speaking **2** *n* **les hispanophones** Spanish-speaking people

hispide [ispid] *adj Bot* hairy, *Spéc* hispid

***hisser** [ise] **1** *vt* to hoist (up), to pull up; *Naut* (*embarcation*) to hoist in; **hissez!** hoist away!; *Naut* up sails!; **oh! hisse!** (yo-)heave-ho!; **h. une échelle par-dessus un mur** to haul a ladder over a wall; **h. qn vers soi** to lift sb up (towards one); **h. qn sur ses épaules** to hoist *or* lift sb onto one's shoulders **2 se hisser** *vpr* **se h. jusqu'à la fenêtre** to pull *or* hoist oneself up to the window; **se h. sur la pointe des pieds** to stand on tiptoe; *Fig* **se h. jusqu'au pouvoir/gouvernement** to rise to a position of power/a position in government

histogramme [istɔgram] *nm* bar chart, histogram

histoire [istwar] *nf* **(a)** history; **l'h. seule jugera** history *or* posterity alone will be the judge; **h. du moyen âge/naturelle** medi(a)eval/natural history; **étudiant en h. de l'art** history of art student *or* art history student; **l'h. des sciences** the history of science; **la petite h.** sidelights on history, footnotes of history; **sachez, pour la petite h., qu'elle fut la maîtresse du roi** let me tell you, by the way *or* for the record, that she was the king's mistress; **l'h. de (la) France** the history of France, French history; *Fig* **tout cela, c'est de l'h. ancienne** that's all ancient history *or* dead and buried; **livre d'h.** history book

(b) (*livre*) history book; **une h. d'Allemagne** a history of Germany

(c) (*récit*) story, tale; *F* (*mensonge*) fib, story; **histoires pour enfants** children's stories; **auteur d'histoires pour enfants** children's author, author of children's stories; **j'ai l'impression que tu es en train de me raconter une h.** I have a feeling that you're pulling my leg *or* telling me a tall story; **je t'assure, je ne te raconte pas d'histoires!** I assure you, I'm not making it up!; **h. de marin** sailor's yarn; **livre d'histoires** story book; **c'est toujours la même h.** it's (always) the same old story; **c'est une autre h.** it's quite a different matter *or* story; **tout ça, ce sont des histoires** that's all nonsense *or* rubbish; **tu crois encore ses histoires?** do you still believe his nonsense?; **le plus beau de l'h., c'est que ...** the best part of the story is that ...; **se fourrer dans une sale/drôle (d')h.** to get mixed up in a nasty/funny business; **il m'est arrivé une drôle d'h./une sale h.** a funny thing/a nasty thing happened to me; **figure-toi qu'il m'est arrivé une h. incroyable!** believe it or not, something incredible has happened to me!; *F* **il est sorti, h. de prendre un peu l'air** he went out just to get a breath of fresh air; **h. de rire un peu** just for a laugh, just for fun; **ce que j'en dis, c'est h. de parler** you can take or leave what I've said; **elle l'a dit, h. de dire qch** she said it just for the sake of saying something; **c'est toute une h.** (*à raconter*) it's a long story; (*pour faire qch*) it's no end of a job, it's quite a business; **en voilà une h. pour pas grand-chose** what a fuss about nothing; *F* **en voilà une h.!** what a fuss!, what a song and dance!; (*c'est incroyable*) that's quite a story; **quelle h.!** that's quite a story!; *F* **faire des histoires** *ou* **un tas d'histoires** to make a fuss *or* a to-do; **tu fais bien des histoires!** you're making *or* kicking up such a fuss!; **s'attirer des histoires** to get oneself into trouble; **faire des histoires à qn** to make trouble for sb; **il faut éviter d'avoir des histoires** you/we/*etc* must keep out of trouble; *F* **pas d'histoires!** no fuss!; **au lit, et pas d'histoires** off to bed now, and I don't want any fuss

▶ **histoire**: **h. de fous** shaggy dog story; **c'est une h. de fous!** it's crazy!; **l'H. sainte** Biblical history

histologie [istɔlɔʒi] *nf* histology

histologique [istɔlɔʒik] *adj* histological

historicité [istɔrisite] *nf* historicity

historié [istɔrje] *adj* that tells a story; (*initiales, bible*) illuminated

historien, -ienne [istɔrjɛ̃, -jɛn] *n* historian; **h. de l'histoire de l'art** art historian

historiette [istɔrjɛt] *nf* anecdote, short story; **c'est une jolie petite h.** it's a nice little story

historiographe [istɔrjɔgraf] *nm* historiographer

historiographie [istɔrjɔgrafi] *nf* historiography

historique [istɔrik] **1** *adj* (*qui concerne l'histoire*) historical; (*important, décisif*) historic; *Gram* **présent h.** historic present; **être classé monument h.** (*d'un monument*) to be listed *or* classified as an ancient monument *or* as a place of historic interest; **liste des monuments historiques français** list of ancient French monuments; **c'est un événement h. dans la famille** it's a historic event *or* a red-letter day for the family

2 *nm* historical record *or* account; *Ordinat* (*de document*) log; **faire l'h. des événements** to give a chronological account of events; **faire l'h. d'une assocation/d'un gouvernement/d'un mot** to trace the history of an association/a government/a word; **h. d'entretien** (*d'une voiture etc*) service history

historiquement [istɔrikmɑ̃] *adv* historically

histrion [istrijɔ̃] *nm Th Arch* play actor; *Litt Péj* second-rate actor

hi-tech [aitɛk] *adj* hi-tech

hitlérien, -ienne [itlerjɛ̃, -jɛn] **1** *adj* Hitlerite; **le gouvernement h.** the Hitler government **2** *n* Hitlerite

hitlérisme [itlerism] *nm* Hitlerism

***hit-parade** [itparad] *nm* charts, hit parade; **chanteur nº 1 au h.** chart-topping singer; **chanson nº 1 au h.** chart-topper, number 1 in the charts *or* hit parade; **être au h. de l'élégance** to be the height of elegance; **être au h. de l'actualité** to be a big news item, to be headline news

***hittite** [itit] *Antiq* **1** *adj* Hittite **2** *n* **H.** Hittite

HIV [aʃive] *nm* HIV

hiver [ivɛr] *nm* [①A6,d,v] winter; **l'h. sera doux/rude** it will be a mild/severe winter; **en h.** in winter; **temps d'h.** wintry weather; **depuis une semaine, il fait un temps d'h.** it's been like winter this last week; **vêtements/sports d'h.** winter clothes/sports; **jardin d'h.** winter garden; *F* **le bonhomme H.** Jack Frost

▶ **hiver**: *Fig* **h. nucléaire** nuclear winter

hivernage [ivɛrnaʒ] *nm* **(a)** (*du bétail, de navires, d'une expédition polaire etc*) wintering **(b)** (*endroit*) winter quarters; *Naut* winter harbour **(c)** (*fourrage*) winter fodder

hivernal, -ale, -aux, -ales [ivɛrnal, -o] *adj* (*froid etc*) winter; (*temps*) wintry; **station hivernale** winter sports resort, ski resort

hivernant, -ante [ivɛrnɑ̃, -ɑ̃t] *n* (*dans un lieu de vacances etc*) winter visitor *or* tourist

hiverner [ivɛrne] **1** *vi* to winter; (*d'un navire*) to lie up (for the winter) **2** *vt* (*bétail*) to winter

HLM [aʃɛlɛm] *n* (*abrév* **habitation à loyer modéré**) *Br* ≈ council flat, house, *US* public housing unit; **vivre dans une** *ou F* **un HLM** to live in a council flat
***ho** [o] *int* (*appel*) hey!; (*surprise*) oh!
***hobby** [ɔbi] *nm* hobby
***hobereau, -eaux** [ɔbro] *nm* **(a)** *souvent Péj* (*gentilhomme*) (country) squire **(b)** *Orn* hobby
***hochement** [ɔʃmɑ̃] *nm* **h. de tête** (*négatif*) shake of the head; (*affirmatif*) nod (of the head)
***hochepot** [ɔʃpo] *nm Culin* meat and vegetable stew
hochequeue [ɔʃkø] *nm Zool* wagtail
***hocher** [ɔʃe] *vt* **h. la tête** (*de dédain*) to toss one's head; (*pour dire non*) to shake one's head; (*pour dire oui*) to nod (one's head); (*d'un cheval*) to toss its head
***hochet** [ɔʃɛ] *nm* (*d'enfant*) (child's) rattle; *Fig* bauble, toy
***hockey** [ɔkɛ] *nm Sp* (*jeu*) (field) hockey; *Can* (*sur glace*) ice hockey; *Can* (*crosse*) (ice) hockey stick; **h. sur gazon** (field) hockey; **h. sur glace** ice hockey, *Am* hockey; **partie de h.** hockey game *or* match; **jouer au h.** to play hockey
***hockeyeur, -euse** [ɔkejœr, -øz] *n* hockey player
hoirie [wari] *nf Jur* **avance** *ou* **avancement d'h.** advancement
***holà** [ɔla] **1** *int* (*pour appeler*) stop!, hold on!; **h., on se calme, hein!** hey, quieten down, OK?; **h., je ne suis pas tout à fait d'accord avec vous, moi!** now hold on, I don't quite agree with you there! **2** *nm* **mettre le h. à qch** to put a stop to sth
***holding** [ɔldiŋ] *n Fin* holding company
***hold-up** [ɔldœp] *nm inv F* hold-up, *surtout Am* stick-up; **faire un h.** to carry out a hold-up
***hollandais, -aise** [ɔlɑ̃dɛ, -ɛz] **1** *adj* Dutch **2** *nm Ling* Dutch **3** *n* **H.** Dutchman, *f* Dutchwoman; **les H.** the Dutch
***Hollande** [ɔlɑ̃d] *nf* Holland
***hollande** [ɔlɑ̃d] **1** *nm* (*fromage*) Dutch cheese **2** *nf Tex* holland
***hollywoodien, -ienne** [ɔliwudjɛ̃, -jɛn] *adj* (*acteur*) Hollywood; (*maison, cadre*) Hollywood-style
holmium [ɔlmjɔm] *nm Ch* holmium
holocauste [ɔlɔkost] *nm* **(a)** (*sacrifice*) sacrifice; (*avec immolation*) burnt offering; **l'H.** (*des Juifs*) the Holocaust **(b)** (*victime*) sacrifice
hologramme [ɔlɔgram] *nm* hologram
holographe [ɔlɔgraf] *nf* holograph
holographie [ɔlɔgrafi] *nf* holography
holothurie [ɔlɔtyri] *nf Zool* sea cucumber, *Spéc* holothurian
***homard** [ɔmar] *nm* lobster; **manger du h.** to eat lobster; **pinces de h.** lobster claws; **bisque de h.** lobster soup *or* bisque; *F* **rouge comme un h.** (*de honte, de gêne*) as red as a beetroot; (*après un coup de soleil*) as red as a lobster
***hombre** [ɔ̃br] *nm Cartes Arch* (game of) ombre
***home** [om] *nm* home; **h. d'enfants** residential leisure centre for children, summer camp
homélie [ɔmeli] *nf* homily
homéopathe [ɔmeɔpat] *Méd* **1** *adj* homeopathic **2** *n* homeopath
homéopathie [ɔmeɔpati] *nf* homeopathy; **se soigner à l'h.** to take homeopathic medicine, to have homeopathic treatment
homéopathique [ɔmeɔpatik] *adj* homeopathic
Homère [ɔmɛr] *nm* Homer
homérique [ɔmerik] *adj* Homeric
homicide [ɔmisid] **1** *adj Arch, Litt* homicidal; (*arme*) murderous **2** *n Litt* (*personne*) homicide, murderer, *f* murderess **3** *nm Jur* (*crime*) homicide; **commettre un h.** to commit homicide
▶ **homicide**: **h. involontaire** *ou* **par imprudence** manslaughter (*through negligence*); **h. sans préméditation** culpable homicide; **h. volontaire** wilful homicide, murder
hominidés [ɔminide] *nmpl* hominids
hommage [ɔmaʒ] *nm* **(a)** homage; **rendre h. à qn** to pay homage *or* (a) tribute to sb; **nous rendons h. à votre courage** we are paying tribute to your courage **(b)** **hommages** respects, compliments; **présenter ses hommages à une dame** to pay one's respects to a lady; **transmettez-lui mes hommages** give him my respects *or* regards **(c)** (*de respect, d'estime*) tribute, token; **faire h. de qch à qn** to offer sth to sb as a token of (one's) esteem; **h. de l'éditeur** complimentary copy, presentation copy; **h. de l'auteur** with the author's compliments
hommasse [ɔmas] *adj Péj* (*femme*) masculine, mannish; **elle a des manières hommasses** she acts like a man
homme [ɔm] *nm* **(a)** [①A14,12,c] man, *pl* men; **l'h. et la femme** man and woman; **jeune h.** young man; **je ne suis plus un jeune h.** I'm not as young as I was; **merci jeune h.** thank you, young man; **h. âgé** old man, elderly man; *Com* **rayon hommes** men's department, menswear; **parler à qn d'h. à h.** to talk to sb man to man, to have a man-to-man talk with sb; **un bel h.** a handsome man; **soyez un h.!** be a man!; *F* **mon h.** my man/husband

(b) (*individu*) (*pl* **hommes** *ou* **gens**) man, *pl* men; **j'ai trouvé ton h., je pense qu'il fera tout à fait l'affaire** I've found just the man for you, I think he'll do nicely; **trouver son h.** to meet one's match; **il n'est pas h. à laisser passer cela** he's not one to *or* the kind of man to let that happen; *Mil* **les officiers et les hommes** the officers and (the) men; **les hommes du président/du directeur** the President's/director's men; **les hommes (d'équipage)** the crew, the ship's company; **un h. de goût** a man of taste; **un h. de droite** a right winger; **l'abominable h. des neiges** the abominable snowman

(c) (*genre humain*) man, mankind; **tous les hommes** all men, all mankind; **de mémoire d'h.** within living memory; **les droits de l'h.** human rights; **comme un seul h.** as one man, in unison; *Prov* **l'h. propose, Dieu dispose** man proposes, God disposes
▶ **homme**: **h. d'affaires** businessman; *Naut* **h. de barre** helmsman; **h. de confiance** right-hand man; **h. d'église** man of the church; **h. d'entretien** maintenance man; **h. d'État** statesman; **h. à femmes** ladies' man; **h.-grenouille**, *pl* **hommes-grenouilles** frogman; **h. de journée** (day) labourer; **h. de lettres** man of letters; **h. de loi** man of law, lawyer; **h. de main** henchman; **h. de métier** professional; **h. du monde** man of the world; **h.-orchestre**, *pl* **hommes-orchestres** one-man band; **h. de paille** figurehead; **h. de parole** man of his word; **h. de peine** (day) labourer; *Litt* **h. de peu** worthless individual; *Naut* **h. de quart** watch; **l'h. de la rue** the man in the street; **h.-sandwich**, *pl* **hommes-sandwich(e)s** sandwich man; **h. à tout faire** odd-job man, handyman; **h. de troupe** ordinary soldier, private
homo [ɔmo] *adj, n* gay
homocentrique [ɔmɔsɑ̃trik] *adj Math* homocentric
homogène [ɔmɔʒɛn] *adj* homogeneous
homogénéisation [ɔmɔʒeneizasjɔ̃] *nf* homogenization
homogénéiser [ɔmɔʒeneize] *vt* to homogenize; **lait homogénéisé** homogenized milk
homogénéité [ɔmɔʒeneite] *nf* homogeneousness, homogeneity
homographe [ɔmɔgraf] **1** *nm* homograph **2** *adj* homographic
homologation [ɔmɔlɔgasjɔ̃] *nf Jur* (*d'un accord etc*) confirmation; (*d'un testament*) probate; *Sp* (*d'un record etc*) ratification
homologie [ɔmɔlɔʒi] *nf* homology
homologue [ɔmɔlɔg] **1** *adj Biol etc* homologous **2** *nm Biol etc* homologue **3** *n* counterpart, opposite number
homologuer [ɔmɔlɔge] *vt Jur* (*accord etc*) to confirm, to endorse; *Jur* (*testament*) to prove; (*décision*) to ratify; (*comptes*) to approve; *Sp* (*record*) to ratify; *Admin* **prix homologués** authorized charges; *Sp* **record homologué** official record
homoncule [ɔmɔ̃kyl] *nm* = **homuncule**
homonyme [ɔmɔnim] **1** *adj Ling* homonymous **2** *nm* (*mot*) homonym; (*personne*) namesake
homonymie [ɔmɔnimi] *nf Ling* homonymy
homophone [ɔmɔfɔn] **1** *adj Ling, Mus* homophonic, homophonous **2** *nm Ling* homophone
homophonie [ɔmɔfɔni] *nf* homophony
homosexualité [ɔmɔsɛksɥalite] *nf* homosexuality
homosexuel, -elle [ɔmɔsɛksɥɛl] *adj, n* homosexual
homuncule [ɔmɔ̃kyl] *nm Arch* homunculus; *Fig Péj* manikin, dwarf
***hondurien, -ienne** [ɔ̃dyrjɛ̃, -jɛn] **1** *adj* Honduran **2** *n* **H.** Honduran
***hongre** [ɔ̃gr] **1** *adj* (*cheval*) gelded, castrated **2** *nm* gelding
***hongrer** [ɔ̃gre] *vt Vét* to geld, to castrate
***Hongrie** [ɔ̃gri] *nf* Hungary
***hongrois, -oise** [ɔ̃grwa, -waz] **1** *adj* Hungarian **2** *nm Ling* Hungarian **3** *n* **H.** Hungarian
honnête [ɔnɛt] *adj* **(a)** (*intègre*) (*personne etc*) honest, honourable, *US* honorable; **ce n'est pas très h. de sa part** that isn't very honest of him; **homme h., h. homme** honest man, man of honour *or US* honor; **h. homme** (*au dix-huitième siècle etc*) man of culture, gentleman; **peu h.** dishonourable; **moyens honnêtes** fair *or* honest means; **être h. avec soi-même** to be honest with oneself

(b) (*décent*) (*comportement etc*) decent, seemly, becoming; **attitude peu h.** unseemly *or* unbecoming attitude; **je suis une femme h., moi, monsieur!** I'm not that sort of woman!

(c) (*acceptable*) (*prix etc*) reasonable, moderate, fair; **une note plus qu'h.** a more than reasonable mark; **un repas h. sans plus** a reasonable *or* an OK meal, but nothing more *or* nothing to write home about

(d) *Arch* courteous, polite, well-bred
honnêtement [ɔnɛtmɑ̃] *adv* **(a)** (*avec intégrité*) honestly, honourably, *US* honorably; **h., je pense que tu fais une erreur** honestly *or* to be honest, I think you're making a mistake; **conseiller qn h.** to give someone honest advice; **se comporter**

h. en affaires to be an honest businessman/businesswoman **(b)** (*raisonnablement*) reasonably, fairly **(c)** *Arch* (*avec courtoisie*) courteously, politely

honnêteté [ɔnɛtte] *nf* **(a)** (*intégrité*) honesty, integrity; **(b)** (*décence*) decency, propriety, decorum **(c)** (*dans les rapports*) fairness, fair dealing **(d)** *Arch* (*courtoisie*) courtesy, politeness

honneur [ɔnœr] *nm* **(a)** honour, *US* honor; **homme d'h.** man of honour, honourable *or US* honorable man; **mettre** *ou* **se faire un point d'h. à faire qch** to make it a point of honour to do sth; **déclarer/jurer sur l'h. que ...** to state/swear on one's honour that ...; **forfaire** *ou* **manquer à l'h.** to act dishonourably; **il faut sauver l'h.** honour must be saved; **l'h. est sauf** our/his/*etc* honour is safe; **non, je ne l'ai pas vu, parole d'h.** no, I haven't seen him, I give you my word (of honour) *or* cross my heart; **se faire un h. de qch/de faire qch** to be proud of sth/to do sth; **en tout bien tout h.** (*proposition, affaire*) (fair and) aboveboard; **nous nous sommes vus en tout bien tout h.** it was all aboveboard, there was nothing underhand about it; **affaire d'h.** matter of honour; (*duel*) duel; **garçon d'h.** best man; **demoiselle d'h.** bridesmaid

(b) (*hommage*) **réception en l'h. de qn** reception in honour *or US* honor of sb *or* in sb's honour; **assis à la place d'h.** in the seat of honour; **cour d'h.** main courtyard; *Univ* main quadrangle; **escalier d'h.** main staircase, main stairs; *Mil etc* **garde d'h.** guard of honour, *US* honor guard; **hôte d'h.** guest of honour; **président d'h.** honorary president; **faire h. à qn** to do honour to sb, to honour sb; **vous me faites un grand h.** you are doing me a great honour; **me ferez-vous l'h. de m'accompagner?** will you do me the honour of accompanying me?; **à qui ai-je l'h. (de parler)?** to whom have I the honour *or* the pleasure of speaking?; **j'ai l'h. de vous faire savoir que ...** I beg to inform you that ...; **j'ai l'h. de vous demander la main de votre fille** I have the honour of asking for the hand of your daughter; *F* **en quel h. vous voit-on ici?** to what do I/we/*etc* owe the honour (of your visit)?; *F* **et en quel h. me demandes-tu ma voiture?** just who do you think you are, asking me for my car?; *F* **et en quel h. devrais-je t'aider?** give me one good reason why I should help you!; **à vous l'h.** after you; **jouer pour l'h.** to play for love; **être à l'h.** to have the place of honour; **le cricket est à l'h. en Angleterre** cricket holds a place of honour *or* holds pride of place in England; **les lignes floues sont en h. cette année en France** loose-fitting clothes are all the fashion in France this year

(c) *Golf* **avoir l'h.** to have the honour *or US* honor

(d) (*gloire*) credit; **c'est à elle que revient tout l'h. de l'affaire** she must take all the credit for the matter; **être l'h. de son pays** to be an honour *or US* honor *or* a credit to one's country; **son attitude lui fait h.** his attitude is a credit to him *or* does him credit; **on doit dire à leur h. que ...** it must be said to their credit that ...; **il en est sorti à son h.** he came out of it with flying colours; **son refus est tout à son h.** it speaks well for him *or* it is greatly to his credit that he did not accept; **avec h.** creditably

(e) honneurs (*marques d'estime*) honours, *US* honors; **rendre les derniers honneurs** *ou* **les honneurs suprêmes à qn** to pay a last tribute *or* one's last respects to sb; **rendre de grands honneurs aux vainqueurs** to hail the returning victors; *Mil* **rendre les honneurs à qn** to present arms to sb, to give *or* pay (military) honours to sb; **avec tous les honneurs de la guerre** with all the honours of war; **rechercher les honneurs** to be looking for honours; **avoir les honneurs de la première page** to appear on the front page; **faire (à qn) les honneurs de la maison** to (do the honours and) show sb round the house; **rendre les honneurs funèbres à qn** to bury sb with due ceremony; **honneurs militaires** military honours

(f) faire h. à sa signature to honour *or US* honor one's signature; **faire h. à ses engagements** to honour one's commitments; *Com* **faire h. à une traite** to honour *or* meet a bill; *F* **faire h. au dîner** to do justice to the dinner

(g) *Cartes* **les honneurs** honours, *US* honors; **quatre d'honneurs** four by honours; **honneurs partagés** honours even

***honnir** [ɔnir] *vt* to disgrace, to dishonour, *US* to dishonor; **honni soit qui mal y pense** honni soit qui mal y pense, evil be to him who evil thinks; **honni de tous** spurned by all

honorabilité [ɔnɔrabilite] *nf* honourableness, *US* honorableness, worthiness; (*d'une famille, une profession etc*) respectability; **porter atteinte à l'h. de qn/qch** to bring dishonour on sb/sth; **l'h. de ses intentions ne fait aucun doute** his intentions are completely honourable; **c'est quelqu'un d'une très grande h.** he/she is a person of great integrity

honorable [ɔnɔrabl] *adj* **(a)** (*sentiments, personne*) honourable, *US* honorable; (*famille, profession etc*) honourable, respectable; **mes intentions sont honorables** my intentions are honourable; **vieillesse h.** respected old age; *Euph* **un h. correspondant** a secret agent, a special operative **(b)** (*performance*) creditable; **doctorat avec mention h.** = doctorate awarded with distinction; **des résultats plus qu'honorables** more than satisfactory results

honorablement [ɔnɔrabləmɑ̃] *adv* **(a)** honourably, *US* honorably, with honour, *US* with honor; **famille h. connue** family of good reputation; **gagner h. sa vie** to earn an honest living; **vivre h.** to lead a respectable life **(b) s'acquitter h. de qch** to acquit oneself creditably in sth; **il s'en est h. tiré** he did quite creditably

honoraire [ɔnɔrɛr] **1** *adj* (*fonction, membre etc*) honorary; **professeur h.** emeritus professor **2** *nmpl* **honoraires** fee(s); (*d'une profession libérale*) fee, *Spéc* honorarium; (*d'un avocat*) retainer; **honoraires d'agréé en douane** customs broker's fees; **honoraires fixes** fixed fees

honorariat [ɔnɔrarja] *nm* honorary membership

honoré, -ée [ɔnɔre] **1** *adj* honoured, *US* honored; **mon h. confrère** my respected colleague **2** *nf* **votre honorée du ...** (*dans une lettre*) yours of the ...

honorer [ɔnɔre] **1** *vt* **(a)** to honour, *US* to honor; (*qualités de qn etc*) to respect

(b) (*gratifier*) (*personne*) to do honour *or US* honor to; **h. qn de sa confiance** to honour sb with one's confidence; *aussi Iron* **h. une cérémonie de sa présence** to honour *or* grace a ceremony with one's presence

(c) *Com* (*facture*) to honour, *US* to honor, to meet; *Com, Jur* **refuser d'h. (un contrat)** to repudiate (a contract); **h. ses engagements** to honour one's commitments

(d) (*valoir de l'estime à*) (*personne, chose*) to be an honour *or US* honor to, to do credit to, to be a credit to; **c'est un sentiment qui vous honore** the sentiment does you credit

(e) (*sexuellement*) (*d'un animal*) to mate with; *Hum* (*d'un homme*) to make love to

2 s'honorer *vpr* **s'h. de qch/d'avoir fait qch** to be proud of sth/of having done sth; **notre ville s'honore de ses peintres** our town is proud of its painters *or* takes pride in its painters

honorifique [ɔnɔrifik] *adj* (*titre, rang etc*) honorary; **président à titre h.** honorary president

honoris causa [ɔnɔriskoza] *loc adj* honoris causa; **docteur h.** doctor honoris causa, honorary doctor

***honte** [ɔ̃t] *nf* **(a)** shame; **avoir perdu toute h.** *ou* **tout sentiment de h., avoir toute h. bue** to have lost all sense of shame, to have no (sense of) shame, to be lacking in any sense of shame; **faire qch toute h. bue** to do sth quite shamelessly; **h. à vous!** shame on you!; **à ma grande h.** to my shame; **sans h.** (*comme adjectif*) shameless; (*comme adverbe*) shamelessly; **avoir h.** to be ashamed (of oneself); **avoir h. de faire qch, avoir** *ou* **éprouver de la h. à faire qch** to be *or* feel ashamed to do sth *or* of doing something; **il ne faut pas avoir h. de le dire** you shouldn't be ashamed to say it; **avoir h. pour qn** to be ashamed of sb; **faire h. à qn** to make sb ashamed, to put sb to shame; **elle me faisait h., posant sans cesse ses questions ridicules** she made me so ashamed, continually asking her ridiculous questions; **couvrir qn de h., jeter la h. sur qn** to bring shame *or* disgrace (up)on sb; **fausse** *ou* **mauvaise h.** self-consciousness, bashfulness; **se cacher la visage de h.** to hide one's face in shame; **rougir de h.** to blush with shame

(b) (*cause*) (cause of) shame, disgrace, dishonour, *US* dishonor; **faire** *ou* **être la h. de qn** to be a disgrace to sb; **quelle h.!,** what a disgrace!; **c'est une h.** it's a disgrace; *F* **eh, t'as vu ses chaussures? la h.!** *ou* **oh là là, la h.!** have you seen his shoes? they're an absolute disgrace!

***honteusement** [ɔ̃tøzmɑ̃] *adv* shamefully, disgracefully; **il a fui h.** he fled in shame; **il a h. fui** to his shame, he fled

***honteux, -euse** [ɔ̃tø, øz] *adj* **(a)** ashamed; **être h. de qch/d'avoir fait qch** to be ashamed of sth/having done sth **(b)** (*après une erreur*) shamefaced, sheepish **(c)** *Péj* (*conduite etc*) shameful, disgraceful, ignominious; *Vieilli* **maladie honteuse** venereal disease; **c'est h.!** it's a disgrace!, it's shameful!; **si c'est pas h. de voir des choses pareilles!** isn't it terrible!

***hooligan** [uligan] *nm* hooligan

***hooliganisme** [uliganism] *nm* hooliganism

***hop** [ɔp] *int* **allez h.!** (*saute!*) jump!; (*pars!*) off you go!; **allez h., tout le monde dehors!** come on, everybody out!; **h.-là!** oops(-a-daisy)!

hôpital, -aux [ɔpital, -o] *nm* hospital; **il est très bien soigné à l'h.** he is being very well cared for in hospital; **être emmené à l'h.** to be taken to hospital *or Am* the hospital; **chambre d'h.** hospital room; *Naut* **navire-h.** hospital ship

▶ **hôpital**: **h. des armées** military hospital; **h. de campagne** field hospital; **h. militaire** military hospital; **h. psychiatrique** psychiatric hospital

***hoquet** [ɔkɛ] *nm* **(a)** *Physiol* hiccup, hiccough; **avoir le h.** to have (the) hiccups; **que faire contre le h.?** how can you get rid of hiccups? **(b)** (*de surprise, de terreur etc*) gasp; **avoir un h. de surprise** to catch one's breath, to gasp in surprise; **le moteur eut un dernier h. et rendit l'âme** the engine gave a final splutter and died

***hoqueter** [ɔk(ə)te] *vi* **(je hoquette, n. hoquetons; je hoquetterai)** to hiccup, to hiccough; **le moteur hoqueta puis se décida à partir** the engine spluttered into life

horaire [ɔrɛr] **1** *adj* **(a)** (*qui correspond à une heure*) hourly; **salaire h.** hourly rate *or* wage; *Ind* **débit h.** hourly output, output per hour

(b) fuseau h. time zone

2 *nm* timetable, schedule; (*à l'école, pour les moyens de transport*) timetable, *US* schedule; (*d'un magasin*) opening hours; **avoir un h. chargé** to have a busy schedule *or* full timetable; **être en retard sur l'h.** to be behind schedule; **h. flexible** flexible hours, flexitime; **h. variable** flexible hours, flexitime; **h. fixe/flottant** fixed/variable working hours; **h. mobile** *ou* **à la carte** flexitime, flexible working hours; **horaires d'été** summer timetable; **horaires de départ** departure schedule; (*de bateau*) sailing schedule

***horde** [ɔrd] *nf* horde

***horion** [ɔrjɔ̃] *nm* blow

horizon [ɔrizɔ̃] *nm* **(a)** horizon; (*des toits d'une ville etc*) skyline; **la ligne d'h.** the horizon; **à l'h.** on the horizon, on the skyline; **personne à l'h.? on peut y aller** nobody around *or* nobody in sight? let's go; **le soleil descend sur l'h.** the sun goes down beneath the horizon

(b) *Fig* horizon; **se profiler à l'h.** to loom up on the horizon; **l'h. se vide de toute espérance** the future is bleak; **à l'h. 2000** in the year 2000; **ouvrir des horizons nouveaux** to open up new horizons *or* vistas; **tour d'h.** overview, survey; **faire un tour d'h. de la situation du nucléaire en France** to give a general overview of nuclear power in France; **h. intellectuel** intellectual horizons *or* boundaries

▶ **horizon**: *Av* **h. artificiel** artificial horizon

horizontal, -ale, -aux, -ales [ɔrizɔ̃tal, -o] **1** *adj* horizontal; **c'est la position horizontale qui me convient le mieux** I'm most comfortable lying down **2** *nf* **horizontale (a)** horizontal; **le livre est posé à l'horizontale** the book is lying flat **(b)** (*droite*) horizontal line

horizontalement [ɔrizɔ̃talmɑ̃] *adv* horizontally; (*dans les mots croisés*) across

horizontalité [ɔrizɔ̃talite] *nf* horizontality

horloge [ɔrlɔʒ] *nf* clock; **il est deux heures à l'h.** it's two by the clock; **j'ai attendu une bonne heure d'h.** I waited a full *or* solid hour by the clock; **réglé comme une h.** as regular as clockwork

▶ **horloge**: **h. atomique** atomic clock; **h. biologique** biological clock; **h. contrôleuse** time clock; **h. normande** grandfather clock; **l'h. parlante** the speaking clock; **h. de parquet** grandfather clock; **l'h. physiologique** biological clock; **h. pointeuse** time clock; **h. à quartz** quartz clock; *Ordinat* **h. du système** system clock; *Ordinat* **h. en temps réel** real-time clock

horloger, -ère [ɔrlɔʒe, -ɛr] **1** *adj* **l'industrie horlogère** the clock and watchmaking industry **2** *n* clock and watchmaker; *Fig* **le grand h.** the Creator

horloger-bijoutier, *pl* **horlogers-bijoutiers** *nm* jeweller *or* *US* jeweler and watchmaker

horlogerie [ɔrlɔʒri] *nf* (*fabrication*) clock and watchmaking; (*magasin*) clockmaker's *or* watchmaker's (shop); **l'h.** (*ouvrages*) clocks and watches; **mouvement d'h.** clockwork

***hormis** [ɔrmi] *Litt* **1** *prép* (*no liaison*, **h. elle** [ɔrmiɛl]) except, but, save; **personne h. vous** no one but you, no one besides yourself **2** *conj* **h. que** except *or* save that

hormonal, -ale, -aux, -ales [ɔrmɔnal, -o] *adj Méd* hormonal; **insuffisance hormonale** hormone deficiency; **traitement/dosage h.** hormone treatment/test

hormone [ɔrmɔn] *nf* hormone; **veaux aux hormones** hormone-fed calves

hormonothérapie [ɔrmɔnoterapi] *nf Méd* hormone therapy

***hornblende** [ɔrnblɛ̃d] *nf Minér* hornblende

horodatage [ɔrodataʒ] *nm* time and date stamping

horodaté [ɔrɔdate] *adj* pay and display; **stationnement h.** pay and display parking; **ticket h.** pay and display sticker

horodateur [ɔrɔdatœr] *nm* time and date stamp; (*dans la rue*) pay and display machine

horoscope [ɔrɔskɔp] *nm* horoscope; **faire l'h. de qn** to cast sb's horoscope; **consulter son h.** to read *or* consult one's horoscope

horreur [ɔrœr] *nf* **(a)** (*effroi*) horror; **à ma grande h.** to my unspeakable horror; **frappé** *ou* **glacé** *ou* **saisi d'h.** horror-stricken, horror-struck; **paralysé d'h.** paralysed *or* helpless with horror; **une indicible h. me gagnait** I was overcome by an indescribable sense of horror

(b) (*répugnance*) horror, repugnance, disgust, abhorrence; **faire h. à qn** to horrify sb, to fill sb with horror; **tous ces gens me font une sainte h.** all these people make me sick, I can't stand all these people; **avoir qn/qch en h., avoir h. de qn/qch** to have a horror of sb/sth, to hate *or* detest *or* loathe sb/sth; **j'ai h. que l'on me dérange pendant le repas** I hate being disturbed during meals; **considérer qch dans toute son h.** to see sth in all its horror *or* in its full horror

(c) (*chose horrible*) horrible thing; **sa voiture/montre est une h.** his car/watch is hideous *or* dreadful; **tu la trouves belle?, c'est une h.!** you think she's beautiful? she's hideous!; **quelle h.!** that's horrible!, how horrible!; *F* **le lycée, c'est l'h.!** school is the pits!

(d) les horreurs de la guerre the horrors of war; **commettre des horreurs** to commit atrocities; **dire des horreurs de qn** to say horrid *or* horrible *or* dreadful things about sb

horrible [ɔribl] *adj* (*effrayant*) horrible, dreadful, horrid, ghastly; (*répugnant*) gruesome; **spectacle h.** ghastly *or* hideous *or* gruesome sight; **une soif h.** a terrible thirst; **il est h. sans sa moustache** he looks awful *or* horrible without his moustache; **elle a été h. avec lui** she was horrible to him

horriblement [ɔribləmɑ̃] *adv* awfully, dreadfully, horribly; **h. mal habillé** appallingly dressed; **il nous a h. déçus** he let us down very badly; **il a été h. déçu** he was dreadfully disappointed

horrifiant [ɔrifjɑ̃] *adj* horrifying, shocking, appalling

horrifier [ɔrifje] *vt* to horrify; **être horrifié de qch** to be horrified at sth

horrifique [ɔrifik] *adj F Hum* horrific

horripilant [ɔripilɑ̃] *adj* exasperating, maddening

horripilation [ɔripilasjɔ̃] *nf* exasperation

horripiler [ɔripile] *vt* to exasperate; **qu'est-ce qu'il m'horripile avec ses histoires** he really gets on my nerves with his stories

***hors** [ɔr] *prép* (*liaison with* **r**, **h. elle** [ɔrɛl]) **(a) h. de** out of; **h. d'usage** out of action *or* service *or* use; **h. de l'eau** out of the water; **tomber h. du lit** to fall out of bed; **h. de la ville** out of town, outside the town; **dîner h. de chez soi** to dine out; **h. d'ici!** get out (of here)!; **h. d'haleine** out of breath; **h. de combat** (*arme, navire, homme*) out of action; *Fig* **ça l'a mis h. de combat** that put him out of the contest *or* game *or* running; **être h. d'affaire** to be out of the woods; (*d'un malade*) to be out of danger, to be out of the woods; **te voilà h. d'affaire!** that's you over the worst; **h. de portée** out of *or* beyond reach; **à garder h. de portée des enfants** keep out of the reach of children; **h. d'atteinte** out of *or* beyond reach; **h. de danger** out of danger, out of harm's reach; **h. de question** out of the question; **h. de là** apart from that, otherwise; **être h. de soi** (*de colère etc*) to be beside oneself; **ça l'a mis h. d'elle-même** that infuriated her; **c'est h. de prix** the price is prohibitive, it's too expensive; **des produits h. de prix** prohibitively expensive goods; *Archit* **h. d'œuvre** out of alignment, projecting

(b) *Fb* **h. jeu** (*joueur*) offside; **le joueur était h. jeu** the player was offside *or* in an offside position; **skier h. piste** to ski off piste; **longueur h. tout** overall length; **h. taxe** net of tax; (*exempt de taxe*) tax free; **boutique h. taxe** duty-free shop; **mettre qn/qch h. la loi** to outlaw sb/sth

(c) *Litt* (*sauf*) except, save, but; **tous h. un seul** all but one; **h. des gens avec qui je travaille** except (for) *or* apart from the people I work with

▶ **hors**: *TV, Rad* **h. antenne** off-air; *Compta* **h. bilan** off-balance sheet; *TV, Cin* **h. caméra** off-camera; **h. champ** out of vision, out of shot; **h. comptabilité** off-balance sheet; **h. concours: être (mis) h. concours** to be disqualified; *Fig* **il est h. concours** he's in a class of his own; *Fin* **h. cote** unlisted; **h. d'état** out of order; *Journ* **h. enregistrement** off the record; *Rad* **h. fréquence** out-of-band; *TV, Cin* **h. plan** off-shot; *TV, Rad* **h. programmme** unscripted; **h. saison** off-season; *Journ* **h. série** *nm* special edition; **numéro h. série** special issue; *Fig* **un talent h. série** an exceptional talent, a talent (that is) out of the ordinary; **h. studio** remote; (*répétition*) pre-studio rehearsal; **h. synchronisation** out of sync; **h. TVA** net of VAT

***hors-bord** *nm inv* motor boat *or* speedboat (*with outboard motor*); **moteur h.** outboard motor

***hors-concours** *nm inv* = person/exhibit ineligible for competition (because of superiority)

***hors-d'œuvre** [ɔrdœvr] *nm inv* **(a)** *Culin* hors d'œuvre, starter **(b)** *Fig* starter, taster **(c)** *Archit* annexe, outwork

***horse power** [ɔrspawœr] *nm inv* horsepower

***hors-jeu** *nm inv Sp* offside

***hors-la-loi** *nm inv* outlaw
***hors-piste** *nm inv Ski* off piste; **faire du h.** to go ski-ing off piste
***hors-route** *adj inv* off-highway
***hors-texte** *nm inv* (inset) plate
hortensia [ɔrtɑ̃sja] *nf Bot* hydrangea
horticole [ɔrtikɔl] *adj* horticultural; **exposition h.** flower show
horticulteur [ɔrtikyltœr] *nm* horticulturist
horticulture [ɔrtikyltyr] *nf* horticulture
***hosanna** [ozana] **1** *int* hosanna! **2** *nm* hosanna
hospice [ɔspis] *nm* **(a)** (*maison*) (*de Saint-Bernard etc*) hospice **(b)** (*foyer*) (old people's/children's) home; **mourir à l'h.** to die in the poorhouse **(c)** (*hôpital*) hospice
hospitalier[1], -ière [ɔspitalje, -jɛr] *adj* hospitable; *Litt* (*rive, ombre*) welcoming
hospitalier[2], -ière 1 *adj* **(a)** hospital; **personnel h.** hospital staff **(b)** *Rel* **religieux h.** hospitaller; **sœur hospitalière** Sister of Charity **2** *n Rel* Hospitaller
hospitalisation [ɔspitalizasjɔ̃] *nf* (*admission, séjour*) hospitalization; **h. à domicile** home care
hospitalisé, -ée [ɔspitalize] *n* (*à l'hôpital*) (in-)patient
hospitaliser [ɔspitalize] *vt* to hospitalize; **faire h. qn** to hospitalize sb, to send sb to hospital; **il est resté hospitalisé de longs mois** he was in hospital for several months
hospitalité [ɔspitalite] *nf* hospitality; **offrir l'h. à qn** to offer sb hospitality; **donner l'h. à qn pour la nuit** to put sb up for the night; **avoir le sens de l'h.** to be hospitable
hospitalo-universitaire [ɔspitaloyniversitɛr] *adj* **centre h.** university *or* teaching hospital
hostellerie [ɔstɛlri] *nf* (fashionable) country inn
hostie [ɔsti] *nf Rel* host
hostile [ɔstil] *adj* hostile; (*action*) unfriendly; **être h. à qn/qch** to be hostile *or* opposed to sb/sth; **tenir des propos hostiles à qn** to make hostile *or* unfriendly remarks to sb
hostilement [ɔstilmɑ̃] *adv* hostilely, in a hostile manner
hostilité [ɔstilite] *nf* **(a)** hostility **(contre, envers** to(wards)); **acte d'h.** act of war **(b) hostilités** hostilities
hosto [ɔsto] *nm F* (*abrév* **hôpital**) hospital; **aller à l'h.** to go to hospital
***hot-dog** [ɔtdɔg], *pl* **hot-dogs** *nm* hot dog
hôte [ot] **1** *nm* host; *Vieilli* (*dans une taverne etc*) landlord; **dîner à la table d'h.** to have the set menu *or* the table d'hôte **2** *n* **(a)** (*invité*) guest, visitor; **h. de marque** VIP guest; **h. payant** paying guest **(b)** *Biol* (*d'un parasite*) host **(c)** *Litt* (*habitant*) dweller; **les hôtes des bois** the woodland creatures, the creatures of the woods; **les souris et les araignées sont les hôtes de mon grenier** my attic is inhabited by mice and spiders
hôtel [otɛl] *nm* **(a)** hotel; **h. de luxe/miteux** luxury/seedy hotel; **h. deux/trois étoiles** two/three star hotel; **une chambre d'h.** a hotel room; **descendre à l'h.** to stay at *or* put up at a hotel; **j'habitais un petit h. de banlieue** I was staying in a little hotel on the outskirts of town; **h. meublé** residential hotel (*providing lodging but not board*); **on n'est pas à l'h. ici!** this isn't a hotel, you know!; **rat d'h.** hotel thief **(b) h. (particulier)** mansion, town house **(c)** *Admin* public building
▶ **hôtel**: **h. d'aéroport** airport hotel; **h. balnéaire** seaside hotel; **h. classe touriste** tourist class hotel; **h.-club** leisure hotel; **h. de congrès** hotel with conference facilities; **h. familial** family-run hotel; **h. de gare** railway hotel; **h. homologué** hotel classified by the 'préfecture de région'; **h. des impôts** tax office; **h. médicalisé** spa hotel; **l'H. de la Monnaie** ≈ the Royal Mint; **h. non homologué** simple, basic hotel classified by the 'préfectures'; **h. de passe** (hotel used as a) brothel; **h. de préfecture** quite small and basic hotel classified by the 'préfectures'; **h. quatre étoiles luxe** five-star hotel, luxury hotel; **h. de tourisme** hotel classified by the ministry of Tourism; **h. de vacances** holiday hotel; **h. des ventes** auction rooms *or* salerooms; **h. de ville** town hall, *Am* city hall
hôtel-Dieu, *pl* **hôtels-Dieu** *nm* hospital
hôtelier, -ière [otəlje, -jɛr] **1** *n* hotel keeper, hotelier **2** *adj* **l'industrie hôtelière** the hotel industry *or* trade
hôtellerie [otɛlri] *nf* **(a)** (*hôtel*) inn **(b)** (*secteur*) **l'h.** the hotel trade *or* industry *or* business, the hospitality business; **crise de l'h.** crisis in the hotel trade; **h. de plein air** camping and caravaning **(c)** (*dans un couvent*) guest quarters
hôtel-restaurant, *pl* **hôtels-restaurants** *nm* hotel-restaurant
hôtesse [otɛs] *nf* **(a)** hostess; *Vieilli* (*dans une taverne etc*) landlady **(b)** *Av* hostess, stewardess
▶ **hôtesse**: **h. d'accueil** (*dans une entreprise, une foire etc*) receptionist; (*à une exposition*) hostess; **h. d'accueil téléphonique** switchboard operator; **h. de l'air** air hostess, cabin *or* flight attendant
hot rod [ɔtrɔd], *pl* **hot rods** *nm Aut* hot rod
***hotte** [ɔt] *nf* **(a)** (*sur le dos*) basket; (*de maçon*) (bricklayer's) hod; **la h. du Père Noël** Father Christmas's *or* Santa's sack **(b)** (*dans un laboratoire, au-dessus d'une cuisinière, dans une forge*) hood; **h. aspirante** extractor hood
***hottentot, -ote** [ɔtɑ̃to, -ɔt] **1** *adj* Hottentot **2** *n* **H.** Hottentot
***hou** [u] *int* boo!; **h.! la vilaine!** tut-tut, you naughty girl!
***houblon** [ublɔ̃] *nm* hop
***houblonnier, -ière** [ublɔnje, -jɛr] **1** *adj* **région houblonnière** hop(-growing) district **2** *nm* hop grower **3** *nf* **houblonnière** hop field
***houe** [u] *nf* hoe
***houille** [uj] *nf* coal; **mine de h.** coalmine, colliery; **h. blanche** hydroelectric power; **h. bleue** wave power
***houiller, -ère** [uje, -ɛr] **1** *adj* carboniferous, coal-bearing; **dépôt** *ou* **bassin h.** coal bed *or* basin; **production houillère** coal output **2** *nf* **houillère** coalmine, colliery
***houle** [ul] *nf* (*de la mer*) swell, surge; **grosse h.** heavy swell
***houlette** [ulɛt] *nf* **(a)** (*de berger*) (shepherd's) crook; (*crosse*) (bishop's) crosier; *Fig* **sous la h. de notre guide** under the leadership of our guide **(b)** (*petite bêche*) trowel, spud
***houleux, -euse** [ulø, -øz] *adj* (*mer*) swelling, surging; *Fig* (*assemblée*) surging, tumultuous; **réunion houleuse** stormy meeting
***houp** [up, *occ* hup] *int* = **hop**
***houppe** [up] *nf* (*de poils etc*) tuft; (*de plumes*) crest, tuft; **h. à poudrer** powder puff
***houppelande** [uplɑ̃d] *nf* cloak
***houppette** [upɛt] *nf* (*de plumes etc*) small tuft; (*à poudre*) powder puff
***hourdage** [urdaʒ] *nm Constr* roughcasting
***hourder** [urde] *vt Constr* to roughcast
***houri** [uri] *nf Rel* houri
***hourra** [ura] **1** *int* hurrah!; **hip, hip, hip, h.!** hip, hip, hooray! **2** *nm* hurrah; **pousser trois hourras** to give three cheers
***hourvari** [urvari] *nm Litt* uproar, tumult
***houspiller** [uspije] *vt* **h. qn** (*le réprimander*) to reprimand sb, *F* to tell sb off
***housse** [us] *nf* **(a)** (*de meubles*) cover; (*contre la poussière*) dust sheet; (*dans une voiture*) seat cover; **h. à vêtements** garment bag **(b)** (*pour cheval*) trappings
***houx** [u] *nm* holly
***hovercraft** [ɔvɛrkraft] *nm* hovercraft
HT *abrév* **(a) (haute tension)** ht **(b) (hors taxe)** before tax, exclusive of tax; **le montant HT de la facture** the net amount of the invoice, the invoice net of tax
H. TVA (*abrév* **hors TVA**) net of VAT
***huard, huart** [ɥar] *nm* **(a)** osprey, *Am* fish hawk **(b)** *Can* black-throated diver
***hublot** [yblo] *nm* porthole; (*dans un avion, une machine à laver*) window; *Aut* scuttle; *Fig F* **des hublots** (*lunettes*) thick *or F* milk-bottle glasses; **h. de contrôle** sight glass
***huche** [yʃ] *nf* (*pétrin*) kneading trough; (*coffre*) bin; **h. à pain** bread bin
***hue** [y, hy] *int* (*à un cheval*) gee up!; **tirer à h. et à dia** to pull in opposite *or* different directions; **l'un tire à h. et l'autre à dia** they're pulling in opposite *or* different directions
***huée** [ɥe] *nf* (*usu pl*) **huées** booing, jeering; **quitter la scène sous les huées** to be booed off the stage
***huer** [ɥe] **1** *vt* (*acteur etc*) to boo; (*orateur etc*) to barrack **2** *vi* (*d'un hibou*) to hoot
***huerta** [wɛrta] *nf* = irrigated plain in Spain
***huguenot, -ote** [yg(ə)no, -ɔt] *Hist* **1** *adj* Huguenot **2** *n* **H.** Huguenot
huilage [ɥilaʒ] *nm* oiling, lubrication
huile [ɥil] *nf* oil; **frit à l'h.** fried in oil; **tache d'h.** oil stain; *Fig* **faire tache d'h.** to spread; **évidemment, ça a fait tache d'h. et tout le monde l'a su** obviously it spread like wildfire and everyone knew about it; *Fig* **jeter** *ou* **verser de l'h. sur le feu** to add fuel to the fire; *Fig* **mettre de l'h. dans les rouages** to oil the wheels; **une mer d'h.** a glassy sea; *Arg* **les huiles** the big shots, the top brass; *Beaux-Arts* **peinture à l'h.** oil painting; **faire de la peinture à l'h.** to paint in oils; **des tubes de peinture à l'h.** tubes of oil paint; **portrait à l'h.** portrait in oils; **une de ses huiles** one of his oil paintings
▶ **huile**: **h. de bras** elbow grease, *Can* **h. de chauffage** heating oil; **h. de coude** elbow grease; *Aut* **h. de damper** damper oil, hydraulic fluid; **h. détergente** detergent oil; **h. essentielle** essential oil; **h. de foie de morue** cod liver oil; **h. de graissage** lubricating *or* lubrication oil; **h. de lin** linseed oil; **h. lourde** heavy-duty oil; **h. de lubrification** lubricating *or* lubrication oil; **h. de machine** machine oil; **h. minérale** mineral oil; **h. moteur** engine oil; **h. multigrade** multi-grade *or* cross-grade oil; **h. d'olive** olive oil; **h. de paraffine** paraffin oil; **h. réfrigérante** refrigerant oil; **h. de ricin** castor

oil; **h. solaire** suntan oil; **h. synthétique** synthetic oil; **h. de table** salad oil; **h. de tournesol** sunflower (seed) oil; **h. végétale** vegetable oil

huiler [ɥile] *vt* to oil, to lubricate

huilerie [ɥilri] *nf Ind* oil works; *Com* oil trade; **il s'est enrichi dans l'h.** he made his money in the oil business

huileux, -euse [ɥilø, -øz] *adj* oily, greasy

huilier [ɥilje] *nm* **(a)** (*de table*) oil and vinegar cruet **(b)** *Ind* oil manufacturer

huis [ɥi] *nm Arch* door; **entretien à h. clos** conversation behind closed doors; *Jur* **entendre une cause à h. clos** to hear a case in camera; **ordonner le h. clos** to order a case to be heard in camera

huisserie [ɥisri] *nf Constr* (*d'une porte, d'une fenêtre*) frame

huissier [ɥisje] *nm* **(a)** *Jur* process server, ≈ sheriff's officer, bailiff; **h. audiencier** court usher **(b)** (*portier*) usher

***huit** [ɥit] **1** *adj inv* (*as cardinal adj before a noun or adj beginning with a consonant sound* [ɥi]) eight; **h. (petits) garçons** [ɥi(pti)garsɔ̃] eight (little) boys; **h. hommes** [ɥitɔm] eight men; **j'en ai h.** [ɥit] I have eight (of them); **le h. mai** [ɥimɛ] the eighth of May, May the eighth; **h. jours** a week; **aujourd'hui/demain en h.** a week today/tomorrow, *Fml* today/tomorrow week; **donner ses h. jours à qn** to give sb a week's notice; *Ordinat* **à h. éléments binaires** eight-bit

2 *nm inv* eight; (*figure de patinage*) figure of eight; **elle habite au h. de la rue ...** she lives at number eight, ... Street; **le h. de carreau** the eight of diamonds; **la route fait un h. dans les collines** the road snakes round the hills; **l'ivrogne avançait en faisant des huit** the drunk was reeling *or* staggering along

***huitain** [ɥitɛ̃] *nm Littér* octet

***huitaine** [ɥitɛn] *nf* **(a)** (about) eight **(b)** (*une semaine*) week; **il faut compter une bonne h. (de jours) pour que le paquet arrive** you must allow a good week for the parcel to get there; **dans une h. de jours** in a week or so; **affaire remise à h.** case adjourned for a week

***huitante** [ɥitɑ̃t] *num adj inv Suisse* eighty

***huitantième** [ɥitɑ̃tjɛm] *num adj, n Suisse* eightieth

***huitième** [ɥitjɛm] **1** *adj, n* eighth **2** *nm* (*fraction*) eighth; *Sp* **être en h. de finale** to be through to the last sixteen **3** *nf Sch* **(classe de) h.** ≈ third form of junior school, *US* ≈ eighth grade

***huitièmement** [ɥitjɛmmɑ̃] *adv* eighthly, in eighth place

huître [ɥitr] *nf* **(a)** oyster; **h. perlière** pearl oyster **(b)** *F* (*idiot*) fool, mug

***huit-reflets** [ɥir(ə)flɛ] *nm inv* top hat

huîtrier, -ère [ɥitrije, -ɛr] **1** *adj* **industrie huîtrière** oyster farming **2** *nm Orn* oyster catcher **3** *nf* **huîtrière** oyster bed

***hulotte** [ylɔt] *nf* tawny owl

***hululement** [ylylmɑ̃] *nm* hoot; **l'h. d'un hibou** the hoot *or* hooting of an owl; **des hululements** hooting

***hululer** [ylyle] *vi* (*du hibou*) to hoot

***hum** [œm] *int* hem!, h'm!

humain [ymɛ̃] **1** *adj* **(a)** human; **il est h. après tout** he's only human; **c'est h.** it's only human; **le genre h.** mankind; **tu ne vas pas t'en prendre au genre h.** you can't put the blame on the whole human race; **les êtres humains** human beings, humans; **c'est un être h., après tout** he's a human being, after all; **des pertes humaines énormes** a huge loss of life; **à l'échelle humaine** on a human scale; **sciences humaines** social sciences; *Mus* **voix humaine** (*d'un orgue*) vox humana; **ressources humaines** human resources; **l'erreur est humaine** to err is human

(b) (*compréhensif*) humane; **elle a toujours été très humaine avec moi** she has always treated me very considerately

2 *nm* human (being)

humainement [ymɛnmɑ̃] *adv* **(a)** humanly; **si c'est h. possible** if humanly possible **(b)** (*avec bonté*) humanely

humanisation [ymanizasjɔ̃] *nf* humanization, humanizing

humaniser [ymanize] **1** *vt* **(a)** to humanize, to make human **(b)** (*rendre plus charitable*) **h. qn** to make sb more human *or* humane **2 s'humaniser** *vpr* **(a)** to become more human **(b)** (*devenir plus charitable*) to become more human *or* humane

humanisme [ymanism] *nm Litt, Phil* humanism

humaniste [ymanist] **1** *n* humanist **2** *adj* humanist(ic)

humanitaire [ymanitɛr] *adj* humanitarian; **organisation/aide h.** humanitarian organization/aid

humanitarisme [ymanitarism] *nm* humanitarianism

humanité [ymanite] *nf* **(a)** (*genre humain*) humanity, mankind; **tu rendrais service à l'h.** you'd be doing mankind *or* humanity a favour **(b)** (*du Christ*) human nature **(c)** (*bonté*) humanity, humaneness; **traiter qn avec h.** to treat sb humanely **(d) humanités** humanities, classics; **faire ses humanités** to study the classics

humanoïde [ymanɔid] *nm* humanoid

humble [œ̃bl] *adj* humble, lowly; **à mon h. avis** in my humble opinion

humblement [œ̃bləmɑ̃] *adv* humbly

humectage [ymɛktaʒ] *nm* dampening, moistening

humecter [ymɛkte] **1** *vt* to dampen, to moisten **2 s'humecter** *vpr* **s'h. les lèvres** to moisten one's lips; *F* **s'h. le gosier** to wet one's whistle

***humer** [yme] *vt* **(a)** (*aspirer*) to inhale; (*sentir*) to sniff; **h. l'air frais** to inhale *or* breathe in the fresh air; **h. le parfum d'une fleur** to smell a flower **(b)** (*liquide*) to suck in *or* up

huméral, -ale, -aux, -ales [ymeral, -o] *adj Anat* humeral

humérus [ymerys] *nm Anat* humerus

humeur [ymœr] *nf* **(a)** (*disposition*) mood, spirits, humour, *US* humor; **être de bonne h.** to be in a good mood *or* in good spirits; **un livre/film plein de bonne h.** a good-humoured book/film; **être de mauvaise h.** to be in a bad mood; **une personne de mauvaise h.** an ill-humoured person; **passer sa mauvaise h. sur qn/qch** to take one's bad mood out on sb/sth; **de méchante h.** in a (bad) temper; **être d'une h. massacrante** *ou F* **de chien** to be in a foul *or* filthy mood *or* temper; **être d'une h. noire** (*déprimé*) to be depressed; (*mécontent*) to be in a (bad) temper; **il est rentré d'h. noire** he came home in a bad temper; **être** *ou* **se sentir d'h. à refuser** to be in the mood to refuse

(b) (*caractère*) temper, temperament; **avoir l'h. vive** to be quick-tempered; **il y a incompatibilité d'h. entre nous** we are temperamentally unsuited; **homme d'h. égale** even-tempered man

(c) *Litt* (*mauvaise humeure*) ill humour *or US* humor, bad mood; **mouvement d'h.** outburst of temper; **geste d'h.** ill-tempered gesture; **montrer de l'h.** to show (ill) temper; **avec h.** testily, irritably; **je redoute ses sautes d'h.** I dread his changes of mood; **épancher son h. sur qn** to vent one's spleen on sb

(d) *Méd Arch* humour, *US* humor

▶ **humeur**: *Anat* **h. aqueuse** aqueous humour; **h. vitrée** vitreous humour

humide [ymid] *adj* (*maison, linge*) damp; (*climat*) damp, humid; **il fait h.** it *or* the weather is damp *or* humid; **couloir sombre et h.** dark, dank passage; **temps h. et chaud** muggy *or* close weather; **temps h. et froid** raw weather; **les yeux humides (de larmes)** eyes moist with tears; **elle me lançait des regards humides** she looked at me with moist eyes

humidificateur [ymidifikatœr] *nm* (*à usage domestique*) humidifier; (*pour les cigares*) humidor

humidification [ymidifikasjɔ̃] *nf* (*fait de rendre humide*) dampening, moistening; (*contre le dessèchement*) humidification; **pour l'h. des cigares** to prevent cigars drying out

humidifier [ymidifje] *vt* to dampen, moisten; (*contre le dessèchement*) to humidify

humidité [ymidite] *nf* (*d'une maison, du linge*) dampness; (*du climat*) humidity, dampness; **il faut beaucoup d'h. à cette plante** this plant needs a lot of moisture; **h. absolue/relative** absolute/relative humidity; **craint l'h.** (*sur un paquet*) keep dry, store in a dry place; **taches d'h.** damp patches, mildew; **teneur en h.** moisture content; **il y a de l'h. dans l'air** it's going to *or* it feels like rain; (*au bord de la mer*) there is moisture *or* dampness in the air

humiliant [ymiljɑ̃] *adj* humiliating, mortifying; **il lui fit des reproches humiliants** he upbraided her in a humiliating fashion

humiliation [ymiljasjɔ̃] *nf* humiliation, mortification; **elle en fut malade d'h.** she was totally mortified

humilier [ymilje] **1** *vt* (*abaisser*) to humiliate; *Vieilli, Rel* (*rendre humble*) to humble **2 s'humilier** *vpr* (*s'abaisser*) to humiliate oneself; (*devenir humble*) to humble oneself; **je ne veux pas m'h. devant eux** I'm not going to go grovelling to them; **s'h. jusqu'à faire qch** to stoop to doing sth

humilité [ymilite] *nf* humility, humbleness; **ton d'h.** humble tone, tone of humility; **ce fut une grande leçon d'h.** it was a lesson in humility

humoral, -ale, -aux, -ales [ymɔral, -o] *adj Méd* humoral

humoriste [ymɔrist] **1** *adj* (*écrivain etc*) humorous **2** humorist

humoristique [ymɔristik] *adj* (*orateur, écrivain etc*) humorous; **dessin h.** cartoon

humour [ymur] *nm* humour, *US* humor; **faire preuve d'h.** to keep smiling, to keep one's sense of humour, *F* to grin and bear it; **avoir (le sens) de l'h.** to have a (good) sense of humour; **h. noir** sick humour, black humour; **h. anglais** English humour

humus [ymys] *nm* humus

***Hun** [œ̃] *nm Hist* Hun

***hune** [yn] *nf Naut* top; **h. de vigie** crow's nest

***hunier** [ynje] *nm Naut* topsail

***huppe[1]** [yp] *nf Orn* hoopoe
***huppe[2]** *nf (d'un oiseau)* tuft, crest
***huppé** [ype] *adj* **(a)** *(oiseau)* tufted, crested **(b)** *F* high-class, *Br F* posh; **les classes huppées** the upper classes, *Br F* the toffs; **des gens huppés** the upper crust, *Br F* toffs, posh folk; **ce quartier est des plus huppés** this is a very high-class *or Br F* posh area
***hure** [yr] *nf* **(a)** *(de sanglier etc)* head **(b)** *Culin* brawn, *Am* headcheese
***hurlement** [yrləmɑ̃] *nm (d'un loup, d'un chien)* howl; *(d'une personne)* yell, scream; *(du vent)* howling; *(d'une sirène d'alarme)* shriek, wail; **hurlements** *(d'un loup etc)* howling; *(d'une personne)* yelling, screaming; **pousser un h.** to give a howl; **pousser des hurlements** to howl
***hurler** [yrle] **1** *vi (d'un loup, d'un chien)* to howl; *(du vent, de la tempête)* to howl, to roar; *(d'une alarme)* to shriek, to wail; *(d'une personne)* to howl, to roar, to yell; **elle faisait h. sa radio dans la cuisine** she had her radio blaring in the kitchen; **h. de douleur** to howl *or* scream (out) with pain; **c'est à h. de rire** it was screamingly funny, it was a scream; **h. à la lune** to bay at the moon; **il faut h. avec les loups** when in Rome, do as the Romans do; **couleurs qui hurlent** colours that clash (with one another)
2 *vt (chanson, discours etc)* to roar out, to bawl out; **elle me hurlait une recette par téléphone** she bawled a recipe down the telephone at me
***hurleur, -euse** [yrlœr, -øz] **1** *adj* howling, yelling **2** *n* howler, yeller **3** *nm (singe)* howler (monkey)
hurluberlu [yrlybɛrly] *nm* eccentric (person); **cet h. de Michel** that oddball Michel; **quel h., celui-là!** he's really odd *or* strange
***huron, -onne** [yrɔ̃, ɔn] *adj, n* Huron
husky [œski] *nm* husky
***hussard** [ysar] *nm Mil* hussar
***hussarde** [ysard] *nf* **à la h.** roughly, in a cavalier fashion, cavalierly; **partir à la h.** to leave unceremoniously
***hussite** [ysit] *nm Hist, Rel* Hussite
***hutte** [yt] *nf* hut
hyacinthe [jasɛ̃t] *nf* **(a)** *Arch (fleur)* hyacinth **(b)** *(pierre)* hyacinth, jacinth
hyalin [jalɛ̃] *adj* transparent, glassy; *Minér* **quartz h.** rock crystal
hybridation [ibridasjɔ̃] *nf Bot* hybridization; *Biol* cross-breeding
hybride [ibrid] *adj, nm* hybrid
hybrider [ibride] *vt Bot* to hybridize; *Biol* to cross(-breed)
hybridité [ibridite] *nf* hybridity, hybridism
hydracide [idrasid] *nm Ch* hydracid
hydratant [idratɑ̃] **1** *adj (crème)* moisturizing **2** *nm* moisturizer
hydratation [idratasjɔ̃] *nf* **(a)** *Ch* hydration **(b)** *(de la peau)* moisturizing
hydrate [idrat] *nm Ch* hydrate; **h. de potasse** caustic potash; **h. de carbone** carbohydrate
hydrater [idrate] **1** *vt* **(a)** *Ch* to hydrate **(b)** *(peau)* to moisturize **2 s'hydrater** *vpr* to hydrate, to become hydrated *or* moisturized
hydraulicien [idrolisjɛ̃] *nm* hydraulic engineer
hydraulique [idrolik] **1** *adj* hydraulic; **roue h.** waterwheel **2** *nf* **(a)** *(science)* hydraulics **(b)** *(technique)* hydraulic engineering
hydravion [idravjɔ̃] *nm* seaplane
hydre [idr] *nf* hydra
hydrique [idrik] *adj* hydrous
hydrocarbure [idrɔkarbyr] *nm Ch* hydrocarbon
hydrocéphale [idrɔsefal] *Méd* **1** *adj* hydrocephalic, hydrocephalous **2** *n* hydrocephalic *or* hydrocephalous patient
hydrocortisone [idrɔkɔrtizɔn] *nf* hydrocortisone
hydrocracking, hydrocraquage [idrɔkrakiŋ, -kaʒ] *nm Pétr* hydrocracking
hydrocution [idrɔkysjɔ̃] *nf* = form of hypothermia subsequent on immersion in very cold water
hydrodynamique [idrɔdinamik] **1** *adj* hydrodynamic **2** *nf* hydrodynamics
hydro-électricité [idrɔelɛktrisite] *nf* hydroelectricity
hydro-électrique [idrɔelɛktrik] *adj* hydroelectric
hydrofoil [idrɔfɔil] *nm* hydrofoil
hydrofuge [idrɔfyʒ] *adj (vêtement, tissu)* waterproof
hydrofuger [idrɔfyʒe] *vt* **(j'hydrofugeai(s); n. hydrofugeons)** *(vêtement, tissu)* to waterproof
hydrogénation [idrɔʒenasjɔ̃] *nf* hydrogenation
hydrogène [idrɔʒɛn] *nm Ch* hydrogen; **h. lourd** heavy hydrogen
hydrogéné [idrɔʒene] *adj* hydrogenated
hydrogéner [idrɔʒene] *vt* to hydrogenate
hydroglisseur [idrɔglisœr] *nm* jetfoil
hydrographe [idrɔgraf] *adj, nm* **(ingénieur) h.** hydrographer
hydrographie [idrɔgrafi] *nf* hydrography
hydrographique [idrɔgrafik] *adj* hydrographic(al)
hydrologie [idrɔlɔʒi] *nf* hydrology
hydrologique [idrɔlɔʒik] *adj* hydrological
hydrologiste [idrɔlɔʒist], **hydrologue** [idrɔlɔg] *n* hydrologist
hydrolyse [idrɔliz] *nf Ch* hydrolysis
hydrolyser [idrɔlize] *vt Ch* to hydrolize, to hydrolyse
hydromel [idrɔmɛl] *nm* mead
hydromètre [idrɔmɛtr] **1** *nm* hydrometer; *(d'océan)* depth gauge **2** *nf Ent* water spider
hydrométrie [idrɔmetri] *nf Phys* hydrometry
hydrométrique [idrɔmetrik] *adj* hydrometric
hydrominéralisme [idromineralism] *nm* water cures
hydrophile [idrɔfil] *adj (coton etc)* absorbent
hydrophobe [idrɔfɔb] **1** *adj* hydrophobic **2** *n Méd* hydrophobic patient
hydrophobie [idrɔfɔbi] *nf Méd* hydrophobia
hydropique [idrɔpik] *Méd* **1** *adj* dropsical **2** *n* dropsical patient
hydropisie [idrɔpizi] *nf Méd* dropsy
hydroptère [idrɔptɛr] *nm* hydrofoil
hydroquinone [idrɔkinɔn] *nf Ch, Phot* hydroquinone
hydrosol [idrɔsɔl] *nm Ch* hydrosol
hydrosoluble [idrɔsɔlybl] *adj* water-soluble
hydrospeed [idrɔspid] *nm Sp* = type of water sport consisting of shooting the rapids on a board
hydrosphère [idrɔsfɛr] *nf* hydrosphere
hydrostatique [idrɔstatik] **1** *adj* hydrostatic **2** *nf* hydrostatics
hydrothérapie [idrɔterapi] *nf Méd (traitement)* hydrotherapy, water cure; *(science)* hydrotherapeutics
hydrothérapique [idrɔterapik] *adj* hydrotherapeutic
hydrothermal, -ale, -aux, -ales [idrɔtɛrmal, -o] *adj* hydrothermal
hydrothermalisme [idrɔtɛrmalism] *nm Méd* water therapy
hydroxyde [idrɔksid] *nm Ch* hydroxide
hydrure [idryr] *nm Ch* hydride
hyène [jɛn] *nf (when aspirated* **la hyène**, *when silent* **l'hyène**) hyena
hygiaphone [iʒjafɔn] *nm (au guichet)* grill; **parlez dans l'h.** to speak through the grill
hygiène [iʒjɛn] *nf* hygiene; **h. publique/mentale** public/mental health; **produits d'h. courante** cleaning *or* cleansing products; **prendre des mesures d'h.** to take steps to deal with a hygiene problem; **mauvaise h. alimentaire** bad eating habits, poor diet; **vous devriez surveiller votre h. alimentaire** you should watch your diet *or* what you eat
hygiénique [iʒjenik] *adj* **(a)** *(sanitaire)* hygienic, sanitary; **peu h.** unhygienic; **papier h.** toilet paper; **serviette h.** sanitary towel *or US* napkin **(b)** *(bon pour la santé)* healthy; **une promenade h.** a healthy walk, a constitutional
hygiéniquement [iʒjenikmɑ̃] *adv* **(a)** hygienically **(b)** *(bon pour la santé)* healthily
hygrométrie [igrɔmetri] *nf Phys* hygrometry
hygroscope [igrɔskɔp] *nm Phys* hygroscope
hygroscopique [igrɔskɔpik] *adj Phys* hygroscopic
hymen [imɛn] *nm* **(a)** *Litt* marriage **(b)** *Anat* hymen
hyménée [imene] *nm Litt* marriage
hyménoptère [imenɔptɛr] *Ent* **1** *adj* hymenopterous **2** *nmpl* **hyménoptères** Hymenoptera
hymne [imn] **1** *nm (de louanges)* song (of praise); **un h. à la beauté** a hymn to beauty; **l'h. à la joie** the Ode to Joy; **h. national** national anthem **2** *n Rel* hymn
hyoïde [jɔid] *adj, nm Anat* **(os) h.** hyoid (bone)
hyper- [ipɛr] *préf Arg* mega-; **hypercool** hyper- *or* mega-cool; **hyperchiant** mega-boring
hyperacidité [ipɛrasidite] *nf Méd* hyperacidity
hyperbare [ipɛrbar] *adj Tech* hyperbaric; **caisson h.** decompression chamber
hyperbole [ipɛrbɔl] *nf* **(a)** *Littér* hyperbole **(b)** *Math* hyperbola
hyperbolique [ipɛrbɔlik] *adj Littér, Math* hyperbolic(al)
hyperboliquement [ipɛrbɔlikmɑ̃] *adv Littér* hyperbolically
hyperboloïde [ipɛrbɔlɔid] *Math* **1** *adj* hyperboloidal **2** *nm* hyperboloid
hyperboréen, -enne [ipɛrbɔreɛ̃, -ɛn] *adj Litt* hyperborean
hypercritique [ipɛrkritik] *adj* hypercritical, overcritical
hyperémotivité [ipɛremɔtivite] *nf Méd* hyperemotionalism, hyperemotivity
hyperfréquence [ipɛrfrekɑ̃s] *nf Rad* ultra high frequency
hyperglycémie [ipɛrglisemi] *nf Méd* hyperglyc(a)emia
hypermarché [ipɛrmarʃe] *nm* hypermarket, superstore
hypermétrope [ipɛrmetrɔp] *adj Méd* hypermetropic
hypermétropie [ipɛrmetrɔpi] *nf Méd* hypermetropia
hypernerveux, -euse [ipɛrnɛrvø, -øz] **1** *adj* highly strung **2** *n* highly strung person
hyperpack [ipɛrpak] *nm* multipack

hyperréalisme [ipɛrrealism] *nm Beaux-Arts* hyperrealism
hypersensibilité [ipɛrsɑ̃sibilite] *nf* hypersensitivity
hypersensible [ipɛrsɑ̃sibl] *adj* hypersensitive
hypertendu [ipɛrtɑ̃dy] *Méd* **1** *adj* hypertensive, suffering from high blood pressure **2** *n* hypertensive patient, person suffering from high blood pressure
hypertensif, -ive [ipɛrtɑ̃sif, -iv] *adj, n Méd* hypertensive
hypertension [ipɛrtɑ̃sjɔ̃] *nf Méd* hypertension, high blood pressure
hypertexte [ipɛrtɛkst] *nm Ordinat* hypertext
hyperthyroïdie [ipɛrtirɔidi] *nf Méd* hyperthyroidism
hypertrophie [ipɛrtrɔfi] *nf Méd* hypertrophy; **h. des amygdales** enlarged tonsils; *Fig* **l'h. urbaine** urban sprawl; **elle souffre d'h. du moi** she's got a swollen ego
hypertrophier [ipɛrtrɔfje] *Méd* **1** *vt* to hypertrophy; **amygdales hypertrophiées** enlarged tonsils **2 s'hypertrophier** *vpr* to hypertrophy, to become too large; *Fig* (*de sentiments*) to become strong, to grow
hypertrophique [ipɛrtrɔfik] *adj Méd* hypertrophic
hypervitaminose [ipɛrvitaminoz] *nf Méd* hypervitaminosis
hypnose [ipnoz] *nf* hypnosis, (hypnotic) trance; **être en état d'h.** to be under hypnosis, to be in a hypnotic trance
hypnotique [ipnɔtik] *adj, n* hypnotic
hypnotiser [ipnɔtize] *vt* to hypnotize
hypnotiseur [ipnɔtizœr] *nm* hypnotist
hypnotisme [ipnɔtism] *nm* hypnotism
hypoallergénique [ipɔalɛrʒenik] *adj* hypoallergenic
hypocalcémie [ipɔkalsemi] *nf Méd* hypocalcaemia
hypocalorique [ipɔkalɔrik] *adj* **régime h.** low-calorie diet
hypocentre [ipɔsɑ̃tr] *nm Géol* focus, hypocentre
hypocondre [ipɔkɔ̃dr] **1** *nm Anat* hypochondrium **2** *n* hypochondriac
hypocondriaque [ipɔkɔ̃drijak] **1** *adj* hypochondriac **2** *n* hypochondriac
hypocondrie [ipɔkɔ̃dri] *nf* hypochondria; **être atteint d'h.** to have hypochondria, to be (a) hypochondriac
hypocras [ipɔkras] *nm Arch* hippocras
hypocrisie [ipɔkrizi] *nf* hypocrisy
hypocrite [ipɔkrit] **1** *adj* hypocritical **2** *n* hypocrite; **faire l'h.** to be a hypocrite
hypocritement [ipɔkritmɑ̃] *adv* hypocritically
hypodermique [ipɔdɛrmik] *adj* hypodermic
hypogastrique [ipɔgastrik] *adj Anat* hypogastric; *Méd* **ceinture h.** abdominal belt
hypogée [ipɔʒe] *nm Archéol* underground (burial) vault, *Spéc* hypogeum
hypoglycémiant [ipoglisemjɑ̃] *adj Pharm* hypoglycemic
hypoglycémie [ipɔglisemi] *nf Méd* hypoglycemia; **être en h.** to be hypoglycemic, to have low blood sugar
hypoïd [ipɔid] *adj* (*engrenage*) hypoid
hypolipidémiant [ipolipidemjɑ̃] *Pharm* **1** *adj* lipid-lowering **2** *nm* lipid-lowering drug
hypophosphite [ipɔfɔsfit] *nm Ch* hypophosphite
hypophyse [ipɔfiz] *nf Anat* pituitary gland, *Spéc* hypophysis
hypostase [ipɔstaz] *nf* hypostasis
hypostatique [ipɔstatik] *adj Phil, Rel* hypostatic
hypostyle [ipɔstil] *adj Archit* hypostyle, pillared
hypotendu, -ue [ipɔtɑ̃dy] *Méd* **1** *adj* hypotensive, suffering from low blood pressure **2** *n* hypotensive patient, person suffering from low blood pressure
hypotenseur [ipɔtɑ̃sœr] *nm Méd* hypotensive
hypotension [ipɔtɑ̃sjɔ̃] *nf Méd* low blood pressure, *Spéc* hypotension
hypoténuse [ipɔtenyz] *nf* hypotenuse
hypothalamus [ipɔtalamys] *nm* hypothalamus
hypothécable [ipɔtekabl] *adj* mortgageable
hypothécaire [ipɔtekɛr] *adj* **prêt h.** mortgage (loan); **contrat h.** mortgage deed; **créancier h.** mortgagee; **débiteur h.** mortgager
hypothécairement [ipɔtekɛrmɑ̃] *adv Jur* by *or* on mortgage
hypothèque [ipɔtɛk] *nf* mortgage; **franc** *ou* **libre d'hypothèques** unmortgaged; **prendre une h.** to take out a mortgage; **prêt sur h.** mortgage (loan); **h. de premier rang** first legal mortgage; **purger une h.** to pay off *or* clear *or* redeem a mortgage; *Fig* **ces difficultés font peser une lourde h. sur son avenir** these difficulties are posing a great threat to his future
hypothéquer [ipɔteke] *vt* **(j'hypothèque; j'hypothéquerai) (a)** (*propriété etc*) to mortgage; *Fig* **h. son avenir** to sign away one's future **(b) h. une dette** to secure a debt by mortgage
hypothermie [ipɔtɛrmi] *nf Méd* hypothermia
hypothèse [ipɔtɛz] *nf* [①A14,10] hypothesis; **émettre une h.** to venture a hypothesis; **nous pouvons faire l'h. que …** we can assume *or* make the assumption that …; **en être réduit aux hypothèses** to be reduced to making hypotheses *or* to hypothesizing; **selon cette h.** on this assumption
hypothétique [ipɔtetik] *adj* hypothetical
hypothétiquement [ipɔtetikmɑ̃] *adv* hypothetically
hypothyroïdie [ipɔtirɔidi] *nf Méd* thyroid deficiency, *Spéc* hypothyroidism
hypovitaminose [ipɔvitaminoz] *nf Méd* vitamin deficiency, *Spéc* hypovitaminosis
hypsomètre [ipsɔmɛtr] *nm* hypsometer
hypsométrie [ipsɔmetri] *nf* hypsometry
hypsométrique [ipsɔmetrik] *adj* hypsometric(al); **courbe h.** contour line; **carte h.** contour map
hysope [izɔp] *nf Bot* hyssop
hystérectomie [isterɛktɔmi] *nf Chir* hysterectomy
hystérie [isteri] *nf Méd* hysteria; **je ne veux pas de crise d'h.** I don't want any hysterics; *F* **c'est de l'h.** it's sheer hysterics ▶ **hystérie**: **h. collective** mass hysteria
hystérique [isterik] *Méd* **1** *adj* hysterical **2** *n* hysterical person, hysteric
hystérotomie [isterɔtɔmi] *nf Chir* hysterotomy; **h. abdominale** caesarean *or US* cesarean section

I

I, i [i] *nm (lettre)* I, i
IA [ia] *nf Ordinat (abrév* **intelligence artificielle**) AI
iambe [jɑ̃b] *nm Littér* **(a)** *(pied)* iamb, iambus **(b)** *(vers)* iambic **(c) iambes** *(poème satirique)* iambics
iambique [jɑ̃bik] *adj (vers, strophe)* iambic
IATA [jata] *nf (abrév* **Association Internationale des Transporteurs Aériens**) IATA
ibère [ibɛr] **1** *adj* Iberian **2** *n* **I.** Iberian
ibérique [iberik] *adj* Iberian; **la péninsule i.** the Iberian peninsula
ibidem, ibid, ib [ibidɛm] *adv* ibid., ib.
ibis [ibis] *nm (oiseau)* ibis
Icare [ikar] *nm* Icarus
iceberg [ajsbɛrg, isbɛrg] *nm* iceberg; **la partie visible de l'i.** the part of the iceberg above water; *Fig* the tip of the iceberg; **la partie cachée de l'i.** the part of the iceberg under water; *Fig* **quand tu réaliseras ce qu'est la partie cachée de l'i.** when you realize the true scale of the task/problem
icelui [isəlɥi], **icelle** [isɛl], **iceux** [isø], **icelles** [isɛl] *pron dém, adj Arch, Jur, Hum* = **celui(-ci) , celle(-ci) , ceux(-ci), celles(-ci)**
ichtyocolle [iktjɔkɔl] *nf* fish glue, isinglass
ichtyologie [iktjɔlɔʒi] *nf* ichthyology
ichtyologique [iktjɔlɔʒik] *adj* ichthyologic(al)
ichtyologiste [iktjɔlɔʒist] *n* ichthyologist
ichtyophage [iktjɔfaʒ] **1** *adj* fish-eating, ichthyophagous **2** *n* ichthyophagist
ici [isi] *adv* **(a)** *(dans l'espace)* here; **i. et là** here and there; **i. même** on this very spot, in this very place; **les gens d'i.** the people (who live) here, the locals; **je ne suis pas d'i.** I'm not from (round) here; **d'i., on a un très beau point de vue** there is a very good view from here; **M. Leblanc, i. présent** Mr Leblanc, who is here; *F* **je vois ça d'i.!** I can just see it!, I can see it coming!; *F* **tu vois d'i. les problèmes!** you can see the problems there are going to be!; **i.-bas** here below, on earth; **il y a vingt kilomètres d'i. à Paris** it's twenty kilometres from here to Paris; **c'est à dix minutes d'i.** it's ten minutes away *or* from here; **c'est loin d'i.** it's a long way away (from here); **viens par i.** come (over) here; *(en entrant)* come in here; *(en sortant)* come out here; **regarde par i.** look (over) here; **c'est par i. que ça se passe** it's happening (over) here; *(dans cette pièce etc)* it's happening in here; *(dans le jardin etc)* it's happening out here; **il habite par i.** *ou* **près d'i.** he lives near here *or* around here; **passez par i.** (come) this way, please; **par i. la sortie** this way out, the exit is this way; **par i. la monnaie** (over) here with the money; **c'est i.** this is the place; **c'est i. que ça s'est passé/que je veux habiter** this is where it happened/where I want to live; **le car vient jusqu'i.** the bus comes as far as here *or* as far as this; *Fig* **je reprends i. ses propres paroles** and here I'm using his own words; *Tél* **i. Thomas** (it's) Thomas speaking, Thomas here; *Rad* **i. France Inter** this is France Inter; **i. le Palais de l'Elysée, à vous les studios (Jean Lô au micro)** this is Jean Lô at the Elysée Palace handing you back to the studio
(b) *(dans le temps)* **jusqu'i.** until now, up to now; **d'i. lundi/la semaine prochaine/demain** by Monday/next week/ tomorrow; **d'i. lundi, il peut se passer tellement de choses!** so many things can happen between now and Monday *or* before Monday!; **d'i. là** by that time, by then; **mais d'i. là, on a le temps** but we've got time until then; **d'i. peu** before long; **d'i. à ce que vous ayez fini, je serai parti** by the time you've finished, I'll have gone; **d'i. à ce qu'il la quitte, il n'y a pas loin** *ou* **il n'y a qu'un pas** it won't be long before he leaves her; **d'i. à ce qu'on y arrive, on a quelques efforts à faire** we've quite a bit to do before we get there; **ce voyage est tentant, mais d'i. à ce que j'ai la somme nécessaire!** this trip is tempting, but it's going to take me forever to get the money together
icône [ikon] *nf Rel* icon, ikon; *Ordinat* icon; *Ordinat* **i. contrastée** highlighted icon; *Ordinat* **i. de la corbeille** wastebasket icon, *Am* trash icon
iconoclasme [ikɔnɔklasm] *nm* iconoclasm
iconoclaste [ikɔnɔklast] **1** *adj* iconoclastic **2** *n* iconoclast
iconographe [ikɔnɔgraf] *n* **(a)** iconographer **(b)** *(dans l'édition)* art *or* picture editor
iconographie [ikɔnɔgrafi] *nf* **(a)** iconography **(b)** *(dans l'édition)* illustrations, art work
iconographique [ikɔnɔgrafik] *adj* iconographic(al)
iconoscope [ikɔnɔskɔp] *nm TV* iconoscope
ictère [iktɛr] *nm Méd* icterus, jaundice; **i. du nouveau-né** neonatal jaundice
ictérique [ikterik] *Méd* **1** *adj* **(a)** *(personne, yeux etc)* jaundiced **(b)** *(troubles)* icteric(al) **2** *n* jaundice sufferer
idéal, -als, -aux, -ales [ideal, -o] **1** *adj* ideal; *Litt* **devenir i.** to become a shadow of its former self **2** *nm* **(a)** ideal; **avoir un i.** to have an ideal; **l'i. de la beauté chez les Grecs** the Greek ideal of beauty **(b) l'i.** the ideal thing; **c'est l'i. pour se remettre en forme** it's the ideal thing for getting back into shape; **l'i., c'est de pouvoir s'exprimer** the ideal thing is to be able to express oneself; **l'i. serait que tu y ailles tout seul** ideally, you should go alone
idéalement [idealmɑ̃] *adv* ideally; **elle est i. belle** she is beauty itself
idéalisation [idealizasjɔ̃] *nf* idealization, idealizing
idéaliser [idealize] *vt* to idealize
idéalisme [idealism] *nm* idealism
idéaliste [idealist] **1** *adj* idealistic **2** *n* idealist
idée [ide] *nf* **(a)** idea; **je n'ai pas eu l'i. de lui téléphoner** the idea of phoning him didn't occur to me, I didn't have the idea of phoning him; **as-tu une i. de ce qu'on pourrait faire ce soir?** (do you have) any idea what we could do this evening?; **je n'arrive pas à avoir d'idées pour ma dissertation** I can't get any ideas for my essay; **i. de génie, i. lumineuse** brilliant idea, *Br* brainwave, *Am* brainstorm; **bonne i.!** good idea!; **c'était une bonne i. de l'emmener au restaurant** it was a good idea to take him out to eat; **j'ai une i. de pièce de théâtre** I've got an idea for a play; **avoir la bonne i. de faire qch** to have the bright idea of doing sth; **j'ai du mal à accepter l'i. que tu vas partir** I'm finding it hard to accept the idea that *or* to come to terms with the fact that you're leaving; **qu'est-ce qui vous a donné l'i. de venir?** what gave you the idea *or* made you think of coming?; **l'i. ne te viendrait pas à l'esprit qu'elle a peut-être ses problèmes?** doesn't it occur to you that she has problems too?; **à l'i. de.../que ...** at the idea of.../that ...; **je me sens très triste à l'i. de te voir partir** I feel very sad at the idea of seeing you go; **se faire à l'i. de.../que ...** to get used to the idea of.../that ...; **je n'arrive pas à me faire à cette i.** I can't get used to the idea; **l'i. de Pierre était de ...** Pierre's idea was to ...; **avoir une i. derrière la tête** to be up to something; **donner des idées à qn** to put ideas into sb's head, to give sb ideas; **ce livre me donne des idées de voyage** the book gives me some ideas for holidays; **c'était juste une i. en l'air** it was just an idea; **avoir sa petite i. sur qch** to have one's own little ideas about sth; **il ne manque pas d'idées!** he's got some good ideas; **il a des idées** he's quite imaginative, he comes up with good ideas; **il y a de l'i.** it's got something; **il y a de l'i. mais le plan de devoir laisse à désirer** the idea is good but your presentation leaves something to be desired; **quelle (drôle d')i.!, en voilà une i.!** what an idea!, what a thought!, the very idea!; **où a-t-elle pu prendre** *ou F* **pêcher cette i.?** where did she get that idea from?; **se faire des idées** to imagine things
(b) *(notion)* idea, notion; **l'i. qu'il a du travail** his idea *or* notion of work; **il a une i. un peu étrange de l'amour** he has rather a strange idea of love; **juste pour vous donner une i. de la situation** just to give you an idea of the situation; **vous avez trois jours pour vous faire une i. de la situation** you've got three days to get a handle on the situation; **je me faisais une autre i. du métier de journaliste** I imagined the journalist's profession to be different; **as-tu (une) i.** *ou* **la moindre i. du prix que ça coûte?** have you any idea of the price of it?; **je n'en ai pas la moindre i.** I haven't the least *or*

faintest idea, *F* I haven't a clue; **aucune i.!** no idea!; **j'ai (comme une) i. qu'il va venir ce soir** I've an idea he'll come tonight; *F* **on n'a pas i. de faire des choses pareilles!** whoever heard of doing things like that!; *F* **on n'a pas i.!** whoever heard of that!; **tu n'as pas i. du monde qu'il peut y avoir!** you've no idea how crowded it can be!; *F* **elle est belle, t'as pas i.!** she's incredibly beautiful!

(c) (*opinion*) view, opinion; **avoir une haute i. de qn/qch** to have a high opinion of sb/sth; **se faire une i. de qch** to get an *or* some idea of sth; **je préfère me faire une i. (par) moi-même** I prefer to make up my own mind; **avoir des idées arrêtées sur qch** to have set ideas *or* very decided views on sth; **il a les idées très à gauche** he has very left-wing ideas *or* views *or* opinions; **on a tous une i. différente sur la question** we all have a different opinion *or* view on the matter; **avoir les idées larges/étroites** to be broad-/narrow-minded; **combattre pour ses idées** to fight for one's ideas

(d) (*esprit*) **ça ne m'est jamais venu à l'i.** it's never occurred to me, it's never entered my head *or* mind; **elle n'est pas bien ici? ça ne m'était même pas venu à l'i.** she's not happy here? the possibility never even crossed my mind; **il ne me viendrait pas à l'i. de le lui reprocher** it wouldn't occur to me to reproach him for it; **il me vient à l'i. que ...** it occurs to me that ...; **j'ai dans l'i. que ...** I have an idea that ...; **elle a dans l'i. d'ouvrir un magasin** she's thinking of opening a shop; **je ne peux pas lui ôter cela de l'i.** I can't get it out of his mind *or* head; **on ne m'ôtera pas de l'i. que c'est elle qui a volé le sac** you won't get me to believe that it wasn't her who stole the bag; **se mettre dans l'i. que ...** to get it into one's head that ...; **il s'est mis dans l'i. de repeindre la cuisine en bleu** he got it into his head to repaint the kitchen blue; **cela m'était sorti de l'i.** it had gone right out *or* clean out of my mind *or* head; **il me revient à l'i. que ...** now I remember that ...

(e) (*goût, avis*) **agir à son i.** to act as one likes; **fais à ton i.** do as you like; **elle n'en fait qu'à son i.** she does just as she likes; **elle n'agit qu'à son i.** she acts just as she likes; **à ton i., je me coupe les cheveux?** you think I should cut my hair?; **changer d'i.** to change one's mind

(f) (*suggestion*) **i.-...** ... -idea; **des idées-vacances/-cadeaux** holiday/gift ideas; **ce livret contient des idées-repas** this booklet offers ideas for meals; **une i.-rangement astucieuse** a clever storage idea

▶ **idée: i. fixe** obsession, idée fixe; **i. reçue** generally accepted idea; **idées noires** gloomy *or* black thoughts

idem [idɛm] *adv* idem, ditto; *F* **je suis venu en voiture et lui i.** I came by car and so did he *or* and he did too; *F* **je veux une glace à la fraise – i. pour moi** I'd like a strawberry ice cream – me too *or* the same for me

identifiable [idɑ̃tifjabl] *adj* identifiable

identificateur [idɑ̃tifikatœr] *nm Ordinat* identifier; *Mktg* **i. de marque** brand identifier

identification [idɑ̃tifikasjɔ̃] *nf* identification **(avec, à** with); *Méd* **i. des types (de bactéries/de virus)** typing (of bacteria/viruses); *Ordinat* **i. de l'utilisateur** user identification; *Mktg* **i. de marque** brand recognition

identifier [idɑ̃tifje] **1** *vt* (*confondre*) to identify **(avec, à** with); (*reconnaître*) to identify; **i. des empreintes digitales** to identify fingerprints **2 s'identifier** *vpr* to identify (oneself), to become identified **(avec, à** with)

identique [idɑ̃tik] **1** *adj* identical; **je l'ai trouvé i. à lui-même** I found him the same as ever **2** *adv* **à l'i.** identically; **j'en ai fait un à l'i.** I made an identical one; **à l'i. de** identical to; **je fais refaire mon salon à l'i. du précédent** I'm having my lounge redecorated in exactly the same way as the last one

identiquement [idɑ̃tikmɑ̃] *adv* identically; **les candidats ont répondu i.** the candidates gave identical answers

identité [idɑ̃tite] *nf* identity; **bracelet d'i.** identity bracelet; *Admin* **carte d'i.** identity card; **papiers** *ou* **pièces d'i.** identity papers; **avez-vous une pièce d'i.?** do you have some identification *or F* ID?; **l'I. judiciaire** ≈ the Criminal Records Office; *Mktg* **i. graphique** logo

idéogramme [ideɔgram] *nm Ling* ideogram, ideograph

idéographie [ideɔgrafi] *nf Ling* ideography

idéographique [ideɔgrafik] *adj Ling* ideographic(al)

idéologie [ideɔlɔʒi] *nf* ideology

idéologique [ideɔlɔʒik] *adj* ideological

idéologue [ideɔlɔg] *n* ideologist, ideologue

idiolecte [idjɔlɛkt] *nm Ling* idiolect

idiomatique [idjɔmatik] *adj* **(①A3; B2)** *Ling* idiomatic; **expression i.** idiom; **utiliser des tournures idiomatiques** to speak/write idiomatically

idiome [idjom] *nm Ling* idiom

idiosyncrasie [idjɔsɛ̃krazi] *nf* idiosyncrasy

idiot, -ote [idjo, -ɔt] **1** *adj* idiotic, stupid; (*accident*) stupid, silly; *Méd* idiotic, imbecilic; **ce système n'est pas i. du tout** this system is pretty clever *or* smart; **si tu es assez i. pour le croire** if you're stupid enough to believe it; **tu as été i. de refuser son offre** you were stupid to refuse his offer; **ce serait i. de ne pas le faire** it would be stupid *or* idiotic not to; *Hum* **dis-moi son nom/comment faire, je ne veux pas mourir i.** tell me his name/how to do it or I'll die of suspense

2 *n* idiot, fool; *Méd* idiot, imbecile; *F* **l'i. du village** the village idiot; **faire l'i.** (*faire des bêtises*) to act *or* play the fool; (*feindre de ne pas comprendre*) to act stupid; **elle me prend pour un i.** she takes me for an idiot *or* a fool; **c'est loin d'être un i.** he's far from stupid

3 *adv F* **bronzer i.** to sunbathe like a moron

idiotement [idjɔtmɑ̃] *adv* idiotically, stupidly

idiotie [idjɔsi] *nf* **(a)** (*bêtise*) stupidity, idiocy; (*chose, parole idiote*) idiotic *or* stupid thing; **c'est de l'i. d'avoir fait ça** it's stupid *or* idiotic to have done that; **ne dites pas d'idioties!** don't talk rubbish *or* nonsense!; **faire une i.** to do something stupid *or* idiotic; **ne va pas voir cette i.!** don't go and see that rubbish! **(b)** *Méd* idiocy, imbecility, mental deficiency

idiotisme [idjɔtism] *nm Ling* idiom, idiomatic expression

idoine [idwan] *adj Arch, Hum, Jur* appropriate; *Jur* **apte et i. à tester** fit and competent to make a will

idolâtre [idɔlɑtr] **1** *adj* idolatrous **2** *n* idolater, *f* idolatress

idolâtrer [idɔlɑtre] *vt* (*qn*) to idolize; (*qch*) to be passionately fond of

idolâtrie [idɔlɑtri] *nf* idolatry

idolâtrique [idɔlɑtrik] *adj* idolatrous

idole [idɔl] *nf* idol; **il en a fait son i.** he idolized him; **c'est l'i. des jeunes** he's/she's a teenage idol

IDS [ideɛs] *nf Mil* (*abrév* **initiative de défense stratégique**) SDI

idylle [idil] *nf* (*aventure*) romance; *Littér* idyll

idyllique [idilik] *adj* idyllic

if [if] *nm* **(a)** (*arbre*) yew (tree) **(b)** (*pour bouteilles*) draining rack

IGF [iʒeɛf] *nm inv* (*abrév* **impôt sur les grandes fortunes**) wealth tax

igloo, iglou [iglu] *nm* igloo

igname [iɲam] *nf* yam

ignare [iɲar] **1** *adj* ignorant **2** *n* ignoramus

ignifugation [ignifygasjɔ̃] *nf* fireproofing

ignifuge [ignifyʒ] **1** *adj* non-(in)flammable, fireproof; (*qui retarde l'embrasement*) fire-resistant, flame-retardant **2** *nm* fireproof material

ignifugé [ignifyʒe] *adj* (*matériau*) fireproofed

ignifugeant [ignifyʒɑ̃] *adj* = **ignifuge 1**

ignifuger [ignifyʒe] *vt* **(j'ignifugeai(s); n. ignifugeons)** to fireproof

ignoble [iɲɔbl] *adj* **(a)** (*personne*) ignoble, base; (*conduite, attitude etc*) vile, disgraceful, unspeakable; **tu as vraiment été i. avec elle** you were really vile to her **(b)** (*habitation, quartier etc*) wretched, filthy

ignoblement [iɲɔbləmɑ̃] *adv* (*se conduire*) ignobly, basely, disgracefully; **une maison i. sale** a disgracefully dirty house

ignominie [iɲɔmini] *nf* **(a)** (*caractère*) ignominy, shame, disgrace; **se couvrir d'i.** to cover oneself in ignominy *or* shame, to bring ignominy *or* shame *or* disgrace upon oneself **(b)** (*action*) shameful *or* disgraceful action; **c'est une i.!** it's a disgrace!, it's shameful!; **s'abaisser aux pires ignominies** to stoop to the lowest kinds of behaviour

ignominieusement [iɲɔminjøzmɑ̃] *adv* ignominiously

ignominieux, -ieuse [iɲɔminjø, -jøz] *adj* (*conduite*) ignominious, shameful, disgraceful; (*vie, mort, destin*) ignominious; (*accusation*) shameful, disgraceful

ignorance [iɲɔrɑ̃s] *nf* **(a)** ignorance; **par i.** through *or* out of ignorance; **être/tenir qn dans l'i.** to be/keep sb in the dark; **être/tenir qn dans l'i. de qch** to be/keep sb in the dark about *or* in ignorance of sth; *F* **il est d'une i. crasse** he is incredibly ignorant **(b) ignorances** gaps in one's knowledge

ignorant, -ante [iɲɔrɑ̃, -ɑ̃t] **1** *adj* **(a)** (*inculte*) ignorant; **être i. en latin** not to know (any) Latin **(b)** (*non informé*) **i. de qch** ignorant *or* unaware of sth **2** *n* ignoramus; **faire l'i.** to pretend one doesn't know; **ne fais pas l'i., je suis sûr que c'est toi** don't pretend you don't know what I'm talking about *or* don't know anything about it, I'm sure it was you

ignoré [iɲɔre] *adj* unknown; (*négligé*) ignored; **vivre i.** to live in obscurity; **i. de** *ou* **par ses contemporains** unknown to his contemporaries; (*négligé*) ignored by his contemporaries

ignorer [iɲɔre] **1** *vt* **(a)** (*ne pas savoir*) not to know (about), to be ignorant *or* unaware of; **il ignore tout de ...** he knows nothing whatever about ...; **nul n'est censé i. la loi** ignorance of the law is no excuse; **je n'ignore pas les difficultés** I am not unaware *or* I'm well aware of the difficulties; **je n'ignore rien de ses activités** I'm perfectly well aware of what he's up to; **elle ignorait vous avoir blessé** she hadn't the least idea that she had hurt you; **elle ignore qui je suis** she doesn't know who I am; **i. que** + *sub or* + *ind* not to know that, to be unaware that; **il ignore que vous avez déjà travaillé** he doesn't know *or* he's unaware that you've already got work experience; **il ignorait que vous le connaissiez** he didn't know *or* wasn't aware (that) you knew him; *Litt* **il ignorait que nous fussions déjà arrivés** he was not aware that we had already arrived; **personne n'ignore que ...** everybody knows that ...; **j'ignorais si vous viendriez** I didn't know whether you would come; **j'ignore comment il est venu/où il habite** I don't know how he came/where he lives; **un fusil qu'il ignorait être chargé** a gun which he didn't know was loaded

(b) *(mépriser) (personne, conseil, panneau, interdiction etc)* to ignore

2 s'ignorer *vpr* **(a)** *(se mépriser l'un l'autre)* to ignore each other

(b) *(se méconnaître)* **c'est un artiste/un homosexuel qui s'ignore** he is unaware of his artistic talents/his homosexuality

iguane [igwan] *nm* iguana

il, *pl* **ils** [il] *pron pers* [①A26-7,a-c; B17,1; B63,2] **(a)** *(personne)* he; *(bébé, animal)* it, he; *(chose)* it; *(bateau, pays)* it, she; **ils** they; **sont-ils arrivés?** have they come?; **ton père a-t-il ouvert la bouteille?** has your father opened the bottle?

(b) *(interrogatif, emphatique)* **viendra-t-il?** will he come?; **ton père est-il toujours à l'hôpital?** is your father still in hospital?; **le lave-vaisselle est-il toujours en panne?** is the dishwasher still broken?; **qu'il est joli, ce foulard!** what a pretty scarf (that is)!; **ton cousin, il n'est pas prêt de me revoir** your cousin's not likely to see me again in a hurry

(c) [①A27,d,i; B27-8,E] *(impersonnel)* it; **il est/il doit être six heures** it is/it must be six o'clock; **il est facile de s'en assurer** it's easy to make sure; **il est vrai que j'étais là** it's true that I was there; **il était une fois une fée** once upon a time there was a fairy; **il pleut/neige** it's raining/snowing; **il faut partir** it's time to go, we must go; **il y a quelqu'un à la porte** there's someone at the door

île [il] *nf* island; **habiter dans une î.** to live on an island; **î. coralienne** coral island; **î. déserte** desert island; **l'Î de France** = greater Paris; **les îles Anglo-Normandes** the Channel Islands

▶ **île**: *Culin* **î. flottante** floating island

iléon [ileɔ̃] *nm Anat* ileum

Iliade (l') [iljad] *nf* the Iliad

iliaque [iljak] *adj Anat* iliac; **os i.** ilium

illégal, -ale, -aux, -ales [ilegal, -o] *adj* illegal, unlawful

illégalement [ilegalmɑ̃] *adv* illegally, unlawfully

illégalité [ilegalite] *nf (d'une action)* illegality, unlawfulness; **commettre une i.** to break the law; **vivre dans l'i.** to live outside the law; **être** *ou* **entrer dans l'i.** to break *or* flout the law; **ils ont fait tout cela dans la plus parfaite i.** they did all that in complete defiance of the law

illégitime [ileʒitim] *adj (enfant)* illegitimate; *(mariage)* unlawful; *(demande)* unwarranted; *(soupçons)* unfounded, groundless; **il était vraiment i. de ne pas lui faire confiance** it was completely unwarranted not to trust him

illégitimement [ileʒitim(ə)mɑ̃] *adv (hériter, bénéficier de qch)* illegitimately, unlawfully; *(se marier)* unlawfully; **faire un enfant i.** to have an illegitimate child

illégitimité [ileʒitimite] *nf (d'un enfant)* illegitimacy; *(d'un mariage)* unlawfulness; *(d'une demande)* unwarranted nature

illettré, -ée [iletre] **1** *adj* illiterate **2** *n* illiterate (person); **les illettrés** illiterate people

illettrisme [iletrism] *nm* illiteracy

illicite [ilisit] *adj* illicit, unlawful; *Sp* **coup i.** foul

illicitement [ilisitmɑ̃] *adv* illicitly, unlawfully

illico [iliko] *adv F* **i. (presto)** at once, pronto

illimité [ilimite] *adj (pouvoirs)* unlimited, limitless; *(moyens, fortune, crédit)* unlimited; *(empire)* limitless, boundless; *(confiance, mépris)* boundless, limitless, unbounded; **congé i.** indefinite leave

illisibilité [ilizibilite] *nf* illegibility

illisible [ilizibl] *adj* **(a)** *(qu'on ne peut pas déchiffrer)* illegible, unreadable; *Ordinat (fichier, disquette)* unreadable **(b)** *(qu'on ne peut pas comprendre)* unreadable

illisiblement [ilizibləmɑ̃] *adv* illegibly

illogique [ilɔʒik] *adj* illogical

illogiquement [ilɔʒikmɑ̃] *adv* illogically

illogisme [ilɔʒism] *nm* illogicality; **procéder de cette manière est un i.** to proceed like that is illogical

illumination [ilyminasjɔ̃] *nf* **(a)** *(action d'illuminer)* lighting up, illumination; **i. (par projecteurs)** floodlighting **(b)** *(lumière)* **illuminations** lights, illuminations **(c)** *(inspiration)* (flash of) inspiration; **j'ai eu une i.** I've had an inspiration *or* a brilliant idea

illuminé, -ée [ilymine] **1** *adj (éclairé)* lit up, illuminated; *(par projecteur)* floodlit **2** *n* visionary, *Péj* fanatic, *F* loony

illuminer [ilymine] **1** *vt* **(a)** *(éclairer)* to light up, to illuminate; *(par projecteur)* to floodlight; *Fig (visage, yeux)* to light up; **un superbe sourire illumina son visage** a radiant smile lit up his face; **une étrange lueur illuminait ses yeux** a strange glow lit up his eyes; **cette nouvelle a illuminé la journée** this news brightened up the day **(b)** *Rel, Phil* to enlighten **2 s'illuminer** *vpr* to light up **(de** with)

illusion [ilyzjɔ̃] *nf* illusion; **se nourrir d'illusions, se bercer d'illusions, se faire des illusions** to delude oneself, to live in a fool's paradise; **je ne me fais aucune i. sur ses intentions** I have no illusions about his intentions; **elle l'a entretenu dans cette i.** she encouraged him in this illusion; **ces paroles lui ont enlevé** *ou* **ôté toutes ses illusions** these words completely disillusioned him; **perdre ses illusions** to become disillusioned; **faire perdre ses illusions à qn** to disillusion sb; **donner des illusions à qn** to raise sb's hopes *or* expectations; **faire i.** to take people in, to delude people; **cela n'a pas fait i.** no-one was taken in; **cet éclairage donne une i. de lumière naturelle** the lighting gives an *or* the impression of natural light; **ces espoirs n'étaient qu'i.** the hopes were illusory

▶ **illusion**: *Phys* **i. d'optique** optical illusion

illusionner [ilyzjɔne] **1** *vt* to delude **2 s'illusionner** *vpr* to delude oneself, to deceive oneself **(sur** about)

illusionnisme [ilyzjɔnism] *nm* conjuring

illusionniste [ilyzjɔnist] *n* illusionist, conjurer

illusoire [ilyzwar] *adj* illusory, illusive

illusoirement [ilyzwarmɑ̃] *adv* illusorily

illustrateur, -trice [ilystratœr] *n* illustrator; *Journ* picture editor; *TV, Cin* **i. sonore** sound effects supervisor

illustration [ilystrasjɔ̃] *nf* **(a)** *(action)* illustration; *(dans l'édition)* picture editing **(b)** *(dessin)* illustration; **illustrations** *(dans l'édition)* artwork; **i. en couleur** coloured illustration; **l'i. du livre** the illustrations *or* the artwork in the book; **texte et illustrations de ...** text and illustrations by ...

illustre [ilystr] *adj* illustrious, renowned, famous; *Hum* **un i. inconnu** somebody no-one has ever heard of

illustré [ilystre] **1** *adj* illustrated; **abondamment i.** copiously illustrated **2** *nm* illustrated magazine; *(pour enfant)* comic

illustrer [ilystre] **1** *vt* **(a)** *(livre etc)* to illustrate; **illustré de nombreux exemples** illustrated with numerous examples **(b)** *Arch, Litt (rendre illustre)* to make illustrious **2 s'illustrer** *vpr (d'une personne)* to distinguish oneself **(par** by)

îlot [ilo] *nm (petite île)* islet, small island; *(groupe d'immeubles)* block of buildings; *Com* gondola; *Fig* **î. de verdure** island of greenery; *Fig* **î. de résistance** pocket of resistance

▶ **îlot**: **î. directionnel** *(sur une route)* traffic divider

îlotage [ilɔtaʒ] *nm* division of a town into blocks

ilote [ilɔt] *n Hist* Helot; *Fig Litt* slave

îlotier [ilɔtje] *nm* = community policeman

ILV [iɛlve] *nf (abrév* **information sur le lieu de vente)** point-of-sale information

image [imaʒ] *nf* **(a)** *(dans l'eau, dans un miroir etc)* reflection, image; *Cin (de la pellicule)* frame; *Cin, TV (sur l'écran)* picture; *Opt* **i. réelle/virtuelle** real/virtual image; *Cin, TV* **25 images par seconde** 25 frames per second; **nous avons le son mais pas l'i.** *ou* **pas les images** we've got the sound but no picture; **nous n'avons plus d'i.** the picture's gone; **à l'i.** on-camera; **être à l'i.** to be on camera; **images en direct** live pictures; **i. à l'écran** screen image; **soigner son image** to try hard to present one's image; **i. par i.** single frame

(b) *Fig* image; **l'i. de son père** the image of his father; **Dieu créa l'homme à son i.** God created man in his own image; **ils sont l'i. du bonheur/de la réussite** they are the picture of happiness/success; **donner une bonne/mauvaise i. de qch** to present a good/bad image of sth

(c) *(dessin)* picture; **livre d'images** picture book; **récit en images** pictorial record; **images pieuses** holy pictures; *Scol* **voici une i.** *(récompense)* ≈ here's a gold star; *Mktg* **images à compléter** picture completion

(d) *(représentation)* image, picture; **i. visuelle forte** strong visual image *or* picture *or* impression; **garder l'i. d'une personne en mémoire** to keep an image *or* a picture of sb in one's memory; **la première i. qui vient à l'esprit** the first image that comes to mind; **i. fidèle** truthful account; *Compta* true and fair view

(e) *Littér* image; **images** imagery; **il parle avec des images** he talks in images

▶ **image**: *TV, Cin* **i. animée** moving picture; *TV, Cin* **i. d'archives** stock shot, library shot; *TV, Cin* **i. arrêtée** hold frame; *Ordinat* **i. bitmap** bitmap image; *TV, Cin* **i. chassée** pushover wipe; *Ordinat* **i. digitalisée** digitized image; *TV, Cin* **i. divisée en quatre** quad split; *Mktg* **i. de l'entreprise** corporate image; *TV, Cin* **i. fixe** still frame, stop frame, photostill; **i. institutionnelle** corporate image; **i. de marque** (*d'un produit*) brand image; (*d'un homme politique, d'une société etc*) (public) image; **i. en négatif** negative image; *Mktg* **i. du produit** product image; **i. publique** public image; **images de synthèse** computer-generated images, CGI; *Ordinat* **i. vectorielle** outline image

imagé [imaʒe] *adj* (*style, langage*) vivid, full of imagery; (*expression*) vivid

imager [imaʒe] *vt* **(j'imageai(s); n. imageons)** *Litt* (*style, discours*) to colour, *US* to color

imagerie [imaʒri] *nf* **(a)** *Littér* imagery **(b)** *Com* colour *or US* color print trade; (*usine*) colour *or US* color print works **(c)** *Méd* **i. par résonance magnétique** magnetic resonance imaging

imageur [imaʒœr] *nm Ordinat* imager; **i. documentaire** document imager

imagier [imaʒje] *nm* **(a)** (*peintre*) painter; (*sculpteur*) sculptor, carver **(b)** (*dessinateur*) drawer of pictures **(c)** (*imprimeur*) colour *or US* color print maker; *Com* colour *or US* color print seller

imaginable [imaʒinabl] *adj* imaginable, conceivable; **cela n'était pas i. il y a quelques années** it was unimaginable *or* inconceivable a few years ago; **toutes les solutions possibles et imaginables** every conceivable solution, every solution imaginable

imaginaire [imaʒinɛr] **1** *adj* (*personnage, pays, animal etc*) imaginary; *Hum* **malade i.** hypochondriac **2** *nm* imagination; **toute cette histoire relève de l'i.** the whole story is a product of the imagination, the story is entirely imaginary

imaginatif, -ive [imaʒinatif, -iv] *adj* imaginative

imagination [imaʒinasjɔ̃] *nf* imagination; **faire preuve d'i.** to show some imagination; **avoir de l'i.** to have imagination, to be imaginative; **avoir une i. débordante** to have a very active imagination; **tu manques d'i.!** you have no imagination!; **tu as vraiment trop d'i.!** you imagine things!; **ces histoires sortent de son i.** these stories are a product *or Pej* figment of his imagination; **voir qch en i.** to see sth in one's mind's eye *or* in one's imagination; **vivre qch en i.** to experience sth in one's imagination

imaginer [imaʒine] **1** *vt* **(a)** (*inventer*) (*méthode, système, stratagème*) to devise, to think up; (*machine, dispositif*) to devise; **bien imaginé** well thought out; **j'imaginais que nous étions sur la lune** I pretended we were on the moon

(b) (*concevoir*) to imagine; **imaginez un peu mon étonnement** just imagine my surprise; **tu l'imagines avec des enfants!** just think of *or* imagine *or* picture him/her with children!; **j'imagine qu'il viendra vers 9 heures** he'll come about 9 o'clock I should think; **je n'imaginais pas que cela soit faisable** I didn't think it could be done; **tout ce qu'on peut i. de plus beau** the finest thing imaginable; **que vas-tu i. là?** how can you think such a thing?; **vous plaisantez, j'imagine** you must be joking!

2 s'imaginer *vpr* **(a)** (*croire à tort*) **elle s'imagine que tout le monde l'admire** she imagines *or* thinks (that) everyone admires her; **elle s'est imaginé qu'il allait tout lui dire** she imagined *or* got it into her head that he would tell her everything; **il s'imagine tout savoir** he thinks he knows everything

(b) (*se figurer*) to imagine; **tu t'imagines la tête qu'il va faire** you can imagine how he'll take it; **comme on peut se l'i.** as you can (well) imagine; **je m'imagine que je pars sur un bateau** I pretend that I'm sailing away; **je me l'imaginais bien plus grand** I imagined him much taller; **il est bien plus grand que je ne me l'imaginais** he's much taller than I imagined

(c) (*se voir*) to picture *or* see oneself; **je m'imagine sur la scène/à quarante ans** I can (just) picture *or* see myself on the stage/at forty

imago [imago] *n* imago

imam [imam] *nm*, **iman** [imɑ̃] *nm* imam

imbattable [ɛ̃batabl] *adj* (*champion*) invincible, unbeatable; (*record*) unbeatable, unbreakable; (*prix*) unbeatable

imbécile [ɛ̃besil] **1** *adj* idiotic, stupid; *Méd* imbecilic, idiotic **2** *n* idiot, fool, imbecile; *Méd* imbecile, idiot; **le premier i. venu vous dira cela** any fool will tell you that; **c'est un i. heureux** he's a bit simple-minded; **faire l'i.** (*faire des bêtises*) to play *or* act the fool; (*feindre de ne pas comprendre*) to act stupid

imbécilement [ɛ̃besilmɑ̃] *adv* idiotically, stupidly

imbécillité [ɛ̃besilite] *nf* **(a)** (*stupidité*) idiocy, stupidity; *Méd* imbecility, idiocy **(b)** (*parole, chose stupide*) idiotic *or* stupid thing; **dire des imbécillités** to talk nonsense *or* rubbish

imberbe [ɛ̃bɛrb] *adj* beardless

imbibé [ɛ̃bibe] *adj F* drunk

imbiber [ɛ̃bibe] **1** *vt* **i. qch (de qch)** to soak sth (in *or* with sth); **imbibé d'eau** saturated (with water); (*terrain*) waterlogged; **chiffon imbibé d'huile** oil-soaked rag **2 s'imbiber** *vpr* **(a)** to become soaked **(de** with) **(b)** *F* **s'i. d'alcool** to hit the bottle; **s'i. d'alcool pour oublier ses problèmes** to drown one's sorrows (in drink)

imbit(t)able [ɛ̃bitabl] *adj très F* unfathomable, incomprehensible

imbrication [ɛ̃brikasjɔ̃] *nf* (*de tuiles, d'écailles etc*) overlap(ping); *Ordinat* embedding; (*de commandes*) nesting; **se dépêtrer d'une i. de problèmes** to extricate oneself from a mesh *or* web of problems; **je ne m'y retrouve pas dans cette i. de personnages** I can't get my bearings in this complex web of characters

imbriqué [ɛ̃brike] *adj Ordinat* embedded; (*commande*) nested

imbriquer [ɛ̃brike] **1** *vt* to overlap; *Ordinat* to embed; (*commandes*) to nest **2 s'imbriquer** *vpr* (*de tuiles, d'écailles etc*) to overlap; (*de questions, problèmes, situations*) to be interwoven; **tous ces problèmes s'imbriquent les uns dans les autres** all these problems are interwoven

imbroglio [ɛ̃brɔljo] *nm* imbroglio

imbu [ɛ̃by] *adj* **i. de sa personne** *ou* **de soi-même** full of one's own importance *or* of oneself

imbuvable [ɛ̃byvabl] *adj* undrinkable; *Fig* (*personne*) insufferable, unbearable

imitable [imitabl] *adj* imitable; **sa voix est facilement i.** his voice is easy to imitate *or* easily imitated

imitateur, -trice [imitatœr, -tris] **1** *n* imitator; *Th* impersonator **2** *adj* imitative

imitatif, -ive [imitatif, -iv] *adj* imitative

imitation [imitasjɔ̃] *nf* **(a)** (*fait de copier*) (*de produit, style etc*) imitation, imitating, copying; **à l'i. de qn/qch** in imitation of sb/sth **(b)** (*de personne*) imitation, mimicking, mimicry; *Th* impersonation; (*de cri d'animal, de chant d'oiseau*) imitation; **elle fait d'excellentes imitations** she does excellent imitations, she is an excellent mimic **(c)** (*de signature, de papier officiel etc*) forgery, forging; (*d'argent*) counterfeiting **(d)** (*copie*) imitation, copy; **bijoux en i. argent** imitation silver jewellery; **manteau (en) i. loutre** imitation sealskin coat; *Péj* **une pâle i.** a pale imitation

imiter [imite] *vt* (*personne*) to imitate, to mimic, *F* to take off; *Th* to impersonate; (*faire comme*) to imitate, to copy; (*cri d'animal, chant d'oiseau*) to imitate; (*style*) to imitate, to copy; (*signature*) to forge; (*money*) to counterfeit; **il leva son verre et tout le monde l'imita** he raised his glass and everyone followed suit *or* did the same; **matière qui imite le cuir/le bois** material that simulates leather/wood; **je voudrais une table qui imite celle des bistrots parisiens** I'd like a table that looks like those used in Parisian cafés

immaculé [imakyle] *adj* (*draps, linge, blanc*) spotless, immaculate; (*réputation*) spotless; *Rel* **l'Immaculée Conception** the Immaculate Conception

immanence [imanɑ̃s] *nf* immanence

immanent [imanɑ̃] *adj* immanent; **justice immanente** divine retribution

immangeable [ɛ̃mɑ̃ʒabl] *adj* inedible, uneatable

immanquable [ɛ̃mɑ̃kabl] *adj* (*événement, conséquence etc*) inevitable; *Vieilli* (*moyen, astuce etc*) infallible

immanquablement [ɛ̃mɑ̃kabləmɑ̃] *adv* inevitably, without fail

immatérialité [imaterjalite] *nf Phil* immateriality

immatériel, -ielle [imaterjɛl] *adj Phil* immaterial; *Fin* (*actif*) intangible; *Litt* (*pâleur, minceur etc*) ethereal

immatriculation [imatrikylasjɔ̃] *nf* (*d'acte, de voiture etc*) registration, registering; (*d'étudiant*) registration, enrolment; (*à la Sécurité Sociale*) registration **(à** with); **numéro d'i.** registration number

immatriculer [imatrikyle] *vt* (*document, voiture etc*) to register; (*étudiant*) to register, to enrol; (*à la Sécurité Sociale*) to register **(à** with); **voiture immatriculée SPF 342 T/dans le Var** car with the registration number SPF 342 T/with a Var number plate *or Am* license plate; *Com* **i. des marchandises** to register goods

immature [imatyr] *adj* immature

immaturité [imatyrite] *nf* immaturity

immédiat [imedja] **1** *adj* **(a)** (*cause, successeur etc*) immediate, direct; (*sentiment*) direct; *Ch* **analyse immédiate** proximate analysis **(b)** (*proximité*) close; **être en contact i. avec le feu/le patron** to be in direct contact with the fire/the boss **(c)** (*dans le temps*) (*changement*) immediate, instant; (*résultat*) immediate; **la mort a été immédiate** death was instantaneous;

(mécanisme) à action immédiate quick-acting (mechanism) **2** *nm* **dans l'i.** for the moment, for the time being
immédiatement [imedjatmɑ̃] *adv* immediately
immédiateté [imedjat(ə)te] *nf Phil* immediacy
immémorial, -ale, -aux, -ales [imemɔrjal, -o] *adj Litt* age-old; **de temps i.** from *or* since time immemorial; **en des temps immémoriaux** in ancient times
immense [imɑ̃s] *adj* (*maison, forêt, foule etc*) immense, vast, huge; (*tâche, sacrifice*) huge, immense; (*joie, soulagement*) tremendous, great; (*succès*) huge, great; **c'est un i. acteur/écrivain** he's a tremendous *or* great actor/writer
immensément [imɑ̃semɑ̃] *adv* **i. grand/riche/généreux** immensely big/rich/generous; **ce cadeau me fait i. plaisir** this gift gives me tremendous *or* great pleasure, this gift pleases me greatly; **j'ai eu i. peur** I was terribly afraid
immensité [imɑ̃site] *nf* (*de parc, maison etc*) vastness, hugeness, immenseness; (*de tâche*) immensity, hugeness; **les yeux perdus dans l'i.** gazing into the far distance *or* into space
immergé [imɛrʒe] *adj* submerged; **plante immergée** aquatic plant; **bateau i. par 200 mètres de fond** boat lying 200 metres under(water)
immerger [imɛrʒe] **(j'immergeai(s); n. immergeons) 1** *vt* to immerse, to submerge (**dans** in); (*câble*) to lay underwater; (*déchets*) to get rid of *or* dispose of *or* dump at sea; (*mort*) to bury at sea **2 s'immerger** *vpr* (*d'un sous-marin*) to submerge, to dive
immérité [imerite] *adj* unmerited, undeserved
immersion [imɛrsjɔ̃] *nf* immersion; (*de câble*) laying underwater; (*de déchets*) disposal *or* dumping at sea; (*d'un sous-marin*) submersion, submergence; (*de mort*) burial at sea
immettable [ɛ̃mɛtabl] *adj* unwearable
immeuble [imœbl] **1** *nm* **(a)** (*bâtiment*) building; (*de bureaux*) office block; (*d'appartements*) block of flats, *Am* apartment block; **i. de 10 étages** 10-storey building; **i. de rapport, i. locatif** rental property **(b)** *Jur* real estate **2** *adj Jur* real, fixed; **biens immeubles** real estate
immigrant, -ante [imigrɑ̃, -ɑ̃t] *adj, n* immigrant; *Can* **i. reçu** landed immigrant
immigration [imigrasjɔ̃] *nf* immigration; **agent du service de l'i.** immigration officer
immigré, -ée [imigre] *adj, n* immigrant
immigrer [imigre] *vi* to immigrate; **i. en Europe/aux États-Unis** to immigrate to Europe/the United States
imminence [iminɑ̃s] *nf* imminence
imminent [iminɑ̃] *adj* imminent, impending; **être i.** to be imminent
immiscer (s') [simise] *vpr* **(je m'immisçai(s); n. n. immisçons)** to interfere, to meddle (**dans** in); **il faut toujours qu'elle s'immisce dans les conversations** she always has to interrupt
immixtion [imikstjɔ̃] *nf* interference, meddling (**dans** in)
immobile [imɔbil] *adj* **(a)** (*personne, mer etc*) motionless, still; (*pièce de machine*) fixed, immobile; (*visage*) immobile, set; **rester complètement i.** to remain totally still **(b)** *Fig* (*institution, dogme etc*) unchanging, changeless
immobilier, -ière [imɔbilje, -jɛr] *Jur, Com* **1** *adj* property, real-estate; **biens immobiliers** real estate, *esp Am* realty; **vente immobilière** sale of property; **société immobilière** property company; **agence immobilière** estate agency, *Am* real estate office; **agent i.** estate agent, *Am* real estate agent, realtor **2** *nm* real estate, property, *Am* realty; **i. de loisir** holiday property
immobilisation [imɔbilizasjɔ̃] *nf* **(a)** (*fait de ne plus bouger*) immobilization; **l'i. du malade est essentielle** it is essential to immobilize the patient; **attendre l'i. complète du train** wait until the train comes to a complete stop *or* standstill
(b) *Jur* conversion into real estate
(c) *Fin* (*de capital*) locking up, tying up, immobilization
(d) *Compta* asset; **immobilisations** fixed *or* capital assets; **i. de capitaux** tied-up capital, capital assets; **immobilisations corporelles** tangible fixed assets; **immobilisations financières** long-term investments; **immobilisations incorporelles** intangible fixed assets; **immobilisations non financières** physical fixed assets
immobiliser [imɔbilize] **1** *vt* **(a)** (*rendre immobile*) (*blessé*) to immobilize; (*train*) to bring to a standstill; **i. un véhicule** (*avec sabot*) to clamp a vehicle **(b)** *Jur* to convert into real estate **(c)** *Fin* (*capital*) to lock up, to tie up, to immobilize; *Fin* **i. des actifs** to freeze assets **2** *vpr* **s'immobiliser** (*d'un véhicule*) to come to a stop *or* a standstill; (*d'un corps en mouvement*) to come to rest
immobilisme [imɔbilism] *nm* opposition to progress, ultra-conservatism
immobiliste [imɔbilist] **1** *adj* opposed to progress, ultra-conservative **2** *n* ultra-conservative
immobilité [imɔbilite] *nf* (*d'un animal, de l'eau, des feuilles, des arbres etc*) stillness, motionlessness; (*d'un visage*) immobility; **être condamné à l'i. pour une semaine** (*d'un malade*) to be kept immobile for a week
immodération [imɔderasjɔ̃] *nf* immoderation, immoderateness
immodéré [imɔdere] *adj* immoderate, excessive, inordinate
immodérément [imɔderemɑ̃] *adv* immoderately, excessively, inordinately
immodeste [imɔdɛst] *adj Vieilli* immodest
immodestement [imɔdɛstəmɑ̃] *adv Vieilli* immodestly
immodestie [imɔdɛsti] *nf Vieilli* immodesty
immolateur [imɔlatœr] *nm Arch, Litt* immolator, sacrificer
immolation [imɔlasjɔ̃] *nf Litt* immolation, sacrifice
immoler [imɔle] *Litt* **1** *vt* to immolate, to sacrifice **2 s'immoler** *vpr* to immolate *or* sacrifice oneself; **s'i. par le feu** to die by setting fire to oneself
immonde [imɔ̃d] *adj* **(a)** (*sale*) (*quartier, maison etc*) foul, filthy, vile **(b)** (*ignoble*) (*acte, comportement etc*) foul, vile **(c)** (*laid*) (*personne, objet*) vile **(d)** *Rel* unclean
immondices [imɔ̃dis] *nfpl* refuse, rubbish
immoral, -ale, -aux, -ales [imɔral, -o] *adj* immoral
immoralement [imɔralmɑ̃] *adv* immorally
immoralisme [imɔralism] *nm Phil* immoralism
immoraliste [imɔralist] *adj, n Phil* immoralist
immoralité [imɔralite] *nf* immorality
immortaliser [imɔrtalize] **1** *vt* to immortalize **2 s'immortaliser** *vpr* to gain immortality, to win everlasting fame (**par** through, with)
immortalité [imɔrtalite] *nf* immortality; **entrer dans l'i.** to gain immortality, to win everlasting fame
immortel, -elle [imɔrtɛl] **1** *adj* (*dieu, être*) immortal; (*réputation, amour etc*) everlasting, undying **2** *n* (*membre de l'Académie française*) member of the Académie Française **3** *nf* **immortelle** (*plante*) everlasting (flower), immortelle
immotivé [imɔtive] *adj* (*action, renvoi*) unmotivated; (*peur*) groundless, baseless
immuabilité [imɥabilite] *nf* immutability
immuable [imɥabl] *adj* (*vérité*) unchanging, immutable; (*passion*) undying; (*opinion*) fixed, set; (*sourire*) fixed, perpetual
immuablement [imɥabləmɑ̃] *adv* immutably, unalterably, perpetually
immun [imœ̃] *adj* immune
immunisant [imynizɑ̃] *adj* immunizing
immunisation [imynizasjɔ̃] *nf Méd* immunization
immuniser [imynize] *vt Méd* to immunize; **être immunisé contre qch** *Méd* to be immunized against sth; *Fig* to be immune to *or* from sth; *Fig* **je suis immunisé** I'm immune
immunitaire [imynitɛr] *adj Méd* **système i.** immune system; **réactions immunitaires** immune reactions *or* responses; **défenses immunitaires** immune defences
immunité [imynite] *nf* immunity; **i. parlementaire** parliamentary privilege *or* immunity; **i. diplomatique** diplomatic immunity; **i. naturelle/acquise** natural/acquired immunity
immunodéficience [imynɔdefisjɑ̃s] *nf Méd* immunodeficiency
immunodéficitaire [imynɔdefisitɛr] *adj Méd* immunodeficient
immunodépresseur [imynɔdeprɛsœr] *adj, nm Méd* immunosuppressive
immunodépressif, -ive [imynɔdeprɛsif -iv] *adj Méd* immunosuppressive
immunodéprimé, -ée [imynɔdeprime] *Méd* **1** *adj* with a weakened immune system **2** *n* person with a weakened immune system
immunogène [imynɔʒɛn] *adj Méd* immunogenic
immunoglobuline [imynɔglɔbylin] *nf Méd* immunoglobulin
immunologie [imynɔlɔʒi] *nf* immunology
immunologique [imynɔlɔʒik] *adj* immunological
immunologiste [imynɔlɔʒist] *n* immunologist
immunosuppresseur [imynɔsyprɛsœr] *nm Méd* immunosuppressive, immunosuppressant
immunothérapie [imynɔterapi] *nf Méd* immunotherapy
immutabilité [imytabilite] *nf* immutability
impact [ɛ̃pakt] *nm* impact; *Fig* **avoir un i. sur qch** to have an impact on sth, to impact on sth; **point d'i.** point of impact; **étude d'i.** impact study; **i. sur les ventes** sales impact, impact on sales
impair [ɛ̃pɛr] **1** *adj* (*nombre, fonction etc*) odd, uneven; (*jour*) odd; (*côté de la rue*) odd-numbered; (*vers*) with an uneven number of syllables; (*organe*) unpaired; **2** *nm* **(a)** (*aux jeux*) odd numbers **(b)** (*gaffe*) blunder; **faire** *ou* **commettre un i.** to make a blunder, *F* to put one's foot in it
impala [ɛ̃pala] *nm* impala
impalpable [ɛ̃palpabl] *adj* impalpable, intangible

impaludation [ɛ̃palydasjɔ̃] *nf* infection with the malaria virus

impaludé [ɛ̃palyde] *adj (personne)* suffering from malaria; *(région)* infected with malaria

imparable [ɛ̃parabl] *adj (tir, coup, botte etc)* unstoppable; *Fig (argument, logique)* irrefutable, unanswerable

impardonnable [ɛ̃pardɔnabl] *adj* unforgivable, unpardonable; **il serait i. de ne pas les aider** it would be unforgivable not to help them; **c'est vraiment i. d'avoir oublié l'anniversaire de ta femme** it's really unforgivable of you to have forgotten your wife's birthday; **j'ai encore pris votre parapluie, je suis i.** I've taken your umbrella again, I'm hopeless

imparfait [ɛ̃parfɛ] **1** *adj* **(a)** *Litt (qui n'est pas achevé)* unfinished, uncompleted; **avoir une connaissance imparfaite de qch** to have an imperfect knowledge of sth **(b)** *(qui a des défauts)* imperfect, defective **2** *nm* [①**B28**,F,2] *Gram* imperfect (tense); **à l'i.** in the imperfect (tense)

imparfaitement [ɛ̃parfɛtmɑ̃] *adv* imperfectly

impartial, -iale, -iaux, -iales [ɛ̃parsjal, -jo] *adj* impartial, unbias(s)ed

impartialement [ɛ̃parsjalmɑ̃] *adv* impartially, without bias

impartialité [ɛ̃parsjalite] *nf* impartiality, lack of bias

impartir [ɛ̃partir] *vt Jur, Litt (droit, faveur)* to grant (**à** to); *(tâche)* to assign (**à** to); *(don)* to bestow (**à** on); **délai imparti** time limit, time allowed; **le temps qui vous est imparti** the time allotted to you

impasse [ɛ̃pas] *nf* **(a)** *(cul-de-sac)* dead end, cul-de-sac; *(sur panneau)* no through road

(b) *Fig* impasse, deadlock; **être** *ou* **se trouver dans une i.** to be at a dead end; **il faut sortir de l'i.** the deadlock has to be broken; **les négociations sont dans l'i.** the talks have reached an impasse *or* a deadlock *or* are deadlocked; **aboutir à une i.** to reach an impasse

(c) *Fin Vieilli* **i. budgétaire** budget deficit

(d) *Cartes* **faire une i.** to finesse; **faire l'i. au roi** to finesse against the king; *Scol* **faire une i. sur un sujet** to give a subject a miss when revising for an exam; **j'ai fait (l')i. sur le Japon en géographie** I gave Japan a miss in my geography revision

impassibilité [ɛ̃pasibilite] *nf* impassiveness, impassivity

impassible [ɛ̃pasibl] *adj* impassive

impassiblement [ɛ̃pasibləmɑ̃] *adv* impassively

impatiemment [ɛ̃pasjamɑ̃] *adv* impatiently

impatience [ɛ̃pasjɑ̃s] *nf* **(a)** impatience; **avec i.** impatiently; **montrer des signes d'i.** to show signs of impatience; **elle brûle d'i. de te le dire** she's dying to tell you; **avoir une grande i.** *ou* **être dans l'i. de faire qch** to be really impatient to do sth **(b)** *Litt* **impatiences** fits of impatience

impatient, -ente [ɛ̃pasjɑ̃, -ɑ̃t] **1** *adj* impatient; **d'un air i.** impatiently; **être i. de faire qch** to be impatient *or* eager to do sth; **être i. avec qn** to be impatient with sb **2** *nf (plante)* **impatiente** Busy Lizzie, *Spéc* impatiens

impatienter [ɛ̃pasjɑ̃te] **1** *vt (qn)* to annoy, to irritate; **tes questions m'impatientent** I'm getting impatient with your questions, you're annoying *or* irritating me with your questions **2 s'impatienter** *vpr* to get impatient, to lose patience (**de qch** at sth; **contre** *ou* **avec qn** with sb)

impavide [ɛ̃pavid] *adj Fml* composed, unruffled, impassive

impayable [ɛ̃pɛjabl] *adj F (blague, histoire etc)* priceless; **elle est i.!** she's priceless!, she's a scream!

impayé, -ée [ɛ̃peje] **1** *adj (dette, facture)* unpaid; *(paiement)* outstanding **2** *nm* outstanding payment; **j'ai un tas d'impayés** I've got a stack of unpaid bills

impec [ɛ̃pɛk] *adj, adv F* = **impeccable**

impeccable [ɛ̃pɛkabl] **1** *adj (propre) (costume, personne, chambre, voiture)* impeccable; *(parfait) (traduction, voiture, repassage)* impeccable, perfect; **un travail i.** an impeccable *or* a perfect piece of work; **d'une propreté i.** impeccably clean **2** *adv F* **i.!** great!

impeccablement [ɛ̃pɛkabləmɑ̃] *adv* impeccably

impécunieux, -euse [ɛ̃pekynjø, -øz] *adj Litt* impecunious

impédance [ɛ̃pedɑ̃s] *nf Él* impedance

impedimenta [ɛ̃pedimɛ̃ta] *nmpl* impedimenta

impénétrabilité [ɛ̃penetrabilite] *nf* **(a)** *(densité) (d'une forêt)* impenetrability; *(à l'eau)* imperviousness **(b)** *(mystère)* inscrutability

impénétrable [ɛ̃penetrabl] *adj* **(a)** *(forêt, citadelle, murs etc)* impenetrable; **i. à l'eau** impervious to water **(b)** *(visage, caractère)* inscrutable; *(mystère, secret, énigme)* unfathomable, impenetrable; *(texte)* impenetrable; **prendre un air i.** to adopt an inscrutable air; **les voies du Seigneur sont impénétrables** God works in a mysterious way

impénitence [ɛ̃penitɑ̃s] *nf Rel* impenitence

impénitent [ɛ̃penitɑ̃] *adj Rel* impenitent, unrepentant; *Fig* **un fumeur/buveur i.** an unrepentant *or* a confirmed smoker/drinker

impensable [ɛ̃pɑ̃sabl] *adj* unthinkable, inconceivable; **il est i. de faire/que ...** it's unthinkable *or* inconceivable to do/that ...

impense [ɛ̃pɑ̃s] *nf Fin* property improvement expense

imper [ɛ̃pɛr] *nm F* (= **imperméable**) raincoat, *Br* mac(k)

impératif, -ive [ɛ̃peratif, -iv] **1** *adj (ton, geste etc)* imperious, imperative, peremptory; *(nécessité, besoin)* imperative; *Jur (loi, disposition)* mandatory; **il est i. de connaître l'anglais pour ce poste** it is imperative to know English for this post **2** *nm* **(a)** *(exigence)* requirement; **savoir nager est un i.** it is essential to be able to swim; **les impératifs de la mode** the dictates *or* demands of fashion; *Hum* **ce sont les impératifs du direct** that's what you have to contend with when you're broadcasting live **(b)** [①**A39**,8; **B32**,4] *Gram* imperative (mood); **à l'i.** in the imperative (mood)

impérativement [ɛ̃perativmɑ̃] *adv* imperatively; **il faut i. que je la voie** it is imperative that I see her

impératrice [ɛ̃peratris] *nf* empress

imperceptibilité [ɛ̃pɛrsɛptibilite] *nf* imperceptibility

imperceptible [ɛ̃pɛrsɛptibl] *adj* imperceptible; **i. par l'oreille humaine** imperceptible to the human ear; **elle eut un sourire i.** she gave a barely perceptible smile

imperceptiblement [ɛ̃pɛrsɛptibləmɑ̃] *adv* imperceptibly; **sourire i.** to give a barely perceptible smile

imperdable [ɛ̃pɛrdabl] *adj* **le match/le procès est i.** the match/the case can't be lost; **le match est i. pour la France** France can't lose

imperfectible [ɛ̃pɛrfɛktibl] *adj* that cannot be perfected, imperfectible

imperfectif, -ive [ɛ̃pɛrfɛktif, -iv] *adj Gram* imperfective

imperfection [ɛ̃pɛrfɛksjɔ̃] *nf (état imparfait)* imperfection; *(défaut) (de texte)* imperfection, flaw; *(de peau)* imperfection, blemish; *(de prototype)* imperfection, defect, fault; *(d'une personne)* shortcoming, failing, fault

impérial, -ale, -aux, -ales [ɛ̃perjal, -o] **1** *adj* **(a)** *(relatif à l'empire)* imperial; **prendre un air i.** to adopt an imperial *or* a magisterial air **(b)** *(de qualité supérieure)* imperial **2** *nf* **impériale (a)** *(de bus, wagon etc)* top (deck), upper deck; **autobus à i.** doubledecker (bus) **(b)** *(barbe)* imperial

impérialement [ɛ̃perjalmɑ̃] *adv* imperially

impérialisme [ɛ̃perjalism] *nm* imperialism

impérialiste [ɛ̃perjalist] **1** *adj* imperialist(ic) **2** *n* imperialist

impérieusement [ɛ̃perjøzmɑ̃] *adv* **(a)** *(avec autorité)* imperiously **(b)** *(de façon pressante)* urgently; **il a i. besoin de manger** he is urgently in need of *or* urgently needs something to eat

impérieux, -euse [ɛ̃perjø, -øz] *adj* **(a)** *(autoritaire)* imperious, domineering **(b)** *(impératif) (nécessité, désir etc)* urgent, pressing; **j'ai un besoin i. de voir le patron** I need to see the boss urgently

impérissable [ɛ̃perisabl] *adj (œuvre)* imperishable; *(gloire)* everlasting, eternal; *(vérité, valeur)* eternal, imperishable; *(souvenir)* unforgettable, enduring, indelible; **cette aventure lui a laissé un souvenir i.** this adventure made an unforgettable impression on him *or* stayed in his mind forever; **ce film/mec ne me laissera pas un souvenir i.** that film's/guy's pretty forgettable

imperméabilisant [ɛ̃pɛrmeabilizɑ̃] **1** *adj* waterproofing **2** *nm* waterproofing agent

imperméabilisation [ɛ̃pɛrmeabilizasjɔ̃] *nf* waterproofing

imperméabiliser [ɛ̃pɛrmeabilize] *vt* to waterproof

imperméabilité [ɛ̃pɛrmeabilite] *nf* impermeability; *Fig* imperviousness (**à** to)

imperméable [ɛ̃pɛrmeabl] **1** *adj* impermeable; *Fig* impervious (**à** to); **i. (à l'eau)** waterproof; **i. à la poussière** dustproof; *Fig* **être i. à la critique** to be impervious to criticism **2** *nm* raincoat, *Br* mackintosh

impersonnalité [ɛ̃pɛrsɔnalite] *nf* impersonality

impersonnel, -elle [ɛ̃pɛrsɔnɛl] *adj* [①**A27**,d; **B27-8**,E] impersonal

impersonnellement [ɛ̃pɛrsɔnɛlmɑ̃] *adv* impersonally

impertinemment [ɛ̃pɛrtinamɑ̃] *adv* impertinently

impertinence [ɛ̃pɛrtinɑ̃s] *nf* impertinence; **dire des impertinences à qn** to speak impertinently to sb; **répondre avec i.** to answer impertinently

impertinent, -ente [ɛ̃pɛrtinɑ̃, -ɑ̃t] **1** *adj* impertinent **2** *n* impertinent person; **un petit i.** an impertinent little boy

imperturbabilité [ɛ̃pɛrtyrbabilite] *nf* imperturbability

imperturbable [ɛ̃pɛrtyrbabl] *adj (personne)* imperturbable; *(optimisme)* unshakeable; **il restait i.** he remained impassive *or* unruffled

imperturbablement [ɛ̃pɛrtyrbabləmɑ̃] *adv* imperturbably

impétigo [ɛ̃petigo] *nm Méd* impetigo

impétueusement [ɛ̃petɥøzmɑ̃] *adv Litt* impetuously

impétueux, -euse [ɛ̃petɥø, -øz] *adj* **(a)** *(fougueux) (personne)*

impetuous, hotheaded, impulsive; (*tempérament*) fiery; (*amour*) impetuous **(b)** *Litt* (*torrent, flot etc*) raging, wild
impétuosité [ɛ̃petɥozite] *nf* **(a)** (*fougue*) impetuosity, impetuousness **(b)** *Litt* **l'i. du torrent/des flots** the raging *or* wild torrent/waves
impie [ɛ̃pi] **1** *adj* impious, ungodly **2** *n* impious *or* ungodly person
impiété [ɛ̃pjete] *nf* **(a)** (*caractère impie*) impiety, ungodliness **(b)** (*acte, parole impie*) impiety
impitoyable [ɛ̃pitwajabl] *adj* pitiless, merciless, ruthless **(envers, pour** towards)
impitoyablement [ɛ̃pitwajabləmɑ̃] *adv* pitilessly, mercilessly, ruthlessly
implacable [ɛ̃plakabl] *adj* (*personne*) implacable, unrelenting; (*haine, vengeance, logique*) implacable; (*avancée*) relentless
implacablement [ɛ̃plakabləmɑ̃] *adv* implacably; (*avancer*) relentlessly
implant [ɛ̃plɑ̃] *nm* **(a)** *Méd* implant; **i. dentaire** dental implant; **implants capillaires** hair graft; **il s'est fait faire des implants** he had a hair graft **(b)** (*bureau de voyages*) in-house travel agency, *Am* in-plant agency
implantation [ɛ̃plɑ̃tasjɔ̃] *nf* (*d'un système, d'une mode, d'une coutume*) introduction; (*d'une industrie, d'une filiale, d'un parti politique etc*) setting up, establishment; *Méd* implantation; (*des cheveux, des dents*) line; **i. commerciale** business operation
implanter [ɛ̃plɑ̃te] **1** *vt* (*système, mode, coutume*) to introduce; (*idée*) to implant; (*industrie, filiale, parti politique etc*) to set up, to establish; *Méd* to implant; **cette habitude est bien implantée chez eux** this habit is well established with them; **solidement implanté** (*croyance*) firmly established **2 s'implanter** *vpr* (*d'un usage, d'un sport, d'un parti etc*) to become established; (*d'une société, d'une industrie*) to set up, to become established **(dans** in); **s'i. à l'étranger** to set up overseas
implémentation [ɛ̃plemɑ̃tasjɔ̃] *nf Ordinat* implementation
implémenter [ɛ̃plemɑ̃te] *vt Ordinat* to implement
implication [ɛ̃plikasjɔ̃] *nf* **(a)** (*engagement*) involvement; *Jur* implication **(dans** in) **(b) implications** (*conséquences*) implications
implicite [ɛ̃plisit] *adj* implicit, implied
implicitement [ɛ̃plisitmɑ̃] *adv* implicitly
impliquer [ɛ̃plike] **1** *vt* **(a)** (*compromettre*) to implicate **(dans** in); **véhicule impliqué (dans un accident)** vehicle involved (in an accident)

(b) (*entraîner*) to involve, to entail, to mean; **la carrière de chanteur implique de nombreux déplacements** a singing career involves *or* entails *or* means a lot of travelling; **s'occuper d'enfants implique d'être très disponible** looking after children means having a lot of free time; **i. que ...** + *ind* to imply that ...; **je n'implique pas que vous deviez vous sentir responsable** I'm not implying that you should feel responsible

(c) (*engager*) to involve **(dans** in)

2 s'impliquer *vpr* to become *or* get involved **(dans** in); **il s'est beaucoup impliqué** he became *or* got heavily *or* deeply involved
implorant [ɛ̃plɔrɑ̃] *adj* imploring; **d'un ton i.** imploringly
imploration [ɛ̃plɔrasjɔ̃] *nf* entreaty, plea; **i. de Dieu** entreaty *or* plea to God
implorer [ɛ̃plɔre] *vt* (*personne, Dieu, le Ciel*) to implore, to beseech, to entreat; **i. le pardon de qn** to beg sb's forgiveness; **i. qn du regard** to give sb an imploring look; **i. qn de faire qch** to implore *or* beseech *or* entreat sb to do sth
imploser [ɛ̃ploze] *vi* to implode
implosion [ɛ̃plozjɔ̃] *nf* implosion
impoli [ɛ̃pɔli] *adj* impolite, rude, *Fml* discourteous
impoliment [ɛ̃pɔlimɑ̃] *adv* impolitely, rudely, *Fml* discourteously
impolitesse [ɛ̃pɔlitɛs] *nf* **(a)** (*caractère impoli*) rudeness, impoliteness, *Fml* discourtesy; **avec i.** rudely, impolitely **(b)** (*acte*) impolite act, act of rudeness; (*remarque*) rude *or* impolite remark; **dire des impolitesses** to be impolite *or* rude, to say impolite things; **dire une i. à qn** to make an impolite *or* rude remark to sb, to say something impolite *or* rude to sb; **c'est une i. de quitter la table avant la fin du repas** it is impolite *or* rude to leave the table before the end of the meal
impolitique [ɛ̃pɔlitik] *adj* impolitic, ill-advised
impondérabilité [ɛ̃pɔ̃derabilite] *nf* imponderability
impondérable [ɛ̃pɔ̃derabl] **1** *adj* imponderable **2** *nmpl* **les impondérables** the imponderables
impopulaire [ɛ̃pɔpylɛr] *adj* unpopular
impopularité [ɛ̃pɔpylarite] *nf* unpopularity
import [ɛ̃pɔr] *nm* (*action d'importer*) import; *Ordinat* **i. de données** data import
importable[1] [ɛ̃pɔrtabl] *adj* (*marchandises*) importable
importable[2] *adj* (*vêtement*) unwearable
importance [ɛ̃pɔrtɑ̃s] *nf* **(a)** importance; **avoir de l'i.** to be important, to matter; **cela/elle a beaucoup d'i. pour moi** it's/she's very important to me, it/she matters a lot to me; **sans i.** unimportant; **c'est sans i.** it's not important, it doesn't matter; **cela n'a pas d'i.** it's not important, it doesn't matter, it's of no importance *or Fml* of no consequence; **cela n'a aucune i.** it doesn't matter one bit *or* in the slightest, it's not at all important; **c'est d'une i. capitale** it's extremely important; **événement de la première** *ou* **de la plus haute i.** event of outstanding importance, all-important event; **attacher de l'i. à qch** to attach importance to sth; **tu attaches** *ou* **tu donnes trop d'i. à cela** you attach too much importance to it; **et alors? quelle i.?** so what?; **affaire d'i.** important matter; **l'affaire est d'i.** the matter is of some importance; **de peu d'i.** of little importance, of no great significance; **se donner de l'i.** to give oneself airs

(b) (*d'une ville, d'un campus etc*) size; (*de dommages, d'une catastrophe etc*) extent; (*d'une somme, d'un projet*) size, magnitude; **i. d'une blessure** seriousness of a wound; **on ne connaît pas encore l'i. de ses blessures** the extent of his injuries is not yet known; **prendre de l'i.** (*d'une société etc*) to expand; **le mouvement prend de l'i.** the movement is gaining ground; **i. d'un crédit** size of a loan
important, -ante [ɛ̃pɔrtɑ̃, -ɑ̃t] **1** *adj* **(a)** important, significant; **ce n'est pas i.** it's not important, it doesn't matter; **cette maison est très importante pour moi** this house is very important to me; **il est très i. que vous le sachiez** it is very important that you should know *or Am* that you know; **ce qui est vraiment i., c'est que ...** what is really important *or* what really matters is that ...; **peu i.** unimportant, immaterial; **rien d'i.** nothing important, nothing of any importance *or* significance; **personnage i.** important *or* influential person; **c'est quelqu'un d'i.** he is (somebody) important; **se donner des airs importants** to give oneself airs

(b) (*ville, société, projet etc*) large, major; (*somme d'argent, dégâts etc*) considerable, significant; **la recette a atteint un chiffre i.** the takings reached a high *or* a considerable figure; **un retard i.** a considerable delay

2 *n Péj* **faire l'i.** to act important *or* big, to put on airs

3 *nm* **l'i.** the important thing, the main point; **l'i., c'est que tu sois satisfait** the important *or* main thing is for you to be satisfied; **ce n'est pas là le plus i.** that's not the most important thing, that's not what matters most
importateur, -trice [ɛ̃pɔrtatœr, -tris] **1** *n* importer **2** *adj* (*firme, pays etc*) importing; **les pays importateurs de pétrole** oil-importing countries, oil importers
importation [ɛ̃pɔrtasjɔ̃] *nf* **(a)** (*de marchandises*) import, importation, importing; **articles** *ou* **produits d'i.** imports; **licence d'i.** import licence; **l'i. de la cuisine japonaise** the introduction of Japanese cooking **(b)** (*produit*) import; **i. grise** grey import; **importations invisibles** invisible imports
importer[1] [ɛ̃pɔrte] *vt* **(a)** (*marchandises, coutume*) to import **(b)** *Ordinat* to import; **i. qch depuis qch** to import sth from sth
importer[2] (*used only in the third person, participles and inf*) *vi* **(a)** (*compter*) to matter, to be of importance; **les choses qui importent** (the) things that matter *or* that are important; **est-ce que cela importe vraiment?** does it really matter?, is it really of any importance?; **ton opinion m'importe beaucoup** your opinion is very important *or* matters a lot to me; **les vacances lui importent peu** holidays don't matter much to him; **ce qui importe, c'est que tu viennes** the important thing is for you to come; **que m'importe la vie!** what is life to me!; **les diplômes importent de moins en moins** degrees are becoming less and less important, degrees matter less and less

(b) il importe que... + *sub* it is important that ...; **il importe qu'elle soit consciente de ses responsabilités** it is important that she should be *or Am* she be aware of her responsibilities; **je vais être en retard – peu importe** I'm going to be late – no matter *or* it doesn't matter; **tu veux aller au cinema ou au restaurant? – peu importe** do you want to go to the cinema or to the restaurant? – I don't mind; **peu importe que le voile soit blanc ou écru** it doesn't matter much whether the veil is white or beige; **peu m'importe** I don't mind, it's all the same to me; **peu m'importe s'il vienne ou pas** it doesn't matter to me whether he comes or not; **peu m'importe le temps que ça prendra** I don't mind *or* care how long it takes; **peu importe le prix** the price isn't important *or* doesn't matter; **qu'importe?** what does it *or* that matter?; **qu'importe qu'il vienne ou non?** what does it matter whether he comes or not?; **que m'importe?** what do I care?

(c) **faire qch n'importe où/quand** to do sth no matter where/when, to do sth anywhere/(at) any time; **tu l'as fait n'importe comment** you did it any old how; *F* **n'importe comment, c'est trop tard** anyway, it's too late; **tu peux venir n'importe quand** you can come at any time, you can come when you like, it doesn't matter when you come; **mets-le n'importe où** put it anywhere *or* wherever you like; **tu arrives n'importe quand et tu t'attends à ce que je sois là** you arrive at all hours *or* no matter when and expect to find me here; **n'importe** never mind; **le vert ou le bleu? n'importe** the blue or the green? either *or* it doesn't matter; **n'importe quel gamin aurait pu faire ce travail** any child could have done the work; **n'importe quelle autre personne** anybody else; **venez n'importe quel jour** come any day; **donnez-moi n'importe lequel** give me any of them, give me whichever you like; **n'importe qui** anybody, anyone, no matter who; **n'importe qui d'autre aurait compris** anybody else would have understood; **n'importe qui réagirait de la même manière** anyone would have the same reaction; **coucher avec n'importe qui** to sleep around; **je ne suis pas n'importe qui, je suis ta femme** I'm not just anybody, I'm your wife; *F* **ce n'est pas n'importe qui** he isn't just anybody; **n'importe quoi** anything (at all); **elle ferait n'importe quoi pour avoir le poste** she would do anything *or* no matter what to get the job; *Péj* **il dit n'importe quoi!** he's talking nonsense!; *F* **n'importe quoi!** rubbish!

import-export *nf Com* import-export (business); **il fait de l'i.** he works in the import-export business

importun, -une [ɛ̃pɔrtœ̃, -yn] *Fml* **1** *adj* (*personne*) troublesome, tiresome, *Fml* importunate; (*visiteur*) unwelcome; (*arrivée, remarque*) ill-timed; (*question*) tiresome; **je crains de vous être i.** I'm afraid I'm disturbing you **2** *n* (*personne*) nuisance; **les importuns de son espèce** tiresome people like him

importunément [ɛ̃pɔrtynemɑ̃] *adv Fml* importunately

importuner [ɛ̃pɔrtyne] *vt* (*ennuyer*) to bother, to pester, to badger; (*déranger*) to disturb, to trouble, to inconvenience; **ses questions m'importunent au plus haut point** I find his questions extremely annoying; **j'espère que je ne vous importune pas** I hope I'm not disturbing you; **la fumée/la musique m'importune** the smoke/the music bothers me

importunité [ɛ̃pɔrtynite] *nf Fml* importunity

imposable [ɛ̃pozabl] *adj* (*personne, revenu*) taxable; (*propriété*) rateable, assessable

imposant [ɛ̃pozɑ̃] *adj* (*figure, cérémonie*) imposing; (*personne*) commanding, stately, dignified; **d'une stature imposante** of imposing stature; **une imposante majorité** an impressive majority

imposé, -ée [ɛ̃poze] *adj* **(a)** *Sp* **figures imposées** compulsory figures; *Com* **prix i.** fixed price **(b)** (*personne*) taxed

imposer [ɛ̃poze] **1** *vt* **(a)** (*une punition, un travail etc*) to impose; (*tâche*) to set; **i. des conditions** to impose *or* dictate conditions; **le règlement nous impose le secret absolu** the rules compel us to absolute secrecy; **i. une règle** to lay down a rule; **i. (le) silence à qn** to impose silence on sb; **elle veut toujours i. ses caprices à tout le monde** she always wants to force her whims on everyone; **i. sa présence à qn** to impose *or* force one's presence on sb; **i. sa manière de voir les choses à qn** to force one's opinions on sb; **cela nous a été imposé par les circonstances** it was forced on us by circumstances; **il a imposé son chouchou dans le service** he foisted his favourite on the department; **i. sa loi** to lay down the law; **i. le respect** to command *or* compel respect; **i. un blocage des prix** to impose a price freeze

(b) *Admin* (*soumettre à l'impôt*) (*personne, objet*) to tax; **i. des droits sur qch** to impose *or* put a tax on sth, to tax sth; **être lourdement imposé** to be heavily taxed; **i. un immeuble** to levy a rate on *or* to assess a building

(c) *Typ* (*feuille*) to impose

(d) *Rel* (*mains*) to lay on

2 *vi* **en i.** to command *or* inspire respect, to be awe-inspiring; **en i. à qn** to impress sb

3 s'imposer *vpr* **(a)** (*faire reconnaître sa valeur*) to assert oneself; **elle s'est imposée par sa compétence** she made a name for herself through sheer ability; **le coureur kenyan s'est imposé sans difficulté dans le 110 m haies** the Kenyan runner easily dominated the 110m hurdles; **la joueuse espagnole s'est imposée face à la Japonaise en 2 sets** the Spanish player powered her way past the Japanese player in straight sets; **il s'est imposé comme le meilleur boxeur de sa génération** he has stood out *or* made a name for himself as the best boxer of his generation; **le libéralisme économique s'impose comme la seule doctrine viable** free enterprise stands out as the only viable doctrine

(b) (*déranger*) **je ne voulais pas m'i.** I didn't want to impose; **s'i. à qn** to foist *or* thrust *or* force oneself on sb; (*importuner*) to impose on sb

(c) (*être nécessaire*) to be essential; **la discrétion s'impose** discretion is imperative *or* essential; **prendre les mesures qui s'imposent** to take the necessary steps; **s'i. à l'attention** to command attention; **la conviction s'imposa à mon esprit que ...** the conviction forced itself upon me that ...; **une visite au Louvre s'impose** you/we/*etc* must visit the Louvre, *F* a visit to the Louvre is a must; *Hum* **cette gifle ne s'imposait peut-être pas** maybe that slap wasn't called for; **cette solution/décoration s'est imposée d'elle-même** it seemed the obvious solution/style of decoration, the solution/decor suggested itself

(d) (*se contraindre*) **s'i. un labeur** to set oneself a task; **s'i. un sacrifice** to force oneself to make a sacrifice; **s'i. de faire qch** to make it a rule to do sth; **s'i. un régime sévère** to follow a strict diet; **elle s'impose plusieurs heures de sport par jour/de travailler huit heures par jour** she makes it a rule to do several hours sport a day/to work eight hours a day

imposition [ɛ̃pozisjɔ̃] *nf* **(a)** *Fin* taxation; **avis d'i.** notice of assessment; **avis de non-i.** notice of exemption; **tranche d'i.** tax bracket **(b)** *Typ* imposing, imposition **(c)** *Rel* **i. des mains** laying on of hands

impossibilité [ɛ̃pɔsibilite] *nf* impossibility; **être** *ou* **se trouver dans l'i. de faire qch** to find it impossible to do sth; **je suis dans l'i. de quitter mon lit** I can't get out of bed; **vu l'i. dans laquelle je me trouve de vous téléphoner** since it has been impossible to reach you by telephone; **en cas d'i.** if that is not possible

impossible [ɛ̃pɔsibl] **1** *adj* **(a)** (*irréalisable*) impossible; **i. à déchiffrer** impossible to decipher; **c'est i. à faire** it can't be done, it's impossible; **il est i. qu'il revienne avant lundi** he can't possibly be back before Monday; **il est i. de croire ce qu'il dit** you can't believe what he says; **c'est matériellement i.** it's (physically) impossible; **la résolution du problème est i.** it is impossible to solve the problem, the problem cannot be solved; **cela m'est i.** it's not possible for me, I can't (possibly); **il m'est i. de le faire** I can't (possibly) do it, it's impossible for me to do it; **il n'est pas i. que je vous rende visite** you might well get a visit from me, a visit from me is not out of the question; **est-ce que tu vas venir? – ce n'est pas i.** are you going to come? – it's not impossible; **i. n'est pas français** there's no such word as can't *or* impossible

(b) (*insupportable*) (*situation*) intolerable, impossible; **il a fallu nous lever à une heure i.** we had to get up at an unearthly *or* a ridiculous hour; **avoir des horaires impossibles** to work ridiculous hours; **vous lui rendez la vie i.** you're making life impossible for him, you're making his life a misery; **tu es i.!** you're impossible!

(c) (*farfelu, F chapeau etc*) extravagant, absurd, ridiculous; **encore une de tes histoires impossibles!** another one of your incredible *or* ridiculous stories!

2 *nm* **(a)** **l'i.** the impossible; **tenter l'i.** to attempt the impossibe; **il a fait l'i. pour nous secourir** he did his utmost *or* did everything possible to help us; *Prov* **à l'i. nul n'est tenu** you can't do the impossible

(b) **si par i. il est encore vivant** if, by some remote chance *or* some miracle, he is still alive

imposte [ɛ̃pɔst] *nf Archit* **(a)** impost; (*d'arcade*) springer **(b)** (*fenêtre*) fanlight, *US* transom (window)

imposteur [ɛ̃pɔstœr] *nm* impostor

imposture [ɛ̃pɔstyr] *nf* imposture; **c'est une i.!** he's/she's an impostor!; **rendu célèbre par ses impostures** famed as an impostor

impôt [ɛ̃po] *nm* tax; (*taxes*) taxes, taxation; **je ne paie pas d'impôts** I don't pay any tax; **déductible des impôts** tax deductible; **payer mille francs d'impôts** to pay a thousand francs in tax(es); **déclaration d'impôts** income tax form *or* statement *or* return; **faire sa déclaration d'impôts** to fill out one's income tax form, *F* to do one's taxes; **frapper qch d'un i.** to tax sth, to put a tax on sth; *F* **les impôts m'ont envoyé une lettre** the tax man has sent me a letter; *F* **il faut que j'aille aux impôts** I have to see the tax man *or* go to the tax offices; **i. retenu à la source** tax deducted at source, ≈ pay as you earn, PAYE, *Am* ≈ pay as you go

▶ **impôt**: **i. sur les bénéfices** corporation tax; **i. sur le capital** capital tax; **i. sur le chiffre d'affaires** turnover tax, sales tax; **i. direct** direct tax; **i. foncier** land *or* property tax; **i. sur les grandes fortunes** wealth tax; **i. sur l'hôtellerie** hotel tax; **i. indirect** indirect tax; **impôts locaux** local taxes, *Br* council tax, *Br formerly* rates; **i. sur les plus-values** capital gains tax; **i. progressif** graduated income tax; **i. sur le revenu** income tax; **i. sur les sociétés** corporation tax; **i. de solidarité sur la fortune** wealth tax; **i. sur les traitements et salaires** tax on wages and salaries

impotence [ɛpɔtɑ̃s] *nf* disability; (*causée par la vieillesse*) infirmity

impotent, -ente [ɛ̃pɔtɑ̃, -ɑ̃t] **1** *adj* crippled; **être i. de la jambe gauche** to have lost the use of the left leg **2** *n* disabled person, cripple

impraticabilité [ɛ̃pratikabilite] *nf* impracticability

impraticable [ɛ̃pratikabl] *adj* **(a)** (*où l'on ne peut pas passer*) impassable; **chemin i. aux** *ou* **pour les automobiles** road unfit for motor vehicles **(b)** *Sp* (*terrain*) unplayable, unfit for play; **annulé pour cause de terrain i.** cancelled because of the state of the pitch **(c)** (*irréalisable*) impractical

imprécation [ɛ̃prekasjɔ̃] *nf Litt* curse, oath, *Fml* imprecation

imprécatoire [ɛ̃prekatwar] *adj Litt* imprecatory

imprécis [ɛ̃presi] *adj* **(a)** (*vague*) (*témoignage, proposition, rapport, contours*) vague, imprecise, indefinite; (*souvenir*) vague **(b)** (*tir, balance*) inaccurate

imprécision [ɛ̃presizjɔ̃] *nf* **(a)** (*caractère vague*) imprecision, looseness; (*d'un témoignage, souvenir, rapport*) vagueness; (*de contours*) lack of definition **(b)** (*de tir, d'une balance*) inaccuracy

imprégnation [ɛ̃preɲasjɔ̃] *nf* impregnation, permeation; **imprégnation: i. alcoolique** blood alcohol content

imprégner [ɛ̃preɲe] **(j'imprègne; j'imprégnerai) 1** *vt* to impregnate, to permeate (**de** with); *Fig* **imprégné de préjugés** full of prejudice; **ses vêtements sont imprégnés de l'odeur de fumée** his clothes stink of smoke; **leur famille est imprégnée des idées du grand-père** the grandfather's ideas have been imprinted on the family **2 s'imprégner** *vpr* to become impregnated *or* permeated (**de** with); **s'i. d'eau** to be saturated *or* soaked with water; *Fig* **s'i. d'un auteur** to immerse oneself in an author

imprenable [ɛ̃prənabl] *adj* impregnable; **vue i.** unobstructed view (**sur** of)

impréparation [ɛ̃preparasjɔ̃] *nf* unpreparedness

impresario [ɛ̃presarjo] *nm* manager

imprescriptibilité [ɛ̃prɛskriptibilite] *nf Jur* imprescriptibility, indefeasibility

imprescriptible [ɛ̃prɛskriptibl] *adj Jur* imprescriptible, indefeasible

impression [ɛ̃prɛsjɔ̃] *nf* **(a)** (*sensation*) impression; **il nous a donné l'i. que …** he gave us the impression that …; **elle nous donne** *ou* **nous fait l'i. de** *ou* **d'être quelqu'un d'intelligent** she impresses us as an intelligent woman, she gives us the impression that she is intelligent; **il me donne l'i. de rêver/d'être heureux** he gives me the impression *or* he makes me feel that I'm dreaming/that I'm happy; **il me fait l'i. de rêver/d'être heureux** he gives me the impression that he's dreaming/happy; **il donne toujours l'i. d'être ailleurs** he always gives the impression that he's miles away; **faire i.** to make an impression, to be impressive; **il ne fait pas assez i.** he doesn't make enough of an impression, he's not impressive enough; **faire forte i.** to have *or* make a strong impression; **faire bonne/mauvaise i. (sur qn)** to make a good/bad impression (on sb); **c'est quelqu'un de très sympathique mais qui fait mauvaise i.** he's extremely nice but he gives people the wrong impression; **pour faire bonne i. chez mes parents** to make a good impression on my parents, to impress my parents; **il ne m'a pas fait une grande i.** he did not make a great impression on me; **elle m'a fait une i. favorable** she made a favourable impression on me, she impressed me favourably; **ça fait une drôle d'i. de s'entendre parler** it's a funny feeling, hearing yourself speak; **j'ai l'i. de l'avoir déjà vue** *ou* **que je l'ai déjà vue** I've an idea *or* a feeling that I've seen her before; **j'ai l'i. qu'elle est assez timide** I have the impression that *or* my impression of her is that she's rather shy; **l'i. que j'ai d'elle n'est pas excellente** I do not have an excellent opinion of her; **quelles sont vos impressions?** what are your impressions?

(b) (*action d'imprimer*), *Typ, Tex* printing; (*copie*) printout, computer printout; **livre à l'i.** book in (the) *or* at press; **faute d'i.** misprint; **troisième i. d'un livre** third impression *or* printing of a book; **i. en couleurs** colour *or US* color printing; *Phot* **double i.** double exposure; *Ordinat* **i. rapide** draft; *Typ* **i. continue** web-offset printing; **i. en arrière-plan** background (mode) printing, spooling; *Ordinat* **i. en continu** continuous printout; **i. en deux couleurs** two-tone printing; **i. en qualité brouillon** draft quality printing; (*copie*) draft printout; **i. laser** laser printing; (*copie*) laser printout; **i. ombrée** shadow print; **i. proportionnelle** proportional printing; **i. recto-verso** double-sided printing; **i. sans presse** plateless printing; *Ordinat* **i. écran** screen dump; **i. à jet d'encre** ink-jet printing; (*copie*) ink-jet printout

(c) (*image*) print; **i. en couleurs** colour print

(d) (*première couche de peinture*) primer, undercoat

(e) (*motif*) **tissu à impressions florales** material with a flower pattern *or* print

(f) *Vieilli* (*sur cire, sol etc*) impression, imprint; **i. de pas** footprint

impressionnabilité [ɛ̃prɛsjɔnabilite] *nf* **(a)** (*sensibilité*) impressionability **(b)** *Phot* sensitivity

impressionnable [ɛ̃prɛsjɔnabl] *adj* **(a)** (*sensible*) impressionable **(b)** *Phot* (*plaque etc*) sensitive

impressionnant [ɛ̃prɛsjɔnɑ̃] *adj* impressive; **tout ce sang partout était très i.** the sight of all that blood made a strong impression *or* was extremely upsetting

impressionner [ɛ̃prɛsjɔne] *vt* **(a)** (*frapper, bouleverser*) to impress, to make an impression on; (*d'une mauvaise nouvelle, d'un accident*) to upset; **ils ont été très impressionnés par les trapézistes** they were very impressed by *or* with the trapeze artists; **il ne faut pas se laisser i.** don't let yourself be overawed; **vision** *ou* **vue qui impressionne** impressive sight; **j'ai été très impressionné** it/he/etc made a strong impression on me

(b) *Opt* (*rétine*) to act on; *Phot* (*papier sensibilisé etc*) to produce an image on; (*film*) to expose

impressionnisme [ɛ̃prɛsjɔnism] *nm Beaux-Arts* impressionism

impressionniste [ɛ̃prɛsjɔnist] *Beaux-Arts* **1** *adj* impressionist(ic) **2** *n* impressionist

imprévisibilité [ɛ̃previzibilite] *nf* unpredictability; **elle est d'une telle i. que …** she is so unpredictable that …

imprévisible [ɛ̃previzibl] *adj* (*temps, réaction, personne*) unpredictable; (*événement, circonstances*) unforeseeable; **ce qu'il aime surtout chez elle, c'est son caractère i.** what he especially likes about her is her unpredictability *or* is that she's unpredictable

imprévoyance [ɛ̃prevwajɑ̃s] *nf* lack of foresight, improvidence

imprévoyant [ɛ̃prevwajɑ̃] *adj* lacking in foresight, improvident

imprévu [ɛ̃prevy] **1** *adj* unexpected, unforeseen; **leur arrivée était tout à fait imprévue** they arrived quite unexpectedly **2** *nm* **(a)** (*caractère*) (*d'événement*) unexpectedness; **elle aime l'i.** she likes the unexpected **(b)** (*incident*) unexpected *or* unforeseen event; **sauf i., à moins d'un i.** barring accidents, unless something unforeseen *or* unexpected happens; **en cas d'i.** in (case of) an emergency; **en cas d'i., on se retrouve à la répétition** if something crops up *or* failing that, we'll see each other at the rehearsal

imprimable [ɛ̃primabl] *adj* printable

imprimante [ɛ̃primɑ̃t] *nf* printer; **i. à aiguilles** dot matrix printer; **i. 24 aiguilles** 24-pin printer; **i. à bulles** bubble-jet printer; **i. feuille à feuille** sheet-fed printer; **i. à grand chariot** wide carriage printer; **i. graphique** graphics printer; **i. à impact** impact printer; **i. à jet d'encre** ink-jet (printer); **i. (à) laser** laser printer; **i. ligne, i. par lignes** line printer; **i. à marguerite** daisywheel (printer); **i. page par page** page printer; **i. par pages** page printer; **i. par points** *ou* **matricielle** dot matrix (printer); **i. à petit chariot** narrow carriage printer; **i. de qualité courrier** letter quality printer, LQ printer; **i. sans impact** non-impact printer; **i. (à transfert) thermique** thermal (transfer) printer

imprimatur [ɛ̃primatyr] *nm inv* imprimatur

imprimé [ɛ̃prime] **1** *adj* printed; **tissu imprimé** printed fabric, print; *Électron* **circuit imprimé** printed circuit **2** *nm* **(a)** (*formulaire*) form; **imprimés** (*journaux etc*) printed matter; **département/catalogue des imprimés** (*dans une bibliothèque*) department/catalogue of printed books; **i. fiscal** tax return; **i. sans adresse** mailshot **(b)** *Ordinat* **i. ligne par ligne** line print out **(c)** *Tex* print; **un i. à fleurs/à motifs géométriques** a flower/geometric print

imprimer [ɛ̃prime] *vt* **(a)** (*marquer*) to (im)print, to impress, to stamp; *Tex* (*tissu*) to print; *Fig* **un moment imprimé dans mon cœur/ma mémoire** a moment imprinted *or* stamped *or* engraved on my heart/in my memory; **(b)** *Typ* (*livre*) to print; *Ordinat* to print (off), to print (out); *Ordinat* **i. un écran** to do a print screen; **presse à i.** printing press **(c)** (*direction*) to communicate; **i. un mouvement à un corps** to impart *or* transmit motion to a body

imprimerie [ɛ̃primri] *nf* **(a)** (*technique*) (art of) printing **(b)** (*atelier, usine*) printing house, printing works, (printing) press; **l'I. nationale** *Br* ≈ HMSO (Her Majesty's Stationery Office), *US* ≈ Government Printing Office

imprimeur [ɛ̃primœr] *nm* printer; **i.-éditeur** printer and publisher

improbabilité [ɛ̃prɔbabilite] *nf* improbability

improbable [ɛ̃prɔbabl] *adj* improbable, unlikely; **son retour est très i.** he/she is very unlikely to come back, it's very improbable that he/she will come back; **dans le cas, très i., où …** in the very unlikely event that …

improbité [ɛ̃prɔbite] *nf Litt* dishonesty, lack of integrity

improductif, -ive [ɛ̃prɔdyktif, -iv] **1** *adj* unproductive; (*capital*) non-productive, idle **2** *n* administrative employee

(*as opposed to one working on the production side*); **les improductifs** (*d'une compagnie*) the administrative staff, management; (*d'une nation*) the unwaged
improductivité [ɛ̃prɔdyktivite] *nf* unproductiveness
impromptu [ɛ̃prɔ̃pty] **1** *adj* (*départ, arrivée, visite, réflexion*) impromptu, unexpected; (*repas*) impromptu; (*discours*) impromptu, off the cuff, *Fml* extempore; **il a fait une arrivée impromptue** he turned up unexpectedly; **sa réflexion était si impromptue qu'elle a laissé tout le monde sans voix** the remark was so unexpected that it left everyone speechless; **je vais lui faire une visite impromptue un de ces jours** I'll drop in on him unannounced one of these days
2 *adv* (*parler*) off the cuff, impromptu; (*répondre*) off the cuff; **elle est venue i. hier soir** she turned up unexpectedly last night
3 *nm Th, Mus* impromptu
imprononçable [ɛ̃prɔnɔ̃sabl] *adj* unpronounceable
impropre [ɛ̃prɔpr] *adj* **(a)** (*terme*) inappropriate, incorrect **(b)** **i. à qch** unfit *or* unsuitable for sth; **i. à la consommation** unfit for human consumption
improprement [ɛ̃prɔprəmɑ̃] *adv* improperly, incorrectly
impropriété [ɛ̃prɔprijete] *nf* (*mot*) inappropriate *or* incorrect term; (*de mot*) inappropriateness, incorrectness
improuvable [ɛ̃pruvabl] *adj* unprovable
improvisateur, -trice [ɛ̃prɔvizatœr, -tris] *n* improviser; **avoir un talent d'i.** to have a talent for improvising
improvisation [ɛ̃prɔvizasjɔ̃] *nf* improvisation; (*remarque, trait d'esprit*) ad-lib; **en cuisine, elle adore l'i.** she loves to improvise in the kitchen; **i. sur un thème** improvisation on a theme; **faire une i.** to improvise; **être doué pour l'i.** to be good at improvising; (*d'un comique*) to be good at ad-libbing
improvisé [ɛ̃prɔvize] *adj* (*discours, remarque*) improvised, extempore, off-the-cuff; (*sketch, siège*) improvised; *Sp* (*équipe*) scratch; **nous avons fait un barbecue i.** we had an impromptu barbecue
improviser [ɛ̃prɔvize] **1** *vt* to improvise; **i. un discours** to make an impromptu *or* extempore speech, to speak off the cuff, to ad-lib; **je dus m'i. infirmière pour la circonstance** I had to act as nurse **2** *vi* to improvise; (*de comique*) to ad-lib; **i. à l'orgue** to improvise on the organ **3 s'improviser** *vpr* **l'organisation, ça ne s'improvise pas** organization isn't something you can improvise; **on ne s'improvise pas danseur étoile comme ça** you don't just become a lead dancer overnight
improviste (à l') [alɛ̃prɔvist] *adv* unexpectedly, without any warning; **prendre qn à l'i.** to take *or* catch sb unawares *or* by surprise; **visite à l'i.** surprise visit
imprudemment [ɛ̃prydamɑ̃] *adv* imprudently, rashly, unwisely; (*conduire*) recklessly
imprudence [ɛ̃prydɑ̃s] *nf* **(a)** (*caractère*) imprudence, foolhardiness, rashness, recklessness; *Jur* **homicide par i.** = manslaughter **(b)** (*action*) **commettre une i.** to act rashly *or* imprudently; **j'ai peur qu'il fasse une i.** I'm afraid he may do something rash; **(ne fais) pas d'imprudences** don't do anything rash *or* silly
imprudent, -ente [ɛ̃prydɑ̃, -ɑ̃t] **1** *adj* imprudent, foolhardy, rash, reckless, unwise; **il serait très i. de la laisser partir seule** it would be very unwise to let her go off on her own; **c'est un peu i. de ne pas mettre sa ceinture de sécurité** it's rather rash not to wear a safety belt **2** *n* imprudent *or* rash *or* reckless person
impubère [ɛ̃pybɛr] **1** *adj* impubescent **2** *n Jur* impubescent minor
impubliable [ɛ̃pyblijabl] *adj* unpublishable
impudemment [ɛ̃pydamɑ̃] *adv* impudently; (*avec cynisme*) brazenly, shamelessly; **il ment i.** he's a brazen *or* shameless liar
impudence [ɛ̃pydɑ̃s] *nf* **(a)** (*caractère*) impudence; (*effronterie*) effrontery; (*cynisme*) shamelessness; **quelle i.!** what impudence!; **il est d'une telle i. que ...** he is so impudent that ...; **il n'aura pas l'i. de revenir** he won't have the impudence *or* be impudent enough to come back **(b)** (*action, parole*) impudent action/remark
impudent [ɛ̃pydɑ̃] *adj* impudent; (*cynique*) shameless, brazen
impudeur [ɛ̃pydœr] *nf* shamelessness, immodesty
impudicité [ɛ̃pydisite] *nf* shamelessness; (*obscénité*) lewdness
impudique [ɛ̃pydik] *adj* shameless; (*obscène*) lewd
impudiquement [ɛ̃pydikmɑ̃] *adv* shamelessly; (*d'une manière obscène*) lewdly
impuissance [ɛ̃pɥisɑ̃s] *nf* **(a)** (*incapacité*) powerlessness, helplessness, impotence; **i. à faire qch** powerlessness *or* inability to do sth; **en geste d'i., il leva les bras au ciel** in a gesture of helplessness, he raised his arms to the heavens **(b)** *Méd* impotence
impuissant [ɛ̃pɥisɑ̃] **1** *adj* **(a)** (*incapable*) powerless, helpless, impotent; **i. devant sa douleur** powerless *or* helpless in the face of his pain; **i. à faire qch** powerless *or* unable to do sth **(b)** *Méd* impotent **2** *nm Méd* impotent man
impulsif, -ive [ɛ̃pylsif, -iv] **1** *adj* impulsive **2** *n* person who acts on impulse; **c'est une impulsive** she's impulsive
impulsion [ɛ̃pylsjɔ̃] *nf* **(a)** (*influence*) impulse; **faire qch sous l'i. de la colère/de l'enthousiasme** to do sth in a fit of anger/enthusiasm **(b)** (*élan*) impulse, impetus, boost; **donner de l'i. au commerce** to give a boost to trade; **les affaires ont reçu une nouvelle i.** business has received fresh impetus *or* shows renewed activity **(c)** *Tech* impulse; **force d'i.** impulsive force; *Él* **i. de courant** current impulse; **radar à impulsions** pulse radar; **i. électrique** electrical impulse
impulsivité [ɛ̃pylsivite] *nf* impulsiveness
impunément [ɛ̃pynemɑ̃] *adv* with impunity; **tu ne crois tout de même pas qu'on va te laisser faire tes bêtises i.** I hope you don't think you're going to get away with being so stupid
impuni [ɛ̃pyni] *adj* unpunished
impunité [ɛ̃pynite] *nf* impunity; **agir en toute i.** to act with impunity
impur [ɛ̃pyr] *adj* impure; (*personne*) (morally) impure; *Rel* (*viande*) unclean
impureté [ɛ̃pyrte] *nf* **(a)** (*état*) impurity; (*d'une personne*) (moral) impurity; *Rel* uncleanness **(b)** (*saletés*) **impuretés** impurities
imputabilité [ɛ̃pytabilite] *nf* imputability
imputable [ɛ̃pytabl] *adj* **(a)** attributable, ascribable, imputable (**à** to); **erreur i. à la distraction** mistake attributable to *or* caused by absent-mindedness; **cet accident ne m'est pas i.** I cannot be held responsible for the accident **(b)** *Fin* chargeable; **frais imputables sur un compte** expenses chargeable to an account
imputation [ɛ̃pytasjɔ̃] *nf* **(a)** (*accusation*) charge, imputation **(b)** *Com* (*des dépenses etc*) charge, charging; *Fin* **i. à** charge to; **i. d'une somme au crédit/débit d'un compte** crediting/debiting an amount to an account
imputer [ɛ̃pyte] *vt* **(a)** (*crime etc*) to ascribe, to attribute (**à** to); **ils ont imputé cette erreur à son ignorance** they attributed the mistake to *or* put the mistake down to his ignorance **(b)** *Com* **i. des frais sur un compte** to charge expenses to an account
imputrescibilité [ɛ̃pytrɛsibilite] *nf* **l'i. du bois/du plastique fait que ...** the fact that the wood/plastic does not rot means ...
imputrescible [ɛ̃pytrɛsibl] *adj* which is not subject to rot
in [in] *adj inv F* in; **l'endroit le plus in de Paris** the most in spot in Paris; **être in** to be in
inabordable [inabɔrdabl] *adj* (*endroit*) unapproachable, inaccessible; (*prix*) unaffordable; (*fruits, légumes etc*) overpriced; *Vieilli* (*personne*) unapproachable
inabrogeable [inabrɔʒabl] *adj Jur* unrepealable
inaccentué [inaksɑ̃tɥe] *adj* (*voyelle*) unaccented; (*syllabe etc*) unstressed
inacceptable [inaksɛptabl] *adj* unacceptable; (*conduite, méthodes*) unacceptable, objectionable
inaccessibilité [inaksesibilite] *nf* inaccessibility
inaccessible [inaksesibl] *adj* **(a)** (*inabordable*) inaccessible; **ils vivent dans un coin i.** they live in an out-of-the-way place; **se fixer un objectif i.** to set oneself an unattainable goal; **i. au grand public** (*livre*) not accessible to the general public **(b)** (*personne*) unapproachable; **cette femme belle et i.** that beautiful, unapproachable woman **(c)** **i. à la pitié** incapable of pity; **i. à la flatterie** impervious to flattery
inaccompli [inakɔ̃pli] *adj Litt* (*tâche*) unaccomplished; (*rêve, vœu*) unfulfilled
inaccoutumé [inakutyme] *adj* **(a)** (*inhabituel*) unusual **(b)** *Litt* (*inhabitué*) unaccustomed, unused (**à** to)
inachevé [inaʃ(ə)ve] *adj* unfinished, uncompleted
inachèvement [inaʃɛvmɑ̃] *nm* incompletion
inacquitté [inakite] *adj* unpaid
inactif, -ive [inaktif, -iv] **1** *adj* (*personne*) inactive, idle; *Écon* **la population inactive** the non-working population, *Br* the unwaged; *Com* **marché i.** sluggish *or* dull *or* slack market **2** *n* *Écon* **un i.** a person without paid employment; **les inactifs** the non-working population, *Br* the unwaged
inaction [inaksjɔ̃] *nf* inaction, idleness; **c'est l'i. qui est parfois responsable de la délinquance** (*due aux circonstances*) a lack of things to do can be a cause of delinquency; (*due à la paresse*) idleness can be a cause of delinquency; **je ne supporte pas l'i.** I can't bear being idle *or* having nothing to do
inactivité [inaktivite] *nf* inactivity; *Com* (*du marché*)

sluggishness, dullness; **sa maladie l'a réduit à l'i. pendant plusieurs mois** his illness put him out of action for several months; **j'ai été forcée à l'i. à cause de mon accident** I've had to give up all forms of activity *or* give up doing anything active since I had my accident; **elle ne supporte pas l'i.** she can't bear being idle *or* having nothing to do; **période d'i.** period of inactivity; *Com* dead period; **en i.** *Admin* (temporarily) unemployed; *Mil* not on the active list

inadaptation [inadaptasjɔ̃] *nf* (*sociale*) maladjustment; (*physique, mentale*) handicap; **i. familiale/scolaire** inability to adjust to family life/school

inadapté, -ée [inadapte] **1** *adj* (*personne*) (*socialement*) maladjusted; (*physiquement, mentalement*) handicapped; (*matériel*) unsuitable; **l'enfance inadaptée** handicapped children, children with special needs; **matériel i. à ses besoins** equipment unsuited to *or* unsuitable for one's needs **2** *n* (*socialement*) maladjusted person; (*physiquement, mentalement*) handicapped person; **les inadaptés** the maladjusted/the handicapped

inadéquat [inadekwa] *adj* (*salaire, ressources*) inadequate; (*remède, matériel*) unsuitable

inadéquation [inadekwasjɔ̃] *nf* unsuitability; (*d'une mesure*) inadequacy; **étant donné l'i. des moyens au problème** since the means are not suited *or* are unsuited to the problem

inadmissibilité [inadmisibilite] *nf* inadmissibility

inadmissible [inadmisibl] *adj* (*attitude, négligence, erreur*) unacceptable, inadmissible; (*demande, proposition*) unacceptable; **il est i. qu'on ne l'ait pas reçu à l'examen** it's unacceptable that they should have failed him

inadvertance [inadvɛrtɑ̃s] *nf* **par i.** inadvertently, by mistake

inaliénabilité [inaljenabilite] *nf Jur* (*d'un droit*) inalienability, indefeasibility

inaliénable [inaljenabl] *adj Jur* (*droit*) inalienable, indefeasible

inalliable [inaljabl] *adj Métal* that cannot be alloyed, non-alloyable

inaltérabilité [inalterabilite] *nf* (*d'un matériau, un revêtement*) resistance to deterioration, permanence

inaltérable [inalterabl] *adj* **(a)** (*métal, revêtement*) that does not deteriorate, permanent; (*couleur*) fast; **i. à l'air/l'eau** unaffected by air/water **(b)** *Fig* (*bonne humeur*) unfailing, unvarying; (*espoir*) steadfast, unwavering; (*calme*) unwavering; **sa croyance en sa propre réussite semblait i.** his belief in his own success never seemed to waver *or* seemed steadfast

inaltéré [inaltere] *adj* (*bois, pierre*) unweathered

inamical, -ale, -aux, -ales [inamikal, -o] *adj* unfriendly; **avoir un geste i. envers qn** to act in an unfriendly way towards sb

inamovibilité [inamɔvibilite] *nf Admin* fixity of tenure; (*d'un juge, magistrat*) irremovability

inamovible [inamɔvibl] *adj* (*four, autoradio*) built-in; *Jur* (*juge, magistrat*) holding appointment for life; (*poste*) held for life; *F* **il est vraiment i.** he's a permanent fixture

inanimé [inanime] *adj* **(a)** (*matière*) inanimate, lifeless **(b)** (*personne, corps*) (*mort*) lifeless; (*inconscient*) motionless; *Fig* (*marché boursier*) sluggish; **tomber i.** to faint, to fall down in a faint

inanité [inanite] *nf* (*futilité*) (*de conversation*) inanity; (*inutilité*) (*d'effort*) futility; **des conversations d'une i. terrifiante** incredibly inane conversations

inanition [inanisjɔ̃] *nf* starvation; **tomber d'i.** to faint from hunger; **mourir d'i.** to die of starvation, to starve to death

inapaisable [inapɛzabl] *adj* (*faim*) unappeasable; (*soif*) unquenchable; (*chagrin*) that nothing can assuage

inapaisé [inapeze] *adj* (*faim*) unappeased; (*soif*) unquenched; (*désir*) unassuaged

inaperçu [inapɛrsy] *adj* **passer i.** to escape notice, to pass unnoticed; *Euph* **cet événement ne passa pas i.** the event did not go unnoticed

inappétence [inapetɑ̃s] *nf Méd* (*manque d'appétit*) lack of appetite; (*manque de désir*) lack of desire

inapplicable [inaplikabl] *adj* unenforceable

inapplication [inaplikasjɔ̃] *nf* **(a)** (*défaut d'application*) **i. d'une loi** failure to put a law into effect **(b)** (*manque de soin*) (*d'une personne*) lack of application

inappliqué, -ée [inaplike] *adj* **(a)** (*non mis en service*) (*méthode, procédé, technique*) not applied; (*loi*) in abeyance **(b)** (*peu soigneux*) (*personne*) lacking in application

inappréciable [inapresjabl] *adj* **(a)** (*impossible à évaluer*) (*quantité etc*) inappreciable; (*différence etc*) imperceptible **(b)** (*inestimable*) (*qualité, avantage, don*) invaluable, priceless, inestimable

inapprécié [inapresje] *adj* unappreciated

inapprivoisable [inaprivwazabl] *adj* untamable

inapte [inapt] **1** *adj* **(a)** (*non apte*) (*personne*) (*pour raisons médicales*) unfit (**au travail** for work); (*intellectuellement*) unsuited (**à** to); **i. à faire qch** incapable of doing sth; **i. à travailler** unfit to work **(b)** *Mil* unfit (*for military service*) **2** *nmpl surtout Mil* **les inaptes** the unfit

inaptitude [inaptityd] *nf* (*intellectuelle*) inaptitude; (*médicale, militaire*) unfitness (**au travail** for work); **son i. à travailler a été prouvée à maintes reprises** it has been proved many times over that he is unfit for *or* to work

inarticulé [inartikyle] *adj* (*difficilement audible*) (*son, cris*) inarticulate

inassimilable [inasimilabl] *adj* which cannot be assimilated, unassimilable

inassouvi [inasuvi] *adj* (*faim*) unappeased, unsatisfied; (*soif*) unslaked, unquenched; (*désir*) ungratified, unfulfilled; **ma vengeance est restée inassouvie pendant longtemps** my desire for revenge remained unsatisfied for a long time

inassouvissable [inasuvisabl] *adj Litt* insatiable

inattaquable [inatakabl] *adj* (*position, forteresse, tour, argumentation, projet de loi*) unassailable; (*personne*) unassailable, *F* untouchable; (*testament*) incontestable; (*preuves*) unimpeachable; *Ch* **i. par les acides** acid-proof, acid-resisting

inattendu [inatɑ̃dy] *adj* (*visite, réponse, lettre, nouvelle, comportement*) unexpected; (*événement*) unexpected, unforeseen; **ce qui était très i. de leur part** which was very unexpected of them, which I wasn't/we weren't/*etc* expecting at all

inattentif, -ive [inatɑ̃tif, -iv] *adj* inattentive; **il est i. à tout ce qu'on lui dit** he doesn't pay any attention *or* heed to what you say to him; **i. aux conseils** heedless of advice

inattention [inatɑ̃sjɔ̃] *nf* inattention, carelessness; **faute d'i.** slip, careless mistake; **l'accident est dû à un moment d'i. du conducteur** the accident was due to a lapse of concentration by the driver

inaudible [inodibl] *adj* inaudible

inaugural, -ale, -aux, -ales [inogyral, -o] *adj* (*discours, séance*) inaugural; **voyage i.** maiden voyage

inauguration [inogyrasjɔ̃] *nf* (*d'une usine, d'un bâtiment, d'une route*) (official) opening, inauguration; (*d'une statue, d'un monument*) unveiling; **discours d'i.** inaugural speech; **depuis l'i. du nouveau tronçon d'autoroute** since the new section of the motorway was opened

inaugurer [inogyre] *vt* (*édifice, hôpital, route*) to (officially) open, to inaugurate; (*statue, monument*) to unveil; *Fig* (*nouvelle politique*) to inaugurate; (*époque*) to usher in

inauthenticité [inotɑ̃tisite] *nf* unauthentic nature

inauthentique [inotɑ̃tik] *adj* (*document*) not authentic, not genuine, unauthentic; (*fait*) incorrect; (*ouvrage*) inaccurate

inavouable [inavwabl] *adj* shameful

inavoué [inavwe] *adj* unconfessed

INC [iɛnse] *nm* (*abrév* **Institut national de la consommation**) national consumer institute

inca [ɛ̃ka] **1** *adj inv* Inca **2** *n* **I.** Inca

incalculable [ɛ̃kalkylabl] *adj* (*conséquences, risques*) incalculable; **un nombre i. de vieux journaux/de gens** countless old newspapers/people

incandescence [ɛ̃kɑ̃desɑ̃s] *nf* incandescence; *Él* **lampe à i.** incandescent lamp

incandescent [ɛ̃kɑ̃desɑ̃] *adj* incandescent; *Fig* (*imagination*) ardent

incantation [ɛ̃kɑ̃tasjɔ̃] *nf* incantation

incantatoire [ɛ̃kɑ̃tatwar] *adj* incantatory

incapable [ɛ̃kapabl] **1** *adj* **(a)** (*personne*) incapable, incompetent; *Jur* (legally) incompetent

(b) être i. de faire qch to be incapable of doing sth; (*par impossibilité physique*) to be unable to do sth; **i. de mentir/d'en vouloir à qn** incapable of lying/being cross with sb; **elle est i. de se détendre** she is incapable of relaxing, she cannot relax; *F* **il est i. de se faire cuire un œuf** he can't boil *or* he's incapable of boiling an egg; **i. de lâcheté/d'honnêteté/de mensonge** incapable of cowardice/of honesty/of lying

2 *n* **(a)** (*personne incompétente*) idiot, fool; **c'est un i.** he's incompetent, he's useless *or* no use

(b) *Jur* person who is legally incompetent

incapacité [ɛ̃kapasite] *nf* **(a)** (*incompétence*) (*d'une personne*) incompetence; **i. de faire qch** incapability of doing sth, incapacity to do sth, inability to do sth; **il est dans l'i. de vous répondre** he is incapable of giving *or* unable to give you an answer **(b)** (*invalidité*) **i.** (**de travail**) disability; *Admin* **i. permanente** permanent disablement **(c)** *Jur* (legal) incompetence

incarcération [ɛ̃karserasjɔ̃] *nf* imprisonment, *Fml* incarceration

incarcérer [ɛ̃karsere] *vt* (**j'incarcère; j'incarcérerai**) to imprison, *Fml* to incarcerate; **il a été incarcéré à la prison des Baumettes** he has been sent to Baumettes prison; **il est**

incarcéré à la prison des Baumettes he is (being held) in Baumettes prison
incarnat [ɛ̃karna] **1** *adj* pinkish red; *Bot* **trèfle i.** red clover **2** *nm* (*de l'aurore*) rosy tint; (*du teint*) rosiness
incarnation [ɛ̃karnasjɔ̃] *nf Rel, Myth* (*de personne*) incarnation; *Fig* (*du mal, de l'honnêteté*) incarnation, embodiment (**de** of)
incarné [ɛ̃karne] *adj* **(a)** *Rel* incarnate; *Fig* **la vertu/méchanceté incarnée** virtue/nastiness incarnate *or* personified; **c'est le diable i.!** he's the devil incarnate! **(b)** *Méd* (*ongle*) ingrowing
incarner [ɛ̃karne] **1** *vt* **(a)** *Rel* to incarnate; *Fig* to embody, to personify **(b)** *Th, Cin* **i. qn** *ou* **le rôle de qn** to play (the part of) sb; **il incarne magistralement Hamlet** he is an authoritative Hamlet, he gives an authoritative performance as Hamlet **2 s'incarner** *vpr* **(a)** *Rel* to become incarnate **(b)** *Méd* (*d'un ongle*) to become ingrown
incartade [ɛ̃kartad] *nf* **(a)** (*léger écart de conduite*) indiscretion **(b)** *Équitation* (*de cheval*) sudden swerve
incassable [ɛ̃kasabl] *adj* unbreakable
incendiaire [ɛ̃sɑ̃djɛr] **1** *adj* (*bombe*) incendiary; *Fig* (*discours*) inflammatory **2** *n* (*personne*) arsonist, fire raiser
incendie [ɛ̃sɑ̃di] *nm* (outbreak of) fire, *Fml* conflagration; **i. de forêt** forest fire; **i. volontaire** *ou* **criminel** arson; **provoquer un i.** (*d'une personne*) to start a fire; *Jur* to commit arson; (*d'une explosion, un court-circuit etc*) to cause *or* start a fire; **la police pense qu'il s'agit d'un i. volontaire** the police suspect arson; **70% des incendies de forêt sont en fait des incendies volontaires** 70% of forest fires are caused by arson; **le nombre d'incendies volontaires** the number of cases of arson; *Litt* **l'i. du soleil couchant** the blaze of the setting sun
incendié, -ée [ɛ̃sɑ̃dje] **1** *adj* (*détruit par les flammes*) (*villa, ville*) destroyed by fire, burnt to the ground *or* down **2** *n* victim of a/the fire
incendier [ɛ̃sɑ̃dje] *vt* **(a)** (*mettre le feu à*) to set on fire, to set fire to; *Litt* (*le ciel, les nuages*) to set ablaze *or* on fire; *Fig* (*imagination*) to fire; **toute la ville a été incendiée** (*détruite*) the entire city was burnt down *or* burnt to the ground; **la nouvelle risque d'i. les esprits** the news may well have an inflammatory effect **(b)** *F* (*accabler de reproches*) **i. qn** to tell sb off, to tear sb off a strip; **se faire i.** to get a telling off, to get torn off a strip; **on m'a incendié de reproches** I was bitterly reproached
incertain [ɛ̃sɛrtɛ̃] **1** *adj* (*fait, donnée*) uncertain, doubtful; (*résultat*) uncertain; (*temps*) unsettled; (*mémoire*) unreliable; (*personne*) indecisive; (*démarche, pas*) unsteady; **couleur incertaine** vague colour; **d'un âge i.** of uncertain age; **à une date incertaine** (*passée*) at some uncertain date; (*future*) at a date still to be decided *or* specified; **i. de qch** (*d'une personne*) uncertain *or* unsure of *or* about sth; **l'époque où a été écrit ce texte reste incertaine** there is still some uncertainty as to when the text was written; **ma démarche était très incertaine** I was very unsteady (on my feet); **il avançait d'un pas i. en direction de sa mère** he walked unsteadily *or* tottered towards his mother
2 *nm Fin* **coter l'i.** to quote on the exchange rate
incertitude [ɛ̃sɛrtityd] *nf* (*d'une personne, de l'avenir etc*) uncertainty; (*de caractère*) indecisiveness; **être dans l'i.** to be uncertain *or* in a state of uncertainty (**quant à** about); **nager dans l'i.** to be completely uncertain; **depuis le début de cette affaire, on nage dans l'i.** there has been constant uncertainty since the business started; **il reste encore bien des incertitudes dans cette affaire** there are still a great many uncertainties *or* unresolved questions in the matter; **i. du marché** market uncertainty; **son i. a charmé l'auditoire** his/her timidity charmed the public; **je comprends votre i.** I understand your uncertainty *or* indecision
incessamment [ɛ̃sesamɑ̃] *adv* **(a)** (*sans attendre*) immediately, without delay, at once; **elle arrivera i.** she'll be arriving (at) any moment now *or* very shortly *or US* momentarily; *Hum* **i. sous peu** in the very near future, any moment now **(b)** *Arch* (*sans cesse*) unceasingly, incessantly
incessant [ɛ̃sesɑ̃] *adj* incessant, constant
incessibilité [ɛ̃sesibilite] *nf Jur* inalienability; *Fin* non-transferability
incessible [ɛ̃sesibl] *adj* (*pension, titre de propriété*) non-transferable, not negotiable; *Jur* (*droit*) inalienable
inceste [ɛ̃sɛst] *nm* incest
incestueux [ɛ̃sɛstɥø] *adj* (*personne, relation*) incestuous; **enfant i.** child of an incestuous relationship
inchangé [ɛ̃ʃɑ̃ʒe] *adj* (*prix, plan, emploi du temps, situation*) unchanged
inchangeable [ɛ̃ʃɑ̃ʒabl] *adj* unchangeable
inchantable [ɛ̃ʃɑ̃tabl] *adj* unsingable
inchauffable [ɛ̃ʃofabl] *adj* (*pièce, maison, voiture*) impossible to heat
inchavirable [ɛ̃ʃavirabl] *adj* (*bateau*) uncapsizable, self-righting
inchoatif, -ive [ɛ̃kɔatif -iv] *adj, nm Ling* inceptive
incidemment [ɛ̃sidamɑ̃] *adv* (*apprendre une nouvelle*) in passing, incidentally; (*demander qch*) in passing; **il a été i. question du problème des retards** the problem of lateness came up in passing *or* incidentally
incidence [ɛ̃sidɑ̃s] *nf* **(a)** (*répercussion*) repercussion; (*impact*) effect, impact; **cette action qu'il pensait sans i.** this action which he thought would have no repercussions; **quelle i. aura la démission du ministre sur la situation?** what effect *or* impact will the Minister's resignation have on the situation?, how will the Minister's resignation affect the situation?; **i. fiscale** tax implications **(b)** *Méd* (*d'une maladie*) incidence **(c)** *Tech* incidence; *Phys* **angle d'i.** angle of incidence
incident [ɛ̃sidɑ̃] **1** *nm* **(a)** (*événement sans conséquence*) hitch, difficulty; **se dérouler sans i.** to go off without a hitch *or* without incident *or* smoothly; **c'est juste un i.** it's nothing much, it's just a slight mishap **(b)** (*événement plus grave*) incident; **l'i. est clos** the incident is closed; **i. à la frontière** border incident **(c)** *Jur* point of law **2** *adj* **(a)** (*par hasard*) (*question, remarque*) incidental **(b)** *Phys* (*rayon*) incident
▸ **incident**: **i. diplomatique** diplomatic incident; **i. de parcours** minor setback; **i. technique** technical hitch *or* problem
incinérateur [ɛ̃sineratœr] *nm* incinerator
incinération [ɛ̃sinerasjɔ̃] *nf* (*de déchets*) incineration; (*d'une personne*) cremation
incinérer [ɛ̃sinere] *vt* (**j'incinère; j'incinérerai**) (*objets, déchets*) to incinerate; (*personne*) to cremate
incirconcis [ɛ̃sirkɔ̃si] *adj* uncircumcised
incise [ɛ̃siz] *nf Gram* interpolated clause, incidental clause
inciser [ɛ̃size] **1** *vt* (*gencive*) to incise, to make an incision in; (*abcès, furoncle*) to lance; (*arbre*) to tap (*for resin*) **2** *vi* to incise
incisif, -ive [ɛ̃sizif, -iv] **1** *adj* **(a)** (*remarque*) incisive, sharp, cutting; (*personne, style*) incisive **(b)** **dent incisive** incisor tooth **2** *nf* **incisive** incisor
incision [ɛ̃sizjɔ̃] *nf* **(a)** (*action*) (*de gencive*) incision; (*d'un furoncle, d'un abcès*) lancing; (*d'un arbre*) tapping (*for resin*) **(b)** (*coupure*) incision
incitation [ɛ̃sitasjɔ̃] *nf* (*à la violence, l'émeute*) incitement; (*encouragement*) stimulus, incentive; **i. fiscale** tax incentive; **i. à l'achat** incentive to buy; **i. à la débauche** corruption; **i. de mineurs à la débauche** corruption of minors
inciter [ɛ̃site] *vt* to encourage, *Péj* to incite (**qn à faire qch** sb to do sth); **i. au crime** to incite crime; **tu incites tes petits camarades à bavarder** you're encouraging your friends *or* egging your friends on to chatter; **il faut i. les jeunes à travailler** young people must be encouraged *or* given incentives to work; **cette réponse m'incite à la prudence** the answer inclines me to be cautious; **son attitude n'incite pas à l'aider** his attitude does not incline you to help him
incivil [ɛ̃sivil] *adj Litt* uncivil, rude
incivilisable [ɛ̃sivilizabl] *adj* which cannot be civilized
incivilité [ɛ̃sivilite] *nf Litt* **(a)** (*manque de politesse*) incivility, rudeness **(b)** (*remarque/action impolie*) rude remark/action
incivique [ɛ̃sivik] *adj Vieilli* with no sense of civic duty
inclassable [ɛ̃klasabl] *adj* unclassifiable; **un film/peintre i.** a film/painter that/who cannot be classified *or* pigeonholed; **elle est vraiment i.** she's in a class all of her own
inclémence [ɛ̃klemɑ̃s] *nf* inclemency
inclément [ɛ̃klemɑ̃] *adj* inclement
inclinable [ɛ̃klinabl] *adj* (*siège*) reclining; (*table, plan*) tilting
inclinaison [ɛ̃klinɛzɔ̃] *nf* (*état de ce qui est incliné*) (*de colline*) incline, gradient, slope; (*de ligne*) inclination; (*de toit*) pitch, slant, cant; (*de tête, chapeau*) tilt; (*de bateau*) heel, list; (*de mât*) rake; (*d'aiguille magnétique*) dip; (*de trajectoire*) angle; **comble à forte/faible i.** high-/low-pitched roof; **degré d'i. d'une courbe** steepness of a curve
▸ **inclinaison**: **i. magnétique** (magnetic) declination, magnetic variation
inclination [ɛ̃klinasjɔ̃] *nf* **(a)** *Fig* (*tendance naturelle*) inclination, tendency; **suivre ses inclinations** to follow one's inclinations; **montrer de l'i. pour la musique/le français** to show an inclination for music/French; **avoir de l'i. pour qch** to have a liking for sth *or* an inclination for sth; **avoir de l'i. pour la musique** to have an inclination for music, to be musically inclined, *Fml* to have a musical bent; *Vieilli* **mariage d'i.** love match
(b) (*du corps*) angle; (*de la tête*) angle, tilt; **on note une légère i. de la tête du personnage central du tableau** the

head of the central figure in the painting is slightly tilted *or* is at a slight angle

incliné [ɛ̃kline] *adj* (*penché*) (*poteau, mât*) at an angle *or* slope, sloping; (*plan de travail*) tilted; **la tête inclinée** (*sur le côté*) with one's head (tilted) to one side; (*en avant*) with bowed head; **plan i.** inclined plane; **le poteau est légèrement i.** the stake is at a bit of an angle; **le mur était i.** the wall sloped

incliner [ɛ̃kline] **1** *vt* **(a)** (*pencher*) (*poteau, barre, tablette, dossier de siège*) to tilt; *Constr* (*toit*) to slant, to slope, to cant; (*planche*) to tip up, to tilt; **i. le buste en avant** to bend forward *or* from the waist; **i. la tête** (*en avant*) to bow one's head; (*en signe de salut*) to nod (one's head); (*sur le côté*) to tilt one's head to one side; **il inclina la tête dans ma direction** he nodded in my direction

(b) *Fig* **i. qn à faire qch** to incline sb to do sth; **i. qn à la prudence** to incline sb to be cautious, *Fml* to predispose sb to caution; **la vue de tous ces malheureux l'inclinait à la pitié** the sight of all these wretched people inclined him towards pity; **être incliné à faire qch** to be *or* feel inclined to do sth

2 *vi* **(a)** (*d'un mur etc*) to lean, to slope

(b) (*être enclin à*) **i. à la pitié** to be inclined to feel pity; **i. à la modération** to be moderate

3 s'incliner *vpr* **(a)** (*d'un terrain*) to slant, to slope; (*d'un bateau*) to heel (over); (*d'un avion*) to bank

(b) (*se pencher*) (*en avant*) to bend over *or* forward; (*sur le côté*) to bend to one side; (*pour saluer*) to bow (**devant** before); *Fig* **s'i. devant qn/le génie de qn** to bow down before sb/sb's genius

(c) (*se soumettre*) **s'i. devant les arguments de qn** to bow *or* yield to sb's arguments; **j'ai dû m'i.** I had to give in; **s'i. devant son adversaire** to yield to one's opponent, to admit defeat

(d) (*être battu*) (*d'une équipe, d'un club*) to admit defeat, to lose; **s'i. face à** *ou* **devant qn** to be beaten by sb, to lose to sb; **l'équipe de France a dû s'i.** the French team had to admit defeat

inclinomètre [ɛ̃klinɔmɛtr] *nm Av* inclinometer

inclure [ɛ̃klyr] *vt* (*conj like* **conclure** *except pp* **inclus**) **(a)** (*document, cassette, pièces de dossier*) to enclose **(b)** *Jur* (*clause, condition, disposition*) to insert, to include (**à** in), to add (**à** to); **l'accord inclut les conditions suivantes** the agreement includes the following conditions

inclus [ɛ̃kly] *adj* **(a)** (*compris*) **jusqu'à la page 5 incluse** up to and including page 5; **je serai absente jusqu'au mardi i.** I will be away until Wednesday, *US* I will be away through Tuesday; **du 7 au 18 i.** from the 7th to the 18th inclusive; **ils seront 35, professeurs i.** there will be 35 of them, including the teachers; **le service est-il i.?** is service included?; *Math* **A est i. dans B** A is included in B **(b) dent incluse** impacted tooth

inclusif, -ive [ɛ̃klyzif, -iv] *adj Ling* inclusive

inclusion [ɛ̃klyzjɔ̃] *nf* **(a)** (*fait d'inclure qch*) inclusion, insertion; (*d'un document dans une lettre etc*) enclosure (**dans** with); **on a décidé l'i. d'un nouveau paragraphe au traité** we decided to add a new clause to the treaty **(b)** (*objet décoratif*) = flower, shell etc set into plastic and used as paperweight, ornament, jewellery etc **(c)** *Math* inclusion **(d)** (*d'une dent*) impacting **(e)** *Ordinat* (*de fichier*) insertion

inclusivement [ɛ̃klyzivmɑ̃] *adv* **du vendredi au mardi i.** from Friday to Tuesday inclusive, *US* from Friday through Tuesday; **jusqu'au 14 mars i.** up to and including 14th March, *US* through March 14th

incoercible [ɛ̃kɔɛrsibl] *adj Litt* (*toux*) uncontrollable; (*rire*) irrepressible

incognito [ɛ̃kɔɲito] **1** *adv* (*venir, voyager*) incognito **2** *nm* **garder l'i.** to remain incognito

incohérence [ɛ̃kɔerɑ̃s] *nf* (*d'une personne, dans un film, une histoire*) inconsistency; (*d'un discours*) disjointedness, incoherence; (*d'idées*) disjointedness; **le film est plein d'incohérences** the film is full of inconsistencies; **le discours était un tissu d'incohérences** the speech was totally incoherent; **d'une i. ahurissante** dreadfully inconsistent *or* incoherent

incohérent [ɛ̃kɔerɑ̃] *adj* (*personne, histoire, attitude*) inconsistent; (*idées, argumentation*) disjointed; (*discours*) incoherent, disjointed; **tenir des propos incohérents** to speak incoherently

incollable [ɛ̃kɔlabl] *adj* **(a)** (*riz*) non-stick **(b)** *F* **elle est i. sur la question/en histoire** you can't catch her out on the subject/on history

incolore [ɛ̃kɔlɔr] *adj* colourless, *US* colorless

incomber [ɛ̃kɔ̃be] *vt ind* (*used only in third person*) **les devoirs qui lui incombent** the duties which fall on him, *Fml* the duties incumbent on him; **la responsabilité incombe à l'auteur** the responsibility lies *or* rests with the author, it is the author's responsibility; **il m'incombe de pourvoir à leurs besoins** it is my duty *or Fml* it is incumbent on me to provide for their needs; **il incombe au gouvernement d'indemniser les sinistrés** the onus is on the government to compensate the victims

incombustibilité [ɛ̃kɔ̃bystibilite] *nf* incombustibility

incombustible [ɛ̃kɔ̃bystibl] *adj* incombustible, non-(in)flammable, fireproof

incommensurable [ɛ̃kɔmɑ̃syrabl] *adj* **(a)** (*immense*) (*richesse*) immeasurable; (*rage*) tremendous; **il est d'une bêtise i.** his stupidity knows no bounds **(b)** *Math* incommensurate, incommensurable (**avec** with); **racine i.** irrational root

incommensurablement [ɛ̃kɔmɑ̃syrabləmɑ̃] *adv* **(a)** (*immensément*) (*riche*) immeasurably; (*bête*) tremendously **(b)** *Math* incommensurably

incommodant [ɛ̃kɔmɔdɑ̃] *adj* (*odeur, promiscuité*) unpleasant, disagreeable; (*bruit*) annoying

incommode [ɛ̃kɔmɔd] *adj* (*horaire, arrangement*) inconvenient, awkward; (*situation*) awkward, uncomfortable; (*chaise*) uncomfortable; (*outil*) clumsy, awkward; (*appartement*) inconvenient; *Vieilli* (*personne*) unwelcome

incommodé [ɛ̃kɔmɔde] *adj* (*gêné*) **être i.** to feel unwell *or* off colour; **être i. par la chaleur** to feel *or* be bothered by the heat; **être i. par une odeur/un bruit** to be bothered by a smell/noise

incommodément [ɛ̃kɔmɔdemɑ̃] *adv* uncomfortably, awkwardly

incommoder [ɛ̃kɔmɔde] *vt* (*gêner*) to bother

incommodité [ɛ̃kɔmɔdite] *nf* (*d'une situation*) uncomfortableness, awkwardness; (*d'un arrangement, un horaire*) inconvenience, awkwardness; (*d'un appartement*) inconvenience; (*d'un outil*) awkwardness, clumsiness; **en raison de l'i. des horaires** because the timetables are so inconvenient *or* awkward

incommunicabilité [ɛ̃kɔmynikabilite] *nf Litt* (*d'un secret*) strict confidentiality; **l'i. des sentiments est souvent à l'origine de nombreuses incompréhensions** the fact that people don't talk about *or* aren't open about their feelings gives rise to numerous misunderstandings; **nous en étions arrivé à un point d'i. tel que …** we had stopped communicating to the point where …

incommunicable [ɛ̃kɔmynikabl] *adj* (*secret*) which cannot be revealed; (*sentiment*) indescribable; **ce que j'ai ressenti est i.** I cannot describe my feelings *or* how I felt

incommutable [ɛ̃kɔmytabl] *adj Jur* (*propriété*) non-transferable; (*droit*) indefeasible

incomparable [ɛ̃kɔ̃parabl] *adj* (*qualité, cuisinière*) incomparable, beyond compare, matchless; **vous sentez la différence? – c'est i.!** do you feel the difference? – there's just no comparison

incomparablement [ɛ̃kɔ̃parabləmɑ̃] *adv* incomparably

incompatibilité [ɛ̃kɔ̃patibilite] *nf* incompatibility; **i. d'humeur** *ou* **de caractère** incompatibility of temperament; **il y a i. entre nous** we are incompatible

▶ **incompatibilité**: *Pharm* **i. médicamenteuse** incompatibility of drugs; *Méd* **i. sanguine** incompatibility of blood groups

incompatible [ɛ̃kɔ̃patibl] *adj* (*caractère, idée*) incompatible, inconsistent, at variance (**avec** with); (*fonctions, méthodes, Méd groupes sanguins, Pharm médicaments*) incompatible

incompétence [ɛ̃kɔ̃petɑ̃s] *nf* **(a)** (*manque de compétence*) incompetence; **son i. en informatique/matière de voitures** his ignorance about *or* lack of knowledge of computers/cars **(b)** *Jur* (*d'une personne, d'un tribunal*) incompetence, incompetency

incompétent [ɛ̃kɔ̃petɑ̃] *adj* **(a)** incompetent; **je suis i. en cuisine** I'm an incompetent cook, I know nothing about cooking; **je suis i. en informatique/en matière de voitures/en matière de droit** I know nothing *or* I am ignorant about computers/cars/the law **(b)** *Jur* (*non habilité*) (*tribunal*) not qualified, unqualified

incomplètement [ɛ̃kɔ̃plɛtmɑ̃] *adv* incompletely

incomplet, -ète [ɛ̃kɔ̃plɛ, -ɛt] *adj* incomplete

incomplétude [ɛ̃kɔ̃pletyd] *nf Psy* **sentiment d'i.** (sense of) inadequacy *or* non-fulfilment

incompréhensibilité [ɛ̃kɔ̃preɑ̃sibilite] *nf Litt* incomprehensibility

incompréhensible [ɛ̃kɔ̃preɑ̃sibl] *adj* incomprehensible; **c'est i., je les avais posées là!** I don't understand it, I put them right there!

incompréhensif, -ive [ɛ̃kɔ̃preɑ̃sif, -iv] *adj* (*père, médecin, parents*) unsympathetic, lacking in understanding; (*esprit*) unsympathetic

incompréhension [ɛ̃kɔ̃preɑ̃sjɔ̃] *nf* lack of understanding *or* sympathy

incompressible [ɛ̃kɔ̃prɛsibl] *adj Phys (matériau)* incompressible; *Jur (peine)* to be served in full; **dépenses incompressibles** expenditure which cannot be reduced *or* pared down; **il existe un chômage i.** there is a level below which unemployment cannot be reduced

incompris, -ise [ɛ̃kɔ̃pri, -iz] **1** *adj* misunderstood **2** *n* **je suis un i.** I am misunderstood, nobody understands me

inconcevable [ɛ̃kɔ̃s(ə)vabl] *adj* inconceivable, unthinkable, unimaginable; **il est i. que ...** it's inconceivable that ...; **c'est totalement i.** it's quite unthinkable

inconcevablement [ɛ̃kɔ̃s(ə)vabləmɑ̃] *adv* inconceivably

inconciliable [ɛ̃kɔ̃siljabl] *adj (théorie)* irreconcilable (**avec** with); **le métier est i. avec une vie de famille** the profession is incompatible with family life

inconditionnalité [ɛ̃kɔdisjɔnalite] *nf (d'un partisan)* unwavering *or* unquestioning support

inconditionné [ɛ̃kɔ̃disjɔne] *adj Psy (réflexe, stimulus)* unconditioned

inconditionnel, -elle [ɛ̃kɔ̃disjɔnɛl] **1** *adj (soutien, retrait etc)* unconditional; *(obéissance)* unquestioning, unconditional; *(supporter)* staunch, unwavering **2** *n* fan(atic), enthusiast; **c'est un i. de la pêche/du hard rock** he's a fishing/hard rock fanatic, he's fanatical about fishing/hard rock; **je suis une inconditionnelle de Prévert** I am a great fan of Prévert, I am mad about Prévert; **je suis une inconditionnelle de l'Espagne/des îles grecques** I am mad about *or* I adore Spain/the Greek islands

inconditionnellement [ɛ̃kɔ̃disjɔnɛlmɑ̃] *adv (soutenir qn)* unconditionally, without question; *(obéir)* unquestioningly, without question; **être i. favorable à qn/qch** to support sb/sth wholeheartedly

inconduite [ɛ̃kɔ̃dɥit] *nf Litt* loose living; *Jur* misconduct

inconfort [ɛ̃kɔ̃fɔr] *nm (manque de confort matériel)* discomfort; *(malaise moral)* uncomfortableness

inconfortable [ɛ̃kɔ̃fɔrtabl] *adj (siège, voiture, Fig situation)* uncomfortable

inconfortablement [ɛ̃kɔ̃fɔrtabləmɑ̃] *adv* uncomfortably

incongru [ɛ̃kɔ̃gry] *adj (remarque, réponse)* incongruous, inappropriate, out of place; *(question, comportement)* inappropriate, improper, unseemly; *(bruit)* rude, unseemly; **il allait travailler dans une tenue des plus incongrues** he wore a really extravagant outfit to work

incongruité [ɛ̃kɔ̃grɥite] *nf* **(a)** *(caractère déplacé) (d'une remarque, réponse)* incongruity, inappropriateness; *(d'un comportement, d'une question)* inappropriateness, unseemliness, impropriety; *(de vêtements)* extravagance **(b)** *(remarque déplacée)* inappropriate *or* improper remark; *(action qui choque)* inappropriate *or* improper action

incongrûment [ɛ̃kɔ̃grymɑ̃] *adv Litt (répondre, parler)* in an unseemly fashion

inconnaissable [ɛ̃kɔnɛsabl] *adj, nm* unknowable

inconnu, -ue [ɛ̃kɔny] **1** *adj (auteur, civilisation, destination)* unknown (**de, à** to); **se retrouver dans un lieu i.** to find oneself in a strange place; **il m'était i.** I didn't know him, he was a stranger to me; **il était i. de tout le monde** nobody knew him, he was a stranger to everybody; **né de père i.** *(sur document administratif)* father unknown; **elle est née de père i.** she doesn't know who her father was; **visages inconnus** strange faces; **c'est un problème qui lui est totalement i.** the problem is totally foreign to him, it's a problem he knows absolutely nothing about; **i. à cette adresse** not known at this address; *F* **Durand? i. au bataillon!** Durand? never heard of him!

2 *n (étranger)* stranger; **c'est un i. qui a remporté le prix Nobel** someone no-one has ever heard of has won the Nobel prize

3 *nm* **l'i.** the unknown; **la peur de l'i.** the fear of the unknown; **faire un saut dans l'i.** to take a leap in the dark

4 *nf Math* **inconnue** unknown (quantity); *Fig* **il y a beaucoup trop d'inconnues dans cette affaire** there are two many unknowns in the matter

inconsciemment [ɛ̃kɔ̃sjamɑ̃] *adv* **(a)** *(dans l'inconscient)* subconsciously **(b)** *(sans réfléchir)* without thinking, thoughtlessly; **il a signé un peu i.** he signed without giving it too much thought

inconscience [ɛ̃kɔ̃sjɑ̃s] *nf* **(a)** *(physique)* unconsciousness; **sombrer** *ou* **tomber dans l'i.** to lapse into unconsciousness, to become unconscious **(b)** *(manque de jugement)* recklessness, irresponsibility; **faire preuve d'i.** to be reckless *or* irresponsible; **c'est de l'i. pure et simple!** it's sheer madness!, how irresponsible can you get!

inconscient, -ente [ɛ̃kɔ̃sjɑ̃, -ɑ̃t] **1** *adj* **(a)** *(sans connaissance) (personne, blessé)* unconscious **(b)** *(irréfléchi) (personne)* irresponsible; *(geste)* rash, *Fml* ill-considered; **c'est i. ce que tu as fait là** it was irresponsible of you **(c)** *(non conscient) (acte)* unconscious; **i. de ce qui se passe autour de lui** oblivious to *or* unaware of what is going on around him **2** *n* irresponsible person; **tu n'es qu'une inconsciente!** you really are irresponsible! **3** *nm Psy* **l'i.** the unconscious, the subconscious

▶ **inconscient: l'i. collectif** the collective unconscious

inconséquence [ɛ̃kɔ̃sekɑ̃s] *nf (caractère inconséquent)* thoughtlessness; *(action inconséquente)* rash *or* irresponsible act; **on me blâmait pour mes inconséquences** I was reproached for being rash *or* irresponsible

inconséquent [ɛ̃kɔ̃sekɑ̃] *adj* **(a)** *(illogique, versatile) (argument, personne)* inconsistent; **être i. dans ses propos** to contradict oneself, to speak illogically; **il dit des choses inconséquentes** he speaks incoherently **(b)** *(irréfléchi) (personne, démarche)* thoughtless, rash

inconsidéré [ɛ̃kɔ̃sidere] *adj* **(a)** *(acte, remarque)* thoughtless, rash, *Fml* ill-considered; *(dépenses)* rash, reckless; **faire des dépenses inconsidérées** to spend recklessly **(b)** *Vieilli (personne)* inconsiderate

inconsidérément [ɛ̃kɔ̃sideremɑ̃] *adv (agir, parler)* thoughtlessly, without thinking, rashly; *(dépenser)* recklessly

inconsistance [ɛ̃kɔ̃sistɑ̃s] *nf* **(a)** *(manque de consistance) (d'une pâte)* runniness; *(de la boue)* softness; *(du sol)* looseness **(b)** *(d'une personne, d'un acte)* inconsistency; *(d'une intrigue)* thinness, flimsiness; *(d'un film, d'un roman)* thinness; *(d'une accusation)* flimsiness, insubstantial nature; **le film/roman était d'une i. telle que ...** the film/novel was so lacking in substance that ...

inconsistant [ɛ̃kɔ̃sistɑ̃] *adj* **(a)** *(liquide) (pâte, crème)* thin, runny; *(boue)* soft; *(sol)* loose **(b)** *(manquant de logique) (conduite, personne)* inconsistent **(c)** *(manquant de matière) (intrigue)* thin, flimsy, insubstantial; *(film)* insubstantial; *(accusation)* flimsy, without substance

inconsolable [ɛ̃kɔ̃sɔlabl] *adj (personne, chagrin, tristesse)* inconsolable

inconsolé [ɛ̃kɔ̃sɔle] *adj* unconsoled

inconsommable [ɛ̃kɔ̃sɔmabl] *adj* unfit for consumption

inconstance [ɛ̃kɔ̃stɑ̃s] *nf* **(a)** *(d'une personne) (de caractère)* changeableness; *(en amour)* fickleness, *Fml* inconstancy **(b)** *Litt (du temps, de la mode)* fickleness, changeableness

inconstant [ɛ̃kɔ̃stɑ̃] *adj* **(a)** *(personne) (caractère)* changeable; *(en amour)* fickle, *Fml* inconstant; **être i. en amour** to be fickle **(b)** *Litt (mode)* fickle, changeable

inconstatable [ɛ̃kɔ̃statabl] *adj* unascertainable, unverifiable

inconstitutionnalité [ɛ̃kɔ̃stitysjɔnalite] *nf Jur* unconstitutionality

inconstitutionnel, -elle [ɛ̃kɔ̃stitysjɔnɛl] *adj Jur* unconstitutional

inconstitutionnellement [ɛ̃kɔ̃stitysjɔnɛlmɑ̃] *adv Jur* unconstitutionally

inconstructible [ɛ̃kɔ̃stryktibl] *adj (zone, terrain)* that cannot be developed

incontestabilité [ɛ̃kɔ̃tɛstabilite] *nf Jur* incontestability

incontestable [ɛ̃kɔ̃tɛstabl] *adj (fait, preuve, victoire)* undeniable, indisputable, *Fml* incontestable; *(vérité)* undeniable, indisputable; **il est i. que ...** it is undeniable that ..., it cannot be denied that ...

incontestablement [ɛ̃kɔ̃tɛstabləmɑ̃] *adv* undeniably, indisputably, beyond all doubt, *Fml* incontestably

incontesté [ɛ̃kɔ̃tɛste] *adj (droit)* uncontested, undisputed; *(maître, victoire)* undisputed

incontinence [ɛ̃kɔ̃tinɑ̃s] *nf* **(a)** *Méd* incontinence; **i. nocturne** bedwetting **(b)** *Vieilli, Litt (luxure)* incontinence, lack of restraint; **souffrir d'i. verbale** to have verbal diarrhoea

incontinent[1] [ɛ̃kɔ̃tinɑ̃] *adj* **(a)** *Méd* incontinent **(b)** *Arch, Litt (dans vie sexuelle)* incontinent, unrestrained; **être i. dans ses propos** to talk far too much; **un orateur complètement i. dans ses propos** an orator who goes on and on *or* who doesn't know when to stop

incontinent[2] *adv Arch, Litt* at once, forthwith

incontournable [ɛkɔ̃turnabl] *adj* **c'est i.** you can't get away from it; **son argument était i.** there was no getting away from his argument; **Harrods/la tour penchée de Pise est un magasin/un monument i.** Harrods/the leaning tower of Pisa should not be missed, Harrods/the leaning tower of Pisa is a must; **son dernier film est absolument i.** his latest film is an absolute must

incontrôlable [ɛ̃kɔ̃trolabl] *adj* **(a)** *(affirmation)* difficult to verify *or* to check, unverifiable **(b)** *(incendie, supporter)* uncontrollable; **très vite, l'incendie fut i.** the fire very quickly got out of control *or* out of hand; **des éléments incontrôlables** the rowdy elements

incontrôlé [ɛ̃kɔ̃trole] *adj* **(a)** *(non vérifié)* unchecked, unverified **(b)** *(non surveillé)* uncontrolled

inconvenance [ɛ̃kɔ̃v(ə)nɑ̃s] *nf (caractère inconvenant)* impropriety; **comme si j'avais dit/commis une i.** as if I had said/done something improper *or* out of place *or* out of turn

inconvenant [ɛ̃kɔ̃v(ə)nɑ̃] *adj (propos, remarque, acte)* improper, out of place, out of turn; **il est vraiment i.** he doesn't know how to behave, he has no manners; **il serait totalement i. d'aller à un enterrement habillé de rouge** it would be totally inappropriate to go to a funeral dressed in red

inconvénient [ɛ̃kɔ̃venjɑ̃] *nm* drawback, disadvantage; **les inconvénients qu'il y a à vivre si loin de la ville** the disadvantages *or* drawbacks *or* inconvenience of living so far from town; **le seul i., c'est que …** the only drawback is that …; **l'i. c'est que …** the problem is that …; **je n'y vois pas d'i.** I can't see any objection(s) (to it), I've got nothing against it; **si vous n'y voyez aucun i., je voudrais …** if you have no objection, I'd like to …; **si je t'emprunte ta voiture, est-ce que tu y vois un i.?** would you have any objections if I borrowed your car?; **il n'y a pas d'i. à cela** that doesn't pose any problem; **nous pouvons sans i. modifier notre itinéraire** we can easily change our route

inconvertible [ɛ̃kɔ̃vɛrtibl] *adj (monnaie)* inconvertible, non-convertible

incoordination [ɛ̃kɔɔrdinasjɔ̃] *nf* lack of coordination; *Méd* ataxia

incorporable [ɛ̃kɔrpɔrabl] *adj (rare) (appelé)* eligible for military service

incorporation [ɛ̃kɔrpɔrasjɔ̃] *nf* **(a)** *(mélange)* incorporation, blending, mixing (**de qch dans qch** of sth into *or* with sth); **opérer l'i. d'une poudre à un mélange** to incorporate a powder into a mixture; *Fin* **i. des réserves au capital** capitalization of reserves **(b)** *Mil* conscription; **sursis d'i.** deferment of call-up

incorporéité [ɛ̃kɔrpɔreite] *nf* incorporeity, incorporality

incorporel, -elle [ɛ̃kɔrpɔrɛl] *adj (qui n'a pas de corps)* incorporeal; *Jur* **biens incorporels** intangible property

incorporer [ɛ̃kɔrpɔre] **1** *vt* **(a)** *(amalgamer)* **i. qch à** *ou parfois* **avec qch** to incorporate *or* blend *or* mix sth into *or* with sth **(b)** *(intégrer) (terrain)* to incorporate (**dans un domaine** in(to) an estate); *(paragraphe)* to incorporate (**à** in(to)), to insert (**à** in); **le flash est incorporé à l'appareil photo** the flash is built into the camera; **un magnétophone avec micro incorporé** a tape recorder with a built-in microphone **(c)** *Mil (troupes)* to draft **2 s'incorporer** *vpr* **chercher à s'i. dans un groupe** to try to join a group

incorrect [ɛ̃kɔrɛkt] *adj* **(a)** *(impropre) (emploi d'un mot, réponse, traduction)* incorrect, wrong **(b)** *(défectueux) (montage)* defective, faulty; *(tracé)* incorrect, wrong **(c)** *(d'une façon inconvenante)* contrary to etiquette; **tenue incorrecte** *(débraillée)* slovenly clothes; *(déplacée)* unsuitable clothes **(d)** *(personne)* impolite, ill-mannered, rude; *(attitude)* improper; **être i. en affaires** to be unscrupulous in business

incorrectement [ɛ̃kɔrɛktəmɑ̃] *adv* **(a)** *(en faisant des erreurs) (employer, écrire, traduire)* incorrectly, wrongly **(b)** *(d'une façon défectueuse) (monté)* defectively; *(tracé)* incorrectly, wrongly **(c)** *(habillé) (de façon débraillée)* in a slovenly manner; *(de façon déplacée)* unsuitably, incorrectly **(d)** *(avec impolitesse) (agir, se comporter)* improperly; **se conduire i. avec qn, agir i. avec qn** to behave improperly towards sb

incorrection [ɛ̃kɔrɛksjɔ̃] *nf* **(a)** *(impolitesse)* rudeness, impoliteness, lack of (good) manners; **pour i. envers ses professeurs** for being rude to his teachers; **elle est d'une i. avec les gens!** she is incredibly rude to people **(b)** *Gram* incorrect expression; **le mot était considéré comme une i.** the word used to be considered incorrect **(c)** *(action incorrecte)* impolite *or* rude action; *(propos incorrect)* impolite *or* rude remark; **à la suite d'une grave i. envers un professeur** after being extremely rude to a teacher

incorrigibilité [ɛ̃kɔriʒibilite] *nf* incorrigibility

incorrigible [ɛ̃kɔriʒibl] *adj* incorrigible; **d'une gourmandise i.** incorrigibly greedy

incorrigiblement [ɛ̃kɔriʒibləmɑ̃] *adv (rare)* incorrigibly; **elle est i. bavarde** she is an incorrigible chatterbox

incorruptibilité [ɛ̃kɔryptibilite] *nf* incorruptibility

incorruptible [ɛ̃kɔryptibl] **1** *adj* incorruptible **2** *n* incorruptible person

incoté [ɛ̃kɔte] *adj Fin* unquoted

incoterms [ɛ̃kɔtɛrm] *nmpl Com* incoterms

incrédibilité [ɛ̃kredibilite] *nf* incredibility

incrédule [ɛ̃kredyl] **1** *adj (sceptique)* incredulous; *Rel* unbelieving; **il hochait la tête d'un air i.** he shook his head in disbelief *or* incredulously; **je suis très i. quant à la véracité de ce qu'il raconte** I'm very sceptical about what he says, I'm very incredulous about the truth of what he says **2** *n (personne sceptique)*, *Rel* unbeliever

incrédulité [ɛ̃kredylite] *nf* incredulity; *Rel* unbelief; **avec i.** incredulously

incrémenter [ɛ̃kremɑ̃te] *Ordinat* to increment

increvable [ɛ̃krəvabl] *adj* **(a)** *(pneu)* puncture-proof **(b)** *F (personne)* full of energy *or F* beans, tireless; *(personne âgée, voiture, moteur)* indestructible; **les enfants sont increvables** it's impossible to tire children out

incriminé [ɛ̃krimine] *adj Jur (personne)* accused, charged

incriminer [ɛ̃krimine] *vt (personne) Jur* to accuse, to charge, to indict; *(tenir responsable)* to blame, to accuse; *(actions, paroles de qn)* to condemn

incrochetable [ɛ̃krɔʃtabl] *adj (serrure)* unpickable; *(coffre)* burglar-proof

incroyable [ɛ̃krwajabl] **1** *adj (histoire, chance, paresse)* incredible, unbelievable, extraordinary; *(chapeau)* incredible, extraordinary; **une histoire tout à fait i.** an altogether incredible story; **il est d'une paresse i.** he's incredibly lazy; **j'ai eu une chance i.** I was incredibly lucky, I had incredible luck; **je trouve ça i. que …** I think it's incredible *or* extraordinary that …; **tu es vraiment i.!** you're the limit!, I don't believe you!; **c'est i. ça!** I don't believe it! **2** *n Hist Fr* incroyable *(beau or belle of the French Directoire period)*

incroyablement [ɛ̃krwajabləmɑ̃] *adv (beau, vulgaire)* incredibly, unbelievably, extraordinarily; *(vêtu, maquillée)* incredibly, extraordinarily; **il s'est i. bien comporté** he behaved incredibly well

incroyance [ɛ̃krwajɑ̃s] *nf Rel* unbelief

incroyant, -ante [ɛ̃krwajɑ̃, -ɑ̃t] **1** *adj* unbelieving **2** *n* unbeliever, non-believer

incrustation [ɛ̃krystasjɔ̃] *nf* **(a)** *(action)* encrusting; *Menuis* inlaying **(b)** *(dépôt) (dans une chaudière, une bouilloire)* fur, scale **(c)** *(ornement)* encrustation, inlay, inlaid work; **i. de dentelle** lace inlay; **avec incrustations de nacre** inlaid with mother of pearl **(d)** *Couture* insertion **(e)** *TV* matting, keying

incruster [ɛ̃kryste] **1** *vt* **(a)** *Menuis* to inlay (**de** with) **(b)** *(former un dépôt)* to encrust; *(d'une eau calcaire) (tuyaux, chaudière, bouilloire)* to scale, to fur (up) **(c)** *(pour orner)* to encrust **(d)** *TV* to overlay **2 s'incruster** *vpr* **(a)** *(adhérer)* to become encrusted **(b)** *(d'une chaudière, une bouilloire)* to fur up **(c)** *F (s'imposer)* **quand on l'invite, il s'incruste** once you invite him you can't get rid of him; **je ne voudrais pas m'i.** I wouldn't want to overstay my welcome; **ils font une fête, on s'incruste?** they're having a party, let's gatecrash

incubateur, -trice [ɛ̃kybatœr, -tris] **1** *adj (appareil etc)* incubating **2** *nm* incubator

incubation [ɛ̃kybasjɔ̃] *nf* **(a)** *(d'œufs)* incubation; *(de poules)* sitting **(b)** *Méd* incubation; **période d'i.** incubation period

incube [ɛ̃kyb] *nm* incubus

incuber [ɛ̃kybe] *vt (œufs)* to incubate, to hatch (out)

inculcation [ɛ̃kylkasjɔ̃] *nf Litt* inculcating, inculcation

inculpation [ɛ̃kylpasjɔ̃] *nf* indictment; **depuis son i.** since his indictment, since he was indicted *or* charged; **le juge lui a notifié son i.** the judge informed him that he was being charged; **sous l'i. d'assassinat** charged with murder; **i. de trois responsables du club de football pour détournement de fonds** *(titre de journal)* three football club managers charged with embezzlement

inculpé, -ée [ɛ̃kylpe] *n Jur* **l'i.** the accused, the defendant

inculper [ɛ̃kylpe] *vt* to indict, to charge (**de, pour** with); **les trois hommes inculpés pour trafic de drogue** the three men charged with drug trafficking, the three defendants in the drug trafficking trial

inculquer [ɛ̃kylke] *vt* to instil, *Fml* to inculcate (**à qn** in sb)

inculte [ɛ̃kylt] *adj (non cultivé) (jardin)* uncultivated, wild; *(terre)* waste; *(non soigné) (barbe)* unkempt; *(ignorant) (personne)* uneducated

incultivable [ɛ̃kyltivabl] *adj (terre)* untillable, irreclaimable

incultivé [ɛ̃kyltive] *adj (terre)* untilled, uncultivated

inculture [ɛ̃kyltyr] *nf* lack of culture

incunable [ɛ̃kynabl] *nm Hist, Typ* incunabulum *pl* incunabula

incurable [ɛ̃kyrabl] **1** *adj* incurable; **d'une paresse/bêtise i.** incurably lazy/stupid **2** *n* person with an incurable disease

incurablement [ɛ̃kyrabləmɑ̃] *adv (atteint, paresseux, bête)* incurably

incurie [ɛ̃kyri] *nf Fml* negligence; **faire preuve d'i.** to be negligent, to be guilty of negligence

incursion [ɛ̃kyrsjɔ̃] *nf* **(a)** *(invasion)* raid, foray, incursion **(b)** *Fig (entrée soudaine)* intrusion, interruption; **faire une i. dans une pièce/une réunion** to burst into a room/a meeting

incurvation [ɛ̃kyrvasjɔ̃] *nf* bend, curve

incurvé [ɛ̃kyrve] *adj* bent, curved

incurver [ɛ̃kyrve] **1** *vt* to bend, to curve **2** s'incurver *vpr* to bend, to curve

indatable [ɛ̃databl] *adj* that cannot be dated

Inde [ɛ̃d] *nf* India; *Vieilli* **les Indes** the Indies; *Hist* **les Indes**

occidentales the West Indies; **les Indes orientales** the East Indies
inde [ɛ̃d] *nm* dark blue
indébrouillable [ɛ̃debrujabl] *adj* (*situation*) inextricable, tangled; (*histoire*) tangled
indécemment [ɛ̃desamɑ̃] *adv* indecently
indécence [ɛ̃desɑ̃s] *nf* indecency
indécent [ɛ̃desɑ̃] *adj* (*tenue, décolleté, jupe*) indecent; (*gaspillage*) sinful, immoral; (*luxe, étalage de richesses*) obscene
indéchiffrable [ɛ̃deʃifrabl] *adj* **(a)** (*qu'on ne peut pas lire*) (*inscription, message*) indecipherable; (*écriture*) illegible; (*partition*) impossible to sight-read **(b)** (*incompréhensible*) unintelligible, incomprehensible; (*personne*) impenetrable, inscrutable
indéchirable [ɛ̃deʃirabl] *adj* tearproof, impossible to tear
indécis, -ise [ɛ̃desi, -iz] **1** *adj* **(a)** (*peu net*) (*question*) undecided, unsettled; (*victoire*) indecisive, doubtful; (*bataille*) undecided; (*contour*) vague, blurred; (*flamme*) wavering **(b)** (*personne*) (*de caractère*) indecisive, *Fml* irresolute; (*ponctuellement*) undecided; **être i. quant à l'attitude à adopter/sur le choix des couleurs** to be undecided *or* in two minds about what attitude to adopt/about the choice of colour; **je suis encore indécise** I still haven't decided *or* made my mind up **2** *n* **c'est un i.** he can never make his mind up; *Pol* **les indécis** the undecided voters; (*dans un sondage*) the don't knows
indécision [ɛ̃desizjɔ̃] *nf* (*de caractère*) indecisiveness; (*ponctuelle*) indecision; **l'i. n'est pas possible dans un travail comme le vôtre** you cannot afford to be indecisive in a job like yours
indécollable [ɛ̃dekɔlabl] *adj* (*papier peint*) that cannot be removed *or* peeled off
indécomposable [ɛ̃dekɔ̃pozabl] *adj* (*élément etc*) irresolvable
indécrottable [ɛ̃dekrɔtabl] *adj* **(a)** *F* (*personne, cancre, ignorance*) hopeless; **être d'une ignorance/une bêtise i.** to be hopelessly ignorant/stupid; **c'est un i. paresseux** he's hopelessly *or* incurably lazy; **elle est vraiment i.** she's a hopeless case, there's no hope for her **(b)** (*difficile à nettoyer*) impossible to clean
indéfectibilité [ɛ̃defɛktibilite] *nf Rel* (*de l'Église etc*) indefectibility
indéfectible [ɛ̃defɛktibl] *adj* **(a)** *Rel* indefectible **(b)** *Litt* (*amitié, attachement etc*) everlasting, indestructible; (*mémoire*) unfailing
indéfendable [ɛ̃defɑ̃dabl] *adj* indefensible
indéfini [ɛ̃defini] *adj* **(a)** (*illimité*) indefinite **(b)** (*non précis*) (*nombre*) indefinite; (*tristesse, malaise*) vague, undefined **(c)** [①**A4-5**,A-C; **A34-8**; **B4**,B; **B14-5**,B] *Gram* (*pronom, article*) indefinite
indéfiniment [ɛ̃definimɑ̃] *adv* (*ajourner une réunion, attendre*) indefinitely, for ever; **répéter qch i.** to say sth over and over again, to keep repeating sth
indéfinissable [ɛ̃definisabl] *adj* (*terme*) indefinable, undefinable; (*goût, sentiment, charme, personne*) indefinable, impossible to describe
indéformable [ɛ̃defɔrmabl] *adj* (*chapeau, tissu*) that keeps its shape; (*acier*) that does not buckle
indéfrisable [ɛ̃defrizabl] *nf Vieilli* permanent wave, perm
indélébile [ɛ̃delebil] *adj* (*encre, Fig souvenir*) indelible; (*tache*) permanent, indelible
indélicat [ɛ̃delika] *adj* **(a)** (*personne, réflexion, action, démarche*) tactless, insensitive; **il est i. au possible** he's an insensitive lout **(b)** (*malhonnête*) dishonest, unscrupulous
indélicatement [ɛ̃delikatmɑ̃] *adv* **(a)** (*avec un manque de délicatesse*) tactlessly, insensitively **(b)** (*malhonnêtement*) unscrupulously
indélicatesse [ɛ̃delikatɛs] *nf* **(a)** (*manque de tact*) (*d'une action, une personne*) tactlessness, insensitivity, *Fml* indelicacy; (*acte indélicat*) tactless action **(b)** (*malhonnêteté*) unscrupulousness; (*acte malhonnête*) unscrupulous action; **commettre une i.** to behave dishonestly
indémaillable [ɛ̃demajabl] **1** *adj* (*bas*) non-run, run-proof, *Br* ladderproof **2** *nm* non-run *or* run-proof fabric
indemne [ɛ̃dɛmn] *adj* (*sauf*) uninjured, unhurt, unharmed, unscathed; **elle est sortie i. de l'accident** she escaped uninjured
indemnisable [ɛ̃dɛmnizabl] *adj* (*personne*) entitled to compensation; (*dommages, dégâts*) compensable
indemnisation [ɛ̃dɛmnizasjɔ̃] *nf* (*de victimes, sinistrés*) compensation, *Fml* indemnification; **avoir droit à une i.** to be entitled to compensation
indemniser [ɛ̃dɛmnize] *vt* (*victime, sinistré*) to compensate, *Fml* to indemnify; **i. qn d'une perte** to compensate sb for a loss; **i. qn en argent** to pay sb compensation in cash
indemnitaire [ɛ̃dɛmnitɛr] *adj* **prestation i.** compensation
indemnité [ɛ̃dɛmnite] *nf* **(a)** (*pour perte encourue*) compensation, indemnity; (*pour délai, non-livraison etc*) compensation to other party, penalty **(b)** *Admin* allowance, grant
▶ **indemnité**: **i. de chômage** unemployment benefit; *Fin* **i. de clientèle** compensation for loss of custom; **i. compensatrice** compensation; **i. compensatrice de congés payés** pay in lieu of holidays; **i. complémentaire** additional allowance; **i. conventionnelle** contractual allowance; **i. de déménagement** relocation grant *or* allowance; **i. de départ** *ou* **de licenciement** severance pay, redundancy payment; **i. de déplacement** *ou* **de transport** travel *or* transport allowance; **i. de guerre** war indemnity; **i. journalière** daily allowance; **i. kilométrique** = mileage allowance; **i. de logement** accommodation allowance; **i. de maladie** sickness benefit; **i. parlementaire** = MP's salary; **i. de représentation** entertainment allowance; **i. de résidence** housing allowance; *Fin* **i. de retard** late payment penalty; *Fin* **i. de rupture** severance pay; *Fin* **i. de rupture abusive** compensation for breach of contract; **i. de séjour** living expenses; *Can* **i. de la vie chère** cost of living allowance
indémodable [ɛ̃demɔdabl] *adj* **un tailleur i.** a classic suit, a suit that will never go out of fashion
indémontable [ɛ̃demɔ̃tabl] *adj* (*serrure, armoire*) which cannot be dismantled; **c'est i.** it doesn't dismantle
indémontrable [ɛ̃demɔ̃trabl] *adj* unprovable, undemonstrable
indéniable [ɛ̃denjabl] *adj* undeniable; **il est i. que …** it cannot be denied that …, there's no denying that …
indéniablement [ɛ̃denjabləmɑ̃] *adv* undeniably
indentation [ɛ̃dɑ̃tasjɔ̃] *nf Litt* indentation; *Typ* **i. à droite/gauche** right/left indent
indenter [ɛ̃dɑ̃te] *vt Typ* to indent
indépassable [ɛ̃depasabl] *adj* (*limite*) which cannot be exceeded
indépendamment [ɛ̃depɑ̃damɑ̃] *adv* independently **(de** of); **i. de l'ancienneté** irrespective *or* regardless of seniority; **i. de ce que je t'ai dit hier** regardless of *or* despite what I said to you yesterday; **i. des avantages que cette méthode comporte** leaving aside the advantages of this method
indépendance [ɛ̃depɑ̃dɑ̃s] *nf* independence; **accéder à l'i.** to gain independence; **guerre d'i.** war of independence; **on note chez lui une grande i. d'esprit et de caractère** he is very independently minded, he thinks for himself
indépendant [ɛ̃depɑ̃dɑ̃] **1** *adj* **(a)** (*personne, pays, vie*) independent **(de** of); (*travailleur*) self-employed; (*traducteur, photographe etc, profession*) freelance; (*appartement*) self-contained; **circonstances indépendantes de ma volonté** circumstances beyond my control; **député i.** independent (MP); *Aut* **roues (avant) indépendantes** independent (front-wheel) suspension **(b)** *Gram* **proposition indépendante** main clause **2** *n* (*travailleur*) self-employed worker; (*traducteur/photographe*) freelancer, freelance (translator/photographer); *Pol* independent
indépendantisme [ɛ̃depɑ̃dɑ̃tism] *nm Pol* independence movement; **l'i. fait entendre sa voix** the desire for independence is making itself felt
indépendantiste [ɛ̃depɑ̃dɑ̃tist] *n Pol* (*membre actif*) freedom fighter; (*supporter de l'indépendance*) supporter of independence
indéracinable [ɛ̃derasinabl] *adj* (*arbre*) impossible to uproot; *Fig* (*personne*) impossible to move; (*préjugés*) deep-rooted, deep-seated, *Fml* ineradicable
indéréglable [ɛ̃dereglabl] *adj* (*mécanisme*) foolproof
indescriptible [ɛ̃dɛskriptibl] *adj* indescribable
indésirable [ɛ̃dezirabl] *adj, n* undesirable; *Méd* **effets indésirables: assoupissements, nausées** may cause drowsiness or nausea
indestructibilité [ɛ̃dɛstryktibilite] *nf* indestructibility
indestructible [ɛ̃dɛstryktibl] *adj* indestructible
indétectable [ɛ̃detɛktabl] *adj* undetectable
indéterminable [ɛ̃detɛrminabl] *adj* indeterminable
indétermination [ɛ̃detɛrminasjɔ̃] *nf* **(a)** (*d'idées*) vagueness **(b)** (*d'une personne*) indecisiveness, *Fml* irresoluteness; **faire preuve d'i.** to be indecisive
indéterminé [ɛ̃detɛrmine] *adj* **(a)** (*vague*) (*date, heure*) unspecified; (*idées*) indefinite, vague, *Fml* indeterminate; **pour une raison indéterminée** for some unknown reason; **la réunion est reportée à une date qui reste encore indéterminée** the meeting has been postponed to a date which has still to be decided **(b)** (*personne*) undecided; **elle est encore indéterminée sur ce point** she still has not made her mind up on the issue
index [ɛ̃dɛks] *nm* [①**A14**,9] **(a)** *Anat* forefinger, index finger **(b)** (*aiguille*) (*de balance*) pointer, needle **(c)** (*de livre*) index; *Cathol* **l'I.** the Index; *Fig* **mettre qn/qch à l'i.** to blacklist sb/sth **(d)** *Ordinat* index; **i. de totalisation** hashed index

indexage [ɛ̃dɛksaʒ] *nm* indexing
indexation [ɛ̃dɛksasjɔ̃] *nf Écon* (*des salaires etc*) indexation, index-linking; *Ordinat* indexing
indexé [ɛ̃dɛkse] *adj* (*salaire etc*) index-linked
indexer [ɛ̃dɛkse] *vt* **(a)** *Écon* (*prix, salaires*) to index-link, to peg, to index; **salaires indexés sur le coût de la vie** salaries indexed to the cost of living **(b)** (*ajouter un index à*) (*ouvrage, collection*), *Ordinat* to index
indic [ɛ̃dik] *n Arg* grass, informer
indicateur, -trice [ɛ̃dikatœr, -tris] **1** *adj* **poteau i.** signpost; **panneau i. (de route)** road sign
2 *nm* **(a)** *Péj* (*informateur*) informer
(b) (*livre*) **i. des rues de Paris** Paris (street) directory *or* street finder; **i. horaire** timetable; **i. des chemins de fer** (railway) timetable
(c) (*instrument*) **i. de niveau (de carburant)** (fuel) gauge; **i. de pression** pressure gauge; **i. de vitesse** speed indicator, tachometer; *Aut* speedometer; *Av* airspeed indicator; *Av* **i. d'altitude** altimeter; *Rad* **i. de direction** direction finder; *Aut* **i. (de changement) de direction** (directional) indicator, direction indicator; *Aut* **i. d'usure** (*de pneu*) tread depth gauge, tread depth safety indicator, tread wear indicator; *Aut* **i. de pression d'huile** oil pressure gauge; *Aut* **i. de pression de pneu** tyre pressure gauge; *Aut* **i. de température** temperature indicator *or* gauge; *Aut* **i. lumineux de porte ouverte** door-open warning light; **i. à diodes électroluminescentes** LED indicator
(d) *Ch* indicator
(e) **i. économique** economic indicator; *Fin* **i. de tendance** market indicator
indicatif, -ive [ɛ̃dikatif, -iv] **1** *adj* **(a)** (*qui indique*) (*signe*) indicative (**de** of); **à titre i.** as an indication, *F* to give me/you/*etc* an idea; **ces prix/chiffres ne sont fournis qu'à titre i.** these prices/figures are supplied for information only **(b)** *Gram* **mode i.** indicative (mood) **2** *nm* **(a)** [ⓘ**A39**,8] *Gram* indicative (mood); **à l'i.** in the indicative **(b)** *Tél* dialling code; *TV, Rad* ident; *Ordinat* prompt; *Ordinat* **i. (du) DOS** DOS prompt; **i. d'appel** *Rad* call sign; (*téléphonique*) dialling code; *Rad* **i. (musical)** (*de programme*) signature tune, theme tune; **i. de générique** theme tune; *Rad* **i. de station** station ident(ification)
indication [ɛ̃dikasjɔ̃] *nf* **(a)** (*action*) indication, indicating, pointing out; **l'i. de la date de péremption est obligatoire** the use-by date must be shown *or* indicated; **i. d'origine** indication of origin
(b) (*renseignement*) (piece of) information; **sauf i. contraire** unless otherwise specified; **sauf i. contraire de ta mère** unless your mother says otherwise *or F* different; **donne-lui quelques indications pour se servir de l'ordinateur** can you show him how to use the computer; **une de tes indications était fausse ce qui fait que je me suis perdue** I got lost because one of your directions was wrong; **à titre d'i.** as an indication, *F* to give me/you/*etc* an idea
(c) (*signe*) sign, token
(d) **indications topographiques** survey marks *or* data
(e) **indications** (*sur mode d'emploi*) instructions; (*sur notice pharmaceutique*) for (*tonsillitis etc*); **indications du mode d'emploi** directions for use; **indications spéciales** special indications; **quelles sont les indications pour ce médicament?** what is this medicine for?
▶ **indication**: *Th* **indications scéniques** stage directions
indice [ɛ̃dis] *nm* **(a)** (*signe*) sign, indication; (*d'un crime*) clue; **les indices du crime** the clues to the crime; **c'est l'i. de la reprise** it's the sign of a recovery; **j'ai vu là un i. de ta fatigue** to me that was a sign *or* an indication you were tired **(b)** [ⓘ**A14**,9] (*chiffre indicateur*), *Math* index (number); *Typ* subscript; **3 en i.** subscript 3
▶ **indice**: *Mktg* **i. ad hoc** specific indicator; **i. boursier** share index; *Fin* **i. CAC 40** ≈ FTSE; *Aut* **i. de cétane** cetane number; *Écon* **i. corrigé des variations saisonnières** seasonally adjusted index; **i. des cours d'actions** share price index; *Écon* **i. du coût de la vie** cost of living index; *Écon* **i. de croissance** index of growth; **i. d'écoute** *Rad* ratings; *TV* ratings, viewing figures; *Rad, TV* **avoir un bon i. d'écoute** to stand high in the ratings, to attract a large listening/viewing audience; **l'i. d'écoute a baissé** the ratings have dropped; **i. hiérarchique** salary scale code; **i. inférieur** suffix; *Écon* **i. non-corrigé des variations saisonnières** non-seasonally adjusted index; *Ch* **i. d'octane** octane rating *or* number; *Aut* **i. d'octane méthode moteur** motor octane number, MON; **i. de popularité** (popularity) rating; **l'i. de popularité du Président est en baisse** the President has dropped in the popularity ratings; **i. des prix** price index; **i. des prix à la consommation** consumer price index; **i. des prix de détail** retail price index; **i. des prix de gros** wholesale price index; **i. des prix et des salaires** wage and price index; **i. de profit** profit indicator; **i. de protection** (*d'une crème solaire*) protection factor; **i. spécifique** specific indicator; *Aut* **i. de viscosité** viscosity index
indiciaire [ɛ̃disjɛr] *adj Fin* **impôt i.** wealth tax
indicible [ɛ̃disibl] *adj Litt* (*plaisir, joie, bonheur*) indescribable; (*chagrin, rage, peur*) indescribable, unspeakable; **d'une saleté i.** indescribably *or* unspeakably filthy
indiciblement [ɛ̃disibləmɑ̃] *adv Litt* (*d'une façon inexprimable*) inexpressibly
indien, -ienne [ɛ̃djɛ̃, -jɛn] **1** *adj* **(a)** Indian; **l'océan i.** the Indian Ocean **(b)** **en** *ou* **à la file indienne** in single *or* Indian file **2** *n* **I.** (*d'Inde, d'Amérique*) Indian **3** *nf* **indienne** *Tex* cotton print, *surtout US* printed calico; **nage (à l')indienne** overarm stroke
indifféremment [ɛ̃diferamɑ̃] *adv* **(a)** (*sans faire de différence*) indiscriminately, equally; **vous pouvez prendre i. la route de gauche ou celle de droite** you can take either the left-hand or the right-hand road *or* it doesn't really matter which road you take (they're equally good); **il va i. dans l'un ou l'autre de ces restaurants** it doesn't matter to him which restaurant he goes to; **traduire i. en chinois et en russe** to translate into Chinese and Russian equally well; **elle mange de tout i.** she'll eat anything, she doesn't have any fads **(b)** *Vieilli* (*avec froideur*) indifferently
indifférence [ɛ̃diferɑ̃s] *nf* indifference; **répondre avec i.** to answer with indifference *or* indifferently; **i. à (l'égard de)** *ou* **pour** *ou* **face à** (*pour la politique*) indifference to, lack of interest in; (*devant la misère du monde*) indifference to, lack of concern about; **elle est d'une i. totale face à tout ce qui ne concerne pas son métier** she is totally indifferent to anything that is not work-related
indifférenciable [ɛ̃diferɑ̃sjabl] *adj* indistinguishable; **ces jumeaux sont absolument indifférenciables** it's impossible to tell the twins apart
indifférenciation [ɛ̃diferɑ̃sjasjɔ̃] *nf* lack of differentiation
indifférencié [ɛ̃diferɑ̃sje] *adj* undifferentiated
indifférent, -ente [ɛ̃diferɑ̃, ɑ̃t] **1** *adj* **(a)** (*peu ou pas intéressé*) indifferent (**à** to); (*sans émotion*) indifferent, cold, emotionless; **être i. au sort de qn** to be indifferent to sb's fate; **il m'est i.** I'm indifferent to him; **il a été i. à tous mes arguments** he was unmoved by my arguments; **rester i. à tout** to take no interest in anything; **toutes ses avances l'ont laissée indifférente** she was indifferent to his advances, *F* his advances left her cold; **elle ne le laisse pas i.** he is not indifferent *or* unattracted to her; **cela ne peut vous laisser i.** it can't leave you indifferent *or* unmoved; **ta requête ne pourra pas le laisser i.** he can't fail to respond to your request
(b) (*sans importance*) immaterial, unimportant; **recherchons baby-sitter, sexe i.** baby-sitter wanted, male or female; **cela m'est i.** it's all the same *or* it's quite immaterial to me, I don't care either way; **cela m'est complètement i.** I couldn't care less, it's all the same to me; **il m'est i. de faire cela ou autre chose** it doesn't matter to me *or* it's all the same to me whether I do that or something else; **parler de choses indifférentes** to chat (about nothing in particular)
2 *n* uncaring person; **c'est un i.** he doesn't care about people, he's very uncaring; **elle se plaint que son mari est un i.** she complains that her husband doesn't care about her *or* is indifferent to her; **jouer les indifférents** to pretend to be indifferent, to put on a show of indifference
indifférer [ɛ̃difere] *vt used with pronoun complement only* (**il indiffère; il indifférera**) **cela m'indiffère** I couldn't care less (about it); **mon sort l'indiffère complètement** he couldn't care less what happens to me
indigence [ɛ̃diʒɑ̃s] *nf* **(a)** (*dénuement*) destitution; **être/tomber dans l'i.** to be/become destitute; **vivre dans l'i.** to live in dire poverty **(b)** *Fml Fig* (*manque*) **faire preuve d'une i. d'idées** to be totally devoid of ideas; **l'i. de ses idées** the poverty of his ideas; **l'i. d'esprit dont fait preuve la télévision** the dearth of intelligent programmes on television
indigène [ɛ̃diʒɛn] **1** *adj Zool, Bot* indigenous (**à** to); (*population*) native, indigenous; (*coutume*) native **2** *n* native
indigent, -ente [ɛ̃diʒɑ̃, -ɑ̃t] **1** *adj* **(a)** (*personne*) destitute, poverty-stricken, *Fml* indigent **(b)** *Fig* (*esprit*) impoverished, poor; **avoir une imagination indigente** to be totally lacking in imagination **2** *n* person who is destitute; **les indigents** the destitute
indigeste [ɛ̃diʒɛst] *adj* (*nourriture, Fig livre*) indigestible, difficult to digest
indigestion [ɛ̃diʒɛstjɔ̃] *nf* indigestion; **avoir une i.** to have (an attack of) indigestion; **j'ai mangé tellement de chocolat**

que je m'en suis donné une i., j'ai mangé du chocolat jusqu'à l'i. I ate so much chocolate I gave myself indigestion; *Fig F* **j'en ai une i.** I'm fed up with it, I've had my fill of it

indignation [ɛ̃diɲasjɔ̃] *nf* indignation; **faire éclater** *ou* **crier son i.** to give one's indignation free rein; **éclater** *ou* **exploser d'i.** to explode in indignation; **avec i.** (*parler, protester etc*) indignantly, with indignation

indigne [ɛ̃diɲ] *adj* **(a)** (*qui n'est pas digne*) (*personne*) unworthy, undeserving; **ces bassesses sont indignes de vous** such behaviour is unworthy of you; **i. de notre confiance** unworthy of our confidence; **je suis i. de votre dévouement** I don't deserve such devotion; **cet auteur est i. de figurer aux programmes des écoles** this author is not fit to be included in the school syllabus; **il est i. de vivre** he doesn't deserve to live, he's not fit to live; **être i. d'un poste/d'une tâche** to be unworthy of a position/a task; **ce travail est i. de lui** this work is not good enough for him *or* is beneath him; **conduite i. d'une sœur/d'un père** unsisterly/unfatherly conduct

(b) (*méprisable*) (*action, conduite*) shameful; **c'est une mère i.** she's not a fit mother

indigné [ɛ̃diɲe] *adj* indignant; **je suis absolument i. par votre manque de sérieux** I am quite indignant about *or* at your lack of professionalism; **d'un air/ton i.** indignantly

indignement [ɛ̃diɲmɑ̃] *adv* shamefully

indigner [ɛ̃diɲe] **1** *vt* **i. qn** to make sb indignant, to outrage sb **2 s'indigner** *vpr* to become *or* get *or* be indignant; **je m'indigne de voir ce crime impuni** it makes me indignant to see this crime go unpunished; **s'i. de** *ou* **contre qch/qn** to be indignant at *or* about sth/with sb; **s'i. que** + *sub ou* **de ce que** + *ind ou sub* to be indignant that

indignité [ɛ̃diɲite] *nf* **(a)** (*d'une personne*) unworthiness; (*d'une action*) baseness, vileness **(b)** (*action*) shameful act

▶ **indignité**: *Jur* **i. nationale** deprivation of citizenship rights (*imposed on those who collaborated with the Germans in World War II*)

indigo [ɛ̃digo] *nm, adj inv* indigo(-blue)

indiqué [ɛ̃dike] *adj* (*recommandé*) advisable; **un sujet de plaisanterie tout i.** an obvious subject for jokes; **il est tout à fait i. pour ce poste** he's the very man *or* just the man for the job; **dans votre cas, un séjour à la montagne me paraît tout à fait i.** a stay in the mountains seems to me to be just the thing you need; **il n'est pas très i. de mélanger l'alcool et les médicaments** it's not very advisable to mix alcohol and medication

indiquer [ɛ̃dike] *vt* **(a)** (*montrer*) (*de personne*) to show, to point out, to indicate; **i. qch du doigt** to point to *or* at sth, to point sth out, to indicate sth; **i. le chemin à qn** to show sb the way, to direct sb; **tu peux m'i. le chemin** *ou* **la route pour aller au cinéma?** can you show me the way *or* direct me to the cinema?; **i. une rue à qn** to tell sb where a street is; **indique-lui où ça se trouve** show him where it is; **elle m'indiqua comment utiliser cet outil** she showed me how to use the tool

(b) (*marquer*) to show, to indicate; **le compteur indique cent** the meter reads *or* shows one hundred; **point indiqué sur la carte** point shown *or* marked on the map; **la maison indiquée sur le bordereau ci-joint** the firm shown *or* given *or* mentioned on the enclosed slip; **le panneau vert indique la sortie** the green panel indicates the exit; **suivre les pontillés comme indiqué** follow the dotted line as shown *or* indicated; **la loi oblige à i. le prix des marchandises en vitrine** by law, you have to show the price of goods displayed in the window; **le prix n'est pas indiqué** there's no price on it

(c) (*recommander*) **elle m'a indiqué un dentiste/garage qui est vraiment excellent** she told me about *or* recommended a really excellent dentist/garage; **s'il vous plaît, indiquez-moi un bon médecin** can you recommend a (good) doctor?

(d) (*dénoter*) to point to, to indicate; **ce genre d'attitude indique un manque de professionnalisme total** this sort of attitude points to *or* indicates a total lack of professionalism; **tout dans la maison indique un goût raffiné** everything in the house indicates *or* shows good taste

(e) (*donner*) (*jour, date*) to give, to indicate; (*ligne d'action etc*) to prescribe, to lay down; **à l'heure indiquée** at the appointed *or* agreed time; **veuillez i. vos nom et adresse** please give your name and address; **pourriez-vous m'i. le prix de ce vase?** could you tell me how much the vase is?; **i. un prix** to quote a price

indirect [ɛ̃dirɛkt] *adj* **(a)** (*non direct*) (*itinéraire, critique*) indirect; (*chemin*) roundabout; (*attaque*) indirect, covert; *Jur* (*héritiers*) collateral; **éclairage i.** indirect *or* concealed lighting; **elle l'a dit d'une façon indirecte** she said it in an indirect *or* a roundabout way; **je l'ai appris de manière indirecte** I learned of it indirectly; **contributions indirectes** indirect taxation **(b)** [①B17-8,2] *Gram* (*objet*) indirect; **discours i.** indirect speech, reported speech; **au discours i.** in indirect *or* reported speech **(c)** *Jur* (*preuves*) circumstantial

indirectement [ɛ̃dirɛktəmɑ̃] *adv* indirectly; **dire les choses i.** to say things in an indirect *or* a roundabout way

indiscernable [ɛ̃disɛrnabl] *adj* indiscernible, imperceptible

indiscipline [ɛ̃disiplin] *nf* indiscipline, lack of discipline; **faire acte** *ou* **preuve d'i.** to show a lack of discipline

indiscipliné [ɛ̃disipline] *adj* (*élève*) undisciplined, unruly; (*soldat*) undisciplined; *Fig* **cheveux indisciplinés** unruly *or* unmanageable hair

indiscret, -ète [ɛ̃diskrɛ, -ɛt] **1** *adj* (*personne, remarque, question, bavardage*) indiscreet; (*inquisiteur*) inquisitive; **serait-il i. de vous demander où vous allez?** would it be indiscreet to ask you where you're going?; **à l'abri des regards indiscrets** safe from prying eyes; **une question fort indiscrète** a very personal question; **je ne voudrais pas être i., mais ...** I don't want to be indiscreet but ...; **je me méfie des oreilles indiscrètes** I'm on my guard against eavesdroppers **2** *n* indiscreet person, *F Péj* nosy parker; **à l'abri des indiscrets** away from eavesdroppers *or* prying eyes

indiscrètement [ɛ̃diskrɛtmɑ̃] *adv* indiscreetly

indiscrétion [ɛ̃diskresjɔ̃] *nf* **(a)** (*manque de discrétion*) indiscretion, indiscreetness; (*curiosité excessive*) inquisitiveness; **peut-on vous demander sans i. ...?** would it be indiscreet *or* rude to ask ...?; **elle a eu l'i. de venir elle-même vérifier** she was so indiscreet as to come and see for herself; **il a poussé l'i. jusqu'à demander des détails** he was so indiscreet as to ask for details **(b)** (*action, remarque*) indiscretion; **commettre une i.** to commit an indiscretion, to be indiscreet

indiscutable [ɛ̃diskytabl] *adj* indisputable, unquestionable; **il est i. que vous ayez raison** you're indisputably *or* unquestionably right; **il est i. qu'il faille améliorer la production** there's no question but that production needs to be improved

indiscutablement [ɛ̃diskytabləmɑ̃] *adv* indisputably, unquestionably

indiscuté [ɛ̃diskyte] *adj* undisputed, unquestioned

indispensable [ɛ̃dispɑ̃sabl] **1** *adj* indispensable (**à qn** to sb; **à** *ou* **pour qch** for sth; **pour faire qch** for doing sth), essential (**à qch** for sth, to sth); **une condition i.** an essential condition; **il est i. que j'aie/d'avoir votre autorisation écrite** it is essential that I have/it is essential to have your authorization in writing; **anglais i.** (*dans une offre d'emploi*) English indispensable *or* essential; **votre aide m'est i.** your help is indispensable (to me); **tu te crois donc i.?** so you think you're indispensable?; **personne n'est i.** no-one is indispensable; **il nous est i.** he is indispensable to us, we can't do without him

2 *nm* **l'i.** the essentials, what is/was strictly necessary; **ne prenez que l'i.** only take the essentials *or* what you really need *or* what is strictly necessary

indisponibilité [ɛ̃dispɔnibilite] *nf* **(a)** (*d'une personne*) unavailability **(b)** *Jur* inalienability

indisponible [ɛ̃dispɔnibl] *adj* **(a)** (*personne, argent*) unavailable, not available **(b)** *Jur* (*biens*) inalienable; (*domaine*) entailed

indisposé [ɛ̃dispoze] *adj* (*fatigué*) indisposed, unwell, *F* out of sorts; **se sentir vaguement i.** to feel unwell *or Br* off colour; *Euph* **elle est indisposée** she's indisposed, it's her time of the month

indisposer [ɛ̃dispoze] *vt* **(a)** (*rendre légèrement malade*) **i. qn** to make sb unwell; (*de la nourriture*) to upset sb, to disagree with sb; **cette odeur m'indispose** that smell makes me (feel) sick **(b)** (*contrarier*) to antagonize, to annoy; **i. qn contre qn** to set sb against sb; **tout l'indispose** everything annoys him; **elle indispose tout le monde par son attitude** her attitude antagonizes everybody

indisposition [ɛ̃dispozisjɔ̃] *nf* indisposition, slight illness, upset; *Euph* **souffrir d'une i. passagère** to be temporarily indisposed

indissociable [ɛ̃disɔsjabl] *adj* indissociable

indissolubilité [ɛ̃disɔlybilite] *nf* (*du mariage*) indissolubility

indissoluble [ɛ̃disɔlybl] *adj* (*lien, amitié*) indissoluble

indissolublement [ɛ̃disɔlybləmɑ̃] *adv* indissolubly

indistinct [ɛ̃distɛ̃(kt)] *adj* (*voix, bruits*) indistinct; (*visuellement*) (*contour, lumière, forme*) vague, indistinct

indistinctement [ɛ̃distɛ̃ktəmɑ̃] *adv* **(a)** (*indifféremment*) without distinction **(b)** (*voir*) indistinctly, vaguely; (*parler*) indistinctly

individu [ɛ̃dividy] *nm* **(a)** *Biol* individual **(b)** (*être humain*) individual; **tout i. est unique** every individual is unique; *F* **soigner son i.** to look after number one **(c)** *souvent Péj* (*homme*) individual, fellow; **i. louche** shady customer, suspicious character; **quel drôle d'i.!** what an odd person!, what a funny individual!; **un triste i.** a sad character

individualisation [ɛ̃dividɥalizasjɔ̃] *nf* individualization; **i. de l'enseignement/des peines** adapting *or* tailoring of education/sentences to individual needs

individualiser [ɛ̃dividɥalize] **1** *vt* to individualize; **i. l'enseignement/les peines** to adapt *or* tailor education/sentences to individual needs; **i. les salaires** to award salaries on an individual basis **2 s'individualiser** *vpr* (*d'une personne*) to develop a personality of one's own; *Biol* to take on individual characteristics

individualisme [ɛ̃dividɥalism] *nm* individualism

individualiste [ɛ̃dividɥalist] **1** *adj* (*attitude, comportement, morale*) individualistic **2** *n* individualist

individualité [ɛ̃dividɥalite] *nf* individuality

individuel, -elle [ɛ̃dividɥɛl] *adj* (*cas, qualité*) individual; (*liberté, responsabilité, opinion*) personal; (*maison*) detached; (*chambre*) single; **faire qch à titre i.** to do sth as an individual; **fiche individuelle** personal record card; **secrétaire i.** personal *or* private secretary; *Sp* **épreuve individuelle** individual event

individuellement [ɛ̃dividɥɛlmɑ̃] *adv* individually

indivis [ɛ̃divi] *adj Jur* (*domaine, succession*) undivided, joint; (*propriétaires*) joint; **par** *ou* **en i.** jointly

indivisaire [ɛ̃divizɛr] *n Jur* joint owner

indivisément [ɛ̃divizemɑ̃] *adv Jur* jointly

indivisibilité [ɛ̃divizibilite] *nf* indivisibility

indivisible [ɛ̃divizibl] *adj* indivisible

indivisiblement [ɛ̃diviziblәmɑ̃] *adv* indivisibly

indivision [ɛ̃divizjɔ̃] *nf Jur* joint possession; **propriété en i.** jointly held property

Indochine [ɛ̃dɔʃin] *nf* Indochina

indochinois, -oise [ɛ̃dɔʃinwa, -waz] **1** *adj* Indochinese **2** *n* **I.** Indochinese

indocile [ɛ̃dɔsil] *adj* intractable, disobedient; **une mèche i.** a cowlick

indocilité [ɛ̃dɔsilite] *nf* intractability, disobedience

indo-européen, -enne [ɛ̃dɔøʀɔpeɛ̃, -ɛn], *pl* **indo-européens, -ennes 1** *adj* (*langue*) Indo-European **2** *n* **I.** Indo-European **3** *nm Ling* Indo-European

indolemment [ɛ̃dɔlamɑ̃] *adv* indolently

indolence [ɛ̃dɔlɑ̃s] *nf* indolence

indolent [ɛ̃dɔlɑ̃] *adj* **(a)** (*nonchalant*) indolent; **démarche indolente** slow *or* lazy walk **(b)** *Méd* (*tumeur*) indolent, painless

indolore [ɛ̃dɔlɔr] *adj* painless

indomptable [ɛ̃dɔ̃ptabl] *adj* **(a)** (*animal*) untam(e)able; (*nation*) unconquerable **(b)** *Fig* (*orgueil, caractère*) indomitable; (*passion*) ungovernable, uncontrollable

indompté [ɛ̃dɔ̃pte] *adj* (*animal*) untamed; (*nation*) unconquered; *Fig* (*passion, orgueil*) uncontrolled; (*esprit*) unbroken

Indonésie [ɛ̃dɔnezi] *nf* Indonesia

indonésien, -ienne [ɛ̃dɔnezjɛ̃, -jɛn] **1** *adj* Indonesian **2** *n* **I.** Indonesian

indou, -oue [ɛ̃du] *Rel* **1** *adj* Hindu **2** *n* **I.** Hindu

in-douze *adj inv, nm inv Typ* duodecimo, twelvemo

indu [ɛ̃dy] *adj* (*hâte*) undue; (*remarque, protestation*) unwarranted; **à une heure indue** at an ungodly hour; **il rentre à des heures indues** he comes home at all hours of the night

indubitable [ɛ̃dybitabl] *adj* (*preuves, détails*) indisputable, indubitable; **c'est lui le vainqueur, c'est i.** he's the winner, there's no doubt about it *or* it's beyond doubt; **il est i. que ...** there's no doubt that ...

indubitablement [ɛ̃dybitablәmɑ̃] *adv* undoubtedly, indubitably, unquestionably

inductance [ɛ̃dyktɑ̃s] *nf Él* inductance; *Aut* induction

inducteur, -trice [ɛ̃dyktœr, -tris] **1** *adj Él* (*capacité, champ*) inductive; (*courant*) inducing **2** *nm Él* inductor; (*de dynamo*) field magnet

inductif, -ive [ɛ̃dyktif, -iv] *adj* inductive

induction [ɛ̃dyksjɔ̃] *nf* **(a)** (*en logique*) induction; **raisonner par i.** to reason by induction **(b)** *Él* **courant d'i.** induced current; **bobine d'i.** induction coil

induire [ɛ̃dɥir] *vt* (*prp* **induisant**; *pp* **induit**; *pr ind* **j'induis, n. induisons, ils induisent**; *p hist* **j'induisis**; *fu* **j'induirai**) **(a)** (*entraîner*) **i. qn à faire qch** to induce sb to do sth; **i. qn en erreur** to mislead sb, to lead sb astray; *Litt* **i. qn au mal** to lead sb astray **(b)** (*conclure*) to infer, to induce; **que pouvez-vous en i.?** what can you infer from that?

induit [ɛ̃dɥi] *Él* **1** *adj* (*circuit*) induced, secondary; **courant i.** induction current **2** *nm* (*circuit*) induced circuit; (*de dynamo*) armature, rotor; **charge d'i.** induced charge

indulgence [ɛ̃dylʒɑ̃s] *nf* **(a)** (*tolérance*) indulgence, leniency; **avec i.** indulgently, leniently; **avoir** *ou* **montrer de l'i. pour** *ou* **envers qn, faire preuve d'i. envers qn** to be indulgent with sb, to make allowances for sb; **regard plein d'i.** indulgent look; **par avance, je demande votre i.** I request your indulgence in advance; **rires sans i.** merciless laughter; **il me fit d'elle une portrait sans i.** he described her to me warts and all **(b)** *Rel* indulgence

indulgent [ɛ̃dylʒɑ̃] *adj* (*personne, attitude*) indulgent, lenient; (*regard*) indulgent; **être i. avec** *ou* **envers qn** to be indulgent *or* lenient with sb; **être trop i. avec lui-même** to be easy on oneself

indûment [ɛ̃dymɑ̃] *adv* (*protester*) unduly; (*facturé*) incorrectly; **s'ingérer i. dans les affaires d'autrui** to interfere unduly *or* without justification in other people's affairs

industrialisation [ɛ̃dystrijalizasjɔ̃] *nf* industrialization; **économie en voie d'i.** industrializing economy

industrialiser [ɛ̃dystrijalize] **1** *vt* to industrialize **2 s'industrialiser** *vpr* to become industrialized

industrialisme [ɛ̃dystrijalism] *nm Hist* industrialism

industrie [ɛ̃dystri] *nf* **(a)** *Écon* (*secteur*) industry, manufacturing; (*entreprise*) industry; **travailler dans l'i.** to work in industry *or* in manufacturing; **être à la tête d'une i.** to head an industry; **capitaine d'i.** captain of industry **(b)** *Arch, Litt* (*activité*) activity; (*des abeilles*) industry; (*ingéniosité*) ingenuity, cleverness

▶ **industrie**: **i. alimentaire** food industry; **l'i. automobile** the motor *or* automotive industry; **l'i. du bâtiment** the building trade, the construction industry; **i. de fabrication** manufacturing industry; **i. de haute technologie** high-tech(nology) industry, sunrise industry; **i. hôtelière** *ou* **de l'hôtellerie** hotel industry, professional hospitality industry; **i. de l'hôtellerie et de la restauration** hotel and catering industry; *Ling* **les industries de la langue** the language professions; **l'i. légère** light industry; **i. des loisirs** leisure industry; **l'i. lourde** heavy industry; **l'i. pharmaceutique** the pharmaceutical industry, pharmaceuticals; **i. de pointe** high-tech *or* state-of-the-art industry; **i. de la restauration** catering industry; **i. de service** service industry; **i. des services** service industry; **l'i. du spectacle** the entertainment industry, show business; **i. de transformation** processing industry; **i. de volume** volume industry

industriel, -elle [ɛ̃dystrijɛl] **1** *adj* (*produit, secteur, fabrication*) industrial; **zone industrielle** (*d'une ville*) industrial area; *F* **des magazines en quantité industrielle** vast quantities of magazines **2** *nm* manufacturer, industrialist

industriellement [ɛ̃dystrijɛlmɑ̃] *adv* industrially; **vins produits i.** mass-produced wines

industrieux, -euse [ɛ̃dystrijø, -øz] *adj Litt* (*qui travaille beaucoup*) industrious; (*qui montre de l'habileté*) skilful, ingenious

inébranlable [inebrɑ̃labl] *adj* (*mur, pilier, rocher*) immovable, solid, firm; *Fig* (*personne, foi, amitié*) unshakeable, steadfast; (*confiance*) unshakeable; (*courage*) unwavering; **il en a une conviction i.** he is firmly convinced of it, his conviction is unshakeable

inébranlablement [inebrɑ̃lablәmɑ̃] *adv* unshakeably

inéchangeable [inɛʃɑ̃ʒabl] *adj* non-exchangeable; *Fin* (*devise*) non-convertible

inécoutable [inekutabl] *adj* unbearable, impossible to listen to

inécouté [inekute] *adj* unheeded

inédit [inedi] **1** *adj* **(a)** (*non publié*) (*livre, disque, nouvelles*) unpublished **(b)** (*original*) (*spectacle, projet*) new, original; **elle a des idées inédites** she has some original ideas **2** *nm* **(a)** (*texte*) unpublished work; **un i. de Gide** an unpublished work by Gide **(b) l'i.** the new, the original

ineffable [inefabl] *adj* ineffable, unutterable

ineffablement [inefablәmɑ̃] *adv* ineffably

ineffaçable [inefasabl] *adj* (*marque, tache, mémoire*) indelible, ineffaceable

ineffaçablement [inefasablәmɑ̃] *adv* ineffaceably

inefficace [inefikas] *adj* (*personne*) ineffective, ineffectual; (*dans son travail*) inefficient; (*remède, méthode, loi*) ineffective, ineffectual

inefficacement [inefikasmɑ̃] *adv* ineffectively; (*travailler*) inefficiently

inefficacité [inefikasite] *nf* (*de personne*) ineffectiveness, ineffectualness; (*dans son travail*) inefficiency; (*d'un remède*) ineffectiveness, ineffectualness, inefficacy

inégal, -ale, -aux, -ales [inegal, -o] *adj* **(a)** (*non égal*) (*parts,* *partage, segments, force, lutte*) unequal; **force est de constater que les citoyens sont inégaux face à la loi** we have to recognize that not all citizens are equal in the eyes of the law **(b)** (*irrégulier*) (*sol*) uneven; (*pouls*) irregular; (*vent*) changeable; *Fig* (*travail, écrivain, style*) inconsistent, erratic; (*qualité*) inconsistent, varying; **être d'une humeur inégale** to be as changeable as the weather

inégalable [inegalabl] *adj* incomparable, matchless; (*record*) unbeatable

inégalé [inegale] *adj* unequalled, unmatched; **le record reste jusqu'à ce jour i.** the record remains unbeaten to this day

inégalement [inegalmɑ̃] *adv* **(a)** (*injustement*) unequally, unevenly; **i. partagé** unequally *or* unevenly shared **(b)** (*irrégulièrement*) unevenly; **carreaux i. disposés** unevenly arranged tiles; **son cœur battait i.** his heart was beating irregularly; **le film a été i. apprécié par les critiques** the film received mixed reviews from the critics

inégalité [inegalite] *nf* **(a)** (*injustice*) inequality **(entre** between); **inégalités sociales** social inequalities **(b)** (*différence*) disparity, difference **(de** between); **les inégalités de salaire sont énormes dans cette entreprise** the differences in salary are huge in this company **(c)** (*du sol*) unevenness; **les inégalités du chemin** the bumps in the road, the unevenness of the road; *Fig* **i. d'humeur** capriciousness **(d)** *Math* inequality

inélastique [inelastik] *adj Phys* inelastic

inélégamment [inelegamɑ̃] *adv Litt* inelegantly

inélégance [inelegɑ̃s] *nf Litt* inelegance

inélégant [inelegɑ̃] *adj Litt* inelegant; **il eût été i. d'insister** it would have been inappropriate to insist; **une action inélégante** an improper *or* unfitting act

inéligibilité [ineliʒibilite] *nf* ineligibility

inéligible [ineliʒibl] *adj* ineligible

inéluctable [inelyktabl] *adj* inescapable, *Fml* ineluctable

inéluctablement [inelyktabləmɑ̃] *adv* inescapably, *Fml* ineluctably

inemployable [inɑ̃plwajabl] *adj* unusable

inemployé [inɑ̃plwaje] *adj* unused; (*ressources*) untapped; (*forces*) unchannelled

inénarrable [inenarabl] *adj* comical, funny; **dommage que vous ne l'ayez pas vu, c'était i.!** it was a shame you didn't see it, it was priceless!

inentamé [inɑ̃tame] *adj* intact; (*pain, camembert, gâteau*) uncut; (*fortune*) intact, untouched

inéprouvé [inepruve] *adj* **(a)** (*non mis à l'épreuve*) untried, untested **(b)** (*non ressenti*) not yet experienced *or* felt

inepte [inɛpt] *adj* (*remarque, réponse*) inept, foolish, idiotic

ineptie [inɛpsi] *nf* **(a)** (*caractère stupide*) ineptitude, ineptness **(b)** (*action, remarque*) **dire des inepties** to talk nonsense *or* rubbish; **ce traité est une i.** this treaty is nonsense *or* an absurdity; **c'est une i. de dire que ...** it's idiotic *or* absurd to say that ...

inépuisable [inepɥizabl] *adj* (*réserves, sujet, curiosité*) inexhaustible; **un stock i. d'histoires drôles** an inexhaustible supply of funny stories; **une imagination i.** a limitless imagination; **sur ce sujet-là, il est i.** you can never get him off the subject

inéquation [inekwasjɔ̃] *nf Math* inequation

inéquitable [inekitabl] *adj* inequitable, unfair

inerte [inɛrt] *adj* (*masse, corps, matière*) inert; (*nature*) sluggish; (*personne déprimée*) in state of inertia; **elle gisait par terre, i.** she lay on the ground, motionless; **un visage i.** an expressionless face; **le visage i.** (*écouter etc*) impassively

inertie [inɛrsi] *nf* **(a)** *Phys* inertia; **force d'i.** force of inertia; **moment d'i.** moment of inertia **(b)** (*manque de réaction*) passivity, inertia; (*de l'esprit, du corps*) sluggishness, inertness

inescomptable [inɛskɔ̃tabl] *adj Fin* undiscountable

inespéré [inɛspere] *adj* unexpected, unhoped-for

inesthétique [inɛstetik] *adj* unaesthetic

inestimable [inɛstimabl] *adj* (*dégâts, coût, richesse*) incalculable, inestimable; **bijoux d'une valeur i.** priceless jewels; **votre aide a été i.** your help was invaluable; **être en bonne santé est une chance i.** good health is something to be treasured

inévitable [inevitabl] *adj* (*accident, contretemps*) unavoidable; (*résultat, conséquences*) inevitable, inescapable, unavoidable; **c'est i.** it's inevitable; *Hum* **l'i. Lulu était là** Lulu was there as per usual; *Hum* **nous eûmes droit à l'i. gâteau aux cerises** we were treated to the inevitable *or* the usual cherry cake

inévitablement [inevitabləmɑ̃] *adv* inevitably, unavoidably; **si on passe par là, il va i. nous voir** if we go that way he's bound to see us

inexact [inɛgzakt] *adj* **(a)** (*incorrect*) (*réponse, données, description, version, détail*) inaccurate, incorrect, inexact; (*somme, calcul*) wrong, incorrect; **des renseignements inexacts** inaccurate *or* incorrect information; **mais c'est i.** but that's wrong *or* incorrect **(b)** (*manquant de ponctualité*) (*personne*) unpunctual

inexactement [inɛgzaktəmɑ̃] *adv* inaccurately, incorrectly

inexactitude [inɛgzaktityd] *nf* **(a)** (*caractère erroné, imprécision*) (*de renseignement, données*) inaccuracy, incorrectness; (*faute*) mistake, inaccuracy; **relever des inexactitudes dans une traduction** to find mistakes *or* inaccuracies in a translation **(b)** (*manque de ponctualité*) unpunctuality

inexaucé [inɛgzose] *adj* (*prière*) unanswered; (*désir*) unfulfilled

inexcusable [inɛkskyzabl] *adj* (*action, retard, négligence*) inexcusable, unforgivable; **vous êtes i.!** you're unforgivable!

inexécutable [inɛgzekytabl] *adj* (*projet*) impracticable, impractical, unworkable; (*ordre*) that cannot be carried out *or* executed

inexécuté [inɛgzekyte] *adj* (*promesse*) unfulfilled; **l'ordre de tirer sur les civils resta i.** the order to shoot civilians was not carried out; **le projet resta i.** the project did not go ahead

inexécution [inɛgzekysjɔ̃] *nf* (*d'un contrat*) non-performance; (*d'une promesse*) non-fulfilment

inexercé [inɛgzɛrse] *adj* **(a)** (*sans entraînement*) untrained **(b)** (*sans expérience*) (*œil, oreille*) unpractised, untrained

inexhaustible [inɛgzostibl] *adj Litt* inexhaustible

inexigible [inɛgziʒibl] *adj Fin* not due

inexistant [inɛgzistɑ̃] *adj* non-existent; *F* **il est totalement i.** he's a complete non-entity; *F* **lors de la réunion, il a été i.** at the meeting he just merged into the wallpaper; *F* **Becker a été quasiment i. pendant le premier set** Becker seemed totally out of it in the first set

inexistence [inɛgzistɑ̃s] *nf* non-existence; (*absence d'importance*) worthlessness

inexorabilité [inɛgzɔrabilite] *nf* inexorability

inexorable [inɛgzɔrabl] *adj* (*volonté, rigueur, fatalité*) inexorable; (*juge*) unrelenting, inflexible, inexorable

inexorablement [inɛgzɔrabləmɑ̃] *adv* inexorably

inexpérience [inɛksperjɑ̃s] *nf* inexperience

inexpérimenté [inɛksperimɑ̃te] *adj* **(a)** (*sans expérience*) (*personne, pilote*) inexperienced; (*main etc*) unpractised, unskilled **(b)** (*non testé*) (*procédé*) untried, untested

inexpert [inɛkspɛr] *adj Litt* inexpert, unpractised

inexpiable [inɛkspjabl] *adj* (*faute, péché, crime*) inexpiable, irremissible; (*qu'on ne peut apaiser*) merciless

inexpié [inɛkspje] *adj* unexpiated, unatoned

inexplicable [inɛksplikabl] *adj* (*comportement, accident, peur, joie*) inexplicable, unexplainable; **le sentiment que j'ai est i.** I can't explain the feeling I have

inexplicablement [inɛksplikabləmɑ̃] *adv* inexplicably, unaccountably

inexpliqué [inɛksplike] *adj* unexplained

inexploitable [inɛksplwatabl] *adj* (*mine, terre*) unworkable, inexploitable

inexploité [inɛksplwate] *adj* (*mine*) unworked; (*terre*) undeveloped, unworked; **ressources inexploitées** untapped resources

inexplorable [inɛksplɔrabl] *adj* inexplorable

inexploré [inɛksplɔre] *adj* unexplored

inexplosible [inɛksplozibl] *adj* non-explosive

inexpressif, -ive [inɛkspresif, -iv] *adj* inexpressive; (*visage, personne*) expressionless

inexprimable [inɛksprimabl] *adj* inexpressible

inexprimé [inɛksprime] *adj* unexpressed

inexpugnable [inɛkspygnabl] *adj* (*forteresse, position*) impregnable; (*force, âme*) invincible, unassailable

inextensible [inɛkstɑ̃sibl] *adj* (*tissu*) nonstretch; (*matière*) inextensible

in extenso [ɛkstɛ̃so] *adv* in full, in extenso

inextinguible [inɛkstɛ̃g(ɥ)ibl] *adj* (*feu, vengeance, haine*) inextinguishable, unquenchable; (*rire*) irrepressible, uncontrollable

in extremis [ɛkstremis] *adv* at the (very) last minute; **baptiser/marier qn i.** to baptize/marry sb on his/her deathbed

inextricable [inɛkstrikabl] *adj* inextricable; **nous nous trouvâmes dans un i. labyrinthe** we found ourselves in an impassable maze

inextricablement [inɛkstrikabləmɑ̃] *adv* inextricably

infaillibilité [ɛ̃fajibilite] *nf* infallibility

infaillible [ɛ̃fajibl] *adj* infallible

infailliblement [ɛ̃fajibləmɑ̃] *adv* infallibly

infaisable [ɛ̃fəzabl] *adj* not feasible, impossible; **ces mots croisés sont vraiment infaisables** this crossword is just impossible *or* just can't be done

infamant [ɛ̃famɑ̃] *adj* **(a)** (*déclaration, accusation*) defamatory, slanderous **(b)** *Jur* **peine infamante** penalty involving loss of civil rights

infâme [ɛ̃fɑm] *adj* (*mensonge, trafic*) infamous; (*acte, crime, créature*) foul, vile, unspeakable; (*taudis*) vile, squalid; (*odeur, nourriture*) vile, foul, revolting

infamie [ɛ̃fami] *nf* **(a)** (*caractère infâme*) infamy **(b)** (*action infâme*) foul *or* vile action; (*remarque infâme*) piece of slander; **dire des infamies à** *ou* **de qn** to vilify *or* slander sb

infant, -ante [ɛ̃fɑ̃, -ɑ̃t] *n Hist* infante, *f* infanta

infanterie [ɛ̃fɑ̃tri] *nf Mil* infantry; **soldat d'i.** infantryman, foot soldier; **i. aéroportée** *ou* **de l'air** airborne infantry; **i. de marine** marine corps, marines

infanticide [ɛ̃fɑ̃tisid] **1** *n* (*personne*) infanticide, child killer **2** *adj* infanticidal **3** *nm* (*crime*) infanticide, child murder

infantile [ɛ̃fɑ̃til] *adj* **(a)** (*maladie, affection*) infantile; **mortalité i.** infant mortality; **psychiatrie i.** child psychiatry **(b)** *Péj* (*attitude, réaction, personne*) infantile, childish

infantiliser [ɛfɑ̃tilize] *vt Péj* **la télévision infantilise les gens** television reduces people to the level of two-year-olds

infantilisme [ɛ̃fɑ̃tilism] *nm* **(a)** *Méd* infantilism, retarded development **(b)** *Péj* **c'est de l'i.** how infantile!, how childish!

infarctus [ɛ̃farktys] *nm Méd* infarct, infarction; **i. du myocarde** myocardial infarction, coronary thrombosis

infatigable [ɛ̃fatigabl] *adj* indefatigable, tireless, untiring

infatigablement [ɛ̃fatigabləmɑ̃] *adv* tirelessly, untiringly, indefatigably

infatuation [ɛ̃fatɥasjɔ̃] *nf* (*suffisance*) self-conceit, self-importance

infatué [ɛ̃fatɥe] *adj* **(a)** (*suffisant*) conceited; **i. (de soi-même)** conceited, full of oneself *or* of one's own importance **(b)** *Vieilli* infatuated

infatuer [ɛ̃fatɥe] **1** *vt Vieilli* to infatuate **2 s'infatuer** *vpr* **(a)** **s'i. (de soi-même)** to become conceited, to become full of oneself *or* of one's own importance **(b)** *Vieilli* **s'i. de qn/qch** to become infatuated with sb/sth

infécond [ɛ̃fekɔ̃] *adj* (*femelle, femme, esprit*) infertile, sterile, barren; (*terre*) barren, infertile

infécondité [ɛ̃fekɔ̃dite] *nf* (*de femelle, femme, d'esprit*) infertility, sterility, barrenness; (*de terre*) barrenness, infertility; **période d'i.** (*de femelle, femme*) period of infertility

infect [ɛ̃fɛkt] *adj* (*nourriture, repas*) vile, revolting; (*air*) foul; (*goût*) foul, revolting; **odeur infecte** foul *or* revolting smell, stench, stink; **taudis i.** filthy hovel; **temps i.** filthy *or* foul weather; **elle a été infecte avec sa sœur** she was vile *or* rotten to her sister; **c'est quelqu'un d'i.** he's/she's a vile person *or* really obnoxious

infectant [ɛ̃fɛktɑ̃] *adj Méd* (*virus*) infectious

infecter [ɛ̃fɛkte] **1** *vt* **(a)** *Méd, Ordinat* to infect **(b)** (*atmosphère, air*) to poison, to contaminate, to pollute; (*eau, sol*) to contaminate, to taint, to pollute **2 s'infecter** *vpr* (*de blessure, plaie, pied etc*) to become infected, to turn *or* go septic

infectieux, -euse [ɛ̃fɛksjø, -øz] *adj Méd* infectious

infection [ɛ̃fɛksjɔ̃] *nf* **(a)** *Méd, Ordinat* infection; **i. virale** viral infection **(b)** (*puanteur*) stench, stink; **quelle i. dans cette pièce!** this room stinks!

inféodation [ɛ̃feɔdasjɔ̃] *nf* **(a)** *Pol* allegiance **(à** to) **(b)** *Hist* (*d'un vassal*) enfeoffment; (*d'une terre*) giving in fief

inféoder [ɛ̃feɔde] **1** *vt* **(a)** (*soumettre*) to subjugate **(b)** *Hist* (*vassal*) to enfeoff; (*terre*) to give in fief **2 s'inféoder** *vpr Pol* **s'i. à un groupe/un parti** to give one's allegiance to a group/ a party; **être inféodé à** to be subservient to

inférence [ɛ̃ferɑ̃s] *nf* inference

inférer [ɛ̃fere] *vt* **(j'infère; j'inférerai)** to infer, to gather **(de** from)

inférieur, -eure [ɛ̃ferjœr] **1** *adj* **(a)** (*qui est en bas*) (*étagère, niveau*) bottom; (*étages*) lower; (*lèvre, paupière, mâchoire*) lower, bottom; **partie inférieure** lower part, bottom (part); **membres inférieurs** lower limbs; **allez voir à l'étage i.** go and look on the floor below *or* the next floor down; *Astron* **planète inférieure** inferior planet; *Géog* **le cours i. d'un fleuve** the lower course of a river; **i. au niveau de la mer** below sea level

(b) (*dans une hiérarchie*) (*qualité, marchandises*) inferior, poor; (*intelligence*) inferior; *Bot, Zool* (*plante, animal*) lower; **d'un rang i.** of a lower rank, lower in rank; **être rétrogradé à l'échelon i.** to be demoted to the grade below; **elle ne lui est pas inférieure** she is his equal, she's not inferior to him; **elle n'est en rien inférieure à ses collègues** she is in no way inferior to her colleagues

(c) (*dans une comparaison*) **6 est i. à 8** 6 is less than 8; **a est i. ou égal à 3** a is less than or equal to 3; **note inférieure à douze** mark below twelve; **vitesse i. à 500 km/h** speed below *or* under 500 km/h; **température i. à -30** temperature below -30; **i. en nombre** fewer in number; **i. à la normale** (*de la température*) below normal; **i. à la moyenne** below average; **ce mois-ci la production est inférieure à celle des mois précédents** this month production is lower than *or* less than *or* below that of previous months; **son dernier roman est i. aux précédents** his latest novel is inferior to *or* not as good as his previous ones; *Litt* **il est i. à sa tâche** he is not equal to the task, he is not up to the job

2 *n* inferior

inférieurement [ɛ̃ferjœrmɑ̃] *adv* **(a)** (*en bas*) in a lower position **(b)** (*moins bien*) in an inferior manner **(à** to), less well **(à** than)

infériorité [ɛ̃ferjɔrite] *nf* inferiority; **i. numérique** *ou* **en nombre** numerical inferiority, inferiority in numbers; *Psy* **avoir un complexe d'i.** to have an inferiority complex; **i. de niveau** difference *or* drop in level; **se sentir/être en position d'i. (par rapport à qn)** to feel/be in a position of inferiority *or* in an inferior position (in relation to sb)

infernal, -ale, -aux, -ales [ɛ̃fɛrnal, -o] *adj* **(a)** (*de l'enfer*) infernal, of hell; *Fig* **cruauté/méchanceté infernale** diabolical cruelty/wickedness **(b)** *F* (*insupportable*) (*chaleur, bruit*) infernal; **nous dévalions la pente à une vitesse infernale** we hurtled down the slope at (a) breakneck speed; **la direction nous impose des cadences infernales** the management wants us to work at an impossible speed; **cet enfant est i.** this child's a little devil; **elle est infernale, à toujours se plaindre** she's really awful, she's always complaining; **c'est i.!** it's hellish!, it's sheer hell!

infertile [ɛ̃fertil] *adj* (*terre, imagination, esprit*) infertile, barren

infertilité [ɛ̃fɛrtilite] *nf* infertility

infestation [ɛ̃fɛstasjɔ̃] *nf Méd* infestation

infester [ɛ̃fɛste] *vt* (*de la vermine etc*) to infest, to overrun; **infesté d'insectes/de pirates** infested *or* overrun with insects/pirates

infeutrable [ɛ̃føtrabl] *adj* which does not felt *or* mat

infibulation [ɛ̃fibylasjɔ̃] *nf* infibulation

infichu [ɛ̃fiʃy] *adj F* (*incapable*) incapable **(de** of)

infidèle [ɛ̃fidɛl] **1** *adj* **(a)** (*déloyal*) (*ami*) unfaithful, disloyal **(à** to); (*mari, femme*) unfaithful **(à** to); *Litt* **être i. à sa promesse** to be false or untrue to one's promise, to break one's promise **(b)** (*inexact*) (*traduction, rapport etc*) inaccurate, incorrect; (*mémoire, témoignage*) unreliable, untrustworthy; **c'est une traduction i.** it is not an accurate *or* a faithful translation **(c)** *Rel* infidel **2** *n Rel* infidel

infidèlement [ɛ̃fidɛlmɑ̃] *adv* **(a)** (*déloyalement*) unfaithfully **(b)** (*inexactement*) inaccurately, incorrectly

infidélité [ɛ̃fidelite] *nf* **(a)** (*déloyauté*) (*d'ami*) unfaithfulness, disloyalty **(à** to); (*de mari, femme*) unfaithfulness, infidelity **(à** to); **faire des infidélités à sa femme** to be unfaithful to one's wife; *Hum* **faire une i. à son boucher/son coiffeur** to be unfaithful to one's butcher/hairdresser, to go to a different butcher/hairdresser (*just for once*) **(b)** (*manque d'exactitude*) (*dans une traduction, un compte-rendu, un rapport*) inaccuracy; **infidélités** inaccuracies

infiltration [ɛ̃filtrasjɔ̃] *nf* **(a)** (*d'un liquide*) (*dans qch*) infiltration **(dans** into), seepage; (*à travers qch*) seepage, percolation **(à travers** through); **il y a des infiltrations dans le plafond** there are some leaks in the ceiling **(b)** *Fig* (*de nouvelles idées, coutumes, espions etc*) infiltration **(c)** *Méd* (*injection*) injection; **faire des infiltrations à qn** to give sb injections

infiltrer [ɛ̃filtre] **1** *vt* **(a)** (*noyauter*) (*parti, pays etc*) to infiltrate **(b)** *Méd* to inject **(dans** into) **2 s'infiltrer** *vpr* **(a)** (*d'un fluide*) **s'i. dans qch** to seep into sth, to infiltrate (into) sth; **s'i. à travers qch** to seep through sth, to percolate through sth **(b)** *Fig* (*d'une idée, d'une théorie etc*) to infiltrate; **s'i. dans** to infiltrate **(c)** **s'i. dans un groupuscule/ une organisation** to infiltrate a group/an organization; *Mil* **s'i. dans un pays** to infiltrate a country

infime [ɛ̃fim] *adj* **(a)** (*quantité, nombre, proportion, pourcentage, différence*) tiny, minute, infinitesimal **(b)** (*rang etc*) lowly, mean

infini [ɛ̃fini] **1** *adj* (*espace, univers*) infinite, boundless; (*soin, bonté, patience etc*) infinite; (*bonheur*) (*intense*) utter, intense; (*arguments etc*) innumerable; **prendre d'infinies précautions** to take innumerable *or* countless precautions; **être d'une** *ou* **avoir une patience infinie** to be infinitely patient, to have infinite patience; **vous m'avez fait un plaisir i. en venant me voir** you have given me enormous pleasure in coming to see me; **auriez-vous l'infinie bonté de me donner l'heure, monsieur?** would you do me the great kindness of telling me the time, sir?; **il est resté au téléphone un temps i.** he stayed on the phone for an eternity; *Math* **ensemble i.** infinite set

2 *nm* **l'i.** *Phil* the infinite; *Phys* infinity; *Phot* **mettre au point sur l'i.** to focus on infinity; **à l'i.** (*s'étendre, se refléter*) to infinity; (*discutailler*) ad infinitum

infiniment [ɛ̃finimɑ̃] *adv* (*bon, généreux, patient*) infinitely; **i. plus intelligent** infinitely more intelligent; **i. petit** infinitesimally small; **l'i. petit** the infinitesimal; **l'i. grand** the infinitely great; **i. grand** enormously large; **se donner i. de peine** to give oneself an infinite *or* an enormous amount of trouble; **il parle à ses enfants avec i. de douceur** he is enormously gentle when speaking to his children; **je regrette i.** I'm extremely sorry; **je vous suis i. reconnaissant de m'avoir aidé** I'm extremely *or* enormously grateful to you for helping me

infinité [ɛ̃finite] *nf* **(a)** *Math, Phys* infinity; **l'i. de l'espace** the infinity *or* boundlessness of space **(b)** (*grand nombre*) **une i. de personnes/raisons** an infinite number of people/reasons

infinitésimal, -ale, -aux, -ales [ɛ̃finitezimal, -o] *adj* infinitesimal

infinitif, -ive [ɛ̃finitif, -iv] [①**A40-2**,C,1; **B32-5**,H] *Gram* **1** *adj* infinitive **2** *nm* infinitive; **à l'i.** in the infinitive

infirmation [ɛ̃firmasjɔ̃] *nf Jur* invalidation, nullification, quashing

infirme [ɛ̃firm] **1** *adj* disabled, crippled, *Arch, Litt* weak; **i. du bras gauche** crippled in the left arm; **il est resté i. à la suite de son accident** his accident left him disabled *or* crippled *or* a cripple **2** *n* cripple, disabled person; **les infirmes** the disabled, the crippled

infirmer [ɛ̃firme] *vt* **(a)** (*montrer la faiblesse de*) (*théorie*) to pinpoint the weakness of; (*contredire*) (*témoignage*) to invalidate; (*information, nouvelle*) to refute **(b)** *Jur* (*jugement*) to invalidate, to nullify, to quash

infirmerie [ɛ̃firməri] *nf* (*de prison, caserne etc*) infirmary; (*à l'école, dans un bateau*) sick bay

infirmier [ɛ̃firmje] *nm* (male) nurse; **i. militaire** medical orderly

infirmière [ɛ̃firmjɛr] *nf* nurse; *Mil* medical orderly; **i. diplômée** ≈ state-registered nurse, *US* registered nurse; **i. en chef** nursing officer, *US* quality control officer; **i. visiteuse** district nurse, *US* home health nurse

infirmité [ɛ̃firmite] *nf* (*invalidité*) (physical) disability, *Arch, Litt* weakness, frailty

inflammabilité [ɛ̃flamabilite] *nf* inflammability, flammability

inflammable [ɛ̃flamabl] *adj* inflammable, flammable

inflammation [ɛ̃flamasjɔ̃] *nf Méd* inflammation

inflammatoire [ɛ̃flamatwar] *adj Méd* inflammatory

inflation [ɛ̃flasjɔ̃] *nf Écon* inflation; **politique d'i.** inflationary policy; **i. rampante/galopante** rampant/galloping inflation; **l'i. du nombre des ...** the marked increase in the number of ...; **i. des prix** price inflation; **i. des salaires** wage inflation; **i. par la demande** demand-pull inflation; **i. par les coûts** cost-push inflation

inflationniste [ɛ̃flasjɔnist] **1** *n* inflationist **2** *adj Écon* inflationary

infléchi [ɛ̃fleʃi] *adj* **(a)** *Gram* (*voyelle*) inflected **(b)** (*rayon etc*) inflected, bent

infléchir [ɛ̃fleʃir] **1** *vt* **(a)** (*rayon*) to bend, to inflect, to curve **(b)** (*politique*) to change the direction of; **i. le cours des événements** to change *or* alter the course of events **2 s'infléchir** *vpr* **(a)** (*dévier*) (*d'une route, d'une ligne etc*) to bend, to curve; *Opt* (*d'un rayon*) to be inflected *or* bent **(b)** (*d'un plancher, d'une poutre*) to sag, to bow **(c)** (*changer*) (*de politique*) to change direction, to shift

inflexibilité [ɛ̃flɛksibilite] *nf* inflexibility, rigidity

inflexible [ɛ̃flɛksibl] *adj* (*personne*) inflexible, rigid, unyielding; (*règle, loi*) inflexible, rigid, hard and fast; **une volonté i.** an iron *or* inflexible *or* unbending will; **demeurer i. dans une résolution** to remain firm in *or* stick to a resolution

inflexiblement [ɛ̃flɛksibləmɑ̃] *adv* inflexibly, rigidly

inflexion [ɛ̃flɛksjɔ̃] *nf* **(a)** (*mouvement*) **i. du corps** bend(ing) of the body; (*pour saluer*) bow; **i. de (la) tête** tilt(ing) of the head; (*pour saluer, acquiescer*) nod **(b)** (*de la voix*) inflection, modulation **(c)** (*de courbe, rayon*) inflection **(d)** *Ling* inflection

infliger [ɛ̃fliʒe] **(j'infligeai(s); n. infligeons) 1** *vt* (*correction, punition, musique pénible etc*) to inflict (**à** on); **i. une peine/une amende à qn** to impose a penalty/a fine on sb; **i. des épreuves à qn** to bring hardship on sb; **il nous a infligé sa présence** he inflicted himself *or* his presence on us **2 s'infliger** *vpr* **s'i. des privations** *ou* **des épreuves** to bring hardship on oneself

inflorescence [ɛ̃flɔresɑ̃s] *nf Bot* inflorescence

influençable [ɛ̃flyɑ̃sabl] *adj* easily influenced

influence [ɛ̃flyɑ̃s] *nf* influence (**sur** on); **avoir une bonne/mauvaise i. sur qn** to have a good/bad influence on sb; **exercer une i. bénéfique/néfaste sur qch/qn** to have a beneficial/harmful influence *or* effect on sth/sb; **sous l'i. de l'alcool/la drogue** under the influence of drink/drugs; *F* **être sous i.** to be under the influence of drugs; **agir sous l'i. de la colère/la jalousie** to act in a fit of anger/jealousy; **sous ton i.** under your influence; **il a beaucoup d'i.** he has a lot of influence, he's very influential; **cet incident n'a eu aucune i. sur ma décision** this incident had no influence on *or* didn't influence my decision; **sphère d'i.** sphere of influence; **trafic d'i.** corrupt practice

influencer [ɛ̃flyɑ̃se] *vt* **(j'influençai(s); n. influençons)** to influence, to have an influence on; (*opinion publique*) to influence, to sway, to have an influence on; **ce peintre a beaucoup été influencé par le cubisme** this painter was greatly influenced by cubism; **il ne faut pas te laisser i. par ce type-là!** you mustn't let yourself be influenced by that fellow!; **il se laisse facilement i.** he's easily influenced

influent [ɛ̃flyɑ̃] *adj* influential

influer [ɛ̃flye] *vi* **i. sur qch/qn** to have influence on sth/sb, to influence sth/sb; **le temps influe sur son humeur** the weather affects *or* has an effect on his mood

influx [ɛ̃fly] *nm* **(a)** *Physiol* **i. nerveux** nerve impulse **(b)** (*fluide*) influx

info [ɛ̃fo] *nf Journ, Rad, TV F* (*nouvelle*) news item; **les infos** the news

infographe [ɛ̃fograf] *n* graphics artist, graphics designer

infographie [ɛ̃fɔgrafi] *nf* computer graphics

infographiste [ɛ̃fografist] *n* graphics artist, graphics designer

in-folio *adj inv, nm inv* folio

informateur, -trice [ɛ̃fɔrmatœr, -tris] *n* informant; (*de police*) informer; (*de journaliste*) inside source

informaticien, -ienne [ɛ̃fɔrmatisjɛ̃, -jɛn] **1** *n* computer scientist **2** *adj* **ingénieur i.** computer engineer

informatif, -ive [ɛ̃fɔrmatif, -iv] *adj* informative

information [ɛ̃fɔrmasjɔ̃] *nf* **(a)** (*renseignement*) (piece of) information; **informations** information; **pour votre i.** for your information; **à titre d'i.** for information; **une i. de première importance** a very important piece of information; **c'est la seule i. dont je dispose** it's the only information I have; **je vous envoie pour votre i. ...** I'm sending you for your information ...; **assurer l'i. du public en matière de santé** to ensure that the public is (kept) informed about matters of health; **le droit à l'i.** freedom of information; **centre d'i.** information centre; *Mktg* **i. sur le lieu de vente** point-of-sale information; *Mktg* **informations primaires** primary data

(b) *Journ, Rad, TV* (*nouvelle*) news (item), item *or* piece of news; **une i. de dernière minute** some late news, a late (news) item; *Journ* **informations de dernière minute** stop press (news); **cette i. n'est pas confirmée** this news is unconfirmed; **un journal d'i.** a serious *or* quality newspaper; *Rad, TV, Journ* **les informations** the news

(c) (*médias*) **l'i.** the media; **mettre la main sur l'i.** to take control of the media

(d) *Ordinat* data, information; **traitement de l'i.** data processing; **théorie de l'i.** information theory

(e) *Jur* (*enquête*) inquiry; (*instruction préparatoire*) preliminary investigation; **ouvrir une i.** to begin legal proceedings

informatique [ɛ̃fɔrmatik] **1** *nf* (*traitement de l'information*) data processing, DP; (*science*) computer science, computing, information science *or* technology, IT; **travailler dans l'i.** to work *or* be in computers; **société/magazine d'i.** computer company/magazine; **cours d'i.** computer *or* data-processing course; **i. à domicile** home computing **2** *adj* (*mobilier, réseau etc*) computer

informatiquement [ɛ̃fɔrmatikmɑ̃] *adv* by *or* on computer; **toutes les données sont traitées i.** all the data is processed by *or* on computer

informatisation [ɛ̃fɔrmatizasjɔ̃] *nf* computerization

informatiser [ɛ̃fɔrmatize] *vt* to computerize; **service informatisé** computerized department

informe [ɛ̃fɔrm] *adj* (*masse, amas, objet*) shapeless, formless; (*chapeau, pull, chaussures*) shapeless; (*plan*) crude, rough; (*monstre, être*) misshapen, ill-formed

informé [ɛ̃fɔrme] **1** *adj* informed; **dans les milieux informés** in informed circles **2** *nm Jur* inquiry; **ordonner un plus ample i.** to order a broadening of the inquiry; **jusqu'à plus ample i.** until we have further information *or* are better informed

informel, -elle [ɛ̃fɔrmɛl] *adj* informal

informer [ɛ̃fɔrme] **1** *vt* **i. qn de qch** to inform sb of sth, to tell sb *or* let sb know about sth; **i. qn d'un fait** to inform sb of *or* acquaint sb with a fact, to tell sb a fact; **personne ne m'a informé du fait qu'il devait rester plusieurs jours!** no one informed me (of the fact) that *or* told me that *or* let me know that he was to stay several days!; **veuillez m'en i.** please let me know, please inform me, please tell me; **i. qn que ...** to inform *or* tell sb that ..., to let sb know that ...; **nous informons les voyageurs que ...** we would like to inform passengers that ...; **bien informé** well informed; **mal informé** ill-informed; **on vous a mal informé, vous avez été mal informé** you've been misinformed *or* wrongly informed

2 *vi Jur* **i. sur un crime** to investigate a crime, to inquire into a crime; **i. contre qn** to begin legal proceedings against sb

3 s'informer *vpr* (*se renseigner*) to inquire, to ask, to make inquiries (**de qch** about sth; **au sujet de qn** about sb); (*se tenir au courant*) to inform oneself, to get to know about things; **s'i. de l'état de santé de qn** to inquire *or* ask after *or* about sb's health

informulé [ɛ̃fɔrmyle] *adj* unformulated

infortune [ɛ̃fɔrtyn] *nf surtout Litt* misfortune; **compagnons d'i.** companions in adversity, fellow sufferers; **tomber dans l'i.** to meet with misfortune

infortuné [ɛ̃fɔrtyne] **1** *adj* unfortunate, unlucky, wretched **2** *n* (poor *or* unfortunate) wretch; **les infortunés** the unfortunate, the wretched

infoutu [ɛ̃futy] *adj très F* downright incapable (**de** of)

infraction [ɛ̃fraksjɔ̃] *nf* (*à un règlement, une règle*) infringement, contravention; (*à la loi*) infringement, breach; (*à une coutume*) violation (**à** of); (*délit*) offence; **i. au code de la route** traffic offence, *Am* traffic violation; **être en i.** to be committing an offence, to be breaking the law

infranchissable [ɛ̃frɑ̃ʃisabl] *adj* (*rivière, col, gouffre*) impassable; (*obstacle, difficulté*) insurmountable, insuperable

infrangible [ɛ̃frɑ̃ʒibl] *adj Litt* infrangible

infrarouge [ɛ̃fraruʒ] *adj, nm Phys* infrared

infrason [ɛ̃frasɔ̃] *nm Phys* infrasonic vibration

infra(-)sonore [ɛ̃frasɔnɔr], *pl* **infra(-)sonores** *adj* infrasonic

infrastructure [ɛ̃frastryktyr] *nf* (**a**) *Constr* substructure (**b**) *Écon, Tech* (*de chemins de fer, d'hôpitaux etc*) infrastructure; **i. routière/touristique** road/tourist infrastructure; **i. organisationnelle** organizational infrastructure

infréquentable [ɛ̃frekɑ̃tabl] *adj* **gens infréquentables** people one doesn't want to associate with

infroissable [ɛ̃frwasabl] *adj Tex* crease-resistant, uncrushable

infructueux, -euse [ɛ̃fryktɥø, -øz] *adj* (**a**) (*effort, tentative*) fruitless, unfruitful, unsuccessful; (*investissement*) unprofitable (**b**) *Vieilli* (*terre etc*) unfruitful, barren

infumable [ɛ̃fymabl] *adj* unsmokable

infus [ɛ̃fy] *adj* (*connaissance*) inborn, innate; **je n'ai pas la science infuse!** I can't be expected to know everything!

infuser [ɛ̃fyze] **1** *vt* (**a**) (*faire pénétrer*) to instil, to infuse (**dans** into); **i. le doute dans l'esprit de qn** to instil *or* infuse doubt into sb's mind; *Fig* **i. un sang nouveau à un organisme** to inject new blood into an organization (**b**) (*herbes*) to infuse; **le thé est assez infusé** the tea has brewed for long enough **2** *vi* **faire i. le thé** to brew *or Fml* infuse the tea; **laisser i. le thé** to let the tea brew *or Fml* infuse

infusible [ɛ̃fyzibl] *adj* infusible, non-fusible

infusion [ɛ̃fyzjɔ̃] *nf* (**a**) (*action*) (*d'herbes, de thé*) infusion; (*plantes etc*) steeping (**b**) (*boisson*) herb tea, infusion; **une i. de camomille** some camomile tea, an infusion of camomile

ingagnable [ɛ̃gaɲabl] *adj* impossible to win; **la partie est i. pour l'Angleterre** England can't win (the game)

ingambe [ɛ̃gɑ̃b] *adj Vieilli* (*physiquement*) nimble, sprightly; (*esprit*) alert

ingénier (s') [sɛ̃ʒenje] *vpr* **s'i. à faire qch** to strive *or* make great efforts to do sth; **il s'ingénie à me rendre la vie impossible/de me contredire** he goes out of his way to make my life impossible/to contradict me

ingénierie [ɛ̃ʒeniri] *nf* engineering; **i. assistée par ordinateur** computer-aided engineering; **i. inverse** reverse engineering; **i. financière** corporate finance

ingénieur [ɛ̃ʒenjœr] *nm* engineer; **femme i.** female *or* woman engineer

▶ **ingénieur**: **i. civil** civil engineer; **i. commercial** sales engineer; *Naut* **i. des constructions navales** naval constructor; **i. de diffusion** broadcasting engineer; **i. éclairagiste** lighting director; **i. électricien** electrical engineer; **i. électronicien** electronics engineer; *Mil* **Corps des Ingénieurs géographes** ≈ Ordnance Survey; **i. magnétoscope** videotape engineer; **i. mécanicien** mechanical engineer; **i. des mines** mining engineer; **i. des ponts et chaussées** = (government) civil engineer; **i. du son** sound *or* audio *or* recording engineer; (*chargé du mixage ou doublage*) dubbing mixer; **i. technico-commercial** sales engineer *or* technician; **i. des télécommunications** telecommunications engineer; **i. des travaux publics** civil engineer; **i. des ventes** sales engineer; **i. de la vision** vision control operator, vision mixer, vision engineer; **i. de vol** flight engineer

ingénieur-conseil, *pl* **ingénieurs-conseils** *nm* consulting engineer

ingénieusement [ɛ̃ʒenjøzmɑ̃] *adv* ingeniously, cleverly

ingénieux, -euse [ɛ̃ʒenjø, -øz] *adj* ingenious, clever

ingéniosité [ɛ̃ʒenjozite] *nf* ingenuity, cleverness

ingénu, -ue [ɛ̃ʒeny] **1** *adj* (*personne*) ingenuous, artless, simple; (*regard*) ingenuous **2** *n* ingenuous *or* artless *or* simple person; **faire l'i.** to affect simplicity **3** *nf Th* **ingénue** ingénue

ingénuité [ɛ̃ʒenɥite] *nf* ingenuousness, artlessness, simplicity

ingénument [ɛ̃ʒenymɑ̃] *adv* ingenuously, artlessly

ingérence [ɛ̃ʒerɑ̃s] *nf* interference, meddling (**dans** in); **politique de non i.** policy of non-interference

ingérer [ɛ̃ʒere] (**j'ingère; j'ingérerai**) **1** *vt Physiol* (*nourriture*) to ingest **2 s'ingérer** *vpr* **s'i. dans qch** to interfere *or* meddle in sth

ingestion [ɛ̃ʒɛstjɔ̃] *nf Physiol* ingestion

ingouvernable [ɛ̃guvɛrnabl] *adj* (*nation etc*) ungovernable; (*bateau etc*) unmanageable

ingrat, -ate [ɛ̃gra, -at] **1** *adj* (*personne*) ungrateful (**envers** to, towards); (*sol, terre*) unproductive, barren; (*matière*) intractable; (*tâche*) thankless; (*travail, sujet*) unrewarding; (*apparence, visage etc*) unattractive, unpleasant; **l'âge i.** the awkward age **2** *n* ungrateful person

ingratement [ɛ̃gratmɑ̃] *adv Litt* ungratefully

ingratitude [ɛ̃gratityd] *nf* ingratitude, ungratefulness

ingrédient [ɛ̃gredjɑ̃] *nm* ingredient

inguérissable [ɛ̃gerisabl] *adj Méd* incurable; (*chagrin*) inconsolable

ingurgitation [ɛ̃gyrʒitasjɔ̃] *nf* ingurgitation

ingurgiter [ɛ̃gyrʒite] *vt* (*manger*) to gulp down, to swallow (down); (*boire*) to gulp down, to knock back; **faire i. qch à qn** to force sb to swallow sth, to make sb swallow sth; *Fig F* to cram sth into sb's head; **le prof nous a fait i. toutes les déclinaisons en une semaine** the teacher crammed all the declensions into our heads in a week; **j'ai ingurgité tout le programme d'histoire la veille de l'examen** I crammed the whole history syllabus into my head the day before the exam

inhabile [inabil] *adj Litt* (*malhabile*) unskilled (**à** in), unskilful, clumsy; *Jur* **i. à tester** incompetent to make a will

inhabileté [inabilte] *nf* lack of skill (**à faire qch** in doing sth); **c'est quelqu'un d'une grande i. en matière de commerce** he is extremely unskilful in commercial matters

inhabilité [inabilite] *nf Jur* incapacity, disability; **i. à succéder** incompetency to succeed

inhabitable [inabitabl] *adj* uninhabitable

inhabité [inabite] *adj* (*maison*) unoccupied, uninhabited; (*région*) uninhabited; *Astron* **vol i.** unmanned flight

inhabituel, -elle [inabitɥɛl] *adj* unusual; **c'est i. de ne pas les trouver à la maison le dimanche** it's unusual not to find them at home on a Sunday

inhalateur, -trice [inalatœr, -tris] **1** *adj* (*appareil*) inhaling **2** *nm Méd* inhaler

inhalation [inalasjɔ̃] *nf Physiol* inhalation; *Méd* **faire des inhalations** to inhale

inhaler [inale] *vt* to inhale

inharmonieux, -ieuse [inarmɔnjø, -jøz] *adj* (*son*) inharmonious, discordant

inhérence [inerɑ̃s] *nf* inherence, inherency

inhérent [inerɑ̃] *adj* inherent (**à** in)

inhiber [inibe] *vt* to inhibit

inhibiteur, -trice [inibitœr, -tris] **1** *adj Biol, Physiol* (*réflexe, nerf etc*) inhibitory **2** *nm Pharm* inhibitor; *Aut* **i. d'oxydation** oxidation inhibitor; *Aut* **i. de corrosion** corrosion inhibitor

inhibition [inibisjɔ̃] *nf* inhibition

inhospitalier, -ière [inɔspitalje, -jɛr] *adj* inhospitable

inhumain [inymɛ̃] *adj* inhuman

inhumainement [inymɛnmɑ̃] *adv Litt* inhumanly

inhumanité [inymanite] *nf Litt* inhumanity

inhumation [inymasjɔ̃] *nf* burial, interment

inhumer [inyme] *vt* to bury, to inter

inimaginable [inimaʒinabl] *adj* unimaginable, inconceivable, unbelievable

inimitable [inimitabl] *adj* inimitable

inimité [inimite] *adj* matchless; **un artiste extraordinaire resté i. à ce jour** an extraordinary artist whose like has never been seen since

inimitié [inimitje] *nf* enmity, hostility, ill feeling

ininflammable [inɛ̃flamabl] *adj* non-(in)flammable, fireproof

inintelligemment [inɛ̃teliʒamɑ̃] *adv* unintelligently

inintelligence [inɛ̃teliʒɑ̃s] *nf* (**a**) (*manque d'intelligence*) lack of intelligence; **elle a eu l'i. d'accepter son invitation** she rather unwisely accepted his invitation (**b**) (*incompréhension*) **son i. du problème** his inability to understand *or* his lack of understanding of the problem

inintelligent [inɛ̃teliʒɑ̃] *adj* unintelligent
inintelligibilité [inɛ̃teliʒibilite] *nf* unintelligibility
inintelligible [inɛ̃teliʒibl] *adj* unintelligible
inintelligiblement [inɛ̃teliʒibləmɑ̃] *adv* unintelligibly
inintéressant [inɛ̃terɛsɑ̃] *adj* uninteresting
ininterrompu [inɛ̃tɛrɔ̃py] *adj* (*efforts*) continued, uninterrupted, unremitting; (*discussions*) uninterrupted; (*sommeil, pluie*) uninterrupted, unbroken; (*progrès*) steady, continued; (*suite*) uninterrupted; **le flot i. des voitures** the steady *or* unbroken stream of cars; **deux heures de musique ininterrompue** two hours of non-stop *or* uninterrupted *or* continuous music
inique [inik] *adj* iniquitous
iniquement [inikmɑ̃] *adv* iniquitously
iniquité [inikite] *nf* iniquity
initial, -iale, -iaux, -iales [inisjal, -jo] **1** *adj* (*lettre, coût etc*) initial; **vitesse initiale** (*d'un projectile*) muzzle velocity **2** *nf* **initiale** initial (letter); **il a signé le document de ses initiales** he signed the document with his initials, he initialled the document
initialement [inisjalmɑ̃] *adv* initially
initialisation [inisjalizasjɔ̃] *Ordinat nf* initialization; **i. du compteur** counter initialization, zeroing of the counter
initialiser [inisjalize] *vt Ordinat* (*disque*) to initialize; (*ordinateur*) to boot (up)
initiateur, -trice [inisjatœr, -tris] **1** *n* (*d'un projet, d'une réforme etc*) initiator, originator; **elle fut son initiatrice** she initiated him into it **2** *adj* initiatory
initiation [inisjasjɔ̃] *nf* initiation (**à** into); **une i. à la musique** an introduction to music; **rite d'i.** initiation rite
initiatique [inisjatik] *adj* initiatory
initiative [inisjativ] *nf* initiative; **sur l'i. de qn** on sb's initiative; **prendre l'i. d'une réforme** to initiate a reform; **prendre l'i. de faire qch** to take the initiative in doing sth; **faire qch de sa propre i.** to do sth on one's own initiative; **faire preuve d'i.** to show initiative; **manquer d'i.** to lack initiative; **il n'a aucune i.** he's got no initiative; **syndicat d'i.** tourist information bureau; *Mil* **i. de défense stratégique** strategic defence initiative
initié, -ée [inisje] *n Rel, Fig* initiate; **les initiés** the initiated, the initiates; *Bourse* **délit d'i.** insider trading
initier [inisje] **1** *vt* to initiate (**à** into); **i. qn au grec/aux échecs/à l'harmonica** to introduce sb to Greek/chess/the harmonica **2 s'initier** *vpr* **s'i. à** (*matière, discipline*) to start learning; (*sport*) to start to play
injectable [ɛ̃ʒɛktabl] *adj* injectable
injecté [ɛ̃ʒɛkte] *adj* (*visage*) congested; **yeux injectés de sang** bloodshot eyes
injecter [ɛ̃ʒɛkte] **1** *vt* (*substance*) to inject (**dans** into); **i. des capitaux dans une entreprise** to inject capital into a business **2 s'injecter** *vpr* (*des yeux*) to become bloodshot
injecteur, -trice [ɛ̃ʒɛktœr, -tris] *Tech* **1** *adj* (*tube*) injecting **2** *nm* injector; *Av* nozzle; *Aut* **i. de carburant** fuel injector; **i. multitrous** multi-hole injector, multi-hole nozzle
injection [ɛ̃ʒɛksjɔ̃] *nf* (*de pénicilline, de capital etc*) injection; **moteur à i.** fuel injection engine; *Aut* **i. diesel** diesel injection; *Aut* **i. directe** direct injection; *Aut* **i. monopoint** single-point fuel injection; *Aut* **i. multipoint** multi-point injection, multi-port fuel injection
injoignable [ɛ̃ʒwaɲabl] *adj* (*personne*) unreachable; **elle est i. au téléphone** she can't be reached *or* is unreachable on the *or* by phone
injonction [ɛ̃ʒɔ̃ksjɔ̃] *nf* injunction; *Jur* injunction, order; **recevoir l'i. de faire qch** to get the order to do sth; **faire qch sur l'i. de qn** to do sth on sb's orders
injure [ɛ̃ʒyr] *nf* (*insulte*) insult; *Jur* (*délit*) = slander without object; **injures** abuse, insults; **en venir aux injures** to start insulting *or* abusing each other; **couvrir qn d'injures** to hurl insults *or* abuse at sb; **faire i. à qn** to insult sb; **elle m'a fait l'i. de ne pas venir à ma soirée** she insulted me by not coming to my party; *Litt* **l'i. des ans** the ravages of time
injurier [ɛ̃ʒyrje] *vt* to abuse, to insult
injurieux, -euse [ɛ̃ʒyrjø, -øz] *adj* insulting, abusive
injuste [ɛ̃ʒyst] **1** *adj* unjust, unfair (**envers, avec** to, towards) **2** *nm* **le juste et l'i.** right and wrong
injustement [ɛ̃ʒystəmɑ̃] *adv* unjustly, unfairly
injustice [ɛ̃ʒystis] *nf* (**a**) (*iniquité*) injustice, unfairness (**envers** to, towards); **i. sociale** social injustice; **lutter contre l'i.** to fight (against) injustice (**b**) (*acte, parole*) injustice
injustifiable [ɛ̃ʒystifjabl] *adj* unjustifiable
injustifié [ɛ̃ʒystifje] *adj* unjustified, unwarranted
inlassable [ɛ̃lasabl] *adj* (*efforts, patience*) untiring, unflagging; (*personne*) tireless
inlassablement [ɛ̃lasabləmɑ̃] *adv* untiringly, tirelessly; (*répéter*) ceaselessly
inné [ine] *adj* innate, inborn
innervation [inɛrvasjɔ̃] *nf Physiol* innervation
innerver [inɛrve] *vt Physiol* to innervate
innocemment [inɔsamɑ̃] *adv* innocently; **j'ai posé la question i.** I asked the question in all innocence, I meant no harm by my question
innocence [inɔsɑ̃s] *nf* innocence; (*d'une plaisanterie*) harmlessness; **prouver l'i. de qn** to prove sb innocent, to prove sb's innocence; **il a posé la question/l'a invitée en toute i.** he asked the question/invited her in all innocence, he meant no harm by his question/by inviting her
innocent, -ente [inɔsɑ̃, -ɑ̃t] **1** *adj* (*non coupable, pur, naïf*) innocent; (*plaisanterie, remarque*) harmless, innocent; **i. comme l'enfant qui vient de naître** as innocent as a newborn babe; **il est i. du crime dont on l'accuse** he is innocent of the crime of which he is accused **2** *n* (*non coupable*) innocent person; (*idiot*) simpleton; **les (saints) Innocents** the Holy Innocents; **ne fais pas l'i.!** don't act so innocent *or* the innocent!; **l'i. du village** the village idiot; *Prov* **aux innocents les mains pleines** fortune favours fools
innocenter [inɔsɑ̃te] *vt* (**a**) **i. qn (d'une accusation/d'un crime)** to clear sb (of a charge/of a crime); (*d'un juge, d'un jury*) to find sb not guilty *or* to clear sb (of a charge/of a crime) (**b**) (*justifier*) (*conduite*) to excuse, to justify
innocuité [inɔkɥite] *nf* harmlessness, innocuousness; **il est d'une i. totale** he's completely harmless
innombrable [inɔ̃brabl] *adj* innumerable, countless; (*foule*) huge, vast
innommable [inɔmabl] *adj Péj* (*comportement, conduite, actes*) unspeakable; (*nourriture, odeur*) vile, revolting; **des monstres innommables** loathsome monsters
innom(m)é [inɔme] *adj* unnamed, nameless
innovateur, -trice [inɔvatœr, -tris] **1** *adj* innovative, innovatory **2** *n* innovator; *Mktg* **i. continu** continuous innovator
innovation [inɔvasjɔ̃] *nf* innovation; *Mktg* **i. continue** continuous innovation; **i. de produit** product innovation
innover [inɔve] **1** *vi* to introduce innovations, to break new ground, to innovate; **il a beaucoup innové en matière de musique contemporaine** he has broken a lot of new ground *or* has introduced many innovations *or* has been a great innovator in the field of contemporary music **2** *vt* to introduce, to invent
inobservable [inɔpsɛrvabl] *adj* unobservable
inobservance [inɔpsɛrvɑ̃s] *nf* non-observance, inobservance
inobservation [inɔpsɛrvasjɔ̃] *nf Jur* non-observance (**de** of), non-compliance (**de** with)
inobservé [inɔpsɛrve] *adj* (**a**) (*non observé*) unobserved; (*non remarqué*) unobserved, unnoticed (**b**) (*loi, règlement*) unobserved
inoccupé [inɔkype] *adj* (**a**) (*libre*) (*siège, poste*) unoccupied, vacant; (*maison*) unoccupied, empty, uninhabited (**b**) (*personne*) idle, unoccupied
inoculation [inɔkylasjɔ̃] *nf Méd* inoculation
inoculer [inɔkyle] *vt* (**a**) **i. un virus/un vaccin à qn** to inoculate sb with a virus/a vaccine; **i. une maladie à qn** to infect sb with a disease; *Fig* **elle nous a inoculé sa gaieté** she infected us with her gaiety (**b**) **i. qn (contre une maladie)** to inoculate sb (against a disease)
inodore [inɔdɔr] *adj* odourless, *Am* odorless; *Hum Péj* **incolore, i. et sans saveur** (*personne*) totally colourless, *F* wishy-washy
inoffensif, -ive [inɔfɑ̃sif, -iv] *adj* (*personne*) inoffensive, harmless; (*drogue, livre, jeu, action*) harmless, innocuous
inondable [inɔ̃dabl] *adj* (*terre*) liable to flooding
inondation [inɔ̃dasjɔ̃] *nf* flood, *Fml* inundation; (*action*) flooding, *Fml* inundation; *Fig* (*invasion*) deluge, flood
inondé, -ée [inɔ̃de] **1** *adj* flooded; **populations inondées** flood victims; **visage i. de larmes** face streaming with tears; **i. de lumière** flooded *or* bathed with light; **i. d'invitations** inundated *or* swamped with invitations **2** *n* flood victim
inonder [inɔ̃de] **1** *vt* (*champs, route, maison, habitant*) to flood, *Fml* to inundate; *Fig* (*marché*) to flood, to inundate, to swamp (**de** with); **être inondé d'invitations/de prospectus** to be inundated with invitations/brochures; **i. un pays de voitures bon marché** to flood a country with cheap cars; **le soleil inonda la chambre de son insoutenable clarté** blinding sunlight flooded *or* poured into the room; **un bonheur ineffable m'inonda le coeur** an indescribable happiness flooded my heart **2 s'inonder** *vpr* **s'i. de parfum** to perfume oneself heavily
inopérable [inɔperabl] *adj Chir* inoperable
inopérant [inɔperɑ̃] *adj* ineffective, inoperative
inopiné [inɔpine] *adj* unexpected
inopinément [inɔpinemɑ̃] *adv* unexpectedly
inopportun [inɔpɔrtœ̃] *adj* inopportune, untimely, ill-

timed; **le moment est i.** it isn't the best *or* most opportune moment

inopportunément [inɔpɔrtynemɑ̃] *adv* inopportunely

inopportunité [inɔpɔrtynite] *nf Litt* inopportuneness, untimeliness

inorganique [inɔrganik] *adj Ch* inorganic

inorganisé [inɔrganize] *adj* (*personne, entreprise, service etc*) disorganized; (*main-d'œuvre*) unorganized, non-union; *Biol, Ch* inorganic; (*pas encore structuré*) unorganized

inoubliable [inublijabl] *adj* unforgettable

inouï [inwi] *adj* **(a)** (*nouveau*) unheard of, unprecedented **(b)** (*ahurissant*) incredible, extraordinary; **avec une violence inouïe** with incredible *or* extraordinary violence; **il lui est arrivé une histoire inouïe** something incredible *or* extraordinary happened to him; **c'est/vous êtes i.!** it's/you're incredible *or* unbelievable!

inox [inɔks] **1** *adj inv* **acier i.** stainless steel **2** *nm* stainless steel; **évier en i.** stainless steel sink

inoxydable [inɔksidabl] **1** *adj* rustproof, rust-resistant; **acier i.** stainless steel **2** *nm* stainless steel

INPI [iɛnpei] *nm* (*abrév* **Institut national de la propriété industrielle**) ≈ Patent Office

input [input] *nm Ordinat* input

inqualifiable [ɛ̃kalifjabl] *adj* (*comportement, propos*) unspeakable

in-quarto [inkwarto] **1** *adj inv* quarto **2** *nm inv* quarto

inquiet, -ète [ɛ̃kjɛ, -ɛt] **1 (a)** *adj* (*anxieux*) (*personne, air, regard*) worried, anxious, uneasy (**au sujet de** about); (*voix*) worried, anxious; (*attente*) anxious, uneasy; **elle est inquiète de ne pas avoir de nouvelles** she's worried *or* anxious at not having any news; **sommeil i.** uneasy *or* troubled *or* broken sleep; **i. sur qch/de qn** uneasy *or* worried about sth/sb **(b)** *Litt* (*agité*) restless **2** *n* worrier

inquiétant [ɛ̃kjetɑ̃, -ɑ̃t] *adj* **(a)** (*alarmant*) (*nouvelles, situation etc*) worrying, disturbing; (*état de santé*) worrying **(b)** (*qui effraie*) (*air, sourire*) frightening

inquiéter [ɛ̃kjete] **(j'inquiète; j'inquiéterai) 1** *vt* to worry, to trouble, to make anxious; (*ennemi, adversaire*) to harass, to worry; (*tranquillité de qn etc*) to disturb; **la santé de ma mère m'inquiète** I'm worried *or* anxious about my mother's health, my mother's health is worrying me *or* troubling me *or* making me anxious; **l'homme n'a pas été inquiété par la police** the man wasn't harassed *or* bothered *or* troubled by the police; **il n'a pas assez d'expérience pour vraiment i. le champion du monde** he doesn't have enough experience to give the world champion any real trouble, he doesn't have enough experience really to trouble *or* worry the world champion

2 s'inquiéter *vpr* **(a)** (*s'en faire*) to worry, to get worried; **il n'y a pas de quoi s'i.** there's nothing to get worried *or* to worry about; **je ne m'inquiète pas pour lui** I'm not worried *or* bothered about him; **il s'inquiète de ce qu'elle n'ait pas donné de nouvelles** he's worried that she hasn't been in touch

(b) (*s'occuper de, faire attention à*) to bother; **ne vous inquiétez pas de cela** don't worry *or* don't bother about that; **elle ne s'est jamais inquiétée de savoir si j'avais besoin de quelque chose** she never bothered *or* troubled *or* took the trouble to find out if I needed anything; **sans s'i. de rien** without a care in the world

inquiétude [ɛ̃kjetyd] *nf* **(a)** (*souci*) anxiety, uneasiness; **dissiper les inquiétudes de qn** to set sb's mind at rest; **état d'i.** state of anxiety, anxious state of mind; **sujet d'i.** cause for concern *or* worry; **sois sans i., je m'en occupe** don't worry (about a thing), I'll take care of it; **éprouver quelques inquiétudes** to have a few worries, to feel a bit worried *or* anxious **(b)** *Arch, Litt* (*agitation*) agitation, restlessness

inquisiteur, -trice [ɛ̃kizitœr, -tris] **1** *nm* inquisitor **2** *adj* (*regard*) inquisitive, prying

inquisition [ɛ̃kizisjɔ̃] *nf* inquisition; *Hist* **l'I.** the Inquisition

inquisitorial, -iale, -iaux, -iales [ɛ̃kizitɔrjal, -jo] *adj* inquisitorial

inracontable [ɛ̃rakɔ̃tabl] *adj* (*trop complexe*) not easily describable; (*trop scabreux ou insoutenable*) unrepeatable

insaisissable [ɛ̃sezisabl] *adj* **(a)** (*que l'on ne peut attraper*) (*fugitif, voleur*) difficult to catch, elusive; (*son, différence, nuance*) imperceptible **(b)** *Jur* (*biens*) not distrainable, not attachable

insalissable [ɛ̃salisabl] *adj* dirt-proof

insalubre [ɛ̃salybr] *adj* (*climat*) insalubrious, unhealthy; (*occupation*) unhealthy; (*habitation, pays*) insalubrious

insalubrité [ɛ̃salybrite] *nf* (*de climat*) insalubrity, unhealthiness; (*d'habitation, de pays*) insalubrity

insanité [ɛ̃sanite] *nf* (*de raisonnement, propos*) insanity; **proférer des insanités** to talk insanely; **sa dissertation est un tissu d'insanités** his essay is a mishmash of complete nonsense

insatiabilité [ɛ̃sasjabilite] *nf* insatiability

insatiable [ɛ̃sasjabl] *adj* (*soif*) insatiable, unquenchable; (*appétit, curiosité*) insatiable; **d'une curiosité i.** insatiably curious

insatiablement [ɛ̃sasjabləmɑ̃] *adv* insatiably

insatisfaction [ɛ̃satisfaksjɔ̃] *nf* dissatisfaction

insatisfaisant [ɛ̃satisfəzɑ̃] *adj* unsatisfactory

insatisfait [ɛ̃satisfɛ] **1** *adj* (*personne*) dissatisfied; (*désir*) unsatisfied **2** *n* **c'est un (éternel) i.** he's never satisfied (with anything), he's always dissatisfied (with things)

inscriptible [ɛ̃skriptibl] *adj Ordinat* writable

inscription [ɛ̃skripsjɔ̃] *nf* **(a)** (*action*) (*d'un nom, d'une date etc*) writing down, noting down; (*dans un journal, un registre*) entering, recording; (*immatriculation*) registration, enrolment; *Univ* **les inscriptions auront lieu ...** registration *or* enrolment will take place ...; *F* **faire son i. à l'université** to register *or* enrol at university; **depuis son i. au club** since he joined the club; **avez-vous fait votre i. sur les listes électorales?** have you registered to vote?, have you put your name down on the electoral roll?; **droit/feuille d'i.** registration fee/form; (*pour concours*) entry *or* entrance fee/form; (*pour club, association*) enrolment fee/form; **prendre une i.** (*s'incrire*) to enter one's name

(b) (*sur une tombe, un mur etc*) inscription; (*dans un livre de comptes*) entry; (*sur un poteau indicateur*) directions; *Compta* **i. comptable** accounting entry

▶ **inscription**: *Jur* **i. de** *ou* **en faux** plea of forgery; *Jur* **i. hypothécaire** registry *or* registration of mortgages; *Fin* **inscriptions nominatives** registered shares; **i. sur le registre du commerce** registration in the trade register

inscrire [ɛ̃skrir] (*prp* **inscrivant**; *pp* **inscrit**; *pr ind* **j'inscris, il inscrit, n. inscrivons**; *p hist* **j'inscrivis**; *fu* **j'inscrirai**) **1** *vt* **(a)** (*renseignements, date etc*) to write down, to note down; (*dans un journal, registre etc*) to enter, to record; **i. une adresse sur qch** to address sth; **i. une question à l'ordre du jour** to put *or* place a question on the agenda; **i. une dépense au budget** to include an item in the budget; **inscrivez la date en haut à droite** write the date in the top right-hand corner

(b) i. un enfant à un club to enrol a child in a club; **i. un enfant à une école** to put a child *or* a child's name down for a school; **i. qn à une activité** to put sb's name down *or* enrol sb for an activity; **il m'a inscrit au marathon** he put me *or* my name down for the marathon, he entered me *or* put me in for the marathon

(c) (*dans la pierre*) (*épitaphe etc*) to inscribe, to engrave; **il a inscrit ses initiales dans l'écorce de l'arbre** he inscribed *or* carved his initials in the bark of the tree; *Fig* **cette date restera inscrite dans ma mémoire à tout jamais** that date will remain etched *or* inscribed on my memory for all time

(d) *Géom* (*triangle, carré*) to inscribe (**dans** in)

2 s'inscrire *vpr* (*à l'université, à une école*) to register, to enrol (**à** at); (*à la Sécurité sociale, au chômage*) to register (**à** with); (*sur les listes électorales*) to have one's name put on the electoral roll; (*à un tournoi, un concours*) to put oneself *or* one's name down, to enter (**à** for); (*au macramé, à des cours d'informatique etc*) to put oneself *or* one's name down, to enrol (**à** for); **s'i. dans un club/à un parti** to join a club/party, to enrol in a club/party; **s'i. en faux contre qch** to deny sth; *Jur* to contest the validity of sth; *Fin* **s'i. en baisse** to fall; *Fin* **s'i. en hausse** to rise; **cette décision s'inscrit dans le cadre de la politique gouvernementale** this decision is in keeping with the general pattern of government policy; **noter l'adresse qui va s'i. sur vos écrans** note down the address which is coming up on your screens

inscrit, -ite [ɛ̃skri, -it] **1** *adj* **(a)** (*électeur, candidat*) registered **(b)** *Géom* inscribed **2** *n* (*à l'université*) registered student; (*dans un club, parti*) registered member; (*à un concours*) registered entrant; (*électeur*) registered voter **3** *nm Naut* **i. maritime** = certified navigator

insécable [ɛ̃sekabl] *adj* indivisible; *Ordinat* hard

insecte [ɛ̃sɛkt] *nm* insect

insecticide [ɛ̃sɛktisid] **1** *adj* insecticidal; **poudre i.** insect powder **2** *nm* insecticide

insectifuge [ɛ̃sɛktifyʒ] *nm* insect repellent

insectivore [ɛ̃sɛktivɔr] *Zool* **1** *adj* insectivorous **2** *nm* insectivore; **insectivores** insectivores, *Spéc* Insectivora

insécurité [ɛ̃sekyrite] *nf* **(a)** lack of safety **(b)** *Psy* insecurity

inséminateur, -trice [ɛ̃seminatœr, -tris] **1** *adj* inseminating **2** *nm* inseminator

insémination [ɛ̃seminasjɔ̃] *nf* insemination; **i. artificielle** artificial insemination

inséminer [ɛ̃semine] *vt* to inseminate

insensé, -ée [ɛ̃sɑ̃se] **1** *adj* (*action, geste*) extravagant, wild; (*projet, idée*) crazy, harebrained; (*espoir*) wild; (*dépenses*) extravagant, wild; *Vieilli* (*fou*) mad, insane; **il m'a dit des paroles insensées** what he said to me was mad; **c'est i.!** it's crazy!; **c'est i. ce qu'il peut boire!** it's crazy the amount he can drink! **2** *nm* madman **3** *nf* **insensée** madwoman

insensibilisation [ɛ̃sɑ̃sibilizasjɔ̃] *nf* anaesthetization, *Am* anesthetization

insensibiliser [ɛ̃sɑ̃sibilize] *vt* to anaesthetize, *Am* to anesthetize

insensibilité [ɛ̃sɑ̃sibilite] *nf* insensitivity (**à** to)

insensible [ɛ̃sɑ̃sibl] *adj* **(a)** (*à la douleur, au froid etc*) insensitive (**à** to); **i. à la critique** impervious to criticism; **il demeura i. à leurs larmes** he remained unmoved by their tears **(b)** (*différence, changement*) imperceptible, hardly perceptible

insensiblement [ɛ̃sɑ̃sibləmɑ̃] *adv* imperceptibly

inséparable [ɛ̃separabl] **1** *adj* inseparable **2** *nmpl* **inséparables** (*oiseaux*) lovebirds; **ce sont deux inséparables** (*de personnes*) they are inseparable

inséparablement [ɛ̃separabləmɑ̃] *adv* inseparably

insérable [ɛ̃serabl] *adj* insertable

insérer [ɛ̃sere] **(j'insère; j'insérerai) 1** *vt* to insert (**dans** in); *TV, Cin* to edit in, to intercut; **i. une annonce dans un journal** to insert *or* put an advertisement in a paper; **prière d'i.** (*formule*) for publication (in your columns); (*feuille*) publication details **2 s'insérer** *vpr* **(a)** (*s'attacher*) to be attached (**sur** to) **(b)** (*s'intégrer*) (*réformes, politique etc*) to fit (**dans** into); (*immigrés*) to integrate (**dans** into); **ces mesures s'insèrent dans le cadre des nouvelles réformes** these measures fit into the general pattern of the new reforms

insert [ɛ̃sɛr(t)] *nm TV, Cin* cut-in, insert

insertion [ɛ̃sɛrsjɔ̃] *nf* insertion; **l'i. sociale des immigrés** the (social) integration of immigrants; **l'i. professionnelle des jeunes** the integration of young people into the job market; *Ordinat* **mode d'i.** insert mode; **i. de caractère** character insert; **i. de ligne** line insert; **i. publicitaire** advertisement

insidieusement [ɛ̃sidjøzmɑ̃] *adv* insidiously

insidieux, -euse [ɛ̃sidjø, -øz] *adj* insidious

insigne¹ [ɛ̃siɲ] *adj* **(a)** (*remarquable*) remarkable; **faveur i.** signal favour; **j'ai eu l'honneur i. d'être invité à sa table** I had the great honour of being invited to his table **(b)** *Péj* (*indiscrétion, erreur, maladresse*) glaring; (*menteur, escroc etc*) notorious

insigne² *nm* (*de club, parti, militaire*) badge; **insignes de la royauté** insignia of royalty

insignifiance [ɛ̃siɲifjɑ̃s] *nf* insignificance, unimportance

insignifiant [ɛ̃siɲifjɑ̃] *adj* insignificant, unimportant; (*perte, somme*) trivial, trifling

insincère [ɛ̃sɛ̃sɛr] *adj Litt* insincere

insinuant [ɛ̃sinɥɑ̃] *adj* ingratiating

insinuation [ɛ̃sinɥasjɔ̃] *nf* insinuation, innuendo; **par insinuations** by insinuation, by innuendo; **il procède toujours par i.** he always speaks in innuendos

insinuer [ɛ̃sinɥe] **1** *vt* to insinuate, to suggest, to hint at; **que voulez-vous i.?** what are you insinuating *or* implying *or* hinting at?

2 s'insinuer *vpr* **le lierre s'insinuait dans les moindres fissures** the ivy was creeping (its way) into the smallest of cracks; **le froid s'insinue dans la pièce par tous les interstices** the cold is creeping into the room through all the cracks; **s'i. dans les bonnes grâces de qn** to insinuate oneself *or* worm one's way into sb's good books; **il a réussi à s'i. jusque dans les plus hautes sphères du pouvoir** he managed to worm his way into the higher reaches of power; **le doute/l'idée qui s'insinue dans mon esprit** the doubt/the idea that is creeping into my mind; **s'i. entre les voitures** to thread one's way through the traffic

insipide [ɛ̃sipid] *adj* (*personne, conversation, histoire, film etc*) insipid, dull, uninteresting; (*nourriture, boisson*) insipid, tasteless; (*fin*) tame

insipidité [ɛ̃sipidite] *nf* insipidness, dullness; (*de nourriture, boisson*) insipidness, tastelessness

insistance [ɛ̃sistɑ̃s] *nf* insistence (**à faire qch** on doing sth); **avec i.** insistently

insistant [ɛ̃sistɑ̃] *adj* insistent

insister [ɛ̃siste] *vi* to insist; **i. sur un fait** to stress a fact; **nous insistons particulièrement sur la ponctualité** we lay particular stress *or* emphasis on punctuality; **elle a beaucoup insisté** she was very insistent; **i. pour faire qch** to insist on doing sth; **elle a insisté pour que nous restions la nuit** she insisted on our staying the night; **i. auprès de qn** to take up a matter strongly with sb; **n'insistez pas trop** don't push it; **j'insiste là-dessus** I insist on it; **n'insistez pas trop là-dessus** don't put too much emphasis on it, don't overstress it; **elle a essayé la planche à voile mais elle n'a pas insisté** she tried windsurfing but soon gave (it) up; **j'ai dit non! n'insistez pas!** *ou* **inutile d'i.!** I said no! don't go on (about it)!; **ça ne répond pas – insiste encore un peu** there's no answer – hang on a bit; **j'ai essayé de la convaincre puis je me suis aperçu que ça ne servait à rien d'i.** I tried to convince her, then I realized that it was useless to keep on (trying); **insiste sinon la tache ne partira jamais** keep rubbing or the stain will never come out

in situ [insity] *adj, adv* in situ

insociabilité [ɛ̃sɔsjabilite] *nf* unsociability

insociable [ɛ̃sɔsjabl] *adj* unsociable

insolation [ɛ̃sɔlasjɔ̃] *nf* **(a)** (*exposition au soleil*) exposure to the sun; *Méd* sunstroke; (*d'une région etc*) hours of sunshine; **attraper une i.** to get sunstroke; **tu risques l'i. si ...** you'll risk getting sunstroke if ... **(b)** *Phot* exposure

insolemment [ɛ̃sɔlamɑ̃] *adv* insolently, impertinently

insolence [ɛ̃sɔlɑ̃s] *nf* **(a)** (*impertinence*) insolence, impertinence, impudence; **répondre avec i.** to answer insolently *or* impertinently *or* impudently; **cet enfant est d'une i.!** that child is so insolent *or* impertinent *or* impudent! **(b)** (*remarque, action*) impertinence

insolent [ɛ̃sɔlɑ̃] **1** *adj* **(a)** (*impertinent*) insolent, impertinent, impudent (**envers, avec** to); **répondre sur un ton i.** to answer insolently *or* impertinently *or* impudently **(b)** (*dans la victoire*) haughty, arrogant **(c)** (*succès*) outrageous; (*luxe*) unashamed, blatant, indecent; **il a une chance insolente** he's got the luck of the devil **2** *n* insolent person; **petit i./petite insolente!** you insolent little boy/girl!

insolite [ɛ̃sɔlit] **1** *adj* unusual, strange **2** *nm* **l'i.** the unusual

insolubilité [ɛ̃sɔlybilite] *nf* (*de substance*) insolubility; (*de problème*) insolvability

insoluble [ɛ̃sɔlybl] *adj* **(a)** (*substance*) insoluble **(b)** (*problème*) insoluble, insolvable

insolvabilité [ɛ̃sɔlvabilite] *nf Com* insolvency

insolvable [ɛ̃sɔlvabl] *adj Com* insolvent

insomniaque [ɛ̃sɔmnjak] *adj, n* insomniac

insomnie [ɛ̃sɔmni] *nf* insomnia, sleeplessness; **nuit d'i.** sleepless night; **souffrir d'i., avoir des insomnies** to have insomnia

insondable [ɛ̃sɔ̃dabl] *adj* **(a)** (*océan, gouffre*) unfathomable, fathomless **(b)** (*mystère*) unfathomable, impenetrable **(c)** (*stupidité, désespoir*) immense, unbelievable

insonore [ɛ̃sɔnɔr] *adj* (*studio, matériau*) soundproof

insonorisation [ɛ̃sɔnɔrizasjɔ̃] *nf* (*de studio, d'appartement*) soundproofing

insonoriser [ɛ̃sɔnɔrize] *vt* (*studio, appartement*) to soundproof

insouciance [ɛ̃susjɑ̃s] *nf* (*absence de soucis*) carefreeness, freedom from care; (*détachement*) unconcern, lack of concern, *Litt* insouciance; **vivre dans l'i.** to live a carefree life

insouciant [ɛ̃susjɑ̃] *adj* (*sans soucis*) carefree; (*détaché*) unconcerned; (*léger*) thoughtless, casual, happy-go-lucky; **i. de son avenir** unconcerned about his future; **i. du danger/des conséquences possibles** heedless of the danger/the possible consequences; **ils sont jeunes et insouciants** they are young and carefree

insoucieux, -euse [ɛ̃susjø, -øz] *adj Litt* (*attitude, air*) unconcerned, casual; (*humeur*) carefree; **il est i. de l'avenir/du qu'en-dira-t-on** he is unconcerned about *or* pays no heed to the future/what people say; **i. du danger, il ...** heedless of the danger, he ...

insoumis, -ise [ɛ̃sumi, -iz] **1** *adj* **(a)** (*gens, peuple, tribus*) unsubdued **(b)** (*personne*) insubordinate, rebellious, refractory **(c)** *Mil* (*soldat*) absentee **2** *n* rebellious *or* insubordinate person **3** *nm Mil* absentee

insoumission [ɛ̃sumisjɔ̃] *nf* **(a)** (*indiscipline*) insubordination, rebelliousness **(b)** *Mil* absence without leave

insoupçonnable [ɛ̃supsɔnabl] *adj* (*personne*) beyond *or* above suspicion; **il est d'une probité i.** his probity is unquestionable *or* beyond question

insoupçonné [ɛ̃supsɔne] *adj* unsuspected (**de** by)

insoutenable [ɛ̃sutnabl] **1** *adj* **(a)** (*opinion, théorie*) untenable; (*affirmation*) unwarrantable; (*position*) indefensible, untenable **(b)** (*agonie, pression, tension, spectacle, odeur*) unbearable **2** *nm* **l'i.** the unbearable; **à la limite de l'i.** verging on the unbearable

inspecter [ɛ̃spɛkte] *vt* (*troupes, école, établissement*) to inspect; (*champ de bataille*) to survey; (*travail, bagages*) to examine, to inspect; **i. des marchandises** to examine goods

inspecteur, -trice [ɛ̃spɛktœr, -tris] *n* inspector; (*des travaux*) overseer; (*des mines*) surveyor

▶ **inspecteur**: *Scol* **i. d'Académie** school inspector, *Br* ≈ HMI; **i. des contributions directes/indirectes** inspector of taxes, tax inspector; **i. des finances** ≈ senior Treasury official; **i. de police** police inspector; **i. (de l'Enseignement) primaire** primary school inspector; **i. d'une société d'assurances** insurance inspector; **i. de la sûreté** detective inspector; **i. du travail** factory inspector; *Hum* **i. des travaux finis** idler, *Br* skiver (*who arrives after the work has been done*); **i. des ventes** sales coordinator

inspection [ɛ̃spɛksjɔ̃] *nf* **(a)** (*examen*) inspection; (*de bagages*) examination, inspection; **faire l'i. de** to inspect; *Mil* **faire l'i. des armes** to inspect arms; *Mil* **passer l'i. d'une compagnie** to inspect a company; **passer à l'i.** to undergo an inspection; **une i. en règle** a thorough inspection **(b)** (*fonction*) inspectorship, inspectorate **(c)** (*service*) inspectorate

▶ **inspection**: *Admin* **i. académique** school inspectorate; **entrer à l'i. académique** to become a school inspector; *Admin* **i. générale des finances** department responsible for auditing public bodies; **i. de la Sécurité sociale** Social Security Inspectorate; **i. du travail** factory inspectorate

inspectorat [ɛ̃spɛktɔra] *nm Admin* inspectorship, inspectorate

inspirateur, -trice [ɛ̃spiratœr, -tris] **1** *adj* **(a)** (*pensée, idée*) inspiring **(b)** *Anat* (*muscle*) inspiratory **2** *n* (*d'activité créatrice*) inspiration; (*d'une intrigue*) instigator; **c'était elle mon inspiratrice** she was my inspiration

inspiration [ɛ̃spirasjɔ̃] *nf* **(a)** (*créatrice*) inspiration; **avoir de l'i.** to be inspired, to have inspiration; **un poème d'i. romantique** a poem in the romantic style; **elle est pour lui une source d'i.** (*d'une femme*) she's his muse; (*d'une ville etc*) it's a source of inspiration for him **(b)** (*influence*) instigation, prompting; **sous l'i. de qn** at sb's instigation *or* prompting **(c)** *Physiol* inspiration, breathing in **(d)** (*idée*) inspiration; **i. soudaine** sudden inspiration, *F Br* brainwave, *Am* brainstorm; **elle a eu la lumineuse i. de venir me chercher** she had the bright idea to come for me; **selon l'i. du moment** on the spur of the moment

inspiré, -ée [ɛ̃spire] **1** *adj* **(a)** (*style, poète, artiste, air*) inspired; **une toile inspirée de Bosch** a painting inspired by Bosch **(b) il serait bien/mal i. de changer de métier** he'd be well-advised *or* he'd do well/he'd be ill-advised to change profession; **tu as été bien/mal i. de l'inviter à ta soirée** it was a good/bad idea of yours to invite him to your party **2** *n* mystic, visionary

inspirer [ɛ̃spire] **1** *vt* **(a)** (*suggérer*) **i. confiance/le respect** to inspire confidence/respect; **i. confiance à qn** to inspire sb with confidence, to inspire confidence in sb; **i. le respect à qn** to command *or* win sb's respect; **i. de l'admiration à qn** to fill sb with admiration; **spectacle qui inspire l'horreur/le dégoût** horrific/disgusting spectacle; **cet enfant ne peut i. que de la tendresse** you can't help but feel affectionate towards the child; **l'état du malade nous inspire la plus grande inquiétude** the patient's condition is giving us great cause for concern; **votre discours m'a inspiré plusieurs réflexions** your speech has given me food for thought *or* has set me thinking; **inspiré par la jalousie** prompted by jealousy

(b) (*artiste, poète etc*) to inspire; **cet événement m'a inspiré une chanson/un poème** this event inspired me to write a song/a poem; **la vie de sa grand-mère lui a inspiré ce roman** his grandmother's life was the inspiration for the novel; **l'histoire est largement inspirée de la vie du grand homme** the story is largely drawn from *or* based upon the great man's life; *Iron* **cette question ne m'inspire guère** the subject doesn't exactly inspire me

(c) *Physiol* (*air*) to breathe in, *Spéc* to inspire

2 *vi Physiol* to breathe in, *Spéc* to inspire

3 s'inspirer *vpr* **s'i. de qn/qch** to take *or* draw one's inspiration from sb/sth, to be inspired by sb/sth

instabilité [ɛ̃stabilite] *nf* (*de caractère, situation, gouvernement etc*) instability; (*du temps*) changeability, unsettled nature; *Ch* instability; *Naut* (*d'un bateau*) crank; **i. des cours** unsteadiness of prices; **i. mentale** mental instability

instable [ɛ̃stabl] *adj* **(a)** (*branlant*) (*échafaudage, plateau etc*) unstable, unsteady, wobbly; (*marché boursier*) unsettled; **équilibre i.** unsteady balance **(b)** (*personne, nature*) unstable **(c)** (*temps*) unsettled, changeable; *Naut* (*bateau*) crank; (*situation politique*) unstable, uncertain; (*gouvernement*) unstable; **la paix est encore i.** the peace is still fragile *or* uncertain **(d)** *Ch* (*solution, mélange*) unstable

installateur [ɛ̃stalatœr] *nm* fitter

installation [ɛ̃stalasjɔ̃] *nf* **(a)** (*fait d'installer*) (*d'une machine, d'un ascenseur etc*) installation; (*de cuisinière, réfrigérateur*) installation, putting in; (*d'une machine à laver*) plumbing in, installation; (*de chauffage, téléphone etc*) putting in, installation; (*électricité, gaz, eau*) putting in, *Br* laying on; (*d'une usine, d'un atelier*) fitting up *or* out, equipping; (*d'appartement, de cuisine*) fitting out; (*de rideaux*) putting up, hanging; (*de fenêtres*) fitting, installation; (*d'un ecclésiastique, magistrat*) installation, induction

(b) (*emménagement*) **fêter son i.** to celebrate moving in; **prévoir son i. dans une région** to plan to settle in an area; **comment s'est passée votre i. dans votre nouvelle maison?** how did the move into your new house go?

(c) *Ordinat* **programme d'i.** installation program; **i. en réseau** network installation

(d) installations (*d'une maison*) fixtures and fittings; (*d'un atelier*) fittings, equipment; *Ind* plant; **installations portuaires** port installations; **installations sanitaires** sanitary installations *or* fittings; (*tuyauterie*) plumbing; **installations techniques** plant and machinery; **installations touristiques** tourist facilities, visitor facilities; **l'i. électrique n'est pas conforme** the wiring is not up to standard; **installations de lavage** washing bay; **installations au sol** (*dans un aérodrome*) ground installations

installé [ɛ̃stale] *adj Ordinat* (*RAM*) on board

installer [ɛ̃stale] **1** *vt* (*sa famille, son fils etc*) to settle; (*machine, ascenseur etc*) to install; (*cuisinière, réfrigérateur*) to install, to put in; (*machine à laver, lave-vaisselle*) to plumb in, to install; (*chauffage, téléphone etc*) to put in, to install; (*électricité, gaz, eau*) to put in, *Br* to lay on; (*usine, atelier*) to fit up *or* out, to equip; (*appartement, cuisine*) to fit out; (*rideaux, tenture*) to put up, to hang; (*fenêtres*) to fit, to install; (*ecclésiastique, magistrat*) to install, to induct; **i. le câble** to install cable television; **où va-t-on i. le buffet?** where are we going to put the sideboard?; **il a installé son ordinateur dans sa chambre à coucher** he set up *or* put his computer in his bedroom; **i. qn dans un fauteuil/son lit** to settle sb comfortably *or* make sb comfortable in an armchair/in his/her bed; **i. qn devant la télévision** to settle sb down *or* install sb in front of the television; **je les ai installés dans la chambre bleue** I've put them in the blue room; **les nouveaux bureaux sont très bien installés** the new offices are very well fitted out *or* equipped; **i. la cuisine/la salle de bain dans une pièce** to turn a room into a kitchen/bathroom; **il a installé son bureau au grenier** he set up his office in the attic, he turned the attic into his office; **ils ont installé le musée dans une ancienne gare** they set up the museum in a former station; **i. son cabinet** (*d'un médecin*) to set up (in) practice

2 s'installer *vpr* (*de supermarché, cirque*) to set up; (*de personne*) (*devant la télé*) to settle down, to install oneself; (*dans la vie*) to settle (down); (*chez qn*) to make oneself at home; **confortablement installé dans un fauteuil** comfortably settled in an armchair; **s'i. au bar** to install oneself at the bar; **s'i. à la campagne/à Madagascar** to settle in the country/in Madagascar; **des bourgeois bien installés** comfortably off middle-class people; **s'i. comme médecin** to set (oneself) up as a doctor; **s'i. à son compte** to set up in business on one's own (account); **un climat d'insécurité s'est installé dans le pays** a climate of insecurity has taken hold of the country

instamment [ɛ̃stamɑ̃] *adv* (*recommander*) earnestly; **je vous demande i. de revenir sur votre décision** I beg *or* urge you to reconsider your decision; **elle l'a prié i. de la suivre** she begged him to follow her

instance [ɛ̃stɑ̃s] *nf* **(a)** (*insistance*) **demander qch à qn avec i.** to beg *or* plead with sb for sth; **c'est avec i. qu'ils m'ont demandé d'accepter** they begged *or* urged me to accept

(b) instances entreaties, pleas; **j'ai dû plier devant ses instances** I had to give in to his entreaties *or* pleas; **sur** *ou* **devant les instances de son frère** in the face of his brother's entreaties *or* pleas

(c) *Jur* process, suit; **introduire une i. (en justice)** to institute an action; **tribunal d'i.** *Eng* ≈ magistrates' court, *Scot* ≈ sheriff court; **tribunal de grande i.** *Eng* ≈ county court, *Scot* ≈ sheriff court; **tribunal de première i.** court of first instance; **acquitté en seconde i.** acquitted on appeal

(d) (*autorité*) authority; **les instances internationales** the international authorities; **l'i. compétente/supérieure** the relevant/higher authority; **instances dirigeantes** governing body

(e) (*cours*) **ils sont en i. de divorce** they are waiting for a divorce, their divorce proceedings are under way; **être en i. de départ** to be on the point of departure *or* about to leave; **courrier en i.** mail waiting *or* ready to go out; **tout est encore en i.** everything is still pending

instant¹ [ɛ̃stɑ̃] *adj Litt* **(a)** (*imminent*) (*péril*) pressing **(b)** (*d'une manière pressante*) (*prière etc*) insistent

instant² *nm* moment, instant; **à chaque** *ou* **tout i.** continually, all the time; **par instants** now and then; **il a eu un i. d'inattention** he had a momentary lapse of concentration;

pendant un i. for a moment; **pendant un i., j'ai cru que j'allais gagner** for a moment *or* for one instant I thought I was going to win; **j'ai cru l'espace d'un i. que ...** I thought for a *or* one (split) second that ...; **un i.!** one moment!; **nous n'avons pas un i. à perdre** we don't have a moment to lose; **profiter de chaque i.** to profit from every moment; **nous avons vécu ensemble des instants de bonheur parfait** we've shared some blissfully happy moments; **elle va arriver d'un i. à l'autre** she'll be arriving any moment now *or* at any moment; **à l'i.** (*dans le passé*) (just) a moment ago; (*tout de suite*) immediately, instantly, at once; **il vient de partir à l'i.** he has just this minute gone, he went (just) a moment ago; **j'en reviens à l'i.** I've just come back from there; **on m'apprend à l'i. que ...** I've just (this minute) found out that ...; **il est entré dans le bureau à l'i. même où ...** he went into the office at the very *or* exact moment that ...; **pour l'i.** for the moment, for the time being; **dans un i.** in a moment; **en un i.** in no time (at all); **un soin de tous les instants** unremitting *or* ceaseless care; **dès l'i. où je l'ai vue** (*dès que*) from the moment I saw her; **dès l'i. que tu as réussi tous tes examens** (*du moment que*) since you've *or* seeing that you've passed all your exams

instantané [ɛ̃stɑ̃tane] **1** *adj* (*mort*) instantaneous; (*riposte*) instantaneous, immediate; (*café, thé, soupe, bouillie*) instant **2** *nm Phot* snapshot, *F* snap

instantanément [ɛ̃stɑ̃tanemɑ̃] *adv* instantaneously

instar de (à l') [alɛ̃stardə] *adv Litt* following the example of; **à l'i. de son père il a choisi d'être facteur** following his father's example *or* following in his father's footsteps, he chose to be a postman

instaurateur, -trice [ɛ̃stɔratœr, -tris] *n Litt* establisher

instauration [ɛ̃stɔrasjɔ̃] *nf* establishment, institution

instaurer [ɛ̃stɔre] **1** *vt* to establish; (*usage*) to institute; (*mode de scrutin, système*) to introduce; **i. des mesures** to bring in new measures **2 s'instaurer** *vpr* to be established

instigateur, -trice [ɛ̃stigatœr, -tris] *n* instigator

instigation [ɛ̃stigasjɔ̃] *nf* instigation, incitement; **agir à l'i. de qn** to act at *or* on sb's instigation

instillation [ɛ̃stilasjɔ̃] *nf Méd* instillation

instiller [ɛ̃stile] *vt Méd, Fig* to instil (**dans** into, in); **i. le doute dans l'esprit de qn** to instil doubt into *or* in sb's mind

instinct [ɛ̃stɛ̃] *nm* instinct; **se fier à/suivre son i.** to trust to/follow one's instinct(s); **i. maternel** maternal instinct; **i. de conservation** instinct of self-preservation; **faire qch d'i.** to do sth by instinct *or* instinctively; **avoir l'i. du commerce** to have an instinct *or* a feel for business; **être guidé par un heureux i.** to be well guided by one's instinct

instinctif, -ive [ɛ̃stɛ̃ktif, -iv] *adj* (*personne, réaction etc*) instinctive

instinctivement [ɛ̃stɛ̃ktivmɑ̃] *adv* instinctively

instit [ɛ̃stit] *n F* (*abrév* **instituteur, -trice**) (primary school) teacher

instituer [ɛ̃stitɥe] *vt* **1** (**a**) (*établir*) (*un impôt, un règlement, le suffrage universel*) to introduce, *Fml* to institute; (*une commission d'enquête*) to set up, *Fml* to institute (**b**) (*fonctionnaire, héritier*) to appoint **2 s'instituer** *vpr* (*climat de confiance, relations commerciales*) to become established; **il s'est institué juge/arbitre dans cette affaire** he has appointed himself judge/referee in the matter

institut [ɛ̃stity] *nm* (**a**) (*établissement*) institute, institution; **i. de crédit** credit institution; **i. national de recherche** national research institute (**b**) **l'I. (de France)** the Institute (*composed of the five Académies*)

▸ **institut: i. de beauté** beauty salon *or* parlour; **i. médico-légal** forensic laboratory; **I. national de la consommation** national consumer institute; **I. national de la propriété industrielle** ≈ Patent Office; **I. universitaire de technologie** technical college (*conferring two-year degrees*), *Br* ≈ polytechnic

instituteur, -trice [ɛ̃stitytœr, -tris] **1** *n Scol* (primary school) teacher **2** *nf Arch* **institutrice** governess

institution [ɛ̃stitysjɔ̃] *nf* (**a**) (*établissement*) institution, institute; **i. de crédit** credit institution; *F* **c'est devenu une véritable i.** it has become an institution (**b**) *Jur* (*d'héritier*) appointing (**c**) *Pol* **institutions** institutions (**d**) (*coutume*) institution; **le mariage est une i. menacée** the institution of marriage is under threat (**e**) (*d'enseignement*) establishment

institutionnalisation [ɛ̃stitysjɔnalizasjɔ̃] *nf* institutionalization

institutionnaliser [ɛ̃stitysjɔnalize] *vt* (*pratique, procédure*) to institutionalize

institutionnel, -elle [ɛ̃stitysjɔnɛl] *adj* institutional

instructeur [ɛ̃stryktœr] **1** *nm* instructor, teacher; *Mil* **sergent i.** drill sergeant **2** *adj Jur* **juge i.** examining magistrate

instructif, -ive [ɛ̃stryktif, -iv] *adj* instructive

instruction [ɛ̃stryksjɔ̃] *nf* (**a**) **instructions** instructions, directions; **il faut suivre les instructions à la lettre** you must follow the instructions to the letter; **conformément aux instructions** as directed; **conformément à vos instructions** in accordance with your instructions, as instructed; **instructions de facturation** invoicing instructions; **instructions pour l'expédition** shipping instructions
(**b**) *Ordinat* instruction; **i.-machine** machine instruction; **i. d'entrée-sortie** input/output instruction; **i. de code machine** machine code instruction
(**c**) *Scol* education, schooling; *Mil* training (of troops); *Scol* **i. primaire/secondaire** primary/secondary education; **i. professionnelle** vocational training; **avoir de l'i.** to be well educated; **sans i.** uneducated; **i. religieuse** religious instruction; **i. musicale/militaire** musical/military training; **i. civique** civics
(**d**) *Jur* (*d'une affaire*) preliminary investigation; **juge d'i.** examining magistrate
(**e**) (*circulaire*) (official) memo, circular

instruire [ɛ̃strɥir] (*prp* **instruisant**; *pp* **instruit**; *pr ind* **j'instruis, il instruit, n. instruisons**; *p hist* **j'instruisis**) **1** *vt* (**a**) (*enseigner à*) to teach, to educate, to instruct; **lisez Jünger, ça vous instruira** read Jünger, that will educate you
(**b**) (*informer*) **i. qn de qch** to inform sb of sth
(**c**) (*troupes*) to train, to drill
(**d**) *Jur* (*affaire*) to examine, to investigate
2 *vi* to teach; **i. par le jeu/l'exemple** to teach through play/by example
3 s'instruire *vpr* to educate oneself, to improve one's mind; **s'i. de** to find out *or* get information about; **il s'instruisit des événements survenus pendant son absence** he brought himself up to date on what had happened during his absence; *Fml* **je viens m'i. de la santé de Madame votre femme** I've come to inquire after your wife's health

instruit [ɛ̃strɥi] *adj* educated, learned, well-read

instrument [ɛ̃strymɑ̃] *nm* instrument, implement, tool; *Mus* instrument; *Jur* (legal) instrument; **i. de mesure/de précision** measuring/precision instrument; **i. de travail** work instrument; **i. de navigation** navigation(al) instrument; *Av* **atterrissage aux instruments** instrument landing; *Av* **naviguer aux instruments** to fly on instruments; **i. de chirurgie** surgical instrument; **i. de crédit** credit instrument; **i. de paiement** payment instrument; *Fig* **servir d'i. à la vengeance de qn** to serve as the instrument of sb's revenge; **elle fut l'i. de sa vengeance** she was the instrument of his revenge; **il n'a été qu'un i.** he was merely a tool; **être l'i. de qn** to be sb's tool *or* instrument; **sa femme a été l'i. de sa réussite** his success was solely due to his wife; *Mus* **jouer d'un i.** to play an instrument; **i. à anche/clavier/vent/cordes** reed/keyboard/wind/string instrument

instrumentaire [ɛ̃strymɑ̃tɛr] *adj Jur* **témoin i.** witness to a deed

instrumental, -ale, -aux, -ales [ɛ̃strymɑ̃tal, -o] **1** *adj* (*musique etc*) instrumental **2** *nm Ling* instrumental

instrumentation [ɛ̃strymɑ̃tasjɔ̃] *nf Mus* scoring, instrumentation, orchestration

instrumenter [ɛ̃strymɑ̃te] **1** *vi Jur* to draw up a document; **i. contre qn** to order proceedings to be taken against sb **2** *vt Mus* (*opéra*) to score, to orchestrate

instrumentiste [ɛ̃strymɑ̃tist] *n Mus* instrumentalist

insu [ɛ̃sy] *nm* (*used in the phrase*) **à l'i. de** without the knowledge of; **à l'i. de ses parents** without his parents' knowledge, unbeknownst to his parents; **à mon i.** without my knowledge, unbeknownst to me

insubmersible [ɛ̃sybmɛrsibl] *adj* unsinkable

insubordination [ɛ̃sybɔrdinasjɔ̃] *nf* insubordination

insubordonné [ɛ̃sybɔrdɔne] *adj* insubordinate

insuccès [ɛ̃syksɛ] *nm* lack of success, failure

insuffisamment [ɛ̃syfizamɑ̃] *adv* insufficiently, inadequately; **cette pièce est i. éclairée** there's not enough light in this room; **être i. affranchi** to have insufficient postage

insuffisance [ɛ̃syfizɑ̃s] *nf* (**a**) (*manque*) insufficiency, deficiency; (*de personnel, de réserves en devises*) shortage; (*de moyens*) inadequacy; **l'i. de nos ressources est telle que ...** our resources are so inadequate that ...; **i. de provision** insufficient funds (**b**) *Méd* (*d'un organe*) failure; **i. respiratoire** respiratory insufficiency; **i. cardiaque** cardiac insufficiency, *F* heart failure; **i. rénale** kidney failure (**c**) (*incompétence*) incompetence, inefficiency; **son travail révèle de graves insuffisances** his work shows serious shortcomings

insuffisant [ɛ̃syfizɑ̃] *adj* (**a**) (*quantité*) insufficient; (*moyens, mesures*) inadequate, insufficient; **nous disposons de médicaments mais en quantité insuffisante** we have drugs at our disposal but not enough of them *or Fml* but in insufficient quantity; **nos soldats sont en nombre i.** we do not have enough *or* sufficient soldiers; **vos résultats en physique sont insuffisants!** your physics results are not good enough!; **notre chiffre d'affaires est i. pour que l'on puisse envisager de recruter davantage de personnel** our sales aren't good enough to allow us to take on more staff (**b**) *Fml* (*incapable*) incapable, incompetent

insufflateur [ɛ̃syflatœr] *nm Méd* insufflator

insufflation [ɛ̃syflasjɔ̃] *nf Méd* insufflation

insuffler [ɛ̃syfle] *vt* (**a**) to blow, to breathe; *Méd* to insufflate; *Méd* **i. de l'air dans les poumons d'un malade** to insufflate a patient; *Fig* **i. une confiance/un respect à qn** to inspire sb with confidence/respect; **i. du dégoût à qn** to fill sb with disgust; **ce succès a insufflé un nouvel élan à l'entreprise** this success gave the company a new lease of life *or* breathed new life into the company (**b**) *Méd* (*gorge etc*) to spray

insulaire [ɛ̃sylɛr] **1** *adj* island, *Spéc* insular; *Péj* (*mentalité*) insular **2** *n* islander

insularité [ɛ̃sylarite] *nf* insularity; **l'i. du pays a grandement contribué à sa puissance maritime** the fact that the country is an island has a great deal to do with its status as a maritime power; **leur i. leur donne un complexe de supériorité** the fact that they are an island race gives them a superiority complex

insuline [ɛ̃sylin] *nf Méd* insulin

insulinodépendant [ɛ̃sylinodepɑ̃dɑ̃] *adj Méd* insulin-dependent

insulinothérapie [ɛ̃sylinɔterapi] *nf Méd* insulin therapy

insultant [ɛ̃syltɑ̃] *adj* insulting; **c'est i.!** it's insulting!, it's an insult!; **il s'est comporté de façon insultante à mon égard** he behaved insultingly to me

insulte [ɛ̃sylt] *nf* insult; **insultes** insults, abuse; **c'est la pire des insultes** that's the worst possible insult; **il lui a lancé les pires insultes** he called him every name under the sun; **faire i. à qn** to insult sb; **une i. à notre intelligence/au bon goût** an insult to our intelligence/to good taste

insulté, -ée [ɛ̃sylte] **1** *adj* insulted **2** *n* injured party

insulter [ɛ̃sylte] **1** *vt* to insult **2** *vi* **i. au malheur** to jeer at misfortune; **i. au bon goût** to insult good taste

insupportable [ɛ̃sypɔrtabl] *adj* (*douleur, chaleur, froid*) unbearable, unendurable; (*vacarme*) unbearable, intolerable; (*conduite*) intolerable; (*personne*) unbearable, insufferable; **la luminosité du soleil était i.** the sun was unbearably bright; **il fait une chaleur i.** it's unbearably hot; **cette pensée m'était i.** the thought was unbearable

insupportablement [ɛ̃sypɔrtabləmɑ̃] *adv* unbearably

insurgé, -ée [ɛ̃syrʒe] *adj, n* rebel, *Fml* insurgent

insurger (s') [sɛ̃syrʒe] *vpr* (**je m'insurgeai(s); n. n. insurgeons**) to rise up (in rebellion), to revolt, to rebel; **il s'est insurgé contre ces mesures** he rebelled against these measures

insurmontable [ɛ̃syrmɔ̃tabl] *adj* (*difficulté, obstacle*) insurmountable, insuperable; (*aversion, dégoût*) unconquerable; **il m'inspire un dégoût i.** I cannot overcome *or* conquer the disgust I feel for him

insurmontablement [ɛ̃syrmɔ̃tabləmɑ̃] *adv* insurmountably

insurpassable [ɛ̃syrpasabl] *adj* unsurpassable

insurrection [ɛ̃syrɛksjɔ̃] *nf* uprising, rebellion, insurrection; **en état d'i.** (*paysans, étudiants*) up in arms, in a state of rebellion; (*pays*) in a state of insurrection *or* rebellion

insurrectionnel, -elle [ɛ̃syrɛksjɔnɛl] *adj* (*troupes, mouvement, gouvernement*) rebel, *Fml* insurrectionary

intact [ɛ̃takt] *adj* intact

intaille [ɛ̃taj] *nf Spéc* intaglio

intangibilité [ɛ̃tɑ̃ʒibilite] *nf* intangibility

intangible [ɛ̃tɑ̃ʒibl] *adj* intangible; (*loi, institution*) sacred

intarissable [ɛ̃tarisabl] *adj* (*puits, imagination*) inexhaustible; (*bavardage*) endless; **le puits/la source est i.** the well/the spring never dries up; **quand il commence à parler de football, il est i.** once he starts to talk about football he never shuts up

intarissablement [ɛ̃tarisabləmɑ̃] *adv* (*parler*) endlessly, inexhaustibly

intégrable [ɛ̃tegrabl] *adj Math* integrable; *Ordinat* (*lecteur etc*) integratable

intégral, -ale, -aux, -ales [ɛ̃tegral, -o] **1** *adj* (**a**) **paiement/remboursement i.** payment/refund in full, full payment/refund; **après le versement i. de la rançon** after the ransom has been paid in full; **nous demandons le maintien i. des prestations de la Sécurité sociale** we ask that social security benefits be maintained at their current levels; **texte i.** complete and unabridged; **édition intégrale** (complete and) unabridged edition; *Cin* **version intégrale** uncut *or* full-length version; **elle pratique le bronzage i.** she goes in for an all-over tan, she sunbathes in the nude; **nu i.** total nudity; **un spectacle de nu i.** a nude show; *F* **un fumiste i.** an out-and-out clown *or* joker; *F* **un crétin i.** a complete (and utter) idiot, an unmitigated idiot; *F* **un menteur i.** an absolute *or* unmitigated liar; *F* **c'est un profiteur i.** he's just out for what he can get

(**b**) *Math* **calcul i.** integral calculus

2 *nf* **intégrale** (**a**) *Math* integral

(**b**) **l'intégrale des symphonies de Beethoven** the complete set of Beethoven symphonies; **l'intégrale des œuvres de Shakespeare** the complete works of Shakespeare

intégralement [ɛ̃tegralmɑ̃] *adv* (*citer, rembourser*) fully, in full; **il a vidé i. son compte épargne pour s'acheter une moto** he took all the money out of his savings account to buy a motor bike; *F* **se moquer i. de qch** not to give a damn about sth; *Fin* **i. libéré** fully paid up

intégralité [ɛ̃tegralite] *nf* **l'i.** the whole; **l'i. de son salaire** the whole of his salary, his entire salary; **ils lui ont remboursé l'i. de ses dépenses** they refunded his expenses in full; **dans son i.** in its entirety, in full

intégrante [ɛ̃tegrɑ̃] *adj f* **une partie i. de** an integral part of; **faire partie i. de** to be an integral part of, *F* to be part and parcel of

intégrateur [ɛ̃tegratœr] *nm Ordinat* integrator

intégration [ɛ̃tegrasjɔ̃] *nf* (*d'une population*) (social) integration; *Math* integration; **i. d'un candidat à Polytechnique** admission of a candidate to the Ecole Polytechnique

▶ **intégration**: *Écon* **i. en amont** backward integration; *Écon* **i. en aval** forward integration; *Ordinat* **i. à grande échelle** large-scale integration; *Écon* **i. horizontale** horizontal integration; *Ordinat* **i. à moyenne échelle** medium-scale integration; *Ordinat* **i. à petite échelle** small-scale integration; *Ordinat* **i. à très grande échelle** very large scale integration; *Écon* **i. verticale** vertical integration; *Écon* **i. verticale en amont** vertical backward integration; *Écon* **i. verticale en aval** vertical forward integration

intégré [ɛ̃tegre] **1** *adj Ordinat* integrated; *Aut* built-in; *Ordinat* **commandes intégrées** embedded commands; *Can* **système i. de gestion** management information system **2** *nm Ordinat* integrated package

intègre [ɛ̃tɛgr] *adj* upright, honest; **une femme i.** a woman of integrity

intégrer [ɛ̃tegre] (**j'intègre; j'intégrerai**) **1** *vt* (**a**) to integrate (**à, dans** into); **i. une somme dans une facture** to include a sum in an invoice (**b**) *Ordinat* (*commande*) to embed **2 s'intégrer** *vpr* to become integrated (**à, dans** into, with)

intégrisme [ɛ̃tegrism] *nm Rel* fundamentalism

intégriste [ɛ̃tegrist] *adj, n Rel* fundamentalist

intégrité [ɛ̃tegrite] *nf* (**a**) (*totalité*) integrity, completeness, entirety; *Ordinat* **i. des données** data integrity (**b**) (*honnêteté*) integrity, uprightness, honesty

intellect [ɛ̃telɛkt] *nm* intellect

intellectualiser [ɛ̃telɛktɥalize] *vt* to intellectualize

intellectualisme [ɛ̃telɛktɥalism] *nm* intellectualism

intellectualiste [ɛ̃telɛktɥalist] *adj, n* intellectualist

intellectualité [ɛ̃telɛktɥalite] *nf Litt* intellectuality

intellectuel, -elle [ɛ̃telɛktɥɛl] **1** *adj* intellectual, *Péj* highbrow; (*fatigue, effort*) mental; (*travail, travailleur*) white-collar, non-manual **2** *n* intellectual, *Péj* highbrow

intellectuellement [ɛ̃telɛktɥɛlmɑ̃] *adv* intellectually

intelligemment [ɛ̃teliʒamɑ̃] *adv* intelligently

intelligence [ɛ̃teliʒɑ̃s] *nf* (**a**) (*compréhension*) understanding, comprehension; **avoir l'i. des affaires** to have a good head for business; **pour l'i. de ce qui va suivre** in order to understand what follows

(**b**) (*intellect*) intelligence, intellect, mind; **aiguiser l'i. de qn** to sharpen sb's wits; **le développement de l'i.** intellectual development; **un homme d'une vive i.** an extremely intelligent man, *Fml* a man of lively intelligence; **d'une i. extraordinaire** extraordinarily intelligent; **elle a eu l'i. de se taire** she had the intelligence *or F* the wits *or* the brains to keep quiet

(**c**) (*connivence*) **un regard/sourire d'i.** a knowing look/smile; **faire des signes d'i. à qn** to signal to sb; **être d'i. avec qn** to be in collusion with sb; **entretenir des intelligences avec qn** to keep up a secret correspondence with sb; **avoir des intelligences avec l'ennemi** to have (secret) dealings with the enemy

(**d**) (*entente*) **vivre en bonne/mauvaise i. avec qn** to be on good/bad terms with sb

▶ **intelligence**: **i. artificielle** artificial intelligence; **i. mercatique** marketing *or* market intelligence

intelligent [ɛ̃teliʒɑ̃] *adj* intelligent, bright, clever, *F* brainy; *Ordinat* smart, intelligent; **une femme intelligente** an intelligent woman, a woman of intelligence; *Iron* **ah, franchement, c'est i.!** that's really clever!

intelligentsia [inteliḍʒɛnsja] *nf* **l'i.** the intelligentsia
intelligibilité [ɛ̃teliʒibilite] *nf* intelligibility
intelligible [ɛ̃teliʒibl] *adj* (*compréhensible*) intelligible, understandable; (*clair*) clear, distinct; **à haute et i. voix** in a loud, clear voice
intelligiblement [ɛ̃teliʒibləmɑ̃] *adv* intelligibly
intello [ɛ̃telo] *n F souvent Péj* intellectual, highbrow, egghead
intempérance [ɛ̃tɑ̃perɑ̃s] *nf* intemperance
intempérant [ɛ̃tɑ̃perɑ̃] *adj* intemperate
intempérie [ɛ̃tɑ̃peri] *nf* **(a) intempéries** bad weather; **exposé aux intempéries** exposed to the elements **(b)** *Arch* (*du temps*) inclemency
intempestif, -ive [ɛ̃tɑ̃pestif, -iv] *adj* untimely, ill-timed, inopportune; **pas de démarches intempestives!** don't let's rush into this, let's not be hasty
intemporalité [ɛ̃tɑ̃pɔralite] *nf* timelessness
intemporel, -elle [ɛ̃tɑ̃pɔrɛl] *adj* (*hors du temps*) timeless
intenable [ɛ̃t(ə)nabl] *adj* (*chaleur, situation*) intolerable, unbearable; (*position*) untenable; *F* **enfant i.** uncontrollable child
intendance [ɛ̃tɑ̃dɑ̃s] *nf* **(a)** *Scol* bursary; (*bureau*) bursar's office **(b)** *Mil* Commissariat **(c)** *Hist Fr* (*d'une province*) administration **(d)** *Arch* (*d'un domaine*) stewardship
intendant, -ante [ɛ̃tɑ̃dɑ̃, -ɑ̃t] **1** *nm* **(a)** *Scol* bursar **(b)** *Mil* senior Commissariat officer **(c)** *Hist Fr* (*d'une province*) administrator **(d)** *Arch* (*d'un domaine*) steward **2** *nf* **intendante (a)** *Scol* (woman) bursar **(b)** *Hist Fr* (*d'une province*) wife of the administrator **(c)** *Rel* Mother Superior **(d)** *Arch* steward's wife
intense [ɛ̃tɑ̃s] *adj* (*plaisir, froid, chaleur, activité*) intense; (*douleur*) intense, severe; (*couleur*) intense, deep; (*circulation*) dense, heavy; (*tir*) heavy; **temps d'un froid i.** intensely cold weather; **des yeux d'un bleu i.** intensely blue eyes, deep blue eyes
intensément [ɛ̃tɑ̃semɑ̃] *adv* (*vivre*) intensely; (*regarder qn*) intently, intensely
intensif, -ive [ɛ̃tɑ̃sif, -iv] *adj* (*entraînement, cours, soins, bombardement*) intensive; *Agr* **culture intensive** intensive farming *or* cultivation
intensification [ɛ̃tɑ̃sifikasjɔ̃] *nf* intensification; **l'i. des échanges commerciaux** the strengthening of trade links, the increase in trade
intensifier [ɛ̃tɑ̃sifje] **1** *vt* (*bombardements*) to intensify, *F* to step up; (*échanges commerciaux*) to increase, *F* to step up **2 s'intensifier** *vpr* to intensify, to become more intense; (*de lueur*) to get brighter *or* stronger; (*de douleur*) to become more intense, to get worse
intensité [ɛ̃tɑ̃site] *nf* **(a)** (*d'un sentiment*) intensity; (*d'un regard*) intentness, intensity; (*de la lumière*) intensity, brightness; (*du vent*) force; (*d'une couleur*) intensity, depth; (*du froid*) severity, intensity; *Él* (*du courant*) strength; (*d'un champ magnétique*) density; **i. acoustique** loudness; **i. lumineuse** light intensity; **l'i. de la lumière était telle que ...** the light was so intense *or* bright that ...; **donner plus d'i. à un morceau de musique** to give more feeling to a piece of music; **il y a dans ce spectacle des moments d'une grande i.** there are some very intense moments in the show **(b)** *Ling* **accent d'i.** stress mark
intensivement [ɛ̃tɑ̃sivmɑ̃] *adv* (*répéter, s'entraîner etc*) intensively
intenter [ɛ̃tɑ̃te] *vt Jur* **i. une action/un procès à** *ou* **contre qn** to bring an action against sb, to institute proceedings against sb
intention [ɛ̃tɑ̃sjɔ̃] *nf* **(a)** (*projet*) intention, purpose, design; *Jur* intent; *Jur* **avec i. délictueuse** with malicious intent; **sans mauvaise i.** with no ill intent; **dans l'i. de nuire** with intent to harm; **sans i. de nuire** with no intent to harm, without malice; *Mktg* **i. d'achat** intention to buy, purchase intention; **avoir l'i. de faire qch** to intend *or* mean to do sth; **il n'a pas l'i. de se laisser faire** he doesn't intend to be cheated; **je n'ai nullement l'i. d'accepter** I have no *or* not the slightest intention of accepting; **à cette i.** with that in mind, to that end; **dans l'i. de faire qch** with a view to *or* with the intention of doing sth; **il a de bonnes intentions** he means well, his intentions are good; **il est plein de bonnes intentions** he's full of good intentions; **c'est l'i. qui compte** it's the thought that counts; *Prov* **l'enfer est pavé de bonnes intentions** the road to hell is paved with good intentions

(b) ils ont organisé un banquet à l'i. de leurs invités they organized a banquet in honour of their guests; **une messe à l'i. des disparus** a mass for the dead; **voici une écharpe que j'ai achetée à votre i.** here's a scarf I bought especially for you; **c'était une remarque à mon i.** the remark was meant for me; **livres écrits à l'i. des enfants** books for children, books aimed at children; *Com* **à l'i. de ...** for the attention of ...

intentionné [ɛ̃tɑ̃sjɔne] *adj* **bien/mal i.** well-/ill-disposed (**envers** towards); **personne bien intentionnée** well-intentioned *or* well-meaning person; **c'était une démarche bien intentionnée** it was well-intentioned
intentionnel, -elle [ɛ̃tɑ̃sjɔnɛl] *adj* intentional, deliberate; **mon geste n'était pas i.** I didn't do it deliberately *or* intentionally *or* on purpose; **de façon intentionnelle** deliberately, intentionally
intentionnellement [ɛ̃tɑ̃sjɔnɛlmɑ̃] *adv* deliberately, intentionally; **c'est i. que je ne l'ai pas invitée** I deliberately didn't invite her, I didn't invite her on purpose
inter [ɛ̃tɛr] *nm* **(a)** *Fb* **i. droit/gauche** inside right/left **(b)** *Tél Vieilli* trunk (line)
interactif, -ive [ɛ̃tɛraktif, -iv] *adj Ordinat* interactive
interaction [ɛ̃tɛraksjɔ̃] *nf* interaction
interactivité [ɛ̃tɛraktivite] *nf* interactivity, interactiveness
interallié [ɛ̃teralje] *adj* allied
interarmées [ɛ̃terarme] *adj inv Mil* **état-major i.** joint staff
interarmes [ɛ̃tɛrarm] *adj inv Mil* (*opération, manœuvre*) combined
interastral, -ale, -aux, -ales [ɛ̃tɛrastral, -o] *adj* (*rare*) interstellar
interbancaire [ɛ̃tɛrbɑ̃kɛr] *adj* interbank
interblocage [ɛ̃tɛrblɔkaʒ] *nm Ordinat* deadlock
intercalaire [ɛ̃tɛrkalɛr] **1** *adj* **(a) feuille i.** interpolated sheet; **feuillet i.** insert **(b) carte i.** (*de fichier*) guide (card) **(c)** (*jour*) intercalary **2** *nm* insert, interpolated sheet; (*dans classeur*) divider
intercalation [ɛ̃tɛrkalasjɔ̃] *nf* (*dans un texte*) insertion; *Él* (*d'une résistance*) switching in
intercaler [ɛ̃tɛrkale] **1** *vt* (*dans un texte, un film*) to insert, to include; (*dans un programme, entre deux événements*) to slot in; *Él* (*résistance*) to cut in, to switch in; (*jour dans une année bissextile*) to intercalate; **i. des citations dans un discours** to intersperse *or* sprinkle a speech with quotations; **i. un court métrage entre les deux grands films** to slot a short in between the two features; **i. un mot dans un texte** to insert a word in a text **2 s'intercaler** *vpr* to come in between
intercéder [ɛ̃tɛrsede] *vt* (*conj like* **céder**) to intercede (**auprès de** with)
intercepter [ɛ̃tɛrsɛpte] *vt* (*lettre, avion, ballon, personne etc*) to intercept; (*bruit, lumière*) to shut *or* cut out
intercepteur [ɛ̃tɛrsɛptœr] *nm Av* interceptor
interception [ɛ̃tɛrsɛpsjɔ̃] *nf* (*d'une lettre, d'un avion, d'un ballon*) interception; (*du bruit, de la lumière*) cutting *or* shutting out; **avion d'i.** interceptor (aircraft)
intercesseur [ɛ̃tɛrsesœr] *nm Litt* mediator; **il fut mon i. auprès du patron** he interceded with the boss on my behalf
intercession [ɛ̃tɛrsesjɔ̃] *nf Litt* intercession
interchangeable [ɛ̃tɛrʃɑ̃ʒabl] *adj* interchangeable
interclasse [ɛ̃tɛrklas] *nm Scol* (short) break (between classes)
interclassement [ɛ̃tɛrklasmɑ̃] *nm Ordinat* **i. du courrier** mail merge
interclasseuse [ɛ̃tɛrklasøz] *nf* (*de documents*) collator
intercom [ɛ̃tɛrkɔm] *nm TV etc* **i. de production** production talkback system
intercommunication [ɛ̃tɛrkɔmynikasjɔ̃] *nf* intercommunication
interconnexion [ɛ̃tɛrkɔnɛksjɔ̃] *nf Él* interconnection
intercontinental, -ale, -aux, -ales [ɛ̃tɛrkɔ̃tinɑ̃tal, -o] *adj* intercontinental; **fusée intercontinentale** intercontinental ballistic missile
intercooler [ɛ̃tɛrkulœr] *nm Aut* intercooler
intercostal, -ale, -aux, -ales [ɛ̃tɛrkɔstal, -o] *Anat* **1** *adj* (*muscle*) intercostal; **des douleurs intercostales** pains in the side **2** *nm* intercostal muscle
interdépartemental, -ale, -aux, -ales [ɛ̃tɛrdepartəmɑ̃tal, -o] *adj* interdepartmental
interdépendance [ɛ̃tɛrdepɑ̃dɑ̃s] *nf* interdependence
interdépendant [ɛ̃tɛrdepɑ̃dɑ̃] *adj* interdependent; (*problèmes*) linked, related
interdiction [ɛ̃tɛrdiksjɔ̃] *nf* **(a)** (*défense*) prohibition, banning, forbidding; **i. des essais atomiques** atomic test ban; **i. de fumer/stationner** no smoking/parking, smoking/parking prohibited; **i. de tourner à droite** no right turn; **i. d'un livre par la censure** banning of a book by the censor; **i. absolue de toucher aux objets exposés** please do not touch the exhibits; **i. absolue de toucher à mon ordinateur** don't touch my computer, *F* hands off my computer **(b)** *Jur* state of minority declared by court, deprival of control over money; **i. d'un aliéné** certifying of an insane person **(c)** *MecE* inhibit
▶ **interdiction: i. de commerce** trade ban; **i. d'exportation** export ban; **i. d'importation** import ban; **i. légale**

suspension *or* (temporary) deprivation of civil rights; *Admin, Pol* **i. de séjour** ban(ning order), exclusion order; **i. de vol** aircraft grounding

interdigital, -ale, -aux, -ales [ɛ̃tɛrdiʒital, -o] *adj* (*espace, pli*) between the fingers, *Spéc* interdigital

interdire [ɛ̃tɛrdir] (*conj like* **dire,** *except pr ind* **v. interdisez** *and imp* **interdisez) 1** *vt* **(a)** (*défendre*) (*parti politique*) to ban; (*la vente d'un produit, un meeting etc*) to ban, to prohibit; **i. qch à qn** to forbid sb sth; **il est interdit de marcher sur l'herbe** keep off the grass; **nos parents nous interdisaient les sorties** our parents forbade us to go out; **le centre-ville est interdit aux camions** lorries are banned from *or* are not allowed in the centre of town, the centre of town is closed to lorries; **la passerelle est interdite aux voyageurs** passengers are not allowed on the bridge; **le médecin lui a interdit l'alcool** the doctor has forbidden him to drink; **ils ont décidé d'interdire l'accès du club aux femmes/aux mineurs** they've decided to ban women/minors from the club; **il nous est interdit de révéler ...** we are not allowed to reveal ...; **i. à qn de faire qch** to prohibit sb from doing sth, to forbid sb to do sth; **je t'interdis de fumer/de toucher à mes affaires/de parler à des étrangers** I forbid you to smoke/to touch my things/to talk to strangers; **i. à un pilote de voler** to ground a pilot

(b) *Jur* **faire i. qn** to have sb declared incapable of managing his own affairs

(c) (*empêcher*) to prevent, to stop; **le temps nous interdit de sortir** the weather is preventing *or* stopping us from going out *or* is making it impossible for us to go out; **son propre père lui a interdit sa porte** his own father has forbidden him the house

2 s'interdire *vpr* **s'i. l'alcool/le tabac** to give up drinking/smoking; **il s'interdit d'y penser** he doesn't let himself think about it

interdisciplinaire [ɛ̃tɛrdisiplinɛr] *adj* interdisciplinary

interdit, -ite [ɛ̃tɛrdi, -it] **1** *adj* **(a)** (*non autorisé*) forbidden; **(il est) i. de fumer** no smoking; **entrée interdite (au public)** no admittance, no entry; **affichage i.** billposters will be prosecuted; **passage/stationnement i.** no thoroughfare/parking; **c'est un sujet i. ici** it's a forbidden *or* taboo subject here; **film i. aux moins de 18 ans** *Br* ≈ (18); **i. de séjour** (*dans un pays*) banned; **il est i. de séjour en France** he is banned from France, he is persona non grata in France; **être i. de chéquier** to have had one's cheque book withdrawn; **être i. bancaire** to have had all banking facilities withdrawn; *Ordinat* **i. d'écriture** (*disquette*) write-protected; **avion i. de vol** grounded aircraft

(b) (*déconcerté*) disconcerted, nonplussed, taken aback

2 *n Jur* **(aliéné) i.** certified person; **i. de séjour** ex-convict prohibited from entering a certain area

3 *nm* (*dans la société*) taboo; *Rel* interdict; **elle fait fi de tous les interdits** she flouts all the conventions; **fumer en public constituait un i. pour les femmes** it used to be frowned on *or* to be taboo for women to smoke in public; *Rel* **des interdits alimentaires** food forbidden by dietary law; **frapper qn/qch d'i.** to impose a ban on sb/sth

intéressant, -ante [ɛ̃teresɑ̃, -ɑ̃t] **1** *adj* **(a)** (*attirant*) interesting; **peu i.** dull, uninteresting; **il n'y a pas grande chose d'i. à la télévision** there's not much of interest on television, *F* there's not much on television; **chercher à se rendre i.** to try to make oneself interesting, to draw attention to oneself **(b)** (*avantageux*) worthwhile; (*prix*) attractive; (*placements*) profitable **2** *n F* **faire l'i.** to show off, to draw attention to oneself

intéressé [ɛ̃terese] **1** *adj* **(a)** (*concerné*) **les parties intéressées** the interested parties, the persons concerned *or* involved **(b)** (*égoïste*) selfish, self-seeking; **amour i.** cupboard love; **son amour pour lui est i.** his/her love for him is self-interested; **une amitié intéressée** a self-interested friendship; **agir dans un but i.** to have an axe to grind; **encore un conseil i.!** another piece of biased advice! **2** *npl* **les intéressés** the interested parties, the persons concerned *or* involved; **les premiers intéressés** those most directly affected; **c'est vous le premier i.** you're the one most affected *or* most closely concerned

intéressement [ɛ̃terɛsmɑ̃] *nm Com, Ind* **i. (aux résultats)** employee profit-sharing scheme

intéresser [ɛ̃terese] **1** *vt* **(a)** (*captiver*) to interest, to be interesting to; **un sujet qui m'intéresse beaucoup** a subject which interests me greatly; **la politique/l'astronomie m'intéresse beaucoup** I am very interested *or* I take a great deal of interest in politics/astronomy; **ceci peut vous i.** this may interest you *or* be of interest to you; **savoir i. les enfants** to know how to get children's interest; **i. qn à qch** to interest sb in sth; **le sort des réfugiés n'intéresse personne** no-one is interested in the fate of the refugees; **on va au cinéma, est-ce que ça t'intéresse?** we're going to the cinema, are you interested?; *Iron* **continue** *ou* **cause toujours, tu m'intéresses** how interesting!

(b) (*concerner*) to concern, to affect; **question qui intéresse le monde entier** question of worldwide interest *or* of concern to the entire world

(c) *Ind, Com* **i. les employés (aux bénéfices)** to initiate a profit-sharing scheme; **être intéressé dans une affaire** to have a share in a business

2 s'intéresser *vpr* **s'i. à qn/qch** to take an interest in sb/sth, to be interested in sb/sth; **un jeune romancier qui mérite qu'on s'intéresse à lui** a young novelist who merits some attention; **il s'intéresse beaucoup à elle** he's very interested in her, he's showing a great deal of interest in her

intérêt [ɛ̃terɛ] *nm* **(a)** (*dans une affaire etc*) share, stake; **avoir des intérêts dans une affaire** to have financial interests in a business; **il y a de gros intérêts en jeu** there's a lot at stake; **les intérêts économiques de notre pays dans cette région** our country's economic interests in that region

(b) (*avantage*) interest; **j'ai i. à le faire, c'est dans mon i. de le faire** it's in my interest to do it; **tu aurais tout i. à le faire** you would be well advised to do it; **on a i. à réserver si on veut avoir des places** it is advisable to book if we want seats; *F* **tu n'as pas i. à recommencer!** you'd better not do it again!; **agir dans son i.** to act in one's own interest(s); **agir dans/contre l'i. de qn** to act in/against sb's interest(s); **ce n'est pas dans mon i. (de le faire)** it's not in my interest (to do it); **je n'ai aucun i. à le faire** it's not at all in my interest; **quel i. aurait-elle à te nuire?** why should she want to harm you?; **agir par i. personnel** to act out of self-interest; **son i. personnel** his/her own interests; **il a fait un mariage d'i.** he married for money; **il sait où se trouve son i.** he knows where his advantage lies *or F* which side his bread is buttered on; **l'i. des vacances en groupe, c'est de faire des rencontres** the advantage of *or F* the great thing about group holidays is that you meet people; *Rail* **ligne d'i. local** branch line, local line; *très F* **tu viens à la réunion du syndicat? – y'a i.!** are you coming to the union meeting? – you bet (I am)!

(c) (*attention, curiosité*) interest; **d'i. historique/architectural** of historical/architectural interest; **ressentir de l'i. pour qn/qch** to feel interested in sb/sth; **prendre de l'i. à qch** to take an interest in sth; **montrer un i. pour qch** to show an interest in sth; **livre sans i.** *ou* **dépourvu d'i.** uninteresting book, book devoid of interest; **elle a perdu tout son i. pour son travail/cet ami** she has lost all interest in her work/friend

(d) (*importance*) importance; **du plus haut i.** of the greatest importance; **quelques paroles sans i.** some unimportant words; **c'était sans i.** it wasn't important

(e) *Fin* interest; **i. simple/composé** simple/compound interest; **placer son argent à 12% d'i.** to invest one's money at 12% interest; **prêt à i.** interest-bearing loan

▶ **intérêt: i. bancaire** bank interest; *Fin* **intérêts compensatoires** damages; **i. du consommateur** consumer welfare; **intérêt(s) couru(s)** accrued interest; *Fin* **intérêts dus** interest due; *Fin* **intérêts à échoir** accruing interest; *Fin* **intérêts échus** accrued interest; *Fin* **intérêts exigibles** interest due and payable; *Fin* **i. fixe** fixed interest; *Fin* **intérêts moratoires** default interest, penalty interest; **i. public** public interest; **c'est dans l'i. du public** it's in the public interest; *Bourse* **i. de report** contango; *Fin* **i. de retard** interest on arrears; *Fin* **i. variable** variable-rate interest

interfaçage [ɛ̃tɛrfasaʒ] *nm Ordinat* interfacing

interface [ɛ̃tɛrfas] *nf Ordinat* interface; **i. pour petit système informatique** small computer system interface; **i. utilisateur** user interface; *Ordinat* **i. d'imprimante** printer interface; *Ordinat* **i. graphique** graphic interface; *TV, Cin* **i. numérique** digital interface; *Ordinat* **i. parallèle** parallel interface; *Ordinat* **i. série** serial interface; *Ordinat* **i. utilisateur graphique** graphical user interface, GUI; *TV, Cin* **interface vidéo numérique** digital video interface

interfacer [ɛ̃tɛrfase] *vt Ordinat* to interface

interférence [ɛ̃tɛrferɑ̃s] *nf* **(a)** *Phys, Rad* interference; *Rad, Tél* **à cause des interférences** because of the interference; **i. électrique** electrical interference **(b)** (*d'événements*) combination

interférent [ɛ̃tɛrferɑ̃] *adj Phys* (*rayons etc*) interfering

interférer [ɛ̃tɛrfere] *vi* **(il interfère; il interférait; il interférera) (a)** *Phys* (*des ondes lumineuses etc*) to interfere **(b)** (*d'un projet*) to interfere **(avec** with); (*de projets, politiques*) to interfere with each other

interféron [ɛ̃tɛrferɔ̃] *nm Biol* interferon

interfolier [ɛ̃tɛrfɔlje] *vt Tech* to interleave, to interpage

intergalactique [ɛ̃tɛrgalaktik] *adj* intergalactic

intergouvernemental, -ale, -aux, -ales [ɛ̃tɛrguvɛrnəmɑ̃tal, -o] *adj* intergovernmental

intérieur [ɛ̃terjœr] **1** *adj* **(a)** (*dans l'espace*) (*escalier*) interior, inner, inside; (*cour*) inner; (*poche*) inside; (*partie*) inside, internal; (*mer*) inland

(b) (*national*) (*administration, politique, marché, dette, commerce*) domestic, internal, home; **vol i.** domestic flight; **(tarif d')affranchissement en régime i.** inland postage rate

(c) (*vie, sentiments, force*) inner

2 *nm* **(a)** (*dedans*) (*d'une maison, d'une voiture*) inside, interior; (*d'un four, d'un récipient, d'une boîte etc*) inside; **à l'i.** inside, on the inside; (*à la maison*) inside, indoors; **à l'i. de la gare/de la malle** inside the station/the trunk; **à l'i. du parti** within *or* inside the party; **à l'i. de lui-même il savait que …** deep down he knew that …; **la porte était verrouillée de l'i.** the door was bolted on *or* from the inside; **il veut transformer le parti de l'i.** he wants to change the party from the inside *or* from within; *Cin* **tourné en i.** shot indoors *or* inside; **l'i. du pays** the interior of the country; **dans l'i. du pays** inland; **avancer vers l'i. du pays** to advance inland; **Ministère de l'I.** Ministry of the Interior, *Br* ≈ Home Office, *US* ≈ Department of the Interior; **i. cuir** (*de voiture*) leather trim; **i. sport** (*de voiture*) sports trim

(b) (*maison*) interior, home; **un i. douillet** a cosy interior *or* home; **vie d'i.** home life, domestic life; **femme d'i.** houseproud housewife; **elle est très femme d'i.** she's very houseproud; **vêtements d'i.** indoor clothes

(c) *Fb* **i. gauche/droit** inside left/right

intérieurement [ɛ̃terjœrmɑ̃] *adv* (*savoir*) inwardly, inside, within oneself; (*maudire qn*) inwardly; **rire i.** to laugh to oneself *or* inwardly

intérim [ɛ̃terim] *nm* interim; (*travail intérimaire*) temporary work, temping; **dans l'i.** in the interim, (in the) meantime; **par i.** (*président*) acting **secrétaire par i.** acting *or* temporary secretary; **faire de l'i.** to do temporary work, to temp; **assurer l'i. (de qn)** to deputize *or* stand in (for sb); *Méd* to act as locum (for sb)

intérimaire [ɛ̃terimɛr] **1** *adj* (*fonction, fonctionnaire etc*) temporary; *Pol* **cabinet i.** caretaker cabinet; **directeur i.** acting manager; **dividende/rapport i.** interim dividend/report **2** *n* (*travailleur*) temporary worker; (*secrétaire*) temporary secretary, temp; *Méd* locum (tenens); **travailler comme i.** to temp, to work as a temp

intériorisation [ɛ̃terjɔrizasjɔ̃] *nf* internalization, interiorization

intérioriser [ɛ̃terjɔrize] *vt* to internalize, to interiorize

interjectif, -ive [ɛ̃tɛrʒɛktif, -iv] *adj* interjectional

interjection [ɛ̃tɛrʒɛksjɔ̃] *nf* **(a)** *Gram* interjection **(b)** *Jur* (*d'appel*) lodging

interjeter [ɛ̃tɛrʒəte] *vt* (*conj like* **jeter**) *Jur* **i. appel** to lodge an appeal, to give notice of appeal

interlettrage [ɛ̃tɛrlɛtraʒ] *nm Ordinat* intercharacter spacing

interlignage [ɛ̃tɛrliɲaʒ] *nm Typ* leading, line spacing; **i. simple** single spacing

interligne [ɛ̃tɛrliɲ] **1** *nm Typ* leading, interline spacing, line spacing; *Mus* (*sur une portée*) space; **dans les interlignes** between the lines; **tapé en simple/double i.** typed with single/double spacing, single-/double-spaced **2** *nf Typ* (*lame*) lead

interligner [ɛ̃tɛrliɲe] *vt* **(a)** (*insérer*) (*mot*) to write between the lines, *Spéc* to interline **(b)** *Typ* (*séparer*) to lead out

interlinéaire [ɛ̃tɛrlineɛr] *adj* (*notes*) interlinear

interlocuteur, -trice [ɛ̃tɛrlɔkytœr, -tris] *n* speaker, *Fml* interlocutor; **mon i.** the person I was/am speaking to, *Fml* my interlocutor; **i. privilégié** = person/country with whom one/a country has a special relationship; **les États-Unis ont toujours été un i. privilégié pour la Grande-Bretagne** the United States has always had a special relationship with Great Britain; **un i. valable** (*de négociation*) an acceptable negotiating partner

interlocutoire [ɛ̃tɛrlɔkytwar] *Jur* **1** *adj* interlocutory **2** *nm* interlocutory judgement

interlope [ɛ̃tɛrlɔp] *adj* (*établissement*) suspect, dubious, shady; *Rare* (*commerce*) unauthorized, illegal; **c'était le lieu de rendez-vous de tout un monde i.** it was the meeting place of the underworld

interloqué [ɛ̃tɛrlɔke] *adj* dumbfounded, flabbergasted, taken aback

interloquer [ɛ̃tɛrlɔke] *vt* (*personne*) to take aback, to dumbfound

interlude [ɛ̃tɛrlyd] *nm Mus, Th, TV* interlude

intermède [ɛ̃tɛrmɛd] *nm Th, Fig* interlude

intermédiaire [ɛ̃tɛrmedjɛr] **1** *adj* (*état, temps etc*) intermediate, intermediary; **couleur i. entre le bleu et le vert** colour halfway between blue and green; **sentiment i. entre la tristesse et le désespoir** feeling halfway between sadness and despair; **trouver une solution i.** to find a solution somewhere in-between; **une pointure i.** a size in-between; *MecE* **arbre i.** countershaft **2** *n* (*personne*) intermediary, go-between; *Com* middleman; **i. commercial** merchant middleman **3** *nm* **par l'i. de qn/qch** through sb/sth; **par l'i. de la presse** through (the medium of) the press; **sans i.** directly; **sans l'i. de** without the intermediary of

intermezzo [ɛ̃tɛrmɛdzo] *nm Mus* intermezzo

interminable [ɛ̃tɛrminabl] *adj* never-ending, endless, interminable

interminablement [ɛ̃tɛrminabləmɑ̃] *adv* endlessly, interminably

interministériel, -ielle [ɛ̃tɛrministerjɛl] *adj* (*entre ministres*) interministerial; (*entre ministères*) interdepartmental, interministerial

intermission [ɛ̃tɛrmisjɔ̃] *nf Méd* intermission

intermittence [ɛ̃tɛrmitɑ̃s] *nf* **(a)** (*irrégularité*) intermittence, intermittency; (*de la production, du pouls etc*) irregularity; **par i.** sporadically, intermittently; **il a plu par i.** it rained on and off **(b)** *Méd* (*intermission*) intermission

intermittent, -ente [ɛ̃tɛrmitɑ̃, -ɑ̃t] **1** *adj* intermittent, sporadic; (*pouls*) irregular; **travail i.** casual work; *Él* **courant i.** make-and-break current **2** *n* casual worker

intermoléculaire [ɛ̃tɛrmɔlekylɛr] *adj* intermolecular

internat [ɛ̃tɛrna] *nm* **(a)** *Scol* (*système*) boarding; (*pensionnat*) boarding school **(b)** *Méd* (*concours*) entrance examination for a housemanship *or Am* an internship; (*formation*) clinicals, *Am* internship; **faire l'i.** to be a house doctor *or* a houseman *or Am* an intern

international, -ale, -aux, -ales [ɛ̃tɛrnasjɔnal, -o] **1** *adj* international **2** *n Sp* (*joueur*) international; **il a été trois fois i. de rugby** he played rugby three times for his country *or* at international level, *Br* he was capped three times *or* he won three caps at rugby **3** *nf* **l'Internationale** (*groupement*) the International; (*chant*) the Internationale

internationalement [ɛ̃tɛrnasjɔnalmɑ̃] *adv* internationally

internationalisation [ɛ̃tɛrnasjɔnalizasjɔ̃] *nf* internationalization

internationaliser [ɛ̃tɛrnasjɔnalize] **1** *vt* to internationalize **2 s'internationaliser** *vpr* to become international

internationalisme [ɛ̃tɛrnasjɔnalism] *nm* internationalism

internationaliste [ɛ̃tɛrnasjɔnalist] *adj, n* internationalist

internationalité [ɛ̃tɛrnasjɔnalite] *nf* internationality

internaute [ɛ̃tɛrnot] *n* Internet surfer, net surfer

interne [ɛ̃tɛrn] **1** *adj* (*structure, paroi, hémorragie*) internal; (*de l'entreprise*) in-house; (*côté*) inner; *Math* (*angle*) interior; **le gouvernement connaît des difficultés internes** the government is experiencing internal difficulties; *Anat* **face i. du bras** inside of the arm; *Scol* **élève i.** boarder **2** *n Scol* boarder; *Méd* **i. (des hôpitaux)** *Br* house doctor, houseman, *Am* intern

interné, -ée [ɛ̃tɛrne] *n Pol* internee; *Méd* inmate

internement [ɛ̃tɛrnəmɑ̃] *nm* (*d'un étranger*) internment; (*des malades mentaux*) confinement

interner [ɛ̃tɛrne] *vt* (*étranger*) to intern; (*les malades mentaux*) to commit

Internet [ɛ̃tɛrnɛt] *nm* Internet

interocéanique [ɛ̃tɛrɔseanik] *adj* interoceanic

interparlementaire [ɛ̃tɛrparləmɑ̃tɛr] *adj Pol* interparliamentary; **commission i.** joint committee

interpellateur, -trice [ɛ̃tɛrpelatœr, -tris] *n* heckler; *Pol* questioner

interpellation [ɛ̃tɛrpelasjɔ̃] *n* (*appel*) calling out; (*par sentinelle*) challenge; *Pol* (*question*) question; **répondre à une i.** (*au Parlement*) to answer a question; **interpellation(s)** (*à une réunion, à un spectacle*) heckling; **la police a procédé à plusieurs interpellations** the police took several people in for questionning

interpeller [ɛ̃tɛrpele] **1** *vt* **(a)** (*appeler*) to call (out) to; *Pol* (*ministre*) to question, to put a question to; (*à une réunion politique, un spectacle*) to heckle; (*d'une sentinelle*) to challenge; **se faire i. par la police** to be questioned by the police; **i. le ministre pour qu'il s'explique sur sa politique** to call on *or* challenge the Minister to explain his policy

(b) *F* (*toucher*) **ce film/roman m'interpelle vraiment** I can really relate to this film/novel, this film/novel really says something to me

2 s'interpeller *vpr* to call (out) to each other; **les deux automobilistes s'interpellaient grossièrement** the two drivers were exchanging insults *or* shouting insults at each other

interpénétration [ɛ̃tɛrpenetrasjɔ̃] *nf* (*de phénomènes, domaines, cultures*) interpenetration

interpénétrer (s') [sɛ̃tɛrpenetre] *vpr* to interpenetrate

interphone [ɛ̃tɛrfɔn] *nm* (*dans un bureau*) intercom; (*à l'entrée d'un immeuble*) entryphone; *TV, Rad* talkback; **à l'i.** on the intercom; *TV, Rad* **i. commuté** switched talkback; **i. de studio** studio talkback

interplanétaire [ɛ̃tɛrplanetɛr] *adj* interplanetary; **voyage i.** space flight

interpolation [ɛ̃tɛrpɔlasjɔ̃] *nf* interpolation

interpoler [ɛ̃tɛrpɔle] *vt* to interpolate

interposé [ɛ̃tɛrpoze] *adj* **agir par personnes interposées** to act through intermediaries; **il m'a contacté par personne interposée** he contacted me through an intermediary

interposer [ɛ̃tɛrpoze] **1** *vt* to interpose (**entre** between) **2 s'interposer** *vpr* (*se mettre entre*) to come between; (*intervenir*) to intervene

interposition [ɛ̃tɛrpozisjɔ̃] *nf* **(a)** (*intervention*) intervention **(b)** (*situation*) interposition

interprétable [ɛ̃tɛrpretabl] *adj* interpretable; **c'est i. de plusieurs façons** it can be interpreted in several ways

interprétariat [ɛ̃tɛrpretarja] *nm* interpreting

interprétatif, -ive [ɛ̃tɛrpretatif, -iv] *adj* (*note, déclaration*) interpretative, explanatory

interprétation [ɛ̃tɛrpretasjɔ̃] *nf* (*explication*) (*de texte, déclaration, discours, rêves*) interpretation; (*métier*) interpreting; *Mus* interpretation, performance, rendering, rendition; *Th, Cin* interpretation, performance; **selon l'i. que l'on donne au texte** according to the interpretation put on the text, according to how the text is interpreted; **i. erronée** misinterpretation; **donner une i. erronée d'un passage** to misinterpret a passage; **i. d'un contrat** interpretation of a contract; *TV, Cin* **i. visuelle** visual interpretation

interprète [ɛ̃tɛrprɛt] *n* (*dans une autre langue*) interpreter; *Th, Mus, Cin* interpreter, performer; **i. de conférence** conference interpreter; *Th* **les interprètes** the cast; **servir d'i. à qn** *Ling* to act as interpreter to sb, to interpret for sb; (*porte-parole*) to act as sb's spokesman/spokeswoman; **se faire l'i. de qn** to act as sb's spokesman/spokeswoman; **il s'est fait l'i. des paysans auprès du gouvernement** he spoke with the government on behalf of the peasants; **je ne suis que son i.** I'm just passing on what he said

interpréter [ɛ̃tɛrprete] *vt* (**j'interprète; j'interpréterai**) **(a)** *Mus, Th* to perform, to interpret; **un morceau de musique magistralement interprété** a brilliantly performed *or* interpreted piece of music; **i. les grands rôles/Cinna** to perform the great roles/Cinna; **il a interprété tous ses grands succès** he performed all his great hits; **elle va maintenant nous i. un concerto** she will now perform *or* play a concerto for us

(b) (*texte, déclaration, discours, geste, rêves*) to interpret; **ils ont interprété mon silence/son sourire comme ...** they interpreted my silence/his smile as ...; **mal i. les paroles de qn** to misinterpret sb's words; **mal i. un signe** to misread a sign

interpréteur [ɛ̃tɛrpretœr] *nm Ordinat* interpreter; **i. de commande** command interpreter

interprofessionnel, -elle [ɛ̃tɛrprɔfɛsjɔnɛl] *adj* interprofessional

interrègne [ɛ̃tɛrrɛɲ] *nm* interregnum

interrogateur, -trice [ɛ̃tɛrɔgatœr, -tris] **1** *adj* (*air, regard*) questioning, inquiring; **d'un air i.** inquiringly, questioningly **2** *n* questioner, interrogator; *Scol* (oral) examiner

interrogatif, -ive [ɛ̃tɛrɔgatif, -iv] **1** *adj* **(a)** (*air, ton*) inquiring, questioning **(b)** *Gram* (*pronom, phrase etc*) interrogative **2** *nm* [①**A31**; **B15-6**,**C**] *Gram* interrogative (word/pronoun/adjective) **3** *nf Gram* **interrogative** interrogative (clause)

interrogation [ɛ̃tɛrɔgasjɔ̃] *nf* **(a)** (*d'un prisonnier, d'un suspect etc*) questioning, interrogation; **les yeux emplis d'une secrète i.** with secretly enquiring eyes **(b)** (*question*) question; **i. directe/indirecte** direct/indirect question; *Scol* **i. orale/écrite** oral/written test **(c)** *Ordinat* (*d'une base de données*) inquiry, enquiry, query; (*activité*) interrogation; **i. à distance** remote interrogation

interrogativement [ɛ̃tɛrɔgativmɑ̃] *adv* interrogatively, questioningly

interrogatoire [ɛ̃tɛrɔgatwar] *nm Jur* (*de prisonniers, d'inculpé*) questioning, interrogation; (*au tribunal*) cross-examination; **pendant l'i. le témoin a dit ...** under cross-examination, the witness stated ...; **subir un i. en règle** to undergo a thorough questioning *or* interrogation; **faire subir un i. en règle à qn** to question *or* interrogate sb thoroughly

interrogeable [ɛ̃tɛrɔʒabl] *adj Ordinat* **i. en langage naturel** which can be interrogated using natural language; **i. à distance** with a remote interrogation facility; *Tél* **répondeur i. à distance** answering machine with remote-access facility

interroger [ɛ̃tɛrɔʒe] (**j'interrogeai(s); n. interrogeons**) **1** *vt* **(a)** (*de la police*) to question, to interrogate; *Jur* (*au tribunal*) to cross-examine; (*candidat, élève*) to examine; *Mktg* to interview; (*les faits, l'histoire etc*) to consult; (*sa conscience*) to examine; **il m'a longuement interrogé à ton sujet** he asked me a lot of questions about you; **la moitié des personnes interrogées a répondu oui** half the people questioned answered yes; **i. qn du regard** to look at sb questioningly *or* inquiringly, to give sb a questioning *or* an inquiring look; **il a interrogé les élèves oralement/par écrit** he gave the pupils an oral/a written test

(b) *Ordinat* (*base de données*) to query, to interrogate

2 s'interroger *vpr* to ask oneself, to wonder (**sur** about; **si** whether, if)

interrompre [ɛ̃tɛrɔ̃pr] (*conj like* **rompre**) **1** *vt* (*couper la parole à*) to interrupt, to cut in on; (*au cours d'une réunion, au travail etc*) to interrupt; (*conversation, représentation, match etc*) to interrupt; (*trafic*) to hold up, to stop; (*négociations, tournée, traitement médical etc*) to break off; (*voyage*) to break; (*courant d'une rivière etc*) to intercept, to interrupt; *Él* (*courant*) to break, to switch off; **je ne voulais pas vous i. dans votre travail** I didn't want to interrupt you while you were working; **prière de ne pas nous i.** please don't interrupt (us); **le match a été interrompu par la pluie** rain stopped play; *Rad, TV* **nous interrompons nos programmes pour un flash spécial d'information** we interrupt our programmes for a special newsflash; **toutes les nuits, mon sommeil est interrompu par les cris du bébé** every night my sleep is broken by the baby's cries

2 s'interrompre *vpr* to break off, to stop

interrupteur, -trice [ɛ̃tɛryptœr, -tris] **1** *n* interrupter **2** *nm Él* (*commutateur*) switch; **i. marche-arrêt** on-off switch; **i. à bascule** toggle switch; **i. à gradation de lumière** dimmer (switch); **i. d'escalier** two-way switch; *Ordinat* **i. DIP** *ou* **à plusieurs positions** DIP switch; *Aut* **i. d'allumage** ignition cut-off switch, ignition switch; *Aut* **i. de démarrage** starter switch; *Ordinat* **i. à effleurement** touch-sensitive switch

interruption [ɛ̃tɛrypsjɔ̃] *nf* interruption; (*de négociations*) breaking off; *Él* (*de courant*) disconnection, switching off, breaking; **sans i.** (*travailler, parler, lire etc*) without a break, nonstop, continuously; **le magasin sera ouvert de 9h à 22h sans i.** the shop will be open all day from 9 a.m. to 10 p.m.; **des avions cargo assureront le ravitaillement, et ce, sans i.** cargo planes will ensure the continuous provision of fresh supplies; *Rad, TV* **nous nous excusons pour cette i. momentanée de l'image/du son** we apologize for the momentary loss of picture/of sound; *Ordinat* **fonction d'i.** interrupt fonction

▶ **interruption:** *Méd* **i. de grossesse** termination (of pregnancy); *Méd* **i. de grossesse spontanée** spontaneous abortion, miscarriage; *Méd* **i. volontaire de grossesse** voluntary termination of pregnancy

interscolaire [ɛ̃tɛrskɔlɛr] *adj* inter-school

intersecté [ɛ̃tɛrsekte] *adj* **(a)** *Archit* intersecting, interlacing **(b)** *Math* (*ligne etc*) intersected

intersection [ɛ̃tɛrseksjɔ̃] *nf* intersection, junction; **à l'i. des deux rues** at the junction of the two streets, where the two streets meet; **à l'i. de deux écoles de pensée** where two schools of thought converge; **point d'i.** point of intersection

intersidéral, -ale, -aux, -ales [ɛ̃tɛrsideral, -o] *adj* intersidereal, interstellar; **l'espace i.** outer space

interstellaire [ɛ̃tɛrstelɛr] *adj Astron* interstellar; **l'espace i.** outer space

interstice [ɛ̃tɛrstis] *nm* chink, crack, *Fml* interstice

interstitiel, -ielle [ɛ̃tɛrstisjɛl] *adj* interstitial

intersyndical, -ale, -aux, -ales [ɛ̃tɛrsɛ̃dikal, -o] **1** *adj* interunion **2** *nf* **intersyndicale** interunion group; (*réunion*) interunion meeting

intertexte [ɛ̃tɛrtɛkst] *nm Littér* intertext

intertextualité [ɛ̃tɛrtɛkstɥalite] *nf Littér* intertextuality

intertitre [ɛ̃tɛrtitr] *nm Journ* subheading, crosshead; *Cin* caption, subtitle

intertropical, -ale, -aux, -ales [ɛ̃tɛrtrɔpikal, -o] *adj* intertropical

interurbain [ɛ̃tɛryrbɛ̃] **1** *adj* interurban; *Tél Vieilli* **lignes interurbaines** long-distance *or Br* trunk lines; **c'est pour une communication interurbaine?** is it a long-distance *or Br* trunk call? **2** *nm Tél Vieilli* long-distance *or Br* trunk service; **il faut passer par l'i.** you have to go through the long-distance operator

intervalle [ɛ̃tɛrval] *nm* **(a)** (*dans le temps*) interval; **un i. d'une heure** an hour's interval, an interval of an hour, a one-hour interval; **visites à de longs intervalles** visits at long intervals; **à intervalles réguliers** at regular intervals; **à deux mois d'i.** two months apart; **par intervalles** at intervals, now and then; **dans l'i.** in the meantime, meanwhile

(b) *(dans l'espace, entre des paragraphes etc)* gap, space; *Mus* interval; **à deux mètres d'i.** two metres apart; **laissez deux mètres d'i. entre chaque piquet** leave a gap *or* space of two metres *or* a two-metre gap *or* space between each stake

(c) *Math* interval; **i. ouvert/fermé** open/closed interval

intervenant, -ante [ɛ̃tɛrvənɑ̃, -ɑ̃t] **1** *adj Jur* intervening **2** *n* **(a)** *Jur* intervening party **(b)** *(dans une conférence, un débat)* participant, contributor

intervenir [ɛ̃tɛrvənir] *vi (conj like* **venir**, *aux* **être) (a)** *(agir)* to intervene **(dans** in); *(dans une discussion, un débat)* to intervene **(dans** in), to cut in **(dans** on); **i. pour faire qch** to intervene *or* step in to do sth; **elle va i. en ta faveur** she will intervene *or* intercede on your behalf; **i. auprès de qn** to intercede with sb; **au besoin, je pourrais i.** I could intervene if necessary; **faire i. la force armée** to call out the military, to bring in the army

(b) *(arriver) (de facteurs, d'éléments, de considérations)* to arise, to come up; **un accord est intervenu** an agreement has been reached; **les changements intervenus depuis 1981** the changes that have occurred since 1981

(c) *(jouer un rôle)* to play a part **(dans** in); **ces facteurs n'interviennent pas dans le processus de l'inflation** those factors have no effect *or* bearing on the rise in inflation

(d) *Méd* to operate

intervention [ɛ̃tɛrvɑ̃sjɔ̃] *nf* **(a)** *(dans une crise etc)* intervention; **i. divine** divine intervention; **i. en faveur de qn** intervention on behalf of sb; **i. auprès de qn** intervention with sb; **par son i.** through his intervention; **offre d'i.** offer of mediation; **il a fallu l'i. de la police pour séparer les deux hordes de supporters** the police had to intervene *or* step in to separate the two hordes of supporters; **i. de l'État** state intervention; *Mil, Av* **i. aérienne** air strike

(b) *(prise de parole)* intervention; **l'i. du premier ministre à l'Assemblée nationale** the Prime Minister's speech to the National Assembly

(c) *Méd* **i. (chirurgicale)** operation, surgery

(d) *CE* **prix d'i.** intervention price

interventionnisme [ɛ̃tɛrvɑ̃sjɔnism] *nm Pol* interventionism

interventionniste [ɛ̃tɛrvɑ̃sjɔnist] *adj, n Pol* interventionist

interversion [ɛ̃tɛrvɛrsjɔ̃] *nf (de termes, dates etc)* inversion, transposition, reversal

intervertébral, -ale, -aux, -ales [ɛ̃tɛrvɛrtebral, -o] *adj Anat* intervertebral; **disque i.** (intervertebral) disc

intervertir [ɛ̃tɛrvɛrtir] *vt (l'ordre de qch)* to invert, to reverse; *(objets, éléments)* to switch (round); **maintenant les rôles sont intervertis** now the roles are reversed

interview [ɛ̃tɛrvju] *nf* interview; **i.-déclaration** interpretative interview; **i.-document** documentary interview; **i.-explanation** interpretative interview; **i. question-réponse** question-and-answer interview; **i. téléphonique** telephone interview; **i.-témoignage** informational interview

interviewé, -ée [ɛ̃tɛrvjuve] *n* interviewee

interviewer [ɛ̃tɛrvjuve] *vt* to interview

intervieweu(u)r [ɛ̃tɛrvjuvœr] *nm* interviewer

intervocalique [ɛ̃tɛrvɔkalik] *adj Ling* intervocalic

intestat [ɛ̃tɛsta] *adj inv Jur* **mourir i.** to die intestate

intestin¹ [ɛ̃tɛstɛ̃] *adj* internal; *(guerre)* internecine; **luttes intestines** infighting

intestin² *nm Anat* intestine; **intestins** intestines, bowels; **gros i.** large intestine; **i. grêle** small intestine

intestinal, -ale, -aux, -ales [ɛ̃tɛstinal, -o] *adj* intestinal

intifada [intifada] *nf* intifada

intimation [ɛ̃timasjɔ̃] *nf Jur* notification; *(citation devant un tribunal)* summons; **i. de vider les lieux** notice to quit

intime [ɛ̃tim] **1** *adj (relations, endroit, atmosphère etc)* intimate; *(pièce)* cosy; *(dîner, fête)* intimate, quiet; *(ami)* intimate, close; **être i. avec qn** to be close to sb, to be intimate with sb; **hygiène** *ou* **toilette i.** personal hygiene; **avoir la conviction i. de qch** to be thoroughly convinced of sth; **elle a l'i. conviction** *ou* **la conviction i. que …** she is thoroughly convinced that …; **pensées intimes** intimate *or* inmost *or* innermost thoughts; **journal i.** (private *or* personal) diary; *Phys* **la structure i. de la matière** the intimate *or* innermost structure of matter

2 *n* close *or* intimate friend, intimate; **Solange, Sosso pour les intimes** Solange, Sosso to my/her friends

intimé, -ée [ɛ̃time] *n Jur* respondent, defendant

intimement [ɛ̃timmɑ̃] *adv* intimately; **i. liés** *(amis)* very close; *(phénomènes)* closely *or* intimately linked; **je suis i. persuadé que …** I'm thoroughly convinced that …

intimer [ɛ̃time] *vt* **(a) i. à qn l'ordre de faire qch** to order sb to do sth **(b)** *Jur* **i. qn** to summons sb to appear before the Court of Appeal

intimidable [ɛ̃timidabl] *adj* easily intimidated; **ce n'est pas qn de facilement i.** he's/she's not someone to be *or* who can be easily intimidated

intimidant [ɛ̃timidɑ̃] *adj* intimidating

intimidateur, -trice [ɛ̃timidatœr, -tris] *adj (paroles, propos)* intimidating

intimidation [ɛ̃timidasjɔ̃] *nf* intimidation; **ils ont usé d'i. pour lui faire signer la déclaration** they intimidated him into signing *or* used intimidation to make him sign the declaration

intimider [ɛ̃timide] *vt (effrayer)* to intimidate; *surtout Jur* to exert undue influence on; **elle ne se laisse pas facilement i.** she is not easily intimidated; **nullement intimidé** nothing daunted

intimisme [ɛ̃timism] *nm Littér, Beaux-Arts* intimism

intimiste [ɛ̃timist] *adj, n Littér, Beaux-Arts* intimist

intimité [ɛ̃timite] *nf* **(a)** *(vie privée)* privacy; *(entre amis)* intimacy, closeness; **dans l'i.** in private (life); **dans l'i. de notre foyer** in the privacy of our own home; **dans l'i. conjugale** in one's private married life; **il vit dans l'i. des grands de ce monde** he is on close *or* intimate terms with people in high places; **le mariage a été célébré dans la plus stricte i.** only close family attended the wedding **(b) dans l'i. de son être** in the depths of one's being; **dans l'i. de sa conscience** in one's innermost conscience, in the depths of one's conscience

intitulé [ɛ̃tityle] *nm (de document, livre etc)* title; *(de chapitre)* heading, title; *(d'un article)* catchline; **i. de compte** account particulars

intituler [ɛ̃tityle] **1** *vt (livre, film, opéra)* to give a title to; **livre intitulé …** book entitled …, book with the title of …; **article intitulé …** article headed …, article with the heading …; **pourquoi avez-vous intitulé votre livre 'Colère'?** why did you give your book the title 'Anger'?, why did you call your book 'Anger'? **2 s'intituler** *vpr (de livre, morceau de musique etc)* to be entitled, to be called; *(de personne)* to call oneself; **ce livre s'intitule 'Reflets'** this book is entitled *or* called 'Reflections'

intolérable [ɛ̃tɔlerabl] *adj* intolerable, insufferable

intolérablement [ɛ̃tɔlerabləmɑ̃] *adv* intolerably

intolérance [ɛ̃tɔlerɑ̃s] *nf* intolerance; *Méd* **i. à une substance** intolerance to a substance

intolérant [ɛ̃tɔlerɑ̃] *adj* intolerant

intonation [ɛ̃tɔnasjɔ̃] *nf* intonation; **une voix aux intonations très douces** a very soft voice

intouchable [ɛ̃tuʃabl] *adj, n* untouchable

intox [ɛ̃tɔks] *nf Pol F* brainwashing; *(par la presse)* managed news

intoxicant [ɛ̃tɔksikɑ̃] *adj Méd* poisonous, toxic

intoxication [ɛ̃tɔksikasjɔ̃] *nf Méd* poisoning; *Fig F* indoctrination, brainwashing; **i. alimentaire** food poisoning

intoxiqué, -ée [ɛ̃tɔksike] *n* addict

intoxiquer [ɛ̃tɔksike] **1** *vt Méd* to poison; *F* **les médias intoxiquent le public** the media indoctrinate *or* brainwash people; **intoxiqué par la publicité** brainwashed by advertising **2 s'intoxiquer** *vpr* to poison oneself; **il s'est intoxiqué avec des champignons** he got food poisoning from (eating) mushrooms

intracellulaire [ɛ̃traselylɛr] *adj Biol* intracellular

intradermique [ɛ̃tradɛrmik] *Méd* **1** *adj* intradermic, intradermal **2** *nf* intradermic *or* intradermal injection

intrados [ɛ̃trado] *nm Archit (d'une voûte)* intrados; *Av (d'une aile)* undersurface

intraduisible [ɛ̃tradɥizibl] *adj* untranslatable

intraitable [ɛ̃trɛtabl] *adj* uncompromising, inflexible; **il est i. sur le chapitre de la propreté** he is a stickler for cleanliness, he is uncompromising *or* inflexible where cleanliness is concerned

intra-muros [ɛ̃tramyros] *adv (habiter)* within the town/city, in the town/city itself; **Londres/Paris i.** inner London/Paris

intramusculaire [ɛ̃tramyskylɛr] *Méd* **1** *adj* intramuscular **2** *nf* intramuscular injection

intransigeance [ɛ̃trɑ̃ziʒɑ̃s] *nf* intransigence; **faire preuve d'i.** to be intransigent *or* uncompromising

intransigeant, -ante [ɛ̃trɑ̃ziʒɑ̃, -ɑ̃t] **1** *adj (personne)* intransigent, uncompromising, inflexible; *(code moral, ligne de conduite)* uncompromising, strict; *(ton)* peremptory; **il est très i. avec les gens qui ne pensent pas exactement comme lui** he takes a hard line with those who don't exactly share his views **2** *n Pol* hardliner, intransigent

intransitif, -ive [ɛ̃trɑ̃zitif, -iv] *adj, nm Gram* intransitive

intransitivement [ɛ̃trɑ̃zitivmɑ̃] *adv Gram* intransitively

intransitivité [ɛ̃trɑ̃zitivite] *nf Gram* intransitivity

intransmissible [ɛ̃trɑ̃smisibl] *adj* intransmissible, untransferable

intransportable [ɛ̃trɑ̃spɔrtabl] *adj (objet)* untransportable; *(blessé)* unfit to travel

intra-utérin [ɛ̃trayterɛ̃], *pl* **intra-utérins, -rines** *adj Anat* intra-uterine; **la vie i.** life in the womb

intraveineux, -euse [ɛ̃travɛnø, -øz] *Méd* **1** *adj* intravenous **2** *nf* **intraveineuse** intravenous injection

intrépide [ɛ̃trepid] **1** *adj* **(a)** *(courageux)* intrepid, fearless **(b)** *(que rien ne rebute)* **buveur i.** hardened drinker; **menteur i.** barefaced liar **2** *n* fearless *or* intrepid person

intrépidement [ɛ̃trepidmɑ̃] *adv* fearlessly, intrepidly

intrépidité [ɛ̃trepidite] *nf* fearlessness, intrepidity; **avec i.** fearlessly, intrepidly

intrigant, -ante [ɛ̃trigɑ̃, -ɑ̃t] **1** *adj* scheming, plotting, conniving **2** *n* schemer, intriguer

intrigue [ɛ̃trig] *nf* *(machination)* intrigue; *(liaison amoureuse)* (love) affair, intrigue; *Th, Cin, Littér* plot; **déjouer/ourdir une i.** to foil/hatch a plot

intriguer [ɛ̃trige] **1** *vt* to intrigue **2** *vi* to scheme, to intrigue

intrinsèque [ɛ̃trɛ̃sɛk] *adj* intrinsic

intrinsèquement [ɛ̃trɛ̃sɛkmɑ̃] *adv* intrinsically

intro [ɛ̃tro] *nf F* intro; *(musicale)* theme tune

introducteur, -trice [ɛ̃trɔdyktœr, -tris] *n* *(d'une mode, d'un courant)* initiator; **il fut l'i. du tabac en France** he introduced tobacco (in)to France; **il fut mon i. auprès de la comtesse** he introduced me to the countess; *Ordinat* **i. feuille à feuille** sheet feeder; *Ordinat* **i. manuel** manual feed

introductif, -ive [ɛ̃trɔdyktif, -iv] *adj Jur* introductory

introduction [ɛ̃trɔdyksjɔ̃] *nf* **(a)** *(d'un livre, d'une dissertation, d'un morceau de musique)* introduction; *TV etc* introduction, lead-in; **quelques mots/pages d'i.** a few introductory words/ pages, a few words/pages of introduction

(b) *(de nouvelles techniques, du suffrage universel etc)* introduction

(c) *(présentation)* introduction; **ce roman constitue une bonne i. à la littérature russe** this novel is a good introduction to Russian literature; **après mon i. auprès de quelques personnages influents** after I was introduced to a few influential people; **lettre d'i.** letter of introduction **(de la part de** from; **auprès de** to)

(d) *(insertion)* insertion, *Fml* introduction **(dans** into)

(e) *Rugby* put-in

▶ **introduction: i. en Bourse** listing on the stock market

introduire [ɛ̃trɔdɥir] *(prp* **introduisant**; *pp* **introduit**; *pr ind* **j'introduis, il introduit, n. introduisons**; *p hist* **j'introduisis**; *fu* **j'introduirai)** **1** *vt* *(coutume, réforme, mesures etc)* to introduce; *(clé dans une serrure, doigt dans un trou etc)* to insert, to put, *Fml* to introduce **(dans** into); *Ordinat* *(données)* to enter, to input; *(marchandises)* to bring in; *(mode)* to introduce, to initiate; *(étranger, visiteur)* to show in, to usher in; **i. des marchandises en contrebande dans un pays** to smuggle goods into a country, to bring goods illegally into a country; **i. le tabac/la mode des cheveux longs en France** to introduce tobacco/the fashion for long hair (in)to France; **introduisez ce monsieur** show the gentleman in; **il fut introduit dans une salle d'attente** he was shown into a waiting room; **i. qn auprès de qn** to show sb in to see sb; *(présenter)* to introduce sb to sb; **il est bien introduit dans les milieux de la finance** he is well established *or* has a firm foothold in the financial world; **i. en Bourse** to list on the stock market, to introduce on the Stock Exchange; **i. sur le marché** to bring onto the market, to launch; **i. une action en justice** to start legal proceedings, to bring action; **i. une instance** to start legal proceedings

2 s'introduire *vpr* **s'i. dans une maison** *(d'un intrus)* to get into *or* enter a house; **s'i. dans un tunnel/tuyau** to work *or* worm one's way into a tunnel/pipe; **s'i. dans un club très fermé** to get into a very exclusive club; **l'eau s'introduit partout** water is getting in everywhere

intromission [ɛ̃trɔmisjɔ̃] *nf* intromission

intronisation [ɛ̃trɔnizasjɔ̃] *nf* **(a)** *(d'un évêque, d'un roi)* enthronement, enthroning **(b)** *(d'un système, d'une politique nouvelle)* establishment

introniser [ɛ̃trɔnize] *vt* *(roi, évêque)* to enthrone

introspectif, -ive [ɛ̃trɔspɛktif, -iv] *adj* introspective

introspection [ɛ̃trɔspɛksjɔ̃] *nf* introspection

introuvable [ɛ̃truvabl] *adj* *(produit, denrées)* unobtainable; **mes clés sont introuvables** my keys are nowhere to be found, I can't find my keys anywhere; **l'assassin reste i.** the murderer is still at large *or* still hasn't been found

introversion [ɛ̃trɔvɛrsjɔ̃] *nf Psy* introversion

introverti, -ie [ɛ̃trɔvɛrti] *Psy* **1** *adj* introverted **2** *n* introvert

intrus, -use [ɛ̃try, -yz] *n aussi Ordinat* intruder; *(dans une réception, une soirée)* gatecrasher; *Jur* trespasser

intrusion [ɛ̃tryzjɔ̃] *nf* intrusion; *(dans une affaire)* interference **(dans** in), intrusion **(dans** into); **il fit i. dans la salle en plein milieu de la réunion** he came into the room and interrupted the meeting; *Géol* **roches d'i.** intrusive rocks

intubation [ɛ̃tybasjɔ̃] *nf Méd* intubation

intuber [ɛ̃tybe] *vti* to intubate

intuitif, -ive [ɛ̃tɥitif, -iv] **1** *adj* intuitive **2** *n* **c'est un i.** he's an intuitive sort *or* person

intuition [ɛ̃tɥisjɔ̃] *nf* intuition; **par i.** intuitively, by intuition; **avoir une i.** to have an intuition; **avoir l'i. que ...** to have a hunch *or* a feeling that ...

intuitivement [ɛ̃tɥitivmɑ̃] *adv* intuitively

intuitivité [ɛ̃t ɥitivite] *nf Ordinat* *(de logiciel, interface)* intuitiveness

intumescence [ɛ̃tymɛsɑ̃s] *nf* intumescence

intumescent [ɛ̃tymɛsɑ̃] *adj* intumescent

inusable [inyzabl] *adj* *(souliers, veste, tissu, ustensile, thème, explication)* hard-wearing; **ces chaussures sont pratiquement inusables** these shoes will last for ever *or* never wear out

inusité [inyzite] *adj* *(mots)* uncommon, not in common use; *Rare* *(bruit, sensation, parfum etc)* unusual

inutile [inytil] *adj* *(qui ne sert à rien)* useless; *(effort)* vain, pointless, useless; *(non nécessaire)* *(précautions, démarche)* pointless, unnecessary; *(bagages)* unnecessary; **je suis i. ici** I'm (of) no use here; **c'est i.!** it's pointless!; *(ce n'est pas la peine)* you needn't bother; **bouches inutiles** unproductive people; **i. de dire que ...** needless to say ...; **i. de vous dire que ...** I don't have to tell you that ...; **i. d'attendre/de retenir** it's pointless waiting/booking, there's no point in waiting/booking; **i. d'insister, je ne viens pas, un point, c'est tout** don't go on about it, I'm not coming and that's that; **c'est complètement i. de lui demander, jamais il n'acceptera** it's totally pointless asking him *or* there's absolutely no point in asking him, he'll never accept; **il n'est pas i. de préciser que ...** it is useful to point out that ...; **quelques leçons particulières ne seraient pas inutiles** a few private lessons wouldn't go amiss *or* would be useful

inutilement [inytilmɑ̃] *adv* needlessly, unnecessarily; **se déranger i.** to put oneself out needlessly *or* unnecessarily, to go to unnecessary trouble; **c'est i. que je lui ai parlé** it was pointless talking to him, talking to him served no purpose

inutilisable [inytilizabl] *adj* unusable, useless; **sans la prise adéquate, cet appareil est i.** without the right plug this machine is useless; **ces statistiques sont trop vieilles, elles sont inutilisables** these statistics are too old, they are unusable

inutilisé [inytilize] *adj* unused; *(ressources, talent)* untapped, unused

inutilité [inytilite] *nf* uselessness, pointlessness, needlessness

invaincu [ɛ̃vɛ̃ky] *adj* *(pays)* unconquered, undefeated; *(armée)* unvanquished, undefeated; *Sp* unbeaten, undefeated

invalidant [ɛ̃validɑ̃] *adj* incapacitating, disabling

invalidation [ɛ̃validasjɔ̃] *nf Jur* *(de document, d'élection)* invalidation; *(d'un membre élu)* unseating

invalide [ɛ̃valid] **1** *adj* *(personne)* disabled; *Jur Vieilli* *(loi, mariage etc)* invalid **2** *n* disabled person, invalid; **les grands invalides** the severely disabled

▶ **invalide: i. de guerre** disabled *or* invalid ex-serviceman/ex-servicewoman; **i. du travail** = person disabled in an industrial accident

invalider [ɛ̃valide] *vt Jur* *(testament, élection etc)* to invalidate; *(membre élu)* to unseat

invalidité [ɛ̃validite] *nf* *(de personne)* disability, invalidity; *(d'une procédure, d'un contrat etc)* invalidity; **pension d'i.** disability pension

invariabilité [ɛ̃varjabilite] *nf* invariability

invariable [ɛ̃varjabl] *adj* invariable, unvarying; *Gram* invariable; **être i. dans ses opinions** to be unwavering in one's opinions

invariablement [ɛ̃varjabləmɑ̃] *adv* invariably

invasif, -ive [ɛ̃vazif, -iv] *adj Méd* *(traitement)* invasive

invasion [ɛ̃vazjɔ̃] *nf* invasion; **i. de sauterelles** invasion of locusts; *Fig* **l'i. des touristes** the tourist invasion

invective [ɛ̃vɛktiv] *nf* invective; **invectives** abuse; **se répandre en invectives contre** to let out *or* let loose a stream of abuse at

invectiver [ɛ̃vɛktive] **1** *vi* **i. contre qn** to inveigh *or* rail against sb **2** *vt* *(qn)* to hurl abuse at; **il s'est fait i. par des manifestants** he had abuse hurled at him by the demonstrators

invendable [ɛ̃vɑ̃dabl] *adj* unsaleable, unsellable

invendu [ɛ̃vɑ̃dy] **1** *adj* unsold **2** *nm* **invendus** unsold goods; *(journaux)* unsold copies; *(livres)* unsold copies; *(revendus moins cher)* remainders

inventaire [ɛ̃vɑ̃tɛr] *nm* **(a)** *(liste)* inventory; **faire** *ou* **dresser un i.** to draw up *or* make an inventory; **sous bénéfice d'i.** conditionally, with reservations; *Jur* **accepter une succession sous bénéfice d'i.** to accept an estate without liability to debts beyond the assets descended

(b) *Com* stocklist, inventory; **(établissement** *ou* **levée d')i.** stocktaking; **faire** *ou* **dresser l'i.** to take stock, to stocktake; **fermé pour cause d'i.** closed for stocktaking; *Compta* **i. comptable** book inventory; **i. de stock** physical inventory; **i. des marchandises** inventory of goods; **i. effectif** physical inventory; **i. intermittent** periodical inventory; **i. permanent** perpetual inventory; **i. physique** physical inventory; **i. théorique** theoretical inventory

(c) (*de monuments anciens, peintures, richesses artistiques*) survey

inventer [ɛ̃vɑ̃te] **1** *vt* (*machine etc*) to invent, to devise; (*imaginer*) (*concept, moyen*) to think up, to dream up; (*histoire, excuse*) to make up, to think up; (*expression*) to coin; *F* **il n'a pas inventé la poudre** *ou* **l'eau chaude** *ou* **l'eau tiède** *ou* **le fil à couper le beurre** he'll never set the Thames on fire; **il ne sait plus quoi i. pour la distraire** he doesn't know what else he can think up *or* dream up to keep her amused; **non, il ne dit pas de mal de toi derrière ton dos, qu'est-ce que tu vas i.?** no, he doesn't criticize you behind your back, you're making it (all) up!; **mais qu'est-ce qu'il va i. là?** what's he on about?; **cette histoire a été inventée de toutes pièces** this story has been completely fabricated *or* is a complete fabrication; **i. de faire qch** to hit on the idea of doing sth; **je n'invente rien** (*c'est vrai*) I'm not making anything up

2 s'inventer *vpr* **ça ne s'invente pas** (*ce don etc*) you've either got it or you haven't; (*des détails comme ça etc*) you can't make something like that up; **il s'inventa un nouveau passé** he invented a new past for himself

inventeur, -trice [ɛ̃vɑ̃tœr, -tris] *n* **(a)** (*d'une machine, d'un processus etc*) inventor **(b)** *Jur* (*d'un objet perdu*) finder

inventif, -ive [ɛ̃vɑ̃tif, -iv] *adj* inventive

invention [ɛ̃vɑ̃sjɔ̃] *nf* **(a)** (*action*) invention, inventing; (*faculté*) inventiveness, invention; **nécessité est mère d'i.** necessity is the mother of invention; **c'est encore une plaisanterie de son i.!** it's another one of his jokes! **(b)** (*découverte*) invention; (*mensonge*) fabrication, invention; **brevet d'i.** patent (*for an invention*); **pure i. (que) tout cela!** that's sheer fabrication *or* invention!; **i. de produit** product invention; *Mktg* **i. rétrograde** backward invention **(c)** *Jur* **i. d'un trésor** finding of treasure trove

inventivité [ɛ̃vɑ̃tivite] *nf* inventiveness

inventorier [ɛ̃vɑ̃tɔrje] *vt* (*marchandises*) to make an inventory of, to inventory

invérifiable [ɛ̃verifjabl] *adj* unverifiable, uncheckable

inverse [ɛ̃vɛrs] **1** *adj* inverse; **en sens i. (de qch)** in the opposite direction (to sth); **dans l'ordre i.** in (the) reverse order; **dans le sens i. des aiguilles d'une montre** *Br* anticlockwise, *Am* counterclockwise; *Math* **en raison i. de qch** in inverse proportion to sth; *Math* **fonction i.** inverse function

2 *nm* **(a) l'i.** the opposite, the reverse; **faire l'i.** to do the opposite *or* the reverse **(de** of**)**; **c'est parce qu'il était déprimé qu'il s'est mis à boire et non l'i.** he started drinking because he was depressed and not the other way round *or* and not vice versa; **dans mon cas, c'est l'i. qui se passe** it's the reverse *or* the opposite in my case; **c'est quelqu'un de très renfermé, à l'i., son frère est très exubérant** he's very withdrawn, whereas his brother is very exuberant; **à l'i. de** unlike; **à l'inverse de ce que nous avions prévu** contrary to our predictions

(b) *Math* **l'i. d'un nombre** the inverse *or* reciprocal of a number

inversé [ɛ̃vɛrse] *adj Ordinat* inverse; **vidéo inversée** reverse video

inversement [ɛ̃vɛrsəmɑ̃] *adv Math* inversely; *Fig* conversely; **… ou i.** … or the other way round, … or vice versa

inverser [ɛ̃vɛrse] *vt* (*ordre*) to reverse, to invert; (*deux mots d'une phrase*) to invert, to change round; (*tendance*) to reverse; *Él* (*courant*) to reverse; (*dans l'impression*) to reverse out; **carburateur inversé** down-draught carburettor

inverseur [ɛ̃vɛrsœr] *nm* reverser, reversing device; *Él* **i. du courant** current reverser, change-over switch

inversion [ɛ̃vɛrsjɔ̃] *nf* **(a)** [(i)A72-3,17] *Gram, Mus etc* inversion **(b)** (*du courant électrique*) reversal, reversing; **i. de marche** reverse gear; **i. de chiffres** inversion of figures; *Ordinat* **i. vidéo** reverse video **(c)** *Psy* inversion

invertébré [ɛ̃vɛrtebre] *adj, nm* invertebrate; **les invertébrés** the invertebrates, *Spéc* the Invertebrata

inverti, -ie [ɛ̃vɛrti] **1** *adj* **sucre i.** inverted sugar **2** *n* homosexual, *Fml* invert

invertir [ɛ̃vɛrtir] *vt* (*chiffres*) to invert

investigateur, -trice [ɛ̃vɛstigatœr, -tris] **1** *adj* investigative; (*regard*) searching, inquiring **2** *n* investigator

investigation [ɛ̃vɛstigasjɔ̃] *nf* investigation

investir [ɛ̃vɛstir] **1** *vt* **(a)** (*argent, Fig temps, énergie*) to invest **(dans** in**)** **(b)** (*encercler*) (*ville, édifice*) to besiege, to encircle; (*occuper*) (*ville, pays, bâtiment, locaux*) to occupy **(c) i. qn d'une fonction** to invest *or* vest sb with an office; **i. qn d'une mission** to entrust sb with a mission **2** *vi Fin* to invest **(dans** in**)**; **i. à court terme** to make a short-term investment; **i. à long terme** to make a long-term investment **3 s'investir** *vpr* **il ne s'investit pas assez dans son travail** he doesn't put enough effort into his work; **il s'investit beaucoup dans son club de théâtre** he puts a lot of time and effort into his drama club

investissement [ɛ̃vɛstismɑ̃] *nm* **(a)** *Fin, Psy* investment; (*action*) investing; **i. de l'étranger** inward investment; **i. à l'étranger** outward *or* overseas *or* foreign investment; **i. de capitaux** capital investment; **i. direct** direct investment; **i. à court terme** short-term investment; **investissements productifs** interest-bearing investments **(b)** (*encerclement*) (*d'une ville, d'un édifice*) besieging, encircling; (*occupation*) occupation

investisseur [ɛ̃vɛstisœr] *nm Fin* investor; **i. institutionnel** institutional investor; **i. privé** private investor

investiture [ɛ̃vɛstityr] *nf* investiture; (*d'un évêque*) induction, investiture; *Pol* (*d'un candidat*) nomination

invétéré [ɛ̃vetere] *adj* **(a)** (*haine, manie, orgueil etc*) inveterate, deeply rooted **(b)** (*ivrogne, criminel, menteur*) inveterate, confirmed, habitual

invincibilité [ɛ̃vɛ̃sibilite] *nf* invincibility

invincible [ɛ̃vɛ̃sibl] *adj* (*armée, adversaire etc*) invincible; (*courage*) invincible, indomitable; (*difficulté, obstacle*) insuperable, insurmountable

invinciblement [ɛ̃vɛ̃sibləmɑ̃] *adv* invincibly

inviolabilité [ɛ̃vjɔlabilite] *nf* inviolability; (*d'un office*) immunity, inviolability; **i. diplomatique** diplomatic immunity

inviolable [ɛ̃vjɔlabl] *adj* inviolable; (*office*) immune, inviolable

inviolé [ɛ̃vjɔle] *adj Litt* inviolate, inviolated; (*sommet*) unconquered; (*forêt*) virgin

invisibilité [ɛ̃vizibilite] *nf* invisibility

invisible [ɛ̃vizibl] **1** *adj* invisible; *Fig* **il restait i.** he was nowhere to be seen; **un danger i.** a hidden danger **2** *nm* **l'i.** the invisible

invisiblement [ɛ̃viziblәmɑ̃] *adv* invisibly

invitant [ɛ̃vitɑ̃] *adj* attractive, inviting; **gouvernement i.** host country

invitation [ɛ̃vitasjɔ̃] *nf* invitation; **venir sur l'i. de qn** to come at sb's invitation; **venir sans i.** to come uninvited; **lettre d'i.** letter of invitation; **carton d'i.** invitation card; **envoyer une i. à qn** to send sb an invitation; **une i. à dîner** an invitation to dinner; **être une i. à la réflexion** to be thought-provoking; **ce roman est une i. au voyage** this novel takes you out of yourself

invite [ɛ̃vit] *nf* **(a)** invitation; **répondre à l'i. de qn** to respond to sb's advances **(b)** *Ordinat* prompt; **i. du DOS** DOS prompt; **i. du système** system prompt

invité, -ée [ɛ̃vite] *n* guest

inviter [ɛ̃vite] **1** *vt* **(a)** (*convier*) to invite; **i. qn à dîner** to invite *or* ask sb to dinner; **elle m'a invité à aller avec elle au théâtre** she invited me (to go) to the theatre with her; **personne ne l'invite jamais à sortir** no one ever asks her out; **être déjà invité** to have a previous engagement

(b) (*inciter*) **i. qn à faire qch** to ask sb to do sth; **j'invite tous les locataires à signer la pétition** I urge all tenants to sign the petition; **les passagers à destination de Rome sont invités à se présenter à la porte d'embarquement numéro deux** passengers for Rome are requested to proceed to gate number two; **i. qn à entrer** to ask sb (to come) in; **d'un geste de la tête, il m'invita à le suivre** he motioned with his head that I should follow him; **i. à la réflexion** to be thought-provoking; **tout l'invitait à partir** everything indicated *or* suggested to him that he should leave

2 *vi* (*payer*) **ce soir, c'est moi qui invite!** it's my treat this evening!, I'm paying this evening!

3 s'inviter *vpr* to invite oneself; **s'i. à dîner** to invite oneself to dinner

in vitro [vitro] *adv, adj* in vitro; **fécondation i.** in vitro fertilization

invivable [ɛ̃vivabl] *adj* unbearable, intolerable; (*existence*) not worth living, unbearable; *F* (*personne*) impossible to live with, unbearable

in vivo [vivo] *adj, adv* in vivo

invocation [ɛ̃vɔkasjɔ̃] *nf* invocation

invocatoire [ɛ̃vɔkatwar] *adj Litt* invocatory

involontaire [ɛ̃vɔlɔ̃tɛr] *adj* **(a)** (*machinal*) (*mouvement, geste etc*) involuntary **(b)** (*pas intentionnel*) (*erreur, réaction etc*) unintentional; **le témoin i. d'une scène de ménage** the unwilling witness of a domestic dispute

involontairement [ɛ̃vɔlɔ̃tɛrmɑ̃] *adv* involuntarily; (*vexer qn*) unintentionally; **je lui ai i. donné des renseignements confidentiels sur le projet** I unwittingly gave him confidential information about the project
involution [ɛ̃vɔlysjɔ̃] *nf* involution
invoquer [ɛ̃vɔke] *vt* (**a**) (*raison, prétexte*) to put forward; (*loi, texte*) to refer to; **il a invoqué l'étourderie/la maladresse pour expliquer son erreur** he pleaded absentmindedness/clumsiness to explain his mistake (**b**) (*Dieu, divinité*) to call upon, to invoke; (*esprit*) to invoke, to call forth; **i. l'aide de la justice** to appeal to the law; **i. l'aide de ses amis** to call upon the help of one's friends
invraisemblable [ɛ̃vrɛsɑ̃blabl] *adj* unlikely, improbable; (*excuses, alibi*) implausible; (*aventure*) incredible, unbelievable; **histoire i.** tall *or* unlikely story; **chapeau i.** incredible hat; **ces gens-là sont invraisemblables** those people are extraordinary *or* incredible
invraisemblablement [ɛ̃vrɛsɑ̃blabləmɑ̃] *adv* incredibly, improbably
invraisemblance [ɛ̃vrɛsɑ̃blɑ̃s] *nf* (**a**) (*improbabilité*) unlikelihood, unlikeliness, improbability; (*d'un récit, d'alibi*) implausibility (**b**) (*dans une déclaration etc*) implausibility
invulnérabilité [ɛ̃vylnerabilite] *nf* invulnerability
invulnérable [ɛ̃vylnerabl] *adj* invulnerable; **i. à la fatigue** immune to fatigue; **i. à l'injure** immune *or* impervious to insults
iode [jɔd] *nm* iodine; **teinture d'i.** tincture of iodine; **lampe à i.** halogen lamp
iodé [jɔde] *adj* (*eau, air*) iodized
ioder [jɔde] *vt* to iodize
iodique [jɔdik] *adj Ch* iodic
iodler [jɔdle] *vi* to yodel
iodoforme [jɔdɔfɔrm] *nm Ch* iodoform
iodure [jɔdyr] *nm Ch* iodide
ion [jɔ̃] *nm Phys* ion
ionien, -ienne [jɔnjɛ̃, -jɛn] **1** *adj* Ionian; (*dialecte*) Ionic **2** *n* **I.** Ionian
ionique¹ [jɔnik] *adj Archit* (*ordre*) Ionic
ionique² *adj Phys* ionic; **accélération i.** ion acceleration
ionisant [jɔnizɑ̃] *adj Phys* ionizing
ionisation [jɔnizasjɔ̃] *nf Phys* ionization
ioniser [jɔnize] *vt Phys, Ch* to ionize
ionosphère [jɔnɔsfɛr] *nf* ionosphere
iota [jɔta] *nm* iota; *F* **on n'y a pas changé un i.** not an iota of it has been changed; **j'ai accepté de faire des compromis mais lui n'a pas bougé d'un i.** I accepted the need for compromise but he didn't shift an inch
iourte [jurt] *nf* yourt, yurt
ipéca(cuana) [ipeka(kwana)] *nm Pharm* ipecac(uanha)
ipso facto [ipsofakto] *adv* ipso facto
Irak [irak] *nm* Iraq, Irak
irakien, -ienne [irakjɛ̃, -jɛn] **1** *adj* Iraqi **2** *nm Ling* Iraqi **3** *n* **I.** Iraqi
Iran [irɑ̃] *nm* Iran
iranien, -ienne [iranjɛ̃, -jɛn] **1** *adj* Iranian **2** *nm Ling* Iranian **3** *n* **I.** Iranian
Iraq [irak] *nm* Iraq, Irak
iraquien, -ienne [irakjɛ̃, -jɛn] *adj, n* = **irakien**
irascibilité [irasibilite] *nf Litt* irascibility, irritability, testiness
irascible [irasibl] *adj* irascible, irritable
ire [ir] *nf Litt* ire, wrath
iridescent [iridesɑ̃] *adj Litt* iridescent
iridié [iridje] *adj* iridic; **platine i.** iridioplatinum
iridium [iridjɔm] *nm Ch* iridium
iris [iris] *nm* (**a**) *Anat* (*de l'œil*) iris (**b**) *Bot* (*plante*) iris, flag; **i. jaune** *ou* **des marais** yellow iris; **racine d'i.** orris root (**c**) *Opt* iris; *Phot* (**diaphragme**) **i.** iris (diaphragm)
irisation [irizasjɔ̃] *nf* iridescence, irisation
irisé [irize] *adj* iridescent
iriser [irize] **1** *vt* to make iridescent **2 s'iriser** *vpr* to become iridescent
irlandais, -aise [irlɑ̃dɛ, -ɛz] **1** *adj* Irish **2** *nm Ling* Irish **3** *n* **I.** Irishman; **Irlandaise** Irishwoman; **les I.** the Irish; **un I. du Nord** a Northern Irishman, an Ulsterman; **les I. du Nord** the Northern Irish
Irlande [irlɑ̃d] *nf* Ireland; **I. du Nord** Northern Ireland, Ulster; **I. du Sud** Southern Ireland, Eire
IRM [iɛrɛm] *nf Méd* (*abrév* **imagerie par résonance magnétique**) MRI
ironie [irɔni] *nf* irony; **avec une pointe d'i.** with a touch *or* note of irony; **par une i. du sort** by an irony of fate; **avec i.** ironically, with irony
ironique [irɔnik] *adj* ironic(al)
ironiquement [irɔnikmɑ̃] *adv* ironically
ironiser [irɔnize] *vi* to be ironical (**sur** about)
ironiste [irɔnist] *n* ironist
iroquois, -oise [irɔkwa, -waz] **1** *adj* Iroquois, Iroquoian; **coiffure iroquoise** mohican (hairstyle) **2** *nm Ling* Iroquoian **3** *n* **I.** Iroquois, Iroquoian
irrachetable [iraʃtabl] *adj* (*obligation*) irredeemable
irradiation [iradjasjɔ̃] *nf Phys, Méd* (ir)radiation
irradier [iradje] **1** *vi* to (ir)radiate; (*d'une douleur*) to radiate, to spread **2** *vt* (**a**) to irradiate, to expose to radiation; **aliments irradiés** irradiated food (**b**) (*illuminer*) to illuminate; *Fig* (*paix, joie etc*) to radiate **3 s'irradier** *vpr* to glow
irraisonné [irɛzɔne] *adj* (*action*) unreasonable; (*peur*) irrational
irrationalisme [irasjɔnalism] *nm* irrationalism
irrationalité [irasjɔnalite] *nf* irrationality
irrationnel, -elle [irasjɔnɛl] **1** *adj* irrational **2** *nm* **l'i.** the irrational
irrationnellement [irasjɔnɛlmɑ̃] *adv* irrationally
irrattrapable [iratrapabl] *adj* (*retard*) that cannot be made up; (*erreur*) irredeemable; **une gaffe i.** a blunder you cannot do anything about
irréalisable [irealizabl] *adj* (*rêve*) unrealizable, unachievable; (*projet*) impracticable, unfeasible
irréalisé [irealize] *adj* unrealized
irréalisme [irealism] *nm* lack of realism; **faire preuve d'i.** to be unrealistic
irréaliste [irealist] *adj* (*personne, proposition, projet*) unrealistic
irréalité [irealite] *nf* unreality
irrecevabilité [irəsəvabilite] *nf Jur* inadmissibility
irrecevable [irəsəvabl] *adj Jur* (*preuve, demande*) inadmissible; (*théorie*) unacceptable
irréconciliable [irekɔ̃siljabl] *adj* irreconcilable; (*haine*) implacable
irrécouvrable [irekuvrabl] *adj* irrecoverable, unrecoverable
irrécupérable [irekyperabl] **1** *adj* (*argent*) irrecoverable; (*personne*) irredeemable, incorrigible; **cette machine à laver est i.** this washing machine is beyond repair *or* unrepairable **2** *n* **c'est un i.** he's beyond redemption, he's irredeemable; **les irrécupérables** those beyond redemption
irrécusable [irekyzabl] *adj* (**a**) (*indéniable*) (*preuve, signe*) indisputable, undeniable (**b**) *Jur* (*témoignage, juge*) unimpeachable
irréductibilité [iredyktibilite] *nf* (*d'opposition*) implacability; *Math* irreducibility
irréductible [iredyktibl] **1** *adj* (**a**) (*personne, optimisme*) indomitable, invincible; (*attachement à qn*) unshakeable; (*opposition*) unyielding, relentless, implacable; **un ennemi i. du parti** an inveterate *or* implacable enemy of the party (**b**) *Math, Méd* (*équation, fraction, dislocation*) irreducible **2** *n* **une poignée d'irréductibles** a handful of die-hards
irréel, -elle [ireɛl] **1** *adj* unreal **2** *nm* **l'i.** the unreal; *Gram* **l'i. du présent/passé** the hypothetical present/past
irréfléchi [irefleʃi] *adj* (*personne*) hasty, rash, unthinking; (*action, réponse*) thoughtless, unconsidered; **avoir un mouvement/geste i.** to make an instinctive movement/gesture
irréflexion [ireflɛksjɔ̃] *nf* thoughtlessness; **faire preuve d'i.** to be thoughtless
irréformable [irefɔrmabl] *adj Jur* (*décision etc*) irrevocable
irréfragable [irefragabl] *adj* indisputable, irrefragable
irréfutabilité [irefytabilite] *nf* irrefutability
irréfutable [irefytabl] *adj* indisputable, irrefutable; **il a prouvé de manière i. que ...** he proved irrefutably *or* indisputably that ...
irréfutablement [irefytabləmɑ̃] *adv* indisputably, irrefutably
irréfuté [irefyte] *adj* unrefuted
irrégularité [iregylarite] *nf* (*du sol, d'un terrain*) unevenness; (*du pouls, de traits, d'horaires etc*) irregularity; **les irrégularités d'une élection** the irregularities of an election; **on a relevé quelques irrégularités dans les comptes** a few irregularities have been found in the accounts
irrégulier, -ière [iregylje, -jɛr] **1** *adj* (**a**) (*verbe*) irregular; (*sol, terrain*) uneven; (*sommeil*) fitful, irregular; (*rythme, horaire*) irregular; (*pouls, respiration*) irregular, erratic; (*visage, traits*) irregular; (*résultats, athlète*) inconsistent, erratic; (*efforts*) uneven, inconsistent; (*marché boursier*) unsteady; **troupes irrégulières** irregular troops, irregulars

(**b**) (*peu honnête*) (*procédure, situation*) irregular; **il a été i. dans cette affaire** he acted irregularly in this business; **il est en situation irrégulière, il risque l'expulsion si on le retrouve** he's in the country illegally, he risks being deported if he's discovered; **les voyageurs en situation irrégulière devront payer une amende** passengers without a valid ticket will have to pay a fine

2 *nmpl Mil* **irréguliers** irregulars
irrégulièrement [iregyljɛrmɑ̃] *adv* (**a**) (*respirer, disposer etc*) irregularly; **il n'assiste que très i. aux réunions** he attends

the meetings only very irregularly *or* only on a very irregular basis **(b)** (*pas légalement*) irregularly
irréligieux, -ieuse [ireliʒjø, -jøz] *adj* irreligious
irréligion [ireliʒjɔ̃] *nf* irreligion
irremboursable [irɑ̃bursabl] (*obligation*) irredeemable
irrémédiable [iremedjabl] **1** *adj* (*préjudice, perte, problème*) irreparable; (*désastre*) irremediable; (*maladie*) incurable **2** *nm* **l'i.** the inevitable
irrémédiablement [iremedjabləmɑ̃] *adv* irreparably; **être i. hors d'usage** to be beyond repair
irrémissible [iremisibl] *adj Litt* **(a)** (*crime*) unpardonable, irremissible **(b)** (*irrémédiable*) irreversible
irremplaçable [irɑ̃plasabl] *adj* irreplaceable
irréparable [ireparabl] **1** *adj* (*tort, perte, erreur*) irreparable; (*affront*) unpardonable; (*souliers, voiture, télévision etc*) beyond repair, unrepairable **2** *nm* **commettre l'i.** to go beyond the point of no return; **éviter l'i.** to stop before (one has reached) the point of no return
irréparablement [ireparabləmɑ̃] *adv* irreparably
irrépréhensible [irepreɑ̃sibl] *adj* blameless
irrépressible [irepresibl] *adj* irrepressible
irréprochable [ireprɔʃabl] *adj* (*personne, conduite*) irreproachable; (*tenue, travail*) impeccable; **une nappe d'une propreté i.** an impeccably clean tablecloth
irréprochablement [ireprɔʃabləmɑ̃] *adv Litt* irreproachably; (*vêtu*) impeccably
irrésistible [irezistibl] *adj* irresistible; (*envie, besoin etc*) irresistible, compelling; **elle était i. avec son petit chapeau** she was irresistible in that hat
irrésistiblement [irezistibləmɑ̃] *adv* irresistibly
irrésolu [irezɔly] *adj* **(a)** (*personne, nature*) irresolute, indecisive; (*pas*) faltering, unsteady, uncertain **(b)** (*problème*) unresolved, unsolved
irrésolution [irezɔlysjɔ̃] *nf* irresolution, irresoluteness, indecisiveness, indecision
irrespect [irɛspɛ] *nm* disrespect (**envers** to, towards)
irrespectueusement [irɛspɛktɥøzmɑ̃] *adv* disrespectfully
irrespectueux, -euse [irɛspɛktɥø, -øz] *adj* disrespectful (**envers** to, towards)
irrespirable [irɛspirabl] *adj* unbreathable; **aère ta chambre, c'est i. ici!** air your room, it's stifling in here!; *Fig* **l'atmosphère du bureau est devenue i.** the atmosphere in the office has become unbearable
irresponsabilité [irɛspɔ̃sabilite] *nf* **(a)** (*inconscience*) irresponsibility; **c'est de l'i.!** that's irresponsible! **(b)** *Jur* irresponsibility
irresponsable [irɛspɔ̃sabl] **1** *adj* irresponsible; **avoir une conduite i.** to behave irresponsibly **2** *nm* irresponsible person; **espèce d'i.!** you irresponsible idiot!
irrétrécissable [iretresisabl] *adj* unshrinkable, non-shrink
irrévérence [ireverɑ̃s] *nf* **(a)** (*caractère*) irreverence, disrespect **(b)** (*acte, propos*) irreverence; **il lui a fait l'i. de ne point la raccompagner après le bal** he paid her the irreverence of not taking her home after the ball
irrévérencieusement [ireverɑ̃sjøzmɑ̃] *adv* irreverently, disrespectfully
irrévérencieux, -euse [ireverɑ̃sjø, -øz] *adj* irreverent, disrespectful
irréversibilité [ireversibilite] *nf* irreversibility
irréversible [ireversibl] *adj* irreversible
irréversiblement [ireversibləmɑ̃] *adv* irreversibly
irrévocabilité [irevɔkabilite] *nf* irrevocability
irrévocable [irevɔkabl] **1** *adj* irrevocable; (*accord*) binding; *Jur* **décret i.** decree absolute **2** *nm* **l'i.** the irrevocable
irrévocablement [irevɔkabləmɑ̃] *adv* irrevocably
irrigable [irigabl] *adj* irrigable
irrigateur [irigatœr] *nm* **(a)** (*pour arrosage*) irrigator **(b)** *Méd* (*pour blessures*) irrigator
irrigation [irigasjɔ̃] *nf* **(a)** *Agr* irrigation; **canal d'i.** irrigation canal **(b)** *Méd* irrigation, supply of blood
irriguer [irige] *vt* **(a)** *Agr* to irrigate; **si le cerveau n'est pas irrigué pendant plus de 3 minutes ...** if there is no blood supply to the brain for more than 3 minutes ... **(b)** *Méd* (*blessure*) to irrigate
irritabilité [iritabilite] *nf* irritability
irritable [iritabl] *adj also Méd* irritable
irritant [iritɑ̃] **1** *adj* **(a)** (*énervant*) irritating, annoying **(b)** *Méd* irritant (**pour** to) **2** *nm Méd* irritant
irritation [iritasjɔ̃] *nf* irritation, annoyance; *Méd* irritation
irrité [irite] *adj* **(a)** (*en colère*) irritated, annoyed (**contre** with) **(b)** *Méd* (*blessure*) inflamed; **avoir la gorge irritée** to have an inflamed throat
irriter [irite] **1** *vt* **(a)** (*agacer*) to irritate, to annoy **(b)** (*provoquer une inflammation de*) (*les yeux, la peau*) to irritate **(c)** *Litt* (*passions etc*) to excite; **i. la curiosité de qn** to excite sb's curiosity **2 s'irriter** *vpr* **(a)** **s'i. contre qn/de qch** to get irritated *or* annoyed with sb/at sth **(b)** (*s'enflammer*) to become irritated *or* inflamed
irruption [irypsjɔ̃] *nf* (*arrivée brusque*) (*de barbares etc*) invasion; **les forces de l'ordre ne purent empêcher l'i. de la foule sur le terrain/sur la place** the police couldn't stop the crowd from pouring on to the pitch/into the square; **il a fui juste avant l'i. de la police dans la boîte de nuit** he fled just before the police burst into the nightclub; **faire i. dans une salle** to burst into a room; **elle a fait i. chez nous à deux heures du matin** she burst in on us at two o'clock in the morning; **l'eau a fait i. dans les champs** the water flooded the fields; **l'i. de nouveaux fondamentalismes religieux** the upsurge of new (religious) fundamentalist groups
IRSM [iɛrɛsɛm] *nm* (*abrév* **impact sur la rentabilité de la stratégie mercatique**) PIMS
ISA [iɛsa] *nm* (*abrév* **imprimé sans adresse**) mailshot
isabelle [izabɛl] **1** *adj inv* biscuit- *or* cream-coloured; **cheval i.** light-bay horse, light bay **2** *nm* light-bay horse, light bay
Isaïe [izai] *nm Bible* Isaiah
isard [izar] *nm* izard
ISBN [iɛsbeɛn] *nm* (*abrév* **International Standard Book Number**) ISBN
ISF [iɛsɛf] *nm abrév* **impôt de solidarité sur la fortune**
Islam [islam] *nm Rel* Islam
islamique [islamik] *adj* Islamic
islamisation [islamizasjɔ̃] *nf* Islamization
islamiser [islamize] *vt* to Islamize
islamisme [islamism] *nm* Islamism
islamiste [islamist] *n* Islamic fundamentalist
islandais, -aise [islɑ̃dɛ, -ɛz] **1** *adj* Icelandic **2** *nm Ling* Icelandic **3** *n* **I.** Icelander
Islande [islɑ̃d] *nf* Iceland
isobare [izɔbar] *Météo* **1** *adj* isobaric **2** *nf* isobar
isocèle [izɔsɛl] *adj Math* (*triangle*) isosceles
isochrone [izɔkrɔn] *adj Spéc* isochronous, isochronal
isoclinal, -ale, -aux, -ales [izɔklinal, -o] *adj Géol* isoclinal
isocline [izɔklin] *Math, Phys* **1** *adj* (*ligne*) isoclinal **2** *nf* isocline, isoclinal line
isolable [izɔlabl] *adj Ch* isolable
isolant [izɔlɑ̃] **1** *adj* **(a)** *Constr, Él* insulating; **bouteille isolante** vacuum flask; **matériau i.** (*contre le froid*) insulation, insulating material; (*contre le bruit*) soundproofing (material); *Él* insulating material; **ruban i.** insulating tape **(b)** *Ling* (*langues*) isolating **2** *nm* (*contre le froid*) insulation, insulating material; (*contre le bruit*) soundproofing (material); *Él* insulating material; *Aut* insulator
isolateur, -trice [izɔlatœr, -tris] *Él* **1** *adj* insulating **2** *nm* insulator
isolation [izɔlasjɔ̃] *nf* **(a)** *Él* insulation **(b)** **i. acoustique** *ou* **phonique** soundproofing; **i. contre le froid** *ou* **thermique** insulation; **i. thermique** thermal insulation **(c)** *Psy* isolation
isolationnisme [izɔlasjɔnism] *nm Pol* isolationism
isolationniste [izɔlasjɔnist] *adj, n Pol* isolationist
isolé, -ée [izɔle] **1** *adj* **(a)** (*personne*) isolated; (*endroit, maison*) isolated, lonely, remote; (*cas*) isolated; *Pol* (*pays*) isolated; **se sentir i.** to feel isolated; **il vit trop i.** he lives too much in isolation, he leads too isolated a life; **quelques arbres isolés au milieu du champ** a few isolated trees in the middle of the field; **l'attentat est l'œuvre de quelques activistes isolés** the attack is the work of a few isolated *or* lone activists **(b)** *Él* (*câble*) insulated **2** *n* (*dans un parti, un mouvement etc*) maverick
isolement [izɔlmɑ̃] *nm* **(a)** (*de personne, maison etc*) isolation; **vivre dans un i. complet** to live in complete isolation; *Pol* **l'i. diplomatique d'un pays** the diplomatic isolation of a country **(b)** *Él* insulation
isolément [izɔlemɑ̃] *adv* (*interroger des gens*) separately, individually; (*employer un mot*) in isolation; **le malfaiteur a agi i.** the criminal acted in isolation *or* on his own
isoler [izɔle] **1** *vt* **(a)** (*malade, dissident etc*) to isolate (**de** from); *Méd, Phys* (*virus, gène, corps*) to isolate; **sa maladie/son handicap l'isole** her illness/her handicap cuts her off from other people; **se trouver isolé** to find oneself isolated **(b)** *Él* to insulate **(c)** (*protéger du bruit*) to soundproof **2 s'isoler** *vpr* **(a)** (*se séparer*) to isolate oneself; **avoir besoin de s'i. quelques instants** to need to be alone for a few moments **(b)** (*vivre seul*) to cut oneself off, to isolate oneself
isoloir [izɔlwar] *nm* polling booth
isomère [izɔmɛr] *Ch* **1** *adj* isomeric **2** *nm* isomer
isométrique [izɔmetrik] *adj Math* isometric(al)
isomorphe [izɔmɔrf] *adj Math, Ch* isomorphous, isomorphic
isomorphisme [izɔmɔrfism] *nm Math, Ch* isomorphism
isorel® [izɔrɛl] *nm Constr* hardboard

isotherme [izɔtɛrm] *Météo* **1** *adj* isothermal; **sac i.** cool bag **2** *nf* isotherm
isotope [izɔtɔp] *nm Ch* isotope
isotrope [izɔtrɔp] *adj Ch, Phys* isotropic
Israël [israɛl] *nm* Israel
israélien, -ienne [israeljɛ̃, -jɛn] **1** *adj* Israeli **2** *n* **I.** Israeli
israélite [israelit] **1** *adj* Jewish; *Bible* Israelite **2** *n* **I.** Jew, *f* Jewess; *Bible* Israelite
issu [isy] *adj* **il est i. d'une grande famille périgourdine/d'un milieu artistique** he was born into an important family from the Perigord/into an artistic milieu; **cousins issus de germains** second cousins; **enfant i. d'un second mariage** child from a second marriage; *Fig* **être i. de** to stem from, to derive from
issue [isy] *nf* **(a)** (*sortie*) exit, way out; (*de tunnel, de conduit etc*) outlet; **i. de secours** emergency exit; **voie sans i.** cul-de-sac, dead end; (*sur panneau*) no through road; *Fig* dead end; *Fig* **en faisant ça, tu t'engages sur une voie sans i.** doing that will get you absolutely nowhere; **ses études l'ont mené sur une voie sans i.** his studies led to a dead end; *Fig* **la seule i. possible** the only possible solution; **il n'y a pas d'autre i.** there is no other way out; **elle est dans une situation sans i.** there's no way out of her situation; *Fig* **se ménager une i.** to leave oneself a way out
(b) (*fin*) (*de match, conférence de paix etc*) outcome; **l'affaire a eu une i. heureuse** the matter had a happy ending *or* conclusion *or* outcome, the matter ended happily; **à l'i. de la réunion** at the end *or* close *or* conclusion of the meeting
Istanbul [istɑ̃bul] *n* Istanbul
isthme [ism] *nm Géog, Anat* isthmus
isthmique [ismik] *adj* isthmian
italianisant, -ante [italjanizɑ̃, -ɑ̃t] *n* expert on Italy, Italianist; *Ling* Italian specialist, Italianist
italianiser [italjanize] *vt* to Italianize
italianisme [italjanism] *nm Ling* Italianism
Italie [itali] *nf* Italy
italien, -ienne [italjɛ̃, -jɛn] **1** *adj* Italian **2** *nm Ling* Italian **3** *n* **I.** Italian **4** *nf Ordinat* **italienne: imprimer à l'italienne** to print landscape
italique [italik] **1** *adj* **(a)** *Typ* (*caractère*) italic **(b)** *Hist* Italic **2** *nm* **(a)** *Typ* italics; **en italique(s)** in italics **(b)** *Ling* Italic **3** *n Hist* **I.** Italic
item [itɛm] **1** *adv Com* ditto, item **2** *nm Ling, Psy* item
itératif, -ive [iteratif, -iv] *adj* **(a)** *Jur* (*interdiction etc*) reiterated, repeated **(b)** *Gram* (*verbe*) iterative **(c)** *Ordinat* iterative
itération [iterasjɔ̃] *nf Math, Ordinat, Psy* iteration
Ithaque [itak] *nf* Ithaca
itinéraire [itinerɛr] *nm* route, itinerary; **tracer un i.** to map out a route *or* an itinerary; **changer d'i.** to change one's route *or* itinerary; **i. touristique** tourist route; **il a eu un i. sentimental mouvementé** his love life has had its ups and downs
▸ **itinéraire:** *Aut* **i. bis: prendre un i. bis** to take a less busy route
itinérant [itinerɑ̃] *adj* (*prédicateur*) itinerant; **ambassadeur i.** roving ambassador; **camp (de marche) i. de deux semaines** two-week camping hike
itou [itu] *adv F Vieilli* likewise, also, too; **et moi i.!** (and) me too!
IUFM [iyɛfɛm] *nm* (*abrév* **Institut universitaire de formation des maîtres**) ≈ teacher training college
IUT [iyte] *nm abrév* **Institut universitaire de technologie**
IV *adj Méd* (*abrév* **intra-veineux**) IV
I.V.C. [ivese] *nf Can* (*abrév* **indemnité de la vie chère**) COLA
I.V.G. [iveʒe] *nf Méd abrév* **interruption volontaire de grossesse**
ivoire [ivwar] *nm* **(a)** (*matière*) ivory; **crucifix d'i.** *ou* **en i.** ivory crucifix; **noir d'i.** ivory black; *Fig* **dents d'i.** teeth like ivory; *Géog* **la Côte d'I.** the Ivory Coast; *Fig* **tour d'i.** ivory tower **(b)** (*statuette etc*) ivory
ivoirien, -ienne [ivwarjɛ̃, -jɛn] **1** *adj* of/from the Ivory Coast **2** *n* **I.** (*natif*) native of the Ivory Coast; (*habitant*) inhabitant of the Ivory Coast
ivoirier, -ière [ivwarje, -jɛr] *n* worker in ivory
ivraie [ivrɛ] *nf Bot* **i. vivace, fausse i.** rye grass; *Fig* **séparer l'i. d'avec le bon grain** to separate the wheat from the chaff
ivre [ivr] *adj* drunk; **i. mort** blind *or* dead drunk; **i. de joie** beside oneself with joy, wild with joy; **i. de colère** raging, wild with anger
ivresse [ivrɛs] *nf* drunkenness; (*extase*) exhilaration, intoxication; **se laisser griser par l'i. du succès** to become intoxicated by success, to let success go to one's head; **dans l'i. du moment** in the excitement of the moment; *Jur* **conduite en état d'i.** drunken driving, drink driving
▸ **ivresse:** *Méd* **i. des profondeurs** bends
ivrogne [ivrɔɲ] *n* drunkard
ivrognerie [ivrɔɲri] *nf* drunkenness

J

J, j [ʒi] *nm* (*lettre*) J, j; **le jour J** D-day
j' [ʒ] *pron pers* (*used before a verb beginning with a vowel or h mute; also before* **en, y**) = **je**
jabot [ʒabo] *nm* **(a)** (*d'un oiseau*) crop **(b)** (*de chemise, blouse*) frill, ruffle, jabot
jacasse [ʒakas] *nf* magpie
jacassement [ʒakasmɑ̃] *nm* (*d'une pie, d'une personne*) chatter(ing); **leurs incessants jacassements** their constant chatter(ing)
jacasser [ʒakase] *vi* (*d'une pie, d'une personne*) to chatter
jacasserie [ʒakas(ə)ri] *nf* chatter(ing); **leurs incessantes jacasseries** their incessant chatter(ing)
jachère [ʒaʃɛr] *nf* fallow (land); **champ en j.** fallow field; **laisser en j.** (*champ*) to leave fallow, to let lie fallow; *Fig* (*talent*) to leave undeveloped, to ignore; *Fig* **laisser qn en j.** to ignore sb's talents
jacinthe [ʒasɛ̃t] *nf* hyacinth; **j. sauvage** *ou* **des bois** bluebell, wild hyacinth
jack [(d)ʒak] *nm Él, Tél etc* jack
Jacob [ʒakɔb] *nm* Jacob
jacobin, -ine [ʒakɔbɛ̃, -in] **1** *nm* **(a)** *Hist* **J.** Jacobin **(b)** *Rel* Dominican friar **2** *nf Rel* **jacobine** Dominican nun **3** *adj* Jacobin
jacobite [ʒakɔbit] *adj, nm Hist* Jacobite
jacquard [ʒakar] **1** *nm* (*métier à tisser*) Jacquard loom; (*tissu*) Jacquard (weave); (*pull*) Jacquard **2** *adj* **pull j.** Jacquard sweater
jacquerie [ʒakri] *nf* peasant revolt; *Hist* **J.** Jacquerie; *Fig* **la j. des agriculteurs français** the rising up of French farmers
Jacques [ʒak] *nm* **Maître J.** factotum; *Hist* **J. (Bonhomme)** the French peasant; *F* **faire le J.** to act *or* play the fool
jacquet [ʒakɛ] *nm* backgammon
Jacquot [ʒako] *nm* (*perroquet gris*) grey parrot
jactance [ʒaktɑ̃s] *nf* **(a)** *Litt* (*vanité*) boastfulness **(b)** *F* (*bavardage*) chatter
jacter [ʒakte] *vi F* to chatter, *Péj* to spout; **t'as trop jacté, maintenant, ils savent tout** you've been opening your mouth too much, now they know everything
jacuzzi® [ʒakyzi] *nm* jacuzzi
jade [ʒad] *nm* **(a)** *Minér* jade **(b)** (*statuette etc*) jade object
jadis [ʒadis] **1** *adv Litt* in times past, formerly; **les chevaliers de j.** the knights of old **2** *adj* **le temps j.** the olden days, days gone by; **contes du temps j.** tales of long ago *or* of days gone by
jaguar [ʒagwar] *nm* jaguar
jaillir [ʒajir] *vi* **(a)** (*de l'eau, du pétrole, du sang*) to gush (out), to spurt (out); (*de source*) to gush (out); (*d'étincelles*) to fly (out), to shoot out; (*de flammes*) to shoot out *or* up; (*de la lumière*) to flash

(b) (*apparaître soudainement*) (*concrètement*) **des pierres jaillirent de tous côtés** stones flew from all sides; **une foule de gens jaillit soudain de la rue** a crowd of people suddenly shot out of the street; **des curieux jaillissaient de toutes les maisons** inquisitive people were shooting out of all the houses; **tout à coup, on vit j. des mitraillettes des buissons environnants** suddenly the surrounding bushes sprouted submachine guns

(c) (*abstraitement*) (*rires, cris*) to burst out; **des idées très bizarres jaillissent parfois de son cerveau** some very strange ideas pop out of his head sometimes; **on ne peut pas dire que les bonnes réponses aient jailli** correct answers didn't exactly fly thick and fast; **la vérité jaillira d'elle-même** the truth will out

jaillissant [ʒajisɑ̃] *adj* (*liquide*) gushing, spurting; (*étincelles*) flying, shooting
jaillissement [ʒajismɑ̃] *nm* (*d'un liquide*) gush(ing) (out), spurt(ing) (out); *Él* **j. d'étincelles** sparking
jaïnisme [ʒainism] *nm Rel* Jainism
jais [ʒɛ] *nm Minér* jet; **yeux (noirs) de j.** jet-black eyes
jalon [ʒalɔ̃] *nm* (*piquet*) (surveyor's) staff *or Am* rod; *Fig* **poser** *ou* **planter des jalons** *ou* **les premiers jalons** to prepare the ground; **poser les jalons d'un accord** to pave the way for *or* to prepare the ground for an agreement
jalonnement [ʒalɔnmɑ̃] *nm* marking out, staking out
jalonner [ʒalɔne] *vt* (*délimiter*) (*ligne, parcelle, piste d'atterrissage etc*) to mark out, to stake out; **de petits panneaux jalonnent le parcours** small signs mark out the course; *Fig* **la route est jalonnée de jolies maisons** the road is lined with pretty houses; **événements qui jalonnent la vie de qn** events that stand out as landmarks *or* milestones in sb's life; **sa vie est jalonnée de rencontres déterminantes/drames** his life has been punctuated with decisive encounters/drama
jalousement [ʒaluzmɑ̃] *adv* (*regarder, garder etc*) jealously
jalouser [ʒaluze] *vt* to be jealous of
jalousie [ʒaluzi] *nf* **(a)** (*sentiment*) jealousy, envy; (*en amour*) jealousy; **éprouver de la j. envers qn** to be *or* feel jealous of sb; **j'en crève** *ou* **j'en suis malade de j.** I'm green with envy; **ce sont de petites jalousies** they're just petty jealousies **(b)** (*store*) Venetian blind
jaloux, -ouse [ʒalu, -uz] **1** *adj* (*envieux*) jealous, envious **(de** of); (*en amour*) jealous; **il est j. comme un tigre** he's wildly jealous; **j. de sa réputation** jealous of one's reputation; **il exerce une surveillance jalouse sur son trésor** he guards his treasure jealously **2** *n* **c'est un j.** he's a jealous man; **faire des j.** to make people jealous
jamaïcain, -aine, jamaïquain, -aine [ʒamaikɛ̃, -ɛn] **1** *adj* Jamaican **2** *n* **J.** Jamaican
Jamaïque [ʒamaik] *nf* Jamaica
jamais [ʒamɛ] *adv* **(a)** (*positif*) ever; **plus que j.** more than ever; **plus cher que j.** dearer than ever; **pire que j.** worse than ever; **si j. il revenait** if he ever came back; **avez-vous j. entendu chose pareille?** did you ever hear such a thing?; **avez-vous j. été à Rome?** have you ever been to Rome?; **c'est le film le plus drôle que j'aie j. vu** it's the funniest film I've ever seen; **c'est la maison la plus chère qui ait j. été construite** it's the most expensive house ever (to have been) built; **il désespère de j. avoir raison** he despairs of ever being right; **c'est à se demander s'il a j. vu un peigne** he doesn't seem to know what a comb's for *or* what a comb is; **à (tout) j.** for good, for ever; **je te quitte à j.** I'm leaving you for good; **ils sont séparés à tout j.** they've parted for good; **ils sont unis à tout j.** they are united for ever(more) *or* for ever and ever; **elle a renoncé à écrire à j.** she's given up ever writing again; **je renonce à tout j. à connaître le fin mot de l'histoire** I've given up ever trying to get to the bottom of the matter

(b) [①**A23**,3,a,ii; **B60**,B] (*négatif*) never; **je ne l'ai j. vu** I've never seen him; **n'a-t-il j. appris à conduire?** has he never learnt to drive?; **je n'ai j. pu supporter ce genre d'individus** I've never been able to bear *or* I never could bear that sort of individual; **je suis heureuse comme j. je ne l'avais été** I'm happier than I ever have been; **je ne partirai j. sans ma femme** I'll never go without my wife; **il a passé toute sa vie sans j. boire un verre d'alcool** he's gone all his life without touching a drop of alcohol; **sans j. y avoir pensé** without ever having thought of it; **vous prenez un petit verre, commissaire? – j. pendant le service!** you'll have a quick one, superintendent? – not while I'm on duty!; **on ne sait j.** you never know; **j. homme ne fut plus admiré** never was a man more admired; **j. je n'aurais pensé ça de lui** I would never have thought it of him; **j. le dimanche** never on a Sunday; **c'est maintenant ou j., c'est le moment ou j.** it's now or never; **c'est le moment ou j. d'investir dans la pierre** now's the time (if ever there was one) to invest in bricks and mortar; **on ne le voit presque j.** we hardly ever see him; **on ne le verra plus j.** *ou* **j. plus** we shall never see him again; **tu vas refaire du bateau? – j. plus** *ou* **plus j.** are you going sailing again? – never; **elle n'a j. fait que se plaindre toute sa vie** she's done nothing *or* never done anything but complain all her life; **cela ne fait j. qu'une semaine que nous attendons ce colis** we've been waiting for this parcel for no more than a week; **il n'a j. que dix minutes de retard** he's only ten minutes late (at the most); **ce n'est j. qu'une faute de frappe** it's only *or* just a typing error (after all); **tu vas accepter son offre? – j. de la vie!** are you going to accept his offer? – never (in a million years)! *or* not on your life! *or* certainly not!; **tu as bu! – j. de la vie!** you've been drinking! – I certainly have not!; **t'es amoureuse de lui, hein? – j. de la vie!** you're in love with him, aren't you? – certainly not!; **je n'ai j. fait ça de ma vie** I've never done that in my life; **j. de ma vie, je n'ai été aussi heureuse** I've never been so happy in (all) my life; **j. de sa vie, il n'avait vu un spectacle aussi bête** never in his life had he seen anything so stupid; *Prov* **mieux vaut tard que j.** better late than never; **il n'est j. trop tard** it's never too late; **il n'est j. trop tard pour bien faire** it's never too late to mend; **j., au grand j., je n'admettrai cela** I shall never, (repeat) never, admit it; **j. deux sans trois** it never rains but it pours; *F* **j. tu t'excuses/frappes avant d'entrer?** don't you ever say sorry/knock before coming in?

jambage [ʒɑ̃baʒ] *nm* **(a)** (*de porte, fenêtre, cheminée etc*) jamb **(b)** (*de lettre*) downstroke; *Ordinat* descender

jambe [ʒɑ̃b] *nf* **(a)** *Anat, Zool* leg; **être jambes nues** to be bare-legged; **aux longues jambes** long-legged, with long legs; **être tout en jambes** to be all legs; **avoir de bonnes jambes** to have a good pair of legs, to be a good walker; **je n'ai plus mes jambes de vingt ans** I'm not as young as I was; **il tire** *ou* **traîne la j.** (*de fatigue*) he's dragging his feet *or* heels; (*en boitant*) he's dragging one foot behind him; **se mettre en jambes** to limber up, to warm up; **il s'est sauvé à toutes jambes** he ran off as fast as his legs could carry him, he ran off at full *or* top speed; **la peur/la faim lui donnait des jambes** fear/hunger gave him wings; *F* **prendre ses jambes à son cou** to take to one's heels, to show a clean pair of heels; **il est toujours dans mes jambes** he's always under my feet *or* in my way; **tirer dans les jambes de qn** to make things *or* life difficult for sb, to create problems for sb; *F* **travail fait par-dessous** *ou* **par-dessus la j.** sloppy *or* slipshod work; **traiter qn par-dessous** *ou* **par-dessus la j.** to treat sb in an offhand manner, to be offhand with sb; *F* **ça me/lui fait une belle j.!** a (fat) lot of good that will do me/him!; *Fig F* **j'en avais les jambes sciées** you could have knocked me over with a feather, I was absolutely flabbergasted; **avoir dix kilomètres dans les jambes** to have walked ten kilometres; *Fig F* **n'avoir plus de jambes** to be tired out *or* worn out *or* exhausted; **je ne tiens plus sur mes jambes** my legs are giving way, I can't keep on my feet; *F* **tenir la j. à qn** to bore sb with one's talk; *F* **lâche-moi la j.** get off my back, leave me alone; *F* **en avoir plein les jambes** to be on one's last legs, to be absolutely worn out *or* exhausted; **j'avais les jambes en coton** my legs were like jelly
(b) (*de pantalon, compas*) leg

▶ **jambe**: *Naut* **j. de chien** sheepshank; **j. de force** *Constr* strut, prop, brace; *Aut* stay (rod), torque rod

jambier, -ière [ʒɑ̃bje, -jɛr] **1** *adj, nm Anat* **(muscle) j.** leg muscle **2** *nf* **jambière** *Cr* pad; *Fb* (shin) pad *or* guard; (*d'armure*) greave; **jambières** (*grandes chaussettes*) leggings; (*sans pied, en laine*) legwarmers

jambon [ʒɑ̃bɔ̃] *nm* **(a)** *Culin* ham **(b)** *très F* (*cuisse*) thigh

▶ **jambon**: **j. de Bayonne** Bayonne ham; **j. blanc** boiled ham; **j. braisé** braised ham; **j. cru** raw ham; **j. fumé** smoked ham; **j. de montagne** raw ham; **j. à l'os** ham on the bone; **j. de Paris** boiled ham; **j. de Parme** Parma ham; **j. de pays** raw ham

jambonneau, -eaux [ʒɑ̃bɔno] *nm* knuckle of ham

jamboree [ʒɑ̃bɔre, ʒɑ̃bɔri] *nm* jamboree

janissaire [ʒanisɛr] *nm Hist Mil* janissary, janizary

jansénisme [ʒɑ̃senism] *nm Hist Rel* Jansenism

janséniste [ʒɑ̃senist] *adj, n Hist Rel* Jansenist

jante [ʒɑ̃t] *nf* (*de vélo, de roue de voiture*) rim; *Aut* **j. (en) alliage** alloy wheel; *Aut* **j. en aluminium, j. alu** aluminium wheel; *Aut* **j. de roue** wheel rim; *Fig F* **rouler sur la j.** to be going round the bend, to be losing one's marbles

janvier [ʒɑ̃vje] *nm* [①**A75-6**,B-C; **B58-9**,B-C] January; **en j.** in January; **au mois de j.** in (the month of) January; **le sept j.** (on) the seventh of January, (on) January the seventh, *Am* (on) January seventh

Japon [ʒapɔ̃] *nm* **(a)** Japan; **être au J.** to be in Japan; **aller au J.** to go to Japan **(b)** (*porcelaine*) Japanese porcelain **(c)** (*papier*) Japanese vellum

japonais, -aise [ʒapɔnɛ, -ɛz] **1** *adj* Japanese; **2** *nm Ling* Japanese **3** *n* **J.** Japanese; **les J.** the Japanese

japonaiserie [ʒapɔnɛzri] *nf*, **japonerie** [ʒapɔnri] *nf* piece of Japanese art; (*bibelot*) Japanese curio

japonisant, -ante [ʒapɔnizɑ̃, -ɑ̃t] *n* expert on Japan; *Ling* Japanese specialist

jappement [ʒapmɑ̃] *nm* yelp(ing), yap(ping); **jappements** yelping, yapping

japper [ʒape] *vi* to yelp, to yap

jaquette [ʒakɛt] *nf* **(a)** (*d'homme*) morning coat, cutaway; (*de femme*) jacket; *Can* (*chemise de nuit*) nightdress **(b)** (*de livre*) (dust) jacket, (dust) cover; (*d'une fiche*) jacket **(c)** (*de dent*) crown, cap

jardin [ʒardɛ̃] *nm* garden; *Fig* **c'est mon j. secret** I keep it very much to myself; *Fig* **ça, c'est une pierre dans mon j.** that's a dig at me, that's aimed *or* directed at me, that's meant for me

▶ **jardin**: **j. d'acclimatation** zoological garden(s); **j. d'agrément** pleasure garden; **j. à l'anglaise** landscape(d) garden; **j. botanique** botanical garden(s); *Scol* **j. d'enfants** kindergarten; **j. à la française** formal garden; **j. fruitier** orchard; **j. d'hiver** winter garden; **j. japonais** miniature Japanese garden; **jardins ouvriers** allotments; **j. potager** kitchen garden; **j. public** (public) park, public gardens; **j. de rapport** market garden; **jardins suspendus** hanging gardens; **j. zoologique** zoological garden(s)

jardinage [ʒardinaʒ] *nm* gardening

jardiner [ʒardine] *vi* to do some gardening, to do the garden, to garden; **j'aime j.** I like gardening; **je n'ai pas peur de me salir quand je jardine** I'm not afraid of getting dirty when I do the garden(ing)

jardinerie [ʒardinri] *nf* garden centre

jardinet [ʒardinɛ] *nm* small garden

jardinier, -ière [ʒardinje, -jɛr] **1** *adj* **plantes jardinières** garden plants **2** *n* (*personne*) gardener; (*d'un parc etc*) groundskeeper **3** *nf* **jardinière** **(a)** (*pour le balcon*) window box; (*à l'intérieur*) jardinière **(b)** *Culin* **jardinière (de légumes)** mixed vegetables, jardinière **(c)** *Scol* **jardinière d'enfants** kindergarten teacher

jargon [ʒargɔ̃] *nm* **(a)** (*argot*) jargon, lingo; **le j. du palais** legal jargon, legalese; **j. journalistique** journalese, newspaper jargon; **j. administratif** official jargon, officialese; **j. du métier** professional jargon **(b)** (*baragouin*) gibberish

jargonner [ʒargɔne] *vi* **(a)** to talk jargon **(b)** (*baragouiner*) to talk gibberish

Jarnac [ʒarnak] *voir* **coup**

jarre [ʒar] *nf* (earthenware) jar

jarret [ʒarɛ] *nm* **(a)** (*de personne*) back of the knee, *F* ham; (*de cheval, zèbre etc*) hock; **avoir des jarrets d'acier** to have a good *or* sturdy pair of legs **(b)** *Culin* (*de veau*) knuckle; (*de bœuf*) shin

jarretelle [ʒartɛl] *nf* suspender, *Am* garter

jarretière [ʒartjɛr] *nf* **(a)** garter **(b)** *Naut* gasket

jars [ʒar] *nm* gander

jas [ʒa] *nm Naut* (*d'ancre*) stock; **sans j.** stockless

jaser [ʒaze] *vi* **(a)** *Vieilli, Can* (*bavarder*) to chatter, to prattle **(de** about) **(b)** (*médire*) to gossip; **cela va faire j.** that'll set tongues wagging *or* people talking **(c)** (*moucharder*) to grass, to talk

jaseur, -euse [ʒazœr, -øz] **1** *adj* gossiping; **ce qu'il est j.** what a gossip he is **2** *n* gossip **3** *nm* (*oiseau*) waxwing

jasmin [ʒasmɛ̃] *nm* jasmine

jaspe [ʒasp] *nm* **(a)** *Minér* jasper; **j. noir** touchstone; **j. sanguin** bloodstone **(b)** (*statuette etc*) jasper object

jasper [ʒaspe] *vt* to marble, to mottle

jaspiner [ʒaspine] *F* **1** *vt* **il jaspine bien l'anglais** he speaks English well **2** *vi* to chatter, *Br* to natter; **qu'est-ce qu'il jaspine bien!** he's got the gift of the gab

jaspure [ʒaspyr] *nf* marbling, mottling

JAT [ʒiate] *Com* (*abrév* **juste à temps**) JIT

jatte [ʒat] *nf* bowl

jattée [ʒate] *nf* bowlful

jauge [ʒoʒ] *nf* **(a)** (*de tonneau, réservoir etc*) gauge, capacity **(b)** *Naut* (*de navire*) tonnage **(c)** *Tech* (*instrument*) gauge; *Aut etc* **j. d'essence** petrol gauge; **j. de niveau d'huile** oil-level indicator; (*manuelle*) dipstick; **j. de vapeur** steam gauge; **robinet de j.** gauge cock; **j. de carburant** fuel gauge; *Aut* **j. manuelle** dipstick; *Aut* **j. à flotteur** float indicator **(d)** *Com* **j. brute** gross registered tonnage; **j. nette** net registered tonnage

jaugeage [ʒoʒaʒ] *nm* (*de tonneau, réservoir etc*) gauging

jauger [ʒoʒe] *vt* **(je jaugeais; n. jaugeons)** **(a)** (*mesurer*) (*tonneau, réservoir etc*) to gauge, to measure the capacity of; (*navire*) to measure the tonnage of **(b)** *Fig* (*personne, situation*) to size up **(c)** (*d'un navire*) **j. 300 tonneaux** to be of 300 tons burden; **pétrolier qui jauge quarante mille tonneaux** forty-thousand-ton tanker; **j. deux mètres d'eau** to draw two metres of water

jaunâtre [ʒonɑtr], **jaunasse** [ʒonas] *adj* yellowish; (*teint*) sallow, yellowish

jaune [ʒon] **1** *adj* **(a)** yellow; **avoir le teint j.** to have a sallow complexion; **avoir les dents jaunes** to have yellow teeth; **j. comme un coing** *ou* **comme un citron** as yellow as a lemon; **la race j.** the yellow-skinned race(s) (**b**) *Can* (*lâche*) yellow(-bellied)

2 *adv* **rire j.** to force a laugh, to give a forced laugh; **elle a ri, mais j.** she laughed, but it was forced

3 *nm* (**a**) (*couleur*) yellow; **tirer sur le j.** to be yellowish; **porter du j.** to wear yellow

(**b**) (*colorant*) **j. d'ocre** yellow ochre; **j. de chrome** chrome yellow

(**c**) **j. d'œuf** (egg) yolk

(**d**) *Ind F* scab, rat, *Br* blackleg, *Am* fink

(**e**) *Can* (*lâche*) yellowbelly

4 *n Péj* (*terme injurieux*) **J.** (*Asiatique*) Asian; (*Chinois*) Chink(ie); (*Japonais*) Jap, Nip

▶ **jaune**: **j. canari** canary yellow; **j. citron** lemon yellow; *F* **j. cocu** garish yellow; **j. moutarde** mustard yellow; **j. d'or** golden yellow; **j. paille** straw-coloured; *F* **j. pipi** piss yellow; **j. safran** saffron (yellow); **j. serin** canary yellow

jauni [ʒoni] *adj* (*par le temps, le soleil etc*) yellowed

jaunir [ʒonir] **1** *vt* to turn yellow, to yellow **2** *vi* to turn *or* become yellow, to yellow

jaunissant [ʒonisɑ̃] *adj* yellowing; **blés jaunissants** ripening corn

jaunisse [ʒonis] *nf Méd* jaundice; *Fig F* **en faire une j.** to get into a state about it, to get worked up about it; **il n'y a pas de quoi en faire une j.** there's nothing to get into a state about *or* to get worked up about

jaunissement [ʒonismɑ̃] *nm* yellowing; (*du blé*) ripening

Java [ʒava] *nf* Java

java [ʒava] *nf* (**a**) (*danse*) = type of popular waltz (**b**) *F* (*fête*) **faire la j.** to live it up, to have a wild time

javanais, -aise [ʒavanɛ, -ɛz] **1** *adj* Javanese **2** *nm Ling* (**a**) Javan(ese) (**b**) (*argot*) = a form of slang consisting of introducing 'av' or 'va' into words; *F* **c'est du j.** (*baragouin*) it's gibberish *or Br* double Dutch **3** *n* **J.** Javanese; **les J.** the Javanese

Javel (eau de) [odʒavɛl] *nf* bleach

javeline [ʒavlin] *nf* javelin

javelle [ʒavɛl] *nf Agr* (*de blé etc*) swath

javellisation [ʒavelizasjɔ̃] *nf* chlorination

javelliser [ʒavelize] *vt* to chlorinate

javelot [ʒavlo] *nm* javelin; *Sp* **le (lancer de) j.** the javelin

jazz [dʒaz] *nm* jazz

jazzman [dʒazman] *nm Mus* jazzman, jazz musician

J.-C. (*abrév* **Jésus-Christ**) JC; **av. J.-C.** BC; **ap. J.-C.** AD

je, j' [ʒ(ə)] **1** *pron pers* [①**A26**,a; **B17**,1,a] (**a**) (*non accentué*) I; **je vois** I see; **j'ai** I have, I've; **j'en ai** I have some; **que vois-je** [vwaʒ] ? what do *or* can I see?; (**b**) *F* **et je tourne sans mettre de clignotant** and he/she goes and turns without indicating; **et que je te marche sur les pieds et que je te dis pas pardon!** fancy treading on your toes and not saying sorry! (**c**) *Admin* **je, soussigné ...** I, the undersigned ... **2** *nm* **employer le je** (*dans un récit*) to use the first person

Jean [ʒɑ̃] *nm* **(saint) J.-Baptiste** [batist] (St) John the Baptist; **la Saint-J.** Midsummer('s) Day; *Can* **la Saint-J.-Baptiste** (*public holiday in Quebec*) Saint-Jean-Baptiste Day

jean [dʒin] *nm* (*pantalon*) (pair of) jeans; (*tissu*) denim; **j. en velours** velvet trousers; (*côtelé*) cord(uroy) jeans, corduroys, cords; **veste en j.** denim jacket

jean-foutre [ʒɑ̃futr] *nm inv Vieilli très F* good-for-nothing, ne'er-do-well

Jeanne [ʒan] *nf* **J. d'Arc** Joan of Arc; **cheveux à la J. d'Arc** bobbed hair with a fringe *or Am* bangs

jeannette [ʒanɛt] *nf* (**a**) (*croix*) gold cross (**b**) (*de planche à repasser*) sleeveboard (**c**) (*plante*) **j. jaune** daffodil (**d**) (*scout*) Brownie (Guide)

Jeannot [ʒano] *nm F* **J. lapin** bunny (rabbit)

jeep [(d)ʒip] *nf* jeep

Jéhovah [ʒeɔva] *nm* Jehovah

jéjunum [ʒeʒynɔm] *nm Anat* jejunum

je-m'en-fichisme [ʒmɑ̃fiʃism] *nm F* couldn't-care-less attitude; **faire preuve de j.** to show one couldn't care less

je-m'en-fichiste [ʒmɑ̃fiʃist] *n F* couldn't-care-less type

je-m'en-foutisme [ʒmɑ̃futism] *nm très F* couldn't-give-a-damn attitude; **ce n'est pas parce que tu ne savais pas le faire, c'est du j.** it's not because you didn't know how to do it, it's because you couldn't give a damn

je-m'en-foutiste [ʒmɑ̃futist] *n très F* couldn't-give-a-damn type

je(-)ne(-)sais(-)quoi [ʒənsɛkwa] *nm inv* **un j.** a certain *or* an indefinable something; **il y a un j. qui ne me plaît pas** there's something about it I don't like

jennérien, -ienne [ʒɛnerjɛ̃, -jɛn] *adj Méd* Jennerian

jenny [ʒeni] *nf Tex* spinning jenny

jérémiades [ʒeremjad] *nfpl* whining, complaining, moaning

Jérémie [ʒeremi] *nm Bible* Jeremiah

jerez [xerɛs, kserɛs, gzerɛs] *nm* **(vin de) j.** sherry

Jéricho [ʒeriko] *n* Jericho

jerk [djɛrk] *nm* (*danse*) jerk

jéroboam [ʒerɔbɔam] *nm* jeroboam

jerrican(e), jerrycan [(d)ʒerikan] *nm* jerry can

Jersey [ʒɛrzɛ] *nf* Jersey

jersey [ʒɛrzɛ] *nm* (*tissu*) jersey; **j. de laine** wool jersey; **j. de soie** silk jersey; *Tricot* **point (de) j.** stocking stitch

jersiais, -aise [ʒɛrzjɛ, -ɛz] **1** *adj* of *or* from Jersey; **vache jersiaise** Jersey cow **2** *n* **J.** (*natif*) native of Jersey; (*habitant*) inhabitant of Jersey **3** *nf* **jersiaise** Jersey cow

jésuite [ʒezɥit] **1** *nm Rel* Jesuit **2** *adj* (**a**) *Rel* Jesuit; **prêtre j.** Jesuit priest (**b**) *Péj* Jesuitical, jesuitical

jésuitique [ʒezɥitik] *adj* (**a**) *Rel* Jesuitic (**b**) *Péj* Jesuitical, jesuitical

jésuitisme [ʒezɥitism] *nm* (**a**) *Rel* Jesuitism (**b**) *Péj* Jesuitry, jesuitry

Jésus [ʒezy] *nm* Jesus; **J.-Christ** [ʒezykri] Jesus Christ; **en l'an 44 avant/après J.-Christ** in the year 44 BC/AD

jésus [ʒezy] *nm* (**a**) (*statue*) statue of the baby Jesus *or* of the Christ Child (**b**) *Typ* = super-royal, long royal paper; **grand j.** = imperial (**c**) *Culin* **j. (de Lyon)** = salami

jet[1] [ʒɛ] *nm* (**a**) (*action*) (*de pierre, balle, grenade etc*) throwing; *Arch, Litt* (*de filet, dé*) casting; (*résultat*) (*de pierre, balle, grenade etc*) throw; *Arch, Litt* (*de filet, dé*) cast; **à un j. de pierre de nous** a stone's throw away from us, within a stone's throw of us; **force de j.** impetus; **armes de j.** projectiles, missiles

(**b**) *Métal* cast, casting; **couler qch d'un seul j.** to cast sth in one piece; *Fig* **faire qch d'un seul j.** to do sth at *or* in one go; **premier j.** *Beaux-Arts* first *or* rough sketch; *Littér* first *or* rough draft

(**c**) **j. (de marchandises) à la mer** jettisoning (of cargo), throwing overboard (of cargo)

(**d**) (*de liquide*) jet; (*de sang*) spurt, gush; (*de lumière*) flash; (*de flamme*) jet, burst; **j. de vapeur** jet of steam; **j. d'incendie** jet of water from a fire hose; **j. d'eau** (*fontaine*) fountain; **il parle à j. continu** he talks non-stop *or* continuously; *Tech* **j. de sable** sand blast; **j. d'encre** ink jet

(**e**) *Bot* (*d'arbre*) young shoot; **elle est tout d'un j.** she is tall and slender

(**f**) (*de tuyau*) nozzle; (*de pompe, d'arrosoir etc*) spout; **j. de gaz** gas jet; **diriger le j. de la douche vers le mur** to turn the shower-head towards the wall

jet[2] [dʒɛt] *nm Av F* jet

jetable [ʒətabl(ə)] *adj* disposable, throwaway

jeté [ʒ(ə)te] **1** *nm* (**a**) (*en danse*) jeté (**b**) *Tricot* wool over *or* forward; **j. simple/double** make one/two (**c**) *Sp* (*en haltérophilie*) jerk (**d**) **j. de table** (table) runner; **j. de lit** bedspread **2** *adj F* crazy, nuts

jetée [ʒ(ə)te] *nf* jetty, pier

jeter [ʒ(ə)te] **(je jette, n. jetons; je jetterai) 1** *vt* (**a**) (*lancer*) to throw; (*plus fort*) to fling, to hurl; *Arch, Litt* (*filets, dés*) to cast; (*faire tomber*) to throw down; **j. qch à qn** to throw sb sth, to throw sth to sb; **j. qn à la porte** *ou* **dehors** to throw sb out; **j. qch à la tête de qn** to throw sth at sb; *Fig* **elle nous jette ses diplômes à la tête** she harps on to us about her qualifications, she rams her qualifications down our throats; **j. qch à terre** *ou* **par terre** to throw sth to *or* on the ground; **j. qn à terre** to throw sb to the ground; **j. qn en prison/à la rue** to throw sb in jail/out (into the street); **j. qch à la mer** *ou* **par-dessus bord** to jettison sth, to throw sth overboard; **objets jetés à la mer** jetsam; **navires jetés à la côte par la tempête** ships driven ashore by the storm; **il rêve de j. bas le gouvernement** he dreams of bringing down *or* overthrowing the government; *Boxe, Fig* **j. l'éponge** to throw in the sponge *or* towel; *Fig F* **n'en jetez plus (la cour est pleine)!** enough, enough!, you're making me blush!

(**b**) (*se défaire de*) to throw away, to throw out; **j. qch à la poubelle** to throw sth in the (dust)bin *or Am* garbage can, *Br* to bin sth; **j. qch au panier** to throw sth in the wastepaper basket, *Br* to bin sth; **j. qch au** *ou* **dans le feu** to throw sth on *or* in the fire; **à j.** to be thrown away *or* out; *Fig F* **ce devoir/livre est (bon) à j.** this homework/book is trash *or* rubbish; **elle est vraiment à j., cette fille** that girl's really the pits; *F* **il n'y a rien à j. dans ce livre** this book's as good as you'll get; **j. son argent par la fenêtre** to throw (one's) money away, to throw (one's) money down the drain; *très F* **se faire j.** to get chucked out (**de** of); **quand je l'ai invitée à danser, elle m'a jeté/je me suis fait j.** when I asked her to dance she gave me the brush-off/I was given the brush-off; **j. le bébé avec l'eau du bain** to throw the baby out with the bath water

(**c**) (*émettre*) **j. un cri** to utter a cry; **j. un regard sur qn** to glance at sb, to throw *or* cast a glance at sb; **elle lui jetait des regards désespérés** she glanced at him despairingly *or* in despair, she threw *or* cast despairing glances at him; **j. un (coup d')œil** to have a (quick) glance (**sur** at)

(d) (*dire*) **j. des reproches à la tête de qn** to hurl reproaches at sb; **j. des insultes à qn** to hurl abuse at sb; **elle m'a jeté à la figure que je n'étais qu'une pauvre idiote** she told me straight to my face that I was just a stupid fool; **'bien vu', lui jeta-t-il en passant** 'well done', he called out to him as he went by

(e) (*construire*) **j. un pont sur une rivière** to hastily construct a bridge over a river; **j. les fondements d'un édifice** to lay the foundations of a building

(f) (*mettre*) **j. qn dans l'embarras** to throw sb into confusion; **j. qn dans le désespoir** to plunge sb into despair; **j. qn dans l'angoisse** to throw sb into a state of distress; **j. le discrédit sur qn/qch** to bring discredit on sb/sth, to bring sb/sth into disrepute; **sa remarque a jeté le doute/le trouble dans mon esprit** his remark cast *or* sowed doubt in my mind/troubled *or* disturbed me; **ça a jeté un froid** it cast a chill

(g) (*mettre rapidement*) to throw; **j. quelques affaires dans un sac** to throw a few things in a bag; **j. un châle sur ses épaules** to throw a shawl over one's shoulders, to throw on a shawl; **j. une lettre à la boîte** to pop a letter in the postbox *or Am* mailbox; **j. quelques notes sur une feuille** to jot down a few notes on a sheet of paper

(h) (*faire un mouvement du corps*) **j. la tête/les épaules en arrière** to throw one's head/shoulders back; **j. ses bras autour du cou de qn** to throw *or* fling one's arms around sb's neck

2 se jeter *vpr* to throw oneself; **cours d'eau qui se jette dans la Seine** stream that flows into the Seine; **se j. à l'eau** to throw oneself *or* plunge into the water; *Fig* to take the plunge; **se j. par la fenêtre** to throw oneself out of the window; **elle s'est jetée du troisième étage de la tour Eiffel** she threw herself from the third level of the Eiffel Tower; **il s'est jeté sous le métro/dans la Seine** he threw himself beneath an underground train/in the Seine; **se j. aux pieds de qn** to throw oneself at sb's feet; **se j. sur qn** to throw oneself upon *or* at sb; **elle s'est jetée sur moi** *ou* **dans mes bras pour m'embrasser** she rushed up to me and kissed me; *Fig* **se j. à la tête de qn** (*draguer outrageusement*) to throw oneself at sb; **il s'est jeté sur le buffet/le champagne** he pounced on the buffet/the champagne; **se j. (à corps perdu) dans une entreprise** to throw oneself (body and soul *or* wholeheartedly) into an undertaking; *F* **s'en j. un (derrière la cravate)** to have a quick one *or* a quickie

3 *vi F* **ça jette!** it's really something!, it's brilliant!; **elle en jette, ta bagnole** your car's really something, that's some car you've got

jeteur, -euse [ʒ(ə)tœr, -øz] *n* **j. /jeteuse de sort** wizard/witch

jeton [ʒ(ə)tɔ̃] *nm* **(a)** *Cartes etc* counter, chip; (*pour téléphone, autos tamponneuses etc*) token; **j. de présence** (*objet*) tally, token (*issued as voucher for attendance at meeting*); *Com* (*honoraires*) director's fees; **toucher ses jetons** to draw one's fees

(b) *très F* (*coup de poing*) whack, thump; **il s'est pris un j. pendant la bagarre** he got a whack *or* a thump during the brawl; **dans l'accident, ma bagnole a pris quelques jetons** (*coups*) my car got a bit of a bashing *or* got a few dents in the accident

(c) *très F* (*peur*) **avoir les jetons** to have the jitters, to be scared stiff; **j'ai les jetons que mon père apprenne que j'ai séché** I'm scared stiff my father'll find out I've skipped school; **ça/il m'a donné les jetons** it/he gave me the jitters, it/he put the wind up me

jet-set [dʒɛtsɛt] *nf*, **jet-society** [dʒɛtsɔsajti] *nf* jet-set

jet-ski [dʒɛski] *nm* jet-skiing

jet-stream, *pl* **jet-streams** [dʒɛtstrim] *nm Météo* jet stream

jeu, *pl* **jeux** [ʒø] *nm* **(a)** (*amusement*) **le j.** play; **salle de jeux** playroom; (*dans hôtel etc*) games room; **j. de main** horseplay, rough and tumble; *Prov* **jeux de mains, jeux de vilains** all this fooling around is going to end in tears; *Fig* **c'est un j. d'enfant** it's child's play; **se faire (un) j. de (faire) qch** to make light work *or* easy work of (doing) sth; *Fig* **à quel j. joues-tu?** what's your game?, what are you playing at?; **faire qch par j.** to do sth for fun; **cessez ce j. cruel!** stop this cruel game!; **les jeux de l'amour** *ou* **amoureux** love-play

(b) (*activité comportant un gagnant*) game; *Ordinat* **jeux électroniques** computer games; **les jeux du cirque** (*antiquité*) the games of the circus; **la règle du j.** the rules of the game; *F* **ce n'est pas du j.** that's not fair; **jouer le j.** to play the game; **on aurait beau j. de répondre** it would be quite easy to answer that; *Fig* **faire le j. de qn** to play into sb's hands; **entrer dans le j. de qn** to go along with sb; **le j. n'en vaut pas la chandelle** the game isn't worth the candle; **se prendre** *ou* **se laisser prendre au j.** to get caught up in it; **se piquer au j.** to get into it; **être pris à son propre j.** to be caught out at one's own game, *Fml* to be hoist with one's own petard; **jouer un j. dangereux** to play a dangerous game; **voir clair/lire dans le jeu de qn** to see through sb's game; **jouer franc j. (avec qn)** to play fair (and square) (with sb); **se prêter au jeu** to join in with *or* to go along with the game; **j. grand public** game(s) show

(c) (*cartes que le joueur a en main*) hand; **avoir un beau j.** *ou* **du j.** to have a good hand, to have good cards; **cacher son j.** *Cartes* to hide one's hand *or* one's cards; *Fig* to keep one's cards close to one's chest; *Cartes, Fig* **montrer/laisser voir son j.** to show one's hand *or* one's cards; *Fig* **sortir le grand j.** to go all out, to pull out all the stops

(d) (*activité soumise au hasard*) **le j.** (*au casino etc*) gambling, *Fml* gaming; **j. de bourse** stock market gamble; **maison de j.** gaming house; **perdre une fortune au j.** to gamble away a fortune, to lose a fortune gambling; **se ruiner au j.** to ruin oneself gambling; **dettes de j.** gambling debts; **table de j.** card table, gaming table; **jouer gros j.** to play for high stakes; **les jeux sont faits** (*à la roulette*) les jeux sont faits; *Fig* the die is cast; (*situation critique*) the chips are down; **faites vos jeux!** place your bets!; **mettre qch en j.** (*argent, voiture, carrière etc*) to stake sth; *Fig* **mettre tout en j.** to stake one's all, to risk everything; **être en j.** to be at stake; **les intérêts en j.** the interests at stake *or* at issue *or* involved; **les forces en j.** the forces at work, the forces involved

(e) *Tennis* (*division d'une partie*) game; **j., set et match** game, set and match; **j. Noah** game (to) Noah; *Fb* **être hors j.** (*ballon*) to be out of play; (*joueur*) to be offside; **où en est le j.?** what's the score?; **terrain de jeux** playing field, sports ground; **en j.** in play; **mettre la balle en j.** to bring the ball into play; *Hockey* to bully off

(f) *Fig* (*système*) **le j. de l'offre et de la demande** the system of supply and demand; **j. du marché** market forces; *Fig* **le j. des alliances** the interplay *or* interaction of alliances; **il a obtenu cette faveur par le j. des relations diplomatiques** he obtained this favour through the exercise of diplomatic relations; **le j. des événements** the turn of events; **entrer en j.** to come into play

(g) *Th, Mus* (*d'un acteur*) acting; (*d'un musicien*) playing; **il a un j. très subtil** *Mus* his playing is very subtle, he has a very subtle manner of playing; *Th* his acting is very subtle; *Th* **jeux de scène** stage business; **le j. de main d'un pianiste** a pianist's technique

(h) (*ensemble*) (*d'outils, de clés etc*) set; **j. d'échecs/de dominos** chess set/set of dominoes; **j. de boules/quilles** set of bowls/skittles *or* ninepins; **j. de cartes** pack *or* deck of cards; *Typ* **j. de caractères** character set; *Com* **j. complet de connaissements** full set of bills of lading; **j. de fiches** card index; **j. de lettres de change** set of bills of exchange

(i) *Tech* (*fonctionnement d'un mécanisme*) **j. d'une serrure** action of a lock; **j. d'un piston** length of stroke of a piston

(j) *MecE, Aut* play; *MecE* **j. (utile)** play; **il faut rattraper le j.** it needs to be tightened up; **il y a du j.** it's rather loose, there's a bit of play; **donner du j. à qch** to ease *or* loosen sth; **j. (nuisible)** play, looseness; **prendre du j.** to work free *or* loose; *Vieilli Fig* **donner du j. à des négociations** to allow (some) scope for negotiations

▶ **jeu**: **jeux d'adresse** games of skill; **j. d'arcade** arcade game; *Tennis* **j. blanc** love game; **j. d'eau** fountain; *Fin* **j. d'écritures** creative accounting; **jeux éducatifs** educational games; **j. électronique** computer game; *Aut* **j. d'embouts** socket set; *Aut* **j. d'engrenages** gearing; **j. d'esprit** witticism; **jeux de hasard** games of chance; *Sp* **j. de jambes** (*d'un boxeur, d'un joueur de tennis etc*) footwork; **j. de lumière** play of light; *Th* **jeux de lumière** lighting effects; **j. de mots** play on words, pun; *Sp* **Jeux olympiques** Olympic Games, Olympics; **j. d'ombre et de lumière** interplay of light and shade; *Mus* **j. d'orgue** (organ) stop; *Sp* **Jeux paralympiques** special olympics; **j. de rôles** role-playing, role play; **jeux de société** (*charades, devinettes etc*) parlour games; (*petits chevaux, jeu de l'oie etc*) board games; *Aut* **j. de soupapes** valve clearance; **j. télévisé** (television) game show; (*avec questions*) (television) quiz (show); **j. vidéo** video game

jeu-concours, *pl* **jeu-concours** [ʒøkɔ̃kur] *nm Rad, TV, Journ* competition; (*émission*) game show; (*avec questions*) quiz (show)

jeudi [ʒødi] *nm* [①**A75-6**,B-C; **B58-9**,B-C] Thursday; **j. saint** Maundy Thursday; *F* **la semaine des quatre jeudis** when pigs fly

jeun (à) [aʒœ̃] *adj* (*pas ivre*) sober; **être à j.** (*sans avoir* *mangé ni bu*) to have eaten or drunk nothing; **boire à j.** to drink on an empty stomach

jeune [ʒœn] **1** *adj* **(a)** (*personne, âge*) young; (*apparence, allure etc*) youthful; (*coiffure, vêtement*) young, that makes one look young; **j. homme** young man, youth; **elle n'est plus très** *ou* **toute j.** she's not as young as she was; **j. fille** girl, young woman; **jeunes gens** young people; (*hommes*) young men, youths; **j. aveugle** blind boy/girl; **un j. Français/Anglais** a French/an English boy; **une j. Indienne** an Indian girl; **j. détenu** juvenile offender; **j. délinquant** juvenile delinquent; **le plus j. de mes frères** my youngest brother, the youngest of my brothers; **je suis plus j. que lui de quatre ans** I'm four years younger than him *or* than he is; **dans son j. âge** in his younger days, when he was younger; **être j. d'allure** to be young-looking, to be youthful-looking, to have a youthful appearance; **j. d'esprit** young at heart, youthful in outlook; **il est trop j. dans la société pour qu'on lui confie de telles responsabilités** he hasn't been with the firm long enough to be given such responsibilities; **faire j.** (*de personne*) to look young; **faire** *ou* **paraître plus j. que son âge** to look younger than one's age *or* one's years *or* one is

(b) (*en comparaison*) younger; **mon j. frère** my younger brother; **M. Martin J.** Mr Martin junior, young Mr Martin

(c) (*vert*) (*vin, industrie*) young, new; (*fromage*) young

(d) *F* (*juste*) **c'est un peu j.!** it's a bit on the short side!; **c'est un peu j. pour le vin, on est un peu j. en vin** the wine's a bit on the short side; **je trouve ses arguments un peu jeunes** I find his arguments a bit flimsy *or* thin

2 *n* **(a)** (*personne jeune*) **un j.** a youngster, a youth; **une j.** a girl; *F* **un petit j.** a young guy; **les jeunes** (the) young people; **les jeunes d'aujourd'hui** *ou* **de maintenant** the young people *or* the youth of today, young people today

(b) (*d'un animal*) young animal; **jeunes** young

3 *adv* **ça fait j.** it makes you/her/*etc* look young(er); **s'habiller j.** to wear young clothes, to dress in a youthful style; **se coiffer j.** to wear one's hair in youthful styles/in a youthful style

jeûne [ʒøn] *nm* **(a)** (*période*) fast; **rompre le j.** to break one's fast; **j. de protestation** hunger strike **(b)** (*pratique*) fasting; **jour de j.** day of fasting, fast day

jeûner [ʒøne] *vi* to go without food, to fast; *Rel* to fast

jeunesse [ʒœnɛs] *nf* **(a)** (*période*) youth; **dans ma j.** in my youth, in my younger days, when I was young; **ne pas être de (la) première j.** (*de personne*) not to be as young as one was, to be no longer in one's first flush of youth, to be getting on; (*d'objet*) to have seen better days; **erreurs/péchés de j.** errors of youth/youthful indiscretions; *prov* **il faut que j. se passe** youth will have its fling

(b) (*fraîcheur*) youthfulness; **j. de peau** youthful appearance of the skin; **j. d'esprit** youthful outlook

(c) (*du vin*) newness

(d) [①A11,f,ii] (*les jeunes*) young people; **il aime se retrouver au milieu de la j.** he likes to be surrounded by young people; **la j. nous rejoindra plus tard** the young people will join us later; **la j. dorée** the bright young things, *Litt* gilded youth; **club pour la j.** youth club; **livres pour la j.** books for young people; **la j. du village** the young people *or* the youth of the village; *F* **salut la j.!** hi (there), guys!; *F* **roulez j.!** let's go!; *Prov* **si j. savait, si vieillesse pouvait** if youth but knew, if age but could

(e) *Vieilli* (*jeune fille*) girl

jeunet, -ette [ʒœnɛ, -ɛt] *adj F* youngish; **elle est un peu jeunette pour faire ce travail** she's a bit on the young side to do this job

jeûneur, -euse [ʒønœr, -øz] *n* faster

jeunot, -otte [ʒœno, -ɔt] *F* **1** *adj* youngish, on the young side **2** *nm Péj* youngster; **un petit j.** a young little fellow

JF *n abrév* **jeune fille/femme**

JH *nm abrév* **jeune homme**

jingle [dʒingəl] *nm Rad* jingle

jiu-jitsu [ʒ(j)yʒitsy] *nm inv Sp* j(i)ujitsu

JJ [ʒiʒi] *Bourse* (*abrév* **au jour le jour**) overnight

Jne (*abrév* **jeune**) jr, jnr, jun

JO [ʒio] **1** *nm abrév* **Journal officiel 2** *nmpl abrév* **Jeux olympiques**

joaillerie [ʒoajri] *nf* **(a)** (*magasin*) jeweller's *or US* jeweler's shop **(b)** (*marchandises*) jewellery, *US* jewelry **(c)** (*commerce*) jewellery *or US* jewelry trade

joaillier, -ière [ʒoaje, -jɛr] *n* jeweller, *US* jeweler

Job [ʒɔb] *nm Bible* Job; **pauvre comme J.** poor as a church mouse

job [dʒɔb] *nm F* job

jobard, -arde [ʒɔbar, -ard] *F* **1** *adj* gullible, naive **2** *n* sucker, *Br* mug

jobarderie [ʒɔbard(ə)ri] *nf*, **jobardise** [ʒɔbardiz] *nf F* gullibility; **c'est de la j.** it's a mug's game

JOC [ʒɔk] *nf abrév* **Jeunesse ouvrière chrétienne**

jockey [ʒɔkɛ] *nm Courses de chevaux* jockey; *Arch* outrider

Joconde (la) [laʒɔkɔ̃d] *nf* the Mona Lisa

jodler [ʒɔdle, jɔ-] *vi* to yodel

joggeur, -euse [(d)ʒɔgœr, -øz] *n* jogger

jogging [(d)ʒɔgiŋ] *nm* **(a)** (*vêtement*) jogging suit, tracksuit **(b)** (*activité*) jogging; **faire du j.** to go jogging, to jog

joie [ʒwa] *nf* joy, delight; **plein de j.** full of joy; **dans la j. et la bonne humeur** happily and cheerfully; **elle était folle de j.** she was wild with joy *or* delight; **être au comble de la j.** to be overjoyed; **mettre qn au comble de la j.** to make sb deliriously happy; **sauter de j.** to jump for joy; **ne plus se sentir de j.** to be beside oneself with joy; *F* **c'est pas la j.!** it's no fun; **à ma grande j.** to my great delight; **une j. profonde** great pleasure; **accepter avec j.** to accept with pleasure, to accept gladly; **ça me met en j.** I'm delighted by it; **aller au concert ce soir me met en j.** I'm delighted *or* thrilled about going to the concert this evening; **ma fille faisait ma j.** my daughter was my (pride and) joy; **le film a fait la j. de Simon** the film delighted Simon; **c'est une j. de le voir rétabli** it's a joy *or* a delight to see him on his feet again; **se faire une j. de faire qch** to delight *or* take a delight in doing sth; **quand vais-je avoir la j. de faire sa connaissance?** when will I have the pleasure of making his acquaintance?; **pour ma plus grande j.** much to my delight, to my great delight; **feu de j.** bonfire; **j. de vivre** joy of living, joie de vivre; **il se faisait une j. de vous voir** he was looking forward (so much) to seeing you; **il se fera une j. de vous guider** he'll be only too pleased to guide you; **elle vous a fait une fausse j.** she gave you false cause for celebration; *Iron* **les joies de la famille/la plomberie!** the joys of family life/plumbing!

joignable [ʒwaɲabl] *adj* contactable

joindre [ʒwɛ̃dr] (*prp* **joignant**; *pp* **joint**; *pr ind* **je joins, il joint, n. joignons, ils joignent**; *impf* **je joignais**; *p hist* **je joignis**; *fu* **je joindrai**) **1** *vt* **(a)** (*réunir*) to join; **j. les mains** to clasp one's hands, to put one's hands together; **j. deux tuyaux bout à bout/un tuyau au bout d'un autre** to join two pipes end to end/one pipe to the end of another; **j. nos efforts** to combine *or* unite our efforts; *F* **j. les deux bouts** to make ends meet

(b) (*ajouter*) to add (**à** to); (*dans une lettre, un colis etc*) to enclose (**à** with); **le bon sens joint à l'intelligence** common sense combined with intelligence; **j. le geste à la parole** to suit the action to the word; **j. l'utile à l'agréable** to combine business with pleasure; **j. sa voix aux protestations** to add one's voice to *or* join in the protests; **l'échantillon joint à votre lettre** the sample enclosed with *or* attached to your letter; **j. une carte à un bouquet de fleurs** to attach a card to a bouquet of flowers

(c) (*contacter*) (*qn*) to contact, to get in contact *or* in touch with, to reach

2 *vi* (*de planches, tuiles etc*) to meet, to fit; **fenêtre qui joint mal** window that doesn't shut properly

3 se joindre *vpr* **se j. à** to join; **se j. à la conversation** to join in the conversation; **voulez-vous vous j. à nous?** would you like to join us?; **Marie se joint à moi pour vous remercier** Marie joins me in thanking you; **je voudrais me j. à vous pour le cadeau de Marie** I'd like to contribute to Marie's present

joint [ʒwɛ̃] **1** *pp de* **joindre 2** *adj* joined; **sauter à pieds joints** to do a standing jump, to jump from a standing position; **les mains jointes** with clasped hands, with hands together; **efforts joints** combined *or* united efforts; **pièces jointes** (*dans une lettre*) enclosures **3** *nm* **(a)** *Menuis, MecE, Aut* joint, join; (*de réservoir*) seam; (*produit d'étanchéité*) sealant **(b)** *F* **chercher/trouver le j. pour faire qch** to look for/find a way of doing sth; **faire le j. (entre deux personnes)** to act as a go-between (between two people) **(c)** *F* (*drogue*) joint

► **joint**: **j. en about** butt joint; **j. abouté** butt joint; **j. articulé** knuckle (joint); **j. biseauté** scarf joint; **j. à brides** flange joint; **j. brisé** universal *or* cardan joint, coupling; **j. de cardan** universal *or* cardan joint, coupling, constant-velocity joint; **j. carré** butt joint; **j. en charnière** knuckle (joint); *Aut* **j. de culasse** cylinder head gasket, head gasket; **j. d'étanchéité** gasket, seal; *Aut* **j. d'huile** oil seal; *Aut* **j. moteur** engine gasket; **j. plat** butt joint; **j. à rotule** ball(-and socket) joint; **j. sphérique** ball(-and socket) joint; *Aut* **j. de transmission** universal joint; **j. universel** universal *or* cardan joint, coupling

jointif, -ive [ʒwɛ̃tif, -iv] *adj Tech* joined, placed edge to edge, contiguous

jointure [ʒwɛ̃tyr] *nf Anat* joint; *Tech* joint, join; (*d'un cheval*) (*boulet*) fetlock (joint); (*paturon*) pastern; **les jointures des doigts** the knuckles

joint venture *nf Fin* joint venture
jojo [ʒoʒo] *F* **1** *nm* **affreux j.** little horror *or* monster **2** *adj inv* **il n'était pas j.** he wasn't a pretty sight
jojoba [ʒoʒoba] *nm Bot* jojoba
joker [ʒɔkɛr] *nm Cartes* joker; *Ordinat* wildcard; *Fig* **sortir son j.** to play one's trump card
joli [ʒɔli] **1** *adj* (*enfant, fille*) pretty, attractive, good-looking; (*ville, tableau*) pretty, attractive; (*voix, chanson*) pretty, lovely; (*promenade, histoire, image*) lovely, nice; (*expression*) attractive; **le j. mois de mai** the merry month of May; **j. comme un cœur, j. à croquer** pretty as a picture; **il est j. garçon** he's good-looking, he's attractive; **faire le j. cœur** to flirt; **il a une jolie fortune** he's pretty well off; **c'est bien j. tout ça mais …** that's all well and good *or* all very well but …; **c'est bien j. de vouloir acheter un bateau, mais avec quels sous?** it's all well and good *or* all very well to want to buy a boat, but where's the money coming from?; *F Iron* **c'est pas j. j.** (*blâmable*) that's not very nice; (*laid*) it's not a pretty sight; **ah te voilà dans une jolie situation!** what a fine mess you've got yourself into!; **une jolie pagaille/merde** a fine old shambles/mess
2 *nm* **le j. de l'affaire, c'est que …** the best thing (about it) *or* the beauty of the thing is that …; *Iron* **c'est du j.!** that's marvellous *or* wonderful!; **c'est du j., de mentir** that's nice, lying; **faire du j.** to make a mess of everything; **faire du j. avec qch** to make a mess of sth
joliesse [ʒɔljɛs] *nf Litt* prettiness
joliment [ʒɔlimɑ̃] *adv* **(a)** (*bien*) nicely; **c'est j. dit!** that's neatly *or* nicely put; **elle parle très j. de sa fille** she talks quite charmingly about her daughter **(b)** *F* (*extrêmement*) really; **vous avez j. raison** you're dead right; **on s'est j. amusé(s)** we had a great *or* marvellous time; **elle s'est j. fait engueuler** she got a right telling-off **(c)** *F Iron* (*très mal*) **te voilà j. arrangé!** you're in a right mess *or* state!; **on a été j. reçu** we got a less than warm welcome; **il a été j. arrangé par la critique** the critics didn't leave a hair on him
jonc [ʒɔ̃] *nm* **(a)** (*plante*) rush; **(canne de) j.** Malacca cane **(b)** (*en vannerie*) rush; (*baguette*) malacca cane, rattan (walking stick) **(c)** (*bague*) ring; (*bracelet*) bangle
▸ **jonc**: *Aut* **j. d'enjoliveur** wheel trim; *Bot* **j. fleuri** flowering rush; *Bot* **j. d'Inde** rattan; *Bot* **j. des marais** bulrush
joncher [ʒɔ̃ʃe] *vt* to strew; **j. la terre de fleurs** to strew the ground with flowers; **les débris de la statue jonchaient le pavé** fragments of the statue lay strewn about the pavement; **plancher jonché de débris** floor strewn *or* littered with rubbish
jonchets [ʒɔ̃ʃɛ] *nmpl* jackstraws, spillikins, pick-up sticks
jonction [ʒɔ̃ksjɔ̃] *nf* junction; (*fait de joindre*) joining; **point de j.** meeting point, junction; **j. de deux routes** junction of two roads; *Tech* **tuyau de j.** joint pipe; *Mil* **opérer une j.** (*de troupes*) to join forces; *Jur* **j. d'instance** joinder; *Ordinat* **j. physique** physical interface
jongler [ʒɔ̃gle] *vi* to juggle (**avec** with); *Fig* **j. avec les concepts/les chiffres/les problèmes** to juggle with concepts/figures/problems
jonglerie [ʒɔ̃gləri] *nf* juggling
jongleur, -euse [ʒɔ̃glœr, -øz] *n* **(a)** (*acrobate*) juggler **(b)** *Hist* (*ménestrel*) jongleur, (wandering) minstrel
jonque [ʒɔ̃k] *nf Naut* junk
jonquille [ʒɔ̃kij] **1** *nf* daffodil, jonquil **2** *nm* bright yellow, daffodil (yellow) **3** *adj inv* bright yellow, daffodil (yellow)
Jordanie [ʒɔrdani] *nf* Jordan
jordanien, -ienne [ʒɔrdanjɛ̃, -jɛn] **1** *adj* Jordanian **2** *n* **J.** Jordanian
joseph [ʒozɛf] *adj* **papier j.** fine transparent filter paper
Josué [ʒozɥe] *nm Bible* Joshua
jouable [ʒwabl] *adj* playable
joual [ʒwal] *nm Can Ling* joual (*French Canadian dialect*)
joubarbe [ʒubarb] *nf* houseleek
joue [ʒu] *nf* **(a)** (*de personne, cheval*) cheek; **elle sentit le rouge lui monter aux joues** she felt herself going red in the face; **fard à joues** blusher; **danser j. contre j.** to dance cheek to cheek; **tendre la j.** to offer *or* present one's cheek; *Fig* **tendre** *ou* **présenter l'autre j.** to turn the other cheek; *Culin* **j. de bœuf** ox cheek
(b) mettre *ou* **coucher qn en j.** to aim at sb, to take aim at sb; **mettre** *ou* **coucher un fusil en j.** to aim a gun, to take aim with a gun; **tenir qn en j.** to keep sb in one's sights; *Mil* **en j.!** take aim!
(c) (*de fauteuil etc*) side; (*de palier, mortaise etc*) cheek; (*de roue etc*) flange; (*de poutre etc*) web
(d) *Arch* **joues** (*d'un bateau*) bows
jouer [ʒwe] **1** *vi* **(a)** (*s'amuser*) to play; **va j. ailleurs** go and play somewhere else; **j. avec ses lunettes** to play *or* fiddle *or* toy with one's glasses; **j. sur les mots** to play with words; **j. avec une idée** to toy with an idea; *Fig* **j. avec les sentiments de qn** to play *or* toy *or* trifle with sb's feelings; **j. avec qn** (*s'en moquer*) to play games with sb; **il joue avec son avenir** he's gambling with *or* risking his future
(b) *Sp etc* to play; **j. à qch** to play (at) sth; **j. au tennis/aux cartes** to play tennis/cards; **j. aux soldats/charades** to play (at) soldiers/charades; **j. au docteur** to play doctors and nurses; **j. aux gendarmes et aux voleurs** to play cops and robbers; **j. à la marchande** to play (at) shops; **j. à faire des pâtés** to make sandcastles *or* sandpies; **j. au détective** (*quand on n'en est pas un*) to play detective; *Sp* **j. en finale** to play in the final; **j. dans l'équipe de France** to play in *or* for the French team; **je ne joue plus!** I'm not playing any more!; **c'est à qui de j.?** whose turn *or* go is it?; (*aux échecs, dames etc*) whose move is it?; *Cartes, Fig* **à vous de j.** it's your turn; *Fig* **j. au plus malin/au plus fort avec qn** to try to outwit/outdo sb; *très F* **j. au con** to act like a prat
(c) *Mus* to play; **j. du piano/de la harpe** to play the piano/the harp; **j. dans un groupe** (*d'un musicien*) to play in a group
(d) (*manier avec habileté*) (*éventail*) to wave; (*couteau, pistolet, hache etc*) to wield *or* brandish
(e) *Th, Cin, TV* (*d'un acteur*) to act; (*d'une troupe*) to perform; **il joue très mal** he's a very bad actor, he acts very badly; **je joue/cette troupe joue demain à Paris** I'm playing *or* performing *or* acting/this company is playing *or* performing in Paris tomorrow
(f) (*parier*) to gamble; *Bourse* to speculate; **j. en Bourse** to speculate on the Stock Market; **j. aux courses** to bet on *or* back horses; **j. 500 F sur un cheval** to bet *or* stake 500 F on a horse; **j. à la hausse** to gamble on a rise in prices, to bull the market; **j. à la baisse** to gamble on a fall in prices, to bear the market
(g) (*fonctionner*) to work, to function; **clef qui ne joue pas bien** key that is hard to turn; **faire j. un ressort** to work *or* trigger *or* release a spring; *Fig* **faire j. ses relations pour obtenir qch** to pull a few strings to get sth; **faire j. la corde sensible** to strike *or* touch a chord
(h) (*intervenir*) **l'augmentation des salaires joue depuis le 1er janvier** the rise in salaries has been effective since January 1; **cette considération ne joue pas** that consideration doesn't apply *or* is irrelevant; **votre situation a joué dans l'obtention de ce dédommagement** your situation has been a factor *or* has played a role in obtaining this compensation; **cela jouera en sa faveur/défaveur** that will work in his favour/against him; **cela a joué contre lui** that worked against him
(i) (*du bois*) to warp; (*d'une pièce*) to fit loosely, to have too much play
(j) (*locutions*) **j. des coudes** to elbow one's way through; *Fig* to do some manoeuvring; **une fille qui joue de l'œil** a girl who's making eyes at sb *or* who's giving sb the eye; **elle joue de son expérience/de sa maladie** she's playing on her experience/her illness
2 *vt* **(a)** (*parier*) to stake; (*cheval*) to back, to bet on; **j. cinq francs** to stake five francs; **j. la revanche** to play the return match; **j. sa tête** to risk one's neck; **j. un cheval gagnant et placé** to back a horse each way
(b) *Sp* **j. la finale** to play in the final
(c) (*carte*) to play; (*pion*) to move, to play; *Cartes* **j. trèfle** to play clubs; (*au début*) to lead clubs; *Échecs* **j. une pièce** to move *or* play a piece
(d) *Th, Cin, TV* (*rôle*) to act, to play, to perform; **j. (du) Genet** (*d'une troupe*) to perform *or* put on a Genet play; (*d'un acteur*) to act in a Genet play; **j. Phèdre** (*d'une actrice*) to play Phaedra; *Fig* **j. un rôle dans l'affaire** to play a part in the affair; **j. la surprise** to feign surprise, to pretend to be surprised; **j. les héros/les séducteurs** to play the hero/the seducer; **arrête de j. les incompris** stop acting as though no one understands you; **qu'est-ce qu'on joue?** what's on?
(e) *Mus* **j. un air au piano/à la flûte** to play a tune on the piano/flute; **j. du Bach** to play (some) Bach
(f) (*duper*) (*qn*) to trick, to fool, to make a fool of
3 se jouer *vpr* **(a) c'est un jeu qui se joue à plusieurs** it's a game played by several people; **le match se jouera la semaine prochaine** the match will be played next week; **des sommes énormes se jouent au casino tous les soirs** huge sums are gambled in the casino every night
(b) (*se décider*) **son sort est en train de se jouer** his fate is hanging in the balance
(c) faire qch (comme) en se jouant to do sth easily *or* without any difficulty, to make child's play of sth
(d) se j. de qn to trifle with sb; (*se moquer*) to mock sb, to make fun of sb; **se j. des lois/des difficultés** to make a mockery of the law/to make light of difficulties; **il se joue de**

tous les chasseurs de prime lancés à ses trousses he makes a mockery of all the bounty hunters at his heels

(e) *Litt* (*de la brise, de la lumière, d'un filet de lune*) to play; **une brise légère se jouait dans ses cheveux** a gentle breeze caressed her hair

(f) *Th* **qu'est-ce qui se joue actuellement?** what's on *or* playing at the moment?

jouet [ʒwɛ] *nm* **(a)** (*d'enfant*) toy; (*terme plus général*) plaything **(b)** *Fig* **son mari n'est qu'un j. pour elle** her husband is just her plaything; **être le j. d'une illusion/des événements** to be the victim of an illusion/of events

jouette [ʒwɛt] *adj Belg* **enfant j.** child who loves playing

joueur, -euse [ʒwœr, -øz] **1** *n* **(a)** (*d'un jeu*) player; **j. de tennis** tennis player; **j. de golf/cricket** golfer/cricketer; **j. de cartes** card player; **être bon j.** to be a good player; **être beau/mauvais j.** to be a good/bad loser **(b)** *Mus* player **(c)** (*au casino etc*) gambler; *Bourse* speculator **2** *adj* (*enfant, chien*) playful

joufflu [ʒufly] *adj* (*bébé, angelot*) chubby-cheeked; (*visage*) chubby

joug [ʒu] *nm* **(a)** *Agr* yoke; **mettre les bœufs sous le j.** to yoke the oxen; *Fig* **être sous le j. d'un tyran** to be under the yoke of a tyrant; **secouer le j., s'affranchir du j.** to throw off the yoke **(b)** (*d'une balance*) beam

jouir [ʒwir] *vi* **(a)** (*avoir du bon temps*) to enjoy oneself, to have a good time **(b)** (*sexuellement*) to have an orgasm, *F* to come; *Fig* **ça le fait j. de nous voir peiner** he gets a kick out of seeing us struggle **(c)** (*profiter*) **j. de la vie** to enjoy life **(d)** (*être en possession*) **j. de toutes ses facultés** to be in full possession of one's faculties; **j. d'une bonne réputation** to have a good reputation; **j. d'une bonne santé** to enjoy good health

jouissance [ʒwisɑ̃s] *nf* **(a)** (*plaisir*) enjoyment, pleasure; (*sexuel*) orgasm, climax; **il tire une véritable j. du travail** he gets real enjoyment *or* pleasure from work **(b)** *Jur* (*possession*) possession, tenure; **avoir la j. de certains droits** to enjoy certain rights; **entrer en j. de ses biens** to enter into possession of one's property; **maison à vendre avec j. immédiate** house for sale with vacant possession; **avec j. de la cuisine** (*d'un logement*) with use of kitchen; *Fin* **j. d'intérêts** entitlement to interest

jouisseur, -euse [ʒwisœr, -øz] *n* sensualist, *Litt* sybarite

jouissif, -ive [ʒwisif, -iv] *adj F* really great; **tirer un plaisir j. de faire qch** to get a great kick out of doing sth

joujou, -oux [ʒuʒu] *nm F* toy; (*terme plus général*) plaything; **faire j.** to play; **faire j. avec une poupée/des explosifs** to play with a doll/explosives

joule [ʒul] *nm Phys* joule

jour [ʒur] *nm* **(a)** (*clarté*) day, (day)light; **au petit j.** at daybreak, at break of day, at dawn; **avant le j.** before dawn, before daybreak, before break of day; **en plein j.** in broad daylight; **à la tombée du j.** at nightfall; **il fait j.** it's (getting) light; **l'été, il fait j. à 4h30** in the summer it gets light at 4. 30; **il fait à peine j.** it's hardly light; **vous me cachez le j.** you're in my light; **mets-toi face au j.** face the light; **le j. se fit dans mon esprit** I began to understand *or* to see daylight; **la vérité se fait j. dans son esprit** the truth is dawning on him; **voyager le** *ou* **de j.** to travel by day *or* in the day(time); **travailler j. et nuit** to work day and night *or* night and day; *Min* **travail au j.** surface work; *Fig* **elle et son mari c'est le j. et la nuit** she and her husband are like chalk and cheese; **elle est belle comme le j.** she's a real beauty

(b) [①**A75-6**,B-C; **B58-9**,B-C] (*journée*) day; **huit jours** a week; **quinze jours** two weeks, *Br* a fortnight; **à quelques jours de là** a few days after (that); **500 francs/trois pages par j.** 500 francs/three pages a day; **une à deux fois par j.** once or twice a day; **c'est à un j. de voyage** it's a day's journey (away); **quel j. sommes-nous?** (*de la semaine*) what day (of the week) is it (today)?; *Prov* **les jours se suivent et ne se ressemblent pas** who knows what tomorrow holds?; *F* **il y a les jours avec et les jours sans** there are good days and (there are) bad days, there are days when everything goes right and others when everything goes wrong; **je l'ai vu l'autre j.** I saw him the other day; **un j. ou l'autre** one day, some time (or other); **de j. en j.** day by day, from day to day; **nous l'attendons d'un j. à l'autre** we're expecting him any day (now); **un j. que je me promenais** one day when I was out walking; **un (beau) j. je vous le dirai** one day *or* some day I'll tell you; **un beau j. il décida de …** one day he decided to …; **du j. au lendemain** overnight, from one day to the next; **tous les jours** every day, each day; **mes vêtements de tous les jours** my everyday clothes; **vivre au j. le j.** (*sans faire de prévisions sur l'avenir*) to live from day to day; (*financièrement*) to live from hand to mouth; *Bourse* **argent au j. le j.** overnight money; **leur beauté n'est que d'un j.** their beauty is ephemeral *or* short-lived; **à j.** up to date; **mettre à j.** to update, to bring up to date; **tenir à j.** to keep up to date; **un de ces jours** one of these days; **j. de présence/d'absence** day at/off work; *F* **à un de ces jours!** I'll be seeing you!, see you soon!

(c) (*date*) day; **quel j. (du mois) sommes-nous?** what's the date (today)?, what's today's date?; **un j. d'été** a summer('s) day; **j. de Noël** Christmas Day; **le j. de mes 20 ans** my 20th birthday; **fixer un j. pour qch/pour faire qch** to fix a day *or* date for sth/for doing sth; **il y a six ans j. pour j.** six years ago to the (very) day; **à ce jour nous n'avons toujours pas reçu votre lettre** to date we still have not received your letter; **le journal du j.** today's paper; **quelles sont les nouvelles du j.?** what is today's news?; **le grand j.** the big day; **plat du j.** (*au restaurant*) dish of the day, *F* today's special; **jours de consultation: mardi et jeudi de 9h à 18h** consulting *or* surgery hours: Tuesday and Thursday, 0900 to 1800; **ce n'est pas le j. du boucher, aujourd'hui** this isn't the day the butcher comes; **décidément ce n'est pas mon j.!** it really isn't my day today!; **vas-y, je suis dans un bon j.** go ahead, I'm in a good mood today; **je t'invite, c'est mon j. de bonté** my treat, I'm feeling generous today

(d) (*époque*) **de nos jours** these days, nowadays; **l'homme du j.** the man of the moment; **les beaux jours** the fine days of summer; **ils ont connu des jours difficiles** they've been through *or* seen hard times; **vieux jours** old age; **je l'ai connue dans ses beaux jours** I knew her in her prime

(e) (*vie*) **donner le j. à un enfant** to give birth to a child; **il vit le j. à Paris** he was born in Paris; **mettre fin à ses jours** to put an end to one's life

(f) (*éclairage*) light; *Fig* **jeter le j. sur une affaire** to throw (some) light on a matter; **voir qch sous un j. nouveau/sous son vrai j.** to see sth in a new light/in its true light; **se montrer sous son vrai j.** to show one's true colours; **présenter une affaire sous un j. favorable** to present a matter in a favourable light

(g) (*ouverture*) (*entre des planches, tuiles, rideaux etc*) gap, chink; (*d'un escalier*) well; **pratiquer un j. dans un mur** to cut an opening *or* a hole in a wall; *Fig* **percer qn/qch à j.** to see through sb/sth; *Fig* **mettre qch au j.** to bring sth to light; *Fig* **au grand j.** publicly

(h) *Couture* **à jours** (*passementerie, tricot, chemisier*) openwork; **draps ornés de jours** sheets decorated with openwork

(i) *Mil* **service de j.** day duty; **officier de j.** duty officer; **être de j.** to be on (day) duty; **travailler de j.** to work days; **hôpital de j.** day hospital, *Am* outpatient clinic; **infirmière de j.** day nurse

(j) *Beaux-Arts* (*d'un tableau*) light

▶ **jour**: **j. de bourse** trading day; **j. chômé** public holiday; **j. de congé** day off; **j. férié** public holiday, *Br* bank holiday; **j. franc** clear day; *Com* **j. de grâce** day of grace; *Fin* **jours d'intérêt** interest days; *Fin* **j. de liquidation** settlement day; **j. ouvrable** *or* **ouvré** working day; **j. de paiement** payment day; **j. de repos** day off; *Fin* **j. de valeur** value date

Jourdain [ʒurdɛ̃] *nm* **le J.** the Jordan

journal, -aux [ʒurnal, -o] *nm* **(a)** (*publication*) (news)paper; **j. du matin/du soir** morning/evening paper; **j. gratuit** free paper, free sheet, giveaway paper; **les journaux** (*la presse*) the newspapers, the press; **marchand de journaux** newsagent, *Am* news dealer; (*dans la rue*) (news)paper seller *or* vendor, newsvendor; **livreur de journaux** paperboy, *Am* newsboy; **dans du (papier) j.** (wrapped) in newspaper; *Rad Vieilli* **j. parlé** radio news; *TV* **j. (télévisé)** (television) news

(b) (*lieu de rédaction, équipe de rédaction*) office; **le j. va déménager** the (news)paper will be moving (office)

(c) (*récit d'événements, d'expériences*) journal, record; *Fin* ledger; *Ordinat* log; *Vieilli* **(livre) j.** account book; **tenir un j.** to keep a journal

▶ **journal**: *Compta* **j. des achats** purchase ledger; *Compta* **j. analytique** analysis ledger; *Fin* **j. de banque** bank book; *Naut* **j. de bord** log (book); *Compta* **j. de caisse** cash book; **j. sur CD-Rom** CD-Rom newspaper; **j. à diffusion contrôlée** controlled circulation newspaper; **j. à diffusion nationale** national newspaper, national; *Compta* **j. des effets à payer** bills payable ledger; *Compta* **j. des effets à recevoir** bills receivable ledger; **j. électronique** electronic newspaper; **j. factures-clients** sales invoice ledger; *Compta* **j. factures-fournisseurs** purchase invoice ledger; **j. d'information** newspaper; **j. interne d'entreprise** in-house *or* staff news-sheet *or* newsletter, company magazine; **j. intime** diary; *Ordinat* **j. logique** logical log; **j. de mode** fashion magazine; *Admin* **J. officiel** = French government publication giving information to the public about new laws, government business, new companies etc, *Br* ≈ the gazette; *Compta* **j. de paie** wages ledger; **j. de petites annonces** advertising magazine; **j. plein format** broadsheet newspaper; **j. professionnel** trade journal; *Compta* **j. des rendus** returns ledger *or* book; **j. sportif** sports paper; *Compta* **j. des ventes** sales ledger

journaleux [ʒurnalø] *nm F Péj* hack (journalist)

journalier, -ière [ʒurnalje, -jɛr] **1** *adj* (*tâche, salaire, souci*) daily **2** *nm Br* day labourer, *US* day laborer

journalisme [ʒurnalism] *nm* journalism; **faire du j.** to be a journalist; **j. d'enquête** investigative journalism; **j. de radiodiffusion** broadcast journalism; **j. de télévision** television journalism, broadcast journalism; **j. engagé** campaigning journalism; **j. militant** politically-orientated journalism; **j. sportif** sports journalism; **j. électronique** electronic journalism, EJ; **j. électronique de télévision** electronic news gathering

journaliste [ʒurnalist] *n* journalist; **j. politique/sportif/économique** political/sports/economics correspondent *or* journalist; **elle est j. au Monde** she's a journalist for *or* with Le Monde; **les journalistes de la rédaction** the editorial staff; **j. d'investigation** investigative journalist; **j. de télévision** television journalist; (*présentateur*) newscaster; **j. indépendant** freelance journalist; **j. parlementaire** parliamentary reporter; **j. permanent(e)** staff reporter

journalistique [ʒurnalistik] *adj* journalistic; **style j.** journalistic style, *Péj* journalese

journée [ʒurne] *nf* **(a)** (*par opposition à nuit*) day(time); **pendant la j.** in the daytime, during the day; **dans la j.** in the course of the day, during the day; **toute la j.** all day (long), the whole day; **il ne fait rien de la j.** he does nothing all day (long); **elle soupire/bavarde à longueur de j.** she sighs/chats for days on end; **par une belle j. d'été** on a fine summer's day

(b) [①B58,B,3] (*ensemble des activités*) day; **quelle j., je suis épuisée!** what a day, I'm exhausted!; **j'ai eu une j. bien remplie/mouvementée** I've had a very full *or* busy/eventful day; **j. de travail** (*jour non chômé*) working day, workday; (*quantité de travail*) day's work; **j. de huit heures** eight-hour day; **faire la j. continue** (*d'une personne*) to work through lunch(time); (*d'un magasin*) to remain open at lunchtime; **travailler à la j.** to work by the day; *Vieilli* **homme de j.** (day) labourer; *Vieilli* **femme de j.** cleaning lady, *Br* char(woman), *Br* daily (help); *Vieilli* **faire des journées** (*d'une femme de ménage*) to do cleaning work, to work as a cleaning lady

(c) (*salaire*) day's pay *or* wages; **tu as gagné ta j.** you've earned your (day's) pay *or* wages; *Iron* **j'ai gagné ma j.!** it's not my day!

(d) *Vieilli* (*distance*) day's journey; **Valence était à une j. de Lyon** Valence was a day's journey from Lyons

▸ **journée**: *Aut* **j. jaune** day with no serious motorway congestion; *Aut* **j. noire** day with very severe motorway congestion; *Aut* **j. orange** day with some motorway congestion; **j. portes ouvertes** open day, *Am* open house; *Aut* **j. rouge** day with heavy motorway congestion

journellement [ʒurnɛlmɑ̃] *adv* daily, every day

joute [ʒut] *nf* **(a)** (*combat médiéval*) joust, tilt **(b)** (*jeu actuel*) **j. nautique** *ou* **lyonnaise** water joust; *Fig* **j. oratoire** verbal sparring (match) **(c)** *Can Sp* game, match; (*duel*) joust, duel

jouter [ʒute] *vi* **(a)** (*combattre*) (*à cheval*) to joust, to tilt; (*sur l'eau*) to joust **(b)** (*rivaliser*) to spar (**avec qn** with sb)

jouteur, -euse [ʒutœr, -øz] *n* **(a)** (*dans une discussion, un débat*) adversary **(b)** (*à cheval*) jouster, tilter; (*sur l'eau*) jouster

jouvence [ʒuvɑ̃s] *nf Litt* **cela a été une bain** *ou* **une cure de j.** it has rejuvenated me, it has made me feel years younger

jouvenceau, -eaux [ʒuvɑ̃so] *nm Arch* stripling, youth, lad

jouvencelle [ʒuvɑ̃sɛl] *nf Arch* maiden, damsel

jouxter [ʒukste] *vt Litt* to adjoin, to be adjacent to

jovial, -iale, -iaux, -iales [ʒɔvjal, -o] *adj* jovial, jolly

jovialement [ʒɔvjalmɑ̃] *adv* jovially

jovialité [ʒɔvjalite] *nf* joviality, jolliness

joyau, -aux [ʒwajo] *nm* jewel, gem; **les joyaux de la couronne** the crown jewels; *Fig* **j. de la civilisation italienne** jewel (in the crown) of Italian civilization; **le Tadj Mahall est un véritable j. de l'art indien** the Taj Mahal is a real jewel *or* gem of Indian art

joyeusement [ʒwajøzmɑ̃] *adv* joyfully, *Litt* joyously

joyeux, -euse [ʒwajø, -øz] *adj* (*personne, équipe*) joyful, *Litt* joyous; (*cris, nouvelles, mine*) joyful, cheerful; **une bande de joyeux drilles** a group of cheerful fellows; **joyeuses Pâques!** Happy Easter!; **j. anniversaire Louis!** Happy Birthday, Louis!; **j. Noël!** Happy *or* Merry Christmas!

jubé [ʒybe] *nm Archit* rood loft *or* screen, jube

jubilaire [ʒybilɛr] *adj* **année j.** jubilee year

jubilation [ʒybilasjɔ̃] *nf* jubilation

jubilé [ʒybile] *nm* jubilee

jubiler [ʒybile] *vi* to be jubilant; (*méchamment*) to gloat; **il jubilait de me voir humilié** he gloated over my humiliation

jucher [ʒyʃe] **1** *vt* to perch **2** *vi* (*d'oiseaux*) (*pour dormir*) to roost **3 se jucher** *vpr* (*d'oiseaux, de personnes*) to perch

juchoir [ʒyʃwar] *nm* roost(ing place); (*perche*) perch

judaïcité [ʒdaisite] *nf Rel* Jewishness

judaïque [ʒydaik] *adj Rel* (*loi, héritage*) Judaic, Jewish

judaïser [ʒydaize] *vi* to Judaize

judaïsme [ʒydaism] *nm* Judaism

judas [ʒyda] *nm* **(a)** *Bible* **J.** Judas; **baiser de J.** Judas kiss **(b)** (*traître*) Judas, traitor, betrayer **(c)** (*ouverture*) peephole, spyhole, judas (hole); **j. (optique)** (*avec lentille*) peephole

Judée [ʒyde] *nf Bible* Judaea; **arbre de J.** Judas tree

judéité [ʒydeite] *nf* Jewishness

judéo-allemand, *pl* **judéo-allemand(es)** [ʒydeɔalmɑ̃(d)] **1** *adj* Yiddish **2** *nm Ling* Yiddish

judéo-chrétien, -ienne, *pl* **judéo-chrétien(nes)** [ʒydeɔkretjɛ̃, -jɛn] *n, adj* Jud(a)eo-Christian

judiciaire [ʒydisjɛr] *adj Jur* (*pouvoir, enquête, acte*) judicial; (*aide, autorité*) legal; (*vente*) court-ordered; **frais judiciaires** legal charges; **erreur j.** miscarriage of justice; **vente j.** sale by order of the court; **poursuites judiciaires** legal proceedings

judiciairement [ʒydisjɛrmɑ̃] *adv* judicially

judicieusement [ʒydisjøzmɑ̃] *adv* judiciously

judicieux, -euse [ʒydisjø, -øz] *adj* (*remarque, choix, personne, esprit*) sensible, *Fml* judicious; **peu j.** injudicious; **il serait j. de téléphoner avant d'y aller** it would be sensible *or* wise to phone before going

judo [ʒydo] *nm* judo

judoka [ʒydɔka] *n Sp* judoka

juge [ʒyʒ] *nm* **(a)** *Jur* judge; **Monsieur le J.** Your Honour, *US* Your Honor, *Br* M'Lord, M'Lud; **les juges** the bench **(b)** (*arbitre*) judge **(c) je vous en fais j., je vous laisse j.** judge for yourself, I leave it to you to judge; **on ne peut pas à la fois être j. et partie** you can't be (the) judge in your own case; **tu es seul j.** you alone can judge, only you can (be the) judge

▸ **juge**: **j. aux affaires matrimoniales** divorce court judge; **j. de l'application des peines** = judge responsible for supervising the way a sentence is carried out; **j. consulaire** commercial court judge; **j. des enfants** juvenile court judge; **j. d'instance** police court magistrate, ≈ Justice of the Peace; **j. d'instruction** examining magistrate, *Arch* conciliation magistrate (*in commercial cases*); *Tennis* **j. de ligne** line judge; *Arch* **j. de paix** police court magistrate, ≈ Justice of the Peace, *Arch* conciliation magistrate (*in commercial cases*); **j. rapporteur** inquiry judge; **j. des référés** = judge sitting in chambers to deal provisionally with matters of special urgency; **j. de touche** *Fb* linesman; *Rugby* touch judge

jugé [ʒyʒe] *nm* **tirer au j.** to fire blind; **calculer/estimer au j.** to calculate/estimate roughly

jugeable [ʒyʒabl] *adj Jur* subject to a legal decision

jugement [ʒyʒmɑ̃] *nm* **(a)** *Jur* (*d'une affaire*) trial; **faire passer qn en j.** to bring sb to trial, to put sb on trial; **mettre en j.** to commit for trial, to arraign; **mise en j.** committal for trial, arraignment; **passer en j.** to be brought to trial, to stand trial, to go on trial; **j. par défaut** judg(e)ment by default

(b) *Jur* (*décision*) decision, award; (*dans des affaires criminelles*) sentence; **prononcer un j.** to pass judg(e)ment; **rendre un j. arbitral** to make an award; **j. provisoire** decree nisi; **j. déclaratif de faillite** adjudication in bankruptcy

(c) (*opinion*) judg(e)ment, opinion; **porter un j. sur qch** to pass judg(e)ment *or* give an opinion on sth; **j. de valeur** value judg(e)ment; **soumettre qch au j. de qn** to submit sth to sb for his/her judg(e)ment

(d) (*discernement*) judg(e)ment; **montrer du j.** to show (sound) judg(e)ment *or* good sense; **manquer de j.** to lack (good) judg(e)ment; **erreur de j.** error of judg(e)ment

▸ **jugement**: **J. dernier** Last Judg(e)ment; **le jour du J. dernier** Judg(e)ment Day, Doomsday; *Hist* **J. de dieu** (*ordalie*) ordeal

jugeote [ʒyʒɔt] *nf F* common sense, *Br* gumption, *Br* nous; **avoir de la j.** to have one's head screwed on (the right way), to know what's what; **il n'a pas deux sous de j.** he hasn't got a scrap of common sense, *Br* he's got no gumption at all

juger[1] [ʒyʒe] **(je jugeai(s); n. jugeons) 1** *vt* **(a)** *Jur* (*affaire*) to try, to judge; (*prévenu*) to try; (*demande, litige*) to adjudicate, to arbitrate

(b) (*donner son avis sur*) (*situation, candidat, qualités de qn, livre etc*) to judge; (*condamner*) (*personne*) to judge; **j. les gens sur la mine** to judge people by *or* from appearances

(c) (*croire*) **j. que** to think *or* consider that, to be of the opinion that; **on le jugeait fou** people thought *or* considered him mad; **j. à propos/nécessaire/superflu de faire qch** to think *or* consider it advisable/necessary/superfluous to do sth; **j'ai jugé bon de vous prévenir** I thought *or* considered it right *or* a good idea to warn you

2 *vt ind* **j. de qch** to judge sth; **j. de qn** to form an opinion of sb, to judge sb; **j. favorablement d'un candidat** to form a favourable opinion of a candidate, to judge a candidate favourably; **jugez de ma surprise** imagine my surprise; **à en j. par …** to judge by …, judging *or* going by …; **autant que je puisse en j.** as far as I can judge, to the best of my judg(e)ment; **à vous d'en j.** it's up to you to judge

3 *vi* to judge; **à toi de j.** it's up to you to judge; **tu ne peux pas j.** you're in no position to judge

4 **se juger** *vpr* to be judged; **un homme se juge par ses actions** a man is judged by his actions

juger² *nm* = **jugé**

jugulaire [ʒygylɛr] **1** *adj Anat (veine)* jugular **2** *nf* **(a)** *Anat* jugular (vein) **(b)** *(de casque)* chin strap

juguler [ʒygyle] *vt* **(a)** *(révolte, rébellion)* to put down, to suppress, to stifle; *(inflation)* to curb, to damp down, to check; *(épidémie)* to arrest, to halt **(b)** *Arch* to strangle, to throttle

juif, juive [ʒɥif, ʒɥiv] **1** *adj* Jewish **2** *n* **J.** Jew; **Juive** Jewish woman/girl, Jew(ess); **le J. errant** the Wandering Jew **3** *nm Anat F* **le petit j.** the funny bone

juillet [ʒɥijɛ] *nm* [**①A75-6**,B-C; **B58-9**,B-C] July; **en j.** in July; **au mois de j.** in (the month of) July; **le sept j.** (on) the seventh of July, (on) July the seventh, *Am* (on) July seventh; **le 14 j.** Bastille Day *(day of national celebration in France)*

juilletiste [ʒɥijɛtist] *n* July holiday-maker *or Am* vacationer

juin [ʒɥɛ̃] *nm* [**①A75-6**,B-C; **B58-9**,B-C] June; **en j.** in June; **au mois de j.** in (the month of) June; **le sept j.** (on) the seventh of June, (on) June the seventh, *Am* (on) June seventh

juiverie [ʒɥivri] *nf Arch (juifs, quartier juif)* Jewry

jujube [ʒyʒyb] *nm Bot, Pharm* jujube

jujubier [ʒyʒybje] *nm Bot* jujube (tree)

juke-box, *pl* **juke-boxes** [(d)ʒykbɔks] *nm* jukebox

julep [ʒylɛp] *nm Pharm* julep

Jules [ʒyl] *nm* Julius; **J. César** Julius Caesar

jules [ʒyl] *nm* **(a)** *très F (mari, petit ami)* man, guy **(b)** *très F (vase de nuit)* chamber pot, *Br* jerry

julien, -ienne¹ [ʒyljɛ̃, -jɛn] *adj Antiq* Julian; **année julienne** Julian year

julienne² [ʒyljɛn] *nf* **(a)** *(plante)* rocket **(b)** *Culin (soupe)* julienne; **j. de légumes** vegetables julienne, julienne of vegetables **(c)** *Zool (poisson)* ling

jumbo(-jet), *pl* **jumbo-jets** [(d)ʒœmbo(dʒɛt)] *nm F* jumbo (jet)

jumeau, -elle [ʒymo, -ɛl] **1** *adj* **(a)** **frères jumeaux/sœurs jumelles** twin brothers/sisters; **lits jumeaux** twin beds; **maisons jumelles** semi-detached houses **(b)** *(fruits)* double **2** *nm Anat* gemellus muscle **3** *n (frère)* twin (brother); *(sosie)* double, twin; **jumelle** twin (sister); **vrais jumeaux** identical twins; **faux jumeaux** fraternal twins

jumelage [ʒymlaʒ] *nm* **(a)** *(assemblage) (de poutres, roues)* coupling, pairing **(b)** *(de villes)* twinning; **j. d'entreprises** twinning of companies

jumelé [ʒymle] *adj* **maison jumelée** semi-detached house; **villes jumelées** twin(ned) towns; *Aut* **pneus jumelés** twin *or* dual tyres; *Courses de chevaux* **pari j.** dual forecast *(of first two horses in a race)*

jumeler [ʒymle] *vt* **(je jumelle, n. jumelons; je jumellerai)** *(villes)* to twin **(avec** with); *(mât, poutre)* to fish, to reinforce

jumelles [ʒymɛl] *nfpl* **(a)** [**①A10**,e] *Opt* **(paire de) j.** (pair of) binoculars; **j. de théâtre** opera glasses; **j. de campagne** field glasses **(b)** *Aut* (spring) shackles

jument [ʒymɑ̃] *nf* mare; **j. poulinière** brood mare

jumping [(d)ʒœmpiŋ] *nm Equitation* show jumping

jungle [ʒɔ̃gl, ʒœ̃gl] *nf* jungle; *Fig* **c'est une vraie j.** *(le monde du travail etc)* it's a jungle out there, it's a real rat race, it's dog eat dog; **la j. de la haute finance** the financial jungle; **la loi de la j.** the law of the jungle

junior [ʒynjɔr] **1** *adj inv* junior; *Hum* **M. Martin j.** Mr Martin junior; *Com* **style** *ou* **mode j.** junior fashion **2** *n Sp* junior

junkie [dʒœnki] *n F* junkie

Junon [ʒynɔ̃] *nf Astron, Myth* Juno

junte [ʒœ̃t] *nf Mil* junta

jupe [ʒyp] *nf* **(a)** skirt; **j. à fleurs/à carreaux** floral/checked skirt; **j. droite/plissée** straight/pleated skirt; *F* **pendu aux jupes de sa mère** tied to his mother's apron strings; *Vieilli* **retrousser ses jupes** to hitch up one's skirts **(b)** *Tech* skirt; *Aut* **j. de pare-chocs** bumper skirt

jupe-culotte, *pl* **jupes-culottes** *nf* culotte(s), divided skirt

jupette [ʒypɛt] *nf* skirt; *Sp* **j. de tennis** tennis skirt

Jupiter [ʒypitɛr] **1** *nm Myth* Jupiter, Jove **2** *nf Astron* Jupiter

jupon [ʒypɔ̃] *nm* **(a)** underskirt, slip, (waist) petticoat **(b)** *Vieilli, Péj* **courir le j.** to chase after women, to chase the girls; **coureur de j.** womanizer

Jura [ʒyra] *nm (massif)* **le J.** the Jura (Mountains)

jurassien, -ienne [ʒyrasjɛ̃, -jɛn] **1** *adj* of *or* from the Jura **2** *n* **J.** *(natif)* native of the Jura; *(habitant)* inhabitant of the Jura

jurassique [ʒyrasik] *Géol adj, nm* Jurassic

juratoire [ʒyratwar] *adj Jur* **caution j.** guarantee given on oath

juré, -ée [ʒyre] **1** *adj (qui a prêté serment)* sworn; **expert j.** sworn expert; *Fig* **ennemi j.** sworn enemy **2** *n* juror, juryman; **jurée** juror, jurywoman; **les jurés** the jury; **mesdames, messieurs les jurés** ladies and gentlemen of the jury; **un des jurés** one of the jury, a member of the jury

jurer [ʒyre] **1** *vt* to swear; **j. sa foi** to pledge one's word; **j. sur la Bible** to swear on the Bible; **j. fidélité à qn** to swear *or* pledge loyalty to sb; **faire j. le secret à qn** to swear sb to secrecy; **j. de faire qch** to swear *or* vow to do sth; **j. de se venger** to swear *or* vow (to take) revenge; **je vous jure que c'est vrai** I swear (to you) that it's the truth; *F* **je le jure sur la tête de ma mère/mon père** cross my heart and hope to die; **j. ses grands dieux** to swear blind, to swear to God; **j'en jurerais** I would swear to it; **c'est drôle, j'aurais juré que la voiture était bleue** that's funny, I could have sworn that the car was blue; *Prov* **il ne faut j. de rien** you never can tell

2 *vi* **(a)** *(blasphémer)* to swear, to curse; *F* **j. comme un charretier** to swear like a trooper

(b) *(des couleurs, vêtements etc)* to clash **(avec** with)

3 **se jurer** *vpr* **(a)** *(l'un l'autre)* **se j. un éternel amour** to swear eternal love; **les époux se sont juré fidélité** the married couple swore to be faithful to each other

(b) *(soi-même)* **se j. de faire qch** to swear *or* vow to do sth; **se j. que** to swear *or* vow that

juridiction [ʒyridiksjɔ̃] *nf (compétence)* jurisdiction; *(tribunaux)* courts (of law); **sous la j. de …** within the jurisdiction of …; **j. nationale** national jurisdiction

juridictionnel, -elle [ʒyridiksjɔnɛl] *adj* jurisdictional

juridique [ʒyridik] *adj* legal; **conseiller j.** legal adviser; **il a une formation j.** he has studied law

juridiquement [ʒyridikmɑ̃] *adv* legally

jurisconsulte [ʒyriskɔ̃sylt] *nm* jurisconsult, legal expert

jurisprudence [ʒyrisprydɑ̃s] *nf (doctrine)* jurisprudence; *(décision)* precedent *(of a case)*; *(ensemble des décisions)* case law; **faire j.** to set a precedent

juriste [ʒyrist] *n (spécialiste du droit)* jurist, legal expert; *(étudiant)* law student

juron [ʒyrɔ̃] *nm* oath, curse; *(gros mot)* swearword; **lâcher** *ou* **pousser un j.** to curse, to swear

jury [ʒyri] *nm* **(a)** [**①A11**,g,i] *Jur* jury; **dresser la liste du j.** to draw up the jury list; **membre du j.** member of the jury, juror **(b)** *(d'une exposition, d'un jeu-concours, d'un prix)* (panel of) judges; **j. (d'examen)** examining board, board of examiners; **j. de concours d'entrée** board for the entrance examination; *Mktg* **j. de consommateurs** consumer jury

jus [ʒy] *nm* **(a)** *(de pamplemousse, de tomate etc)* juice; **j. de fruit** fruit juice; **j. de fruit pressé** freshly squeezed fruit juice; **j. de poire/d'abricot** pear/apricot juice; **plein de j.** juicy, full of juice; **un j. d'orange, s'il vous plaît!** an orange juice, please

(b) *Culin (de viande)* juice(s); *(sauce)* gravy; **j. de viande** juice(s) from the meat, meat juices; **mon rôti n'a pas fait beaucoup de j.** my roast hasn't given off *or* produced much juice; **cuire** *ou* **mijoter dans son j.** *(de volaille, rôti)* to stew in its own juice; *Fig F* to stew in one's own juice

(c) *Arg* **il est tombé au j.** he fell in(to) the water; **au j.!** into the water with him/her!

(d) *Arg (café)* coffee

(e) *F (courant électrique)* juice; **j'ai pris du j.!** I got an electric shock!; **mets le j.!** switch on!

(f) *F (essence)* juice

(g) *F* **ça vaut le j.** it's really something

▶ **jus**: *F* **j. de chaussettes** *(café)* dishwater

jusant [ʒyzɑ̃] *nm* ebb (tide)

jusqu'au-boutisme [ʒyskobutism] *nm inv F* hard-line attitude; **je n'aime pas son j.** I don't like the way he always has to go the whole hog *or* his hard-line attitude

jusqu'au-boutiste, *pl* **jusqu'au-boutistes** [ʒyskobutist] *n F* hard liner, extremist; *(fidèle à un parti, des principes)* diehard

jusque [ʒysk(ə)] **1** *prép* **(a)** *(espace, mesure)* up to, as far as; **jusqu'ici** up to here, as far as here; **venez jusqu'ici** come over here; **j.-là** up to *or* as far as there *or* that point; **jusqu'où?** how far?; **depuis Londres jusqu'à Paris** all the way from London to Paris; **avoir de l'eau jusqu'à la taille** to have water (coming) right up to one's waist, to be waist-deep in water; **jusqu'au bout (de la rue)** (right) to the end (of the street); *Fig* **aller jusqu'au bout d'un raisonnement/d'une action** to follow an argument/action through; *Fig* **jusqu'à un**

certain point up to a certain point, to a certain extent; *Fig* **jusqu'où ira-t-il?** how far will he go?; **aller jusqu'à faire qch** to go so far as to do sth; **il a poussé la curiosité/le culot jusqu'à me demander si . . .** he was so curious/cheeky as to ask me if ..., his curiosity/cheek was such that he asked me if ...; **j. chez lui** (up) to his door; **rougir jusqu'aux oreilles** to blush to the roots of one's hair, to go as red as a beetroot; **la nouvelle est venue jusqu'à lui** the news reached him; **ce scandale va remonter jusqu'au directeur** this scandal will go as far up as the director, this scandal will go right to the top; **nous avions de la paille j. dans nos sous-vêtements** the straw even got inside our underwear; **compter jusqu'à dix** to count (up) to ten; **je veux bien mettre jusqu'à 200 francs** I'm prepared to put in up to 200 francs; **jusqu'à concurrence de 5 000 francs** (up) to 5,000 francs; **jusqu'à 250 gr** not exceeding 250g, up to 250g

(b) (*temps*) until, till; **attendez jusqu'après les vacances** wait until *or* till after the holidays; **jusqu'ici, jusqu'à maintenant, jusqu'à présent, j.-là** (*en référence au présent*) until now, up to now, to date, as yet, so far; **j.-là, jusqu'alors** (*en référence au passé*) until then, up to then; **jusqu'ici** *ou* **j.-là, c'est très bien** so far so good; **jusqu'à hier/dix heures** until *or* up to yesterday/ten o'clock; **jusqu'à (l'âge de) 15 ans** up to the age of 15, up to 15 (years old); **jusqu'à aujourd'hui** until today; **jusqu'à fin mai** until the end of May; **jusqu'à nouvel ordre** until further notice; **jusqu'à plus ample informé** pending further information, until further information is available; **jusqu'à mon dernier jour** to my dying day; **jusqu'au jour** *ou* **moment où ...** until the time when ..., until ...; **si nous remontons jusqu'en** *ou* **jusqu'à 1800** if we go back as far as 1800, if we go right back to 1800

(c) (*indique un point extrême*) **tous jusqu'au dernier** every last one (of them); **jusqu'à dix personnes l'ont vu** as many as ten people saw it; **tout en lui, jusqu'à son sourire, a changé** everything about him, right down to *or* even his smile, has changed; **il se montrait sévère jusqu'à la cruauté** he was severe to the point of cruelty

2 *conj* **jusqu'à ce que ...** *+sub, Vieilli* **jusqu'à tant que ...** *+sub* until ..., till ...; **jusqu'à ce que les portes soient fermées** until *or* till the doors are shut

jusques [ʒyskə] *prép Arch, Litt* = **jusque**; **j. et y compris . . .** [ʒyskəzeikɔ̃pri] up to and including . . .

justaucorps [ʒystokɔr] *nm* **(a)** (*pour la gymnastique*) leotard **(b)** (*pourpoint*) jerkin

juste [ʒyst] **1** *adj* **(a)** (*équitable*) (*personne, décision, punition, revendication*) fair, just; **ce n'est pas j.** it's not fair, it's unfair; **il est en colère, et à j. titre!** he's angry, and quite rightly (so) *or* and with good reason!; **ce n'est que j. récompense** it's nothing more than he/she/*etc* deserves, he/she/*etc* thoroughly deserves it; **ce n'est que j. récompense s'il a eu le premier prix** it's only right that he got first prize, he thoroughly deserves his first prize; **j. indignation** righteous indignation; **j. colère** righteous *or* justifiable anger; **elle se mit dans une j. colère** she became justifiably angry; **être j. avec** *ou* **vis-à-vis de** *ou* **envers qn** to be fair to sb; **pour être j. envers elle** to be fair to her, to give her her due; *Vieilli* **j. ciel!** heavens above!

(b) (*exact*) (*calcul, réponse, données*) right, accurate, correct; (*raisonnement*) sound; **quelle est l'heure j.?** what is the right *or* exact time?; **le mot j.** the exact *or* right word; **se faire une idée j. de la situation** to get a true *or* an accurate picture of the situation; **j. milieu** happy medium; **votre réponse n'est pas j.** your answer is not right *or* is wrong *or* is incorrect; **c'est j.** that's right; **c'est très j. ce que vous dites-là** what you say is quite right; **balance j.** accurate scales; **ma balance/ma montre n'est pas très j.** my scales are not/my watch is not very accurate *or* exact *or* precise; **ma montre est j.** my watch is right *or* accurate; **arriver à l'heure j.** to arrive right on time, *F* to arrive on the dot

(c) *Mus* (*en accord*) (*note*) right; **quarte j.** perfect fourth

(d) (*qui suffit à peine*) (*indemnité*) scanty; **c'est bien j.** (*plat, boisson etc*) there's barely *or* scarcely enough to go round; **un aussi petit gâteau pour six, tu ne trouves pas que c'est trop j.?** do you think such a little cake is anywhere near enough for six?; **une bouteille de champagne pour sept, c'est j.** one bottle of champagne for seven is cutting it a bit fine; **deux cents francs pour une semaine, c'est un peu j.!** 200 francs for one week, it's a bit on the short side *or* it's not a lot!; *Com* **au plus j. prix** at a rock bottom price, at a keen price; **ses résultats sont trop justes pour qu'elle passe dans la classe supérieure** she is not quite good enough to move up a class

(e) (*trop petit*) (*chaussures*) tight(-fitting); (*vêtement*) tight(-fitting), skimpy; **je te donne cette veste, moi elle m'est un peu j.** you can have this jacket, it's a bit tight on me

(f) *F* (*gêné financièrement*) **on est un peu justes en ce moment** we're a bit pushed for money *or* strapped for cash at the moment

2 *adv* **(a)** (*avec exactitude*) (*viser, parler*) accurately, **frapper j.** to land a perfect blow; *Fig* to strike *or* hit home; **je ne pouvais pas frapper plus j. en mentionnant ce sujet** I couldn't have struck *or* hit home harder when I mentioned this subject; **chanter j.** to sing in tune; **elle ne chante pas très j.** she can't sing in tune very well; **sonner j.** (*cloche, carillon*) to ring in tune; *Fig* (*discours, arguments*) to ring true; *Fig* **voir j.** to guess correctly *or* right; **raisonner j.** to argue soundly; **deviner** *ou F* **tomber j.** to guess right; **tout j.!** you said it!, that's right!

(b) (*précisément*) exactly, precisely, just; **il est midi j.** it's exactly *or* precisely twelve o'clock; **arriver à dix heures j.** to arrive on the stroke of ten, to arrive at ten o'clock sharp *or F* on the dot; **c'est j. au coin/en face/à côté** it's just *or* right on the corner/opposite/next door; **j. au milieu** right in the middle; **ça fait dix francs (tout) j.** that's ten francs exactly; **c'est j. l'homme qu'il nous faut** he's just the man *or* he's the very man we want *or* need; **c'est j. ce qu'il me fallait** it's just what I wanted, it's the very thing, it's just the job; *Iron* **un coup de téléphone de ma mère, c'est j. ce qu'il me fallait!** a phone call from my mother, that's all I needed!

(c) (*seulement, à peine*) just, only; **j'ai bu j. une gorgée pour goûter** I just *or* only drank a mouthful to get the taste; **mets-m'en j. un fond s'il te plait** give me just *or* only give me a drop, please; **c'est tout j. s'il sait lire** he can only just *or* he can barely read; **il ne manque jamais son train, mais c'est tout j.** he never misses his train, but he cuts it fine *or* it's a close thing; **c'est tout j. si elle ne m'a pas raccroché au nez!** she very nearly hung up on me!; **avoir j. le temps (de faire qch)** to have just (enough) time (to do sth); **vous avez tout j. le temps** you haven't a moment to spare; **j. à temps** just in time, in the nick of time; *Ind* just in time; **je suis arrivée j. à temps pour le voir** I arrived just in time to see him; **arriver j. à l'heure** to arrive just in time *or* in the nick of time; **il échappa tout j. à la mort** he narrowly escaped death; **on a tout j. évité la catastrophe** we narrowly avoided a catastrophe; **ils ont tout j. fini de manger** they've only just finished eating

(d) (*trop peu*) **voir** *ou* **prévoir** *ou* **calculer trop j.** not to allow enough, to allow too little (**pour** for)

(e) au j., tu fais quoi cet été? by the way, what are you doing this summer?; **je ne sais pas au j. si ...** I don't exactly know whether ...; **comme de j.** of course, as usual, naturally, as one would expect

3 *n Bible* **les justes** the just, the righteous

justement [ʒystəmɑ̃] *adv* **(a)** (*avec justesse*) rightly; **comme tu le disais si j. hier** as you so rightly said yesterday; **je lui ai j. fait remarquer que ...** I rightly pointed out to him that ...

(b) (*avec justice*) justly, rightly; **être j. récompensé** to be justly rewarded

(c) (*précisément*) exactly, precisely; **je vais faire des courses – tiens, j., si tu pouvais m'acheter ...** I'm going shopping – oh, well, if you could buy me ...; **voici j. la lettre que j'attendais** this is exactly *or* precisely the letter *or* here is the very letter I was waiting for; **j'ai toujours voulu voir Venise – j., on y va** I've always wanted to visit Venice – well that's just *or* exactly *or* precisely where we're going; **tu ne vas pas partir sans lui dire au revoir? – si, j.!** you're not going without saying goodbye to him? – that's precisely *or* exactly what I'm doing! *or* indeed I am!; **c'est drôle, on parlait de lui et j. le voilà** that's funny, we were just talking about him and here he is; **j., à ce propos, je voulais te dire que ...** well, while we're on the subject, I wanted to tell you that ...; **ah, vous tombez bien, j. je voulais vous parler de ...** ah, you've come at the right moment, I was just wanting to talk to you about ...

justesse [ʒystɛs] *nf* **(a)** (*précision*) (*d'une balance, d'un instrument de mesure*) accuracy, precision, exactness; (*d'une opinion*) soundness; (*d'une expression*) aptness, appropriateness; (*d'une comparaison*) exactness; **raisonner avec j.** to argue soundly **(b) de j.** (only) just; **j'ai eu mon train de j.** I (only) just got my train

justice [ʒystis] *nf* **(a)** (*équité*) justice; **c'est j., ce n'est que j.** it's only right *or* fair *or* just; *Hum* **il n'y a pas de j.!** there's no justice (in the world)!; **demander j. /que j. soit faite** to demand justice/that justice be done; **faire régner la j.** to establish justice; **en toute** *ou* **bonne j.** in all fairness; **avec j.** (*agir*) justly, in a just manner; **faire** *ou* **rendre j. à qn** to do justice to sb, to give sb his/her due; **se faire j. (à soi-même)** to take the law into one's own hands; (*se suicider*) to take one's own life, to commit suicide; **faire j. de qch** to judge sth for what it is

(b) *Jur* **la j.** the law; **la j. civile/militaire/administrative** civil/military/administrative law; **gens de j.** (*juges*) magistrates; (*avocats*) lawyers; **action en j.** action at law; **aller en j.** to go to law; **poursuivre qn en j.** to bring proceedings against sb, to take legal action against sb, to take sb to court; **traduire qn en j.** to bring sb before the courts

justiciable [ʒystisjabl] **1** *adj Jur* **j. d'un tribunal** justiciable to *or* in a court, amenable to a court; *Méd* **cas j. d'un certain traitement** case in which a certain treatment is indicated **2** *n* person subject to be tried

justicier, -ière [ʒystisje, -jɛr] *n* (a) dispenser of justice, righter of wrongs (b) *Jur Vieilli* dispenser of justice, justiciary

justifiable [ʒystifjabl] *adj* justifiable; **peu j.** unjustifiable

justificateur, -trice [ʒystifikatœr, -tris] **1** *adj* justifying, *Fml* justificatory **2** *n Typ* justifier

justificatif, -ive [ʒystifikatif, -iv] **1** *adj* justificatory; **pièce justificative** *Com* voucher (copy); *Admin* (*document écrit*) written proof; *Jur* relevant document; **pièces justificatives** (*pour une inscription*) supporting documents **2** *nm* (a) *Admin* written proof; *Jur* relevant document (b) (*exemplaire d'un journal*) free copy (*of newspaper sent to those who have an advertisement or a review etc in it*); **j. de paiement** proof of payment

justification [ʒystifikasjɔ̃] *nf* (a) (*explication*) justification; **demander/chercher des justifications** to demand/seek justification; **avez-vous une j. de votre absence d'hier?** is there any justification for *or* can you justify your absence yesterday?; **cela ne doit pas être une j. de la violence** that cannot be a justification for *or* of violence; **son livre est une j. du régime** his book is a justification of the regime; **il n'y a pas de j. possible à un acte aussi barbare** there is no possible justification for such a barbaric act

(b) (*preuve*) (*de fait, d'identité*) proof

(c) *Typ, Ordinat* (*de lignes*) justification; **j. à droite/gauche** right/left justification

justifié [ʒystifje] *adj* (a) (*action, comportement, réponse, colère etc*) justified, justifiable; **peu j.** unjustified, unwarranted (b) *Jur* **préjudice j.** proved damages (c) *Typ* justified; **j. à droite** flush right, right justified; **j. à gauche** flush left, left justified

justifier [ʒystifje] (*impf, pr sub* **n. justifiions, v. justifiiez**) **1** *vt* (a) (*faire apparaître comme légitime*) (*action, conduite, erreur, décision etc*) to justify; (*dépenses*) (*de personne*) to justify; (*de voyage, activité professionnelle*) to warrant, to justify; **les faits ont justifié nos craintes** the facts have justified *or* borne out *or* vindicated our fears; **son échec ne justifie pas cette crise de nerfs** his failure doesn't justify *or* warrant such hysterics

(b) *Typ, Ordinat* (*ligne de caractères*) to justify; **j. à droite/gauche** to right-/left-justify

(c) *Jur* **j. de ses mouvements** to account for one's movements; **j. de son identité** to prove one's identity

3 se justifier *vpr* (a) to justify oneself; **se j. d'une accusation** to clear oneself *or* one's name of an accusation; **inutile de te j.** there's no point in trying to justify yourself

(b) *Typ* to justify

jute [ʒyt] *nm* jute; **toile de j.** hessian

juter [ʒyte] *vi* to be juicy, to drip (with) juice

juteux, -euse [ʒytø, -øz] **1** *adj* (*fruit*) juicy; *F* **une affaire juteuse** a juicy *or* lucrative piece of business **2** *nm Mil Arg* warrant officer

juvénile [ʒyvenil] *adj* youthful; **délinquance j.** juvenile delinquency

juvénilité [ʒyvenilite] *nf Litt* youthfulness

juxtalinéaire [ʒykstalineɛr] *adj* **traduction j.** parallel translation

juxtaposer [ʒykstapoze] *vt* to juxtapose, to place side by side

juxtaposition [ʒykstapozisjɔ̃] *nf* juxtaposition

K

K, k [kɑ] *nm (lettre)* K, k; *Phys* **échelle K** (= **Kelvin**) Kelvin *or* absolute scale (*of temperatures*)
k (*abrév* **kilo**) k
K7 [kaset] *nf* (*abrév* **cassette**) tape
Kaboul [kabul] *n* Kabul
kabyle [kabil] **1** *adj* Kabyle **2** *nm Ling* Kabyle **3** *n* **K.** Kabyle
Kabylie [kabili] *nf* (**la Grande/Petite**) **K.** (Great/Lesser) Kabylia
kafkaïen, -ïenne [kafkajɛ̃, -jɛn] *adj* Kafkaesque
kaiser [kajzɛr] *nm* kaiser
kakatoès [kakatɔɛs] *nm* = **cacatoès**
kaki[1] [kaki] *adj inv, nm* (*couleur*) khaki, *Am* olive-drab
kaki[2] *nm* (*arbre, fruit*) persimmon
kalachnikov [kalaʃnikɔf] *nm* kalashnikov
Kalahari [kalaari] *nm* **le** (**désert du**) **K.** the Kalahari (Desert)
kaléidoscope [kaleidɔskɔp] *nm Opt, Fig* kaleidoscope
kaléidoscopique [kaleidɔskɔpik] *adj Opt, Fig* kaleidoscopic
kalmouk, -ouke [kalmuk] **1** *adj* Kalmuck **2** *nm Ling* Kalmuck **3** *n* **K.** Kalmuck
kamikaze [kamikaz] **1** *nm* kamikaze; *Fig* **être k.** to have a death wish **2** *adj inv* kamikaze; **opération k.** kamikaze operation, suicide mission
Kampuchéa [kɑ̃mputʃea] *nm* Kampuchea
kanak [kanak] *adj, n* = **canaque**
kangourou [kɑ̃guru] *nm* **(a)** *Zool* kangaroo; **k. de rochers** wallaby; *Géog* **île des Kangourous** Kangaroo Island **(b)** **(sac) k.** baby carrier; **slip k.** Y-fronts® **(c)** *Com* **exportation k.** piggybacking
kantien, -ienne [kɑ̃tjɛ̃, -jɛn] *adj Phil* Kantian
kantisme [kɑ̃tism] *nm Phil* Kantianism
kaolin [kaɔlɛ̃] *nm* kaolin
kaolinisation [kaɔlinizasjɔ̃] *nf Géol* kaolinization
kapok [kapɔk] *nm* kapok
kapokier [kapɔkje] *nm* kapok tree
Kaposi [kapozi] *nm Méd* **maladie** *ou* **sarcome de K.** Kaposi's sarcoma
karakul [karakyl] *nm* (*animal, laine*) caracul, karakul
karaté [karate] *nm* karate; **faire du k.** to do karate
karateka [karateka] *nm* karate expert, karateka
karbau [karbo] *nm* water buffalo
kardex [kardɛks] *nf* (*d'un client dans un hôtel*) guest history card
karité [karite] *nm* (*arbre*) shea (tree); **beurre de k.** shea butter
karma [karma] *nm Rel* karma
Karpathes [karpat] *nfpl* = **Carpates**
karst [karst] *nm Géol* karst
karstique [karstik] *adj Géol* karstic
kart [kart] *nm* (go-)kart, (go-)cart
karting [kartiŋ] *nm* karting, go-kart racing; **faire du k.** to go karting
kasba(h) [kazba] *nf* = **casba(h)**
kascher [kaʃɛr] *adj inv Rel* kosher
Katmandou [katmɑ̃du] *n* Katmandu
kava, kawa [kava] *nf* (*arbuste, boisson*) kava
kayac, kayak [kajak] *nm* **(a)** canoe, kayak; **faire du k.** to go canoeing, to canoe **(b)** (*embarcation des Esquimaux*) kayak
kayakiste [kajakist] *n* canoeist
Kazakhstan [kazakstɑ̃] *nm* Kazakhstan
keffieh [kefje] *nm* keffiyeh
kéfir [kefir] *nm Culin* kefir
kelvin [kɛlvin] *Phys* **1** *adj inv* **échelle K.** Kelvin *or* absolute scale (*of temperatures*) **2** *nm* kelvin
kendo [kɛndo] *nm* kendo
Kenya [kenja] *nm* Kenya
kenyan, -ane [kenjɑ̃, -an] **1** *adj* Kenyan **2** *n* **K.** Kenyan
képhir [kefir] *nm Culin* kefir
képi [kepi] *nm* kepi
kérabau [kerabo] *nm* water buffalo
kératine [keratin] *nf* keratin, ceratin
kératite [keratit] *nf Méd* keratitis
kératoplastie [keratɔplasti] *nf Chir* keratoplasty, corneal grafting
kératose [keratoz] *nf Méd, Vét* keratosis
Kerguelen [kɛrgelɛn] *nfpl* **les (îles) K.** Kerguelen
kermesse [kɛrmɛs] *nf* **(a)** (*dans les Flandres*) kermis, village fair **(b)** (*fête de bienfaisance*) (charity) fête; **la k. de l'école** the school fête
kérosène [kerozɛn] *nm Av* kerosene; *Ch* paraffin (oil), *Am* kerosene
ketch [kɛtʃ] *nm Naut* ketch
ketchup [kɛtʃœp] *nm Culin* (tomato) ketchup
keufs [kœf] *nmpl très F* **les k.** the fuzz, the cops
kevlar® [kevlar] *nm* kevlar
keynésien, -ienne [kenezjɛ̃, -jɛn] *adj, n Écon* Keynesian
KF [kaɛf] *nm* (*abrév* **kilofrancs**) thousand francs; **poste de directeur à 500 KF** director's post, salary 500 K
kg (*abrév* **kilogramme**) kg
KGB [kagebe] *nm* KGB
khâgne [kaɲ] *nf* = **cagne**
khâgneux, -euse [kaɲø, -øz] *n F* = **cagneux**
khalifat [kalifa] *nm* = **califat**
khalife [kalif] *nm* = **calife**
khamsin [xamsin] *nm Météo* khamsin
khan [kɑ̃] *nm* khan
khédive [kediv] *nm* khedive
khmer, khmère [kmɛr] **1** *adj* Khmer **2** *nm Ling* Khmer **3** *n* **K.** Khmer; *Pol* **les Khmers rouges** the Khmer Rouge
khôl [kol] *nm* kohl
kibboutz, *pl* **kibbouts** [kibuts], **kibboutzim** [kibutsim] *nm* [①A14,11] kibbutz
kick-down [kikdawn] *nm Aut* kick-down
kick(-starter), *pl* **kick(-starter)s** [kik(startɛr)] *nm* (*pour moto etc*) kick-starter; **démarrer une moto au k.** to kick-start a motorbike; **donner un coup de k.** to kick the starter
kidnapper [kidnape] *vt* to kidnap
kidnappeur, -euse [kidnapœr, -øz] *n* kidnapper
kidnapping [kidnapiŋ] *nm* kidnapping
kievien, -ienne [kjevjɛ̃, -jɛn] **1** *adj* Kievan; *Hist* **Russie kievienne** Kievan Russia, Kiev Rus **2** *n* **K.** Kievan
kif[1] [kif] *nm* cannabis, hemp
kif[2], **kif-kif** *adj inv F* **c'est k., c'est k-k. (bourricot)** it's all the same, it makes no difference *or Br* no odds
kiki [kiki] *nm F* **(a)** (*cou*) neck, throat; **serrer le k. à qn** (*de personne*) to throttle sb, to wring sb's neck; **couper le k. à qn** (*lui couper le sifflet*) to shut sb up **(b)** *Région F* (*petit ruban*) bow **(c)** (*sexe des petits garçons*) willy **(d)** **c'est parti mon k.!** here we go!
kil [kil] *nm F* litre, *US* liter; **un k. de rouge** a litre of red (wine)
Kilimandjaro [kilimɑ̃dʒaro] *nm* **le K.** (Mount) Kilimanjaro
kilo [kilo] *nm* kilo
kilobaud [kilɔbo] *nm Ordinat* kilobaud
kilocalorie [kilɔkalɔri] *nf* kilocalorie
kilocycle [kilɔsikl] *nm* kilocycle
kilofranc [kilɔfrɑ̃] *nm Fin* thousand francs
kilogramme [kilɔgram] *nm* kilogram(me)
kilohertz [kilɔɛrts] *nm* kilohertz
kilojoule [kilɔʒul] *nm* kilojoule
kilométrage [kilɔmetraʒ] *nm* **(a)** (*d'une route*) marking off with milestones **(b)** (*distance*) ≈ mileage; **location de voiture avec k. illimité** car rental with unlimited mileage; **k. maximal autorisé** maximum permitted mileage
kilomètre [kilɔmɛtr] *nm* kilometre, *US* kilometer; **k. carré/cube** square/cubic kilometre; **100 kilomètres à l'heure, 100 kilomètres-heure** 100 kilometres per *or* an hour; *F* **bouffer** *ou* **avaler du k.** *ou* **les kilomètres** to eat up the miles; *F* **des kilomètres de pellicule** miles of film; **taper du texte** *ou* **faire de la saisie de texte au k.** to type text straight in (*and leave the formatting etc until later*); *Cyclisme* **k. arrêté** standing-start kilometre
kilomètre-passager, *pl* **kilomètres-passagers** *nm Admin, Av* passenger-kilometre, *US* passenger-kilometer
kilométrer [kilɔmetre] *vt* (**je kilomètre, n. kilométrons**; **je kilométrerai**) (*route*) to mark off with kilometre *or US* kilometer stones

kilomètre-voyageur, *pl* **kilomètres-voyageurs** *nm Admin* passenger-kilometre, *US* passenger-kilometer
kilométrique [kilɔmetrik] *adj* **borne k.** kilometre *or US* kilometer stone, ≈ milestone; **distance k.** distance in kilometres *or US* kilometers
kilo-octet, *pl* **kilo-octets** *nm Ordinat* kilobyte
kilotonne [kilɔtɔn] *nf* kiloton
kilovolt [kilɔvɔlt] *nm Vieilli* kilovolt
kilowatt [kilɔwat] *nm Vieilli* kilowatt
kilowattheure [kilɔwatœr] *nm Phys* kilowatt-hour
kilt [kilt] *nm* kilt; (*de femme*) pleated tartan skirt
kimono [kimɔno] *nm* kimono; **manche k.** kimono sleeve
kinase [kinaz] *nf Biol, Ch* kinase
kiné [kine] *n F* (*abrév* **kinésithérapeute, kinésithérapie**) physio
kinéscope [kineskɔp] *nm* kinescope
kinésithérapeute [kineziterapøt] *n* physiotherapist
kinésithérapie [kineziterapi] *nf* physiotherapy
kinesthésie [kinɛstezi] *nf* kinaesthesia, *US* kinesthesia
king-charles [kiŋʃarl] *nm inv* King Charles spaniel
kinkajou [kɛ̃kaʒu] *nm* kinkajou, honey bear
kiosque [kjɔsk] *nm* **(a)** (*pavillon*) pavilion; (*où l'on vend qch*) kiosk; **k. de** *ou* **à musique** bandstand; **k. à journaux** newspaper kiosk, newsstand **(b)** *Naut* (*d'un sous-marin*) conning tower; **k. de la barre** (*d'un navire*) wheelhouse; **k. de veille/de navigation** pilot house/chart house *or* room **(c)** *Télécom* **k. télématique**® Minitel information service
kip [kip] *nm Fin* kip
kippa [kipa] *nf* kippa
kipper [kipœr] *nm* kipper
kir [kir] *nm* kir
kirghise, kirghize [kirgiz] **1** *adj* Khirghiz **2** *nm Ling* Khirgiz **3** *n* **K.** Khirgiz
Kirghizistan [kirgizistɑ̃] *nm*, **Kirghizie** [kirgizi] *nf* Kirghizia
kirsch [kirʃ] *nm* kirsch
kit [kit] *nm* (home- *or* self-assembly) kit; **étagère vendue en k.** shelf unit sold in kit form, shelf unit sold for home- *or* self-assembly; **acheter une table en k.** to buy a table in kit form; *Pharm* **k. de dépistage** home testing kit; **k. développeur** (*pour imprimante*) developer kit; *Ordinat* **k. d'extension** *ou* **d'évolution** upgrade kit; **k. de téléchargeur** download kit
kitchenette [kitʃənɛt] *nf* kitchenette
kit(s)ch [kitʃ] *adj inv, nm inv* kitsch
kiwi [kiwi] *nm* **(a)** (*oiseau*) kiwi **(b)** (*fruit*) kiwi fruit, Chinese gooseberry
klaxon [klaksɔn] *nm Aut* horn; **donner un coup de k.** to sound one's horn, *Br* to hoot (one's horn); **k. italien** tune-playing horn
klaxonner [klaksɔne] **1** *vi Aut* to sound one's horn, *Br* to hoot (one's horn) **2** *vt* **k. qn** to sound one's horn at sb, *Br* to hoot (one's horn) at sb
klebs [klɛp(s)] *nm très F* = **clebs**
kleenex® [klinɛks] *nm inv* Kleenex®, (paper) tissue, paper hanky
kleptomane [klɛptɔman] *adj, n* kleptomaniac
kleptomanie [klɛptɔmani] *nf* kleptomania
klystron [klistrɔ̃] *nm Électron* klystron
km (*abrév* **kilomètre(s)**) km
km/h (*abrév* **kilomètres (à l')heure**) km./h, kph
knicker [nikœr] *nm*, **knickers** [nikœr] *nmpl* knickerbockers, *Am* knickers
knock-out [nɔkawt] *Boxe* **1** *adj inv* **mettre qn k.** to knock sb out; **être k.** to be knocked out **2** *nm inv* knockout
knout [knut] *nm Hist Russe* knout
Ko *nm* (*abrév* **kilo-octet**) K, KB
k-o [kao] **1** *nm Boxe abrév* **knock-out 2** *adj inv* **(a)** *Boxe abrév* **knock-out (b)** *F* (*fatigué*) shattered; **mettre qn k.** to shatter sb
koala [kɔala] *nm* koala (bear)
kobold [kɔbɔld] *nm Myth* kobold
koch [kɔk] *n Méd* **bacille de k.** Koch's bacillus
kola [kɔla] *nm* (*fruit*) **(noix de) k.** cola *or* kola nut
kolatier [kɔlatje] *nm* cola (tree), kola (tree)
kolkhoze [kɔlkoz] *nm* kolkhoz, collective farm
kolkhozien, -ienne [kɔlkɔzjɛ̃, -jɛn] **1** *adj* kolkhoz **2** *n* kolkhoznik
Komintern [kɔmintɛrn] *nm Hist Pol* Comintern
kommandantur [kɔmɑ̃dɑ̃tur] *nf Hist* German military command
komsomol [kɔmsɔmɔl] *nm Hist Pol* Komsomol member
kopeck [kɔpɛk] *nm* kopeck; *F* **ça ne vaut pas un k.** it's not worth a bean
Koran (le) [ləkɔrɑ̃] *nm* the Koran
korrigan, -ane [kɔrigɑ̃, -an] *n* (*en Bretagne*) goblin
Kosovo [kosovo] *nm* Kosovo
kouglof [kuglɔf] *nm Culin* kugelhopf
koukri [kukri] *nm* kukri, Gurkha knife
koulak [kulak] *nm* kulak
Kouriles [kuril] *nfpl* **les (îles) Kouriles** the Kuril(e) Islands
Koweït [kɔwɛ(j)t] **1** *nm* (*État*) Kuwait **2** *n* (*ville*) Kuwait
koweïtien, -ienne [kɔwɛ(j)tjɛ̃, jɛn] **1** *adj* Kuwaiti **2** *n* **K.** Kuwaiti
kraal [kral] *nm* kraal
krach [krak] *nm* **k. (boursier)** (Stock Market) crash
kraft [kraft] *nm* **(papier) k.** brown (wrapping) paper, manil(l)a paper; **enveloppe en papier k.** manil(l)a envelope
kraken [krakɛn] *nm* kraken
Kremlin (le) [ləkrɛmlɛ̃] *nm* the Kremlin
kremlinologie [krɛmlinɔlɔʒi] *nf* Kremlinology
kremlinologue [kremlinɔlɔg] *n* Kremlinologist, *F* Kremlin-watcher
kriss [kris] *nm* kris, Malay dagger
kroumir [krumir] *nm* (*chausson*) pump
krypton [kriptɔ̃] *nm Ch* krypton
ksar, *pl* **ksour** [ksar, ksur] *nm* fortress, fortified village (*in North Africa*)
kumquat [kɔmkwat, kum-] *nm* (*fruit*) kumquat, cumquat
kung-fu [kuŋfu] *nm inv* kung fu; **faire du k.** to do kung fu
kurde [kyrd] **1** *adj* Kurdish **2** *nm Ling* Kurdish **3** *n* **K.** Kurd
Kurdistan [kyrdistɑ̃] *nm* Kurdistan
kvas [kvas] *nm* kvas(s)
kW *Él* (*abrév* **kilowatt**) kW
kwas [kvas] *nm* kvas(s)
k-way® [kawɛ] *nm* cagoule, waterproof jacket, *Am* K-way; **pantalon de k.** waterproof leggings
kWh *Él* (*abrév* **kilowatt(s)-heure**) kWh
kyat [kjat] *nm* kyat
kymographe [kimɔgraf] *nm Méd* kymograph
kymrique [kimrik] *adj, nm* Cymric, Kymric
kyrie [kirje] *nm Rel* Kyrie (eleison)
kyrielle [kirjɛl] *nf* (*de mots, raisons, mensonges*) string; (*de reproches*) string, stream; (*d'enfants*) swarm, crowd; **une k. d'insultes** a stream *or* torrent of abuse; **une k. de pièces/de photos** a whole series of rooms/photos; **elle a une k. d'amis** she has masses *or* a mass of friends; **il m'a fait une k. de reproches** he reproached me again and again
kyste [kist] *nm Méd* cyst; **k. synovial** ganglion
kystique [kistik] *adj Méd* cystic

L

L, l [ɛl] *n* **(a)** (*lettre*) L, l **(b)** *Ling* **l mouillé(e)** liquid l, palatal(ized) l **(c)** *Fin* **L** £

l *abrév* **(a)** (**litre**) l **(b)** (**la livre**) lb

l', la¹ [la] *art déf, pron f voir* = **le¹,²**

la² *nm inv Mus* **(a)** (*note*) A; **donner le la** to give the *or* an A; *Fig* to set the tone **(b)** (*tonalité*) (*au solfège*) la

là [la] **1** *adv* **(a)** (*endroit où se trouve celui qui parle*) here; (*là-bas*) there; **là où vous êtes** where you are; **il est là** (*présent*) he's here; **viens là!** come here!; **quand il n'est pas là** when he isn't here/there, when he's away; **le patron n'est jamais là le jeudi** the boss isn't here/there on Thursdays; **est-ce que le patron est là?** is the boss in?; **de là au village il y a un kilomètre** it's one kilometre from there to the village; **à cinq pas de là se tenait l'agent de police** five paces away stood the policeman; **c'est là qu'il demeure** that's where he lives; *F* **ôtez-vous de là!** get out of there!; **si tu vas par là** (*dans cette direction*) if you're going that way; *Fig* **si tu vas par là, pourquoi ne pas rétablir le travail des enfants?** why not bring back child labour while you're at it?; **quelque part par là** somewhere around here/there; **là, en bas/en haut** down/up there

(b) (*à ce point*) **les choses en sont là** that's how things stand at the moment; **restons-en là** let's leave it at that; **la question n'est pas là** that's not the point; **c'est bien là le problème** that's the problem; **c'est là où nous ne sommes plus d'accord/que nos opinions divergent** that's where we disagree/where we *or* our opinions differ; **c'est là qu'elle fut interrompue** that's when she was interrupted, it was at that moment that she was interrupted; *Fig* **je m'en suis mis jusque-là** (*j'ai beaucoup et bien mangé*) I'm full up to here; *F* **j'en ai jusque-là de vos histoires** I've had it up to here with your stories, I've had your stories up to here

(c) (*ici, à ce moment*) **qu'est-ce que je vois là? mais ce sont mes gants!** if it isn't my gloves!; **mais qu'est-ce que je vois là? ma fille avec un garçon** what's this (I see)? my daughter with a boy?; *Mil* **halte! qui va là?** halt! who goes there?; **que dites-vous là?** what's that you're saying?; (*qu'est-ce que vous voulez dire?*) what are you saying?, what do you mean?; **là tu exagères** now you're exaggerating; **je ne vois là aucune raison de s'inquiéter** I don't see that there's anything to worry about; **il n'y a là rien d'étonnant** there's nothing surprising about that

(d) (*ce moment*) then; **d'ici là** between now and then, in the meantime; **en l'an 2036, mais d'ici là …** in the year 2036, but by then …; **à quelques jours de là** some days after (that), a few days later

(e) (*ceci, ça*) **de là à croire que tout est facile, il y a une marge!** but to conclude from that that everything's easy!; **mais de là à dire qu'ils sont tous antipathiques!** but to conclude from that that they're all unpleasant!; **mais de là à ce qu'il nous donne son accord …** but as to giving us his agreement …; **qu'entendez vous par là?** what do you mean by that?; **de là on peut conclure que …** from this *or* hence, it may be concluded that …; **de là sa réaction** hence his reaction

(f) ce …-là that …; **ces …-là** those …; **ces gens-là sont ennuyeux** those people are boring; **il est taré ce mec-là!** the guy's crazy!; **il est bête à ce point-là?** is he (really) that stupid?; **je savais qu'il buvait beaucoup, mais pas à ce point-là!** I knew he drank a lot but not that much *or* not to that extent!; *voir* **ce², celui-là, celle-là**

(g) *Iron* **il se pose (un peu) là, comme plombier!** he's an absolutely hopeless plumber!

2 *int* **(a)** (*doucement*) **hé là! doucement!** gently does it!; **là, là!** there now, there there

(b) oh là là! oh dear!; **oh là là! ce qu'il fait chaud!** goodness, it's warm!

(c) alors là, ce n'est pas étonnant! well, <u>that's</u> not surprising!

(d) oh là! il a failli tomber! oh dear *or* goodness, he almost fell!; **oh là doucement! je n'ai pas dit ça!** now wait a minute *or F* hang about a bit, I didn't say that

là-bas *adv* over there; (*dans cette région, ce pays*) there; **tiens! le voilà l.** there he is over there

label [labɛl] **1** *nm* **(a)** *Com* quality label; **l. NF** *ou* **norme française** (*délivré par l'AFNOR*) French industry standards label; **l. d'exportation** export label; **le produit porte un l. de qualité** the product carries a quality label; *Fig* **il fera probablement campagne sous le l. socialiste** he will probably campaign as a Socialist **(b)** *Ordinat* **l. de volume** volume label **2** *adj inv Com* which carries a seal of approval

labelisé [labɛlize] *adj* which carries a seal of approval

labeur [labœr] *nm* **(a)** *Litt* labour, *US* labor, toil, hard work **(b)** *Typ* **imprimerie de l.** book printing works

labial, -iale, -iaux, -iales [labjal, -jo] **1** *adj* **(a)** *Anat* (*muscle etc*) labial **(b)** *Ling* **consonne labiale** labial **2** *nf Ling* **labiale** labial

labialisation [labjalizasjɔ̃] *nf Ling* labialization

labialiser [labjalize] *vt Ling* to labialize

labié [labje] *adj Bot* lipped, *Spéc* labiate

labiodental, -ale, -aux, -ales [labjodɑ̃tal, -o] *Ling* **1** *adj* labiodental **2** *nf* **labiodentale** labiodental

labo [labo] *nm F* lab; **l. photo** darkroom; **l. de langues** language lab; **les élèves qui font du l.** the pupils doing lab work

laborantin, -ine [labɔrɑ̃tɛ̃, -in] *n* laboratory *or F* lab assistant

laboratoire [labɔratwar] *nm* laboratory; **l. de recherche/de langues** research/language laboratory; **l. d'analyses (médicales)** pathology laboratory; **l. spatial/orbital** spacelab/orbiting laboratory; **l. d'essai de produits** testing laboratory; **l. de développement** processing lab; **l. de film** film laboratory

laborieusement [labɔrjøzmɑ̃] *adv* laboriously; **gagner l. sa vie** to work hard for a living

laborieux, -euse [labɔrjø, -øz] *adj* **(a)** (*difficile*) laborious; *Péj* (*style*) laboured, *US* labored; *Péj* **ce roman a quelque chose de l.** the novel is rather laboured; *F* **il n'a pas encore fini? c'est l.!** hasn't he finished yet? it's taking a long time *or* he's making heavy weather of it!; **j'ai réussi à la convaincre, mais ça a été l.!** I managed to convince her but it was a laborious task *or* but it was heavy going! **(b)** (*travailleur*) hard-working; *Litt* **les masses laborieuses** the toiling masses

labour [labur] *nm Agr* **(a)** (*labourage*) ploughing, *US* plowing, tilling; **l. à la bêche** digging; **cheval de l.** plough *or US* plow horse **(b) labours** ploughed *or US* plowed land; **le semeur dans les labours** the sower in his ploughed fields

labourable [laburabl] *adj Agr* (*terre*) ploughable, *US* plowable

labourage [laburaʒ] *nm Agr* ploughing, *US* plowing, tilling

labourer [labure] **1** *vt* **(a)** (*terre*), *Agr* to plough, *US* to plow, to till; (*de char, moto*) to churn up; **l. la terre à la bêche** to dig the soil; **un petit vent méchant labourait la mer** a sharp breeze was furrowing the surface of the sea

(b) *Naut* **l. le fond** (*d'un bateau*) to graze the bottom; (*d'une ancre*) to drag

(c) visage labouré de rides face furrowed with wrinkles; **les griffes du tigre lui ont labouré la poitrine** his chest was lacerated by the tiger's claws; **mon sac à dos me laboure le bas du dos** my rucksack is digging into my back; *F* **les flics lui ont labouré les côtes (de coups)** the cops gave him a going-over *or* roughed him up

2 se labourer *vpr* **se l. les mains** to lacerate one's hands

laboureur [laburœr] *nm Agr* ploughman, *US* plowman

Labrador [labradɔr] *nm Géog* Labrador

labrador [labradɔr] *nm* Labrador

labyrinthe [labirɛ̃t] *nm* **(a)** maze, labyrinth; *Fig* maze **(b)** *Anat* (*de l'oreille*) labyrinth

labyrinthique [labirɛ̃tik] *adj* labyrinthine

lac [lak] *nm Géog* lake; **l. de cirque** tarn; **les lacs d'Écosse** the Scottish lochs; **le l. Léman** *ou* **de Genève** Lake Geneva; **l. artificiel** artificial lake; (*pour fournir de l'eau*) reservoir; **l. de montagne** mountain lake; *Fig* **être dans le l.** to have fallen through

laçage [lasaʒ] *nm* (*de chaussures, bottes*) tying (up); (*de corset*) lacing (up)
lacer [lase] (**je laçai(s); n. laçons**) **1** *vt* (*corset*) to lace up; **l. ses chaussures/ses bottes** to tie one's shoe/boot laces, to tie up *or* do up one's shoes/boots **2 se lacer** *vpr* (*de chaussures, bottes*) to tie up, to do up; **ce corset se lace sur le côté** this corset laces (up) at the side
lacération [laserasjɔ̃] *nf* **(a)** (*action*) laceration; (*avec un couteau*) slashing **(b)** (*blessure*) laceration; (*faite avec un couteau, des ciseaux*) slash
lacérer [lasere] *vt* (**je lacère, n. lacérons, je lacérerai**) *Méd* to lacerate; **il s'est lacéré les jambes avec un couteau** he slashed his legs with a knife; **le chat a lacéré le fauteuil avec ses griffes** the cat has clawed the armchair to pieces; **la douleur lui lacère le dos** the pain is like a knife in his back, he has a lacerating pain in his back
lacet [lasɛ] *nm* **(a)** (*de chaussure*) (shoe)lace; (*de botte*) (boot)lace; (*de corset*) lace; **chaussures à lacets** lace-up shoes, lace-ups; **faire ses lacets** to tie one's laces **(b)** (*tournant*) (hairpin) bend, sharp bend; **sentier en lacets** winding *or* twisting *or* zigzag path; **la route monte en lacets** the road winds steeply up; **la route fait des lacets** the road zigzags, the road twists and turns **(c)** *Tech, Av* yaw(ing) **(d)** (*collet*) (*pour lapins, oiseaux etc*) noose, snare; **tendre un l.** to set a snare **(e)** *Couture* braid
lâchage [lɑʃaʒ] *nm* (*d'un parachutiste etc*) dropping; **un l. de vivres** a supply drop; *Fig* **ce n'est pas le l. de quelques-uns qui nous forcera à abandonner** we're not going to give up just because one or two people have backed out
lâche [lɑʃ] **1** *adj* **(a)** (*non serré, large*) (*ressort, nœud etc*) loose, slack; (*vêtement*) loose-fitting; (*discipline*) lax; (*style*) woolly **(b)** *Péj* (*peureux*) cowardly **(c)** *Péj* (*vil*) (*acte, attitude, attaque*) cowardly **(d)** *Litt Péj* (*mou*) (*personnage*) weak, feeble **2** *n* coward
lâchement [lɑʃmɑ̃] *adv* **(a)** (*non serré*) loosely, slackly **(b)** (*sans courage*) like a coward; **un crime l. perpétré** a cowardly act
lâcher[1] [lɑʃe] **1** *vt* **(a)** (*donner du mou à*) (*corde*) to slacken, to loosen; *Aut* **l. la pédale du frein** to take one's foot off the brake
(b) (*ne plus tenir*) (*corde etc*) to let go of; (*laisser tomber*) to drop; *Av* (*bombe*) to release, to drop; (*parachutiste*) to drop; **lâchez-moi!** let me go!, let go of me!; **l. sa proie** (*d'un animal*) to drop its prey; **l. prise** to let go; *F* **il ne m'a pas lâché d'une semelle** he stuck to me like a leech; *F* **l. des sous,** *très F* **les l.** to fork out; **il a du mal à les l., il ne les lâche pas facilement** he hates putting his hand in his pocket; **il les lâche avec un élastique** he's a real Scrooge *or Am* tightwad
(c) *F* (*abandonner*) (*associé, mari, famille, société*) to walk out on; (*amant*) to drop, to ditch; (*fiancé*) to jilt; (*ami*) to drop; (*emploi*) to chuck in; **la voiture nous a lâchés** the car died on us *or* packed in on us; **l. ses études** to drop out (of university)
(d) (*distancer*) (*reporter, poursuivant etc*) to shake off; **il vient de l. le peloton** he has just left the rest of the field behind *or* gone way out in front
(e) *F* (*cesser d'importuner*) to leave alone; **lâche-moi les baskets** *ou Vulg* **la grappe** give it a rest, get off my back
(f) (*libérer*) to release; **le sergent nous lâchait toujours à la dernière minute** the sergeant never used to let us go until the last minute; **l. un chien** to unleash a dog, to let a dog loose; (*à la chasse*) to slip a dog; **l. le chien contre qn** to set the dog on sb
(g) *Ordinat* (*icône*) to drop
(h) (*laisser échapper*) (*juron, cri de surprise, Vulg pet, rot*) to let out; (*sottise, plaisanterie*) to come out with; (*phrase*) to say; *Arg* **l. le paquet** *ou* **le morceau** to spill the beans, to come clean
2 *vi* (*d'une corde, d'un câble*) to break; (*d'un mécanisme, d'une pièce*) to go; (*d'un moteur*) to die, to pack in; *F* (*d'un organe*) to give out, to pack in; **mes freins ont lâché** my brakes failed; *Fig* **ses nerfs ont lâché** he broke down, his nerves gave way
lâcher[2] *nm* (*de pigeons, ballons etc*) release; *Ordinat* **l. d'icônes** icon drop
lâcheté [lɑʃte] *nf* **(a)** (*couardise*) cowardice, cowardliness; **il se tait par l.** he is keeping quiet out of cowardice **(b)** *Litt* (*faiblesse, mollesse*) weakness **(c)** (*acte lâche*) act of cowardice
lâcheur, -euse [lɑʃœr, -øz] *n F* (*traître*) rat
lacis [lasi] *nm* (*de nerfs, fils etc*) network; **un fin l. de veines bleutées** a delicate web of blue veins; **l. de ruelles** maze of back streets; **un l. d'intrigues** a web of intrigue
laconique [lakɔnik] *adj* laconic; **répondre de façon l.** to answer laconically
laconiquement [lakɔnikmɑ̃] *adv* laconically
laconisme [lakɔnism] *nm* (*d'une réponse*) laconicism; **elle ne supporte pas son l.** she cannot bear the fact that he is so taciturn
lacrymal, -ale, -aux, -ales [lakrimal, -o] *adj* (*conduit*) tear, *Spéc* lachrymal; **glande lacrymale** tear gland
lacrymogène [lakrimɔʒɛn] *adj* **gaz/grenade l.** tear-gas/tear-gas grenade
lacs [lɑ] *nm* **(a)** (*motif décoratif*) **l. d'amour** love knot **(b)** *Arch, Litt* (*piège*) noose, snare; *Fig Litt* **tomber dans le l.** to fall into the trap
lactaire [laktɛr] **1** *adj* lacteal **2** *nm* (*champignon*) lactarius; **l. délicieux** saffron milk cap
lactation [laktasjɔ̃] *nf Physiol* lactation
lacté [lakte] *adj* (*sécrétion*) lacteal; (*produit*) which contains milk; (*régime*) milk; *Litt* (*chair*) milky
lactescent [laktesɑ̃] *adj* milky
lactifère [laktifɛr] *adj Anat* lactiferous; (*conduit*) lacteal
lactique [laktik] *adj Ch* (*acide*) lactic
lactose [laktoz] *nf Ch* lactose
lacunaire [lakynɛr] *adj* **(a)** (*documentation, informations*) incomplete **(b)** *Anat, Bot* (*incomplet*) lacunar(y), lacunal
lacune [lakyn] *nf* **(a)** (*manque*) (*dans un texte, un dictionnaire, ses connaissances, ses souvenirs*) gap, *Fml* lacune; (*de mémoire*) blank; **cette liste comporte plusieurs lacunes** there are several gaps in the list, the list is incomplete; **cette loi n'est pas sans lacunes** there are loopholes in this law; **malgré ses lacunes en physique** despite his shortcomings in physics **(b)** *Biol, Anat* lacuna; *Bot* air cell
lacuneux, -euse [lakynø, -øz] *adj* = **lacunaire**
lacustre [lakystr] *adj* (*flore, faune, habitat*) lakeside, lakeshore, *Spéc* lacustrine; **habitation l.** lake dwelling, pile dwelling; **cité l.** lake village, collection of lake dwellings
lad [lad] *nm* stable lad, boy
là-dedans [lad(ə)dɑ̃] *adv* inside; (*dans un lieu, objet indiqué*) in there; (*dans une boîte, un sac*) in it, in this; **il y a l. quelque chose que je ne comprends pas** there's something here I don't understand; **ça ne m'étonnerait pas qu'elle soit impliquée l.** it wouldn't surprise me if she was involved (in it); **il n'a rien à voir l.!** he's got nothing to do with it!; *F* **debout l.!** rise and shine!; *F* **il y en a l.!** he's/she's got a lot up top
là-dessous [latsu] *adv* under that, under there, underneath; *Fig* **il y a quelque chose l.** there's something behind it; **il y a un secret l.** something is being kept secret
là-dessus [latsy] *adv* on that, on it; **tout le monde est d'accord l.** everybody agrees about that; **l., il est sorti** with that *or Fml* thereupon, he went out; **nous reviendrons l.** we'll come back to that; **c'est l. qu'il faut se concentrer** that's what you/we/*etc* have to concentrate on
ladre [ladr] **1** *adj* **(a)** *Vét* (*porc*) measly, measled **(b)** *Arch* (*lépreux*) leprous **(c)** *Arch, Litt* (*avare*) miserly **2** *n Arch* **(a)** (*lépreux*) leper **(b)** *Litt* (*avare*) miser
ladrerie [ladrəri] *nf* **(a)** *Vét* (*des porcs*) measles **(b)** *Arch* (*léproserie*) leprosy **(c)** *Arch, Litt* (*avarice*) miserliness
lagon [lagɔ̃] *nm Géog* lagoon
lagopède [lagɔpɛd] *nm Orn* lagopus; **l. des Alpes** ptarmigan; **l. d'Écosse** red grouse
lagune [lagyn] *nf Géog* lagoon
là-haut *adv* up there; (*à un étage supérieur*) upstairs; (*dans cette région, ce pays*) there
lai[1] [lɛ] *nm Littér* lay
lai[2] *adj Rel* **frère/sœur lai(e)** lay brother/sister
laïc [laik] *adj, nm* = **laïque**
laîche [lɛʃ] *nf Bot* sedge
laïcisation [laisizasjɔ̃] *nf* secularization, laicization
laïciser [laisize] *vt* to secularize, to laicize
laïcisme [laisism] *nm* secularism, laicism
laïcité [laisite] *nf* (*des écoles*) secularity; *Pol* secularism
laid, laide [lɛ, lɛd] **1 (a)** *adj* (*personne, visage*) ugly; (*imperfection, tache, édifice*) ugly, unsightly; *F* **l. comme un pou** *ou* **à faire peur** as ugly as sin, *F* plug ugly **(b)** (*méprisable*) (*action etc*) despicable; **c'est l. de mentir** (*à un enfant*) it's very naughty to tell lies; **comme c'est l. de faire des grimaces!** it's not nice to make faces! **2** *n* (*physiquement*) ugly person **3** *nm* **le l.** ugly things; **le l. et le beau** the ugly and the beautiful; **c'est d'un l.!** it's so ugly!
laidement [lɛdmɑ̃] *adv* **(a)** (*sans goût, mal*) in an ugly way **(b)** (*ignoblement*) meanly, dishonestly
laideron [lɛdrɔ̃] *nm Péj* ugly girl/woman; **un petit l.** an ugly duckling
laideur [lɛdœr] *nf* **(a)** (*physique*) (*d'une personne, d'un visage*) ugliness; (*d'une imperfection, d'une tache, d'un édifice*) ugliness, unsightliness; **d'une l. épouvantable** horrifically

ugly **(b)** *(bassesse) (d'une conduite etc)* meanness, lowness, nastiness **(c) les laideurs de la vie** the ugly side of life

laie[1] [lɛ] *nf Zool* (wild) sow

laie[2] *nf (sentier)* forest track, ride

laie[3] *nf Tech* bush hammer

lainage [lɛnaʒ] *nm* **(a)** *(étoffe)* woollen fabric **(b)** *(vêtement en laine)* woollen garment *or* article, *F* woolly; *Com* **lainages** woollen goods, woollens **(c)** *Tex* teaseling, napping **(d)** *(toison)* fleece

laine [lɛn] *nf* **(a)** wool; **jupe en** *ou* **de l.** woollen skirt; **tapis de haute l.** thick-pile wool carpet; **pure l.** pure wool; **ensemble pure l.** pure wool outfit; *Fig* **se laisser manger** *ou* **tondre la l. sur le dos** *(voler)* to (let oneself) be fleeced; *(exploiter)* to (let oneself) be taken advantage of **(b)** *(vêtement)* **mettre une petite l.** to put on something warm

▶ **laine**: **l. de bois** wood fibre *or US* fiber; **l. cardée** carding wool; **l. à matelas** stuffing; **l. peignée** worsted; **l. perlée** crochet wool; **l. à tricoter** knitting wool; **l. de verre** glass wool

lainer[1] [lene] *vt Tex (tissu)* to teasel, to nap

lainer[2] *nm Tex (d'un tissu)* nap

lainerie [lɛnri] *nf* **(a)** *(fabrication)* manufacture of woollens **(b)** *(usine, atelier)* woollen mill **(c)** *(magasin de gros)* (wholesale) wool shop

laineur, -euse [lɛnœr, -øz] *n Tex* teaseler, napper

laineux, -euse [lɛnø, -øz] *adj (tissu etc)* fleecy; *(mouton, cheveux)* woolly

lainier, -ière [lɛnje, -jɛr] **1** *adj (commerce, industrie)* wool **2** *n Ind (ouvrier)* worker in a woollen mill, wool worker

laïque [laik] **1** *adj* lay; *(vie, état)* secular; **école/enseignement l.** = (non-religious) state school/education **2** *n* layman/laywoman, lay person; **les laïques** the laity

lais [lɛ] *nm (laisse)* foreshore

laisse[1] [lɛs] *nf* leash, lead; *(à la chasse)* slip; **tenir un chien en l.** to keep a dog on a lead *or* on the leash; *F* **mener** *ou* **tenir qn en l.** to keep a tight rein on sb

laisse[2] *nf Géog* foreshore; **l. de haute/basse mer** high-water/low-water mark

laissé(e)-pour-compte, *pl* **laissé(e)s-pour-compte** [lesepurkɔ̃t] **1** *adj* **(a)** *Com (article)* rejected, returned **(b)** *(non désiré, non voulu) (personne)* rejected, unwanted **2** *nm Com* reject **3** *n (personne)* unwanted person, castoff; **les laissés-pour-compte** the castoffs of society; **les ouvriers métallurgiques sont les laissés-pour-compte du redéploiement industriel** industrial redeployment is throwing steel workers on the scrap heap

laisser [lese] **1** *vt* **(a)** [①**A40**,B,1,a; **B33**,2,b,i] *(permettre)* to let; **il le laissa partir** he let him go, he allowed him to go; **laissez-moi passer** let me past; **laisse-le passer devant** let him (go) in front; **laisse sortir les gens avant de monter** let the people out before you get in; **je les ai laissés dire** I let them speak; **l. dire** to let people talk; *F* **il ne m'a laissé en placer une** he wouldn't let me get a word in edgeways; **je vous laisse libre d'agir** you are free to do as you like; **le toit laissait passer la pluie** the roof let the rain in; **l. voir son mécontentement** to show one's displeasure *or* disapproval; **ne rien l. deviner** to give nothing away; **l. tomber qch/qn** to drop sth/sb; *F* **laissez-moi rire!** don't make me laugh!; **l. sécher la peinture** to let the paint dry, to allow the paint to dry; **laissez-les boire un verre de vin** let them have a glass of wine; **laisse faire** never mind, don't bother; **laissez-le faire!** leave it to him, let him get on with it; **laisse-moi faire, ça ira plus vite** just leave me to it *or* let me get on with it and it'll soon be done; *F* **l. courir** to leave (things) alone

(b) *(quitter) (mari, femme)* to leave, *F* to walk out on; **vous n'allez pas me l. tout seul?** you're not going to leave me (all) on my own?; **bon, je vous laisse!** well, I'm going *or* I'm off; **merci, vous pouvez nous l.** thank you, that will be all; **il a laissé une veuve et trois enfants** he left a widow and three children; **nous l'avions laissé pour mort** we had left him for dead; **laissez-moi!** let me go!; *(ne me dérangez pas)* I don't want to be disturbed!; **laissez-moi tranquille!** leave me alone!; **elle a laissé son mari planté sur le trottoir** she left her husband standing on the pavement looking like a fool; **l. là qn** to leave sb in the lurch

(c) *(ne pas prendre)* **l. qch de côté** to put sth aside *or* to one side; **laissez-lui du gâteau** leave *or* save some cake for him; **l. le meilleur pour la fin** to leave *or* save the best till last; *F* **c'est à prendre ou à l.** take it or leave it

(d) *(vélo, traces, cicatrices etc)* to leave; **ne laisse pas traîner tes affaires partout dans la maison** don't leave your things lying everywhere about the house; **l. qn derrière soi** *(dans une matière etc)* to leave sb behind; **l. la fenêtre ouverte** to leave *or* keep the window open; **laissons cela jusqu'à demain** let's leave that until tomorrow; **laissez (, c'est moi qui paie)** leave that, I'm paying; **laisse, je m'en occupe** don't bother about that, I'll look after it

(e) *(donner)* **je vous laisse le soin de le faire** I'll leave it to you (to do it), I'll leave you to do it; **je vous laisse le soin de décider** I'll leave it (up) to you to decide; **cela nous laisse le temps de ...** that leaves *or* gives us time to ...; **il m'a laissé entendre que ...** he gave me to understand that ...; **je te laisse imaginer la suite** I'll leave the rest to your imagination; **elle ne m'a pas laissé le choix** she left *or* gave me no choice; **l. à qn un héritage** to leave sb a legacy; **laissez-moi vos clefs** leave me your keys, let me have your keys; **ils ont laissé les enfants à la grand-mère** they left the children with their grandmother; **partir sans l. d'adresse** to go away without leaving one's address; **je vous le laisse pour 100 francs** I'll let you have it *or* you can have it for 100 francs; **je laisse maintenant la parole à mon collègue** I now hand over to my colleague

(f) *(perdre) (fortune, vie, membre)* to lose

(g) *Litt* **il ne laissera pas d'y aller** he won't fail to go; **cela ne laisse pas de m'inquiéter** nevertheless, I cannot help worrying about it; **cela n'a pas laissé de le surprendre** it could not fail to surprise him

2 se laisser *vpr* **elle se laisse vivre** she takes life as it comes; **se l. aller** to let oneself go; **ne vous laissez pas aller comme ça!** pull yourself together!; **se l. aller au découragement** to let oneself become discouraged; **se l. aller au pessimisme** to give way to pessimism; **je me suis laissé aller à reprendre trois fois du gâteau** I went so far as to have three pieces of cake; **se l. décourager** to let oneself be discouraged; **se l. emporter par la colère/l'enthousiasme** to get carried away by anger/enthusiasm; **elle se laissa embrasser** she allowed herself to be kissed, she let herself be kissed, she let him/her/*etc* kiss her; **je me suis laissé dire que ...** I hear that ...; *F* **ce vin se laisse boire** this wine is definitely quite drinkable; **ce livre n'est pas de la grande littérature mais il se laisse lire** it's not great literature but it's quite readable *or* pleasant enough

3 *vi* **je vous laisse à penser quel fut son bonheur en apprenant ...** you can imagine how happy he was when he learned ...; **tout laisse à penser que l'affaire aura des suites** there is every indication that the affair will have repercussions; **cela laisse (beaucoup) à désirer** it leaves much to be desired

laisser-aller *nm inv* **(a)** *(désinvolture)* casualness **(b)** *Péj (relâchement) (de l'apparence, la tenue etc)* carelessness, slovenliness; *(du travail)* carelessness, sloppiness; **il règne trop de l. dans ce bureau** things are too slack in this office

laisser-faire, laissez-faire *nm inv Pol* laisser-faire, laissez-faire

laissez-passer [lesepase] *nm inv* pass, permit; *Naut* sea pass; *(de douane)* transire

lait [lɛ] *nm* **(a)** milk; **petit l.** whey; *Fig F* **boire du petit l.** to lap it up; **ce punch se boit comme du petit l.** this punch is very moreish; **vache à l.** dairy cow; *F* **je ne suis pas une vache à l.** I'm not made of money; **pot à l.** milk jug; **frère/sœur de l.** foster brother/sister; **cochon de l.** suckling *or* sucking pig **(b)** *(cosmétique)* **l. démaquillant** cleansing lotion, cleanser; **l. bronzant** suntan lotion; **l. hydratant** moisturising lotion, moisturiser

▶ **lait**: **l. caillé** curd, curdled milk; **l. de chaux** limewater, whitewash; **l. de coco** coconut milk; **l. concentré** evaporated milk; **l. condensé** condensed milk; **l. cru** unpasteurized milk; **l. demi-écrémé** semi-skimmed milk; **l. écrémé** skimmed milk; **l. entier** whole milk; **l. de ferme** unpasteurized milk; **l. longue conservation** long-life milk; **l. maternel** mother's milk; **l. en poudre** powdered *or* dried milk; *Am (pour bébé)* formula; **l. de poule** egg flip, egg nog

laitage [lɛtaʒ] *nm* dairy product

laitance [lɛtɑ̃s] *nf*, **laite** [lɛt] *nf (de poisson)* milt; *Culin* soft roe

laité [lete] *adj (poisson)* soft-roed

laiterie [lɛtri] *nf* **(a)** *(dans la ferme)* dairy **(b)** *(usine)* factory producing dairy products; *(industrie)* dairy industry **(c)** *Vieilli (crémerie)* dairy

laiteron [lɛtrɔ̃] *nm Bot* sow thistle, milkweed

laiteux, -euse [lɛtø, -øz] *adj (teint)* creamy; *(couleur)* milky; *(lumière)* milky(-white)

laitier[1], **-ière** [lɛtje, -jɛr] **1** *adj (industrie, produit, vache)* dairy **2** *nf* **laitière** dairy cow; **ces vaches sont de bonnes laitières** these cows are good milkers **3** *n* **(a)** *(livreur, -euse)* milkman/milkwoman **(b)** *(crémier, -ière)* dairyman/dairywoman

laitier[2] *nm Métal etc* dross, slag

laiton [lɛtɔ̃] *nm* brass; **(fil de) l.** brass wire

laitue [lɛty] *nf (légume)* lettuce; **l. romaine** cos (lettuce), *Am* romaine (lettuce)

laïus [lajys] *nm* **(a)** *F* (*discours*) speech; (*long et ennuyeux*) long-winded speech; **faire un l.** to make a speech; (*long et ennuyeux*) to hold forth, to make a long-winded speech (**sur** about) **(b)** *Péj* (*baratin*) **quel l.!, venons-en au fait!** what a lot of waffle! let's get to the point!
lama[1] [lama] *nm Rel* lama; **le Grand l., le dalaï-l.** the Dalai Lama
lama[2] *nm Zool, Tex* llama
lamantin [lamɑ̃tɛ̃] *nm Zool* manatee, sea cow
lamaserie [lamazri] *nf Rel* lamasery
lambada [lɑ̃mbada] *nf Mus* lambada
lambda [lɑ̃bda] *adj inv F* average; **un garçon l.** an average boy; **le contribuable l.** the average *or* ordinary taxpayer
lambeau, -eaux [lɑ̃bo] *nm* (*de tissu, papier, viande etc*) scrap, bit, shred; (*de musique, conversation etc*) scrap, fragment; **vêtements en lambeaux** clothes in rags *or* in tatters; **mettre qch en lambeaux** to tear sth to shreds *or* to pieces; **réduire qch en lambeaux** to reduce sth to shreds; **tomber en lambeaux** to fall to pieces
lambin, -ine [lɑ̃bɛ̃, -in] *F* **1** *adj* slow; **ce qu'il peut être l., celui-là!** what a dawdler *or* slowcoach *or Am* slowpoke that one is! **2** *n* dawdler, slowcoach, *Am* slowpoke
lambiner [lɑ̃bine] *vi F* to dawdle
lambourde [lɑ̃burd] *nf* **(a)** (*d'arbre*) fruit shoot **(b)** *Constr* (*pour parquet*) bridging joist; (*de plancher*) wall plate, bearing joist
lambrequin [lɑ̃brəkɛ̃] *nm* **(a)** *Hér* mantling, lambrequin **(b)** (*de rideau*) valance, pelmet
lambris [lɑ̃bri] *nm Constr* (*en bois*) panelling, wainscot(t)ing; (*en marbre, stuc*) lining; **l. d'appui** dado
lambrissage [lɑ̃brisaʒ] *nm Constr* (*de bois*) panelling, wainscot(t)ing; (*de marbre, stuc*) lining
lambrisser [lɑ̃brise] *vt Constr* **(a)** (*revêtir de lambris*) (*de bois*) to panel, to wainscot; (*de marbre, stuc*) to line; **plafond lambrissé** panelled ceiling **(b)** (*avec du plâtre*) (*mur, plafond*) to plaster
lambswool [lɑ̃bswul] *nm Tex* lambswool; **un pull en l.** a lambswool sweater
lame [lam] *nf* **(a)** (*d'épée, de couteau etc*) blade; (*épée*) sword, blade; **l. de rasoir** razor blade; **l. ressort** spring blade; *Fig Litt* **c'est une fine l.** he's a fine swordsman; **visage en l. de couteau** hatchet face **(b)** (*bande plate*) (*de métal, verre etc*) strip; (*de ressort*) leaf; (*de microscope*) slide; (*de store*) slat; **l. de parquet** strip of parquet flooring **(c)** *Anat, Bot* lamina; (*de champignon*) gill **(d)** (*vague*) wave; **l. de fond** ground swell; **le creux de la l.** the trough of the wave
lamé [lame] **1** *adj* lamé; **robe lamée d'or** gold lamé dress **2** *nm* lamé; **une robe en l.** a lamé dress
lamellaire [lamelɛr] *adj Minér etc* lamellar, lamellate, foliated
lamelle [lamɛl] *nf* **(a)** (*de fer, plastique etc*) thin strip; (*de mica*) scale, flake; *Bot* (*de champignon*) lamella, gill; *Culin* **couper en (fines) lamelles** to cut into (wafer-)thin slices **(b)** (*de microscope*) cover glass
lamellé [lamɛle], **lamelleux, -euse** [lamɛlø, -øz] *adj* lamellate(d)
lamentable [lamɑ̃tabl] *adj* **(a)** (*déplorable*) (*histoire, fait divers etc*) appalling, dreadful, terrible, awful; **sort l.** terrible fate **(b)** *Péj* (*mauvais*) appalling, awful; (*personne*) hopeless, pathetic **(c)** (*triste*) (*voix, ton*) mournful, woeful
lamentablement [lamɑ̃tabləmɑ̃] *adv* (*échouer*) miserably, lamentably
lamentation [lamɑ̃tasjɔ̃] *nf* **(a)** (*cri de douleur extrême*) lament, lamentation; **cri de l.** wail; **les lamentations d'une femme qui a perdu son enfant** the wailing of a woman who has lost her child **(b)** *Péj* (*plainte, jérémiades*) moaning, complaining; **elle ne cesse de se répandre en lamentations** she never stops complaining *or* moaning
lamenter (se) [səlamɑ̃te] *vpr* **se l. sur son sort** to bemoan *or* lament one's fate; **se l. de son ignorance** to deplore *or* regret one's ignorance; **se l. d'avoir laissé passer sa chance** to moan about missing one's chance; **cesse donc de te l.!** stop feeling sorry for yourself!
lamento [lamɛnto] *nm Mus* lament
laminage [laminaʒ] *nm* **(a)** *Métal* lamination, rolling, flatt(en)ing; **l. à chaud/à froid** hot-/cold-rolling **(b)** *Fig* (*de parti politique*) near annihilation
laminaire [laminɛr] *nf* oarweed
laminer [lamine] *vt* **(a)** *Métal* to laminate, to roll **(b)** *Fig* (*écraser, diminuer*) to erode; (*personne*) to destroy, to annihilate; **ses revenus sont laminés par les impôts** his income is swallowed up *or* gobbled up by taxes; **la gauche a été laminée aux législatives** the left were nearly annihilated in the parliamentary elections
lamineur [laminœr] *Métal* **1** *adj m* **cylindre l.** roller **2** *nm* rolling mill operator
laminoir [laminwar] *nm* **(a)** *Métal* rolling mill, flatting mill; **l. de finissage** finishing rolls; *Fig* **faire passer qn au l.** to put sb through the mill **(b)** (*pour le papier*) plate glazing calender
lampadaire [lɑ̃padɛr] *nm* **(a)** (*lampe sur haut support*) standard lamp, *Am* floor lamp **(b)** (*réverbère*) lamp post
lampant [lɑ̃pɑ̃] *adj* **pétrole l.** paraffin (oil), *Am* kerosene
lamparo [lɑ̃paro] *nm Pêche* lamp (*used to attract fish*); **aller à la pêche au l.** to go fishing by lamplight
lampe [lɑ̃p] *nf* **(a)** (*appareil d'éclairage*) lamp; *Él* lamp, light; **à (la lumière de) la l.** by lamplight **(b)** *Électron* **l. (de radio)** (radio) valve *or* tube; **l. d'amplification** amplifying tube **(c)** *Arg* **s'en mettre plein la l.** to have a good blowout
▶ **lampe**: **l. à alcool** spirit lamp; **l. à arc** arc light *or* lamp; **l. à bronzer** sun lamp; **l. de bureau** desk lamp *or* light; **l. de camping** camping gas lamp; **l. de chevet** bedside lamp; **l. à gaz** gas lamp; **l. halogène** halogen lamp; **l. à huile** oil lamp; **l. à incandescence** incandescent lamp; *Aut* filament lamp; *Aut* **l. de lecture** reading light, map light; **l. de mineur** miner's (safety) lamp; **l. murale** wall light *or* lamp; **l. au néon** neon light *or* lamp; **l. à pétrole** oil lamp, paraffin lamp, *Am* kerosene lamp; **l. de poche** torch, *Am* flashlight; **l. à souder** blowlamp, *Am* blowtorch; *Mil Arg* machine gun; **l. de sûreté** miner's (safety) lamp; **l. témoin** warning light *or* lamp; **l. tungstène halogène au quartz** tungsten-halogen lamp
lampée [lɑ̃pe] *nf F* (*d'eau, de vin etc*) gulp, swig; (*de soupe*) gulp; **finir son verre d'une seule l.** to down (the rest of) one's drink in one; **boire qch à grandes lampées** to gulp sth down
lamper [lɑ̃pe] *vt F* (*eau, vin etc*) to gulp down, to swig (down)
lampe-tempête, *pl* **lampes-tempêtes** *nf* hurricane lamp, storm lantern
lampion [lɑ̃pjɔ̃] *nm* (*lanterne*) paper lantern, Chinese lantern; *F* **crier sur l'air des lampions** (*slogan*) to chant
lampiste [lɑ̃pist] *nm* **(a)** *Tech* light maintenance man; *Rail* lampman **(b)** *Fig F* (*subalterne*) underling; (*dupe*) scapegoat, fall guy; **ce sont toujours les lampistes qui trinquent** it's always the little man that gets the blame; **s'en prendre au l.** to bully one's subordinate(s) **(c)** *Arch* (*fabricant*) lamp maker; (*vendeur*) lamp seller
lampisterie [lɑ̃pistəri] *nf Rail etc* lamp room
lamproie [lɑ̃prwa] *nf Zool* lamprey; (*de rivière*) river lamprey
lance [lɑ̃s] *nf* **(a)** (*pique*) spear; **percer un animal d'un coup de l.** to spear an animal **(b)** *Fig Litt* **rompre une l.** *ou* **des lances avec** *ou* **contre qn** to cross swords with sb; **rompre des lances pour qn** to take up the cudgels for sb **(c)** (*tuyau*) **l. d'arrosage** water hose; **l. d'incendie** fire hose
lance-bombes *nm inv Av* bomb launcher
lancée [lɑ̃se] *nf* momentum, impetus; **continuer sur sa l.** to forge ahead, to press on; **je ne voulais pas t'interrompre sur ta l.** I didn't want to interrupt you (while you were) in full flow; **j'ai fait les exercices 5, 6, et 7 et sur ma l. j'ai fait le 8** I did exercises 5, 6 and 7 and while I was at it I did 8 as well
lance-flammes *nm inv Mil* flamethrower
lance-fusées *nm inv Mil* rocket launcher
lance-grenades *nm inv Mil* grenade launcher
lancement [lɑ̃smɑ̃] *nm* **(a)** (*projection*) throwing; (*de missile, fusée*) launch(ing); (*de bombe*) dropping, releasing; (*de grenade*) throwing, launching; **rampe de l.** launching ramp; **dégager l'aire de l.** to clear the launch(ing) area
(b) *Sp* **l. du javelot/du disque/du marteau** throwing the javelin/the discus/the hammer; **l. du poids** putting the shot; **il a gagné au l. du poids/du javelot** he won (in) the shot/the javelin
(c) (*de bateau*) launching
(d) (*de moteur*) starting (up)
(e) (*de projet, d'attaque*) launch(ing)
(f) *Com* (*de compagnie, produit, modèle*) launch(ing); *Bourse* (*de compagnie*) floating; **l. de produit** product launch; *Mktg* **l. sur le marché** market entry; **l. parallèle/tardif** parallel/late entry; **campagne de l.** launch campaign
(g) *Ordinat* (*d'impression*) start; (*de programme*) running
lance-missiles *nm inv Mil* missile launcher
lancéolé [lɑ̃seɔle] *adj Bot* lanceolate
lance-pierre(s) *nm inv* catapult, *Am* slingshot; *Fig F* **manger avec un l.** to wolf one's food (down); *F* **être payé au l.** to be paid a pittance, to be paid next to nothing
lancer[1] [lɑ̃se] (**je lançai(s); n. lançons**) **1** *vt* **(a)** (*projeter*) to throw, *Litt* to cast; (*violemment*) to fling, to hurl; (*flèche*) to shoot; (*fusée, torpille*) to launch; (*bombe*) to drop, to release; (*grenade*) to throw, to launch; **l. des pierres à qn** to throw stones at sb; **l. de la fumée** to send out smoke; **l. des étincelles** to shoot out sparks; **les joyaux lançaient mille feux** the jewels were sparkling brightly; **l. ses bras en avant** to throw one's arms out in front; *Pêche* **l. la ligne** to cast the line; **l. qch/qn en l'air** to throw *or* toss sth/sb into the air;

Constr **l. un pont sur une rivière** to throw a bridge over a river; **une proposition que j'ai lancée à tout hasard** a suggestion that I threw out just on the off-chance; **l. une idée** to throw out an idea; **l. un coup d'œil à qn** to dart *or* shoot a glance at sb; **l. un regard plein de haine à qn** to shoot a look of hatred at sb; **l. un mandat d'arrêt contre qn** to issue a warrant for sb's arrest; **l. un ultimatum** to issue an ultimatum; **l. un juron** to let out a swearword; **l. un mot d'esprit/une remarque désagréable** to come out with a witty remark/an unpleasant remark; **l. une bordée d'injures** to let fly *or* let loose a torrent of abuse; **l. une plaisanterie** to crack *or* make a joke

(b) *Sp* (*balle*) to throw; *Baseball* to pitch; **l. le disque/le javelot/le marteau** to throw the discus/the javelin/the hammer; **l. le poids** to put the shot

(c) (*envoyer*) (*signaux de détresse, SOS*) to send out; **l. un cheval** to start a horse off at full gallop; **l. un chien contre qn** to set a dog on sb; *Fig* **si vous le lancez sur ce sujet il ne s'arrêtera plus** if you start him (off) on this subject he'll never stop; **une fois lancé sur ce sujet il est intarissable** once he's (off) on this subject *or* once he's launched on this subject he can go on for ever

(d) (*navire, projet, attaque, compagnie, produit*) to launch; *Bourse* (*compagnie*) to float; (*acteur, carrière etc*) to launch; (*mode*) to start, to launch; **l. une souscription** to start a fund; **l. qn (dans les affaires)** to give sb a start *or* set sb up (in business); **maintenant qu'il est lancé il pourra demander plus cher** now that he's made a name for himself he can ask for more money; *Fin* **l. des titres sur le marché** to issue shares; *Fin* **l. un emprunt** to issue a bond

(e) (*faire démarrer*) (*moteur*) to start (up); **une fois lancés, les skieurs ...** once they got going, the skiers ...; **le train lancé à toute vapeur ne put freiner à temps** the train was rushing along at full speed and couldn't brake in time

(f) *Ordinat* (*impression*) to start; (*programme*) to run, to start (up)

2 *vi F* **ma jambe/mon abcès m'a lancé toute la nuit** my leg/my abscess has been giving me shooting pains *or* has been giving me twinges all night; **ça me lance dans le bras** I've got shooting pains in my arm, I've got twinges in my arm

3 se lancer *vpr* **(a)** (*se jeter*) **le malheureux s'est lancé dans le vide** the poor wretch threw himself into the abyss; **se l. en avant** to rush *or* dash *or* shoot forward; **se l. à l'attaque** to throw oneself into the attack; **se l. à l'assaut d'une place forte** to launch an assault on a fortress; **se l. à la poursuite de qn** to dash off *or* rush off in pursuit of sb

(b) (*s'engager*) **se l. dans** (*affaire, discussion*) to embark on, to get involved in; (*aventure*) to embark on; (*dépenses*) to get involved in; **se l. dans les affaires** to launch out into the world of business; **se l. sur le marché** to enter the market; **il s'est lancé dans des digressions interminables** he went off into endless digressions

(c) (*se faire connaître*) **elle veut se l.** she wants to make a name for herself

lancer^2 *nm* **(a) (pêche au) l.** rod-and-reel fishing **(b)** *Sp* throw; *Baseball* pitch; **l. du javelot/du disque/du marteau** throwing the javelin/the discus/the hammer; **l. du poids** putting the shot; **l. franc** (*au basket*) free throw

lance-roquettes *nm inv Mil* rocket launcher

lance-satellites *nm inv* satellite launcher

lance-torpilles *nm inv Mil* **(tube) l.** torpedo tube

lancette [lɑ̃sɛt] *nf* **(a)** *Chir* lancet **(b)** *Archit* **(arc à) l.** lancet (arch)

lanceur, -euse [lɑ̃sœr, -øz] **1** *n Cr* bowler; *Baseball* pitcher; **l. de javelot/disque/marteau** javelin/discus/hammer thrower; **l. de poids** shot putter **2** *nm* (*de satellite, vaisseau spatial etc*) launcher; **l. d'engins** underwater missile launcher

lancier [lɑ̃sje] *nm* **(a)** *Mil* lancer **(b) (quadrille des) lanciers** lancers

lancinant [lɑ̃sinɑ̃] *adj* **(a)** (*douleur*) shooting **(b)** (*obsédant*) (*souvenir*) haunting; (*regret*) nagging; (*air, musique*) insistent, haunting

lanciner [lɑ̃sine] **1** *vi Litt* (*d'une douleur*) to shoot; (*d'un doigt etc*) to throb **2** *vt* (*d'une idée, des remords etc*) to haunt, to trouble, to plague

lançon [lɑ̃sɔ̃] *nm Zool* sand eel, launce

landais, -aise [lɑ̃dɛ, -ɛz] **1** *adj* of/from the Landes (region); **le paysage l.** the landscape of the Landes (region); **race landaise** breed of cattle from the Landes (region) **2** *n* **L.** (*natif*) native of the Landes (region); (*habitant*) inhabitant of the Landes (region)

landau [lɑ̃do] *nm* **(a)** (*voiture d'enfant*) pram, *Am* baby carriage **(b)** (*sorte de fiacre*) landau

lande [lɑ̃d] *nf* **(a)** (*terre*) moor, heath **(b) les Landes** the Landes (region) (*in south-west France*)

landier [lɑ̃dje] *nm* andiron, fire dog

land rover® [landrɔvɛr] *nf Aut* Land Rover

langage [lɑ̃gaʒ] *nm* **(a)** *Ling* language; **l'étude du l.** the study of language; **l'apprentissage du l.** language learning, the acquisition of language; *Méd* **troubles du l.** speech problems *or* difficulties

(b) (*style, façon de s'exprimer*) language; **l. administratif/scientifique** official/scientific language *or Péj* jargon; **l. enfantin** children's language; **l. populaire** popular speech; **tenir un l. grossier à qn** to speak rudely to sb; **il a un l. très grossier** his language is very coarse; **vous tenez là un drôle de l.** that's a strange way to talk; **changer de l.** to change one's tune; **en voilà un l.!** that's no way to talk!; **surveillez votre l.!** watch your language!

(c) (*code*) **le l. des fleurs/de l'amour** the language of flowers/of love; **l. chiffré** cipher, code; **l. du corps** body language; **parler le l. de la raison** to be reasonable

(d) *Ordinat* language; **l. assembleur** *ou* **d'assemblage** assembly language; **l. utilisateur** user language; **l. machine** machine language; **l. de programmation** programming language; **l. interactif** interactive language; **l. d'imprimante par pages** page printer language; **l. d'interrogation** query language; **l. de description de page** page description language; **l. de procédures** procedural language; **l. naturel** natural language; **l. à objets** object-oriented language

langagier, -ière [lɑ̃gaʒje, -jɛr] **1** *adj* linguistic **2** *n Can* language professional

lange [lɑ̃ʒ] *nm* **(a)** (*pour emmailloter*) (baby) blanket, *Arch* **langes** swaddling clothes **(b)** (*couche*) nappy, *Am* diaper **(c)** *Fig* **être encore dans les langes** to be still in its infancy

langer [lɑ̃ʒe] *vt* **(je langeai(s); n. langeons)** (*bébé*) (*mettre une couche à*) to put a nappy *or Am* diaper on; *Arch* (*emmailloter*) to wrap in swaddling clothes

langoureusement [lɑ̃gurøzmɑ̃] *adv* languorously

langoureux, -euse [lɑ̃gurø, -øz] *adj* languorous

langouste [lɑ̃gust] *nf* crayfish, spiny *or* rock lobster

langoustine [lɑ̃gustin] *nf* Dublin Bay prawn; *Culin* **langoustines** scampi

langue [lɑ̃g] *nf* **(a)** *Anat* tongue; **se mordre/se brûler la l.** to bite/burn one's tongue; **coup de l.** lick; **la vache me donna un coup de l.** the cow gave me a lick *or* licked me; **tirer la l.** to stick out one's tongue **(à qn** at sb); *F* (*avoir soif*) to be very thirsty; *F* (*être dans le besoin*) to be strapped for cash; **après dix kilomètres de marche, je tirais drôlement la l.** after walking ten kilometres, my tongue was really hanging out; *F* **j'ai tiré la l.** (*peiné*) it was hard *or* tough going; **l. pâteuse** *ou* **chargée** coated *or* furred tongue; **ils me regardaient manger mon sandwich la l. pendante** they watched me eating my sandwich with their tongues hanging out; *Culin* **l. de bœuf** ox tongue

(b) (*parole*) **délier la l. à qn** to loosen sb's tongue; **avoir la l. bien pendue** to have the gift of the gab; **ne pas avoir la l. dans sa poche** never to be at a loss for words; **elle a la l. trop longue** she can't keep her mouth shut, she talks too much; **il ne sait pas tenir sa l.** he can't keep a secret; **tiens ta l.** keep quiet about it; **je l'avais sur le bout de la l.** I had it on the tip of my tongue; **je donne ma l. au chat** (*par référence à une devinette etc*) I give up, I can't guess; **tu donnes ta l. au chat?** give up?; **tu ne dis plus rien? tu as avalé** *ou* **perdu ta l.?** you've gone all quiet, (has the) cat got your tongue?; **alors, tu as retrouvé ta l.?** well, have you found your tongue?; *F* **se mordre la l.** (*pour ne pas parler*) to bite one's tongue; *F* **s'en mordre la l.** to be kicking oneself for having spoken; **tourner sept fois la l. dans sa bouche** to take one's time *or* think before one speaks

(c) [①A7,d,xi; B4,3,d] *Ling* language, *Litt* tongue; **langues étrangères** foreign languages; **elle parle deux langues couramment** she speaks two (foreign) languages fluently; **avoir le don des langues** to be a good linguist, to have a gift for languages; *Rel* to have the gift of tongues; **peuples/pays de l. anglaise** English-speaking people/countries; **l. diplomatique** language of diplomacy; **l. officielle** official language

(d) (*manière de s'exprimer*) language; **l. parlée/écrite** spoken/written language; **la l. bien reconnaissable de Proust** the easily recognizable language of Proust

(e) (*jargon*) language; *Péj* jargon; **l. scientifique** scientific language *or Péj* jargon

(f) (*personne*) **une mauvaise l.** a backbiter, a scandalmonger; **une l. de vipère** a spiteful gossip

(g) (*chose allongée*) **l. de terre** strip *or* spit of land

► **langue**: **l. d'arrivée** target language; **l. de bois** platitudes, clichés; **les politiciens qui parlent la l. de bois** politicians who mouth platitudes *or* clichés; **l. cible** target language; **l. de départ** source language; **l. maternelle** mother tongue; **l.**

morte dead language; **l. verte** slang; **langues de feu** tongues of flame; **langues O** Oriental languages; (*institut*) = centre for Oriental studies in Paris, *Br* ≈ School of Oriental Studies; **langues vivantes** living languages; (*comme matière*) modern languages

langue-de-bœuf, *pl* **langues-de-bœuf** *nf* **(a)** (*champignon*) beefsteak fungus **(b)** (*outil*) (heart-shaped) trowel

langue-de-chat, *pl* **langues-de-chat** *nf Culin* (flat) finger biscuit, langue de chat

languedocien, -ienne [lɑ̃gdɔsjɛ̃, -jɛn] **1** *adj* of/from the Languedoc; **la région languedocienne** the Languedoc region (*of southern France*) **2** *n* **L.** (*natif*) native of the Languedoc (region); (*habitant*) inhabitant of the Languedoc (region)

languette [lɑ̃gɛt] *nf* **(a)** (*objet en forme de petite langue*) (*de bois, métal, terre etc*) tongue; (*de papier*) strip; (*de soulier*) tongue; *Menuis* **assemblage à rainure et l.** tongue-and-groove (joint) **(b)** *Él* **contact à l.** snap contact

langueur [lɑ̃gœr] *nf* **(a)** (*apathie*) listlessness, *Litt, Arch* **se mourir de l.** to pine away **(b)** *Litt* (*mélancolie douce, rêverie*) languor, languidness; **regard plein de l.** languishing look **(c)** *Litt, Arch* **(maladie de) l.** wasting disease

languide [lɑ̃gid] *adj Litt* languid

languir [lɑ̃gir] **1** *vi* **(a)** (*se mourir*) to languish, to pine, to waste away; (*d'une plante*) to wilt; **l. d'amour** to be lovesick **(b)** (*désirer, attendre avec impatience*) **ne nous faites pas l.** don't keep us on tenterhooks *or* in suspense; *Litt* **je languis d'être avec vous** I am longing *or* pining *or* yearning to be with you; *Litt* **l. après qn/qch** to long *or* pine *or* yearn for sb/sth; **la conversation languit** the conversation is flagging; **les affaires languissent** business is slack **2 se languir** *vpr* to languish; *Litt* **se l. d'amour** to be lovesick; *Litt* **je me languis de toi** I am longing *or* pining for you

languissamment [lɑ̃gisamɑ̃] *adv Litt* languidly

languissant [lɑ̃gisɑ̃] *adj Litt* **(a)** (*sans énergie*) (*conversation, récit*) flagging, dragging; (*santé*) failing; (*économie*) slack, inactive; (*foi*) declining, dwindling **(b)** (*amoureux*) (*yeux, regard*) languishing, lovesick

lanière [lanjɛr] *nf* strap; (*de fouet*) lash; **découper qch en lanières** to cut sth in(to) strips

lanifère [lanifɛr], **lanigère** [laniʒɛr] *adj* wool-bearing

lanoline [lanɔlin] *nf* lanolin(e)

lanterne [lɑ̃tɛrn] *nf* **(a)** (*lampe*) lantern; *Fig* **elle veut nous faire prendre des vessies pour des lanternes** she's trying to pull the wool over our eyes; *F* **éclairer la l. de qn** to enlighten sb **(b)** (*de véhicule*) (side)light, *Am* parking light; **se mettre en lanternes** to put one's (side)lights *or Am* parking lights on **(c)** *Hist* (*pendant la Révolution*) **à la l.!** string them up! **(d)** *Archit* lantern

▶ **lanterne**: **l. chinoise** Chinese lantern; **l. magique** magic lantern; **l. de projection** (slide) projector; **l. rouge** (*d'un convoi*) rear *or* tail light; *Arch* (*d'un bordel*) red light; **la l. rouge** *Sp, Fig* the back-marker, the tail-ender; (*dans un classement*) the one at the bottom; **l. sourde** dark lantern; **l. vénitienne** paper lantern, Chinese lantern

lanterneau, -eaux [lɑ̃tɛrno] *nm* (*au-dessus d'un escalier*) skylight

lanterner [lɑ̃tɛrne] *vi F* (*traînailler*) to dawdle; **faire l. qn** to keep sb hanging about *or* waiting

laotien, -ienne [laɔsjɛ̃, -jɛn] **1** *adj* Laotian **2** *n* **L.** Laotian

La Palice [lapalis] *nm* **vérité de L.** truism, statement of the obvious

lapalissade [lapalisad] *nf* truism, statement of the obvious

laparoscopie [laparɔskɔpi] *nf Méd* laparoscopy

lapement [lapmɑ̃] *nm* (*de lait etc*) lapping (up); (*bruit*) lapping

laper [lape] **1** *vt* (*d'un chien, chat etc*) (*eau, lait etc*) to lap up **2** *vi* to lap

lapereau, -eaux [lapro] *nm* young rabbit

lapidaire [lapidɛr] **1** *adj* (*inscription*) lapidary; (*concis*) (*style, formule*) concise, succinct **2** *nm* lapidary

lapidation [lapidasjɔ̃] *nf* stoning

lapider [lapide] *vt* (*jeter des pierres à*) to stone, to throw stones at; (*mettre à mort*) to stone to death; *Fig* (*critiquer*) to criticize severely

lapin [lapɛ̃] *nm* rabbit; *Culin* **un civet de l.** (a) rabbit stew, jugged rabbit; *Com* **peau de l.** rabbit(skin), cony (skin); **manteau en (peau de) l.** rabbitskin coat; *F* **poser un l. à qn** to stand sb up; *F* **un chaud l.** a randy devil; *F* **c'est un fameux l.** he's quite a guy; **se sauver** *ou* **courir** *ou F* **détaler comme un l.** to run like hell; **coup du l.** rabbit punch; (*dans un accident de la circulation*) whiplash injury; **mon petit l.** my pet, sweetheart

▶ **lapin**: **l. domestique** rabbit (*bred for food*); **l. de garenne** wild rabbit

lapine [lapin] *nf* doe (rabbit)

lapiner [lapine] *vi* (*d'un lapin*) to litter

lapinière [lapinjɛr] *nf* rabbit hutch

lapis [lapis], **lapis-lazuli** [lapislazyli] **1** *nm inv Minér* lapis lazuli **2** *adj* **ciel l.** bright blue sky

lapon, -one [lapɔ̃, -ɔn] **1** *adj* Lapp **2** *nm Ling* Lapp, Lappish **3** *n* **L.** Lapp, Laplander

Laponie [lapɔni] *nf* Lapland

laps [laps] *nm* **un l. de temps** a period of time; **un l. de temps de trois heures** a period of three hours

lapsus [lapsys] *nm* (*oral*) slip of the tongue; (*par écrit*) slip of the pen; **l. de mémoire** lapse of memory; **faire un l.** to make a slip (of the tongue/pen); **un l. révélateur** a Freudian slip

laquage [lakaʒ] *nm* lacquering

laquais [lakɛ] *nm* footman, lackey; *Fig Péj* lackey, flunkey

laque [lak] **1** *nf* **(a)** (*naturelle*) lac; **l. en feuilles** shellac **(b)** (*vernis*) lacquer **(c)** (*pour les cheveux*) (hair) lacquer, hair spray **(d)** (*peinture*) gloss (paint) **2** *nm* **(a)** (*vernis*) lacquer; **de** *ou* **en l.** lacquered; **l. de Chine** japan **(b)** (*objet d'art*) **des laques** lacquerware; **un l.** a piece of lacquerware

laqué [lake] *adj* **(a)** (*de laque naturelle*) lacquered **(b)** (*vaporisé de fixateur*) (*cheveux*) lacquered **(c)** *Culin* **canard l.** Peking duck

laquelle *voir* **lequel**

laquer [lake] *vt* **(a)** (*de laque naturelle*) to lacquer **(b)** (*de vernis*) to lacquer; (*de peinture*) to paint with gloss; **meubles laqués blanc** furniture painted with *or* in white gloss

larbin [larbɛ̃] *nm F souvent Péj* flunky; **je ne suis pas ton l., débrouille-toi tout seul!** I'm not your servant, sort it out yourself!

larcin [larsɛ̃] *nm* **(a)** (*vol*) (petty) theft **(b)** *Vieilli* (*objet volé*) loot; **ses larcins** his loot

lard [lar] *nm* **(a)** (*morceau de viande*) bacon; (*gras du cochon*) fat; **l. maigre** streaky bacon; **l. gras** fatty bacon; **l. fumé** smoked bacon; **omelette au l.** bacon omelette **(b)** *Arg* (*graisse*) **(se) faire du l.** to (sit around and) get fat; **gros l.** big fat slob **(c)** *Fig* **se demander si c'est du l. ou du cochon** to wonder what to make of it; **c'est une vraie tête de l.** he is so pigheaded; *Fig F* **rentrer dans le l. à qn** to lay into sb, to let sb have it

larder [larde] *vt* (*morceau de viande*) to lard; *F* **l. qn de coups de couteau** to hack at sb with a knife; *F* **l. un texte de citations** to lard *or* pepper a text with quotations; *Tech* **l. un morceau de bois** to stud a piece of wood with nails

lardoire [lardwar] *nf* **(a)** *Culin* larding needle *or* pin **(b)** *F* (*épée*) sword

lardon [lardɔ̃] *nm* **(a)** *Culin* lardon; **lardons** diced bacon fat **(b)** *Arg* (*enfant*) kid **(c)** *Vieilli* (*raillerie*) jibe, cutting remark

lare [lar] *Antiq* **1** *adj* **les dieux lares** lares, the household gods **2** *nm* household god; **les lares** lares, the household gods

largable [largabl] *adj Av* (*container, équipement*) releasable

largage [largaʒ] *nm Av* (*de parachutistes, vivres etc*) dropping; (*de bombe*) releasing, dropping

large [larʒ] **1** *adj* **(a)** (*grand, étendu*) (*route, rivière, table, porte, chaussures etc*) wide; (*visage, nez, mains*) broad; **l. d'épaules** broad-shouldered; **elle a les hanches larges** she has broad hips, she is broad in the hips; **chapeau à larges bords** wide-brimmed *or* broad-brimmed hat; **route l. de dix mètres** road ten metres wide; **vêtements larges** loose-fitting clothes; **d'un geste l.** with a (broad) sweeping gesture; **terme employé dans son sens l.** term used in its wide *or* broad sense; **avoir l'esprit l.** to be broad-minded; *Beaux-Arts* **style l.** broad *or* bold *or* free style

(b) (*important, considérable*) large; **de larges ressources** ample resources; **dans une l. mesure** to a large extent; **avoir une l. part de responsabilité dans qch** to bear a large part of the responsibility for sth; **ils font une part très l. à l'esprit d'initiative** they give a lot of importance to the spirit of enterprise; **dans son spectacle il fait une l. part à l'improvisation** improvization plays a large part in his show, he devotes a lot of his show to improvization

(c) (*généreux*) **mener une vie l.** to spend freely; **il n'a pas été très l.** he wasn't very generous

2 *nm* **(a)** (*espace*) room, space; **être au l.** to have plenty of room; (*financièrement*) to be well off

(b) *Naut* open sea; **brise du l.** sea breeze; **prendre le l.** to take to the open sea; *F* (*s'enfuir*) to beat it, to clear off; **gagner le l.** to get to the open sea; **au l.!** keep away!; **au l. de Cherbourg** off Cherbourg; **trop au l.** too far from the shore

(c) (*largeur*) width, breadth; **avoir** *ou* **faire dix mètres de l.** to be ten metres wide; **se promener de long en l.** to walk up and down *or* to and fro; **il parcourait la pièce en long et en l.** he was walking up and down the room; *F* **il examina la question en long et en l.** *ou* **en long, en l. et en travers** he examined the question from every angle, he looked into every aspect of the question

3 *adv* **calculer l.** to allow a margin for error; **compter l.** to allow for more; **cette robe habille** *ou* **taille l.** this dress is loose-fitting; **ces chaussures chaussent l.** these shoes are wide-fitting; **voir l.** to think big; **il n'en mène pas l.** he has his heart in his boots

largement [larʒəmɑ̃] *adv* **(a)** (*dans l'espace*) widely, broadly; **la porte était l. ouverte** the door was wide open; **opinion l. répandue** widely held opinion; **l. critiqué** widely criticized; *Beaux-Arts* **peindre l.** to paint in a free *or* broad style

(b) (*amplement*) amply; (*généreusement*) generously; **on l'a l. récompensé** he has been amply *or* handsomely rewarded; **si tu aimes les musées il y a l. de quoi faire à Paris** if you like museums there's more than enough to do in Paris; **dépasser l. qch** to exceed sth by a long way, to go way *or* far beyond sth; **le quota est l. dépassé** the quota has been greatly exceeded; **il a été l. devancé par ses adversaires** he was left far *or* a long way behind by his opponents; **il s'est l. inspiré de Rabelais pour écrire son roman** he drew a great deal of inspiration from Rabelais in writing his novel; **avoir l. de quoi vivre** to have ample means; **services l. rétribués** highly paid services; **avoir l. le temps** to have plenty of time; **c'est l. suffisant, ça suffit l.** it's more than enough *or* sufficient; **elle a l. quarante ans** she's at least *or* easily forty (if not more); **il en a eu l. assez** he's had more than enough; **je me suis l. servi** I've taken a generous helping

largesse [larʒɛs] *nf* **(a)** (*générosité*) generosity, largesse **(envers** towards); **avec l.** generously **(b) largesses** generous gifts; **faire des largesses** to make generous gifts

largeur [larʒœr] *nf* **(a)** width, breadth; (*de voie ferrée*) gauge; (*de bateau*) breadth, beam; **avoir** *ou* **faire trois mètres de l.** to be three metres wide; **en l., dans la l.** widthwise, breadthwise; **distance en l.** distance across; **les policiers barraient la rue sur toute sa l.** the policemen blocked off the whole width of the street; *Rad* **l. de bande** bandwidth; *Ordinat* **l. de papier** paper width; *Aut etc* **l. aux coudes** elbow room; *Aut* **l. de faisceau** beamwidth **(b)** *Fig* **l. de vues** broadness of outlook; **l. d'esprit** broadmindedness, broadness of mind; *F* **dans les grandes largeurs** in a big way, well and truly

largo [largo] *Mus* **1** *adv* largo **2** *nm* largo

largue [larg] **1** *adj* (*cordage*) loose, slack; (*vent*) free; **naviguer vent l.** to sail free **2** *nm* **grand l.** quartering (wind), (wind) on the quarter

largué [large] *adj F* (*qui ne comprend pas/plus*) lost; (*qui n'est plus à la page*) out of touch

larguer [large] *vt* **(a)** (*cordage*) to let go *or* loose; **l. les amarres** to cast off *or* to slip the mooring ropes; *Fig* to slip one's moorings; **l. la grand-voile** to unfurl the mainsail **(b)** *Av* (*parachutiste, vivres etc*) to drop; (*bombe*) to release, to drop **(c)** *F* (*se débarrasser de*) (*qn*) to chuck, to ditch, to dump; **il a tout largué et est parti vivre aux Caraïbes** he dropped everything *or* chucked everything in and went to live in the Caribbean

larme [larm] *nf* **(a)** (*des yeux*) tear; **fondre en larmes** to burst into tears, to break down in tears; **verser des larmes de joie** to weep tears of joy; **pleurer à chaudes larmes** to weep bitterly; **avoir les larmes aux yeux** to have tears in one's eyes; **mettre les larmes aux yeux** to bring tears to one's eyes; **elle était en larmes** she was in tears; **avec des larmes dans la voix** in a tearful voice; **au bord des larmes** on the verge of tears, close to tears; *F* **avoir toujours la l. à l'œil** to cry easily, to be easily moved to tears; **un rien lui met la l. à l'œil** he cries over nothing; **il a ri (jusqu')aux larmes** he laughed till he cried *or* till the tears rolled down his face; **pleurer toutes les larmes de son corps** to cry one's eyes *or* heart out; **larmes de crocodile** crocodile tears

(b) *F* (*petite quantité*) drop; **une l. de rhum** a drop of rum

larmier [larmje] *nm* **(a)** *Anat* inner corner of the eye, *Spéc* inner canthus **(b)** (*de cerf*) tear bag; (*de cheval*) temple **(c)** *Archit* drip(stone)

larmoiement [larmwamɑ̃] *nm* **(a)** *Méd* (*des yeux*) watering **(b)** *Péj* (*pleurnicheries*) snivelling

larmoyant [larmwajɑ̃] *adj* **(a)** *Méd* **yeux larmoyants** watering eyes **(b)** (*pleurnicheur*) (*voix, ton*) tearful, snivelling **(c)** *Péj* (*histoire, film, sentimentalité etc*) maudlin, mawkish; *Hist, Littér* (*comédie, drame*) sentimental

larmoyer [larmwaje] *vi* **(je larmoie, n. larmoyons; je larmoierai)** **(a)** (*des yeux*) to water **(b)** (*pleurnicher*) to snivel

larron [larɔ̃] *nm Arch* thief; *F* **s'entendre comme larrons en foire** to be as thick as thieves; **l'occasion fait le l.** opportunity makes the thief; *Bible* **le bon l. et le mauvais l.** the thief that was saved and the thief that was damned

larvaire [larvɛr] *adj* **(a)** *Zool* larval **(b)** *Fig* (*stade, état etc*) rudimentary, embryonic

larve [larv] *nf* **(a)** **[①A13,6]** larva; (*d'insecte*) grub; *Fig* worm; *Péj* **vivre comme une l.** to live like the lowest of God's creatures **(b)** *F* (*personne apathique*) wimp **(c)** *Litt* spectre

larvé [larve] *adj* **(a)** *Méd* (*fièvre etc*) larvate **(b)** *Fig* (*non déclaré*) (*guerre, conflit etc*) latent

laryngé [larɛ̃ʒe] *adj Anat* laryngeal

laryngectomie [larɛ̃ʒɛktɔmi] *nf Chir* laryngectomy

laryngien, -ienne [larɛ̃ʒjɛ̃, -jɛn] *adj Méd, Anat* laryngeal

laryngite [larɛ̃ʒit] *nf Méd* laryngitis

laryngologie [larɛ̃gɔlɔʒi] *nf Méd* laryngology

laryngologiste [larɛ̃gɔlɔʒist], **laryngologue** [larɛ̃gɔlɔg] *n Méd* laryngologist

laryngoscope [larɛ̃gɔskɔp] *nm Méd* laryngoscope

laryngotomie [larɛ̃gɔtɔmi] *nf Chir* laryngotomy

larynx [larɛ̃ks] *nm Anat* larynx

las[1] [lɑs] *int Arch* alack!, alas!

las[2]**, lasse** [lɑ, lɑs] *adj* tired, weary; **être l. de qch** to be tired *or* weary of sth; **de guerre lasse il consentit** tired of resisting, he agreed; **être l. de vivre** to be tired *or* weary of life *or* of living

lasagnes [lazaɲ] *nfpl Culin* lasagne, lasagna

lascar [laskar] *nm F* smart *or* streetwise character; **c'est un sacré l.** he's really smart *or* streetwise; **un drôle de l.** a shady *or* dubious character; **à nous deux mon l.!** you rascal!

lascif, -ive [lasif, -iv] *adj* **(a)** (*sensuel*) sensual, lascivious **(b)** (*lubrique*) (*comportement*) lascivious, lewd, lecherous

lascivement [lasivmɑ̃] *adv* lasciviously, lustfully

lasciveté [lasivte], **lascivité** [lasivite] *nf* lasciviousness, lustfulness

laser [lazɛr] *nm Phys* laser; **disque l.** compact disc; **rayon l.** laser beam; **faire qch au l.** to do sth using a laser

lassant [lɑsɑ̃] *adj* wearisome, tedious

lasser [lɑse] **1** *vt* to tire, to weary; **ses explications me lassent** I find his/her excuses so tiresome; *Litt* **l. la patience de qn** to try *or* tax sb's patience **2 se lasser** *vpr* to tire; **se l. de qn/de qch/de faire qch** to get tired of sb/of sth/of doing sth, to tire *or* weary of sb/of sth/of doing sth; *Litt* **faire qch sans se l.** to do sth without tiring

lassitude [lɑsityd] *nf* weariness, lassitude

lasso [laso] *nm* lasso; **prendre au l.** to lasso

latence [latɑ̃s] *nf* latency; **une période** *ou* **un temps de l.** a period of latency, a latent period

latent [latɑ̃] *adj* (*maladie, chaleur etc*) latent; **état l.** latent state, latency

latéral, -ale, -aux, -ales [lateral, -o] **1** *adj* **(a)** (*de côté*) (*vent, choc*) lateral; **entrée/rue latérale** side entrance/street; *Th* **projecteurs latéraux** side projectors **(b)** *Ling* **consonne latérale** lateral (consonant) **2** *nf Ling* **latérale** lateral

latéralement [lateralmɑ̃] *adv* (*se déplacer*) sideways, laterally; (*être situé*) at *or* on the side, laterally; **le vent soufflait l.** the wind was blowing from the side

latéralisation [lateralizasjɔ̃] *nf* **l. à droite/à gauche** right-/left-handedness

latex [latɛks] *nm Bot, Ind* latex

latifundium, *pl* **latifundia** [latifɔ̃djɔm, latifɔ̃dja] *nf Agr* large farm

latin, -ine [latɛ̃, -in] **1** *adj* **(a)** (*qui parle une langue romane*) (*peuple*) Latin; **les langues latines** the Romance languages; **le caractère l.** the Latin temperament **(b)** *Naut* **voile latine** lateen sail **(c)** *Ling* Latin; **une tournure latine** a Latin expression; **une version latine** a translation from Latin **2** *nm Ling* Latin; **l. classique** classical Latin; **bas l.** low Latin; **l. de cuisine** dog Latin; *Fig* **j'y perds mon l.** I can't make head (n)or tail of it **3** *n* **L.** Latin

latinisation [latinizasjɔ̃] *nf* Latinization

latiniser [latinize] *vt* to Latinize

latinisme [latinism] *nm* Latinism

latiniste [latinist] *n* (*spécialiste*) Latinist, Latin scholar; (*étudiant*) Latin student, student of Latin

latinité [latinite] *nf* (*civilisation*) Latin civilization *or* world; (*caractère*) Latin character

latino [latino] *nm F* latino

latino-américain, -aine, *pl* **latino-américain(e)s** **1** *adj* Latin-American **2** *n* **L.** Latin-American

latitude [latityd] *nf* **(a)** *Géog* latitude; (*région*) latitude, region; **à 30° de l. nord** at latitude 30° North; **il faut vivre différemment sous ces latitudes** you have to adopt a different way of life in this part of the world *or* in these latitudes **(b)** (*liberté*) latitude, scope, freedom; **avoir/donner à qn toute l. pour agir** to have/give sb total freedom of action *or* full discretion to act; **vous avez toute l. de dire oui ou non** you are completely free *or* at liberty to say yes or no

latitudinaire [latitydinɛr] *adj, n* latitudinarian

latrines [latrin] *nfpl* latrines

lattage [lataʒ] *nm* (*du plafond, mur etc*) lathing

latte [lat] *nf* **(a)** lath, batten, slat; **l. volige** slate lath, roof batten **(b)** *F (pied)* foot; *(chaussure)* shoe; **donner un coup de l. à qn** to kick sb, to give sb a kick; **prendre un coup de l.** to get kicked, to get a kick

latter [late] *vt* **(a)** *(toit, plancher)* to lath; *(jointures, tuiles)* to batten **(b)** *Arg* **l. qn** to give sb a kicking

lattis [lati] *nm* lathing, lathwork

laudanum [lodanɔm] *nm Pharm* laudanum

laudateur, -trice [lodatœr, -tris] *n Litt* lauder, praiser

laudatif, -ive [lodatif, -iv] *adj (discours, article etc)* laudatory; **il a été très l.** he was full of praise

lauréat, -ate [lɔrea, -at] **1** *adj (élève, candidat etc)* (prize)winning **2** *n* (prize)winner; **les lauréats du prix Nobel** the Nobel prizewinners

lauréole [lɔreɔl] *nf* daphne

laurier [lɔrje] *nm* **(a)** *(plante)* laurel; **l. commun** bay laurel, sweet bay; *Culin* **feuille de l.** bay leaf; *Culin* **du l.** (some) bay leaves **(b)** *Fig (gloire)* **lauriers** laurels; **les lauriers du vainqueur** the victor's laurels; **couronne de lauriers** laurel wreath; **se reposer** *ou* **s'endormir sur ses lauriers** to rest on one's laurels; **il est revenu de ses campagnes militaires couvert de lauriers** he returned from his military campaigns covered with glory

laurier-rose, *pl* **lauriers-roses** *nm (plante)* common oleander, rose laurel

laurier-sauce, *pl* **lauriers-sauce** *nm* bay

LAV [lɑv] *nm Méd abrév* **lymphadenopathy associated virus**

lavable [lavabl] *adj* washable; **l. en machine/à la main** machine-washable/washable by hand

lavabo [lavabo] *nm* **(a)** *(appareil sanitaire)* washbasin **(b)** *(salle de bain)* bathroom, washroom **(c)** *Euph* **lavabos** *(toilettes)* toilets **(d)** *Rel* lavabo

lavage [lavaʒ] *nm* washing; *(avec une brosse)* scrubbing; **toutes mes affaires sont au l.** all my things are in the wash; **ma chemise a rétréci/déteint au l.** my shirt has shrunk/run in the wash; **il a fallu trois lavages pour venir à bout des taches** it took three washes to get rid of the stains

▶ **lavage**: **l. auto** carwash; **l. de cerveau** brainwashing; **faire subir un l. de cerveau à qn** to brainwash sb; *Méd* **l. d'estomac** pumping out of the stomach; **faire un lavage d'estomac à qn** to pump out sb's stomach; *F* **l. de tête** dressing-down, telling-off

lavage-balayage, *pl* **lavages-balayages** *nm Aut* wash-wipe

lavallière [lavaljɛr] *nf* **(cravate) l.** necktie with a large bow, *Spéc* lavallière

lavande [lavɑ̃d] *nf Bot (fleur)* lavender; **(eau de) l.** lavender water; **bleu l.** lavender blue

lavandière [lavɑ̃djɛr] *nf* **(a)** *(blanchisseuse)* washerwoman, laundress **(b)** *(oiseau)* wagtail

lavaret [lavarɛ] *nm Région (poisson)* lavaret, pollan

lavasse [lavas] *nf F Péj (boisson)* dishwater; **son café, c'est de la l.** his coffee tastes like dishwater

lave [lav] *nf Géol* lava

lavé [lave] *adj (couleur)* pale, faint; *(délavé)* washed-out, faded; *Tech, Beaux-Arts* **dessin l.** wash drawing

lave-auto, *pl* **lave-autos** *nm Can* carwash

lave-essuie-phare, *pl* **lave-essuie-phares** *nm Aut* headlamp wash/wipe

lave-glace, *pl* **lave-glaces** *nm Aut* windscreen *or Am* windshield washer, screen wash

lave-linge *nm inv* washing machine

lave-mains *nm inv* (small) handbasin

lavement [lavmɑ̃] *nm Méd* enema; **l. baryté** barium enema

lave-phares *nm inv Aut* headlamp washer

lave-projecteurs *nm inv Aut* headlamp washers

laver [lave] **1** *vt* **(a)** *(nettoyer avec un liquide)* to wash; **l. qch à l'eau froide** to wash sth in cold water; **l. à grande eau** *(plancher, bateau, voiture)* to swill down; *(cuisine, atelier)* to swill out, to sluice down; **l. à la brosse** to scrub; **l. qch à l'éponge** to sponge sth (down); **l. qch au jet** to hose sth (down); *(pièce, cuve etc)* to hose sth (out); **l. la vaisselle** to wash *or* do the dishes, *Br* to wash up, *Br* to do the washing-up; **l. une tache** to wash out a stain; **l. une plaie** to bathe *or* cleanse a wound; *Fig F* **l. la tête à qn** to tell sb off, to haul sb over the coals; *Fig* **il faut l. son linge sale en famille** one shouldn't wash one's dirty linen in public; *Fig* **l'affront a été lavé dans le sang** the insult was paid for *or* avenged in blood

(b) *Fig Litt (disculper)* **l. qn d'une accusation/de tout soupçon** to clear sb of an accusation/of all suspicion

(c) *(mélanger d'eau) (peinture)* to dilute, to water down; **l. un dessin** to wash a drawing

(d) *Tech* **l. un minerai** to wash an ore

2 *vi* **cette lessive lave très bien** this powder washes very well

3 se laver *vpr* **(a)** *(se nettoyer)* to wash (oneself), to have a wash, *Am* to wash up; **se l. les dents** to clean *or* brush one's teeth; **se l. les cheveux** *ou* **la tête** to wash one's hair; **se l. les mains** to wash one's hands; *Fig* **je m'en lave les mains** I wash my hands of it

(b) *(pouvoir être lavé)* **ce tissu ne se lave pas** this material won't wash *or* isn't washable; **comment ça se lave, la viscose?** how should viscose be washed?

laverie [lavri] *nf* **(a)** *Ind* washing plant, washery **(b) l. automatique** launderette, *Am* laundromat

lavette [lavɛt] *nf* **(a)** *(de vaisselle)* dishcloth **(b)** *Belg, Suisse (gant de toilette)* face cloth *or* flannel, *Am* washcloth **(c)** *Fig F (homme)* spineless creature, drip, wet

laveur, -euse [lavœr, -øz] **1** *n (personne)* washer; **laveuse (de linge)** washerwoman; **l. de vaisselle** dishwasher, *Br* washer-up; **l. de vitres** window cleaner **2** *nm* scrubber

lave-vaisselle *nm inv* dishwasher

lave-vitre, *pl* **lave-vitres** *nm Aut* windscreen washer, *Am* windshield washer

lavis [lavi] *nm* **(a)** *(procédé) (de dessin)* washing, tinting **(b)** *(dessin)* wash drawing

lavoir [lavwar] *nm* **(a)** *(établissement)* **l. (public)** (public) washhouse **(b)** *(bassin)* (cement) washtub **(c)** *Tech, Ind (machine)* washer; *(atelier)* washing plant

lavomatic [lavomatik] *nm* launderette, *Am* laundromat

laxatif, -ive [laksatif, -iv] *adj, nm Méd* laxative

laxisme [laksism] *nm* **(a)** *Rel* latitudinarianism **(b)** *(manque de fermeté)* laxness, laxity

laxiste [laksist] **1** *adj* **(a)** *(qui manque de fermeté)* lax **(b)** *Rel* latitudinarian **2** *n* **(a)** *(qui manque de fermeté)* lax person **(b)** *Rel* latitudinarian

layette [lɛjɛt] *nf* baby clothes, layette; *Com* babywear; **bleu/rose layette** baby blue/pink

layon [lɛjɔ̃] *nm* forest track *or* trail; *(pour monter à cheval)* bridle path

lazaret [lazarɛ] *nm* lazaret(to)

lazariste [lazarist] *nm* Lazarist (priest)

lazulite [lazylit] *nm* lazulite, blue spar

lazzi [lazi, ladzi] *nmpl* gibes

l/c *nf, Fin (abrév* **lettre de crédit**) L/C

LCR [ɛlseɛr] *nf, Fin (abrév* **lettre de change relevé**) bills of exchange statement

LDL-cholestérol [ɛldeɛlkɔlɛsterɔl] *nm Méd (abrév* **low-density lipoprotein-cholesterol**) LDL-cholesterol

le[1] [lə], **la**[1] [la], **les**[1] [le] *art déf* [①**A6-8; B3-4,A**] **(le** *and* **la** *are elided to* **l'** *before a vowel or h mute*; **le** *and* **les** *contract with* **à, de** *into* **au, aux, du, des) (a)** *(précisant le nom ou pronom)* the; **ouvrez la porte** open the door; **il est venu la semaine dernière** he came last week; **j'apprends le français** I'm learning French; **j'étudie l'économie/la physique** I'm studying economics/physics; **la ville a perdu le quart/le tiers de ses habitants** the city has lost a quarter/a third of its inhabitants; **l'un ... l'autre** the one ... the other; **mon livre et le tien** my book and yours; **j'ai l'impression qu'il ne dit pas tout** I have the impression *or* a *or* the feeling that there's something he's not saying; **j'ai la certitude qu'il ment** I'm certain *or* sure that he's lying; **il est arrivé le lundi 12** he arrived on Monday the 12th; **ça s'est passé la veille de Noël** it happened on Christmas Eve; **oh! le beau chat!** what a beautiful cat!; **debout, les enfants!** time to get up, children!; **voilà le livre que j'ai préféré** this is the book that I liked best; **ce n'est plus la Claire que je connaissais** she's no longer the Claire I used to know; **le Paris de l'après-guerre/que nous aimions** post-war Paris/the Paris we knew and loved; **l'Amérique de Mark Twain n'existe plus** Mark Twain's America no longer exists

(b) *(noms de lieux)* **la France** France; **l'Afrique** Africa; **le Mont Blanc** Mont Blanc; **les Alpes** the Alps; **la Seine** the Seine; **le lac de Constance** Lake Constance; **les Maldives** the Maldives; **la Réunion** Réunion (Island); **l'île de Pâques** Easter Island; **la vallée du Rhône** the Rhône Valley; **dans le Berry** in the Berry (region)

(c) *(noms de personnes)* **l'empereur Guillaume** the Emperor William; **le roi Édouard** King Edward; **le cardinal Richelieu** Cardinal Richelieu; **le roi de France** the king of France; *F* **la Marie** Marie; *F* **le Pierre** Pierre

(d) *(avec certains noms italiens, certains noms d'actrices et de cantatrices)* **le Tasse** Tasso; **la Callas** Callas; **le Caravage** Caravaggio

(e) *(devant un nom déposé)* **la Renault® de mon père** my father's Renault

(f) *(noms de villes)* **Le Havre** Le Havre; **je reviens du Havre** I'm just back from le Havre; **La Rochelle** La Rochelle; **Le Mans** Le Mans; **Le Caire** Cairo; **La Havane** Havana; **La Nouvelle-Orléans** New Orleans; **La Haye** The Hague

(g) *(noms de famille)* **les tableaux de Le Brun** Le Brun's pictures; **les Curie** the Curies; **comment vont les Dupond?** how are the Duponds?

(h) (*avec la plupart des jours de fête*) **la Toussaint** All Saints' Day; **quand tombe la Saint Simon?** what day does Saint Simon's day fall on?; *F* **à la Noël** at Christmas

(i) (*parties du corps*) **j'ai mal à la gorge** I've got a sore throat; **elle a les yeux bleus** she has blue eyes; **elle a les cheveux longs/blonds** she has long/blond hair; **elle a les hanches larges** she has wide hips; **hausser les épaules** to shrug one's shoulders; **elle ferma les yeux** she closed her eyes; **il s'est coincé le doigt dans la porte** he caught his finger in the door; **le bras me fait mal** my arm hurts

(j) *F* (*environ*) **il a téléphoné vers les trois heures** he phoned (at) about *or* around three o'clock; **ça fera dans les 500 francs** it'll come to about *or* to something in the region of 500 francs

(k) (*formant les superlatifs*) **les jours les plus longs** the longest days; **le meilleur vin de sa cave** the best wine in his cellar; **mon amie la plus intime** my closest friend; **c'est elle (qui est) la plus jolie** she's the prettiest; (*avec des adverbes*) **c'est elle qui travaille le mieux** she's the one who works (the) best; (*avec un superlatif absolu*) **c'est lorsqu'elle est seule qu'elle est le plus heureuse** she's happiest when she's by herself

(l) (*généralisant le nom*) **je préfère le café au thé** I prefer coffee to tea; **aimer la musique/la littérature/le football** to like music/literature/football; **aller au théâtre/au cinéma** to go to the theatre/the cinema; **ils ne vont jamais au restaurant** they never go to a restaurant, they never eat out; **il méprise les pauvres** he scorns poor people *or* the poor; **l'homme est un animal social** man is a social animal; **le dauphin est un mammifère marin** the dolphin is a marine mammal; **il fume la pipe/la cigarette** he smokes a pipe/cigarettes; **je n'ai pas eu la patience d'attendre/le courage de refuser** I didn't have the patience to wait/the courage to refuse; **il a eu le culot de me réclamer de l'argent** he had the cheek to demand money from me; **j'ai le droit de vivre** I have a right to live; **donner l'exemple** to set an example; **la paresse est un des septs péchés capitaux** sloth is one of the seven deadly sins; **demander le divorce** to sue for (a) divorce; **la belle excuse!** a fine excuse!

(m) (*distributif*) **trois fois l'an** three times a year; **cinq francs la livre** five francs a pound; **il vient le jeudi/(tous) les jeudis** he comes on Thursdays/every Thursday; **il a passé le samedi chez ses parents** he spent Saturday at his parents' house; **il a passé la nuit dehors** he spent the night outdoors; **il a bu toute la nuit** he drank all night; **je n'ai pas mangé de la journée** I haven't eaten all day

(n) (*avec un adjectif*) **je vous donne les livres neufs et je reprends les vieux** I'll give you the new books and take back the old ones; **tu préfères la rouge ou la jaune?** do you prefer the red (one) or the yellow (one)?

(o) **à la française/l'italienne** in the French/Italian fashion *or* style *or* way; **champignons à la grecque** mushrooms à la grecque; **un travail fait à la va-vite** *ou* **à la hâte** a piece of work done in a hurry; **encore une blague à la Marie** another one of Marie's little jokes

(p) *partitif* **du, de la, des** *voir* **de** [2]

le[2], la[2], les[2] *pron pers* **(a)** (*remplaçant le nom*) (*pour un homme*) him; (*pour une femme*) her; (*pour un bébé, un animal*) it, him, her; (*pour une chose, une idée*) it; (*pour un navire*) it, her; (*au pluriel*) them; **je vous le/la présenterai** I'll introduce him/her to you; **je ne le lui ai pas donné** I didn't give it to him/her; **les voilà!** there they are!; **ne l'abîmez pas!** don't spoil it!; **ce pays, je le connais** I know this country

(b) (*remplaçant l'adjectif ou le nom utilisé adjectivement*) **malheureux, je l'étais certainement** I certainly was unhappy; **son frère est médecin, il voudrait l'être aussi** his brother is a doctor, he would like to be one too; **j'étais fatigué mais maintenant je ne le suis plus** I was tired, but now I'm not

(c) (*remplaçant une proposition*) **il me l'a dit** he told me so; **je le pense aussi** I think so too; **il est plus riche que vous (ne) le pensez** he's richer than you think (he is); **tiens-le-toi pour dit** I'm telling you once and for all; **tu le sais aussi bien que moi** you know (it) as well as I do

lé [le] *nm* (*de tissu*) width, breadth; (*de papier peint*) strip

leader [lidœr] *nm* **(a)** *Pol, Sp, Mktg* leader; **cette entreprise est le l. mondial de la micro-informatique** this firm is the world leader in microcomputing **(b)** *Journ* **(article) l.** editorial, *Br* leader, leading article

leasing [liziŋ] *nm* leasing; **acheter une auto en l.** to buy a car on a leasing basis, to lease a car

léchage [leʃaʒ] *nm* licking; *F* **l. de bottes** bootlicking

lèche [lɛʃ] *nf très F* bootlicking; **faire de la l.** to be a bootlicker; **faire de la l. à qn** to suck up to sb, to lick sb's boots

lèche-bottes *F* **1** *adj inv* **elle est l.** she's a bootlicker **2** *n inv* bootlicker, *Am* apple polisher

lèche-cul *nm inv Vulg* arse-licker, *Am* ass-licker, *Am* brown-nose

lèchefrite [lɛʃfrit] *nf Culin* dripping pan

lécher [leʃe] **(je lèche, n. léchons; je lécherai) 1** *vt* **(a)** (*glace, cuiller, plaies etc*) to lick; **l. le beurre d'une tartine** to lick the butter off a slice of bread; *Fig* **l. les vitrines** to go window-shopping; *Péj* **l. les bottes** *ou Vulg* **le cul de** *ou* **à qn** to lick sb's boots, *Vulg* to lick *or* kiss sb's arse *or Am* ass

(b) (*fignoler*) (*travail, style*) to polish; **trop léché** overpolished, overdone

(c) (*effleurer*) (*des vagues*) to lap against; (*des flammes*) to lick; **les vagues léchaient le sable** the waves were lapping on the sand

2 se lécher *vpr* **se l. les doigts** to lick one's fingers; *F* **il s'en léchait les doigts** *ou* **les babines** he licked his lips *or* his chops over it; *F* **quel beau gâteau, c'est à s'en l. les doigts** *ou* **les babines** what a lovely cake, it's really mouthwatering

lécheur, -euse [leʃœr, -øz] *n F Péj* bootlicker, toady

lèche-vitrines *nm F* window-shopping; **faire du l.** to go window-shopping

lécithine [lesitin] *nf Ch* lecithin

leçon [ləsɔ̃] *nf* **(a)** *Scol* (*cours*) lesson, class; (*ce qu'on doit étudier, apprendre*) lesson; **il ne connaît pas sa/ses leçon(s)** he hasn't learned his lesson(s); **réciter sa l.** to recite one's lesson; *Fig* to recite one's answers/*etc* parrot-fashion; *Fig* **ils avaient bien appris leur l.** they had learnt their lines well, they had rehearsed what to say very well; **leçons de chant** singing lessons; **le bricolage en dix leçons** DIY in ten (easy) lessons

(b) (*conseil*) **leçon(s)** advice; **faire la l. à qn** (*le guider*) to give sb instructions, to tell sb what to do; (*le réprimander*) to lecture sb, to give sb a lecture; **faire une l.** *ou* **des leçons de morale à qn** to lecture sb (on his/her morals); **je n'ai pas de l. à recevoir de toi** I don't need your advice *or* (any) advice from you; **je n'ai de l. à recevoir de personne** I don't need anybody's advice *or* (any) advice from anybody

(c) (*enseignement*) lesson; **donner une l. à qn** to teach sb a lesson; **espérons qu'il en aura tiré une l.** let's hope he's learnt his lesson; **que cela vous serve de l.** let that be a lesson *or* a warning to you

(d) (*de manuscrit*) reading

(e) *Rel* lesson

▶ **leçon**: **l. de choses** general science (*in primary school*); **leçons particulières** private lessons, private tuition

lecteur, -trice [lɛktœr, -tris] **1** *n* **(a)** (*personne qui lit*) reader; **c'est un grand l. de romans** he reads a lot of novels, he's a great novel reader

(b) (*dans l'édition*) (publisher's) reader

(c) *Univ* foreign language assistant, lector

2 *nm* **(a)** *TV etc* (*dispositif*) player, playback deck, reproducer; **l. de badges** badge reader; **l. de carte** *Aut* map light, spot lamp; (*de cartes de crédit*) credit card reader; **l. de carte à puce** smartcard reader; **l. de cartes à mémoire** smartcard reader, card reader; **l. de cartouche** cartridge player; **l. de cassettes** cassette player; **l. de codes barres** bar code reader *or* scanner; **l. de disques compacts** compact disc player, CD player; **l. optique** optical reader, visual scanner, optical drive; *Cin etc* **l. de ruban perforé** punchtape reader; **l. de son** sound head, sound reader; **l. de télé-cinéma** film scanner; **l. de vidéodisque** video disc player

(b) *Ordinat* **l. (de disquettes)** (disk) drive, floppy (disk) drive; **l. de CD-Rom** *ou* **de disque optique** CD-Rom drive; **l. de disque dur** hard disk drive; **l. de bandes** tape drive *or* reader; **l. de destination** destination drive; **l. de lignes/de pages** line/page scanner

lecteur-encodeur, *pl* **lecteurs-encodeurs** *nm Ordinat* reader-encoder

lectorat [lɛktɔra] *nm* **(a)** *Univ* assistantship **(b)** (*lecteurs*) readership

lecture [lɛktyr] *nf* **(a)** (*action de lire*) reading; **enseigner la l. à qn** to teach sb to read; **livre de l.** reading book, reader; **livre d'une l. agréable** book that makes pleasant reading; **salle de l.** (*de bibliothèque*) reading room; **méthode de l. rapide** rapid-reading method; *Mus* **l. à vue** sight-reading; **s'informer par la l. des journaux** to keep oneself informed by reading the newspapers; **l. à haute voix** *ou* **à voix haute** reading aloud; **faire la l. à qn** to read aloud to sb; **à la l. de sa lettre, j'ai souri** on reading his letter, I smiled; *Fml* **donner l.**

d'un document to read out a document (**à qn** to sb); *Pol* **projet repoussé en deuxième l.** bill rejected at the second reading; **l. des épreuves** proof-reading

(**b**) (*ce qu'on lit*) reading, reading material; **l. pour la jeunesse** reading *or* books for young people; **Balzac fait partie de mes lectures** Balzac is part of my reading; **il m'a apporté de la l.** he brought me something to read; **avoir de saines/mauvaises lectures** to read the right/wrong things, to read wholesome/unwholesome books

(**c**) (*interprétation*) reading, interpretation; **une nouvelle l. de Balzac** a new reading *or* interpretation of Balzac; **l. marxiste/psychanalytique** Marxist/psychoanalytic(al) reading *or* interpretation; **tous les sociologues n'ont pas la même l. des faits** not all sociologists read *or* interpret the facts in the same way; **grille de l.** interpretative framework

(**d**) *Ordinat* read(ing); **en l. seule** in read-only mode; **mettre un fichier en l. seule** to make a file read-only; **l. optique** optical reading; **l. au scanneur** scan; **l. destructive** destructive read; **l. non destructive** non-destructive read; **l. sur disque** reading to disk

(**e**) *Cin* **l. du son** sound reproduction

ledit, ladite, *pl* **lesdits, lesdites** [lədi, ladit, ledi, ledit] *adj* (*contractions avec* **à** *et* **de**: *voir* **le**[1]) the aforesaid, the aforementioned, the said

légal, -ale, -aux, -ales [legal, -o] *adj* legal; (*action*) legal, lawful; **avoir recours aux moyens légaux** to take legal action, to institute legal proceedings; **suivre la procédure légale** to follow the legal procedure; **par les voies légales** legally, by legal means; *Fin* **taux l.** official rate of interest; **monnaie légale** legal tender

légalement [legalmɑ̃] *adv* legally, lawfully

légalisation [legalizasjɔ̃] *nf* legalization; (*de signature*) authentication, certification

légaliser [legalize] *vt* (*rendre légal*) (*pratique, drogue etc*) to legalize; (*authentifier*) (*signature, procuration*) to authenticate, to certify; **l. des documents** to certify documents

légalisme [legalism] *nm* legalism

légaliste [legalist] *adj, n* legalist

légalité [legalite] *nf* (**a**) (*de mesure, décision, licenciement etc*) legality, lawfulness (**b**) (*situation légale*) **la l.** the law; **rester dans/respecter la l.** to keep within/respect the law; **cet acte l'a fait sortir de la l.** this act has brought *or* put him/her outside the law; **agir en toute l.** to act within the law; **il l'a ainsi dépouillé de ses biens en toute l.** he thus stripped him of his possessions quite legally

légat [lega] *nm Rel, Antiq* legate; **l. du Pape** papal legate

légataire [legatɛr] *n Jur* legatee, heir; **l. universel** sole legatee; **l. d'une succession** heir to an estate

légation [legasjɔ̃] *nf* legation

legato [legato] *adv Mus* **jouer l.** to play legato

légendaire [leʒɑ̃dɛr] *adj* legendary

légende [leʒɑ̃d] *nf* (**a**) (*histoire, fable*) legend; *Fig* (*mensonge*) fairy tale *or* story; **entrer dans la l.** to become a legend; **entrer vivant dans la l.** to become a living legend *or* a legend in one's own lifetime; **la l. napoléonienne** the Napoleonic legend; **pays/personnage de l.** legendary country/character (**b**) (*sur une pièce, médaille*) inscription, legend; (*de dessin, photo*) caption; (*de diagramme, carte etc*) key, legend; **consulter la l.** to refer to the key

légender [leʒɑ̃de] *vt* (*photo, dessin etc*) to provide with a caption; (*plan, carte etc*) to provide with a key; **voir photo légendée** see photo with caption

léger, -ère [leʒe, -ɛr] **1** *adj* (**a**) (*de peu de poids*) light; **l. comme une plume** as light as a feather; **armes légères** light weaponry; **un croiseur l.** a light cruiser; **industrie légère** light industry; **repas l.** light meal; **avoir le cœur l.** to be light-hearted; **partir le cœur l.** to leave with a light heart; **marcher d'un pas l.** to walk with a light step *or* with a spring in one's step; *Fig* **je me sens plus l. depuis que je lui ai tout avoué** telling him everything has taken a (great) weight off my mind *or* shoulders

(**b**) (*faible*) (*douleur, erreur, blessure*) slight; (*brise*) light, gentle; (*couche de peinture, vin, parfum*) light; (*tabac*) mild; (*thé, café*) weak; (*goût, odeur*) slight, light, faint; (*son, nuance*) faint; **avoir le sommeil l.** to be a light sleeper; **il y a eu quelques blessés légers** some people were slightly injured; *Jur* **peine légère** light sentence, mild punishment; **il y a un l. mieux** there is a slight improvement; **perte légère** slight *or* small *or* trivial loss; **une légère pointe d'ail/d'ironie** a slight *or* little touch of garlic/irony; **elle a eu un l. sourire** she gave a slight *or* little smile

(**c**) (*insuffisant*) (*preuves, arguments*) thin, lightweight; **c'est un peu l.** it's a bit on the thin side; **c'est un peu l. comme résultat** there's not much to show for it; **la musique légère** light music, easy listening music; **c'est un film l.** it's a light film

(**d**) (*désinvolte, frivole*) (*personne*) thoughtless; (*en amour*) fickle; **le responsable s'est montré un peu l.** the person in charge was quite offhand about it; **femme légère** *ou* **de mœurs légères** woman of easy virtue, loose woman; **avoir la cuisse légère** to sleep around; **propos légers** frivolous *or* idle talk

2 *nf* **agir à la légère** to act without due consideration *or* thoughtlessly; **parler à la légère** to speak unthinkingly *or* thoughtlessly; **ce nouveau parti est un danger pour la démocratie, je ne parle pas à la légère** this new party is a danger to democracy, and I'm not saying that lightly *or* I mean that very seriously; **prendre** *ou* **traiter qch à la légère** to make light of sth, not to take sth seriously, to treat sth lightly

3 *adv* **manger l.** to eat lightly *or* light meals/a light meal; **s'habiller l.** to wear light clothes; *F* **il faut y aller l. avec les tranquillisants** you have to go easy with tranquillizers

légèrement [leʒɛrmɑ̃] *adv* (**a**) (*avec légèreté*) (*habillé, armé*) lightly; **manger l.** to eat lightly *or* light meals/a light meal (**b**) (*un peu*) (*ennuyeux, surpris, plus grand etc*) slightly, somewhat; (*blessé*) slightly; **ça sent l. le moisi** there's a slight smell of mildew; **pourrais-tu reculer l.?** could you go back slightly *or* a bit? (**c**) (*avec souplesse*) nimbly, gracefully; **elle se déplace l.** she moves gracefully (**d**) (*avec désinvolture*) **agir l.** to act without due consideration *or* thoughtlessly; **traiter qch l.** to make light of sth, not to take sth seriously, to treat sth lightly

légèreté [leʒɛrte] *nf* (**a**) (*poids faible*) lightness; (*d'un danseur, sportif, cheval*) agility; **l. de main** (*d'un pianiste, d'une infirmière*) lightness of touch (**b**) (*faiblesse*) (*de blessure*) slightness; (*de brise*) lightness, gentleness; (*du tabac*) mildness; (*de vin*) lightness; (*du thé, café*) weakness; (*de son, nuance*) faintness (**c**) (*désinvolture*) thoughtlessness; **agir avec l.** to act without due consideration *or* thoughtlessly; **parler avec l.** to speak unthinkingly *or* thoughtlessly (**d**) (*en amour*) fickleness; (*des mœurs*) looseness

leggings [legiŋz] *nmpl* leggings

légiférer [leʒifere] *vi* (**je légifère, n. légiférons; je légiférai**) to legislate (**sur** on)

légion [leʒjɔ̃] *nf* legion; **la L. (étrangère)** the Foreign Legion; **la L. d'honneur** the Legion of Honour *or US* Honor; *Fig* **l. de moucherons/touristes** host *or* swarm of gnats/tourists; **elle a une l. d'oncles et tantes** she has a huge number of uncles and aunts; **ils sont l.** they are legion

légionnaire [leʒjɔnɛr] *nm* (**a**) *Hist* legionary (**b**) (*à la Légion étrangère*) legionnaire, Foreign Legionary (**c**) (*membre de La Légion d'honneur*) member of the Legion of Honour *or US* Honor (**d**) *Méd* **maladie du l.** legionnaire's disease

législateur, -trice [leʒislatœr, -tris] *Jur* **1** *n* (*personne qui fait les lois*) legislator, lawmaker **2** *nm* (*corps législatif*) legislature **3** *adj* legislative, lawmaking; **puissance législatrice** legislative power

législatif, -ive [leʒislatif, -iv] **1** *adj Jur* legislative; *Hist Fr* **l'Assemblée législative** the Legislative Assembly; **élections législatives** parliamentary elections; **le pouvoir l.** the legislature **2** *nm Pol* **le l.** legislative power **3** *nf* (**a**) *Hist Fr* **la Législative** the Legislative Assembly (**b**) *Pol* **législatives** parliamentary elections

législation [leʒislasjɔ̃] *nf Jur* legislation, law(s); **l. criminelle/fiscale/du travail** criminal/tax/employment legislation *or* law; **l. française/anglaise** French/English legislation *or* laws; **l. commerciale** commercial legislation *or* law; **l. douanière** customs legislation; **l. financière** financial legislation; **l. sur la consommation** consumer legislation; **l. sur la sécurité** safety legislation

législature [leʒislatyr] *nf Jur* (**a**) (*durée*) term of office (*of legislative body*) (**b**) (*corps*) legislature, legislative body

légiste [leʒist] **1** *nm Jur* jurist **2** *adj* **médecin l.** pathologist

légitimation [leʒitimasjɔ̃] *nf* (**a**) (*d'enfant*) legitimization (**b**) (*de délégué, titre etc*) official recognition (**c**) *Litt* (*de conduite*) justification

légitime [leʒitim] **1** *adj* (**a**) (*légal*) legitimate; (*action*) lawful; **propriétaire l.** legal owner; **union l.** marriage (*as opposed to living together*); **héritier l.** rightful heir; **enfant l.** legitimate child; *Jur* **l. défense** self-defence; **il était en état de l. défense** he was acting in self-defence (**b**) (*juste*) (*récompense, motif, désir etc*) legitimate, justified, justifiable; **il est tout à fait l. qu'il soit en colère, sa colère est tout à fait l.** he is quite justified in his anger, it's quite legitimate *or* justifiable for him to be angry, his anger is quite justified *or* legitimate **2** *nf Arg* **ma l.** the wife, the missus, *Br Arg* her indoors

légitimement [leʒitimmɑ̃] *adv* legitimately; (*en colère*) justifiably; (*appartenir à qn*) rightfully; *Jur* lawfully

légitimer [leʒitime] *vt* (**a**) *Jur* (*enfant, union etc*) to legitim(at)ize, to legitimate (**b**) (*action, demande etc*) to justify (**c**) (*titre, pouvoir*) to recognize

légitimiste [leʒitimist] *adj, n Hist* legitimist
légitimité [leʒitimite] *nf* **(a)** *Jur* (*d'un enfant, d'une union etc*) legitimacy **(b)** (*bien-fondé*) (*de démarche, conduite etc*) legitimacy, justifiability; **tes soupçons sont sans l.** your suspicions are unjustified *or* without foundation
legs [lɛ, lɛg] *nm* **(a)** *Jur* legacy, bequest; **l. universel** universal bequest; **l. particulier** specific bequest; **faire un l. particulier à son neveu** to make a specific bequest to one's nephew; **faire un l. à qn** to leave sb a legacy, to make a bequest to sb **(b)** *Fig Litt* (*héritage*) **le l. du passé** the legacy of the past
léguer [lege] *vt* **(je lègue, n. léguons; je léguerai)** **(a)** *Jur* to bequeath, to leave (**à qn** to sb) **(b)** (*transmettre*) (*tradition, qualité etc*) to hand down, to pass on (**à** to)
légume [legym] **1** *nm* **(a)** [①**A9**,b,ii] vegetable **légumes verts** green vegetables, greens; **soupe de légumes** vegetable soup; **légumes secs** pulses **(b)** *Fig F* (*personne végétative*) vegetable; **il est devenu un vrai l. après son accident** he's become a complete vegetable since his accident **2** *nf F* **grosse l.** bigwig, big shot
légumier, -ière [legymje, -jɛr] **1** *adj* **culture légumière** vegetable growing **2** *nm* (*plat*) vegetable dish **3** *n Belg* (*commerçant*) greengrocer
légumineux, -euse [legyminø, -øz] *Bot* **1** *adj* leguminous **2** *nf* **légumineuse** leguminous plant; **les légumineuses** Leguminosae
leitmotiv, *pl* **leitmotive** [lajtmɔtiv, lɛmɔtiv] *nm Mus, Fig* leitmotif, leitmotiv, recurring theme
lem [lɛm] *nm Astron* lunar exploration module, LEM, *F* moon buggy
Léman [lemɑ̃] *nm* **le lac L.** Lake Geneva
lemme [lɛm] *nm Math, Phil* lemma
lemming [lemiŋ] *nm* lemming
lémure [lemyr] *nm Antiq* lemur
lémurien [lemyrjɛ̃] *nm Zool* lemur
lendemain [lɑ̃dmɛ̃] *nm* **(a)** (*jour suivant*) **le l.** the next day, the following day; **le l. de la bataille** the day after the battle; **le l. matin** the next morning, the morning after; **le l. après-midi, (dans) l'après-midi du l.** the next afternoon, the afternoon after; **il devint célèbre du jour au l.** he became famous overnight; *F* **un l. de cuite** *ou* **de fête** the morning after (the night before)

(b) (*avenir*) **il faut penser au l.** one must think of the future *or* of tomorrow; **des lendemains prometteurs** a promising future; *Hum* **des lendemains qui chantent** a better *or* bright(er) future; **avoir d'heureux lendemains** to have happy consequences; **des succès/aventures (amoureuses) sans l.** short-lived successes/(love) affairs

(c) (*période qui suit*) **au l. de la guerre/de ce scandale** soon after *or* in the days following the war/this scandal
lénifiant [lenifjɑ̃] *adj Méd, Fig* soothing
lénifier [lenifje] *vt* (*pr sub, impf* **n. lénifiions, v. lénifiiez**) **(a)** *Méd* to soothe, to alleviate **(b)** *Fig* (*apaiser*) to soothe, to calm
Lénine [lenin] *nm* Lenin
léninisme [leninism] *nm Pol* Leninism
léniniste [leninist] *adj, n Pol* Leninist
lénitif, -ive [lenitif, -iv] *adj, nm* lenitive
lent [lɑ̃] *adj* (*mouvement, développement etc*) slow; (*poison*) slow(-acting); (*tortue etc*) slow-moving; **mort lente** slow *or* lingering death; **être l. à faire qch** to be slow to do sth; **vous êtes l. à faire la vaisselle** you're slow at *or* taking your time doing the dishes; **vous êtes l. à manger** you're a slow eater, you eat slowly; **vous êtes l. à comprendre** you're slow to understand *or F* slow on the uptake; **avoir l'esprit l.** to be slow-witted, to be slow in understanding, *F* to be slow on the uptake
lente [lɑ̃t] *nf* nit
lentement [lɑ̃tmɑ̃] *adv* slowly; **ruisseau qui coule l.** slow-flowing stream; **l. mais sûrement** slowly but surely
lenteur [lɑ̃tœr] *nf* **(a)** (*développement lent*) slowness; **avec l.** slowly **(b)** **lenteurs** (*actions lentes*) slowness; **les lenteurs de la justice** the slowness of the law
lentigo [lɑ̃tigo] *nm Méd* lentigo
lentille [lɑ̃tij] *nf* **(a)** *Culin, Bot* lentil **(b)** *Bot* **l. d'eau** duckweed, *Spéc* lemna **(c)** *Opt* lens; **lentilles de contact** *ou* **cornéennes** contact lenses; **lentilles souples/dures** soft/hard lenses
lento [lɛnto] *adv, nm Mus* lento
léonin, -ine [leɔnɛ̃, -in] *adj* leonine; **partage l.** lion's share
léopard [leɔpar] *nm* **(a)** leopard; **manteau de l.** leopard skin coat **(b)** *Hér* leopard
LEP [ɛlpe, lɛp] *nm* **(a)** (*abrév* **Lycée d'Enseignement Professionnel**) ≈ technical college **(b)** (*abrév* **livret d'épargne populaire**) general savings account
lépidoptère [lepidɔptɛr] **1** *adj* lepidopterous **2** *nm* (*insecte*) lepidopteran
lèpre [lɛpr] *nf* **(a)** *Méd* leprosy **(b)** *Fig* (*pourriture, ce qui ronge*) **mur rongé par la l.** peeling *or* flaking *or* crumbling wall **(c)** *Litt* (*mal*) canker, scourge; **l'envie le ronge comme une l.** envy eats away at him like a cancer
lépreux, -euse [leprø, -øz] **1** *adj* **(a)** *Méd* leprous **(b)** *Fig* (*mur*) peeling, flaking, crumbling; (*quartier*) dilapidated, rundown **2** *n* leper; **traiter qn comme un l.** to treat sb like a leper
léproserie [leprozri] *nf* leper hospital
lequel, laquelle, lesquels, lesquelles [ləkɛl, lakɛl, lekɛl] (*contracted with* **à** *and* **de** *to* **auquel, auxquel(le)s, duquel, desquel(le)s**) **1** [①**A32**,a-f; **B20-21**,d] *pron rel* (*personne*) who; (*après prép*) whom; (*chose*) which; **le père de cette jeune fille, l. est très riche** this girl's father, who is very rich; **le père de cette jeune fille, laquelle est très riche** the father of this girl, who is very rich; **ont comparu trois témoins, lesquels ont déclaré ...** three witnesses appeared, who stated ...; **la dame avec laquelle elle était sortie** the lady with whom she had gone out; **les deux officiers entre lesquels elle était assise** the two officers between whom she was sitting; **j'ai retrouvé mon parapluie, l. était sous mon lit** I've found my umbrella, which was under my bed; **l'adresse à laquelle il devait m'écrire** the address at which he was to write to me; **la farine avec laquelle j'ai fait ce gâteau** the flour (that) I used to make this cake *or* with which I made this cake; **l'actrice à laquelle je pense est plus jeune** the actress (that) I'm thinking of *or* of whom I'm thinking is younger; **la personne par laquelle il faut passer pour obtenir ce dossier** the person (that) you have to go through to get this file; **décision par laquelle ...** decision whereby ...; **n'importe l. fera l'affaire** any (one) of them will do; **il y avait beaucoup de gens, parmi lesquels mon cousin Paul** there were a lot of people, among whom was my cousin Paul; **la dame chez laquelle je l'ai rencontré** the lady at whose house I met him; **l'homme sans l'avis duquel on ne peut rien faire** the man without whose advice one can do nothing; **la maison sur la porte de laquelle vous trouverez une plaque** the house with a plaque on the door; **le roman d'après l. il a tiré son film** the novel he took his film from *or* on which he based his film

2 [①**A31**,c; **B16**,3,a] *adj rel* **voici cent francs, laquelle somme vous était due par mon père** here's a hundred francs, (which was) the sum my father owed you; **j'ai vu son adversaire, l. adversaire est impressionnant** I've seen his opponent, (who is) an impressive one; **il écrira peut-être, auquel cas ...** perhaps he will write, in which case ...

3 *pron interr* which (one); **lesquel(le)s** which; **l. (de ces chapeaux) préférez-vous?** which (one) (of these hats) do you prefer?; **l. d'entre nous?** which (one) of us?; **de laquelle de ces deux régions êtes-vous originaire?** which (one) of these two regions do you come from?; **auquel de ces deux hommes faites-vous confiance?** which (one) of these two men do you trust?
lerch(e) [lɛrʃ] *adv Arg* **pas l.** damn all, *Br* bugger all
lérot [lero] *nm* lerot, garden dormouse
les [le] *voir* **le**[1, 2]
lesbianisme [lɛsbjanism] *nm* lesbianism
lesbien, -ienne [lɛsbjɛ̃, -jɛn] **1** *adj* lesbian **2** *nf* **lesbienne** lesbian
lèse-majesté [lɛzmaʒɛste] *nf inv Jur* high treason, lese-majesty
léser [leze] *vt* **(je lèse, n. lésons; je léserai)** **(a)** (*désavantager*) to wrong; (*intérêts de qn*) to harm, to damage; *Jur* **l. les droits de qn** to encroach *or* infringe upon sb's rights; **la partie lésée** the injured party **(b)** *Méd* (*organe*) to injure
lésine [lezin] *nf Litt, Vieilli* stinginess
lésiner [lezine] *vi* to skimp (**sur** on); **ils n'avaient pas lésiné sur le vin** they hadn't skimped on the wine; **ne pas l. sur les moyens** not to go in for penny-pinching; (*pour une fête, en vacances etc*) to really push the boat out
lésineur, -euse [lezinœr, -øz] *n Vieilli* niggard, miser
lésion [lezjɔ̃] *nf Méd, Jur* lesion
lessivable [lesivabl] *adj* (*papier peint, tissus etc*) washable
lessivage [lesivaʒ] *nm* (*de linge, mur etc*) washing; *Ch* leaching; *Fig* **c'est le grand l. dans la compagnie** there's a big clear-out (of personnel) going on in the company
lessive [lesiv] *nf* **(a)** (*produit*) (*en poudre*) washing powder; (*liquide*) liquid detergent; *Ch* lye **(b)** (*action de laver*) wash(ing); **faire la l.** to do the washing; **jour de l.** wash(ing) day; **j'ai fait trois lessives ce matin** I've done three washes this morning; **une l. de blanc et une l. de couleurs** one wash of whites and one wash of coloureds **(c)** (*linge sale*) (dirty) washing **(d)** (*linge propre*) (clean) washing; **une l.** a batch of washing **(e)** *Fig* (*assainissement*) shake-out, clear-out (operation); **il faut faire une grande l. dans cette famille** this family really needs sorting out

lessivé [lesive] *adj F (fatigué)* washed out, worn out, done in
lessiver [lesive] *vt* **(a)** *(nettoyer) (sol, mur etc)* to wash **(b)** *Ch* to leach **(c)** *Fig très F (battre)* to lick, to wipe the floor with; **se faire l.** *(au jeu)* to be cleaned out **(d)** *Fig F (fatiguer)* to wear out, to do in; **ce match m'a lessivé** this match has worn me out *or* done me in
lessiveuse [lesivøz] *nf* boiler, *Br* copper
lessiviel [lesivjɛl] *adj m* **produit l.** detergent (product)
lest [lɛst] *nm, no pl (de bateau, ballon)* ballast; *Naut* **naviguer sur son l.** to sail in ballast *or* without a cargo; **jeter** *ou* **lâcher du l.** to discharge ballast; *Fig (faire des concessions)* to make concessions
lestage [lɛstaʒ] *nm (de bateau, ballon)* ballasting
leste [lɛst] *adj* **(a)** *(agile) (personne, animal)* nimble, agile; *(mouvement)* brisk, nimble **(b)** *Fig (grivois) (manières, gestes, mot)* crude; *(plaisanteries, roman etc)* risqué
lestement [lɛstəmɑ̃] *adv* nimbly, smartly; *(avec une légèreté choquante)* offhandedly, casually
lester [lɛste] **1** *vt* **(a)** *(bateau, ballon)* to ballast **(b)** *F (poche, portefeuille etc)* to stuff, to fill; **l. son estomac** to fill one's stomach **2 se lester** *vpr* **(a)** *(plongeur etc)* to weigh oneself down **(b)** *F* **se l. (l'estomac)** to stuff oneself; **se l. les poches de petite monnaie/de bonbons** to stuff *or* fill one's pockets with small change/sweets
létal, -ale, -aux, -ales [letal, -o] *adj* lethal; *Biol* **gène l.** lethal gene; **dose létale** lethal dose
letchi [lɛtʃi] *nm Bot* lychee, litchi
léthargie [letarʒi] *nf* lethargy; *Méd* coma; *Méd* **tomber en l.** to sink into a coma; *Fig* **en l.** in a state of lethargy
léthargique [letarʒik] *adj* lethargic
lette [lɛt] *nm Ling* Lettish, Latvian
letton, -onne [lɛtɔ̃, -ɔn] **1** *adj* Latvian; *(personne)* Lett, Latvian **2** *nm Ling* Lettish, Latvian **3** *n* **L.** Latvian, Lett
Lettonie [lɛtɔni] *nf* Latvia
lettrage [lɛtraʒ] *nm Typ* lettering
lettre [lɛtr] *nf* **(a)** *(de l'alphabet)* letter; **l. majuscule/minuscule** capital/small letter; **mot de sept lettres** seven-letter word, word of seven letters; **écrire qch en toutes lettres** to write sth out in full; **écrire une somme en (toutes) lettres** to write an amount in words; *Fig* **c'est écrit en toutes lettres** it's there in black and white; **je l'ai vu écrit en toutes lettres dans les journaux** I saw it in black and white in the newspapers; *Typ* **le corps de la l.** the body of the letter; *Fig Litt* **c'est gravé en lettres d'or** it will remain in my/our/*etc* memory for all time; **c'est gravé en lettres de feu** it's written in letters of fire; **écrit/gravé en lettres de sang** written in blood

(b) *(missive)* letter; **petite l.** note, short letter; **mettre une l. à la poste** *ou* **la boîte** to mail *or Br* to post a letter; *Vieilli* **c'est pour moi lettres closes** it's a mystery to me; *F* **c'est passé comme une l. à la poste** it went off without a hitch, it went off smoothly; **ce couscous est passé comme une l. à la poste** this couscous went down with no trouble; **la nouvelle est passée comme une l. à la poste** the news was received without any fuss

(c) selon la l. de la loi according to the letter of the law; **au pied de la l.** literally; **traduire à la l.** to translate word for word; **il prend les choses à la l.** he takes everything literally; **j'ai suivi vos instructions à la l.** I've followed your instructions to the letter; **il fut surréaliste avant la l.** he was a surrealist before the word had been invented

(d) lettres *(littérature)* literature, *Litt* letters; *Univ* arts subjects, humanities; *Litt* **les belles lettres** literature; **homme/femme de lettres** man/woman of letters; **avoir des lettres** to be well read; *Univ* **faculté de lettres** faculty of arts *or* humanities

▶ **lettre**: **l. d'accompagnement** covering letter; **l. d'affaires** business letter; **l. d'amour** love letter; **l. anonyme** anonymous letter; **l. par avion** airmail letter; **l. d'avis** advice note; *Hist* **l. de cachet** = order under the King's private seal; *Fin* **l. de change** bill of exchange, B/E; **l. de change relevé** bills of exchange statement; **l. circulaire** circular; **lettres classiques** ≈ classics; **l. commerciale** business letter; **l. de confirmation** letter of confirmation; *Pol* **lettres de créance** credentials; *Banque, Com* **l. de crédit** letter of credit; **émettre une l. de crédit** to open a letter of credit; **l. de crédit documentaire** documentary letter of credit; **l. de crédit irrévocable** irrevocable letter of credit; **l. de démission** letter of resignation; **l. d'excuse** letter of apology; **l. exprès** express letter; **l. de félicitations** letter of congratulations, congratulatory letter; *Fin* **l. de garantie** letter of guarantee; **l. de garantie bancaire** bank guarantee; **l. de grâce** reprieve; **l. d'injures** abusive letter; *Jur* **l. d'intention** letter of intent; **l. de licenciement** letter of dismissal; **l. de menace** threatening letter; *Jur* **l. missive** letter missive; **lettres modernes** *(section scolaire ou universitaire)* French; *Belg* **l. de mort** death announcement; **ce règlement est resté l. morte** this regulation was not enforced *or* stayed a dead letter; **ce projet est resté l. morte** this project was never put into operation; **toutes ses bonnes résolutions sont restées l. morte** he never put any of his good resolutions into practice; **l. de motivation** letter explaining why one is interested in the post *or* in support of one's application; **lettres de noblesse** letters patent of nobility; *Fig* **donner ses lettres de noblesse à qch** to establish *or* prove the worth of sth; *Fig* **conquérir** *ou* **gagner ses lettres de noblesse** to establish *or* prove its worth; *Journ* **l. ouverte** open letter **(à** to); *Hist* **lettres patentes** letters patent; **l. de poursuite** letter threatening legal action, chasing letter; **l. de rappel** reminder; **l. de réclamation** letter of complaint; **l. de recommandation** letter of recommendation, reference; **l. recommandée** registered letter; **l. recommandée avec accusé de réception** registered letter with confirmation of receipt; **l. de relance** follow-up letter; **l. de relance des impayés** debt chasing letter; **lettres supérieures** = preparatory classes for the *Normale Supérieure littéraire*; **l.-transfert,** *pl* **lettres-transferts** transfer *or Am* decal letter; *Com* **l. de transport aérien** air waybill; **l. type** *(pour mailing)* form letter; **l. de vente** sales letter; *Com* **l. de voiture** waybill, consignment note; *Com* **l. de voiture CIM** CIM waybill; *Com* **l. de voiture CMR** CMR waybill; *Com* **l. de voiture fluviale** inland waterway waybill
lettré, -ée [letre] **1** *adj (personne)* well-read, cultured **2** *n* well-read person
lettrine [letrin] *nf Typ (au début des chapitres etc)* dropped initial; *(dans un dictionnaire)* running head(line)
leu[1], *pl* **lei** [lø, lɛ] *nm (monnaie)* leu *(pl* lei)
leu[2] *nm* **à la queue l. l.** in single file, in Indian file
leucémie [løsemi] *nf Méd* leukaemia, *US* leukemia
leucémique [løsemik] *Méd* **1** *adj* leukaemic, *US* leukemic **2** *n* leukaemia *or US* leukemia sufferer
leucocytaire [løkositɛr] *adj Physiol* leucocytic
leucocyte [løkosit] *nm Physiol* leucocyte, leukocyte
leucocytose [løkositoz] *nf Méd* leucocytosis
leucome [løkom] *nm Méd* leucoma, albugo
leucorrhée [løkɔre] *nf Méd* leucorrh(o)ea
leucose [løkoz] *nf Méd* leukaemia, *US* leukemia
leur[1] [lœr] **1** [①A30,8; B19-20,E,1] *adj poss* their; **l. oncle et l. tante** their uncle and (their) aunt; **l. père et l. mère,** *Litt* **leurs père et mère** their mother and father; **ils ont mis l. chapeau et leurs gants** they put on their hat and (their) gloves; **elles ont pris l. sac** *(il n'y a qu'un sac)* they took their bag; *(chacune a son sac)* they took their bags; **elles ont pris leurs sacs** they took their bags; **un(e) de leurs ami(e)s** a friend of theirs, one of their friends; **un professeur de leurs amis** a teacher friend of theirs; *F* **ils auront l. chambre à eux** *(il n'y a qu'une chambre)* they'll have their own room; *(chacun aura sa chambre)* they'll have their own rooms; *F* **l. imbécile de frère** their idiot of a brother; *F* **leurs artistes de mari** their artist husbands; *F* **ils ont eu l. vendredi** they got Friday off

2 [①A30,8; B20,E,2] *pron poss* **le l., la l., les leurs** theirs; **ils me prêtent le l.** I can borrow theirs; **tu n'as qu'à prendre le l.** just take theirs; **il ressemble au l.** it looks like theirs; **ils veulent bien te donner du l.** you can have some of theirs; **ils n'en ont pas besoin, ils ont le l.** they don't need it, they've got their own; **je n'en ai pas besoin, j'ai le l.** I don't need it, I've got theirs; **les deux leurs** their two, the two *or* both of theirs; *(en insistant)* their own two; **ils nous ont laissé deux des leurs** they gave us two of theirs; *(ils en ont sacrifié deux)* they gave us two of their own; *très F* **le l. bébé est plus intelligent** their baby is more intelligent; *F* **à la l.!** *(en buvant)* let's drink to them!

3 *nm* **le l.** *(ce qui leur appartient)* theirs; **ils devraient y mettre du l.** they should really do their share

4 *nmpl* **les leurs** *(leur famille)* their family, *F* their folks; *(leurs partisans)* their followers; *(leurs coéquipiers)* their team-mates; **ils font leurs vos principes** they have adopted these principles of yours; **ils font leurs les félicitations que je vous adresse** they join me in congratulating you
leur[2] *pron voir* **lui**[1]
leurre [lœr] *nm* **(a)** *(pour faucons)* lure; *(pour gibier)* decoy; *(pour poissons)* (artificial) bait, lure **(b)** *(illusion)* illusion, delusion **(c)** *Mil* chaff
leurrer [lœre] **1** *vt* **(a)** *(en fauconnerie) (faucon)* to lure **(b)** *(tromper)* to deceive, to delude; **l. qn par des promesses** to deceive sb with promises; **il se laisse facilement l.** he is easily taken in **2 se leurrer** *vpr* to delude oneself **(sur** about)
lev, *pl* **leva** [lɛv, leva] *nm (monnaie)* lev *(pl* leva)

levage [ləvaʒ] *nm* **(a)** *Tech* lifting (up), hoisting, raising; **câble de l.** hoisting cable; **appareil de l.** lifting apparatus; **cric de l.** lifting jack **(b)** *Culin* (*de pâte etc*) rising

levain [ləvɛ̃] *nm* leaven; **pain au/sans l.** leavened/unleavened bread; *Fig Litt* **ils furent le l. de la révolte/du changement** they sowed the seeds of revolt/change

levant [ləvɑ̃] **1** *adj* **soleil l.** rising sun; **il est parti au soleil l.** he left at sunrise *or Am* at sun-up **2** *nm* **(a)** *Litt* **le l.** the east, the orient; **du l. au couchant** from East to West **(b)** *Vieilli* **le L.** the Levant

levantin, -ine [ləvɑ̃tɛ̃, -in] *Vieilli* **1** *adj* Levantine **2** *n* **L.** Levantine

levé [ləve] **1** *adj* **(a)** (*en l'air*) (*main, poing*) raised; **voter à mains levées** to vote by a show of hands; **dessin à main levée** freehand drawing; **pierre levée** standing stone **(b)** *Culin* **pâte bien levée** well-risen dough **(c)** (*debout*) up, out of bed; (*du soleil etc*) up; **je suis l. de bonne heure tous les jours** I'm up early every day **2** *nm* **(a)** (*de terrain*) plan, survey; **l. aérophotogrammétrique** aerial survey; **faire le l. d'un terrain** to survey a piece of land **(b)** *Mus* up beat

levée [ləve] *nf* **(a)** (*action de faire cesser*) (*d'embargo, de peine, d'interdiction, de sanctions etc*) lifting; (*de séance*) adjournment; (*d'immunité parlementaire*) stripping; *Mil* (*de siège*) raising; (*de scellés*) removal, breaking; *Jur* **demander la l. de la séance** to ask for an adjournment

(b) (*enrôlement*) (*de troupes*) levy(ing)

(c) (*collecte*) (*de lettres*) collection; **heures de l.** collection times; **la l. est faite** the post has been collected *or* has gone; **il y a trois levées par jour** there are three collections a day; *Vieilli* **la l. d'un impôt** the levying of a tax; **l. des impôts** tax collection, collection of taxes; *Fin* **l. des titres** taking delivery of shares; *Fin* **l. des actions** taking up of stock

(d) *Cartes* trick; **faire une l.** to take a trick

▶ **levée**: **l. de boucliers** general outcry; **l. du corps** = removal of the coffin; **pendant la l. du corps la veuve s'est évanouie** the widow fainted as the coffin was being removed *or* carried out; *Jur* **l. d'écrou** release from prison; *Jur* **l. de jugement** transcript of the verdict; **l. en masse** levy en masse; *Jur* **l. d'option** exercising of an option; **l. de terre** levee

lève-glace(s) [lɛvglas] *nm inv Aut* window winder

lever[1] [ləve] (**je lève, n. levons; je lèverai**) **1** *vt* **(a)** (*objet*) to lift, to raise; (*filet de pêche*) to raise; (*store*) to open; (*vitre*) to wind up; **l. son verre (à qn/qch)** to raise one's glass (to sb/sth); **je lève mon verre à votre réussite/aux futurs époux** here's to your success/the happy couple; **l. un étendard** to raise a standard; *Fig Litt* **l. l'étendard de la révolte** to raise the standard of revolt; *Naut* **l. l'ancre** to weigh *or* lift anchor; *Fig F* to take off, to hit the road, to go

(b) (*parties du corps*) to raise, to lift; **l. la tête** to look up, to raise one's head; *Fig Litt* (*se montrer digne*) to hold one's head high; **l. les yeux (sur qn)** to look up (at sb); **lève les yeux quand je te parle!** look at me when I'm talking to you!; **l. les yeux au ciel** to raise one's eyes to heaven *or* the heavens; **l. les sourcils** to raise one's eyebrows; **l. les bras au ciel** to throw up one's hands; *Fig F* **l. le coude** to (be able to) knock it back; **l. la main droite** to raise one's right hand; *Fig* **l. la main sur qn** to raise *or* lift one's hand to sb; **l. le doigt** (*à l'école*) to put one's hand up; **il n'a pas levé le petit doigt** he didn't lift a finger, he didn't do a thing; **lève les pieds quand tu marches** lift your feet up when you walk; *F* **on conseille aux automobilistes de l. le pied ce soir** motorists are advised to drive slowly this evening; *F* **lève le pied** (*ralentis*) slow down; **ça me lève le cœur** it makes my stomach turn; *très F* **lève ton cul!** move your arse!; *F* **l. la patte** (*d'un chien*) to cock *or* lift its leg

(c) (*faire cesser*) (*embargo, peine, interdiction*) to lift; (*difficulté, doute, ambiguïté, inhibitions*) to remove; (*audience*) to adjourn; *Mil* (*siège*) to raise; **l. la séance** to close a/the meeting; *Jur* to adjourn; **l. le camp** to strike *or* break camp; *Fig F* to take off, to hit the road, to go; *Fig* **cet article lève le voile sur l'affaire des diamants** this article reveals the truth about the affair of the diamonds

(d) (*enlever*), *Jur* **l. les scellés** to break the seals

(e) (*débusquer*) (*perdrix*) to flush; *Arg* (*femme*) to pull; (*de prostituée*) (*client*) to pick up; **l. un lièvre** to start a hare; *Fig* to open a can of worms

(f) (*faire sortir du lit*) (*enfant, malade*) to get up

(g) (*collecter*) (*lettres, courrier*) to collect; *Fin* (*actions, titres, options*) to take up; **l. des impôts** to collect *ou Vieilli* levy taxes

(h) (*enrôler*) (*troupes, armée*) to raise, to levy

(i) *Cartes* **l. les cartes** to pick up a trick

(j) (*plan*) to make, to draw

(k) *Culin* **l. les filets** to remove the fillets

2 *vi* **(a)** *Litt* (*du blé, du grain*) to shoot

(b) (*de la pâte*) to rise

(c) *Cartes* to pick up a trick

3 se lever *vpr* **(a)** (*se mettre debout*) to stand up, to get up, to rise; **levez-vous** stand up, get up; **se l. de sa chaise** to get up (from one's chair), to rise (from one's chair), to stand up; *Jur* **accusé, levez-vous** the accused will rise; **va aider grand-mère à se l.** go and help grandma (to get) up; **se l. de table** to leave the table; **le peuple se leva en masse ou en foule contre l'oppresseur** the nation rose up as one against the oppressor

(b) (*quitter le lit*) to get up, to get out of bed; **je me lève de bonne heure** I'm an early riser, I get up early; *F* **se l. du pied gauche** to get out of bed on the wrong side

(c) (*apparaître*) (*du soleil, d'un astre, de la lune*) to rise; (*de la brise, du vent*) to rise, to get up; **le jour se lève** day is breaking *or* dawning; *Fig Litt* **le désespoir/la tristesse se lève dans mon cœur** despair/sadness is welling up inside me

(d) (*s'éclaircir*) (*du temps*) to clear up; (*de la brume*) to lift, to clear up

(e) (*se mouvoir vers le haut*) (*des mains*) to go up; *Th* (*du rideau*) to go up, to rise; (*vitre*) to wind up

lever[2] *nm* **(a)** (*du lit*) getting up, *Fml* rising; *Hist* (*du roi*) levee; **programme de la journée: l. 6h30, petit-déjeuner 7h30** today's schedule: rise *or* get up 6.30, breakfast at 7.30; **au l., il est bon de boire un jus d'orange** first thing in the morning, it's good to have a drink of orange juice **(b)** (*apparition*) **l. du soleil** sunrise; **l. du jour** daybreak **(c)** (*montée*), *Th* (*du rideau*) rising, rise; **le l. du rideau est à 19h** the curtain rises at 7 pm; *Fig* **un l. de rideau** a curtain raiser **(d)** (*croquis*) = **levé 2(a)**

lève-tard [lɛvtar] *nm inv F* late riser

lève-tôt [lɛvto] *nm inv F* early riser

lève-vitre [lɛvvitr], *pl* **lève-vitres** *nm Aut* window winder

levier [ləvje] *nm* **(a)** (*outil*) crowbar, lever; **soulever/ouvrir qch avec un l.** to prize *or* prise *or* lever sth up/open

(b) *Phys* lever; **bras de l.** lever arm; **force de l.** leverage; **faire l.** to act as a lever; **ce poids fait l. et permet de bouger la caisse** this weight acts as a lever and allows the crate to be moved

(c) (*commande*) lever, handle; *MecE* **l. d'arrêt** shut-off lever; **l. de frein** brake lever; **l. de commande** control lever; *Fig* **être aux leviers de commande** to be in control *or* in command; **l. de dégagement du chariot** (*de machine à écrire*) carriage release arm; **l. de dégagement du papier** (*de machine à écrire*) paper release arm; *Aut* **l. (de changement) de vitesse** gear lever, gear stick, *Am* gearshift; *Aut* **l. de direction** steering lever; *Aut* **l. de débrayage** clutch release lever; *Aut* **l. de vitesses au plancher** floor shift; *Aut* **l. de vitesses sur colonne de direction** column change; *Aut* **l. sélecteur** selector lever; *Aut* **l. à fourche** forked lever

(d) *Fig* (*motif d'action*) spur, lever

(e) *Econ* **l. financier** financial leverage

lévitation [levitasjɔ̃] *nf* levitation; **être en l.** to be levitating

lévite [levit] *nm Rel* Levite

levraut [ləvro] *nm* leveret

lèvre [lɛvr] *nf* **(a)** *Anat* lip; **avoir les lèvres charnues** *ou* **pleines/minces** to have thick *or* full/thin lips; **la l. inférieure** the lower lip; **se mettre du rouge à lèvres** to put on lipstick; **il avait un cigare aux lèvres** he had a cigar in his mouth; **le sourire aux lèvres** with a smile on his lips; **j'ai son nom sur les lèvres** *ou* **le bord des lèvres** his name is on the tip of my tongue; **son nom est sur toutes les lèvres** his name is on everybody's lips; **manger du bout des lèvres** to nibble *or* pick at one's food; **il accepta, mais du bout des lèvres** he grudgingly accepted; **rire du bout des lèvres** to force a laugh; *Fig* **nous étions tous suspendus à ses lèvres** we were all hanging on his every word; **pincer les lèvres** (*pour ne pas rire, pour exprimer son dédain*) to purse one's lips

(b) *Anat* (*de la vulve*) **lèvres** lips, labia; **les grandes/petites lèvres** the labia majora/minora

(c) (*bord*) (*de plaie*) lip; (*de cratère*) rim

(d) *Bot* lip, *Spéc* labium

levrette [ləvrɛt] *nf* **(a)** greyhound bitch; **l. (d'Italie)** (small) Italian greyhound **(b)** **en l.** doggy fashion

lévrier [levrije] *nm* greyhound; **l. irlandais** *ou* **d'Irlande** Irish wolfhound; **l. d'Italie** Italian greyhound; **l. afghan** Afghan hound; **l. à poil long** borzoi; **courses de lévriers** greyhound racing

levure [ləvyr] *nf* yeast; **l. de boulanger** fresh *or* baker's yeast; **l. de bière** brewer's yeast; **l. chimique** = baking powder; **l. en sachet** yeast in a packet *or* sachet

lexème [lɛksɛm] *nm Ling* lexeme

lexical, -ale, -aux, -ales [lɛksikal, -o] *adj* lexical
lexicalisation [lɛksikalizasjɔ̃] *nf* lexicalization
lexicalisé [lɛksikalize] *adj* lexicalized
lexicographe [lɛksikɔgraf] *n* lexicographer
lexicographie [lɛksikɔgrafi] *nf* lexicography
lexicographique [lɛksikɔgrafik] *adj* lexicographical
lexicologie [lɛksikɔlɔʒi] *nf* lexicology
lexicologique [lɛksikɔlɔʒik] *adj* lexicological
lexicologue [lɛksikɔlɔg] *n* lexicologist
lexie [lɛksi] *nf* lexical unit
lexique [lɛksik] *nm* **(a)** *(dictionnaire)* lexicon, small dictionary; *(glossaire)* glossary; **l. financier** financial glossary **(b)** *(à la fin d'un livre)* list of terms **(c)** *(mots d'un auteur)* vocabulary, *Spéc* lexis
lézard [lezar] *nm* **(a)** *(reptile)* lizard; **l. gris/des murailles** grey/wall lizard; **l. vert** green lizard; *F* **faire le l.** to bask *or* lounge in the sun **(b)** *(cuir)* lizard skin **(c)** *F* **il y a un l.** there's a catch, there's something fishy about it; **il n'y a pas de l.** there's no catch, it's kosher
lézarde [lezard] *nf* crack
lézardé [lezarde] *adj (mur, plâtre)* cracked, full of cracks
lézarder [lezarde] **1** *vt (plâtre, ciment)* to crack **2 se lézarder** *vpr (de mur)* to crack **3** *vi F* to bask *or* lounge in the sun
LFAJ [ɛlɛfaʒi] *nf (abrév* **Ligue Française des Auberges de Jeunesse**) French youth hostel association
liais [ljɛ] *nm Minér* hard limestone
liaison [ljɛzɔ̃] *nf* **(a)** *(enchaînement logique)* connection; **il y a un manque de l. dans l'expression de vos idées** you express your ideas in a disjointed fashion; **des idées sans l.** unconnected ideas; **en l. avec ce qui a été dit** in connection with *or* leading on from what has been said
(b) *Télécom* communications link; **l. radio/téléphonique** radio/telephone link; **l. par satellite** satellite link *or* link-up; **la l. est mauvaise** it's a bad connection; **la l. est coupée entre la plateforme et le continent** all shore contact with the rig has been lost; **établir une l. radio** to establish radio contact; *Ordinat* **l. alternat** half duplex; *Ordinat* **l. par modem** modem link; *Ordinat* **l. spécialisée** dedicated line
(c) *(entre des personnes)* close contact *or* relationship; **assurer la l. entre deux personnes/services** to liaise between two people/departments; **les différents services sont en (étroite) l.** the various departments are in close contact *or* liaise closely (with each other); **les différents services sont en l. permanente** the various departments are constantly in touch with each other; **être en l. avec qn** to be in touch with sb; **rester en l.** to stay in touch; **se mettre en l. avec qn** to get in touch with sb; **travailler en l. (étroite) avec qn** to work (closely) with sb; *esp Mil* to liaise with sb; **l. (amoureuse)** (love) affair, *Fml* liaison; **agent de l.** go-between; *Mil* liaison officer
(d) *(dans les transports)* **l. aérienne/maritime/ferroviaire/routière** air/sea/rail/road link; **toutes les liaisons Paris-Téhéran sont suspendues** all services between Paris and Teheran have been suspended; **une navette assure la l. entre l'aéroport et le centre-ville** there is a shuttle service between the airport and the town centre; **un avion hebdomadaire assure la l. entre Paris et Moscou** there is one flight a week between Paris and Moscow; **les liaisons sont bonnes entre ces deux villes, que ce soit par le train ou par la route** there are good rail and road services between the two towns
(e) *Ling* liaison (= *sounding of final consonant before initial vowel sound*); **faire la l.** to make *or* sound the liaison; *Gram* **mot** *ou* **terme de l.** linkword
(f) *Constr (de briques etc)* bonding; *(produit)* mortar, cement; **maçonnerie en l.** bonded masonry; *MecE* **l. élastique** rubber joint; *Aut* **l. transversale** cross-tie
(g) *Mus (pour lier deux notes)* slur; *(pour lier une suite de notes)* tie, ligature
(h) *Ch* bond
(i) *Culin (pour sauce)* thickening
liaisonner [ljɛzɔne] *vt Constr (briques)* to bond; *(en maçonnerie)* to grout, to point
liane [ljan] *nf Bot* creeper, *Spéc* liana
liant [ljɑ̃] **1** *adj* sociable, friendly; **il est très l.** he's quick to make friends **2** *nm* **(a)** *Tech* binder, binding agent **(b)** *Litt (sociabilité)* **avoir du l.** to be sociable **(c)** *(souplesse)* flexibility, pliability
liard [ljar] *nm Arch* half farthing; **il n'a pas un l.** he hasn't (got) a farthing, he hasn't (got) a penny to his name
lias [ljas] *nm Géol* lias
liasse [ljas] *nf (de lettres)* bundle, packet; *(de billets)* wad; *(de papiers)* bundle; **l. carbonée** print-through paper
libage [libaʒ] *nm Constr* bastard ashlar
Liban [libɑ̃] *nm* **le L.** (the) Lebanon
libanais, -aise [libanɛ, -ɛz] **1** *adj* Lebanese **2** *n* **L.** Lebanese; **les L.** the Lebanese
libation [libasjɔ̃] *nf* **(a)** *Antiq, Rel* libation **(b)** *Fig* **faire des libations** to partake of libations
libelle [libɛl] *nm Litt* lampoon, scurrilous satire
libellé [libele] *nm (de document)* wording, terms used; **le l. du chèque/de la pièce comptable est incorrect** the cheque/voucher is not made out correctly
libeller [libele] *vt Admin (document, acte, contrat)* to word, to draw up; *Fin* to denominate; **l. un chèque** to make out *or* write out a cheque; **chèque libellé à l'ordre de Y. Mourier** cheque made out *or* payable to Y. Mourier; **télégramme libellé comme suit ...** telegram worded as follows ... *or* that reads as follows ...; **l. une facture** to make out an invoice; **libellé au porteur** *(chèque)* made out to bearer; **libellé en** *(chèque)* made out in; *(cours)* quoted *or* given in; *Fin* **libellé en dollars** denominated in dollars
libellule [libɛlyl] *nf (insecte)* dragonfly
libérable [liberabl] *Mil* **1** *adj (soldat)* dischargeable, who can be demobbed; **congé** *ou* **permission l.** demob leave **2** *nm* soldier about to finish his military service
libéral, -ale, -aux, -ales [liberal, -o] **1** *adj* **(a)** *(tolérant) (personne, éducation)* lenient, liberal; *(idées)* liberal **(b)** *(indépendant)* **il exerce une profession libérale** he's a professional man; **défendre la médecine libérale** to defend private medicine **(c)** *(généreux)* generous **(d)** *Pol* liberal; **le parti l.** the Liberal Party **2** *n Pol* liberal
libéralement [liberalmɑ̃] *adv* **(a)** *(généreusement)* liberally **(b)** *(avec tolérance)* leniently, liberally
libéralisation [liberalizasjɔ̃] *nf Écon (de l'économie, des échanges commerciaux)* liberalization; **la l. de la presse** the liberalization of the press, the easing of restrictions on the press; **l. du commerce** liberalization of trade; **l. du cours du franc** freeing of the franc
libéraliser [liberalize] *vt (économie)* to liberalize
libéralisme [liberalism] *nm Pol, Écon* liberalism
libéralité [liberalite] *nf* **(a)** *(libéralisme)* liberality **(b)** *(générosité)* generosity **(c)** *(cadeau)* generous gift; *Litt* **faire des libéralités à qn** to give liberally *or* freely to sb; **vivre des libéralités de ses amis** to live off the generosity of one's friends
libérateur, -trice [liberatœr, -tris] **1** *adj (soldats, force)* liberating; **guerre libératrice** war of liberation; **le pouvoir l. du rire** the liberating power of laughter **2** *n* liberator
libération [liberasjɔ̃] *nf* **(a)** *(mise en liberté)* liberation, freeing, release; *(de prisonnier)* discharge, release; *(de soldat)* discharge; **l. conditionnelle** release of prisoner on parole
(b) *(d'un joug)* liberation; **le mouvement de l. de la femme** the women's liberation movement, *F* women's lib; *Hist Fr* **la L.** the Liberation *(from the Germans in 1944-45)*
(c) *(dérèglementation) (des prix, des échanges commerciaux)* freeing; *(de dette)* payment in full, discharge; *Fin* **l. d'une action** paying up of a share; **l. des échanges commerciaux** deregulation of trade
(d) *Phys (émission)* liberation, release; **la l. de chaleur/d'hormones** the liberation *or* release of heat/hormones; *Astronaut* **vitesse de l.** escape *or* parabolic velocity
libératoire [liberatwar] *adj Jur* **paiement l.** payment in full discharge from debt
libéré [libere] **1** *adj* **(a)** *(physiquement)* liberated, free; **jeune homme l. des obligations militaires** young man who has carried out his national service duties **(b)** *(moralement)* liberated **(c)** *Fin (action)* (fully) paid-up **2** *nm* released prisoner
libérer [libere] **(je libère, n. libérons, je libérerai) 1** *vt* **(a)** *(rendre sa liberté à) (otage, prisonnier)* to free, to set free, to release; *(pays, peuple)* to liberate; *(soldat)* to discharge; **l. qn de ses chaînes** to free sb from his chains; **le prof a libéré les élèves plus tôt** the teacher let the children go *or* let the children out early; **l. qn de sa promesse** to release sb from his promise
(b) *(soulager)* **l. sa conscience** to salve one's conscience; **cela me libérera d'un souci** *ou* **poids** that will take a load off my mind; **l. les jeunes des tabous sexuels** to free *or* liberate young people from sexual taboos
(c) *(rendre disponible) (appartement, chambre d'hôtel)* to vacate
(d) *(débloquer)*, *Fin (prix, échanges commerciaux)* to free; *(cran de sûreté, mécanisme)* to release; *(instincts, passions)* to unleash; **l. le passage** to clear the way
(e) *(décharger) (d'une dette)* to free; *(d'un engagement)* to release; **l. entièrement une action** to make a share fully paid-up, to pay up a share in full; **l. un débiteur** to discharge a debtor, to release a debtor

(f) (*émettre*) (*gaz, hormone, énergie, chaleur*) to release
2 se libérer *vpr* (a) (*de liens, chaînes, oppresseur, passion*) to free oneself
(b) (*se rendre disponible*) (*d'une personne*) to get away; **je n'ai pas pu me l. plus tôt** I couldn't get away any earlier; **se l. pour deux jours** to (arrange to) take two days off; **il y a une place de parking qui vient juste de se l.** someone's just left a parking space; **il y a un poste qui vient de se l.** a job vacancy has just come up
(c) (*se dégager*) **se l.** (**d'une dette**) to redeem *or* liquidate a debt

Libéria [liberja] *nm* Liberia

libérien, -ienne [liberjɛ̃, -jɛn] **1** *adj* Liberian **2** *n* **L.** Liberian

libertaire [libɛrtɛr] *adj, n* libertarian

liberté [libɛrte] *nf* (a) (*de personne, d'animal*) liberty, freedom; **l'assassin est toujours en l.** the murderer is still at large; **animaux en l.** animals in the wild, animals running free; **vivre en l.** (*d'un animal*) to live in the wild; **rendre sa l. à qn** (*fiancé etc*) to let sb go; **rendre sa l. à un animal** to let an animal go, to set an animal free; **reprendre sa l.** (*de conjoint*) to regain one's freedom; **être mis en l.** to be set free, to be released, to be allowed to go free; (*d'un inculpé*) to be discharged; **(re)mettre qn en l.** to set sb free, to free *or* release sb; *Jur* **mise en l.** (*d'un prisonnier*) release; *Jur* **(mise en) l. provisoire** *ou* **sous caution** (release on) bail; **mettre qn en l. provisoire** to release sb on bail; *Jur* **l. conditionnelle** parole; **mettre qn en l. conditionnelle** to release sb on parole; *Jur* **l. surveillée** probation; **mettre qn en l. surveillée** to release sb on probation
(b) *Pol* (*droit de l'individu*) freedom, liberty; **la l. civile** civil liberty; **atteinte aux libertés individuelles** infringement of one's individual freedom; **l., égalité, fraternité** liberty, equality, fraternity
(c) (*absence de contrainte*) freedom; **l. d'entreprise** free enterprise; **avoir toute** *ou* **pleine l. d'action** to have complete freedom of action, to have a free hand; **vous avez toute l. pour organiser la rencontre** you have a free hand *or* complete freedom to organize the meeting as you wish; **vous avez pleine (et entière) l. d'agir comme bon vous semble** you are quite free *or* you are completely at liberty to act as you see fit; **parler en toute l.** to speak freely *or* without restraint; **j'ai pris la l. de dire ...** I took the liberty of saying ...; **si je puis prendre une telle l.** if I may be so bold
(d) (*temps libre*) **jour de l.** free day, day off; **un moment de l.** a spare *or* free moment; **avec tout ce travail je n'ai pas beaucoup de l.** with all this work I haven't (got) much spare *or* free time
(e) *Fin, Écon* (*dérèglementation*) (*de prix, échanges*) freeing; *Av* **libertés commerciales** commercial freedoms
(f) (*familiarités*) **prendre** *ou* **se permettre des libertés avec qn/un texte** to take liberties with sb/a text; **se permettre des libertés de langage** to be rather free in one's use of language
▶ **liberté**: **l. de conscience** freedom of conscience; **l. du culte** freedom of worship; **l. d'enseignement** freedom of educational choice; **l. d'expression** freedom of expression *or* of speech; **l. de mouvement** freedom of movement; **l. d'opinion** freedom of opinion; **l. de pensée** freedom of thought; **l. de la presse** freedom of the press; **l. de réunion** freedom of assembly; **l. syndicale** freedom of association

libertin, -ine [libɛrtɛ̃, -in] **1** *adj* (a) (*aux mœurs libres*) (*personne*) libertine, dissolute; (*livre, propos*) licentious (b) *Hist* free-thinking **2** *n* (a) (*de par ses mœurs*) libertine (b) *Hist* free-thinker

libertinage [libɛrtinaʒ] *nm* (a) (*débauche*) licentiousness (b) *Hist* free-thinking

liberty [libɛrti] *nm* liberty fabric; **une housse de coussin en l.** a liberty cushion cover

libidineux, -euse [libidinø, -øz] *adj* libidinous, lustful; **des regards libidineux** lustful *or* lascivious glances

libido [libido] *nf* libido; **avoir une forte l.** to be highly sexed

libraire [librɛr] *n Com* bookseller

libraire-éditeur, *pl* **libraires-éditeurs** *nm Com* publisher and bookseller

librairie [librɛri] *nf* (a) (*magasin*) bookshop, *Am* bookstore; **l. d'art** art bookshop; **l.-papeterie** bookshop and stationer's (b) *Com* (*activité*) bookselling; **ouvrages en l.** published books

libre [libr] *adj* (a) (*non soumis*) (*personne, pays*) free; **le monde l.** the free world; *Hist Fr* **zone l.** unoccupied France; *Hist Fr* **la France l.** Free France; **l'homme est l.** man is a free agent; **laisser qn l. d'agir** to leave sb a free hand, to leave sb free to act; **laisser qn l. de choisir** to leave sb free to choose; **il nous laisse l. de partir** he lets us go when we want; **vous êtes l. de le faire, l. à vous de le faire** you are quite free *or* at liberty to do it; **l. à vous d'essayer** you're free *or* welcome to try; **donner l. cours à son enthousiasme/sa curiosité/son imagination** to give one's enthusiasm/curiosity/imagination free rein; **être l. de tout souci** to be free from care, to be carefree; **l. de préjugés** free from prejudice
(b) (*disponible*) (*personne*) free, not tied down; (*sentimentalement*) unattached; (*temps*) free, spare; (*appartement, maison, chambre*) available; (*toilettes*) (*sur la porte*) vacant; (*table, place de parking, fauteuil*) free, unoccupied; **vous êtes l.?** (*à un taxi*) are you free?; **vous êtes l. ce soir?** are you free this evening?; **avoir du temps (de) l.** to have some free *or* spare time, to have some time free *or* to spare; **je suis l. de onze heures à midi** I'm free between eleven and twelve; *F* **le lundi est mon jour de l.** Monday is my day off, I have Mondays free; **je n'ai pas eu une minute de l. aujourd'hui** I haven't had a spare minute today; **être l. comme l'air** to be as free as the air *or* a bird; **j'ai les mains libres** I'm not carrying anything; *Fig* I'm a free agent; *Fig* **laisser les mains libres à qn** to give sb a free rein *or* hand; **studio à louer, l. de suite** (*annonce*) one-room flat to rent, available immediately; **j'ai trouvé une place l. pour me garer** I found a place to park; *Tél* **la ligne n'est pas l.** the line is engaged *or esp Am* busy
(c) (*non attaché*) (*mouvement etc*) unrestrained; **robe qui laisse la taille l.** dress which fits loosely round the waist; **elle a les cheveux libres** she wears her hair down *or* loose
(d) **être l. avec qn** to be free with sb, to treat sb in a familiar way; **allures** *ou* **manières libres** free and easy manner
(e) (*non bloqué*) (*route*) clear, open; **laisser le champ l.** to leave the field clear; **je vous laisse le champ l.** I'll leave you to it, you're free to do as you think best; *Fig* **la voie est l.** the coast is clear; *Rail* **voie l.** line clear
(f) (*non imposé*) (*adaptation, traduction, vers*) free; *Scol* **sujet l., texte l.** free choice of subject
(g) (*privé*) **enseignement l.** independent Catholic education system; **école l.** independent Catholic school; **radio l.** independent radio
(h) *Tech* disengaged; **roue l.** (*de bicyclette, voiture*) freewheel; **descendre une côte en roue l.** to freewheel *or* coast down a hill; *Fig* **être en roue l.** to be coasting
(i) *Com* **entrée l.** (*dans un magasin*) please come in and look around, no obligation to buy; (*entrée gratuite*) admission free
(j) *Sp* free, freestyle; **les figures libres** freestyle skating; **escalade l.** free climbing
(k) (*non réglementé*) (*prix*) free; **le l. jeu de la concurrence** the free play of competition; **défendre la l. entreprise** to defend free *or* private enterprise; **il pratique les honoraires libres** = he's in private practice; **bibliothèque en l. accès** public library; **l. circulation des personnes** freedom of movement; **l. circulation des marchandises** free movement of goods; **l. échange international** international free trade
▶ **libre**: **l. arbitre** free will; *Écon* **l.-échange** free trade; *Écon* **l.-échangisme** free trade; *Écon* **l.-échangiste,** *pl* **l-échangistes 1** *adj* (*politique, théorie*) free trade **2** *n* free trader; **l. parole** free speech; **l. pensée** free thinking, free thought; **l. penseur/penseuse** free thinker

librement [librəmɑ̃] *adv* freely

libre-service, *pl* **libres-services** *nm* (a) (*principe*) self-service; **magasin/restaurant en l.** self-service shop *or Am* store/restaurant; **station-service en l.** self-service petrol *or Am* gas station (b) (*magasin, restaurant*) self-service

librettiste [librɛtist] *n Mus* librettist

libretto, *pl* **libretti, librettos** [librɛto, librɛti] *nm Mus* libretto

Libye [libi] *nf* Libya

libyen, -yenne [libjɛ̃, -jɛn] **1** *adj* Libyan **2** *n* **L.** Libyan

lice [lis] *nf Hist* (*barrière, enclos*) lists *pl*; *Fig* **entrer en l.** to enter the lists *or* the fray; **les athlètes français entreront en l. à 10 heures pour les épreuves de saut en hauteur** the French high jumpers will enter the competition at 10 am; **trois concurrents sont en l.** there are three competitors, three people are in contention

licence [lisɑ̃s] *nf* (a) (*permis*) licence, *US* license; **accorder une l. à qn** to license sb; **accorder une l. sur un nom** to license a name; **l. d'utilisation** user licence; **l. de brevet** patent licence; **l. de fabrication** manufacturing licence; **l. de vente** sales licence; **l. exclusive** exclusive licence; **fabriqué sous l.** made under licence; **l. d'importation/d'exportation** import/export licence; **l. de logiciel** software licence
(b) *Sp* permit, certificate (*giving right of entry into competition*)
(c) *Univ* bachelor's degree; **l. ès** *ou* **de lettres/ès** *ou* **de sciences/en droit** bachelor's degree in arts/in science/in law, arts/science/law degree; **passer sa l.** to sit *or* take one's degree exams *or* one's finals; **faire une l.** to do a degree

(d) (*liberté*) licence, *US* license; **l. poétique** poetic licence; **l. syntaxique** syntactic licence; **donner** *ou* **laisser à qn la l. de faire qch** to give sb licence to do sth; **je vous laisse toute l. pour la décoration du stand** I leave the decoration of the stand entirely up to you, you can decorate the stand as you like; *Arch* **prendre des licences avec qn** to take liberties with sb

(e) *Vieilli* (*dérèglement*) licentiousness

licencié, -ée [lisɑ̃sje] **1** *adj* (a) *Univ* **il est l.** he's a graduate; **professeur l.** graduate teacher (b) (*renvoyé*) (made) redundant; **un ouvrier l.** (*pour raisons économiques*) a redundant worker; (*pour faute professionnelle*) a dismissed worker **2** *n* (a) *Univ* **l. ès lettres/ès** *ou* **en sciences/en droit** bachelor of arts/of science/of law, arts/science/law graduate (b) *Sp* member

licenciement [lisɑ̃simɑ̃] *nm* (*pour raisons économiques*) redundancy; (*pour faute professionnelle*) dismissal; *Mil* (*de troupes*) disbanding; **recevoir une lettre de l.** to receive a redundancy notice/notice of dismissal; **il y a eu beaucoup de licenciements** many (people) were made redundant, there were a lot of redundancies; **l. économique** redundancy; **l. collectif** mass redundancies; **l. abusif** unfair dismissal; **l. avec/sans préavis** dismissal with/without notice

licencier [lisɑ̃sje] *vt* (*pr sub, impf* **n. licenciions, v. licenciiez**) (*pour raisons économiques*) to make redundant; (*pour faute professionnelle*) to dismiss; *Mil* (*troupes*) to disband

licencieusement [lisɑ̃sjøzmɑ̃] *adv Litt* licentiously

licencieux, -euse [lisɑ̃sjø, -øz] *adj Litt* licentious

lichen [likɛn] *nm* lichen

lichette [liʃɛt] *nf F* (*de pain, fromage etc*) tiny bit, smidgen; (*de vin*) drop, smidgen

licite [lisit] *adj* licit, lawful, permissible

licitement [lisitmɑ̃] *adv* licitly, lawfully

licol [likɔl] *nm* halter

licorne [likɔrn] *nf* (a) *Myth, Hér* unicorn (b) *Zool* **l. de mer** sea unicorn, narwhal

licou [liku] *nm* halter

licteur [liktœr] *nm Antiq* lictor

lido [lido] *nm Géog* sand bar

lie [li] **1** *nf* (*dépôt*) dregs *pl*; **l. (de vin)** lees *or* sediment of wine; *Fig* **la l. de la société** the dregs of society **2** *adj inv* **l. (-)de (-)vin** purplish red, wine-coloured

lié [lje] *adj* (a) (*attaché*) bound; **avoir les mains liées** to have one's hands tied; *Fig* **j'ai les mains liées** my hands are tied (b) (*en relation étroite*) **être (très) l. avec qn** to be (great) friends *or* intimately acquainted with sb; **nous sommes très liés** we are great friends, we are very close; **avoir partie liée avec qn** to be in league with sb (c) *Mus* **notes liées** slurred notes; (*deux notes différentes*) tied notes

lied, *pl* **lieder** [lid, lidœr] *nm Mus* lied, song

liège [ljɛʒ] *nm* (*matière naturelle*) cork; **semelle de l.** cork sole; **cigarette à bout (de) l.** cork-tipped cigarette; **bouchon de l.** cork

liégeois, -oise [ljeʒwa, -waz] **1** *adj* (a) of/from Liège (b) *Culin* **café/chocolat l.** coffee/chocolate ice cream topped with crème Chantilly **2** *n* **L.** (*natif*) native of Liège; (*habitant*) inhabitant of Liège

lien [ljɛ̃] *nm* (a) (*attache*) tie, *esp Litt* bond; **il s'est libéré de ses liens** he freed himself (from his bonds)

(b) *Fig* **liens du sang** blood ties; **l. de parenté** *ou* **de famille** family relationship; **il y a un l. de parenté entre ces deux familles** the two families are related; **des liens de famille avec le PDG expliquent sa nomination à ce poste** the fact that he is related to the Chairman *or* is a relation of the Chairman's accounts for his appointment; **les liens du mariage** the bonds of marriage *or* matrimony; **je vous déclare unis par les liens du mariage** = I now pronounce you man and wife; **l. d'amitié** bond of friendship; *Ordinat* **l. hypertexte** hypertext link

(c) (*relation*) link, connection; **j'ai du mal à faire le l. avec ce qu'il a dit avant** I can't see the connection with what he said before; **il y a un l. entre ces événements** there's a connection *or* link between these events

lier [lje] (*pr sub, impf* **n. liions, v. liiez**) **1** *vt* (a) (*attacher*) to bind, to fasten, to tie, to tie up; (*d'un contrat*) to be binding on; **l. qch avec une corde** to bind sth *or* tie sth up with a rope; **l. les pieds et les mains à qn** to bind sb hand and foot; **l. un fagot** to tie up a bundle of sticks; **on l'a lié à un arbre** he was tied (up) to a tree; **vous êtes lié par ce contrat** you are bound by this agreement, this agreement binds you *or* is binding on you; **l'intérêt nous lie** we have common interests; **cela les a intimement liés** that has formed a close bond between them; **un même amour de l'art les lie** they are united by a mutual love of art; **l. les paragraphes** to connect *or* link the paragraphs; **tout est lié** everything is connected; **ce jardin est lié au souvenir de sa grand-mère** the garden is linked to the memory of his grandmother; **l. deux mots** to link two words (in pronunciation), to sound the liaison; *Mus* **l. deux notes** to slur (two notes); (*deux notes différentes*) to tie two notes

(b) *Culin* (*sauce*) to thicken

(c) **l. amitié/conversation avec qn** to strike up a friendship/conversation with sb

2 se lier *vpr* (a) (*socialement*) **se l. avec qn** to form *or* strike up a friendship with sb; **il se lie facilement** he makes friends easily; **je me suis lié d'amitié avec son père** I have made friends with his father

(b) (*se mélanger*) **le lait et le jaune d'œuf se lient facilement** milk and egg yolk blend easily

lierre [ljɛr] *nm* ivy; **l. terrestre** ground ivy

liesse [ljɛs] *nf Arch, Litt* jubilation, gaiety; *Litt* **en l.** jubilant, in celebratory mood

lieu[1], *pl* **lieux** [ljø] *nm* (a) (*endroit*) place; **mettre qch en l. sûr** to put sth in a safe place; *Litt* **en tous lieux** everywhere; *Litt* **en aucun l.** nowhere; **visiter les lieux saints** to visit the Holy Places; **elle y a ses lieux de promenade** she goes for walks there; **c'est un drôle de l. de promenade** it's a funny place for a walk; **les mendiants se mettent de préférence sur les lieux de passage** beggars prefer busy areas *or* areas where there are lots of people going past; **cette ville n'est qu'un l. de passage** people merely pass through the town

(b) (*dans l'espace ou le temps*) **en premier l.** in the first place, first of all, first(ly); **c'est le saumon que je mettrais en premier l.** I would put salmon first; **peut-être devrais-tu lui poser la question en premier l.** perhaps you should put the question to him first; **en troisième l.** third(ly); **en dernier l.** last of all, last(ly), finally; **en temps et l.** at the proper time and place; **en son l.** in due course

(c) **lieux** (*local*) premises; (*d'un accident, d'un crime*) scene; **avant de quitter ces lieux** before leaving the premises; **quitter** *ou* **vider les lieux** to vacate the premises; **la police est sur les lieux de l'accident** the police are at the scene of the accident; **quand je suis arrivé sur les lieux (du crime)** when I arrived on the scene/at the scene of the crime; **j'étais sur les lieux bien avant vous** I was there well before you; **rendez-vous immédiatement sur les lieux** go there immediately; *Litt* **il vous faut prendre congé du maître de ces lieux** it's time to bid your host farewell; *Litt* **ces lieux de tristesse** this place of sorrow

(d) **avoir l.** to take place; **la réunion aura l. à ...** the meeting will take place *or* be held at ...

(e) (*raisons*) **il y a (tout) l. /j'ai tout l. de supposer que ...** + *ind* there are/I have (good) grounds for supposing that ..., there is/I have (every) reason to suppose that ...; **il y a l. d'attendre** it would be advisable *or* as well to wait; **je vous écrirai s'il y a l.** I'll write to you if necessary; **donner l. à** (*une querelle, des problèmes*) to cause, to give rise to; **son retour a donné l. à une réunion de famille** his return was the occasion for a family gathering; **donner l. à des désagréments** to cause inconvenience; **tout donne l. de croire que** ... everything leads me/us/*etc* *or* there is every reason to believe that ...

(f) (*fonction*) **tenir l. de qch** to take the place of sth; **elle lui a tenu l. de mère** she has been a mother to him

(g) **au l. de** instead of, *Fml* in lieu of; **au l. de te plaindre** instead of complaining; **et au l. de cela, elle** ... but instead she ...; *Litt* **au l. que** + *sub* instead of + *gerund*

▶ **lieu[1]**: *Vieilli* **lieux (d'aisances)** lavatory; **l. commun** commonplace; **l. de départ** point of departure; **l. de destination** destination; **l. d'émission** place of issue; *Math* **l. géométrique** locus; **l. de livraison** point of delivery; **l. de naissance** place of birth; *Fin* **l. de paiement** place of payment; **l. public** public place; **l. de rassemblement** assembly point; **l. de réception** place of receipt; **l. de rencontre** meeting place; **l. de rendez-vous** meeting place; **quel est le l. de rendez-vous?** where are we/they/*etc* meeting?; **l. de travail** place of work; **sur le l. de travail** in the workplace; **l. de vacances** holiday resort

lieu[2], *pl* **lieus** *nm* (*poisson*) **l. jaune** pollack, pollock; **l. noir** coalfish

lieu(-)dit, *pl* **lieux(-)dits** *nm* (named) place, locality

lieue [ljø] *nf* league (= 4 kilometres); *Naut* **l. marine** = 52 kilometres; **j'étais à cent** *ou* **mille lieues de penser/croire que** ... I would never (in a million years) have dreamt/ believed that ...; *Vieilli* **il sent son docteur d'une l.** you can tell he's a doctor a mile off

lieur, -euse [ljœr, -øz] *Agr* **1** *n Arch* (*de gerbes, de bottes etc*) binder **2** *nf* **lieuse** (*machine*) (mechanical) sheaf binder

lieutenant [ljøtnɑ̃] *nm Mil* lieutenant; *Av* flying officer, *US* first lieutenant; (*dans la marine marchande*) mate; *Naut* **premier l.** second mate; *Naut* **l. de vaisseau** lieutenant

lieutenant-colonel, *pl* **lieutenants-colonels** *nm Mil* lieutenant-colonel; *Av* wing commander

lièvre [ljɛvr] *nm* hare; *Fig* **courir deux lièvres à la fois** to try to do two things at once; *Culin* **pâté de l.** hare pâté

lift [lift] *nm Sp* topspin; **faire un l.** to give a ball topspin, to put topspin on a ball

lifter [lifte] *vt Sp* **l. une balle** to give a ball topspin, to put topspin on a ball

liftier [liftje] *nm* lift attendant, *Am* elevator operator

lifting [liftiŋ] *nm Chir, Fig* face lift; **elle s'est fait faire un l.** she's had a face lift

ligament [ligamɑ̃] *nm Anat* ligament

ligature [ligatyr] *nf* **(a)** *(fait d'attacher)* tying, binding; **la l. des greffes** the binding of (the) grafts **(b)** *Él (au moyen d'un fil, câble)* splice **(c)** *Chir, Typ* ligature; **l. des trompes** the tying of tubes

ligaturer [ligatyre] *vt (attacher)* to bind; *Él (câble, fil)* to splice; *Chir* to ligature, to tie; *Typ* **ligaturé** ligatured

lige [liʒ] *adj Hist* liege

lignage[1] [liɲaʒ] *nm Arch* lineage, descent

lignage[2] *nm Typ* linage

ligne [liɲ] *nf* **(a)** *(trait)* line; **l. droite** straight line; **l. brisée** broken line; **tracer une l. à main levée** to draw a line freehand; **les lignes de la main** the lines of the hand; **votre l. de vie/de cœur est courte** you have a short life-/heart-line; **avancer en l. droite** to advance in a straight line; *Mus* **l. supplémentaire** ledger line; *Naut* **la l. (équatoriale)** the line, the Equator; **passer la l. (équatoriale)** to cross the line; *TV* **définition de 625 lignes** definition of 625 lines

(b) *(d'écriture)* line; **le prof m'a donné cent lignes** *(en punition)* the teacher gave me a hundred lines; **elle m'a juste envoyé deux lignes** she just dropped me a line; **je vous envoie ces quelques lignes pour vous donner les dernières nouvelles** this is just a note to give you the latest news; *Fig* **lire entre les lignes** to read between the lines; **aller à la l.** to begin a new line *or* a new paragraph; **à la l.** *(en dictant)* new paragraph, new line; **passer** *ou* **sauter une l.** to leave a line; **être payé à la l.** to be paid by the line; **tirer à la l.** *(délayer)* to pad it out; *Fig* **mettre sur la même l.** to compare; **sa rapidité et son intelligence sont à mettre sur la même l.** he is as quick as he is intelligent, his speed is matched by his intelligence; *Fig* **entrer en l. de compte** to be taken into consideration; **les sentiments ne doivent pas entrer en l. de compte dans ton jugement** feelings should not influence *or* enter into your decision; **cela n'entre pas en l. de compte** that doesn't come *or* enter into it; **faire entrer un facteur en l. de compte** to take a factor into account; **c'est un facteur à faire entrer en l. de compte** it's something to be considered *or* taken into account *or* consideration

(c) *(contour, silhouette)* (out)line; **la l. du nez** the line *or* contour of the nose; **la pureté des lignes** purity of line; **la l. élégante d'une voiture** the elegant lines of a car; **garder/soigner sa l.** to keep/watch one's waistline *or* one's figure; **avoir la l.** to have a good figure; **perdre la l.** to lose one's figure

(d) *(rangée)* line; **se mettre en l.** to line up; **plantés en l.** planted in a line *or* row; *Mil, Fig* **en première l.** in the front line; *Fig* **sur toute la l.** all along the line

(e) *(direction, règle)* line; **redéfinir sa l. d'action** to adopt a different line *or* course of action; **la l. du parti communiste** the communist party line; *Fig* **grandes lignes d'une œuvre** broad *or* general outline(s) of a work; **je vais vous expliquer le projet dans ses grandes lignes** I'll explain the broad outline(s) of the project to you

(f) *(transports)*, *Av (destination)* route; *Rail* line; *Rail* **grandes lignes** main lines; **l. maritime/aérienne** shipping line/airline; *Av* **lignes intérieures** domestic services; *(destinations)* domestic routes; *Av* **nous espérons vous revoir sur nos lignes** we hope we will soon have the pleasure of welcoming you on board again; **l. d'autobus** bus service; *(parcours)* bus route; **il n'y a que deux lignes de bus qui fonctionnent la nuit** there are only two late-night bus services; **l. de banlieue** commuter service; *Av* **l. radiale** minor domestic air route; *Av* **l. transversale** domestic or international air route not serving the capital

(g) *Él* (power) line; **l. télégraphique** telegraph line

(h) *Tél* **l. téléphonique** telephone line; **être en l.** *(téléphonique)* to be on a call; **la l. est occupée** the line is engaged *or esp Am* busy; **la l. a été coupée** I've/we've/*etc* been cut off; **il y a quelqu'un sur la l.** there's someone on the line; **vous êtes en l.** you're connected, you're through; **il est déjà en l.** he's on another line; **l. commutée** switched line; **l. directe accessible 24 heures sur 24** twenty-four-hour hotline; **l. extérieure** outside line; **l. ouverte** open line; **l. principale** switchboard line, main line; **l. privée** private line; **l. spécifique** dedicated line; **l. téléphonique directe** direct dial telephone

(i) *(fil)* line; *Pêche* (fishing) line; **planter des arbres à la l.** to plant trees straight by using a line *or* a cord

(j) *Com* line, range; **l. de produits** line of products, product line; **BOTÉ lance une nouvelle l. de cosmétiques** BOTÉ are launching a new line *or* range of cosmetics; **l. pour hommes** range for men

(k) *(filiation)* **descendre en l. directe** *ou* **en droite l. de ...** to be directly descended from ..., to be descended in a direct line from ...

(l) *Can (mesure)* eighth of an inch (= 3. 175 mm)

(m) *Ordinat* line; **en l.** on line; **sur l.** on line; **hors l.** off line; **changer de l.** to do a line feed; **l. de commande** command line; *(type de commande)* line command; **l. d'état** status line; **l. vide** blank line

▶ **ligne**: **l. d'arrivée** finishing line; **l. d'attaque** line of attack; **l. de bataille** line of battle, fighting line; *Aut* **l. blanche** white line, *Am* yellow line; **l. de changement de date** *ou* **de jour** International Date Line; *Naut* **l. de charge** load line; **l. de coke** line of coke; **l. de combat** line of battle, fighting line; **l. continue** *(aussi sur la route)* continuous line; *Fin* **l. de démarcation** demarcation line; **l. de départ** starting line; **l. directrice** keynote, thrust; **l. discontinue** *(sur la route)* broken line; *Aut* **l. d'échappement** exhaust system; *Ordinat* **l.-écran**, *pl* **lignes-écran** screen line; *Naut* **l. de flottaison** waterline; **l. de fond** *Pêche* ledger line; *Tennis* base line; *Phys* **l. de force** line of force; *Mil* **l. de front** front line; **l. à haute tension** high tension wire *or* line; **l. d'horizon** (line of the) horizon; *Aut* **l. jaune** white line, *Am* yellow line; *Hist* **L. Maginot** Maginot Line; **l. magnétique** magnetic *or* black strip; *Com* **l. maritime de conférence** conference line; **l. médiane** centre line; **l. de mire** line of sight; *F (d'un fusil à lunette)* sights; *Fig* **avoir qn dans sa l. de mire** to have sb in one's sights; **l. du partage des eaux** watershed; *Typ* **l. de pointillé** dotted line; *Mus* **l. de portée** stave line; **l. de sonde** plumb line; **l. de tir** line of fire; *Fb* **l. de touche** touch line; *Mil* **l. de visée** line of sight

lignée [liɲe] *nf* (line of) descendants; *(origine)* line, lineage; **une nombreuse l.** a large number of descendants; **ce clan est très fier de sa nombreuse l. de combattants** the clan is very proud of its many warrior descendants; **de bonne l. allemande** of good German stock; *Fig* **un philosophe dans la l. de Russell** a philosopher in the tradition of Russell

ligneux, -euse [liɲø, -øz] *adj* ligneous, woody

lignite [liɲit] *nm Minér* lignite, brown coal

ligoter [ligɔte] *vt* to tie up; **être ligoté à qch** to be tied to sth

ligue [lig] *nf* league, confederacy; *Hist Fr* **la (Sainte) L.** the (Holy Catholic) League; *Hist Fr* **L. des droits de l'homme** = organization set up in 1898 to defend Dreyfus

liguer [lige] **1** *vt (nations, clans etc)* to league together; **être ligué avec qn** to be in league with sb **2 se liguer** *vpr* to form a league (**avec** with, **contre** against); **ils se liguent contre moi** they're ganging up on me

ligueur, -euse [ligœr, -øz] *n* member of a league

lilas [lila] **1** *nm Bot* lilac **2** *adj inv* lilac

lilliputien, -ienne [lilipysjɛ̃, -jɛn] **1** *adj* Lilliputian **2** *n* **L.** Lilliputian

lillois, -oise [lilwa, -waz] **1** *adj* of/from Lille **2** *n* **L.** *(natif)* native of Lille; *(habitant)* inhabitant of Lille

limace [limas] *nf* **(a)** *(mollusque)* slug; *F* **c'est une vraie l.** he's such a slowcoach *or Am* slowpoke, *Am* he's as slow as molasses in winter **(b)** *Arg (chemise)* shirt

limaçon [limasɔ̃] *nm* **(a)** *Vieilli* snail **(b)** *Anat (de l'oreille)* cochlea

limage [limaʒ] *nm* filing (down)

limaille [limaj] *nf* filings; **l. de fer** iron filings

limande [limɑ̃d] *nf (poisson)* dab; **l.-sole** lemon sole; *F* **plate comme une l.** *(d'une femme)* as flat as a pancake

limbe [lɛ̃b] *nm* **(a)** *Astron, Math* limb **(b)** *Bot (de feuille)* lamina, limb **(c)** *Rel* **les Limbes** limbo; *Fig* **dans les limbes** in (a state of) limbo

lime[1] [lim] *nf* **(a)** *(outil)* file; **l. sourde** dead-smooth file; **l. à ongles** nail file; **l. émeri** emery board; **aiguiser un outil à la l.** to file up a tool **(b)** *(mollusque)* lima

lime[2] *nf Bot* lime

limer [lime] **1** *vt (réduire)* to file (down); *(polir)* to file (up); **l. les barreaux** to file through the bars **2 se limer** *vpr* **se l. les ongles** to file one's nails **3** *vi Vulg (baiser)* to screw, to have one's end away

limier [limje] *nm (chien)* bloodhound; *Fig* sleuth; *Bourse* investigator

liminaire [liminɛr] *adj (note, remarque etc)* introductory

limitatif, -ive [limitatif, -iv] *adj* limiting, restrictive, restricting; **dispositions limitatives** restrictions; **une liste**

non limitative an open-ended list; **la liste n'est pas limitative** the list is not exhaustive

limitation [limitasjɔ̃] *nf* limitation, restriction; **l. des armements** arms limitation; **l. des naissances** birth control, family planning; **l. des salaires** imposition of wage restraints; (*volontaire*) (voluntary) wage restraint; **l. de vitesse** speed limit; **ce test se fait sans l. de temps** there is no time limit for the test; **l. de poids** weight limit; **l. de responsabilité** limitation of responsibility

limite [limit] **1** *nf* **(a)** (*de pays, champ etc*) boundary; **les limites d'un terrain de football** the boundary (lines) of a football pitch; **marquer les limites du terrain** to mark out the ground; **à la l. du jardin, il y a une forêt** just beyond the garden there is a forest

(b) (*de pouvoir, compréhension etc*) limit; **fixer** *ou* **imposer des limites à l'autorité de qn** to set limits *or* bounds on sb's authority; **son ambition/sa générosité/son amour pour elle ne connaît pas de limites** his ambition/his generosity/ his love for her knows no bounds; **je connais mes limites** I know my limits; **il y a des limites!** there are limits!; **ma patience a des limites!** there are limits to my patience!, my patience is wearing thin!; **la bonté a des limites** there are limits to my/her/*etc* kindness; **mettre une l. /des limites à qch** to set a limit/limits to sth, to limit sth; **franchir** *ou* **dépasser les limites** to go too far, to be out of line; **Sarajevo a franchi les limites de l'horreur** the horror of what is happening in Sarajevo is beyond belief; **vous avez vraiment dépassé les limites du supportable** what you did is quite intolerable; **c'est à la l. de la vulgarité/du supportable** it's bordering on vulgarity/the unacceptable; **je vous aiderai dans les limites du possible** I'll do everything possible *or* everything I possibly can to help you, I'll help you as far as is humanly possible; **dans les limites du raisonnable** within reasonable limits; **dans les limites du sujet** within the limits of the subject; **veuillez rester dans les limites du sujet** please keep to the subject; **dans la l. des places disponibles** subject to availability; **dans la l. des stocks disponibles** while stocks last; **dans une certaine l.** up to a point, to a certain extent; **je suis prêt à vous prêter de l'argent dans une certaine l.** I am ready to lend you money up to a point; **à la l., j'accepterais de le voir** if pushed *or* if I have to, I'll agree to see him; **ça va? — oui, à la limite** is that OK? — yes, just about; **se battre/résister/travailler jusqu'à la dernière l.** to fight/resist/work to the last; **il est à la l. de ses forces** he's completely exhausted, he's at the limit of his endurance; **sans limites** unbounded, limitless; *Boxe* **gagner avant la l.** to win inside the distance

(c) *Math* limit, limiting value

2 *adj* **cas l.** borderline case; **vitesse l.** maximum speed; **charge l. d'un pont** maximum load of a bridge; **date l.** deadline; (*pour candidature etc*) deadline, closing date; *F* **50 francs, c'est le prix l. que j'accepterais de payer** 50 francs is my top price; *F* **je ne lui ai pas mis une claque, mais c'était l.** I didn't slap him but I came very close to it *or* but it was touch and go; *F* **elle est l., ta dissertation** your essay's a borderline case *or* only just this side of acceptable; *F* **je suis un peu l. financièrement** I'm a bit short (of cash), my bank account's not very healthy; *F* **j'ai trouvé qu'il était l. avec elle** I thought he was a bit hard on her

▶ **limite**: **l. d'âge** age limit; **l. de crédit** credit limit; *Tech* **l. d'élasticité** elastic limit; *MecE* **l. élastique** yield point; **l. d'endettement** borrowing limit; **l. de poids** weight limit; *Bourse* **l. de position** position limit; **l. de rupture** breaking *or* yield point

limité [limite] *adj* limited; **vitesse limitée à 60 km/heure** speed restricted to 60km/hour; **en temps l.** in a limited amount of time; **n'avoir qu'une confiance limitée dans une machine/l'honnêteté de qn** to have a limited amount of confidence in a machine/a person's honesty; **avec lui, la conversation est limitée** conversation is limited with him, you can't have much of a conversation with him; *F* **il est un peu l. ce mec** the guy's a bit thick

limiter [limite] **1** *vt* **(a)** (*délimiter*) (*pays, territoire etc*) to bound, to mark the bounds of

(b) (*restreindre*) to limit, to restrict; (*pouvoir, droits etc de qn*) to set bounds *or* limits to; *F* **l. les dégâts** to limit the damage; **je ne connaissais pas vraiment le sujet de l'examen, mais j'ai limité les dégâts** I didn't really know anything about the exam subject but I managed to make something of it; **l. la production** to limit production

2 se limiter *vpr* **il faut apprendre à se l.** you have to learn to limit yourself *or* to keep within limits; **quand il commence à boire, il est incapable de se l.** once he starts drinking he doesn't know when to stop; **se l. à ...** to limit *or* restrict *or* confine oneself to ...; **elle se limita à dire que ...** she confined herself to saying that ...

limiteur [limitœr] *nm Aut* limiter; **l. de freinage** (*correcteur*) pressure limiter; **l. de régime** over-run valve, rev limiter

limitrophe [limitrɔf] *adj* adjacent (**de** to), bordering (**de** on); **les pays limitrophes** the neighbouring *or US* neighboring countries; **être l. d'un autre pays** to border on another country

limogeage [limɔʒaʒ] *nm* (*d'officier*) superseding; (*de fonctionnaire*) dismissal

limoger [limɔʒe] *vt* (*officier*) to supersede; (*fonctionnaire*) to dismiss

limon[1] [limɔ̃] *nm* **(a)** (*alluvion*) silt, *Spéc* alluvium; **le l. employé comme engrais** silt used as a fertilizer **(b)** *Géol* limon

limon[2] *nm* **(a)** (*brancard*) shaft **(b)** *Constr* (*d'escalier*) stringboard, stringer

limon[3] *nm Bot, Arch* lemon

limonade [limɔnad] *nf* (*boisson gazeuse*) (fizzy) lemonade

limonadier, -ière [limɔnadje, -jɛr] *n* **(a)** *Ind* soft drinks manufacturer **(b)** *Arch* (*cafetier*) keeper *or* owner of a café

limoneux, -euse [limɔnø, -øz] *adj* (*eau etc*) muddy, silty; *Géol* alluvial

limousin, -ine[1] [limuzɛ̃, -in] **1** *adj* of/from (the province of) Limousin **2** *n* **L.** (*natif*) native of (the province of) Limousin; (*habitant*) inhabitant of (the province of) Limousin **3** *nm Ling* Limousin dialect

limousine[2] *nf Aut* limousine

limpide [lɛ̃pid] *adj* (*quartz, eau etc*) limpid, clear; (*explication*) clear, lucid; (*style*) limpid, lucid; **un regard l.** clear *or Litt* limpid expression

limpidité [lɛ̃pidite] *nf* (*de quartz, eau*) clarity, limpidity; (*d'explication*) clarity, lucidity; (*de style*) limpidity, lucidity; (*de regard*) limpidity

lin [lɛ̃] *nm* **(a)** (*plante*) flax; **graine de l.** linseed; **huile de l.** linseed oil **(b)** *Tex* **(tissu/toile de) l.** linen

linceul [lɛ̃sœl] *nm* winding sheet, shroud

linéaire [lineɛr] *adj* **1 (a)** *Math* linear **(b) dessin l.** geometrical drawing **(c)** *Fig Litt* **récit l.** linear narrative **2** *nm* (*dans un magasin*) shelf-space

linge [lɛ̃ʒ] *nm* **(a)** (*draps etc*) linen; **gros l.** household linen; **armoire à l.** linen cupboard **(b)** (*dessous*) **(petit) l.** underwear; *Fig F* **c'est du beau l.** they're society people **(c)** (*vêtements*) clothes **(d)** (*lessive*) washing; **corde à l.** clothesline; **corbeille à l.** laundry basket **(e)** (*morceau de tissu*) cloth

▶ **linge**: **l. de corps** underwear; *Can* **l. de maison** household linen; **l. de table** table linen

lingère [lɛ̃ʒɛr] *nf* linen-keeper

lingerie [lɛ̃ʒri] *nf* **(a)** (*dessous féminins*) underwear, lingerie **(b)** (*pour rangement*) linen room; (*pour entretien*) laundry

lingot [lɛ̃go] *nm* **(a)** (*masse de métal*) ingot; **l. d'or** gold bar *or* ingot; *Fin* **or/argent en lingots** (gold/silver) bullion **(b)** *Typ* slug

lingual, -ale, -aux, -ales [lɛ̃gwal, -o] *adj Anat, Ling* lingual

linguiste [lɛ̃gɥist] *n* linguist

linguistique [lɛ̃gɥistik] **1** *adj* linguistic; **un séjour l.** a stay in a foreign country (*for the purposes of learning the language*); **une communauté l.** a speech community **2** *nf* linguistics

linguistiquement [lɛ̃gɥistikmɑ̃] *adv* linguistically

liniment [linimɑ̃] *nm Méd* liniment

lino [lino] *nm F* (*abrév* **linoléum**) lino

linoléum [linɔleɔm] *nm* linoleum

linon [linɔ̃] *nm Tex* lawn

linotte [linɔt] *nf* (*oiseau*) linnet; *F* **tête de l.** scatterbrain

linotype® [linotip] *nf Typ* Linotype®

linotypie [linotipi] *nf Typ* setting by Linotype®

linotypiste [linotipist] *n Typ* Linotype® operator

linteau, -eaux [lɛ̃to] *nm Constr* lintel

lion [ljɔ̃] *nm* **(a)** [①**A12,1,g**] lion; **la part du l.** the lion's share; *F* **il a mangé** *ou Arg* **bouffé du l.** he's being all hyper; **tourner comme un l. en cage** to prowl around; *Arch, Litt* celebrity; (*littéraire*) lion **(b)** *Astron, Astrol* **le L.** Leo; **être (du signe du) L.** to be (a) Leo

lionceau, -eaux [ljɔ̃so] *nm* lion cub

lion de mer [ljɔ̃dmɛr] *nm* sea lion

lionne [ljɔn] *nf* lioness; *Vieilli Fig* **une lionne** a handsome *or* elegant-looking woman

lipase [lipaz] *nf Biol, Ch* lipase

lipide [lipid] *nm Biol, Ch* lipid

liposome [lipozom] *nm Biol, Ch* liposome

liposuccion [liposysjɔ̃] *nf* liposuction

lippe [lip] *nf* (thick) lower lip; **faire la l.** (*faire la moue*) to pout; (*bouder*) to sulk

lippu [lipy] *adj* (*personne*) thick-lipped; (*lèvre*) thick

liquéfaction [likefaksjɔ̃] *nf* liquefaction

liquéfiable [likefjabl] *adj* liquefiable

liquéfiant, -iante [likefjɑ̃] *adj* liquefactive, liquefying

liquéfier [likefje] (*pr sub, impf* **n. liquéfiions, v. liquéfiiez**) **1** *vt* to liquefy **2 se liquéfier** *vpr* to liquefy; *Fig* to be drained (of energy); (*avoir peur*) to turn to jelly
liquette [likɛt] *nf F* T-shirt, tee shirt
liqueur [likœr] *nf* **(a)** (*spiritueux*) liqueur; **verre à l.** liqueur glass; **l. de cassis** blackcurrant liqueur **(b)** *Can* **l. (douce)** soft drink **(c)** *Ch* solution; **l. titrée** standard solution; *Méd* **l. de Dakin** Dakin's solution
liquidateur, -trice [likidatœr, -tris] *n Jur* liquidator
liquidation [likidasjɔ̃] *nf* **(a)** *Jur* liquidation; **l. forcée/volontaire** compulsory/voluntary liquidation; **l. judiciaire** official receivership; **l. des biens** liquidation of assets; **entrer en l.** to go into liquidation **(b)** (*de comptes*) settlement, clearing; *Bourse* settlement; *Bourse* (*d'une position*) liquidation; *Bourse* **l. en espèces** cash settlement; **chambre de l.** (bankers') clearing house; *Compta* **l. de fin de mois/de quinzaine** end-of-month/fortnightly settlement **(c)** *Com* (*de stocks*) selling off **(d)** *F* (*fait de tuer*) liquidation, elimination
liquide [likid] **1** *adj* liquid; **la soupe est trop l.** the soup is too watery *or* too thin; **argent l.** cash, ready money, hard cash; *Fin* **actif l.** liquid asset; *Fin* **peu l.** illiquid **2** *nm* **(a)** (*substance*) liquid, fluid; **il ne pourra prendre que des liquides pendant une semaine** he'll be on liquids for a week **(b)** *Fig* (*espèces*) (ready) cash; **je n'ai pas assez de l.** I haven't enough (ready) cash; **vous payez par chèque ou en l.?** are you paying by cheque or (in) cash? **3** *nf Ling* liquid
▶ **liquide**: *Méd* **l. céphalo-rachidéen** cerebrospinal fluid; **l. correcteur** correction fluid; *Aut* **l. de direction assistée** power steering fluid; **l. de frein** brake fluid; **l. hydraulique de frein** hydraulic brake fluid; **l. de nettoyage** cleaning fluid; **l. de refroidissement** coolant, coolant fluid; *Méd* **l. synovial** synovial fluid; *Aut* **l. pour transmission automatique** automatic transmission fluid
liquider [likide] *vt* **(a)** *Jur* (*affaire*) to liquidate, to wind up **(b)** (*compte*) to settle, to clear; *Bourse* (*une position*) to liquidate, to close out; **l. une dette** to pay off a debt **(c)** *F* (*tuer*) to liquidate, to eliminate; **l. une tâche** to get through a task, to get a task finished **(d)** (*stock*) to sell off; **ils liquident chez Martin** they're selling off stock at Martin's
liquidité [likidite] *nf* liquidity; *Fin* **liquidités** liquid assets
liquoreux, -euse [likɔrø, -øz] *adj* (*vin*) liqueur-like
lire[1] [lir] (*prp* **lisant**; *pp* **lu**; *pr ind* **je lis, il lit**; *impf* **je lisais**; *p hist* **je lus**; *fu* **je lirai**) **1** *vt* **(a)** (*livre, auteur, disquette, données, musique etc*) to read; (*bande son, image*) to reproduce; **elle sait l.** she can read; **l. tout haut** *ou* **à haute voix** to read aloud; **l. en diagonale** to scan, to cast a quick eye over, to skim through; **l. qch dans un livre** to read sth in a book; **l. qch à qn** to read sth (out) to sb; **avoir beaucoup lu** to be well read; **c'est un auteur qui est très lu** he's a widely read author; **lu et approuvé** read and approved; **dans l'attente de vous l.** (*dans une lettre*) hoping to hear from you soon; *Fig* **l. entre les lignes** to read between the lines; *Ordinat* **l. au scanneur** to scan; **l. les épreuves de tirage** to proof-read

(b) (*interpréter*) to read; **on peut le l. de deux façons différentes** you can read it two different ways

(c) (*déchiffrer*) **l. dans la pensée de qn** to read sb's thoughts; **l. dans le jeu de qn** to know sb's game, to know what sb is up to; **elle a voulu me l. les lignes de la main** she wanted to read my hand; **l. dans une boule de cristal** to read a crystal ball; **l. dans le marc de café** ≈ to read the tea leaves

2 se lire *vpr* **(a) ce livre se lit bien** *ou* **se laisse l.** it's a readable book, this book is very readable *or* a good read; **ce roman se lit en une soirée** this novel can be read in an evening; **ce genre de fautes se lit couramment** you read this sort of mistake a lot

(b) (*se deviner*) **cela se lit sur votre visage/dans vos yeux** it shows in your face/in your eyes, it's written all over your face/you can read it in your eyes
lire[2] *nf* (*monnaie*) lira
lis [lis] *nm* lily; **l. blanc** white lily; **l. des vallées** lily of the valley; **l. d'eau** *ou* **d'étang** water lily; **teint de l.** lily-white complexion
Lisbonne [lizbɔn] *nf* Lisbon
liseré [lizre] *nm*, **liséré** [lizere] *nm Couture* border, edging
liseron [lizrɔ̃] *nm* bindweed, convolvulus
liseur, -euse [lizœr, -øz] **1** *n* reader **2** *nf* **liseuse (a)** (*couverture amovible*) book cover **(b)** (*vêtement de femme*) (lady's) bed jacket **(c)** (*en train, en avion*) reading light
lisibilité [lizibilite] *nf* **(a)** (*d'une écriture*) legibility **(b)** (*d'un texte, fichier informatique*) readability
lisible [lizibl] *adj* **(a)** (*qu'on peut déchiffrer*) legible, readable; **l. par ordinateur** machine-readable **(b)** (*qu'on peut comprendre*) readable
lisiblement [lizibləmɑ̃] *adv* legibly
lisière [lizjɛr] *nf* **(a)** (*de champ, forêt*) edge, border **(b)** (*bande de tissu*) selvage, selvedge
lissage [lisaʒ] *nm* (*de pierre etc*) smoothing, polishing; (*de cuir*) sleeking; (*de papier etc*) glazing; *Ordinat* **l. de courbes/des caractères** curve/character smoothing
lisse[1] [lis] *nf Naut* **(a)** (*de coque*) ribband; **lisses de l'avant** harpings **(b)** (*du bastingage*) handrail
lisse[2] *adj* smooth; (*poli*) polished; (*pneu*) bald; **cheveux lisses** sleek hair
lisser [lise] **1** *vt* (*cheveux*) to smooth down, to sleek down; (*pli*) to smooth out; (*pierre etc*) to smooth, to polish; (*cuir*) to sleek; (*papier etc*) to glaze **2 se lisser** *vpr* **se l. les plumes** (*d'un oiseau*) to preen its feathers *or* itself
lisseur [lisœr] *nm* **l. de fontes** font smoother
listage [listaʒ] *nm Ordinat* listing, printout
liste [list] *nf* list; **dresser/faire une l.** to draw up/make (out) a list; **être en tête/en fin de l.** to be at the top/the bottom of the list; **l. officielle des taux** schedule of charges; *Tél* **être sur (la) l. rouge** to be ex-directory, *Am* to have an unlisted number, to be unlisted
▶ **liste**: **l. des actionnaires** list of shareholders; **l. d'adresses** mailing list, address list; **l. des arrivées** arrivals list; **l. d'attente** waiting list, waitlist; **l. civile** civil list; **l. de clients** customer *or* client list; (*d'hôtel*) guest list; *Com* **l. de colisage** packing list; **l. des correspondants** list of correspondents; **l. des départs** departure list; **l. électorale** electoral roll; **l. d'envoi** mailing list; *Ordinat* **l. de fichiers à imprimer** print list, print queue; **l. de mariage** wedding list; **l. noire** blacklist; *TV, Cin* **l. des prises (de vue)** take sheet, shot list; **l. de prix** price list; *Ordinat* **l. rapide** draft; **l. récapitulative** checklist; **l. des réservations** reservations list; **l. des signatures autorisées** authorized signatory list; **l. des tarifs** price list, tariff; (*de transport*) fare list
listel, -els, -eaux [listɛl, -o] *nm* **(a)** *Archit etc* listel, fillet **(b)** (*de pièce de monnaie*) rim
lister [liste] *vt Ordinat* to list
listériose [listerjoz] *nf Méd* listeriosis
listing [listiŋ] *nm Ordinat* listing, printout
lit [li] *nm* **(a)** (*meuble*) bed; **l. moelleux/dur** soft/hard bed *or* mattress; **l. de fer** iron bedstead; **aller au l.** to go to bed; **se mettre au l.** to get into bed; **l. pour deux personnes, grand l.** double bed; **mettre un enfant au l.** to put a child to bed; **au l. les enfants!** time for bed, children!, bedtime, children!; **au saut du l.** just after one has got up; **être au l.** to be in bed; **prendre le l.** to take to one's bed; **garder le l.** to stay in bed; **tirer qn du l.** to get sb out of bed; **je ne te tire** *ou* **sors pas du l. au moins?** I hope I didn't get you out of bed; **faire le l.** to make the bed; *Fig* **faire le l. de** to pave the way for; **faire l. à part** to sleep in separate beds; **un hôtel de 200 lits** a 200-bed hotel, a hotel with 200 beds; **chambre à un l. /à deux lits** single-/twin-bedded room; **mourir dans son l.** to die in (one's) bed; **bois de l.** bedstead

(b) *Jur* **enfant du second l.** child by one's second marriage

(c) (*couche*) (*d'argile, de pierre etc*) bed, layer; **l. de cendres** bed of ashes; *Culin* **placer les filets sur un l. d'épinards** place the fillets on a bed of spinach

(d) (*de rivière etc*) bed; **la rivière est sortie de son l.** the river has burst its banks

(e) *Naut* (*de marée etc*) set; **être dans le l. de marée** to be in the tideway; **dans le l. du vent** in the wind's eye
▶ **lit**: **l. à baldaquin** canopied four-poster (bed), tester bed; **l.-bateau,** *pl* **lits-bateaux** = bed with curved sides, higher at the ends; **l.-cage,** *pl* **lits-cages** cot, *Am* crib; **l. de camp** camp bed, *Am* cot; **l. en cathédrale** = bed placed upright with sleeper in it; **l. clos** box bed; **l. à colonnes** four-poster (bed); **l. conjugal** marriage bed; *Litt* **l. de douleur** sick bed; **l. d'enfant** cot, *Am* crib; **l. escamotable** Murphy bed; **l. de long séjour** (*dans un hôtel*) long-stay bed; **l. majeur** (*d'un fleuve*) flood plain; *HydE* high water *or* bed; *HydE* **l. mineur** mean water *or* bed; *Vieilli* **l. de misère** childbed; **l. de mort: être sur son l. de mort** to be on one's death bed; **l.-nacelle,** *pl* **lits-nacelles** carry cot; **l. pliant** folding *or* foldaway bed; **l. en portefeuille** apple-pie bed; **l. de repos** couch; **l. une place** single bed; **lits gigognes** beds that fit into each other; **lits jumeaux** twin beds; **lits superposés** bunk beds, bunks
litanie [litani] *nf* **(a)** *Rel* **litanies** litany **(b)** *Péj* (*de griefs, plaintes*) litany; **c'est toujours la même l.** it's the same old story
litchi [litʃi] *nm* (*fruit*) lychee, litchi
liteau, -eaux [lito] *nm* **(a)** *Constr* batten, rail, ribband **(b)** *Tex* (*sur linge de table etc*) band, stripe
litée [lite] *nf* (*d'animaux*) litter

literie [litri] *nf* bedding
lithiase [litjaz] *nf Méd* lithiasis
lithine [litin] *nf Ch* lithia
lithiné [litine] **1** *adj* **eau lithinée** lithia water **2** *nmpl* **lithinés** lithium salts
lithium [litjɔm] *nm Ch* lithium
litho [lito] *nf F* (*abrév* **lithographie**) litho
lithographe [litograf] *n* lithographer
lithographie [litografi] *nf* (**a**) (*technique*) lithography; **l. offset** offset lithography (**b**) (*résultat*) lithograph
lithographier [litografje] *vt* (*pr sub & impf* **n. lithographiions, v. lithographiiez**) to lithograph
lithographique [litografik] *adj* lithographic
lithosphère [litɔsfɛr] *nf Géol* lithosphere
Lithuanie [litɥani] *nf* Lithuania
lithuanien, -ienne [litɥanjɛ̃, -jɛn] *adj, n* = **lituanien, -ienne**
litière [litjɛr] *nf* (**a**) (*d'écurie*) litter; **la l. du chat** the cat's litter (**b**) *Hist* (*palanquin*) litter; **être porté en l.** to be carried in a litter
litige [litiʒ] *nm* dispute; (*poursuite*) lawsuit; (*recours à la loi*) litigation; **objet** *ou* **point de l.** bone of contention; *Jur* subject of the action; **être en l.** to be in dispute, to be disputed
litigieux, -euse [litiʒjø, -øz] *adj* (*affaire, héritage, contrat*) disputed, in dispute; (*question, cas*) contentious
litote [litɔt] *nf Littér* litotes, understatement
litre [litr] *nm* (**a**) (*mesure*) litre, *US* liter (**b**) (*récipient d'un litre*) litre *or US* liter bottle
litron [litrɔ̃] *nm F* litre *or US* liter of wine
littéraire [literɛr] **1** *adj* (**a**) (*critique, prix, langue etc*) literary; **la vie l.** the literary world, literary life; **avoir l'esprit l.** to have a literary turn of mind (**b**) *Litt Péj* (*développements, contritions*) insincere, affected **2** *n* (**a**) (*personne douée pour la littérature*) literary person (**b**) (*étudiant*) student of literature (**c**) (*professeur*) teacher of literature
littérairement [literɛrmɑ̃] *adv* in literary terms; (*intéressant*) from a literary point of view
littéral, -ale, -aux, -ales [literal, -o] *adj* (**a**) (*traduction, sens etc*) literal; *Math* **coefficient l.** literal coefficient (**b**) (*par écrit*), *Jur* **preuve littérale** documentary evidence; **arabe l.** written Arabic
littéralement [literalmɑ̃] *adv* literally
littéralité [literalite] *nf Litt* literality, literalness
littérateur [literatœr] *nm* literary man, man of letters, *Péj* literary hack
littérature [literatyr] *nf* literature; **se lancer dans la l.** to embark on a literary career; **faire carrière dans la l.** to make a career in writing; **l. commerciale** sales literature; *Fig Péj* **tout ça c'est de la l.** all that's of trifling importance; **on a publié une importante l. sur le sujet** a considerable amount of literature has been published on the subject
littoral, -ale, -aux, -ales [litɔral, -o] **1** *adj* coastal, *Spéc* littoral **2** *nm* coast(line), *Spéc* littoral
Lituanie [litɥani] *nf* Lithuania
lituanien, -ienne [litɥanjɛ̃, -jɛn] **1** *adj* Lithuanian **2** *nm Ling* Lithuanian **3** *n* **L.** Lithuanian
liturgie [lityrʒi] *nf Rel* liturgy
liturgique [lityrʒik] *adj Rel* liturgical
livarde [livard] *nf Naut* sprit; **voile à l.** spritsail
livarot [livaro] *nm Culin* Livarot (cheese)
livide [livid] *adj* (**a**) (*teint*) pallid (**b**) *Litt* (*bleuâtre*) livid
lividité [lividite] *nf* pallor, pallidness; *Méd* **l. cadavérique** livor mortis, post-mortem lividity
living(-room), *pl* **living(-room)s** [liviŋ(rum)] *nm* living room
livrable [livrabl] *adj* (**a**) *Com* that can be delivered; **marchandises livrables à domicile** goods delivered to your home (**b**) *Fin* deliverable
livraison [livrɛzɔ̃] *nf* (**a**) (*de marchandises etc*) delivery; **l. gratuite,** *Spéc* **l. franco** free delivery, delivered free; **l. franco par nos soins** carriage paid; **payable à la l.** payable on delivery; **l. contre remboursement, paiement à la l.** cash on delivery, *Am* collect on delivery; **faire une l.** to make a delivery; **faire la l. de qch** to deliver sth; **faire la l. de pain/journaux** to deliver the bread/the newspapers; **prendre l. de qch** to take delivery of sth; **défaut de l.** non-delivery; **voiture de l.** delivery van; *Fin* **l. des titres** delivery of securities; *Com* **l. immédiate** available for delivery, ready delivery; **l. le jour même** same-day delivery; *Com* **l. à terme** future delivery, forward delivery; *Com* **l. à domicile** door-to-door delivery, home delivery; (*de journaux*) direct door delivery; **'l. à domicile'** home deliveries; **la l. est arrivée** (*marchandise*) the delivery has arrived
(**b**) (*d'ouvrage publié en fascicules*) part
livre¹ [livr] *nf* (**a**) [①A12,1,h,ii] (*poids*) half kilo, = pound; *Can* pound (= 0.453kg) (**b**) [①A12,1,h,ii] **l.** (**sterling**) pound (sterling) (**c**) *Hist Fr* (*monnaie*) livre

livre² *nm* (**a**) (*objet*) book; **un l. sur les papillons** a book on *or* about butterflies; **connaître qch par les livres** to know sth from *or* through books; **elle a toujours le nez dans les livres** she's always got her nose in a book; **l. relié** bound book; **l. de classe** *ou* **scolaire** schoolbook; **l. de grammaire** grammar (book); **l. de lecture** reader, reading book; **l. de cuisine** cookery book, cookbook; **l. d'images/d'enfant** picture/children's book; **l. musical** musical book; **parler comme un l.** to talk like a book; **traduire un passage à l. ouvert** to translate a passage at sight; **il lit Cicéron à l. ouvert** he can read Cicero at sight
(**b**) (*édition*) **l'industrie du l., le l.** the book trade; **les ouvriers du l.** book-trade workers
(**c**) *Com* (*registre*) **grand l.** ledger; **tenir les livres** to keep the accounts *or* the books; **tenue des livres** book-keeping
(**d**) (*de la Bible etc*) book; **le premier l. des 'Fables' de la Fontaine** the first book of La Fontaine's Fables
▶ **livre²**: *Compta* **l. d'achats** purchase ledger; **l. d'actionnaires** register of shareholders; **l. blanc** official report; **l. de bord** *Naut* log(book); *Scol* (teacher's) record book; (*à la maison*) housekeeping book; **l. de caisse** cashbook; **l. de chevet** bedside book; **l. de commandes** order book; **l. de comptes** journal, ledger, account book; **l. de coupures de presse** cuttings book; *Compta* **l. des créanciers** accounts payable ledger; *Compta* **l. des débiteurs** accounts receivable ledger; *Compta* **l. de dépenses** cash book; *Compta* **l. des effets à payer** bills payable ledger; *Compta* **l. des effets à recevoir** bills receivable ledger; *Compta* **l. des entrées** purchase ledger; **l. d'heures** book of hours; *Compta* **l. des inventaires** stock book; *Com* **l. journal** daybook, journal; *Compta* book of original entry; **l. de la Loi** book of the Law; **l. de messe** missal, prayer book; **l. d'or** visitors' book; **l. de paie** payroll; *Compta* wages ledger; **l. de poche** paperback; **l. de prières** prayer book; **l. de prix** prize book; *Arch* **l. de raison** family record book; **l. des réclamations** claims book; *Compta* **l. des rendus** returns ledger; **l. de réservation** reservations book, hotel register; *Compta* **l. des sorties** sales ledger; *Compta* **l. de trésorerie générale** general cash book; **l. des ventes** sales ledger; **livres de comptes** account books, books
livre-cassette, *pl* **livres-cassettes** *nm* spoken word cassette; (*pour les aveugles*) talking book
livrée [livre] *nf* (**a**) (*habit de domestique*) livery; **valet en l.** servant in livery, liveried servant (**b**) (*pelage*) coat; (*plumage*) plumage
livre-jeu, *pl* **livres-jeux** *nm* game in the form of a book
livrer [livre] **1** *vti* (**a**) (*marchandises etc*) to deliver; **nous avons bien été livrés** we have received the delivery; **l. une commande** to fulfill an order; *Com* **l. à terme fixe** to deliver at a fixed term; **nous livrons à domicile** we deliver (anywhere) *or* to your door; **vous serez livrés dès demain** you'll receive delivery tomorrow; *Com* **livré franco domicile** delivered free at domicile
(**b**) (*abandonner*) to abandon; (*remettre*) to deliver (**à** to); **l. un village au pillage/un pays à l'anarchie** to abandon a village to pillage/a country to anarchy; **l. qn à la justice** to deliver *or* hand over sb to justice *or* to the authorities; **il a finalement livré ses complices** he finally delivered up his accomplices; **l. une place forte à l'ennemi** to give up a fortress to the enemy; **l. qn à la mort** to send sb to his death; **l. qn/qch aux flammes** to commit sb/sth to the flames; *Litt* **un épouvantail livré aux vents** a scarecrow left to the mercy of the four winds; **bateau livré à la tempête** boat at the mercy of the storm; **livré à soi-même** left to oneself *or* to one's own devices
(**c**) (*donner, dévoiler*) **l. un secret** to divulge a secret (**à** to); **je vous livre un secret ...** I'll let you in on a secret ...; **l. ses secrets à qn** to confide one's secrets to sb; **l. un peu/beaucoup de soi-même** to reveal a little/a lot of oneself, to open up a bit/a lot; **elle livre peu d'elle-même au bureau** she doesn't reveal much of herself *or* doesn't open up much at the office
(**d**) **l. passage à qn** to let sb pass; **l. bataille** *ou* **combat** to join battle (**à** with), to give battle (**à** to); *Fig* **l. bataille à la pauvreté/à la famine** to battle against poverty/famine
2 se livrer *vpr* (**a**) (*se rendre*) to give oneself up (**à** to); **se l. à la justice** to surrender to the authorities, to give oneself up
(**b**) (*se confier*) to open up; **se l. à qn** to confide in sb
(**c**) (*s'abandonner à*) **se l. à un vice/à des pratiques ignobles** to indulge in a vice/disgraceful practices; **se l. à des spéculations/des plaisirs coupables** to indulge in *or* give oneself over to speculation/guilty pleasures; **se l. au désespoir** to give way to despair; **se l. à la violence** to behave violently, to turn violent; *Litt* **elle s'est livrée à son amant** she gave *or* offered herself (up) to her lover; *Arch, Litt* **se l. à la boisson** to take to drink

(d) (*s'occuper à*) **se l. à des recherches** to be engaged in research; **se l. à ses occupations habituelles** to indulge in one's usual activities; **se l. à une enquête** to set up *or* hold an inquiry; **se l. à l'étude/à la lecture** to devote oneself to study/reading; **se l. à un sport** to practise a sport

livresque [livrɛsk] *adj* (a) (*théorique*) acquired from books; **connaissances livresques** book learning (b) *Péj* (*esprit*) bookish

livret [livrɛ] *nm* (a) (*petit livre*) booklet; **l. (de caisse) d'épargne** bankbook, passbook; **compte sur l.** savings account (b) *Mus* (*d'opéra*) libretto, book

▶ **livret**: *Banque* **l. de compte** bankbook; *Banque* **l. de dépôts** deposit book, passbook; *Admin* **l. de famille** family record book for registration of births and deaths; **l. militaire** service record; **l. scolaire** school report book

livreur [livrœr] *nm* delivery man/boy

livreuse [livrøz] *nf* delivery girl/woman

LJM [ɛlʒiɛm] *nf Com* (*abrév* **livraison le jour même**) same-day delivery

LOA [ɛloa] *nf* (*abrév* **location avec option d'achat**) lease purchase

lob [lɔb] *nm Tennis* lob; **faire un l.** to hit a lob, to lob

lobby, *pl* **lobbies** [lɔbi] *nm Pol* lobby

lobbying [lɔbiiŋ] *nm Pol* lobbying; **faire du l.** to lobby

lobe [lɔb] *nm* (a) *Anat, Bot* lobe; **l. de l'oreille** ear lobe (b) *Archit* foil

lobé [lɔbe] *adj* (a) *Bot* lobed, lobate (b) *Archit* foiled

lobectomie [lɔbɛktɔmi] *nf Chir* lobectomy

lobélie [lɔbeli] *nf Bot* lobelia

lober [lɔbe] **1** *vi Tennis, Fb* to lob **2** *vt Fb* **l. le gardien de but** to lob the goalkeeper

lobotomie [lɔbɔtɔmi] *nf Chir* lobotomy; **on lui a fait une l.** he's had a lobotomy, he's been lobotomized

lobulaire [lɔbylɛr] *adj Anat* lobular

lobule [lɔbyl] *nm Anat* lobule

local, -ale, -aux, -ales [lɔkal, -o] **1** *adj* (*autorité, radio, administration etc*), *Méd* local; **coutumes locales** local customs; **averses locales demain dans la matinée** scattered showers tomorrow morning; **le journal l.** the local paper; **anesthésie locale** local anaesthetic

2 *nm* (a) (*lieu, endroit*) (*de société, d'organisation*) premises; **l. d'habitation** dwelling; **l. professionnel** premises used for professional purposes; **locaux commerciaux** business premises

(b) (*bureau, permanence*) office(s), premises; **rendez-vous au l. à dix heures pour préparer le matériel** meeting at the office at ten o'clock to prepare the material

(c) *Can Tél* extension

3 *nf Journ* **locale** local column

localement [lɔkalmɑ̃] *adv* locally

localier [lɔkalje] *nm Journ* local reporter

localisable [lɔkalizabl] *adj* locatable; (*appel téléphonique*) traceable

localisation [lɔkalizasjɔ̃] *nf* (a) (*circonscription*) localization, confinement (b) (*repérage*) location, locating; (*d'un appel téléphonique*) tracing; **l. de logiciel** software localization

localisé [lɔkalize] *adj* localized

localiser [lɔkalize] **1** *vt* (a) (*circonscrire*) (*épidémie, incendie etc*) to localize, to confine (b) (*repérer*) (*bruit, gène etc*) to locate; (*appel téléphonique*) to trace; **l. qch dans sa mémoire** to place sth; **ne quittez pas, je vais essayer de le l.** hold the line, I'll try and locate him *or* find out where he is **2** **se localiser** *vpr* to confine itself (**à** to)

localité [lɔkalite] *nf* (*ville*) town; (*village*) village

locataire [lɔkatɛr] *n* (*de propriété louée, de locaux commerciaux*) tenant; (*chez le propriétaire*) lodger, *Am* roomer; (*avec bail*) lessee, leaseholder

locateur [lɔkatœr] *nm Jur* lessor

locatif¹, -ive [lɔkatif, -iv] *adj* concerning the renting of premises; **risques locatifs** = tenant's obligations and responsibilities (*as regards damage etc*); **valeur locative** rental value; **réparations locatives** repairs incumbent upon the tenant; **le marché l.** the property rental market

locatif², -ive *Gram* **1** *adj* locative **2** *nm* locative (case)

location [lɔkasjɔ̃] *nf* (a) (*de voiture, d'équipement, de costume etc*) (*par le locataire*) renting, *Br* hiring; (*par le propriétaire*) renting (out), rental, *Br* hiring (out); **prendre qch en l.** to rent sth, *Br* to hire sth; **donner qch en l.** to rent sth (out), *Br* to hire sth (out); **l. de voitures (sans chauffeur)** (self-drive) car rental *or Br* hire; **voiture de l.** rented *or Br* hire car, *Am* rental car; **vélos en l.** bikes for *Br* hire *or Am* rent

(b) (*de logement*) (*par le locataire*) renting; (*par le propriétaire*) renting (out), *Br* letting (out); **prix de l.** rent; **dans cette agence ils ne font pas la l.** they don't rent (out) *or Br* let (out) property in this agency, they don't deal with rented property in this agency

(c) (*propriété à louer*) rented property; (*pour y vivre uniquement*) rented accommodation; **nous n'avons pas trouvé de l. pour cet été** we haven't found anywhere to rent this summer

(d) (*de places*) booking, reservation; **(bureau de) l.** box office, booking office

▶ **location**: **l.-bail,** *pl* **locations-bails** leasing, lease purchase; **l. gérance** rented business; **l. avec option d'achat** lease purchase; **l.-vente,** *pl* **locations-ventes** hire purchase, *US* installment plan, *Can* instalment plan

loch [lɔk] *nm Naut* (ship's) log; **ligne de l.** log line; **livre de l.** log

loche [lɔʃ] *nf* (a) (*poisson*) loach (b) (*mollusque*) grey slug

lock-out [lɔkawt] *nm inv Ind* lockout

lock(-)outer [lɔkawte] *vt Ind* to lock out

locks [lɔks] *nfpl F* dreadlocks

lock-up [lɔkœp] *nm inv Aut* lock-up

loco [loko] *nf F* (*abrév* **locomotive**) loco

locomoteur, -trice [lɔkɔmɔtœr, -tris] **1** *adj* (*organe, troubles etc*) locomotor **2** *nf Rail* **locomotrice** electric engine

locomotion [lɔkɔmɔsjɔ̃] *nf* locomotion; **moyens de l.** means of transport

locomotive [lɔkɔmɔtiv] *nf* (a) *Rail* locomotive, engine; **l. diesel (à transmission) électrique** diesel electric locomotive (b) *Fig* (*élément moteur*) motive force; (*leader*) pacemaker, pacesetter; (*en politique*) dynamic *or* forceful leader

locus [lɔkys] *nm Biol* locus

locuteur, -trice [lɔkytœr, -tris] *n Ling* speaker; **l. natif** native speaker

locution [lɔkysjɔ̃] *nf* (*expression*) expression, phrase, locution; **l. figée** set phrase *or* expression; **l. vicieuse** incorrect expression; *Gram* **l. adverbiale** adverbial phrase; **l. conjonctive** complex conjunction

loden [lɔdɛn] *nm Tex* loden; (*manteau*) loden coat

lœss [løs] *nm Géol* loess

lof [lɔf] *nm Naut* windward side; **venir** *ou* **aller au l.** to sail into the wind, to luff; **virer l. pour l.** to wear

lofer [lɔfe] *vi Naut* to luff

loft [lɔft] *nm* converted warehouse/garage/*etc*

logarithme [lɔgaritm] *Math* **1** *nm* logarithm, log; **table de logarithmes** log(arithm) table **2** *adj* **fonction l.** logarithmic function

logarithmique [lɔgaritmik] *adj Math* logarithmic

loge [lɔʒ] *nf* (a) (*d'artiste*) dressing room (b) (*de spectateur*) box; **première l.** first-tier box; *Fig* **être aux premières loges** to have a ringside seat (c) (*de franc-maçon, de concierge*) lodge (d) *Beaux-Arts, Mus* individual exam room (*for the Prix de Rome*) (e) *Archit* loggia (f) *Bot* cell

logeable [lɔʒabl] *adj* (*habitable*) habitable, fit for occupation

logement [lɔʒmɑ̃] *nm* (a) (*habitation*) accommodation, *Am* accommodations; (*maison*) house; (*appartement*) flat, *Am* apartment; **chercher un l.** to look for somewhere to live, to look for accommodation; **l. garni** *ou* **meublé** furnished rooms *or* flat *or Am* apartment; **l. collectif** block of flats, *Am* apartment block; **l. à demeure** live-in accommodation (b) (*action*) (*de gens*) housing; (*de troupes*) quartering; (*dans maison privée*) billeting; (*de chevaux*) stabling; **crise du l.** housing shortage (c) *Mil* (*local*) quarters; (*dans maison privée*) billet (d) (*de pièce de machine*) seating; (*de manche*) housing

loger [lɔʒe] **(je logeai(s); n. logeons)** **1** *vi* to live; (*de troupes*) to be quartered; (*dans maison privée*) to be billeted; **l. à l'hôtel** to stay *or* put up at *or* in a hotel; *Mil* **l. chez l'habitant** to be billeted in private houses; **je compte l. chez l'habitant pendant les vacances** I'm intending to stay in a private house when I go on holiday; **être logé et nourri** to have board and lodging *or* bed and board

2 *vt* (a) (*héberger*) (*étudiants, touristes etc*) to accommodate; (*troupes*) to quarter; (*dans maison privée*) to billet; (*chevaux*) to stable; **l. un ami pour la nuit** to put a friend up for the night; **l'auberge de jeunesse peut l. jusqu'à 200 personnes** the youth hostel can accommodate up to 200 people; **crois-tu qu'on arrivera à l. tous les invités dans la salle à manger?** do you think we'll manage to accommodate all the guests in the dining room?

(b) (*placer*) to put; **l. une balle dans qch** to put *or* lodge a bullet in sth; **j'ai réussi à l. ton sac entre les deux valises** I managed to put your bag between the two cases; **il faudra bien l. toutes nos affaires dans ce placard** we'll have to put all our belongings in that cupboard

3 se loger *vpr* (a) (*pour s'installer*) to find accommodation, to find somewhere to live; (*pour la nuit*) to find accommodation, to find somewhere to stay; **nous avons trouvé à nous l.**

we've found accommodation, we've found somewhere to live/stay

(b) (*se placer*) **mon ballon est allé se l. entre l'antenne de télé et la cheminée** my ball got stuck *or* lodged itself between the television aerial and the chimney; **où a-t-il bien pu aller se l.?** where has it got to?; **la balle se logea dans le mur** the bullet embedded itself in the wall; **la poignée repliée se loge dans un creux spécialement prévu à cet effet** the folded handle fits into a hollow specially designed for the purpose; **la jalousie s'est logée dans son cœur** jealousy filled his heart; **la souris s'est logée sous le lit** the mouse went and hid under the bed; **on a réussi à tous se l. dans son canapé** we all managed to fit *or* squeeze on to his sofa

logeur [lɔʒœr] *nm* landlord (*of furnished apartments*)

logeuse [lɔʒøz] *nf* landlady (*of furnished apartments*)

loggia [lɔdʒja] *nf Archit* loggia

logiciel [lɔʒisjɛl] *nm Ordinat* software; **un l.** a software package, a package; (*programme*) a piece of software, a computer program; **un l. très utile** a very useful software package; **l. d'application** application software; **l. bureautique** business software (package); **l. de communication** communications package, comms package, communications software; **l. de compression de données** data compression software; **l. de comptabilité** accounts package, accounts software; **l. contributif** shareware; **l. à contribution volontaire** shareware; **l. de décompression** decompression software, decompressor; **l. de dessin** art package, drawing program; **l. d'exploitation** operating system software; **l. grapheur** graphics package, graphics software; **l. de groupe** groupware; **l. de jeu** games software; **l. ludique** games software; **l. de mise en page** desktop publishing package; **l. monoposte** single-user software package; **l. multi-utilisateur** multi-user software; **l. de présentation** presentation software; **l. public** freeware; **l. de reconnaissance de caractères** OCR software, character recognition software; **l. de reconnaissance vocale** voice recognition software; **l. de récupération** recovery program; **l. de réseau** network software; **l. de SGBD** DBMS software; **l. système** system software; **l. de télémaintenance** remote access software; (*pour base de données*) server software; **logiciels de traitement de texte** word-processing software, word-processing software packages, WP packages; **l. utilisateur** user software

logicien, -ienne [lɔʒisjɛ̃, -jɛn] *n* logician

logique [lɔʒik] **1** *adj* (**a**) (*cohérent*) (*raisonnement, déduction, esprit etc*) logical; **voyons, soyons logiques** come on, let's be logical about this; **il est tout à fait l. que tu n'aies pas envie de le revoir** it's quite natural that you don't want to see him again; **c'est l.** it stands to reason, it's only natural; **je trouve ça l.** it sounds logical to me; **tu n'es pas l.!** you're being illogical!; **il faut être l. avec soi-même** you have to be logical; **le candidat doit avoir l'esprit l.** the candidate must have a logical mind

(**b**) (*analytique*) logical, methodical; *Ordinat* **analyseur l.** logic analyser; *Gram* **analyse l.** (*de phrase*) analysis

2 *nf* (**a**) *Phil, Math* logic; **faire de la l.** to do logic; **l. formelle/pure** formal/pure logic

(**b**) (*cohérence, raisonnement*) logic; **la l. de la passion/de la folie** the logic of passion/madness; **la l. des enfants** children's logic, the way children's minds work; **nous sommes entrés dans une l. de guerre** war is inevitable, war is the next logical step; **en toute l., voilà ce qui devrait se passer** logically, that's what ought to happen; **c'est dans la l. des choses que les enfants ne vivent pas éternellement chez leurs parents** it's logical *or* natural that children shouldn't live with their parents for ever; **ça manque de l.** there's no logic in it, it's illogical; **là, vous manquez de l.** you're not being very logical

▶ **logique**: *Ordinat* **l. câblée** wired logic; **l. floue** fuzzy logic

logiquement [lɔʒikmɑ̃] *adv* (*rationnellement*) logically; (*normalement*) all going well, all things being equal; **l., il devrait déjà être là** he should already be here, there's no reason why he shouldn't already be there

logis [lɔʒi] *nm Vieilli, Litt* (*maison*) home, dwelling, abode; **trouver un l.** to find accommodation

logistique [lɔʒistik] **1** *adj* logistic; **soutien l.** logistic(al) support **2** *nf Mil etc* logistics

logo [logo] *nm* (*abrév* **logotype**) logo; *Rad etc* **l. audio/sonde** audio/sound logo; *Journ* **l. de page** page logo

logomachie [lɔgɔmaʃi] *nf* logomachy; (*assemblage de mots, vide de sens*) verbiage, verbosity; **une l.** a lot of verbiage

logorrhée [lɔgɔre] *nf Psy* logorrhea; *Hum* verbal diarrhoea; *Hum* **j'ai tendance à la l.** I tend to witter on

loi [lwa] *nf* (**a**) *Jur* **la l.** (*le droit*) the law; **tomber sous le coup de la l.** to come under the law; **avoir la l. pour soi** to have the law on one's side; **je suis désolé mais c'est la l.** I'm sorry but that's the law *or* the law's the law; **respecter la l.** to respect *or* obey the law; **nul n'est censé ignorer la l.** ignorance is no defence in (a court of) law; **homme de l.** lawyer, legal practitioner

(**b**) (*prescription de l'État*) **une l.** a law, an act (of Parliament); **projet de l., proposition de l.** bill; **la l. anti-tabac n'est pas très respectée** not many people respect *or* abide by the anti-smoking laws; **l. fiscale** tax law, fiscal law; **l. bancaire** banking law

(**c**) (*autorité individuelle*) law; **faire la** *ou* **sa l.** to lay down the law; **dicter sa l.** to lay down the law, to impose one's will; **faire la l. chez qn** to lay down the law *or* dictate to sb; **c'est lui qui fait la l.** he's the master *or F* the boss; **la l. du plus fort** might is right; **dans la cour de récréation c'est la l. du plus fort** it's the law of the jungle in the playground; *Litt* **ce qu'il dit fait l.** his word is law; **nécessité fait l.** needs must when the devil drives; *Litt* **se faire une l. de faire qch** to make a rule *or* a point of doing sth; *Litt* **subir la l. de qn** to be ruled by sb, to be under sb's thumb

(**d**) (*règle qui s'impose*) law; **l. de la nature** law of nature; **l. de la jungle** law of the jungle; **les lois économiques** the laws of economics; **l. phonétique** law of phonetics; **l. de l'offre et de la demande** law of supply and demand; **lois de l'esthétique** rules of aesthetics; **lois de la mode** dictates of fashion; **les lois de la politesse/de l'honneur** the rules of etiquette/the code of honour

(**e**) *Phys, Math* law

(**f**) *Rel* **la l. divine** divine law, the law of God; *Fig* **c'est la l. et les prophètes** its/his/*etc* word is law

▶ **loi**: *Pol, Jur* **l. d'amnistie** amnesty law; *Pol, Jur* **l. de finances** Finance Act; *Pol, Jur* **l. d'habilitation** enabling act; **L. Informatique et Libertés** Data Protection Act; **l. naturelle** natural law; **l. sur les sociétés anonymes** public company law; **la l. du talion** an eye for an eye (and a tooth for a tooth)

loi-cadre, *pl* **lois-cadres** *nf* outline law

loin [lwɛ̃] **1** [ⓘA19,g,i] *adv* (**a**) (*dans l'espace ou le temps*) far (**de** from); **c'est encore l. le théâtre/Annecy?** is it far to the theatre/Annecy?; **est-ce l. d'ici?** is it far from here?; **ce n'est pas l.** it's not far; **la poste est l.** the post office is a long way off, it's a long way to the post office; **plus l.** farther *or* further (on); **moins l.** less far, not so far; **il y a l. d'ici à Paris** it's a long way to Paris; **l. de moi la prétention de vous apprendre quelque chose** far be it from me to tell you what to do; *Fig aussi Iron* **l. de moi cette idée!** I wouldn't dream of it!, the thought never entered my head!; **l. de moi l'idée d'insinuer que …** far be it from me to insinuate that …, I wouldn't dream of insinuating that …; **le prisonnier s'est échappé mais il n'est pas allé très l.** the prisoner escaped but he didn't get very far; **la voiture est vieille, elle n'ira pas l.** the car is old and on its last legs; *Fig* **ce jeune homme ira l.** this young man will go far; *Fig* **tu n'iras pas l. avec des théories pareilles!** you won't get very far with theories like that!; *Fig* **on pourrait même aller plus l. et dire que …** you could even go further and say that …; *Fig* **ça va (très) l. ce que vous dites** that's taking things a bit far; *Fig* **vous allez trop l.** you're going too far; **ça peut aller très l.** you don't realize what you're getting into; **si je m'en mêle ça peut aller très l.** if I decide to do something about it they'd better watch out; **voir l.** to be far-sighted; *Fig* to be far-sighted *or* shrewd; **voir plus l.** (*dans un texte*) see below/see following pages; *Fig* to look further ahead, to look to the future; **l. derrière lui** far *or* way behind him; *Fig* **laisser ses souvenirs l. derrière soi** to leave one's memories far behind; **j'étais l. de la vérité, ça m'a coûté £300!** I was way out (in my calculations), it cost me £300!; *Prov* **l. des yeux, l. du cœur** out of sight, out of mind; *Fig* **de là à l'accuser de mensonge il n'y a pas l.** that's not far from *or* it's close to calling him a liar; **il ne voit pas plus l. que le bout de son nez** he can't see any further than the end of his nose, he can't see beyond the end of his nose; *Prov* **il y a l. de la coupe aux lèvres** there's many a slip 'twixt the cup and the lip; **nous étions l. de penser/croire/d'imaginer que …** we never thought/believed/imagined for a moment that …; **je ne suis pas l. de penser que …** I've more or less come to the conclusion that …; **elle est l. d'être bête** she is far from stupid; **il est l. d'avoir compris** he still hasn't understood by a long chalk; **je suis encore l. d'avoir fini** I'm still far from finished; **ne pas être l. d'une découverte** to be on the brink of a discovery; **je ne suis pas fâché, l. de là!** I'm not angry, far from it *or* anything but!; **cette époque est bien l.** those days are long gone; **c'est l. tout ça** (*c'est du passé*) that all happened a long time ago; **ça remonte à l. maintenant** it happened a long time *or* years *or* ages ago; **leur brouille remonte à l.** their quarrel is of long standing, they quarrelled a long time ago; **comme c'est l., tout ça!** that all happened such a long time ago!, that's ancient history!; **ce jour est encore l.** that day is still a long way off *or Fml* is still distant; **c'est encore l. les vacances?** is it still a long time (to go) till the holidays?; **il ne devait pas être l. de midi** it must have been getting on for twelve (o'clock)

(b) (*dans locutions*) **je l'ai reconnu de l.** I recognized him from a distance *or* from a long way off; **admirer qn de l.** to admire sb at *or* from a distance *or* from afar; **ils sont parents, mais de l.** they are only distantly related; *Litt* **d'aussi l.** *ou* **du plus l. qu'il se souvienne** as far back *or* for as long as he can remember; *Fig* **de l.** (*de beaucoup*) by far; **il est de l. plus intelligent que moi** he is far more intelligent than I am; **c'est de l. son meilleur roman** it's by far his best novel; **l. de l'affoler** far from upsetting him; **de l. en l.** (*de temps en temps*) at long intervals, now and then

2 *nm* **au l.** in the distance; **apercevoir qn au l.** to see sb a long way off *or* a long way away *or* in the distance

lointain [lwɛ̃tɛ̃] **1** *adj* distant, far off, faraway; (*île*) remote; (*ressemblance*) vague; **mes souvenirs les plus lointains** my earliest recollections; **dans un avenir l.** in the distant future; **elle avait l'air l.** she looked as if she was miles away, she had a faraway look on her face; **elle écoutait la conversation, l'air l.** she was listening to the conversation with a faraway look on her face **2** *nm* distance; **dans le l.** in the distance; **regard plongé dans le l.** faraway look; *Beaux-Arts* **les lointains** the distances

loi-programme, *pl* **lois-programmes** *nf Fin Pol* = law providing framework for long-term government programme

loir [lwar] *nm* (*mammifère*) dormouse; **dormir comme un l.** to sleep like a log

loisible [lwazibl] *adj Litt* **il lui est l. de refuser** he is at liberty *or* entitled to refuse

loisir [lwazir] *nm* **(a)** (*temps libre*) leisure; **dans mes heures de l., pendant mes loisirs** in my spare time; **activités de loisir** leisure *or* spare-time activities; **avoir des loisirs** to have some spare time

(b) (*activité*) **le l., les loisirs** leisure *or* spare-time activities; **un professionnel du l.** *ou* **des loisirs** = specialist travel agency; **le ski/la lecture est mon l. préféré** skiing/reading is my favourite pastime; **société de loisirs** leisure society; **les loisirs sportifs** sporting activities

(c) (*possibilité, temps nécessaire*) opportunity; **je n'ai pas encore eu le l. de lui parler/de le lire** I haven't had a chance *or* (the) time to speak to him/to read it; *Litt* **donner** *ou* **laisser à qn le l. de faire qch** to give sb the opportunity to do sth, to allow sb to do sth; **on ne m'a pas laissé le l. de me reposer** I wasn't given the opportunity *or* any time to rest; **on ne m'a pas laissé le l. de donner mon avis** I wasn't given a chance *or* an opportunity to express my opinion; *Litt* **examiner qch à l.** to examine sth at one's leisure

lolo [lolo] *nm F* **(a)** *Enf* (*lait*) milk **(b)** (*sein*) booby

lombaire [lɔ̃bɛr] *Anat* **1** *adj* (*douleur, région, vertèbre*) lower back, *Spéc* lumbar; **ponction l.** lumbar puncture **2** *nf* lumbar

lombalgie [lɔ̃balʒi] *nf Méd* lower back pain

lombard, -arde [lɔ̃bar, -ard] **1** *adj* Lombard, of/from Lombardy; *Hist* **la ligue lombarde** the Lombard League **2** *nm Ling* Lombard dialect **3** *n* **L.** Lombard

Lombardie [lɔ̃bardi] *nf* Lombardy

lombes [lɔ̃b] *nfpl Anat* loins

lombric [lɔ̃brik] *nm* earthworm

londonien, -ienne [lɔ̃dɔnjɛ̃, -jɛn] **1** *adj* London **2** *n* **L.** Londoner

Londres [lɔ̃dr] *nm* London

londrès [lɔ̃drɛs] *nm* Havana cigar

long, longue [lɔ̃, lɔ̃g] **1** *adj* **(a)** (*dans l'espace*) long; **avoir un l. nez/de longues jambes** to have a long nose/long legs; **elle a les cheveux longs** she has long hair; **corde longue de 5 mètres** rope 5 metres long, 5-metre rope; **prendre le chemin le plus l.** to go the longest way (round); **un vieillard l. et maigre le regardait fixement** an old man, tall and slim, was staring at him; *Vieilli* **il est l. comme un jour sans pain** he's a real beanpole; **ce voyage/discours est l. comme un jour sans pain** this journey/speech seems to be lasting for ever *or* dragging on for ever; *Fig* **avoir le bras l.** to be able to pull strings, *F* to have pull; **phare longue portée** high-intensity light; **navigation au l. cours** deep-sea navigation

(b) (*dans le temps*) long; **les jours sont de plus en plus longs** the days are getting longer (and longer); **dix jours, c'est l.** ten days is a long time; **pendant de longues années** for many years; **discours un peu l.** rather long *or* somewhat lengthy speech; **c'est une longue histoire** it's a long story; **je trouve le temps l.** time seems to drag; **je trouve les jours longs** I find the days long, time seems to drag; **l. soupir** long-drawn *or* lengthy sigh; **un ami de longue date** an old friend, a friend of long standing; **projet à longue échéance** long-term project; **à l. terme** long-term; **longue durée** (*chômage*) long-term; (*pile*) long-life; (*cassette*) extended play; (*disque*) long-playing; **à plus ou moins longue échéance, à plus ou moins l. terme** sooner or later

(c) (*lent*) slow; **être l. à faire qch** to take a long time to do sth, to be slow to do sth; **qu'est-ce que tu es l.!** you're so slow!, you're taking forever!; **il est l. ce feu** these lights take forever to change; **être l. à réagir** to be slow to react; **j'ai été l. à comprendre** it took me a long time to understand; **je ne serai pas l.** I won't be long; **ce ne sera pas l.** it won't take long; **c'est un travail l. à faire** it's slow work, this work takes a long time; **il s'en sortira, mais ce sera l.** he'll recover but it'll take a long time *or* it will be a slow process

(d) *Ling* **une voyelle longue** a long vowel; **'a' l.** long 'a'

(e) *Culin* **sauce longue** thin sauce

2 *nm* **(a)** (*dans l'espace*) length; **table qui a 2 mètres de l.** table 2 metres long *or* in length; **le l. de** along; **se faufiler/grimper le l. du mur** to creep along/to climb up the wall; **tout le l. du rivage** all along the shore; **en l.** (*couper, fendre*) lengthwise; **de l. en large** up and down, to and fro; **il arpentait la pièce de l. en large** he paced up and down the room; *F* **expliquer qch en l. et en large** *ou* **en l. en large et en travers** to explain sth in great detail *or* at great length; **étendu de tout son l.** stretched out (at) full length; **tomber de tout son l.** to fall flat on one's face

(b) (*dans le temps*) **tout le l. du jour/de la nuit** all day/night long, throughout the day/night; **tout au** *ou* **du l. de l'entretien** throughout *or* all through the conversation

3 *adv* **(a)** (*beaucoup*) **je crois qu'il est inutile que j'en dise plus l.** need I say more?; **regard qui en dit l.** meaningful *or* eloquent look, look that speaks volumes; **cette action en dit l. sur ...** this action speaks volumes for ...; **en savoir l. /plus l. /trop l.** to know a lot/more/too much; **j'en sais l. /je pourrais en dire l. sur cette affaire** I know/I could say quite a lot about this business

(b) **s'habiller l.** to wear long clothes

4 *nf* **longue (a)** *Ling* long syllable

(b) **à la longue** in time, in the end, eventually

(c) *Mus* long note

(d) *Cartes* **longue à pic/trèfles** long suit of spades/clubs

longanime [lɔ̃ganim] *adj Litt* forbearing

longanimité [lɔ̃ganimite] *nf Litt* forbearance

long-courrier, *pl* **long-courriers** **1** *adj* (*navire*) ocean-going; (*avion*) long-haul, long-range **2** *nm Naut* ocean-going ship, ocean-goer, ocean liner; *Av* long-haul *or* long-range aircraft

longe[1] [lɔ̃ʒ] *nf* (*pour mener le cheval*) leading rein, halter; (*pour l'attacher*) tether; (*pour le dresser*) lunge, longe

longe[2] *nf Culin* (*de veau, porc*) loin

longer [lɔ̃ʒe] *vt* **(je longeai(s); n. longeons)** **(a)** (*suivre*) (*de personne, voiture*) (*route, rivière*) to follow, to go along; (*mur, côte*) to follow, to hug **(b)** (*s'étendre le long de*) (*de sentier, canal, voie ferrée*) to follow, to run alongside, to border; **la route longe un bois/la côte/la rivière** the road skirts a wood/follows *or* hugs the coastline/follows the river

longeron [lɔ̃ʒrɔ̃] *nm* **(a)** *Constr* (*de pont de chemin de fer*) stringer, longitudinal girder; (*maîtresse poutre*) beam, member **(b)** *Aut* (*de châssis*) side member, side sill **(c)** *Av* (*sur fuselage*) longeron; (*d'aile*) spar

longévité [lɔ̃ʒevite] *nf* (*durée de vie*) longevity; (*longue vie*) long life; (*de produit*) life; **table de l. d'une population** life-expectancy table of a population

longiligne [lɔ̃ʒiliɲ] *adj* willowy

longitude [lɔ̃ʒityd] *nf Géog* longitude; **par 10° de l. ouest** at 10° longitude west

longitudinal, -ale, -aux, -ales [lɔ̃ʒitydinal, -o] *adj* longitudinal, lengthwise

longitudinalement [lɔ̃ʒitydinalmɑ̃] *adv* longitudinally, lengthwise, lengthways

longrine [lɔ̃grin] *nf* **(a)** *Constr* longitudinal beam *or* girder *or* member **(b)** *Rail* longitudinal sleeper

longtemps [lɔ̃tɑ̃] *adv* **(a)** (*pendant un long moment*) a long time; **attendre l.** to wait (for) a long time; **ça fait l. que tu attends?** have you been waiting long?; *Iron* **tu peux attendre l.** you'll have a long wait; **cela ne pouvait pas durer l.** it couldn't last (for) long; **est-ce que ça va durer l.?** will it take long?; **ça va durer encore l. ce vacarme?** is this racket going to go on for much longer?; **ça ne va plus durer l. maintenant** it won't be long now; **rester trop l.** to stay too long

(b) (*long espace de temps*) **il y a l.** long ago, a long time ago; **il n'y a pas l.** not long ago; **il y a l. qu'il est mort** he has been dead (for) a long time *or F* for ages; **il y a l. que je ne l'ai vu** it's a long time *or F* ages since I saw him; **pendant l.** for a long time; **(pendant) l. j'ai cru qu'elle reviendrait** I believed for a long time that she would come back; **mettre l. à faire qch** to take a long time *or F* ages to do sth; **je n'en ai pas pour l.** I shan't be long, it won't take me long; **tu en as encore pour l.?** are you going to be much longer?; **il n'en a plus pour l.** he hasn't much longer (to live); **cela existe depuis l.** it has existed for a long time *or F* for ages; **l. avant/après** long before/after; **avant l.** before long; **cela ne se fera pas avant l.** it won't happen for a long time (to come); **je ne pensais pas vous revoir avant** *ou* **de l.** I didn't expect to see you again for a long time

longuement [lɔ̃gmɑ̃] *adv (pendant longtemps) (attendre, réfléchir, s'attarder)* for a long time; *(parler)* for a long time, at great length; *(expliquer)* at great length, lengthily; **il la regarda l.** he gazed earnestly at her; **parler l. avec qn** to have a (good) long talk with sb; **il a l. insisté pour que je vienne** he kept on insisting *or* was extremely insistent that I should come; **il faudrait analyser plus l. les personnages** the characters must be analysed in greater detail

longuet, -ette [lɔ̃gɛ, -ɛt] **1** *adj F (livre, discours, spectacle, attente)* rather long, longish; **c'est un peu l.** it's a bit long **2** *nm Région* bread stick

longueur [lɔ̃gœr] *nf* **(a)** *(dimension)* length; **l. totale, l. hors tout** length over all, overall length; **mesures de l.** linear measures; **unité de l.** unit of length; **jardin de cent mètres de l.** *ou* **d'une l. de cent mètres** garden a hundred metres long; **couper/scier qch en l.** *ou* **dans le sens de la l.** to cut/saw sth lengthwise; *Sp* **mener/gagner d'une l.** to lead/win by a length; **le cheval A prend une l. d'avance sur le cheval B** horse A is now one length ahead of horse B; *Fig* **la ville de Grenoble avait une l. d'avance sur les autres pour la prévention du sida** Grenoble had a clear lead over other cities as regards preventive measures against Aids; *Fig* **cette entreprise a plusieurs longueurs d'avance** this company has a good lead *or* is way ahead; *Péj* **traîner en l.** *(de discours, repas etc)* to drag (on), to drag on for ever; **faire traîner qch en l.** to drag sth out; *Typ* **l. de ligne** line width; *Typ* **l. de page** page length

(b) *(état de ce qui est long)* **son discours/le film était d'une l.!** his speech/the film was incredibly long *or* dragged on for ever; **d'une l. incroyable/excessive** incredibly/excessively long

(c) *Péj* **à l. de journée/de semaine/d'année** all day/week/year long; **je n'entends que ça à l. de journées** that's all I hear day after day

(d) *Péj (développement trop long)* **roman plein de longueurs** novel full of long drawn-out passages

(e) *(en nageant)* length; **faire des longueurs** to do lengths

▶ **longueur**: *Rad, Fig* **l. d'ondes** wavelength; *Fig* **nous ne sommes pas sur la même l. d'ondes** we're not on the same wavelength

longue-vue, *pl* **longues-vues** [lɔ̃gvy] *nf* telescope, field glass

look [luk] *nm F* look; **soigner son l.** to cultivate one's image; **changer de l.** to change one's look *or* image; *très F* **il a un l. d'enfer** he looks out of this world

looping [lupiŋ] *nm Av* loop; **faire un l. /des loopings** to loop the loop

lopin [lɔpɛ̃] *nm* **l. de terre** piece *or* patch *or* plot of ground

loquace [lɔkas] *adj* talkative, *Fml* loquacious

loquacité [lɔkasite] *nf* talkativeness, *Fml* loquacity; **elle a retrouvé sa l. d'antan** she's her old talkative self again

loque [lɔk] *nf* **(a)** rag; **être en loques** to be in rags *or* in tatters; **ses vêtements tombent en loques** his clothes are falling to pieces **(b)** *Fig (personne)* **l. (humaine)** wreck; **l'alcool a fait de lui une l.** alcohol has turned him into a human wreck

loquet [lɔkɛ] *nm (de porte)* latch; *Arch* **fermer la porte au l., pousser le l.** to put the latch on the door, to latch the door

loqueteau, -eaux [lɔkto] *nm (pour volet)* small latch, catch

loqueteux, -euse [lɔktø, -øz] **1** *adj (personne)* in rags, in tatters; *(vêtements)* ragged, tattered; **un vieillard l.** an old man (dressed) in rags, a ragged old man **2** *n* ragamuffin

lord [lɔr(d)] *nm* lord; **la Chambre des lords** the House of Lords

lord-maire, *pl* **lords-maires** *nm (de Londres etc)* Lord Mayor

lordose [lɔrdoz] *nf Méd* hollow-back, *Spéc* lordosis

lorgner [lɔrɲe] *vt* **(a)** *(regarder indiscrètement) (personne, décolleté)* to eye; **l. une femme** to eye up *or* ogle a woman; **l. qch/qn du coin de l'œil** to keep eyeing sth/sb, to cast a sidelong glance at sth/sb **(b)** *(convoiter) (héritage, poste etc)* to have one's eye on

lorgnette [lɔrɲɛt] *nf* (pair of) opera glasses; *Fig* **regarder/voir qch par le petit bout de la l.** take a narrow-minded *or* blinkered view of things

lorgnon [lɔrɲɔ̃] *nm (avec une tige)* lorgnette; *(avec ressort)* pince-nez

loriot [lɔrjo] *nm* **l. (jaune)** (golden) oriole

lorrain, -aine [lɔrɛ̃, -ɛn] **1** *adj* from/of Lorraine **2** *nm Ling* Lorraine dialect **3** *n* **L.** *(habitant)* inhabitant of Lorraine; *(natif)* native of Lorraine **4** *nf* **la Lorraine** Lorraine

lorry [lɔri] *nm Rail* (platelayer's) trolley, pushcar

lors [lɔr] *adv* **(a)** *Litt* **depuis l.** from that time, ever since then; **dès l.** *(à partir de ce moment-là)* from that moment on; **dès l. que tu refuses, tu es mis à la porte** should you *or* if you should happen to refuse, you're dismissed; **l. même qu'il souffre, il ne le dit pas** even though he is in pain, he says nothing; **espérez l. même qu'il n'y a plus d'espoir** you must hope against hope **(b) l. de** *(pendant)* during; **l. de mon séjour à Hawaï** during my stay in Hawaii, while I was in Hawaii; **l. de mon accident** at the time of my accident

lorsque [lɔrsk(ə)] *conj* [①**B29-30**] *(becomes* **lorsqu'** *before* **il(s), elle(s), on, en, un(e)**) when

losange [lɔzɑ̃ʒ] *nm* **(a)** *(forme)* diamond; *Géom* rhomb(us) **(b)** *Hér* lozenge

losangé [lɔzɑ̃ʒe] *adj (boucle d'oreille etc)* diamond-shaped; *(frise)* with a diamond pattern; *Hér* lozengy

loser [luzœr] *nm F* loser

lot [lo] *nm* **(a)** *(à une loterie)* prize; **gros l.** first prize, jackpot; *Fig F* **en l'épousant, tu as gagné le gros l.** by marrying him you've hit the jackpot; **l. de consolation** consolation prize; *Fin* **emprunt à lots** lottery loan

(b) *(articles vendus ensemble) (de marchandises etc)* batch; *(de serviettes, casseroles)* set; *(de chaussettes, collants, savonnettes etc)* pack; *(aux enchères)* lot; **vendus par lots** *(casseroles, serviettes)* sold in sets; *(chaussettes, collants)* sold in packs; *Fig* **dans le l. il y en aura au moins un de bon** *(choses, personnes)* at least one out of this lot *or* batch should be some good; *Fig* **se détacher** *ou* **être au dessus du l.** to stand out from the crowd

(c) *(dans un partage)* share; **diviser un terrain en lots** to divide a piece of land into plots, to parcel up a piece of land

(d) *Litt (sort)* lot, fate; **la souffrance est son l.** suffering is his lot; **son l. est d'être toujours seul** he is destined to remain alone all his life; **chacun son l.** we all have our cross to bear

(e) *Ordinat* **traitement par lots** batch processing

loterie [lɔtri] *nf* lottery; **l. nationale** national lottery; **gagner à la l.** to win the lottery; *Fig* **c'est une l.** it's a lottery *or* matter of chance, it's the luck of the draw

lotion [losjɔ̃] *nf* lotion; **l. tonique** toning lotion, toner; **l. capillaire** hair lotion; **l. après-rasage** after-shave (lotion)

lotionner [losjɔne] *vt (épiderme, cuir chevelu)* to apply lotion to

lotir [lɔtir] *vt* **(a)** *(diviser en lots) (terrain)* to divide into plots; *(immeubles)* to divide into lots; **terrains à l.** development site, building land **(b)** *(donner)* **l. qn de qch** to allot sth to sb; *Fig* **être bien/mal loti** to be well/badly off

lotissement [lɔtismɑ̃] *nm* **(a)** *(résidence)* housing estate *or* development **(b)** *(mise en lots) (de terrain)* parcelling out; *(de marchandises etc)* dividing into lots

loto [lɔto] *nm* **(a)** *(jeu de hasard)* lotto; **un (jeu de) l.** *(matériel)* a lotto set; *Fig* **il me regarda avec des yeux en boules de l.** he looked at me with eyes like saucers **(b)** *(jeu national)* national lottery; **il joue au l. tous les mercredis** he buys a lottery ticket *or* takes part in *or* enters the national lottery every Wednesday; **le l., c'est facile, c'est pas cher et ça peut rapporter gros!** ≈ it could be you!

lotte [lɔt] *nf (poisson)* burbot; *(de mer)* monkfish, anglerfish

lotus [lɔtys] *nm* **(a)** *(plante)* lotus; **l. sacré** Indian lotus **(b)** *(arbre)* lotus tree **(c)** *Myth* Lotus

louable[1] [lwabl] *adj (acte, courage)* laudable, praiseworthy, commendable; *(intentions, efforts)* laudable; **c'est tout à fait l. de ta part** it is highly laudable of you, it is highly commendable on your part

louable[2] *adj (appartement, magasin etc)* rentable; **appartement difficilement l.** apartment that is difficult to rent

louage [lwaʒ] *nm* **contrat de l.** rental agreement *or* contract; **l. de services** contract of employment; **voiture de l.** hired carriage

louange [lwɑ̃ʒ] *nf (éloge)* praise; **digne de louange(s)** *(personne)* praiseworthy; *(action)* praiseworthy, commendable; **chanter les louanges de qn** to sing sb's praises; **couvrir qn de louanges** to shower sb with praise, to heap praise on sb; **faire un discours à la l. de qn** to make a speech in praise of sb; **c'est tout à sa l.** *(à son honneur)* it's to his credit, it's very commendable of him

louanger [lwɑ̃ʒe] *vt Litt* to sing the praises of

louangeur, -euse [lwɑ̃ʒœr, -øz] *adj Litt (poème, paroles)* laudatory

loubar(d), -arde [lubar, -ard] *n F* yob(bo), lout, *surtout Am* hoodlum

louche[1] [luʃ] **1** *adj* **(a)** *(conduite, caractère, personne)* shady, suspicious, shifty; *(situation)* dubious; *(quartier, bar)* sleazy; *(passé)* shady; **c'est l.** there's something suspicious *or F* fishy about it; **il n'y a rien de l. là-dedans** it's all fair and above board, *F* there's nothing fishy about it **(b)** *(lumière, éclairage)* murky **2** *nm* **il y a du l. dans cette affaire** this business is a bit shady *or F* fishy

louche[2] *nf* (soup) ladle

loucher [luʃe] *vi* to squint; *(être atteint de strabisme)* to be cross-eyed, to have a squint; **l. de l'œil gauche** to have a squint in the left eye; *F* **l. vers** *ou* **sur qch** to eye *or* ogle sth; *Fig F* **l. sur l'héritage** to have one's eye on the inheritance

loucherie [luʃri] *nf* squint(ing)

loucheur, -euse [luʃœr, -øz] *n* cross-eyed *or* squint-eyed person

louer[1] [lwe] **1** *vt* **(a)** *(donner en location) (chambre, maison etc)* to rent (out), *Br* to let (out); *(équipement, véhicule, costume etc)* to rent (out), *Br* to hire (out) **(à** to); **maison à l.** house *Br* to let *or* for rent; **l. une ferme à bail** to lease out a farm

(b) *(prendre en location) (chambre, maison etc)* to rent **(à** from); *(voiture, équipement, costume etc)* to rent, *Br* to hire; *(place de théâtre etc)* to reserve, to book; **l. une maison pour l'été** to take *or* rent a house for the summer

2 se louer *vpr* **(a)** *(être à louer) (de maison, chambre etc)* to be for rent, *Br* to be to let; *(d'équipement)* to be for rent *or Br* for hire; **cet appartement se loue très cher** this flat is very expensive to rent

(b) *Arch (d'ouvrier agricole)* to hire oneself out

louer[2] **1** *vt (qn, courage de qn)* to praise; *(officiellement)* to commend; **il n'a pas cessé de l. tes qualités** he has had nothing but praise for your qualities; **l. qn de** *ou* **pour qch** to praise sb for sth; **louons le seigneur!** praise the Lord!; **Dieu soit loué!** thank God!; **loués soient les philanthropes qui ...** praise be to the philanthropists who ...

2 se louer *vpr* **se l. de qch** to be pleased *or* well satisfied with sth; **je me loue chaque jour de notre collaboration** not a day goes by without my realizing the value of our collaboration; **je n'ai qu'à me louer de lui/de ses services** I have nothing but praise for him/for his services; **je n'ai qu'à me l. de mon choix** I must congratulate myself on my choice; **se l. d'avoir fait qch** to congratulate oneself on having done sth

loueur, -euse [lwœr, -øz] *n Jur* lessor; **l. de bateaux/chevaux/costumes** person who rents (out) *or Br* hires (out) boats/horses/costumes

loufiat [lufja] *nm Arg Vieilli (dans un café)* waiter

loufoque [lufɔk] *F* **1** *adj* loony, barmy, w(h)acky **2** *n* crackpot, nut, *Am* screwball

loufoquerie [lufɔkri] *nf F* **(a)** *(absurdité)* craziness, barminess **(b)** *(acte)* crazy act; **loufoqueries** crazy behaviour

lougre [lugr] *nm Naut* lugger

louis [lwi] *nm Hist* **l. (d'or)** louis (d'or)

Louisiane [lwizjan] *nf* Louisiana

loukoum [lukum] *nm* **(rahat-)l.** Turkish delight; **j'ai mangé quatre loukoums** I've eaten four pieces of Turkish delight

loulou, -oute [lulu, -ut] **1** *n* **(a)** *F (chéri, chérie)* dear, darling **(b)** *F (voyou)* lout, yob(bo), *Am* hoodlum **2** *nm (chien)* spitz; **l. de Poméranie** Pomeranian (dog), *F* pom

loup [lu] *nm* **(a)** [①A12,1,d] wolf **une meute de loups** a pack of wolves; **à pas de l.** stealthily; **marcher à pas de l.** to creep along, to steal along, to walk stealthily; *Fig* **avoir une faim de l.** to be absolutely starving, to be ravenous; *Fig* **il fait un froid de l.** it's freezing (cold), it's bitterly cold; *Fig* **faire entrer le l. dans la bergerie** to set the fox to mind the geese; *Fig F* **se jeter dans la gueule du l.** to throw oneself into the lion's mouth; *Fig* **il est connu comme le l. blanc** everybody knows him; *Prov* **quand on parle du l. on en voit la queue** talk of the devil; *Fig* **avoir vu le l.** to have lost one's virginity; *Fig* **l'homme est un l. pour l'homme** it's dog eat dog in this world; *Prov* **les loups ne se mangent pas entre eux** there is honour among thieves; *Fig* **jeune l.** young go-getter; *(en politique)* Young Turk; *Fig F* **mon petit l., mon gros l.** *(terme d'affection)* (my) darling, (my) pet

(b) *(poisson)* sea perch, sea dace

(c) *Tech (dans le bois etc)* flaw; *Ind* defect

(d) *(demi-masque)* eye mask, domino

loup-cervier, *pl* **loups-cerviers** [lusɛrvje] *nm* lynx

loup de mer [ludmɛr] *nm (poisson)* sea perch, sea dace; *Fig F (marin)* old salt, seadog; *(tricot rayé)* striped tee-shirt

loupe [lup] *nf* **(a)** *Opt* magnifying glass; **regarder qch à la l.** to look at sth through *or* with a magnifying glass; *Fig* to put sth under a *or* the microscope; **étudions-en tous les aspects à la l.** let's look at it very closely from every angle **(b)** *Méd* wen **(c)** *(sur arbre)* burr, burl; **un meuble en l. de noyer** a piece of furniture made of burr walnut

louper [lupe] *F* **1** *vi* **tu n'as pas voulu m'écouter et ça n'a pas loupé, tu t'es coupé** you wouldn't listen to me and sure enough you've cut yourself; **je lui ai dit qu'il attraperait froid et ça n'a pas loupé** I told him he would catch cold and sure enough he did; **si tu continues comme ça tu vas tout faire l.** if you carry on like that you'll mess everything up *or* make a mess of everything

2 *vt* **(a)** *(ne pas réussir) (travail, discours, tarte etc)* to botch, to bungle, to make a botch *or* a mess of; *(examen)* to fail, *Am* to flunk; *Th* **l. son entrée** to fluff one's entrance; **loupé!** missed!; **la soirée est loupée** the party's a flop; **la fin du film est complètement loupée** the end of the film is completely botched *or* bungled

(b) *(ne pas prendre) (son tour, occasion, train)* to miss; **il n'en loupe pas une!** it's one stupid thing after another!; *(en parlant)* he's always opening his big mouth!; *F* **je ne vais pas le l.** I won't let him get away with it

3 se louper *vpr* **il a déjà fait plusieurs tentatives de suicide et cette fois-ci, il ne s'est pas loupé** he's made several suicide attempts in the past and this time he didn't bungle it; **tu as vu son maquillage? – elle ne s'est pas loupée!** have you seen her make-up? – she's put it on with a trowel

loup-garou, *pl* **loups-garous** [lugaru] *nm* **(a)** *Myth* werewolf **(b)** *(pour les enfants)* = bogeyman; **si tu ne manges pas ta soupe, attention au l.!** if you don't eat your soup, the bogeyman will get you!

loupiot [lupjo] *nm F (enfant)* kid

loupiote [lupjɔt] *nf F (lampe)* small light *or* lamp

lourd, lourde [lur, lurd] **1** *adj* **(a)** *(objet, chargement, nourriture, repas etc)* heavy; *(sommeil)* heavy, deep; **démarche lourde** heavy gait; **artillerie/industrie lourde** heavy artillery/industry; **sol l.** heavy soil; **le terrain est l. aujourd'hui** *Sp* the ground *or Horseracing* the going is heavy *or* soft today; **marcher/quitter la pièce d'un pas l.** to walk/leave the room with a heavy tread *or* step; **yeux lourds de fatigue** eyes heavy with tiredness; **avoir le sommeil l.** to be a heavy *or* deep sleeper; **j'ai la tête lourde** I've got a thick head, my head feels fuzzy; **avoir l'estomac l.** to feel bloated; **c'est l. à digérer** it's difficult to digest, it's heavy on the stomach; **avoir le cœur l.** to feel very sad, *Litt* to have a heavy heart; **avoir la main lourde** *(punir)* to mete out punishment with a heavy hand; *(verser en quantité généreuse)* to be overgenerous; **ce travail est trop l. pour elle** this work is too much for her

(b) *(à l'aspect pesant) (personne)* heavily-built; *(forme, silhouette, tentures etc)* heavy; **un visage aux traits lourds** a face with heavy features

(c) *(qui manque de subtilité) (personne, comique, scène)* unsubtle, heavy-handed; *(plaisanterie)* unsubtle, obvious, clumsy; *(mouvement, style)* heavy, ponderous; **un gros garçon pataud aux mouvements lourds** a big fat lumbering oaf; **avoir l'esprit l.** to be slow(-witted) *or* dull-witted

(d) *(sérieux, grave) (erreur)* serious, grave; *(perte)* heavy, severe, serious; *(dépenses, charges)* heavy; *(tâche, responsabilité)* heavy, weighty; **une lourde hérédité** a history of mental/physical illness in the family

(e) *(temps)* close, sultry, muggy; **un parfum l.** a heavy *or* strong fragrance; **il fait l.** it's close *or* sultry *or* muggy

(f) incident/refus l. de conséquences incident/refusal fraught with consequences; **silence/nuages lourd(s) de menaces** ominous silence/clouds; **un discours l. de sous-entendus** a speech packed *or* loaded with innuendos

2 *adv* **peser l.** to weigh a lot, to be heavy; *Fig* **peser l. (dans la balance)** to count for a lot; *Fig* **ça ne pèse pas l.** that doesn't count for much; **en avoir l. sur le cœur** to have a heavy heart, to feel very sad; *F* **il n'en reste pas l.** there isn't much left; *(dénombrable)* there aren't many left; **je n'en fais pas l.** I don't exactly overwork; **il n'en sait pas l. sur l'histoire de son pays** he doesn't know much about the history of his country; **il travaille beaucoup mais ne gagne pas l.** he works a lot but doesn't earn much; **ça ne fait pas l.** it's not much to show for it

3 *nf Arg* **lourde** door; **ferme la l.** put the wood in the hole

lourdaud, -aude [lurdo, -od] *Péj* **1** *adj (maladroit)* awkward, clumsy; *(bête)* oafish **2** *n* oaf

lourdement [lurdəmɑ̃] *adv* **(a)** *(avec un matériel pesant)* heavily; **l. chargé/équipé** heavily laden/equipped

(**b**) (*pesamment*) (*se déplacer*) heavily; **elle avance l.** she lumbers forward; **il est tombé l.** he fell heavily
(**c**) (*grandement*) heavily; **se tromper l.** to be greatly mistaken; **ces changements vont peser l. sur notre budget** these changes will weigh heavily on our budget; **elle insistait l.** she would keep on insisting; **il insiste toujours l. sur les défauts de ses collègues** he always lays great stress on his colleagues' failings
(**d**) *Péj* (*sans finesse*) (*rire*) coarsely

lourder [lurde] *vt F* **l. qn** to give sb the boot *or* the elbow; **se faire l. par sa petite amie** to get the boot *or* the elbow from one's girlfriend, to be given the boot *or* the elbow by one's girlfriend

lourdeur [lurdœr] *nf* (*d'objet, de charge etc*) heaviness; (*de bâtiment, d'architecture*) heaviness, massiveness; (*de traits de visage*) heaviness; (*d'administration, de bureaucratie*) unwieldiness, cumbersomeness; (*de personne*) (*dans les mouvements, de style*) clumsiness, awkwardness; (*manque de vivacité d'esprit*) slow(-witted)ness, dull-wittedness; (*de responsabilité*) weight; (*du temps*) sultriness, closeness; **l. d'esprit** slow(-witted)ness, dull-wittedness; *Vieilli* **avoir des lourdeurs de tête** to have fits of drowsiness, to feel headachy; **j'ai des lourdeurs d'estomac** my stomach feels heavy

lourdingue [lurdɛ̃g] *adj F* (*style*) heavy; (*personne, plaisanterie*) unsubtle

loustic [lustik] *nm* (**a**) *F* (*farceur*) joker; **il fait le l.** he's playing the fool, he's fooling around (**b**) **c'est un drôle de l.** (*louche*) he's a strange guy, he's an oddball

loutre [lutr] *nf* otter; (*fourrure*) otter (skin); **manteau de l.** otter-skin coat; **l. marine** *ou* **de mer** sea otter

louve [luv] *nf* she-wolf

louveteau, -eaux [luvto] *nm* (**a**) *Zool* wolf cub (**b**) (*jeune scout*) cub (scout)

louvoiement [luvwamɑ̃] *nm Naut* tacking; *Fig* hedging

louvoyer [luvwaje] *vi* (**je louvoie, n. louvoyons, je louvoierai**) *Naut* to tack, to beat about, to beat to windward; *Fig* to hedge, to beat about the bush

lover [lɔve] **1** *vt* (*corde*) to coil; **lové dans un canapé** curled up on a couch **2 se lover** *vpr* (*de serpent, d'anguille etc*) to coil up; **se l. dans un canapé moelleux** to curl up on a soft couch

loxodromique [lɔksɔdrɔmik] *adj Naut* (*courbe, navigation*) loxodromic; **navigation l.** plane sailing

loyal, -ale, -aux, -ales [lwajal, -o] **1** *adj* (**a**) (*honnête*) (*personne*) honest, fair, upright; (*procédés*) honest; (*combat*) clean; **être l. en affaires** to be straightforward *or* honest in one's business dealings; **il a été l. avec moi** he was honest *or* straight with me; **jeu l.** fair play; **ce n'est pas un adversaire l.** he doesn't play fair (**b**) (*serviteur, ami*) loyal, faithful, trusty; **après 25 ans de bons et loyaux services** after 25 years of good and faithful service **2** *nf F* **se battre à la loyale** to fight cleanly

loyalement [lwajalmɑ̃] *adv* (**a**) (*honnêtement*) (*agir*) honestly, fairly; (*se battre*) fairly (**b**) (*fidèlement*) (*servir*) loyally, faithfully

loyalisme [lwajalism] *nm Pol* loyalty

loyaliste [lwajalist] *adj, n Pol* loyalist

loyauté [lwajote] *nf* (**a**) (*honnêteté*) honesty, fairness, uprightness (**b**) (*fidélité*) loyalty, faithfulness (**envers** to)

loyer [lwaje] *nm* (**a**) rent; *Arch* **prendre une maison à l.** to rent a house; *Arch* **donner à l.** to rent (out), *Br* to let (out); **vous êtes encore en retard pour payer votre l.** you're late with your rent again; **j'ai trois loyers de retard** I'm three months behind with my rent; **l. arriéré** rent arrears; **l. commercial** commercial rent; **l. nominal** nominal rent (**b**) *Fin* **l. de l'argent** cost of money

LSD [ɛlɛsde] *nm Ch* LSD

LTA [ɛltea] *nf* (*abrév* **lettre de transport aérien**) AWB

lubie [lybi] *nf* whim, fad, craze; **il a des lubies, il lui prend des lubies** he has whims *or* fads *or* crazes; **il lui prit la l. de manger à 4 heures du matin** he took it into his head *or* got the crazy idea to have something to eat at 4 o'clock in the morning

lubricité [lybrisite] *nf* (*de personne, de regard*) lustfulness, lechery; (*de propos*) lewdness

lubrifiant [lybrifjɑ̃] **1** *adj* lubricating **2** *nm* lubricant; **l. EP** EP lubricant; **l. extrême pression** extreme pressure lubricant

lubrification [lybrifikasjɔ̃] *nf* lubrication

lubrifier [lybrifje] *vt* (*pr sub & impf* **n. lubrifiions, v. lubrifiiez**) to lubricate

lubrique [lybrik] *adj* (*homme, regard*) lustful, lecherous; (*propos*) lewd

lubriquement [lybrik(ə)mɑ̃] *adv* (*regarder*) lustfully, lecherously; (*parler*) lewdly

Luc [lyk] *nm* **saint L.** Saint Luke

lucane [lykan] *nm Ent* stag beetle

lucarne [lykarn] *nf* (**a**) (*fenêtre dans un toit*) dormer (window); (*tabatière*) skylight; **l. rampante** dormer (window) (**b**) *Fb* (*de filet*) top corner

lucide [lysid] *adj* (**a**) (*perspicace*) (*esprit, raisonnement etc*) lucid, clear; (*personne*) lucid, clear-headed; **il jette sur la société contemporaine un regard très l.** he casts a very lucid *or* clear gaze *or* eye on contemporary society; **elle ne se fait pas d'illusion sur ce qui l'attend, elle est l.** she has no illusions about what awaits her, she sees things clearly (**b**) (*conscient*) lucid

lucidement [lysidmɑ̃] *adv* lucidly, clearly

lucidité [lysidite] *nf* (**a**) (*perspicacité*) (*d'analyse, d'exposé*) lucidity, clearness; (*de personne*) lucidity, clear-headedness (**b**) (*état conscient*) lucidity; **elle a encore toute sa l.** she still has all her wits about her *or* all her faculties; **elle a des moments de l., puis se remet à délirer** she has lucid moments *or* moments of lucidity, then sinks back into delirium

Lucifer [lysifɛr] *nm* Lucifer

luciférien, -ienne [lysiferjɛ̃, -jɛn] **1** *adj* (*propre à Lucifer*) Luciferian **2** *n Hist* Satanist

luciole [lysjɔl] *nf* firefly, *Spéc* luciola

lucratif, -ive [lykratif, -iv] *adj* (*entreprise, opération*) lucrative, profitable; (*emploi*) well-paid, lucrative; **à but l.** profit-making; **sans but l.** non-profit-making, *Am* not-for-profit

lucrativement [lykrativmɑ̃] *adv* lucratively

lucre [lykr] *nm Péj* lucre

ludiciel [lydisjɛl] *nm Ordinat* games software, gameware; **un l.** a games package

ludion [lydjɔ̃] *nm Phys* Cartesian diver; *Fig* (*jouet des circonstances*) plaything, toy

ludique [lydik] *adj* play; **activité l.** play activity; **il doit y avoir une dimension l. dans ...** there has to be an aspect of play in ...

ludothèque [lydɔtɛk] *nf* toy and game library

luette [lɥɛt] *nf Anat* uvula

lueur [lɥœr] *nf* (**a**) (*lumière faible*) (*de lampe, feu, allumette, soleil etc*) glow, glimmer; (*de couteau, épée*) gleam; **à la l. d'une bougie** by candlelight; **à la l. des étoiles** by starlight; **à la l. des derniers événements** in the light of recent events; **les premières lueurs de l'aube** the first light of dawn (**b**) (*lumière soudaine*) **l. soudaine** flash; **l'allumette jeta une dernière l. avant de s'éteindre** the match flared one last time, then went out (**c**) *Fig* (*moment bref*) (*de lucidité, colère*) flash; (*d'intelligence*) spark, glimmer; (*d'espoir*) glimmer, gleam

luge [lyʒ] *nf* toboggan, sledge, *Am* sled; *Sp* luge; **faire de la l.** to go tobogganing *or* sledging *or Am* sledding; *Sp* to luge

lugeur, -euse [lyʒœr, -øz] *n Sp* luger

lugubre [lygybr] *adj* (*atmosphère, humeur, personne, récit*) lugubrious, gloomy, dismal; (*endroit*) gloomy, grim; (*son, cri*) doleful, mournful

lugubrement [lygybrəmɑ̃] *adv* lugubriously, gloomily

lui[1], *pl* **leur** [lɥi, lœr] *pron pers* (*pour un homme*) (to) him; (*pour une femme*) (to) her; (*pour un bébé, un animal*) (to) it, (to) him, (to) her; (*pour une chose, une idée*) (to) it; (*pour un pays, navire*) (to) it, (to) her; (*au pluriel*) (to) them; **je le l. donne** I give it (to) him/her, I give him/her it; **donnez-l.-en** give him/her some; **donnez-le-l.** give it (to) him/her, give him/her it; **cette maison leur appartient** this house belongs to them, this house is theirs; **je le leur ai reproché** I reproached them for it; **je l. trouve mauvaise mine** I think he/she looks ill; **je l. ai serré la main** I shook his/her hand; **je l. ai entendu dire ...** I heard him/her say that ...; **il l. vint une envie de tout l. dire** he/she felt a desire to tell him/her everything; **il leur jeta une pierre** he threw a stone at them; **montrez-le-leur** show it (to) them, show them it

lui[2], *pl* **eux** [lɥi, ø] *stressed pron pers m* (**a**) (*sujet*) (*pour un homme*) he; (*pour un bébé, un animal*) it, he; (*pour une chose*) it; (*pour un pays, navire*) it, she; (*au pluriel*) they; **ce sont eux,** *F* **c'est eux** it's them; **c'est l.** it's him; (*en le désignant*) that's him; **c'est l. qui nous a présentés** he's the one who introduced us, he introduced us; **c'est l. le coupable** he's the culprit *or* guilty one, he's guilty; **elle est blonde, l. est brun** she's blonde, he's dark-haired; **eux deux/tous** the two of/all of them; **Jacques et l. l'ont fait** he and Jacques did it, *F* Jacques and him did it; **l., au moins, il a fait un effort** he, at least, made an effort; **elle veut vendre la maison, mais est-ce que l. est d'accord?** she wants to sell the house, but does he agree to it?; **si j'étais l., je me méfierais** if I were him I'd be careful; **l.? il ne ferait jamais ça!** him? he'd never do that!; **mon frère, l., n'est pas venu** as for my brother, he didn't come; **il doit suivre un régime: il**

est malheureux, l. qui est si gourmand! he has to go on a diet, and loving his food as he does, he's not happy about it; **ils jouent tous les deux au tennis, elle très bien, l. plutôt mal** they both play tennis, she very well, he rather badly; **elle aime le cinéma, l. non** she likes the cinema, he doesn't

(**b**) (*objet*) (*pour un homme*) him; (*pour un bébé, un animal*) it, him; (*pour une chose*) it; (*pour un pays, un navire*) it, her; (*au pluriel*) them; **j'accuse son frère et l.** I accuse him and his brother; **l., je le connais, je le connais, l.** I know him; **l., je le connais, les autres non** him I know *or* I know him but not the others; **des deux frères, c'est l. que je connais le mieux** of the two brothers I know him *or* it's him I know best; **elle est plus grande que l.** she's taller than him *or* than he is; **elle gagne plus que l.** she earns more than him *or* than he does; **j'ai plus bu que l.** I've drunk more than him *or* than he has; **j'apprécie Marie plus que l.** (*plus qu'il ne l'apprécie*) I like Marie more than he does *or* than him; (*je préfère Marie*) I like Marie more than him; **elle m'a présenté à l.** she introduced me to him; **elle pense encore à l.** she still thinks about him; **ce livre est à l. /à eux** this book is his/theirs; **à l. tout seul, il n'y arrivera pas** on his own he won't manage it; **à l. seul, il possède la moitié de la ville** he owns half of the town himself; **voilà une photo de l.** here's a photo of him; **c'est pour l.** it's for him; **c'est par l. que je l'ai su** it's *or* it was through him that I found out; **j'ai confiance en l.** I trust him; **c'est à l. de décider** it's for him to decide; **c'est un ami à l.** it's *or* he's a friend of his; **l'enfant n'est pas de l.** the child is not his; **maintenant tout le monde va vouloir faire comme eux** now everyone will want to do as they do

(**c**) (*réfléchi*) (*pour un homme*) him(self); (*pour un bébé, un animal*) it(self), him(self); (*pour une chose*) it(self); (*pour un pays, un navire*) it(self), her(self); (*au pluriel*) them(selves); **il les rassembla autour de l.** he gathered them round him; **il ne pense qu'à l.** he thinks only of himself

lui-même *pron pers* (*pour un homme*) himself; (*pour un bébé, un animal*) itself, himself; (*pour un objet*) itself; **c'est l. qui me l'a dit** he told me so himself; **chacun d'eux travaille pour l.** each of them works for himself; *voir* = **même 1**(**c**)

luire [lɥir] *vi* (*prp* **luisant**; *pp* **lui**, *invariable in feminine*; *pr ind* **il luit, ils luisent**; *p hist* **il luit, ils luirent,** *parfois* **il luisit**; *fu* **il luira**) (*de métal, surface propre*) to gleam, to shine; (*de surface de l'eau, trottoirs mouillés etc*) to glisten; (*d'étoile, de soleil*) to shine; (*de feu, bougie*) to glow; (*d'yeux*) to gleam; (*de cheveux*) to be shiny, to shine; **l. au soleil** to gleam *or* shine in the sun

luisant [lɥizɑ̃] **1** *adj* (*étoile, métal etc*) shining, bright; (*surface, pelage, peau*) shiny, glossy; (*yeux*) gleaming; (*braise*) glowing; **front l. de sueur** forehead glistening with sweat; **manteau l. d'usure** coat shiny with wear **2** *nm* (*d'étoffe, de vernis*) shine, sheen

lumbago [lɔ̃bago] *nm Méd* lumbago

lumen [lymɛn] *nm* lumen

lumière [lymjɛr] *nf* (**a**) (*clarté*) light; **l. du jour** daylight; **l. du soleil** sunlight; **l. des étoiles** starlight; **l. électrique** electric light; **il n'y a plus de l.** the light's gone out; **la fenêtre donne de la l.** the window lets in (the) light; **à la l. de la lune** by moonlight; **allume la l., on n'y voit rien** put the light on, we can't see anything in here; **il y a de la l. chez lui** there's a light on *or* there are lights on at his place; **as-tu pensé à éteindre toutes les lumières?** did you remember to switch off all the lights?; **les lumières de la ville** the lights of the city, the city lights; *Aut F* **allume tes lumières, il y a du brouillard** put your lights on, it's foggy; **l. d'ambiance** floodlight; **l. stroboscopique** strobe light; **l. tamisée** soft light

(**b**) *Fig* (*compréhension*) light; **à la l. de son exposé, tout paraît évident** in the light of his presentation, everything seems clear; **mettre qch en l.** to bring sth out; **jeter une l. nouvelle sur qch** to throw *or* shed new light on sth; **faire (toute) la l. sur qch** to get (right) to the bottom of sth

(**c**) (*connaissances rationnelles*) **les lumières de la raison** the light of reason; **avoir des lumières sur qch** to have some knowledge about sth; **j'ai besoin de tes lumières** I need the benefit of your knowledge; **le siècle des lumières** the Age of Enlightenment

(**d**) (*homme de savoir*) **une des lumières de la science moderne/de son époque** one of the leading lights of modern science/of his age; *F* **ce n'est pas une l.** he's not very bright

(**e**) *MecE* (*ouverture*) (*d'admission etc*) port; (*de mire*) aperture; **l. d'admission/d'échappement** inlet/exhaust port

(**f**) *Phys, Astron* **l. oxhydrique** limelight; *Phys* **l. blanche** white light; **l. noire** *ou* **de Wood** black light; *Astron* **l. cendrée** earthlight, earthshine

lumignon [lymiɲɔ̃] *nm* (**a**) (*lampe*) dim light *or* lamp (**b**) (*bout de mèche*) candle end

luminaire [lyminɛr] *nm* (**a**) (*lampe*) light (**b**) (*dans une église*) lights

luminescence [lyminɛsɑ̃s] *nf* luminescence

luminescent [lyminɛsɑ̃] *adj* luminescent

lumineusement [lyminøzmɑ̃] *adv* luminously, brightly; *Fig* (*expliquer*) lucidly, clearly

lumineux, -euse [lyminø, -øz] *adj* (**a**) (*corps, cadran*) luminous; (*pièce*) bright, filled with light; (*ciel*) bright, luminous; *Ordinat* (*bloc etc*) highlighted; **montre à cadran l.** watch with a luminous dial, luminous watch; **enseigne lumineuse** illuminated sign; **couleur très lumineuse** very bright *or* intense colour; *Phys* **onde lumineuse** light wave (**b**) *Fig* (*explication, propos*) lucid, clear; **regard l.** radiant look *or* expression; **c'est une idée lumineuse** it's a brilliant idea *or* a brainwave *or Am* a brainstorm; **il est d'une intelligence lumineuse** he is extremely bright

luminosité [lyminozite] *nf* (**a**) (*de ciel*) brightness, luminosity; (*de regard*) radiance; **la l. est insuffisante pour prendre une photo** there is insufficient light (available) for taking a photo (**b**) *Ordinat* brightness; (*mise en relief*) highlighting

lump [lœp] *nm* lumpfish; **œufs de l.** lumpfish roe

lunaire [lynɛr] **1** *adj* (*de la lune*) lunar; (*pareil à la lune*) moonlike; **paysage l.** lunar landscape; *Fig* **un visage l.** a moon-face **2** *nf* (*plante*) honesty, moonwort, *Spéc* lunaria

lunaison [lynɛzɔ̃] *nf Astron* lunation, lunar month

lunatique [lynatik] *adj* (*personne*) whimsical, quirky, temperamental

lunch, *pl* **lunches, lunchs** [lœntʃ] *nm* buffet lunch

lundi [lœ̃di] *nm* Monday; **le l. de Pâques/de la Pentecôte** Easter/Whit Monday

lune [lyn] *nf* (**a**) *Astron* moon; **la pleine l.** the full moon; **la nouvelle l.** the new moon; **les phases de la l.** the phases of the moon; **(au) clair de l.** (in the) moonlight; **nuit sans l.** moonless night; **la l. se lève** the moon is rising; **face de l., visage de pleine l.** moon-face, moonlike face; *Fig* **demander la l.** to ask for the moon; **je ne te demande pas la l.** I'm not asking for the moon; *Fig* **promettre la l.** to promise the moon; **je ne vous promets pas la l.** I can't promise you the moon; *Fig F* **être dans la l.** to be miles away, to be in the clouds; *Fig très F* **être con comme la l.** to be dead from the neck up, *Br* to be as thick as two short planks; *Fig F* **tomber de la l.** to look flabbergasted

(**b**) *Arch, Litt* (*mois*) moon, month

(**c**) *F* (*derrière*) bottom, backside

(**d**) **vieilles lunes** old-fashioned *or* outmoded ideas

(**e**) *Vieilli* **il est dans une bonne/mauvaise l.** (*humeur*) he is in one of his good/bad moods; **lunes** vagary, caprice, whim

(**f**) **l. de mer, poisson l.** (ocean) sunfish

(**g**) **pierre de l.** moonstone

▶ **lune**: *Bot* **l. d'eau** white water-lily; **l. de miel** honeymoon; **l. rousse** April moon

luné [lyne] *adj F* **être bien/mal l.** to be in a good/bad mood

lunetier, -ière [lyntje, -jɛr] **1** *n* (*fabricant*) spectacle manufacturer **2** *adj* **industrie lunetière** spectacle industry

lunette [lynɛt] *nf* (**a**) [①A10,e] **(paire de) lunettes** (pair of) glasses *or* spectacles *or F* specs *or Am* eyeglasses; **porter (des) lunettes** to wear glasses *or* spectacles *or F* specs; *F* **c'est un type à lunettes, facile à reconnaître** he wears specs, he's easy to recognize; *F* **c'est le type à lunettes** he's the guy in specs; **lunettes de vue** corrective glasses; **lunettes d'écaille** horn-rimmed glasses

(**b**) *Opt* **l. (d'approche)** telescope, field glass; *Mil* **l. de pointage** sighting telescope; **l. de fusil** gun sight(s); **fusil à l.** gun with sights; **l. astronomique** astronomical telescope

(**c**) *Archit* lunette

(**d**) (*de guillotine*) lunette

(**e**) (*siège des W.-C.*) seat

▶ **lunette**: *Aut* **l. arrière** rear window; **lunettes noires** dark glasses, *F* shades; **lunettes de plongée** swimming goggles; **lunettes de protection** goggles; **lunettes de soleil** sunglasses, *F* shades

lunetterie [lynɛtri] *nf* spectacle trade

lunule [lynyl] *nf* (**a**) *Math* lune (**b**) *Anat* (*d'ongle*) half-moon, *Spéc* lunula

lupanar [lypanar] *nm Litt Vieilli* brothel

lupin [lypɛ̃] *nm* (*plante*) lupin

lupus [lypys] *nm Méd* lupus

lurette [lyrɛt] *nf F* (*utilisé seulement dans*) **il y a belle l.** a long time ago, *F* ages ago; **il y a belle l. que je ne t'ai pas vu** I haven't seen you for a long time *or F* for ages, *F* it's been ages since I saw you

luron, -onne [lyrɔ̃, -ɔn] *n F* **c'est un gai** *ou* **un joyeux l.** he's quite *or* a bit of a lad, *Vieilli* he's a gay dog; **c'est une sacrée luronne** she's quite a girl

lusitanien, -ienne [lyzitanjɛ̃, -jɛn] *Antiq* **1** *adj* Lusitanian **2** *n* **L.** Lusitanian

lustrage [lystraʒ] *nm* (*de tissu, cuir*) glossing, glazing, lustring; (*de verre*) polishing; **l. des fourrures** lustring of furs

lustre[1] [lystr] *nm* **(a)** (*lampe*) chandelier **(b)** (*brillant, éclat*) lustre, *US* luster, gloss **(c)** *Litt* (*éclat*) lustre, *US* luster; **il faut redonner du l. à cette ancienne demeure** some of the lustre needs to be brought back to this stately old dwelling; **redonner du l. à un parti politique** to give a political party a facelift

lustre[2] *nm Litt* (*cinq ans*) lustrum; *Fig* **ça fait des lustres qu'on t'attend!** we've been waiting ages for you!; *Fig* **depuis des lustres** for ages

lustré [lystre] *adj* (*poterie*) glazed; (*fourrure, tissu, barbe, robe d'un cheval, cheveux*) glossy; **étoffe lustrée par l'usure** cloth shiny with wear

lustrer [lystre] *vt* (*glace, meuble, voiture*) to polish (up); (*par l'usure*) to make shiny; *Tech* (*tissu, cuir*) to glaze, to gloss, to lustre; **ce tissu se lustre facilement** this material gets shiny very quickly

lustrerie [lystrəri] *nf Ind, Com* lighting industry

lustrine [lystrin] *nf* cotton lustre

lut [lyt] *nm Cér, Ind* lute, luting

Lutèce [lytɛs] *nf Antiq* Lutetia

lutéine [lytein] *nf Biol, Ch* lutein

luter [lyte] *vt Cér, Ind* to lute, to seal with luting

luth [lyt] *nm* **(a)** *Mus* lute **(b)** *Zool* **l.** *ou* **tortue l.** leatherback (turtle)

luthéranisme [lyteranism] *nm Rel* Lutheranism

lutherie [lytri] *nf Mus* **(a)** (*fabrication*) stringed instrument making **(b)** (*instruments*) stringed instruments

luthérien, -ienne [lyterjɛ̃, -jɛn] *adj, n Rel* Lutheran

luthier [lytje] *nm* stringed instrument maker

luthiste [lytist] *n Mus* lutanist, lutenist, lute player

lutin [lytɛ̃] **1** *nm* **(a)** (*créature de conte etc*) imp, elf, goblin; (*irlandais*) leprechaun **(b)** (*enfant*) imp **2** *adj* mischievous, impish

lutiner [lytine] *vt* **(a)** (*femme*) to fondle, to tickle **(b)** (*à la manière d'un lutin*) to plague, to torment; (*avec espièglerie*) to tease

lutrin [lytrɛ̃] *nm* **(a)** *Rel* lectern **(b)** (*pour soutenir un livre, des feuilles*) reading *or* book stand **(c)** (*endroit où se tient le chœur*) choir stall

lutte [lyt] *nf* **(a)** *Sp* wrestling; **l. libre** all-in *or* freestyle wrestling; **l. gréco-romaine** Graeco-Roman wrestling; **faire de la l.** to wrestle

(b) (*combat, action violente*) fight, struggle; (*morale, de guerre*) conflict; **entrer/être en l. contre qn** to enter into/to be in conflict with sb; **après plusieurs années de l.** after several years of struggle; **la l. doit continuer!** the fight *or* struggle must go on!; **il faut soutenir les travailleurs en l.** we must support the workers in their fight *or* struggle; **les partis en l. pour le pouvoir** the opposing parties fighting for power; **luttes intestines** infighting; **l. d'influence** struggle for influence; **luttes parlementaires** parliamentary clashes; **l. armée** armed struggle; **se livrer à une l. acharnée pour qch** to be engaged in a desperate struggle for sth; **gagner de haute l.** to win by sheer force; **l. à mort** life-and-death struggle, fight to the death

(c) (*pour venir à bout d'un mal*) **l. contre l'alcoolisme/le cancer** fight against alcoholism/cancer; **l. pour la liberté** struggle for freedom; **l. antipollution** fight against pollution

(d) *Biol, Fig* **l. pour la vie** struggle *or* fight for survival; (*d'un malade*) fight for life

(e) (*antagonisme*) conflict; **la l. entre le devoir et la passion/le bien et le mal** the conflict between duty and passion/good and evil; **l. d'intérêts** conflict *or* clash of interests; **la l. des classes** the class struggle *or* conflict

lutter [lyte] *vi* **(a)** *Sp* to wrestle (**avec, contre** with) **(b)** (*se battre*) to struggle, to fight; **l. contre la maladie** to fight (against) *or* to combat disease; **l. contre le vent** to battle with *or* against the wind; **l. contre un incendie** to fight a fire; **l. pour l'indépendance** to fight for independence; **l. contre le sommeil** to fight off sleep; **l. contre la tentation** to fight (against) temptation; **l. contre l'alcoolisme** to fight (against) alcoholism **(c)** (*rivaliser*) **l. de vitesse avec qn** to race sb; **elles luttent d'adresse** they're using all their skills to outdo each other

lutteur, -euse [lytœr, -øz] *n* **(a)** *Sp* wrestler **(b)** (*pour une cause etc*) fighter; **un tempérament de l.** a fighting *or* fighter's temperament

lux [lyks] *nm Phys* lux

luxation [lyksasjɔ̃] *nf Méd* (*d'articulation*) dislocation, *Spéc* luxation; **l. congénitale** congenital dislocation

luxe [lyks] *nm* **(a)** (*abondance, richesse*) luxury; (*de maison, pièce, ameublement etc*) luxuriousness, sumptuousness; **vivre dans le l.** to live in luxury; **goûts de l.** luxurious *or* extravagant tastes; **un l. tapageur** a flashy display of wealth; **étaler son l.** to flaunt one's wealth

(b) (*qualité*) luxury, luxuriousness; **articles de l.** luxury articles; **édition de l.** de luxe edition; **voiture de l.** de luxe car, luxury car; **boutique de l.** luxury goods shop; **taxe (sur les produits) de l.** tax on luxury goods

(c) (*bien superflu, coûteux*) luxury; **mon seul l., c'est d'aller au cinéma** my only luxury *or* indulgence is going to the cinema; **elle ne peut pas s'offrir le l. de refuser cet emploi** she can't afford the luxury of turning this job down; **je me suis payé le l. de le lui dire** I gave myself the pleasure of telling him so; **se payer le l. d'un cigare** to indulge in (the luxury of) a cigar; **je vais faire nettoyer ce vieil imperméable, ce ne sera pas du l.** I'm going to have this old raincoat cleaned, it really needs it; **j'ai acheté un nouveau tapis, ce n'était pas du l.** I bought a new carpet, it had to be done *or* it was an essential purchase

(d) (*profusion*) abundance; **un l. de précautions** a wealth of precautions; **l. de détails** wealth *or* abundance of details

Luxembourg [lyksɑ̃bur] *nm* (*pays, ville*) Luxembourg

luxembourgeois, -oise [lyksɑ̃burʒwa, -waz] **1** *adj* of/from Luxembourg **2** *n* **L.** Luxembourger

luxer [lykse] **1** *vt* (*articulation, coude etc*) to dislocate, *Spéc* to luxate **2 se luxer** *vpr* **se l. un membre** to dislocate a limb; **se l. l'épaule** to dislocate one's shoulder, to put one's shoulder out

luxueusement [lyksɥøzmɑ̃] *adv* luxuriously, sumptuously

luxueux, -euse [lyksɥø, -øz] *adj* luxurious, sumptuous

luxure [lyksyr] *nf Litt* lust

luxuriance [lyksyrjɑ̃s] *nf* luxuriance

luxuriant [lyksyrjɑ̃] *adj* (*végétation, forêt etc*) luxuriant, lush; (*chevelure*) luxuriant; (*imagination*) fertile; *Archit, Littér* **un style l.** a luxuriant style

luxurieux, -euse [lyksyrjø, -øz] *adj* lascivious, lewd, lustful, sensual

luzerne [lyzɛrn] *nf* (*plante*) lucerne, alfalfa

lycée [lise] *nm* **(a)** *Scol* = *Br* secondary school, *Am* high school (*for pupils aged 15 to 18*); **l. (d'enseignement) professionnel** technical school; **l. technique** technical high school; **l. technique hôtelier** hotel school; **il se souvient du l. comme de ses meilleures années** he looks back on his schooldays as the best years of his life **(b)** *Antiq* **le L.** the Lyceum

lycéen, -éenne [liseɛ̃, -eɛn] **1** *n* = *Br* secondary school *or Am* high school pupil **2** *adj* = *Br* secondary school, *Am* high school

lycra® [likra] *nm* Lycra®; **pantalon en l.** Lycra trousers

lymphatique [lɛ̃fatik] **1** *adj* **(a)** (*glande etc*) lymphatic **(b)** (*personne*) lethargic, apathetic **2** *nm* lymphatic (duct)

lymphe [lɛ̃f] *nf* lymph

lymphocyte [lɛ̃fɔsit] *nm* lymphocyte

lymphoïde [lɛ̃fɔid] *adj* (*cellules, tissu*) lymphoid

lynchage [lɛ̃ʃaʒ] *nm* lynching

lyncher [lɛ̃ʃe] *vt* to lynch

lynx [lɛ̃ks] *nm* lynx; *Fig* **avoir des yeux de l.** to have eyes like a hawk, to be hawk-eyed

Lyon [ljɔ̃] *n* Lyons

lyonnais, -aise [ljɔnɛ, -ɛz] **1** *adj* of/from Lyons **2** *n* **L.** (*natif*) native of Lyons; (*habitant*) inhabitant of Lyons **3** *nm* **le L.** (*région*) Lyonnais

lyophilisation [ljɔfilizasjɔ̃] *nf Tech* freeze-drying

lyophiliser [ljɔfilize] *vt Tech* (*café, soupe etc*) to freeze-dry; **café lyophilisé** freeze-dried coffee

lyre [lir] *nf Mus* lyre; *F* **toute la l.** the whole lot (of them), the whole shoot; **(oiseau-)l.** lyre bird

lyrique [lirik] **1** *adj* **(a)** *Littér* (*poème, poète etc*) lyric **(b)** (*mis en musique*) **art l.** opera; **artiste l.** opera singer; **drame l.** lyric drama, opera; **comédie l.** comic opera, operetta; **théâtre l.** opera house **(c)** (*poétique, passionné*) lyrical; **des envolées lyriques** flights of lyricism; **parler de qch/qn d'une façon l.** (*avec lyrisme*) to wax lyrical about sth/sb **2** *nm* lyric poet

lyrisme [lirism] *nm* **(a)** lyricism; **parler avec l. de qch** to wax lyrical about sth; **s'exprimer avec l.** to wax lyrical **(b)** (*exaltation*) excessive enthusiasm

lys [lis] *nm Arch* = **lis**

lysergique [lizɛrʒik] *adj Ch* lysergic

M

M, m [ɛm] *nm* (*lettre*) M, m
m *abrév* **(a) M (Monsieur)** Mr **(b) (mètre)** m; **1m 50** 1. 5m **(c)** *Gram* **(masculin)** m
m' *voir* **me**
ma [ma] *voir* **mon**
maboul [mabul] *F* **1** *adj* (*fou*) crazy, nuts, loony **2** *n* nut, loony
mac [mak] *nm Arg* (*maquereau*) pimp
macabre [makabr] *adj* (*découverte, histoire*) macabre, gruesome, grisly; (*humour*) macabre; **danse m.** dance of death, danse macabre
macache [makaʃ] *adv F* (*absolument pas*) no way!, nothing doing!, not likely!; (*absolument rien*) not a sausage, *surtout Am* zilch
macadam [makadam] *nm* **(a)** (*revêtement*) macadam; **m. goudronné** tarmac(adam) **(b)** (*route*) road
macadamisage [makadamizaʒ] *nm,* **macadamisation** [makadamizasjɔ̃] *nf* (*de route*) tarmacking
macadamiser [makadamize] *vt* (*route*) to tarmac
macaque [makak] **1** *nm* (*singe*) macaque; **m. rhésus** rhesus monkey **2** *n F* (*personne*) ugly ape
macareux [makarø] *nm* puffin
macaron [makarɔ̃] *nm* **(a)** *Culin* macaroon **(b) macarons** (*coiffure*) coils (*over the ears*); *F* earphones **(c)** (*badge*) badge; (*décoration*) rosette; (*autocollant*) sticker; *Journ* **m. de presse** press badge
macaroni [makarɔni] *nm* **(a)** [①A13,7] *Culin* piece of macaroni; **des macaronis** macaroni **(b)** *Arg Péj* (*Italien*) wop, *Br* Eyetie
Mac(c)abées [makabe] *nmpl Bible* Maccabees
macchabée [makabe] *nm très F* (*mort*) stiff, corpse
Macédoine [masedwan] *nf* Macedonia
macédoine [masedwan] *nf* **(a)** *Culin* **m. de fruits** fruit salad; **m. de légumes** mixed vegetables, *Spéc* macedoine of vegetables **(b)** *Vieilli F* (*mélange*) medley, miscellany, *Péj* hotchpotch
macédonien, -ienne [masedɔnjɛ̃, -jɛn] **1** *adj* Macedonian **2** *n* **M.** Macedonian
macération [maserasjɔ̃] *nf* **(a)** steeping, soaking **(b)** *Rel* mortificaiton
macérer [masere] **(je macère; je macérerai) 1** *vt* **(a)** to steep, to soak; **laisser m. qch** to leave something to steep *or* soak **(b)** *Rel* (*chair*) to mortify **2** *vi* to steep, to soak; **la viande doit m. plusieurs jours** the meat should be left to steep *or* soak for several days; *Fig F* **laissons-le m. quelques jours** let's leave him stewing for a few days
Mach [mak] *nm Av* **(nombre de) M.** Mach (number)
mâche [mɑʃ] *nf Bot* corn salad, lamb's lettuce
mâchefer [mɑʃfɛr] *nm Tech* clinker, slag
mâchement [mɑʃmɑ̃] *nm Rare* chewing, *Fml* mastication
mâcher [mɑʃe] *vt* (*nourriture*) to chew, *Fml* to masticate; (*quelque chose qui croustille ou qui croque*) to munch; (*d'un animal*) (*fourrage*) to champ, to chomp; **m. le mors** (*d'un cheval*) to champ at the bit; **ne pas m. ses mots** not to mince (one's) words; **m. le travail** *ou* **la besogne à qn** to spoon-feed sb; **m. le bois** (*d'un outil émoussé etc*) to chew up the wood
machette [maʃɛt] *nf* machete
Machiavel [makjavɛl] *nm* Machiavelli
machiavélique [makjavelik] *adj* (*ruse etc*) Machiavellian
machiavélisme [makjavelism] *nm* Machiavellianism
mâchicoulis [mɑʃikuli] *nm Archit* machicolation; **à m.** machicolated
machin [maʃɛ̃] *nm F* **(a)** (*objet*) thing(ummy), thingumajig, thingumabob, whatsit(sname), what-d'you-call-it; **qu'est-ce que c'est que ce m-là?** what's that thing(ummy) *or* thingumajig *or* thingumabob? **(b)** (*personne*) **monsieur M.** Mr Whatshisname, what-d'you-call-him, Thingummy; **madame M.** Mrs Whatshername, what-d'you-call-her, Thingummy; **j'ai vu m-chouette aujourd'hui** I saw whatshisname *or* what-d'you-call-him *or* thingummy today
machinal, -aux [maʃinal, -o] *adj* (*action, geste*) mechanical, unconscious; (*réaction*) automatic, instinctive; (*travail*) mechanical; **faire qch de façon machinale** to do sth mechanically *or* unconsciously
machinalement [maʃinalmɑ̃] *adv* (*agir*) mechanically, unconsciously; (*réagir, répondre etc*) automatically
machination [maʃinasjɔ̃] *nf* plot, machination
machine [maʃin] *nf* **(a)** (*appareil*) machine; *Ind* **les machines** the machinery, the plant; **machines agricoles** agricultural machinery *or* machines; **écrire une lettre à la m.** to type a letter; **écrit à la m.** typed, typewritten; **travailler le métal à la m.** to machine metal; **fait à la m.** (*objets*) machine-made; (*opération*) done by machine; **laver qch en m.** to machine-wash sth, to wash sth in a machine; *Fig* **la m. administrative/judiciaire** the administrative/judicial machinery *or* machine; *Fig* **la m. est usée/fatiguée** (*corps humain*) the old body has had it/is tired out; *Fig Péj* **il n'est qu'une m. à penser/à faire de l'argent** he's nothing but a thinking/money-making machine; *Th* **pièce à machines** play with stage effects

(b) (*locomotive*) locomotive, engine; *F* (*moto*) machine; **m. volante** flying machine

(c) *Naut* (*moteur*) engine; **salle des machines** engine room; **stopper les machines** to stop the engines; **faire m. arrière** to reverse the engine; *Fig* to backtrack

▶ **machine**: **m. à adresser** addressing machine; **m. à affranchir** franking machine; **m. agrafeuse** stapling machine, stapler; **m. à aléser** boring machine, fine borer; **m. à battre** threshing machine; **m. de bureau** office machine; **m. à café** coffee machine; **m. à calculer** calculator; (*plus grande*) adding machine, calculating machine; *Typ* **m. à composer** typesetting machine; **m. comptable** accounting machine; **m. à coudre** sewing machine; **m. à écrire** typewriter; **m. à écrire à mémoire** memory typewriter; *Aut* **m. d'équilibrage des roues** wheel-balancing machine; **m. à fraiser** milling machine; **m. de guerre** engine of war; **m. infernale** explosive device; **m. interprète de cartes perforées** punch card reader; **m. à laver** washing machine, washer; **m. à laver la vaisselle** dishwasher; **m. à plier les documents** paper folding machine; **m. poinçonneuse** (*de cartes perforées*) punch; **m. à polycopier** duplicating machine; **m. à rayons X** X-ray machine; *MecE* **m. de rectification** grinding machine; **m. à repasser** ironing machine; **m. à sous** slot machine, *F* one-armed bandit, *Br* fruit machine; **m. de traitement de l'information** data processor; **m. à** *ou* **de traitement de texte** word processor; **m. à tricoter** knitting machine; **m. trieuse** sorter; **m. à vapeur** steam engine
machine-outil, *pl* **machines-outils** *nf* machine tool
machiner [maʃine] *vt Vieilli* to plot, to scheme; (*complot*) to hatch; **affaire machinée d'avance** put-up job; **qu'est-ce qu'il machine?** what's he plotting?; **c'est lui qui a tout machiné pour les faire accuser** he's the one who fixed *or* engineered everything so that they'd be blamed
machinerie [maʃinri] *nf* **(a)** (*machines*) machinery; *Ind* machinery, plant **(b)** (*salle*), *Ind* machine room; *Naut* engine room
machinisme [maʃinism] *nm* mechanization
machiniste [maʃinist] *nm* **(a)** *Th* sceneshifter, stagehand; *Cin, TV* grip; **m. de plateau** grips, grip, floor man, stagehand; **m. caméra** dolly operator; **m. de travelling** tracker **(b)** (*chauffeur*) (*d'autobus, de tramway*) driver; **'faire signe au m.'** 'request stop'
machisme [ma(t)ʃism(ə)] *nm Péj* (*virilité*) machismo; (*phallocratie*) male chauvinism
machiste [ma(t)ʃist] *adj, nm Péj* = **macho**
machmètre [makmɛtr] *nm Av* Machmeter
macho [matʃo] *Péj* **1** *nm* (*phallocrate*) male chauvinist (pig) **2** *adj inv* (*comportement, attitude*) male chauvinist, macho
mâchoire [mɑʃwar] *nf* **(a)** *Anat* (*d'une personne, d'un animal*) jaw; *F* **jouer** *ou* **travailler des mâchoires** (*manger avec appétit*) to get stuck in **(b) mâchoires** (*d'un étau, d'une tenaille, d'une pince*) jaws; *Tech* **m. d'une poulie** flange of a pulley; *Aut* **mâchoires de frein** brake shoes
mâchonnement [mɑʃɔnmɑ̃] *nm* chewing; *Méd* tooth-grinding, *Spéc* bruxism

mâchonner [mɑʃɔne] *vt* **(a)** *(nourriture, cigare)* to chew (on); *(d'un cheval)* to chew on, to munch; **m. son crayon** to chew (the end of) one's pencil **(b)** *(marmonner)* *(menace)* to mutter; *(prière)* to mumble, to mutter
mâchouiller [mɑʃuje] *vt F* to chew away at *or* on
mâchure [mɑʃyr] *nf Tex (dans velours, drap)* flaw
mâchurer¹ [mɑʃyre] *vt (noircir)* to soil, to dirty; *Typ (feuille)* to smudge, to mackle, to blur
mâchurer² *vt Tech (partie métallique d'un étau)* to dent, to bruise
macis [masi] *nm Bot, Culin* mace
macle [makl] *nf Bot* water chestnut
maçon [masɔ̃] **1** *nm* **(a)** *(artisan)* bricklayer; *(avec des pierres)* (stone)mason **(b)** *(franc-maçon)* Mason, freemason **2** *adj* **abeille maçonne** [masɔn] mason bee
mâcon [mɑkɔ̃] *nm* **m., vin de M.** Mâcon (wine)
maçonnage [masɔnaʒ] *nm (action)* bricklaying; *(avec des pierres)* laying of stones; *(ouvrage)* masonry
maçonner [masɔne] *vt (construire)* to build; *(recouvrir de pierres) (mur)* to face with stone; *(condamner) (porte, fenêtre)* to wall up; *(avec des briques)* to brick up
maçonnerie [masɔnri] *nf* **(a)** *(avec des briques)* brickwork, masonry; *(avec des pierres)* masonry, stonework; **grosse m.** work on the superstructure; **petite m.** interior building work; **entreprise de m.** building *or* construction firm **(b)** *(organisation secrète)* (free)masonry
maçonnique [masɔnik] *adj* masonic
macramé [makrame] *nm* macramé; **faire du m.** to do macramé; **un set de table en m.** a set of macramé table-mats
macre [makr] *nf Bot* water chestnut
macreuse [makrøz] *nf* **(a)** *(oiseau)* scoter (duck) **(b)** *Culin* shoulder of beef
macrobiotique [makrobjɔtik] **1** *adj* macrobiotic **2** *nf* macrobiotics
macrocéphale [makrosefal] *adj* macrocephalic
macro-commande, *pl* **macro-commandes** [makrokɔmɑ̃d] *nf Ordinat* macro (command)
macrocosme [makrɔkɔsm] *nm* macrocosm
macroéconomie [makroekɔnɔmi] *nf* macroeconomics
macroéconomique [makrekɔnɔmik] *adj* macroeconomic
macro-environnement, *pl* **macro-environnements** *nm* macro-environment
macro-instruction, *pl* **macro-instructions** [makroɛ̃stryksjɔ̃] *nf Ordinat* macro instruction
macrolangage [makrolɑ̃gaʒ] *nm Ordinat* macro language
macromarketing [makromarketiŋ] *nm* macromarketing
macromercatique [maɔromɛrkatik] *nf* macromarketing
macromolécule [makromɔlekyl] *nf Ch* macromolecule
macroordinateur [makroɔrdinatœr] *nm* mainframe
macrophotographie [makrofɔtɔgrafi] *nf Phot* macrophotography
macropode [makrɔpɔd] *nm (poisson)* paradise fish
macroscopique [makrɔskɔpik] *adj* macroscopic
macula [makyla] *nf Anat* macula
maculage [makylaʒ] *nm (action de salir)* soiling, staining; *Typ* off-setting, mackling; *(tache)* stain, spot
maculature [makylatyr] *nf Typ (pour l'emballage)* waste sheet, heavy wrapping paper; *(feuille intercalaire)* interleaf
macule [makyl] *nf* **(a)** *Typ (pour l'emballage)* waste sheet **(b)** *Arch, Litt (tache)* stain, spot **(c)** *Méd* macula **(d)** *Typ (salissure)* mackle, blur
maculer [makyle] *vt Litt (de sang)* to stain, to spot; *(de boue)* to spatter, to spot (**de** with); *Typ* to mackle, to blur; **maculé de taches d'encre** smeared with ink stains
Madagascar [madagaskar] *nm* Madagascar; **aller à Madagascar** to go to Madagascar
madame, *pl* **mesdames** [madam, medam] *nf* **(a)** *(titre)* Mrs; **M. Martin** Mrs Martin; **Mesdames Martin** the Mrs Martin; **M. Veuve Martin** Mrs Martin, widow of David/*etc* Martin; **m. la marquise/la comtesse de X** the Marchioness/the Countess of X; **je voudrais parler à m. la directrice** *(du magasin)* I would like to speak to the manageress; *(d'un service)* I would like to speak to the manager; *(d'une école)* I would like to speak to the headmistress; *Fml* **comment va m. votre mère?** how is your mother?
(b) *(utilisé seul)* **voici le chapeau de m.** here is your hat, madam; **M. se plaint que ...** *(dit par vendeur)* the lady *or* this lady *or Fml* madam is complaining that ...; *(dit par un domestique)* the mistress *or Fml* madam is complaining that ...; **M. est sortie** Madam is not at home; **M. a sonné?** you rang, madam?; **M. est servie** dinner is served(, madam); **occupez-vous de M.** *(à un employé de magasin)* see to the *or* this lady
(c) *(apostrophe)* madam, *surtout Am* ma'am; *(à une dame titrée)* your ladyship; *(dans la police, l'armée etc)* ma'am; **non/au revoir, m.** no/goodbye, *Fml* no/goodbye, madam; *(à une femme qui s'appelle Martin)* no/goodbye, Mrs Martin; **oui, m. la colonelle** yes, colonel; *(épouse du colonel Martin)* yes, Mrs Martin; **entrez, mesdames** come in, ladies; **m.?** *(dans un magasin)* can I help you?, *Fml* can I help you madam?
(d) *(dans une lettre) (always written in full)* **Madame** Dear Madam; **chère Madame** *(qui s'appelle Martin)* Dear Mrs Martin
(e) *F (dame)* **jouer à la m.** to put on airs (and graces)
Madeleine [madlɛn] *nf* **(a)** *Bible* Magdalen(e); *F* **pleurer comme une M.** to cry one's eyes *or* heart out **(b)** *Culin* **m.** madeleine
mademoiselle, *pl* **mesdemoiselles** [madmwazɛl, medmwazɛl] *nf* **(a)** *(titre)* Miss; **M. Martin** Miss Martin; **Mesdemoiselles Martin et Durand** the Misses Martin and Durand, Miss Martin and Miss Durand; *Fml Vieilli* **comment va m. votre cousine?** how is your cousin?
(b) *(utilisé seul)* **M. se plaint que ...** *(dans un magasin)* the *or* this young lady is complaining that ...
(c) *(apostrophe)* **merci m.** thank you, *Fml* thank you, miss; *(à une femme qui s'appelle Martin)* thank you, Miss Martin; **m. est servie** dinner is served(, madam); *Fml (à Caroline)* dinner is served, Miss Caroline; **m., avez-vous choisi?** *(au restaurant)* are you ready to order(, miss)?; **mesdemoiselles, un peu de silence je vous prie!** *(dans une classe)* let's have some quiet, girls, please!
(d) *(dans une lettre) (always written in full)* **Mademoiselle** Dear Madam; **chère Mademoiselle** *(qui s'appelle Martin)* Dear Miss Martin
Madère [madɛr] **1** *nf Géog* Madeira **2** *nm* **m., vin de M.** Madeira (wine)
madone [madɔn] *nf* madonna; *Fig* **un visage de m.** a madonna-like face
madras [madrɑ(s)] *nm (tissu)* madras (cotton); *(foulard)* (cotton) headscarf
madré, -ée [madre] *Litt* **1** *adj* sly, crafty, wily **2** *n* sly fox, crafty devil
madrépore [madrepɔr] *nm Zool* madrepore
madrier [madrije] *nm* (piece of) timber; *(façonné)* thick board *or* plank; *(poutre)* beam
madrigal, -aux [madrigal, -o] *nm Mus* madrigal
madrilène [madrilɛn] **1** *adj* of/from Madrid **2** *n* **M.** *(natif)* native of Madrid; *(habitant)* inhabitant of Madrid
maelstrom [malstrɔm] *nm* maelstrom
maestria [maɛstrija] *nf* mastery; **avec m.** in a masterly manner, brilliantly
maestro [maɛstro] *nm Mus* maestro
maf(f)ia [mafja] *nf* **(a) la M.** the Mafia **(b)** *(groupe aux intérêts communs)* gang; **le monde du spectacle est une vraie m.** show business is a real Mafia
maf(f)ieux, -ieuse [mafjø, -jøz] **1** *adj* Mafia **2** *n* mafioso
maf(f)ioso, -si [mafjozo, -zi] *nm* mafioso
mafflu [mafly] *adj Arch, Litt (personne)* chubby-cheeked, chubby-faced; *(visage)* chubby
magasin [magazɛ̃] *nm* **(a)** *(boutique)* shop, *surtout Am* store; **grand m.** department store; **chaîne de magasins** chain of shops *or* stores; **employé(e) de m.** shop assistant, *Am* salesclerk; **courir** *ou* **faire les magasins** to go shopping; **m. bon marché** bargain store
(b) *(entrepôt)* store, warehouse, storeroom; *TV etc* **m. de décors** scene dock; **marchandises en m.** stock in hand; **nous n'avons pas cet article en m.** we don't have that item in stock
(c) *(de fusil, projecteur)* magazine; **m. à papier** *(d'une imprimante etc)* paper tray
▶ **magasin**: **m. d'alimentation** grocery shop *or* store; **m. d'armes** armoury, *US* armory; **m. discompte** discount store; **magasins généraux** (public) bonded warehouse(s); *Mktg* **m. laboratoire** model test-shop used to monitor consumer behaviour; **m. à libre service** self-service store; **m. minimarge** discount store; **m. de proximité** convenience store; **m. à succursales multiples** chain store; **m. d'usine** factory retail outlet, factory shop
magasinage [magazinaʒ] *nm* **(a)** *Com (de marchandises)* warehousing, storing **(b) (droits de) m.** warehouse dues, storage (charges) **(c)** *Can* **faire du m.** to go shopping
magasiner [magazine] *vi Can* to go shopping
magasinier [magazinje] *nm* warehouseman, storekeeper
magazine [magazin] *nm* **(a)** *(journal)* magazine; **un m. féminin** a women's magazine; **un m. hebdomadaire/mensuel** a weekly/monthly (magazine); **m. d'information** news magazine; **m. en couleur** colour magazine **(b)** *Rad, TV* magazine (programme); **m. d'information/culturel** current affairs/arts magazine (programme)

magdalénien, -ienne [magdalenjẽ, -jɛn] *adj, nm Hist* Magdalenian

mage [maʒ] *nm* **(a)** *Antiq* magus; *Bible* **les (trois) Rois Mages** the Three Wise Men, the (Three) Magi **(b)** (*voyant*) seer

magenta [maʒẽta] *adj inv, nm* magenta

Maghreb [magrɛb] *nm* **le M.** the Maghreb (*French-speaking North Africa*)

maghrébin, -ine [magrebẽ, -in] **1** *adj* of/from the Maghreb **2** *n* **M.** person from the Maghreb

magicien, -ienne [maʒisjẽ, -jɛn] *n* **(a)** (*qui pratique la magie*) magician, sorcerer, *f* sorceress **(b)** (*illusioniste*); *Fig* magician

magie [maʒi] *nf* magic; **c'est de la m.!** it's magic!; **comme par m.** as if by magic; *Fig* **la m. du verbe** the magic of language *or* words

▶ **magie**: **m. blanche** white magic; **m. noire** black magic

magique [maʒik] *adj* **(a)** (*pouvoirs*) magic(al); (*mot, formule*) magic; **c'est m.!** it's magic! **(b)** *Fig* (*formidable*) (*spectacle, musique etc*) magical

magiquement [maʒikmɑ̃] *adv* magically

magister [maʒistɛr] *nm* **(a)** *Arch* (*maître d'école*) (village) schoolmaster **(b)** *Péj* (*pédant*) pedant

magistère [maʒistɛr] *nm* **(a)** *Univ* post-graduate vocational qualification **(b)** *Fig* (*autorité*) authority **(c)** (*titre*) Grand Master; **M. de l'Ordre de Malte** Grand Master of the Order of Malta

magistral, -ale, -aux, -ales [maʒistral, -o] *adj* **(a)** (*admirable*) (*œuvre, interprétation, démonstration*) masterly, authoritative; (*réussite*) brilliant, resounding; *Fig* (*rossée, engueulade*) sound, proper, thorough; (*gifle*) resounding; (*erreur*) colossal, monumental; **il s'est fait rembarrer de façon magistrale** he was told in no uncertain terms where to go; **réussir un coup m.** to pull off a master stroke **(b)** (*docte*) (*ton*) magisterial, authoritative **(c)** *Univ* **cours m.** lecture; **enseignement m.** lecturing **(d)** *Pharm* **préparation magistrale** prescribed medication specially made up by the pharmacist for the particular patient

magistralement [maʒistralmɑ̃] *adv* authoritatively

magistrat [maʒistra] *nm* **(a)** magistrate; **il est m.** he's a magistrate, he sits on the Bench; **m. du parquet** public prosecutor **(b) premier m. de France** supreme judicial officer of France

magistrature [maʒistratyr] *nf* **(a)** (*personnes*) magistrature; **la m. assise** = the judges, the Bench; **la m. debout** = the (body of) public prosecutors; **entrer dans la m.** (*devenir juge*) to be appointed a judge; (*devenir fonctionnaire public*) to be appointed a public prosecutor **(b)** (*période*) magistrature

magma [magma] *nm Ch, Géol* magma; **un m. informe de boue et de pierres** a shapeless heap *or* pile of mud and stones; *Fig* **un m. d'idées confuses** a jumble of confused ideas

magnanerie [maɲanri] *nf* **(a)** (*élevage*) silkworm breeding, *Spéc* sericulture **(b)** (*bâtiment*) silkworm house

magnanier, -ière [maɲanje, -jɛr] *n* silkworm breeder, *Spéc* sericulturist

magnanime [maɲanim] *adj* magnanimous; **se montrer m.** to show magnanimity, to be magnanimous

magnanimement [maɲanimmɑ̃] *adv* magnanimously

magnanimité [maɲanimite] *nf* magnanimity

magnat [magna] *nm* **(a)** *Com, Ind* magnate, tycoon; **magnats du pétrole** oil magnates *or* tycoons; **m. de la presse** press baron *or* tycoon **(b)** *Hist* (*de Pologne, Hongrie*) magnate, grandee

magner (se) [s(ə)maɲe] *vpr F* to get a move on, to get one's skates on; *très F* **magne-toi le train!** get your backside into gear!

magnésie [maɲezi] *nf Ch, Pharm* magnesia, magnesium oxide; *Pharm* **sulfate de m.** Epsom salts

magnésite [maɲezit] *nf* (*carbonate de magnésium*) magnesite; (*silicate de magnésium*) meerschaum

magnésium [maɲezjɔm] *nm Ch* magnesium; **éclair de m.** magnesium light *or* flash

magnétique [maɲetik] *adj* magnetic; **champ m.** magnetic field; **enregistrement sur bande m.** recording on magnetic tape, tape-recording; *Fig* **exercer un pouvoir m.** to exert a hypnotic *or* magnetic power (**sur** on, over)

magnétisable [maɲetizabl] *adj* magnetizable; (*personne*) hypnotizable

magnétisation [maɲetizasjɔ̃] *nf* **(a)** *Phys* magnetization **(b)** (*d'une personne*) hypnotizing, mesmerizing

magnétiser [maɲetize] *vt* **(a)** (*fer etc*) to magnetize **(b)** (*personne*) to hypnotize, to mesmerize; *Fig* **auditoire magnétisé** hypnotized *or* spellbound audience; **orateur qui magnétise les foules** speaker who hypnotizes *or* mesmerizes the crowds, speaker who holds the crowds in his spell

magnétiseur [maɲetizœr] *nm* (*guérisseur*) healer; (*hypnotiseur*) hypnotist

magnétisme [maɲetism] *nm* **(a)** *Phys* magnetism; **le m. terrestre** the earth's magnetism; **m. rémanent** residual magnetism **(b)** (*hypnotisme*) hypnotism, mesmerism; *Fig* **m. personnel** personal magnetism; **une personne qui a beaucoup de m.** a person with a great deal of charisma *or* personality; **m. animal** animal magnetism

magnétite [maɲetit] *nf Minér* magnetite, lodestone

magnéto [maɲeto] **1** *nf Él* magneto **2** *nm F* (*magnétophone*) tape recorder

magnétocassette [maɲetokasɛt] *nm Ordinat* **m. numérique** digital cassette recorder

magnétomètre [maɲetɔmɛtr] *nm Tech* magnetometer

magnétophone [maɲetɔfɔn] *nm* tape recorder; **m. (enregistreur) à cassettes** cassette recorder; **m. à bande** audio tape recorder; **m. à bobines** reel-to-reel tape recorder

magnétoscope [maɲetɔskɔp] *nm* video recorder, video; **enregistrer un film au m.** to video a film, to record a film on video, to make a video of a film; **m. d'enregistrement** recording deck; **m. de lecture** playback deck; **m. de standard professionel** video(tape) recorder, VTR; **m. à cassette** video cassette recorder, VCR; **m. à cassette vidéo numérique** digital video(tape) recorder

magnétoscoper [maɲetɔskɔpe] *vt* to video, to record on video, to make a video of

magnificat [magnifikat] *nm inv Rel* magnificat

magnificence [maɲifisɑ̃s] *nf* (*richesse, éclat*) magnificence, *Br* splendour, *US* splendor; *Litt* (*générosité*) munificence, lavishness

magnifier [maɲifje] *vt* (*pr sub & impf* **n. magnifiions, v. magnifiiez**) **(a)** (*exalter*) to magnify, to glorify **(b)** (*idéaliser*) to idealize

magnifique [maɲifik] *adj* **(a)** (*château, palais, meubles etc*) magnificent, splendid; (*temps*) glorious, superb, splendid, magnificent; (*corps*) superb, magnificent; (*film, tableau, fruits, cadeau etc*) splendid, marvellous, wonderful; **on a une vue m. depuis le deuxième étage** there is a magnificent *or* superb view from the second floor; **(c'est) m.!** (it's) marvellous *or* great *or* fantastic!; **elle était m. dans sa robe de mariée** she looked magnificent *or* wonderful *or* superb in her wedding dress; **un bébé m.** a bonny (little) *or* lovely (little) baby; **il est m. dans le rôle** he is magnificent *or* superb *or* brilliant in the role

(b) *Vieilli* (*généreux, prodigue*) (*personne*) liberal, munificent; **Laurent le Magnifique** Lorenzo il Magnifico; **Gatsby le m.** the Great Gatsby

magnifiquement [maɲifikmɑ̃] *adv* (*décoré, vêtu*) magnificently, splendidly; (*réussir*) brilliantly; **un morceau de musique m. exécuté** a brilliantly performed piece of music; **la soirée s'est m. passée** the party went splendidly *or* marvellously *or* wonderfully

magnitude [maɲityd] *nf Astron, Géol* magnitude; **un séisme de m. 5 sur l'échelle de Richter** an earthquake measuring 5 on the Richter scale

magnolia [maɲɔlja] *nm*, **magnolier** [maɲɔlje] *nm* magnolia (tree)

magnum [magnɔm] *nm* magnum

magot[1] [mago] *nm F* (*d'argent*) hoard, pile; (*économies*) savings, nest egg; **il a dû amasser un joli m.** he must have built up a nice little nest egg *or* a nice little pile; **dis-nous où tu as mis le m.!** tell us where you've stashed the loot!

magot[2] *nm* **(a)** (*singe*) Barbary ape **(b)** (*figurine*) magot

magouillage [magujaʒ] *nm*, **magouille** [maguj] *nf F* scheming, shady dealing; **faire des magouillages** to scheme; **magouillages électoraux** pre-election scheming

magouiller [maguje] *F* **1** *vt* to scheme; **il magouille un mauvais coup** he's cooking up a dirty trick **2** *vi* **il magouille pour avoir des ordinateurs gratuits** he's trying to wangle some free computers, he's scheming to get some free computers; **il a dû m. pour avoir ce poste** he had to do some scheming to get the job

magouilleur, -euse [magujœr, -øz] *n F* schemer

magret [magrɛ] *nm Culin* (*d'oie, de canard*) fillet, breast

magyar, -are [magjar] **1** *adj* Magyar **2** *n* **M.** Magyar

maharajah [maaradʒa] *nm* maharaja(h)

maharani [maarani] *nf* maharanee

mahatma [maatma] *nm* mahatma

mah-jong [maʒɔ̃g] *nm* mah-jong(g)

Mahomet [maɔmɛ] *nm* Mohammed, Mahomet

mahométan, -ane [maɔmetɑ̃, -an] *adj, n Vieilli* Mohammedan, Mahometan

mahométisme [maɔmetism] *nm Vieilli* Mohammedanism
mai [mɛ] *nm* [①A75-6,B-C; B58-9,B-C] May; **en m.** in May; **au mois de m.** in (the month of) May; **le sept m.** (on) the seventh of May, (on) May the seventh, *Am* (on) May seventh; **le premier m.** the first of May; *Admin* May Day
MAIF [maif] *nf abrév* **Mutuelle assurance des instituteurs de France**
maigre [mɛgr] **1** *adj* (*personne, animal, bras, cou*) thin, *Péj* skinny; (*viande*) lean; (*revenu, récolte, résultats*) meagre, *US* meager, poor; (*végétation*) sparse, scanty; (*barbe*) straggly, sparse; (*conclusions, explication*) thin; (*succès*) very limited; **m. comme un clou** as thin as a rake; **homme grand et m.** a tall, thin man; **fromage m.** low-fat cheese; **m. filet d'eau** thin trickle of water; **m. repas** scanty *or* frugal meal; **jour m.** day of abstinence; *Typ* **caractères maigres** lightfaced type
2 *n* (*personne*) **un grand m.** a tall, thin man; **c'est une fausse m.** she's not as thin as she looks
3 *nm* **(a) maigres** (*de rivière*) shallows **(b)** (*viande*) **un morceau de m.** a piece of lean (meat)
4 *adv* **manger** *ou* **faire m.** not to eat meat, to abstain from meat
maigrelet, -ette [mɛgrəlɛ, -ɛt] *Péj* **1** *adj* skinny **2** *n* skinny person
maigrement [mɛgrəmɑ̃] *adv* meagrely, *US* meagerly, poorly; **il est m. payé** he's poorly paid, he gets a meagre pay
maigreur [mɛgrœr] *nf* (*de personne*) thinness, *Péj* skinniness; *Fig* (*de végétation*) sparseness, scantiness; (*de récolte, salaire*) meagreness, *US* meagerness, poorness; **d'une m. effrayante** frighteningly thin
maigrichon, -onne [megriʃɔ̃, -ɔn], **maigriot, -otte** [megrijo, -ɔt] *adj, n F* = **maigrelet**
maigrir [mɛgrir] **1** *vi* to get thin(ner), to lose weight; **elle essaie de m.** she's trying to lose weight, she's slimming; **j'ai maigri de dix kilos** I've lost ten kilos; **régime pour m.** (weight-loss) diet **2** *vt* **(a) m. qn** (*d'une maladie*) to make sb thin(ner); (*d'un vêtement*) to make sb look thin(ner) **(b)** (*pièce de bois*) to thin
mail [maj] *nm* **(a)** *Vieilli* (*allée*) mall, avenue, promenade **(b)** *Hist* (*jeu, lieu*) pall-mall **(c)** *Arch* (*marteau*) mallet
mailing [mɛliŋ] *nm* mailshot; **faire un m.** to do a mailshot
maillage [majaʒ] *nm* networking
maille[1] [maj] *nf* **(a)** (*en tricot etc*) stitch; **m. (à l')endroit** plain (stitch); **m. (à l')envers** purl (stitch); **une m. à l'endroit, une m. à l'envers** knit one, purl one; **m. qui file** ladder, *Am* run **(b)** (*tissu tricoté*) knitwear; **une robe en m. de coton** a knitted cotton dress **(c)** (*d'une chaîne*) link; **j'aime la m. de son bracelet** I like the style of link in her bracelet; **cotte de mailles** coat of mail **(d)** (*de filet, de grillage etc*) mesh; **filet à larges mailles** wide-mesh net; **passer entre** *ou* **à travers les mailles du filet** to slip through the net
maille[2] *nf* **avoir m. à partir avec qn** to have a set-to with sb; **avoir m. à partir avec la justice** to have a brush with the law
maillechort [majʃɔr] *nm* nickel silver
maillet [majɛ] *nm* **(a)** (*outil*) mallet **(b)** *Sp* (*au polo*) stick, mallet; (*au croquet*) mallet
mailloche [majɔʃ] *nf* **(a)** (*outil*) beetle, large mallet **(b)** *Mus* bass drumstick
maillon [mɑjɔ̃] *nm* **(a)** (*de chaîne*) link; **m. tournant** swivel; *Fig* **n'être qu'un m. de la chaîne** to be just one link in the chain **(b)** *Naut* shackle
maillot [majo] *nm* **(a)** (*tee-shirt*) T-shirt, tee shirt; (*pour la danse*) leotard; *Sp* (*de footballeur, d'équipe*) shirt, jersey; (*de coureur, rameur*) vest, singlet; **m. (de bain)** (*pour femme*) swimsuit, *Br* swimming *or* bathing costume; (*pour homme*) (swimming *or* bathing) trunks; **leur nouvelle collection de maillots** their new swimwear collection; **m. de corps** (*pour homme*) vest, *Am* undershirt; **m. une pièce/deux pièces** one-piece/two-piece swimsuit; **être m. jaune** to be the overall leader of the Tour de France; **m. de marin** striped tee shirt; (*pull*) striped sweater **(b)** *Hist* (*pour bébé*) swaddling clothes
main [mɛ̃] **1** *nf* **(a)** hand; **faire qch de la m. droite/gauche** to do sth right-handed/left-handed *or* with one's right/left hand; **faire qch à la m.** to do sth by hand; (*fabriquer*) to make sth by hand; **fait à la m.** (*pull etc*) handmade; **travailler de ses mains** to work with one's hands; **écrire une lettre de sa propre m.** to write a letter in one's own hand; **notes écrites à la m.** handwritten notes; **d'une (seule) m.** with one hand; **je n'ai que deux mains** I only have one pair of hands; **prendre un plateau/son courage à deux mains** to take a tray/one's courage in both hands; *Fig* **signer qch des deux mains** to sign sth eagerly; *Fig* **souscrire à deux mains à qch** to subscribe unreservedly to sth; **je lui ai serré la m.** I shook hands with him, I shook his hand; **dire adieu de la m. à qn** to wave goodbye to sb; **donner la m. à qn** to hold sb's hand; **donne la m. à Philippe** (*pour traverser la rue*) give Philippe your hand, take *or* hold Philippe's hand; **ils se tenaient (par) la m., ils se donnaient la m.** they were holding hands; *Fig* **se donner la m.** to give each other a helping hand; *Fig* **ces deux-là peuvent se donner la m.** they're two of a kind, those two are as bad as each other; **prendre qn par la m.** to take sb's hand, to take sb by the hand; *Fig* **tu n'as qu'à ne prendre par la m.** just go for it, just do it; **il n'a qu'à se prendre par la m. et le faire** he just has to do it; *Fig* **se prendre en m.** to take oneself in hand; **prendre qn en m.** to take sb in hand; **prendre une affaire/une situation en m.** to take a matter/a situation in hand; **il a sa voiture bien en m.** he's got the feel of his car; **j'ai la situation en m.** I've got the situation in hand *or* under control; **la m. dans la m.** hand in hand; **avoir/tenir qch dans la m.** to have/hold sth in one's hand; **avoir une canne/une craie à la m.** to have a stick/a piece of chalk in one's hand; **mourir les armes à la m.** to die on the battlefield; **ne rien savoir faire de ses mains** to be hopeless with one's hands; **je ne suis pas très adroite de mes mains** I'm not very good with my hands; **la bouteille m'a échappé des mains** the bottle slipped out of *or* from my hands; **de m. en m.** from hand to hand; **passer de m. en m.** (*d'un objet*) to pass *or* be passed from hand to hand *or* from person to person; *Fig* (*d'une maison, d'un livre etc*) to go *or* pass through several hands; **passer aux mains de …** to pass *or* fall into the hands of …; **haut les mains!, les mains en l'air!** hands up!; **faire qch d'une m. habile** *ou* **experte** *ou* **exercée** to do sth with a skilled *or* an expert hand, to do sth skilfully; **en venir aux mains** to come to blows; **se battre à main(s) nue(s)** to fight with bare hands *or* fists; **combat à mains nues** bare-fisted *or* bare-knuckle fight; **attaque/vol à m. armée** armed attack/robbery; **venir/repartir les mains vides** to come/return empty-handed; *Fig* **arriver les mains dans les poches** to arrive unprepared; **donner d'une m. et reprendre de l'autre** to give with one hand and take back with the other; **demander la m. d'une jeune fille à ses parents** to ask a girl's parents for her hand (in marriage); **accorder/refuser sa m. à qn** (*d'une femme*) to give/refuse sb one's hand in marriage; **tendre la m. (à qn)** to hold *or* stretch out one's hand (to sb); *Fig* (*pour l'aider*) to hold *or* stretch out a hand (to sb); **tendre à qn une m. secourable** to hold *or* stretch out a helping hand to sb; *Fig* **on le soupçonna de vouloir tendre la m. aux Protestants** he was suspected of making conciliatory moves towards the Protestants; *Fig* **passer la m. dans le dos à qn** to butter sb up; **porter la m. à son chapeau** (*pour saluer*) to touch one's hat, to tip one's hat; *Fig* **on ne le voit pas souvent mettre la m. à son portefeuille** you don't often see him putting his hand in his pocket; **porter** *ou* **lever la m. sur qn** to lift *or* raise one's hand to sb; *F* **tu veux ma m. sur la figure?** do you want my hand across your face?; **mettre la m. sur qn** *ou* **au collet de qn** (*de la police*) to catch sb, *F* to collar *or* nab sb; (*le trouver*) to find sb; **mettre la m. sur qch** (*trouver qch que l'on cherchait*) to lay one's hands on sth, to put one's hand on sth; (*trouver par hasard*) to come across, to find; **je n'en mettrais pas ma m. au feu** *ou* **à couper** I shouldn't like to swear to it; **j'en mettrais ma m. au feu** *ou* **à couper** I'd swear to it; **mettre la m. à la pâte** *ou* **à l'ouvrage** to lend a hand; **mettre la dernière m. à qch** to put the finishing touches to sth; *Arg* **mettre la m. au panier de qn** to grope sb's behind; **prendre qn la m. dans le sac** to catch sb red-handed; **ne pas y aller de m. morte** (*en frappant, insultant qn*) not to pull one's punches; (*exagérer*) to overdo it; **faire m. basse sur qch** to get one's hands on sth; **avoir qch sous la m.** *ou* **à portée de (la) m.** to have sth handy *or* within easy reach *or* close at hand; **le premier objet qui lui est tombé sous la m.** the first object that came to hand; **faire qch en sous m.** to do sth in an underhand way; **ne pas laisser ce produit à portée de m. des enfants** keep out of the reach of children; *F* **donner un coup de m. à qn** to lend *or* give sb a hand; **prêter la m. à qn pour faire qch** to lend sb a hand to do sth; **prêter la m. à qch** to have a hand in sth; **se faire la m.** to get one's hand in; **pour garder la m.** in order to keep your hand in; **il avait gardé la m.** he hadn't lost the knack *or* his touch; **il a perdu la m.** he's lost the knack *or* his touch; (*d'un sportif, musicien*) he's out of practice; **avoir le coup de m. (pour faire qch)** to have the knack (of doing sth); **ce n'est pas à mettre entre toutes les mains** it mustn't fall into the wrong hands; **une m. de fer dans un gant de velours** an iron hand *or* fist in a velvet glove; **d'une m. de fer** with an iron hand; **il empoigna la Kalashnikov à pleines mains** he grabbed the Kalashnikov with both hands; **il puise à pleines mains dans la caisse** he's got his hand in the till; **il a puisé à**

pleines mains dans les caisses de l'état he liberally helped himself from the state coffers; **donner de l'argent à pleine(s) main(s)** to dish out money by the handful; **prendre qch à pleines mains** to take handfuls of sth; **il prit le livre à pleines mains** he took the book in both hands; **payer de la m. à la m.** to pay cash in hand; **tomber entre les mains** *ou* **aux mains** *ou* **sous la m. de qn** to fall into sb's hands *or* clutches; **tomber aux mains de l'ennemi** to fall into enemy hands; **l'affaire est entre les mains du juge Martin** the case is in the hands of Mr Justice Martin; **mon avenir est entre vos mains** my future is in your hands; **la décision est entre vos mains** the decision is in your hands *or* is up to you *or* is yours; **être en** *ou* **entre (de) bonnes mains** to be in good hands; **remettre qch à qn en mains propres** to deliver sth to sb in person; **acheter qch en première/seconde m.** to buy sth firsthand/secondhand; **article de seconde m.** secondhand article; **renseignements de première m.** firsthand information; **avoir la m. verte** to have green fingers *or Am* a green thumb; **ça nous laisse les mains libres pour agir** that gives us a free hand; **garder les mains libres** to keep a free hand; **j'ai les mains liées** my hands are tied; **avoir la m. légère** to have a delicate touch; *Litt (être habile)* to be clever with one's hands; *(être délicat)* to act with restraint *or* discretion; *(ne pas faire sentir son autorité)* to rule with a light hand; *(ne pas assaisonner suffisamment)* to underseason; **tu as eu la m. légère avec la crème/le sucre** you haven't put enough cream/sugar in; **avoir la m. lourde** *(avec le poivre, le whisky etc)* to be overgenerous, to be a bit heavy-handed (**avec** with); *(punir)* to mete out punishment with a heavy hand; **ce commerçant a la m. un peu lourde** this shopkeeper always gives you a bit over the weight; **avoir la m. leste** *(baladeuse)* to have wandering hands; *(être prompt à gifler)* to be a bit too quick with one's hands; **avoir la m. heureuse** to be lucky; **j'ai eu la m. heureuse** I was *or* got lucky, I had a lucky break; **mains criminelles/sacrilèges** criminal/sacrilegious hands; **dessin à m. levée** freehand drawing; **voter à m. levée** to vote by a show of hands; **gagner haut la m.** to win easily *or* hands down; *Vieilli* **de longue m.** for a long time (past); *Fig* **se laver les mains de qch** to wash one's hands of sth; *Fig* **se frotter les mains** to be rubbing one's hands with glee; **grand comme la m.** tiny; **leur maison est grande comme la m.** their house isn't big enough to swing a cat in; *Prov* **aux innocents les mains pleines** fortune favours fools, beginners have all the luck; *Mus* **morceau à quatre mains** piece for four hands, duet; **m. de maître** master hand; **de m. de maître** by a master('s) hand; **un concerto exécuté de m. de maître** a masterfully performed concerto; **la cérémonie a été organisée de m. de maître** the ceremony was a masterpiece of organization; **c'est fait de m. de maître** it's a masterpiece; **on reconnaît la m. du maître** this is obviously the work of a master; **reconnaître la m. d'un peintre** to recognize a painter's style; **à m. droite/gauche** on the right-hand/left-hand side

(b) *Cartes* lead; **avoir/perdre la m.** to have/lose the lead; **passer la m.** *Cartes* to pass the lead; *Fig* to stand aside, to give someone else a chance; **passer la m. à son fils** to hand over the reins to one's son

(c) *Couture* **petite m.** junior assistant

2 *adv* **tricoté/fait/cousu m.** hand-knitted/made/sewn

▶ **main**: **m. d'accoucheur** claw-like hand; **m. courante** *(d'escalier)* handrail; *Com* daybook; **m. courante de justice** incident book; **m. de Fatma** hand of Fatima; *Typ* **m. de papier** quire of paper

mainate [mɛnat] *nm* myna(h) (bird)

main-d'œuvre [mɛ̃dœvr] *nf (personnes, travail)* manpower, workforce; *Écon* labour, *US* labor; **embaucher de la m.** to take on workers; **m. étrangère** foreign labour(ers); **frais de m.** labour costs; **m. qualifiée** skilled labour; **m. temporaire** temporary labour

main-forte [mɛ̃fɔrt] *nf inv* **prêter m. à qn** to come to sb's assistance *or* aid

mainlevée [mɛ̃lve] *nf Jur (d'un acte)* lifting; **m. de saisie** restoration of goods *(taken in distraint)*

mainmise [mɛ̃miz] *nf* seizure (**sur** of); *Fig* **la m. du gouvernement sur les médias** the government's appropriation *or* takeover of the media

maint [mɛ̃] *adj Litt* many a; **m. auteur** many an author; **maintes et maintes fois, à maintes reprises, en m. (et m.) occasion** time and (time) again

maintenance [mɛ̃tnɑ̃s] *nf* **(a)** *Ind (entretien)* maintenance, service; **m. sur site** on-site maintenance **(b)** *Mil* keeping up to strength

maintenant [mɛ̃tnɑ̃] *adv* [①A23,3,a,i] now; **vous devriez être prêt m.** you ought to be ready by now; **à vous m.** now it's your turn; **dès m., à partir de m.** from now on(wards), in future, *Fml* henceforth; **m. que tu es grand** now (that) you're a big boy; **je vous donne ce conseil, m. vous en faites ce que vous voulez** that's my advice to you, (now) take it or leave it; **m. reste à savoir si les employés voudront reprendre le travail** the question now is whether the employees will be willing to go back to work; **les jeunes de m.** young people today *or* nowadays, the young people *or* the youth of today

mainteneur [mɛ̃tnœr] *nm Bourse* **m. de marché** market maker

maintenir [mɛ̃tnir] *(conj like* **tenir) 1** *vt* **(a)** *(soutenir, retenir, tenir fermement)* to keep *or* hold in position; **colonnes qui maintiennent la voûte** columns that hold up *or* support the vault; **m. la foule** to hold back the crowd; **m. son cheval** to keep one's horse under control

(b) *(entretenir, garder) (tradition)* to maintain, to keep, to uphold; *(discipline)* to maintain, to keep; *(paix)* to keep, to maintain, to preserve; *(décision)* to abide by; **m. qn dans ses fonctions** to maintain *or* keep sb in office; **m. sa position** to maintain one's position; **je maintiens que c'est faux** I maintain that it's untrue; **les médecins font tout pour le m. en vie** the doctors are doing everything possible to keep him alive; **m. qch à température constante** to keep *or* maintain sth at a constant temperature; **nos programmes sont maintenus malgré la grève** the station is maintaining normal service despite the strike

2 se maintenir *vpr (de prix, dollar, taux de change, cours de la Bourse)* to remain steady, to hold up *or* steady; **se m. dans les bonnes grâces de qn** to keep in favour with sb, to stay in sb's good books; *F* **comment ça va? – je me maintiens** how are you? – (I'm) bearing up; **cela ne peut pas se m. longtemps** it can't last long; **le temps se maintient** the weather is holding

maintien [mɛ̃tjɛ̃] *nm* **(a)** *(fait de conserver dans le même état)* maintenance; *(de la loi, d'un principe)* upholding; *(de la discipline)* maintenance, keeping; **m. de l'ordre** policing, maintenance of law and order; *Mil* **force de m. de la paix** peacekeeping force; *Jur* **m. dans les lieux** right(s) of occupancy, security of tenure; *Ordinat* **m. majuscule** caps lock **(b)** *(allure, posture)* bearing, deportment; **leçons de m.** lessons in deportment

maire [mɛr] *nm* mayor; *(en Écosse)* provost; **monsieur/madame le m.** the Mayor, His/Her Worship (the Mayor); *(en s'adressant à lui/elle)* Your Worship; *Hum* **passer devant (monsieur) le m.** to tie the knot, to get hitched

mairesse [mɛrɛs] *nf Vieilli (femme du maire)* mayoress; *Rare (femme maire)* mayor

mairie [mɛri] *nf (lieu)* town hall, *Am* city hall; *(administration municipale)* town *or* city council, *Am* city hall; **la m. a organisé un voyage pour les personnes âgées de la ville** the council has organized a trip for the town's senior citizens; **c'est un employé de m.** he works for the council, he's a council worker

mais [mɛ] **1** *adv Litt* **n'en pouvoir m.** to be unable to do anything about it

2 *conj* **(a)** *(marque l'opposition)* but; **famille riche m. honnête** rich but honest family; **il n'est pas très intelligent m. il est très travailleur** he's not very intelligent but he's a hard worker; **non seulement ..., m. aussi** *ou* **encore ...** not only ... but also ...

(b) *(emphatique)* **m. oui!** oh yes!, of course!, *Am* sure!; **m. non!** oh no!, not at all!, of course not!; **m. c'est vrai!** but it's true!, it really is true!; **m. enfin!** well really!; **m. enfin je te l'avais bien dit!** I told you!; **elle ne fait rien de la journée, m. vraiment rien** she does nothing all day, absolutely nothing

(c) *(transition)* **m. qu'avez-vous donc?** whatever's the matter?; **m. à quoi penses-tu?** whatever's got into you?; **m. tu l'as déjà vu?** what, you've already seen it?; **m. j'y pense, je ne l'ai pas encore appelé!** I've just thought, I haven't rung him yet!

3 *nm* **il y a un m.** there's one snag; **il n'y a pas de m. (qui tienne)** there are no buts about it

maïs [mais] *nm (plante)* maize, *Am* corn; *(légume)* (sweet) corn; **farine de m.** cornflour, *Am* cornstarch

maison [mɛzɔ̃] **1** *nf* **(a)** *(habitation)* house; **m. individuelle** detached house; **m. bourgeoise** luxurious house; **il porte des pantoufles dans la m.** he wears slippers indoors *or* around the house

(b) *(foyer)* home; **tenir la m. de qn** to keep house for sb; **à la m.** at home; **retournons à la m.** let's go home, let's go back to the house; **elle travaille à la m.** she works at *or* from home; **ça fait longtemps que tu n'es pas venu à la m.** it's a long time since you came to our house; **dépenses de (la) m.**

household expenses; **ça ne va pas fort à la m. en ce moment** things aren't too good at home just now; **toute la m. dort** the whole house is asleep; **le fils de la m.** the son of the house; **ami de la m.** friend of the family; **chez eux, c'est la m. du Bon Dieu** they keep open house, their door is always open

(c) (*entreprise*) firm, company; **cela fait vingt ans qu'elle est dans la m., elle a vingt ans de m.** she's been with the firm *or* company for twenty years; **la m. décline toute responsabilité en cas de perte ou de vol** we accept no responsibility for loss or theft; **la m. ne fait pas crédit** we do not give credit; **la M. du Stylo** the Pen Shop; **l'esprit de la m.** the company spirit

(d) (*lignée*) **la m. de Bourbon** the House of Bourbon

(e) (*domestiques*) household, staff; **la m. du Roi** the Royal Household; **gens de m.** servants, (domestic) staff

(f) *Astrol* house

2 *adj inv* **(a)** home-made; **spécialité m.** speciality of the house

(b) *F* (*énorme*) colossal; **on s'est pris une engueulade m.** we got an almighty telling-off

(c) *F* (*très réussi*) fantastic

▶ **maison**: *Banque* **m. d'acceptation** accepting house; **m. d'arrêt** = remand centre; **m. de campagne** (*résidence secondaire*) house in the country, country house; (*de style campagnard*) country cottage; **m. centrale** prison; **m. close** brothel; **m. de commerce** business; **m. de convalescence** convalescent home; *Vieilli* **m. de correction** reformatory; **m. de couture** fashion house; **m. de la culture** = arts centre; **m. de détail** retail business; **M. de Dieu** house of God; **m. d'édition** publishing house; **m. d'éducation surveillée** approved school, *Am* reformatory; **m. d'enfants** children's holiday centre, *Am* camp; **m. familiale** holiday *or Am* vacation home (*for families on low incomes*); *Fig F* **m. de fous** madhouse; **m. de gros** wholesale business; **m. des jeunes et de la culture** = youth club and arts centre; **m. de jeux** gambling club, gaming club; **m. de maître** large luxurious house; **m. mère** parent company; *Rel* mother house; **m. de passe** brothel; **m. de poupées** doll's house; **m. de rapport** rental property; **m. de redressement** reformatory; **m. religieuse** convent; **m. de rendez-vous** love nest; **m. de repos** rest home; **m. de retraite** old people's home; **m. de santé** (*établissement hospitalier*) nursing home; (*psychiatrique*) mental home; **M. du Seigneur** house of God; **m. à succursales multiples** multiple outlet company; *Fin* **m. de titres** securities firm; **m. de tolérance** brothel; **m. de vente par correspondance** mail order firm *or* house

Maison-Blanche (la) [lamɛzɔ̃blɑ̃ʃ] *nf* the White House

maisonnée [mɛzɔne] *nf* household, family

maisonnette [mɛzɔnɛt] *nf* small house; (*à la campagne*) cottage

maistrance [mɛstrɑ̃s] *nf Naut* petty officers

maître, maîtresse [mɛtr, mɛtrɛs] **1** *nm* **(a)** (*personne qui contrôle*) master, *f* mistress; **je veux être m. chez moi** I insist on being master in my own house; **ce chien n'obéit qu'à son m.** the dog obeys nobody but its master; **agir/parler en m.** to act/speak authoritatively; **être m. de la situation** to be master of *or* in control of the situation; **un dictateur fou qui veut devenir le m. du monde** a mad dictator who wants to take over *or* rule the world; **trouver son m.** to meet one's match; **être/rester son propre m.** to be/remain one's own master; **être/rester m. de soi** to be/remain self-possessed, to be/remain in control of one's emotions; **il n'était plus m. de lui-même** he lost control (of himself); **être m. de son véhicule** to be in control of one's vehicle; **le conducteur n'était plus m. de son véhicule** the driver (had) lost control of the car; **se rendre m. de qch** to take possession of sth; **tableau de m.** masterpiece; **les grands maîtres de la peinture flamande/de la musique** the great masters of Flemish painting/the great composers; **coup de m.** masterstroke; **être passé m. dans l'art de (faire) qch** to be a past master at (doing) sth; *Naut* **second m.** petty officer; **premier m.** chief petty officer; **être le seul m. à bord** to be sole master on board; *Fig* to be free to choose, to be free to do whatever one wants; *Fig* **c'est toi le seul m. à bord** you're the boss, you're in charge

(b) *Scol* (school)teacher, *Old-fashioned* (school)master

(c) *Jur* (*forme d'adresse*) (*pour un avocat qui s'appelle Martin*) Mr/Mrs/Miss Martin, *US* counsellor; **M. Dupont s'occupera de l'affaire** Mr/Mrs/Miss Dupont will be dealing with the case

(d) (*titre octroyé à un peintre etc*) Maestro

2 *adj* chief, principal, main; **m. mot** key word; **poutre maîtresse** (*en métal*) main girder; (*en bois*) main beam; **cheville maîtresse** kingpin; **idée maîtresse d'un ouvrage** governing *or* key idea of a work; **maîtresse femme** capable woman; **carte maîtresse** *Cartes, Ordinat* master card; *Fig* (*principal atout*) trump card

▶ **maître**: *Constr* **m. d'armes** fencing master; *Univ* **m. assistant** = assistant lecturer; *Rel* **m-autel**, *pl* **maîtres-autels** high altar; *Scol* **m. auxiliaire** supply *or Am* substitute teacher; **m. de cérémonies** master of ceremonies; **m. chanteur** blackmailer; **m. de chapelle** choirmaster; **m. charpentier** master carpenter; **m. chien**, *pl* **maîtres-chiens** dog-handler; *Univ* **m. de conférence** ≈ (senior) lecturer, *Am* assistant professor; **m-coq**, *pl* **maître-coqs** executive chef; *Aut* **m-cylindres**, *pl* **maîtres-cylindres** master cylinder; **m. de danse** dancing master; **m. d'école** primary school *or Am* elementary school teacher; **m. d'équipage** boatswain; **m. de forges** ironmaster; **m. d'hôtel** (*dans une maison*) butler; (*dans un restaurant*) head waiter, *Am* maitre d' [ˈmetr(ə)diː]; *Naut* chief steward; **m. d'internat** = housemaster; **m. maçon** master mason; **m. de maison** (*pour un invité*) host; **pourrais-je parler au m. de maison?** could I speak to the man *or* the master of the house?; **m. de manège** riding instructor *or* master; **m. nageur** swimming instructor; **m. d'œuvre** prime contractor, project manager, master of works; **m. d'ouvrage** *ou* **de l'ouvrage** contracting authority; **m. queux** chef

maîtresse [mɛtrɛs] *nf* **(a)** (*personne qui contrôle*) *voir* **maître 1**(*a*) **(b)** (*d'un homme*) mistress; **avoir une m.** to have a mistress; **être la m. de qn** to be sb's mistress **(c)** *Scol* (school) teacher, *Old-fashioned* (school) mistress

▶ **maîtresse**: **m. d'école** primary school *or Am* elementary school teacher; **m. de maison** (*pour un invité*) hostess; (*ménagère*) lady of the house; **pourrais-je parler à la m. de maison?** could I speak to the lady of the house?

maîtrisable [mɛtrizabl] *adj* controllable

maîtrise [mɛtriz] *nf* **(a)** *Univ* ≈ master's degree, MA; **une m. d'anglais** ≈ a master's degree in English, an MA in English **(b)** (*contrôle*) (*de ses passions, d'un art, un sujet etc*) mastery, command; **m. de soi** self-control; *Mil* **m. des mers** command *or* control of the seas **(c)** *Ind* supervisory staff **(d)** (*école*) choir school; (*chorale*) choir; (*poste*) post of choirmaster

maîtriser [mɛtrize] **1** *vt* (*agresseur*) to overpower; (*élèves, animal*) to control; (*flammes, opposition*) to subdue; (*incendie, épidémie*) to control, to get under control; (*passion, impatience*) to control, to curb, to contain; (*ses nerfs*) to control; (*ses peurs*) to master, to overcome; (*langue, sujet etc*) to master; **il ne maîtrise pas la langue** he has no command of the language **2 se maîtriser** *vpr* to control oneself; **ne pas savoir se m.** to have no self-control

maïzena® [maizena] *nf Culin* cornflour, *Am* cornstarch

majesté [maʒɛste] *nf* **(a)** (*souverain*) majesty; **Sa M. le Roi/la Reine** His Majesty the King/Her Majesty the Queen; **Leurs Majestés** their Majesties; *Gram* **pluriel de m.** royal we **(b)** (*de port*) majesty, dignity, stateliness; (*de style, paysage*) majesty, grandeur

majestueusement [maʒɛstɥøzmɑ̃] *adv* majestically

majestueux, -euse [maʒɛstɥø, -øz] *adj* (*port*) majestic, stately; (*silhouette*) majestic, imposing; **paysage m.** majestic *or* magnificent landscape

majeur, -eure [maʒœr] **1** *adj* **(a)** (*plus grand*) (*préoccupation, intérêt, difficulté*) major; **la majeure partie de** the greater part of, the major part of; **en majeure partie** for the most part; **prémisse majeure** major premise; *Rel* **les ordres majeurs** the major orders; **raison majeure de qch** chief reason for sth; **il n'y a pas de raison majeure pour que vous veniez** there's no real reason for you to come; **être absent pour raison majeure** to be unavoidably absent; *Cartes* **couleur majeure** major suit

(b) *Jur* **être m.** to be of age; **le jour où il a été m.** the day he came of age; *Fig* **il est m., il sait ce qu'il fait** he's old enough *or* grown up, he knows what he's doing; *Hum* **je suis m. et vacciné** I'm old enough to look after myself; *Fig* **un peuple m.** a mature *or* responsible nation; *Jur* **m. incapable** mentally incompetent person

(c) *Mus* (*clé etc*) major; **en sol bémol m.** in G flat major

2 *n* (*personne*) person who has come of age *or* reached the age of majority

3 *nm* (*doigt*) middle finger

4 *nf Cartes* **majeure** major suit

majolique [maʒɔlik] *nf Cér* majolica

major [maʒɔr] *nm* **(a)** *Mil* regimental adjutant (*with administrative duties*); **m. général** chief of staff (*of a commander-in-chief in the field*); **m. du camp** camp commandant; **(médecin) m.** medical officer, M.O. **(b)** *Univ* **être m. de promotion** = to be top of one's year

majoration [maʒɔrasjɔ̃] *nf* **(a)** (*surestimation*) (*de biens*) overestimation, overvaluation **(b)** (*augmentation*) (*d'une facture*) surcharge, additional charge (**de** on); (*d'un prix*) increase (**de** in); (*pour plus de bénéfices*) markup; **m. pour retard de paiement** additional charge *or* surcharge for late payment

majordome [maʒɔrdɔm] *nm* major-domo

majorer [maʒɔre] *vt* **(a)** (*surestimer*) (*biens*) to overestimate, to overvalue **(b)** (*augmenter*) (*facture*) to put a surcharge *or* an additional charge on; (*prix*) to raise, to put up, to increase; (*pour faire plus de bénéfices*) to mark up; (*salaires*) to increase; **m. les prix de dix pour cent** to raise *or* put up *or* increase prices by ten per cent; **m. une facture de dix pour cent** to put a surcharge of ten per cent on an invoice, to increase an invoice by ten per cent

majorette [maʒɔrɛt] *nf* (drum) majorette

majoritaire [maʒɔritɛr] **1** *adj* majority; *Pol* **vote/parti m.** majority vote/party; *Fin* **actionnaire m.** majority shareholder; **être majoritaires** to be in the *or* a majority; **c'est un métier où les hommes ont toujours été largement majoritaires** it's a profession where men have always been in a large majority *or* where there has always been a large majority of men **2** *npl* **majoritaires** *Pol* members of the majority (party); *Fin* majority (shareholders)

majorité [maʒɔrite] *nf* **(a)** [①**A11**,g,i] (*supériorité en nombre*) majority; **la m. silencieuse** the silent majority; **la m. des personnes interrogées ...** the majority of (the) people *or* most of the people questioned ...; **être en m., avoir la m.** to be in a *or* the majority; **les citoyens pensent en m. que ...** the majority of citizens *or* most citizens think that ...; **dans la m. des cas** in the majority of cases, in most cases; **nous sommes une m. à vouloir combattre ce fléau** the *or* a majority of us want to fight against this scourge

(b) (*dans des élections*) majority; **remporter la m. des suffrages** to win a *or* the majority of the votes, to win a majority; **élu avec dix voix de m.** elected by a majority of ten; **m. relative/absolue** relative/absolute majority; **décision prise à la m. (des voix)** decision taken by a majority, majority decision

(c) *Parl* (*parti*) majority party; **m. gouvernementale** parliamentary majority; **être dans la m.** to be a member of the majority party

(d) *Jur* majority, coming of age; **atteindre la m.** to come of age, to attain one's majority; **m. légale** (minimum) voting age; **m. pénale** = minimum age in law at which a person is deemed capable of distinguishing between right and wrong

Majorque [maʒɔrk] *nf* Majorca

majorquin, -ine [maʒɔrkɛ̃, -in] **1** *adj* Majorcan **2** *n* **M.** Majorcan

majuscule [maʒyskyl] **1** *adj* (*lettre*) capital **2** *nf* capital letter; *Typ* upper-case letter; **en majuscules** in capitals; **majuscules** caps; **majuscules d'imprimerie** block letters, block capitals

majuscule-clic, *pl* **majuscules-clics** *nm Ordinat* shift-click

majuscule-glisser, *pl* **majuscules-glisser** *nm Ordinat* shift-drag

mal[1]**, maux** [mal, mo] *nm* **(a)** (*douleur, sensation désagréable*) pain, ache; (*maladie*) illness, sickness; **souffrir d'horribles maux de ventre** to suffer from *or* to have terrible stomach pains; *F* **prendre** *ou* **attraper (du) m.** to catch cold, to catch a chill; **avoir m. à l'estomac/à la tête/au dos** to have stomach ache *or* a sore stomach/a headache *or* a sore head/backache *or* a sore back; **avoir m. à la gorge/au bras** to have a sore throat/arm; **avoir m. aux dents** to have toothache; *F* **avoir m. aux cheveux** to have a hangover; **où avez-vous m.?** where does it hurt?, where is the pain?; **vous me faites (du) m.** you're hurting me; **mon genou me fait m.** my knee hurts; **se faire m.** to hurt oneself; **spectacle qui fait m. (au cœur** *ou* **au ventre)** painful sight; **ça fait m. au ventre de voir des choses pareilles!** it makes you sick *or* it's sickening to see things like that!; *Fig F* **ça me ferait m. (au ventre)!** it would make me sick!; *très F* **ça me ferait m. aux seins!** it would really piss me off!; *F* **tu vas lui prêter ta robe? – ça me ferait m.** are you going to lend her your dress? – no way!; **être en m. de qch** to be yearning *or* desperate for sth, to be badly in need of sth; **je ne me laisserai pas calomnier par des journalistes en m. de copie** I'm not going to be slandered by journalists, with nothing better to write about *or* who're short of copy; **femme en m. d'enfants** woman desperate for children *or* to have children

(b) (*préjudice, tort, souffrance*) harm, hurt; **faire du m.** to do harm; **faire du m. à qn** to harm sb, to do sb harm; **ne bougez pas et aucun m. ne vous sera fait** don't move and nobody will get hurt; **allez, un p'tit coup de gnôle, ça n'a jamais fait de m. à personne!** go on, a little tipple never did anyone any harm!; **mettre qch à m.** to damage sth; *Fig Vieilli* **il avait mis à m. toutes les servantes** he had ravished all the maidservants; **il fait plus de bruit que de m.** (*chien, personne*) his bark is worse than his bite; **s'en tirer sans aucun m.** to escape uninjured *or* unhurt *or* unscathed; **il ne ferait pas de m. à une mouche** he wouldn't hurt a fly; **je ne lui veux pas de m.** I mean him no harm; **cela fera plus de m. que de bien** it will do more harm than good; **le m. est fait** the harm *or* damage has been done; *Prov* **aux grands maux les grands remèdes** desperate situations call for desperate remedies; **souffrir de trois grands maux** to suffer from three great evils; **entre deux maux il faut choisir le moindre** you have to choose the lesser of two evils; **entre deux maux j'ai choisi le moindre** it was the lesser of two evils; **un m. nécessaire** a necessary evil; **il n'y a pas de m. à cela** there's no harm in that; **quel m. y a-t-il à cela?** what harm can that do?, what harm is there in it?; *F* **il n'y a pas de m.** (*à qn qui s'excuse*) there's no harm done; **m. lui en a pris** he has had cause to regret it *or* to rue it; **dire du m. de qn, parler en m. de qn** to speak ill of sb; **il a changé en m.** he has changed for the worse

(c) (*contraire au bien*) wrong; (*vice*) evil; (*mauvaises actions*) wrongdoing; **le bien et le m.** right and wrong, good and evil; **faire la différence entre le bien et le m.** to know the difference between right and wrong; **rendre le m. pour le m.** to answer evil with evil, to render evil for evil; **il ne pense pas à m.** he doesn't mean any harm; **voir le m. partout** to see bad in everything; *Rel* **délivre-nous du m.** deliver us from evil; **les forces du m.** the forces of evil; **faire le m.** to do evil

(d) (*difficulté*) **non sans m.** not without difficulty; **se donner du m. pour faire qch** to go to a lot of trouble to do sth, to take pains to do sth; **je me suis vraiment donné du m. pour que la soirée soit réussie** I really went to a lot of trouble *or* I took great pains to make the party a success; **je me suis donné beaucoup de mal pour faire cette traduction** I worked really hard on this translation; *F* **se donner un m. de chien** to go to a hell of a lot of trouble; **donner du m. à qn** to give sb (some) trouble; **avoir du m. à faire qch** to have difficulty *or* trouble (in) doing sth; **avoir le plus grand m. à faire qch** to have the utmost *or* a great deal of difficulty doing sth; **avoir de plus en plus de m. à faire qch** to find it harder and harder to do sth; **tu ne peux pas savoir le m. que j'ai eu pour trouver cet objet** you don't know the trouble I've had finding this thing; *F* **avoir un m. de chien à faire qch** to have a hell of a job to do sth; **prendre son m. en patience** to try to put up with it, to be patient; **on n'a rien sans m.** you don't get anything easily

▶ **mal**: **m. de l'air** airsickness; **avoir le m. de l'air** to be airsick; **m. blanc** whitlow; **m. de cœur** sickness, nausea; **m. de dents** toothache; **m. de gorge** sore throat; **m. de mer** seasickness; **avoir le m. de mer** to be seasick; **m. des montagnes** altitude sickness; *Arch* **m. napolitain** pox; **m. du pays** homesickness; **avoir le m. du pays** to be homesick; **m. des rayons** radiation sickness; **m. de la route** carsickness; **avoir le m. de la route** to be carsick; *Litt* **m. du siècle** world-weariness; **la dépression est le nouveau m. du siècle** depression is the new scourge of the century; **m. de tête** headache; **m. des transports** travel-sickness; **m. de vivre** weariness with life; **avoir le m. de vivre** to be tired of life

mal[2] *adv* **(a)** (*jouer, nager, traiter qn, se conduire etc*) badly; (*payer*) poorly, badly, badly; **tout cela finira m.** it will all end in tears; **leur histoire a m. fini** their story had a sad *or* an unhappy ending; **je n'aime pas ce livre, il finit m.** I don't like this book, it's got a sad *or* an unhappy ending; **si tu crois qu'elle va accepter, c'est m. la connaître!** if you think she's going to say yes, you don't know her very well!; **tout va m. en ce moment** everything's going wrong at the moment; **je dors très m. en ce moment** I'm sleeping very badly *or* I'm not sleeping at all well just now; **qu'est-ce qu'on mange m. ici** the food's really bad here; **cette cafetière verse m.** this coffee pot doesn't pour properly; **m. à l'aise** ill at ease; **vous avez m. agi** you did wrong, you acted badly; **je ne pensais pas m. faire** I didn't think I was doing anything wrong; **il se tient m. à table** he has bad table manners; **redresse-toi, tu te tiens m.** straighten up, you're not standing/sitting properly; *Prov* **bien m. acquis ne profite jamais** nobody ever profits by ill-gotten gains; **cette robe lui va m.** that dress doesn't suit her; **ça lui va m. de traiter les autres de paresseux** he's got a nerve calling other people lazy; **travail m. fait** badly done work, shoddy work; **tant bien que m.** as best one can/could; (*réussir*) after a fashion; **on a tout rangé tant bien que m.** we tidied everything up as best we could; **aller de m. en pis** to go from bad to worse; **s'y prendre m.** to go about it the wrong way; **s'y prendre m. avec qn** to handle sb the wrong way; **tu t'y es m. pris pour assembler la bibliothèque** you've gone the wrong way about assembling the bookcase; **m. choisir** to make the wrong choice, to choose wrongly; **tu as m. choisi ton jour pour te plaindre** you've chosen the wrong day to complain; **m. tourner** (*d'une situation*) to turn sour; (*d'une dispute*) to turn ugly; (*d'une personne*) to go to the dogs; **avoir l'esprit m. tourné** to have a dirty *or* one-track mind; **m. comprendre** to misunderstand; **m. interpréter qch** to misinterpret sth, to misconstrue sth; **on voit m. d'ici** you can't see (very) well *or* properly from here; **on voit m. comment** ... it's difficult *or* not easy to see how ...; **m. informé** ill-informed; **m. embouché** foul-mouthed; **m. famé** disreputable, of ill repute; **il a très m. pris la chose, il l'a très m. pris** (*cela l'a blessé, chagriné, irrité*) he took it very badly; **se mettre m. avec qn** (*se brouiller*) to fall out with sb; *F* **être m. avec qn** to be on bad terms with sb; **vous ne feriez peut-être pas m. de** ... it wouldn't be a bad thing (if you were) to ..., it might not be a bad idea to ...

(**b**) (*en mauvaise santé*) **se sentir m.** to feel ill; (*avoir la nausée*) to feel sick; (*sur le point de s'évanouir*) to feel faint; **se trouver m.** to faint; **aller** *ou* **se porter m.** to be in poor health, to be ill; **être au plus m.** to be critically ill *or* at death's door; **elle est** *ou* **elle va très m.** she's in a very bad way

(**c**) (*une certaine quantité*) **pas m. (de qch)** quite a lot (of sth); **il (n')y en a pas m.** there is quite a lot of it/there are quite a lot of them; **cela m'a pris pas m. de temps** it took me quite a time, it took me a fair time

(**d**) (*avec fonction adjectivale*) **vous savez ce qui est bien et ce qui est m.** you know what's right and what's wrong, you know the difference between right and wrong; **c'est très m. de faire ça** (*en parlant à un enfant*) it's very naughty to do that; **c'est pas m.** it's not bad, it's quite good; **ce n'était pas m. du tout** it wasn't at all bad; **elle n'est pas m.** she's quite good-looking; **qu'est-ce que tu penses de ce pull? – pas m.** what do you think of this pullover? – it's not bad *or* it's OK; *F* **il déconne pas m. en ce moment** he's really arsing about at the moment; **nous ne sommes pas m. ici** we're quite comfortable *or* not badly off here

malachite [malakit] *nf Minér* malachite

malade [malad] **1** *adj* (**a**) (*souffrant*) (*personne*) ill, *Am* sick, unwell; *F* poorly; (*organe*) diseased; (*dent*) bad; (*jambe*) bad, *F* gammy; *Fig* (*industrie*) ailing; **tomber m.** to fall *or* be taken ill; **m. de la fièvre typhoïde** ill with typhoid; **être m. d'inquiétude/de jalousie** to be sick with worry/jealousy; **il a été m. comme un chien** *ou* **une bête** he was as sick as a dog; *très F* **j'ai été m. à crever** I was horribly *or* dreadfully ill; **être m. du cœur, avoir le cœur m.** to have heart trouble, to have a bad heart; **être m. de l'estomac, avoir l'estomac m.** to have stomach trouble; **ça me rend m. de le voir gâcher sa vie** it makes me sick to see him waste his life; *F* **il en est m.** he feels sick *or* he's sick about it; **à l'idée de le voir demain, j'en suis m.** I feel *or* I'm sick at the thought of seeing him tomorrow; *Mil etc* **se faire porter m.** to report *or* go sick

(**b**) (*fou*) mad, crazy; **esprit m.** sick *or* unhealthy mind; *F* **t'es pas un peu m.?** are you right in the head?, are you off your rocker?

2 *n* (**a**) *Méd* patient; **un grand m.** a seriously ill person; **un m. mental** a mentally ill *or* sick person; (*dans un hôpital*) a mental patient; **les malades** the sick; **m. imaginaire** hypochondriac; **faire le m.** to pretend to be ill, to malinger

(**b**) (*mentalement*) **c'est un m.** he's mentally ill; *F* **c'est un m., ce mec!** that guy isn't right in the head!; *F* **comme un m.** (*travailler, courir, pousser*) like mad *or* crazy; (*conduire*) like a lunatic *or* a madman; *F* **un m. de Schubert/de ski** a Schubert/skiing fanatic; *F* **c'est un m. des films de Fellini/de la bouffe indienne** he's mad about Fellini's films/Indian food

maladie [maladi] *nf* (**a**) [①A10,d] illness, disease; **c'est une petite m.** it's just a minor illness; **m. bénigne** minor illness; **m. grave** serious illness; **m. mortelle** fatal illness *or* disease; **m. contagieuse** contagious disease *or* illness; **m. mentale** mental illness; **attraper une m.** to catch a disease; **cet hiver, le petit nous a fait toutes les maladies** this winter our boy's had all the diseases under the sun; **maladies des plantes** plant diseases; **par suite de m.** through illness; **congé de m.** sick leave; *Fig F* **il en fait une m.** he's making a song and dance about it; *F* **c'est quoi, cette m. de toujours tout critiquer?** what's with this mania for *or* obsession with criticizing everything?; *F* **c'est une m. chez toi, le piment/le foot** chilli's/football's an obsession with you

(**b**) *Vét* (*des chiens*) (canine) distemper

▶ **maladie**: **m. d'Alzheimer** Alzheimer's (disease); **m. de Basedow** Graves' *or* Basedow's disease; **m. bleue** blue disease; **m. de Carré** (canine) distemper; **m. des chiens** (canine) distemper; **m. de cœur** heart complaint *or* disease; **m. de Crohn** Crohn's disease; **m. cutanée** skin disease; **m. du foie** liver complaint *or* disease; **m. de Hodgkin** Hodgkin's disease; *Vieilli* **m. honteuse** venereal disease; **m. infantile** child's illness *or* complaint; **m. du légionnaire** legionnaire's disease; **m. de Parkinson** Parkinson's (disease), Parkinsonism; **m. de peau** skin disease; **m. professionnelle** occupational illness; **m. sexuellement transmissible** sexually transmitted disease; **m. du sommeil** sleeping sickness; *Vét* **m. de la vache folle** mad cow disease; **m. vénérienne** venereal disease

maladif, -ive [maladif, -iv] *adj* (*enfant*) sickly; (*curiosité, pensées*) morbid, unhealthy; **elle était d'une pâleur maladive** she was unhealthily pale; **sa maniaquerie est presque maladive** his fussiness is almost pathological; **être d'une jalousie maladive** to be pathologically jealous; **la propreté, chez lui, c'est m.** cleanliness is an obsession with him

maladivement [maladivmɑ̃] *adv* (*jaloux*) pathologically; (*inquiet, ordonné*) obsessively

maladresse [maladrɛs] *nf* (*inhabileté*) clumsiness, awkwardness; (*manque de tact*) tactlessness; (*bévue, impair*) blunder; **quelle m. de lui avoir dit que tu n'aimais pas sa robe** how tactless of you to tell her that you didn't like her dress; **il y a quelques maladresses de style** there are a few awkward *or* clumsy turns of phrase

maladroit, -oite [maladrwa, -wat] **1** *adj* (*inhabile*) clumsy, awkward; (*qui manque de tact*) tactless **2** *n* (*personne inhabile*) awkward *or* clumsy person; (*personne sans tact*) tactless person

maladroitement [maladrwatmɑ̃] *adv* (*de façon gauche*) clumsily; (*sans tact*) tactlessly

malais, -aise [malɛ, -ɛz] **1** *adj*, Malaysian, Malay(an) **2** *nm Ling* Malay **3** *n* **M.** Malaysian, Malay(an)

malaise [malɛz] *nm* (**a**) (*moral*) uneasiness, discomfort; (*social, politique*) unrest; **sa remarque a provoqué un certain m.** his remark aroused a certain uneasiness; **sentiment de m.** uneasy feeling, feeling of unease (**b**) (*physique*) feeling of sickness *or* ill-health; (*étourdissement*) dizzy spell; **avoir un m.** to feel faint

malaisé [malɛze] *adj* difficult; **certains auteurs sont d'une traduction malaisée** certain authors are difficult to translate

malaisément [malɛzemɑ̃] *adv* with difficulty

Malaisie [malɛzi] *nf* Malaysia

malandrin [malɑ̃drɛ̃] *nm Vieilli, Litt* brigand, robber

malappris, -ise [malapri, -iz] *Vieilli* **1** *adj* uncouth, ill-bred, loutish **2** *n* uncouth *or* ill-bred person, lout

malard [malar] *nm* drake

malaria [malarja] *nf* malaria

malavisé [malavize] *adj Vieilli, Litt* (*action*) ill-advised, unwise; (*personne*) unwise, injudicious; **être m. de faire qch** to be ill-advised *or* unwise to do sth

malaxage [malaksaʒ] *nm* (*de pâte, d'argile*) kneading; (*de beurre*) creaming; (*de ciment*) mixing

malaxer [malakse] *vt* (*pâte, argile*) to knead; (*beurre*) to cream; (*ciment*) to mix

malaxeur [malaksœr] *nm* mixer, mixing machine; (*pour beurre*) butter creamer; (*pour ciment*) cement mixer

malchance [malʃɑ̃s] *nf* (**a**) (*guigne*) bad luck, ill luck; **par m.** as ill luck would have it; **vous jouez de m.** you're not having much luck (**b**) (*mésaventure*) mishap, misfortune

malchanceux, -euse [malʃɑ̃sø, -øz] **1** *adj* unlucky **2** *n* unlucky person

malcommode [malkɔmɔd] *adj* (*appareil*) impractical; (*vêtement*) unsuitable

maldonne [maldɔn] *nf Cartes* misdeal; **faire (une) m.** to misdeal; *Fig F* **il y a m.** something's gone wrong somewhere

mâle [mɑl] **1** *adj* (**a**) *Biol* male; (*oiseau*) cock; (*lapin, lièvre, antilope*) buck; (*renard, loup*) dog; (*éléphant*) bull; **un ours m.** a he-bear; **héritier m.** male heir (**b**) (*courage, assurance*) manly; (*style*) virile (**c**) *Él* male; **prise m.** plug; *Tech* **pièce m.** male component **2** *nm* male; **un beau m.** (*animal*) a beautiful male specimen; *Hum* (*homme*) a real he-man

malédiction [malediksjɔ̃] **1** *nf Litt* (*imprécation*) curse, *Fml* malediction; **une m. pèse sur elle** she is under a curse, a curse is hanging over her **2** *int Vieilli* **m.! nous sommes enfermés** curses! *or* curse it! we're locked in

maléfice [malefis] *nm* evil spell

maléfique [malefik] *adj Litt* maleficent; (*étoile*) unlucky; (*influence, pouvoirs*) evil

malencontreusement [malɑ̃kɔ̃trøzmɑ̃] *adv* unfortunately

malencontreux, -euse [malɑ̃kɔ̃trø, -øz] *adj* (*événement, *remarque*) unfortunate, untoward; **par un hasard m.** by a stroke of bad luck

mal(-)en(-)point [malɑ̃pwɛ̃] *adj* in a bad way; **être très/un peu m.** to be in a very bad/a bit of a bad way

malentendant, -ante [malɑ̃tɑ̃dɑ̃, -ɑ̃t] **1** *n* person who is hard of hearing, hearing-impaired person; **les malentendants** the hard of hearing, the hearing-impaired **2** *adj* **enfant m.** child who is hard of hearing, hearing-impaired child

malentendu [malɑ̃tɑ̃dy] *nm* misunderstanding, *Fml* misapprehension

malfaçon [malfasɔ̃] *nf* (*défaut*) defect

malfaisance [malfəzɑ̃s] *nf Litt* maleficence, evil-mindedness

malfaisant [malfəzɑ̃] *adj* (*personne*) evil-minded, harmful; (*influence*) evil, harmful; (*propos*) harmful

malfaiteur, -trice [malfɛtœr, -tris] *n* criminal, lawbreaker, *Litt* wrongdoer, *Fml, Vieilli* malefactor; **un dangereux m.** a dangerous criminal; **association de malfaiteurs** criminal conspiracy

malformation [malfɔrmasjɔ̃] *nf* malformation

malfrat [malfra] *nm F* crook

malgache [malgaʃ] **1** *adj* Madagascan, Malagasy **2** *nm Ling* Malagasy **3** *n* **M.** Madagascan, Malagasy

malgracieux, -ieuse [malgrasjø, -jøz] *adj* **(a)** *Vieilli* (*qui manque de politesse*) ungracious, churlish, rude **(b)** *Litt* (*qui manque d'élégance*) inelegant, ungainly, clumsy

malgré [malgre] **1** *prép* in spite of, despite, *Fml* notwithstanding; **m. tout** in spite of *or* despite everything; (*pourtant*) all the same, nevertheless; **m. sa fortune** for all his wealth; **je l'ai fait m. moi** I did it in spite of myself *or* against my better judgment **2** *conj* (*seulement dans* **m. que j'en aie/que tu en aies/***etc*) **m. que vous en ayez** whether you like it or not

malhabile [malabil] *adj* clumsy, awkward; **mains malhabiles** unskilled hands

malhabilement [malabilmɑ̃] *adv* clumsily, awkwardly

malheur [malœr] **1** *nm* **(a)** (*drame, catastrophe*) misfortune; (*accident*) (serious) accident; **la disparition de sa femme a été son plus grand m.** the death of his wife was the greatest misfortune ever to afflict him; **depuis quelques années, je n'ai que des malheurs** for some years now I've had nothing but misfortune; **ils ont eu des malheurs** they have been through difficult times; **il n'arrête pas de me raconter ses petits malheurs** he's forever telling me (about) all his petty cares and woes; *Prov* **un m. n'arrive** *ou* **ne vient jamais seul** misfortunes never come singly, it never rains but it pours; **un m. est si vite arrivé** accidents happen so easily; **l'argent qu'il met de côté en cas de m.** the money he puts aside just in case something should happen; **quel m.!** what a tragedy!; **le m. c'est que ...** the unfortunate thing is that ...; *Prov* **à quelque chose m. est bon** it's an ill wind that blows nobody any good; *F* **je crois qu'on va déménager à Londres – parle pas de m.!** I think we're moving to London – God forbid!; **faire un m.** (*tuer qn*) to commit murder; *F* **s'il entre ici je fais un m.!** if he comes in here I'll say something I'll regret!; *F* **sa nouvelle pièce a fait un m.** his latest play was a big hit; *F* **les pantalons pattes d'éléphant font un m. en France** bell-bottomed trousers are all the rage in France

(b) (*chagrin, infortune*) adversity, misfortune; **ils sont dans le m.** they are going through hard times; **il est resté très digne dans le m.** he remained very dignified in (his) adversity; **c'est dans le m. qu'on reconnaît ses amis** it's when things are going badly that you find out who your friends are; *Prov* a friend in need is a friend indeed; **enfant qui fait le m. de ses parents** child who brings sorrow to his parents; *Prov* **le m. des uns fait le bonheur des autres** one man's joy is another man's sorrow

(c) (*malchance*) bad luck, ill luck; **par m.** unfortunately; **quel m. que je ne l'aie pas su** what a pity I didn't know (about it); **je le connais pour mon m.** unfortunately for me *or* unluckily for me I know him; **porter m. à qn** to bring sb bad luck; **ceux qui ont le m. de le connaître** those who are unfortunate *or* unlucky enough to know him; **j'ai eu le m. de lui dire que je n'étais pas d'accord avec lui** I made the (big) mistake of telling him that I didn't agree with him; **jouer de m.** to be unlucky *or* out of luck; *F* **ces lettres de m.!** these blasted letters!; **m. à eux!** woe betide them!

2 *int* hell!

malheureusement [malørøzmɑ̃] *adv* unfortunately

malheureux, -euse [malørø, -øz] **1** *adj* **(a)** (*triste*) (*personne, enfance*) unhappy, miserable; (*expression, air, regard*) unhappy, sad, miserable; (*affaire*) unfortunate, unhappy; **m. comme les pierres** wretched, utterly miserable

(b) (*malchanceux*) (*personne*) unlucky; (*candidat*) unsuccessful, unlucky; (*tentative*) unsuccessful; **avoir la main malheureuse** to be unlucky; **m. au jeu** unlucky at gambling; *Prov* **heureux au jeu, m. en amour** lucky at cards, unlucky in love; **amour m.** unrequited love; **amours malheureuses** unhappy love affairs

(c) (*regrettable*) (*geste, mot*) unfortunate; **c'est bien m. pour vous!** it's hard for you!; **il est bien m. que ...** + *sub* it's very unfortunate *or* a great pity that ...; *F* **si ça n'est** *ou* **très** *F* **si c'est pas m. tout de même de voir ces enfants obligés de travailler!** it's such a terrible pity *or* shame to see these children having to work; *F* **le voilà enfin, ce n'est pas m.!** here he comes at last, and a good job too!

(d) *F* (*négligeable*) miserable, wretched, paltry; **tout ça pour une malheureuse faute!** all that because of a stupid little mistake

2 *n* **les m.** the poor, the needy; **une famille de m.** a poor family; **le m./la malheureuse!** poor man/woman!, poor wretch!; **m.! qu'avez-vous fait?** you wretch! what have you done

malhonnête [malɔnɛt] *adj* **(a)** (*employé, commerçant etc*) dishonest; *F* crooked; **des procédés malhonnêtes** underhand *or* dishonest methods **(b)** *Vieilli* (*impoli*) (*personne*) rude, impolite **(c)** *Vieilli* (*indécent*) (*geste*) indecent; (*suggestion*) improper

malhonnêtement [malɔnɛtmɑ̃] *adv* dishonestly

malhonnêteté [malɔnɛtte] *nf* **(a)** dishonesty; **la m. de ses procédés** the underhandedness *or* the dishonesty of his methods **(b)** *Vieilli* (*manque de politesse*) rudeness, impoliteness; (*remarque impolie*) rude remark

malice [malis] *nf* **(a)** (*ruse, espièglerie*) mischief, mischievousness, roguishness; **plein de m.** full of mischief, mischievous; **la m. de ses réflexions** the mischievousness of his remarks **(b)** *Vieilli* (*méchanceté*) malice, spitefulness; **ne pas entendre m. à qch** (*ne voir rien de mal à qch*) to see no harm in sth; (*ne pas avoir l'intention de faire du mal*) to mean no harm by sth; **il ne faut pas y entendre m.** he/she/*etc* didn't mean any harm; **être sans m.** to be harmless **(c) sac/boîte à malices** bag/box of tricks

malicieusement [malisjøzmɑ̃] *adv* mischievously

malicieux, -ieuse [malisjø, -jøz] *adj* **(a)** (*espiègle*) (*personne, sourire, remarque*) mischievous, roguish, impish; (*solution*) clever, smart **(b)** *Vieilli* (*méchant*) malicious

malien, -ienne [maljɛ̃, -jɛn] **1** *adj* Malian **2** *n* **M.** Malian

malignement [maliɲmɑ̃] *adv* maliciously

malignité [maliɲite] *nf* **(a)** malice, spite(fulness) **(b)** *Méd* (*d'une maladie, d'un tumeur*) malignancy

malin, -igne [malɛ̃, -iɲ] **1** *adj* **(a)** (*espiègle, fûté*) shrewd, cunning, crafty; **regard m.** knowing look; **il est plus m. que ça** he knows better; **il est m. comme un singe** he's a crafty devil; (*d'un enfant*) he's a little monkey; **elle n'est pas bien maligne** *ou F* **maline** she's not very clever *or* not all that bright; **ce n'est pas la peine de jouer au plus m.** there's no point in trying to outwit *or* outsmart each other; **bien m. qui le trouvera!** it will take a smart one to find that!; **tu te crois m.?** do you think you're clever?; **ce n'était pas très m. (de ta part)** that wasn't very bright, was it?; *Iron* **c'est m.! tu as tout gâché!** that was clever! now you've spoiled everything!; *F* **c'est pas bien m.!** that's dead easy!, that's simple!

(b) (*plaisir, joie*) malicious; *Arch* (*influence*) malignant, evil; **l'esprit m.** the Evil One, the Devil; **éprouver un m. plaisir à faire souffrir qn** to take a sadistic *or* malicious pleasure in making sb suffer

(c) *Méd* (*cancer*) malignant

2 *n* **c'est un m.** he has his wits about him, *F* he knows what's what; **un petit m.** a crafty one, *Péj* a smart Aleck; **c'est une petite maligne** *ou F* **maline** she's a sly one, she's a little imp; **faire le m.** to show off, to try to be smart; *Iron* **gros m.!** smarty-pants!, smart aleck!, *Br* clever Dick!; *Prov* **à m., m. et demi** there's always somebody cleverer than you

3 *nm* **le M.** the Evil One, the Devil

malingre [malɛ̃gr] *adj* (*personne, corps*) puny

malintentionné [malɛ̃tɑ̃sjɔne] *adj* (*personne*) ill-intentioned

mal-jugé, *pl* **mal-jugés** [malʒyʒe] *nm Jur* miscarriage of justice

malle [mal] *nf* **(a)** (*valise*) trunk, *Vieilli* box; **faire sa m.** *ou* **ses malles** to pack (one's trunk); *F* **se faire la m.** to clear off, *Br* to scarper, *Br* to do a runner **(b)** *Aut* boot, *Am* trunk; **m. arrière** luggage compartment, load area **(c)** *Hist* (*voiture de la poste*) mail coach; **la m. des Indes** the Indian mail **(d)** *Can* **mettre une lettre à la m.** to post *or surtout Am* mail a letter

malléabilité [maleabilite] *nf* malleability

malléable [maleabl] *adj* malleable

malle-poste, *pl* **malles-poste(s)** *nf Hist* (*voiture de la poste*) mail coach

mallette [malɛt] *nf* overnight bag; (*valise*) small (suit)case; (*porte-documents*) attaché case, briefcase; **une m. en osier** a wicker (picnic) basket

malmener [malməne] *vt* (*conj like* **mener**) (*brutaliser*) (*qn*) to manhandle, to treat roughly; *Fig* (*en paroles*) to run down; (*qch*) to handle *or* treat roughly; **il malmène sa voiture** he's really rough with his car; **il a été malmené par la critique** he was slated by the critics; **notre équipe a été malmenée durant tout le match** our team was given a rough time *or* ride all through the match; **m. la grammaire** to misuse grammar, to make grammatical mistakes

malnutrition [malnytrisjɔ̃] *nf* malnutrition

malodorant [malɔdɔrɑ̃] *adj* foul-smelling, smelly, *Fml* malodorous

malotru, -ue [malɔtry] *n* lout, *Br* yob

malouin, -ine [malwɛ̃, -in] **1** *adj* of/from Saint-Malo **2** *n* **M.** (*natif*) native of Saint-Malo; (*habitant*) inhabitant of Saint-Malo

Malouines [malwin] *nfpl* **les (îles) M.** the Falkland Islands, the Falklands; **la guerre des M.** the Falklands War *or* conflict; **un habitant des îles M.** a Falkland Islander

malpoli, -ie [malpɔli] *F* **1** *adj* rude, impolite **2** *n* rude *or* impolite person; **petit m.** rude *or* impolite (little) boy

malpropre [malprɔpr] **1** *adj* **(a)** (*sale*) (*mains*) dirty, grubby; (*apparence*) slovenly, untidy; (*travail*) slovenly, slipshod **(b)** (*inconvenant*) (*histoire, attitude etc*) smutty **(c)** (*malhonnête*) (*individu, conduite etc*) despicable **2** *n* **se faire traiter comme un m.** to be treated like dirt; **se faire renvoyer comme un m.** to be sent packing

malproprement [malprɔprəmɑ̃] *adv* (*manger*) messily; (*se conduire*) despicably

malpropreté [malprɔprəte] *nf* dirtiness; *Fig* (*d'histoire*) smuttiness

malsain [malsɛ̃] *adj* (*maladif*) (*personne*) unhealthy(-looking); (*dangereux pour la santé*) (*nourriture*) unhealthy, unwholesome; (*climat, maison*) unhealthy; (*pernicieux*) (*littérature, atmosphère etc*) unhealthy, unwholesome; (*personne*) unwholesome; (*curiosité, attitude*) unhealthy; **c'est très m. de vivre près des marécages** it's very unhealthy to live close to marshland; *Fig* **ça devient m. par ici** things are *or* it's looking a bit dodgy round here

malséant [malseɑ̃] *adj Litt* unseemly, unbecoming; **il serait tout à fait m. que tu m'accompagnes** it would be quite unseemly *or* unbecoming for you to accompany me

malsonnant [malsɔnɑ̃] *adj* offensive; (*malséant*) unseemly

malt [malt] *nm* malt

maltage [maltaʒ] *nm* (*procédé*) malting

maltais, -aise [maltɛ, -ɛz] **1** *adj* Maltese **2** *nm Ling* Maltese **3** *n* **M.** Maltese

Malte [malt] *nf* Malta; **croix de M.** Maltese cross

malter [malte] *vt* (*houblon*) to malt

malterie [maltəri] *nf* (*usine*) malt house, malting

malthusianisme [maltyzjanism] *nm* Malthusianism

malthusien, -ienne [maltyzjɛ̃, -jɛn] *adj, n* Malthusian

maltose [maltoz] *nm Ch, Ind* maltose

maltraiter [maltrɛte] *vt* **(a)** (*brutaliser*) to maltreat, to mistreat, to handle *or* treat roughly; **enfants maltraités** abused *or* maltreated children **(b)** (*en paroles*) to run down; **il a été maltraité par la critique** he was slated by the critics **(c)** (*grammaire, langue*) to misuse

malus [malys] *nm* (*assurance*) loss of no-claims bonus

malveillance [malvɛjɑ̃s] *nf* (*hostilité, animosité*) spite, malice, malevolence; **avec m.** spitefully, maliciously, malevolently; **un incident dû à la m.** malicious incident

malveillant [malvɛjɑ̃] *adj* spiteful, malicious, malevolent

malvenu [malvəny] *adj* **(a)** (*déplacé*) out of place, inappropriate; **elle serait malvenue de se plaindre** she's scarcely in a position to complain; **il serait tout à fait m. de le critiquer** it would be quite inappropriate to criticize him **(b)** (*mal développé*) (*plante*) malformed

malversation [malvɛrsasjɔ̃] *nf* **malversation(s)** misappropriation of funds, embezzlement

malvoisie [malvwazi] *nm* **m., vin de M.** malmsey (wine)

maman [mamɑ̃] *nf* mum(my), *Am* mom; **les mamans regardent** the mothers *or* mums *or* moms are watching

mambo [mɑ̃mbo] *nm* mambo

mamelle [mamɛl] *nf* **(a)** (*de vache*) udder; (*de chienne, truie etc*) teat, dug; *Prov* **labourage et pâturage sont les deux mamelles de la France** ploughing and grazing are the lifeblood of France **(b)** *Anat, Vieilli* (*sein*) breast; **enfant à la m.** child at the breast

mamelon [mamlɔ̃] *nm* **(a)** *Anat* (*de femme*) nipple **(b)** *Géog* hillock, knoll

mamelonné [mamlɔne] *adj* (*paysage*) hillocky

mamel(o)uk [mamluk] *nm Hist* Mameluke

m'amie, mamie¹ [mami] *nf F Arch* (*mon amie*) my dear

mamie² *nf F* **(a)** (*grand-mère*) gran(ny), *Br F* nan **(b)** (*vieille dame*) old lady

mamillaire [mamilɛr] *adj Anat* mamillary

mammaire [mamɛr] *adj* mammary

mammalogie [mamalɔʒi] *nf* mammalogy

mammectomie [mamɛktɔmi] *nf Méd* mastectomy

mammifère [mamifɛr] **1** *adj* mammalian **2** *nm* mammal

mammographie [mamɔgrafi] *nf Méd* mammography

mammouth [mamut] *nm* mammoth

mamours [mamur] *nmpl F* **faire des m. à qn** to caress *or* fondle sb

mam'selle, mam'zelle [mamzɛl] *nf F* miss

MAN [ɛmaɛn] *n Can Pol* (*abrév* **Membre de l'Assemblée Nationale**) MNA

manade [manad] *nf* (*dans le dialecte provençal*) (*taureaux*) herd of bulls; (*chevaux*) herd of horses

management [manaʒmɛnt] *nm* management

manager¹, manageur [manadʒɛr] *nm Ind, Sp etc* manager; *Cin, Th* agent

manager² [mana(d)ʒe] *vt* to manage

manant [manɑ̃] *nm* **(a)** *Hist* (*villageois*) villager; (*paysan*) peasant **(b)** *Litt* (*mufle*) churl, boor

manceau, -elle [mɑ̃so, -ɛl] **1** *adj* of/from Le Mans **2** *n* **M.** (*natif*) native of Le Mans; (*habitant*) inhabitant of Le Mans

manche¹ [mɑ̃ʃ] *nf* **(a)** (*de vêtement*) sleeve; **manches longues/courtes** long/short sleeves; **robe sans manches** sleeveless dress; **être en manches de chemise** to be in one's shirtsleeves; **relever** *ou* **retrousser ses manches** to roll up one's sleeves; *Fig* to roll up one's sleeves, to get down to work; *Fig* **avoir qn dans sa m.** to have sb in one's pocket; *F* **ça, c'est une autre paire de manches** that's quite another matter, that's a different kettle of fish; *F* **faire la m.** to busk **(b)** *Av* (*de ballon*) neck **(c)** (*en athlétisme*) heat; *Boxe* round; *Tennis* set; *Cartes* hand, game

manche² *nm* **(a)** (*de marteau, casserole etc*) handle; (*de poignard*) handle, haft; (*de club de golf*) shaft; (*de fouet*) stock; (*de violon, guitare etc*) neck; **couteau à m. d'ivoire** ivory-handled knife, knife with an ivory handle; *F* **être du côté du m.** to be well in with those who count; **branler dans le m.** to have a loose handle; *Fig* to be shaky

(b) *Ordinat* joystick, control column *or* stick; *Av* joystick

(c) *Culin* (*de gigot*) knuckle; **m. à gigot** leg-of-mutton holder (*for carving*)

(d) *F* (*personne maladroite*) clumsy idiot; **s'y prendre comme un m.** to make a right mess of things; **avec les femmes, il s'y prend comme un m.** he's absolutely useless with women; **il conduit/danse comme un m.** he's a lousy *or* hopeless driver/dancer

▶ **manche**: **m. à air** *Av* wind sock; *Naut* windsail; *Tech* **m. d'arrosage** hose (pipe); **m. de** *ou* **à balai** broomstick; **m. à balai** *Ordinat* joystick, control column *or* stick; *Av* joystick; **manches ballon** puff sleeves; *Tech* **m. à eau** hose (pipe); **manches gigot** leg-of-mutton sleeves; **m. à incendie** fire hose; **manches kimono** kimono sleeves; **manches raglan** raglan sleeves; **manches trois-quarts** three-quarter sleeves; *Av* **m. à vent** wind sock

Manche (la) [lamɑ̃ʃ] *nf* **(a)** the (English) Channel **(b)** (*en Espagne*) La Mancha

manchette [mɑ̃ʃɛt] *nf* **(a)** (*extrémité de la manche*) cuff **(b)** (*pour protéger les vêtements*) oversleeve, cuff protector **(c)** *Sp* (*au catch*) forearm smash; (*au volley-ball*) dig **(d)** *Typ* (*de journal*) (banner) headline

manchon [mɑ̃ʃɔ̃] *nm* (*vêtement*) muff; *Tech* (*pour axe, arbre etc*) sleeve; (*de palier*) bush(ing); (*pour pivot etc*) socket; **m. d'accouplement** coupling sleeve; *Aut etc* **m. d'embrayage** clutch; **m. à incandescence** incandescent (gas) mantle

manchot¹, -ote [mɑ̃ʃo, -ɔt] **1** *adj* (*privé d'un bras*) one-armed; (*privé d'une main*) one-handed; (*privé des deux bras*) armless, with no arms; (*privé des deux mains*) with no hands; *F* **il n'est pas m.** (*adroit*) he's clever with his hands; (*il peut le faire lui-même*) he's got hands, hasn't he? **2** *n* (*privé d'un bras*) one-armed person; (*privé d'une main*) one-handed person; (*privé des deux bras*) armless person, person with no arms; (*privé des deux mains*) person with no hands

manchot² [mɑ̃ʃo] *nm Zool* penguin

mandala [mɑ̃dala] *nm* mandala

mandale [mɑ̃dal] *nf très F* clout, slap (in the face)

mandant [mɑ̃dɑ̃] *nm* **(a)** *Jur* (*dans une transaction*) principal **(b)** *Pol* **le député et ses mandants** the member and his constituents

mandarin [mɑ̃darɛ̃] *nm* **(a)** *Hist* mandarin; *Fig Péj* (*fonctionnaire, intellectuel*) mandarin **(b)** *Ling* Mandarin (Chinese) **(c)** (*oiseau*) **(canard) m.** mandarin duck

mandarinal, -aux [mɑ̃darinal, -o] *adj* mandarin

mandarinat [mɑ̃darina] *nm Hist* mandarinate; *Fig Péj* **le m.** the establishment; **les jeunes médecins s'opposent au m.** young doctors are against the medical establishment

mandarine [mɑ̃darin] **1** *nf* **(a)** mandarin (orange) **(b)** *TV, Cin* (*éclairage*) redhead **2** *adj inv* tangerine(-coloured)

mandarinier [mɑ̃darinje] *nm Bot* mandarin (orange) tree

mandat [mɑ̃da] *nm* **(a)** (*autorité*), *Hist* mandate; **territoires sous m.** mandated territories; **m. de député** member's (electoral) mandate; **m. présidentiel** president's *or* presidential term of office **(b)** *Jur* (*procuration*) power of attorney, proxy **(c)** *Jur* (*ordre*) warrant **(d)** *Fin* (*mode de paiement*) order (to pay), money order; (*mandat-poste*) postal order, *surtout Am* money order

▶ **mandat**: **m. d'amener** = summons; **m. d'arrêt** arrest warrant; **m-carte**, *pl* **mandats-cartes** postal order, *surtout Am* money order (*in postcard form*); **m. de comparution** summons (to appear), subpoena; **m. de dépôt** committal order; **placer qn sous m. de dépôt** to commit sb; **m. d'expulsion** eviction order; **m. international** international money order; **m.-lettre**, *pl* **mandats-lettres** postal order, *surtout Am* money order (*in letter card form*); **m. de paiement** order to pay; **m. de perquisition** search warrant; **m. postal** postal order, *surtout Am* money order; **m.-poste**, *pl* **mandats-poste** postal order, *surtout Am* money order; **m. télégraphique** telegraphic money order; **m. de virement** transfer order

mandataire [mɑ̃datɛr] *n* (*représentant*) (*d'électeurs etc*) representative; (*à une réunion*) proxy; *Com* agent

mandater [mɑ̃date] *vt* **(a)** (*charger d'une mission*) (*représentant etc*) to commission; (*membre parlemententaire*) to give a mandate to **(b) m. des frais** (*payer par mandat*) to pay expenses by money order

mandchou, -oue [mɑ̃dʃu] **1** *adj* Manchurian **2** *nm Ling* Manchu **3** *n* **M.** Manchurian

Mandchourie [mɑ̃dʃuri] *nf* Manchuria

mandement [mɑ̃dmɑ̃] *nm* **(a)** *Arch* (*ordre*) mandate, order **(b)** *Rel* pastoral (letter)

mander [mɑ̃de] *vt Arch* **(a)** (*personne*) to summon **(b) m. une nouvelle à qn** to convey *or* send news to sb (*by letter*)

mandibule [mɑ̃dibyl] *nf Anat, Zool* mandible; *F* **jouer des mandibules** to feed one's face

mandoline [mɑ̃dɔlin] *nf Mus* mandolin(e)

mandragore [mɑ̃dragɔr] *nf* mandrake

mandrill [mɑ̃dril] *nm* mandrill

mandrin [mɑ̃drɛ̃] *nm MecE* (*de tour*) chuck; (*de vilebrequin*) pad; (*pour faire un trou*) punch; (*pour élargir un trou*) drift

manécanterie [manekɑ̃tri] *nf* choir school

manège [manɛʒ] *nm* **(a)** *Équitation* (*exercices*) exercises; (*dressage*) (*de cheval*) training, breaking in; **(salle de) m.** riding school; **m. découvert** open-air riding school **(b) m. (de chevaux de bois)** merry-go-round, roundabout, *surtout Am* carousel; **aller aux manèges** (*fête foraine*) to go to the fair **(c)** (*manigances*) ploy, trick; **j'observais leur m.** I was watching their little game

mânes [mɑn] *nmpl Antiq, Rel* manes, shades, spirits (*of the dead*); **les m. de mes ancêtres** the spirits of my ancestors

maneton [mantɔ̃] *nm Aut* crankpin

manette [manɛt] *nf* (hand) lever; *Aut* stalk; (*ouverture capot*) lever; *Av* **m. des gaz** throttle lever; **m. de jeux** joystick

manganate [mɑ̃ganat] *nm Ch* manganate

manganèse [mɑ̃ganɛz] *nm Ch* manganese

manganite [mɑ̃ganit] *nm Ch* manganite

mangeable [mɑ̃ʒabl] *adj* **(a)** (*comestible*) edible, eatable **(b)** (*médiocre*) (just about) eatable

mangeaille [mɑ̃ʒaj] *nf* **(a)** *Arch* (*pour animaux domestiques*) feed **(b)** *F* (*nourriture*) grub, *Br* nosh

mange-disque, *pl* **mange-disques** [mɑ̃ʒdisk] *nm* slot-feed record player

mangeoire [mɑ̃ʒwar] *nf Agr* (feeding) trough; (*pour chevaux, bétail*) manger; (*de canari*) feeding dish

manger[1] [mɑ̃ʒe] **(je mangeai(s), n. mangeons) 1** *vt* to eat; **qu'est-ce qu'on mange?** what are we having to eat?, what's for lunch/dinner/*etc*?; **il a tout mangé** he's eaten everything (up); **il mange de tout** he'll eat anything; **je ne mange pas de viande** I don't eat meat; **mange ta soupe** eat (up) *or* drink (up) your soup; **j'ai faim, je mangerais bien un morceau** I'm hungry, I could do with a bite to eat; *Fig* **il est conscient d'avoir mangé son pain blanc le premier** he knows that he had it easy for a while; **je me rends compte que je mange mon pain blanc le premier** *ou* **avant mon pain noir** I realise that I had it easy to start with; **ça ne mange pas de pain** it doesn't cost anything; *F* **je ne mange pas de ce pain-là** I don't go in for that sort of thing; *F* **m. du curé** to be violently anticlerical; *F* **elle ne vous mangera pas** she won't eat you; **la rouille mange l'acier** rust eats into steel; *F* **chaudière qui mange beaucoup de charbon** boiler that is very heavy on coal *or* that eats up coal; **mangé aux** *ou* **par les mites** moth-eaten; **ses yeux lui mangent le visage** his eyes seem to fill his face; **ses cheveux lui mangent le visage** her face is almost hidden by her hair; **m. ses mots** to mumble; *Arg* **m. le morceau** to spill the beans, to talk; *F* **m. son argent** to squander one's money, to run through one's money; *F* **il a mangé du lion aujourd'hui** he's full of beans today; *F* **m. de la vache enragée** to have a hard time of it; *F* **m. la laine sur le dos de qn** to sponge shamelessly off sb; *F* **tu vas bientôt me m. la soupe sur la tête** you'll soon be taller than me; **m. qn/qch des yeux** to look at sb/sth longingly; **m. qn de baisers** to smother sb with kisses; *F* **m. les pissenlits par la racine** to be pushing up the daisies

2 *vi* to eat; **je les ai invités à m.** I've invited them for something to eat *or* for a meal; **m. dans une assiette** to eat off *or* from a plate; **c'est tellement propre chez elle qu'on mangerait par terre** her house is so clean you could eat off the floor; **bon à m.** good to eat; **m. sur le pouce** to have a (quick) snack, to have a bite to eat; **maman, je vais être obligé de m. sur le pouce** I'm going to have to eat and run, Mum; **m. au restaurant** to eat out, to go out for a meal; **m. dehors** (*dans le jardin*) to eat outside; (*ailleurs que chez soi*) to eat out, to go out for a meal; **donner à m. à qn** to feed sb, to give sb something to eat; **donner à m. à un animal/bébé** to feed an animal/a baby; **m. comme quatre** *ou* **comme un ogre** to eat like a horse; **m. comme un oiseau** *ou* **un moineau** to eat like a sparrow; **m. du bout des dents** to pick at one's food; **m. à sa faim** to eat one's fill; **m. léger** to eat a light meal; **nous avons bien mangé** we had a very good meal; **d'habitude on mange très bien en France** you usually eat very well in France; **l'appétit vient en mangeant** you only realize how hungry you are once you start eating, *Litt Prov* the appetite grows by what it feeds on

3 se manger *vpr* to be eaten; **le fromage se mange avec du pain** cheese is eaten with bread

manger[2] *nm* food; **chez eux, vous aurez le boire et le m.** you'll get something to eat and drink *or* you'll get food and drink at their place; **je ne pourrai pas rentrer avant m.** I won't be able to get back before lunch/dinner/*etc*; **à prendre après m.** to be taken after meals

mange-tout [mɑ̃ʒtu] *adj inv, nm inv* **(pois)**, **m.** mange-tout, sugar pea; **(haricot) m.** runner bean, *Am* string bean

mangeur, -euse [mɑ̃ʒœr, -øz] *n* eater; **gros** *ou* **grand m.** big eater; **c'est un gros m. de pommes de terre** he eats a lot of potatoes, he's a big potato eater; **mangeurs d'hommes** cannibals, man-eating savages; **tigre m. d'hommes** man-eating tiger

manglier [mɑ̃glije] *nm Bot* mangrove (tree)

mangoustan [mɑ̃gustɑ̃] *nm* (*arbre, fruit*) mangosteen

mangouste [mɑ̃gust] *nf* **(a)** *Zool* mongoose **(b)** (*fruit*) mangosteen

mangue [mɑ̃g] *nf* mango

manguier [mɑ̃gje] *nm* mango (tree)

maniabilité [manjabilite] *nf* (*d'outil*) handiness; (*d'avion*) manoeuvrability, *US* maneuverability; (*de véhicule*) handling ability; (*d'un logiciel*) user-friendliness

maniable [manjabl] *adj* (*valise etc*) manageable; (*outil*) handy; (*véhicule*) easy to handle *or* control *or* drive; (*avion*) easy to control, easy to manoeuvre *or US* maneuver

maniaco-dépressif, -ive, *pl* **maniaco-dépressifs** [manjakodeprɛsif, -iv] *adj, n* manic-depressive

maniaque [manjak] **1** *adj* fussy, finicky, pernickety **2** *n* **(a)** (*fou*) maniac, raving lunatic, *m* madman, *f* madwoman; **m. sexuel** sex maniac **(b)** (*pointilleux*) fusspot, *US* fussbudget; (*capricieux*) crank; **c'est une m. de l'hygiène/de l'ordre** she's fanatical about *or* obsessed with hygiene/tidiness

maniaquerie [manjakri] *nf* fussiness, finickiness

manichéen, -enne [manikeɛ̃, -ɛn] *adj* Manichean

manichéisme [manikeism] *nm* Manicheism

manicle [manikl(ə)] *nf* = **manique**

manie [mani] *nf* **(a)** *Psy* mania, obsession; **m. de la persécution** persecution mania *or* complex

(b) (*passion*) mania, craze; (*habitude, petite obsession*) odd habit; **avoir la m. de la propreté** to have a mania for cleanliness, to be fanatical about *or* obsessed with cleanliness; **elle a la m. de tout ranger** she has a compulsive habit of tidying everything up; **il a ses petites manies** he has his little ways *or* his little fads; **c'est ta nouvelle m., de fumer la pipe?** is that your latest fad *or* craze, smoking a pipe?; **c'est une m. chez lui de dire du mal des autres** it's become a habit with him to run other people down; **mais quelle m. de claquer les portes!** why do people always have to slam doors?

(c) *Méd Arch* mental derangement

maniement [manimɑ̃] *nm* (*d'outils, d'affaires, de langue etc*) handling; *Mil* **m. d'armes** drill

manier [manje] (*impf & pr sub* **n. maniions, v. maniiez**) **1** *vt*

(a) *(outil, corde, armes etc)* to handle (b) *(diriger, contrôler)* *(hommes, cheval etc)* to handle, to manage; *(avion)* to control, to manoeuvre, *US* to maneuver; **m. les avirons** to ply *or* pull the oars; **savoir m. la parole** to know how to handle words, to be good with words (c) *Arch (tissu)* to feel **2 se manier** *vpr F (seulement à l'infinitif) (se dépêcher)* to get a move on, to get one's skates on

manière [manjɛr] *nf* (a) *(façon)* way, manner; **d'une m. assez particulière** in a rather unusual way *or* manner; **sa m. de s'habiller, la m. dont elle s'habille** the way she dresses, her way of dressing; **la m. qu'elle a de regarder les gens par en dessous** the furtive way she has of looking at people; **c'est sa m. d'être** that's the way he is; **laissez-moi faire à ma m.** let me do it my (own) way; **m. de voir** *ou* **de penser** way of looking at things; **s'y prendre de la bonne m.** to set about it the right way; **je comprends qu'il t'ait critiqué, mais il y a la m.** I can understand him criticizing you, but there are ways of doing these things; **employer la m. forte** to use strong-arm tactics, to use force; **de cette m.** (in) this way, (in) that way; **d'une m. ou d'une autre** one way or another; **de m. à ce que** so that, in such a way that; **de telle m. que** in such a way that; **d'une** *ou* **de m. générale** generally speaking; **en aucune m.** under no circumstances, not under any circumstances; **de toute m.** in any case; **d'une certaine m.** in a manner of speaking, in a sense; **de la même m.** in the same way

(b) *(conduite)* **manières** manners; **avoir de bonnes** *ou* **de belles manières** to have good manners, to be well mannered; **avoir de mauvaises manières** to have bad manners, to be ill-mannered; **en voilà des manières!** what a way *or* that's no way to behave!; *Fig* **apprendre les bonnes manières à qn** to teach sb some manners; **faire des manières** *(être poseur)* to put on airs and graces; *(se faire prier)* to stand on ceremony, to make a fuss; **elle est sans manières** she is unaffected, she doesn't give herself airs and graces; **elle a accepté notre invitation sans (faire de) manières** she accepted our invitation just like that *or* without any fuss; **venez dîner ce soir, mais vous savez, ce sera sans manières** come and have dinner tonight, but you know, it'll only be a simple meal

(c) *Beaux-Arts, Littér etc* **tableau à la m. de Degas** painting after (the manner of) Degas

maniéré [manjere] *adj* (a) *(poseur) (personne, politesse etc)* affected (b) *Beaux-Arts, Littér (style)* mannered

maniérisme [manjerism] *nm* (a) affectation (b) *Beaux-Arts, Littér* mannerism

manieur, -euse [manjœr, -øz] *n (d'hommes, d'affaires etc)* manager; **m. d'argent** financier

manif [manif] *nf F* demo

manifestant, -ante [manifɛstɑ̃, -ɑ̃t] *n* demonstrator

manifestation [manifɛstasjɔ̃] *nf* (a) *(de sentiment, tendance, opinion etc)* expression; **avec de grandes manifestations de joie** with a great show of joy, with great expressions of joy (b) *(politique)* demonstration (c) *Rel* revelation (d) *(événement)* event; **m. sportive/culturelle** sporting/cultural event

manifeste¹ [manifɛst] *adj* obvious, manifest; **il est m. que ses études ne l'intéressent pas** it's obvious that he isn't interested in his studies; **il est d'une incompétence m.** he is obviously *or* manifestly incompetent

manifeste² *nm* (a) *Pol* manifesto (b) *Naut, Av* manifest; **m. de douane** customs manifest

manifestement [manifɛstəmɑ̃] *adv* obviously, manifestly

manifester [manifeste] **1** *vt (ses intentions, ses sentiments, son étonnement etc)* to show, to reveal; *(de l'intérêt)* to show, to manifest; *(son courage)* to show, to display; **m. sa volonté** to make one's wishes clear; **il m'a manifesté sa sympathie** he expressed his sympathy to me

2 *vi Pol* to demonstrate

3 se manifester *vpr* (a) *(de personne)* to turn up, to show up, to appear; **ça fait très longtemps qu'il ne s'est pas manifesté** he hasn't been in touch for ages, I/we/*etc* haven't heard from him for ages; **je n'ai pas osé me m.** I didn't dare (to) show myself

(b) *(de sentiment, maladie etc)* to show *or* manifest itself (**par** in)

manigance [manigɑ̃s] *nf* scheme, plot; **manigances** scheming, schemes

manigancer [manigɑ̃se] *vt* (**je manigançai(s), n. manigançons**) to scheme, to plot; **qu'est-ce qu'ils manigancent?** what's their (little) game?, what are they up to?; **je ne sais pas ce que je vais pouvoir m. pour ne pas le rencontrer** I don't know what I'll be able to come up with to avoid meeting him

Manille [manij] *n* Manila

manille¹ [manij] *nm (cigare)* Manila (cigar)

manille² *nf Cartes* = type of game in which the ten is the highest card

manille³ *nf* shackle

manillon [manijɔ̃] *nm Cartes* ace *(at manille)*

manioc [manjɔk] *nm* manioc, cassava

manip [manip] *nf F* experiment

manipulateur, -trice [manipylatœr, -tris] **1** *n* (a) *(de machine)* operator; *(d'argent, de biens etc)* handler; **m. radio(graphe)/de laboratoire** X-ray/lab(oratory) technician *or* assistant (b) *Péj (de personne)* manipulator (c) *(prestidigitateur)* conjuror **2** *nm* (a) *(en robotique)* manipulator (b) *Télécom* (sending) key

manipulation [manipylasjɔ̃] *nf* (a) *(de produits chimiques)* handling; **m. génétique** genetic engineering (b) *Méd* manipulation; **m. vertébrale** manipulation of the spine; **un ostéopathe m'a fait des manipulations** an osteopath manipulated my spine (c) *Scol* **manipulations** *(surtout en science)* experiments, practical work (d) *(en prestidigitation)* sleight of hand (e) *Péj* manipulation; *Pol* **manipulations électorales** vote-rigging (f) *Ordinat* **m. de colonnes** column handling; **m. de données** data manipulation

manipuler [manipyle] *vt* (a) *(outil compliqué)* to manipulate; *(appareil, produits chimiques, marchandise)* to handle; *Télécom* to operate; **m. un colis avec précaution** to handle a parcel with care (b) *Péj (personne, électeurs)* to manipulate; *(statistiques)* to massage

manique [manik] *nf (pour la cuisine)* oven glove; *Tech* protective glove

manitou [manitu] *nm* (a) *(d'Indiens d'Amérique)* manitou (b) *Fig F* (**grand**) **m.** big shot, big noise; *(patron)* big boss

manivelle [manivɛl] *nf* (a) *MecE* crank; *(pour un vélo)* pedal crank; *(pour un moteur)* crank (handle); *Aut* starting handle; *(de lève-glace)* window winder; **retour de m.** backfire; *Fig* **il y eut un retour de m.** it backfired (b) *Cin (sur les anciennes caméras)* winding handle; *Fig* **dès le premier tour de m.** as soon as shooting started

manne¹ [man] *nf Bible* manna; *Fig (don inespéré)* godsend, manna from heaven

manne² *nf (panier)* basket, hamper

mannequin¹ [mankɛ̃] *nm* (a) *Beaux-Arts* manikin, lay figure; *Couture* dress stand; *(qui a la forme du corps)* (dress-maker's) dummy (b) *(personne)* model, *Vieilli* mannequin; **elle est m. chez Chanel** she works for Chanel as a model, she models for Chanel

mannequin² *nm (panier)* small (wicker) basket

manocontact [manoktakt] *nm Aut etc* pressure switch

manœuvrabilité [manœvrabilite] *nf* manoeuvrability, *US* maneuverability

manœuvrable [manœvrabl] *adj* manoeuvrable, *US* maneuverable; **cette voiture est peu m.** the car is not at all easy to manoeuvre *or* handle

manœuvre¹ [manœvr] *nf* (a) *(conduite, direction) (de machine, grue etc)* operation; *(de véhicule)* manoeuvring, *US* maneuvering; **m. de stationnement** parking manoeuvre; **est-ce que tu connais les manœuvres pour allumer la chaudière?** do you know how to go about lighting the boiler?; *Aut* **faire une m.** to (do a) manoeuvre *or US* maneuver; **faire une fausse m.** *Fig* to do something wrong; *Aut* to manoeuvre badly; *Fig* **il n'a pas fait une seule fausse m.** he didn't put a foot wrong; *Fig* **vous avez toute liberté de m.** you have a completely free hand, you have complete freedom of action

(b) *Naut (action)* manoeuvre, *US* maneuver; **m. d'accostage** docking manoeuvre

(c) *Mil* drill, exercise; *(dans une bataille)* manoeuvre, *US* maneuver; **en manoeuvres** on manoeuvres; **grandes manœuvres** army manoeuvres *or* exercises; **m. d'encerclement** encircling movement

(d) *Rail (de trains)* shunting, marshalling; **voie de m.** shunting *or Am* switching track

(e) *Fig* manoeuvre, *US* maneuver; **m. électorale** vote-catching manoeuvre; **manœuvres** scheming, manoeuvring; *Jur* **manœuvres frauduleuses** embezzling

(f) *Naut (cordage)* rope; **manœuvres dormantes** standing rigging; **manœuvres courantes** running rigging

manœuvre² *nm* unskilled worker; **travail de m.** unskilled work

manœuvrer [manœvre] **1** *vt (faire fonctionner) (machine, grue etc)* to operate; *(conduire, diriger) (véhicule)* to manoeuvre, *US* to maneuver, to handle; *Rail (wagons à plateforme)* to shunt, to marshal **2** *vi* to manoeuvre, *US* to maneuver; *Fig* to manoeuvre, to scheme; **il se laisse m. par sa femme** he lets himself be manipulated *or* manoeuvred by his wife

manœuvrier, -ière [manœvrije, -jɛr] *n* **(a)** (*soldat, marin etc*) tactician **(b)** *Fig Vieilli* manoeuvrer, *US* maneuverer

manoir [manwar] *nm* (*petit château*) manor; (*grande maison*) manor (house), country house

manomètre [manɔmɛtr] *nm* pressure gauge; (*en forme d'U*) manometer; *Aut* **m. de compression** cylinder compression gauge; *Aut* **m. de pression d'huile** oil pressure gauge

manométrique [manɔmetrik] *adj Phys* manometric(al); **hauteur m.** head of water

manouche [manuʃ] *n Péj* gipsy, gypsy

manquant[1], -ante [mɑ̃kɑ̃, -ɑ̃t] **1** *adj* (*personne*) (*dans une classe, une réunion*) absent, missing; (*objet*) missing; **une pièce manquante d'un puzzle** a piece missing from *or* a missing piece of a jigsaw **2** *n* (*personne*) absentee; **les manquants** the absentees, those absent, those missing

manquant[2] *nm Com* **manquants** shortages; **éviter des manquants dans la marchandise** to prevent short delivery

manque [mɑ̃k] *nm* **(a)** (*carence*) (*de nourriture, d'argent, de main-d'œuvre, d'information etc*) lack, shortage; (*de vitamines, calcium etc*) lack, deficiency; (*par rapport à un total désiré*) shortfall; (*de courage, goût, sommeil, d'humour, d'enthousiasme etc*) lack; **par m. de** through lack of; **m. de chance** *ou F* **de pot** *ou F* **de bol!** bad luck!; *F* **m. de bol j'ai du travail** it's just (my) tough *or* rotten luck that I've got work to do; *Méd* **(crise de) m.** withdrawal symptoms; **il est en m.** (*de drogue*) he's got withdrawal symptoms; *très F* **elle est en m. ou quoi, celle-là!** (*sexuellement*) is she not getting enough, or what?

(b) (*vide*) emptiness; **je ressens un grand m. depuis sa mort** I feel a great emptiness since his death; **elle souffre d'un m. affectif** she suffers from a lack of affection

(c) *F* **à la m.** lousy, pathetic; **espèce d'électricien à la m.!** call yourself an electrician!; **quelle voiture à la m.!** what a pile of scrap *or* junk this car is!; **toi et tes idées à la m.!** you and your useless ideas!

(d) (*lacunes*) **avoir conscience de ses manques** to be aware of one's shortcomings *or* failings

(e) (*au casino*) manque

▶ **manque**: *Compta* **m. de caisse** cash unders; **m. de fonds** lack of funds; *Com, Fin* **m. à gagner** loss of earnings *or* profit *or* revenue

manqué [mɑ̃ke] **1** *adj* (*occasion*) missed, lost; (*rendez-vous*) missed; (*tentative, expérience*) unsuccessful, abortive; (*photo*) unsuccessful; **coup m.** (*tir etc*) miss; **vie manquée** wasted life; **c'est un médecin m.** he ought to have been a doctor **2** *nm Culin* = biscuit with almond-flavoured or fruit-flavoured icing; **moule à m.** (round) cake tin

manquement [mɑ̃kmɑ̃] *nm* **m. à une règle** breach *or* violation of a rule; **m. à la discipline** breach of discipline; **m. au devoir** breach *or* dereliction of duty

manquer [mɑ̃ke] **1** *vi* **(a) m. de** (*argent, main-d'œuvre*) to be short of, to lack; (*courage, bon sens, charme etc*) to lack, to be lacking in; **nous manquons de sucre/vin** we're short of sugar/wine; (*nous n'en avons plus*) we're out of sugar/wine; **m. de temps** to be short of time; **nous manquons de l'essentiel** we lack *or* we're short of the basics; **ne m. de rien** to have all that one needs; **elle m'a manqué de respect** she showed a lack of respect towards me; **la chambre manque de lumière** the room doesn't get enough light, the room is lacking in *or* lacks light; **on manque d'air ici** there isn't enough air *or* there's no air in here; **ils ont fini par m. d'air et mourir** they finally ran out of air and died; **tu ne manques pas d'audace** *ou* **de culot** *ou F* **d'air!** you're not lacking in nerve!; **elle ne manque pas d'admirateurs** she's not short of *or* not lacking in admirers

(b) je sera là sans m. I'll be there without fail; *Vieilli* **il a manqué (de) tomber** he nearly *or* almost fell

(c) (*faire défaut*) to be lacking, to be in short supply; **commencer à m.** (*de vivres, d'eau etc*) to begin to run short *or* run out; **quand l'eau vint à m.** when the water ran short; **le bouton qui manque à ma veste** the button that's missing from my jacket, the missing button on my jacket; **une pièce manque au puzzle** there's a piece missing from the jigsaw puzzle, a piece of the jigsaw puzzle is missing; **les mots me manquent pour exprimer ...** I'm at a loss for words to express ...; **la voix me manqua** words failed me; **le pied lui manqua** he lost his footing; **le temps nous manque pour finir ce projet** we don't have enough time *or* the time to complete this project; **la place me manque** I don't have enough room; **ce n'est pas l'envie qui m'en manque** it's not that I don't want to, I would if I could; *Litt* **le cœur lui manqua** his heart failed him; **les occasions ne manquent pas, ce ne sont pas les occasions qui manquent** there's no lack of opportunity (**de faire** to do)

(d) (*dans une classe, une réunion*) to be absent, to be missing; (*avoir disparu*) to be missing; **m. à l'appel** to be absent from rollcall; *Scol* **elle a beaucoup manqué le mois dernier** she was off (school) a lot *or* missed a lot of classes last month

(e) (*être regretté*) **tu me manques** I miss you; **est-ce que je t'ai manqué?** did you miss me?; **sa mère/sa maison lui manque** he's missing his mother/his house; **c'est au parti qu'il manque le plus** it's the party that's missing him most

(f) (*faillir à qch*) **m. à** (*son devoir, son honneur*) to fail in; (*sa parole, ses promesses*) to break; *Hum* **je manque à tous mes devoirs** I'm neglecting my duties; **m. à la consigne** to disregard orders; **m. à une règle** to break *or* violate a rule; **m. à la livraison** to miss a delivery; **m. à ses engagements financiers** to fail to meet one's financial liabilities

(g) (*échouer*) to fail

(h) (*à la forme négative*) **personne ne peut m. d'avoir observé ...** no one can fail to have noticed ...; **il n'a pas manqué d'être étonné** he couldn't help but be surprised; **cela ne pouvait m. d'arriver** it was bound to happen, it had to happen; **j'étais sûr qu'il allait casser l'assiette, et bien sûr, ça n'a pas manqué** I was sure he'd break the plate, and sure enough, he did; **ne manquez pas de nous écrire** don't forget to *or* be sure to write to us; **elle ne manquera pas de t'en faire la remarque** she'll be quite sure *or* she's bound to point it out to you; **remerciez bien votre mère! – je n'y manquerai pas** be sure to thank your mother! – I won't forget *or* I'll do that

2 *v impers* [①B27,E,2,d] **il ne manque pas de candidats** there's no lack *or* no shortage of candidates; **il manque quelques pages** there are a few pages missing; **il me manque dix francs** I'm ten francs short, I need another ten francs; **il lui manque un bras** he has only one arm, he has lost an arm; **il ne lui manque que la parole** (*d'un animal*) the only thing it can't do is speak; *F* **il lui manque une case** he's got a screw loose; **il s'en manque de beaucoup** far from it; **il ne manquait plus que cela!** that's all I/he/*etc* needed!; *F* **il ne manquerait plus que ça!** that'd be all I'd/he'd/*etc* need!; **il ne manquerait plus que ça, qu'il vienne avec sa nouvelle maîtresse!** it'd be the last straw if he came with his new mistress!

3 *vt* (*rater*) (*cible, train etc*) to miss; (*occasion*) to miss, to lose; **j'ai manqué le train de trois minutes** I missed the train by three minutes; **M. Martin? vous l'avez manqué de peu** Mr Martin? you('ve) just missed him; **un film superbe, à ne m. sous aucun prétexte** a superb film, not to be missed under any circumstances; *Fig Hum* **je crois que j'ai manqué une étape** *ou* **un épisode** I think I've missed something; **il ne faut surtout pas m. ça** you really mustn't miss it; *F* **tu as manqué le coche** you've missed your chance *or* opportunity, *Br F* you've missed the bus; *F* **tu as encore manqué une occasion de te taire** *ou très F* **de fermer ta gueule** why didn't you just keep your big mouth shut for once?; **m. son coup** to miss; *Fig* to miss one's chance; **elle a manqué son coup, elle n'a pas réussi à le convaincre** she failed (in her attempt) to convince him; *F* **il n'en manque pas une** he's always putting his foot in it; **m. sa vocation** to miss one's vocation

4 se manquer *vpr* **(a)** to miss each other (*by not being in the same place at the same time*)

(b) (*rater son suicide*) to fail in one's suicide attempt

mansarde [mɑ̃sard] *nf* (*chambre*) attic; *Archit* (**toit** *ou* **comble en) m.** mansard roof

mansardé [mɑ̃sarde] *adj* **chambre mansardée** attic (room)

mansuétude [mɑ̃sɥetyd] *nf Litt* leniency

mante [mɑ̃t] *nf* mantis; **m. religieuse** praying mantis; *Fig* (*femme*) man-eater

manteau, -eaux [mɑ̃to] *nm* **(a)** (*vêtement*) coat; **m. de pluie** raincoat; **m. de fourrure** fur coat; *Fig* **m. de neige** mantle *or* blanket of snow; **sous le m. de la nuit** under (the) cover of darkness; **faire qch sous le m.** to do sth secretly *or Fml* clandestinely **(b)** *Zool* (*de mollusque*) mantle

▶ **manteau**: *Th* **m. d'Arlequin** proscenium arch; **m. de cheminée** mantel(piece)

mantelé [mɑ̃tle] *adj Zool* (*corbeau*) hooded

mantelet [mɑ̃tlɛ] *nm* **(a)** *Rel* mantelletta **(b)** (*de femme*) cape

mantille [mɑ̃tij] *nf* mantilla

manucure [manykyr] **1** *n* (*personne*) manicurist **2** *nf* (*technique*) manicure; **se faire faire une m.** to have a manicure

manucuré [manykyre] *adj* manicured

manuel[1], -elle [manɥɛl] **1** *adj* (*travail, activité etc*) manual; **je ne suis pas m. pour deux sous** I'm no good at all with my hands; **un cours de travaux manuels** a handicrafts class; **commande manuelle** manual controls; **corrections manuelles** corrections by hand, manual corrections **2** *n* **(a)**

(*adroit de ses mains*) **c'est un m.** he is good with his hands **(b)** (*qui exerce une profession manuelle*) manual worker

manuel² *nm* (*livre*) manual, handbook; **un m. scolaire/d'histoire** a school/history textbook; **m. de l'utilisateur, m. d'utilisation** user *or* instruction manual; **m. d'entretien** service manual, maintenance manual, workshop manual; **m. d'installation** installation manual; **m. de référence** reference manual

manuellement [manɥɛlmɑ̃] *adv* manually; **m., je ne vaux rien** I'm useless with my hands

manufacture [manyfaktyr] *nf* **(a)** *Vieilli* (*usine*) factory; **la M. de porcelaine de Sèvres** the Sèvres porcelain factory **(b)** *Arch* (*fabrication*) manufacture

manufacturer [manyfaktyre] *vt* to manufacture; **produits manufacturés** manufactured goods, manufactures

manufacturier, -ière [manyfaktyrje, -jɛr] **1** *adj* manufacturing **2** *n Vieilli* manufacturer

manu militari [manymilitari] *adv* by force

manuscrit [manyskri] **1** *adj* handwritten **2** *nm* (*texte écrit à la main*) handwritten text; *Littér* manuscript; **m. (dactylographié)** typescript; **un m. du XIIIe siècle** a 13th-century manuscript; **les manuscrits de la mer Morte** the Dead Sea Scrolls

manutention [manytɑ̃sjɔ̃] *nf* **(a)** (*action*) handling (of goods); **il fait de la m.** he's a goods handler **(b)** (*lieu*) storehouse, store(s)

manutentionnaire [manytɑ̃sjɔnɛr] *n* goods handler; (*dans un entrepôt*) storekeeper, storeman

manutentionner [manytɑ̃sjɔne] *vt* (*marchandises*) to handle

maoïsme [maɔism] *nm Pol* Maoism

maoïste [maɔist] *adj, n Pol* Maoist

maori, -ie [maɔri] **1** *adj* Maori **2** *nm Ling* Maori **3** *n* **M.** Maori

maous, maousse [maus] *adj F* ginormous, enormous

mappemonde [mapmɔ̃d] *nf* (*carte*) map of the world in two hemispheres; (*globe*) globe

maquer [make] *très F* **1** *vt* **je pense pas qu'elle soit maquée** I don't think she's got a man; **on va essayer de le m.** we're going to try and fix him up (with a woman); **elle est maquée avec lui** she's shacked up with him; **on a réussi à les m. ensemble** we managed to fix them up with each other **2 se maquer** *vpr* **se m. avec qn** to be shacked up with sb; **depuis qu'elle s'est maquée ...** since she got herself a man ...

maquereau¹, -eaux [makro] *nm* [①**A12**,1,g] (*poisson*) mackerel

maquereau², -eaux *nm Arg* (*souteneur*) pimp

maquerelle [makrɛl] *nf Arg* **(mère) m.** madam

maquette [makɛt] *nf* **(a)** *Beaux-Arts* model **(b)** *Th* (*de mise en scène*) model **(c)** (*de livre*) dummy; (*de page*) paste-up, layout **(d)** *Ind* scale model **(e)** (*jouet*) model; **il fait des maquettes** he makes models; **m. d'avion/de bateau** model plane/boat

maquettiste [maketist] *n* **(a)** model maker **(b)** *Typ* layout compositor, make-up compositor

maquignon [makiɲɔ̃] *nm* **(a)** (*marchand de chevaux*) horse trader *or* dealer **(b)** *Fig* (*entremetteur malhonnête*) dishonest *or* crooked dealer

maquignonnage [makiɲɔnaʒ] *nm* **(a)** (*vente de chevaux*) horse trading, horse dealing **(b)** (*trafic*) sharp practice

maquignonner [makiɲɔne] *vt Péj* **(a)** (*cheval*) to trade dishonestly **(b)** *Fig* (*affaire*) to conduct dishonestly; **affaire maquignonnée** put-up job

maquillage [makijaʒ] *nm* **(a)** (*action*) (*de visage*) making up; **elle met beaucoup de soin dans son m.** she takes a lot of care with her make-up **(b)** (*produits*) make-up; **m. correcteur** corrective make-up **(c)** (*modification frauduleuse*) (*de voiture volée*) disguising; (*de documents*) forging; (*de photos*) faking; (*de comptes*) falsification, doctoring, *Br F* fiddling

maquiller [makije] **1** *vt* **(a)** (*qn, visage*) to make up **(b)** (*déguiser, falsifier*) (*voiture volée*) to disguise; (*documents*) to forge; (*photos*) to fake; (*comptes*) to falsify, to doctor, *Br F* to fiddle **2 se maquiller** *vpr* to put (one's) make-up on, to make up; **elle se maquille trop** she uses too much make-up, she puts too much make-up on

maquilleur, -euse [makijœr, -øz] *n Th etc* make-up artist *or* man/woman; *Cin, TV* **elle est maquilleuse de studio** she works at a studio as a make-up artist

maquis [maki] *nm* **(a)** *Géog* maquis; *Fig* **le m. de la procédure** the jungle of legal procedure **(b)** *Fr Hist* maquis, underground movement (*in WW II*); **les m. d'Afghanistan** the Afghan freedom fighters; **prendre le m.** to go underground; (*fuir à la campagne*) to take to the hills

maquisard [makizar] *nm Fr Hist* member of the maquis, Resistance fighter (*in WWII*)

marabout [marabu] *nm* **(a)** *Rel* (*ermite, tombeau*) marabout **(b)** (*sorcier*) witchdoctor **(c)** (*oiseau, plume*) marabou

marabouter [marabute] *vt* to put a spell on

maraîchage [marɛʃaʒ] *nm* market gardening, *Am* truck farming

maraîcher, -ère [mareʃe, -ɛr] **1** *adj* **culture maraîchère** market gardening, *Am* truck farming; **produits maraîchers** market garden produce, *Am* truck **2** *n* market gardener, *Am* truck farmer

marais [marɛ] *nm* **(a)** marsh; (*dans un pays chaud*) swamp; (*dans l'est de l'Angleterre*) fen; (*terres marécageuses*) marshland; **m. salant** salt marsh; **m. tourbeux** peat bog **(b)** (*terrain consacré à la culture maraîchère*) market garden, *Am* truck farm **(c)** *Fig* **le m. d'une vie sans surprises** a humdrum, uneventful existence **(d)** *Météo* **m. barométrique** shallow depression

marasme [marasm] *nm* **(a)** *Méd* emaciation, *Spéc* marasmus; *Fig* **il était en plein m.** he was totally drained (*of energy, inspiration*) **(b)** *Écon* stagnation, slump; **dans le m. économique actuel** in the present economic slump

marasque [marask] *nf* = type of cherry

marasquin [maraskɛ̃] *nm* maraschino; **cerise au m.** maraschino cherry

marathon [maratɔ̃] *nm Sp, Fig* marathon; *Fig* **m. de danse** dance marathon; **c'est toujours le m. entre la famille, les amis, les expos** it's always an endless round of family, friends, exhibitions

marathonien, -ienne [maratɔnjɛ̃, -jɛn] *n* marathon runner

marâtre [marɑtr] *nf* (*belle-mère*) stepmother; (*mère dénaturée*) cruel mother

maraud, -aude [maro, -od] *n Arch* villain, rascal, rogue

maraudage [marodaʒ] *nm* = **maraude (a)**

maraude [marod] *nf* **(a)** (*vol*) pilfering, petty thieving (*from orchards etc*) **(b) taxi en m.** cruising taxi

marauder [marode] *vi* **(a)** (*voler*) to thieve, to pilfer (*from orchards etc*) **(b)** (*de taxi*) to cruise (for fares)

maraudeur, -euse [marodœr, -øz] **1** *n* pilferer, petty thief **2** *adj* **(a) taxi m.** cruising taxi **(b) loup m.** prowling wolf

marbre [marbr] *nm* **(a)** (*roche*) marble; **un escalier/une statue en m.** a marble staircase/statue; *Fig* **elle est restée de m.** she remained impassive **(b)** (*statue*) marble (statue); (*de cheminée, commode etc*) marble top **(c)** (*en reliure*) marbling **(d)** *MecE* surface plate, face plate **(e)** *Typ* (*de presse*) imposing stone *or* bed; *Journ* reserve feature; **livre sur le m.** book in type *or* at press; **ne vous inquiétez pas pour l'édition de demain, j'ai du m.** don't worry about tomorrow's edition, I've got some items left over (from today)

marbré [marbre] *adj* (*surface, couverture de livre*) marbled, mottled; (*peau*) mottled, blotchy; (*pierre*) veined, mottled; **il avait la peau toute marbrée de coups** his skin was all marked with bruises; **gâteau m.** marble cake

marbrer [marbre] *vt* (*surface*) to marble, to mottle; (*peau*) to mottle; **le froid lui avait marbré la peau** his skin was mottled *or* blotchy from the cold

marbrerie [marbrəri] *nf* **(a)** (*art*) marble working *or* cutting; **m. funéraire** monumental sculpture *or* masonry **(b)** (*lieu*) marble mason's yard

marbrier, -ière [marbrije, -ijɛr] **1** *adj* (*industrie etc*) marble **2** *nm* monumental sculptor *or* mason **3** *nf* **marbrière** marble quarry

marbrure [marbryr] *nf* **(a)** (*jaspure*) marbling, veining **(b)** (*de peau*) mottling; (*d'ecchymose*) mark, blotch

marc¹ [mar] *nm* **(a)** (*mesure*) mark; **un m. d'or/d'argent** a gold/silver mark (coin) **(b)** *Jur Vieilli* **au m. le franc** pro rata

marc² *nm* **(a)** (*de raisins, d'olives etc*) marc **(b) (eau de vie de) m.** marc (brandy) **(c) m. de café** coffee grounds; **lire dans le m. de café** ≈ to read the tea leaves

marcassin [markasɛ̃] *nm* young wild boar

marcassite [markasit] *nf Minér* marcasite

marchand, -ande [marʃɑ̃, -ɑ̃d] **1** *n* (*dans un magasin*) shopkeeper, *Am* storekeeper; (*de vin*) merchant; **m. de chevaux/tableaux/meubles** horse/picture/furniture dealer **2** *adj* **(a)** *Com* commercial, market; **denrées marchandes** saleable *or* marketable goods; **prix m.** trade price; **un tableau sans aucune valeur marchande** a painting of no saleable *or* marketable value **(b) galerie marchande** shopping centre, *Am* mall **(c) marine marchande** merchant navy *or* marine

▶ **marchand**: **m. ambulant** hawker; *Péj* **m. de canons** arms dealer; **m. de couleurs** *Br* ironmonger, hardware dealer; **m. au détail** retailer; **m. en gros** wholesaler; **m. de journaux** newsagent; **m. de légumes** greengrocer; **m. des quatre saisons** street merchant (*selling fruit and vegetables*), *Br* barrow boy, *Vieilli* costermonger; **m. de sable: le m. de sable est passé** the sandman's on his way; *Péj* **m. de sommeil** slum landlord; *Fig Péj* **m. de soupe** (*restaurateur*) second-rate restaurant owner; (*directeur d'institution*) =

money-grubbing headmaster of a private school; **m. de tabac** tobacconist; **m. de tapis** carpet dealer; *Fig Péj* haggler; **des discussions de marchands de tapis** haggling; **m. de vin** wine merchant, vintner; *Culin* in a red wine sauce

marchandage [marʃɑ̃daʒ] *nm* **(a)** bargaining, haggling; *Fig Péj* horse-trading **(b)** *Jur* subcontracting

marchander [marʃɑ̃de] **1** *vt* **(a) m. qch avec qn** to haggle *or* bargain with sb over sth **(b)** *Jur* to subcontract **2** *vi* to haggle, to bargain

marchandeur, -euse [marʃɑ̃dœr, -øz] *n* **(a)** haggler **(b)** *Jur* subcontractor

marchandisage [marʃɑ̃dizaʒ] *nm* merchandising; **m. du distributeur/producteur** distributor/manufacturer merchandising

marchandise [marʃɑ̃diz] *nf* (*denrée*) commodity, piece of merchandise; **marchandises** goods, merchandise, *Vieilli* wares; **la m. est bien arrivée** the goods have arrived safely; **vanter** *ou* **étaler** *ou* **faire valoir sa m.** to show one's wares to good *or* best advantage; *Fig* to make the most of oneself; *Fig* **je remballe ma m.** forget I said it; **tromper qn sur la m.** (*fournir un article de qualité inférieure*) to sell sb a dud; (*fournir un article différent*) to sell sb the wrong thing; *Fig* **j'ai été trompée sur la m.** he/they/*etc* didn't live up to my expectations; **train de marchandises** goods train, freight train; **gare de m.** goods station

▶ **marchandise**: **marchandises acquittées** duty-paid goods; **marchandises avariées** spoiled *or* damaged goods; **marchandises franches de douane** duty-free goods; **m. hors taxes** duty-free goods; **m. libérée** duty-paid goods; **m. libre à la sortie** goods free of exit duty; **marchandises périssables** perishable goods, perishables; **m. prohibée** prohibited goods; **marchandises en transit** goods in transit

marchandiseur [marʃɑ̃dizœr] *nm* merchandiser; **m. de grande distribution** mass merchandiser

marchant [marʃɑ̃] *adj* **aile marchante** *Mil* outer flank (*of wheeling movement*); *Fig* (*de groupement politique*) leading wing

marche[1] [marʃ] *nf Géog* march(es), border country

marche[2] *nf* **(a)** step; (*d'escalier*) step, stair; *Tech* (*pédale*) (*de métier à tisser etc*) treadle; (*d'orgue etc*) pedal; **la m. du bas** the bottom step *or* stair; **volée de marches** (*à l'extérieur*) flight of steps; (*à l'intérieur*) flight of stairs; **attention à la m.!** mind the step!; **rater une m.** to miss a step

(b) (*action de marcher*) walking; (*promenade*) walk; **aimer la m.** to be fond of walking; **nous avons fait une longue m. dans la campagne** we went for a long walk in the country; **ralentir sa m.** to slacken one's pace; **continuer sa m.** to walk on; **se mettre en m.** to set off *or* out, to start off *or* out; **deux heures de m.** two hours' walk(ing); **une m. lente/rapide** a slow/rapid pace; **elle a réglé sa m. sur celle de la vieille dame** she adjusted her pace to the old lady's; **chaussures de m.** walking shoes

(c) (*défilé, manifestation*) march; **une m. silencieuse pour protester contre la mort d'un de leurs camarades** a silent protest march following the death of one of their comrades; **ouvrir la m.** to lead the way; **fermer la m.** to bring up the rear; **colonne en m.** column on the march; **ordre(s) de m.** marching orders; *Hist* **la Longue M.** the Long March; **en avant, m.!** forward, march!; *Mus* **m. nuptiale/funèbre/militaire** wedding/funeral/military march

(d) (*mouvement*) (*de trains, d'autobus etc*) running; (*de bateaux*) sailing, running; *Aut* **m. avant** forward gear; **m. arrière** (*pour un véhicule*) reversing, reverse, reverse gear; *Fig* backtracking; **faire m. arrière** (*de voiture*) to reverse; *Fig* to backtrack; **entrer dans le garage en m. arrière** to back *or* reverse into the garage; **en m.** moving, in motion; **navire en m.** ship under way; **se mettre en m.** (*de véhicule*) to move off; **assis dans le sens de la m.** (*dans un train*) sitting facing the engine; (*dans un bus*) sitting facing forward; **assis dans le sens contraire de la m.** (*dans un train*) sitting with one's back to the engine; (*dans un bus*) sitting facing backwards

(e) (*fonctionnement*) (*de machine*) running, working; **être en m.** (*de machine*) to be running; (*de fourneau*) to be in blast; **(re)mettre une machine en m.** to (re)start a machine; **en état de m.** in working order; **se mettre en m.** (*de machine*) to start; **il est responsable de la bonne m. de l'entreprise** he is responsible for the smooth running of the firm

(f) (*des événements, de l'histoire etc*) course; **la m. du temps** the march of time; **m. à suivre** procedure

marché [marʃe] *nm* **(a)** (*accord*) deal, bargain; (*plus officiel*) contract; **faire** *ou* **conclure un m.** to strike a deal *or* bargain; **m. conclu!** it's a deal!, *F* done!; **mettre à qn le m. en main** to invite sb to take it or leave it; **par-dessus le m.** into the bargain, on top of (all) that; **acheter/vendre qch (à) bon m.** to buy/sell sth cheaply *or* cheap; **(à) meilleur m.** more cheaply, cheaper; **articles bon m.** cheap *or* inexpensive articles

(b) (*lieu public de vente*) market; **jour de m.** market day; **m. aux fleurs/à la volaille** flower/poultry market; **m. couvert** covered market; **aller au m.** to go to (the) market; **faire son m.** to go shopping *or* to do one's shopping (at the market)

(c) *Com* market; **lancer un produit sur le m.** to launch a product; **produit qui n'a pas de m.** product for which there is no market; **conquérir un m.** to break into a market; **le m. mondial des bijoux** the world market in precious stones; *Bourse* **le m. de Londres** the London (Stock) Market; **économie de m.** market economy; **étude de m.** market research

▶ **marché**: **m. d'acheteurs** buyers' market; *Bourse* **m. actions** securities market; *Bourse* **m. des actions** share market; **m. amont** market from which a company buys; **m. aval** sales market; **m. à la baisse** sellers' market; *Bourse* **m. baissier** bear market; **m. boursier** stock market; **marchés de capitaux** capital markets; **m. captif** captive market; *Bourse* **m. des changes** currency (exchange) market, foreign exchange market; **m-cible** target market; **M. commun** Common Market; **m. compensatoire** compensation deal; *Fin* **m. au comptant** spot market; **m. des consommateurs** *ou* **de consommation** consumer market; **m. de la grande consommation** mass market; **m. effectif** available market; **m. des entreprises** business market; **m. environnant** substitution market; **m. de l'eurodevise** *ou* **des eurodevises** euromarket; **m. à l'export** *ou* **à l'exportation** export market; **m. extérieur** foreign market, overseas market; **m. ferme** steady *or* strong *or* firm market; **m. financier** money *or* financial market; **m. grand public** consumer market; **m. de gré à gré entre banques** interbank wholesale market; **m. gris** grey market; **m. à la hausse** buyers' market; *Bourse* **m. haussier** bull market; *Bourse* **m. hors cote** unlisted securities market, USM, over-the-counter market, OTC market; **m. industriel** industrial market, business market; **m. interbancaire** interbank market; **m. intérieur** home market, domestic market, national market; **m. libre** free market; **m. monétaire** money market; **m. monopolitique** monopoly market; **m. national** national market, home market; *Bourse* **m. du neuf** primary market; **m. noir** black market; *Bourse* **m. des nouvelles émissions** new issue market; *Bourse* **m. obligataire** bond market; **m. officiel** official market; **m. orienté à la hausse** bull market; **marchés d'outre-mer** overseas markets; **m. principal** core market; **m. aux puces** flea market; **m. de référence** core market; **m. régional** regional market, area market; **m. à règlement mensuel** monthly settlement market; **m. secondaire** secondary market; **m. témoin** control market, test market; **m. à terme** futures market; **m.-test** test market; *Bourse* **m. des titres** securities market; **m. du travail** labour market; **M. unique (européen)** Single (European) Market; **m. utile** adressable market; **m. des valeurs mobilières** share market; **m. visé** target market

marchéage [marʃeaʒ] *nm Mktg* marketing mix spectrum; **m. de distribution** retailing mix

marchéisation [marʃeizasjɔ̃] *nf* marketization

marchepied [marʃəpje] *nm* (*d'autel*) steps; (*de train*) step; *Vieilli* (*de voiture*) running board; (*escabeau*) (pair of) steps; (*avec plusieurs marches*) stepladder; *Fig* **servir de m. à qn** to serve as a stepping-stone for sb

marcher [marʃe] *vi* **(a)** (*se déplacer à pied*) to walk; **l'enfant ne marche pas encore** the child isn't walking yet; **il boite en marchant** he walks with a limp; **façon de m.** way of walking, gait; **m. à quatre pattes/sur les mains** to walk on all fours/on one's hands; **m. sur les pieds de qn** to tread on sb's toes; *Fig* **ne te laisse pas m. sur les pieds** don't let them walk all over you, don't let yourself be taken advantage of; **défense de m. sur les pelouses** keep off the grass; *Fig* **m. droit** to keep on the straight and narrow; *Fig* **m. sur les traces** *ou* **les pas de qn** to follow in sb's footsteps; **m. sur des œufs** (*avoir une démarche ralentie*) to walk gingerly; (*devoir être prudent*) to tread carefully *or* gently; **l'État marche à la ruine** the State is heading for ruin; **un peuple qui marche vers la liberté** a people marching *or* on the march towards liberty *or* freedom; *Mil* **m. contre l'ennemi** to advance on *or* move against the enemy; *F* **c'est marche ou crève!** it's do or die!, it's sink or swim!; *Fig F* **faire m. qn** to pull sb's leg, to have *or Am* put sb on, *Br* to wind sb up; *F* **et il a marché** and he fell for it, and he swallowed it

(b) (*fonctionner*) (*de machine*) to work, to run, to go; (*de plans etc*) to work; **ma montre ne marche plus** my watch isn't working *or* going; **faire m. une machine** to work *or* operate a machine; **comment ça marche?** how does it work?; *Fig* **les affaires marchent (bien)** business is going *or* doing well, business is brisk; **les affaires ne marchent plus** business is at a standstill *or* is (very) slack; **cela fait m. le commerce** it's good for business; **ça marche pour ce soir? – ça marche!** is it OK for this evening *or* are we on for this evening? – definitely *or* sure!; *F* **m. (dans la combine)** to get involved; **tu es sûr qu'il va m. dans la combine?** are you sure he'll come in on it?; *F* **on vole une voiture ce soir? – OK, je marche!** how about stealing a car tonight? – OK, count me in!; *F* **je ne marche pas** I'm having nothing to do with it, count me out; **on partage les bénéfices 50/50, ça marche?** we'll share the profits 50/50, (is that) agreed *or* OK?; **ça marche comme sur des roulettes** it's going like clockwork *or* like a dream *or* really smoothly; **ça ne marche pas si mal** we're not doing too badly; **la répétition a bien/mal marché** the rehearsal went well/badly

marcheur, -euse [marʃœr, -øz] **1** *n* walker **2** *adj* **(a)** *Zool* **oiseaux marcheurs** flightless birds **(b) navire bon m.** fast ship

marcottage [markɔtaʒ] *nm Bot* formation of runners; (*artificiel*) layering

marcotte [markɔt] *nf Bot* layer

marcotter [markɔte] *vt Bot* to layer

mardi [mardi] *nm* [①A75-6,B-C; B58-9,B-C] Tuesday; **M. gras** Shrove Tuesday, *Br* Pancake Day; *Iron* **ce n'est pas m. gras aujourd'hui** are you going to a fancy-dress ball?

mare [mar] *nf* pool; (*dans un parc, une ferme*) pond; **m. aux canards** duck pond; **m. de sang** pool of blood

marécage [marekaʒ] *nm* marsh, bog; (*dans un pays chaud*) swamp; (*dans l'est de l'Angleterre*) fen; (*terres marécageuses*) marshland

marécageux, -euse [marekaʒø, -øz] *adj* **(a)** (*de la nature des marécages*) marshy, boggy; (*dans un pays chaud*) swampy **(b)** (*qui vit dans les marécages*) marsh; **une plante marécageuse** a marsh plant

maréchal, -aux [mareʃal, -o] *nm* **(a) m. (de France)** *Mil* ≈ field marshal; *Hist* (*de maison royale etc*) ≈ marshal **(b)** *Mil* **m. des logis** sergeant; **m. des logis-chef** sergeant-major

maréchalat [mareʃala] *nm Mil* ≈ rank of field marshal

maréchale [mareʃal] *nf Mil* field marshal's wife

maréchalerie [mareʃalri] *nf* (*métier*) horse-shoeing, *Br* farriery; (*atelier*) smithy, forge

maréchal-ferrant, *pl* **maréchaux-ferrants** [mareʃalferɑ̃] *nm* blacksmith, *Br* farrier

maréchaussée [mareʃose] *nf Hist* mounted constabulary; *F Hum* **la m.** the boys in blue, the constabulary, the police

marée [mare] *nf* **(a)** (*mouvement de la mer*) tide; **à m. haute/basse** at high/low tide; **m. montante/descendante** flood/ebb tide; **grande m.** spring tide; **horaire des marées** tide tables; **fleuve à m.** tidal river; *Fig* **m. humaine** surging mass of people, human tidal wave; **m. noire** oil slick **(b)** *Pêche* fresh (sea) fish; **arriver comme m. en carême** to come as surely as night follows day

marelle [marɛl] *nf* (*jeu*) hopscotch; (*figure*) (set of) hopscotch squares

marémoteur, -trice [maremɔtœr, -tris] *adj* (*énergie*) tidal; **usine marémotrice** tidal power station

marengo [marɛ̃go] **1** *nf Culin* **poulet/veau (à la) m.** chicken/veal marengo **2** *nm* (*tissu*) = black cloth with white speckles

marennes [marɛn] *nf* Marennes oyster

mareyage [marɛjaʒ] *nm* fish trade

mareyeur, -euse [marɛjœr, -øz] *n* fish wholesaler

margarine [margarin] *nf* margarine

marge [marʒ] *nf* **(a)** (*de livre, de page manuscrite*) margin; **écrire qch dans la m.** to write sth in the margin; **laissez une m. de trois centimètres** leave a margin of three centimetres; **note en m.** marginal note, note in the margin; **m. de droite/gauche** right-/left-hand margin, right/left margin; **m. du haut** *ou* **supérieure** top margin; **m. inférieure** *ou* **du bas** bottom margin; **m. de reliure** inside margin

(b) *Fig* **accorder** *ou* **donner de la m. à qn** to allow sb some latitude *or* leeway *or* scope; (*temps*) to allow sb extra time; **avoir de la m.** to have plenty of scope; (*temps*) to have time in hand *or* to spare; **m. de négociation/manoeuvre** room for negotiation/manoeuvre

(c) en m. de on the fringe(s) of; **il y a une grande exposition de photos en m. du festival** there's a big exhibition of photographs as a fringe event; **en m. de cet enseignement, les élèves sont censés avoir des activités culturelles nombreuses** in addition, the pupils are supposed to have many extracurricular cultural activities; **rester en m. de l'histoire** to remain a footnote in history; **vivre en m. (de la société)** to live on the fringe(s) of society

(d) *Com* margin; *Bourse* **appel de m.** margin call

▶ **marge**: **m. avant impôt** pretax margin; **m. bénéficiaire** profit margin; *Compta* **m. brute d'autofinancement** cashflow, funds generated by operations; **m. commerciale (brute)** gross profit margin; **m. commerciale moyenne** average gross profit margin; *Compta* **m. sur coûts variables** contribution; **m. de crédit** credit margin; **m. du détaillant** retailer margin; **m. du distributeur** distributor's margin; **m. d'erreur** margin of error; **m. du grossiste** wholesaler margin; **m. de l'importateur** importer margin; **m. nette** net margin; **m. de profit** profit margin; **m. supplémentaire** additional margin; **m. de sécurité** safety margin; *Ind* **m. de tolérance** tolerance (margin)

margelle [marʒɛl] *nf* (*de puits*) coping, curb

marger [marʒe] **1** *vt Typ* to feed in; *Ordinat* **m. une page** to set the page margins **2** *vi* to set the margin(s); **m. à droite/à gauche** to set the right/left margin

margeur [marʒœr] *nm* (*de machine à écrire*) margin stop

marginal, -ales, -aux, -ales [marʒinal, -o] **1** *adj* **(a)** *Écon* (*coût, revenu*) marginal **(b)** *Fig* (*secondaire*) marginal; **occupations marginales** side lines; **ce problème n'a qu'une importance marginale** this problem is of only marginal importance **(c)** *Géog* (*récif*) fringing **2** *n* dropout; **les marginaux** the fringe(s) of society

marginalisation [marʒinalizasjɔ̃] *nf* marginalization

marginaliser [marʒinalize] **1** *vt* to marginalize; **un groupe social marginalisé** a marginalized social group, a group on the fringe(s) of society **2** *vpr* **se marginaliser** to become marginalized

marginalité [marʒinalite] *nf* nonconformism; **vivre dans la m.** to live on the fringe(s) of society

marginer [marʒine] *vt* to make margin notes in

margoulette [margulɛt] *nf F* **se casser la m.** to fall flat on one's face, to come a cropper

margoulin [margulɛ̃] *nm* rogue; (*homme d'affaires*) swindler

marguerite [margərit] **(a)** *nf Bot* **(petite) m.** daisy; **grande m.** marguerite; **effeuiller la m.** to play she/he loves me, she/he loves me not **(b)** (*pour machine à écrire*) daisy wheel

marguillier [margije] *nm Vieilli* churchwarden

mari [mari] *nm* husband; *F* **son petit m.** her hubby

mariable [marjabl] *adj* marriageable

mariage [marjaʒ] *nm* **(a)** (*cérémonie*) wedding; **anniversaire de m.** wedding anniversary; **ils ont fêté leurs vingt-cinq ans de m.** they celebrated their 25th wedding anniversary *or* their silver wedding; **liste de m.** wedding list

(b) (*union*) marriage; (*état*) marriage, matrimony; **elle a fait un mauvais m.** she made a bad marriage; **le m. ne lui a pas réussi** marriage *or* married life didn't suit him; **leur première année de m.** their first year of married life *or* marriage; **né hors m.** born out of wedlock; **demande en m.** proposal (of marriage); **acte de m.** marriage certificate

(c) *Fig* (*d'esprit et de beauté etc*) combination, marriage; (*de couleurs*) blend(ing); **cette fille, c'est le m. de l'intelligence et de la beauté** this girl is a combination of *or* combines intelligence and beauty; *F* **c'est le m. de la carpe et du lapin** they make strange bedfellows

(d) *Cartes* king and queen (*of a suit*)

▶ **mariage**: **m. d'amour** love match; **faire un m. d'amour** to marry for love; **m. d'argent: faire un m. d'argent** to marry for money; **m. en blanc** white wedding; **m. blanc** unconsummated marriage; **faire une m. blanc** to enter into a marriage of convenience (*primarily in order to acquire nationality*); **m. civil** civil wedding, *Br* registry office wedding; **m. de convenance** marriage of convenience; **m. mixte** mixed marriage; **m. de raison** marriage of convenience; **m. religieux** church wedding

Marianne [marjan] *nf Fig* = the (French) Republic

Marie [mari] *nf Rel* Mary

marié, -ée [marje] **1** *adj* married; **non m.** unmarried, single **2** *n* (*homme*) (bride)groom; (*femme*) bride; **féliciter les mariés** to congratulate the bride and groom *or* the married couple; **jeune m. /mariée** (*le jour du mariage*) (bride)groom/bride; (*dans les premiers temps*) newly married man/woman; **jeunes mariés** newly married couple, newlyweds; **robe de mariée** wedding dress; *Prov* **se plaindre que la mariée est trop belle** not to know how lucky one is

marie-couche-toi-là [marikuʃtwala] *nf inv Péj* harlot, strumpet

marier [marje] (*pr sub & impf* **n. mariions, v. mariiez**) **1** *vt* **(a)** (*de prêtre etc*) (*homme et femme*) to marry; (*de père*) (*fille*) to marry (off); **je suis marié depuis trois ans** I've been married for three years; *Fig F* **nous ne sommes pas mariés!** we're not married to each other!, we're not Siamese twins!

(b) (*deux qualités*) to combine; (*deux sociétés*) to merge; (*couleurs, senteurs*) to blend, to harmonize; (*vêtements, styles de meubles*) to harmonize; **il marie l'égoïsme à la**

plus parfaite indifférence he is a combination of selfishness and total indifference

2 se marier *vpr* **(a)** (*de personnes*) to get married, to marry; **se m. avec qn** to marry sb

(b) (*de couleurs, senteurs*) to blend, to harmonize (**avec** with); (*de vêtements, styles de meubles*) to go together, to harmonize; **le jaune se marie très bien avec le noir** yellow goes very well with black

marie-salope, *pl* **maries-salopes** [marisalɔp] *nf* **(a)** *Vulg* slut, *Br* slag **(b)** *Naut* (mud) dredger

marieur, -ieuse [marjœr, -jøz] *n F* matchmaker

marigot [marigo] *nm* (*dans les régions tropicales*) backwater (*of river*)

marihuana [marirwana] *nf*, **marijuana** [mariʒɥana] *nf* marijuana

marin, -ine [marɛ̃, -in] **1** *adj* **(a)** (*en relation avec la mer*) (*air, brise*) sea; (*plante, animal*) marine; **algues marines** seaweed, *Spéc* marine algae; **sel m.** sea salt; **monstres marins** sea monsters **(b)** (*destiné à la navigation*) **carte marine** sea chart; **mille m.** nautical mile; **avoir le pied m.** to be a good sailr **2** *nm* sailor, seaman, *Litt* seafarer, mariner; (*dans la flotte*) (able) seaman; **simple m.** ordinary seaman, rating; **costume m.** sailor suit

▶ **marin**: **m. d'eau douce** landlubber; **m. pêcheur** (deep-sea) fisherman

marina [marina] *nf* marina

marinade [marinad] *nf Culin* **(a)** (*saumure*) pickle; (*avant de faire cuire*) marinade; **m. de poissons/de gibier** marinaded fish/game **(b)** *Can* **marinades** pickles

marine [marin] **1** *nf* **(a)** (*flotte*) navy; **la m. marchande** the merchant navy; **la m. de guerre** the navy; **officier de m.** naval officer **(b)** (*navigation*) seamanship; **terme de m.** nautical term **(c)** *Beaux-Arts* seascape **2** *adj* (**bleu**) **m.** navy (blue); **un chapeau bleu m.** a navy(-blue) hat; **une jupe m.** a navy(-blue) skirt **3** *nm Mil Br* (Royal) Marine, *US* marine

mariné [marine] *adj Culin* (*pour conserver*) pickled; (*avant cuisson*) marinaded

mariner [marine] *Culin* **1** *vt* (*pour conserver*) to pickle; (*avant cuisson*) to marinade, to marinate **2** *vi* to marinade, to marinate; **un poisson qui doit m. tout une nuit** a fish that should be left to soak *or* to marinate overnight; *Fig F* **il m'a fait m. pendant deux heures dans son bureau** he kept me hanging around in his office for two hours; **ça fait déjà six mois que je marine en attendant une lettre de lui** I've been hanging on for six months now waiting for a letter from him

maringouin [marɛ̃gwɛ̃] *nm* (*sous les tropiques, au Canada*) mosquito

marinier [marinje] **1** *adj* **officier m.** petty officer **2** *nm* bargee, *Am* bargeman

marinière [marinjɛr] *nf* **(a)** (*vêtement*) blouse **(b)** *Culin* **moules (à la) m.** moules (à la) marinière (*mussels cooked in white wine*)

mariol(le) [marjɔl] *nm F* sly *or* clever devil; **faire le m.** to try to be clever

marionnette [marjɔnɛt] *nf* **m. (à fil)** puppet, marionette; **m. à gaine** glove puppet; *Fig* **je ne suis pas une m.** I'm not a puppet; **spectacle/théâtre de marionnettes** puppet show/theatre; **faire les marionnettes** = to move one's hands and sing in order to amuse a young child

marionnettiste [marjɔnetist] *n* puppeteer

marital, -ale, -aux, -ales [marital, -o] *adj* (*union*) marital

maritalement [maritalmɑ̃] *adv* **ils vivent m.** they're living as husband and wife, they're cohabiting; **vivre m. avec qn** to cohabit with sb

maritime [maritim] *adj* (*navigation, plante etc*) maritime; **ville m.** seaside town; **commerce m.** seaborne trade; **assurance m.** marine *or* shipping insurance; **courtier m.** shipbroker; **agent m.** shipping agent; **arsenal m.** naval dockyard; *Rail* **gare m.** harbour station; *Can Géog* **les Provinces Maritimes** the Maritime Provinces

maritorne [maritɔrn] *nf Vieilli* slattern, slut, sloven

marivaudage [marivodaʒ] *nm Litt* (*badinage*) light-hearted banter

marivauder [marivode] *vi Litt* to engage in light-hearted banter

marjolaine [marʒɔlɛn] *nf Bot* marjoram

mark [mark] *nm* (German) mark

marketing [marketiŋ] *nm* marketing; **m. direct** direct marketing; **faire du m.** (*étudier*) to do marketing; (*avoir pour profession*) to be in marketing; **elle est chef du m.** she's (the) head of marketing; **m. 'à la carte'** customized *or* tailored marketing; **m. après-vente** after-sales marketing; **m. ciblé** target marketing; **m. mix** marketing mix; **m. vert** green marketing

marlou [marlu] *nm Arg* pimp

marmaille [marmɑj] *nf F* (noisy) kids, brats; **rue pleine de m.** street swarming with (noisy) kids *or* brats; *Péj* **elle est venue avec toute sa m.** she brought the whole brood with her

marmelade [marməlad] *nf* **m. (d'oranges)** (orange) marmalade; *Fig F* **mettre qch en m.** to reduce sth to a pulp; **en m.** reduced to a pulp

marmite [marmit] *nf* **(a)** (*récipient*) (cooking) pot, pan; (*contenu*) potful, panful; **m. autoclave** pressure cooker; *Fig* **faire bouillir la m.** to bring home the bacon **(b)** *Mil F Vieilli* heavy shell **(c)** *Géol* **m. de géants** pothole

marmiton [marmitɔ̃] *nm* kitchen boy

marmonnement [marmɔnmɑ̃] *nm* mumbling, muttering

marmonner [marmɔne] *vti* to mumble, to mutter; **qu'est-ce que tu marmonnes encore?** what's that you're muttering *or* mumbling (now)?

marmoréen, -enne [marmɔreɛ̃, -ɛn] *adj Litt* marmoreal, marmorean; **blancheur marmoréenne** marble whiteness

marmot [marmo] *nm F* (*enfant*) kid, *Péj* brat

marmotte [marmɔt] *nf* marmot; *Fig* sleepyhead; *Fig* **dormir comme une m.** to sleep like a log *or* a baby

marmottement [marmɔtmɑ̃] *nm* mumbling, muttering

marmotter [marmɔte] *vti* **m. (entre ses dents)** to mumble, to mutter

marnage[1] [marnaʒ] *nm Agr* (*de sol*) marling

marnage[2] *nm Naut* tidal range

marne [marn] *nf Géol* marl

marner [marne] **1** *vt Agr* (*sol*) to marl **2** *vi* **(a)** *Arg Vieilli* (*travailler dur*) to slave, to slog **(b)** (*de la mer*) to rise

Maroc [marɔk] *nm* Morocco

marocain, -aine [marɔkɛ̃, -ɛn] **1** *adj* Moroccan **2** *n* **M.** Moroccan

maronite [marɔnit] *adj, n* Maronite

maronner [marɔne] *vi F* to grouse, to grumble

maroquin [marɔkɛ̃] *nm* **(a)** (*cuir*) morocco (leather) **(b)** *Fig* (minister's) portfolio

maroquinerie [marɔkinri] *nf* **(a)** *Ind* (*fabrication du maroquin*) morocco-leather tanning; (*du cuir*) leather working **(b)** (*atelier*) morocco-leather tannery **(c)** *Com* (*articles*) (fancy) leather goods; (*magasin*) (fancy) leather goods shop

maroquinier [marɔkinje] *nm* **(a)** (*tanneur*) morocco-leather tanner; (*personne qui fabrique des objets en cuir*) leather worker **(b)** (*commerçant*) dealer in (fancy) leather goods; **chez le m.** at the leather goods shop

marotte [marɔt] *nf* **(a)** (*manie, folie*) fad, craze; (*passe-temps*) hobby **(b)** (*de modiste, coiffeur*) dummy head

marouflage [maruflaʒ] *nm Beaux-Arts* re-mounting

maroufler [marufle] *vt Beaux-Arts* to re-mount

marquage [markaʒ] *nm aussi Sp* marking; *Com* branding; **m. de marchandises** marking of goods; *Aut* **m. au sol** road markings; **m. en zig-zag** zig-zag marking

marquant [markɑ̃] *adj* (*incident, personne, journée*) remarkable, outstanding; **un épisode m. de son adolescence** a significant episode in his adolescence; *Cartes* **carte marquante** card that counts

marque [mark] *nf* **(a)** (*signe, trace*) mark; *Ling* mark, sign; **la m. du pluriel** the mark *or* sign of the plural; **faire une m. dans la marge** to put a mark in the margin; **faire une m. au couteau sur qch** to make a mark with a knife *or* a knife mark on sth, to mark sth with a knife; **le cintre a fait une m. sur ce vêtement** the coat-hanger has left a mark on this garment; **les roues avaient laissé des marques sur le sable** the wheels had left marks in the sand; **on voit encore la m. du coup qu'elle a reçu** you can still see where she was hit; *Com* **marques d'expédition** shipping marks; *Fig* **marques d'amitié** tokens of friendship

(b) *Com* brand; (*de voiture*) make; (*sur l'article*) trademark; **j'ai eu des voitures de trois marques différentes** I've had three different makes of car; **les grandes marques d'électroménager** the main brands of electrical appliance(s); *Fig* **personnage de m.** person of distinction, distinguished *or* prominent person; **produits de m.** branded goods; **produits de m. courante** well-known branded goods; **vin de m.** wine from a well-known vineyard, choice *or* vintage wine; **produits sans m.** unbranded goods; **m. dominante** dominant brand; **m. milieu de gamme** middle brand, middle-of-the-range brand; **m. numéro un** number-one brand; **m. ombrelle** umbrella brand; **m. économique** (*bon marché*) budget *or* economy brand

(c) *Com* (*cachet*) stamp; **un produit qui porte la m. de la douane** goods that have been stamped at customs

(d) *Sp* **à vos marques! prêts? partez!** on your marks! get set! go!

(e) (*aux jeux*) score; **tenir la m.** to keep (the) score; **où en est la m.?** what's the score?

(f) *Ordinat* marker, flag, tag; **m. d'insertion** insertion marker

(g) *Naut* **la m. de l'amiral** the admiral's flag

▶ **marque**: **m. commerciale** *ou* **de commerce** brand, brand name, trademark; **m. déposée** registered trademark; **m. de détaillant** retailer brand; **m. de distributeur** distributor brand, retailer brand, private brand, private-label brand, own brand; **m. d'enseigne** retailer brand, shop's own brand; **m. de fabricant** manufacturer brand; **m. de fabrique** brand; (*de voiture*) make; (*sur l'article*) trademark; *Fig* **m. du génie: porter la m. du génie** to bear the stamp *or* the hallmark of genius; **m. de magasin** shop's own brand, store brand; **m. d'orfèvre** hallmark; **m. d'origine** origin of goods label; **m. pilote** brand leader; **m. de revendeur** dealer brand

marqué [marke] *adj* **(a)** (*qui porte une marque, un signe*) marked, bearing a mark; **être m.** (*de personne*) to have a lined *or* furrowed face; **visage m. par la petite vérole/l'âge** pockmarked face/face lined with age; *F* **qu'est-ce qui est m.** *ou* **qu'est-ce qu'il y a de m. sur l'enveloppe?** what does it say on the envelope?, what's written on the envelope?; *Fig* **j'ai été très m. par ce film** the film made a strong impression on me; **il est m. à vie par cette expérience** he has been marked for life by the experience; **elle guérira mais restera marquée toute sa vie** she'll get better, but she'll carry *or* bear the marks of it *or* the scars for the rest of her life

(b) (*prononcé*) (*différence, penchant etc*) marked, decided, distinct; (*traits*) pronounced; **robe à la taille marquée** dress with a fitted waist

marque-page, *pl* **marque-pages** *nm* bookmark

marquer [marke] **1** *vt* **(a)** (*faire une marque, un signe sur*) to mark; (*écrire*) to write; (*enregistrer en écrivant*) to make a note of, to note down; **m. les prix** to mark prices; **m. du bétail (au fer)** to brand cattle; **tous les prisonniers ont été marqués au fer** all the prisoners were branded; *Fig* **c'est un événement/jour à m. d'une pierre blanche** it was a remarkable event/red-letter day; **marquez votre nom en haut à gauche** write your name in the top left-hand corner; **il est** *ou* **c'est marqué qu'il faut une pièce d'identité** it says that some form of identification is required

(b) (*délimiter*) to mark; **cette clôture marque l'extrémité de la propriété** this fence marks the boundary of the property; **m. sa place** (*dans un train etc*) to reserve *or F* bag one's seat; *Fig* **cet événement a marqué la fin de son adolescence** this event marked the end of his adolescence

(c) *Sp* **m. un adversaire** (*le surveiller*) to mark an opponent; **m. un but** to score a goal; **m. les points** to keep (the) score; **m. trente points** to score thirty (points); **ne m. aucun point** to fail to score (a single point); *Fig* **m. un point** (*dans une discussion*) to make a good point; **tu as raison, tu marques un point** you're right, one up to you; **tu as marqué plusieurs points** you scored several points

(d) (*indiquer*) to indicate, to show; **la pendule marque dix heures** the clock says ten o'clock; **le thermomètre marque 25°** the thermometer shows *or* registers 25°; **elle n'a pas marqué beaucoup d'intérêt pour l'exposition** she didn't show much interest in the exhibition; *Mus* **m. la mesure** to beat time; **m. le pas** to mark time; **manteau qui marque bien la taille** coat that shows off the figure; *Fig* **m. le coup** to mark the occasion

(e) (*laisser une forte impression sur*) to mark; **la guerre l'a beaucoup marqué** the war certainly left its mark on him *or* left a deep impression on him; **le film ne m'a pas marqué** I wasn't very struck by the film

(f) *Ordinat* to mark, to flag, to tag

2 *vi* **(a)** (*écrire*) **crayon qui ne marque pas** pencil that won't write

(b) (*laisser une impression*) (*d'un événement*) to stand out; (*d'une personne*) to leave *or* make one's mark

(c) le verre a marqué sur la table the glass left a mark on the table, the glass marked the table

marqueté [markəte] *adj* (*bois*) inlaid; (*fourrure*) speckled

marqueterie [markətri] *nf* inlaid work, marquetry; **guéridon en m.** inlaid pedestal table; **bois de m.** marquetry wood

marqueteur [markətœr] *nm* worker in marquetry, inlayer

marqueur, -euse [markœr, -øz] **1** *n* **(a)** (*de documents*) stamper; (*de bétail*) brander **(b)** (*aux jeux*) scorekeeper, scorer; *Fb etc* **m. (de but)** (goal) scorer; *Billard* **m. automatique** scoreboard **2** *nm* **(a)** (felt-tip) marker; **m. surligneur** highlighter **(b)** *Ordinat* marker, flag; **m. de fin de texte** end of text marker **(c)** (*biologique*) marker

marquis [marki] *nm* marquis, marquess

marquisat [markiza] *nm* marquisate

marquise [markiz] *nf* **(a)** (*noble*) marchioness **(b)** (*véranda*) (*de toile, tissu*) awning, canopy; (*de verre*) glass awning *or* canopy; (*de gare*) glass roof **(c)** (*canapé*) sofa, settee (*for two people*), *Am* love seat **(d)** (*bague*) marquise (ring) **(e)** *Culin* **m. au chocolat** = chocolate charlotte russe

Marquises [markiz] *nfpl* **les (îles) M.** the Marquesas Islands

marraine [marɛn] *nf* **(a)** (*d'enfant*) godmother; (*de bateau*) christener **(b)** *Hist* **m. de guerre** = female correspondent of soldier at the front

marrant, -ante [marɑ̃, -ɑ̃t] *F* **1** *adj* **(a)** (*drôle*) funny; **je ne vois pas ce qu'il y a de m. là-dedans** I can't see anything funny in it, I can't see what's so funny about it; **tu n'es vraiment pas m., tu ne veux jamais sortir** you're not much fun, you never want to go out **(b)** (*bizarre*) funny, odd, strange; **vous êtes m., vous, alors!** you're the limit! **2** *n* **c'est un m., celui-là** that guy's a scream, that guy's hilarious; **le nouveau directeur, c'est vraiment pas un m.** the new manager doesn't fool around; **il a épousé une petite marrante** the woman he married is a real scream

marre [mar] *adv F* **en avoir m. de qch/qn** to be fed up with *or* sick of sth/sb, to have had enough of sth/sb; **j'en ai m.!** I'm fed up!, I'm sick of it!, I've had enough (of it)!; **j'en ai m. de venir à pied tous les jours** I'm fed up with *or* I'm sick of walking here every day; **j'en ai m. que ce soit toujours moi qui fasse les courses** I'm fed up with always having to do the shopping; **il y en a m.** that's enough **(de** of); **il y en a m. de te voir ne rien faire** I'm sick (and tired) of seeing you laze around; **et c'est m.** and that's that

marrer (se) [səmare] *vpr F* to have a good laugh; **elle ne doit pas se m. tous les jours avec ce type-là** she can't have much fun with that guy; **quand elle me dit qu'elle va chercher du boulot, je me marre** when she tells me she's going to look for a job, I have to laugh; **faire m. qn** to make sb laugh; *Iron* **qu'est-ce qu'on se marre!** this is great fun, I don't think!

marri [mari] *adj Arch* grieved, sad

marron[1] [marɔ̃] **1** *adj inv* brown **2** *nm* **(a)** *Bot, Culin* chestnut; **m. d'Inde** horse chestnut; **crème de m.** chestnut purée; **marrons glacés** candied *or* sugared chestnuts, marrons glacés; **marrons chauds** roast chestnuts; *Fig* **tirer les marrons du feu pour qn** to pull sb's chestnuts out of the fire; **c'est Pierre qui va tirer les marrons du deu** (*s'assurer tous les avantages*) it'll be Pierre who'll reap the benefits **(b)** *F* (*coup*) thump, wallop; **il s'est pris de ces marrons!** he got a real thumping *or* walloping!; **il s'est pris de ces marrons pendant son enfance** he took some real thumpings *or* wallopings as a kid **(c)** (*couleur*) brown

marron[2]**, -onne** [marɔ̃, -ɔn] *adj* **(a)** *Hist* **esclave m.** runaway slave **(b)** (*médecin, homme de loi*) quack

marronnier [marɔnje] *nm* chestnut tree; **m. d'Inde** horse chestnut tree

Mars [mars] **1** *nm Myth* Mars **2** *nf Astron* Mars

mars [mars] *nm* [①A75-6,B-C; B58-9,B-C] March; **en m.** in March; **au mois de m.** in (the month of) March; **le sept m.** (on) the seventh of March, (on) March the seventh, *Am* (on) March seventh; **blé de m., les m.** spring wheat; **arriver comme m. en carême** to come as surely as night follows day

marseillais, -aise [marsɛjɛ, -ɛz] **1** *adj* (of/from) Marseilles **2** *n* **M.** (*natif*) native of Marseilles; (*habitant*) inhabitant of Marseilles **3** *nf* **la Marseillaise** the Marseillaise

Marseille [marsɛj] *n* Marseilles

marsouin [marswɛ̃] *nm* **(a)** (*mammifère*) porpoise **(b)** *Mil F Arch* marine

marsupial, -ale, -iaux, -ales [marsypjal, -jo] *adj, nm* marsupial

marteau, -eaux [marto] **1** *nm* (*outil*), *Sp* hammer; (*de commissaire-priseur*) hammer, gavel; (*de porte*) (door) knocker; (*d'horloge*) striker; **coup de m.** hammer stroke *or* blow; *Fig* **être entre le m. et l'enclume** to be stuck in the middle; *Sp* **lanceur de m.** hammer thrower; **être premier au lancer de m.** to come first in the hammer; **requin m.** hammerhead (shark) **2** *adj F* nuts, crazy; **elles sont complètement marteaux** they're completely nuts *or* crazy

▶ **marteau**: **m. à panne fendue** claw hammer; **m.-perforateur**, *pl* **marteaux-perforateurs** hammer drill; *Métal* **m.-pilon**, *pl* **marteaux-pilons** power hammer; **m.-piolet**, *pl* **marteaux-piolets** (*en alpinisme*) piton hammer; **m.-piqueur**, *pl* **marteaux-piqueurs** pneumatic drill; **m. pneumatique** pneumatic drill

martel [martɛl] *nm* **se mettre m. en tête** to be anxious, to worry

martelage [martəlaʒ] *nm* hammering

martelé [martəle] *adj* hammered; **argent m.** beaten silver; **paroles martelées** hammered-out words

martèlement [martɛlmɑ̃] *nm* hammering

marteler [martəle] *vt* **(je martèle; je martèlerai)** to hammer; *Métal* **m. à froid** to cold-hammer; *Fig* **m. ses mots** to hammer out one's words; *Fig* **m. un air** to hammer out *or* pound out a tune; **la douleur martelait ma tempe** the pain was hammering away at my temple

martial, -ale, -aux, -ales [marsjal, -o] *adj* (*musique*) martial; **arts martiaux** martial arts; *Mil* **loi martiale** martial law; *Mil* **code m.** articles of war; *Mil* **cour martiale** court martial; **passer devant la cour martiale pour haute trahison** to be court-martialled for high treason

martialement [marsjalmɑ̃] *adv* martially

martien, -ienne [marsjɛ̃, -jɛn] *adj, n* Martian; **les martiens ont débarqué** the Martians have landed

martinet[1] [martinɛ] *nm* **(a)** *Métal* tilt hammer, drop stamp **(b)** (*fouet*) strap; **tu vas avoir six coups de m.** you'll get six of the strap *or* of the best

martinet[2] *nm* (*oiseau*) swift

martingale [martɛ̃gal] *nf* **(a)** (*pour un cheval*) martingale; (*sur un vêtement*) half belt **(b)** (*au jeu*) (*façon de jouer*) doubling-up, martingale; (*combinaison*) (winning) formula

martin-pêcheur, *pl* **martins-pêcheurs** [martɛ̃pɛʃœr] *nm* (*oiseau*) kingfisher

martre [martr] *nf* marten; **m. zibeline** sable; **m. du Canada** mink

martyr, -yre [martir] **1** *n* martyr; **m. d'une cause** martyr to a cause; **se donner des airs de m., jouer les martyrs** to act the martyr, to put on a martyred expression *or* look; **ne prends pas cet air de m.** don't act the martyr **2** *adj* **un enfant m.** an abused child; **un peuple m.** a martyred people

martyre [martir] *nm* martyrdom; **souffrir le m.** to suffer martyrdom; *Fig* to suffer agonies; **sa vie de couple a été un vrai m.** his married life was pure agony *or* a real martyrdom; **mettre qn au m.** to torture sb

martyriser [martirize] *vt Rel* to martyr; *Fig* (*faire souffrir*) to torture; **il a été martyrisé par ses parents** he was abused by his parents; **il martyrise sa petite sœur** he bullies his little sister

marxisme [marksism] *nm* Marxism

marxisme-léninisme [marksism(ə)leninism] *nm* Marxism-Leninism

marxiste [marksist] *adj, n* Marxist

marxiste-léniniste [marksist(ə)leninist] *adj, n* Marxist-Leninist

mas [mɑ(s)] *nm* (*en Provence*) (*ferme*) farm; (*maison*) farmhouse

mascara [maskara] *nm* mascara; **se mettre du m.** to put on mascara

mascarade [maskarad] *nf* masquerade; *Fig* sham, masquerade; **cette élection n'est qu'une m.** the election is nothing but a sham

mascaret [maskarɛ] *nm* (*dans un estuaire*) bore, tidal wave

mascaron [maskarɔ̃] *nm Archit* (*sur une clef de voûte etc*) grotesque mask

mascotte [maskɔt] *nf* mascot

masculin [maskylɛ̃] **1** *adj* **(a)** (*sexe, voix, mode, métier etc*) male; (*qui a les caractères de l'homme*) (*orgueil, vanité etc*) masculine; (*femme*) masculine, mannish; **mes collègues masculins** my male colleagues **(b)** *Gram* masculine; **nom m.** masculine noun **(c)** (*en poésie*) **rime masculine** masculine rhyme **2** *nm* (①B5-6,A) *Gram* masculine (gender); **ce mot est du m.** this word is masculine; **au m.** in the masculine

masculinisation [maskylinizasjɔ̃] *nf Méd* masculinization; **la m. d'une profession** the increase in the number of men in a profession

masculiniser [maskylinize] *vt* **m. qn** (*de vêtement, coupe etc*) to make sb look masculine; (*de médicaments*) to produce male characteristics in sb, to masculinize sb; **m. une profession** to increase the number of men in a profession

masculinité [maskylinite] *nf* masculinity

maskinongé [maskinɔ̃ʒe] *nm Can* (*poisson*) muskellunge; *F* muskie

maso [mazo] *n, adj inv F* (*masochiste*) masochist; **tu es complètement m. d'avoir accepté!** you must be a masochist *or* a glutton for punishment if you agreed!

masochisme [mazɔʃism] *nm* masochism

masochiste [mazɔʃist] **1** *adj* masochistic **2** *n* masochist

masquage [maskaʒ] *nm Ordinat* masking

masque [mask] *nm* **(a)** mask; **un m. de carnaval** a carnival mask; *Fig* **sa gentillesse n'est qu'un m.** his kindness is only a façade *or* front; **ôter** *ou* **arracher le m. à qn** to unmask sb; **lever le m.** to throw off one's mask; **m. (de beauté)** (*pour la peau*) face pack **(b)** *Ordinat* mask; **m. d'entrée, m. de saisie** input mask; **m. d'écran** screen mask **(c)** *Mil* (*dispositif de camouflage*) (*d'arme*) shield, hood

▶ **masque**: *Méd* **m. de chirurgien** operating *or* surgeon's mask; **m. à gaz** gas mask; **m. de grossesse** brown patches on the skin, *Spéc* chloasma; **m. mortuaire** death mask; *Méd* **m. à oxygène** oxygen mask; **m. de plongée** diving mask; **m. de soudeur** welding mask

masqué [maske] *adj* (*personne*) masked; (*porte*) concealed, hidden; **bal m.** masked ball; *Mil* **tir m.** hidden *or* concealed fire

masquer [maske] **1** *vt* (*mettre un masque à*) (*qn*) to put a mask on, to mask; (*cacher à la vue*) (*paysage etc*) to mask, to hide, to conceal; (*sentiments, amour*) to hide, to conceal; (*déguiser*) (*goût, odeur, peine*) to disguise, to mask; (*lumière*) to shade; *Naut* (*navire*) to darken; *Mil* **m. une batterie** to conceal *or* hide a battery; *Naut* **naviguer à feux masqués** to sail without lights; **on ne peut m. la vérité plus longtemps** the truth cannot be (kept) hidden any longer; **m. ses véritables intentions** to conceal *or* disguise one's true intentions **2 se masquer** *vpr* to put a mask on

massacrante [masakrɑ̃t] *adj* **être d'une humeur m.** to be in a filthy *or* vile temper

massacre [masakr] *nm* **(a)** (*tuerie*) massacre, slaughter; (*d'animaux*) slaughter; *Hist* **le m. de la Saint-Barthélemy** the St Bartholomew's Day Massacre; **envoyer des soldats au m.** to send soldiers to the slaughter *or* to be slaughtered; *Fig* **le match a été un vrai m.** the match was a real massacre; **jeu de m.** ≈ Aunt Sally; *Fig* demolition job

(b) *F* (*travail mal fait*) mess; **ils ont voulu faire un gâteau, c'est un véritable m.** they wanted to make a cake but they've made a right mess of it *or* it's a right mess!; **jouer Shakespeare comme cela, c'est un m.** it's absolutely massacring *or* murdering Shakespeare to perform him like that!

(c) *F* (*grand succès*) **cette pièce va faire un m.** the play will be a smash hit

(d) (*tête de daim, de cerf*) stag's head (*displayed as a hunting trophy*)

massacrer [masakre] *vt* **(a)** (*tuer, exterminer*) to massacre, to slaughter; (*animaux*) to slaughter; *Fig* **notre équipe s'est fait m.** our team was massacred; **le film a été massacré par les critiques** the film was torn to pieces *or* savaged by the critics; **lors du débat, il s'est vraiment fait m. par son interlocuteur** he was really savaged by his opponent in the debate **(b)** *F* (*travail*) to bungle, to botch, to make a mess *or* hash of; (*musique, texte*) to murder, to massacre; (*vêtements*) to ruin

massacreur, -euse [masakrœr, -øz] *n* **(a)** (*tueur*) slaughterer, butcher **(b)** *F* (*gâcheur*) bungler, botcher

massage [masaʒ] *nm* massage; **se faire faire un m.** to have a massage

▶ **massage**: *Méd* **m. cardiaque** cardiac *or* heart massage; **m. thaïlandais** Thai massage: **faire des massages thaïlandais** to work in a massage parlour

masse[1] [mas] *nf* **(a)** *Phys, MecE* mass; **le kilogramme est l'unité de m.** the kilogram is the unit of mass

(b) (*grande quantité*) mass; (*de gens*) mass, crowd; **m. d'eau** body of water; (*en mouvement*) mass of water; *Météo* **m. d'air** mass of air, air mass; **tomber comme une m.** to fall in a heap; **taillé dans la m.** carved from the block; *F* **un grand type taillé dans la m.** a big, heavily-built sort of chap; **en m.** (*en grand nombre*) in large numbers, en masse; **'arrivée en m. des estivants sur les plages'** 'holidaymakers invade the beaches *or* take to the beaches in droves'; **les villageois se préparent à une arrivée en m. des touristes** villagers are bracing themselves for a tourist invasion; **la m. des connaissances** the total sum of knowledge; **la grande m. des employés** the vast majority of employees, virtually all employees; **les masses** the masses; **culture de m.** mass *or* popular culture; *F* **il y avait des masses de livres** there were masses (and masses) of books; *F* **il y a une m. de gens qui votent pour lui** masses of people *or* a whole mass of people are voting for him; *F* **il n'y avait pas des masses de gens** there weren't exactly masses of people there; *F* **il n'y en a pas des masses** (*objets*) there aren't masses of them; (*sucre, farine etc*) there isn't masses (of it); *F* **t'as faim? – pas des masses!** are you hungry? – not really

(c) *Fin* fund, stock; **il faut établir la m. d'équipment dans le budget de cette année** we have to establish the total amount of (money allowed for) capital goods in this year's budget

(d) *Él* earth, *Am* ground; **mettre le courant à la m.** to earth *or Am* ground the current; *Fig F* **être à la m.** to be mad, to be off one's head

▶ **masse**: *Fin* **m. active** assets; *Phys, Nucl* **m. critique** critical mass; **masses laborieuses** (working) masses, *Litt* toiling masses; *Fin* **m. monétaire** money supply, (total amount of) money in circulation; *Fin* **m. passive** liabilities; **m. salariale** wage bill, staff costs; **faire partie de la m. salariale** to be on the payroll; *Phys* **m. spécifique** *ou* **volumique** density

masse[2] *nf* **(a)** (*marteau*) sledgehammer; **m. en bois** beetle; *Fig F* **coup de m.** (*dû à une émotion*) crushing blow; (*dû à un* *prix exorbitant*) (very) nasty shock (*when one sees the bill*); **il a reçu le coup de m.** (*quand il a appris qu'il était renvoyé*) it came as a crushing blow; **ça a été le coup de m.** (*quand il nous a annoncé le total*) it came as a (very) nasty shock **(b)** (*d'huissier*) (ceremonial) mace; **m. (d'armes)** (*arme ancienne*) mace

masselotte [maslɔt] *nf MecE* bob weight; (*de régulateur*) flyweight

massepain [maspɛ̃] *nm* marzipan

masser¹ [mase] **1** *vt* (*réunir*) (*personnes*) to gather together, to assemble; (*soldats*) to mass; *Beaux-Arts* (*figures etc*) to group; **elle massait ses cheveux dans sa nuque** she gathered her hair (together) at the back of her neck **2 se masser** *vpr* to gather, to form a crowd; **la foule s'est massée devant le tribunal** the crowd gathered in front of the courtroom

masser² *vt* (*frotter*) to massage; **il m'a massé le dos** he massaged my back; **elle a massé le patient** she gave the patient a massage, she massaged the patient; **se faire m.** to have a massage, to be massaged

massette [masɛt] *nf* **(a)** (*outil*) two-handed hammer **(b)** *Bot* bulrush, reed mace, cat's tail

masseur, -euse [masœr, -øz] **1** *n* (*personne*) masseur, *f* masseuse **2** *nm* (*appareil*) (vibro)massager

masseur-kinésithérapeute, *pl* **masseurs-kinésithérapeutes** *n* physiotherapist

massicot¹ [masiko] *nm Ch* massicot

massicot² *nm Tech* guillotine, trimmer

massicoter [masikɔte] *vt Tech* to guillotine

massif, -ive [masif, -iv] **1** *adj* **(a)** (*gros, épais*) massive, bulky; (*homme*) heavily built; **des traits massifs** heavy features **(b)** (*plein*) (*argent, acajou etc*) solid; **bijoux en or m.** solid gold jewellery **(c)** *Fig* (*en masse, en grande quantité*) (*dose, bombardements*) massive; **départs massifs** mass exodus; **un 'oui' franc et m.** a clear and overwhelming 'yes' **2** *nm* **(a)** (*d'arbustes, d'arbres*) clump; **m. de fleurs** bed of flowers, flower bed **(b)** *Géog* massif; **le M. central** the Massif Central (*mountain range in central France*)

massique [masik] *adj Phys* mass; **puissance m.** power-to-weight ratio

massivement [masivmɑ̃] *adv* (*répondre, voter etc*) en masse, in large numbers

mass media [masmedja] *nmpl* mass media

massue [masy] *nf* club, bludgeon; **coup de m.** blow with a club; *Fig* **ça a été le coup de m.** (*prix excessif*) it was a rip-off; (*qch d'imprévu*) it was a bolt from the blue, it was a staggering blow; **quand on a reçu la facture, ça a été le coup de m.** when we got the invoice we had a (very) nasty shock; **argument m.** sledgehammer argument

mastard [mastar] *nm F* hefty man

mastectomie [mastɛktɔmi] *nf* mastectomy

master [mastɛr] *nm TV etc* master; **m. monté** edited master

mastère [mastɛr] *nm Univ* (*d'ingénieur*) DEng; (*de commerce*) MBA

mastic [mastic] **1** *nm* **(a)** (*résine*) mastic (resin); (*pour fenêtres etc*) putty; (*pour bois etc*) filler, mastic; **m. de colmatage** filler paste **(b)** *Typ* **faire un m.** to (accidentally) transpose characters **2** *adj inv* putty-coloured *or US* -colored

masticage [mastikaʒ] *nm* (*de fenêtre*) puttying; (*de bois*) filling

masticateur, -trice [mastikatœr, -tris] *adj* masticatory

mastication [mastikasjɔ̃] *nf* chewing, *Fml* mastication

masticatoire [mastikatwar] *adj, nm* masticatory

mastiquer¹ [mastike] *vt* (*mâcher*) to chew, *Fml* to masticate

mastiquer² **1** *vt* (*fissures etc*) to fill (in); (*fenêtre, vitre*) to putty **2** *vi* **couteau à m.** putty knife

mastite [mastit] *nf Méd* mastitis

mastoc [mastɔk] *adj inv F* (*personne*) hulking, lumpish; (*construction*) clumsy

mastodonte [mastɔdɔ̃t] *nm* **(a)** *Zool* mastodon **(b)** *F* (*véhicule*) juggernaut; (*personne*) colossus

mastoïde [mastɔid] *nf Anat* mastoid

mastoïdien, ienne [mastɔidjɛ̃, -jɛn] *adj Anat* mastoid

mastose [mastoz] *nf Méd* mastosis

mastroquet [mastrɔkɛ] *nm Vieilli F* **(a)** (*cafetier*) bar owner, *Br* publican **(b)** (*bistro*) bar, *Br* pub

masturbation [mastyrbasjɔ̃] *nf* masturbation; **c'est de la m. intellectuelle** it's intellectual self-indulgence *or* masturbation

masturber [mastyrbe] **1** *vt* to masturbate **2 se masturber** *vpr* to masturbate

m'as-tu-vu, -vue [matyvy] *n inv F* show-off; **qu'est-ce qu'elle est m'as-tu-vue** what a show-off she is; **ce genre de voiture, ça fait très m.** it's a really flashy type of car

masure [mazyr] *nf* tumbledown cottage, *Péj* hovel

mat¹ [mat] *adj* (*métal*) mat(t), unpolished, dull; (*couleur*) mat(t), flat; **teint m.** mat(t) complexion; **son m.** dull sound, thud

mat² *Échecs* **1** *adj inv* checkmated; **le roi est m.** the king is checkmated *or* in checkmate **2** *nm inv* (check)mate; **faire m. en trois coups** to mate in three

mât [mɑ] *nm* **(a)** *Naut* mast; **grand m.** mainmast; **m. d'artimon** mizzenmast; **m. de misaine** foremast; **m. de hune** topmast; **m. de charge** cargo boom, derrick; **navire à trois mâts** three-masted ship, three-master **(b)** (*poteau*) pole; **m. de tente** tent pole; **m. de cocagne** greasy pole; *Rail* **m. de sémaphore** signal post, signal mast

matador [matadɔr] *nm* matador

mataf [mataf] *nm Arg* (*matelot*) tar, sailor

matamore [matamɔr] *nm* braggart, boaster; **faire le m.** to boast, to brag

match, *pl* **matchs, matches** [matʃ] *nm Sp* match; **disputer un m.** to play a match; **on fait un m.?** shall we have *or* play a match?; **il est impitoyable en m.** he's ruthless when he's playing (a match); **m. de boxe** boxing match; *Fb* **m. de championnat (professionel)** league match; **m. aller** first leg; **m. retour** return match, second leg; **m. amical** friendly (match); **m. nul** draw; **faire m. nul** to draw, to tie; **ils ont fait m. nul** they drew, the match ended in a draw

maté [mate] *nm* maté

matelas [matla] *nm* **(a)** mattress; **m. à ressorts** spring mattress; **m. pneumatique** inflatable mattress, air bed, *Br* Lilo®; **toile à m.** ticking; *Constr* **m. d'air** air space **(b)** *F* (*fortune*) pile (of money); **un m. de billets de banque** a wad of banknotes

matelassé [matlase] **1** *adj Tex* quilted; **blouson m.** quilted *or* padded jacket; **enveloppe matelassée** padded envelope, Jiffy bag® **2** *nm* quilted material; **du m. de soie** quilted silk

matelasser [matlase] *vt* (*meuble*) to upholster; (*tissu*) to quilt; (*recouvrir de tissu matelassé*) to cover with quilted material

matelassure [matlasyr] *nf* (*de matelas, selle etc*) padding, stuffing

matelot [matlo] *nm Naut* **(a)** (*personne*) sailor; **m. (breveté) de première classe** leading seaman; **m. de deuxième classe** able seaman; **servir comme simple m.** to sail before the mast **(b)** (*bateau*) consort (ship); **m. d'avant/d'arrière** next ship ahead/astern

matelotage [matlɔtaʒ] *nm* **(a)** (*connaissances*) seamanship **(b)** (*paye*) sailor's pay

matelote [matlɔt] *nf Culin* matelote, fish stew; **m. de morue** cod stew; **sauce m.** red wine and onion sauce

mater¹ [mate] *vt* **(a)** *Échecs* to (check)mate **(b)** *Fig* (*dresser, dompter*) (*qn, chien*) to bring to heel, to subdue, to tame

mater² *vt* **(a)** (*métaux, verre etc*) to mat(t), to dull **(b)** (*joints de chaudière etc*) to caulk, to hammer

mater³ *F* **1** *vt* to ogle, to eye up; **mate un peu la gonzesse!** just take a look at *or* get an eyeful of that chick!; **se faire m.** to be ogled, to be eyed up **2** *vi* to eye up *or* ogle (the) women; **qu'est-ce que ça mate, ici!** all these men eyeing us up!

mâter [mɑte] *vt* (*navire*) to mast

matérialisation [materjalizasjɔ̃] *nf* (*d'espoir, de projet*) materialization, realization; **la m. de Dieu sur terre** the materialization of God on earth

matérialisé [materjalize] *adj Admin* **voie matérialisée** = section of road delimited by a white line

matérialiser [materjalize] **1** *vt* (*idée, espoir, projet*), *Fin* to realize **2 se matérialiser** *vpr* to materialize

matérialisme [materjalism] *nm* materialism

matérialiste [materjalist] **1** *adj* materialistic **2** *n* materialist

matérialité [materjalite] *nf* **(a)** (*caractère de ce qui est réel, matériel*) materiality **(b)** (*matérialisme*) materialism

matériau [materjo] *nm Constr* material; **m. composite** composite

matériaux [materjo] *nmpl* **(a)** *Constr* material(s); **m. de construction** building *or* construction material(s) **(b)** *Fig* material; **il n'a pas tellement de m. pour rédiger sa thèse** he doesn't have much material for his thesis

matériel¹, -elle [materjɛl] *adj* (*confort, besoins, aide etc*) material; (*financier*) financial; **tu n'en as pas la preuve matérielle** you don't have material *or* solid *or* firm proof of it; **l'organisation matérielle de la fête a posé de gros problèmes** the practical organization of the party posed great problems; **je n'ai pas le temps m. de le faire** I simply don't have time to do it; **être dans l'impossibilité matérielle de bouger** to find it physically impossible to move

matériel² *nm* **(a)** equipment; (*d'usine*) plant; *Mil* equipment, *Spéc* matériel; *Mil* **service du m.** ordnance; **m. de camping/de laboratoire** camping/labaratory equipment; **m. d'exploitation** working plant; **m. de guerre** weaponry; **m. d'emballage** packaging; **m. de bureau** office equipment; **m. industriel** plant; *Rail* **m. roulant** rolling stock **(b)** *Ordinat* hardware; **m. de composition** film setting hardware; **m. informatique** computer hardware

matériellement [materjɛlmɑ̃] *adv* materially; (*financièrement*) financially; **avoir de quoi vivre m.** to have enough for one's material needs; **chose m. impossible** physical impossibility; **je ne peux m. pas accepter un travail à temps complet** it is physically impossible for me to take on a full-time job; **je n'ai m. pas le temps de venir te voir** I simply don't have time to come and see you

maternage [materna3] *nm* mothering

maternel, -elle [matɛrnɛl] *adj* maternal; (*soins, gestes*) motherly; **lait m.** mother's milk; **allaitement m.** breast-feeding; **l'instinct m.** the maternal instinct; **elle est très maternelle avec ses collègues** she acts in a very maternal *or* motherly way towards her colleagues; **un cousin du côté m.** a cousin on one's mother's side; **grand-père m.** maternal grandfather; **langue maternelle** mother tongue, native tongue; **centre de protection maternelle et infantile** mother-and-baby clinic; **école maternelle** nursery (school)

maternelle [matɛrnɛl] *nf* nursery (school)

maternellement [matɛrnɛlmɑ̃] *adv* maternally, in a motherly way

materner [matɛrne] *vt* to mother

maternisé [matɛrnize] *adj* **lait m.** milk suitable for infants

maternité [matɛrnite] *nf* **(a)** (*fait d'être mère*) motherhood; **un corps déformé par des maternités successives** a body misshapen by one pregnancy after another; **en congé de m.** on maternity leave **(b)** (*hôpital*) maternity hospital **(c)** *Beaux-Arts* Madonna and Child

mateur, -euse [matœr, -øz] *n très F* ogler

mathématicien, -ienne [matematisjɛ̃, -jɛn] *n* mathematician

mathématique [matematik] **1** *adj* mathematical; *Fig* (*esprit*) (very) logical; (*rigueur*) mathematical; **c'est m.!** it's perfectly obvious! **2** *nfpl* [①A10,c] **mathématiques** mathematics; **mathématiques pures/appliquées** pure/applied mathematics

mathématiquement [matematikmɑ̃] *adv* mathematically; **m., je ne pourrai pas être à l'heure** it's physically impossible for me to be on time

matheux, -euse [matø, -øz] *n F* mathematician; (*élève, étudiant*) maths *or Am* math student

math(s) [mat] *nfpl F* maths, *Am* math; *Univ* **m. sup/spé** = first-/second-year maths class (*for candidates for the grandes écoles*)

Mathusalem [matyzalɛm] *nm* **(a)** Methuselah; *F* **ça date de M.** (*objet*) it's as old as the hills; (*nouvelle*) it's ancient history **(b) m.** (*bouteille*) Methuselah

matière [matjɛr] *nf* **(a)** (*substance*) material; **en quelle m. est ton pantalon?** what material are your trousers made of?; **matière(s) plastique(s)** plastic(s); **sachet en m. plastique** plastic bag; **matières consommables** consumables

(b) *Phys, Phil* matter; **m. inanimée** inanimate matter; **m. solide inflammable** flammable solid; **la désintégration de la m.** the disintegration of matter; *Biol* **m. vivante** living matter

(c) *Fig* (*sujet, contenu*) (*de discours*) subject (matter); (*pour discussion*) subject, topic, theme; (*pour en faire un film, un livre, une étude etc*) material; *Scol* subject; **table des matières** (table of) contents; **faire une entrée en m.** to give an introduction; **il n'y a pas m. à rire** it's no laughing matter; **cela donne m. à réflexion** it's food for thought; **il y a m. à procès/dispute** there are grounds for going to court/ for contesting it; **il n'y avait pas m. à discuter** there was nothing to be said about it; **en m. de** as regards; **être bon juge en m. de musique** to be a good judge of music; **être bon juge en la m.** to be a good judge of the subject

▶ **matière**: *Méd* **m. fécale** fecal matter; **matières grasses** fat; **fromage à 20 % de matières grasses** cheese with a 20% fat content; **m. grise** grey matter; *Ind* **matière(s) première(s)** raw material(s)

Matif [matif] (*nm abrév* **marché à terme des instruments financiers**) (French) international financial futures market

Matignon [matiɲɔ̃] *n* = French Prime Minister's offices; **M. a décidé que ...** the Prime Minister's office has decided that ...

matin [matɛ̃] **1** *nm* [①A75,A,e; B58,A,e] morning; **du m. au soir** from morning till night; **quatre heures du m.** four o'clock in the morning, 4 a. m. ; **le jeudi deux au m.** on the morning of Thursday the second; **c'est le m. que je travaille le mieux** I work best in the morning; **elle travaille seulement le m.** she only works mornings, she only works in the morning; **demain m.** tomorrow morning; **tous les lundis m.** every Monday morning; **de grand** *ou* **bon m., le m. de bonne heure** early in the morning, in the early morning; **être du m.** to be an early bird *or* an early riser; **rentrer au petit m.** to come home in the small *or* early hours; **un de ces (quatre) matins, un beau m.** one of these (fine) days

2 *adv* early in the morning; **se lever très m.** to get up very early

mâtin, -ine [mɑtɛ̃, -in] **1** *nm* (*chien*) mastiff, watchdog **2** *n Arch F* (*coquin*) sly dog, *f* minx **3** *int Arch* by Jove!

matinal, -ale, -aux, -ales [matinal, -o] **1** *adj* **(a)** (*brise*) morning; **à cette heure matinale** at this early hour; **promenade matinale** morning walk **(b) être m.** to be an early riser; **comme tu es m. aujourd'hui!** you're an early bird! **2** *n* early riser

mâtiné [mɑtine] *adj* crossbred; (*chien*) mongrel, crossbred; **un teckel m. de caniche** a cross between a dachshund and a poodle

matinée [matine] *nf* **(a)** [①B58,B,3] (*matin*) morning; **dans la m.** in (the course of) the morning; **en fin de m.** towards the end of the morning; **j'ai passé toute ma m. à l'attendre/au lit** I spent the whole morning waiting for him/in bed; **je ne l'ai pas vu de toute la m.** I haven't seen him all morning; **une m. de lecture** a morning (spent) reading; *F* **faire la grasse m.** to have a lie-in **(b)** *Th* matinée (performance), afternoon performance; *Cin* matinée, afternoon showing *or* screening; **on joue ce film en m.** the film is showing as a matinée

matines [matin] *nfpl Rel* matins

matir [matir] *vt* = **mater²**

matité [matite] *nf* (*de son*) dullness

matois, -oise [matwa, -waz] *Litt* **1** *adj* sly, cunning, crafty **2** *n* crafty person; **fin m.** sly devil

maton, -onne [matɔ̃, -ɔn] *n Arg* (*de prison*) screw

matos [matos] *nm F* equipment

matou [matu] *nm* tom (cat)

matraquage [matraka3] *nm* bludgeoning, *Br* coshing, *Am* blackjacking; *Fig* **m. idéologique** ideological brainwashing; **m. publicitaire** (publicity) hype; **on n'échappe pas au m. publicitaire** there's no escaping the constant bombardment of adverts; **c'est vraiment du m. qu'ils font pour la sortie de ce film** they're really hyping *or* plugging the release of this film; **avec les élections, ça va être le m. à la télé!** with the elections it'll be total overkill on TV!

matraque [matrak] *nf* bludgeon, *Br* cosh, *Am* blackjack; (*d'agent de police*) *surtout Br* truncheon, *Am* billy (club); *Fig F* **c'est le coup de m.** it's a rip-off

matraquer [matrake] *vt* (*frapper*) to bludgeon, *Br* to cosh; *Fig F* **m. le client** to rip off *or* fleece the customer; *Fig* **la radio matraque ses annonces/cette chanson toute la journée** the radio churns out its announcements/that song all day long; **m. le public par des campagnes répétitives** to bombard the public with continuous campaigning

matriarcal, -ale, -aux, -ales [matrjarkal, -o] *adj* matriarchal

matriarcat [matrjarka] *nm* matriarchy

matrice [matris] *nf* **(a)** [①A14,9] *Math* matrix; *Tech* matrix, die; *Typ* matrix, type mould; (*de disque*) matrix **(b)** *Ordinat* array; **m. active/passive** active/passive matrix; **m. d'aiguilles** dot matrix; **m. de vérité** truth table **(c)** *Admin* (*du rôle des contributions*) original **(d)** *Anat* uterus, womb

matricide [matrisid] **1** *adj* matricidal **2** *n* matricide **3** *nm* (*crime*) matricide

matriciel, -ale, -ielle, -ales [matrisjɛl] **1** *adj Math* matrix; *Ordinat* **imprimante matricielle** dot matrix printer **2** *nf Ordinat* dot matrix

matricule [matrikyl] **1** *adj Mil, Admin* **numéro m.** number **2** *nm Mil, Admin* number; *F* **ça va chauffer pour ton m.** you'll be in hot water **3** *nf* **(a)** (*liste*) (*de prison, d'hôpital*) roll, register, list; *Mil* (regimental) roll; (*immatriculation*) registration **(b)** (*extrait*) registration certificate

matrimonial, -iaux [matrimɔnjal, -jo] *adj* matrimonial; **agence matrimoniale** marriage agency *or* bureau; **régime m.** marriage settlement; **juge des affaires matrimoniales** divorce court judge

matrone [matrɔn] *nf Antiq* matron; *Péj* (*femme imposante*) stout *or* portly woman; **vieille m.** fat old woman

maturation [matyrasjɔ̃] *nf* maturation; (*de fruit, céréale, fromage*) ripening; (*de tabac*) maturing; *Physiol* **m. sexuelle** sexual maturation

mature [matyr] *adj* mature

mâture [mɑtyr] *nf Naut* masts (and spars); **dans la m.** aloft

maturité [matyrite] *nf* (*de personne, d'animal*) maturity; (*de fruit, fromage*) ripeness; **arriver** *ou* **venir à m.** to come to maturity, to mature; **cette jeune femme ne manque pas de m.** that young woman is very mature; **elle manque totalement de m.** she's totally immature; **sa m. d'esprit est remarquable** he has a remarkably mature mind

matutinal, -ale, -aux, -ales [matytinal, -o] *adj Litt* morning

maudire [modir] *vt* (*prp* **maudissant**; *pp* **maudit**; *pr ind* **je maudis, n. maudissons, v. maudissez, ils maudissent**; *pr sub* **je maudisse**; *p hist* **je maudis**; *fu* **je maudirai**) to curse; *Litt* **maudit sois-tu!** a curse on you!

maudit, -ite [modi, -it] **1** *adj* **(a)** (*crime, science*) accursed **(b)** (*before noun*) (*voiture, ville etc*) damn(ed), blasted, cursed; **quel m. temps!** what filthy weather! **2** *n* **le M.** the Devil; **les maudits** the damned, the accursed

maugréer [mogree] *vi* to grumble, to grouse (**contre** about, at)

maure [mɔr] **1** *adj* Moorish **2** *n* **M.** Moor

mauresque [mɔrɛsk] **1** *adj* (*architecture, motif etc*) Moorish **2** *nf* **(a) M.** Moorish woman **(b)** (*boisson*) = pastis with barley water and water

Maurice [mɔris] *n* **l'île M.** Mauritius

mauricien, -ienne [mɔrisjɛ̃ -jɛn] **1** *adj* Mauritian **2** *n* **M.** Mauritian

Mauritanie [mɔritani] *nf* Mauritania

mauritanien, -ienne [mɔritanjɛ̃, -jɛn] **1** *adj* Mauritanian **2** *n* **M.** Mauritanian

mausolée [mozɔle] *nm* mausoleum

maussade [mosad] *adj* **(a)** (*de mauvaise humeur*) sullen, morose; (*triste*) glum; **ça l'a rendu m.** (*amer*) that disgruntled him **(b)** (*temps*) dull, gloomy; **paysage m.** gloomy countryside

maussaderie [mosadri] *nf Litt* sullenness, moroseness

mauvais [mɔvɛ] **1** *adj* **(a)** (*repas, haleine, rêve, avis, organisation, qualité etc*) bad; **m. pour la santé/la digestion** bad for one's health/the digestion; **de plus en plus m.** worse and worse; **le plus m.** the worst; **m. temps** bad weather; **mer mauvaise** rough sea; **être en mauvaise posture** to be in a difficult situation; **cela a fait m. effet** it looked bad, it made a bad impression; **elle a reçu une mauvaise nouvelle** she has had some bad news; **ce n'est pas m.** (*c'est bon*) it's not bad; **je l'ai trouvé mauvaise** I didn't appreciate it; **il risque de la trouver mauvaise quand il apprendra** he's not going to be very happy when he finds out; **elle a mauvaise mine** she doesn't look well; **avoir une mauvaise santé** to be in bad *or* poor health; **mauvaise vue** bad *or* poor eyesight; **il a fait une mauvaise bronchite** he's had a bad attack of bronchitis; **faire de mauvaises affaires** to be involved in some bad business deals; **la récolte sera mauvaise** it will be a bad *or* poor harvest; **les freins sont m.** the brakes are defective; **c'est un m. banquier** he's a poor *or* bad banker; **m. en anglais** bad *or* poor at English; **une mauvaise excuse** a poor excuse

(b) (*inapproprié*) wrong; **c'est la mauvaise clef** it's the wrong key; **arriver au m. moment** to come at a bad *or* an inconvenient time *or* at a bad *or* an awkward moment; *Tél* **m. numéro** wrong number

(c) (*méchant*) (*personne*) bad, nasty; (*augure*) bad, ill; **être m. avec qn** to be nasty to sb; **qu'est-ce qu'elle est mauvaise aujourd'hui!** she's in a nasty mood today!; **mauvaise action** wrong(doing); **avoir l'air m.** (*de personne*) to look nasty; (*de chien*) to look fierce *or* vicious; **c'est un m. sujet** *ou* **un m. garçon** he's a bad lot; **né sous une mauvaise étoile** born under an unlucky star; **elle n'a pas un m. fond** deep down she's not bad, she's not bad at heart; **elle a vraiment un m. fond!** she's a really nasty character!

2 *adv* **sentir m.** to smell (bad), to stink; **il fait m.** the weather's bad

3 *n* villain; *F* baddie; **dans le film, il joue le rôle du m.** he plays the baddie in the film

▶ **mauvais**: **mauvaise langue** (spiteful) gossip; **c'est vraiment une mauvaise langue** he's got a really spiteful *or* nasty tongue; **ce que tu peux être mauvaise langue, alors!** you can be a real gossip!; **m. œil** evil eye; **elle est persuadée d'avoir le m. œil** she's convinced that somebody has put the evil eye on her; **m. plaisant** practical joker

mauve [mov] **1** *nm* (*couleur*) mauve **2** *nf Bot* mallow **3** *adj* mauve

mauviette [movjet] *nf F* (*physiquement*) wimp, *Br* weed; (*moralement*) wimp, drip, *Br* wet; **quelle m. tu fais!** you're such a wimp

MAV [ɛmave] *nf* (*abrév* **mercatique après-vente**) after-sales marketing

max [maks] *nm inv* (*abrév* **maximum**) **(a)** (*dans annonce*) max **(b)** *F* **un m.** loads, lots; **ça lui plaît un m.** he likes it loads *or* lots; **on s'est éclaté un m. à la soirée de Caroline** we had a really fantastic time at Caroline's party

maxi [maksi] *F* **1** *adj inv* maxi; **une m.(-)bouteille** a giant-size *or* jumbo-size bottle **2** *nm Vieilli* (*manteau*) maxi (coat); **la mode du m.** the maxi fashion **3** *nf Vieilli* (*jupe*) maxi (skirt)

maxillaire [maksilɛr] *Anat* **1** *adj* maxillary; **os m.** jawbone, *Spéc* maxilla **2** *nm* jawbone, *Spéc* maxilla

maximal, -ale, -aux, -ales [maksimal, -o] *adj* (*effet, excitation, peine etc*) maximum; (*température*) maximum, top; **vitesse maximale autorisée: 60 km/h** speed limit: 60 kmph

maxime [maksim] *nf* maxim

maximisation [maksimizasjɔ̃] *nf* **m. du profit** profit optimization

maximiser [maksimize] *vt* to maximize

maximum [maksimɔm], *pl* **maximums, maxima** [maksima] **1** *nm* maximum; **faire le m. (pour faire qch)** to do one's utmost *or* one's best (to do sth); **m. de rendement** maximum output; **porter la production au m.** to increase production to a maximum, to maximize production; **je vais essayer de t'aider au m.** I'll try my very hardest *or* my very best to help you; **thermomètre à maxima** maximum thermometer; **on sera 20 au m.** there will be 20 of us at (the) most; **nous avons de la place pour 20 personnes au m.** we have room for a maximum of 20 (people) *or* for 20 (people) at (the) most; *F* **un m.** (*beaucoup*) loads, lots; *F* **ça lui plaît un m.** he likes it loads *or* lots

2 *adj souvent inv* maximum; **rendement m.** maximum *or* peak output

maya [maja] **1** *adj* Maya, Mayan **2** *nm Ling* Mayan **3** *n* **M.** Maya, Mayan

Mayence [majɑ̃s] *nf* Mainz

mayonnaise [majɔnɛz] *nf Culin* mayonnaise; *Fig F* **faire monter la m.** to stir things up; *Fig F* **la m. n'a pas pris** it didn't work

mazagran [mazagrɑ̃] *nm* (*en verre, faïence*) goblet

mazout [mazut] *nm* (fuel) oil; **chauffage central au m.** oil-fired central heating; **poêle à m.** oil stove

mazouté [mazute] *adj* (*plage*) oil-polluted, polluted with oil; (*oiseau*) oil-covered, covered in oil, oiled

mazurka [mazyrka] *nf* mazurka

mb *nm Météo abrév* **millibar**

MBA [embea] *nf Compta* (*abrév* **marge brute d'autofinancement**) cashflow, funds generated by operations

Mbps *Ordinat* (*abrév* **mégabits par seconde**) mbps

m. d. *Mus* (*abrév* **main droite**) R.H.

me *before a vowel sound* **m'** [mə] *pron pers* [①**A26**,a-b; **B17-18**,2] **(a)** (*objet direct*) me; **il m'aime** he loves me; **me voici** here I am **(b)** (*objet indirect*) (to) me; **il m'a écrit** he wrote to me; **il me l'a dit** he told me (so); **donnez-m'en** give me some; *F* **tu veux bien m'éteindre la lumière?** would you switch off the light (for me)? **(c)** [①**A29**,d; **B26**,D] (*verbe pronominal*) myself; **je m'amusais** I was enjoying myself; **je ne m'en souviens plus** I don't remember any more; **je me suis dit que ...** I said to myself that ...

mea-culpa [meakylpa] *nm inv* **faire** *ou* **dire son m.** to own up *or* to confess (to one's mistake)

méandre [meɑ̃dr] *nm* (*de rivière*) meander, loop; (*de route*) bend; *Fig* **se perdre dans les méandres d'un raisonnement** to get lost in the intricacies of an argument

mec [mɛk] *nm F* guy, *Br* bloke; **t'en fais pas, m.!** don't worry about it, mate *or* pal *or esp Am* man; **son nouveau m.** her new guy *or* man; **eh les mecs! venez voir!** hey guys! come and have a look!

mécanicien, -ienne [mekanisjɛ̃, -jɛn] **1** *n* **(a)** *Aut* (garage *or* motor) mechanic; *Naut* engineer; *Av* **m. de bord** *ou* **navigant** flight engineer; **c'est une bonne mécanicienne** she's a good mechanic; **ouvrier m.** mechanic; **ingénieur m.** mechanical engineer **(b)** *Rail* engine driver, *Am* engineer **2** *nf Couture* **mécanicienne** machinist

mécanicien-dentiste, *pl* **mécaniciens-dentistes** *nm Vieilli* dental technician

mécanique [mekanik] **1** *adj Tech etc* (*fonctionnement, système*) mechanical; (*dentelle, tuiles etc*) machine-made; **jouet m.** clockwork toy; **métier à tisser m.** power loom; **atelier(s) de constructions mécaniques** engineering works; **nous avons eu des ennuis mécaniques en route** we had mechanical problems on the way; **moyens mécaniques de contraception** barrier methods of contraception; *Fig* **un geste m.** a mechanical *or* an automatic movement; **c'est devenu m. pour lui** it's become automatic for him; **c'est un travail très m.** it's very mechanical work

2 *nf* **(a)** (*science du mouvement*) mechanics; **m. des fluides** fluid mechanics; **m. quantique** quantum mechanics

(b) (*des moteurs, machines*) mechanical engineering; *Aut* **il adore la m.** he likes fiddling about with cars/motorbikes

(c) (*mécanisme*) mechanism, piece of machinery; (*d'une imprimante laser*) engine; **c'est une belle m., cette moto** that motorbike's a lovely piece of machinery

mécaniquement [mekanikmɑ̃] *adv* mechanically

mécanisation [mekanizasjɔ̃] *nf* mechanization

mécaniser [mekanize] *vt* to mechanize

mécanisme [mekanism] *nm* **(a)** mechanism; (*de montre*) works; **le m. du corps humain** the workings of the human body; **m. de défense** defence mechanism; *CE* **m. des taux de change** Exchange Rate Mechanism; *Aut* **m. d'avance automatique** automatic advance mechanism; *Aut* **m. d'avance centrifuge** centrifugal advance mechanism; *Aut*

m. de basculement tipping gear; *Aut* **m. de direction** steering gear **(b)** (*de la pensée, parole*) mechanics

mécano [mekano] *nm F* mechanic, grease monkey

mécanographe [mekanɔgraf] *n* punch card operator

mécanographie [mekanɔgrafi] *nf* (*procédé*) (mechanical) data processing; (*service*) data processing department

mécanographique [mekanɔgrafik] *adj* **service m.** data processing department; **fiche m.** punch(ed) card

mécénat [mesena] *nm* sponsorship; (*des arts*) sponsorship, patronage; **m. d'entreprise** corporate *or* business sponsorship

mécène [mesɛn] *nm* sponsor; (*des arts*) sponsor, patron

méchamment [meʃamɑ̃] *adv* **(a)** (*de façon méchante*) spitefully, nastily, maliciously **(b)** *F* (*vrai, bon etc*) damn(ed); (*trompé, déçu*) horribly, terribly; **il avait m. bu** he'd drunk a hell of a lot; **ça a m. cartonné hier au bar** there was one hell of a punch-up in the bar yesterday; **ce qu'il m'a dit m'a m. refroidi** what he said really put me off *or Br* didn't half put me off

méchanceté [meʃɑ̃ste] *nf* **(a)** (*de personne, remarque etc*) spitefulness, nastiness, maliciousness; (*d'enfant*) naughtiness; **faire qch par m.** to do sth out of spite *or* malice; **il l'a dit sans m.** he didn't mean to be unkind; **je dis ça sans m. aucune** I say that without any malice **(b)** (*action, parole*) spiteful *or* nasty action/remark; **quelle m.!** what a spiteful *or* nasty thing to do/say!

méchant, -ante [meʃɑ̃, -ɑ̃t] **1** *adj* **(a)** (*personne, remarque etc*) spiteful, nasty, malicious; (*enfant*) naughty; (*animal*) vicious, bad-tempered; **attention chien m.** (*sur panneau*) beware of the dog; **il n'est pas si m. que ça!** he's not as bad as all that!; *F* **pas m.** harmless

(b) (*désagréable*) (*affaire*) unpleasant, disagreeable; (*blessure, grippe*) nasty, bad; **être de méchante humeur** to be in a foul mood

(c) *F* (*sacré*) terrific, incredible; **avoir une méchante dégaine** to look incredible; **j'avais une méchante envie de dormir/lui casser la figure** I had an incredible urge to sleep/ to smash his face in

(d) *Arch* (*résidence etc*) miserable, wretched, poor, sorry; **un m. billet de cent francs** a paltry hundred-franc note; **méchante excuse** lame excuse

2 *n* **petit m./petite méchante!** you naughty little boy/ girl!; *F* **les bons et les méchants** the goodies and the baddies

mèche¹ [mɛʃ] *nf* **(a)** (*de bougie, lampe*) wick; (*pour mettre le feu à des explosifs*) match; (*de mine*) fuse; *F* **vendre la m.** to give the game away, to spill the beans; **éventer** *ou* **découvrir la m.** to uncover the plot **(b)** (*de cheveux*) lock; (*de laine*) wisp, tuft; **elle se fait faire des mèches tous les mois** she has streaks *or* highlights put in her hair every month; **m. postiche** hairpiece **(c)** *Chir* dressing **(d)** (*de câble etc*) core, heart; *Él* **charbon à m.** cored carbon **(e)** *Menuis* auger, gimlet; **m. anglaise** *ou* **à trois pointes** centre bit; **m. hélicoïdale** twist bit, twist drill

mèche² *n inv F* **(a) être de m. (avec qn)** to be in cahoots (with sb) **(b) il n'y a pas m.** nothing doing

méchoui [meʃwi] *nm Culin* spit-roasted lamb

mécompte [mekɔ̃t] *nm* **(a)** *Litt* (*désillusion*) disappointment; **il a eu un grave m.** he has had a serious disappointment, he has been badly let down **(b)** *Vieilli* (*erreur*) miscalculation, error

méconium [mekɔnjɔm] *nm Physiol* meconium

méconnaissable [mekɔnɛsabl] *adj* unrecognizable

méconnaissance [mekɔnɛsɑ̃s] *nf* **(a)** *Litt* (*du talent de qn*) lack of recognition; (*de faits, situation*) ignorance, lack of knowledge; **elle a toujours fait preuve d'une m. totale de la politique** she has never had any grasp *or* understanding of politics whatsoever **(b)** (*refus de reconnaître comme valable*) (*d'un droit, d'une loi*) disregard

méconnaître [mekɔnɛtr] *vt* (*conj like* **connaître**) **(a)** (*talent de qn, écrivain etc*) to fail to appreciate, to fail to recognize; (*les faits*) to fail to take account of; (*l'importance d'une découverte*) to underrate, to misjudge **(b)** (*devoir*) to disregard

méconnu [mekɔny] *adj* (*talent, écrivain etc*) unrecognized, unappreciated

mécontent, -ente [mekɔ̃tɑ̃, -ɑ̃t] **1** *adj* (*insatisfait*) displeased, dissatisfied, discontented (**de** with); (*fâché*) annoyed; **je ne suis pas m. de mon sort** I am not discontented with my lot; **être m. que ...** + *sub* to be annoyed that ... **2** *n* grumbler, moaner; *Pol* **les mécontents** the discontented

mécontentement [mekɔ̃tɑ̃tmɑ̃] *nm* (*insatisfaction*) discontent, dissatisfaction; (*contrariété*) annoyance; **c'est un sujet de m.** it's a source of discontent *or* dissatisfaction; **marquer** *ou* **exprimer son m.** to show *or* express one's annoyance *or* displeasure

mécontenter [mekɔ̃tɑ̃te] *vt* to displease

Mecque (la) [lamɛk] *nf* Mecca

mécréant, -ante [mekreɑ̃, -ɑ̃t] *Vieilli* **1** *adj* infidel, unbelieving **2** *n* infidel, unbeliever; **c'était une petite crapule, un mécréant** he was a rogue and a heathen

médaille [medaj] *nf* **(a)** (*récompense*) medal; *Sp* **la m. d'or/ d'argent/de bronze** the gold/silver/bronze (medal); **détenir la m. du 60 mètres** to hold the medal for the 60 metres; **être m. d'or** (*de sportif*) to be a gold medallist, to be a gold medal winner; **m. du travail** medal for long service, long-service medal; *Fig* **le revers de la m.** the other side of the coin; *Fig* **je ne lui donnerais pas la m. du courage!** he wouldn't win any medals for bravery! **(b)** (*en hommage à qn*) medal; **m. pieuse** holy medal **(c)** (*insigne*) (official) badge; (*plaque d'identité*) (*de chat, chien*) identity disc *or* tag

médaillé, -ée [medaje] **1** *adj* holding a medal; (*soldat*) decorated **2** *n Mil* medal-holder; *Sp* medallist; **le m. du 400 mètres nage libre** the 400 metres freestyle medallist; **un m. du travail** a holder of a long-service medal

médaillier [medaje] *nm* medal collection (*in cabinet*)

médaillon [medajɔ̃] *nm* **(a)** (*médaille*) medallion **(b)** *Culin* medallion **(c)** (*bijou*) medallion; (*avec photo*) locket **(d)** *TV, Cin, Journ* inset

médecin [medsɛ̃] *nm* doctor, *Fml* physician; **aller chez le m.** to go to the doctor('s); **femme m.** woman doctor

▶ **médecin**: **m. de bord** ship's doctor; **m. de campagne** country doctor; **m.-conseil**, *pl* **médecins-conseils** medical consultant *or* adviser; **m. consultant** consultant; **m. de famille** family doctor; **m. généraliste** general practitioner, G. P; **m. légiste** forensic pathologist, *US* medical examiner; **m. militaire** army medical officer, M.O.; **Médecins Sans Frontières** = charitable organization providing medical aid, especially to Third World countries; **m. traitant** consulting physician; **qui est votre m. (traitant)?** who is your (regular) doctor?; **m. du travail** = doctor who carries out the annual examination, required by law, of a company's employees

médecine [medsin] *nf* **(a)** (*science*) medicine; *F* **elle fait m.** she's doing medicine; **docteur en m.** doctor of medicine, M.D. ; **étudiant en m.** medical student, *F* medic, **école de m.** medical school **(b)** (*profession du médecin*) medicine; **exercer la m.** to practise medicine

▶ **médecine**: **m. douce** alternative medicine; **m. générale** general medicine; **m. légale** forensic medicine, *F* forensics; **service de m. légale** forensic department, *F* forensics; **m. naturelle** natural medicine; **m. parallèle** alternative medicine; **m. préventive** preventive medicine; **m. sportive** sports medicine; **m. du travail** industrial medicine

média [medja] *nm* [①A13,3,a] medium *pl* media; **le pouvoir des médias** the power of the media; **la télévision est un m. privilégié** television is the most efficient medium; **m. grand public** mass media; **m. planneur** media planner; **médias de télécommunication** telecommunications media; **médias numériques interactifs** interactive digital media; **médias électroniques** electronic media

médial, -ale, -aux, -ales [medjal, -o] **1** *adj Ling* (*lettre*) medial **2** *nf* **médiale** (*en statistique*) median

médian, -iane [medjɑ̃, -jan] **1** *adj* (*nerf, ligne etc*) median **2** *nf* **médiane (a)** *Ling* mid vowel **(b)** (*en statistique*) median

médiateur, -trice¹ [medjatœr, -tris] **1** *adj* mediating, mediatory **2** *n* (*personne*) *Ind* mediator; *Admin* ≈ Ombudsman; **agir en tant que m., servir de m.** to act as (a) mediator

médiathèque [medjatɛk] *nf* media library

médiation [medjasjɔ̃] *nf* mediation

médiatique [medjatik] *adj* (*couverture, personnalité etc*) media; **d'un intérêt m.** newsworthy; **événement m.** media event; **c'est quelqu'un de très m.** he/she is well suited to *or* comes over well in the media

médiatisation [medjatizasjɔ̃] *nf* **la m. d'un événement** the media coverage *or* attention given to an event; **à cause de la m. de la politique** because politics is becoming a media event

médiatiser [medjatize] *vt* (*événement*) to give media coverage to

médiator [medjatɔr] *nm Mus* plectrum

médiatrice² [medjatris] *nf Géom* median

médical, -ale, -aux, -ales [medikal, -o] *adj* medical; **examen m. (complet)** medical examination, check-up; **certificat m.** medical certificate

médicalement [medikalmɑ̃] *adv* medically

médicalisation [medikalizasjɔ̃] *nf* (*de population*) provision of medical care (**de** for); **la m. de la grossesse** the treatment of pregnancy as a medical matter, the medicalization of pregnancy; **m. à outrance** pill-pushing

médicalisé [medikalize] *adj* **logement m.** nursing home

médicaliser [medikalize] *vt* (*personne*) to give medical care to; (*population*) to provide with medical care, to make medical care available to; (*la ménopause, la grossesse*) to treat as a medical matter, to medicalize
médicament [medikamɑ̃] *nm* medicine, drug, medication; **tu as pris tes médicaments?** have you taken your medicine?; **est-ce que vous prenez des médicaments?** are you on any kind of medication?; **m. de confort** palliative
médicamenteux, -euse [medikamɑ̃tø, -øz] *adj* medicinal
médication [medikasjɔ̃] *nf* medication, medical treatment
médicinal, -ale, -aux, -ales [medisinal, -o] *adj* medicinal
medicine-ball, *pl* **medicine-balls** [medisinbol] *nm* medicine ball
médico-légal, -ale, -aux, -ales [medikolegal, -o] *adj* forensic
médico-pédagogique, *pl* **médico-pédagogiques** [medikopedagɔʒik] *adj* **institut m.** special school (*for children with special learning needs*)
médico-social, -aux [medikosɔsjal, -o] *adj* **centre m.** health centre
médiéval, -ale, -aux, -ales [medjeval, -o] *adj* medieval
médiéviste [medjevist] *n* medievalist
médina [medina] *nf* medina
médiocre [medjɔkr] **1** *adj* mediocre; *Scol* (*appréciation*) poor **2** *n* (*personne*) nonentity **3** *nm* (*médiocrité*) mediocrity
médiocrement [medjɔkrəmɑ̃] *adv* indifferently, poorly; **m. riche** not very rich; **elle chante très m.** she's a very mediocre singer; **il a m. réussi ses examens** he scraped through his exams
médiocrité [medjɔkrite] *nf* mediocrity
médire [medir] *vi* (*conj like* **dire**, *except pr ind and imp* **médisez**) **m. de qn** to speak ill of sb, to run sb down; **il médit facilement** he is always ready to run people down; **je ne voudrais pas m., mais ...** I don't like to gossip, but ...
médisance [medizɑ̃s] *nf* **(a)** (*action*) scandalmongering, slander **(b)** (*propos*) (bit of) scandal *or* gossip; **médisances** scandal, gossip
médisant [medizɑ̃] **1** *adj* (*paroles*) slanderous; (*personne*) scandalmongering; **qu'est-ce que tu peux être m.!** what a scandalmonger you are!; **je ne voudrais être m. mais ...** I don't like to gossip but ... **2** *n* scandalmonger, slanderer
méditatif, -ive [meditatif, -iv] *adj* meditative, thoughtful
méditation [meditasjɔ̃] *nf* meditation; **plongé dans la m.** lost in thought; **entrer en m.** to start to meditate; **faire de la m.** to meditate; **m. transcendantale** transcendental meditation
méditer [medite] **1** *vi* to meditate (**sur** on); **m. de faire qch** to be contemplating doing sth; **m. de prendre sa revanche** to plot one's revenge **2** *vt* to contemplate; **m. un projet** to reflect on *or* mull over a plan; **m. une vengeance** to contemplate vengeance
Méditerranée [mediterane] *nf* **la (mer) M.** the Mediterranean (sea), *F* the Med; **en M.** in the Mediterranean
méditerranéen, -enne [mediteraneɛ̃, -ɛn] **1** *adj* Mediterranean **2** *n* **M.** **(a)** (*natif*) native of a Mediterranean country; (*habitant*) inhabitant of a Mediterranean country **(b)** (*en France*) Southerner
médium [medjɔm] *nm* **(a)** *Mus* (*de voix*) middle register **(b)** [①**A13,5**] (*en parapsychologie*) medium
médius [medjys] *nm Anat* middle finger
médoc [medɔk] *nm* Médoc (wine)
médullaire [medylɛr] *adj Anat, Bot* medullary
méduse [medyz] *nf* **(a)** *Zool* jellyfish, *Spéc* medusa **(b)** *Myth* **M.** Medusa
méduser [medyze] *vt* to transfix, to dumbfound
meeting [mitiŋ] *nm Pol, Sp etc* meeting; **m. aérien** air show; **m. d'athlétisme** athletics meeting *or* meet
méfait [mefɛ] *nm* misdeed; *Jur* misdemeanour, *US* misdemeanor; (*d'un orage*) damage; **les méfaits de l'alcoolisme** the ill effects of *or* the damage done by alcoholism; **les méfaits de la surinformation** the evils of over-information; **se déclarer l'auteur du m.** to own up (to the deed)
méfiance [mefjɑ̃s] *nf* (*manque de confiance*) distrust; (*suspicion*) mistrust, suspicion; **m.!** be on your guard; **avoir de la m. envers qn** to distrust sb; (*avoir de la suspicion*) to mistrust sb; **avec m.** distrustfully; (*avec suspicion*) mistrustfully, suspiciously; *Prov* **m. est mère de sûreté** better safe than sorry
méfiant [mefjɑ̃] *adj* distrustful; (*suspicieux*) mistrustful, suspicious (**à l'égard de, avec** of)
méfier (se) [səmefje] *vpr* (*impf & pr sub* **n. n. méfiions, v. v. méfiiez**) to be on one's guard, to take care; **se m. de qn** to distrust sb; (*avoir de la suspicion*) to mistrust sb; **méfiez-vous des pickpockets** beware of pickpockets; **se m. de qch** to be wary of sth, to be on one's guard against sth; **il faut se m. des apparences** you shouldn't trust appearances
méforme [mefɔrm] *nf Sp* poor form, lack of form; **être en m.** to be off form
méga[1] [mega] *nm Ordinat* megabyte, meg
méga[2] *adj inv Arg* mega
mégacycle [megasikl] *nm Él* megacycle
mégahertz [megaɛrts] *nm Él* megahertz
mégalithe [megalit] *nm* megalith
mégalithique [megalitik] *adj* megalithic
mégalomane [megalɔman], *F* **mégalo** [megalo] *adj, n* megalomaniac
mégalomanie [megalɔmani] *nf* megalomania
mégalopole [megalɔpɔl] *nf* megalopolis
mégamercatique [megamɛrkatik] *nf* mega-marketing
méga-octet, *pl* **méga-octets** *nm Ordinat* megabyte
mégaphone [megafɔn] *nm* megaphone; (*électrique*) loud-hailer, *Am* bullhorn
mégarde (par) [parmegard] *adv* inadvertently, accidentally
mégatonne [megatɔn] *nf* megaton
mégawatt [megawat] *nm Phys* megawatt
mégère [meʒɛr] *nf* shrew, termagant
mégot [mego] *nm F* (*de cigarette*) (cigarette) butt, *Br* fag end; (*de cigare*) stump, butt
mégotage [megɔtaʒ] *nm F* skimping
mégoter [megɔte] *vi F* to skimp (**sur, pour** on)
méhari [meari], *pl* **méhara** [meara], **méharis** *nm* racing camel, mehari
méhariste [mearist] *nm* camel driver, meharist; *Mil Arch* member of the camel corps (*in the Sahara*)
meilleur, -eure [mɛjœr] **1** *adj* **(a)** (*comp de* **bon**) better; **elle est meilleure que lui** she is better than him *or* than he is; **il est m. en anglais qu'en allemand** he is better at English than German; **il est m. danseur que coureur** he is a better dancer than he is a runner, he is better at dancing than running; **les fraises, c'est m. avec de la crème** strawberries are better with cream; **rendre qch m.** to make sth better, to improve sth; **devenir m.** to get better, to improve; **je ne connais rien de m.** I don't know anything better; **les choses prennent une meilleure tournure** things are taking a turn for the better; **m. marché** cheaper

(b) (*superl de* **bon**) **le m./la meilleure** (*de plusieurs*) the best; (*de deux*) the better; **m. ami** best friend; **nous sommes les meilleurs amis du monde** we're the best of friends; **meilleurs vœux** (*dans une lettre*) with all good wishes, (with) best wishes

2 *n* **que le m. gagne** may the best man win; **j'en passe et des meilleures** and that's the least of it, and that's not the half of it, and I could go on; *F* **tu connais la meilleure? elle va se marier!** you know the best bit? she's going to get married!; *F* **c'est la meilleure (de l'année)!** that's the best (one) I've heard in a long time!

3 *nm* **le m.** the best; **garder le m. pour la fin** to keep the best till last; **pour le m. et pour le pire** for better or (for) worse; **donner le m. de soi-même** to give of one's best; **le m. de son temps/de la journee** the best part of one's time/of the day; **il a passé le m. de sa vie à l'aider** he spent the best years of his life helping him; *Sp* **prendre le m. sur son adversaire** to get the better of one's opponent

4 *adv* **il fait m.** it's warmer
méiose [mejoz] *nf Biol* meiosis
méiotique [mejɔtik] *adj Biol* meiotic
méjuger [meʒyʒe] (*conj like* **juger**) **1** *vi* **m. de qn/qch** to underestimate sb/sth **2** *vt* to underestimate **3** *vpr* **se méjuger** to underestimate oneself
mélna [melena], **méléna** *nm Méd* melaena
mélamine [melamin] *nf Ch* melamine
mélaminé [melamine] *adj Ch* melamine-covered
mélancolie [melɑ̃kɔli] *nf* melancholy, gloom; *Méd* melancholia; **elle a un accès de m.** she's (feeling) a bit down *or* a bit gloomy; **ne pas engendrer la m.** to be great fun
mélancolique [melɑ̃kɔlik] *adj* melancholy, gloomy; *Méd* melancholic
Mélanésie [melanezi] *nf* Melanesia
mélanésien, -ienne [melanezjɛ̃, -jɛn] **1** *adj* Melanesian **2** *nm Ling* Melanesian **3** *n* **M.** Melanesian
mélange [melɑ̃ʒ] *nm* **(a)** (*action*) mixing; (*de thés, vins, tabacs*) blending; (*d'espèces*) crossing

(b) (*résultat*) mixture; (*de thés, vins, tabacs*) blend; (*de ciment, de plâtre*) mix; **m. pharmaceutique** pharmaceutical mixture; **m. explosif** *ou* **détonant** explosive mixture; **m. air/carburant** fuel/air mixture; *Aut* **m. carburé** explosive mixture; *Aut* **m. gazeux** gas mixture; **pas de whisky après le vin, je ne fais pas de mélanges** no whisky after my wine, I don't mix my drinks; **un curieux m. de timidité et d'orgueil** a strange mixture *or* blend of shyness and arrogance; *Fig* **sans m.** unadulterated, unalloyed

(c) (*ouvrage*) **mélanges** miscellany

mélangé [melɑ̃ʒe] *adj* (*coton, laine*) mixed; **en coton m.** in a cotton mixture

mélanger [melɑ̃ʒe] (**je mélangeai(s), n. mélangeons**) **1** *vt* (*ingrédients etc*) to mix; (*thés, vins, tabacs*) to blend; (*confondre*) (*idées, documents etc*) to mix up; **m. le citron à la crème** to mix the lemon (in) with the cream; *Cartes* **m. les cartes** to shuffle the cards **2 se mélanger** *vpr* (**a**) to mix; **l'eau et l'huile ne se mélangent pas bien** water and oil don't mix well (**b**) *F* **se m. les pédales** *ou* **les pinceaux (dans qch)** to get (oneself) into a muddle (with sth), to get (sth) muddled up

mélangeur [melɑ̃ʒœr] *nm* mixer; (**robinet**) **m.** mixer tap, *Am* mixing faucet; *Électron* **m.** (**de son**) mixer, production switcher; *TV etc* **m.** (**de production**) production mixer *or* switcher; *TV etc* **m. de son** dubbing *or* sound mixer; *TV etc* **m. numérique 16 entrées** 16-source digital mixer; *TV, Cin* **m. vidéo** vision mixer

mélanine [melanin] *nf* melanin

mélanome [melanom] *nm Méd* melanoma

mêlant [mɛlɑ̃] *adj Can* **c'est pas m.** there's no doubt about it

mélasse [melas] *nf* (black) treacle, *Am* molasses; **m. raffinée** golden syrup; *F* **être dans la m.** to be in a mess *or* in the soup; *F* **quelle m.!** what a mess!

Melba [mɛlba] *adj inv Culin* Melba; **pêche/poire M.** peach/pear melba

mêlé [mele] *adj* (**a**) (*mélangé*) (*sentiments, compagnie*) mixed; (*sons*) mingled; **du rouge m. d'un peu de bleu** red mixed with a bit of blue; **fierté mêlée d'une certaine crainte** pride mixed *or* mingled with fear (**b**) (*emmêlé*) (*affaires*) involved, tangled; **dans cette histoire, la politique et le crime sont très mêlés** politics and crime are closely linked in this business; **tout est mêlé dans son suicide: la drogue, sa célébrité déclinante ...** everything played a part in his suicide: drugs, his declining fame ...

mêlée [mele] *nf* (**a**) (*conflit*) fray, mêlée; *F* (*bagarre*) scuffle, tussle, free-for-all; *Fig* **au dessus de la m.** above the fray; **entrer dans la m.** to enter the fray (**b**) *Rugby* scrum(mage); **m. ouverte** ruck

mêler [mele] **1** *vt* (**a**) (*ingrédients, substances etc*) to mix; (*sons différents, plusieurs cultures etc*) to combine; **m. qch à** *ou* **avec qch** to mix/combine sth with sth; **m. son vin d'eau** to put water in one's wine; **m. deux races de chien** to cross two breeds of dog

(**b**) **m. qn à qch** to involve sb in sth; **il est mêlé à plusieurs scandales financiers** he's involved in *or* mixed up in several financial scandals; **m. qn à la conversation** to bring sb into the conversation; **il est mêlé à tout** he's got a finger in every pie

(**c**) (*mettre en désordre*) (*papiers*) to mix up, to muddle (up); (*idées etc*) to confuse, to mix up; *Cartes* **m. les cartes** to shuffle the cards

2 se mêler *vpr* (*de sons, parfums*) to blend; (*de substances*) to mix, to blend; **se m. à la foule** to mingle with *or* blend into the crowd; **se m. à la conversation** to join in the conversation; **quand l'amour propre se mêle à la colère** when self-esteem is mingled *or* combined with anger; **mêlez-vous de ce qui vous regarde** mind your own business; *F* **mais de quoi je me mêle?** what's it got to do with you?, what business is it of yours?; **ce n'est pas à moi de m'en m.** it's not for me to interfere; **se m. de politique** to dabble in politics

mélèze [melɛz] *nm* larch (tree)

méli-mélo, *pl* **mélis-mélos** [melimelo] *nm F* (*d'objets*) jumble; (*de faits*) jumble, hotchpotch, *Am* hodgepodge; (*de gens*) mix, mixture; **quel m.!** what a mess!

mélioratif, -ive [meljɔratif, -iv] *adj* meliorative

mélisse [melis] *nf Bot* balm

mélo [melo] *F* **1** *nm* melodrama **2** *adj* melodramatic

mélodie [melɔdi] *nf* (**a**) *Mus* melody, tune (**b**) (*de vers, d'une langue etc*) melodiousness

mélodieusement [melɔdjøzmɑ̃] *adv* melodiously, tunefully

mélodieux, -ieuse [melɔdjø, -jøz] *adj* melodious, tuneful

mélodique [melɔdik] *adj Mus* melodic

mélodiste [melɔdist] *n* melody writer

mélodramatique [melɔdramatik] *adj* melodramatic

mélodrame [melɔdram] *nm* melodrama

mélomane [melɔman] **1** *adj* music-loving **2** *n* music lover

melon [məlɔ̃] *nm* (**a**) (*fruit*) melon; **m. cantaloup** cantaloup(e) (melon), *Am* rock melon; **m. d'hiver** *ou* **de garde** honeydew melon; **m. d'eau** watermelon (**b**) (**chapeau**) **m.** bowler (hat), *Am* derby (**c**) (*terme raciste*) Arab, *Br* wog

melonnière [məlɔnjɛr] *nf* melon bed

mélopée [melɔpe] *nf Mus* (**a**) (*chant récitatif*) chant, recitative (**b**) (*chant monotone*) threnody

MEM [mɛm] *nf Ordinat* (*abrév* **mémoire morte**) ROM

membrane [mɑ̃bran] *nf* (**a**) *Anat, Biol* membrane (**b**) *Tech* (*dans un microphone etc*) diaphragm

membraneux, -euse [mɑ̃branø, -øz] *adj Anat, Méd* membranous

membre [mɑ̃br] *nm* (**a**) *Anat* limb, *Fml* member; **m. supérieur/inférieur** upper/lower limb

(**b**) (*d'une association, d'une classe etc*) member; **membres** membership, members; **les membres de l'ONU/du Parlement Européen** the members of the UN/of the European Parliament; **être/devenir m. de ...** to be/become a member of ...; **m. du comité** committee member; **m. du conseil d'administration** member of the board, board member; **m. fondateur** founding *or* founder member; **m. honoraire** honorary member; **m. perpétuel** life member; **les états membres** the member states; *Can* **Membre de l'Assemblée Nationale** Member of the National Assembly; **carte de m.** membership card, member's card

(**c**) (*part constituante*), *Ling, Archit* member; *Math* **premier/second m. d'une équation** lefthand/righthand side of an equation

(**d**) (*de bateau*) rib, timber

▶ **membre**: *Bourse* **m. de compensation** clearing member; *Méd* **m. fantôme** phantom limb; **m. viril** (male) member, penis

membré [mɑ̃bre] *adj* limbed; **bien/mal m.** strong-/weak-limbed; *Hum* **bien m.** (*homme*) well-hung

membrure [mɑ̃bryr] *nf* (**a**) (*d'édifice etc*) frame(work); (*de bateau*) ribs, timbers (**b**) *Litt* (*de personne*) limbs; **homme à forte m.** strong-limbed *or* powerfully built man

même [mɛm] **1** *adj* (**a**) [①**B14**,B,1,b] (*avant le nom*) (*semblable, identique*) same; **j'ai la m. voiture qu'elle** I have the same car as her *or* as she does; **une seule et m. chose** one and the same thing; **ils sont du m. âge** they're the same age; **ce m. jour** that same day; **tous rassemblés en un m. lieu** all gathered in the same place; **en m. temps** at the same time

(**b**) [①**B10**,D,3] (*après le nom*) very; **aujourd'hui m.** this very day; **il habite ici m.** he lives in this very place/house; **c'est cela m.** that's right; **donner les chiffres mêmes** to give the actual figures; **c'est le titre m. que vous avez à traduire** it's the title itself *or* the actual title that you have to translate; **elle est la bonté/la beauté m.** she's kindness/beauty itself *or* personified

(**c**) **...-m.** self; **moi-m.** myself; **toi-m.** yourself; **lui-m.** himself/itself; **elle-m.** herself/itself; **soi-m.** oneself; **nous-mêmes** ourselves; **vous-mêmes** yourselves; **eux-mêmes/elles-mêmes** themselves; **moi-m., quand j'y pense, j'en ai des frissons** I get shivers myself when I think about it; **par toi-m.** by yourself; **j'ai dû y aller car elle-m. ne peut plus se déplacer** I had to go because she can't get about herself any more; **il l'a fait lui-m.** he did it himself; **faire qch de soi-m.** to do sth of one's own accord; **c'est lui-m. qui me l'a dit, il me l'a dit lui-m.** he told me himself; **je l'ai trouvée pareille à elle-m.** I found she hadn't changed, I found her the same as ever; **rester/être égal à soi-m.** to remain/be true to form; **égale à elle-m., elle est restée très calme** typically *or* true to form, she remained calm; *Enf* **menteur! – toi-m.!** liar! – liar yourself!; **la chose n'est pas mauvaise en elle-m.** the thing is not bad in itself *or* per se; **un autre lui-m.** a second self; **je pensais en moi-m. que ...** I was thinking to myself that ...

2 *adv* (**a**) even; **je le pense et m. j'en suis sûr** I think so, in fact I am sure of it; **je n'ai pas m.** *ou* **je n'ai m. pas le prix de mon voyage** I haven't even enough to pay my fare; **m. lui l'affirme** even he says so; **m. si je le savais** even if I knew; *F* **il va venir, m. qu'il me l'a promis!** he'll come, what's more he promised me he would!

(**b**) **je vous souhaite le bonsoir – moi de m.** I wish you goodnight – likewise; **la France a privatisé ses banques et la Grande-Bretagne de m.** France has privatized its banks and so has Great Britain *or* and Great Britain has too; **la France a privatisé ses banques et ses compagnies d'assurance de m.** France has privatized its banks and its insurance companies too; **faire de m.** to do likewise, to do the same; **il en est de m. des autres** it's the same for the others, the same is true *or* holds good for the others; **il a refusé de travailler pour eux, de m. qu'il avait refusé de le faire pour moi** he refused to work for them, just as *or* just like he had refused to for me; **je déteste la Bretagne de m. que la Normandie** I hate Britanny just as much as Normandy; **tout de m., quand m.** all the same, even so; **je trouve que tu aurais quand m. pu t'excuser** all the same *or* even so I think you could have apologized; **mais tout de m.!, enfin quand m.!** well really!

(**c**) **boire à m. la bouteille** to drink (straight) from *or* out of the bottle; **couché à m. le sable** lying on the bare sand; **banc taillé à m. la pierre** bench cut out of the rock; **à m. la peau** next to the skin; **être à m. de faire qch** to be able *or* in a position to do sth; **il n'est pas à m. de faire le voyage** he's not up to making the journey; **cela me met à m. de le faire** that enables me *or* puts me in a position to do it

3 *pron indéf* **on prend les mêmes et on recommence** it's the mixture as before; **tu n'es plus le m.!** you're not the same!; **cela revient au m.** it comes (down) *or* amounts to the same thing; *F* **c'est du pareil au m.** it's all the same, it comes to the same thing, it makes no difference

mémé [meme] *nf F* (*grand-mère*) grandma, gran(ny), *Br F* nan; (*vieille dame*) old dear; *F Péj* **ça fait m. cette robe!** that dress makes you look ancient!

mémento [memɛ̃to] *nm* **(a)** (*de service*) memo(randum), note **(b)** (*pour se souvenir*) memo, reminder **(c)** (*livre*) handbook; *Scol* **m. de chimie** chemistry revision notes

mémère [memɛr] *nf F* **(a)** (*grand-mère*) grandma, gran(ny), nan **(b)** *Péj* **une grosse m.** a fat middle-aged woman; **tu fais m. avec cette robe** that dress makes you look fat and middle-aged; **qu'est-ce qu'elle est m., cette fille!** she looks so dowdy, that girl!; **le petit chien-chien à sa m.** mummy's little doggie-woggie

mémo [memo] *nm* memo

mémoire¹ [memwar] *nf* **(a)** (*faculté*) memory; **je n'ai pas la m. des noms/dates** I've no memory for names/dates; **tu perds la m.?** are you losing your memory?; **il n'a pas de m.** he's got a bad memory; **avoir la m. courte** to have a short memory; **je n'ai plus son nom en m.** his name has slipped my memory, his name escapes me; **son nom est resté dans toutes les mémoires** his name is remembered by everyone; **c'est gravé dans ma m.** it's engraved in my memory; **rappeler qch à la m. de qn** to remind sb of sth; **je vais lui rafraîchir la m.** I'll refresh his memory; **réciter qch de m.** to recite sth from memory; **si j'ai bonne m.** if I remember rightly, if my memory serves me right; **avoir une m. d'éléphant** to have a long memory *or* a memory like an elephant; **m. collective** collective memory

(b) (*souvenir*) memory; **de m. d'homme** within living memory; **de m. de pêcheur, je n'avais jamais vu de si gros poisson** in all my years as an angler, I've never seen such a big fish; **à la m. de qn** (*de monument etc*) in memory of sb, to the memory of sb; **faire qch à la m. de qn** to do sth in memory of sb; **je signale, pour m., que …** I might mention, for the record, that …; **je vous signale pour m. que …** I would remind you that …; **de sinistre m.** of evil memory

(c) *Ordinat* memory; **m. de 40 méga-octets** 40 megabyte memory; **mettre un dossier en m.** to write a file to memory; **carte d'extension de m.** memory expansion card; **m. bloc-notes** scratchpad memory; **m. à bulles** bubble memory; **m. cache** cache memory; **m. centrale** main memory; **m. à disque** disk memory, RAM disc; **m. écran** screen memory; **m. étendue** extended memory; **m. expansée** expanded memory; **m. haute** high memory; **avoir chargé en m. haute** to have memory loaded high; **m. d'images** picture memory; **m. de masse** mass storage; **m. morte** read-only memory, ROM; **m. morte masquée** masked ROM; **m. non effaçable** non-erasable memory; **m. paginée** expanded memory; **m. tampon** buffer store, buffer (memory); **m. tampon de données** data buffer; **m. tampon d'imprimante** *ou* **pour imprimante** printer buffer; **m. tampon de sortie** output buffer; **m. tampon de texte** text buffer; **m. vidéo** video memory; **m. vive** random access memory, RAM; **m. vive dynamique** DRAM, dynamic random access memory; **m. vive statique** SRAM, static RAM, static random access memory

mémoire² *nm* **(a)** (*rapport*) report; *Jur* (*de procès*) (written) statement; *Univ* thesis, dissertation; **m. de maîtrise** ≈ master's thesis *or* dissertation **(b)** (*d'entrepreneur*) account; (*de coûts*) bill **(c)** *Littér* **mémoires** memoirs; **écrire ses mémoires** to write one's memoirs **(d)** **mémoires** (*de société savante etc*) transactions

mémorable [memɔrabl] *adj* memorable

mémorandum [memɔrɑ̃dɔm] *nm* **(a)** [①A13,5] (*note*) memorandum, note, memo; *Naut* **m. de combat** battle orders **(b)** (*carnet*) notebook

mémorial, -iaux [memɔrjal, -jo] *nm* **(a)** (*monument*) memorial **(b)** (*mémoires*) memoir **(c)** *Com* daybook

mémorisation [memɔrizasjɔ̃] *nf* memorization, memorizing; *Ordinat* writing to memory; *Mktg* **m. de la marque** brand awareness; **m. un jour après** day after recall

mémoriser [memɔrize] *vt* to memorize, to commit to memory; *Ordinat* to write to memory

menaçant [mənasɑ̃] *adj* threatening, menacing; **il fait un temps m.** the weather's looking ominous, it's threatening to rain

menace [mənas] *nf* threat; *Jur* **menaces** intimidation; **obtenir qch par la m.** to obtain sth by threats *or* intimidation; **faire qch sous la m.** to do sth under duress; **mettre ses menaces à exécution** to carry out one's threats; **m. de tempête/d'épidémie** threat of a storm/an epidemic; **m. de guerre** threat of war; **recevoir des menaces de mort** to receive death threats; **silence lourd de menaces** ominous silence

menacé [mənase] *adj* threatened; **vos jours sont menacés** your life is in danger *or* threatened

menacer [mənase] **(je menaçai(s), n. menaçons)** **1** *vt* to threaten, *Fml* to menace; **m. qn du doigt/poing** to shake one's finger/fist at sb; **m. qn d'un procès** to threaten sb with legal proceedings; **cette longue séparation menace leur mariage** this long separation is threatening their marriage *or* is putting their marriage at risk; **m. de faire qch** to threaten to do sth; **le procès menace d'être long** the trial threatens to be lengthy **2** *vi* (*de tempête, d'orage, de révolution*) to be brewing; **la pluie menace** it's threatening to rain, it looks like rain; **l'incendie menace** there's a danger of fire

ménage [menaʒ] *nm* **(a)** (*nettoyage*) **faire le m.** to do the housework, *Am* to clean house; **le grand m.** the spring-cleaning; *Fig* **faire le (grand) m.** (*dans un parti, une entreprise*) to have a shake-up; **faire des ménages** to go out cleaning; **tenir le m. de qn** to keep house for sb; **femme de m.** cleaner, *Br* daily help, *Br F* daily, *Am* cleaning woman

(b) (*meubles*) **monter son m.** to furnish one's house; **m. de poupée** set of doll's furniture

(c) (*couple*) (married) couple; (*famille*) household, family; *Écon* household; **jeune m.** young (married) couple; **se mettre en m.** to live together; **se mettre en m. avec qn** to live with sb, to move in with sb; **heureux en m.** happily married; **faire bon/mauvais m. (ensemble)** to get on well/badly (together); *Écon* **la consommation des ménages** household consumption

(d) *Vieilli* **de m.** (*pain etc*) homemade

ménage à trois *nm* ménage à trois, (matrimonial) triangle

ménagement [menaʒmɑ̃] *nm* care, caution, circumspection; (*tact*) consideration; **avec ménagement(s)** carefully, cautiously; (*avec tact*) considerately, tactfully; **parler/annoncer une nouvelle sans m.** to speak/break a piece of news bluntly; **traiter qn sans m.** to treat sb unceremoniously *or* without consideration

ménager¹, -ère [menaʒe, -ɛr] **1** *adj* (*équipement*) household; **appareils ménagers** household appliances; **travaux ménagers** housework; **arts ménagers** domestic science; **eaux ménagères** waste water; **Salon des Arts Ménagers** ≈ Ideal Home Exhibition **2** *nf* **ménagère (a)** (*femme*) housewife; **elle est bonne ménagère** she's a good housekeeper; *Écon* **le panier de la ménagère** the shopping basket **(b)** (*service de couverts*) canteen of cutlery

ménager² **(je ménageai(s), n. ménageons)** **1** *vt* **(a)** (*utiliser avec parcimonie*) to use sparingly, to be sparing with; **essayez de m. vos jambes pendant quelques jours** try not to use your legs too much for a few days; **sans m. ses paroles** without mincing one's words; **ne pas m. sa peine** to put in a lot of effort

(b) (*traiter avec soin*) **m. sa santé** to take care of one's health; **m. qn** to treat sb tactfully *or* with consideration; **ne le ménagez pas** don't spare him; **ses parents le ménagent trop** his parents are too soft with him; **elle cherche toujours à m. les uns et les autres** she always tries to do right by everybody; *Fig* **m. la chèvre et le chou** to keep everyone happy, *Prov* to run with the hare and hunt with the hounds

(c) (*arranger*) (*entrevue, réunion etc*) to arrange, to organize; (*réconciliation*) to bring about; **m. une surprise à qn** to prepare a surprise for sb; **m. une ouverture pour les fils** to make an opening for the wires; **m. une sortie** to provide an exit

2 se ménager *vpr* **(a)** (*prendre soin de soi*) to take care of oneself, to look after oneself, *Péj* to coddle oneself

(b) (*disposer*) **se m. une sortie** to provide oneself with a way out; **se m. une petite place dans le train** to make some space for oneself to sit down in the train

ménagerie [menaʒri] *nf* menagerie

mendélien, -ienne [mɛ̃deljɛ̃, -jɛn] *adj Biol* Mendelian

mendélisme [mɛ̃delism] *nm Biol* Mendelism

mendiant, -ante [mɑ̃djɑ̃, -ɑ̃t] **1** *adj* (*moine, ordre*) mendicant **2** *n* beggar; *Culin* **les (quatre) mendiants** = almonds, raisins, hazelnuts and figs (*served as dessert*)

mendicité [mɑ̃disite] *nf* begging; **réduit à la m.** reduced to begging *or* beggary

mendier [mɑ̃dje] (*impf, pr sub* **n. mendiions, v. mendiiez**) **1** *vi* to beg **2** *vt* (*du pain, des bonbons, des caresses*) to beg for; *Fig Péj* (*votes*) to canvass; **m. des compliments** to fish for compliments

mendigo(t), -ote [mɑ̃digo, -ɔt] *n Arg* beggar
meneau, -eaux [məno] *nm Archit* **m. vertical** mullion; **m. horizontal** transom
menées [məne] *nfpl* scheming, machinations; **déjouer les m. de qn** to thwart *or* outwit sb
mener [məne] **(je mène; je mènerai) 1** *vt* **(a)** *(accompagner)* to take; **m. qn à sa chambre** to take *or* show sb to his room; **m. qn à sa dernière demeure** to accompany sb to his final resting place; **m. une ligne entre deux points** to draw a line between two points
(b) *(être devant)* to lead, to be at the head of; **m. le deuil** to be chief mourner; *Sp* **la France mène la Belgique (par) 2 à 1** France is leading Belgium (by) 2 to 1; **m. la danse** *ou* **le bal** to lead the dance; *Fig* to call the tune
(c) *Fig* *(conduire)* to lead; **cette petite somme ne te mènera pas bien loin** that won't get you very far; **cela nous mène à croire que ...** this leads us to believe that ...; **cette affaire peut le m. loin** this business could get him into deep water
(d) *(diriger)* *(entreprise)* to run, to manage; *(personnel)* to manage, to control; **m. les débats** to lead *or* chair the discussions; **mari mené par sa femme** henpecked husband; **m. son personnel au doigt et à l'œil** *ou* **à la baguette** to have one's staff under one's thumb; **m. qn par le bout du nez** to lead sb by the nose; **elle se laisse m. par le bout du nez par son fiancé** her fiancé has got her under his thumb; **chez eux, c'est elle qui mène la barque** she wears the trousers in their house
(e) *(bateau)* to steer; *Fig* **m. qn en bateau** to take sb for a ride; **m. de front plusieurs affaires** to have several irons in the fire; **comment peux-tu m. de front tes études et ton engagement politique?** how do you manage to fit in both your studies and your political commitments?; *MecE* **roue menée** driven wheel
(f) *(affaire, enquête, campagne)* to conduct; **m. à bonne fin** *ou* **à bien** to bring to a successful conclusion; *(plan)* to carry through, to carry out; **m. un combat de tous les instants contre qch** to wage a constant fight against sth; **m. une vie triste** to lead a sad life; **m. la vie dure à qn** to give sb a hard time; **m. grand train** to live in grand style
2 *vi* **chemin qui mène à la ville** road that leads to the town; **cela ne mène à rien** this is getting us nowhere; *Fig* **elle n'en menait pas large** her heart was in her mouth
ménestrel [menɛstrɛl] *nm* minstrel
ménétrier [menetrije] *nm* (strolling) fiddler
meneur, -euse [mənœr, -øz] **1** *n* *(de parti politique etc)* leader; *(de révolte, chahuteurs)* ringleader **2** *nf* **meneuse de revue** principal chorus girl; *Can Sp* **meneuse de claques** cheerleader, pom-pom girl
▶ **meneur**: **m. de bœufs** cattle drover; **m. d'hommes** leader of men; **le grand m. d'hommes que fut De Gaulle** De Gaulle, that great leader of men; **m. de jeu** *(de spectacle)* master of ceremonies, *F* emcee, *Br* compère; *TV Rad* *(de jeu)* question master, quiz master; *Fb* play maker
menhir [menir] *nm* menhir
méninge [menɛ̃ʒ] *nf Anat* meninx; *F* **se creuser les méninges** to rack one's brains; **il ne se fatigue pas les méninges** he doesn't exactly overtax his brain
méningé [menɛ̃ʒe] *adj Anat* meningeal
méningite [menɛ̃ʒit] *nf Méd* meningitis; *Fig* **il ne risque pas d'attraper une m.!** there's no risk of him overtaxing his brain!
ménisque [menisk] *nm Anat, Phys* meniscus
ménopause [menɔpoz] *nf Physiol* menopause; **faire sa m.** to go through the menopause
ménopausée [menɔpoze] *adj f* poste-menopausal; **des femme ménopausées** women who hav gone through the menopause
ménorragie [menɔraʒi] *nf Méd* menorrhagia
menotte [mənɔt] *nf* **(a)** *Enf* little hand **(b)** **menottes** handcuffs; *Hist* manacles; **mettre** *ou* **passer les menottes à qn** to handcuff sb, to put handcuffs on sb
mensonge [mɑ̃sɔ̃ʒ] *nm* **(a)** *(propos)* lie; **faire** *ou* **dire un m.** to tell a lie; **petit m., pieux m.** white lie; **gros m.** downright lie; *F* whopper, *Br F* porky; *Hum* **c'est vrai, ce m.?** do you expect me to believe that?, pull the other one *or* leg! **(b)** *(acte)* lying; **vivre dans le m.** to live a lie; **détester le m.** to hate lying *or* lies
mensonger, -ère [mɑ̃sɔ̃ʒe, -ɛr] *adj* *(histoire)* untrue; *(regard)* deceitful, false; *(promesse)* false, empty; *(publicité)* false
menstruation [mɑ̃stryasjɔ̃] *nf Physiol* menstruation
menstruel, -elle [mɑ̃stryɛl] *adj Physiol* menstrual
menstrues [mɑ̃stry] *nfpl Physiol* menses
mensualisation [mɑ̃sɥalizasjɔ̃] *nf* *(du personnel, des salaires, des impôts)* monthly payment; **remboursement par mensualisations** repayment in monthly instalments
mensualiser [mɑ̃sɥalize] *vt* to pay monthly *or* on a monthly basis, to make payable by the month; **je me suis fait m. pour tout** I pay everything monthly *or* on a monthly basis
mensualité [mɑ̃sɥalite] *nf* monthly payment; **payer par mensualités** to pay monthly *or* by monthly instalments
mensuel, -elle [mɑ̃sɥɛl] **1** *adj* monthly **2** *nm* *(publication)* monthly (magazine) **3** *n* employee paid monthly
mensuellement [mɑ̃sɥɛlmɑ̃] *adv* monthly, every month
mensuration [mɑ̃syrasjɔ̃] *nf* *(action)* measurement, measuring; **prendre les mensurations de qn** to take sb's measurements; **mensurations** *(de femme)* vital statistics; *Jur* **mensurations judiciaires** height and weight (as shown on criminal record)
mental, -ale, -aux, -ales [mɑ̃tal, -o] **1** *adj* *(activité)* mental; **calcul m.** *(matière)* mental arithmetic; *(opération)* mental calculation; **maladie mentale** mental illness; **aliénation mentale** insanity **2** *nm* mental attitude; **un m. d'acier** a positive mental attitude
mentalement [mɑ̃talmɑ̃] *adv* mentally; *(calculer)* in one's head, mentally; *(prier)* silently; **j'ai préparé m. ce que j'allais lui répondre** I prepared in my head the answer I was going to give him; **se dire m. que** to tell oneself that
mentalité [mɑ̃talite] *nf* mentality; **elle a une m. de petite bourgeoise** she has a lower middle-class mentality; **avoir une sale m.** to have a nasty mind; **il vole chez ses copains: jolie m.!** he steals from his friends: very nice!
menteur, -euse [mɑ̃tœr, -øz] **1** *adj* *(personne)* untruthful, lying; *(discours, compliments)* deceitful **2** *n* liar
menthe [mɑ̃t] *nf* *(plante)* mint; **m. verte** spearmint, garden mint; **m. anglaise** *ou* **poivrée** peppermint; **pastilles de m.** (pepper)mints; **boire une m. à l'eau** to drink a glass of peppermint cordial; **sirop à la m.** peppermint cordial; **thé à la m.** mint tea; **gigot à la m.** leg of lamb with mint
menthol [mɑ̃tɔl] *nm* menthol; **bonbons/cigarettes au m.** menthol(ated) sweets/cigarettes
mentholé [mɑ̃tɔle] *adj* menthol(ated)
mention [mɑ̃sjɔ̃] *nf* mention; **faire m. de qn/qch** to mention *or* refer to sb/sth; **m. écrite** written indication; **mentions obligatoires** *(sur étiquette)* essential information; *Scol* **reçu avec m.** ≈ passed with distinction; **décrocher la m. bien** ≈ to get a distinction
mentionner [mɑ̃sjɔne] *vt* to mention; **mentionné ci-dessus** above-mentioned, aforesaid; *TV, Cin* **m. au générique** to acknowledge in the credits, to give a credit to
mentir [mɑ̃tir] *(prp* **mentant**; *pp* **menti**; *pr ind* **je mens, il ment, n. mentons, ils mentent**; *p hist* **je mentis**; *fu* **je mentirai) 1** *vi* to lie **(à qn** to sb); **sans m.!** honestly!; **tu mens comme tu respires** you're a compulsive liar; **m. à sa réputation** not to live up to one's reputation; **elle ment à son mari** she is deceiving her husband **2 se mentir** *vpr* to fool oneself
menton [mɑ̃tɔ̃] *nm* chin; **m. en galoche** jutting chin; **m. fuyant** receding chin; **double m.** double chin
mentonnier, -ière [mɑ̃tɔnje, -jɛr] **1** *adj* of the chin **2** *nf* **mentonnière** *Mil* chin strap; *Hist* *(de casque)* chinpiece; *Mus* chin rest
mentor [mɑ̃tɔr] *nm Litt* mentor
menu[1] [məny] **1** *adj* **(a)** *(petit)* small; *(gravier)* fine; *(silhouette)* slender, slim, slight; *(fragment)* tiny; **m. plomb** small shot, bird shot; **menue monnaie** small change; *Compta* **menus frais** petty expenses, incidental expenses **(b)** *(incident)* trifling, petty; **menues réparations** minor repairs; **menus détails** minute details; **menus frais, menues dépenses** minor expenses; **menus propos** small talk **2** *adv* *(piler)* small, fine; **hacher m.** to chop fine *or* small; *(très fin)* to mince; **écrire m.** to write small **3** *n* **raconter qch par le m.** to relate sth in detail
menu[2] *nm* **(a)** *(repas)* meal; **composer son m.** to plan one's meal; **m. équilibré** balanced meal
(b) *(liste)* *(au restaurant)*, menu; **prendre le m. (à 75 francs)** to have the (75-franc) set meal; **m. touristique/gastronomique** economy/gourmet menu; **m. déjeuner** lunch menu; **m. enfant** children's menu; **m. table d'hôte** table d'hôte menu; **m. à prix fixe** set menu, fixed-price menu
(c) *Ordinat* menu; **contrôlé par menu(s)** menu-driven; **m. primaire/secondaire/principal** primary/secondary/main menu; **m. d'impression** print menu; **m. déroulant** pull-down menu; **m. d'aide** help menu; **m. de césure** hyphenation menu; **m. fichier** file menu; **m. local** pop-up menu, pop-up; **menus en cascade** pull-down menus, cascading menus
menuet [mənɥɛ] *nm* minuet
menuiserie [mənɥizri] *nf* **(a)** *(travail)* joinery, woodwork **(b)** *(atelier)* (joiner's) workshop **(c)** *(résultat)* joinery, woodwork
menuisier [mənɥizje] *nm* joiner
méphistophélique [mefistofelik] *adj* Mephistophelean

méphitique [mefitik] *adj* foul, noxious
méplat [mepla] *nm* flat surface; (*de rocher*) ledge
méprendre (se) [səmeprɑ̃dr] *vpr* (*conj like* **prendre**) to be mistaken (**sur, quant à** about); **il imitait le maître à s'y m.** he could give a lifelike imitation of the master
mépris [mepri] *nm* contempt, scorn, disdain; **m. des richesses** contempt for wealth; **avoir le m. de l'argent/des conventions** to scorn *or* despise money/convention; **avoir du m. pour qn** to despise sb; **je n'éprouve que du m. à son égard** I have nothing but contempt for him; **au m. de qch** regardless of sth; **avec m.** scornfully, contemptuously; **sourire de m.** contemptuous *or* scornful smile
méprisable [meprizabl] *adj* contemptible, despicable
méprisant [meprizɑ̃] *adj* contemptuous, scornful
méprise [mepriz] *nf* mistake; **il y a m. sur le destinataire** it has been delivered to the wrong person; **par m.** by mistake
mépriser [meprize] *vt* (*personne, argent*) to despise, to scorn; (*conseil, offre, danger*) to scorn
mer [mɛr] *nf* **(a)** (*étendue d'eau*) sea; **en haute** *ou* **pleine m.** (out) at sea; **m. fermée** *ou* **intérieure** inland sea, landlocked sea; **la m. Rouge/Noire** the Red/Black Sea; **la m. Baltique** the Baltic (Sea); **la m. du Nord** the North Sea; **m. d'huile** sea as calm as a millpond; **au bord de la m.** at *or* by the seaside, by the sea; **aller à la m.** to go to the seaside; **une maison à la m.** a house by the sea(side); **grosse m.** heavy sea; **par grosse m.** when the sea is heavy; **il y a de la m.** the sea is running high, there's a heavy sea; **essuyer un coup de m.** to be struck by a heavy sea; **un homme à la m.!** man overboard!; **servir sur m.** to serve afloat *or* at sea; **voyager par m.** to travel by sea; **prendre la m.** to set sail, to put (out) to sea; **ce capitaine/navire n'a pas pris la m. depuis vingt ans** this captain/boat hasn't been to sea for twenty years; **mettre une embarcation à la m.** to get out a boat; (*d'un navire*) to lower a boat; **tenir la m.** (*rester au large*) to remain at sea; (*la contrôler*) to hold the seas, to rule the waves; **navire qui tient bien la m.** ship that behaves well in a heavy sea; **droit de la m.** maritime law; *F* **ce n'est pas la m. à boire** it's no big deal; *Fig* **m. de sable** vast expanse of sand
(b) (*marée*) tide; **m. haute, pleine m.** high tide; **basse m.** low tide
mer-air *adj inv Mil* **missile m.** sea-to-air missile
mercanti [mɛrkɑ̃ti] *nm* (*marchand*) bazaar-keeper, *Péj* profiteer, shark
mercantile [mɛrkɑ̃til] *adj* **(a)** *Péj* **esprit m.** money-grabbing mentality **(b)** *Arch* (*opération etc*) mercantile, commercial
mercantilisme [mɛrkɑ̃tilism] *nm* **(a)** *Péj* money-grabbing, profiteering **(b)** *Écon Hist* mercantilism
mercaphonie [mɛrkafoni] *nf Mktg* telemarketing, telephone marketing
mercaticien, -ienne [mɛrkatisjɛ̃] *n Mktg* marketeer, marketer, marketing expert
mercatique [mɛrkatik] *nf Écon* marketing; **m. après-vente** after-sales marketing; **m. ciblée** niche *or* target marketing; **m. commerciale** trade marketing; **m. de contact** direct marketing; **m. de grande consommation** mass marketing; **m. de la valeur** value marketing; **m. de relance** remarketing; **m. de stimulation** stimulation *or* incentive marketing; **m. défensive** defensive marketing; **m. expansionniste** rollout marketing; **m. indifférenciée** undifferentiated marketing; **m. non lucrative** not-for-profit marketing; (*résultats insatisfaisants*) unprofitable marketing; **m. relationnelle** relationship *or* direct marketing; **m. stratégique** strategic marketing; **m. sur mesure** customized marketing; **m. test dirigé** controlled test marketing; **m. téléphonique** telephone marketing; **m. écologique** green marketing
mercenaire [mɛrsənɛr] *adj, n* mercenary
mercerie [mɛrsəri] *nf* **(a)** (*marchandise*) haberdashery, *Am* notions **(b)** (*magasin*) haberdasher's (shop), *Am* notions store
merceriser [mɛrsərize] *vt Tex* to mercerize; **coton mercerisé** mercerized cotton
merchandising [mɛrʃɑ̃dajziŋ] *nm Écon* merchandising
merci [mɛrsi] **1** *int* thank you, thanks; (*refus*) no thank you, no thanks; **dire m.** to say thank you *or* thanks; **il ne m'a pas dit m.** he didn't say thank you to me; **m. bien, m. beaucoup** thank you very much, thanks a lot; **m. de** *ou* **pour votre offre** thank you for your offer; *F* **m. qui? m. mon chien!** don't bother to say thank you!; **grand m.!** no thank you!; *Iron* **m'excuser? m. bien, après ce qu'il m'a fait!** apologize? no way *or* no thanks, not after what he did to me!; *Iron* **m. du compliment!** thanks for the compliment!; **mille mercis de** *ou* **pour votre invitation** thank you so much *or* many thanks for your invitation
2 *nm* thank you; **il a pris le livre sans un m.** he took the book without a word of thanks *or* without saying thank you *or* without so much as a thanks
3 *nf* mercy; **être à la m. de qn/qch** to be at the mercy of sb/sth; **tenir qn à sa m.** to have sb at one's mercy; **crier m.** to cry for mercy; **sans m.** *adj* merciless, pitiless, ruthless; *adv* mercilessly, pitilessly, ruthlessly
mercier, -ière [mɛrsje, -jɛr] *n* haberdasher, *Am* notions dealer
mercredi [mɛrkrədi] **1** *nm* [①A75-6,B-C; B58-9,B-C] Wednesday; **le m. des Cendres** Ash Wednesday **2** *int Euph* sugar!
mercure [mɛrkyr] **1** *nm* **(a)** *Ch* mercury **(b)** *Myth* **M.** Mercury **2** *nf Astron* **M.** Mercury
mercuriale[1] [mɛrkyrjal] *nf Bot* mercury
mercuriale[2] *nf Litt* (*réprimande*) reprimand, rebuke
mercuriale[3] *nf Com* commodity price list
mercuriel, -ielle [mɛrkyrjɛl] *adj Pharm* mercurial
mercurochrome® [mɛrkyrɔkrom] *nm* mercurochrome®
merde [mɛrd] *Vulg* **1** *nf* (*excrément*) shit, crap; (*étron*) turd; **j'ai marché dans une m. de chien** I've trodden in a dog turd *or* in some dog shit; **il y a une m. d'oiseau sur le pare-brise** there's some bird shit on the windscreen; *Fig* **il est dans la m.** he's in the shit; **il ne se prend pas pour de la m.** he thinks he's God's gift to the world, *Br Vulg* he thinks the sun shines out of his arse; **c'est de la m.** (*ce qu'il vient de dire*) that's a load of shit *or* crap; (*ce tissu, ce film etc*) it's crap; **c'est une vraie m.** it's a right load of crap; **une m. à 50 francs** some cheap rubbish costing 50 francs; **de m.** (*voiture, idée etc*) shitty, crappy; **c'est la m.** things are shitty, *Am* this sucks
2 *int* shit!; **m. alors, je ne m'attendais pas à ça** oh shit, I didn't expect that; **et m., j'en ai marre!** to hell with it *or Br* sod it, I've had enough!; **et m. au boulot, je vais au ciné** to hell with work *or Br* sod work, I'm off to the cinema; **t'es d'accord, oui ou m.?** are we agreed or not, for Christ's sake?; **je te dis m.** (*bonne chance!*) ≈ break a leg!
merder [mɛrde] *vi F* **ma bagnole merde depuis huit jours** my car's been playing up for the past week; **j'ai envie de partir en vacances, mais j'ai l'impression que ça va m.** I want to go on holiday, but I've a feeling it'll all come to nothing; **j'ai complètement merdé dans les explications que je t'ai données** I made a real hash *or* mess of the instructions I gave you; **ils ne savent pas trop ce qui a merdé entre eux** they don't really know what screwed things up between them
merdeux, -euse [mɛrdø, -øz] *Vulg* **1** *adj* (*linge etc*) shitty; *Arch* **c'est un bâton m.** he's a shit; **elle se sent merdeuse** she feels shitty **2** *n* (*personne*) shit; **un petit m.** a little shit
merdier [mɛrdje] *nm Vulg* (*désordre*) mess; **je ne sais pas par quel bout ranger tellement c'est le m.** it's such a mess *or* pigsty I don't know where to start tidying up; **c'est le m. dans ma vie** my life's (in) a real mess; **je suis dans un sacré m.** I'm really in the shit
merdique [mɛrdik] *adj Vulg* shitty, crappy
merdoyer [mɛrdwaje] *vi* (**je merdoie, n. merdoyons; je merdoierai**) *Vulg* to make a cockup *or* balls-up *or US* ball-up, *Br* to cock up
mère [mɛr] *nf* **(a)** (*parent*) mother; *Zool* dam; **elle est m. de famille** she is a wife and mother; **elle est m. de trois enfants** she is the mother of three children, she is a mother of three; **elle a été une vraie m. pour son frère** she's been like a mother to her brother; **sœur par la m.** half-sister on the mother's side; *F* **la m. Martin** old Mrs Martin; *F* **et dites donc, la petite m.!** well, missus!
(b) (*source, origine*) **l'oisiveté est (la) m. de tous les vices** the devil finds work for idle hands (to do)
(c) *Beaux-Arts, Cér* (*pour moules en plâtre etc*) mould, *US* mold, matrix
(d) **langue m.** mother tongue; *Biol* **cellule m.** mother cell; *Com* **maison m.** parent company; **la Reine M.** the Queen Mother
▶ **mère**: *Rel* **m. abbesse** abbess; **m. biologique** natural *or* biological mother; **m. célibataire** single *or Vieilli* unmarried mother; **m. d'emprunt** surrogate mother; **m. génétique** natural *or* biological mother; **m. nourricière** foster mother; **m. patrie** mother country, motherland; **m. porteuse** surrogate mother; **m. poule** mother hen; **m. de substitution** surrogate mother; *Rel* **M. supérieure** Mother Superior (*of convent*); **m. de vinaigre** mother of vinegar
merguez [mɛrgɛz] *nf* merguez (*spicy North African sausage*)
méridien, -ienne [meridjɛ̃, -jɛn] **1** *adj* (*ligne etc*) meridian, meridional; **chaleur méridienne** midday heat; **ombre méridienne** shadow at noon **2** *nm* meridian; **sous le m. de vingt degrés à l'ouest de Greenwich** twenty degrees West of Greenwich **3** *nf* **méridienne (a)** *Astron* meridian line; (*altitude*) meridian altitude **(b)** *Arch* (*sieste*) midday siesta *or* nap **(c)** (*canapé*) day bed

méridional, -ale, -aux, -ales [meridjɔnal, -o] **1** *adj* (*du Sud*) southern; (*du Sud de la France*) Southern French **2** *n* (*du Sud*) southerner; (*du Sud de la France*) Southern Frenchman, *f* Frenchwoman; **méridionaux** (*du Sud de la France*) Southern French people
meringue [mərɛ̃g] *nf Culin* meringue
meringuer [mərɛ̃ge] *vt Culin* to cover with meringue; **tarte à la rhubarbe meringuée** rhubarb meringue pie
mérinos [merinos] *nm* (*mouton, laine, tissu*) merino; *Arg* **laisse pisser le m.!** don't let it get to you!
merise [məriz] *nf* (*fruit*) wild cherry
merisier [mərizje] *nm* (*arbre*) wild cherry (tree); (*bois*) cherry (wood)
méritant [meritɑ̃] *adj* deserving; **peu m.** undeserving
mérite [merit] *nm* (*qualité estimable*) merit; (*honneur*) credit; (*valeur*) worth; **ses remarques avaient le m. d'être franches** his remarks had the merit of being frank; **tu n'as même pas le m. de l'avoir fait tout seul** you can't even take credit for doing it yourself; **je n'ai aucun m.** I deserve no credit, I can't take any credit (for it); **s'attribuer le m. de qch** to take the credit for sth; **tout le m. lui revient** the credit is all his, all the credit is due to him; **son m. est grand d'avoir tout accepté, il a le grand m. d'avoir tout accepté** it is greatly to his credit that he accepted everything; **au seul m.** on merit alone; **augmentation au m.** merit increase; **par ordre de m.** in order of merit; **selon ses mérites** according to one's merits; **homme de m.** man of merit *or* talent *or* ability
mériter [merite] *vt* **(a)** to deserve, to merit; **il mérite des baffes** he deserves to be slapped; **il n'a que ce qu'il mérite** he's got what he deserves, it serves him right; **livre qui mérite d'être lu** book worth reading; **cela mérite réflexion** it's worth thinking about; **tu mérites qu'on te fasse la même chose** you deserve to have the same thing happen to you; **tu mériterais que je te laisse là tout seul** it would serve you right if I left you there on your own **(b) voilà ce qui lui a mérité cette renommée** this is what earned him this fame; **bien m. de la patrie** to deserve well of one's country
méritocratie [meritokrasi] *nf* meritocracy
méritoire [meritwar] *adj* commendable, praiseworthy, meritorious
merlan [mɛrlɑ̃] *nm* **(a)** (*poisson*) whiting; *F* **faire des yeux de m. frit à qn, regarder qn avec des yeux de m. frit** (*parce qu'on n'a pas compris*) to gape at sb; (*parce qu'on est amoureux de lui*) to make sheep's eyes at sb **(b)** *Arg* (*coiffeur*) (*pour hommes*) barber, hairdresser; (*pour femmes*) hairdresser
merle [mɛrl] *nm* (*oiseau*) blackbird; *Fig* **vilain m.**; *Iron* **beau m.** nasty customer, *Br* nasty piece of work; **m. blanc** rare bird; **chercher le m. blanc** to ask for the moon
merlin[1] [mɛrlɛ̃] *nm Naut* marline
merlin[2] *nm* (*hache*) axe, *US* ax; (*pour abattre les arbres*) felling axe; (*pour abattre le bétail*) poleaxe
merlu [mɛrly] *nm* hake
merluche [mɛrlyʃ] *nf* **(a)** [①A12,1,g] (*poisson*) hake **(b)** *Culin* dried (unsalted) cod, stockfish
mer-mer *adj inv Mil* **missile m.** sea-to-sea missile
mérou [meru] *nm* (*poisson*) grouper
mérovingien, -ienne [merɔvɛ̃ʒjɛ̃, -jɛn] *Hist* **1** *adj* Merovingian **2** *nm* **M.** Merovingian
mer-sol *adj inv Mil* **missile m.** sea-to-ground missile
merveille [mɛrvɛj] *nf* **(a)** marvel, wonder; **les merveilles de la technologie** the marvels *or* wonders of technology; **les sept merveilles du monde** the seven wonders of the world; **ma nouvelle machine à laver est une m.** my new washing machine is a marvel; **faire m.** to work *or* do wonders (**sur** with, for); **faire des merveilles** to work *or* do *or* perform wonders; **c'est m. que vous soyez à l'heure** it's a wonder that you're on time; **à m.** perfectly, wonderfully (well); **se porter à m.** to be in excellent health *or* in the best of health; **ce chèque tombe à m.** this cheque has arrived at exactly the right moment
(b) *Culin* = sweet fritter
merveilleusement [mɛrvɛjøzmɑ̃] *adv* marvellously, wonderfully; **il fait m. beau** it's marvellous *or* wonderful weather, the weather's marvellous *or* wonderful; **aller m. bien** to be wonderfully well, to be in excellent health; **elle a m. réussi son examen** she passed her exam with excellent results
merveilleux, -euse [mɛrvɛjø -øz] **1** *adj* marvellous, wonderful; **il a fait un temps m.** it was marvellous *or* wonderful weather, the weather was marvellous *or* wonderful; **c'est m. ce qu'il a changé** it's marvellous how he's changed **2** *nm* **le m.** the supernatural **3** *nf Hist* **merveilleuse** fashionable lady

mes [me] *voir* **mon**
mésalliance [mezaljɑ̃s] *nf* unsuitable marriage; **faire une m.** to marry beneath oneself
mésallier (se) [səmezalje] *vt* (*conj like* **allier**) to marry beneath oneself
mésange [mezɑ̃ʒ] *nf* tit; **m. bleue** bluetit; **m. charbonnière** great tit; **m. noire** coaltit
mésaventure [mezavɑ̃tyr] *nf* misadventure, mishap, misfortune
mescal [mɛskal] *nm* mescal
mescaline [mɛskalin] *nf* mescalin(e)
mésentente [mezɑ̃tɑ̃t] *nf* disagreement; **climat de m.** coolness
mésestimation [mezɛstimasjɔ̃] *nf Litt* underestimation, underrating, undervaluing
mésestime [mezɛstim] *nf Litt* low esteem; **tenir qn en m.** to hold sb in low esteem
mésestimer [mezɛstime] *vt* to underestimate
mésintelligence [mezɛ̃teliʒɑ̃s] *nf Litt* disagreement; **être en m. avec qn** to be at loggerheads with sb
mesmérisme [mɛsmerism] *nm* mesmerism
Mésopotamie [mezɔpɔtami] *nf* Mesopotamia
mésopotamien, -ienne [mezɔpɔtamjɛ̃, -jɛn] **1** *adj* Mesopotamian **2** *n* **M.** Mesopotamian
mésothérapie [mezoterapi] *nf Méd* mesotherapy
mésozoïque [mezɔzɔik] *adj, nm Géol* Mesozoic
mesquin [mɛskɛ̃] *adj* (*méchant*) mean, petty; (*avare*) mean, stingy, niggardly; (*excuse*) paltry, petty; **un coup m.** a mean *or* shabby trick; **il a vraiment un esprit m.** he's really small-minded *or* mean *or* petty
mesquinement [mɛskinmɑ̃] *adv* meanly
mesquinerie [mɛskinri] *nf* (*de caractère, procédé*) meanness, pettiness; (*avarice*) meanness, stinginess, niggardliness; **je ne te savais pas capable de telles mesquineries** I would never have thought you capable of such meanness *or* pettiness, I didn't think you could be so mean *or* petty
mess [mɛs] *nm Mil* mess; **m. des officiers** officers' mess
message [mesaʒ] *nm* message; **prendre un m.** to take a message; **chanson/pièce à m.** song/play with a message; **m. codé** coded message; **m. subliminal** subliminal message; **m. télex** telex (message); **m. téléphonique** telephone message; **m. de détresse** distress message; **m. publicitaire** advertisement, advertising message; *Ordinat* **m. d'accueil** welcome message; *Ordinat* **m. d'alerte** warning message, alert box; *Ordinat* **m. d'attente (du système)** (system) prompt; *Ordinat* **m. d'erreur** error message; *Ordinat* **m. d'invite** (*du système*) prompt; *Ordinat* **m. guide-opérateur** prompt
messager, -ère [mesaʒe, -ɛr] **1** *n* messenger; **m. de malheur** bearer of bad news; *Litt* **m. du printemps** harbinger of spring **2** *nm* (*de colis, cargaison*) carrier
messagerie [mesaʒri] *nf* **service de messageries** parcel delivery service; **m. électronique** electronic mail service, e-mail; **m. de presse** newspaper distributing service; **m. rose** = interactive Minitel service for those seeking romantic and sexual contacts; **messageries maritimes** shipping line; **messageries aériennes** air freight company; **bureau de(s) messageries** *Naut* shipping office; *Rail* parcel(s) office; *Hist* stagecoach office
messe [mɛs] *nf Rel* mass; **aller à la m.** to go to mass; **célébrer** *ou* **dire la m.** to celebrate *or* say mass; **faire dire une m. pour qn** to have a mass said for sb; *Mus* **m. en si mineur** mass in B minor
► **messe**: **m. basse** low mass; *Fig F* **pas de messes basses!** stop whispering!; **m. de minuit** midnight mass; **m. des morts** requiem mass; **m. noire** black mass
messeoir [meswar] *vi* (*prp* **messeyant**; *pp is lacking*; *pr ind* **il messied, ils messeyent**; *pr sub* **il messeye**; *impf* **il messeyait**; *p hist is lacking*; *fu* **il messiéra**) *Arch, Litt* to be unbecoming *or* unseemly; **il lui messied de …** it ill becomes him to …
messianique [mesjanik] *adj* Messianic
messianisme [mesjanism] *nm* Messianism
messidor [mesidɔr] *nm Hist* tenth month of the French Republican calendar (*19-20 June—19-20 July*)
Messie [mesi] *nm* Messiah; **on l'a attendu comme le M.** we were waiting eagerly for him
messin, -ine [mesɛ̃, -in] **1** *adj* of/from Metz **2** *n* **M.** (*natif*) native of Metz; (*habitant*) inhabitant of Metz
messire [mesir] *nm Arch* Sir, Master
mesurable [məzyrabl] *adj* measurable, *Spéc* mensurable
mesurage [məzyraʒ] *nm* measuring, measurement
mesure [məzyr] *nf* **(a)** [①B56-7,D,1] (*dimension*) measurement; (*action*) measurement, measuring; **appareil de m.** measuring apparatus; **prendre les mesures de qn** to take sb's measurements, to measure sb; **prendre les mesures de qch** to measure sth; *Fig* **prendre la m. de qn** to size sb up, to

get the measure of sb; **sur m.** made to measure, tailor-made; **complet (fait) sur mesure(s)** made-to-measure *or Am* custom-made suit; **faire faire un complet sur mesure** to have a suit made to measure *or* tailor-made; *Fig* **être en m. de faire qch** to be in a position to do sth; **le producteur lui a trouvé un rôle sur m.** the producer found him a role that was tailor-made for him; *Fig* **donner toute sa m.** to show what one is capable of; *Fig* **être à la m. de qn/qch** to measure up to sb/sth; *Sp, Fig* **trouver un adversaire à sa m.** to meet one's match

(**b**) **dans une certaine m.** to some *or* a certain extent *or* degree; **dans une large m.** to a large extent *or* degree, in large measure; **dans la m. où** insofar as; **je vous aiderai dans la m. de mes forces** *ou* **du possible** I'll help you to the best of my ability *or* as much as I can *or* as best I can; **ces dépenses ne sont pas dans la m. de mes moyens** this expenditure is beyond my means

(**c**) **(au fur et) à m.** as one goes along; **je vérifie les chiffres (au fur et) à m.** I check the figures as I go along; **à m. que** as; **à m. que je reculais, il s'avançait** as I retreated he advanced

(**d**) (*action*) measure, step, action; **m. de sécurité** safety measure *or* precaution; **par m. de sécurité/d'hygiène** for reasons of safety/hygiene, as a safety/hygiene measure; **par m. d'économie** as a cost-saving measure, for reasons of economy; **prendre des mesures** to take measures *or* steps *or* action; **prendre des mesures pour faire qch/pour que ...** to take measures *or* steps to do sth/so that ...; **prendre des mesures contre qch** to take action against sth; **prendre ses mesures** to make arrangements; **j'ai pris mes mesures pour que les enfants soient gardés** I've made arrangements for the children to be looked after

(**e**) (*quantité, unité*) measure; **verser une m. de vin à qn** to pour sb out a measure of wine; **faites-moi bonne m.** give me good measure; *Fig* **il n'y a pas commune m. entre ces deux vins** there is no comparison between the two wines; **sans commune m.** unrivalled; **m. de longueur** measure of length; **m. de surface** *ou* **de superficie** square measure; **m. de volume** cubic measure; **poids et mesures** weights and measures

(**f**) **pièces qui ne sont pas de m.** pieces that are not the right size *or* that are not to size; **rester dans la juste m.** to keep within bounds; **elle n'a pas le sens de la m.** she has no sense of moderation; **(dé)passer la m.** to overstep the mark, to go too far; **ne garder aucune m., oublier toute m.** to fling aside all restraint, to lose all sense of moderation *or* proportion; **ambition sans m.** unbounded *or* limitless ambition

(**g**) *Escrime* measure, reach, distance

(**h**) *Mus* (*temps*) time; (*division*) bar; **m. à quatre temps** four-four time, common time; **battre la m.** to beat time; **barre de m.** bar line; **en m.** in (strict) time; **aller en m.** to keep time; **deux mesures plus loin** two bars further on

(**i**) *Littér* (*de vers*) metre, *US* meter

mesuré [məzyre] *adj* (*pas*) measured; (*langage, personne*) moderate, restrained

mesurément [məzyremɑ̃] *adv* in moderation

mesurer [məzyre] **1** *vt* (**a**) (*dimensions, taille*) to measure; (*farine, sucre etc*) to measure out; (*bois, terre*) to measure (up); (*tissu*) to measure off; (*carburant*) to meter; *Fig* (*qn, qch*) to size up; **m. deux mètres** (*de personne*) to be two metres tall; **la colonne mesure dix mètres** the column measures ten metres *or* is ten metres high; **on mesure le travail au résultat** the work is measured by results; **m. la nourriture à qn** to ration sb's food; **le temps vous sera mesuré pour cette épreuve** you will have a limited amount of time for this test; **m. sa dépense sur ses profits** to cut one's coat according to one's cloth; **m. la distance à la vue** to judge *or* estimate *or* gauge the distance with one's eyes

(**b**) (*ménager, régler*) **m. le châtiment à l'offense** to make the punishment fit the crime; **m. ses paroles** *ou* **son vocabulaire** to moderate one's language; **il ne mesure pas la portée de ses paroles** he says things without thinking

2 se mesurer *vpr* **se m. avec** *ou* **à qn** to measure one's strength against sb, to measure *or* pit oneself against sb; **vous n'êtes pas de force** *ou* **de taille à vous m. avec lui** you're no match for him; **les adversaires se mesurèrent des yeux** the opponents sized each other up

mesureur [məzyrœr] *nm* (*personne, appareil*) measurer; **m. de pression** pressure gauge

mésuser [mezyze] *vi* **m. de son bien** to misuse one's wealth; **m. de son pouvoir** to abuse one's power

métabolique [metabɔlik] *adj* metabolic

métabolisme [metabɔlism] *nm* metabolism

métacarpe [metakarp] *nm Anat* metacarpus

métacarpien, -ienne [metakarpjɛ̃, -jɛn] *adj, nm Anat* metacarpal

métairie [metɛri] *nf* small farm (*worked by share-cropper*)

métal, -aux [metal, -o] *nm* (**a**) metal; **métaux précieux** precious metals; **m. blanc** white metal; **m. antifriction** Babbit metal, bearing metal (**b**) *Fin* **m. en barres** bullion

métalangage [metalɑ̃gaʒ] *nm* metalanguage

métalangue [metalɑ̃g] *nf* metalanguage

métallifère [metalifɛr] *adj* metal-bearing, metalliferous

métallique [metalik] *adj* metallic; **câble m.** wire rope; **plume m.** metal nib; **rendre un son m.** to clang, to clank; *Fin* **réserve m.** bullion reserve

métallisation [metalizasjɔ̃] *nf* metallization

métallisé [metalize] *adj surtout Aut* (*peinture*) metallic; **voiture bleu m.** metallic blue car

métalliser [metalize] *vt* to metallize

métallo [metalo] *nm F* metalworker

métallurgie [metalyrʒi] *nf* metallurgy; **crise dans la m.** crisis in the metallurgical industry

métallurgique [metalyrʒik] *adj* metallurgical

métallurgiste [metalyrʒist] *nm* (**a**) (*scientifique*) metallurgist (**b**) (*ouvrier*) metalworker

métamorphique [metamɔrfik] *adj Géol* metamorphic

métamorphiser [metamɔrfize] *vt Géol* to metamorphose

métamorphisme [metamɔrfism] *nm Géol* metamorphism

métamorphose [metamɔrfoz] *nf* transformation, metamorphosis; *Fig* transformation; *Fig* **quelle m.!** what a transformation!

métamorphoser [metamɔrfoze] **1** *vt* to transform, to metamorphose; *Fig* to transform **2 se métamorphoser** *vpr* to change completely, to be transformed

métaphore [metafɔr] *nf* metaphor; **parler par métaphores** to speak in metaphors; **elle parle beaucoup par métaphores** she is very metaphorical in her speech, she uses a lot of metaphor(s) when she speaks

métaphorique [metafɔrik] *adj* (*expression, style*) metaphorical, figurative; **cela n'a qu'une valeur m.** it's purely metaphorical *or* figurative

métaphoriquement [metafɔrikmɑ̃] *adv* metaphorically, figuratively

métaphysicien, -ienne [metafizisjɛ̃, -jɛn] *n* metaphysician, metaphysicist

métaphysique [metafizik] **1** *adj* metaphysical **2** *nf* metaphysics

métaphysiquement [metafizikmɑ̃] *adv* metaphysically

métapsychique [metapsiʃik] **1** *adj* (*phénomène*) psychic **2** *nf* parapsychology

métastase [metastɑz] *nf Méd* metastasis, secondary cancer; **former des métastases** to metastasize

métatarse [metatars] *nm Anat* metatarsus

métatarsien, -ienne [metatarsjɛ̃, -jɛn] *adj, nm Anat* metatarsal

métathèse [metatɛz] *nf Ling* metathesis

métayage [metɛjaʒ] *nm Agr* sharecropping

métayer, -ère [metɛje, -ɛr] *n Agr* sharecropper

métazoaire [metazɔɛr] *nm Biol* metazoan; **métazoaires** Metazoa

métempsycose [metɑ̃psikoz] *nf* transmigration of the soul, *Spéc* metempsychosis

météo [meteo] *F* **1** *nf* (**a**) weather forecast *or* report; **la m. est mauvaise pour toute la semaine** the weather forecast is bad for the whole week; **je n'ai pas eu le temps d'écouter/de regarder la m.** I didn't have time to listen to/to look at the weather (forecast) (**b**) (= **bureau central de météorologie**) weather office, met office **2** *nm* **Monsieur M.** the weather man **3** *adj* weather, meteorological; **bulletin m.** weather report *or* forecast; **station m.** meteorological *or* weather station; **frégate** *ou* **navire m.** weather ship

météore [meteɔr] *nm* meteor

météorique [meteɔrik] *adj* meteoric

météorite [meteɔrit] *n* meteorite

météorologie [meteɔrɔlɔʒi] *nf* meteorology; **le bureau central de m.** = the meteorological *or* weather office

météorologique [meteɔrɔlɔʒik] *adj* = **météo 3**

météorologiste [meteɔrɔlɔʒist], **météorologue** [meteɔrɔlɔg] *n* meteorologist

métèque [metɛk] *nm* (*terme injurieux*) wog

méthane [metan] *nm Ch* methane

méthanier [metanje] *nm Naut* methane tanker

méthanol [metanɔl] *nm* methanol

méthode [metɔd] *nf* (**a**) (*démarche*) method, way; **m. pour faire qch** method *or* way of doing sth; **une bonne m. pour apprendre les langues** a good method for *or* way of learning languages; **c'est quoi ta m. pour rester aussi mince?** how do you manage to stay so slim?; **elle a sa m.** she has her own method *or* way of doing things; **je vais changer de m.** I'm going to change my methods; **tu as suivi quelle m.?** which method did you use?; **c'est la seule m. à suivre** it's the only way to do it; **il n'y a pas 36 méthodes** it's the only way; *F* **je n'ai pas la m. avec lui** I don't know how to handle him; **tu as vraiment la m. avec les enfants!** you really have a way with *or* know how to handle children!; *F* **trouver la m. pour faire qch** to find out how to do sth, to find a way of doing sth; **m. de lecture** reading method; **m. de financement** funding method; **m. de gestion** management technique; **m. de travail** work method; *Compta* **m. par** *ou* **à échelles** daily balance interest calculation

(b) (*ordre*) method; **il a beaucoup de m.** he's very methodical *or* systematic; **avec m.** methodically, systematically; **sans m.** unmethodically, without method, unsystematically

(c) (*livre*) primer, grammar; **m. de piano** piano tutor

méthodique [metɔdik] *adj* methodic(al), systematic

méthodiquement [metɔdikmɑ̃] *adv* methodically, systematically

méthodisme [metɔdism] *nm Rel* Methodism

méthodiste [metɔdist] *adj, n Rel* Methodist

méthodologie [metɔdɔlɔʒi] *nf* methodology

méthodologique [metɔdɔlɔʒik] *adj* methodological

méthyle [metil] *nm Ch* methyl

méthylène [metilɛn] *nm Ch* methylene

méthylique [metilik] *adj Ch* methyl(ic)

méticuleusement [metikyløzmɑ̃] *adv* meticulously

méticuleux, -euse [metikylø, -øz] *adj* meticulous; **par trop m.** over-meticulous; **elle est d'une propreté méticuleuse** she keeps everything immaculate *or* everything spotless(ly clean)

méticulosité [metikylozite] *nf Litt* meticulousness; **d'une m. exaspérante** exasperatingly meticulous

métier [metje] *nm* **(a)** [①**B4**,B,2,b,i] (*travail*) trade, profession, occupation; **les métiers artistiques** the artistic professions; **j'ai fait tous les métiers** I've done a bit of everything; **quel est votre m.?** what do you do (for a living)?, what's your job?; **exercer** *ou* **faire un m.** to carry on a trade *or* a profession; **j'exerce le m. de journaliste** I'm a journalist (by profession); **quel m. veux-tu faire plus tard?** what do you want to be when you grow up?; **il n'est pas** *ou* **il n'y a pas de sot m.** a job's a job; **m. de banquier** banking profession, banking; *Euph* **le plus vieux m. du monde** the oldest profession in the world; **il est charpentier de son m.** he's a carpenter by trade; **elle a un bon m.** she has a good job; **il sent qu'il est temps de changer de m.** he feels it's time he changed his job; **ils sont du m.** they're in the business *or* trade; *Fig* **ce n'est pas mon m.** it's not my job; **il connaît son m.** he knows what he's doing; **ce n'est pas toi qui vas m'apprendre mon m.** don't teach me my business, I know what I'm doing; **ils font leur m.** they're only doing their job; **parler m.** to talk shop; *F* **quel m.!** what a life!; **quel m. de fou!** you don't have to be crazy to do this job but it helps!; **chacun son m. (et les vaches seront bien gardées)** you do your job and I'll do mine; **terme de m.** technical term

(b) (*savoir-faire, expérience*) experience; **il a du m.** he has experience, he is experienced; **elle a plusieurs années de m.** she has several years' experience; **homme de m.** professional; **gens de m.** experts, professionals; **ficelles** *ou* **trucs du m.** tricks of the trade; *Fig* **c'est le m. qui rentre** put it down to experience, that's how you learn

(c) *Tex* **m. à tisser** loom; **m. mécanique** power loom; **m. à filer** spinning frame; **m. à tapisserie** tapestry frame; **m. à broder** embroidery frame, tambour frame; *Fig* **avoir un ouvrage sur le m.** to have a piece of work in hand

métis, -isse [metis] **1** *adj* **(a)** (*personne*) halfcaste; (*animal*) crossbreed; (*chien*) mongrel; **plante métisse** hybrid plant **(b)** *Tex* **tissu m.** linen-cotton mixture **2** *n* (*personne*) halfcaste, *Péj* halfbreed; (*animal*) crossbreed; (*chien*) mongrel **3** *nm Tex* linen-cotton mixture

métissage [metisaʒ] *nm* crossbreeding

métisser [metise] *vt* to cross(breed); **une population très métissée** a highly intermixed population

métonymie [metɔnimi] *nf Ling* metonymy

métrage [metraʒ] *nm* **(a)** (*action*) measuring, measurement; *Constr* quantity surveying **(b)** (*longueur*) (metric) length; **grand/petit m.** (*tissu*) cut lengthways/crossways; **des métrages de lin** lengths of linen; **vous le voulez en quel m.?** what width would you like? **(c)** *Cin* footage, length; **long m.** feature film; **moyen m.** medium length film; **court m.** short

mètre[1] [mɛtr] *nm* **(a)** metre, *US* meter; **m. carré/cube** square/cubic metre; *Sp* **elle se prépare à courir un 200 mètres (haies)** she's training for the 200 metres (hurdles); **l'épreuve du 400 mètres** the 400 metres (race) **(b)** (*pour mesurer*) tape measure; (*en bois*) rule; **m. pliant** folding rule; **m. à ruban** tape measure

mètre[2] *nm Littér* metre, *US* meter

métré [metre] *nm Constr* (*de terrain à construire etc*) measurement(s); (*devis*) bill of quantities

métrer [metre] *vt* **(je mètre; je métrerai) (a)** to measure (by the metre *or US* meter) **(b)** *Constr* to survey (for quantities)

métreur, -euse [metrœr, -øz] *n* **m. (vérificateur)** quantity surveyor

métrique[1] [metrik] *adj* metric; **adopter le système m.** to adopt the metric system; *F* to go metric

métrique[2] *Littér* **1** *adj* metric(al) **2** *nf* prosody, metrics

métro [metro] *nm* underground, *Am* subway; **le m. de Paris/de Montréal** the Paris/Montreal metro; **le m. de Londres** the London underground (system), *F* the tube; **aller quelque part en m.** to go somewhere by metro/underground/tube/subway; **il y a un m. direct de la gare jusque chez moi** you can get a metro/tube/subway directly from the station to my place; **au m. Charonne** at Charonne metro (station); *F* **avoir un m. de retard** to be behind the times; *F* **m., boulot, dodo** the daily grind, the daily routine; **depuis que j'habite à Paris, ma vie c'est vraiment m., boulot, dodo** life has become very humdrum *or* routine since I moved to Paris

métrologie [metrɔlɔʒi] *nf* metrology

métrologique [metrɔlɔʒik] *adj* metrological

métrologiste [metrɔlɔʒist] *n* metrologist

métronome [metrɔnɔm] *nm Mus* metronome

métropole [metrɔpɔl] *nf* **(a)** (*grande ville*) metropolis; **faire de Marseille une m. d'équilibre** to turn Marseilles into a second capital **(b)** (*état*) mother country; **les Français de la M.** the French of Metropolitan France **(c)** *Rel* metropolis; (*d'archevêque*) see

métropolitain, -aine [metrɔpɔlitɛ̃, -ɛn] **1** *adj* **(a)** *Admin* metropolitan; **armée métropolitaine** home army **(b)** *Rel* metropolitan; (*église etc*) archiepiscopal **2** *nm* **(a)** *Admin* underground (railway), *Am* subway **(b)** *Rel* archbishop; (*de l'Église orthodoxe*) metropolitan

mets [mɛ] *nm* food

mettable [mɛtabl] *adj* (*vêtements etc*) wearable; **pas m.** not fit to wear; **elle dit n'avoir plus rien de m.** she says she has nothing to wear

metteur, -euse [mɛtœr, -øz] *n Typ* compositor, comp; **m. en scène** *Cin* director; *Th* director, *Br* producer; *Rad* **m. en ondes** producer; *Typ* **m. en pages** compositor, comp; **m. en œuvre** (*de bijoux etc*) mounter

mettre [mɛtr] (*prp* **mettant**; *pp* **mis**; *pr ind* **je mets, il met, n. mettons, ils mettent**; *p hist* **je mis**; *fu* **je mettrai**) **1** *vt* **(a)** (*placer*) to put; **ne mets pas les coudes sur la table!** don't put your elbows on the table!; **m. qn au lit/dans le train** to put sb to bed/on the train; **il a mis le pied sur une peau de banane** he stepped on a banana skin; **il mit la main sur mon épaule** he put *or* laid his hand on my shoulder; **m. genou à terre** to go down on one knee; **mettez tout cela par terre** put all that on the floor; **m. qch debout** to stand sth upright; **mets les livres debout** stand the books on end; **m. qch à plat** to put *or* lay sth down flat; **m. un manche à un balai** to put a handle on *or* fit a handle to a broom; **m. une annonce dans les journaux** to put an advertisement in the (news)papers; **il a mis de la boue sur le tapis** he's got mud on the carpet; **m. une lettre à la poste** to post a letter; **m. de l'argent sur un compte** to put money into an account; **qu'est-ce qui vous a mis cela dans la tête?** what put that into your head?; **il met ses parents avant tout le reste** he puts his parents first; *Sp* **m. le ballon au fond des filets** to put the ball in the back of the net; **nous avons mis 3 kms entre nous et nos poursuivants** we put 3 km between us and our pursuers

(b) (*appliquer*) (*fond de teint, maquillage, parfum, pansement, couche de peinture etc*) to put on

(c) (*consacrer*) **m. du temps à faire qch** to take time to do sth; **j'ai mis deux ans à faire cela** I took *or* it took me two years to do that; *F* **tu y as mis le temps, pour comprendre** it took you a while to catch on; **combien de temps met-on pour aller de Paris à Marseille en voiture?** how long does it take to get from Paris to Marseilles by car?; **le train met deux heures pour le trajet** the trip takes two hours by train, it takes the train two hours to do the trip; **m. toute son énergie/tout son enthousiasme à faire qch** to put all one's energy/enthusiasm into doing sth; **j'y mettrai tous mes soins** I'll give it my full attention

(d) (*dépenser une somme d'argent*) to spend; (*investir*) to sink; **m. 500 francs dans qch** to spend 500 francs on sth; **il faudra m. dans les 5000 francs** you'll have to spend about 5,000 francs; **m. 100000 francs dans une affaire** to sink 100,000 francs into a business venture; **je serais prêt à m. tout ce que j'ai dans cette entreprise** I'd be willing to put everything I have into this venture; *F* **y m. le prix** to pay for it; **mais il faudra que vous y mettiez le prix** but it'll cost you; **m. un enjeu** to lay a stake; **m. de l'argent sur un cheval** to put money on a horse, to back a horse

(e) (*revêtir*) (*vêtements, lunettes, chaussures etc*) to put on; **qu'est-ce que je vais m.?** what shall I wear?; **mettez votre robe bleue** put your blue dress on; **elle ne met que des mini-jupes** all she wears is mini-skirts; **je n'ai plus rien à m.** I've nothing to wear; **je ne mets plus cette robe** I don't wear this dress any more, I've stopped wearing this dress; **j'ai du mal à m. mes souliers** I find it difficult to get my shoes on; **n'oubliez pas de m. un collier anti-puce à votre chien** don't forget to put a flea collar on your dog

(f) (*faire fonctionner*) (*gaz, chauffage, lumière, radio, télévision etc*) to put on, to turn on, to switch on; **m. en marche** (*machine à laver, télévision etc*) to turn on; (*moteur*) to turn on, to start (up); **m. une machine en route** to turn a machine on, to set a machine going; *Aut* **m. le contact** to start the engine *or* car; **m. un peu le chauffage** to put *or* turn the heating on low; **m. la radio plus fort** to turn up the radio; **m. de la musique** to put on some music, to put some music on; **mets le film de la deux** put on the film that's on Channel 2; **m. sa montre à l'heure** to set one's watch to the correct time; **m. le réveil à cinq heures** to set the alarm for five o'clock

(g) (*installer*) (*moquette, parquet, gazon*) to lay; (*papier peint, étagères*) to put up; **elle a décidé de (faire) m. le chauffage central/l'électricité** she decided to have central heating/electricity put in; **m. la table** *ou* **le couvert** to lay *or* set the table; **m. des rideaux aux fenêtres** to put curtains at the windows, to put up curtains

(h) (*placer dans une situation, un état*) (*en prison, en pension, à l'asile etc*) to put; **m. qn au désespoir** to cause sb to despair; **m. qn au régime/sous antibiotiques** to put sb on a diet/on antibiotics; **m. qn à la torture** to subject sb to torture; **m. qn à la porte** to throw sb out; (*le renvoyer*) to dismiss *or F* sack sb; **m. ses enfants à l'école publique** to send one's children to a state school; **m. le feu à qch** to set fire to sth, to set sth on fire; **m. du linge à sécher, m. à sécher du linge** to hang some washing up *or* out (to dry); **m. du linge à tremper** to put some washing in to soak; **m. de l'eau à chauffer** to put some water on to heat (up); **ça le met dans tous ses états** that gets him into a state; **m. qn dans l'embarras** to embarrass sb; **m. qn dans l'angoisse** to cause sb great anxiety; **m. qn dans l'obligation de faire qch** to force *or* compel sb to do sth; **m. qn en colère** to make sb angry; **la réunion l'a mise d'une humeur exécrable** the meeting put her in a very bad mood *or* made her very bad-tempered; **m. qch en œuvre** to implement sth; **m. une pièce en scène** to direct a play; **m. des vers en musique** to set verse to music; **il a fallu m. le texte en espagnol** the text had to be put into Spanish; **m. le nom au pluriel** to put the noun into the plural; **m. de la gaieté** to brighten up; **ça mettra de la couleur dans la pièce** it will give the room a bit of colour

(i) (*admettre*) **ça va prendre, mettons, trois mois** it'll take, say, three months; **mettons que vous avez** *ou* **ayez raison** suppose *or* let's say you're right; **mettons que ça fasse cent francs** (let's) call it *or* say a hundred francs; **mettons qu'il en soit ainsi** let's assume that that's the case; **mettez que je n'ai rien dit** pretend I didn't say anything

(j) (*écrire*) to write; **que faut-il m. dans les cases de droite?** what do you have to put *or* write in the right-hand boxes?; **mettez votre signature au bas de la page** put your signature at the bottom of the page; **qu'est-ce qu'elle met, dans sa lettre?** what does she say in her letter?; **tu veux lui m. un petit mot?** (*sur la carte, lettre*) do you want to write him a little note?; **tu n'as qu'à m. que je le remercie** (*dans une lettre*) tell him thanks; **m. un texte au propre** to make a fair copy of a text; **m. qch par écrit** to put sth in writing; **tu as oublié de m. une virgule** you forgot to put a comma; **je t'ai mis sur la liste des invités** I've put you on the guest list

(k) (*flanquer*) **j'ai bien envie de lui m. une gifle** I feel like slapping him *or* giving him a slap; **m. son poing dans la figure de qn** to punch sb's face, to give sb a punch in the face; **m. douze balles dans la peau de qn** to put twelve bullets in sb; *F* **on va leur m. la pâtée** (*les battre, les frapper*) we're going to hammer them *or* beat the living daylights out of them; **qu'est-ce qu'il leur a mis!** he gave them a real roasting!

(l) *Arg* **il va falloir m. les bouts** *ou* **les voiles, il va falloir les m.!** we'd better make a move

(m) *Naut* **m. une voile au vent** to hoist *or* set a sail

2 se mettre *vpr* **(a)** (*se placer*) to go, to get; **se m. derrière un arbre** to go *or* get behind a tree; **se m. au lit** to get into bed; **se m. à table** to sit down at the table; **se m. au soleil/à l'ombre** to sit in the sunshine/shade; **se m. à l'abri** to take shelter; **mettez-vous auprès du feu** sit (down) by the fire; **mettez-vous autour de grand-mère pour la photo** gather round grandmother for the photo; **se m. contre un mur** to stand *or* lean against a wall; **se m. debout** to stand up; **mets-toi là et ne bouge plus** stand/sit there and don't move; **où dois-je me m.?** where do you want me to stand/sit?; *Fig* **je ne savais plus où me m.** I didn't know where to put myself; **se m. sur le dos/le ventre** to lie on one's back/stomach; **les tasses se mettent dans le placard de droite** the cups go in the right-hand cupboard; **cette pièce se met facilement/se met dans cette case** this piece goes *or* fits in easily/goes *or* fits in this box

(b) se m. dans (*situation, état*) to get into; **se m. en rage** to get into a rage; **je me suis mis de la peinture dans les cheveux/de la confiture sur les doigts** I've got paint in my hair/jam on my fingers; **se m. dans tous ses états** to get into a state; **se m. au service de qn** to enter sb's service; **se m. en avant** to push oneself forward; **se m. une idée dans la** *ou* **en tête** to get an idea into one's head; **elle s'est mis dans la tête l'idée que …** she's got it into her head that …; **on a fini par se m. d'accord** we finally reached agreement; **se m. au vert** to go to the country, to get some fresh air; **se m. nu** to undress, to strip off

(c) (*commencer*) **se m. à (faire) qch** to begin *or* start *or* set about (doing) sth; **se m. à rire/chanter/pleurer** to begin *or* start to laugh/sing/cry, to start laughing/singing/crying; **il s'est mis à boire après le dessert** he started drinking after dessert; **c'est quand sa femme est morte qu'il s'est mis à boire** he started drinking *or* took to drink after his wife died; **il s'est mis à pleuvoir** it began *or* started to rain, the rain came on; **se m. au travail** to set to work; **il est temps de s'y m.** we'd better get down to it *or* get on with it; **se m. au régime** to put oneself on a diet, to go on a diet; **se m. à l'allemand** to start (learning) German; **se m. à la politique** to go in for *or* take up politics; **se m. en route** to start off, to set off; **se m. au pas** (*dans un défilé*) to fall into step; *F* **elle est insupportable quand elle s'y met** she's unbearable once she gets started *or* going; *F* **si tu t'y mets aussi** if you join in, if you start on me/her/*etc* too

(d) (*revêtir*) (*vêtement*) to wear; (*vernis à ongles, fard à paupières*) to put on; **se m. un pull chaud** to put on a warm pullover; **je n'ai rien à me m.** I haven't got anything to wear, I haven't a thing to wear; **elle ne se met jamais en pantalon/en rouge** she never wears trousers/red; **pourquoi ne te mets-tu pas en jupe ce soir?** why don't you put on *or* wear a skirt this evening?

(e) le temps se met au beau the weather's turning out fine; **le temps se met à la pluie** it's turning to rain

(f) (*se grouper*) **on a dû se m. à trois pour bouger l'armoire** it took three of us to move the wardrobe; **ils se sont mis à trois pour écrire ce livre** the three of them wrote the book together; **on a préféré se m. à cinq pour faire l'exposé** we thought it preferable if five of us gave the presentation; **se m. avec qn** (*faire équipe*) to team up with sb; *F* (*vivre*) to move in *or* live with *or Am F* to shack up with sb

(g) *F* **qu'est-ce qu'ils se sont mis!** they went at it hammer and tongs!, they really laid into each other!

3 *vi* **(a)** *Naut* **m. à la voile** to set sail

(b) *Vulg* **se faire m.** to get shagged; **va te faire m.!** sod off!

meublant [mœblɑ̃] *adj Jur* **meubles meublants** movables

meuble [mœbl] **1** *adj* movable; *Jur* **biens meubles** movables, personal estate, chattels; *Agr* **terre m.** light soil **2** *nm* **(a)** piece of furniture; **meubles** furniture; **être dans ses meubles** to have a place of one's own; *F* **faire partie des meubles** to be part of the furniture; **je manque de meubles de rangement** I don't have much storage space; **m. d'angle** corner unit; **meubles de bureau** office furniture; **m. hi-fi** hi-fi unit **(b)** *Jur* movable, chattel

meublé [mœble] **1** *adj* (*chambre etc*) furnished; **non m.** unfurnished **2** *nm* furnished room; (*appartement*) furnished flat *or Am* apartment; **habiter en m.** to live in lodgings; (*dans un appartement*) to live in a furnished flat

meubler [mœble] **1** *vt* (*pièce*) to furnish; (*ferme*) to stock (**de** with); **ils sont entièrement meublés en Empire/en chêne** all their furniture is Empire style/oak; **m. la conversation** to make conversation **2** *vpr* **se meubler** to furnish one's home; **je me meuble chez IKEA** I buy *or* get my furniture at IKEA

meuf [mœf] *nf très F* bird, female, *Am* chick, dame; (*épouse*) old woman, better half, *Am* old lady

meuglement [møgləmɑ̃] *nm* (*de vache*) lowing, mooing; (*de sirène*) moaning, wailing

meugler [møgle] *vi* (*de vache*) to low, to moo; (*de sirène*) to moan, to wail

meulage [mølaʒ] *nm* grinding (down)

meule [møl] *nf* **(a)** (*de foin, de paille*) stack, rick; (*fumier*)

mushroom compost; **mettre le foin en m.** to stack *or* rick the hay; **m. de foin** haystack, hayrick **(b)** *(de moulin)* millstone; **m. à aiguiser** grindstone; **m. à polir** buff(ing) wheel **(c) m. de fromage** (whole) cheese **(d)** *F* **les meules** *(les fesses)* *(d'une femme)* arse, *Am* ass; *(d'un homme)* buns; **elle/il a de belles meules** she's got a great arse *or Am* ass/he's got nice buns **(e)** *F (mobylette)* moped
meuler [møle] *vt (burin etc)* to grind; *(lentille etc)* to grind (down)
meulette [mølɛt] *nf* small haystack
meulière [møljɛr] **1** *adj f* **pierre m.** millstone (grit) **2** *nf* **(a)** *(carrière)* millstone quarry **(b)** *(pierre)* millstone (grit)
meunerie [mønri] *nf* **(a)** *(activité)* (flour) milling **(b)** *Ind* milling trade
meunier, -ière [mønje, -jɛr] **1** *nm* miller **2** *nf* **meunière (a)** miller's wife **(b)** *(oiseau)* long-tailed tit **3** *adj* **(a)** *(industrie, méthode etc)* (flour-)milling **(b)** *Culin* **truite/sole m.** trout/sole meunière *(coated with flour and fried in butter)*
meurtre [mœrtr] *nm* murder; **au m.!** murder!
meurtri [mœrtri] *adj (bras, fruit etc)* bruised; **visage m.** bruised *or* battered face; *(par la fatigue)* ravaged face; **être tout m.** to be black and blue all over; **elle est sortie très meurtrie de cette expérience** she was bruised by the experience, it was a very bruising experience for her; **je suis m. dans mon cœur** *ou* **âme** I am heartbroken
meurtrier, -ière [mœrtrije, -ijɛr] **1** *adj* **(a)** *(guerre, attentat, colère)* murderous; *(arme)* deadly, lethal; *(épidémie)* lethal; **ce croisement est m.** this junction is a death trap; **l'imprudence rend la route meurtrière** reckless driving turns roads into death traps; **le lundi de Pâques est souvent m.** there are often a lot of deaths on the road on Easter Monday **(b)** *Arch (personne)* murderous, guilty of murder **2** *n* murderer, murderess **3** *nf Archit, Mil* **meurtrière** loophole
meurtrir [mœrtrir] *vt (son bras, fruit etc)* to bruise; **m. qn de coups** to beat sb black and blue; **tu as meurtri mon cœur** you broke my heart
meurtrissure [mœrtrisyr] *nf* bruise
Meuse [møz] *nf* **la M.** the Meuse, the Maas
meute [møt] *nf (de chiens courants)* pack; *Fig* mob, pack, crowd; **chiens de m.** hounds; **lancer la m.** to loose the pack *or* hounds
MEV [mɛv] *nf Ordinat (abrév* **mémoire vive)** RAM
mévente [mevɑ̃t] *nf* **(a)** *(des affaires)* slump, stagnation **(b)** *Vieilli (de biens)* sale at a loss
mexicain, -aine [mɛksikɛ̃, -ɛn] **1** *adj* Mexican **2** *n* **M.** Mexican
Mexico [mɛksiko] *n* Mexico City
Mexique (le) [ləmɛksik] *nm* Mexico
mézigue [mezig] *pron pers Arg (moi)* yours truly; **c'est pour m.** it's for yours truly; **les plaintes c'est pour m.** yours truly has to cope with the complaints; **et m.?** what about me?
mezzanine [mɛdzanin] *nf* **(a)** *(étage)* mezzanine (floor) **(b)** *(fenêtre)* mezzanine window **(c)** *Th* dress circle, *Am* mezzanine
mezzo(-soprano), *pl* **mezzo-sopranos** [mɛdzosɔprano], **-soprani** *Mus* **1** *nm* mezzo(-soprano) (voice) **2** *nf (femme)* mezzo(-soprano)
mezzo-tinto [mɛdzotinto] *nm inv* mezzotint
MF [ɛmɛf] *nf Rad (abrév* **modulation de fréquence)** FM
mg *(abrév* **milligramme)** mg
MGP [ɛmʒepe] *nm (abrév* **marché grand public)** consumer market
Mgr *Rel (abrév* **Monseigneur)** Mgr
mi[1] [mi] *adv* **la mi-avril/-mai** mid-April/-May; **à mi-hauteur** halfway up *or* down; **elle avait de l'eau jusqu'à mi-jambe/mi-cuisse** the water was halfway up her legs/thighs; **il la regardait, mi-amusé, mi-intrigué** he was looking at her half-amused, half-puzzled *or* with a mixture of amusement and puzzlement; **m-figue, m-raisin** half one thing and half another; **un petit sourire mi-f., mi-raisin** a half-hearted *or* wry *or* forced smile; **ton mi-f., mi-raisin** tone (of voice) half in jest and half in earnest; **acier mi-doux** semi-mild steel; **tissu mi-laine mi-soie** wool-silk mixture
mi[2] *nm inv Mus* **(a)** *(note)* E; *(de solfège)* mi; **morceau en mi** piece in E **(b)** *(d'un violon)* first string, E string
miam-miam [mjammjam] *int* yum, yum
miaou [mjau] *nm* miaow, mew; **faire m.** to miaow, to mew
miasmatique [mjasmatik] *adj Litt* miasmic
miasme [mjasm] *nm* miasma
miaulement [mjolmɑ̃] *nm* mewing, miaowing; *(plus aigu)* caterwauling
miauler [mjole] *vi* to mew, to miaow; *(de façon plus aiguë)* to caterwaul
miauleur, -euse [mjolœr, -øz] *adj* mewing, miaowing
mi-bas *nm inv* knee-high; *(tricoté)* knee(-length) sock, *Com* half-hose
mica [mika] *nm Minér* mica
mi-carême, *pl* **mi-carêmes** *nf* mid-Lent
micaschiste [mikaʃist] *nm Minér* mica schist
miche [miʃ] *nf* **(a)** *(pain)* round loaf, *Br* cob (loaf) **(b)** *F* **miches** *(fesses)* bum, *Am* butt; **vire tes miches** move yourself, move your backside; **gare à tes miches** look out, mind yourself
Michel-Ange [mikɛlɑ̃ʒ] *nm* Michelangelo
micheline [miʃlin] *nf Rail* railcar *(invented and equipped by the Michelin Tyre Company)*
mi-chemin (à) [amiʃmɛ̃] *adv* halfway, midway; **on est à m.** we're halfway there
micheton [miʃtɔ̃] *nm Arg* trick, *Am* john; **elle s'est fait cinq michetons dans la soirée** she turned five tricks that evening
michetonner [miʃtɔne] *vi Arg* to turn the occasional trick
mi-clos, *pl* **mi-clos(es)** *adj (yeux, lèvres etc)* half-closed, half-shut
micmac [mikmak] *nm F* scheme; *(résultat)* put-up job; *(désordre)* muddle; **j'en ai assez de tes micmacs** I've had enough of your schemes *or* scheming
mi-corps (à) *adv* **portrait à m.** half-length portrait; **avoir de l'eau jusqu'à m.** to be in water up to one's waist
mi-côte (à) *adv* halfway up the hill
mi-course (à) *adv* at the halfway mark
micro [mikro] **1** *nm F* **(a)** *(microphone)* mike; *(tenu à la main)* baton *or* stick mike; **parler dans le m.** to speak into the mike; **m. caché** concealed microphone **(b)** *Ordinat* micro(computer) **2** *nf Ordinat* microcomputing
▶ **micro**: **m. canon** rifle *or* gun mike; **m. sur casque** headphone talkback; **m. à condensateur** condenser mike; **m-cravate**, *pl* **micros-cravates** lapel mike; **m. directionnel** directional mike; **m. électro-dynamique** dynamic mike; **m. sur perche** fishpole *or* boom mike; **m. portatif** hand microphone; **m. suspendu** hung *or* hanging *or* slung mike; **m. de table** desk mike
microanalyse [mikroanaliz] *nf Ch* microanalysis
microbalance [mikrobalɑ̃s] *nf Phys* microbalance
microbe [mikrɔb] *nm* microbe; *(bactérie)* germ; *F* bug; **je ne veux pas que tu me donnes tes microbes** I don't want your germs; *Fig* **écrase-toi, m.!** push off, you little squirt!
microbicide [mikrɔbisid] **1** *adj* germ-killing, *Spéc* microbicidal **2** *nm* germ-killer, *Spéc* microbicide
microbien, -ienne [mikrɔbjɛ̃, -jɛn] *adj (maladie, culture etc)* microbial, microbic
microbiologie [mikrobjɔlɔʒi] *nf* microbiology
microbiologique [mikrobjɔlɔʒik] *adj* microbiological
microbiologiste [mikrobjɔlɔʒist] *n* microbiologist
microcéphale [mikrosefal] **1** *adj* microcephalous, microcephalic **2** *n* microcephalic
microchirurgie [mikroʃiryrʒi] *nf Méd* microsurgery
microcircuit [mikrosirkɥi] *nm Ordinat* microcircuit; **microcircuits** microcircuitry
microclimat [mikroklima] *nm* microclimate
microcosme [mikrɔkɔsm] *nm* microcosm
microcosmique [mikrokɔsmik] *adj* microcosmic
microcoupure [mikrokupyr] *nf Électron* power blip
microdisquette [mikrodiskɛt] *nf Ordinat* microfloppy
microéconomie [mikroekɔnɔmi] *nf* microeconomics
microéconomique [mikroekɔnɔmik] *adj* microeconomic
microédition [mikroedisjɔ̃] *nf Ordinat* desktop publishing, DTP
microélectronique [mikroelɛktrɔnik] *nf* microelectronics
micro-environnement, *pl* **micro-environnements** *nm* micro-environment
micro(-)espace, *pl* **micro(-)espaces** *nm Ordinat* micro-space
microfiche [mikrofiʃ] *nf* microfiche
microfilm [mikrofilm] *nm* microfilm
microfilmer [mikrofilme] *vt* to microfilm
micrographie [mikrɔgrafi] *nf* micrography
micrographique [mikrɔgrafik] *adj* micrographic
micro-informatique *nf Ordinat* microcomputing
micro-interrupteur, *pl* **micro-interrupteurs** *nm Ordinat* microswitch
micromarché [mikromarʃe] *nm* micromarket
micromarketing [mikromarketiŋ] *nm* micromarketing
micromercatique [mikromɛkatik] *nf* micromarketing
micromètre [mikrɔmɛtr] *nm* micrometer
micrométrique [mikrɔmetrik] *adj* micrometric(al); **vis m.** micrometer screw
micron [mikrɔ̃] *nm* micron
micronisation [mikrɔnizasjɔ̃] *nf Ordinat* downsizing
microniser [mikrɔnize] *vt Ordinat* to downsize
micro-onde, *pl* **micro-ondes** [mikrɔɔ̃d] *nf* micro-wave; **four à micro-ondes** microwave oven
micro-ondes *nm inv* microwave (oven); **faire cuire qch au m.** to cook sth in the microwave, to microwave sth

micro-ordinateur, *pl* **micro-ordinateurs** *nm Ordinat* micro(computer)
micro-organisme, *pl* **micro-organismes** *nm* micro-organism
microphone [mikrɔfɔn] *nm* microphone; (*de téléphone*) mouthpiece; **m. à condensateur** condenser microphone; **m. sur girafe** sound-boom microphone; **m. sur pied** stand microphone
microphotographie [mikrofɔtɔgrafi] *nf* **(a)** (*activité*) microphotography, photomicrography **(b)** (*résultat*) microphotograph, photomicrograph
microphotographique [mikrofɔtɔgrafik] *adj* microphotographic, photomicrographic
microphysique [mikrofizik] *nf* microphysics
micropilule [mikropilyl] *nf Pharm* minipill
microplaquette [mikroplakɛt] *nf Électron* chip
microprocesseur [mikroprɔsesœr] *nm Ordinat* microprocessor; **m. en tranches** bit slice microprocessor
microprogramme [mikroprɔgram] *nm Ordinat* microprogram
microscope [mikrɔskɔp] *nm* microscope; **regarder au m.** to look through a microscope; **regarder qch au m.** to look at sth through *or* under a microscope; **visible au m.** visible under the microscope; **m. électronique** electron microscope; **m. électronique à balayage** electron scanning microscope; **m. optique** light microscope
microscopie [mikrɔskɔpi] *nf* microscopy
microscopique [mikrɔskɔpik] *adj* microscopic
microseconde [mikrosəgɔ̃d] *nf* microsecond
microsillon [mikrɔsijɔ̃] *nm* **(a)** (*sillon*) microgroove **(b)** **(disque) m.** long-playing record, LP
microsociété [mikrosɔsjete] *nf* miniature society, society in miniature
microsociologie [mikrosɔsjɔlɔʒi] *nf* = sociology of small groups
microtome [mikrɔtɔm] *nm* microtome
miction [miksjɔ̃] *nf* urination, *Spéc* micturition
midi [midi] **1** *nm no pl* **(a)** (*heure*) midday, (twelve) noon, twelve o'clock; **il est m.** it's twelve o'clock; **avant/après m.** before/after twelve (o'clock); **m. et demi** half-past twelve; **entre m. et deux** at lunch time; *Fig* **chercher m. à quatorze heures** to look for difficulties where there are none, to complicate matters
(b) (*moment du déjeuner*) lunch time; **tu fais quoi, ce m.?** what are you doing at lunch time *or* for lunch?; **à m.** at lunch time; **à m., j'ai mangé des frites** I had chips at lunch time *or* for lunch; **repas de m.** midday meal
(c) (*milieu du jour*) **en plein m.** at the height of noon
(d) (*sud*) south; **chambre au m.** room facing south; **le M. (de la France)** the South of France
2 *adj inv* (*de taille moyenne*) **chaîne m.** midi system
midinette [midinet] *nf* **(a)** silly young girl; **des lectures de m.** slushy novels **(b)** *Vieilli* (*ouvrière*) shop girl; (*couturière*) young dressmaker
mi-distance (à) *adv* halfway, midway; **nous sommes à m. de notre but** we are halfway to our goal
midship, *pl* **midships** [mitʃip] *nm* midshipman
mie¹ [mi] *nf* crumb (*of loaf, as opposed to crust*); **pain de m.** sandwich loaf
mie² *nf Arch, Litt* (= **amie**) **ma m.** my pet, my love, darling, sweetheart
miel [mjɛl] **1** *nm* honey; **une tartine de m.** a slice of bread and honey; **m. rosat** rose honey; *Fig* **faire son m. de qch** to make capital out of sth; *Fig* **elle était (tout sucre et) tout m.** she was all sweetness and light **2** *int F* **et m.!** oh, sugar!
miellé [mjele] *adj Litt* (*parfum*) honeyed; (*boisson*) tasting of honey
mielleusement [mjɛløzmɑ̃] *adv Péj* (*dire*) in honeyed tones; **sourire m.** to give a sweet, sugary smile
mielleux, -euse [mjɛlø, -øz] *adj* **(a)** (*boisson, bonbon etc*) tasting of honey **(b)** *Péj* (*discours, sourire etc*) sugary; (*personne*) sugary, smooth
mien, mienne [mjɛ̃, mjɛn] **1** *pron poss* [①A30,8; C20,E,2] **le mien, la mienne, les miens, les miennes** mine; **je te prête le m.** you can borrow mine; **tu n'as qu'à prendre la mienne** just take mine; **il ressemble au mien** it looks like mine; **je veux bien te donner du m.** please have some of mine; **tu n'en as pas besoin, tu as le m.** you don't need it, you've got mine; **les deux miens** my two, both of mine; (*en insistant*) my own two; **je lui ai laissé deux des miens** I gave him two of mine; *très F* **le m. de bébé est plus intelligent** my baby is more intelligent; *F* **à la mienne!** (*en buvant*) here's to me!
2 *nm* **le m.** (*ce qui m'appartient*) mine; **je devrais y mettre du m.** I should really do my share
3 *nmpl* **les miens** (*ma famille*) my family, *Am* my folks; (*mes partisans*) my followers; (*mes coéquipiers*) my team-mates
4 *adj poss Litt* mine; **un m. cousin** a cousin of mine; **je fais miens tes principes** I've adopted your principles as my own; **je fais miennes les félicitations qu'il vous adresse** I join (with) him in congratulating you
miette [mjɛt] *nf* (*de pain*) crumb; (*morceau*) morsel, scrap; **miettes de crabe/thon** flaked crab/tuna; **elle m'a laissé quelques miettes de son gâteau** she left me a few crumbs of her cake; **ils n'en ont pas laissé une m.** they didn't leave a crumb, they scoffed the lot; **mettre** *ou* **réduire qch en miettes** (*objet*) to smash sth to pieces *or* bits *or* smithereens; **je n'en prendrai qu'une m.** I'll just have a morsel *or* a very little *or F* a smidgeon; *Fig* **elle n'a pas perdu une m. de la conversation** not one scrap of the conversation escaped her *or* passed her by
mieux [mjø] **1** *adv* **(a)** [①A40,C,1,a] (*comp*) better; **elle danse m. que moi** she dances better than I do; **j'avais espéré m.** I had hoped for better *or* more; **je ne peux pas m. dire** *ou* **dire m.** that's all I can say, what more can I say?; **il ne parle pas m. l'italien que l'espagnol** his Italian isn't any *or* is no better than his Spanish, he speaks Italian no better than he does Spanish; **on va vivre ensemble, m. on va se marier!** we're going to live together, better still, we're getting married!; **je ne demande pas m.!** I'd be delighted, there's nothing I'd like better; **je ne demande pas m. que (de) te rendre service** I'd be delighted to help, there's nothing I'd like better than to help; **il vaut m. les surveiller** you should watch them more closely; **vous feriez m. de m'écouter** you'd do better to *or* you'd be well advised to listen to me, you'd better listen to me; *Prov* **m. vaut tard que jamais** better late than never; *Prov* **m. vaut prévenir que guérir** prevention is better than cure; **elle va m. que jamais** she has never been better; **il va m.** he's (feeling) better; **il ne va pas m.** he is no better, he isn't any better; **ça va m.** things are improving; *F* **ça va m.?** feeling better?; *F* **j'ai l'impression que, Bernard, ça va m. aujourd'hui** I'm under the impression that Bernard is feeling better today; **comment ça va, la santé/l'école/avec ton mari? – ça va m.** how are you/things at school/things with your husband? – better; **ça ira m. demain** it'll *or* things'll be better tomorrow; *Hum* **je vois que ça ne va pas m.!** you've not improved one bit!, there hasn't been any change for the better!; *Scol* **'peut m. faire'** can do better; **moins je travaille, m. je me porte** the less I work, the better I feel; **plus je le vois, m. je l'apprécie** the more I see of him, the more I appreciate him *or* the better I like him; **de m. en m.** better and better; **au bureau, ça va de m. en m.** it's getting better and better at the office, things are improving all the time at the office; **m. encore ...** better still ...; **m. encore, je dirais que c'est un artiste** I'd go even further and describe him as an artist; **on dirait m. 'pallier les inconvénients'** 'pallier les inconvénients' is more correct; **qui dit m.?** (*pour faire monter les enchères*) any advance?; **elle va on ne peut m.** she's in the best of health; **ce travail est on ne peut m. fait** no-one could have done better, he has/you have/*etc* done a perfect job; **elle coud on ne peut m.** no-one sews better than she does; **faire qch à qui m. m.** to vie with one another in doing sth; **ils criaient à qui m. m.** it was a case of who could shout the loudest
(b) le m., la m., les m. (the) best; **la femme la m. habillée de Paris** the best-dressed woman in Paris; **c'est à Paris que les femmes sont le m. habillées** you find the best-dressed women in Paris; **c'est à ce bureau que je travaille le m.** I work best at this desk; **le plus tôt sera le m.** the sooner the better; **il s'en est acquitté le m. du monde** nobody could have done it better; **un service des m. organisés** an extremely well organized department; **fais du m. que tu peux** do the best you can
2 *adj* **vous serez m. dans ce fauteuil** you'll be more comfortable *or* better in this armchair; **il est m.** he's (feeling) better; **vous ne trouverez pas m. comme hôtel** you won't find a better hotel; **tu ne trouveras rien de m.** you won't find anything better; *F* **c'est ce qu'il y a de m., c'est ce qu'on fait de m.** it's the best there is; **ce qu'il y a de m. sur le marché** the best (there is) on the market; **c'est ce qu'il y a de m. si ...** it's ideal if ...; **c'est ce qu'il y a de m. (à faire) dans votre cas** that's the best thing to do (in your case); **ce que vous avez de m. à faire c'est de ...** the best thing you can do is to ...; **si tu n'as rien de m. à faire** if you've nothing better to do; **tu ne crois pas que tu as m. à faire que ...** don't you think there are better things to do than ...; *Iron* **elle n'a rien trouvé de m. que d'aller le répéter à sa mère** what did she do but go and tell her mother; **c'est m. comme ça** its better like that; *F* **c'était la m. des trois sœurs** she was the best of the three sisters; (*la plus jolie*) she was the best-looking of the three sisters

3 *nm* **le m. est l'ennemi du bien** leave well (enough) alone, *F* if it ain't broke don't fix it; **faute de m.** for want *or* lack of anything better; **il y a un m.** *ou* **du m.** there's been a change for the better, there's been an improvement; **faire** *ou* **agir pour le m.** to act for the best; **mais on fera pour le m.** but we'll do our best, but we'll do the best we can; **le m. serait de ...** the best thing would be to ..., it would be best to ...; **le m. serait qu'il se désiste de lui-même** it would be best if he withdrew of his own accord; **(en mettant les choses) au m., je ferai ce travail en deux mois** I can do the job in two months at best; **(en mettant les choses) au m., je ne pourrai pas être là avant six heures** I can't be there before six o'clock at the earliest; **au m., il la vendra 100 francs** he'll get a hundred francs at most for it; **agir au m. des intérêts de qn** to act in sb's best interests; **être au m. avec qn** to be on the best of terms with sb; **faire de son m.** to do one's best, to do the best one can

mieux-disant, *pl* **mieux-disants** [mjødizɑ̃] *nm* elite

mieux-être [mjøzɛtr] *nm no pl* improved condition; **les progrès techniques doivent servir au m. des hommes** technical progress must improve the human condition

mieux-vivre *nm no pl* better *or* higher standard of living; **la lutte pour le m.** the struggle for a better *or* higher standard of living

mièvre [mjɛvr] *adj Péj* (*fille*) insipid; (*ton*) simpering; **des trucs mièvres à la télé** stupid things on TV

mièvrerie [mjɛvrəri] *nf Péj* insipidness; **d'une m. exaspérante** exasperatingly insipid; **ces mièvreries qu'on nous sert à la télé** these stupid programmes *or* the pap they show on TV

mi-fin, *pl* **mi-fins** *adj Com* medium

mignard [miɲar] *adj* = **mignon**; *Péj* affected

mignardise [miɲardiz] *nf* **(a)** (*caractère mignon*) charm, *Péj* affectedness **(b) (œillet) m.** garden pink

mignon, -onne [miɲɔ̃, -ɔn] **1** *adj* delightful, charming; (*enfant*) darling, *surtout Am* cute; **un mec super m.** a great looking guy; **est-elle mignonne!** isn't she a darling!; **c'est m. comme tout chez eux** they have a delightful *or* charming home; **sois m., va me chercher mes cigarettes** be a dear *or* an angel and get my cigarettes **2** *n* **(a)** (*terme d'affection*) pet, darling, dear **(b)** *Arch* (*favori*) minion

mignonnette [miɲɔnɛt] *nf* **(a)** (*plante*) (*saxifrage ombreuse*) London pride; (*chicorée sauvage*) wild chicory; (*œillet mignardise*) garden pink **(b)** *Tex* mignonette lace **(c)** (*poivre*) coarse-ground pepper **(d)** (*gravier*) gravel **(e)** (*flacon*) miniature

migraine [migrɛn] *nf* migraine; *F* (*mal de tête*) headache; **elle a des migraines** she has migraines; **elle a la m.** she has a headache; **migraine ophtalmique** headache caused by eyestrain

migraineux, -euse [migrɛnø, -øz] *n* migraine sufferer

migrant, -ante [migrɑ̃, -ɑ̃t] **1** *adj* migrant **2** *n* migrant

migrateur, -trice [migratœr, -tris] *adj* (*animaux*) migrating, migratory; (*personnes*) migrant

migration [migrasjɔ̃] *nf Orn* migration; *Fig* exodus; **au moment des vacances, les migrations sont impressionnantes** the number of people on the move at holiday time is staggering

migratoire [migratwar] *adj* migratory

migrer [migre] *vi* to migrate (**vers** to); *Ordinat* **faire m.** to transmit

mi-jambe(s) (à) *adv* halfway up the leg(s)

mijaurée [miʒɔre] *nf Péj* conceited *or* affected woman; **ne fais pas la** *ou* **ta m.!** don't give yourself such airs!

mijoter [miʒɔte] **1** *vt Culin* to simmer, to let simmer; *Fig* (*projet, vengeance*) to mull over; **elle mijote avec amour de bons petits plats à son mari** she lovingly prepares wonderful meals for her husband; **m. un complot** to hatch a plot; **qu'est-ce que vous mijotez encore?** now what are you scheming *or* up to? **2** *vi* to simmer; *Fig* **je vois bien que ça mijote dans sa tête** I know he's up to something **3 se mijoter** *vpr Fig* **il se mijote quelque chose** there's something in the wind, something's brewing

mikado [mikado] *nm* Mikado

mil[1] [mil] *adj* (*used only in writing out dates AD*) thousand; **l'an m. neuf cent quatre-vingt-un** (the year) nineteen hundred and eighty-one

mil[2] [mij, mil] *nm* (*céréale*) millet

milady, *pl* **miladys** [miledi] *nf* (*titre*) my Lady; (*noble*) titled (English) lady

milan [milɑ̃] *nm* (*oiseau*) kite

mildiou [mildju] *nm* mildew; (*de la vigne*) brown rot; **atteint de m.** mildewed

mildiousé [mildjuze] *adj* (*vigne etc*) mildewed

mile [majl] *nm* mile

miliaire [miljɛr] *Méd* **1** *adj* (*glande, fièvre etc*) miliary **2** *nf* prickly heat, *Spéc* miliaria

milice [milis] *nf* militia

milicien, -ienne [milisjɛ̃, -jɛn] *n* member of a/the militia, *m* militiaman

milieu, -ieux [miljø] *nm* **(a)** (*centre*) middle; **couper/plier qch en son m.** to cut sth through/to fold sth in the middle; **il est entré en plein m. d'une discussion** he came in right in the middle of a discussion; **au m. de** in the middle of, *Litt* amid(st), in the midst of; **au beau m. de la rue/la cour** right in the middle of the street/the yard; **au m. du courant** in midstream; **au m. de l'été** in the middle *or* at the height of summer; **au m. de l'hiver** in the middle *or* depth(s) of winter; **au m. de la nuit** in the middle of the night, *Litt* at dead of night; **vers le m. du mois** about the middle of the month; **la table du m.** the middle table

(b) (*environnement*) (*physique*) environment, surroundings, milieu; (*social*) (social) sphere, circle; *Phys* medium; **le m. familial** the home environment, family surroundings; **les animaux dans leur m.** animals in their environment *or* natural surroundings; **je n'appartiens pas à leur m., je ne suis pas de leur m.** I don't belong to *or* I'm not part of their set *or* circle, I don't move in their circles; **dans les milieux bien informés** in well informed circles *or* quarters; **elle ne tient pas à changer de m.** she's not keen on a change of surroundings; **c'est parce qu'elle n'est pas dans son m.** it's because she's not in her usual surroundings

(c) le m., les gens du m. the underworld; **c'est un type du m.** he's a member of the underworld

(d) (*moyenne*) middle course; **il n'y a pas de m.** there's no middle course; **le juste m.** the happy medium, the golden mean; **tenir le m. entre ... et ...** to steer a middle course between ... and ...

militaire [militɛr] **1** *adj* (*discipline, service, hôpital, opération etc*) military; **véhicule m.** military *or* army vehicle; **à huit heures, heure m.** at eight o'clock sharp; **la marine m.** the Navy; **port m.** naval port **2** *nm* serviceman, soldier; **les militaires** the military, the armed forces, the services; **m. de carrière** career *or* professional soldier

militairement [militɛrmɑ̃] *adv* militarily; **saluer m.** to give a military salute; **occuper une ville m.** to occupy a town by force of arms

militant, -ante [militɑ̃, -ɑ̃t] **1** *adj* militant **2** *n* militant; (*d'un parti*) member; **m. de base** grassroots member

militantisme [militɑ̃tism] *nm* militancy

militarisation [militarizasjɔ̃] *nf* militarization

militariser [militarize] *vt* to militarize

militarisme [militarism] *nm* militarism

militariste [militarist] *adj, n* militarist

militer [milite] *vi* to militate (**pour, en faveur de** in favour of, **contre** against); **m. au PS** to be a member of the Socialist Party

milk-shake, *pl* **milk-shakes** [milkʃɛk] *nm* milk shake; **m. à la vanille** vanilla milk shake

millage [milaʒ] *nm Can* mileage

mille[1] [mil] **1** *adj inv* [①**A12**,1,h,i; **B56**,A] **(a)** thousand; **m. hommes** a thousand men, one thousand men; **deux m.** two thousand; **trois cent m. hommes** three hundred thousand men; **m. un** a thousand and one, one thousand and one; **Les M. et une Nuits** the Arabian Nights, the Thousand and One Nights; **l'an m.** the year one thousand; **l'an m. neuf cent avant J-C.** (the year) nineteen hundred B.C.

(b) *Fig* (*beaucoup de*) (*exemples, raisons*) countless, numerous, many; **je vous l'ai dit m. fois** I've told you a thousand times, I've told you time and time again; **vous avez m. fois raison** you are so right; **m. baisers** much love; **m. mercis** many thanks, thank you so much; **m. pardons** *ou* **regrets** I am so sorry; **c'est m. fois trop grand** it's miles *or* *Am* way too big; **casser qch en m. morceaux** to smash sth to smithereens; **souffrir** *ou* **endurer m. morts** (*physiquement*) to suffer agonies, to go through hell; (*moralement*) to go through hell, to die a thousand deaths; **j'étais à m. lieues de me douter que ...** I never for a moment suspected that ...; **je te le donne en m.** you'll never guess in a million years

2 *nm inv* **(a)** (*chiffre*) thousand; **m. plus m.** a thousand plus a thousand, one thousand plus one thousand; **par m. de briques vendu(es)** per thousand bricks sold, for every thousand bricks sold; **un habitant sur m.** one inhabitant in a thousand; **les chances de guérison sont de dix pour m.** there's a one in a hundred chance of a cure; **un taux de natalité de 5 pour m.** a birthrate of 0.5 per cent; **ils sont morts par centaines de m.** they died in (their) hundreds of thousands

(b) *Fig* **mettre** *ou* **donner dans le m.** to hit the bull's eye; *F* **il gagne des m. et des cents** he makes a mint

mille[2] *nm* (*mesure*) mile (= 1.609 m); **m. (marin** *ou* **nautique)** nautical mile

mille(-)feuille, *pl* **mille-feuilles** [milfœj] **1** *nf Bot* milfoil, yarrow **2** *nm Culin* millefeuille, *US* napoleon
millénaire 1 *adj* (*arbre, monument*) a thousand years old; **cette superstition est plusieurs fois m.** the superstition has existed for several thousands of years **2** *nm* [①A13,5] thousand years, millenium; (*anniversaire*) millennium, millenary; **dater du premier m. av. J-C.** to date from the first millenium BC; **cette tradition est vieille d'au moins un m.** the tradition has existed for at least a thousand years
millénarisme [milenarism] *nm* millenarianism
millénariste [milenarist] *adj, n* millenarian, millenary
millénium [milenjɔm] *nm* [①A13,5] millennium
mille-pattes [milpat] *nm inv* centipede, millipede
mille(-)pertuis [milpɛrtɥi] *nm inv Bot* St John's wort
mille-raies [milrɛ] **1** *nm* needlecord **2** *adj* **velours m.** needlecord
millésime [milezim] *nm* (*de voiture*) year of manufacture; (*de vin*) year, vintage; (*sur pièce, timbre*) date; **il ne boit que de grands millésimes** he only drinks vintage wine
millésimé [milezime] *adj* (*vin*) vintage; (*pièce*) dated
millet [mijɛ] *nm Bot* millet; **(grains de) m.** birdseed, canary seed
milliampère [miliɑ̃pɛr] *nm* milliamp(ere)
milliard [miljar] *nm* [①A70,16,1] billion, *Br Vieilli* one thousand million(s), milliard; **dès que j'aurai un m., je prends ma retraite** I'll retire as soon as I make my million *or* fortune
milliardaire [miljardɛr] *adj, n* billionaire
milliardième [miljardjɛm] *adj, n* billionth, *Br Vieilli* one thousand millionth
millibar [milibar] *nm Météo* millibar
millième [miljɛm] *adj, n* thousandth
millier [milje] *nm* thousand; **un m. de personnes** a thousand people; **des milliers de personnes** thousands of people; **par milliers** in thousands
milligramme [miligram] *nm* milligram(me)
millilitre [mililitr] *nm* millilitre, *US* milliliter
millimètre [milimɛtr] *nm* millimetre, *US* millimeter
millimétré [milimetre], **millimétrique** [milimetrik] *adj* **échelle millimétrée** millimetre *or US* millimeter scale; **papier m.** graph paper
million [miljɔ̃] *nm* [①A12,1,h,i] million; **quatre millions d'hommes** four million men; **riche à millions** worth millions; **il n'y en a pas des millions à s'appeler comme ça** there can't be too many people with a name like that
millionième [miljɔnjɛm] *adj, n* millionth
millionnaire [miljɔnɛr] *adj, n* millionaire
milliseconde [milis(ə)gɔ̃d] *nf* millisecond
millivolt [milivɔlt] *nm* millivolt
milord, [milɔr] *nm* **(a)** (*titre*) my Lord; (*noble*) (English) nobleman; *Fig* immensely wealthy man **(b)** *Arch* (*voiture*) victoria
mi-lourd *pl* **mi-lourds** *adj, nm Boxe* **(poids) m.** light heavyweight (boxer)
mime [mim] **1** *nm* mime, (art of) miming; **faire du m.** to mime, to do mime; **spectacle de m.** mime show **2** *n* (*personne*) mime; (*imitateur*) mimic
mimer [mime] *vt* **(a)** to mime; **m. une scène** to mime a scene, to act a scene in dumb show **(b)** (*imiter*) to mimic
mimétique [mimetik] *adj Zool* mimetic; **le pouvoir m. de sa voix** his ability to imitate other people's voices
mimétisme [mimetism] *nm Zool* mimicry, *Spéc* mimesis; **par m., elle a fini par faire aussi de la peinture** taking the attitude that, 'if you can't beat 'em, join 'em', she ended up doing painting too; **ils le font tous par m.** they can't help copying each other, they can't help mimicking each other
mimi [mimi] **1** *nm Enf* **(a)** (*chat*) pussy (cat), kitty; **mon petit m.** my darling, my pet **(b)** (*baiser*) kiss; **fais m. à ta sœur** give your sister a kiss; **faire un gros m. à qn** to give sb a big kiss; **elle adore faire des mimis à son petit frère** she loves cuddling her little brother **2** *adj F* (*mignon*) gorgeous, *surtout Am* cute
mimique [mimik] **1** *adj* **langage m.** sign language **2** *nf* (*expression*) expression; (*grimace*) grimace; (*de sourd-muet*) sign language; **il s'exprime beaucoup par m.** he uses his face to convey his feelings
mimodrame [mimɔdram] *nm Th* mime
mimolette [mimɔlɛt] *nf Culin* = type of firm cheese
mimosa [mimoza] *nm* mimosa
mi-moyen, *pl* **mi-moyens** *adj, nm Boxe* **(poids) m.** welterweight (boxer)
min (*abrév* **minimum**) min
minable [minabl] *Péj* **1** *adj* (*appartement, apparence*) shabby, seedy; (*personne*) pathetic; **salaire m.** mere pittance (of a wage), miserable *or* pathetic wage; **c'est m., ce que tu lui as fait** that was a rotten trick you played on him **2** *n* failure, loser; **quelle bande de minables** what a pathetic *or* useless bunch
minaret [minarɛ] *nm* minaret
minauder [minode] *vi* to simper
minauderie [minodri] *nf* simpering; **minauderies** simpering (manner)
minaudier, -ière [minodje, -jɛr] *adj* (*personne*) simpering, affected
mince [mɛ̃s] **1** *adj* **(a)** (*fin*) (*planche, étoffe, tranche, mur etc*) thin; (*personne*) slim, slender

(b) (*insuffisant*) (*prétexte*) slim, thin; (*preuves*) slim, thin, scant; (*profit*) small, slight; (*chance*) slight; **mes connaissances dans ce domaine sont trop minces** I know too little about this field, my knowledge in this field is too scanty; **d'un intérêt un peu m.** of little interest; **m. revenu** slender *or* small *or* scanty income; **tes arguments sont un peu minces** your arguments are a bit poor *or* feeble; *F* **ce n'est pas une m. affaire** it's not an easy job, it's not easy

2 *int F* **m. (alors)!** (*surprise*) well, I'm blowed; (*déception*) blast (it)!

3 *adv* thinly
minceur [mɛ̃sœr] *nf* **(a)** (*de couche, de peau*) thinness; (*de personne*) slimness, slenderness; **elle est d'une m. extraordinaire** she is extraordinarily slim **(b)** (*insuffisance*) scantiness; **étant donné la m. de mes revenus** since my income is so small
mincir [mɛ̃sir] *vi* to get thinner *or* slimmer, to lose weight
mine[1] [min] *nf* **(a)** (*gisement*) mine; **travailler à la m.** to work in the mine, to be a miner; **exploitation des mines** mining; **m. de charbon** coalmine, colliery, pit; **m. d'or** goldmine; *Fig* **ce travail est loin d'être une m. d'or** you won't get rich doing this job; **m. à ciel ouvert** opencast mine; *Fig* **une m. de renseignements** a mine of information

(b) *Admin* **les Mines** = government department responsible for supervising all construction projects involving tunnelling; **École des Mines** = university level institute for geological engineers; **ingénieur des Mines** = geological engineer (who has graduated from the École des Mines); **service des Mines** = government department which verifies the roadworthiness of cars which have been involved in accidents

(c) m. (de crayon) (pencil) lead; **crayon à m. grasse/dure** soft/hard pencil; **m. de plomb** graphite, blacklead

(d) *Mil, Constr etc* mine; **poser** *ou* **mouiller une m.** to lay a mine; **faire jouer une m.** to fire a blast *or* a mine; **coup de m.** blast; **attention aux coups de m.!** (*sur panneau*) danger, blasting; **m. flottante** floating mine; **mouilleur de mines** minelayer; **champ de mines** minefield; **m. terrestre** landmine
mine[2] *nf* (*de personne*) appearance, look; **mines** (*de bébé*) gestures, expressions; **avoir bonne/mauvaise m.** to look well/ill; *Iron* **nous avons bonne m. maintenant!** we do look good *or* silly!; **plat qui a bonne m.** dish that looks good *or* appetizing; **sa bonne m. fait plaisir à voir** it's a pleasure to see him/her looking so well; **avoir une m. resplendissante** to look in the best of health; **vous avez meilleure m.** you're looking better; **il en a une (sale) m.!** he does look ill; **avoir une m. de papier mâché** *ou* **de déterré** to look like death warmed up; **m. boudeuse** sulky expression; **elle a toujours une m. réjouie** she always looks happpy; **prendre une m. contrite** to look offended; **ne fais pas cette m.** don't look like that; **faire** *ou* **avoir triste m.** to look down in the dumps; **faire bonne m.** to put a good face on it *or* on things; **faire bonne m. à** *ou* **devant qn** to be pleasant to sb, to greet sb pleasantly *or* with a smile; **faire grise m.** to look miserable *or* po-faced; **faire grise m. à qn** to give sb a cool reception; **juger les gens sur la m.** to judge people by *or* on appearances; **sous sa m. d'homme rangé** behind that sober exterior of his; **il ne faut pas vous fier à sa m. de petite fille sage** don't trust that butter-wouldn't-melt-in-my-mouth expression of hers; *Fig* **ça/il ne paie pas de m.** it/he isn't much to look at; **faire m. d'être fâché** to pretend to be *or* look as though one is angry; **il a fait m. de me suivre** he made as if to follow me; *F* **m. de rien, essaie de vérifier** try to check on it without letting on (what you're up to); *F* **m. de rien, l'affaire progresse** the work is progressing, though you wouldn't think so to look at it; *Péj* **faire des mines** to simper; **elles font des mines devant le miroir** they're making faces in the mirror
miner[1] [mine] *vt* **(a)** (*saper*) (*forteresse etc*) to mine; **la mer mine les falaises** the sea is undermining the cliffs *or* is eating the cliffs away **(b)** *Fig* **la fièvre l'a miné** fever has undermined *or* sapped his strength; **ses soucis la minent** her worries are wearing her down; **miné par l'envie** eaten up *or* consumed with envy
miner[2] *vt* (*poser des mines dans*) to mine

minerai [minrε] *nm* ore; **m. de fer** iron ore
minéral, -ale, -aux, -ales [mineral, -o] **1** *adj* mineral **2** *nm* mineral
minéralier [mineralje] *nm* ore tanker
minéralisation [mineralizasjɔ̃] *nf* mineralization
minéraliser [mineralize] *vt* to mineralize
minéralogie [mineralɔʒi] *nf* mineralogy
minéralogique [mineralɔʒik] *adj* **(a)** *Géol* mineralogical **(b)** *Aut Admin* **numéro m.** registration number, *US* license *or Can* licence number; **plaque m.** number plate, *US* license *or Can* licence plate
minéralogiste [mineralɔʒist] *n* mineralogist
Minerve [minεrv] *nf Myth* Minerva
minerve *nf Méd* (surgical) collar
minestrone [minεstrɔn] *nm Culin* minestrone
minet, -ette [minε, -εt] *n F* **(a)** (*chat*) pussy (cat), kitty; **mon m. /ma minette** (*terme d'affection*) my darling, my pet **(b)** *Péj F* (*jeune*) trendy; **tu as vu la minette là-bas!** look at that bimbo over there
mineur[1] [minœr] *nm* **(a)** (*ouvrier*) (coal) miner, collier; **m. de fond** underground worker **(b)** *Mil* sapper
mineur[2]**, -eure** [minœr] **1** *adj* **(a)** (*inférieur*) minor, lesser; **Asie Mineure** Asia Minor **(b)** *Jur* under age **(c)** *Mus* (*note, gamme etc*) minor; **en ut m.** in C minor **(d)** (*de moindre importance*) minor; **ce sont des soucis mineurs** these are minor worries **2** *n Jur* minor; **ce film est interdit aux mineurs** this film is restricted to over-18s; **cet établissement est interdit aux mineurs** these premises are banned to persons under 18 **3** *nm Mus* minor key
mini [mini] *F* **1** *adj inv* mini; **la mode m. est de retour** the mini is back (in fashion) **2** *nf* mini(skirt) **3** *adv* **s'habiller m.** to wear miniskirts
miniature [minjatyr] **1** *nf* miniature; **peintre de miniatures** miniature painter, miniaturist; **en m.** in miniature, on a small scale; **c'est tout sa mère en m.** she's a miniature version of her mother **2** *adj inv* miniature
miniaturisation [minjatyrizasjɔ̃] *nf* miniaturization; **la m. de l'informatique** computer (circuitry) miniaturization
miniaturiser [minjatyrize] **1** *vt* to miniaturize; **un téléviseur miniaturisé** a mini *or* miniature television **2** *vpr* **se miniaturiser** to become miniaturized; **la hi-fi se miniaturise** sound systems are getting much smaller
miniaturiste [minjatyrist] *n* miniaturist, miniature painter
minibar [minibar] *nm* **(a)** (*dans le train*) trolley; **un service de m. est assuré dans ce train** there is a trolley service on the train **(b)** (*à l'hôtel*) minibar; **avez-vous consommé au m.?** did you have anything from the minibar?
minibus [minibys] *nm* minibus
minicassette [minikasεt] **1** *nf* mini-cassette **2** *nm* portable tape recorder
minichaîne [miniʃεn] *nf* mini-hifi
mini-disquette, *pl* **mini-disquettes** *nf* minidisk, mini-floppy
minier, -ière [minje, -jεr] **1** *adj* (*industrie, région etc*) mining **2** *nf* **minière** surface *or* opencast mine
minigolf [minigɔlf] *nm* crazy-golf
mini(-)jupe, *pl* **mini(-)jupes** *nf* miniskirt
minimal, -aux [minimal, -o] *adj* (*température, durée*) minimum; (*art*) minimal; *Ling* **paire minimale** minimal pair
minimalisme [minimalism] *nm Beaux-Arts* minimalism
minimaliste [minimalist] *adj, n Beaux-Arts* minimalist
minime [minim] **1** *adj* (*dégâts, implication*) minimal; (*rôle*) minor; (*perte*) trivial; (*valeur*) trifling **2** *n* **(a)** *Sp* junior (*to 15 years old*) **(b)** *Rel Hist* Minim friar
minimisation [minimizasjɔ̃] *nf* minimization; **ce n'est pas la m. de nos problèmes qui va les résoudre** we won't solve our problems by minimizing them *or F* by playing them down
minimiser [minimize] *vt* to minimize, to reduce to the minimum; *Fig* (*rôle, situation, problème*) to play down, to downplay
minimum [minimɔm], *pl* **minima** [minima], **minimums 1** *nm* minimum; **avec un m. d'efforts** with a minimum of effort; **un m. de temps** a minimum amount of time; **en un m. de temps** in as short a time as possible; **nous exigeons un m. de garanties** we demand the minimum guarantees; **trois mois, c'est un m. pour s'habituer au climat** three months is the minimum it takes *or* it takes at least three months to get used to the climate; **c'est vraiment le m. que tu puisses faire pour elle** it's the least you can do for her; **il ne fait même plus le m. pour donner le change à sa femme** he's stopped making even the slightest attempt to keep his wife in the dark; **m. vital** minimum living wage; **réduire les frais au m.** to reduce expenses to a minimum; *F* **je n'y resterai que le m. de temps** I'll make it as brief as I can; **dépenser le m.** to spend as little as possible; *F* **bouger le** *ou* **au m.** to move as little as possible; **au m. 200 francs/cinq ans d'expérience** at least 200 francs/five years' experience, a minimum of 200 francs/five years' experience

2 *adj* minimum; **les largeurs minimums** *ou* **minima** the minimum widths; **vitesse m.** minimum speed; **prix m.** (*à une vente aux enchères*) reserve price; *Él* **charge m.** (*de génératrice*) base load
mini-ordinateur, *pl* **mini-ordinateurs** *nm* minicomputer, mini
minipilule [minipilyl] *nf* minipill
mini-séjour, *pl* **mini-séjours** *nm* mini-break, short break
mini-série, *pl* **mini-séries** *nf TV etc* mini-series
ministère [ministεr] *nm* **(a)** (*département*) government department; **m. de l'Intérieur** ≈ Home Office; **m. des Affaires étrangères** ≈ Foreign (and Commonwealth) Office, *US* ≈ State Department, *Can* ≈ External Affairs Department; **m. de l'Éducation nationale** ≈ Department of Education; **m. de la Défense (nationale)** ≈ Ministry of Defence; **m. des Travaux publics** *Can* ≈ Department of Public Works; *Br Hist* Ministry of Public Works; **m. de l'Environnement** ≈ Department of the Environment; **m. du Commerce** ≈ Department of Trade; **m. de la Communication** ministry for communications; **m. du Commerce extérieur** foreign trade department; **m. de l'Economie et des Finances** Treasury; **m. des Finances** Ministry of Finance, *Br* Exchequer; **m. du Commerce et de l'Industrie** Department of Trade and Industry, DTI; **m. du Tourisme** Ministry of Tourism

(b) (*gouvernement*) office; **entrer dans un m.** to take office; **former un m.** to form a government; **sous le m. Giscard** under Giscard d'Estaing's government

(c) *Jur* **le m. public** ≈ the (Department of the) Director of Public Prosecutions

(d) *Rel* **le (saint) m.** the ministry

(e) *Arch, Litt* (*aide*) agency; **user du m. de qn** to make use of sb's services; *Jur* **l'accusé a droit au m. d'un avocat** the accused has the right to counsel *or Am* a lawyer
ministériel, -ielle [ministerjεl] *adj* (*arrêté, décret, entourage*) ministerial; (*crise, remaniement*) cabinet; *Vieilli* **journal m.** newspaper supporting the government, government organ; *Jur* **officier m.** (*avoué, huissier, notaire*) officer of the court
ministrable [ministrabl] *Pol* **1** *adj* likely to become a minister **2** *n* likely choice as minister, ministerial hopeful
ministre [ministr] *nm* **(a)** (*de gouvernement*) minister; **Premier m.** Prime Minister; *Can* (*d'une province*) Premier; **m. de l'Intérieur** *Br* ≈ Home Secretary, *US* ≈ Secretary of the Interior; **m. des Affaires étrangères** *Br* ≈ Foreign Secretary, *US* ≈ Secretary of State, *Can* ≈ Secretary of State for External Affairs; **m. de l'Éducation nationale** ≈ Secretary of State for Education; **m. de la Défense (nationale)** ≈ Secretary of State for Defence, Minister of Defence; **m. sans portefeuille** Minister without Portfolio; **m. des Travaux publics** *Br Hist, Can* ≈ Minister of Public Works; **m. de l'Environnement** ≈ Secretary of State for the Environment; **m. des Finances** *Br* ≈ Chancellor of the Exchequer, *US* ≈ Secretary of the Treasury, *Can* ≈ Minister of Finance; **m. de la Justice** *Br* ≈ Lord Chancellor, *US* ≈ Attorney General, *Can* ≈ Minister of Justice and Attorney General; **m. du Commerce** ≈ Secretary of State for Trade and Industry; **m. de la Communication** minister for communications; **m. du Tourisme** Minister for Tourism; **papier m.** ≈ official foolscap

(b) *Rel* (Protestant) minister, clergyman

(c) *Arch, Litt* (*de Dieu, d'un prince etc*) servant, agent
minitéliste [minitelist] *n* Minitel user
minitel® [minitεl] *nm* = small terminal, connected to telephone, used to consult data banks etc, *Br* ≈ Prestel®; **m. rose** = electronic equivalent of lonely hearts column
mini-tour, *pl* **mini-tours** *nf Ordinat* mini tower
minium [minjɔm] *nm Ch* red lead, minium; (*antirouille*) red lead paint
minivague [minivag] *nf* body wave
minois [minwa] *nm* (*d'enfant, de jeune femme*) (pretty) face; **une jeune fille au frais m.** a fresh-faced young girl
minoration [minɔrasjɔ̃] *nf* (*de tarifs, temps de travail*) reduction, decrease
minorer [minɔre] *vt* (*minimiser*) (*incident*) to downplay, (*faire baisser*) (*chiffre, somme, prix, impôt etc*) to lower, to reduce
minoritaire [minɔritεr] **1** *adj* (*parti, participation*) minority; **ils sont minoritaires à l'Assemblée** they are in the minority in the Assembly; **très minoritaires** very much in the minority **2** *n* member of a minority
minorité [minɔrite] *nf* [①A11,g,i] minority; *Jur* minority, infancy, nonage; **le service ne fonctionne qu'avec une m. de gens** the department is run by a skeleton staff; **être en**

m. to be in the *or* in a minority; **mettre en m.** to defeat; **la gauche a été mise en m. lors des dernières élections** the left became the minority party at the last elections; **m. ethnique** ethnic minority; **m. de blocage** blocking minority vote
Minorque [minɔrk] *nf* Minorca
minorquin, -ine [minɔrkɛ̃, -in] **1** *adj* Minorcan **2** *n* **M.** Minorcan
minoterie [minɔtri] *nf* (*moulin*) (large) flour mill; (*activité*) flour-milling
minotier [minɔtje] *nm* (flour) miller
minou [minu] *nm F* (*chat*) pussy (cat), kitty; **mon m.** my darling, my pet
minuit [minɥi] *nm* midnight, twelve (o'clock) (at night); **m. et demi** half-past twelve at night
minuscule [minyskyl] **1** *adj* **(a)** (*très petit*) tiny, minute, minuscule **(b) lettre m.** small letter; *Typ* lower-case letter **2** *nf* small letter; *Typ* lower-case letter; **en minuscules** (in) lower case
minus (habens) [minys(abɛ̃s)] *nm inv F* half-wit, moron
minutage [minytaʒ] *nm* timing; **faire un m. exact de qch** to time something to the minute
minute [minyt] *nf* **(a)** [①**A75**,A,d; **B58**,A,d] (*d'heure, degré*) minute; **à deux minutes près, vous le ratiez** a couple of minutes later and you would have missed him/it; **toutes les vingt minutes** every twenty minutes; **de dernière m.** last-minute; **faire qch à la m.** to do sth at a minute's *or* a moment's notice; *F* **on n'est pas à la m.** we've got plenty of time, there's no rush; **il sera là d'une m. à l'autre** he'll be here any minute now; *F* **m. (papillon)!** just a minute!, hold on!

(b) (*court moment*) minute; **ne pas avoir une m. à perdre/de répit** not to have a moment *or* minute to lose/a moment's *or* minute's rest; **ne pas avoir une m. à soi** not to have a minute *or* a moment to oneself; **nettoyage-m.** dry-cleaning while you wait; **talons/clés m.** heel/key bar; **réparations (à la) m.** repairs while you wait; **repas-m.** convenience meal; **steak m.** minute steak

(c) (*de contrat etc*) minute, draft; (*d'acte, de jugement*) record; **faire la m. d'un acte** to draft an act; **faire la m. d'une réunion** to draw up the minutes of *or* to minute a meeting

▶ **minute**: **une m. de silence** a moment's silence; **la m. de vérité** the moment of truth
minuter [minyte] *vt* **(a)** (*dans le temps*) to time; **sa journée est soigneusement minutée** every minute of his day is carefully planned *or* accounted for **(b)** (*accord etc*) to minute, to draw up, to draft; (*acte, jugement*) to record, to enter
minuterie [minytri] *nf* **(a)** (*appareil*) (*de lumière*) timer, (automatic) time switch **(b)** (*mécanisme*) (*d'une horlogerie*) motionwork, train of wheels; **as-tu mis en route la m. du four?** did you set the oven timer?
minuteur [minytœr] *nm* timer
minutie [minysi] *nf* **(a)** (*caractère*) meticulousness, attention to detail; **avec m.** meticulously; **d'une m. remarquable** remarkably meticulous **(b)** *Vieilli* (*détail*) minute detail; **minuties** trifles, petty details, *Fml* minutiae
minutieusement [minysjøzmɑ̃] *adv* meticulously, with attention to detail; **très m.** very meticulously, with great attention to detail; **examiner qch m.** to examine sth minutely, to scrutinize sth
minutieux, -ieuse [minysjø, -jøz] *adj* (*personne*) meticulous; (*inspection, examen*) close, thorough, minute, detailed; (*dessin, sculpture*) detailed; **la broderie est un travail très m.** embroidery demands close work *or* attention to detail
miocène [mjɔsɛn] *adj, nm Géol* Miocene
mioche [mjɔʃ] *n F* kid(die), tot, *Péj* brat
mi-pente (à) *adv* halfway up/down the hill
MIPS [mips] *nm Ordinat* (*abrév* **million d'instructions par seconde**) MIPS
mirabelle [mirabɛl] *nf* mirabelle plum
mirabellier [mirabelje] *nm* mirabelle plum tree
miracle [mirɑkl] **1** *nm* **(a)** miracle; **ne t'attends pas à un m.** don't expect any miracles; **faire un m.** to perform *or* work a miracle; *Fig* **faire des miracles** to work miracles *or* wonders; **croire aux miracles** to believe in miracles; **cela tient du m.** it's miraculous; **m. d'architecture** marvel *or* miracle of architecture; **le m. industriel français** the French industrial miracle; **par m.** miraculously, by a miracle; **échapper par m.** to have a miraculous escape; **c'est (un) m. que ...** + *sub* it's a miracle *or* a wonder that ...; **crier (au) m.** to go into raptures

(b) *Hist, Littér* miracle (play)

2 *adj inv F* **produit m.** miracle *or* wonder product; **une crème m. contre la cellulite** a cream that works miracles *or* wonders on cellulite; **je ne crois pas aux solutions m.** I don't believe in miracle cures; **elle a toujours des solutions m.** she can always come up with a solution

miraculé [mirakyle] **1** *adj* (*personne*) miraculously cured/saved, cured/saved by a miracle **2** *n* **je suis un m.** I'm lucky to be alive; **l'explosion n'a laissé que quelques miraculés** only a few people escaped death in the explosion; **les miraculés de Lourdes** the miracle cures of Lourdes
miraculeusement [mirakyløzmɑ̃] *adv* by a miracle, miraculously; **m. vite** miraculously quickly
miraculeux, -euse [mirakylø, -øz] *adj* miraculous, wonderful; **remède m.** miracle cure; **cette crème est miraculeuse contre les rides** this cream works miracles *or* wonders on wrinkles
mirador [miradɔr] *nm* **(a)** *Archit* mirador, belvedere **(b)** *Mil* (*dans un arbre etc*) observation post; (*de camp de prisonniers*) watchtower
mirage [miraʒ] *nm* mirage
mire [mir] *nf* **(a)** (*de fusil*) foresight **(b)** (*signal*) sighting mark; *TV* **m. (de réglage)** test card, test chart *or* pattern **(c)** (*piquet*) (surveyor's) ranging pole
mirer [mire] **1** *vt* **(a)** *Vieilli* (*viser*) to aim at, to take aim at **(b)** *Litt* (*refléter*) to reflect, to mirror **(c)** (*œufs*) to candle **2 se mirer** *vpr* (*dans un miroir, l'eau etc*) to look *or* gaze at oneself; *Litt* **les arbres se mirent dans l'eau** the trees are reflected in the water
mirettes [mirɛt] *nfpl F* (*yeux*) peepers, *Am* baby blues; **on s'en est pris plein les mirettes** we feasted our eyes on it
mirifique [mirifik] *adj F* wonderful, fabulous
mirliflor(e) [mirliflɔr] *nm Hum, Vieilli Fig* dandy, fop
mirliton [mirlitɔ̃] *nm* (*sifflet*) kazoo, mirliton; **des vers de m.** doggerel, bad verse
mirmidon [mirmidɔ̃] *nm Vieilli F* whippersnapper, pipsqueak, little runt
mirobolant [mirɔbɔlɑ̃] *adj F* fabulous, wonderful, marvellous; **son travail n'est vraiment pas m.** his work is not exactly brilliant
miroir [mirwar] *nm* mirror, *Fml* (looking) glass; **m. (pliant) à trois faces** triple mirror; **m. grossissant** magnifying mirror; **m. déformant** distorting mirror; *Fig* **le m. d'une société** the mirror of a society; **ce journal est-il réellement le m. de ce que pensent les gens?** does this newspaper really mirror *or* reflect what people think?

▶ **miroir**: **m. aux alouettes** = lure for attracting birds; *Fig* snare, delusion; **m. de courtoisie** vanity mirror
miroitant [mirwatɑ̃] *adj* (*argent*) glistening, gleaming, flashing; (*lac, soie*) shimmering; (*bijou*) sparkling
miroité [mirwate] *adj* (*cheval*) dappled bay
miroitement [mirwatmɑ̃] *nm* (*d'argent*) glistening, gleam(ing), flash(ing); (*de lac, de soie*) shimmer(ing); (*de bijou*) sparkle, sparkling
miroiter [mirwate] *vi* (*d'argent*) to glisten, to gleam, to flash; (*de lac, de soie*) to shimmer; (*de bijou*) to sparkle; *Fig* **faire m. l'avenir à qn** to lure sb with bright prospects, to hold out *or* dangle the prospect of a bright future in front of sb; **ils m'ont fait m. une promotion/un voyage** they dangled the prospect of promotion/a trip in front of me
miroton [mirɔtɔ̃] *nm Culin* **(boeuf) m.** beef boiled in sauce with onions
mis [mi] *adj Vieilli* **être bien/mal m.** to be well/badly attired
misaine [mizɛn] *nf Naut* **(voile de) m.** (square) foresail; **mât de m.** foremast
misanthrope [mizɑ̃trɔp] **1** *nm* misanthropist, misanthrope **2** *adj* misanthropic
misanthropie [mizɑ̃trɔpi] *nf* misanthropy
misanthropique [mizɑ̃trɔpik] *adj Litt* misanthropic
miscible [misibl] *adj* miscible
mise [miz] *nf* **(a)** (*placement*) placing, putting in place; **m. à l'eau** (*d'un bateau*) launch, launching; **m. en bouteilles/boîtes** bottling/canning; **m. à terre** (*de marchandises*) landing; **m. en pratique** carrying out, putting into practice; **m. en musique d'un poème** setting a poem to music; **m. en eau (d'un barrage)** filling (of a reservoir); **m. au net** (*d'un document etc*) finalizing; **m. à exécution** (*d'une mesure*) implementation; **toute une série de mesures avec m. à exécution immédiate** a whole series of measures to be implemented immediately; **on craint la m. à exécution des menaces** there is concern that the threats will be carried out; **m. en italiques** italicization; **m. en valeur** (*d'un terrain, d'arguments*) development; **pour assurer la m. en valeur de sa collection** to show his collection off to better advantage *or* better effect; **m. en vigueur** implementation; **m. en application** (*d'un règlement, d'une décision*) implementation, application; **la m. en application du règlement avait connu quelques difficultés** there had been some difficulties in implementing *or* applying the regulation; **m. en place** setting up, putting into place; **nous avons dû retarder la m. en place du nouveau système** we have had

to postpone setting up the new system; **la m. en place du nouveau réseau demandera plusieurs mois** it will take several months to set up the new system *or* to get the new system up and running; **m. en vente** putting up for sale, putting on the market; **elle attend la m. en vente de sa maison pour commencer à en chercher une autre** she's waiting for her house to go on the market before she starts looking for another; **j'ai confié la m. en vente de la maison à un notaire** I put the sale of the house in the hands of a notary; **m. en exploitation** (*d'une machine*) commissioning; **m. en veille** putting on standby; *Télécom* **m. en attente d'appels** call holding; *Ordinat* **m. en attente des fichiers à imprimer** printer spooling; *Ordinat* **m. en mémoire** saving; **la m. en mémoire n'a pas été faite** it hasn't been saved; *Ordinat* **m. en relief** highlighting; *Ordinat* **m. en réseau** networking; **m. sur pied** setting up

(**b**) (*habillement*) dress, clothing, *Fml* attire; **elle est simple dans sa m.** she dresses simply; **on voit à sa m. qu'elle n'est pas très riche** you can see from the way she dresses *or* the clothes she wears that she's not very rich

(**c**) *Cartes* stake; (*à une vente aux enchères*) bid; **m. à prix** reserve price, upset price; *Fig* **son arrivée m'a sauvé la m.** his arrival got me out of a tight spot

(**d**) **être de m.** to be obligatory; **le tutoiement n'est pas de m.** it's not the done thing to say "tu"; **si tu y vas, sache que la cravate est de m.** if you go, you'll have to wear a tie, mind

▶ **mise**: **m. en accusation** committal (for trial); *Fig* **on a assisté à une véritable m. en accusation du président du club** accusations were hurled at the club chairman; **m. bas** (*d'animal*) dropping (*of young*); **m. en bière: assister à la m. en bière** to be present when the body is placed in the coffin; **m. en cause** (*de l'honnêteté etc de qn*) questioning; (*dans une affaire*) involvement; **m. en circulation** (*de billets*) issue; **m. en demeure** summons; (*de paiement*) formal demand; **m. en disponibilité** leave of absence; *Can Ind* layoff; **demander sa** *ou* **une m. en disponibilité** to ask for leave of absence; **m. sur écoutes (téléphoniques)** bugging; **c'est pourquoi ils ont décidé de la m. sur écoutes** that's why they decided to bug his/her phone; *Jur* **m. en examen** indictment; **m. à feu** (*de fusée etc*) firing; *Com* **m. de fonds** investment; *Typ, Ordinat* **m. en forme** formatting; **m. en garde** warning, caution; **m. hors tension** power-down; **m. en jeu** (*au début*), *Fb, Rugby* kick off; *Hockey* bully-off; (*à la touche*), *Fb* throw-in; *Rugby* line-out; **m. à jour** (*réactualisation*) (*action*) updating, update, bringing up to date; (*résultat*) update, updated version; (*d'un secret etc*) bringing to light; **m. en liberté** release; *Jur* **m. en liberté provisoire** = remand; **m. en marche** (*de moteur etc*) starting, start up; **m. à mort** killing; *Ordinat* **m. à niveau** upgrade; *Scol* **faire une m. à niveau en maths** = to catch up in maths; (*after switching to another specialization*); **m. en œuvre** (*d'un projet*) implementation; *Rad* **m. en ondes** production; *Astronaut* **m. en orbite** putting into orbit; **depuis sa m. en orbite** since it was put into orbit; **la m. en orbite est prévue pour 15h** the satellite is scheduled to be sent into orbit at 3pm; *Typ* **m. en page(s)** page make-up; **m. à pied** (*disciplinaire*) (*permanent*) dismissal; (*temporaire*) suspension; *Can* (*chômage*) layoff; **donner trois jours de m. à pied à qn** to give sb three days suspension, to suspend sb for three days; **m. en plis** set; **faire une m. en plis à qn** to set sb's hair, to give sb a set; **shampooing et m. en plis** shampoo and set; **m. au point** (*d'un objectif*) focussing; (*d'une technique*) perfecting; (*d'un moteur*) tuning; (*d'un mécanisme*) adjustment; (*d'un document, d'un rapport*) finalization, finalizing; *Journ* correction; **je voudrais faire une m. au point** I'd like to clarify something; *Ordinat* **m. en relation** (*avec un service*) log-on; *Typ* **m. en retrait** indent; **m. à la** *ou* **en retraite** pensioning (off), retirement on a pension; **il y aura 50 mises en retraite** 50 people will be retired; **m. en route** start-up; **m. à sac** (*par des soldats*) sacking; (*par des voleurs*) ransacking; **après la m. à sac de la maison** after the house was ransacked; **se livrer à une m. à sac** (*de voyous*) to go on a looting spree; **m. en scène** (*d'une pièce*) staging, production; (*d'un film*) direction; **c'est elle qui fera la m. en scène** she'll be responsible for staging the play; *Fig* **toute cette histoire n'était en fait qu'une vaste m. en scène** the entire story was just one big set-up; **m. en service** (*d'une machine*) commissioning; **mais sa m. en service ne se fera qu'en septembre** but it won't come into service until September; *Ordinat, Él* **m. sous tension** (*d'un ordinateur, d'une turbine*) power-up; **m. en train** (*d'un projet etc*) start-up; **quelques minutes d'exercice pour assurer sa m. en train** a few minutes exercise to get oneself started *or* going in the morning

miser [mize] **1** *vt* to stake (**sur** on) **2** *vi* **m. sur un cheval** to back a horse, to (put a) bet on a horse; *Fig* **m. sur les deux tableaux** to try to have it both ways; *F* **m. sur qn** to count *or* bank on sb

misérabilisme [mizerabilism] *nm* sordid realism

misérabiliste [mizerabilist] *adj* sordidly realistic

misérable [mizerabl] **1** *adj* (**a**) (*indigent*) poor, wretched, impoverished, miserable; (*condition, existence*) wretched; **quartier m.** poor *or* poverty-stricken district (**b**) (*insignifiant*) wretched, miserable, worthless; **un m. salaire** a miserable wage, a mere pittance (of a wage); **pour la m. somme de 50 francs** for a paltry 50 francs (**c**) *Vieilli* (*action etc*) despicable, mean **2** *n Arch* (*malheureux*) poor wretch; *Vieilli* (*fripouille*) scoundrel, wretch, villain; **comment as-tu pu faire une chose pareille, m.?** how could you have done such a thing, you scoundrel *or* wretch?

misérablement [mizerabləmɑ̃] *adv* miserably

misère [mizɛr] **1** *nf* (**a**) (*indigence*) extreme poverty, destitution; **être dans la m.** to be poverty-stricken *or* destitute; **ils sont dans une m. noire** they have nothing, they are quite destitute; **vivre dans la m.** to live in poverty; **tomber dans la m.** to become destitute; **réduire qn à la m.** to reduce sb to penury; **crier** *ou* **pleurer m.** to plead poverty; **salaire de m.** starvation wage

(**b**) (*ennui*) trouble, misfortune; **les misères de l'âge** the afflictions of old age; **faire des misères à qn** to tease sb unmercifully

(**c**) *Vieilli* (*malheur*) misery; **reprendre son collier de m.** to get back to the treadmill; **c'est vraiment une m. de la voir si malheureuse!** it is dreadful to see her so unhappy!; **lit de m.** sick bed

(**d**) (*vétille*) **une m.** a trifle; **cent francs? une m.!** a hundred francs? a mere nothing!; **je l'ai eu pour une m.** I got it for a song

(**e**) *Cartes* misère

(**f**) *Bot* tradescantia

2 *int* **m.!** damn!, blast!

miserere, miséréré [mizerere] *nm inv Rel, Mus* miserere

miséreux, -euse [mizerø, -øz] **1** *adj* poverty-stricken, destitute **2** *n* poverty-stricken *or* destitute person

miséricorde [mizerikɔrd] **1** *nf* mercy **2** *int Vieilli* mercy on us!, mercy me!

miséricordieux, -ieuse [mizerikɔrdjø, -jøz] *adj* merciful (**envers** to)

misogyne [mizɔʒin], *F* **miso** [mizo] **1** *adj* misogynous **2** *n* misogynist, woman-hater

misogynie [mizɔʒini] *nf* misogyny; **d'une m. invraisemblable** incredibly misogynous

miss, *pl* **miss(es)** [mis] *nf* (**a**) (*reine de beauté*) beauty queen; **M. Monde/France** Miss World/France (**b**) *F* **voilà, m.** there you are (miss); **et comment va m. Martin?** and how is Miss Martin?; (*en s'adressant directement à la personne*) and how are we today Miss Martin? (**c**) *Arch* (*gouvernante*) (English) governess

missel [misɛl] *nm Rel* missal

missile [misil] *nm Mil* missile; **m. à tête chercheuse à infrarouge** heat-seeking missile; **m. ballistique de moyenne portée** *ou* **de portée intermédiaire** intermediate-range ballistic missile; **m. de courte/longue portée** short-/long-range missile; **m. de croisière** cruise missile; **m. stratégique** strategic missile; **m. tactique** tactical missile; **m. anti-sous-marins** anti-submarine missile

mission [misjɔ̃] *nf* (**a**) (*tâche*), *Pol, Mil etc* mission; (*d'employé*) job, task, assignment; **j'ai (pour) m. de faire qch** my job *or* task is to do sth; **ministre en m. spéciale à Paris** minister on a special mission to Paris; **chargé de m.** representative; **envoyer qn en m. aux Etats-Unis** to send sb to the United States; **partir en m.** (*d'un cadre*) to go away on business; (*d'un diplomate*) to go off on a mission; *Mil* **en m. de reconnaissance** on a reconnaissance mission, on reconnaissance; **m. accomplie** mission accomplished; **m. vous avait été confiée de faire ...** you were given the job of doing ..., *Fml* you were assigned the task of ...; **il s'était donné pour m. de sauver les enfants** he had taken it upon himself to save the children; *Hum* **viens ici, j'ai une m. à te confier!** (*à un enfant*) come here, there's something I'd like you to do for me

(**b**) (*groupe*) delegation; *Pol* delegation, mission; **m. scientifique** scientific expedition; **partir en m. au pôle Nord** to go on an expedition to the North Pole

(**c**) *Rel* (*vocation, organisation*) mission; (*bâtiment*) mission (station)

(**d**) (*rôle*) (*de l'art etc*) task, rôle, function; **la m. civilisatrice de l'école** the civilizing mission of schools

▶ **mission**: **m. commerciale** business assignment; (*gouvernementale*) trade mission; **m. diplomatique** diplomatic mission

missionnaire [misjɔnɛr] *adj, n* missionary
missive [misiv] *nf Litt, Hum* missive, letter
mistigri [mistigri] *nm F (chat)* puss
mistoufle [mistufl] *nf F Vieilli* **(a) être dans la m.** to be broke *or* hard up *or* skint **(b) faire des mistoufles à qn** to annoy *or* tease *or* plague sb
mistral [mistral] *nm Météo* mistral
mitaine [mitɛn] *nf Can, Vieilli (moufle)* mitten; *(qui laisse les doigts nus)* fingerless glove
mite [mit] *nf* **(a)** mite; **m. du fromage** cheese mite **(b)** *(petit papillon)* moth; **mangé des** *ou* **aux mites, troué aux mites** moth-eaten
mité [mite] *adj* moth-eaten
mi-temps 1 *nf inv Fb etc* half-time, interval; **première/ seconde m.** first/second half; **la police craint la troisième m.** the police fear after-match trouble *or* violence **2** *nm* part-time job; **l'emploi à m.** part-time work *or* employment; **travailler** *ou* **être à m.** to work part-time, to have a part-time job; *Scol* **m. pédagogique** part-time teaching position; **l'avantage d'un m.** the advantage of a part-time job *or* of working part-time
miter (se) [səmite] *vpr* to become moth-eaten
miteux, -euse [mitø, -øz] **1** *adj (vêtements, quartier, boîte)* seedy, shabby, tatty; *(personne)* seedy-looking, shabby, down-at-heel **2** *n F* shabby *or* down-at-heel *or* seedy-looking person; **tes amis, c'est une bande de miteux!** your friends are a seedy lot!
Mithridate [mitridat] *nm* Mithridates
mithridatiser [mitridatize] *vt* **m. qn** to make sb immune (to poison)
mitigation [mitigasjɔ̃] *nf Jur* mitigation
mitigé [mitiʒe] *adj (enthousiasme)* moderate, *Fml* mitigated; *(sentiments, impressions)* mixed; **le public était assez m.** the public was quite mixed in its reaction; **morale mitigée** lax morals; *Jur* **peine mitigée** reduced sentence
mitiger [mitiʒe] *vt* **(je mitigeai(s), n. mitigeons)** *Vieilli (mal)* to mitigate; *(peine)* to reduce, to mitigate; *(règlement, loi)* to relax
mitigeur [mitiʒœr] *nm* mixer tap
mitochondrie [mitokɔ̃dri] *nf* mitochondrion
mitonner [mitɔne] **1** *vt* **(a)** *Culin* to prepare, to cook; *(cuire à feu doux)* to simmer **(b)** *Fig (projet etc)* to concoct, to cook up **(c)** *Litt (enfant)* to coddle, to pamper, to cosset **2** *vi Culin* to simmer
mitose [mitoz] *nf Biol* mitosis
mitoyen, -enne [mitwajɛ̃, -jɛn] *adj* intermediate; **mur m.** party wall; **cloison mitoyenne** dividing wall *(between two rooms)*; **maisons mitoyennes** semi-detached houses; *(plus de deux)* terraced houses
mitoyenneté [mitwajɛnte] *nf Jur (de mur, de haie)* joint ownership
mitraillade [mitrajad] *nf* (volley of) shots, machine-gun fire; **une m.** a burst of machine-gun fire
mitraillage [mitrajaʒ] *nm* machine-gunning
mitraille [mitraj] *nf* **(a)** *Mil (projectiles)* case shot, canister shot, grapeshot; *(décharge)* hail of bullets **(b)** *F (monnaie)* small change
mitrailler [mitraje] *vt* to machine-gun; *Phot F* to click away at, to snap away at, to take snaps of; **les vedettes ont été abondamment mitraillées** lots of photographs were taken of the film stars; *Fig* **m. qn de questions** to fire questions at sb, to bombard sb with questions
mitraillette [mitrajɛt] *nf* submachine gun, *F* tommy gun
mitrailleur [mitrajœr] **1** *nm* machine-gunner; *Mil, Av* **m. arrière** rear gunner **2** *adj* **fusil m.** Bren gun
mitrailleuse [mitrajøz] *nf* machine gun
mitral, -aux [mitral, -o] *adj Anat* mitral
mitre [mitr] *nf* **(a)** *(d'évêque)* mitre, *US* miter **(b)** *Tech (de cheminée)* cowl
mitré [mitre] *adj (abbé)* mitred, *US* mitered
mitron [mitrɔ̃] *nm* baker's boy
mi-voix (à) *adv* in an undertone, under one's breath; **ils parlaient à m.** they were speaking in undertones
mix [miks] *nm Mktg (marchéage)* mix; **m. de produits** product mix
mixage [miksaʒ] *nm Cin etc (de sons)* mixing, dubbing; **m. magnétique final** master soundtrack
mixer [mikse] *vt* **(a)** *Cin* to mix **(b)** *Culin* to blend, to liquidize
mixe(u)r [miksœr] *nm* mixer; *(pour rendre liquide)* liquidizer
mixité [miksite] *nf Scol* co-education
mixte [mikst] *adj* **(a)** *(des deux sexes)* mixed; **école m.** mixed *or* co-educational school; *Tennis* **double m.** mixed doubles **(b)** *(combiné)* **train m.** composite train *(goods and passengers)*; **commission m.** joint commission; **billet m.** combined rail and road ticket; **mariage m.** mixed marriage; **cuisinière m.** gas and electric cooker

mixtion [mikstjɔ̃] *nf Pharm (action) (de drogues etc)* compounding; *(médicament)* mixture
mixture [mikstyr] *nf* **(a)** *Pharm* mixture **(b)** *Culin; Fig* concoction
ml *(abrév* **millilitre)** ml
MLF [ɛmɛlɛf] *nm abrév* **Mouvement de libération des femmes**
Mlle *(abrév* **mademoiselle)** Miss
Mlles *(abrév* **mesdemoiselles)** Misses
MM *(abrév* **Messieurs)** Messrs
mm *(abrév* **millimètre(s))** mm
Mme *(abrév* **Madame)** Mrs
Mmes *abrév* **Mesdames**
mnémonique [mnemɔnik] *adj, nf* mnemonic
mnémotechnie [mnemɔtɛkni] *nf* mnemonics
mnémotechnique [mnemɔtɛknik] **1** *adj* mnemonic; **un moyen m.** a mnemonic **2** *nf* mnemonics
Mo *nm Ordinat (abrév* **méga-octet)** Mb
mob [mɔb] *nf F* = **mobylette**
mobile [mɔbil] **1** *adj* **(a)** *(qui peut être mû) (cloison)* mobile, movable; *(feuillets)* loose; **album à feuilles mobiles** loose-leaf album
(b) *(expression, regard)* shifting, changing; *(visage)* lively, expressive; *(organe, cartilage)* mobile, having freedom of movement; *(cible)* moving; *(personne âgée)* mobile; *(employé, main d'œuvre)* willing to move *or* relocate; *(population)* mobile, shifting; **dans les pays pauvres les populations ont tendance à être plus mobiles** people in poor countries tend to move around more; **le boxeur est très m.** the boxer is very nimble *or* quick on his feet; *Tech* **organes mobiles** sliding *or* working *or* moving parts
(c) *Mil* **gendarmerie m.** = flying squad; **gendarme** *ou* **garde m.** = member of the flying squad; *Hist* **garde nationale m.** *(de 1848, de 1868-71)* militia; *Hist* **la garde républicaine m.** = the (State) security police
(d) *Vieilli (humeur)* changeable
2 *nm* **(a)** *(motif) (du crime)* motive **(de** for)
(b) *Phys etc* moving body, body in motion
(c) *(en décoration), Beaux-Arts* mobile
mobile home, *pl* **mobile homes** [mɔbilom] *nm* mobile home
mobilier, -ière [mɔbilje, -jɛr] **1** *adj Jur* movable, personal; **biens mobiliers** personal property, chattels; *Fin* **valeurs mobilières** stocks and shares, transferable securities **2** *nm (ameublement)* furniture; **m. de bureau** office furniture; **m. de présentation** display stands
▶ **mobilier**: **m. national** government property; **m. urbain** street furniture
mobilisable [mɔbilizabl] *adj* **(a)** *Mil (troupes)* which can be mobilized; **les jeunes de moins de 18 ans ne sont pas mobilisables** young people under 18 are not eligible for call-up **(b)** *(créance)* discountable
mobilisateur, -trice [mɔbilizatœr, -tris] *adj* motivating; **slogan m.** rallying cry; **un appel m.** a call to rally the troops
mobilisation [mɔbilizasjɔ̃] *nf (de troupes)* mobilization; *Fin (de capital)* raising; **m. de fonds** raising of funds; *Mil* **ordre de m. générale** general mobilization order; **les syndicats comptent beaucoup sur la m. des enseignants contre ce projet de réforme** the unions are relying heavily on the teachers rallying to fight this proposed reform; **nous avons besoin d'une m. des électeurs/consommateurs pour dire non à ...** we need voters/consumers to mobilize *or* rally and say no to ...; **on sent un manque de m. total chez les étudiants en faveur de/contre ces nouvelles mesures** students seem to be totally unwilling to rally in order to support/fight these new measures
mobilisé, -ée [mɔbilize] **1** *adj (troupes)* mobilized; *(réservistes)* called up **2** *n* serviceman, *f* servicewoman; **un m. de la guerre de 14** a soldier in the First World War; **les mobilisés de la dernière guerre** those who served in the last war
mobiliser [mɔbilize] **1** *vt (troupes)* to mobilize; *(réserviste)* to call up; *(syndicat, électorat)* to rally; *(ressources)* to mobilize; *(créances)* to discount; *(capital, argent)* to raise; **m. toute son énergie** to summon up all one's energy; *(de son travail, ses enfants)* to use up all one's energy; **il faut m. les énergies** we'll have to mobilize people **2** *vpr* **se mobiliser** to mobilize; **se m. contre/en faveur de qch** to rally against/in support of sth
mobilité [mɔbilite] *nf (de la population etc)* mobility; *(dans le travail)* willingness to move *or* relocate; *(des organes)* freedom of movement; *Fig (de caractère, d'humeur)* changeability; **la m. de son visage est remarquable** he has a remarkably lively face; **personnes à m. réduite** people of reduced mobility; **la m. de la mâchoire inférieure est affectée** the movement of the lower jaw is affected; *Écon* **m. sociale** upward mobility
mobylette® [mɔbilɛt] *nf* moped; **faire de la m.** to ride a moped; **elle y va en** *ou* **à m.** she goes there on her moped

mocassin [mɔkasɛ̃] *nm* mocassin

moche [mɔʃ] *adj F* **(a)** (*individu, chose*) hideous, ugly; **qu'est-ce qu'elle est m. aujourd'hui!** she looks a real sight today!; **c'est m. ces rideaux bleus avec ce canapé rose!** those blue curtains look really hideous with that pink sofa; **je ne trouve pas qu'il soit m.** I don't think he's bad-looking **(b)** (*appréciation morale*) rotten, nasty; **c'est m. ce qu'ils t'ont fait** it's rotten what they did to you; **c'est trop m. de mourir à vingt ans** it's terrible to die at twenty

mocheté [mɔʃte] *nf F* (*laideur*) ugliness; **c'est d'une m.!** what an eyesore!, it's absolutely hideous!; **la mode de cet été est d'une m.!** this summer's fashions are hideous; **quelle m., cette fille!** that girl's such a dog!

modal, -ale, -aux, -ales [mɔdal, -o] *adj, nm* [①**A55-9**,18; **B36-7**,K] *Ling* modal

modalité [mɔdalite] *nf* **(a)** method, mode; (*d'application d'une loi*) mode; *Jur* **modalités** (restrictive) clauses; **modalités de paiement** (*liquide, chèque etc*) methods of payment; (*conditions*) terms *or* conditions of payment; **modalités d'examen** examination procedure; *Fin* **modalités d'une émission** terms and conditions of an issue **(b)** *Phil, Mus, Gram* modality

mode¹ [mɔd] **1** *nf* **(a)** fashion; **la m. est aux couleurs pastel** pastels are in (fashion); **la m. des pantalons pattes d'éléphants est revenue** flares are back (in fashion); **la m. du long est passée** long skirts are out (of fashion); **lancer la m. de qch** to set the fashion for sth, to make sth fashionable; **être à la m.** to be in fashion *or* in vogue, to be all the rage; **ta sœur est très à la m.** your sister's very fashionable *or F* trendy; **robe à la m.** fashionable *or* stylish dress; **revenir à la m.** to come back (into fashion); **passer de m.** to go out of fashion; **tu ne trouves pas que c'est un peu passé de m.?** don't you think it's a bit old-fashioned?; **à l'ancienne m.** in the old style; **journal de m.** fashion magazine; **un professionnel de la m.** a fashion professional; **à la m. de ...** after the style *or* manner of ...; **neveu/nièce à la m. de Bretagne** first cousin once removed

(b) *Arch* **modes** (*vêtements*) fashions; **gravures de modes** fashion plates; **magasin de modes** milliner's shop

2 *adj inv* **le coloris m.** fashionable shades *or* colours, the shades *or* colours in fashion; **elle est toujours habillée très m.** she's always dressed very fashionably; **c'est très m.** it's very fashionable, it's very much in fashion

mode² *nm* **(a)** (*d'éducation etc*) method, mode; **m. d'emploi** instructions; **m. de vie** life style, way of life; **m. de cuisson** cooking instructions; **m. opératoire** modus operandi; **m. de gestion** management method *or* style; **m. d'expression** means of expression; **m. d'expédition** method of delivery; **m. de classement** filing system; **m. de codification** coding method; **m. de paiement** *ou* **de réglement** method of payment; **m. de transport** method of transport; *Aut* **m. de conduite hiver** winter driving mode; *Aut* **m. de sélecteur de vitesses** gear selector; *Aut* **m. dégradé** limp-home mode

(b) [①**A39**,8; **B30-2**,G] *Gram* mood; *Mus, Ordinat* mode

▶ **mode**: *Ordinat* **m. ajout** append mode; **m. amélioré** enhanced mode; **m. brouillon** draft mode; **m. continu** continuous mode; (*de transmission*) burst mode; **m. conversationnel** (*d'un modem*) conversation mode; **m. dialogue** (*d'un modem*) dialog(ue) mode; **m. différé** non real-time mode, off-line mode; **m. direct** real time mode; *Typ* **m. 'à la française'** portrait mode; **m. insertion** insert mode; *Typ* **m. 'à l'italienne'** landscape mode; **m. lecture seule** read-only mode; **m. machine à écrire** typewriter mode; **m. multitâche** multitask(ing) mode; **m. point** bitmap; **m. survol** browse mode; **m. sélectif** veto mode; **m. texte** text mode

modelage [mɔdlaʒ] *nm* (*action*) (*de l'argile etc*) modelling; (*résultat*) model

modèle [mɔdɛl] **1** *nm* **(a)** (*exemple*) model; **m. d'écriture** handwriting copy; **m. de lettre** standard letter; **machines toutes bâties sur le même m.** machines all built to one pattern *or* on *or* along the same lines; **faites un résumé de ce texte en vous aidant du m.** summarize this text along the same lines; **voiture dernier m.** car of the latest design; **prendre qn pour m.** to take sb as one's (role) model, to model oneself on sb; **Anne n'est pas un m. (à suivre)** don't follow Anne's example *or* lead; **m. de générosité/fidélité** model of generosity/fidelity; **m. de vertu** paragon *or* model of virtue

(b) *Couture* (*de robe*) style; (*de tricot*) pattern; *Beaux-Arts* (artist's) model; **vous n'auriez pas un plus grand m.?** do you have it in a larger size?; **dessiné d'après m.** drawn from life; **servir de m. à un artiste** to sit *or* model for an artist

(c) *Écon, Math, Ling* (*représentation schématique*) model; **m. de décision** decision model; **m. de décision en arborescence** decision-tree model; **m. du chemin critique** critical path model; **m. décisionnel** *ou* **déterministe** decision model; **m. mathématique** mathematical model

2 *adj* **époux m.** model *or* exemplary husband; **l'employé m.** the model employee; **adopter une conduite m.** to behave in an exemplary manner; **appartement/maison m.** show flat/house

▶ **modèle**: *Com, Ind* **m. déposé** registered pattern *or* model; **m.-phare** flagship; **m. réduit** scale mode; **m. réduit de yacht/d'avion** model yacht/airplan; **amateurs de modèles réduits** model enthusiasts

modelé [mɔdle] *nm* **(a)** *Beaux-Arts* relief; (*de sculpture*) contours **(b)** *Géog* relief

modeler [mɔdle] **(je modèle; je modèlerai) 1** *vt* (*argile, cire*) to model, to mould, *US* to mold; *Fig* (*caractère*) to shape, to mould; (*destinée*) to shape; **il avait un corps d'athlète, modelé par l'exercice physique** he had the body of an athlete, shaped by physical exercice; **un lobe d'oreille délicatement modelé** a delicately shaped earlobe; **l'eau/l'érosion a modelé le relief de la côte** water/erosion has shaped the coastline; **m. sa personnalité sur celle de qn** to model oneself on sb **2 se modeler** *vpr* **se m. sur qn** to take sb as one's model, to model oneself on sb

modeleur, -euse [mɔdlœr, -øz] *n Beaux-Arts* modeller; *Tech, Ind* pattern maker

modélisation [mɔdelizasjɔ̃] *nf* modelling

modélisme [mɔdelism] *nm* model-making; **un passionné de m.** a keen model-maker

modéliste [mɔdelist] *n* **(a)** (*de maquette*) model-maker **(b)** (*de vêtements*) dress designer

modem [mɔdɛm] *nm Ordinat* modem; **carte m.** modem card; **m. nul** null modem; **envoyer qch à qn par m.** to modem sth to sb, to send sth to sb by modem

modem-télécopieur, *pl* **modems-télécopieurs** *nm* fax-modem

modérateur, -trice [mɔderatœr, -tris] **1** *adj* moderating, restraining **2** *n* moderating influence **3** *nm* (*de moteur etc*) regulator, governor; *Nucl* moderator

modération [mɔderasjɔ̃] *nf* **(a)** (*retenue*) moderation, restraint; **sa réponse était pleine de m.** his answer was very restrained; **tu devrais faire preuve d'un peu plus de m. dans tes propos** you should curb your tongue a bit more; **avec m.** in *or* with moderation **(b)** (*réduction*) (*de prix*) restriction; (*fiscale*) reduction; **promettre une m. des impôts** to promise lower taxes

modéré, -ée [mɔdere] **1** *adj* (*personne, propos*) moderate, restrained; (*ton, attitude*) restrained; (*température*) moderate; (*prix etc*) reasonable, moderate; (*acclamations*) subdued **2** *n Pol* moderate

modérément [mɔderemɑ̃] *adv* moderately, in moderation; **j'aime m. le whisky** I'm moderately fond of whisky; **il fume, mais m.** he smokes, but in moderation; *Iron* **j'ai m. apprécié sa conduite** I was less than overwhelmed by his behaviour; **j'ai m. apprécié qu'il dise que je ronflais!** I didn't exactly appreciate him saying I snored!; **j'apprécie m. qu'on mette le nez dans mes affaires** I'm not very keen on people sticking their noses into my business

modérer [mɔdere] **(je modère; je modérerai) 1** *vt* **(a)** (*passions, désirs, envies*) to moderate, to restrain, to curb; (*vitesse*) to reduce, to slacken; *Ind* **m. les cadences** to reduce *or* lower production rates; **m. ses ambitions** to lower one's sights, to be less ambitious; **je te prie de m. ton langage!** please mind your tongue! **(b)** (*réduire*) (*prix*) to restrict **2 se modérer** *vpr* (*s'apaiser*) to control oneself, to calm down; (*faire preuve de sobriété*) to restrain oneself

moderne [mɔdɛrn] **1** *adj* (*concept, monde, médecine, musique, danse*) modern; (*équipement, méthode, technologie, idée, pensée*) modern, up-to-date; **studio équipé de tout le confort m.** studio flat with all modern conveniences; **découverte m.** recent discovery; **la femme m. travaille** the modern woman goes out to work; *Hist* **la période m.** the modern period, recent history; **grec m.** modern Greek; **étudier les lettres modernes** (*en France*) to study French language and literature

2 *nm* **le m.** (*style*) (the) modern style; **nous avons tout meublé en m.** all our furniture is modern; **mélanger le m. et l'ancien** to mix old and new

3 *n* (*personne*) modern

modernisation [mɔdɛrnizasjɔ̃] *nf* modernization; **les efforts de m. de l'enseignement** the attempts to modernize education

moderniser [mɔdɛrnize] *vt* to modernize, to bring up to date

modernisme [mɔdɛrnism] *nm* modernism

moderniste [mɔdɛrnist] *adj, n* modernist

modernité [mɔdɛrnite] *nf* modernity; **on est tout d'abord frappé par sa m.** the first thing that strikes you is how modern it is; **il a toujours été un défenseur de la m.** he has always defended what is modern

modern style [mɔdɛrnstil] **1** *nm* art nouveau **2** *adj inv* art nouveau; **balcon m.** art nouveau balcony

modeste [mɔdɛst] **1** *adj* **(a)** (*sans orgueil*) (*personne*) modest, unassuming, self-effacing **(b)** (*sans faste*) (*revenu, hôtel, appartement, repas*) modest; (*milieu*) modest, humble; (*personne*) humble, simple; **avoir un train de vie m.** to have a modest lifestyle *or* way of life; **être d'une origine m.** to be of humble origin; **une pièce aux dimensions modestes** a small room, a room of modest dimensions **(c)** *Litt Vieilli* (*pudique*) modest **2** *n* **ne faites pas le/la m.** don't be (so) modest; **elle joue les modestes** she's acting modest

modestement [mɔdɛstəmɑ̃] *adv* (*sourire, parler*) modestly; **être m. logé** to live in modest surroundings

modestie [mɔdɛsti] *nf* **(a)** (*de personne, revenu*) modesty; **fausse m.** false modesty **(b)** *Litt Vieilli* (*pudeur*) modesty

modicité [mɔdisite] *nf* (*de moyens, revenus*) slenderness; (*de prix*) moderateness, lowness, reasonableness; **la m. de ses revenus l'empêchait de partir en vacances** his income was too small *or* low to allow him to go on holiday; **malgré la m. du loyer** despite the low rent

modifiable [mɔdifjabl] *adj* modifiable; **jouet m.** Transformer®; **après cela le texte ne sera plus m.** after that the text cannot be amended

modificateur, -trice [mɔdifikatœr, -tris] **1** *adj* modifying **2** *nm* modifier

modificatif, -ive [mɔdifikatif, -iv] *adj* modifying

modification [mɔdifikasjɔ̃] *nf* (*à un discours, un texte, une déclaration*) alteration, change, amendment, modification; (*à une loi, une convention, un contrat*) amendment; (*à un plan, un programme, une carte*) alteration, change; (*physique*) change; **apporter** *ou* **faire une m. à qch** to make an alteration to *or* modify sth

modifier [mɔdifje] (*pr sub, impf* **n. modifiions, v. modifiiez**) **1** *vt* **(a)** (*texte, discours, déclaration*) to alter, to change, to amend, to modify; (*projet de loi, convention*) to amend; (*plan, programme, façon de faire*) to alter, to change; **ne modifiez rien** don't change anything, don't make any changes *or* alterations; **j'ai modifié la disposition des meubles** I've moved *or* changed the furniture around; *Naut* **m. la route** to alter course **(b)** *Gram* (*verbe*) to qualify, to modify **2 se modifier** *vpr* to alter, to be modified *or* altered

modique [mɔdik] *adj* (*coût, prix etc*) moderate, modest, reasonable; (*revenu*) modest, slender; **pour la m. somme de 50 francs** for the modest sum of 50 francs, for a mere 50 francs; *Iron* **sa voiture a coûté la m. somme de 100 000 francs** his car cost a cool hundred thousand

modiquement [mɔdikmɑ̃] *adv* **m. payé** poorly paid

modiste [mɔdist] *nf* milliner

modulable [mɔdylabl] *adj* (*horaires, tarif*) flexible; (*salle*) multi-purpose; (*espace intérieur*) adjustable

modulaire [mɔdylɛr] *adj* modular

modulateur, -trice [mɔdylatœr, -tris] *Rad etc* **1** *adj* (*valve etc*) modulating **2** *nm* modulator

modulation [mɔdylasjɔ̃] *nf* **(a)** *Mus* modulation, transition; *Fig* **une m. des paiements serait souhaitable pour les nouveaux adhérents** it would be desirable to adjust the rate of payment for new members **(b)** (*de la voix*) modulation, inflexion **(c)** *Rad etc* modulation, mod; **m. d'amplitude** amplitude modulation; **m. de fréquence** frequency modulation **(d)** *Ling* modulation

module [mɔdyl] *nm* (*élément constitutif d'un tout*) unit; *Archit, Astronaut, Ordinat* module; *Math, MecE, Phys* modulus; *Univ* **m. (d'enseignement)** module; *Astronaut* **m. lunaire/de commande** lunar/command module; *Ordinat* **m. d'aide** help module

moduler [mɔdyle] **1** *vt* (*des sons, Phys amplitude etc*) to modulate; (*sa voix*) to inflect, to modulate; *Fig* **m. des paiements** to adjust the rate of payment; **m. la thérapeutique en fonction des résultats obtenus** to adjust the treatment in the light of results **2** *vi Mus* to modulate

modus vivendi [mɔdysvivɛ̃di] *nm inv* modus vivendi

moelle [mwal] *nf* **(a)** (*d'os*) marrow, *Spéc* medulla; **m. épinière** spinal cord; **m. osseuse** bone marrow; **greffe de m. osseuse** bone marrow transplant; **os à m.** marrowbone; *Fig* **anglais jusqu'à la m.** English to the core; *Fig* **glacé jusqu'à la m.** frozen to the bone *or* to the marrow; *Fig* **corrompu** *ou* **pourri jusqu'à la m.** rotten to the core **(b)** *Bot* pith

moelleusement [mwaløzmɑ̃] *adv* snugly; **s'enfoncer m. dans un coussin de plumes** to snuggle down into a feather cushion; **être m. installé dans son lit** to be snuggled up in bed, to be snugly tucked up in bed; **être m. installé dans un fauteuil/sous une couette** to be snuggled up in an armchair/under an eiderdown

moelleux, -euse [mwalø, -øz] **1** *adj* (*tapis, étoffe, pull*) (velvety) soft; (*coussin, lit*) soft; (*couverture, couette*) soft, downy; (*caramel, substance*) smooth; (*gâteau*) moist; (*vin, voix*) mellow, smooth **2** *nm* (*d'un tapis, d'une étoffe, d'un pull*) (velvety) softness, velvetiness; (*d'un lit, de coussins*) softness; (*d'une couverture*) softness, downiness; (*d'une voix, d'un vin*) mellowness, smoothness; **un vin qui a du m.** a mellow *or* smooth wine

moellon [mwalɔ̃] *nm* quarry stone; **m. brut** rubble(stone); **m. d'appareil** ashlar

mœurs [mœr(s)] *nfpl* **(a)** (*coutumes*) (*de gens*) manners, customs; (*de pays, d'époque etc*) customs, *Fml* mores; (*d'animaux*) habits; **vivre avec les m. de son temps** to be in tune with the times; **il a de drôles de m.!** he's got some funny habits *or* ways; **entrer** *ou* **paser dans les m.** to become part of everyday life

(b) (*conduite en matière sexuelle*), *Jur* **certificat de bonne vie et m.** certificate of good character; **la brigade des m.**, *F* **les M.** = the vice squad; **attentat aux m.** sexual offence; **affaire de m.** sex case; **il a des m. spéciales** *ou* **particulières** he's the other way inclined; **femme de m. légères** *ou* **faciles** woman of easy virtue

(c) (*sens moral*) morals; **gens sans m.** unprincipled people; *Arch* **bonnes m.** morality; **c'est contraire aux bonnes m.** it is immoral *or* indecent; *Arch* **avoir des m.** to be of good moral character

mofette [mɔfɛt] *nf* (*mammifère*) skunk

mohair [mɔɛr] *nm Tex* mohair; **laine m.** mohair wool; **un pull en m.** a mohair sweater

Mohican [mɔikɑ̃] *nm* Mohican

moi [mwa] **1** *pron pers* [①**A26**,a; **B19**,5,a-b] **(a)** (*sujet*) I; **c'est m.** it's me, *Fml* it is I; **il est plus âgé que m.** he is older than me *or* than I am; **elle est invitée et m. aussi** she's invited and so am I; **qui vient avec nous? – m.** who's coming with us? – I am, me; **m. m'sieur, m. m'sieur je connais la réponse!** me sir, me sir, I know the answer; **m., je veux bien (le faire)** I don't mind (doing it); **m. qui vous parle** I'm telling you; **m., quand je serai grand** when I grow up; *très F* **m., les femmes, c'est fini** I've had my fill of women

(b) (*objet*) me; **il nous accuse mon frère et m.** he accuses my brother and me; **et m.? vous m'oubliez?** what about me? have you forgotten me?; **vous me soupçonnez, m.!** you suspect <u>me</u>!; **avec m.** with me; **venez à m.** come to me; **à m.!** help!; **à m., au secours!** help!, help!; **ce livre est à m.** this book is mine *or* belongs to me; **un ami à m.** a friend of mine; **ces vers ne sont pas de m.** these verses are not mine; **de vous à m.** between you and me, between ourselves, *F* between you, me and the gatepost

(c) (*après impératif*) **laissez-m. tranquille** leave me alone; **donnez-le-m.** give it to me; **dis-m., où est-ce que tu as mis le dossier bleu?** (by the way *or* by the by *or Am* say,) where have you put the blue file?; **dites-m. Jérôme, si nous allions à la mer cet été?** how about going to the seaside this year, Jérôme?, *Am* say, Jérôme, how about going to the seaside this year?

2 *nm* [①**A12**,1,d] ego, self; **culte du m.** egoism; **la psychanalyse nous aide à découvrir notre vrai m.** psychoanalysis helps us discover our true self

moignon [mwaɲɔ̃] *nm* (*de membre amputé etc*) stump

moi-même *pron pers* myself; *voir* **moi, même**

moindre [mwɛ̃dr] **1** *adj* **(a)** [①**A19**,g,iii] (*comp*) less(er); (*prix*) lower; (*quantité*) smaller; (*vitesse*) slower, lower; **question de m. importance** question of less(er) importance *or* of minor importance; **deux sur dix c'est un m. mal** two out of ten is not as bad as it might have been; **ce qui est un m. mal** so things aren't as bad as they might have been; **s'il arrive à s'en sortir avec seulement une jambe cassée ce sera un m. mal** if he comes out of it with just a broken leg, well, things might have been a lot worse

(b) (*superl*) **le/la m.** the least; **pas la m. chance** not the slightest *or* remotest *or* faintest chance; **c'est la m. des choses** *ou* **politesses** it's the least I/he/*etc* can do; **au m. reproche, il se met à pleurer** he bursts into tears at the slightest reproach; **au m. sourire il s'imagine qu'on s'intéresse à lui** the least little smile and he thinks you're interested in him; **il n'y a pas le m. espoir de les retrouver vivants** there isn't the slightest hope of finding them alive; **je ne lui ai pas fait le m. reproche** I didn't reproach him in the slightest *or* in the least

2 *n* **de deux maux il faut choisir le m.** you have to choose the lesser of two evils; **un expert, et non des moindres** no mean expert

moindrement [mwɛ̃drəmɑ̃] *adv Litt* (*souvent avec nég*) **sans être le m. intéressé/gêné** without being in the least bit interested/embarrassed; **je vous dérange? – pas le m.** am I disturbing you? – not at all *or* not in the slightest *or* not in the least

moine [mwan] *nm* **(a)** *Rel* monk, friar; *Prov* **l'habit ne fait pas le m.** clothes do not make the man; *Fig* **être gras comme un m.** to be fat, *esp Am* to be a real butterball; **mener une vie de m.** to live like a monk **(b)** *Arch* (*bassinoire*) bed warmer

moineau, -eaux [mwano] *nm* (*oiseau*) sparrow; *F* **c'est un vilain m.** he's a bad lot *or* a nasty piece of work; *Com* **têtes de m.** nuts (*of coal*)

moinillon [mwanijɔ̃] *nm F* young monk

moins [mwɛ̃] **1** *adv* **(a)** [①A10,b,iii; A19,g,iii] (*comparatif*) less; **je gagne m. que vous** I earn less than you (do); **elle gagne peu et lui m. encore** she doesn't earn much and he earns even less *or Fml* still less; **elle est m. intelligente que sa sœur** she's not as intelligent as her sister, she's less intelligent than her sister; **il est m. pingre qu'économe** he's not so much stingy as thrifty; **beaucoup m. long** much shorter; **m. d'argent** less money, not so much money, not as much money; **m. d'hommes/d'occasions** fewer *or* not so many men/opportunities; **j'ai eu m. de remords** I felt less remorse; **un peu m. de fierté** a little less pride; **plus on le punit, m. il travaille** the more he's punished the less he works; **plus il vieillit m. il a de cheveux** the older he gets the less hair he has; *F* **m. je le vois, mieux je me porte** the less I see of him the better; **il travaille de m. en m.** he's working less and less; **m. de dix francs** less than *or* under ten francs; **celui-ci coûte dix francs de m. que l'autre** this is ten francs less than the other one; **il y a eu 20% de visiteurs de m.** *ou* **en m.** there have been 20% fewer visitors; **je ne peux pas vous le laisser à m.** I can't let you have it for less; **il a m. de trente ans** he's less than *or* under thirty; **les m. de trente ans** the under-thirties; **les jeunes et les m. jeunes** the young and the not so young; **vous compterez cela en m.** you can deduct that, you can take that off the total; **il est revenu avec un œil/un bras/une jambe en m.** he came back minus an eye/an arm/a leg; **nous étions à m. d'un kilomètre de l'église** we were less than a kilometre from the church, we were within one kilometre of the church; **en m. de dix minutes** in less than ten minutes; **en m. de temps qu'il ne faut pour le dire,** *F* **en m. de deux** in no time (at all); *F* **c'était m. une** it was a close shave, it was a close *or* near thing; **il est on ne peut m. soigneux/honnête** he is extremely untidy/dishonest, *Fml* he is untidy/dishonest in the extreme; **je n'en suis pas m. décidée à le faire** I'm still going to do it nonetheless; **il est gentil mais il n'en est pas m. vrai que …** he's very nice but it's true nonetheless that …; **pas m. de 200 personnes** no fewer than 200 people; *F* no less than 200 people; **pas m. de 2 000 francs/trois jours** no less than 2,000 francs/three days; **rien m. que** nothing less than; **ce n'est rien m. qu'un héros** he's nothing less than a hero; **ce n'est rien (de) m. qu'un miracle** it's nothing short of a miracle; **elle mérite des éloges non m. que son frère** she deserves no less praise than her brother, she deserves praise quite as much as her brother

(b) à m. d'avis contraire unless I/you/*etc* hear to the contrary; **à m. d'un imprévu/un miracle/une catastrophe** barring something unforeseen/a miracle/a catastrophe, unless something unforeseen happens/a miracle happens/ there's a catastrophe; **à m. de partir tout de suite** unless I/ you/*etc* leave at once; **à m. que … +** *sub* unless …; **à m. que vous (ne) l'ordonniez** unless you order it

(c) (*superlatif*) **le m.** the least; **les élèves les m. appliqués** the least industrious pupils; **le m. de gens possible** the smallest possible number of people, as few people as possible; **pas le m. du monde** not in the least *or* slightest, by no means; *Prov* **qui peut le plus peut le m.** you've/he's/*etc* done much more complicated things in your/his/*etc* time

(d) du m. at least, that is to say, at all events; **c'est (tout) du m. ce qu'il dit** that's what he says, at least; **au m.** at least; **gagner 100 000 francs par an au m.** to earn 100, 000 francs a year at (the very) least; *F* **tu as fait ton travail, au m.?** you've done your work, I hope?; **c'est pour le m. surprenant** it's surprising to say the least

2 *prép* minus, less; **une heure m. cinq** five (minutes) to *or Am* of one; **six m. quatre égale deux** six minus four equals two; **il fait m. dix (degrés)** it's minus ten (degrees)

3 *nm Math* minus (sign)

4 *n F* **un/une m. que rien** a rat

moins-disant, *pl* **moins-disants** [mwɛ̃dizɑ̃] *nm* lowest bidder

moins-perçu, *pl* **moins-perçus** *nm Fin* outstanding amount, amount due *or* owing

moins-value, *pl* **moins-values** [mwɛ̃valy] *nf Fin* depreciation, drop in value; (*après une vente*) capital loss

moirage [mwaraʒ] *nm* (*de soie etc*) (*action de moirer*) watering

moire [mwar] *nf* **(a)** *Tex* moire, moiré; **m. de soie** watered silk **(b)** (*reflet*) shimmer

moiré [mware] *Tex* **1 (a)** *adj* (*soie etc*) watered, moiré **(b)** (*aux reflets changeants*) shimmering **2** *nm* = **moirure**

moirer [mware] *vt* **(a)** *Tex* (*soie etc*) to water **(b)** *Litt* to make shimmer

moirure [mwaryr] *nf* **(a)** *Tex* watered effect, moiré **(b)** *Litt* shimmer, shimmering

mois [mwa] *nm* **(a)** [①A75-6,B-C; B58-9,B-C] month; **au m. d'août** in (the month of) August; **louer qch au m.** to hire sth by the month; **pendant deux m.** for two months; **cent francs par m.** a hundred francs a month; **un m. de vacances/salaire** a month's holiday/wages; **le treizième m.** = one month's salary paid as a bonus; *Bourse* **m. d'échéance** trading month **(b)** (*de paie*) month's wages *or* salary; **je n'ai pas encore touché mon m.** I still haven't received this month's wages *or* salary; **je dois deux m. à l'épicier** I haven't paid the grocer for two months

moïse [mɔiz] *nm* **(a)** (*berceau*) Moses basket **(b)** *Bible* **M.** Moses

moisi [mwazi] **1** *adj* (*pain, gâteau, fromage*) mouldy, *US* moldy; (*mur, tissu etc*) mildewed, mildewy; (*goût*) musty; (*odeur*) musty, fusty **2** *nm* (*sur pain, confiture, fromage*) mould, *US* mold; (*sur mur, tissu*) mildew; **odeur de m.** musty *or* fusty smell; **avoir un goût de m.** to taste mouldy *or* musty; **sentir le m.** to smell musty *or* fusty

moisir [mwazir] **1** *vi* (*de pain*) to go mouldy *or US* moldy; (*de raisins*) to go mouldy, to mildew; (*de linge*) to mildew; *Fig* **j'avais l'impression de m. dans cette ville** I felt I was mouldering away in that town; **il m'a laissé m. deux heures** he left me cooling my heels for two hours; *Fig F* **on ne va pas m. ici** (*partons*) let's not hang about here **2** *vt* (*pain*) to make mouldy *or US* moldy; (*raisins, linge*) to mildew

moisissure [mwazisyr] *nf* **(a)** (*partie moisie*) mould, *US* mold; **moisissures** mouldy bits, mould **(b)** (*processus*) (formation of) mould *or US* mold; **une forte odeur de m.** a strong musty smell

moisson [mwasɔ̃] *nf* **(a)** (*action*) (*de céréales*) harvest(ing); (*époque*) harvest time; **faire la m.** *ou* **les moissons** to harvest; *Fig* **une m. de documents** a pile *or* sheaf of documents; **une m. d'idées** a wealth of ideas **(b)** (*récolte*) crop, harvest; **rentrer la m.** to bring in the crops *or* the harvest

moissonnage [mwasɔnaʒ] *nm* harvesting, reaping

moissonner [mwasɔne] *vt* **(a)** (*céréales*) to reap, to harvest; (*champ*) to reap; (*récoltes*) to harvest, to gather (in); **lundi prochain, on commence à m.** we'll start harvesting next Monday; *Litt Fig* **m. des informations** to gather a wealth of information; **m. des lauriers** to reap *or* win laurels **(b)** *Litt* **la guerre moissonne les vies humaines** war cuts short many lives

moissonneur, -euse [mwasɔnœr, -øz] **1** *n* harvester, reaper **2** *nf* **moissonneuse** (*machine*) reaper, reaping machine

moissonneuse-batteuse, *pl* **moissonneuses-batteuses** [mwasɔnøzbatøz] *nf* combine (harvester)

moissonneuse-lieuse, *pl* **moissonneuses-lieuses** [mwasɔnøzljøz] *nf* reaper-binder

moite [mwat] *adj* (*mains, front*) sweaty, clammy; (*atmosphère, air*) muggy; (*chaleur*) moist; **j'avais les mains moites de sueur** my hands were sweaty, my hands were damp with sweat

moiteur [mwatœr] *nf* (*de mains, du front*) sweatiness, clamminess; (*de terre*) wetness; (*d'atmosphère, d'air*) mugginess

moitié [mwatje] **1** *nf* **(a)** [①A5,B; A12,1,d] half; **quelle est la m. de dix?** what is half of ten?; **la m. de la production** half (of) the production; **qui veut la m. d'une banane?** who wants half (of) a banana?; **la bouteille était à m. pleine/vide** the bottle was half full/empty; **deux moitiés** two halves; **partagé en deux moitiés** divided into two halves, halved; **vendre qch à m. prix** to sell sth (at) half price; **réduit de m.** reduced by half; *F* **m.-m.** fifty-fifty; **faire m.-m.** to go halves *or* fifty-fifty; **ça devrait faire à peu près m.-m.** that should be us just about even; **se mettre** *ou* **être de m. avec qn** to go halves with sb, to go fifty-fifty with sb; **il est pour m. responsable** he is equally *or* just as much to blame, half the responsibility is his; **à m.** half; **à m. mort/cuit/nu/endormi** half-dead/-cooked/-naked/-asleep; **faire les choses à m.** to do things by halves; **elle ne fait pas les choses à m.** she doesn't do things by halves

(b) *Hum F* (*époux, épouse*) **ma (chère) m.** my better half

2 *adv* half; **m. riant, m. pleurant** half laughing, half crying; **m. Anglaise, m. Écossaise** half English, half Scottish; **m. plus** half as much again; **il y a m. de plus de**

monde que l'année dernière there are half as many people again as there were last year; **m. moins gros/cher/de monde** fifty percent smaller/cheaper/fewer people; **c'est m. moins gros que l'autre** it's half the size of the other one; **ça m'a coûté m. moins cher** it cost me half the price; **il y a m. moins de monde qu'à la première représentation** there are half the people there were at the first performance

moitir [mwatir] *vt Vieilli Tech* (*papier etc*) to moisten

moka [mɔka] **1** *nm* (*café*) mocha (coffee); (*gâteau*) mocha *or* coffee cake; **glace au m.** coffee ice-cream **2** *n Géog* **M.** Mocha, Mokha

mol *voir* **mou**[1]

molaire[1] [mɔlɛr] *nf* molar

molaire[2] *adj Phys* molar

molasse [mɔlas] *nf* = **mollasse 2**

moldave [mɔldav] **1** *adj* Moldavian **2** *n* **M.** Moldavian

Moldavie [mɔldavi] *nf* Moldavia

mole [mɔl] *nf Phys* mole

môle [mol] *nm* (*brise-lames*) breakwater, mole; (*quai*) pier

moléculaire [mɔlekylɛr] *adj* molecular

molécule [mɔlekyl] *nf* molecule

molécule-gramme, *pl* **molécules-grammes** *nf Phys* gram(me) molecule

molène [mɔlɛn] *nf Bot* mullein

moleskine [mɔlɛskin] *nf* imitation leather; (*coton*) moleskin

molester [mɔlɛste] *vt* **m. qn** to rough sb up; **se faire m. par la police** to be roughed up by the police

moletage [mɔltaʒ] *nm* milling, knurling

moleter [mɔlte] *vt* (**je molette; je moletterai**) to mill, to knurl

molette [mɔlɛt] *nf* **(a)** (*d'éperon*) rowel; (*de briquet*) wheel; (*de jumelles*) focus wheel; **m. de réglage** control knob **(b)** (*pour le verre etc*) cutting wheel

moliéresque [moljerɛsk] *adj* (*situation, verve*) reminiscent of Molière

mollah [mɔla] *nm Rel* mullah

mollard [mɔlar] *nm Vulg* gob of spit

mollarder [mɔlarde] *vi Vulg* to gob

mollasse [mɔlas] **1** *adj* flabby; *Fig F* (*personne*) (*physiquement*) lethargic; (*moralement*) spineless **2** *n F* **un/une m.** a lazy lump (of a man/woman)

mollasson, -onne [mɔlasɔ̃, -ɔn] *F* **1** *adj* (*personne*) (*physiquement*) lethargic; (*moralement*) spineless **2** *n* **un m./une mollassonne** a lazy lump (of a man/woman)

molle *voir* **mou**[1]

mollement [mɔlmɑ̃] *adv* **(a)** (*avec abandon*) languidly; (*avec lenteur*) gently; **les barques se balançaient m. sur l'eau** the small boats were bobbing gently on the water; **m. étendu sur sa couche** stretched out languidly on his couch **(b)** (*sans énergie*) (*répondre, se déplacer*) feebly, weakly; (*serrer la main*) limply; (*protester, réagir*) feebly

mollesse [mɔlɛs] *nf* **(a)** (*manque d'énergie*) lethargy; (*de tissus, muscles*) flabbiness; (*de style*) flabbiness, limpness; (*de gouvernement*) laxity, laxness; *Beaux-Arts* **la m. du trait** the lack of vigour in the brushstrokes **(b)** (*de coussin, matelas, chaise etc*) softness

mollet[1] [mɔlɛ] *adj m* (*œuf*) soft-boiled; **pain m.** (soft) bread roll

mollet[2] *nm* [①A12,1,d] *Anat* calf; **des mollets de coq** spindly legs

molletière [mɔltjɛr] **1** *adj f* **bandes molletières** puttees **2** *nf* puttee

molleton [mɔltɔ̃] *nm* (*en coton*) flannelette; (*en laine*) flannel; (*de table*) table felt

molletonné [mɔltɔne] *adj* (*gants, veste*) fleece-lined

molletonner [mɔltɔne] *vt* to line with fleece

mollir [mɔlir] **1** *vi* (*du vent*) to die down, to abate; (*de courage, enthousiasme*) to flag, to slacken; **je sentis mes jambes m.** I felt my legs give way (beneath me); **le sol mollissait sous mes pieds** the ground was giving way beneath my feet **2** *vt Naut* (*cordage*) to slacken, to ease, to slack off; (*barre*) to ease

mollusque [mɔlysk] *nm* **(a)** *Zool* mollusc, *US* mollusk **(b)** *F* (*personne*) lazy lump

molosse [mɔlɔs] *nm* watchdog, guard dog

molybdène [mɔlibdɛn] *nm Minér* molybdenum

môme [mom] **1** *n F* (*enfant*) kid **2** *nf Arg* (*femme, fille*) chick; (*petite amie*) girl **3** *adj* **quand j'étais (tout) m.** when I was (just) a kid

moment [mɔmɑ̃] *nm* **(a)** (*espace de temps*) moment; **le m. venu** (*passé*) when the time came; (*futur*) when the time comes; **à ce m.-là** then; *Fig* (*dans ces conditions*) if that's the case, in that case; **s'il ne peut pas te ramener, à ce m.-là tu m'appelles et je passerai** if he can't bring you back, then ring me and I'll come and get you; **à un m. donné** at one point; **c'est le bon m. pour ...** now is the (right) time to ...; **c'est le m. ou jamais** it's now or never; **c'est le m. ou jamais de lui dire ce que tu penses** now's the time (if ever there was one) to tell him what you think; **un m.!** one moment!, just a moment!; **je suis à vous dans un m.** I'll be with you in a moment; **en ce m.** at the moment, just now, at present; **à quel m. de l'année/la semaine?** at what time of the year/the week?; **à quel m. de l'histoire/sa vie?** at what stage of *or* point in the story/his life?; **il ne me faut rien pour le m.** I don't need anything at the moment *or* for the moment *or* for the time being; **sur le m.** at the time; **dans ces moments, on ne réfléchit pas** at times like that you don't think; **passer un bon m.** to have a good time; **attendre le m. opportun** to wait for an opportune moment *or* the right moment; **arriver au bon m.** to arrive at just the right time; **ce n'est qu'un mauvais m. à passer** it'll soon be over with; **j'ai eu un m. de honte** for a moment I felt ashamed; **elle n'a pas eu un m. de repos aujourd'hui** she hasn't had a moment's rest today; **elle n'a pas un m. à elle** she hasn't a moment *or* minute to herself; **elle en a pour un m. avec ce travail** the work'll keep her busy for a (good) while; **par moments** at times, now and again; **d'un m. à l'autre** (at) any moment *or* time *or* minute; **à tout m., à tous moments** (*sans cesse*) constantly; (*n'importe quand*) at any moment; **il vaut mieux lui demander dans un de ses bons moments** it's better to ask him when he's in one of his good moods; **dans un m. de bonté** in a moment of kindness; **au m. de partir** just as I/he/ *etc* was leaving *or* was about to leave; **il attend toujours le dernier m. pour nous dire ce qu'il a décidé** he always waits till the last moment *or* minute to tell us what he's decided; **les derniers moments de sa vie** the last moments of his life; **au m. de sa naissance/de l'accident/des élections** at the time of his birth/of the accident/of the elections; **jusqu'au m. où ...** until ...

(b) du m. que ... seeing that ..., since ...

(c) (*temps présent*) **le m.** the moment; **c'est le disque/la star du m.** it's the record/she's the star of the moment

(d) *Phys* (*de force, d'inertie etc*) moment

momentané [mɔmɑ̃tane] *adj* (*effort, coup de cafard*) brief; (*absence, interruption*) brief, temporary; (*panne*) temporary; **je suis bloqué chez moi mais c'est m.** I'm stuck at home, but it won't be for long; **je prends ce bureau mais ce n'est que m.** I'm taking this office, but it's only a temporary measure

momentanément [mɔmɑ̃tanemɑ̃] *adv* (*perdre connaissance, s'assoupir*) momentarily, for a moment, briefly; (*être absent, arrêter de fumer*) temporarily; *TV* **nos programmes sont m. interrompus** there is a temporary break in transmission

momerie [momri] *nf Litt Vieilli* mummery; (*pratique insincère*) insincerity

mômerie [momri] *nf* (*enfantillage*) childishness, childish behaviour; **cesse tes mômeries** stop being so childish

momie [mɔmi] *nf* mummy

momification [mɔmifikasjɔ̃] *nf* mummification

momifier [mɔmifje] (*impf & pr sub* **n. momifiions, v. momifiiez**) **1** *vt* to mummify **2 se momifier** *vpr* to become mummified; *Fig* to become fossilized

mon, ma, mes [mɔ̃, ma, me] *adj poss* [①A30,8; B19-20,E,1] (**mon** *is used instead of* **ma** *before f words beginning with vowel or mute h*) **(a)** my; **m. ami/amie** my friend; **m. meilleur ami/ma meilleure amie** my best friend; **m. oncle et ma tante** my uncle and (my) aunt; **m. père et ma mère**, *Litt* **mes père et mère** my mother and father; **j'ai mis m. chapeau et mes gants** I put on my hat and (my) gloves; **un(e) de mes ami(e)s** one of my friends, a friend of mine; **un professeur de mes amis** a teacher friend of mine; *F* **j'aurai ma chambre à moi** I'll have my own room; *F* **m. imbécile de frère** my idiot of a brother; *F* **m. artiste de mari** my husband, the artist; *F* **alors, tu veux le recontrer, m. artiste?** do you want to meet this artist of mine, then?; *F* **et voilà m. Simon qui se met à rouspéter** then old Simon starts grumbling; *F* **j'ai eu m. vendredi** I got Friday off

(b) (*pour s'adresser à qn*) **non, m. général/capitaine** no, General/Captain; *Rel* **oui, ma sœur/mère, oui, m. père** yes, Sister/Mother, yes Father; *Fml* **m. oncle, je vous écris pour demander ...** I'm writing to you, uncle, to ask you ...; **viens, m. enfant** come here, child;

monacal, -ale, -aux, -ales [mɔnakal, -o] *adj* (*vie, calme*) monastic

monachisme [mɔnaʃism] *nm* monasticism

monade [mɔnad] *nf Phil* monad

monarchie [mɔnarʃi] *nf* monarchy; **m. constitutionnelle** *ou* **tempérée/absolue** constitutional/absolute monarchy

monarchique [mɔnarʃik] *adj* monarchic(al)

monarchisme [mɔnarʃism] *nm* monarchism

monarchiste [mɔnarʃist] *adj, n* monarchist

monarque [mɔnark] *nm* monarch

monastère [mɔnastɛr] *nm* (*de moines*) monastery; (*de religieuses*) convent

monastique [mɔnastik] *adj* monastic

monaural, -ale, -aux, -ales [mɔnɔral, -o] *adj* monaural

monceau, -eaux [mɔ̃so] *nm* heap, pile

mondain, -aine [mɔ̃dɛ̃, -ɛn] **1** *adj* **(a)** (*lieu*) fashionable; **réunion/soirée mondaine** society gathering/evening; *Journ* **carnet m., rubrique** *ou* **chronique mondaine** society news, gossip column; **écrivain/chroniqueur m.** society writer/ columnist; **la brigade mondaine** = the vice squad **(b)** *Péj* (*qui aime les mondanités*) **il est très m.** he likes moving in fashionable circles, he's a great socialite **(c)** *Rel* (*plaisirs etc*) worldly, earthly **2** *n* socialite **3** *nf F* **la Mondaine** = the vice squad

mondanité [mɔ̃danite] *nf* **(a)** society life; **je ne supporte pas sa m.** I can't bear his love of society **(b) mondanités** social gatherings; (*politesses, conversations superficielles*) social niceties; *Journ* society news, gossip column **(c)** *Rel* worldliness

monde [mɔ̃d] *nm* **(a)** (*univers, humanité*) world; **le m. entier** the whole world; **dans le m. entier** (*connu, en vente*) worldwide, all over the world, the world over; **(que) le m. est petit!** it's a small world!; **faire le tour du m.** to go round the world; **faire le tour du m. à la voile** to sail round the world; **les quatre coins du m.** the four corners of the world *or* globe; **il est allé/a travaillé aux quatre coins du m.** he's been/worked all over the world; **parcourir** *ou* **courir le m.** to travel the world; **mettre qn au m.** to bring sb into the world, to give birth to sb; **être seul au m.** to be alone in the world; **il est encore de ce m.** he is still with us, he is still alive; **je ne te ferais souffrir pour rien au m.** I wouldn't hurt you for (anything in) the world; *F* **c'est un m.!, c'est quand même un m.!** that's a bit much!; **c'est tout de même** *ou* **quand même un m. de ne pas pouvoir faire ce qu'on veut chez soi!** it's a bit much if you can't do what you want in your own home!; *F* **elle se fait toujours un m. de tout** she always gets worked up about everything; **il n'y a pas de quoi s'en faire un m.** it's not worth getting worked up about, it's no big deal; **personne au m. ne me fera changer d'avis** no one in the world will make me change my mind; **un des seuls êtres en ce m. qui …** one of the few people in the world who …; **les meilleurs amis du m.** the best friends in the world; **vieux comme le m.** (as) old as the hills; **depuis que le m. est m.** since time began, since the beginning of time; **elle a volé à la face du m.** she stole things right under everybody's nose; *Fig* **c'est le m. à l'envers** the world's gone mad, the whole world's topsy-turvy; **le bout du m.** the ends of the earth; **ils habitent au bout du m.** they live at the back of beyond; *Fig F* **ce n'est pas le bout du m.!** (*c'est faisable*) it's not the end of the world!, it's no big deal!; *Fig F* **c'est le bout du m. s'il me faut deux jours pour terminer ce travail** I'll finish the job in two days at the outside *or* at the very most; **il faut de tout pour faire un m.** it takes all sorts (to make a world); **ainsi va le m.** it's the way of the world; **refaire le m.** to put the world to rights; *Iron* **tout est pour le mieux dans le meilleur des mondes** everything is for the best in the best of all possible worlds; **l'autre m.** the next world; **il vit dans un autre m.** he lives in another world; **elle est dans son m.** she's in her own little world; **en ce bas m.** here on earth

(b) (*milieu*) world; **le m. de la haute finance** the world of high finance; **je ne suis pas de leur m.** I'm not in their set *or* crowd; **le (beau) m.** (fashionable) society, *F* the glitterati; **le grand m.** high society; **aller (beaucoup) dans le m.** to go out a great deal, to move in fashionable circles; **homme du m.** society man; *Iron* **embarquez-moi tout ce joli m. dans le panier à salade** throw this bunch *or* crew into the back of the van

(c) (*gens*) people; **tout le m.** everybody, everyone; **il y a du m.** (*le lieu n'est pas désert*) there are some people; (*il y a foule*) there are a lot of people; *très F* **il y a du m. au balcon** she's well-endowed; **il y a trop de m.** it's too crowded, there are too many people; **peu de m., pas grand m.** not many people, not a large crowd; **avoir du m. à dîner** to have people to dinner; **tu te moques du m.? je te demande d'arriver à 9h et …** what do you take me for? I asked you to be here by 9 o'clock and …; *F* **les politiciens se fichent vraiment du m.** politicians really must think we're stupid; *très F* **je n'aime pas qu'on se foute du m.! quand on me dit une chose un jour …** I don't like being taken for a bloody idiot! if I'm told one thing one day …; **il connaît son m.** he knows the people he has to deal with; **comment va tout votre m.?** how is your *or* the family?

(d) *Arch* (*domestiques*) servants, men, hands

(e) (*vie séculière*) **se retirer du m.** to withdraw from the world

mondial, -ale, -iaux, -ales [mɔ̃djal, -jo] **1** *adj* (*crise, conflit, problème, ampleur*) worldwide, global; **à l'échelle mondiale** on a world(wide) scale, on a global scale; **la première/ deuxième guerre mondiale** the First/Second World War, World War One/Two **2** *nm Fb* **le M.** the World Cup

mondialement [mɔ̃djalmɑ̃] *adv* throughout the world, universally; **m. reconnu pour son génie** known throughout the world *or* universally for his genius; **m. célébré** world-famous, celebrated throughout the world

mondialisation [mɔ̃djalizasjɔ̃] *nf* globalization

mondialiser [mɔ̃djalize] **1** *vt* to globalize **2 se mondialiser** *vpr* to become globalized; **l'utilisation du Minitel se mondialise** the use of Minitel is spreading worldwide

mond(i)ovision [mɔ̃d(j)ovizjɔ̃] *nf TV, Télécom* satellite *or* world television

monégasque [mɔnegask] **1** *adj* Monacan, Monegasque **2** *n* **M.** Monacan, Monegasque

monème [mɔnɛm] *nm Ling* moneme

MONEP [mɔnɛp] *nm* (*abrév* **marché des options négociables à Paris**) MONEP

monétaire [mɔnetɛr] *adj* (*unité, système, questions*) monetary; **quelle est l'unité m. du Pérou?** what is the currency of Peru?; **marché m.** money market; **masse m.** money supply; *CE* **le serpent m.** the (currency) snake

monétarisme [mɔnetarism] *nm Écon* monetarism

monétariste [mɔnetarist] *adj, n Écon* monetarist

monétique [mɔnetik] *nf Fin* electronic money, e-money; *Banque* electronic banking

monétiser [mɔnetize] *vt* to monetize

mongol, -ole [mɔ̃gɔl] **1** *adj* **(a)** (*de Mongolie*) Mongol, Mongolian **(b)** *F Péj* moronic **2** *nm Ling* Mongolian **3** *n* **(a)** *Géog* **M.** Mongol, Mongolian **(b)** *F Péj* moron

Mongolie [mɔ̃gɔli] *nf* Mongolia

mongolien, -ienne [mɔ̃gɔljɛ̃, -jɛn] *Méd* **1** *adj* **bébé m.** Down's syndrome baby, *Vieilli* mongol baby **2** *n* (*bébé*) Down's syndrome baby, *Vieilli* mongol (baby); (*personne*) person with Down's syndrome, *Vieilli* mongol

mongolique [mɔ̃gɔlik] *adj* Mongol(ian)

mongolisme [mɔ̃gɔlism] *nm Méd* Down's syndrome, *Vieilli* mongolism

mongoloïde [mɔ̃gɔlɔid] *Méd* **1** *adj* (*traits*) mongoloid; (*individu*) affected by Down's syndrome **2** *n Vieilli* mongoloid

moniteur, -trice [mɔnitœr, -tris] **1** *n* **(a)** *Sp* instructor, *f* instructress, coach; **m. d'auto-école/de ski** driving/ski instructor **(b)** (*dans une colonie de vacances*) assistant, *US* (camp) counselor **2** *nm Ordinat, Tech, Méd, TV* monitor; *Méd* **m. cardiaque** cardiac *or* heart monitor; *Ordinat* **m. SVGA** SVGA monitor; *Ordinat* **m. basse radiation** low-radiation monitor; **m. couleur** colour monitor; *Ordinat* **m. pleine page** A4 monitor; **m. à cristaux liquides** liquid crystal monitor; *Ordinat* **m. à tube cathodique** cathode ray tube monitor; **m. à écran plat** flat screen monitor

monitorage [mɔnitɔraʒ] *nm* monitoring; **écran de m.** monitor

monitorat [mɔnitɔra] *nm* (*fonction*) instructorship; (*période de formation*) instructor training; **m. sportif** sports instruction

monitoring [mɔnitɔriŋ] *nm* monitoring

monnaie [mɔnɛ] *nf* **(a)** [①**A12**,1,b] *Fin* (*argent*) money; (*d'un pays*) currency; **pièce de m.** coin; **m. électronique** plastic money, electronic money *or* methods of payment, e-money; **m. légale** legal tender; **m. scripturale** bank money, deposit money; **fausse m.** counterfeit money; **frapper la m., battre m.** to coin *or* mint money; **(l'hôtel de) la M.** ≈ the Royal Mint; **m. de papier** paper money; **m. de compte (convertible)** (convertible) money of account; **m. de réserve** reserve currency; *F* **m. de singe** worthless currency; *F* **c'est de la m. de singe!** it's worthless; *F* **payer qn en m. de singe** to fob sb off, to let sb whistle for his/her money; **c'est m. courante dans ce milieu** it's common in these circles

(b) (*pièces etc*) change; **petite m.** small change; **vous auriez de la m. pour le parcmètre?** do you have some change for the parking meter?; **vous auriez la m. de cent francs?** could you give me change for a hundred-franc note, could you change a hundred-franc note for me?; **faire de la m.** to get some change; **pourriez-vous me faire de la m.?** could you give me some change?; **faire la m. de mille francs** to get change for a thousand-franc note; (*du commercant*) to give change for a thousand-franc note; *Fig* **rendre à qn la m. de sa pièce** to pay sb back in his/her own coin *or* in kind

monnaie-du-pape, *pl* **monnaies-du-pape** *nf Bot* honesty

monnayable [mɔnɛjabl] *adj* convertible into money; *Fig* **cette formation/son expérience est m.** this training/his experience is worth money; **ce diplôme n'est pas m.** this diploma is of no value financially

monnayage [mɔnɛjaʒ] *nm* minting, coining

monnayer [mɔneje] **(je monnaye, je monnaie; je monnayerai, je monnaierai) 1** *vt* **(a)** (*argent*) to coin, to mint **(b)** *Fig* (*son influence, son talent etc*) to capitalize on, to cash in on; **il refusa de m. son silence** he refused to put a price on his silence **2 se monnayer** *vpr* **ça se monnaye** there's money to be made out of it, there's money in it; **je veux bien faire ce que vous me demandez mais ça se monnaye** I'm happy to do what you ask, but it'll cost you; **ici tout se monnaye** money can buy (you) anything here, everything here has its price
monnayeur [mɔnɛjœr] *nm* coiner, minter; **faux m.** counterfeiter
mono¹ [mɔno] *adj inv F* (*disque*) mono; **en m.** in mono
mono² *n F* = **moniteur, -trice 1**
monoacide [mɔnoasid] *adj Ch* monoacid(ic)
monobloc [mɔnoblɔk] *adj inv* (*cylindres, châssis*) made in one piece, cast solid
monocaméra [mɔnokamera] *nf* single camera
monochrome [mɔnokrom] **1** *adj* monochrome; *Ordinat* **écran m.** monochrome screen **2** *nm Beaux-Arts* monochrome
monochromie [mɔnokromi] *nf* monochromaticity
monocle [mɔnɔkl] *nm* monocle
monocoque [mɔnokɔk] **1** *adj* **avion m.** monocoque; **carrosserie m.** (*de voiture*) monocoque body; **bateau m.** monohull **2** *nm* (*bateau*) monohull
monocorde [mɔnokɔrd] **1** *adj* **(a)** *Mus* (*instrument*) single-stringed **(b)** (*son, ton, voix*) monotonous **2** *nm* monochord
monocotylédone [mɔnokɔtiledɔn] *nf Bot* monocotyledon
monoculaire [mɔnɔkylɛr] *adj* (*jumelles, vision, microscope*) monocular; **cécité m.** blindness in one eye
monoculture [mɔnokyltyr] *nf Agr* monoculture
monocycle [mɔnosikl] *nm* unicycle, monocycle
monocylindre [mɔnosilɛ̃dr] *nm Aut* single-cylinder engine
monocylindrique [mɔnosilɛ̃drik] *adj Aut* (*moteur*) single-cylinder
monoéthylèneglycol [mɔnoetilɛnglikɔl] *nm* monoethylene glycol
monogame [mɔnɔgam] *adj* monogamous
monogamie [mɔnɔgami] *nf* monogamy
monogamique [mɔnɔgamik] *adj* monogamous
monogramme [mɔnɔgram] *nm* monogram
monographie [mɔnɔgrafi] *nf* monograph
monoï [mɔnɔj] *nm* scented coconut oil
mono-insaturé [mɔnoɛ̃satyre] *adj* (*lipide*) mono-unsaturated
monokini [mɔnokini] *nm* monokini; **faire du m.** to wear a monokini, to go topless
monolingue [mɔnɔlɛ̃g] *adj* monolingual
monolinguisme [mɔnɔlɛ̃gɥism] *nm* monolingualism
monolithe [mɔnɔlit] **1** *adj* monolithic **2** *nm* monolith
monolithique [mɔnɔlitik] *adj* monolithic; *Fig* (*organisation, parti*) monolithic; (*caractère, personne*) uncompromising
monologue [mɔnɔlɔg] *nm* monologue; *Th* (*de Hamlet etc*) soliloquy, monologue; **m. intérieur** interior monologue
monologuer [mɔnɔlɔge] *vi* (*parler seul*) to talk to oneself; *Th* to soliloquize, to talk to oneself
monomanie [mɔnomani] *nf Vieilli* monomania
monôme [mɔnom] *nm Math* monomial, single term
monométallisme [mɔnometalism] *nm Fin* monometallism
monomoteur [mɔnomɔtœr] **1** *adj* single-engined **2** *nm* single-engined aircraft
mononucléose [mɔnonykleoz] *nf Méd* mononucleosis; **m. infectieuse** glandular fever, *Spéc* infectious mononucleosis
monoparental, -ale, -aux, -ales [mɔnoparɑ̃tal, -o] *adj* (*famille*) single-parent, one-parent
monophasé [mɔnofɑze] *Él* **1** *adj* (*courant*) single-phase **2** *nm* single-phase current
monophonique [mɔnofɔnik] *adj* monoaural
monoplace [mɔnoplas] **1** *adj* (*avion, voiture*) single-seater **2** *nm ou f Aut* single-seater (car) **3** *nm Av* single-seater (plane)
monoplan [mɔnoplɑ̃] *nm Av* monoplane
monopole [mɔnɔpɔl] *nm* monopoly; **m. d'État** State monopoly; **m. d'exploitation** operating monopoly; **m. de vente** sales monopoly; **avoir le m. de qch** *Écon* to have the monopoly of sth, to have a monopoly on sth; *Fig* to have a monopoly on sth
monopoleur [mɔnɔpɔlœr] *nm* monopolist
monopolisateur, -trice [mɔnɔpɔlizatœr, -tris] **1** *n* monopolizer, monopolist **2** *adj* monopolizing
monopolisation [mɔnɔpɔlizasjɔ̃] *nf* monopolization
monopoliser [mɔnɔpɔlize] *vt* to monopolize; **m. la parole** not to let anyone else speak
monoposte [mɔnopɔst] *nm Ordinat* standalone
monorail [mɔnorɑj] **1** *adj* monorail **2** *nm* monorail
monoski [mɔnoski] *nm Sp* monoski; **faire du m.** to monoski
monospace [mɔnospas] *nm Aut* people carrier
monosyllabe [mɔnosilab] **1** *adj* monosyllabic **2** *nm* monosyllable
monosyllabique [mɔnosilabik] *adj* monosyllabic
mono-tâche *adj inv Ordinat* single-tasking
monothéisme [mɔnoteism] *nm* monotheism
monothéiste [mɔnoteist] **1** *adj* monotheistic **2** *n* monotheist
monotone [mɔnɔtɔn] *adj* monotonous; (*existence*) monotonous, humdrum
monotonie [mɔnɔtɔni] *nf* monotony; **rompre la m.** to break the monotony
monotype® [mɔnotip] *nf Typ* Monotype (machine)
monovalent [mɔnovalɑ̃] *adj Ch* monovalent, univalent
monoxyde [mɔnɔksid] *nm* **m. de carbone** carbon monoxide
monseigneur [mɔ̃sɛɲœr] *nm* **(a)** *pl* **nosseigneurs** *ou* **messeigneurs** (*référence à un prince*) His Royal Highness; (*à un cardinal*) His Eminence; (*à un duc, archevêque*) His Grace; (*à un évêque*) His Lordship; **m. l'évêque de ...** the Lord Bishop of ... **(b)** *pl* **messeigneurs** (*en s'adressant au prince*) Your Royal Highness; (*au cardinal*) Your Eminence; (*au duc, à l'archevêque*) Your Grace; (*à l'évêque*) My Lord (Bishop), Your Lordship
monsieur, *pl* **messieurs** [məsjø, mesjø] *nm* **(a) M. Robert Marceau** Mr Robert Marceau; **Messieurs Marceau et Cie** Messrs Marceau and Co; **m. le duc/le comte de Montignac** the Duke/the Earl of Montignac; **m. le duc/le comte est servi** dinner is served, your Grace/my Lord

(b) *Vieilli* (*à un petit garçon*) **M. Robert** Master Robert

(c) *Fml* (*utilisé seul*) **voici le chapeau de m.** (*en s'adressant à lui*) here's your hat, sir; (*sans s'adresser à lui*) here's the gentleman's hat; (*à quelqu'un qui s'appelle Martin*) here's Mr Martin's hat; **m. n'est pas là** Mr Martin/*etc* is out; **m. a sonné?** you rang, sir?

(d) (*à un homme*) sir; (*à un duc*) sir, Your Grace; (*à un comte*) sir, Your Lordship; **au revoir, m.** goodbye, *Fml* goodbye sir; **bonsoir, messieurs** goodnight, gentlemen; **que prendront ces messieurs?** what will you have, gentlemen?; **Mesdames, Messieurs** ladies and gentlemen; **bonjour, Messieurs-Dames!** good morning/afternoon!

(e) (*dans une lettre*) **M.** (*à un étranger*) (Dear) Sir; **M. et cher Confrère, M. et cher Collègue** (*qui s'appelle Martin*) Dear Mr Martin; **Cher M.** (*à une connaissance qui s'appelle Martin*) Dear Mr Martin

(f) (*sur enveloppe*) **M.T. Marceau** Mr T. Marceau, *Fml* T. Marceau Esq

(g) (*homme*) (gentle)man; *Enf* **dis bonjour au m.** say hello (to the gentleman); **il y a un m. qui veut vous parler** there is a (gentle)man here who wants to speak to you; **c'est un vilain m.** he's a nasty piece of work

▶ **monsieur**: **m. je-sais-tout** Mr Know(-it)-all; **il va encore nous jouer son m. je-sais-tout** here he goes again, the know(-it)-all; *TV etc* **M. météo** the weatherman; **m. tout-le-monde** the man in the street, *Am* Joe Public, Joe Blow
monstre [mɔ̃str] **1** *nm Myth*; *Fig* monster; **les monstres marins** the monsters of the deep; *Fig* **m. d'ingratitude/d'égoïsme** ungrateful/selfish monster *or* brute, *Fml* monster of ingratitude/selfishness; *Fig F* **petit m.!** you little monster *or* horror! **2** *adj F* huge, colossal, mammoth; (*succès*) enormous, huge, wild; **un travail m.** a mammoth task; **j'ai eu une chance m.** I was incredibly lucky; **elle avait une trouille m.** she was scared stiff *or* to death

▶ **monstre**: **m. sacré** (*du cinéma, de la danse etc*) giant, idol; **le m. de la réforme soviétique** the leading light of Soviet reform
monstrueusement [mɔ̃stryøzmɑ̃] *adv* (*laid, gros*) monstrously, hideously; (*égoïste*) horrendously, outrageously
monstrueux, -euse [mɔ̃stryø, -øz] *adj* **(a)** (*malformé*) monstrous, deformed **(b)** (*énorme*) (*erreur, gaffe*) huge, colossal; (*prix*) extortionate, exorbitant **(c)** (*scandaleux*) monstrous; **elle est d'un égoïsme m.** she is a selfish monster
monstruosité [mɔ̃stryozite] *nf* **(a)** (*difformité*) monstrosity **(b)** (*de crime, criminel etc*) monstrousness, monstrosity
mont [mɔ̃] *nm* **(a)** mountain; **le m. Sinaï/Everest** Mount Sinai/Everest; **le m. des Oliviers** the Mount of Olives; **le m. Blanc** Mont Blanc; *Fig* **par monts et par vaux** up hill and down dale; *Fig* **être toujours par monts et par vaux** to be always on the move; *Fig* **promettre monts et merveilles à qn** to promise sb the earth *or* the moon **(b)** *Anat* **m. de Vénus** mons veneris
montage [mɔ̃taʒ] *nm* **(a)** (*pose*) (*de bijou*) setting, mounting; (*de pneu*) fitting (on); (*d'appareil, de meuble etc*) assembling, assembly; (*d'atelier etc*) fitting out; (*de porte*) hanging; *Ind* **chaîne de m.** assembly line; **atelier de m.** assembly shop; *MecE* **m. serré** push fit; *MecE* **m. à la presse** press fit

(b) *Cin, Rad, TV* editing; *Phot, Cin, TV* (*image truquée*) montage; *Typ* make-up; **m. original** edited master; **m. vidéo**

video(tape) editing, tape editing; *Cin, TV, Rad* **m. sonore** sound editing; (*avec truquage*) sound montage; *Cin* **salle de m.** cutting room; *Cin* **film de m.** film montage

(c) *Écon* **le m. financier d'un projet** the financial arrangements for a project; **le m. financier a été difficile** it wasn't easy getting the money together; **le m. financier du projet sera le suivant** money for the project will be provided as follows

(d) *Él* connecting (up), wiring (up)

(e) (*de matériaux de construction etc*) taking up, carrying up

montagnard, -arde [mɔ̃taɲar, -ard] **1** *adj* mountain, highland **2** *n* **(a)** (*habitant*) mountain dweller, highlander **(b)** *Hist Fr* member of the Mountain

montagne [mɔ̃taɲ] *nf* **(a)** mountain; (*région*) mountains, mountain region; **la haute/moyenne m.** the high mountains/the uplands; **passer ses vacances à la m.** to spend one's holiday in the mountains; **aimer les paysages de montagnes** to like mountain scenery; *Fig* **une m. de choux/repassage** a huge pile of cabbages/ironing; *Fig* **se faire une m. de qch** to make a great song and dance *or* a great to-do about sth; **tu t'en fais une m.!** you're making a mountain out of a molehill!; *Fig* **c'est la m. qui accouche d'une souris** what a lot of fuss for nothing, *Litt* the mountain laboured and brought forth a mouse

(b) *Sp* **faire de la m.** (*alpinisme*) to go mountain climbing; (*randonnée*) to go hill walking; **sports de m.** mountain sports

(c) *Hist Fr* **la M.** the Mountain

▶ **montagne**: *CE* **m. de beurre** butter mountain; **montagnes russes** (*à la foire*) big dipper, roller coaster; *Fig* **faire des montagnes russes** (*d'une route*) to switchback; **m. à vaches** hills

montagneux, -euse [mɔ̃taɲø, -øz] *adj* mountainous

montant [mɔ̃tɑ̃] **1** *adj* rising; **chemin m.** uphill road; **marée montante** rising tide, flood tide; **col m.** high *or* stand-up collar; *Rail* **train/quai m.** up train/platform; *Mil* **garde montante** new guard, relieving guard

2 *nm* **(a)** (*somme*) amount, sum; **cinq versements d'un m. de 500 francs** five payments of 500 francs (each); **j'ignore le m. de mes dettes** I don't know what my debts amount to; **m. brut/total** gross/total (amount); **m. du retour net** net return; **m. exonéré de TVA** VAT exempt amount; **m. maximum/minimum** maximum/minimum (amount); **m. net** net (total); **m. prévisionnel des ventes** forecast sales level; *CE Écon* **montants compensatoires (monétaires)** subsidies, *Spéc* compensatory amounts

(b) (*partie verticale*) (*d'échelle*) upright; (*de lit*) post; (*de fenêtre*) jamb; (*de portail*) post; (*de bride*) cheek strap; *Sp* **les montants** (*de but*) the goalposts; *Aut* **m. de pare-brise** screen pillar, windscreen pillar, A-pillar; *Aut* **m. de porte** door pillar, B-pillar

mont-de-piété, *pl* **monts-de-piété** *nm Arch* pawnshop; **mettre qch au m.** to pawn sth

monte [mɔ̃t] *nf* **(a)** *Courses de chevaux* (*action*) mounting; **jockey qui a eu trois montes dans la journée** jockey who has ridden three times *or* who has had three mounts *or* rides in the day **(b)** (*façon de monter à cheval*) horsemanship; **m. à l'obstacle** jumping **(c)** (*accouplement*) covering; (*époque de l'accouplement*) breeding *or* mating season

monté [mɔ̃te] *adj* **(a)** (*à cheval*) (*police, troupes*) mounted **(b)** (*bijou*) set, mounted; **m. sur or** gold-mounted; **médaille montée en pendentif** medal mounted as a pendant; **photographies non montées** unmounted photographs; **cave/boutique bien montée** well-stocked cellar/shop **(c)** *F* **il était m.** *ou* **il avait la tête montée contre elle** he had it in for her; **il est drôlement m., ce matin, le patron!** the boss is really worked up *or* wound up this morning! **(d)** *Arg* **bien m.** (*homme*) well-hung

monte-charge, *pl* **monte-charges** *nm* hoist, *Br* goods lift, *Br* service lift, *Am* goods elevator

montée [mɔ̃te] *nf* **(a)** (*mouvement*) rise, rising; (*ascension*) ascent; *Fig* (*du nationalisme, fascisme etc*) rise, growth, increase; **pendant la m. du col** as he was/we were/*etc* going uphill; *HydE etc* **tuyau de m.** uptake pipe, riser; **m. des eaux** (*dans un réservoir*) inflow; **la m. des prix** the rise in prices, rising prices; *Physiol* **m. de lait** onset of lactation **(b)** *Aut, Av* **essai de m.** climbing test; **vitesse en m.** *Av* climbing speed; *Aut, Rail* speed on a gradient **(c)** (*côte*) (*sur une route*) slope, hill; **en haut de la m.** at the top of the slope *or* hill; **il y a une méchante m. avant d'arriver chez lui** there's a stiff climb before you reach his house

monte-en-l'air *nm inv F Vieilli* cat burglar

monte-plats *nm inv* (*au restaurant*) dumbwaiter

monter [mɔ̃te] **1** *vi* (*aux souvent* **être**, *parfois* **avoir**) **(a)** (*se déplacer vers le haut*) to go up, to climb (up); (*en haut de l'escalier*) to go up(stairs); (*d'un oiseau*) to soar, to fly up; (*d'un avion*) to climb, to fly up; **m. à** *ou* **sur un arbre/une échelle** to climb (up) (into) a tree/(on to) a ladder; **m. en haut d'une colline** to climb *or* go up (right) to the top of a hill; **m. en courant/en rampant** to run/crawl up; **m. se coucher** to go (up) to bed; **faire m. qn** to show sb up; **montez chez moi** come up to my place; **après ses études, il est monté à Paris** after college, he moved up to Paris; **elle monte souvent à Paris pour voir sa sœur** she often goes up to Paris to see her sister; *Aut* **m. en régime** to rev; *Mil* **m. en ligne** to go to the front (line); **m. à l'assaut** to go into the attack; *Tennis* **m. au filet** to come up/go up to the net; *Naut* **faire m. tous les hommes** to order all hands on deck

(b) (*pour s'installer etc*) to climb *or* get on/in; (*dans le train, l'autobus etc*) to get on; **où êtes-vous monté?** where did you get on?; **m. sur une chaise** to stand *or* get on a chair; **m. en chaire** to ascend the pulpit; **m. à cheval** to get on a horse, to mount (a horse); (*faire de l'équitation*) to ride, to go riding; **montez-vous (à cheval)?** do you ride?; *F* **m. sur ses grands chevaux** to get on one's high horse; **m. à** *ou* **en bicyclette** to ride a bicycle; **m. en voiture** to get into a car; *Naut, Av* **m. à bord** to go on board, to board; **faire m. qn (en voiture) avec soi** to give sb a lift; *Th* **m. sur les planches** to go on the stage

(c) (*d'un ballon, du soleil etc*) to rise; (*d'un prix, du baromètre etc*) to rise, to go up; (*de la marée*) to rise, to come in; **les frais montent** the costs are mounting (up); **la somme monte à cent francs** the total amounts to *or* comes to a hundred francs; **m. en flèche** (*de prix*) to soar; **faire m. les prix** to put up *or* increase *or* raise prices; **empêcher les prix de m.** to keep prices down, to stop prices rising; **le sang lui monta à la tête** the blood rushed to his head; **faire m. les larmes aux yeux de qn** to bring tears to sb's eyes

(d) (*d'une route etc*) to climb, to go up, to rise; **la rue va en montant** the street climbs

(e) m. dans l'estime de qn to go up *or* rise in sb's estimation; **faire m. qn dans l'estime de qn** to raise sb in sb's estimation

2 *vt* (*aux* **avoir**) **(a)** (*colline, escalier etc*) to go/come up, to climb (up); **m. la rue en courant** to run up the street

(b) (*porter*) to bring up; **m. du vin de la cave** to fetch *or* bring wine up from the cellar; **m. le courrier** to bring the post; **m. le son** to turn up the volume; *Fig* **m. (la tête à) qn contre qn** to set sb against sb

(c) (*bijou*) to set, to mount; (*photo, hameçon etc*) to mount; (*pneu*) to fit (on); (*appareil, machine*) to set up, to erect; (*porte*) to hang; (*atelier*) to fit out, to equip; *Th* (*scène*) to set; (*pièce*) to put on, to stage, to produce; *Cin* (*film*) to edit; *Couture* (*vêtement*) to make up; (*en imprimerie*) to paste up; **m. une entreprise** to set up a business; **m. un magasin** to set up *or* open a shop; **elle commence à m. son trousseau** she's beginning to put her trousseau together; **m. un complot/un coup** to hatch a plot/to plan a job; *F* **m. le coup à qn** to take sb in, to take sb for a ride; *F* **m. qch en épingle** to blow sth up out of all proportion; *Tricot* **m. les mailles** to cast on (the stitches)

(d) *Mil etc* **m. la garde** to mount *or* keep guard

(e) (*cheval*) to ride

(f) être bien monté en vaisselle to be well-supplied with crockery; *Vulg* **il est bien monté** he's hung like a donkey

(g) *Él* to connect up, to wire (up)

3 se monter *vpr* **(a)** (*d'un prix etc*) **se m. à** to come to, to add up to, to amount to; **à combien se monte tout cela?** how much does all this come to *or* add up to *or* amount to?

(b) (*s'équiper*) to equip oneself, to fit oneself out (**en** with); **se m. en vaisselle** to supply oneself with crockery; **se m. en affaires** to set up (in business) on one's own

(c) *F* (*s'énerver*) to get worked up *or* wound up; **elle s'est montée contre lui** she's got it in for him

(d) (*d'un cheval*) to be ridden; **Flicka se monte facilement** Flicka is easy to ride

monteur, -euse [mɔ̃tœr, -øz] *n* (*de bijoux*) setter; (*d'images*) mounter; *Cin* editor; *MecE* fitter; *Aut* engine fitter; *TV, Cin* **m. vidéo** videotape editor, VT editor

montgolfière [mɔ̃gɔlfjɛr] *nf* hot-air balloon

monticule [mɔ̃tikyl] *nm* (*petite colline*) hillock, mound; (*plus petit*) hummock; *Can Baseball* mound

montoir [mɔ̃twar] *nm* (*de cheval*) mounting block; **côté (du) m.** nearside; **côté hors (du) m.** offside

montrable [mɔ̃trabl] *adj* presentable, fit to be seen

montre [mɔ̃tr] *nf* **(a)** (*instrument*) watch; **m. (de poignet)** (wrist)watch; **m. de plongée** diver's watch; **m. à quartz** quartz watch; **à ma m. il est midi** by my watch it's twelve o'clock; **cela lui a pris dix minutes m. en main** it took him exactly ten minutes; **course contre la m.** race against the clock; *Fig* **on est dans une course contre la m.** we're racing against time *or* the clock

(**b**) (*preuve*) show, display; **faire m. de patience/d'un grand courage** to show *or* display patience/great courage; *Litt* **faire qch pour la m.** to do sth merely for show

(**c**) (*vitrine*) shop window, display window; (*dans meuble*) showcase; **mettre qch en m.** to put sth in the window *or* on show *or* on display

Montréal [mɔ̃real] *n* Montreal

montréalais, -aise [mɔ̃realɛ, -ɛz] **1** *adj* (of/from) Montreal **2** *n* **M.** Montrealer

montre-bracelet, *pl* **montres-bracelets** *nf* wristwatch

montrer [mɔ̃tre] **1** *vt* (*révéler*) to show; (*désigner*) to show, to point out; (*faire preuve de*) to show, to display; **elle nous a montré où nous allions dormir** she showed us *or* pointed out to us where we were to sleep; **il a montré un grand courage** he showed *or* displayed great courage; **il faudrait que tu montres ta fille/cette vilaine blessure à un médecin** you should let a doctor have a look at *or* see your daughter/ that nasty wound; **une robe décolletée qui montre les épaules** a low-cut dress which leaves the shoulders bare *or* which exposes the shoulders; **elle a montré une jolie paire de jambes en s'asseyant** she showed a pretty pair of legs as she sat down; **elle adore m. ses charmes** she loves showing off *or* displaying her charms; **il n'y montre jamais le nez** he never shows his face there; **m. qn/qch du doigt** to point sb/ sth out, to point to *or* at sb/sth; *Fig* to point the finger at sb/ sth; **m. le chemin à qn** to show sb the way; **m. la ville à qn** to show sb round the town; **il a réussi à ne pas m. qu'il était au courant** he managed not to show that he knew about it; **cela te montre qu'il faut être prudent** that (just) shows that you have to be careful; **montre-lui la manière de le faire** *ou* **comment le faire** show him how to do it *or* how it's done; **peux-tu me m. comment ça marche?** can you show me how it works?; **m. le poing à qn** to shake one's fist at sb; **m. les dents** to show *or* bare one's teeth; **m. la porte à qn** to show sb the door

2 se montrer *vpr* (**a**) (*se présenter*) to show oneself, to appear; **il n'ose plus se m.** he doesn't dare show himself *or* his face

(**b**) (*se révéler*) **il s'est montré très gentil/courageux** he was very kind/courageous, he showed great kindness/ courage; **il s'est montré incapable de faire face à la situation** he proved (to be) *or* he was incapable of facing up to the situation

montreur, -euse [mɔ̃trœr, -øz] *n* (*dans une foire etc*) (*de bêtes sauvages*) exhibitor; **m. d'ours** bear leader; **m. de marionnettes** puppeteer

montueux, -euse [mɔ̃tɥø, -øz] *adj* hilly

monture [mɔ̃tyr] *nf* (**a**) (*de bijou*) setting; (*de scie, parapluie, lunettes etc*) frame; (*de fusil, revolver*) stock; (*d'épée*) guard; **lunettes sans m.** rimless spectacles (**b**) (*cheval etc*) mount

monument [mɔnymɑ̃] *nm* (**a**) (*statue etc*) monument, memorial; **élever un m. à la mémoire de qn** to erect a monument in memory of *or* to the memory of sb; **m. funéraire** monument (*over a tomb*); **m. aux morts** war memorial (**b**) (*édifice public*) monument; **m. historique** historic monument *or* building; **être classé m. historique** to be a listed building (**c**) *F* **cette armoire est un m.** this cupboard's enormous; **être un m. d'absurdité** to be monumentally absurd (**d**) *Fig* (*livre, film*) masterpiece

monumental, -ale, -aux, -ales [mɔnymɑ̃tal, -o] *adj* monumental; **une erreur monumentale** a monumental blunder; **elle est d'une bêtise monumentale** she's monumentally stupid

mope [mɔp] *nf Can* (*balai*) mop

moquer [mɔke] **1** *vt Arch* to mock

2 se moquer *vpr* (**a**) (*railler*) **se m. de qn/qch** to make fun of *or* laugh at *or* poke fun at *or* mock sb/sth; **vous vous moquez?** what are you laughing at?, what's so funny?

(**b**) (*ne pas faire cas*) **se m. de qch** not to care *or* not to give a damn about sth; **je me moque de ce que les gens pensent** I don't care *or* I don't give a damn what people think; **je m'en moque** I don't care, I don't give a damn; **elle s'en moque éperdument** she doesn't give a damn, she just couldn't care less; **il se moque du tiers comme du quart** he doesn't care *or* give a damn about anybody or anything; *F* **je m'en moque comme de l'an quarante** *ou* **comme de ma première chemise** I don't give a damn, I don't care two hoots *or* a tinker's cuss

(**c**) (*tromper*) **vous vous moquez** *ou* **c'est se m. du monde!** you've got a nerve!

moquerie [mɔkri] *nf* mockery, jeering, ridicule; **leurs moqueries continuelles** their constant mockery *or* jeering *or* ridicule

moquette [mɔkɛt] *nf* (**a**) fitted carpet, wall-to-wall carpet; **faire poser une** *ou* **de la m.** to have a (fitted *or* wall-to-wall) carpet laid (**b**) *Tex* moquette

moquetter [mɔkəte] *vt* to carpet

moqueur, -euse [mɔkœr, -øz] **1** *adj* (**a**) (*remarque, rires etc*) mocking, jeering, derisive (**b**) (*personne*) given to mockery **2** *n* (*personne*) mocker, scoffer **3** *nm* (*oiseau*) mockingbird

moqueusement [mɔkøzmɑ̃] *adv* mockingly

moraillon [mɔrajɔ̃] *nm* (*de serrure*) hasp

moraine [mɔrɛn] *nf Géol* moraine

moral, -ale, -aux, -ales [mɔral, -o] **1** *adj* (**a**) (*conduite, sens, certitude, courage, victoire*) moral; **cette histoire n'est pas morale** this is not a very edifying story; **facultés morales** ability to distinguish between right and wrong; **je me fais une obligation morale de le faire** I'm under a moral obligation *or* I'm morally obliged to do it

(**b**) *Jur* **personne morale** legal entity, corporation

2 *nm* morale; **c'est bon pour le m.** it's good for morale; **le m. est bas** morale is low; **son m. est bas** his spirits are low, he's in low spirits; **je n'ai pas le m. en ce moment** I'm feeling down just now; **avoir le m. au beau fixe** to be in fine spirits; **elle a un m. d'acier** nothing gets her down; *F* **avoir le m. à zéro** to feel down in the dumps; **remonter le m. de** *ou* **à qn** to raise sb's spirits, to cheer sb up; **il se marie avec elle? il a le m.!** he's marrying her? he's got guts *or* he's a brave chap!

morale [mɔral] *nf* (**a**) (*bien*) morals, morality; **contraire/ conforme à la m.** immoral/moral (**b**) (*règles*) morality, ethics; **tu ne vas quand même pas me faire une leçon de m.?** you're not going to start lecturing me, are you now?; **faire la m. à qn** to lecture sb; **adopter une m. d'ascète** to adopt an ascetic philosophy *or* way of life (**c**) (*d'une histoire*) moral

moralement [mɔralmɑ̃] *adv* morally; **m. tu ne peux pas lui faire ça** morally (speaking) you can't do that to him

moralisant [mɔralizɑ̃] *adj* moralizing

moralisateur, -trice [mɔralizatœr, -tris] **1** *adj* (**a**) (*personne*) moralizing (**b**) (*principes*) elevating, edifying **2** *n* moralizer

moralisation [mɔralizasjɔ̃] *nf* moralization

moraliser [mɔralize] **1** *vi* to moralize **2** *vt* (**a**) (*politique, le marché financier etc*) to clean up (**b**) (*personne*) to lecture

moraliste [mɔralist] **1** *adj* moralistic **2** *n* moralist

moralité [mɔralite] *nf* (**a**) (*mérite*) morality, (good) moral conduct; **certificat de m.** character reference (**b**) (*attitude*) morals, morality; **elle est d'une m. douteuse** her morals are dubious, she has dubious morals, she is of dubious morality; **quelqu'un d'une haute m./d'une m. au-dessus de tout soupçon** someone with high/impeccable moral standards (**c**) (*d'une histoire*) moral; **m.: rien ne sert de courir, il faut partir à point** the moral of the story is that it's better to start on time than to try to catch up later; **il n'a pris aucune précaution, m.: il est mort** he didn't take any precautions and as a result he's dead (**d**) *Hist, Littér* morality (play)

morasse [mɔras] *nf Typ* (*de journal*) brush proof

moratoire [mɔratwar] *Jur* **1** *adj* (*accord etc*) moratory; (*paiement*) delayed by agreement; **intérêts moratoires** interest on overdue payments **2** *nm* moratorium

moratorium [mɔratɔrjɔm] *nm Jur* moratorium

morbide [mɔrbid] *adj* morbid

morbidement [mɔrbidmɑ̃] *adv* morbidly

morbidité [mɔrbidite] *nf* morbidness, morbidity

morbleu [mɔrblø] *int Arch* 'sdeath!, zounds!

morceau, -eaux [mɔrso] *nm* (**a**) (*de nourriture*) piece, bit; **m. de choix** choice morsel; **bas morceaux** (*de viande*) cheap(er) cuts; **aimer les bons morceaux** to like good things (to eat); *F* **manger** *ou* **prendre un m.** to have a bite to eat *or* a snack; *Fig F* **emporter le m.** to win (the day) (*in deal, court case etc*); *Fig F* **lâcher** *ou* **cracher le m.** to spill the beans

(**b**) (*de savon, tissu, laine, ficelle etc*) piece, bit; (*de papier*) piece, bit, scrap; (*de sucre*) lump; (*de terre*) piece, patch; *Mus* piece; **en morceaux** in pieces; **sucre en morceaux** lump sugar, cube sugar; **mettre qch en morceaux** to pull *or* tear sth to pieces *or* to bits; **il va me mettre en morceaux** he'll tear me limb from limb; **tomber en morceaux** to fall to pieces *or* bits; *Mus* **m. pour trombone** piece for trombone; *Littér* **morceaux choisis** selected passages *or* extracts; **m. d'anthologie** anthology piece; **m. de bravoure** purple passage, purple patch; *F* **cette fille, c'est un beau m.** she's a bit of all right, that girl

morceler [mɔrsəle] *vt* (**je morcelle; je morcellerai**) to divide (up); **m. une propriété** to break up *or* parcel out *or* divide (up) an estate

morcellement [mɔrsɛlmɑ̃] *nm* division

mordacité [mɔrdasite] *nf Litt* (*de critique*) mordancy

mordant [mɔrdɑ̃] **1** *adj* (*esprit, ironie, discours*) biting, caustic, scathing, *Fml* mordant; (*remarque, ton*) cutting, caustic, scathing; (*personne*) scathing; **froid m.** biting cold **2**

nm (*d'esprit, d'ironie*) bite, *Litt* mordancy; (*d'analyse*) scathing nature; (*de troupes, d'équipe etc*) keenness; (*d'outil*) bite; (*pour teinture*) mordant; **le m. de son ton** his cutting *or* caustic *or* scathing tone

mordicus [mɔrdikys] *adv F* stubbornly, doggedly; **elle l'affirme m.** she's quite stubborn *or* dogged about it

mordieu [mɔrdjø] *int Arch* 'sdeath!, zounds!

mordillage [mɔrdijaʒ] *nm,* **mordillement** [mɔrdijmɑ̃] *nm* nibbling

mordiller [mɔrdije] *vt* to nibble

mordoré [mɔrdɔre] *adj, n* (*couleur*) bronze

mordorer [mɔrdɔre] *vt Litt* to bronze

mordorure [mɔrdɔryr] *nf* (*couleur*) bronze

mordre [mɔrdr] **1** *vt* (**a**) (*d'une personne, d'un chien etc*) to bite; **m. une pomme** to bite into an apple; **m. qn au bras** to bite sb's arm, to bite sb on the arm; **elle s'est fait m. par un rat** she was bitten by a rat; **approche, je ne vais pas te m.** come on, I won't bite you; **le froid lui mordait les doigts** the cold was nipping *or* biting his fingers; *Fig F* **m. la poussière** to bite the dust

(**b**) (*accrocher*) to bite into; **acide qui mord les métaux** acid that eats into metals; **l'angoisse me mord le cœur** I'm gnawed by anxiety

2 *vi* (**a**) (*d'une personne, d'un chien etc*) to bite; **m. dans une pomme** to bite into *or* take a bite out of an apple; *Fig* **m. sur qch** to encroach (up)on sth; **la route mord sur mon terrain** the road encroaches on my land; *Tennis* **m. sur la ligne** to have one's foot (just) over the line; *Pêche, Fig* **m. à l'appât** *ou* **à l'hameçon** to rise to *or* swallow the bait; **le public a bien mordu** the public responded well; *F* **il mord au latin** he's taking to Latin; *Pêche* **ça mord** I've got a bite

(**b**) (*accrocher*) to bite; **lime/vis qui mord** file/screw that bites *or* has a good bite; **l'ancre ne mord pas** the anchor won't hold *or* grip

(**c**) *Beaux-Arts* **m. une planche** to etch a plate

3 se mordre *vpr* to bite oneself; **se m. la langue** to bite one's tongue; **se m. la langue d'avoir parlé** to regret bitterly having spoken; **se m. les lèvres pour ne pas rire/pour ne pas hurler** to bite one's lips so as not to laugh/scream; *Fig* **il s'en mord les doigts** he's kicking himself; **si vous outrepassez mes ordres, vous vous en mordrez les doigts** if you exceed my orders, you'll be sorry *or* you'll regret it

mordu, -e [mɔrdy] **1** *adj* bitten; *Fig F* madly in love; *Fig F* **elle est mordue de ski/tricot** she's been bitten by the skiing/knitting bug, she's mad on skiing/knitting **2** *n F* enthusiast; **m. du bridge/cinéma** bridge/film fanatic *or* enthusiast

more [mɔr] = **maure**

morelle [mɔrɛl] *nf Bot* nightshade

moresque [mɔrɛsk] = **mauresque**

morfal, -als [mɔrfal] *n F* greedy-guts, *Br F* gannet; **il a un appétit de m.** he eats like a horse

morfondre (se) [səmɔrfɔ̃dr] *vpr* (*s'ennuyer*) to be bored to death; (*être triste*) to mope; (*en attendant qch*) to fret

morfondu [mɔrfɔ̃dy] *adj* gloomy, dejected

morganatique [mɔrganatik] *adj* morganatic

morgue¹ [mɔrg] *nf* (*insolence*) pride, haughtiness, arrogance; **regard plein de m.** haughty *or* arrogant look

morgue² *nf* (*dans un hôpital*) mortuary, morgue

moribond, -onde [mɔribɔ̃, -ɔ̃d] **1** *adj* dying, *Fml* moribund **2** *n* dying man, *f* woman; **les moribonds** the dying

moricaud, -aude [mɔriko, -od] *F Péj* **1** *adj* dark-skinned, dusky, swarthy **2** *n* dark-skinned person; (*terme raciste*) darky, darkie

morigéner [mɔriʒene] *vt* (**je morigène**; **je morigénerai**) to lecture, to take to task, to give a good talking-to

morille [mɔrij] *nf Culin* morel

morillon [mɔrijɔ̃] *nm* (**a**) (*oiseau*) tufted duck (**b**) (*pierre précieuse*) rough emerald

mormon, -one [mɔrmɔ̃, -ɔn] *adj, n* Mormon

mormonisme [mɔrmɔnism] *nm* Mormonism

morne [mɔrn] *adj* (*personne, regard*) gloomy, glum; (*silence*) gloomy; (*temps, vacances*) dismal, dreary, dull; **parler d'un ton m.** to speak drearily *or* in a dreary voice

mornifle [mɔrnifl] *nf F* clout, slap

morose [mɔroz] *adj* (*personne, humeur*) morose, sullen, glum; (*temps, année*) miserable

morosité [mɔrozite] *nf* (*de personne*) moroseness, sullenness; (*de climat*) miserableness; (*du paysage*) gloominess

Morphée [mɔrfe] *nm* Morpheus; **dans les bras de M.** in the arms of Morpheus

morphème [mɔrfɛm] *nm Ling* morpheme

morphine [mɔrfin] *nf* morphine, morphia

morphinisme [mɔrfinism] *nm Méd* morphinism

morphinomane [mɔrfinɔman] **1** *adj* addicted to morphine **2** *n* morphine addict

morphinomanie [mɔrfinɔmani] *nf* addiction to morphine

morphologie [mɔrfɔlɔʒi] *nf* morphology

morphologique [mɔrfɔlɔʒik] *adj* morphological

morphologiquement [mɔrfɔlɔʒikmɑ̃] *adv* morphologically

morphopsychologie [mɔrfopsikɔlɔʒi] *nf* = study of the relationship between people's morphology and their psychological make-up

morpion [mɔrpjɔ̃] *nm* (**a**) *Arg* (*pou*) crab (**b**) *Arg* (*gamin*) kid (**c**) (*jeu*) noughts and crosses, *US* tick-tack-toe

mors [mɔr] *nm* (**a**) (*d'un étau*) jaw (**b**) (*de livre*) joint (**c**) (*de harnais*) bit; **prendre le m. aux dents** (*d'un cheval*) to take the bit in its teeth; *Fig* (*d'une personne*) to take the bit between one's teeth

morse¹ [mɔrs] *nm Zool* walrus

morse² *nm* (*code*) Morse (code)

morsure [mɔrsyr] *nf* (**a**) bite; **une m. de chien** a dog bite (**b**) (*d'acide*) biting

mort¹, morte [mɔr, mɔrt] **1** *adj* (**a**) (*personne, peau, feuille, langue etc*) dead; (*doigt*) dead, numb; **m. et enterré** dead and buried, dead and gone; **je le veux m. ou vif** I want him dead or alive; **plus m. que vif** (*à demi mort*) more dead than alive; (*très effrayé*) half-dead with fright; **il est m.** he's dead; **il est m. hier** he died yesterday; **si tu fais un geste, tu es un homme m.** one move and you're a dead man; **m. pour la France** who died for France; *Prov* **morte la bête, m. le venin** dead men tell no tales; **m. de peur/d'inquiétude/de froid** frightened/worried/frozen to death; *F* **je n'en peux plus, je suis m. (de fatigue)** I can't go on, I'm dead tired; **elle avait le regard m.** her eyes were lifeless; **la mer Morte** the Dead Sea; **au mois d'août, la ville semble morte** in August the town seems dead

(**b**) **temps m.** *Sp* (*dans un match*) injury time, stoppage time; (*dans le travail, la conversation*) lull; **poids m.** *MecE* dead weight; *Constr* dead load; **point m.** (*de la course d'un piston*) dead centre *or US* center; (*d'un levier etc*) neutral position; *Aut* neutral; *Aut* **mettre le levier au point m.** to put the (gear) lever into neutral; *Fig* **arriver à un point m.** to come to a standstill; **angle m.** (*dans une voiture etc*) blind spot; **eau morte** stagnant water; *Beaux-Arts* **nature morte** still life; **balle morte** spent bullet

(**c**) *F* (*hors d'usage*) (*piles, appareil etc*) finished; **ma voiture est morte** my car's had it

2 *n* dead person, dead man, *f* woman; **les morts** the dead; **le nombre des morts sur la route** the number of deaths on the roads; **cet accident a fait trois morts** the accident claimed three lives, three people died *or* were killed in the accident; **la drogue fait de nombreux morts chaque année** drugs claim many lives each year, many people die from drugs each year; *Rel* **jour** *ou* **fête des Morts** All Souls' Day; **l'office des morts** the burial service; **faire le m.** to pretend to be dead, to play dead; **je lui ai écrit il y a trois semaines, mais depuis, il fait le m.** I wrote to him three weeks ago but since then he's been as silent as the grave *or* I haven't heard a thing; *Aut* **la place du m.** the passenger *or Am F* the death seat; *Fig* **c'est un m. vivant** he's half dead, he's more dead than alive; *Fig* he's a zombie, he's more dead than alive; *Fig* **les morts vivants** the walking dead, the zombies

3 *nm Cartes* dummy; **faire le m.** to be dummy

mort² *nf* death; **m. accidentelle/violente/clinique** accidental/violent/clinical death; **trouver la m. dans un accident** to die in an accident; **se donner la m.** to take one's (own) life; *F* **vous allez attraper la m.!** you'll catch your death (of cold)!; *F* **c'est pas la m.!** it won't kill you/him/*etc*!; **mourir de sa belle m.** *ou* **de m. naturelle** to die a natural death, to die of natural causes; **être à la m.** *ou* **à l'article de la m.** to be at death's door; **à la m. de son père** on his father's death; **pâle comme la m.** as pale as death, deathly pale; **il n'y a pas eu m. d'homme** there was no loss of life; **mettre qn à m.** to put sb to death; **condamner qn à m.** to condemn *or* sentence sb to death; **sentence** *ou* **arrêt de m.** death sentence, sentence of death; **à m. les traîtres!** death to the traitors!; *Arg* **m. aux vaches!** down with the cops!; **blessé à m.** fatally *or Litt* mortally wounded; **lutte à m.** fight to the death *or* the end; *F* **freiner à m.** to jam on the brakes; **haïr qn à m.** to hate sb's guts, to loathe and detest sb; *Arg* **s'emmerder à m.** to be bored to death *or* out of one's mind, to be bored rigid; **nous sommes fâchés à m.** we are at daggers drawn; **en vouloir à qn à m.** to have a huge grudge against sb; **je lui en veux à m. d'avoir dit ça** I'll never forgive him for saying that; **ennemis à m.** deadly enemies; **silence de m.** deadly *or* deathlike silence *or* hush; **il avait la m. dans l'âme** he was sick at heart, he had a heavy heart; **partir la m. dans l'âme** to leave with a heavy heart; **souffrir m. et passion** to suffer agonies; **je m'en souviendrai jusqu'à la m.** I'll remember it until my dying day; **à la vie, à la m.** for ever, for life; **jamais je ne**

t'abandonnerai, à la vie, à la m. I'll never leave you, we're in this together; **le monopole est la m. de l'industrie** monopoly means the end *or* is the ruin of industry; **ce fut un arrêt de m. pour notre entreprise** it spelt the end *or* was the deathknell for our company

▶ **mort**: *Bot* **m. aux loups** wolfsbane; *Bot* **m. aux poules** henbane

mortadelle [mɔrtadɛl] *nf* mortadella

mortaise [mɔrtɛz] *nf Menuis* mortise; **assemblage à tenon et à m.** mortise (and tenon) joint

mortaiser [mɔrteze] *vt Menuis* to mortise

mortalité [mɔrtalite] *nf* **(a)** mortality, death rate; **taux de m.** mortality *or* death rate; **m. infantile** child *or* infant mortality **(b)** *Arch* (*condition mortelle*) mortal nature

mort-aux-rats [mɔrora] *nf inv* rat poison

mort-bois, *pl* **morts-bois** *nm* underwood, brushwood

morte-eau, *pl* **mortes-eaux** *nf* neap tide

mortel, -elle [mɔrtɛl] **1** *adj* **(a)** (*sujet à la mort*) mortal

(b) (*qui tue*) (*blessure, maladie, accident*) fatal; (*coup*) fatal, lethal, *Fml* mortal; (*dose*) lethal; (*champignon*) poisonous, deadly; **poison m.** deadly poison; **rayon m.** death ray; **il a fait une chute mortelle de 100 mètres** he fell 100 metres to his death; *F* **il fait un froid m. dans cette chambre!** it's freezing in this bedroom, you could freeze to death in this bedroom

(c) (*haine, péché*) deadly; (*silence*) deathly; **ennemi m.** deadly enemy, mortal enemy; **d'une pâleur mortelle** deathly pale

(d) *F* (*ennuyeux*) deadly dull, dead boring; **je l'ai attendu deux mortelles heures** I waited two solid *or* whole hours for him; **le sport, je trouve ça m.** I find sport deadly dull; **d'un ennui m.** deadly dull, dead boring

2 *n* mortal

mortellement [mɔrtɛlmɑ̃] *adv* (*blessé*) fatally, *Fml* mortally; **m. pâle** deathly pale; **m. offensé** mortally offended; *F* **s'ennuyer m.** to be bored to death, to be bored rigid; **m. ennuyeux** deadly dull, dead boring; *Rel* **pécher m.** to commit a mortal sin

morte-saison, *pl* **mortes-saisons** *nf Com* slack period, off season

mortier [mɔrtje] *nm* **(a)** *Culin* mortar; **pilon et m.** mortar and pestle **(b)** *Mil* mortar; **obus/tirs de m.** mortar shell/fire; **attaque au m.** mortar attack **(c)** *Constr* mortar; **m. liquide** *ou* **clair** grout(ing); **planche à m.** mortarboard

mortifiant [mɔrtifjɑ̃] *adj* mortifying, humiliating

mortification [mɔrtifikasjɔ̃] *nf* **(a)** (*de la chair, des passions etc*) mortification **(b)** (*humiliation*) mortification, humiliation; **il a subi une terrible m.** he felt mortified *or* humiliated; **infliger une m. à qn** to mortify *or* humiliate sb **(c)** *Culin* (*de gibier*) hanging **(d)** *Méd Vieilli* (*de membre*) gangrene, mortification

mortifié [mɔrtifje] *adj* **(a)** mortified, humiliated **(b)** *Méd Vieilli* gangrenous

mortifier [mɔrtifje] (*pr sub, impf* **n. mortifiions, v. mortifiiez**) **1** *vt* **(a)** (*chair, passions*) to mortify **(b)** (*humilier*) to mortify, to humiliate; **elle en a été mortifiée** she was mortified **(c)** *Culin* (*gibier etc*) to hang **(d)** *Méd Vieilli* (*membre*) to make gangrenous **2 se mortifier** *vpr* to mortify oneself

mortinatalité [mɔrtinatalite] *nf* **(taux de) m.** stillbirth rate, number of stillbirths

mort-né, -née, *pl* **mort-né(e)s 1** *adj* (*enfant, animal*) stillborn; *Fig* **projet m.** plan destined to fail **2** *n* stillborn child

mortuaire [mɔrtɥɛr] *adj* **drap m.** pall; **masque m.** death mask; **registre m.** register of deaths; **la maison m.** the house of the deceased; **chambre m.** death chamber; **dépôt m.** mortuary; **cérémonie m.** funeral; **couronne m.** funeral wreath

morue [mɔry] *nf* **(a)** [①A12,1,g] (*poisson*) cod; **huile de foie de m.** cod-liver oil **(b)** *Vulg* (*prostituée*) tart

morutier, -ière [mɔrytje, -jɛr] **1** *adj* (*industrie*) cod-fishing **2** *nm* **(a)** (*bateau*) cod-fishing boat **(b)** (*pêcheur*) cod-fisher(man)

morve [mɔrv] *nf* **(a)** (*de nez*) (nasal) mucus; *F* snot; **ce gamin a toujours la m. qui lui coule du nez** that kid has always got a snotty nose **(b)** *Vét* glanders

morveux, -euse [mɔrvø, -øz] **1** *adj* **(a)** (*enfant etc*) runny-nosed; *F* snotty-nosed; (*nez*) runny, *F* snotty; *Prov* **qui se sent m. se mouche** if the cap fits wear it **(b)** *Vét* glandered **2** *n F* (*gamin*) kid, *Péj* brat; (*plus âgé*) snot, (little) jerk, snotty-nosed kid

MOS [mɔs] *nm* (*abrév* **métal-oxyde-semiconducteur**) *Ordinat* **M. complémentaire** complementary MOS

mosaïque[1] [mɔzaik] *adj Bible* (*loi*) Mosaic

mosaïque[2] *nf Beaux-Arts, Fig* mosaic; **dallage en m.** mosaic flooring; *Fig* **une m. de couleurs** a kaleidoscope of colours

mosaïste [mɔzaist] *n Beaux-Arts* worker in mosaic

Moscou [mɔsku] *n* Moscow

moscovite [mɔskɔvit] **1** *adj* Muscovite **2** *n* **M.** Muscovite

mosquée [mɔske] *nf* mosque

mot [mo] *nm* word; **les mots me manquent pour t'exprimer ma gratitude** I cannot find the words to express my gratitude; **les mots me manquent!** words fail me!; **manger** *ou* **avaler ses mots** to mumble; **répéter qch m. pour m.** to repeat sth word for word *or* verbatim; **traduire m. à m., faire du m. à m.** to translate word for word *or* literally; **prendre qn au m.** to take sb at his/her word; **groupe de mots** word group; **sans m. dire** without (saying) a word; **il n'a pas dit un m. de toute la soirée** he didn't say a (single) word the entire evening; **qui ne dit m. consent** silence is tantamount to consent; **ne pas souffler m. de qch** not to breathe a word about sth; **dire un m.** *ou* **deux mots à qn** to have a word with sb; **il n'a pas dit un seul m. en ta faveur** he didn't put in a single good word for you; **avoir des mots avec qn** to have words with sb; **lâche? en effet, je crois que c'est le m.** a coward? yes, I think that's just the word for him; **avoir le dernier m.** to have the last word; **je ne sais pas un (traître) m. de russe** I don't know a word of Russian; **sur ces mots, il se leva** and with these words *or* so saying, he got up; **en un m. /quelques mots** in a word/a few words; **en un m. comme en cent** in a nutshell; **il faut compter au bas m. trois heures/3 000 francs** you'll have to allow at least three hours/3,000 francs; **gros m.** swear word; **ne dis pas de gros mots!** don't swear!; **des mots doux, des mots d'amour** loving words, *F* sweet nothings; **il ne dit jamais un m. plus haut que l'autre** he never raises his voice, he never utters a cross word; **voilà le fin m. de l'affaire!** so that's what's at the bottom of it!; **on ne saura jamais le fin m. de l'affaire** we'll never get to the bottom of it, we'll never know the truth of the matter; **dire qch à mots couverts** to hint at sth, to say sth in a roundabout manner; **faire comprendre qch à qn à mots couverts** to give sb to understand sth in a roundabout manner; **se donner le m.** to pass *or* give the word; **ils ont dû se donner le m.** they must have agreed on it, they must have passed the word around; **envoyer** *ou* **écrire un (petit) m. à qn** to drop sb a line, to write sb a note; **il m'a laissé un m. sur mon bureau** he left a note on my desk; **un m. d'excuse pour l'institutrice** a note for the teacher; **je lui en toucherai un m.** I'll have a word with him about it, I'll mention it to him; **avoir son m. à dire** to have one's say; **tu n'as qu'un m. à dire** just say the word, you just have to say the word; **je ne pouvais pas placer un m.** I couldn't get a word in edgeways; **il a toujours le m. pour rire** he's always ready with a joke; **m. historique** historic remark, memorable saying; **bon m.** witty remark, witticism; *Ordinat* **m. de 6 bits** 6-bit byte; *Ordinat* **m. binaire** binary word

▶ **mot**: **m.-clé**, *pl* **mots-clé(s)** keyword; **mots croisés** crossword puzzle, crossword; **faire des mots croisés** to do crosswords *or* crossword puzzles; **m. d'ordre** *Mil* password; (*de politique*) keynote; (*de parti politique, organisation*) watchword, slogan; **m. de passe** password; *Mil* **m. de ralliement** password

motard [mɔtar] *nm F* **(a)** biker **(b)** (*de police*) motorcycle policeman

motel [motɛl] *nm* motel

motet [mɔtɛ] *nm Mus* motet

moteur, -trice [mɔtœr, -tris] **1** *adj* **(a)** *Tech* **arbre m.** drive shaft, main shaft; *MecE* **unité motrice** power pack *or* unit; **force motrice** driving force; **roue motrice** driving wheel; **voiture à roues avant motrices** car with front-wheel drive; **temps m.** power stroke

(b) *Anat* (*nerve*) motor; **troubles moteurs** motor deficiences; **un handicapé m.** a person with motor deficiencies

2 *nm* **(a)** motor, engine; *Cin* **m.!** camera!, action!, roll!; **à m.** motor(-driven), power(-driven); **bateau à m.** motor boat; **caméra à m.** motor-driven camera; **commandé par m.** motor(-driven), power(-driven); **à moteurs multiples, à plusieurs moteurs** (*aircraft etc*) multi-engine(d)

(b) *Fig* **c'est lui le m. de l'entreprise** he's the driving force behind the undertaking; *Fig* **le m. principal de la pensée hégélienne** the mainspring of Hegelian thought; **sans autre m. que l'amour de la gloire** for no other reason than love of glory

3 *nf Rail* **motrice** motor coach, *surtout US* motor car

▶ **moteur**: **m. ACT** ohc engine; **m. à allumage par bougie** spark-ignition engine; **m. à allumage par compression** compression-ignition engine; **m. alternatif à combustion interne** internal combustion (reciprocating) engine; **m. d'avion** aero-engine; **m. carré** square engine; **m. à combustion interne** internal combustion engine; **m. à**

cylindres à plat boxer engine; **m. à deux temps** two-stroke engine; **m. diesel** diesel engine; **m. électrique** electric motor; **m. à explosion** internal combustion engine; **m. à gaz** gas engine; **m. hydrogène** hydrogen engine; **m. d'impression** (*d'une imprimante laser*) printer engine; **m. à injection** fuel-injected engine; **m. 'lean burn'** lean-burn engine; **m. en ligne** in-line engine; **m. multicylindre** multi-cylinder engine; **m. multisoupape** multi-valve engine; **m. pas à pas** stepper motor; **m. à pistons** piston engine; **m. à plat** flat engine; **m. polycarburant** multi-fuel engine; **m. polycylindre** multi-cylinder engine; **m. à quatre temps** four-stroke engine; **m. à réaction** jet engine; **m. à refroidissement par air** air-cooled engine; **m. rénové** reconditioned engine, recon; **m. seize soupapes** sixteen-valve engine; **m. turbocompressé** turbocharged engine; **m. turbo-diesel** turbo-diesel engine; **m. en V** vee engine; **m. V6** V6 (engine); **m. à vapeur** steam engine

motif [mɔtif] *nm* **(a)** motive, reason; **un m. valable** a valid reason; **m. de mécontentement** cause *or* grounds for discontent; **m. de réclamation** reason for claim; **avoir un m. pour faire qch** to have a motive *or* a reason for doing sth; **c'est un faux m.** that's not the real reason; **pour quel m. a-t-il été puni?** what was the reason for punishing him?, why was he punished?; *F Vieilli* **courtiser qn pour le bon m.** to court sb with honourable intentions; **quel est le m. de ce coup de téléphone?** what is the reason for *or* behind this telephone call?; **quel m. avez-vous de vous plaindre?** what cause *or* grounds have you for complaint?; **soupçons sans m.** groundless *or* unfounded suspicions; **il s'est fâché sans m.** he got angry for no reason at all *or* without any reason; **insulter qn sans m.** to insult sb for no reason at all *or Fml* gratuitously; **il semble que l'individu ait agi sans m.** it seems that he acted without any motive; **le crime avait-il un m.?** did the crime have a motive?, was there a motive to the crime?; *Jur* **motifs d'un jugement** grounds upon which a judgment has been delivered

(b) *Beaux-Arts* motif; *Couture* (*pour la broderie*) design, pattern, motif; *Mus* theme, motto, figure; **m. à fleurs** flower(ed) pattern; **papier peint à m. à fleurs** flowered wallpaper; **une veste avec des motifs noirs et blancs** a jacket with a black and white design

motion [mosjɔ̃] *nf* motion; **proposer une m.** to propose a motion, to move a proposal; **la m. a été adoptée** the motion was carried; **présenter une m.** to table a motion; **m. de censure** motion of censure

motivant [mɔtivɑ̃] *adj* (*travail*) motivating; (*salaire, rémunération*) worthwhile

motivation [mɔtivasjɔ̃] *nf Psy* motivation; **quelles sont vos motivations?** what motivates you?; **joindre une lettre de m. à votre C.V.** send a covering letter with your CV telling them why you're interested in the job *or* what prompted you to apply; **m. d'achat** buying motivation

motivé [mɔtive] *adj* **(a)** (*personne*) motivated; **élève très m.** very keen *or* motivated pupil **(b)** (*action*) justified; **refus m.** justifiable refusal; **non m.** unjustified, unwarranted; *Jur* **sentence arbitrale motivée** = award stating the reasons on which it is based; *Jur* **avis m.** counsel's opinion

motiver [mɔtive] *vt* **(a)** (*causer, stimuler*) (*action, personne*) to motivate; **l'ambition les motivent** they are motivated by ambition; **des crimes motivés par l'argent** crimes motivated by money *or* with money as the motive **(b)** (*justifier*) to justify, to warrant; (*refus etc*) to state the reason for; **la situation motive nos craintes** the situation gives us (just) cause for concern

moto [moto] *nf F* motorbike; **aller au travail à** *ou* **en m.** to go to work on a motorbike, to ride a motorbike to work; **faire de la m.** to ride a motorbike; **m. tout terrain** motocross bike

motocross [motokrɔs] *nm Sp* motocross

motoculteur [motokyltœr] *nm Agr* motor cultivator

motoculture [motokyltyr] *nf* mechanized farming

motocycle [motosikl] *nm Admin* motorcycle

motocyclette [motosiklɛt] *nf* motorcycle; *F* motorbike

motocycliste [motosiklist] *nm* motorcyclist, *F* biker; *Mil* dispatch rider

motonautique [motonotik] *adj* **sport m.** motorboating

motonautisme [motonotism] *nm* motorboating

motoneige [motonɛʒ] *nf* snowmobile, *surtout Can* skidoo

motopompe [motopɔ̃p] *nf* motor(-driven) pump

motorisation [mɔtɔrizasjɔ̃] *nf* mechanization

motorisé [mɔtɔrize] *adj* mechanized; *Mil* **troupes motorisées** mechanized troops; *F* **vous êtes m.?** have you got a car *or* transport *or Am F* wheels?, are you mobile?

motoriser [mɔtɔrize] *vt* to mechanize

motoriste [mɔtɔrist] *nm* engine manufacturer

mot-outil, *pl* **mots-outils** *nm Ling* form word, link word

motrice [mɔtris] *nf voir* **moteur**

motricité [mɔtrisite] *nf Physiol* motor function

motte [mɔt] *nf* **(a)** (*de terre*) clod, clump; (*sur les racines d'un arbre*) root ball; **m. de gazon** sod, turf; **m. de tourbe** (turf of) peat; **m. de beurre** pat *or* block of butter; **du beurre à la m.** butter in blocks **(b)** *Archéol* motte

motteux [mɔtø] *nm* (*oiseau*) wheatear, stonechat

motus [mɔtys] *int* **m. (et bouche cousue)!** mum's the word!

mou[1], *f* **molle** [mu, mɔl] **1** *adj* (*the masc form* **mol** *is used before vowel or h mute*) (*beurre, matelas, substance*) soft; (*personne*) spineless; (*gouvernement, chef*) spineless, lax, soft; (*geste*) lifeless, limp; (*corde*) slack; (*pédale*) slack, spongy; (*chair, main, ventre*) flabby, soft; (*poignée de main*) limp, flabby, feeble; (*muscle*) soft, *Fml* flaccid; (*style*) feeble, flabby; **ce que tu peux être m.!** God you're feeble *or* useless!; **j'ai les jambes molles** my legs are like cotton wool; **m. au toucher** soft to the touch; **un mol (et doux) oreiller** a (soft and) downy pillow; **des collines molles, des collines au relief m.** rolling hills; *F* **il est m. comme une chiffe** *ou* **comme une chique** he's an absolute wimp; *F* **je ne me sens pas bien, je suis** *ou* **je me sens tout m.** I'm not well, I feel like a wet rag; **il m'a fait de molles excuses** he gave me some lame *or* feeble excuses

2 *n F* wimp

3 *nm* (*de corde, fil*) slack; **donne-moi un peu de m.** give me some slack; **donner du m. à un cordage** to slacken a rope; **prendre du m.** (*d'une corde*) to slacken

4 *adv* **(a) elle joue trop m.** she doesn't put enough verve into her playing

(b) *très F* **vas-y m.!** go easy!, take it easy!; **vas-y m. avec le whisky** go easy on the whisky

mou[2] *nm* lights, lungs (*of slaughtered animal*); *Fig F* **il est en train de te bourrer le m.** he's spinning you a yarn *or* handing you a line; *Fig F* **je vais lui rentrer dans le m.** I'll punch him one

mouchage [muʃaʒ] *nm* **(a)** (*de nez*) wiping, blowing **(b)** (*de chandelles*) snuffing (out)

mouchard [muʃar] *nm F* **(a)** (*informateur*) grass, informer, stool pigeon; *Scol* sneak **(b)** *Tech* (*tachymètre*) spy in the cab **(c)** (*contrôleur*) watchman's clock **(d)** *Av* observation plane **(e)** (*dans une porte*) peephole

moucharder [muʃarde] *vt F* (*qn*) to grass on *or* up, to squeal on; *Scol* to sneak on; **tu n'as pas intérêt à m.** you'd better not grass *or* squeal

mouche [muʃ] *nf* **(a)** (*insecte*) fly; **on aurait entendu une m. voler** you could have heard a pin drop; **gober les mouches, regarder les mouches voler** to gaze *or* stare into space; *F* **prendre la m.** to fly off the handle; *F* **quelle m. vous pique?** what's up with you?, what's bitten you?, who rattled your cage?; **elle ne ferait pas de mal à une m.** she wouldn't hurt a fly; **tomber comme des mouches** to be dropping like flies; **c'est une fine m.** he's a sharp customer, he's a fly one; **j'ai des mouches devant les yeux** I've got spots before my eyes; *Pêche* **m. mouillée** wet fly; *Pêche* **m. à saumon** salmon fly; **pêche à la m. sèche** dry-fly fishing; *Boxe* **poids m.** flyweight

(b) (*de cible*) bull's eye; **faire m.** to hit the bull's eye, to score a bull; *Fig* **il a fait m. avec cette proposition** he hit the jackpot *or* he scored with that suggestion

(c) bateau m. river bus, bateau mouche

(d) (*grain de beauté*) beauty spot; *Hist* (*sur visage*) patch; (*sur menton*) tuft of hair

(e) *Escrime* button

(f) *Arch* (*tache*) spot, speck; (*sur vêtement etc*) stain

▶ **mouche**: **m. bleue** bluebottle, blowfly; **m. domestique** housefly; **m. à merde** (*bleue*) bluebottle; (*verte*) greenbottle; **m. à miel** honey bee; **m. tsé-tsé** tsetse fly; **m. de la viande** blowfly, bluebottle

moucher [muʃe] **1** *vt* **(a)** (*nez*) to wipe, to blow; **m. un enfant** to wipe a child's nose; **je mouche du sang** there's blood on my handkerchief when I blow my nose **(b)** (*chandelle*) to snuff (out); *F* **m. qn** to put sb in his/her place **2 se moucher** *vpr* to blow one's nose; *F* **il ne se mouche pas du coude** *ou* **du pied** he thinks a lot *or* he's got a high opinion of himself

moucheron [muʃrɔ̃] *nm* gnat, midge

moucheronner [muʃrɔne] *vi* (*de poisson*) to be rising, to be on the rise

moucheté [muʃte] *adj* **(a)** (*poisson, œuf*) speckled; (*robe de cheval*) dappled; **mer mouchetée d'écume** foam-flecked sea; **nez moucheté de taches de rousseur** freckled nose; **une écharpe blanche mouchetée de noir** a white scarf flecked *or* specked with black, a white scarf with black flecks **(b)** *Escrime* (*fleuret*) buttoned

moucheter [muʃte] *vt* (**je mouchette**; **je mouchetterai**) **(a)** (*étoffe, papier*) to speckle, to fleck **(b)** *Escrime* to button, to put a button on

mouchette [muʃɛt] *nf* **(a) mouchettes** (*pour chandelles*) (pair of) snuffers **(b)** *Archit* (*de larmier*) outer fillet

moucheture [muʃtyr] *nf* speck, speckle; **une écharpe blanche avec des mouchetures noires** a white scarf with black flecks, a white scarf specked *or* flecked with black

mouchoir [muʃwar] *nm* handkerchief; (*autour du cou*) kerchief; **m. en papier** paper handkerchief, tissue; **m. en tissu** handkerchief; *Fig* **je vais faire un nœud à mon m.** I'll tie a knot in my handkerchief; **jardin grand comme un m. (de poche)** pocket handkerchief (of a) garden; **arriver dans un m. de poche** to come in neck and neck

mouchure [muʃyr] *nf* (*du nez*) mucus

moudjahiddin [mudʒaidin] *nm* mujaheddin, mujahedeen

moudre [mudr] *vt* (*prp* **moulant**; *pp* **moulu**; *pr ind* **je mouds, il moud, n. moulons, ils moulent**; *pr sub* **je moule**; *p hist* **je moulus**; *fu* **je moudrai) (a)** (*grain*) to grind, to mill; (*café, poivre*) to grind; *Fig* **m. qn de coups** to beat sb to a pulp **(b)** *Vieilli* (*air*) (*sur orgue de Barbarie*) to grind out

moue [mu] *nf* pout; **faire la m.** to pout, to look sulky; **faire une m.** to purse one's lips; **m. boudeuse** sulk; **il eut une m. désapprobatrice** he looked disaproving; *Fig* **le public fit la m. et la pièce fit un four** the public stayed away in droves and the play flopped; **les critiques firent la m.** the critics turned up their noses

mouette [mwɛt] *nf* (sea)gull

mouf(f)ette [mufɛt] *nf* skunk

moufle [mufl] **1** *nf* (*gant*) mitten, mitt **2** *n Tech* **(a)** tackle block, pulley block **(b)** (*palan*) (block and) tackle

mouflet, -ette [muflɛ, -ɛt] *n F* (*enfant*) kid, *Péj* brat

mouflon [muflɔ̃] *nm* mouf(f)lon, wild sheep

mouillage [mujaʒ] *nm* **(a)** (*de tissu, linge*) moistening, damping; (*du vin*) (fraudulent) watering down **(b)** *Naut* (*de bateau*) anchoring; (*de mine*) laying; (*de bouée*) putting down **(c)** *Naut* (*emplacement*) anchorage, moorage; **être au m.** to be riding at anchor; **prendre son m.** to anchor

mouillé [muje] *adj* **(a)** wet; **tout m.** soaked; **m. jusqu'aux os** wet through, soaked to the skin; **elle avait les yeux mouillés de larmes** her eyes were wet with tears **(b)** *Ling* (*consonne*) palatalized

mouillement [mujmɑ̃] *nm Ling* palatalization

mouiller [muje] **1** *vt* **(a)** (*rendre humide*) to wet; (*linge à repasser*) to moisten, to damp(en); *Culin* (*ragoût*) to add liquid to; (*vin, boisson alcoolisée, lait*) to dilute, to water down; **il a mouillé le bas de son pantalon en traversant la rivière à gué** he got the bottom of his trousers wet wading across the river; **l'averse a mouillé le linge** the clothes got wet in the rain; **on s'est fait m. par l'averse** we got soaked in the downpour; *Fig* **m. sa chemise** to put one's back into it, to work up a sweat, to get stuck in; **ce n'est pas avec le travail qu'il fournit qu'il risque de m. sa chemise** *ou* **son maillot** he's not likely to break into a sweat with the amount of work that he does

(b) *Naut* (*ancre*) to cast, to drop

(c) *Naut* (*mine*) to lay; (*bouée*) to put down

(d) *F* (*compromettre*) to involve, to drag in

(e) *Ling* (*consonne*) to palatalize

2 *vi Naut* to anchor; (*de navire*) to lie at anchor; **mouillez!** let go (the anchor)!

3 se mouiller *vpr* **(a)** to get wet; (*des yeux*) to fill with tears; **se m. les pieds** to get one's feet wet

(b) *F* (*dans un crime, une affaire louche*) to get involved; **il ne veut pas se m.** (*prendre parti*) he doesn't want to stick his neck out

mouillette [mujɛt] *nf* (*de pain*) finger, *surtout Br* soldier

mouilleur [mujœr] *nm* **(a)** *Naut* **m. de mines** minelayer **(b)** (*pour timbres*) damper

mouillure [mujyr] *nf* **(a)** (*marque*) damp mark, stain **(b)** *Ling* (*de consonne*) palatalization

mouise [mwiz] *nf Arg* poverty; **être dans la m.** to be hard up *or* in dire straits; **tirer qn de la m.** to get sb out of a hole

moujik [muʒik] *nm* moujik

moujingue [muʒɛ̃g] *n Arg* (*enfant*) kid, *Péj* brat

moukère [mukɛr] *nf* (*femme maghrébine*) Maghrebi woman; *Arg* (*femme*) female; (*prostituée*) pro

moulage¹ [mulaʒ] *nm* (*du grain*) grinding, milling

moulage² *nm* **(a)** (*fait de mouler*) casting, moulding, *US* molding; (*de fer*) founding; **m. à cire perdue** lost wax process **(b) m. au** *ou* **en plâtre** plaster cast

moule¹ [mul] *nm* **(a)** mould, *US* mold; *Tech* mould, *Spéc* matrix; **m. à gelée** jelly mould; **m. à gâteaux** cake tin; **m. à beurre** butter mould *or* print **(b)** *Fig* **on n'en fait plus des comme lui, on a cassé le m.** they broke the mould when they made him; **elle a rejeté le m. de son éducation** she has broken out of the mould of her upbringing; **ils ont été coulés dans le même m.** they're cast in the same mould; they're out of the same mould; **l'école est un m. qui étouffe la créativité de l'enfant** school stifles children's creativity by forcing them into a mould; **une fille faite au m.** a girl with a great figure

moule² *nf* **(a)** *Zool Culin* mussel **(b)** *Arg* (*personne molle*) wimp, drip; (*idiot*) fool, idiot **(c)** *Vulg* (*sexe de femme*) pussy, cunt

moulé [mule] *adj* cast, moulded, *US* molded; **statue de plâtre m.** plaster cast; **pain m.** tin loaf; **écriture moulée** copperplate handwriting; **lettres moulées** printing; **je me trouve trop moulée dans cette robe** this dress clings too much

mouler [mule] **1** *vt* to mould, *US* to mold; *Métal* to cast; **robe qui moule la taille** tightly fitting *or* figure-hugging dress; *Fig* **m. sa conduite sur qn** to model one's behaviour on sb **2 se mouler** *vpr Fig* (*prendre pour modèle*) to model oneself **(sur** on)

mouleur [mulœr] *nm* caster, moulder, *US* molder

moulière [muljɛr] *nf* mussel bed

moulin [mulɛ̃] *nm* **(a)** mill; **roue de m.** millwheel; **on y entre comme dans un m.** people *or* all and sundry can just walk in; **ce n'est pas un m. ici!** you can't just walk in *or* breeze in as if you owned the place!; *Fig* **se battre contre des moulins à vent** to tilt at windmills **(b)** *F* (*de voiture*) engine

▶ **moulin**: **m. à café** coffee grinder; (*manuel*) coffee mill; **m. à eau** watermill; **m. à légumes** food mill; **m. à minerai** ore crusher; *Fig* **m. à paroles** chatterbox, gasbag; **m. à poivre** pepper mill; *Rel* **m. à prières** prayer wheel; **m. à vent** windmill

mouliner [muline] *vt* **(a)** *Culin F* to pass through a food mill **(b)** *Pêche* (*ligne*) to reel in

moulinet [mulinɛ] *nm* **(a)** *Tech* winch; *Pêche* reel **(b) faire des moulinets (avec sa canne)** to twirl one's (walking) stick; **faire des moulinets (avec les bras)** to wave one's arms around

moulinette® [mulinɛt] *nf* food mill; **passer la soupe à la m.** to put the soup through the food mill; *Fig* **il m'a passé à la m.** he put me through it *or* through the mill; **passer qch à la m.** to tear sth to shreds

moult [mult] *adj Hum, Vieilli* a multitude of; **avec m. remerciements** with many thanks

moulu [muly] *adj* (*café, poivre*) ground; *Fig* (*personne*) shattered, worn-out, dead-beat; **m. (de coups)** black and blue

moulure [mulyr] *nf Archit, Menuis* (ornamental) moulding, *US* molding

moulurer [mulyre] *vt Constr* to cut a moulding *or US* molding on; **profils moulurés** mouldings

mourant, -ante [murɑ̃, -ɑ̃t] **1** *adj* dying; (*voix*) faint **2** *n* dying man, *f* dying woman; **les mourants** the dying

mourir [murir] (*prp* **mourant**; *pp* **mort**; *pr ind* **je meurs, il meurt, n. mourons, ils meurent**; *pr sub* **je meure, n. mourions**; *p hist* **il mourut**; *fu* **je mourrai** [murre]; *aux* **être) 1** *vi* **(a)** (*de personne, d'animal, de plante*) to die; **il est mort hier** he died yesterday; **il est mort assassiné** he was murdered; **il est mort de vieillesse** he died of old age; **m. de faim** to die of starvation, to starve to death; (*avoir très faim*) to be starving; **m. de soif/chaleur/épuisement** to die of thirst/heat/exhaustion; **m. de froid** to freeze to death; **m. accidentellement** to die in an accident; **elle l'aimait à en m.** she was desperately in love with him; **m. avant l'âge** to die before one's time; **m. à la tâche** to die in harness, *F* to die with one's boots on; **au moment de m.** in the hour of death; **au moment de m. il a fait venir toute sa famille** just before he died, he sent for his entire family; **faire m. qn** to put sb to death; **faire m. qn à petit feu** to kill sb by inches; *F* **il me fera m.** he'll be the death of me; **vous me faites m. d'impatience** the suspense is killing me; **je mourais de peur** I was dying of fright, I was frightened to death; **m. d'inquiétude** to be worried to death; **elle me fera m. d'inquiétude** she'll worry me to death, she'll be the death of me; **m. de chagrin** to be weighed down with grief, to be grief-stricken; (*littéralement*) to die of grief; **m. d'ennui** to die of boredom; **ennuyer qn à m.** to bore sb to death; **être à m. d'ennui** (*de film, roman, conversation*) to be deadly boring; **m. d'envie de faire qch** to be dying to do sth; **j'ai cru m. de rire** I thought I would die laughing, I nearly died laughing; **être à m. de rire** (*de film, roman, personne*) to be uproariously funny; *très F* **plus bête/avare que lui, tu meurs** there's nobody on God's earth who's as stupid/mean as he is; *Fig* **tu ne vas pas en m., tout de même** it won't kill you, you know!

(b) (*d'un feu, d'une coutume, d'une industrie, d'une civilisation*) to die out; (*d'une région*) to die; **la plainte s'enfla, envahit l'espace, puis finit par m.** the wailing grew, filled the whole space, then finally died away *or* faded away; **les vagues qui viennent m. sur la plage** the waves which break and spend themselves on the beach

2 se mourir *vpr Litt* to be dying; (*d'une habitude*) to die out; (*d'un feu*) to die down; **je sens que je me meurs** I feel that I am dying; **la lampe se mourait** the lamp was fading *or* giving out

3 *v impers* **il meurt des milliers d'enfants chaque jour** thousands of children die every day

mouroir [murwar] *nm F Péj* old people's home; **ces foyers de personnes âgées sont des mouroirs** these homes are just places where old people are left to die

mouron [murɔ̃] *nm F* **se faire du m.** to worry; **je commence à me faire du m.** I'm beginning to worry *or* get worried

mousquet [muskɛ] *nm* musket

mousquetaire [muskətɛr] *nm* musketeer; **gants (à la) m.** gauntlets

mousqueterie [muskətri] *nf* musketry; **feu de m.** musket fire

mousqueton [muskətɔ̃] *nm* **(a)** *Mil* (*fusil court*) carbine **(b)** (*d'escalade etc*) (*anneau*) karabiner; (*système d'accrochage*) snaphook

moussage [musaʒ] *nm* foaming

moussaillon [musajɔ̃] *nm F* ship's boy

moussaka [musaka] *nf Culin* moussaka

moussant [musɑ̃] *adj* (*gel*) foaming; **être très m.** to produce a lot of lather; **il est peu m.** it doesn't produce *or* give much of a lather

mousse[1] [mus] *nf* **(a)** *Bot* moss; **couvert de m.** covered with moss, moss-grown, mossy; *Prov* **pierre qui roule n'amasse pas m.** a rolling stone gathers no moss; *Tricot* **point m.** moss stitch

(b) (*de mer, dans cours d'eau pollué, de cappucino*) froth, foam; (*sur verre de bière*) head; (*de savon*) lather; *Culin* mousse; **les assiettes sont encore pleines de m.** the plates are still covered in suds; **les vêtements sont encore pleins de m.** the clothes are still full of soap; *F* **une m.** (*bière*) a beer; *F* **se faire de la m.** to fret, to worry; *Culin* **m. au chocolat/de saumon** chocolate/salmon mousse; **m. à raser** shaving foam

(c) (caoutchouc) m. foam rubber; **matelas en m.** foam rubber mattress

mousse[2] *nm* ship's boy

mousse[3] *adj Tech* (*lame, pointe etc*) blunt

mousseline [muslin] *nf* **(a)** *Tex* muslin; **m. de soie** chiffon **(b)** *Culin* **pommes (de terre) m.** puréed potatoes

mousser [muse] *vi* (*de bière*) to froth, to foam; (*d'eau savonneuse, de savon, lessive*) to lather; (*de vin, eau gazeuse*) to sparkle, to fizz; **ce savon/cette lessive ne mousse pas beaucoup** this soap/washing powder doesn't lather very well *or* doesn't give much of a lather; **ce champagne mousse beaucoup** there are a lot of bubbles in this champagne, this champagne is very fizzy; *Arg* **faire m. qn** (*mettre en colère*) to make sb lose his/her temper *or* flare up; (*faire valoir*) to boast about sb, to sing sb's praises; **se faire m.** to show off

mousseron [musrɔ̃] *nm* edible mushroom, *surtout* St George's agaric

mousseux, -euse [musø, -øz] **1** *adj* **(a)** (*écumeux*) (*eau*) frothy, foaming; (*chocolat, cappucino, crème*) frothy; (*bière*) frothy, with a lot of head **(b)** (*vin, cidre*) sparkling **2** *nm* sparkling wine

moussoir [muswar] *nm* whisk

mousson [musɔ̃] *nf* monsoon

moussu [musy] *adj* mossy, mossgrown

moustache [mustaʃ] *nf* **(a) m., moustaches** moustache; **m. à la gauloise** walrus moustache; **m. en brosse** toothbrush moustache; **porter la m., avoir une m.** to have a moustache **(b)** (*de chat, rongeur*) whiskers

moustachu [mustaʃy] **1** *adj* (*homme*) with a moustache; **être m.** to have a moustache **2** *nm* man with a moustache

moustiquaire [mustikɛr] *nf* mosquito net; *Can* (*à la fenêtre*) screen

moustique [mustik] *nm* **(a)** [①**A12**,1,c] (*insecte*) mosquito **(b)** *F* (*personne maigrichonne*) weed; (*enfant*) kid, nipper

moût [mu] *nm* (*de raisins*) must; (*de bière*) wort

moutard [mutar] *nm Arg* (*enfant*) kid, nipper

moutarde [mutard] **1** *nf* mustard; **m. forte** *ou* **de Dijon** strong *or* Dijon mustard; **graine de m.** mustard seed; *Fig* **la m. lui est montée au nez** he lost his temper *or* flared up; **je sens la m. qui me monte au nez** I'm beginning to lose my temper, I'm doing a slow burn **2** *adj inv* **gaz m.** mustard gas; **(jaune) m.** mustard (yellow)

moutardier [mutardje] *nm* **(a)** (*fabricant*) mustard maker; (*vendeur*) mustard seller; *F* **il se croit le premier m. du pape** he thinks he's the cat's pyjamas *or* the bee's knees **(b)** (*pot*) mustard pot

moutier [mutje] *nm Arch* monastery

mouton, -onne [mutɔ̃, -ɔn] **1** *nm* **(a)** [①**A12**,1,g] *Zool* sheep; *Culin* mutton; *Culin* **ragoût de m.** mutton stew; **(peau de) m.** sheepskin; **éleveur de moutons** (*pour la viande*) sheep farmer; (*pour la laine*) woolgrower; *Fig* **doux comme un m.** as meek as a lamb; **être frisé comme un m.** to have curly hair; *Fig* **revenons à nos moutons** let's get back to the subject; **ils ont tous suivi comme des moutons** they all followed like sheep; **compter les moutons** (*pour s'endormir*) to count sheep; *Fig* **c'est un m. à cinq pattes** he's a rare breed; **vous recherchez le m. à cinq pattes** you're looking for something that doesn't exist, you want the impossible

(b) *F* (*dans les prisons*) grass

(c) moutons (*sur les vagues*) white horses; (*dans le ciel*) fluffy *or* fleecy white clouds; **la mer fait des moutons** there are white horses on the sea

(d) moutons (*sous les meubles*) fluff, *Am* dust bunnies

(e) *Constr* drop hammer

2 *adj Fig* sheeplike

moutonnant [mutɔnɑ̃] *adj* (*mer*) covered with white horses

moutonné [mutɔne] *adj* (*ciel*) dotted with fleecy clouds; **tête moutonnée** curly head of hair

moutonnement [mutɔnmɑ̃] *nm* (*de la mer*) breaking into white horses, frothing; **m. du ciel** dotting of fleecy clouds in the sky

moutonner [mutɔne] *vi* (*de la mer*) to break into white horses, to froth; (*du ciel*) to become dotted with fleecy clouds

moutonneux, -euse [mutɔnø, -øz] *adj* **(a)** (*mer*) foam-flecked, covered with white horses **(b)** (*ciel*) dotted with fleecy clouds

moutonnier, -ière [mutɔnje, -jɛr] *adj* (*élevage*) sheep; *Fig* (*foule*) sheeplike; (*personne*) easily led

mouture [mutyr] *nf* **(a)** (*de blé*) grinding, milling; (*de café*) grinding; **avec ce moulin à café la m. est excellente** this mill grinds the coffee really well; **si la m. était plus fine** if it were ground more finely; **vous voulez quelle m.?** how would you like it ground?; *Fig Vieilli* **tirer deux moutures d'un sac** to profit twice over from sth **(b)** (*d'un ouvrage, un livre*) version, *Péj* rehash; **c'est la deuxième m. du texte** this is the second version of *or* draft of *or F* go at the text

mouvance [muvɑ̃s] *nf* **(a)** (*de pays*) sphere of influence; **elle a été dans la m. surréaliste pendant un temps** she moved in surrealist circles for a time; **il se situe davantage dans la m. du parti socialiste** he is closer to *or* tends more towards the socialist party **(b)** *Litt* (*instabilité*) flux, constant change; **tout est en m.** everything is in a state of flux

mouvant [muvɑ̃] *adj* (*terrain*) unstable; (*cible*) moving; (*feuillage, herbe*) swaying; **les blés mouvants sous le ciel d'orage** the swaying corn under the stormy sky; *Fig* **être sur un terrain m.** to be on shifting *or* unsteady ground

mouvement [muvmɑ̃] *nm* **(a)** movement, motion; (*geste*) gesture; **m. vers l'arrière** backward movement *or* motion; **il tomba du cheval et resta sans m.** he fell from his horse and lay motionless on the ground; **il y eut un m. de panique dans la foule** the crowd panicked; **il y eut un m. de foule** a ripple ran through the crowd; **il y eut un m. de foule, et je perdis mon frère de vue** I lost sight of my brother in the crush; **un m. de panique à la Bourse** panic *or* a panicky reaction on the Stock Exchange; **faire un m.** to move; **faire un faux m.** (*qui provoque une douleur*) to move the wrong way; **j'ai fait un faux m. et j'ai renversé le verre de vin** I clumsily knocked the glass of wine over; **surveiller les mouvements de qn** to monitor sb's movements; **il aime le m.** (*voyager*) he likes change, he likes to move around, he can't stay in one place; **être toujours en m.** (*d'une personne*) to be always on the move; **répondre d'un m. de tête** (*pour dire non*) to answer with a shake of the head, to shake one's head; (*pour dire oui*) to answer with a nod, to nod; **elle me fit signe d'entrer d'un m. de tête** she signalled to me to come in; **avoir un m. de dégoût** to recoil in disgust; **il a eu un m. de recul** he recoiled, he started backwards; **mettre un mécanisme en m.** to set a machine in motion, to start a machine; **se mettre en m.** to start off, to move off; **c'est une ville toujours en m.** it's a bustling *or* very lively city; **quelques mouvements de gymnastique** a few exercises; **des mouvements pour soulager son mal de dos** exercises to relieve backache; **on ne pouvait pas faire un m.** you couldn't move; **un film d'action où il y a beaucoup de m.** an action film with lots going on; **pièces en m.** (*de machine*) moving parts; **contrôler le m. des marchandises/des capitaux** to monitor the flow *or* movement of goods/capital; *Aut* **m. de caisse** body roll; *Mil* **m. de troupes** troop movement; **guerre de m.** mobile warfare; **amorcer un m. de repli** to start falling back; *F* **il faut accélérer le m.** we'll have to get a move on; **m. perpétuel** perpetual motion

(b) (*changement*) **m. de terrain** undulation; **un m. de**

personnel staff changes; **suivre le m.** to go with the flow; **le m. des idées** the evolution of ideas; **le m. des naissances** the trend in the birthrate; *F* **être dans le m.** to be with it, to be abreast of the times *or* up to date; *Bourse* **connaître un m. à la hausse/à la baisse** to move up/down; **m. ascensionnel** upward movement; **m. de baisse** downward movement; **m. boursier** stock market movement; **m. d'un compte** account movement; **m. des capitaux** movement of capital; **m. des cours/des prix** price fluctuation; **m. des devises** currency fluctuation; **m. des valeurs** share movements; **mouvements monétaires** monetary fluctuations

(c) (*élan*) **mon premier m. fut de ...** my first impulse was to ...; **m. d'humeur** outburst (of temper); **dans un m. de colère** in a fit of anger; **de son propre m.** of one's own accord; **avoir un bon m.** to act on a kindly impulse; **allez! un bon m.!** be a good sort

(d) *Pol etc* movement; **le m. syndical/ouvrier** the union/labour movement; **M. de libération des femmes** Women's Liberation Movement; *F* Women's Lib; **m. pacifiste** peace movement; **m. consumériste** consumer movement; **les cheminots vont reconduire leur m. de grève** the railwaymen want to extend their strike action; **lancer un m. de grève/révolte** to instigate a strike/revolt; **m. insurrectionnel** uprising

(e) (*aspect*) (*de draperies, cou, reins*) line(s); (*de terrain*) contours

(f) (*dans un port, un aéroport, une gare*) traffic; **un quartier où il y a toujours beaucoup de m.** a very busy area, an area with a lot of traffic; *Rail* **mouvements des trains** train arrivals and departures; *Rail* **chef de m.** traffic manager; **mouvements des navires** shipping intelligence

(g) *Mus* movement; **symphonie à trois mouvements** symphony in three movements; **presser/ralentir le m.** to quicken/slow the tempo

(h) (*d'horloge*) works, movement; **m. d'horlogerie** clockwork

mouvementé [muvmɑ̃te] *adj* (a) (*discussion, débat*) animated, lively; (*journée, voyage, traversée, vie*) eventful; **une partie mouvementée** an exciting game (b) **terrain m.** undulating ground

mouvoir [muvwar] (*prp* **mouvant**; *pp* **mû, mue**; *pr ind* **je meus, il meut, n. mouvons, ils meuvent**; *pr sub* **je meuve, n. mouvions, ils meuvent**; *p hist* **je mus** (*rare*); *fu* **je mouvrai**) **1** *vt* (a) (*machine*) to drive, to actuate; (*bateau*) to propel; **mû par la vapeur** steam-driven; **mû par un ressort** spring-loaded; *Fig* **mû par la colère/l'intérêt** moved *or* prompted by anger/prompted by interest (b) (*objet*) to move **2 se mouvoir** *vpr* to move

moyen[1], -enne [mwajɛ̃, -ɛn] *adj* (a) (*du milieu*) middle; **les classes moyennes** the middle class(es); *Scol* **cours m.** intermediate class; **cours m. première/deuxième année** ≈ primary IV/V, *Am* ≈ fourth/fifth grade; *Géog* **le cours m. d'un fleuve** the middle reaches of a river; **moyenne saison** (*en tourisme*) shoulder period

(b) (*coût, prix, durée, consommateur, élève, altitude etc*) average; (*pression, vitesse, température, temps de réaction*) average, *surtout Spéc* mean; (*qualité*) average, medium; **la durée moyenne de travail du Français** the average hours of work in France; **le Français m.** the average Frenchman, the man in the street; **à m. terme** in the medium term; **choisir un m. terme** to choose a middle course; **entre la passivité et la guerre, il doit y avoir un m. terme** there must be a middle ground between passiveness and war; **de taille** *ou* **grandeur moyenne** medium-sized; **femme de taille moyenne** woman of average height; *Péj* **travail/vin d'une qualité très moyenne** very average work/wine, work/wine of a very indifferent quality; **il est trop m. en physique** his physics marks aren't good enough

moyen[2] *nm* [①**A13,3,b**] (a) means; *Prov* **la fin justifie les moyens** the end justifies the means; *Prov* **qui veut la fin veut les moyens** you can't make an omelette without breaking eggs; **par tous les moyens** any way I/you/*etc* can, *Péj* by fair means or foul; **j'emploierai tous les moyens** I'll use whatever means *or* do whatever I have to; **employer les grands moyens** to take extreme measures; **au m.** *ou* **par (le) m. de qch** by means of *or* with the help of sth; **il a calé la table au moyen d'un ticket de métro** he used a metro ticket as a wedge for the table, he wedged the table with a metro ticket; **y a-t-il m. de le faire?** is there any way it can be done?, is it possible (to do it)?; **y a-t-il m. d'éviter le centre-ville?** is there any way of avoiding the centre of town?; **y aurait-il m. de s'arrêter cinq minutes?** would it be possible to *or* could we stop for five minutes?; **y aurait-il m. d'avoir un vol moins cher/d'avoir un peu de pain avec mon fromage?** is there any chance of a cheaper flight/a bit of bread with my cheese?; **il y a m. de la contacter par l'intermédiaire de ses parents** she can be contacted through her parents; **il n'y a pas m.** it can't be done, it's impossible; **j'ai essayé d'ouvrir le pot, il n'y a pas m.** I've tried to open the jar but it's impossible, *F* I've tried but no way can I get the jar open; **il n'y a pas m. de le lui faire comprendre** there's no way of making him understand, it's impossible to *or F* no way can you make him understand; **j'ai essayé de le convaincre mais il n'y a pas eu m.** I tried to convince him but it was impossible *or* but I couldn't budge him; *F* **j'ai essayé de lui faire entendre raison/de le faire changer d'avis: pas m.!** I tried to make him see reason/change his mind but no way!; **j'ai essayé de le joindre au téléphone tout l'après-midi: pas m.!** I tried all afternoon to get him on the phone but it was impossible *or* but nothing doing; **trouver un m. de faire qch** to find a way *or* means of doing sth; **trouver le m. de faire qch** to discover *or* find out how to do sth; **il a encore trouvé le m. de se faire dispenser** he's managed to get out of it again; *Iron* **elle a trouvé le m. de se mettre mal avec tous ses collègues** she's managed to get *or* she's succeeded in getting on bad terms with all her colleagues; **inventer un m. de s'échapper** to come up with a way of escaping; **faire qch par ses propres moyens** to do sth on one's own *or* unaided; **elle est venue par ses propres moyens** she came under her own steam; [①**A26-27,c**] **m. de transport** means of transport; **disposes-tu d'un m. de transport?** do you have transport?; **moyens de production** means of production; **moyens de communication** means of communication; **avec les moyens du bord** with the means at one's disposal; **nous avons fait avec les moyens du bord** we made do with what we had; **si tu veux réussir il faut t'en donner les moyens** if you want to succeed you have to equip yourself to do so; **dans la mesure de mes moyens** to the best *or* to the utmost of my ability, as best I can; **enfant qui a des moyens** bright *or* talented child; **il a peu de moyens** he's not very bright; **perdre tous ses moyens** to lose one's head, to go to pieces; **faire perdre tous ses moyens à qn** to make sb lose his/her head

(b) *Fin* **moyens** means; **moyens de paiement** means of payment; **moyens financiers** financial means; **moyens liquides** liquid resources; **vivre au-dessus de ses moyens** to live beyond one's means; **il a largement les moyens de faire construire** he can well afford to build; **je n'en ai pas les moyens** I can't afford it; **ils ont les moyens** they're well off, they can afford it; **dans la mesure de mes moyens** as best I can, as far as my finances permit

moyen(-)âge [mwajɛnɑʒ] *nm* **le m.** the Middle Ages; **le haut m.** the early Middle Ages; **coutumes du m.** medieval customs

moyenâgeux, -euse [mwajɛnɑʒø, -øz] *adj* medieval; *Fig Péj* medieval, old-fashioned, outdated

moyen-courrier, *pl* **moyens-courriers** *adj, nm* **(avion) m.** medium-range *or* medium-haul (aircraft)

moyennant [mwajɛnɑ̃] *prép* (in return) for; **louer qch m. cent francs par jour** to hire sth for *or* at (a charge of) a hundred francs a day; **m. paiement** in exchange for payment, subject to payment; **faire qch m. finance** to do sth in return for payment *or* for a consideration; **je veux bien nettoyer ton jardin, mais m. finance** I'm willing to tidy up your garden but I'll want to be paid for it; **m. dix francs** for ten francs, on payment of ten francs; **m. quoi** in return for which, *Fml* in consideration of which; **je l'ai aidé à faire son devoir d'anglais, m. quoi il ...** I helped him with his English homework and in return he ...

moyenne [mwajɛn] *nf* average; *Math* mean; *Scol* pass mark; **j'ai 8/20 de moyenne en mathématiques** ≈ I averaged 40% in maths; *Scol* **améliorer sa m. de français** to improve one's average (mark) in French; **en m.** on (an) average; **m. (horaire)** (hourly) average; *Aut* average (speed); **faire du 100 de m.** to do an average of *or* to average 100 kilometres per hour; **supérieure/inférieure à la m.** above/below average, higher/lower than average; **enfant d'une intelligence au-dessus/au-dessous de la m.** child of above/below average intelligence; **m. de temps entre deux pannes** mean time between failures, MTBF

moyennement [mwajɛnmɑ̃] *adv* moderately, fairly; **travailler m.** to work fairly well

Moyen-Orient [mwajɛnɔrjɑ̃] *nm* **le M.** the Middle East

moyen-oriental, -ale, -aux, -ales [mwajɛnɔrjɑ̃tal, -o] *adj* Middle Eastern

moyette [mwajɛt] *nf Agr* (*de blé*) shock

moyeu, -eux [mwajø] *nm* (*de roue de voiture*) hub; (*de roue de charrette*) nave; (*d'hélice*) boss

mozzarella [mɔdʒarɛla] *nm* mozzarella

MST[1] [ɛmɛste] *nf Méd* (*abrév* **maladie sexuellement transmissible**) STD

MST[2] *nf* (*abrév* **Maîtrise de Sciences Techniques**) **M. hôtellerie-restauration** higher vocational qualification in hotel management and catering
mû *voir* **mouvoir**
muance [mɥɑ̃s] *nf Arch* (*à la puberté*) breaking of the voice
mucilage [mysilaʒ] *nm* mucilage, gum
mucilagineux, -euse [mysilaʒinø, -øz] *adj* mucilaginous, viscous
mucosité [mykozite] *nf* mucus, mucosity
mucoviscidose [mykovisidoz] *nf Méd* cystic fibrosis
mucus [mykys] *nm* mucus
mue [my] *nf* **(a)** (*d'oiseaux, de mammifères, de crustacés*) moult(ing), *US* molt(ing); (*de cerf*) shedding *or* casting of the antlers; (*de reptiles*) sloughing; (*époque*) moulting season; (*dépouille*) (*d'oiseau*) discarded feathers; (*de crustacé*) discarded shell; (*de cerf*) discarded antlers; (*de serpents*) slough; **serin en m.** moulting canary **(b)** *Physiol* (*à la puberté*) breaking of the voice **(c)** (*cage*) (*pour faucons*) mew; (*pour volaille*) coop
muer [mɥe] **1** *vt Litt* **m. sa tête** (*de cerf*) to shed *or* cast its antlers **2** *vi* **(a)** (*d'oiseau, de mammifère, de crustacé*) to moult, *US* to molt; (*de cerf*) to shed *or* cast its antlers; (*de reptile*) to slough, to cast its skin **(b)** (*de voix*) (*à la puberté*) to break; **il commence à m.** his voice is breaking **3 se muer** *vpr* **se m. en** to change (in)to
müesli [myɛsli, mysli] *nm* muesli
muet, -ette [mɥɛ, -ɛt] **1** *adj* (*personne*) (*privé de l'usage de la parole*) dumb; (*silencieux*) silent, dumb, mute; (*film, réprobation, complicité*), *Ling* silent; (*rôle*) non-speaking; (*carte géographique*) blank; (*clavier de machine à écrire*) blank, unmarked; **m. de naissance** born dumb, dumb from birth; *Fig* **la stupeur m'a rendu m.** I was struck dumb with astonishment; **j'écoutais, m. d'étonnement** I listened speechless with astonishment *or* in mute astonishment; **m. de colère** speechless with anger; **rester m.** to remain silent; **m. comme une tombe** (as) silent as the grave; **il est resté m. comme une carpe** (*il n'a pas répondu à la question*) he didn't say a word, he clammed up; **tu es resté m. comme une carpe toute la soirée** you didn't open your mouth *or* say a word all evening; **les grandes douleurs sont muettes** great sorrow is often silent; **le cinéma m.** silent cinema *or* films
2 *n* mute
3 *nm Cin* **le m.** silent films
mufle [myfl] *nm* **(a)** (*du bœuf, bison etc*) (hairless part of) muzzle, muffle; (*de lion, taureau etc*) nose, *F* snout **(b)** *F* (*homme*) boor, lout
muflerie [myflǝri] *nf F* **(a)** (*caractère*) boorishness **(b)** (*action*) boorish behaviour; **lassée de ses mufleries** tired of his boorish behaviour *or* boorishness **(c)** (*parole*) boorish remark
muflier [myflije] *nm Bot* antirrhinum, snapdragon
mufti [myfti] *nm Rel* mufti
muge [myʒ] *nm* (*poisson*) mullet
mugir [myʒir] *vi* **(a)** (*de vache*) to low, to moo; (*de taureau*) to bellow **(b)** (*du vent*) to moan, to howl; (*d'un torrent*) to roar; (*d'une sirène*) to wail
mugissement [myʒismɑ̃] *nm* **(a)** (*de vache*) lowing, mooing; (*de taureau*) bellowing **(b)** (*du vent*) moaning, howling; (*d'un torrent*) roaring; (*d'une sirène*) wailing
muguet [mygɛ] *nm* **(a)** (*plante*) lily of the valley **(b)** *Méd* thrush
mulâtre [mylɑtr] **1** *adj* mulatto, half-caste **2** *n* (*f* **mulâtre, mulâtresse** [mylɑtrɛs]) mulatto
mule[1] [myl] *nf Zool* mule
mule[2] *nf* (*pantoufle*) mule; **la m. du Pape** the Pope's slipper; **baiser la m. du Pape** to kiss the Pope's toe
mulet[1] [mylɛ] *nm Zool* mule
mulet[2] *nm* (*poisson*) grey mullet
muletier, -ière [myltje, -jɛr] **1** *adj* (*chemin, sentier*) mule; **équipage m.** mule train **2** *nm* mule driver, muleteer
mulot [mylo] *nm* field mouse
multibancarisation [myltibɑ̃karizasjɔ̃] *nf* growth in the number of banks
multicarte [myltikart] *adj, n* **(représentant) m.** rep for several companies
multicellulaire [myltiselylɛr] *adj* multicellular
multicolonnage [myltikɔlɔnaʒ] *nm Ordinat* multicolumn working
multicolore [myltikɔlɔr] *adj* multicoloured, *US* multicolored
multicoque [myltikɔk] *nm Naut* multihull
multicritère [myltikritɛr] *nm Ordinat* multicriterion
multiculturalisme [myltikyltyralism] *nm* multiculturalism
multiculturel, -elle [myltikyltyrɛl] *adj* multicultural
multidevise [myltidǝviz] *adj* multicurrency
multidimensionnel, -elle [myltidimɑ̃sjɔnɛl] *adj* multidimensional; *Fig* (*expérience, compétence etc*) multifaceted
multidisciplinaire [myltidisiplinɛr] *adj* multidisciplinary
multidistribution [myltidistribysjɔ̃] *nf* multidistribution
multi-écran, *pl* **multi-écrans** [myltiekrɑ̃] *TV etc nm* multi-screen, split screen
multiflore [myltiflɔr] *adj Bot* multiflora
multifonctions [myltifɔ̃ksjɔ̃] *adj* multi-functional; *Ordinat* **clavier m.** multi-functional keyboard
multiforme [myltifɔrm] *adj* multiform; *Fig* (*pays, problème etc*) multifaceted
multigrade [myltigrad] *adj* (*huile*) multi-grade
multi-image [myltiimaʒ] *adj TV etc* multi-image
multilatéral, -ale, -aux, -ales [myltilateral, -o] *adj* (*accord*) multilateral
multimédia [myltimedja] *adj nm* multimedia
multimilliardaire [myltimiljardɛr], **multimillionnaire** [myltimiljɔnɛr] *adj, n* multimillionaire
multimode [myltimɔd] *adj Ordinat* multimode
multinational, -ale, -aux, -ales [myltinasjɔnal, -o] **1** *adj* multinational **2** *nf* **multinationale** multinational (company)
multinorme [myltinɔrm] *adj TV* multistandard
multipare [myltipar] **1** *adj* multiparous **2** *nf* multipara
multipassage [myltipasaʒ] *adj Ordinat* multistrike
multipiste [myltipist] *adj* multitrack
multiplace [myltiplas] *adj, nm* **(avion) m.** = passenger aircraft
multiple [myltipl] **1** *adj* **(a)** (*raisons, résidences, talents, dangers*) many, numerous; *Psy* (*personnalité*) multiple; **les causes sont multiples** the reasons are many *or Fml* manifold; **à usages multiples** multipurpose; **maison à succursales multiples** multiple store, chain store; *Scol* **question à choix multiples** multiple-choice question; **nous avons essayé de vous joindre à de multiples reprises** we tried repeatedly to contact you; *Ordinat* **à accès m.** multi-access **(b)** (*complexe*) (*monde, âme etc*) complex, multi-faceted **2** *nm Math* multiple; **le plus petit commun m.** the lowest common multiple
multiplex [myltiplɛks] *adj inv, nm Rad, TV* multiplex
multiplexage [myltiplɛksaʒ] *nm* multiplexing
multiplexé [myltiplɛkse] *adj* multiplex
multiplexer [myltiplɛkse] *vt* to multiplex
multiplexeur [myltiplɛksœr] *nm* multiplexer, multiplexor
multipliable [myltiplijabl] *adj* multipliable; **tout nombre est m.** any number can be multiplied
multiplicande [myltiplikɑ̃d] *nm Math* multiplicand
multiplicateur, -trice [myltiplikatœr, -tris] **1** *adj* multiplying; **engrenage m.** step-up gear **2** *nm Math, Él* multiplier
multiplicatif, -ive [myltiplikatif, -iv] *adj* multiplicative, multiplying
multiplication [myltiplikasjɔ̃] *nf* **(a)** *Math* multiplication; **la m. des vols de voitures/des clubs sportifs** the increase in car theft/in the number of sports clubs; *Bible* **la m. des pains** the miracle of the loaves and fishes **(b)** *MecE* gear (ratio); **grande/petite m.** high/low gear; **m. du levier** leverage
multiplicité [myltiplisite] *nf* multiplicity
multiplier [myltiplije] (*pr sub, impf* **n. multipliions, v. multipliiez**) **1** *vt* **(a)** *Math* to multiply **(par** by)
(b) (*répéter*) **m. les mises en garde** to issue repeated warnings; **m. les erreurs** to make mistake after mistake; **le chef de l'état a multiplié les appels au calme** the head of state has called repeatedly for calm; **ses erreurs/efforts multiplié(e)s** his repeated mistakes/efforts
(c) *MecE* **m. la vitesse de révolution** to gear up
2 se multiplier *vpr* **(a)** to increase; **les crimes se multiplient** crime is on the increase; **les lapins se multiplient rapidement** rabbits multiply rapidly
(b) *Fig* to be in half a dozen places at once; **se m. pour aider qn** to bend over backwards to help sb
multipolaire [myltipɔlɛr] *adj Él, Biol* multipolar
multipostage [myltipɔstaʒ] *nm* bus-mailing
multiposte [myltipɔst] *adj Ordinat* multi-station
multiprocesseur [myltiprɔsesœr] *nm Ordinat* multiprocessor
multiprogrammation [myltiprɔgramasjɔ̃] *nf Ordinat* multiprogramming
multipropriété [myltiprɔprijete] *nf* time-share, multi-ownership; **acheter un appartement/une maison en m.** to buy a time-share (flat/house)
multiracial, -ale, -aux, -ales [myltirasjal, -o] *adj* multiracial
multirisque [myltirisk] *adj* **assurance m.** comprehensive insurance
multisalles [myltisal] **1** *adj inv* **complexe m.** multiplex (cinema) **2** *nm inv* multiplex (cinema)
multisectoriel [myltisektɔrjɛl] *adj* multisector

multisoupape [myltisupap] *nm Aut* multi-valve (engine)
multistandard [myltistɑ̃dar] *adj inv TV* multistandard
multitâche [myltitɑʃ] *adj Ordinat* multitasking
multitraitement [myltitrɛtmɑ̃] *nm Ordinat* multiprocessing
multitude [myltityd] *nf* **(a)** multitude (**de** of); **une m. de gens** hosts *or* crowds *or* swarms of people; **il y avait sur la cheminée une m. de bibelots** the mantelpiece was crowded with ornaments **(b)** *Litt Péj* **la m.** the masses
multi-utilisateur [myltiytilizatœr] *adj Ordinat* multi-user
multivision [myltivizjɔ̃] *nf TV* multivision
munichois, -oise [mynikwa, -waz] **1** *adj* of/from Munich **2** *n* **(a) M.** (*natif*) native of Munich; (*habitant*) inhabitant of Munich **(b)** *Hist Pol* (*partisan des accords de Munich*) Munich supporter
municipal, -ale, -aux, -ales [mynisipal, -o] **1** *adj* (*élection, employé*) municipal, local-government; (*bibliothèque, stade, patinoire, piscine*) municipal, local; **conseil m.** town council, local council; **arrêté m.** by-law; *Hist* **la garde municipale** the military police (*of Paris*) **2** *nfpl* **les municipales** municipal *or* local(-government) elections
municipalisation [mynisipalizasjɔ̃] *nf* municipalization; **la m. des sols a été votée** there has been a vote in favour of placing land under municipal control
municipaliser [mynisipalize] *vt* to municipalize
municipalité [mynisipalite] *nf* **(a)** (*ville*) municipality, town **(b)** (*région*) local administrative area **(c)** (*maire et conseillers municipaux*) (local) council, corporation
munificence [mynifisɑ̃s] *nf Litt* munificence
munificent [mynifisɑ̃] *adj Litt* munificent
munir [mynir] **1** *vt* (*personne*) to supply, to provide, *Fml* to furnish (**de** with); (*voiture, chambre*) to fit, to equip (**de** with); **muni des sacrements de l'Église** fortified with the rites of the Church **2 se munir** *vpr* (*de vêtements chauds, cartes routières, provisions*) to equip *or* provide oneself (**de** with); (*de crème solaire, d'un parapluie*) to take; **il faut se m. d'un passeport** you need (to take) a passport
munition [mynisjɔ̃] *nf* **(a) munitions (de guerre)** ammunition, munitions; **des armes et des munitions** arms and ammunition **(b)** *Arch* (*d'armée*) munitioning, provisioning; **munitions de bouche** provisions
muphti [myfti] *nm Rel* mufti
muqueux, -euse [mykø, -øz] **1** *adj* (*membrane*) mucous **2** *nf* **muqueuse** mucous membrane
mur [myr] *nm Constr, Fig* (*d'eau, de policiers*) wall; **m. de clôture** surrounding wall; **m. d'appui** low wall; **m. de soutènement** retaining wall; **m. de refend** partition (wall); **m. mitoyen** party wall; **m. porteur** load-bearing wall; **m. d'escalade, m. de varappe** climbing wall; **gros murs** main walls; *F* **les cambrioleurs n'ont laissé que les (quatre) murs** the burglars took everything but the kitchen sink, the burglars stripped the place bare; **rester entre quatre murs** (*en prison*) to be inside; **j'en ai marre de rester entre quatre murs toute la journée** I'm tired of being cooped up all day; *Fig* **mettre qn au pied du m.** to put sb on the spot, to drive sb into a corner, to have sb with his back to the wall; **être au pied du m.** to have one's back to the wall; **l'ennemi est dans nos murs** the enemy is within the gates; *Fig* **il est à présent dans nos murs** (*en visite dans notre ville*) he is in town at the moment; (*dans nos locaux*) he is on the premises at the moment; *Fig* **c'est à se taper la tête contre les murs** it's enough to drive *or* send you up the wall; *Fig* **se heurter à un m.** to come up against a brick wall; **se heurter à un m. d'incompréhension** to come up against a wall *or* a barrier of incomprehension; *Fig* **j'ai l'impression de parler à un m.** it's like talking to a brick wall; *Fig* **les murs ont des oreilles** walls have ears; **faire le m.** to sneak out
▶ **mur**: *Hist* **le m. de Berlin** the Berlin wall; **le M. des Lamentations** the Wailing Wall; **m. du son** sound barrier; **franchir le m. du son** to break the sound barrier
mûr [myr] *adj* **(a)** (*fruit*) ripe; (*vin*) mellow; (*personne, esprit*) mature; **trop m.** (*fruit*) overripe; **il est très m. pour son âge** he is very mature for his age; **l'abcès est m.** the abscess has come to a head; **l'âge m.** maturity; **homme d'âge m.** man of mature years; **après mûre réflexion** after careful *or Fml* mature consideration; **m. pour qch** ripe *or* ready for sth; *Litt* **les temps sont mûrs** the time has come, the time is ripe **(b)** *Arg* (*saoul*) plastered, canned
murage [myraʒ] *nm* (*de porte, fenêtre*) walling up, blocking up
muraille [myrɑj] *nf* **(a)** (*mur*) (high) wall; **la Grande M. de Chine** the Great Wall of China; **les murailles de la ville** the town walls **(b)** (*de bateau*) side
mural, -ale, -aux, -ales [myral, -o] *adj* wall; **peinture murale** mural; **pendule murale** wall clock; **carte murale** wall map; *Archit* **console murale** wall bracket
mûre [myr] *nf* **(a) m. (sauvage** *ou* **de ronce)** blackberry **(b)** (*fruit du mûrier*) mulberry
mûrement [myrmɑ̃] *adv* **après avoir m. réfléchi** after careful *or Fml* mature consideration; **un plan m. réfléchi** a carefully thought-out plan; **tout cela a été m. préparé** it was all very carefully planned
murène [myrɛn] *nf* (*poisson*) moray (eel)
murer [myre] **1** *vt* **(a)** (*entourer de murs*) (*ville, cité*) to wall in **(b)** (*bloquer*) (*porte, fenêtre*) to wall up, to block up; (*personne*) to wall up **2 se murer** *vpr* to shut oneself away; **elle se mure dans le silence/la solitude** she has retreated *or* withdrawn into silence/solitude; **muré chez soi** shut away at home
muret [myrɛ] *nm,* **murette** [myrɛt] *nf* low wall; (*de pierres posées les unes sur les autres*) dry-stone wall
mûrier [myrje] *nm Bot* mulberry (tree *or* bush); **m. (sauvage)** blackberry bush, bramble
mûrir [myrir] **1** *vt* (*fruit*) to ripen; *Fig* (*projet, pensées*) to nurture; **les épreuves l'ont beaucoup mûri** his hardships have made him much more mature; **laisser m. un abcès** to let an abscess come to a head **2** *vi* (*de fruit*) to ripen; (*d'abcès*) to come to a head; (*de projet, processus*) to evolve, to develop; (*de sentiment*) to ripen; **cet enfant a beaucoup mûri** the child has become much more mature *or* has greatly matured
mûrissant [myrisɑ̃] *adj* (*fruit*) ripening; (*personne*) of mature years
mûrissement [myrismɑ̃] *nm* (*de fruits*) ripening; *Fig* (*de projet*) development
murmure [myrmyr] *nm* (*à voix basse*) murmur, murmuring; (*de ruisseau*) babbling; **murmures** murmuring, murmurs; (*plaintes*) murmuring, muttering, grumbling; **un m. d'approbation** a murmur of approval; **ce fut accepté sans un m. (de réprobation)** this was accepted without a murmur
murmurer [myrmyre] **1** *vt* to murmur; **on murmure qu'il va démissionner** rumour has it *or* there are rumours that he's going to resign **2** *vi* (*à voix basse*) to murmur; (*se plaindre*) to grumble, to complain; (*cancaner*) to say things, to talk; (*de ruisseau*) to babble; **m. entre ses dents** to mutter
mûron [myrɔ̃] *nm Bot* wild raspberry
musaraigne [myzarɛɲ] *nf Zool* shrew
musard, -arde [myzar, -ard] *F Vieilli* **1** *adj* dawdling **2** *n* dawdler
musarder [myzarde] *vi* to dawdle, to amble; (*fainéanter*) to dither
musc [mysk] *nm* musk
muscade [myskad] *nf* **(a)** *Bot* **(noix) m.** nutmeg; **fleur de m.** mace **(b)** (*d'escamoteur*) vanishing ball; **passez m.!** hey presto!
muscadier [myskadje] *nm Bot* nutmeg (tree)
muscadin [myskadɛ̃] *nm Arch* dandy, fop
muscardin [myskardɛ̃] *nm Zool* dormouse
muscat [myska] *Agr* **1** *adj* muscat; **raisin m.** muscat grape, muscatel grape; **vin m.** muscatel (wine) **2** *nm* (*raisin*) muscat *or* muscatel grape; (*vin*) muscatel (wine)
muscle [myskl] *nm* muscle; **avoir des muscles** to be muscular, to be brawny; **il est tout en muscles** he's all muscle; **m. antagoniste** antagonistic muscle; **m. biceps** biceps
musclé [myskle] *adj* (*personne, bras, jambes*) muscular, brawny; **il est bien m.** he is very muscular, he has well developed muscles; *Fig* **cet écrivain écrit dans un style m.** this author has a sinewy *or* robust style; **un café m.** a good strong coffee; **une campagne électorale musclée** a punchy electoral campaign; **un discours m.** a punchy *or* forceful speech; **l'intervention musclée de la police** the strong-arm tactics of the police; **un régime m.** a strong-arm regime; **politique musclée** hardline *or* tough policy
muscler [myskle] **1** *vt* to develop the muscles of; **il faut te m. les jambes** you must develop your leg muscles; *Fig* **tout faire pour m. l'industrie française** to do everything to give French industry some muscle *or* to beef up French industry **2** *vi F* **le sport, ça muscle** sport builds up your muscles **3 se muscler** *vpr* to develop one's muscles
muscu [mysky] *nf F* = **musculation**
musculaire [myskylɛr] *adj* (*système, tissu, force*) muscular; **fibre m.** muscle fibre
musculation [myskylasjɔ̃] *nf* body-building; **faire de la m.** to do body-building
musculature [myskylatyr] *nf* musculature; **il a une belle m.** he has a fine set of muscles
musculeux, -euse [myskylø, -øz] *adj aussi Anat* muscular
muse [myz] *nf* muse; *Myth* **les Muses** the Muses; **invoquer sa m.** to invoke *or* call on one's muse; **taquiner la Muse** to write the odd bit of verse
museau, -eaux [myzo] *nm* **(a)** (*d'animal*) muzzle, snout;

Culin **m. vinaigrette** = brawn in vinaigrette **(b)** *F* *(visage)* face; **vilain m.** ugly mug
musée [myze] *nm* museum; **m. (de peinture** *ou* **d'art)** art gallery; **m. des arts et traditions populaires** folk museum; **m. des transports** transport museum; **Venise, ville-m.** the historical city of Venice; *F* **chez eux c'est le m. des horreurs!** their place is full of things I wouldn't give house room to; *Arg* **tu as vu le m. des horreurs!** *(ce groupe)* what an ugly looking crew!
museler [myzle] *vt* **(je muselle; je musellerai)** *(animal)* to muzzle; *Fig (qn, la presse, l'opposition)* to muzzle, to gag
muselière [myzəljɛr] *nf* muzzle; **mettre une m. à** *(un chien, Fig la presse)* to muzzle
musellement [myzɛlmɑ̃] *nm* *(d'animal)* muzzling; *(de personne, la presse)* muzzling, gagging
muser [myze] *vi Arch, Litt* to idle (about); *(flâner)* to dawdle, to amble
muserolle [myzrɔl] *nf Équitation* noseband
musette [myzɛt] **1** *nf* **(a)** *Mus (instrument)* musette *(type of bagpipe)*; **orchestre m.** accordion band; **bal m.** dance to an accordion band; *(lieu)* dance hall with an accordion band **(b)** *(de cheval)* **m. (mangeoire)** nosebag **(c)** *(sac)* bag; *Mil* haversack; *Arch (d'écolier)* satchel **2** *nm Mus F* **le m.** accordion music
muséum [myzeɔm] *nm* natural history museum
musical, -ale, -aux, -ales [myzikal, -o] *adj (son, soirée)* musical; **l'art m.** music; **avoir l'oreille musicale** to have an ear *or* a good ear for music
musicalement [myzikalmɑ̃] *adv* musically
musicalité [myzikalite] *nf* musicality, musical quality
music-hall, *pl* **music-halls** [myzikol] *nm (spectacle)* variety, *Br* music hall, *Am* vaudeville; *(salle)* variety theatre, *Br* music hall, *Am* vaudeville theater; **faire du m.** to do variety *or Br* music hall *or Am* vaudeville; **numéros de m.** variety turns
musicien, -ienne [myzisjɛ̃, -jɛn] **1** *adj* musical **2** *n* musician
musicographe [myzikɔgraf] *n* musicographer
musicologie [myzikɔlɔʒi] *nf* musicology
musicologue [myzikɔlɔg] *n* musicologist
musicothérapie [myzikoterapi] *nf* music therapy
musique [myzik] *nf* music; **mettre des paroles en m.** to set words to music; **instrument de m.** musical instrument; **boîte à m.** music(al) box; **chef de m.** bandmaster; **m. classique** classical music; **m. légère** light music; **m. folklorique** folk music; **m. pop** pop music; **m. religieuse** church music; **m. de chambre** chamber music; **m. d'ambiance** *ou* **de fond** background music; **m. de supermarché** Muzak®, piped music; **m. militaire** *(formation)* military band; *(composition)* military music; **faire de la m.** to make music, to play; **lire la m.** to read music; *F* **je connais la m.** I've heard it all before, it's the same old story; **il veut acheter la m. du film** he wants to buy the soundtrack of the film; *F* **en avant la m.!** let's get started; *Can* **faire face à la m.** to face the music; *TV etc* **m. d'archives** stock music; *TV etc* **m. de générique** title music, theme tune; *TV etc* **m. (de générique) de fin** playout music; *TV etc* **m. d'ouverture** introductory music
musiquette [myzikɛt] *nf Péj* piped music, Muzak®
musoir [myzwar] *nm* pierhead, jetty head
musqué [myske] *adj* **(a)** *(odeur, parfum)* musky **(b) bœuf m.** musk ox; **rat m.** muskrat, musquash; **canard m.** Muscovy duck, musk duck **(c)** *Arch (poète, style etc)* affected
must [mœst] *nm F* must
mustang [mystɑ̃g] *nm* mustang
musulman, -ane [myzylmɑ̃, -an] *adj, n* Moslem, Muslim
mutabilité [mytabilite] *nf* mutability
mutable [mytabl] *adj* mutable
mutant, -e [mytɑ̃] *adj, n* mutant
mutation [mytasjɔ̃] *nf* **(a)** *(de personnel)* transfer; **il a demandé/obtenu sa m. pour raison de santé** he asked for/obtained a transfer for health reasons **(b)** *(changement)* change, alteration; *Biol* mutation; *Ling (de voyelle)* gradation; *(de consonne)* shift; *Jur* change of ownership; *(de propriété)* transfer; **l'Europe de l'Est est en pleine m. politique** Eastern Europe is undergoing profound political change; **le secteur sidérurgique a subi de profondes mutations** the steel industry has undergone extensive change(s)
muter [myte] **1** *vt (personnel)* to transfer **2** *vi Biol* to mutate
mutilateur, -trice [mytilatœr, -tris] **1** *n* mutilator **2** *adj Fig (expérience)* crippling
mutilation [mytilasjɔ̃] *nf (de personne)* mutilation, maiming; *(de statue, objet d'art)* mutilation, defacement; *(de texte)* mutilation; **m. volontaire** self-mutilation
mutilé, -ée [mytile] **1** *adj (personne)* mutilated, maimed; **il est m. du bras** he's lost an arm; **m. au visage** disfigured **2** *n* **mutilés de guerre** disabled ex-servicemen
mutiler [mytile] **1** *vt (qn)* to mutilate, to maim; *(statue, objet d'art)* to mutilate, to deface; *(arbre, texte)* to mutilate; *(paysage)* to disfigure; **il a eu les deux jambes mutilées à la guerre** he lost both legs in the war; **il a eu la main mutilée dans un accident du travail** his hand was badly injured in an industrial accident **2 se m.** *vpr* to mutilate oneself
mutin, -ine [mytɛ̃, -in] **1** *adj* **(a)** *(malicieux)* mischievous, impish, playful **(b)** *Arch (désobéissant)* disobedient, unruly, unbiddable **2** *nm (rebel)* mutineer
mutiné [mytine] **1** *adj* rebellious; *(troupes)* mutinous **2** *nm* mutineer
mutiner (se) [səmytine] *vpr* to rebel **(contre** against); *Naut, Mil* to mutiny
mutinerie [mytinri] *nf* rebellion; *Naut, Mil* mutiny
mutique [mytik] *adj Méd (personne)* suffering from mutism
mutisme [mytism] *nm* **(a)** silence; **les responsables observent un m. absolu** the officials are maintaining (a) total silence; **s'enfermer dans le m.** to maintain a stubborn silence **(b)** *Méd* mutism
mutité [mytite] *nf Méd* mutism
mutualisme [mytɥalism] *nm* **(a)** *Biol* symbiosis, mutualism **(b)** *Écon* mutual insurance
mutualiste [mytɥalist] **1** *adj* **(a)** *Biol* symbiotic, mutualistic **(b)** *Écon* **pharmacie m.** = chemist associated with private insurance company, which may offer reduced rates on certain items to members of the company **2** *n Écon* member of a mutual insurance company
mutualité [mytɥalite] *nf Écon* mutual insurance; **société de m.** mutual insurance company, *Br* friendly society
mutuel, -elle [mytɥɛl] **1** *adj (amour etc)* mutual; **société d'assurance mutuelle** mutual insurance company, *Br* friendly society **2** *nf* **mutuelle** *(société)* mutual insurance company, *Br* friendly society; *(assurance)* private insurance; **prendre une mutuelle** to take out private insurance
mutuellement [mytɥɛlmɑ̃] *adv* each other, one another; **ils se sont aidés/critiqués m.** they helped/criticized each other *or* one another
Mycènes [misɛn] *n Hist* Mycenae
mycénien, -ienne [misenjɛ̃, -jɛn] *adj Hist* Mycenaean
mycologie [mikɔlɔʒi] *nf Bot* mycology
mycose [mikoz] *nf Méd* fungal infection, *Spéc* mycosis; *(sur les pieds)* athlete's foot
myéline [mjelin] *nf Anat* myelin(e)
myélite [mjelit] *nf Méd* myelitis
myélome [mjelom] *nm Méd* myeloma
mygale [migal] *nf* trapdoor spider
myocarde [mjɔkard] *nm Anat* myocardium
myocardite [mjɔkardit] *nf Méd* myocarditis
myologie [mjɔlɔʒi] *nf Anat* myology
myome [mjom] *nm Méd* myoma
myopathe [mɔpat] *n Méd* person with muscular dystrophy
myopathie [mjɔpati] *nf Méd* muscular dystrophy
myope [mjɔp] **1** *adj* shortsighted, *Spéc* myopic; *Fig* **m. comme une taupe** as blind as a bat **2** *n* shortsighted person, *Spéc* myope
myopie [mjɔpi] *nf Méd* shortsightedness, *Spéc* myopia; *Mktg* **m. mercatique** marketing myopia
myosotis [mjɔzɔtis] *nm (fleur)* forget-me-not, *Spéc* myosotis
myriade [mirjad] *nf* myriad; **des myriades d'étoiles** myriads of stars, a myriad stars
myrmidon [mirmidɔ̃] *nm F* pipsqueak
myrrhe [mir] *nf* myrrh
myrte [mirt] *nm (plante)* myrtle; **m. des marais** bog myrtle
myrtille [mirtij] *nf (baie)* bilberry, whortleberry
mystère [mistɛr] *nm* **(a)** mystery; **rester un m.** to remain a mystery; **on n'a jamais pénétré ce m.** no one has ever got to the bottom of this mystery; **si tu veux réussir il faut travailler, il n'y a pas de m.!** if you want to succeed you have to work, there's no mystery about it *or* it's as simple as that!; **ce garçon est un m. pour moi** that boy's a mystery to me; *F* **m. et boule de gomme** *(je n'en ai aucune idée)* I've no idea; *F* search me; *Fig* **ne fais pas tant de mystères!** don't be so mysterious!; **je n'en fais pas m.** I make no secret of it **(b)** *Hist, Littér* mystery (play); **m. de la Passion** Passion play **(c)** *Antiq, Myth* mystery
mystérieusement [misterjøzmɑ̃] *adv* mysteriously
mystérieux, -euse [misterjø, -øz] **1** *adj* mysterious; *(secret)* secret; **un rendez-vous m.** a secret rendezvous **2** *nm* **(a) jouer le(s) m.** to behave very mysteriously **(b) le m.** the mysterious
mysticisme [mistisism] *nm* mysticism
mystifiable [mistifjabl] *adj* gullible
mystifiant [mistifjɑ̃] *adj* deceiving
mystificateur, -trice [mistifikatœr, -tris] **1** *adj (coup de téléphone, lettre, annonce)* hoax; **avoir un côté m.** to have a mischievous streak **2** *n* hoaxer

mystification [mistifikasjɔ̃] *nf Péj* (*tromperie*) deception; (*farce*) hoax; **m. collective** mass deception
mystifier [mistifje] *vt* (*pr sub & impf* **n. mystifiions, v. mystifiiez**) **m. qn** (*faire marcher*) to pull sb's leg; (*beurrer*) to fool sb, to take sb in; **se laisser m. par qch** to (let oneself) be taken in *or* fooled by sth
mystique [mistik] **1** *adj* mystical **2** *n* mystic **3** *nf* mystique
mystiquement [mistikmɑ̃] *adv* mystically
mythe [mit] *nm* myth
mythique [mitik] *adj* mythical
mythologie [mitɔlɔʒi] *nf* mythology
mythologique [mitɔlɔʒik] *adj* mythological
mythologiquement [mitɔlɔʒikmɑ̃] *adv* mythologically
mythologue [mitɔlɔg] *n* mythologist
mythomane [mitɔman] **1** *adj* **être m.** to be a pathological liar **2** *n* pathological liar; *Psy* mythomaniac
mythomanie [mitɔmani] *nf Psy* mythomania
mytiliculteur, -trice [mitilikyltœr, -tris] *n* mussel farmer
mytiliculture [mitilikyltyr] *nf* mussel farming
myxœdème [miksedɛm] *nm Méd Br* myxoedema, *US* myxedema
myxomatose [miksɔmatoz] *nf* myxomatosis

N

N, n [ɛn] *nm* N, n

na [na] *int F* **(et) na!** so there!

nabab [nabab] *nm* nabob

nabot, -ote [nabo, -ɔt] *Péj* **1** *n* dwarf, midget **2** *adj* (*personne*) dwarfish, tiny

Nabuchodonosor [nabykɔdɔnɔzɔr] *nm* **(a)** *Bible, Hist* Nebuchadnezzar **(b)** (*bouteille de champagne*) Nebuchadnezzar

nacelle [nasɛl] *nf* **(a)** (*de montgolfière*) basket; (*de dirigeable*) gondola, car; (*d'avion*) nacelle; (*de moteur d'avion*) pod; (*de laveur de carreau*) cradle, aerial work platform **(b)** (*de landau, poussette*) (*détachable*) carrycot; (*fixe*) carriage **(c)** *Vieilli* (*bateau*) skiff, wherry

nacre [nakr] *nf* mother-of-pearl; **un collier de** *ou* **en n.** a mother-of-pearl necklace

nacré [nakre] *adj* pearlescent

nacrer [nakre] *vt* **(a) n. qch** to give sth a pearly finish **(b)** *Litt* to cast a pearly glimmer onto

nadir [nadir] *nm Astron* nadir

nævus [nevys] *nm Méd* nævus, *US* nevus

nage [naʒ] *nf* **(a)** swimming; (*style*) stroke; **atteindre le rivage à la n.** to swim to the shore; **traverser une rivière à la n.** to swim across a river; **je pratique trois nages** I can do three strokes; **épreuve du 100 m quatre nages** 4 x 100 m relay; **n. libre** freestyle; **n. sur le dos** backstroke; **n. (à l')indienne** overarm stroke **(b) être (tout) en n.** to be bathed in perspiration **(c)** (*aviron*) rowing, sculling; **banc de n.** thwart; **chef de n.** stroke **(d)** *Culin* **à la n.** poached in white wine

nageoire [naʒwar] *nf* **(a)** (*de poisson*) fin; (*de dauphin, cétacé etc*) flipper; **n. caudale** caudal fin, tail fluke; **n. dorsale** dorsal fin; **n. anale** anal fin; **n. pelvienne** pelvic fin; **n. pectorale** pectoral fin **(b)** (*d'hydravion*) fin

nager [naʒe] **(je nageais, n. nageons) 1** *vi* **(a)** to swim; (*de bois, bouchon etc*) to float; **on va n.?** shall we go for a swim?; **tu sais n.?** can you swim?; *Fig* **savoir n.** to know one's way around, to know how to take care of oneself; **n. vers la côte** to swim for the shore; **n. sous l'eau/sur le dos** to swim underwater/on one's back; **n. comme un poisson** to swim like a fish; **n. comme un fer à repasser** to swim like a brick; **n. entre deux eaux** to be floating beneath the surface; *Fig* not to commit oneself; **légumes qui nagent dans le beurre** vegetables swimming in butter; *Fig* **n. dans son sang** to be bathed in blood; **n. dans l'abondance** to be rolling in money; **on ne peut pas dire que la région nage dans l'abondance** the region is not exactly well-off *or* blessed with prosperity; **n. dans le bonheur** to be blissfully happy; *F* **tu nages dans ce costume** the suit drowns you; **tu nages vraiment trop dans ce short** the shorts really are far too big for you; **depuis qu'il a perdu 20 kg il nage dans tous ses vêtements** his clothes just hang on him since he lost 20 kilos; *Fig F* **je nage** I'm all at sea; **je nage complètement!** I'm totally at sea *or* lost!

(b) *Fig Litt* (*vapeurs, nuages, effluves*) to drift

(c) *Naut* to row; **nagez partout!** pull away!; **n. en arrière** *ou Spéc* **à culer** to back water; **n. plat** to feather; **n. à** *ou* **en couple** to (double) scull; **n. en pointe** to row

2 *vt* **(a)** (*la brasse, le crawl etc*) to do, to swim

(b) (*disputer*) **n. le 100 mètres/le quatre fois 100 mètres** to swim (in) the 100 metres/the 4 x 100 metres relay

nageur, -euse [naʒœr, -øz] **1** *n* **(a)** swimmer; **être bon/mauvais n.** to be a good/bad swimmer, to swim well/badly; *Mil* **n. de combat** frogman **(b)** *Naut* (*rameur*) oarsman, oarswoman, rower; **n. de l'arrière** stroke; **n. de l'avant** bow (oar) **(c)** (*maillot de bain*) swimsuit, swimming costume **2** *adj* (*animal*) swimming

naguère [nagɛr] *adv Litt* not long ago, a short time ago, lately; (*autrefois*) formerly

naïade [najad] *nf* naiad, water nymph

naïf, -ïve [naif, -iv] **1** *adj* (*innocent*) naive, ingenuous, innocent; **elle était assez naïve pour croire ses mensonges** she was naive enough to believe his lies; *Beaux-Arts* **un peintre n.** a naive painter **2** *n* **(a) vous me prenez pour un n.!** what sort of a fool do you take me for?; **jouer les naïfs/les naïves** to act *or* play the innocent **(b)** *Beaux-Arts* naive (painter)

nain, naine [nɛ̃, nɛn] **1** [ⓘA12,1,d] *n* **(a)** dwarf, midget; (*étoile*) dwarf **(b)** *Arg* (*enfant*) kid, brat **2** *adj* (*personne, étoile*) dwarf; **haricots nains** dwarf beans; **poule naine** bantam; **caniche n.** toy poodle; **étoile naine** dwarf star; **rosier n.** miniature rosebush

▶ **nain**: *Cartes* **N. jaune** Pope Joan

naissain [nɛsɛ̃] *nm* (*d'huître, de moule*) spawn, spat

naissance [nɛsɑ̃s] *nf* **(a)** *aussi Fig* birth; **date de n.** date of birth; **lieu de n.** birthplace; **acte de n.** birth certificate; **extrait de n.** = (copy of) birth certificate; **contrôle** *ou* **limitation** *ou* **régulation des naissances** birth control; **donner n. à un enfant** to give birth to a child; **à sa n., il avait les cheveux blonds** his hair was blond when he was born; **sourd/aveugle de n.** deaf/blind from birth, born deaf/blind; **paresseux de n.** bone idle; **qu'est-ce que tu es paresseuse! – oui, je sais, chez moi, c'est de n.** you're so lazy! – I know, I was born that way *or* I've been like that since the day I was born; **français de n.** French by birth; **de haute/d'obscure n.** of high *or* noble/humble birth; *Fig Litt* **la n. du printemps** the birth of spring; *Litt* **la n. du jour** dawn, daybreak, the break of day; **donner n. à une rumeur/de nouvelles habitudes de vie** to give rise to a rumour/new lifestyles

(b) (*de langue, d'ongle etc*) root; (*de rivière*) source; *Archit* (*de pilier, d'arche*) spring; **n. du cou** base of the neck; **cicatrice à la n. des cheveux** scar just where the hair begins *or* at the hairline; **à la n. des seins** at the top of one's cleavage; **prendre n.** to originate, to start; (*d'une rivière*) to rise

naissant [nɛsɑ̃] *adj* **(a)** (*jour*) dawning; (*beauté*) nascent; **à l'aube naissante** at break of day; **une barbe naissante** the beginnings of a beard; **ses seins naissants** her budding breasts; **les rondeurs naissantes de sa gorge** the blossoming curves of her breasts **(b)** *Ch* **à l'état n.** nascent

naître [nɛtr] *vi* (*prp* **naissant**; *pp* **né**; *pr ind* **je nais, il naît, n. naissons, ils naissent**; *pr sub* **je naisse**; *p hist* **je naquis**; *fu* **je naîtrai**; *aux* **être**) **(a)** to be born; **il naquit** *ou* **est né en 1880** he was born in 1880; **enfant/poussin qui vient de n.** newly-born child/newly-hatched chick; **je l'ai vu n.** I have known him from birth *or* since he was a baby; **né de parents anglais** born of English parents, of English parentage; **né de parents inconnus** of unknown parentage; **enfant à n.** unborn child; **il naît plus de filles que de garçons** more girls are being born than boys, there's a higher level of female births than male birth; **Casanova était né pour l'amour** Casanova was destined to be a great lover; **il est né pour être musicien/réussir/diriger** he was born *or* destined to be a musician/to succeed/to be a manager; **elle est née pour emmerder le monde** it seems to be her mission in life to get up people's noses; *Litt* **n. à l'amour** to know love for the first time, to awaken to love; **il est né poète/bricoleur** he is a born poet/handyman; **Christine Thomas, née Martin** Christine Thomas, née Martin; **je ne suis pas né d'hier** *ou* **de la dernière pluie** I wasn't born yesterday; **il n'est pas encore né, celui qui me fera manger des escargots!** the man who can make me eat snails hasn't been born yet!

(b) (*d'espoirs*) to spring up, to (a)rise, to be born; (*de peur*) to (a)rise; (*de projet, d'idée*) to originate (**de** in), to arise (**de** out of); **faire n.** (*espoir, doute*) to give rise to, to raise; (*soupçon*) to give rise to, to arouse, to cause; (*sourire*) to provoke, to raise; **cette peur du noir est née du fait qu'enfant, il avait été laissé seul** his fear of the dark originates *or* arises from his being left alone as a child; **l'espoir de paix est né de la rencontre des deux présidents** the meeting between the two presidents has given rise to hopes of peace

(c) (*de plantes*) to begin to grow *or* come up, to appear; (*du jour*) to dawn

naïvement [naivmɑ̃] *adv* naively

naïveté [naivte] *nf* **(a)** (*innocence*) naivety; **elle a eu la n. de**

croire à ses promesses she was naive enough to believe his promises (**b**) (*remarque*) naive remark
Namibie [namibi] *nf* Namibia
namibien, -ienne [namibjɛ̃, -jɛn] **1** *adj* Namibian **2** *n* **N.** Namibian
nana [nana] *nf F* (**a**) (*jeune fille*) girl, bird, *Am* chick; **une n. qu'elle a rencontrée cet été** a girl she met last summer; **c'est là qu'on trouve les plus belles nanas** that's where the best-looking birds *or* chicks are; **c'est plein de nanas, mais il n'y a pas un seul mec** it's full of women/girls but there isn't a single man (**b**) (*petite amie*) girlfriend
nandou [nɑ̃du] *nm Zool* Rhea
nanisme [nanism] *nm Méd* dwarfism
Nankin [nɑ̃kɛ̃] **1** *n* (**a**) Nanking (**b**) *Tex* **n.** nankeen **2** *adj inv Tex* **n.** nankeen
nanoseconde [nanosəgɔ̃d] *nf* nanosecond
nansouk [nɑ̃zuk] *nm Tex* nainsook
nanti, -ie [nɑ̃ti] **1** *adj* (*personne, pays*) well-off, rich **2** *n* **les nantis** the well-off, the rich
nantir [nɑ̃tir] **1** *vt* (**a**) **n. qn de qch** to provide sb with sth; **être bien nanti** to be well off *or* well provided for (**b**) *Jur* (*créancier*) to give security to; **n. des valeurs** to deposit shares as security; **n. un prêt** to secure a loan **2 se nantir** *vpr Litt* **se n. d'un parapluie** to provide *or* arm oneself with an umbrella
nantissement [nɑ̃tismɑ̃] *nm* security; (*pour prêt*) collateral, security; **déposer des titres en n.** to lodge stock as security; *Banque* **n. flottant** *ou* **général** floating charge
napalm [napalm] *nm* napalm; **bombe au n.** napalm bomb
naphtaline [naftalin] *nf*, **naphtalène** [naftalɛn] *nm* naphthalene; *Can Fig* **sortir qch de la n.** to take sth out of mothballs; **boules de n.** mothballs
naphte [naft] *nm* naphtha, mineral oil; **n. de goudron** coal-tar naphtha
Napoléon [napɔleɔ̃] *nm* (**a**) Napoleon (**b**) **n.** (*pièce*) twenty-franc piece (*bearing the effigy of Napoleon*)
napoléonien, -ienne [napɔleɔnjɛ̃, -jɛn] *adj* (*guerre, empire*) Napoleonic
napolitain, -aine [napɔlitɛ̃, -ɛn] **1** *adj* Neapolitan **2** *nm* (*dialecte*) Neapolitan **3** *n* **N.** Neapolitan
nappage [napaʒ] *nm Culin* coating, covering
nappe [nap] *nf* (**a**) (*de table*) tablecloth; **mettre/ôter la n.** to lay/remove the cloth; **n. à thé** tea cloth; *Rel* **n. d'autel** altar cloth (**b**) *Fig* (*vaste étendue*) (*de glace*) sheet; **n. de feu** sea of flames
▶ **nappe**: **n. d'armature** belt; **n. de brouillard** fog patch; **n. carcasse** casing ply; **n. croisée** cross-ply; *Géog* **n. d'eau** water table; **n. éruptive** lava flow; *Géog* **n. phréatique** water table; **n. de pétrole** oil slick; **n. pétrolifère** oil layer
napper [nape] *vt* (**a**) *Culin* to coat, to cover (**de** with); **glace à la vanille nappée de chocolat** vanilla ice cream topped with chocolate *or* with chocolate topping (**b**) *Vieilli* (*recouvrir*) (*table*) to cover with a cloth
napperon [naprɔ̃] *nm* mat
Narcisse [narsis] *nm Myth* Narcissus
narcisse [narsis] *nm* (**a**) (*plante*) narcissus; **n. des poètes** pheasant's eye; **n. sauvage** *ou* **des prés** daffodil (**b**) *Psy* narcissist
narcissique [narsisik] *adj Psy* narcissistic
narcissisme [narsisism] *nm Psy* narcissism
narcodollars [narkodɔlar] *nmpl* drug money
narcolepsie [narkolɛpsi] *nf Méd* narcolepsy
narcose [narkoz] *nf Méd* narcosis
narcotique [narkɔtik] *Méd* **1** *adj* narcotic **2** *nm* narcotic, drug; **faire prendre un n. à qn** to give sb a narcotic, to drug sb
narcotrafiquant, -ante [narkotrafikɑ̃, -ɑ̃t] *n* drug trafficker
nard [nar] *nm Bot, Pharm* spikenard, nard
narguer [narge] *vt* to taunt, to scoff at; (*la mort, le danger*) to flout
narguilé, narghilé, narghileh [nargile] *nm* hookah, narghile
narine [narin] *nf* nostril
narquois [narkwa] *adj* (*ton, sourire*) taunting, mocking
narquoisement [narkwazmɑ̃] *adv* tauntingly, mockingly
narrateur, -trice [naratœr, -tris] *n* (*de roman etc*) narrator; (*conteur*) storyteller
narratif, -ive [naratif, -iv] *adj* (*style, contenu*) narrative
narration [narasjɔ̃] *nf* (**a**) narration; *Gram* **présent de n.** historic present (**b**) (*d'événement*) narrative, account; *Scol Vieilli* narrative composition
narrer [nare] *vt Litt* to narrate, to relate
narval, -als [narval] *nm* narwhal, unicorn whale
nasal, -ale, -aux, -ales [nazal, -o] **1** *adj* (*os, son, cloison*) nasal **2** *nf Ling* **nasale** nasal
nasaliser [nazalize] *vt* (*son*) to nasalize
nase [naz] *F* **1** *adj* (**a**) (*fatigué*) (*personne*) shattered, whacked, dead beat; (*voiture etc*) clapped out (**b**) (*idiot*) thick; **il est tout n. ce mec** the guy's a complete idiot (**c**) (*nul*) bloody useless *or* hopeless **2** *n* **c'est un n., ce mec** this guy's rubbish, this guy's bloody useless
naseau, -eaux [nazo] *nm* (*de cheval, bœuf*) nostril; *F* **les naseaux** the hooter, the conk
nasillard [nazijar] *adj* nasal; (*vieux disque etc*) tinny; **ton n.** (nasal) twang; **parler d'une voix nasillarde** to talk through one's nose
nasillement [nazijmɑ̃] *nm* (*son nasillard*) (nasal) twang
nasiller [nazije] *vi* to speak through one's nose *or* with a twang; (*radio, vieux disque*) to make a tinny sound; (*du canard*) to quack
nasique [nazik] *nm* (*singe*) proboscis monkey
nasse [nas] *nf* lobster pot; (*pour oiseaux*) hoop net; (*pour rats*) trap; *Fig Vieilli* **tomber dans la n.** to fall into the trap
natal, -ale, -als, -ales [natal] *adj* (*village*) native; **ville natale** birthplace; *F* home town; **mon pays n.** my native land; **mon Écosse/ma France natale** my native Scotland/ France; **ma maison natale** the house where I was born
nataliste [natalist] *adj* **politique n.** policy to increase the birthrate, pro-birth policy
natalité [natalite] *nf* (**taux de**) **n.** birthrate; **forte n.** high birthrate; **courbe de n.** birthrate
natation [natasjɔ̃] *nf* swimming; **club de n.** swimming club; **faire de la n.** to swim; **n. synchronisée** synchronized swimming
natatoire [natatwar] *adj Zool* (*organe, membrane*) natatory, natatorial; **vessie n.** (*de poisson*) swim bladder, air bladder
natif, -ive [natif, -iv] **1** *adj* (**a**) native; **je suis n. de Londres** I'm a native Londoner, I'm a Londoner (by birth) (**b**) *Minér* (*or etc*) native, virgin (**c**) *Litt* (*inné*) natural, inborn; **bon sens n.** mother *or* native wit **2** *n* native
nation [nasjɔ̃] *nf* nation; **Nations Unies** United Nations
national, -ale, -aux, -ales [nasjɔnal, -o] **1** *adj* (*équipe, gloire*) national; **l'hymne n.** the national anthem; **à l'échelle nationale et internationale** nationally and internationally **2** *npl* **nationaux** nationals **3** *nf Aut* **nationale** main road, *Br* ≈ A road, *Am* highway
nationalement [nasjɔnalmɑ̃] *adv* nationally
nationalisation [nasjɔnalizasjɔ̃] *nf* nationalization
nationaliser [nasjɔnalize] *vt* (*industrie*) to nationalize; **nationalisé** nationalized, state-owned
nationalisme [nasjɔnalism] *nm Pol* nationalism
nationaliste [nasjɔnalist] **1** *n Pol* nationalist **2** *adj* nationalist, *Péj* nationalistic; **la Chine n.** Nationalist China
nationalité [nasjɔnalite] *nf* [①**A20-21**,d; **B10**,**D**,1] nationality; *Naut* **acte de n.** (ship's) certificate of registry; **les personnes de n. française** people of French nationality, French nationals; **il est de quelle n.?** what nationality is he?; **n. à la naissance** nationality at birth; **code de la n.** = rules and regulations defining entitlement to French nationality
national-socialisme *nm Hist Pol* National Socialism
nativité [nativite] *nf Rel, Beaux-Arts* nativity; *Beaux-Arts* nativity scene
natron [natrɔ̃] *nm*, **natrum** [natrɔm] *nm Minér* natron
natte [nat] *nf* (**a**) (*de cheveux, fil d'or etc*) plait, braid; **porter des nattes** to wear one's hair in plaits *or* pigtails, to have plaits *or* pigtails; **porter** *ou* **avoir une n.** to have a pigtail (**b**) (*de jonc, paille*) mat
natter [nate] *vt* (**a**) (*cheveux, paille etc*) to plait, to braid (**b**) (*mur etc*) to cover with mats
naturalisation [natyralizasjɔ̃] *nf* (**a**) *Admin* naturalization (**b**) (*de plante, d'animal*) naturalization; (*de mot*) adoption, naturalization (**c**) (*de spécimen botanique etc*) preservation, mounting; **n. d'animaux** taxidermy
naturalisé, -ée [natyralize] **1** *adj* naturalized **2** *n* naturalized subject *or* citizen
naturaliser [natyralize] *vt* (**a**) *Admin* to naturalize; **se faire n. français** to become a naturalized Frenchman (**b**) (*plante, animal*) to naturalize, to acclimatize; (*mot*) to adopt, to naturalize (**c**) (*préserver*) (*spécimen botanique etc*) to preserve, to mount; (*empailler*) (*animal*) to stuff
naturalisme [natyralism] *nm* naturalism
naturaliste [natyralist] **1** *n* (**a**) (*savant*) naturalist (**b**) (*artisan*) taxidermist **2** *adj* naturalistic
nature [natyr] **1** *nf* (**a**) (*univers*) nature; **les lois de la n.** the laws of nature; **une merveille de la n.** a wonder of nature; **une force de la n.** a force of nature; **laisser faire la n.** to let nature take its course; **tous les goûts sont dans la n.** everyone to his own taste; **vice contre n.** unnatural vice; **c'est contre n. qu'une femme ait des enfants après la ménopause** it's unnatural *or* it's against nature for a woman to have children after the menopause; **la n. fait bien les**

choses *ou* **est bien faite** Mother Nature does wonderful things, isn't nature wonderful?; *F* **la pauvre fille n'est pas gâtée par la n.** nature hasn't been kind to the poor girl; **à l'état de n.** in the natural state

(**b**) (*milieu végétal et animal*) nature; **une n. luxuriante s'offrit à nos yeux** a luxuriant landscape opened up before us; **les amoureux de la n.** nature lovers; **protection de la n.** protection of the environment; **maison en pleine n.** house deep in the country; **se promener dans la n.** to go for a walk in the country; *Fig* **se perdre** *ou* **disparaître dans la n.** to vanish into thin air; *Aut F* **partir dans la n.** to run into a ditch/a field; *Beaux-Arts* **n. morte** still life

(**c**) (*caractère*) nature; **n. du climat/du sol** nature of the climate/soil; **ce n'est pas dans ma n.** it's not in my nature; **c'est dans la n. des choses** it's in the nature of things; **une découverte de n. à révolutionner la science** a discovery likely to revolutionize science; **ce genre de détail n'est pas de n. à les inquiéter** that kind of detail is unlikely to bother them; **faits de n. à nous étonner** facts of an astonishing nature, astonishing facts; **un programme de cette n.** a programme of this kind *or* nature; **être d'une n. douce** to have a gentle nature; **être timide de** *ou* **par n., être d'une n. timide** to be naturally shy, to be shy by nature; **c'est une bonne n.** he's/she's a kind soul *or* a kindly (sort of) man/woman; **c'est une n. violente** he's/she's a violent sort; **c'est une n.** he's/she's a real character; *F* **c'est une petite n.** (*n'a pas une santé solide*) he's/she's got a weak constitution

(**d**) (*réalité*) **plus grand que n.** larger than life; **peindre d'après n.** to paint from nature *or* from life; **payer en n.** (*avec des marchandises*) to pay in kind

2 *adj inv* (**a**) *Culin* (*yaourt, omelette*) plain; **riz n.** (plain) boiled rice; **thé n.** tea without milk

(**b**) (*conforme à la réalité*) **grandeur n.** full-scale, life-size(d)

(**c**) *F* (*personne*) natural, unaffected

naturel, -elle [natyrɛl] **1** *adj* (**a**) (*inhérent à la nature*) (*phénomène, loi, frontière, gaz*) natural; (*besoin, fonction*) bodily; **mort naturelle** death from natural causes; **il est mort de mort naturelle** he died from natural causes; **les défenses naturelles de l'homme** the body's natural defences

(**b**) (*inné*) (*don, tendance*) natural, innate; **il a des dispositions naturelles pour la peinture** painting comes naturally to him; **il a une grâce naturelle** he is naturally graceful

(**c**) (*non artificiel*) (*procréation, couleur de cheveux, jus de fruit etc*) natural; **soie naturelle** pure *or* real silk

(**d**) (*normal*) natural; **son inquiétude est tout à fait naturelle** it's only natural that he should be worried; **c'est n. de le faire** it's only natural *or* reasonable to do so; **mais c'est tout n.** don't mention it, you're welcome

(**e**) (*non affecté*) (*personne, air, style*) natural, unaffected; (*réponse*) simple, straightforward; **vin n.** unfortified wine

(**f**) *Mus* **note naturelle** natural

2 *nm* (**a**) (*tempérament*) nature, character, disposition; **d'un bon n.** kind, of a kind disposition; **elle est d'un n. généreux/peureux/jaloux** she has a generous/timid/jealous nature, she is generous/timid/jealous by nature; *Prov* **chassez le n., il revient au galop** what's bred in the bone (will come out in the flesh)

(**b**) (*simplicité, spontanéité*) naturalness; **elle joue la comédie avec beaucoup de n.** she's a natural (as a) comic actor; **parler avec n.** to speak naturally

(**c**) *Culin* **thon au n.** tuna (packed) in brine; **poires au n.** pears in natural fruit juice

naturellement [natyrɛlmɑ̃] *adv* naturally; **n. timide** naturally shy, shy by nature; **se conduire n.** to behave naturally *or* without affectation; **vous vous en êtes fâché? – n.!** you resented it? – naturally! *or* of course (I did)!

naturisme [natyrism] *nm* naturism; **adepte du n.** naturist, nudist

naturiste [natyrist] **1** *n* naturist, nudist **2** *adj* naturist

naufrage [nofraʒ] *nm* (ship)wreck; *Fig* (*d'entreprise*) failure; **lors du n. du Titanic** when the Titanic sank; **faire n.** (*de bateau*) to be wrecked; (*de marin*) to be shipwrecked; *Fig* (*d'entreprise, de mariage*) to collapse; **périr dans un n.** to be lost at sea; *Fig* **le pays va vers le n.** the country is heading for disaster; *Fig* **le n. de ses ambitions** the collapse of his ambitions

naufragé, -ée [nofraʒe] **1** *adj* (*bateau*) wrecked; (*marin*) shipwrecked, castaway **2** *n* castaway, shipwrecked man/woman

naufrageur, -euse [nofraʒœr, -øz] *n* (*de bateaux*) wrecker; **bateau n.** wrecker

naupathie [nopati] *nf Méd* seasickness

nauséabond [nozeabɔ̃] *adj* (*odeur*) nauseating, foul; (*personne, pièce*) foul-smelling; *Fig* (*thèses etc*) sickening, nauseating

nausée [noze] *nf* (**a**) (*envie de vomir*) nausea; (*chez la femme enceinte*) morning sickness; **avoir la n.** *ou* **des nausées** to feel sick *or* nauseous; **avoir des nausées** (*d'une femme enceinte*) to have morning sickness; **donner des nausées à qn** to make sb feel sick (**b**) *Fig* disgust; **l'hypocrisie me donne la n.** hypocrisy makes me sick *or* nauseates me

nauséeux, -euse [nozeø, -øz] *adj* (**a**) (*odeur*) nauseating; **se sentir n.** to feel sick *or* nauseous (**b**) *Fig* (*hypocrisie etc*) nauseating, sickening

nautile [notil] *nm Zool* nautilus

nautique [notik] *adj* (*terme, instrument etc*) nautical; **sports nautiques** water sports; **carte n.** (sea) chart; **salon n.** boat show

nautisme [notism] *nm Sp* water sports

naval, -ale, -als, -ales [naval] **1** *adj* (*architecture, base, combat*) naval; **termes navals** nautical *or* sailing terms; **construction navale** shipbuilding; **chantier n.** shipyard; **les forces navales** the navy; **l'École navale** the Naval College **2** *nf F* **Navale: faire N.** to attend Naval College

navarin [navarɛ̃] *nm Culin* lamb stew *or* casserole

navet [navɛ] *nm* (**a**) turnip (**b**) *F* (*film, pièce de théâtre*) **c'est un n.** it's a load of rubbish *or* nonsense

navette[1] [navɛt] *nf* (**a**) *Tex* shuttle (**b**) *Av etc* shuttle (service); **navettes fréquentes entre la gare et la ville** frequent (shuttle) service between station and town; **faire la n. entre deux endroits/services** (*de véhicule, personne, dossier etc*) to shuttle back and forth between two places/two departments; **je fais la n. entre Glasgow et Édimbourg tous les jours** I commute between Glasgow and Edinburgh; **n. de transfert** transfer bus; **n. gratuite** courtesy bus (**c**) (*fusée*) shuttle (**d**) *Rel* incense box

▶ **navette: n. spatiale** space shuttle

navette[2] *nf Bot* rape; **(huile de) n.** rape (seed) oil, colza oil

navigabilité [navigabilite] *nf* (**a**) (*de rivière etc*) navigability (**b**) **(état de) n.** (*de bateau*) seaworthiness; (*d'avion*) airworthiness; **en (bon) état de n.** (*bateau*) seaworthy; (*avion*) airworthy

navigable [navigabl] *adj* (**a**) (*rivière, voie*) navigable (**b**) (*bateau*) seaworthy; (*avion*) airworthy

navigant, -ante [navigɑ̃, -ɑ̃t] **1** *adj* **personnel n.** navigation crew, flight crew **2** *n* **les navigants** the navigation crew, the flight crew

navigateur [navigatœr] **1** *nm* (**a**) (*de bateau, d'avion etc*) navigator (**b**) (*voyageur sur mer*) navigator, seafarer; **n. solitaire** lone *or* single-handed yachtsman *or* sailor (**c**) **n. de l'Internet** Internet surfer **2** *adj* **peuple n.** seafaring people

navigation [navigasjɔ̃] *nf* navigation; **école de n. (de la marine marchande)** nautical school; **compagnie de n.** shipping company; **compagnie de n. aérienne** airline; **permis de n.** ship's passport, sea letter; **après un mois de n.** after a month at sea

▶ **navigation**: **n. côtière** coastal navigation; **n. à l'estime** dead reckoning; **n. extérieure** deep-sea navigation; **n. fluviale** inland navigation; **n. hauturière** deep-sea *or* ocean navigation; *Av* **n. aux instruments** instrument flying; **n. intérieure** inland navigation; **n. au long cours** deep-sea *or* ocean navigation; **n. maritime** deep-sea *or* maritime navigation; **n. de plaisance** sailing, yachting, pleasure cruising; *Astronaut* **n. spatiale** space navigation, astronautics; **n. à voile** sailing; *Av* **n. à vue** visual flying

naviguer [navige] **1** *vi* (**a**) (*de bateau, marin*) to sail (**vers** to); **navire qui navigue bien** ship that handles well at sea *or* that behaves well; **n. au compas** to sail *or* navigate by the compass; *Fig F* **savoir n.** to know the ropes (**b**) (*se déplacer*) (*de personne, dossier*) to move around; **le dossier a navigué entre les différents responsables du projet** the file moved around *or* was passed from project manager to project manager (**c**) **n. dans l'Internet** to surf the Internet *or* the Net **2** *vt* (*bateau, avion*) to navigate

navire [navir] *nm* ship, vessel; **les navires du port** the ships *or* shipping in the harbour

▶ **navire**: **n. amiral** flag ship; **n.-citerne** tanker; **n. de combat** battleship; **n. de commerce** merchant ship, merchantman; **n. de conférence** conference ship; **n.-école** training ship; **n. de guerre** warship; **n.-hôpital** hospital ship; **n.-jumeau** twin ship; **n. au long cours** ocean-going ship; **n. marchand** merchant ship, merchantman; **n. porte-conteneurs** container ship; **n. à voiles** sailing ship

navrant [navrɑ̃] *adj* (*nouvelle, attitude etc*) distressing, upsetting; **un film n. de bêtise** an incredibly stupid film; **un contretemps n.** an unfortunate *or* regrettable mishap

navré [navre] *adj* (*personne, expression, ton*) distressed; **être n. de qch** to be very *or* terribly sorry about sth; **je suis n. (de**

l'apprendre) I'm terribly *or* very sorry (to hear that); **n. de vous avoir fait attendre** sorry to have kept you waiting
navrer [navre] *vt* to distress, to upset
nazaréen, -enne [nazareẽ, -ɛn] *adj, n Bible* Nazarene
naze [naz] *adj F* = **nase**
nazi, -e [nazi] *adj, n Hist Pol* Nazi
nazisme [nazism] *nm Hist Pol* Nazism
NB [ɛnbe] (*abrév* **nota bene**) NB
NbP *Typ* (*abrév* **note de bas de page**) footnote
NC [ɛnse] *nm* (*abrév* **network computer**) NC
NCM [ɛnseɛm] (*abrév* **négociations commerciales multilatérales**) multilateral trade negotiations
NDLR *nf* (*abrév* **note de la rédaction**) editor's note
NdT *nf* (*abrév* **note du traducteur**) translator's note
ne, n' [n(ə)] *adv* [①B60,B] **(a)** (*forming neg verb with* **pas**) **je ne la connais pas** I don't know her; (*emphatique*) I do not know her; **il ne m'avait pas vu** he hadn't seen me (**NOTE** *for the use of* **ne** *in conjunction with* **aucun, aucunement, goutte, guère, jamais, mie, mot, personne, plus, point, que (ne ... que), rien,** *see these words*)
(b) (*used alone, chiefly in literary style with* **cesser, oser, pouvoir, savoir, importer** *and often as an archaism with other verbs*) **il ne cesse de parler** he is for ever *or* always talking, he doesn't stop *or* never stops talking; **je n'ose lui parler** I dare not speak to him/her; **je ne puis vous le promettre** I cannot promise you that; **je ne sais que faire** I do not know what to do; **je ne saurais vous le dire** I cannot tell you
(c) (*in the following constructions*) **qui ne connaît cette œuvre célèbre?** who does not know this famous work?; **que ne ferait-elle pour vous?** what would she not do for you?; **je n'ai d'autre désir que celui de vous plaire** I have no other desire than to please you; **si je ne me trompe** *ou* **m'abuse** if I am not mistaken, unless I am mistaken; **voilà six mois que je ne l'ai vue** it is now six months since I (last) saw her, I haven't seen her for six months; **il n'y a personne à qui il ne se soit adressé** there is no one whom he didn't speak to; **il n'eut garde d'y aller** he took good care not to go, he made quite sure he did not go; **qu'à cela ne tienne!** never mind (about) that!, that's no problem!; **je n'ai que faire de votre aide** I have no need of your help
(d) (*used optionally in literary style with a vague negative connotation*) **je crains qu'elle (ne) prenne froid** I am afraid she may catch cold; **évitez** *ou* **prenez garde qu'on (ne) vous voie** take care not to be seen; **peu s'en fallut qu'elle (ne) tombât** she very nearly fell; **je ne nie pas que cela (ne) soit vrai** I don't deny that it's true; **il est plus vigoureux qu'il n'y paraît** he is stronger than he looks; **elle agit autrement qu'elle ne parle** her actions belie *or* don't match her words
né [ne] *adj* born; *Litt* **c'est un conteur/conducteur né** he's a born story-teller/driver; **enfant né d'un premier mariage** child from a first marriage; **né d'une famille bourgeoise** born into a middle-class family; *Fig* **un film né de la rencontre d'un réalisateur et d'une actrice** a film born of *or* that grew out of a meeting between a director and an actress; **Mme Martin, née Dupond** Mrs Martin, née Dupond; *Arch* **être bien né** to be well born *or* of noble birth
néanmoins [neɑ̃mwɛ̃] *adv* nevertheless, nonetheless, yet; **il est sérieux mais n. décontracté** he's serious but nevertheless *or* but nonetheless *or* yet relaxed
néant [neɑ̃] *nm* **(a)** (*ce qui n'existe pas*) nothingness, void; **sortir du n.** to rise from nothing; **réduire qch à n.** to reduce sth to nothing, to destroy sth; **tous ses espoirs furent réduit à n.** all his hopes were dashed **(b)** (*de qn, qch*) worthlessness, uselessness; **le n. des grandeurs humaines** the vanity of human greatness **(c)** (*sur formulaire, feuille de déclaration d'impôts etc*) none, nil; **signes particuliers: n.** distinguishing marks: none
nébuleux, -euse [nebylø, -øz] **1** *adj* (*ciel, vue*) cloudy, hazy, misty; (*idées, raisonnement, explications*) vague, hazy, nebulous; (*écrivain, théorie, propos*) obscure **2** *nf Astron* **nébuleuse** nebula; *Fig* **toute une n. de sociétés-écrans** a whole cluster of umbrella companies
nébuliseur [nebylizœr] *nm* nebulizer
nébulosité [nebylozite] *nf* **(a)** *Météo* (*nuage très fin*) wispy cloud; (*ciel couvert*) cloud cover; **forte n.** heavy cloud cover **(b)** (*d'une idée etc*) vagueness, haziness
nécessaire [nesesɛr] **1** *adj* **(a)** necessary; **cela ne sera pas n.** that won't be necessary; **n. à** *ou* **pour qch/qn** necessary *or* required for sth/sb; **n. pour faire qch** necessary to do sth; **avoir l'argent/le temps/la patience n.** to have the necessary money/time/patience; **il est n. de bien lire les instructions** the instructions need to be read properly, it is necessary to read the instructions properly; **il n'est pas n. d'être impoli** there is no need to be rude; **il n'est pas n. de passer par le standard** there is no need *or* it is not necessary to go through the switchboard; **ils n'ont pas jugé n. de venir s'excuser** they didn't think *or* consider it necessary to come and apologize; **il est n. que vous teniez compte de cela/procédiez de cette manière** you need to *or* you must take notice of this/proceed like this; **peu n.** unnecessary, needless
(b) *Phil* necessary
2 *nm* **le strict n.** the bare necessities *or* essentials; **il ne fait que le strict n.** he does no more than that which is strictly necessary; **manquer du n.** to lack the necessities *or* basics of life; **faire le n.** to do what is necessary, *F* to do the necessary; **je vais faire le n.** I'll see to it; **pour les billets ne t'inquiète pas, je ferai le n.** don't worry about the tickets, I'll see to them; **merci de faire le n. pour qu'il soit accueilli à l'aéroport** thank you for arranging for him to be met at the airport
▶ **nécessaire**: **n. à chaussures** shoe-cleaning kit; **n. de couture** sewing kit; **n. à ongles** manicure set; **n. de toilette** (set of) toiletries; **n. de voyage** overnight bag
nécessairement [nesesɛrmɑ̃] *adv* necessarily; **ce n'est pas n. une mauvaise idée** it's not necessarily a bad idea; **mais c'est complètement idiot! – pas n.** but it's completely stupid! – not necessarily
nécessité [nesesite] *nf* **(a)** (*caractère nécessaire*), *Phil* necessity; **être dans la n. de faire qch** to have no choice but to do sth; **c'est une n.** it's essential; **quelle n. y avait-il de faire cela?** what need was there to do that?; **faire qch par n.** to do sth out of necessity, to be compelled to do sth; **faire de n. vertu** to make a virtue (out) of necessity; *Vieilli* **de (toute) n.** necessarily, of necessity; **il est de toute n. de faire quelque chose** it is essential that we do something, we simply must do something
(b) (*chose nécessaire*) necessity; **les nécessités de la vie** the necessities of life; **à cause des nécessités du service** due to operational requirements; **objets** *ou* **articles de première n.** essential items, essentials; **denrées de première n.** essential commodities; **être dans la n.** (*être pauvre*) to be in need
nécessiter [nesesite] *vt* to require, to need, to necessitate; **une telle question nécessite qu'on prenne le temps de réfléchir** such a question requires *or* needs time to be considered
nécessiteux, -euse [nesesitø, -øz] **1** *adj* needy, in need **2** *n* **les n.** the needy, the poor, the destitute
nec plus ultra [nɛkplyzyltra] *nm inv* **le n.** the best there is; **le n. des voitures** the best car there is; **le n. du confort/luxe** the last word in comfort/luxury
nécrologe [nekrɔlɔʒ] *nm* necrology, death roll
nécrologie [nekrɔlɔʒi] *nf* (*notice*) obituary (notice); (*liste*) deaths (column), obituary column, obituaries
nécrologique [nekrɔlɔʒik] *adj* **avis/rubrique n.** obituary notice/column
nécromancie [nekrɔmɑ̃si] *nf* necromancy
nécromancien, -ienne [nekrɔmɑ̃sjɛ̃, -jɛn] *n* necromancer
nécrophage [nekrɔfaʒ] *adj* necrophagous
nécrophile [nekrɔfil] *adj* necrophiliac
nécrophilie [nekrɔfili] *nf* necrophilia
nécrophore [nekrɔfɔr] *nm* carrion beetle
nécropole [nekrɔpɔl] *nf* necropolis
nécrose [nekroz] *nf Biol* necrosis
nécroser [nekroze] *Biol* **1** *vt* (*tissu*) to necrose **2 se nécroser** *vpr* to necrose
nectaire [nɛktɛr] *nm Bot* nectary
nectar [nɛktar] *nm* (*jus de fruit, Litt boisson exquise*), *Myth, Bot* nectar; **n. de poire/d'abricot** pear/apricot nectar
nectarine [nɛktarin] *nf* (*fruit*) nectarine
néerlandais, -aise [neɛrlɑ̃dɛ, -ɛz] **1** *adj* Dutch, (of the) Netherlands; **le gouvernement n.** the Dutch Government, the Government of the Netherlands **2** *nm Ling* (*aux Pays-Bas*) Dutch; (*en Belgique*) Flemish **3** *n* **N.** Dutchman, Dutchwoman
nef [nɛf] *nf* **(a)** (*d'église*) **n. (centrale)** nave; **n. latérale** aisle **(b)** *Litt* (*navire*) ship
néfaste [nefast] *adj* (*effet, conséquence, influence*) harmful; **jour n.** ill-fated *or* evil day
nèfle [nɛfl] *nf* (*fruit*) medlar; *Fig F* **des nèfles!** no fear!, nothing doing!; **n. du Japon** loquat
néflier [neflije] *nm* medlar (tree); **n. du Japon** loquat (tree)
négateur, -trice [negatœr, -tris] *Litt* **1** *adj* **une doctrine négatrice** a negative doctrine **2** *n* denier
négatif, -ive [negatif, -iv] **1** *adj* negative; *Phot* **épreuve négative** negative **2** *nm Phot* negative **3** *nf Gram* **négative** negative; **je réponds par la négative** my answer is in the negative
négation [negasjɔ̃] *nf* **(a)** (*fait de nier*) negation, denial **(b)** [①A46-47,9; B60,B] *Gram* negative

négativement [negativmɑ̃] *adv* (*réagir*) negatively; (*répondre*) in the negative
négativisme [negativism] *nm* negativism
négligé [negliʒe] **1** *adj* **(a)** (*peu soigné*) (*tenue, apparence, personne*) slovenly, untidy, scruffy; (*travail, devoir, style*) slovenly, careless **(b)** (*auquel on ne porte pas assez d'attention*) (*enfant, femme etc*) neglected **2** *nm* **(a)** (caractère) slovenliness, untidiness **(b)** (*vêtement*) negligee, negligée
négligeable [negliʒabl] *adj* (*détail, risque, quantité*) negligible, insignificant; **un avantage non n.** a not inconsiderable advantage; **une quantité non n. de** a significant quantity of; **il me traite comme (une) quantité n.** he treats me as if I'm not there *or* as if I don't exist
négligemment [negliʒamɑ̃] *adv* **(a)** (*habillé*) carelessly, untidily, scruffily **(b)** (*répondre, lire*) casually, nonchalantly; (*pour feindre l'inattention*) casually; **elle était n. installée dans le canapé** she was draped over the sofa
négligence [negliʒɑ̃s] *nf* **(a)** (*manque de soin*) negligence, carelessness; (*de qn, d'un devoir*) neglect; **avec n.** (*travailler*) carelessly
(b) (*insouciance*) casualness, nonchalance; **il me répondit avec n. qu'il viendrait peut-être** he casually *or* nonchalantly replied that he would perhaps come
(c) (*acte négligent*) act of carelessness, careless act; (*oubli*) oversight; **l'accident est dû à une n.** the accident was due to carelessness; **par (pure) n.** through (sheer) carelessness *or* negligence; **je reconnais que c'est une n. de notre part** I admit that it is an oversight on our part; **n. de style** stylistic error, error of style; *Jur* **n. coupable** *ou* **criminelle** criminal negligence
négligent [negliʒɑ̃] *adj* (*parent, touriste, campeur*) negligent, careless; (*remarque, attitude, coup d'œil*) casual
négliger [negliʒe] **(je négligeai(s); n. négligeons) 1** *vt* **(a)** (*délaisser*) (*sa santé, son devoir, ses enfants*) to neglect, to be neglectful of; (*son apparence, sa tenue*) not to care about **(b)** (*omettre, oublier*) (*avis, conseil*) to disregard; (*occasion*) to miss; (*élément, détail*) to overlook, to disregard; **il ne faut jamais rien n.** you must never leave anything to chance; **n. de faire qch** to neglect *or* fail to do sth **2 se négliger** *vpr* to neglect one's appearance, to let oneself go
négoce [negɔs] *nm* trade; *Arch* **faire du n.** to be in trade; *Bourse* **n. de titres** share dealing
négociabilité [negɔsjabilite] *nf Fin* negotiability
négociable [negɔsjabl] *adj* (*salaire, prix, conditions d'emploi*) negotiable; *Fin* (*bon, traite*) negotiable, transferable, trad(e)able
négociant, -ante [negɔsjɑ̃, -ɑ̃t] *n* (*en gros*) merchant, dealer; **n. en gros** wholesaler; **n. en vins** wine merchant; **n. exportateur** export merchant
négociateur, -trice [negɔsjatœr, -tris] *n* (*de traité, marché etc*) negotiator
négociation [negɔsjasjɔ̃] *nf* **(a)** (*de traité, paix*) negotiation **(sur** on); **entamer des négociations** to enter into negotiations; **négociations collectives** joint negotiations; (*au sein d'une entreprise*) collective bargaining; **négociations commerciales multilatérales** multilateral trade negotiations; **négociations précontractuelles** precontractual negotiations; **en n.** (*conditions etc*) under negotiation; **nous sommes en n. avec la direction** we are negotiating *or* we are in negotiation with management
(b) *Com* negotiation, transaction; **n. d'un effet** negotiation of a bill of exchange; **négociations au comptant** spot trading; **négociations à prime** options trading; **négociations à terme** futures trading
négocier [negɔsje] (*impf & pr sub* **n. négociions) 1** *vi* **(a)** (*traiter, discuter*) to negotiate **(avec** with) **(b)** *Arch* (*faire du commerce*) to trade **2** *vt* **(a)** (*prêt, traite, salaire, paix*) to negotiate; *Bourse* to trade; **modalités du contrat: à n.** terms negotiable **(b)** *Aut* **n. un virage** to negotiate a bend
nègre [nɛgr] **1** *nm* **(a)** [①**A12**,1,c] *Péj* (*Noir*) Negro; **la traite des nègres** the slave trade; *F* **travailler comme un n.** to work like a slave **(b)** *Fig* (*écrivain*) ghost (writer); **être le n. de qn** to ghost for sb **2** *adj* **(a)** (*art*) Negro **(b)** *Péj* (*race*) Negro **(c)** *inv* (*couleur*) nigger(-brown)
▶ **nègre**: **n. blanc** White Negro; **propos n. blanc** double talk; *Culin* **n. en chemise** chocolate dessert with whipped cream
négresse [negrɛs] *nf Péj* Negress
négrier [negrije] **1** *nm* **(a)** (*trafiquant d'esclaves*) slave trader; (*employeur, surveillant*) slave driver **(b)** (*bateau*) slave ship, slaver **2** *adj* **vaisseau n.** slave ship, slaver
négrillon, -onne [negrijɔ̃, -ɔn] *n Péj* piccaninny
négritude [negrityd] *nf* negritude
négroïde [negrɔid] *adj* (*traits, type*) Negroid
neige [nɛʒ] *nf* **(a)** snow; **tempête de n.** blizzard, snowstorm; *Can* **banc de n.** snow bank; **être bloqué par la n.** to be snowed up *or* snowbound; **aller à la n.** to go on a skiing holiday; **sports de n.** winter sports; **fondre comme n. au soleil** to melt away (like snow in the sun); **blanc comme (la) n.** white as snow, snow-white; *Fig* **être blanc comme n.** to be as pure as the driven snow; *Culin* **blancs d'œufs battus en n.** stiffly beaten egg whites **(b)** *Arg* (*cocaïne*) snow
▶ **neige**: **n. artificielle** artificial snow; **n. carbonique** dry ice, (carbon dioxide) snow; **n. fondue** (*qui tombe*) sleet; (*par terre*) slush; **n. fraîche** freshly fallen snow; **n. poudreuse** powdery snow; *Ski* **n. pourrie** hazardous *or* crumbly snow; *Ski* **n. tôlée** crusted snow; **neiges éternelles** perpetual snow
neiger [neʒe] *v impers* **(il neigeait)** to snow
neigeux, -euse [nɛʒø, -øz] *adj* **(a)** (*pic, temps*) snowy; (*toit, pente etc*) snow-covered **(b)** *Fig* (*barbe*) snow-white, snowy
nem [nɛm] *nm Culin* spring roll
nématode [nematɔd] *nm Zool* nematode (threadworm)
néné [nene] *nm F* tit, boob
nénette [nenet] *nf F* **(a)** (*jeune fille*) bird, *Am* chick **(b)** (*petite amie*) girl **(c)** (*tête*) **se casser la n.** to rack one's brains; **tu ne t'es pas trop cassé la n. pour faire ta rédaction** you didn't exactly strain yourself *or* exert yourself over your essay
nénuphar [nenyfar] *nm* waterlily; **n. des étangs, n. jaune** yellow pond lily
néo- [neo] *préf* neo-
néo-calédonien, -ienne, *pl* **néo-calédoniens, -iennes 1** *adj* New Caledonian **2** *n* **N.** New Caledonian
néocapitalisme [neokapitalism] *nm* neocapitalism
néocapitaliste [neokapitalist] *adj, n* neocapitalist
néoclassicisme [neoklasisism] *nm* neoclassicism
néoclassique [neoklasik] *adj* (*style, architecture*) neoclassical
néocolonialisme [neokɔlɔnjalism] *nm* neocolonialism
néofascisme [neofasism, -ʃism] *nm* neofascism
néofasciste [neofaʃist] *adj, n* neofascist
néogothique [neogɔtik] *adj, nm Archit* neogothic
néo-hébridais, -aise [neoebridɛ, -ɛz], *pl* **néo-hébridais, -aises 1** *adj* of the New Hebrides **2** *n* **N.** (*natif*) native of the New Hebrides; (*habitant*) inhabitant of the New Hebrides
néo-impressionnisme *nm Beaux-Arts* neo-impressionism
néolibéralisme [neoliberalism] *nm* neo-liberalism
néolithique [neolitik] *adj, nm* Neolithic
néologisme [neɔlɔʒism] *nm* neologism
néon [neɔ̃] *nm Ch* neon; **tube au n.** neon tube
néonatal, -ale, -als, -ales [neonatal] *adj Méd* neonatal
néonazi, -ie [neonazi] *adj, n* neo-Nazi
néonazisme [neonazism] *nm* neo-Nazism
néophyte [neɔfit] *n* **(a)** *Rel* (*converti*) neophyte **(b)** *Fig* (*novice*) novice, tyro; **je suis totalement n.** I'm a complete novice
néoprène® [neɔprɛn] *nm Tech* neoprene
néoréalisme [neorealism] *nm* neorealism
néoréaliste [neorealist] *adj* (*film, cinéaste*) neorealist
néo-zélandais, -aise, *pl* **néo-zélandais, -aises** [neozelɑ̃dɛ, -ɛz] **1** *adj* New Zealand **2** *n* **N.** New Zealander
népalais, -aise [nepalɛ -ɛz] **1** *adj* Nepalese, Nepali **2** *nm Ling* Nepali **3** *n* **N.** Nepalese, Nepali
népérien, -ienne [neperjɛ̃, -jɛn] *adj* (*logarithmes*) Napierian
néphrétique [nefretik] **1** *adj* **colique n.** renal colic **2** *n* sufferer from nephritis
néphrite [nefrit] *nf* **(a)** *Méd* nephritis; **n. chronique** Bright's disease **(b)** *Minér* nephrite, jade
néphrologie [nefrɔlɔʒi] *nf Méd* nephrology
néphron [nefrɔ̃] *nm Méd* nephron
népotisme [nepɔtism] *nm* nepotism
néréide [nereid] *nf* nereid, sea nymph
nerf [nɛr] *nm* **(a)** (*optique, spinal*) nerve; **viande pleine de nerfs** meat full of gristle, gristly meat; *F* **il a les nerfs en pelote** *ou* **à vif** *ou* **en boule** his nerves are *or* he is on edge; *F* **porter** *ou* **taper** *ou Can* **tomber sur les nerfs à qn** to get on sb's nerves; **avoir les nerfs à fleur de peau** to be all on edge; **je suis à bout de nerfs** I'm at the end of my tether; *F* **c'est un paquet** *ou* **une boule de nerfs** he is a bundle *or* bag of nerves; **être** *ou* **vivre sur les nerfs** to live on one's nerves; **passer ses nerfs sur qn/qch** to take it out on sb/sth; **guerre des nerfs** war of nerves; *F* **avoir les nerfs** to be really fed up; **avoir les nerfs solides** to have strong *or* steady nerves, to have nerves of steel; **être malade des nerfs** to suffer from nerves, to have bad nerves
(b) *Vieilli* (*tendon*) sinew, tendon, ligament; **un grand athlète tout en n.** a tall sinewy athlete
(c) (*force*) **un peu de n.!/du n.!** put some energy into it!; **avoir du n.** (*d'un moteur, d'une voiture*) to be responsive *or* lively; (*d'une personne*) to have some go about one; **l'argent est le n. de la guerre** money is the sinews of war
(d) (*de reliure*) band, cord
▶ **nerf**: **n. de bœuf** *F* cosh, *Am* blackjack; *Anat* **n. crânien** cranial nerve; *Anat* **n. sciatique** sciatic nerve

nerprun [nɛrprœ̃] *nm Bot* buckthorn
nervation [nɛrvasjɔ̃] *nf Bot, Zool* nervation, venation
nervé [nɛrve] *adj Bot* nervate, veined
nerveusement [nɛrvøzmɑ̃] *adv* (**a**) nervously (**b**) (*avec énergie*) energetically
nerveux, -euse [nɛrvø, -øz] **1** *adj* (**a**) (*relatif aux nerfs*) (*système, maladie*) nervous; **centre n.** nerve centre; **dépression nerveuse** nervous breakdown; **influx n.** nerve impulse
(**b**) (*émotif*) (*personne, tempérament*) nervous, excitable, highly-strung, *Br F* nervy; (*en un moment précis, avant un examen etc*) nervous, tense; (*rire, toux*) nervous; **être d'une nature nerveuse** to be of a nervous disposition; **rendre qn n.** to make sb nervous
(**c**) (*aux tendons apparents*) (*corps, mains*) sinewy; (*viande*) stringy
(**d**) (*dynamique*) (*personne*) dynamic, energetic; (*style*) vigorous, terse; *Aut* (*conduite*) dynamic; **votre conduite est trop nerveuse** your driving is jerky; **moteur n.** responsive *or* lively engine **2** *n* nervous person
nervi [nɛrvi] *nm* henchman, thug
nervosité [nɛrvozite] *nf* nervousness; (*irritabilité*) irritability; **donner des signes de n.** to show signs of agitation
nervure [nɛrvyr] *nf* (*de feuille, d'aile d'insecte*) nervure, vein, rib; *Tech* flange, rib; (*de radiateur etc*) gill; *Av* (*d'aile*) rib; (*au dos d'un livre*) rib, raised band; *Archit* **voûte à nervures** ribbed vault; **plafond à nervures** filleted ceiling; *Couture* **nervures** pin tucks
nervuré [nɛrvyre] *adj* (*feuille, aile*) veined; (*vêtement*) ribbed
n'est-ce-pas [nɛspa] *adv* [ⓘA46,8b; B61,3b] **tu viendras, n.?** you'll come, won't you?; **tu l'as déjà vue, n.?** you've already seen her, haven't you?; **n., qu'elle est mignonne?** she's cute, isn't she?; **le problème n., c'est qu'elle est un peu prude cette petite** the problem is that she's something of a prude, don't you think?
net, nette [nɛt] **1** *adj* (**a**) (*propre*) (*assiette, pièce, miroir, mains*) clean; *Fig* (*conscience*) clear; **j'ai la conscience nette** I have a clear conscience, my conscience is clear; *Fig* **j'ai les mains nettes** my hands are clean; **faire place nette** to clear everything out; *Cartes etc* **faire tapis n.** to sweep the board
(**b**) (*clair, précis*) (*vue, idée, style*) clear; (*contour*) sharp; (*réponse*) plain, straight; **je n'ai pas les idées très nettes aujourd'hui** I'm not quite with it today; **écriture nette** neat handwriting; **il fait plus froid ici, c'est très n.** it's noticeably *or* definitely colder here; *Phot, TV, Opt* **image nette** sharp image; **cassure nette** clean break; **division nette** clear-cut division; **elle a gardé des souvenirs très nets de sa petite enfance** she remembers her childhood quite clearly *or* vividly
(**c**) (*différence, amélioration, refroidissement etc*) clear, marked, distinct
(**d**) *F* **il n'est pas n.** (*un peu dérangé*) he's not all there; (*louche*) he's a bit shady
(**e**) (*poids, prix, salaire*) net; (*profit*) net, clear; **n. d'impôt** net of tax; **le montant n.** the net amount, the net
2 *adv* (**a**) (*de manière précise, brutale*) (*parler*) plainly, frankly; **refuser (tout) n.** to refuse point-blank *or* flatly; **je lui ai dit tout n. ma façon de penser** I told him plainly *or* frankly what I thought; **s'arrêter n.** to stop dead; **se casser n.** to break clean through; **coupé n.** cut clean through; **tué n.** killed outright; **mets ton exercice au n.** copy the exercise out neatly
(**b**) *Com* **cent francs n.** a hundred francs net; **gagner mille francs n.** to earn a thousand francs net, to net a thousand francs
▶ **net**: *Compta* **n. commercial** net profit; **n. financier** net interest income; (*à payer*) net interest charges; **n. à payer** net payable
netsurfer [nɛtsœrfœr] *nm Ordinat* net surfer
nettement [nɛtmɑ̃] *adv* (**a**) (*distinctement*) (*voir, se dessiner*) clearly, distinctly; **profil n. découpé** clear-cut profile (**b**) (*incontestablement*) distinctly, markedly; **ce livre est n. pacifiste** this book is distinctly *or* markedly pacifist (**c**) (*beaucoup*) much, distinctly; **ça va n. mieux comme ça** it's a lot *or* much better like this; **elle est n. moins bonne que lui** she's not nearly as good as him; **il est arrivé n. en retard** he was more than a little late, he arrived quite late
netteté [nɛtte] *nf* (**a**) (*propreté*) cleanliness, cleanness (**b**) (*précision*) (*de rupture*) cleanness; **s'exprimer avec n.** to express oneself clearly (**c**) (*clarté*) (*de pensée, style*) clearness, clarity; (*de vision, d'objet*) distinctness; (*d'image*) sharpness; (*de mémoire*) vividness; (*de refus*) flatness; **l'image manque de n.** the picture isn't very sharp; *Phot* **régler la n.** to focus
nettoiement [nɛtwamɑ̃] *nm* (*de rues*) cleaning; (*du sol*) cleaning, clearing; (*de forêt*) clearing; **service du n.** refuse collection service
nettoyage [nɛtwajaʒ] *nm* (**a**) cleaning; **faire le n.** to do the cleaning; **grand n. de printemps** spring cleaning; **produit de n.** cleaning product; **entreprise de n.** cleaning firm (**b**) (*par la police*) cleaning *or* clearing out; **les policiers ont opéré un véritable n. du quartier** the police officers really cleaned out *or* cleared out the district; *Mil* **opérations de n.** mopping-up operations
▶ **nettoyage**: *Pol* **n. ethnique** ethnic cleansing; **n. par le vide** vacuum cleaning; *Fig* **faire le n. par le vide** to throw everything out; **n. à sec** dry cleaning
nettoyant [nɛtwajɑ̃] **1** *adj* cleaning **2** *nm* cleaning product
nettoyer [nɛtwaje] (**je nettoie; je nettoierai**) **1** *vt* (**a**) (*pièce, vêtements, casserole, blessure*) to clean; (*bouteille*) to wash out; *Naut* (*pont*) to swab; **n. à sec** to dry-clean
(**b**) *Fig F* (*de cambrioleur*) (*maison*) to strip, to clean out; **se faire n. au jeu** to be *or* get cleaned out gambling; **la police est en train de n. le quartier** the police are cleaning out *or* clearing out the district; *Mil* **n. les poches de résistance** to mop up
(**c**) *F* (*tuer*) to wipe out; **se faire n.** to be *or* get wiped out
2 se nettoyer *vpr* **se n. les oreilles/les mains** to clean one's ears/hands; **le four se nettoie automatiquement** the oven cleans itself automatically *or* is self-cleaning
nettoyeur, -euse [nɛtwajœr, -øz] **1** *n* (*personne*) cleaner **2** *nf* **nettoyeuse** (*machine*) cleaning machine, cleaner
neuf[1] [nœf, *before* **ans** *and* **heures** nœv] **1** *adj* nine; **les n. dixièmes du total** nine-tenths of the total; **n. fois sur dix** nine times out of ten **2** *nm* (*nombre, numéro*) nine; **le n. mai** the ninth of May, May the ninth; **Louis N.** Louis the Ninth; **deux neufs** two nines; **le n. de carreau** the nine of diamonds; *Math* **faire la preuve par n.** to cast out the nines
neuf[2] [nœf, nœv] **1** *adj* new; **à l'état n.** in new condition, as new; (*timbre postal, livre*) in mint condition, unused; **'état n.'** (*dans petite annonce*) as new; **tout n.** brand new; **comme n.** as good as new; **aborder/considérer/regarder qch d'un œil n.** to approach/consider/look at sth with a fresh eye; **la curiosité (toute) neuve d'un enfant** a child's newly awakened curiosity; **être n. dans un métier** to be new to a job; **quoi de n.?** what's new?; **il n'y a rien de n.** there's nothing new
2 *nm* **vendre du n. et de l'occasion** to sell new and second-hand goods; **habillé de n.** wearing new clothes; **meublé en n.** newly furnished; **acheter du n.** (*dans l'immobilier*) to buy new; **refaire/repeindre une maison à n.** to redo/repaint a house completely; **remettre qch à n.** to make sth as good as new; (*machine*) to recondition sth, to renovate sth; **tu as du n. pour ton visa?** any developments on the visa front?, have you heard anything about your visa?
neurasthénie [nørasteni] *nf Méd* neurasthenia; *Vieilli* **faire de la n.** (*dépression*) to be depressed
neurasthénique [nørastenik] **1** *adj Vieilli* depressed; *Méd* neurasthenic **2** *n Vieilli* depressive, depressed person; *Méd* neurasthenic
neurobiologie [nørobjɔlɔʒi] *nf* neurobiology
neuroblaste [nøroblast] *nm Biol* neuroblast
neurochirurgie [nøroʃiryrʒi] *nf Chir* neurosurgery
neurochirurgien, -ienne [nøroʃiryrʒjɛ̃, -jɛn] *n Chir* neurosurgeon
neuroleptique [nørolɛptik] *Méd* **1** *adj* (*médicament*) neuroleptic **2** *nm* neuroleptic, *F* tranquillizer; **être sous neuroleptiques** to be on tranquillizers
neurologie [nørɔlɔʒi] *nf Méd* neurology
neurologiste [nørɔlɔʒist] *n*, **neurologue** [nørɔlɔg] *n Méd* neurologist, nerve specialist
neuronal, -ale, -aux, - ales [nørɔnal, -o] *adj* neuronal; **réseau n.** neural net
neurone [nørɔn, -ron] *nm Biol, Ordinat* neuron, neurone
neuronique [nørɔnik] *adj* neuronic
neuropathologie [nøropatɔlɔʒi] *nf* neuropathology
neuropsychiatrie [nøropsikjatri] *nf* neuropsychiatry
neuropsychologie [nøropsikɔlɔʒi] *nf* neuropsychology
neurovégétatif, -ive [nøroveʒetatif, -iv] *adj Anat* (*système*) neurovegetative
neutralisation [nøtralizasjɔ̃] *nf* (*de pays, d'acide etc*) neutralization, neutralizing; *Mil* **tir de n.** neutralizing fire
neutraliser [nøtralize] **1** *vt* (*pays, acide*) to neutralize; (*efforts, concurrence, agents ennemis etc*) to thwart; (*agresseur*) to overpower; (*circulation*) to stop **2 se neutraliser** *vpr* (*s'annuler réciproquement*) to cancel each other out
neutralisme [nøtralism] *nm Pol* neutralism
neutraliste [nøtralist] *adj, n Pol* neutralist
neutralité [nøtralite] *nf Pol, Ch, Él etc* neutrality; **garder la n.** to remain neutral; **sortir de sa n.** to take sides; *Pol* to abandon one's neutrality *or* one's neutral position; **violer la n. d'un État** to violate a state's neutrality
neutre [nøtr] **1** *adj* (**a**) (*ni masculin, ni féminin*) neuter; *Gram*

pronom n. neuter pronoun; **abeille n.** neuter *or* worker bee **(b)** (*qui n'a pas pris position*) (*nation, navire, position, article de presse*) neutral; *Mil* **la zone n.** no-man's land; **rester n.** to remain neutral, not to take sides **(c)** (*sans caractéristique distinctive*) (*ton de voix, couleur*) neutral **(d)** *Ch, Él* (*sel, fil*) neutral **2** *nm* **(a)** *Gram* neuter; **au n.** in the neuter **(b)** *Can Aut* neutral; **se mettre sur le n.** to go into neutral

neutrino [nøtrino] *nm Phys* neutrino

neutron [nøtrɔ̃] *nm Phys* neutron; **bombe à neutrons** neutron bomb

neuvaine [nøvɛn] *nf Rel* novena

neuvième [nœvjɛm] **1** *adj* ninth **2** *n* (*personne, chose*) ninth; **la n. de Beethoven** Beethoven's Ninth **3** *nm* (*fraction*) ninth **4** *nf Mus* ninth; *Scol* (*d'école primaire*) *Br* ≈ third year of primary school, *Am* ≈ third grade

neuvièmement [nœvjɛmmɑ̃] *adv* ninthly

névé [neve] *nm Géol* névé, firn

neveu, -eux [nœvø] *nm* nephew; *F* **un peu mon n.!** [nvø] you bet!

névralgie [nevralʒi] *nf* neuralgia; **avoir des névralgies** to suffer from neuralgia

névralgique [nevralʒik] *adj* neuralgic; *Fig* **point n.** (*d'une situation*) sensitive area

névrite [nevrit] *nf Méd* neuritis

névritique [nevritik] *adj* neuritic

névropathe [nevrɔpat] *n Vieilli* neuropath

névrose [nevroz] *nf Méd* neurosis; **n. post-traumatique** post-traumatic stress disorder

névrosé, -ée [nevroze] *adj, n* neurotic

névrotique [nevrɔtik] *adj Psy* (*désordre etc*) neurotic

new-look [njuluk] *nm inv, adj inv* New Look

new-yorkais, -aise [njujɔrkɛ, -ɛz] **1** *adj* (of/from) New York; **un bar/théâtre n.** a bar/theatre in New York **2** *n* **N.** New Yorker

nez [ne] *nm* **(a)** nose; **parler/respirer du n.** to speak/breathe through one's nose; **j'ai le n. bouché** my nose is stuffed up *or* blocked; **se casser le n.** to break one's nose; *Fig* (*trouver porte close*) to find nobody at home; (*échouer*) to come a cropper; **le bout du n.** the tip of the nose; *Fig* **elle ne voit pas plus loin que le bout de son n.** she can't see beyond the *or* further than the end of her nose; **montrer (le bout de) son n.** to show oneself *or* one's face, to put in an appearance; **mener qn par le bout du n.** to push sb around; **se laisser mener par le bout du n.** to let oneself be pushed around; **avoir le n. en l'air** to look up in the air; *Fig* (*rêvasser*) to have one's head in the clouds; **partir/se promener le n. au vent** to stroll *or* dawdle off/along; **où est mon dictionnaire? – il est sous ton n.** *ou* **tu as le n. dessus** where's my dictionary? – it's (right) under your nose; **avoir le n. dans son journal/ses bouquins** to have one's nose in one's newspaper/one's books; **sans lever le n.** (*lire, travailler*) without a break; **ça se voit comme le n. au milieu de la figure** it's as plain as the nose on your face; **se trouver n. à n. avec qn** to find oneself face to face with sb; **fourrer** *ou* **mettre son n. dans les affaires d'autrui** to poke one's nose *or* pry into other people's affairs; **je n'aime pas qu'on mette le n. dans mes affaires** I don't like people poking their noses *or* prying into my affairs; **baisser le n.** to hang one's head, to look sheepish; **cela lui pend au n.** he's got it coming (to him); *Arg* **je l'ai dans le n.** I can't stand him, *Br* he gets up my nose; **avoir un verre** *ou* **un coup dans le n.** to be a bit merry *or* tipsy; **ça m'est passé sous le n.** it slipped through my fingers; **regarder qn sous le n.** to stare sb in the face; **dire qch au n. de qn** to say sth to sb's face; **rire au n. de qn** to laugh in sb's face; **raccrocher au n. de qn** to hang up on sb, to put the phone down on sb; **s'évader au n. et à la barbe des gendarmes** to escape right under the police's noses; **dérober qch au n. et à la barbe de qn** to steal sth from right under sb's nose; *F* **se manger** *ou* **se bouffer le n.** to be at each other's throats; **fermer** *ou* **claquer la porte au n. de qn** to shut the door in sb's face; **je n'ai pas mis le n. dehors de la journée** I didn't set foot outside the door all day; **il fait un temps à ne pas mettre le n. dehors** it's not the kind of weather to be out in; **ton n. remue** *ou* **s'allonge!** (*tu mens*) your nose is getting longer!; **sentir l'ail à plein n.** to smell strongly of garlic; **sentir le renfermé à plein n.** to smell very musty; *Fig* **ça sent le discours préparé à plein n.** you can tell it's a well-rehearsed speech; *Fig* **ça sent l'entourloupe à plein n.** there's some dirty business going on

(b) (*odorat*) sense of smell; (*de chiens*) scent; **avoir le n. fin** (*avoir un bon odorat*) to have a good nose *or* a keen sense of smell; *Fig* **avoir le n. fin** *ou* **creux, avoir du n.** (*avoir de l'intuition*) to be shrewd

(c) (*de bateau*) nose, bow, head; (*d'avion*) nose; (*de marche*) nosing; (*de moteur*) nosepiece; *Com* **n. de caisse** checkout display; **piquer du n.** (*d'un avion*) to nosedive; (*s'endormir*) to nod off, to doze off

▶ **nez**: **n. en pied de marmite** bulbous nose; **n. en trompette, n. retroussé** turned-up *or* snub nose

NfD *nf Typ* (*abrév* **note de fin de document**) endnote

NGP [ɛnʒepe] *Com* (*abrév* **nomenclature générale des produits**) customs nomenclature

ni [ni] *conj* [①B60,B] (**ne** *is either expressed or implied*) nor; **ni moi** nor me (either), *Fml* nor I, *F* me neither; **sans argent ni bagages** without money or luggage, with neither money nor luggage; **il ne mange ni ne boit** he neither eats nor drinks; **il est parti sans manger ni boire** he left without (either) eating or drinking; **ni ... ni** neither ... nor; **ni Pierre ni Henri ne sont** *ou* **n'est là** neither Pierre nor Henri is there; **je n'ai ni femme ni enfant ni amis** I have neither wife nor child nor friends; **ni l'un ni l'autre ne se souvient** neither (of them) remembers; **lequel a été pris sur les deux? – ni l'un ni l'autre** which of the two was taken? – neither of them *or* neither one nor the other; **ni plus ni moins** neither more nor less

niais, -aise [njɛ, -ɛz] **1** *adj* (*personne, réponse, air*) simple, foolish, silly; (*sourire*) inane, silly **2** *n* fool, simpleton; **espèce de n.!** you silly fool!

niaisage [njezaʒ] *nm Can* idleness

niaisement [njɛzmɑ̃] *adv* foolishly; **rire n.** to give a silly laugh, to laugh inanely

niaiser [njeze] *Can* **1** *vt* **n. qn** (*faire tourner en bourrique*) to drive sb crazy; (*se moquer de*) to laugh at; (*raconter des histoires à*) to pull sb's leg **2** *vi* (*ne rien faire*) to hang around doing nothing

niaiserie [njɛzri] *nf* **(a)** (*caractère stupide*) silliness, foolishness **(b)** (*une bêtise, une ânerie*) silly thing; **dire des niaiseries** to talk nonsense

niaiseux, -euse [njɛzø, -øz] *Can F* **1** *adj* idiotic, stupid **2** *n* idiot

Nicaragua [nikaragwa] *nm Géog* Nicaragua

nicaraguayen, -enne [nikaragwajɛ̃, -ɛn] **1** *adj* Nicaraguan **2** *n* **N.** Nicaraguan

Nicée [nise] *nf Antiq* Nicaea; **le symbole de N.** the Nicene Creed

niche[1] [niʃ] *nf* **(a)** (*renfoncement*) niche, recess, alcove **(b)** (*de chien*) kennel **(c)** *Mktg* niche (market)

niche[2] *nf F Vieilli* (*farce*) trick, prank

nichée [niʃe] *nf* (*d'oisillons*) nest(ful), brood; (*de souris, de chiots*) litter; *Hum* (*d'enfants*) brood

nicher [niʃe] **1** *vi* (*d'oiseaux*) to nest, to build a nest (**dans** in); *F* (*de personnes*) to hang out; **maison nichée dans la montagne** cottage nestling in *or* hidden away in the mountains; **niché dans un fauteuil** curled up in an armchair **2 se nicher** *vpr* **(a)** (*d'oiseaux*) to nest, to build a nest **(b)** (*se cacher*) **où est-il allé se n.?** where's he hiding (himself)?, where's he got to?; **où ce chat a-t-il bien pu se n.?** where's the cat got to? **3** *vt* (*blottir*) **n. sa tête au creux de l'épaule de qn** to nuzzle *or* nestle one's head against sb's shoulder

nichet [niʃɛ] *nm* (*œuf factice*) nest egg

nichoir [niʃwar] *nm* nesting box

nichon [niʃɔ̃] *nm F* (*sein*) boob, tit

nickel [nikɛl] **1** *nm Métal* nickel **2** *adj inv F* (*propre*) clean as a whistle

nickelage [niklaʒ] *nm* nickel plating

nickelé [nikle] *adj* nickel-plated, nickelled; *Vieilli F* **avoir les pieds nickelés** to sit tight, to refuse to budge

nickeler [nikle] *vt* (**je nickelle, n. nickelons; je nickellerai**) to nickel

nickélifère [nikelifɛr] *adj* nickel-bearing

niçois, -oise [niswa, -waz] **1** *adj* of/from Nice **2** *n* **N.** (*natif*) native of Nice; (*habitant*) inhabitant of Nice

nicotine [nikɔtin] *nf Ch* nicotine

nictation [niktasjɔ̃] *nf*, **nictitation** [niktitasjɔ̃] *nf* nictation, nictitation

nictitant [niktitɑ̃] *adj Zool* (*membrane*) nictitating

nid [ni] *nm* **(a)** (*d'oiseaux, de souris, de fourmis etc*) nest; *aussi Fig* **n. d'aigle** eyrie; *Fig* **n. de brigands/d'espions** den of ruffians/of spies; *Mil* **n. de mitrailleuses** nest of machine guns; *Prov* **petit à petit l'oiseau fait son n.** slow and steady wins the race **(b)** (*logis confortable*) nest; **un petit n. douillet** a cosy little nest; **n. d'amour(eux)** love nest

▶ **nid**: *Couture* **nid(s) d'abeilles** smocking, honeycomb stitch; **un torchon nid(s) d'abeilles** a honeycomb cloth; **n. d'ange** (*pour les bébés*) (baby's) sleeping bag, *Am* bunting (bag); **n. à poussière** dust trap

nid-de-pie, *pl* **nids-de-pie** *nm Naut* crow's nest; *Mil* (*retranchement*) lodg(e)ment

nid-de-poule, *pl* **nids-de-poule** *nm* pothole

nièce [njɛs] *nf* niece
nielle¹ [njɛl] *nf* (*maladie du blé*) smut, blight
nielle² *nf* (*fleur*) **n. des blés** corncockle
nielle³ *nm Beaux-Arts* niello
niellé [njele] *adj* **blé n.** blighted wheat
nieller [njele] *vt Beaux-Arts* to inlay with niello
niellure [njelyr] *nf Beaux-Arts* niello work
nier [nje] (*impf & pr sub* **n. niions**) **1** *vt* (*un fait, l'existence de qch*) to deny; **je nie l'avoir vue** I deny having seen her; **je nie qu'il m'ait vu** I deny that he saw me; **n. l'évidence** to deny the obvious *or* what's obvious; **je ne nie pas que j'ai parfois tort** I don't deny that I'm sometimes wrong; **on ne peut pas n. que ...** there's no denying *or* one can't deny *or* it's undeniable that ... **2** *vi* **l'accusé nie** the accused denies the charge
nigaud, -aude [nigo, -od] **1** *n* ninny, fool; **gros n.!** you great *or* big ninny! **2** *adj* (*sourire, réponse*) silly
nigelle [niʒɛl] *nf* (*fleur*) nigella, love-in-a-mist
Niger [niʒɛr] *nm* Niger
Nigéria [niʒerja] *nm* Nigeria
nigérian, -ane [niʒerjɑ̃, -an] **1** *adj* Nigerian **2** *n* **N.** Nigerian
nigérien, -ienne [niʒerjɛ̃ -jɛn] **1** *adj* of/from Niger, Nigerien **2** *n* **N.** Nigerien
nihilisme [niilism] *nm Phil* nihilism
nihiliste [niilist] *Phil* **1** *adj* nihilist(ic) **2** *n* nihilist
Nil [nil] *nm* **le N.** the Nile; **vert N.** (*couleur*) eau-de-nil
nilgau(t) [nilgo] *nm* (*mammifère*) nilgai
nilotique [nilɔtik] *adj* of the Nile, Nilotic
nimbe [nɛ̃b] *nm* halo, nimbus
nimbé [nɛ̃be] *adj* haloed
nimbus [nɛ̃bys] *nm Météo* nimbus
ninas [ninas] *nm inv* small cigar
nipper [nipe] *F* **1** *vt* (*habiller*) to deck out; **bien nippé** well turned out **2 se nipper** *vpr* (*s'habiller*) to dress; **je me nippe chez Tati** I get my clothes at Tati's
nippes [nip] *nfpl F* (*vêtements*) gear, togs; **à part les n., rien ne l'intéresse** he isn't interested in anything apart from clothes
nippon, -one [nipɔ̃, -ɔn] **1** *adj* Japanese **2** *n* **N.** Japanese
nique [nik] *nf F* **faire la n. à qn** to cock a snook at sb
niquer [nike] *vt* **(a)** *Vulg* to screw, to shag **(b)** *F* (*bousiller*) to knacker, to bugger
nitrate [nitrat] *nm Ch* nitrate
nitre [nitr] *nm Ch* nitre, saltpetre, *US* niter, saltpeter
nitré [nitre] *adj Ch* nitrated; **composé n.** nitro compound
nitrer [nitre] *vt Tech* to nitrate
nitreux, -euse [nitrø, -øz] *adj* nitrous
nitrifier [nitrifje] *vt Ch* to nitrify
nitrique [nitrik] *adj Ch* (*acide*) nitric
nitrobenzène [nitrobɛ̃zɛn] *nm Ch* nitrobenzene
nitroglycérine [nitrogliserin] *nf Ch* nitroglycerine
nitrure [nitryr] *nm Ch* nitride; **n. de fer** iron nitride
nitrurer [nitryre] *vt* to nitride
niveau, -eaux [nivo] *nm* **(a)** (*hauteur*) level; **n. d'eau/d'huile** water/oil level; **n. de l'eau/de la mer** water/sea level; **au n. de la mer** at sea level; **n. des basses/hautes eaux** low-water/high-water mark; **elle a une cicatrice au n. de la cuisse** she has a scar on her leg at about thigh-level; **l'eau nous arrivait au n. de la taille** the water came up to our waists; **les deux encadrements ne sont pas au même n.** the two frames are not level (with each other) *or* are not on the same level; **la Saône/la production n'avait jamais atteint un n. aussi haut** the Saône/production had never reached such a high level *or* had never been so high; **quand tu arrives au n. de la place des Jacobins, prends à gauche** when you get to the Place des Jacobins, turn left; **au n. régional/local** at regional/local level; **au n. matériel/du travail** on the financial/work front, financewise/workwise, where finance/work is concerned; **au n. sentimental** as far as one's love life is concerned; **se mettre au n. de qn** *aussi Fig* to come down to sb's level; **être de n.** to be level; **mettre qch de n.** to make sth level

(b) (*étage*) level; **jardin à trois niveaux** garden on three levels; **immeuble à dix niveaux** ten-storey building; **le supermarché se trouve au troisième n.** the supermarket is on the third level; **n. arrivée** (*d'un aéroport*) arrivals level; **n. départ** (*d'un aéroport*) departures level

(c) (*degré*) level; *Scol* standard; **n. de pollution** pollution level; **n. sonore** noise level; *Rad* **n. de transmission** transmission level; **n. scolaire** academic standard; **tous les élèves ne sont pas du** *ou* **n'ont pas le même n.** not all the pupils are of *or* have reached the same (academic) standard, not all the pupils are of the same level of ability; **quel est son n. en anglais?** what is her standard in English?; **il a un très bon n. en physique** his physics is of a very high standard; **avoir le n. (requis), être au n.** to be up to standard, *F* to be up to scratch; **votre fils n'a pas le n. pour passer le concours** your son is not of a high enough standard to take the examination; **évaluer le n. des candidats** to evaluate the candidates' level of ability; **test de n.** assessment; **être au n. de qch/qn, être de n. avec qch/qn** to be on a level *or* on a par with sth/sb; **nous recherchons un candidat n. baccalauréat/maîtrise** we are looking for a candidate of baccalauréat/master's degree standard; **ils sont d'un n. social différent** they are from different social backgrounds; **au plus bas n. de l'échelle** at the very bottom of the ladder; **au plus haut n. de la hiérarchie** at the highest level of the hierarchy, at the very top; **les salaires augmentent régulièrement à tous les niveaux** there are regular salary increases for all grades *or* at all levels; **n. d'occupation** (*d'un hôtel*) occupancy level; **n. des prix** price levels; **n. des salaires** salary levels; **n. des stocks** inventory *or* stock level; **n. record** record level

▶ **niveau**: *Ordinat* **n. d'accès** (*dans un réseau*) access level; **n. à bulle d'air** spirit level; *Bourse* **n. de dépôt requis** margin requirement; *Ordinat* **n. de gris** grey scale; *Ling* **n. de langue** register, language level; *Tech* **n. à lunette** surveyor's level; *Tech* **n. de maçon** vertical *or* plumb level; *Tech* **n. à plomb** vertical *or* plumb level; **n. tarifaire** fare level; *Écon* **n. de vie** standard of living
nivelage [niv(ə)laʒ] *nm Constr* levelling
niveler [nivle] *vt* **(je nivelle; je nivellerai) (a)** (*aplanir*) (*sol, terrain*) to level, to make level **(b)** (*les fortunes*) to level, to even out *or* up; **n. les prix** to level prices; **n. par le bas** to level down
niveleuse [niv(ə)løz] *nf Constr* grader
nivellement [nivɛlmɑ̃] *nm* (*de terrain, des classes sociales*) levelling; **n. par le bas** levelling down; **repère de n.** (*dans l'arpentage*) bench mark
nivéole [niveɔl] *nf* (*plante*) snowflake
nivôse [nivoz] *nm Hist Fr* = fourth month of Republican calendar (*Dec-Jan*)
nobélisable [nɔbelizabl] **1** *adj* (*chercheur, écrivain*) potential Nobel prizewinning **2** *n* potential Nobel prizewinner
nobiliaire [nɔbiljɛr] **1** *adj* **titre n.** title; **particule n.** nobiliary particle **2** *nm* peerage (list)
noble [nɔbl] **1** *adj* **(a)** (*famille, origine*) noble **(b)** (*imposant*) (*air, allure*) noble, stately **(c)** (*hautement apprécié*) (*cause, motif, entreprise*) noble; **il n'est animé que par de nobles sentiments** he is acting out of noble sentiments; **le n. art** (*boxe*) the noble art **(d)** (*précieux*) noble; **la soie est une matière n.** silk is a noble fabric **2** *nm* nobleman, noble; **les nobles** the nobility, the nobles **3** *nf* noblewoman, noble
noblement [nɔbləmɑ̃] *adv* nobly
noblesse [nɔblɛs] *nf* **(a)** (*par la descendance*) nobility; **famille de n. récente** recently ennobled family; **la haute et la petite n.** the nobility and the gentry; **se marier dans la n.** to marry into nobility, to marry a title; **n. oblige** noblesse oblige **(b)** (*de style, de conduite*) nobility, nobleness; **agir avec beaucoup de n.** to act very nobly

▶ **noblesse**: *Hist* **n. d'épée** old nobility; *Hist* **n. de robe** noblesse de robe
nobliau, -iaux [nɔblijo] *nm Péj* lesser noble(man)
noce [nɔs] *nf* **(a)** (*cérémonie du mariage*) wedding; (*fête*) wedding festivities; (*ensemble des assistants*) wedding party; **repas de n.** wedding breakfast; **noces d'argent/de vermeil/d'or/de diamant** silver/ruby/golden/diamond wedding; **il l'avait épousée en secondes noces** she was his second wife **(b)** *F* **faire la n.** to go on a binge, to live it up; **je n'étais pas à la n.** it was no picnic
noceur, -euse [nɔsœr, -øz] *n F* fast liver, *Br* raver, *Arch* Carouser
nocif, -ive [nɔsif, -iv] *adj* (*produit, émanation*) harmful, noxious
nocivité [nɔsivite] *nf* harmfulness, noxiousness
noctambule [nɔktɑ̃byl] *n* (*qui aime sortir la nuit*) night owl, night bird
noctuelle [nɔktɥɛl] *nf Ent* noctua, owlet moth
nocturne [nɔktyrn] **1** *adj* (*animal*) nocturnal; (*attaque, visite*) night; *Bot* night-flowering; **évasion n.** escape by night **2** *nm* **(a)** (*rapace*) nocturnal bird (of prey) **(b)** *Rel* nocturn **(c)** *Beaux-Arts, Mus* nocturne **3** *nf* (*d'un magasin etc*) late-night opening; *Sp* **match (disputé) en n.** evening game
nodal, -ale, -aux, -ales [nɔdal, -o] **1** *adj* (*point, ligne*) nodal **2** *nm TV etc* master control room
nodosité [nɔdɔzite] *nf Bot, Méd* (*nodule*) node, nodule; (*état*) nodosity
nodule [nɔdyl] *nm Géol, Méd etc* nodule
Noé [noe] *nm Bible* Noah
Noël [nɔɛl] *nm* **(a)** (*fête*) Christmas; **à N.**, *Région* **à la N.** at

Christmas (time); **le jour de N.** Christmas Day; **la nuit** *ou* **la veillée de N.** Christmas Eve; **bûche de N.** yule log; **vacances de N.** Christmas holidays, *Am* Christmas vacation; **arbre** *ou* **sapin de N.** Christmas tree; **joyeux N.!** Happy *or* Merry Christmas! **(b)** *(chanson)* (Christmas) carol **(c)** *(cadeau)* **offrir qch à qn pour son (petit) n.** to give sb sth for Christmas *or* as a Christmas present

nœud [nø] *nm* **(a)** *(entrecroisement)* knot; *Naut* hitch, bend; **corde à nœuds** knotted rope; **faire** *ou* **serrer un n.** to make *or* tie a knot; *Fig* **faire un n. à son mouchoir** to tie a knot in one's handkerchief; *Fig* **avoir un n. dans l'estomac** to have a knot in one's stomach; *Fig* **avoir un n. dans la gorge** to have a lump in one's throat; *Fig* **le n. du problème** the crux of the problem *or* matter; *Fig* **quel sac de nœuds!** what a muddle!

(b) *(ornement)* bow; **faire un n.** to tie a bow; **mettre un n. dans ses cheveux** to put a bow in one's hair; **n. de diamants** diamond cluster

(c) *(de serpent)* coil

(d) *(d'orbite, de courbe, d'oscillation)*, *Ordinat* node

(e) *(sur un arbre, une planche)* knot, knur(l)

(f) *(carrefour de grandes lignes)* **n. autoroutier/ferroviaire** major road/rail junction *or* intersection

(g) *Naut* *(vitesse)* knot; **filer** *ou* **faire vingt nœuds** to do *or* make twenty knots

(h) *Littér, Th* knot, crux

(i) *Vulg* *(pénis)* prick, dick, cock

▶ **nœud**: **n. coulant** *(pour serrer)* slipknot; *(pour étrangler)* noose; **n. de cravate** tie knot; **faire son n. de cravate** to knot one's tie; **n. gordien** Gordian knot; **trancher le n. gordien** to cut the Gordian knot; *Tech* **n. de grappin** fisherman's bend; *Anat* **n. lymphatique** lymph node; **n. papillon**; *F* **n. pap** bow tie; **n. plat** reef knot; *Tech* **n. de vache** carrick bend; **n. de vipères** nest of vipers

noir, noire [nwar] **1** *adj* **(a)** *(couleur)* black; **n. comme de l'encre** as black as ink, inky black; *Litt* **n. comme (de) l'ébène** as black as ebony, ebony black; *Litt* **n. comme (du) jais** jet black; *Litt* **n. comme de la poix** pitch-black; **n. d'ivoire** ivory black

(b) *(très sombre)* *(cheveux, yeux, ciel, lunettes)* dark; **il est rentré n. de ses vacances** he was incredibly brown when he came back from his holidays

(c) *(relatif à la race)* *(peau, race, origine, quartier, chanteuse)* black

(d) *(plongé dans l'obscurité)* *(nuit, cellule)* dark; **il fait n.** it's dark; **il faisait nuit noire** *ou* **n. comme dans un four** it was pitch-dark *or* pitch-black; **la place était noire de monde** the square was thick *or* swarming with people

(e) *(pessimiste)* *(pensées, vision)* black, gloomy; **avoir des idées noires** to be down in the dumps; **il m'a fait un tableau très n. de la situation** he painted a very black *or* gloomy picture of the situation; **le lundi/jeudi n.** Black Monday/Thursday; **rien n'est tout blanc ou tout n.** nothing is completely black and white

(f) *(sale)* *(visage, mains, ongles, linge)* black, filthy, dirty; **tu es tout n.** you're all black *or* filthy *or* dirty; **être n. de crasse** to be black with grime; **être n. comme du charbon** to be as black as soot

(g) *(inspiré par la colère)* *(regard)* black; *Litt* *(crime)* heinous, foul; *(ingratitude)* utter; *(calomnie)* wicked; **regarder qn d'un œil n.** to give sb a black look; *Litt* **de noirs desseins** evil designs; **être d'une humeur noire** to be in a black *or* foul mood

(h) *(illicite)* **le marché n.** the black market

(i) *(intense)* **colère noire** towering rage; **se mettre dans une colère noire** to fly into a towering rage; **misère noire** dire *or* abject poverty, utter destitution; **être dans une misère noire** to be utterly destitute

(j) *Arg* *(ivre)* blind drunk

(k) *Cin, Littér* **film n.** film noir, gangster thriller; **roman n.** gangster novel

2 *n* **N.** Black (man); **Noire** Black (woman); **il est N.** he's (a) Black; *Hist* **traite des Noirs** slave trade

3 *nm* **(a)** *(couleur)* black; **j'aime le n.** I like black; **en n. et blanc** *(film, photographie)* black and white; **être vêtu de n., être en n.** to be dressed (all) in black; *F* **se mettre du n. aux yeux** to put eyeliner on; **d'un n. d'ébène** as black as ebony, ebony black; **c'était écrit n. sur blanc** it was there in black and white

(b) *(obscurité)* dark, darkness; **avoir peur du n.** *ou* **dans le n.** to be afraid of the dark

(c) *(trace de salissure)* **tu as du n. sur le visage** you've got a black mark on your face; **j'ai mis plein de n. sur mon pantalon** I've got black marks all over my trousers

(d) *(pessimisme)* **voir tout en n.** to look on the black side of everything; **broyer du n.** to be down in the dumps

(e) *F* *(travail illicite)* **le travail au n.** moonlighting, work on the side; **il a été engagé au n.** he was employed illegally; **il est chauffeur de taxi au n.** he moonlights *or* works on the side as a taxi-driver; **faire des petits boulots au n.** to do some little jobs on the side

(f) *(d'une cible)* bull's-eye

(g) *(café)* **un (petit) n.** a (small) black coffee

4 *nf Mus* **noire** crotchet, *Am* quarter note

▶ **noir**: *Typ* **n. au blanc** reverse printing, white-on-black; **n. de Chine** Indian ink, *Am* India ink; **n. de fumée** lampblack; *Typ* **n. au gris** black-on-tone, BOT

noirâtre [nwarɑtr] *adj* blackish

noiraud, -aude [nwaro, -od] **1** *adj* dark, swarthy **2** *n* dark *or* swarthy person, *Péj* darky, darkie

noirceur [nwarsœr] *nf* **(a)** *(d'encre etc)* blackness; *Litt* *(d'un crime)* heinousness, foulness **(b)** *Can* *(obscurité)* dark, darkness; **dans la n.** in the dark *or* darkness; **avoir peur dans la n.** to be afraid of the dark

noircir [nwarsir] **1** *vi* to turn *or* go black, to darken

2 *vt* *(mur, pierres etc)* to blacken, to make black; **n. du papier** to write a lot *or* screeds; **n. du papier, n. des pages et des pages** to write page after page; **il a noirci trois feuilles sans s'interrompre** he covered three sheets of paper without stopping; **tout ce qu'il est capable de faire, c'est n. du papier** the only thing he's good at is putting ink on paper; **n. qn** *ou* **la réputation de qn** to blacken sb's reputation; **n. le tableau** *ou* **la situation** to paint things blacker than they are

3 se noircir *vpr* *(de métal, pierre, mur etc)* to turn *or* go black, to darken; *(du ciel)* to darken, to become overcast; *Fig F* *(se soûler)* to get blind drunk **(à la vodka** on vodka); **se n. le visage** to black one's face; *Th* to black up

noircissement [nwarsismɑ̃] *nm* blackening

noircissure [nwarsisyr] *nf* black mark

noise [nwaz] *nf Litt* **chercher n.** *ou* **des noises à qn** to try to pick a quarrel with sb

noisetier [nwaztje] *nm* hazel (tree *or* bush); *(bois)* hazel (wood)

noisette [nwazɛt] **1** *nf* **(a)** *Bot, Culin* hazel(nut) **(b)** *(petite quantité)* *(de beurre)* knob; *(de mousse coiffante)* small ball **(c)** *Culin* **n. d'agneau** noisette of lamb **2** *adj inv* **yeux n.** hazel eyes

noix [nwa] *nf* **(a)** *(fruit)* walnut **(b)** *F* **quelle n.!** *(imbécile)* what a twerp!; **comment vas-tu, vieille n.?** how are you, old thing?; *Fig F* **à la n. (de coco)** rubbishy, lousy; **excuses à la n.** paltry *or* trivial excuses **(c)** *Culin* **n. de bœuf, n. de côtelette, n. de gigot** pope's eye; **un rôti dans la n., n. de veau** cushion *or* topside of veal **(d)** *(petite quantité)* **n. de beurre** knob of butter

▶ **noix**: **n. d'acajou** cashew nut; **n. du Brésil** Brazil nut; **n. de cajou** cashew nut; **n. de coco** coconut; **n. de Pécan** pecan; **n. vomique** nux vomica

nolisation [nɔlizasjɔ̃] *nf* chartering

nolisement [nɔliz(ə)mɑ̃] *nm* chartering

noliser [nɔlize] *vt* to charter

nom [nɔ̃] *nm* **(a)** [①B8,10] *(de personne)* name; **quel est votre n.?** what's your name?; **n. … prénom** *(sur formulaire)* surname … first name; **n. et prénoms** full name; **vos n., prénoms et adresse** your full name and address; **quelqu'un dont je tairai le n.** someone who shall remain nameless; **je porte le n. de ma grand-mère** I'm called after my grandmother; **tu porteras le n. de ton mari ou pas?** will you take your husband's name or not?; **je la connais de n. seulement** I only know her by name; **je n'arrive pas à mettre un n. sur sa tête/sur sa voix** I can't put a name to him; **voyager sous un faux n.** to travel under a false name *or* an alias; **on le connaissait sous le n. de Leduc** he went by *or* was known by the name of Leduc; **appeler les choses par leur n.** to call a spade a spade; **impolitesse sans n.** unspeakable rudeness; *F* **n. de n.!, n. d'une pipe!, n. d'un chien!, n. de Dieu!** hell!; **se faire un n.** to make a name for oneself; **un grand n. de la musique** one of the great names of music; **les grands noms de la littérature russe** the great names of Russian literature; **il n'est médecin que de n.** he's a doctor in name only; **au n. de la loi** in the name of the law; **faire qch au n. de l'amitié/la justice** to do sth in the name of friendship/justice; **faire une proposition au n. de qn** to make a proposal for sb *or* on behalf of sb; **parler en son n.** to speak for oneself; **je parlerai en votre n.** I'll speak for you *or* in your name; **un homme du n. de Pierre** a man by the name of *or* named Pierre; **Louis, treizième du n.** Louis, thirteenth king of that name; **traiter qn de tous les noms** to call sb names; **je lui ai donné tous les noms d'oiseaux** I called him every name under the sun; *F* **avoir un n. à coucher dehors** to have a totally unpronounceable name

(b) *(de plantes, d'animaux, d'objets etc)* name; **c'est quoi le n. de ta rue?** what's the name of your street?; **le porte-**

bébé, comme son n. l'indique, permet de porter un bébé a baby carrier, as the name indicates, allows you to carry a baby **(c)** [①**A8-16; B5-8**] *Gram* noun

▶ **nom**: **n. de baptême** first name, Christian name, *Am* given name; *Ordinat* **n. de champ** field name; **n. commercial** company *or* trade name; *Gram* **n. commun** common noun; *Gram* **n. composé** compound (noun); *Com* **n. déposé** (registered) trade mark; **n. d'emprunt** assumed name; **n. de famille** surname; *Mktg* **n. de famille global** blanket family name; *Ordinat* **n. de fichier** file name; **n. de guerre** assumed name, pseudonym; *(d'un écrivain, d'un journaliste)* pseudonym, pen name; *(d'un acteur)* stage name; **n. de jeune fille** maiden name; **n. de marque** brand name; **n. à particule** = name with a nobiliary particle; **n. de plume** nom de plume, pen name, pseudonym; *Gram* **n. propre** [①**B8**,10] proper noun; *F* **n. à rallonges** long aristocratic surname, double-barrelled name; **n. de scène** stage name; **n. de théâtre** stage name; *F* **n. à tiroirs** long aristocratic surname

nomade [nɔmad] **1** *adj (vie, tribu)* nomadic, wandering **2** *n (du désert)* nomad; *Jur (gitan)* traveller

nomadisme [nɔmadism] *nm* nomadism

nombre [nɔ̃br] *nm* **(a)** [①**A70-2**,16; **B56-57**] number; **(bon) n. de gens, un certain n. de gens, un assez grand n. de gens** a number of people *or* a good many people; **le plus grand n. est de cet avis** the majority are of this opinion; **un grand/petit n. d'entre nous** many/a few of us; **ils finirent par succomber sous le n. des assaillants** they were finally overcome by the sheer number of their attackers; **n. de mots** word count, number of words; *Litt* **surpasser en n.** to outnumber; **supérieur en n.** superior in number(s); **nous sommes en n. suffisant** there are enough of us; *(dans une réunion)* we have a quorum; **sans n.** *(foule)* huge, vast; **venez pour faire n.** come and make up the numbers; **venir/se précipiter en n.** to come/rush in large *or* great numbers; **les voitures/manifestants convergeaient en (très) grand n. vers le centre de la ville** the cars/demonstrators were converging in huge numbers on the town centre; *Litt* **en n. écrasant** by an overwhelming majority; **ils sont au n. de huit** there are eight of them; **être au n.** *ou* **du n. des élus** to be one of *or* among the elect; *Fml* **mettre** *ou* **compter qn au n. de ses intimes** to number sb among one's friends; **sur le n.** among *or* out of (all) those; *Bible* **Le Livre des Nombres** (the Book of) Numbers

(b) *Gram* number; **s'accorder en genre et en n.** to agree in gender and number

▶ **nombre**: **n. atomique** atomic number; *Phys* **n. d'Avogadro** Avogadro number; *Math* **n. complexe** complex number; *Math* **n. décimal** decimal (number); *Math* **n. entier** whole number, integer; **n. d'or** golden section; *Math* **n. premier** prime number

nombreux, -euse [nɔ̃brø, -øz] *adj (membres, objets)* numerous, many; *(famille, armée, groupe)* large; **auditoire peu n.** small audience; **pendant de nombreuses générations** for many generations; **nous sommes peu n.** there are not many of us, there are very few of us; **n. sont ceux qui ...** there are/were many who ...; **venir (très) n.** to come in (very) large numbers; **venez n.!** all (are) welcome!, everyone (is) welcome!

nombril [nɔ̃bri(l)] *nm* **(a)** *Anat* navel; *F Hum* **être décolletée jusqu'au n.** to be showing a lot of cleavage; **il avait une chemise ouverte jusqu'au n.** his shirt was open to the waist; *F* **il se prend pour le n. du monde** *ou* **de la terre** he thinks the whole world revolves around him; *Fig* **se regarder le n.** to contemplate one's navel **(b)** *Bot* hilum

nombrilisme [nɔ̃brilism] *nm* self-absorption, self-centredness; **faire du n.** to contemplate one's navel

nombriliste [nɔ̃brilist] *adj* self-absorbed, self-centred

nomenclature [nɔmɑ̃klatyr] *nf (ensemble de termes techniques)* nomenclature; *(liste des objets d'une collection etc)* list, catalogue; *(d'un dictionnaire)* word list; *(d'une voiture etc)* parts list; **n. douanière** *ou* **n. générale des produits** customs nomenclature

nominal, -ale, -aux, -ales [nɔminal, -o] **1** *adj* **(a)** *(prix, puissance en chevaux, autorité)* nominal; *Fin* nominal, par; *Fin* **valeur nominale** face value; *Él* **courant n.** *(d'une machine)* rated current **(b)** *(relatif au nom de famille)* **appel n.** roll call; **liste nominale** list of names, name list; **vérification** *ou* **contrôle nominal(e)** name check **(c)** *Gram (emploi, fonction)* nominal **2** *nm (d'une action)* nominal value; *(d'une obligation)* par value

nominalement [nɔminalmɑ̃] *adv* **(a)** *(appeler qn)* by name; **rester n. propriétaire d'un immeuble** to remain the owner of an apartment block in name only **(b)** *Gram (comme un nom)* nominally, as a noun

nominalisme [nɔminalism] *nm Phil* nominalism

nominatif, -ive [nɔminatif, -iv] **1** *adj* **(a)** *(qui comporte un nom) (carte d'adhérent, billet)* nontransferable; **état n.** list of names, name list; **votre carte bancaire est nominative** *(inscription sur carte)* this banker's card may be used only by the authorized signatory *or* by the person whose name it bears; **les places de concert ne sont pas nominatives** the seats for the concert are transferable **(b)** *Fin* **titres nominatifs** registered securities **2** *nm Gram* nominative (case); **au n.** in the nominative (case)

nomination [nɔminasjɔ̃] *nf* **(a)** *(à un poste)* appointment **(à** to**)**; **attendre sa n.** to expect to be appointed; **n. à un grade supérieur** promotion **(b)** *(pour une remise de récompense)* nomination, recommendation; **ce film a trois nominations pour les Césars** this film has received three César nominations **(c)** *Phil* naming

nominativement [nɔminativmɑ̃] *adv* by name

nominé [nɔmine] *adj (film etc)* nominated **(à une récompense** for an award**)**

nommé, -ée [nɔme] **1** *adj (personne, objet)* named **2** *n* **le n. Antoine** the man named *or* called Antoine; **la nommée Chantal** the woman named *or* called Chantal; **un n. Bertrand a appelé** someone named *or* called Bertrand rang

nommément [nɔmemɑ̃] *adv* **(a) accuser/dénoncer/désigner qn n.** to accuse/denounce/refer to sb by name **(b)** *(spécialement)* especially, in particular

nommer [nɔme] **1** *vt* **(a)** *(appeler)* to name, to give a name to; **on le nomma Paul** they named *or* called him Paul; **on nomme aumôniers les prêtres attachés à un régiment** priests attached to a regiment are called chaplains

(b) *(désigner) (personne)* to name, to mention by name; **un homme que je ne nommerai pas** a man who shall remain nameless *or* whom I won't (mention by) name; *Hum* **M. Dutronc, pour ne pas le n.** without mentioning any names *or* naming no names, Mr Dutronc; *Vieilli* **à jour nommé** on the appointed day; **elle est arrivée à point nommé** she arrived just at the right moment *or* just when she was needed

(c) *(à un poste)* to appoint **(à** to**)**; *Mil (un officier)* to commission; **n. qn directeur** to appoint sb manager; **n. des experts** to appoint experts; **elle a été nommée responsable des ventes** she was appointed sales director; **être nommé au grade supérieur** to be promoted; **être nommé à Lille** to be posted to Lille

2 se nommer *vpr* **(a)** *(avoir pour nom)* to be called *or* named; **comment vous nommez-vous?** what is your name? **(b)** *(s'identifier)* to give one's name

non [nɔ̃] **1** [①**B60**,B] *adv* **(a)** [①**B61**,D,1] *(en réponse)* no; **répondre par oui ou n.** to answer yes or no; **n., n. et n.!** no, no, no!; **c'est dégoûtant, n., tu ne trouves pas?** it's disgusting, isn't it?; **il est pas mal, n. (tu ne trouves pas)?** he's not bad-looking, is he?; **il a commencé comme éboueur – n.!** *(c'est pas possible!)* he started as a dustman – no! *or* really!; **alors, ton augmentation? – c'est n.** what about your pay rise? – I didn't get it; **mais n.!, dame n.!, mon Dieu n.!,** *Hum* **que n.!** certainly not!, definitely not!; **n. mais! je ne te permets pas** no, really! I can't allow that; **tu es content? – ma foi n.** *ou* **certes n.!** are you happy? – certainly not! *or* far from it!; *Litt* **n. pas!** not so!, not at all!; **n., je vous en prie** please don't!; **je pense que n.** I don't think so, I think not; **je dis que n.** I say no; **faire signe que n.** *(de la tête)* to shake one's head; *(avec le doigt)* to indicate no; **il voulait traverser la rue, mais sa mère lui fit signe que n.** he was about to cross the road, but his mother signalled to him not to; **tu viens oui ou n.?** are you coming, yes or no?; **qu'elle vienne ou n.** whether she comes or not

(b) [①**A25**,f] *(pas)* not; **n. loin de la ville** not far from the town; **n. sans raison** not without reason; **n. seulement ..., mais encore** *ou* **aussi ...** not only ..., but also ...; **moi n. plus** me neither; **le problème est cette fois n. plus d'ordre économique mais social** the problem is now not economic but social; **ton frère est studieux, toi n.** your brother is studious, but you're not *or* unlike you; **il faut que ce soit toi qui lui parles et n. l'inverse** it's you who have to talk to him and not the other way round; **n. content de conduire sans permis, l'individu était ivre** not content with driving without a licence, the man was also drunk; **n. coupable** not guilty; **n. solvable** insolvent; **n. (pas) que je le craigne** not that I fear him; **n. que je ne vous plaigne** not that I don't pity you

2 *nm inv* no; **répondre par un n.** to answer with a no *or* in the negative; **les n. l'emportent** the noes have it; **se fâcher/pleurer pour un oui, pour un n.** to flare up/cry at the least (little) thing

non-activité [nɔnaktivite] *nf Admin* **mettre en n.** *(employé)* to suspend; *Mil (officier)* to put on half pay; **mise en n.** *(d'un employé)* suspension; *Mil (d'un officier)* putting on half pay

nonagénaire [nɔnaʒenɛr] *adj, n* nonagenarian, ninety-year-old
non-agression [nɔnagresjɔ̃] *nf* non-aggression; **pacte de n.** non-aggression pact
non-alcoolisé [nɔnalkɔlize] *adj* non-alcoholic
non-aligné, *pl* **non-alignés** [nɔnaliɲe] *Pol* **1** *adj* (*pays*) nonaligned **2** *nm* **les non-alignés** the nonaligned countries
non-alignement [nɔnaliɲ(ə)mɑ̃] *nm Pol* nonalignment
nonante [nɔnɑ̃t] *adj, nm inv Belg, Suisse* ninety
non-assistance [nɔnasistɑ̃s] *nf Jur* **n. à personne en danger** failure to render assistance to a person in danger
non-autorisé [nɔnɔtɔrize, nɔ̃-] *adj Ordinat* (*nom de fichier etc*) illegal
non-banque *adj* non-bank
non-belligérance *nf* nonbelligerence
non-belligérant, -ante, *pl* **non-belligérant(e)s** *adj, n* nonbelligerent
nonce [nɔ̃s] *nm* **n. du Pape** Papal Nuncio
non-cessible *adj* (*billet etc*) not transferable
nonchalamment [nɔ̃ʃalamɑ̃] *adv* nonchalantly; **marcher n.** to saunter along
nonchalance [nɔ̃ʃalɑ̃s] *nf* nonchalance
nonchalant [nɔ̃ʃalɑ̃] *adj* nonchalant
nonciature [nɔ̃sjatyr] *nf* **(a)** (*charge d'un nonce*) nunciature **(b)** (*résidence*) nuncio's residence
non-combattant, *pl* **non-combattants** *adj, nm* non-combatant
non-comparution *nf* non-appearance
non-conciliation *nf* failure to settle out of court
non-confirmé *adj* unconfirmed
non-conformisme *nm Rel, Fig* nonconformism
non-conformiste, *pl* **non-conformistes** *adj, n Rel, Fig* nonconformist
non-conformité *nf* **n. d'un produit** non-conformity of a product, product non-conformity
non-connecté *adj Ordinat* off-line
non-cumul *nm* **n. des peines** concurrence of sentences
non-dit, *pl* **non-dits** *nm* **le n.** what is unspoken *or* unvoiced; **non-dits** unspoken *or* unvoiced comments; **un film riche en non-dits** a film full of meaningful silences
none [nɔn] *nf Antiq* (*heure*) ninth hour; **nones** (*jour*) nones
non-engagé, *pl* **non-engagés** [nɔnɑ̃gaʒe] *Pol* **1** *adj* neutral **2** *nm* neutral country
non-engagement [nɔnɑ̃gaʒmɑ̃] *nm Pol* neutrality
non-être [nɔnɛtr] *nm Phil* nonbeing, nonexistence
non-exécution [nɔnɛgzekysjɔ̃] *nf* (*d'un accord*) non-fulfilment; (*d'un contrat*) nonperformance
non-existence [nɔnɛgzistɑ̃s] *nf* nonexistence
non-ferreux, -euse *adj Métal* nonferrous
non-figuratif, -ive, *pl* **non-figuratifs, -ives** *Beaux-Arts* **1** *adj* nonfigurative **2** *n* nonfigurative artist
non-formaté *adj Ordinat* unformatted
non-fumeur, -euse, *pl* **non-fumeurs, -euses 1** *adj* nonsmoking; **fumeur ou n.?** smoking or nonsmoking? **2** *n* nonsmoker
non-gage *nm Aut* **certificat de n.** certificate of ownership
non-ingérence [nɔnɛ̃ʒerɑ̃s] *nf* noninterference
non-initialisé [nɔninisjalize, nɔ̃-] *adj Ordinat* uninitialized
non-initié, -ée, *pl* **non-initié(e)s** [nɔninisje] **1** *adj* uninitiated **2** *n* uninitiated person; **les non-initiés** the uninitiated
non-inscrit, -ite, *pl* **non-inscrit(e)s** [nɔnɛ̃skri] *n Pol* independent
non-intervention [nɔnɛ̃tɛrvɑ̃sjɔ̃] *nf* non-intervention
non-interventionniste, *pl* **non-inverventionnistes** [nɔnɛ̃tɛrvɑ̃sjɔnist] *adj, n* non-interventionist
non-jouissance *nf Jur* (*d'un bien*) nonenjoyment
non-justifié *adj Typ* unjustified, non-justified; **n. à droite** ragged right; **n. à gauche** ragged left
non-lieu, *pl* **non-lieux** *nm Jur* **bénéficier d'un n.** to be discharged through lack of evidence; **ordonnance** *ou* **arrêt de n.** nonsuit
non-modifiable *adj* (*billet etc*) not alterable
nonne [nɔn] *nf Rel* nun
non-négociable *adj* non-negotiable
nonnette [nɔnɛt] *nf* **(a)** *Rel F* young nun **(b)** *Culin* small iced gingerbread cake **(c)** (*oiseau*) tit
non-nuisible *adj* **n. à l'environnement** environmentally friendly, environment-friendly
nono, -ote [nono, -ɔt] *n Can F* idiot
nonobstant [nɔnɔpstɑ̃] *prép, adv Vieilli* notwithstanding; **ce n.** this notwithstanding
non-paiement *nm* nonpayment
nonpareil, -eille [nɔ̃parɛj] *adj Vieilli* peerless
non-polluant *adj* environmentally friendly
non-prolifération *nf* nonproliferation
non-recevoir *nm* **opposer une fin de n. à une réclamation** to refuse; *Jur* to put in a plea in bar of a claim
non-récupérable *adj Ordinat* non-recoverable
non-relationnel, elle *adj Ordinat* non-relational
non-remboursable *adj* non-refundable
non-représentation *nf Jur* **n. d'enfant** refusal to comply with the access *or* visiting rights of a child
non-résident, -ente, *pl* **non-résident(e)s** *n* nonresident
non-respect *nm Jur* (*d'une loi*) nonobservance
non-retour *nm* **point de n.** point of no return
non-salarié[1], -ée, *pl* **non-salarié(e)s 1** *adj* unsalaried **2** *n* self-employed person; **les non-salariés** the self-employed
non-sens *nm inv* **(a)** *Scol* (*dans une traduction*) meaningless word *or* phrase **(b) c'est un n.** it's (a) nonsense
non-spécialiste, *pl* **non-spécialistes** *n* nonspecialist
non-stop [nɔnstɔp] *adj inv, adv F* nonstop
non-structuré [nɔ̃stryktyre] *adj Ordinat* unstructured
non-suspendu *adj Aut* (*freins*) outboard
non-syndiqué, -ée, *pl* **non-syndiqués, -ées 1** *adj* (*employé*) non-union, *Am* non-unionized **2** *n* non-union *or Am* non-unionized worker
non-taxable *adj* non-dutiable
non-tissé [nɔ̃tise] *nm Tex* nonwoven material
non-trié [nɔ̃trije] *adj Ordinat* unsorted
non-usage [nɔnyzaʒ] *nm* non-use
non-valeur, *pl* **non-valeurs** *nf Jur* (*état*) unproductiveness; (*bien*) unproductive asset; *Fin* bad debt; (*créance*) worthless amount; **terres en n.** unproductive land
non-vérifié [nɔ̃verifje] *adj Compta* unaudited
non-viable *adj Méd* nonviable
non-violence *nf* nonviolence
non-violent, -ente, *pl* **non-violent(e)s 1** *n* supporter of nonviolence **2** *adj* nonviolent
non-voyant, -ante, *pl* **non-voyant(e)s** *n* unsighted person; **les non-voyants** the unsighted
nopal, -als [nɔpal] *nm Bot* nopal
nord [nɔr] **1** *nm, no pl* north; **au n., dans le n.** in the north; **au n. de Madrid** (to the) north of Madrid; **dans le n. de Madrid** in North Madrid; **borné au n. par la Belgique** bounded on the north by Belgium; **maison exposée au n.** house facing north; **les fenêtres sont orientées plein n.** the windows face directly north; **voyager vers le n.** to travel north *or* northward(s); **du n.** of/from the north; (*province*) northern; (*vent*) northerly, north; **elle est du n.** she's from the North; **le N. canadien** the Canadian North; **le grand N.** the frozen North; *F* **perdre le n.** (*s'égarer*) to lose one's bearings; (*paniquer*) to lose one's head; **gens du N.** northerners; **industriels du N.** northern industrialists

2 *adj inv* north; (*partie, quartier*) northern; **le pôle N.** the North Pole
nord-africain, -aine, *pl* **nord-africains, -aines 1** *adj* North African **2** *n* **N.** North African
nord-américain, -aine, *pl* **nord-américains, -aines 1** *adj* North American **2** *n* **N.** North American
nord-coréen, -enne, *pl* **nord-coréens, -ennes 1** *adj* North Korean **2** *n* **N.** North Korean
nord-est 1 *nm* **(a)** (*région, point cardinal*) northeast **(b)** (*vent*) northeast wind, northeaster, *F* nor'easter **2** *adj inv* northeast
nordique [nɔrdik] **1** *adj* Nordic; *Hist* Norse; **langues nordiques** Nordic *or* Scandinavian languages **2** *nm Ling* Norse **3** *n* **N.** Scandinavian
nordir [nɔrdir] *vi Naut* (*du vent*) to veer north(ward)
nordiste [nɔrdist] **1** *adj* **(a)** *US Hist* Northern **(b)** *Sp* (*club*) northern **2** *nm US Hist* Northerner
nord-nord-est *nm, adj inv* north-northeast
nord-nord-ouest *nm, adj inv* north-northwest
nord-ouest 1 *nm* **(a)** (*région, point cardinal*) northwest **(b)** (*vent*) northwest wind, northwester, *F* nor'wester **2** *adj inv* northwest
nord-vietnamien, -ienne, *pl* **nord-vietnamiens, -iennes 1** *adj* North Vietnamese **2** *n* **N.** North Vietnamese
NOREX [nɔrɛks] *Com* = source of information on standards and rules governing goods for export
noria [nɔrja] *nf* **(a)** (*machine*) noria **(b)** (*véhicules qui vont et viennent*) endless stream
normal, ale, -aux, -ales [nɔrmal, -o] **1** *adj* **(a)** (*dans la norme*) (*état, cours*) normal; **elle n'est pas dans son état n.** she's not her normal *or* usual self; **en temps n.** in *or* under normal circumstances

(b) (*naturel*) normal; **c'est tout à fait n. que la jeunesse se rebelle** it's only normal *or* natural for young people to rebel; **c'est bien n.** it's quite normal *or* natural; **tu trouves ça n. toi?** do you think that's all right *or* OK?; **ce n'est pas n.** it's not right **(que** that)

(c) (*moyen*) (*poids, taille*) standard; **cet enfant n'a pas encore atteint la taille normale pour son age** this child is still below average height for his age; **vitesse normale** normal, *or Spéc* rated speed

(d) (*intellectuellement*) (*personne*) normal
(e) *Typ* roman
2 *nf* **normale (a) la normale** normal, the norm; **la température est revenue à la normale** the temperature is back to normal; **intelligence/température au-dessus/au-dessous de la normale** above-/below-average intelligence/temperature; **température au-dessous des normales saisonnières** temperature below the seasonal norm *or* average
(b) *Univ F* **Normale Sup** = École normale supérieure

normalement [nɔrmalmɑ̃] *adv* normally

normalien, -ienne [nɔrmaljɛ̃, -jɛn] *n Scol* student/former student of a teacher training college; *Univ* student/former student of the École normale supérieure

normalisation [nɔrmalizasjɔ̃] *nf* **(a)** *Pol* normalization **(b)** *Ind* standardization

normalisé [nɔrmalize] *adj* (*produit*) standard

normaliser [nɔrmalize] *vt* (*relations*) to normalize; (*équipement*) to standardize

normalité [nɔrmalite] *nf* normality

normand, -ande [nɔrmɑ̃, -ɑ̃d] **1** *adj* **(a)** (*de Normandie*) Norman, (of) Normandy; **armoire normande** large rustic wardrobe **(b)** *Hist* Norman; **la conquête normande** the Norman Conquest **2** *n* **(a) N.** Norman; **c'est un fin N.** he's shrewd; **réponse de N.** non-committal *or* equivocal *or* evasive answer **(b)** *Hist* **les Normands** the Normans

Normandie [nɔrmɑ̃di] *nf* Normandy

norme [nɔrm] *nf* **(a)** (*règle*) norm, standard; **échapper à la n.** to be an exception; **être d'une intelligence qui échappe à la n.** to be exceptionally intelligent
(b) *Ind, Com* standard; **normes européennes** European standards; **jouet conforme aux normes de sécurité** toy which conforms to safety standards; **n. de production** production norm; **n. de productivité** productivity norm; **n. de travail** work standard; **n. technique** technical standard; **n. d'application** relevant standard; **normes d'application obligatoires** compulsory standards; **normes d'application volontaires** voluntary standards; **normes publicitaires** advertising standards
(c) *Math* norm

normographe [nɔrmɔgraf] *nm* stencil

norois, noroît [nɔrwa] *nm* (*vent*) northwest wind, northwester, nor'wester

Norvège [nɔrvɛʒ] *nf* Norway

norvégien, -ienne [nɔrveʒjɛ̃, -jɛn] **1** *adj* Norwegian **2** *nm Ling* Norwegian **3** *n* **N.** Norwegian **4** *nf* **norvégienne** round-stemmed boat

nos *voir* **notre**

nostalgie [nɔstalʒi] *nf* nostalgia; (*mal du pays*) homesickness; **j'ai la n. de ces temps-là** I look back on that time with nostalgia, I feel nostalgia for that time; **avoir la n. de son foyer** to long *or* yearn for home, to be homesick; **avoir la n. du pays** to be homesick; **penser à qch avec n.** to think of sth nostalgically *or* with nostalgia

nostalgique [nɔstalʒik] **1** *adj* (*humeur, souvenirs, sentiments, personne*) nostalgic **2** *n* nostalgic person

nostalgiquement [nɔstalʒikmɑ̃] *adv* nostalgically

nota [nɔta] *nm inv* (*en bas de texte*) footnote; (*en marge*) marginal note; **n. bene** [nɔtabene] nota bene, NB

notabilité [nɔtabilite] *nf* (*personne, caractère*) notability

notable [nɔtabl] **1** *adj* **(a)** (*remarquable*) notable, worthy of note; **sans variation n.** without appreciable change **(b)** (*personne*) notable, distinguished **2** *nm* notable (person), distinguished person, person of note *or* distinction; **les notables de la ville** the leading citizens, *Hum* the local worthies

notablement [nɔtabləmɑ̃] *adv* notably, appreciably

notaire [nɔtɛr] *nm Jur* notary (public); **par-devant n.** before a notary

notamment [nɔtamɑ̃] *adv* notably

notarié [nɔtarje] *adj Jur* certified by a notary; **acte n.** notarized deed

notation [nɔtasjɔ̃] *nf* **(a)** *Scol* (*d'un travail, d'un élève*) marking **(b)** (*par des symboles*) notation; *Ordinat* **n. hexadécimale** hex *or* hexadecimal code **(c)** *Fin* rating; *Bourse* **n. AAA** triple-A rating

note [nɔt] *nf* **(a)** (*mots, phrases*) note; **prendre des notes** to take (down) notes; **jeter quelques notes sur le papier** to jot down a few notes; **prendre n. de qch, prendre qch en n.** to note sth, to make a note of sth; **prendre bonne n. de qch** to take due note of sth; *Typ* **n. de** *ou* **en** *ou* **au bas de la page** footnote, footer; **n. de couverture** cover note; *Typ* **n. de fin de document** endnote; **n. marginale** note in the margin; **n. de renvoi** cross reference; **n. de la rédaction** editor's note; **notes prises en sténo(graphie)** shorthand notes
(b) *Scol, Univ* (*appréciation*) mark, *Am* grade; **bonne/mauvaise n.** good/bad mark; **notes trimestrielles** (end-of-term) report; **carnet** *ou* **relevé de notes** school report
(c) *Mus* note; **fausse n.** wrong note; *Fig* false note; *Mus* **donner la n.** (*aux chanteurs etc*) to sound the keynote; *Fig* **forcer la n.** to exaggerate; (*faire du zèle*) to overdo it; **sa robe n'était pas/ses blagues n'étaient pas dans la n.** her dress/his jokes struck the wrong note; **une n. d'originalité/de gaieté** a touch *or* note of originality/gaiety
(d) (*facture*), *Com* bill; (*dans un hôtel etc*) bill, *Am* check; **n. de téléphone** phone bill; *Fin* **n. de commission** commission note, fee note; **n. de crédit** credit note; **n. de débit** debit note; **n. de rappel** reminder

▶ **note: n. diplomatique** diplomatic note; **n. de frais** expense account; (*présentée après coup*) expenses; **mettre qch sur sa n. de frais** to put sth on one's expense account; *Admin* **n. de service** memorandum, memo

noté [nɔte] *adj* **(a) être bien/mal n.** (*d'élève, employé*) to have a good/bad record; (*de devoir*) to have received a good/poor mark **(b)** *Bourse* **n. triple "A"** triple A rated

notebook [nɔtbuk] *nm Ordinat* notebook

noter [nɔte] *vt* **(a)** (*mettre par écrit*) to note *or* put *or* jot down, to make a note of; **vas-y, je note** go ahead, I've got something to write with; **n. un passage** to mark a passage; **n. une commande** to log *or* to note an order; **n. la consommation de combustible** to keep a note of fuel consumption; **n. que** to note down *or* make a note that
(b) (*remarquer*) to note, to take notice of; **à n. : les bus ne circulent pas le dimanche** note: there are no buses on Sundays; **notez bien cela** take good note of this, note this well; **il est à n. que ...** it is to be noted that ...; **c'est bon à n.** it's worthy noting *or* making a note of; **notez bien ce que je vous dis** mark my words; **note bien que cela n'a pas d'importance/je pourrais faire autrement** but it really doesn't matter/I could always do something else; **très bien, chef, c'est noté** *ou* **je note** OK boss, I've got it
(c) *Scol, Univ* (*travail*) to mark, *Am* to grade

notice [nɔtis] *nf* **(a)** (*notes sommaires*) note **(b)** (*préface de livre*) note **(c)** (*mode d'emploi*) instructions, directions; (*livret*) instruction book(let), handbook, manual; **n. bibliographique** bibliographical note; **n. explicative** directions for use, explanatory leaflet; **n. du constructeur** manufacturer's instructions; **n. technique** technical specification

notification [nɔtifikasjɔ̃] *nf Jur* notification, notice; **recevoir n. de qch** to receive notification *or* be notified of sth

notifier [nɔtifje] *vt* (*impf, pr sub* **n. notifiions**) (*faire savoir*) **n. qch à qn** to notify sb of sth; *Jur* **n. son consentement** to signify one's consent **(à qn** to sb); **on lui notifia qu'il aurait à déménager dans les vingt-quatre heures** he received notice to quit within twenty-four hours

notion [nosjɔ̃] *nf* **(a)** (*concept*) notion, concept; **l'amitié est une n. abstraite** friendship is an abstract notion *or* concept; **perdre la n. du temps/de la réalité** to lose track of time/all sense of reality **(b)** (*connaissance succincte*) **des notions de** a smattering of, the basics of; **avoir des notions de chimie/russe** to have a smattering of *or* to know the basics of chemistry/Russian

notoire [nɔtwar] *adj* (*connu de tous*) well-known, *Péj* notorious; **son avarice est n.** his miserliness is notorious *or* legendary

notoirement [nɔtwarmɑ̃] *adv* manifestly, *Péj* notoriously; **fait n. faux** manifestly false fact; **un malfrat n. connu** a notorious gangster

notoriété [nɔtɔrjete] *nf* **(a)** (*d'un fait, d'une personne*) reputation; **avoir de la n.** to be well known, to have a (good) reputation; **cela lui a valu une certaine n.** that brought *or* earned him a certain reputation; **il est de n. publique que ...** it is public *or* common knowledge that ...; *Mktg* **n. de la marque** brand awareness **(b)** *Jur* **acte de n.** attested affidavit

notre, nos [nɔtr, no] *adj poss* [①A30,8; B19-20,E,1] our; (*de roi, de reine*) Our; **n. oncle et n. tante** our uncle and (our) aunt; **n. père et n. mère**, *Litt* **nos père et mère** our father and mother; **ils ont mis n. chapeau et nos gants** they put on our hats and (our) gloves; **nous avons pris n. sac** (*il n'y a qu'un sac*) we took our bag; (*chacun a son sac*) we took our bags; **nous avons pris nos sacs** we took our bags; *F* **nous aurons n. chambre à nous** (*il y a une chambre*) we will have our own room; *F* **n. imbécile de frère** our idiot of a brother; *F* **nos artistes de maris** our artist-husbands; **nous retrouvons n. héros dix ans plus tard ...** we meet our hero again ten years later ...; *F* **nous avons n. vendredi** we've got Friday off

nôtre [notr] **(a)** *pron poss* [①A30,8; B20,E,2] **le n., la n., les nôtres** ours; **il ressemble au n.** it looks like ours; **nous voulons bien te donner du n.** you can have some of ours; **nous n'en**

avons pas besoin, nous avons le n. we don't need it, we've got our own; **tu n'en as pas besoin, tu as le n.** you don't need it, you've got ours; **les deux nôtres** our two, the two of ours, both of ours; (*en insistant*) our own two; *F* **le n. de bébé est plus intelligent!** our baby is more intelligent!; *F* **à la n.!** (*en buvant*) here's to us!

(**b**) *nm* **le n.** (*ce qui nous appartient*) ours; **nous devrions y mettre du n.** we should do our share

(**c**) *nmpl* **les nôtres** (*notre famille*) our family, *Am* our folks; (*nos partisans*) our followers; (*nos coéquipiers*) our team-mates; **est-il des nôtres?** (*de notre côté*) is he one of us?; **vous serez des nôtres, n'est-ce-pas?** (*pour dîner*) you will join us, won't you?

(**d**) *adj poss Litt* ours; **un n. cousin** a cousin of ours; **nous ferons nôtres ses principes** we shall adopt these principles of his; **nous faisons nôtres les félicitations qu'ils vous adressent** we join them in congratulating you

Notre-Dame [nɔtrədam] *nf Rel* Our Lady; **la fête de N.** the feast of the Assumption

nouba [nuba] *nf* (**a**) *F* party; **faire la n.** to party (**b**) (*musique*) (Algerian) military band

noue¹ [nu] *nf* (*terre grasse*) marshy meadow, water meadow

noue² *nf Constr* (**a**) (*arête*) valley (**b**) (*tuile*) gutter tile; (*bande de plomb*) flashing

nouer [nwe] **1** *vt* (*ficelle, corde, ruban*) to tie, to knot; **n. qch serré** to knot sth tightly, to make a tight knot in sth; **n. ses cheveux** to tie up one's hair; **n. sa cravate** to knot one's tie; **n. ses lacets** to tie (up) one's laces; **n. son tablier** to tie one's apron; **elle noua ses bras autour du cou de son ami** she wrapped her arms around her friend's neck; **avoir la gorge nouée** to have a lump in one's throat; **avoir l'estomac noué** to have a knot in one's stomach; **n. conversation avec qn** to enter into conversation with sb; **n. des relations avec qn** to establish relations with sb; **n. l'intrigue d'un roman** to bring the action of a novel to a head *or* climax

2 *vi* (*de fleur*) to set

3 se nouer *vpr* (**a**) **se n. les cheveux** to tie up one's hair

(**b**) (*se faire*) **des amitiés qui se nouent** friendships which are formed *or* which form

(**c**) *Littér, Th, Cin* to take shape; **l'intrigue se noue dès le premier acte** the plot takes shape right from Act One

noueux, -euse [nwø, -øz] *adj* (*ficelle, bois*) knotty; (*tronc d'arbre, mains, doigts*) gnarled

nougat [nuga] *nm* nougat

nougatine [nugatin] *nf* nougatine

nouille [nuj] *nf* (**a**) *Culin* noodle (**b**) *F* (*personne molle*) drip; (*bébête*) dimwit, noodle

noumène [numɛn] *nm Phil* noumenon

nounou [nunu] *nf Enf F* nanny

nounours [nunurs] *nm* teddy (bear)

nourri [nuri] *adj* (**a**) (*alimenté*) fed; **bien n.** well fed; **mal n.** undernourished, underfed (**b**) (*riche*) (*style*) rich; (*ligne en dessin*) broad, firm; (*ton, son*) full; (*applaudissements*) sustained, prolonged; **discussion nourrie** heated debate, lively discussion; *Mil* **feu n.** heavy *or* sustained fire

nourrice [nuris] *nf* (**a**) (*assistante maternelle*) child minder; **n. agréée** registered child minder (**b**) (*personne qui allaite*) (wet) nurse; **mettre un enfant en n.** to put a child out to nurse (**c**) *Tech* auxiliary tank, service tank; *Aut* (*de carburant*) spare can

nourricier, -ière [nurisje, -jɛr] **1** *adj Bot* (*sève, suc*) nutritive; *Anat* (*artère, canal*) nutrient; *Litt* (*terre*) nourishing **2** *n* **père n.** foster father; **mère nourricière** foster mother

nourrir [nurir] **1** *vt* (**a**) (*donner à manger à*) (*personnes, animaux*) to feed (**de, avec** with, on); **nourri au biberon/sein** bottle-/breast-fed; **n. sa famille** to provide for *or* feed one's family; **j'ai cinq personnes à n.** I've five mouths to feed; **être logé (et) nourri (blanchi)** to get (one's) bed and board; **avoir 3 000 francs par mois logé et nourri** to get 3000 francs a month with board and lodging; **travail qui nourrit son homme** job that provides a living; **le lait nourrit** milk is nourishing; *Fig* **lectures qui nourrissent l'esprit** reading that improves the mind; *Mus* **n. le son** to give fullness *or* body to the tone

(**b**) (*de crème, lotion*) (*peau, visage, cuir*) to nourish; (*feu*) to feed

(**c**) *Litt* (*entretenir*) (*haine*) to foster; (*idées de vengeance, illusion etc*) to harbour, *US* to harbor; (*espoir*) to cherish, to harbour, to entertain; (*projet*) to nurse; **je nourris l'espoir de le revoir** I cherish the hope of seeing him again

2 se nourrir *vpr* (*manger*) to eat; **il refuse de se n.** he won't eat; **chasser pour se n.** to hunt for one's food; **il gagne juste de quoi se n.** he earns just enough to live on; **se n. de lait/fruits** to live on milk/fruit

nourrissant [nurisɑ̃] *adj* (*repas, aliments*) nourishing, nutritious; (*crème pour le visage, le cuir*) nourishing

nourrisseur [nurisœr] *nm* (**a**) (*de bétail, de boucherie*) stockbreeder; (*de vaches laitières*) dairyman (**b**) *Tech* (*pour l'alimentation des animaux*) feed roll

nourrisson [nurisɔ̃] *nm* young baby, infant

nourriture [nurityr] *nf* (*aliments*) food; **retrouver une n. saine et équilibrée** to get back to a healthy and balanced diet; **priver qn de n.** to starve sb, to deprive sb of food; **il refuse toute n. depuis trois jours** he has been refusing food *or* refusing to eat for three days; **n. de l'esprit** food for the mind; **les nourritures terrestres** the fruits of the earth

nous [nu] *pron pers* [①**A26**,a-b; **B17-18**,1-2] (**a**) (*sujet*) we; *F* **n. sommes allés au restaurant avec mon mari** (*lui et moi*) me and my husband went to the restaurant

(**b**) (*objet direct*) us; (*objet indirect*) to us; **il ne n. connaît pas** he does not know us; **lisez-le-n.** read it to us; **elle n. en a parlé** she spoke to us about it

(**c**) [①**A29**; **B26**,D] (*réfléchi*) **n. n. réchauffons** we are warming ourselves; **n. n. sommes versé du vin** we poured ourselves some wine; **n. n. battions avec l'ennemi** we were fighting the enemy

(**d**) (*réciproque*) **n. n. connaissons** we know each other

(**e**) **n. deux/tous** (*sujet*) both/all of us, we two/all; (*objet*) both/all of us, us two/all; **c'est n. qui sommes fautifs** we are to blame, it is us *or surtout Fml* we who are to blame; **n. autres Anglais** we English; **un ami à n.** a friend of ours; **ce livre est à n.** that book is ours *or* belongs to us; **bon, à n. maintenant** so, we can have a talk now; **à n. deux** (*sur ton menaçant*) let's have a little talk; (*avant de se battre*) let's fight it out; **c'est à n. de jouer** it's our turn; **il était avec n.** he was with us; **entre n. (soit dit)** (this is) between ourselves

(**f**) (**nous** *de majesté ou de modestie, employé pour* **je**) we; **n. sommes désolé de l'apprendre** we are grieved to hear it

nous-même *pron pers* (*après* **nous** *de majesté, de modestie*) ourself *voir* **même**

nous-mêmes *pron pers* ourselves; **nous l'avons fait n.** we did it ourselves *voir* **même**

nouveau, -el, -elle, -eaux [nuvo, -ɛl] **1** *adj* (**nouvel** *is used before m sing nouns beginning with a vowel or h mute*) (**a**) (*récent*) new; **nouvelles voitures** new cars; **livres nouveaux** new books; **il est n., ce manteau?** is this coat new?; **techniques nouvelles** new *or* up-to-date techniques; **je suis n. dans ce métier** I'm new to this business; *F* **tu sais ce que c'est, tout n. tout beau, ça lui passera** you know what it's like, it's all new and exciting at first, but she'll get over it; **il n'y a rien de n.** there's nothing new, there are no new developments; **il y a quelqu'un de n. au bureau** there's someone new in the office; **c'est n. ça!** that's new!; **il n'y a rien de n. sous le soleil** there's nothing new under the sun; **nouvel utilisateur** first-time user

(**b**) (*qui succède à un autre*) (*télévision, directeur, épisode, gouvernement, adresse, collection*) new; **les nouveaux pères** modern(-day) fathers; **nouvelle technologie** new technology; *Fin* **nouvelle émission** (*d'actions*) new issue; **nouveaux emprunts** new borrowings; *Cin etc* **nouvelle version** remake; **faire une nouvelle version de** to do a remake of, to reversion; **jusqu'à nouvel ordre** until further notice; **que font-ils au sujet des enfants? – jusqu'à nouvel ordre, rien** what are they doing about the children? – they haven't decided yet; **la nouvelle Marilyn Monroe** the new Marilyn Monroe; **la nouvelle mode** the latest fashion; **la nouvelle génération** the new *or* rising generation; **j'ai besoin d'une nouvelle voiture** I need a new car; **il met tous les jours une nouvelle chemise** he wears a clean *or* different shirt every day; **n. et amélioré** (*sur emballage*) new improved

(**c**) (*autre*) new; **sous un jour n.** in a new light; **un n. chapitre** a new *or* fresh chapter; **une nouvelle raison/hausse des prix** a further *or* an additional *or* another reason/price rise; **se faire de nouveaux amis** (*supplémentaires*) to make new friends; **elle a eu un nouvel enfant** she has had another child; **faire de nouveaux efforts** to make new *or* fresh efforts; *Jur* **n. procès** retrial

(**d**) (*nouvellement produit*) (*carotte, pomme de terre*) new; **du vin n.** new *or* young wine; **le beaujolais n.** the new Beaujolais *or* Beaujolais nouveau; **herbe nouvelle** young grass

(**e**) (*avec une fonction adverbiale*) **le nouvel arrivé** the newcomer; **les nouveaux arrivés** the newcomers; **les nouveaux élus** those newly elected; **les nouveaux convertis** the new converts, the newly converted; **n. pays industrialisé** newly industrialized country

(**f**) **à n., de n.** (once *or* over) again; **recommencer à n.** to start afresh; **elle est de n. malade** she is ill again; **la terre a à n.** *ou* **de n. tremblé en Californie** there has been another earthquake in California

2 *nm* **il y a du n.** there's been a new development; **j'ai du n. au sujet de ...** I've got news about ...; **tu as du n. pour ton billet d'avion?** have you heard anything more about your plane ticket?

3 *n* (*personne*) new person; *Scol* new pupil

▶ **nouveau: n. franc** new franc; *Beaux-Arts* **n. réalisme** New Realism; **n. réaliste** New Realist; *Péj* **n. riche** *n, adj* nouveau riche; **n. roman** nouveau roman, new novel; **nouvelle cuisine** nouvelle cuisine; **N. Monde** New World; **N. testament** New Testament; **nouveaux pauvres** new poor; **Nouvel An** New Year; **passer le Nouvel An chez des amis** to spend New Year's Eve at friends'; *Cin* **la Nouvelle Vague** the New Wave

nouveau-né, -née, *pl* **nouveau-nés, -nées 1** *adj* newborn **2** *n* newborn child

nouveauté [nuvote] *nf* **(a)** (*caractère nouveau*) newness, novelty; *F* **tu sais qu'il trompe sa femme? – c'est pas une n.!** do you know he's cheating on his wife? – that's nothing new!; **recherche constante de la n.** constant search for something new *or* for novelty

(b) (*produit récent*) (*livre*) new publication; (*invention*) new invention; **le cinéma n'est plus une n.** the cinema is no longer a novelty *or* anything new; **vous trouverez ce disque/livre au rayon des nouveautés** you'll find that record in the new releases rack/that book on the new titles shelf

(c) *Vieilli* **magasin de nouveautés** draper's shop, *Am* dry goods store; **les nouveautés de printemps** the new spring fashions

nouvelle [nuvɛl] *nf* **(a)** [①**A10**,d] (*annonce d'un événement*) (piece of) news; **nouvelles** news (**de qn** of sb, about sb); **bonne/mauvaise n.** good/bad news; **j'ai une bonne n.!** (I've) good news!; **une n. plutôt décevante** a rather disappointing piece of news; **première n.!** that's news to me!, that's the first I've heard of it!; **la n. de sa mort** the news of his death; **la n. a été confirmée par le gouvernement** the news *or* report was confirmed by the government; **vous connaissez la n.?** have you heard the news *or* the latest?

(b) (*informations*) **nouvelles (de qch/qn)** news (of *or* about sth/sb); **demander** *ou* **(aller) prendre des nouvelles de (la santé de) qn** to inquire *or* ask about sb('s health); **j'ai eu des nouvelles de Pierre** (*par lui-même*) I've had news from *or* I've heard from Pierre; (*par qn d'autre*) I've had news about *or* of Pierre; **envoyez-moi de vos nouvelles** let me know how you're doing; **on n'eut plus jamais de leurs nouvelles** they were never heard of again; **je suis sans nouvelles de lui** (*directement*) I've had no news from him, I've not heard from him; (*indirectement*) I've had no news of *or* about him; **aux dernières nouvelles il était à Lima** he was last heard of in Lima; **les nouvelles vont vite!** news travels fast!; **goûtez cela, vous m'en direz des nouvelles** taste this, I'm sure you'll like it; **vous aurez de mes nouvelles!** you'll be hearing from me!; **pas de nouvelles, bonnes nouvelles** no news is good news

(c) *Journ* news item; **les nouvelles** the news; **dernières nouvelles** late news; **nouvelles de dernière minute** stop press

(d) *Littér* short story

Nouvelle-Angleterre *nf* New England

Nouvelle-Calédonie [nuvɛlkaledɔni] *nf* New Caledonia

Nouvelle-Écosse *nf* Nova Scotia

Nouvelle-Galles du Sud *nf* New South Wales

Nouvelle-Guinée *nf* New Guinea

nouvellement [nuvɛlmɑ̃] *adv* newly, recently

Nouvelle-Orléans [nuvɛlɔrleɑ̃] *nf* New Orleans

Nouvelles-Hébrides [nuvɛlzebrid] *nfpl* New Hebrides

Nouvelle-Zélande [nuvɛlzelɑ̃d] *nf* New Zealand

nouvelliste [nuvelist] *n* short-story writer

nova, *pl* **novæ** [nɔva, -ə] *nf Astron* nova

novateur, -trice [nɔvatœr, -tris] **1** *adj* innovative **2** *n* innovator

novembre [nɔvɑ̃br] *nm* [①**A75-6**,B-C; **B58-9**,B-C] November; **en n.** in November; **au mois de n.** in (the month of) November; **le premier n.** (on) the first of November, (on) November the first

novice [nɔvis] **1** *n* (*personne sans expérience*) novice, beginner; (*au couvent*) novice; (*jeune marin*) junior seaman **2** *adj* **être n. à** *ou* **dans qch** to be new to *or* inexperienced in sth

noviciat [nɔvisja] *nm Rel* noviciate, novitiate

noyade [nwajad] *nf* **(a)** drowning; **sauver qn de la n.** to save sb from drowning; **mort par n.** death by drowning **(b)** *Hist Fr* execution by drowning

noyau, -aux [nwajo] *nm* **(a)** (*de fruit*) stone, *Am* pit; **fruit à n.** stone fruit; **enlever** *ou* **retirer le n. d'un fruit** to stone *or Am* pit a fruit; **n. de cerise** cherry stone *or Am* pit

(b) [①**A13**,8] (*centre*) (*d'atome, de cellule, de comète*) nucleus; (*de la terre*) core; **n. de bombe nucléaire** nuclear bomb core

(c) (*petit groupe*) **un n. de joueurs** a small group of players; **un n. d'opposants/d'irréductibles** a small group of opponents/hardliners; **un n. d'amis** a small circle of friends; **le n. dur** the hard core; *Bourse* group of stable shareholders chosen for a company by the government on its flotation; **noyaux de résistance** pockets of resistance

(d) *Archit* (*d'escalier*) newel; **escalier à n. plein** winding staircase

(e) (*Él d'armature, Métal de moule*) core; *Ordinat* node; *Géol* **n. volcanique** volcanic bomb

noyautage [nwajotaʒ] *nm Pol* infiltration

noyauter [nwajote] *vt Pol* (*syndicat, parti, organisation*) to infiltrate

noyé, -ée [nwaje] **1** *adj* (*par noyade*) **mourir n.** to die by drowning; *Fig* **être n.** to be out of one's depth **2** *n* drowned person; **secours aux noyés** first aid for the drowning; **on a repêché un n. dans la rivière** a drowned man was fished out of the river

noyer[1] [nwaje] *nm* (*arbre*) walnut (tree); (*bois*) walnut; **n. (blanc) d'Amérique** hickory

noyer[2] **(je noie, n. noyons; je noierai) 1** *vt* **(a)** (*personne, animal*) to drown; (*la terre etc*) to swamp, to inundate, to deluge; (*soute*) to flood; **les polders ont été noyés sous des mètres cubes d'eau** the polders were submerged under several cubic metres of water; **n. une rébellion dans le sang** to quash a rebellion with bloodshed; *Fig* **n. son chagrin (dans l'alcool)** to drown one's sorrows (in drink); **noyé dans la foule** lost in the crowd; **n. le poisson** (*à la ligne*) to play the fish; *Fig* to confuse the issue deliberately, to muddy the waters

(b) *Aut* **n. le moteur** to flood the engine

(c) (*mouiller abondamment*) **les larmes noyaient son visage/ses joues** his face was/his cheeks were drenched with tears, tears poured down his face/cheeks; **yeux noyés de larmes** eyes brimming with tears; **elle avait les yeux noyés de larmes** her eyes were brimming with tears; **n. la sauce** to make the sauce too thin; **n. le vin** to drown the wine

(d) (*recouvrir entièrement*) (*de brouillard, brume*) to shroud, to envelop; **le village était noyé dans la brume** *ou* **noyé de brume** the village was shrouded *or* enveloped in mist; **la chambre était noyée dans la pénombre/de lumière** the room was shrouded in darkness/bathed in light; **les points essentiels sont noyés dans le détail** the essential points are buried *or* lost in too many details

(e) (*contours, couleurs*) to blend, to blur

(f) *Constr* to sink in cement; (*vis*) to countersink; (*clou*) to drive in flush

2 se noyer *vpr* (*mourir par noyade*) (*accidentellement*) to be drowned, to drown; (*volontairement*) to drown oneself; *Fig* **se n. dans les détails/des explications** to get bogged down in details/in explanations; **elle se noierait dans un verre d'eau** she makes a mountain out of a molehill

NPI [ɛnpei] *nm* (*abrév* **nouveau pays industrialisé**) NIC

nu [ny] **1** *adj* **(a)** (*dévêtu*) (*personne*) naked; (*épaules, bras, jambe*) bare; *Beaux-Arts* nude; **mettez-vous torse nu** strip to the waist; **il était torse nu** *ou* **nu jusqu'à la ceinture** he was stripped to the waist; **être tout nu** to be stark naked; **se baigner tout nu** to bathe in the nude; **avoir les seins nus** to be topless, to have bare breasts; **nu comme la main** *ou* **comme un ver** stark naked, in the buff; **danseuse nue** striptease artist; **(NOTE nu** *before the noun that it qualifies is invariable and is joined to the noun by a hyphen*) **aller tête nue** *ou* **nu-tête** to go bareheaded *or* without anything on one's head; **aller pieds nus** *ou* **nu-pieds** to go barefoot; **se battre à main(s) nue(s)** to fight with bare fists; **la boxe à main(s) nue(s)** bare-knuckle boxing

(b) *Fig* (*style*) plain, unadorned; (*épée*) unsheathed, naked; **la vérité (toute) nue** the plain *or* naked truth; *Él* **fil nu** bare wire

(c) (*dégarni*) (*paysage, arbre, pièce, mur*) bare

2 *nm Beaux-Arts* (*personne, œuvre*) nude; **le nu** (*genre*) the nude; **mettre à nu** to lay bare, to expose, to uncover; (*fil électrique*) to strip; **il a mis son cœur à nu** he laid bare his heart; *Équitation Vieilli* **monter un cheval à nu** to ride (a horse) bareback

nuage [nɥaʒ] *nm* cloud; **nuages pommelés** fleecy *or* fluffy clouds; **nuages en flocons** fluffy clouds; **ciel couvert** *ou* **chargé de nuages** overcast *or* cloudy sky; **n. de poussière/fumée/sauterelles** cloud of dust/smoke/locusts; **n. radioactif** cloud of radioactive dust; **sans nuages** (*ciel*) cloudless; *Fig* (*vie, avenir*) unclouded; *Fig* **bonheur sans nuages** perfect bliss; *Fig* **un n. de tristesse assombrissait**

son front her face was clouded with sadness; *Fig* **être dans les nuages** to have one's head in the clouds, to be daydreaming; **n. de lait** drop *or* dash of milk

nuageux, -euse [nɥaʒø, -øz] *adj* (*temps*) cloudy; (*ciel*) overcast, cloudy; **masse nuageuse** cloud mass

nuance [nɥɑ̃s] *nf* **(a)** (*de couleur*) shade, hue; **toutes les nuances de bleu** all shades of blue

(b) (*légère trace*) **une n. d'amertume/de mépris/de regrets** a touch *or* hint *or* suggestion of bitterness/contempt/regret

(c) (*subtilité*) nuance; (*légère différence*) slight *or* subtle difference; **les nuances de la langue** the nuances of the language; **récit tout en nuances** story full of nuances; **je ne saisis pas la n.** I don't quite see the difference; **il y a une n.!** there's a slight difference!; **j'ai dit peut-être, pas oui, n.!** I said perhaps, not yes, there's a slight difference!; *Fig* **il est sans nuances** he sees everything in black and white

(d) *Mus* nuance; **il joue sans nuances** he plays without any light and shade

nuancé [nɥɑ̃se] *adj* (*couleur, ton*) subtle; *Fig* (*discours, propos, attitude*) full of nuances; **ses réponses sont toujours très nuancées** he always qualifies his answers a lot

nuancer [nɥɑ̃se] *vt* **(je nuançai(s); n. nuançons)** **(a)** (*en dessin, peinture*) (*couleurs*) to shade; (*mélanger*) to blend **(de** with); **n. une couleur avec une autre** to shade one colour into another **(b)** (*modérer*) (*pensée, jugement, propos*) to qualify **(c)** *Mus* **n. son jeu** to introduce light and shade into one's playing

nuancier [nɥɑ̃sje] *nm* (*de couleurs*), *Com* sample card *or* chart; *Phot* colour chart; *Aut* graduated tint shadeband

nubile [nybil] *adj* nubile, marriageable; *Sociol* **âge n.** age of nubility

nubilité [nybilite] *nf* nubility

nucléaire [nykleɛr] **1** *adj* **(a)** *Phys, Mil* (*énergie, fission, armes*) nuclear; **particule n.** elementary particle **(b)** *Biol* (*membrane*) nuclear **(c)** *Sociol* **la famille n.** the nuclear family **2** *nm* **le n.** nuclear power

nucléé [nyklee] *adj Biol* (*cellule*) nucleate

nucléique [nykleik] *adj* (*acide*) nucleic

nucléole [nykleɔl] *nm Biol* nucleolus

nucléon [nykleɔ̃] *nm Phys* nucleon

nucléonique [nykleɔnik] *Phys* **1** *adj* nucleonic **2** *nf* nucleonics

nucléus [nykleys] *nm Biol* nucleus

nudisme [nydism] *nm* nudism

nudiste [nydist] *n* nudist

nudité [nydite] *nf* **(a)** (*de personne*) nudity, nakedness; (*de rocher, de mur*) bareness; *Fig* **l'horreur étalée dans toute sa n.** the horror displayed in all its starkness **(b)** *Beaux-Arts* nude (figure)

nue [ny] *nf Arch, Litt* high cloud(s); **nues** skies; **l'oiseau fendait les nues** the bird was cleaving its way through the skies; *Fig* **porter qn/qch aux nues** to laud *or* praise sb/sth to the skies; *Litt* **se perdre dans les nues** to have one's head (completely) in the clouds, to be lost in the clouds *or* in daydreams; *Fig* **tomber des nues** to be flabbergasted, to be thunderstruck

nuée [nɥe] *nf Litt* cloud, storm cloud; (*d'insectes, de criquets*) cloud, swarm; *Fig* **une n. de journalistes/touristes** a horde *or* swarm of journalists/tourists; **n. ardente** nuée ardente (*cloud of ash, gas etc*)

nu(e)-propriétaire, *pl* **nu(e)s-propriétaires** *n* reversionary owner

nue-propriété, *pl* **nues-propriétés** *nf* reversionary ownership

nuire [nɥir] (*ppr* **nuisant**; *pp* **nui**; *pr ind* **je nuis, n. nuisons**; *pr sub* **je nuise**; *p hist* **je nuisis**; *fu* **je nuirai**) **1** *vi* (*desservir*) **n. à qn/à qch** (*de personne*) to harm sb/sth; (*de chose*) to harm *or* be harmful to sb/sth; **cela ne nuira en rien** it won't do any harm; **cela nuira à sa réputation** it will damage *or* harm *or* be harmful to his reputation; **n. aux intérêts de qn** to prejudice *or* harm *or* damage sb's interests; **le tabac nuit gravement à la santé** smoking seriously damages your health; **dans l'intention de n.** maliciously; *Prov* **abondance de biens ne nuit pas** you can't have too much of a good thing; *Prov* **trop parler nuit** too much talking is harmful

2 se nuire *vpr* to do oneself (a great deal of) harm

nuisance [nɥizɑ̃s] *nf* nuisance; **nuisances acoustiques** noise pollution; **nuisances chimiques** chemical pollution

nuisette [nɥizɛt] *nf* baby doll (nightie)

nuisibilité [nɥizibilite] *nf* harmfulness

nuisible [nɥizibl] **1** *adj* harmful (**à** to); **plantes nuisibles** noxious plants; **animaux nuisibles** vermin, pests **2** *nm* pest; **les nuisibles** vermin, pests

nuit [nɥi] *nf* **(a)** night; **la n. dernière** last night; **cette n.** tonight; (*passée*) last night; **cela s'est passé dans la n. de samedi à dimanche** it happened during Saturday night *or* the night of Saturday to Sunday; **la n. où il est mort** the night (when) he died; **bonne n.!** good night; **as-tu passé une bonne n.?** did you have a good night?; **veiller jusqu'à une heure avancée de la n.** to sit up far into the night; **passer la n. à faire qch** to stay up *or* spend all night doing sth; **on a passé la n. à faire la fête** we made a night of it; **passer la n. chez des amis** to stay overnight *or* the night with friends; **passer la n. à l'hôtel** to spend *or* stay the night at a hotel; **une chambre à 200 francs la n.** a room at 200 francs a *or* per night; **le train/bateau/voyage de n.** the night train/boat *or* ferry/journey; **vêtements de n.** nightwear; **médecin de n.** night doctor; *Beaux-Arts* **effet de n.** night effect; **être de n.** to be on night shift *or* night duty *or F* nights; **voyager de n.** *ou* **la n.** to travel by night *or* at night; **conduire de n.** to drive at night *or* in the dark; **n. et jour** [nɥiteʒur] night and day; **il ne passera pas la n.** he won't last the night; **je n'ai pas dormi de la n.** I didn't sleep a wink all night; **le bébé fait ses nuits** the baby sleeps through the night; **il commence à faire n.** night is falling, it is growing *or* getting dark; **il fait déjà n.** it is dark already; **à la n. tombante** at nightfall, at dusk; **une fois la n. tombée, à (la) n. tombée** after dark; **la n. porte conseil** it would be best to sleep on it; *Prov* **la n. tous les chats sont gris** all cats are grey in the dark

(b) *Fig* darkness; *Litt* **la n. de l'ignorance** the darkness of ignorance; **perdu dans la n. des temps** lost in the mists of time; **c'est le jour et la n.** they're (like) chalk and cheese

▶ **nuit**: *Cin* **n. américaine** day for night; **n. blanche** sleepless night; **passer une n. blanche** (*par insomnie*) to spend a sleepless night; (*volontairement*) to stay up all night; **n. bleue** night of terror; **n. d'hôtel** (*hôtellerie*) bed-night; **payer une n. d'hôtel** to pay for a night at a hotel; *Hist* **la N. des longs couteaux** the Night of the Long Knives; **n. de noces** wedding night; **la n. de la Saint-Jean** Midsummer Night

nuitamment [nɥitamɑ̃] *adv Litt* by night

nuitée [nɥite] *nf* (*hôtellerie*) overnight stay, bed-night; **deux nuitées pour quatre personnes** two nights for four people; **la n. va de midi à midi le lendemain** a night runs from noon to noon the next day

nul, nulle [nyl] **1** *adj* **(a)** (*inexistant*) (*différence, risques, écart, récolte*) nil; (*élection*) null and void, invalid; **rendre n.** to nullify, to annul; *Sp* **score n. zéro (à) zéro** (*en fin de match*) match drawn nil-nil; (*à la mi-temps*) score nil-nil; **le score est n.** (*en fin de match*) the game is drawn, the result is a draw; (*à la mi-temps*) neither team has scored yet, the game so far is drawn; **match n.** draw, drawn match; **faire match n.** to draw, to tie; **bulletin (de vote) n.** spoilt (ballot) paper; **le solde est n.** the balance is nil; *Phys* **tension nulle** zero tension; *Jur* **n. et non avenu** invalid, null and void

(b) *F* (*qui ne vaut rien*) (*réponse, personne*) useless, hopeless; (*film, livre, chanson, blague*) rubbish, *très F* crap; (*argument*) useless; *Vulg* **c'est n. à chier!** it's a load of crap!

(c) *F* (*incompétent*) (*élève, employé*) hopeless, useless; **être n. en qch** to be hopeless *or* useless at sth

2 *adj indéf* [①B60,B] (*avec* **ne** *exprimé ou compris*) no; *Litt* **n. espoir** no hope; **il n'a nulle raison de se plaindre** he has no reason to complain; **sans nulle vanité** without boasting; **n. doute qu'il y serait parvenu** there's no doubt that he would have managed it; *Litt* **à nul(le) autre pareil(le)** unparalleled; **n. autre que moi ne le sait** I alone know of it

3 *pron indéf* no one, nobody; *Prov* **n. n'est prophète en son pays** no man is a prophet in his own country; **à l'impossible n. n'est tenu** you can't be expected to do the impossible

nullard, -arde [nylar, -ard] *très F* **1** *adj* (*personne*) useless, hopeless **2** *n* dimwit, plonker

nullement [nylmɑ̃] *adv* (*avec* **ne** *exprimé ou compris*) not at all, by no means; **cela vous dérange-t-il? – n.!** does that bother you? – not at all! *or* by no means!; **nous ne sommes n. surpris** we are not in the least *or* at all surprised; **je n'ai n. l'intention d'y aller** I haven't the slightest *or* least intention of going; **il n'est n. sot** he is no fool

nulle part *adv* nowhere; **je ne les vois n.** I can't see them anywhere; **je n'ai vu ça n. (ailleurs)** I've not seen that anywhere (else), I've seen that nowhere (else)

nullification [nylifikasjɔ̃] *nf* nullification

nullité [nylite] *nf* **(a)** *Jur* (*de contrat, de mariage etc*) nullity, invalidity; **frapper une clause de n.** to render a clause void; **lors d'un mariage, la bigamie est une cause de n.** bigamy is grounds for the annulment of a marriage **(b)** (*stupidité*) (*de personne*) uselessness, hopelessness; (*de remarque, plaisanterie*) crassness; **elle est d'une n.!** she's totally useless!; **cette blague est d'une n. totale** that joke is completely pathetic **(c)** *F* (*personne incompétente*) dead loss

nûment [nymɑ̃] *adv Litt* frankly, without embellishment

numéraire [nymerɛr] **1** *adj* (*monnaie*) legal; **valeur n.** cash value **2** *nm* specie, (current) coin; **payer en n.** to pay in cash *or Spéc* in specie

numéral, -ale, -aux, -ales [nymeral, -o] *adj, nm* numeral

numérateur [nymeratœr] *nm Math* numerator

numération [nymerasjɔ̃] *nf Math* numeration, notation; *Méd* **n. globulaire** blood count; **n. et formule sanguine** full blood count

numérique [nymerik] *adj* **(a)** (*valeur, supériorité etc*) numerical **(b)** *Ordinat* (*ordinateur, donnée*) digital; **balance à affichage n.** digital scales; **enregistrement/disque n.** digital recording/record

numériquement [nymerikmɑ̃] *adv* **(a)** numerically **(b)** *Ordinat* digitally

numérisation [nymerizasjɔ̃] *Ordinat nf* digitization

numériser [nymerize] *vt Ordinat* to digitize

numériseur [nymerizœr] *nm Ordinat* digitizer; **n. d'image** image digitizer

numéro [nymero] *nm* **(a)** (*chiffre*) number; **tirer le bon n.** to draw the lucky *or* winning number; *Fig* to strike (it) lucky; **le n. gagnant** the winning number; **le n. un/deux du parti** the number one/two in the party; **j'habite au n. 10** I live at number 10; **l'ennemi public n. un** public enemy number one; **la chambre n. 20** room (number) 20

(b) (*de périodique*) issue, number (**sur** on, about); (*d'émission*) edition; **n. du jour/de la semaine/du mois, dernier n.** current issue *or* number; **ancien n., n. déjà paru** back issue *or* number; **n. spécial** (*d'un magazine etc*) special issue; **vente au n.** single copies sold; **la suite au prochain n.** (*dans magazine*) (to be) continued in the next issue, to be continued; *Fig F* watch this space

(c) *Th* act, number, turn; **n. de cirque** circus act; *F* **il aime faire son petit n.** he likes doing his little act

(d) (*personne*) **quel n.!** what a character!

▶ **numéro**: **n. d'appel** telephone number; **n. d'appel gratuit** freephone number, *Am* toll-free number; *Tél* **n. azur** = type of 0800 *or Am* toll-free number in which costs are shared between caller and company; **n. de chambre** room number; *Aut* **n. de châssis** chassis *or* commission number; **n. de commande** order number; *Journ* **n. de commission paritaire** publication registration number; **n. de compte** account number; **n. d'enregistrement** booking number; **n. d'identification** identification number; **n. d'identité bancaire** bank sort code; **n. d'immatriculation** registration number; **n. d'ordre** running *or* serial *or* order number; *Tél* **n. de poste** extension number; **n. de référence** reference number; **n. de sécurité sociale** social security number; **n. de série** serial number; **n. de sociétaire** (*d'une assurance*) insurance *or* policy number; **n. de téléphone** [①A71,5] telephone number; *Tél* **n. d'urgence** hot-line; *Tél* **n. vert** Freefone®, 0800 number, *Can* Zenith, *Am* ≈ 0800 number, toll-free number; **n. de vol** flight number

numérologie [nymerɔlɔʒi] *nf* numerology

numérotage [nymerɔtaʒ] *nm* (*des maisons, pages de livre etc*) numbering

numérotation [nymerɔtasjɔ̃] *nf* numbering; (*téléphone*) dialling, *US* dialing; *Tél* **n. abrégée** short code dialling; *Ordinat* **n. alphanumérique** alphanumeric numbering; *Ordinat* **n. décimale** decimal numbering

numéroter [nymerɔte] **1** *vt* (*maisons, pages de livre etc*) to number; **les places ne sont pas numérotées** the seats are not numbered; *Mil* **numérotez-vous (à partir de la droite)!** (from the right) number! **2** *vi Tél* to dial

numéroteur [nymerɔtœr] *nm* numbering device

numismate [nymismat] *n* numismatist

numismatique [nymismatik] **1** *adj* numismatic **2** *nf* numismatics, numismatology

nummulaire [nymylɛr] *nf Bot* moneywort, creeping Jenny

nunuche [nynyʃ] *adj F* silly

nu-pieds *nm inv* sandal

nuptial, -ale, -iaux, -ales [nypsjal, -jo] *adj* wedding; **anneau/marche n.** wedding ring/march; **chambre nuptiale** bridal suite; **cortège n.** bridal procession; **robe nuptiale** wedding dress, bridal gown; **messe nuptiale** nuptial mass

nuptialité [nypsjalite] *nf* marriage rate

nuque [nyk] *nf* nape *or* back of the neck; **elle veut une coupe de cheveux qui dégage bien la n.** she wants her hair cut short at the back; **saisir qn par la n.** to catch hold of sb by the scruff of the neck

nurse [nœrs] *nf Vieilli* nanny, (children's) nurse

nursery [nœrsəri], *pl* **nurseries** *nf* (*d'hôpital*) nursery

nutation [nytasjɔ̃] *nf* nutation

nutritif, -ive [nytritif, -iv] *adj* nutritive; (*aliment*) nutritious, nourishing; **valeur nutritive** food *or* nutritional value

nutrition [nytrisjɔ̃] *nf* nutrition; **une mauvaise n.** a bad *or* an unbalanced diet

nutritionniste [nytrisjɔnist] *n* nutritionist

nyctalope [niktalɔp] *adj* day-blind, *Spéc* hemeralopic

nylon [nilɔ̃] *nm* nylon; **des bas (de) n.** nylon stockings, nylons

nymphe [nɛ̃f] *nf* **(a)** *Myth* nymph **(b)** *Ent* nymph, pupa, chrysalis

nymphéa [nɛ̃fea] *nm* nymphea, white waterlily

nymphette [nɛ̃fɛt] *nf* nymphet

nymphomane [nɛ̃fɔman] *adj, nf* nymphomaniac

nymphomanie [nɛ̃fɔmani] *nf* nymphomania

O

O, o [o] *nm* **(a)** *(lettre)* O, o **(b)** *(abrév* **ouest)** W

ô [o] *int Litt* O!

OAA [oaa] *nf (abrév* **Organisation de l'alimentation et l'agriculture)** FAO

OACI [oasei] *nf (abrév* **Organisation de l'aviation civile internationale)** ICAO

OAS [oaɛs] *n Hist abrév* **Organisation de l'armée secrète**

oasien, -ienne [oazjɛ̃, -jɛn] **1** *adj* oasis **2** *n* oasis dweller

oasis [ɔazis] *nf (parfois m)* [①A14,10] oasis; *Fig* **une o. de calme/bonheur** a haven of peace/happiness

obédience [ɔbedjɑ̃s] *nf* **(a)** *Cathol* obedience **(b)** *(fidélité)* **musulman/catholique de stricte o.** strict *or* devout Moslem/Catholic; **pays d'o. communiste** countries under Communist rule; **des communistes d'o. trotskiste** Communists of the Trotskyist tendency **(c)** *Litt (obéissance)* obedience

obéir [ɔbeir] *vi* to obey; **o. à qn** to obey sb; **o. à qn au doigt et à l'œil** to be at sb's beck and call; **mes enfants m'obéissent peu** my children aren't very obedient; **il est obéi de ses enfants** he is obeyed by his children; **un prof pas du tout obéi de ses élèves** a teacher with no control over his pupils; **se faire o.** to command obedience; **o. à un règlement/une loi** to obey a rule/a law, to abide by a rule/a law; **o. à un ordre** to obey an order, to comply with an order; **o. à la force/une contrainte** to yield to force/a constraint; **o. à son instinct** to follow *or* obey one's instinct; **o. à une impulsion** to act on *or* follow an impulse; **o. à une envie très forte** to give in to a very strong desire; **o. à sa conscience** to follow the dictates of *or* to obey one's conscience; **o. à la mode** to follow (the dictates of) fashion; *Naut* **o. à la barre** to answer the helm; *Av* **o. aux commandes** to respond to the controls

obéissance [ɔbeisɑ̃s] *nf* obedience **(à** to); **refus d'o.** insubordination; **devoir o. à qn** to owe sb obedience *or* allegiance; **jurer o. au roi** to swear allegiance to the king

obéissant [ɔbeisɑ̃] *adj* obedient

obélisque [ɔbelisk] *nm Archit* obelisk

obérer [ɔbere] *vt* **(j'obère; j'obérerai)** *Fml (personne, secteur etc)* to burden with debt; **très** *ou* **fort obéré** heavily burdened with debt, deeply in debt, debt-ridden

obèse [ɔbɛz] **1** *adj* obese **2** *n* obese person

obésité [ɔbezite] *nf* obesity

obier [ɔbje] *nm* guelder rose, snowball tree

objecter [ɔbʒɛkte] *vt (rétorquer)* to raise as an objection; **je n'ai rien à o. à la proposition** I have no objection to the proposal, I have nothing (to say) against the proposal; **qu'avait-il à o.?** what was his objection?, what did he have against it?; **o. des arguments à une théorie** to put forward arguments against a theory; **o. qch à qn** to put sth forward as an argument to sb; **que puis-je lui o.?** how can I answer him? what can I say in response?; **tout ce qu'il m'a objecté, j'y avais déjà réfléchi** I'd already given some thought to what arguments he might use; **o. que …** to object that …; **on vous objectera que …** they will object that …; **on lui objecta sa jeunesse** they took exception to his youth, his youth counted *or* was held against him

objecteur [ɔbʒɛktœr] *nm* **o. de conscience** conscientious objector

objectif, -ive [ɔbʒɛktif, -iv] **1** *adj (impartial)* objective; **observateur o.** neutral *or* objective observer

2 *nm* **(a)** *(but)* object(ive), aim; *Mil* objective; *(cible)* target; **atteindre son o.** to attain one's object(ive); **o. de chiffre d'affaires** sales target; **o. de vente** sales target *or* objective; **o. à terme** short-term objective

(b) *Phot* lens; *Phys (d'un microscope)* object glass, objective; *Phot* **régler l'o.** to adjust the focus; *Phot* **braquer son o. sur qn** to train one's lens *or* camera on sb; **devant l'o.** in front of the camera; *Phot* **o. fish eye** fish-eye lens; *Phot* **o. grand angle** wide-angle lens; *Phot* **o. normal** normal angle lens; *Phot* **o. ultra grand angle** fish-eye lens; *Phot* **o. zoom** zoom lens; *TV, Cin* **o. à courte focale** short-focus lens; *TV, Cin* **o. à distance focale variable** zoom lens; *TV, Cin* **o. à focale fixe** prime lens

objection [ɔbʒɛksjɔ̃] *nf* objection; **faire** *ou* **formuler** *ou* **soulever une o.** to make *or* raise an objection, to object **(à qch** to sth); **on me fit l'o. que …** they objected *or* argued that …; **voyez-vous une o. à son départ/à ce que je lui en parle?** do you have any objection to his leaving/to my talking to him about it?; *Jur* **o. (votre honneur)!** objection *or* I object, m'lud *or US* your honor!

▶ **objection: o. de conscience** conscientious objection

objectivement [ɔbʒɛktivmɑ̃] *adv* objectively

objectiver [ɔbʒɛktive] *vt* to objectivize

objectivisme [ɔbʒɛktivism] *nm* objectivism

objectivité [ɔbʒɛktivite] *nf* objectivity, objectiveness

objet [ɔbʒɛ] *nm* **(a)** *(chose)* object, thing; **o. de luxe** luxury article *or* item; **o. de première nécessité** essential *or* basic item; **objets trouvés** lost-property office, *Am* lost and found

(b) [①A73,b; B49-50,2-4] *Gram* object; **o. direct/indirect** direct/indirect object

(c) *Phil* object; **femme-o.** woman as an object

(d) *(sujet) (d'une dispute, colloque)* subject; *(d'une conversation)* topic, subject; **l'o. du litige** the matter at issue; **o. d'un contrat** subject matter of a contract; **quel est l'o. de l'anthropologie?** what does anthropology cover?; **les enfants sont l'o. de nombreux soins** children receive a lot of care; **votre requête sera l'o. de toute notre attention** your request will receive our full attention; **cela fera l'o. de ma conférence/d'une recherche approfondie** this will be the subject of my lecture/of a thorough investigation; **o. de pitié/haine** object of pity/hatred

(e) *(but) (d'une action)* object, aim, purpose; **l'o. de ma visite** the purpose of my visit; **remplir son o.** to achieve *or* fulfil its object *or* aim *or* purpose; **cet appareil/cette nouvelle mesure remplit tout à fait son o.** the device/the new measure does exactly what it's supposed to; **sans o.** *(remarque, réclamation, préoccupation)* unjustified

(f) *Ordinat* object

▶ **objet: o. d'art** objet d'art; *Astron* **o. volant non identifié** unidentified flying object; **objets de valeur** valuable items, valuables; **aucun o. de valeur n'a disparu** nothing valuable was taken; **ne laissez pas d'o. de valeur dans votre voiture** don't leave valuables in your car

objurgation [ɔbʒyrgasjɔ̃] *nf* objurgation

oblat, -ate [ɔbla, -at] *n Rel* oblate

oblation [ɔblasjɔ̃] *nf Rel* oblation, offering

obligataire [ɔbligatɛr] *Fin* **1** *n* bondholder, debenture holder **2** *nm* debenture bond **3** *adj* **emprunt/marché o.** debenture *or* bond loan/market

obligation [ɔbligasjɔ̃] *nf* **(a)** [①A58-9,e-f; B36,K,1,a] *(contrainte, devoir)* obligation; **tu viens si tu veux, mais ce n'est pas une o.** you can come if you want, but you're not obliged to *or* you don't have to; **avoir l'o. de faire qch** to be under an obligation to do sth, to be obliged to do sth; **être dans l'o. de faire qch** to be obliged to do sth; **je me sens dans l'o. de vous avertir** I feel obliged to warn you; **je me vois dans l'o. de me taire** I find myself obliged to keep silent; **sans o. d'achat** no purchase necessary; **sans o. de votre part** without any obligation (on your part); **tu manques à toutes tes obligations** you're not facing up to any of your responsibilities; *Fin* **honorer ses obligations** to honour *or* meet one's obligations; **remplir ses obligations** to meet one's obligations; **avoir/se sentir des obligations envers qn** to be/feel under an obligation to sb; **avoir des obligations (familiales)** to have (family) obligations; **obligations militaires** liability to military service; **ayant rempli ses obligations militaires** having completed one's military service; **o. contractuelle** contractual obligation

(b) *Jur (acte)* recognizance, bond; **o. alimentaire** maintenance order; **contracter une o. irrévocable** to enter into a binding agreement

(c) *Fin* bond, debenture; **obligations** bonds, loan stock *or* notes; **o. cautionnée** secured bond; **o. convertible** *ou* **échangeable** convertible bond; **o. garantie** guaranteed bond; **o. hypothécaire** mortgage bond; **o. indexée** index-linked bond; **o. à intérêt variable** floating rate bond; **o. nominative** registered bond; **o. au porteur** bearer bond; **o. à revenu fixe** fixed rate bond; **o. à revenu variable** floating rate bond; **o. à taux progressif** step-up bond

obligatoire [ɔbligatwar] *adj* obligatory, compulsory, mandatory; **école laïque, gratuite et o.** free, compulsory and non-religious education; **l'uniforme est o.** uniform is compulsory *or* obligatory *or* must be worn; *F* **c'était o.** (*c'était forcé*) it had to happen, it was bound to happen, it was inevitable

obligatoirement [ɔbligatwarmɑ̃] *adv* **vous devez o. montrer votre passeport** you are required to show your passport; *F* **elle lui demandera o. des comptes sur ce qui s'est passé** she's bound to ask him for an explanation of what happened; **est-ce qu'il faut porter une robe habillée? – pas o.** do you have to wear an evening dress? – not necessarily

obligé, -ée [ɔbliʒe] **1** *adj* **(a)** (*contraint*) obliged, compelled (**de faire qch** to do sth); **tu y es allé? – (bien) o.!** did you go? – I had to! **(b)** (*indispensable*) necessary; **c'est un passage o.** it's something that has to be done **(c)** *F* (*inévitable*) inevitable; **c'est o. qu'il rate son examen** he's bound to fail his exam **(d)** *Fml* (*reconnaissant*) obliged, grateful (**de** for); **je vous serais très o. de ...** (*dans une lettre*) I would be most obliged *or* grateful (to you) if you would ... **(e)** *Mus* **récitatif o.** recitative ob(b)ligato **2** *n* person under an obligation; *Jur* obligee; *Vieilli* **je suis votre o.** I am in your debt

obligeamment [ɔbliʒamɑ̃] *adv* obligingly; **il m'a o. aidé à porter ma valise** he obligingly helped me to carry my suitcase

obligeance [ɔbliʒɑ̃s] *nf* obligingness; **ayez** *ou* **veuillez avoir l'o. de fermer la porte** would you oblige me by closing the door, would you be so kind as to close the door

obligeant [ɔbliʒɑ̃] *adj* obliging, helpful, kind

obliger [ɔbliʒe] **(j'obligeai(s); n. obligeons) 1** *vt* **(a)** (*contraindre*) **o. qn à faire qch** (*d'une personne*) to compel *or* force sb to do sth, to make sb do sth; (*d'une situation etc*) to force *or* oblige sb to do sth; **ce travail m'oblige à me lever à cinq heures tous les matins** this job means I have to get up at five o'clock every morning; **ne m'oblige pas à me mettre en colère** don't force me to lose my temper; **personne ne t'oblige à aller travailler à l'étranger** nobody's forcing you to go and work abroad; **son état de santé l'oblige à de longs moments de repos** the state of his health means he has to rest for long periods; **le temps nous oblige à rester enfermés** the weather is keeping us indoors; **ma signature m'y oblige** my signature binds me *or* holds me to it; **la loi m'y oblige** I'm required to by law, the law requires me to; **votre devoir/honneur vous y oblige** you are duty/honour bound to do it; **être obligé de faire qch** to be obliged *or* compelled to do sth, to have to do sth; **ne te sens pas obligé de le faire** don't feel obliged *or* compelled to do it, don't feel you have to do it; **ne te crois pas obligé de tout manger** don't feel you have to eat everything; **rien ne t'y oblige** you don't have to, nobody's forcing you

(b) *Fml* (*rendre service à*) **o. qn** to oblige sb; **vous m'obligeriez en fermant la porte** I'd be obliged if you would close the door, you would oblige me by closing the door

2 s'obliger *vpr* **s'obliger à faire qch** (*ne pas manquer de*) to make a point of doing sth; (*se forcer de*) to force oneself to do sth

oblique [ɔblik] **1** *adj* (*ligne*) oblique; (*rayon*) slanting, oblique; **regard o.** sideways *or* sidelong glance; **manœuvre o.** (*malhonnête*) underhand move; *Gram* **cas o.** oblique case **2** *nm Anat* oblique muscle **3** *nf* oblique (line); **en o.** diagonally; **se stationner en o.** to angle park

obliquement [ɔblikmɑ̃] *adv* obliquely, slantwise; **regarder qn o.** to look sideways *or* sidelong at sb

obliquer [ɔblike] *vi* **obliquez à gauche/à droite!** bear left/right!

obliquité [ɔblikɥite] *nf* obliqueness

oblitérateur, -trice [ɔbliteratœr, -tris] **1** *adj Tech* cancelling **2** *nm* (*pour timbres*) franker

oblitération [ɔbliterasjɔ̃] *nf* **(a)** *Méd* obstruction **(b)** (*de timbres*) cancellation, cancelling; **(cachet d')o.** postmark

oblitérer [ɔblitere] **(j'oblitère, n. oblitérons; j'oblitérerai) 1** *vt* **(a)** (*timbre*) to cancel, to frank; **timbre oblitéré** used stamp; **la lettre n'a pas été oblitérée** the letter hasn't been postmarked **(b)** *Méd* (*obstruer*) to obstruct **(c)** *Litt Fig* (*souvenirs, le passé etc*) to obliterate **2 s'oblitérer** *vpr Litt* **peu à peu le passé s'oblitérait dans sa mémoire** little by little, every trace of the past disappeared from his memory

oblong, -ongue [ɔblɔ̃, -ɔ̃g] *adj* **(a)** oblong; **un coquillage de forme oblongue** an oblong shell **(b)** *Typ* **format o.** oblong format

obnubiler [ɔbnybile] *vt* (*obséder*) to obsess; **elle est obnubilée par l'idée que ...** she is obsessed by the idea that ...

obole [ɔbɔl] *nf* **(a)** (*argent*) small offering; (*dans la Bible*) widow's mite; **apporter** *ou* **verser son o. (à qch)** to make a contribution (to sth); *esp Litt* **il ne m'a pas fait l'o. d'un sourire** he didn't deign to smile at me **(b)** *Hist* (*monnaie grecque*) obol(us); (*monnaie française*) obole

OBSA [ɔpsa] *nm Fin* (*abrév* **obligation avec bon de souscription d'actions**) bond with share warrant attached

obscène [ɔpsɛn] *adj* (*langage, livre*) obscene; (*geste*) obscene, lewd

obscénité [ɔpsenite] *nf* (*d'un langage, d'un livre*) obscenity, smuttiness; (*d'un geste*) obscenity, lewdness; **dire des obscénités** to make obscene remarks

obscur [ɔpskyr] *adj* **(a)** (*sombre*) (*nuit, chambre*) dark **(b)** (*inexplicable, confus*) obscure **(c)** (*vague*) (*pressentiment*) vague, dim; (*impression*) vague **(d)** (*inconnu*) (*écrivain, peintre etc*) obscure; (*humble*) (*naissance*) lowly, humble

obscurantisme [ɔpskyrɑ̃tism] *nm* obscurantism

obscurantiste [ɔpskyrɑ̃tist] *adj, n* obscurantist

obscurcir [ɔpskyrsir] **1** *vt* **(a)** (*assombrir*) (*lumière*) to obscure; (*chambre, ciel*) to darken; **yeux obscurcis par les larmes** eyes misty *or* dim with tears **(b)** (*rendre confus*) **il avait le jugement/les idées obscurci(es) par l'alcool/la douleur** his judgment/thinking was clouded by alcohol/pain **2 s'obscurcir** *vpr* (*d'une pièce, du paysage*) to darken, to grow dark; (*du ciel*) to darken, to grow dark, to cloud over; (*de l'esprit, de la vue*) to grow dim; **son regard s'obscurcit** his face clouded over *or* darkened

obscurcissement [ɔpskyrsismɑ̃] *nm* (*du sens*) obscuring; (*d'une chambre, du ciel*) darkening; (*de l'esprit, de la vue*) dimming

obscurément [ɔpskyremɑ̃] *adv* obscurely, dimly; (*sentir*) vaguely; **j'ai o. l'impression que ...** I've a vague impression that ...; **mourir o.** to die in obscurity

obscurité [ɔpskyrite] *nf* **(a)** (*noirceur*) darkness; **dans l'o.** in the dark; **j'ai peur dans l'o.** I'm scared in the dark; **elle doit rester dans l'o.** she has to stay in darkness *or* in a darkened room; **soudain, l'o. se fit** everything suddenly went dark **(b)** (*caractère complexe, confusion*) obscurity; **la solution de cette énigme restera à jamais dans l'o.** the answer to this enigma will for ever remain shrouded in obscurity **(c)** (*anonymat*) obscurity; **vivre dans l'o.** to live in obscurity; **sortir de l'o.** to emerge from obscurity, to become known

obsédant [ɔpsedɑ̃] *adj* (*souvenir, musique*) haunting; (*pensée*) obsessive

obsédé, -ée [ɔpsede] *n* fanatic; **un o. du cinéma/du rangement** a film/tidiness fanatic *or* freak; **un o. (sexuel)** a sex maniac

obséder [ɔpsede] *vt* **(j'obsède; j'obséderai)** (*d'une pensée, d'un souvenir*) to obsess; **son souvenir m'obsède** I'm obsessed by his memory; **être obsédé par qch** to be obsessed by *or* with sth; **elle est obsédée par ses enfants** she is obsessed with her children; **c'est un problème, mais ne te laisse pas o.** it's a problem, but don't become obsessed by it *or* don't let it become an obsession

obsèques [ɔpsɛk] *nfpl* funeral; **avoir droit à des o. nationales** to be given a state funeral; **les o. se feront dans la plus stricte intimité** the funeral will be strictly private

obséquieusement [ɔpsekjøzmɑ̃] *adv* obsequiously

obséquieux, -euse [ɔpsekjø, -øz] *adj* obsequious

obséquiosité [ɔpsekjozite] *nf* obsequiousness

observable [ɔpsɛrvabl] *adj* observable; **un fait o. uniquement dans certaines couches de la population** a phenomenon that can be observed only in certain segments of the population

observance [ɔpsɛrvɑ̃s] *nf* (*d'un règlement*) observance; **communiste de stricte o.** hardline communist; **un bénédictin d'ancienne o.** a Benedictine of the old school

observateur, -trice [ɔpsɛrvatœr, -tris] **1** *n* **(a)** (*d'événements, d'un phénomène, des mouvements de l'ennemi, etc*) observer; *Mil* (*qui règle les tirs*) spotter; **o. des Nations Unies** United Nations observer **(b)** (*des réglements, des lois*) observer, keeper **2** *adj* observant

observation [ɔpsɛrvasjɔ̃] *nf* **(a)** (*surveillance*) observation; **être en o.** to be under observation; **mettre/(main)tenir qn en o.** to put/keep sb under observation; **malade en o.** patient under observation; **poste d'o.** observation *or* lookout post; **avion d'o.** spotter plane; **observations par satellite** satellite observations; **il a l'esprit d'o.** he is very observant

(b) (*remarque*) observation, remark, comment; (*critique*) remark; **faire des observations** to make observations *or* remarks *or* comments; (*critiques*) to make *or* pass remarks; **je peux faire une petite o.?** can I make one tiny remark?; **si je puis me permettre une o.** if I may make an observation *or* say something; **il faisait toujours des observations à ses élèves** he was always finding fault with his pupils; **à la**

moindre o. de ma part, elle se met en colère the slightest remark from me and she gets angry, she gets angry if I make the slightest remark; **observations sur un auteur** comments on an author

(c) (*respect*) (*des lois*) observance, keeping

(d) (*étude*) (*des étoiles, des insectes, des oiseaux etc*) observation

observatoire [ɔpsɛrvatwar] *nm Astron* observatory; *Mil* observation post

observer [ɔpsɛrve] **1** *vt* **(a)** (*surveiller, regarder*) (*personne, chose*) to watch, to observe; **on nous observe** we are being watched; **se sentir observé** to feel one is being watched; **elle adore o. les gens dans le métro** she loves watching people *or* she loves to people-watch in the metro

(b) (*remarquer*) to notice; **nous observons un retour à …** we are seeing *or* witnessing a return to …; **faire o. qch à qn** to draw sb's attention to sth, to point sth out to sb; **faire o. à qn que …** to point out to sb that …; **je vous ferai o. que …** I must point out to you that …

(c) (*suivre, respecter*) (*réglements, lois etc*) to observe, to keep (to), to comply with; (*promesse*) to keep; **o. le silence** to keep silent; **o. une minute de silence** to observe a minute's silence; **o. la loi** to observe the law; **faire o. la loi** to enforce (obedience to) the law; **o. un contrat** to comply with a contract

(d) (*étudier*) (*les étoiles, les insectes, les peuplades etc*) to observe; (*un angle*) to take, to read; **il passait des heures à o. les oiseaux** he spent hours bird-watching; *Naut* **o. le soleil** to take the sun, to take a sight at the sun

2 s'observer *vpr* **(a)** (*d'un phénomène, d'une attitude*) to be seen; **ce phénomène ne s'observe que dans les pays tropicaux** this phenomenon can be seen only in tropical countries

(b) (*de deux personnes*) to watch *or* observe each other

(c) (*d'une personne*) to keep a check on oneself

obsession [ɔpsɛsjɔ̃] *nf* obsession; **mais c'est une o.** *ou* **de l'o.!** you're/he's/*etc* obsessed (with the idea)!; **il ne faudrait pas en faire une o., il ne faudrait pas que cela devienne de l'o.** it shouldn't become an obsession; **avoir l'o. de qch** to be obsessed with sth

obsessionnel, -elle [ɔpsɛsjɔnɛl] *Psy* **1** *adj* obsessional; **une névrose obsessionnelle** an obsessional neurosis **2** *n* **c'est un o.** he's obsessive, he has *or* is an obsessive personality

obsidienne [ɔpsidjɛn] *nf Minér* obsidian

obsolescence [ɔpsɔlɛsɑ̃s] *nf* obsolescence

obsolescent [ɔpsɔlɛsɑ̃] *adj* obsolescent

obsolète [ɔpsɔlɛt] *adj* obsolete; **un mot devenu o.** a word that has become obsolete, an obsolete word

obstacle [ɔpstakl] *nm* obstacle; *Courses de chevaux* fence, jump; *Sp* hurdle; *Fig* obstacle, hindrance, impediment; **il continua sa route/il a atteint son but sans rencontrer d'o.** he continued on his way/he achieved his aim without meeting any obstacles; **se heurter à un o.** to come up against an obstacle; **venir à bout d'un o.** to overcome an obstacle; **faire o. à qch** to be an obstacle to sth, to stand in the way of sth; **plus rien ne faisait o. à mon départ** *ou* **à ce que je parte** there was no longer any reason for me not to go; **je n'y vois pas d'o.** I don't see any difficulty *or* problem (about it); **course d'obstacles** *Courses de chevaux* steeplechase; *Sp* hurdle race

obstétrical, -ale, -aux, -ales [ɔpstetrikal, -o] *adj* obstetric

obstétricien, -ienne [ɔpstetrisjɛ̃, -jɛn] *n* obstetrician

obstétrique [ɔpstetrik] *nf* obstetrics

obstination [ɔpstinasjɔ̃] *nf* obstinacy, stubbornness; *F Péj* pigheadedness

obstiné [ɔpstine] *adj* (*personne, caractère*) obstinate, stubborn; *F Péj* pigheaded; (*résistance*) stubborn, dogged; (*travail*) determined, dogged

obstinément [ɔpstinemɑ̃] *adv* obstinately, stubbornly; (*travailler, avancer*) determinedly, doggedly; (*répondre*) stubbornly

obstiner (s') [sɔpstine] *vpr* to persist; **obstine-toi!** be persistent!, don't give up!; **s'o. à faire qch** (*continuer*) to persist in doing sth; (*vouloir*) to be set *or Fml* bent on doing sth; **elle s'obstine sur cette question** she won't let go, she won't give up, *F* she's like a dog with a bone; **s'o. dans son silence** to remain stubbornly *or* obstinately silent; **s'o. dans ses idées/convictions** to cling stubbornly *or* doggedly to one's ideas/convictions

obstruction [ɔpstryksjɔ̃] *nf* (*d'une rue, d'un passage*) blocking, obstruction; (*d'un égout*) blocking; *Méd* **o. intestinale** obstruction of the bowels; **faire de l'o.** *Pol* to be obstructive, to use obstructive tactics; *Sp* to obstruct

obstructionnisme [ɔpstryksjɔnism] *nm Pol* obstructionism

obstructionniste [ɔpstryksjɔnist] *adj, nm Pol* obstructionist

obstruer [ɔpstrye] *vt* (*rue, passage*) to block, to obstruct; (*tuyau*) to block; **il a des artères obstruées** he has blocked arteries; **le tuyau est obstrué par des cheveux** the pipe is clogged up with hair

obtempérer [ɔptɑ̃pere] *vt, ind* **(j'obtempère, n. obtempérons; j'obtempérerai) o. à** (*ordre, assignation*) to obey, to comply with; *Jur* **refus d'o.** obstruction

obtenir [ɔptənir] (*conj like* **tenir**) **1** *vt* (*biens, permission, réponse etc*) to obtain, to get; (*promesse*) to obtain, to secure, to get; (*le consentement de qn*) to obtain, to gain, to get; (*résultat*) to obtain, to achieve, to get; **o. la libération des otages** to obtain the release of the hostages; **si on mélange ces deux substances, qu'obtient-on?** what do you get if you mix these two substances?; **si on ajoute les deux, on obtient 500** if you add the two together, you get 500; **j'ai travaillé sur ce dossier pendant trois mois et qu'ai-je obtenu? — rien!** I've worked on this case for three months and what have I got to show for it *or* what have I achieved? — nothing!; **o. qch de qn** to obtain *or* get sth from sb; **n'espère plus rien o. de moi** don't expect (to get) anything else from me; **c'est lui qui m'a fait o. ces renseignements** he's the one who got (hold of) *or* obtained the information for me; **j'ai obtenu de le voir** I obtained *or* got permission to see him; **j'ai obtenu d'elle qu'elle vérifie tout** I got her to agree to check everything; **j'ai obtenu qu'elle revienne** I arranged for her to come back

2 s'obtenir *vpr* **où cela s'obtient-il?** where can you get it?

obtention [ɔptɑ̃sjɔ̃] *nf* obtaining; **depuis l'o. de son diplôme** since obtaining his/her diploma, since he/she got his/her diploma; **ajoutez du blanc jusqu'à o. de la couleur désirée** add white until the desired colour is obtained; **pour l'o. de qch** (in order) to obtain sth; **o. d'un prêt** obtaining of a loan

obturateur, -trice [ɔptyratœr, -tris] **1** *adj* closing; *Anat* (*membrane, muscle*) obturator **2** *nm* **(a)** *Anat, Chir* (*d'une ouverture*) obturator **(b)** (*clapet*) shutter, stop valve; *Aut* throttle; *Phot* shutter; *Phot* **o. de plaque** focal-plane shutter; *Phot* **o. au diaphragme** diaphragm shutter; *Aut* **o. de bloc** core plug; *Aut* **o. papillon** throttle valve

obturation [ɔptyrasjɔ̃] *nf* (*d'un tuyau, d'une ouverture*) sealing; (*d'une dent*) filling

obturer [ɔptyre] *vt* (*tuyau, ouverture*) to seal; (*dent*) to fill

obtus [ɔpty] *adj* **(a)** (*angle*) obtuse **(b)** (*personne*) obtuse, dim-witted

obus [ɔby, oby] *nm Mil* shell; **o. à balles** *ou* **à mitraille** shrapnel (shell); **o. de mortier** mortar shell; **o. traçant** tracer shell

obusier [ɔbyzjɛ] *nm Mil* howitzer

obvier [obvje] *vi* (*impf, pr sub* **n. obviions**) *Litt* **o. à qch** to obviate sth; **o. à un accident** to take precautions *or* to guard against an accident

OC [ose] *nfpl Rad* (*abrév* **ondes courtes**) SW

oc [ɔk] *adv Hist Ling* **langue d'oc** langue d'oc (*language of southern France*)

ocarina [ɔkarina] *nm* ocarina

occase [ɔkaz] *nf F* **(a)** (*affaire*) bargain **(b)** (*article de seconde main*) secondhand item; **elle est neuve ta voiture? – non, c'est une o.** is your car new? – no, it's secondhand; **je cherche une o. pas trop chère** I'm looking for a secondhand one, not too expensive; **acheter qch d'o.** to buy sth secondhand

occasion [ɔkazjɔ̃] *nf* **(a)** (*circonstance favorable*) opportunity, chance; (*moment*) occasion; **saisir l'o.** to take *or* seize the opportunity; *F* **sauter sur l'o.** to jump at the chance *or* the opportunity; *F* **c'est l'o. ou jamais** it's now or never; *F* **c'est l'o. ou jamais de le faire** now's the time to do it; *F* **c'était l'o. ou jamais de changer de boulot!** if ever there was a time to change jobs it was then!; **avoir l'o. de faire qch** to have the opportunity *or* chance of doing *or* to do sth; **tout le monde n'a pas l'o. de faire ça** not everybody gets the chance *or* opportunity to do that; **je n'ai jamais eu l'o. de le regretter** I've never had cause *or* reason to regret it, I've never had any cause for regret; **donner à qn l'o. de faire qch** to give sb the *or* an opportunity *or* a *or* the chance to do sth; **si l'o. se présente** if you get the chance, if the opportunity arises, *Fml* should the opportunity arise; **laisser passer l'o.** to let the opportunity slip (by); **profiter de l'o. pour faire qch** to take the opportunity to do sth; *Iron* **tu as encore perdu l'o. de te taire** why can't you keep your mouth shut?; *Iron* **il ne perd jamais une o. d'être désagréable/de se faire remarquer** he never misses an opportunity to be unpleasant/to get himself noticed; **attendre l'o.** to bide one's time; **à l'o.** when the opportunity presents itself; **voir qn à l'o.** to see sb occasionally *or* from time to time; **venez boire un coup à l'o.** come for a drink when you get a *or* the chance; **elle sait être très virulente à l'o.** she can be very harsh on occasions; **il faudra que je m'en assure, à l'o.** I'll have to check it myself, when I get the chance; **à la première o.** at the first *or* earliest opportunity; **je m'en débarrasserai à la premiere o.** I'll get rid of it the first chance I get; **à** *ou* **en plusieurs occasions** on several occasions; **s'habiller pour l'o.** to dress for the occasion; **on a bu du champagne pour l'o.** we drank champagne to celebrate, we drank champagne to mark the occasion; **à l'o. de son mariage** on the occasion of his marriage; **je l'ai rencontré à l'o. d'un concert** I met him at a concert; **je m'en suis rendu compte à l'o. d'une visite de routine** I realized it during a routine visit; **à l'o. de sa venue** upon his arrival; **en pareille o.** in circumstances like these, in similar circumstances; **à cette o.** on that occasion; **dans/pour les grandes occasions** on/for great occasions; *Prov* **l'o. fait le larron** opportunity makes the thief; **être l'o. de qch** to be the occasion of sth; **ce sera l'o. de faire la fête** that will be a good excuse for a party; *Fin* **o. de profit** profit opportunity

(b) (*affaire*) bargain; **le marché de l'o.** the secondhand market; **faire le neuf et l'o.** to sell new and secondhand goods; **marchandises/voitures/livres/meubles d'o.** secondhand goods/cars/books/furniture; **elle est neuve ta voiture? – non, c'est une o.** is your car new? – no, it's secondhand; **je l'ai acheté d'o.** I bought it secondhand; **ça, c'est une o.!** it's a bargain!

occasionnel, -elle [ɔkazjɔnɛl] *adj* occasional; (*rencontre*) chance; (*aide*) casual; **je vais parfois au restaurant mais cela reste très o.** I sometimes go to the restaurant but only very occasionally; **cause occasionnelle d'une révolte** event that triggered *or Fml* occasioned a revolt

occasionnellement [ɔkazjɔnɛlmɑ̃] *adv* occasionally

occasionner [ɔkazjɔne] *vt* to cause, to give rise to, *Fml* to occasion; **un bébé occasionne de nombreux frais** having a baby is a costly business

occident [ɔksidɑ̃] *nm* west, *Fml* occident; *Pol* **l'O.** the West

occidental, -ale, -aux, -ales [ɔksidɑ̃tal, -o] **1** *adj* west, western; **côte occidentale** west coast; **l'Europe occidentale** Western Europe; **les Indes occidentales** the West Indies **2** *n* Westerner, *Fml* Occidental

occidentalisation [ɔksidɑ̃talizasjɔ̃] *nf* westernization

occidentaliser [ɔksidɑ̃talize] **1** *vt* to westernize **2 s'occidentaliser** *vpr* to become westernized

occipital, -ale, -aux, -ales [ɔksipital, -o] *Anat* **1** *adj* occipital **2** *nm* occipital (bone)

occiput [ɔksipyt] *nm Anat* occiput

occire [ɔksir] *vt* (*used only in inf & pp* **occis**) *Arch, Hum* to slay; **se faire o.** to be slain

occlusif, -ive [ɔklysif, -iv] *Ling* **1** *adj* occlusive **2** *nf* **occlusive** occlusive consonant, stop

occlusion [ɔklyzjɔ̃] *nf* occlusion; *Méd* **o. intestinale** intestinal obstruction, *Spéc* ileus

occultation [ɔkyltasjɔ̃] *nf Astron* occultation; *Fig* concealment

occulte [ɔkylt] *adj* (*surnatural*) occult; (*secret*) (*comptabilité*) secret; (*cause*) hidden; (*rôle*) clandestine, covert; **les sciences occultes** the occult, the occult sciences

occulter [ɔkylte] *vt Astron* to occult; (*signal lumineux*) to block out, *Spéc* to occult; *Fig* (*informations, intentions etc*) to conceal

occultisme [ɔkyltism] *nm* occultism

occupant, -ante [ɔkypɑ̃, -ɑ̃t] **1** *adj* (*locataire, armée*) occupying **2** *n* (*d'une maison*) occupier, occupant; (*d'un poste*) occupant; *Jur* **premier o.** occupant; *Mil* **l'o.** the occupying forces

occupation [ɔkypasjɔ̃] *nf* **(a)** (*fait d'être ou de rester quelque part*) occupancy, occupation; (*fait de posséder ou d'entrer en possession*) (*d'une maison*) possession; *Mil* (*d'un territoire conquis*) occupation; **armée d'o.** army of occupation; *Hist* **l'O.** the Occupation; **grève avec o. des lieux** sit-down strike, sit-in; **manifestation estudiantine avec o. des locaux** student sit-in; **o. des chambres/des lits** (*dans un hôtel*) room/bed occupancy; **o. double** double occupancy; **o. maximale** capacity occupancy

(b) (*besogne, ouvrage*) occupation; **avoir de l'o.** to be busy, to have things to do; **être sans o., ne pas avoir d'o.** to have nothing to do; **j'ai bien assez d'occupations comme cela!** I've got enough to do *or* enough on my plate already!; **vaquer à ses occupations** to go about one's business; *Admin* **o. principale** main occupation

occupé [ɔkype] *adj* **(a)** (*personne*) (*travaillant*) busy; (*avec un autre client*) busy, engaged; **o. aux préparatifs du départ** busy with the preparations for departure, busy getting ready to leave; **o. à relire le texte** busy rereading the text; **c'est un homme fort o.** he's a very busy man; **elle a des journées/semaines très occupées en ce moment** her days/weeks are very full at present **(b)** (*place*) taken; *Tél* (*ligne*) engaged, *Am* busy; (*sur la porte des toilettes*) engaged; **en territoire o.** in occupied territory

occuper [ɔkype] **1** *vt* **(a)** (*maison*) to occupy; (*place*) to take up, to occupy; **ce lit occupe beaucoup trop de place** this bed takes up *or* occupies far too much room; **les livres d'art occupent trois étagères de la bibliothèque** the art books take up *or* occupy *or* fill three shelves of the bookcase; **le magasin n'occupe que le rez-de-chaussée** the shop takes up *or* occupies only the ground floor

(b) *Mil etc* (*par la force*) (*ville, bâtiment*) to occupy; **les ouvriers ont décidé d'o. l'usine** the workers have decided to occupy the factory; **o. le terrain** *Mil* to hold the field; *Com* to make one's presence felt in the market

(c) (*remplir*) (*temps*) to fill, to occupy; **faire qch pour o. le temps** to do sth to fill *or* occupy the time; **o. ses loisirs** to fill *or* occupy one's free time; **les enfants occupent la majeure partie de mon temps** the children take up the greater part of my time; **o. sa journée à faire qch** to spend one's day doing sth; **fais un peu de ménage, ça occupe!** *ou* **ça t'occupera!** do a bit of housework, that'll pass *or* fill the time!

(d) (*poste etc*) to have, to hold

(e) o. qn (*employer*) to employ sb; (*donner une activité à*) to keep sb busy *or* occupied, to give sb something to do, to occupy sb; **la lecture de ce livre m'a occupé toute la soirée** reading this book took up my entire evening *or* kept me busy all evening; **ces problèmes m'ont occupé pendant un certain temps** these problems have kept me busy *or* kept me occupied *or* given me something to think about for some time

2 s'occuper *vpr* **(a)** to keep oneself busy *or* occupied; **s'o. à faire qch** to be busy doing sth, to be occupied in doing sth; **s'o. en lisant** to spend one's time reading; **on a toujours de quoi s'o.** there's always something to keep you busy *or* occupied, there's always something that needs doing; **je trouverai bien de quoi m'o. en attendant** I'll find something to keep me busy *or* to occupy myself with while I wait

(b) s'o. de (*être intéressé par*) (*photographie, littérature etc*) to be interested in; (*se charger de*) (*qch*) to deal with, to take care of, to attend to; (*qn, ses enfants*) to take care of, to look after; **s'o. de faire qch** to see about doing sth; **cette maison s'occupe surtout d'argenterie** this firm specializes in silverware; **nous allons maintenant nous o. du bilan** we will now turn (our attention) to the balance sheet; **ce n'est pas la peine de vous o. de cela pour l'instant** it's not worth worrying *or* bothering about that at the moment; **il s'occupe de trop de choses** he takes on too much, he has too many irons in the fire; **je m'en occuperai** I'll see to it, I'll deal with it, I'll take care of it; *F* **occupe-toi de ce qui te regarde** *ou* **de tes affaires** *ou* **de tes oignons!** mind your own business!; **de quoi tu t'occupes?** what business is it of yours?, what's it got to do with you?; *F* **t'occupe (pas)!** keep your nose out!, mind your own business!; *Iron* **je vais m'o. de lui** I'll take care of him; *Com* **est-ce qu'on s'occupe de vous?** are you being attended to *or* being served?

occurrence [ɔkyrɑ̃s] *nf* **(a)** (*circonstance*) **en l'o.** in this case, as it happens/happened; **et en l'o. il s'agissait d'une ville romaine** and as it happened *or* as it turned out, it was a Roman town; **mais en l'o. tu as tort** but in this case *or* but this time *or* but as it happens, you're wrong **(b)** *Ling* (*apparition*) occurrence

OCDE [osedeə] *nf* (*abrév* **Organisation de coopération et de développement économique**) OECD

océan [ɔseɑ̃] *nm* ocean; **l'o. Atlantique** the Atlantic (Ocean); **l'o. Indien** the Indian Ocean; **l'o. Pacifique** the Pacific (Ocean); **l'o. Antarctique** *ou* **Austral** the Antarctic Ocean; **l'o. Arctique** the Arctic Ocean; **d'un o. à l'autre** from coast to coast; *Fig* **un o. de fleurs/couleurs** a sea of flowers/colour

Océanie [ɔseani] *nf* Oceania

océanien, -ienne [ɔseanjɛ̃, -jɛn] **1** *adj* Oceanian **2** *n* **O.** Oceanian; (*de Polynésie, Mélanésie*) South Sea Islander

océanique [ɔseanik] *adj* (*courant, climat*) ocean, oceanic

océanographe [ɔseanɔgraf] *n* oceanographer

océanographie [ɔseanɔgrafi] *nf* oceanography

océanographique [ɔseanɔgrafik] *adj* oceanographic(al)

océanologie [ɔseanɔlɔʒi] *nf* oceanology

ocelle [ɔsɛl] *nm Zool* (*d'un insecte*) simple eye, *Spéc* ocellus; (*d'une plume, de l'aile d'un insecte*) eye, *Spéc* ocellus

ocelot [ɔslo] *nm* ocelot

ocre [ɔkr] *nf, adj inv* ochre, *US* ocher

ocré [ɔkre] *adj* ochre(-coloured), *US* ocher(-colored)

ocreux, -euse [ɔkrø, -øz] *adj* ochreous

octaèdre [ɔktaɛdr] **1** *adj* octahedral **2** *nm* octahedron

octaédrique [ɔktaedrik] *adj* octahedral

octal, -ale, -aux, -ales [ɔktal, -o] *adj Ordinat* octal

octane [ɔktan] *nm Ch* octane; **essence à haut indice d'o.** high-octane petrol *or Am* gasoline

octante [ɔktɑ̃t] *adj inv Région* eighty

octave [ɔktav] *nf* octave; **jouer à l'o.** (*plus haut*) to play an octave higher; (*plus bas*) to play an octave lower

octet [ɔktɛ] *nm Ordinat* (eight-bit) byte; **milliard d'octets** gigabyte; **o. de contrôle** check byte

octobre [ɔktɔbr] *nm* [①**A75-6**,B-C; **B58-9**,B-C] October; **en o.** in October; **au mois d'o.** in (the month of) October; **le premier o.** (on) October the first, (on) the first of October, *Am* (on) October first

octogénaire [ɔktɔʒenɛr] *adj, n* octogenarian

octogonal, -ale, -aux, -ales [ɔktɔgɔnal, -o] *adj* octagonal

octogone [ɔktɔgɔn] *nm* octagon

octopode [ɔktɔpɔd] *adj, nm* octopod

octosyllabe [ɔktɔsilab] **1** *adj* octosyllabic **2** *nm* octosyllable

octosyllabique [ɔktɔsilabik] *adj* octosyllabic

octroi [ɔktrwa] *nm* **(a)** (*concession*) (*d'une faveur*) concession, granting; *Com* **o. de licence** licensing **(b)** *Hist* (*impôt*) town dues, city toll; (*bureau*) tollhouse

octroyer [ɔktrwaje] (**j'octroie, n. octroyons; j'octroierai**) **1** *vt* **o. qch à qn** to grant *or* concede sth to sb; **o. du temps à qn** to allow sb time; **o. une permission à qn** to give *or* grant sb leave; **o. sa grâce à un condamné a mort** to reprieve a condemned man; **o. des faveurs à qn** to bestow favours on sb; **o. un prêt** to grant a loan **2 s'octroyer** *vpr* **il s'est octroyé un jour de vacances supplémentaire** he gave himself *or* awarded himself an extra day's holiday

octuor [ɔktɥɔr] *nm Mus* octet

octuple [ɔktypl] **1** *adj* octuple; (*montant*) eightfold **2** *nm* octuple

oculaire [ɔkylɛr] **1** *adj* **(a)** (*visuel*) **témoin o.** eyewitness **(b)** (*de l'œil*) **hygiène o.** eye care, care of the eyes; **globe o.** eyeball **2** *nm Opt* eyepiece, *Spéc* ocular; **o. de visée** (*d'une caméra*) eyepiece

oculiste [ɔkylist] *n* eye specialist, ophthalmologist

odalisque [ɔdalisk] *nf* odalisque, odalisk

ode [ɔd] *nf* ode

odeur [ɔdœr] *nf* (*généralement désagréable*) smell, odour, *US* odor; (*agréable*) scent, smell; **il a une drôle d'o., ce poisson** this fish has a funny smell *or* smells funny; **o. de brûlé** smell of burning; **je sentais une o. de brûlé** I could smell something burning; **sans o.** odourless, *US* odorless; **bonne o.** lovely *or* pleasant smell; **mauvaise o.** bad *or* unpleasant smell, *F* stink; *Fig* **mourir en o. de sainteté** to die in the odour of sanctity; *Fig* **être en o. de sainteté auprès de qn** to be in sb's good books; *Fig* **ne pas être en o. de sainteté auprès de qn** to be in sb's bad books; **je ne suis pas en o. de sainteté** I'm not popular, *F* I'm in the doghouse, *F* I'm not flavour of the month; *Prov* **l'argent n'a pas d'o.** money has no smell

odieusement [ɔdjøzmɑ̃] *adv* odiously, hatefully

odieux, -euse [ɔdjø, -øz] *adj* (*personne*) odious, hateful; (*crime, vice*) odious, abominable

odomètre [ɔdɔmɛtr] *nm* (*pour véhicule*) odometer; (*pour piéton*) pedometer

odontologie [ɔdɔ̃tɔlɔʒi] *nf Méd* odontology

odorant [ɔdɔrɑ̃] *adj* (*agréable*) sweet-smelling, fragrant; (*désagréable*) strong-smelling, *F* smelly

odorat [ɔdɔra] *nm* (sense of) smell; **avoir l'o. développé** to have a keen sense of smell

odoriférant [ɔdɔriferɑ̃] *adj* sweet-smelling, *Litt* odoriferous

odyssée [ɔdise] *nf* **(a)** *Littér* **l'O.** the Odyssey **(b)** *Fig* odyssey; **ce voyage a été une véritable o.** it was a truly epic journey

œcuménique [ekymenik, ø-] *adj Rel* ecumenical

œcuménisme [ekymenism, ø-] *nm Rel* ecumenicalism

œcuméniste [ekymenist, ø-] *n, adj Rel* ecumenalist

œdème [edɛm, ø-] *nm Méd* oedema, *US* edema; **avoir un o. aux poumons** to have pulmonary oedema

Œdipe [edip, ø-] *nm Littér* Oedipus; *Psy* **complexe d'O.** Oedipus complex

œil, *pl* **yeux** [œj, jø] *nm* **(a)** *Anat* eye; **avoir de grands/petits yeux** to have large/small eyes; **avoir les yeux bleus** to have blue eyes; **avoir les yeux globuleux/enfoncés** to have protruding/deep-set eyes; **j'ai le soleil dans les yeux** *ou* **dans l'o.** the sun's in my eyes, I've got the sun in my eyes; **se maquiller** *ou* **se faire les yeux** to do one's eyes, to put on one's eye make-up; **visible à l'o. nu** visible to the naked eye; **voir qch de ses (propres) yeux** to see sth with one's own eyes; **je l'ai de mes yeux vu** I saw it with my (very) own eyes; *F* **avoir un o. qui dit zut** *ou* **merde à l'autre, avoir un o. qui joue au billard et l'autre qui compte les points, avoir les yeux qui se croisent les bras** to be cross-eyed, to have a squint; **avoir un o. de verre** to have a glass eye; *F* **avoir une coquetterie dans l'o.** to have a cast in one's eye; **avoir les yeux injectés de sang** to have bloodshot eyes; **fermer/ouvrir les yeux** to close/open one's eyes; **je n'ai pas fermé l'o. de la nuit** I didn't sleep a wink all night; **ne dormir que d'un o.** to sleep with one eye open; **j'étais tellement inquiète que je n'ai pu dormir que d'un o.** I was so worried I couldn't sleep properly; *Fig* **je pourrais le faire les yeux fermés** I could do it with my eyes shut *or* closed; **chez eux, j'achète les yeux fermés** I buy things from them with complete confidence; **ouvrir un o.** to half-open one's eyes; **ouvrir de grands yeux** to look surprised; **faire les gros yeux (à qn)** to glare (at sb); **lever les yeux au ciel** to raise one's eyes heavenward *or* to heaven; **baisser les yeux** to lower one's eyes *or* gaze, to look down; *F* **avoir de petits yeux** to look tired; **j'ai les yeux qui se ferment (tout seuls), je ne peux plus garder les yeux ouverts** I can't keep my eyes open; **avoir un o. au beurre noir** *ou* **un o. poché** to have a black eye; **regarder qn dans les yeux** to look sb in the eye; *F* **entre quat'z'yeux** [katzjø] in private; (*avec franchise*) man to man/woman to woman; **les yeux dans les yeux** face to face, facing each other; (*amoureusement*) gazing into each other's eyes; **n'avoir d'yeux que pour une personne** to have eyes for only one person; *Prov* **o. pour o., dent pour dent** an eye for an eye, a tooth for a tooth; **épouser une femme pour ses beaux yeux** to marry a woman for her (good) looks; **je ne travaille pas pour les beaux yeux de mon patron!** I don't do this job for the love of it!; **je ne le fais pas pour ses beaux yeux** I'm not doing it just to please him; *F* **avoir des yeux de merlan frit** to look like a lovesick calf; **coûter les yeux de la tête** to cost a fortune *or* an arm and a leg; **tu as les yeux plus gros** *ou* **grands que le ventre** your eyes are bigger than your belly; **n'avoir plus que les** *ou* **ses yeux pour pleurer** to have nothing left apart from the clothes on one's back; **ça saute aux yeux** it's glaringly obvious; **ça crève les yeux qu'il est amoureux d'elle** it's glaringly obvious that he's in love with her; *F* **je m'en bats l'o.** I don't give a damn, I couldn't care less; *F* **mon o.!** my eye!; **tourner de l'o.** to keel over, to faint; *F* **à l'o.** free, gratis, for nothing; **le mauvais o.** the evil eye; **porter un o. critique sur qch** to be critical about sth; **nous voyons ça du même o.** we see eye to eye (with each other) about it; **nous ne voyons pas du tout les choses de cet o-là** we don't see things in that light at all; **voir** *ou* **regarder qn/qch d'un bon o.** to look favourably *or* approvingly on sb/sth; **voir** *ou* **regarder qn/qch d'un mauvais o.** to look unfavourably *or* disapprovingly on sb/sth, to frown on sb/sth; **je n'en croyais pas mes yeux** I couldn't *or* didn't believe my eyes; **faire les yeux doux à qn** to make eyes at sb; *F* **faire de l'o. à qn** to give sb the eye; *F* **taper dans l'o. à qn** to take sb's fancy

(b) (*vue*) (eye)sight *or* eyes; **avoir de bons/mauvais yeux** to have good/bad (eye)sight; **je n'ai plus mes yeux de 20 ans** I can't see as well as I used to; **s'user** *ou* **s'abîmer les yeux** to ruin one's eyes *or* eyesight; **fatiguer les yeux** to strain one's eyes; **cette lumière me fatigue les yeux** I'm straining my eyes in this light; **dès que j'eus jeté les yeux sur lui** as soon as I had set eyes on him; **chercher qn des yeux** to look around for sb; **suivre qn des yeux** to follow sb with one's eyes; **couver** *ou* **manger** *ou* **dévorer qn des yeux** to look lovingly *or* fondly at sb; **regarder qn avec les yeux de l'amour** to look at sb through the eyes of love; *F* **se rincer l'o.** to get an eyeful; **elle n'a pas froid aux yeux** she's not afraid of anything; **aux yeux de la loi/de Dieu** in the eyes of the law/in the eyes *or* sight of God; **à mes yeux** in my eyes, in my opinion; **l'accident s'est déroulé sous mes yeux** the accident happened right before my eyes; **sous l'o. jaloux/inquisiteur/bienveillant de qn** under the jealous/inquisitive/kindly eye of sb; **avoir qch sous les yeux** to have sth right in front of one *or* one's eyes; **je n'ai pas encore eu leur projet sous les yeux** I haven't had sight of *or* I haven't seen their plan yet

(c) (*attention*) **avoir** *ou* **garder l'o. ouvert** *ou* **les yeux ouverts** to keep one's eyes open; **avoir l'o. sur qch** to keep an eye on sth; **avoir l'o. sur qn, avoir qn à l'o.** to keep an eye on sb; **avoir l'o. à tout** to keep an eye on everything; *F* **ouvrir l'o. (et le bon)** to keep one's eyes open *or* peeled *or* skinned; **ne pas avoir les yeux en face des trous** to be half-asleep; *F* **elle n'a pas les yeux dans sa poche** she keeps her eyes open, she's very observant; **fermer les yeux sur qch** (*par indulgence*) to turn a blind eye to sth; (*par refus de la réalité*) to close one's eyes to sth; **ouvrir les yeux à qn sur qch** to open sb's eyes to sth; **coup d'o.** glance; **au** *ou* **du premier coup d'o., d'un seul coup d'o.** at a glance; **jeter un coup d'o. sur qch** to have a quick look at sth, to have a glance at sth; **il y a un joli coup d'o. d'ici** there's a lovely view from here; **avoir le coup d'o.** to have a good eye (for things); **ça vaut** *ou* **ça mérite le coup d'o.** it's worth a look

(d) (*d'une aiguille etc*) eye; (*d'une charnière*) (screw-)hole; (*sur une corde*) eye (splice); (*dans du pain, du gruyère*) hole; (*dans la soupe*) globule *or* speck of fat; **piton à o.** eye bolt (**e**) *Typ* (*pl* **œils**) typeface, face

(**f**) *Él, TV* **o. électrique** electric eye; *Rad* **o. magique, o. cathodique** magic eye

(**g**) *Météo* (*d'un cyclone*) eye

œil-de-bœuf, *pl* **œils-de-bœuf** *nm* bull's-eye (window)

œil-de-chat, *pl* **œils-de-chat** *nm Minér* cat's-eye

œil-de-perdrix, *pl* **œils-de-perdrix** *nm* (*au pied*) (soft) corn

œillade [œjad] *nf* glance; **lancer** *ou* **jeter une o. à qn** to give sb the eye; **lancer des œillades à qn** to make eyes at sb, to give sb the eye

œillère [œjɛr] *nf* (**a**) (*pour un cheval*) blinker, *Am* blinder; *Fig* **avoir des œillères** (*être borné*) to be narrow-minded; (*ignorer la réalité*) to wear blinkers (**b**) *Méd* eyebath, *Am* eyecup

œillet [œjɛ] *nm* (**a**) (*fleur*) carnation; **o. des fleuristes** carnation, clove pink; **o. de poète** sweet william; **o. des prés** ragged robin; **o. d'Inde** French marigold (**b**) (*trou*) (*d'une botte, d'une voile etc*) eyelet (**c**) (*en papeterie*) (gummed) reinforcement

œilleton [œjtɔ̃] *nm* (**a**) *Opt* (*d'un viseur*) eyepiece (**b**) (*d'une plante*) eye (bud)

œillette [œjɛt] *nf* oil poppy, opium poppy; **huile d'o.** poppy seed oil

œnologie [enɔlɔʒi, ø-] *nf* wine-making, *Spéc* oenology, *US* enology; **cours d'o.** wine appreciation course

œnologique [enɔlɔʒik, ø-] *adj* wine, *Spéc* oenological, *US* enological; **croisière o.** wine-tasting cruise

œnologue [enɔlɔg, ø-] *n* wine expert, *Spéc* oenologist, *US* enologist

œsophage [ezɔfaʒ, ø-] *nm Anat* oesophagus, *US* esophagus

œstre [østr] *nm* (*mouche*) gadfly, warble fly

œstrogène [ɛstrɔʒɛn, ø-] *adj, nm Physiol* oestrogen, *US* estrogen

œstrus [ɛstrys] *nm Physiol* oestrus, *US* estrus

œuf, *pl* **œufs** [œf, ø] *nm* (**a**) egg; **blanc/jaune d'o.** egg white/yolk; **o. du jour** freshly-laid egg; **o. frais** fresh egg; **œufs battus** *ou* **montés en neige** beaten egg whites; **en forme d'o.** egg-shaped; *Fig* **mettre tous ses œufs dans le même panier** to put all one's eggs in one basket; *Fig F* **marcher sur des œufs** to tread warily; **il tondrait un o.** he's a skinflint; *Prov* **qui vole un o. vole un bœuf** he that will steal a penny will steal a pound; **tuer la poule aux œufs d'or** to kill the goose that lays the golden egg(s); *F* **quel o.!** what an idiot *or* fool!; *F* **une tête d'o.** an egghead; *F* **va te faire cuire un o.!** take a running jump!, go jump in the lake!; **c'est comme l'o. de Christophe Colomb, il fallait y penser** it's easy when you know how

(**b**) *Biol* egg; (*d'écrevisse, de homard*) berry; (*d'insecte*) egg; **œufs** (*de grenouille*) spawn; (*de poisson*) spawn, hard roe; *F* **étouffer** *ou* **tuer qch dans l'o.** to nip sth in the bud

(**c**) *Ski* (*télécabine*) cable car

▶ **œuf**: **œufs brouillés** scrambled eggs; **o. en chocolat** chocolate egg; **o. à la coque** boiled egg; **o. dur** hard-boiled egg; **œufs au lait** egg custard; **œufs à la liqueur** small liqueur-filled Easter eggs; **œufs de lump** lumpfish roe; **œufs mimosa** eggs mimosa (= *egg whites filled with mayonnaise and crushed egg yolk*); **o. (au) miroir** fried egg; **o. mollet** soft-boiled egg; **œufs à la neige** floating islands; **o. de Pâques** Easter egg; **o. au plat** *ou* **sur le plat** fried egg; *Péj Fig F* **elle n'a que des œufs sur le plat** she's as flat as a pancake; **o. poché** poached egg; **o. en poudre** dried *or* dehydrated *or* powdered egg; *Couture* **o. à repriser** darning egg

œufrier [œfrije] *nm* egg holder *or* stand (*for boiling eggs*)

œuvre [œvr] **1** *nf* (**a**) (*travail*) work; **faire o. utile** to do useful work; **leur rencontre était son o.** (*grâce à lui*) it was thanks to him that they met; (*à cause de lui*) it was because of him that they met; **être à l'o.** to be at work; **mettre qn à l'o.** to set sb to work; **se mettre à l'o.** to get down to *or* set to work; **quand le médecin arriva, la mort avait déjà fait son o.** by the time the doctor arrived the patient had already died; **la maladie/cette idée néfaste a déjà fait son o.** the disease/this dangerous idea has already done its work; **mettre en o.** to use, to make use of; (*traité, loi, système*) to implement; **mettre tout en o.** to do everything possible; **les bonnes œuvres** charitable work; **quête au profit d'une o.** collection in aid of a charity

(**b**) (*création*) work; **œuvres d'un peintre** works of a painter; **œuvres complètes/choisies** complete/selected works

2 *nm Constr* **gros o.** (**d'un bâtiment**) fabric (of a building); **à pied d'o.** on site; *Fig* ready to start work

3 *nm ou f Beaux-Arts, Littér* (*ensemble de créations*) works; **l'o. entière** *ou* **entier de Beethoven** the complete works of Beethoven

▶ **œuvre**: **o. d'art** work of art; **o. de bienfaisance** charity, charitable institution; **o. cinématographique** work of cinema; **o. de charité** charity, charitable institution; *Naut* **œuvres mortes** dead works, upper works, topsides; *Naut* **œuvres vives** quick works, vitals

œuvrer [œvre] *vi Litt* to work

off [ɔf] **1** *adj inv* (**a**) (*hors champ*) **voix o.** voice off (**b**) (*festival*) fringe **2** *nm* fringe festival

offensant [ɔfɑ̃sɑ̃] *adj* offensive, insulting

offense [ɔfɑ̃s] *nf* (**a**) (*affront*) insult; **faire (une) o. à qn** to offend sb; **o. envers un chef d'État** insult to a head of state; **soit dit sans o.** with all due respect; *F* **il n'y a pas d'o.** no offence taken (**b**) *Rel* transgression, trespass; **pardonne-nous nos offenses** forgive us our trespasses

offensé, -ée [ɔfɑ̃se] **1** *adj* offended, insulted **2** *n* offended *or* injured party

offenser [ɔfɑ̃se] **1** *vt* (**a**) **o. qn** to offend sb, to give offence *or US* offense to sb; **sans (vouloir) vous o. monsieur le ministre** with all due respect Minister; **sans vouloir t'o. Jean-Pierre, j'ai bien l'impression que …** no offence (intended) Jean-Pierre *or* I don't wish to offend Jean-Pierre but I get the feeling that … (**b**) *Litt* (*bon goût, délicatesse etc*) to offend against; **o. les regards** to be an eyesore, *Litt* to offend the eye **2 s'offenser** *vpr* to be offended (**de** by), to take offence *or US* offense (**de** at)

offenseur [ɔfɑ̃sœr] *nm* offending person *or* party

offensif, -ive [ɔfɑ̃sif, -iv] *adj* (*guerre, arme*) offensive

offensive [ɔfɑ̃siv] *nf* offensive; **passer à l'o.** to go on the *or* over to the offensive; *Fig* **l'o. de l'hiver est particulièrement précoce cette année** winter has come particularly early this year; **o. du froid** sudden cold spell, cold snap; **o. diplomatique** diplomatic offensive

offertoire [ɔfɛrtwar] *nm Rel, Mus* offertory

office [ɔfis] **1** *nm* (**a**) (*charge*) office; **le secrétaire n'a pas rempli son o.** the secretary didn't carry out his duties; **la pénicilline a rempli son o.** the penicillin did its job; **faire o. de secrétaire/témoin** to act as secretary/witness; **une robe blanche toute simple a fait o. de robe de mariée** a simple white dress served as a wedding gown; **d'o.** automatically, as a matter of course; *Jur* **nommé** *ou* **commis d'o.** appointed by the court

(**b**) (*assistance*) **accepter les bons offices de qn** to accept sb's good offices; **proposer ses bons offices** to offer to act as mediator; *F* **monsieur bons offices** mediator

(**c**) *Rel* service, office; **l'o. des morts** the burial service, the Office for the Dead; **livre d'o.** prayer book; **aller à l'o.** to go to church

2 *nf Vieilli* back kitchen, scullery

▶ **office**: **O. du commerce extérieur** foreign trade Office; **O. national de la navigation** French national shipping and inland waterways office; **o. de publicité** advertising agency; **o. du tourisme(-syndicat d'initiative)** tourist information centre *or US* center

officialisation [ɔfisjalizasjɔ̃] *nf* officialization, officializing

officialiser [ɔfisjalize] *vt* to officialize

officiant [ɔfisjɑ̃] *Rel* **1** *adj* (*prêtre*) officiating **2** *nm* officiant

officiel, -ielle [ɔfisjɛl] **1** *adj* (*déclaration, langage, visite, source*) official; **la version officielle est le suicide** the official version is suicide; **c'est o.** it's official; **à titre o.** officially, formally; **le Journal o.** *CE* the Official Journal; *Br* = the (official) Gazette **2** *nm* (**a**) official (**b**) **l'O.** = the (official) Gazette

officiellement [ɔfisjɛlmɑ̃] *adv* officially; **o. il a donné sa démission** officially, he resigned; **il a donné sa démission o.** he formally resigned

officier[1] [ɔfisje] *nm* (**a**) (*fonctionnaire*) official, officer (**b**) *Mil* officer; **o. de marine** naval officer

▶ **officier**: **o. d'état civil** = registrar (of births, marriages and deaths); **o. général** *Mil* general officer; *Naut* flag officer; **O. de la Légion d'Honneur** Officer of the Legion of Honour *or US* Honor; *Jur* **o. ministériel** (*notaire*) notary (public); (*huissier*) officer of the court; *Naut* **o. de pont** deck officer; **o. de port** harbour *or US* harbor master; *Mil* **o. supérieur** field officer

officier[2] *vi* (*impf & pr sub* **n. officiions**) to officiate; *Hum, Fig* to do the honours *or US* honors

officieusement [ɔfisjøzmɑ̃] *adv* unofficially

officieux, -euse [ɔfisjø, -øz] *adj* unofficial; *Journ* **note d'origine officieuse** inspired piece; **à titre o.** unofficially

officinal, -ale, -aux, -ales [ɔfisinal, -o] *adj Pharm* (*plante*) medicinal; **préparation officinale** patent medicine

officine [ɔfisin] *nf* (**a**) *Pharm* dispensary, pharmacy (**b**) *Fig* (*d'une intrigue*) hotbed; (*d'espions*) nest

off-line [ɔflajn] *adj Ordinat* off-line

offrande [ɔfrɑ̃d] *nf* (**a**) offering, gift; **apporter son** *ou* **une o.**

to make a donation (**à** to) (**b**) *Rel* (*don*) offering; (*cérémonie*) offertory; **o. votive** votive offering

offrant [ɔfrɑ̃] *nm* **le plus o.** the highest bidder; **vendre au plus o.** to sell to the highest bidder; **on me propose deux emplois et j'ai décidé de dire oui au plus o.** I've got two job offers and I've decided to accept the one offering the most money

offre [ɔfr] *nf* offer; (*dans un appel d'offres*) tender, bid; (*dans une vente aux enchères*) bid; **faire o. de qch** to offer sth; **recevoir/accepter une o.** to receive/accept an offer; **faire des offres de service à qn** to offer to help sb; *Com* to solicit orders from sb; *Écon* **l'o. et la demande** supply and demand

▶ **offre**: *Mktg* **o.-ami** introduce-a-friend scheme; **o. de base** basic offer; **o. de bon de réduction** coupon offer; **o. commerciale** bid; **o. d'emploi** job offer, offer of employment; *Journ* **offres d'emploi** situations vacant; **o. d'essai** trial offer; **o. export** export bid; **o. promotionnelle** promotional offer; **o. publique** takeover bid; *Fin* **o. publique d'achat** takeover bid; **faire** *ou* **lancer une o. publique d'achat** to make a takeover bid (**sur** for); *Fin* **o. publique d'échange** takeover bid for shares; **o. publique de vente** public offering, public share offer; **o. de remboursement** money-back offer; **o. de service** offer of services; **o. spéciale** special offer, price special, bargain offer; **o. de vente** offer for sale

offrir [ɔfrir] (*prp* **offrant**; *pp* **offert** [ɔfɛr]; *pr ind* **j'offre, n. offrons**; *p hist* **j'offris**; *fu* **j'offrirai**) **1** *vt* (**a**) (*cadeau*) to give; (*sacrifice*) to offer up; **c'est pour o.** it's a gift *or* present; **c'est pour o.?** would you like it giftwrapped?; **o. à déjeuner à qn** to offer sb lunch; **essaie de te faire o. un repas au restaurant** try to get yourself invited out for a meal; **je t'offre un verre** I'll buy *or* stand you a drink; **on lui a offert une place de mécanicien** he was offered a job as a mechanic; **o. la main de sa fille à qn** to offer one's daughter's hand in marriage to sb

(**b**) (*proposer*) to offer; **o. de faire qch** to offer to do sth; **o. mille francs (pour** *ou* **de qch)** to offer a thousand francs (for sth); (*aux enchères*) to bid a thousand francs (for sth); **combien t'en a-t-il offert?** how much did he offer you for it?; **o. des marchandises** to offer goods for sale; **o. un prix** to offer a price

(**c**) (*présenter*) **o. une résistance acharnée** to put up stiff *or* fierce resistance; **la campagne offre des vues splendides** the countryside offers *or Fml* affords magnificent views; **l'histoire en offre plusieurs exemples** history gives *or Fml* affords several examples of it

2 s'offrir *vpr* (**a**) **s'o. comme guide** to offer to act as a guide, to offer oneself *or* one's services as a guide; **s'o. pour faire qch** to offer to do sth; **s'o. à faire qch** to offer *or* volunteer to do sth; **s'o. aux regards** (*d'un spectacle, d'une vue*) to meet *or* greet the eyes; (*d'une personne*) to expose oneself to the public gaze, *Péj* to flaunt oneself

(**b**) **s'o. un bon cigare/une semaine de vacances** to treat oneself to a good cigar/a week's holiday; **tu ne peux vraiment pas t'o. une soirée au cinéma?** can you really not afford a night out at the cinema?; **je ne peux pas m'o. une secrétaire** I can't afford (the luxury of) a secretary

off-set [ɔfset] *nm Typ* offset

off-shore [ɔfʃɔr] **1** *adj* (**a**) *Sp* **bateau o.** speedboat, powerboat; **course o.** speedboat *or* powerboat race; *Pétr* **plate-forme/forage o.** offshore oil rig/drilling (**b**) *Fin* **placement o.** offshore investment **2** *nm* (*bateau*) speedboat, powerboat; (*course*) speedboat *or* powerboat racing

offusquer [ɔfyske] **1** *vt* (*personne*) to offend, to shock **2 s'offusquer** *vpr* **s'o. de qch** to take offence *or US* offense at sth; **il s'offusque d'un rien** he takes offence at the slightest thing

ogival, -ale, -aux, -ales [ɔʒival, -o] *adj Archit* ogival

ogive [ɔʒiv] *nf* (**a**) *Archit* (diagonal) rib; **voûte d'ogives** ribbed vault (**b**) *Mil* (*d'un obus*) head; (*d'une roquette*) nose cone; **o. nucléaire** nuclear warhead

ogre [ɔgr] *nm* ogre; **manger comme un o.** to eat like a horse

ogresse [ɔgrɛs] *nf* ogress

oh [o] *int* oh!; **oh! hisse!** (yo-)heave-ho!

ohé [ɔe] *int* hey!; **o. du bateau!** ahoy!

ohm [om] *nm Él* ohm

ohmique [omik] *adj Él* ohmic

ohmmètre [ommɛtr] *nm Él* ohmmeter

oie [wa] *nf* goose; **o. sauvage** wild goose; *Culin* **confit d'o.** = goose preserved in goose fat; **graisse d'o.** goose fat; **conte de ma mère l'O.** Mother Goose story; **pas de l'o.** goose step; **jeu de l'o.** ≈ snakes and ladders

▶ **oie**: *F* **o. blanche** naive young girl; **je ne suis pas une o. blanche** I'm no innocent

oignon [ɔɲɔ̃] *nm* (**a**) (*légume*) onion; **petits oignons** (*pour les salades*) spring onions; (*pour les conserves*) pickling onions; **aux petits oignons** *Culin* with baby onions; *Fig F* (*parfait*) first-rate; *Fig F* **chez eux, je suis toujours soigné aux petits oignons** I always get the VIP treatment when I'm with them; **en rang d'oignons** in a row *or* line; **se mettre en rang d'oignons** to form up in a row *or* line, to line up; *F* **occupe-toi** *ou* **mêle-toi de tes oignons** mind your own business; *F* **ce ne sont pas tes oignons** it's none of your business (**b**) *Bot* bulb; **oignons de tulipe** tulip bulbs (**c**) *Méd* bunion (**d**) (*montre*) turnip (watch)

oïl [ɔjl] *adv Hist Ling* **langue d'o.** langue d'oïl (*language of northern France*)

oindre [wɛ̃dr] *vt* (*conj like* **craindre**) (**a**) *Vieilli* (*enduire*) to (rub with) oil (**b**) *Rel* (*roi etc*) to anoint

oint [wɛ̃] *adj, nm* anointed; **l'O. du Seigneur** the Lord's anointed

oiseau, -eaux [wazo] *nm* bird; *Prov* **petit à petit l'o. fait son nid** slow and steady wins the race; **avoir un appétit d'o., manger comme un o.** to eat like a bird; **à vol d'o.** as the crow flies; *Fig F* **l'o. s'est envolé** the bird has flown; *Fig F* **c'est un drôle d'o.** he's an odd type *or* sort *or* customer, he's a funny old bird; **mon petit o.** my pet; **donner à qn des noms d'o.** to call sb names

▶ **oiseau**: **oiseaux de basse-cour** poultry; *Fig* **o. de malheur, o. de mauvais augure** bird of ill omen; **o. de nuit** nocturnal bird; *Fig* nightowl; **o. de passage** bird of passage; **o. de proie** bird of prey; **o. rare: c'est l'o. rare** he's/she's a rare bird; **elle cherche l'o. rare** (*comme époux*) she's looking for the ideal man; (*comme employé*) she's looking for the ideal employee

oiseau-lyre, *pl* **oiseaux-lyres** *nm* lyrebird

oiseau-mouche, *pl* **oiseaux-mouches** *nm* hummingbird

oiseleur [wazlœr] *nm* bird catcher

oiselier [wazəlje] *nm* bird seller

oiselle [wazɛl] *nf* hen bird; *Fig F* naive young girl

oisellerie [wazɛlri] *nf* (*élevage*) bird breeding; (*vente*) bird selling

oiseux, -euse [wazø, -øz] *adj* (*conversation*) idle; (*débat*) pointless; **explication oiseuse** unsatisfactory explanation

oisif, -ive [wazif, -iv] **1** *adj* idle, unoccupied; (*capital*) idle; **vie oisive** idle life, life of idleness **2** *n* person of leisure

oisillon [wazijɔ̃] *nm* fledgling

oisivement [wazivmɑ̃] *adv* idly

oisiveté [wazivte] *nf* idleness; *Prov* **l'o. est (la) mère de tous les vices** the Devil finds work for idle hands to do

oison [wazɔ̃] *nm* gosling

OIT [oite] *nf* (*abrév* **Organisation internationale du travail**) ILO

OK [ɔkɛ] *F* **1** *adv* OK, okay **2** *adj* OK, okay; **c'est OK en ce qui me concerne!** that's OK *or* fine by me!

okapi [ɔkapi] *nm* okapi

olé [ɔle] *int* olé!

oléagineux, -euse [ɔleaʒinø, -øz] **1** *adj* oleaginous, oil-yielding; **graines oléagineuses** oilseeds **2** *nmpl* oleaginous *or* oil-yielding plants

oléiculteur, -trice [ɔleikyltœr, -tris] *n* olive grower

oléiculture [ɔleikyltyr] *nf* olive growing

oléifère [ɔleifɛr] *adj* oil-producing

oléine [ɔlein] *nf* olein, triolein

oléique [ɔleik] *adj Ch* (*acide*) oleic

oléoduc [ɔleɔdyk] *nm* pipeline

olé-olé *adj inv F* (*propos, spectacle*) risqué; (*robe*) daring; (*gens, soirée*) wild; **elle est très o. depuis qu'elle a divorcé** she's been leading a pretty wild life since her divorce; **il y a quelques scènes o.** some of the scenes are a bit close to the bone *or* risqué *or Br* near the knuckle

oléopneumatique [ɔleopnømatik] *adj* air/hydraulic

olfactif, -ive [ɔlfaktif, -iv] *adj* (*nerfs, sens, bulbe*) olfactory

olibrius [ɔlibrijys] *nm F Péj* oddball

olifant [ɔlifɑ̃] *nm* (ivory) horn

oligarchie [ɔligarʃi] *nf* oligarchy

oligarchique [ɔligarʃik] *adj* oligarchic(al)

oligarque [ɔligark] *nm* oligarch

oligo-élément, *pl* **oligo-éléments** [ɔligoelemɑ̃] *nm Biol* trace element

oligopole [ɔligɔpɔl] *nm Écon Pol* oligopoly

oliphant [ɔlifɑ̃] *nm* (ivory) horn

olivaie [ɔlivɛ] *nf* olive grove *or* plantation

olivâtre [ɔlivatr] *adj* olive-greenish; (*teint*) sallow

olive [ɔliv] **1** *nf* (**a**) olive; **huile d'o.** olive oil (**b**) *Él* switch **2** *adj inv* olive (green)

oliveraie [ɔlivrɛ] *nf* olive grove *or* plantation

olivette [ɔlivɛt] *nf* (**a**) (*raisin*) = variety of grape; (*tomate*) plum tomato (**b**) (*olivaie*) olive plantation *or* grove

olivier [ɔlivje] *nm* (**a**) (*arbre*) olive (tree); *Bible* **le Mont des**

Oliviers the Mount of Olives; **se présenter un rameau d'o. à la main** to hold out the olive branch **(b)** *(bois)* olive (wood); **saladier en o.** olive-wood salad bowl

olographe [ɔlɔgraf] *adj Jur* **testament o.** holograph will

OLP [oɛlpe] *nf* (*abrév* **Organisation de libération de la Palestine**) PLO

Olympe [ɔlɛ̃p] *nm Myth* (Mount) Olympus; **les dieux de l'O.** the gods of Olympus

olympiade [ɔlɛ̃pjad] *nf* Olympiad

olympien, -ienne [ɔlɛ̃pjɛ̃, -jɛn] **1** *adj* Olympian; *Fig* **calme o.** Olympian calm **2** *n* **O.** Olympian

olympique [ɔlɛ̃pik] *adj (jeux, champion, flamme)* Olympic; **Comité international o.** International Olympic Committee; **stade/piscine o.** Olympic stadium/pool

ombelle [ɔ̃bɛl] *nf Bot* umbel; **en o.** umbellate

ombellifère [ɔ̃belifɛr] *Bot* **1** *adj* umbelliferous **2** *nfpl* **ombellifères** Umbelliferae, umbellifers

ombilic [ɔ̃bilik] *nm Anat* navel, *Spéc* umbilicus

ombilical, -ale, -aux, -ales [ɔ̃bilikal, -o] *adj* umbilical; *Obst, Astronaut* **cordon o.** umbilical cord; *Fig* **couper le cordon o.** to cut the apron strings

omble [ɔ̃bl] *nm* **o. (-chevalier)** char

ombrage [ɔ̃braʒ] *nm* **(a)** *(des arbres)* shade **(b)** *Ordinat* shading **(c)** *Fig* **prendre o. de qch** to take umbrage *or* offence *or US* offense at sth; **porter** *ou* **faire o. à qn** to give offence to sb

ombragé [ɔ̃braʒe] *adj* shaded, shady

ombrager [ɔ̃braʒe] *vt* **(il ombrageait)** *(d'un arbre)* to shade

ombrageux, -euse [ɔ̃braʒø, -øz] *adj (personne)* touchy, easily offended, quick to take offence *or US* offense; *(cheval)* skittish

ombre¹ [ɔ̃br] *nf* **(a)** *(forme)* shadow; **projeter une o.** to cast a shadow; *Fig* **suivre qn comme son o.** to stick to sb like glue; *(espionner)* to shadow sb; **avoir peur de son o.** to be afraid of one's own shadow; **lâcher la proie pour l'o.** to catch at shadows

(b) *(d'un arbre)* shade; **se reposer à l'o. d'un arbre** to rest in the shade of a tree; **quarante degrés à l'o.** forty degrees in the shade; **elle a grandi à l'o. de la Tour Eiffel** she grew up in the shadow of *or* within a stone's throw of the Eiffel Tower; *Fig F* **mettre qn à l'o.** to put sb inside, to put sb behind bars; *Fig* **jeter une o. sur la fête** to cast a shadow *or* a gloom over the festivities; *Fig* **vivre dans l'o. de qn** to live in sb's shadow, to be (always) overshadowed by sb; **faire de l'o. à qn** to be in sb's light; *Fig* to put sb in the shade

(c) *(obscurité)* darkness; *Fig (anonymat)* obscurity; **ils disparurent dans l'o. de la nuit** they were swallowed up by the darkness; **leurs agissements délictueux se faisaient dans l'o. de la nuit** their criminal schemes were carried out under cover of darkness; *Fig* **rester dans/sortir de l'o.** to remain in/emerge from obscurity; *Fig* **laisser qch dans l'o.** to keep sth dark; *Fig* **travailler dans l'o.** to work behind the scenes

(d) *(être de l'au-delà)* ghost, *Litt* shade; **le royaume des ombres** the nether world; *Fig* **n'être plus que l'o. de soi-même** to be a mere shadow of one's former self

(e) *(trace)* **vous n'avez pas l'o. d'une chance** you haven't the ghost of a chance; **il n'y a pas l'o. d'un doute** there isn't the *or* a shadow of a doubt; **elle n'a pas l'o. d'un scrupule!** she's totally unscrupulous *or* without scruples!; **une o. de méchanceté/jalousie** a hint of malice/jealousy

(f) *Astron* umbra

(g) *Beaux-Arts* **l'o. et la lumière** light and shade; *Fig* **il y a une o. au tableau** there's a fly in the ointment

▶ **ombre: ombres chinoises** shadow play; **théâtre d'ombres chinoises** shadow theatre; **o. à paupières** eye shadow

ombre² *nf* **terre d'o.** umber

ombre³ *nm (poisson)* **o. (-chevalier)** char; **o. de rivière** grayling

ombré [ɔ̃bre] *nm Ordinat* shading

ombrelle [ɔ̃brɛl] *nf* sunshade, parasol; *Zool (d'une méduse)* umbrella

ombrer [ɔ̃bre] *vt (serre, dessin)* to shade; **o. ses paupières de bleu** to put blue eye shadow on

ombreux, -euse [ɔ̃brø, -øz] *adj Litt (promenade, bosquet)* shady

Ombrie [ɔ̃bri] *nf* Umbria

OMCI [oɛmsei] *nf* (*abrév* **Organisation de la navigation maritime consultative et intergouvernementale**) IMCO

oméga [ɔmega] *nm* omega

omelette [ɔmlɛt] *nf* omelette, *US* omelet; **o. au jambon** ham omelette; **o. norvégienne** baked Alaska; *Fig* **on ne fait pas d'o. sans casser des œufs** you can't make an omelette without breaking eggs

omettre [ɔmɛtr] *vt (conj like* **mettre***) (mot, détail)* to omit, to miss out, to leave out; **o. de faire qch** to fail *or* omit *or* neglect to do sth

OMI [oɛmi] *nf* (*abrév* **Organisation maritime internationale**) IMO

omission [ɔmisjɔ̃] *nf (d'un mot, détail)* omission; *(oubli)* oversight; **péché/mensonge par o.** sin/lie of omission; *Typ* **signe d'o.** caret

omnibus [ɔmnibys] **1** *nm* **(a)** *(train)* slow train, *Br* stopping train **(b)** *Arch (bus)* omnibus **2** *adj inv* **train o.** slow train, *Br* stopping train; *Él* **barre o.** busbar

omnidirectionnel, -elle [ɔmnidirɛksjɔnɛl] *adj (antenne)* omnidirectional

omnipotence [ɔmnipɔtɑ̃s] *nf* omnipotence

omnipotent [ɔmnipɔtɑ̃] *adj* omnipotent, all-powerful

omnipraticien, -ienne [ɔmnipratisjɛ̃, -jɛn] *n Méd* general practitioner, GP

omniprésence [ɔmniprezɑ̃s] *nf* omnipresence

omniprésent [ɔmniprezɑ̃] *adj* omnipresent

omniscience [ɔmnisjɑ̃s] *nf* omniscience

omniscient [ɔmnisjɑ̃] *adj* omniscient

omnisports [ɔmnispɔr] *adj inv* **stade/centre o.** sports stadium/centre

omnium [ɔmnjɔm] *nm* **(a)** *Écon* combine; *Bourse* **o. de valeurs** = investment trust **(b)** *Sp* open; *Courses de chevaux* open handicap

omnivore [ɔmnivɔr] **1** *adj* omnivorous **2** *nm* omnivore

omoplate [ɔmɔplat] *nf* shoulder blade, *Spéc* scapula

OMS [oɛmɛs] *nf* (*abrév* **Organisation mondiale de la santé**) WHO

on [ɔ̃] *pron indéf (sometimes becomes* **l'on***, especially after vowel sound)* [①**A27-8**,e-h; **A54**,16,iv; **B15**,2,C; **B36**,J] **(a)** *(indéterminé)* you, people, *Fml* one; *(quelqu'un)* someone, somebody; **on ne sait jamais** you never know, *Fml* one never knows, you *or Fml* one never can tell; **on n'en sait rien** nobody knows anything about it; **on n'aime pas être traité comme ça** people don't like to be treated like that; **on dit qu'elle est folle** it's said *or* they say *or* people say that she's mad, she's said to be mad; **on le dit dans les milieux autorisés** that's what is being said in official circles; **partout où l'on trouve de ces fossiles** wherever these fossils are found; **on ne connaît jamais son bonheur** you never know how lucky you are, *Fml* one never knows how lucky one is; **quand on demande à une femme de vous épouser** when a man asks a woman to marry him, when you ask a woman to marry you; **on était le sept mars** it was the seventh of March; **on frappe à la porte** someone's *or* somebody's (knocking) at the door, there's a knock at the door; **on sonne** there's the (door)bell, there's someone *or* somebody at the door; **on a enfoncé la porte** the door was burst open; **on m'a volé mon sac** my bag has been stolen, someone's stolen my bag; **on demande une bonne cuisinière** *(annonce)* wanted, a good cook

(b) *(précisé) (a following adj, noun or pp agrees in gender and number as the sense requires)* **on parlait très peu au déjeuner** we didn't talk much over lunch; **on ne s'était jamais séparés** we had never been separated; **on n'est pas toujours jeune et belle** women can't be young and beautiful forever; **où va-t-on?** where are we going?; **alors, on s'en va comme ça?** are you really leaving just like that?; **on est dix en tout** there are ten of us in all; *F* **nous, on est tous égaux** we're all equal here; *F* **on est allés au cinema avec les parents** we went to the pictures with our parents

onagre¹ [ɔnagr] *nf Bot* evening primrose

onagre² *nm Zool* onager, wild ass

onanisme [ɔnanism] *nm* onanism

once¹ [ɔ̃s] *nf (mesure)* ounce; **il n'a pas une o. de bon sens** he doesn't have an ounce of common sense

once² *nf Zool* ounce, snow leopard

oncle [ɔ̃kl] *nm* uncle; **o. à la mode de Bretagne** first cousin once removed; **o. d'Amérique** rich uncle; **o. à héritage** rich uncle *(from whom one expects to inherit)*; **O. Sam** Uncle Sam

oncogène [ɔ̃kɔʒɛn] *adj Méd* oncogenic

onction [ɔ̃ksjɔ̃] *nf Rel, Fig* unction; *Méd Vieilli* = massage or rubbing with oil

onctueusement [ɔ̃ktɥøzmɑ̃] *adv Péj* unctuously

onctueux, -euse [ɔ̃ktɥø, -øz] *adj (yaourt, sauce)* smooth, creamy; *Péj (manières, paroles)* smooth, unctuous

onctuosité [ɔ̃ktɥozite] *nf (de yaourt, d'une sauce)* smoothness, creaminess

onde [ɔ̃d] *nf* **(a)** *Phys* wave; **o. calorifique/lumineuse/sonore** heat/light/sound wave; *Rad* **ondes** airwaves; **sur les ondes** on the air *or* the radio; **passer sur les ondes** *(d'une émission)* to be broadcast; *(d'une personne)* to be on air *or* radio; **petites ondes** short wave; **grandes ondes** long wave; **sur grandes ondes** on long wave; *Fig F* **nous ne sommes pas sur la même longueur d'o.** we're not on the same wavelength **(b)** *Métal* corrugation **(c)** *Litt* (*eau*) waters; **sur la terre et sur l'o.** on land and water

▶ **onde**: **o. de choc** shock wave; *Rad* **ondes courtes** short wave; **ondes hertziennes** terrestrially-relayed waves; **ondes longues** long wave; **ondes moyennes** medium wave; **ondes radio** radio waves; **ondes très courtes** very high frequency; **ondes ultra-courtes** ultra high frequency

ondé [ɔ̃de] *adj Litt* (*cheveux*) wavy; (*soie*) watered

ondée [ɔ̃de] *nf* sudden downpour

ondemètre [ɔ̃dmɛtr] *nm Rad* wavemeter

ondin, -ine [ɔ̃dɛ̃, -in] *n Myth* water sprite

on-dit *nm inv* rumour, *US* rumor, hearsay; **il ne faut pas croire à ces o.** you shouldn't believe these rumours; **ce ne sont que des o.** it's only hearsay

ondoiement [ɔ̃dwamɑ̃] *nm* **(a)** (*des roseaux, du maïs etc*) swaying, undulation **(b)** *Rel* summary baptism (*conducted in cases of emergency*)

ondoyant [ɔ̃dwajɑ̃] *adj* **(a)** (*sol*) undulating; (*cheveux*) wavy; (*foule, mouvement*) swaying; (*roseaux*) swaying, undulating **(b)** *Litt* (*personne, caractère*) changeable

ondoyer [ɔ̃dwaje] **(j'ondoie; j'ondoierai) 1** *vi* (*des blés*) to sway, to undulate; (*d'un drapeau*) to wave; (*de la surface de l'eau*) to undulate; (*de flammes*) to flicker **2** *vt Rel* to baptize summarily (*in cases of emergency*)

ondulant [ɔ̃dylɑ̃] *adj* (*courbe, ligne*) undulating; (*plaine*) rolling, undulating; (*roseaux*) swaying, undulating; (*crinière*) flowing; **avoir une démarche ondulante** to swing one's hips

ondulation [ɔ̃dylasjɔ̃] *nf* (*de l'eau, du sol etc*) undulation; (*dans les cheveux*) wave; *TV* **o. de l'image** picture weave

ondulatoire [ɔ̃dylatwar] *adj* undulatory; *Phys* **mouvement o.** wave motion

ondulé [ɔ̃dyle] *adj* (*sol*) undulating; (*cheveux*) wavy; (*tôle, carton*) corrugated; **route ondulée** switchback road; **trait o.** wavy line

onduler [ɔ̃dyle] **1** *vi* to undulate; (*cheveux*) to be wavy **2** *vt* (*cheveux*) to wave

onduleur [ɔ̃dylœr] *nm Ordinat* uninterruptible power supply, UPS

onduleux, -euse [ɔ̃dylø, -øz] *adj* = **ondulant**

onéreux, -euse [ɔnerø, -øz] *adj* (*dépense*) heavy; (*achat*) expensive, costly; **à titre o.** subject to payment

ONG [oɛnʒe] *nf* (*abrév* **organisation non gouvernementale**) NGO

ongle [ɔ̃gl] *nm* (finger)nail; (*des orteils*) (toe)nail; (*d'un animal*) claw; (*d'un oiseau de proie*) talon, claw; **coup d'o.** scratch; **se faire les ongles** to do one's nails; *F* **avoir les ongles en deuil** to have dirty nails; *Méd* **o. incarné** ingrowing nail; **se ronger les ongles** to bite one's nails; *Fig* **avoir les ongles crochus** to be mean *or* tight-fisted; **connaître** *ou* **savoir qch sur le bout des ongles** to know sth perfectly; **il est français jusqu'au bout des ongles** he's French to his fingertips, he's every inch a Frenchman

▶ **ongle**: *Méd* **o. incarné** ingrowing nail

onglée [ɔ̃gle] *nf* tingling, aching (*of numbed fingertips*); **j'ai l'o.** my fingers are numb with cold

onglet [ɔ̃glɛ] *nm* **(a)** (*d'un répertoire*) tab; (*d'un canif*) thumbnail groove; **dictionnaire à onglets** thumb-indexed dictionary; **o. à fenêtre** (*d'une fiche etc*) window tab **(b)** *Typ* (*d'un livre*) guard **(c)** *Menuis* mitre, *US* miter; **boîte à onglets** mitre box; **tailler à o.** to mitre **(d)** *Culin* flank of beef

onglier [ɔ̃glije] *nm* manicure set

onguent [ɔ̃gɑ̃] *nm Litt* ointment, unguent

ongulé [ɔ̃gyle] *adj, nm Zool* ungulate

onirique [ɔnirik] *adj Litt* dreamlike

onirisme [ɔnirism] *nm* (state of) hallucination

onirologie [ɔnirɔlɔʒi] *nf* interpretation of dreams

ONN [oɛnɛn] *nm* (*abrév* **Office national de la navigation**) French national shipping and inland waterways office

onomasiologie [ɔnɔmazjɔlɔʒi] *nf Ling* onomasiology

onomastique [ɔnɔmastik] *Ling* **1** *nf* onomastics **2** *adj* onomastic

onomatopée [ɔnɔmatɔpe] *nf* onomatopoeia

onomatopéique [ɔnɔmatɔpeik] *adj* onomatopoeic

ontogenèse [ɔ̃tɔʒənɛz] *nf* ontogenesis, ontogeny

ontogénétique [ɔ̃tɔʒenetik] *adj* ontogenetic, ontogenic

ontologie [ɔ̃tɔlɔʒi] *nf Phil* ontology

ontologique [ɔ̃tɔlɔʒik] *adj Phil* ontological

ONU [ony, oɛny] *nf* (*abrév* **Organisation des Nations unies**) UN

onusien, -ienne [ɔnyzjɛ̃, -jɛn] **1** *adj* (of the) UN; **la politique onusienne** UN policy **2** *n* UN official

onyx [ɔniks] *nm Minér* onyx

onze [ɔ̃z] (*the* **e** *of* **le** *and* **de** *is not, as a rule, elided before* **onze** *and its derivatives*) **1** *adj inv* eleven; **o. cent trente** eleven hundred and thirty; **nous n'étions que o.** [kəɔ̃z] **nous n'étions qu'o.** there were only eleven of us; **le o. avril** the eleventh of April, *Am* April eleventh; **Louis O.** Louis the Eleventh **2** *nm inv Fb* **le o. de France** the French team, the French eleven

onzième [ɔ̃zjɛm] **1** *adj* eleventh; **le o. jour** the eleventh day **2** *n* (*personne, chose*) eleventh **3** *nm* (*fraction*) eleventh **4** *nf Mus* eleventh

onzièmement [ɔ̃zjɛmmɑ̃] *adv* in the eleventh place

oolithe [ɔɔlit] *nm Minér* oolite

oolithique [ɔɔlitik] *adj Minér* oolitic

OPA [opea] *nf* (*abrév* **offre publique d'achat**) takeover bid; **lancer une O.** to make a takeover bid (**sur** for); **O. amicale/inamicale** friendly/hostile takeover bid; **être l'objet d'une O.** to be the subject of a takeover bid

opacification [ɔpasifikasjɔ̃] *nf* making opaque

opacifier [ɔpasifje] *vt* to make opaque

opacité [ɔpasite] *nm* (*d'un corps, d'un liquide*) opacity, opaqueness; (*d'une forêt*) darkness, denseness; (*d'un texte*) opaqueness, impenetrability

opale [ɔpal] **1** *nf* opal **2** *adj inv* **verre o.** opal glass; *Él* **ampoule o.** pearl bulb

opalescence [ɔpalesɑ̃s] *nf* opalescence

opalescent [ɔpalɛsɑ̃] *adj* opalescent

opalin, -ine [ɔpalɛ̃, -in] **1** *adj* (*nuance, reflet*) opaline **2** *nf* opaline

opaque [ɔpak] *adj* opaque; (*forêt*) dark, dense; *Fig* (*texte, explications*) opaque, impenetrable; **collant o.** opaque tights; **o. aux rayons X** impervious to X-rays; *Ling* **mot o.** opaque word

OPCVM [opeseveɛm] *nm Bourse* (*abrév* **organisme de placement collectif en valeurs mobilières**) unit trust, *Am* mutual fund; **O. actions** equity-based unit trust

OPE [opeə] *nf abrév* **offre publique d'échange**

opéable [ɔpeabl] *adj* ripe for takeover

opeamania [opeamanja] *nf Fin* takeover fever

open [ɔpɛn] **1** *adj inv* open; **une compétition o.** an open competition; **un billet o.** an open ticket **2** *nm Sp* open; **un o. de tennis** a tennis open

OPEP [ɔpɛp] *nf* (*abrév* **Organisation des pays exportateurs de pétrole**) OPEC

opéra [ɔpera] *nm* **(a)** (*genre, œuvre*) opera; **il aime beaucoup l'o.** he loves opera; **c'est une chanteuse d'o.** she's an opera singer; **grand o.** grand opera **(b)** (*lieu*) opera house; **je vais rarement à l'o.** I rarely go to the opera; **l'O. (de Paris)** the Paris Opera House; **les petits rats de l'O.** = the ballet pupils at the Paris Opera House

▶ **opéra**: **o. bouffe** comic opera, opera buffa

opérable [ɔperabl] *adj Chir* (*tumeur*) operable; (*malade*) who can be operated on, operable

opéra-comique, *pl* **opéras-comiques** *nm* opéra comique (*opera with spoken dialogue*)

opérande [ɔperɑ̃d] *nm Ordinat* operand

opérant [ɔperɑ̃] *adj* effective; **les mesures ont été opérantes** the measures (taken) were effective

opérateur, -trice [ɔperatœr, -tris] **1** *n* (*personne*) (machine) operator; *Typ* machine setter; *Journ* copytaker; *Fin* trader; *Tél* operator; *Cin* cameraman **2** *nm* **(a)** *Math* operator **(b)** (*d'une machine*) working piece

▶ **opérateur**: *TV, Cin* **o. banc-titre** rostrum cameraman; *Ordinat* **o. booléen** Boolean operator; *Fin* **o. boursier** stock-exchange dealer; *Ordinat* **o. de comparaison** comparator; *Ordinat* **o. logique** logical operator; *TV, Cin* **o. magnétoscope** videotape operator; *TV, Cin* **o. de prise de vue** camera(man), camera operator; **o. de radio** radio operator; *Ordinat* **o. relationnel** relational operator; *Ordinat* **o. de saisie** keyboard operator, keyboarder; *TV, Cin* **o. steadicam** steadicam operator; *Com* **o. de transport multimodal** multi-modal operator; **o. vidéo** video operator; *TV, Cin* **o. de la vision** video control operator

opération [ɔperasjɔ̃] *nf* **(a)** *Chir* **o. (chirurgicale)** operation; **subir une o.** to have *or* undergo an operation; **salle d'o.** operating theatre *or Am* room

(b) *Math, Mil, Ordinat* operation; *Com, Fin, Banque* deal, transaction; **o. financière** financial transaction; **o. imposable** taxable transaction; **opérations militaires** military operations; **o. de police** police operation; **o. publicitaire** advertising campaign; *Fin* **opérations fermes** firm transactions; *Scol* **j'ai des opérations à faire pour demain** I've got some calculations to do for tomorrow

(c) (*démarche*) operation, process; **par l'o. du Saint-Esprit** by the working of the Holy Ghost; *Fig F* by magic

▶ **opération**: **opérations de Bourse** Stock Exchange dealings *or* business *or* transactions; *Banque* **opérations de caisse** counter transactions; *Compta* **o. en capital** capital transaction; *Méd* **o. à chaud** emergency operation (*for* *appendicitis etc*); *Chir* **o. à cœur ouvert** open-heart surgery; *Com* **opérations en commun** joint ventures; *Compta* **o. courante** normal business transaction; *Compta* **opérations courantes** ordinary activities; **o. escargot** go-slow *or Am* slow-down by lorry/bus/car drivers; *Bourse* **o. de journée** day trade; *Bourse* **o. jumbo** jumbo trade; *Ordinat* **o. 'si-alors'** if-then operation

opérationnel, -elle [ɔperasjɔnɛl] *adj* operational

opératoire [ɔperatwar] *adj Chir* (*procédure*) operating; **médecine o.** surgery; **choc o.** post-operative shock

opercule [ɔpɛrkyl] *nm Tech* cover, lid, cap; *Biol* (*d'un poisson, d'un mollusque*) operculum; *Naut* **o. de hublot** deadlight

operculé [ɔpɛrkyle] *adj Biol* operculate(d)

opéré, -ée [ɔpere] *n* patient (who has had an operation)

opérer [ɔpere] **(j'opère; j'opérerai) 1** *vt* **(a)** (*accomplir, faire*) (*réforme*) to carry out; (*multiplication, Ch synthèse*) to perform; **o. une retraite** to (effect a) retreat; **o. un sondage** *Tech* to sink a borehole; (*d'opinion*) to carry out *or* conduct an opinion poll; *Banque* **o. un virement** to make a transfer

(b) *Chir* to operate on; **être opéré de l'appendicite** to be operated on for appendicitis, to have an operation for appendicitis; **o. qn des amygdales** to take sb's tonsils out; **se faire o.** to have *or* undergo an operation; **se faire o. des amygdales** to have one's tonsils taken out; **tu t'es déjà fait o.?** have you been operated on *or* had an operation before?

2 *vi* (*d'un médicament*) to take effect, to work; **laisser o. la nature** to let nature take its course; **laissons les choses o. par elles-mêmes** let's allow things to take their own course; **son éloquence/charme opéra sur la foule** his eloquence/charm had an effect on *or* worked on the crowd; **la façon dont les cambrioleurs ont opéré** the way the burglars went to work, *F* the burglars' M.O. ; **je ne sais pas comment il opère en de telles circonstances** I don't know how he proceeds in such circumstances

3 s'opérer *vpr* (*d'un changement, d'une transformation*) to come about, to take place; **un changement complet s'est opéré dans sa vie** there's been a complete change in his life, his life has changed completely

opérette [ɔperɛt] *nf* operetta; **chanteuse d'o.** operetta singer; *Fig* **héros d'o.** cardboard *or* two-dimensional hero

ophidien, -ienne [ɔfidjɛ̃, -jɛn] *adj, nm* ophidian

ophite [ɔfit] *nm Minér* ophite, serpentine

ophrys [ɔfris] *nm Bot* ophrys; **o. abeille** bee orchid; **o. araignée** spider orchid

ophtalmie [ɔftalmi] *nf Méd* ophthalmia; **o. des neiges** snow blindness

ophtalmique [ɔftalmik] *adj Méd* ophthalmic

ophtalmo [ɔftalmo] *n Méd F* ophthalmologist

ophtalmologie [ɔftalmɔlɔʒi] *nf Méd* ophthalmology

ophtalmologiste [ɔftalmɔlɔʒist], **ophtalmologue** [ɔftalmɔlɔg] *n Méd* ophthalmologist

ophtalmoscope [ɔftalmɔskɔp] *nm Méd* ophthalmoscope

opiacé [ɔpjase] *Pharm* **1** *adj* containing opium, opiate **2** *n* opiate

opiner [ɔpine] *vi* **o. pour/contre qch** to come down in favour of/against sth; **o. du chef** *ou* **de la tête** *ou* **du bonnet** to nod (one's) assent, to nod in agreement

opiniâtre [ɔpinjɑtr] *adj* (*tenace*) (*personne*) obstinate, stubborn; (*toux*) stubborn, persistent; (*opposition*) stubborn, unyielding; (*résistance*) stubborn, dogged

opiniâtrement [ɔpinjɑtrəmɑ̃] *adv* obstinately, stubbornly; (*résister*) stubbornly, doggedly

opiniâtreté [ɔpinjɑtrəte] *nf Vieilli* (*obstination*) obstinacy, stubbornness; (*persévérance*) perseverance, determination

opinion [ɔpinjɔ̃] *nf* opinion (**de** of; **sur** about, on); **opinions politiques/religieuses** political/religious opinions *or* views; **liberté d'o.** freedom of thought *or* opinion; **journal d'o.** = political weekly/monthly (with a particular stance); **créer un mouvement d'o.** to create a groundswell of opinion; **sondage d'o.** opinion poll; **se faire une o. sur qch** to make up one's mind about sth, to form an opinion about sth; **mon o. est faite** I've made up my mind; **émettre** *ou* **exprimer une o.** to express an opinion; **sans o.** (*dans un sondage*) don't know; **les opinions sont partagées** opinion is divided; **partager l'o. de qn** to agree with sb, to share sb's opinion; **partager les opinions de qn** to share sb's opinions *or* views, to think the same way as sb; **avoir le courage de ses opinions** to have the courage of one's convictions; **amener qn à son o.** to bring sb round to one's way of thinking; **avoir bonne/mauvaise o. de qn/qch** to have a good/bad opinion of sb/sth; **donner bonne o. de soi** to make a good impression

▶ **opinion**: **o. publique** public opinion

opiomane [ɔpjɔman] *n* opium addict

opium [ɔpjɔm] *nm* opium; *Fig* **la religion est l'o. du peuple** religion is the opium of the people; *Hist* **guerre de l'o.** opium war

opossum [ɔpɔsɔm] *nm* opossum

opportun, -une [ɔpɔrtœ̃, -yn] *adj* (*arrivée*) timely, opportune, well-timed; (*moment, jour*) right; **arriver au moment o.** to come at the right time *or* an opportune moment

opportunément [ɔpɔrtynemɑ̃] *adv* at the right time, opportunely

opportunisme [ɔpɔrtynism] *nm* opportunism

opportuniste [ɔpɔrtynist] **1** *adj* opportunist; (*maladie*) opportunistic **2** *n* opportunist

opportunité [ɔpɔrtynite] *nf* (*d'une arrivée*) timeliness, *Fml* opportuneness; (*d'un projet, d'une décision*) advisability; **o. commerciale** market opportunity; **o. mercatique** marketing opportunity

opposable [ɔpozabl] *adj* opposable (**à** to); **rien n'est o. à ses arguments** there is no answer to his arguments, nothing can be said against his arguments

opposant, -ante [ɔpozɑ̃, -ɑ̃t] **1** *adj* (*minorité*) opposing **2** *n* opponent (**à** of); *Pol* member of the Opposition

opposé [ɔpoze] **1** *adj* **(a)** (*armées, caractères etc*) opposing; (*côtés, rivage, direction*) opposite; (*intérêts, conseil*) conflicting; **angles opposés par le sommet** vertically opposite angles; **leurs opinions sont diamétralement opposées** their views are poles apart *or* diametrically opposed; **elle est plutôt artiste, lui est diamétralement o.** she is rather artistic, he is the exact opposite; **tons opposés** contrasting colours

(b) être o. à une mesure to oppose *or* be opposed to *or* be against a measure; **je suis opposé à ce qu'une centrale soit construite dans cette région** I'm opposed to *or* I'm against a power station being built in this area

2 *nm* **(a)** (*contraire*) **l'o.** the opposite, the reverse; **à l'o.** (*dans l'espace*) opposite, on the other side; *Fig* on the other hand; **le deuxième film de ce réalisateur est vraiment l'o. du premier** the director's second film is the complete opposite of *or* is in complete contrast to his first; **mon avis est à l'o. du sien** my opinion is the opposite of his; **à l'o. de ce que nous attendions** contrary to expectation *or* to what we expected; **cela va à l'o. de ce que l'on m'avait promis/de notre politique** that goes against what I was promised/our policy

(b) la gare est à l'o. the station is in the opposite direction; **à l'o. de la gare** opposite the station

opposer [ɔpoze] **1** *vt* (*deux adversaires*) to bring into conflict (with each other); **o. des arguments valables à une théorie** to put forward valid arguments against a theory; **je n'ai rien à o. à ce raisonnement** I cannot counter this argument; **que peut-il t'o.?** what objection can he have to that?, what can he say against that?; **o. une résistance vigoureuse** to put up *or* offer vigorous resistance; *F* to resist tooth and nail; **o. un farouche refus à qch** to be fiercely opposed to sth; **o. son veto** to exercise one's veto; **o. des idées/théories l'une à l'autre** to contrast ideas/theories; **o. Mozart à Debussy** to contrast Mozart with Debussy; **cette course oppose les meilleurs athlètes de toute l'Europe** this race brings together Europe's finest athletes; **ce match opposera le joueur français au joueur américain** this match will pit the French player against the American; **la finale opposera la France à l'Italie** France will meet Italy *or* come up against Italy in the final

2 s'opposer *vpr* **s'o. à qch** to oppose sth, to be opposed to sth, to be against sth; **nous nous opposons à ce que la centrale soit construite** we oppose the building of the power station, we are opposed to *or* are against the power station being built; **nous nous opposons à ce qu'il arrête ses études** we are against *or* we are opposed to the idea of him giving up his studies; **il n'y a pas de loi qui s'y oppose** there is no law against it; **rien ne s'oppose à votre succès** nothing stands between you and success; **rien ne s'oppose à votre projet** nothing stands in the way of your plan; **rien ne s'oppose à ce que vous fassiez ce que vous souhaitez** there's nothing to stop you doing what you want to; **les meilleurs joueurs d'échecs s'opposent dans ce tournoi** this tournament pits the best chess players against one another, the best chess players come up against each other in this tournament

opposite [ɔpozit] *nm* **à l'o. de** opposite, facing; *Fig* opposed to

opposition [ɔpozisjɔ̃] *nf* **(a)** (*résistance*) opposition; *Pol* **l'o.** the Opposition; **faire o. à un chèque** to stop a cheque, to stop payment of a cheque; **à chaque fois qu'on parle d'un nouveau projet, il fait de l'o.** every time there is talk of a new plan, he is opposed to it *or* against it

(b) *Jur* caveat; **o. sur titre** attachment against securities; **jugement susceptible d'o.** judgment liable to stay of execution

(c) (*contraste*) contrast; **c'est en o. totale avec les**

principes qu'il expose dans ses livres it is in complete contrast to *or* is totally at odds with *or* totally contradicts the principles that he puts forward in his books; **tout cela est en o. totale avec ce que je pense** all that is the complete opposite of what I think; **par o. à qch** as opposed to sth; **couleurs en o.** contrasting colours
(**d**) *Astron* (*des planètes*) opposition

oppressant [ɔpresɑ̃] *adj* (*chaleur, sentiment*) oppressive

oppresser [ɔprese] *vt* (**a**) (*d'une situation, d'une atmosphère etc*) to oppress (**b**) (*de problèmes, responsabilités*) to weigh down (**c**) *Litt* = **opprimer**

oppresseur [ɔpresœr] **1** *nm* oppressor **2** *adj m* oppressive

oppressif, -ive [ɔpresif, -iv] *adj* (*gouvernement, autorité etc*) oppressive

oppression [ɔpresjɔ̃] *nf* (**a**) (*d'un peuple*) oppression (**b**) *Méd* **o. de la poitrine** tightness of the chest, difficulty in breathing

opprimé, -ée [ɔprime] **1** *adj* oppressed, down-trodden **2** *npl* **les opprimés** the oppressed

opprimer [ɔprime] *vt* (*peuple, nation*) to oppress; (*liberté*) to suppress

opprobre [ɔprɔbr] *nm Litt* opprobrium; **jeter l'o. sur qn** to cast opprobrium on sb; **accabler** *ou* **couvrir qn d'o.** to heap opprobrium on sb

optatif, -ive [ɔptatif, -iv] *adj, nm Ling* optative

opter [ɔpte] *vi* **o. entre deux choses** to choose between two things; **o. pour qch** to opt for sth

opticien, -ienne [ɔptisjɛ̃, -jɛn] *n* optician

optimal, -ale, -aux, -ales [ɔptimal, -o] *adj* optimum, optimal

optimisation [ɔptimizasjɔ̃] *nf aussi Ordinat* optimization

optimiser [ɔptimize] *vt Ordinat, Mktg etc* to optimize

optimiseur [ɔptimizœr] *nm Ordinat* optimizer

optimisme [ɔptimism] *nm* optimism; **avec o.** optimistically

optimiste [ɔptimist] **1** *adj* optimistic; **sois un peu o.,** try to be optimistic, try to look on the bright side; **nous ne sommes pas très optimistes quant à la guérison de ce malade** we're not very optimistic about the patient's chances of recovery *or* that the patient will recover **2** *n* optimist

optimum [ɔptimɔm], *pl* **optimums,** *parfois* **optima 1** *adj* (*conditions*) optimum; **la température o.** *ou* **optima ne dépasse pas 5 degrés** the optimum temperature does not exceed 5 degrees **2** *nm* optimum

option [ɔpsjɔ̃] *nf* option, choice (**de** of; **entre** between); **prendre une o. sur qch** to take (out) an option on sth; **le flash est en o.** the flash is optional *or* is an optional extra; *Bourse* **jour d'o.** option day; *Scol* **matières à o.** optional *or* elective subjects; **il avait le latin en o. au baccalauréat** he took Latin as an option *or* an optional subject *or* an elective subject for the baccalauréat

▶ **option**: *Bourse* **o. d'achat** call (option), option to buy; *Bourse* **o. sur actions** option on shares; *Bourse* **o. américaine** American-style option; *Fin* **o. de change** foreign currency option; *Bourse* **o. européenne** European-style option; *Ordinat* **o. d'impression** print option; *Bourse* **o. sur indice** index option; *Ordinat* **o. de menu** menu option; *Bourse* **o. négociable** traded option; *Ordinat* **o. de sauvegarde** save option; *Bourse* **o. de vente** put (option), option to sell

optionnel, -elle [ɔpsjɔnɛl] *adj* optional

optique [ɔptik] **1** *adj* (*nerf*) optic; (*angle*) visual; (*verre*) optical; **télégraphie o.** visual signalling **2** *nf* (**a**) (*science*) optics; **instruments d'o.** optical instruments; **o. électronique** electron optics; **transmettre par o.** to communicate by visual signals (**b**) (*perspective*) perspective; **nous ne travaillons pas dans la même o.** we're working towards different aims; **o. du théâtre** stage perspective; *Mktg* **o. mercatique** marketing orientation; *Mktg* **o. produit** product orientation; *Mktg* **o. vente** sales orientation, sales philosophy (**c**) (*d'un projecteur*) optical system

optométrie [ɔptɔmetri] *nf* optometry

optométriste [ɔptɔmetrist] *n* optometrist

opulence [ɔpylɑ̃s] *nf* opulence, affluence; *Fig* (*de la poitrine, des formes etc*) fullness, ampleness; **nager** *ou* **être dans l'o.** to be rolling in money; **vivre dans l'o.** to have an opulent lifestyle, to live in opulence

opulent [ɔpylɑ̃] *adj* (*mobilier, environs*) opulent; (*personne*) opulent, wealthy, affluent; *Fig* (*moisson, pâturage*) abundant; **une poitrine opulente** an ample *or* full bosom

opuscule [ɔpyskyl] *nm* opuscule

or[1] [ɔr] *nm* (**a**) (*métal*) gold; **or pur/fin** pure/fine gold; **la ruée vers l'or** the gold rush; **chercheur d'or** gold-prospector; *Fig* gold-digger; *Min, Fig* **mine d'or** gold mine; *Fig* **cette boutique est une véritable mine d'or pour les collectionneurs** this shop is a real gold mine *or* treasure trove for collectors; **or en barre** *ou* **en lingots** (gold) bullion; *Fig* **c'est de l'or en barre** it's as safe as the Bank of England *or* as houses; *Fin* **étalon or** gold standard; **poudre d'or** gold dust; **montre en or** *ou* **d'or** gold watch; **bracelet doré à l'or fin** a fine gold(-plated) bracelet; **en or massif** (in) solid gold; **or en feuille(s)** gold leaf *or* foil; **feuille d'or** gold leaf; **payer qch à prix d'or** to pay a fortune for sth; **revendre qch à prix d'or** to resell sth for a fortune; **affaire en or** (*achat*) excellent bargain; (*commerce, combine*) lucrative line of business; *F* **j'ai une femme en or** I've a wonderful wife; **il/ça vaut son pesant d'or** he's worth his/it's worth its weight in gold; **pour tout l'or du monde** for all the money in the world, for all the tea in China; **l'âge d'or** the golden age; **cœur d'or** heart of gold; **parler d'or** to speak words of wisdom; **livre d'or** (official) visitors' book; **rouler sur l'or, être (tout) cousu d'or** to be rolling in money, to have money coming out of one's ears; **il ne roule pas sur l'or** he isn't exactly rolling in it; *Prov* **tout ce qui brille n'est pas or** all that glitters *or* glistens is not gold; **le silence est d'or** silence is golden
(**b**) (*couleur*) gold; *Hér* or; **vieil or** old gold; **murs/voiture vieil or** old gold walls/car; **chevelure d'or** golden hair

▶ **or**: **or blanc** *ou* **gris** white gold; **o. noir** black gold, oil; **or rouge** red gold

or[2] *conj* now; (*pour conclure*) well; **or, pour revenir à ce que nous disions** now to come back to what we were saying; **or ..., donc ...** now ..., therefore ...; **avant de le lire, je pensais que le livre était bon — or, il ne l'était pas** before reading it, I thought the book was good — well, it wasn't; **il n'achète jamais de chocolats, or ...** he never buys chocolates, but ...

oracle [ɔrɑkl] *nm* oracle; **parler d'un ton d'o.** to speak with assurance

orage [ɔraʒ] *nm* (thunder)storm; **temps d'o.** thundery *or* stormy weather; **le temps est à l'o.** there's thunder in the air, there's a storm brewing; *Fig* **l'atmosphère est à l'o. au bureau** there's trouble *or* a storm brewing in the office; **il va faire de l'o., il y a de l'o. dans l'air** there's a storm brewing; *Fig* there's trouble *or* a storm brewing, there's trouble in the air; *Fig* **laisser passer l'o.** to let the storm blow over

▶ **orage**: **o. magnétique** magnetic storm

orageusement [ɔraʒøzmɑ̃] *adv* stormily

orageux, -euse [ɔraʒø, -øz] *adj* (*temps*) thundery, stormy; (*saison, mer*) stormy; *Fig* (*vie*) stormy, tempestuous; (*discussion*) stormy, heated

oraison [ɔrɛzɔ̃] *nf* prayer; **faire** *ou* **dire** *ou* **réciter une o.** to say a prayer; **o. funèbre** funeral oration

oral, -ale, -aux, -ales [ɔral, -o] **1** *adj* (*tradition, enseignement, examen*) oral; (*déposition, communication*) oral, verbal; *Anat* (*cavité*) oral; **par voie orale** orally; *Psy* **stade o.** oral stage **2** *nm* oral examination; *surtout Univ* oral *or* viva voce examination, *F* oral, viva

oralement [ɔralmɑ̃] *adv* orally

orange [ɔrɑ̃ʒ] **1** *nf* (*fruit*) orange; **peau d'o.** orange peel; *Fig* orange-peel skin **2** *nm* (*couleur*) orange; *Aut* **passer à l'o.** to go through (the lights) on amber; **le feu était à l'o.** the lights were at amber **3** *adj inv* orange; *Aut* **feu o.** amber light; **carte o.** (*pour les transports parisiens*) = monthly season ticket

▶ **orange**: **o. amère** bitter orange, Seville orange; **o. givrée** orange sorbet; **o. pressée** freshly-squeezed orange juice; **o. sanguine** blood orange

orangé [ɔrɑ̃ʒe] **1** *adj* orange-coloured *or US* -colored **2** *nm* orange colour *or US* color

orangeade [ɔrɑ̃ʒad] *nf* orangeade

oranger [ɔrɑ̃ʒe] *nm* orange tree; **fleur d'o.** orange blossom; **eau de fleur d'o.** orange-flower water

orangeraie [ɔrɑ̃ʒrɛ] *nf* orange grove

orangerie [ɔrɑ̃ʒri] *nf* orangery

orang-outan(g) [ɔrɑ̃utɑ̃], *pl* **orangs-outan(g)s** *nm* orang-outang, orang-utan

orateur, -trice [ɔratœr, -tris] *n* orator; (*dans un dîner*) speaker

oratoire[1] [ɔratwar] *adj* oratorical; **l'art o.** (the art of) oratory, public speaking; **il a pris des précautions oratoires** he chose his words carefully; **joutes oratoires** verbal sparring matches

oratoire[2] *nm Rel* (**a**) (*chapelle*) oratory, chapel for private prayer (**b**) **l'O.** the Oratory

oratorio [ɔratɔrjo] *nm Mus* oratorio

orbe[1] [ɔrb] *nm* orb

orbe[2] *adj* **mur o.** blind wall

orbitaire [ɔrbitɛr] *adj Anat* orbital

orbital, -ale, -aux, -ales [ɔrbital, -o] *adj Astron* orbital

orbite [ɔrbit] *nf* (**a**) (*d'une planète, d'un vaisseau spatial, d'un électron*) orbit; **en** *ou* **sur o.** in orbit; **mettre** *ou* **placer un satellite en** *ou* **sur o.** to put a satellite into orbit (**b**) (*sphère d'influence*) orbit, (sphere of) influence (**c**) *Anat* (*de l'œil*) socket, orbit

orbiter [ɔrbite] *vi* to orbit
Orcades (les) [lezɔrkad] *nfpl* the Orkneys, the Orkney Islands
orchestral, -ale, -aux, -ales [ɔrkɛstral, -o] *adj* orchestral
orchestration [ɔrkɛstrasjɔ̃] *nf* **(a)** *Mus* orchestration; **faire une nouvelle o. d'un morceau** to re-orchestrate a piece **(b)** *Fig (d'une campagne électorale ou commerciale)* orchestration, organization
orchestre [ɔrkɛstr] *nm* [①A11,g,i] *Mus* orchestra; **diriger un o.** to conduct an orchestra; **chef d'o.** conductor; **o. de jazz** jazz band; **o. de chambre** chamber orchestra; *Th* **(fauteuil d')o.** seat in the stalls *or Am* orchestra; **deux fauteuils d'o., deux orchestres** two stalls, two stall *or Am* orchestra seats
orchestrer [ɔrkɛstre] *vt Mus* to orchestrate; *Fig (organiser) (campagne électorale ou commerciale etc)* to orchestrate, to organize
orchidée [ɔrkide] *nf* orchid
ordalie [ɔrdali] *nf Hist* ordeal; **o. par l'eau/le feu** ordeal by water/fire
ordinaire [ɔrdinɛr] **1** *adj (habituel)* ordinary, usual, normal; **vêtements ordinaires** ordinary *or* everyday clothes; **vin o.** table *or US* jug wine; **peu** *ou* **pas o.** unusual, uncommon, out of the ordinary; **gens ordinaires** ordinary people; **elle est vraiment o.** she's so ordinary; *F* **voilà une chose qui n'est pas o.!** that's not something you see every day; *Math* **fractions ordinaires** vulgar fractions; *Fin* **actions ordinaires** ordinary shares, *US* common stock; **votre fournisseur o.** your normal *or* regular *or* usual supplier; **votre médicin o.** your usual doctor; **médecin o. du roi** physician in ordinary to the king; **évêque o.** diocesan bishop; **de taille o.** ordinary-sized, normal-sized, *Am* regular-sized; *(personne)* of average height; **vin très o.** very ordinary wine; **une vie très o.** a very ordinary *or* run-of-the-mill life

2 *nm* **(a)** *(habitude)* **d'o., à l'o.** usually, as a rule; **plus en forme qu'à l'o.** fitter than usual; **comme à l'o., comme d'o.** as usual

(b) *(moyenne)* **cela sort de l'o.** it's unusual, it's out of the ordinary; **beauté/intelligence qui sort de l'o.** exceptional beauty/intelligence

(c) *(au restaurant)* standard fare; *Mil* (company) mess; **auberge où l'o. est excellent** inn where the food is excellent; *Mil* **fonds d'o.** mess fund

(d) *Cathol* **l'o. de la messe** the ordinary of the Mass
ordinairement [ɔrdinɛrmɑ̃] *adv* ordinarily, usually, as a rule
ordinal, -ale, -aux, -ales [ɔrdinal, -o] *adj* [①A70,16,1; B56,B] ordinal
ordinateur [ɔrdinatœr] *nm* **(a)** *Ordinat* computer; **o. autonome** stand alone (computer); **o. bloc-notes** notebook (computer); *Aut* **o. de bord** trip computer; **o. de bureau** business computer, desktop (computer); **o. central** mainframe (computer); **o. domestique** home computer; **o. à écran tactile** touch-screen computer; **o. frontal** front end computer *or* processor, front end; **o. individuel** personal computer; **o. de poche** palmtop (computer), pocket computer; **o. portable** *ou* **portatif** portable (computer), laptop (computer); **o. de réseau** network computer; **o. sans clavier** keyboardless computer; **o. serveur** host computer, server; **o. de table** desktop (PC) **(b)** *Rel* ordainer
ordination [ɔrdinasjɔ̃] *nf Rel* ordination
ordinogramme [ɔrdinɔgram] *nm* flow chart
ordonnance [ɔrdɔnɑ̃s] *nf* **(a)** *(disposition) (d'un bâtiment)* layout, (general) arrangement; *(d'un tableau)* organization **(b)** *(ordre)* order; *Jur* order, ruling; **o. d'amnistie** amnesty order; *Fin* **o. de paiement** order *or* warrant for payment, order to pay **(c)** *Méd* prescription; **délivré seulement sur o.** available only on prescription **(d)** *Mil* orderly; **bottes d'o.** standard issue boots; **revolver d'o.** service revolver; **officier d'o.** aide-de-camp; *Naut* flag lieutenant
ordonnancement [ɔrdɔnɑ̃smɑ̃] *nm* **(a)** *Fin* order to pay **(b)** *Ind (de production)* scheduling
ordonnancer [ɔrdɔnɑ̃se] *vt* **(j'ordonnançai(s); n. ordonnançons)** *Fin* to authorize; **o. un paiement** to order *or* authorize a payment
ordonnancier [ɔrdɔnɑ̃sje] *nm (du pharmacien)* prescription book; *(du médecin)* prescription pad
ordonnateur, -trice [ɔrdɔnatœr, -tris] *n* **(a)** organizer; *(d'un spectacle)* master of ceremonies; **o. des pompes funèbres** funeral director *(at the funeral itself)* **(b)** *Admin* person authorized to pass accounts; *Fin* payer; *Bourse* giver *or* placer of an order
ordonné, -ée [ɔrdɔne] **1** *adj* **(a)** *(vie, rangement)* orderly, (well-)ordered; *Ordinat* **traitement non o.** random processing **(b)** *(personne)* tidy, orderly **2** *nf Math* **ordonnée** ordinate; **axe des ordonnées** Y-axis
ordonner [ɔrdɔne] *vt* **(a)** *(mettre de l'ordre dans)* to organize, to arrange; *Math* to arrange in order; **il faut davantage o. votre argumentation** you need to organize your arguments a bit more, you need to get more order into your arguments **(b)** *(commander)* to order; **o. à qn de faire qch** to order sb to do sth; **o. à qn de se taire** to tell sb to be quiet; **o. une grève** to call a strike; **o. une enquête** to order an enquiry; *Méd* **o. un remède à qn** to prescribe a remedy for sb **(c)** *Jur (statuer)* to ordain, to rule; *Rel* **o. qn prêtre** to ordain sb
ordre [ɔrdr] *nm* **(a)** *(organisation)* order; **o. alphabétique/chronologique** alphabetical/chronological order; **par o. alphabétique** in alphabetical order; **o. croissant/décroissant** ascending/descending order; **rangé par o. de grandeur** arranged in order of size; **procéder par o.** to do things in order; *Th* **distribution par o. d'entrée en scène** *ou Cin, TV* **par o. d'apparition à l'écran** cast in order of appearance; **numéro d'o.** serial number; **l'o. de classement des livres/dossiers est le suivant** books/files are arranged as follows; *Fig* **c'est dans l'o. des choses** it's in the nature of things; **avec o.** *(travailler)* methodically; **manque d'o.** untidiness; **manquer d'o.** to be untidy; **en bon o.** *(de façon réglée)* in an orderly manner; *(comme cela doit être)* in good order; **mettre bon o. à qch** to sort sth out; **homme d'o.** orderly man; *(qui est pour l'ordre public)* law-and-order man; **avoir de l'o.** *(ranger ses affaires)* to be tidy; *(être méthodique)* to be methodical; **(re)mettre de l'o. dans sa vie** to put *or* get one's life (back) in order; **(re)mettre de l'o. dans ses souvenirs** to get one's memories into some kind of order; **mettre de l'o. dans sa chambre, mettre sa chambre en o.** to tidy (up) one's room; **laisser une maison en o.** to leave a house tidy; **mettre de l'o. dans ses affaires, mettre ses affaires en o.** *(arranger, régler)* to put one's affairs in order, to settle one's affairs; *Fig* to set one's house in order; **tout est en o.** everything is in order; **en o. de marche** *(machine etc)* in working order

(b) *(discipline)* order; **assurer l'o.** to preserve (law and) order; **maintenir l'o.** to maintain order; **rétablir l'o.** to restore order; **les forces de l'o.** the police, the forces of law and order *(especially at demonstration etc)*; **rappeler qn à l'o.** to call sb to order; **tout est rentré dans l'o.** everything has returned to normal; *(après une émeute etc)* order has been restored; **idées qui renversent l'o. établi** ideas that upset the established order (of things); **retour à l'o. moral** return to traditional moral values

(c) *(catégorie), Biol, Archit* order; **o. des carnivores** order of carnivores; **ordres grecs** classical orders; *Hist* **les trois ordres (de l'État)** the three orders *or* classes (of the State); **de premier o.** first-class, first-rate; **tireur de premier o.** crack shot; **un crétin de premier o.** a first-class cretin; **hôtel de troisième o.** third-rate hotel; **renseignements/idées d'o. général** general information/ideas; **d'o. privé** of a private nature; **dans un tout autre o. d'idées** in a quite different connection; **du même o.** of the same order; **de l'o. de dix tonnes** in the order of *or* in the region of *or* about ten tonnes

(d) *(communauté)* order; **o. religieux** religious *or* monastic order; *Rel* **les ordres** holy orders; **entrer dans les ordres** to take holy orders

(e) *(acte d'autorité)* order; *Mil* order, command; **o. d'exécution** death warrant; *Ind etc* instruction to proceed; **donner l'o. à qn de faire qch** to order sb to do sth; **donner des ordres à qn** to give sb orders, to order sb about; **recevoir des ordres** to be given orders; **je n'ai d'ordres à recevoir de personne** I don't take orders from anyone; **je ne reçois** *ou* **prends mes ordres que de mes supérieurs** I only take orders from my superiors; **se mettre aux ordres de qn** to put oneself at sb's disposal; **être aux ordres de qn** to be at sb's disposal; **je ne suis pas à tes ordres!** I don't take orders from you!; **à vos ordres, mon général!** yes sir!; *Hum* **à vos ordres!** yes sir!; **c'est un o.!** that's an order!; **par o.** *ou* **sur l'o. de qn** on the order of sb; **jusqu'à nouvel o.** until further notice; *(pour le moment)* for the time being; **sauf o. contraire** unless otherwise stated; **mot d'o.** watchword

(f) *Fin, Com* order; **payez à l'o. de J. Martin** pay to the order of J. Martin; **faites votre chèque à l'o. de ...** make your cheque out to ..., make your cheque payable to ...; **c'est à quel o.?** who should I make it out to?, who should I make it payable to?; **à l'o. de ...** payable to (the order of) ...; **billet à o.** bill of exchange payable to order

▶ **ordre**: **o. d'achat** *Com* purchase order; *Bourse* buy order; *Mil* **o. d'appel (sous les drapeaux)** call-up papers, *US* draft notice; **o. des avocats** Bar Association; *Mil* **o. de bataille** battle order *or* array; *Bourse* **o. de bourse** Stock Exchange order; **o. de chevalerie** order of knighthood; *Jur* **o. de comparaître** summons; *Fin* **o. au comptant** cash order; *Bourse* **o. conditionnel** contingent order; *Bourse* **o. environ** discretionary order; *Fin* **o. ferme** firm order; **O. de la Jarretière** Order of the Garter; **o. du jour** *(du comité etc)* agenda; *Mil* general orders, order of the day; *Mil* **cité à l'o. du jour** = mentioned in despatches; *Fig* **le mariage de la princesse est à l'o. du jour** the princess's marriage is very much in the news; **o. de la Légion d'Honneur** Order of the Legion of Honour *or US* Honor; **o. des médecins** the (British/ American/*etc*) Medical Association; *Bourse* **o. au mieux** market order; *Bourse* **o. aux mieux** at best order, at the market order; *Bourse* **o. de négociation** trading order; *Fin* **o. de paiement** payment order; *Banque* **o. permanent** standing order; *Banque* **o. de prélèvement automatique** direct debit mandate; **o. public** law and order, public order; **atteinte à l'o. public** breach of the peace; **troubler l'o. public** to cause a breach of the peace; *Bourse* **o. à révocation** good-till-cancelled order; *Bourse* **o. stop à cours limité** stop-limit order; *Fin* **o. à terme** futures order; *Bourse* **o. 'tout ou rien'** all-or-none order; **o. de vente** order to sell; *Fin* **o. de virement** transfer order

ordure [ɔrdyr] *nf* (a) (*saleté*) dirt, filth, muck; **faire ses ordures sur le trottoir** (*d'un chien*) to make a mess on the pavement
(b) (*objets*) **ordures** refuse, *Br* rubbish, *Am* garbage; **boîte à ordures** dustbin, *Am* garbage *or* trash can; **jeter *ou* mettre qch aux ordures** to throw sth in the dustbin *or* garbage *or* trash can; **c'est bon à mettre aux ordures** it's fit for the dustbin *or Am* garbage can *or Am* the trash
(c) (*dans un échange*) filth, dirt, smut; **dire/écrire des ordures** to talk/write filth *or* dirt *or* smut; *Litt* **se vautrer dans l'o.** to wallow in filth
(d) *Fig Péj très F* **il exploite tout le monde, c'est vraiment une o.** he exploits everybody, he's a real shit *or* bastard
▶ **ordure**: **ordures ménagères** household refuse *or Br* rubbish *or Am* garbage

ordurier, -ière [ɔrdyrje, -jɛr] *adj* (*livre, chanson, langage*) filthy, dirty, smutty

orée [ɔre] *nf* **à l'o. de la forêt/du bois** on the edge of the forest/wood

oreillard [ɔrɛjar] *nm* (a) *Zool* long-eared bat (b) (*d'un fauteuil*) wing

oreille [ɔrɛj] *nf* (a) (*d'une personne, d'un animal*) ear; **il a les oreilles décollées** his ears stick out, he has protruding ears; *F* **avoir les oreilles en feuilles de chou** to have huge protruding ears; **avoir mal à l'o./aux oreilles** to have earache; **chien aux oreilles courtes/longues** short-eared/ long-eared dog; **mettre *ou* porter son chapeau sur l'o.** to wear one's hat over one ear; *Fig* **baisser l'o., avoir l'o. basse** to be crestfallen; **il partit l'o. basse** he went off with his tail between his legs; **coucher les oreilles** (*d'un cheval*) to set *or* lay its ears back; **tirer les oreilles à qn** to pull *or* tweak sb's ears; *Fig* to give sb a telling off; *Fig* **tu vas te faire tirer les oreilles** you'll get told off, you'll get a telling-off; *F* **il s'est (bien) fait tirer l'o.** he took a lot of coaxing; *F* **il ne s'est pas fait tirer l'o.** he didn't have to be asked twice; *Fig* **montrer le bout de l'o.** to show one's true colours; **rougir jusqu'aux oreilles** to go as red as a beetroot; **n'écouter que d'une o., écouter d'une o. distraite** to listen with half an ear; *F* **ça lui entre par une o. et ça sort par l'autre** it goes in one ear and out the other; **dire *ou* souffler qch à l'o. de qn *ou* dans le creux de l'o. de qn** to whisper sth in sb's ear; **dresser *ou* tendre l'o.** to prick up one's ears; **être tout oreilles** to be all ears; **prêter l'o.** to lend an ear; **je n'en crois pas mes oreilles** I can't believe my ears *or* what I'm hearing; **faire la sourde o. (à qch)** to turn a deaf ear (to sth); **ce n'est pas tombé dans l'o. d'un sourd** it did not fall on deaf ears; **il n'entend pas de cette o.-là** he is deaf in that ear; *Fig* **il ne l'entend pas de cette o.** he won't hear of it; *F* **(é)chauffer les oreilles à qn** to get on sb's nerves, to annoy sb; **casser les oreilles à qn** (*en faisant du bruit*) to deafen sb; (*en posant des questions ennuyeuses*) to drive sb crazy; **c'est le bouche à o. qui a fait le succès de ce film** it was word of mouth that made the film a hit; **quand ça m'est venu *ou* arrivé aux oreilles** when I got to hear of it; **mettre la puce à l'o. à qn** to set sb thinking, to make sb suspicious; **rebattre les oreilles à qn de qch** to go on and on to sb about sth; **être dur d'o.** to be hard of hearing; *Fig* **vous pouvez dormir sur vos deux oreilles** you can sleep easy in your bed; **avoir de l'o.** (*pour la musique*) to have a good ear, to have an ear for music; **avoir l'o. absolue** to have perfect pitch
(b) (*d'un fauteuil*) wing; (*d'un plat, d'un vase*) handle; (*d'une casquette*) ear flap; **écrou à oreilles** wing *or* butterfly nut
(c) *Journ* position to right/left of headline
▶ **oreille**: *Anat* **o. externe** outer ear; *Anat* **o. interne** inner ear; *Anat* **o. moyenne** middle ear

oreiller [ɔrɛje] *nm* pillow; **taie d'o.** pillowcase, pillowslip; **sur l'o.** in bed; **confidences sur l'o.** pillow talk

oreillette [ɔrɛjɛt] *nf* (a) *Anat* (*du cœur*) auricle, atrium (b) **fauteuil à oreillettes** wing chair; **casquette à oreillettes** cap with ear flaps

oreillons [ɔrɛjɔ̃] *nmpl* [①A10,d] *Méd* mumps

Orénoque (l') [lɔrenɔk] *nm* the Orinoco

ores [ɔr] *adv* **d'o. et déjà** already

orfèvre [ɔrfɛvr] *nm* goldsmith/silversmith; *Fig* **être o. en la matière** to be an expert in the matter

orfèvrerie [ɔrfɛvrəri] *nf* (*métier*) goldsmith's/silversmith's trade; (*magasin*) goldsmith's/silversmith's shop; (*objets*) plate

orfraie [ɔrfrɛ] *nf Orn* sea eagle; *F* **pousser des cris d'o.** to shriek at the top of one's voice

organdi [ɔrgɑ̃di] *nm Tex* organdie

organe [ɔrgan] *nm* (a) *Physiol* organ; **les organes génitaux** the genital organs, the genitals, the genitalia (b) (*élément*) (*d'une machine*) part, component; **organes de transmission** transmission system; *Ordinat* **o. d'entrée** input unit; *Ordinat* **o. périphérique** peripheral device (c) *Fig* (*instrument*) organ; **o. de publicité** advertising agency; **o. de presse** (*publication*) organ of the press; **l'o. officiel du parti** the official organ of the party (d) (*voix*) voice; **o. mâle et sonore** manly voice; *Hum* **il a un bel o.** he has a fine voice

organigramme [ɔrganigram] *nm* organization chart; *Ordinat* (data) flow chart; **o. de production** production flowchart

organique [ɔrganik] *adj* (*maladie, chimie, loi*) organic

organiquement [ɔrganikmɑ̃] *adv* organically

organisateur, -trice [ɔrganizatœr, -tris] **1** *adj* organizing **2** *n* organizer; (*d'une rencontre sportive*) promoter, organizer; **o. de conférences/de congrès** conference organizer; **o. de voyages** tour operator

organisation [ɔrganizasjɔ̃] *nf* (a) (*planification*) organization; **qualités d'o.** organizing *or* organizational ability; *Ordinat* **o. des données** data organization (b) (*groupement*) organization; **o. à but non lucratif** non profit-making organization, *Am* not-for-profit organization; **o. politique/ syndicale** political/trade-union organization (c) *Biol* (*du corps humain*) structure
▶ **organisation**: **O. de l'alimentation et l'agriculture** Food and Agriculture Organization; *Hist* **O. de l'armée secrète** Secret Army Organization (= *right-wing group opposed to Algerian independence*); **O. de l'aviation civile internationale** International Civil Aviation Authority; **O. de coopération et de développement économique** Organization for Economic Cooperation and Development; **O. internationale de normalisation** International Standards Organization; **O. internationale du travail** International Labour Organization; **O. de libération de la Palestine** Palestine Liberation Organization; **O. maritime internationale** International Maritime Organization; **O. mondiale de la santé** World Health Organization; **O. des Nations unies** United Nations Organization; **O. des Nations unies pour l'éducation, la science et la culture** United Nations Educational, Scientific and Cultural Organization; **O. de la navigation maritime consultative et intergouvernementale** Intergovernmental Maritime Consultative Organization; **o. non gouvernementale** non-governmental organization; **O. des pays exportateurs de pétrole** O. of Petroleum Exporting Countries; **o. scientifique du travail** organization and methods, time and motion studies; **O. du traité de l'Atlantique Nord** North Atlantic Treaty Organization; **O. de l'unité africaine** Organization of African Unity

organisationnel, -elle [organizasjɔnɛl] *adj* organizational

organisé [ɔrganize] *adj* (a) (*planifié*) organized; **voyage o.** package tour; *F* **c'est du vol o.** it's a rip-off, *Br* it's daylight robbery; **il est bien o.** he is (well-)organized; **les manifestants n'étaient pas organisés** the demonstrators were not organized (b) *Biol* (*être*) organic

organiser [ɔrganize] **1** *vt* (*réunion, affaires, fête, voyage etc*) to organize, to arrange; (*temps, emploi du temps*) to organize, to plan **2 s'organiser** *vpr* to get organized

organiseur [ɔrganizœr] *nm* **o. personnel** (*logiciel*) personal organizer; **o. électronique** electronic organizer

organisme [ɔrganism] *nm* (a) *Biol* organism; *Anat* system; **le tabac est mauvais pour l'o.** tobacco is bad for the system (b) (*organisation*) organization, body; **o. de crédit** credit institution; **o. international** international organization; **o. professionnel** professional body

organiste [ɔrganist] *n Mus* organist

orgasme [ɔrgasm] *nm* orgasm

orge [ɔrʒ] **1** *nf* barley; **sucre d'o.** barley sugar **2** *nm* **o. mondé** hulled barley; **o. perlé** pearl barley

orgeat [ɔrʒa] *nm* **sirop d'o.** barley water

orgelet [ɔrʒəlɛ] *nm Méd* sty(e)

orgiaque [ɔrʒjak] *adj* orgiastic
orgie [ɔrʒi] *nf* (*sexuelle*) orgy; (*avec excès de boissons*) drunken feast; *Fig* **j'ai fait une o. de foie gras** I gorged myself on foie gras; **une o. de couleurs** a riot of colour; **une o. de lumières** a profusion of lights
orgue [ɔrg] *nm* (*pl souvent f*) **(a)** *Mus* organ; **un bel o., de belles orgues** a fine organ; **tenir l'o.** *ou* **les orgues** to be at *or* to be playing the organ; **o. électrique/électronique** electric/electronic organ; **joueur d'o.** organ grinder; **point d'o.** pause; *Fig* **le point d'o. de la réunion** the climax *or* high point of the meeting **(b)** *Géol* **orgues de basalte** basalt columns
▸ **orgue**: **o. de Barbarie** barrel organ
orgueil [ɔrgœj] *nm* pride; *Péj* pride, arrogance; **péché d'o.** sin of pride; **être gonflé** *ou* **bouffi d'o.** to be puffed up *or* swollen with pride; **tirer o. de qch** to take pride in sth; **être l'o. (et la joie) de qn** to be sb's pride and joy; **par o.** out of pride; **par o., il ne veut pas admettre son erreur** he is too proud to admit his error
orgueilleusement [ɔrgœjøzmɑ̃] *adv* proudly; *Péj* proudly, arrogantly
orgueilleux, -euse [ɔrgœjø, -øz] **1** *adj* proud; *Péj* proud, arrogant **2** *n* proud person; *Péj* arrogant person
oriel [ɔrjɛl] *nm* oriel (window), bay window
orient [ɔrjɑ̃] *nm* **(a)** (*est*) east, *Litt* orient; **l'O.** the East, the Orient; **le moyen/l'extrême O.** the Middle/Far East; **en O.** in the East; **pays/peuples d'O.** Oriental nations/peoples; **tapis d'O.** oriental carpet; *Hist* **l'Empire d'O.** the Eastern (Roman) Empire **(b)** (*dans la franc-maçonnerie*) **Grand-O.** Grand Lodge
orientable [ɔrjɑ̃tabl] *adj* (*grue*) swivelling; (*lampe, antenne*) adjustable
oriental, -ale, -aux, -ales [ɔrjɑ̃tal, -o] **1** *adj* (*région*) eastern; (*côte*) east; (*langue*) oriental; *Hist* **les Indes orientales** the East Indies **2** *n* **O.** Oriental
orientalisme [ɔrjɑ̃talism] *nm* Orientalism
orientaliste [ɔrjɑ̃talist] *n* Orientalist
orientateur, -trice [ɔrjɑ̃tatœr, -tris] *n* = **orienteur, -euse 1**
orientation [ɔrjɑ̃tasjɔ̃] *nf* **(a)** (*détermination de position*) orientation; **table d'o.** orientation *or* panoramic table; **avoir le sens de l'o.** to have a (good) sense of direction; **course d'o.** orienteering course
(b) *Scol* **choisir une o.** to choose a course of study; **o. en fin de cinquième** = determination of future course of studies at the end of one's second year; **conseiller d'o.** course and careers adviser
(c) (*d'une grue, d'une antenne*) positioning; **o. d'un canon** training of a gun; **à o. libre** free-moving, adjustable; *Aut* **o. de la roue** wheel alignment, tracking
(d) (*d'une maison*) aspect, orientation; (*d'une politique*) thrust; **o. des voiles** set *or* trim of the sails; **o. de la Bourse** stock market trend; **o. du marché** market orientation; **o. stratégique de la société** corporate strategic orientation
▸ **orientation**: **o. professionnelle** careers advice *or* guidance
orienté [ɔrjɑ̃te] *adj* **(a)** (*disposé*) **maison/pièce orientée au sud** house/room facing south, house/room with a southerly aspect; **le jardin est mal o.** the garden is badly positioned; *Bourse* **o. à la baisse** (*marché*) falling; **o. à la hausse** (*marché*) rising **(b)** (*peu objectif*) bias(s)ed, slanted; **ouvrage o. politiquement** work with a political bias *or* slant **(c)** *Ordinat* **o. bloc** block-orientated; **o. ligne** line-orientated; **o. objet** object-orientated; **o. problème** problem-orientated; **o. procédure** procedure-orientated
orienter [ɔrjɑ̃te] **1** *vt* **(a)** (*bâtiment*) to orient(ate); (*canon, fusil*) to train (**vers** on); (*télescope*) to point, to direct; (*voile*) to trim
(b) (*mener*) to direct, to guide; *Scol* **o. un élève vers la chimie** to steer a pupil towards chemistry, to advise a pupil to take up chemistry; *Scol* **on l'a mal/bien orienté** he was given the wrong/right academic advice; **o. la conversation vers d'autres sujets** to steer *or* turn the conversation to other topics; **j'ai essayé d'o. la conversation sur toi** I tried to bring *or* steer the conversation round to you
(c) (*carte*) to orient(ate)
(d) *Math* **o. une droite** to indicate the direction of a straight line
2 s'orienter *vpr* **(a)** to get *or* find one's bearings, to orientate oneself; (*avec une boussole*) to take one's bearings
(b) (*se destiner*) **elle veut s'o. vers le droit** she wants to go in for *or* specialize in law; **il a décidé de s'o. vers la carrière diplomatique** he has decided on a career in the diplomatic service; **cette politique s'oriente vers le communisme** this policy is tending *or* moving towards Communism; **s'o. vers la vente de produits écologiques** to specialize in the sale of environmentally-friendly products; **s'o. en fonction des cours** to move in relation to prices
orienteur, -euse [ɔrjɑ̃tœr, -øz] **1** *n* careers adviser **2** *nm* (*instrument*) orientator **3** *adj Mil* **officier o.** interviewing officer (*for candidates for military service*)
orifice [ɔrifis] *nm* opening, aperture; (*du corps*) orifice; (*d'un puits, d'une galerie*) mouth; *MecE* port; *Aut* **o. d'admission** inlet port; *Aut* **o. d'air** air port; *Aut* **o. d'alimentation** feed hole; *Aut* **o. d'arrivée d'essence** petrol port; *Aut* **o. d'écoulement d'huile** oil drain hole; *Aut* **o. de sortie** outlet port
oriflamme [ɔriflam] *nf* **(a)** *Hist* oriflamme **(b)** (*bannière*) banner
origami [ɔrigami] *nm* origami
origan [ɔrigɑ̃] *nm* oregano
originaire [ɔriʒinɛr] *adj* **(a)** **o. de** (*personne*) originating from, coming from; **il est o. de Russie/du Havre** he is a native of *or* he comes from Russia/Le Havre; **le haggis est o. d'Écosse** haggis originates in *or* comes from Scotland **(b)** (*initial*) (*membre*) original, founding
originairement [ɔriʒinɛrmɑ̃] *adv* originally
original, -ale, -aux, -ales [ɔriʒinal, -o] **1** *adj* **(a)** (*premier*) (*texte, manuscrit*) original; (*bande etc*) master; **édition originale** first edition; *Cin* **copie originale (du film)** master print **(b)** (*nouveau*) (*style, idée*) original **(c)** (*excentrique*) odd, eccentric **2** *nm* (*œuvre, document*) original; (*d'un fichier, d'une disquette*) master copy; **copier qch d'après l'o.** to copy sth from the original **3** *n* (*excentrique*) eccentric; **c'est un o.** he's (quite) a character, he's an eccentric
originalité [ɔriʒinalite] *nf* **(a)** (*nouveauté*) originality **(b)** (*excentricité*) eccentricity, oddness **(c)** (*trait original*) original feature; (*de personne*) eccentricity
origine [ɔriʒin] *nf* **(a)** (*création, début*) origin; **l'o. de l'univers** the origin of the universe; **dès l'o.** from the very beginning, from the outset; **à l'o.** originally, in the beginning, at first; **à l'o. de** at the origin of; **des origines à nos jours** from the earliest times to the present day
(b) (*ascendance*) origin; **être d'o. illustre/ouvrière** to be of noble/working-class descent; **être d'o. modeste** to be of humble origin *or* descent; **il est d'o. anglaise, il est anglais d'o.** he is English by birth; **il a des origines anglaises** he is of English extraction *or* has English origins; **d'o. française** (*produit, mot*) of French origin; **la colonie devait son o. aux baleiniers** the colony was founded by *or* owed its origins to whalers
(c) (*source*) origin, source; (*d'un mot*) origin, derivation; (*d'une tradition*) origin; **l'o. de cette coutume est ...** the custom has its origins in ...; **tirer son o. de qch** to originate from sth, to have its origins in sth; **le mot tire son o. du latin** the word originates *or* derives from the Latin; **bureau d'o.** office of dispatch; **certificat d'o.** certificate of origin; **vins d'o.** vintage wines; **appellation d'o. contrôlée d'un vin** = official quality guarantee of a wine
(d) *Math* **(point) o.** zero point
originel, -elle [ɔriʒinɛl] *adj* (*péché, forme*) original; (*cause, sens*) original, primary
originellement [ɔriʒinɛlmɑ̃] *adv* (*à l'origine*) originally; (*dès l'origine*) from the outset
orignal, -aux [ɔriɲal, -o] *nm Zool* moose
oripeaux [ɔripo] *nmpl* (*haillons*) rags, tatters; (*vêtements voyants*) loud *or* gaudy clothes
ORL [oɛrɛl] *n Méd* (*abrév* **oto-rhino-laryngologiste**) ENT specialist
orléaniste [ɔrleanist] *adj, n Hist Fr* Orleanist
Orlon® [ɔrlɔ̃] *nm* Orlon
ormaie [ɔrmɛ] *nf* elm grove
orme [ɔrm] *nm* **(a)** (*arbre*) elm (tree); **o. blanc, o. de(s) montagne(s)** wych elm; **o. champêtre** *ou* **à petites feuilles** common elm, English elm; **maladie des ormes** Dutch elm disease **(b)** (*bois*) elm (wood)
ormeau, -eaux [ɔrmo] *nm* (*arbre*) (young) elm
orné [ɔrne] *adj* (*style*) ornate, florid; **lettre ornée** illuminated letter
ornement [ɔrnəmɑ̃] *nm* ornament; (*détail*) embellishment; (*parure*) adornment; **sans o.** plain, unadorned; **plantes d'o.** ornamental plants; *Rel* **ornements sacerdotaux** vestments; *Mus* **notes d'o.** grace notes, ornaments
ornemental, -ale, -aux, -ales [ɔrnəmɑ̃tal, -o] *adj* ornamental
ornementation [ɔrnəmɑ̃tasjɔ̃] *nf* ornamentation, decoration
ornementer [ɔrnəmɑ̃te] *vt* to ornament, to decorate
orner [ɔrne] *vt* to decorate (**de** with); **o. une robe de dentelles** to trim a dress with lace
ornière [ɔrnjɛr] *nf* rut; *Fig* **sortir de l'o.** to get out of trouble; **tirer qn de l'o.** to get sb out of trouble
ornithologie [ɔrnitɔlɔʒi] *nf* ornithology

ornithologique [ɔrnitɔlɔʒik] *adj* ornithological
ornithologiste [ɔrnitɔlɔʒist] *n*, **ornithologue** [ɔrnitɔlɔg] *n* ornithologist
ornithorynque [ɔrnitɔrɛ̃k] *nm Zool* duck-billed platypus, *Spéc* ornithorhynchus
orogénèse [ɔrɔʒenɛz] *nf Géol* orogenesis
orogénie [ɔrɔʒeni] *nf Géol* orogeny
orogénique [ɔrɔʒenik] *adj Géol* orogenic
orographie [ɔrɔgrafi] *nf* orography
oronge [ɔrɔ̃ʒ] *nf Bot* royal agaric, Caesar's mushroom; **fausse o.** fly agaric
orpaillage [ɔrpajaʒ] *nm* gold washing *or* panning
Orphée [ɔrfe] *nm Myth* Orpheus
orphelin, -ine [ɔrfəlɛ̃, -in] **1** *n* orphan **2** *adj* orphan(ed); **o. de père** fatherless; **o. de mère** motherless **3** *nf Typ* **orpheline** orphan
orphelinat [ɔrfəlina] *nm* orphanage
orphéon [ɔrfeɔ̃] *nm* **(a)** *(fanfare)* band **(b)** *Arch* *(chorale)* choral society
orphéoniste [ɔrfeɔnist] *n* **(a)** *(d'une fanfare)* band member **(b)** *Arch* *(d'une chorale)* choral society member
orphie [ɔrfi] *nf Zool* garfish, garpike
orpiment [ɔrpimɑ̃] *nm Tech* orpiment
orque [ɔrk] *nf Zool* killer whale, orc, grampus
Orsay [ɔrsɛ] **le Quai d'O.** = the French Foreign Office
orteil [ɔrtɛj] *nm* toe; **(gros) o.** big toe; **petit o.** little toe
ORTF [ɔɛrteɛf] *nm* (*abrév* **Office de la radiodiffusion et télévision française**) = French broadcasting corporation (*until 1974*)
orthochromatique [ɔrtokrɔmatik] *adj Phot* orthochromatic
orthodontie [ɔrtodɔ̃ti] *nf* orthodontics
orthodontiste [ɔrtodɔ̃tist] *n* orthodontist
orthodoxe [ɔrtɔdɔks] **1** *adj* *(église, doctrine, opinion)* orthodox; **peu o.** unorthodox, unconventional **2** *n Rel* person of orthodox beliefs; *(de l'Église orthodoxe)* member of the Orthodox Church; *Pol* follower of the (official) party line
orthodoxie [ɔrtɔdɔksi] *nf* orthodoxy
orthogénie [ɔrtɔʒeni] *nf Méd* birth control, family planning
orthogonal, -ale, -aux, -ales [ɔrtɔgɔnal, -o] *adj* orthogonal
orthogonalement [ɔrtɔgɔnalmɑ̃] *adv* orthogonally, at right angles
orthographe [ɔrtɔgraf] *nf* [①A74] spelling; **je ne connais pas l'o. de ce mot** I don't know how to spell this word *or* how this word is spelt; **mot qui a deux orthographes** word that has two spellings, word that can be spelt in two ways; **faute d'o.** spelling mistake; **réforme de l'o.** spelling reform; **o. d'usage/d'accord** literal/grammatical spelling; **être bon en o., avoir une bonne o.** to be good at spelling
orthographier [ɔrtɔgrafje] *vt* *(impf, pr sub* **n. orthographiions***)* to spell; **mal o. un mot** to spell a word incorrectly, to misspell a word
orthographique [ɔrtɔgrafik] *adj Gram* orthographic(al); **réforme o.** spelling reform
orthopédie [ɔrtɔpedi] *nf* orthopaedics, *US* orthopedics
orthopédique [ɔrtɔpedik] *adj* orthopaedic, *US* orthopedic; **chaussures/semelles orthopédiques** orthopaedic *or US* orthopedic shoes/built-up soles
orthopédiste [ɔrtɔpedist] *n* **(a)** *(médecin)* orthopaedist, *esp US* orthopedist; **chirurgien o.** orthopaedic *or esp US* orthopedic surgeon **(b)** *(fabricant)* maker of orthopaedic *or esp US* orthopedic apparatus
orthophonie [ɔrtɔfɔni] *nf* speech therapy
orthophoniste [ɔrtɔfɔnist] *n* speech therapist
orthoptie [ɔrtɔpsi] *nf* orthoptics
orthoptiste [ɔrtɔptist] *n* orthoptist
ortie [ɔrti] *nf* nettle; **o. brûlante** stinging nettle; **o. blanche** dead nettle
ortolan [ɔrtɔlɑ̃] *nm Orn* ortolan (bunting)
orvet [ɔrvɛ] *nm Zool* slow-worm, blindworm
OS [oɛs] *nm abrév* **ouvrier spécialisé**
os [ɔs, *pl* o] *nm* bone; **avoir de gros/petits os** to be big-boned/small-boned; **viande avec os** meat on the bone; **viande sans os** meat off the bone, boned meat; **cuiller en os** bone spoon; **n'avoir que la peau sur les os, n'être qu'un sac** *ou* **un paquet d'os** to be nothing but skin and bone, to be just a bag of bones; **elle est tellement maigre qu'on lui voit les os** she's a bag of bones; **voir qn en chair et en os** to see sb in the flesh; **mouillé** *ou* **trempé jusqu'aux os** soaked to the skin, wet through; **pourri jusqu'à l'os** thoroughly corrupt; **se rompre les os** to break one's neck; **il ne fera pas de vieux os** he's not long for this world, he won't make old bones; *Fig* **donner** *ou* **jeter un os à ronger à qn** to give sb something to keep him/her happy; *F* **tomber sur un os** to run up against *or* hit a snag; *F* **il y a un os** there's a snag *or* hitch; *très F* **je l'ai dans l'os** I've been shafted *or* screwed
▶ **os**: *Anat* **os malaire** cheek bone; **o. à moelle** marrowbone; **o. de seiche** cuttlebone
oscar [ɔskar] *nm Cin* Oscar
oscillant [ɔsilɑ̃, -jɑ̃] *adj* *(pendule, Él décharge)* oscillating; *(tige)* rocking; *Rad* **circuit o.** oscillatory circuit; *Méd* **fièvre oscillante** irregular fever
oscillateur [ɔsilatœr] *nm Rad, Électron* oscillator
oscillation [ɔsilasjɔ̃] *nf* **(a)** *(d'un pendule)* swing, oscillation; *Phys, Él* oscillation; *Phys* **oscillations amorties/entretenues** damped/sustained oscillations **(b)** *(d'un bateau)* rocking **(c)** *MecE* vibration **(d)** *Fig* *(du marché, de l'opinion etc)* fluctuation
oscillatoire [ɔsilatwar] *adj* *(mouvement, circuit)* oscillatory
osciller [ɔsile, -je] *vi* **(a)** *(d'un pendule)* to swing, to oscillate; *(de l'aiguille d'un compteur de vitesse)* to flicker; *(d'un bateau)* to rock; *Phys, Él* to oscillate **(b)** *(hésiter)* **o. entre deux opinions/positions** to waver between two opinions/positions **(c)** *Fin* *(du marché)* to fluctuate
oscillogramme [ɔsilɔgram] *nm* oscillogram
oscillographe [ɔsilɔgraf] *nm* oscillograph; **o. cathodique** cathode ray tube
oscilloscope [ɔsilɔskɔp] *nm* oscilloscope
osé [oze] *adj* *(tentative, démarche, geste)* daring, bold, audacious; *(plaisanterie, scène d'un film)* daring, risqué; *(demande)* bold; **c'est vraiment o. de sa part** that's really daring *or* bold *or* audacious of him
oseille [ozɛj] *nf* **(a)** *Bot* sorrel **(b)** *Arg* *(argent)* dough, bread, *Br* lolly; **avoir de l'o.** to have bags *or* pots of money, to be loaded; **prends l'o. et tire-toi** take the money and run
oser [oze] *vt* [①A40,C,1,a; A59,19; B33,2,b,i] **o. faire qch** to dare (to) do sth; **elle n'ose (pas) le faire** she daren't do it, she doesn't dare (to) do it; **les mots qu'il n'a jamais osé dire** the words he never dared (to) say; **comment oses-tu répondre à ton père!** how dare you answer your father back!; **j'ose croire que je recevrai le paquet mardi** I dare say I'll get the parcel on Tuesday; **je voudrais qu'il vienne mais je n'ose l'espérer** I'd like him to come but I daren't hope *or* I don't dare hope that he will; **si j'ose dire** if I may (venture to) say so; *Litt* **o. qch** to dare sth; **il faut o.** nothing ventured, nothing gained; **comment osez-vous?** how dare you!; **approchez si vous osez!** come over here if you dare!; **il veut me parler? qu'il ose un peu!** he wants to talk to me? just let him dare!; **vous n'oseriez (pas)!** you wouldn't dare!
oseraie [ozrɛ] *nf* osier bed
osier [ozje] *nm* **(a)** *Bot* osier; **brin d'o.** withy **(b)** *(en vannerie)* wicker; *(objets en osier)* wickerwork; **panier d'o.** wicker basket
osmonde [ɔsmɔ̃d] *nf Bot* **o. royale** royal fern
osmose [ɔsmoz] *nf aussi Fig* osmosis; *Fig* *(entre des personnes)* total empathy
ossature [ɔsatyr] *nf* **(a)** *Biol* *(d'un homme, d'un animal)* frame, skeleton; **d'une o. puissante** powerfully built, of powerful build **(b)** *Fig* *(structure)* *(d'un bâtiment)* frame(work); *(d'un pont)* main girders; *(d'un texte, d'une démocratie etc)* framework, structure
osselet [ɔslɛ] *nm* *(de mouton)* knucklebone; **jouer aux osselets** to play at knucklebones; *Anat* **les osselets de l'oreille** the ossicles of the ear, the otic bones
ossements [ɔsmɑ̃] *nmpl* bones
osseux, -euse [ɔsø, -øz] *adj* *(visage, main)* bony; *(tissu)* bone, *Spéc* osseous; **système o.** bone structure; **greffe osseuse** bone graft
ossification [ɔsifikasjɔ̃] *nf Méd* ossification
ossifier [ɔsifje] **1** *vt* to ossify **2 s'ossifier** *vpr* to ossify, to become ossified
ossu [ɔsy] *adj* big-boned, raw-boned
ossuaire [ɔsɥɛr] *nm* ossuary, charnel house
OST [oɛste] *nf Com* (*abrév* **organisation scientifique du travail**) organization and methods, time and motion studies
ostensible [ɔstɑ̃sibl] *adj* open; *(mépris)* clear, patent
ostensiblement [ɔstɑ̃sibləmɑ̃] *adv* openly
ostensoir [ɔstɑ̃swar] *nm Rel* monstrance
ostentation [ɔstɑ̃tasjɔ̃] *nf* ostentation, show, display; *Litt* **faire o. de sa misère** to parade one's poverty; **agir par** *ou* **avec o.** to act ostentatiously; **sans o.** unostentatiously
ostentatoire [ɔstɑ̃tatwar] *adj* ostentatious
ostéologie [ɔsteɔlɔʒi] *nf* osteology
ostéomyélite [ɔsteɔmjelit] *nf Méd* osteomyelitis
ostéopathe [ɔsteɔpat] *n Méd* osteopath
ostéoporose [ɔsteɔpɔroz] *nf Méd* osteoporosis
ostracisme [ɔstrasism] *nm* **(a)** *(exclusion)* ostracism; **frapper qn d'o.** to ostracize sb **(b)** *(hostilité, attitude de rejet)* hostility
ostréicole [ɔstreikɔl] *adj* **l'industrie o.** oyster farming; **parc o.** oyster bed; **la région est l'un des plus grands parcs**

ostréicoles de la France it is one of the largest oyster-producing regions in France
ostréiculteur, -trice [ɔstreikyltœr, -tris] *n* oyster farmer
ostréiculture [ɔstreikyltyr] *nf* oyster farming
ostrogot(h), -ot(h)e [ɔstrɔgo, -ɔt] **1** *n Hist* **O.** Ostrogoth **2** *nm (homme malappris)* boor
OT *nm (abrév* **Office du Tourisme***)* tourist office
otage [ɔtaʒ] *nm* hostage **(de** for**)**; **prendre qn en o.** to take sb hostage; **une prise d'o.** a hostage-taking
otalgie [ɔtalʒi] *nf Méd* earache, *Spéc* otalgia
OTAN [ɔtɑ̃] *nf (abrév* **Organisation du traité de l'Atlantique Nord***)* NATO
otarie [ɔtari] *nf* sea lion, *Spéc* otary, eared seal
ôter [ote] **1** *vt* to remove, to take away; *(vêtement)* to take off; *(tache)* to remove, to take out; *(assiettes)* to clear away; **ô. le couvert** to clear away, to clear the table; **ô. qch à qn** to take sth away from sb; **il faudrait leur ô. ces armes des mains** these weapons should be taken away from them; **ô. ses illusions à qn** to rid sb of his/her illusions; **ça lui a ôté ses illusions** that shattered his illusions; **cela lui a ôté l'appétit** it has taken away his appetite; **cela lui a ôté toute sa force** it has drained him of all his strength; **ô. à qn l'espoir/l'envie de faire qch** to deprive sb of all hope/all desire of doing sth; **tu ne m'ôteras pas de l'idée que …** I'm quite convinced that …; **cela n'ôte rien à sa valeur/à notre amitié** that in no way detracts from its value/from our friendship; **ô. qch à** *ou* **de qch** to remove sth from sth; **ôtez trois de cinq** take (away) *or* subtract three from five; **cela me l'a ôté tout à fait de l'esprit** that drove *or* put it right out of my head; **ô. le pain de la bouche à qn** to take the bread out of sb's mouth; **ô. la vie à qn** to take sb's life

2 s'ôter *vpr F* **ôtez-vous de là!** get out of the way!, move (yourself)!; **ôte-toi de mon chemin!** get out of my way!; **ôte-toi de là que je m'y mette!** get out and make room for me!; **il faut qu'il s'ôte cette idée de la tête** he has to get that idea out of his head; **elle ne peut pas s'ô. de l'idée que …** she can't get it out of her head that …
otique [ɔtik] *adj Anat* otic
otite [ɔtit] *nf Méd* otitis
OTM [oteɛm] *nm Com (abrév* **opérateur de transport multimodal***)* multi-modal operator
otologie [ɔtɔlɔʒi] *nf* otology
oto-rhino [otorino], *pl* **oto-rhinos** *n Méd F* ENT specialist
oto-rhino-laryngologie *nf Méd* ear, nose and throat medicine, *Spéc* otolaryngology, otorhinolaryngology
oto-rhino-laryngologiste, *pl* **oto-rhino-laryngologistes** *n Méd* ear, nose and throat specialist, *Spéc* otolaryngologist
otoscope [ɔtɔskɔp] *nm Méd* otoscope, ear speculum
OTSI *nm (abrév* **Office du tourisme-syndicat d'initiative***)* tourist office
ottoman, -ane [ɔtɔmɑ̃, -an] **1** *adj Hist* Ottoman **2** *n Hist* **O.** Ottoman **3** *nm (étoffe)* ottoman **4** *nf* **ottomane** *(meuble)* ottoman
ou [u] *conj* or; **voulez-vous du bœuf ou du jambon?** would you like beef or ham?; **trois ou quatre fois par jour** three or four times a day; **l'un ou l'autre** one or the other; **entrez ou sortez** either come in or go out; **qu'il vienne ou non, nous irons** whether he comes or not, we'll go; **vous ou moi, nous lui en parlerons** (either) you or I will speak to him about it; **lui ou son frère va** *ou* **vont vous aider** he or his brother will help you; **l'un ou l'autre devait forcément être le chef** one or the other was bound to take the lead; **j'appelle tout de suite ou j'attends demain?** shall I call straight away or wait till tomorrow?; **ou … ou (bien) …** either … or (else) …; **ou vous payez ou j'appelle la police** either you pay up or (else) I call the police; *Ordinat* **circuit OU** OR circuit
où [u] *adv* **(a)** *(dans l'espace) (interr)* where; **où habite-t-il?** where does he live?; **où allez-vous?** where are you going?; **où en êtes-vous?** how far have you got (with it)?; **par où est-il passé?** which way did he go?; **jusqu'où les a-t-il suivis?** how far did he follow them?; **qui peut dire où nous vivrons dans dix ans** who can tell where we'll be living in ten years' time?

(b) [①**B21**,f] *(dans l'espace) (rel)* where; **j'irai où vous voudrez** I'll go where(ever) you wish; **partout où il va** wherever he goes, everywhere he goes; **vous le trouverez là où vous l'avez laissé** you'll find it where you left it; **d'où on conclut qu'il est coupable** from which one concludes that he is guilty; **d'où sa tristesse** hence her sadness; **où que vous soyez** wherever you may be; **mettez-le n'importe où** put it down anywhere; **nous cherchons un studio où passer quelques jours** we're looking for a studio flat for a few days *or* where we can spend a few days; **dans l'état où elle est** in the state she's in; **au train où vont les choses** at this rate, at the rate things are going

(c) *(temps)* when; **à l'époque où il était jeune** in the days when he was young

(d) *(= dans lequel, auquel etc)* **la maison où il habite** the house he lives in, the house in which he lives
OUA [oya] *nf (abrév* **Organisation de l'unité africaine***)* OAU
ouache [waʃ] *nf Can* bear's den
ouah [wa] *int* woof
ouaille [wɑj] *nf Bible, Litt* sheep; **le pasteur et ses ouailles** the minister and his flock
ouais [wɛ] *int F* yeah!, yep!; *(sceptique)* oh yeah?
ouananiche [wananiʃ] *nf Can* freshwater salmon
ouaouaron [wawarɔ̃] *nm Can* bullfrog
ouate [wat] *nf (souvent* **la ouate,** *parfois* **l'ouate) (a)** *(pour rembourrage)* padding, wadding; **doublé d'o.** quilted **(b)** *(pour soins)* cotton wool, *US* absorbent cotton; **o. hydrophile** absorbent cotton wool *or* cotton; *Fig* **avoir été élevé dans la o.** to have been brought up in cotton wool
ouaté [wate] *adj (vêtement)* quilted; *Fig (bruit de pas)* muffled, soft; *(contours)* vague, fuzzy
ouater [wate] *vt* to quilt
ouatine [watin] *nf Tex* quilting (material)
ouatiné [watine] *adj (tissu)* quilted; *Fig (vie)* cosy
oubli [ubli] *nm* **(a)** *(acte d'oublier)* forgetting; *(défaillance de la mémoire)* forgetfulness; *(négligence) (du devoir)* neglect; **l'o. de soi** selflessness **(b)** *(général)* oblivion; **tomber dans l'o.** to sink *or* fall into oblivion, to be forgotten; **sortir de l'o.** to emerge from oblivion **(c)** *(trou de mémoire)* oversight; *(lacune)* omission; **réparer un o.** to rectify an oversight/omission; **je suis désolée de ne pas l'avoir fait, c'est un o.** I'm sorry I've not done it, it's an oversight on my part
oublier [ublije] *(impf, pr sub* **n. oubliions) 1** *vt* **(a)** [①**A43**,b,iii] *(ne pas se rappeler)* to forget; **j'ai oublié son nom** I've forgotten his name, his name has slipped my mind; **j'ai oublié son visage** I've forgotten what he looks like; **o. où/quand/qui …** to forget where/when/who …; **j'ai complètement oublié que nous avions rendez-vous aujourd'hui** I completely forgot that we'd agreed to meet today; **o. le passé** to forget the past; **oublions le passé** let's let bygones be bygones; **faire o. son passé** to live down one's past; **o. de faire qch** to forget to do sth; **on ne nous le laissera pas o.** we'll never hear the last of it *or* be allowed to forget it, we'll never live it down; **il mourut oublié de tous** he died forgotten by all, he died in obscurity; **n'oubliez pas à qui vous vous adressez** remember who you're talking to

(b) *(ne pas prendre)* to forget, to leave (behind); *(omettre)* to leave out; *(rendez-vous)* to overlook; *(devoir)* to neglect; **j'ai oublié mes lunettes chez toi** I've left my glasses (behind) at your place; **o. l'heure** to forget the time, to lose track of the time

2 s'oublier *vpr* **(a)** *(se relâcher)* to forget oneself, to forget one's manners; **le chien s'est oublié sur le tapis** the dog's made a mess on the carpet; *F* **il ne s'oublie pas** he always looks after himself, he always takes care of number one

(b) *(sortir de la mémoire)* **les langues étrangères s'oublient facilement quand on ne les pratique pas** foreign languages are easily forgotten when you don't use them; **des choses pareilles ne doivent jamais s'o.** things like that must never be forgotten; **c'est comme le vélo, ça ne s'oublie pas!** it's like riding a bike, once you learn you never forget
oubliette [ublijɛt] *nf* dungeon, oubliette; *F* **mettre qch aux oubliettes** to shelve sth indefinitely; **cet homme politique fut mis aux oubliettes pendant dix ans** this politician was condemned to ten years in the wilderness
oublieux, -euse [ublijø, -øz] *adj* forgetful; **o. de** forgetful of; *(devoir)* neglectful of, forgetful of
oued [wɛd] *nm Géog* wadi
Ouessant [wɛsɑ̃] *nm* Ushant
ouest [wɛst] **1** *nm* west; **les provinces de l'o.** the western provinces; **vent d'o.** westerly wind; **le vent d'o.** the west wind; **à l'o. de qch** (to the) west of sth, westward of sth; **à l'o., dans l'o.** in the west; **A l'O. rien de nouveau** All Quiet on the Western Front; **vers l'o.** westward(s); **une pièce exposée plein o.** a room that faces due west; *Pol* **l'O.** the West; **les rapports entre l'Est and l'O. sont moins tendus qu'ils ne l'ont été** East-West relations are less tense than they were **2** *adj inv (côte, côté)* west; *(vent)* westerly; *(région)* western
ouest-allemand, -ande, *pl* **ouest-allemand(e)s 1** *adj* West German **2** *n* **O.** West German
ouf [uf] **1** *int* whew!, phew!; *F* **il n'a pas eu le temps de dire o.!** he didn't even have time to catch his breath **2** *nm* **pousser un o. de soulagement** to heave a sigh of relief
Ouganda [ugɑ̃da] *nm* Uganda
ougrien, -ienne [ugrijɛ̃ -jɛn] *Ling* **1** *adj* Ugric **2** *nm* Ugric

oui [wi] **1** *adv* [①B61,D] yes; **vient-il? – o.** is he coming? – yes (he is); **je crois que o.** I think so; **faire signe que o., faire o. de la tête** to nod (one's head); **mais o., bien sûr que o.** (yes,) of course; **o., o., allez toujours** yes, (yes,) get on with it; **êtes-vous content de partir? – o. et non** are you happy to be leaving? – yes and no; **eh o.! c'est encore moi!** yes! it's me again!; *Naut* **o., commandant!** aye, aye, sir!; **ah, o.?** really?, is that so?; *F* **tu viens, o.?** you're coming, aren't you?; *F* **tu viens, o. ou non** *ou très F* **o. ou merde?** are you coming or not?, are you coming or aren't you?, are you coming, yes or no?

2 *nm inv Pol* **deux cents o. et trois cents non** two hundred ayes and three hundred noes; *F* **se quereller/pleurer pour un o. pour un non** to quarrel/cry over the slightest thing; **changer d'avis pour un o. pour un non** to change one's mind at the drop of a hat

ouï-dire [widir] *nm inv* hearsay; **ce sont des o.** it's hearsay; **je ne le sais que par o.** I know it only by *or* from hearsay

ouïe [wi] *nf* **(a)** (*sens*) (sense of) hearing; **avoir l'o. fine** to have keen *or* sharp ears, to have excellent hearing; **avoir l'o. défectueuse** to be hard of hearing; **à portée de l'o.** within earshot, within hearing distance; **être tout o.** to be all ears *or* all attention **(b)** *Mus* **ouïes** (*de violon*) sound holes **(c)** *Tech* (*d'un ventilateur*) ear **(d)** *Zool* **ouïes** gills

ouille [uj] *int* ouch!, ow!

ouïr [wir] *vt* (*only used in inf, pp* **ouï,** *compound tenses, prp* **oyant** *and imp* **oyez**; *p hist* **j'ouïs** *and fu* **j'ouïrai** *sometimes used*) *Arch* to hear; **nous l'avons ouï dire à notre père** we have heard our father say so; **j'ai souvent ouï dire que ...** I have often heard it said that ...; *Jur* **o. les témoins** to hear the witnesses; *Arch* **oyez, oyez braves gens ...** oyez, oyez *or* now hear this, good people ...

ouistiti [wistiti] *nm Zool* marmoset; *Fig F* **un drôle de o.** an odd character

ouragan [uragɑ̃] *nm* hurricane; **entrer comme un o. dans une pièce** to burst into a room; **sa déclaration a déclenché un o. de protestations** his statement caused a storm of protest *or* an uproar

Oural (l') [lural] *nm* **(a)** (*fleuve*) the Ural **(b)** (*montagnes*) the Urals, the Ural Mountains

ourdir [urdir] *vt* **(a)** *Tex* (*lin, tissu*) to warp **(b)** (*paille*) to plait **(c)** *Fig* (*complot*) to hatch, to weave

ourdissage [urdisaʒ] *nm Tex* warping

ourdou [urdu] *nm Ling* Urdu

ourlé [urle] *adj Couture* hemmed; **des oreilles délicatement ourlées** delicately shaped ears

ourler [urle] *vt* **(a)** *Couture* to hem; **o. à jour** to hemstitch **(b)** (*border*) to edge (**de** with) **(c)** *Tech* (*feuilles de métal*) to lap-joint

ourlet [urlɛ] *nm* **(a)** *Couture* hem; **o. à jour** hemstitched hem; **faux o.** false hem; **point d'o.** hemstitch **(b)** (*repli, rebord*) (*d'un cratère*) edge; (*de l'oreille*) rim, *Spéc* helix **(c)** *Tech* (*de feuilles de métal*) lap joint, hem

ours, ourse [urs] **1** *n* **(a)** bear, *f* she bear; **il vit comme un o.** he's a grumpy, unsociable sort; *Fig* **quel o.!** what a boor; *Prov* **il ne faut pas vendre la peau de l'o. avant de l'avoir tué** don't count your chickens before they're hatched; *Arg* **avoir ses o.** (*d'une femme*) to have the curse, to have one's period **(b)** *Journ* masthead **2** *nf Astron* **la Grande Ourse** (*constellation*) the Great Bear; (*sept étoiles*) the Plough, *Am* the Big Dipper; **la Petite Ourse** the Little Bear, *Am* the Little Dipper

▶ **ours**: **o. blanc** polar bear; **o. brun** brown bear; **o. gris d'Amérique** grizzly bear; *F* **o. mal léché** uncouth individual; **o. marin** sea bear, fur seal; **o. en peluche** teddy bear; **o. polaire** polar bear

oursin [ursɛ̃] *nm* sea urchin

ourson [ursɔ̃] *nm* bear cub

oust(e) [ust] *int F* **allez o.!** (*avance!*) get a move on!; (*va-t'en!*) scram!, *Br* hop it!

out [aʊwt] *adj inv* **(a)** (*personne*) out (of fashion); **ce chanteur est déjà o.** that singer is already out of fashion **(b)** *Tennis* out

outarde [utard] *nf Orn* **(a)** bustard **(b)** *Can* Canada goose

outil [uti] *nm* **(a)** (*d'un ouvrier, artisan*) tool; (*d'un jardinier*) tool, implement; **o. coupant** *ou* **de coupe** *ou* **tranchant** cutting tool; (*pour bords ou bordures*) edging tool **(b)** (*moyen*) tool; **outils pédagogiques** teaching aids; *Bourse* **o. de spéculation** trading instrument; **o. de travail** tool, work instrument; **o. d'aide à la décision** decision-making tool; **o. de gestion** management tool; **o. de recherche** research tool

outillage [utijaʒ] *nm* **(a)** (*ensemble d'outils*) (set of) tools **(b)** (*équipement*) (*d'une usine*) plant, equipment

outiller [utije] **1** *vt* (*ouvrier*) to equip *or* supply with tools; (*usine*) to equip, to fit out, to tool up; **nous ne sommes pas outillés pour ce genre de réparation** we're not equipped *or* we don't have the tools for that sort of repair **2 s'outiller** *vpr* (*d'une usine*) to equip itself; (*d'un bricoleur*) to equip oneself with tools

outrage [utraʒ] *nm* (*injure*) (*au bon goût etc*) insult (**à** to); **c'est un o. aux convenances/à la morale** it offends against propriety/against morality; *Euph* **faire subir les derniers outrages à une femme** to violate a woman; *Litt Fig* **l'o. des ans** *ou* **du temps** the ravages of time

▶ **outrage**: *Jur* **o. à agent** insulting behaviour; **o. aux bonnes mœurs** affront to public decency; **o. à magistrat** = contempt of court; **o. à la pudeur** public indecency

outrageant [utraʒɑ̃] *adj* (*proposition, refus*) insulting; (*plaisanterie, propos*) offensive; (*accusation*) outrageous

outrager [utraʒe] *vt* (**j'outrageai(s)**) **(a)** (*insulter*) to insult; **o. un homme dans son honneur/sa dignité** to offend against a man's honour/dignity **(b)** *Vieilli* (*porter atteinte à*) (*la vérité*) to violate; (*la raison, le bon sens, le bon goût*) to offend against

outrageusement [utraʒøzmɑ̃] *adv* **(a)** (*excessivement*) excessively, outrageously **(b)** *Vieilli* insultingly

outrageux, -euse [utraʒø, -øz] *adj Vieilli* insulting

outrance [utrɑ̃s] *nf* excess; (*d'une tenue, d'une attitude, de propos*) extravagance; **faire des outrances de langage** to use outrageous language; **agressif/méfiant à o.** excessively aggressive/mistrustful; **combat à o.** fight to the death; **attaque/industrialisation à o.** all out attack/industrialization; **travailler à o.** to work excessively *or* to excess

outrancier, -ière [utrɑ̃sje, -jɛr] *adj* (*personnalité, propos*) extreme

outre[1] [utr] *nf* wine skin; (*en peau de chèvre*) goatskin bottle

outre[2] **1** *prép* **(a) o. mesure** (*travailler*) excessively; (*se soucier, s'exposer etc*) unduly, excessively; **se fatiguer o. mesure** to tire oneself out unduly, to overtire oneself; **je ne me sens pas fatigué o. mesure** I don't feel unduly *or* overly tired; **il n'est pas scrupuleux o. mesure** he's not excessively *or* overly scrupulous

(b) (*en plus de*) besides, in addition to; **o. cette somme** besides *or* in addition to that sum; **o. cela** besides that, in addition to that

2 *adv* **passer o., aller o.** to go on *or* further; *Fig* **passer o.** to carry on regardless; **passer o. à une interdiction/la loi** to disregard *or* take no notice of *or* ignore a ban/the law; **en o.** besides, moreover; **j'ai, en o., deux neveux** I have two nephews besides

3 *conj* **o. (le fait) qu'il est riche** apart from the fact that he's rich, apart from *or* besides *or* in addition to being rich; **o. qu'il est riche il est extrêmement aimable** he's not only rich, he's also very nice

outré [utre] *adj* **(a)** (*indigné*) outraged, indignant; **j'ai été o. par son attitude** I was outraged by *or* at his attitude; **je suis outré de voir que ...** I'm outraged to see that ... **(b)** *Litt* (*excessif*) (*éloge*) exaggerated, extravagant, overdone; **comédien dont le jeu est o.** actor who overacts, actor whose acting is overdone

outre-Atlantique *adv* on the other side of the Atlantic, across the Atlantic

outrecuidance [utrəkɥidɑ̃s] *nf* **(a)** (*orgueil*) presumptuousness **(b)** (*insolence*) impertinence, effrontery; **il a eu l'o. de me dire que ...** he had the impertinence *or* effrontery to tell me that ...

outrecuidant [utrəkɥidɑ̃] *adj* **(a)** (*orgueilleux*) presumptuous **(b)** (*insolent*) impertinent

outre-Manche [utrəmɑ̃ʃ] *adv* on the other side of the Channel, across the Channel

outremer [utrəmɛr] **1** *nm* **(a)** *Minér* lapis lazuli **(b) (bleu d')o.** ultramarine **2** *adj* ultramarine

outre-mer [utrəmɛr] *adv* overseas; **commerce d'o.** overseas trade; *Admin* **territoires d'o.** overseas territories

outrepasser [utrəpase] *vt* (*une limite, ses droits*) to exceed, to go beyond

outrer [utre] *vt* **(a)** (*exagérer*) to exaggerate; (*rôle*) to overdo **(b)** (*mettre en colère*) to outrage, to infuriate

outre-Rhin [utrərɛ̃] *adv* beyond *or* across the Rhine

outre-tombe (d') [dutrətɔ̃b] *adv* from beyond the grave; *Fig* **une voix d'o.** a sepulchral voice

outsider [awtsajdœr] *nm Courses de chevaux, Fig* outsider

ouvert [uvɛr] *adj* **(a)** (*porte, fenêtre, tiroir*) open; **entre, la porte est ouverte** *ou* **c'est o.** come in, the door's open; **porte grande ouverte** wide-open door; **plaie ouverte** open *or* gaping wound; **fracture ouverte** open fracture; **il a le crâne/le genou ouvert** he has a gaping wound in his skull/knee, his skull/knee has been split open; *Chir* **opérer qn à cœur o.** to perform open-heart surgery on sb; **accueillir qn à bras ouverts** to welcome sb with open arms; **il était dans son lit, les yeux ouverts** he was lying in bed with his eyes open; **tu ne peux pas les recevoir chemise ouverte** you can't greet them with your shirt open *or* undone; **manteau qui se porte le col o.** coat that is worn with the collar open *or* undone; **voyelle ouverte** open vowel; *Fb* **jeu o.** open play; **traduire à livre o.** to translate at sight *or* off the cuff; **elle lit le grec à livre o.** she can read Greek at sight; **ville ouverte** open *or* unfortified town; **o. de 10 heures à 5 heures** open (from) 10 to 5; *F* **l'épicier du coin reste o. jusqu'à minuit** the grocer on the corner stays open till midnight; **collection ouverte au public** collection open to the public; **o. à la navigation** open to navigation; *Banque* **compte o.** open account; **c'est la guerre ouverte contre les fumeurs** it's open war on smokers; **être en guerre ouverte avec qn** to be openly at war with sb; **le gaz/robinet est o.** the gas/tap is on; **la séance est ouverte** I declare the meeting open; **la chasse/la campagne électorale est ouverte depuis ce matin** the hunting season/the election campaign began *or* started this morning; **les paris sont ouverts** *Courses de chevaux* bets are being taken; *Fig* it's anyone's guess

(**b**) *Fig* (*franc, sans préjugé*) (*personne, caractère*) open, frank; **être o. à toute proposition** to be open to suggestions; **avoir l'esprit o.** to be open-minded; **parler à cœur o.** to speak openly *or* frankly

ouvertement [uvɛrtəmɑ̃] *adv* openly; (*parler*) openly, frankly

ouverture [uvɛrtyr] *nf* (**a**) (*d'une porte, d'un livre, d'une séance etc*) opening; (*de la saison de chasse, d'une campagne*) opening, start; **pour ne pas faire la queue, j'étais là avant même l'o.** to avoid queuing I was there even before it *or* the doors opened; **elle travaille dans cette boutique depuis l'o.** she has worked in the shop since it opened; **j'ai fait l'o. de la galerie** I was at the opening of the gallery; *Bourse* **à l'o., le dollar était à 5,98 francs** at the start of trading, the dollar was at 5.98 francs, the dollar opened at 5.98 francs; **l'o. des portes du musée est prévue pour janvier** the museum is scheduled to open (its doors) in January; **l'o. des portes du lycée se fait tous les jours à huit heures** the school doors are opened every day at eight o'clock; **o. d'un compte** opening of an account; *Fin* **o. d'un crédit** granting of a loan; **o. des hostilités** outbreak of hostilities; *Ordinat* **o. de session** logon; *Aut* **o. sans clé** keyless entry; **conférence/discours d'o.** opening lecture/speech; *Bourse* **cours d'o.** opening price; **heures d'o.** opening hours; *Rugby* **il est demi d'o.** he plays stand-off *or* fly-half

(**b**) **ouvertures** (*avances*) overtures; **faire des ouvertures à qn** to make overtures to sb; **des ouvertures de paix** peace overtures

(**c**) *Mus* overture

(**d**) (*accès*) (*dans un mur etc*) opening, aperture; (*d'une caverne*) mouth; (*d'une haie*) gap, break

(**e**) (*écartement*) (*d'une voûte etc*) width, span; (*des branches d'un compas*) spread; *Él* **o. d'induit** armature gap

(**f**) *Phot* aperture

(**g**) *Fig* **o. de cœur** openness, frankness; **o. d'esprit** open-mindedness; *Pol* **le Président pratique une politique d'o.** the President is following a policy of conciliation

(**h**) *Cartes, Échecs* opening

(**i**) *Mktg* window of opportunity

ouvrable [uvrabl] *adj* **jour o.** working day; **heures ouvrables** business hours, working hours

ouvrage [uvraʒ] **1** *nm* (**a**) (*travail*) work; **se mettre à l'o.** to set to work, to get down to work; **avoir du cœur à l'o.** to put one's heart into one's work, to work with a will; **je n'ai pas le cœur à l'o. aujourd'hui** I haven't the heart for work today, I don't feel like working today

(**b**) *Constr* work; **entreprise spécialisée dans les ouvrages de maçonnerie** firm specializing in masonry work; **ouvrages d'art** civil engineering works

(**c**) (*livre*) work, book; **o. en prose** prose work; **un o. de philosophie** a work of philosophy, a philosophy book; **un o. de géographie** a geography book; **o. de référence** reference work *or* book, work of reference

(**d**) (*résultat*) piece of work, product; *Vieilli* **o. de dames** needlework; **corbeille/boîte à o.** workbasket/workbox; **une rencontre qui est l'o. du hasard** a meeting which is due to chance, a chance meeting; **l'o. du temps** the work of time

2 *nf F* **c'est de la belle o.** that's a nice bit of work

ouvragé [uvraʒe] *adj* (**a**) = **ouvré** (**b**) (*orné*) elaborate

ouvrager [uvraʒe] *vt* (**j'ouvrageai(s)**) (*métal, bijou*) to work; (*orner*) (*brocart*) to figure

ouvrant [uvrɑ̃] **1** *adj Aut* **toit o.** sun roof, sliding roof **2** *nm Beaux-Arts* (*d'un triptyque*) panel

ouvré [uvre] *adj* (**a**) *Tech* (*fer*) wrought; **produits ouvrés et semi-ouvrés** finished and semi-finished products (**b**) *Litt* (*orné*) decorated; (*nappe*) embroidered

ouvre-boîte(s) [uvrəbwat], *pl* **ouvre-boîtes** *nm* can opener, *Br* tin opener; **o. électrique** electric can *or* tin opener

ouvre-bouteille(s) [uvrəbutɛj], *pl* **ouvre-bouteilles** *nm* bottle opener

ouvre-huître(s) [uvrɥitr], *pl* **ouvre-huîtres** *nm* oyster knife

ouvrer [uvre] *vt* (**a**) *Tech* (*bois, cuivre etc*) to work (**b**) (*orner*) (*nappe etc*) to work, to embroider

ouvreur¹, -euse [uvrœr, -øz] *n Cartes* opener

ouvreuse² [uvrøz] *nf Th, Cin* usherette

ouvrez-moi [uvremwa] *Ordinat nm inv* read-me document

ouvrier, -ère [uvrije, -ɛr] **1** *adj* (**a**) (*prolétaire*) (*quartier, tradition*) working-class; **la classe ouvrière** the working class(es); **agitation ouvrière** industrial unrest, labour unrest; **syndicat o.** trade union (**b**) *Zool* **abeille ouvrière** worker bee; **fourmi ouvrière** worker ant **2** *n* worker; (*prolétaire*) working man/woman; (*de réparation, de travaux publics*) workman; (*d'une machine*) operative; **o. en bois/sur métaux** woodworker/metalworker; **une famille d'ouvriers** a working-class family; *Litt Fig* **il est l'o. de sa fortune** he is a self-made man **3** *nf Zool* **ouvrière** worker

▶ **ouvrier**: **o. agricole** farm worker *or* hand, agricultural labourer; **o. non qualifié** unskilled manual worker; **o. qualifié** skilled worker; **o. spécialisé** semi-skilled worker

ouvriérisme [uvrijerism] *nm Pol* (*autogestion*) worker control; (*syndicalisme*) trade unionism

ouvrir [uvrir] (*prp* **ouvrant**; *pp* **ouvert**; *pr ind* **j'ouvre**; *p hist* **j'ouvris**) **1** *vt* (**a**) (*porte, fenêtre, boîte, bouteille etc*) to open; (*verrou*) to draw; (*loquet*) to unfasten; (*avec une clef*) to unlock; (*rideaux*) to open, to draw (back); **o. sa maison** *ou* **sa porte à qn** to throw open one's house to sb; *Fig* **o. la porte à qch** to open the door to sth; **il n'a pas ouvert la bouche,** *F* **il ne l'a pas ouverte** he didn't open his mouth; **o. le lit** to turn down the bed(clothes); **o. un robinet/le gaz** to turn on a tap/the gas; **o. l'électricité** to switch on (the electricity); *F* **o. le poste** to put on *or* switch on the radio; *Él* **o. le circuit** to switch off *or* break the current

(**b**) *Fig* (*découvrir*) **o. son cœur à qn** to open one's heart to sb, to unburden oneself to sb; **cette expérience lui a ouvert l'esprit** the experience broadened his mind; **cela ouvre l'appétit** it sharpens *or* whets the appetite

(**c**) (*percer*) (*mur*) to cut through; (*mine*) to open up; (*canal*) to cut; *Méd* (*abcès*) to lance; **le chirurgien lui a ouvert l'estomac** the surgeon opened (up) his stomach

(**d**) (*commencer, lancer*) (*une école, une boutique*) to open; (*un débat, une discussion*) to open, to start; **o. un compte chez qn** to open an account with sb; **o. un col en montagne** to open up a pass through *or* in the mountains; **cette discussion m'a ouvert de nouvelles perspectives** the discussion opened (up) new horizons for me; **ce sont des professions que nous voulons o. aux femmes** they are professions that we want to open up to women; **o. le bal** to open the ball; **o. boutique** to set up shop; **o. la marche** to lead the way; *Fin* **o. un crédit** to grant a loan; *Com* **o. un débouché à un produit** to open up a new outlet for a product; *Ordinat* **o. une session** to log in, to log on

2 *vi* to open; (*ouvrir la porte*) to open the door; **o. à qn** to open the door to sb, to let sb in; **les magasins n'ouvrent pas les jours de fête** the shops don't open *or* aren't open on public holidays; **la fenêtre n'ouvre plus** the window doesn't *or* won't open any more; **la porte n'ouvre que de l'intérieur** the door can only be opened from the inside, the door only opens from the inside; **la scène ouvre par un chœur** the scene opens with a chorus; **le salon/la fenêtre ouvrait sur le jardin** the drawing room/the window opened on(to) the garden; *TV, Cin* **o. en fondu** to fade in; *TV, Cin* **o. par un volet** to wipe on

3 s'ouvrir *vpr* (**a**) (*devenir ouvert*) (*d'une porte, d'une fenêtre, des yeux etc*) to open; (*d'une fleur*) to come out, to open; **la porte s'ouvrit en coup de vent** the door flew open; **les fenêtres s'ouvrent sur le jardin** the windows open on(to) the garden; *Fig* **un gouffre s'ouvrait sous mes pieds** a chasm opened up *or* yawned under my feet; **s'o. un chemin à travers la foule** to push one's way through the crowd; **les possibilités/nouvelles perspectives qui s'ouvrent aux jeunes diplômés** the possibilities/new horizons that are opening up for young graduates; **carrières qui s'ouvrent de plus en plus aux femmes** careers that are opening up more and more to women; **s'o. à de nouvelles technologies** to open (up) one's mind to new technologies; **tu ne peux pas ne pas t'o. à l'informatique** you can't afford to close yourself off to computer technology, you have to be open to computer technology; **la séance s'ouvre par un discours** the meeting opens with a speech; **le bal s'ouvrit par une valse** the ball opened *or* began *or* started with a waltz

(**b**) (*se couper*) **s'o. la main/le menton** to cut open one's hand/chin; **s'o. les veines** to slash one's wrists

(**c**) (*se confier*) **s'o. à qn** to unburden oneself to sb, to

confide in sb; **s'o. à qn de qch** to open one's heart to sb about sth, to confide in sb about sth
ouvroir [uvrwar] *nm* workroom, sewing room
ovaire [ɔvɛr] *nm Anat, Bot* ovary; **kyste de l'o.** ovarian cyst
ovale [ɔval] **1** *adj* oval; *Sp* **ballon o.** rugby ball; *(le rugby)* rugby; **les adeptes du ballon o.** rugby fans **2** *nm* oval; **en o.** oval
ovalisation [ɔvalizasjɔ̃] *nf Tech (des cylindres)* ovalization
ovalisé [ɔvalize] *adj Tech (cylindre)* ovalized
ovaliser [ɔvalize] *vt Tech* **l'usure ovalise les cylindres** cylinders become ovalized through wear
ovariectomie [ɔvarjɛktɔmi] *nf Méd* ovariectomy, oophorectomy
ovarien, -ienne [ɔvarjɛ̃, -jɛn] *adj Anat, Bot* ovarian
ovation [ɔvasjɔ̃] *nf* ovation; **faire une o. à qn** to give sb an ovation
ovationner [ɔvasjɔne] *vt* **o. qn** to give sb an ovation
ové [ɔve] *adj (fruit)* egg-shaped, ovate
overdose [ɔvœrdoz] *nf Méd, Fig* overdose; **mourir d'une o.** to die of *or* from an overdose; *Fig* **j'ai fait une o. de films japonais** I've overdosed on *or* I've had an overdose of Japanese films
overdrive [ɔvœrdrajv] *Aut nm* overdrive
ovidés [ɔvide] *nmpl Zool, Agr* Ovidae
oviducte [ɔvidykt] *nm* oviduct
ovin [ɔvɛ̃] *Agr* **1** *adj* ovine **2** *nmpl* **ovins** sheep
ovipare [ɔvipar] *Zool* **1** *adj* oviparous **2** *nm* oviparous animal
ovni [ɔvni] *nm (abrév* **objet volant non identifié)** UFO
ovoïde [ɔvɔid] *adj* ovoid, egg-shaped; *Él* **maillon o.** egg insulator
ovovivipare [ɔvɔvivipar] *Zool* **1** *adj* ovoviviparous **2** *nm* ovoviviparous animal
ovulaire [ɔvylɛr] *adj* ovular
ovulation [ɔvylasjɔ̃] *nf* ovulation
ovule [ɔvyl] *nm* **(a)** *Biol* ovum **(b)** *Pharm* **ovules gynécologiques** (vaginal) pessaries
ovuler [ɔvyle] *vi* to ovulate
oxalate [ɔksalat] *nm Ch* oxalate
oxalide [ɔksalid] *nf,* **oxalis** [ɔksalis] *nm Bot* oxalis, wood sorrel
oxalique [ɔksalik] *adj Ch* **acide o.** oxalic acid
oxford [ɔksfɔrd] *Tex* **1** *nm* **une chemise en o.** an Oxford shirt **2** *adj* **de la flanelle o.** Oxford
oxhydrique [ɔksidrik] *adj* oxyhydrogen
oxyacétylénique [ɔksiasetilenik] *adj Tech (gaz, soudure)* oxyacetylene
oxycoupage [ɔksikupaʒ] *nm Métal* oxygen cutting
oxydable [ɔksidabl] *adj* **(a)** *Ch* oxidizable **(b)** *(d'un métal)* liable to rust
oxydant [ɔksidɑ̃] **1** *adj* oxidizing **2** *nm* oxidizer, oxidizing agent
oxydation [ɔksidasjɔ̃] *nf Ch* oxidization, oxidation
oxyde [ɔksid] *nm Ch* oxide; **o. de carbone** carbon monoxide; **o. d'azote** nitrogen oxide; **o. nitrique** nitric oxide
oxyder [ɔkside] **1** *vt* to oxidize **2 s'oxyder** *vpr* to oxidize
oxygénation [ɔksiʒenasjɔ̃] *nf* **(a)** *Ch* oxygenation **(b)** *(application d'eau oxygénée)* **les méfaits de l'o. sur les cheveux** the damaging effects of bleach on the hair
oxygéné [ɔksiʒene] *adj Ch* oxygenated; **eau oxygénée** hydrogen peroxide; **cheveux oxygénés** peroxide blonde hair, bleached hair
oxygène [ɔksiʒɛn] *nm* **(a)** *Ch* oxygen; *Méd* **tente à o.** oxygen tent **(b)** *F* **j'ai besoin d'o.** I need a change of air
oxygéner [ɔksiʒene] **(il oxygène; il oxygénera) 1** *vt* **(a)** *Ch (liquide, tissu vivant)* to oxygenate, to oxygenize; *(élément, produit chimique)* to oxidize **(b)** *(cheveux)* to bleach, to peroxide **2 s'oxygéner** *vpr F (respirer)* to take *or* get a breath of fresh air; **partir à la campagne pour une quinzaine pour s'o.** to go off to the countryside for two weeks to get some good clean air (in one's lungs)
oxyton [ɔksitɔ̃] *nm Ling* oxytone
oxyure [ɔksjyr] *nm Méd* oxyuris
oyat [ɔja] *nm Bot* marram grass
ozalid® [ɔzalid] *nm Typ* ozalid
ozone [ɔzon] *nm Ch* ozone; **couche d'o.** ozone layer
ozonisation [ɔzɔnizasjɔ̃] *nf Ch, Tech* ozonization
ozoniser [ɔzɔnize] *vt* to ozonize

P

P, p [pe] *nm (lettre)* P, p
PAC [pak] *nf (abrév* **Politique Agricole Commune)** CAP
pacage [pakaʒ] *nm Agr* **(a)** *(champ)* pasture(land); **p. d'été** summer pasture **(b)** *(action de faire paître)* pasturing, grazing; *Jur* **droit(s) de p.** grazing rights
pacager [pakaʒe] **(je pacageai(s); n. pacageons) 1** *vt (troupeau)* to pasture, to graze **2** *vi (d'un troupeau)* to graze
pacane [pakan] *nf* pecan (nut); *Culin* **tarte aux pacanes** pecan pie
pacemaker [pɛsmɛkœr] *nm Sp, Méd* pacemaker
pacha [paʃa] *nm* pasha; *F* **mener une vie de p.** to live like a lord; **tu ne vas pas faire le p. tout le week-end!** don't expect to be waited on hand and foot all weekend!
pachyderme [paʃidɛrm] *nm* pachyderm; *Fig F (personne)* great *or* fat lump, tub of lard; **de p.** *(allure, démarche)* elephantine, lumbering; *(grâce)* elephantine
pacificateur, -trice [pasifikatœr, -tris] **1** *adj* pacifying **2** *n* peacemaker
pacification [pasifikasjɔ̃] *nf* pacification
pacifier [pasifje] *vt (impf, pr sub* **n. pacifiions, v. pacifiiez)** to pacify
pacifique [pasifik] **1** *adj (coexistence, manifestation etc)* peaceful; *(qui aime la paix)* peace-loving; **mesure à but p.** measure intended to bring about peace; **mener une existence p.** to lead a quiet *or* peaceful life; **l'océan P.** the Pacific (Ocean); *Jur* **possesseur p.** uncontested owner **2** *n Bible* **bienheureux les pacifiques** blessed are the peacemakers **3** *nm* **le P.** *(océan)* the Pacific
pacifiquement [pasifikmɑ̃] *adv* peacefully; **le meeting s'est déroulé p.** the meeting went off peacefully *or* quietly
pacifisme [pasifism] *nm Pol* pacifism
pacifiste [pasifist] *adj, n Pol* pacifist
pack [pak] *nm* **(a)** *(des mers polaires)* pack ice, ice pack **(b)** *Rugby* pack **(c)** *(lot)* pack; **des cannettes de bière en p. de 6** a six-pack (of beer); **lait vendu en p.** milk sold in multipacks
package [pakɛdʒ] *nm Com, Ordinat* package
packaging [pakɛdʒiŋ] *nm* packaging
pacotille [pakɔtij] *nf Péj* **(marchandises de) p.** shoddy goods; **c'est de la p.** it's junk; **de p.** shoddy, third-rate; **bijoux de p.** paste jewellery; **exotisme de p.** third-rate exoticism
pacson [paksɔ̃] *nm F (argent, paquet)* packet; **toucher le p.** to win a packet
pacte [pakt] *nm* pact; **conclure** *ou* **faire** *ou* **sceller un p. avec/contre qn** to enter into a pact with/against sb; **signer un p. avec le diable** to sign a pact with the Devil
▶ **pacte**: **p. de non-agression** non-aggression pact; **p. à quatre** four-power pact; **le P. de Varsovie** the Warsaw Pact
pactiser [paktize] *vi* **p. avec qn** to come to terms with sb; **p. avec le diable** to make a pact with the devil; *Fig* **p. avec sa conscience** to come to terms with one's conscience; *Jur* **p. avec un crime** to compound a felony
pactole [paktɔl] *nm* **(a)** *Litt (qui enrichit)* gold mine; **ce travail est un vrai p.** this type of work is a real gold mine **(b)** *F (argent mis en jeu)* kitty; **il rêvait de gagner le p.** *(au loto)* he dreamt of winning the lottery; **son job lui rapporte un sacré p.** his job brings in megabucks; **elle a touché un joli p. quand son grand-père est mort** she came in for a nice little sum when her grandfather died
paddle [padœl] *nm Sp* paddle tennis
paddock [padɔk] *nm* paddock; *F (lit)* bed; *F* **se mettre** *ou* **aller au p.** *(se coucher)* to hit the sack *or* hay
paddy [padi] *nm inv* paddy
Padoue [padu] *nf* Padua
paella [paɛla, paɛja] *nf Culin* paella
PAF [paf] *nm abrév* **paysage audiovisuel français**
paf [paf] **1** *int* slap!, bang! **2** *adj F* **être p.** *(saoul)* to be pissed; **il est complètement p.** he's as pissed as a newt
PAG [peaʒe] *nf Com (abrév* **procédure accélérée générale de dédouanement)** accelerated customs clearance procedure
pagaie [pagɛ] *nf (rame)* paddle
pagaïe, pagaille [pagaj] *nf F (d'objets)* disorder, clutter; **il y a une drôle de p. dans ce bureau** this office looks as if a bomb has hit it *or* is in a fine old mess; **c'est la p. dans les rues de Paris** the streets of Paris are completely snarled up; **quelle p.!** what a mess!, what a shambles!; *(à cause des embouteillages)* what a snarl-up!; **quelle p. dans cette pièce!** this room's (in) a real mess!; **en p.** *(maison, chambre)* in a mess; *(affaires, papiers)* all jumbled up, in a mess; **ses affaires étaient en p. avec les miennes/dans le sac** his things were jumbled up with mine/in the bag; **j'ai mis mes papiers en p. dans mon cartable** I stuffed my papers into my briefcase any old how; **je les ai mis en p.** *(ces livres etc)* I've just bundled them up, they're not in any particular order; **évite de mettre tout en p.** don't get things all jumbled *or* mixed up; **avec des cadeaux en p.** with presents galore, with masses *or* loads of presents; **il y en a en p.** there's masses *or* lots *or* loads of it/them; **semer la p.** to cause trouble **(parmi** among; **dans** in); **il adore semer la p.** he likes causing trouble, *Br F* he's a real stirrer
paganisme [paganism] *nm* paganism
pagayer [pageje] *vi* **(je pagaie, je pagaye)** to paddle
pagayeur, -euse [pagɛjœr, -øz] *n* paddler
page¹ [paʒ] *nf (d'un livre etc)* page; **feuilleter les pages d'un magazine** to flick through a magazine; **un livre de 250 pages** a 250-page book; **être payé à la p.** to be paid by the page; **je gagne 50 F de la p.** I earn 50 francs a page; **en première p. des journaux** on the front page of the newspapers; **faire la première p. des journaux** to hit the headlines; *Journ* **photo sur une double p.** two-page photo spread; *Journ* **article sur une double p.** two-page spread; **ouvrez vos livres à la p. 10** open your books at page 10 *or* and turn to page 10; **j'ai perdu la p.** I've lost my place; **je voudrais finir la p.** I'd like to finish the page I'm on; *Typ* **mettre en page(s)** to make up; **mise en page(s)** pagination, page make-up; *Ordinat* **logiciel de mise en p.** desktop publishing package; *Typ* **fausse p.** dummy; **une des plus belles pages de Victor Hugo** one of Victor Hugo's finest passages; *Fig* **une des plus célèbres pages de l'histoire** one of the most famous pages *or* chapters in history; **une nouvelle p. de l'histoire de France était tournée** a new chapter had begun in the history of France; *F* **être à la p.** to be up to date; **je ne suis plus vraiment à la p. en matière de musique** I'm pretty out of touch with what's happening in music; **ne pas être à la p.** to be behind the times; **tu n'es plus du tout à la p.** you're totally behind the times *or* out of it; **il faut te mettre à la p.** you're going to have to get with it; **rester à la p.** to keep up to date
▶ **page¹**: *Ordinat* **p. d'accueil** logo page; *Journ* **p. d'actualités** news page; *Journ* **p. centrale** centre page; *Journ* **p. centrale dépliante** centre spread, centrefold; **p. de couverture** cover page; *Typ* **pages de départ** prelims; *Ordinat* **p.-écran** screen page; *Journ* **p. féminine** women's page; *Journ* **pages financières** financial *or Br* City pages; *Typ* **p. de garde** endpaper; *(d'un fax)* cover(ing) sheet; **les pages jaunes (de l'annuaire)** the yellow pages; *Journ* **p. de mode** fashion page; *Ordinat* **p. précédente** page up; **p. de publicité** *Journ* full-page advert; *Rad, TV* commercial break; *Ordinat* **p. suivante** page down; *Typ* **p. de titre** title page; **p. volante** slip page
page² *nm* page(boy)
page³, pageot [paʒo] *nm F (lit)* sack, *Br* pit; **se mettre au p.** to hit the sack *or* hay, to crawl between the sheets
pageux [paʒø] *nm Typ* compositor, comp
pagination [paʒinasjɔ̃] *nf* pagination, page numbering
paginer [paʒine] *vt* to paginate
pagne [paɲ] *nm* loincloth; *(en paille)* grass skirt
pagnoter (se) [səpaɲɔte] *vpr F (se coucher)* to hit the sack *or* hay
pagode [pagɔd] *nf* **(a)** *Archit* pagoda; **toit en p.** pagoda roof; **manches pagodes** pagoda sleeves **(b)** *(figurine à tête mobile)* mandarin
paie [pɛ] *nf* pay; *(par semaine)* wages; **feuille** *ou* **bulletin de p.** pay (advice) slip; **jour de p.** pay day; **faire la p.** to pay (out) the wages; **toucher sa p.** to get paid, to get one's pay; *Fig F*

ça fait une p. que je ne l'ai pas vu I haven't seen him in a month of Sundays; **quand vous êtes-vous rencontrés? – ça fait une p.!** when did you meet? – donkey's years ago!

paiement [pɛmɑ̃] *nm* payment; **p. mensuel** monthly payment; **p. du solde** payment of the balance; **demander des délais de p.** to ask for time to pay; *aussi Fig* **c'est tout ce qu'il reçut en p. de son travail** that's all he got (as payment) for his work; *Fig* **voilà donc le p. de mon aide!** so that's what I get (in return) for helping you!

▶ **paiement**: **p. anticipatif** *ou* **anticipé** advance payment, payment in advance, prepayment; **p. par anticipation** payment in advance; **p. arriéré** payment in arrears; **p. d'avance** payment in advance, advance payment, prepayment; *TV* **p. à la carte** (*des programmes*) payment by card; *Banque* **p. par carte** card payment, payment by card; **p. par chèque** payment by cheque; **p. à la commande** cash with order, CWO; **p. (au) comptant** cash payment, payment in cash; *TV* **p. à la consommation** *ou* **à la séance** pay as you view, pay per view; **p. contre documents** payment against documents; **p. différé** deferred payment; **p. échelonné** staged *or* staggered payments; **p. électronique** electronic payment, payment by electronic transfer; **p. en espèces** payment in cash, cash payment; **p. intégral** payment in full; **p. à la livraison, p. contre livraison** cash on delivery, COD; **p. en nature** payment in kind; **p. partiel** partial *or* part payment; **paiements périodiques** periodic payments; **p. préalable** prepayment; **p. progressif** graduated *or* increasing payments; **p. en souffrance** overdue *or* outstanding payment; **p. à termes** *ou* **par acomptes** payment by *or* in instalments

païen, -ïenne [pajɛ̃, -jɛn] *adj, n* pagan, heathen; **jurer comme un p.** to swear like a trooper

paierie [pɛri] *nf* local government finance office

paillage [pɑjaʒ] *nm Agr* mulching

paillard, -arde [pajar, -ard] **1** *adj* (*personne, chanson, plaisanterie*) bawdy, ribald; **regard p.** leer **2** *n* debauchee; (*homme*) debauchee, rake

paillardise [pajardiz] *nf* **(a)** (*d'une personne, chanson etc*) bawdiness, ribaldry **(b)** *Vieilli* (*histoire*) bawdy story

paillasse [pajas] **1** *nf* **(a)** (*matelas*) straw mattress, paillasse, palliasse **(b)** (*de l'évier*) draining board; (*de laboratoire*) (laboratory) bench **(c)** *F* **crever** *ou* **trouer la p. à qn** to stab sb in the stomach (and kill him/her) **(d)** *F Vieilli* (*prostituée*) floozy, tart **2** *nm* clown, buffoon

paillasson [pajasɔ̃] *nm* (*tapis-brosse*) (door)mat; *Agr* straw matting; *Fig* (*personne*) doormat; *Fig* **mettre la clef sous le p.** to clear out, *Br F* to scarper

paille [paj] **1** *nf* **(a)** straw; **p. de litière** loose straw; **menue p., p. d'avoine** chaff; **p. de riz** *ou* **d'Italie** rice straw; **chapeau de p.** straw hat; **chaise de p.** straw-bottomed chair; **vin de p.** straw wine (*wine made from grapes dried on straw mats before pressing*); *Fig* **homme de p.** man of straw, *Am* straw man; **il leur fallait un homme de p.** they needed a front man *or* a figurehead; *Fig* **feu de p.** flash in the pan; **ce ne fut qu'un feu de p.** (*leur amour*) it was just a flash in the pan; (*ce scandale*) it was just a nine-days wonder; **cela leur passera comme un feu de p.** they'll soon get over it, it'll be a flash in the pan; **sur la p. humide des cachots** behind bars; *Fig* **sur la p.** destitute, *F* on one's uppers, down and out; **voilà ce qui t'a mis sur la p.** that's what put you on your uppers; **mourir sur la p.** to die destitute; **vieillir sur la p.** to be old and destitute; **c'est facile de voir la p. dans l'œil du voisin (et ne pas voir la poutre dans le sien)** it's easy to criticize, you/he/*etc* should take the mote out of your/his/*etc* own eye first; **c'est la p. et la poutre** you/he/*etc* should take the mote out of your/his/*etc* own eye first; **tirer à la courte p.** to draw lots; **on tira à la courte p. qui irait faire du café** we drew lots to see who would make the coffee; **on tira à la courte p. le nom du gagnant** the winner was chosen by lot, the name of the winner was drawn out of a hat

(b) (*pour boire*) (drinking) straw; **boire qch avec une p.** to drink sth through *or* with a straw; **tirer sur une p.** to suck on a straw

(c) p. de fer steel wool

(d) (*défaut*) (*dans une pierre précieuse etc*) flaw

2 *adj inv* **(a)** straw-coloured *or US* -colored; **jaune p.** pale yellow

(b) *Culin* **pommes p.** = deep-fried straw potatoes

paillé[1] [paje] *nm* stable litter

paillé[2] *adj* **(a)** (*couleur*) straw-coloured *or US* -colored **(b)** (*chaise*) straw-bottomed **(c)** (*métal, pierre précieuse etc*) flawed

pailler[1] [paje] *nm* (*hangar*) farmyard, straw yard; (*meule*) straw stack

pailler[2] *vt* **(a)** (*arbuste*) to protect *or* mulch with straw **(b)** (*chaise*) to put a straw bottom in

paillet [pajɛ] *nm Naut* mat, fender; **p. d'abordage, p. makarov** collision mat

pailleté [pajte] *adj* spangled (**de** with), sequined

pailleter [pajte] *vt* (**je paillette; je pailletterai**) to sequin, to spangle

paillette [pajɛt] *nf* **(a)** sequin, spangle; **à paillettes** sequined **(b)** (*d'or*) grain of gold dust; (*de mica etc*) flake; **savon en paillettes** soap flakes **(c)** (*d'une pierre précieuse*) flaw

pailleux, -euse [pajø, -øz] *adj* **(a)** *Agr* **fumier p.** manure which has not rotted down sufficiently **(b)** *Tech* (*acier*) flawed

paillis [paji] *nm Agr* mulch

paillote [pɑjɔt] *nf* straw hut

pain [pɛ̃] *nm* **(a)** [①A12,1,d] (*aliment*) bread; (*unité*) loaf, *pl* loaves; **achète deux pains** buy two loaves; **quelle sorte de p. devrais-je acheter?** what kind of bread should I buy?; *Rel* **le p. et le vin** the bread and wine; *Rel* **le/notre p. quotidien** our daily bread; **mettre qn au p. (sec) et à l'eau/au p. sec** to put sb on bread and water/on dry bread; **bon comme du bon p.** *ou* **comme le p.** extremely kind-hearted; **long comme un jour sans p.** interminable; *Fig* **c'est p. bénit** it serves him/her/them right but it's a godsend for us; **acheter qch pour une bouchée de p.** to buy sth for a song *or* for next to nothing; **il ne vaut pas le p. qu'il mange** he isn't worth his salt; **avoir du p. sur la planche** to have a lot on one's plate, to have plenty of work to do; **gagner son p. (à la sueur de son front)** to earn one's *or* make a living (by the sweat of one's brow); **ôter le p. de la bouche à qn** to take the bread out of sb's mouth; **je ne mange pas de ce p.-là** I'm not getting involved in that, I'm not having any of that; **ça ne mange pas de p.** it won't cost you/him/*etc* anything; **du p. et des jeux** bread and circuses; *Bot* **arbre à p.** breadfruit tree

(b) petit p. (bread) roll; *Fig* **ça part** *ou* **se vend comme des petits pains** it sells/it's selling like hot cakes; **ces foulards sont partis comme des petits pains** those scarves went *or* sold like hot cakes; *Culin* **p. de poisson** fish loaf

(c) (*de savon*) bar, cake; (*de cire*) stick

(d) *F* (*coup de poing*) punch; **flanque-lui un p.** sock him one, *Br* give him a bunch of fives; **il a pris un p. dans la gueule** he got socked in the kisser

▶ **pain**: **p. azyme** unleavened bread; **p. bis** brown bread/loaf; *Fig* **p. blanc: il a mangé son p. blanc le premier** he was lucky to start with; **fais attention à ne pas manger ton p. blanc le premier** remember that tomorrow always comes, always keep something to fall back on; **p. brioché** = bread closely resembling brioche in texture; **p. de campagne** farmhouse loaf; **p. au chocolat** chocolate-filled pastry; **p. complet** wholemeal bread/loaf; **p. d'épices** ≈ gingerbread; **p. de Gênes** Genoa cake; **p. grillé** toast; **p. au lait** sweet roll; **p. au levain** sourdough bread/loaf; **p. de ménage** homemade bread/loaf; **p. de mie** sandwich loaf; **p. noir** black bread; **p. parisien** short French stick; **p. paysan** farmhouse loaf; **p. perdu** (*cuit à la poêle*) French toast; (*cuit au four*) = dessert consisting of stale bread soaked in milk and cooked with eggs, sugar and raisins; **p. aux raisins** currant bun; **p. de seigle** rye bread/loaf; **p. au** *ou* **de son** bran bread/loaf; **p. de sucre** sugar loaf; *Géog* **(montagne en) p. de sucre** sugar loaf (mountain); **p. viennois** Viennese bread/loaf

pair [pɛr] **1** *adj* (*nombre*) even; **jours pairs** even dates; *Ordinat* **parité paire** even parity; **organes pairs** paired organs

2 *nm* **(a)** (*égal*) equal, peer; **être jugé par ses pairs** to be judged by one's peers; *Litt* **être avec qn** *ou* **traiter qn de p. à compagnon** to treat sb as an equal; **hors (de) p.** (*habileté, talent, efficacité etc*) unequalled, unrivalled, beyond compare; (*personne*) unequalled; **c'est un traducteur hors p.** as a translator he's second to none *or* in a class by himself; **pour ce qui est de l'informatique, elle est hors p.** there is no-one to equal *or* match her *or* she is unequalled when it comes to computers; **aller de p.** (*de deux choses*) to go together, to go hand in hand; **aller de p. avec qch** to go hand in hand with sth; **le chômage va de p. avec les crises économiques** unemployment and economic crises go hand in hand; **ça va de p.** the two go hand in hand

(b) (*noble*) peer (of the realm); *Br* **Chambre des Pairs** House of Lords

(c) *Fin* par; *Com* **p. commercial** par; *Com* **p. du change** par of exchange; **au-dessous/au-dessus du p.** below/above par; **au p.** at par

(d) au p.: travailler au p. to work au pair, to do au pair work; **jeune fille au p.** au pair (girl); **elle est au p. dans une famille bordelaise/chez un médecin** she's working (as an) au pair for a family in Bordeaux/for a doctor; **elle envoie**

des jeunes filles au p. aux États-Unis she sends girls to work au pair in the United States

(e) **jouer p./impair** to bet on the even/odd numbers

paire [pɛr] *nf* [①A10,e] (*de chaussures, de lunettes, de ciseaux etc*) pair; (*de draps*) set; (*de gibier à plumes, de pistolets*) brace; **p. de bœufs** yoke of oxen; **une belle p. de seins** a great pair, *Arg* great boobs *or* tits; *F* **une belle p. de fesses** (*de femme*) a nice ass; (*d'homme*) nice buns; **il a reçu une p. de claques** he got his face slapped; *Fig F* **ça, c'est une autre p. de manches** that's another matter, that's a different kettle of fish; **quant à lui faire comprendre cela, c'est une autre p. de manches** it's another matter *or* a different kettle of fish getting him to understand; *F* **ils font la p.** they're two of a kind; *F* **se faire la p.** to clear out, to beat it, *Br* to scarper; *Tech* **p. torsadée** twisted pair

pairesse [pɛrɛs] *nf Br* peeress

pairie [pɛri] *nf* peerage

paisible [pɛzibl] *adj* peaceful; (*silence, sommeil*) peaceful, undisturbed; (*personne*) quiet; (*eau*) calm; *Jur* **p. possesseur d'un bien** uncontested owner of a piece of property; **dormir d'un sommeil p.** to sleep peacefully; **retrouver un sommeil p.** to sleep peacefully again

paisiblement [pɛzibləmɑ̃] *adv* peacefully

paître [pɛtr] (*prp* **paisant**; *pr ind* **je pais, il paît, n. paissons**; *pr sub* **je paisse**; *impf* **je paissais**; *fu* **je paîtrai**; *no p hist*) **1** *vt* (*des animaux*) (*feuilles etc*) to feed on; (*herbe*) to crop; *Arch, Litt* (*bétail*) to feed, to graze **2** *vi* (*des animaux*) to feed; (*manger de l'herbe*) to graze, to pasture; (*manger des feuilles*) to browse; *Fig F* **je l'ai envoyé p.** I sent him packing, I sent him off with a flea in his ear

paix [pɛ] *nf* (a) (*entre états*) peace; **en temps de p.** in peacetime, in times of peace; **demander la p.** to sue for peace; **troubler la p.** to break the peace; **faire la p.** to make peace (**avec** with); *Fig* **faire la p. avec qn** to make one's peace with sb, to make it up with sb; *Fig* **on fait la p.?** let's make up, let's be friends again; *Fig* **faire la p. avec son passé** to come to terms with one's past; **rester en p. avec un pays** to remain at peace with a country; **vivre en p. avec ses voisins** to live at peace with one's neighbours; *Fig* **je souhaite vivre en p. avec ma conscience/mon passé** I want to be able to live with my conscience/my past; *Jur* **juge de p.** magistrate, justice of the peace; **climat de p. sociale** (*absence de grève*) climate of industrial peace

(b) *Rel* (*sérénité*) peace; **la p. du tombeau** the quiet of the grave; **p. à son âme** may his/her soul rest in peace; **qu'il repose en p.** may he rest in peace; **allez en p.** go in peace

(c) (*tranquillité*) peace; **dormir en p.** to sleep peacefully; **avoir besoin de p. pour se concentrer** to need peace and quiet to concentrate; **troubler la p. de qn** to disturb sb; (*moralement*) to disturb sb's peace of mind; **troubler la p. de ce petit matin** to break the peace of the early morning; **il ne m'a pas laissé en p. tant que …** he gave me no peace until …; **laissez-moi en p.** leave me alone *or* in peace; **je suis pour la p. des ménages** I'm a great believer in marital harmony; *F* **avoir la p.** to get peace (and quiet); **impossible d'avoir la p. quand il est là** it's impossible to get any peace (and quiet) when he's around; **je peux avoir la p. cinq minutes?** can I have five minutes' peace (and quiet)?, can't I be left alone for five minutes?; *F* **je veux qu'on me fiche** *ou* **foute la p.** I want to be left alone; *F* **il faut lui ficher** *ou* **fiche** *ou* **foutre la p. avec tes questions** stop pestering him with your damn questions; *F* **fiche-moi** *ou* **fous-moi la p.!** leave me alone!, stop pestering me!, get off my back!; **fous-lui la p.!** bloody leave him alone!; *F* **la p.!** hush!, be quiet!

▶ **paix**: **p. armée** armed peace; **p. séparée** separate peace; **p. universelle** universal peace

Pakistan [pakistɑ̃] *nm* Pakistan

pakistanais, -aise [pakistanɛ, -ɛz] **1** *adj* Pakistani **2** *n* **P.** Pakistani

PAL [pal] *nm TV* PAL

pal, -als [pal] *nm* (a) (*pieu*) pale, stake; *Arch* **le (supplice du) p.** impalement (b) (*plantoir*) planter, dibber

palabre [palabr] *n* (*souvent pl*) **palabres** palaver, (endless) discussion; **après de long(ue)s palabres** after a long discussion; **s'éterniser en palabres** to drag on for ever

palabrer [palabre] *vi* to palaver, to talk endlessly

palace [palas] *nm* luxury hotel

paladin [paladɛ̃] *nm* paladin; (*itinérant*) knight-errant

palais¹ [palɛ] *nm* (a) (*d'un roi etc*) palace (b) *Jur* **le p. de Justice, le p.** the law courts; **les gens du** *ou* **de p., le p.** the legal profession; **terme de p.** legal term; **le style du p.** legal language *or* jargon, the language of the courts

▶ **palais**: **le P. Bourbon** = home of the French Parliament; **le P. Brongniart** = the Paris Stock Exchange; **p. des congrès** convention centre; **le P. de l'Élysée** the Élysée (Palace) (*official residence of the French President*); **le P. Garnier** = the Paris Opera House; **le Grand P.** = science museum in Paris originally built as part of the 1900 World Fair; **le P. du Luxembourg** = home of the French Senate; **le P. des Papes** = papal palace in Avignon, now the centre of a large arts festival; **le Petit P.** = art museum in Paris originally built as part of the 1900 World Fair; **p. des sports** sports centre

palais² *nm* (a) *Anat* palate; **voûte du p., p. dur** hard palate; **voile du p., p. mou** soft palate; **p. fendu** cleft palate (b) (*goût*) (sense of) taste; **avoir le p. fin** to have a fine palate; **flatter le p.** to please the palate

palan [palɑ̃] *nm Tech* hoist, hoisting gear; *Naut* pulley block, purchase tackle, whip; *Com* **sous p.** under ship's tackle

palanche [palɑ̃ʃ] *nf* (*pour porter des seaux etc*) yoke

palanque [palɑ̃k] *nf* (timber) stockade

palanquer [palɑ̃ke] *vt* to stockade

palanquin [palɑ̃kɛ̃] *nm* palanquin

palatal, -ale, -aux, -ales [palatal, -o] **1** *adj* (a) *Ling* (*consonne*) palatal; (*voyelle*) front (b) *Anat* (*os etc*) palatal **2** *nf Ling* **palatale** (*consonne*) palatal (consonant); (*voyelle*) front vowel

palatalisation [palatalizasjɔ̃] *nf Ling* palatalization

palataliser [palatalize] *Ling* **1** *vt* to palatalize **2 se palataliser** *vpr* to be palatalized

palatin, -ine [palatɛ̃, -in] **1** *adj* (a) *Hist* palatine; **Comte p.** Count Palatine (b) *Géog* **le Mont P.** the Palatine Hill **2** *n Hist* palatine **3** *nf Hist* **La Palatine** the Princess Palatine

Palatinat (le) [ləpalatina] *nm Hist* the Palatinate

pale¹ [pal] *nf* (a) (*d'une rame, d'une hélice, d'un ventilateur etc*) blade; **hélice à trois/quatre pales** three-/four-bladed propeller (b) (*vanne*) sluice (gate)

pale² *nf Rel* chalice cover, pall(a)

pâle [pɑl] *adj* (a) (*livide, blafard*) pale; *Litt, Méd* pallid; **p. comme un linge** as white as a sheet; **p. comme la mort** deathly pale, ashen, as pale as death; **p. de colère** livid with rage; **p. de jalousie** green with envy; *Mil F* **se faire porter p.** to report sick; **les Visages pâles** the Palefaces (b) (*couleur, ciel*) pale; (*lumière*) pale, faint; (*sourire*) wan, faint; (*style*) colourless; **une p. imitation de Vermeer** a pale *or* poor imitation of Vermeer; **mes aventures semblent bien pâles auprès des vôtres** my adventures pale by comparison with yours; *F* **c'est un p. crétin** he's a complete idiot *or* fool

palefrenier [palfrənje] *nm* groom; *Arch* (*d'auberge*) ostler

palefroi [palfrwa] *nm Hist* palfrey

paléographe [paleɔgraf] *n* palaeographer, *surtout US* paleographer

paléographie [paleɔgrafi] *nf* palaeography, *surtout US* paleography

paléographique [paleɔgrafik] *adj* palaeographic, *surtout US* paleographic

paléolithique [paleɔlitik] **1** *adj* Palaeolithic, *surtout US* Paleolithic **2** *nm* Palaeolithic age, *surtout US* Paleolithic age

paléontologie [paleɔ̃tɔlɔʒi] *nf* palaeontology, *surtout US* paleontology

paléontologique [paleɔ̃tɔlɔʒik] *adj* palaeontological, *surtout US* paleontological

paléontologiste [paleɔ̃tɔlɔʒist], **paléontologue** [paleɔ̃tɔlɔg] *n* palaeontologist, *surtout US* paleontologist

paleron [palrɔ̃] *nm* (*de cheval, de bœuf etc*) shoulder blade, blade bone; *Culin* neck, *Am* chuck; *Culin* **p. de bœuf** chuck

Palestine [palɛstin] *nf Géog* Palestine

palestinien, -ienne [palɛstinjɛ̃, -jɛn] **1** *adj* Palestinian **2** *n* **P.** Palestinian

palet [palɛ] *nm* (a) (*anneau*) quoit; **jouer au(x) palet(s)** to play quoits (b) (*pour hockey sur glace*) puck; (*pour curling*) stone

paletot [palto] *nm* (short) overcoat; *Fig F* **tomber sur le p. à qn** (*l'attaquer*) to jump sb; (*d'un voleur*) to mug sb; (*pour lui parler*) to buttonhole sb, to nab sb

palette [palɛt] *nf* (a) (*de peintre*) palette; *Fig* (*éventail*) (*d'activités, de produits etc*) range; *Fig* **la p. de Matisse** the range of colours used by Matisse, Matisse's palette; *Ordinat* **p. d'outils** tool palette (b) (*pour la manutention*) pallet; **p. (en) bois** wooden pallet; *Com* **p.-avion** air freight pallet (c) *Culin* (*de mouton, de porc*) shoulder (d) (*d'une roue à aubes*) paddle (e) *Sp* (*raquette de bois*) (wooden) battledore (f) (*pour le linge*) (washerwoman's) beetle

palettisation [palɛtizasjɔ̃] *nf Tech* palletization

palettiser [palɛtize] *adj Tech* to palletize

palettiseur [palɛtizœr] *nm Com* palletizer

palétuvier [paletyvje] *nm* mangrove

pâleur [pɑlœr] *nf* (*du teint*) paleness, pallor; (*de la lumière*) faintness; (*du style*) colourlessness, *US* colorlessness; **d'une p. mortelle** deathly pale

pâlichon, -onne [pɑliʃɔ̃, -ɔn] *adj F* pale, green around the gills

palier [palje] *nm* **(a)** *Archit* (*d'escalier*) landing; **nous sommes voisins de p.** we live on the same floor; **tu connais tes voisins de p.?** do you know the people who live on the same floor as you?, do you know your next-door neighbours?; **p. intermédiaire** half-landing

(b) (*étape*) stage; **par paliers** in stages

(c) *Aut, Rail etc* level stretch; *Math etc* (*d'un graphique*) plateau; **atteindre un p.** (*devenir plat*) to reach a plateau; **le taux des naissances a atteint un p.** the birthrate has reached a plateau *or* has levelled off; **à partir d'un certain p., le taux change** the rate changes at a certain point; *Aut, Rail etc* **vitesse en p.** speed on the level *or* on the flat; *Av* **voler en p.** to fly level

(d) *Tech* bearing; **p. d'arbre** shaft bearing; **p. d'appui** mounting; **p. de tête de bielle** big-end bearing

palière [paljɛr] *adj* **porte p.** landing door, door opening onto the landing; **marche p.** top step

palimpseste [palɛ̃psɛst] *nm* palimpsest

palindrome [palɛ̃drom] *nm Ling* palindrome

palinodie [palinɔdi] *nf* **(a)** *Littér* palinode **(b)** *Péj* volte-face

pâlir [pɑlir] **1** *vi* (*d'une personne*) to turn *or* become *or* grow pale, to pale; (*d'une lumière, d'une étoile etc*) to fade, to grow dim; (*d'une couleur, d'un souvenir*) to fade; **ses joues ont pâli** his cheeks have lost their colour; **p. d'horreur/de peur** to turn pale *or* go white with horror/fright; **p. de rage/de colère** to become livid with rage/anger; **p. de jalousie** to turn green with envy; **faire p. qn de jalousie** to make sb green with envy; **à faire p.** (*cauchemar, histoire*) terrifying; (*revenus, succès, maison*) amazing, unbelievable; **ils ont une maison à faire p. (d'envie)** they have a house that would make you green (with envy); *Fig* **p. sur un travail** to slave over a piece of work

2 *vt Litt* **p. qn** (*d'une couleur, un maquillage etc*) to make sb look pale

palis [pali] *nm* **(a)** (*clôture*) (picket) fence **(b)** (*espace clôturé*) enclosure **(c)** (*pieu*) picket

palissade [palisad] *nf* **(a)** (*clôture*) fence; *Mil* palisade **(b)** (*haie*) hedge

palissader [palisade] *vt* to fence in, to rail in, to enclose; *Mil* to palisade

palissandre [palisɑ̃dr] *nm* (*bois*) Brazilian rosewood

pâlissant [pɑlisɑ̃] *adj* (*visage*) turning pale; (*lumière*) fading, waning; (*couleur*) fading

palladium [paladjɔm] *nm Ch* palladium

palliatif, -ive [paljatif, -iv] **1** *adj* palliative **2** *nm Méd* palliative; *Fig* stopgap measure, *Litt* palliative

pallier [palje] (*impf, pr sub* **n. palliions, v. palliiez**) **1** *vt* (*atténuer*) (*douleur, maladie*) to alleviate, *Fml* to palliate; (*faute, erreur*) to lessen the impact of **2** *vi* **p. à** (*un manque de qch*) to compensate for, to make up for; (*conséquences, problèmes*) to lessen the impact of

palmarès [palmarɛs] *nm Scol etc* honours *or US* honors list; (*à une distribution de prix*) (list of) prize winners; *Sp* (list of) winners; *Mus, Rad etc* **le p. (de la chanson)** the charts, the top twenty/thirty; **être** *ou* **figurer au p.** to be among the (prize) winners; *Mus* to be in the charts; **une chanteuse qui ne figure plus au p.** a singer who's dropped out of the charts; **il est au p. des hommes les plus séduisants de France** he's been voted one of the most attractive men in France; **avoir un beau p.** (*d'un sportif*) to be having a good season *or* year; **il a** *ou* **compte 50 victoires à son p.** he has fifty wins to his credit, he has notched up fifty wins

palme [palm] *nf* **(a)** (*de palmier*) palm (branch); *Fig* (*symbole de la victoire*) palm; **le dimanche des Palmes** Palm Sunday; **p. du martyre** martyr's crown, crown of martyrdom; **avec p.** (*decoration*) ≈ with bar; **décerner la p. de qch** to award the prize for sth; **remporter la p.** to win, to be victorious, *Litt* to carry off the palm of victory; **la p. lui revient** he's the winner, the victory goes to him; *Fig* **pour ce qui est de la cuisine, c'est lui qui remporte la p.** when it comes to cooking, there's no-one to beat him; *Hum* **on peut lui décerner la p. de la paresse** he takes the biscuit for sheer laziness

(b) *Arch* (*arbre*) palm (tree); **huile/vin de p.** palm oil/wine **(c)** (*pour nager*) flipper

▶ **palme**: **la P. d'or (du festival de Cannes)** the Palme d'or (of the Cannes Film Festival); *Admin* **les palmes (académiques)** = decoration awarded to teachers; **décerner les palmes académiques à qn** to decorate sb for services to teaching

palmé [palme] *adj* **(a)** *Bot* (*feuille*) palmate **(b)** *Orn* web-footed; **pied p.** webbed foot

palmer [palmɛr] *nm Tech* micrometer

palmeraie [palmərɛ] *nf* palm grove

palmier [palmje] *nm* **(a)** (*arbre*) palm (tree); **p. dattier** date palm; **cœur de p.** palm (tree) heart **(b)** *Culin* = small sweet heart-shaped pastry

palmipède [palmipɛd] *Orn* **1** *adj* web-footed, *Spéc* palmiped(e) **2** *nm* web-footed bird, *Spéc* palmiped(e)

palmiste [palmist] *nm* (*plante*) cabbage palm *or* tree; **chou p.** palm tree heart

palombe [palɔ̃b] *nf Région* ringdove, wood pigeon

palonnier [palɔnje] *nm Av* rudder bar; *Aut* **p. de freinage** compensator

pâlot, -otte [pɑlo, -ɔt] *adj* rather pale, peaky

palourde [palurd] *nf* (*mollusque*) clam

palpable [palpabl] *adj* **(a)** (*que l'on peut toucher*) palpable, tangible **(b)** (*réel, vérifiable*) (*erreur, mensonge*) palpable; (*vérité etc*) obvious, plain

palpation [palpɑsjɔ̃] *nf Méd* palpation

palper [palpe] **1** *vt* **(a)** (*objet*) to feel (with one's hands); *Méd* to palpate **(b)** *F* (*somme*) to be paid, to get **2** *vi F* to get one's money, to get paid; **qu'est-ce qu'il a dû p.!** he must have made a mint! **3** *nm Méd* palpation

palpeur [palpœr] *nm* (heat) sensor; *Ordinat* sensor; *Aut* **p. de détonation** knock sensor

palpitant [palpitɑ̃] **1** *adj* (*cœur, pouls*) fluttering; (*plus fort*) throbbing; *Méd* palpitating; (*personne*) (*d'émotion etc*) quivering; **p. (d'intérêt)** (*roman, film etc*) exciting, thrilling **2** *nm Arg* (*cœur*) ticker

palpitation [palpitasjɔ̃] *nf* (*du cœur, pouls*) fluttering; (*plus fort*) throbbing; *Méd* palpitation; (*d'une paupière*) fluttering; **avoir des palpitations** to have palpitations; *F* **elle me donne des palpitations** she gives me palpitations

palpiter [palpite] *vi* (*du cœur, pouls*) to flutter; (*plus fort*) to throb; *Méd* to palpitate; (*d'une paupière*) to flutter; (*d'une lumière etc*) to flicker; (*d'une personne*) (*de peur, rage*) to quiver (**de** with); **p. de froid** to tremble with cold

paltoquet [paltɔkɛ] *nm F Vieilli* jackanapes

paluche [palyʃ] *nf très F* (*main*) mitt, paw

paludéen, -enne [palydeɛ̃, -ɛn] *adj* (*plante, terrain etc*) marsh; *Méd* malarial

paludisme [palydism] *nm* malaria

palustre [palystr] *adj* (*plante etc*) marsh; *Méd* malarial

pâmer (se) [səpɑme] *vpr Vieilli* (*s'évanouir*) to swoon, to faint; *Fig Hum* to (practically) swoon; *Fig* **se p. devant qn** to practically swoon over sb; **se p. (d'aise)** to be blissfully happy; **se p. de rire** to be convulsed with laughter; **ça la faisait se p. de rire, cette histoire** the story sent her into hysterics; **se p. d'admiration** to be in raptures (**sur** over), to be overcome with admiration (**sur** for); **se p. d'amour** to be head over heels in love

pâmoison [pɑmwazɔ̃] *nf Vieilli* swoon; *Iron* **tomber en p.** to swoon; **tomber en p. devant qch** to go into raptures *or* to swoon over sth

pampa [pɑ̃pa] *nf* (*d'Amérique du Sud*) pampas

pamphlet [pɑ̃flɛ] *nm* satirical tract, lampoon

pamphlétaire [pɑ̃fletɛr] *n* pamphleteer

pamplemousse [pɑ̃pləmus] *nm* (*fruit*) grapefruit

pampre [pɑ̃pr] *nm Litt* vine branch (*with grapes*)

Pan [pɑ̃] *nm Myth* Pan

pan[1] [pɑ̃] *nm* **(a)** (*de chemise, manteau*) tail; (*de jupe*) panel; **relever les pans de son manteau** to hitch up one's coat; **il l'a enveloppée des pans de son manteau** he wrapped his coat around her; **se promener en p. de chemise** to wander about in one's shirt-tails **(b)** (*morceau*) section, piece; *Fig* (*d'enfance, d'une époque*) section, portion; **p. de mur** section of wall; **p. de ciel** patch of sky **(c)** (*d'un polyèdre etc*) face, side; **tour à huit pans** eight-sided *or* octagonal tower; **p. coupé** cant; **en p. coupé** with the corner cut off

pan[2] *int* **(a)** bang!, crash!, wham!; **et p.! je te tue!** bang bang you're dead!; **et p., le voilà qui entre!** and then, would you believe it, in he comes! **(b)** *Enf* **je vais te faire p. p. (cucul)!** I'll smack you!

panacée [panase] *nf* panacea

panachage [panaʃaʒ] *nm* **(a)** (*de couleurs etc*) mixing **(b)** *Pol* **p. électoral** splitting one's vote between candidates from different parties

panache [panaʃ] *nm* **(a)** (*aigrette*) plume, panache; (*de plumes etc*) plume, tuft; **p. de fumée** plume *or* wreath *or* trail of smoke **(b)** (*brio, éclat*) panache; **avec p.** with panache; **il avait le goût du p.** he did things in style *or* with panache

panaché [panaʃe] **1** *adj* **(a)** (*oiseau, fleur*) multicoloured, *US* multicolored; (*feuillage*) variegated; (*foule*) motley; **p. de blanc** streaked with white, with white streaks; *Culin* **salade panachée** mixed salad; **glace panachée** = selection of various flavours of ice cream; **demi p.** shandy **(b)** *Pol* **liste (électorale) panachée** = ballot paper in which votes are split among candidates from different parties **2** *nm* shandy

panacher [panaʃe] *vt* **(a)** (*bigarrer*) (*couleurs*) to mix; **p. un bouquet** to put together a mixed bouquet **(b)** *Pol* **p. une liste**

électorale to split one's votes (*among candidates from different parties*)
panade [panad] *nf Culin* = soup made from bread; *Fig F* **être dans la p.** to be in the soup *or* in a real fix; (*ne pas avoir d'argent temporairement*) to be short of cash; **ça m'a mise dans la p.** I was really up the creek; **quelle p.!** what a mess!
panafricain [panafrikɛ̃] *adj Pol* Pan-African
panafricanisme [panafrikanism] *nm Pol* Pan-Africanism
panais [panɛ] *nm* (*légume*) parsnip
Panama [panama] *nm Géog* (a) Panama; **le canal de P.** the Panama Canal (b) **p.** (*chapeau*) panama hat
Paname [panam] *nm Géog très F* Paris
panaméen, -enne [panameɛ̃, -ɛn] **1** *adj* Panamanian **2** *n* **P.** Panamanian
panaméricain [panamerikɛ̃] *adj Pol* Pan-American
panaméricanisme [panamerikanism] *nm Pol* Pan-Americanism
panarabe [panarab] *adj Pol* Pan-Arab
panarabisme [panarabism] *nm Pol* Pan-Arabism
panard [panar] **1** *adj* (*cheval*) knock-kneed **2** *nm très F* (*pied*) foot; **panards** feet, *Br* plates (of meat); *Fig* **quel p.!** great!, terrific!, fantastic!; **tu imagines, vivre au bord de la mer, quel p.!** just imagine how great *or* terrific *or* fantastic it would be to live at the seaside!; **ce n'est pas le p.** it's not exactly a load of laughs *or* a barrel of fun
panaris [panari] *nm Méd* whitlow
panavision [panavizjɔ̃] *nf* panavision
pan-bagnat, *pl* **pans-bagnats** [pɑ̃baɲa] *nm* = snack consisting of a roll sliced and served with salade niçoise
pancarte [pɑ̃kart] *nf* sign, notice; (*affiche*) placard
pancréas [pɑ̃kreas] *nm Anat* pancreas
pancréatique [pɑ̃kreatik] *adj Anat* pancreatic
panda [pɑ̃da] *nm* panda
pandémie [pɑ̃demi] *nf Méd* pandemic
pandémique [pɑ̃demik] *adj Méd* pandemic
pandémonium [pɑ̃demɔnjɔm] *nm* (*lieu de corruption*) den of vice *or* iniquity; (*lieu de désordre*) pandemonium
pandit [pɑ̃di] *nm* (*titre indien*) pandit, pundit
Pandore [pɑ̃dɔr] *nf Myth* Pandora; **boîte de P.** Pandora's box
pané [pane] *adj Culin* coated with breadcrumbs, breaded
panégyrique [paneʒirik] *nm* eulogy, *Litt* panegyric; **faire le p. de qn** to extol sb's virtues *or* merits, to eulogize sb
panégyriste [paneʒirist] *nm* eulogist, *Litt* panegyrist
panel [panel] *nm* (*groupe*) panel; (*échantillon*) sample (group); *Mktg* **p. de consommateurs** consumer panel, shopping panel; *Mktg* **p. de distributeurs** distributor panel; *Mktg* **p. de détaillants** retail panel; *Mktg* **p. d'essayeurs de produits** product testing panel; **p. de téléspectateurs** *Mktg* television viewing panel; *TV, Rad* television opinion panel
panéliste [panelist] *n Mktg* panellist, panel member
paner [pane] *vt Culin* to cover *or* coat with breadcrumbs, to bread
panetière [pantjɛr] *nf* bread bin
paneuropéanisme [panøropeanism] *nm Pol* Pan-Europeanism
paneuropéen, -enne [panøropeɛ̃, -ɛn] *adj Pol* Pan-European
pangermanisme [pɑ̃ʒɛrmanism] *nm Pol* Pan-Germanism
pangermaniste [pɑ̃ʒɛrmanist] *adj, n Pol* Pan-Germanist
panier [panje] *nm* (a) (*corbeille*) basket; (*de fruits etc*) basket(ful); **p. à anse(s)** basket; **un plein p. de fruits** a basketful of fruit; **mettre** *ou* **jeter qch au p.** to throw sth in the wastepaper basket; *Fig* to throw sth away *or* out, *Br F* to bin sth; **ton pantalon est bon à mettre au p.** your trousers aren't fit to be seen, your trousers should be thrown out; *Fig* **mettre tous ses œufs dans le même p.** to put all one's eggs in one basket; *Fig* **moi, les hommes, je les mets tous dans le même p.** men are all alike *or* the same, as far as I'm concerned; *Fig* **il ne faut pas tous les mettre dans le même p.** you can't lump them all together, they're not all tarred with the same brush; *Fig* **le dessus du p.** the elite; *Scol, Univ* the pick of the bunch, the cream of the crop; **il ne fréquente que le dessus du p.** he only mixes with the very best people; **faire partie du dessus du p.** to be out of the top drawer; *Scol, Univ* to be one of the best

(b) (*nasse*) lobster pot

(c) *Sp* (*basketball*) basket; **réussir** *ou* **marquer un p.** to score (a basket)

(d) (*de tondeuse*) grass box

(e) (*pour diapositives*) slide magazine

(f) (*de crinoline*) hoop

▶ **panier**: *Bourse* **p. d'actions** basket of shares; **p. à bouteilles** bottle carrier; *Fig* **p. de crabes: c'est un p. de crabes** they're constantly at each other's throats, they're always trying to stick knives in each other's backs; *Fin* **p. des devises** basket of currencies; **p. à légumes** (*pour cuisson vapeur*) steamer insert; (*de cocotte-minute*) food basket; **p. à linge** linen basket; *Écon* **le p. de la ménagère** the shopping basket; **avec des conséquences sur le p. de la ménagère** with consequences for the food bill; **p. de monnaies** basket of currencies; **p. à ouvrage** sewing basket; *F* **p. percé** spendthrift; *Mktg* **p. de présentation en vrac** dump bin; **p. à provisions** shopping basket; **p. à salade** salad shaker; *F* (*convoi cellulaire*) police van *or US* wagon, *Br Vieilli* Black Maria
panier-repas, *pl* **paniers-repas** *nm* (*panier*) lunch basket; (*repas*) packed lunch
panifiable [panifjabl] *adj* (*céréale*) suitable for making bread; **farine p.** bread flour
panifier [panifje] *vt* (*impf, pr sub* **n. panifiions, v. panifiiez**) **p. de la farine** to make bread
panique [panik] **1** *adj* **peur p.** panic

2 *nf* panic; **pris de p.** panic-stricken; **pris de p., ils s'enfuirent** they fled in (a) panic; **pris de p., je ne trouvais plus mes mots** I was panic-stricken and couldn't say a word; **être pris de p.** to panic; **p. boursière** stock market panic; **ne pas céder à la p.** not to let oneself be panicked, not to give way to panic; **la police recommande à la population de ne pas céder à la p.** the police are urging people not to panic; *F* **pas de p., ce n'est pas la fin du monde!** don't panic, it's not the end of the world!; **c'était la p. totale** it was panic stations; **il y a eu un début de p.** people started to panic; **il y a eu un mouvement de p.** there was a stampede, there was panic; **la p. était générale** there was a general state of panic
paniqué [panike] *adj F* in a panic, panicky; **complètement p.** in a complete panic
paniquer [panike] *F* **1** *vt* **p. qn** to get sb into a panic, to panic sb, to put the wind up sb **2** *vi* to (get into a) panic, to get panicky **3 se paniquer** *vpr* to (get into a) panic, to get panicky
panislamique [panislamik] *adj Pol* Pan-Islamic
panislamisme [panislamism] *nm Pol* Pan-Islamism
panne¹ [pan] *nf* (a) *Tex* panne, plush (b) (*gras*) fat, lard; *Fig* (*d'une personne*) flab; *Fig* **tu prends/tu as de la p.** you're getting/you're flabby
panne² *nf* (a) (*arrêt de fonctionnement*) (mechanical) breakdown; *Aut* breakdown; *Él* (power) failure, outage; *Ordinat* failure, crash; **p. de courant** *ou* **d'électricité** power failure *or* cut, blackout; *Rad, TV* **p. d'émission** technical fault *or* hitch; **p. de moteur** engine failure; **nous avons eu plusieurs pannes de moteur avec cette auto** the engine on the car has failed several times; **p. de secteur** power failure *or* outage, mains failure; *Ordinat* **p. du système** system crash; *Ordinat* **p. matérielle** hardware crash; **tomber en p.** (*d'une voiture, une machine*) to break down; (*d'un automobiliste*) to break down, to have a breakdown; **tomber en p. d'essence, tomber en p. sèche** to run out of petrol *or Am* gas; **en p.** (*ascenseur etc*) out of order; **je suis en p.** (*d'automobiliste*) I've broken down; *F* **rester en p. devant une difficulté** to be put off *or* floored by a difficulty; *F* **laisser qn en p.** to leave sb in the lurch, to let sb down; *F* **je suis en p. d'allumettes/de café/d'idées** I've run out of matches/coffee/ideas; **trouver la p.** to find the problem, to find the cause of the problem; **soudain, ce fut la p.** suddenly, we/they/it/*etc* broke down; *F Hum* **j'ai eu une p. d'oreiller** I overslept; *F* **il m'a fait le coup de la p.** he pretended we'd run out of petrol, he tried to pull the old 'we've run out of petrol' trick

(b) *Naut* **en p.** hove to; **mettre un navire en p.** to bring a ship to
panne³ *nf Constr* (*d'un toit*) purlin
panne⁴ *nf Tech* (*d'un marteau*) peen, pane
panneau, -eaux [pano] *nm* (a) (*pour afficher*) board (b) (*élément plan*) (*de bois, contre-plaqué etc*) panel; **panneaux** panelling, panels; **porte à panneaux** panelled door; **p. vitré** glass panel; **p. mobile/coulissant** movable/sliding panel (c) (*pour le gibier*) snare, net; *Fig* **tomber** *ou* **donner dans le p.** to fall into the trap (d) *Aut* signpost, direction sign

▶ **panneau**: **p. d'affichage** notice *or Am* bulletin board; *Ordinat* bulletin board; *Naut* **p. de cale** hatch cover; *Aut* **p. de carrosserie** body panel; *Mktg* **p. à crochets** (*présentoir*) pegboard; *Naut* **p. d'écoutille** hatch cover; *Aut* **p. indicateur** signpost; **p. publicitaire** hoarding, *Am* billboard; **p. de signalisation (routière)** roadsign; **p. solaire** solar panel; **panneaux électoraux** noticeboards for election posters
panneton [pantɔ̃] *nm* (*d'une clé*) web, bit
pano [pano] *nm* (*abrév* **panoramique**) *TV, Cin* **p. de poursuite** following pan; **p. filé** whip *or* zip pan
panonceau, -eaux [panɔ̃so] *nm* (a) (*de notaire etc*) plaque (b) (*pancarte*) sign (c) *Hist* escutcheon
panoplie [panɔpli] *nf* (*armure*) panoply; (*assortiment*) (*d'outils*) set; *Fig* (*de raisons*) array, multitude; (*d'arguments*) battery; (*de dettes*) multitude, *F* pile; **p. de soldat/**

d'infirmière (*pour enfants*) soldier's/nurse's outfit *or* costume; **toute la p. du parfait bricoleur** a whole array of DIY equipment; *Iron* **j'ai eu droit à toute la p.** I got the works

panorama [panɔrama] *nm* panorama; *Fig* overview

panoramique [panɔramik] **1** *adj* (*écran etc*) panoramic; (*restaurant*) with panoramic views; *Méd* (*radiographie*) all-over, total; **voiture avec carrosserie p.** car with panoramic *or* wrap-round windows; **vue p.** panoramic view; *Fig* overview; *Cin* **prise p.** panning shot **2** *nm Cin, TV* panning; **faire un p.** to pan; **p. filé** blur *or* zip pan; **p. horizontal** wipe pan; **faire un p. vers le bas/le haut** to pan down/up; **faire un p. vertical** to tilt

panoramiquer [panɔramike] *vi TV, Cin* to pan; **p. vers le bas/le haut** to pan down/up

pansage [pɑ̃saʒ] *nm* (*d'un cheval etc*) grooming

panse [pɑ̃s] *nf* **(a)** *F* (*ventre*) belly, paunch, pot; **s'en mettre plein la p.** to gorge *or* stuff oneself; **manger à s'en faire crever la p.** to stuff oneself *or* one's face, to eat until one is fit to burst **(b)** (*d'un ruminant*) first stomach, paunch, rumen **(c)** (*d'une bouteille etc*) belly, bulge

pansement [pɑ̃smɑ̃] *nm Méd* **(a)** (*action*) (*d'une blessure*) dressing **(b)** (*élément protecteur*) dressing; (*enroulé autour d'une blessure*) bandage; **p. (adhésif)** (sticking) plaster; **faire un p.** to dress a wound, to apply a dressing; **refaire un p.** to change a dressing; **faire/refaire un p. à qn** to dress sb's wound(s)/to change sb's dressing(s); **il est couvert de pansements** he's all bandaged up; **il faut mettre un p.** it needs a plaster

▶ **pansement**: **p. gastrique** (*liquide*) = milk of magnesia; (*poudre*) stomach powder

panser [pɑ̃se] *vt* **(a)** (*blessure*) to dress, to put a dressing on; (*membre*) to bandage; (*avec un sparadrap*) to put a plaster on; **p. un blessé** to dress somebody's wounds; *Fig* **p. ses blessures** to lick one's wounds; **six mois lui suffiront pour p. ses blessures** six months will be long enough for him to get over it **(b)** (*cheval*) to groom, to rub down

panslavisme [pɑ̃slavism] *nm Pol* Pan-Slavism

pansu [pɑ̃sy] *adj* (*personne*) potbellied, paunchy; (*bouteille*) potbellied

pantagruélique [pɑ̃tagryelik] *adj* (*repas, appétit*) enormous, gigantic

pantalon [pɑ̃talɔ̃] *nm* **(a)** [①A10,e] (pair of) trousers *or Am* pants; **mettre un p.** to put on a pair of trousers; **mettre son p.** to put on one's trousers; **un p. neuf** a new pair of trousers, some new trousers; **p. cigarette** drainpipes; **p. fuseau** tapering trousers *or Am* pants, ski pants; **p. de golf** plus-fours; **p. à pattes d'éléphant** flared trousers *or Am* pants, flares; **p. à pinces** pleated trousers *or Am* pants; **p. de pyjama** pyjama trousers *or Am* pants; **p. de ski** ski pants; **p. de toile** canvas trousers *or Am* pants; **p. de velours côtelé** corduroy trousers *or Am* pants, cords; **elle porte un p.** *ou Vieilli* **des pantalons** she wears trousers; *Fig* **c'est elle qui porte le p.** she wears the trousers *or Am* pants

(b) *Th* **P.** Pantaloon

pantalon-jupe, *pl* **pantalons-jupes** *nm* palazzo pants

pantalonnade [pɑ̃talɔnad] *nf* **(a)** *Hist Th* burlesque farce **(b)** (*hypocrisie*) piece of hypocrisy

pantelant [pɑ̃tlɑ̃] *adj* **(a)** panting, gasping (**de** with); **tout p.** gasping for breath, out of breath; **la nouvelle m'a laissé p.** the news left *or* had me gasping **(b)** (*homme ou animal à l'agonie*) quivering, twitching; **chair pantelante** (*d'un animal à l'agonie*) twitching flesh

panteler [pɑ̃tle] *vi* (**je pantelle, n. pantelons; je pantellerai**) *Vieilli* (*respirer*) to pant; *Fig* (*d'émotion*) to gasp (**de** with); (*palpiter*) to quiver

panthéisme [pɑ̃teism] *nm Phil* pantheism

panthéiste [pɑ̃teist] *Phil* **1** *adj* pantheistic(al) **2** *n* pantheist

panthéon [pɑ̃teɔ̃] *nm* pantheon; **faire partie du p. des hommes célèbres** to have a place in the hall of fame; **le p. cinématographique** the film industry's hall of fame; **elle fait partie du p. cinématographique** she is one of the all-time movie greats; **mettre qn au p. des musiciens** to consider sb a great musician, to rank sb among the best musicians

panthère [pɑ̃tɛr] *nf* leopard; **p. noire** panther; **manteau en (peau de) p.** leopard-skin coat

pantin [pɑ̃tɛ̃] *nm* (*poupée*) jumping jack; *Péj* (*fantoche*) puppet, stooge; **elle a fait de son époux un p.** she has turned her husband into a puppet

pantographe [pɑ̃tɔgraf] *nm Rail* pantograph; *Aut* scissor jack

pantois [pɑ̃twa] *adj* astounded, *F* flabbergasted; **j'en suis tout p.** I'm astounded *or* speechless *or F* flabbergasted; **en rester p.** to be speechless *or F* flabbergasted

pantomime [pɑ̃tɔmim] *nf* **(a)** *Th* (*art*) mime; (*spectacle*) mime show **(b)** *Péj* (*comédie*) scene; **que signifie cette p.?** what is all this nonsense?

pantouflard, -arde [pɑ̃tuflar, -ard] *adj, n F* stay-at-home; **ils sont très pantouflards** they're real homebodies, they never go out; **ce qu'il est p.!** he's a real stay-at-home

pantoufle [pɑ̃tufl] *nf* slipper; **il était en pantoufles** he was wearing slippers, he was in his slippers; **les pantoufles de vair** *ou* **de verre de Cendrillon** Cinderella's glass slippers; *Fig* **passer sa vie dans ses pantoufles** to live a quiet life; *Fig F* **raisonner comme une p.** to talk through one's hat

pantoufler [pɑ̃tufle] *vi Arg* (*d'un fonctionnaire*) to join the private sector

panure [panyr] *nf Culin* breadcrumbs

Panurge [panyrʒ] *nm* **agir comme les moutons de P.** to follow the herd

PAO [peao] *nf Ordinat* (*abrév* **publication assistée par ordinateur**) DTP

paon [pɑ̃] *nm* **(a)** (*oiseau*) peacock; **pousser des cris de p.** to screech like a peacock; *Fig* **se parer des plumes du p.** to take all the credit; **être vaniteux comme un p.** to be as vain as a peacock; **faire le p.** to strut about **(b)** (*insecte*) peacock butterfly

paonne [pan] *nf* peahen

paonneau, -eaux [pano] *nm* peachick

papa [papa] *nm* dad, *surtout Enf* daddy, *surtout Am* pop; **jouer au p. et à la maman** to play mothers and fathers; **c'est un fils à p.** he's a daddy's boy; *F* **faire qch à la p.** to do sth in a leisurely fashion; *F* **l'amour à la p.** boring sex; **nous allons faire ça à la p.** we'll take it easy, we won't rush things; *Aut* **aller à la p.** to potter along; *F Péj* **de p.** old-fashioned, behind the times; *F* **le cinéma/l'armée de p.** the films/army of the past; **p. gâteau** indulgent father; **p. poule** doting father

papal, -ale, -aux, -ales [papal, -o] *adj* papal

paparazzi [paparadzi] *nmpl* paparazzi

paparazzo [paparadzo] *nm* paparazzo

papauté [papote] *nf* papacy

papaye [papaj] *nf* pa(w)paw, papaya

papayer [papaje] *nm* pa(w)paw *or* papaya (tree)

pape [pap] *nm* **(a)** *Rel* pope; *F* **heureux comme un p.** happy as a sandboy, happy as Larry; *F* **sérieux comme un p.** deadly serious, very solemn; **le P. Jean-Paul II** Pope John Paul II **(b)** (*d'une association, un mouvement etc*) leading light

papelard[1], -arde [paplar, -ard] *Péj* **1** *adj* (*voix etc*) sanctimonious; **il a un air p.** he looks as if butter wouldn't melt in his mouth; **dit-il, d'un air p.** he said sanctimoniously **2** *n* sanctimonious *or* self-righteous person, hypocrite

papelard[2] *nm F* (*petit papier*) (piece of) paper; (*journal*) (news)paper; **j'ai oublié mes papelards** I've forgotten my (identity) papers *or F* my ID

paperasse [papras] *nf Péj* papers, *Br F* bumf, bumph; (*fiches à remplir*) forms; **il y a plein de p. sur mon bureau** my desk is covered in paper; **c'est de la p.!** it's just a load of bumph!; **j'ai horreur de toutes ces paperasses** I hate all this red tape; **je passe mon temps à m'occuper de paperasses** I spend all my time doing paperwork

paperasserie [paprasri] *nf Péj* (accumulation of) papers, *Br F* bumf, bumph; (*à remplir*) forms; **la p. (administrative)** red tape; **il y a trop de p.** (*dans ce travail*) there's too much paperwork; (*pour obtenir un visa etc*) there's too much paperwork *or* red tape (involved)

paperassier, -ière [paprasje, -jɛr] *Péj* **1** *adj* (*personne*) fond of paperwork; (*procédure*) cluttered up with red tape **2** *n* **(a)** (*personne qui amasse les papiers*) hoarder of (old) papers, *Am F* pack rat **(b)** (*fonctionnaire*) bureaucrat

papeterie [papɛtri] *nf* **(a)** (*fabrication*) paper manufacturing; (*usine*) paper mill; **la p.** (*industrie*) the paper industry **(b)** (*magasin*) stationer's (shop); (*articles*) stationery

papetier, -ière [pap(ə)tje, -jɛr] **1** *n* **(a)** *Ind* paper manufacturer **(b)** *Com* stationer **2** *adj* paper

papetier-libraire, *pl* **papetiers-libraires** *nm Com* bookseller and stationer

papier [papje] *nm* **(a)** (*matière*) paper; **pâte à p.** pulp; **un p.** a sheet *or* piece of paper; **notez plutôt cela dans votre carnet que sur un p.** put it down in your notebook rather than on a scrap of paper; **son bureau est couvert de papiers** his desk is covered in paper(s); **classer ses papiers** to put one's papers in order; **jeter des idées sur le p.** to put some ideas down on paper; **ça n'est pas ce qui est dit sur le p.** that's not what it says here; *Fig* **sur le p.** on paper, in theory; **gratter du p.** (*comme métier*) to be a pen-pusher; (*en utiliser beaucoup*) to use a lot of paper; *Fig F* **être dans les petits papiers de qn** to be in sb's good books; *Fig F* **rayez cela de vos papiers** don't count on it, (you can) forget it

(b) **papiers** (*documents*) papers, documents; *Jur* **papiers d'une affaire** documents relating to a case; **les papiers de la vente/de la voiture** the sale/car documents; *Admin* **papiers**

(d'identité) identity papers; *F* ID; **mes papiers sont en règle** my papers are in order; **vos papiers, s'il vous plaît!** can I see your identity papers, please?; *Aut* can I see your driving licence *or Am* driver's license, please?; **faux papiers** false ID
(c) *Jur* **p. timbré** stamped paper (*for official and legal documents*)
(d) *Fin* bill(s); **p. de commerce** commercial *or* trade paper; **p. long** *ou* **à long terme** long(-dated) bill
(e) *Journ* article; **j'ai fini mon p.** I've finished writing my report *or* my copy

▶ **papier**: *F* **p. alu** (kitchen *or* aluminium) foil; **p. d'aluminium** aluminium foil, tinfoil; **p. d'argent** silver foil *or* paper; **p. avion** airmail paper; *Fin* **p. bancable** bankable paper; *Ordinat* **p. à bandes perforées** perforated paper; **p. bible** Bible paper; **p. de bonbon** sweet wrapper; **p. buvard** blotting paper; **p. cadeau** gift wrap, wrapping paper; **mettre un p. cadeau à qch** to giftwrap sth; **p. calque** tracing paper; **p. carbone** carbon paper; *Ordinat* **p. Caroll** perforated paper; **p. à cigarettes** cigarette paper; **fin comme du p. à cigarettes** (*usé*) like tissue paper; **un voile fin comme du p. à cigarettes** a gossamer-thin veil; *Fin* **p. commercial** commercial paper; *Ordinat* **p. continu** continuous paper *or* stationery; *Ordinat* **p. continu plié en accordéon** fanfold paper; **p. couché** coated paper; *Beaux-Arts* art paper; *Vulg* **p. cul** bog paper; **p. à dessin** drawing paper; **p. d'emballage** wrapping *or* packing paper; **p. émeri** emery paper; **p. à en-tête** headed notepaper; **p. d'étain** tinfoil; **p. à étiquettes** sheets of labels; **p. filtre** filter paper; **p. glacé** glazed paper; **papiers gras** litter; **p. hygiénique** toilet paper, *Br F* loo paper, *Com* bathroom tissue; **p. journal** newsprint; (*vieux journaux*) newspaper; **p. kraft** brown paper, *Spéc* kraft (paper); **p. à lettres** notepaper, writing paper; *Ordinat* **p. listing** listing paper; **p. mâché** papier mâché; **poupées en p. mâché** papier mâché doll; **avoir une mine de p. mâché** to look green about the gills; **p. machine** typing paper; **p. ministre** foolscap; *Fin* **p.-monnaie** paper money; *Ordinat* **p. multiple** multi-part stationery; **p. à musique** manuscript paper; **être réglé comme du p. à musique** to be as regular as clockwork; **une vie réglée comme du p. à musique** a very orderly life; **un emploi du temps réglé comme du p. à musique** a very strict routine; **chez nous, le matin, c'est réglé comme du p. à musique** there's a strict routine in our house in the morning; *Fin* **p. négociable** negotiable paper; *Fin* **p. à ordre** instrument to order; **p. parcheminé** greaseproof paper; *aussi Ordinat* **p. peint** wallpaper; **p. pelure** India paper; *Fin* **p. au porteur** bearer paper; **p. réglé** ruled *or* lined paper; *Phot* **p. sensible** sensitized paper; **p. de soie** tissue paper; *Ordinat* **p. thermique** thermal paper; **p. toilette** toilet paper, *Br F* loo paper, *Euph* bathroom tissue; *Fin* **papiers valeurs** securities; **p. de verre** glasspaper, sandpaper; *Fin* **p. à vue** sight paper

papillaire [papilɛr] *adj Anat etc* papillary

papille [papij, -il] *nf Anat, Bot* papilla; **p. gustative** taste bud

papillon [papijɔ̃] *nm* **(a)** (*insecte*) butterfly; **p. de nuit** moth; *Fig* **être un p.** to be flighty; *F* **minute p.!** just a minute!, hold on a minute!; *Natation* **(brasse) p.** butterfly (stroke); **nager le p.** to do the butterfly **(b)** (*dans un livre*) inset; (*prospectus*) handbill; (*sur document*) flag; **p. publicitaire** advertising leaflet, *Am* flier **(c)** (*contravention*) (parking) ticket **(d)** *Tech* (*de réglage*) butterfly valve, throttle; (*écrou*) thumb screw, butterfly *or* wing nut; *Aut* **p. des gaz** throttle

papillonnant [papijɔnɑ̃] *adj* fluttering, flitting; *Fig* (*personne*) flighty, fickle

papillonnement [papijɔnmɑ̃] *nm* fluttering; (*d'un lieu à un autre, d'une personne à une autre*) flitting; *Fig* (*d'une personne*) flightiness, fickleness

papillonner [papijɔne] *vi* (*des paupières*) to flutter; (*d'une personne à une autre*) to flit about; (*d'un sujet à un autre*) to pass rapidly; **les yeux des enfants papillonnaient devant le spectacle** the children blinked (in astonishment) at the sight

papillotage [papijɔtaʒ] *nm* **p. des yeux** blinking (of the eyes)

papillote [papijɔt] *nf* **(a)** *Culin* (*pour faire cuire les côtelettes etc*) buttered paper; (*en papier alu*) silver foil; **cailles en papillotes** quails en papillote **(b)** (*papier*) twist of paper; (*autour d'un jambon etc*) frill; *Fig* **tu peux en faire des papillotes** you can throw it away; *Fig* **ta dissertation, tu peux en faire des papillotes** your essay is rubbish, your essay isn't worth the paper it's written on **(c)** *Arch* (*pour les cheveux*) paper **(d)** *Région* (*bonbon*) = special kind of sweet with bright shiny wrappings available at Christmas

papillotement [papijɔtmɑ̃] *nm* (*des yeux*) blinking; (*d'une lumière*), *Cin, TV* flickering

papilloter [papijɔte] **1** *vi* **(a)** (*des yeux*) to blink; (*d'une lumière*), *Cin, TV* to flicker **(b)** (*scintiller*) to glitter; (*plus brillamment*) to dazzle **2** *vt Arch* **p. ses cheveux** to put one's hair in curl papers

papisme [papism] *nm* (Roman) Catholicism, *Péj* popery, papistry

papiste [papist] *n* (Roman) Catholic, *Péj* papist

papoter [papɔte] *vi F* to chat, to have a natter; **nous avons passé la journée à p.** we spent the day nattering *or Am* shooting the breeze

papou, -oue, *pl* **papous, -oues** [papu] **1** *adj* Papuan **2** *nm Ling* Papuan **3** *n* **P.** Papuan

papouille [papuj] *nf F* **faire des papouilles à qn** to cuddle *or* squeeze sb; **se faire des papouilles** to have a bit of a cuddle *or Br* of slap and tickle; **il aime les papouilles** he likes a little cuddle

paprika [paprika] *nm Bot, Culin* paprika

papule [papyl] *nf* pimple; *Méd* papule; (*d'urticaire*) weal

papyrus [papirys] *nm* [①A13,8] papyrus; (*feuille*) sheet of papyrus; **écrire sur des p.** to write on papyrus

paqson [paksɔ̃] *nm Arg* = **pacson**

pâque [pɑk] **1** *nf Rel* **P., la P. Juive** Passover **2** *nfpl* **pâques** Easter; **faire ses pâques** to take the sacrament at Easter **3** *nm* (*contraction of* **jour de Pâques**, *used without article*) **Pâques** Easter; **le lundi de Pâques** Easter Monday; **œufs de Pâques** Easter eggs; *Fig F* **remettre qch à Pâques ou à la Trinité** to put sth off indefinitely; **il le fera, enfin, à Pâques ou à la Trinité** he'll never do it in a month of Sundays; **île de Pâques** Easter Island

paquebot [pakbo] *nm Naut* (steam)ship; (*gros*) liner; **p. de ligne** liner; **p. de haute mer** ocean liner

paquégique [pakeʒik] *nf Mktg* packaging

pâquerette [pɑkrɛt] *nf* daisy

paquet [pakɛ] *nm* **(a)** (*de thé, pâtes*) packet; (*de café, sucre, riz*) bag, packet; (*de cigarettes*) packet, *Am* pack; (*postal*) parcel, package; (*ballot, liasse*) bundle; **expédier** *ou* **envoyer un p.** to send (off) a parcel; **faire un p.** to make up a parcel; **faire son p.** *ou* **ses paquets** to pack one's bags; **p. de billets** wad of notes; *F* **il a touché un joli p.** he's made a packet; **du riz/du café en p.** pre-packed *or* packaged rice/coffee; **il fume un p. (de cigarettes) par jour** he smokes twenty *or* a packet *or Am* a pack a day; **il est tombé un p. de neige** it snowed heavily, there was a lot of snow; **des paquets d'eau tombaient** the rain was coming down in sheets; **c'est un p. d'os** he's all skin and bone; **c'est un p. de nerfs** he's a bag *or* bundle of nerves; *Fig F* **mettre le p.** to go all out, to pull out all the stops; *Fig F* **risquer le p.** to risk *or* chance everything one's got *or* the lot; *Fig F* **lâcher le p.** to spill the beans
(b) *Rugby* **p. (d'avants)** pack

▶ **paquet**: *Fin* **p. d'actions** parcel *or* block of shares; *Mktg* **p. économique** economy pack; *Mktg* **p. familial** family-size packet; **p. de mer** (*vague*) big wave; **embarquer des paquets de mer** (*d'un bateau*) to take on a lot of water; **p. postal** parcel; *Mktg* **p. de présentation** display pack; *Fin* **p. de valeurs** parcel *or* block of shares

paquetage [paktaʒ] *nm Mil etc* (soldier's) pack; **faire son p.** to get one's kit ready

paquet-cadeau, *pl* **paquets-cadeaux** *nm* gift-wrapped parcel; **je vous fais un p.?** would you like it gift-wrapped?; **dans un joli p.** prettily gift-wrapped

par [par] **1** *prép* [①B53] **(a)** (*à travers*) (*porte, hall, trou de la serrure*) through; **il entra p. la fenêtre** he came in through *or* by the window; **regarder p. la fenêtre** (*de l'intérieur*) to look out (of) the window; (*de l'extérieur*) to look (in) through the window; **passer p. Calais** to travel *or* go through *or* via Calais *or* by way of Calais; **venez p. ici** come this way; **allez p. là** go that way; **p. ici la sortie** this is the way out, it's this way out; **p. où est-il passé?** which way did he go?; **p. où passe ce cordon électrique?** where does this wire go?; **p. où est-il entré?** how did he get in?; **il court p. les rues** he runs through the streets; **de p. le monde** all over the world
(b) (*position*) **p. ici** round (about) here; **p. 10° de latitude nord** at a latitude of 10° North; **j'ai mal p. ici** it hurts round about here; **ça doit être p. là quelque part** it must be over there somewhere
(c) (*pendant, durant*) **p. un jour d'hiver** on a winter's day; **p. cette chaleur/ces temps de pluie** in this heat/rainy weather; **p. le passé** in the past; **je l'ai averti p. trois fois** I warned him three times; *Litt* **p. trois fois, il fut blessé** he was wounded on three separate occasions
(d) (*agent*) by; **tu as été appelé p. M. Alain** Mr Alain called you, you had a call from Mr Alain; **accablé p. l'inquiétude** overcome by *or* with anxiety; **soulagé p. cette nouvelle** relieved by *or* at the news; **faire qch p. soi-même** (*seul*) to do sth by oneself *or* on one's own; (*de sa propre volonté*) to do sth on one's own initiative; **examiner/juger/voir qch p. soi-même** to examine/judge/see sth for oneself; **elle est remarquable p. sa beauté** she is remarkable for her

beauty; **elle est unique p. sa générosité/son intelligence** there is no-one to equal her for generosity/intelligence; **j'ai appris p. les Martin que vous étiez malade** I heard through *or* from the Martins that you were ill; *F* **tu le sais p. qui, toi?** who did you get that from?, who told you that?; **faire faire qch p. qn** to have sth done by sb; **as-tu vu Don Juan p. Planchon?** have you seen Planchon's Don Juan?

(e) (*motif*) (*habitude, négligence, curiosité, amitié etc*) out of; **j'ai fait cela p. amitié/respect pour vous** I did it out of friendship/respect for you; **p. pitié!** for pity's sake!; **p. hasard/erreur** by chance/mistake; **p. malheur** unfortunately, as bad luck would have it

(f) (*au moyen de*) (*clou, chaîne etc*) with, by (means of); (*train, avion, voiture, bateau*) by; **il fut salué p. des acclamations** he was hailed with *or* by cheers; **remercié p. un bouquet** thanked with a bouquet; **conduire/prendre qn p. la main** to lead/take sb by the hand; **tenir qn p. la taille** to hold sb round the waist; **envoyer qch p. la poste** to send sth by post *or* through the post; **répondre p. oui ou p. non** to answer yes or no; **commencer** *ou* **débuter/finir** *ou* **achever** *ou* **terminer p. qch/faire qch** to begin/end with sth/by doing sth; **se terminer p. un divorce/une dispute** to end in divorce/an argument; **commençons p. le commencement** let's begin at the beginning; **il a essayé p. tous les moyens** he tried (by) every possible means, he tried everything; **il est monté p. l'escalier** he took the stairs up; **il a dû monter p. l'échelle** he must have climbed the ladder; **mon cousin p. alliance** my cousin by marriage; **société p. actions** joint-stock company; **obtenir qch p. la force** to obtain sth by force; **p. la seule volonté** by sheer force of will; **appeler qn p. son nom** to call sb by his/her name; *Fig* **appeler les choses p. leur(s) nom(s)** to call a spade a spade; **p. route** by road

(g) (*selon*) according to; **p. taille, p. ordre de grandeur** according to size; **p. ordre alphabetique/chronologique** in alphabetical/chronological order

(h) (*distributif*) **entrer deux p. deux** to come in two by two, to come in in twos; **deux jours p. semaine** two days a week; **il gagne 1 000 francs p. semaine** he earns 1,000 francs a *or* per week; **10 000 francs p. an** 10,000 francs a year *or* per annum; **un siège p. personne** one seat per person; **un guide p. groupe de six** one guide per group of six *or* for each group of six; **actualité transmise heure p. heure** hourly news broadcasts

(i) *Arch* (*au nom de*) **de p. le Roi** by order of the King, in the name of the King

2 *adv Litt* **p. trop** far too, much too; **vous êtes p. trop aimable** you are much too kind

para [para] *nm F* (*abrév* **parachutiste**) para

parabole [parabɔl] *nf* **(a)** (*allégorie*) parable; **parler par paraboles** to speak in parables **(b)** *Géom* parabola **(c)** *Télécom* (*antenne*) (parabolic) dish

parabolique [parabɔlik] **1** *adj* (*miroir, Géom courbe*) parabolic; *Télécom* **antenne p.** dish (antenna); **radiateur p.** electric fire (with parabolic reflector) **2** *nm* electric fire (with parabolic reflector)

paracétamol [parasetamɔl] *nm* paracetamol; **prendre du p.** to take some paracetamol; **deux cachets de p.** two paracetamol

parachèvement [paraʃɛvmɑ̃] *nm* completion, finishing; (*perfectionnement*) perfecting, perfection

parachever [paraʃ(ə)ve] *vt* (*conj like* **achever**) to complete, to finish off; (*perfectionner*) to perfect

parachutage [paraʃytaʒ] *nm* parachuting, dropping (by parachute); *Pol F* (*d'un candidat*) parachuting in; *Fig F* **son p. dans le bureau** the way he was foisted on the office

parachute [paraʃyt] *nm* (*appareil de saut*) parachute; *F* chute; **p. dorsal/ventral** back(-pack)/lap-pack parachute; **saut en p.** parachute jump; **sauter en p.** to make a parachute jump; **faire du p.** to go parachuting; **p. ascensionnel** parascending

parachuter [paraʃyte] *vt* (*vivres*) to drop by parachute, to parachute in; (*soldats*) to parachute in; *Pol F* (*nommer*) to parachute in; *Fig F* **la façon dont il s'est fait p. dans le service** the way he was foisted on *or* parachuted into the department; *Fig F* **j'ai été parachuté à ce poste** I've been pitchforked into this job

parachutisme [paraʃytism] *nm* parachuting, parachute jumping

parachutiste [paraʃytist] **1** *n* parachutist, parachute jumper **2** *nm Mil* paratrooper; **parachutistes** (*corps d'armée*) paratroops **3** *adj* parachute

parade¹ [parad] *nf* **(a)** (*défilé*) parade; **faire la p.** to parade; **comme à la p.** (*facilement*) like clockwork; **p. de cirque** circus parade **(b)** (*exhibition*) show, ostentation; **faire p. de** (*ses bijoux, ses connaissances*) to parade, to display, to show off; (*sa beauté*) to flaunt; **habits de p.** full-dress *or* ceremonial clothes; *Fig* **de p.** (*sourire, air etc*) insincere, forced **(c)** *Équitation* (*de cheval*) stopping, pulling up **(d)** *Zool* display; **p. nuptiale** (*des animaux*) courtship dance *or* ritual

parade² *nf* **(a)** *Escrime* parade, parry; *Boxe* parry **(b)** (*réplique*) riposte; **faire une p.** to riposte, to parry; **je n'ai pas encore trouvé la p.** I haven't come up with a way of handling it/them yet

parader [parade] *vi* to show off; (*en se promenant*) to strut about; *Zool* to display

paradigmatique [paradigmatik] *Ling* **1** *adj* paradigmatic **2** *nf* study of paradigmatic relationships

paradigme [paradigm] *nm Ling* paradigm

paradis [paradi] *nm* paradise, heaven; *Fig* paradise; **un p. terrestre** heaven on earth, an earthly paradise; **l'enfer et le p.** heaven and hell; **aller au** *ou* **en p.** to go to heaven *or* paradise; **il ne l'emportera pas au** *ou* **en p.** he won't get away with it, he'll be sorry; **un p. pour les enfants** a paradise for children; **c'est le p. des pêcheurs** it's a fisherman's paradise *or* idea of heaven; *Th F* **le p.** the gods; **oiseau de p.** bird of paradise

▶ **paradis**: **p. fiscal** tax haven; **le P. terrestre** the Garden of Eden

paradisiaque [paradizjak] *adj* of paradise, *Fml* paradisiac(al), paradisaical; *Fig* (*vacances, lieu*) heavenly

paradisier [paradizje] *nm* (*oiseau*) bird of paradise

paradoxal, -ale, -aux, -ales [paradɔksal, -o] *adj* paradoxical; **c'est complètement p.** it's totally illogical

paradoxalement [paradɔksalmɑ̃] *adv* paradoxically

paradoxe [paradɔks] *nm* paradox

parafe [paraf] *nm* = **paraphe**

parafer [parafe] *vt* = **parapher**

paraffinage [parafinaʒ] *nm* paraffining, waxing

paraffine [parafin] *nf Ch* paraffin; *Com* paraffin (wax); *Méd* **huile de p.** liquid paraffin

paraffiner [parafine] *vt* to paraffin

parafiscal, -ale, -aux, -ales [parafiskal, -o] *adj* (*taxe*) exceptional, special

parafiscalité [parafiskalite] *nf* indirect taxation, special taxation

parage¹ [paraʒ] *nm Arch* **de haut p.** of high lineage, high-born

parage² *nm* **(a)** *Naut* (*souvent pl*) **parages** waters, region(s); **les parages du Cap Horn** the waters off Cape Horn; **se trouver dans les parages du Cap Horn** to be off Cape Horn **(b)** (*toujours pl*) **dans les parages de ...** in the vicinity of ..., near ...; **que faites-vous dans ces parages?** what are you doing here *or* in this neck of the woods?; **est-ce qu'il est dans les parages?** is he around?; **il est dans les parages** he's around somewhere; **elle habite dans les parages** she lives round about here

paragraphe [paragraf] *nm* **(a)** paragraph; *Journ* par; (*d'un texte de loi*) subsection **(b)** *Typ* section mark, paragraph

Paraguay [paragwɛ] *nm Géog* Paraguay

paraguayen, -enne [paragwɛjɛ̃, -ɛn] **1** *adj* Paraguayan **2** *n* **P.** Paraguayan

para-hôtellerie *nf* serviced accommodation industry

paraître¹ [parɛtr] *nm* **l'être et le p.** appearance and reality; **s'intéresser davantage au p.** to be more interested in appearances; **juger sur le p.** to judge by appearances

paraître² (*prp* **paraissant**; *pp* **paru**; *pr ind* **je parais, il paraît, n. paraissons**; *impf* **je paraissais**; *p hist* **je parus**; *fu* **je paraîtrai**) **1** *vi* **(a)** (*se montrer*) to appear; (*d'une étoile, de la lune etc*) to appear, to come out; (*d'un acteur*) to appear, to come on; **le jour commençait à p.** day was dawning; **il n'a pas** *ou* **n'est pas paru de la journée** he hasn't appeared all day; **lorsque l'enfant paraît** when the baby arrives; **laisser p. ses sentiments/sa déception** to show one's feelings/disappointment, to let one's feelings/disappointment show; **il ne pouvait pas s'empêcher de laisser p. un certain agacement** he couldn't help showing *or* betraying a degree of annoyance; **un faible sourire a paru sur ses lèvres** he/she smiled weakly; **p. en public** to appear in public; *Th* **c'est alors qu'elle parut sur la scène** it was at that moment that she appeared on stage *or* she came on (stage); **elle aime un peu trop p.** she likes to show off; **elle ne pense qu'à p.** all she thinks about is impressing people

(b) (*d'un livre etc*) to come out, to appear, to be published; (*d'un périodique*) to appear, to come out; **faire p. un livre** to publish a book, to bring out a book; **vient de p.** just out; (*livre*) just published; **le dernier San Antonio vient de p.** the latest San Antonio has just come out

(c) (*sembler*) to seem, to look, to appear

(d) **il paraissait furieux** he looked furious; (*à l'entendre*) he sounded furious; **cette décision me paraît bizarre** it seems a strange decision to me, it strikes me as a strange decision; **cela me paraît (être) une très bonne idée** it sounds to me like *or* strikes me as a very good idea; **ça ne te paraît pas une bonne idée?** don't you think that's a good idea?; **l'endroit lui parut familier** the place seemed familiar to him; **il ne paraît pas remarquer leur présence** he doesn't seem *or* appear to notice their presence; **il paraît (avoir) trente ans** he looks about thirty; (*d'une personne plus âgée*) he looks no more than thirty; **elle a quarante ans, mais elle ne les paraît pas** she's forty, but she doesn't look it; **p. son âge** to look one's age; (*se faire passer pour*) to pass for, to appear to be; **il veut p. ce qu'il n'est pas** he wants to pass for *or* he wants to appear to be something that he isn't; **pourquoi ce besoin de p.?** why this need to appear to be what you're/he's/*etc* not?

2 *v impers* [①B27,E,2,e] **(a)** (*sembler*) **je suis très mal – il n'y paraît pas** I'm very ill – you don't look it *or* it doesn't look as if you are; **demain, il n'y paraîtra plus** there'll be no trace of it tomorrow; **sans qu'il n'y paraisse** without it *or Fml* its being apparent; **il faut l'aider sans qu'il n'y paraisse** we must help him without making it obvious *or* without making it look as if we are doing; **il me paraît que ...** it seems to me *or* it strikes me that ...; **il me paraît utile de ...** I think it would be useful to ...

(b) il paraît que (*on dit que*) it seems *or* appears that; **il paraît qu'elle s'en va, elle s'en va, paraît-il** it seems *or* appears *or* would appear that she's leaving, she's leaving apparently; **il paraît que ça fait maigrir** apparently it helps you lose weight; **à ce qu'il paraît** apparently, it would seem so; **à ce qu'il paraît, c'est plus rapide par la route que par avion** apparently *or* seemingly *or* it would appear that it's quicker by road than by air; **il paraît (que oui)** so it appears *or* would appear, it appears *or* seems so, apparently; **il paraît que non** it appears *or* would appear not, it seems not, apparently not

paralittéraire [paraliterɛr] *adj* **œuvre p.** work of popular literature; **écriture p.** popular writing

paralittérature [paraliteratyr] *nf* popular literature

parallaxe [paralaks] *nf Astron etc* parallax; *Opt etc* **erreur de p.** parallax error

parallèle [paralɛl] **1** *adj Géom* parallel (**à** to, with); *Fig* (*expériences, destinées, carrières etc*) very similar; *Ordinat* **imprimante/interface p.** parallel printer/interface; *Gym* **barres parallèles** parallel bars; **faire des barres parallèles** to do exercises on the parallel bars; **rue qui est p. à la rivière** street that is *or* runs parallel to *or* with the river; **droites parallèles à l'infini** parallel straight lines extending into infinity; **mener une action p.** to take parallel *or* similar action; **mener une vie p.** to lead a secret life; **circuits parallèles de vente** parallel sales networks; **police p.** illegally constituted police force; *Écon* **marché p.** unofficial *or* illegal market

2 *nf* parallel (line)

3 *nm Géog* (*d'une latitude*) parallel; (*comparaison*) comparison, parallel; **en p.** (*employé adjectivement*) parallel; (*employé adverbialement*) in parallel; **mettre qch en p. avec qch** to compare sth with sth; **mettre deux événements/réactions en p.** to compare two events/reactions, to set two events/reactions side by side; **établir un p. entre ... et ...** to establish *or* draw a parallel between ... and ...

parallèlement [paralɛlmɑ̃] *adv* parallel (**à** to, with); (*en même temps*) at the same time, *Fml* concurrently; (*de la même façon*) in the same way; **p. à la route** parallel to the road, alongside the road

parallélépipède [paralelepipɛd] *nm Géom* parallelepiped

parallélisme [paralelism] *nm* parallelism; *Aut* **p. (des roues)** (wheel) alignment; *Aut* **il y a un défaut de p.** there's something wrong with the alignment, the wheels aren't properly aligned

parallélogramme [paralelɔgram] *nm Géom* parallelogram

paralysant [paralizɑ̃] *adj Méd, Fig* (*peur*) paralysing; (*timidité*) crippling, paralysing

paralysé, -ée [paralize] **1** *adj Méd* paralysed; *Fig* (*pays*) crippled; *Fig* **p. de peur** paralysed with fear; *Fig* **je suis resté p.** I was paralysed *or* petrified; **nous sommes paralysés par l'absence de fonds suffisants** we are hamstrung by a lack of funds **2** *n* person who is paralysed; **les paralysés** the paralysed

paralyser [paralize] *vt* (*rendre infirme*) to paralyse; *Fig* (*empêcher d'agir, de fonctionner*) to paralyse, to incapacitate; *Fig* (*économie, pays*) to cripple; *Fig* (*circulation*) to bring to a standstill; **paralysé des deux jambes** paralysed in both legs; **le froid paralyse ses mains** his hands are numb with the cold; **ce genre de situation me paralyse** I'm petrified in that kind of situation; **paralysé par la peur** paralysed *or* helpless with fear

paralysie [paralizi] *nf Méd* (*d'une partie du corps*) paralysis; *Fig* state of paralysis; **p. agitante** Parkinson's disease; **p. générale (progressive)** creeping paralysis; **p. cérébrale** cerebral palsy; **p. faciale** facial palsy

paralytique [paralitik] **1** *adj* paralytic **2** *n* person who is paralysed, paralytic

paramédical, -ale, -aux, -ales [paramedikal, -o] **1** *adj* paramedical; **personnel p.** paramedics **2** *nm* **emplois du p.** jobs in paramedics, paramedic jobs

paramétrable [parametrabl] *adj Ordinat* configurable; **p. par l'utilisateur** user-definable

paramétrage [parametraʒ] *nm Ordinat* configuration

paramètre [paramɛtr] *nm Math, Fig* parameter; *Ordinat* parameter, setting; (*du DOS*) switch

paramétrer [parametre] *vt Ordinat* to configure

paramilitaire [paramilitɛr] *adj* paramilitary

parangon [parɑ̃gɔ̃] *nm Litt* paragon; **p. de vertu** paragon of virtue

parano [parano] *F* **1** *adj* paranoid **2** *nf* paranoia; **elle fait de la p.!** she's being paranoid!; **tu es en pleine p.!** you're being completely paranoid!; **arrête ta p.!** stop being paranoid!

paranoïa [paranɔja] *nf Psy* paranoia; *Fig* **tu es en pleine p.** you're being completely paranoid

paranoïaque [paranɔjak] *adj, n Psy* paranoiac

paranoïde [paranɔid] *adj* paranoid

paranormal, -ale, -aux, -ales [paranormal, -o] *adj* paranormal

parapente [parapɑ̃t] *nf* (*activité*) paragliding; (*parachute*) paraglider; **faire du p.** to go paragliding

parapet [parapɛ] *nm* parapet

paraphe [paraf] *nm* **(a)** (*ajouté à la signature*) flourish **(b)** (*de son nom*) initials

parapher [parafe] *vt* to initial; (*signer*) to sign

parapheur [parafœr] *nm* signature book

paraphrase [parafraz] *nf* paraphrase; **faire de la p.** to paraphrase

paraphraser [parafraze] *vt* to paraphrase

paraplégie [parapleʒi] *nf Méd* paraplegia

paraplégique [parapleʒik] *adj, n Méd* paraplegic

parapluie [paraplɥi] *nm* umbrella, *Br F* brolly; **p. de golf** golf umbrella; *Fig* **p. nucléaire** *ou* **atomique** nuclear umbrella

parapsychologie [parapsikɔlɔʒi] *nf* parapsychology

parapublic, -ique [parapyblik] *adj* (*entreprise*) part government-owned

parasciences [parasjɑ̃s] *nfpl* sciences of the paranormal

parascolaire [paraskɔlɛr] *adj* extracurricular

parasismique [parasismik] *adj* anti-earthquake

parasitaire [parazitɛr] *adj* parasitic(al)

parasite [parazit] **1** *nm Biol* parasite; *Fig* parasite, *F* sponger, freeloader; **un p. social** a social parasite; *Rad, TV* **parasites** interference; (*causés par des phénomènes atmosphériques*) atmospherics **2** *adj Biol* (*insecte, plante etc*) parasitic; *Fig* (*mot*) unnecessary, superfluous; *Rad, TV* **bruits parasites** interference

parasiter [parazite] *vt Biol* to parasitize; *Fig F* **p. la société** to be a parasite on society

parasitique [parazitik] *adj* parasitic(al)

parasitisme [parazitism] *nm* parasitism

parasitologie [parazitɔlɔʒi] *nf Méd* parasitology

parasitologique [parazitɔlɔʒik] *adj Méd* parasitological

parasitose [parazitoz] *nf Méd* disease caused by a parasite

parasol [parasɔl] *nm* parasol, sunshade; (*sur la plage*) beach umbrella; **pin p.** parasol *or* umbrella pine

parasympathique [parasɛ̃patik] *adj Anat* parasympathetic

paratonnerre [paratɔnɛr] *nm* lightning conductor

paratyphoïde [paratifɔid] *adj, nf Méd* **(fièvre) p.** paratyphoid fever

paravalanche [paravalɑ̃ʃ] **1** *adj* **mur** *ou* **installation p.** avalanche barrier *or* wall **2** *nm* avalanche barrier *or* wall

paravent [paravɑ̃] *nm* screen; *Fig* **ce n'est qu'un p.** it's just a smoke screen *or* a front; **cette société leur sert de p. pour d'autres activités** the company is a screen *or* front for their other activities

parbleu [parblø] *int Vieilli* good Lord!

parc [park] *nm* **(a)** (*jardin*) park; (*d'un château etc*) grounds, park **(b)** (*pour enfant*) playpen **(c)** (*ensemble*) (*de bus, de voitures etc*) fleet; *Rail* rolling stock; **p. automobile** number of cars on the roads; **le p. automobile français** the number of cars in France; **le p. des téléviseurs couleurs** the total number of colour televisions owned by the population; *Ordinat* **p. de micros** computer park; *Ordinat* **p. informatique** computer park; **p. immobilier** housing stock; **le p. nucléaire de la France** France's nuclear power stations

▶ **parc**: **p. aquatique** water park; **p. d'attractions** theme park; **p. à bestiaux** cattle pen; *Aut* **p. d'exposition** forecourt; **p. des expositions** exhibition centre; **p. à huîtres** oyster bed; **p. de loisirs** leisure park; **p. à moules** mussel bed; **p. à moutons** sheep pen, sheepfold; **p. national** national park; **p. naturel** nature reserve; **p. régional** regional park; **p. résidentiel de loisirs** chalet park, holiday camp; **p. de stationnement** car park, *Am* parking lot; **p. de stationnement à plusieurs niveaux** multi-storey car park, *Am* multi-story parking garage; **p. à thème** theme park; **p. zoologique** zoo, *Fml* zoological gardens

parcage [parkaʒ] *nm* **(a)** *(du bétail, de moutons)* penning, enclosing **(b)** *Télécom* hold; **mettre en p.** *(correspondant)* to put on hold; *Ordinat (disque dur)* to park

parcellaire [parsɛlɛr] *adj (terrain)* divided into small portions *or* into parcels; **travail p.** work divided into sections

parcelle [parsɛl] *nf* (small) fragment, morsel; *(de terrain)* piece, parcel; *Fig* **pas la moindre p. de jugement/d'intelligence/de vérité** not an ounce of common sense/intelligence/truth; **il n'a pas la moindre p. de générosité** he doesn't have a generous bone in his body; **il ne cèdera pas la moindre p. de son indépendance/sa liberté** he will not give up the least little bit of his independence/freedom

parcellisation [parsɛlizasjɔ̃] *nf (du terrain)* parcelling up; **p. du travail** breaking work down into sections

parcelliser [parsɛlize] *vt (terrain)* to divide into small portions, to parcel up; *(travail)* to break down into sections

parce que [pars(ə)kə] *conj* because; **p. c'est vrai** because it's true; **ce n'est pas p. tu n'aimes pas la cervelle que ...** just because you don't like brains doesn't mean that ...; **p. qu'on lui dit de le faire, il le fait** he does it (just) because he's told to do it; **pourquoi ne viens-tu pas? – p.** why aren't you coming? – (just) because (I'm not); **mais pourquoi pleures-tu comme ça? – p.** why are you crying? – just because; **ce chandelier vous intéresse? p. je pourrais ...** are you interested in the chandelier? because if you are *or* if so, I could ...; **je le ferai, mais p. c'est vous!** I'll do it, but just because it's you!

parchemin [parʃəmɛ̃] *nm* parchment; *(de livre)* vellum; **papier p.** parchment paper; **un p.** a parchment; *Univ* a diploma; **des parchemins** *(titres de noblesse)* titles of nobility

parcheminé [parʃəmine] *adj* parchment-like; *Fig (visage)* wizened, wrinkled

parcheminer [parʃəmine] **1** *vt (papier)* to give a parchment finish to **2 se parcheminer** *vpr (de la peau)* to shrivel up, to become shrivelled

parcimonie [parsimɔni] *nf* thrift; **avec p.** sparingly; **elle distribue les conseils avec p.** she is sparing with her advice

parcimonieusement [parsimɔnjøzmɑ̃] *adv* sparingly; **distribuer les compliments p.** to be sparing with one's compliments

parcimonieux, -euse [parsimɔnjø, -øz] *adj (personne, action)* thrifty; **une distribution parcimonieuse du pain** a sparing distribution of bread

par-ci, par-là *adv (dans l'espace)* here and there; *(dans le temps)* now and then, from time to time; **une virgule par-ci, un point d'exclamation par-là** a comma here, an exclamation mark there

parcmètre [parkmɛtr], **parcomètre** [parkɔmɛtr] *nm* (parking) meter; **ma voiture est au p.** I'm on a meter

parcourir [parkurir] *vt (conj like* **courir***)* **(a)** *(région, quartier)* to roam, to travel through; *(les rues)* to roam, to wander (through); **p. les mers** to sail the seas; **p. le pays de long en large** to travel the length and breadth of the country; **p. un endroit à la recherche de qn** to scour a place for sb; **p. une distance de plusieurs kilomètres** to cover a distance of several kilometres; **il reste deux kilomètres/un long chemin à p.** there are two kilometres/there is a long way to go; **le pays est parcouru de canaux** the country has a network of canals; **mesurer le chemin parcouru** to measure the distance covered; *Fig* to measure one's progress; *Fig* **un frisson me parcourut** a shiver went through me; *Fig* **un frisson me parcourut l'échine** *ou* **le dos** a shiver ran down my spine; *Fig* **un murmure a parcouru la foule** a murmur ran through the crowd

(b) *(regarder) (texte, document)* to look at briefly, to read *or* run through *or* over; *(lettre, journal)* to skim, to glance at; *(livre)* to skim (through), to glance through; *Ordinat* to scroll through; **p. qch des yeux** *ou* **du regard** to glance at *or* over sth, to run one's eyes over sth; **p. ses notes avant une réunion** to go over *or* look over one's notes before a meeting

parcours [parkur] *nm (d'un défilé, de bus etc)* route; *(d'un fleuve)* course; *Sp (de voitures, motos etc)* circuit; *(de chevaux), Golf* course; *(distance)* distance covered; *(voyage en avion)* leg; *(itinéraire)* route; *Av* **p. à vide** deadhead flight, empty leg; **les chevaux font un p. de 20 kilomètres** the horses run over a distance of 20 kilometres; *Golf* **un p. dix-huit trous** an eighteen-hole golf course; **le car fait le p. entre la ville et la côte** the bus runs between the town and the coast; **elle fait plusieurs fois le p. dans la journée** she does the journey several times a day; **je fais le p. à pied dans les deux sens** I walk both ways; **payer le p.** *(dans un taxi)* to pay the fare; **le prix du p.** the fare; **je ne connais pas le prix du p. pour aller à l'aéroport** I don't know the fare to the airport *or* how much it costs to get to the airport; *Courses de chevaux* **reconnaître le p.** to walk the course; **faire un p. sans faute** *(d'un cheval)* to have a clear round; *Fig (dans une carrière)* to have a copybook career; *Mil, Fig* **p. du combattant** obstacle course; **faire le p. du combattant** to do an obstacle course

par-delà *prép, adv* beyond

par-derrière **1** *adv (attaquer qn)* from behind; *(se boutonner)* at the back; **entrer p.** to come in the back way, to come in the back door; **des coups p.** underhand tricks; **elle a toujours fait des coups p.** she's always been underhand; **dire des choses p.** to say things behind people's backs; **mais p. je suis sûr qu'il dit autre chose** but I'm sure he says something quite different behind my back **2** *prép* behind

par-dessous **1** *prép* under, beneath, underneath **2** *adv* underneath; **je suis passé p.** I crept underneath; **prendre qch p.** to get hold of sth underneath

pardessus [pardəsy] *nm* overcoat

par-dessus **1** *prép* over (the top of); **sauter p. la table** to leap over the table; **jeter qch p. bord** to throw sth overboard; *Fig* **p. le marché** into the bargain; **p. tout** above all; *(le comble)* to crown it all, on top of it all; *Fig F* **j'en ai p. la tête** I've had just about enough; **regarder p. l'épaule de qn** to look over sb's shoulder **2** *adv* over

par-devant **1** *prép* in front of; **passer p. la maison** to pass the house; *Jur* **acte signé p. (le) notaire** deed signed in the presence of a lawyer **2** *adv* in front

par-devers *prép* **(a) p. soi** in one's possession **(b) p. le juge** before the judge

pardi [pardi] *int F* of course!, naturally!

pardieu [pardjø] *int Arch* zounds!

pardon [pardɔ̃] *nm* **(a)** *(grâce)* forgiveness; **accorder son p. à qn** to forgive *or* pardon sb; **demander p. à qn** to apologize to sb, to say sorry to sb; **demander p. à Dieu pour ses péchés** to ask God's forgiveness for one's sins; **mille pardons** a thousand apologies; **arrête de toujours (me) demander p.** stop apologizing; **c'est à lui de te demander p.** it's up to him to apologize, he should apologize to <u>you</u>; **(je vous demande) p.** (I'm) sorry, I beg your pardon; *(pour passer, avertir, attirer l'attention de qn)* excuse me; **j'ai fait une grosse bêtise, je vous demande p.** I'm sorry *or* I <u>do</u> apologize, I've done something very stupid; **je vous demande p., quel est votre nom?** I'm sorry, what is your name?; **p., ce n'est pas ce que j'ai dit!** *(pour contredire)* excuse *or* pardon me, but that's <u>not</u> what I said; **p.(, qu'as-tu dit)?** what did you say?, excuse me?, (I beg your) pardon?; *F* **on dit qu'il n'est pas très malin, mais son fils, p.!** he's not very bright, it seems, but his son is even worse!; **la mère est jolie, mais la fille, p.!** the mother's pretty, but the daughter, wow!

(b) *Rel (en Bretagne)* religious festival; *Rel Juive* **Grand P., jour du P.** Day of Atonement, Yom Kippur

pardonnable [pardɔnabl] *adj (faute, erreur)* forgivable, excusable, pardonable; **il s'est trompé mais c'est p.** he made a mistake, but he can be forgiven *or* excused *or* it's excusable; **tu es p. d'avoir oublié** you can be forgiven for forgetting; **vous n'êtes pas p.!** it's unforgivable *or* inexcusable of you!

pardonner [pardɔne] **1** *vt (erreur, faute)* to forgive, to excuse, to pardon; *(personne)* to forgive; **est-ce que tu me pardonnes?** do you forgive me?, am I forgiven?; **p. qch à qn** to forgive sb sth; **elle m'a pardonné d'avoir oublié** she forgave me for forgetting; **pardonnez-moi si je vous contredis** I'm sorry to contradict you, excuse *or* forgive *or* pardon me for contradicting you; **pour me/te/***etc* **faire p.** to make it up; **pour se faire p. son retard** as a way of saying sorry for being late; **tu es tout pardonné** you are forgiven

2 *vi* to forgive; **elle pardonne vite** she is quick to forgive; **maladie/faute qui ne pardonne pas** fatal illness/mistake; **ça ne pardonne pas** you don't get a second chance

3 se pardonner *vpr* **je ne me le pardonnerai jamais** I'll never forgive myself (for it); **c'est une erreur qui ne se pardonne pas** it's an unforgivable mistake; **ils se sont pardonné leurs paroles de colère** they forgave each other for being angry

paré [pare] *adj* **(a)** *(prêt)* ready (**à** for); **être p. contre** *(le froid, les attaques etc)* to be prepared for; **vous voilà p.!** you're all set!; *Naut* **p. à virer!** ready about! **(b)** *(orné)* decorated, ornamented (**de** with); *(personne) (vêtu)* dressed (up) (**de** in); *(couvert de bijoux)* wearing jewels, covered in jewels **(c)** *Culin (viande)* dressed

pare-avalanches [paravalɑ̃ʃ] *nm inv* avalanche barrier *or* wall
pare-balles [parbal] *adj inv* bullet-proof; **gilet p.** bullet-proof vest
pare-boue [parbu] *nm inv* mudflap
pare-brise [parbriz] *nm inv Aut etc* windscreen, *Am* windshield; **p. feuilleté** laminated windscreen
pare-chocs [parʃɔk] *nm inv Aut* bumper, *Am* fender; **on roulait p. contre p.** it *or* the traffic was bumper to bumper; **p. bouclier** bumper; **p. circonférenciel** *ou* **enveloppant** wrap-around bumper; **p. à absorption d'énergie** energy-absorbing bumper
pare-éclats [parekla] *nm inv Mil* splinter-proof shield (*on trench parapet etc*)
pare-étincelles [paretɛ̃sɛl] *nm inv* fireguard
pare-feu [parfø] *nm inv* **(a)** (*dans la forêt*) firebreak **(b)** (*de cheminée*) fireguard; **porte p.** fire door; *Aut* **p. de moteur** engine bulkhead, *Am* firewall
pare-flammes [parflam] *nm inv Aut* flame arrester
parégorique [paregɔrik] *adj Pharm* paregoric
pareil, -eille [parɛj] **1** *adj* **(a)** (*semblable*) alike, similar; **elles sont presque pareilles** they are almost the same; **ce n'est pas p.** it's not the same (thing); **une erreur et un oubli, ce n'est pas p.** a mistake and an oversight are not the same (thing); **ce n'est pas p. que l'année dernière** it's not the same as last year; **en voici un tout p.** here's one exactly the same *or* exactly like it; **il est vraiment p.** it's very similar; **l'an dernier à pareille époque** this time last year; *Litt* **à nul autre p.** without equal, unparalleled; **p. que** *ou* **à** the same as, just like; **et lui, qu'est-ce qu'on lui donne? – p., une orange** and what will we give him? – the same (thing), an orange; **ses deux chaussettes ne sont pas pareilles** his socks don't match; **ces bougeoirs ne sont pas pareils** these candlesticks aren't alike *or* the same; **il n'y en a pas deux (de) pareils** no two are alike; **les gens sont partout pareils** people are the same the world over; *F* **si ça ne te plaît pas, c'est p.** too bad if you don't like it; **toujours p. à lui-même** the same as always; **c'est toujours p. avec lui** it's always the same with him
(b) (*tel*) such; (*suivant le nom*) like that; **en p. cas** in a case like this, in such cases; **dans de pareils moments, dans des moments pareils** at times like these; **dans pareille situation** in a similar situation; **par un temps p.** in weather like this; **comment a-t-elle pu faire une chose pareille!** how could she do such a thing!; **je n'ai jamais vu (une) chose pareille** I've never seen anything like it; **mais je n'ai jamais dit une chose pareille!** but I never said any such thing!; **tu ne vas pas croire une chose pareille!** you're not going to believe something like that!; **qu'a-t-il donc fait pour avoir une chance pareille?** how did he manage to get so lucky?; **j'ignorais que tu y portais un p. intérêt** I didn't realize you were so interested; **a-t-on idée de rentrer à des heures pareilles!** what kind of time is this to come home at?
2 *n* (*pair*) **il n'a pas son p. au monde** there's no one like him, he's second to none; **un cuisinier qui n'a pas son p. au monde** a chef in a class of his own; **cet endroit n'a pas son p. au monde** there's nowhere else like this; **comme sage-femme elle n'a pas sa pareille** there's no one to equal *or* match her as a midwife; **elle n'a pas son p. pour faire le cassoulet** nobody can make cassoulet like her *or* the way she can; **sans p.** (*occasion, méchanceté*) unparalleled; (*richesse, beauté*) unparalleled, unrivalled, unequalled; (*gentillesse, imagination*) unparalleled, unequalled; **une soirée sans pareille** a wonderful evening; **c'est une cuisinière sans p.** she's a superb cook, no-one can match her when it comes to cooking; **mes pareils** my equals; **lui et ses pareils** him and people like him
3 *nf* **rendre la pareille à qn** (*se venger*) to retaliate, to get one's own back on sb; (*faire preuve de reconnaissance*) to repay sb, to pay sb back; **elle ne manquera pas de lui rendre la pareille** she'll get her own back (on him); **si on me frappe, je rends la pareille** if any one hits me I hit back
4 *nm F* **c'est du p. au même** it's six of one and half a dozen of the other, it comes (down) to the same thing
5 *adv F* **faire p.** to do the same thing; **je ne fais pas p.** that's not how I do it; **ils s'habillent/écrivent p.** they dress/write the same (way); **ils mangent/lisent p.** they eat/read the same kind of things; **elles se coiffent p.** they have the same hairdo, they do their hair the same way; **elle se coiffe p. depuis 10 ans** she's had the same hairdo for the past 10 years
pareillement [parɛjmɑ̃] *adv* **(a)** (*de la même manière*) in a similar manner, in the same way; **p. habillé** dressed the same **(b)** (*aussi*) also, likewise; (*en réponse à des vœux*) the same to you!; **et moi p.!** same here!; **ravi de vous rencontrer – et moi p.!** pleased to meet you – likewise!
parement [parmɑ̃] *nm* **(a)** (*décoration*) ornament, decoration; *Couture* (*de manche, col*) facing; *Rel* **p. d'autel** (altar) frontal **(b)** *Constr* (*d'un mur*) facing; (*de la pierre*) (dressed) face
parent, -ente [parɑ̃, -ɑ̃t] **1** *nm* **(a)** (*always pl*) **parents** (*père et mère*) parents, mother and father; **les parents sortent ce soir** my parents *or surtout Am* my folks *or F* (my) mum and dad are going out this evening; **tu as prévenu les parents?** have you told mum and dad?; **la relation parents-enfant** the parent-child relationship
(b) *Litt* (*always pl*) **parents** (*ancêtres*) forefathers, forebears
(c) *Biol* parent
2 *n* (*personne appartenant à la proche famille*) relative, relation, *Arch* kinsman, *f* kinswoman; **c'est mon seul p.** he's my only living relative; *Jur* **le p. survivant** the last surviving relative; **proche p./p. éloigné** close/distant relative; **être (proches) parents** to be (closely) related; **être p. avec qn, être un p. de qn** to be related to sb; **nous sommes parents par alliance/par mon père** we are related by marriage/on my father's side; *Fig* **p. pauvre** poor relation; *Fig* **traiter qn en p. pauvre** to treat sb like a poor relation
3 *adj* related; (*semblable*) similar; **sciences parentes** related sciences; **leurs œuvres révèlent des intelligences/sensibilités parentes** their work shows a similar intelligence/sensitivity
▶ **parent**: **parents adoptifs** adoptive parents; **parents biologiques** biological parents; **parents d'élèves: association de parents d'élèves** parent teacher association, PTA
parental, -ale, -aux, -ales [parɑ̃tal, -o] *adj* (*autorité etc*) parental
parenté [parɑ̃te] *nf* **(a)** *aussi Fig* (*rapport*) relationship; *Spéc* (*en sociologie*) kinship; **il n'y a entre eux aucune p.** they are not related in any way; **quel est le lien de p. entre eux?** what relation are they to each other?, how are they related?; **as-tu un lien de p. avec ...?** are you related to *or* any relation of ...?; **liens de p.** family connections **(b)** (*famille*) family, relations
parenthèse [parɑ̃tɛz] *nf* [①A14,10] bracket, parenthesis; *Fig* (*dans un discours*) digression; *Typ* **p. fermante/ouvrante** closing/opening bracket; *Fig* **cette époque a été une p. dans sa vie** that period was an interlude in his life; *Fig* **c'est une p. dans ma routine quotidienne** it's a break from my daily routine; **je voudrais ouvrir une p.** (*pour aborder cette question*) I would like to digress for a moment; **je voudrais vous dire, dans une p.** *ou* **par p., que ...** I would like to say by way of digression *or* parenthetically that ...; **il est temps de fermer la p. et de revenir à notre sujet** enough of this digression, let's get back to our subject; **entre parenthèses** (*mot etc*) in brackets *or* parentheses, bracketed; *Fig* incidentally, by the way; **mettre un mot entre parenthèses** to put a word in brackets, to bracket a word; *Fig* **il faut mettre ce problème entre parenthèses** (*de côté*) this problem has to be put aside *or* to one side
paréo [pareo] *nm* pareo; **jupe-p.** sarong (skirt)
parer[1] [pare] **1** *vt* **(a)** (*éviter*) (*attaque, coup*) to fend off, to ward off; *Escrime, Boxe, Fig* (*question*) to parry; (*en esquivant*) (*coup*) to dodge; *Naut* (*abordage*) to avoid, to fend off; *Fig* **ils savaient qu'une OPA se préparait et ils ont réussi à p. le coup** they knew a takeover was in the offing and managed to ward it off; *Naut* **p. un cap** to clear *or* double a headland
(b) (*protéger*) to protect (**contre** against); **je suis paré contre le froid/l'hiver** I'm ready for *or* to face the cold/the winter
2 *vi* **p. à** (*accident*) to prevent, to guard against; (*difficulté, problème*) to avoid; (*défaite, désastre*) to ward off, to stave off; **pour p. à toute difficulté/à tout retard** in order to guard against any difficulties/delay; **p. à toute éventualité** to be prepared for anything; **on ne peut pas p. à tout** you can't guard against everything; **p. au plus pressé** to attend to the most urgent things first; **nous devons p. au plus pressé** first things first
parer[2] **1** *vt* **(a)** (*arranger*) (*viande, cuir*) to dress; *Naut* (*câble, ancre etc*) to clear
(b) (*vêtir*) (*personne*) to deck out, to adorn (**de** with); (*décorer*) to decorate with taste; **p. la mariée** to dress the bride; *Fig* **p. qn de toutes les vertus/qualités** to endow sb with every virtue/quality
2 se parer *vpr* to dress oneself up; **se p. de bijoux** to deck oneself out in jewels, to adorn oneself with jewels; **elle ne sort pas sans s'être parée de bijoux** she never goes out without her jewellery on; **se p. d'un faux titre** to assume a false title; **je me suis paré contre le froid** I've made sure that I'm not going to feel the cold
pare-soleil [parsɔlɛj] *nm inv Aut* sun visor; *Phot* lens hood

paresse [parɛs] *nf* **(a)** (*indolence*) laziness, idleness; **par pure p.** out of sheer laziness; **d'une p. incroyable/incurable** incredibly/ incurably lazy **(b)** (*lenteur*) **p. d'esprit** *ou* **intellectuelle** sluggishness of mind; *Méd* **p. intestinale** sluggishness of the bowels

paresser [parese] *vi* to laze (about *or* around)

paresseusement [parɛsøzmɑ̃] *adv* lazily; **le fleuve coule p.** the river moves slowly *or* sluggishly

paresseux, -euse [parɛsø, -øz] **1** *adj* **(a)** (*nonchalant*) lazy, *Fml* indolent; **p. comme une couleuvre** *ou* **un loir** bone idle; **il est p. le matin** he moves at a snail's pace in the morning **(b)** (*lent*) (*intestins*) sluggish; (*geste*) lazy; (*fleuve*) sluggish, slow-moving; **c'est un esprit p.** he won't use the brains God gave him, he's mentally lazy **2** *n* lazy person, *F* lazybones **3** *nm Zool* sloth

parfaire [parfɛr] *vt* (*conj like* **faire**; *used chiefly in inf and pp*) (*travail etc*) to finish off, to complete; (*technique, compétences etc*) to perfect

parfait [parfɛ] **1** *adj* **(a)** (*irréprochable*) perfect; (*performance*) faultless, perfect; (*diamant*) flawless; (*réputation*) unsullied; **en ordre p.** in perfect order; **le tout était rangé dans un ordre p.** there was not a thing out of place; **il est p. en toute occasion** he always knows what to do; **personne n'est p.** nobody's perfect; **il est loin d'être p.** he's far from perfect, he's no saint; **vous avez été p.** you were wonderful *or* splendid *or* marvellous; *Iron* you were just great; **(c'est** *ou* **voilà qui est) p.!** (that's) splendid! *or* fine! *or* wonderful!, *F* great!; *Iron* (that's just) great!; **p., passons à autre chose** fine *or* good, let's go on to something else

(b) (*complet*) (*bonheur*) perfect, complete; (*réussite*) complete; (*ressemblance*) exact; **un p. orateur** an accomplished speaker; **un p. meneur d'hommes** a wonderful leader; *F* **un p. imbécile** a perfect *or* complete idiot, an utter fool; **en p. accord** in full *or* perfect agreement; **je suis en p. accord avec ce qu'il a dit** I quite *or* totally agree with what he said; **nous travaillons en p. accord** *ou* **en parfaite harmonie l'un avec l'autre** we work in perfect harmony with each other; **être dans l'ignorance la plus parfaite de qch** to be completely ignorant of sth; *Mus* **accord p.** perfect chord

2 *nm* **(a)** [①**A48-9**,d-e; **B28**,F,3] *Gram* perfect (tense)

(b) *Culin* parfait; **p. au café** coffee parfait

parfaitement [parfɛtmɑ̃] *adv* **(a)** (*admirablement*) perfectly, to perfection; **cela m'ira p.** that will suit me perfectly *or* just fine; **elle s'occupe p. de ses enfants** she looks after her children wonderfully well; **un vin qui accompagne p. le poisson** a wine that is the perfect accompaniment for fish; **elle parle p. (l')anglais** she speaks English perfectly, she speaks perfect English

(b) (*totalement*) completely, thoroughly; (*compréhensible, clair, heureux*) perfectly; **elle est p. qualifiée pour faire le travail** she's perfectly *or* ideally qualified for the job; **il connaît p. son domaine** he knows his field thoroughly; **je comprends p.** I quite *or* perfectly understand; **il est p. idiot** he's a perfect idiot; **il a p. le droit de le dire** he has a perfect right *or* he is perfectly entitled to say so; **ceci m'est p. égal** it's really all the same to me; **j'ai p. conscience de …** I'm fully aware of …; **il a p. raison** he's perfectly right

(c) (*tout à fait*) certainly, exactly; **vous dites que vous l'avez vu? – oui, p.** you say you saw it? – indeed I did *or* yes, I most definitely did; **oui, p., j'y étais** yes indeed, I was there

parfois [parfwa] *adv* sometimes, at times; (*moins souvent*) occasionally, (every) now and then; **p. elle lit, p. elle tricote** sometimes she reads, other times she knits

parfum [parfœ̃] *nm* **(a)** (*senteur, odeur*) (*de fleurs*) perfume, fragrance, scent; (*d'un vin*) bouquet, aroma; *Fig* **un p. de scandale** a whiff of scandal **(b)** (*à base d'essences*) perfume, *Br* scent **(c)** *Culin* (*de glace, yaourt*) flavour, *US* flavor **(d)** *Fig F* **être au p.** to be in the know; **il n'était pas au p.** he didn't know anything (about it); **mettre qn au p.** to fill sb in, to put sb in the picture

parfumé [parfyme] *adj* (*fleur*) scented, fragrant, sweet-smelling; (*savon*) perfumed, scented; (*vin, air*) fragrant; (*au goût*) sweet-tasting; **des fruits très parfumés** fruit that is full of flavour *or US* flavor; **glace parfumée au café** coffee-flavoured ice-cream; **l'air p. du soir** the balmy evening air; **elle est trop parfumée** she's wearing too much perfume *or Br* scent

parfumer [parfyme] **1** *vt* **(a)** (*embaumer*) to scent, to perfume; **les fleurs parfument la pièce** the flowers scent the room; **un pot-pourri pour p. vos pièces** potpourri to scent *or* fragrance your rooms; **le gâteau parfume la cuisine** the kitchen smells of cake **(b)** *Culin* to flavour, *US* to flavor **(à** with) **(c)** (*mettre du parfum sur*) (*mouchoir*) to scent; (*armoire à linge*) to perfume; (*eau de bain*) to scent, to fragrance; **je vous parfume?** (*à une cliente*) would you like to try some (perfume)? **2 se parfumer** *vpr* to wear *or* use perfume *or Br* scent

parfumerie [parfymri] *nf* (*magasin*) perfume shop, perfumery; (*rayon*) perfume counter; (*produits*) perfumes, perfumery; (*industrie*) perfume industry

parfumeur, -euse [parfymœr, -øz] *n* perfumer

pari [pari] *nm* **(a)** (*convention*) bet, *Vieilli* wager; **faire un p.** to make *or* lay a bet; **faire un p. avec qn** to make a bet with sb; **je suis prêt à faire le p. que …** I'm willing to bet that …; **tenir un p.** to take a bet; *Fig* **les paris sont ouverts** it's anyone's guess **(b)** (*jeu*) betting; **p. mutuel** *Br* ≈ totalizator system, *F* tote, *Am* ≈ pari-mutuel

paria [parja] *nm* (*en Inde*) pariah; *Fig* pariah, (social) outcast

parier [parje] (*impf, pr sub* **n. pariions, v. pariiez)** **1** *vt* to bet, *Fml* to wager; **je parie une bouteille de vin qu'il ne viendra pas** I bet a bottle of wine he won't come; **je parie qu'il viendra** I bet he'll come, it's my bet he'll come; **tu veux p. qu'il te le reprochera?** what's the betting he'll blame you?; **il y a gros** *ou* **fort à p. que …** it's virtually certain that …, the odds are that …, it's odds on that …; **je te parie tout ce que tu veux …** I bet you anything (you like) …; **je l'aurais parié** I might have known (it) *or* guessed; *F* **tu en as assez, je parie?** I bet you've had enough

2 *vi* to bet; **p. avec qn/sur qch** to bet with sb/on sth; **p. sur un cheval** to bet on *or* back a horse; **on a parié gros** the betting ran high; **je te dis qu'il viendra – on parie?** he'll come I tell you – (do you) want a bet?

pariétal, -ale, -aux, -ales [parjetal, -o] **1** *adj* **(a)** *Anat* (*os*) parietal **(b)** *Beaux-Arts* **art p.** cave painting **2** *nm Anat* parietal bone

parieur, -euse [parjœr, -øz] *n* better, *F* punter; *Sp, surtout Courses de chevaux* backer; **c'est un p.** he'll bet on anything

parigot, -ote [parigo, -ɔt] *F Péj* **1** *adj* Parisian **2** *n* **P.** Parisian

Paris [pari] *nm* Paris

parisianisme [parizjanism] *nm Ling* = expression particular to Paris, Parisienism

parisien, -ienne [parizjɛ̃, -jɛn] **1** *adj* Parisian; *Péj* **esprit p.** superior Parisian outlook; **le Bassin p./la banlieue parisienne** the Paris Basin/suburbs **2** *n* **P.** Parisian

paritaire [paritɛr] *adj Ind* with parity of representation; **commission p.** = board on which management and unions are equally represented

parité [parite] *nf* **(a)** (*égalité*) parity; (*de rang, de valeur*) equality; *Fin* **p. des monnaies** monetary parity; *Fin* **p. franc-mark** franc-mark parity; *Bourse* **à p.** at the money; *Bourse* **au voisinage de la p.** close to par; **p. du pouvoir d'achat** purchasing power parity; **parités du change** exchange rate parity **(b)** *Math, Ordinat* parity; **p. paire/impaire** even/odd parity; **pas de p.** no parity

parjure [parʒyr] **1** *nm* perjury; **commettre un p.** to commit perjury, to perjure oneself **2** *n* (*personne*) perjurer **3** *adj* (*personne*) who does not keep his/her word

parjurer (se) [səparʒyre] *vpr* to perjure oneself, to be guilty of *or* to commit perjury

parka [parka] *nm ou f* parka

parking [parkiŋ] *nm* (*stationnement*) parking; (*emplacement*) car park, *Am* parking lot; **place de p.** parking place *or* spot, place to park; **il y a encore des places de p. derrière le restaurant** there's more parking space behind the restaurant; **mettre sa voiture au p.** to put one's car in the car park

▶ **parking**: **p. courte durée** short-stay car park; **p. gratuit** free car park; **p. longue durée** long-stay car park; **p. payant** paying car park; **p. privé** private car park; **'p. privé'** private parking

parkinsonien, -ienne [parkinsɔnjɛ̃, -jɛn] *Méd* **1** *adj* Parkinson's **2** *n* person with Parkinson's (disease), Parkinson's sufferer

parlant [parlɑ̃] *adj* **(a)** (*doué de parole*) speaking; (*portrait*) lifelike; (*geste*) eloquent, meaningful; (*description*) vivid; **cinéma p.** talking pictures, *F* talkies; **film p.** talking picture, *F* talkie; *Tél* **l'horloge parlante** the speaking clock, *Br F* Tim; **être p.** (*d'une réaction, de preuve*) to speak for itself **(b)** *F* (*bavard*) talkative

parlé [parle] **1** *adj* **l'anglais/le français p.** colloquial English/ French; **ça se dit dans la langue parlée** it's a colloquial term, it's used colloquially; *TV, Rad* **journal p.** news (broadcast *or* programme); **présenter le journal p.** to present the news **2** *nm* (*dans un opéra*) spoken part

parlement [parləmɑ̃] *nm* **(a)** [①**A11**,g,i] **le P.** Parliament **(b)** *Hist Jur* high judicial court (*in Paris and provinces*)

▶ **parlement**: **le P. européen** the European Parliament; **membre du P. européen** member of the European Parliament, MEP, Euro-MP

parlementaire¹ [parləmɑ̃tɛr] **1** *adj Pol* (*gouvernement, immunité, débat etc*) parliamentary **2** *n Pol* member of Parliament, *US* Congressman, *f* Congresswoman

parlementaire² *n Mil* negotiator, mediator

parlementarisme [parləmɑ̃tarism] *nm Pol* parliamentary government

parlementer [parləmɑ̃te] *vi* (*négocier*) to negociate **(avec** with), *Vieilli* to parley, to hold a parley **(avec** with); **nous avons dû p. avant de pouvoir quitter le poste de police** we had to talk our way out of the police station

parler¹ [parle] **1** *vi* **(a)** to speak, to talk; (*avouer*) to talk; **je ne peux pas le faire p.** I can't get him to talk, I can't get a word out of him; **parlons peu mais parlons bien** let's be brief and to the point; **elle a perdu sa voix à force de p.** she lost her voice from talking so much; **s'enrouer à force de p.** to talk oneself hoarse; **son fils ne parle pas encore** her son isn't talking yet; **est-ce que ton perroquet parle?** can your parrot talk?; **le président va p.** the president is about to speak; **laissez-le p.** (*ne l'interrompez pas*) let him speak *or* have his say *or* say what he has to say; (*ne faites pas attention à ce qu'il dit*) let him talk; **elle aime s'écouter p.** she likes the sound of her own voice; **il parle bien/avec style** (*d'un orateur*) he's a good/stylish speaker; **p. haut/bas** to talk *or* speak loudly/quietly; **parlez plus haut** *ou* **plus fort!** speak up!; **il faut p. moins haut** don't speak so loud; **parle plus bas** lower your voice; **p. par signes** to sign, to use sign language; **p. avec les mains** to gesticulate, to talk with one's hands; **p. par gestes** (*des muets*) to use sign language; to gesture **(à qn** to sb); **p. entre ses dents** to mumble; **p. du nez** to talk through one's nose; **parlez-vous sérieusement?** are you serious?, do you really mean it?; **p. pour ne rien dire** to talk for the sake of talking, *Br F* to rabbit on; **p. en l'air** to make empty promises; **p. à tort et à travers** to talk drivel; **parlons franc** let's be frank, let's talk frankly; **généralement parlant** generally speaking; **on parlait très peu au petit déjeuner** there was very little talking over breakfast; **ils parlent très peu entre eux** they don't talk much to each other, they don't do much talking; **elle parle peu, ta sœur** your sister isn't very talkative, your sister doesn't have much to say for herself; **(c'est une) façon de p.** so to speak; **enfin, c'est une façon de p.** well, that's one way of putting it; **elle connaît six langues étrangères, enfin c'est une façon de p.** she can speak six languages more or less; *F* **tu peux (bien) p.!** you can talk!, you're a fine one to talk!; *F* **ses ambitions? parlons-en!** his ambitions? who are you kidding? *or* you've got to be joking!; *F* **tu parles!** you're telling me!, you bet!; (*pas question*) you must be joking!, no way!; *F Iron* **des progrès? tu parles!** progress? you must be joking!; *F Iron* **tu parles comme c'était intéressant!** talk about interesting!; *F* **tu parles d'une occasion/d'un idiot!** talk about an opportunity/an idiot!; *F* **parle pour toi!** speak for yourself!; *F* **tu parles d'un athlète!** some athlete!; **que tu m'aides, tu parles!** you? help me? you must be joking!; **tu parles si je te la prêterai!** no way will I lend it to you!, you must be joking if you think I'll lend it to you!; **tu parles si c'est utile!** a fat lot of use that is!; *F* **voilà qui est parlé!** now you're talking!; **il trouvera à qui p.** he'll get more than he bargained for; **mais je parle, je parle, qu'en pense notre cher ami?** but I'm talking too much *or* I really mustn't go on so much, what do you think about it?; **je parle en toute connaissance de cause** I know what I'm talking about

(b) p. à qn to talk *or* speak to sb; **p. de qn/qch** to talk about sb/sth; **je ne lui parle plus** (*je me suis disputé avec lui*) I'm not talking to him, I'm not on speaking terms with him; **je ne lui parle plus depuis cette date** I haven't said a word to him since; **je l'avais déjà rencontré, mais je ne lui avais jamais parlé** I'd met him but I'd never spoken to him; *F* **moi qui vous parle, je peux vous aider** I'm the one who can help you; **moi qui vous parle, j'ai fait trois guerres** listen, I've been in three wars; **c'est (comme) p. à un mur** it's like talking to a brick wall; *Fig* **cette peinture parle à l'imagination** this painting fires the imagination; *Fig F* **cette peinture ne me parle pas beaucoup/du tout** the painting doesn't do much/does absolutely nothing for me; **il est temps que nous parlions de ta conduite** it's time we had a talk about your behaviour; **je sais de quoi je parle** I know what I'm talking about; **nous avons dû p. de cette question une douzaine de fois!** we must have gone over this point a dozen times!; **son dernier film/livre parle de la guerre** his latest film/book is about the war; **ce tableau parle de …** the subject of the painting is …; **ça parle de quoi?** what's it about?; **on ne parle que de cela** everyone's talking about it, that's all people are talking about; **les journaux ne parlent que de ça** the newspapers are full of it; **faire p. de soi** to become famous; **il a beaucoup fait p. de lui dans les années 50** he was very much to the fore in the 50s; **tu lui en as parlé?** have you talked *or* spoken to him about it?, have you mentioned it to him?; **ne lui en parle surtout pas!** don't mention it to him, don't say a word about it to him; **nous en parlerons après déjeuner** we'll talk about it *or* discuss it after lunch; **toute la ville en parle** the whole town is talking about it, it's the talk of the town; *Fig* **ici, tout me parle de toi** everything here reminds me of you; **il n'en parle jamais** he never talks about *or* refers to *or* mentions it; **n'en parlez à personne** don't tell anyone about it, don't mention it to anyone; *F* **ne m'en parlez pas!** you're telling me!; **les voisins? ne m'en parlez pas!** the neighbours? don't mention them *or* their name to me!; **n'en parlons plus** let's drop the subject, let's say no more about it; **vacances, n'en parlons plus** let's drop the subject of holidays, let's say no more about holidays; **cela ne vaut pas la peine d'en p.** it isn't worth talking about, it's nothing to speak of; **on parle d'organiser une fête** there's some talk about *or* they're talking about (organizing) a party; **elle parle de déménager** she's talking about moving; **sans p. de …** to say nothing of …, not to mention …; **pour ne p. que des …** to mention only the …; **les résultats/faits parlent d'eux-mêmes** the results/facts speak for themselves; **mal p. de qn** to criticize sb, to run sb down; **p. pour/contre qn** to speak for/against sb; **j'entends beaucoup p. de lui** I hear a lot about him; **mon père ne veut pas en entendre p.** my father won't hear of it; **on m'a beaucoup parlé de vous** I've heard a lot about you; **elle ne veut pas entendre p. d'informatique** she doesn't want to hear a word about computers; **il veut p. de moi à son patron** he's going to mention *or* recommend me to his boss; **je n'en ai jamais entendu p.** I've never heard of it/him/her/*etc*

2 *vt* **p. (le) français** to speak French; **p. le langage des sourds-muets** to know (how to use) sign language *or* how to sign; **elle parlait français** she was speaking French *or* talking (in) French; **ici on parle français** (*dans un magasin*) French spoken; **p. chiffons/cuisine/vacances** to talk about *or* discuss clothes/cooking/holidays; **p. affaires/boutique/politique** to talk business/shop/politics

3 se parler *vpr* **(a)** (*d'une langue*) to be spoken; **l'anglais se parle partout** English is spoken everywhere

(b) se p. à soi-même to talk to oneself; **ils ne se parlent plus** (*ils se sont disputés*) they're not speaking *or* talking to each other, they're not on speaking terms; **nous ne nous parlons plus** (*de conjoints*) we've stopped communicating, we don't talk any more; **ils ne s'étaient jamais parlé** they had never spoken (to each other)

parler² *nm* speech; (*régional*) dialect; **il a un p. rude** he's got a coarse way of speaking

parleur, -euse [parlœr, -øz] *n Péj* **beau p.** smooth talker; **c'est un beau p.** he's all talk, *F* he's got the gift of the gab; (*il est enjôleur*) he's a smooth talker, *F* he's got the gift of the gab

parloir [parlwar] *nm* , visiting room; *Rel* parlour, *US* parlor

parlot(t)e [parlɔt] *nf F* gossip, *Br* natter; **faire la p.** to gossip, to chat; **faire la p. avec qn** to have a chat *or Br* natter with sb; **j'en ai assez de ces parlottes** I've had enough of this chitchat *or* gossiping *or* chattering

Parme [parm] *nf* Parma; **jambon de P.** Parma ham

parmesan [parməzɑ̃] *nm Culin* parmesan (cheese)

parmi [parmi] *prép* (①**A64**) among; **p. la foule** among *or* in the crowd; **nous souhaitons vous voir bientôt p. nous** we hope that you'll soon be with us; **c'est une solution p. d'autres** that's one solution; **il figure p. les meilleurs** he's one of the best, he's among the best

Parnasse (le) [ləparnas] *nm* **(a)** *Antiq* Parnassus **(b)** *Hist Littér* the Parnassian School (of poetry)

parnassien, -ienne [parnasjɛ̃, -jɛn] *adj, nm Hist Littér* Parnassian

parodie [parɔdi] *nf* (*pastiche*) parody; (*simulacre*) parody, mockery; **c'est une p. de procès** this trial is a mockery *or F* a joke

parodier [parɔdje] *vt* (*impf, pr sub* **n. parodiions, v. parodiiez**) (*personne, pièce de théâtre*) to parody

parodique [parɔdik] *adj Littér* parodic(al)

parodiste [parɔdist] *n Littér* parodist

paroi [parwa] *nf* **(a)** (*cloison*) (*entre des pièces*) partition (wall) **(b)** (*mur*) (*d'une tente etc, Biol d'une cellule*) wall; (*d'une maison*) (inner) wall; (*d'une falaise*) face; **p. artérielle** artery wall **(c)** (*face intérieure*) (*d'un tunnel*) lining; (*de l'estomac*) lining, wall; (*d'un vase etc*) inner side *or* surface; *Aut* **p. des cylindres** cylinder wall

paroisse [parwas] *nf* **(a)** (*territoire*) parish; **il n'est pas de la p.** he's not from here **(b)** (*habitants*) parishioners

paroissial, -ale, -aux, -ales [parwasjal, -o] *adj* parish;

église paroissiale parish church; **salle paroissiale** church hall

paroissien, -ienne [parwasjɛ̃, -jɛn] **1** *n* parishioner; *Vieilli* **un drôle de p.** a queer bird **2** *nm* (*livre*) prayer book

parole [parɔl] *nf* **(a)** (*mot*) word; **paroles** (*d'une chanson*) lyrics, words; **elle n'a pas dit une p. de la journée** she hasn't said a word *or* spoken all day; **c'est la seule p. qu'il a prononcée** that's all he said; **ce sont ses propres paroles** those are his very words; **assez de paroles! des actes!** that's enough talk(ing)! let's see some action!; **être courageux en paroles** to be all talk, to talk big; **histoire sans paroles** cartoon without a caption; *TV, Cin* short silent film; **p. blessante** hurtful remark; *Iron* **belles paroles** fine words; **ce sont encore de belles paroles, mais …** that's all very well and good but …; **sur ces belles paroles …** on this note …; **voilà une bonne p.!** well said!, *US F* right on!

(b) *Fig* (*engagement*) promise, word; **tenir (sa) p.** to keep one's promise *or* word; **nous vous obligerons à tenir p.** we'll keep you to that *or* to your word; **manquer à sa p.** to break one's promise *or* word; **il est (homme) de p., il a sa p., il n'a qu'une p.** he's a man of his word; **donner sa p. d'honneur à qn que …** to give sb one's word that …, to promise sb that …; **(ma) p. d'honneur!** (on) my word of honour!; **non, je ne l'ai pas vu, p. d'honneur** no, I haven't seen him, I give you my word (of honour); **je vous en donne ma p.** I give you my word, (you can) take my word for it; **je vous crois sur p.** I'll take your word for it; **il a promis de m'aider et je l'ai cru sur p.** he promised to help me and I took him at his word; **c'est votre p. contre la sienne** it's your word against his; **prisonnier sur p.** prisoner on parole

(c) la p. (*faculté de parler*) speech; (*manière, diction*) delivery; **avoir le don de la p.** to be a good speaker; **perdre la p.** to lose the power of speech; *Hum* **tu as perdu l'usage de la p.?** cat got your tongue?; **usage de la p.** power of speech; **si les animaux avaient l'usage de la p.** if animals could speak *or* talk *or* had the power of speech; **il ne lui manque que la p.** (*d'un chien*) the only thing he can't do is talk; **retrouver l'usage de la p.** to be able to speak again; **adresser la p. à qn** to speak to sb, to address sb; **elle ne m'a pas adressé la p. de toute la soirée** she didn't say a word to me *or* speak to me the entire evening; **couper la p. à qn** to interrupt sb, to cut sb short; **prendre la p.** to speak; **je vous rends la p.** (*dans un débat*) the floor is yours again; *Rad, TV* back *or* over to you; *Rad, TV* **nous passons maintenant la p. à …** we now hand over *or* go over to …; **taisez-vous, vous n'avez pas la p.** be quiet, it's not your turn to speak; (*dans un débat*) be quiet, you don't have the floor; **la p. est à M. Renault** Mr Renault will now speak, Mr Renault has the floor; **la p. de Dieu** the word of God

(d) *Cartes* **p.!** pass!; (*au bridge*) no bid!

parolier, -ière [parɔlje, -jɛr] *n* lyric writer, lyricist; (*d'opéra*) librettist

paronyme [parɔnim] *nm* paronym

paronymie [parɔnimi] *nf* paronymy

paroxysme [parɔksism] *nm* (*de colère, violence, plaisir*) height, peak; *Méd* (*d'une maladie*) crisis (point); **être au p. de la joie** to be ecstatically happy; **être au p. de la douleur** to be in agony; **il était au p. de la colère** he was blazingly angry *or Fml* in a paroxysm of rage; **être au p. de la solitude** to be agonizingly lonely; **être au p. de l'angoisse** to be in anguish; **l'incendie était à son p.** the fire was at its height; **cela va pousser la crise à son p.** that's going to take the crisis to breaking point; **atteindre son p.** to reach a climax, to peak *or* climax; **la crise/la douleur a atteint son p.** the crisis/the pain is at its height *or* its worst

parpaing [parpɛ̃] *nm Constr* breeze block

Parque [park] *nf Myth* **les Parques** the Fates

parquer [parke] **1** *vt* (*voiture, Ordinat disque*) to park; (*bétail, moutons*) to pen; (*prisonniers*) to confine, to pack in; **on nous a parqués comme des moutons dans la salle d'attente** we were herded into the waiting room; **des étudiants parqués dans des salles de cours trop petites** students packed into lecture theatres that are too small **2 se parquer** *vpr Aut* to park

parquet [parkɛ] *nm* **(a)** *Jur* public prosecutor's office; **(membres du) p.** public prosecutor and his deputies; **déposer une plainte au p.** to lodge a complaint in court **(b)** *Bourse* **le P.** the floor *or* trading floor, *Am* the pit **(c)** *Constr* (wooden *or* parquet) floor *or* flooring; **lame de p.** floorboard

parquetage [parkətaʒ] *nm* **(a)** (*installation*) laying of wooden *or* parquet floors **(b)** (*sol*) wooden *or* parquet flooring *or* floor

parqueter [parkəte] *vt* **(je parquette, n. parquetons; je parquetterai) p. une pièce** to lay a wooden *or* parquet floor in a room, to parquet a room

parqueterie [parketri, -kətri] *nf* (*installation*) laying of (wooden *or* parquet) floors; (*fabrication*) making of (wooden *or* parquet) floors

parqueteur [parkətœr] *nm* (*fabricant*) parquet maker; (*installateur*) ≈ flooring contractor

parrain [parɛ̃] *nm Rel, Fig Péj* godfather; (*d'un enfant du tiers monde, d'un sportif, d'une manifestation sportive*) sponsor; (*d'un nouveau membre d'un club*) sponsor, proposer; (*d'une fondation*) patron; *Mktg* promoter, sponsor; *Rel* **être p.** to be *or* stand godfather (**de** to); **être le p. d'un navire** to name a ship

parrainage [parɛnaʒ] *nm* (*d'un enfant du tiers monde*) sponsorship, sponsoring; (*d'un nouveau membre*) sponsorship, sponsoring, proposing; (*d'un navire*) naming; (*d'une fondation*) patronage; *Mktg* **p.-partenariat** partnership sponsoring; *Mktg* **p.-télévision** television sponsorship *or* sponsoring

parrainer [parene] *vt Rel* (*enfant*) to act as godfather/ godmother to; (*enfant du tiers monde*) to sponsor; (*nouveau membre*) to sponsor, to propose; (*navire*) to name; (*fondation*) to act as patron of; *Mktg* to sponsor

parricide [parisid] **1** *n* parricide **2** *nm* (*crime*) parricide; **commettre un p.** to commit parricide **3** *adj* parricidal

parsemé [parsəme] *adj* **ciel p. d'étoiles** sky studded *or* spangled with stars; **champ p. de pâquerettes** field dotted with daisies; **texte p. de coquilles** text littered with misprints; **un visage p. de taches de rousseur** a freckled face; **ses affaires sont parsemées sur le sol de sa chambre** his things are scattered *or* strewn all over the floor of his room

parsemer [parsəme] *vt* (*conj like* **semer**) (*de papiers*) to strew (**de** with); (*de sucre*) to sprinkle (**de** with); (*de graines*) to scatter (**de** with); **des feuilles parsemaient le chemin** the path was scattered *or* strewn with leaves, leaves were scattered *or* strewn all over the path

parsi, -ie [parsi] *adj, n Rel* Parsee

part [par] *nf* **(a)** (*portion*) share, part, portion; **diviser un gâteau en parts égales** to divide a cake into equal portions; **combien de parts de gâteau faut-il faire?** how many pieces should I cut (the cake into)?; **une p. de gâteau** a piece of cake; *Fig* **avoir/vouloir sa p. du gâteau** to have/want one's share of the cake *or* slice of the cake; **sa p. des bénéfices** his share of the profits; **elle a eu sa p. de malheurs** she's had her share of misfortune; **professeur à p. entière** fully qualified teacher, *F* fully fledged *or* full-fledged teacher; **ils viennent pour une bonne p. des environs de Lille** a good many of them come from *or* they come very largely from the Lille area; **une grande/petite p. d'entre elles** a large/small proportion *or* number of them; **pour ma p.** for my part, as for me, as far as I am concerned, speaking for myself; *Fig* **prendre qch en bonne/mauvaise p.** to take sth in good/bad part, to take sth the right/wrong way, to take sth well/badly; *Fig* **ne le prends pas en mauvaise p., mais …** don't take this the wrong way but …; *Fig* **comment veux-tu que je ne le prenne pas en mauvaise p.?** how else should I react?

(b) (*participation*) share, part; **avoir p. à qch** to have a hand *or* a share in sth; **avoir p. aux bénéfices** to have a share of the profits; **prendre p. à** to take part in; (*conversation, débat, jeu*) to take part in, to join in; (*honneurs*) to share (in); (*la joie, la douleur, la déception de qn*) to share; **je n'y ai pris aucune p.** I had nothing to do with it, I had no part in it; **faire p. de qch à qn** to inform sb of sth, to tell sb about sth; **qui t'a fait p. de cette information?** who gave you this information?; **je tenais à vous faire p. de notre joie** I wanted to let you know how happy we are; **lettre de faire-p.** (*de mariage, de décès etc*) announcement; **faire la p. de qch** to take sth into account *or* into consideration, to make allowance(s) for sth; **faire la p. des choses** to make allowances

(c) [ⓘB60,B] **nulle p.** nowhere; **je ne les ai vus nulle p.** I couldn't see them anywhere; **nulle p. ailleurs** nowhere else; **elle ne veut partir nulle p. ailleurs** she doesn't want to go anywhere else; **autre p.** somewhere else, *Fml* elsewhere; **quelque p.** somewhere; **de p. et d'autre** here and there; **faire des concessions de p. et d'autre** to make concessions on both sides; **de toute(s) part(s)** on all sides; **de p. en p.** through and through, right through; **d'une p. …, d'autre p. …** on the one hand … on the other hand …

(d) de la p. de from; **je viens de la p. de Madame Dubol** (*c'est elle qui m'envoie*) I've come on behalf of Madame Dubol; (*c'est elle qui m'a parlé de vous*) Madame Dubol gave me your name; **une indiscrétion de la p. de …** an indiscretion on the part of …; *Tél* **c'est de la p. de qui?** who's speaking *or* calling?; **dites-lui de ma p. que …** tell him from me that …; **ce serait bien aimable de votre p.** it would be very kind of you; **cela m'étonne de sa p.** that surprises me, coming from him; **je n'aurais jamais cru ça de sa p.** I would never have believed it of him (**e**) **à p.** apart, separately; **prendre qn à p.** to take sb aside; **il m'en a parlé à p.** he spoke to me about it in private; **mettre de l'argent à p.** to put money by *or* aside; **plaisanterie à p.** joking apart; **c'est une femme à p.** she's an exceptional woman, she's one of a kind; **un cas à p.** a special case, a case apart; **et à p. lui?** who besides him?, who apart from him?; **tu aimes le foot, et à p. ça?** what else do you like apart from *or* besides football?; **je me disais à p. moi que …** I was saying to myself that …; **à p. quelques exceptions/ quelques pages** with a few exceptions/with the exception of a few pages; **à p. quelques fautes d'inattention** apart from *or* except for a few careless mistakes; **à p. cela tout va bien** apart from that everything is fine; *F* **à p. que …** apart from the fact that …

▶ **part**: **p. du feu: faire la p. du feu** to cut one's losses; *Fin* **p. de fondateur** founder's share(s); **la p. du lion** the lion's share; *Com* **p. de marché** market share, share of the market; *Fin* **p. sociale** share of capital, capital share

partage [partaʒ] *nm* (**a**) (*action*) (*d'une fortune, d'un domaine, d'une propriété etc*) division, sharing out; *Pol, Jur* (*d'un pays, de biens*) partition; **faire le p. de qch** to divide sth up, to share sth out; **sans p.** (*amour, engagement etc*) total; **il y a p. d'opinions** opinions are divided; *Géog* **ligne de p. des eaux** watershed, *Am* divide

(**b**) (*lot*) share, portion; **donner qch en p.** to give sth away (*as part of one's fortune*); **recevoir qch en p.** to receive sth (*as part of one's inheritance*); **il leur donna cet argent en p.** he gave them the money (as their share of his fortune); **ce que les hommes reçurent en p. de la nature** nature's gifts to mankind; **la pauvre n'a pas reçu la beauté en p.** the poor girl isn't one of nature's beauties; **la souffrance est le p. du genre humain** suffering is the lot of mankind; **cela fait partie du p. de chacun** it's something we all have to put up with

▶ **partage**: *Ordinat* **p. d'imprimantes** printer sharing; **p. du travail** job-sharing; **p. des voix** distribution of votes; **regardons le p. des voix** let's look at how people voted; **en cas de p. des voix** in the event of a tied vote

partagé [partaʒe] *adj* (**a**) (*incertain*) **elle est partagée** (*elle a du mal à décider, à choisir*) she's torn; **je suis très p. sur ce point** I have very mixed feelings on the subject; **je suis partagée entre la tristesse et la joie** I don't know whether to feel sad or happy; **être p. entre son devoir et ses sentiments** to be torn between one's duty and one's feelings; **les avis sont partagés** opinions are divided (**b**) (*entre plusieurs personnes*) (*convictions, sentiments, impressions*) shared; **amour p.** mutual love; *Ordinat* **travail en temps p.** timesharing

partageable [partaʒabl] *adj* divisible, which can be divided

partager [partaʒe] (**je partageai(s); n. partageons**) **1** *vt* (**a**) (*terrain, groupes etc*) to divide (up); (*biens etc*) to divide (up), to apportion; (*butin etc*) to divide (up), to share (out); **p. son temps entre deux occupations** to divide *or* split one's time between two occupations; **p. qch en deux** to divide sth in two, to halve sth; **le fleuve partage le pays en deux** the river divides *or* splits *or* cuts the country in two; **ce débat partage l'opinion** people are divided *or* split over the issue

(**b**) (*avoir ou mettre en commun*) to share; **nous partageons la même chambre** we share a room; **je partage un appartement avec mon amie** I share a flat *or* I flat-share with a friend; **je ne partage vraiment rien avec ces gens-là** I really have nothing in common with those people; **p. l'avis de qn** to share sb's opinion; **p. la joie/la douleur de qn** to share (in) sb's joy/sorrow; **p. le repas de qn** to share sb's meal, to share a meal with sb; **je lui ai proposé de p. mon croissant** I offered him a share of my croissant

2 *vi* to share; **elle n'aime pas p.** she doesn't like sharing

3 se partager *vpr* (**a**) (*être partagé*) to divide, to be divided; **le gâteau peut se p. en quatre morceaux** the cake can be cut into four portions

(**b**) (*se communiquer*) **ces expériences ne se partagent pas si facilement** it's not very easy to share such experiences; **ça ne se partage pas** it's not something you can share

(**c**) (*faire un partage entre soi*) to share; **ils se sont partagé les bénéfices** they shared *or* divided the profits between them

(**d**) (*partager son temps*) to divide one's time; **elle se partage entre ses enfants et son travail** she divides her time between her children and her work

partageur, -euse [partaʒœr, -øz] *adj* willing to share; **il n'est pas p.** he doesn't like *or* he's not very good at sharing; **on ne lui a jamais appris à être p.** he's never been taught to share

partance [partɑ̃s] *nf* **en p.** (*train*) about to leave; (*avion*) about to take off; (*navire*) about to sail; **en p. pour Bordeaux** bound for Bordeaux; **train en p. pour Londres** train for London, London train

partant[1] [partɑ̃] *adv Litt* consequently, therefore

partant[2], **-ante** [-ɑ̃t] **1** *adj* departing; *F* **je suis p.** you can count me in, I'm game; *F* **êtes-vous toujours p.?** are you still game?, can I/we/*etc* still count you in?; *F* **elle est toujours partante pour aller au restaurant** she's always game for a meal out **2** *n Sp* starter; (*en athlétisme*), *Courses de chevaux* runner, starter

partenaire [partənɛr] *n* partner; **partenaires commerciaux** trading partners; **les partenaires sociaux** employers and trade unions *or US* labor unions, workers and management; **je suis son p. au tennis** I partner him at tennis, I'm his tennis partner

partenariat [partənarja] *nm* partnership; *Mktg* **p. télévision** television tie-in

parterre [partɛr] *nm* (**a**) *F* (*sol*) floor (**b**) (*de fleurs*) (flower) bed; (*plate-bande*) border (**c**) *Th* (*places, le public*) pit

Parthe [part] *nm* **la flèche du P.** the Parthian shot

parthénogénèse [partenɔʒenɛz] *nf Biol* parthenogenesis

parthénogénétique [partenɔʒenetik] *adj Biol* parthenogenetic

Parthénon (le) [ləpartenɔ̃] *nm Antiq* the Parthenon

parti[1] [parti] *nm* (**a**) (*camp*) party, side; **prendre le p. de qn, se mettre** *ou* **se ranger du p. de qn** to take sb's side *or* part, to take sides with sb, to side with sb; **prendre p. pour qn** to side with sb, to take sb's side; **prendre p. contre qn** to side *or* take sides against sb; **je ne prends p. pour ou contre personne** I'm not taking sides; **j'hésite à prendre p.** I'm reluctant to come down on one side or the other; **il faut que tu prennes p. pour ou contre l'un ou l'autre** you're going to have to make your mind up one way or the other; **il ne faut pas que tu prennes p. contre l'un ou l'autre** you mustn't take sides

(**b**) *Pol* party; **le P. (communiste)** the Communist Party; **prendre sa carte du** *ou* **au p.** to join the party, to become a card-carrying member; **un p. unique** a single party

(**c**) (*personne bonne à marier*) **un bon** *ou* **beau p.** a good match *or F* catch

(**d**) (*choix, décision*) **prendre un p.** to decide, to make up one's mind, to come to a decision; **prendre le p. de faire qch** to decide *or* resolve to do sth; **il ne savait quel p. prendre** he didn't know what course to take; **en prendre son p.** to resign oneself, to make the best of it *or F* the best of a bad job

(**e**) (*profit*) **tirer p. de qch** to take advantage of sth, to make (good) use of sth, to turn sth to (good) account; **il n'a jamais cherché à tirer p. de cet avantage** he's never tried to take advantage of it; **tirer le meilleur p. possible de …** to make the best possible use of …

(**f**) **faire un mauvais p. à qn** to treat sb badly; **la presse lui fit un mauvais p.** he got rough treatment from the press

(**g**) **p. pris** (*pour ou contre un concurrent etc*) bias; (*préjugé*) prejudice; **avoir un p. pris contre qch/qn** to be prejudiced about sth/sb, to have a prejudice towards sth/sb; **avoir un p. pris pour qn** to be bia(s)sed in sb's favour; **faire preuve de p. pris** to show bias; **sans p. pris** unbias(s)ed; **sans p. pris, elle est vraiment mauvaise dans son domaine, non?** speaking impartially, she's really bad in her field, isn't she?

parti[2] *adj F* (*ivre*) tipsy, tight; (*sous l'effet de la drogue*) high, spaced out; **il est complètement p.** (*ivre*) he's sozzled; (*sous l'effet de la drogue*) he's totally spaced out

partial, -ale, -aux, -ales [parsjal, -o] *adj* (*personne*) bias(s)ed, *Fml* partial; (*opinion, article*) bias(s)ed, one-sided

partialement [parsjalmɑ̃] *adv* in a bias(s)ed way, with bias

partialité [parsjalite] *nf* bias (**envers** in favour of; **contre** against), *Fml* partiality (**envers** for, to); **il juge toujours avec p.** he's always bia(s)sed in his judgments; **s'exprimer avec p.** to be bia(s)sed

participant, -ante [partisipɑ̃, -ɑ̃t] **1** *adj* participating; **les personnes participantes** the participants, the people taking part **2** *n* (*à une réunion, une action*) participant (**à** in); (*à un concours*) participant, contestant; (*d'un club*) member; *Sp etc* competitor; **les participants à la manifestation** those taking part in the demonstration; **le nombre croissant des participants aux manifestations sportives** the increase in the number of people taking part in sporting activities

participation [partisipasjɔ̃] *nf* (**a**) (*collaboration*) participation (**à** in); (*aux élections*) turnout; (*à un cadeau*) contribution; **cela s'est fait sans ma p.** I didn't take any part in it, I had no part *or* hand in it; **cela s'est fait avec ma p.** I was involved in it; *Cin, TV* **avec la p. de Jean Martin (dans le rôle de …)** with *or* featuring Jean Martin (as …); **nous avons pu réaliser ce film grâce à la p. des Transports Dubout** our thanks to the Dubout Transport Company for helping us make this film; **sans la p. de M. Martin, rien de tout cela**

n'aurait vu le jour none of this would have been possible without the help of Mr Martin; **représentation avec la p. de plusieurs vedettes** show with appearances by several stars; *Scol* **mauvaise p. d'un élève en classe** poor level of participation by a pupil; *Scol* **doit faire des efforts de p.** must try to take part more; **p. aux frais** (financial) contribution; **la p. aux frais est de 200 francs par personne** each person will contribute 200 francs; **taux de p.** level of participation; (*à un marathon, un jeu télévisé*) entries; **taux de p. électorale** voter turnout

(**b**) *Com, Fin* share, interest (**à** in); *Fin* holding

▶ **participation**: **p. active** active participation; **p. aux bénéfices** profit sharing; **p. croisée** cross-holding; **p. majoritaire** major shareholding, majority holding; **p. ouvrière** worker participation; **p. des salariés** employees' holdings

participe [partisip] *nm* [①A44-45; B35-36,l] *Gram* participle

participer [partisipe] *vi* (**a**) **p. à** (*réunion, jeu etc*) to take part in; (*discussion etc*) to take part in, to participate in; (*concours*) to take part in, to enter; (*marathon*) to take part in, to enter, to run in; (*complot etc*) to be involved in, to be (a) party to; (*d'un acteur*) (*spectacle*) to appear in; **p. à la joie/au chagrin de qn** to share (in) sb's joy/sadness; **elle participe activement au projet** she takes an active part in the project

(**b**) **p. à** (*financièrement*) to contribute (money) to

(**c**) **p. à** (*partager*) (*bénéfices etc*) to share in, to have a share in; *Fin* **p. à une entreprise** to have an interest in a business

(**d**) *Fml* **p. de qch** to partake of sth, to have some of the characteristics of sth; **sa théorie participe plus de la philosophie que des sciences exactes** his theory bears more of a resemblance to philosophy than to the exact sciences

participial, -ale, -aux, -ales [partisipjal, -o] *Gram* **1** *adj* (*proposition etc*) participial **2** *nf* **participiale** participial clause

particularisation [partikylarizasjɔ̃] *nf* particularization

particulariser [partikylarize] **1** *vt* (*définir par ses particularités*) to particularize **2 se particulariser** *vpr* to stand out; **il se particularise par ses cheveux roux** his red hair makes him stand out, he stands out by virtue of his red hair; **il s'habille toujours en noir pour se p.** he always wears black to make himself different *or* to make himself stand out

particularisme [partikylarism] *nm Pol, Rel etc* particularism

particularité [partikylarite] *nf* (**a**) (*spécificité*) (*de qch*) particularity, special nature (**b**) (*trait caractéristique*) characteristic, (distinctive) feature; (*qui sort de l'ordinaire*) peculiarity; **la p. de cette imprimante, c'est que ...** what distinguishes this printer (from all the rest) *or* what is special about this printer is that ... (**c**) *Litt* (*détail*) detail, particular

particule [partikyl] *nf* (**a**) (*de poussière, sable etc*), *Nucl* particle; **panneau de particules** particle board; *Nucl* **p. élémentaire** elementary particle; *Nucl* **p. alpha/bêta** alpha/beta particle; *Nucl* **physique des particules** particle physics (**b**) *Gram* particle; **avoir un nom à p.** = to have a double-barrelled name; **dictionnaire des particules nobiliaires** *Br* ≈ Burke's Peerage®

particulier, -ière [partikylje, -jɛr] **1** *adj* (**a**) (*spécial*) particular, special; (*propre*) characteristic (**à** of), peculiar (**à** to); **signes particuliers** (*sur passeport*) distinguishing features; **il a un humour qui lui est p.** he has his own special brand of humour; **sa démarche bien particulière** his own particular way of walking; **la saveur très particulière du citron vert** the very distinctive taste of the lime; **les besoins particuliers à l'enfant** the special *or* specific *or* particular needs of children; **revenir sur un point p.** to come back to a specific *or* particular point

(**b**) (*remarquable*) unusual, exceptional; (*soin, attention, patience, intérêt*) particular; *Péj* (*style, gens, mœurs etc*) peculiar; **le médecin s'est occupé de lui avec une patience toute particulière** the doctor was particularly patient with him; **cas p.** special case; *Hum* **elle, c'est un cas p.** she's a real oddball

(**c**) (*privé*) (*maison, voiture etc*) private; (*compte*) personal; (*salle de bain*) en-suite; **secrétaire p./particulière** private secretary; **cours particuliers, leçons particulières** private lessons, tuition; **j'ai des raisons particulières pour le désirer** I have my own (private *or* particular) reasons *or* I have reasons of my own for wishing it; **à titre p.** in a private capacity; **il a pris la voiture de l'entreprise pour s'en servir à titre p.** he took the company car for his own personal use

(**d**) **en p.** (*spécialement*) in particular, particularly; **ses frères et en p. son frère cadet** his brothers, particularly his younger brother, his brothers and his younger brother in particular; **ce livre en p.** this book in particular

(**e**) (*en privé*) **en p.** privately, in private; **recevoir qn en p.** to see sb privately *or* in private; **demander à être reçu en p.** to ask for a private meeting; **prendre qn en p.** to take sb aside; **je ne pourrai pas m'occuper de vous en p.** I won't be able to deal with you in person

2 *n* (private) individual; *F Péj Vieilli* individual; **simple p.** ordinary person, private citizen; *Vieilli* **que nous veut cette particulière?** what does she *or* that woman want?

3 *nm* **le p. ne l'intéresse pas** he's not interested in details; **aller du p. au général** to go from the specific to the general

particulièrement [partikyljɛrmɑ̃] *adv* (**a**) (*surtout*) particularly, (e)specially; **il aime tous les arts et p. la peinture** he is fond of all the arts, especially painting *or* and painting in particular

(**b**) (*spécialement*) (*intelligent, beau, bête etc*) particularly, outstandingly, exceptionally; **j'attire tout p. votre attention sur cette question** I would particularly like to draw your attention to this question; **cela ne me fait pas p. plaisir** I'm not particularly happy about it; **je sais que cela lui fera p. plaisir** I know it will give him particular pleasure; **pas p.** not particularly

(**c**) (*d'une façon intime*) intimately; **je ne la connais pas p.** I don't know her very *or* particularly well

partie [parti] *nf* (**a**) (*morceau*) (*d'un tout*) part; **certaines parties ne sont pas mauvaises** it's not bad in parts, parts *or* bits of it aren't bad; **une p. de la maison est à louer** part of the house is to let; **une bonne p. du papier est abîmée** a good *or* great deal of the paper is damaged; **une bonne p. du personnel est en grève** a good portion of the staff *or* a good many of the employees are on strike; **une bonne p. des pistes de ski** a good many of the ski runs; **la plus grande p. du chemin** the best part of the way; **la plus grande p. de mon temps/du travail** the greatest part of *or* most of *or* the majority of my time/the work; **il dépense la plus grande p. de son argent** he spends most of *or* the best part of his money; **les parties communes** (*d'une maison*) the communal areas; [①B20,1,b,iv] **les parties du corps** the parts of the body; **les parties génitales,** *Vieilli* **les parties honteuses,** *F* **les parties** the genitals, *F* the private parts, *F* the privates; **une dissertation en trois parties** a dissertation in three parts *or* sections; *Hum* **je ne vais pas te faire une démonstration en trois parties** I won't go into the sordid details; **parties par million** parts per million

(**b**) **en p.** partly, in part; **en p. responsable** partly responsible, responsible in part; **refait en p.** (*appartement*) partly redecorated; **nous avons été en p. remboursés** we got a part refund, we were partially refunded; **j'étais en p. surprise/déçue** I was slightly surprised/disappointed; **en grande** *ou* **majeure p.** largely, to a great extent, for the most part; **ce sont en grande p. des adolescents** most of them are teenagers, they are teenagers for the most part

(**c**) **faire p. de qch** to be *or* form part of sth; **cela fait p. de mes intentions** that's one of the things I intend to do; **cela ne fait pas p. de mes responsabilités** that isn't part of *or* one of my responsibilities; **cela ne fait pas p. des choses qui nous occupent aujourd'hui** that's not one of the things that concern us today; **je ne fais plus p. de ce cercle** I don't belong to this club any longer; **elle ne fait plus p. de nos amis** she is no longer a friend of ours; **faire p. de la famille** to be part of *or* one of the family; **tu fais un peu p. de la famille, maintenant** you're like one of the family now; **je n'ai pas l'impression de faire p. de cette famille** I don't feel like (I'm) part *or* a member of this family; *F* **faire p. des meubles** to be part of the furniture

(**d**) *Fin* **p. double** double entry; **comptabilité en p. simple/double** single-/double-entry book-keeping

(**e**) (*domaine*) field, subject; (*d'une entreprise, une profession*) line, particular branch; **ce n'est pas (de) ma p., je ne suis pas de la p.** that's not (in) my line, that's not up my street

(**f**) *Mus* (*d'une voix, un instrument*) part; **parties d'orchestre** orchestral parts

(**g**) (*fête, réunion*) party; *Fig* **voulez-vous être de la p.?** will you join us?; *Fig* **s'il voulait être de la p., nous pourrions bénéficier de ses conseils** if he was willing to come in with us we could benefit from his advice; **je n'étais pas de la p.** I wasn't invited; **elle ne pouvait pas être de la p. car ...** she couldn't be here *or* join us because ...

(**h**) (*jeu*) (*de cartes, échecs, tennis*) game; (*de golf*) game, round; **faire une p. de cartes/d'échecs** to have *or* play a game of cards/chess; **p. nulle** draw; **gagner la p.** to win the game; **après 30 minutes de jeu, elle avait la p. gagnée** the match was hers *or* she had the match won after 30 minutes; *Fig* **ce n'est que p. remise** we'll do it soon, *Am* let's take a rain check (**i**) (*combat*) struggle; (*pour un point d'honneur*) duel; **p. inégale** uneven struggle

(**j**) *Jur* (*d'un litige, dans un contrat etc*) party; **la p. adverse** the other side; **entendre les avocats des deux parties** to hear counsel on both sides; *Fig* **être juge et p.** to be judge and jury; **p. prenante** party concerned; (*dans un projet*) participant

(**k**) (*adversaire*) opponent; **les parties belligérantes** the belligerent parties, the belligerents; **avoir affaire à forte p.** to have a tough opponent on one's hands

(**l**) **prendre qn à p.** to tell sb off; **il nous a pris à p. en nous reprochant de faire trop de bruit** he told us off for making too much noise

(**m**) **avoir p. liée avec qn** to have joined forces with sb

▶ **partie**: **p. de campagne** picnic; *F* **p. carrée** foursome (*in bed*); **p. de chasse** shooting party; *Jur* **p. civile** plaintiff claiming damages (in criminal case); **se constituer** *ou* **se porter p. civile** to take civil action, to sue; *Gram* **parties du discours** parts of speech; *F* **p. de jambes en l'air** roll in the hay; **ils commencent à m'énerver avec leurs parties de jambes en l'air en pleine nuit** they're beginning to get on my nerves doing it in the middle of the night; **p. de plaisir: ce n'est pas une p. de plaisir!** it's no picnic!, it's not my idea of fun!

partiel, -elle [parsjɛl] **1** *adj* partial; **paiement p.** part payment; *Pol* **élection partielle** by-election; *Univ* **épreuve partielle** class exam **2** *nm Univ* class exam **3** *nf Pol* **partielle** by-election

partiellement [parsjɛlmɑ̃] *adv* (*cuit*) part, partly, partially; (*fini, guéri, satisfait etc*) partly, partially, in part

partir [partir] *vi* (*prp* **partant**; *pp* **parti**; *pr ind* **je pars, il part, n. partons, ils partent**; *pr sub* **je parte**; *impf* **je partais**; *p hist* **je partis**; *fu* **je partirai**) (*aux* **être**) (**a**) (*s'en aller*) to leave, *Fml* to depart; (*commencer un voyage*) to start, to set out, to set off; (*sans destination particulière*) to go off, to go away; (*à pied*) to walk off *or* away; (*d'un bateau*) to leave, to sail; (*d'un avion*) to leave, to take off; *Aut* (*d'un moteur*) to start; (*d'un fusil, un pétard*) to go off; *Euph* (*mourir*) to pass away; **nous partons demain** we're leaving tomorrow; **il est temps que je parte** it's time I went *or* I left *or* I was off; **partez!** get out!; *Sp* go!; **je pars de la maison à huit heures** I leave home at eight o'clock; **l'avion va p. dans une heure** the plane leaves *or* takes off in an hour; **toutes les heures un bus part pour le centre-ville** a bus leaves for the town centre every hour; **le train/bus est parti à temps** the train/bus left *or* pulled out on time; **la voiture est partie** the car drove away *or* off; **p. pour Paris/le Canada/la France/la campagne, p. à Paris/au Canada/en France/à la campagne** to leave *or F* take off for Paris/Canada/France/the country; **p. en vacances** to go (away *or* off) on holiday; **p. en promenade** *ou F* **en balade** to go for a stroll; **p. en excursion** to go off on a trip; **p. faire ses courses** to go and do one's shopping, to go out (to do one's) shopping; **p. chez qn** to go to sb's house *or F* place; **p. au front** to go off to war *or* to fight; *Fig* **p. de ce monde** *ou* **pour un monde meilleur** to die, to depart this life; **p. du bon/mauvais pied** to get off to a good/bad start; **p. à toute vitesse** *ou* **comme une flèche** *ou* **en courant** to shoot *or* speed off; **s'il m'en reparle, je pars à toute vitesse** *ou* **en courant** if he mentions it again, I'll be off like a shot *or* he won't see me for dust; **p. à la renverse** to fall over backwards; **la gifle est partie toute seule** I just slapped him/her automatically; **la réponse est partie trop vite** I/you/*etc* didn't take the time to think, I/you/*etc* should have thought first; **il est parti avec la femme de son meilleur ami** he's gone off with his best friend's wife; **p. gagnant** to think like a winner, to think positive; **p. perdant** to think like a loser; **si tu pars perdant, tu n'as aucune chance de réussir** if you think you won't win then you won't, if you think you'll be beaten you will be; **cette affaire est bien/mal partie** the business has got off to a good/bad start; **elle est mal partie si elle veut faire la paix avec moi** if she wants to make her peace with me she's not going the right way about it; **je voulais lui faire une surprise, mais c'est mal p.** I wanted to give him a surprise but it might not work now; *F* **c'est parti, mon kiki!** here we go!; *Vieilli* **p. d'un éclat de rire, p. à rire** to burst out laughing; **il est parti d'une longue tirade contre les ...** he burst into *or* came out with a long tirade about the ...; **p. de zéro** (*dans sa carrière*) to start from nothing; **je suis parti de zéro et j'ai lu tous les grands écrivains de la littérature anglaise** I started from scratch and read all the English classics; **on est bien partis pour se faire mouiller** we're in for a soaking; **on est partis pour se faire attraper** we're going to get caught, we'll end up getting caught; **il est parti pour être malheureux** he'll end up being unhappy; **nous sommes partis pour une période de prospérité** we're in for a period of prosperity; **quand elle part sur ce sujet, on ne l'arrête pas** once she's off on *or* started on the subject, there's no stopping her; **faire p.** (*fusil*) to fire; (*feux d'artifice*) to let off; (*mine*) to set *or* touch off; (*moteur*) to start; (*courrier*) to send off; **p. c'est mourir un peu** you always leave a bit of yourself *or* your heart behind

(**b**) (*disparaître*) (*de la douleur, d'un bleu*) to go (away), to disappear; (*d'une tache*) to come out *or* off; (*de la peinture, du vernis etc*) to peel, to come off; **la tache ne part pas** the stain won't come off *or* out; **ça part difficilement sur la soie** it's not easy to get it off silk *or* out of silk; **p. au lavage** to wash out; **faire p. une tache** to get a stain out, to remove a stain

(**c**) (*émaner, sortir*) to spring, to emanate, to proceed (**de** from); **mot qui part du cœur** word (which comes) from the heart; **en partant du principe qu'il a raison** assuming that he's right; **si l'on part de l'idée que ...** if we start from the assumption that ...; **j'étais parti sur l'idée que ...** I had assumed that ...; **le chemin part du village** the path starts at the village; **ça partait pourtant d'un bon sentiment** it was for the best of motives; **ça partait des meilleures intentions** he/she/*etc* meant well, it was well meant; **et partant de là ...** on that assumption ...

(**d**) **à p. d'aujourd'hui** from today (onwards); **à p. du 15** from the 15th (onwards), on and after the 15th; **à p. de maintenant** from now on, starting now; **à p. de cette date, les billets ne seront plus valables** tickets will not be valid from that date; **à p. de cette rencontre/discussion, ma vie a changé** my life changed after that meeting/discussion; **à p. de la route, tu peux courir** you can start running when you get to the road; **à p. de la haie, le champ est à lui** his part of the field starts at the hedge; **robes à p. de 200 francs** dresses from 200 francs (upwards); **c'est fait à p. de céréales** it's made from cereals

partisan, -ane [partizɑ̃, -an] **1** *n* (*d'un homme politique*) supporter, follower; (*d'une politique, d'une cause etc*) supporter, advocate **2** *nm Mil* partisan; **guerre de partisans** guer(r)illa warfare **3** *adj* (*esprit*) partisan; **querelles partisanes** sectarian quarrels; **être p. de (faire) qch** to be in favour *or US* favor of (doing) sth; **je suis p. de cette réforme** I'm in favour of *or F* all for the reform

partitif, -ive [partitif, -iv] *adj, nm* [①**B4-5**,C] *Gram* partitive

partition [partisjɔ̃] *nf* (**a**) *Pol* partition, division (**b**) *Mus* score; **p. d'orchestre** full score; **elle joue sans p.** she plays without music

partitionner [partisjɔne] *vt Ordinat* (*disque dur*) to partition

partouse [partuz] *nf très F* orgy

partout [partu] *adv* (**a**) [①**A23**,3,b] everywhere; **chercher qch p.** to look everywhere for sth, to hunt high and low for sth; **p. où** wherever; **p. où je suis allé** wherever I went, everywhere *or* every place I went; **p. ailleurs** everywhere else; **un peu p.** all over (the place); **souffrir de p.** to feel pain all over; **j'ai mal p.** I ache all over; **je ne peux pas être p. à la fois** I can't be everywhere *or* in two places at once (**b**) *Sp* all; **trois buts p.** three (goals) all; *Tennis* **15/30 p.** 15/30 all; *Tennis* **40 p.** deuce

partouze [partuz] *nf très F* orgy

partouzer [partuze] *vi très F* to have an orgy

parturiente [partyrjɑ̃t] *nf Méd* woman in childbirth *or Spéc* parturition

parturition [partyrisjɔ̃] *nf Méd* childbirth, *Spéc* parturition

parure [paryr] *nf* (**a**) (*décoration*) ornament; (*vêtements et bijoux*) costume, finery; *Fig* **une peau éclatante sera votre seule p.** a superb complexion will be your sole adornment (**b**) (*ensemble*) (*de bijoux, de diamants, de lingerie etc*) set; **p. de table/lit** set of table linen/bed linen

parution [parysjɔ̃] *nf* (*d'un livre, d'un article*) appearance, publication; (*d'une revue*) issue; **date de p.** (*d'un livre, article*) date of publication, publication date; (*d'une revue*) date of issue; **p. variable** occasional publication

parvenir [parvənir] *vi* (*conj like* **venir**; *aux* **être**) (**a**) (*arriver*) to arrive; **p. à un endroit** to arrive at *or* reach *or* come to a place; **quand le sang parvient au visage** when the blood reaches the face; **la lettre leur est parvenue** they received the letter, the letter reached them; **votre demande doit nous p. avant le 4** your application must be in *or* reach us by the 4th; **faire p. qch à qn** to send *or* forward sth to sb; **écrits anciens qui sont parvenus jusqu'à nous** ancient writings which have come down to us

(**b**) (*atteindre*) **p. à** (*un grand âge etc*) to attain, to reach; (*la gloire, la célébrité*) to achieve; **p. à faire qch** to manage to do sth, to succeed in doing sth; **je croyais p. à le convaincre** I thought I could convince him; **p. à ses fins** to achieve one's ends

(**c**) (*s'élever socialement*) to succeed *or* get on (in life)

parvenu, -ue [parvəny] *n Péj* upstart, *Fml* parvenu, *f* parvenue

parvis [parvi] *nm Archit* (*devant une église*) square, *Spéc* parvis

pas[1] [pa] *nm* **(a)** (*enjambée*) step, pace; (*plus long*) stride; (*allure*) pace; (*de danse*), *Mil* step; **à chaque p.** at every step; **p. à p.** step by step; (*progresser*) step by step, little by little; **allonger le p.** to lengthen one's stride; **à p. de loup** stealthily; **j'entrai à p. de loup dans la maison** I crept into the house; **aller à p. comptés** to walk with measured tread; **aller** *ou* **avancer** *ou* **marcher à grands p.** to stride along; *Fig* **avancer à grands p.** to make great strides (forward), to make great progress; **marcher à petits p.** (*d'un enfant etc*) to toddle (along); **aller** *ou* **marcher d'un p. lourd/léger/hésitant** to walk heavily/lightly/hesitantly; **faire un p.** to take a step (**vers** towards, in the direction of); *Fig* **elle a fait un p. vers la réussite/son but** she is one step closer to *or* nearer success/her goal; *Fig* **je ne peux pas faire un p. sans que ...** I can't do a thing without ...; *Fig* **faire le(s) premier(s) p.** to take the first step, to make the first move; **faire ses premiers p.** to take one's first steps; *Fig* **il n'y a que le premier p. qui coûte** the longest journey starts with a single step; **faire un p. en avant/en arrière** to step forward/back, to take a step forward/back; *Fig* **un p. en avant et deux p. en arrière** one step forward and two back; *Fig* **elle a fait un grand p. en avant** she has made great progress; **faire deux p. en avant** to take two steps *or* paces forward; **faire les cent p.** to pace up and down; *Fig* **c'est un grand p. de fait** it's a big step forward; *Fig* **il n'y a qu'un p.** it's a short step; *Fig* **et de là à conclure que Martin savait, il n'y a qu'un p.** and it doesn't take much (doing) to work out from that that Martin knew; **j'y vais de ce p.** I'll do it right now *or* right away; **il faut lui en parler, et j'y vais de ce p.** somebody has to talk to him and I'm going to do it right now; **entendre des p.** *ou* **un bruit de p.** to hear footsteps; **je l'ai reconnu à son p.** I knew him by his step, I recognized his footstep; **ils habitent à deux p. d'ici** they live a few yards away *or* (within) a stone's throw from here; **c'est à deux p. d'ici** it's not very far away, it's a stone's throw away; **il était à deux p. de nous** he was a couple of paces *or* feet away from us; **à quelques p. de Piccadilly** just off Piccadilly; **aller d'un bon p.** to step out; **au p.** (*lentement*) at a walking pace; **avancer au p.** (*de la circulation*) to move at a crawl; **roulez au p.** (*sur panneau*) dead slow; **aller** *ou* **rouler au p.** (*en voiture*) to crawl along; **mettre son cheval au p.** to walk one's horse; *Fig* **mettre qn au p.** to bring sb into line; *Mil* **marcher au p.** to march in step *or* in time; **se mettre au p.** *Mil* to get in step; *Fig* to fall in line; **marquer le p.** to mark time; **allez! au p. de course!** go on! run!; *Mil* **changer le p.** to change step; **hâter** *ou* **presser le p.** to quicken one's pace; **ralentir le p.** to slow down; **avoir/prendre le p. sur qn/qch** to have/take precedence over sb/sth; **céder le p. à qn** to give way to sb; **je vais là où me conduisent mes p.** I just follow my nose, I just go where the fancy takes me

(b) (*trace*) footprint; **marcher sur les p. de qn** to follow in sb's wake; *Fig* to follow in sb's footsteps; **arriver sur les p. de qn** to arrive just after sb *or* on sb's heels; **revenir** *ou* **retourner sur ses p.** to retrace one's steps

(c) *Vieilli* (*d'un escalier*) step; **p. de la porte** doorstep; **il est sur le p. de la porte** he's standing on the doorstep

(d) (*passage*) passage; (*de montagne*) (mountain) pass; (*détroit*) strait; *Fig* **tirer qn d'un mauvais p.** to get sb out of a hole *or* fix; *Fig* **sauter le p.** to take the plunge; *Litt* (*mourir*) to die

(e) *Tech* (*d'une vis*) pitch, thread; (*d'une hélice*) pitch; (*entre les sièges d'un avion, d'un car etc*) distance, spacing; *Typ* (*des caractères*) pitch; **sièges au p. de 980 mm** seats 980 mm apart

▶ **pas: p. de bourrée** (*en danse*) pas de bourrée; *Mil* **p. cadencé: marcher au p. cadencé** to march in quick time; **le p. de Calais** the Straits of Dover; **p. de deux** (*en danse*) pas de deux; *Typ* **p. d'écriture** pitch; **p. de gymnastique** jog trot; *Mil* double time; **p. de l'oie** goose step; *Mil* **p. ordinaire** normal pace; *Jur* **p. de porte** (*d'appartement*) key money; *Com* **p. de porte à vendre** business for sale; *Mil* **p. redoublé** double time; **p. de valse** waltz step

pas[2] *adv* [①**A25**,f; **B60**,B] **(a)** not; (*avant un nom*) no; **je ne sais p.** I don't know; **je ne l'ai p. encore vue** I haven't seen her yet; **je n'en dis p. plus** I won't say another word; **je n'en sais p. plus** that's all I know, I don't know any more; **elle ne te le dira p.** she won't tell you; **ça ne te suffit donc p.?** isn't that enough for you?; **prière de ne p. parler au conducteur** (please) do not speak to the driver; **prière de ne p. fumer** no smoking; **il est difficile de ne p. le lui dire** it's difficult not to tell him; **comment va-t-elle? – p. mieux** how is she? – no better; **p. du tout, absolument p.** not at all, absolutely not, *F* not a bit of it; **pourquoi p.?** why not?; **p. moi** not me; **qu'il vienne ou p. cela m'est égal** it's all the same to me whether he comes or not; **alors, c'est d'accord ou p.?** so, is that agreed or not?; **elle est libre, lui p.** *ou* **p. lui** she's free, he isn't; **il a de l'argent, elle p.** *ou* **p. elle** he has money, she hasn't; **elle le peut, moi p.** she can (do it), I can't; **il n'y a p. que ça** that's not all; **p. tant que ça** not that much, not as much as that; **jolie, mais p. tant que ça** pretty but not that pretty; **est-ce que ça a coûté beaucoup? – p. tant que ça** did it cost a lot? – not all that much; **p. si fort, la radio!** turn that radio down!; **p. si vite, quand tu manges/conduis/parles!** slow down when you eat/drive/talk, don't eat/drive/talk so fast; **p. si vite!** (*pas d'emballement*) steady on!, hold on!, not so fast!; **déçu, non p. découragé** disappointed but not discouraged; **ce n'est p. qu'il soit beau, mais il a énormément de charme** he's not exactly handsome *or* he's not what you would call handsome but he's very charming; **ce n'est p. que j'y tienne particulièrement mais ...** it's not that I'm particularly keen on it but ...; **p. d'argent, p. de voiture** no money, no car; **allez, p. d'histoires!** come on, don't make a fuss!; **viendra?, viendra p.?/passera?, passera p.?/***etc* will he come or won't he?, will he or won't he (come)?/will he make it or won't he?, will he or won't he (make it)?/*etc*; *F* **tu es heureuse, p. vrai?** you're happy, aren't you?; *F* **c'est magnifique, p. vrai?** it's wonderful, isn't it?; *F* **c'est p. vrai!** you're kidding!, no kidding!; *F* **c'est p. vrai, la presse a déjà les photos!** I don't believe it, the press has already got hold of the photos!; *F* **connais p.!** I don't know him/her/*etc*; **lui, la propreté, connaît p.!** he doesn't know what the word 'clean' means; *F* **si c'est p. malheureux!** isn't that a shame!; **p. possible!** no! incredible!

(b) (*qualifying an adj*) **des lilas p. fleuris** lilac not yet in bloom; **des fruits p. mûrs** unripe fruit; **p. décidé** undecided; **je déteste les gens p. sûrs d'eux** I hate people who are unsure of themselves

(c) p. un mot ne fut dit not a word was spoken; **p. un n'a réagi** not a single person *or* not one reacted; **fier comme p. un** prouder than anyone; **il fait les omelettes comme p. un** he makes omelettes better than anybody else *or F* like nobody else can; **il est menteur comme p. un** he's a terrible liar

pascal[1], -ale, -aux, -ales [paskal, -o] *adj Rel* (*agneau*) paschal; (*de la fête de Pâques chrétienne*) (*communion etc*) Easter

pascal[2] *nm Phys* pascal; *F* (*billet de 500 francs*) 500 franc note

pascalien, -ienne [paskaljɛ̃, -jɛn] *adj Phil* Pascal's; **la théorie pascalienne du pari** Pascal's wager

pasionaria [pasjɔnarja] *nf Pol* (political) militant

paso-doble [pasɔdɔbl] *nm* paso doble

passable [pasabl] *adj* fair, passable, acceptable; *Scol* **mention p.** ≈ (average to below average) pass; **c'est p.** it's not too bad

passablement [pasabləmɑ̃] *adv* (*ivre, fatigué, déçu etc*) fairly; **dessiner p.** to draw tolerably well; **il a p. voyagé** he's done a bit of travelling, he's travelled a bit

passade [pasad] *nf* (*engouement*) passing fancy, whim; (*liaison courte*) passing fancy

passage [pasaʒ] *nm* **(a)** (*d'une route, d'une rivière*) crossing; (*d'une région*) passing through *or* across; (*d'une porte*) passing through; (*d'un lieu*) passing, going past; *Naut* passage; **p. de frontière** border crossing; *Él* **p. du courant** flow of current; *Aut* **p. de l'huile** oil passage; *Aut* **p. de rapports** *ou* **de vitesses** gear shifting; **p. en douane** customs clearance; **p. à la télévision** (*de spot publicitaire, film*) screening; (*de personne*) screen appearance; **la rivière est de p. facile** the river is easy to cross; **elle guette le p. du facteur** she's watching for *or* on the lookout for the postman; **j'attends le p. de l'autobus** I'm waiting for the bus (to come); **chacun sourit sur son p.** everyone smiles as he goes by; **les hommes se retournaient sur son p.** she made heads turn; **les soldats ont tout détruit sur leur p.** the soldiers destroyed everything in their path *or* everything they came across; **après le p. des sauterelles, il ne restait plus rien dans les champs** there was nothing left in the fields after the locusts had been there; **il y a toujours du p. ici** there are always a lot of people (coming and going) here; **livrer p. (à qn)** to make way (for sb); **lieu de p.** busy area; **de p.** (*client*) passing, *Am* transient; **oiseau de p.** bird of passage; **droit de p.** right of way; **être de p. dans une ville** to be passing through a town; **voyageur de p. à Paris** traveller passing through Paris; **la clientèle de p.,** *F* **le p.** passing *or* casual trade; *Mus* **note de p.** passing note; **j'ai pris un prospectus au p.** I picked up a brochure as I went past; *Fig* **et au p. je te**

ferai remarquer ceci … and incidentally, let me draw your attention to this …; *Naut* **payer son p.** to pay for one's passage; **p. du jour à la nuit** transition *or* change from day to night; **avec le p. du temps** with the passage of time, as the days passed, as time went on *or* by; *Scol* **le p. d'un élève en classe supérieure** the moving up of a child into a higher class; **examen de p.** end-of-year exam, *Am* final exam

(b) (*chemin*) passage, way; (*ruelle*) alley(way); (*magasins*) (shopping) arcade, *Am* mall; *Naut* channel; **se frayer un p.** to force *or* push one's way through; **barrer le p. à qn** to stand in *or* block sb's way, to block sb's passage; *Fig* to stand in sb's way

(c) (*extrait*) (*d'un livre*) passage; (*d'un morceau de musique*) passage, piece

(d) *Météo* **p. nuageux/pluvieux** cloudy/rainy spell

▶ **passage**: *Psy* **p. à l'acte** living out of a fantasy/fantasies; *Aut* **p. d'air de roue** wheel vent; *Ordinat* **p. automatique à la ligne suivante** wordwrap; **p. clouté** pedestrian crossing, ≈ zebra crossing, *Am* crosswalk; *Aut* **p. d'huile** oil gallery, oilway; **p. interdit (au public)** no entry, no thoroughfare; *Rail* **p. à niveau** level crossing, *Am* grade crossing; **p. piéton** *ou* **pour piétons** pedestrian crossing, ≈ zebra crossing, *Am* crosswalk; (*sous-terrain*) pedestrian subway; *Aut* **p. protégé** priority over secondary roads; *Aut* **p. de roue** wheel arch; **p. souterrain** subway, underpass, *Am* underground passage; *F* **p. à tabac** beating up; **p. à vide: avoir un p. à vide** to go through a bad patch; *Sp* **il a eu un p. à vide dans la côte** (*d'un cycliste, d'un coureur*) he lost it on the hill

passager, -ère [pasaʒe, -ɛr] **1** *adj* (*beauté, bonheur*) fleeting, short-lived, transitory; (*douleur, malaise*) momentary; **état p.** passing phase; **pluies passagères** occasional showers; **elle se crut amoureuse de lui, mais ce ne fut que p.** she thought she was in love with him, but it was a passing thing; **ils ont eu une petite brouille passagère** they fell out momentarily

2 *n* (*par bateau, par avion*) passenger; **p. clandestin** stowaway; *Aut* **p. arrière** back-seat passenger; **p. direct** through passenger; **p. en correspondance** transfer passenger; **p. en transit** transit passenger; **p. piéton** *ou* **à pied** foot passenger

passagèrement [pasaʒɛrmɑ̃] *adv* temporarily, for a short while

passant, -ante [pasɑ̃, -ɑ̃t] **1** *adj* (*rue*) busy **2** *n* passer-by **3** *nm* (*de ceinture, jean*) loop; **p. de courroie** strap loop

passation [pasasjɔ̃] *nf Jur* (*d'un accord*) signing; *Compta* (*d'écritures*) entering; *Pol* **p. des pouvoirs** transfer of power; *Fin* **p. d'un dividende** payment of a dividend; *Compta* **p. d'écriture** journal entry; *Fin* **p. de commande** placing of an order

passavant [pasavɑ̃] *nm* **(a)** *Naut* (fore-and-aft) gangway, catwalk **(b)** *Jur* transire; *Com* transire, transit bill

passe[1] [pas] *nf* **(a)** *Fb* pass; *Escrime* pass, thrust; *Escrime, Fig* **p. d'armes** passage of arms; *Fb* **p. en avant/en retrait** forward/back pass

(b) (*manipulation*) **passes magnétiques** mesmeric *or* hypnotic passes

(c) *Métal* (*sur un tour*) cut

(d) (*d'une prostituée*) trick; **c'est combien la p.?** how much is it a time?; **j'ai fait dix passes** I've had ten clients *or* *Br* punters; **maison de p.** brothel; **hôtel de p.** = hotel used by prostitutes and their clients

(e) (*à la roulette*) passe (*any number above 18*)

(f) *Naut* (*chenal*) pass, channel; **p. étroite** narrows

(g) *Fig* **être en p. de faire qch** to be on the way to doing sth; **être dans une mauvaise p.** to be in a fix *or* a tight corner; **tirer qn/se sortir d'une mauvaise p.** to get sb out of/ get out of a tight corner; **elle est dans une bonne p.** everything's going right for her

(h) *Typ* **(main de) p.** overs, over sheets, overplus; **exemplaires de p.** surplus copies, over copies

(i) *Fin* **p. de caisse** cashier error allowance

passe[2] *nm F* (*clé*) skeleton *or* master *or* pass key

passé [pase] **1** *adj* **(a)** (*écoulé*) (*temps*) past; **la semaine/ l'année passée** last week/year; **lundi p.** last Monday; **il est quatre heures passées** it's gone four, it's after four; **il a quarante ans passés** he's over forty; **à quinze ans passés, il ne savait toujours pas lire** he was over fifteen and he still couldn't read; **ça fait deux ans passés que je ne l'ai pas vu** it's over two years now since I saw him; **p. de mode** out of fashion

(b) (*fini*) over; **l'orage/la crise est passé(e)** the storm/the crisis is over; **penser à son enfance/sa beauté passée** to think of one's vanished childhood/beauty

(c) (*éteint, décoloré*) (*couleur, tissu etc*) faded; **mon salon est tout p.** my living room is looking old and drab

2 *nm* **(a) le p.** the past; **dans le p.** in the past; **comme par le p.** as in the past; **tout ça, c'est du p.** that's all in the past; **avoir un p. chargé** *ou* **un lourd p.** to have a shady past; **oublier le p.** to forget the past; **oublions le p.** let bygones be bygones; **avoir honte/être fier de son p.** to be ashamed/ proud of one's past

(b) [①A48-9,11; B28,F,2-4] *Gram* past (tense); **les temps du p.** the past tenses; **p. simple** preterite, past historic; **p. composé** perfect (tense); **au p.** in the past (tense); **p. progressif** past continuous

3 *prép* after; **p. les arbres …** after *or* beyond the trees …; **p. cette date** after this date; **p. la première impression** once *or* after the first impression has worn off

passe-crassane, *pl* **passe-crassanes** [paskrasan] *nf* passe crassane (*type of pear*)

passe-droit, *pl* **passe-droits** *nm* (undeserved) privilege, favour, *Am* favor; **le fils du patron a eu un p., on a fait un p. au fils du patron** the boss's son got preferential treatment

passéisme [paseism] *nm Péj* attachment to the past, backward-looking attitude

passéiste [paseist] *Péj* **1** *adj* backward-looking **2** *n* backward-looking person

passe-lacet, *pl* **passe-lacets** *nm* bodkin; *Fig F* **raide comme un p.** stony broke, *Am* stone broke

passement [pasmɑ̃] *nm* braid, braiding

passementer [pasmɑ̃te] *vt* to braid

passementerie [pasmɑ̃tri] *nf* **(a)** *Com Br* haberdashery trade, *Am* notions trade **(b)** (*accessoire décoratif*) braid

passementier, -ière [pasmɑ̃tje, -jɛr] **1** *adj* (*commerce, industrie*) haberdashery, *Am* notions **2** *n* haberdasher, *Am* dealer in notions

passe-montagne, *pl* **passe-montagnes** *nm* balaclava (helmet)

passe-partout 1 *nm inv* **(a)** (*clef*) skeleton *or* master *or* pass key **(b)** (*scie*) cross-cut saw **(c)** (*cadre*) passe-partout **(d)** *Journ* filler **2** *adj inv* all-purpose; **réponse p.** stock *or* all-purpose reply *or* answer; **tenue p.** all-purpose outfit

passe-passe *nm inv* **tour de p.** (conjuring *or* magic) trick; *Fig* (*tromperie*) trick

passe-plat, *pl* **passe-plats** *nm* serving hatch

passepoil [paspwal] *nm* (*pour vêtements*) piping

passepoiler [paspwale] *vt* (*vêtement*) to pipe; **poche passepoilée** welted pocket

passeport [paspɔr] *nm Admin, Fig* passport; *Naut* passport, sea letter; **les enfants sont sur le p. de leur mère** the children are on their mother's passport

passer [pase] **1** *vi* (*aux* **être**) **(a)** (*se déplacer, circuler*) to pass, to go/come past, *Fml* to proceed; **par où est-il passé?** which way did he go?; **je regardais p. la procession** I was watching the procession go by; **p. sur un pont** to cross (over) a bridge; **il est passé devant le magasin** he went/came by *or* passed (by) the shop; **p. par-dessus/par-dessous qch** to get over/ under sth; **la voiture lui est passée** *ou* **lui a passé sur les jambes** the car ran over his legs; *Fig* **p. sur le corps de qn pour parvenir à qch** to trample all over sb to attain sth; **il faudrait me p. sur le corps pour que je dise oui** if you get me to say yes it'll be over my dead body; **la bouteille est passée** *ou* **a passé de main en main** the bottle was passed round; **faire p. les gâteaux/photos** to hand round *or* pass round the cakes/photos; **p. sur une difficulté** to pass over a difficulty; **passons!** let's leave it at that!; **en passant** in passing; **dire qch en passant** to mention sth in passing; **soit dit en passant** by the way, incidentally

(b) (*aller d'un lieu à un autre, changer*) **p. à l'ennemi** to go over to the enemy; (*d'un espion*) to defect; **le chiffre d'affaires est passé de deux à trois millions** the turnover has gone up from two to three million; **p. à table** to sit up at the table; **passons à table!** would everybody like to sit up at the table, food's ready; **passons à la salle à manger** let's go into the dining room; **il nous fit p. dans le bureau** he showed us into the office; *Scol* **p. dans la classe supérieure** to move up *or* be moved up (a class); *Sp* **p. en seconde division** (*être promu*) to go up to the second division; (*être relégué*) to go down to the second division; **passons à autre chose** let's move on to other matters; (*changeons de sujet*) let's change the subject; *Aut* **p. en seconde/troisième** to go *or* change into second/third (gear); **il est passé du rire aux larmes** his laughter turned to tears

(c) (*se transmettre*) **p. à la postérité** to go down to posterity; **l'héritage est passé à sa fille** the inheritance went to his daughter; **le mot est passé dans l'usage/dans le vocabulaire général** the word passed into common usage/ into the general vocabulary; **c'est passé dans la tradition/ les coutumes** it passed into tradition/custom; **c'est passé dans la langue** it's entered the language; **l'alcool passe très rapidement dans le sang** alcohol goes *or* gets into the bloodstream very quickly

(d) (*traverser*) **la route passe par le village** the road runs *or* goes through the village; **passez par la fenêtre** go through the window; **on est passé par Bourges/la Belgique** we went through *or* via Bourges/Belgium; **mon dîner ne passe pas** my dinner won't go down; *Fig* **ce qu'il m'a dit, ça ne passe pas** what he told me sticks in my throat; **je ne peux pas p.** I can't get by *or* past; **empêcher qn de p.** to stop sb from getting by *or* past; **on ne passe pas** you're not allowed through; **laisser p.** (*lumière, air etc*) to let in; (*personne etc*) to let through; *Fig* **laisser p. une erreur** to overlook a mistake; **faire p. un tuyau à travers le mur** to run a pipe through the wall; **faire p. des gens d'un pays à un autre** to smuggle people out of one country and into another; *Fig* **il est passé par l'université** he did a university course; **il dit tout ce qui lui passe par la tête** he says anything *or* the first thing that comes into his head; **la première chose qui m'est passée** *ou* **m'a passé par la tête** the first thing that came into my head; **une idée m'est passée par la tête ...** an idea has occurred to me ..., I've had an idea ...; **il faut que le café passe très lentement** the coffee has to filter very slowly; *Can* **j'ai passé tout droit** I overslept

(e) *Cin* to be on, to be showing; *Rad, TV* to be on; **cette chanson n'est pas passée à la radio** this song hasn't been played on the radio; **ça ne passe jamais à la radio/télévision** it's never on the radio/on television; **ce film est passé la semaine dernière** the film was on last week; **qu'est-ce qui passe ce soir?** what's on this evening?

(f) (*aller*) **p. chez qn** to call on sb; **p. au pressing/à la boucherie** to call (in) at *or F* pop in at the dry cleaner's/butcher's; **je passerai chez vous ce soir** I'll come round *or* drop round this evening; **je passerai vous prendre vers 18 h** I'll pick you up *or* call for you *or* fetch you at about 6 o'clock; **en passant, je suis entré dire bonjour** I just looked in *or* dropped in on my way past; **il est passé prendre le courrier** he dropped by to pick up the mail; **je ne fais que p.** I'm not stopping; **est-ce que le facteur est passé?** has the postman been?, has the post come?

(g) (*subir*) **elle est passée par des périodes vraiment difficiles** she has been *or* gone through some really difficult periods; **je suis passé par là** I've been through it, it's happened to me; *F* **quand il se met en colère, tout le monde y passe** when he gets angry, everybody bears the brunt of it; *F* **il a failli y p.** he nearly died; **toute sa fortune y est passée** he spent his entire fortune on it

(h) (*disparaître, finir*) to disappear; **la douleur est passée** the pain has gone *or* passed *or* disappeared; **cela fera p. la douleur** that will get rid of the pain; **cela a fait p. mon mal de tête** it has cured my headache; **le vert est passé de mode** green is out of fashion; **le plus dur est passé** the worst is over; **ça lui passera (avec l'âge)** he'll grow out of it; **j'ai été un peu déprimé mais maintenant c'est passé** *ou* **ça m'a passé** I was a bit down but it's over now *or* I've got over it now *or* that's all in the past now; **couleurs qui passent** colours that fade; **le soleil a fait p. les couleurs** the sun faded the colours; **il faut laisser p. l'orage** we must let the storm blow over; **la crise est passée** the crisis is over *or* past; **il fallait bien laisser p. cette période difficile** we just had to get through that difficult period; **laisser p. sa dernière chance** to miss one's last chance; **laisser p. une occasion** to miss *or* let slip an opportunity

(i) (*s'écouler*) to go by, to pass; **des** *ou* **les années ont passé depuis ...** years have passed *or* it's been years since ...; **à mesure que les années passent** as the years go by; **comme le temps passe (vite)!** how time flies!; **faire p. le temps** to pass the time; **tout passe, tout lasse, tout casse** nothing lasts, everything comes to an end

(j) (*être considéré*) **p. pour riche** to be considered rich, to pass for rich; **p. pour avoir fait qch** to be credited with having done sth; **ceci passe pour vrai** everyone believes this is true; **se faire p. pour ...** to pass oneself off as ...; **tu veux me faire p. pour un imbécile ou quoi?** do you want me to be taken for a fool or what?

(k) (*être accepté*) to be accepted; **la loi est passée** the law has been passed *or* has gone through; **passe encore qu'il revienne demain, mais ..., qu'il revienne demain, passe encore mais ...** if he comes back tomorrow that's one thing *or* (that's all) well and good, but ...; **cela peut p./cela ne passe pas** it will/won't do; *F* **cette excuse ne passera pas** that excuse won't wash; **alors, c'est passé, il a accepté?** well, did it work, did he accept?, *F* well, any joy, did he accept?

(l) *Jur* **p. en jugement** to come up for judgment; **l'affaire passera demain/en janvier** the case will be heard tomorrow/in January

(m) *Cartes* **passe!** pass!; (*au bridge*) no bid!

2 *vt* (*aux* **avoir**) **(a)** (*pont, rivière, frontière*) to cross, to go over; (*porte, barrière*) to go through, to pass through; (*douanes*) to go through, to clear; *Fig* (*limite*) to pass, to go beyond, to exceed; **vous avez passé la maison** you've gone past the house; *Fig* **il a passé la soixantaine** he's in his sixties; *Fig* **cela passe les limites** *ou* **les bornes** that's going too far; *Fig* **le vieux ne passera pas l'hiver** the old man won't last the winter (out); **p. son chemin** to carry on one's way

(b) (*transporter*) to convey across, to carry across; **p. des marchandises en fraude** to smuggle goods

(c) (*mettre en circulation*) to pass; **p. des faux billets** to pass forged banknotes

(d) (*donner*) **p. qch à qn** to pass *or* give sth to sb; **voulez-vous me p. l'eau, s'il vous plaît** would you pass me the water, please; **est-ce que tu peux me p. ton stylo?** (*prêter*) could you lend me your pen?; **voulez-vous me p. le volant?** do you want me to drive?; **p. un message (à qn)** to pass on a message (to sb); **il m'a passé son rhume** he gave me his cold, I caught his cold; *Sp* **p. le ballon** to pass the ball; **p. la parole à qn** to hand over to sb; *Tél* **allô, je vous passe Paris/M. Robert** hello, I'm putting you through to Paris/Mr Robert; *Tél* **passez-moi M. Robert** put me through to *or* give me Mr Robert; *Tél* **passez-moi un coup de fil demain** call me tomorrow, give me a call *or Br* a ring tomorrow; **p. son tour** (*en jouant*) to miss one's go; (*exprès*) to pass

(e) (*mettre, faire aller*) **p. l'éponge sur le tableau** to wipe the blackboard; *Fig* **passons l'éponge là-dessus** let's say no more about it; **p. l'aspirateur sur le tapis** to vacuum *or Br* hoover the carpet; **p. un coup de chiffon sur les meubles** to give the furniture a quick dust; **p. sa tête par la fenêtre** to put *or* stick one's head out of the window; **p. sa main dans qch** to put *or* slip one's hand in sth; **je lui ai passé mon bras autour de la taille** I put *or* slipped my arm round his/her waist; **p. une chemise/une robe** to slip on a shirt/a dress; *Aut* **p. la seconde/la troisième** to go into *or* change into second/third (gear); *Naut* **p. une manœuvre** to reeve a rope; **p. sa colère sur qn** to vent one's anger on sb; **p. ses nerfs sur qn** to take it out on sb; **qu'est-ce que je vais lui p.!** I won't half tell him off!, he won't half catch it!; *F* **il s'est fait p. un savon** he got a telling-off; **je l'ai senti p.** I really caught it; **p. un couteau à la meule** to sharpen a knife; **p. un parquet à la cire** to polish a (parquet) floor; **p. des troupes en revue** to inspect *or* review troops

(f) *Cin, TV* (*film*) to show; **p. un disque** to put on *or* play a record; **p. une vidéo** to put on a video; **qu'est-ce qu'ils passent au cinéma cette semaine?** what's on *or* showing at the cinema this week?, what are they showing at the cinema this week?

(g) (*temps, sa vie, vacances*) to spend, to pass; **p. l'après-midi à faire qch** to spend the afternoon doing sth; **la secrétaire qui passe son temps à ne rien faire** the secretary who sits there doing nothing; **on y passera le temps nécessaire** we'll spend as much time on it as necessary; **pour p. le temps** (in order) to while away *or* pass the time

(h) (*pardonner*) to excuse; **on ne lui passe rien** he doesn't get away with anything; **elle lui passe tout** she lets him get away with everything; **passez-moi l'expression** (if you'll) pardon the expression

(i) (*omettre*) to leave out, to omit; **p. qch sous silence** to make no mention of sth; (*fait gênant, secret inavouable*) to keep quiet about sth; **(et) j'en passe, et des meilleures** and that's not all, and that's not the half of it; **il est beau, intelligent, instruit, et j'en passe** he's handsome, intelligent, cultured, and that's not all

(j) *Jur* (*accord, contrat*) to enter into, to sign; **p. un marché** to sign a deal; *Fin* **p. un montant** to post an amount; **p. une commande** to place an order (**de qch à qn** for sth with sb); **p. une loi** to pass a law

(k) *Compta* **p. un article en compte** to post an entry; **p. par pertes et profits** to transfer to profit and loss

(l) **p. un examen** to take *or* sit an exam; **p. le permis de conduire** to take one's driving test

(m) (*liquide*) to strain; (*farine*) to sift; **p. le café** to filter the coffee

(n) (*devenir*) **p. capitaine** to be promoted to captain; **elle est passée maître dans l'art du collage/l'art de mentir** *ou* **du mensonge** she's a past master at collage/lying

3 se passer *vpr* **(a)** [①**B27**,E,2,c] (*se produire, arriver*) to happen; **cela s'est passé il y a dix ans** it happened ten years ago; **que se passe-t-il?, qu'est-ce qui se passe?** what's going on?, what's happening?; **tout s'est bien passé** everything went (off) smoothly; **comment ça c'est passé?** how did it go?; **mon histoire se passe en France** my story is set in France; *F* **ça ne se passera pas comme ça** I won't stand for it (**b**) (*cesser*) (*du temps*) to go by, to pass; **nos ennuis finiront par se p.** our troubles will come to an end eventually; **mon mal de tête se passe** my headache is going

(**c**) **se p. de qn/qch** to do without sb/sth, to dispense with sb/sth; **je m'en passerai** I'll do *or* manage without it/them; **je m'en passerais** I can well do without it/them; **ces faits se passent de commentaires** these facts need no comment

(**d**) **se p. la main dans les cheveux** to run one's fingers through one's hair; **se p. un mouchoir sur le visage** to wipe one's face with a handkerchief

(**e**) **se p. une fantaisie** to indulge a whim

passereau, -eaux [pasro] *nm Orn* passerine; *Arch* (*moineau*) sparrow

passerelle [pasrɛl] *nf* (**a**) (*au-dessus d'une rue, d'un ruisseau*) footbridge (**b**) *Naut* boarding bridge; (*escalier*) boarding steps; (*de ferry*) linkspan, boarding ramp; **p. (de commandement)** bridge; **p. de navigation** navigation bridge (**c**) (*pont incliné*) **p. de débarquement** *ou* **d'embarquement** *Naut* gangway, gangplank; *Av* (*amovible*) steps; (*fixe*) passenger bridge (**d**) *Fig* (*intermédiaire*) link; **ce cours est une p. entre les deux niveaux** this course bridges the two levels (**e**) *Ordinat* **p. (de connexion)** gateway (**avec** to)

passe-temps *nm inv* pastime, hobby

passe-thé *nm inv* tea strainer

passeur, -euse [pasœr, -øz] *n* ferryman, *f* ferrywoman; **il est p.** (*de marchandises*) he's a smuggler; (*de gens*) he smuggles people across the border

passible [pasibl] *adj* liable (**de** to, for); **p. d'une amende** liable to a fine; **p. de l'impôt** liable for tax; **p. de taxe** liable to tax

passif, -ive [pasif, -iv] **1** *adj* passive; **rester p.** to remain passive; *Pol* **faire de la résistance passive** to offer passive resistance; *Gram* **forme passive** passive form; *Com* **dettes passives** liabilities; *Mil* **défense passive** civil defence **2** *nm* (**a**) [①A53-4,16; B36,J] *Gram* passive; **au p.** in the passive (**b**) *Fin* liabilities; **p. exigible** *ou* **circulant** current liabilities

passiflore [pasiflɔr] *nf Bot* passionflower

passing-shot, *pl* **passing-shots** [pasiŋʃɔt] *nm Sp* passing shot; **faire un p.** to play a passing shot

passion [pasjɔ̃] *nf* (**a**) passion; **avoir une p. pour la musique** to have a passion for music; **il a la p. des voitures** he has a passion for cars; **la moto est sa p., la moto est une p. chez lui** he's mad about motorbikes; **vivre une p.** to have a passionate love affair, to be passionately in love; **avec p.** passionately; **aimer qn à la** *ou* **avec p.** to love sb passionately; **parler avec/sans p.** to speak passionately/ dispassionately; **lutter contre ses passions** to struggle against one's passions; **déchaîner les passions** to unleash passions *or* strong emotions

(**b**) *Rel* **la P.** the Passion (of Christ); **la semaine de la P.** Passion Week; *Mus* **la P. selon saint Jean** the St John Passion

passionnant [pasjɔnɑ̃] *adj* (*histoire, livre, film*) gripping, fascinating; (*aventure*) thrilling, exciting; (*personne*) fascinating; **ce boulot n'est vraiment pas très p.** this job's really not very exciting

passionné, -ée [pasjɔne] **1** *adj* passionate; **débat p.** heated *or* impassioned debate; **p. de** *ou* **pour qn/qch** passionately fond of sb/sth **2** *n* enthusiast; **c'est une passionnée de moto(s)** she's mad about motorbikes, she's a motorbike fanatic

passionnel, -elle [pasjɔnɛl] *adj* passionate; **état p.** state of passion, passionate state; **crime p.** crime of passion

passionnément [pasjɔnemɑ̃] *adv* passionately

passionner [pasjɔne] **1** *vt* (**a**) (*inspirer un intérêt très vif à*) (*d'un livre, film etc*) to fascinate, to grip; **ce livre m'a passionné** I found this book fascinating *or* gripping, this book fascinated *or* gripped me; **le sport/travailler avec les enfants la passionne** sport/working with children is a passion with her; **son métier le passionne** he finds his job fascinating (**b**) (*animer*) (*débat*) to inflame **2 se passionner** *vpr* **se p. de** *ou* **pour qch** to be passionately fond of sth, to have a passion for sth

passivement [pasivmɑ̃] *adv* passively

passivité [pasivite] *nf* passivity, passiveness

passoire [paswar] *nf Culin* sieve; (*pour liquides*) strainer; **p. (à légumes)** colander; **sa mémoire est une (vraie) p., il a la tête comme une p.** he's got a memory *or* a head like a sieve; **cette frontière est une vraie p.** this border doesn't keep anyone in or out; *Fb* **ce gardien est une vraie p.!** this goalkeeper is really useless *or* lets everything in

pastel [pastɛl] **1** *nm* (**a**) *Beaux-Arts* pastel; (*dessin*) pastel (drawing); **tableau au p.** picture in pastels (**b**) *Bot* woad **2** *adj inv* pastel; **bleu p.** pastel blue; **tons pastel** pastel shades

pastelliste [pastɛlist] *n Beaux-Arts* pastellist

pastèque [pastɛk] *nf* watermelon; *F* **j'ai la tête comme une p.** my head is buzzing

pasteur [pastœr] *nm* (**a**) *Litt* (*berger*) shepherd; **peuple p.** pastoral people; *Rel* **le bon P.** the Good Shepherd (**b**) *Rel* pastor, minister

pasteurisation [pastœrizasjɔ̃] *nf* pasteurization

pasteuriser [pastœrize] *vt* to pasteurize

pastiche [pastiʃ] *nm* pastiche

pasticher [pastiʃe] *vt* to do a pastiche of

pasticheur, -euse [pastiʃœr, -øz] *n* writer of pastiches

pastille [pastij] *nf* (**a**) (*bonbon, pilule*) (*molle*) pastille; (*dure*) lozenge; **p. contre la toux** cough drop *or Br* sweet; **p. de menthe** (pepper)mint; **p. pour purifier l'eau** water sterilizing tablet (**b**) (*motif*) circle

pastis [pastis] *nm* (**a**) (*boisson*) pastis (**b**) *Fig F* **être dans le p.** to be in a fix; **quel p.!** what a mess!

pastoral, -ale, -aux, -ales [pastɔral, -o] **1** *adj* pastoral **2** *nf* **pastorale** *Littér* pastoral; *Mus* pastorale

pastorat [pastɔra] *nm* pastorate

pastoureau, -elle, -eaux, -elles [pasturo, -ɛl] **1** *n Arch, Litt* shepherd lad, *f* shepherd lass **2** *nf* **pastourelle** *Mus* pastourelle; (*danse*) fourth figure of the quadrille

pat [pat] *nm inv Échecs* stalemate; **les Noirs sont p.** Black is stalemated

patachon [pataʃɔ̃] *nm Arg* **mener une vie de p.** to lead a wild life

Patagonie [patagɔni] *nf* Patagonia

patapouf [patapuf] **1** *int* flop! **2** *nm Enf* **gros p.** fat lump

pataquès [patakɛs] *nm* (**a**) (*faute de liaison*) incorrect liaison (**b**) (*faute de langage*) serious mistake (*in pronunciation etc*) (**c**) *F* (*gaffe*) boo-boo, *Br* boob

patata [patata] *int voir* **patati**

patate [patat] *nf* (**a**) *F* (*pomme de terre*) spud; *Fig* (*imbécile*) clot, idiot; **la corvée de patates** peeling the spuds; *Mil* spud-bashing; *Fig* **en avoir gros sur la p.** to be down in the mouth *or* down in the dumps (**b**) **p. (douce)** sweet potato (**c**) *Math* = set diagram

patati [patati] *int F* **et p. et patata** and so on and so forth

patatras [patatra] *int F* crash!

pataud, -aude [pato, -od] **1** *nm* (*chiot*) puppy with big paws **2** *n Vieilli* lump **3** *adj F* (*personne*) lumpish, clumsy; (*apparence, démarche*) clumsy, awkward

pataugas® [patogas] *nm* = canvas walking shoe

pataugeoire [patoʒwar] *nf* paddling pool

patauger [patoʒe] *vi* (**je pataugeai(s)**; **n. pataugeons**) (*dans la boue*) to squelch; (*dans l'eau*) to paddle; *Fig F* (*s'embrouiller*) (*en parlant, dans une situation, en maths etc*) to flounder

patch [patʃ] *nm* (**a**) *Pharm* patch (*for administering substance through the skin*) (**b**) *Él* jackfield

patchouli [patʃuli] *nm* patchouli

patchwork [patʃwɔrk] *nm* patchwork

pâte [pɑt] *nf* (**a**) *Culin* (*à tarte*) pastry; (*à pain*) dough; (*à gâteau*) mixture; **pâtes (alimentaires)** pasta; **pâtes fraîches** fresh pasta; *Fig* **c'est une bonne p.** he's a good sort; *Fig* **mettre la main à la p.** to lend a hand; *Fig* **être comme un coq en p.** to be in clover; *Fig* **une p. molle** a drip, a wimp (**b**) (*mélange, composition*) **fromage à p. dure/molle** hard/soft cheese (**c**) *Beaux-Arts* paint, colours, *Am* colors; (*plus épais*) paste (**d**) *Typ* (printer's) pie; **caractères tombés en p.** pied type

▸ **pâte**: **p. d'amandes** almond paste; **p. brisée** short(crust) pastry; **p. à choux** choux pastry; **p. à crêpes** pancake batter; **p. dentifrice** toothpaste; **p. feuilletée** flaky pastry; **p. à frire** batter; **p. de fruits** fruit jelly; **p. à modeler** modelling clay; **p. à pain** bread dough; **p. à papier** pulp; **p. sablée** rich shortcrust pastry; **p. à tarte** pastry

pâté [pɑte] *nm* (**a**) *Culin* (*terrine*) pâté; **p. de foie** liver pâté; **p. de campagne** pâté de campagne (*coarse pâté made with pork*); **p. en croûte** = meat pie; **p. impérial** spring roll (**b**) **p. (de sable)** sandpie (**c**) (*tache d'encre*) blot; **faire un p. sur sa copie** to blot one's paper (**d**) (*bloc*) **p. de maisons** block of houses

pâtée [pɑte] *nf* (**a**) (*pour volaille, cochon*) mash; (*pour chat/ chien*) cat/dog food (**b**) *F* (*défaite*) **prendre la p.** to get a thrashing *or* a good hiding; **on leur a mis** *ou* **foutu la p.** they got a thrashing, they were thrashed

patelin [patlɛ̃] **1** *adj Litt Péj* (*personne, manière, air*) unctuous **2** *nm F* village; **quel sale p.!** what a dump!, what a hole!

patelle [patɛl] *nf* (**a**) (*mollusque*) limpet (**b**) *Archéol* patella

patène [patɛn] *nf Rel* paten

patenôtre [patnotr] *nf F* prayer, *Arch* paternoster; *Fig* (*paroles incompréhensibles*) gibberish

patent [patɑ̃] *adj* (**a**) (*clair*) (*erreur, injustice*) obvious, patent; **il est p. que ...** it is patently obvious that ... (**b**) **lettres patentes** letters patent

patentable [patɑ̃tabl] *adj Admin* subject to a licence, requiring a licence

patente [patɑ̃t] *nf* (a) *Com* (*licence*) licence (*to exercise a trade or profession*); (*impôt*) tax (*paid by traders and professional men*); **payer p.** to be duly licensed (b) *Naut* **p. (de santé)** bill of health

patenté [patɑ̃te] *adj Com* licensed; *Fig F* **spécialiste/graphiste p.** recognized specialist/graphic designer; **imbécile/menteur/voleur p.** out-and-out fool/liar/thief

patenter [patɑ̃te] *vt Com* to license

pater [patɛr] *nm inv* (a) *Rel* Paternoster (b) *F* (*père*) old man; **le p.** the old man, *Am* pop, *Br Vieilli, Hum* pater

patère [patɛr] *nf* (coat) peg

paternalisme [patɛrnalism] *nm* paternalism

paternaliste [patɛrnalist] *adj* paternalistic

paterne [patɛrn] *adj Litt* benevolent

paternel, -elle [patɛrnɛl] **1** *adj* paternal; (*protecteur, bienveillant*) (*ton, conseil*) fatherly, kindly; (*attention*) fatherly; **du côté p.** on the father's side; **ma grand-mère paternelle** my grandmother on my father's side; **le domicile p.** (the family) home; **image paternelle** father figure; **l'amour p.** paternal *or* fatherly love **2** *nm F* (*père*) old man; **le p.** the old man, *Br Vieilli, Hum* pater, *Am* pop

paternellement [patɛrnɛlmɑ̃] *adv* paternally, in a fatherly way

paternité [patɛrnite] *nf* paternity, fatherhood; *Jur* **p. légitime/naturelle** legitimate/natural paternity; *Jur* **recherche de p.** affiliation; **il vit mal sa p.** he's finding fatherhood difficult, he's finding it difficult being a father; *Fig* **revendiquer/désavouer la p. d'un livre** to claim/to repudiate authorship of a book; **la p. d'une découverte/d'une invention** the paternity of a discovery/an invention

pâteux, -euse [pɑtø, -øz] *adj* (a) (*substance, crème*) pasty; (*pain*) doughy; **j'ai la langue pâteuse** my tongue is all furry; **j'ai la bouche pâteuse** my mouth is all dry *or F* is like the bottom of a parrot's cage (b) (*trop épais*) (*encre*) thick; *Péj* **style p.** woolly style

pathétique [patetik] **1** *adj* (a) *Litt* (*histoire, situation, ton*) pathetic, touching, moving (b) *Anat* **nerf p.** pathetic nerve **2** *nm Litt* pathos

pathétiquement [patetikmɑ̃] *adv* pathetically, movingly

pathétisme [patetism] *nm Litt* pathos

pathogène [patɔʒɛn] *adj Méd* pathogenic

pathologie [patɔlɔʒi] *nf Méd* pathology

pathologique [patɔlɔʒik] *adj Méd* pathological; **c'est un cas p.** he/she's a pathological case; *F* **c'est p. chez lui** it's a neurosis with him, it's pathological

pathologiquement [patɔlɔʒikmɑ̃] *adj Méd* pathologically

pathologiste [patɔlɔʒist] *n Méd* pathologist

pathos [patos] *nm Litt* pathos

patibulaire [patibylɛr] *adj* (a) (*sinistre*) **avoir une mine p.** to have a sinister look, to look sinister (b) *Vieilli* **fourches patibulaires** gibbet

patiemment [pasjamɑ̃] *adv* patiently

patience[1] [pasjɑ̃s] *nf* (a) patience; **avoir de la p., prendre p.** to be patient, to have patience; **avoir de la p. avec qn** to be patient with sb; **prendre son mal en p.** to suffer patiently; **faire preuve de p.** *ou* **montrer de la p. envers qn** to be patient with sb; **avoir une p. d'ange** to have the patience of a saint *or* of Job; **avec p.** patiently; **ma p. est à bout, je suis à bout de p.** my patience is exhausted *or* is at an end; **ma p. a des limites!** there are limits to my patience!; **s'armer de p.** to be as patient as one can; **(prenez) p.!** be patient!; **perdre p.** to lose (one's) patience; *Prov* **p. et longueur de temps (font plus que force ni que rage)** all things must take their time; **jeu de p.** (jigsaw) puzzle; *Fig* painstaking business

(b) *Cartes* patience, *Am* solitaire; **faire des patiences** to play patience *or Am* solitaire

patience[2] *nf Bot* patience (dock)

patient, -ente [pasjɑ̃, -ɑ̃t] **1** *adj* patient; (*qui endure une épreuve*) long-suffering **2** *n Méd* patient

patienter [pasjɑ̃te] *vi* to wait; **faire p. qn** to ask sb to wait; *Tél* to ask sb to hold; **pour vous faire p. je vais vous passer un film** I'll show you a film while you're waiting *or* to pass the time for you; **p. en lisant le journal** to read the newspaper to while away *or* pass the time

patin [patɛ̃] *nm* (a) (*de patineur*) skate; (*de traîneau*) runner; **patins à glace/à roulettes** ice/roller skates; **nous allons faire du p. à glace** we're going (ice)skating; **sais-tu faire du p. à glace/à roulettes?** can you (ice)skate/(roller)skate? (b) (*sur parquet*) cloth pad; *Arch* (*chaussure*) patten (c) *Tech* shoe; **p. (de frein)** (brake) shoe; *Aut* **p. amortisseur** damping slipper (d) *très F* (*baiser*) French kiss; **rouler un p. à qn** to French kiss sb; **ils n'ont pas arrêté de se rouler des patins toute la soirée** they had their tongues down each other's throats the whole evening

patinage[1] [patinaʒ] *nm* (a) *Sp* skating; **p. artistique** figure skating; **p. de vitesse** speed skating (b) (*d'une roue*) spinning; *Aut* **p. de l'embrayage** clutch slip; **p. des roues** wheel spin

patinage[2] *nm Tech* patination

patine [patin] *nf* patina; *Fig* **la p. du temps** the patina of age *or* time

patiner[1] [patine] *vi* (a) (*faire du patinage*) to skate (b) *Aut* to skid; (*d'une roue*) to spin; (*d'une courroie, de l'embrayage*) to slip; *Fig* (*stagner*) to get nowhere; **ça patine!** it's slippery!; **faire p. l'embrayage** to slip the clutch

patiner[2] **1** *vt Tech* to give a patina to **2** *vpr* **se patiner** to develop a patina

patinette [patinɛt] *nf* scooter

patineur, -euse [patinœr, -øz] *n* skater

patinoire [patinwar] *nf* skating *or* ice rink; **cette route est une vraie p.** this road is like a skating rink *or* an ice rink

patio [patjo] *nm* patio

pâtir [pɑtir] *vi* to suffer (**de** because of); **c'est moi qui vais en p.** I'm the one that's going to suffer

pâtis [pɑti] *nm Agr* grazing ground, pasture

pâtisserie [pɑtisri] *nf* (a) *Culin* (*gâteau*) pastry, (small) cake; (*gâteaux*) pastries (b) (*confection de gâteaux*) pastry-making; **apprendre à faire de la p.** to learn pastry-making; **elle fait de la bonne p.** she makes good cakes (c) (*magasin*) cake shop; **p.-confiserie** confectioner's

pâtissier, -ière [pɑtisje, -jɛr] **1** *n* (*de restaurant*) pastrycook; (*commerçant*) confectioner; **Papa est très bon p.** Dad makes very good cakes **2** *adj* **crème pâtissière** confectioner's custard

patois [patwa] **1** *nm* patois, (local) dialect **2** *adj* patois

patoisant, -ante [patwazɑ̃, -ɑ̃t] **1** *adj* (*personne*) patois- *or* dialect-speaking; **histoire patoisante** story in patois *or* dialect **2** *n* patois *or* dialect speaker

patouiller [patuje] *F* **1** *vi* to flounder **2** *vt* to paw

patraque [patrak] *adj F* (*personne*) out of sorts, under the weather

pâtre [pɑtr] *nm Litt* (*pour bétail*) herdsman; (*pour moutons*) shepherd

patriarcal, -ale, -aux, -ales [patriarkal, -o] *adj* patriarchal

patriarcat [patriarka] *nm* (a) patriarchy (b) *Rel* patriarchate

patriarche [patriarʃ] *nm* patriarch

patricien, -ienne [patrisjɛ̃, -jɛn] *adj, n* patrician

patrie [patri] *nf* (*nation*) homeland; (*localité de naissance*) birthplace; **mère p.** mother country; **mourir pour la p.** to die for one's country; **une seconde p.** my/his/*etc* second home; *Fig* **la p. des arts/de la musique** the cradle of the arts/of music

patrimoine [patrimwan] *nm* heritage; (*d'un ancêtre*) patrimony, inheritance; *Fin* property, wealth, personal assets; (*actif net*) net worth; **faire partie du p.** to be part of our/one's/*etc* heritage; **p. familial** family wealth *or* heritage; *Fig* family heritage; *Banque* **p. social** social assets; **p. artistique** artistic heritage; **p. culturel** cultural heritage; *Biol* **p. héréditaire** *ou* **génétique** genotype

patrimonial, -ale, -aux, -ales [patrimɔnjal, -o] *adj Jur* patrimonial

patriotard, -arde [patrijɔtar, -ard] *Péj* **1** *adj* jingoistic **2** *nm* jingoist

patriote [patrijɔt] **1** *adj* (*personne*) patriotic **2** *n* patriot

patriotique [patrijɔtik] *adj* patriotic

patriotisme [patrijɔtism] *nm* patriotism

patron, -onne [patrɔ̃, -ɔn] **1** *n* (a) (*d'une usine, d'une entreprise, d'un hôtel*) (*personne qui dirige*) boss; (*propriétaire*) owner; *F* **c'est moi le p.!** I'm the boss!, I'm in charge!; **eh la patronne, une bière!** a beer please, landlady!; **être son propre p.** to be one's own boss; **oui, p.** yes, boss, *Am* yes, chief; **il faut en parler au p.** you'll have to speak to the boss about it; *Univ* **p. de thèse** thesis supervisor

(b) (*protecteur*) (*d'une association, des arts, d'un artiste*) patron, *f* patroness; **le p. d'un club** the patron of a club

(c) *Rel* patron saint; **le saint p.** the patron saint; **la patronne des musiciens** the patron saint of musicians

(d) *Méd* (*dans un hôpital universitaire*) senior consultant; **les grands patrons** the leading specialists *or* consultants

2 *nm Couture* pattern; **p. (ajuré)** stencil (plate)

patronage [patrɔnaʒ] *nm* (a) (*parrainage*) patronage; *Com* sponsoring; **placé sous le p. de ...** sponsored by ...; **sous le p. de** under the sponsorship of (b) (*organisation, siège*) youth club; *Fig Péj* **roman de p.** moralizing *or F* preachy novel

patronal, -ale, -aux, -ales [patrɔnal, -o] *adj* (a) (*de l'employeur*) employers', of employers; **syndicat p.** employers' association (b) (*relatif au saint patron*) patronal

patronat [patrɔna] *nm* employers; (*syndicat*) employers' organization, ≈ Confederation of British Industry, CBI; **le p. français** French employers

patronner [patrɔne] *vt* (*hôpital, charité etc*) to support; (*artiste, candidat*) to sponsor; **p. une candidature** to support a candidacy; (*avec aide financière*) to sponsor a candidacy; **p. une entreprise** to back a business

patronnesse [patrɔnɛs] *adj, nf souvent Iron* **(dame) p.** patroness

patronyme [patrɔnim] *nm* patronymic

patronymique [patrɔnimik] *adj* patronymic

patrouille [patruj] *nf Mil etc* patrol; **aller en p.** to go on patrol; **être de p.** to be on patrol; *Av* **p. de chasse** fighter patrol

patrouiller [patruje] *vi* to patrol, to be on patrol

patrouilleur [patrujœr] *nm* soldier/guard/*etc* on patrol; *Av* patrol plane; *Naut* patrol boat

patte [pat] *nf* **(a)** (*de chien, chat etc*) paw; (*d'oiseau*) foot; (*d'insecte*) leg; *F* (*jambe*) pin, leg; *F* (*main*) hand, *Péj* paw; **se dresser sur ses pattes** to sit up and beg; **pattes de devant** forelegs; (*partie griffue*) forepaws; **pattes de derrière** hind legs; (*partie griffue*) back paws; **marcher/se mettre à quatre pattes** to walk/get down on all fours; *Fig* **retomber sur ses pattes** to land on one's feet; *Fig* **tirer dans les pattes de qn** to give sb a hard time; **court/haut sur pattes** short/long-legged; **coup de p.** blow with the paw; *Fig* cutting remark, *F* dig; *F* **pattes (de lapin)** (*cheveux*) sideboards, sideburns; *F* **avoir le coup de p.** (*d'un peintre*) to have talent; *F* **tomber dans les pattes de qn** to fall into sb's clutches; *F* **bas les pattes!** hands off!; *Fig F* **graisser la p. à qn** to grease sb's palm

(b) (*rabat*) (*d'une poche, d'une enveloppe*) flap; (*d'un portefeuille, d'une chaussure*) tongue

(c) (*attache*) clamp, clip, fastening; *Naut* (*d'une ancre*) fluke, palm; (*d'un grappin*) claw

(d) *Couture* (*sur un vêtement*) strap; **pattes d'épaule** shoulder straps

▶ **patte**: **p. blanche**: *Fig* **montrer p. blanche** to show one's credentials; **pattes d'éléphant: pantalon à pattes d'éléphant** bell-bottom(ed) *or* flared trousers; **p. folle: avoir une p. folle** to have a gammy *or Am* gimpy leg; **p. de lapin** rabbit foot; *F* **pattes de mouche(s)** cramped handwriting; **p. de velours**: **faire p. de velours** (*d'un chat*) to draw in its claws; *Fig* to be all sweetness and light

patte-d'oie, *pl* **pattes-d'oie** *nf* **(a)** (*carrefour*) crossroads **(b)** (*ride*) crow's-foot **(c)** *Bot* goosefoot

pattemouille [patmuj] *nf* damp cloth (*for ironing clothes*)

pâturage [pɑtyraʒ] *nm* **(a)** (*action*) grazing; *Jur* (*droit*) grazing rights **(b)** (*endroit*) pasture; **pâturages** pasture land

pâture [pɑtyr] *nf* **(a)** (*nourriture*) (*pour animaux*) food, feed, fodder; *Fig* **p. intellectuelle** food for the mind; *Fig* **donner qn/qch en p. au public** to serve sb/sth up for public consumption **(b)** (*pâturage*) pasture; *Jur* **vaine p.** (right of) common

pâturer [pɑtyre] *vi* (*du bétail*) to graze

paturon [patyrɔ̃] *nm* pastern

paume [pom] *nf* **(a)** *Anat* (*de la main*) palm **(b) (jeu de) p.** real tennis; **jeu de p.** (*terrain*) real-tennis court

paumé, -ée [pome] *F* **1** *adj* (*perdu*) lost; (*dans une explication*) all at sea, lost; *Fig* **il est complètement p.** he hasn't got a clue; **un bled complètement p.** a godforsaken hole **2** *n* (*personne*) loser

paumelle [pomɛl] *nf* **(a)** *Naut* (sailmaker's) palm **(b)** (*des gonds d'une porte*) plate

paumer [pome] *F* **1** *vt* to lose **2 se paumer** *vpr* to get lost

paupérisation [poperizasjɔ̃] *nf* impoverishment

paupériser [poperize] *vt* to impoverish

paupérisme [poperism] *nm* pauperism

paupière [popjɛr] *nf Anat* eyelid

paupiette [popjɛt] *nf Culin* (meat) olive; **paupiettes de veau** veal olives

pause [poz] *nf* **(a)** (*arrêt*) (*dans une activité*) break; (*en parlant*) pause; (*pour déjeuner*) meal break; **faire une p.** to have a break; (*en parlant*) to pause; **p. de midi** lunch break **(b)** *Mus Br* semibreve *or Am* whole-note rest

▶ **pause**: **p.-café** coffee break; **p.-cigarette** break for a cigarette; **p.-repas** meal break

pauvre [povr] **1** *adj* [①B10,D,3] **(a)** (*qui manque de biens*) poor; **p. comme Job** poor as a church mouse; **minerai p. en métal** ore with a low metal content; **p. en vitamine C** with a low vitamin C content; *Aut* **mélange p.** weak mixture

(b) (*malheureux*) poor, unfortunate; **le p. homme!** poor chap!; **p. de moi!** poor old me!; **p. Pierre** poor (old) Pierre; **p. vieux/vieille** poor old thing

(c) (*misérable*) (*robe, meubles etc*) shabby; (*excuse*) paltry, poor, weak; (*sourire*) weak, thin; (*argument*) pathetic, weak, poor; (*orateur*) poor, bad; **c'est un p. type** he's pathetic, *Br très F* he's a poor sod; **p. idiot!** silly fool!; *très F* **p. con!** poor bastard!, *Br* poor sod!

(d) (*stérile*) (*sol*) poor; **des terres pauvres** barren lands

2 *n* poor man/woman; **les pauvres et les riches** the poor and the rich; *Fig* **p. d'esprit** half-wit; *Rel* **les pauvres d'esprit** the poor in spirit; **le p., il n'a pas de chance!** poor chap, he doesn't have much luck!; **la p., elle a encore loupé son examen** poor girl/woman, she's failed her exam again; **mon p.!** you poor thing!

pauvrement [povrəmɑ̃] *adv* poorly; **p. vêtu/meublé** poorly *or* shabbily dressed/furnished

pauvresse [povrɛs] *nf* poor girl/woman

pauvret, -ette [povrɛ, -ɛt] *n F* **le p./la pauvrette** the poor little thing

pauvreté [povrəte] *nf* poverty; *Fig* (*du langage*) poverty, poorness; (*d'un style*) poverty, baldness; *Rel* **vœu de p.** vow of poverty; **p. du sol** poorness of the soil

pavage [pavaʒ] *nm* **(a)** (*action*) paving; (*aux pavés ronds*) cobbling **(b)** (*revêtement*) paving; (*rond*) cobbles, cobblestones

pavane [pavan] *nf Mus* pavan(e)

pavaner (se) [səpavane] *vpr* to strut about

pavé [pave] *n* **(a)** (*morceau de grès*) paving stone; (*rond*) cobblestone; *Journ F* prominent article; *F Péj* (*livre, thèse*) massive tome; *Fig* **un p. dans la mare** a bombshell; *Fig* **avoir un p. sur l'estomac** to have a weight on one's stomach; *Culin* **p. (de bœuf)** slab of beef; *Journ* **p. publicitaire** display ad

(b) (*revêtement*) pavement, paving; (*rond*) cobbles; *Fig* **le p.** (*rues*) the street, the streets; **brûler le p.** to tear along; *Fig* **tenir le haut du p.** to be at the top; *Fig* **céder le haut du p. à qn** to give pride of place to sb; **battre le p.** to loaf about the streets; **être sur le p.** to be on the street; **sous les pavés, la plage** (*slogan dating from the 1968 student riots and referring both to the paving stones thrown at the police and to the ultimately pacifist ideals behind the acts of violence*) *par ex.* la manifestation a été très violente, mais souviens-toi, sous les pavés, la plage

(c) *Ordinat* keypad; *Ordinat* **p. numérique** numeric keypad

(d) *Typ* box

pavement [pavmɑ̃] *nm* paving

paver [pave] *vt* to pave; (*avec des pavés ronds*) to cobble; **cour pavée** paved/cobbled yard; *Fig* **l'enfer est pavé de bonnes intentions** the road to hell is paved with good intentions

paveur [pavœr] *nm* paver

pavillon [pavijɔ̃] *nm* **(a)** (*petite maison*) (small) bungalow; **p. d'entrée** (gate) lodge; **p. de jardin** summerhouse, pavilion; **p. de chasse** hunting *or* shooting lodge

(b) (*d'un hôpital*) pavilion, block, wing

(c) (*partie évasée*) (*d'un klaxon, d'un haut-parleur, d'une sirène*) horn; (*d'un entonnoir*) mouth; *Mus* (*de cuivres*) bell; *Tél* **p. d'écouteur** earpiece; *Anat* **p. de l'oreille** auricle, pinna, external ear

(d) *Naut* (*drapeau*) flag; **hisser** *ou* **arborer son p.** to hoist one's colours; **battre p. britannique** to fly the British flag; **baisser p.** to strike one's flag, to surrender; *Fig* (*céder*) to admit defeat, to give in

(e) *Mil Arch* pavilion, tent

(f) *Aut* roof, roof panel

▶ **pavillon**: **p. de complaisance** flag of convenience; **p. de départ** *ou* **de partance** Blue Peter; **p. de détresse** flag of distress; **p. noir** Jolly Roger; **p. de quarantaine** yellow flag

pavillonnaire [pavijɔnɛr] *adj* **banlieue p.** suburbia

pavois [pavwa] *nm* **(a)** *Naut* (*d'un navire*) bulwark **(b)** *Naut* **petit/grand p.** flags (*for dressing ship*), dressing; **mettre** *ou* **hisser le grand p.** to dress over all **(c)** *Hist* (*grand bouclier*) (body) shield, pavis(e)

pavoiser [pavwaze] **1** *vt* (*décorer*) (*rue, maison*) to deck with flags *or* bunting; *Naut* (*navire*) to dress **2** *vi* (*décorer*) to put out the flags; *Naut* to dress ship; *F* (*se réjouir*) to crow; *F* **il n'y a vraiment pas de quoi p.!** there's nothing to crow about!

pavot [pavo] *nm* (*fleur*) poppy; **p. somnifère** opium poppy; **tête de p.** poppyhead; **graine(s) de p.** poppy seed

payable [pɛjabl] *adj* payable; *Com* **p. à la livraison** payable on delivery; **p. à vue** payable at *or* on sight; **p. comptant** payable in cash; **p. à l'arrivée** payable on arrival; **p. à l'échéance** payable at maturity; **p. à la banque** payable at the bank; **p. à la commande** payable with order

payant [pɛjɑ̃] *adj* (*qui paie*) (*hôte, élève*) paying; (*où il faut payer*) with charge for admission; **spectateur p.** ticket-holder who pays (for admission); **spectacle p.** show with charge for admission; **l'entrée est payante** there is an admission charge *or* a charge for admission; *Fig* **affaire payante** (*bénéfique*) paying proposition; *Fig* **ça s'est avéré p.** it turned out to be worth it

payement [pɛjmɑ̃] *nm* = **paiement**

payer [peje] **(je paye, je paie; je payerai, je paierai) 1** *vt* **(a)** (*somme*) to pay; **p. qn** to pay sb; **payez au porteur** pay to bearer; **tu l'as payé combien pour qu'il fasse tout cela?** how much did you pay him to do all that?; **je ne suis pas payé pour ça** that's not my job; **combien vous a-t-il fait p.?** how much did he charge you?; **elle ne nous/m'/***etc* **a pas fait p. cher** she didn't charge a lot; **p. qn de ses services** to pay sb for his services; **trop peu/trop payé** underpaid/ overpaid; **ce travail est peu payé** this work isn't paid *or* doesn't pay very well; **se faire p.** to get *or* be paid; **il a accepté de nous aider mais il veut se faire p.** he has agreed to help us but he wants paying *or* he wants to be paid; **p. qn de paroles** *ou* **de mots** to put sb off with fine words; **il les méprise et il est payé de retour** he despises them and the feeling is mutual

(b) (*acquitter, régler*) (*dette*) to pay, to settle, to discharge; **p. son loyer** to pay one's *or* the rent; **p. la note** to pay the bill; *Com* **p. un effet** to honour *or US* to honor a bill; **la prime de déplacement ne paie pas tous les frais de voyage** the relocation allowance doesn't cover all the travel costs; **congés payés** paid holidays, *Admin* paid leave; **tu as les congés payés?** do you get holiday pay?

(c) (*acquérir contre de l'argent*) to pay for; **la viande a été payée** the meat's (been) paid for; **combien tu l'as payé?** how much did you pay for it?; **elle ne l'a pas payé très cher** she didn't pay a lot for it; **je ne vous fais pas p. le transport** I'm not charging you for transport; **je le lui ai payé cent francs** I paid him a hundred francs for it; **p. qch à qn** (*lui offrir*) to buy sth for sb; **ses parents lui paient tout ce qu'il veut** his parents pay for everything he wants, his parents buy him anything he wants; **elle va se le faire p. par son mari** she's going to get her husband to buy it for her; **p. le dîner à qn** to treat sb to dinner; **c'est moi qui paie la tournée** it's my round; **payé d'avance** prepaid; **port payé** post(age) paid; *Tél* **réponse payée** answer prepaid

(d) *Fig* (*expier*) to pay for; **il a payé sa témérité de sa vie** he paid for his rashness with his life; **faire p. ses méfaits à qn** to bring sb to account; **vous me le paierez!** you'll pay for it!; *F* **je suis payé pour le savoir** I've learnt (it) the hard way; **il l'a payé cher** he paid dearly for it; **il paya cher son insolence** he paid dearly for his rudeness, his rudeness cost him

2 *vi* **(a)** (*verser de l'argent*) to pay; **vous payez comment?** how are you paying?, how would you like to pay?; **p. cash** *ou* **comptant** to pay cash; **p. en liquide/par carte (de crédit)** to pay (in) cash/by credit card; **p. par chèque** to pay by cheque *or Am* check; **p. de sa poche** to pay out of one's own pocket; **c'est toujours moi qui paie** I'm always the one who pays, it's always me who pays; **p. rubis sur l'ongle** to pay on the nail

(b) p. de ses dernières économies to sacrifice the last of one's savings; *Fig* **p. de sa personne** to put oneself out; **il lui fallut p. d'audace** he had to be bold; **il ne paie pas de mine, mais il est doué** he doesn't look it, but he's very clever, he doesn't look very clever but he is

(c) (*rapporter*) to pay; **le crime ne paie pas** crime doesn't pay; **la traduction en free-lance, ça ne paie pas** freelance translation doesn't pay; **ça a payé** (*cette affaire*) it was worth it

3 se payer *vpr* **(a) voilà monsieur, payez-vous** here you are, take it out of that; *Fig* **se p. de mots** to talk a lot of fine words

(b) (*s'offrir*) **je me suis payé une glace/une semaine de vacances** I treated myself to an ice cream/a week's holiday; **se p. le luxe de sortir deux fois par semaine** to treat oneself to two nights out a week; *Fig* **se p. le culot de partir sans régler ses dettes** to have the nerve to leave without paying one's debts; *Fig* **se p. la tête de qn** to make fun of sb; **je n'aime pas qu'on se paie ma tête** I don't like being made fun of; *F* **se p. un arbre/un mur** to crash into a tree/a wall; *F* **je me suis payé un bon rhume** I got a nasty cold; *F* **s'en p. une tranche** to have a good time

payeur, -euse [pɛjœr, -øz] *n* payer; *Admin* pay clerk; *Mil* paymaster; **mauvais p.** bad payer

pays[1] [pei] *nm* **(a)** [①A27,c,iii] (*nation*) country; **un p. lointain** a faraway country *or* land; **l'Espagne, p. de la corrida** Spain, land of the bullfight; **visiter des p. étrangers** to visit foreign countries *or* lands

(b) (*région*) region, district, locality; **voir du p.** to travel around; **p. du rêve** dreamland; **vous n'êtes donc pas du p.?** so you're not from these parts *or* from round here?; **être en p. de connaissance** to be among friends; (*sur un sujet*) to be on familiar *or* home ground; **vin de p.** *ou* **du p.** local wine; **miel/fruits du p.** locally produced honey/fruit; **c'est un gars/une coutume du p.** he's a local lad/it's a local custom; **revenir au p.** to go back home; **avoir le mal du p.** to be homesick; **p. de montagne(s)/lacs** mountain/lake country; **p. de chasse/pêche** hunting/fishing country

▶ **pays**: **p. de destination** country of destination; **p. exportateur** exporting country; **p. hors communauté** non-EC country; **p. importateur** importing country; **p. industrialisé** industrialized *or* developed country; **p. d'origine** country of origin; **p. de provenance** country of export; **p. riche** affluent country; **p. du tiers-monde** Third World country; **p. en voie de développement** developing country; **p. en voie d'industrialisation** industrializing country

pays[2]**, payse** [pei, peiz] *n Région* fellow-countryman/ -woman; **nous sommes p.** we're from the same area *or* place

paysage [peizaʒ] *nm* **(a)** landscape; (*vue*) scenery; *Fig* (*ensemble*) scene, set-up; **cette région offre de merveilleux paysages** this area has marvellous scenery; *F* **cela fait bien dans le p.** it looks good; **le p. urbain** the urban landscape; *Fig* **le p. audiovisuel français** the broadcasting scene *or* set-up in France; *Fig* **le p. politique** the political scene **(b)** *Beaux-Arts* landscape (painting) **(c)** *Ordinat* **mode p.** landscape mode

paysager, -ère [peizaʒe, -ɛr] *adj* (*jardin, espace*) landscaped; **bureau p.** open-plan office

paysagiste [peizaʒist] *n* **(a)** (*peintre*) landscape painter **(b)** (**jardinier**) **p.** landscape gardener

paysan, -anne [peizɑ̃, -an] **1** *adj* (*vie, famille*) peasant; (*façon de vivre, manières*) rustic, country **2** *n* (small) farmer, *Péj* peasant, *Hum Péj* rustic; *Hist* peasant; *Agr* **p. (propriétaire)** farmer; *Hist* **les paysans** the peasants, the peasantry

paysannerie [peizanri] *nf Hist* peasantry

Pays-Bas (les) [lepeibɑ] *nmpl* the Netherlands

PC [pese] *abrév* **1** *nm* **(a) (parti communiste)** CP **(b) poste de commandement (c)** *Ordinat* PC **2** *nf Fin* (*abrév* **pièce de caisse**) cash voucher

PCC, Pcc [pesese] *abrév* **pour copie conforme**

PCG [peseʒe] *nm Compta* (*abrév* **plan comptable général**) chart of accounts

PCS [peseɛs] (*abrév* **professions et catégories sociales**) socio-economic categories

PCV [peseve] *nm Tél* (*abrév* **payable chez vous**) **(appel en) P.** collect call, *Br* reverse-charge call; **appeler en P., faire un appel en P.** to call collect, *Br* to make a reverse-charge call

pd *Com abrév* **port dû**

PDG [pedeʒe] *nm inv* (*abrév* **Président-directeur général**) chairman and managing director, CEO, chief executive officer, *Am* President

PDM [pedeɛm] *nf* (*abrév* **part de marché**) market share

PDV [pedeve] *nm* (*abrév* **point de vente**) POS

PEA [peøa] *nm Fin* (*abrév* **plan d'épargne en actions**) PEP

péage [peaʒ] *nm* **(a)** (*droit*) toll; **pont à p.** toll bridge; *Hist* **barrière de p.** turnpike, tollgate **(b)** (*installation*) *Aut* tollbooth; *Hist* tollhouse **(c)** *TV* **chaîne (de télévision) à p.** pay channel; **p. à la consommation** pay per view, PPV

péagiste [peaʒist] *n Aut* tollbooth attendant

peau, peaux [po] *nf* **(a)** (*derme*) skin; **avoir la p. blanche/ noire** to be white/black; **une belle p.** a beautiful skin *or* complexion; **avoir la p. grasse/sèche/mixte** to have greasy/ dry/combination skin; **peaux mortes** dead skin; *Fig* **p. de pêche** (soft and) velvety skin; **avoir une p. de pêche** to have (soft and) velvety skin; *Fig* **avoir la p. dure** (*d'une personne*) to have a thick skin, to be thick-skinned; **ce genre de croyances stupides a la p. dure** this sort of stupid belief takes a long time to die out; *Fig* **attraper** *ou* **prendre qn par la p. du cou** *ou* **du dos** *ou F* **des fesses** *ou Vulg* **du cul** to grab *or* take sb by the scruff of the neck; *Fig* **faire p. neuve** (*d'une personne*) to turn over a new leaf; (*d'une entreprise, d'un parti etc*) to get a new image, to modernize itself; **elle n'a que la p. et les os** she's nothing but skin and bone; **je ne voudrais pas être dans sa p.** I wouldn't like to be in his shoes; **se mettre dans la p. de qn** to put oneself in sb's shoes; *Th* **entrer dans la p. d'un personnage** to get right inside a character, to get under the skin of a character; *Fig* **j'ai ça dans la p.** it's in my blood; *Fig F* **avoir qn dans la p.** to be crazy about sb; *F* **se sentir bien/mal dans sa p.** to feel/ not to feel good about oneself; *F* **craindre pour/tenir à sa p.** to fear for/value one's life; *F* **risquer sa p.** to risk one's neck *or* one's life; *F* **sauver sa p.** to save one's skin *or* bacon; *F* **se faire trouer** *ou* **crever la p.** to get bumped off, to get killed; *F* **recevoir** *ou* **prendre douze balles dans la p.** to be shot by firing squad; *F* **faire la p. à qn** to kill sb; *F* **j'aurai sa p.!** I'll get *or* have him!; *F* **la p.!, p. de balle** *ou Vulg* **de zébi!** nothing doing!, no way!; *F* **ce qu'on nous a donné? p. de balle!** what did we get? *Br* bugger all! *or surtout Am* zilch!; *Arg Vieilli* **vieille p.** old hag

(b) (*dépouille*) (*d'un animal*) skin, hide; (*d'un animal à*

fourrure) pelt, fur; **p. de lapin** rabbit skin, cony(skin); **vêtu de peaux de bête** dressed in (animal) skins
(c) (*cuir*) hide, leather; **p. de chamois** shammy (leather), chamois leather; **p. de chevreau** kid; **p. de daim** buckskin; **p. de mouton** sheepskin; **p. de requin** shagreen; **p. de serpent** snakeskin; **p. de veau** calfskin, box calf
(d) (*de fruit*) skin, peel; **enlever la p. d'un fruit** to peel a fruit; *aussi Fig* **p. de banane** banana skin; **p. d'orange** orange peel; *Fig* orange-peel skin
(e) (*pellicule*) (*du lait*) skin
(f) (*autour des ongles*) hangnail
▶ **peau**: *F* **p. d'âne** diploma; *Fig F* **p. de chagrin** diminishing asset; **diminuer comme une p. de chagrin** to dwindle away; *Arg* **p. de vache: c'est une p. de vache** (*cet homme*) he's a bastard; (*cette femme*) she's a cow *or* a bitch

peaucier [posje] *adj, nm Anat* **(muscle) p.** platysma

peaufiner [pofine] *vt* to clean with a shammy leather; *Fig F* (*fignoler*) (*texte*) to polish up, to add the final touches to

Peau-Rouge, *pl* **Peaux-Rouges** *adj, n Vieilli* (*amérindien*) Red Indian, redskin

peausserie [posri] *nf* (a) (*commerce*) skin trade (b) (*marchandise*) leatherwear

peaussier [posje] *nm* skinner, skin dresser

pébroc, pébroque [pebrɔk] *nm F* umbrella, *Br* brolly

pécari [pekari] *nm* peccary

peccadille [pekadij] *nf* peccadillo

pechblende [pɛʃblɛ̃d] *nf Minér* pitchblende

pêche[1] [pɛʃ] **1** *nf* (a) (*fruit*) peach; **p.-abricot, p. jaune** yellow peach; **p. blanche** white peach; **p. Melba** peach Melba (b) *F* (*coup*) clout, blow; **se prendre une p.** to get a clout (c) *F* **se fendre la p.** (*rire*) to split one's sides (laughing); (*s'amuser*) to have a good laugh (d) *F* (*forme*) feeling of being on top of the world; **avoir la p.** to be feeling on top of the world, to be on top form; **ça va te donner la p.** it'll make you feel on top of the world **2** *adj inv Br* peach(-coloured), *US* peach (-colored)

pêche[2] *nf* (a) (*activité*) fishing; **aller à la p.** to go fishing; **p. à la truite** trout fishing; **p. aux crevettes** shrimping; **grande p.** deep-sea fishing; **canne à p.** fishing rod (b) (*produits pêchés*) catch; **faire une heureuse** *ou* **bonne p.** to get a good haul (c) (*endroit*) fishing ground(s); **p. gardée** restricted fishing area; **p. privée** private fishing ground
▶ **pêche**: **p. côtière** coastal *or* inshore fishing; **p. au large** deep-sea fishing; **p. à la ligne** angling; **la p. miraculeuse** *Bible* the miraculous draught of fishes; (*à la fête foraine*) ≈ the lucky dip; **p. à la mouche** fly fishing

péché [peʃe] *nm* sin, *Fml* transgression; **les sept péchés capitaux** the seven deadly sins; **vivre dans le p.** *Rel* to live in a state of sin, to lead a sinful life; *Hum* (*de concubins*) to live in sin; **à tout p. miséricorde** there is no sin that cannot be forgiven; *F* **ce n'est pas un p.!** it's not a crime!
▶ **péché**: **p. de jeunesse** youthful indiscretion; **p. mignon: les éclairs au chocolat, c'est son p. mignon** chocolate éclairs are his weakness; **p. mortel** mortal sin; **le p. originel** original sin

pécher [peʃe] *vi* (**je pèche, n. péchons; je pécherai**) to sin, *Fml* to transgress; **p. par orgueil** to commit the sin of pride; **il pèche par excès de timidité/trop d'humilité** he is excessively shy/humble; **p. par manque de confiance** to lack sufficient confidence; **cette enquête pèche sur un point** the inquiry falls down on one point; **p. par excès/défaut** to exceed/fall short of what is required; **p. par omission** to sin by omission; **p. contre l'honnêteté** to act dishonestly; **p. contre le bon goût** to break the rules of good taste

pêcher[1] [pɛʃe] *nm* peach tree

pêcher[2] **1** *vt* (a) (*truite etc*) to fish for; **p. le corail** to dive for coral; **p. la baleine** to hunt whales, to go whaling (b) *F* (*trouver*) **où avez-vous (été) pêché cela?** where did you pick that up?, where did you get hold of that?; **je ne sais pas où elle a (été) pêché que nous allions nous marier** I don't know where she got hold of the idea that we're getting married **2** *vi* to fish, to go fishing; **p. à la ligne** to go angling; **p. à la mouche** to go fly-fishing; **p. en mer** to go sea fishing; *Fig* **p. en eau trouble** to fish in troubled waters

pêcherie [pɛʃri] *nf* fishery, fishing ground

pécheur, pécheresse [peʃœr, peʃrɛs] *Rel* **1** *n* sinner, *Fml* transgressor **2** *adj* sinful

pêcheur, -euse [pɛʃœr, -øz] **1** *n* fisherman, *f* fisherwoman; **p. à la ligne** angler; **p. de baleines** whaler; **p. de perles** pearl diver **2** *adj* **bateau p.** fishing boat

pécore [pekɔr] *nf F* silly stuck-up girl/woman

pectine [pɛktin] *nf* pectin

pectique [pɛktik] *adj* (*acide*) pectic

pectoral, -ale, -aux, -ales [pɛktɔral, -o] **1** *adj* (*muscle, nageoire etc*) pectoral; *Méd* **sirop p.** expectorant; *Méd* **pâte pectorale** cough lozenge **2** *nm Anat* pectoral muscle; **travailler ses pectoraux** to work on one's pecs

pécule [pekyl] *nm* (a) (*économies*) savings, nest egg (b) *Mil, Naut* gratuity (*on discharge*)

pécuniaire [pekynjɛr] *adj* (*avantage*) financial, *Fml* pecuniary; (*position*) financial

pécuniairement [pekynjɛrmɑ̃] *adv* financially

pédagogie [pedagɔʒi] *nf* pedagogy, pedagogics; **manquer de p.** to lack teaching skills

pédagogique [pedagɔʒik] *adj* (*voyage, sortie etc*) educational; (*méthode*) teaching, *Fml* pedagogical

pédagogiquement [pedagɔʒikmɑ̃] *adv* pedagogically

pédagogue [pedagɔg] *n* educationalist, *Fml, Arch* pedagogue

pédale [pedal] *nf* (a) (*de vélo, de voiture, de piano etc*) pedal; *MecE* (*de tour*) pedal, treadle; **appuyer sur les pédales** (*à vélo*) to pedal hard; **p. d'embrayage** clutch pedal; **p. d'accélérateur** accelerator pedal; **p. de frein** brake pedal; *Fig F* **perdre les pédales** to get all mixed up; (*s'affoler*) to lose one's head, to get in a tizzy (b) *Mus* **(note de) p.** pedal (note); *Fig F* **mettre la p. douce** to go easy (c) *F Péj* (*homosexuel*) queer, poof(ter); **il est de la p.** he's queer

pédaler [pedale] *vi* (a) to pedal (b) *F* **je pédale dans la choucroute** *ou* **la semoule** it's like swimming in treacle

pédaleur, -euse [pedalœr, -øz] *n* pedaller

pédalier [pedalje] *nm* (a) (*de vélo*) crank gear (b) (*clavier d'orgue*) pedal board

pédalo [pedalo] *nm* pedal boat, pedalo

pédant, -ante [pedɑ̃, -ɑ̃t] **1** *n* pedant **2** *adj* pedantic

pédanterie [pedɑ̃tri] *nf* pedantry

pédantesque [pedɑ̃tɛsk] *adj* pedantic

pédantisme [pedɑ̃tism] *nm* pedantry

pédé [pede] *nm F Péj* (*homosexuel*) queer, poof(ter)

pédéraste [pederast] *nm* (a) pederast (b) (*homosexuel*) homosexual

pédérastie [pederasti] *nf* (a) pederasty (b) (*homosexualité*) homosexuality

pédestre [pedɛstr] *adj* (*voyage*) on foot; **chemin p.** footpath; **randonnée p.** hike

pédiatre [pedjatr] *n Méd* paediatrician, *US* pediatrician

pédiatrie [pedjatri] *nf Méd* paediatrics, *US* pediatrics

pedibus [pedibys] *adv F Hum* **p. (cum jambis)** on foot, on shanks's *Br* pony *or Am* mare

pédicelle [pedisɛl] *nm Biol, Bot* pedicel, pedicle

pédicule [pedikyl] *nm Biol, Anat* pedicle, peduncle

pédicure [pedikyr] *n* chiropodist

pédieux, -euse [pedjø, -øz] *adj Anat* pedal

pedigree [pedigre] *nm* (*d'un animal, Fig d'une personne*) pedigree

pédomètre [pedɔmɛtr] *nm* pedometer

pédoncule [pedɔ̃kyl] *nm Biol* peduncle

pédophile [pedɔfil] *adj* paedophile, *US* pedophile

pédophilie [pedɔfili] *nf* paedophilia, *US* pedophilia

pedzouille [pedzuj] *nm F* peasant, country bumpkin

PEE [peøø] *nm, abrév Fin* **(plan d'épargne d'entreprise)** company savings scheme

peeling [piliŋ] *nm* (*gommage*) facial scrub; *Méd* exfoliation treatment; **se faire un p.** to give oneself a facial scrub; *Méd* **se faire faire un p.** to have one's skin peeled

pègre [pɛgr] *nf* **la p.** the underworld

peignage [pɛɲaʒ] *nm Tex* carding, combing

peigne [pɛɲ] *nm* (a) (*démêloir, barrette*) comb; **p. fin** fine-tooth comb; *Fig* **passer qch au p. fin** to go through sth with a fine-tooth comb; **se donner un coup de p.** to run a comb through one's hair, to give one's hair a comb; **sale comme un p.** filthy (b) *Tex* (*pour la laine*) card, comb; (*pour le chanvre*) hackle; **p. de métier à tisser** reed (c) (*mollusque*) pecten, scallop

peigné [peɲe] **1** *adj* (a) (*personne*) combed; **bien p.** (*personne*) well groomed; (*cheveux*) tidy; **mal p.** (*personne*) unkempt; (*cheveux*) tousled (b) *Tex* (*fil*) worsted **2** *nm* worsted (yarn)

peigne-cul, *pl* **peigne-culs** *nm Péj très F* creep

peignée [peɲe] *nf* (a) *Tex* (*de laine, de lin, de chanvre*) cardful (b) *F* (*raclée*) thrashing, good hiding

peigner [peɲe] **1** *vt* (a) (*coiffer*) (*cheveux*) to comb; **p. un enfant** to comb a child's hair; *Fig F* **p. la girafe** to waste one's time (b) *Tex* (*laine*) to card, to comb; (*chanvre*) to hackle **2 se peigner** *vpr* to comb one's hair

peignoir [pɛɲwar] *nm* (a) (*vêtement d'intérieur*) housecoat; (*robe de chambre*) dressing gown; **p. (de bain)** bath robe (b) (*chez le coiffeur*) cape, overall

peinard [pɛnar] *adj F* (*poste, situation*) cushy; **rester p.** to take it *or* things easy; **tiens-toi p.** keep quiet, keep your nose clean; **il est bien p.** he's having an easy time of it

peindre [pɛ̃dr] (*prp* **peignant**; *pp* **peint**; *pr ind* **je peins, il peint, n. peignons**; *impf* **je peignais**; *p hist* **je peignis**; *fu* **je**

peindrai) 1 *vt* to paint; **p. qch en vert** to paint sth green; **p. au pinceau/au rouleau/à la brosse** to paint with a brush/a roller/a brush; **papier peint** wallpaper; *Fig* **elle peint la situation avec justesse** she portrays *or* depicts the situation accurately; *Fig* **p. tout en rose** to paint everything in rosy colours **2** *vi* to paint **3 se peindre** *vpr Fig* **l'innocence se peint sur son visage** innocence is written on his face

peine [pɛn] *nf* **(a)** (*sanction*) punishment, penalty; **p. capitale** capital punishment; **la p. de mort** the death penalty; **condamné à la p. capitale** *ou* **de mort** sentenced to death; **p. de prison** prison sentence; **p. incompressible** sentence without remission; **p. de substitution** non-custodial sentence; **défense d'entrer sous p. d'amende** *ou* **de poursuites** trespassers will be prosecuted; **pour la** *ou* **ta p., tu vas descendre la poubelle** (just) for that you can take the bin down

(b) (*chagrin*) sorrow, sadness; (*tourment*) distress; **j'ai beaucoup de p.** I feel very upset, I'm very distressed; **faire de la p. à qn** to upset *or* distress sb, to cause sb distress; **je m'en suis séparé avec beaucoup de p.** I was very sorry to part with it; **cela fait p. à voir** it's painful *or* distressing to see; **elle fait p. à voir** she's a pitiful sight; **être dans la p.** to be in distress; **p. de cœur** heartache; **raconter ses peines de cœur à qn** to tell sb about one's troubled love life

(c) (*effort*) trouble, pains; **se donner de la p. pour faire qch** to take trouble *or* pains to do sth; **se donner beaucoup de p. pour faire qch** to go to a lot of trouble *or* take great pains to do sth; **ils se sont donné beaucoup de p. pour leurs enfants** they went to a lot of trouble *or* they really put themselves out for their children; **ils se sont donné beaucoup de p. pour la décoration** they took a lot of trouble with *or* over the decoration; **en vous donnant un peu de p. vous y arriverez** with a little effort you'll manage it; **donnez-vous** *ou* **prenez la p. d'entrer** please come in; **si au moins tu te donnais la p. de lui en parler** if you at least made the effort to talk to him about it; **ne vous donnez pas cette p.** don't bother; **se mettre en p. pour qn/qch** to put oneself out *or* put oneself to a lot of trouble for sb/sth; **c'est p. perdue** it's a waste of time; **elle n'est pas au bout de ses peines** her troubles aren't over yet; **en être pour sa p.** to have nothing to show for one's trouble; **il lui a donné 100 francs pour sa p.** he gave him 100 francs for his trouble; **cela vaut la p. d'essayer** it's worth trying; **cela vaut la p. que tu viennes** it's (well) worth your while coming; **ça ne vaut pas la p. qu'on y aille à trois** it's not worth all three of us going; **cela ne vaut pas la p.** it's not worth it, it's not worth the trouble; **non, ce n'est pas la p.** no, don't bother; **ce n'est pas la p. d'aller voir cette pièce/de lui en parler** it's not worth *or* it's a waste of time going to see that play/talking to him about it; **ce n'est pas la p. de changer de robe** you needn't bother to change *or* it's not worth changing your dress; *Iron* **c'était bien la p. de venir!** we might just as well have stayed at home!; *Iron* **c'était bien la p. que je me dérange!** I'm glad I went to so much trouble!

(d) (*difficulté*) difficulty; **j'ai eu toutes les peines du monde à le trouver** I had a real *or* terrible job finding it; **elle a de la p. à parler** (*après une opération*) she has difficulty speaking, she finds it difficult to speak; **elle a de la p. à en parler** it's difficult for her to talk about it, she finds it difficult to talk about; **j'ai (de la) p. à croire que ... +** *sub* I find it hard to believe that ...; **avoir p. à retenir ses larmes** to have difficulty holding back one's tears; **ne jamais être en p. de trouver une excuse** never to be at a loss for an excuse; **elle serait bien en p. de t'expliquer comment ça marche** she'd be hard put *or* hard pushed to explain *or* she'd have great difficulty explaining to you how it works; **elle n'est pas en p. pour trouver des amis avec qui sortir** she has no trouble *or* difficulty finding friends to go out with; **avec p.** with difficulty; **à grand-p.** with great difficulty; **faire qch sans p.** to do sth without difficulty *or* easily; **l'anglais sans p.** English made easy, English without tears; **cela n'a pas été sans p.** it was no easy matter; **sans p. aucune** without any difficulty *or* trouble

(e) [①B59,12,7] **à p.** hardly, barely, scarcely; **on tient à p. debout tellement il y a de vent!** it's so windy, we can hardly *or* barely *or* scarcely stay on our feet!; **c'est à p. si je le connais** I hardly know him; **il est à p. 3 heures** it's barely 3 o'clock; **à p. étions-nous sortis qu'il se mit à pleuvoir** we had only just gone out when it began to rain, we were scarcely out of the door before it started to rain; **j'arrive à p.** I've only just arrived, I've arrived just this minute; **à p. arrivée, elle se mit à se plaindre** no sooner had she arrived than she began to complain; *Iron F* **à p.!** hardly!, not much!

peiner [pene] **1** *vt* (*qn*) to upset, to sadden, to distress; **cette nouvelle m'a beaucoup peiné** I was very upset *or* saddened by the news; **d'un ton peiné** in a sad tone **2** *vi* to toil, to labour, *Am* to labor; *Aut* (*d'un moteur*) to labour; **il peinait sur son travail** he was toiling at *or* over his work; **p. à marcher** to have trouble *or* difficulty walking

peintre [pɛ̃tr] *nm* **(a) (artiste) p.** painter, artist; **une femme p.** a woman artist **(b)** (*ouvrier, artisan*) **p. en bâtiment(s)** (house) painter; **p.(-)décorateur** painter and decorator; *TV etc* scenic artist **(c)** *Fig* portrayer; **cet auteur est un p. de la société parisienne** this author is a portrayer of *or* portrays Parisian society

peinture [pɛ̃tyr] *nf* **(a)** (*art, action*) painting; **musée de p.** art *or* picture gallery; **faire de la p.** to paint

(b) (*tableau*) painting, picture; *Fig* **p. des mœurs de l'époque** portrayal *or* description of the customs of the period; *Fig* **je ne peux pas le voir en p.** I can't stand the sight of him

(c) (*matière*) paint; **attention p. fraîche!, attention à la p.!** wet paint; **p. à la colle/en détrempe** size/distemper; **p. mate** matt emulsion (paint); **p. brillante** *ou* **laquée** gloss (paint); *Péj* **c'est un vrai pot de p.!** she wears make-up an inch thick!

(d) (*surface peinte*) paintwork; **il faudra refaire les peintures** the paintwork will have to be done; **c'est moi qui ai fait la p. de la cuisine** I did the paintwork in the kitchen

▶ **peinture**: **p. en bâtiments** (house) painting; **p. à l'eau** watercolour *or US* watercolor (painting); **p. figurative** figurative painting; **p. à l'huile** oil painting; **p. au pistolet** spray painting

peinturlurer [pɛ̃tyrlyre] *vt F* (*toile, mur, morceau de papier etc*) to daub (with paint)

péjoratif, -ive [peʒɔratif, -iv] **1** *adj* (*mot, sens*) pejorative; (*remarque, ton*) disparaging **2** *nm* pejorative

péjoration [peʒɔrasjɔ̃] *nf* pejoration

péjorativement [peʒɔrativmɑ̃] *adv* pejoratively

Pékin [pekɛ̃] *nm* Peking, Beijing

pékin [pekɛ̃] *nm* **(a)** *Tex* Pekin (fabric) **(b)** *Mil F* civilian; **être en p.** to be in civvies

pékinois, -oise [pekinwa, -waz] **1** *adj* of/from Peking *or* Beijing **2** *nm* **(a)** (*chien*) pekin(g)ese, *F* peke **(b)** (*dialecte*) Mandarin (Chinese), Pekinese **3** *n* **P.** Pekin(g)ese

pelade [pəlad] *nf Méd* alopecia

pelage [pəlaʒ] *nm* (*d'un animal*) coat, fur

pélagique [pelaʒik] *adj* pelagic, pelagian

pélargonium [pelargɔnjɔm] *nm* pelargonium, *F* geranium

pelé, -ée [pəle] **1** *adj* (*personne, fourrure*) bald; *Fig* (*paysage*) bare; (*tissu*) threadbare **2** *n F* baldie; **il n'y avait que trois pelés et un tondu** there was hardly anyone there

pêle-mêle [pɛlmɛl] **1** *adv* higgledy-piggledy; **tout est entassé p.** everything is piled up higgledy-piggledy *or* any old how; **mettre tout p.** to jumble everything up **2** *nm inv* jumble; (*cadre*) multiple (photo) frame

peler [pəle] **1** *vt* (*légumes, fruit*) to peel, to skin **2 se peler** *vpr* to peel; **la pêche se pèle facilement** peaches peel easily *or* are easy to peel; *Fig F* **on se pèle (de froid)** it's freezing (cold) **3** *vi* (*de la peau etc*) to peel; **j'ai le nez qui pèle** my nose is peeling; *Fig F* **je pèle (de froid)** I'm freezing (cold)

pèlerin, -ine[1] [pɛlrɛ̃, -in] **1** *n* pilgrim **2** *nm* **(a) (requin) p.** basking shark **(b) (faucon) p.** peregrine falcon

pèlerinage [pɛlrinaʒ] *nm* (*action*) pilgrimage; (*lieu*) place of pilgrimage; **faire un p.** to go on a pilgrimage

pèlerine[2] [pɛlrin] *nf* cape; (*à capuche*) hooded cape

pélican [pelikɑ̃] *nm* pelican

pelisse [pəlis] *nf* pelisse

pellagre [pelagr] *nf Méd* pellagra

pelle [pɛl] *nf* (*d'enfant, de jardinier*) spade; (*pour charbon, cendres*) shovel; (*pour céréales, noix etc*) scoop; **ramasser qch à la p.** to shovel sth up; *Fig* **à la p.** by the bucketful; *Fig* **il y en a à la p., on les ramasse à la p.** there's masses *or* loads (of it/them); **remuer/ramasser l'argent à la p.** to be rolling in money/to be raking it in; **ça ne se trouve pas à la p. des mecs comme lui** guys like him are few and far between; *F* **ramasser** *ou* **se prendre une p.** to fall flat on one's face; *F* **rouler une p. à qn** to French kiss sb; **ils étaient en train de se rouler une p.** they had their tongues down each other's throats

▶ **pelle**: **p. à charbon** coal shovel; *Constr etc* **p. mécanique** mechanical shovel; (*drague*) shovel dredger; **p. à ordures** dustpan; **p. à tarte** cake *or* tart slice

pelle-pioche, *pl* **pelles-pioches** *nf* combined pick and shovel

pelletée [pɛlte] *nf* shovelful, spadeful; *Fig F* **une p. d'injures** a stream of insults

pelleter [pɛlte] *vt* **(je pellette** [pɛlt], **n. pelletons; je pelletterai** [pɛltre]) to shovel (up)

pelleterie [pɛltri] *nf* **(a)** (*fourrure*) pelt **(b)** (*confection*) fur making; (*commerce*) fur trade, furriery

pelleteuse [pɛltøz] *nf Constr* mechanical shovel
pelletier, -ière [pɛltje, -jɛr] *n* furrier
pellicule [pelikyl] *nf* **(a)** (*de glace, peinture*) thin layer; (*sur un liquide*) film **(b)** (*enveloppe du raisin*) grape skin **(c)** *Phot* film; **p. en bobine** roll film; **p. inversible** reversal film **(d)** (*dans les cheveux*) **pellicules** dandruff; **avoir des pellicules** to have dandruff; **shampooing contre les pellicules** dandruff shampoo
Péloponnèse (le) [ləpelɔpɔnɛz] *nm* the Peloponnese
pelotage [p(ə)lɔtaʒ] *nm F* petting
pelotari [p(ə)lɔtari] *nm* pelota player
pelote [p(ə)lɔt] *nf* **(a)** (*de laine, de ficelle*) ball; **p. (à épingles)** pincushion; *Fig F* **faire sa p.** to make one's pile; (*aux dépens d'autrui*) to feather one's nest; *Fig* **avoir les nerfs en p.** to be on edge, to be nervy; *Vieilli F* **envoyer qn aux pelotes** to send sb packing **(b)** *Sp* **p. (basque)** pelota
peloter [p(ə)lɔte] *F* **1** *vt* to pet **2 se peloter** *vpr* to pet
peloteur, -euse [p(ə)lɔtœr, -øz] **1** *n* **(a)** *F* **c'est un sacré p.** he's got wandering hands, he can't keep his hands to himself **(b)** *Tex* (*ouvrier*) ball winder **2** *nf Tex* **peloteuse** (*machine*) balling machine
peloton [p(ə)lɔtɔ̃] *nm* **(a)** (*de laine, de ficelle etc*) (small) ball **(b)** (*de gens*) group; (*d'abeilles, de chenilles*) cluster; *Sp* **le p.** the pack, the bunch; **le p. de tête** *Sp* the leaders, the leading bunch, the front pack; *Fig* the front runners, the leaders **(c)** *Mil* (*de cavalerie*) troop; (*de tanks*) platoon
▶ **peloton**: **p. de discipline** punishment squad; **p. d'exécution** firing squad; **p. d'instruction** training unit; **p. de punition** punishment squad
pelotonner [p(ə)lɔtɔne] **1** *vt* (*laine, ficelle etc*) to wind into a ball **2 se pelotonner** *vpr* to curl up; (*pour avoir chaud*) to huddle up; **se p. dans un fauteuil** to curl up in an armchair; **se p. contre la cheminée** to huddle up to the fire; **se p. dans les bras de qn** to snuggle up in sb's arms
pelouse [p(ə)luz] *nf* lawn; *Courses de chevaux* **la p.** the public enclosure
peluche [p(ə)lyʃ] *nf* **(a)** *Tex* plush; **jouet en p.** soft *or* cuddly toy **(b)** (*flocon, poil*) (piece of) fluff; **mon pull est plein de peluches** my sweater is all pilled
peluché [p(ə)lyʃe] *adj* (*tissu*) pilled
pelucher [p(ə)lyʃe] *vi* (*d'un tissu usé*) to pill
pelucheux, -euse [p(ə)lyʃø, -øz] *adj* fluffy
pelure [p(ə)lyr] *nf* **(a)** (*peau*) (*de fruit*) peel, skin; (*de légumes*) peelings; **p. d'oignon** (*vin*) dark rosé wine; *Com* **(papier) p.** flimsy **(b)** *F* (*vêtement*) coat
pelvien, -ienne [pɛlvjɛ̃, -jɛn] *adj Anat* pelvic
pelvis [pɛlvis] *nm Anat* pelvis
pénal, -ale, -aux, -ales [penal, -o] *adj* (*code*) penal; **clause pénale** penalty clause
pénalement [penalmɑ̃] *adv* penally
pénalisation [penalizasjɔ̃] *nf Sp* penalization, penalizing; **point de p.** penalty point
pénaliser [penalize] *vt Sp* to penalize
pénalité [penalite] *nf Jur, Sp etc* (*sanction*) penalty; *Fb* **coup de pied de p.** penalty (kick); **donner le coup de pied de p.** to take the penalty (kick); *Fin* **p. de retard** late payment penalty; (*pour livraison tardive*) late delivery penalty; *Fin* **p. libératoire** full and final penalty payment
penalty, *pl* **penalties** [penalti] *nm Fb* penalty; **point de p.** penalty point; **tirer/marquer/manquer un p.** to take/score/ miss a penalty; **siffler un p.** to award *or* give a penalty
pénates [penat] *nmpl* (*dieux domestiques*) penates; *Fig* **regagner ses p.** to return home
penaud [pəno] *adj* sheepish; **d'un air p.** sheepishly
penchant [pɑ̃ʃɑ̃] *nm* **(a)** (*tendance*) propensity **(pour qch** for sth), tendency; (*préférence*) leaning **(vers** towards), penchant **(vers** for); **p. à faire qch** (*tendance*) tendency to do sth; (*préférence*) inclination to do sth, penchant for doing sth; **un p. pour la boisson** a fondness *or* partiality for drink; **avoir un p. pour qn** to be fond of sb **(b)** *Arch, Litt* (*pente*) slope; **p. de la colline** hillside
penché [pɑ̃ʃe] *adj* (*incliné*) leaning; (*écriture*) sloping, slanting; **la Tour penchée de Pise** the leaning Tower (of Pisa); *Fig* **prendre des airs penchés** to look pensive; **d'un air p.** pensively
pencher [pɑ̃ʃe] **1** *vt* (*assiette, bouilloire, verre etc*) to tilt; **p. la tête en avant/en arrière** to bend *or* lean forward/ backwards; **p. la tête à droite** to lean one's head to the right

2 *vi* (*s'écarter de la position verticale*) to lean (over); **le navire penche sur le côté** the ship is listing; **le tableau penche vers la droite** the picture is tilting to the right; *Fig* **faire p. la balance** to tip the scales; *Fig* **p. vers** *ou* **pour qch** to incline *or* lean towards sth; *Fig* **p. pour une solution** to prefer *or* favour *or US* favor a solution; **il pencherait plutôt pour des vacances en Italie** he would prefer to take his holidays in Italy

3 se pencher *vpr* to lean over, to bend over; **se p. en avant/en arrière/sur le côté** to bend *or* lean forward/ backwards/to the side; **se p. (en** *ou* **au) dehors** to lean out; **se p. à** *ou* **par la fenêtre** to lean out (of) the window; *Fig* **se p. sur un problème/cas** to look into a problem/case
pendable [pɑ̃dabl] *adj* (*coup, histoire*) outrageous; *Arch* (*crime*) for which the penalty is hanging; *Vieilli* **cas p.** reprehensible action; **jouer un tour p. à qn** to play a rotten trick on sb; **ce n'est pas un cas p.!** it's not a hanging matter!
pendaison [pɑ̃dɛzɔ̃] *nf* hanging; **p. de crémaillère** housewarming (party)
pendant[1] [pɑ̃dɑ̃] **1** *adj* **(a)** (*qui pend*) hanging, *Fml* pendent; (*jambes*) dangling; **oreilles pendantes** floppy ears; **le chien le regardait, la langue pendante** the dog looked at him with its tongue hanging out **(b)** (*en attente*) pending **2** *nm* **(a) p. (d'oreille)** drop earring; *Mil* **p. de ceinturon** sword-belt sling, frog **(b)** (*d'un tableau, d'un bibelot etc*) matching piece **(de** to); **ces deux tableaux (se) font p.** these two pictures make a pair
pendant[2] **1** *prép* [①A66; B53] during; **p. l'été** during the summer, in summer; **p. toute ma jeunesse** all through my youth, during the whole of my youth; **restez là p. quelques minutes/un quart d'heure** stay there for a few minutes/a quarter of an hour; **il a été silencieux p. tout le trajet** he was silent throughout the journey *or* for the whole journey; **route bordée d'arbres p. un kilomètre** road lined with trees for a kilometre; **j'irai faire les courses p. ce temps** I'll go shopping in the meantime; **et p. ce temps-là, tu ne penseras pas à tes problèmes** it will take your mind off your problems for a while; **avant la classe et p.** before and during the class, before the class and during it; **il te l'a dit après la réunion? – non, p.** did he tell you after the meeting? – no, during it

2 *conj* [①B29-30,11] **p. que** while, *Fml* whilst; **elle lisait p. que je repassais** she was reading while I was ironing, she read while I ironed; **p. que j'y pense** while I think of it; **p. que vous y êtes** while you're at *or* about it
pendard, -arde [pɑ̃dar, -ard] *n F Arch* rogue, scoundrel
pendeloque [pɑ̃dlɔk] *nf* (*de bijou*) pendant; (*de lustre*) pendant, crystal
pendentif [pɑ̃dɑ̃tif] *nm* **(a)** (*bijou*) pendant **(b)** *Archit* pendentive
penderie [pɑ̃dri] *nf* wardrobe, *Am* closet
pendiller [pɑ̃dije] *vi* to dangle
pendoir [pɑ̃dwar] *nm* (meat) hook
pendouiller [pɑ̃duje] *vi F* to dangle
pendre [pɑ̃dr] **1** *vt* **(a)** (*accrocher*) to hang (up); **p. le linge (pour le faire sécher)** to hang the washing out (to dry); **p. la crémaillère** to have a housewarming (party)

(b) (*mettre à mort*) to hang; **p. qn haut et court** to hang sb (by the neck); *Fig F* **qu'il aille se faire p. ailleurs** let him go hang *or* go to hell; *Fig* **je veux être pendu si ...** I'll be hanged if ...

2 *vi* to hang; (*des cheveux*) to hang down; (*de la langue d'un animal*) to hang out; **les voiles pendaient le long des mâts** the sails were flapping idly against the masts; **jupe qui pend par derrière** skirt that hangs down *or* dips at the back; *F* **ça lui pend au nez** he's got it coming to him

3 se pendre *vpr* **(a)** (*se suicider*) to hang oneself

(b) (*s'accrocher*) **se p. à qch** to hang from sth; **se p. au cou de qn** to hug sb
pendu, -ue [pɑ̃dy] **1** *adj* hung up, hanging (up); (*personne*) hanged; **p. aux jupes de sa mère** clinging to his mother's skirts; *Fig* **avoir la langue bien pendue** to be a great talker, to be very talkative; **il est toujours p. au téléphone** he's never off the phone, he spends all his time on the phone; **elle est restée deux heures pendue au téléphone** she spent two hours on the phone **2** *n* hanged man/woman; **le p.** (*jeu*) hangman
pendulaire [pɑ̃dylɛr] *adj* swinging, pendular
pendule [pɑ̃dyl] **1** *nm* pendulum **2** *nf* clock; **p. à coucou** cuckoo clock; *Fig* **remettre les pendules à l'heure** to get things straight; *F* **tu ne vas pas en faire** *ou* *Vulg* **chier une p.** you're not going to make a big fuss *or* a song and dance about it
pendulette [pɑ̃dylɛt] *nf* small clock; (*réveil-matin*) travelling clock, travel alarm
pêne [pɛn] *nm* bolt
pénéplaine [peneplɛn] *nf Géol* peneplain
pénétrabilité [penetrabilite] *nf* penetrability
pénétrable [penetrabl] *adj* **(a)** (*perméable*) penetrable **(à** by) **(b)** (*compréhensible*) understandable
pénétrant, -ante [penetrɑ̃, -ɑ̃t] **1** *adj* penetrating; (*vent, froid*) piercing; (*pluie*) drenching; (*odeur*) penetrating, pervasive, obtrusive; (*regard*) penetrating, searching, keen;

(*esprit*) penetrating, shrewd, acute **2 pénétrante** *nf* = dual carriageway or motorway leading into the centre of a city

pénétration [penetrasjɔ̃] *nf* **(a)** (*d'un produit chimique, d'une balle etc*) penetration; *Fig* **la p. d'idées nouvelles** the penetration of new ideas **(b)** (*clairvoyance*) (*d'une personne*) penetration, insight, shrewdness; (*de l'esprit*) acuteness **(c)** (*sexuellement*) penetration

pénétré [penetre] *adj* **p. d'humidité** (*mur etc*) riddled with damp; *Fig* **p. d'un sentiment/d'une idée** imbued with a feeling/an idea; *Péj* **il est p. de son importance** he's full of his own importance; **un candidat/orateur p. de son sujet** a candidate/speaker who is completely immersed in his subject; **d'un ton p.** in an earnest tone, earnestly; **d'un air p.** with an earnest air, earnestly

pénétrer [penetre] **(je pénètre, n. pénétrons; je pénétrerai) 1** *vi* to penetrate; **la baïonnette pénétra jusqu'au poumon** the bayonet penetrated to the lung; **un cambrioleur a pénétré dans la maison** a burglar got into the house; **ils pénétrèrent par la force** (*de policiers, soldats etc*) they broke in, they forced their way in; **l'armée a pénétré en territoire ennemi** the army penetrated enemy territory; **l'eau avait pénétré partout** the water had penetrated everywhere *or* got in everywhere; **le vent pénètre dans toute la maison** the wind gets into the whole house

2 *vt* to penetrate; **la balle pénétra l'os** the bullet penetrated *or* pierced the bone; **p. un secret** to penetrate *or* fathom a secret; **p. la pensée/les intentions de qn** to fathom sb's thoughts/intentions; *Com* **p. un marché** to penetrate a market; **le froid nous pénètre (jusqu'aux os)** the cold goes right through us, the cold chills us to the bone

3 se pénétrer *vpr* **se p. d'une idée** to let an idea sink in; **se p. de l'importance de qch** to be fully aware of the importance of sth

pénible [penibl] *adj* **(a)** (*qui demande de l'effort*) (*tâche*) laborious, arduous, hard; (*respiration, style*) laboured, *US* labored, heavy; (*route*) rough; (*hiver, froid*) severe; **vie p.** hard *or* difficult life **(b)** (*dérangeant, insupportable*) (*spectacle, nouvelles etc*) painful, distressing; **l'idée m'est trop p.** the idea is too painful; **il m'est p. de devoir vous annoncer que ...** it is my painful duty to inform you that ...; **p. à voir** painful to see **(c)** *F* (*personne*) **ce qu'elle est p.!** she's such a pain!

péniblement [penibləmɑ̃] *adv* with difficulty, laboriously; (*douloureusement*) painfully; **avancer** *ou* **marcher p.** to struggle along; **respirer p.** to breathe heavily

péniche [peniʃ] *nf* **(a)** (*de transport fluvial*) barge; (*pour embarquer des marchandises*) lighter; **il vit sur une p.** he lives on a houseboat *or* barge; *Mil* **p. de débarquement** landing craft **(b)** *F* **péniches** (*chaussures*) clodhoppers

péniche-hôtel, *pl* **péniches-hôtels** *nf* botel (*moored*)

pénicilline [penisilin] *nf Pharm* penicillin

péninsulaire [penɛ̃sylɛr] *adj* peninsular

péninsule [penɛ̃syl] *nf* peninsula; **la p. Ibérique** the Iberian Peninsula

pénis [penis] *nm Anat* penis

pénitence [penitɑ̃s] *nf* **(a)** *Rel* (*repentir*) penitence, repentance; (*peine*) penance; **pour votre p.** as a penance; **faire p.** to do penance **(de** for) **(b)** (*punition*) punishment; **mettre un enfant en p.** to punish a child; **il est en p.** he's in disgrace; **pour ta p.** as a punishment **(c)** *Vieilli* (*aux jeux*) forfeit

pénitencier [penitɑ̃sje] *nm* **(a)** *Rel* **grand p.** penitentiary (priest) **(b)** (*maison d'arrêt*) prison, *Am* penitentiary

pénitent, -ente [penitɑ̃, -ɑ̃t] *adj, n Rel* penitent

pénitentiaire [penitɑ̃sjɛr] *adj* **système p.** prison system

pénitentiel, -ielle [penitɑ̃sjɛl] *Rel* **1** *adj* penitential **2** *nm* penitential (book)

penne [pɛn] *nf* (*d'un oiseau*) quill, *Spéc* penna; (*d'une flèche*) flight

Pennsylvanie [pɛnsilvani] *nf* Pennsylvania

pénombre [penɔ̃br] *nf* (*lumière faible*) half-light, semi-darkness, shadowy light; *Astron, Phys* penumbra; *Fig* **rester dans la p.** to remain in the background

pensable [pɑ̃sabl] *adj* thinkable; **ce n'est pas p.** it's unthinkable

pensant [pɑ̃sɑ̃] *adj* (*créature*) thinking; **mal p.** unorthodox

pense-bête, *pl* **pense-bêtes** [pɑ̃sbɛt] *nm F* memory jogger, reminder; *TV, Cin* goof sheet, idiot board

pensée[1] [pɑ̃se] *nf* (*fleur*) pansy

pensée[2] *nf* (*réflexion*) thought; (*esprit*) thought, mind; (*opinion*) thought, view; **absorbé** *ou* **perdu** *ou* **plongé dans ses pensées** lost in thought *or* in one's thoughts; **se représenter clairement qch par la p.** to have a clear conception *or* a clear idea of sth; **entrer dans la p. de qn** to understand sb's thinking; **deviner les pensées de qn** to read sb's mind, to guess what sb is thinking; **dire sa p.** to speak one's mind, to say what one thinks; **dire le fond de sa p.** to say what one really thinks; **saisir la p. de qn** to grasp sb's meaning; **il partage ma p.** he shares my opinion, he thinks the same way I do; **libre p.** free thought *or* thinking; **à la p. des vacances, ...** at the thought of the holidays, ...; **la seule p. de ce repas me met l'eau à la bouche** just thinking about *or* just the thought of this meal makes my mouth water; **la p. que tu seras là** the thought that you will be there; **la p. marxiste/bouddhiste** Marxist/Buddhist thought *or* thinking; **en p., par la p.** in one's mind; **voyager par la p.** to be an armchair traveller; **je suis avec vous en p.** *ou* **par la p.** my thoughts are with you; **avoir une p. pour qn** to think of sb; **ayons une p. émue pour elle** let's spare a thought for her; **pensées affectueuses** (*dans une lettre*) fond(est) regards

penser[1] [pɑ̃se] *nm Arch, Litt* thought

penser[2] **1** *vi* **(a)** (*songer, réfléchir*) to think; **p. à qn/qch** (*songer à*) to think of *or* about sb/sth; **il pense à elle tout le temps** he's always thinking about her; **il pense par lui-même** he thinks for himself; **à quoi pensez-vous?** what are you thinking of *or* about?, what's going through your mind?; (*où avez-vous la tête?*) what are you thinking of?, how could you (think of such a thing)?; **p. tout haut** to think aloud; **je l'ai fait sans y p.** I did it without thinking; **pensez-vous!** what an idea!; **est-ce qu'il a donné un bon pourboire? – pensez-vous!** did he give a good tip? – what do you think? *or* you're joking! *or* what, him!; **pensez donc!** just fancy!; **vous n'y pensez pas!** you're not serious!; **n'y pensons plus** let's forget (about) it; **ce n'est même pas la peine d'y p.** it's not even worth thinking about; **ah, j'y pense!** by the way!; **rien que d'y p., ça me donne des frissons** just thinking about *or* of it gives me the shivers, I shiver at the mere thought (of it); **elle l'a fait sans p. à mal** she didn't mean any harm by it; **je lui ai parlé de toi sans p. à mal** I didn't mean any harm by speaking to him about you

(b) (*se souvenir*) **p. à tout** to think of everything; **p. à faire qch** to remember to do sth; **c'est toujours moi qui dois penser à tout** I'm the one who always has to think of *or* remember everything; **tu penses à tout!** you think of everything!; **pourrais-tu me faire p. à vérifier que ...?** could you remind me to check that ...?; **il me fait p. à mon frère** he reminds me of my brother; **ça me fait p. à du Proust/de la banane** it reminds me of Proust/banana

(c) (*estimer*) to think; **je pense comme vous** I think like you *or* as you do, I agree with you; **voilà ma façon** *ou* **manière de p.** that's my way of thinking, that's the way I see it; **je ne partage pas sa façon de p.** I don't share his way of thinking

(d) p. vacances to think (about) holidays; **il faut p. européen** we must think European

2 *vt* **(a)** (*estimer*) to think, to believe; (*imaginer*) to imagine, to picture; **est-ce que tu penses réellement ce que tu viens de dire?** do you really believe what you've just said?; **je le pensais bien** I thought as much, I thought so; **comment peux-tu p. une chose pareille?** how can you think such a thing?; **je pense que oui/non** I think/don't think so; **pensez si j'étais furieux** you can imagine how angry I was; **je ne savais plus que p.** I no longer knew what to think; **je le pense fou** I think he's mad

(b) p. qch de qn/qch to think sth of sb/sth; **qu'est-ce que tu penses de lui?** what do you think of him?; **je ne pense rien de ce genre de gens** I think nothing *or* I don't think anything of these sort of people; **qu'en penses-tu?** what do you think (of it)?; **j'en pense le plus grand bien** I have a very high opinion of him/her/it; **p. du mal de qn** to have a poor opinion of sb, not to think much of sb; **je lui ai dit carrément ce que j'en pensais** *ou* **ce que je pensais** I told him straight out what I thought; (*en se fâchant*) I gave him a piece of my mind

(c) p. faire qch (*espérer*) to expect *or* hope to do sth; (*avoir l'intention*) to be thinking of doing sth; **je pensais le voir demain** I was expecting to see him tomorrow; *Litt* **j'ai pensé mourir de rire** I thought I would die laughing

(d) (*concevoir*) **p. qch** to think sth out; **p. la ville en fonction des habitants** to think of the city in terms of its inhabitants; **les plans ont été mal pensés** the plans were badly thought out; **p. l'actualité en démocrate** to view current events from a democratic standpoint

penseur, -euse [pɑ̃sœr, -øz] *n* thinker; **libre p.** free thinker

pensif, -ive [pɑ̃sif, -iv] *adj* thoughtful, pensive

pension [pɑ̃sjɔ̃] *nf* **(a)** (*allocation*) pension, allowance; *Fin* **mise en p.** borrowing against securities pledging **(b) être en p. chez qn** to board with sb; **prendre qn en p.** to take sb in as a lodger; **prendre p. chez qn** to take board and lodging with sb; *Hum* **tu es toujours fourré chez eux, tu prends p.**

ou quoi? you're always round at their place, are you moving in with them or what?; **chambre et p.** board and lodging **(c)** (*pensionnat*) boarding school; (*élèves*) boarders; **mettre un enfant en p.** to send a child to boarding school

▶ **pension**: *Fin* **p. alimentaire** maintenance, alimony; **verser/recevoir une p. alimentaire** to pay/get alimony; **demander 10 000 francs de p. alimentaire** to claim 10,000 francs' maintenance *or* alimony; **p. complète** full board, *US* American plan; **sept jours en p. complète** seven days full board *or US* American plan; **p. de famille** boarding house; *Fin* **p. de retraite** (retirement *or* old age) pension; *Fin* **p. de réversion** survivor's pension; *Fin* **p. viagère** life annuity

pensionnaire [pɑ̃sjɔnɛr] *n* **(a)** (*dans une pension de famille, à l'école*) boarder; (*à l'hôtel*) resident; (*dans une maison privée*) lodger, paying guest; (*dans une maison pour personnes âgées*) resident; *F* (*d'une prison*) inmate **(b)** (*personne qui reçoit une pension*) pensioner; **p. de la Comédie-Française** member of the Comédie Française company; **p. de la Villa Médicis** = scholarship student at the Villa Medicis

pensionnat [pɑ̃sjɔna] *nm Scol* (*établissement*) boarding school; (*élèves*) boarders

pensionné, -ée [pɑ̃sjɔne] **1** *adj* (*soldat, employé*) pensioned **2** *n* pensioner

pensionner [pɑ̃sjɔne] *vt* to pension

pensivement [pɑ̃sivmɑ̃] *adv* pensively, thoughtfully

pensum [pɛ̃sɔm] *nm Scol Vieilli* imposition; (*lignes*) lines; *Fig* chore

pentagonal, -ale, -aux, -ales [pɛ̃tagɔnal, -o] *adj Math* pentagonal

pentagone [pɛ̃tagɔn] *nm* **(a)** *Math* pentagon **(b)** *US Mil* **le P.** the Pentagon

pentamètre [pɛ̃tamɛtr] *adj, nm Littér* pentameter

Pentateuque (le) [ləpɛ̃tatøk] *nm Bible* the Pentateuch

pentathlon [pɛ̃tatlɔ̃] *nm Sp* pentathlon

pentatonique [pɛ̃tatɔnik] *adj Mus* pentatonic

pente [pɑ̃t] *nf* **(a)** (*inclinaison*) slope; *Spéc* (*d'une colline*) gradient, *Am* grade; **p. ascendante/descendante** upward/downward slope *or Spéc* gradient; **à faible/forte p.** gently/steeply sloping; **p. à 10%** slope of 10%, 1-in-10 hill; **en p.** sloping; (*plage, côte*) shelving; **rue en p.** street on a slope; **p. d'une rivière** fall of a river; *Arg* **avoir la dalle en p.** to be a bit of a boozer; *Fig F* **être sur une mauvaise p.** to be going downhill, to be on a slippery slope, to be on a downward path; *Fig* **remonter la p.** to get back on one's feet
(b) (*cambrure*) (*de la route*) camber; (*du toit*) pitch; *Math* (*d'une courbe*) slope; **angle de p.** (*sur un plan*) angle of slope **(c)** *Av* (*de la trajectoire de vol*) slope

Pentecôte [pɑ̃tkot] *nf Rel* Pentecost; (*jours fériés*) Whitsun(tide); **dimanche de la P.** Whit Sunday

penthotal® [pɛ̃tɔtal] *nm Pharm* truth drug, *Spéc* penthotal

pentu [pɑ̃ty] *adj* sloping

penture [pɑ̃tyr] *nf Tech* (*de porte etc*) strap hinge; **p. et gond** hook and hinge; *Naut* **pentures du gouvernail** rudder braces

pénultième [penyltjɛm] *adj, nf* penultimate

pénurie [penyri] *nf* shortage, scarcity (**de** of); **p. de capitaux** shortage of capital; **p. de main-d'œuvre** labour shortage; **organiser la p.** to maximize available resources in times of shortage

Pep [pɛp] *nm Fin* (*abrév* **plan d'épargne personnel**) popular savings scheme

pep [pɛp] *nm F* pep; **avoir du p.** to be full of pep

pépé [pepe] *nm F* grandad, grandpa, *Am* gramp(s); (*vieil homme*) grandad

pépée [pepe] *nf F* (*fille*) chick, *Br* bird, *Am* broad

pépère [pepɛr] *F* **1** *nm* **(a) c'est un gros p.** he's an old fatty; (*d'un enfant*) he's a chubby little fellow **(b)** (*grand-père*) grandad, grandpa, *US* gramp(s) **2** *adj* **(a)** (*endroit*) quiet; (*repas*) quiet, relaxed; **un petit coin p.** a nice quiet little spot **(b) il est p.** (*dans une situation confortable*) he's got it easy; **un travail p.** a cushy little job *or* number **3** *adv Aut* **rouler p.** to potter along

pépettes, pépètes [pepɛt] *nfpl très F* (*argent*) dough, bread, *Br* lolly

pépie [pepi] *nf* (*d'oiseau*) pip; *F* **avoir la p.** (*avoir soif*) to be parched

pépiement [pepimɑ̃] *nm* cheep(ing), chirp(ing)

pépier [pepje] *vi* to cheep, to chirp

pépin[1] [pepɛ̃] *nm* **(a)** (*de pomme, de raisin etc*) pip; **sans pépins** seedless **(b)** *F* (*ennui*) hitch; **avoir un p.** to be in trouble *or* in difficulties; **elle a eu un gros p.** she had some trouble *or* problems

pépin[2] *nm F* (*parapluie*) umbrella, *Br* brolly

pépinière [pepinjɛr] *nf* **(a)** (*d'arbustes*) nursery **(b)** *Fig* training ground (**de** for)

pépiniériste [pepinjerist] *n* nursery gardener

pépite [pepit] *nf* (*d'or*) nugget; **pépites de chocolat** chocolate chips

péplum [peplɔm] *nm F* (*film*) epic (*set in the ancient world*)

PEPS [peøpeɛs] *Com* (*abrév* **premier entré, premier sorti**) FIFO

pepsine [pɛpsin] *nf Biol, Ch* pepsin

peptide [pɛptid] *nm Biol, Ch* peptide

peptique [pɛptik] *adj* peptic

peptone [pɛptɔn] *nf Physiol, Ch* peptone

péquenaud, -aude [pekno, -od] *n F* peasant, country bumpkin, yokel

péquenot [pekno] *nm F* = **péquenaud**

péquiste [pekist] *Can Pol* **1** *adj* (of the) Parti Québécois, PQ **2** *n* member/supporter of the Parti Québécois *or* PQ

PER [peøɛr] *nm, Fin* (*abrév* **plan d'épargne de retraite**) retirement savings scheme

perborate [pɛrbɔrat] *nm Ch* perborate

perçage [pɛrsaʒ] *nm* (*de tissu, de la peau*) piercing; (*d'un grand trou*) boring; (*d'un plus petit trou*) drilling

percale [pɛrkal] *nf Tex* percale

percaline [pɛrkalin] *nf Tex* percaline

perçant [pɛrsɑ̃] *adj* (*regard, cri*) piercing; (*voix*) penetrating, *Péj* shrill; **vue perçante** sharp eyesight

perce [pɛrs] *nf* **(a)** (*machine*) borer; (*outil*) drill; (*poinçon*) punch **(b)** (*d'un instrument à vent*) hole **(c) mettre en p.** to broach, to tap

percé [pɛrse] *adj* pierced; (*chaussures, poche*) with a hole/holes in; **p. de vers** (*fruit, bois*) worm-eaten; **oreilles percées** pierced ears; **pantalon p. au genou** trousers with a hole in the knee, trousers out at the knee; **mes chaussures sont percées** I've got holes in my shoes

percée [pɛrse] *nf* **(a)** (*ouverture*) opening; (*dans un mur*) opening, breach, gap; (*dans une forêt*) clearing; **ouvrir** *ou* **faire une p. dans un bois** to cut a passage through a wood **(b)** *Mil, Sp, Fig* breakthrough; **faire une p.** to make a breakthrough, to break through; **p. technologique** technological breakthrough

percement [pɛrs(ə)mɑ̃] *nm* (*d'un trou, d'un passage*) boring; (*d'une avenue*) opening; (*d'un canal*) cutting; (*d'un tunnel*) driving

perce-muraille, *pl* **perce-murailles** *nf Bot* wall pellitory

perce-neige *n inv Bot* snowdrop

perce-oreille, *pl* **perce-oreilles** *nm* earwig

perce-pierre, *pl* **perce-pierres** *nf* (*plante*) samphire, sea fennel, saxifrage

percepteur, -trice [pɛrsɛptœr, -tris] **1** *adj* (*organe*) of perception **2** *nm Admin* tax collector, *F* tax man

perceptibilité [pɛrsɛptibilite] *nf* perceptibility

perceptible [pɛrsɛptibl] *adj* **(a)** (*que l'on peut percevoir*) perceptible (**à** to), discernible; **p. à l'oreille** audible **(b)** *Admin* (*impôt*) collectable

perceptiblement [pɛrsɛptibləmɑ̃] *adv* perceptibly; (*à l'oreille*) audibly

perceptif, -ive [pɛrsɛptif, -iv] *adj* perceptive

perception [pɛrsɛpsjɔ̃] *nf* **(a)** (*par les sens*) perception **(b)** *Admin* (*d'impôts, de droits, de loyer*) collection; (**bureau de**) **p.** tax office; *Fin* **p. de dividende** receipt of a dividend; *Com* **p. douanière** collection of customs duties; *Fin* **p. à la source** tax deduction at source

perceptoscope [pɛrsɛptɔskɔp] *nm Mktg* perceptoscope

percer [pɛrse] (**je perçai(s)**; **n. perçons**) **1** *vt* **(a)** (*transpercer*) to pierce, to go through; *Fig* **ça me perce les oreilles** it's ear-splitting; *Litt* **p. la foule** to make *or* elbow one's way through a crowd; **p. un abcès** to lance an abscess; **le soleil perce les nuages** the sun is breaking through *or* piercing the clouds; **p. le cœur/bras à qn d'un coup de couteau** to stab sb through the heart/in the arm; *Fig* **p. un complot** to uncover a plot; **p. un mystère/une énigme** to solve a mystery/a riddle; **p. qch à jour** to see through sth; **ses yeux perçaient l'obscurité** his eyes penetrated the darkness
(b) (*trouer*) to make a hole in, to pierce; (*trou*) to make, to pierce; (*avec une perceuse*) to drill, to bore; (*tunnel*) to drive; (*avenue*) to open; (*canal*) to cut; **p. un mur** to make a hole in a wall; **p. un tonneau** to broach *or* tap a cask; **p. une porte dans un mur** to make *or* open a door in a wall; **se faire p. les oreilles** to have one's ears pierced
2 *vi* to come *or* break through; **le soleil commence à p.** the sun is breaking through *or* coming out; **ses dents percent** his teeth are coming through, he is cutting his teeth; **l'abcès a percé** the abscess has burst; *Fig* **rien n'a percé de leur entretien** nothing has emerged about *or* got out about their meeting; **auteur qui commence à p.** author who is beginning to make a name (for himself); **il laissa p. son impatience/sa jalousie** he let his impatience/jealousy show

perceur, -euse [pɛrsœr, -øz] **1** *n* (*de feuille de métal etc*) driller, puncher **2** *nf* **perceuse** (*machine*) boring *or* drilling machine; (*outil*) drill; **perceuse à percussion** hammer drill; **perceuse électrique** electric drill **3** *nm* **p. de coffres-forts** safe breaker

percevable [pɛrsəvabl] *adj Admin* (*impôt*) collectable

percevoir [pɛrsəvwar] *vt* (*prp* **percevant**; *pp* **perçu**; *pr ind* **je perçois, n. percevons, ils perçoivent**; *pr sub* **je perçoive, n. percevions, ils perçoivent**; *impf* **je percevais**; *p hist* **je perçus**; *fu* **je percevrai**) **(a)** (*prendre conscience de*) (*par les sens, l'intellect*) to perceive, to discern; **p. un bruit** to hear *or* catch a sound; **je ne perçois pas la différence** I can't make out *or* see the difference; **je n'ai pas perçu, dans sa voix, qu'elle était désespérée** I didn't sense, from her voice, that she was desperate; **être bien/mal perçu** to be well/badly thought of; (*d'une information*) to be well/badly received; (*d'un produit*) to be well/badly perceived; **risque perçu** perceived risk

(b) *Admin* (*impôts, loyers*) to collect; (*intérêts*) to receive, to be paid; **p. l'allocation chômage** to receive unemployment benefit; **p. une commission** to receive a commission

perche[1] [pɛrʃ] *nf* (*pièce de bois*) pole; *Rail* coupling pole; **p. à houblon** hop pole; *Sp* **saut à la p.** pole vault(ing); *Cin, TV* **p. (à son)** boom; **conduire un bateau à la p.** to punt a boat; *Fig* **tendre la p. à qn** to give sb a helping hand; (*donner une indication*) to give sb a broad hint; *F* **une grande p.** (*personne*) a beanpole

perche[2] *nf* (*poisson*) perch

perch(e)man [pɛrʃman] *nm* ski-lift attendant; *Cin, TV* boom operator

percher [pɛrʃe] **1** *vi* (*des oiseaux*) to perch; (*des poules*) to roost; *Fig F* **il perche au quatrième** he lives up on the fourth floor; **où perchez-vous?** where's your pad? **2** *vt F* to perch, to stick; **p. un vase sur une armoire** to perch *or* stick a vase on top of a wardrobe **3 se percher** *vpr* **se p. sur une branche** (*d'un oiseau*) to perch on a branch; *F* **il s'est perché sur le mur pour mieux voir** he perched himself on the wall to see better

percheron [pɛrʃərɔ̃] *nm* (*cheval*) Percheron

perchette [pɛrʃɛt] *nf TV, Cin* fishing rod

percheur, -euse [pɛrʃœr, -øz] *adj* (*oiseau*) perching

perchiste [pɛrʃist] *n Sp* pole vaulter; *Cin, TV* boom operator

perchlorate [pɛrklɔrat] *nm Ch* perchlorate

perchlorique [pɛrklɔrik] *adj Ch* perchloric

perchoir [pɛrʃwar] *nm* perch; (*pour la volaille*) roost; *Fig* perch; *Pol* = raised seat for the President of the French National Assembly; *Pol* **obtenir le p.** to become President of the (French) National Assembly

perclus [pɛrkly] *adj* paralysed, *US* paralyzed; **p. de rhumatismes** crippled with rheumatism; *Fig* **p. de terreur/froid/timidité** paralysed with fright/cold/shyness

perçoir [pɛrswar] *nm* (*outil*) awl, gimlet, broach

percolateur [pɛrkɔlatœr] *nm* (coffee) percolator

perçu [pɛrsy] *adj* **(a)** (*valeur, importance*) perceived **(b)** (*somme, traitement, intérêt*) received

percussion [pɛrkysjɔ̃] *nf Tech* percussion; *Méd* sounding (by percussion), percussion; **fusil à p.** percussion gun; *Mus* **instruments à p.** percussion instruments; *Mus* **aux percussions, Jack** on percussion, Jack

percussionniste [pɛrkysjɔnist] *n Mus* percussionist

percutané [pɛrkytane] *adj Méd* percutaneous

percutant [pɛrkytɑ̃] **1** *adj* **(a)** (*qui percute*) percussive; *Mil* **obus p.** percussion fuse shell **(b)** *Fig* (*discours, argument*) forceful, powerful; (*style*) incisive **2** *nm Mil* percussion fuse shell

percuter [pɛrkyte] **1** *vt* **(a)** (*heurter violemment*) (*voiture, avion etc*) to crash into; **p. l'amorce** (*sur une arme*) to strike the primer **(b)** *Méd* to sound by percussion, to percuss **2** *vi* **l'avion percuta contre le sol** the plane crashed to the ground; **la voiture est allée p. contre un arbre** the car crashed into a tree

percuteur [pɛrkytœr] *nm* (*d'une arme à feu, d'un fusible*) striker, hammer; (*d'un fusil*) needle; (*d'une mitrailleuse*) firing pin

percutiréaction [pɛrkytireaksjɔ̃] *nf Méd* percutaneous reaction

perdant, -ante [pɛrdɑ̃, -ɑ̃t] **1** *adj* losing; **partir p.** to start out with low hopes **2** *n* loser; **être bon/mauvais p.** to be a good/bad loser

perdition [pɛrdisjɔ̃] *nf* **(a)** *Rel* perdition; **lieu de p.** den of vice *or* iniquity **(b)** *Naut* **navire en p.** ship in distress; *Fig* **entreprise en p.** company in difficulties *or* in trouble

perdre [pɛrdr] **1** *vt* **(a)** to lose; **j'ai perdu mes clés** I've lost my keys; **vous êtes en train de p. votre écharpe** you're losing your scarf; **p. un ami** (*après une dispute, Euph après sa mort*) to lose a friend; **p. du terrain** to lose ground; **p. pied** (*d'un nageur*), *Fig* to get out of one's depth; (*d'un grimpeur*) to lose one's footing; **p. la partie** to lose the game; **il perd son pantalon** his trousers are too big for him; **p. ses cheveux** to lose one's hair, to go bald; **le chien perd ses poils** the dog is losing *or* shedding his hair; **p. une dent/un bras** to lose a tooth/an arm; **p. du poids/quelques kilos** to lose weight/a few pounds; **p. la raison** *ou* **la tête** *ou F* **la boule** to go mad, *F* to go off one's head, to go round the bend; **faire p. la tête à qn** (*le rendre fou*) to drive sb mad *or F* round the bend; (*de passion*) to drive sb crazy; *F* **il ne perd pas le nord!** he's no fool!; *F* **il n'en perd pas une** he doesn't miss a trick; **p. son calme** to lose one's composure; **p. la face** to lose face; **p. le fil (de ses pensées)** to lose the thread; **courir à p. haleine** to run until one is out of breath; **p. courage/patience/espoir/confiance** to lose heart/patience/hope/confidence; **p. connaissance** to lose consciousness; **p. une habitude** to shake off *or* get rid of a habit; **j'aimerais bien que tu perdes l'habitude de m'appeler 'ma vieille'** I wish you'd get out of the habit of calling me 'old girl'; **faire p. une habitude à qn** to break sb of a habit; **tu ne perds rien pour attendre!** just you wait!; **n'avoir rien à p.** to have nothing to lose; **p. son chemin** to lose one's way; **p. son temps** to waste (one's) time; **p. du temps** to waste time; (*dans un programme de travail, un horaire*) to lose time; **faire qch sans p. de temps** to do sth without losing *or* wasting any time, to lose no time in doing sth; **il n'y a pas de temps à p.** there is no time to lose; **il n'y a pas un instant** *ou* **une minute** *ou* **une seconde à p.** there isn't a moment to lose; **elle ne perd pas un mot** *ou* **une miette** *ou* **une bouchée de la conversation** she isn't missing a (single) word of the conversation; **p. une occasion** to miss an opportunity; **p. qn/qch de vue** to lose sight of sb/sth; **vous n'y perdez rien** you're not missing anything

(b) (*ruiner*) to ruin; **l'ambition l'a perdu** ambition was his undoing *or* his downfall; *Hum* **ce qui te perdra, toi, c'est la gourmandise** your greed will be your undoing; **des lectures qui perdent la jeunesse** the kind of reading that is ruining our youth

(c) *Obst* **elle a perdu les eaux** her waters have broken

2 *vi* **(a) la marée perd** the tide is ebbing

(b) *Naut* to fall *or* drop astern

(c) (*ne pas remporter une partie, bataille etc*) to lose

(d) y p. (*dans un échange*) to lose out; (*dans une vente*) to make a loss; **p. au change** to lose out on the deal

3 se perdre *vpr* **(a)** (*disparaître*) to disappear, to be lost; **le navire se perdit corps et biens** the ship was lost with all hands; **se p. dans la foule** to disappear into the crowd, to lose oneself in the crowd; **cela se perd facilement** it's easily lost, it's easy to lose; **cet usage se perd** this custom is dying out; *Fig* **se p. de vue** to lose touch *or* contact with each other

(b) (*d'une puissance mécanique*) to be wasted

(c) (*de la nourriture*) to go bad

(d) il y a des fessées qui se perdent he/she needs a good spanking

(e) (*s'égarer*) to lose one's way, to get lost; **il s'est perdu dans le bois** he got lost in the wood; **se p. en conjectures** to get lost in conjecture; **se p. dans des explications/dans les détails** to get bogged down in explanations/details; **se p. dans ses pensées** to be lost in thought; *F* **je m'y perds** I can't make head (n)or tail of it, I'm confused; **on s'y perd** it's confusing

perdreau, -eaux [pɛrdro] *nm* young partridge

perdrix [pɛrdri] *nf* [①A12,1,g] partridge; **p. des neiges** ptarmigan

perdu, -ue [pɛrdy] **1** *adj* **(a)** lost; (*égaré*) lost, missing; (*que l'on ne gagne pas*) lost; **p. dans ses pensées** lost in thought; **je suis p.** I'm lost; *Fig* (*je n'y comprends rien*) I'm lost, I'm confused; **les causes perdues d'avance** causes lost right from the start; **un match p.** a lost match, a defeat; **il habite un trou p.** he lives at the back of beyond *or* in the middle of nowhere; **à mes moments perdus, à mes heures perdues** in my spare time; *Com* **emballage p.** non-returnable *or* throw-away *or* disposable packaging; **ce n'est pas p. pour tout le monde** (*objet*) somebody's making good use of it

(b) (*abîmé*) ruined; (*ruiné, fini*) (*personne*) ruined; **il est perdu** (*de malade*) there's no hope for him; *Litt* **il est p. de réputation** his reputation is ruined; **âme perdue** lost soul

(c) à corps p. without restraint, recklessly; **se jeter à corps p. dans une activité** to throw oneself into an activity; **se jeter à corps p. dans la mêlée** to hurl oneself into the fray

2 *n* **crier comme un p.** to shout like a madman

perdurer [pɛrdyre] *vi Litt* to continue

père [pɛr] *nm* **(a)** (*géniteur*) father; **de p. en fils** from father to son, from generation to generation; *Prov* **tel p. tel fils** like father like son; **M. Martin p.** Mr Martin senior; **nos pères** our forefathers, our ancestors; *F* **un gros p.** a chubby fellow; *F* **c'est un p. tranquille** he's a quiet sort; *F* **(mon) petit p.** old chap, *Am* old buddy; **le p. Jean** old John; **il a été un vrai p. pour moi** he was like a father to me; *Fig* **le p. du cubisme/de l'infographie** the father of cubism/computer graphics

(b) *Rel* father; **le Saint-P.** the Holy Father; **le (Révérend) P. Martin** Father Martin; **mon p.** father; **notre P. qui êtes aux cieux** our Father who art in heaven; **le P., le Fils et le Saint Esprit** the Father, the Son and the Holy Ghost

(c) *(dans un élevage)* sire

▶ **père**: **p. de famille** father, family man; **en bon p. de famille** wisely; **p. naturel** natural father; *Th* **p. noble** heavy father; **le P. Noël** Father Christmas, Santa Claus; **croire au P. Noël** to believe in Father Christmas *or* Santa Claus; *Fig F* to believe in Father Christmas *or* Santa Claus *or* fairies; **p. spirituel** *Rel* father confessor; *Fig (d'un mouvement)* father; **les Pères Blancs** the White Friars, the Carmelites

pérégrination [peregrinasjɔ̃] *nf Litt* peregrination

péremption [perɑ̃psjɔ̃] *nf* **(a)** *Jur* lapsing; *(dans un procès)* time limitation **(b) date de p.** use-by date

péremptoire [perɑ̃ptwar] *adj* **(a)** *(ton)* peremptory; **argument p.** unanswerable argument **(b)** *Jur* **délai p.** strict time limit

péremptoirement [perɑ̃ptwarmɑ̃] *adv* peremptorily

pérenniser [perenize] *vt* to perpetuate

pérennité [perenite] *nf (d'une théorie, d'une tradition, d'une vérité)* timelessness; *(de fournisseur)* permanence

péréquation [perekwasjɔ̃] *nf Admin, Écon (d'impôts, de salaires)* equalization; *Rail (des charges de fret, de tarifs)* standardizing; *Can Admin* **fonds de p.** equalization fund

perestroïka [perɛstrɔika] *nf Pol* perestroika

perfectibilité [pɛrfɛktibilite] *nf Litt* perfectibility

perfectible [pɛrfɛktibl] *adj* perfectible

perfectif, -ive [pɛrfɛktif, -iv] *adj, nm Gram* perfective

perfection [pɛrfɛksjɔ̃] *nf* **(a)** *(qualité)* perfection; **atteindre la p.** to achieve perfection; **à la p.** to perfection, perfectly **(b)** *F* **une p.** a gem

perfectionné [pɛrfɛksjɔne] *adj* sophisticated

perfectionnement [pɛrfɛksjɔnmɑ̃] *nm* **(a)** *(action)* perfecting; *(amélioration)* improving; *(formation)* (further) training; **brevet de p.** patent relating to improvements; *Scol* **cours de p.** proficiency course **(b)** *(résultat)* improvement

perfectionner [pɛrfɛksjɔne] **1** *vt* to perfect; *(améliorer)* to improve **2 se perfectionner** *vpr* to improve; **se p. en allemand** to improve one's German

perfectionnisme [pɛrfɛksjɔnism] *nm* perfectionism

perfectionniste [pɛrfɛksjɔnist] *adj, n* perfectionist; **elle n'est pas assez p.** she is not enough of a perfectionist

perfide [pɛrfid] **1** *adj* treacherous **(envers** to), *Litt* perfidious; **la p. Albion** perfidious Albion **2** *n Arch, Litt* traitor

perfidement [pɛrfidmɑ̃] *adv* treacherously, *Litt* perfidiously

perfidie [pɛrfidi] *nf Litt* **(a)** *(déloyauté)* perfidiousness **(b)** *(action)* perfidy

perforage [pɛrfɔraʒ] *nm (de cuir)* punching; *(de papier)* perforation; *(à travers du bois, un mur etc)* boring

perforant [pɛrfɔrɑ̃] *adj* perforating; **obus p.** armour-piercing *or US* armor-piercing shell

perforateur, -trice [pɛrfɔratœr, -tris] **1** *adj* perforating **2** *n (personne)* punch card operator **3** *nf* **perforatrice (a)** *Constr* rock drill **(b)** *(pour papier)* (hole) punch; *(pour cuir)* punch; **(pince) perforatrice** ticket punch **(c)** *Ordinat* card punch, (key) punch; **perforatrice de bande** tape punch **4** *nm Chir* perforator

perforation [pɛrfɔrasjɔ̃] *nf* **(a)** *(action)* perforation, perforating; *Ordinat* punching **(b)** *(trou)* perforation; *Ordinat* punch (hole); *Méd* **p. intestinale** perforation of the intestine

perforer [pɛrfɔre] *vt* **(a)** *(trouer) (papier)* to perforate; *(bois, mur)* to bore (through), to drill; *(cuir)* to punch **(b)** *Ordinat (carte, bande)* to punch; **carte perforée** punch card; **bande perforée** punched tape

perforeuse [pɛrfɔrøz] *nf* perforator; *Ordinat* card punch

performance [pɛrfɔrmɑ̃s] *nf Sp* performance; *Fig (exploit)* feat, achievement; *Tech* **les performances d'une voiture/d'un ordinateur** a car's/computer's performance; **moteur (à) haute p.** high-performance engine; **la p. éblouissante d'un acteur** the dazzling performance of an actor

performant [pɛrfɔrmɑ̃] *adj (machine)* high-performance; *(entreprise)* high-performance, efficient; **des résultats performants** outstanding *or* impressive results

perfuser [pɛrfyze] *vt Méd* to put on a drip; *(organe)* to attach a drip to

perfusion [pɛrfyzjɔ̃] *nf Méd* drip, *Spéc* perfusion; **être sous p.** to be on a drip

pergola [pɛrgɔla] *nf* pergola

péricarde [perikard] *nm Anat* pericardium

péricardite [perikardit] *nf Méd* pericarditis

péricliter [periklite] *vi (d'une affaire, d'une entreprise)* to be in jeopardy; **ses affaires périclitent** his business is about to collapse

péridot [perido] *nm (pierre)* peridot, chrysolite

péridural, -ale, -aux, -ales [peridyral, -o] *Méd* **1** *adj* epidural; **anesthésie péridurale** epidural anaesthesia *or US* anesthesia, *F* epidural **2** *nf* **péridurale** epidural; **accoucher sous péridurale** to give birth under an epidural

périgée [periʒe] *nm Astron* perigee

périglaciaire [periglasjɛr] *adj Géog* periglacial

périhélie [perieli] *nm Astron* perihelion

péri-informatique [periɛ̃fɔrmatik] *nf Tech* computer-related technologies

péril [peril] *nm* peril, danger; *(particulier)* risk, hazard; **au p. de sa vie** at the risk of one's life; **en p.** in peril, in danger; **il y aurait p. à sortir en mer aujourd'hui** it would be unsafe to go out to sea today; **mettre qch en p.** to imperil *or* endanger *or* jeopardize sth; **les périls de cette affaire** the risks involved in this affair; **à ses risques et périls** at one's own risk; **il y a/il n'y a pas p. en la demeure** it's a matter of great urgency/there's no urgency about it; *Péj* **le p. jaune** the yellow peril

périlleusement [perijøzmɑ̃] *adv* perilously

périlleux, -euse [perijø, -øz] *adj* perilous, dangerous, hazardous; **saut p.** somersault

périmé [perime] *adj (billet, passeport, coupon)* out of date, no longer valid; *(mandat)* lapsed; *(nourriture, marchandises)* past its/their sell-by date; **votre passeport est p.** your passport has expired *or* is out of date *or* is no longer valid; *Fig* **conceptions périmées** outdated *or* outmoded concepts

périmer [perime] **1** *vi* **laisser p. un passeport** to let a passport expire; **laisser p. de la nourriture** to let food go off *or* bad **2 se périmer** *vpr Jur* to lapse; *(d'un passeport, d'un billet)* to expire

périmètre [perimɛtr] *nm Géom* perimeter; **dans un p. de 50 km** within a 50-km radius; **p. de vision** zone of vision

périnatal, -ale, -aux, -ales [perinatal, -o] *adj Méd* perinatal

périnatologie [perinatɔlɔʒi] *nf Méd* perinatal medicine

périnée [perine] *nm Anat* perineum

période [perjɔd] *nf* **(a)** *(de temps)* period; **p. de changements sociaux** period of social change; **longue p. de beau temps** long spell of fine weather; **la p. bleue de Picasso** Picasso's Blue Period; **elle a eu sa p. jazz** she went through a jazz period; *Beaux-Arts* **la p. classique** the Classical Period *or* Age; **première p. de l'existence** early stages of life; *Mil* **p. (d'instruction)** training; **pendant la p. électorale** during the elections; **aller en France en pleine p. électorale** to go to France in the middle of elections; **pendant la p. de Noël** *ou* **des fêtes** during the Christmas period; **p. de fêtes** holiday period; **p. estivale** summer season; **p. de pointe** peak period

(b) *(d'un phénomène récurrent, d'un cycle)* period; **nombre de périodes par seconde** *(d'une onde sonore etc)* frequency; *Math* **p. d'une fraction décimale** repetend of a (recurring) decimal; *Phys* **p. d'une onde** period of a wave

(c) *Gram* period, complete sentence; *Mus* **p. (musicale)** phrase

▶ **période**: *Fin* **p. d'amortissement** depreciation period; *Rail* **p. blanche/bleue/rouge** moderately busy/slackest/busiest period on the French rail system; **p. comptable** financial *or Am* fiscal period; **p. d'essai** trial period; **p. d'essai gratuit** free trial period; *Biol* **p. d'incubation** incubation period; *Ch* **p. de radioactivité** half-life; **p. de référence** reference period

périodicité [perjɔdisite] *nf* periodicity

périodique [perjɔdik] **1** *adj* **(a)** periodic; **phases périodiques de récession et de progrès** periodic *or* cyclical phases of recession and economic progress; *Journ* **presse p.** periodical publications; *Math* **fraction p.** recurring decimal; *Math* **fonction p.** periodic function; *Méd* **fièvre p.** recurrent fever **(b)** *(hygiénique)* **tampons périodiques** tampons; **serviettes** *ou* **garnitures périodiques** sanitary towels *or Am* napkins **2** *nm* periodical

périodiquement [perjɔdikmɑ̃] *adv* periodically, every so often

périoste [perjɔst] *nm Anat* periosteum

péripatéticien, -ienne [peripatetisjɛ̃, -jɛn] **1** *adj Phil* peripatetic **2** *n Phil* peripatetic **3** *nf F* **péripatéticienne** streetwalker, prostitute

péripétie [peripesi] *nf Litt* **(a)** *(dans un roman, dans la vie)* sudden change of fortune **(b) péripéties** adventures, incidents; *(de la vie)* ups and downs, vicissitudes

périph [perif] *nm F abrév* **périphérique 2 (a)**

périphérie [periferi] *nf* **(a)** periphery; *Géom* circumference **(b)**

(*banlieue*) outskirts; **vivre à la p. de Paris** to live on the outskirts of Paris

périphérique [periferik] **1** *adj* **(a)** (*situé autour*) peripheral; **boulevard p.** ring road, *Am* beltway; *Rad* **radio p.** = radio station broadcasting from outside national territory; *Anat* **système nerveux p.** peripheral nervous system **(b)** *Ordinat* peripheral **2** *nm* **(a)** (*ceinture routière*) ring road, *Am* beltway **(b)** *Ordinat* peripheral; **p. d'entrée** input device; **p. externe** external device; **p. d'impression** printer peripheral; **p. de sortie** output device

périphrase [perifraz] *nf* circumlocution; *Gram* periphrasis, periphrase

périphrastique [perifrastik] *adj* circumlocutory; *Gram* periphrastic

périple [peripl] *nm* (*voyage*) (long) tour, journey; (*par mer*) (sea) voyage

périr [perir] *vi* (*aux* **avoir**) (*d'une personne*) to perish, to die; (*de la gloire, d'une réputation*) to be destroyed; (*d'un empire*) to fall; **p. dans un incendie/accident** to die *or* perish in a fire/an accident; **p. noyé** to drown, to be drowned; *Fig Litt* **p. d'ennui** to die of boredom; *Fig Litt* **s'ennuyer à p.** to be bored to death; **son nom ne périra pas** his name will live (on); **la démocratie ne peut p.** democracy cannot be destroyed

périscolaire [periskɔlɛr] *adj* extracurricular

périscope [periskɔp] *nm* periscope

périscopique [periskɔpik] *adj* periscopic

périssabilité [perisabilite] *nf* perishability

périssable [perisabl] *adj* perishable; **denrées périssables** perishable foodstuffs

périssoire [periswar] *nf* canoe

péristaltique [peristaltik] *adj Physiol* (*mouvement*) peristaltic

péristaltisme [peristaltism] *nm Physiol* peristalsis

péristyle [peristil] *nm Archit* peristyle

péritéléphonie [peritelefɔni] *nf Tech* peripheral telephone equipment

péritel® [peritɛl] *adj inv* **prise p.** scart plug; (*qui reçoit*) scart socket

péritoine [peritwan] *nm Anat* peritoneum

péritonite [peritɔnit] *nf Méd* peritonitis

périurbain [periyrbɛ̃] *adj* (*cité, lotissement*) suburban; (*parking, shopping*) out-of-town

perle [pɛrl] *nf* **(a)** (*naturelle*) pearl; (*de verre, de métal etc*) bead; *Fig* (*personne*) gem, treasure; **rang de perles** row *or* string of pearls; *Fig* **jeter des perles aux pourceaux** to cast pearls before swine; **c'est la p. des frères** he's the best brother in the world; **ma bonne est une p. (rare)** my maid is a (real) gem *or* treasure; *Fig F* **enfiler des perles** to waste one's time on trivia; **p. de rosée** dewdrop; **perles de sang** drops of blood; **perles de sueur** beads of sweat **(b)** *Scol* howler

▶ **perle**: **p. de culture** cultured pearl; **p. fine** real pearl

perlé [pɛrle] *adj* **(a)** (*orné de perles*) set with pearls; (*de perles de verre*) beaded; **riz p.** husked *or* polished rice; **orge p.** pearl barley; **coton p.** pearl cotton; *Fig* **rire p.** rippling laughter **(b)** (*travail*) exquisitely done; *Mus* clear-cut

perler [pɛrle] **1** *vt* (*travail*) to execute to perfection; *Mus* to play in clear-cut fashion **2** *vi* (*des larmes, de la sueur etc*) to form in beads; **la sueur perlait sur son front** sweat beaded his forehead, beads of sweat stood out on his forehead

perlier, -ière [pɛrlje, -jɛr] *adj* **huître perlière** pearl oyster; **industrie perlière** pearl industry

perlimpinpin [pɛrlɛ̃pɛ̃pɛ̃] *nm* **poudre de p.** magic *or* miracle powder

perlingual, -ale, -aux, -ales [pɛrlɛ̃gwal, -o] *adj Méd* **à prendre par voie perlinguale** place under the tongue

perlouse, perlouze [pɛrluz] *nf Arg* pearl

perm [pɛrm] *nf F* **(a)** *Mil* leave **(b)** *Scol* study room; **aller en p.** to go to the study room; **avoir deux heures de p.** to have two hours' private study

permanence [pɛrmanɑ̃s] *nf* **(a)** (*continuité*) permanence; **en p.** permanently, continuously **(b)** (*service d'accueil d'un organisme*) reception; **la p. est assurée le dimanche** there is someone on duty on Sundays; **être de p.** to be on duty; **p. électorale** committee rooms **(c)** *Scol* study room; **aller en p.** to go to the study room; **avoir deux heures de p.** to have two hours' private study

permanent, -ente [pɛrmanɑ̃, -ɑ̃t] **1** *adj* (*ordre, commission*) standing; (*spectacle*) continuous; (*tribunal*) permanent; **en direct de notre envoyé p. à New York** live from our New York correspondent *or* from our permanent correspondent in New York; *Ordinat* **mémoire permanente** permanent memory; **cinéma p.** (*concept*) continuous showings; (*bâtiment*) cinema *or Am* movie theater with continous showings **2** *nf* **permanente** perm, permanent wave; **se faire une permanente** to have a perm, to have one's hair permed **3** *n Pol* official

permanenter [pɛrmanɑ̃te] *vt* to perm; **se faire p.** to have a perm, to have one's hair permed

permanganate [pɛrmɑ̃ganat] *nm Ch* permanganate

perméabilité [pɛrmeabilite] *nf* permeability, perviousness; *Fig* (*à une influence*) susceptibility

perméable [pɛrmeabl] *adj* permeable, pervious (**à** to); *Fig* susceptible (**à** to)

permettre [pɛrmɛtr] (*conj like* **mettre**) **1** *vt* to allow, to permit; **p. qch à qn** to allow sb sth; **les médecins ne lui permettent pas l'alcool/le sport** the doctors don't allow *or* permit him to drink/to do sport; **p. à qn de faire qch** to allow *or* permit sb to do sth, to let sb do sth; **mes moyens ne me le permettent pas** I can't afford it; **est-il permis d'entrer?** may I come in?; **s'il est permis de s'exprimer ainsi** if I/we may (be allowed to) say so; **il n'est pas permis de stationner là** you're not allowed *or* permitted to park there, parking there isn't allowed *or* permitted; **est-ce qu'il est permis de rapporter six bouteilles de vin?** am I allowed to bring back six bottles of wine?, are six bottles of wine allowable?; **cela ne devrait pas être permis** it shouldn't be allowed; *Hum* **être aussi beau/riche que ça, ça ne devrait pas être permis** nobody's got a right to be that good-looking/rich; **est-il permis de se montrer aussi insolent?** how can anyone be so insolent?; *F* **il est égoïste comme ce n'est pas permis!** he's incredibly selfish!; *F* **il boit comme c'est pas permis!** he drinks like there's no tomorrow; **autant qu'il est permis d'en juger** as far as one can tell; **il se croit tout permis** he thinks he can do anything he likes *or* whatever he likes; **il n'est pas permis à tout le monde de …** not everyone can …; **permettez-moi de vous dire que vous avez tort** excuse me, but you're wrong; **permettez-moi de vous présenter ma sœur** allow me to introduce you to my sister, may I introduce you to my sister?; **permettez!** excuse me!, if you don't mind!; **vous permettez?** may I?, do you mind?; **si le temps le permet** weather permitting; **si mon emploi du temps le permet** if my schedule allows it

2 se permettre *vpr* **(a) se p. de faire qch** to take the liberty of doing sth; **je me permets d'attirer votre attention sur …** may I draw your attention to …; **tu ne t'es pas servi un verre? – je ne me serais pas permis!** didn't you get yourself a drink? – I didn't like to!

(b) se p. qch to allow oneself sth; **il se permet bien des choses** he takes a lot of liberties

permis [pɛrmi] **1** *adj* allowed, permitted **2** *nm Admin* permit, licence, *US* license

▶ **permis**: **p. de chasse** hunting permit; *Aut* **p. de conduire,** *F* **p.** driving licence, *Can* driver's licence, *US* driver's license; (*examen*) driving test; **p. de conduire international** international driving licence; **p. de construire** planning permission; **p. de débarquement** unloading note *or* permit; **p. de douane** customs permit; **p. d'embarquement** shipping note *or* permit; **p. d'exportation** export licence; **p. d'importation** import licence; **p. d'inhumer** burial certificate; **p. provisoire** = temporary licence issued after passing driving test; **p. de séjour** residence permit; **p. tous véhicules** full licence; **p. de travail** work permit

permissif, -ive [pɛrmisif, -iv] *adj* permissive

permission [pɛrmisjɔ̃] *nf* **(a)** [ⓘ**A57**,c-d; **B37**,K,2] (*autorisation*) permission; *Jur* leave; **demander/donner la p. à qn de faire qch** to ask/give sb permission to do sth; **il n'a pas même demandé la p.** he didn't even ask permission; **avec votre p.** with your permission, if I may **(b)** *Mil* (*congé*) leave (of absence); (*certificat*) pass; **en p.** on leave; **il s'est marié pendant sa p.** he got married during his leave *or* while (he was) on leave

permissionnaire [pɛrmisjɔnɛr] **1** *nm* **(a)** *Mil* man on leave; *Naut* liberty man **(b)** (*détenteur d'un permis*) permit holder **2** *adj* **officier p.** officer on leave

permissivité [pɛrmisivite] *nf* permissiveness

permutabilité [pɛrmytabilite] *nf* permutability, interchangeability

permutable [pɛrmytabl] *adj* permutable, interchangeable

permutation [pɛrmytasjɔ̃] *nf* **(a)** (*échange*) exchange of posts; *Mil* transfer **(b)** (*de lettres, de chiffres*) transposition; *Math* permutation **(c)** *Ling* metathesis

permuter [pɛrmyte] **1** *vt* **(a)** (*lettres, chiffres*) to transpose; *Math* to permute **(b)** *Vieilli* (*poste*) to exchange (**avec qn** with sb) **2** *vi* to exchange posts

pernicieusement [pɛrnisjøzmɑ̃] *adv* perniciously

pernicieux, -ieuse [pɛrnisjø, -jøz] *adj* pernicious, harmful; *Méd* **anémie pernicieuse** pernicious anæmia *or US* anemia

péroné [perɔne] *nm Anat* fibula

péronnelle [perɔnɛl] *nf F Péj* silly goose

péroraison [perɔrɛzɔ̃] *nf* peroration
pérorer [perɔre] *vi Péj* to hold forth, to speechify, to spout
Pérou [peru] *nm* Peru; *Fig* **ce n'est pas le P.** it's not great
peroxyde [perɔksid] *nm Ch* peroxide
perpendiculaire [pɛrpɑ̃dikylɛr] **1** *adj* perpendicular (**à, sur** to) **2** *nf Géom* perpendicular; **tirer une p.** to drop *or* draw a perpendicular (**à, sur** to)
perpendiculairement [pɛrpɑ̃dikylɛrmɑ̃] *adv* perpendicularly; **p. à** perpendicular to
perpète [pɛrpɛt] *adv F* (a) (*perpétuité*) **condamné à p.** sentenced to life; **il a pris p.** he got life; **je ne vais pas t'attendre jusqu'à p.!** I'm not going to wait for you for ever! (b) (*distance*) **envoyer qn à p.** (*très loin*) to send sb miles away; **vivre à P. (-les-Oies)** to live at the back of beyond *or* in the sticks *or Am* in the boonies
perpétration [pɛrpetrasjɔ̃] *nf Jur* perpetration
perpétrer [pɛrpetre] *vt* (**je perpètre; je perpétrerai**) to perpetrate
perpette [pɛrpɛt] = **perpète**
perpétuation [pɛrpetɥasjɔ̃] *nf* perpetuation
perpétuel, -elle [pɛrpetɥɛl] *adj* perpetual; (*Dieu, amour*) everlasting; (*secrétaire, membre*) permanent; **rente perpétuelle** perpetuity; **mouvement p.** perpetual motion; **crainte perpétuelle** perpetual *or* constant fear; **de perpétuels reproches** perpetual *or* constant *or* endless reproaches
perpétuellement [pɛrpetɥɛlmɑ̃] *adv* perpetually
perpétuer [pɛrpetɥe] **1** *vt* (*nom, réputation*) to perpetuate; (*tradition*) to carry on, to perpetuate; **p. le souvenir de qn** to perpetuate sb's memory, to keep sb's memory alive **2 se perpétuer** *vpr* to survive; *Fig* (*d'un problème*) to survive, to live on; **se p. dans son œuvre** to live on in one's work
perpétuité [pɛrpetɥite] *nf* perpetuity; **à p.** (*concession*) in perpetuity; (*emprisonnement*) for life; **être condamné (à la réclusion) à p.** to be sentenced to life (imprisonment)
perplexe [pɛrplɛks] *adj* perplexed, puzzled; **laisser qn p.** to perplex *or* puzzle sb
perplexité [pɛrplɛksite] *nf* perplexity; **être dans la plus grande p.** to be completely baffled *or* utterly perplexed; **plonger qn dans la plus grande p.** to completely baffle *or* utterly perplex sb; **avoir un air de p.** to look confused; **la p. se lisait sur son visage** you could see that he was confused
perquisition [pɛrkizisjɔ̃] *nf Jur* search; **mandat de p.** search warrant; **faire une p. chez qn** to search sb's premises; **procéder à une p.** to carry out a search
perquisitionner [pɛrkizisjɔne] **1** *vi Jur* to make *or* conduct *or* carry out a search; **p. au domicile de qn** to search sb's house **2** *vt* to search
perré [pere] *nm Constr* (*d'une route, d'une digue*) stone pitching *or* facing
perron [pɛrɔ̃] *nm Archit* (flight of) steps (*leading to building*), *Spéc* perron
perroquet [perɔkɛ] *nm* (a) *Orn* parrot; **p. de mer** puffin; **répéter qch comme un p.** to repeat sth parrot-fashion (b) (*boisson*) pastis with mint (c) *Naut* (*voile*) topgallant (d) (*crochet*) hook
perruche [peryʃ] *nf* (a) (*oiseau*) budgerigar, *F* budgie; *Vieilli* (*femelle du perroquet*) hen parrot; *F* (*femme bavarde*) chatterbox, chatterer (b) *Naut* mizzen topgallant sail
perruque [peryk] *nf* (a) (*postiche*) wig; *Hist* periwig, peruke (b) *Pêche* tangled line, *F* bird's nest
perruquier, -ière [perykje, -jɛr] *n* wig maker
pers [pɛr] *adj Litt* blue-green
persan, -ane [pɛrsɑ̃, -an] **1** *adj* Persian; **chat p.** Persian cat; **tapis p.** Persian carpet *or* (*plus petit*) rug **2** *nm Ling* Farsi; *Hist* Persian **3** *n* **P.** Persian
perse [pɛrs] **1** *nf Géog* **la P.** Persia; **tapis de P.** Persian carpet *or* (*plus petit*) rug **2** *adj* of/from ancient Persia, (ancient) Persian **3** *n* **P.** Persian **4** *nm Hist, Ling* Persian **5** *nf Tex* chintz
persécuté, -ée [pɛrsekyte] **1** *adj* (*personne*) persecuted **2** *n* (a) *Psy* sufferer from persecution mania (b) (*victime*) victim of persecution
persécuter [pɛrsekyte] *vt* (*minorité, peuple*) to persecute; (*harceler*) to harass; (*élève, enfant*) to bully; **se sentir persécuté** to feel persecuted
persécuteur, -trice [pɛrsekytœr, -tris] **1** *n* persecutor **2** *adj* persecuting
persécution [pɛrsekysjɔ̃] *nf* persecution; *Psy* **manie** *ou* **délire de p.** persecution mania *or* complex; *Psy* **avoir la manie de la p.** to have a persecution complex
persévérance [pɛrseverɑ̃s] *nf* perseverance
persévérant [pɛrseverɑ̃] *adj* persevering
persévérer [pɛrsevere] *vi* (**je persévère, n. persévérons; je persévérerai**) to persevere (**dans** in); **p. dans une attitude de refus** to remain stubbornly opposed; **il persévère dans l'erreur** he refuses to admit that he is wrong; **il n'a guère persévéré** he didn't show much perseverance; *Litt* **p. à faire qch** to persevere in doing sth
persicaire [pɛrsikɛr] *nf Bot* persicaria, lady's thumb
persienne [pɛrsjɛn] *nf* (slatted) shutter
persiflage [pɛrsiflaʒ] *nm* mockery
persifler [pɛrsifle] *vt* to mock, to ridicule
persifleur, -euse [pɛrsiflœr, -øz] **1** *n* mocker **2** *adj* mocking, derisive
persil [pɛrsi] *nm* parsley
persillade [pɛrsijad] *nf Culin* = sauce seasoned with parsley, garlic etc; (*plat*) beef seasoned with 'persillade' sauce
persillé [pɛrsije] *adj Culin* (a) **fromage à pâte persillée** veined cheese (b) (*viande*) marbled (c) (*assaisonné de persil*) sprinkled with chopped parsley
persique [pɛrsik] *adj* (ancient) Persian; **le Golfe P.** the Persian Gulf
persistance [pɛrsistɑ̃s] *nf* (a) (*constance*) persistence, persistency (**à faire qch** in doing sth); **avec p.** persistently; **p. dans le mensonge** persistent lying (b) (*continuité*) (*de la fièvre etc*) persistence, continuance
persistant [pɛrsistɑ̃] *adj* (*parfum, toux, fièvre etc*) persistent; *Bot* (*feuilles*) persistent, indeciduous
persister [pɛrsiste] *vi* (a) (*persévérer*) to persist; **il faut p.** you must persevere, you must keep at it; **p. dans sa résolution** to persist in one's resolve; **p. dans sa décision/son choix** to stick to one's decision/choice; **p. à faire qch** to persist in doing sth; **p. à croire qch** to persist in thinking sth, to continue to believe sth; **je persiste et signe** I'm sticking to it (b) (*continuer*) (*de fièvre, mécontentement etc*) to persist, to continue; **(il) persiste un doute/une interrogation** there remains a doubt/question
perso [pɛrso] *adj inv F* personal; **pour un ailier, il est trop p.** for a winger, he hogs the ball too much *or* he is too much of a solo artist
persona [pɛrsɔna] *adj inv* **p. grata/non grata** persona grata/ non grata; **déclarer qn p. grata/non grata** to declare sb persona grata/non grata
personnage [pɛrsɔnaʒ] *nm* (a) (*personne importante*) important person, *Fml* personage; **p. connu** *ou* **célèbre** celebrity; **p. officiel** VIP; **un grand p.** a great figure; **un grand p. de l'État** a State dignitary; **les grands personnages de l'histoire** the great names of history; **c'est devenu un p.** he's become an important person *or F* a big shot

(b) (*individu*) individual, character; **un curieux p.** an odd (sort of) character; **c'est un triste p.** he's a poor specimen; **cet homme-là, c'est un p.!** he's quite a character, that man!

(c) (*image publique*) (public) image, persona; **il s'est construit un p.** he's created an image for himself

(d) *Th, Littér* character; **p. principal** main *or* principal character; **jouer un p.** to play a part *or* role; *Fig* to play a part *or* role, to put on an act

(e) *Beaux-Arts* (*de tableau*) figure
personnalisation [pɛrsɔnalizasjɔ̃] *nf* personalization; *Mktg* customization
personnalisé [pɛrsɔnalize] *adj* personalized; (*voiture, crédit*) customized; **nous vous promettons un accueil p.** we promise you a welcome with a personal touch
personnaliser [pɛrsɔnalize] *vt* to personalize; (*chambre, appartement, bureau etc*) to give a personal touch to; **p. une voiture** to customize a car; **p. sa retraite** to adapt one's pension to one's personal needs; **p. l'image de marque du personnel** to give the staff a corporate identity; **nous devons p. l'accueil** we must welcome our guests/clients/*etc* in a more personal manner
personnalité [pɛrsɔnalite] *nf* (a) (*caractère*) personality; **trouble de la p.** personality disorder; **avoir de la p.** to be full of personality; **manquer de p.** to have no personality; **elle ne manque pas de p.** she's got plenty of personality, she doesn't lack personality; **c'est une forte p.** he/she has a strong personality; *F* **il a une sacrée p.** he's got one hell of a personality; *Pol* **culte de la p.** personality cult (b) (*personnage important*) personality, VIP, Very Important Person; **les personnalités politiques** the key political figures; **c'est une p.** he's/she's an important man/woman (c) *Jur* **p. juridique** legal personality *or* status
personne [pɛrsɔn] **1** *nf* (a) (*individu*) person; **trois personnes** three people; **le respect de la p. (humaine)** respect for the individual's rights; **une tierce p.** a third party; **par p. interposée** through a third person *or* party; **toute p. intéressée doit** *ou* **toutes les personnes intéressées sont priées de me contacter au …** all interested parties *or* all those interested should contact me at …; **p. interrogée** respondent; **cela coûte 20 francs par p.** it costs 20 francs a head *or* per head *or* per person; **il y a deux oranges par p.**

there are two oranges per person *or* each; **une p. âgée** an elderly person; **les personnes âgées** the elderly, elderly people, senior citizens; **p. handicapée** disabled person; **une grande p.** a grown-up; **une jeune p.** a young lady; **il y a erreur sur la p.** you've got the wrong person; **personnes à charge** dependants

(b) *Jur* **p. morale** body corporate, corporate body, legal entity; **p. physique** natural person; **personnes physiques ou morales** individual and legal entities

(c) *(soi-même)* **être satisfait/faire grand cas de sa (petite) p.** to be self-satisfied/to be full of (one's own) self-importance; **prendre soin de sa (petite) p.** to look after oneself; **il ne pense qu'à sa petite p.** he only thinks about number one, he's all self; **en p.** in person, personally; **le roi est venu en p.** the king came in person, the king himself came; **il est la bonté en p.** he is kindness itself, he is kindness personified; **elle est bien de sa p.** she's got a good figure; **il est bien/mal fait de sa p.** he's well/badly proportioned; **exposer sa p.** to expose oneself to danger, to risk one's life; **y aller** *ou* **donner de sa p.** to give everything one has

(d) *(personnalité)* person; **la gentillesse émane de toute sa p.** his/her whole person *or* being radiates kindness; **j'apprécie le cinéaste, mais je n'aime pas la p.** I like him as a film maker, but not as a person

(e) *Gram* person; **écrire à la troisième p. du singulier** to write in the third person singular

2 *pron indéf* [①B15,B,2] **(a)** *(quiconque)* anyone, anybody; **il le sait aussi bien** *ou* **mieux que p.** nobody knows it better than he does; **il est exclu que p. parle** nobody is allowed to speak; **elle danse comme p.** no-one dances *or* can dance like her, she dances *or* can dance better than anyone; **sans nommer p.** without naming anybody, naming no names, without naming names

(b) [①B60,B] *(with* **ne** *expressed or understood)* no-one, nobody; **p. n'est venu, il n'est venu p.** no-one *or* nobody has come; **qui est là? – p.** who's there? – no-one *or* nobody; **que p. ne sorte** no-one *or* nobody is to leave; **il n'y a p. de blessé** no-one *or* nobody has been injured, there are no casualties; **il n'y avait p. d'intéressé** no-one *or* nobody was interested; **p. d'autre n'était à bord** there was no-one else *or* nobody else on board; **je ne peux le dire à p. d'autre** I can't tell anyone *or* anybody else; **je ne dois rien à p.** I don't owe anyone anything; **dans cette maison p. ne se connaissait** in this house no-one knew anyone else *or* nobody knew anybody else; **je n'y suis pour p.** I'm not at home to anybody *or* anyone, if anybody *or* anyone calls I'm not at home; **je ne connais p. de plus hypocrite** I don't know anybody *or* anyone (who is) more hypocritical; **ne connaissez-vous p. qui puisse nous aider?** do you *or* don't you know anybody who could help us?; *F* **dès qu'il s'agit de travailler, il n'y a plus p.** as soon as there's work to be done, you can't see anyone for dust

personnel, -elle [pɛrsɔnɛl] **1** *adj* **(a)** *(lettre, entreprise, idées etc)* personal; *(titre de transport)* non-transferable; **objets personnels** personal belongings; **fortune personnelle** personal *or* private fortune; [①A26-28; B16-19,D] *Gram* **pronom p.** personal pronoun

(b) *(égoïste)* selfish; *Sp* **joueur p.** selfish player; **il avait un intérêt p. à voir se détériorer les choses** he had a personal *or* vested interest in seeing things get worse; **elle a des intérêts personnels dans cette affaire** she has a vested interest in the matter

2 *nm* [①A11,g,iii] *(d'une institution, d'une firme)* personnel, staff, employees; *(d'une école)* staff; *(d'une usine, dans l'industrie)* workforce, employees; *Mil* personnel, manpower; *Naut* complement; **faire partie du p. de ...** to be on the staff of ...; **p. réduit** reduced *or* skeleton staff; **manquer de p.** to be understaffed; **un membre du p.** a member of staff, *surtout US* a staffer; **directeur du p.** personnel manager; **service du p.** personnel (department); **le p. politique/artistique** the political/artistic staff

▶ **personnel**: **p. administratif** administrative staff; *Banque* **p. de back-office** back-office staff; **p. de bureau** office *or* clerical staff; *Av* **p. de cabine** flight personnel, cabin staff; **p. d'encadrement** management; *(animateurs)* activity organizers; *(moniteurs)* instructors; **p. extra** relief staff; *Av* **p. navigant** flight personnel *or* staff *or* crew; *TV etc* **p. de plateau** floor crew; *Av* **p. au sol** ground personnel *or* staff *or* crew; *Mktg* **p. de soutien commercial** sales support staff; **p. de vente** sales personnel

personnellement [pɛrsɔnɛlmɑ̃] *adv* personally

personnification [pɛrsɔnifikasjɔ̃] *nf* personification, embodiment

personnifier [pɛrsɔnifje] *vt (impf, pr sub* **n. personnifiions, v. personnifiiez)** *(objet, vertu, vice etc)* to personify; **elle personnifie toute la bonté humaine** she is the embodiment *or* personification of all human kindness; **il est la bêtise personnifiée** he is stupidity personified, he is stupidity itself; **il personnifie son pays** he typifies his country

perspectif, -ive¹ [pɛrspɛktif, -iv] *adj (plan)* perspective

perspective² [pɛrspɛktiv] *nf* **(a)** *(avenir, idée)* prospect; **en p.** in prospect; **avoir qch en p.** to have sth in prospect *or* in view; **quels sont les projets en p.?** what projects are there lined up *or* in prospect?; **perspectives de reprise** outlook for recovery; **elle était très excitée à la p. de faire ce voyage** she was very excited at the prospect of going on the journey; **j'envisage avec plaisir la p. de le revoir** I am looking forward to seeing him again; **des perspectives d'avenir** future prospects

(b) *Beaux-Arts etc* perspective; **p. à vol d'oiseau** bird's-eye view; **dessin en p.** drawing in perspective

(c) *(point de vue)* viewpoint, point of view; **ce roman est analysé sous des perspectives différentes** this novel is analysed from several different viewpoints *or* points of view; **dans une p. marxiste** from a Marxist viewpoint *or* point of view

perspicace [pɛrspikas] *adj* shrewd, perspicacious

perspicacité [pɛrspikasite] *nf* shrewdness, insight, perspicacity

persuader [pɛrsɥade] **1** *vt* **(a) p. qn** to persuade *or* convince sb; **p. qn de qch/de faire qch** to persuade *or* convince sb of sth/to persuade sb to do sth; **j'ai fini par les p.** I convinced *or* persuaded them in the end, I talked them round in the end; **être persuadé de qch** to be convinced of sth; **être persuadé que ...** to be sure *or* convinced that ...; **j'en suis tout à fait persuadé** I'm quite convinced (of it); **je n'en suis pas persuadé** I'm not convinced (of it)

(b) *Vieilli* **p. qch à qn** to persuade sb of sth, to make sb believe sth

2 se persuader *vpr (se convaincre)* to persuade *or* convince oneself; **ils se sont persuadé(s) que ...** they have persuaded *or* convinced themselves that ...

persuasif, -ive [pɛrsɥazif, -iv] *adj* persuasive

persuasion [pɛrsɥazjɔ̃] *nf* **(a)** *(fait ou action de persuader)* persuasion; **à force de p.** through (the use of) persuasion; **agir par (la) p.** to use persuasion, to persuade; **avoir un grand pouvoir de p.** to have great powers of persuasion **(b)** *(conviction, certitude)* conviction, belief

perte [pɛrt] *nf* **(a)** *(d'argent, d'un proche, d'un procès, de la vue, de la raison etc)* loss; **des pertes importantes** considerable *or* significant losses; **de lourdes pertes en hommes et en matériel** heavy losses of men and equipment; *Fig F* **elle a été renvoyée avec p. et fracas** she was thrown out of her job; *Fig F* **il est sorti avec p. et fracas** he made a big scene when he left; **à p. de vue** as far as the eye can see; **ce n'est pas une grosse p.** it's no great loss; **p. de pouvoir d'achat** loss of purchasing power; **pertes et profits** profit and loss; *aussi Fig* **passer qch par pertes et profits** to write sth off; **vendre qch à p.** to sell sth at a loss

(b) *(gaspillage)* waste; **une p. de temps** a waste of time; **en pure p.** to no purpose, fruitlessly; **expliquer qch à qn en pure p.** to waste one's time *or* one's breath trying to explain sth to sb; **une dépense en pure p.** wasteful expenditure

(c) *(déperdition)* loss; *(de tuyau, récipient)* leakage; **p. de chaleur** heat loss, loss of heat; *Él* **p. de charge** drop in voltage; *Él* **p. à la terre** earth *or Am* ground leakage; *Av* **avion en p. de vitesse** plane that is losing speed; *Fig* **le président/le cinéma semble en p. de vitesse** the President/the film industry seems to be running out of steam; **pertes de mémoire** memory losses; *Méd* **pertes de sang** bleeding

(d) *(destruction)* ruin; **jurer la p. de qn** to swear to ruin sb; **il/l'entreprise court à sa p.** he/the company is heading for disaster

▶ **perte**: **p. de bénéfice** loss of profit; **p. brute** gross loss; **p. en capitaux** capital loss; *Fin* **p. de change** (foreign) exchange loss; **p. de connaissance** loss of consciousness; *Ordinat* **p. de données irréparable** irretrievable data loss; **p. envisagée** estimated loss; *Fin* **p. d'intérêts** loss of interest; *Fin* **p. latente** unrealized loss; *Fin* **p. nette** net loss; *Fin* **p. sèche** dead loss; *Compta* **p. supportée** loss attributable; *Fin* **p. totale** total loss; *Compta* **p. transférée** loss transferred; *Méd* **pertes blanches** vaginal discharge, *Spéc* leucorrhoea, *surtout US* leukorrhea; **pertes humaines** loss of life

pertinemment [pɛrtinamɑ̃] *adv* **(a)** *Litt (s'exprimer)* pertinently, to the point **(b) savoir qch p.** to know sth for a fact

pertinence [pɛrtinɑ̃s] *nf* pertinence, pertinency, relevance

pertinent [pɛrtinɑ̃] *adj* pertinent, relevant

pertuis [pɛrtɥi] *nm* **(a)** *(canal)* sluice **(b)** *(d'un fleuve)* narrows; *(détroit)* strait(s), (narrow) channel

perturbant [pɛrtyrbɑ̃] *adj* disturbing, upsetting
perturbateur, -trice [pɛrtyrbatœr, -tris] **1** *adj* disruptive **2** *n* troublemaker
perturbation [pɛrtyrbasjɔ̃] *nf* (*de services publics*) disruption; *Astron* perturbation; **p. (atmosphérique)** (atmospheric) disturbance; **perturbations du service aérien** disruption of air travel
perturber [pɛrtyrbe] *vt* (*services publics, trains, métro*) to disrupt; (*personne*) to perturb, to upset; *Astron* to perturb
péruvien, -ienne [peryvjɛ̃, -jɛn] **1** *adj* Peruvian **2** *n* **P.** Peruvian
pervenche [pɛrvɑ̃ʃ] *nf* **(a)** (*plante*) periwinkle; **(bleu) p.** periwinkle blue **(b)** *F* (*contractuelle*) (female) traffic warden, *Am* meter maid
pervers, -erse [pɛrvɛr, -ɛrs] **1** *adj* (*idée*) perverse; (*esprit, pratiques sexuelles*) perverted; **goûts p.** unnatural *or* perverted tastes; **conseils p.** evil advice; **effet p.** perverse effect **2** *n* twisted person; (*vicieux*) pervert
perversion [pɛrvɛrsjɔ̃] *nf* (*des goûts, de la morale*) perversion; (*de l'esprit*) warping; *F* **c'est de la p.!** that's twisted *or* perverted!; **p. sexuelle** sexual perversion
perversité [pɛrvɛrsite] *nf* perversity, depravity
perverti, -ie [pɛrvɛrti] **1** *adj* (*personne*) perverted, depraved **2** *n* pervert
pervertir [pɛrvɛrtir] **1** *vt* (*goût, sens*) to pervert; (*personne*) to pervert, to deprave, to corrupt; (*morale*) to corrupt **2 se pervertir** *vpr* (*d'un goût, d'un sens*) to become perverted; (*d'une personne*) to become perverted *or* depraved *or* corrupt(ed); (*d'une morale*) to become corrupt(ed)
pesage [pəzaʒ] *nm* **(a)** (*pesée*) weighing **(b)** *Courses de chevaux* weigh-in; (*lieu*) weighing room
pesamment [pəzamɑ̃] *adv* heavily; **marcher p.** to walk with a heavy tread *or* heavily
pesant [pəzɑ̃] **1** *adj* (*valise, pas*) heavy; (*style, écrivain*) heavy, ponderous; (*esprit*) slow, sluggish; (*sommeil*) deep; (*ambiance*) oppressive; **silence p.** heavy silence; **marcher à pas pesants** to walk with a heavy step *or* heavily; **le temps me semble p.** time hangs heavy on my hands **2** *nm* **cela vaut son p. d'or** *ou F* **de moutarde** *ou F* **de cacahuètes** it's worth its weight in gold
pesanteur [pəzɑ̃tœr] *nf* **(a)** *Phys* gravity; **p. spécifique** specific gravity **(b)** (*lourdeur*) heaviness; (*d'un mouvement, d'une démarche*) inelegance, unwieldiness; (*de l'esprit*) slowness, sluggishness; **j'ai une p. d'estomac** there's something lying heavy on my stomach; *Fig* **pesanteurs intellectuelles** intellectual baggage *or* impedimenta; *Fig* **pesanteurs économiques** economic impedimenta
pèse-alcool, *pl* **pèse-alcools** [pɛzalkɔl] *nm* alcoholometer
pèse-bébé, *pl* **pèse-bébés** [pɛzbebe] *nm* baby scales
pesée [pəze] *nf* **(a)** weighing; *Boxe, Courses de chevaux* weigh-in; **faire la p. de qch** to weigh sth; **cette balance a une p. de 150 kilos** the scale(s) can weigh up to 150 kilos **(b)** (*pression*) force, effort; **exercer une p. sur une porte** to try to force a door
pèse-lait [pɛzlɛ], *pl* **pèse-laits** *nm* lactometer
pèse-lettre(s), *pl* **pèse-lettres** [pɛzlɛtr] *nm* letter scales
pèse-personne, *pl* **pèse-personnes** [pɛzpɛrsɔn] *nm* scales
peser [pəze] **(je pèse, n. pesons; je pèserai) 1** *vt* to weigh; **p. à vide** to tare; *Fig* **p. ses mots** *ou* **ses paroles** to weigh one's words, to think before one speaks; **et je pèse mes mots!** and I don't say it lightly!; **réponse bien pesée** considered *or* careful answer; *Fig* **tout bien pesé** all things considered; **p. tous les éléments** to weigh (up) all the facts; **p. une décision** to weigh up *or* ponder a decision; **p. le pour et le contre** to weigh (up) the pros and cons; *Sp* **se faire p.** to weigh in

2 se peser *vpr* to weigh oneself

3 *vi* (*faire ou avoir comme poids*) to weigh; (*être lourd*) to be heavy; (*d'un argument*) to carry weight; **ce paquet pèse deux kilos** this parcel weighs two kilos; **il ne pèse pas lourd** he doesn't weigh much, he's not very heavy; *Fig* he doesn't carry much weight *or* count for much; **mon avis ne pèse pas lourd** my opinion doesn't carry much weight *or* count for much; **cela me pèse de vous le demander** it isn't easy for me to ask you; **le temps lui pèse** time hangs heavy on his hands; **l'isolement/votre absence me pèse** this isolation/your absence gets me down *or* is a strain; **cette ambiance me pèse un peu** I'm finding this atmosphere a bit oppressive; **toutes ces discussions lui pèsent** all these discussions are a strain on him; **p. sur qch** to press on sth; **p. sur un levier** to press down *or* push down on a lever; *Can* **p. sur un bouton** to push a button; **aliment qui pèse sur l'estomac** food that lies heavy on the stomach; **p. sur le cœur à qn** to give sb a heavy heart; **un silence pesait sur l'assemblée** a heavy silence hung over the meeting; **une lourde responsabilité pèse sur lui** he is weighed down by a heavy responsibility; **une menace qui pèse sur nous** a threat that is hanging over us; **ça lui pèse sur la conscience** it lies heavy on his conscience; **p. sur un choix** to weigh up *or* mull over a choice; **p. sur** *ou* **dans une décision** to carry weight in a decision; **p. sur un mot** to lay stress on *or* to stress a word
peseta [pezeta] *nf* peseta
pèse-vin, *pl* **pèse-vins** [pɛzvɛ̃] *nm* oenometer
peson [pəzɔ̃] *nm* balance
pessaire [pesɛr] *nm Méd* pessary
pesse [pɛs] *nf,* **pessereau** [pɛsro] *nm* (*plante*) horse tail, *Spéc* equisetum
pessimisme [pesimism] *nm* pessimism
pessimiste [pesimist] **1** *adj* pessimistic **2** *n* pessimist
peste [pɛst] *nf* **(a)** *Méd* plague, *Litt, Arch* pestilence; **être atteint de la p.** to have the plague, to be stricken with the plague; *F* **fuir qch/qn comme la p.** to avoid sth/sb like the plague; **je me méfie de lui/ça comme de la p.** I don't trust him/it one little bit, I wouldn't trust him/it as far as I could throw him/it; *Litt, Vieilli* **p.!** good gracious!, heavens!; *Litt, Arch* **(la) p. soit du vieux fou!** a plague on the old fool!; *Vieilli* **que la p. t'étouffe!** a plague on you!

(b) *Fig Péj* (*enfant*) pest, nuisance; **une petite p.** a little devil *or* pest

(c) *Litt Péj* (*chose dangereuse*) curse; **ces livres sont la p. de nos consciences** these books are a blight upon our souls
▶ **peste: p. bovine** cattle plague; **la p. bubonique** *ou* **noire** the bubonic plague; *Hist* the Black Death; **p. porcine** swine fever
pester [pɛste] *vi* **p. contre qn/qch** to curse sb/sth, to rave at sb/sth; **il pestait** he was cursing
pesticide [pɛstisid] **1** *adj* pesticidal **2** *nm* pesticide
pestiféré, -ée [pɛstifere] **1** *adj* plague-stricken **2** *n* plague victim; **fuir qn comme un p.** to avoid sb like the plague
pestilence [pɛstilɑ̃s] *nf* stench, stink
pestilentiel, -elle [pɛstilɑ̃sjɛl] *adj* stinking, fetid
pet [pɛ] *nm F* **(a)** (*vent*) fart; **faire** *ou* **lâcher un p.** to fart; **ça ne vaut pas un p. (de lapin)** it isn't worth a monkey's fart *or* a damn; *Fig* **il a toujours un p. de travers** there's always something wrong with him *or* the matter with him **(b)** *Arg Vieilli* (*grabuge*) **il va y avoir du p.** there's going to be trouble **(c)** (*choc*) [pɛt] **ta voiture a pris un p.** your car's had a bash; **j'ai fait un p. à la voiture** I've put a dent in the car; **plein de pets** all bashed up, full of dents
pétainiste [petenist] *Hist* **1** *adj* Pétainist **2** *n* follower of Pétain, Pétainist
pétale [petal] *nm* petal
pétanque [petɑ̃k] *nf* ≈ bowls (*played in the South of France*)
pétant [petɑ̃] *adj F* **à neuf heures pétantes** at nine o'clock sharp *or* on the dot, on the stroke of nine
pétaradant [petaradɑ̃] *adj* (*moto, camion etc*) spluttering, sputtering
pétarade [petarad] *nf* **(a)** (*d'un cheval*) (succession of) farts **(b)** (*de feux d'artifice, d'armes à feu*) crackling **(c)** (*de voiture, mobylette etc*) backfiring, backfire
pétarader [petarade] *vi* **(a)** (*d'un cheval*) to let off a succession of farts **(b)** (*de feux d'artifice, d'armes à feu*) to crackle **(c)** (*de voiture, mobylette etc*) to backfire
pétard [petar] *nm* **(a)** (*feu d'artifice*) (fire)cracker, *Br* banger; *Min* shot, blast; *Mil* explosive charge, *Arch* petard; *Rail* fog signal; **faire partir** *ou* **claquer un p.** to let off a (fire)cracker *or Br* banger; *Fig* **p. mouillé** damp squib **(b)** *F* (*grabuge*) **il va y avoir du p.** there's going to be a hell of a row; **faire du p.** to raise a stink; **être en p.** (*en colère*) to be raging **(contre** against), to be in a flaming temper **(c)** *F* (*pistolet*) shooter, *US* gat **(d)** *F* (*derrière*) bum, *Am* ass, fanny **(e)** *F* (*joint*) joint, reefer, spliff
pétasse [petas] *nf très F* (*terme injurieux*) bitch, cow
pétaudière [petodjɛr] *nf* bedlam, bear garden; **la réunion a tourné en p.** the meeting turned into a bear garden
pet-de-nonne, *pl* **pets-de-nonne** *nm Culin* fritter
pété [pete] *adj F* (*ivre*) smashed, plastered
péter [pete] **(je pète, n. pétons; je péterai) 1** *vi* **(a)** *F* (*d'une personne*) to fart; *Fig* **il l'a envoyé p.** he told him to piss off; *Fig* **p. dans la soie** to be stinking rich, to be loaded; *Fig* **il pète plus haut que son derrière** *ou* **son cul** he thinks he's really somebody *or* really it, he thinks he's God's gift to humanity

(b) *F* (*exploser*) to blow up; **faire p. des pétards** to set off (fire)crackers; *Fig* **il faut que ça pète** let's have it all out in the open; **ça va p. entre eux** they're going to have one hell of a row

(c) (*de bois qui brûle*) to crack, to crackle; (*d'un bouchon*) to pop

(d) *F* (*casser*) to break; (*d'une ficelle, d'une branche, d'un *câble*) to snap, to break; **ça va lui p. entre les mains** it'll break in his hands; **tous les boutons étaient prêts à p.** all the buttons were about to pop off

(**e**) *F* **p. de joie/santé** to be jumping for joy/bouncing with health; **et je veux que ça pète!** chop, chop!, *Arg* and get your finger out!; **on a enfin l'impression que ça pète!** things seem to be moving at last!, we're seeing a bit of action at last!

2 *vt F* (**a**) **p. le feu** *ou* **la forme** to be bursting with energy *or* vitality; **ça va p. des flammes** there's going to be a hell of a row

(**b**) (*casser*) to bust; *F* **je vais lui p. la gueule** I'll smash his face in

3 se péter *vpr F* (*d'une machine etc*) to break; **il s'est pété la gueule** (*il est tombé*) he came a cropper; (*il s'est saoulé*) he got smashed *or* plastered

pète(-)sec [pɛtsɛk] *F* **1** *nm inv* petty tyrant **2** *adj inv* curt

péteux, -euse [petø, -øz] *F Péj* **1** *n* (*lâche*) yellowbelly, coward; **c'est un petit p.** he's yellow **2** *adj* cowardly

pétillant [petijɑ̃] *adj* (*feu*) crackling; (*vin*) sparkling; (*eau*) fizzy; *Fig* (*yeux*) sparkling; *Fig* **esprit p.** sparkling wit

pétillement [petijmɑ̃] *nm* (*du bois qui brûle*) crackling; (*du champagne*) sparkling, fizzing, bubbling; (*des yeux*) sparkling

pétiller [petije] *vi* (*de bois qui brûle*) to crackle; (*d'une boisson*) to sparkle, to fizz, to bubble; *Fig* (*des yeux*) to sparkle; *Fig* **p. d'esprit** to sparkle with wit; **elle pétillait de joie** she was bubbling over with joy; **un regard qui pétille de joie/d'intelligence** a look that sparkles with joy/with intelligence

pétiole [pesjɔl] *nm Bot* petiole

petiot, -ote [pətjo, -ɔt] *F* **1** *adj* tiny, wee **2** *n* tiny child; **ma petiote** my little girl; **viens ici, p.** come here, little fellow

petit, -ite [p(ə)ti, -it] **1** *adj* (**a**) [①A17,3,a] (*de taille réduite*) small, little; **un p. homme** a small *or* short *or* little man; **c'est un homme p.** he's small *or* short *or* little; **jouer avec des petits soldats/des petites voitures** to play with toy soldiers/toy cars; **une toute petite maison/boîte/entreprise** a tiny little house/box/firm; **petite distance** short distance; **un p. nombre de gens** a small number of people; **ces chaussures sont trop petites (pour moi)** these shoes are too small (for me); **faire de petits profits** to make a small profit; **rouler à petite vitesse** to drive slowly; **pendant un p. moment** for a little while; *F* **nous avons attendu un bon p. moment** we waited quite a time; *F* **j'y suis resté une petite demi-heure** I stayed there just under half an hour; *Fig* **se faire tout p.** to make oneself as inconspicuous as possible; **il s'est fait tout p. devant elle** he tried to do everything to please her; *Fig* **comme le monde est p.** it's a small world

(**b**) (*méprisant*) **p. crétin/con!** little idiot/bastard!

(**c**) (*affectueux*) little; **mais ma petite Louise ...** but my dear Louise ...; **Ma chère petite maman** (*dans une lettre*) Dear Mummy; **un p. coup de rouge** a drop of red wine; **et si on se regardait une petite cassette vidéo?** how about watching a video?; **je prendrais bien une petite cigarette** I'd love a cigarette; **on s'en fume une petite?** shall we have a quick smoke *or Br* fag?

(**d**) (*de niveau inférieur*) lesser, minor; *Scol* **les petites classes** the lower classes; **le p. personnel** the junior staff; **la petite industrie** light industry; **les petits propriétaires** the small landowners; *Com* **petite caisse** petty cash

(**e**) (*de moindre importance*) (*problème, erreur etc*) small, minor, insignificant; (*fait*) insignificant, unimportant; *Péj* (*plainte, affaire*) petty; (*événement*) minor; **petites routes** minor roads; **entrer par la petite porte** to start off at the bottom; **ce n'est pas une petite affaire** it's no small matter; **p. accident** minor accident; **j'ai un p. rhume** I've a slight cold *or* a bit of a cold; **les petites gens** ordinary people

(**f**) (*jeune*) little, young; **p. enfant** little *or* young child; **petite fille** little girl; **mon p. frère** my little brother; **tu es trop p. pour ça** you're too young for that; **quand tu étais p.** when you were little *or* small *or* young; **un p. Anglais** an English boy; **les petits Thomas** the Thomas children

(**g**) (*faible*) **il a une petite santé** he's delicate; **une petite voix** a small voice

(**h**) (*borné*) narrow-minded; (*mesquin*) petty; (*remarque, acte*) mean, petty; (*dans ses compliments, ses défaites*) ungenerous; **c'est vraiment p.** that's really mean *or* petty; **c'est un p. esprit** he's petty-minded

2 *n* (*enfant*) (little) boy, *f* (little) girl; **pauvre petit(e)** poor little thing; *Scol* **les petits** the juniors; **le p.** (*dans une famille*) the youngest (boy); *F* **bonjour, mon p.** (*à une femme, un enfant*) good morning, my dear

3 *nm* (*d'un animal*) young; **petits du chien/du chat** (dog's) puppies/(cat's) kittens; **faire** *ou* **avoir des petits** to have young; (*d'une chienne*) to have pups, *Spéc* to pup, to whelp; (*d'une lionne*) to have cubs, *Spéc* to whelp; (*d'une truie*) to have piglets, *Spéc* to farrow; (*d'une chatte*) to have kittens, *Spéc* to kitten; (*d'une louve*) to have cubs, *Spéc* to cub; *Fig F* **faire des petits** (*de l'argent*) to increase, to multiply

4 *adv* **p. à p.** little by little, bit by bit, gradually; **en p.** on a small scale, in miniature; **le même mais en plus p.** the same only smaller

▶ **petit**: **p. ami** boyfriend; **petite amie** girlfriend; *Journ* **petite annonce** classified advertisement, small ad; *Journ* **petites annonces personnelles** personal column; **p. bois** kindling wood; *Typ* **petite capitale** small cap; *F* **le p. coin** the toilet, *Br* the loo, *Am* the john; **p. commerçant** small shopkeeper; *F* **p. copain** boyfriend; *F* **petite copine** girlfriend; *Typ* **petits corps** small type; **p. cousin/petite cousine** second cousin; **p. déjeuner** breakfast; **p. déjeuner américain** American breakfast; **p. déjeuner à l'anglaise** English breakfast; **p. déjeuner continental** Continental breakfast; **p. doigt** little finger, *Am, Scot* pinkie; **la petite enfance** early childhood, infancy; **petits fours** petits fours; **la petite mort** orgasm; **petites et moyennes entreprises** small (and medium-sized) businesses; **petites et moyennes industries** small (and medium-sized) industries; *F* **p. nom** first *or Br* Christian name; *Fig* **petites phrases** (*des hommes politiques*) soundbites; **il est connu pour ses petites phrases très médiatiques** he's the master of the soundbite; **petits pois** (garden) peas; *Fin* **p. porteur** small investor *or* shareholder; *Culin* **p. salé** = streaky bacon; **petits salariés** low wage-earners

petit-beurre, *pl* **petits-beurre** *nm Culin* butter biscuit *or Am* cookie

petit-bourgeois, petite-bourgeoise, *pl* **petit(e)s-bourgeois(es)** **1** *adj aussi Péj* lower middle class, petit-bourgeois **2** *n* member of the lower middle class; **les petits-bourgeois** the petty bourgeoisie

petit-déj' [p(ə)tidɛʒ] *nm F* = **petit déjeuner**

petite-fille, *pl* **petites-filles** [p(ə)titfij] *nf* granddaughter

petitement [pətitmɑ̃] *adv* (**a**) (*dans la pauvreté*) poorly (**b**) (*à l'étroit*) **elle est logée p.** she lives in cramped accommodation (**c**) (*bassement*) meanly, pettily

petite-nièce, *pl* **petites-nièces** [p(ə)titnjɛs] *nf* great-niece

petitesse [p(ə)titɛs] *nf* (**a**) (*d'un objet*) smallness, small size; (*d'une silhouette*) slenderness (**b**) *Péj* (*mesquinerie*) meanness, pettiness; (*d'un repas, d'une somme d'argent*) paltriness; **p. d'esprit** narrow-mindedness; **p. de cœur** small-mindedness (**c**) *Péj* (*action mesquine*) shabby deed

petit-fils, *pl* **petits-fils** *nm* grandson

petit-gris, *pl* **petits-gris** *nm* (**a**) (*écureuil*) Siberian squirrel; (*fourrure*) squirrel (fur) (**b**) *Culin* = edible brown snail

pétition [petisjɔ̃] *nf* (**a**) petition; **adresser une p. à qn** to petition sb; **faire signer une p. à qn** to get sb to sign a petition (**b**) **p. de principe** begging the question, *Spéc* petitio principii

pétitionnaire [petisjɔnɛr] *n* petitioner

petit-lait, *pl* **petits-laits** *nm* whey; **cela se boit comme du p.** it goes down *or* slips down a treat; *Fig* **boire du p.** to lap it up

petit-maître, *pl* **petits-maîtres** *nm Arch* fop, dandy

petit-nègre *nm* (*no pl*) *Ling F* (**a**) (*mauvais français*) bad French; **c'est du p.** it's gibberish (**b**) *Vieilli* (*français parlé dans les colonies*) pidgin French

petit-neveu, *pl* **petits-neveux** *nm* great-nephew

petits-enfants [p(ə)tizɑ̃fɑ̃] *nmpl* grandchildren

petit-suisse, *pl* **petits-suisses** *nm Culin* petit-suisse (*small cream cheese dessert*)

pétochard, -arde [petɔʃar, -ard] *n F* yellowbelly, coward

pétoche [petɔʃ] *nf F* jitters; **avoir la p.** to have the jitters, to be scared stiff; **ficher** *ou* **flanquer** *ou très F* **foutre la p. à qn** to give sb the jitters, to scare sb stiff

pétoire [petwar] *nf* (**a**) (*sarbacane*) peashooter (**b**) (*mauvais fusil*) popgun (**c**) (*moto*) motorbike; (*mobylette*) moped

peton [pətɔ̃] *nm Enf* tootsy(-wootsy); **petons** tootsies, tootsy-wootsies

pétoncle [petɔ̃kl] *nm* scallop

Pétrarque [petrark] *nm* Petrarch

pétrel [petrɛl] *nm* petrel; **p. tempête** storm(y) petrel

pétri [petri] *adj* kneaded, moulded, *US* molded (**de** out of); **un homme p. d'orgueil** a man puffed up with pride; **p. d'ignorance** steeped in ignorance; **p. de contradictions** riddled with contradictions

pétrifiant [petrifjɑ̃] *adj* (*eau*) petrifying, petrifactive; (*nouvelle*) stupefying

pétrification [petrifikasjɔ̃] *nf* petrification, petrifaction; *Fig* **p. du cœur** hardening of the heart; **p. de l'esprit** sclerosis of the mind

pétrifier [petrifje] (*impf, pr sub* **n. pétrifiions, v. pétrifiiez**) **1** *vt* (**a**) *Minér* to petrify; *Fig* **pétrifié de peur** petrified, paralysed *or US* paralyzed with fear; **pétrifié de froid** frozen stiff **(b)** (*couvrir de calcaire*) to encrust with lime **2 se pétrifier** *vpr Minér* to petrify, to become petrified; *Fig* **son sourire se pétrifia** his smile froze; **son esprit se pétrifiait** he was developing sclerosis of the mind; **en entendant son nom, elle s'est pétrifiée** hearing his name, she froze

pétrin [petrɛ̃] *nm* kneading trough; **p. mécanique** kneading machine; *F* **mettre qn/se mettre dans le p.** to get sb/get into a mess *or* a fix; *F* **laisser qn dans le p.** to drop sb in it, to leave sb in a mess; *F* **être dans le p.** to be in a mess *or* a fix; **nous voilà dans un beau** *ou* **joli** *ou* **sale p.** that's a fine *or* right mess we're in

pétrir [petrir] *vt* (*brasser*) (*pâte à pain*) to knead; (*façonner*) (*argile*) to knead, to shape, to mould, *US* to mold; *Fig* **p. l'esprit de qn** to mould *or* shape sb's mind; **il lui pétrissait le bras** he was kneading her arm; **il pétrissait son chapeau avec nervosité** he was nervously fiddling *or* toying with his hat; *Méd* **p. un muscle** to knead a muscle

pétrissage [petrisaʒ] *nm* kneading

pétrisseur, -euse [petrisœr, -øz] **1** *n* **(ouvrier) p.** dough mixer **2** *nf* **pétrisseuse** (*machine*) kneading machine

pétrochimie [petroʃimi] *nf* petrochemistry

pétrochimique [petroʃimik] *adj* petrochemical

pétrochimiste [petroʃimist] *n* petrochemist

pétrodollar [petrodɔlar] *nm Fin* petrodollar

pétrographie [petrɔgrafi] *nf Géol* petrography

pétrole [petrɔl] *nm* oil, petroleum; **p. brut** crude (oil); **p. lampant** paraffin (oil), *Am* kerosene; **gisement de p.** oil deposit, oilfield; **puits de p.** oil well; **lampe à p.** oil lamp; **bleu p.** *inv* petrol blue; **vert p.** *inv* deep turquoise

pétrolette [petrɔlɛt] *nf F* moped

pétroleuse [petrɔløz] *nf* activist; *Hist* female incendiary (*during the Paris Commune of 1871*)

pétrolier, -ière [petrɔljɛ, -jɛr] **1** *adj* **l'industrie pétrolière** the oil *or* petroleum industry; **société pétrolière** oil company; **pays p.** oil-producing country; **navire p.** (oil) tanker; **choc p.** oil crisis **2** *nm* **(a)** (*financier, industriel*) oil magnate, oilman; (*technicien*) petroleum engineer **(b)** (*navire*) (oil) tanker

pétrolifère [petrɔlifɛr] *adj* oil-bearing, *Spéc* petroliferous; **gisement p.** oilfield

pétulance [petylɑ̃s] *nf* liveliness, exuberance

pétulant [petylɑ̃] *adj* lively, exuberant

pétunia [petynja] *nm* petunia

peu [pø] **1** *adv* **(a)** ((*en*) *petite quantité*) little; **très/trop p.** very/too little; **de l'instruction, il en avait p. ou pas** he had little or no education, he had precious little education; **p. ou point** little or none; **manger p. (ou point)** to eat little (or nothing); **p. à p.** bit by bit, little by little, gradually; **c'est p. dire** that's an understatement; **c'est p. dire qu'il était content** it's an understatement to say that he was content; **ce n'est pas p. dire** that's saying a good deal *or* a lot; **il a p. fait pour nous** he has done (very) little for us; **quelque p.** somewhat, rather; **je suis quelque p. surpris** I am somewhat *or* rather surprised; **si tu m'aimais tant soit p.** if you loved me at all *or* even a little; **si tu es tant soit p. fatigué** if you're at all *or* the least bit tired; **p. s'en faut** *ou* **il s'en faut de p. pour que je me mette en colère** I'm on the verge of losing my temper, it won't take much to make me lose my temper; **p. s'en est fallu qu'il fasse tout rater, il s'en est fallu de p. qu'il fasse tout rater** he very nearly ruined everything; **pour p. qu'il soit de mauvaise humeur, on va passer une sacrée soirée** if he's in a bad mood at all, we're in for one hell of an evening; **il ne s'est pas découragé pour si p.** he didn't get discouraged by such a small thing; **p. de viande** not much meat, very little meat; **c'est p. de chose** it's nothing; **nous en savons p. de choses** we know little about it, we don't know much about it; **il suffirait de p. de choses pour que ça fonctionne** it wouldn't need much *or* it would take very little to get it to work; **nous sommes bien p. de choses** life is so fragile; **fort p.** (*de sucre etc*) very little, not much; *F* **très p. pour moi!** not for me!

(b) [①A5,C,d] (*nombre*) few; **p. en garderont un souvenir** few (people) will remember it; **p. de gens** *ou* **monde** few people; **très p. de gens** very few people, not very many people; **p. d'entre eux avaient voyagé** few of them had travelled; **en p. de mots** in a few words

(c) (*pas* (*très*)) not very; **p. utile** not very useful; **p. intelligent** unintelligent, not very intelligent; **p. enviable** unenviable; **p. honnête** dishonest; **p. profond** shallow; **p. souvent** not very often, infrequently; **elle n'est pas p. séduisante** she's more than a little seductive

(d) (*de temps*) **il reste p. de temps** there's not much time left; **très p. de temps** very little time, not very much time; **en très p. de temps** very quickly, in no time at all; **p. après** shortly after(wards), not long after(wards); **sous p., dans p., avant p., d'ici p.** soon, shortly, before long; **depuis p.** lately, recently; **j'ai manqué le train de p.** I (only) just missed the train; **il y a p.** not (very) long ago, recently; **j'ai p. de temps à vous accorder** I don't have much time

2 *nm* **(a)** (*petite quantité*) little; **le p. qu'il y a est à votre disposition** you are welcome to the little there is; **le p. que je sais de lui** the little I know about him; **le p. d'argent qu'il me reste** what little money I have left; **finis le plat, pour le p. qu'il reste** finish the dish, there's only a little bit left; **son p. d'instruction** what little education he has had

(b) [①A5,C,d] **un p.** a little, a bit; **un p. de** a little, a bit of; **il nous reste un p. de temps/sucre** we still have a little time/sugar left *or* a bit of time/sugar left; **elle a un p. moins/un p. plus de quarante ans** she's a little under/over forty; **j'en veux un p. plus/moins** I want a little *or* a bit more/less; **un tout petit p.** a tiny bit, a very little; **un tout petit p. de beurre** a tiny bit of butter, a very little butter; **encore un p.** a bit more, a little more; (*encore quelques-uns*) a few more; **encore un p. de lait** a bit *or* a little more milk; **j'ai besoin d'un petit p. de temps avant de donner une réponse** I need a little bit of time before giving an answer; **il sait un p. d'anglais** he knows a little English *or* a bit of English, he has a smattering of English; **vous êtes allé un p. loin!** you went a bit far!; **je suis un p. en retard** I'm a bit *or* a little late; **il est un p. artiste** he's something of an artist; *F* **ça, c'est un p. fort!** that's a bit much!; **un p. plus et il tombait dans l'eau** he very nearly fell in the water; **pour un p. je l'aurais jeté dehors** I all but *or* I very nearly threw him out; **écoutez un p.** just listen; **viens un p. ici** come here a minute; **regarde un p. ce que tu as fait!** just look what you've done!; **il m'aime un p., beaucoup, passionnément, à la folie, pas du tout** (*en effeuillant une marguerite*) = he loves me, he loves me not; *très F* **t'as vu un p. comment il m'a parlé?** did you see the way he spoke to me?; *F* **je vous demande un p.!** I ask you!; *F* **tu ferais ça? – un p.!** you'd do that? – you bet!; *F* **un p. mon neveu!** you bet!, sure!

(c) (*de temps*) **restez encore un p.** stay a bit longer, stay a little (while) longer; **j'aurais voulu prolonger encore un p. mon séjour** I would have liked to extend my stay a bit *or* a little

peuchère [pøʃɛr] *int Région* heavens!, *Br* strewth!

peuh! [pø] *int* pooh!, bah!

peuplade [pœplad] *nf* (small) tribe

peuple [pœpl] **1** *nm* [①A11,g,iii] **(a)** (*nation*) people, nation; **le p. français** the French people; **le p. élu** the chosen people

(b) (*ensemble des citoyens*) people (*considered as a political entity*); **dans une démocratie le p. gouverne** in a democracy it is the people who govern; **le roi et son p.** the king and his people *or* subjects; **les gens du p.,** *Vieilli* **le bas** *ou* **petit p.** the lower classes

(c) (*foule*) *Vieilli* crowd (of people); *F* **quel p.!** what a crowd!, what a lot of people!; *F* **ça fait du p.** that's a lot of people; *F* **elle se fiche** *ou* **se fout** *ou* **se moque du p.** who does she think she is!

2 *adj inv F Péj* common, vulgar; **ça fait p.** that's common, that's vulgar

peuplé [pœple] *adj* inhabited; **p. de** inhabited by; **très/peu p.** densely/sparsely populated

peuplement [pœpləmɑ̃] *nm* (*d'une région*) populating; (*d'un vivier, d'un parc à gibier etc*) stocking; (*d'une forêt*) planting (with trees); **régions à faible p.** sparsely populated areas

peupler [pœple] **1** *vt* **(a)** (*pourvoir d'habitants*) (*pays*) to populate, to people; (*vivier, parc à gibier etc*) to stock; (*forêt*) to plant (with trees) **(b)** (*occuper*) to inhabit; **rue peuplée de gens** street crowded with people, crowded street; *Fig* **ville peuplée de souvenirs** town full of memories **2 se peupler** *vpr* (*d'une région, ville*) to become populated; **la rue s'est peuplée peu à peu** the street gradually filled (up) with people

peupleraie [pøplərɛ] *nf* poplar grove *or* plantation

peuplier [pøplije] *nm* poplar; **p. tremble** aspen

peur [pœr] *nf* fear; (*subite*) fright; **avoir p.** to be afraid *or* frightened; **avoir p. des chiens** to be afraid *or* frightened of dogs; *Fig* **n'ayons pas p. des mots** let's call a spade a spade, let's not mince our words; **ne pas avoir p. de mourir** not to be afraid *or* frightened of dying; **il ne faut pas avoir p. de le lui dire** you mustn't be afraid *or* frightened of telling him so; **j'avais p. de vous gêner** I was afraid I might be in your way; **elle n'a pas p. de déplaire** she doesn't care if she's not liked; **j'ai p. pour lui** I'm afraid *or* frightened for him; **n'ayez pas p.!** don't be afraid!; **n'aie pas p., tout va s'arranger** don't worry, everything will be all right; *F* **vous n'avez pas p.!** you've got a *or* some nerve!; **prendre p.** to take fright; **je n'avais qu'une p., qu'il dise oui** my only fear was that he might say yes; *F* **avoir une p. bleue** to be scared to death;

avoir une p. bleue des abeilles/de parler en public to be scared to death of bees/of speaking in public; **avoir une p. panique des voyages en avion** to be terrified of flying; **avoir la p. au ventre** to be terrified *or* petrified; **en être quitte pour la p.** to get off with a fright; **il a eu plus de p. que de mal** he was more frightened than hurt; **il me fait p.** he frightens me; **tu m'as fait p.!** you frightened *or* startled me!, you gave me a fright!; **il m'a fait une de ces peurs** he gave me such a fright!; **être laid à faire p.** to be as ugly as sin; **c'était d'un ennui à faire p.** it was dreadfully boring; **sans p.** *adj* fearless; *adv* fearlessly; **un chevalier sans p. et sans reproche** ≈ a very parfitt gentle knight; **j'en ai bien p.** I'm afraid so; **j'ai p. qu'il (ne) soit en retard** I'm worried in case he is *or Fml* should be late; **la p. des élèves (devant leur professeur)** the children's fear (of their teacher); *F* **la p. du gendarme** the fear of being caught; **c'est par p. des représailles que ...** it's for *or* through fear of reprisals that ...; **la p. de s'engager** the fear of committing oneself; **de p. de faire qch** for fear of doing sth; **de p. que ... (ne) +** *sub* in case ..., for fear that ...; **elle ne t'en a pas parlé de p. que tu ne t'offenses** she didn't tell you about it in case you *or* for fear that you took *or Fml* should take offence

peureusement [pœrøzmɑ̃] *adv* fearfully

peureux, -euse [pœrø, -øz] **1** *adj* (*personne, regard*) timid, fearful, *Fml* timorous **2** *n* fearful *or* timid person; **quel p.!** what a coward!, *F* what a wimp!

peut-être [pøtɛtr] *adv* [①**B59-60**,7] perhaps, maybe, possibly; **p. que oui, p. que non** perhaps, perhaps not, maybe, maybe not; **elle est p. rentrée chez elle** perhaps *or* maybe she has gone home, she may have gone home; **je ne suis p. pas riche, mais j'ai mon honneur** I may not be rich *or* perhaps I'm not rich, but I have my honour; **p. bien qu'il viendra** he may (very) well come; *Iron* **tu le sais mieux que moi, p.?** you think you know better, do you?; **je ne sais pas faire la cuisine, p.?** you think I can't cook?

p. ex. (*abrév* **par exemple**) eg

pèze [pɛz] *nm Arg* (*argent*) dough, *Br* lolly

pff [pf], **pfft** [pft], **pffut** [pfyt] *int* pooh!

PgPr *Ordinat* (*abrév* **page précédente**) PgUp

PgSv *Ordinat* (*abrév* **page suivante**) PgDn

phacochère [fakɔʃɛr] *nm* warthog

phaéton [faetɔ̃] *nm* phaeton

phagocyte [fagɔsit] *nm Biol* phagocyte

phagocyter [fagɔsite] *vt Fig* to swallow up, to engulf; **les zones industrielles phagocytent la banlieue** the suburbs are being swallowed up *or* engulfed by industrial estates

phagocytose [fagɔsitoz] *nf Biol* phagocytosis; *Fig* swallowing up

phalange [falɑ̃ʒ] *nf* **(a)** *Antiq Mil* phalanx; *Litt* (*armée*) host, army; *Hist Pol* **la P.** the Falange, the Falangist party **(b)** *Anat* phalanx

phalangette [falɑ̃ʒɛt] *nf Anat* (*du doigt, de l'orteil*) top joint, *Spéc* ungual phalanx

phalangien, -ienne [falɑ̃ʒjɛ̃, -jɛn] *adj Anat* phalangeal

phalangiste [falɑ̃ʒist] *n Hist Pol* Falangist

phalanstère [falɑ̃stɛr] *nm Hist Écon* phalanstery; *Fig* **un p. de philosophes** a community of philosophers

phalène [falɛn] *nf* (*parfois nm en poésie*) geometrid (moth)

phallique [falik] *adj* phallic

phallo [falo] *nm F Péj* (*abrév* **phallocrate**) MCP

phallocrate [falɔkrat] *nm Péj* male chauvinist (pig)

phallocratie [falɔkrasi] *nf* male chauvinism

phalloïde [falɔid] *adj Biol* phalloid; **amanite p.** (*champignon vénéneux*) death cap, *Spéc* amanita phalloides

phallus [falys] *nm* phallus

phantasme [fɑ̃tasm] *nm* = **fantasme**

pharamineux, -euse [faraminø, -øz] *adj F* phenomenal, staggering

pharaon [faraɔ̃] *nm* **(a)** *Hist* Pharaoh **(b)** *Cartes* faro

pharaonique [faraɔnik], **pharaonien, -ienne** [faraɔnjɛ̃, -jɛn] *adj Hist* Pharaonic

phare [far] *nm* **(a)** (*tour lumineuse*) lighthouse; **p. à éclats** flashing light; **p. à feu fixe/à feu tournant** fixed/revolving light; **gardien de p.** lighthouse keeper **(b)** *Av* beacon; **p. d'atterrissage** landing light **(c)** *Aut* headlight, headlamp; **faire un appel de phares** to flash one's headlights; **mettre ses phares** to switch on one's headlights; **se mettre en phares** to dip *or Am* dim one's headlights; **rouler (en) pleins phares** to drive on full headlights *or Br* on full beam *or Am* on high beams; **p. anti-brouillard** foglight; **p. de recul** reversing *or Am* backup light

-phare [far] *suff* **personnalité-p.** leading light; **film-p.** seminal film

pharisaïque [farizaik] *adj* **(a)** *Péj* (*hypocrite*) hypocritical, *Litt* pharisaic(al) **(b)** *Hist Rel* Pharisaic(al)

pharisien, -ienne [farizjɛ̃, -jɛn] **1** *n* **(a)** *Péj* (*hypocrite*) hypocrite, *Vieilli, Litt* pharisee **(b)** *Hist Rel* Pharisee **2** *adj* **(a)** *Péj* (*pointilleux*) self-righteous **(b)** *Hist Rel* Pharisaic(al)

pharmaceutique [farmasøtik] *adj* pharmaceutical

pharmacie [farmasi] *nf* **(a)** (*science*) pharmacy, pharmaceutics **(b)** (*magasin*) pharmacy; chemist's (shop), *Am* drugstore; (*dispensaire*) dispensary; **la p. de l'hôpital** the hospital dispensary **(c)** (*médicaments*) pharmaceuticals; **(armoire à) p.** medicine chest *or* cabinet; **p. de premiers soins** first-aid kit; **p. de voyage** travelling *or Am* traveling first-aid kit

pharmacien, -ienne [farmasjɛ̃, -jɛn] *n* (*vendeur*) pharmacist, *Br* (dispensing) chemist, *Am* druggist; (*d'un laboratoire pharmaceutique, dans l'industrie*) pharmacist, *Br* chemist

pharmacodépendance [farmakodepɑ̃dɑ̃s] *nf* drug dependency

pharmacologie [farmakɔlɔʒi] *nf* pharmacology

pharmacologique [farmakɔlɔʒik] *adj* pharmacological

pharmacopée [farmakɔpe] *nf* pharmacopoeia

pharmacorésistance [farmakorezistɑ̃s] *nf* resistance to drugs

pharmacovigilance [farmakoviʒilɑ̃s] *nf* drug testing and control

pharyngé [farɛ̃ʒe], **pharyngien, -ienne** [farɛ̃ʒjɛ̃, -jɛn] *adj Méd, Anat* pharyng(e)al

pharyngite [farɛ̃ʒit] *nf Méd* pharyngitis

pharynx [farɛ̃ks] *nm Anat* pharynx

phascolome [faskɔlɔm] *nm Zool* wombat

phase [fɑz] *nf* (*période*) phase, stage; *Astron, Ch, Phys* phase; **cancer en p. terminale** terminal cancer; **cancéreux en p. terminale** terminal cancer patient; *Ind* **p. de production** stage of production; *Phys* **en p.** in phase; *Fig* **être en p.** to be on the same wavelength; *Phys* **décalage de p.** difference of phase, phase displacement; *Él* **(conducteur de) p.** phase conductor

phatique [fatik] *adj Ling* **fonction p.** phatic function

Phébus [febys] *nm Myth* Phoebus

Phèdre [fɛdr] *nf Myth* Phaedra

Phénicie [fenisi] *nf* Phoenicia

phénicien, -ienne [fenisjɛ̃, -jɛn] *Hist* **1** *adj* Phoenician **2** *nm Ling* Phoenician **3** *n* **P.** Phoenician

phénix [feniks] *nm Myth* phoenix; *Fig Litt* (*personne unique en son genre*) paragon

phénol [fenɔl] *nm Ch* phenol; *Com* carbolic acid

phénoménal, -ale, -aux, -ales [fenɔmenal, -o] *adj Phil, F* (*incroyable*) phenomenal

phénoménalement [fenɔmenalmɑ̃] *adv* phenomenally

phénomène [fenɔmɛn] *nm* (*expérience, fait, personne*) phenomenon, *pl* phenomena; (*dans les foires*) freak; **quel p.!** (*excentrique*) what a character!; **c'est un drôle de p.!** he's quite a character!

phénoménologie [fenɔmenɔlɔʒi] *nf Phil* phenomenology

philanthrope [filɑ̃trɔp] *n* philanthropist

philanthropie [filɑ̃trɔpi] *nf* philanthropy

philanthropique [filɑ̃trɔpik] *adj* philanthropic

philatélie [filateli] *nf* philately, stamp collecting

philatélique [filatelik] *adj* philatelic

philatéliste [filatelist] *n* philatelist, stamp collector

philharmonie [filarmɔni] *nf* philharmonic society

philharmonique [filarmɔnik] *adj* (*société, orchestre etc*) philharmonic

philhellène [filelɛn] **1** *nm* philhellene **2** *adj* philhellenic

philhellénisme [filelenism] *nm* philhellenism

philippin, -ine [filipɛ̃, -in] **1** *adj* Filipino, Philippine **2** *n* **P.** Filipino

Philippines (les) [lefilipin] *nfpl* [①**A11**,g,ii] the Philippines

philistin [filistɛ̃] *adj m, nm Péj* philistine

philo [filo] *nf Scol F* philosophy

philodendron [filɔdɛ̃drɔ̃] *nm* philodendron

philologie [filɔlɔʒi] *nf* philology

philologique [filɔlɔʒik] *adj* philological

philologiquement [filɔlɔʒikmɑ̃] *adv* philologically

philologue [filɔlɔg] *n* philologist

philosophale [filɔzɔfal] *adj f* **la pierre p.** the philosophers' stone

philosophe [filɔzɔf] **1** *n* philosopher; **prendre les choses en p.** to take things philosophically **2** *adj* philosophical; **se montrer p. face à une déception** to react philosophically to a disappointment

philosopher [filɔzɔfe] *vi* to philosophize

philosophie [filɔzɔfi] *nf* (*science*) philosophy; **la p. de l'histoire/des sciences** the philosophy of history/science; **supporter une épreuve avec p.** to suffer a hardship philosophically; *F* **c'est ma p.** that's my philosophy, that's my outlook on life; *Scol Vieilli* **(classe de) p.** final year arts and humanities class

philosophique [filɔzɔfik] *adj* philosophical
philosophiquement [filɔzɔfikmɑ̃] *adv* philosophically
philtre [filtr] *nm* philtre, *US* philter; **p. d'amour** love potion
phlébite [flebit] *nf Méd* phlebitis
phlébologie [flebɔlɔʒi] *nf Méd* phlebology
phlébologue [flebɔlɔg] *n Méd* vein specialist
phlébotomie [flebɔtɔmi] *nf Méd* phlebotomy
phlegmon [flɛgmɔ̃] *nm Méd* phlegmon
phlox [flɔks] *nm* phlox
pH-mètre [peaʃmɛtr] *nm Tech* pH meter
phobie [fɔbi] *nf Psy, Méd* phobia, morbid fear; **avoir la p. de qch** to have a phobia about sth
phobique [fɔbik] *adj, n Psy, Méd* phobic
phocéen, -enne [fɔseɛ̃, -ɛn] *adj* Marseilles
phonation [fɔnasjɔ̃] *nf Physiol, Ling* phonation
phonatoire [fɔnatwar] *adj* phonatory
phone [fɔn] *nm Phys* phon
phonématique [fɔnematik] *adj Ling* phonemic
phonème [fɔnɛm] *nm Ling* phoneme
phonémique [fɔnemik] *adj Ling* phonemic
phonéticien, -ienne [fɔnetisjɛ̃, -jɛn] *n* phonetician
phonétique [fɔnetik] **1** *adj* phonetic **2** *nf* phonetics
phonétiquement [fɔnetikmɑ̃] *adv* phonetically
phoniatre [fɔnjatr] *n Méd* speech therapist
phoniatrie [fɔnjatri] *nf Méd* speech therapy
phonie [fɔni] *nf Rad, Électron* wireless telegraphy, radiotelegraphy
phoning [foniŋ] *nm Mktg* telesales
phonique [fɔnik] *adj* acoustic, *Vieilli* phonic; **isolation p.** soundproofing, sound insulation
phono [fono] *nm F Vieilli* = **phonographe**
phonographe [fɔnɔgraf] *nm (gramophone) Vieilli* gramophone, *Am, Arch* phonograph
phonographique [fɔnɔgrafik] *adj* phonographic
phonologie [fɔnɔlɔʒi] *nf Ling* phonology
phonologique [fɔnɔlɔʒik] *adj Ling* phonological
phonologue [fɔnɔlɔg] *n Ling* phonologist
phonothèque [fɔnɔtɛk] *nf* sound archives, audio library
phoque [fɔk] *nm* **(a)** *(animal)* seal; **souffler comme un p.** to (puff and) wheeze *or* (puff and) blow like a grampus; *Vulg* **il est pédé comme un p.** he's a real queer *or Br* poofter **(b)** *(fourrure)* sealskin
phosgène [fɔsʒɛn] *nm Ch* phosgene (gas)
phosphatage [fɔsfataʒ] *nm Agr* treating with phosphates
phosphate [fɔsfat] *nm Ch* phosphate; **sans phosphates** phosphate-free
phosphaté [fɔsfate] *adj Ch* phosphatic, phosphated; *(engrais etc)* phosphate-enriched
phosphater [fɔsfate] *vt* to treat with phosphates, to phosphate
phosphène [fɔsfɛn] *nm Physiol* phosphene
phosphore [fɔsfɔr] *nm Ch* phosphorus
phosphoré [fɔsfɔre] *adj Ch* phosphorated
phosphorer [fɔsfɔre] *vi F* to have one's thinking cap on; **alors, ça phosphore?** working hard, are we?
phosphorescence [fɔsfɔresɑ̃s] *nf* phosphorescence
phosphorescent [fɔsfɔresɑ̃] *adj* phosphorescent
phosphoreux, -euse [fɔsfɔrø, -øz] *adj Ch* phosphorous
phosphorique [fɔsfɔrik] *adj Ch* phosphoric
phosphure [fɔsfyr] *nm Ch* phosphide
phot [fɔt] *nm Phys* phot
photo [foto] *nf* photo, snap(shot); *(tirée d'un film, du tournage)* still, photostill; **prendre qn en p.** to take a photo *or* snap(shot) of sb; **se faire prendre en p. par qn** to have one's photo taken by sb; **il est bien en p.** he photographs well; *F* **tu veux ma p.?** who do you think you're staring at?, what are you staring at?; **appareil p.** camera; **p. d'identité** identity photo, passport-sized photograph; **p. souvenir** souvenir photo; **p. de mode** fashion photo
photobiologie [fotobjɔlɔʒi] *nf* photobiology
photochimie [fotoʃimi] *nf* photochemistry
photochimique [fotoʃimik] *adj* photochemical
photocomposer [fotokɔ̃poze] *vti* to filmset, to photoset, *Am* to photocompose
photocomposeur [fotokɔ̃pozœr] *nm* = **photocompositeur**
photocomposeuse [fotokɔ̃pozøz] *nf (machine) Br* filmsetter, photosetter, *Am* photocomposer
photocompositeur [fotokɔ̃pozitœr] *nm* filmsetter, photosetter, *Am* photocomposer
photocomposition [fotokɔ̃pozisjɔ̃] *nf* filmsetting, photosetting, *Am* photocomposition
photoconducteur, -trice [fotokɔ̃dyktœr, -tris] *adj* photoconductive
photoconductivité [fotokɔ̃dyktivite] *nf* photoconductivity
photocopie [fotokɔpi] *nf* photocopy
photocopier [fotokɔpje] *vt (conj like* **copier**) to photocopy
photocopieur [fotokɔpjœr] *nm,* **photocopieuse** [fotokɔpjøz] *nf* photocopier
photodiode [fotodjɔd] *nf* photodiode
photoélectricité [fotoelɛktrisite] *nf* photoelectricity
photoélectrique [fotoelɛktrik] *adj (cellule, effet)* photoelectric
photo-finish, *pl* **photos-finish** *nm Sp* photo finish; *(appareil)* photo-finish camera; **l'arrivée a dû être vérifiée au p.** it was a photo finish
photogénique [fotoʒenik] *adj* photogenic
photogrammétrie [fotogrametri] *nf* photogrammetry
photographe [fotograf] *n (professionnel de la photo)* photographer; **reporter p.** photojournalist; **p. de mode** fashion photographer; **p. de plateau** unit photographer; **p. de presse** press photographer; **p. indépendant(e)** freelance photographer
photographie [fotografi] *nf* **(a)** *(technique, hobby etc)* photography; **p. journalistique** press photography; **p. par téléobjectif** long-lens photography; **faire de la p.** to take photographs **(b)** *(cliché)* photograph; **prendre une p. de qn** to take sb's photograph *or* a photograph of sb; **p. aérienne** aerial photograph
photographier [fotografje] *vt (impf, pr sub* **n. photographiions, v. photographiiez**) to photograph, to take a photograph of; **se faire p.** to have one's photograph taken
photographique [fotografik] *adj (reproduction, description etc)* photographic; **appareil p.** camera
photographiquement [fotografikmɑ̃] *adv* photographically
photograveur [fotogravœr] *nm* photoengraver
photogravure [fotogravyr] *nf (procédé, épreuve)* photogravure, photoengraving
photo-interprétation *nf Tech* = photomapping
photojournalisme [fotoʒurnalism] *nm* photojournalism
photojournaliste [fotoʒurnalist] *n* photojournalist
photolithographie [fotolitɔgrafi] *nf* photolithography
photolyse [fotoliz] *nf Ch* photolysis
photomaton® [fotomatɔ̃] *nm* (automatic) photo machine *or* booth
photomécanique [fotomekanik] *adj Tech (procédé)* photomechanical
photomètre [fotomɛtr] *nm Tech* photometer
photométrie [fotometri] *nf Phys* photometry
photométrique [fotometrik] *adj Phys* photometric
photomontage [fotomɔ̃taʒ] *nm* photomontage
photon [fotɔ̃] *nm* photon
photopériode [fotoperjɔd] *nf Bot* photoperiod
photopériodique [fotoperjɔdik] *adj Bot* photoperiodic
photopériodisme [fotoperjɔdism] *nm Bot* photoperiodism
photophobie [fotofɔbi] *nf Méd* photophobia
photophore [fotofɔr] *nm* **(a)** *(lampe)* reflective lamp *(esp of miner)* **(b)** *(pour bougie)* candle holder with glass shade
photopile [fotopil] *nf Tech* solar cell
photoreportage [fotorəpɔrtaʒ] *nm* **(a)** *(discipline)* photojournalism **(b)** *(reportage)* photo report
photo-robot, *pl* **photos-robots** *nm* Identikit® *or* Photofit® (picture)
photosensible [fotosɑ̃sibl] *adj* photosensitive
photosphère [fotosfɛr] *nf Astron* photosphere
photostat [fotosta] *nm Tech* photostat
photostoppeur, -euse [fotostɔpœr, -øz] *n* street photographer
photostyle [fotostil] *nm Ordinat* light pen
photosynthèse [fotosɛ̃tɛz] *nf Biol* photosynthesis
photothèque [fototɛk] *nf* photo(graphic) *or* picture library, photographic archives; **p. électronique** electronic still store
photothérapie [fototerapi] *nf Méd* phototherapy
phototransistor [fototrɑ̃zistɔr] *nm* phototransistor
phototypie [fototipi] *nf Tech* collotype (process)
photovoltaïque [fotovɔltaik] *adj* photovoltaic; **cellule p.** photovoltaic cell; **effet p.** photovoltaic effect
phragmite [fragmit] *nm* **(a)** *Bot* reed **(b)** *Orn* sedge warbler
phrase [frɑz] *nf* [ⓘ**A72-73**; **B59-61**] *Gram* sentence; *Mus* phrase; **p. toute faite** stock phrase; *Fig* **faire des phrases, faire de grandes phrases** to use high-flown language; **phrases à compléter** sentence completion; **sans phrases** straight out, without mincing one's words; *Gram* **membre de p.** phrase
phrasé [frɑze] *nm Mus* phrasing
phraséologie [frazeɔlɔʒi] *nf (syntaxe)* phraseology; *Péj (verbiage)* flowery *or* high-flown language
phraser [frɑze] **1** *vt Mus* to phrase **2** *vi* to use high-flown language
phraseur, -euse [frɑzœr, -øz] *n Péj* phrasemonger
phrastique [fraztik] *adj Gram* sentence
phréatique [freatik] *adj Géol* **nappe p.** ground water
phrénologie [frenɔlɔʒi] *nf* phrenology

phrénologique [frenɔlɔʒik] *adj* phrenological
phrénologiste [frenɔlɔʒist] *nm* phrenologist
Phrygie [friʒi] *nf Antiq* Phrygia
phrygien, -ienne [friʒjɛ̃, -jɛn] **1** *adj Antiq* Phrygian; *Hist* **bonnet p.** Phrygian cap (*in French Revolution*) **2** *n Antiq* **P.** Phrygian
phtisie [ftizi] *nf Méd Arch* consumption, *Spéc* phthisis; **p. galopante** galloping consumption
phylactère [filaktɛr] *nm* **(a)** *Rel Juive* phylactery **(b)** *Beaux-Arts* scroll **(c)** (*de bande dessinée*) speech balloon
phylloxéra, phylloxera [filɔksera] *nm Ent* phylloxera
physicien, -ienne [fizisjɛ̃, -jɛn] *n* physicist; **p. de l'atome** nuclear physicist
physicochimie [fizikoʃimi] *nf* physical chemistry
physicochimique [fizikoʃimik] *adj* physicochemical
physicomathématique [fizikomatematik] **1** *nf* mathematical physics **2** *adj* relating to mathematical physics
physiocrate [fizjɔkrat] *nm Écon Hist* physiocrat
physiocratie [fizjɔkrasi] *nf Écon Hist* physiocracy
physiologie [fizjɔlɔʒi] *nf* physiology
physiologique [fizjɔlɔʒik] *adj* physiological
physiologiquement [fizjɔlɔʒikmɑ̃] *adv* physiologically
physiologiste [fizjɔlɔʒist] *n* physiologist
physionomie [fizjɔnɔmi] *nf* **(a)** (*traits du visage*) facial appearance, features, *Litt, Hum* physiognomy; **il a une p. joviale** he has a jolly face; **il ne faut pas juger les gens sur leur p.** you shouldn't judge by appearances **(b)** (*aspect*) face; **la p. de l'Europe va changer** the face of Europe will change
physionomiste [fizjɔnɔmist] **1** *adj* **je ne suis pas p.** I've no memory for faces; **elle est très p.** she has a very good memory for faces **2** *n* **c'est un p.** he's got a good memory for faces
physiopathologie [fizjopatɔlɔʒi] *nf Méd* physiopathology
physiothérapie [fizjɔterapi] *nf Méd* natural medicine
physique [fizik] **1** *adj* physical; **culture p.** physical training; *Scol* **éducation p.** physical education; **le monde p.** the physical *or* material world; *F* **je ne le supporte pas, c'est p.** I can't stand him, it's a physical thing

2 *nf* [①**A10**,c] (*science*) physics; *Scol Vieilli* (*livre*) physics (text)book; **p. nucléaire** nuclear physics; *Géog* **p. du globe** geophysics **3** *nm* (*d'une personne*) physique; (*apparence*) external appearance; **avoir un p. avantageux** to have a fine physique; **soigner son p.** to take care of *or* look after oneself; **il a le p. de l'emploi** he looks the part; **le p. et le moral** the mind and the body; **au p.** physically
physiquement [fizikmɑ̃] *adv* physically
phytobiologie [fitobjɔlɔʒi] *nf* phytology
phytogéographie [fitoʒeɔgrafi] *nf* phytogeography
phytoplancton [fitoplɑ̃ktɔ̃] *nm* phytoplankton
phytosanitaire [fitosanitɛr] *adj* **produits phytosanitaires** = fertilizers, herbicides etc
phytothérapie [fitoterapi] *nf* herbal medicine
pi [pi] *nm* (*lettre*) *Math* pi
piaf [pjaf] *nm F* sparrow
piaffement [pjafmɑ̃] *nm* (*d'un cheval*) pawing (the ground)
piaffer [pjafe] *vi* (*d'un cheval*) to paw the ground; *Fig* (*trépigner*) to stamp one's feet; **p. d'impatience** to fidget impatiently
piaillard, -arde [pjɑjar, -ard] *adj, n F* = **piailleur, -euse**
piaillement [pjɑjmɑ̃] *nm F* (*d'un oiseau*) cheeping; *Fig* (*d'un enfant*) squealing, squalling
piailler [pjɑje] *vi F* (*de petits oiseaux*) to cheep; *Fig* (*des enfants*) to squeal, to squall
piaillerie [pjɑjri] *nf F* = **piaillement**
piailleur, -euse [pjɑjœr, -øz] *F* **1** *adj* (*oiseau*) cheeping; (*enfant*) squealing, squalling **2** *n* cheeping bird; *Fig Péj* (*enfant*) squealer, squaller
piane-piane [pjanpjan] *adv F* **allez-y p.** gently does it, go easy
pianiste [pjanist] *n* pianist; **un p. (de) jazz** a jazz pianist
piano[1] [pjano] *nm* (*instrument*) piano; **jouer** *ou* **faire du p.** to play the piano
▶ **piano**: *F* **p. à bretelles** squeeze-box; **p. de concert** concert grand; **p. crapaud** boudoir grand; **p. demi-queue** baby grand; **p. droit** upright piano; **p. mécanique** player piano; **p. quart de queue** miniature grand; **p. à queue** grand piano
piano[2] *adv Mus* piano; *Fig F* **allez-y p.** gently does it, go easy; **allez-y p. avec lui** go easy with *or* on him; **vas-y p. avec le café** go easy with *or* on the coffee
piano-bar, *pl* **pianos-bars** *nm* piano bar
pianoforte [pjanofɔrte] *nm Hist Mus* fortepiano
pianotage [pjanɔtaʒ] *nm F* (*sur le piano*) tinkling (away); (*des doigts*) drumming
pianoter [pjanɔte] *vi F* **(a)** (*mal jouer du piano*) to tinkle away (on the piano) **(b)** (*tapoter*) to drum one's fingers; **ses doigts pianotent sur la nappe** he's drumming his fingers *or* his fingers are drumming on the tablecloth
piastre [pjastr] *nf* piastre; *Can Arg* (*dollar*) buck
piaule [pjol] *nf F* pad
piaulement [pjolmɑ̃] *nm* (*des poussins*) cheeping; *Fig F* (*des enfants*) whimpering, whining
piauler [pjole] *vi* (*des poussins*) to cheep; *Fig F* (*des enfants*) to whimper, to whine
PIB [peibe] *nm Écon* (*abrév* **produit intérieur brut**) GDP
PIBOR [pibɔr] *nm, abrév Bourse* (**Paris interbank offered rate**) PIBOR; **P. 3 mois** three-month PIBOR
pic[1] [pik] *nm* **(a)** (*pioche*) pick, pickaxe, *US* pickax; **p. pneumatique** pneumatic drill; **p. de mineur** miner's pick; **p. à glace** ice pick **(b)** (*sommet*) (mountain) peak; **à p.** (*chute, falaise*) sheer; (*tomber*) straight down; **sentier à p.** steep path; **promontoire à p.** sheer headland, bluff; **couler à p.** to sink like a stone; *Fig F* **tomber à p.** to come at just the right moment
pic[2] *nm* (*oiseau*) woodpecker
pica [pika] *nm Typ* pica
picador [pikadɔr] *nm* picador
picaillons [pikajɔ̃] *nmpl Arg* (*argent*) dough, bread
picard, -arde [pikar, -ard] **1** *adj* (of/from) Picardy; *Culin* **ficelle picarde** = ham and cheese pancake **2** *nm Ling* Picardy dialect **3** *n* **P.** (*natif*) native of Picardy; (*habitant*) inhabitant of Picardy
Picardie [pikardi] *nf* Picardy
picaresque [pikarɛsk] *adj* (*roman*) picaresque
piccolo [pikɔlo] *nm Mus* piccolo
pichenette [piʃnɛt] *nf* flick (of the finger), flip; (*avec le pied*) flick
pichet [piʃɛ] *nm* (small) jug, *Am* pitcher
pickles [pikəlz] *nmpl* pickles
pickpocket [pikpɔkɛt] *nm* pickpocket
pick-up [pikœp] *nm inv* **(a)** (*bras de lecture*) pick-up (arm); *Vieilli* (*éléctrophone*) record player **(b)** (*véhicule*) pick-up (truck)
picoler [pikɔle] *vi F* to booze; **qu'est-ce qu'il peut p.!** he's a real boozer!; **ici, ça picole dur** they're real boozers here!
picoleur, -euse [pikɔlœr, -øz] *n F* boozer
picolo [pikɔlo] *nm Mus* piccolo
picorer [pikɔre] **1** *vi* (*d'un oiseau*) to pick *or* scratch about; *Fig* (*manger à peine*) to pick at one's food **2** *vt* (*d'un oiseau*) to peck (at); (*par manque d'appétit*) (*nourriture*) to pick at; *Fig* (*grignoter*) to nibble; **on a eu des olives à p.** we had olives to nibble, that's all
picot [piko] *nm* **(a)** (*pointe*) splinter (of wood) **(b)** *Tech* (*de roue d'entraînement*) pin **(c)** *Couture* picot **(d)** *Pêche* fishing net (*for flatfish*)
picotement [pikɔtmɑ̃] *nm* (*dans la gorge, le nez*) tickle, tickling; (*dans les yeux*) stinging, smarting; (*sur la peau*) prickling; **j'ai des picotements dans les yeux** my eyes are stinging *or* smarting; **j'ai des picotements dans le nez** my nose is tickling, I've got a tickle in my nose
picoter [pikɔte] *vt* **(a)** (*faire de petits trous dans*) to prick tiny holes in **(b)** (*d'un oiseau*) to peck (at) **(c)** (*irriter*) (*qch*) to produce a tingling sensation in; (*gorge*) to tickle; (*peau*) to prickle; **la fumée me picotait les yeux** the smoke made my eyes sting *or* smart; **j'ai les yeux qui (me) picotent** my eyes are stinging *or* smarting; **j'ai la gorge qui (me) picote** I've a tickle in my throat, my throat is tickling; **j'ai la peau qui (me) picote** my skin is prickling
picotin [pikɔtɛ̃] *nm Agr* (*d'avoine*) (*mesure*) peck; (*ration*) feed, ration
picrate [pikrat] *nm* **(a)** *Arg* (*vin*) cheap red wine, *Br* plonk **(b)** *Ch* picrate
Pictes [pikt] *nmpl Hist* Picts
pictogramme [piktɔgram] *nm* pictogram, pictograph
pictographe [piktɔgraf] *nm* pictogram, pictograph
pictographie [piktɔgrafi] *nf* pictography
pictographique [piktɔgrafik] *adj Ling* pictographic
pictural, -ale, -aux, -ales [piktyral, -o] *adj* pictorial
pic(-)vert, *pl* **pics(-)verts** [pivɛr] *nm* green woodpecker
Pie [pi] *nm* Pius
pie[1] [pi] **1** *nf* magpie; *F* (*personne bavarde*) chatterbox; *F* **être bavard comme une p.** to be a real chatterbox; *Naut* **nid de p.** crow's nest **2** *adj inv* **cheval/jument p.** piebald (horse/mare), *Am* pinto (horse/mare); **vache p.** black and white cow; *Vieilli* **voiture p.** patrol car, *Br* ≈ Panda car
pie[2] *adj* **œuvre p.** good deed, act of charity
pièce [pjɛs] *nf* **(a)** (*salle, chambre*) room; **un appartement de trois pièces, un trois-pièces** a three-room(ed) flat *or Am* apartment; **un trois-pièces cuisine** a three-room(ed) flat with kitchen, *Am* a three and a half

(b) (*élément*) piece; **p. de musée** museum piece; **p. de bétail/gibier** head of cattle/game; **p. de blé** wheatfield; **un service complet de trente-six pièces** a complete thirty-six piece dinner service; **les pièces d'un uniforme** the items of a uniform; **costume deux-pièces/trois-pièces** two-piece/three-piece suit; **un (maillot de bain) une-p./deux-pièces** a one-piece/two-piece swimsuit; **ils coûtent dix francs (la) p.** they cost ten francs each *or* apiece; **ils se vendent à la p.** they are sold singly *or* separately; **travailler aux pièces** to do piece work; *F* **on n'est pas aux pièces** there's no hurry *or* rush

(c) *Fin* coin; **p. de dix francs** ten-franc piece; **donner la p. à qn** to give sb a tip, to tip sb; **je ne vous demanderai qu'une petite p.** (*d'un mendiant*) have you got any loose change you don't need?

(d) *Th* play; **monter une p.** to put on *or* stage a play; **p. radiophonique** radio play, radio drama

(e) *Mus, Littér* piece; **une p. de Couperin/en vers** a piece by Couperin/of verse

(f) tout d'une p. all in one piece; *Fig* **être tout d'une p.** to be straightforward and uncompromising; **une histoire inventée de toutes pièces** a completely made-up story, a complete fabrication; **ce qu'il raconte est forgé de toutes pièces** he's making the whole thing up; **mensonge fait de toutes pièces** out-and-out lie

(g) (*d'une machine, d'une horloge etc*) part, component; **pièces de rechange, pièces détachées** replacement parts, spare parts, spares; **p. de charpente** beam; (*sous le plancher*) joist; *Tech* **p. en croix** crosspiece; *Tech* **p. en mouvement** moving part; *Tech* **p. matricée** pressing

(h) (*raccord*) patch; **mettre** *ou* **poser une p. à un vêtement** to put a patch on *or* to patch a garment

(i) (*morceau, débris*) piece, bit, fragment; **être en pièces** to be in pieces; (*de vêtements*) to be in tatters; **mettre en pièces** (*vase*) to smash to bits *or* to pieces; (*livre*) to pull *or* tear to pieces; (*vêtement*) to tear to pieces; **tailler l'ennemi en pièces** to cut the enemy to pieces; *Fig* **se faire tailler en pièces** to be torn to pieces

(j) *Jur, Admin etc* (*document*) document, paper; **p. justificative** *Admin* written proof; *Jur* relevant document; *Com* voucher (copy); *Compta* **p. de caisse** cash voucher; **p. à l'appui** supporting document; **juger sur pièces** to judge on the evidence; **p. jointe** (*à une lettre*) enclosure; **p. à joindre** (*à une lettre*) enclosure

(k) (*quantité déterminée*) **p. de bœuf** cut *or* piece of beef; **p. d'étoffe** length *or* piece of material

(l) *Échecs* piece; (*aux dames*) draught(sman), *Am* checker

(m) *Mil* **p. (d'artillerie)** gun, *Spéc* piece of ordnance; **p. de campagne** field gun; **chef de p.** number one, squad leader, *US* chief of (piece) section

▶ **pièce:** *Jur* **p. à conviction** exhibit (*in criminal case*); **p. détachée** component; (*de rechange*) spare part; **p. d'eau** ornamental lake; (*plus petite*) water feature, ornamental pond; **p. d'identité** identity paper(s), proof of identity; **p. de monnaie** coin; *Culin* **p. montée** ornamental cake; **p. rapportée** insert; *Couture* patch; *Fig* (*dans une famille*) in-law; **p. de résistance** pièce de résistance, main dish; *Fig* pièce de résistance; **p. de théâtre** play; **p. de vin** barrel *or* cask of wine

piécette [pjesɛt] *nf* small coin

pied [pje] *nm* **(a)** (*d'une personne*) foot; **p. bot/plat** club/flat foot; **doigts de p.** toes; **sauter à pieds joints/sur un p.** to jump with (one's) feet together/to hop (on one foot); **être/marcher pieds nus** to be/walk barefoot(ed), to be/walk in one's bare feet; **elle s'est mise pieds nus** she took off her shoes (and stockings); **il n'avait pas de chaussures aux pieds** he had no shoes on (his feet); **se jeter aux pieds de qn** to throw oneself at sb's feet; **avoir bon p. bon œil** to be hale and hearty; **se lever du p. gauche** to get out of bed on the wrong side; **il ne peut pas mettre un p. devant l'autre** he can hardly put one foot in front of the other; **de la tête aux pieds, de p. en cap** [dəpjetɑ̃kap] from head to toe *or* foot, from top to toe; *Fig* **faire des pieds et des mains pour faire qch** to move heaven and earth to do sth; *F* **être bête comme ses pieds** to be unbelievably stupid, *Br F* to be as thick as two short planks; *F* **faire du p. à qn** to play footsie with sb; *F* **ça lui fera les pieds!** that'll teach him a lesson!; *F* **c'est bien fait pour tes pieds!** it serves you right!; *F* **elle me casse les pieds** (*elle m'ennuie*) she bores the pants off me; (*elle m'agace*) she gets on my nerves *or Br* my wick; **ça fait deux mois qu'elle me casse les pieds pour que je t'en parle** she's been on at me for two months now to talk to you about it; **mettre p. à terre** [pjetatɛr] (*d'un cheval, d'un vélo*) to dismount; (*sans descendre de vélo*) to put one's foot down; *aussi Fig* **tomber sur ses pieds** to fall *or* land on one's feet; **je ne remettrai jamais les pieds chez lui** I'll never set foot in his house again; *F* **mettre les pieds dans le plat** to put one's foot in it; **attention où vous mettez les pieds!** mind where you're treading!, watch your step!; **avoir un p. dans la tombe** to have one foot in the grave; **marcher sur les pieds de qn** to tread on sb's toes; *Fig* **tu ne vas pas te laisser marcher sur les pieds par ton chef de service?** you're not going to let your head of department walk all over you *or* take advantage of you?; *F* **lever le p.** (*partir*) to run off, *Br F* to scarper, to do a runner; (*en voiture*) to ease off; **faire qch au p. levé** to do sth at a moment's notice; **répondre au p. levé** to answer off the cuff; *Fig* **pieds et poings liés** bound hand and foot; **frapper du p.** to stamp (one's foot); **pousser qch du p.** to kick sth; **coup de p.** kick; **donner** *ou* **envoyer un coup de p. à qn** to kick sb, to give sb a kick; **il faut te donner un bon coup de p. (au derrière)** you need a good kick (up the backside); **recevoir un coup de p.** to be kicked, to get a kick; **chasser qn à coups de p.** to kick sb out; **enfoncer une porte à coups de p.** to kick a door in *or* down; **se prendre les pieds dans un tapis** to trip over a carpet

(b) à p. on foot; **aller à p.** to walk, to go on foot; **faire deux kilomètres à p.** to walk two kilometres; **vous en avez pour vingt minutes à p.** it will take you twenty minutes to walk (there) *or* twenty minutes on foot; **course à p.** (running) race; **mettre qn à p.** to suspend sb, *Can* to lay sb off

(c) mettre une affaire sur p. to set up *or* start a business; **il est de nouveau sur p.** he's up and about again, he's getting about again; **portrait en p.** full-length portrait

(d) *F* **jouer/chanter/conduire comme un p.** to be a lousy *or* terrible player/singer/driver; **je m'y suis pris comme un p. pour le réparer** I made a real mess of repairing it

(e) *Fig* **elle a le p. marin** she's a good sailor, she never gets seasick; **avoir p.** to be within one's depth; *aussi Fig* **perdre p.** to get out of one's depth; **prendre p. (sur un marché/un territoire)** to get a foothold (in a market/a territory); **lâcher p.** to give in, to give way; **faire un p. de nez à qn** to cock a snook at sb; **faire un p. de nez au destin** to thumb one's nose at fate

(f) *F* **prendre son p.** to get one's kicks; (*sexuellement*) to come; **c'est le p.!** it's fantastic!, it's great!; **ce n'est pas (vraiment) le p.** it's not much fun

(g) *Fig* (*rang*) **être sur un p. d'égalité avec qn** to be on an equal footing with sb; **vivre sur un grand p.** to live on a grand scale

(h) (*patte*) (*de cheval*) hoof; (*à la chasse*) (*trace*) footprint; (*piste*) track(s); *Culin* **p. de veau/mouton/porc** knuckle of veal/leg of mutton/pigs' trotter

(i) (*partie inférieure*) (*d'un bas, d'un arbre, d'un escalier, d'un lit*) foot; (*d'une colonne, d'un mur*) foot, base; (*bas*) (*d'une montagne*) foot, bottom; *Math* (*d'une perpendiculaire*) foot; *Typ* **p. de page** footer; **à p. d'œuvre** *Constr etc* on site; *Fig* ready to get on with the job

(j) (*support*) (*d'une chaise, d'une table etc*) leg; (*de télescope*) stand, rest; (*d'un verre*) stem; *Phot* foot; **p. (à trois branches)** tripod; **p. de lampe** *ou* **de lampadaire** lampstand; *TV, Cin* **p. de sol** (*d'une caméra*) high hat

(k) (*tige*) stalk; (*de vigne*) stock; **p. de céleri/d'asperges/de salade** (*plant*) head of celery/asparagus/lettuce

(l) *Naut* (*du mât*) step, heel

(m) [ⓘ**A12**,1,h,ii,y] (*mesure*), *Littér* foot; **p. carré/cube** square/cubic foot; **au petit p.** (in) miniature; **p. à p.** [pjeapje] inch by inch; **six pieds sous terre** six foot under; **p. à coulisse** calliper

pied-à-terre [pjetatɛr] *nm inv* pied-à-terre

pied-bot, *pl* **pieds-bots** *nm* club-footed person; *Méd* club foot

pied-d'alouette, *pl* **pieds-d'alouette** *nm Bot* larkspur, delphinium

pied-de-biche, *pl* **pieds-de-biche** *nm* (*poignée de sonnette*) bell pull; (*outil*) nail claw, nail extractor; (*d'une machine à coudre*) presser foot; (*d'une chaise, d'une table etc*) cabriole leg

pied-de-coq, *pl* **pieds-de-coq** *adj, nm Tex* houndstooth

pied-de-poule, *pl* **pieds-de-poule** *adj, nm Tex* houndstooth

pied-de-roi, *pl* **pieds-de-roi** *nm Can* folding rule

pied-droit, *pl* **pieds-droits** *nm Constr* (*d'une voûte, d'un pont*) pier

piédestal, -aux [pjedɛstal, -o] *nm* pedestal

pied-noir, *pl* **pieds-noirs** *F* **1** *n* Algerian-born Frenchman, *f* Frenchwoman **2** *adj inv* French Algerian, Algerian French

piédouche [pjeduʃ] *nm* small pedestal

piédroit [pjedrwa] *nm* = **pied-droit**

piège [pjɛʒ] *nm* **(a)** (*pour les animaux*) trap, snare; **p. à souris** mousetrap; **p. à rats** rat trap; **dresser** *ou* **tendre un p.** to set a trap **(à** for); **prendre un animal au p.** to trap an animal, to catch an animal in a trap **(b)** *Fig* (*embuscade*) trap; **attirer l'ennemi dans un p.** to draw the enemy into a trap; **donner** *ou* **tomber dans un p.** to fall into a trap; **tendre un p. à qn** to set a trap for sb; **être pris à son propre p.** to be caught in one's own trap, *prov* to be hoist by one's own petard; **dictée pleine de pièges** dictation full of pitfalls; *très F* **p. à cons** con

piégeage [pjeʒaʒ] *nm* (*d'animaux*) trapping

piéger [pjeʒe] *vt* (**je piège, n. piégeons; je piégeai(s); je piégerai**) **(a)** (*attraper*) *aussi Fig* to trap; **se faire p.** to be trapped; **se laisser p.** to fall into a trap, to get trapped **(b)** (*munir de pièges*) (*cour, forêt*) to set a trap/traps in **(c)** (*placer un explosif dans*) to booby-trap; **voiture piégée** car bomb, booby-trapped car; **colis piégé** parcel bomb; **lettre piégée** letter bomb

piégeur [pjeʒœr] *nm* trapper

pie-grièche, *pl* **pies-grièches** [pigrijɛʃ] *nf Orn* shrike

pie-mère, *pl* **pies-mères** *nf Anat* pia mater

Piémont [pjemɔ̃] *nm* Piedmont

piémontais, -aise [pjemɔ̃tɛ, -ɛz] **1** *adj* Piedmontese **2** *nm Ling* Piedmont (dialect) **3** *n* **P.** Piedmontese

piéride [pjerid] *nf* pierid; **p. du chou** cabbage white (butterfly)

pierraille [pjɛraj] *nf* loose stones

Pierre [pjɛr] *nm* **P. le Grand** Peter the Great

pierre [pjɛr] *nf* **(a)** (*matière, caillou, bloc rocheux*) stone; (*rocher*) rock, boulder; **pierres de gué** stepping stones; *Prov* **p. qui roule n'amasse pas mousse** a rolling stone gathers no moss; **attaquer qn à coups de pierres** to pelt sb with stones, to throw stones at sb; **on le fit partir à coups de pierres** they drove him away by throwing stones (at him); **jeter une p. à qn** to throw a stone at sb; *Fig* **jeter la p. à qn** to reproach sb; *Fig* **je ne serai pas le premier à lui jeter la p.** I will not be the one to throw the first stone; *Fig* **c'est une p. dans votre jardin** that's a dig at you; *Fig* **faire d'une p. deux coups** to kill two birds with one stone; *Fig* **être malheureux comme les pierres** to be bitterly unhappy; *Fig* **avoir un cœur de p.** to have a heart of stone; **mur de p.** stone wall; **mur en pierres sèches** drystone wall; **maison de** *ou* **en p.** stone(-built) house; **investir (son argent) dans la p.** to invest in bricks and mortar; **aimer les vieilles pierres** to like old buildings; **p. à p.** stone by stone; *Fig* (*progressivement*) bit by bit, little by little; **ils n'ont pas laissé p. sur p.** they didn't leave a stone standing; *Fig* **apporter sa p. à l'édifice** to make a contribution; **poser la première p.** to lay the foundation stone; *Fig* to lay the foundation (**de** for); *Hist* **Âge de p.** Stone Age; **Âge de la p. taillée/polie** Old/New Stone Age; **outils en p.** stone implements

(b) (*en bijouterie*) stone; **p. précieuse** precious stone, gem; **p. fine** *ou* **semi-précieuse** semi-precious stone

(c) (*concrétion*) piece of grit; **des fruits pleins de pierres** fruit full of grit

▶ **pierre**: **p. d'achoppement** stumbling block; *Tech* **p. à aiguiser** whetstone, grindstone; *Constr, Fig* **p. angulaire** cornerstone; *Constr* **p. à bâtir** building stone; **p. à briquet** (lighter) flint; **p. à chaux** limestone; **p. à fusil** gun flint; **p. de lune** moonstone; **p. philosophale** philosopher's stone; **p. ponce** pumice (stone); **p. de taille** dressed stone; *Minér, Fig* **p. de touche** touchstone

pierreries [pjɛr(ə)ri] *nfpl* precious stones, jewels, gems

pierreux, -euse [pjɛrø, -øz] *adj* **(a)** (*couvert de pierres*) (*sol, route etc*) stony; (*lit de rivière*) gravelly **(b)** (*qui contient des concrétions*) (*poire*) gritty **(c)** *Méd* (*formation*) calculous

pierrot [pjɛro] *nm* **(a)** *Th* **P.** Pierrot **(b)** *F* (*oiseau*) sparrow

pietà [pjeta] *nf inv* pietà

piétaille [pjetɑj] *nf F Mil Vieilli* rank and file, infantrymen; *Fig* rank and file; (*piétons*) pedestrians

piété [pjete] *nf* **(a)** (*ferveur religieuse*) piety; **articles de p.** devotional objects **(b)** (*affection*) **p. filiale** filial devotion

piétinement [pjetinmɑ̃] *nm* (*bruit*) stamping; (*marche sur place*) standing around; *Fig* (*stagnation*) lack of progress; **à cause du p. de l'enquête** because the enquiry is at a standstill *or* is marking time

piétiner [pjetine] **1** *vt* **(a)** **p. qch** (*en trépignant*) to stamp on sth; (*en marchant*) to trample on sth; (*écraser*) to trample sth underfoot; **ils sont morts piétinés par la foule** they were trampled to death by the crowd **(b)** *Fig* (*malmener*) (*les convictions de qn, les souhaits de qn, la mémoire de qn etc*) to have no respect for, to trample underfoot **2** *vi* (*frapper des pieds*) **p. d'impatience** to stamp (one's feet) impatiently *or* with impatience; **p. (sur place)** to stand around; *Fig* **l'instruction piétine** the investigation is marking time *or* is making no headway *or* is at a standstill; **je piétine depuis deux mois** I've been marking time for two months

piétisme [pjetism] *nm Hist Rel* Pietism

piétiste [pjetist] *adj, n Hist, Rel* Pietist

piéton, -onne [pjetɔ̃, -ɔn] **1** *n* pedestrian; **passage (pour) piétons** pedestrian crossing, ≈ zebra crossing, *Am* crosswalk **2** *adj* **rue piétonne** pedestrianized street; **zone piétonne** pedestrian precinct

piétonnier, -ière [pjetɔnje, -jɛr] *adj* pedestrian; **rue piétonnière** pedestrianized street; **zone piétonnière** pedestrian precinct

piètre [pjɛtr] *adj Litt* (*compagnon*) wretched, poor; (*excuse*) lame, paltry; **faire p. figure** to cut a poor *or* sorry figure; **p. consolation** cold *or* small comfort

piètrement [pjɛtrəmɑ̃] *adv* wretchedly, poorly

pieu[1], -ieux [pjø] *nm* (*piquet*) stake, post; *Constr* pile; **enfoncer** *ou* **battre un p.** to drive (in) a pile; **p. creux** tubular pile; **p. de fondation** foundation pile

pieu[2] *nm F* (*lit*) bed; **se mettre au p., aller au p.** to hit the hay *or* the sack

pieusement [pjøzmɑ̃] *adv* (*dévotement*) piously, devoutly; (*avec grand respect*) reverently

pieuter (se) [səpjøte] *vpr F* to hit the hay *or* the sack

pieuvre [pjœvr] *nf* (*animal*) octopus; *Fig Péj* (*personne*) leech; *Fig* **la p. bureaucratique** the tentacles of bureaucracy; **la p.** (*la Mafia*) the Mob

pieux, -euse [pjø, -øz] *adj* **(a)** (*religieux*) pious, devout; *Fig* **p. mensonge** white lie; **c'est un vœu p.** it's wishful thinking **(b)** *Litt* (*dévoué*) (*silence*) reverent; (*fils*) devoted

pif[1] [pif] *int* bang!, smack!; **p., paf!** pow!; **p., paf, boum!** slap! bang! wallop!

pif[2] *nm F* **(a)** (*nez*) conk, *Br* hooter **(b)** *Fig* **faire qch au p.** to do sth by guesswork; **j'ai fait ça au p.** it was sheer guesswork, I made it up as I went along; **répondre à une question au p.** to guess at the answer to a question; **au p., je dirais qu'il y en a vingt** at a rough guess I'd say there are twenty; **au lieu d'y aller au p., tu ferais mieux de consulter un plan!** instead of just following your nose, you'd do better to consult a map!

pif(f)er [pife] *vt F* **je peux pas le p.** I can't stand (the sight of) him, I can't stomach him

pifomètre [pifɔmɛtr] *nm F* intuition; **en politique, il n'y a que le p. qui compte** in politics, having a nose for things *or* having intuition is all-important; **au p.** = **au pif**

pige [piʒ] *nf* **(a)** (*mesure*) measuring rod; *Typ* take (= *amount of copy to be set up in a given time*); *Journ* freelance contribution; **être payé à la p.** to be paid by the line; **faire des piges,** *Can* **travailler à la p.** to do freelance work, to work freelance **(b)** *F* (*année*) **il a 45 piges** he's 45; **à 60 piges** at 60 **(c)** *F* **faire la p. à qn** to go one better than sb

pigeon [piʒɔ̃] *nm* **(a)** (*oiseau*) pigeon; **p. mâle/femelle** cock/hen pigeon; **p. voyageur** carrier pigeon, homing pigeon; **p. colombin** *ou* **bleu** stock dove; **p. ramier** ring dove, wood pigeon; **p. paon** fantail (pigeon); **p. d'argile** clay pigeon; **tir aux pigeons d'argile** (*sport*) clay-pigeon shooting; (*événement*) clay-pigeon shoot; **p. vole** = children's game with forfeits, ≈ Simon says **(b)** *F Péj* (*personne*) sucker, mug, *Am* fall guy **(c)** *Constr* builder's plaster; (*morceau de pierre dans la chaux*) hard lump

pigeonnant [piʒɔnɑ̃] *adj F* **poitrine pigeonnante** high bust; **soutien-gorge p.** uplift bra, (lift and) support bra

pigeonne [piʒɔn] *nf* hen pigeon

pigeonneau, -eaux [piʒɔno] *nm* young pigeon, *Spéc* squab

pigeonner [piʒɔne] *vt F* **p. qn** to take sb in; **je me suis laissé** *ou* **fait p.** I've been had, I've been taken for a ride *or* taken in

pigeonnier [piʒɔnje] *nm* **(a)** dovecot(e) **(b)** *F Fig* (*logement très petit*) garret, attic

piger [piʒe] (**je pigeai(s); n. pigeons**) **1** *vt F* (*comprendre*) to get; **tu piges la combine?** do you get what they're/we're/*etc* up to?; **je ne pige rien aux mathématiques** I haven't got a clue about mathematics; **je n'ai rien pigé à ce qu'il a raconté** I didn't get any of what he was on about, I didn't have a clue what he was on about **2** *vi* **tu piges?** get it?; **il a pigé** he's got it, *Br* he's twigged, the penny's dropped; **il ne pige pas** (*chaque fois*) he doesn't get it; (*cette fois-ci*) he hasn't got it

pigiste [piʒist] *n* **(a)** (*journaliste*) freelance journalist, freelancer; **travailler comme p.** to freelance, to work as a freelancer **(b)** *Can* freelancer

pigment [pigmɑ̃] *nm* pigment

pigmentaire [pigmɑ̃tɛr] *adj* pigmentary

pigmentation [pigmɑ̃tasjɔ̃] *nf* pigmentation

pigmenter [pigmɑ̃te] *vt* to pigment

pigne [piɲ] *nf* pine cone; (*graine*) pine nut *or* kernel

pignocher [piɲɔʃe] *vi Vieilli* to pick at one's food

pignon[1] [piɲɔ̃] *nm Constr* gable; **avoir p. sur rue** to have premises in a desirable location; *Fig* to be of some standing

pignon[2] *nm MecE* gear(wheel); (*la plus petite de deux roues*) pinion; **p. de chaîne** sprocket wheel, chain sprocket; **grand p.** (*d'une bicyclette*) front chain wheel; *Tech* **p. conique** bevel gear; **p. d'attaque** (*de différentiel*) driving pinion; **p. de distribution** timing gear; **p. fou** idler; **p. planétaire** planet gear, planet wheel; **p. satellite** (intermediate) planet gear, gearing between sun gear and planet gear

pignon[3] *nm Bot* pine nut *or* kernel
pignoratif, -ive [piɲɔratif, -iv] *adj Fin* with a repurchase option
pignouf [piɲuf] *nm F* slob, *Br* yob(bo)
pilaf [pilaf] *nm Culin* pilaf, pilau; **riz p.** pilau rice
pilage [pilaʒ] *nm* pounding, crushing, grinding
pilaire [pilɛr] *adj* of the hair
pilastre [pilastr] *nm Archit* pilaster; (*au bout d'une rampe*) newel
Pilate [pilat] *nm Hist* **Ponce P.** Pontius Pilate
pilchard [pilʃar] *nm* pilchard
pile[1] [pil] *nf* **(a)** (*tas*) pile, stack; **mettre en p.** to stack (up), to pile (up) **(b)** (*pilier*) (*d'un pont*) pier **(c)** *Él* battery, *Spéc* cell; **p. sèche** dry cell; **p. plate/ronde** square/round battery; **p. bouton** (*pour montre/appareil photo/calculatrice*) watch/camera/calculator battery; **la radio marche aussi avec des piles** the radio also works on *or* off batteries **(d)** *Phys Nucl Vieilli* **p. atomique** atomic pile, nuclear reactor
pile[2] *nf F* **(a)** (*volée de coups*) belting, beating, thrashing; **flanquer** *ou* **donner une p. à qn** to give sb a thrashing *or* belting *or* beating **(b)** (*défaite*) hammering; **recevoir** *ou* **prendre une p.** to take *or* get a hammering, to get hammered; **flanquer une p. à une équipe** to hammer a team, to walk all over a team
pile[3] **1** *nf* (*d'une pièce*) reverse; **p. ou face?** heads or tails?; **jouer** *ou* **tirer à p. ou face** to toss for it; **on tira à p. ou face qui irait chercher de l'eau** we tossed (up) *or* tossed a coin to decide who was going to get some water
2 *adj* **côté p.** (*d'une pièce*) reverse side
3 *adv F* **s'arrêter p.** to stop dead, to come to a dead stop; **vous tombez p.** you've come just at the right moment; **ça tombait p.** that's just what was wanted *or* just what the doctor ordered, that came just at the right time; **tu seras p. à l'heure** you'll be (there) right on time, you'll be (there) on the dot; **à six heures p.** at six on the dot, bang on six; **ma montre est p. à l'heure** my watch is dead on *or* bang on (time); **elle est arrivée p. le même jour que moi** she arrived on exactly the same day as I did; **nous étions p. dix à table** there were exactly ten of us at the table
piler [pile] **1** *vt* **(a)** (*broyer*) to pound, to crush, to grind; (*amandes*) to grind **(b)** *F* (*battre*) to thrash, to hammer; **notre équipe s'est fait p.** our team got a good thrashing *or* hammering **2** *vi F* to slam on the brakes
pilet [pilɛ] *nm* **(canard) p.** pintail (duck)
pileux, -euse [pilø, -øz] *adj Anat* hair, *Spéc* pilose; **follicule p.** hair follicle; **système p.** hair
pilier [pilje] *nm* **(a)** (*colonne*) pillar, column; (*poteau, pieu*) post **(b)** *Rugby* prop (forward) **(c)** *Fig* (*soutien*) **ce point est le p. de notre théorie** that point is the mainstay of our theory, our theory rests on that point; **p. de l'Église/de la démocratie** (*personne, journal*) bastion *or* pillar of the Church/of democracy; *F Péj* **c'est un p. de bar** *ou* **de bistrot** he's always propping up the bar
pillage [pijaʒ] *nm* **(a)** (*ravage*) pillaging, looting, plundering; **mettre une ville au p.** to sack a town **(b)** *Fig* (*d'œuvre*) plagiarism
pillard, -arde [pijar, -ard] **1** *adj* pillaging, looting **2** *n* pillager, plunderer; (*lors d'une émeute*) looter
piller [pije] *vt* **(a)** (*dévaster, ravager*) (*village*) to pillage, to plunder; (*magasin*) to loot; (*Rome etc*) to sack; (*maison, pièce*) to ransack **(b)** *Fig* (*livre, film*) to plagiarize; **p. un auteur** to plagiarize an author, to steal from an author; **p. les idées de qn** to steal sb's ideas
pilleur, -euse [pijœr, -øz] **1** *adj* pillaging, plundering, looting **2** *n* pillager, plunderer; (*lors d'une émeute*) looter; **c'est un p. d'idées** he's always stealing ideas from people; *Naut* **p. d'épaves** plunderer of wrecks
pilon [pilɔ̃] *nm* **(a)** *Pharm etc* pestle; *Tech* (earth) rammer; **p. mécanique** power hammer; *Fig* **mettre un livre au p.** to pulp a book; **tous ces livres iront au p.** all these books will be pulped **(b)** (*cuisse de poulet*) drumstick **(c)** (*jambe de bois*) wooden leg
pilonnage [pilɔnaʒ] *nm* (*de produits pharmaceutiques etc*) pounding; (*de terre, béton etc*) ramming; *Mil* bombardment, shelling
pilonner [pilɔne] *vt* **(a)** (*écraser*) (*produits pharmaceutiques etc*) to pound; (*papier*) to pulp; (*terre, béton etc*) to ram **(b)** *Mil* to bombard, to shell
pilori [pilɔri] *nm* pillory; *aussi Fig* **clouer** *ou* **mettre qn au p.** to pillory sb
pilosébacé [pilosebase] *adj Anat* pilosebaceous
pilosité [pilozite] *nf Anat* hairiness, *Spéc* pilosity; **p. normale/excessive** normal/excessive hair growth; **p. faciale** facial hair
pilot [pilo] *nm* **(a)** *Constr* pile; **p. de pont** bridge pile **(b)** *Tech* (*chiffons*) = cloth used in paper-making
pilotage [pilɔtaʒ] *nm* **(a)** *Naut* piloting; **(droits** *ou* **frais de) p.** pilotage (dues) **(b)** *Av* piloting, flying; **le p. d'un jumbo-jet ne s'apprend pas en un mois** you can't learn to fly a jumbo jet in the space of a month; **poste de p.** cockpit; (*dans un avion plus important*) flight deck; **p. automatique** automatic piloting; **école de p.** flying school **(c)** *Ordinat* control
pilote [pilɔt] **1** *nm* **(a)** *Av, Naut* pilot; (*conducteur*) (*de voiture de course*) driver; (*de moto de course*) rider; *Av* **p. d'essai** test pilot; *Av* **p. de ligne** airline pilot; **p. breveté** *Av* licensed pilot; *Mil Av* certified pilot; **p. automatique** automatic pilot, autopilot, *Br F* George; *Fig* **je vais lui servir de p.** I'll show him round, I'll act as his guide
(b) (*poisson*) pilot fish
(c) *Ordinat* driver; **p. d'affichage** display driver; **p. d'imprimante** printer driver; **p. de logiciel** software driver; **p. de mise en attente des fichiers à imprimer** printer spooler
(d) *TV* pilot
2 *adj* **usine/installation(-)p.** pilot factory/plant; **université (-)p.** experimental university; **bateau(-)p.** pilot boat
piloter [pilɔte] *vt* **(a)** (*navire*) to pilot; (*avion*) to pilot, to fly; (*conduire*) (*voiture de course*) to drive; (*moto de course*) to ride; *Fig* (*projet*) to be in charge of; *Fig* **p. qn dans Londres** to guide *or* show sb round London **(b)** *Ordinat* to drive; **piloté par menu** menu-driven
pilotis [pilɔti] *nm Constr* piling, piles; **bâti sur p.** built on piles
pilou [pilu] *nm Tex* flannelette, cotton flannel
pilulaire [pilylɛr] *adj Pharm* pilular
pilule [pilyl] *nf Pharm* pill, tablet; **la p. (contraceptive** *ou* **anticonceptionnelle)** the pill; **prendre la p.** to be on the pill; **p. abortive** abortion pill; **p. du lendemain** morning-after pill; *Fig* **avaler la p.** to grin and bear it; *Fig* **vous aurez du mal à leur faire avaler la p.** you'll have a hard time getting them to accept that; *Fig* **la p. était amère** it was a bitter pill to swallow; *Fig* **dorer la p. (à qn)** to sugar the pill (for sb); *Fig très F* **on va prendre la p.** *ou* **une de ces pilules!** we'll get a hammering, we'll get hammered
pimbêche [pɛ̃bɛʃ] **1** *nf* stuck-up girl/woman **2** *adj* stuck-up
piment [pimɑ̃] *nm Bot* pimento, capsicum; *Fig* (*piquant*) spice, piquancy; *Culin* **p. rouge** chilli; **p. doux** pepper, *Am* bell pepper, capsicum; **une histoire/vie qui ne manque pas de p.** a story/life that is anything but dull; **donner du p. à une histoire/une soirée** to add spice to a story/a party
pimenté [pimɑ̃te] *adj Culin* spicy, highly spiced, hot; *Fig* (*histoire*) spicy
pimenter [pimɑ̃te] *vt Culin* to spice up; *Fig* (*relever*) (*histoire*) to spice up, to add spice to
pimpant [pɛ̃pɑ̃] *adj* (*personne*) smart, spruce, trim
pimprenelle [pɛ̃prənɛl] *nf Bot* burnet
pin [pɛ̃] *nm* **(a)** (*arbre*) pine (tree); **p. maritime** maritime pine; **p. d'Écosse** *ou* **sylvestre** Scots pine; **p. pignon** *ou* **parasol** umbrella pine; **p. de montagne** silver pine, white pine; **p. de Virginie** scrub pine; **pomme de p.** pine cone; (*de sapin*) fir cone **(b)** (*bois*) pine(wood)
pinacle [pinakl] *nm* pinnacle; *Fig* **porter qn au p.** to praise sb to the skies; **être au p.** to be at the top
pinacothèque [pinakɔtɛk] *nf* picture gallery, art gallery
pinaillage [pinajaʒ] *nm F* quibbling, hair-splitting, nitpicking
pinailler [pinaje] *vi F* to quibble, to split hairs, to nitpick; **p. sur qch** to quibble over sth
pinailleur, -euse [pinajœr, -øz] *F* **1** *adj* nitpicking **2** *n* quibbler, nitpicker
pinard [pinar] *nm F* vino, wine; (*de qualité inférieure*) cheap wine, *Br* plonk
pinasse [pinas] *nf Naut* pinnace, shallop
pinçage [pɛ̃saʒ] *nm* (*de bourgeons*) pinching off, nipping off
pince [pɛ̃s] *nf* **(a)** [①A10,e] (*outil*) pliers; (*aux mâchoires recourbées*) pincers; (*de forgeron*) tongs; *Chir* forceps **(b)** (*patte*) (*de crabe etc*) pincer, claw **(c)** *F* (*main*) paw, mitt; **serrer la p. à qn** to shake hands with sb **(d)** (*d'un animal herbivore*) incisor **(e)** (*du sabot d'un cheval*) toe, point; *F* **aller à pinces** (*à pied*) to foot it; **il est parti à pinces** he left on foot **(f)** *Couture* dart
▶ **pince**: **p. alligator** alligator clip; **p. à becs fins** needle-nosed pliers; **p. à becs pointus** pointed-nose pliers; **p. à circlip** circlip pliers; **pince(s) coupante(s)** cutting pliers, wire cutters; **pince(s) coupante(s) d'électricien** electrician's side cutters; **p. de cravate** tie clip; **p. crocodile** crocodile clip; **p. à épiler** tweezers; *Él* **p. pour fil terminal** terminal clamp; *Chir* **p. hémostatique** artery clip; **p. à linge** clothes peg; **p. multiprise** combination pliers; **p. à ongles** nail clippers; *TV, Cin* **p. pour projecteur** gaffer grip; *Él* **p. de raccordement** connecting clamp, connector; **p. à sucre** sugar tongs; **p. universelle** (universal) pliers, combination pliers; **p. à vélo** bicycle clip

pincé [pɛ̃se] *adj* (*air*) stiff, starchy; **sourire p.** tight-lipped smile; **répondre d'un ton p.** to answer stiffly *or* starchily; **nez p.** thin nose; **les lèvres pincées** with pursed lips *or* lips pursed, tight-lipped; **instrument à cordes pincées** plucked stringed instrument

pinceau, -eaux [pɛ̃so] *nm* **(a)** (*brosse*) (paint)brush; **p. en poils de martre** sable brush; **coup de p.** brush stroke; **on reconnaît facilement le coup de p. de l'artiste** the artist's brushwork is easily recognizable; **elle a un bon coup de p.** she paints well **(b)** *Fig* (*technique, manière*) brushwork **(c)** *F* (*pied*) foot; **s'emmêler les pinceaux** to get into a muddle **(d)** *Opt* **p. de lumière** pencil of light

pincée [pɛ̃se] *nf* (*de sel, de tabac à priser etc*) pinch

pince-fesses *nm inv F Vieilli* knees-up, shindig, bash

pincement [pɛ̃smɑ̃] *nm* **(a)** (*fait de pincer*) pinching, nipping **(b)** *Fig* (*sensation vive, douloureuse*) (*de regret etc*) pang, twinge; **il a eu un p. au cœur** his heart missed a beat **(c)** *Mus* (*des cordes de guitare etc*) plucking **(d)** (*des bourgeons*) pinching off, nipping off

pince-monseigneur, *pl* **pinces-monseigneur** *nf* jemmy, *US* jimmy; **forcer une porte à la p.** to jemmy *or* jimmy a door

pince-nez *nm inv* pince-nez

pincer [pɛ̃se] **(je pinçai(s); n. pinçons) 1** *vt* **(a)** (*serrer*) to pinch, to nip; **son grand-père lui pinça la joue** his grandfather pinched his cheek; **p. les lèvres** to purse one's lips; **non mais pince-moi, je rêve!** pinch me, I'm dreaming!; *F* **ça pince dur ce matin!** it's pretty nippy this morning!

(b) (*bourgeons*) to pinch off, to nip off; (*plante*) to top

(c) *Mus* (*cordes de harpe etc*) to pluck

(d) *Couture* (*vêtement*) to put darts in

(e) *F* (*attraper*) (*personne*) to catch; **se faire p.** to be *or* get caught, to cop it; *F* **en p. pour qn** to be crazy about sb, to be gone on sb

2 se pincer *vpr* **se p. le doigt dans la porte** to catch one's finger in the door; **fais attention, tu vas te p.** watch out, you'll catch yourself; **se p. le nez** to hold one's nose

pince-sans-rire 1 *n inv* person with a dry sense of humour **2** *adj* dry, deadpan; **répondre d'un air p.** to answer drily *or* deadpan

pincette [pɛ̃sɛt] *nf* [①A10,e] (*petite pince*) tweezers; **pincettes** (fire) tongs, pair of (fire) tongs; *Fig F* **il n'est pas à prendre avec des pincettes** (*il est sale*) he's absolutely filthy; (*il est de très mauvaise humeur*) he's like a bear with a sore head

pinçon [pɛ̃sɔ̃] *nm* pinch mark

pindarique [pɛ̃darik] *adj Littér* Pindaric

pinéal, -ale, -aux, -ales [pineal, -o] *adj Anat* pineal

pineau [pino] *nm* pineau (*apéritif made from wine and brandy*)

pinède [pinɛd] *nf*, **pineraie** [pinrɛ] *nf* pine forest *or* wood

pingouin [pɛ̃gwɛ̃] *nm* penguin; (*de la famille des macareux*) auk; **p. royal** king penguin

ping-pong [piŋpɔ̃g] *nm* (*no pl*) ping pong, table tennis

pingre [pɛ̃gr] *Péj* **1** *adj* stingy, niggardly, miserly **2** *n* miser, skinflint, *Am* tightwad

pingrerie [pɛ̃grəri] *nf Péj* stinginess, niggardliness, miserliness

pinot [pino] *nm* Pinot grape

pin's [pinz] *nm inv* lapel badge *or* pin

pinson [pɛ̃sɔ̃] *n* chaffinch; **être gai comme un p.** to be as happy as a lark

pintade [pɛ̃tad] *nf* guinea fowl; **p. mâle** guinea cock; **p. femelle** guinea hen

pintadeau, -eaux [pɛ̃tado] *nm* young guinea fowl, guinea poult

pinte [pɛ̃t] *nf* **(a)** *Arch* pint (*0.93 litres*); *Br, US* pint; *Can* quart **(b)** *F Vieilli* **se payer une p. de bon sang** to have a good time *or* a good laugh

pinter [pɛ̃te] *très F* **1** *vi* to booze **2 se pinter** *vpr* to booze; (*s'enivrer*) to get sozzled *or* plastered; **il s'est pinté (la gueule)** he got plastered, *Am* he tied one on

pin up [pinœp] *nf inv* (*photo*) pin-up; (*jolie fille*) sexy-looking girl

pinyin [pinjin] *nm Ling* Pinyin

pioche [pjɔʃ] *nf* **(a)** (*outil*) pick, pickaxe, *US* pickax; *Agr* mattock; *Fig F* **tête de p.** pig-headed person **(b)** (*dominos*) stock, pile

piocher [pjɔʃe] **1** *vt* **(a)** (*creuser*) to dig (with a pick) **(b)** *Scol F* **p. son allemand** to swot up *or* mug up one's German **2** *vi* **(a)** (*fouiller*) to dig, to delve (**dans** into) **(b)** (*dominos*) to draw from the stock

piocheur, -euse [pjɔʃœr, -øz] *F* **1** *adj* hardworking **2** *n Scol Vieilli* slogger, *Péj* swot, *Am* grind

piolet [pjɔlɛ] *nm* ice axe

pion [pjɔ̃] *nm* **(a)** *Scol F* supervisor (*paid to supervise pupils outside class hours*) **(b)** *Échecs* pawn; (*aux dames*) draught(sman), *US* checker; (*dans d'autres jeux*) piece; *Fig* **n'être qu'un p. (sur l'échiquier)** to be only a pawn in the game **(c)** *MecE* peg

pioncer [pjɔ̃se] *vi* **(je pionçai(s); n. pionçons)** *F* to sleep, *Br* to kip

pionne [pjɔn] *nf Scol F* supervisor (*paid to supervise pupils outside class hours*)

pionnier, -ière [pjɔnje, -jɛr] **1** *n aussi Fig* pioneer **2** *adj* pioneering; **son esprit p.** his pioneering spirit

pipe¹ [pip] *nf* **(a)** (*de fumeur*) pipe; **p. de bruyère/en terre** briar/clay pipe; **fumer la p.** to smoke a pipe; *Fig F* **casser sa p.** to kick the bucket; **nom d'une p.!** heavens above!; *F* **20 francs par tête de p.** 20 francs a head; *F* **se fendre la p.** (*rire*) to split one's sides (laughing); (*s'amuser*) to have a good laugh; *Vulg* **faire** *ou* **tailler une p. à qn** to give sb a blow job **(b)** (*contenu*) pipe(ful) **(c)** *Arg Vieilli* (*cigarette*) ciggy, *Br* fag **(d)** *Région* (*futaille*) (large) cask, barrel

pipe² [pajp] *nm* (*tuyau*) pipe(line) (*for liquid, gas*)

pipeau, -eaux [pipo] *nm Mus* (reed) pipe; **p. de chasse** bird call; **pipeaux** (*pour prendre les oiseaux*) limed twigs; *F* **c'est du p.** it's all claptrap

pipée [pipe] *nf* bird snaring, bird catching (*with bird calls and limed twigs*)

pipelet, -ette [piplɛ, -ɛt] *F* **1** *n Vieilli* concierge, porter, *Am* janitor **2** *nf* **pipelette** (*personne bavarde*) gossip, chatterbox

pipe(-)line, *pl* **pipe(-)lines** [piplin, pajplajn] *nm* pipeline

piper [pipe] *vt* **(a)** (*attraper avec des appeaux*) (*oiseaux*) to lure by means of bird calls **(b)** (*truquer*) (*dés*) to load; (*cartes*) to mark; *Fig* **les dés sont pipés** the dice are loaded **(c)** *F* **ne pas p. (mot)** not to say a word, to keep silent, to keep mum

piperade [pip(ə)rad] *nf*, **pipérade** [piperad] *nf Culin* omelette with peppers and tomatoes

pipette [pipɛt] *nf* pipette

pipi [pipi] *nm F* pee, *Enf* wee(-wee); **faire p.** to pee, *Enf* to wee(-wee), to have a wee(-wee); **aller faire p.** to go to the loo *or Am* john, to go for a pee; **faire p. au lit** to wet the bed; **le chien a fait p. sur le tapis** the dog's made a puddle on the carpet; *F Péj* **c'est du p. de chat** (*boisson*) it's dishwater; (*argument, discours etc*) it's tripe

pipi-room, *pl* **pipi-rooms** [pipirum] *nm F* loo, *Am* rest room; **où sont les pipi-rooms?** where's the loo

pipistrelle [pipistrɛl] *nf Zool* pipistrelle

piquage [pikaʒ] *nm Couture* (machine) stitching; (*d'une surface métallique*) pitting

piquant [pikɑ̃] **1** *adj* **(a)** (*pointu*) (*objet*) pointed; (*plante*) prickly, thorny; (*ortie*) stinging; (*barbe*) bristly, prickly; (*sensation*) prickling

(b) (*vent*) biting

(c) (*goût*) spicy, hot, piquant; **moutarde piquante** hot mustard

(d) *Fig* (*caustique*) (*remarques etc*) cutting, caustic

(e) *Fig* (*qui stimule la curiosité, l'intérêt*) (*beauté*) piquant, striking; **une petite brune piquante** a striking little brunette

2 *nm* **(a)** (*épine*) (*d'une plante*) prickle, thorn; (*d'un porc-épic*) quill, spine; (*d'un hérisson*) bristle; (*de fil de fer barbelé*) spike, barb

(b) *F* (*agrément*) (*d'un style, d'une situation*) piquancy; (*d'une histoire*) spice; **cette fille a du p.** that girl is rather striking *or* is strikingly attractive; **le changement donne du p. à la vie** variety is the spice of life; **c'est ce qui fait tout le p. de la situation** it's what makes the situation so piquant

pique¹ [pik] **1** *nf* (*armement*) pike; (*d'un picador*) lance **2** *nm Cartes* (*carte*) spade; (*couleur*) spades; **valet de p.** jack of spades; **jouer (un) p.** to play spades *or* a spade; **il me reste encore trois piques** I still have three spades left (in my hand)

pique² *nf* **(a)** (*méchanceté*) taunt, spiteful remark, *F* dig; **envoyer** *ou* **lancer des piques à qn** to get at sb, *F* to have a dig *or* a go at sb **(b)** *Vieilli* (*brouille*) tiff

piqué, -ée [pike] **1** *adj* **(a)** (*dessus de lit, vêtement*) quilted; **p. à la machine** machine-stitched; (*matelassé*) machine-quilted

(b) (*marqué par les vers*) (*bois, livre*) wormeaten; (*marqué par l'humidité*) (*miroir*) tarnished; (*page, gravure*) foxed; (*métal*) pitted; *Fig* **ciel p. d'étoiles** sky studded with stars; *F* **une histoire/recette qui n'est pas piquée des hannetons** *ou* **des vers** one heck of a story/recipe

(c) *F* (*fou*) batty, barmy, loony

(d) (*acide*) (*vin*) sour, tart

(e) *Mus* (*notes*) staccato

2 *nm* **(a)** *Av* **descente en p.** vertical dive, nose dive; **bombardement en p.** dive bombing

(b) *Tex* piqué

3 *n F* nutter, loony

pique-assiette, *pl* **pique-assiettes** *n F* scrounger, sponger, freeloader
pique-bœuf, *pl* **pique-bœufs** [pikbø] *nm Orn* oxpecker
pique-feu *nm inv* poker
pique-fleurs *nm inv* flower holder, frog
pique-nique, *pl* **pique-niques** *nm* picnic; **faire un p.** to have a picnic
pique-niquer *vi* to have a picnic, to picnic
pique-niqueur, -euse [piknikœr, -øz], *pl* **pique-niqueurs, -euses** *n* picnicker
pique-notes *nm inv* spike
piquer [pike] **1** *vt* **(a)** (*percer avec une pointe*) to prick; (*d'une guêpe, d'un moustique etc*) to sting; (*d'une puce*) to bite; (*aiguillonner*) (*cheval*) to spur on; (*bœuf*) to goad; *F* **quelle mouche vous a piqué?** what's eating *or* biting you?, what's got into you?, who rattled your cage?; **se faire p. par un insecte** to be bitten by an insect; **p. un cheval de l'éperon** to prick *or* spur a horse; **la fumée me pique les yeux** the smoke makes my eyes sting *or* smart; **ça me pique la gorge/le nez** it tickles my throat/nose

(b) *Méd* **p. qn** to give sb an injection *or Br F* a jab; *F* **se faire p. contre qch** to be vaccinated against sth; *F* **p. un chien** to put a dog down, to put a dog to sleep; **faire p. un chien** to have a dog put down *or* put to sleep

(c) (*offenser, froisser*) to offend, to pique; **p. qn au vif** to cut sb to the quick

(d) (*exciter*) **p. l'attention de qn** to arouse sb's attention; **p. la curiosité de qn** to arouse *or* excite sb's curiosity

(e) (*trouer*) (*d'acide, de vers*) to eat into; (*tacheter*) to spot, to mark; **mains piquées de taches de rousseur** freckled *or* freckly hands

(f) (*coudre*) to (back)stitch; (*dessus de lit etc*) to quilt; **p. (à la machine)** to machine (stitch); **p. du cuir** to stitch leather

(g) *Culin* **p. de la viande** to lard meat; **rôti piqué d'ail** joint stuck with garlic

(h) *Mus* **p. une note** to play a note staccato; *Naut* **p. l'heure** to strike the hour

(i) *F* (*voler*) to pinch, to swipe (**qch à qn** sth from sb); **ils m'ont piqué ma voiture** they pinched *or* swiped my car; **je me suis fait p. mon stylo** my pen got pinched *or* swiped

(j) (*enfoncer*) to stick (**dans** into)

(k) *F* **p. un cent mètres** to sprint off; **p. une tête** to take a header, to dive; **p. un roupillon** to have forty winks *or* a nap *or* a snooze; **p. une crise** to throw a fit; **p. une crise de nerfs** to have hysterics; **p. un soleil** *ou* **un fard** to go bright red, to blush

2 *vi* **(a)** *Av* **p. (du nez)** to nosedive; *Fig* **p. du nez** to nod off, to doze off; (*baisser les yeux*) to look down; *Naut* **p. de l'avant** to go down by the bows

(b) (*picoter*) (*de plat*) to be hot *or* spicy; (*de vin*) to be sour *or* tart; **moutarde qui pique** hot mustard; *F* **eau qui pique** fizzy water; **vent qui pique** keen *or* biting wind; **ça pique** it stings; **tu piques!** (*à un homme mal rasé*) you're all bristly

(c) (*d'une abeille, d'un moustique etc*) to sting; (*d'une puce*) to bite

(d) **p. des deux** to spur on one's horse; (*s'en aller à cheval*) to gallop off; *Fig* to rush *or* dash off

3 se piquer *vpr* **(a)** (*se blesser*) to prick oneself; (*se faire une piqûre*) (*de malade, drogué*) to give oneself an injection, to inject oneself; **il se pique** he's a needle-user

(b) (*se froisser*) to take offence *or US* offense

(c) **se p. de faire qch** to pride oneself on doing sth; **se p. de littérature** to pride oneself on one's knowledge of literature; **se p. au jeu** to get into it

(d) (*se couvrir de taches*) (*de miroir*) to tarnish; (*de métaux*) to pit; (*du bois*) to become wormeaten, to get woodworm; (*des vêtements etc*) to become motheaten; (*de livres*) to become foxed; (*devenir acide*) (*du vin*) to turn acid, to (turn) sour
piquet[1] [pikɛ] *nm* **(a)** (*pieu*) stake, post; (*plus petit*) peg; **mettre** *ou* **attacher les chevaux au p.** to tether the horses; **droit/raide comme un p.** as straight as a ramrod/as stiff as a poker; **rester planté comme un p.** to stand there doing nothing, *Br F* to stand there like a lemon **(b)** *Scol* **mettre** *ou* **envoyer qn au p.** to send sb to stand in the corner; **être au p.** to stand in the corner
▶ **piquet**: *Ind* **p. de grève** strike picket, picket line; **p. d'incendie** fire picket; **p. de tente** tent peg
piquet[2] *nm Cartes* piquet; **faire un p.** to play a hand of piquet
piquetage [piktaʒ] *nm Tech* staking (out)
piqueter [pikte] *vt* (**je piquette, n. piquetons; je piquetterai**) **(a)** (*jalonner*) to stake out, to mark out **(b)** (*marquer*) to spot, to dot; **piqueté de noir** spotted *or* dotted with black
piquette [pikɛt] *nf* **(a)** *Péj* cheap wine, *Br F* plonk **(b)** *F* (*défaite*) hammering, thrashing; **prendre une** *ou* **la p.** to get *or* take a hammering, to get a good thrashing
piqueur, -euse [pikœr, -øz] **1** *nm* **(a)** (*à la chasse*) whipper-in; *Équitation* groom **(b)** *Min* hewer, pickman **(c)** *Rail* platelayer, *US* tracklayer **2** *n Ind* stitcher **3** *adj Zool* **insecte p.** stinging insect
piquouse [pikuz] *nf F* shot, *Br* jab; **se faire un p.** to have a jab
piqûre [pikyr] *nf* **(a)** (*petite blessure*) (*de guêpe etc*) sting; (*de puce*) bite; **p. d'épingle** pinprick **(b)** *Méd* injection, *F* shot, *Br F* jab; **faire une p. à qn** to give sb an injection **(c)** (*trou*) (small) hole; (*dans le métal*) pit; **p. de vers** (*dans bois, livre*) wormhole; **p. d'aiguille** (*dans le cuir*) pinhole **(d)** *Couture* (*d'un tissu, du cuir*) (back)stitching; **(point de) p.** (*d'une machine à coudre*) lockstitch **(e)** (*tache*) (*de rouille, de poussière, de moisi*) spot, speck; **piqûres** (*dans le métal*) pitting
piranha [pirana] *nm* piranha
piratage [pirataʒ] *nm* pirating; **p. informatique** hacking
pirate [pirat] **1** *nm* **(a)** (*des mers*) pirate **(b)** (*voleur, filou*) crook **2** *adj Fig* pirate; *Rad* **station p.** pirate station; **enregistrement p.** pirate *or* bootleg recording
▶ **pirate**: **p. de l'air** hijacker, skyjacker; *Ordinat* **p. informatique** hacker; **p. de la route** robber (*who preys on motorists*)
pirater [pirate] *vt* (*enregistrement, cassette*) to pirate; *Ordinat* to hack
piraterie [piratri] *nf* **(a)** (*sur les mers*) piracy; (*acte*) act of piracy; *Av* **p. aérienne** hijacking, skyjacking **(b)** *Fig* (*escroquerie*) swindling; **p. audiovisuelle** unauthorized copying *or* reproduction, *F* bootlegging; **p. commerciale** illegal copying of brand-name goods, counterfeiting
pire [pir] **1** *adj* **(a)** (*comp*) worse; **cela est bien p.** that's much worse; **c'est p. qu'avant** it's worse than before; **p. que jamais** worse than ever; **le remède est p. que le mal** the cure is worse than the disease; *Prov* **il n'est p. eau que l'eau qui dort** still waters run deep; *Prov* **il n'est p. sourd que celui qui ne veut pas entendre** there is none so deaf as he who will not hear; **rien n'est p. que …** nothing is worse than …, there is nothing worse than …; **ce qui est p.** what is worse; **c'est de p. en p.** it's getting worse and worse

(b) (*superl*) worst; **le p./la p./les pires** the worst; **un voyou de la p. espèce** a lout of the worst kind; **nos pires erreurs** our worst mistakes; **c'est mon p. ennemi** he's my worst enemy

2 *nm* **le p. de l'histoire, c'est que …** the worst thing about it is that …; **pour le meilleur et pour le p.** for better or for worse; **il est capable du meilleur comme du p.** he can be extremely good or extremely bad; **craindre le p.** to fear the worst; **s'attendre au p.** to expect the worst; **(en mettant les choses) au p.** if the worst comes to the worst, at worst
Pirée (le) [ləpire] *nm* Piraeus
piriforme [pirifɔrm] *adj* pear-shaped, *Spéc* pyriform
pirogue [pirɔg] *nf* pirogue, dugout (canoe)
piroguier [pirɔgje] *nm* boatman (*in a pirogue*)
pirouette [pirwɛt] *nf* **(a)** (*de danseuse*), *Équitation* pirouette; *Fig F* **répondre par une p.** *ou* **des pirouettes** to give a flippant answer **(b)** *Fig* (*revirement*) about-turn, volte-face
pirouetter [pirwete] *vi* to pirouette
pis[1] [pi] *nm* (*d'une vache etc*) udder
pis[2] **1** *adv* **aller de mal en p.** to go from bad to worse

2 *adj* **(a)** (*comp*) worse; **cela serait encore p.** that would be worse still *or* even worse; **qui p. est** what is worse; **son état est p. que jamais** his condition is worse than ever

(b) (*superl*) **ce qu'il y a de p.** what is worst

3 *n* **(a)** (*comp*) worse; **il y a p.** there is/are worse; **il a fait tout cela et p.** he did all that and (something even) worse; **dire p. que pendre de qn** to call sb every name under the sun, not to have a good word to say for sb; **on m'en a dit p. que pendre sur ce restaurant** I've heard nothing but bad things about this restaurant

(b) (*superl*) **le p.** the worst; **faire p.** to do the worst; **en mettant les choses au p.** if the worst comes to the worst, at worst; **au p. aller** at the very worst
pis(-)aller [pizale] *nm inv* (*solution temporaire*) stopgap (solution); **on va l'engager mais c'est un p.** we'll take him on but we're scraping the bottom (of the barrel), we'll take him on as the best of a bad lot; **j'ai pris ce travail, mais pour moi, c'est un p.** I took the job as the best thing available in the circumstances *or* although it's far from ideal
piscicole [pisikɔl] *adj* fish-breeding, *Fml* piscicultural
pisciculteur, -trice [pisikyltœr, -tris] *n* fish breeder, *Fml* pisciculturist
pisciculture [pisikyltyr] *nf* fish breeding, *Fml* pisciculture
pisciforme [pisifɔrm] *adj* pisciform
piscine [pisin] *nf* **(a)** (*bassin de natation*) (swimming) pool; **p. couverte/en plein air** indoor/open-air *or* outdoor pool; **p. d'eau de mer** sea-water pool; **p. d'eau douce** freshwater pool; **p. intérieure** indoor pool; **p. publique** (public)

swimming pool, *Br* swimming baths **(b)** *Arg* **la p.** = the French secret service

piscivore [pisivɔr] *adj* fish-eating, *Spéc* piscivorous

Pise [piz] *nf* Pisa

pissaladière [pisaladjɛr] *nf Culin Région* = (open) onion and tomato tart, garnished with anchovies or sardines and olives

pissat [pisa] *nm* (*de cheval, d'âne etc*) urine

pisse [pis] *nf Vulg* piss, pee

pisse-froid *nm inv F* (*personne morose*) wet blanket

pissenlit [pisɑ̃li] *nm* dandelion; *F* **manger les pissenlits par la racine** to be pushing up the daisies, to be six feet under

pisser [pise] **1** *vi* **(a)** *Vulg* to (have a) piss, to (have a) pee; **il a pissé dans sa culotte** he's pissed in *or* peed in *or* wet his pants; **c'est comme si je pissais dans un violon** it's a complete waste of time, *F* it's like pissing in the wind; **laisse p. (le mérinos)!** leave it!, forget it!, don't let it get to you!; **p. de rire** to piss oneself (laughing); **ça/il ne pisse pas loin** it's/he's not up to much; **ça l'a pris comme une envie de p.** he felt a sudden urge to do it, the urge suddenly took him to do it; **je pisse sur les intellectuels** I despise these fucking intellectuals; **ton patron, je lui pisse dessus!** I don't give a shit about your boss!; **je te pisse à la raie!** up yours!

(b) *F* (*fuir*) (*d'un récipient*) to leak; (*d'un liquide*) to squirt out; **tonneau qui pisse** leaky barrel

2 *vt* **son bras pissait le sang** there was blood gushing *or* pouring from his arm, his arm was pouring with blood; **elle pissait le sang** blood was pouring out of her; *Méd F* **p. du sang** to pass blood; **le robinet pisse de l'eau continuellement** the tap is continually leaking

pissette [pisɛt] *nf Ch* wash(ing) bottle

pisseur, -euse [pisœr, -øz] *Vulg* **1** *n* **(a) c'est un p.** he's always going for a piss *or* pee, he's got a weak bladder **(b)** *Journ Péj* **p. de copie** writer who churns out rubbish **2** *nf* **pisseuse** (*petite fille*) little girl, *Péj* brat

pisseux, -euse [pisø, -øz] *adj F* **(a)** (*qui sent l'urine*) smelling of piss; (*taché par l'urine*) stained with piss, piss-stained **(b)** *Fig* (*couleur*) washed out, wishy-washy, yellowy

pisse-vinaigre *nm inv F* (*qui se plaint toujours*) grumbler, grouser

pissoir [piswar] *nm*, **pissotière** [pisɔtjɛr] *nf F* (public) urinal; (*dans la rue*) street urinal

pistache [pistaʃ] **1** *nf* pistachio (nut); *Culin* **glace à la p.** pistachio ice-cream **2** *adj inv* pistachio (green)

pistachier [pistaʃje] *nm* pistachio (tree)

pistage [pistaʒ] *nm* (*d'animal*) tracking, trailing; (*de personne*) tailing

pistard, -arde [pistar, -ard] *n Cyclisme* track racer

piste [pist] *nf* **(a)** (*trace*) track, trail; **suivre la p.** to follow the track *or* the trail; **être sur la p. de qn/qch** to be on the track of sb/sth; **la police a plusieurs pistes** the police have several leads; **brouiller les pistes** to cover one's tracks; *Fig* to confuse the issue; **suivre une fausse p.** to be on the wrong track; **être sur la bonne p.** to be on the right track

(b) *Sp* track; *Courses de chevaux* (race)track; (*course automobile*) (racing) track; *Fig F Dial* **aller en p.** to go clubbing; **p. cendrée** cinder track; **tour de p.** lap; *Aut etc* **p. de vitesse** racing track; **p. d'essai** test track; **p. de patinage** skating rink; **p. de ski** (ski)run, piste; **p. de luge** toboggan run; *Ski* **p. artificielle** artificial *or* dry ski slope; **p. de danse** dance floor; **p. (de cirque)** (circus) ring; **en p.!** into the ring!; *Fig* (*au travail*) get cracking!

(c) *Av* runway; **p. d'envol** take-off runway; **p. d'atterrissage** landing runway; (*dans la brousse etc*) airstrip; **p. de fortune** airstrip, landing strip

(d) (*chemin*) track, trail; **p. cyclable** cycle path; *MecE* **p. des billes** ball race; **p. en terre** dirt track

(e) (*de magnétophone, Ordinat de disque*) track; **magnéto 4 pistes** 4-track tape recorder; *Cin* **p. sonore** soundtrack; **p. audio** sound track; *Ordinat* **p. d'amorçage** boot track; *TV etc* **p. de fond** backing track; **p. magnétique** magnetic track; *Ordinat* magnetic stripe; **p. optique** optical track; *TV, Cin* **p. pilote** control track; *TV, Cin* **p. son** sound track, audio track; **p. son non synchrone** wild track; *TV, Cin* **p. vidéo** video track; *Ordinat* **pistes par pouce** tracks per inch

pister [piste] *vt* (*animal*) to track, to trail; **p. qn** to tail *or* shadow *or* follow sb

pisteur [pistœr] *nm* ski-run attendant *or* supervisor

pistil [pistil] *nm Bot* pistil

pistole [pistɔl] *nf* pistole

pistolet [pistɔle] *nm* **(a)** (*arme à feu*) pistol, gun; *Tech* **peinture au p.** spray painting, spraying **(b)** *Culin* (milk) roll **(c)** (*de dessinateur*) French curve **(d)** *F* (*urinal*) bottle **(e)** (*type bizarre*) **un drôle de p.** a queer *or* an odd sort *or F* fish

▶ **pistolet**: **p. à air comprimé** air pistol *or* gun; *Hist* **p. d'arçon** horse pistol; **p. à bouchon** popgun; **p. à eau** water pistol; *Tech* **p. à peinture** paint gun, spray gun; *Sp* **p. de starter** starting pistol; *Mil etc* **p. de tir** firing pistol; *Tech* **p. vaporisateur** paint gun, spray gun

pistolet-mitrailleur, *pl* **pistolets-mitrailleurs** *nm* submachine gun, tommy gun, sten gun

pistoleur [pistɔlœr] *nm Tech* spray(-gun) painter

piston [pistɔ̃] *nm* **(a)** *MecE* (*de machine, de pompe, de cric etc*) piston; **p. à air/eau** air/water piston; **tête de p.** piston head; **p. plongeur** (*d'une pompe refoulante etc*) plunger; (*d'une presse hydraulique*) ram; **p. de servo** booster piston **(b)** *Fig* (*recommandation*) string-pulling; **avoir du p.** to have friends in the right places; **il a eu la place par p.** someone pulled strings to get him the job; **faire jouer le p.** to pull strings **(c)** *Mus* valve; **(cornet à) p.** cornet

pistonner [pistɔne] *vt F* **p. qn** to pull strings for sb; **il s'est fait p.** he got someone to pull strings for him

pistou [pistu] *nm Culin* pesto; **soupe de** *ou* **au p.** vegetable soup with pesto

pitance [pitɑ̃s] *nf* **(a)** *Arch* (*dans un couvent*) allowance (of food) **(b)** *Péj Vieilli* sustenance

pitchoun, -oune [pitʃun] *n Région* (*enfant*) little one

pitchpin [pitʃpɛ̃] *nm Bot* pitch pine

piteusement [pitøzmɑ̃] *adv* pitifully, miserably

piteux, -euse [pitø, -øz] *adj* **(a)** (*qui suscite la pitié*) *Vieilli* pitiful **(b)** (*médiocre*) **p. résultat** poor *or* miserable *or* pitiful result; **en p. état** in a sorry *or* pitiful state **(c) faire une mine piteuse, faire piteuse mine** to look crestfallen; **il annonça d'un air p. que …** he announced shamefaced that …

pithécanthrope [pitekɑ̃trɔp] *nm* pithecanthrope

pithiviers [pitivje] *nm Culin* = cake made of puff pastry containing rum and almond-flavoured cream

pitié [pitje] *nf* **(a)** (*compassion*) pity, compassion; **avoir p. de qn** to pity sb; (*s'apitoyer*) to take *or* have pity on sb; (*épargner*) to have mercy on sb; **prendre p. de qn, prendre qn en p.** to take pity on sb; **être sans p.** to be pitiless *or* merciless *or* ruthless; **il les a jugés sans p.** he judged them pitilessly *or* mercilessly *or* ruthlessly; **par p.** out of pity; (*en implorant*) for pity's sake; **p.!** (*grâce*) (have) mercy!, have pity on me!; (*arrête ça*) for pity's sake!; **faire p.** to arouse pity; **il me faisait p.** I felt sorry for him; **cela faisait p. à voir** it was pitiful *or Fml* pitiable to see (it); *Vieilli* **c'est p. qu'il soit resté seul** it's pitiful *or* sad that he should have been left alone

(b) (*commisération mêlée de mépris*) pity; **c'est (une) p. de voir des choses pareilles** it's pitiful to see such things

piton [pitɔ̃] *nm* **(a)** *Tech* eye (bolt); **p. (d'alpiniste)** piton, peg; **p. à vis** screw eye; **p. à boucle** ring bolt **(b)** (*sommet de montagne*) **p. (rocheux)** (rocky) peak

pitoyable [pitwajabl] *adj* **(a)** (*digne de pitié*) (*récit, condition etc*) pitiful, *Fml* pitiable, piteous **(b)** *Péj* (*lamentable*) (*excuse, plaisanterie etc*) pathetic, pitiful

pitoyablement [pitwajabləmɑ̃] *adv* pitifully; **échouer p.** to fail miserably

pitre [pitr] *nm* (*clown*) clown; **faire le p.** to clown (around), to play *or* act the fool

pitrerie [pitrəri] *nf* clowning, tomfoolery

pittoresque [pitɔrɛsk] **1** *adj* picturesque; (*description, style*) colourful, *US* colorful, vivid **2** *nm* picturesqueness; (*d'un style, d'une description*) vividness

pituitaire [pitɥitɛr] *adj Anat* pituitary

pituite [pitɥit] *nf Anat* (*vomissement*) bile, *Arch* phlegm

pivert [pivɛr] *nm* green woodpecker

pivoine [pivwan] *nf Bot* peony; *Fig* **rouge comme une p.** red as a beetroot

pivot [pivo] *nm* **(a)** (*axe*) pivot; (*de fusil*) swivel; (*de levier*) fulcrum; (*en dentisterie*) post; (*de compas, de boussole*) centre pin; **p. à rotule** ball pivot; **à p., monté sur p.** pivoted, swivelling; **canon à p.** swivel gun; *Tech* **p. de fusée** swivel pin, king pin **(b)** *Fig* (*élément central*) (*d'un drame*) mainspring, pivot **(c)** *Bot* tap root

pivotant [pivɔtɑ̃] *adj* **(a)** (*qui tourne*) pivoting, swivelling, revolving; **fauteuil p.** swivel chair; **base pivotante** swivel base **(b)** *Bot* **racine pivotante** tap root

pivoter [pivɔte] *vi* **(a)** (*tourner*) to pivot, to swivel, to turn **(sur** (up)on); *Mil* (*des troupes*) to wheel; **faire p. qch** to turn *or* swivel sth round; **p. sur ses talons** to swing round *or* pivot on one's heels **(b)** *Bot* (*d'une plante*) to form a tap root

pixel [piksɛl] *nm Ordinat* pixel

pixélisé [pikselize] *adj Ordinat* bit-mapped, bitmap

pizza [pidza] *nf* pizza

pizzeria [pidzerja] *nf* pizzeria

pizzicato [pidzikato], *pl* **pizzicati** [pidzikati] *nm Mus* pizzicato

P.J.[1] [peʒi] *nf F* (*abrév* **Police Judiciaire**) ≈ CID, *US* ≈ FBI

PJ[2] (*abrév* **pièce jointe**) encl

placage [plakaʒ] *nm* **(a)** (*fait de recouvrir*) (*de bois*) veneering;

(*de métal*) plating; **p. au chrome** chrome *or* chromium plating **(b)** (*matériau*) (*bois*) veneer; (*métal*) plating; **bois de p.** veneer **(c)** *Rugby* tackle

placard [plakar] *nm* **(a)** (*armoire murale*) cupboard; *Fig F* **mettre qn au p.** to sideline sb; **mettre un projet au p.** to put a plan on ice *or* into cold storage, to shelve a project **(b)** (*affiche*) poster; *Journ* **p. publicitaire** *ou* **de publicité** display advertisement **(c)** *Typ* **(épreuve en) p.** galley (proof) **(d)** *Naut* (*sur une voile*) patch **(e)** *Tech* (*d'une porte*) panel **(f)** *F* (*prison*) clink, *Br* nick; **faire 20 ans de p.** to do 20 years inside *or* in the clink

placarder [plakarde] *vt* **(a)** (*affiche*) to stick up, to put up; **p. un mur de posters** to stick *or* put posters (up) on a wall **(b)** *Typ* to run to galley proofs

place [plas] *nf* **(a)** (*lieu, endroit*) place; **changer sa chaise de p.** to move *or* shift one's chair; **mettre qch en p.** to put sth in place; **tout est à sa p.** everything's in its place; **p. de parking** parking place *or* space; **je n'ai pas trouvé de p. en ville** I couldn't find any parking places *or* spaces in town; **remettez vos livres à leur p.** put your books away; **voulez-vous prendre ma p.?** would you like to take my place?; **il ne peut pas rester en p.** he can't keep still; **il ne tient pas en p. aujourd'hui** he is very fidgety today; **sur p.** on the spot; *Constr* on site; *F* **faire du sur p.** to mark time, to stand still; (*en voiture*) to crawl along; *F* **dans cette affaire, j'ai l'impression de faire du sur p.** I've a feeling I'm getting nowhere with this matter; **il lut la lettre sur p.** he read the letter there and then *or* on the spot; **personnel engagé sur p.** staff hired locally; **rester sur p.** to stay put; **la police sera sur p. dans quelques minutes** the police will be on the scene *or* spot in a few minutes; **on trouve tout sur p.** everything we need is here/will be there; **son nom a pris p. dans l'histoire** his name has found a place in history

(b) *Fig* (*condition, situation*) place; **avoir sa p. au soleil** to have one's place in the sun; **il finira par trouver sa p. dans ce milieu** he'll eventually find his place *or* a niche among those people; **prendre sa p. dans la société** to take one's place in society; **je viens à la p. de mon père** I've come instead of my father, I've come in my father's place *or Fml* stead; **parler à la p. de qn** to speak for sb; **remettre qn à sa p.** to put sb in his/her place; **rester à sa p.** to know one's place; **à votre p., je ...** in your place *or* if I were you I ...; **mets-toi à sa p.!** put yourself in his position, look at things from his point of view

(c) (*espace*) room, space; **prendre** *ou* **occuper beaucoup de p.** to take up a great deal of room *or* space; **nous n'avons pas de p. pour mettre un piano** we have no room *or* space for a piano; **gagner de la p.** to gain some (extra) room *or* space; **faire p. à qn/qch** to make way for sb/sth; *Vieilli* **(faites) p.!** stand aside!, make way!; **faites-lui un peu de p.** make room for him; *Fig* **céder la p. aux jeunes** to make way for the younger generation; *Aut* **p. aux pieds** footwell; *Av* **p. pour les jambes** legroom

(d) (*siège*) seat; **céder sa p. à qn** to give up one's seat to sb, to give sb one's seat; **à vos places!** take your seats!; **restez à votre p.** stay in your seat, remain seated; **louer deux places au théâtre** to book two seats at the theatre; **il n'y avait pas une p.** there wasn't a seat to be found *or* to be had; **voiture à deux/à quatre places** two-/four-seater (car); *Aut* **une deux places** a two-seater; **prix des places** (*transports publics*) fares; (*spectacles*) seat prices; **payer p. entière** (*transports publics*) to pay full fare; (*spectacles*) to pay full price; **p. assise** seat; **p. côté couloir** aisle seat; **p. côté fenêtre** window seat; **p. fumeur** smoking seat; **p. non-fumeur** no-smoking seat

(e) (*appartenance, rôle*) place; **la p. de l'homme dans le monde** man's place in the world; **sa famille tient une grande p. dans sa vie** his family has an important place in his life; **il aura toujours une p. dans mon cœur** he'll always have a place in my heart

(f) (*emploi, poste*) job, post; **quitter/perdre sa p.** to leave/ to lose one's job; **le gouvernement en p.** the government in office *or* power; *Fig* **une personne en p.** a person in high office; *Fig* **les gens en p.** people in high places, people with influence

(g) (*lieu public*) square; **la p. Rouge** Red Square; **p. du marché** market place

(h) *Com, Fin* market; **achats sur p.** local purchases; **prix sur p.** loco price; **être bien connu sur la p.** to be a well-known player in the market; **avoir du crédit sur la p.** to have credit (facilities) locally; **affaires sur la p. de Paris** business on the Paris market

(i) *Mil* **p. (forte** *ou* **de guerre)** fortified place; (*ville*) fortress *or* fortified town; **p. d'armes** parade ground, drill ground

(j) (*rang*) place, placing; **il a eu une bonne p. au concours** he was well placed in the competition; **une p. d'honneur** a place of honour

▶ **place**: **p. bancaire** banking centre; **p. boursière** stock market; **p. commerciale** trade centre; **p. financière** financial centre *or* marketplace; **p. marchande** market place; **p. monétaire** money market

placé [plase] *Courses de chevaux* **1** *adj* placed; **arriver p.** to be placed **2** *nm* placed horse

placebo [plasebo] *nm* placebo

placement [plasmɑ̃] *nm* **(a)** (*fait de donner un emploi*) placement, placing; (*fait d'attribuer un siège*) seating; **bureau** *ou* **agence de placement(s)** employment bureau *or* agency, *US* placement bureau **(b)** *Fin* (*d'argent*) investment, investing; (*argent*) investment; **faire des placements** to invest (money), to make investments; **p. avantageux** good investment; *F* **p. de père de famille** blue chip (investment), gilt-edged investment; **p. court terme** short-term investment; **p. temporaire** temporary investment; **p. à revenus fixes** fixed income investment; **p. à revenus variables** variable income investment **(c)** *Mktg* **p. de produit** product placement

placenta [plasɛ̃ta] *nm Obst* placenta; (*expulsé après accouchement*) afterbirth, placenta

placentaire [plasɛ̃tɛr] *adj Obst* placental

placer [plase] **(je plaçai(s); n. plaçons) 1** *vt* **(a)** (*mettre à sa place*) to place, to put; (*spectateurs, invités etc*) to seat; **p. qn** (*au spectacle*) to show sb to his/her seat; *Fig* **vous êtes mieux placés que moi pour en juger** you're better placed than I (am) to judge; *Fig* **vous êtes bien placés pour le savoir** you're in a position to know, you ought to know; **p. une sentinelle** to post a soldier on sentry duty; **maison bien placée** well situated house; **p. l'honnêteté au plus haut rang** to put *or* set *or* place a high value on honesty; **je place le courage au dessus de toutes les valeurs** I put *or* set *or* place courage above all other values; **confiance mal placée** misplaced confidence; *TV etc* **p. les bandes son** to lay tracks

(b) (*procurer un emploi à*) to find a job for; **p. qn comme apprenti chez qn** to apprentice sb to sb

(c) (*vendre*) (*marchandises*) to sell; *Fin* **valeurs difficiles à p.** bills difficult to negotiate

(d) (*situer*) to set; **c'est ici que l'auteur a placé son roman** this is where the author set his novel

(e) (*dire*) to get in; **il voulait à tout prix p. son histoire** he was determined to get his anecdote in (*in the conversation etc*); *F* **avec elle, on ne peut pas en p. une!** you can't get a word in edgeways *or Am* edgewise with her; **je n'ai pas pu p. un mot** I couldn't get a word in edgeways

(f) *Fin* (*argent*) to invest; **p. à court terme** to invest short-term; **p. à intérêts** to invest at interest

2 se placer *vpr* **(a)** (*prendre sa place*) to take one's seat *or* one's place (*at table etc*); *Mil, Sp etc* to take up one's position; **dites-moi où me p.** tell me where to sit/stand; **il faut se p. dans son optique** you have to look at things from his point of view; **se p. sous la protection de qn** to place oneself under sb's protection; **marchandises qui se placent facilement** goods that sell readily

(b) (*trouver un emploi*) to get *or* find a job; **se p. comme vendeuse** to get a job as a salesgirl

placet [plasɛ] *nm* **(a)** *Arch* petition, address **(b)** *Jur* (plaintiff's) claim

placette [plasɛt] *nf* (small) square

placeur, -euse [plasœr, -øz] *n* **(a)** (*personne qui tient un bureau de placement*) employment agent *or* consultant **(b)** (*dans des réunions publiques*) steward; *Cin, Th* usher, *f* usherette

placide [plasid] *adj* placid, calm

placidement [plasidmɑ̃] *adv* placidly, calmly

placidité [plasidite] *nf* placidity, calmness

placier, -ière [plasje, -jɛr] *n Com* **(a)** (*représentant*) travelling salesman, *f* saleswoman, traveller **(b)** (*forain*) = person who allocates stall space in a market

placoplâtre® [plakoplɑtr] *nm* plasterboard

plafond [plafɔ̃] *nm* **(a)** *Archit* ceiling; **p. à caissons** coffered ceiling; **chambre haute/basse de p.** high-/low-ceilinged room; *Fig F* **avoir une araignée au p.** to have bats in the belfry

(b) (*toit*) (*de voiture, de caverne*) roof

(c) (*maximum*) ceiling; **prix p.** maximum price, ceiling (price); **fixer un p. à un budget** to fix *or* put a ceiling on a budget; **p. des charges budgétaires** spending limit, budgetary limit; *Fin* **p. du crédit** credit ceiling; *Banque* **p. d'autorisation** *ou* **de retrait** withdrawal limit; *Banque* **p. de découvert** overdraft limit

(d) *Av* (*d'avion*) ceiling, maximum flying height; *Aut* top *or* maximum speed; *Météo* **p. (nuageux)** (cloud) ceiling

plafonnage [plafɔnaʒ] *nm Constr* ceiling work

plafonnement [plafɔnmɑ̃] *nm* **p. des salaires/cotisations** (*fait de limiter*) fixing *or* putting a ceiling on wages/ contributions; (*fait d'atteindre un plafond*) peaking *or* levelling *or US* leveling off of wages/contributions

plafonner [plafɔne] **1 (a)** *vt* (*pièce*) to put a ceiling in **(b)** (*salaire etc*) to put a ceiling on; *Fin* **être plafonné à** to have a ceiling of **2** *vi* **(a)** *Av* to fly at the ceiling; *Aut* to go at maximum *or* top speed **(b)** *Fig* to peak, to level out, to level off; **la fréquentation des cinémas plafonne** cinema attendance has peaked *or* is levelling off

plafonneur [plafɔnœr] *nm Tech* plasterer of ceilings

plafonnier [plafɔnje] *nm* ceiling light; *Aut* courtesy *or* interior light

plage [plaʒ] *nf* **(a)** (*grève*) beach; **p. de sable/de galets** sandy/ pebble beach; **sac/robe de p.** beach bag/robe

(b) (*lieu touristique*) seaside resort

(c) *Naut* (*d'un cuirassé*) freeboard deck; **p. arrière** *Naut* quarterdeck; *Aut* window shelf, (rear) parcel shelf

(d) (*surface*) area; *Opt* **p. lumineuse** light area, high light

(e) (*laps de temps*) time, period; *TV, Rad* (*d'émissions*) (time) segment; **p. horaire** time slot; **p. horaire très écoutée/regardée** peak listening/viewing time *or* period; *Can* **p. fixe** (*dans un horaire variable*) core time

(f) *Fig* (*éventail*) range; *Rad* **p. de réception** tuning range; *Com* **p. de prix** price range; *Aut* **p. de régime** engine speed range, rev range

(g) (*d'un disque*) track

plagiaire [plaʒjɛr] *n* plagiarist, plagiarizer

plagiat [plaʒja] *nm* plagiarism

plagier [plaʒje] *vt* (*impf, pr sub* **n. plagiions, v. plagiiez**) to plagiarize

plagiste [plaʒist] *n* beach attendant

plaid [plɛd] *nm* travelling rug

plaidable [plɛdabl] *adj Jur* pleadable

plaidant [plɛdɑ̃] *adj Jur* **avocat p.** ≈ lawyer, *Br* barrister; **les parties plaidantes** the litigants

plaider [plede] **1** *vt* to plead; **p. la cause de qn** *Jur* to plead sb's case, to defend sb; *Fig* to speak in favour of *or* defend sb, to plead sb's cause; **p. sa propre cause** *Jur* to conduct one's own defence; *Fig* to speak in one's own defence; **son défenseur va p. la folie** his counsel will plead insanity *or* will put forward a plea of insanity; **p. le faux pour savoir le vrai** to lie in order to get at the truth; **p. coupable/non coupable** to plead guilty/not guilty

2 *vi* (*d'un avocat*) to plead (**pour** for; **contre** against); (*d'un plaignant*) to go to court, to litigate; **p. contre qn** to take sb to court, to take proceedings against sb; *Fig* **p. pour** *ou* **en faveur de qn/qch** to speak for sb/sth, to defend sb/sth

3 se plaider *vpr* **la cause s'est plaidée hier** the case was heard yesterday

plaideur, -euse [plɛdœr, -øz] *n Jur* litigant

plaidoirie [plɛdwari] *nf Jur* speech for the defence *or US* defense

plaidoyer [plɛdwaje] *nm Jur* speech for the defence *or US* defense; *Fig* (*défense passionnée*) plea

plaie [plɛ] *nf* **(a)** (*blessure*); *Fig* wound; (*coupure*) cut; *Fig* **rouvrir d'anciennes plaies** to re-open old wounds; **retourner** *ou* **remuer le couteau** *ou* **le fer dans la p.** to twist *or* turn the knife in the wound; **mettre le doigt sur la p.** to put one's finger on the source of the trouble **(b)** (*fléau*) affliction, scourge; (*personne, chose*) pest, nuisance; **quelle p.!** what a pest *or* nuisance!; *Bible* **les dix plaies d'Égypte** the ten plagues of Egypt; *Prov* **p. d'argent n'est pas mortelle** money isn't everything

plaignant, -ante [plɛɲɑ̃, -ɑ̃t] *Jur* **1** *adj* **partie plaignante** plaintiff, complainant **2** *n* plaintiff, complainant

plain [plɛ̃] **1** *adj Vieilli* (*terrain, surface*) flat, level, even **2** *nm* **le p.** high tide

plain-chant, *pl* **plains-chants** *nm Mus* plainsong, plainchant

plaindre [plɛ̃dr] (*prp* **plaignant**; *pp* **plaint**; *pr ind* **je plains, il plaint, n. plaignons, ils plaignent**; *pr sub* **je plaigne**; *impf* **je plaignais**; *p hist* **je plaignis**; *fu* **je plaindrai**) **1** *vt* **(a)** (*témoigner de la compassion à*) to pity, to feel sorry for; **je vous plains de voyager dans ces conditions** I pity you *or* I feel sorry for you having to travel in those conditions; **il est fort à p.** he is greatly to be pitied; **elle n'est pas à p.** she hasn't anything to worry about, she's got it made; **il est plus à p. qu'à blâmer** he is more to be pitied than blamed

(b) *Région, Arch* (*donner parcimonieusement*) to (be)grudge; **on n'a pas plaint l'argent** there was no stinting of money, no expense was spared; **il ne plaint pas sa peine** he spares himself no trouble

2 se plaindre *vpr* to complain (**à** to); (*se lamenter*) to moan, to groan; **se p. de qn/qch** to complain about sb/sth; **se p. de maux d'estomac** to complain of stomach pains; **il n'y a pas de quoi vous p., vous n'avez pas à vous p.** you've nothing to complain about, you shouldn't grumble; **se p. (de ce) que ... +** *sub* to complain (about the fact) that ...

plaine [plɛn] *nf* **(a)** *Géog* plain **(b)** *Hist* **la P.** the Plain (= *moderate deputies during the French Revolution*)

plain-pied *adv* **de p.** on the same level, on a level; (*au même étage*) on one floor; **salon de p. avec le jardin** sitting room on a level with *or* on the same level as the garden; **deux surfaces de p.** two surfaces flush with each other; *Fig* **nous sommes de p.** we are on an equal footing (with each other)

plainte [plɛ̃t] *nf* **(a)** (*cri, gémissement*) moan, groan **(b)** (*revendication, protestation*) complaint; **un sujet de p.** the subject of a complaint **(c)** *Jur* complaint; **porter p.** *ou* **déposer une p. contre qn** to lodge a complaint against sb (**auprès de** with); **p. en diffamation** action for libel; **p. contre X** complaint against a person or persons unknown

plaintif, -ive [plɛ̃tif, -iv] *adj* (*ton*) plaintive

plaintivement [plɛ̃tivmɑ̃] *adv* plaintively

plaire [plɛr] (*prp* **plaisant**; *pp* **plu**; *pr ind* **je plais, il plaît, n. plaisons, ils plaisent**; *pr sub* **je plaise**; *impf* **je plaisais**; *p hist* **je plus**; *fu* **je plairai**) **1** *vi* **(a) cet homme me plaît** I like this man; **ce livre/film m'a plu** I liked *or* enjoyed this book/film; **elle te plaît, ta nouvelle voiture?** do you like your new car?; **la nouvelle robe lui plaît beaucoup** she's very pleased with *or* she really likes the new dress; **cette offre devrait lui p.** the offer should appeal to him; **il ne plaît pas aux femmes** women don't like him; (*physiquement*) women don't find him attractive; **cela ne me plaît pas du tout** I don't like that at all; **c'est ce qui plaît en ce moment** it's what people seem to like just now; **il plaît** people like him, he's popular; **ça plaît beaucoup** it's very popular; **tu devrais faire une tarte aux pommes, ça plaît toujours** you ought to make an apple tart, that's always popular *or* welcome *or* that always goes down well; **je le ferai, si cela me plaît** I'll do it if I want to *or* if I feel like it; *F* **si ça ne te plaît pas, c'est pareil!** if you don't like it, tough!; **que cela te plaise ou non** whether you like it or not; *F Iron* **tu commences à me p.!** you're beginning to annoy *or* irritate me!

(b) (*se rendre agréable*) **p. à qn** to please sb; **chercher à p. à qn** to try to please sb; **elle veut p.** (*elle veut qu'on l'aime*) she wants to be liked

2 *v impers* **s'il vous plaît** please, *Vieilli* if you please; *F* (*pour insister*) if you please; **s'il te plaît** please; **et pas n'importe qui, s'il vous plaît** and not just anybody, if you please *or* if you don't mind; **elle passe ses vacances à Saint Tropez, s'il vous plaît** she goes to Saint Tropez for her holidays, if you please *or* don't you know; **vous plairait-il de nous accompagner?** would you like to come with us?; *Vieilli, Région* **plaît-il?** I beg your pardon?, what did you say?; **comme il vous plaira** (just) as you like *or* please; **plaise à Dieu qu'il vienne!** please God let him come, *Fml* God grant that he may come!; **à Dieu ne plaise (que ...)** God forbid (that ...); **plût au ciel que ...!** would to heaven that ...!

3 se plaire *vpr* **(a)** (*s'aimer soi-même*) to admire oneself, *F* to fancy oneself; **elle se plaît dans cette robe** she likes wearing that dress, she likes herself in that dress

(b) (*de deux personnes*) to be attracted to each other, *F* to fancy each other

(c) (*se trouver bien*) **je me plais beaucoup à Paris** I'm very happy in Paris; **se p. à faire qch** to enjoy *or* like doing sth; **il ne se plaît pas ici** he doesn't like it here, he's unhappy here; **la vigne se plaît sur les coteaux** the vine does well *or* thrives on hillsides

plaisamment [plɛzamɑ̃] *adv* **(a)** (*agréablement*) pleasantly **(b)** (*drôlement*) funnily, amusingly **(c)** *Litt* (*d'une façon ridicule*) ridiculously

plaisance [plɛzɑ̃s] *nf* **(a) bateau de p.** pleasure boat; **port de p.** marina; **navigation de p., la p.** boating **(b)** *Arch* pleasure

plaisancier, -ière [plɛzɑ̃sje, -jɛr] *n* (amateur) yachtsman, *f* yachtswoman

plaisant [plɛzɑ̃] **1** *adj* **(a)** (*agréable*) pleasant, agreeable; **p. à l'œil** pleasing to *or F* easy on the eye, pleasing to look at **(b)** (*drôle*) funny, amusing; (*d'un humour sec ou ironique*) droll **(c)** (*always before the noun*) *Vieilli* (*ridicule*) (*personne, réponse*) ridiculous, absurd, ludicrous **2** *nm* **(a) le (plus) p. de l'affaire c'est que ...** the funniest thing about it is that ... **(b)** *Arch* wag, joker; **faire le p.** to play *or* act the comedian; **mauvais p.** malicious joker

plaisanter [plɛzɑ̃te] **1** *vi* **(a)** (*s'amuser, rire*) to joke, *Fml* to jest; **elle aime bien p.** she enjoys a joke; **il faut bien p., n'est-ce pas?** we all have to have a joke from time to time, don't we?; **dire qch en plaisantant** to say sth as a joke *or* in jest; **il n'est pas d'humeur à p.** he's not in a joking mood

(b) (*dire par jeu*) to joke; **vous plaisantez!** you're joking!, you're kidding!, you don't mean it!; **je ne plaisante pas** I'm serious, I'm not joking; **c'est un homme avec qui on ne**

plaisante pas he is not a man to be trifled with; **on ne plaisante pas avec la justice** the law is not to be trifled with; **on ne plaisante pas avec la santé** health is a serious matter; **il ne plaisante pas là-dessus** *ou* **sur ces choses-là** he doesn't joke about things like that; **dans leur famille, on ne plaisante pas avec la religion** you don't joke about religion in their family, religion isn't a joking matter in their family

2 *vt* to tease (**sur qch** about sth), to poke fun at, to make fun of

plaisanterie [plɛzɑ̃tri] *nf* (*blague*) joke, *Fml* jest; (*activité*) joking, *Fml* jesting; **une fine p.** a subtle joke; **une mauvaise p.** (*blague*) a bad joke; (*farce*) a nasty trick; **faire des plaisanteries** to tell *or* crack jokes; **les plaisanteries les plus courtes sont les meilleures** brevity is the soul of wit; **tourner qch en p.** to laugh sth off, to make a joke out of sth; **entendre la p.** to know how to take a joke; **par p.** for fun, for a joke; *Fig* **c'est une p.!** it's a joke!, it's ridiculous *or* laughable!; **ce sera une p. pour toi** it'll be child's play for you; **pousser trop loin la p.** to take the joke too far, to go too far

plaisantin [plɛzɑ̃tɛ̃] *nm* joker; *Fig Péj* **c'est un (petit) p.** (*on ne peut pas lui faire confiance*) he's (a bit of) a joker

plaisir [plezir] *nm* **(a)** (*sensation plaisante*) pleasure, delight; **j'apprends avec p. que vous êtes de mon avis** I'm pleased *or* delighted *or* glad to hear you agree with me; **c'est avec p. que j'ai appris la nouvelle** I was pleased *or* delighted *or* glad to hear the news; **faire p. à qn** to please sb; **ça me ferait vraiment p. que tu acceptes ce travail** I would be really pleased *or* delighted if you accepted the job; **fais-moi p., viens danser** do me a favour, come and dance; **cela m'a fait p. de le revoir** I was pleased *or* delighted to see him again, it gave me great pleasure to see him again; **si cela peut te faire p., s'il n'y a que ça pour te faire p.** if it will make you happy; **je viens avec toi, mais c'est bien pour te faire p.!** I'll come with you just to keep you happy!; **cela me fait grand p. de vous voir** I'm delighted to see you; **cela fait p. à voir** it's a pleasure to see; *Iron* **ça fait (toujours) p.!** charming!; **faire à qn le p. de venir** to do sb the pleasure of coming; **voulez-vous me faire le p. de vous taire!** will you please be quiet!; **ils vous prient de leur faire le p. de dîner avec eux** they request the pleasure of your company at dinner; **j'ai le p. de vous apprendre que ...** I have pleasure in informing *or* I am pleased to inform you that ..., I'm pleased to be able to tell you that ...; **tout le p. est pour moi** the pleasure is all mine; **gâcher le p. de qn** to spoil sb's pleasure; **car tel est le bon p. du roi** because that is what His Majesty wishes; **le p. d'offrir/de recevoir** the pleasure of giving/receiving; **au p. de vous revoir** goodbye, I hope we'll meet again; *F* **au p.!** goodbye!, see you (again)!; **pour le plus grand p. de l'assistance/de ses collègues** to the great delight of the audience/of one's colleagues; **prendre (grand) p. à qch** to (really) enjoy sth; **prendre p.** *ou* **avoir du p. à faire qch** to enjoy doing sth; **prendre un malin p. à faire qch** to take a malicious pleasure in doing sth; **il va se faire un p. de te téléphoner demain** he'll be only too pleased to phone you tomorrow; **rougir/frissonner/gémir de p.** to flush/quiver/moan with pleasure; **avec p.!** with pleasure!

(b) (*agrément*) pleasure, fun; **c'est par p. que vous faites cela?** are you doing that because you like it *or* for the fun of it?; **parler pour le p. de parler** to talk for talking's sake *or* for the sake of it; **elle le dit pour le p. de te faire souffrir** she said it because she wants to make you suffer; **elle travaille pour le p.** she works because she enjoys *or* likes it; **se tourmenter à p.** to worry for the sake of worrying *or* for the sake of it; **faire durer le p.** to make the pleasure last; *Iron* to prolong the agony; *Iron* **je vous souhaite bien du p.** the best of luck (to you)!

(c) (*distraction*) pleasure, enjoyment, amusement; **son plus grand p. est de faire des photos** what he likes doing most *or* best is taking photos; **les plaisirs de la table** fine food; **chaque âge a ses plaisirs** every age has its pleasures; **on prend son p. comme on peut** you take your pleasure where you find it; **s'accorder** *ou* **s'offrir un petit p.** to indulge oneself; **faire qch pour le p.** *ou* **pour son p.** to do sth for pleasure *or* for fun; **le planeur est un p. coûteux** gliding's an expensive pastime *or* hobby; *Iron* **ce n'est pas une partie de p.** it's no picnic

(d) *Litt* (*sensuel*) **le p., les plaisirs** dissipation; **lieu de p.** place of amusement; (*où l'on s'amuse la nuit*) night haunt

(e) le p. (sexuel) (sexual) pleasure; **il y prit du p.** he got a (sexual) thrill out of it; **p. solitaire** self-abuse

plan[1] [plɑ̃] **1** *adj* (*terrain, surface*) flat, level, even; *Géom* (*surface etc*) plane

2 *nm* **(a)** *Math etc* plane

(b) *Beaux-Arts etc* **premier p.** foreground; **second p.** middle ground; **au second p.** in the middle distance; *Fig* **ce problème occupe le premier p.** this question is very much to the fore *or* is very much in the foreground; *Fig* **reléguer qn au second p.** to push sb into the background; *Fig* **un artiste de premier p.** an artist of the first rank, a first-rate artist; **sur le même p.** on the same level; **sur le p. politique/économique, au p. politique/économique** on the political/economic level; *Phot, Cin* **faire un gros p.** to take *or* shoot a close-up

(c) *Av* **p. de sustentation** aerofoil, *Am* airfoil; **p. fixe horizontal** tail plane; **p. supérieur** (*d'un biplan*) upper wing *or* plane

plan[2] *nm* **(a)** (*relevé*) plan; *Constr, Tech* blueprint; (*de ville*) plan, map; **tracer un p.** to draw a plan; **relever le p. d'une région** to map out *or* survey an area; **p. de classement** filing method; **p. d'étage** floor plan; **p. géométral** ground plan; *Typ* **p. de maquette** layout card; **p. de mise en page** page plan

(b) (*projet*) plan, scheme, project; **faire** *ou* **arrêter le p. de qch** to plan sth; **quels sont vos plans pour les années à venir?** what are your plans for the future?; *Fig* **tirer** *ou* **faire des plans sur la comète** to build castles in Spain *or* in the air; *F* **t'as un p. pour ce soir?** got any plans for tonight?; **sans p. arrêté** without any set plan; **p. d'études** study plan *or* programme; **p. économique** economic plan, plan for the economy; **p. d'un roman/d'un devoir** plan for a novel/an essay

▶ **plan**: *TV, Cin* **p. accéléré** time-lapse shot; *Mktg* **p. d'activité** business plan; *TV, Cin* **p. américain** medium close-up; *Compta* **p. d'amortissement** depreciation schedule; *TV, Cin* **p. d'archives** stock shot; *TV, Cin* **p. de buste** bust shot; *Ordinat* **p. calcul** = plan to establish a computer industry in France; *TV, Cin* **p. ceinture** waist shot; *Compta* **p. comptable** chart of accounts; *Compta* **p. comptable général** chart of accounts; *Compta* **p. de comptes** chart of accounts; *TV, Cin* **p. en contre-plongée** periscope shot; **p. de cuisson** hob; *TV, Cin* **p. des décors** floor plan; *TV, Cin* **p. de détail** detail *or* insert shot; **p. d'eau** stretch of water; (*d'une rivière*) reach; *TV, Cin* **p. éloigné** long shot; *TV, Cin* **p. d'ensemble** establishing shot, full shot, long shot, wide shot; *Fin* **p. d'épargne** savings scheme *or* plan; *Fin* **p. d'épargne en actions** personal equity plan, PEP; *Fin* **p. d'épargne retraite** retirement savings plan *or* scheme; **p. d'évacuation** escape route; *Compta* **p. de financement** funding plan, financial plan; **p. fixe** static shot; *Opt* **p. focal** focal plane; *TV, Cin* **p. général** wide shot, full-length shot, full shot, long shot; **p. incliné** inclined plane; *MecE* ball ramp; *TV, Cin* **p. en intérieur** interior (shot); *TV, Cin* **p. de longue durée** continuous film sequence; *Mktg* **p. de marchéage** marketing mix; *Mktg* **p. (des) médias** media planning; *Mktg* **p. de mercatique (stratégique)** (strategic) marketing plan; *TV, Cin* **p. moyen** medium close-up, medium shot, mid-shot; **p. d'occupation des sols** land-use plan; *TV, Cin* **p. en plongée** overhead shot; *TV, Cin* **p. de positionnement sur le plateau** staging plan; **p. de production** production plan; **p. quinquennal** five-year plan; *TV, Cin* **p. rapproché** medium close-up, close-up, close shot; *TV, Cin* **p. de réaction** reaction shot; *Constr* **p. de référence** datum plane *or* level; *TV, Cin* **p. refilmé** retake; *TV, Cin* **p. séquence** sequence shot; *TV, Cin* **p. serré** close-up, tight shot; **p. social** (*du gouvernement*) social plan; *Com* = corporate restructuring plan, usually involving job losses; *Mktg* **p. stratégique d'entreprise** strategic business plan; *Mktg* **p. des supports** media planning; *TV, Cin* **p. à la taille** waist shot; **p. de travail** (*d'une cuisine*) work(ing) surface, worktop; **p. de travail créatif** (*publicité*) creative brief; *TV, Cin* **p. travelling** travelling shot; *TV, Cin* **p. très éloigné** extra *or* extreme long shot; *TV, Cin* **p. très rapproché** extreme close-up; **p. très serré** big close-up; *TV, Cin* **p. de visage** face shot; *Av* **p. de vol** flight plan

plan[3] *nm F* **laisser qn en p.** to leave sb in the lurch; (*sans moyen de transport*) to leave sb stranded; **laisser son travail en p.** to leave one's work unfinished; **il a tout laissé en p. et il est rentré** he dropped everything and went home

planage [planaʒ] *nm Tech* (*de bois*) planing; (*de métal*) planishing

planant [planɑ̃] *adj F* out of this world

planche [plɑ̃ʃ] *nf* **(a)** (*pièce de bois*) plank; (*plus large*) board; (*étagère*) shelf; *F* (*ski*) plank; *Fig* **c'est ma p. de salut** it's my sheet anchor; (*dernier espoir*) it's my last hope; *Natation* **faire la p.** to float on one's back; *Fig F* **c'est une p. à pain, elle est plate comme une p. à pain** she's as flat as a pancake; *Fig* **avoir du pain sur la p.** to have a lot on one's plate

(b) *Naut* **p. (de débarquement)** gangplank; **passer à la p.** to walk the plank; **jour de p.** lay day

(c) *Th* **les planches** *Old-fashioned Hum* the stage, the boards; **monter sur les planches** to go on the stage, to tread the boards; **être sur les planches** to be on the stage; **l'amour des planches** love of the stage

(d) (*d'imprimerie, de gravure etc*) plate, block; **planches en couleurs** colour plates

(e) (*de jardin potager*) bed

(f) *Sp* (*de surf*) surfboard; (*à voile*) sailboard

(g) **les planches** (*sur une plage*) the boardwalk

▶ **planche**: **p. à billets** printing press (*for printing banknotes*); *Fig* **faire fonctionner la p. à billets** to print money; *Aut* **p. de bord** dashboard, fascia panel; **p. à découper** chopping board; **p. à dessin** drawing board; **p. à fromage** cheeseboard; **p. à hacher** chopping board; **p. à laver** washboard; **p. à pain** breadboard; **p. à pâtisserie** pastry board; **p. à repasser** ironing board *or Am* table; **p. à roulettes** skateboard; **faire de la p. à roulettes** to go skateboarding, to skateboard; **p. de surf** surfboard; **p. à voile** sailboard; **faire de la p. à voile** to go windsurfing, to windsurf

planchéiage [plɑ̃ʃejaʒ] *nm* (*de cloison, de plancher*) boarding, planking; (*d'une pièce*) flooring

planchéier [plɑ̃ʃeje] *vt* (*impf, pr sub* **n. planchéiions**) (*cloison*) to board, to plank; (*plancher*) to board over, to plank over; (*pièce*) to floor

plancher[1] [plɑ̃ʃe] *nm* **(a)** (*sol*) floor; *F* **le p. des vaches** dry land, terra firma; *F* **débarrassez-moi le p.!** get out!, clear out!, beat it! **(b)** *Fig* (*minimum*) minimum, lower limit; **le p. des versements** the minimum deposit; **prix p.** bottom price **(c)** *Tech* (*de pont*) planking; (*de la salle des machines*) floorplates; (*de tranchée*) flooring; *Aut* floor, floorpan; *Aut* **p. de chargement** load floor; *Aut, Fig* **mettre le pied au p.** to put one's foot down **(d)** *Tech* (*de serrure*) bottom **(e)** *Anat* (*d'une cavité*) floor; **p. pelvien** pelvic floor

plancher[2] *vi Scol F* to be tested, to have a test; **les ministres planchent sur ce problème** the ministers are working on the problem

planchette [plɑ̃ʃɛt] *nf* (*petite planche*) (small) board; (*étagère*) (small) shelf; *Spéc* (*de topographe*) plane table; *Phot* **p. d'objectif** lens panel

planchiste [plɑ̃ʃist] *n Sp* windsurfer

plançon [plɑ̃sɔ̃] *nm* (*jeune arbre*) sapling; (*plante*) set, slip

plan-concave, *pl* **plan-concaves** *adj Opt* (*lentilles*) plano-concave

plan-convexe, *pl* **plan-convexes** *adj Opt* (*lentilles*) plano-convex

plancton [plɑ̃ktɔ̃] *nm* plankton

plané [plane] *adj Av* **vol p.** gliding; **descendre en vol p.** to glide down; *F* **faire un vol p.** (*tomber*) to go flying

planéité [planeite] *nf* flatness, evenness

planer[1] [plane] *vt Tech* (*bois*) to plane; (*métal*) to planish

planer[2] *vi* **(a)** (*d'un oiseau*) to glide, to soar; (*voltiger*) to hover; (*d'un ballon*) to float; (*d'un planeur*) to glide; (*de la brume, fumée*) to hover, to hang; *Fig* **p. sur qch/qn** to hang *or* hover over sth/sb; **la menace plane** there's a sense of threat in the air

(b) *Litt* **son regard planait au-delà des montagnes** he gazed out beyond the mountains; **son esprit planait au-dessus de la ville** his mind soared above the city

(c) *Fig F* (*être particulièrement bien*) to be on cloud nine, to be *or* feel on top of the world; (*perdre le sens des réalités*) to have one's head in the clouds; (*après s'être drogué*) to be high; **ça plane pour moi!** I'm feeling on top of the world!

planétaire [planetɛr] **1** *adj* **(a)** *Astron* (*système*) planetary **(b)** *MecE* **engrenage p.** planetary gear **(c)** *Phys* (*électrons*) orbital, orbiting **(d)** (*expansion, action*) on a worldwide *or* global scale **2** *nm Aut* sun gear

planétairement [planetɛrmɑ̃] *adv* **voir les choses p.** to look at things on a worldwide *or* global basis

planétarisation [planetarizasjɔ̃] *nf* globalization; **la p. économique** the growth of a world economy

planétarium [planetarjɔm] *nm Astron* planetarium

planète [planɛt] *nf Astron* planet; **planètes inférieures/supérieures** inferior/superior planets; **sur toute la p.** over the whole planet, all over the planet

planétisation [planetizasjɔ̃] *nf* = **planétarisation**

planétoïde [planetɔid] *nm Astron* planetoid

planétologie [planetɔlɔʒi] *nf* planetology

planeur[1] [planœr] *nm Av* glider; **faire du p.** to go gliding

planeur[2], -euse [planœr, -øz] *Tech* **1** *n* (*ouvrier*) planisher **2** *nf* **planeuse** (*machine*) planing machine; (*pour métal*) planishing machine

planifiable [planifjabl] *adj Écon* that can be planned

planificateur, -trice [planifikatœr, -tris] *Écon* **1** *adj* (*autorité, mesures*) planning **2** *n* planner

planification [planifikasjɔ̃] *nf Écon* planning; **p. des naissances** population control; *Mktg* **p. de l'entreprise** corporate planning; **p. à long terme** long-term planning

planifier [planifje] *vt* (*impf, pr sub* **n. planifiions**) *Écon* to plan

planigramme [planigram] *nm Mktg* flowchart

planisme [planism] *nm Écon* planning

planisphère [planisfɛr] *nm* planisphere

planning [planiŋ] *nm* plan, schedule; (*programme d'activités, de travail*) schedule; **p. Whitney** (*dans un hôtel*) Whitney rack; **p. d'occupation journalière** (*dans un hôtel*) daily occupancy chart; **p. de fabrication** manufacturing plan *or* schedule; *Compta* **p. des charges** expenditure plan; **p. à gouttières** slot-in planner

planning familial *nm* family planning; (*lieu*) family planning clinic

planque [plɑ̃k] *nf F* **(a)** (*cachette*) (*pour qn*) hideout, hideaway, hiding place; (*pour qch*) hiding place; **la police est en p. devant la maison** the police are staking out the house **(b)** (*travail facile*) cushy job *or* number; **vraiment, ce boulot, c'est la p.!** this job is really cushy!

planqué [plɑ̃ke] *n F Péj* person with a cushy job; *Mil* dodger, shirker; **quelle planquée!** what a cushy job she's got!

planquer [plɑ̃ke] *F* **1** *vt* to hide (away), to stash (away); (*personne*) to hide **2 se planquer** *vpr* to hide; (*se mettre à l'abri*) to take cover **3** *vi* (*de la police*) **p. devant la maison** to stake out the house

plant [plɑ̃] *nm* **(a)** (*pépinière*) (*d'arbres, d'arbustes*) (nursery) plantation **(b)** (*carré*) patch, bed; **p. de choux** cabbage patch **(c)** (*bouture*) (*d'un arbre*) sapling; (*d'une plante*) set, slip; **jeunes plants** seedlings

plantain [plɑ̃tɛ̃] *nm Bot* plantain

plantaire [plɑ̃tɛr] *adj Anat* plantar; **voûte p.** plantar arch

plantard [plɑ̃tar] *nm* = **plançon**

plantation [plɑ̃tasjɔ̃] *nf* **(a)** (*fait de planter*) (*d'arbres, de graines*) planting **(b)** (*exploitation*) (*de sucre, thé*) plantation; **p. d'oranges** orange grove **(c) la p. des cheveux** (*sur le front*) the hairline

plante[1] [plɑ̃t] *nf Anat* **p. du pied** sole (of the foot); **la p. des pieds** the soles (of the feet)

plante[2] *nf Bot* plant; **Jardin des Plantes** Botanical Gardens; *Fig F* **cette fille, quelle belle p.!** she's a stunner, that girl!

▶ **plante**: **p. d'appartement** pot *or* house plant; **p. à fleurs** flowering plant; **p. grasse** succulent (plant); **p. marine** seaweed; **p. potagère** (*herbe*) herb; (*légume*) vegetable; **p. de serre** hothouse plant; **plantes vertes** house plants, foliage

planté [plɑ̃te] *adj* **(a) enfant bien p.** sturdy *or* healthy child; **bien p. sur ses jambes** sturdily built; **avoir les dents bien/mal plantées** to have straight/crooked teeth **(b)** (*debout*) standing; **il était p. au milieu de la pièce** he had planted himself *or* he was standing right in the middle of the room; *F* **ne la laissez pas plantée là** don't leave her standing there; **tu ne vas pas rester p. devant nous à ne rien faire** you're not just going to stand there doing nothing

planter [plɑ̃te] **1** *vt* **(a)** (*graines, fleurs, arbres*) to plant; (*bouture*) to plant, to set out; **colline plantée d'arbres** hill planted with trees

(b) (*clou*) to knock in, to hammer in; **p. un pieu dans le sol** to drive a stake into the ground; **p. un drapeau** to put up *or* hoist *or* raise a flag; **p. une échelle contre le mur** to stand a ladder (up) against the wall; **p. sa tente** to put up *or* pitch one's tent; *Fig* **p. les personnages** to build up the characters, to give substance to the characters; *F* **p. son chapeau sur la tête** to stick *or* put one's hat on one's head; **p. un baiser sur la joue de qn** to plant a kiss on sb's cheek; *Fig* **p. son regard sur qn** to fix one's gaze on sb; *F* **p. là qn** to dump sb; **il veut tout p. là** he wants to drop everything *or* give it all up

2 se planter *vpr* **(a)** (*se tenir immobile*) to plant oneself, to stand; **se p. devant qn** to plant oneself *or* stand in front of sb

(b) *F* (*se tromper*) to get it wrong; **se p. dans ses calculs** to get one's calculations wrong

(c) *F* (*en voiture*) to crash, to have an accident

(d) *F* (*tomber*) to fall, to come a cropper

planteur [plɑ̃tœr] *nm* **(a)** (*exploitant dans un pays tropical*) planter **(b)** (*cocktail*) planter's punch

planteuse [plɑ̃tøz] *nf Agr, Tech* potato planting machine

plantigrade [plɑ̃tigrad] *adj, nm Zool* plantigrade

plantoir [plɑ̃twar] *nm* dibble, dibber

planton [plɑ̃tɔ̃] *nm Mil* orderly; **être de p.** to be on orderly duty; *F* **faire le p.** to kick one's heels, to hang around

plantureusement [plɑ̃tyrøzmɑ̃] *adv* copiously

plantureux, -euse [plɑ̃tyrø, -øz] *adj* **(a)** (*copieux*) (*repas*) copious, lavish; (*femme*) buxom; **poitrine plantureuse** ample bosom **(b)** (*fécond*) (*région*) fertile

plaquage [plakaʒ] *nm* = **placage (c)**

plaque [plak] *nf* **(a)** (*feuille rigide*) (*de métal*) plate, sheet; (*de marbre*) slab; (*de chocolat*) block; (*de glace*) patch, sheet; (*de neige*) layer; *Phot* **appareil à plaques** plate camera

(b) *Rad* plate, anode; **tension de p.** plate voltage, anode voltage

(c) (*portant une inscription*) plaque; (*insigne*) (*d'un bureau*) badge; (*d'un ordre*) star; **p. de porte** door plate; (*avec nom*) name plate; **p. de rue** street name plate, street sign

(d) *Méd* (*sur la peau*) patch, *Spéc* plaque; **p. (dentaire)** (dental) plaque; **plaques muqueuses** mucous plaque; **sclérose en plaques** multiple sclerosis

(e) *Fig F* **être à côté de la p.** to be off-target, to be wide of the mark

▶ **plaque**: *Él* **p. d'accumulateur** accumulator plate; **p. d'auto-école** ≈ L-plate; **p. de blindage** armour *or US* armor plate; **p. chauffante** hotplate; **p. de cheminée** fireback; **p. commémorative** commemorative plaque; *Com* **p. CSC** CSC plate; **p. d'égout** manhole cover; *Tech* **p. de fond** base plate; **p. de four** baking sheet *or* tray, *Am* cookie sheet; **p. funéraire** church brass; **p. à grille** grid plate; **p. d'identification** (*d'une machine*) model identification plate; (*avec nom*) name plate; (*avec numéro*) number plate; **p. d'identité** (*de soldat*) identity disc, *US F* dog tag; *Aut* **p. d'immatriculation** *ou* **minéralogique** number plate, *US* license plate; **p. mortuaire** church brass; *Typ* **p. offset** offset plate; *Aut* **p. oscillante** (*de pompe d'injection rotative*) cam plate; **p. photographique** photographic plate; **p. de propreté** (*sur une porte*) fingerplate; **p. stéréoscopique** stereo slide; *Typ* **p. de tirage** printing plate; *Rail* **p. tournante** turntable; *Fig* **c'est la p. tournante du projet** the plan hinges on it; **cet aéroport est une p. tournante pour les industries régionales** this airport is the hub of industrial activity in the region; **cette ville deviendra la p. tournante de l'Europe** this city will become the hub of Europe

plaqué [plake] **1** *nm* **(a) p. or** gold plate; **montre en p. or** gold-plated watch; **c'est du p.** it's plated **(b)** (*bois*) veneered wood **2** *adj* **p. or/argent** gold-/silver-plated

plaquemine [plakmin] *nf Bot* persimmon

plaqueminier [plakminje] *nm Bot* persimmon (tree)

plaquer [plake] **1** *vt* **(a)** (*appliquer une plaque sur*) (*bois*) to veneer; (*métal*) to plate; (*appliquer*) (*plâtre*) to lay on

(b) (*mettre à plat*) (*cheveux*) to plaster down; **le vent lui plaquait son manteau sur les jambes** the wind blew *or* flattened his coat against his legs; **p. qn contre un mur** to pin sb to a wall; **il avait les épaules plaquées au mur** he had his shoulders pinned *or* pressed to the wall

(c) *Rugby* (*adversaire*) to tackle, to bring down

(d) *Mus* **p. un accord** to strike (and hold) a chord

(e) *F* (*abandonner*) (*amant, petit ami*) to ditch, to chuck; **j'ai envie de tout p.** I feel like chucking it all in

2 se plaquer *vpr* **se p. au sol/contre un mur** to lie flat on the ground/to flatten oneself against a wall

plaquette [plakɛt] *nf* **(a)** (*petite plaque*) (*de métal*) (small) plate; (*portant un nom, une inscription etc*) (small) plaque; (*bloc*) (*de métal*) block; *Ordinat* circuit board; **p. de circuits imprimés** printed circuit board, PCB; *Aut* **p. de frein** brake pad **(b)** (*petit livre*) booklet; **p. publicitaire** advertising brochure **(c) plaquettes (sanguines)** (blood) platelets

plaqueur [plakœr] *nm* **(a)** (*sur métaux*) plater **(b)** (*sur bois*) veneerer

plasma [plasma] *nm* **(a)** *Biol* plasma; **p. sanguin** blood plasma **(b)** *Phys* **p. gazeux** gas plasma

plastic [plastik] *nm* plastic explosive

plasticage [plastikaʒ] *nm* bomb attack **(de** on)

plasticien, -ienne [plastisjɛ̃, -jɛn] *n* **(a)** *Tech* plastics technician **(b)** *Méd* plastic surgeon

plasticité [plastisite] *nf* plasticity

plastie [plasti] *nf Méd* plastic surgery

plastifiant [plastifjɑ̃] *nm* plasticizer

plastifier [plastifje] *vt* (*impf, pr sub* **n. plastifiions**) **(a)** (*recouvrir de plastique*) to laminate; **jaquette plastifiée** laminated jacket **(b)** *Tech* to plasticize

plastiquage [plastikaʒ] *nm* = **plasticage**

plastique [plastik] **1** *adj* **(a)** (*malléable*) plastic, malleable **(b) arts plastiques** plastic arts; **chirurgie p.** plastic surgery; **statue aux formes plastiques** finely formed statue; **beauté p.** fine forms **2** *nf* **(a)** *Beaux-Arts* plastic art, art of modelling **(b)** (*harmonie des formes*) (*d'une actrice, d'un danseur*) figure, physique **3** *nm* plastic

plastiquement [plastikmɑ̃] *adv* from the viewpoint of form; **cet athlète est p. très beau** this athlete has a very fine physique

plastiquer [plastike] *vt* to bomb (*using plastic explosive*)

plastiqueur, -euse [plastikœr, -øz] *n* bomber (*using plastic explosive*)

plastron [plastrɔ̃] *nm* **(a)** (*pièce d'armure*) breastplate, plastron; (*d'escrimeur*) plastron **(b)** (*de vêtement*) front; (*de chemise*) (*fixe*) shirt front; (*amovible*) dick(e)y, false shirt front

plastronner [plastrɔne] **1** *vt* (*qn*) to put a plastron on **2** *vi* to throw out one's chest; *Fig* to strut around, to swagger around

plat [pla] **1** *adj* **(a)** (*qui a peu de relief*) flat, level; **pays p.** flat country; **chaussure plate** low-heeled *or* flat shoe; **avoir la poitrine plate/les pieds plats** to be flat-chested/-footed; *F* **elle est plate comme une limande** she's as flat as a pancake; **cheveux plats** flat hair; **mer plate** smooth *or* still sea; *Naut* **calme p.** dead calm; **c'est le calme p.** there's a dead calm; *Fig* things are dead quiet; **eau plate** still water; **vis à tête plate** flat-head(ed) screw; **assiette plate** dinner plate; *Ordinat* **écran p.** flat screen

(b) *Fig* (*ennuyeux*) (*style, livre, film, intrigue*) flat, dull, *Fml* insipid; **vin p.** wine that lacks body

(c) à p. (*pneu, batterie*) flat; **mettre qch à p.** to lay sth (down) flat; *Fig* **mettre un problème à p.** to look at a problem from all sides; **couché à p. sur le sol** lying flat on the ground; **dormir à p.** to sleep without a pillow; *Fig* **tomber à p.** (*d'une proposition, d'un projet etc*) to fall flat; **se mettre à p. ventre** to lie flat on one's stomach; *Péj Fig* **se mettre à p. ventre (devant qn)** to crawl *or* grovel *or* kowtow (to sb); *F* **être à p.** (*épuisé*) to be exhausted *or* all in; (*en mauvaise santé*) to be run down; *Aut* to have a flat; **cette maladie l'a mis à p.** the illness has taken it out of him

2 *nm* **(a)** (*partie plate*) (*de la main*) flat; (*d'un aviron*) blade; (*d'un marteau*) face

(b) *Sp* **course de p.** flat race; *Natation* **faire un p.** to do a bellyflop

(c) *F* **faire du p. à qn** (*chercher à séduire*) to make advances to sb; (*flatter*) to crawl to sb, *Br* to suck up to sb

(d) *Culin* (*contenant*) dish; **p. à barbe** shaving dish; **p. de quête** (*dans une église*) collection plate; **p. (de service)** serving dish; *Fig* **mettre les petits plats dans les grands** to put on a marvellous spread; *Fig* **mettre les pieds dans le p.** to put one's foot in it; *F* **en faire tout un p.** to make a great fuss about it

(e) *Culin* (*mets*) dish; (*partie du menu*) course; **p. cuisiné** ready-cooked dish; (*à emporter*) takeaway dish; **p. du jour** today's special, dish of the day; **p. principal** main course; **p. de résistance** main course, main dish; *Fig* pièce de résistance

platane [platan] *nm* plane tree; *F* **rentrer dans un p.** to crash into a tree

plat-bord, *pl* **plats-bords** *nm Naut* gunwale, gunnel; **hauteur au-dessus du p.** height above the hull

plate [plat] *nf Naut* punt, flat-bottomed boat

plateau, -eaux [plato] *nm* **(a)** (*plat*) tray; **p. d'argent** silver tray *or* salver; **p. à** *ou* **de fromages** cheeseboard; **p. de fruits de mer** seafood platter; **p. petit déjeuner** breakfast tray; **p. de courtoisie** hospitality tray; *Fig* **(servi) sur un p.** on a plate; *Fig* **ça ne va pas t'arriver servi sur un p.** you're not going to get it handed to you on a plate

(b) (*d'une balance*) pan; (*d'une platine, d'un four micro-ondes*) turntable; (*de table*) top; **p. tournant** (*de tourne-disques*) turntable

(c) *Géog* plateau; **haut p.** high plateau; **p. continental** continental shelf

(d) *Méd* plateau

(e) *Th* stage; *TV, Cin* **p. de tournage** set; **p. fermé** closed set; **p. sonorisé** sound stage; **p. tournant** revolving stage

(f) *Rail* flat truck *or* wagon *or Am* car

(g) *MecE* plate, disc, *Am* disk; *Tech* **p. absorbeur de couple** torque plate; **p. de chargement** load bed, load platform; **p. d'embrayage** clutch plate; *Tech* **p. de friction** friction plate; *Aut* **p. menant** driving plate; *Aut* **p. mené** driven plate; *Aut* **p. oscillant** wobble-plate, swashplate; *Cyclisme* **p. de pédalier** front chain wheel; *Tech* **p. de pression** pressure plate; *Aut etc* **raccordement à plateaux** flange assembly

plateau-repas, *pl* **plateaux-repas** *nm* meal on a tray

plate-bande, *pl* **plates-bandes** *nf* flower bed; *Fig F* **marcher sur les plates-bandes de qn** to trespass on sb's patch; **ne marchez pas sur mes plates-bandes** keep off my patch

plate-forme, *pl* **plates-formes** *nf* **(a)** (*partie ouverte*) (*d'un bus*) platform; (*d'une locomotive*) footplate; **toit en p.** flat roof; **p. de chargement** loading platform; *Aut* load deck; **p.**

de déchargement unloading *or* offloading platform; *TV, Cin* **p. de prise de vue** camera platform **(b)** *Géog* **p. continentale** continental shelf **(c)** *Rail* flat truck *or* wagon *or Am* car **(d)** *Mil* **p. de tir** gun platform; **p. tournante** turntable **(e)** *Pol* platform **(f)** *Ordinat* platform

plate-longe, *pl* **plates-longes** *nf* (*longe*) leading rein

platement [platmɑ̃] *adv* (*s'exprimer, écrire*) in a dull *or* flat way, dully, flatly; **s'excuser p.** to apologize humbly

platinage [platinaʒ] *nm* platinum plating

platine[1] [platin] *nf Tech* (*d'une serrure*) plate; (*d'une presse à imprimer, d'une machine à écrire*) platen; (*d'un microscope*) stage; (*tourne-disque*) (record) deck, (record) turntable; **p. cassettes** cassette *or* tape deck; **p. laser** CD player

platine[2] **1** *nm* platinum **2** *adj inv* platinum; **cheveux (blonds) p.** platinum blond hair

platiné [platine] *adj* **(a)** (*recouvert de platine*) platinum-plated; *Aut* **vis platinées** points **(b)** **cheveux platinés** platinum blond hair; **une blonde platinée** a platinum blond

platiner [platine] *vt* to plate with platinum

platitude [platityd] *nf* **(a)** (*de personnalité, style, discussion*) dullness; **ce film est d'une p.** this film is so dull! **(b)** (*propos*) platitude, trite remark; **débiter des platitudes** to talk in platitudes, *Fml* to platitudinize; *Arch* **faire des platitudes à qn** to grovel to sb

Platon [platɔ̃] *nm* Plato

platonicien, -ienne [platɔnisjɛ̃, -jɛn] **1** *adj* (*école, philosophe*) Platonic **2** *n* Platonist

platonique [platɔnik] *adj* **(a)** (*amour*) platonic **(b)** (*vain*) futile, vain

platoniquement [platɔnikmɑ̃] *adv* (*aimer*) platonically

platonisme [platɔnism] *nm* Platonism

plâtrage [plɑtraʒ] *nm Constr* (*action*) plastering; (*ouvrage*) plasterwork

plâtras [plɑtra] *nm* (*débris*) (plaster) rubble; (*morceau*) lump of plaster

plâtre [plɑtr] *nm* **(a)** *Constr* plaster; **les plâtres** the plasterwork; *Fig F* **essuyer les plâtres** (*d'une maison*) to be the first occupant; (*subir des conséquences fâcheuses*) to put up with the teething problems; *Fig F* **ce camembert, c'est du p.** this camembert is like chalk **(b)** *Beaux-Arts* plaster; (*ouvrage*) plaster cast; **p. de moulage** plaster of Paris **(c)** *Méd* plaster; (*moule*) plaster cast; **poser un p.** to put a plaster cast on; **avoir la jambe dans le p.** to have one's leg in plaster

plâtrer [plɑtre] *vt* **(a)** (*enduire de plâtre*) (*mur, plafond*) to plaster; (*trou, fissure*) to plaster over *or* up **(b)** *Méd* to put in plaster **(c)** *Agr* (*sol*) to dress with sulphate

plâtrerie [plɑtrəri] *nf* (*usine*) plasterworks; **travaux de p.** plasterwork, plastering

plâtreux, -euse [plɑtrø, -øz] *adj* (*mur*) covered with plaster; *Fig* (*camembert*) chalky; **teint p.** pasty *or* chalky complexion

plâtrier [plɑtrije] *nm* plasterer

plâtrière [plɑtrijɛr] *nf* (*carrière*) gypsum quarry; (*four*) plaster kiln, gypsum kiln

plausibilité [plozibilite] *nf* plausibility

plausible [plozibl] *adj* plausible

plausiblement [ploziblәmɑ̃] *adv* plausibly

Plaute [plot] *nm* Plautus

play-back [plɛbak] *nm inv* miming; **chanter en p.** to mime; **c'est du p.** he's/she's/*etc* miming

play-boy, *pl* **play-boys** [plɛbɔj] *nm* playboy

plèbe [plɛb] *nf* **(a)** *Hist* **la p.** the plebs **(b)** *Litt Péj* **la p.** the hoi polloi, the plebs, the common people

plébéien, -ienne [plebejɛ̃, -jɛn] *adj, n* plebeian

plébiscite [plebisit] *nm* plebiscite

plébisciter [plebisite] *vt* **(a)** (*élire par plébiscite*) **p. qn/qch** to vote for sb/sth by plebiscite **(b)** (*élire à une très forte majorité*) **p. qn** to elect sb by a large majority **(c)** *Fig* to heartily approve of, to endorse

plectre [plɛktr] *nm* plectrum

pléiade [plejad] *nf* **(a)** *Astron* **les Pléiades** the Pleiades **(b)** *Littér* **la P.** the Pleiad; *Fig* **une p. de gens célèbres** a galaxy of famous people

plein [plɛ̃] **1** *adj* **(a)** (*rempli*) full **(de** of**)**; **une bouteille pleine** a full bottle; **une pleine bouteille** a whole bottle, a bottleful; **p. comme un œuf** chock-full, chock-a-block; **salle pleine à craquer** room full to bursting; **avoir le ventre p.** to be full (up), to have eaten one's fill; **ne parle pas la bouche pleine** don't speak with your mouth full; **suffit, j'ai la tête pleine!** that's enough, I've had it up to here!; **être p. de courage** to have a lot of courage; **être p. d'espoir** to be full of hope, to be hopeful; **une entreprise pleine de dangers/risques** an enterprise fraught with danger/risk; **il a les doigts pleins d'encre** his fingers are covered with ink; **être p. de certitudes** to be sure of things

(b) (*complet*) (*accord, adhésion*) full, complete; **pleine lune** full moon; **p. sud** due south; **la chambre est (en) p. ouest** the room faces due west; **pleine mer** (*marée haute*) high tide; **en pleine mer** out at sea, on the open sea; **gagner la pleine mer** to reach the open sea; **p. tarif** full price; (*de transports*) full fare; (*dans un hôtel*) rack rate; **trois jours pleins** three full days; **reliure pleine peau** full leather binding; **p. format** (*journal*) text-size format, broadsheet format; **p. pouvoir** full power; *Jur* power of attorney; **avoir les pleins pouvoirs** to have full powers; **de son p. gré** of one's own free will, of one's own accord

(c) (*solide, qui occupe toute la masse*) (*pneu, essieu etc*) solid; (*ligne*) continuous, unbroken; (*visage*) full; **joues pleines** full *or* plump cheeks

(d) (*intense*) **respirer à pleins poumons** to breathe deeply; **crier à pleine gorge** to shout at the top of one's voice; **rire à pleine gorge** to roar with laughter; **ça sent le brûlé à p. nez** there's a strong smell of burning; **apporter des fleurs à pleines brassées** to bring armfuls of flowers; **être en pleine forme** to be on top form; **être en pleine possession de ses moyens** to be in full possession of one's faculties; **à p. temps** full-time; **travailler à p. temps** to work full-time; **un p. temps** a full-time job

(e) (*au milieu de*) **en p. (milieu du) cours** (right) in the middle of the lesson; **en pleine réunion/messe** (right) in the middle of the meeting/of Mass; **s'arrêter en p. milieu de la place** to stop right in the middle of the square; **en pleine figure**, *très F* **en pleine gueule** right *or* bang in the face; **il a reçu la balle en p. cœur/en pleine poitrine** he got the bullet right *or* bang in the heart/in the chest; **en p. hiver** in the depths *or* the middle of winter; **en p. air** in the open (air); **restaurant/piscine en p. air** open-air restaurant/swimming pool; **en p. soleil** in the full heat of the sun; **marché en p. vent** open-air market; **planté en pleine terre** planted in open ground; **en p. jour** in broad daylight; **en pleine nuit** in the middle of the night, at dead of night; **en pleine lumière** in the full light; **en pleine saison** at the height of the season; **prix de la pleine saison** high-season prices; **en p. tribunal** in open court; **être en p. travail** to be hard at work; **être en pleine croissance** to be growing fast; **à pleines voiles** with all sails set, under full sail

(f) (*animal*) pregnant; **jument/brebis pleine** mare in foal/ewe with lamb; **chèvre pleine** goat in kid

(g) *F* **être p.** (*ivre*) to be plastered, to have had a skinful

2 *adv* **il avait des larmes p. les yeux** his eyes were full of tears; **il a des billes/livres p. ses poches** his pockets are full of marbles/stuffed with books; **avoir de l'argent p. les poches** to have plenty of money; **elle avait de la colle p. les mains** her hands were covered with *or* in glue; **elle a des vêtements p. ses armoires** her cupboards are full of *or* stuffed with clothes; **elle en a p. la bouche** she's full of him/it/*etc*, she never shuts up about him/it/*etc*; *F* **en avoir p. le dos** *ou très F* **le cul** to be sick of it, to be fed up with it, *F* to have had a bellyful; *F* **en avoir p. les jambes** *ou* **les bottes** to be on one's last legs; *F* **en mettre p. la vue à qn** to dazzle sb, to impress sb; *F* **s'en mettre p. la lampe** to have a good blowout; **à p.** (*travailler, fonctionner etc*) at full capacity; **l'avion part à p.** the plane is leaving with a full passenger load; **l'argument/la remarque a porté à p.** the argument/remark has had the desired effect; **elle est mignonne tout p.** she's awfully sweet; *F* **p. de gens/magasins/journaux** lots *or* loads of people/shops/newspapers; *Naut* **porter p.** to keep her full

3 *nm* **(a)** (*fait de remplir*) **faire le p. (d'un réservoir)** to fill (up) (a tank); *Aut* **faire le p. (d'essence)** to fill up (with petrol *or Am* gas); **(faites) le p., s'il vous plaît** fill her up, please; **faire le p. d'air pur/de soleil** to get a good dose of fresh air/sunshine; **on fait le p. une fois par semaine chez Casino** we do a big shop *or* stock up once a week at Casino; **avoir son p.** (*d'un bateau*) to be fully laden

(b) (*phase maximale*) **le p. (de la mer)** high tide; **battre son p.** (*de la marée*) to be at the full; *Fig* **la saison bat son p., c'est le p. de la saison** the season is at its height *or* is in full swing; **la fête battait son p.** the party was in full swing

(c) **en p. dans le centre** full *or* right in the middle, *F* slap bang in the middle; **en p. dans le mille** right in the bull's-eye; *Fig* spot on, *F* bang on

(d) (*trait épais*) downstroke; *Typ* thick stroke

pleinement [plɛnmɑ̃] *adv* fully; **je veux en profiter p.** I want to make the most of it *or* to take full advantage of it

plein-emploi [plɛnɑ̃plwa] *nm inv* full employment

pléistocène [pleistɔsɛn] *adj, nm Géol* Pleistocene

plénier, -ière [plenje, -jɛr] *adj* plenary

plénipotentiaire [plenipɔtɑ̃sjɛr] *adj, nm* plenipotentiary

plénitude [plenityd] *nf* (*d'une émotion, d'une expérience etc*) fullness, plenitude; (*d'une victoire etc*) completeness; (*d'un son*) fullness, richness

plénum [plenɔm] *nm* plenum

pléonasme [pleɔnasm] *nm* pleonasm

pléonastique [pleɔnastik] *adj* pleonastic

plésiosaure [plezjɔzɔr] *nm* plesiosaurus

pléthore [pletɔr] *nf* plethora (**de** of)

pléthorique [pletɔrik] *adj* (**a**) *Méd Vieilli* full-blooded, plethoric (**b**) (*très abondant*) superabundant; (*trop*) excessive

pleur [plœr] *nm Litt* tear; **verser des pleurs** to shed tears; **fondre en pleurs** to dissolve into tears; **cessez vos pleurs** dry your tears; **être (tout) en pleurs** to be (bathed) in tears; *Bible* **il va y avoir des pleurs et des grincements de dents** there will be wailing and gnashing of teeth

pleurage [plœraʒ] *nm Tech* wow; **niveau de p.** wow level

pleural, -ale, -aux, -ales [plœral, -o] *adj Anat* pleural

pleurant, -ante [plœrɑ̃, -ɑ̃t] **1** *adj Litt* weeping, crying **2** *n Beaux-Arts* weeper, mourner (*on a tomb*)

pleurard, -arde [plœrar, -ard] *Péj Vieilli* **1** *adj* (*enfant*) whimpering, fractious; (*voix*) whining, whimpering, tearful **2** *n* whiner, *F* crybaby

pleurer [plœre] **1** *vt* (**a**) **p. qn** to mourn (for) sb; **p. la mort de qn** to mourn sb's death; **p. sa jeunesse, p. ses vingt ans** to weep for *or* over one's lost youth; **mourir sans être pleuré** to die unmourned

(**b**) (*laisser couler*) to cry, to shed, to weep; **p. toutes les larmes de son corps** to cry one's eyes out; **p. des larmes de sang** to weep bitterly, to shed bitter tears; **p. des larmes de bonheur** to cry *or* weep for joy; **p. misère** to bemoan one's lot

(**c**) *Fig F Vieilli* (*ménager*) (*argent*) to stint; **elle ne pleure pas ses efforts** *ou* **sa peine/ses conseils** she spares no effort/she's generous with her advice

2 *vi* (**a**) (*verser des larmes*) to cry, to weep (**sur** over; **pour** for); **et puis j'ai vu que je m'étais trompé et j'en aurais pleuré** when I saw I had made a mistake, I could have cried *or* wept; **elle pleure de ne pas avoir eu son examen** she's crying because she hasn't passed her exam; **p. sur soi-même** *ou* **sur son sort** to bewail *or* bemoan one's fate; **p. de joie** to cry *or* weep for joy; **p. à chaudes larmes** *ou F* **comme une madeleine** *ou F* **comme un veau** to sob *or* to cry one's heart out; **s'endormir en pleurant** to cry oneself to sleep; **il était sentimental, c'était à en p.** he was ridiculously sentimental; **c'est à (faire) p.** it's enough to make you weep *or* cry; **bête/méchant à faire p.** terribly stupid/nasty

(**b**) **j'ai les yeux qui pleurent** my eyes are watering *or* running

(**c**) *Fig Péj* (*supplier*) to beg; **aller p. auprès de qn** to go begging to sb; *F* **et qu'il ne vienne pas me p. dans les bras!** and he needn't come begging to me!; **p. après une faveur** to beg for a favour

pleurésie [plœrezi] *nf Méd* pleurisy

pleurétique [plœretik] *adj, n Méd* pleuritic

pleureur, -euse [plœrœr, -øz] **1** *n Péj Vieilli* whimperer **2** *nf* **pleureuse** (*dans un cortège funèbre*) (hired) mourner, *Arch* mute **3** *adj Péj* whimpering; **saule p.** weeping willow

pleurite [plœrit] *nf Méd* dry pleurisy

pleurnichard, -arde [plœrniʃar, -ard] *n, adj* = **pleurnicheur**

pleurnichement [plœrniʃmɑ̃] *nm* = **pleurnicherie**

pleurnicher [plœrniʃe] *vi F* to whine, to snivel, *Br* (*surtout d'un jeune enfant*) to grizzle

pleurnicherie [plœrniʃri] *nf F* whining, snivelling, *Br* (*surtout d'un jeune enfant*) grizzling

pleurnicheur, -euse [plœrniʃœr, -øz] *F* **1** *n* whiner, sniveller; (*qui pleure facilement*) crybaby **2** *adj* whining, snivelling

pleurote [plœrɔt] *nf* oyster mushroom

pleutre [pløtr] *Litt Péj* **1** *adj* cowardly, *Litt* craven **2** *nm* coward, *Litt* craven

pleuvasser [pløvase], **pleuviner** [pløvine] *v impers* to drizzle

pleuvoir [pløvwar] (*prp* **pleuvant**; *pp* **plu**; *pr ind* **il pleut, ils pleuvent**; *impf* **il pleuvait**; *p hist* **il plut**; *fu* **il pleuvra**) **1** *v impers* to rain; **il pleut** it's raining; **il pleut à verse** *ou* **à seaux** it's pouring (down) (with rain); **les jours où il pleut** on wet *or* rainy days; *F* **il pleut des cordes** *ou* **des hallebardes, il pleut comme vache qui pisse** it's raining cats and dogs, it's coming down in buckets, *Br* it's tipping it down; **des cadeaux comme s'il en pleuvait** presents galore; **dépenser de l'argent comme s'il en pleuvait** to spend money as if there's no tomorrow *or* as if it's going out of fashion

2 *vi* **faire p. des coups sur qn** to rain blows (down) on sb, to shower sb with blows; **les invitations pleuvent sur lui** invitations are pouring in to him, he's being inundated with invitations; **ce ne sont pas exactement les compliments qui pleuvent** I'm not exactly being showered with compliments

pleuvoter [pløvɔte] *v impers* = **pleuvasser**

plèvre [plɛvr] *nf Anat* pleura, pleural membrane

plexiglas® [plɛksiglas] *nm* perspex®, *Am* Plexiglas

plexus [plɛksys] *nm Anat* plexus; **p. solaire** solar plexus

pli [pli] *nm* (**a**) (*rabat*) (*de rideaux, tissu*) fold; *Couture* pleat; *Couture* **p. creux** *ou* **rentré** *ou* **inverti, double p.** box pleat, inverted pleat; **p. couché** knife pleat; **petit p.** tuck; **jupe à plis** pleated skirt; **faire** *ou* **marquer le p. d'un pantalon** to put a crease in a pair of trousers; **faire des plis à une robe** to put pleats in a dress, to pleat a dress; (*la froisser*) to crease a dress; (**faux**) **p.** crease

(**b**) **mise en plis** set; **faire une mise en plis à qn** to set sb's hair

(**c**) *Aut* (*d'un pneu*) ply; **p. diagonal** diagonal ply; **p. radial** radial ply

(**d**) *Fig* **ça ne fait pas un p.** (there's) no doubt about it; **j'étais sûr qu'il allait se tromper et ça n'a pas fait un p.!** I was sure he'd make a mistake and I was right!; *Fig* **prendre le p. (de faire qch)** to get into the habit (of doing sth); **il a pris le p.** he got used to it, he got into the habit; **le p. était pris** I/he/*etc* had got used to it; *Fig* **prendre un mauvais p.** to get into a bad habit

(**e**) (*du bras, de la jambe*) bend; (*de peau*) fold; (*petit*) wrinkle; **p. du jarret** hollow of the knee; **les plis du front** the lines on the forehead; **elle a de gros plis sur le ventre** she has big folds of skin on her stomach; **il a de petits plis autour des yeux** he has wrinkles round his eyes

(**f**) (*enveloppe*) envelope; (*lettre*) letter; **sous p. séparé** under separate cover; **sous p. discret** under plain cover, *aussi Hum* in a plain brown wrapper; **nous vous envoyons sous ce p. ...** we are sending you herewith ..., please find enclosed ...; **p. cacheté** sealed envelope; *Naut* sealed orders; **envoyer qch sous p. cacheté** to send sth in a sealed envelope; **p. chargé** registered and insured letter; **p. recommandé** registered letter; **par p. recommandé** by registered mail

(**g**) *Cartes* trick; **faire un p.** to take a trick

(**h**) *Géol* **p. de terrain** fold

pliable [plijabl] *adj* (*chaise, lit*) foldable; **canot p.** folding boat

pliage [plijaʒ] *nm* (*d'un tissu*) folding; (*origami*) paper folding; (*objet*) folded-paper model

pliant [plijɑ̃] **1** *adj* (*chaise, table*) folding, collapsible; **pied p.** folding tripod **2** *nm* folding *or* collapsible stool

plie [pli] *nf* plaice

plié [plije] *nm* (*en danse*) plié

plier [plije] (*impf, pr sub* **n. pliions**) **1** *vt* (**a**) (*mettre en double*) (*draps, vêtements*) to fold; (*page*) to turn down; (*voile*) to furl; (*rabattre*) (*parapluie*) to fold up *or* away; *Fig* **p. bagage** to pack one's bags

(**b**) (*courber*) (*branche, genou etc*) to bend; **plié en deux** (*personne*) bent double, doubled up; *Fig F* **être plié (de rire)** to be doubled up *or* bent double with laughter; **p. qn à la discipline/une règle/une contrainte** to impose discipline/a rule/a constraint on sb; **p. qn à une habitude** to get sb into a habit

2 *vi* (**a**) (*se courber*) to bend (over); **p. sous le poids de qch** (*d'une poutre, de branches etc*) to bend *or* give *or* sag under the weight of sth

(**b**) (*se soumettre*) to submit, to yield; (*des troupes dans une bataille*) to give way; **elle ne pliera pas devant lui** she will not submit to him *or* give in to him

3 se plier *vpr* (*d'un parapluie, d'une chaise*) to fold (up); **se p. aux circonstances** to yield *or* bow *or* submit to circumstances; **se p. à la discipline** to submit to discipline; **se p. aux lois** to obey the law; **se p. aux caprices/volontés de qn** to give in to sb's whims/wishes

plieur, -euse [plijœr, -øz] *Tech* **1** *n* (*personne*) folder **2** *nf* **plieuse** folding machine

Pline [plin] *nm* **P. l'Ancien/le Jeune** Pliny the Elder/the Younger

plinthe [plɛ̃t] *nf* (**a**) (*lame de bois*) skirting (board), *Am* baseboard (**b**) *Archit* (*de colonne*) plinth

pliocène [plijɔsɛn] *adj, nm Géol* Pliocene

plioir [plijwar] *nm* (*coupe-papier*) paper knife

plissage [plisaʒ] *nm* (*d'un tissu*) pleating

plissé [plise] **1** *adj* (**a**) *Couture* pleated (**b**) **front p.** wrinkled brow; **visage tout p.** creased *or* wrinkled face **2** *nm Couture* pleats; **p. soleil** sunray *or Am* sunburst pleats

plissement [plismɑ̃] *nm* (**a**) (*fait de plier*) (*d'un tissu*) pleating; (*de papier*) folding; (*de métal, de carton*) corrugation (**b**) (*froissement*) (*de papier, de tissu*) creasing, crumpling, crinkling (**c**) (*froncement*) (*des yeux*) screwing up (**d**) *Géol* fold; **le p. hercynien** the Armorican *or* Hercynian fold

plisser [plise] **1** *vt* (**a**) (*plier*) (*vêtement*) to pleat; (*papier*) to fold; (*métal, carton*) to corrugate **(b)** (*froisser*) (*papier, tissu*) to crease, to crumple, to crinkle **(c)** (*froncer*) (*front*) to wrinkle; (*lèvres*) to pucker; **p. les yeux** to screw up one's eyes **2** *vi* (*d'un vêtement*) to crease **3 se plisser** *vpr* (*d'une étoffe*) to crease; (*d'une bouche*) to pucker; **la soie se plisse facilement** silk creases easily; **ses yeux se plissent quand elle sourit** her eyes go all crinkly when she smiles; **son front se plissa** he frowned

plisseur, -euse [plisœr, -øz] *Tex* **1** *n* (*personne*) pleater **2** *nf* **plisseuse** pleating machine

plissure [plisyr] *nf* pleats

pliure [plijyr] *nf* (*action*) (*du papier*) folding; (*résultat*) (*d'un tissu*) fold; (*du genou*) bend

ploc [plɔk] *int* plop!

ploiement [plwamɑ̃] *nm* bending

plomb [plɔ̃] *nm* **(a)** (*métal*) lead; **p.-étain** lead-tin; **p. laminé** *ou* **en feuilles** sheet lead; **tuyau de p.** lead pipe; **blanc de p.** white lead; *Fig* **sommeil de p.** deep *or* heavy sleep; **dormir d'un sommeil de p.** to sleep like a log; **ciel de p.** leaden sky; **teint de p.** livid complexion; **soleil de p.** blazing (hot) sun; *Fig* **n'avoir pas de p. dans la tête** to be scatterbrained; **espérons que cela lui mettra un peu de p. dans la tête** *ou* **dans la cervelle** let's hope that will knock some sense into him

(b) (*poids*) lead (weight); *Pêche* sinker; *Naut* **jeter** *ou* **lancer le p. (de sonde)** to heave the lead; **fil à p.** plumb line; **à p.** upright, vertical

(c) *Archit* **plombs** (*de fenêtre*) leadwork, leads; **mise en p.** leading

(d) *Typ* type, metal; (*de chasse*) shot; **petit** *ou* **menu p.** small shot; **gros p.** buckshot; *Fig* **avoir du p. dans l'aile** to be in a bad way

(e) (*sceau*) lead seal (*on meter etc*); *Él* **p. (fusible)** fuse; **faire sauter les plombs** to blow the fuses; *très F* **j'ai pété les plombs** I blew my top

plombage [plɔ̃baʒ] *nm* **(a)** (*fait de garnir avec du plomb*) covering with lead; *Cér* lead glazing **(b)** (*fait de mettre des plombs*) weighting with lead **(c)** (*d'une dent*) filling

plombagine [plɔ̃baʒin] *nf Minér* black lead, graphite

plombe [plɔ̃b] *nf Arg* hour; **quatre plombes, ce n'est pas une heure à rentrer** four o'clock is no time to come home; **on ne va pas l'attendre pendant des plombes** we're not going to wait for him for ever

plombé [plɔ̃be] *adj* (*fenêtre*) leaded; (*toit*) lead(-covered); *Fig* (*teint*) livid; (*ciel*) leaden

plomber [plɔ̃be] **1** *vt* **(a)** (*couvrir de plomb*) to cover with lead; *Cér* to glaze **(b)** (*mettre des plombs à*) to weight with lead **(c)** *Fig* (*rendre livide*) (*teint, ciel*) to turn livid **(d)** (*dent*) to fill, to stop; **le dentiste m'a plombé une dent** the dentist gave me a filling **(e)** *Constr* (*mur*) to plumb **2 se plomber** *vpr* (*du teint*) to become livid; (*du ciel*) to become leaden

plomberie [plɔ̃bri] *nf* (*installations, métier*) plumbing; (*atelier*) plumber's shop

plombier [plɔ̃bje] *nm* (*technicien*) plumber; *Fig F Péj* (*policier spécialiste de l'écoute clandestine*) snooper, eavesdropper; (*au téléphone*) phone-tapper

plombières [plɔ̃bjɛr] *nf Culin* tutti-frutti (ice cream)

plonge [plɔ̃ʒ] *nf F* (*dans un restaurant*) dishwashing, *Br* washing up; **faire la p.** (*dans un restaurant*) to be a dishwasher; (*at home*) to wash the dishes, *Br* to do the washing up

plongeant [plɔ̃ʒɑ̃] *adj* (*tir, décolleté*) plunging; **vue plongeante** bird's-eye view (**sur** onto), view from above

plongée [plɔ̃ʒe] *nf* **(a)** (*de nageur*) diving; **faire de la p.** to dive; **partir en p.** to go diving; **p. sous-marine** skin *or* scuba diving **(b)** (*de sous-marin*) dive, diving, submersion; **effectuer sa p.** to dive, to submerge; **p. raide** crash-dive **(c)** *Cin, TV* elevated shot; (*verticale*) bird's-eye view **(d)** *Aut* **p. (au freinage)** dive

plongeoir [plɔ̃ʒwar] *nm* diving board

plongeon [plɔ̃ʒɔ̃] *nm* **(a)** (*fait de plonger*) dive; **p. de haut vol** high dive; **faire un p.** (*d'un nageur, gardien de but*) to dive; *Fig F* **faire le p.** (*dans les affaires*) to suffer heavy losses, *Am* to take a bath **(b)** (*oiseau*) diver, *Am* loon

plonger [plɔ̃ʒe] (**je plongeai(s); n. plongeons**) **1** *vi* **(a)** (*s'immerger*) (*d'un nageur, sous-marin, avion etc*) to dive (**dans** into)

(b) *Fig* (*descendre*) to plunge; **les murs plongent dans le fossé** the walls plunge into *or* run steeply down into the moat; **son regard plongea sur nous** he gazed down at us; **d'ici on plonge sur la cathédrale** from here you look down on the cathedral *or* you have a view down onto the cathedral; **p. dans le sommeil** to fall into a deep sleep; **p. dans la décadence** to sink rapidly into decline; **p. dans le travail pour oublier** to throw oneself into work *or* immerse oneself in work to take one's mind off things

2 *vt* to plunge, to thrust (**dans** in(to)); **p. la main dans sa poche/un couteau dans le cœur de qn** to plunge *or* thrust one's hand into one's pocket/a knife into sb's heart; **il plongea son regard sur nous** he stared at us

3 se plonger *vpr* to immerse oneself (**dans** in); *Fig* **être plongé dans ses pensées** to be immersed *or* lost *or* deep in thought; **être plongé dans le silence** to be plunged in silence; **être plongé dans le noir/l'angoisse** to be plunged in darkness/to be overcome by anguish; **se p. dans son travail/l'étude** to throw oneself into *or* to immerse *or* bury oneself in one's work/one's studies; **se p. dans Proust** to become absorbed *or* engrossed in Proust; **se p. dans le vice** to plunge into the world of vice

plongeur, -euse [plɔ̃ʒœr, -øz] **1** *n* **(a)** (*personne qui plonge dans l'eau*) diver; **cloche à plongeurs** diving bell; **p. sous-marin** skin *or* scuba diver **(b)** *F* (*dans un restaurant*) dishwasher, *Br* washer-up **2** *nm* **(a)** *Orn* diver, diving bird **(b)** *Tech* (*d'une pompe*) plunger

plot [plo] *nm Él* contact (stud)

plouc [pluk] *Péj* **1** *nm* yokel, (country) bumpkin **2** *adj F* naff; **ça fait p.!** that's really naff!

plouf [pluf] *int* plop!; (*objet plus lourd*) splash!

ploutocrate [plutɔkrat] *nm* plutocrat

ploutocratie [plutɔkrasi] *nf* plutocracy

ploutocratique [plutɔkratik] *adj* plutocratic

ployable [plwajabl] *adj* pliable, flexible

ployer [plwaje] (**je ploie, n. ployons; je ploierai**) **1** *vi* (*courber*) to bend; (*d'un plancher, d'une poutre*) to sag; (*se casser, s'effondrer*) to give (way); (*sous un joug, un fardeau*) to bend, to bow; (*de troupes*) to give way, to submit, to yield **2** *vt* (*branche, genou*) to bend

pluches [plyʃ] *nfpl Mil F* (**corvée de**) **p.** potato-peeling, *Br* spud-bashing; **je suis de p.** I'm on potato-peeling *or* spud-bashing (duty)

pluie [plɥi] *nf* **(a)** rain; **pluies acides** acid rain; **p. battante** driving *or* pelting *or* lashing rain; **p. diluvienne** pouring rain; **p. torrentielle** torrential rain; **p. fine** drizzle; **p. d'orage** cloudburst; **goutte de p.** raindrop; **il n'y a pas eu une goutte de p. dans la région depuis deux mois** the region hasn't had a drop of rain for two months; **eau de p.** rainwater; **le temps est à la p.** it looks like rain; **temps de p.** rainy *or* wet weather; **jour sans p.** dry day; **sous la p.** in the rain; **sous une p. diluvienne** in the pouring rain; **la saison des pluies** the rainy season; **ajoutez la farine en la versant en p.** sprinkle in the flour; *Fig* **parler de la p. et du beau temps** to talk about nothing in particular, to talk of this and that, *Am* to shoot the breeze; *Fig F* **il n'est pas tombé de la dernière p.** he wasn't born yesterday; *Prov* **après la p. le beau temps** it's a long road that has no turning; *F* **faire la p. et le beau temps** to rule the roost, to be the boss

(b) *Fig* (*de coups, balles, pierres*) hail, shower; (*de reproches, compliments*) stream; **p. d'or** shower of gold

plumage [plymaʒ] *nm* (*ensemble des plumes*) plumage, feathers; (*fait de plumer*) plucking

plumard [plymar] *nm F* bed; **aller au p.** to hit the sack *or* the hay, to crash (out)

plume[1] [plym] *nf* **(a)** (*d'oiseau*) feather; **oiseau sans plumes** unfledged bird; **gibier à plumes** game birds; *Fig F* **il y a laissé des plumes** he didn't come out of it unscathed, he didn't get off lightly; *Fig F* **on lui a volé dans les plumes** they laid into him; **léger comme une p.** (as) light as a feather; *Prov* **la belle p. fait le bel oiseau** fine feathers make fine birds; **lit de plume(s)** feather bed; **couette en plumes d'oie** goose-feather duvet; *Fig Hum* **perdre ses plumes** to go thin on top, to go bald; **poids p.** *Boxe* featherweight; *Fig* lightweight; **un poids p. en politique** a political lightweight

(b) (*de stylo*) (pen) nib; **p. (d'oie)** quill (pen); **p. à dessin** drawing pen; **les idées se pressent sous sa p.** he can't write his ideas down quickly enough, his ideas are coming thick and fast; **écrire des mots/ses idées au courant** *ou* **au fil de la p.** to write down words/one's ideas as they come into one's head; **dessin à la p.** pen (and ink) drawing; **trait de p.** stroke of the pen; **prendre la p.** to put pen to paper; **j'ai pris ma plus belle p. pour écrire cette lettre** I made this the most beautiful letter I could; **vivre de sa p.** to make one's living by writing, to live by one's pen; **avoir la p. facile** to have a gift for writing

(c) *Méd* **p. à vaccin** vaccine point

plume[2] *nm* = **plumard**

plumeau, -eaux [plymo] *nm* feather duster

plumer [plyme] **1** *vt* (*volaille*) to pluck; *F* (*personne*) to fleece **2 se plumer** *vpr F* to hit the sack *or* the hay, to crash (out)

plumet [plymɛ] *nm* plume

plumetis [plymti] *nm Couture* **(a) broderie au p.** raised *or* satin stitch **(b)** (*étoffe*) Swiss muslin

plumeux, -euse [plymø, -øz] *adj* feathery

plumier [plymje] *nm* (*ouvert*) pen tray; (*à couvercle*) pencil box, pencil case

plumitif [plymitif] *nm Péj* (*employé de bureau*) penpusher; (*mauvais écrivain*) scribbler

plum-pudding, *pl* **plum(s)-puddings** [plumpudiŋ] *nm* Christmas pudding, *Vieilli* plum pudding

plupart (la) [laplypar] *nf* most, the majority, *Fml* the greater part; **la p. des gens** most people, the majority of people; **la p. de mes clients** most of my customers, the majority of my customers; **la p. d'entre eux** most of them, the majority of them; **la p. du temps** most of the time; (*en général*) in most cases, generally; **il passe la p. du temps à lire** he spends most of his time reading; **dans la p. des cas** in most cases, in the majority of cases; **pour la p.** for the most part, mostly

plural, -ale, -aux, -ales [plyral, -o] *adj* **vote p.** plural voting

pluralisme [plyralism] *nm Pol, Phil* pluralism

pluraliste [plyralist] **1** *adj* pluralist; **élections pluralistes** multi-party elections **2** *n* pluralist

pluralité [plyralite] *nf* (*multiplicité*) plurality, multiplicity; *Rel* **p. des bénéfices** pluralism; *Arch* **élu à la p. des voix** elected by a majority

pluriannuel, -elle [plyrianɥɛl] *adj* **récolte pluriannuelle** crop harvested every few years; **contrat p.** contract valid for a number of years

pluridisciplinaire [plyridisiplinɛr] **1** *adj* (*approche, études*) multidisciplinary **2** *nm* **le technicien doit être un p.** the technician must possess a range of skills; **des pluridisciplinaires** people with a range of skills

pluridisciplinarité [plyridisiplinarite] *nf* multidisciplinary approach; **favoriser la p. dans les études universitaires** to encourage students to take up a range of subjects; **nous visons à une certaine p. dans nos services** we're aiming to widen the range of tasks undertaken in our departments

pluriel, -elle [plyrjɛl] **1** *adj* plural **2** *nm* [①A9-15; B7-8,C] plural; **au p.** in the plural

plurilingue [plyrilɛ̃g] *adj* multilingual

plurilinguisme [plyrilɛ̃gɥism] *nm* multilingualism

plurinational, -ale, -aux, -ales [plyrinasjɔnal, -o] *adj* multinational

pluripartisme [plyripartism] *nm Pol* multi-party system

plus [ply] (*often* [plys] *at the end of a word group*; [plyz] *before a vowel* **plus on est de fous, plus on rit** [plyzɔ̃nɛdfuplyzɔ̃ri]) **1** *adv* **(a)** [①A18,4,a-b; B10,E; B12-13,F] (*davantage*) more; **p. de** (*davantage*) more; (*au-delà de*) more than; **soyez p. réaliste!** be more realistic!; **p. courageux** braver, more courageous; **p. clair/fort** clearer/stronger; **ils sont (beaucoup) p. nombreux** there are (far) more of them; **c'est sa mère, en p. jeune** she's a younger version of her mother, she looks just like her mother, only younger; **le même, en p. petit** the same, only smaller; **il est p. grand que moi** he's taller than I am *or* than me; **je ne suis pas p. grand que lui** I'm no taller than he is *or* than him; **elle écoute p. attentivement** she listens more attentively; **une fenêtre p. haute que large** a window higher than it is wide; **elle est p. jolie que belle** she is pretty rather than beautiful; **deux fois p. grand/rapide (que)** twice as big/fast (as); **c'est mille fois p. adapté pour ce que tu fais** it's a thousand times more suitable for what you're doing; *F* **c'est p. que bien** it's more than just good; **des résultats p. que satisfaisants** more than satisfactory results; **je gagne p. que vous** I earn more than you (do); **p. qu'à moitié** (*souvent* [plyskamwatje]) (*fait etc*) more than half; **en vouloir toujours p.** to be always wanting more; **il a p. de patience/temps que moi** he has more patience/time than I have *or* than me; **p. d'une fois** more than once; **p. de dix hommes** more than ten men; **il a p. de vingt ans** he's over twenty; **pendant p. d'une heure/d'un kilomètre** for over *or* for more than an hour/a kilometre; **p. loin** further *or* farther (on); **p. tôt** earlier; **je n'étais pas p. tôt arrivé que le téléphone sonnait** no sooner had I arrived than the telephone rang; **p. ... (et) p. ...** the more ..., the more ...; **p. on est de fous, p. on rit** the more the merrier; **p. je lis, moins je retiens** the more I read the less I remember; **et qui p. est** [plyzɛ] and what is more, and moreover; **j'en ai trois fois p. qu'il ne m'en faut** I've (got) three times as much/as many as I need; **il y en a tant et p.** there's an awful lot (of it/them); **c'est d'autant p. facile/compliqué que ...** it's all the easier/the more complicated since ..., it's particularly easy/complicated since ...; **c'est d'autant p. vrai qu'il l'a dit lui-même** it must be true, he said so himself

(b) [①A18,4,a-b; B10,E; B12-13,F] **(le) p.** (the) most; **la p. longue rue** *ou* **la rue la p. longue de la ville** the longest street in the town; **la p. belle femme que j'aie jamais vue** the most beautiful woman I've ever seen; **c'est la femme la p. capable de le faire** she's the woman most capable of doing it; **c'est vous qui avez fait le p. de fautes** you've made (the) most mistakes; **le p. vite possible** as quickly as possible; **c'est à trente ans qu'elle a été la p. belle** she was at her most beautiful *or* at her best at thirty; **ce que je désire le p.** what I most desire, what I desire the most; **le p. drôle, ce qu'il y a de p. drôle** the funniest thing; **crier le p. fort** to shout (the) loudest; **faites le p. que vous pourrez** do the most *or* as much as you can; **(tout) au p.** at the (very) most, at the (very) outside; **c'est tout au p. s'il est midi** it's twelve o'clock at the latest; **c'est tout ce qu'il y a de p. simple** nothing could be simpler; **c'était des p. réussi** (*extrêmement*) it was most successful; **un gâteau des p. délicieux** a most delicious cake

(c) [①B60,B] (*négation*) **ne ... p.** not any more, not any longer, no more, no longer; **je ne les vois p.** I don't see them any more *or* any longer, I no longer see them; **je ne le ferai p.** I won't do it again *or* any more; **tu n'iras p.** you won't go again *or* any more; **je ne la verrai p. (jamais)** I'll never see her again; *Litt* **il n'est p.** (*mort*) he is no more; **je ne veux p. de cela** I don't want any more of that; **je n'ai** *ou* *F* **j'ai p. d'argent** I haven't any money left *or* any more money, I've (got) no more money; **nous n'avons p. d'espoir de la retrouver** we no longer have any hope *or* we have no hope any more of finding her; **il n'y a p. aucun espoir** I've/they've/*etc* given up hope; **sans p. attendre** without further ado; **(il n'y a) p. de doute** there is no longer any doubt about it; **il n'y a p. de jeunesse!** young people aren't what they used to be!, honestly, kids nowadays!; **p. de potage, merci** no more soup, thank you; **il (n')y en a p.** there is/are no more (left), there is/are none left; **il (n')y a p. rien** there's nothing left; **p. que dix minutes!** only ten minutes left!; **on procède non p. par ordre alphabétique, mais par thème** we shall no longer proceed in alphabetical order, but according to theme; **pas p. que** no more than; **pas p. qu'on ne doit voler, on ne doit mentir** it is no more acceptable to lie than it is to steal

(d) non p. either (*in negative sentences*); **je n'en ai pas non p.** I haven't got any either; **(ni) moi non p.** neither do I/did I/*etc*, I don't/didn't/*etc* either, *F* me neither; **jamais non p. je n'avais songé à ...** nor had I ever thought of ...; **vous n'en avez guère non p.** you haven't got much/many either

(e) [plys] *surtout Math* plus; **sept p. neuf** seven plus nine; **il fait p. 20 (degrés)** it's plus 20 (degrees); **500 francs d'amende, p. les frais** 500 francs fine and *or* plus costs; *Golf* **p. quatre** [plyskatr] plus four

(f) de p. more; **une journée de p.** one day more, one more day; **il a trois ans de p. que moi** he's three years older than I am *or* than me; **rien de p., merci** nothing else, thank you; **de p. en p.** more and more; **de p. en p. froid** colder and colder

(g) en p. in addition, into the bargain; (*en sus*) extra; **la même maison, avec un balcon en p.** the same house, but with a balcony; (*avec un autre balcon*) the same house, but with an extra *or* additional balcony; **le vin est en p.** wine is extra; **il y en a trois en p. de lui** there are three more besides him; **en p. de ce qu'il me doit** over and above *or* in addition to *or* besides what he owes me; **sans p.** but no more than that; **elle a été aimable, sans p.** she was pleasant, but no more than that

(h) p. ou moins [plyzumwɛ̃] more or less; **elle joue p. ou moins bien** she plays fairly well, she's not a bad player; **c'est un mensonge, ni p. ni moins** it's nothing more nor less than a lie, it's purely and simply a lie

2 *nm* **(a)** *Prov* **qui peut le p. peut le moins** you have/he has/*etc* done more difficult things than that before

(b) *Math* (*signe*) plus (sign)

(c) *Golf* **le p.** [ləplys] the odd

(d) *Fig* (*atout*) plus; **c'est un p. pour vous** that's a plus for you

plusieurs [plyzjœr] *adj, pron* [①B14-15,B] several; **p. personnes l'ont remarqué** several people *or* a number of people have noticed it; **de p. manières** in more ways than one, in several ways; **j'en ai p.** I have several; **on s'y est mis à p.** several of us *or* a number of us got together (to do it)

plus-que-parfait, *pl* **plus-que-parfaits** [plyskəparfɛ] *nm* [①A49,11,e; B28-29,5] *Gram* pluperfect, past perfect

plus-value, *pl* **plus-values** [plyvaly] *nf Écon, Fin* (*de biens, de terrains etc*) capital gain, appreciation, increase in value; (*excédent*) (*d'impôts*) surplus, excess yield; **les recettes présentent une p. de ...** the receipts show an increase of ...; **impôt sur les plus-values** capital gains tax

plutonium [plytɔnjɔm] *nm Ch* plutonium

plutôt [plyto] *adv* **(a)** (*de préférence*) rather; **p. que de faire les choses en cachette** rather than do things in secret; **p. la mort que l'esclavage** death before slavery, rather *or* sooner death than slavery; **p. souffrir que mentir** it is better to suffer than to lie; **il récite p. qu'il ne chante** he recites rather than sings; **p. que de partir** rather than leave, instead of leaving; **demande p. à ta mère** ask your mother instead; **ne te plains pas, travaille p.!** don't complain, just work!; **il faudrait p. en rire** it's best to laugh

(b) (*pour préciser*) rather; **il faisait p. froid (que chaud)** the weather was cold if anything, it was cold rather than anything (else); **elle n'est pas bête, p. étourdie** she's absent-minded rather than stupid, she's not so much stupid as absent-minded, she's not stupid, just absent-minded; **ses parents ou p. son père** his parents, or rather *or* or more precisely his father; **il n'est pas satisfait, mais p., soulagé** he's relieved rather than satisfied

(c) [①A4,B] (*assez*) fairly, quite, rather, *F* pretty, *surtout Fml* somewhat; **son discours était p. long** his speech was fairly *or* quite *or* rather long *or* was on the long side; *F* **il est p. bien, ce type!** he's not bad-looking at all, that guy!; **c'est p. une bonne idée, tu ne trouves pas?** it's rather a good idea isn't it?; **je suis en retard? – oui p.!** am I late? – you can say that again! *or Br* not half!

(d) [①A72,iv] *Litt* (*à peine*) hardly, scarcely; **il ne nous avait pas p. annoncé la venue de son frère ...** hardly *or* scarcely had he announced the arrival of his brother before ..., no sooner had he announced his brother's arrival than ...

pluvial, -iale, -iaux, -iales [plyvjal, -jo] *adj Géog* pluvial; **eau pluviale** rainwater

pluvier [plyvje] *nm Orn* plover

pluvieux, -ieuse [plyvjø, -jøz] *adj* wet, rainy

pluviner [plyvine] *vi* = **pleuvasser**

pluviomètre [plyvjɔmɛtr] *nm Météo* rain gauge, *Spéc* pluviometer

pluviôse [plyvjoz] *nm Hist Fr* = fifth month of the French Republican calendar (*Jan 20, 21—Feb 18, 19*)

pluviosité [plyvjozite] *nf Météo* rainfall

PLV [peɛlve] *nf* (*abrév* **publicité sur le lieu de vente**) point-of-sale promotion

PME [peɛmə] *nf(pl)* (*abrév* **petite(s) et moyenne(s) entreprise(s)**) small business(es), small and medium-sized business(es); **une P.** a small business

PMI [peɛmi] *nf* (*abrév* **petite et moyenne industrie**) small (and medium-sized) industries

PMU [peɛmy] *nm* (*abrév* **Pari Mutuel Urbain**) = state-run betting system, *Br* ≈ tote

PNB [peɛnbe] *nm Écon* (*abrév* **Produit national brut**) GNP

pneu [pnø] *nm* (a) *Aut* tyre, *US* tire; **avoir des pneus lisses** to have worn tyres; **avoir un p. à plat/crevé** to have a flat/a puncture (b) (*lettre exprès*) express letter (*sent through a pneumatic despatch system*)

▶ **pneu**: **p. à architecture radiale** radial-ply tyre; **p. à ceinture** braced *or* belted tyre; **p. à clous, p. clouté** studded tyre; **pneus jumelés** twin tyres; **p. neige** snow tyre; **p. pluie** wet-weather tyre; **p. sans chambre** tubeless tyre; **p. à structure diagonale** cross-ply tyre; **p. à structure radiale** radial tyre; **p. taille basse** low-profile tyre; **p. temps sec** dry-weather tyre; **p. tout-temps** all-weather tyre; **p. tout-terrain** all-terrain tyre; **p. à usage mixte** town-and-country tyre

pneumatique [pnømatik] **1** *adj* pneumatic; (*canoë*) inflatable; **canot p.** rubber dinghy; **matelas/pistolet p.** air mattress/gun **2** *nm* = **pneu**

pneumocoque [pnømɔkɔk] *nm Biol* pneumococcus

pneumologie [pnømɔlɔʒi] *nf Méd* pneumology

pneumologue [pnømɔlɔg] *n Méd* lung specialist

pneumonie [pnømɔni] *nf Méd* pneumonia

pneumothorax [pnømotɔraks] *nm Méd* pneumothorax

Pô (le) [ləpo] *nm Géog* the (River) Po

PO (a) *Com* (*abrév* **par ordre**) by order (b) *Rad* (*abrév* **petites ondes**) MW

pochade [pɔʃad] *nf* quick sketch

pochard, -arde [pɔʃar, -ard] *n F* drunk(ard)

poche¹ [pɔʃ] *nf* (a) (*partie de vêtement*) pocket; **p. intérieure** inside pocket; **p. plaquée** patch pocket; **p. de poitrine** breast pocket; **p. revolver** hip pocket; *F* **faire les poches à qn** to go through *or* rifle sb's pockets; **argent de p.** pocket money; **calculatrice de p.** pocket calculator; **carnet de p.** pocketbook; **livre de p.** paperback; **j'en suis de ma p.** I'm out of pocket (by it); **payer de sa p.** to pay out of one's own pocket; *Fig* **connaître qn/qch comme sa p.** to know sb/sth inside out *or* like the back of one's hand; *Fig F* **se remplir les poches** to make a packet; **j'ai cent francs en p.** I've got a hundred francs on me; **mettre qch dans sa p.** to put sth in one's pocket, to pocket sth; *F* **mettez ça dans votre p. (et votre mouchoir dessus)** put that in your pipe and smoke it; *Fig* **les mains dans les poches** without a care in the world; **il n'a pas sa langue dans sa p.** he's got plenty to say for himself; **ne pas avoir les yeux dans sa p.** to keep one's eyes open; **elle l'a mis dans sa p.** she's got him eating out of her hand; *F* **c'est dans la p.** it's in the bag

(b) (*sac*) bag; **p. à cartes** map case *or* holder; **p. à tabac** tobacco pouch; *Fig* **acheter chat en p.** to buy a pig in a poke

(c) (*amas de substance*) pocket; **p. de pétrole** pocket of oil; **p. d'air** *Av* air pocket; (*dans une pipe*) airlock

(d) (*déformation*) bag; **pantalon qui fait des poches aux genoux** trousers that are baggy *or* that bag at the knees; **poches sous les yeux** bags under the eyes

(e) *Biol, Méd, Anat* sac; (*d'un kangourou etc*) pouch

(f) (*filet de chasse*) purse *or* bag net; **p. de chalut** purse seine

(g) *Fig* (*secteur*) pocket; **p. de résistance/pauvreté** pocket of resistance/deprivation

▶ **poche**: *Tech* **p. à couler** *ou* **de coulée** casting ladle; *Culin* **p. à douille** piping bag; **p. des eaux** amniotic sac

poche² *nm F* (*livre*) paperback; **paru en (collection de) p.** published in paperback

poché [pɔʃe] *adj* (a) *Culin* **œuf p.** poached egg (b) *F* **œil p.** black eye

pocher [pɔʃe] **1** *vt* (a) *Culin* (*œuf, poisson*) to poach (b) *Beaux-Arts* to dash off (c) *F* **p. l'œil à qn** to give sb a black eye; **la ferme ou je te poche un œil!** shut up, or I'll give you one! **2** *vi* (*de vêtements*) to go *or* get baggy, to bag; **mon pantalon poche aux genoux** my trousers are going *or* getting baggy at the knees

pochette [pɔʃɛt] *nf* (a) (*enveloppe*) pouch; (*pour papiers*) envelope; (*pour stylos, articles de toilette*) case; (*d'un disque*) sleeve; (*pour protéger document*) document cover; **p. d'expédition de disquette** disk mailer; **p. matelassée** Jiffy bag®, padded envelope; **p. d'allumettes** book of matches; **p.-surprise** lucky bag; *F* **il a eu son permis dans une p.-surprise** he's a lousy driver (b) (*petit mouchoir*) (breast) pocket handkerchief

pochoir [pɔʃwar] *nm* stencil; **passer qch au p.** to stencil sth; **motifs au p.** stencils, stencil(led) patterns; **brosse à p.** stencil(ling) brush

pochon [pɔʃɔ̃] *nm Région* (a) (*sac*) bag (b) (*grande louche*) ladle

pochothèque [pɔʃɔtɛk] *nf* paperback shop; (*rayon*) paperback section

podagre [pɔdagr] *Vieilli* **1** *nf* gout **2** *n* gout sufferer **3** *adj* suffering from gout

podium [pɔdjɔm] *nm* podium; **monter sur le p.** to mount *or* take to the podium

podologie [pɔdɔlɔʒi] *nf Méd* chiropody, *Am* podiatry

podologue [pɔdɔlɔg] *n Méd* chiropodist, *Am* podiatrist

podomètre [pɔdɔmɛtr] *nm* pedometer

poêle¹ [pwal] *nf* frying pan, *Am* skillet; **passer qch à la p.** to fry sth

poêle² *nm* (*appareil de chauffage*) stove; **p. à feu continu** slow-burning stove; **p. à bois/à mazout** wood(-burning)/oil stove

poêle³ *nm* (a) *Hist* (*dans un mariage catholique*) canopy (b) (*drap*) pall; **tenir les cordons du p.** to be a pallbearer

poêlée [pwale] *nf* panful

poêler [pwale] *vt* to fry

poêlon [pwalɔ̃] *nm* casserole (dish)

poème [pɔɛm] *nm* poem; **p. symphonique/en prose** symphonic/prose poem; *F* **c'est tout un p.** (*personne*) he's quite a character; (*situation*) it's quite a business *or* a palaver *or Br* a carry-on

poésie [pɔezi] *nf* (a) (*art*) poetry; **écrire** *ou* **faire de la p.** to write poetry; *Fig* **la p. du style/film** the poetry of the style/film; **tu manques de p.** you don't have any soul; **une région pleine de p.** a region full of (poetic) charm; **la p. des grandes villes américaines** the romance of the great American cities (b) (*poème*) poem, piece of poetry

poète [pɔɛt] *nm aussi Fig* poet; **elle est devenue le grand p. de son temps** she became the greatest poet of her age

poétesse [pɔetɛs] *nf* woman poet, poetess

poétique [pɔetik] **1** *adj* (*inspiration, licence etc*) poetic; **l'art p.** the art of poetry **2** *nf* poetics

poétiquement [pɔetikmɑ̃] *adv* poetically

poétiser [pɔetize] *vt* to poeticize

pogne [pɔɲ] *nf Arg* (*main*) paw, mitt

pognon [pɔɲɔ̃] *nm F* (*argent*) dough, bread, *Br* lolly

pogrom(e) [pogrom] *nm* pogrom

poids [pwa] *nm* (a) weight; (*lourdeur*) weight, heaviness; **de tout son p.** with all one's weight, with the whole of one's weight; **surveiller son p.** to watch one's weight; **perdre du p.** to lose weight; **vendre au p.** to sell by weight; **être plié sous le p. d'un sac** to be weighed down by a sack; **ajouter qch pour faire le p.** to put sth in to make up the weight; **ne pas faire le p.** to fail to come up to weight *or* to make the (minimum) weight; *Fig F* **il ne fait pas le p.** he's not up to the job *or* up to scratch *or* up to it; **faire le p. face à la**

concurrence to measure up to the competition; **le parti ne fait pas le p. devant le problème** the party does not measure up to the problem

(**b**) (*charge*) (*dans une horloge, sur une balance*) weight; *Sp* shot; **un p. de 20 kilos** a 20-kilo weight; *Admin* **p. et mesures** weights and measures; **étalonnage des p.** standardization of weights; *Sp* **lancer le p.** to put the shot

(**c**) *Fig* (*charge pénible, écrasante*) burden; *Litt* **le p. des ans** the weight of the years; **le p. des impôts** the burden of taxation; **p. de la fiscalité** tax burden; **le p. de ses soucis** the burden of his worries

(**d**) *Fig* (*importance*) weight; **donner du p. à qch** to give weight to sth; **cette région finira par avoir autant de p. que Paris** this region will eventually carry as much weight as Paris; **son opinion a un certain p.** his opinion carries a certain weight

▶ **poids**: **p. atomique** atomic weight; **p. brut** gross weight; **p. en charge** laden weight; *Boxe* **p. coq** bantamweight; **p. embarqué** shipped weight; *Boxe* **p. léger** lightweight; **p. lourd** *Aut* heavy goods vehicle, HGV, heavy lorry *or Am* truck; *Boxe* heavyweight; *Fig* **un p. lourd de la politique** a political heavyweight; *Boxe* **p. mi-moyen** welterweight; *Mktg* **p. mort** cash trap, dog, dodo; *Fig* **c'est un p. mort** he's a dead weight; *Boxe* **p. mouche** flyweight; *Boxe* **p. moyen** middleweight; **p. net** net weight; *Aut* **p. en ordre de marche** kerb weight; **p. plume** *Boxe* featherweight; *Fig* lightweight; **p. remorqué** tow weight; *Com* **p. rendu** delivered weight; **p. spécifique** *Phys* specific weight; *Ch* specific gravity; *Com* **p. de taxation** chargeable weight; **p. total autorisé** maximum permissible weight; **p. utile** live weight; *Av* payload; **p. à vide** *Aut* unloaded weight, kerb weight; *Com* tare; *Boxe* **p. welter** welterweight

poignant [pwaɲɑ̃] *adj* (*moment, pensée*) poignant; (*expérience, spectacle, lecture etc*) harrowing

poignard [pwaɲar] *nm* dagger; **coup de p.** stab; **donner un coup de p. à qn** to stab sb; **recevoir un coup de p. dans le dos** to be stabbed in the back

poignarder [pwaɲarde] *vt* to stab, *F* to knife; **se faire p.** to get stabbed *or F* knifed

poigne [pwaɲ] *nf* grip, grasp; *Fig* **homme à p.** *ou* **qui a de la p.** strong *or* forceful man; *Fig* **un chef d'état à p.** a strong head of state, a head of state with a firm grip

poignée [pwaɲe] *nf* (**a**) (*quantité contenue dans une main*) (*de farine, de bonbons etc*) handful; (*de billets de banque*) fistful; **à** *ou* **par poignées** by the handful, in handfuls (**b**) (*petit nombre*) handful; **p. d'hommes** handful of men (**c**) (*de porte, sac*) handle; (*de pistolet*) grip; (*d'épée*) hilt; *Aut* **p. de maintien** passenger assist handle, grab handle; *Aut* **p. de portière** door handle (**d**) **p. de main** handshake; **donner une p. de main à qn** to shake hands with sb, to shake sb's hand

poignet [pwaɲɛ] *nm* (**a**) *Anat* wrist; *Fig* **faire qch à la force du p.** to do sth by sheer strength *or* brute force; (*à force de travail*) to do sth by sheer hard work (**b**) (*d'un vêtement*) cuff; (*bracelet, brassard*) wristband

poil [pwal] *nm* (**a**) (*d'un animal*) hair; (*pelage*) coat; **poils de chat** cat hairs; **p. de chameau** camelhair; **à p. long/ras** long-/short-haired; **cheval d'un beau p.** sleek horse; **chien au p. rude/à p. dur** wire-haired/rough-coated dog; *Fig* **caresser qn dans le sens du p.** to rub sb up the right way; *Fig F* **tomber sur le p. de qn** to lay into *or* to go for sb; *Arch* **monter un cheval à p.** to ride a horse bareback; **les poils d'une brosse** the bristles of a brush

(**b**) *Tex* (*d'un tissu*) nap; (*du velours*) pile

(**c**) (*d'une personne*) hair; **poils du visage** facial hair; **poils follets** down; *F* **à p.** stark naked, *Br* starkers; *F* **se mettre à p.** to strip off; *F* **avoir un p. dans la main** to be bone idle *or* workshy; *F* **ne pas avoir un p. sur le caillou** to be as bald as a coot; *F* **avoir du p. aux pattes** to have hairy legs; *Fig* **reprendre du p. de la bête** to regain (one's) strength, to pick up, *F* to perk up; *Fig F* **de tous poils** of all sorts *or* kinds; *F* **être de bon/mauvais p.** to be in a good/bad mood; *F* **au quart de p.** perfectly; *F* **à un p. près** very nearly; **à un p. près il ratait son examen** he very nearly failed his exam; **nous avons payé la même chose à un p. près** we paid more or less the same, we paid the same or as near as makes no difference; *F* **un p. plus haut/moins vite** a fraction *or* a touch higher/slower; *F* **au p.** great, fantastic

(**d**) (*d'une plante*) hair

(**e**) **p. à gratter** itching powder

poilant [pwalɑ̃] *adj F* hilarious, screamingly funny

poiler (se) [səpwale] *vpr F* to kill oneself *or* to die laughing

poilu [pwaly] **1** *adj* (*qui a des poils*) hairy; **p. comme un singe** hairy as an ape **2** *nm F* poilu (*French soldier 1914-1918*)

poinçon [pwɛ̃sɔ̃] *nm* (**a**) (*pointeau*) (*de graveur*) style, burin; (*de cordonnier*) awl, bradawl; *Couture* bodkin; **p. à glace** ice pick (**b**) (*matrice*) die, stamp; **p. à chiffrer** number punch (**c**) (*marque*) stamp; **p. de contrôle** hallmark (stamp)

poinçonnage [pwɛ̃sɔnaʒ], **poinçonnement** [pwɛ̃sɔnmɑ̃] *nm* (*de métal, cuir*) punching; (*contrôle par perforation*) punching, clipping; (*estampillage*) stamping; (*d'or, d'argent*) hallmarking

poinçonner [pwɛ̃sɔne] *vt* (*métal, cuir*) to punch; (*contrôler*) to punch, to clip; (*estampiller*) to stamp; (*or, argent*) to hallmark

poinçonneur, -euse [pwɛ̃sɔnœr, -øz] **1** *n* (*personne*), *Ind* puncher; (*à la gare*) ticket puncher **2** *nf* **poinçonneuse** punching machine

poindre [pwɛ̃dr] *vi* (*prp* **poignant**; *pp* **point**; *pr ind* **il point, ils poignent**; *imp* **il poignait**; *p hist* **il poignit**; *fu* **il poindra**; *used esp in third person and in inf*) (*du jour*) to dawn, to break; (*des plantes, des étoiles*) to appear, to come out; **le jour point à l'horizon** day is breaking; **p. à l'horizon** to come into view

poing [pwɛ̃] *nm* fist; **se battre poings nus** to fight with one's bare fists; **sabre/revolver au p.** sword/revolver in hand; **serrer les poings** to clench one's fists; **menacer qn du p., montrer le p. à qn** to shake one's fist at sb; **les poings sur les hanches** hands on hips, arms akimbo; **dormir à poings fermés** to sleep soundly *or* like a log; **coup de p.** punch; **coup de p. (américain)** knuckleduster; **donner un coup de p. à qn** to punch sb; **recevoir un coup de p.** to be punched; *F* **envoyer son p. dans la figure de qn,** *très F* **mettre son p. sur** *ou* **dans la gueule de qn** to give sb a punch in the face, *F* to bash *or* smash sb's face in; **taper du p. sur la table** to bang one's fist (down) on the table, to pound the table; *Fig* to put one's foot down; **lever le p.** to give a raised-fist salute; **ils défilaient le p. levé** they marched past with their fists raised *or* with raised fists

point[1] [pwɛ̃] *nm* (**a**) (*dans l'espace*) point, spot, place; *aussi Fig* **p. de départ** starting point, point of departure; **p. de vue** (*panorama*) view; *Fig* (*opinion*) point of view, viewpoint, standpoint; **au** *ou* **du p. de vue international/économique** from an international/economic point of view *or* viewpoint; *F* **du** *ou* **au p. de vue caractère/rapidité** as far as character/speed is concerned, character-wise/speed-wise; **en tous points** in every way, in all respects; *Tech, Fig* **p. critique** critical point; *Av* **essai au p. fixe** ground run

(**b**) (*dans le temps*) point; **le p. du jour** daybreak, dawn; **être sur le p. de faire qch** to be about to do sth, to be on the point *or* verge of doing sth; **sur le p. de mourir** at *or* on the point of death; **arriver à p. nommé** *ou* **juste à p.** to arrive just at the right moment; **tout vient à p. à qui sait attendre** everything comes to him who waits

(**c**) (*question*) point; **p. de droit** point of law; **le p. capital** the main point; **traiter un problème en trois points** to deal with a problem in three stages; **mettre son** *ou* **un p. d'honneur à ne pas céder** to make it a point of honour not to yield; **n'ayez aucune crainte sur ce p.** don't worry on that score *or* on that count; **je suis d'accord avec vous sur ce p.** I agree with you on that point; **exécuter un ordre p. par p.** to carry out an order exactly *or* to the letter

(**d**) *Couture* stitch; **faire un p. à un vêtement** to put a few stitches in a garment; **p. arrière** backstitch; **p. de Bruxelles** Brussels lace; **p. de chaînette** chainstitch; **p. de chausson** herringbone stitch; **p. de croix** cross-stitch; **p. devant** *ou* **glissé** *ou* **coulé** running stitch; **p. de feston** buttonhole stitch; **p. de languette** blanket stitch; **p. noué** knot stitch; **p. perdu** blind *or* slip stitch; **coudre qch à points perdus** to blindstitch *or* slipstitch sth; **p. roulé** whipping

(**e**) *Tricot* stitch; **p. de riz** moss stitch; **p. mousse** garter stitch

(**f**) **p. de côté** (*douleur*) stitch (in one's side); **avoir un p. au dos** to have a stabbing pain in one's back

(**g**) *Naut, Av* **p. estimé** dead reckoning (position); **faire le p.** to take bearings, to find one's position

(**h**) *Opt* **au p.** in focus; **mettre au p.** (*lentilles, objectif, caméra etc*) to focus; (*moteur*) to tune; (*mécanisme*) to adjust; (*technique*) to perfect; (*projet, stratégie*) to finalize; **mise au p.** (*de lentilles, d'objectif etc*) focusing; (*d'un moteur*) tuning; (*d'un mécanisme*) adjusting; (*d'une technique*) perfecting; (*d'un projet, d'une stratégie*) finalization, finalizing; **leur organisation n'est pas vraiment au p.** their organization is really not up to scratch; **faire le p.** to take stock; **faire le p. sur l'affaire Martin** to take stock of the Martin affair; *Vieilli* **recherche et mise au p.** research and development

(**i**) (*marque*), *Typ* dot; (*sur les dés*) pip; **p. (final)** full stop, *Am* period; **mettre les points sur les i** to dot one's i's; *Fig* to make one's meaning perfectly plain; **deux points** colon; **(trois) points de suspension** suspension points; (*en parlant ou en dictant*) dot, dot, dot; *F* **tu restes ici, un p., c'est tout!**

ou **p. final!** *ou* **p. à la ligne!** you're staying here and that's final *or* that's that!, *Am* you're staying here, period!; *Télécom* **points et traits** (*de l'alphabet Morse*) dots and dashes; *Typ* **caractères de huit points** eight-point type; *Typ* **points par pouce** dots per inch

(j) (*marque visible*) speck, spot, dot; **le navire n'est qu'un p. à l'horizon** the ship is a mere speck on the horizon

(k) (*phase, degré*) point, stage; (*étendue*) degree, extent; *Culin* **(cuit) à p.** done to a turn; (*steak*) medium-rare; **jusqu'à un certain p.** to a certain extent, up to a (certain) point; **au p. où en sont les choses** as matters stand, as things are; **au p. où j'en suis** the stage I've reached; **à ce p. que ..., à tel p. que ..., au p. que ...** to such a point *or* an extent that ..., so much so that ...; **ils étaient déçus au p. qu'ils ont préféré rentrer directement** they were so disappointed that they preferred to return right away; **vous n'êtes pas malade à ce p.-là** you're not as ill as all that; **au dernier p.** to *or* in the last degree

(l) mal en p. in a bad way

(m) (*de jeux*) point; *Scol* mark; **marquer les points** to keep (the) score; **elle a marqué 10 points** she scored 10 points; *Fig* **là, tu marques un p.!** that's one up to you!; *Boxe* **gagner aux points** to win on points; **rendre des points à qn** to give sb points; *Fig* to be more than a match for sb; *Scol* **bon p.** good mark

(n) (*unité*) point; **l'indice des prix gagne/perd deux points** the retail price index has gone up/down (by) two points

▶ **point**: *Aut* **p. allumage** firing point; *Aut* **p. d'ancrage** anchor(age) point; **p. d'appui** *Mil etc* base of operations; *Méd* pressure point; *Tech* (*de levier*) fulcrum; *Fig* (*d'un argument, d'une théorie*) basis; *Naut* **p. d'attache** mooring (post); *Géog* **points cardinaux** cardinal points, points of the compass; *Ordinat* **p. de césure** breakpoint, hyphenation point; **p. chaud** (*pendant une guerre*) hot spot, trouble spot; *Fig* **les points chauds de l'actualité** the most topical issues of the day; *Typ* **points de conduite** dotted leader; **p. de congélation** freezing point; *TV, Cin* **p. diffus** soft focus; *Mktg* **p. de distribution** distribution outlet; **p. d'eau** (*dans le désert*) waterhole; (*dans un camping*) water supply point; **p. d'ébullition à sec** dry boiling point; **p. d'éclair** flash point; *TV etc* **p. d'entrée** (*d'une bande*) inpoint; **p. d'exclamation** exclamation mark *or Am* point; **p. faible** weak point; *TV, Cin* **p. focal** focus; **p. fort** strong point; **p. de fusion** melting point; **p. de graissage** lubricating point; *Aut* **p. d'inflammation** point of ignition; **p. d'interrogation** *Typ, Fig* question mark; *Mktg* (*produit*) question mark; *Fig* **ce qu'il lui a dit? on ne sait pas, c'est le p. d'interrogation** what did he say to him? we don't know, that's the question we're all asking; **p. d'intersection** (point of) intersection; *Aut* **p. de levage** (*au cric*) jacking *or* jack point; *Math* **points limites** limit points; **p. de mire** target; *Fig* **p. de mire de tous les yeux** (*critiqué*) target for criticism; (*admiré*) focus of attention, *Fml* cynosure; *TV, Cin* **p. de montage** edit point; **p. mort** *Aut* neutral; *Fin* breakeven (point); *Fig* **être au p. mort** to be at a standstill; **p. noir** (*comédon*) blackhead; *Fig* problem; (*à l'avenir*) cloud on the horizon; *Aut* accident blackspot; (*embouteillage*) blackspot; *Mus* **p. d'orgue** pause, fermata; *Fig* climax, highpoint; *Aut* **p. de prise** (*d'embrayage*) take-up point; **p. prix** price point; **p. de référence** benchmark; *Com* **p. de saturation** saturation point; *Tech* **p. de soudure** weld spot; **p. de tabulation** *Ordinat* tab marker; *Typ* tab set; *Aut* **p. talon** accelerator heel point; *Com* **p. de vente** point of sale; (*magasin*) sales outlet; **disponible dans votre p. de vente habituel** available at your local stockist; *Com* **p. de vente au détail** retail outlet; *Com* **p. de vente électronique** electronic point-of-sale, EPOS

point² *adv* [①B60,B] *Vieilli, Litt, Dial* = **pas²**; **peu ou p.** little or not at all; **le connaissez-vous? – p.** do you know him? – not at all; **depuis plusieurs semaines, p. de nouvelles** there's been no news (at all) for several weeks

pointage [pwɛ̃taʒ] *nm* **(a)** (*contrôle*) (*de noms sur une liste*) checking, ticking off; (*de votes*) counting; *Naut* (*d'une carte marine*) pricking; (*d'une position sur une carte*) plotting; (*à l'usine*) timekeeping; (*à l'arrivée*) clocking in; (*au départ*) clocking out; **p. des salariés** signing-in of employees **(b)** *Mus* (*d'une note*) dotting **(c)** (*d'un télescope*) pointing, levelling, training; (*de fusil*) aiming, training

pointe [pwɛ̃t] *nf* **(a)** (*extrémité*) (*d'aiguille, de couteau etc*) point; (*de flèche*) tip, head; (*de balle*) nose; (*de chaussure*) toe; (*d'une flèche d'église*) top; (*de sein*) nipple; *Rail* **p. d'une aiguille** point of a switchblade; **à la p. de l'épée** at the point of a sword; *Fig Vieilli* **j'ai obtenu mon contrat à la p. de l'épée** I had to fight hard to get my contract; **en p.** pointed; **partir en p., former une p.** to taper to a point; **tailler en p.** to cut (in)to a point; (*crayon*) to sharpen; *F* **je vais te tailler les oreilles en p.!** I'll box your ears!; **p. de lance** spearhead; **marcher/se tenir sur la p. des pieds** to walk/stand on tiptoe; **entrer sur la p. des pieds** to tiptoe in; **faire des pointes** to go up on points

(b) (*moment d'intensité*), *Math, Él, Méd* (*d'une courbe, d'une charge, de la fièvre*) peak; *Sp* **p. de vitesse** burst of speed, spurt; **faire une p. de vitesse** to put on a burst of speed *or* a spurt; **avec des pointes de vitesse de 160 km/h** with a top speed of 160 km/h; **dans les pointes de vitesse, on peut faire du 200 km/h** at top speed you can do 200 km/h; **vitesse de p.** top *or* highest speed; **heure de p.** rush hour; **période de p.** peak period; *Litt* **p. du jour** daybreak, dawn

(c) *Mil* (*d'une sentinelle avancée*) point; **nous avons poussé une p. jusqu'à** *ou* **sur Paris** we pressed on *or* pushed on to Paris; *Naut* **tir en p.** firing ahead; **être à la p. du progrès/de la recherche** to be in *or* at the forefront of progress/of research, to be at the cutting *or* leading edge of progress/of research; **à la p. de l'actualité** in the headlines, very much in the news; *Fig* **les secteurs de p.** the high-tech industries, the most advanced sectors of industry; **industrie de p.** high-tech *or* state-of-the-art industry; **technologie de p.** state-of-the-art technology, leading-edge technology; **c'est de la technologie de p.** it's very state-of-the-art

(d) (*petite quantité, trace*) hint, touch, tinge; **parler avec une p. d'accent** to speak with a hint of an accent; **p. d'ironie** touch *or* hint *or* tinge of irony; **p. d'ail/de vanille** touch of garlic/dash of vanilla

(e) (*raillerie*) barb, pointed remark; **lancer des pointes à qn** to make digs at sb

(f) *Géog* **p. (de terre)** headland, foreland

(g) (*outil*) (*de maçon*) point; *Menuis* **p. carrée** bradawl; **p. à tracer** scribe

(h) (*clou*) nail; (*pour tapis*) tack; *Sp* (*sur une chaussure*) spike; **chaussures à pointes** spiked shoes, spikes; **casque à p.** spiked helmet

(i) (*lange*) nappy, *Am* diaper; (*écharpe, foulard*) (triangular) scarf

▶ **pointe**: **p. d'asperge** asparagus tip; **p. Bic®** ballpoint (pen), *Br* Biro®; *Méd* **pointes de feu** ignipuncture; *Beaux-Arts* **p. sèche** (dry) point; (*procédé*) dry-point (engraving); *Él* **p. de tension** surge, spike

pointeau, -eaux [pwɛ̃to] *nm* **(a)** *MecE* centre *or US* center punch; (*de carburateur*) needle **(b)** *Vieilli* (*personne*) timekeeper **(c)** (*sur un autocuiseur*) pressure valve

pointer¹ [pwɛ̃te] **1** *vt* **(a)** (*vérifier*) (*noms sur une liste*) to check, to tick off; (*votes*) to count; *Naut* (*carte marine*) to prick; (*position sur une carte*) to plot

(b) (*dresser*) **p. les oreilles** to prick up its ears; **le chien arriva en pointant le bout de son museau** the dog arrived with its muzzle in the air; *Fig* **il pointa son nez à la porte** his face appeared around the door, he peeped around the door; *Fig* **s'il pointe son nez ici, je lui donne une gifle!** if he shows his face here, I'll give him one!; *Fig* **il n'a pas pointé le bout de son nez depuis longtemps** he hasn't looked in *or* been round for a long time

(c) (*diriger*) (*télescope*) to point **(sur** at), to train **(sur** on); (*fusil*) to aim, to level **(sur** at), to train **(sur** on); (*spot, projecteur*) to train **(sur** on); *Ordinat* (*curseur*) to position **(sur** on); *Ordinat* **pointé** (*mot, page*) where the cursor is; **j'ai pointé le doigt vers lui** I pointed (my finger) at him

(d) *Mus* (*note*) to dot; **note pointée** dotted note

(e) *Vieilli* (*piquer*) (*avec une épée*) to stab; (*avec une aiguille*) to prick

2 *vi* **(a)** (*d'employé*) (*en arrivant*) to sign in; (*en partant*) to sign out; **p. (à l'arrivée/à la sortie)** (*à l'usine*) to clock in/out

(b) (*apparaître*) to appear; (*d'une plante*) to come up; (*d'un oiseau*) to soar; (*d'un cheval*) to rear up; (*du jour*) to dawn; **ses seins pointaient sous son corsage** her firm breasts were clearly outlined beneath her bodice; **ses os pointaient** his bones were sticking out; **le clocher de l'église pointait vers un ciel d'azur** the church steeple soared into *or* rose towards a bright blue sky

(c) (*au jeu de boules*) = to get one's ball nearest to the jack

3 se pointer *vpr F* to turn up, to show up

pointer² [pwɛ̃tɛr] *nm* (*chien*) pointer

pointeur, -euse [pwɛ̃tœr, -øz] **1** *n* (*contrôleur*) *Ind* timekeeper; *Sp* scorer, marker **2** *nf* **pointeuse** (*horloge*) (time)clock **3** *nm Ordinat* pointer; **p.-balle** beachball pointer; **p.-croix** crosshair pointer; **p.-montre** watch pointer; **p. de pile** stack pointer; **p. en I** I-beam

pointillage [pwɛ̃tijaʒ] *nm Beaux-Arts* dotting; (*plus serré*) stippling

pointillé [pwɛ̃tije] **1** *adj* (*ligne*) dotted; (*gravure*) stippled; *Tex*

(*tissu*) pinhead **2** *nm* **(a)** (*trait*) dotted line; (*sur une feuille détachable*) perforations; **détacher suivant les pointillés** tear along the dotted line/the perforations **(b)** (*technique de dessin*) stippling; **dessin en p.** stippled design; **ligne en p.** dotted line; *Fig* **on pouvait lire en p. des allusions à son passé glorieux** reading between the lines we saw certain allusions to his glorious past
pointiller[1] [pwɛ̃tije] *vt* **(a)** (*percer de petits trous*) to dot **(b)** *Beaux-Arts* to stipple
pointiller[2] *vi Péj Arch* to cavil (over trifles), to split hairs
pointilleux, -euse [pwɛ̃tijø, -øz] *adj* particular, fussy, finicky, *F* pernickety (**sur** about)
pointillisme [pwɛ̃tijism] *nm Beaux-Arts* pointillism
pointilliste [pwɛ̃tijist] *adj, n Beaux-Arts* pointillist
pointu [pwɛ̃ty] **1** *adj* **(a)** (*en forme de pointe*) pointed; (*aigu*) (*couteau*) sharp, pointed; (*voix*) shrill **(b)** *Fig* (*susceptible*) (*ton de la voix, humeur*) touchy; **prendre un air p.** to bridle **(c)** *Fig* (*spécialisé*) specialized, specialist **2** *adv Région F* **parler p.** to speak with a Parisian accent
pointure [pwɛ̃tyr] *nf* (*de chaussures, de gants, de coiffure*) size; **quelle est votre p. (de gants/de chaussures)?, quelle p. faites-vous?** what size (gloves/shoes) do you take?, what's your (glove/shoe) size?; *Fig F* **une (grosse) p. du cinéma français/de la physique nucléaire** a big name in French cinema/in nuclear physics
point-virgule, *pl* **points-virgules** *nm* semicolon
poire [pwar] *nf* **(a)** (*fruit*) pear; **entre la p. et le fromage** at the end of the meal; *Fig* **garder une p. pour la soif** to put something by for a rainy day; *Fig* **couper la p. en deux** to compromise; (*faire la moyenne entre deux quantités*) to split the difference

(b) (*objet en forme de poire*) (*d'un appareil photo*) (pear-shaped) bulb; (*d'un interrupteur électrique*) (pear-shaped) switch; **en forme de p.** pear-shaped; **p. à lavement** enema bag

(c) *F* (*tête*) mug, face; **il a une bonne p.** he's got a nice enough face, he looks nice enough; **en pleine p.** right in the face

(d) *F* (*idiot*) sucker, mug; **je ne suis pas une p.!** I'm no sucker *or Br* mug!; **je suis vraiment trop bonne p., je lui pardonne toujours tout** I'm a real sucker *or Br* mug, I let him get away with everything; **et moi, bonne p., j'ai accepté** and like the sucker *or* mug that I am, I accepted
poiré [pware] *nm* perry
poireau, -eaux [pwaro] *nm* (*légume*) leek; *F* **faire le p.** to be kept hanging around *or* waiting, to kick *or* cool one's heels
poireauter [pwarote] *vi F* to be kept hanging around *or* waiting, to kick *or* cool one's heels; **faire p. qn** to keep sb hanging around *or* waiting, to leave sb to kick *or* cool his/her heels
poirée [pware] *nf Bot* white beet
poirier [pwarje] *nm* **(a)** (*arbre*) pear tree; *Gym* **faire le p.** to do a headstand, to stand on one's head **(b)** (*bois*) pear-tree wood
pois [pwa] *nm* **(a)** (*plante*) pea; *Culin* **petits p.** (garden) peas; **purée de p.** thick pea soup; *F* (*brouillard*) peasouper **(b)** (*rond*) spot, (polka) dot; **cravate bleue à p. blancs** blue tie with white spots, blue polka-dot tie; **tissu/robe à p.** spotted *or* polka-dot material/dress
▶ **pois**: **p. carré** marrowfat pea; **p. cassés** split peas; **p. chiche** chickpea; **p. de senteur** sweet pea
poiscaille [pwaskɑj] *n F* fish
poison [pwazɔ̃] **1** *nm* **(a)** (*substance fatale*) poison **(b)** *Fig F* **quel p.!** what a drag *or* bind!, how boring! **2** *n F* (*personne, chien etc*) pest, horror
poissard, -arde [pwasar, -ard] **1** *adj* vulgar, coarse **2** *nf Vieilli Péj* **poissarde** fishwife
poisse [pwas] *nf F* bad luck; **c'est la p.!** just my/our luck!; **porter la p. (à qn)** to bring (sb) bad luck
poisser [pwase] **1** *vt* **(a)** (*engluer*) to pitch; **fil poissé** waxed thread **(b)** (*salir avec une matière gluante*) to make sticky **(c)** *F Vieilli* (*personne*) to nab, to collar **2** *vi* (*d'une substance*) to be sticky
poisseux, -euse [pwasø, -øz] *adj* sticky
poisson [pwasɔ̃] *nm* **(a)** [①**A12,1,g**] fish; **p. d'eau douce/de mer** freshwater/saltwater fish; **prendre un/du p.** to catch a/some fish; **je n'aime pas le p.** I don't like fish; **manger du p.** to eat fish; **p. d'avril!** April fool!; **c'est un p. d'avril** it's an April fool's trick; **être (heureux) comme un p. dans l'eau** to be really in one's element; *F* **engueuler qn comme du p. pourri** to give sb a real mouthful; **se faire engueuler comme du p. pourri** to get a real mouthful; *Prov* **petit p. deviendra grand** great oaks from little acorns grow **(b)** *Astron, Astrol* **les Poissons** Pisces; **être (du signe des) Poissons** to be (a) Pisces
▶ **poisson**: *Ent* **p. d'argent** silverfish; **p. chat** catfish; **p. lune** sunfish; **p. pilote** pilot fish; **p. plat** flatfish; **p. rouge** goldfish; **p. volant** flying fish
poissonnerie [pwasɔnri] *nf* (*magasin*) fish shop, *Br* fishmonger's; (*marché*) fish market
poissonneux, -euse [pwasɔnø, -øz] *adj* full of fish
poissonnier, -ière [pwasɔnje, -jɛr] **1** *n Com* fishmonger, *Am* fish merchant **2** *nm* (*bateau*) = small boat used to buy fish direct from fishing boats **3** *nf* **poissonnière** (*ustensile*) fish kettle
poitevin [pwatvɛ̃] *adj* (*de Poitiers*) of/from Poitiers; (*du Poitou*) of/from Poitou
poitrail [pwatraj] *nm* **(a)** (*partie du corps de certains animaux*) breast; *Fig F* (*poitrine*) chest; **un homme au p. découvert** a man with a bare chest **(b)** (*partie de harnais*) breast strap, breastplate
poitrinaire [pwatrinɛr] *adj, n Vieilli* consumptive
poitrine [pwatrin] *nf* **(a)** (*poumons*) chest; **chanter à pleine p.** to sing at the top of one's voice; **être fragile de la p.** to have a weak chest; *Arch* **s'en aller de la p.** to be dying of consumption; *Mus* **voix de p.** chest voice

(b) (*thorax*) chest, *Litt* breast; (*de femme*) bosom, bust, chest; **serrer qn contre** *ou* **sur sa p.** to hold *or* press *or* clasp sb to one's breast; **tour de p.** (*d'un homme, d'un enfant*) chest (measurement); (*d'une femme*) bust (measurement); **avoir une belle/forte p.** to have a shapely bosom/to be well-endowed; **ne pas avoir de p.** to be flat-chested, to have no bust; **ne pas avoir beaucoup de p.** to be small-chested, to have a small bust; **elle n'a pas encore de p.** her bust hasn't started to develop yet

(c) *Culin* (*de veau*) breast; (*de bœuf*) brisket; (*de porc*) belly
poivrade [pwavrad] *nf Culin* (*sauce*) = sauce made by reducing a heavily peppered mixture of wine and vinegar; **manger des artichauts à la p.** to eat artichokes (raw) with salt and pepper
poivre [pwavr] *nm* pepper; **p. blanc/noir** *ou* **gris** white/black pepper; **p. vert/rouge** green/red pepper; **p. de Cayenne** cayenne (pepper); *Culin* **steak au p.** pepper steak; **grain de p.** peppercorn; **des cheveux p. et sel** pepper-and-salt hair; **une femme p. et sel** a woman with pepper-and-salt hair
poivré [pwavre] *adj* **(a)** (*nourriture*) peppery; (*odeur*) pungent, spicy **(b)** *Fig* (*grivois*) (*histoire*) spicy, juicy
poivrer [pwavre] **1** *vt* to put pepper on/in, to (season with) pepper **2 se poivrer** *vpr F* (*boire*) to get plastered *or* smashed
poivrier [pwavrije] *nm* **(a)** *Bot* pepper plant **(b)** (*petit pot*) pepper pot; (*égrugeoir*) pepper mill
poivrière [pwavrijɛr] *nf* **(a)** (*plantation*) pepper plantation **(b)** (*boîte*) pepper pot **(c)** *Archit* pepperpot (turret)
poivron [pwavrɔ̃] *nm Bot* (sweet) pepper, capsicum, *Am* bell pepper; **p. vert/rouge/jaune** green/red/yellow pepper
poivrot, -ote [pwavro, -ɔt] *n F* drunk
poix [pwa] *nf* pitch; **p. sèche** resin; **p. liquide** tar; **noir comme (de la) p.** pitch black; **collant comme de la p.** sticky as glue
poker [pɔkɛr] *nm Cartes* poker; **faire un p.** to have a game of poker; **p. d'as** (*cartes*) four aces; (*dés*) poker dice; **p. menteur** = type of poker; *Fig* **une partie de p.** a poker game, a game of bluff (and counter-bluff); *Fig* **c'est un coup de p.** it's a game of bluff
polaire [pɔlɛr] **1** *adj* polar; **l'étoile p.** the pole star; **froid p.** intense *or* Arctic cold; **expédition p.** polar expedition, expedition to the (North/South) Pole; **laine p.** fleece, fleecy material; **fourrure p.** fleecy jacket **2** *nf Math* polar; *Astron* **la p.** the pole star
polar [pɔlar] *nm F* (*livre, film*) whodunnit
polard, -arde [pɔlar, -ard] *adj, n Arg* swot; **être p.** to be a swot
polarimètre [pɔlarimɛtr] *nm Phys* polarimeter
polarisable [pɔlarizabl] *adj* polarizable
polarisant [pɔlarizɑ̃] *adj* polarizing
polarisation [pɔlarizasjɔ̃] *nf* **(a)** *Phys* (*de la lumière, d'électrodes*) polarization, polarizing; *Électron* **p. de grille** grid bias; **résistance de p. de grille** bias resistor **(b)** *Fig* (*focalisation*) (*d'attention, d'énergies etc*) focusing
polariscope [pɔlariskɔp] *nm Opt* polariscope
polariser [pɔlarize] **1** *vt Phys, Électron* to polarize; *Fig* (*attention*) to attract; **ce phénomène polarise l'attention de tous** this phenomenon is the focus of everybody's attention; **cette décision a polarisé le mécontentement des masses salariales** this decision has become the focus of the workers' discontent; **p. qn** *ou* **p. l'attention de qn sur qch** to focus sb's attention on sth **2 se polariser** *vpr F* (*de l'attention*) to focus; **se p. sur qch** (*d'une personne*) to focus one's attention on sth
polariseur [pɔlarizœr] *nm Opt* polarizer

polarité [pɔlarite] *nf* polarity
polaroïd® [pɔlarɔid] *nm Phot* polaroid (camera)
polatouche [pɔlatuʃ] *nm Zool* flying squirrel
polder [pɔldɛr] *nm Géog* polder
pôle [pol] *nm* **(a)** *Géog* pole; **P. Nord/Sud** North/South Pole; *Phys* **pôles semblables** like poles; **pôles contraires** opposite poles; **pôles magnétiques** magnetic poles **(b)** *Fig* **p. d'intérêt/d'attraction** focus of interest/centre of attention; **un p. d'attraction économique/touristique** a centre of economic/tourist development; *Écon, Pol* **les pôles de croissance** the main centres of economic growth
polémique [pɔlemik] **1** *adj* polemical **2** *nf* argument, controversy, *Fml* polemic; **faire de la p.** to provoke arguments, to be controversial; **chercher la p.** to look for an argument; **une vive p. s'en suivit** a heated argument ensued
polémiquer [pɔlemike] *vi* to argue
polémiste [pɔlemist] *n* polemicist
polémologie [pɔlemɔlɔʒi] *nf* study of war
polenta [pɔlɛnta] *nf Culin* polenta
pole position [polpozisjɔ̃] *nf* (*dans une course automobile*) **être en p.** to be in pole position
poli[1] [pɔli] **1** *adj* **(a)** (*lisse*) (*métal*) polished, burnished, buffed; (*pierre*) polished **(b)** *Vieilli* (*élégant*) (*style, écrivain*) polished, elegant **2** *nm* shine, polish, gloss
poli[2] *adj* (*courtois*) (*personne, réponse, manières*) polite, civil; **être très p. avec qn** to be very polite *or* very courteous to sb; **il est trop p. pour être honnête** he's so polite that I'm suspicious of him; **peu p.** impolite, rude, discourteous
police[1] [pɔlis] *nf* **(a)** (*maintien de l'ordre*) maintenance of law and order; (*par la police*) policing; **exercer** *ou* **faire la p.** to maintain law and order, to keep order; (*au bureau, dans une classe etc*) to keep order; *Aut Vieilli* **numéro de p.** registration *or Am* license number; **intervention des forces de p.** police intervention, intervention by the police; *Jur* **tribunal de (simple) p.** magistrate's court; *Mil* **salle de p.** guardroom

(b) [①A11,f,ii] (*institution*) **la p.** the police (force); **appeler la p.** to call the police; **appeler p. secours** ≈ to dial 999 *or US* 911 (for the police); **être de** *ou* **dans la p.** to be in *or* to be a member of the police (force); *Fig Hum* **tu n'es pas de la p. à ce que je sache!** what is this, the Spanish Inquisition?, what is this, Twenty Questions?; **p.!, les mains en l'air!** police!, hands up!; **remettre qn entre les mains de la p.** to give sb up to the police; **la p. est à vos trousses** the police are after you *or* are (hot) on your heels; **la guerre des polices** = rivalry between different police departments; **toutes les polices de France sont à ses trousses** the entire French police force are hot on his heels; **p. de la circulation** traffic police; **p. administrative** = administrative branch of the police; **p. judiciaire** *Br* ≈ Criminal Investigation Department, *Am* ≈ Federal Bureau of Investigation; **p. municipale** local police; **la p. nationale** = national police force; **p. mondaine** *ou* **des mœurs** ≈ vice squad; **p. de l'air et des frontières** airport and border police; **p. de l'immigration** immigration police; **p. secrète** secret police; *F* **la p. des polices** ≈ Complaints Investigation Bureau, *Am* Internal Investigation Board; **p. montée** mounted police; **p. parallèle** secret police; **agent de p.** police officer; (*de circulation*) traffic policeman; **inspecteur de p.** = (police) inspector; **commissaire de p.** = (police) superintendent; **préfet de p.** = chief commissioner of police
police[2] *nf* **(a)** *Jur* (insurance) policy; **prendre une p.** to take out a policy; **p. d'assurance (sur la) vie/(contre l')incendie** life insurance/fire insurance policy; **p. d'assurance maritime** marine insurance policy; *Com* **p. de chargement** bill of lading; **p. individuelle crédit acheteur** individual buyer credit policy; **p. individuelle crédit fournisseur** individual supplier credit policy; *Com* **p. ouverte** open policy; **p. tous risques** comprehensive policy, all-risks policy; **p. universelle** worldwide policy; **p. au voyage** travel insurance policy

(b) *Typ, Ordinat* **p. (de caractères)** font; **p. bâton** sans serif font; **p. bitmap** *ou* **pixélisée** bit-mapped font, bitmap font; **p. proportionnelle** proportional font; **p. de taille variable** scalable font; **p. vectorielle** outline font
policé [pɔlise] *adj* civilized
policeman [pɔlisman] *nm* (British) policeman
policer [pɔlise] *vt* **(je poliçai(s); n. poliçons)** **(a)** *Arch* (*gouverner*) **p. un pays** to bring a country under orderly government **(b)** *Arch, Litt* (*civiliser*) to civilize
polichinelle [pɔliʃinɛl] *nm* **(a)** (*marionnette*) Punch; **théâtre de p.** ≈ Punch and Judy show; **secret de p.** open secret; *Fig F* **avoir un p. dans le tiroir** (*être enceinte*) to have a bun in the oven, to be in the pudding club **(b)** *Fig Péj* buffoon; **faire le p.** to act *or* play the fool
policier, -ière [pɔlisje, -jɛr] **1** *adj* (*enquête, État, chien etc*) police; (*roman, film*) detective **2** *nm* [①A11,f,ii] **(a)** (*officier de police*) policeman, police officer; **femme p.** woman police officer **(b)** (*roman*) detective novel; (*film*) detective film
policlinique [pɔliklinik] *nf* outpatients' clinic *or* department
poliment [pɔlimɑ̃] *adv* politely
polio [pɔljo] *Méd* **1** *nf* (*maladie*) polio **2** *n* polio victim
poliomyélite [pɔljɔmjelit] *nf Méd* poliomyelitis
poliomyélitique [pɔljɔmjelitik] *Méd* **1** *adj* (*vaccin*) polio; (*personne*) suffering from polio **2** *n* polio victim
polir [pɔlir] **1** *vt* **(a)** (*poncer*) (*métal*) to polish, to burnish, to buff; (*pierre*) to polish; **poli par l'usage** shiny with use; **poli par l'érosion/le temps** made smooth by erosion/the passage of time **(b)** (*perfectionner*) (*style, discours etc*) to polish (up); (*manières*) to refine **2 se polir** *vpr* **se p. les ongles** to polish *or* buff one's nails
Polisario [pɔlisarjɔ] *nm Pol* **le Front P.** the Polisario
polissage [pɔlisaʒ] *nm* (*de métal*) polishing, burnishing, buffing; (*des ongles*) polishing, buffing
polisseur, -euse [pɔlisœr, -øz] **1** *n* polisher **2** *nf* **polisseuse** (*machine*) polishing machine, polisher
polissoir [pɔliswar] *nm Tech* buffing wheel; (*de graveur*) grinding disc; (*pour les ongles*) nail buffer
polissoire [pɔliswar] *nf* **(a)** (*brosse*) (*pour chaussures*) (polishing) brush **(b)** *Ind* (*atelier*) polishing shop
polisson, -onne [pɔlisɔ̃, -ɔn] **1** *n* **(a)** (*enfant espiègle*) rascal, scamp **(b)** *Vieilli* (*gamin des rues*) street urchin **2** *adj* **(a)** (*méchant*) (*enfant*) naughty, mischievous **(b)** (*coquin, grivois*) smutty; **regard p.** leer
polissonner [pɔlisɔne] *vi Vieilli* (*d'un enfant*) to be mischievous *or* naughty
polissonnerie [pɔlisɔnri] *nf* **(a)** (*espièglerie*) mischievous trick **(b)** *Vieilli* (*parole*) smutty remark; (*plaisanterie*) smutty joke
politesse [pɔlitɛs] *nf* politeness, courtesy; **il est toujours d'une grande p. avec les gens** he is always very polite *or* courteous to people; **dire/faire qch par p.** to say/do sth out of politeness *or* to be polite; **brûler la p. à qn** to leave sb abruptly, to leave without saying goodbye to sb; **faire des politesses à qn** to be polite to sb; **faire échange de politesses** to exchange compliments; **ce serait la moindre des politesses de le prévenir** it's only polite to warn him; **rendre la p. à qn** to return the favour *or US* favor; (*invitation*) to return sb's invitation; (*mauvais tour*) to pay sb back; **formule de p.** closure to a letter
politicaillerie [pɔlitikajri] *nf F Péj* political scheming
politicard, -arde [pɔlitikar, -ard] *F Péj* **1** *n* political schemer **2** *adj* scheming
politicien, -ienne [pɔlitisjɛ̃, -jɛn] **1** *n* politician, *Am F* politico **2** *adj Péj* politicking; **politique politicienne** politicking; **faire de la politique politicienne** to politick
politique [pɔlitik] **1** *adj* **(a)** (*de la société, du gouvernement*) political; **homme/femme p.** politician; **ambitionner une carrière p.** to have political ambitions; **le corps p.** the body politic; **détenu p.** political prisoner; **économie p.** economics, *Vieilli* political economy

(b) *Arch, Litt* (*réponse, choix, conduite*) politic

2 *nf* **(a)** (*de gouvernement, d'entreprise*) policy; **p. intérieure/extérieure** domestic/foreign policy; **suivre** *ou* **adopter une nouvelle p.** to follow *or* adopt a new policy; **la p. de l'autruche** burying one's head in the sand; **pratiquer la p. de l'autruche** to bury one's head in the sand; **pratiquer la p. de la chaise vide** to make a political point by not attending meetings; **p. de la main tendue** policy of the outstretched hand; **pratiquer la p. de la main tendue** to make friendly overtures, to be conciliatory; **la p. du pire** = brinkmanship; *Écon* **p. de la porte ouverte** open-door policy; **p. de droite/gauche** right-wing/left wing policy; **la P. Agricole Commune** the Common Agricultural Policy; **p. commerciale** trade policy; *Mktg* **p. de communication** promotional policy; *Fin* **p. de crédit** credit policy; *Journ* **p. de la rédaction** (*principe*) editorial policy; **p. de plein emploi** policy of full employment; *Mktg* **p. de vente** sales policy; **p. des prix** pricing policy; **p. des salaires** wages policy

(b) [①A10,c] (*affaires publiques*) politics; **parler/discuter p.** to talk/discuss politics; **se lancer dans la p.** to go into politics; **faire de la p.** to be in politics; **tu sais, moi, je ne fais pas de p.!** I'm not politically inclined; *Fig* **p.-fiction** political fantasy *or* fiction; **scénario de p.-fiction** scenario belonging to the realms of political fantasy *or* fiction; **un roman de p.-fiction** a political novel

3 *nm* **(a)** (*personne*) politician

(b) *Fig* (*domaine*) politics; **le p. français** French politics
politiquement [pɔlitikmɑ̃] *adv Pol* politically; *Fig Litt* politically, diplomatically; **p. correct** politically correct

politiquer [pɔlitike] *vi Arch F* to talk politics
politisation [pɔlitizasjɔ̃] *nf* politicization
politiser [pɔlitize] *vt* (*chose*) to politicize, to bring politics into; (*personne*) to politicize; **plus/moins/très politisé** more/less/very politically inclined *or* political
politologie [pɔlitɔlɔʒi] *nf* political science
politologue [pɔlitɔlɔg] *n* political scientist
polka [pɔlka] *nf* polka
pollen [pɔlɛn] *nm* pollen
pollinisation [pɔlinizasjɔ̃] *nf* pollination
polluant [pɔlɥɑ̃] **1** *adj* polluting; **produit p.** pollutant **2** *nm* pollutant
pollué [pɔlɥe] *adj* polluted; **région fortement polluée** highly polluted region, region with a high level of pollution
polluer [pɔlɥe] *vt* to pollute
pollueur, -euse [pɔlɥœr, -øz] **1** *n* polluter; **le principe du p.-payeur** the polluter pays principle **2** *adj* polluting
pollution [pɔlysjɔ̃] *nf* **(a)** (*dégradation de l'environnement*) pollution; **p. atmosphérique** atmospheric *or* air pollution; **p. automobile** traffic pollution **(b)** *Méd* **pollutions nocturnes** wet dreams, *Spéc* nocturnal emissions
polo [polo] *nm* **(a)** *Sp* polo **(b)** (*chemise*) polo shirt
polochon [pɔlɔʃɔ̃] *nm F* bolster; **bataille de polochons** pillow fight; **se battre à coups de polochons** to have a pillow fight
Pologne [pɔlɔɲ] *nf Géog* Poland
polonais, -aise [pɔlɔnɛ, -ɛz] [①**A20**,d] **1** *adj* Polish **2** *nm Ling* Polish **3** *n* **P.** Pole; *F* **soûl comme un P.** as drunk as a lord **4** *nf Mus* **polonaise** polonaise
polonium [pɔlɔnjɔm] *nm Ch* polonium
poltron, -onne [pɔltrɔ̃, -ɔn] **1** *adj* cowardly **2** *n* coward
poltronnerie [pɔltrɔnri] *nf* cowardice
polyacide [pɔliasid] *adj, nm Ch* polyacid
polyamide [pɔliamid] *nm Ch* polyamide
polyandre [pɔljɑ̃dr] *adj* polyandrous
polyandrie [pɔljɑ̃dri] *nf* polyandry
polyarthrite [pɔliartrit] *nf Méd* polyarthritis
polychrome [pɔlikrom] *adj* polychrome, polychromatic
polychromie [pɔlikromi] *nf* polychromy
polyclinique [pɔliklinik] *nf Méd* polyclinic
polycopie [pɔlikɔpi] *nf* (*procédé*) duplicating, duplication; (*document*) duplicate
polycopié [pɔlikɔpje] **1** *adj* duplicated **2** *nm* duplicate; *Scol, Univ* (duplicated) course material; (*plus petit*) handout
polycopier [pɔlikɔpje] *vt* to duplicate
polyculture [pɔlikyltyr] *nf Agr* mixed farming
polydactyle [pɔlidaktil] *adj* polydactyl
polyèdre [pɔliɛdr] *Géom* **1** *adj* polyhedral **2** *nm* polyhedron
polyédrique [pɔliedrik] *adj Géom* polyhedral
polyester [pɔliɛstɛr] *nm Ch* polyester
polyéthylène [pɔlietilɛn] *nm* polythene, *surtout Am* polyethylene
polygame [pɔligam] **1** *adj* polygamous **2** *n* polygamist
polygamie [pɔligami] *nf* polygamy
polyglotte [pɔliglɔt] *adj, n* polyglot
polygonal, -ale, -aux, -ales [pɔligɔnal, -o] *adj* polygonal
polygone [pɔligon] *nm* **(a)** *Géom* polygon **(b)** *Mil* shooting range
polyinsaturé [pɔliɛ̃satyre] *adj* (*lipide*) polyunsaturated
polymère [pɔlimɛr] *Ch* **1** *adj* polymeric **2** *nm* polymer
polymérisation [pɔlimerizasjɔ̃] *nf Ch* polymerization
polymorphe [pɔlimɔrf] *adj* polymorphous, polymorphic
polymorphie [pɔlimɔrfi] *nf,* **polymorphisme** [pɔlimɔrfism] *nm* polymorphism
Polynésie [pɔlinezi] *nf Géog* Polynesia
polynésien, -ienne [pɔlinezjɛ̃, -jɛn] **1** *adj* Polynesian **2** *n* **P.** Polynesian
polynôme [pɔlinom] *nm Math* polynomial
polynucléaire [pɔlinykleɛr] *adj Biol* polynuclear
polype [pɔlip] *nm Méd, Zool* polyp
polypétale [pɔlipetal] *adj Bot* polypetalous
polypeux, -euse [pɔlipø, -øz] *adj Méd* polypous
polyphasé [pɔlifaze] *adj Él* (*système*) polyphase, multiphase
polyphonie [pɔlifɔni] *nf Mus* polyphony
polypropylène [pɔlipropilɛn] *nm* polypropylene
polysémie [pɔlisemi] *nf Ling* polysemy
polysémique [pɔlisemik] *adj Ling* polysemous
polysoc [pɔlisɔk] *nm Agr* multiple plough *or US* plow
polystyle [pɔlistil] *adj Archit* (*salle, temple*) polystyle
polystyrène [pɔlistirɛn] *nm Ch* polystyrene; **boîte en p.** polystyrene box
polysyllabe [pɔlisilab] **1** *adj* (*mot*) polysyllabic **2** *nm* polysyllable
polysyllabique [pɔlisilabik] *adj* polysyllabic
polytechnicien, -ienne [pɔlitɛknisjɛ̃, -jɛn] *n* student at the École polytechnique; (*diplômé*) graduate of the École polytechnique
polytechnique [pɔlitɛknik] **1** *adj* **École p.** = university institution specializing in engineering **2** *nf* **P.** = university institution specializing in engineering
polythéisme [pɔliteism] *nm* polytheism
polythéiste [pɔliteist] **1** *n* polytheist **2** *adj* polytheistic
polythène [pɔlitɛn] *nm Ch* polythene
polytransfusé, -ée [pɔlitrɑ̃sfyze] *Méd* **1** *adj* who has received multiple blood transfusions **2** *n* person who has received multiple blood transfusions
polytraumatisé [pɔlitromatize] *adj Méd* suffering from multiple injuries
polyuréthane [pɔliyretan] *nm Ch* polyurethane
polyvalence [pɔlivalɑ̃s] *nf Ch* polyvalency, multivalency; *Fig* (*d'une personne*) versatility
polyvalent [pɔlivalɑ̃] **1** *adj* **(a)** *Ch* polyvalent, multivalent **(b)** *Fig* (*salle*) multi-purpose; (*outil*) versatile, multi-purpose; (*personne*) versatile; *Admin* **inspecteur p.** tax inspector **2** *nm Admin* tax inspector
polyvinyle [pɔlivinil] *nm Ch* polyvinyl; **chlorure de p.** polyvinyl chloride
polyvinylique [pɔlivinilik] *adj Ch* polyvinyl
pomélo [pɔmelo] *nm* pomelo
Poméranie [pɔmerani] *nf Géog* Pomerania; **loulou de P.** Pomeranian, *F* Pom
pommade [pɔmad] *nf Méd* ointment; *Arch* (*pour les cheveux*) pomade; **p. pour les lèvres** lip salve; *Fig F* **passer de la p. à qn** to butter sb up
pommader [pɔmade] *vt Arch* (*cheveux*) to pomade
pomme [pɔm] *nf* **(a)** (*fruit*) apple; **p. à cuire** cooking apple, *Br* cooker; **p. à couteau** eating apple; **p. à cidre** cider apple; **compote de pommes** stewed apples, apple purée; *Fig F* **c'est toujours pour ma p.** it's always yours truly that gets it; *F* **je ne veux pas voir sa p. ici** I don't want to see him/her here; *F* **ramener sa p.** to turn up, to roll up; *F* **haut comme trois pommes** knee-high to a grasshopper; *F* **tomber dans les pommes** to pass out, to faint; *F* **aux pommes** super, great; *Myth* **les pommes d'or du jardin des Hespérides** the golden apples of Hesperides
(b) (*cœur*) (*de salade, de chou*) heart
(c) (*partie arrondie*) (*de bois de lit, de canne etc*) knob; (*d'arrosoir*) rose; *Naut* (*de mât*) truck; **canne à p. d'or** gold-headed stick; **p. de douche** shower head
▶ **pomme**: *Anat* **p. d'Adam** Adam's apple; **pommes allumettes** matchstick chips *or Am* potatoes; **p. d'amour** (*tomate*) love apple; **p. d'api** = type of small red and white apple; **p. cannelle** custard apple; **p. de chêne** oak apple; **pommes chips** (potato) crisps *or Am* chips; **pommes dauphine** dauphine potatoes; *Fig* **p. de discorde** bone of contention; **pommes duchesse** duchesse potatoes; **p. épineuse** thorn apple; **pommes frites** chips, French fried potatoes, *Am* (French) fries; **pommes noisette** = small potato croquettes; **p. de pin** pine cone; (*de sapin*) fir cone; **p. reinette** pippin; **p. sauvage** crab apple; [①**A12**,1,c] **p. de terre** potato; **pommes de terre à l'eau** boiled potatoes; **p. de terre au four** *ou* **en robe de chambre** *ou* **en robe des champs** baked potato, jacket potato; **pommes de terre frites** *Br* chips, French fried potatoes, *Am* (French) fries; **pommes vapeur** steamed potatoes
pommé [pɔme] *adj* **(a)** (*laitue, chou*) hearty, firm (and round) **(b)** *F Vieilli* (*idiot, gaffe*) complete, downright
pommeau, -eaux [pɔmo] *nm* (*d'un sabre, d'une selle*) pommel; (*d'une canne à pêche*) butt; (*d'une canne, d'un levier de vitesse*) knob; **p. de douche** shower head
pommelé [pɔmle] *adj* dappled, mottled; **gris p.** (*cheval*) dapple-grey; **ciel p.** mackerel sky
pommeler (se) [sәpɔmle] *vpr* (**il se pommelle**; **il se pommellera**) **(a)** (*du ciel*) to become covered *or* dappled with small fleecy clouds **(b)** = **pommer**
pommelle [pɔmɛl] *nf* grating (*over drainpipe etc*)
pommer [pɔme] *vi* (*d'un chou, d'une laitue*) to form a head *or* heart
pommeraie [pɔmrɛ] *nf* apple orchard
pommette [pɔmɛt] *nf Anat* cheekbone; **avoir les pommettes saillantes** to have high cheekbones
pommier [pɔmje] *nm* apple tree; **p. sauvage** crab (apple) tree
pompage [pɔ̃paʒ] *nm* pumping; *Aut* (*de moteur*) hunting; *TV, Rad* (*d'une bande*) flutter; **station de p.** pumping station
pompe[1] [pɔ̃p] *nf* (*cérémonie*) pomp, ceremony; **en grande p.** with great (pomp and) ceremony; **las de la cour et de ses pompes** tired of all the pomp and ceremony
pompe[2] *nf* **(a)** (*machine*) pump; **puiser l'eau à la p.** to pump out the water; **prendre de l'eau à la p.** to get water from the pump; *F* **avoir le** *ou* **un coup de p.** to feel done in *or* shattered all of a sudden; **une barre de chocolat pour le coup de p. de onze heures** a chocolate bar for when you get

that sinking feeling; *F* **à toutes pompes** like lightning, at top speed; *Sp F* **faire des pompes** to do push-ups *or Br* press-ups

(b) *Mus* **p. d'accord** (*d'un instrument à vent*) (tuning) slide

(c) serrure à p. high security lock

(d) *F* **pompes** (*chaussures*) shoes; **ça, c'est de la p.!** those are some shoes!; *Fig* **être bien/mal dans ses pompes** to have got it together/be mixed up; *Fig* **il est à côté de ses pompes** he's not with it, he's not himself

(e) *Mil Arg* **(soldat de) deuxième p.** squaddie, *Am* grunt

▶ **pompe**: **p. à air** air pump, pneumatic pump; **p. d'alimentation** *ou* **alimentaire** feed pump; **p. aspirante** suction pump, lift pump; **p. aspirante et foulante** lift-and-force pump; **p. de bicyclette** bicycle pump; **p. à bière** beer pump; **p. à carburant** fuel pump; **p. à chaleur** heat pump; *Aut* **p. distributrice** distributor pump; *Aut* **p. à eau** water pump; **p. à essence** (*de moteur*) fuel pump; (*distributeur*) petrol *or Am* gas pump; (*station-service*) petrol *or Am* gas station; **p. foulante** force pump; **pompes funèbres** undertaker's, funeral director's, *Am* mortician's; **ordonnateur** *ou* **entrepreneur de pompes funèbres** undertaker, funeral director, *Am* mortician; *Aut* **p. de graissage** grease gun; *MecE* **p. à graisse** grease gun; *Aut* **p. à huile** oil pump; **p. à incendie** water pump (*on a fire engine*); *Aut* **p. d'injection** injection pump, injector pump; **p. pneumatique** air *or* pneumatic pump; **p. refoulante** force pump; *Aut* **p. de refoulement** *ou* **de relevage** lift pump; *Aut* **p. de reprise** accelerator *or* acceleration pump; *F* **p. à vélo** bicycle pump; **p. à vide** vacuum pump; *Aut* exhauster

Pompée [pɔ̃pe] *nm* Pompey

Pompéi [pɔ̃pei] *nf* Pompeii

pompéien, -ienne [pɔ̃pejɛ̃, -jɛn] **1** *adj* Pompeiian **2** *n* **P.** Pompeiian

pomper [pɔ̃pe] **1** *vt* **(a)** (*puiser*) (*eau, air*) to pump; (*faire monter*) to pump up; (*évacuer*) to pump out; **p. de l'eau du puits** to pump (up) water from the well; **p. de l'air dans un pneu** to pump air into a tyre; **des parasites qui pompent le sang** parasites that suck blood; *Fig F* **p. qn** (*épuiser*) to do sb in, to wear sb out; *F* **être pompé** to be done in *or* shattered; *F* **tu me pompes l'air** you're getting on my nerves **(b)** *F* (*boisson*) to knock back **(c)** *Scol F* to copy **(sur qn** from sb) **2** *vi* **(a)** (*faire marcher une pompe*) to pump **(b)** *Scol F* to copy **(sur qn** from sb)

pompette [pɔ̃pɛt] *adj F* tipsy, *Br* merry

pompeusement [pɔ̃pøzmɑ̃] *adv Péj* pompously

pompeux, -euse [pɔ̃pø, -øz] *adj Péj* pompous

pompier [pɔ̃pje] *nm* **(a)** fireman, fire fighter; **p. de service** fire officer; **appeler les pompiers** to call the fire brigade *or Am* the fire fighters; *F* **fumer comme un p.** to smoke like a chimney **(b)** *Vulg* (*fellation*) blow job; **faire un p. à qn** to give sb a blow job

pompier, -ière [pɔ̃pje, -jɛr] *Beaux-Arts Péj* **1** *adj* (*art, style, tableau*) pompous **2** *nm* artist with a pompous style

pompiste [pɔ̃pist] *n Aut* (petrol *or Am* gas) pump attendant, forecourt attendant

pompon [pɔ̃pɔ̃] *nm* pompom, bobble; **bonnet à p.** bobble hat; *F* **ça, c'est le p.!** that's the limit!, that's the last straw!; *Iron* **avoir le p.** to be the limit, *Br* to take the biscuit; *F Vieilli* **avoir son p.** to be tipsy

pomponner (se) [səpɔ̃pɔne] *vpr F* to doll oneself up

ponçage [pɔ̃saʒ] *nm* **(a)** (*action de poncer*) (*à la pierre ponce*) pumicing; (*au papier de verre*) sandpapering; (*de peinture*) rubbing down, sanding down; (*avec une ponceuse*) sanding **(b)** *Beaux-Arts* pouncing

ponce [pɔ̃s] *nf* **(pierre) p.** pumice (stone)

Ponce Pilate [pɔ̃spilat] *nm Bible* Pontius Pilate

poncer [pɔ̃se] *vt* **(je ponçai(s); n. ponçons)** **(a)** (*passer à la pierre ponce*) to pumice; (*au papier de verre*) to sandpaper; (*peinture*) to rub down, to sand down; (*avec une ponceuse*) to sand **(b)** *Beaux-Arts* to pounce

ponceur [pɔ̃sœr] *nm* polisher

ponceuse [pɔ̃søz] *nf* sander, sanding machine

poncho [pɔ̃tʃo] *nm* poncho

poncif [pɔ̃sif] *nm* **(a)** *Beaux-Arts* pouncing pattern **(b)** (*banalité, évidence*) cliché, commonplace

ponction [pɔ̃ksjɔ̃] *nf Méd* puncture; (*de poumon*) tapping; **p. lombaire** lumbar puncture; *Fig* **faire une p./des ponctions dans ses économies** to draw on one's savings; *Admin* **p. fiscale** taxation

ponctionner [pɔ̃ksjɔne] *vt Méd* to puncture; (*poumon, malade*) to tap; *Fig F* (*argent*) to draw on

ponctualité [pɔ̃ktɥalite] *nf* punctuality

ponctuation [pɔ̃ktɥasjɔ̃] *nf* punctuation

ponctuel, -elle [pɔ̃ktɥɛl] *adj* **(a)** (*à l'heure*) punctual **(b)** *Phys* **source ponctuelle de chaleur** pinpoint flame; **source lumineuse ponctuelle** point source; **projecteur p.** spotlight **(c)** *Fig* (*qui ne concerne qu'un point*) (*opération, aide*) ad hoc; **intervention ponctuelle du gouvernement** exceptional action by the government; **nous n'avons fait que des changements ponctuels** we have made only selective changes; **débrayage p.** one-off stoppage; **les terroristes ne se livraient qu'à des actions ponctuelles** the terrorists made only sporadic attacks

ponctuellement [pɔ̃ktɥɛlmɑ̃] *adv* (*de façon limitée*) on an ad hoc basis

ponctuer [pɔ̃ktɥe] *vt* (*phrase*) to punctuate; **elle ponctua ses explications de silences** her explanation was punctuated with silences

pondaison [pɔ̃dɛzɔ̃] *nf* egg-laying time

pondérable [pɔ̃derabl] *adj Tech* weighable

pondéral, -ale, -aux, -ales [pɔ̃deral, -o] *adj* weight; **surcharge pondérale** excess weight

pondérateur, -trice [pɔ̃deratœr, -tris] *adj* stabilizing, balancing

pondération [pɔ̃derasjɔ̃] *nf* **(a)** (*d'une personne*) levelheadedness; (*symétrie, équilibre*) balance; **parler/agir avec p.** to speak/act levelheadedly **(b)** *Écon* (*d'un indice*) weighting; *Math* **coefficient de p.** weighting

pondéré [pɔ̃dere] *adj* **(a)** (*équilibré, calme*) (*esprit*) well balanced; (*personne*) levelheaded **(b)** *Écon* **indice p.** weighted index; **moyenne pondérée** weighted average

pondérer [pɔ̃dere] *vt* **(je pondère; je pondérerai)** **(a)** (*équilibrer*) to balance **(b)** *Écon* (*indice, moyenne*) to weight

pondéreux, -euse [pɔ̃derø, -øz] *Tech* **1** *adj* (*marchandises etc*) heavy **2** *nmpl* **les p.** heavy goods

pondeur, -euse [pɔ̃dœr, -øz] **1** *adj* (egg-)laying; **poule pondeuse** laying hen **2** *nf* **pondeuse** (*poule*) (good) layer; *Fig Péj* **quelle pondeuse!** (*femme*) she's like a battery hen **3** *nm Péj* **p. de prose** prolific scribbler; **p. de tableaux** prolific dauber; **c'est un p. d'articles/de romans** he just churns out articles/novels

pondoir [pɔ̃dwar] *nm* nest box

pondre [pɔ̃dr] *vt* **(a)** (*œuf*) to lay; **œuf frais pondu** new(ly)-laid egg, freshly-laid egg **(b)** *Fig F* (*texte, solution*) to come up with; (*articles, romans*) to churn out; **elle a pondu une de ces traductions!** she came out with an awful translation; **p. une lettre tous les jours** to churn out a letter every day

poney [pɔnɛ] *nm* pony

pongiste [pɔ̃ʒist] *n Sp* table tennis player

pont [pɔ̃] *nm* **(a)** *Constr* bridge; *Admin* **les Ponts et Chaussées** = the Roads *or* Highways Department; **École des Ponts et Chaussées** = specialist institute of Civil Engineering; *Mil* **tête de p.** bridgehead; **vivre sous les ponts** to be a tramp; *Fig* **il est passé de l'eau sous les ponts** a lot of water has passed *or* flowed under the bridge; *Fig* **faire le p.** to make a long weekend of it; *Fig* **le p. de la Pentecôte** the (long) Whitsun Bank Holiday weekend; *Fig* **faire un p. d'or à qn** to give sb a golden hello

(b) *Naut* deck; **faux p.** orlop deck; **navire à un p.** single-decker (ship), single-deck ship; **navire à deux/trois ponts** two-/three-decker; **homme** *ou* **matelot de p.** deck hand; (*dans la marine*) upper-deck rating; **sur le p.** on deck; **tout le monde sur le p.!** all hands on deck!; (*dans la marine*) clear lower deck!; *Com* **sur p.** free on board, fob

(c) *MecE* live axle; *Aut* drive axle

(d) *Fig* link; **assurer un p. entre Paris et la province** to provide a link between Paris and the provinces; **couper les ponts (avec qn)** to break off all relations *or* sever all links *or* sever all ties (with sb)

▶ **pont**: **p. aérien** airlift; **p. aux ânes** *Géom* pons asinorum; *Fig* (piece of) common knowledge; **p. arrière** *Aut* rear *or* back axle; *Naut* afterdeck; **p. autoroutier** motorway bridge, overpass; **p. avant** foredeck; **p. basculant** *ou* **à bascule** drawbridge, bascule bridge; **p. de bateaux** floating *or* pontoon bridge; **p. cantilever** cantilever bridge; *Ind* **p. à chariot culbuteur** tipping stage; **p. à consoles** cantilever bridge; *Ind* **p. de décharge** tipping stage; **p. élévateur** (*dans un garage*) (repair) ramp; **p. des embarcations** boat deck; **p. des emménagements** saloon deck; **p. en encorbellement** cantilever bridge; **p. d'envol** (*d'un porte-avion*) flight deck; **p. des gaillards** upper deck; **p. de graissage** (*dans un garage*) ramp; **p. inférieur** lower deck; **p. de manœuvre** hurricane deck; **p. pour piétons** footbridge; **p. pivotant** swing bridge; **p. des premières** saloon deck; **p. principal** main deck; **p. promenade** promenade deck; (*sur un paquebot*) sun deck, hurricane deck; *Ind* **p. roulant** travelling crane; (*support*) gantry; *Ordinat* **p. routeur** routing node; **p. supérieur** upper deck; **p. suspendu** suspension bridge; **p. tournant** swing bridge; **p. tubulaire** box (girder) bridge; **p. volant** flying bridge; *Él* **p. de Wheatstone** Wheatstone bridge

Pont (le) [ləpɔ̃] *nm Antiq* **(a)** the (Kingdom of) Pontus **(b) le P.-Euxin** the Euxine Sea, the Black Sea
pontage [pɔ̃taʒ] *nm* **(a)** *Constr* bridge building; *(travaux)* bridging **(b)** *Naut* decking **(c)** *Méd* bypass (operation); **p. coronarien** heart bypass (operation); **on lui a fait un p.** he's had a bypass, he's had bypass surgery
pont-bascule, *pl* **ponts-bascules** *nm* drawbridge, bascule bridge; *(pour peser les poids lourds)* weighbridge
ponte[1] [pɔ̃t] *nf (action)* (egg) laying; *(œufs)* eggs (laid); **p. ovulaire** ovulation
ponte[2] *nm* **(a)** *(aux jeux de hasard)* punter **(b)** *F (personnage important)* big shot; **un grand p. de la médecine** a big shot in medicine
ponté [pɔ̃te] *adj* decked; **non p.** open
pontée [pɔ̃te] *nf Naut* deck load, deck cargo
ponter[1] [pɔ̃te] *vt Naut (navire)* to lay the deck(s) of, to deck
ponter[2] *vi (aux jeux de hasard)* to punt
pontier [pɔ̃tje] *nm Tech* swing-bridge keeper
pontife [pɔ̃tif] *nm Rel* pontiff; *Fig F* big shot, bigwig; **le souverain p.** the Supreme Pontiff; *Fig F* **les pontifs de l'hôpital** the bigwigs *or* top brass at the hospital
pontifiant [pɔ̃tifjɑ̃] *adj F Péj* pontificating
pontifical, -ale, -aux, -ales [pɔ̃tifikal, -o] **1** *adj* pontifical, papal **2** *nm* pontifical
pontificat [pɔ̃tifika] *nm* pontificate; **sous le p. de Jean-Paul II** during the pontificate of John-Paul II
pontifier [pɔ̃tifje] *vi (impf, pr sub* **n. pontifiions, v. pontifiiez***)* to pontificate
pont-l'Évêque [pɔ̃levɛk] *nm inv* Pont l'Évêque (cheese)
pont-levis, *pl* **ponts-levis** [pɔ̃l(ə)vi] *nm* drawbridge; **p. à fléau** *ou* **à balancier** lever drawbridge
Pont-Neuf [pɔ̃nœf] *nm Fig* **être solide comme le P.** to have the constitution of an ox, to be as fit as a fiddle
ponton [pɔ̃tɔ̃] *nm* **(a)** *(construction flottante)* pontoon; **p. d'incendie** fire float; **p. d'atterrissage** (floating) landing stage **(b)** *Naut Vieilli (prison flottante)* hulk, prison ship
pontonnier [pɔ̃tɔnje] *nm* **(a)** *Mil* pontoneer, pontonier **(b)** *(gardien)* swing-bridge keeper
pool [pul] *nm* **(a)** *Écon* pool **(b)** *(équipe)* **p. de dactylos** typing pool; **p. de secrétaires** secretarial pool
pop [pɔp] *adj inv, nf* **(musique) p.** pop (music); **chanteur p.** pop singer
pop'art [pɔpart] *nm Beaux-Arts* pop art
pop-corn [pɔpkɔrn] *nm inv* popcorn; **on a mangé du p./des p.** we ate (some) popcorn
pope [pɔp] *nm Rel* pope (of the Orthodox church)
popeline [pɔplin] *nf Tex* poplin
popote [pɔpɔt] **1** *nf* **(a)** *F (cuisine)* cooking; **faire la p.** to do the cooking **(b)** *Mil* canteen; *(mess)* officers' mess **2** *adj inv F souvent Péj (personne)* stay-at-home
popotin [pɔpɔtɛ̃] *nm F* bum, *Am* butt; **se manier le p.** to get a move on
populace [pɔpylas] *nf Péj* rabble, riff-raff, mob
populacier, -ière [pɔpylasje, -jɛr] *adj Péj* vulgar, common
populage [pɔpylaʒ] *nm Bot* marsh marigold
populaire [pɔpylɛr] *adj* **(a)** *(du peuple)* popular; **démocratie p.** popular *or* people's democracy; **manifestation p.** mass demonstration **(b)** *(pour le peuple)* **chanson p.** popular song; **expression p.** vernacular expression; **un roman p.** a low-brow novel; **bal p.** (local) dance *(open to the public)*; **la soupe p.** the soup kitchen **(c)** *(ouvrier)* working-class; **les classes populaires** the working classes; **quartier p.** working-class district **(d)** *(qui plaît)* popular; **se rendre p.** to make oneself popular
populairement [pɔpylɛrmɑ̃] *adv (s'exprimer, parler)* in the vernacular
populariser [pɔpylarize] *vt* to popularize
popularité [pɔpylarite] *nf* popularity; **cote de p.** popularity rating
population [pɔpylasjɔ̃] *nf* population
▶ **population**: **p. active** working population, labour force; *Mktg* **p. cible** target population; **p.-mère** basic population; **p. prévue** projected population
populationnisme [pɔpylasjɔnism] *nm* = policy of population growth
populationniste [pɔpylasjɔnist] *adj* **politique p.** policy of population growth; **gouvernement p.** government in favour of population growth
populeux, -euse [pɔpylø, -øz] *adj* populous, densely populated
populisme [pɔpylism] *nm Littér* populism
populiste [pɔpylist] *adj, n Littér* populist
populo [pɔpylo] *nm F* **(a) le p.** ordinary people, *Péj* the riffraff, the rabble **(b)** *(foule)* crowd (of people)
poquet [pɔkɛ] *nm Agr* seed hole

porc [pɔr] *nm* **(a)** *(animal)* pig, *Am* hog; *F (homme grossier)* pig, slob; **gardeur de porcs** pig keeper, pigman, *Arch* swineherd; **p. sauvage** wild boar; **(peau de) p.** pigskin; **sale comme un p.** filthy (dirty); **manger comme un p.** to eat like a pig **(b)** *Culin* pork; **côtelette de p.** pork chop
porcelaine [pɔrsəlɛn] *nf* **(a)** *Cér* porcelain, china; **p. de Chine** china; **p. de Saxe** Dresden china; **p. tendre (anglaise)** bone china **(b)** *(mollusque)* cowrie
porcelainier, -ière [pɔrsəlenje, -jɛr] **1** *adj* **industrie porcelainière** porcelain *or* china industry **2** *nm* porcelain *or* china manufacturer
porcelet [pɔrsəlɛ] *nm* piglet, young pig
porc-épic [pɔrkepik], *pl* **porcs-épics** [pɔrkepik] *nm* porcupine; *F (personne)* prickly person; **c'est un vrai p.** *(il pique)* his face is all bristly
porche [pɔrʃ] *nm* porch
porcher, -ère [pɔrʃe, -ɛr] *n* pig keeper, *Arch* swineherd
porcherie [pɔrʃəri] *nf* piggery; *(enclos)* pigsty, *Am* pigpen; *Fig Péj* **quelle p.!** what a pigsty *or* pigpen!
porcin, -ine [pɔrsɛ̃, -in] **1** *adj* pig, *Fml* porcine; **élevage p.** pig breeding; **peste porcine** swine fever, *Am* hog cholera; *Fig Péj* **un visage p.** a piggy face; **yeux porcins** piggy eyes **2** *nmpl* **porcins** pigs, swine, *Am* hogs
pore [pɔr] *nm (de peau, de plante, de pierre)* pore; **avoir les pores dilatés** to have open pores; *Fig* **il sue la couardise par tous les pores** he exudes cowardice from every pore
poreux, -euse [pɔrø, -øz] *adj* porous
porno [pɔrno] *adj, nm F* porn
pornographe [pɔrnɔgraf] *n* pornographer
pornographie [pɔrnɔgrafi] *nf* pornography
pornographique [pɔrnɔgrafik] *adj* pornographic
porosité [pɔrozite] *nf* porosity, porousness
porphyre [pɔrfir] *nm Minér* porphyry
porridge [pɔridʒ] *nm Culin* porridge
port[1] [pɔr] *nm* **(a)** *(abri)* harbour, *US* harbor; *(plus important)* port; **capitaine de p.** harbour master; **droits de p.** harbour dues, port charges; **entrer dans le p.** to enter harbour; **entrer au p.** to come into port; **quitter le p.** to leave port, to clear the harbour; *Fig* **arriver à bon p.** to arrive safe and sound; **Dunkerque est le premier p. de France** Dunkirk is the largest port in France; *Naut* **les ports de la métropole** the home ports

(b) *Ordinat* port; **p. de communication** comms port, communications port; **p. d'entrée/sortie** input/output port; **p. d'E/S** I/O port; **p. d'extension** expansion port; **p. d'imprimante** printer port; **p. (de connexion pour) jeux** games port; **p. modem** modem port; **p. parallèle** parallel port; **p. SCSI** SCSI port; **p. série** serial port; **p. souris** mouse port
▶ **port**: **p. d'armement** port of registry, *Am* port of documentation; **p. d'arrivée** port of arrival, port of entry; **p. artificiel** artificial port; **p. d'attache** home port, port of commissioning; *Com* port of registry; *Fig* home base; **p. de commerce** commercial port; **p. pour conteneurs** container port; *Com* **p. d'embarquement** port of loading, port of embarkation; **p. d'entrée** port of entry; **p. d'escale** port of call; *Com* **p. de départ** port of departure; **p. pour ferry** ferry port; **p. fluvial** river port; **p. franc** free port; **p. de guerre** naval port, naval base; **p. lacustre** lakeside port; **p. maritime** *ou* **de mer** seaport; *Com* **p. militaire** naval port, naval base; **p. naturel** natural harbour; **p. de pêche** fishing port; **p. de plaisance** marina; **p. de transit** port of transit
port[2] *nm* **(a)** *(fait de porter)* carrying; **permis de p. d'armes** permit for carrying firearms; *Mil* **se mettre au p. d'armes** to shoulder arms

(b) *(fait de revêtir) (de vêtement, lunettes, barbe)* wearing; **le p. du casque est obligatoire** *(sur panneau)* safety helmets must be worn; *(en moto)* crash helmets must be worn

(c) *(transport payant) (de marchandises)* carriage; *(de paquet, de lettre, de télégramme)* delivery; *Com* **ports de lettres, frais de p.** postage, postal charges; **en p. dû** carriage forward, freight collect; *Com* **p. avancé** carriage forward, freight collect, freight forward; **p. débours** carriage forward paid against invoice; **p. en lourd** deadweight, dwt; **p. et emballage** postage and packing, p&p; **p. forfait** carriage forward paid in a lump sum in advance; **p. franc, p. payé, franc(o) de p.** *(de revue, de journal)* postage paid; *(de marchandise)* carriage paid *or* free, freight collect; **p. payé, assurance comprise** carriage insurance paid

(d) *(allure) (d'une personne)* bearing, carriage; **un p. de reine** a regal *or* queenly bearing; **un gracieux p. de tête** a graceful manner of holding one's head

(e) *Bot (d'une plante)* habit

(f) *Naut (d'un navire)* burden, tonnage

port³ *nm* (*dans les Pyrénées*) pass

portabilité [pɔrtabilite] *nf Ordinat* portability

portable [pɔrtabl] **1** *adj* **(a)** (*facilement transportable*) (*machine à écrire, ordinateur etc*) portable **(b)** (*mettable*) (*vêtement*) wearable, presentable **(c)** *Jur* payable at the address of the payee **2** *nm Ordinat* laptop, portable; *Tél* mobile, mobile phone

portage [pɔrtaʒ] *nm* **(a)** (*transport*) (*de marchandises*) porterage, conveyance, transport; (*de bateau*) portage; **frais de p.** porterage **(b)** (*partie d'un fleuve*) portage **(c)** *Banque* piggy-backing

portager [pɔrtaʒe] *vi Can* to portage

portail [pɔrtaj] *nm* portal

portance [pɔrtɑ̃s] *nf Av* lift (per unit area)

portant [pɔrtɑ̃] **1** *adj* **(a)** (*qui soutient*) **mur p.** load-bearing wall; **à bout p.** at point-blank range, point-blank; *Av* **surface portante** aerofoil, *Am* airfoil; *Naut* **vent p.** fair wind **(b)** **être bien p.** to be in good health, to be well; **être mal p.** to be in poor health, to be unwell; **enfants bien/mal portants** healthy/unhealthy children **2** *nm* **(a)** *Tech* upright; (*support*) stay, strut **(b)** *Vieilli* (*anse*) handle **(c)** (*chenille*) (*d'une roue*) tread **(d)** (*présentoir*) (*dans un magasin de vêtements*) rack

portatif, -ive [pɔrtatif, -iv] **1** *adj* (*machine à écrire, ordinateur, radio*) portable; **armes portatives** small arms **2** *nm Ordinat* laptop

porte [pɔrt] *nf* **(a)** (*de maison, de placard etc*) door; **à ma p.** on my doorstep; **aller ouvrir la p.** to answer the door; **le musée ouvrira ses portes (au public) en juin** the museum will open its doors to the public in June; **le théâtre fermera ses portes à la fin du mois** the theatre will close at the end of the month; *F* **ce n'est pas la p. à côté** it's hardly just around the corner; **il y a deux kilomètres/on met deux heures de p. à p.** it's two kilometres/it takes two hours door to door; *F* **je lui ai parlé entre deux portes** I spoke to him for a brief moment *or* briefly, I had a quick word with him; *F* **on s'est vus entre deux portes** we saw each other briefly; **trouver p. close** to find nobody in; **j'ai voulu aller au musée mais j'ai trouvé p. close** I wanted to go to the museum but it was closed; **être à la p.** to be locked out; **mettre qn à la p.** to throw *or* kick sb out; (*d'un emploi*) to fire *or Br* sack sb; *F* **tais-toi ou tu vas prendre la p.** be quiet or I'll turn you out, be quiet or you're out; **qu'il prenne la p. s'il n'est pas content** let him leave *or* he doesn't have to stay if he's not happy; **elle m'a fermé/claqué la p. au nez** she closed/slammed the door in my face; **refuser** *ou* **fermer** *ou* **défendre sa p. à qn** not to allow sb in, to refuse sb admission; *Fig* **vous avez frappé** *ou* **sonné à la bonne/mauvaise p.** you've come to the right/wrong person; *F* **entrer dans une profession par la petite p.** to start at the bottom; *Fig* **c'est la p. ouverte à toutes les atrocités** it leaves the door wide open to all sorts of atrocities; *Fig* **journée portes ouvertes** open day *or Am* house; *Prov* **il faut qu'une p. soit ouverte ou fermée** it has to be either one way or the other; **chassez-le par la p., il reviendra par la fenêtre** get rid of him one way and he'll come back another

(b) (*voie d'entrée*) (*d'un parc*) gate(way); (*d'un immeuble*) doorway, entrance; (*dans un aéroport*) gate; **portes d'une ville** gates of a town; **l'entreprise est installée aux portes de Paris** the company is situated on the outskirts of Paris; **l'ennemi est à nos portes** the enemy is at our gates; **la guerre est à nos portes** the war is on our doorstep; (*temporel*) war is around the corner; **la campagne est à vos portes** the countryside is on your doorstep; **aux portes du désert** at the gateway to the desert; **être aux portes de la mort** to be at death's door; **les portes de l'enfer** the gates of hell; *Hist* **la (Sublime-)P., la P. ottomane** the (Sublime) Porte

(c) (*portière*) (*de voiture, de train*) door; **attendre l'ouverture complète des portes** wait until the doors are fully open; **(voiture) deux/quatre/cinq portes** two-/four-/five-door car

(d) *Ski* gate

(e) (*fente*) (*d'une agrafe*) eye

(f) (*usu pl*) **portes** (*dans la roche*) gorge; (*passage étroit*) defile, pass

(g) *Ordinat* gate; **p. logique** logic gate

▶ **porte**: **p. d'aérage** air gate, trap door; **p. battante** swing door; **p. cochère** carriage entrance; **portes communicantes** inter-connecting doors; **p. coulissante** sliding door; **p. de débarquement** (disembarkation) gate; **p. de derrière** back door; **p. à deux battants** double door; *Tech* **p. d'écluse** (lock) gate; **p. d'embarquement** (boarding) gate; **p. d'entrée** front door; **p. roulante** sliding door; **p. de secours** emergency exit; **p. de service** (*de maison, d'appartement*) (*de derrière*) back door; (*sur le côté*) side door, *Vieilli* tradesman's entrance; **p. de sortie** way out, exit, exit only door; *Fig* way out, means of escape; **p. tournante, p. à tambour** revolving door; *Tech* **p. de visite** inspection door; (*d'égout*) manhole cover; **p. vitrée** glass door

porté [pɔrte] *adj* **être p. à l'indulgence/la compréhension** to be inclined to be indulgent/understanding; **être p. à la discussion** to be inclined *or* prone to argue; **être p. à la colère** to be quick-tempered; **p. à faire qch** inclined to do sth, given to doing sth; **être p. à oublier** to be apt *or* inclined to forget; **p. sur qch** fond of sth; *F* **être p. sur la chose** to be sex-mad, to have a one-track mind

porte(-)à(-)faux *nm inv* overhang; *Constr* cantilever; **en p.** overhanging; *Fig* **être en p.** to be awkwardly placed

porte-affiche(s), *pl* **porte-affiches** *nm* notice *or Am* bulletin board

porte-aiguille, *pl* **porte-aiguille(s)** *nm Chir* needle holder

porte-aiguilles *nm inv Couture* needle case

porte-amarre, *pl* **porte-amarre(s)** *nm Naut* line-throwing apparatus; **flèche p.** line-throwing rocket

porte-à-porte *nm* door-to-door selling; **faire du p.** (*pour vendre*) to sell from door to door, to do door-to-door selling; (*faire des enquêtes etc*) to go from door to door

porte-avions *nm inv Naut* aircraft carrier

porte-bagages *nm inv* luggage rack; (*de bicyclette*) carrier; (*de voiture*) roof rack

porte-baïonnette, *pl* **porte-baïonnette(s)** *nm* bayonet frog

porte-balais *nm inv Él* brush holder

porte-bébé, *pl* **porte-bébés** *nm* baby carrier

porte-billets *nm inv* notecase, *Am* billfold

porte-bombes *nm inv Mil Av* bomb rack

porte-bonheur *nm inv* (lucky) charm; (*animal, enfant*) mascot; **couleur/petit cochon p.** lucky colour/pig

porte-bouteilles *nm inv* (*pour stocker le vin*) wine rack, bottle rack; (*pour porter*) bottle carrier

porte-brosses [pɔrt(ə)brɔs] *nm inv* **p. (à dents)** toothbrush holder

porte-carte(s) [pɔrtəkart] *nm inv* **(a)** (*pour cartes de crédit, de visite*) card holder *or* wallet **(b)** (*pour cartes géographiques*) map case *or* holder

porte-chapeaux *nm inv* hat stand

porte-chars [pɔrtəʃar] *nm inv Mil* tank transporter

porte-chéquier, *pl* **porte-chéquiers** *nm* cheque *or Am* check book holder

porte-cigares *nm inv* cigar case

porte-cigarettes *nm inv* cigarette case

porte-clefs, porte-clés [pɔrtəkle] *nm inv* key ring

porte-conteneurs *nm inv Tech* container ship

porte-copie, *pl* **porte-copie(s)** *nm Typ* copy holder

porte-couteau, *pl* **porte-couteau(x)** *nm* knife rest

porte-croix [pɔrtəkrwa] *nm inv Rel* cross bearer

porte-documents *nm inv* briefcase

porte-drapeau, *pl* **porte-drapeau(x)** *nm Mil, Fig* standard bearer

portée [pɔrte] *nf* **(a)** (*petits*) litter, brood; (*d'une truie*) farrow

(b) (*amplitude*) (*des bras*) reach; (*de la flèche d'une grue*) radius; (*d'un fusil, d'un émetteur*) range; (*d'un traité*) scope; (*de voix*) range, compass; **(à) courte p., (à) petite p.** (at) short range; **(à) grande p., (à) longue p.** (at) long range; **canon à longue p.** long-range gun; **à p. (de tir)** within range; **à p. de fusil** within rifle range, within gunshot; **à p. de canon** within gun range; **à p. de (la) voix** within earshot; **à p. de (la) vue** (with)in sight; **des chaussures à la p. de toutes les bourses** shoes to suit every pocket *or* budget; **ce sport est maintenant à la p. de toutes les bourses** this sport is now within everyone's means, everyone can now afford this sport; **des chaussures à ce prix ne sont pas à la p. de tout le monde** not everyone can afford shoes at that price; **c'est à ma p.** (*cet objet*) it's within my reach; (*ce livre*) I can understand it; (*ce travail*) I can do it; **hors de ma p.** (*dans l'espace*) beyond my reach; *Fig* (*de compréhension*) beyond my understanding, *F* beyond me; **hors de p.** out of reach, beyond reach; **à mettre hors de (la) p. des enfants** keep out of the reach of children; **à p. de (la) main** within reach, to hand; **j'ai toujours un tube d'aspirine à p. de la main** I always have some aspirin handy; **livre à la p. de tout le monde** (*facile à lire*) book that anyone can understand; **cette musique/ce roman n'est pas à la p. de tout le monde** this music/novel is not accessible to everyone

(c) *Mus* stave, staff

(d) *Fig* (*force*) (*d'une déclaration, des mots*) (full) significance *or Fml* import; **conséquences d'une p. incalculable** far-reaching consequences; **un changement/une décision d'une très grande p.** a very significant *or* a far-reaching change/decision

(e) *Constr* (*charge*) bearing; (*distance*) span; *Naut* **p. en lourd** *ou* **en poids** deadweight (capacity)

(f) *MecE* bearing surface; (*point d'appui*) (*d'un arbre*) boss; **portées** (*d'un arbre*) (main) journals

porte-étendard *nm inv Hist* (*dans la cavalerie*) standard bearer

portefaix [pɔrtəfɛ] *nm Hist* (street) porter

porte-fenêtre, *pl* **portes-fenêtres** *nf* French window *or Am* door

portefeuille [pɔrtəfœj] *nm* (a) (*pour l'argent*) wallet, *Am* billfold; *Fig* **avoir un p. bien garni** to be well off, to be rich; **lit en p.** apple-pie bed; **jupe p.** wrapover *or* wraparound *or* wraparound skirt

(b) (*cartable*) portfolio; *Com* **p. d'assurances** (*d'un assureur*) portfolio; **p. d'actions** share portfolio; *Fin* **effets en p.** bills in hand, holdings; **p. (titres)** investments, securities; **p. de titres** securities portfolio; *Mktg* **p. d'activité** business portfolio, portfolio mix

(c) *Pol* (*fonction de ministre*) portfolio; **ministre sans p.** minister without portfolio

(d) *Aut* (*de semi-remorque*) jackknifing

porte-greffe(s) [pɔrtəgrɛf] *nm inv Bot* stock

porte-hélicoptères [pɔrtelikɔptɛr] *nm inv Naut* helicopter carrier

porte-jarretelles *nm inv* suspender *or Am* garter belt

porte-journaux *nm inv* newspaper rack

porte-jupe, *pl* **porte-jupe(s)** [pɔrtəʒyp] *nm* skirt hanger

porte-malheur *nm inv* bringer of bad luck, jinx; **les plumes de paon sont considérées comme un p.** peacock feathers are thought to bring bad luck

portemanteau, -eaux [pɔrtmɑ̃to] *nm* (a) (*accroché au mur*) coat rack; (*sur pied*) coat stand (b) *Arch* (*malle*) portmanteau

portement [pɔrtəmɑ̃] *nm* **p. de croix** (Christ's) bearing of the Cross

porte-menu *nm inv* menu holder

portemine [pɔrt(ə)min] *nm* propelling pencil

porte-monnaie *nm inv* purse; **p. électronique** electronic purse *or* wallet

porte-musique *nm inv* music case

porte-objet, *pl* **porte-objet(s)** *nm* (*de microscope*) (object) slide; (*platine*) stage

porte-outil, *pl* **porte-outil(s)** *nm* (*d'un machine-outil*) tool holder; (*d'une perceuse*) chuck; (*d'un tour*) slide rest

porte-papier *nm inv* **p. (hygiénique)** toilet paper holder; (*pour rouleau*) toilet roll holder

porte-parapluies *nm inv* umbrella stand

porte-parole *nm inv* spokesperson, spokesman, *f* spokeswoman; (*organe d'un parti politique*) organ; **se faire le p. d'un groupe** to speak for a group, to be the spokesperson for a group

porte-pipes [pɔrtəpip] *nm inv* pipe rack

porte-plat, *pl* **porte-plat(s)** [pɔrtəpla] *nm* (dish) stand

porte-plume [pɔrtəplym] *nm inv* penholder

porter [pɔrte] **1** *vt* (a) (*soutenir*) (*valise, enfant etc*) to carry; (*poids, charge*) to bear, to carry; **p. qn en triomphe** to carry sb in triumph *or* shoulder high (in triumph); **p. la tête haute** to hold *or* carry one's head high; **ces abus portent en eux leur propre châtiment** these abuses carry their own punishment; **une réforme qui porte en elle tous les abus** a reform that carries *or* has within it the seed of all sorts of abuse; **elle porte bien son âge** she's wearing well; **elle porte/ne porte pas son âge** she looks/doesn't look her age; **elle a 30 ans? elle ne les porte pas du tout** she's 30? she doesn't look it at all; **mes jambes ne me portent plus** my legs won't carry me any further; **je ne le porte pas dans mon cœur** he's not exactly my favourite *or US* favorite person; *Mil* **portez armes!** shoulder arms!; *Naut* **p. tout dessus** (*d'un voilier*) to have all sails set

(b) (*produire*) to produce; **p. des fruits** to bear fruit; **terres qui portent du blé** wheat-producing land; **p. intérêt** to yield interest; **argent qui porte intérêt** money that brings in *or* bears interest; **cela vous portera bonheur/malheur** that will bring you luck/bad luck; *Prov* **la nuit porte conseil** sleep on it

(c) (*avoir avec ou sur soi*) (*vêtement, chapeau*) to wear; **p. des lunettes/une bague/du noir** to wear glasses/a ring/black; **p. une moustache/la barbe** to have *or* wear a moustache/a beard; **p. les cheveux courts/longs** to wear one's hair short/long, to have short/long hair; **il portait une cicatrice à la joue droite** he had a scar on his right cheek; *Fig* **p. la soutane** to be a priest; *Fig F* **faire p. le chapeau à qn** to make sb take the rap *or Br* carry the can, *Am* to leave sb holding the bag; *Fig F* **dans le ménage, c'est elle qui porte la culotte** she wears the trousers in their house; **il porte le nom de son oncle** he's called after his uncle; **ce produit porte le nom de son inventeur** this product is named after its inventor, this product bears the name of its inventor; **p. le même prénom que qn** to have the same name as sb; **qu'est-ce qu'elle porte comme prénom?** what's her first name?; **elle porte bien/mal son nom/prénom** her name suits/doesn't suit her; **le chameau porte deux bosses** the camel has two humps

(d) (*transporter*) (*là-bas*) to take; (*ici*) to bring; **p. qch dans la maison/dehors** to take/bring sth into the house/outside; **p. une chaise d'une pièce à une autre** to take *or* carry a chair from one room to another; **p. une lettre à la poste** *ou F* **boîte** to post *or Am* mail a letter; **je suis allée lui p. un message** I took him a message; **je suis allé lui p. la nouvelle** I went to give *or* to tell him the news; **p. à domicile** to deliver to domicile; **p. le lait à domicile** to deliver milk to the door; **il porta le verre à ses lèvres** he raised *or* lifted the glass to his lips; **p. qn en terre** to carry sb to his/her grave

(e) (*diriger*) **p. un coup à qn, p. la main sur qn** to strike *or* hit sb; **s'il porte la main une seule fois sur toi, dis-le-moi** if he ever lays a hand on you *or* strikes you, tell me; **p. la main à sa nuque** to touch the back of one's neck; **il porta la main à sa casquette** he touched his cap; **p. la main à son front** to hold one's hand to one's forehead; **p. ses regards sur qn** to direct one's gaze towards sb, to look at sb; **p. son attention sur qch** to turn one's attention to sth, to give sth one's attention; *Fig* **p. qch devant un tribunal/les tribunaux** to take sth to court; **p. plainte** to make a complaint; *Fig* **p. un toast à qn** to drink *or* offer a toast to sb, to toast sb; **p. témoignage** to testify, to give evidence, to bear witness; **p. qch à la connaissance de qn** to bring sth to sb's attention, to make sth known to sb, to let sb know about sth

(f) (*inscrire*) (*noms, chiffres*) to enter, to write; **p. une position sur une carte** to mark a position on a map; **p. une somme au crédit/au débit de qn** to credit/debit sb with a sum; **p. une somme au crédit/débit d'un compte** to credit/debit a sum to an account; **se faire p. malade** *ou F* **pâle** to report sick; *Mil etc* **p. qn manquant à l'appel** to report sb absent from roll call; **p. qn absent** to report sb absent; **p. qn déserteur** to declare sb a deserter; **être porté disparu** to be reported missing; *Naut* **p. un homme au rôle de l'équipage** to enter a seaman on the ship's books

(g) (*être revêtu ou marqué de*) to bear; **la lettre porte la date du 2 juin** the letter is dated June 2nd; **p. une signature** to bear a signature; **p. le titre de …** (*d'un livre*) to be entitled *or* called …

(h) (*inciter à*) **p. qn à qch** to incite sb to sth; **p. qn à faire qch** to induce *or* prompt sb to do sth; **tout me porte à croire que …** everything leads *or* inclines me to believe that …

(i) (*monter, transformer*) to bring; **p. la température à 100°** to raise the temperature to 100°; **p. qn au pouvoir** to bring sb to power; **p. une pièce classique à l'écran** to bring *or* transfer a classical drama to the screen; **p. la production au maximum** to raise *or* increase production to a maximum; **portez le liquide à ébullition** bring the liquid to the boil; **ça porte à dix le nombre des victimes** that brings the number of victims to ten; **cela portera à cent francs le prix du billet** that will bring the price of the ticket up to a hundred francs

(j) (*avoir*) (*intérêt*) to have (**à** in); (*affection, amour*) to have, to feel (**à** for, towards)

(k) (*donner*) **p. secours à un bateau en détresse/à qn** to come to the aid of a boat in distress/of sb; **p. assistance à qn** to come to sb's assistance, to offer assistance to sb

(l) (*mentionner*) **le rapport ne porte aucune mention de tout cela** the report makes no mention of any of that; **la loi porte que cet usage est interdit** this practice is expressly forbidden by law; *Mil etc* **la décision porte que …** it is stated in orders that …

2 *vi* (a) (*appuyer*) to rest, to bear; **tout le poids porte sur cette poutre** all the weight rests *or* bears on this beam; **croyez-vous que la glace porte?** do you think the ice will hold?; **la discussion porte toujours sur le même sujet** the discussion always deals with *or* turns on the same subject; **les questions ont porté sur un chapitre que je n'avais pas revu** the questions dealt with *or* were about a chapter that I hadn't revised; **faire p. son attention sur qch** to turn one's attention to sth, to focus one's attention on sth; **faire p. sa thèse sur qch** to choose sth as the subject for one's thesis

(b) (*atteindre*) **sa tête a porté sur le rebord du trottoir/contre le volant** his head hit *or* struck the kerb/the wheel; **aucun des coups n'a porté** none of the blows struck home *or* hit their target; **ses attaques/critiques n'ont pas porté** his attacks/criticisms had no effect; **chaque mot a porté** every word hit home; **coup qui porte/qui a porté** telling blow; **sa voix porte bien** his voice carries well; **courant qui porte au sud** current that sets to the south; *F* **ce bruit me porte sur les nerfs** that noise gets on my nerves

(c) *Naut* (*d'une voile*) to fill, to draw

(d) *Naut* **laisser p.** to bear away; **laisser p. sur un navire** to bear down upon *or* run down a ship

(e) (*être en gestation*) **les juments portent onze mois** the gestation period of a mare is eleven months

3 se porter *vpr* **(a)** (*aller*) to go, *Fml* to proceed; **se p. au secours de qn** to go to sb's assistance; **se p. au-devant de tout besoin** to anticipate every need; **la foule s'est portée vers la gare** the crowd made for *or* went towards the station

(b) (*se livrer à*) **se p. à des voies de fait/à des extrémités** to commit assault/to go to extremes

(c) (*se diriger*) **son regard se portait vers son frère** his gaze fell on his brother; *Mil* **se p. en avant** to advance; **la conversation s'est portée sur l'Extrême-Orient** the conversation turned to the Far East; **la conversation se porte toujours sur les mêmes sujets** the conversation always turns on *or* revolves around *or* is always about the same subjects

(d) se p. bien to be well, to be in good health; **se p. à merveille** to be in the best of health; **comment vous portez-vous?** how are you?; **je ne m'en porte pas plus mal** I'm none the worse for it; **moins je le vois, mieux je me porte** the less I see him, the better I feel

(e) (*se présenter comme*) **se p. candidat** to put oneself forward *or* up as a candidate, *Br* to stand as a candidate; **se p. caution** to stand surety; **se p. garant envers** to stand guarantor for, to stand surety for

(f) (*devoir être porté*) to be worn; (*être à la mode*) to be fashionable; **le nœud papillon se porte de plus en plus** more and more people are wearing bow-ties, bow-ties are becoming more and more fashionable; **le bleu se porte beaucoup cette année** blue is being worn a lot *or* is very fashionable this year

porte-raclette, *pl* **porte-raclettes** *nm Aut* wiper arm

porte-revues *nm inv* magazine rack

porterie [pɔrtəri] *nf* (*d'un couvent etc*) gatehouse

porte-satellites *nm inv Aut* planet carrier

porte-savon, *pl* **porte-savon(s)** *nm* soapdish

porte-serviettes *nm inv* towel rail

porte-skis [pɔrt(ə)ski] *nm inv Aut* ski carrier, ski rack

porte-toasts [pɔrtətost] *nm inv* toast rack

porteur, -euse [pɔrtœr, -øz] **1** *n* **(a)** (*d'un message*) bearer; **p. de nouvelles** bearer *or* bringer of news; **j'arrivais p. d'heureuses nouvelles** I arrived bringing *or* bearing good news; **par p.** by messenger

(b) (*de gare, d'aéroport etc*) porter; **p. d'eau** water carrier; **chaise à porteurs** sedan chair

(c) *Méd* carrier; **p. de germes** (germ) carrier; **p. sain** unaffected carrier; (*du SIDA*) = carrier who doesn't have the symptoms of AIDS

(d) (*détenteur*) holder; *Fin* (*d'un chèque*) bearer, payee, endorsee; **p. d'actions** shareholder; **p. de papiers volés/de faux papiers** person carrying stolen/false identity papers; **il était p. de faux papiers** he was carrying false papers; **p. d'une procuration** holder of a power of attorney, holder of a proxy; **p. de titres** holder of stock, stockholder; **p. d'une traite** bearer of a bill, holder of a bill; **payable au p.** payable to bearer; **effets au p.** bearer stock(s)

2 *adj* **(a)** *Tech* **essieu p.** bearing axle, carrying axle; **câble p.** suspension cable; *Él* **fréquence porteuse** carrier frequency; **onde porteuse** carrier wave

(b) *Méd* **les individus porteurs du virus** individuals who carry the virus, (individuals who are) carriers of the virus

(c) *Fig* (*industrie, marché, créneau*) growth

3 *nf Télécom* **porteuse** carrier

porte-vélo, *pl* **porte-vélos** *nm Aut* bike carrier

porte-vent [pɔrtəvɑ̃] *nm inv Tech* air duct

porte-voix [pɔrtəvwa] *nm inv* megaphone; (*électrique*) loudhailer, *Am* bullhorn; **mettre ses mains en p.** to cup one's hands round one's mouth

portfolio [pɔrtfoljo] *nm* portfolio

portier, -ière [pɔrtje, -jɛr] **1** *nm* **(a)** (*gardien*) porter, doorman, doorkeeper; (*dans un hôtel*) commissionaire; **p. de nuit** night porter **(b)** *Litt* (*d'un domaine, monastère etc*) gatekeeper **2** *n Rel* **(frère) p.** porter; **(sœur) portière** portress

portière [pɔrtjɛr] *nf* **(a)** (*d'une voiture, d'un wagon*) door **(b)** (*rideau*) door curtain, portière

portillon [pɔrtijɔ̃] *nm* wicket (gate); *Rail* (*dans un passage à niveaux*) side gate; (*dans une gare*) gate, barrier; *Fig F* **cela se bouscule au p.** (*il y a foule*) people are turning up in droves; (*il s'exprime difficilement*) he can't get his words out

portion [pɔrsjɔ̃] *nf* (*d'argent*) portion, share; (*de gâteau, fromage etc*) portion; (*de viande*) portion, helping; (*d'un groupe, d'une population etc*) portion, section; (*d'un livre*) section, part

portique [pɔrtik] *nm* **(a)** *Archit* portico **(b)** *Gym* (*pour accrocher des agrès*) (cross)beam **(c)** *Rail* **p. à signaux** signal gantry **(d)** *Tech* **grue à p.** travelling gantry crane

portland [pɔrtlɑ̃d] *nm Tech* Portland cement

porto [pɔrto] *nm* (*vin*) port

Porto [pɔrto] *n Géog* Oporto

portoricain, -aine [pɔrtɔrikɛ̃, -ɛn] **1** *adj* Puerto Rican **2** *n* **P.** Puerto Rican

Porto Rico [pɔrtoriko] *nm Géog* Puerto Rico

portrait [pɔrtrɛ] *nm* **(a)** (*représentation*) portrait; (*photo*) portrait(-sized photo); **p. en pied/buste** full-/half-length portrait; **faire le p. de qn** to do *or* paint a portrait of sb; (*au crayon*) to do *or* draw a portrait of sb; *Fig* **c'est le p. vivant de son père, c'est tout le p. de son père** he's the spitting image of his father; *F* **se faire tirer le p.** to have one's photo taken; **p. littéraire** character sketch

(b) (*description*) description, portrayal; **faire le p. de qch/qn** to paint a picture of sth/sb, to describe *or* portray sth/sb; **il nous a fait un p. flatteur de la situation/de sa future femme** he painted a flattering picture of the situation/his future wife

(c) *F* (*visage*) face, mug; **il s'est fait abîmer** *ou* **arranger le p.** someone's made a real mess of *or F* someone's re-arranged his face

(d) *Beaux-Arts* **le p.** (*genre*) portrait painting, portraiture; *Ordinat* **mode p.** portrait mode

portraitiste [pɔrtrɛtist] *n* portrait painter, portraitist

portrait-robot, *pl* **portraits-robots** *nm* Photofit® (picture), Identikit® picture; *Fig* **faire le p. du candidat idéal** to draw up a profile of the ideal candidate

portraiturer [pɔrtrɛtyre] *vt Rare* to portray

portuaire [pɔrtɥɛr] *adj* port, harbour, *US* harbor; **installations portuaires** port facilities *or* installations

portugais, -aise [pɔrtygɛ, -ɛz] **1** *adj* Portuguese **2** *nm Ling* Portuguese **3** *n* **P.** Portuguese **4** *nf* **portugaise (a)** (*huître*) Portuguese oyster **(b)** *F* (*oreille*) **tu as les portugaises ensablées ou quoi?** are you deaf or what?

Portugal [pɔrtygal] *nm Géog* Portugal

pose [poz] *nf* **(a)** (*de rideaux*) putting up, hanging; (*d'un tableau*) hanging; (*de briques, de moquette etc*) laying; (*de pierres précieuses*) setting; (*de bombe*) planting; (*de verre de montre etc*) fitting; (*d'appareils*) installation; **p. de câbles** cable laying; *Typ* **p. de marges** margin setting; **p. de tabulations** tabbing, setting of tabs

(b) (*attitude*) pose, posture; *Beaux-Arts, Phot etc* pose; **garder la p.** to hold the pose; **prendre une p.** to assume *or* strike a pose

(c) *Péj* (*airs*) posing, posturing, affectation; **sans p.** *adv* unaffectedly; *adj* unaffected

(d) *Golf* (*d'une balle*) lie

(e) *Phot* exposure; **temps de p.** exposure time; **p. instantanée** instantaneous exposure; **pellicule de 24 poses** 24-exposure film

posé [poze] *adj* **(a)** (*réfléchi, calme*) (*personne*) self-possessed, composed, calm; *Mus* **voix bien posée** even *or* steady voice **(b)** (*en train de couver*) (*oiseau*) sitting

posément [pozemɑ̃] *adv* calmly, with composure; (*avancer, bouger*) steadily, deliberately

posemètre [pozmɛtr] *nm Phot* exposure meter

poser [poze] **1** *vi* **(a)** (*d'une poutre*) to rest, to lie (**sur** on)

(b) (*comme modèle*) to pose; (*pour qu'on fasse son portrait*) to sit, to pose; **p. pour la postérité** to have one's portrait painted for posterity; **p. nu** to pose (in the) nude

(c) *Péj* (*prendre des airs*) to show off, to pose; **p. pour la galerie** to play to the gallery; *F* **je ne pose pas à l'ange** I don't pretend to be an angel; **il pose au grand connaisseur** he plays *or* acts the great connoisseur

2 *vt* **(a)** (*mettre*) to put, to place; **pose-le sur la table** put it (down) on the table; **p. les armes** to lay down one's arms; **p. un avion** to land an aircraft; **p. sa candidature** (*aux élections*) to put oneself forward (as a candidate), *Br* to stand (as a candidate); (*à un poste*) to apply; **à peine avais-je posé la tête sur l'oreiller que ...** no sooner had my head hit *or* touched the pillow than ...; **l'examen est terminé, posez les stylos** the exam is over, put your pens down

(b) (*formuler*) **p. une question** to ask a question; **p. une question à qn** to ask sb a question, to put a question to sb; *Pol* **p. la question de confiance** to table a motion of confidence; **p. un problème (à qn)** to pose a problem (for sb); **bien/mal p. le problème** (*dans une dissertation*) to identify the problem well/poorly; **p. une règle de conduite** to lay down a rule of conduct

(c) *Math* (*écrire*) **p. un chiffre** to put down *or* set down a number; **je pose deux et je retiens un** put down two (and) carry one

(d) (*rideau, papier peint*) to put up, to hang; (*tableau*) to hang; (*briques, moquette, pierre de fondation, rails etc*) to lay; (*pierres précieuses, rivets*) to set; (*bombe*) to plant; (*chaudière*) to install; (*verre de montre etc*) to fit; **p. une vitre** to put in a pane of glass; **faire p. le téléphone** to have a telephone put in *or* installed; *Typ* **p. des tabulations dans** to tab; *Fig* **p. les jalons** to prepare the ground (**de** for); **p. la première pierre à qch** to lay the foundation stone for sth; *Fig* to lay the foundation(s) for sth

(**e**) **p. qn** to establish sb's reputation; **une telle expérience, ça vous pose un homme** an experience like that sets you up for life

(**f**) (*supposer, établir*) (*hypothèse*) to put forward; **p. des principes** to lay down principles; **posons le cas que cela soit** supposing *or* assuming *or* let's suppose *or* let's assume that that is the case; **cela posé** assuming this to be true

(**g**) *Mus* **bien p. la voix** to pitch (one's voice) correctly

(**h**) **p. son regard sur qn/qch** to look at sb/sth; **il posa sur elle ses yeux de myope** he peered at her shortsightedly

3 se poser *vpr* (**a**) (*d'un oiseau*) to land, to settle, to alight (**sur** on); (*d'un avion*) to land

(**b**) (*apparaître*) (*d'une question, d'un problème*) to arise, to come up, to crop up; **un nouveau problème se pose** we are faced with a new problem, a new problem has arisen; **la question se posera toujours** it's a perennial question; **la question qui se pose est la suivante** the question we are faced with is the following

(**c**) (*se prétendre*) **se p. en réformateur/redresseur de torts** to set oneself up as *or* to claim to be a reformer/a righter of wrongs

(**d**) (*devoir être posé*) **cette potiche se pose par terre/dans un coin** this vase should be (placed) *or* this vase goes on the ground/in a corner; **ça se pose comme du papier peint** you put it up *or* it goes on like wallpaper

(**e**) **se p. des questions** to ask oneself questions; **je finis par me p. des questions** I'm beginning to have my doubts; **il se pose la question de savoir si ...** he is wondering whether ...

(**f**) *F* **il se pose un peu là, comme bricoleur/cuisinier!** some handyman/cook(, I don't think)!; **comme enquiquineur, il se pose là!** he's a real pain in the neck!

poseur, -euse [pozœr, -øz] *n* (**a**) *Tech* (*de câble etc*) layer; **p. d'affiches** billsticker, billposter; *Rail* **p. de rails** platelayer, *Am* tracklayer; *Naut* **p. de mines** minelayer; **p. de bombes** bomb planter; **la police recherche activement les poseurs de bombes** the police have launched a manhunt for the people who planted the bombs (**b**) *Péj* (*pédant*) show-off, poser, poseur; **il est p.** he's always putting on airs, he's affected

positif, -ive [pozitif, -iv] **1** *adj* (**a**) (*sûr, certain*) (*résultat, fait*) positive, actual, real; *Méd* (*réaction, test*) positive (**b**) *Math, Él etc* (*nombre, pôle etc*) positive; *Phot* **épreuve positive** positive (**c**) (*pratique*) (*personne, esprit*) practical, pragmatic (**d**) (*enthousiaste*) (*remarque, attitude, personne*) positive (**e**) *Jur* **droit p.** statute law **2** *nm Phot* positive; **p. (en) couleur** colour positive; **p. transparent** transparency

position [pozisjɔ̃] *nf* (**a**) (*emplacement*) (*de navire, d'avion etc*) position; *Golf* (*de la balle*) lie; **le coureur français est en première/deuxième p.** the French runner is in the lead *or* in first place *or* position/in second place *or* position; **prendre la première p.** to take the lead, to go into first place *or* position; **il est arrivé en troisième p.** he came third; *Aut* **feux de p.** sidelights; **p. d'atterrissage** (*d'un avion*) landing attitude; *Aut* **p. nuit anti-éblouissement** (*de rétro intérieur*) anti-glare position; **p. clé** key position; **p. défensive** *ou* **de défense** defensive position; *Mil, Fig* **p. de repli** fall-back position

(**b**) (*attitude corporelle*) position, posture, attitude; (*debout*) stance; (*des pieds*) position; **s'endormir dans une mauvaise p.** to fall asleep in an uncomfortable *or* awkward position; **être/se mettre en p.** to be in/get into position; **la p. du missionnaire** the missionary position; **première/troisième p.** (*en danse*) first/third position; **en p. debout/assise** in a standing/sitting position; **trois cents passagers en p. debout** three hundred standing passengers

(**c**) (*opinion, avis*) position; **quelle est votre p. sur la guerre?** what is your position on the war?, what position do you take on the war?; **expliquer sa p.** to explain one's position; **elle est restée sur ses positions** she refused to back down, she stood her ground, she stood firm; **prendre p.** to take a stand; **prise de p.** stand; **la prise de p. de notre pays** our country's stand, the stand taken by our country; **une prise de p. devient nécessaire** it's becoming necessary to take a stand; **p. politique** political stance; **p. sociale** (*d'un journal*) social stance

(**d**) (*dans la société*) position; **p. sociale** social standing *or* position *or* status

(**e**) (*situation*) position, situation; **voici ma p.** this is how things stand with me, this is my position *or* situation; **être en p. de faire qch** to be in a position to do sth; *F* **être dans une p. intéressante** to be pregnant, *Vieilli* to be in an interesting situation; **p. gênante** embarrassing position *or* situation; **p. concurrentielle** competitive position; **p. sur le marché** market position

(**f**) *Fin* balance; **demander sa p.** to ask for one's balance; **p. d'un compte** balance of an account; *Fin* **p. de compte** balance; **p. créditrice** credit balance; **p. débitrice** debit balance; **p. financière** financial position

(**g**) *Bourse* **p. acheteur** long position; **p. (courte) couverte** covered (short) position; **p. élémentaire** simple position; **p. longue** long position; **p. non couverte** uncovered position; **p. vendeur** short position

positionnement [pozisjɔnmɑ̃] *nm* (**a**) *Tech* positioning (**b**) *Fin* (*d'un compte*) calculation of the balance (**c**) *Com* positioning; *Mktg* **p. concurrentiel** competitive positioning; **p. de la marque** brand positioning; **p. de prix** price positioning; **p. du produit** product positioning

positionner [pozisjɔne] **1** *vt* (**a**) *Tech, Ordinat* (*curseur, graphique etc*) to position (**b**) *Fin* (*compte*) to calculate the balance of (**c**) *Mktg* (*produit*) to position **2 se positionner** *vpr* **se p. à la hausse sur le marché** to move up-market

positivement [pozitivmɑ̃] *adv* positively; **je ne le sais pas p.** I don't know it for certain, I can't be positive about it; *Él* **chargé p.** positively charged

positivisme [pozitivism] *nm Phil* positivism

positiviste [pozitivist] *adj, n Phil* positivist

positivité [pozitivite] *nf Él, Phil, Méd* positivity

positon [pozitɔ̃] *nm,* **positron** [pozitrɔ̃] *nm Nucl* positron

posologie [pɔzɔlɔʒi] *nf Méd* (*de produit pharmaceutique*) dosage; (*science*) posology

possédant, -ante [pɔsedɑ̃, -ɑ̃t] *adj, n* **les possédants, les classes possédantes** the propertied *or* moneyed classes, the wealthy, *F* the haves

possédé, -ée [pɔsede] **1** *adj* (*par la passion, la jalousie etc*) gripped, dominated (**par** by); **p. du diable** *ou* **du démon** possessed by the devil **2** *n* person possessed; *Fig* maniac, madman, *f* madwoman; **hurler comme un p.** to wail like a banshee, *Fml* to scream like one possessed

posséder [pɔsede] (**je possède; je posséderai**) **1** *vt* (**a**) (*avoir*) to possess, to own, to have; **p. un titre** to have a title; **p. un million** to be a millionaire; **je ne possède pas un centime** I don't have a penny (to my name); **p. un grand talent/sens de l'humour** to possess *or* have a great talent/sense of humour; *Fig* **p. le cœur d'une femme** to have won a woman's heart

(**b**) (*connaître*) (*sujet*) to have a thorough knowledge of, to be master of; (*langue, technique*) to have mastered, to have a good mastery of; **tu ne possèdes pas la vérité, tu sais** you don't know everything, you know; **p. son métier** to know one's job inside out; **elle possède maintenant tous les automatismes** now it comes automatically to her

(**c**) (*dominer*) (*d'un démon, du diable etc*) to possess; **ils étaient tous possédés de la même illusion** they all laboured under the same delusion

(**d**) *F* (*tromper*) (*personne*) to take in, to fool; **je me suis fait p.** I've been taken in *or* had

(**e**) **p. une femme** to possess a woman

2 se posséder *vpr* to control oneself; **elle ne se possédait plus de joie/rage** she was beside herself with joy/rage; **elle ne se possède plus!** she's out of her mind

possesseur [pɔsesœr] *nm* owner; (*de titre*) holder, possessor; **il se croit le p. de la vérité** he thinks he knows everything; **p. de valeurs** share owner

possessif, -ive [pɔsesif, -iv] **1** *adj* (**a**) *Gram* possessive (**b**) *Psy* (*mère, mari*) possessive **2** *nm* [①**A30**,8; **B19-20**,E] *Gram* possessive

possession [pɔsesjɔ̃] *nf* (**a**) (*fait de détenir, d'avoir*) ownership; (*de titre*) holding, possession; **être en p. de qch** to be in possession of sth, to possess sth; *Jur, Fml* to be possessed of sth; *Com* **nous sommes en p. de votre lettre du 4 mars** we are in receipt of *or* have received your letter of 4th March; **avoir qch en sa p.** to have sth in one's possession; **entrer en p. d'un héritage** to enter into possession of an inheritance; **entrée en p. d'un patrimoine** accession to an estate; **prendre p. de qch** to take possession of sth; **rentrer en p. de qch** to gain possession of sth; **comment ce manuscrit est-il tombé en votre p.?** how did this manuscript come into your possession?; **p. vaut titre** possession is nine points *or* nine-tenths of the law; **p. de fait** de facto possession

(**b**) (*bien*) (*surtout bien immobilier, domaine*) possession; **avoir quelques possessions** to have a few possessions; *Fin* **possessions d'une société** assets of a company

(c) *Psy, Rel* possession (*by evil spirit*)

(d) (*maîtrise*) self-control, self-possession; **reprendre p. de soi-même** to regain *or* recover one's self-control *or* composure; **être en pleine p. de ses facultés, être en p. de toutes ses facultés** to be in (full) possession of one's faculties; **elle était en pleine p. de ses moyens** she was at the peak of her powers *or* her abilities

possessivité [pɔsesivite] *nf* possessiveness

possessoire [pɔseswar] *Jur* **1** *adj* **intenter une action p.** to undertake an action for possession (of land) **2** *nm* right of possession

possibilité [pɔsibilite] *nf* **(a)** [①A57-8,c-d; B37,K,2] (*éventualité*) possibility; (*d'un projet, d'une opération*) feasibility; **voir la p. de faire qch** to see the possibility of doing sth; **nous ne voyons aucune p. de changement** we can't see any possibility of change; **il faut prendre en compte la p. du rejet (de greffe)** we have to allow for the possibility of rejection *or* for the possibility that the transplant will be rejected

(b) (*cas*) possibility; **c'est une p. que je n'avais pas envisagée** it's a possibility that I hadn't envisaged

(c) (*moyen, occasion*) opportunity, chance; **c'est la première fois qu'elle a la p. de le faire** this is the first opportunity *or* chance she's had to do it *or* of doing it; **on ne m'en a jamais donné la p.** I was never given the opportunity *or* chance; **si j'ai la p. de lui écrire** if it's possible for me *or* if I can manage to write to him; **p. d'emprunter** borrowing power; *Ordinat* **possibilités d'extension** upgradeability

(d) possibilités (*d'une personne*) capabilities; (*financières*) means; **connaître ses possibilités** to be aware of one's (own) capabilities; **chacun doit payer selon ses possibilités** from each according to his means; **la région dispose de nombreuses possibilités de vacances** the region offers many holiday possibilities; **le nombre de touristes dépasse largement les possibilités de l'hôtel** the number of tourists easily exceeds the capacity of the hotel; **quelles sont vos possibilités d'embauche?** what are your plans for taking people on?; **quelles sont vos possibilités de logement?** how many people can you put up?

possible [pɔsibl] **1** *adj* **(a)** (*faisable*) possible; (*projet, opération*) feasible; **c'est (bien) p.** it's (quite) possible, (very) possibly; **est-ce p.?, ce n'est pas p.!**, *F* **pas p.!** it's not possible!, impossible!, I don't believe it!; *F* **c'est pas Dieu p.** it's unbelievable; **si (c'est) p.** if (it's) possible; **est-il p. de faire des fautes pareilles?** how can people make such mistakes?; **il leur est p. de vous héberger** it's possible for them to put you up; **est-ce qu'il te serait p. de travailler demain?** would it be possible for you to work tomorrow?, could you possibly work tomorrow?; **il ne m'est pas p. de le faire** it's impossible *or* not possible for me to do it, I can't possibly do it; **il ne m'est guère p. de le faire** it's a bit difficult for me to do it; **cela lui est tout à fait p.** it's no trouble at all for him; **il est p. qu'il soit mort** it's possible that he's dead, he may *or* might be dead; **il n'est pas p. que j'y aille** (*je ne peux pas*) it's impossible *or* not possible for me to go; (*il n'est pas question*) there's no possibility of my going; **il est bien p. que ...** it's quite possible that ...; **aussitôt que p., dès que p.** as soon as possible; **est-ce que tu viens? – p.** are you coming? – possibly; **il faut absolument qu'il nous conduise à l'aéroport, ce n'est pas p. autrement** he'll have to drive us to the airport, otherwise we'll never make it

(b) (*existant, maximum, minimum*) **le moins souvent p.** as infrequently as possible; **le moins de détails possible(s)** as few details as possible; **elle nous en parle le moins p.** she talks to us about it as little as possible; **tous les détails possibles** every possible detail; **toutes les informations possibles** all available information; **la boîte la plus grande p.** the largest box possible, the largest possible box; **elle a eu tous les ennuis possibles et imaginables** she's had every problem you can think of; **dans la plus large mesure p.** as far as possible; *Fml* **le plus tôt qu'il vous sera p.** at your earliest convenience

(c) (*éventuel*) possible; **danger p.** possible *or* potential danger; **il est p. qu'il y pense à la dernière minute** he may well think of it at the last minute; *F* **c'est dans les choses possibles** it's a possibility

(d) *F* (*supportable*) **cette fille/situation n'est pas p.!** that girl/this situation is impossible!; **ça n'est plus p.** I can't take (it) any more, I've had enough

2 *nm* **(a)** (*ce qui est possible*) what is possible; **dans la mesure du p.** as far as possible; **faire tout son p. pour ...** to do all *or* everything one (possibly) can (do) to ..., to do one's utmost *or* best to ..., to try one's hardest to ...; **il s'est montré aimable au p.** he couldn't have been nicer, he was extremely pleasant

(b) (*chose réalisable*) possibility; **envisageons tous les possibles** let's consider all the possibilities

post-achat [pɔstaʃa] *adj Mktg* postpurchase

post-acheminement [pɔstaʃ(e)minmɑ̃] *nm* transfer from main airport

postal, -ale, -aux, -ales [pɔstal, -o] *adj* (*tarif*) mail, *Br* postal; (*train, camion, wagon*) mail; **code p.** postcode, postal code, *Am* zip code; **sac p.** mailbag, *Br* postbag; **carte postale** postcard; **colis p.** parcel sent by post; **les services postaux** the postal *or Am* mail services; **les services postaux sont assez fiables dans ce pays** the postal service is quite reliable in this country

postcombustion [pɔstkɔ̃bystjɔ̃] *nf Tech* (*d'une fusée, d'un turboréacteur*) afterburning, reheat; **dispositif de p.** afterburner

postcommunion [pɔstkɔmynjɔ̃] *nf Rel* postcommunion

postcommunisme [pɔstkɔmynism] *nm* postcommunism

postcure [pɔstkyr] *nf Méd* aftercare; **elle est en p.** she's in aftercare

postdater [pɔstdate] *vt* to postdate

poste[1] [pɔst] *nf* **(a)** (*service*) *Br* post, mail; **la P.** the *Br* postal *or* mail service, *Br* = the Post Office; **envoyer une lettre par la p.** to send a letter by post *or* mail; **mettre une lettre à la p.** to post *or* mail a letter; **(bureau de) p.** post office; **p. principale, grande p.** main post office; **aller à la p.** to go to the post office; **receveur/receveuse des postes** postmaster/ postmistress; **grève des postes** postal or mail strike **(b)** *Arch* (*relais de chevaux*) post, relay; **chevaux de p.** posthorses; **maître de p.** postmaster; **aller en p.** to travel post; **courir la p.** to go posthaste

▶ **poste**: **p. aérienne** airmail; **p. restante** poste restante, *Am* general delivery

poste[2] *nm* **(a)** (*fonction*) job, position, post; **il y a des postes vacants** there are (job) vacancies; **présenter sa candidature à un p. de technicien** to apply for a job as a technician; **un p. clé** a key position; **occuper un p. de confiance** to hold a position of trust; *Ind* **p. de jour/nuit** day/night shift; **p. à pourvoir** vacancy

(b) *Rad, TV* **p. (de) radio** radio set; **p. de télévision** television set; **p. récepteur** receiver, receiving set; *F* **ouvrir/ fermer le p.** to switch the radio/television on/off; *Rad* **p. émetteur** (*endroit*) broadcasting station; (*équipement*) transmitter

(c) *Tél* extension; **je voudrais le p. 35, s'il vous plaît** I'd like extension 35, please; **le p. est occupé** the extension *or* line is *Br* engaged *or* busy; **je vous passe le p.** I'm putting you through

(d) (*bureau*) post; (*de police*) station; **passer la nuit au p.** to spend the night at the station; **p. de la Croix-Rouge** Red Cross station

(e) (*salle*) quarters; **p. d'équipage** crew's quarters; (*dans la marine marchande*) forecastle; *Naut* **p. des maîtres** warrant officers' wardroom; **p. des aspirants** gunroom

(f) *Compta* entry, item; **p. créditeur/débiteur** credit/debit item; **p. de bilan** balance sheet item; **p. extraordinaire** extraordinary item

(g) *Mil* (*d'un soldat*) post, station; *Mil* **p. avancé** advanced *or* outlying post; *Mil, Naut* **chef de p.** guard commander; **à vos postes!** to your posts!, stand by!; **postes de combat** action stations; **être à son p.** to be at one's post; *Fig* **être solide** *ou* **fidèle au p.** to be still going strong

(h) *Naut* (*emplacement*) berth; **p. de mouillage** anchoring berth; **p. d'amarrage** mooring berth, mooring(s); **mettre les ancres à p.** to stow the anchors

▶ **poste**: *Rail* **p. d'aiguillage** signal box; **p. de commandement** headquarters, command post; *Naut* control room; **p. de contrôle** checkpoint; *Mil* **p. d'écoute** listening station; **p. d'essence** petrol *or Am* gas station, filling station; *Mil* **p. de garde** guardroom; **p. d'incendie** fire point; *Mil* **p. d'observation** observation post; **p. de péage** toll booth; *Av* **p. de pilotage** cockpit; (*dans un avion plus important*) flight deck; **p. de police** (police) station; *Mil* guardroom; **p. de secours** first-aid post; *Ordinat* **p. de travail** workstation

posté, -ée [pɔste] **1** *adj* **travail p.** shift work; **ouvrier p.** shift worker **2** *n* shift worker

poster[1] [pɔste] **1** *vt* (*sentinelle*) to post; (*hommes, troupes*) to station **2 se poster** *vpr* to take up a position, to station oneself

poster[2] *vt* (*courrier*) *Br* to post, to mail

poster[3] [pɔstɛr] *nm* poster

postérieur [pɔsterjœr] **1** *adj* **(a)** (*dans le temps*) later, subsequent; **p. à son décès** after his death; **la rechute est très postérieure à son opération** the relapse came a long time after his operation; **avoir lieu à une date postérieure** to be held at a later date; **être remis à une date postérieure**

to be postponed to a later date; **à une date postérieure à notre coup de téléphone** at a date some time after our phone call **(b)** *(dans l'espace) (pattes)* back, hind, rear; *Anat* posterior; **partie postérieure** back part **2** *nm F (derrière)* behind, backside, *Hum* posterior, *Am* butt

postérieurement [pɔsterjœrmɑ̃] *adv* later, subsequently, at a later date; **p. à** after

postériorité [pɔsterjɔrite] *nf* posteriority

postérité [pɔsterite] *nf* posterity; *(famille, descendance)* posterity, descendants; **mourir sans (laisser de) p.** to die without issue; **nous travaillons pour la p.** we are working for posterity; *Fig* **la p. du nouveau-roman** the legacy of the nouveau roman; **entrer dans la p., passer à la p.** *(d'une personne)* to go down in history; *(d'une œuvre, d'un mot etc)* to be handed down to posterity

postface [pɔstfas] *nf* postscript

postglaciaire [pɔstglasjɛr] *adj Géol* postglacial

posthume [pɔstym] *adj* posthumous

postiche [pɔstiʃ] **1** *adj (cheveux, cils etc)* false **2** *nm* hairpiece

postier, -ière [pɔstje, -jɛr] *n* postal worker, post office employee

postillon [pɔstijɔ̃] *nm* **(a)** *Hist (cocher)* postilion **(b)** *(salive)* **postillons** shower(s) of spit; **envoyer des postillons** to splutter, to sputter

postillonner [pɔstijɔne] *vi (en parlant)* to splutter, to sputter

postindustriel, -ielle [pɔstɛ̃dystrijɛl] *adj* postindustrial

postmoderne [pɔstmɔdɛrn] *adj* postmodern(ist)

postmodernisme [pɔstmɔdɛrnism] *nm* postmodernism

postnatal, -ale, -als, -ales [pɔstnatal] *adj* postnatal

postopératoire [pɔstɔperatwar] *adj Méd* postoperative

postpartum [pɔstpartɔm] *nm Méd* postpartum

postposer [pɔstpoze] *vt Gram* **p. un adjectif/un verbe** to place *or* put an adjective/a verb after; **adjectif postposé** adjective placed after the noun, postpositive adjective

postposition [pɔstpozisjɔ̃] *nf Gram* postposition

post-production [pɔstprɔdyksjɔ̃] *nf TV etc* postproduction

postscolaire [pɔstskɔlɛr] *adj (cours)* continuation; **enseignement p.** further *or* continuing education

post-scriptum [pɔstskriptɔm] *nm inv* postscript, P.S.

postsonorisation [pɔstsɔnɔrizasjɔ̃] *nf Cin* postsynchronization, dubbing

postsonoriser [pɔstsɔnɔrize] *vt Cin* to postsynchronize, to dub

post-synchro [pɔstsɛ̃kro] *nf Cin* post-syncing

postsynchronisation [pɔstsɛ̃krɔnizasjɔ̃] *nf Cin* postsynchronization, dubbing

postsynchroniser [pɔstsɛ̃krɔnize] *vt Cin* to postsynchronize, to dub

postulant, -ante [pɔstylɑ̃, -ɑ̃t] *n* **(a)** *(à un emploi)* applicant, candidate **(b)** *Rel* postulant

postulat [pɔstyla] *nm Phil* postulate, assumption

postuler [pɔstyle] **1** *vt* **(a)** *(demander) (poste, emploi)* to apply for **(b)** *Phil* to postulate **2** *vi* **(a)** *Jur* **p. pour un client** *(d'un avocat)* to act on behalf of *or* represent a client **(b)** **p. à** *ou* **pour un emploi** to apply for a job

posture [pɔstyr] *nf* **(a)** *(attitude du corps)* posture, position, attitude **(b)** **être en p. de faire qch** to be in a position to do sth; **être en bonne/mauvaise p. (pour faire qch)** to be in a good/bad position *or* well/badly placed (to do sth); **être en fâcheuse p.** to be in an awkward situation

pot [po] *nm* **(a)** *(récipient)* pot; **p. de terre** earthenware pot; **p. à tabac** tobacco jar; *Fig F (personne petite et grosse)* tubby person; **p. à eau** water jug; **p. à lait, p. au lait** milk jug; *(en métal)* milk can; **p. de confiture** jam jar; *F* **le p.** *(pour enfant)* the potty; **aller sur le p.** to use the potty; **mettre en p.** *(plante)* to pot; **p. de colle** pot of glue; *Fig F* **quel p. de colle!** he sticks to you like glue!, you can't shake him off *or* get rid of him!; **quel p. de colle tu fais aujourd'hui!** stop annoying *or* bugging me!; **il est gentil mais c'est un p. de colle** he's nice but he tends to cling; *Fig F* **payer les pots cassés** to take the rap, *Br* to carry the can; *Fig* **découvrir le p. aux roses** [potoroz] to find out what's been going on; *F* **c'est le p. de terre contre le p. de fer** he doesn't stand a chance, he's more than met his match

(b) *(contenu)* pot; **finir un p. de confiture** to finish a jar *or* pot of jam; **un p. d'eau** a jug of water; **petit p.** *(pour bébé)* (jar of) baby food; **p. d'accueil** welcoming drink; *F* **allons prendre un p.** let's go for a drink *or Br* jar; *F* **faire un p. (d'adieu/d'anniversaire)** to have a (farewell/birthday) party

(c) *Culin (marmite)* (cooking) pot; **manger à la fortune du p.** to take pot luck; **en trois coups de cuiller à p.** in less than no time, in no time (at all), in two shakes (of a lamb's tail); *Fig* **tourner autour du p.** to beat about the bush; **sourd comme un p.** as deaf as a post

(d) *F (chance)* **avoir du p.** to be lucky; **avoir un coup de p.** to have a stroke of luck; **manque de p., pas de p.** just his/your/*etc* luck; **elle n'a vraiment pas de p.!** she has no luck at all

▶ **pot**: **p. à absorption** absorption silencer; **p. à catalyseur** catalytic converter; **p. catalytique** catalytic converter; **p. de chambre** chamber pot; **p. d'échappement** silencer, *Am* muffler; *(ensemble du système)* exhaust (system); *(tuyau)* exhaust (pipe), *Am* tail pipe; **p. de fleurs** *(récipient)* flowerpot, plant pot; *(plante)* pot of flowers; *Naut* **p. au noir** doldrums; *Aut* **p. de résonance** resonance chamber

potable [pɔtabl] *adj* **(a)** *(que l'on peut boire)* drinkable, fit to drink; **eau p.** drinking water **(b)** *F (correct)* passable, reasonable; *(tenue)* acceptable, decent

potache [pɔtaʃ] *nm Scol F* schoolboy *(attending a collège or lycée)*

potage [pɔtaʒ] *nm* **(a)** *(soupe)* soup; **p. aux légumes** vegetable soup **(b)** *Arch, Litt* **pour tout p.** all told, (all) in all

potager, -ère [pɔtaʒe, -ɛr] **1** *adj* **herbes potagères** herbs for cooking, pot herbs; **plante potagère** vegetable; **jardin p.** vegetable *or* kitchen garden **2** *nm* vegetable *or* kitchen garden

potasse [pɔtas] *nf Ch* potash; **chlorate de p.** potassium chlorate

potasser [pɔtase] *F* **1** *vt* to bone up on, *Br* to swot up **2** *vi* to bone up, *Br* to swot

potassique [pɔtasik] *adj Ch* potassium; *(sel)* potassic

potassium [pɔtasjɔm] *nm Ch* potassium

pot-au-feu [pɔtofø] **1** *nm inv Culin* = boiled beef with vegetables **2** *adj inv F Vieilli (personne)* stay-at-home

pot-de-vin, *pl* **pots-de-vin** *nm* bribe, *F* backhander; **donner un p. à qn** to bribe sb, *F* to give sb a backhander

pote [pɔt] *nm F* pal, chum, *Br* mate, *Am* buddy

poteau, -eaux [pɔto] *nm* **(a)** post; *Min* pit prop; *Sp (de but)* (goal)post; **p. indicateur** signpost; **p. télégraphique** telegraph pole; **p. électrique** electricity pylon; *Sp* **p. de départ** starting post; *Sp* **p. d'arrivée** finishing post, winning post; **rester au p.** to be left at the post; **être coiffé sur le p.** *Br* to be pipped at the post, *Am* to be beaten by a nose; *F* **avoir des jambes comme des poteaux** to have legs like tree-trunks

(b) **p. (d'exécution)** execution post *or* stake *(for sb about to be shot)*; **mettre qn au p.** to put sb up against a wall and shoot him/her; **le général au p.!** down with the general!

(c) *F (ami)* pal, chum, *Br* mate, *Am* buddy

potée [pɔte] *nf Culin* stew *(esp cabbage and carrots with pork)*

potelé [pɔtle] *adj* chubby, plump

potence [pɔtɑ̃s] *nf* **(a)** [①A13,3,b] *(gibet)* gallows, gibbet; **échapper à la p.** to cheat the gallows; **gibier de p.** gallows bird **(b)** *(charpente)* bracket, arm, support; *(de grue)* jib; *(d'un guidon de bicyclette)* stem; *(d'une perfusion)* stand; **en p.** bracket-shaped, L-shaped **(c)** *Naut, Mil* davit

potentat [pɔtɑ̃ta] *nm* potentate

potentialisation [pɔtɑ̃sjalizasjɔ̃] *nf Pharm* potentiation

potentialiser [pɔtɑ̃sjalize] **1** *vt* **(a)** *Pharm* to potentiate **(b)** *Fig* to maximize **2 se potentialiser** *vpr* to maximize one's potential

potentialité [pɔtɑ̃sjalite] *nf* potentiality; **une p. inutilisée** unused potential

potentiel, -elle [pɔtɑ̃sjɛl] **1** *adj* potential; *Gram* **préfixe/sens p.** potential prefix/meaning; *MecE* **énergie potentielle** potential energy **2** *nm* **(a)** potential; **avoir un bon/fort p.** to have good/strong potential; **p. de guerre** war establishment; **p. de vente** sales potential; **p. du marché** market potential **(b)** *Él* potential; *Rad* **p. de grille** grid potential **(c)** *Gram* potential (mood)

potentiellement [pɔtɑ̃sjɛlmɑ̃] *adv* potentially

potentille [pɔtɑ̃tij] *nf Bot* **p. (rampante)** cinquefoil

potentiomètre [pɔtɑ̃sjɔmɛtr] *nm Électron* potentiometer; *Cin (de son)* fader; **p. de micro** microphone fader; **p. vidéo** video fader

poterie [pɔtri] *nf* **(a)** *(usine)* pottery (works); *(atelier)* potter's workshop *or* studio; *(art, techniques)* pottery; **cours de p.** pottery class; **faire de la p.** to do *or* make pottery **(b)** *(objet)* piece of pottery; *(objets)* pottery; **elle achète souvent de la p./des poteries** she often buys pottery; **p. (de terre)** earthenware; **p. de grès** stoneware **(c)** *Tech* **p. d'étain** pewter(ware)

poterne [pɔtɛrn] *nf* postern (gate)

potiche [pɔtiʃ] *nf* **(a)** *(vase)* (large) vase *(esp of Chinese or Japanese porcelain)* **(b)** *Fig* figurehead

potier [pɔtje] *nm* potter

potin [pɔtɛ̃] *nm F* **(a)** **potins** gossip, tittle-tattle; **s'intéresser aux petits potins** to take an interest in idle gossip **(b)** *(bruit)* row, din, rumpus; **faire du p.** to kick up a row *or* rumpus, to make a din

potiner [pɔtine] *vi* to gossip
potion [posjɔ̃] *nf Méd* potion; **p. magique** magic potion
potiron [pɔtirɔ̃] *nm* pumpkin
pot-pourri, *pl* **pots-pourris** *nm Mus* potpourri, medley; (*fleurs séchées*) potpourri
potron-minet [pɔtrɔ̃minɛ] *nm Arch F* **dès p.** at daybreak, at the crack of dawn
pou, *pl* **poux** [pu] *nm* louse, *pl* lice; **p. du pubis** pubic louse, *F* crab (louse); *F* **laid comme un p.** as ugly as sin; **fier** *ou* **orgueilleux comme un p.** as proud as a peacock; **sale comme un p.** filthy dirty; **elle est vexée comme un p.** she's really really upset, *Br* she's really got the hump; *F* **chercher des poux dans la tête à qn** to pick a quarrel with sb (about nothing)
pouah [pwa] *int* ugh!
poubelle [pubɛl] *nf* (dust)bin, *Am* garbage *or* trash can; *Ordinat* wastebasket, *Am* trash; **p. à pédale** pedal bin; **jeter** *ou* **mettre qch à la p.** to throw *or* put sth in the (dust)bin, to throw sth away; *Fig F* to think sth is a load of rubbish; **c'est bon à jeter** *ou* **mettre à la p.** it should be thrown out, it's fit for the dustbin; *Fig* it's a load of rubbish; **qu'est-ce que j'en fais? – p.!** what do I do with this? – just bin it!; **descendre la p.** to take the rubbish *or Am* garbage down; **faire les poubelles** to scrounge in dustbins
pouce [pus] *nm* **(a)** (*doigt*) thumb; **sucer son p.** to suck one's thumb; *F* **donner un coup de p. à qn/qch** to help sb/sth along (a bit); **elle/le projet n'a besoin que d'un coup de p.** she/the project just needs to be helped along a bit; *F* **manger sur le p.** to have a (quick) snack; **se tourner les pouces** to twiddle one's thumbs; **dire p.** to give up; *Scol* **p.!** truce!, *Br* pax! **(b)** (*gros orteil*) big toe **(c)** (*mesure*) inch; **disquette de 3,5/5,25 pouces** 3.5/5.25 inch disk; *aussi Fig* **ne pas bouger d'un p.** not to move an inch; *aussi Fig* **ne pas céder un p. de terrain** not to yield *or* budge an inch
Poucet [pusɛ] *nm* **le Petit P.** Tom Thumb
poucettes [pusɛt] *nfpl Arch* = metal rings attached to the thumbs of prisoners
poucier [pusje] *nm* (*doigtier*) thumbstall
pouding [pudiŋ] *nm* = **pudding (b)**
poudingue [pudɛ̃g] *nm Géol* pudding stone
poudrage [pudraʒ] *nm Tech* powdering
poudre [pudr] *nf* **(a)** (*substance*) powder; **réduire qch en p.** to reduce sth to powder, to pulverize sth, to powder sth; **café en p.** instant coffee; **chocolat en p.** chocolate powder; **lait en p.** powdered milk; **sucre en p.** caster sugar; **lessive en p., p. à laver** washing powder; **savon en p.** soap powder; **p. compacte/libre** (*maquillage*) pressed/loose powder; *F* **prendre la p. d'escampette** to make off, *Br* to do a bunk
(b) (*explosif*) (explosive) powder; **p. à canon** gunpowder; *Fig* **être vif comme la p.** to flare up easily; *Fig* **mettre le feu aux poudres** to spark off a crisis; **la nouvelle s'est répandue comme une traînée de p.** the news spread like wildfire; **faire parler la p.** to let one's guns do the talking; *Fig* **ça sent la p.** there's trouble brewing
(c) *Arch* (*poussière*) dust; *Fig* **jeter de la p. aux yeux de qn** to dazzle *or* impress sb
(d) *F* (*héroïne*) smack
▶ **poudre**: **p. dentifrice** tooth powder; **p. d'encre** toner; **p. à éternuer** sneezing powder; **p. d'or** gold dust; **p. de perlimpinpin** magic *or* miracle powder; **p. à récurer** scouring powder; **p. de riz** face powder
poudrer [pudre] **1** *vt* to powder; **p. ses cheveux** to powder one's hair, to put powder on one's hair; **une femme poudrée** a woman with a powdered face **2** *v impers Can* **il poudre** it's snowing slightly **3 se poudrer** *vpr* to powder one's face *or* nose; **se p. le visage** to powder one's face
poudrerie [pudrəri] *nf* **(a)** (*fabrique de poudre*) (gun)powder factory **(b)** *Can* (*neige*) drifting snow
poudreux, -euse [pudrø, -øz] **1** *adj* **(a)** (*qui a la consistance de la poudre*) powdery; **neige poudreuse** powder snow **(b)** *Vieilli* (*couvert de poussière*) dusty **2** *nf* **poudreuse (a)** (*neige*) powder snow **(b)** (*sucrier*) sugar sprinkler *or* caster
poudrier [pudrije] *nm* powder box; (*porté dans un sac à main etc*) (powder) compact
poudrière [pudrijɛr] *nf* (*entrepôt*) powder magazine; *Fig* (*région*) powder keg
poudrin [pudrɛ̃] *nm* spindrift
poudroiement [pudrwamɑ̃] *nm* dust haze
poudroyer [pudrwaje] *vi Litt* (**il poudroie**; **il poudroiera**) (*du soleil*) to pick out the dust in the air; **la route poudroie** the dust whirls up from the road
pouf [puf] **1** *int* bump!, thud! **2** *nm* **(a)** (*meuble*) pouf(fe) **(b)** *Belg* **à p.** on tick; **taper à p.** (*au hasard*) to make a wild guess
pouffer [pufe] *vi* **p. (de rire)** to burst out laughing
pouffiasse [pufjas] *nf Vulg Vieilli* (*prostituée*) whore, tart; *Péj Vulg* **une grosse p.** a (great) fat cow, *Br* a fat slag; **quelle p.!** what a slag!
pouillerie [pujri] *nf* squalor; (*lieu*) filthy place, lousy hole
pouilleux, -euse [pujø, -øz] **1** *adj* **(a)** (*couvert de vermine*) lousy, flea-ridden, verminous **(b)** (*misérable*) wretched, miserable; (*quartier, maison*) squalid, shabby **(c)** *Géog* **la Champagne pouilleuse** = the barren part of the Champagne region **2** *n* **(a)** (*personne couverte de vermine*) louse-ridden *or* flea-ridden person **(b)** (*clochard*) tramp, *Am* bum
pouillot [pujo] *nm Orn* warbler
poujadisme [puʒadism] *nm Hist Pol* Poujadism (*lower-middle-class, populist movement in the 1950s and 60s*); *Fig Péj* narrow-minded *or* shopkeeper mentality
poujadiste [puʒadist] *nm Hist Pol* Poujadist; *Fig Péj* narrow-minded person
poulailler [pulaje] *nm* **(a)** (*basse-cour*) hen house, hen roost **(b)** *Th F* **le p.** the gods; **places de p.** seats in the gods
poulain [pulɛ̃] *nm* **(a)** (*cheval*) foal **(b)** *Fig* protégé **(c)** *Tech* **p. (de chargement)** (*pour décharger les tonneaux etc*) skid
poulaine [pulɛn] *nf* **(a)** *Naut* (ship's) head; **les poulaines** the latrines (*for crew*) **(b)** **soulier à la p.** long pointed shoe
poularde [pulard] *nf Culin* fattened pullet
poulbot [pulbo] *nm* street urchin (of Montmartre)
poule[1] [pul] *nf* **(a)** *Zool* hen; *Culin* (boiling) fowl; **p. pondeuse** laying hen; **p. au pot** boiled chicken; *Fig* **ma (petite) p.!** my dear!, my pet!; *Fig* **la p. aux œufs d'or** the goose that lays the golden eggs; *Fig* **mère p.** mother hen; *Fig Péj* **p. mouillée** (*personne*) softie, wimp; *surtout Br Pol* wet; **se coucher comme** *ou* **avec les poules** to go to bed early; **lait de p.** (non-alcoholic) egg flip *or* egg nog; *Fig* **quand les poules auront des dents** when pigs can fly; **p. d'eau** moorhen; **p. faisane** hen pheasant; **petite p. de bruyère** grey hen; **nid de p.** (*sur la route*) pothole
(b) *Arg Péj* (*femme légère*) floozy, tart; (*maîtresse*) mistress; **p. de luxe** high-class call girl
poule[2] *nf* **(a)** (*enjeu*) pool, kitty **(b)** *Escrime* pool, tournament; *Rugby* group **(c)** *Courses de chevaux* **p. d'essai** = early-season race for three-year-olds
poulet [pulɛ] *nm* **(a)** *Zool, Culin* chicken; *Culin* **p. fermier** *ou* **de grain** free-range chicken; **p. élevé en batterie** battery (-farmed) chicken; *Culin* **aile de p.** chicken wing; **cuisse de p.** chicken leg; **p. rôti** roast chicken; *très F* **et mon cul, c'est du p.?** oh come on, don't give me that crap! **(b)** **mon (petit) p.** my darling, my pet, *Hum* my little chickadee **(c)** *F* (*policier*) cop **(d)** *Arch F* (*billet doux*) billet-doux
poulette [pulɛt] *nf* **(a)** *Vieilli* (*jeune poule*) pullet, young hen; *Culin* **sauce (à la) p.** = rich white sauce (*with onions, mushrooms, white wine etc*) **(b)** *F Vieilli* (*fille*) girl, *Am* dame **(c)** *F* **ma p.** my darling, my pet
pouliche [puliʃ] *nf* filly
poulie [puli] *nf* pulley; **p. simple/double** single/double block; **p. fixe** fixed pulley, standing block; **p. d'entraînement** drive pulley; **p. folle** loose pulley, idler
pouliner [puline] *vi* (*d'une jument*) to foal
poulinière [pulinjɛr] *adj, nf* **(jument) p.** brood mare
pouliot[1] [puljo] *nm Bot* pennyroyal
pouliot[2] *nm* (*sur charrette*) windlass
poulot, -otte [pulo, -ɔt] *n Enf* (my) pet, (my) darling
poulpe [pulp] *nm* octopus
pouls [pu] *nm* pulse; **tâter le p. de qn** to feel sb's pulse; **prendre le p. à qn** to take sb's pulse; *Fig* **tâter** *ou* **prendre le p. de l'économie** to take the pulse of the economy; *Fig* **tâter** *ou* **prendre le p. de l'opinion** to sound out public opinion
poumon [pumɔ̃] *nm Anat* lung; **p. d'acier** iron lung; **respirer à pleins poumons** to breathe deeply, to take deep breaths/a deep breath; **crier à pleins poumons** to shout at the top of one's voice; **avoir de bons poumons** *ou* **des poumons** (*d'un chanteur etc*) to have good lungs; *F* **cracher ses poumons** to cough one's guts up *or* out
poupard [pupar] **1** *nm* **(a)** *Vieilli* (*gros bébé*) chubby baby **(b)** *Arch* (*poupée*) baby doll **2** *adj Vieilli* chubby(-cheeked); **visage p.** baby face
poupe [pup] *nf Naut* stern, poop; **avoir le vent en p.** to have the wind aft; *Fig* to have the wind in one's sails
poupée [pupe] *nf* **(a)** (*jouet*) doll, *Enf* dolly; **p. mannequin** doll for dressing up; **poupées gigognes** *ou* **russes** Russian dolls; **p. gonflable** inflatable doll; **maison de p.** doll's house; *Fig* doll's house, shoebox; **jouer à la p.** to play with dolls **(b)** *F* (*jolie fille*) doll **(c)** (*pansement au doigt*) finger bandage; (*le doigt lui-même*) bandaged finger; **faire une p. à qn** to bandage sb's finger **(d)** *Naut* **p. de cabestan** capstan head
poupin [pupɛ̃] *adj* (*personne*) chubby(-cheeked); (*air*) baby-like; **visage p.** baby face
poupon [pupɔ̃] *nm* (tiny) baby
pouponner [pupɔne] *vi* to play the doting mother/father

pouponnière [pupɔnjɛr] *nf* nursery (*for children up to three years old*)

pour [pur] **1** *prép* **(a)** (*à la place de*) for; **dis-le lui/allez-y p. moi** tell him/go for me; **agir p. qn** to act for sb *or* on sb's behalf; **p. le Président, son secrétaire ...** on behalf of the President, his secretary ...; *Fin* **p. acquit** received with thanks

(b) (*comme*) for; **il la veut p. femme** he wants her for *or* as his wife; **tenir qn p. fou** to regard sb as mad, to consider sb mad; **prendre qn p. un autre** to take sb for somebody else; **laisser qn p. mort** to leave sb for dead; **une attitude p. le moins étrange** a somewhat strange attitude, a strange attitude to say the least; *F* **c'est p. de bon** *ou* **p. de vrai** I mean it, I'm serious; *F* **ça compte p. du beurre, on rejoue** that doesn't count, let's play again; **avec p. tout bagage ...** with only ... as luggage, taking only ...

(c) (*direction*) for; **je pars p. la France** I'm off to France, I'm leaving for France; **le train/l'avion p. Paris** the Paris train/plane, the train/plane to *or* for Paris

(d) [①A66; B53-54] (*temps*) for; **je vais en Suisse p. quinze jours** I'm going to Switzerland for two weeks; **p. dans trois jours** in three days, in three days' time; **p. toujours** for ever, for good; **p. le moment** for the moment; **il sera ici p. quatre heures** he'll be here for four hours; (*à quatre heures*) he'll be here by four o'clock; **j'en ai p. une heure** it'll take me an hour, I'll be an hour

(e) (*contre*) for; **il a acheté son vélo p. 50 francs** he bought his bike for 50 francs; **il me l'a vendu p. trois fois rien** he sold it to me for next to nothing; **trente p. cent** thirty per cent *or* percent; **10 p. 1000** one per cent *or* percent; **mot p. mot** word for word; **jour p. jour** to the (very) day; **donnez-moi p. 100 francs d'essence** give me 100 francs' worth of petrol; **j'en ai p. mon argent** I've got my money's worth; **être p. beaucoup/peu dans qch** to play a large part/not to play much of a part in sth, to have a great deal to do/not to have much to do with sth; **je n'y suis p. rien!** it's got nothing to do with me!, I've got nothing to do with it!

(f) (*cause, but*) for; **vêtements p. hommes** men's clothes, clothes for men; **livres p. enfants** children's books, books for children; **j'épargne p. quand je serai vieux** I'm saving for my old age *or* for when I'm old; **je le mets de côté p. ce soir** I'm putting it aside for tonight; **je suis ici p. affaires** I'm here on business; **voyager p. le plaisir** to travel for pleasure; **je viens p. la machine à laver** I've come about the washing machine; **je vous téléphone p. l'annonce parue dans le journal** I'm calling about the advertisement in the newspaper; **pommade p. les démangeaisons** ointment to relieve itching; **shampooing p. cheveux secs** shampoo for dry hair; *Ordinat* **moniteur p. graphismes** graphics monitor; **c'est p. cela qu'il est venu** that's why he came, that's the reason he came; **p. l'amour de Dieu** for God's sake, for heaven's sake; **faites-le p. moi** do it for me *or* my sake; **nous devons y réfléchir p. les générations futures** we should think about it for the sake of future generations; **j'avais peur p. lui** I was afraid for him, I feared for him; **elle s'inquiète p. toi** she's worried about you; **il est bon p. les animaux** he's kind to animals; **l'art p. l'art** art for art's sake; **p. la forme** for form's sake; **beaucoup de bruit p. rien** a lot of fuss about *or* over nothing, *Litt* much ado about nothing; **tant pis p. moi** it's just hard luck on me; **tant mieux p. elle** good for her; **p. quoi faire?** what for?; *F* **c'est fait p.** that's what it's there for; *F* **c'est p. quoi?** what's that for?

(g) (*en faveur de*) for, in favour *or US* favor of; **parler p. qn** to speak in favour of sb; **je suis p. la libération de la femme** I'm (all) for *or* in favour of women's liberation; **moi, je suis p.** I'm (all) for it, I'm in favour of it

(h) (*quant à, en ce qui concerne*) for; **p. mon compte (personnel)** for my part, as far as I'm concerned; **il est grand p. son âge** he's tall for his age; **p. ce qui est de ...** as regards ..., with regard to ...; **p. (ce qui est de) moi** as for me, for my part, as far as I'm concerned; **p. moi, c'est absurde** in my opinion it's ridiculous, I think it's ridiculous; **ce ne sera une surprise p. personne** it will come as no surprise to anybody; **il n'en est pas plus intelligent p. cela** he's none the cleverer for all that; **et p. cela ...** and so ...; **en tout et p. tout** all in all, altogether, in total; *F* **p. de la chance, c'est de la chance** you're in luck and no mistake; **p. une surprise, c'est une surprise!** that's a surprise and no mistake!; **p. une déception/un anniversaire, ce fut une déception/un anniversaire!** it was some disappointment/birthday!, *F* it was one hell of a disappointment/birthday!

(i) p. + *inf* (in order) to; **il faut manger p. vivre** one must eat (in order) to live; **p. ainsi dire** so to speak; **p. bien faire** to do things properly; **c'était p. rire** it was just for fun *or* for a laugh; **il s'en va p. ne jamais revenir** he's going away for good, he's leaving never to return; **nous nous sommes dépêchés p. ne pas être en retard** we hurried so as not to be late

(j) p. que + *sub* so that, in order that; **je vous dis cela p. que vous soyez sur vos gardes** I'm telling you this in order to put you on your guard *or* so that you'll be on your guard; **il est trop tard p. qu'elle sorte** it is too late for her to go out; **mettez-le là, p. qu'on ne l'oublie pas** put it there so that it won't be forgotten

(k) (*ayant pour résultat*) **p. notre grand malheur, il nous a quittés bien tôt** most unfortunately for us, he died very young; **cela n'est pas p. me surprendre** that doesn't come as a surprise to me; **cette amitié n'était pas p. lui plaire** the friendship was not to his liking; **des telles remarques ne sont pas pour me déplaire** such remarks are not unwelcome

(l) assez intelligent p. comprendre intelligent enough to understand; **être trop faible p. marcher** to be too weak to walk; **trop beau p. être vrai** too good to be true

(m) *Litt* (*étant donné que*) **il est bien ignorant p. avoir étudié si longtemps** he's very ignorant considering how long he's studied

(n) *Litt* (*concession*) (a)lthough; **p. être petit, il n'en est pas moins brave** though small, he is none the less brave

(o) *F* **être p. partir** to be about to start out *or* set off, to be on the point of starting out *or* setting off

(p) mourir p. mourir if I/we/*etc* must die; **ennuis p. ennuis, je préfère les miens** as troubles go, I prefer my own

(q) p. peu que vous hésitiez, vous êtes fichu if you hesitate at all, you've had it; **p. peu qu'il se trompe, il est mis à la porte** if he makes any sort of mistake, he's out

(r) (*à cause de*) for; **on l'apprécie p. sa gentillesse** he is liked for *or* on account of his kindness; **fermeture p. raisons familiales** closed for family reasons; **congé p. maladie** sick leave; **p. un rien** over nothing; **p. un peu, c'était trop tard** it was very nearly too late; **merci p. tout** thank you for everything; **être puni p. avoir désobéi** to be punished for having disobeyed *or* for disobeying *or* for disobedience; **je le sais p. l'avoir vu** I know from having seen it *or* from seeing it; **il est mort p. avoir trop travaillé** he died from overwork(ing) *or* from working too hard

2 *nm inv* **peser le p. et le contre** to weigh (up) the pros and cons; **entendre le p. et le contre** to hear both sides; **il y a du p. et du contre** there are pros and cons

pourboire [purbwar] *nm* tip, *Fml* gratuity; **donner un p. au porteur** to tip the porter, to give the porter a tip; **laisser 5 francs/10% de p.** to leave a 5 franc/10% tip; **être payé au p.** to depend on tips for one's pay

pourceau, -eaux [purso] *nm* pig, swine, *Am* hog

pourcentage [pursɑ̃taʒ] *nm* percentage; (*d'intérêts*) rate; (*pour représentant*) percentage, commission; **au p.** on a percentage basis, on a commission basis; **un p. fixe** a fixed percentage; **p. de grisé** shading percentage

pourchasser [purʃase] *vt* to pursue; (*criminel*) to pursue, to hunt (down); (*de créanciers, journalistes*) to harry; **pourchassé de rue en rue** hounded from street to street

pourfendeur [purfɑ̃dœr] *nm Litt, Iron* **p. d'injustices** fighter against injustice

pourfendre [purfɑ̃dr] *vt Litt, Iron* (*injustices, crime etc*) to combat, to fight against

pourlécher (se) [səpurleʃe] **(je me pourlèche; je me pourlécherai)** *vpr* **se p. (les babines)** to lick one's lips; **ça sent bon, d'avance, je m'en pourlèche les babines** that smells good, my mouth is watering already

pourparlers [purparle] *nmpl* talks, discussions, negotiations; **entrer en p.** to enter into *or* begin talks *or* discussions *or* negotiations (**avec** with); **nous sommes en p. avec le Japon** we're having talks *or* discussions with Japan, we're in negotiation with Japan

pourpier [purpje] *nm Bot* purslane

pourpoint [purpwɛ̃] *nm Hist* pourpoint, doublet

pourpre [purpr] **1** *nf* **(a)** (*teinte naturelle*) purple (dye) **(b)** *Fig* (*symbole de haute dignité*) purple; **né dans la p.** born in *or* to the purple **2** *nm* **(a)** crimson, rich red; **le p. (de la honte) lui monta au visage** he/she turned crimson (with shame); *Physiol* **p. rétinien** visual purple **(b)** (*animal*) murex **3** *adj* crimson; (*personne*) crimson, purple (**de rage** with rage)

pourpré [purpre] *adj Litt* crimson

pourquoi [purkwa] **1** *adv, conj* [①A40,C,1,a] why; **p. cela?** why?; **p. êtes-vous venu?** why have you come?, what have you come for?; **dis-moi p.** tell me why; **mais p. donc?** but what on earth for?; **je voulais savoir p. (il était parti)** I wanted to know why (he had left); **voilà p.** that's (the reason) why; **c'est p. ...** and that's why ..., and so ...; **p. pas?, p. non?** why (ever) not?; **il a trouvé du travail, p. pas toi?** he's found a job, why haven't you?; **et p. ne pas aller voir un film?** why don't we go to see a film?

2 *nm inv* (*raison*) reason (**de** for); **je ne sais pas le p.** I don't know the reason why; **le p. et le comment** the whys and wherefores; **les p. des enfants** the questions that children ask

pourri [puri] **1** *adj* **(a)** (*fruit*) rotten, bad; (*bois*) rotten; (*dent*) rotten, decayed; (*chair*) putrid; (*œufs*) bad; *F* (*corrompu*) (*chef, gouvernement etc*) corrupt; *F* **il est p. de vices** he's rotten to the core; *F* **ils sont pourris de fric** they're stinking rich, they're rolling in money; *F* **il est p. de talent** he's amazingly talented, he's bursting with talent

(b) *F* (*insupportable*) (*ville, boulot, été, temps etc*) rotten; **cet enfant est p. gâté** that kid is spoiled rotten

2 *nm* **(a)** (*décomposition*) (*d'un fruit*) rotten *or* bad part; **sentir le p.** to smell rotten

(b) *très F* (*terme injurieux*) bastard; **bande de pourris!** you bastards!

pourrir [purir] **1** *vi* to rot; (*d'un corps*) to putrefy, to decompose; (*de fruits, de la nourriture, d'œufs*) to go rotten, to go bad; **faire p.** to rot; *Fig* **p. en prison** to rot in prison; *Fig* **laisser p. les choses/la situation** to allow things/the situation to deteriorate; **laisser p. une grève** to allow a strike to drag on

2 *vt* **(a)** (*gâter*) (*fruits, bois*) to rot

(b) *Fig F* (*corrompre*) to spoil; **elle pourrit ses enfants en leur donnant tant d'argent** she's spoiling her children by giving them so much money; **elle me pourrit la vie** she's ruining my life

pourrissement [purismɑ̃] *nm* (*d'une situation*) deterioration

pourrissoir [puriswar] *nm Litt* muck heap

pourriture [purityr] *nf* **(a)** (*décomposition*) rotting, rot, decay; **p. sèche (du bois)** dry rot **(b)** (*état de décomposition*) rottenness; *Fig F* corruption **(c)** *très F* (*terme injurieux*) bastard

pour-soi *nm inv Phil* pour-soi

poursuite [pursɥit] *nf* **(a)** (*chasse*) pursuit; (*d'un criminel*) hunt (**de** for), pursuit, hunting, tracking (**de** of); **se mettre** *ou* **se lancer à la p. de qn** to set off in pursuit of sb, to chase after sb; **être à la p. de qch** (*bonheur, paix etc*) to be in pursuit *or* search of sth; (*travail, livre etc*) to be looking for sth; *Fig* **la p. du bonheur/de la sagesse** the pursuit of happiness/wisdom; *Cyclisme* **(course) p.** pursuit; *Cin* **scènes de p.** chase scenes

(b) (*continuation*) continuation; **p. d'un travail** carrying on (with) a piece of work; **nous avons décidé de la p. de la grève** we've decided to continue the strike

(c) *Électron* (*d'un avion, d'un missile etc*) tracking; **radar de p.** tracking radar

(d) *Jur* **poursuites (judiciaires)** (legal) proceedings; (*en droit pénal*) prosecution; **engager** *ou* **entamer** *ou* **intenter des poursuites (judiciaires) contre qn** to start *or* institute (legal) proceedings against sb, to take legal action against sb; (*en droit pénal*) to prosecute sb; **s'exposer à des poursuites** to lay oneself open to prosecution

(e) *Th* (*projecteur*) follow spot

poursuiteur [pursɥitœr] *nm Cyclisme* pursuit cyclist

poursuivant, -ante [pursɥivɑ̃, -ɑ̃t] **1** *adj Jur* (*partie*) prosecuting **2** *n* **(a)** *Jur* plaintiff **(b)** (*personne qui poursuit*) pursuer

poursuivre [pursɥivr] (*conj like* **suivre**) **1** *vt* **(a)** (*pourchasser*) (*personne, animal*) to pursue, to go after, to chase, to hunt (down); (*d'un songe, d'une idée, d'une crainte*) to haunt; **poursuivi par la malchance** dogged by bad luck

(b) (*chercher à atteindre*) (*idéal, rêve, but*) to pursue, to chase (after)

(c) (*harceler*) to pester, to plague (**de** with); (*débiteur*) to hound, to harry; *Mil* (*ennemi*) to harry; **p. une femme de ses assiduités** to force one's attentions on a woman; **p. qn de sa colère** to vent *or* unleash one's anger on sb

(d) *Jur* **p. (en justice)** to sue, to bring proceedings against, to take legal action against; (*en droit pénal*) to prosecute

(e) (*continuer*) to pursue, to continue, to go on with, to proceed with; **p. un travail** to carry on (with) a piece of work

2 *vi* to go on, to continue; **poursuivez** (*votre histoire etc*) go on, continue; **bien, je poursuis ...** well, to continue ...

3 se poursuivre *vpr* (*de préparatifs, négociations etc*) to continue, to go on

pourtant [purtɑ̃] *adv* yet, all the same; **un homme mûr et p. plein de fantaisie** a man who, though mature, is full of imagination, a mature man who is nevertheless full of imagination, a man who is mature yet full of imagination; **il t'aime bien et p. s'il savait ...** he likes you and yet if he knew ...; **vous n'allez p. pas nous quitter?** you're surely not going to leave us?, you're not going to leave us though, are you?; **je ne peux p. pas l'empêcher de venir** all the same *or* even so, I can't stop him from coming; **je fume encore, p. j'aimerais bien m'arrêter** I still smoke, but I'd really like to stop; **tout avait p. bien commencé** and yet it all started so well; **ça n'est p. pas compliqué!** it's hardly complicated!; **on t'avait p. bien dit de ne pas y aller!** we did tell you not to go!; **les instructions étaient p. claires** the instructions were quite clear; **je sais que j'ai bien fait, et p. ...!** I know I did the right thing and yet *or* but still ...!

pourtour [purtur] *nm* circumference, perimeter; **les pays du p. méditerranéen** the countries around the Mediterranean; **avec des rosiers sur le p.** with rose bushes around the edges

pourvoi [purvwa] *nm Jur* appeal; **p. en grâce** appeal for clemency; **p. en cassation** appeal to the Supreme Court

pourvoir [purvwar] (*prp* **pourvoyant**; *pp* **pourvu**; *pr ind* **je pourvois, n. pourvoyons**; *pr sub* **je pourvoie**; *impf* **je pourvoyais**; *p hist* **je pourvus**; *fu* **je pourvoirai**) **1** *vi* **p. aux besoins de qn** to provide for *or* cater for *or* supply sb's needs; (*de façon plus immédiate*) to attend to *or* see to sb's needs; **p. à un emploi** to fill a job; **il y a un poste à p. à la comptabilité** there is a vacancy in Accounts; **on n'y a pas pourvu** no provision has been made for it

2 *vt* **p. qn de** to supply *or* provide *or Fml* furnish sb with; (*outils*) to equip sb with; **p. qn d'une charge** to appoint sb to an office; **être pourvu de tout l'équipement nécessaire** to be supplied *or* provided with all the necessary equipment; **nous étions bien pourvus pour la montagne** we were well equipped for the mountains; **p. une maison du chauffage central** to fit out *or* equip a house with central heating; **il est pourvu d'un grand talent** he is endowed with great talent; **la nature l'a pourvu d'une intelligence hors du commun** nature has endowed him with exceptional intelligence

3 se pourvoir *vpr* **(a)** (*se munir*) to provide oneself (**de** with)

(b) *Jur* to appeal, to lodge an appeal; **se p. en grâce** to appeal for clemency; **se p. en cassation** to take one's case to the Supreme Court of Appeal

pourvoyeur, -euse [purvwajœr, -øz] *n* supplier, provider, *Fml* purveyor; *Constr* contractor; **p. de drogue** drug dealer

pourvu que [purvykə] *conj* (**+** *sub*) **(a)** (*exprimant une condition*) provided (that), so *or* as long as; **tu peux y aller p. tu sois rentré pour le dîner** you can go provided (that) *or* so long as *or* as long as you're back for dinner **(b)** (*exprimant un souhait*) **pourvu qu'il ne fasse pas de gaffes!** I just hope/let's just hope he won't make any blunders!; **p. ça dure!** let's just hope it lasts!

poussage [pusaʒ] *nm Tech* pushing

poussa(h) [pusa] *nm* (*jouet*) tumbler; *Fig* (*gros homme*) potbellied man

pousse [pus] *nf* **(a)** (*croissance*) (*des feuilles, des cheveux, des plumes*) growth; (*des dents*) cutting **(b)** *Bot* (*bourgeon*) (young) shoot, sprout; **p. de bambou** bamboo shoot; **cette plante a des pousses** this plant is putting out shoots

poussé [puse] *adj* (*ornementation etc*) elaborate; (*étude*) thorough, searching, extensive; (*connaissances*) extensive; (*interrogatoire*) intensive; **il aboutit à un scepticisme assez p.** he carries scepticism to some lengths *or* rather far; **un pessimisme assez p.** a fairly deep pessimism; **faire des études très poussées** to pursue one's studies to a very advanced level; **des recherches très poussées** very advanced research; **des critiques très poussées** thoroughgoing criticism; *Aut* **moteur p.** hotted-up *or* souped-up engine

pousse-au-crime *F* **1** *adj inv* that invites crime **2** *nm inv* **c'est du p.** it's an invitation to crime

pousse-café *nm inv* (glass of) liqueur (*after coffee*)

poussée [puse] *nf* **(a)** (*pression*), *Phys* thrust; (*de liquide*) buoyancy; (*de la mer*) heave; **p. du vent** wind pressure; *Phys* **centre de p.** aerodynamic centre, centre of pressure; (*de liquide*) centre of buoyancy; *Phys* **axe de p.** aerodynamic axis; *Phys* **force de p.** upward thrust; **la p. de la foule** the pushing and shoving of the crowd

(b) (*geste, fait de pousser qn*) push, shove; **écarter qch d'une p.** to push *or* shove sth aside

(c) (*fait de croître*) growth; *Méd* (*accès*) (*de boutons, d'herpès*) eruption, outbreak; **p. de croissance** spurt of growth; **faire une p. de croissance** to shoot up; **p. de fièvre** sudden rise of *or* in temperature

(d) *Fig* (*augmentation soudaine*) (*des prix, de l'inflation etc*) upsurge (**de** in)

pousse-pousse *nm inv* rickshaw; **en p.** by rickshaw

pousser [puse] **1** *vt* **(a)** (*soumettre à une force*) to push; (*rudement*) to shove; (*bétail*) to drive; (*bicyclette*) to push, to wheel; (*charrette, brouette*) to push (along); (*du vent*) (*embarcation*) to blow, to drive; **p. qn du coude/du genou** to nudge sb (with one's elbow/knee); **p. la porte/les volets**

(*ouvrir*) to push the door/the shutters open; (*fermer*) to push the door/the shutters to; **on a poussé tous les meubles et on a dansé** we pushed all the furniture out of the way *or* aside and danced; **pousse un peu la chaise, je ne vois plus rien** push the chair out of the way *or* move the chair a bit, I can't see anything; **il poussa le moteur encore un peu plus** he pushed the engine a little harder, he squeezed a bit more out of the engine; **p. un pion** (*aux échecs*) to move a pawn; *Fig* **p. l'aiguille** to sew; *Fig F* **p. le bouchon trop loin** to go too far; *Fig F* **faut pas p. Mémé** *ou* **Mémère dans les orties** don't push your luck!; *Fig F* **à la va comme je te pousse** slipshod; **fait à la va comme je te pousse** done in a slipshod way; *F* **pousse tes fesses** *ou très F* **ton cul!** shift yourself!, shove over!

(b) (*inciter*) (*qn*) to push, to urge on; (*cheval*) to urge on; **des élèves qu'il faut p.** pupils who need pushing *or* to be pushed; **il n'a pas fallu le p. beaucoup pour qu'il accepte** he didn't need much pushing *or* convincing to accept; **nous avons dû le p. à la roue pour qu'il ...** we had to push him a bit to get him to ...; **p. qn à faire qch** (*de la faim, la jalousie etc*) to drive sb to do sth, to lead sb to do sth; (*d'une personne*) (*contre son gré*) to push sb into doing sth; (*encourager*) to urge *or* encourage sb to do sth, to egg sb on to do sth; **p. qn à la dépense** to encourage sb to spend money; **les publicités sont faites pour p. à la consommation** advertisements are designed to encourage *or* stimulate consumption; **poussé par la pitié/la curiosité** prompted by pity/curiosity; *très F* **p. qn au cul** to give sb a kick up the backside

(c) (*continuer*) (*travail*) to push on with; (*études*) to pursue, to continue; **p. trop loin une plaisanterie** to take *or* carry a joke too far; **si l'on pousse encore plus loin cette explication/hypothèse** if we take this explanation/ hypothesis further still; **p. qch jusqu'au bout** *ou* **jusqu'à l'extrême** to push *or* take sth to the limit; **il a même p. la générosité jusqu'à ...** he was so generous that he even ...; **p. les enchères** to push up the bidding; **p. le chauffage/le son** to turn up the heating/volume; **p. le feu** to poke the fire; *Tech* **p. les feux** to raise steam, to stoke up

(d) (*produire*) (*feuilles, racines*) to put out, to grow; (*d'un enfant*) (*dents*) to cut

(e) (*exprimer*) **p. un cri** to shout, to give a shout; **p. des cris** to shout; **p. un cri de joie/de douleur** to shout with joy/pain, to give *or Fml* utter a shout of joy/pain; **p. un soupir** to sigh, to give *or* heave a sigh; **p. un gémissement** to groan, to moan, to give a groan *or* moan; **p. des acclamations** to cheer; **p. un juron** to swear; *F* **p. la chansonnette** *ou* **la romance, en p. une** to sing a song; *F* **il nous en a poussé une** he gave us a song; *très F* **p. une gueulante** to raise the roof, to kick up one hell of a stink

2 *vi* **(a)** (*faire un effort pour expulser qch*) to push; **ne poussez pas!** don't push!, don't shove!; *Fig* **p. à la roue** to do some pushing; *Fig F* **faut pas p.!** don't push your luck!; *F* **partir sans prévenir, vraiment, tu pousses!** going without saying anything, really, it's a bit much *or* you're taking things a bit too far!

(b) (*continuer, avancer*) to push on; *Mil* to push forward; **p. jusqu'au bois** to push on as far as the wood

(c) (*croître*) (*d'une plante, des cheveux, des ongles, d'une ville*) to grow; (*d'un bourgeon*) to sprout; (*des dents*) to come through; **laisser p. sa barbe** to grow a beard; **ses dents commencent à p.** his teeth are beginning to come through, he's beginning to cut his teeth; **p. comme du chiendent** to grow like a weed; **des villes qui ont poussé comme des champignons** towns that sprang up like mushrooms, towns that mushroomed; **tous ces enfants poussent** (*grandissent*) these children are all shooting up; **qu'est-ce qu'elle a poussé!** hasn't she grown!

(d) (*inciter*) **p. à** to press *or* push for; **p. au changement** to press *or* push for change; **p. à la manifestation/la grève** to press *or* push for a demonstration/a strike; *Écon* **p. à la hausse/la baisse** to have an inflationary/a deflationary effect; **poussé par les profits** profit-driven

3 se pousser *vpr* **(a)** (*se mettre en vue*) to push oneself forward; (*dans la société etc*) to make one's way

(b) (*se presser*) (*pour faire de la place*) to move *or* shift over *or* up

poussette [pusɛt] *nf* (*voiture d'enfants*) pushchair, *Am* stroller; (*caddie*) shopping trolley *or Am* cart

pousseur [pusœr] *nm* **(a)** (*bateau*) tug **(b)** *Astronaut* booster rocket

poussier [pusje] *nm* coal dust, *Spéc* screenings; (*charbon*) slack

poussière [pusjɛr] *nf* dust; **une p.** a speck of dust; **p. d'or** gold dust; **enlever la p. des meubles** to dust the furniture; *F* **faire la p.** *ou* **les poussières** to do the dusting, to dust; **couvert de p.** dusty, covered in dust; **s'en aller** *ou* **tomber en p.** to crumble (away) to dust; **réduire qch en p.** to reduce sth to dust; *Fig* to demolish sth; **mordre la p.** to bite the dust; **je lui ferai mordre la p.** I'll wipe the floor with him; *F* **dix francs/ jours et des poussières** ten and a bit francs/days, ten francs/days and a bit; **poussières radioactives** radioactive dust

poussiéreux, -euse [pusjerø, -øz] *adj* dusty; *Fig* (*terne*) dull, humdrum; (*dépassé*) outmoded

poussif, -ive [pusif, -iv] *adj* (*personne*) wheezy, short-winded; (*cheval*) broken-winded; (*moteur*) wheezy

poussin [pusɛ̃] *nm Zool* chick; *Culin* spring chicken; *F* **mon p.** pet

poussivement [pusivmɑ̃] *adv* wheezily

poussoir [puswar] *nm* (*d'une sonnerie électrique*) (push) button; *MecE* (*d'une valve*) push rod; *Aut* tappet, cam follower; *Ordinat* (*de souris*) button; **p. à ressort** trigger

poutrage [putraʒ] *nm*, **poutraison** [putrɛzɔ̃] *nf Constr* framework of beams

poutre [putr] *nf* **(a)** (*en bois*) beam; **grosse p.** ba(u)lk; **p. de faîte** ridge piece, roof tree; **p. de plancher** ceiling joist; **poutres apparentes** exposed beams **(b)** (*en métal*) girder; **p. à âme pleine** plate girder; **p. à caisson** box girder; **p. maîtresse** main girder *or* beam

poutrelle [putrɛl] *nf Constr* girder

poutser [putse] *vt Région F* to clean

pouvoir¹ [puvwar] *nm* **(a)** (*possibilité*) power, ability; **il n'est pas en mon p. de ...** it is not within *or* it is beyond my power to ...; **je ferai tout ce qui est en mon p.** I'll do everything (that's) in my power; **avoir le p. de faire qch** to have the power to do sth; **il a des pouvoirs surnaturels** he has supernatural powers

(b) *Ch, Phys etc* (*propriété*) **p. calorifique** calorific value; **p. rayonnant** radiating capacity; *Aut* **p. antidétonant** anti-knock rating; **p. absorbant** absorbency

(c) (*puissance*) power; **p. politique** political power; **p. absolu** absolute power; **avoir un p. absolu sur qn** to have complete power over sb; **avoir un certain p. sur qn** to have (a certain) power over sb; **tenir qn en son p.** to have sb in one's power; **le p. des sens/des images/des mots** the power of the senses/of images/of words; **abuser de son p.** *ou* **de ses pouvoirs** to abuse one's power; **vouloir prendre le p.** to aim for power; **prendre le p.** to assume power; **arriver au p.** to come to power; **le parti au p.** the party in power; **quand les Libéraux sont au p.** when the Liberals are in (power); *Fig* **dans les milieux proches du p.** in the corridors of power; *Fig* **une affaire qui concerne le p.** a government matter; **huit ans de p.** eight years in power; **avoir un p. de décision** to have decision-making power *or* ability; **en vertu des pouvoirs qui me sont conférés ...** by virtue of the powers invested in me ...

(d) *Jur* (*procuration*) power of attorney; **avoir/recevoir plein(s) pouvoir(s) pour agir** to have full powers/to be (fully) empowered *or* authorized to act; **se présenter sans pouvoirs réguliers** to come without full credentials; **bon pour p.** good for proxy

▶ **pouvoir**: *Écon* **p. d'achat** purchasing power, buying power; **p. exécutif** executive power; **p. judiciaire** judicial power; (*les juges*) judiciary; **p. législatif** legislative power; **les pouvoirs publics** the authorities, the public authorities

pouvoir² (*prp* **pouvant**; *pp* **pu**; *pr ind* **je peux, je puis** (*always* **puis-je** [pɥiʒ], **tu peux, il peut, n. pouvons, ils peuvent**; *pr sub* **je puisse, n. puissions**; *impf* **je pouvais**; *p hist* **je pus**; *fu* **je pourrai** [pure]) **1** *vt* [①**A57-8**,c-d; **B37**,**K**,**2**] **(a)** (*être capable*) to be able; **faire tout ce qu'on peut** to do one's best, to do the best *or* all *or* everything one can; **si je peux** if I can, if I'm able to; **je ne peux pas** I can't, I'm unable to; **je ne peux (pas) le faire** I can't *or* cannot do it, I'm unable *or* not able to do it; **cela ne peut (pas) se faire** it can't *or* cannot be done; **comment a-t-il pu dire cela?** how could he say that?; **comment a-t-il pu?** how could he?; **il aurait pu le faire s'il avait voulu** he could have done it if he had wanted to; **si vous aviez pu le voir** if you could have seen him, if you'd been able to see him; **il ne pouvait pas l'accompagner** he couldn't go with him, he wasn't able *or* he was unable to go with him; **j'ai fait toutes les démarches que j'ai pu** I took every step that I possibly could; **j'ai pu le revoir** I managed *or* got *or* was able to see him again; **je n'y peux rien** I can't help it; **on n'y peut rien** it can't be helped, there's nothing that can be done about it; **il a été on ne peut plus grossier** he couldn't have been ruder, he was extremely rude; **des gens on ne peut plus aimables** extremely kind people; **il travaille on ne peut mieux** he's as good a worker as it's possible to be; **il n'en peut plus (de fatigue)** he's quite exhausted *or* worn out *or* tired out; **je n'en peux plus (de ses scènes/des voisins)** I've had enough *or* I can't take any more (of his scenes/the neighbours); **il n'en peut plus** (*d'impatience*) he can't take any more; **elle peut beaucoup** she's very capable; **sauve qui peut** every man for himself; **on ne peut pas ne pas l'admirer** you can't not admire him, you can't help but admire him, you have to admire him; **je viendrai aussitôt que je pourrai** I'll come as soon as I can *or* I'm able; **qu'est-ce qu'il peut bien me vouloir?** what(ever) can he want?; **où pouvait-il bien être à cette heure?** where(ver) could he be at this time?; **la loi ne peut rien contre lui** the law can't touch him; **nous ne pouvons rien pour vous** we can't do anything for you

(b) (*avoir le droit, la permission* (*de*)) to be allowed to; **vous pouvez partir** you can *or Fml* may go; **elle ne peut pas sortir seule** she can't go out alone, she isn't allowed out alone; **puis-je entrer?** can *or Fml* may I come in?; **quand pourrai-je emménager?** when can I move in?, when will I be able to move in?

(c) (*être possible*) **la porte a pu se fermer toute seule** the door may have *or* could have closed on its own; **on peut se tromper, n'est-ce pas?** after all, we may *or* could be wrong; **nous pourrions le trouver si nous nous dépêchions** we might *or* could find him if we hurry; **elle pourrait le rencontrer, si elle le voulait** she could meet him if she wanted to; **elle peut bien s'excuser, je ne lui pardonnerai pas** she can apologize all she likes, but I shan't forgive her; **tout de même vous auriez (bien) pu faire moins de bruit** all the same you could have *or* might have made less noise; **tu peux (bien) me raconter tout ce que tu veux …** you can say what you like …; **il pouvait être trois ou quatre heures du matin** it might have been three or four in the morning; *F* **qu'est-ce que ça peut (bien) te faire?** what's that got to do with you?

(d) *Litt* **puisse-t-il défendre nos lois!** may he defend our laws!

2 *v impers* **cela se peut (bien)** it may be *or* it could well be (the case), it's quite possible, maybe, possibly; **cela ne se peut pas** that's impossible, that's not possible; **ça se pourrait (bien)** that's quite possible; **advienne que pourra** come what may; **autant que faire se peut** as much as can/could be done; **il peut se faire** *ou* **il peut arriver que …** + *sub* it may be *or* may happen that …; **il se peut qu'il vienne** he may *or* might come; **il se peut qu'il ne soit pas coupable** he may not *or* might not be guilty

pp [pepe] (a) *abrév* **port payé** (b) (*abrév* **par procuration**) (*à la fin d'une lettre*) pp

PPCM [pepeseɛm] *nm Math* (*abrév* **plus petit commun multiple**) LCM

ppm [pepeɛm] (a) (*abrév* **parties par million**) ppm (b) (*abrév* **pages par minute**) ppm

PQ [peky] *nm* (a) *Can Pol* (*abrév* **Parti Québécois**) PQ (b) *très F* (*papier hygiénique*) toilet paper, *Br* loo paper, *Br* bog roll

P.R.[1] [peɛr] *abrév* **poste restante**

P.R.[2] *nm abrév* **Parti Républicain**

pragmatique [pragmatik] *adj* pragmatic

pragmatisme [pragmatism] *nm* pragmatism

pragmatiste [pragmatist] *adj, n* pragmatist

praire [prɛr] *nf* clam

prairial [prɛrjal] *nm Hist Fr* = ninth month of the French Republican Calendar (*May 20-June 18*)

prairie [preri] *nf* (*pré, champ*) meadow; (*large étendue*) grassland, *Am* prairie; **p. artificielle** cultivated grassland; *Géog* **la P.** the Prairies

pralin [pralɛ̃] *nm Culin* praline

praline [pralin] *nf Culin* praline, sugared almond; *Péj F* **cucul la p.** silly, idiotic

praliné [praline] *adj Culin* (*chocolat*) praline-filled; (*crème, glace*) praline-flavoured; **amandes pralinées** sugared almonds

praticable [pratikabl] 1 *adj* (*possible, réalisable*), *Th* (*porte, fenêtre*) practicable; (*projet, idée*) feasible, practicable; (*route etc*) passable, negotiable 2 *nm Th* (*décor*) practicable scenery; *Cin, TV* movable platform (*for camera or projectors*)

praticien, -ienne [pratisjɛ̃, -jɛn] *n* (a) *Jur* (legal) practitioner; *Méd* (medical) practitioner (b) (*technicien*) practitioner (c) *Beaux-Arts* (*ouvrier*) sculptor's assistant

pratiquant, -ante [pratikɑ̃, -ɑ̃t] *Rel* 1 *adj* practising; **catholique p.** practising Catholic; **il est très p.** he's very religious, he's a strong believer; (*d'un chrétien*) he's a regular churchgoer, he goes to church regularly 2 *n* religious person; (*chrétien*) (regular) churchgoer

pratique [pratik] 1 *adj* (*méthode, personne etc*) practical; (*gadget, outil etc*) practical, handy; (*date, heure, jour*) convenient; **avoir l'esprit p.** to have a practical turn of mind, to be practically minded; **sens p.** practical common sense; **c'est très p. d'avoir l'école si près de la maison** it's very practical *or* handy to have the school so close to the house; **cette crème n'est pas p. à appliquer** this cream isn't easy to apply

2 *nf* (a) (*application*) practice; **mettre qch en p.** to put sth into practice; **c'est une p. courante** it's common practice, it's quite usual; **la théorie et la p.** theory and practice; **en p.** in practice

(b) (*expérience*) (practical) experience; *Litt* (*de la vertu*) practice; **p. du théâtre** theatrical experience; **la p. du football m'a valu une jambe cassée** I got a broken leg *or* I broke my leg (through) playing football; **la p. d'un sport est encouragée** sporting activity *or* practising a sport is encouraged; **perdre la p. de qch** to lose the knack of sth; (*d'un sport, d'une activité*) to get out of practice at sth; **avoir une grande** *ou* **longue p. de qch** to have a lot of (practical) experience of sth

(c) *Jur* (*de la loi*) practice; **terme de p.** legal term

(d) (*action*) practice; **pratiques religieuses** religious practices; **pratiques clandestines** underhand practices; *Jur* **libre p.** (*de sa religion etc*) free exercise; *Naut* **avoir libre p.** to be out of quarantine

(e) (*d'avocat, de médecin*) practice; (*de fournisseur*) custom, business; *Vieilli* (*clientèle*) (*d'un avocat*) clients; (*d'un médecin*) patients; (*d'un fournisseur*) customers

(f) *Arch* **il avait vécu dans la p. des hauts fonctionnaires** he had associated with high-ranking civil servants

pratiquement [pratikmɑ̃] *adv* (*dans l'expérience*) in practice; (*en fait*) in actual fact; (*presque*) practically, virtually; **il ne vient p. jamais plus** he practically never comes any more

pratiquer [pratike] 1 *vt* (a) (*exercer*) (*activité, sorcellerie, vertu, charité, religion etc*) to practise; (*méthode*) to employ, to use; (*langue*) to use; **il pratique le football** he plays football; **elle pratique la natation** she's a (keen) swimmer, she swims; **elle ne pratique aucun sport** she doesn't do *or* take part in *or* practise any sport; **il a appris le piano mais ne pratique plus beaucoup** he learnt the piano but doesn't play it much any more; *Com* **les cours pratiqués** the ruling prices; **les prix pratiqués ici** the prices being asked here

(b) *Méd* **p. une intervention** to carry out an operation, to operate; **p. une petite incision** to make a small incision

(c) (*ménager*) to make; **p. une ouverture dans un mur** to make an opening in a wall; **p. un sentier** to make a path, to open up a path

(d) (*livre, auteur*) to study

(e) *Arch* (*fréquenter*) to frequent, to associate with

2 *vi* (a) (*travailler*) (*d'un médecin, avocat, conseiller*) to practise; **il ne pratique plus** he's no longer in practice, he no longer practises

(b) *Rel* to observe the practices of one's religion; **ils sont catholiques mais ils ne pratiquent pas** they're Catholics but not practising Catholics

3 **se pratiquer** *vpr* to be practised; **le commerce de l'ivoire se pratique encore** ivory trading still goes on *or* is still practised; **les mariages arrangés ne se pratiquent plus** arranged marriages no longer take place; **voilà comment ça se pratique** that's how it's done

praxis [praksis] *nf* praxis

pré [pre] *nm* meadow; *Arch* **aller sur le p.** to fight a duel

pré-acheminement *nm* transfer to main airport

préadolescence [preadɔlɛsɑ̃s] *nf* preadolescence

préadolescent, -ente [preadɔlɛsɑ̃, -ɑ̃t] *n* preadolescent

préalable [prealabl] 1 *adj* previous, prior (**à** to); (*accord*) prior; **formalités préalables au débat** formalities that precede the debate; **mais il y a quelques formalités préalables** but there are a few formalities to be gone through first 2 *nm* (a) (*condition*) prerequisite, precondition; **préalables d'un accord** pre-contract conditions; **au p.** first, beforehand (b) *Arch* (*préparation*) preliminary

préalablement [prealabləmɑ̃] *adv* first, beforehand; **p. à …** prior to …

pré-allumage *nm Aut* pre-ignition

Préalpes (les) [leprealp] *nfpl* the foothills of the Alps

préalpin [prealpɛ̃] *adj* of the foothills of the Alps

préambule [preɑ̃byl] *nm* (*d'un discours*) preamble (**de** to); (*d'une action*) prelude (**de** to); **il a abordé le sujet sans p.** he (dispensed with preliminaries and) came straight to the point; **sans p., elle lui a demandé son âge** she asked him straight off how old he was

préamplificateur [preɑ̃plifikatœr] *nm Électron* preamplifier

PréAO [preao] *nf Ordinat* (*abrév* **présentation assistée par ordinateur**) computer-assisted presentation

préapprentissage [preaprɑ̃tisaʒ] *nm* pre-apprenticeship training

préau, -aux [preo] *nm* **(a)** (*cour intérieure*) (court)yard **(b)** (*partie couverte*) covered part (of the playground)
préavis [preavi] *nm* (previous *or* advance) notice; **exiger un p. de trois mois** to require three months' notice; **sans p.** without notice *or* warning; **p. de licenciement** notice (of dismissal); **p. de paiement** payment advice; **p. de grève** strike notice; **déposer un p. de grève** to give notice of strike action
prébende [prebɑ̃d] *nf Rel* prebend; *Fig* (*profit*) sizeable income
prébendé [prebɑ̃de] *adj Rel* prebendal
prébendier [prebɑ̃dje] *nm Rel* prebendary
précaire [prekɛr] *adj* (*position, état de santé*) precarious; (*santé*) delicate; (*abri*) precarious, rickety; **être dans un équilibre un peu p.** to be rather precariously balanced
précairement [prekɛrmɑ̃] *adv* precariously
précambrien, -ienne [prekɑ̃brijɛ̃, -ijɛn] *adj Géol* Precambrian, Pre-Cambrian
précarisation [prekarizasjɔ̃] *nf* jeopardizing
précariser [prekarize] *vt* to jeopardize
précarité [prekarite] *nf* precariousness
précaution [prekosjɔ̃] *nf* **(a)** (*mesure*) precaution; **prendre des** *ou* **ses précautions** to take precautions (**pour** for); *Euph* **prendre ses précautions** to go (*to the toilet*); **mesures de p.** precautionary measures; **par (mesure de) p.** as a precaution; **précautions oratoires** carefully chosen remarks; *Prov* **deux précautions valent mieux qu'une** you can never be too sure, better safe than sorry **(b)** (*soin*) caution, wariness, care; **avec p.** cautiously, warily, carefully; **pour plus de p.** to be extra safe, to be on the safe side, to err on the side of caution
précautionner [prekosjɔne] **1** *vt Arch* to warn, to caution (**contre** against) **2 se précautionner** *vpr* to take precautions; **se p. contre qch** to take precautions *or* guard against sth
précautionneusement [prekosjɔnøzmɑ̃] *adv* carefully
précautionneux, -euse [prekosjɔnø, -øz] *adj* careful
précédemment [presedamɑ̃] *adv* previously, before
précédent [presedɑ̃] **1** *adj* previous; **le jour/mois p.** the day/month before, the previous day/month **2** *nm* precedent; **créer un p.** to create *or* set a precedent; **sans p.** unprecedented, without precedent
précéder [presede] (*conj like* **céder**) **1** *vt* to precede; **la musique précède les troupes** the band marches in front of *or* precedes the troops; **il me précédait pour me guider** he went in front of *or* preceded me in order to guide me; **l'antichambre qui précède le salon** the antechamber leading to the drawing room; **je l'ai précédé de 10 minutes** I got there ten minutes before he did *or* before him *or* ahead of him; **nous serons précédés de quelques jours par nos enfants** our children will get there a few days before we do *or* before us *or* ahead of us; **le scandale a précédé la révélation de l'affaire** the scandal occurred before the affair came to light; **sa réputation le précédait** his reputation went before *or* preceded him; **p. qn (en dignité)** to have precedence over sb; **faire p. un concert d'un discours** to preface a concert with a speech
2 *vi* **la page qui précède** the preceding *or* previous page, the page before; **dans les jours qui précèdent** in the days before, in the preceding days; **ce qui précède** the foregoing
précepte [presɛpt] *nm* precept
précepteur, -trice [presɛptœr, -tris] *n* (private) tutor
préceptorat [presɛptɔra] *nm* tutorship
précession [presesjɔ̃] *nf* precession
préchambre [preʃɑ̃br] *nf Tech* (*d'un moteur diesel*) precombustion chamber
précharge [preʃarʒ] *nf Aut* pre-load
préchargé [preʃarʒe] *adj* (*logiciel*) preloaded
préchauffage [preʃofaʒ] *nm* preheating; (*d'un appareil*) warm-up; **p. moteur diesel** pre-heating
préchauffer [preʃofe] *vt* to preheat
prêche [prɛʃ] *nm* sermon
prêcher [preʃe] **1** *vt* (*enseigner*) to preach (**à** to); **p. qn** to preach to sb; **p. l'économie** to preach economy; *Iron* **p. la bonne parole** to spread the good word; **p. un converti** to preach to the converted **2** *vi* (*prononcer un sermon*) to preach; *Fig* (*moraliser*) to preach, to preachify, to sermonize; *Rel, Fig* **p. dans le désert** to be a voice crying in the wilderness; **p. d'exemple** *ou* **par l'exemple** to practise what one preaches; *Fig* **p. pour sa paroisse** to look after one's own interests
prêcheur, -euse [prɛʃœr, -øz] **1** *adj* **(a)** (*moine*) preaching **(b)** (*moralisateur*) (*personne*) sermonizing **2** *n Fig Péj* sermonizer, preacher
prêchi-prêcha [preʃipreʃa] *nm inv F Péj* preaching, preachifying, sermonizing
précieusement [presjøzmɑ̃] *adv* **(a)** (*avec soin*) very carefully; **garder** *ou* **conserver qch p.** to treasure sth **(b)** (*avec préciosité*) preciously, affectedly
précieux, -euse [presjø, -øz] **1** *adj* **(a)** (*d'une grande valeur*) precious; **pierre précieuse** precious stone **(b)** (*conseil, temps etc*) valuable (**à** to) **(c)** *Litt* (*style*) precious, affected, mannered **2** *nf Hist Littér Fr* **précieuse** = pedantic, over-refined woman
préciosité [presjozite] *nf Litt* affectation, affectedness, preciosity
précipice [presipis] *nm* chasm, abyss; (*bord d'une falaise, d'un ravin etc*) precipice; *Fig* abyss; **au bord d'un p.** on the edge of a precipice; *Fig* **être au bord du p.** to be on the brink, to be on the edge of a precipice
précipitamment [presipitamɑ̃] *adv* hurriedly, hastily, *Fml* precipitately; **entrer/sortir p.** to rush *or* hurry *or* dash in/out; **agir trop p.** to be too hasty *or Fml* precipitate, to be overhasty, to act too hastily *or Fml* precipitately
précipitation [presipitasjɔ̃] *nf* **(a)** (*grande hâte*) haste, great hurry, *Fml* precipitation; **avec p.** hurriedly, hastily, *Fml* precipitately; **entrer/sortir avec p.** to hurry *or* rush *or* dash in/out **(b)** *Ch, Phys* precipitation **(c)** *Météo* **précipitations** precipitation
précipité [presipite] **1** *adj* (*action, décision*) hasty, hurried, *Fml* precipitate; (*départ*) hasty, hurried, abrupt; (*pouls*) racing; **s'avancer à pas précipités** to rush forward; **un bruit de pas précipités** (the sound of) hurried *or* quick footsteps **2** *nm Ch* precipitate
précipiter [presipite] **1** *vt* **(a)** (*entraîner*) to throw down, to hurl down; *Fig* to plunge; **p. qn contre un mur/dans le vide** to hurl sb against a wall/over the edge; *Fig* **p. qn dans le désespoir/le malheur** to plunge sb into despair/misfortune; **p. un peuple dans la guerre** to plunge a nation into war
(b) (*dépêcher, hâter*) (*un achat, une embauche, un mariage etc*) to speed up; (*événements*) to precipitate; (*la mort de qn, la perte de qn*) to hasten; **il ne faut rien p.** we mustn't rush things, we mustn't be overhasty
(c) *Ch* (*substance*) to precipitate
2 *vi Ch* (*d'une substance*) to precipitate, to form a precipitate
3 se précipiter *vpr* **(a)** (*se hâter*) to rush, to hurry
(b) (*s'accélérer*) **les événements se sont précipités** things started happening quickly
(c) (*se jeter*) to rush (**sur** at; **vers** towards); **se p. à la fenêtre** to rush to the window; **se p. aux pieds de qn** to throw oneself at sb's feet; **dès qu'il rentre à la maison, il se précipite devant la télévision** as soon as he gets home he throws himself down in front of the television; **le fleuve se précipite dans la mer** the river rushes into the sea
(d) *Ch* to precipitate
précis [presi] **1** *adj* (*description, vocabulaire, plan, but, intention etc*) precise, exact; **à cet instant p.** at this precise *or* exact moment; **exiger d'une façon précise que ...** to call unambiguously for ...; **à deux heures précises** at two o'clock precisely *or* exactly *or* sharp; **je suis parti sans raison précise** I left for no definite reason *or* for no particular reason; **en termes p.** in precise terms, precisely; **il est très p. dans son travail** he's very meticulous *or* precise *or* exact in his work; **des gestes p.** precise movements; **pensez-vous à quelque chose de p.?** do you have something specific in mind?; **pour être plus p.** to be more precise
2 *nm* précis, summary, abstract; (*livre*) handbook; **p. d'histoire de France** short history of France
précisément [presizemɑ̃] *adv* **(a)** (*exactement*) precisely, exactly; **ou plus p. ...** or more precisely ..., or to be more precise ...; **ce n'est pas p. une réussite** it's not exactly a success, it's not (exactly) what you'd call a success; **a-t-il dit cela? – oui p.** did he say that? – yes, those were his very words **(b)** (*justement*) **c'est p. l'homme que je cherche** he's just the man I'm looking for; **c'est p. ce que je lui disais** that's just *or* exactly what I said to him; **p. il m'en fallait un aujourd'hui** as it happens *or* as a matter of fact, I needed one today
préciser [presize] **1** *vt* **(a)** (*déterminer*) (*prix, date, informations*) to specify; **il faut p. vos affirmations/arguments** you must be (more) explicit *or* specific in your statements/arguments
(b) (*rendre plus net*) to clarify; **je tiens à p. que ...** I wish to make it clear that ...; **p. la date de la réunion** to give the exact *or* precise date of the meeting; **la circulaire ne précise pas où aura lieu la réunion** the circular doesn't specify where the meeting will take place; **il n'a pas été précisé qu'il fallait être en tenue de soirée** it wasn't specifically stated that evening dress was to be worn, evening dress wasn't specified

2 *vi* to be (more) precise *or* explicit
3 **se préciser** *vpr* to become clear(er); (*des idées, d'un contrat*) to take shape; **les vacances se précisent** the holiday plans are taking shape
précision [presizjɔ̃] *nf* **(a)** (*exactitude*) (*d'information, d'une description, d'un travail*) accuracy; (*de mouvements*) preciseness, precision; **avec p.** accurately, precisely; **p. de tir** accuracy of fire; *Typ* **p. de frappe** keying accuracy; **instruments de p.** precision instruments **(b) une p.** a (precise) detail, a (point of) clarification; **donner** *ou* **apporter des précisions sur qch** to give precise details about sth; **demander des précisions sur qch** to ask for more *or* further information *or* details about sth; **merci de ces précisions** thank you for this information
précité [presite] *adj* aforesaid, aforementioned; (*plus haut sur une page, dans un document*) above(-mentioned)
préclassique [preklasik] *adj Hist* preclassical
précoce [prekɔs] *adj* (*enfant*) precocious; (*fruit, gel*) early; (*sénilité, calvitie*) premature; **l'été est p. cette année** summer is early this year; **enfant p. pour son âge** child who is advanced *or* precocious for his age; **sexuellement p.** sexually precocious
précocement [prekɔsmɑ̃] *adv Litt* precociously
précocité [prekɔsite] *nf* precociousness, precocity; (*de fruits, d'une saison etc*) earliness; **p. sexuelle** sexual precociousness
précolombien, -ienne [prekɔlɔ̃bjɛ̃, -jɛn] *adj Hist* pre-Columbian
précombustion [prekɔ̃bystjɔ̃] *nf Tech* precombustion
pré-commercialisation *nf Mktg* pre-marketing
précomptabilisation [prekɔ̃tabilizasjɔ̃] *nf* preparation of accounting entries
précompte [prekɔ̃t] *nm* (*d'un compte, d'un salaire*) (advance) deduction
précompter [prekɔ̃te] *vt* to deduct, to withhold (**sur** from)
préconception [prekɔ̃sɛpsjɔ̃] *nf* preconception; (*contre qn, qch*) prejudice
préconçu [prekɔ̃sy] *adj* preconceived; *Péj* **idée préconçue** preconceived idea
préconfiguré [prekɔ̃figyre] *adj Ordinat* preconfigured
préconisation [prekɔnizasjɔ̃] *nf* recommendation
préconiser [prekɔnize] *vt* to recommend, to advocate; (*remède*) to recommend
précontraint [prekɔ̃trɛ̃] *adj, nm Tech* **(béton) p.** prestressed concrete
précouche [prekuʃ] *nf* precoating
précuit [prekɥi] *adj* pre-cooked, ready-cooked
précurseur [prekyrsœr] **1** *nm* precursor, forerunner **2** *adj* precursory; **signe p.** forewarning, portent
prédateur, -trice [predatœr, -tris] **1** *adj* predatory **2** *nm* predator
prédécesseur [predesesœr] *nm* predecessor
prédécoupé [predekupe] *adj* pre-cut, ready-cut
pré-définition *nf Ordinat* **p. des secteurs** hard sectoring
prédélinquant, -ante [predelɛ̃kɑ̃, -ɑ̃t] *n* potential delinquent
prédestination [predɛstinasjɔ̃] *nf* predestination
prédestiné [predɛstine] *adj* predestined, fated (**à faire qch** to do sth); **p. à qch** predestined for sth
prédestiner [predɛstine] *vt* to predestine (**à faire qch** to do sth; **à qch** for sth)
prédétermination [predetɛrminasjɔ̃] *nf* predetermination
prédéterminer [predetɛrmine] *vt* to predetermine
prédicant [predikɑ̃] *nm Rel* preacher
prédicat [predika] *nm Gram* predicate
prédicateur, -trice [predikatœr, -tris] *n* preacher
prédicatif, -ive [predikatif, -iv] *adj Gram* predicative
prédication [predikasjɔ̃] *nf* **(a)** *Rel* preaching; (*sermon*) sermon **(b)** *Gram* predication
prédiction [prediksjɔ̃] *nf* **(a)** (*action de prédire*) prediction, predicting, foretelling **(b)** (*ce qui est prédit*) prediction, forecast
prédigéré [prediʒere] *adj* predigested
prédilection [predilɛksjɔ̃] *nf* predilection, partiality, fondness; **auteur/restaurant de p.** favourite *or US* favorite author/restaurant; **avoir une p. pour qch** to be partial to sth, to have a predilection *or* fondness for sth
prédire [predir] *vt* (*conj like* **dire** *except pr ind & imp* (**v.**) **prédisez**) to predict, to prophesy, to foretell; **p. qch à qn** to predict sth for sb; **p. que** to predict that
prédisposer [predispoze] *vt* to predispose (**à qch** to sth; **à faire qch** to do sth)
prédisposition [predispozisjɔ̃] *nf* predisposition (**à** to)
prédominance [predɔminɑ̃s] *nf* predominance
prédominant [predɔminɑ̃] *adj* predominant
prédominer [predɔmine] *vi* to predominate; (*d'une préoccupation*) to be uppermost; **ce qui prédomine chez lui, c'est la générosité** generosity is his chief quality

préélectoral, -ale, -aux, -ales [preelɛktɔral, -o] *adj Pol* pre-electoral, pre-election
préemballé [preɑ̃bale] *adj* pre-packed
pré-embarquement *nm* (*à un aéroport*) pre-boarding
pré-embarquer *vi* (*à un aéroport*) to pre-board
prééminence [preeminɑ̃s] *nf* pre-eminence
prééminent [preeminɑ̃] *adj* pre-eminent
préempter [preɑ̃pte] *vt Jur* to pre-empt
préemption [preɑ̃psjɔ̃] *nf Jur* pre-emption
préencollé [preɑ̃kɔle] *adj* (*papier peint*) pre-pasted, ready-pasted
pré-enregistré [preɑ̃r(ə)ʒistre] *adj TV, Rad* pre-recorded, *F* canned
pré-enregistrement *nm* (*à un aéroport*) pre-registration; *TV, Rad* pre-recording, prescoring
préétablir [preetablir] *vt* to pre-establish
préexistant [preɛgzistɑ̃] *adj* pre-existing, pre-existent
préexistence [preɛgzistɑ̃s] *nf* pre-existence
préexister [preɛgziste] *vi* to pre-exist; **p. à qch** to exist *or* be in existence before sth
préfabrication [prefabrikasjɔ̃] *nf* prefabrication
préfabriqué [prefabrike] **1** *adj* prefabricated; *Fig Péj* **sourire p.** artificial smile; **candidat p.** packaged candidate **2** *nm* (*maison*) prefabricated house, *F* prefab
préface [prefas] *nf* **(a)** (*avant-propos*) preface, foreword (**à, de** to) **(b)** *Rel* preface
préfacer [prefase] *vt* to write a preface to *or* for, to preface
préfacier [prefasje] *nm* preface writer
préfacturation [prefaktyrasjɔ̃] *nf Compta* prebilling
préfectoral, -ale, -aux, -ales [prefɛktɔral, -o] *adj Admin* prefectorial
préfecture [prefɛktyr] *nf Admin* prefecture; **la P. de police** police headquarters; **p. maritime** = area under command of a port admiral; (*bureau*) naval superintendent's office, port admiral's office
préférable [preferabl] *adj* preferable (**à** to); **il serait p. de le revoir** *ou* **qu'on le revoie** it would be preferable *or* better to see him again
préférablement [preferabləmɑ̃] *adv* preferably
préféré, -ée [prefere] *adj, n* favourite, *US* favorite
préférence [preferɑ̃s] *nf* preference; **de p.** preferably; **de p. à** … in preference to …; **donner** *ou* **accorder la p. à qn** to give sb preference (**sur** over); **il n'a pas de p.** he has no (particular) preference; **par ordre de p.** in order of preference; *Jur* **droits de p.** priority rights; *Fin* **actions de p.** preference shares, *Am* preferred stock
préférentiel, -elle [preferɑ̃sjɛl] *adj* preferential; *Jur* **vote p.** preferential voting (system); **tarif p.** preferential rate
préférer [prefere] *vt* (**je préfère; je préférerai**) to prefer (**à** to); **je préférerais du thé** I'd prefer tea, I'd rather have tea; **je préférerais que vous veniez** I'd prefer it if you came, I'd rather you came; **p. faire qch** to prefer to do sth; **il préféra mourir plutôt que de se rendre** he preferred to die rather than surrender, he died rather than surrender; **je préfère ne pas y aller** I'd rather not go, I'd prefer not to go
préfet [prefɛ] *nm Admin* prefect; **p. de police** = chief commissioner of police; *Naut* **p. maritime** port admiral, commander-in-chief of the port
préfète [prefɛt] *nf Admin* prefect; (*épouse*) prefect's wife
préfiguration [prefigyrasjɔ̃] *nf* prefiguration, foreshadowing
préfigurer [prefigyre] *vt* to prefigure, to foreshadow
préfinancement [prefinɑ̃smɑ̃] *nm Fin* advance funding, pre-financing
préfixal, -ale, -aux, -ales [prefiksal, -o] *adj Gram* prefixal
préfixation [prefiksasjɔ̃] *nf Gram* prefixation
préfixe [prefiks] *nm* prefix
préfixer [prefikse] *vt* to prefix
pré(-)formaté [prefɔrmate] *adj Ordinat* pre-formatted
préglaciaire [preglasjɛr] *adj Géol* pre-glacial
préhellénique [preelenik] *adj* pre-Hellenic
préhenseur [preɑ̃sœr] *adj m* prehensile
préhensile [preɑ̃sil] *adj* prehensile
préhension [preɑ̃sjɔ̃] *nf* gripping, *Spéc* prehension
préhistoire [preistwar] *nf* prehistory
préhistorique [preistɔrik] *adj* prehistoric
pré-impression *nf Typ* pre-press
pré-imprimé *nm* preprinted form
pré-imprimée [preɛ̃prime] *nf* preprinted form
pré-imputation *nf Compta* pre-input preparation
pré-industriel, -ielle *adj* pre-industrial
pré-inscription *nf* pre-check-in
pré(-)installé [preɛ̃stale] *adj Ordinat* pre-installed
préjudice [preʒydis] *nm* (*à une cause, à la situation de qn etc*) prejudice, detriment; (*à une personne*) harm, wrong, injury; (*aux perspectives de qn*) damage; *Jur* tort; **subir un p.**

(matériel) to sustain damage; **subir un p. (moral)** to be wronged; **porter p. à qn** to do sb harm; (*d'une action, d'une déclaration*) to be prejudicial to sb's interests; **au p. de qn** to the prejudice *or* detriment of sb; **au p. de la justice** at the expense of justice; **sans p. de ...** without prejudice to ...

préjudiciable [preʒydisjabl] *adj* prejudicial, detrimental, harmful (**à** to)

préjudiciel, -elle [preʒydisjɛl] *adj Jur* (*question*) interlocutory; (*action*) prejudicial

préjudicier [preʒydisje] *vi* (*pr sub, impf* **n. préjudiciions**) *Arch, Litt* to be detrimental *or* prejudicial (**à** to)

préjugé [preʒyʒe] *nm* (*opinion toute faite*) prejudice, bias; **p. de classe** class prejudice; **préjugés raciaux** racial prejudice; **avoir un p. pour** *ou* **envers/contre qn/qch** to be prejudiced *or* biassed in favour of/against sb/sth; **elle avait un p. favorable à son égard** he had created a favourable impression upon her; **bénéficier d'un p. favorable** (*dans une course*) to look a likely winner; (*avoir bonne réputation*) to be well thought of

préjuger [preʒyʒe] *vi* (*conj like* **juger**) **p. de qch** to prejudge sth; **autant qu'on peut en p.** as far as one can judge beforehand *or* in advance; **il ne faut jamais p. de l'avenir** you can't tell what the future has in store

prélart [prelar] *nm* tarpaulin

prélasser (se) [səprelase] *vpr* to lounge, to loll; (*au soleil*) to bask

prélat [prela] *nm* prelate

prélature [prelatyr] *nf* prelacy

prélavage [prelavaʒ] *nm* prewash

prèle, prêle [prɛl] *nf Bot* horsetail

prélèvement [prelɛvmɑ̃] *nm* **(a)** *Fin* (*action*) deduction, withholding (**sur** from); **p. sur le capital** *ou* **sur la fortune** capital levy; **faire un p. sur un compte** to debit an account; **p. fiscal** tax deduction; **p. salarial** deduction from wages

(b) *Ind* (*action*) sampling; (*échantillon*) sample; **nous procéderons ensuite à un p. d'échantillons** next we shall proceed to take some samples

(c) *Méd* (*action*) sampling; (*échantillon*) sample; (*d'un organe*) removal; (*de sécrétion*) swab; **faire un p. à qn** to take a sample from sb; **faire un p. de sang** *ou* **sanguin à qn** to take a blood sample from sb

▶ **prélèvement**: *Banque* **p. automatique** direct debit

prélever [prelve] *vt* (*conj like* **lever**) **(a)** (*somme d'argent*) to deduct, to withhold (**sur** from); (*impôt*) to levy; **p. des taxes** to withhold taxes, to deduct taxes; **p. une commission de deux pour cent** to deduct *or* charge a commission of two per cent **(b)** (*organe*) to remove; **p. un échantillon** to take a sample; **p. du sang** to take a blood sample; **p. un morceau de tissu organique** to take a sample of organic tissue

préliminaire [preliminɛr] **1** *adj* preliminary **2** *nmpl* **préliminaires** preliminaries; (*discussions*) preliminary talks; *Typ* prelims

prélude [prelyd] *nm Mus, Fig* prelude (**de, à** to)

préluder [prelyde] *vi Mus* to warm up; (*jouer un prélude*) to play a prelude; *Fig* **p. à qch** to serve as *or* be a prelude to sth

prémaquette [premakɛt] *nf* rough layout

prématuré, -ée [prematyre] **1** *adj* premature; (*mort*) premature, untimely; **il est p. de l'annoncer** it's too early to announce it, an announcement would be premature; **être p. de six semaines** (*de bébé*) to be six weeks premature *or* early **2** *n* premature baby

prématurément [prematyremɑ̃] *adv* prematurely

prématurité [prematyrite] *nf* prematureness, prematurity

prémédication [premedikasjɔ̃] *nf Méd* premedication, *F* premed

prémédiquer [premedike] *vt Méd* to premedicate

préméditation [premeditasjɔ̃] *nf* premeditation; *Jur* **avec p.** (*agir, tuer*) with premeditation, with malice aforethought; **meurtre avec p.** premeditated murder; **meurtre sans p.** unpremeditated murder, murder without premeditation

préméditer [premedite] *vt* to premeditate; **elle n'avait pas prémédité de lui demander de rester** she hadn't planned *or* intended to ask him to stay

prémenstruel, -elle [premɑ̃stryɛl] *adj* premenstrual; **syndrome p.** premenstrual tension *or* syndrome, PMT

prémices [premis] *nfpl* **(a)** *Hist* (*fruits*) first fruits **(b)** *Litt* (*début*) early beginnings

premier, -ière [prəmje, -jɛr] **1** *adj* **(a)** [①**B56**,B,a-b] (*initial*) first; **le p. jour du mois** the first day of the month; **les trois premières années** the first three years; **les premières heures du matin** the early hours (of the morning), the (wee) small hours; **enseignement du p. degré** primary education; **professeurs du p. degré** primary(-school) teachers; **les premiers temps, elle n'osait pas parler** at first she didn't dare speak; **en p. (lieu)** in the first place, first, firstly; **la première fois** the first time; **il y a toujours une première fois** there's always a first time, there's a first time for everything; **dès le p. jour** from the first day, from the beginning *or* the outset; **du p. coup** at the first attempt; **les premiers arrivés** the first to arrive; **le p. venu vous dira cela** anybody *or* anyone will tell you that; **je ne vais pas coucher avec le p. venu** I'm not going to sleep with the first man that comes along; **ce n'est pas le p. venu** he isn't just anybody *or* anyone; **il n'a pas le p. sou** *Br* he hasn't (got) two halfpennies to rub together, *Am* he hasn't a cent; *Typ* **première épreuve** first proof; **première diffusion** (*d'un film*) first run; **première exclusivité** (*film*) first showing

(b) (*original*) primary, original; **sens p. d'un mot** primary *or* original meaning of a word; **cause première** prime *or* primary cause; **vérité première** basic truth; *Ind* **matières premières** raw materials

(c) (*dans un ordre*) first; **habiter au p. étage** to live on the first *or Am* second floor; **p. plan** foreground; *Fig* forefront; **une personnalité de tout p. plan** a leading personality; **première marche** bottom stair; *Th* **premières loges** first-tier boxes; *Fig* **être aux premières loges** to have a ringside seat; **s'asseoir au p. rang** to sit in the front row; **ce pays est au p. rang mondial pour l'exportation du nickel** this country is one of the world leaders in the export of nickel; **au tout p. rang** in the forefront; **prendre la première place** to take the lead

(d) (*placé au sommet de la hiérarchie*) **le p. chirurgien de Paris** the leading *or* top surgeon in Paris; **la première dame de France** the First Lady of France; **capitaine en p.** senior captain; *Culin* **du p. choix** prime cuts (of meat); **un morceau de p. choix** a prime cut (of meat); **de première importance** of the highest importance, of prime importance; **de première nécessité** essential; **je suis concerné au p. chef** it affects me first and foremost; **je suis le p. intéressé/concerné** I'm the one with most at stake/the one most affected; **billet de première classe** first-class ticket; **voyager en première classe** to travel first-class; *Th* **p. rôle** leading part, lead

(e) (*en logique*) (*terme*) given; **nombre p.** prime number

2 *n* **(a)** (*dans un classement*) first; **il/elle est le p./la première de sa classe** he's/she's (the) top of his/her class; **arriver le p./la première** *ou* **en p.** to arrive first; **elle était la première à arriver** she was the first to arrive; **nous sommes arrivés les premiers** we were the first to arrive, we arrived first; **arriver bon p.** to come in an easy first; **être le p. à faire qch** to be (the) first to do sth; **au p. de ces messieurs** next, please

(b) *Th* **jeune p./première** (young) romantic lead; *Fig* **il a des airs de jeune p.** he looks like a matinée idol *or* film star

3 *nf* **première (a)** *Couture* head seamstress

(b) *Th* first *or* opening night, first performance, première; *Cin* première, first showing; *Fig* **c'est une première!** it's a first!; *Journ* **première de couverture** *ou Arg* **de couve** front cover

(c) (*ascension*) first ascent

(d) *Av, Rail etc* first class; **billet de première** first-class ticket; **voyager en première** to travel first-class

(e) *Scol Br* ≈ lower sixth (form), *Am* ≈ eleventh grade

(f) (*vitesse*) first (gear), bottom (gear); **passer en première** to go into first (gear)

(g) (*de chaussure*) inner sole, insole

(h) *Fin* **première de change** first of exchange

(i) *F* **de première** first-rate, first-class

4 *nm* **(a)** (*date*) **le p. janvier** the first of January, January (the) first; **le p. de l'an** New Year's Day

(b) (*premier étage*) first floor, *Am* second floor; **les gens du p.** the people on the first *or Am* second floor

▶ **premier**: **p. commis** principal clerk, head clerk; *Sp* **p. de cordée** leader; **p. cycle** *Scol* = first three years of secondary school; *Univ* = first two years of undergraduate course; **première danseuse** leading dancer; *Naut* **p. maître** chief petty officer; **P. Ministre** Prime Minister; *Can* (*d'une province*) Premier; *TV, Cin* **p. montage** rough cut; **p. numéro** first issue; **p. tirage** first run; (*presse*) early edition; **p. violon** first violin; (*qui dirige*) leader, *Am* concertmaster

premièrement [prəmjɛrmɑ̃] *adv* first, firstly, in the first place

premier-né, première-née [prəmjene, prəmjɛrne], *pl* **premiers-nés, premières-nées** *adj, n* firstborn

prémilitaire [premilitɛr] *adj* premilitary

prémisse [premis] *nf Phil* premise, premiss

prémolaire [premɔlɛr] *nf Anat* premolar

prémonition [premɔnisjɔ̃] *nf* premonition

prémonitoire [premɔnitwar] *adj* premonitory

prémunir [premynir] **1** *vt Vieilli* **p. qn contre qch** (*protéger*) to protect sb against sth; (*mettre en garde*) to put sb on his/her guard against sth **2 se prémunir** *vpr* **se p. contre qch** (*être vigilant*) to be on one's guard against sth; **se p. contre le rhume** to take precautions against (catching) a cold

prenable [prənabl] *adj* (*ville, fort*) pregnable

prenant [prənɑ̃] *adj* **(a)** *Fin* **partie prenante** payee; (*d'argent, de biens*) recipient **(b)** *Zool* (*queue*) prehensile **(c)** (*voix*) captivating; (*livre, film, travail*) fascinating, absorbing

prénatal, -ale, -als, -ales [prenatal] *adj* antenatal, prenatal

prendre [prɑ̃dr] (*prp* **prenant**; *pp* **pris**; *pr ind* **je prends, il prend, n. prenons, ils prennent**; *pr sub* **je prenne, n. prenions**; *impf* **je prenais, n. prenions**; *p hist* **je pris, n. prîmes**; *fu* **je prendrai**) **1** *vt* **(a)** (*saisir*) to take; **p. qch dans un tiroir** to take *or* get sth from *or* out of a drawer; **p. qch sur la table** to take sth from *or* off the table; **p. brusquement qch** to snatch sth (up), to seize sth; **je suis allé p. mon parapluie** I went to get my umbrella; **il l'a prise par le bras/ la main** he took her (by the) arm/hand; **p. qn par la taille** to put one's arm round sb's waist; **p. qn par les cheveux** to take *or* grab sb by the hair; **je l'ai prise dans mes bras** I took her in my arms; **p. les armes** to take up arms; **il faut savoir le p.** you have to know how to handle him; **où avez-vous pris cela?** where did you get that (from)?; (*cette idée*) where did you get that idea (from)?; *Tech* **p. en étau** to clamp

(b) p. qch sur soi to take responsibility for sth; **p. sur soi de faire qch** to take it upon oneself to do sth

(c) (*accepter, recevoir*) to take; (*pensionnaire*) to take (in); **vous avez mal pris mes paroles** you took me *or* what I said the wrong way; **il a très mal pris la chose** he took it very badly; **p. une commande** to take an order; **p. qch à bail** to take out a lease on sth, to lease sth

(d) (*enlever*) to take (away); **p. qch à qn** to take sth (away) from sb; (*voler*) to steal sth from sb, to rob sb of sth; (*priver*) to deprive sb of sth; **cela me prend tout mon temps** it takes (up) all my time; **ça m'a pris deux heures** it took me two hours; **mon temps est entièrement pris** I haven't a free minute, my time is completely taken up; **toute sa semaine est déjà prise** his whole week is already taken up; **c'est toujours ça de pris** that's something at least; **j'ai dû p. sur mes économies** I had to draw on my savings

(e) (*en argent*) **prenez ce que je vous offre** take what I'm offering you; **dites-moi ce que vous prenez pour cela** how much do you charge for that?; **il prend combien?** how much does he charge?; *F* **il prend cher** he charges a lot, he's expensive

(f) (*s'approprier*) to take; **c'est à p. ou à laisser** take it or leave it; **il y a à p. et à laisser** there are good things and bad things; **il y a à p. et à laisser dans ce qu'elle dit** some of what she says is right and some of it isn't

(g) (*considérer*) **à tout p.** on the whole, all in all

(h) (*s'emparer de*) (*fugitif, voleur*) to catch, to capture; (*ville, région*) to take, to capture, to seize; (*marchandises illégales*) to seize; (*poisson, lièvre etc*) to catch; **p. une ville d'assaut** to take a town by storm, to storm a town; *Prov* **tel est pris qui croyait p.** it's a case of the biter bit; **se faire p.** to be *or* get caught; **se laisser p.** to let oneself be *or* get caught; *Fig* to let oneself be taken in; **il s'y est laissé p.** he fell into the trap; **p. qn à voler** to catch sb stealing; **être pris à faire qch** to be caught doing sth; **p. qn sur le fait** to catch sb in the act *or* red-handed; **que je vous y prenne!** just *or* don't let me catch you (at it) again!; **on ne m'y prendra plus** I won't be caught (out) *or* taken in again; **être pris par le brouillard/la tourmente** to be caught in the fog/the gale; **il s'est pris le pied dans une racine** he caught his foot on a root

(i) pris de panique panic-stricken; **pris d'un sentiment d'angoisse** overcome by a feeling of anxiety; **être pris d'une faiblesse** to feel suddenly faint; **elle a été prise d'un fou rire** she got (a fit of) the giggles; **l'envie lui a pris** *ou* **il lui a pris l'envie de partir** he got a sudden urge to leave, he was seized with a desire to leave; **si jamais l'envie vous en prenait** if ever you should feel so inclined; *F* **ça te prend souvent?** do you get like that often?; **qu'est-ce qui lui prend?** what's come over him?, what's up with him?; **bien lui en a pris** it was lucky for him that he did; *Fig très F* **ça/il me prend la tête** it/he really gets on my nerves

(j) (*emmener*) to call for, to collect, to fetch; **prends ton frère avec toi** take your brother with you; **le taxi s'est arrêté pour p. un client** the taxi stopped to pick up a fare; **passe me p. vers six heures** call for *or* come for *or* fetch me at about six o'clock; **p. des marchandises** (*d'un bateau*) to take in cargo; **le bateau prend l'eau** the boat is leaking, the boat is letting in water; **les murs prennent l'humidité** the walls are getting damp

(k) (*acheter*) to get, to buy; (*réserver*) to book, to reserve; **p. une chambre** (*dans un hôtel*) to take a room; (*réserver*) to book a room; **j'ai pris un petit studio** I took a little studio flat; **p. une police d'assurance** to take out an insurance policy

(l) p. sa retraite to retire; **il n'a pas pris de vacances l'année dernière** he didn't take *or* have any holidays last year; **tu devrais p. quelques jours (de vacances)** you ought to take a few days off; **p. du repos** to take *or* have a rest

(m) (*s'informer de*) **p. des renseignements** to make enquiries; **tous renseignements pris ...** after (making) thorough enquiries ...

(n) (*noter*) **p. des notes** to take (down) notes; **p. le pouls/ la température de qn** to take sb's pulse/temperature

(o) (*embaucher*) (*personnel*) to take on, *Fml* to engage

(p) p. qn/qch comme exemple to take sb/sth as an example; **p. qn comme modèle** to model oneself on sb

(q) p. qn/qch pour ... to take sb/sth for ...; **on le prenait pour un colonel** we/they/*etc* took him for a colonel, we/they/ *etc* took him to be a colonel

(r) (*nourriture, boisson*) to have; (*médicament*) to take; (*bain*) to take, to have; **qu'est-ce que vous pren(dr)ez?** what will you have (to drink)?; **il prend du sucre dans son thé** he takes sugar in his tea; **il prend toujours un petit verre avant d'aller se coucher** he always has a small glass of something before going to bed

(s) *F* (*recevoir*) **qu'est-ce que tu vas p.!** you're for it!, you'll catch it!; **elle a pris une sacrée raclée** she got a real good hiding *or* thrashing

(t) (*attraper*) (*maladie*) to get; (*accent, habitudes*) to acquire; **p. froid** to catch cold

(u) (*se mettre à avoir*) (*apparence*) to take on, to assume; (*attitude*) to strike, to assume; **elle prit un ton sévère** her voice took on a severe tone; **p. du poids** to put on *or* gain weight; **p. de l'âge** to be getting old *or* on; **p. un coup de vieux** to age

(v) *Méd* **p. du sang** to take a blood sample

(w) (*utiliser*) (*train, bus etc*) to take; **j'ai pris l'avion** I flew, I took the plane; **prenez une chaise** take *or* have a seat, sit down; **p. la route de** *ou* **pour Paris** to take the road to Paris; **il est temps de p. la route** it's time to set off *or F* to hit the road; *Aut* **p. un virage** to take a bend; *Naut* **p. le large** to take to the open sea; **p. le trot** (*d'un cheval*) to break into a trot; *TV, Rad* **p. l'antenne** to go on the air

2 *vi* **(a)** (*du mortier, de la gelée, du ciment, d'un flan etc*) to set

(b) (*d'une plante*) to take (root)

(c) (*du feu*) to take, to catch; (*d'une allumette*) to strike, to light; **le feu a pris à sa robe** her dress caught fire; **le feu a pris vite et s'est propagé** the fire took hold quickly and spread

(d) (*réussir, marcher*) **le vaccin a pris** the vaccine has taken (effect); **cette mode ne prendra pas** this fashion won't catch on; *F* **ce truc-là prend toujours** this trick always works *or* is always successful; *F* **ça ne prend pas avec moi!** you can't fool me!, it won't wash with me!

(e) p. sur soi to restrain *or* contain oneself

(f) (*aller*) **p. à gauche** to bear (to the) left, to go left; **p. par la vieille ville** to go via the old town; **p. à travers champs** to strike across the fields

3 se prendre *vpr* **(a)** (*s'accrocher*) **son manteau s'est pris dans la porte/à un clou** her coat (got) caught in the door/on a nail; **ils se sont pris par la taille/le cou** they put their arms around each other('s waists/necks); **se p. par la main** to hold hands, to take each other by the hand

(b) *Vieilli* (*d'un flan*) to set

(c) (*se saisir*) to be held; (*être attrapé*) to be caught; **le verre se prend par son pied** the glass is held *or* you hold the glass by the stem; **un médicament qui se prend le soir** a medicine which is (to be) taken in the evening

(d) (*se considérer*) **se p. au sérieux** to take oneself seriously; **il se prend pour un héros** he thinks he's a hero

(e) se p. d'amitié pour qn to take a liking to sb; (*devenir ami*) to form a friendship with sb; **se p. de dégoût pour qch** to take a (strong) dislike to sth

(f) *Litt* (*commencer*) **se p. à faire qch** to begin *or* start to do sth, to begin *or* start doing sth

(g) s'en p. à qn (*physiquement, verbalement*) to attack sb; (*moralement*) to blame sb, to put *or* lay the blame on sb; (*passer sa colère sur*) to take it out on sb; **ne t'en prends qu'à toi-même** you've only (got) yourself to blame

(h) il sait comment s'y p. he knows how to go *or* set about it; **je sais comment m'y p. avec lui** I know how to deal with him *or* handle him; **vous vous y prenez mal** you're going about it (in) the wrong way; **il s'y prend bien** he sets *or* goes about it (in) the right way; **elle s'y prend bien pour le faire** she's going *or* setting about it (in) the right way; **s'y p. à deux fois** to make two attempts, to have two goes

(i) *très F* **se p. la tête** to make life difficult for oneself

preneur, -euse [prənœr, -øz] *n* (**a**) *Com, Fin* buyer, purchaser; (*d'un chèque*) payee; **je suis p.** I'll take it; **trouver p.** to find a buyer; *Fin* **p. de lettre de change** payee of a bill of exchange (**b**) *Jur* (*locataire*) lessee, leaseholder (**c**) **p. de son** sound recordist, sound engineer, sound technician (**d**) **p. d'otages** hostage taker

prénom [prenɔ̃] *nm* first *or Am* given name; (*dans les pays chrétiens*) Christian name

prénommé, -ée [prenɔme] **1** *adj* called, named; *Jur* said, abovenamed, aforesaid; **le p. Victor** the man called *or* named Victor **2** *n Jur* **le p./la prénommée** the abovenamed, the aforesaid

prénommer [prenɔme] **1** *vt* to call, to name; **on la prénomma Irma** she was called *or* named Irma **2 se prénommer** *vpr* **il se prénomme Adam** his first *or Am* given name is Adam, he is called *or* named Adam

prénuptial, -ale, -aux, -ales [prenypsjal, -o] *adj* premarital; **examen p.** premarital medical check

préoccupant [preɔkypɑ̃] *adj* worrying

préoccupation [preɔkypasjɔ̃] *nf* (**a**) (*priorité*) concern, preoccupation; **ma seule p. a été d'assurer ...** my sole concern has been to ensure ...; **j'ai d'autres préoccupations** I have other things to worry about (**b**) (*tourment*) worry

préoccupé [preɔkype] *adj* preoccupied; (*inquiet*) worried; **tu as l'air p.** you look worried; **d'un ton p.** (*pensant à autre chose*) absent-mindedly; (*inquiet*) in a worried tone; **d'un air p.** with a worried look (on his/her face)

préoccuper [preɔkype] **1** *vt* (*tracasser*) to worry; (*obséder*) to preoccupy; **être préoccupé par qch** to be concerned *or* preoccupied with sth; **sa santé me préoccupe** I'm worried *or* anxious *or* concerned about his health; **elle a quelque chose qui la préoccupe** she's got something on her mind, something's worrying her; **le foot est tout ce qui le préoccupe** football is all he thinks about **2 se préoccuper** *vpr* **se p. de qch/qn** to concern oneself with sth/with sb; **il ne s'est pas beaucoup préoccupé de savoir si j'allais bien** he didn't bother himself much to find out if I was all right

préopératoire [preɔperatwar] *adj Méd* preoperative

prépa [prepa] *nf Scol F* preparatory class (*for the entrance exam to the grandes écoles*); **faire une p., être en p.** to be studying for the entrance exam to the grandes écoles

pré-paiement *nm* pre-payment

préparamétré [preparametre] *adj Ordinat* (*logiciel*) preconfigured

préparateur, -trice [preparatœr, -tris] *n* (*assistant*) assistant (*in laboratory*); *Ind* demonstrator; **p. en pharmacie** pharmacist's *or Br* (dispensing) chemist's assistant

préparatifs [preparatif] *nmpl* preparations (**de** for); **faire ses p. de départ** to prepare to *or* get ready to leave, to make one's preparations for departure; **j'étais en plein p. de départ quand ...** I was in the middle of preparing *or* getting ready to leave when ...

préparation [preparasjɔ̃] *nf* (**a**) (*fait de préparer, de se préparer*) preparation (**à** for); (*des repas*) preparation, *esp Am F* fixing; **faire un discours sans p.** to make an ad-lib *or* impromptu speech; **annoncer une nouvelle sans p.** to blurt out a piece of news; **tu ne peux pas le lui dire sans p.** you can't tell him without any preparation, you can't blurt it out; **faire une p. militaire** to do a training course in preparation for military service; **p. au mariage** preparation for marriage

(**b**) *Scol* (*à un examen*) preparation (**de** for); (*composition, exercice préparé*) preparation; **faire une p. aux grandes écoles** to prepare for the entrance exam to the grandes écoles

(**c**) *Pharm* preparation; *Culin* **p. pour gâteau/sauce** cake/sauce mix

(**d**) (*organisation*) preparation, planning

préparatoire [preparatwar] *adj* preparatory, preliminary; *Scol* **cours p.** = first year infants' class, *Am* = nursery school; **classes préparatoires** preparatory classes (*for the entrance exam to the grandes écoles*); **école p.** = school that prepares students for higher education

préparer [prepare] **1** *vt* (**a**) (*organiser, apprêter*) to prepare, to get ready; (*réunions*) to make preparations *or* arrangements for, to arrange; (*lit*) to make (up); (*repas*) to prepare, *surtout Am F* to fix; (*poisson, poulet*) to prepare, to dress; *Pharm* (*ordonnance*) to make up; **elle prépare le déjeuner** she's getting lunch ready, she's preparing lunch; **plats (tout) préparés** ready-cooked meals

(**b**) **p. qn à qch** to prepare sb for sth; (*entraîner*) to train *or* coach sb for sth; **p. qn à une nouvelle** to prepare sb for a piece of news; **rien ne m'y avait préparé** nothing had prepared me for this

(**c**) *Univ* (*examen*) to prepare for, to study for

(**d**) (*prévoir, ébaucher*) to plan, to prepare; **p. un coup** to be hatching something, to be cooking something up; **p. ses vacances** to plan *or* arrange one's holidays; **p. un discours** to prepare a speech; **p. son avenir** to prepare for one's future; **cette découverte a été préparée par toute une tradition scientifique** a whole scientific tradition prepared the ground *or* paved the way for this discovery; **je suis sûr qu'il nous prépare quelque chose** I'm sure he's up to something

2 se préparer *vpr* (**a**) (*être imminent*) to be in the offing; **un orage se prépare** a storm is brewing; **il se prépare quelque chose** there's something in the air; (*mauvais coup*) there's something fishy going on

(**b**) (*s'apprêter*) **se p. à qch/à faire qch** to prepare (oneself) *or* to get ready for sth/to do sth; **se p. à** *ou* **pour un voyage** to get ready for a journey, to make preparations for a journey; **se p. au combat** to prepare for action *or* combat; **il est dans la salle de bain, il se prépare** he's in the bathroom getting ready

(**c**) (*se faire*) **se p. un café** to make oneself a coffee; **tu te prépares bien des ennuis/des désillusions** you're in for trouble/a surprise

pré-passerelle *nf* pre-boarding bridge

prépayé [prepeje] *adj* prepaid

pré-planification *nf* pre-planning

prépondérance [prepɔ̃derɑ̃s] *nf* predominance (**sur** over)

prépondérant [prepɔ̃derɑ̃] *adj* predominant; **sa voix sera prépondérante** he will have the casting vote

préposé, -ée [prepoze] *n* (*employé, agent*) employee; *Admin* official; (*dans un vestiaire*) attendant; **p. (des postes)** postman, *f* postwoman, *Am* mailman, *f* mailwoman; **p. des douanes** customs officer; *Jur* **commettant et p.** principal and agent; **p. aux réservations** reservations clerk

préposer [prepoze] *vt* **p. qn à une fonction** to appoint sb to an office; **il a été préposé au poste de chargé des relations publiques** he was put in charge of public relations, he was appointed public relations officer

prépositif, -ive [prepozitif, -iv] *adj Gram* (*locution*) prepositional

préposition [prepozisjɔ̃] *nf* [①**A64-67**; **B51-54**] *Gram* preposition

prépositionnel, -elle [prepozisjɔnɛl] *adj Gram* prepositional

pré-production *nf* preproduction

préprogrammé [preprɔgrame] *adj Ordinat* preprogrammed

pré-publication *nf* prepublication

prépuce [prepys] *nm Anat* foreskin, *Spéc* prepuce

préraphaélisme [prerafaelism] *nm Beaux-Arts* Pre-Raphaelitism

préraphaélite [prerafaelit] *adj, nm Beaux-Arts* Pre-Raphaelite

prérentrée [prerɑ̃tre] *nf Scol* = day before school begins, used by teachers for preparation

préretraite [prer(ə)trɛt] *nf* early retirement; (*pension*) early retirement pension; **partir en p.** to take early retirement; **être en p.** to have taken early retirement; **être mis en p.** to be given early retirement, to be pensioned off, *F* to be put out to grass

préretraité, -ée [prer(ə)trɛte] *n* = person who has taken early retirement; (*mis en préretraite*) person who has been given early retirement

prérogative [prerɔgativ] *nf* prerogative

préromantique [prerɔmɑ̃tik] *adj Hist Littér* pre-Romantic

préromantisme [prerɔmɑ̃tism] *nm Hist Littér* pre-Romanticism

près [prɛ] **1** *adv* (**a**) (*dans l'espace*) near, close; (*dans le temps*) close; **il habite tout p.** he lives very near here *or* very close by; **c'est tout p.** it's very near *or* close; **vous êtes trop p.** you're too close *or* near; **plus p.** nearer, closer; **moins p.** farther away; **à un détail p.** except for *or* apart from one detail; **à cela p. que ...** except that ...; **à quelques exceptions p.** with a few exceptions; **à cinq centimètres p.** to within five centimetres; **il devinerait votre poids à un milligramme p.** he would guess your weight to the nearest milligram; **nous n'en sommes pas à un ou deux jours/dix francs p.** a day or two/ten francs more or less doesn't matter; **je l'ai raté à deux minutes p.** I missed him by two minutes; **à peu de choses p.**, *F* **à quelque chose p.** more or less

(**b**) **à peu p.** (*pas tout à fait*) nearly, almost; (*approximativement*) about, approximately; **le travail est à peu p. achevé** the work is nearly *or* almost *or* just about *or* more or less finished; **il était à peu p. certain que ...** it was fairly certain that ...

(**c**) *Naut* **courir au plus p.** to sail on a wind *or* close to the wind *or* on a bowline

(**d**) **de p.** closely; (*voir qn*) close to, close up; **tirer de p.** to fire at close range; **examiner qch de p.** to examine sth closely; **suivre qn de p.** (*ne pas être loin derrière*) to follow sb closely, to follow close behind sb, to follow hard *or* close on sb's heels; (*d'un médecin, professeur etc*) to follow sb's progress closely; **de p., elles sont très différentes** (seen) close to *or* up, they are very different

2 *prép* **(a) p. de** (*dans l'espace*) near (to), close to; (*dans le temps*) close to; **p. de là** nearby, close by; **p. de chez eux** near (to) *or* close to where they live; **tout p. de moi** very close *or* near to me; *Naut* **courir p. du vent** to sail close to the wind; **il est p. de midi** it's close on *or* nearly *or* almost twelve (o'clock); **il y a p. de dix ans** close on *or* nearly *or* almost ten years ago; **il a fallu p. de deux heures pour ...** we needed close on *or* nearly *or* almost two hours to ...; **être p. de faire qch** to be about to do sth, to be on the point *or* verge of doing sth; **elle était p. d'éclater en sanglots** she was about to burst into tears, she was close to tears *or* on the brink *or* the verge of tears; *Iron* **nous ne sommes pas p. de le revoir** we won't see him again in a hurry; **est-il p. d'avoir fini?** is he anywhere near finished?; *F* **être p. de ses sous** to be tight-fisted, to be mean

(b) *Admin* **ambassadeur p. le gouvernement français** ambassador to France

présage [prezaʒ] *nm* omen, sign, *Litt* presage, portent; (*de malheur*) foreboding; **mauvais p.** bad *or* ill omen

présager [prezaʒe] *vt* **(je présageai(s); n. présageons) (a)** (*annoncer*) to be an omen of, *Litt* to presage, to portend; (*malheur*) to (fore)bode; **cela ne présage rien de bon** it bodes no good, nothing good will come of it **(b)** (*prédire*) (*d'une personne*) to predict; **ces gros nuages noirs laissent p. un orage** those big black clouds are a sure sign of a storm

présalaire [presalɛr] *nm* (student) grant

pré-salé, *pl* **prés-salés** *nm* (*mouton*) salt-meadow sheep; (*viande*) salt-meadow lamb

presbyte [prɛzbit] *adj* long-sighted, *Spéc* presbyopic

presbytère [prɛzbitɛr] *nm* presbytery

presbytérianisme [prɛzbiterjanism] *nm* Presbyterianism

presbytérien, -ienne [prɛzbiterjɛ̃, -jɛn] *adj, n* Presbyterian

presbytie [prɛsbisi] *nf* long-sightedness, *Spéc* presbyopia

prescience [presjɑ̃s] *nf* (*de l'avenir*) foreknowledge, *Fml* prescience

prescient [presjɑ̃] *adj* prescient

préscolaire [preskɔlɛr] *adj* preschool

préscolarisation [preskɔlarizasjɔ̃] *nf* preschool education

prescripteur, -trice [preskriptœr, -tris] **1** *n* (*médecin*) prescriber; **le p. d'une ordonnance** the writer of a prescription **2** *nm Mktg* influencer

prescription [prɛskripsjɔ̃] *nf* **(a)** *Jur* prescription; **invoquer la p.** to raise a defence under the statute of limitations; **après 50 ans, il y a p.** the statute of limitations runs out after 50 years; *Fin* **p. acquisitive** acquisition of a right due to the passage of time; *Fin* **p. extinctive** lapse of a right due to the passage of time **(b)** *Méd* prescription, direction(s) (for treatment) **(c)** (*instruction*) rule, regulation

prescrire [prɛskrir] (*conj like* **écrire**) **1** *vt* **(a)** (*ordonner*) (*conditions*) to stipulate, to lay down, to specify; (*remède*) to prescribe; **à la date prescrite** on the date laid down, on the prescribed date **(b)** *Jur* to prescribe, to bar by the statute of limitations **(c)** (*réclamer*) to demand, to require; **ce que l'honneur prescrit** the demands *or* dictates of honour **2 se prescrire** *vpr Jur* **ces dettes se prescrivent par cinq ans** these debts are barred at the end of five years; *Méd* **ce médicament se prescrit en cas de ...** this medicine is prescribed for ...

préséance [preseɑ̃s] *nf* precedence, priority (**sur** over); **avoir la p. sur qn** to have precedence over sb

présélecteur [preselɛktœr] *nm Tech* preselector

présélection [preselɛksjɔ̃] *nf* **(a)** (*premier choix*) preselection, preselecting; (*pour un emploi*) shortlisting **(b)** *Aut* **boîte de vitesses à p.** preselector gearbox

présélectionner [preselɛksjɔne] *vt Tech* to preselect; (*candidats*) to shortlist

présence [prezɑ̃s] *nf* **(a)** (*fait d'être dans un lieu*) presence; (*aux cours etc*) attendance; **je désire sa p.** I want him to be here; **il ignore votre p.** he doesn't know you're here; **faire acte de p., faire de la p.** to put in an appearance; **feuille de p.** attendance sheet; *Ind* time card; **p. policière** police presence

(b) (*personnalité*) presence; **avoir de la p.** to have great presence; **elle n'a aucune p. sur scène** she has no stage presence

(c) en p. face to face, facing one another; **mettre les deux parties en p.** to bring the two parties face to face *or* together; **en p. de toute la famille** in front of *or* in the presence of the whole family; **je ne parlerai qu'en p. de mon avocat** I'll only speak with my lawyer present; **en p. de la mort** in the presence of death; **en p. de ces faits/cette situation** faced with these facts/this situation, in view of these facts/this situation; **en p. du virus ...** when the virus is present ...; **mis en p. du réactif ...** when placed in the vicinity of the reagent ...; **cela s'est fait en ma p.** it was done in my presence; **cela s'est dit en ma p.** it was said in my presence *or* hearing

(d) (*existence*) presence; **la p. de sang dans les urines** the presence of blood in the urine; **expliquez-moi la p. de cette arme ici** explain to me how this weapon comes to be here; **j'ai senti une p. à côté de moi** I felt a presence beside me

▶ **présence**: **p. d'esprit** presence of mind; **je n'ai pas eu la p. d'esprit de le lui dire** I didn't have the presence of mind to tell him; *Rel* **p. réelle** real presence

présent¹, -ente [prezɑ̃, -ɑ̃t] **1** *adj* **(a)** (*qui est dans le lieu dont on parle*) present; **les personnes présentes** those present; **être p. à un spectacle/un mariage** to be present at a performance/a wedding; **Jacques Martin, ici p., vous le dira** Jacques Martin, who is here with us, will tell you; *Scol* **Tardi? – p.!** Tardi? – here! *or* present!; *Hum* **dès qu'il s'agit de manger, tu peux être sûr qu'il répond p.** as soon as it's a matter of food, you can be sure he'll be there; **cela m'est toujours p. à l'esprit** it's always in my mind; (*d'un conseil, d'un danger etc*) I always keep it in mind; **p. par la pensée** here/there in spirit

(b) (*actuel*) (*situation, moment*) present; **vivre dans l'instant p.** to live for the moment; **la présente convention** this convention; *Jur* **par la présente lettre** hereby, by these presents

(c) *Gram* present; **le temps p.** the present (tense)

2 *n* (*témoin*) person present; **le nom des présents à la réunion** the names of those present at the meeting

3 *nm* **(a)** [ⓘA47-8,10; B28,F,1] *Gram* present (tense); **le p. du subjonctif/de l'indicatif** the present subjunctive/indicative; **mettre le texte au p.** to put the text into the present (tense)

(b) (*partie du temps*) present; **vivre dans le p.** to live for the moment *or* in the present

4 *nf Jur, Admin* **par la présente** *ou* **les présentes** (*par cette lettre, ce texte*) hereby, by these presents

5 *adv* **à p.** at present, (just) now; **jusqu'à p.** up to now, up to the present (time), until now; (*de qch qui ne s'est pas encore produit*) as yet; **dès à p.** from now on, *Fml* henceforth; **à p. que ...** now that ...

présent² [prezɑ̃] *nm Litt* (*cadeau*) present, gift; **faire p. de qch à qn** to make a present of sth to sb

présentable [prezɑ̃tabl] *adj* presentable

présentateur, -trice [prezɑ̃tatœr, -tris] *n Rad, TV* presenter; (*d'un spectacle télévisé*) master of ceremonies, MC; **p. télé** TV presenter; **p. de journal télévisé** newscaster, news reader; *TV, Rad* **p. principal** anchor

présentation [prezɑ̃tasjɔ̃] *nf* **(a)** (*de faits, d'un travail, d'un titre de transport etc*) presentation; **10% de réduction sur p. de la carte** 10% discount on presentation of this card; *Banque* **p. à l'encaissement d'un chèque** paying in, *Br* encashment; *Fml, Admin* presentation for collection; *Com* **payable à p.** payable on demand *or* on presentation *or* at sight; **p. au paiement** presentation for payment; *Fin* **p. à l'acceptation** presentation for acceptance

(b) (*apparence*) (*d'une personne*) appearance; (*d'un document etc*) presentation; **soigner la** *ou* **sa p.** to take care over one's appearance *or* over how one looks; **recherche hôtesses, excellente p.** hostesses required, must have smart, attractive appearance; **livre de bonne p.** well-produced book; **la p. des objets dans une vitrine** the presentation *or* display of items in a shop window; **p. assistée par ordinateur** computer-aided presentation

(c) *Obst* presentation; **p. par les pieds** breech presentation

(d) (*dans un groupe etc*) introduction (**à qn** to sb); (*à la cour*) presentation; **lettre de p.** letter of introduction; **je vous laisse faire les présentations** I'll leave you to make the introductions

(e) *Rel* **la P. de la Vierge** (the Feast of) the Presentation (of the Blessed Virgin Mary)

(f) (*à un public*) (*d'un film*) showing, presentation; *Mil* **p. du drapeau** trooping the colour; *Com* **p. de collections, p. de mode** fashion show; **la p. du nouveau modèle diesel** the unveiling *or* presentation of the new diesel model

présenter [prezɑ̃te] **1** *vt* **(a)** (*montrer*) (*passeport, billet etc*) to show, to produce, to present; (*spectacle, film*) to present; **p. son passeport au douanier** to show one's passport to the customs officer; **p. une pièce d'identité** (*au commissariat etc*) to show *or* produce *or* present proof of identity; **p. des factures** to present invoices; **p. à l'encaissement** to present for collection; **p. sa main à qn** to hold out one's hand to sb; **il m'a présenté son dos** he turned his back on *or* to me; **je lui ai présenté le meilleur fauteuil/des cacahuètes** I offered him the best chair/some peanuts; *Méd* **p. un symptôme** to present a symptom; *Mil* **p. les armes** to present arms; **présentez armes!** present arms!

(b) (*dire, exprimer*) **je vous présente mes excuses** I do apologise; **p. ses condoléances** to offer one's condolences; **p. ses hommages à qn** to pay one's respects to sb; **p. ses arguments/raisons** to present *or* set out one's arguments/ reasons; **p. ses craintes** to express one's fears

(c) (*soumettre*) (*facture, addition*) to present, to submit; **p. sa candidature à un poste** to apply for a job; *Scol* **p. le français (à un examen)** to take *or* offer French (as one of one's exam subjects)

(d) (*faire connaître*) (*motion*) to table; (*spectacle*) to present, to compere, *Am F* to emcee; **il m'a présenté tous les faits** he set out *or* put *or* laid all the facts before me; **p. des conclusions** to submit conclusions; **p. un projet de loi** to bring in *or* introduce a bill; **son travail est bien présenté** his work is well presented *or* set out

(e) p. qn à qn to introduce sb to sb; (*à la cour*) to present sb to sb; **nous n'avons pas été présentés** we haven't been introduced; **je voudrais vous p. ma cousine** I'd like you to meet my cousin, *Fml* allow me to introduce my cousin (to you); **p. qn comme candidat** to put sb forward as a candidate; **il a été présenté pour ce poste** he has been put forward *or* proposed for this post; **p. les meilleurs élèves pour le concours d'entrée** to enter the best pupils *or* put the best pupils forward for the entrance examination

2 *vi F* **il présente bien** he has a good appearance

3 se présenter *vpr* **(a)** (*se produire*) to arise; **si l'occasion se présente** if the opportunity presents itself *or* arises (**de faire qch** to do sth); **si le cas se présente** if the case arises; **un beau spectacle s'est présenté à mes yeux** a beautiful sight met my eyes; **attendre que quelque chose se présente** to wait for something to turn up; **la chose se présente bien** things look promising; **l'affaire se présente sous un jour nouveau** the matter appears in a new light

(b) (*se porter candidat*) to apply; **est-ce que beaucoup de gens se sont présentés?** did many people apply?, were there many applications?; **se p. à un examen** to take *or Br* sit an examination; **se p. aux élections** to be a candidate *or Br* stand (as a candidate) at the elections; **se p. comme candidat** to come forward as a candidate

(c) (*se rendre*) (*au commissariat*), *Mil* to report; **se p. chez qn** to call on sb; **elle s'est présentée ivre chez son nouvel employeur** she arrived drunk at her new employer's; **prière de vous p. chez Monsieur Troc** please go to see Mr Troc, *Fml* please report to Mr Troc; **si vous êtes intéressé, présentez-vous à nos bureaux** if you're interested, come along to our office

(d) (*se faire connaître*) **se p.** to introduce oneself (à); **permettez-moi de me p.** may I introduce myself?

(e) *Méd, Obst* to present; **l'enfant se présente mal** the child is presenting badly; **le bébé s'est présenté par la tête/ les pieds** the baby was in a normal/breech position

présentoir [prezɑ̃twar] *nm Com* display unit, display shelf

présérie [preseri] *nf Tech* test series, pilot series

préservateur, -trice [prezɛrvatœr, -tris] **1** *adj Arch* preservative; (*mesures*) preventive **2** *nm* (*dans la nourriture*) preservative

préservatif, -ive [prezɛrvatif, -iv] **1** *adj Vieilli* (*épaisseur, vêtement*) protective; **des mesures préservatives contre l'épidemie** steps to ward off the epidemic **2** *nm* (*condom*) condom, sheath; **p. féminin** female condom, Femidom®; (*diaphragme*) diaphragm, cap

préservation [prezɛrvasjɔ̃] *nf* (*de l'environnement, des traditions etc*) preservation, protection; (*d'une personne, des récoltes*) protection

préserver [prezɛrve] **1** *vt* to preserve; (*protéger*) to protect (**de** from); **le ciel m'en préserve!** heaven forbid!; **à p. de l'humidité** to be kept dry **2 se préserver** *vpr* to protect oneself (**de** from); **se p. de l'ennui/de la solitude** to guard against boredom/loneliness

présidence [prezidɑ̃s] *nf* **(a)** *Pol* presidency; **sous sa p.** under *or* during his presidency; **un candidat à la p.** a presidential candidate, a candidate for the presidency; **p. d'une société** chairmanship of a company, *Am* presidency of a company **(b)** (*de club etc*) chairmanship; **prendre la p.** (*à une réunion*) to take the chair **(c)** (*habitation*) presidential residence

président, -ente [prezidɑ̃, -ɑ̃t] *n* **(a)** *Pol* president; **le P.** the President; **la Présidente** the President; *Vieilli* (*femme du Président*) the President's wife, *US* the First Lady **(b)** (*d'assemblée, d'un club etc*) chairperson, chairman, *f* chairwoman; **être élu p.** to be voted into the chair, to be elected chairperson; **Monsieur le p./Madame la présidente, permettez-moi de ...** Mr Chairman/Madam Chairwoman, allow me to ... **(c)** (*magistrat*) presiding judge

▶ **président**: *Hist Pol* **p. du Conseil** Prime Minister; *Com* **P. du conseil d'administration** Chairman of the Board; *Ind, Com* **p.-directeur général** chairman and managing director, chief executive officer, CEO; **p. du jury** *Jur* foreman of the jury; (*dans un concours*) chairman of the adjudicating committee

présidentiable [prezidɑ̃sjabl] *n* presidential hopeful

présidentiel, -elle [prezidɑ̃sjɛl] **1** *adj* presidential; **l'élection présidentielle** the presidential election, the election for president; **régime p.** presidency, presidential system of government **2** *nfpl* **présidentielles** presidential elections

présider [prezide] **1** *vt* **(a)** (*diriger*) (*conseil*) to preside over; (*réunion*) to chair **(b)** (*être à la place d'honneur de*) (*banquet*) to be the guest of honour *or US* honor at **2** *vi* **(a)** (*diriger*) to preside, to be in the chair; **p. à une réunion** to preside at *or* over a meeting **(b)** (*veiller*) **p. à** to preside over; **p. aux destinées de ...** to preside over the destinies of ...; **les codes qui président à ces cérémonies** the codes that govern these ceremonies

présomptif, -ive [prezɔ̃ptif, -iv] *adj* **héritier p.** heir presumptive; (*fils aîné*) heir apparent

présomption [prezɔ̃psjɔ̃] *nf* **(a)** (*supposition*), *Jur* presumption; **de fortes présomptions pèsent sur lui** he is under great suspicion; **ce ne sont que des présomptions de votre part** these are just presumptions *or* assumptions of yours; *Jur* **p. de responsabilité** presumption of liability **(b)** (*suffisance*) presumption, presumptuousness

présomptueusement [prezɔ̃ptɥøzmɑ̃] *adv* presumptuously

présomptueux, -euse [prezɔ̃ptɥø, -øz] **1** *adj* presumptuous **2** *n* **un jeune p.** a presumptuous young man

présono [presɔno] *nf TV, Rad* playback

présonorisation [presɔnɔrizasjɔ̃] *nf TV etc* playback

presque [prɛsk(ə)] *adv* **(a)** (*à peu près*) almost, nearly; **c'est p. impossible** it's almost *or* next to *or* all but *or* well-nigh impossible; **c'est p. sûr** it's almost *or* nearly *or* well-nigh certain; **ça n'est pas sûr mais p.** it's not certain, but just about *or* but as good as; **je les ai p. tous** I have nearly *or* almost all of them; **c'est p. de la folie/la répression** it's little short of madness/repression; **il est sourd ou p.** he's deaf or as good as *or* just about; **j'ai vu tout le monde ou p.** I saw everybody or almost *or* nearly *or* just about everybody

(b) (+ *nég*) scarcely, hardly; **p. jamais** scarcely *or* hardly ever, almost never; **p. rien** scarcely *or* hardly anything, next to nothing; **je ne dors p. pas** I hardly *or* scarcely get any sleep; **je ne dors p. plus** I hardly *or* scarcely get any sleep any more; **p. personne** hardly *or* scarcely anyone; **je ne connais p. personne** I hardly *or* scarcely know anyone; **rien ou p.** nothing, or hardly *or* scarcely anything, nothing, or as good as (nothing)

(c) (*devant un nom*) **la p. totalité de son œuvre** nearly *or* almost all (of) his works, the near totality of his works; *Litt* **la p. obscurité** the near darkness; **c'est une p. certitude** it's virtually certain, it's well-nigh certain

presqu'île [prɛskil] *nf* peninsula

pressage [prɛsaʒ] *nm* (*des raisins, du linge, de disques etc*) pressing

pressant [prɛsɑ̃] *adj* (*besoin*) pressing, urgent; (*créancier, demande*) insistent; **cas p.** urgent case; **il se faisait p.** he was very insistent; *Euph F* **avoir un besoin p.** to need to go (*to the toilet*)

press-book, *pl* **press-books** [presbuk] *nm* press book; (*d'un mannequin, d'un artiste etc*) portfolio

presse [prɛs] *nf* **(a)** (*ensemble des imprimés, des textes*) press; **la grande p.** large-circulation newspapers and magazines; **la liberté de la p.** the freedom of the press, press freedom; **délits de p.** infringements of press laws; **je l'ai lu dans la p.** I read it in the papers; **c'est dans toute la p.** it's in all the papers; **photographe de p.** press photographer; **attaché de p.** press attaché; **service de p.** publicity (department); **agence de p.** news *or* press agency; **conférence de p.** press conference; **avoir bonne/mauvaise p.** to have a good/bad press; *Fig* to be well/badly thought of (**auprès de** by); **la p. affaires** business press; **la p. de charme** soft porn magazines; **la p. clandestine** underground press; **la p. du cœur** romance magazines; **la p. de distribution professionnelle** trade press; **la p. économique** the financial press; **la p. écrite** print media, press; **la p. féminine** women's magazines, the women's press; **la p. généraliste** general(-interest) press; **la p. grand public** general press; **la p. d'information** newspapers and magazines; **la p. d'information professionnelle** trade press; **la p. de midinette** romance press; **la p. musicale** music press; **la p. d'opinion** = newspapers and magazines presenting the news from a particular viewpoint; **la p. parlée/télévisée** radio/television news; **la p. périodique** periodicals; **la p. professionnelle** trade press; **la p. de qualité** quality press; **la p. régionale** *ou* **de province** the regional press; **la p. à scandale, la p. à sensation** the popular press, the tabloids,

Péj the gutter press; **la p. du soir** the evening newspapers; **la p. spécialisée** specialist press; **la p. sportive** sports press

(b) *Tech* press; **p. mécanique** power press; **p. à copier** letter press, copying press; **travailler du métal à la p.** to stamp metal; **p. étoupe** gland; **p. à pantalon** trouser-press; **p. monétaire** minting press

(c) *Typ* (printing) press; **p. à imprimer** *ou* **d'imprimerie** printing press; **p. à bras** hand press; **p. à rogner** guillotine; **p. rotative** rotary press; **livre sous p.** book that has gone to press; **prêt à mettre sous p.** (*livre*) ready for press; (*journal*) ready to put to bed; **le livre sera mis sous p. fin septembre** the book will go to press at the end of September; **à l'heure où nous mettons sous p.** at the time of going to press

(d) *Arch, Litt* (*foule*) press, throng, crowd; **fendre la p.** to force one's way through the crowd

(e) *Naut Arch* press (gang)

(f) (*urgence*) **il n'y a pas de p.** there's no hurry *or* rush; **dans les moments de p.** at busy periods

pressé [prɛse] **1** *adj* **(a)** (*comprimé*) pressed; **citron p.** freshly squeezed lemon juice; **p. à froid** cold-pressed

(b) (*serré*) **il était p. contre le mur** he was pressed *or* squashed up against the wall; **pressés les uns contre les autres** pressed *or* crowded *or* packed *or* squashed together; (*objets*) pressed *or* packed *or* squashed together

(c) (*qui a hâte*) in a hurry *or* rush; **je suis très p.** I'm in rather a hurry, I'm very pressed for time; **p. de faire qch** in a hurry to do sth; **être p. par le temps** to be pushed for time; **aller** *ou* **marcher d'un pas p.** to walk hurriedly; **avoir un air p.** to look as though one is in a hurry; **on n'est pas p.** there's no rush, we're not in a hurry

(d) (*urgent*) urgent; **ce n'est pas p.** it's not urgent, there's no hurry *or* rush; **si vous n'avez rien de plus p. à faire** if you've got nothing more urgent to do

2 *nm* **aller** *ou* **parer au plus p.** to deal with the most urgent thing(s) first

presse-agrumes *nm inv* juice extractor, juicer

presse-ail *nm inv* garlic press

presse-bouton *adj inv* push-button

presse-citron *nm inv* lemon squeezer

pressentiment [presɑ̃timɑ̃] *nm* presentiment; (*d'un malheur*) foreboding; **j'ai comme un p. que ...** I have a (funny) feeling that ...; **avoir le p. que quelque chose va se passer** to have the *or* a feeling that something is going to happen

pressentir [presɑ̃tir] *vt* (*conj like* **sentir**) **(a)** (*prévoir*) to have a presentiment *or* premonition of, to sense; (*malheur*) to have a foreboding of; **p. que quelque chose va se passer** to have a (funny) feeling that something is going to happen; **faire** *ou* **laisser p. qch** to foreshadow *or* portend sth; (*malheur*) to forebode sth; **son attitude me fait p. que ...** I get the feeling *or* I can sense from his attitude that ...; **rien ne laissait p. une rage pareille** nothing could have prepared me/us/*etc* for such a rage **(b) p. qn (sur** *ou* **pour qch)** to sound sb out *or* approach sb (about sth); **le candidat pressenti** the likely candidate (for the job)

presse-papiers *nm inv* paperweight; *Ordinat* clipboard

presse-purée *nm inv* potato masher

presser [prɛse] **1** *vt* **(a)** (*citron, éponge etc*) to squeeze; (*raisin, pommes*), *Tech* (*disque*) to press; **p. à froid** to cold-press; **p. qn contre son cœur** to clasp sb in one's arms, to hug sb; **p. le bras à qn** to squeeze sb's arm; **il m'entraînait en me pressant le bras** he dragged me off clutching me by the arm; *F* **ici on vous presse comme un citron** they get as much out of you as they can here

(b) (*appuyer sur*) (*commutateur, bouton*) to press, to push; *Ordinat* to hit

(c) (*harceler*) to press; **pressé par ses créanciers** pressed by his creditors; **p. l'ennemi** to press the enemy; **p. qn de questions** to ply *or* bombard sb with questions; **p. qn de faire qch** to press *or* urge sb to do sth

(d) (*dépêcher*) (*qn*) to hurry (up); (*travail, mouvement*) to speed up, to accelerate; **p. le pas** *ou* **l'allure** to speed up, to quicken one's pace; **p. le départ de qn** to speed up *or* hasten sb's departure; **qu'est-ce qui vous presse?** why are you in such a hurry?, what's the hurry *or* rush?; **rien ne nous presse** we're not in any hurry *or* rush; **allons, pressons!** come on, let's get a move on!

2 *vi* **le temps presse** there isn't much time (left), time is short *or* is pressing; **le temps ne presse pas** there's plenty of time (left), there's no need to hurry; **l'affaire presse** the matter is urgent; **il n'y a rien qui presse, rien ne presse,** *F* **ça ne presse pas** there's no hurry *or* rush

3 se presser *vpr* **(a)** (*s'entasser*) to press, to crowd; (*contre des grilles*) to squash up, to crush; **on s'y presse toujours à six heures** there's always a crowd there at six o'clock

(b) (*se serrer*) **elle s'est pressée contre lui** she pressed (herself) against him; (*de façon affectueuse*) she snuggled (up) against him, she snuggled up to him; **les badauds se pressaient autour de la victime** the on-lookers crowded *or* clustered around the victim; **on se pressa pour entrer** there was a crush to get in; **les mots se pressaient dans sa bouche** he had so much to say he could not express himself clearly

(c) (*se dépêcher*) to hurry (up); **pressez-vous!** hurry (up)!; **presse-toi de répondre à l'annonce** hurry up and reply to the advertisement; **faire qch sans se p.** to take one's time over doing sth; **répondre sans se p.** to answer deliberately *or* leisurely, to give an unhurried answer; **il faut se p. d'oublier** we must forget as quickly as we can

(d) *F* **se p. le citron** to rack one's brains

presse-raquette *nm inv* racket press

pressing [presiŋ] *nm* **(a)** (*repassage à la vapeur*) (steam) pressing **(b)** (*magasin*) dry cleaner's **(c)** *Fig F* pressure; **faire le p.** to put on pressure

pression [prɛsjɔ̃] *nf* **(a)** *Fig* (*action insistante*) pressure; **faire p. sur qn,** *F* **mettre la p. sur qn** to put pressure on sb, to pressure *or* pressurize sb; **ils vont faire p. sur lui pour qu'il signe** they're going to put pressure on him to sign, they're going to pressure *or* pressurize him into signing; **être soumis/céder à des pressions** to be subjected to/to give in to pressure; **faire monter la p.** to pile on *or* increase the pressure; **être sous p.** to be under pressure; **sous la p. des événements, il dut démissionner** the pressure of events was such that he had to resign; **je travaille mieux sous p.** I work better under pressure; **groupe de p.** pressure group; **p. sociale/démographique** social/demographic pressure; **p. fiscale** tax burden

(b) (*action de presser*) pressure; **exercer une p. sur qch, faire p. sur qch** to exert pressure on sth; **faire monter** *ou* **augmenter la p.** to increase the pressure; **en exerçant une simple p. du doigt** by simply pressing with one's finger; **un bouton (à) p., une p.** a press stud, *F* a popper, *Am* a snap fastener

(c) *Tech* pressure; **vis de p.** binding screw; **p. d'huile** oil pressure; *Aut* **p. de gonflage** tyre pressure; *Aut* **p. des pneumatiques** tyre pressure; *Aut* **p. du carburant** fuel pressure; *Aut* **jauge de p.** pressure gauge; *Tech* **machine à haute/basse p.** high-/low-pressure engine; **mettre sous p.** to pressurize; **mettre la chaudière sous p.** to get up steam; **cabine sous p.** pressurized cabin

(d) *Phys* pressure; **p. atmosphérique/artérielle** atmospheric/blood pressure; *Météo* **zone de hautes/basses pressions** area of high/low pressure

(e) bière (à la) p. draught *or Am* draft beer; **une p., s'il vous plaît** ≈ half a pint of lager *or Am* a beer please

pressographe [prɛsɔgraf] *nm* credit card machine, imprinter machine

pressoir [prɛswar] *nm* **(a)** (*presse*) (*pour faire du vin*) wine press; (*pour faire du cidre*) cider press; (*pour huile*) oil press **(b)** (*lieu*) press house, press room

pressurage [prɛsyraʒ] *nm* pressing

pressurer [prɛsyre] *vt* (*fruits*) to press; *Fig* (*exploiter*) to squeeze

pressurisation [prɛsyrizasjɔ̃] *nf* pressurization

pressuriser [prɛsyrize] *vt* to pressurize

prestance [prɛstɑ̃s] *nf* presence; **avoir de la p.** to have (great) presence; **il faut une certaine p. pour porter ces vêtements** you need a certain style to wear these clothes; **un homme de belle p.** a fine-looking man

prestataire [prɛstatɛr] *nm* **(a)** *Admin* person receiving benefits *or* allowances; **p. de service** service provider, service supplier **(b)** *TV* facilities man

prestation [prɛstasjɔ̃] *nf* **(a)** (*allocation*) benefit; *Admin* allowance; **prestations** services; **prestations familiales** family benefits; **prestations sociales** social security benefits; **p. compensatoire** (*en cas de divorce*) compensation; **p. en nature** payment *or* allowances in kind **(b)** *Com* service; **p. de service** provision of a service; **p. de capitaux** provision of capital **(c)** (*résultat, performance*) performance; **la p. d'un homme politique à la télévision** the performance of a politician on television **(d)** *Jur* **p. de serment** oath taking; *Hist* **p. de foi** oath of fealty

preste [prɛst] *adj* nimble; **avoir la main p.** to have nimble fingers

prestement [prɛstəmɑ̃] *adv* promptly

prestidigitateur, -trice [prɛstidiʒitatœr, -tris] *n* conjurer, magician

prestidigitation [prɛstidiʒitasjɔ̃] *nf* conjuring, magic; **tour de p.** conjuring trick, magic trick; *Fig* **c'est de la p.!** it's magic!

prestige [prɛstiʒ] *nm* **(a)** (*d'une personne, d'une société importante etc*) prestige; (*séduction, attrait*) (*d'une star de* *cinéma, d'une façon de vivre etc*) glamour, *US* glamor; **sans p.** undistinguished; **publicité/magazine de p.** prestige advertising/magazine; **le p. de l'uniforme** the glamour of the uniform **(b)** *Arch* (*chose étonnante*) marvel

prestigieux, -euse [prɛstiʒjø, -øz] *adj* **(a)** (*qui a du renom*) (*artiste, nom etc*) prestigious, famous, great; **produits p.** prestige products **(b)** *Litt* (*étonnant*) marvellous, wonderful, amazing

presto [prɛsto] *adv* **(a)** *Mus* presto **(b)** *F* double-quick, at the double

présumable [prezymabl] *adj* presumable

présumer [prezyme] **1** *vt* (*supposer*) to presume, to assume; **tu viens aussi, je présume?, je présume que tu viens aussi?** you're coming too, I presume *or* assume?, I presume *or* assume that you're coming too?; **p. qn innocent** to presume sb (to be) innocent; **le coupable présumé, le présumé coupable** the alleged culprit; **le voleur présumé** the alleged thief; **il est l'auteur présumé de cette œuvre** he is presumed to be the author *or* he is the presumed author of this work; **on présume qu'il est mort** he is assumed *or* presumed (to be) dead

2 *vi* **trop p. de soi** to presume too much, to be overconfident; **trop p. de ses forces** to overestimate *or* overrate one's strength

présupposé [presypoze] **1** *adj* presupposed **2** *nm* presupposition

présupposer [presypoze] *vt* to presuppose

présupposition [presypozisjɔ̃] *nf* presupposition

présure [prezyr] *nf* rennet

prêt¹ [prɛ] *adj* ready; **p. à l'emploi** ready for use; **p. à servir** ready to serve; **se tenir p.** to hold oneself in readiness, to be ready; **être p. à tout** to be ready for anything; (*pour parvenir à son but*) to be prepared to do anything; **je le sens p. à tout** I think he will stop at nothing; **être p. à faire qch** to be ready to do sth, to be all set to do sth; **p. à partir** ready to leave *or* go, *F* ready for the off; **toujours p. à rendre service** always willing *or* ready to help

prêt² *nm* **(a)** (*action*) lending; (*somme*) loan; **p. de 1 000 francs** loan of 1,000 francs; **faire/consentir/obtenir un p.** to make/grant/get *or* obtain a loan; **demander un p.** to ask for *or* apply for a loan; **p. à court/moyen/long terme** short-/medium-/long-term loan; **le service du p.** (*d'une bibliothèque*) the lending department **(b)** *Mil* pay **(c)** (*avance sur salaire*) advance

▶ **prêt** *Banque*: **p. bancaire** bank loan; **p. bonifié** loan at reduced rate of interest, soft loan; **p. à la consommation** consumer loan; **p. à découvert** overdraft loan; **p. sur gage(s)** pawnbroking; **p. garanti** guaranteed loan; **p. d'honneur** loan on trust; **p. hypothécaire** mortgage loan; **p. à intérêts** loan at interest; **p. participatif** equity loan; **p. en participation** syndicated loan; **p. personnalisé** *ou* **personnel** personal loan; **p.-relais** bridging loan; **p. sans intérêt** interest-free loan; **p. en souffrance** non-performing loan; **p. sur titres** loan against securities

prêt-à-diffuser [prɛtadifyze] *nm* master tape

prêt-à-porter [prɛtapɔrte] *nm* **(a)** ready-to-wear clothes; **en p.** off the peg *or Am* rack; **acheter du p.** to buy ready-to-wear *or Br* off-the-peg *or Am* off-the-rack clothes **(b)** (*secteur*) ready-to-wear (clothing business)

prêté [prete] **1** *adj* borrowed **2** *nm* **c'est un p. pour un rendu** it's tit for tat

prétendant, -ante [pretɑ̃dɑ̃, -ɑ̃t] **1** *n* applicant, candidate **(à** for); (*à un bien, à un titre*) claimant **(à** to); (*au trône*) pretender **(à** to) **2** *nm* suitor, admirer; *Mktg* challenger

prétendre [pretɑ̃dr] **1** *vt* **(a)** (*déclarer*) to maintain, to assert, to claim; **je prétends que ce n'est pas vrai** I maintain that it is not true; **on prétend que ...** people say that ..., it is said that ...; **à ce qu'il prétend** according to him; **elle prétend pouvoir guérir le cancer** she claims to be able to cure cancer; **il ne prétend pas être artiste** he doesn't pretend to be artistic, he lays no claim to being an artist; **je ne prétends pas lui faire comprendre** I don't pretend to be able to make him understand; **on le prétend fou** they say he's mad

(b) (*vouloir*) to mean; **je prétends être obéi** I mean to be obeyed

(c) *Vieilli* (*exiger*) to require, to want; **que prétendez-vous de moi?** what do you require *or* want of me?

2 *vi* **p. à qch** to lay claim to sth; **p. aux honneurs** to aspire to honours; *Litt* **p. à la main de qn** to aspire to marry sb

3 se prétendre *vpr* to claim to be; **elle se prétend trompée sur la qualité du produit** she claims to have been misled about the quality of the product

prétendu, -ue [pretɑ̃dy] **1** *adj* (*coupable, voleur etc*) alleged; (*héros, cantatrice etc*) would-be; **un p. baron** a self-styled baron; **prétendus progrès** so-called progress **2** *n Arch, Région* **mon p.** my fiancé; **ma prétendue** my fiancée

prétendument [pretɑ̃dymɑ̃] *adv* supposedly; **cet individu p. architecte nous avait construit une horreur** this so-called architect built us a monstrosity

prête-nom, *pl* **prête-noms** [prɛtnɔ̃] *nm Fig* figurehead; *Fin* (*société*) nominee company

pré-tenseur *nm Aut* **p. de ceinture** seatbelt pre-tensioner

prétentaine [pretɑ̃tɛn] *nf Vieilli* **courir la p.** to chase (after) women

prétentieusement [pretɑ̃sjøzmɑ̃] *adv* pretentiously

prétentieux, -euse [pretɑ̃sjø, -øz] **1** *adj* (*écrivain, personne, style*) pretentious; (*tenue, apparence*) showy **2** *n* pretentious person; **un jeune p.** a conceited young idiot; **regarde-la, quelle prétentieuse!** look at her, she really fancies herself

prétention [pretɑ̃sjɔ̃] *nf* **(a)** (*revendication, ambition*) pretension, claim **(à** to); **je n'ai pas la p. de remporter le prix** I don't for a moment suppose I shall get the prize; **je n'ai pas la p. de vous être supérieur** I don't pretend *or* claim to be better than you are; **renoncer à ses prétentions** to renounce one's claims

(b) (*fait d'être prétentieux*) pretentiousness, pretension; **homme sans prétention(s)** unassuming *or* unpretentious man; **repas/maison sans p.** unpretentious meal/house; **un style plein de p.** a very pretentious style

(c) (*salaire demandé*) **envoyer curriculum vitae et prétentions** send curriculum vitae and state salary required; **quelles sont ses prétentions?** what sort of salary does he want?

prêter [prɛte] **1** *vt* **(a)** (*fournir temporairement*) to lend, *surtout Am* to loan; **p. qch à qn** to lend sth to sb, to lend sb sth; **p. sur gage(s)** to lend against security; **p. de l'argent à 6%** to lend money at 6%; *Prov* **on ne prête qu'aux riches** only lend to those who can repay; *Fig* people are judged according to their reputation; **p. sur titres** to lend against securities; **p. à intérêt** to lend at interest

(b) (*donner*) to lend, to give; **p. son appui** *ou* **son concours à qn** to give *or* lend sb one's support; **p. assistance** *ou* **secours à qn** to lend *or* give assistance to sb; **p. main forte à qn** to lend *or* give sb a hand; **p. l'oreille** to listen, to lend an ear; **p. attention à qch** to pay attention to sth; **p. serment** to take an oath; **p. le flanc à la critique** to lay oneself open *or* expose oneself to criticism; **p. son nom à qch** to lend one's name to sth, to allow one's name to be used for sth; *Vieilli* **si Dieu me prête vie** God willing

(c) (*attribuer*) (*propos, intentions etc*) to attribute, to ascribe **(à** to); **on me prête des discours que je n'ai jamais tenus** I am credited with speeches which I never made

2 *vi* **(a) p. à confusion/la critique** to give rise to confusion/to criticism; **privilège qui prête aux abus** privilege that lends itself to *or* that is open to *or* that invites abuse; **cela prête à rire** that's laughable

(b) (*des gants, d'un tissu etc*) to give, to stretch

3 se prêter *vpr* **(a)** (*consentir*) to lend oneself, to be a party **(à** to); **se p. à un accommodement** to fall in with *or* consent to an arrangement

(b) (*permettre*) to lend itself **(à** to); **roman qui se prête à des interprétations différentes** novel which lends itself to different interpretations; **domaine d'étude qui se prête à des développements variés** area of study that can be developed in different ways; **j'aurais voulu lui parler de ses enfants, mais la situation ne s'y prêtait pas** I'd have liked to talk to him about his children, but it was neither the time nor the place; **attends que la situation s'y prête** wait until the situation is right; **j'aimerais faire une grande fête mais mon appartement ne s'y prête guère** I'd like to have a big party but my flat is hardly the right place

prétérit [preterit] *nm* [①A39,6] *Gram* preterite (tense); **au p.** in the preterite

pré-test *nm* **p. publicitaire** pre-testing advertisement; **pré-tests publicitaires** copy testing; **pré-tests** pre-testing

pré-tester *vt* to pre-test

préteur [pretœr] *nm Antiq* praetor

prêteur, -euse [prɛtœr, -øz] **1** *n* lender; **p. sur gages** pawnbroker **2** *adj* ready *or* willing to lend things; **je ne suis pas p.** I don't like lending things

prétexte [pretɛkst] **1** *nm* pretext, excuse; **ce n'est qu'un p.** it's just a pretext *or* an excuse; **bon/mauvais p.** good/poor excuse; **se chercher des prétextes** to look for excuses; **sous p. de faire qch** on *or* under the pretext of doing sth; **sous p. d'amitié** on *or* under the pretext of friendship; **sous p. que ...** on *or* under the pretext that ...; **sous aucun p.** on no account, under no circumstances; **prendre p. de qch pour faire qch** to use sth as a pretext *or* an excuse for doing sth; **prendre** *ou* **saisir le premier p. pour ...** to take advantage of the first pretext one can to ...; **donner p. à** to provide an excuse for

2 *nf Antiq* toga praetexta

3 *adj Antiq* **toge p.** toga praetexta

prétexter [pretɛkste] *vt* to use *or* give as a pretext *or* an excuse; **il a prétexté qu'il était malade** he gave the excuse that he was ill; **p. la fatigue** to plead fatigue, to give fatigue as a pretext *or* an excuse

prétoire [pretwar] *nm* **(a)** *Jur* court **(b)** *Antiq* praetorium

prétorien, -ienne [pretɔrjɛ̃, -jɛn] **1** *adj Antiq* praetorian **2** *nm Antiq* praetorian; *Fig* (*de dictature*) praetorian guard, military bodyguard

prêtre [prɛtr] *nm* priest; **grand p.** high priest; **se faire (ordonner) p.** to be ordained (a priest), to become a priest

prêtre-ouvrier, *pl* **prêtres-ouvriers** *nm* worker priest

prêtresse [prɛtrɛs] *nf* priestess

prêtrise [prɛtriz] *nf* priesthood; **recevoir la p.** to take (holy) orders

preuve [prœv] *nf* **(a)** (*d'innocence, d'amitié, de courage, de bonnes intentions etc*) proof, evidence; **une p. de mauvaise organisation** evidence *or* proof of poor organization; **ce n'est pas une p.** that proves nothing *or* doesn't prove anything; **il nous faut des preuves** we need proof *or* evidence; **faire la p. de qch** to prove sth; **avoir la p. que/de ...** to have proof that/of ...; **faire p. d'intelligence/de générosité/***etc* to show intelligence/generosity/*etc*; **faire ses preuves** (*d'un élève, employé etc*) to prove oneself, to show what one can do; **cette méthode a fait ses preuves** this method has proved itself *or* has stood the test of time; **jusqu'à p. du contraire** until there's proof to the contrary; **comme p.** by way of proof, as proof; *F* **le directeur est un incapable, à p. le déficit de la maison** the manager is incompetent, witness the firm's deficit; *F* **on ne peut pas compter sur lui, la p. il est encore absent** you can't count on him, as you can see he's absent again; **à p. que ...** which (just) goes to show that ...; **j'en veux pour p. ...** the proof of it is ...; **être la p. vivante que ...** to be living proof that ...; **p. d'achat** proof of purchase

(b) *Math* **faire la p. d'une opération** to prove *or* test the validity of a mathematical operation; **faire la p. par neuf** to cast out nines

(c) *Jur* evidence; **p. directe** direct evidence; **p. indirecte** circumstantial evidence; **preuves testimoniales** (witnesses') evidence; **le soin** *ou* **l'obligation de faire la p.** the onus *or* burden of proof

preux [prø] *Arch, Litt* **1** *adj* gallant, valiant **2** *nm* gallant *or* valiant knight

prévalence [prevalɑ̃s] *nf Méd* prevalence

prévaloir [prevalwar] (*conj like* **valoir** *except pr sub* **je prévale**) **1** *vi* to prevail (**sur** over; **contre** against); **ce principe prévaut sur tous les autres** this principle takes precedence over all others; **faire p. ses droits** to assert one's rights; **faire p. son opinion** to win acceptance for one's opinion **2 se prévaloir** *vpr* **(a) se p. de** (*profiter de*) to take advantage of; (*un droit*) to exercise **(b) se p. de qch** (*s'enorgueillir*) to pride oneself on sth

prévaricateur, -trice [prevarikatœr, -tris] *Jur* **1** *adj* (*fonctionnaire, magistrat*) dishonest **2** *n* dishonest official; (*dans une gestion*) betrayer of trust

prévarication [prevarikasjɔ̃] *nf Jur* breach of trust; (*dans une organisation*) maladministration

prévariquer [prevarike] *vi Jur* to be guilty of a breach of trust

prévenance [prevnɑ̃s] *nf* kindness, consideration; (*d'un geste, d'une bonne idée*) thoughtfulness; **une p.** a thoughtful *or* kind act *or* deed; **entourer qn de prévenances** to show sb great kindness *or* consideration; **avoir des prévenances pour qn** to show sb kindness *or* consideration

prévenant [prevnɑ̃] *adj* (*personne*) kind (**envers, avec** to), considerate (**envers, avec** towards); (*geste*) thoughtful (**envers, avec** towards); (*manière, apparence*) pleasing, prepossessing

prévenir [prevnir] *vt* (*conj like* **venir** *but with aux* **avoir**) **(a)** (*informer*) to inform, to tell, to let know (**de qch** about sth, of sth); (*avertir*) to warn; (*à l'avance*) to forewarn; **les personnes à p. en cas d'accident** those to be informed *or* notified in case of an accident; **je vais le p. que vous êtes ici** I'll tell him *or* let him know that you're here; **on m'avait prévenu que la police était à mes trousses** I had been warned that the police were after me; **vous auriez dû m'en** *ou* **me p.** you should have told me (about it) beforehand; **je l'ai prévenue, si ça ne s'améliore pas, c'est la porte!** I've warned her, if there's no improvement she'll be out of a job; **tu es prévenu!** you've been warned!; **partir sans p.** to leave without telling anyone *or* without warning

(b) (*empêcher*) (*maladie*) to prevent, to ward off, to avert; (*danger, accident*) to avert; *Prov* **mieux vaut p. que guérir** prevention is better than cure

(c) (*devancer*) (*les désirs de qn*) to anticipate; (*question, objection*) to forestall

(d) *Litt* (*agir, influencer*) **p. qn en faveur de qn** to predispose sb *or* bias sb in favour of sb; **p. qn contre qn** to prejudice sb against sb, to bias sb *or* make sb bias(s)ed against sb; **son visage prévient en sa faveur** he has a prepossessing face

préventif, -ive [prevɑ̃tif, -iv] *adj* preventive; **à titre p.** as a preventive (measure); **médecine préventive** preventive medicine; *Cartes* **ouverture préventive** pre-emptive bid; *Jur* **détention préventive** detention awaiting trial; **être en détention préventive** to be in custody

prévention [prevɑ̃sjɔ̃] *nf* **(a)** (*d'une maladie etc*) prevention; **p. routière** road safety; **p. des accidents du travail** prevention of industrial accidents **(b)** *Jur* **mettre qn en p.** to commit sb for trial; **mise en p.** committal for trial **(c)** *Litt* (*opinion, avis*) predisposition, bias (**en faveur de** in favour of), prejudice, bias (**contre** against); **observateur sans p.** unprejudiced *or* unbias(s)ed observer

préventivement [prevɑ̃tivmɑ̃] *adv* **(a)** as a preventive (measure) **(b)** *Jur* **arrêter qn p.** to arrest sb on suspicion; **détenu p.** committed for trial

préventorium [prevɑ̃tɔrjɔm] *nm* tuberculosis sanatorium

prévenu, -ue [prevny] **1** *adj* **(a)** (*qui a une opinion*) prejudiced, bias(s)ed **(b)** *Jur* **p. de vol** charged with theft **2** *n Jur* **le p./la prévenue** the accused

prévisibilité [previzibilite] *nf* foreseeability

prévisible [previzibl] *adj* foreseeable; **c'était difficilement p.** it was hard to foresee

prévision [previzjɔ̃] *nf* forecast; (*activité*) forecasting; (*description d'un événement futur*) forecast, prediction; **en p. de qch** in expectation *or* anticipation of sth; **dépasser les prévisions** to exceed all expectations; **au-delà de toute p.** beyond all expectation; **selon nos prévisions** according to our forecast; **prévisions météorologiques** *ou* **du temps** weather forecast; *Mktg* **prévisions aléatoires** probability forecasting; *Mktg* **p. de la base** grass-roots forecast; *Mktg* **p. depuis la base** bottom-up forecast; *Fin* **p. boursière** stock-exchange forecast; **prévisions budgétaires** budget estimates *or* forecasts; **prévisions de l'entreprise** company forecasting; *Mktg* **p. événementielle** hazard forecast; (*activité*) hazard forecasting; **prévisions hiérarchisées** top-down forecasting; **p. du marché** market forecast; (*activité*) market forecasting; **p. des ventes** sales forecast; (*activité*) sales forecasting; **p. des ventes et profits** sales and profit forecast; (*activité*) sales and profit forecasting

prévisionnel, -elle [previzjɔnɛl] *adj* forecast; (*budget, coûts*) estimated, provisional; (*analyse, étude*) preliminary; **la gestion prévisionnelle des entreprises** management by objectives; **étude prévisionnelle des ventes** sales forecast *or* projection

pré-visionner *vt TV, Cin* to preview

prévisualisation [previzɥalizasjɔ̃] *nf Ordinat* print preview

prévoir [prevwar] *vt* (*conj like* **voir** *except in fu and cond* **je prévoirai, je prévoirais**) **(a)** (*penser, imaginer*) (*futur, désastre*) to foresee; (*météo, prix etc*) to forecast; (*réaction*) to anticipate; (*difficultés, retards*) to foresee, to anticipate; **il est difficile de p. ce qui va arriver** it's difficult to foresee *or* forecast what will happen; **nous n'avions pas prévu toutes ces dépenses** we didn't foresee *or* allow for *or* plan on all this expense; **tout laisse p. ...** everything points *or* all signs point to ...; **rien ne laisse p. un changement de temps** there appears to be no prospect of a change in the weather; **rien ne laissait p. qu'ils prendraient la fuite** there was nothing to indicate *or* suggest that they would run away; **comment aurais-je pu p. que ça n'allait pas me plaire?** how could I have foreseen *or* known in advance *or* anticipated that I wouldn't like it?; **cela n'était pas prévu au programme** that wasn't on the agenda; **ces incidents n'étaient pas prévus au programme** these incidents were totally unplanned

(b) (*organiser*) (*qch*) to provide for; **p. des mesures** to take measures; **p. des changements** to make changes; **dépenses prévues au budget** expenses provided for *or* included in the budget; **la loi n'a pas prévu un cas semblable** the law makes no provision for a case of this kind; **les seuls cas prévus par la loi** the only cases covered by *or* provided for by the law; **le personnel prévu dans le contrat** the personnel provided for *or* laid down *or* stipulated in the contract; **l'argent que nous avions prévu pour le voyage n'a pas suffi** the money we allowed for *or* budgeted for *or* set aside for the trip wasn't enough; **la réunion est prévue pour demain** the meeting is arranged *or* planned *or* scheduled for tomorrow; **on ne peut pas tout p.** you can't think of everything; **elle prévoit de demander une augmentation** she's planning to ask for *or* planning on asking for a rise; **comme prévu** as (was) planned, as expected; **cela s'est passé comme prévu** it went according to plan; **plus tôt/**

tard que prévu sooner/later than expected; **vitesse prévue** (*d'un bateau*) designed speed; **charge prévue** (*d'un poids lourd etc*) specified load

(c) (*préparer*) (*repas, pique-nique*) to provide, to arrange; **il faudra p. des vêtements de pluie** we'll have to take waterproof clothes; **on a prévu une tente en cas de pluie** we've brought a tent in case it rains

prévôt [prevo] *nm* **(a)** *Escrime* **p. de salle** *ou* **d'armes** assistant fencing master **(b)** *Mil* assistant provost marshal; **grand p.** provost marshal **(c)** *Hist, Jur* provost

prévoyance [prevwajɑ̃s] *nf* (*précaution*) precaution; (*dans le futur*) foresight, forethought; *Fin* contingency, provision for the future; **elle a manqué de p. en achetant cette voiture** it was rather short-sighted *or* unwise of her to buy the car; **il ne manque pas de p.** he thinks well ahead, he doesn't lack foresight; **faire preuve de p.** to show foresight, to be far-sighted, to look ahead; **fonds** *ou* **caisse de p.** contingency fund, reserve fund; **société de p.** provident society; **p. sociale** social security provisions

prévoyant [prevwajɑ̃] *adj* far-sighted, *Fml* provident; **un homme p. aurait ...** a man with foresight would have ...; **en bon père p., il avait prévu de ...** as a prudent father should, he had made arrangements to ...

prie-Dieu [pridjø] *nm inv* prie-dieu, prayer stool

prier [prije] (*impf, pr sub* **n. priions, v. priiez**) **1** *vt* **(a)** *Rel* (*Dieu etc*) to pray to; **je prie Dieu qu'il en soit ainsi** I pray (to) God that it may be so

(b) (*supplier*) to beg, *Fml, Litt* to beseech, to entreat; **se faire p.** to need a lot of persuasion *or* persuading *or* coaxing; **après s'être fait un peu p.** after a bit of persuasion *or* persuading *or* coaxing; **il ne s'est pas fait p. pour venir** he didn't need *or* take much persuading to come, he didn't need to be asked twice to come; **sans se faire p.** readily, willingly; **il est parti sans se faire p.** it didn't need any coaxing *or* persuasion to get him to go

(c) *Fml* (*demander*) to ask, to request; **p. qn de faire qch** to ask sb to do sth; **je te prie de ne pas t'occuper de ça!** I'd be obliged if you minded your own business!, kindly *or* please mind your own business!; **taisez-vous, je vous prie!** please be quiet!; **puis-je vous p. de fermer la porte?** would you be so kind as to *or* be kind enough to close the door?; **dites-moi, je vous prie** would you mind telling me; **je te prie de croire qu'elle a été très surprise** she was very surprised, believe you me *or* let me tell you; **je vous en prie** (*faites-le*) please do!, of course!; (*ne le faites pas*) please don't!; (*il n'y a pas de quoi*) it's/it was a pleasure!, you're welcome!, not at all!; *Fml* **je vous prie de bien vouloir recevoir l'assurance de mes sentiments les meilleurs** (*dans une lettre*) yours sincerely *or* truly; **Monsieur et Madame Hugo prient Monsieur et Madame Adam de leur faire l'honneur d'assister à ...** Mr and Mrs Hugo request the pleasure of Mr and Mrs Adam's company at ...; *Arch, Litt* **p. qn à dîner** to invite sb to dine

2 *vi* to pray (**pour qn/qch** for sb/sth); **nous avons prié pour qu'il revienne vivant** we prayed that he might return alive, we prayed for his safe return

prière [prijɛr] *nf* **(a)** (*formule*) prayer; **faire** *ou* **dire ses prières** to say one's prayers; *Hum* **tu peux faire ta p.** *ou* **tes prières** you can say your prayers **(b)** (*acte de prier*) **faire** *ou* **dire la p.** to offer prayer; **c'est l'heure de la p.** it's time for prayers; **être en prières** to be praying *or* at prayer; **aller à la p.** to go to prayers **(c)** (*demande*) request, *Fml, Litt* entreaty; **à la p. de qn** at sb's request; **céder aux prières de qn** to give in to sb, *Fml* to give way to sb's entreaties; **p. de ne pas fumer** no smoking please, thank you for not smoking, you are requested not to smoke; **p. de fermer la porte** please close the door

prieur, -eure [prijœr] *n* prior, *f* prioress

prieuré [prijœre] *nm Rel* priory

prima donna [primadɔna], *pl* **prime donne** [primedɔne], **prima donna** *nf* prima donna

primage [primaʒ] *nm Tech* priming

primaire [primɛr] **1** *adj* **(a)** (*école, couleur etc*), *Géol* (*ère*) primary; *Él, Tech* **circuit p.** primary; *Écon* **secteur p.** primary sector **(b)** *Péj* (*simpliste*) (*personne*) narrow (in outlook), unsophisticated; (*réaction, attitude*) narrow-minded, unsophisticated; (*racisme*) narrow-minded **2** *nm* **(a)** *Scol* primary education; **être en p.** to be at primary school; **les classes du p.** primary school classes **(b)** *Géol* primary era **(c)** *Él* primary (winding) **(d)** *Écon* primary sector **(e)** *Péj* (*personne*) person of narrow outlook

primat [prima] *nm* **(a)** *Rel* primate **(b)** *Phil* primacy

primate [primat] *nm Zool* primate

primauté [primote] *nf* **(a)** *Rel etc* primacy **(b)** (*supériorité*) supremacy; **avoir la p.** to have priority, to come first; **donner à qch la p. sur qch** to give sth priority over sth

prime¹ [prim] **1** *adj Arch, Litt* first; **de p. abord** at first sight; **de p. abord, il a l'air très sympathique** he seems very nice; **dès sa p. jeunesse** since his/her early youth; **elle n'est plus dans sa p. jeunesse!** she's no spring chicken! **2** *nf* **(a)** *Rel* prime; **chanter p.** to sing the prime **(b)** *Math* **B p.** B prime

prime² *nf* **(a)** *Fin* (*d'assurance*) premium; *Bourse* **marché à p.** option market; *Fig* **faire p.** to come first, to take precedence over everything else; **faire p. sur qch** to come before sth, to take precedence over sth

(b) *Com, Admin etc* (*allocation*) grant; (*sur salaire*) bonus

(c) *Com* (*cadeau*) free gift; **et vous aurez droit à un transistor en p.** and you will get a free transistor *or* a transistor as a free gift; *Fig* **en p.** into the bargain

▶ **prime**: **p. d'ancienneté** long service award; **p. annuelle** annual premium; **p. d'assurance** insurance premium; *Mktg* **p. auto-payante** self-liquidator; **p. à la construction** construction grant (*for people building their own homes*); **p. contenant** (*pour bouteille etc*) container premium; **p. de déménagement** relocation allowance; *Mil* **p. de démobilisation** demobilization gratuity; **p. d'éloignement** isolated post allowance; *Bourse* **p. d'émission** bond discount; **p. à l'exportation** export subsidy; **p. familiale** family allowance; **p. de fusion** merger premium; **p. d'intéressement** reversionary bonus; **p. de licenciement** severance allowance; **p. de rendement** *Ind* productivity bonus, performance bonus; (*suite à une mission réussie*) success fee; **p. de renouvellement** renewal premium; **p. de transport** transport allowance; **p. de vie chère** cost of living allowance

primer¹ [prime] **1** *vt* (*avoir la priorité sur*) to take precedence over; **considération qui prime toutes les autres** consideration of the first importance, consideration that outweighs all others

2 *vi Fig* to come first, to take precedence; **le travail prime avant tout** work takes precedence over *or* comes before everything else; **il faut savoir ce qui prime pour toi** you have to know what comes first with you *or* matters most to you, you have to know what your priorities are; **le courage prime sur toutes les autres qualités** courage is the most important quality; **ce qui prime chez lui, c'est l'honnêteté** honesty is his outstanding quality *or* trait

primer² *vt* (*donner un prix honorifique à*) to award a prize to; **primé** (*taureau*) prize; (*roman, film*) prizewinning, award-winning; **vous avez été primé deux fois à Cannes** you have twice won an award *or* you have won two awards at Cannes

primerose [primroz] *nf* (*fleur*) hollyhock

primesautier, -ière [primsotje, -jɛr] *adj* (*personne, réaction, réponse*) spontaneous; (*esprit*) ready, quick; **au risque de paraître un peu trop p.** at the risk of appearing a little impulsive; **répondre de façon primesautière** to answer spontaneously

prime time [prajmtajm] *nm TV, Rad* prime time

primeur [primœr] *nf* **(a) primeurs** (early) fruit and vegetables; **marchand de primeurs** greengrocer (*selling early produce*) **(b)** *Journ* scoop; **avoir la p. d'une nouvelle** to be the first to hear a piece of news; *Journ, TV* **avoir la p. du reportage/de l'information** to be first with *or* to scoop the report/news; *Journ, TV* **c'est un mariage dont le chanteur nous a réservé la p.** the singer gave us a scoop on his forthcoming marriage; **je vous en réserverai la p.** you'll be the first to know; **nous réservons à nos lecteurs la p. de l'interview** this interview is exclusive to our readers

primevère [primvɛr] *nf* (*fleur*) primula; **p. à grandes fleurs** primrose; **p. commune** cowslip; **p. des jardins** polyanthus

primipare [primipar] **1** *adj* primiparous **2** *nf* primipara

primitif, -ive [primitif, -iv] **1** *adj* **(a)** (*qui est le plus près de l'origine*) (*instinct, l'homme*) primitive; *Opt* **couleurs primitives** primary colours; *Géol* **terrains primitifs** primitive strata, primitive terrain; *Gram* **temps primitifs** primary tenses **(b)** (*premier*) (*forme, couleur*) original; **la forme primitive d'une société** the earliest form of a society; **économie primitive** primitive economic system **(c)** *Péj* (*rudimentaire*) (*société, coutumes etc*) primitive; (*outil, méthodes*) primitive, crude **2** *nm* **(a)** *Beaux-Arts* primitive, early master **(b)** (*membre d'une tribu*) primitive tribesman

primitivement [primitivmɑ̃] *adv* originally

primitivisme [primitivism] *nm* primitivism

primo [primo] *adv* first(ly), in the first place

primogéniture [primoʒenityr] *nf Jur* primogeniture

primo-infection, *pl* **primo-infections** *nf Méd* primary infection

primordial, -ale, -aux, -ales [primɔrdjal, -o] *adj* **(a)** (*premier*) primordial; (*instinct, besoin*) primal; **c'est un besoin p. que de communiquer** we have a primal need to communicate, communication is one of our most basic needs

(b) (*capital*) (*question, rôle, point, caractéristique*) of the utmost importance, essential; (*souci, nécessité, importance*) prime; **d'une nécessité/importance primordiale** of prime necessity/importance; **il est p. que tu sois là** you must be there, your presence is essential; **il est p. de s'inscrire à temps** it is of prime *or* the utmost importance to register in time; **l'eau est un élément p. de la vie** water is essential to life

prince [prɛ̃s] *nm* prince; **p. héritier** *ou* **royal** *ou* **impérial** crown prince; **le fait du p.** high-handed government action; **c'est le fait du p., que pouvons-nous y faire?** that's what the government's decided *or* how the government wants it, so what can we do?; *Fig* **comme un p.** (*traité, élevé*) like a prince, like royalty; **il est habillé comme un p.** he's dressed like a prince; *Fig* **être bon p., se montrer bon p.** to be very decent; **il s'est montré bon p. en t'accordant un délai supplémentaire** it was very decent *or* good of him to give you more time; **allez, montre-toi bon p.** be a good sort; **je vais me montrer bon p. et …** I'm going to be very generous *or* kind and …

▶ **prince**: **le p. charmant** Prince Charming; **p. consort** prince consort; **le p. des ténèbres** the Prince of Darkness

prince de galles [gal] *adj, nm inv Tex* Prince of Wales check

princeps [prɛ̃sɛps] *adj inv* **édition p.** first edition

princesse [prɛ̃sɛs] *nf* princess; **p. royale** princess royal

princier, -ière [prɛ̃sje, -jɛr] *adj* princely

princièrement [prɛ̃sjɛrmɑ̃] *adv* (*dîner*) like a prince, in princely fashion; (*accueilli*) like royalty; **nous avons été reçu p.** we were treated like royalty *or* given the red carpet treatment, *Fml* we were given right royal treatment

principal, -ale, -aux, -ales [prɛ̃sipal, -o] **1** *adj* (*personne*) main, principal, chief, leading; (*question, bâtiment, but*) main, principal; (*agent, Gram proposition*) main; (*actionnaire*) main, major; **associé p.** senior partner; **principale compétence** core competence; **les principaux intéressés** those most concerned **2** *nm* **(a) le p.** the main thing, the most important thing **(b)** *Fin* principal, capital sum; (*de l'impôt*) = original amount of tax payable (before surcharges); **p. et intérêts** principal and interest **(c)** *Mus* principal **3** *n* principal, chief; *Scol* (*d'un collège etc*) principal, *Br* head (teacher), headmaster, *f* headmistress

principalement [prɛ̃sipalmɑ̃] *adv* mainly, principally

principauté [prɛ̃sipote] *nf* principality

principe [prɛ̃sip] *nm* **(a)** (*fondement, loi*) principle; **les principes de la géométrie** the principles of geometry; **un accord de p.** an agreement in principle; **poser qch en p.** to lay sth down as a principle; **le p. de nos actions** the principle governing our actions, the mainspring of our actions; **partir du p. que …** to assume that …, to take it as given that …; *Compta* **p. de la partie double** double-entry method; *Bourse* **p. mark to market** mark-to-market principle

(b) *Ch* (*d'une substance*) element, constituent; **p. actif** active principle *or* constituent

(c) principes (*rudiments*) rudiments; **avoir des principes de philosophie** to have a rudimentary knowledge of philosophy

(d) (*règle de conduite*) principle; **déclaration de principes** statement *or* declaration of principle; **ne serait-ce que pour le p.** if only for the principle of the thing; **c'est une question de p.** it's a matter of principle; **par p.** on principle, as a matter of principle; **en p.** in principle, theoretically, in theory; **avoir pour p. de …** to make it a matter of principle to …

(e) principes (moraux) (moral) principles; **avoir des principes** to have (high) principles; **manquer à ses principes** to fail to live up to one's principles; **sans principes** unprincipled

printanier, -ière [prɛ̃tanje, -jɛr] *adj* (*fleurs etc*) spring; (*température, couleur etc*) spring-like; **comme tu es printanière dans cette robe!** how (fresh and) spring-like you look in that dress!

printemps [prɛ̃tɑ̃] *nm* [①A6,d,v] spring; **au p.** in (the) spring(time); *Can F* **avoir la fièvre du p.** to have spring fever; *Fig* **le p. de la vie** the springtime of one's life; *Fig* **elle n'a que 26 p.** she's only 26; **fêter ses 26 p.** to celebrate one's 26th birthday; **ses 26 p.** *Litt* her 26 summers; *Fig* **le p. de la démocratie** the flowering of democracy

prioritaire [prijɔritɛr] **1** *n* (*automobiliste*) person with priority **2** *adj* (that has) priority; **être p.** to have priority; **droits prioritaires** priority rights; *Fin* **actions prioritaires** preference shares, *Am* preferred stock; **le véhicule venant de la droite est p.** the vehicle coming from the right has (the) right of way *or* has priority; **le véhicule p.** the vehicle with the right of way *or* with priority; **votre demande sera p. sur toutes les autres** your application will have priority over the others; **route p.** main road, road which has priority

priorité [prijɔrite] *nf* **(a)** priority; **donner la p. à qn/qch** to give sb/sth priority; **une question qui vient en p.** a question which has priority; **régler une question en p.** to settle a question as a (matter of) priority; **leur dossier sera traité en p.** their file will get priority treatment; **la p. des priorités** top priority; **ce dossier a la p. absolue** this file is top priority; **avoir la p. sur** to have *or* take priority *or* precedence over; **réclamer la p.** to claim the right to speak first; **droits de p.** priority rights; *Fin* **actions de p.** preference shares, *Am* preferred stock; **carte de p.** = pass entitling its holder to move to the head of a queue

(b) *Aut* **p. (de passage)** right of way, priority; **avoir p.** to have priority *or* right of way; **accorder** *ou* **laisser la p. à une voiture** to give way *or Am* to yield to a car; **refuser la p.** to refuse to give way; **p. à droite** (*sur panneau*) ≈ give way to vehicles coming from the right; **route à p.** major road

pris [pri] *adj* **(a)** (*siège*) occupied, taken; **tout est p.** everything is taken; **avoir les mains prises** to have one's hands full; **tu ne vois donc pas que j'ai les mains prises!** can't you see my hands are full?

(b) (*personne*) busy; **je suis très p. ce matin** I'm very busy this morning, I've got a lot on this morning; **je suis déjà p. ce jour-là** I've already got something on that day, that day's booked already; **désolé, toute ma journée est prise** sorry, I'm tied up all day; **désolé, je suis p.** sorry, I'm tied up

(c) p. de peur seized with fear; **p. de panique** panic-stricken, in a panic; **p. de remords** smitten with remorse; **p. de rage** in a rage; **p. de colère, il a déchiré la lettre** he angrily tore up the letter; **p. de boisson** (*ivre*) the worse for drink *or F* wear; *Fml, Jur* under the influence (of alcohol)

(d) (*flan, gelée etc*) set; (*rivière etc*) frozen (over); **avoir le nez p.** to have a blocked nose; **avoir la gorge prise** to have a sore throat

(e) bien p. (*taille*) trim

(f) (*attrapé*) caught, captured

prise [priz] *nf* **(a)** (*fait de prendre*) (*d'une ville, de prisonniers etc*) taking, capture, seizure; (*de minerai etc*) sample; **la p. de la Bastille** the fall *or* storming of the Bastille; **de nombreuses prises de guerre** numerous war trophies; *Échecs* **la p. de la dame par le fou** the capture of the queen by the bishop; *Méd* **faire une p. de sang** to take a blood sample; *Tech* **faire une p. à une rivière/sur un câble** to tap a river/a cable; **la p. du médicament doit se faire à heures régulières** the medication must be taken regularly; **la p. de cette substance peut provoquer des hallucinations** (taking) this substance may cause hallucinations; **p. de conscience** awareness, realization; **sa première p. de conscience de la situation réelle** the first time he realized *or* grasped the truth of the situation; **la p. en considération de facteurs importants** the taking into consideration *or* account of important factors; **la p. de voile se fit à 39 ans** she took the veil at the age of 39

(b) (*quantité*) (*de poissons*) catch; (*de médicament*) dose; (*de tabac à priser*) pinch

(c) *Él* socket, *Am* outlet; (*mâle*) plug; **p. pour rasoir électrique** shaver socket

(d) *Phot, Cin, TV* (*cliché*) shot; (*de filmage continu*) take; *TV, Cin* **p. non-utilisée** outtake; *Cin* **entre les prises** between takes

(e) *Tech* engagement, mesh(ing); **en p.** in gear, engaged; **mettre en p.** to engage, to put into gear; *Tech* **p. constante** constant mesh; **p. câblée** cable connection; **p. directe** direct drive; *Aut* **en p. (directe)** in top (gear); *Fig* **en p. (directe) sur** *ou* **avec qch** in touch *or* in contact with sth; **hors de p.** out of gear

(f) (*solidification*) **faire p.** (*du ciment*) to set; **ciment à p. rapide** fast-setting cement

(g) (*pour se retenir*) hold; (*plus ferme*) grasp, grip; (*en escalade*) hold; (*pour le pied*) foothold; **trouver (une) p. à** *ou* **sur qch** to get a grip *or* a hold on *or* of sth; *Fml, Tech* to gain a purchase on sth; **il faut trouver de bonnes prises** you have to get a good grip; **je n'avais pas de p. (pour me hisser)** I didn't have a good enough grip (to pull myself up); *Fig* **avoir p. sur qn** to have a hold on *or* over sb; **la morale n'a aucune p. sur ce garçon** preaching has no effect *or* makes no impression on that boy; **ce film n'a eu aucune p. sur moi** the film didn't grip me; **lâcher p.** to lose one's grip; *Fig* to give up, to throw in the towel; **donner p. aux reproches/critiques** to lay oneself open to reproach/criticism

(h) (*de judo, de lutte*) hold; **faire une p. de judo à qn** to use a judo throw on sb; *Fig* **être aux prises avec qch** to grapple with sth; **elle est aux prises avec son chef de service** she is at odds with her boss; **leurs intérêts se sont trouvés aux prises** their interests have clashed

▶ **prise**: **p. d'air** air intake; *Tech* **p. d'alimentation** input socket; *Fin* **p. de bénéfices** profit-taking; **p. en charge** (*par taxi*) (*d'un passager*) picking up; *Admin* (*par sécurité sociale*) (guaranteed) reimbursement; **p. de contact** contact; *Ordinat* **p. de contrôle à distance** remote control; *Jur* **p. de corps** arrest; *Fin* charge; **p. de courant** (*mâle*) plug; (*femelle*) socket, plug *or* power point, outlet; **p. de décision** decision-making; *Com* **p. à domicile** receipt at domicile; **p. d'eau** *HydE* intake of water; (*dispositif*) cock, tap, valve; (*à incendie*) (fire) hydrant; (*point d'alimentation*) (*d'un canal, à partir d'une rivière etc*) offtake; *Jur Pol* **p. illégale d'intérêt** = misuse of public office; *TV, Cin* **p. des marques** blocking; *Él* **p. multiple** adaptor; **p. d'otages** hostage-taking; *Ordinat* **p. péri-informatique** connector; **p. péritel** scart connector; **p. de position** stance, position; *Bourse* position taking; **une p. de position est nécessaire** we must take a stand; **p. de notes** note-taking; **la p. de possession de qch** taking possession of sth; *TV, Cin* **p. de repères** camera blocking; *Cin, TV* **p. de son** sound recording; **effectuer une p. de son** to shoot sound; *Él* **p. de terre** earth *or Am* ground (connection); *Él* **avoir une p. de terre** to be earthed *or Am* grounded; **p. de vue(s)** *Phot* photography; *Cin, TV* shooting; **p. de vue de couverture** cover shot; *TV* **p. de vue(s) en direct** live broadcast

prisée [prize] *nf Jur* (*de biens*) valuation

priser¹ [prize] **1** *vt* **p. du tabac** to take snuff; **p. de la cocaïne** to sniff cocaine **2** *vi* to take snuff; **tabac à p.** snuff

priser² *vt* (**a**) *Litt* (*estimer*) to prize, to value (**b**) *Arch* (*biens*) to appraise, to value

priseur, -euse [prizœr, -øz] *n* snuff-taker

prismatique [prismatik] *adj* prismatic

prisme [prism] *nm* prism; *Fig* **elle voit la situation à travers un p.** she has a distorted view of the situation; **jumelles à p.** prismatic binoculars; *TV, Cin* **p. diviseur (de faisceau)** (prism) beam splitter

prison [prizɔ̃] *nf* (**a**) [①**A6**,d,i] (*lieu de détention*) prison, jail; **être/aller en p.** to be in/to go to prison *or* jail; **mettre qn en p.** to put sb in prison *or* jail, *Fml* to imprison sb; **sortir de p.** to come *or* get out (of prison *or* jail), to be released (from prison *or* jail); **s'échapper de p.** to escape from *or* break out of prison *or* jail; *Fig* **cette école est une vraie p.** this school is like a prison; *Péj F* **aimable comme une porte de p.** extremely unpleasant; **gardien de p.** prison officer, prison warder

(**b**) (*peine*) imprisonment; **il risque la p.** he risks going to prison *or* jail; **faire de la p.** to be in prison *or* jail, to serve a prison *or* jail sentence; **cinq ans de p.** five years' imprisonment; **elle a fait deux ans de p.** she spent two years in prison *or* inside; *F* **il a été condamné à cinq ans de p. ferme/avec sursis** he was given a five-year prison *or* jail sentence/a five-year suspended prison sentence; **p. à vie** *ou* **à perpétuité** life imprisonment; **on l'a condamné à la p. à vie** *ou* **à perpétuité** he was sentenced to life imprisonment, he received a life sentence, he was sent to prison for life

prisonnier, -ière [prizɔnje, -jɛr] **1** *n* prisoner; **faire qn p.** to take sb prisoner; **se constituer p.** to give oneself up; **camp de prisonniers** prison camp; **p. condamné à perpétuité** prisoner serving a life sentence, *F* lifer **2** *adj* imprisoned, in prison; (*pris, attrapé*) captive; **ils sont encore prisonniers sous les décombres** they are still trapped in the rubble; *Fig* **être p. de ses principes** to be a slave to one's principles; **être p. de ses habitudes** to be a creature of habit; **je suis p. du confort** I can't do without my creature comforts; **on est toujours p. de son milieu** you can never break free of your environment

▶ **prisonnier**: *Jur* **p. de droit commun** prisoner; **p. de guerre** prisoner of war, POW; *Pol* **p. d'opinion** prisoner of conscience; **p. politique** political prisoner

Prisunic® [prizynik] *nm* = low-priced general goods store; *Péj* **il m'a donné un truc de P.** he gave me a real cheapo present; **le genre Marilyn des P.** the dyed blonde dolly-bird type

privatif, -ive [privatif, -iv] **1** *adj* (**a**) *Gram* privative (**b**) (*particulier*) private **2** *nm Gram* privative prefix

privation [privasjɔ̃] *nf* (**a**) (*perte, manque*) deprivation; **p. d'un droit/de la liberté** loss of a right/of freedom (**b**) **privations** hardship, privation; **une vie de privations** a life of hardship; **s'imposer des privations** to deprive oneself, to go without

privatique [privatik] *nf* home video equipment

privatisable [privatizabl] *adj* which can be privatized, privatizable

privatisation [privatizasjɔ̃] *nf* privatization

privatiser [privatize] *vt* to privatize

privautés [privote] *nfpl* (undue) familiarity; **prendre** *ou* **se permettre des p. avec qn** to be over-familiar with sb

privé [prive] **1** *adj* (**a**) (*individuel*) (*vie, entreprise, chemin, propriété etc*) private; **se réunir en séance privée** to sit in private *or* closed session; **visite privée** (*d'un président etc*) private *or* unofficial visit; **nous avons eu droit à une visite privée du château** we were given a private tour of the castle, we were shown around the castle on our own; *Hist* **le Conseil p.** the Privy Council; *Fig* **c'est un peu son domaine p.** it's his own private domain

(**b**) (*libre*) (*école, patient etc*) private

2 *nm* (**a**) (*vie*) private life; **en p.** (*parler à qn, voir qn*) in private; **connaître qn dans le p.** to know sb in private life; **dans le p., cet acteur est très modeste** off stage he's a very modest man

(**b**) *Ind, Scol, Méd* **le p.** (*secteur libre*) the private sector; **dans le p., les médecins sont plus attentifs** private doctors are more attentive; *Scol* **elle a mis ses filles dans le p.** she sent her daughters to a private school

priver [prive] **1** *vt* **p. qn de qch** to deprive sb of sth; **on l'a privé de sortie, il a été privé de sortie** (*à cause de ce qu'il a fait*) he wasn't allowed to go out, *Am F* he was grounded; **tu seras privé de dessert** you'll go without pudding, there'll be no pudding for you; **j'ai été privé de sommeil** I didn't get any sleep; **je suis privée de télévision depuis un mois** I've been without television for a month; **je ne vous en prive pas?** can you spare it?, I'm not depriving you, am I?; **ça te prive beaucoup si je te l'emprunte pour la nuit?** would it be too much to ask to borrow it overnight?; **ça ne le prive pas du tout de ne plus fumer** he doesn't find it a hardship not to smoke any more; **ce genre de situation me prive de tous mes moyens** I completely lose my head *or* I go completely to pieces in that kind of situation

2 se priver *vpr* to do *or* go without; **se p. de** (*nourriture etc*) to do *or* go without; (*plaisir etc*) to deprive oneself of, to deny oneself; **toi, tu n'aimes pas te p.!** you certainly don't like to go *or* do without, do you!; **il ne se prive pas de le lui dire** he never misses a chance *or* an opportunity to tell her so; **je ne me suis pas privé de lui dire ce que je pensais** I didn't hesitate to tell him what I thought; **tu peux te reposer cinq minutes, elle ne s'en est pas privée!** you can have a rest for five minutes, she did!

privilège [privilɛʒ] *nm* (**a**) (*avantage, droit*) privilege; **jouir du p.** *ou* **avoir le p. de faire qch** to have the privilege of doing sth, to be privileged to do sth; **cette méthode a le p. d'être très rapide** this method has the advantage of being very fast; **le p. de l'âge/de la beauté/de la naissance** the privileges of age/beauty/birth; **c'est le p. de l'âge que de pouvoir dire ce qu'on pense** speaking your mind is one of the privileges of age; **la raison fait partie des privilèges de l'homme** the ability to reason is one of the advantages enjoyed by man; **c'est un triste p.** it's a dubious privilege; *Iron* **il a le p. de me déplaire** I have a particular dislike for him; *Iron* **elle a le p. de nous agacer** we find her particularly annoying; *Hist* **abolition des privilèges** abolition of privilege

(**b**) (*exclusivité*) licence, grant; (*d'une banque*) charter

(**c**) *Jur* preferential claim

privilégié, -ée [privileʒje] **1** *adj* (*favorisé*) (*classe*) privileged; (*situation*) privileged, favourable; **entretenir des relations privilégiées avec un pays** to have a special relationship with a country; **elle est privilégiée par son expérience** she is at *or* has an advantage on account of her experience; **jouir d'un climat p.** to be privileged *or* blessed in its climate; **le moyen d'expression p. de cet artiste** the artist's favourite *or* preferred means of expression, the means of expression favoured by the artist; **banque privilégiée** chartered bank; **créancier p.** preferential *or* preferred creditor; **action privilégiée** preference share

2 *n* privileged person; **quelques privilégiés l'ont vu** a privileged few have seen it; **nous faisons partie des privilégiés** we are among the privileged; **c'est un p.** (*d'un milieu favorisé*) he comes from a privileged background; **tu es un p.** (*tu as de la chance*) you're one of the privileged

privilégier [privileʒje] *vt* (*pr sub, impf* **n. privilégiions, v. privilégiiez**) (*personne, groupe*) to privilege; (*facteur, aspect*) to prioritize; **c'est l'objectif à p.** it's the objective to be prioritized

prix [pri] *nm* (**a**) (*valeur*) value, worth; (*coût*) cost; *Fig* **à tout p.** at all costs, whatever the cost, at any price; **faire qch à p. d'argent** to do sth for money; **se vendre à p. d'or** (*de biens*) to fetch huge prices; **acheter qch à p. d'or** to pay a huge amount *or F* a fortune for sth; **à aucun p.** not on any terms, not at any price; **elle n'ira à aucun p.** she won't go on any terms *or* at any price, nothing will make her go; **à n'importe quel p.** no matter what it costs; **à tout p.** at all costs; **elle veut changer de travail à tout p.** she wants to change jobs no matter what it costs *or* takes; *Fig* **au p. de** at the cost of; **attacher beaucoup de p. à qch** *ou* **un grand p. à qch** to set great store by sth, to set a lot of value on sth; **il attache beaucoup de p.** *ou* **un grand p. à l'apparence de sa voiture** he sets great store by his car's appearance, he prizes his car's appearance

(b) [①B57,D,2] (*en argent*) price; **acheter qch à juste p.** to buy sth at a fair price, to pay a fair price for sth; **je l'ai acheté à bas p.** I didn't pay very much for it, I paid a low price for it; *F* **faire un p. à qn** to give sb a good deal; **vous nous faites un p. si on en prend deux?** will you give us a good price if we take two?; **je vous ferai un p. (d'ami)** I'll let you have it cheap; **une voiture dans mes p.** a car I can afford *or* within my means *or* within my price range; **ce n'est pas du tout dans mes p.** I can't afford it, it's way beyond my means *or* well outside my price range; **c'est plus dans mes p.** that's more in my price range *or* my line; *Bourse* **actions cotées au p. de ...** shares quoted at the rate of ...; **articles de p.** expensive goods; **coûter un p. fou** to cost the earth *or F* an arm and a leg; **hors de p.** prohibitively expensive; **ne pas avoir de p.** to be priceless; **la santé/le bonheur, ça n'a pas de p.** you can't put a price on health/happiness; **mettre à p. la tête de qn** to put a price on sb's head; **mise à p. d'une propriété** upset price of an estate; **mise à p.** (*aux enchères*) (*d'un article*) reserve price; **c'est mon dernier p.** that's my final offer; **votre p. sera le mien** name your price; *F* **au p. où sont les choses, au p. où est le beurre** given the price of things, seeing what things cost; *Écon* **hausse/baisse des p.** rise/fall in prices; **vous pouvez en trouver si vous y mettez le p.** you can get it if you're willing to pay for it; **mais elle a dû y mettre le p.** but it cost her

(c) (*tarif*) charge; (*d'un voyage*) fare; **quel est le p. du billet?** how much do the tickets cost?; (*transports*) what's the fare?, how much is it?

(d) (*récompense*) prize; (*d'une bonne action*) reward; **avoir** *ou* **remporter le p.** to win the prize, to carry off the prize; **distribution des p.** prizegiving, *Br Scol* speech day; **le jour de la distribution des p.** prizegiving day; *Scol* **livre de p.** prize book; **p. de consolation** consolation prize; *Scol* **p. d'excellence** prize for excellence; **le p. Nobel** the Nobel Prize (**de** for); **le p. Nobel de la Paix** the Nobel Peace Prize; **un/le p. Nobel** (*personne*) a/the Nobel prizewinner *or Am* laureate

(e) (*œuvre, ouvrage primé*) prizewinning work; **j'ai lu le dernier p. Médicis** I've read the latest Prix Médicis *or* the latest Médicis prizewinner

(f) *Sp* race; **Grand p. (automobile)** Grand Prix

▶ **prix**: *Mktg* **p. d'acceptabilité** psychological price; **p. d'achat** purchase price; *Bourse* **p. acheteur** bid price; **p. affiché** posted price; **p. avantageux** bargain price; **p. de catalogue** list price; **p. de la chambre** room rate; **p. au comptant** cash price; **p. conseillé** suggested retail price, recommended retail price; **p. contractuel** contract *or* contractual price; **p. courant** current price, market price; **p. coûtant** cost price; **à** *ou* **au p. coûtant, au p. de revient** at cost price; **acheter/vendre qch au p. coûtant** to buy/sell sth at cost; **p. de détail** retail price; **p. élastique** elastic price; **p. de l'essence à la pompe** price of petrol at the pump; *Bourse* **p. d'exercice** (*d'option d'achat*) exercise price, strike price; **p. discompte** discount price; **p. facturé** invoice *or* invoiced price; **p. fixe** fixed rate; **(repas à) p. fixe** set (price) meal; **p. forfaitaire** all-inclusive price; **p. fort** full price; **au p. fort, ça coûte ...** the full price is ...; **p. de gros** wholesale price; **p. indicatif** approximate price; **p. initial** prime cost; *Mktg* **p. magique** odd numbers price (*eg £9.95*); **p. adapté au marché** market-based price; **p. du marché** market price; **p. sur le marché** market price; *Bourse* **p. de négociation** trade price; **p. net** net rate; **p. d'offre** supply price; **p. optimum** optimal price; **p. plafond** price ceiling; **p. plancher** price floor; *Mktg* **p. de prestige** premium price; **p. promotionnels** promotional pricing; *Mktg* **p. psychologique** psychological price; **p. public** posted price; **p. réduit** discount price; **p. de référence** reference price; **p. taxe comprise** price inclusive of tax; **p. de transport** freight price; **p. hors taxe** price net of tax, price before tax; **p. unique** one price, single price; **p. unitaire** unit price; **p. unitaire produit** unit price; **p. d'usine** factory price; **p. départ usine** price ex-works; *Bourse* **p. vendeur** offer price; **p. de vente** selling price

pro [pro] *n Sp etc F* pro; **elle l'a fait en p.** she did it like a pro; **du travail de p.** professional work, the work of a pro; **ils ont fait du travail de p., tous les deux** they both worked like pros

probabilité [prɔbabilite] *nf* [①A56-9; B36-7,K] probability, likelihood; **selon toute p.** in all probability *or* likelihood, most probably; *Math* **calcul des probabilités** theory of probability; **il y a une forte p.** there's a strong probability; **il y a une faible p.** there's little probability *or* likelihood

probable [prɔbabl] *adj* probable, likely; **il est p. qu'elle viendra** she'll probably come; **il est fort p. que ...** it's very probable that ...; **peu p.** improbable, unlikely; **il est peu p.** *ou* **il n'est pas p. qu'elle vienne** she's not likely *or* she's unlikely to come, it's unlikely that she'll come; **c'est très p.** (it's) very likely; **c'est plus que p.** it's more than likely; *F* **tu pourras rester avec nous? – c'est p.** will you be able to stay with us? – probably (I will); *F* **p. qu'elle ne se souvient plus de ce que je lui ai dit** she probably doesn't remember what I told her

probablement [prɔbabləmɑ̃] *adv* probably

probant [prɔbɑ̃] *adj* (*témoignage, argument etc*) convincing, conclusive; (*raison*) convincing; **peu p.** unconvincing; *Jur* **pièce probante** incriminating piece of evidence

probation [prɔbasjɔ̃] *nf Jur, Rel* probation

probatoire [prɔbatwar] *adj* **stage p.** trial *or* probationary period; *Scol* **examen p.** grading examination; *Jur* **délai p.** probation

probe [prɔb] *adj Litt* honest, upright

probité [prɔbite] *nf* probity, integrity

problématique [prɔblematik] **1** *adj* problematic(al) **2** *nf* set of problems; *Phil* problematics

problématiquement [prɔblematikmɑ̃] *adv* problematically

problème [prɔblɛm] *nm* problem; **un p. d'algèbre/de géométrie/de physique** an algebra/geometry/physics problem; **elle a soulevé le p. de la cantine** she brought up *or* raised the problem of the canteen; **poser un p.** to pose a problem; **si cela devait vous poser un p.** if that poses *or* creates a problem for you, if that's a problem for you; **cet emploi du temps pose p.** this schedule is (posing *or* creating) a problem; **ce n'est pas un p.** it's not a problem, that's no problem; **c'est tout un p.!** it's such a problem!; *F* **tu pourras passer me prendre? – oui, sans p.** could you come and pick me up? – sure, no problem; **tu n'auras aucun p. à la convaincre** you won't have any problem convincing her; *F* **(il n'y a) pas de p.** (*bien sûr!*) no problem!; **avoir des problèmes** to have problems; *Psy* **un adolescent qui a des problèmes** a problem teenager; *Scol* **faire des problèmes** to do sums; *F* **il va nous faire des problèmes** he's going to cause *or* give us problems; **peau/cheveux à problèmes** problem skin/hair; *F* **encore un type à problèmes** another guy with problems; **avoir des problèmes familiaux/d'argent** to have family/money problems

procédé [prɔsede] *nm* **(a)** (*façon de faire*) method; **des procédés peu recommandables** dubious methods; **échange de bons procédés** (*de formules de politesse*) exchange of courtesies *or* civilities; **c'est un échange de bons procédés** (*de petits services*) one good turn deserves another; **leur mésentente se traduit par des échanges constants de mauvais procédés** they don't get on and constantly play dirty tricks on each other; **cet échange de mauvais procédés finit par ...** the dirty tricks they played on each other ended up ...

(b) (*technique*) process; (*de travail*) method; **p. de fonctionnement** operating procedure; **p. de fabrication** manufacturing process; *Péj* **ça sent le p.** it seems rather artificial

(c) (*de queue de billard*) tip

(d) *Litt* (*comportement*) conduct

procéder [prɔsede] *vi* (*conj like* **céder**) **(a)** (*venir de*) **p. de** to arise out of, to originate in; **sa maladie procède de l'humidité ambiante** his illness is caused by *or* is attributable to the dampness **(b)** (*agir*) to proceed, to act; **p. par ordre** to do things in order; **p. par tâtonnement** to feel *or* fumble one's way; **p. avec méthode** to proceed methodically **(c) p. à** (*des recherches, une arrestation, une vérification etc*) to carry out; (*des élections*) to hold

procédure [prɔsedyr] *nf* **(a)** (*méthode*) procedure; **il faut suivre la p.** you/we/*etc* have to follow procedure; *Ordinat* **p. de chargement** loading procedure; *Télécom* **p. de connexion** dialup procedure **(b)** *Jur* procedure; (*démarche*) proceedings; **engager une p.** to take *or* institute proceedings; **engager une p. de divorce** to begin *or* institute divorce proceedings; **terme de p.** legal term; **vice** *ou* **incident de p.** procedural irregularity, legal technicality; *Fin* **p. de faillite** bankruptcy proceedings; **p. douanière** customs procedure **(c)** *Ordinat* procedure

procédurier, -ière [prɔsedyrje, -jɛr] **1** *adj* quibbling, *F* nit-picking; (*avocat*) pettifogging **2** *n* quibbler, *F* nit-picker; (*avocat*) pettifogger

procès [prɔsɛ] *nm* **(a)** *Jur* (legal) proceedings, action (at law); **p. civil** lawsuit; **p. criminel** (criminal) trial; **engager un p.** to take legal action; **faire** *ou* **intenter un p. à** (*un particulier*) to sue, to bring an action against, to institute proceedings against; (*un délinquant*) to prosecute; **engager** *ou*

entreprendre un p. to institute proceedings (**contre qn** against sb); **être en p. avec qn** to be involved in legal proceedings with sb; **intenter un p. en divorce à qn** to institute divorce proceedings against sb; **le dossier du p.** the brief; **gagner/perdre son p.** to win/lose one's case; *F* **avoir un p. sur le dos** to be faced with a lawsuit *or* a court case; *Fig* **tu me/lui/***etc* **fais un p. d'intention** you're jumping to conclusions; *Fig* **faire le p. de qn/qch** to attack sb/sth; *Fig* **sans autre forme de p.** without (any) further ceremony, without further ado; **renvoyé sans autre forme de p.** unceremoniously dismissed; *Fig* **c'est un p. contre la société** the whole of society is on trial; *Journ* **p. médiatique** trial by media

(**b**) *Anat Vieilli* process

processeur [prɔsesœr] *nm Ordinat* processor; **p. SQL** SQL engine; **p. audio** audio processor; **p. central** central processing unit, CPU; **p. de données** data processor; **p. en tranches** bit-slice processor

processif, -ive [prɔsesif, -iv] *adj* (*mesures etc*) progressive

procession [prɔsesjɔ̃] *nf aussi Fig* procession; **aller en p.** to walk in procession

processionnaire [prɔsesjɔnɛr] *adj* processionary

processionnel, -elle [prɔsesjɔnɛl] *adj* processional

processionnellement [prɔsesjɔnɛlmɑ̃] *adv Litt* in procession

processus [prɔsesys] *nm* (**a**) (*évolution*) process; **un p. de changement** a process of change; *Méd* **p. pathologique** pathology (**b**) (*méthode*) process, method; **l'introduction de nouveaux p.** the introduction of new methods; **p. industriel** industrial process (**c**) *Anat* process

procès-verbal, *pl* **procès-verbaux** *nm* (**a**) *Jur* policeman's report (*about an offence*); **avoir un p.** to get a (parking) ticket; **dresser le p. d'une contravention à qn, dresser (un) p. à** *ou* **contre qn** to report *or F* book sb (**b**) (*rapport*) (official) report; (*d'une réunion*) proceedings, minutes; (*d'un témoignage etc*) record; **approbation du p.** approval of the minutes; **registre des procès-verbaux** minute book

prochain, -aine [prɔʃɛ̃, -ɛn] **1** *adj* (**a**) [①A7,d,vi] (*qui suit*) next; **dimanche p.** next Sunday; **la semaine prochaine** next week; **le p. numéro** (*d'un magazine*) the next issue; **la prochaine fois** the next time; **ce sera pour une prochaine fois** another time perhaps, *Am* let's take a rain check; **à la prochaine fois!** be seeing you!, *F* see you (soon)!

(**b**) *surtout Litt* (*imminent*) imminent; **son p. départ, son départ p.** his approaching *or* impending *or* imminent departure; **sa fin prochaine** his imminent death; **dans un avenir p.** in the near *or* not too distant future; **un jour p.** one day soon

2 *n* neighbour, *US* neighbor; (*tout être humain*) fellow human being; **aimer son p.** to love one's neighbour

3 *nf F* (**a**) **à la prochaine!** see you (soon)!

(**b**) **je descends à la prochaine** I'm getting off at the next stop

prochainement [prɔʃɛnmɑ̃] *adv* shortly, soon; **p. sur vos écrans** coming soon to a cinema near you

proche [prɔʃ] **1** *adv* **de p. en p.** little by little, step by step, by degrees

2 *adj* near, close (**de** to), neighbouring, *US* neighboring; **la ville la plus p.** the nearest *or* closest town; **tout p.** close at hand, nearby, close by; **le chalet est tout p.** the chalet is not very far away; **dans un avenir tout p.** in the very near future; **sa fin est p.** he is close *or* near to death, the end is not very far away; **la fin est p.** the end is nigh; **l'heure est p.** the hour is near *or* at hand; **cela me paraît pourtant si p.!** (*dans le passé*) it seems like only yesterday!; **p. de la ruine/la catastrophe** on the verge of *or* close to ruin/catastrophe; **p. de mourir** near death, close to death; **l'italien est p. du français** Italian is close to French; **des langues très proches** languages that are very close to each other; **je me sens p. de lui** I feel close to him; **nous sommes devenus très proches** we became very close; **ses proches parents** his near *or* close relations; *Jur, Fml* his next of kin; **nom et adresse des proches parents** name and address of next of kin; **ils sont proches parents** they are closely related; **les gens les plus proches de nous** the people closest to us, our nearest and dearest; **la guerre est p.** war is close; **les gens proches du pouvoir** those close to the seat of power; **une préoccupation p. de la névrose** a worry bordering on neurosis; **une description p. de la réalité** a realistic *or* true-to-life description

3 *n* **réunir ses proches** to gather one's nearest and dearest (around one); **seuls ses proches étaient au courant** only his nearest and dearest *or* those closest to him knew

Proche-Orient (le) [ləprɔʃɔrjɑ̃] *nm* the Middle East, *Vieilli* the Near East

proclamateur, -trice [prɔklamatœr, -tris] *n Litt* proclaimer

proclamation [prɔklamasjɔ̃] *nf* proclamation

proclamer [prɔklame] *vt* to proclaim; **p. le résultat du scrutin** to declare the results of the election; **on proclama que …** it was given out that …; **tu ne vas pas aller p. ça partout, j'espère** you're not going to announce it to all and sundry *or* shout it from the rooftops, I trust; **elle est allée p. partout que …** she went around telling everybody that …; **p. son innocence** to proclaim *or* protest one's innocence; **p. qn roi** to proclaim sb king

proclitique [prɔklitik] *adj, nm Ling* proclitic

proconsul [prɔkɔ̃syl] *nm Hist* proconsul

proconsulaire [prɔkɔ̃sylɛr] *adj Hist* proconsular

proconsulat [prɔkɔ̃syla] *nm Hist* proconsulate

procréateur, -trice [prɔkreatœr, -tris] *Hum, Vieilli* **1** *adj* procreative **2** *n* procreator

procréation [prɔkreasjɔ̃] *nf* procreation; *Arch* (*des enfants*) begetting; **p. médicalement assistée** assisted conception

procréatique [prɔkreatik] *nf* artificial birth technology

procréer [prɔkree] *vt Litt* to procreate, *Arch* to beget

procurateur [prɔkyratœr] *nm Hist* procurator

procuration [prɔkyrasjɔ̃] *nf Com, Fin, Jur* proxy, power of attorney; **par p.** by proxy, *Spéc* per pro(curationem); **voter par p.** to vote by proxy; **vote par p.** proxy vote; **donner (la) p. à qn** to confer powers of attorney on sb, to give sb power of attorney; **elle lui a envoyé une p.** she sent him a power of attorney; *Fig* **elle avait le sentiment de vivre par p.** she felt she was living by proxy

procuratrice [prɔkyratris] *nf Jur* procurator, proxy

procurer [prɔkyre] **1** *vt* **p. qch à qn** to get *or* obtain *or Fml* procure sth for sb; **p. un emploi à qn** to get sb a job; **p. un renseignement à qn** to get hold of information for sb; **le plaisir que cela nous procure** the pleasure that gives us, the pleasure we derive *or* get from that; **son travail lui procure d'importants revenus** his job provides him with *or* brings in a substantial income

2 se procurer *vpr* to get (hold of), to obtain, *Fml* to procure; **se p. de l'argent** to get hold of *or* raise *or* find money; **où peut-on se p. ce livre?** where can you get hold of this book?

procureur [prɔkyrœr] *nm Jur* procurator, proxy; **p. de la République** (*in lower courts*) *Eng* ≈ public prosecutor, *Scot* ≈ procurator fiscal, *US* ≈ district attorney; **p. général** (*in higher courts*) *Eng* ≈ public prosecutor, *Scot* ≈ procurator fiscal, *US* ≈ district attorney

prodigalité [prɔdigalite] *nf* (*défaut*) extravagance, prodigality; **une p. de** (*détails, anecdotes*) a wealth *or* an abundance of; (*objets*) an abundance of; **une p. de richesses** a king's ransom; **donner avec p.** to be extremely generous; **donner son temps avec p.** to be extremely generous with one's time; *Fig* **prodigalités** (*dépenses*) lavish *or* reckless expenditure

prodige [prɔdiʒ] **1** *nm* wonder, marvel; (*personne*) prodigy; **faire des prodiges** to work *or* do wonders, to work miracles; **un p. d'ingéniosité** a marvel of ingenuity; **un p. de courage/patience** wonderful bravery/patience; **déployer des prodiges de courage/patience** to demonstrate wonderful bravery/patience; **tenir du p.** to be extraordinary, to be something of a miracle; (*être impossible*) to be impossible *or* a physical impossibility; **c'est un p.** (*personne*) he's a prodigy; (*fait*) it's amazing *or* incredible **2** *adj* **enfant p.** child prodigy

prodigieusement [prɔdiʒjøzmɑ̃] *adv* prodigiously

prodigieux, -euse [prɔdiʒjø, -øz] *adj* (*quantité, force*) prodigious, extraordinary; *F* (*incroyable*) phenomenal, stupendous; *Iron* **sa bêtise est prodigieuse** his stupidity knows no bounds, he is phenomenally stupid; **d'un courage p.** extraordinarily brave

prodigue [prɔdig] **1** *adj* (**a**) (*généreux*) lavish, unsparing (**de** in, with); **il est p. pour ses enfants** he's very generous towards his children; **être p. d'excuses** to apologise profusely, to be profuse in one's apologies; **être p. de compliments** to be lavish in one's praise; **être p. de son argent** to spend lavishly, to be free with one's money; **il est très p. de conseils** he's very generous with his advice; *Iron* he's very free with his advice (**b**) *Péj* (*dépensier*) wasteful, spendthrift, *Fml* prodigal; *Bible* **l'enfant p.** the prodigal son **2** *n* spendthrift, squanderer

prodiguer [prɔdige] *vt* (**a**) (*donner abondamment*) (*aide*) to be unstinting in, to give unstintingly; (*compliments*) to be lavish *or* unstinting in; (*énergie*) to lavish; **p. sa patience** to show unstinting patience; **p. qch à qn** to lavish sth on sb; **p. ses conseils** to be generous with one's advice; *Iron* to be free with one's advice; **il lui prodigait ses conseils** he was generous *or Iron* free with his advice; **p. son argent à ses enfants** to spend *or* lavish all one's money on one's children;

p. ses talents à qn to treat sb to a display of one's talents (**b**) *Péj* (*gaspiller*) to waste, to squander

prodrome [prɔdrom] *nm* (**a**) (*d'une maladie*) warning symptom (**b**) (*d'un traité*) preamble

producteur, -trice [prɔdyktœr, -tris] **1** *adj* productive (**de** of); **pays p. de blé/pétrole** wheat-growing/oil-producing country; *Cin* **société productrice** production company **2** *n* (*entreprise etc*), *Rad, TV, Cin* producer; **p. associé** associate producer, production associate; **p. délégué** executive producer

productible [prɔdyktibl] *adj* producible

productif, -ive [prɔdyktif, -iv] *adj* productive; *Fin* **p. d'intérêts** interest-bearing

production [prɔdyksjɔ̃] *nf* (**a**) *Ind, Cin* production; (*d'électricité*) production, generation; **la p. textile/automobile** textile/car production; **augmenter la p.** to increase production *or* output; **les conditions de p. des œuvres artistiques** the conditions in which works of art are produced; **moyens de p.** means of production; **coût de p.** cost of production, production cost; *Cin* **directeur de p.** production manager; **assistant de p.** production assistant; *TV, Cin* **p. back-to-back** back-to-back production; **p. à la chaîne** mass production; **p. cinématographique** film production; *TV, Rad* **p. directe** live production; **p. de l'exercice** (*poste de bilan*) production for the period; *Fin* **p. immobilisée** fixed assets produced for use by the company; *Com* **p. JAT** JIT production; *Com* **p. juste à temps** just-in-time production; **p. en masse** mass production; **p. en série** mass production; **p. en studio** studio production; *TV, Cin* **p. à la suite** back-to-back production; *TV* **p. vidéo légère** electronic field production, EFP

(**b**) (*produit*) product; *Cin* production; *Cin* **p. journalière** rushes, dailies; **productions** *Agr* produce; (*de la mine etc*) yield; (*d'une usine*) output; **p. stockée** (*poste de bilan*) stored production, production left in stock; *Compta* **p. vendue** sales; **p. littéraire** literary output; *Cin* **une p. franco-russe** a Franco-Russian (co-)production

(**c**) *Jur* **p. des pièces** exhibition of documents

productique [prɔdyktik] *nf* production engineering

productivisme [prɔdyktivism] *nm Péj* obsession with productivity

productiviste [prɔdyktivist] *adj Péj* that emphasizes productivity to an obsessive degree

productivité [prɔdyktivite] *nf* productivity, productiveness; (*d'une usine*) productive capacity; **accroissement de la p.** increase in productivity

produire [prɔdɥir] (*prp* **produisant**; *pp* **produit**; *pr ind* **je produis, n. produisons**; *impf* **je produisais**; *p hist* **je produisis**; *fu* **je produirai**) **1** *vt* (**a**) *Ind, Agr, Cin, TV, Rad* to produce; (*chaleur, électricité*) to generate, to produce; *Litt* (*descendance etc*) to bring forth, to bear; **argent qui produit de l'intérêt** money that yields *or* bears interest; **p. cent voitures par jour** to produce *or* turn out *or* have an output of a hundred cars a day; **p. une créance** to result in an account receivable; *TV, Cin* **produit par** produced by

(**b**) (*résultat*) to produce, to bring about, to generate; (*effet*) to produce, to bring about; (*sensation*) to create, to generate; (*odeur*) to produce, to generate; (*irritation*) to cause; **p. une impression favorable sur qn** to produce *or* make a favourable impression on sb; **sa déclaration a produit un certain effet** his statement created *or* caused something of a stir; **il a produit son effet en annonçant cela** his announcement had the effect he wanted *or* was hoping for

(**c**) (*créer*) to produce, to turn out; **elle vient de p. son premier roman** she's just produced *or* written *or* turned out her first novel; **les œuvres que ces années de guerre ont produites** the works that were the outcome of the war years *or* that the war years generated

(**d**) *Jur etc* (*témoignage etc*) to produce, to bring forward; **p. des témoins** to produce witnesses

2 se produire *vpr* (**a**) (*d'un événement*) to happen, to take place, to occur; **il pourrait se p. des incidents** there might be trouble; **cela se produit souvent** that often happens, it's a frequent occurrence

(**b**) (*d'un acteur etc*) to appear

3 *vi* (**a**) *Écon* to produce, to be productive

(**b**) *Jur* **sommation de p.** order *or* requirement to present one's ID papers/driving licence/*etc*

produit [prɔdɥi] *nm* (**a**) (*marchandise*) product; *Agr* **produits** produce; **produits agricoles** agricultural produce, farm products; **le p. de la terre** the produce of the land; **vivre du p. de la terre** to live off the land; **les services et les produits** goods and services

(**b**) (*profit*) yield; **p. d'une vente** proceeds of a sale; *Com* **le p. de la journée** the day's takings *or* receipts; **le p. de dix années de travail** the product *or* result of ten years' work

(**c**) *Math* (*d'une multiplication*) product

(**d**) (*création*) product; **c'est le p. de son imagination** it's the *or* a product of his imagination; **toute cette histoire était le plus pur p. de son imagination** the entire story was a figment of his imagination

▶ **produit**: **produits d'achat courant** convenience goods; *Mktg* **produits d'achat impulsif** impulse goods; *Mktg* **p. d'achat non prémédité** impulse item; *Mktg* **produits d'achat réfléchi** shopping goods; **p. alimentaire** food product; *Compta* **produits annexes** incidental income; **p. augmenté** augmented product; *Mktg* **p. d'avenir** rising star, potential market leader; *Banque* **p. bancaire** banking product; **p. de beauté** beauty product; *Compta* **p. brut** gross proceeds, gross income; **p. chimique** chemical; *Mktg* **p. ciblé** niche product; **p. de consommation** consumer product; *Compta* **p. constaté d'avance** prepaid income; *Compta* **produits courants** current income; *Compta* **produits en cours** work in progress; *Mktg* **produits de dépannage** emergency goods; *Mktg* **p. dodo** dodo; *Mktg* **p. drapeau** own-brand product; **p. écologique** green product; **produits d'entretien** (household) cleaning products; **p. d'étanchéité** sealing compound; *Compta* **produits exceptionnels** extraordinary income; *Compta* **produits d'exploitation** income from operations; **p. final** end product; *Compta* **produits financiers** interest dividends and other financial income; **p. fini** finished product; *Mktg* **p. générique** generic, generic product; **produits de gestion courante** income from operations; **p. de grande consommation** mass-market product; *Compta* **produits de grande consommation** consumer goods; **p. hôtelier** hotel product; *Mktg* **p. d'imitation** imitative product; *Écon* **p. intérieur brut** gross domestic product; **produits intermédiaires** semi-finished products; **p. de luxe** luxury product; **p. manufacturé** manufactured product; **p. de marque** branded *or* brand-name product; **produits de marque** designer goods; *Mktg* **p. à marque de distributeur** own-brand product; **produits ménagers** (household) cleaning products; *Écon* **p. national brut** gross national product; *Compta* **p. net** net proceeds, net income; *Compta* **p. net partiel** accrued income; **p. novateur** innovative product; **produits de première nécessité** emergency convenience goods, staple convenience goods; **produits périssables** non-durable goods; **produits 'prêts-à-consommer'** convenience goods; *Compta* **produits à recevoir** accrued income, accruals; *Mktg* **p. sans marque** unbranded product, no-name product; *Mktg* **p. sans nom** no-name product; **produits de second choix** seconds, rejects; **produits semi-finis** semi-finished goods; **produits spécialisés** speciality goods; *Mktg* **p. substituable** substitutable product; **p. de substitution** substitute product; *Ch* **p. de synthèse** product of synthesis, synthesized product; *Mktg* **p. tactique** me-too product; *Mktg* **p. vert** green product

proéminence [prɔeminɑ̃s] *nf* (*état*) prominence; (*ce qui fait saillie*) protuberance

proéminent [prɔeminɑ̃] *adj* prominent; (*pierre*) projecting; (*nez*) prominent, protuberant; (*grosseur*) protuberant

prof [prɔf] *n F* (school)teacher; (*maître de conférences*) prof; (*maître assistant*) lecturer

profanateur, -trice [prɔfanatœr, -tris] *Litt* **1** *adj* profanatory **2** *n* profaner

profanation [prɔfanasjɔ̃] *nf* (*d'une tombe*) desecration, violation, *Fml* profanation

profane [prɔfan] **1** *adj* profane; (*musique etc*) secular; (*cimetière*) unhallowed; *Fig* **elle est p. (en la matière)** she doesn't know much about it **2** *n Fig* layman; **aux yeux du p.** to the layman *or* the uninitiated, to the untrained eye; **je n'ai jamais fait de ski, je suis un p.** I've never skied, I'm a complete beginner

profaner [prɔfane] *vt* (*église*) to desecrate, *Fml* to profane; (*tombe*) to desecrate, to violate, *Fml* to profane; (*innocence*) to defile

proférer [prɔfere] *vt* (**je profère**; **je proférerai**) to utter; **sans p. une (seule) parole** without (so much as) a word

profès, -esse [prɔfɛ, -ɛs] *Rel* **1** *adj* professed **2** *n* professed monk, *f* professed nun

professer [prɔfese] **1** *vt* (**a**) (*religion, opinion*) to profess; (*point de vue*) to hold (**b**) (*enseigner*) to teach; **il professe la physique au lycée** he teaches physics at the lycée **2** *vi* (*être titulaire d'une chaire*) to be a professor; (*comme maître assistant*) to be a lecturer; (*dans une école*) to be a teacher; **il professe à la Sorbonne** he's a professor/lecturer at the Sorbonne, he teaches at the Sorbonne

professeur [prɔfɛsœr] *nm* (school)teacher, *Br Vieilli* master, *f* mistress; (*à l'université*) professor; (*maître assistant*) lecturer; **elle est p. de piano** she's a piano teacher, she teaches (the) piano; **p. de terminale** sixth-form teacher; **c'est un bon/mauvais p.** he's a good/bad teacher; **p. de chant** singing teacher; **p. principal** class *or* form teacher, *Am* homeroom teacher; *Br* (*dans une école privée*) form master, *f* form mistress

profession [prɔfɛsjɔ̃] *nf* **(a)** [①B4,B,2,b,i] (*métier*) profession, occupation; (*pour artisans*) trade; **médecin de (sa) p.** doctor by profession; **menuisier de p.** carpenter by trade; *Fig F* **rouspéteur de p.** professional grumbler, full-time grumbler; **sans p.** unemployed; **je suis sans p.** I don't work, I don't have a job **(b) faire p. de qch** to profess sth

▶ **profession**: **p. de foi** profession of faith; **p. libérale** (liberal) profession; **avoir une p. libérale** to be a professional person; **j'ai décidé d'avoir une p. libérale** I decided to take up a profession

professionnalisation [prɔfɛsjɔnalisasjɔ̃] *nf* professionalization; (*d'un sportif*) turning professional

professionnaliser (se) [səprɔfɛsjɔnalize] *vpr* (*d'un sportif*) to turn professional; (*d'un sport*) to become professional *or* a professional sport

professionnalisme [prɔfɛsjɔnalism] *nm* professionalism

professionnel, -elle [prɔfɛsjɔnɛl] **1** *adj* **(a)** (*personne, attitude*) professional; (*enseignement*) vocational; **avoir des difficultés professionnelles** to have professional problems *or* problems at work; **maladies professionnelles** occupational diseases; **syndicat p.** trade association; **faire preuve de conscience professionnelle** to be conscientious (in one's work); **cela n'est pas très p.** it's not very professional **(b)** (*footballeur*) professional **2** *n* **(a)** *Sp* professional; **passer p.** to turn professional **(b)** *Ind etc* skilled worker; **le travail d'un p.** a professional job

professionnellement [prɔfɛsjɔnɛlmɑ̃] *adv* professionally

professoral, -ale, -aux, -ales [prɔfɛsɔral, -o] *adj aussi Fig* professorial

professorat [prɔfɛsɔra] *nm* teaching profession (*esp in higher education*); **choisir le p.** to choose teaching as a *or* one's profession

profil [prɔfil] *nm* **(a)** (*d'une personne*) profile; **dessiner qn de p.** to draw sb in profile; **se placer** *ou* **se mettre de p.** to turn one's face (*so it is in profile*); **vue de p.** side view; *Fig* **adopter un p. bas** to adopt a low profile; **garder le p. bas** to keep a low profile, to keep one's head down; **le p. de l'employé idéal** the profile of the ideal employee; **p. de poste** job description; **elle a tout à fait le p. de l'emploi** she fits the job description exactly, she's exactly the type of person that's needed (for the job); **elle a le p. de celle que nous recherchons** she's exactly what we're looking for

(b) (*d'un objet*) profile, contour, outline; (*dessin*) section; **p. en travers** cross section; **p. de l'horizon** skyline; *Géol* **le p. d'une rivière** the profile of a river

▶ **profil**: *Mktg* **p. des consommateurs** consumer profile; **p. grec** Greek profile; *Mktg* **p. du marché** market profile; **p. médical** medical history; *Banque* **p. patrimonial** personnel assets profile; **p. psychologique** psychological profile

profilage [prɔfilaʒ] *nm Beaux-Arts* profiling; *Tech* (*de la carrosserie d'une voiture etc*) shaping, streamlining

profilé [prɔfile] *Tech* **1** *adj* (*métal etc*) shaped; (*voiture etc*) streamlined; **fers profilés** sectional irons, iron sections **2** *nm* **profilés en acier** steel sections, sectional steel; *Aut* **p. creux** box frame section; *Aut* **p. creux de châssis** channel frame section; *Aut* **p. en T** T section

profiler [prɔfile] **1** *Tech vt* **(a)** (*représenter de profil*) to draw in section **(b)** (*morceau de métal*) to shape; (*voiture etc*) to streamline **2 se profiler** *vpr* to stand out in profile, to be outlined, to be silhouetted (**à, sur, contre** against); **des nuages se profilent à l'horizon** clouds are looming up on the horizon; *Fig* **les difficultés qui se profilent pour 1996** the difficulties building up for 1996 *or* in the offing for 1996; *Fig* **tout se profile plutôt bien** everything is shaping up pretty well, things look pretty good; *Fig* **ses vacances se profilent** his holiday plans are taking shape

profit [prɔfi] *nm* **(a)** (*avantage*) profit, benefit; **faire (son) p. de qch** to profit by *or* from sth; **mettre qch à p.** to put sth to good use, *Fml* to turn sth to (good) account; **tirer p. de qch** to take advantage of sth, to derive benefit from sth; **tirer p. d'une situation** to take advantage of *or* make the most of a situation; **elle a su tirer p. de son stage** she made the most of her training period; **tirer le p. maximum de qch** to derive maximum benefit from sth; *F* **sa vieille auto m'aura fait du p.** his old car has served me well, I've got a lot of use out of his old car; **j'en ai eu peu de p.** I gained little advantage from it; **il doit y trouver son p.** he must be getting something out of it; **elle ne cherche que son p.** she's only interested in personal gain; **au p. de qn** on behalf of sb, for the benefit of sb; **au p. des pauvres** in aid of the poor; **concert donné au p. des orphelins** benefit concert for orphans; **elle l'a laissé tomber au p. de son frère** she dropped him for his brother; **les socialistes perdront au p. des communistes** votes will swing from the Socialists to the Communists, the Communists will pick up votes from the Socialists

(b) *Écon* **un p.** a profit; **profits et pertes** profit and loss; **vendre à p.** to sell at a profit; **p. fait sur une vente** profit on a sale; **p. de 12%** 12% profit; **p. espéré** anticipated profit; **p. réel** real profit; **il n'y a pas de petits profits** every little helps

profitabilité [prɔfitabilite] *nf* profitability

profitable [prɔfitabl] *adj* profitable; (*situation*) advantageous; (*expérience, exercice*) beneficial

profitablement [prɔfitabləmɑ̃] *adv* profitably

profiter [prɔfite] *vi* **(a) p. de qch** to take advantage of sth, to (derive) benefit from sth, *Fml* to turn sth to (good) account; **il est de bonne humeur aujourd'hui, il faut en p.** he's in a good mood today, we'd better make the most of it; **p. de l'occasion** to make the most of *or* seize the opportunity; **je profite d'un moment de calme pour vous dire que ...** I'm using these few moments of peace and quiet to tell you that ...; **p. de la vie** to make the most of life, to enjoy life (to the full); **p. de sa jeunesse** to make the most of one's youth; **elle n'a pas pu p. de ce moment de vacances** she was not able to benefit from the break; **nous sommes un peu en avance, j'en profite pour ...** let me take advantage of the few moments we have in hand to ...; **il a profité de ce que tout le monde dormait encore pour s'esquiver** he took advantage of the fact that everyone was still asleep to slip away; **il a profité de mon offre** he took me up on my offer; **elle a profité de ses petits-enfants pendant les vacances** she made the most of her grandchildren during the holidays

(b) *Écon* **p. sur une vente** to make a profit on a sale

(c) p. à qn to be to sb's advantage, to be of benefit to sb, to benefit sb; **ses idées révolutionnaires ne lui ont pas profité** his revolutionary ideas didn't do him any good (in the end); *Prov* **bien mal acquis ne profite jamais** ill-gotten goods never prosper; *F* **ces chaussures m'ont bien profité** these shoes have lasted me a long time, I've got a lot of use out of these shoes

(d) *F* (*d'un enfant, d'une plante etc*) to thrive

profiterole [prɔfitrɔl] *nf Culin* profiterole

profiteur, -euse [prɔfitœr, -øz] *n Péj* profiteer; **les profiteurs de guerre** war profiteers

profond [prɔfɔ̃] **1** *adj* **(a)** (*lac, bassin, trou, voix*) deep; **puits p. de six mètres** well six metres deep; **ces étagères ne sont pas profondes** these shelves are not very deep; **un décolleté p.** a plunging neckline; **une forêt profonde** a dense *or* thick forest; **révérence profonde, p. salut** low *or* deep bow; **peu p.** shallow

(b) (*haine*) profound, deep-seated, deep-rooted; (*préjugé*) deep-seated, deep-rooted; (*cause*) underlying, deep-rooted; **des marques profondes, ineffaçables** deep, indelible scars; **cette expérience a laissé en elle des marques profondes** the experience marked her for life

(c) *Fig* (*sagesse, érudition etc*) profound; (*connaissance, discussion*) thorough, in-depth; (*sommeil*) deep, sound; (*paroles*) profound, meaningful; (*personne*) profound, deep; **un bleu p.** a deep blue; **un silence p.** a profound *or* heavy silence; **un p. soupir** a deep *or* heavy sigh; **p. dégoût** profound *or* deep disgust; **un homme p.** a man who thinks deeply, a deep thinker; **elle leur reproche de ne pas être assez profonds** she reproaches them for their shallowness *or* with being shallow; **un esprit p.** a mind of great depth; **plongés dans de profondes discussions** deep in discussion; **ses intentions profondes étaient honorables** deep down his intentions were honourable; **je ne connais pas ses intentions profondes** I don't know what his intentions are deep down

2 *adv* (*plonger, creuser etc*) deep; **ça descend p. sous la cave** it goes a long way down under the cellar

3 *nm* **au plus p. de mon cœur** in my heart of hearts, deep down; **au plus p. de la nuit** at dead of night, in the middle of the night

profondément [prɔfɔ̃demɑ̃] *adv* (*choqué, vexé, déçu, touché*) deeply, profoundly; (*aimer qn*) deeply; **dormir p.** to sleep soundly; **p. endormi** sound *or* fast asleep; **s'incliner p.** to make a deep *or* low bow; **j'en suis p. convaincu** I am quite convinced of it; **se comprendre p.** to have a profound *or* deep understanding of each other; **je ne te demande pas d'aimer p. ma famille mais ...** I don't expect you to like my family, but ...

profondeur [prɔfɔ̃dœr] *nf* **(a)** (*de l'eau, d'un trou dans le sol etc*) depth; (*d'une voix*) deepness; **avoir dix mètres de p.** to be ten metres deep, to be ten metres in depth; **creuser en p.** to dig deep, to go down a long way; **les plongeurs ont effectué des réparations en p.** the divers carried out repairs far beneath the surface; *Fig* **travailler en p.** to be working in depth; **travail en p.** in-depth work; **des changements en p.** in-depth *or* profound changes; **rien n'a changé en p.** deep down nothing has changed, the changes have all been superficial; **peu de p.** shallowness; **de peu de p.** (*trou, Fig échanges*) shallow

(**b**) (*de sentiment*) depth; (*d'esprit, d'un poème, d'une œuvre d'art*) profoundness, profundity; **un film sans p.** a film with no depth, a shallow *or* superficial film

(**c**) **profondeurs** (*de l'esprit*) depths, recesses; **la psychologie des profondeurs** psychoanalysis

▶ **profondeur**: *Mktg* **p. de l'assortiment de produits** product-mix depth; *Phot* **p. de champ** depth of field; *Phot* **p. de foyer** depth of focus; *Mktg* **p. de gamme** depth of product mix; *Mktg* **p. de produit** product depth

pro forma [fɔrma] *adj inv* **facture p.** pro forma invoice

profus [prɔfy] *adj Litt* profuse

profusément [prɔfyzemɑ̃] *adv Litt* profusely

profusion [prɔfyzjɔ̃] *nf* profusion, abundance; **une p. de** a profusion *or* an abundance of; **avec une p. d'exemples** with abundant examples; **à p.** in profusion; **des bouteilles à p.** an abundance of bottles, bottles galore; **donner de l'argent à p.** to give a great deal of money

progéniture [prɔʒenityr] *nf* progeny, offspring; *F Hum* **il nous a présenté sa p.** he introduced his offspring to us

progestatif, -ive [prɔʒɛstatif, -iv] *Biol, Ch* **1** *adj* **corps p.** corpus luteum **2** *nm* progestin, progestogen

progestérone [prɔʒɛsterɔn] *nf Biol, Ch* progesterone

progiciel [prɔʒisjɛl] *nm Ordinat* software package; **p. de communication** comms package; **p. intégré** integrated package

prognathe [prɔgnat] *adj* (*visage*) undershot, underhung, *Spéc* prognathous

programmable [prɔgramabl] *adj Électron* programmable

programmateur, -trice [prɔgramatœr, -tris] **1** *n Rad, TV* programme planner, scheduler, programmer **2** *nm Tech* automatic control (device); *Ordinat* scheduler, programmer

programmation [prɔgramasjɔ̃] *nf* (**a**) *TV etc* programme planning, scheduling, programming; **un changement de p.** a change to the advertised *or* scheduled programme (**b**) *Ordinat* programming; **langage de p.** programming language; **p. orientée objet, p. par objets** object-oriented programming

programme [prɔgram] *nm* (**a**) *TV, Rad etc* programme, *US* program; (*brochure*), *TV* TV guide, listings magazine; *Cin* programme, schedule; **hors p.** unscheduled; **un changement des programmes** a change to the advertised *or* scheduled programme; *Fig F* **changement de p., on ne part plus** there's been a change of plan, we're not going away after all; **quel est ton p. pour les vacances?** what have you got planned *or* arranged for the holidays?; **on n'a pas de p., on verra au jour le jour** we haven't any definite plans *or* anything definite planned, we'll play it by ear; **qu'est-ce que nous avons comme p. aujourd'hui?** what's on the agenda for today?; **nous n'avons rien au p. aujourd'hui** we haven't anything planned for today, *F* we haven't anything on today; **avoir un p. chargé** to have a busy schedule, *F* to have a lot on; **p. d'actualités** current affairs programme; **p. à la demande** programme-on-demand; **p. familial** family programme; **p. minimum** skeleton programme; *TV, Rad* **p. phare** top-rating programme, banker; **p. radiodiffusé** radio programme; **p. radiophonique** radio programme; *TV, Rad* **p. de stock** programme with re-run potential; **p. télé** TV programme

(**b**) [①A13,8] *Scol* **p. (d'études)** curriculum; (*d'un cours*) syllabus; **être** *ou* **figurer au p.** to be on the syllabus; **ne pas sortir du p.** not to depart from the syllabus; **les auteurs au** *ou* **du p.** the set books; **des auteurs hors p.** books that are not on the syllabus; **une question hors p.** a question not covered by the syllabus

(**c**) (*d'un parti politique, d'une entreprise commerciale*) programme, *US* program, platform; **p. de réformes sociales** programme of social reform; **p. électoral** (election) platform; *Fig* **c'est tout un p.** it's quite a job *or* a business *or* an undertaking; *Mktg* **p. d'amélioration de la qualité** quality improvement programme, QIP; **p. de fidélisation** frequent user programme; **p. de formation** training programme; **p. mercatique** marketing programme; *Mktg* **p. mercatique de fidélisation** frequency marketing programme, FMP; *Mktg* **p. de stimulation** incentive scheme; *Mktg* **p. de vente pyramidale** pyramid selling scheme; **p. de voyage de stimulation** incentive travel programme

(**d**) *Ordinat* program; **p. d'amorçage** boot program; **p. antivirus** antivirus program; **p. d'arrière-plan** background program; **p. assembleur** assembler program; **p. d'auto-test** self-test program; **p. de césure** hyphenation program; **p. de commande** driver; **p. de configuration** configuration program; **p. de conversion** conversion program; **p. de dessin** drawing program, paint program; **p. détecteur de virus** virus detection program; **p. éditeur de liens** link program, linker; **p. d'évaluation (de performance)** benchmark program; **p. de formatage** formatter; **p. d'initialisation** initialization program; **p. maître** master program; **p. objet** object program; **p. pilote** driver; **p. prioritaire** foreground program; **p. de publipostage** mailmerge program; **p. en recouvrement** overlay program; **p. résident** resident program; **p. de routage** router; **p. sentinelle** watchdog program; **p. source** source program; **p. système** system program; **p. de test** test program; **p. traducteur** interpreter; **p. de traitement par lots** batch program; **p. utilitaire** utility program; **p. virus** virus program

programmer [prɔgrame] **1** *vt* (**a**) *Ordinat* to program; **p. en assembleur** to program in assembly language (**b**) *TV, Rad* (*émission*) to schedule (**c**) (*organiser, mettre au point*) (*vacances, changements*) to plan, to schedule **2** *vi* (**a**) *TV, Rad* to schedule, to draw up a schedule (**b**) *Ordinat* to program

programmeur, -euse [prɔgramœr, -øz] *n Ordinat* programmer; **analyste-p.** systems analyst

progrès [prɔgrɛ] *nm* (**a**) (*avance*) progress; (*d'une armée*) progress, advance; (*d'une épidémie*) progress, spread; (*d'un incendie, d'une inondation*) spread

(**b**) (*d'un élève, d'un malade*) progress, improvement; (*d'une enquête*) progress; **faire des p.** (*d'un élève, d'un malade*) to make progress, to improve; (*dans une enquête*) to make progress *or* headway; *Scol* **il n'a pas fait beaucoup de p.** he hasn't made much progress *or* hasn't improved much; **le malade fait des p. satisfaisants** the patient is making satisfactory progress *or* is progressing satisfactorily; **on guette les moindres p. du malade** the patient is being watched for the slightest signs of progress *or* improvement; **suivre les p. d'un malade/d'un élève** to follow *or* monitor a patient's/pupil's progress; **la science a fait de grands p.** science has made great progress *or* great strides (forward); **suivre les p. d'une science** to keep abreast of a science; **suivre les p. d'une affaire** *Jur* to monitor *or* keep track of a case; *Com* to monitor *or* keep track of a transaction; **être en p.** to be making progress; **il y a un net p. par rapport à l'an dernier** it's a distinct improvement over last year; **un p. sensible vers la démocratie** a significant step *or* advance towards democracy; *F* **il y a du p.** there's been an improvement

(**c**) **le p.** progress; **croire au p.** to believe in progress; **c'est ça, le p.!** that's progress for you!; *Pol* **un parti de p.** a party of progress, a progressive party; **le parti du p.** the party of progress

progresser [prɔgrese] *vi* (**a**) (*avancer*) (*d'une armée*) to advance, to progress; (*d'un marcheur*) to make progress; **p. lentement/rapidement** to make slow/rapid progress

(**b**) (*évoluer*) (*d'une épidémie, d'un incendie*) to spread, to gain ground; **son cancer progresse** his cancer is spreading

(**c**) (*faire des progrès*) (*d'un élève, d'un malade*) to make progress, to make headway, to improve; (*d'un projet*) to progress, to make progress; (*d'un enquête, d'un policier*) to make progress *or* headway; **p. lentement/rapidement** (*dans une étude/des recherches*) to make slow/rapid progress; **p. lentement/rapidement dans la lecture d'un livre** to make slow/rapid progress with a book, to get through a book slowly/quickly

progressif, -ive [prɔgrɛsif, -iv] *adj* progressive; (*amélioration, expansion*) gradual; (*taux*) graduated, increasing; [①A48-50] *Ling* **la forme progressive en anglais** the progressive *or* continuous form in English; **impôt p.** progressive *or* graduated tax

progression [prɔgrɛsjɔ̃] *nf* (**a**) (*avance*) (*d'une armée*) advance, progress; **la p. des marcheurs** the walker's progress

(**b**) (*évolution*) (*d'un incendie, d'une maladie, d'un cancer, d'une épidémie, du sida*) spread; (*de la délinquance, du chômage*) rise; (*d'un secteur économique*) expansion; *Bourse* (*des actions*) rise, improvement; (*dans une carrière*) progress, advancement; (*dans la société*) advancement; (*amélioration*) upturn; **être en p.** (*d'un secteur économique*) to be growing *or* expanding; (*d'une maladie*) to be spreading; (*du chômage, de la criminalité*) to be increasing *or* rising, to be on the increase *or* rise

▶ **progression**: *Math* **p. arithmétique** arithmetical progression; *Mus* **p. harmonique** harmonic progression

progressiste [prɔgrɛsist] *adj, n Pol* progressive

progressivement [prɔgrɛsivmɑ̃] *adv* progressively

progressivité [prɔgrɛsivite] *nf* progressiveness; (*d'impôt*) graduation

prohiber [prɔibe] *vt* to prohibit, to forbid; **l'alcool est prohibé là-bas** alcohol is prohibited *or* forbidden there; **marchandises prohibées** illegal goods; **le port d'armes est prohibé** it is illegal to carry weapons, people are forbidden to carry weapons

prohibitif, -ive [prɔibitif, -iv] *adj* **(a)** *(prix)* prohibitive **(b)** *(loi etc)* prohibitory

prohibition [prɔibisjɔ̃] *nf* prohibition; **la p. du port d'armes** the ban on carrying weapons; *Hist* **pendant la p.** during Prohibition; **p. d'importation** import ban

prohibitionnisme [prɔibisjɔnism] *nm Écon etc* prohibitionism

prohibitionniste [prɔibisjɔnist] *adj, n Écon etc* prohibitionist

proie [prwa] *nf* prey; *(à la chasse)* quarry; **oiseau de p.** bird of prey; **faire sa p. de qch** *(d'un animal)* to prey on sth; *Fig* **une p. facile/des proies faciles** easy prey *or* meat; **être la p. de qn** to be the prey *or* victim of sb; **une partie de la population est la p. de cette maladie** part of the population has fallen victim *or* prey to the disease; **les enfants sont la p. de la publicité** children are the victims of advertising; **la maison fut vite la p. des flammes** the house was soon devoured *or* consumed by the flames; **être en p. aux remords/au doute** to be racked *or* tormented by remorse/doubt, *Litt* to be prey to remorse/doubt; **une personne en p. à des obsessions/des hallucinations** a person prey to obsessions/hallucinations; **tomber en p. à la tentation** to fall prey to temptation

projecteur [prɔʒɛktœr] *nm* **(a)** *Cin, Phot* projector; **p. de diapositives** slide projector; *TV, Cin* **p. de décors** scenic projector; **p. de films** film projector; **p. de télévision** telejector; **p. à arc** brute, arc light; **p. à faisceau concentré** spotlight **(b)** *(lampe)* searchlight; *(sur un bâtiment, sur un monument)* floodlight; *Th* spotlight; *Aut* headlamp, headlight; **illuminé par des projecteurs** floodlit; *Fig* **sous les projecteurs de l'actualité** in the limelight *or* news; *Aut* **p. antibrouillard** fog lamp; **p. halogène** halogen headlight; **p. polyéllipsoïde** poly-ellipsoid headlight; **p. de poursuite** follow spot

projectif, -ive [prɔʒɛktif, -iv] *adj Géom, Psy* projective

projectile [prɔʒɛktil] *nm* projectile; *(autoguidé)* missile

projection [prɔʒɛksjɔ̃] *nf* **(a)** *(fait de projeter)* projection; *(d'un liquide)* splashing; *(de boue)* splashing, splattering; *(de graisse)* spattering; **des projections de boue** splashes *or* splatters of mud; *Géol* **projections volcaniques** volcanic ash, *Spéc* (volcanic) ejecta; *Aut* **p. de gravillons** loose chippings

(b) *Cin, Phot* projection; *Cin (d'un film)* screening, showing; **une p. de diapositives** a slide show; *Cin* **la p. durera 45 minutes** it will take 45 minutes to show the film, the screening will last 45 minutes; **nous avons vu le film en p. privée** we were given a private screening *or* showing (of the film); **appareil de p.** projector; **cabine de p.** projection booth; **p. par transparence** rear projection; **conférence avec projections** lecture (illustrated) with slides

(c) *(de lumière)* beam

(d) *Math, Archit etc* projection, plan; **p. horizontale** ground plan

(e) *(image)* (outward) manifestation; *Psy* projection **(dans** onto); **cette expression est la p. de sa pensée** that expression reveals what he is thinking; *Psy* **faire une p. sur qn** to project oneself onto sb

projectionniste [prɔʒɛksjɔnist] *n Cin* projectionist

projet [prɔʒɛ] *nm* **(a)** *(plan)* plan, project, scheme; *(travaux)*, *Scol, Univ* project; **quels sont vos projets pour cet été?** what are your plans for the summer?; **avoir d'autres projets** to have other plans; **faire des projets** to make plans; **faire des projets d'avenir** to plan *or* make plans for the future; **faire** *ou* **former le p. de faire qch** to plan to do sth; **nous avons fait le p. de partir en Norvège l'an prochain** we're planning on *or* thinking about going to Norway next year; **p. d'entreprise** business plan; **p. d'OPA sur ...** planned takeover of ...

(b) *(d'un bâtiment)* plan; *(d'une machine)* blueprint; **p. de contrat** draft agreement; **p. de budget** draft budget; **p. de loi** bill; **à l'état de p., en p.** at the planning stage; **ça n'est resté qu'à l'état de p.** it never got off the ground

projeter [prɔʒte] *(conj like* **jeter)** **1** *vt* **(a)** *(lancer)* to project; *(graisse)* to spatter; *(liquide)* to splash; *(boue)* to splatter, to splash; *(d'un volcan) (cendres)* to eject, to spew out; **le train projette des gravillons en passant** the train throws up loose stones as it passes; **la poêle chaude projette de la graisse** grease is spattering from the hot frying pan; **être projeté au sol/contre la vitre** to be thrown *or* flung *or* hurled to the ground/against the windscreen

(b) *(ombre)* to cast, to throw

(c) *Cin (film)* to show, to screen

(d) *(voyage, expédition etc)* to plan, to think about; **p. de faire qch** to plan to do sth, to plan on doing sth

(e) *Psy* to project **(sur** onto)

(f) *Math* to project

2 se projeter *vpr* **une ombre s'est projetée sur le mur** a shadow fell *or* was cast on the wall; *Psy* **il se projette sur son fils** he's projecting himself onto his son

projeteur [prɔʒtœr] *nm Tech* planner; *(d'une machine etc)* designer

projo [prɔʒo] *nm F* projector

prolapsus [prɔlapsys] *nm Méd* prolapse

prolétaire [prɔletɛr] *adj, n* proletarian

prolétariat [prɔletarja] *nm* [①A11,g,i] proletariat

prolétarien, -ienne [prɔletarjɛ̃, -jɛn] *adj* proletarian

prolétarisation [prɔletarizasjɔ̃] *nf* proletarianization

prolétariser [prɔletarize] *vt* to proletarianize

prolifération [prɔliferasjɔ̃] *nf* proliferation

prolifère [prɔlifɛr] *adj Biol* proliferous

proliférer [prɔlifere] *vi* **(il prolifère; il proliférera)** to proliferate; **les affichages illégaux prolifèrent** flyposting is on the increase

prolifique [prɔlifik] *adj* prolific

prolixe [prɔliks] *adj* wordy, verbose, *Fml* prolix

prolixement [prɔliksəmɑ̃] *adv* at great length

prolixité [prɔliksite] *nf* verbosity, *Fml* prolixity

prolo [prɔlo] *Péj F* **1** *adj (accent, goûts)* plebby, working-class **2** *n* pleb, prole, oik

prologue [prɔlɔg] *nm* prologue **(de** to)

prolongation [prɔlɔ̃gasjɔ̃] *nf (de discussions)* prolongation, protraction; *(de congé, séjour)* extension, prolongation; *Fb* **jouer les prolongations** to play extra time *or Am* overtime

prolonge [prɔlɔ̃ʒ] *nf Mil* ammunition wagon; **p. d'artillerie** gun carriage *(at military funeral)*

prolongé [prɔlɔ̃ʒe] *adj (absence, séjour)* prolonged, lengthy; **visite très prolongée** very lengthy visit; **soupir p.** long-drawn-out sigh; **applaudissements prolongés** prolonged *or* sustained applause; **éviter tout séjour p. au soleil** do not stay in the sun too long, avoid prolonged exposure to the sun; **rue Crinas prolongée** = continuation of rue Crinas

prolongement [prɔlɔ̃ʒmɑ̃] *nm* **(a)** *(d'une rue etc)* prolongation, continuation; *(d'un mur, d'une voie de chemin de fer)* extension; **je veux installer le frigidaire dans le p. de l'évier** I want the fridge in line with the sink; *Fig* **ce départ était dans le p. de sa toute première décision** the departure was in line with *or* consistent with his original decision **(b) prolongements** *(d'une action etc)* ramifications **(de** of)

prolonger [prɔlɔ̃ʒe] **(je prolongeai(s); n. prolongeons)** **1** *vt (la vie)* to prolong; *(séjour, absence)* to prolong, to extend; *(débat, discours, repas)* to prolong, to draw *or* spin out; *(mur, route, voie ferrée etc)* to extend **(jusqu'à** to, as far as); *Rail* **p. un billet** to extend a ticket; **des écuries prolongent les murs de la maison** stables are built on to the house; *Math* **p. une droite** to continue *or* produce a line

2 se prolonger *vpr (d'une absence, une réunion)* to be prolonged; *(d'une rue etc)* to continue, to extend; *(d'une guerre, d'un film etc)* to go *or* carry on, to continue; **leur visite s'est prolongée jusqu'à minuit** they stayed until midnight; **la soirée ne s'est pas prolongée très tard** the party didn't go on till very late *or* finished quite early; **mais il ne faudrait pas que cela se prolonge** but it mustn't be for too long

promenade [prɔmnad] *nf* **(a)** *(balade)* walk; *(courte)* stroll; *(en voiture)* drive, outing, trip; **faire une p. (à pied)** to go for a walk; **faire une p. en voiture** to go for a drive *or* a run; **faire une p. à bicyclette** to go for a bike ride; **faire une p. à cheval** to go (horse)riding, to go for a ride; **p. en bateau** *(en canot)* row; *(en voilier)* sail; **être en p.** *(à pied)* to be out walking, to be out for a walk; *(à bicyclette)* to be out on a bike ride; *(à cheval)* to be out riding, to be out for a ride; **ils ne sont pas chez eux, ils sont en p.** they've gone out; **faire faire une p. à qn** to take sb (out) for a walk; **l'heure de la p.** *(d'un détenu)* exercise time; *Mil* **p. militaire** route march; *Mus* **concert p.** promenade concert, *Br* prom

(b) *(avenue) (au bord de la mer)* promenade

promener [prɔmne] **(je promène; je promènerai)** **1** *vt* **(a)** *(faire aller, conduire)* **p. qn** *(à pied)* to take sb (out) for a walk; *(en voiture)* to take sb (out) for a drive; **p. le chien** to take the dog for a walk, to walk the dog, to take the dog out; **p. son cheval** to exercise one's horse; **p. des amis à travers Paris** to show *or* take friends round Paris; *F* **cela vous promènera un peu** it'll get you out (of the house) a bit; **p. sa tristesse** to parade one's sadness; **je promenais toujours les mêmes idées sombres** I couldn't shake off my dark thoughts, the same dark thoughts were always with me; *Fig*

il m'a promené de musée en musée he dragged me from museum to museum; *Fig F* **j'ai vraiment l'impression qu'il me promène** I really get the impression that he's having me on *or* taking me for a ride; **j'en ai assez qu'on me promène** I've had enough of being taken for a ride

(b) (*faire aller*) (*sa main*) to run (**sur** over); **p. ses yeux sur** (*liste, texte*) to run one's eye(s) over, to scan; (*salle, foule*) to scan

2 se promener *vpr* **(a)** (*se balader*) to walk; *Ordinat* to browse; **je vais me p.** I'm going (out) for a walk *or* stroll; **se p. en Auvergne** to tour Auvergne; *Ordinat* **se p. dans** (*texte*) to scroll through; (*base de données*) to browse through; *F* (**se** *omitted*) **mener p. les enfants** to take the children (out) for a walk; *F* **envoyer p. qn** to send sb packing, to send sb off with a flea in his/her ear; **va te p.!** get out!, *F* buzz off!, *Am* take a hike!

(b) (*des yeux, des pensées etc*) to wander; *Fig F* **cette vieille chaise s'est promenée dans toute la maison** that old chair has found its way into *or* has been in every room in the house; *F* **pourquoi ce dossier se promène-t-il sur ton bureau?** why is this file lying about on your desk?; *F* **il laisse se p. ses affaires partout** he leaves his things lying about *or* around all over the place

promeneur, -euse [prɔmnœr, -øz] *n* (*dans un parc etc*) stroller, walker; (*randonneur*) walker, rambler

promenoir [prɔmnwar] *nm* promenade, (covered) walk; (*dans une cour de justice etc*) lobby; *Th Vieilli* promenade

promesse [prɔmɛs] *nf* **(a)** (*serment*) promise; *Mktg* claim; **faire une p.** to make a promise; **je vais te faire une p.** I'm going to make you a promise; **tu pourrais me faire une p.?** will you promise me something?; **elle m'a fait la p. de ne plus en parler** she has promised me not to speak of it again; **elle m'avait fait de grandes promesses** she promised me great things; **tenir sa p.** to keep one's promise; **tu as ma p.** you have my word *or* promise; **manquer à sa p.** to break one's promise; *Com* **p. écrite** written promise, written undertaking; **p. de Gascon** empty *or* hollow promise; *Fig* **la p. d'un avenir meilleur** the promise of a better future; *Fig* **ces réunions sont la p. d'une paix future** these meetings hold out the hope of peace; *Fig* **plein de promesses** full of promise, that shows a great deal of promise, very promising; **un avenir plein de promesses** a very promising *or* bright future; *Mktg* **p. mensongère** false claim

(b) *Com etc* undertaking to pay; **p. d'achat/de vente** agreement *or* undertaking to purchase/undertaking *or* promise to sell

Prométhée [prɔmete] *nm* Prometheus

prométhéen, -enne [prɔmeteɛ̃, -ɛn] *adj Litt* Promethean

prometteur, -euse [prɔmɛtœr -øz] *adj* (*artiste, premier roman etc*) promising, full of promise; (*sourire*) full of promise; **des débuts prometteurs** a promising start; **c'est très p.!** it's very promising!

promettre [prɔmɛtr] (*conj like* **mettre**) **1** *vt* **(a)** to promise; **p. qch à qn** to promise sb sth, to promise sth to sb; **je ne peux rien te p.** I can't promise (you), I can't make any promises, I can't guarantee it; **tu (me) le promets?** (do you) promise?; **je (te) le promets!** I promise (you)!; **je te promets de lui en parler** I promise you that I'll talk to him about it, I promise to talk to him about it; **il m'a promis qu'il le ferait** he promised (me) he'd do it; **on promet une forte récompense** a handsome reward is being offered; **le médecin promet un prompt rétablissement** the doctor predicts a speedy recovery; **je te rembourserai, c'est promis** I'll pay you back, I promise; *F* **tu le regretteras, je te le promets!** you'll regret it, mark my words *or* take my word for it; *F* **je m'en souviendrai du 1er mai, je te le promets!** you can take it from me *or* you can take my word for it that I won't forget the first of May; *F* **je vous promets qu'on s'est amusé** we had a really great time

(b) (*faire espérer*) **il promet d'éclipser tous ses rivaux** he looks set *or* he promises to eclipse all his rivals; **la soirée promet d'être amusante** it promises to be an amusing evening; **ça nous promet de gros orages** it looks as if we're in for some violent storms; **ce vent nous promet une mer agitée** we're in for rough seas judging from this wind; **la hausse des taux d'intérêt ne promet rien de bon pour l'industrie** the rise in interest rates does not look good *or* *Fml* does not augur well for industry

2 *vi* (*d'un projet etc*) to look promising; **un enfant qui promet** a child with promise; *F* **ça promet!** (*avant, au début d'une affaire*) that looks promising!; *Iron* great!, terrific!; *Iron* **eh bien, ça promet pour la fin de la semaine!** well then, it looks as if we're in for a great weekend!; *Iron* **vraiment, ça promet pour le reste de la soirée!** well now, the rest of the evening promises to be rather interesting!

3 se promettre *vpr* **(a)** (*à qn d'autre*) to promise (to) each other; **ils se sont promis de ne plus se disputer** they promised (each other) not to *or* that they wouldn't quarrel any more

(b) se p. qch to promise oneself sth

(c) (*décider*) **se p. de travailler** to make up one's mind *or* to resolve to work; **je me suis promis de ne pas pleurer devant lui** I made up my mind *or* I promised myself that I wouldn't cry in front of him

promis, -ise [prɔmi, -iz] **1** *adj* promised; **la Terre promise** the Promised Land; **p. à** destined for; **il est p. à un grand avenir** he is destined for a great future, he has a great future ahead of him **2** *n Vieilli, Région* fiancé, *f* fiancée, betrothed

promiscuité [prɔmiskɥite] *nf* overcrowding; **vivre dans la p.** to live in crowded accommodation; **je ne supportais plus la p. de cet apartement** I couldn't take the overcrowding in the flat any more; **je déteste la p. des transports en commun** I hate the crowding *or* the crowds on public transport; **je ne supporte pas la p.** I can't bear having people around me, I need to be on my own, I need lots of space

promontoire [prɔmɔ̃twar] *nm* promontory, headland; (*plus grand*) cape

promoteur, -trice [prɔmɔtœr, -tris] *n* **(a)** *nm Com* promoter; **p. (immobilier)** property developer **(b)** (*créateur*) originator (**de** of)

promotion [prɔmosjɔ̃] *nf* **(a)** (*avancement*) promotion; *Rel* preferment; **p. à l'ancienneté** promotion by seniority; **p. interne** internal promotion, promotion from within the company; **p. sociale** upward mobility, *Fml* social advancement

(b) *Univ* (students of the same) year, *Am* class; **camarade de p.** fellow student; **le premier de sa p.** the first in his year

(c) *Com* promotion; **articles en p.** items on promotion *or Am* on special; **notre p. de la semaine** this week's special offer *or Am* special; **faire une p. sur un produit** to promote a product; **faire la p. de** to sell, to promote; **faire de la p. immobilière** to go in for property development; **contrat de p. immobilière** property development contract; **p. (en quatrième de couverture)** (back-cover) blurb; *Mktg* **p. auprès des intermédiaires** trade promotion order; *Mktg* **p. collective** tie-in promotion; *Mktg* **p. d'entreprises** corporate identity; *Mktg* **p. par une personnalité** personality promotion; *Mktg* **p. sur le lieu de vente** point-of-sale promotion; *Mktg* **p. sur point d'achat** point-of-purchase promotion; **p. spéciale** special promotion; **p. des ventes** sales promotion

promotionnel, -elle [prɔmosjɔnɛl] *adj Com* (*brochure*) promotional; (*tarif*) special; **vente promotionnelle** special offer

promouvoir [prɔmuvwar] *vt* (*conj like* **mouvoir**) **(a)** (*donner un avancement à*) to promote; **être promu** to be promoted, to get promotion; **elle a été promue chef du personnel** she's been promoted *or* moved up to personnel manager **(b)** *Fig* (*favoriser*) (*recherche, création d'entreprise, relations entre États*) to promote, to further **(c)** *Com* to promote; (*à prix réduit*) to put on special offer *or Am* on special

prompt [prɔ̃] *adj* (*réaction, condamnation*) prompt, quick, swift; (*vengeance*) swift, speedy; **avoir la main prompte** to be quick with one's hands *or* to raise one's hand; **avoir la repartie prompte** to be always ready with an answer, *Fml* to have a ready wit; **nous vous souhaitons un p. rétablissement** we wish you a speedy recovery, get well soon; **esprit p.** quick mind; (*sens de l'humour*) ready wit; **être d'humeur prompte** to be quick-tempered; **il est p. à la colère** *ou* **à se fâcher** he loses his temper *or* flares up easily, *Fml* he is quick to anger; **p. à agir** quick *or* prompt to act; **p. à décider** decisive; **p. à la riposte** quick with a riposte

promptement [prɔ̃tmɑ̃, prɔ̃ptəmɑ̃] *adv Litt* promptly, quickly, swiftly

prompteur® [prɔ̃ptœr] *nm* teleprompt(er)®, autocue®; **p. déroulant** roller prompter

promptitude [prɔ̃tityd] *nf Litt* (*d'une réaction etc*) promptness, quickness, swiftness; **avec toute la p. possible** with all possible dispatch

promu, -ue [prɔmy] **1** *adj* (who has been) promoted **2** *n* person who has been promoted; *Univ* **les nouveaux promus** = this year's graduates (*of a grande école*)

promulgation [prɔmylgasjɔ̃] *nf* (*d'une loi*) promulgation; (*d'un décret*) publication

promulguer [prɔmylge] *vt* (*loi*) to promulgate; (*décret*) to publish, to issue

prône [pron] *nm Rel* sermon, homily

prôner [prone] *vt* (*patience, indulgence, tolérance*) to strongly recommend, to advocate, to urge; (*méthode*) to strongly recommend, to advocate

pronom [prɔnɔ̃] *nm* (①**A26-38; B13-22,6**) *Gram* pronoun; **p.**

défini/indéfini/interrogatif definite/indefinite/interrogative pronoun

pronominal, -ale, -aux, -ales [prɔnɔminal, -o] *adj Gram* pronominal

pronominalement [prɔnɔminalmɑ̃] *adv* pronominally

prononçable [prɔnɔ̃sabl] *adj* pronounceable

prononcé [prɔnɔ̃se] **1** *adj* (*traits*) strong; (*forme*) strong, definite; (*tendance*) marked; (*accent*) broad, strong, pronounced; **courbe prononcée** sharp curve; **avoir un goût p. pour qch** to have a strong *or* distinct taste for sth; **peu p.** (*accent*) faint, slight; (*forme*) indefinite, vague; (*relief*) flattish; **avoir un goût peu p. pour qch** to have little taste for sth **2** *nm Jur* decision; **p. du jugement** verdict

prononcer [prɔnɔ̃se] **(je prononçai(s); n. prononçons) 1** *vt* **(a)** (*dire*) (*mot*) to say, to utter; **il a prononcé quelques paroles sur ...** he said a few words about ...; **c'est à peine s'il prononça quelques paroles** he hardly said a word; **sans p. un mot** without (uttering) a word; **il a prononcé quelques mots entre ses dents** he muttered a few words; **il ne faut jamais p. son nom** you must never mention him *or* his name

(b) (*déclarer*) (*discours*) to deliver, to make; *Jur* (*arrêt*) to deliver; **p. une sentence** to pass *or* pronounce sentence; **p. un divorce** to pronounce *or* declare a couple divorced; *Rel* **p. ses vœux** to take one's vows

(c) (*articuler*) (*mot*) to pronounce; **mal p. un mot** to mispronounce a word

2 *vi* **(a)** (*articuler*) to pronounce (one's words); **apprendre à p.** to learn to pronounce one's words properly, to learn proper pronunciation; **p. bien/mal** to have good/bad pronunciation

(b) *Jur* (*s'exprimer*) to give one's verdict (**sur qch** on sth); **p. en faveur de qn** to decide *or* declare in favour of sb; **p. sur une question** to adjudge *or* adjudicate a question

3 se prononcer *vpr* **(a)** (*être articulé*) to be pronounced; **ça s'écrit comme ça se prononce** it is written as it is pronounced; **comment se prononce ...?** how do you pronounce ...?; **le s ne se prononce pas** the s isn't pronounced, the s is silent

(b) (*apparaître*) (*de différences*) to become more pronounced; (*de rides*) to become more marked

(c) (*s'exprimer*) to give an opinion; (*d'un juge*) to give a decision; **le médecin ne s'est pas encore prononcé** the doctor has not yet given his prognosis; **j'ai mis longtemps avant de me p.** it took me a long time to make up my mind; **50 pour cent ne se prononcent pas** (*dans un sondage*) 50 per cent are undecided; **se p. pour** *ou* **en faveur de qn/qch** to express one's support for sb/sth; **ils se sont prononcés pour** *ou* **en faveur de/contre la construction du barrage** they said they were in favour of/against the dam being built; **se p. contre qn/qch** to express one's opposition to sb/sth

prononciation [prɔnɔ̃sjasjɔ̃] *nf* **(a)** (*articulation*) pronunciation; **défaut de p.** speech defect; **faute de p.** mispronunciation, mistake in pronunciation; **elle a une très bonne/mauvaise p.** her pronunciation is very good/bad **(b)** (*d'un discours*) delivery; *Jur* (*d'une condamnation*) passing; (*d'un divorce*) pronouncement; (*d'un arrêt*) delivering

pronostic [prɔnɔstik] *nm* **(a)** (*prévision*) forecast, prediction, prognosis; **quel est votre p. pour le match/la course?** what's your forecast for the match/race, who do you tip to win the match/race? **(b)** *Méd* prognosis

pronostiquer [prɔnɔstike] *vt* **(a)** (*prévoir*) to forecast, to predict; **je lui pronostique la première place** I predict that he'll come in first, I tip him for first place; **on pronostique qu'elle prendra la première place** she's being tipped for first place **(b)** *Méd* **p. un prompt rétablissement** to predict a speedy recovery

pronostiqueur, -euse [prɔnɔstikœr, -øz] *n* forecaster, pundit; *Sp* tipster

pronunciamento [prɔnunsjamɛnto] *nm Pol* pronunciamento

propagande [prɔpagɑ̃d] *nf Péj* propaganda; *Pol* **faire de la p. pour qn** to electioneer on behalf of sb; **c'est de la p.!** it's propaganda!

propagandiste [prɔpagɑ̃dist] *adj, n* propagandist

propagateur, -trice [prɔpagatœr, -tris] *n* (*de nouvelles*) spreader; (*d'idées*) disseminator

propagation [prɔpagasjɔ̃] *nf* (*d'une plante, d'une espèce*) propagation; (*d'une épidémie, d'une rumeur, d'une nouvelle*) spreading; (*d'idées, d'une doctrine*) spreading, dissemination, *Fml* propagation; *Phys* **la vitesse de p. d'une onde** the velocity of propagation of a wave

propager [prɔpaʒe] **(je propageai(s); n. propageons) 1** *vt* (*plante, espèce*) to propagate; (*épidémie*) to spread; (*rumeur, nouvelle*) to spread, *Litt* to spread abroad; (*idées, doctrine*) to spread, *Fml* to propagate; **p. une mode** to spread *or* popularize a fashion **2 se propager** *vpr* **(a)** (*d'une épidémie etc*) to spread **(b)** *Phys* (*de la lumière, du son*) to be propagated **(c)** *Biol* (*d'une plante etc*) to propagate, to reproduce

propane [prɔpan] *nm Ch* propane

propanier [prɔpanje] *nm Naut* propane tanker

propédeutique [prɔpedøtik] *nf* **(a)** (*enseignement préparatoire*) propaedeutics **(b)** *Univ Vieilli* = first year of university course

propène [prɔpɛn] *nm Tech* propene

propension [prɔpɑ̃sjɔ̃] *nf* propensity, tendency, inclination (**à** to)

propergol [prɔpɛrgɔl] *nm Tech* (rocket) propellant

prophète, prophétesse [prɔfɛt, prɔfetɛs] *n* prophet, *f* prophetess, *Litt* seer; **parler en p.** to prophesy; **p. de malheur** prophet of doom, Jeremiah; **nul n'est p. en son pays** no man is a prophet in his own country

prophétie [prɔfesi] *nf* prophecy

prophétique [prɔfetik] *adj* prophetic

prophétiquement [prɔfetikmɑ̃] *adv* prophetically

prophétiser [prɔfetize] *vt* to prophesy, to foretell

prophylactique [prɔfilaktik] *adj Méd* prophylactic

prophylaxie [prɔfilaksi] *nf Méd* prophylaxis

propice [prɔpis] *adj* propitious (**à** to); (*signe, commencement*) auspicious; (*conditions*) favourable, *US* favorable; **attendre le moment p. pour faire qch** to wait for the right moment to do sth; **cet endroit est p. au repos** it's a restful spot; **un climat p. à la guérison des malades** a good climate for people who are ill; **ce festival est p. aux rencontres** the festival is a good place to meet people; **si la fortune nous est p.** if Fortune smiles on us; **peu p.** unpropitious; (*signe, commencement*) inauspicious; **c'est arrivé à un moment peu p.** it did not come at a very good time

propitiation [prɔpisjasjɔ̃] *nf Rel* propitiation

propitiatoire [prɔpisjatwar] *adj Rel* propitiatory

proportion [prɔpɔrsjɔ̃] *nf* **(a)** [①B56,C] proportion; *Math* ratio; **il a bien respecté les proportions** he got the proportions right; **la p. du tronc et des jambes** the size of the trunk (as) compared with the legs; **varier en p. directe/inverse** to vary in direct proportion *or* ratio/in indirect proportion *or* inverse ratio (**de** to); **p. d'alcool dans un vin** percentage of alcohol in a wine, alcohol content of a wine; **les bénéfices ont augmenté dans une p. de 30 pour cent** profits have risen by 30 per cent; **à p., en p.** proportionally, proportionately, in proportion; **à p. de, en p. de** in proportion to; **payé en p. du travail fourni/des heures passées** paid in proportion to *or* according to the amount of work done/the number of hours; **tout augmente, et les salaires à p.** everything is going up, and salaries are keeping pace; **hors de (toute) p. avec** out of (all) proportion to; *Fig* **cette dispute est sans p. avec son objet** the argument is out of all proportion to the issue; **des travaux hors de p.** work of huge proportions; **toute(s) proportion(s) gardée(s)** up to a point, in certain respects

(b) proportions size, proportions; **salle de vastes proportions** hall of vast proportions *or* dimensions; **dans de plus vastes proportions** on a much larger scale; **si les commandes diminuent dans de sérieuses proportions** if orders should decrease to any great extent; **cette histoire a pris de sérieuses proportions** this business has assumed serious proportions; **pourquoi les choses ont-elles pris de telles proportions?** why have things escalated to such an extent?

proportionné [prɔpɔrsjɔne] *adj* **(a) bien/mal p.** (*corps etc*) well/badly proportioned **(b)** proportionate, proportional (**à** to); (*de la même échelle, du même degré*) commensurate (**à** with); **la cotisation est proportionée à vos revenus** payment is in proportion *or* proportional *or* proportionate to your income; **salaire p. aux qualifications** salary commensurate with qualifications

proportionnel, -elle [prɔpɔrsjɔnɛl] **1** *adj* proportional (**à** to); *Pol* **représentation proportionnelle** proportional representation; *Ordinat* **espacement p.** proportional spacing; **inversement p.** inversely proportional, in inverse ratio (**à** to); **impôt p. (au revenu)** fixed-rate *or* fixed-percentage income tax **2** *nf* **proportionnelle (a)** *Math* proportional **(b)** *Pol* proportional representation; **élu à la proportionnelle** elected by proportional representation

proportionnellement [prɔpɔrsjɔnɛlmɑ̃] *adv* proportionally, proportionately, in proportion (**à** to)

proportionner [prɔpɔrsjɔne] *vt* to adapt, to adjust, to proportion (**à** to); **p. les dépenses aux ressources** to adjust expenditure to suit resources, *F Prov* to cut one's coat according to one's cloth

propos [prɔpo] *nm* **(a)** (*sujet*) subject, matter; **à ce p.** talking of which, while we're on the subject, in connection with that; **à p., avez-vous lu ce livre?** by the way *or* by the by *or* incidentally, have you read this book?; **à tout p.** constantly, at every turn; **dire qch à p.** to say sth to the point, to say sth suitable *or* appropriate; **elle n'est pas du tout intervenue à p.** what she had to say was entirely irrelevant; **vous avez réagi tout à fait à p.** you reacted quite appropriately; **jeté à p., fait à p.** (*mot, remarque*) timely; **faire qch à p.** to do sth at the right moment; **arriver fort à p.** to arrive at just the right moment *or* in the nick of time; **juger à p. de faire qch** to consider it advisable to do sth, to see fit to do sth; **mal à p.** at the wrong time *or* moment, *Fml* inopportunely; **tu ne pouvais pas tomber plus mal à p.** you couldn't have come at a worse time *or Fml* a more inopportune moment; **hors de p.** (*remarque*) irrelevant; **il est intervenu tout à fait hors de p.** what he had to say was entirely irrelevant; **à p. de** about, in connection with, with regard to, on the subject of; **à p. de rien** (*se disputer, se chamailler, s'agiter*) about nothing, for nothing at all, for no reason whatever; **à p. de tout et de rien** about anything and everything; **à p. de quoi?, à quel p.?** what about?; **à quel p. t'a-t-elle dit cela?** what did she say that to you for?; **c'est à quel p.?** what's it about?; **elle veut te voir – à quel p.?** she wants to see you – what about *or* what for?

(b) (*intention*) purpose, intention, resolution; **avoir le ferme p. de faire qch** to firmly intend to do sth, to have the firm intention of doing sth; **de p. délibéré** deliberately, on purpose; **tel n'est pas mon p.** that is not my intention; **ce n'est pas le p.** that's not the point

(c) (*parole*) **des p.** talk, words; **p. méchants/désagréables** nasty/unpleasant remarks; **les p. qu'ils échangèrent sont restés confidentiels** their talk *or* conversation has remained confidential; **des p. de table** table talk; **changer de p.** to change the subject

proposer [prɔpoze] **1** *vt* (*projet, solution, idée, plan d'action etc*) to propose, to suggest; (*théorie*) to propose, to suggest, *Fml* to propound; (*définition, interprétation, lecture d'un texte*) to suggest, to offer, to propose; (*appartement, somme d'argent, travail*) to offer; *Parl* (*amendement, décret, loi*) to table, to propose, to move, to put forward; **mais que propose-t-il d'autre?** but what else does he have to suggest?; **c'est tout ce que tu proposes comme idée?** is that all you have to offer by way of an idea?; **écoutez, voilà ce que je vous propose** listen, this is what I suggest; **allons boire une bière, proposa-t-elle** let's go for a beer, she suggested; **ils (vous) proposent deux semaines aux Seychelles pour une misère** they're offering two weeks in the Seychelles for next to nothing; **le cinéma le César vous propose cette semaine ...** this week at le César: ...; **aujourd'hui le restaurant vous propose comme plat du jour ...** today's special is ...; **p. ses services à qn** to offer *or* volunteer one's services to sb; **je vous en propose 6 000 francs/un bon prix** I'll give you 6,000 francs/a good price for it; **il m'a proposé un bon prix pour la voiture** he offered me a good price for the car; **p. un candidat** to put forward *or* put up *or* propose a candidate; **être proposé pour un emploi** to be suggested *or* proposed *or* recommended for a job; **son nom a été proposé plusieurs fois** his name has been suggested *or* put forward several times; **puis-je vous p. mon parapluie?** would you like *or* can I offer you my umbrella?; **p. que l'on fasse qch** to suggest *or* propose that sth should be done; **je propose que l'on passe d'abord au marché** I suggest going *or* that we go to the market first; **je propose que nous commencions par le problème du Brésil** (*en ouverture de discours*) I propose to start with the problem of Brazil; **je lui ai proposé de venir avec moi** I suggested (to him) that he should come with me; **je vous propose d'attendre jusqu'à ce que ...** I suggest waiting *or* that you should wait until ...; **elle m'a proposé de m'aider** she offered to help me

2 *vi* to propose; **je le laisse p.** I leave him to make the suggestions; **l'homme propose et Dieu dispose** man proposes and God disposes

3 se proposer *vpr* **(a)** (*se présenter*) to come forward, to offer one's services; **se p. comme secrétaire** to offer to act as secretary, to offer one's services *or* oneself as secretary; **se p. pour faire qch** to offer *or* volunteer to do sth

(b) il s'est proposé cet objectif he set himself this objective; **se p. de faire qch** to propose to do sth

proposition [prɔpozisjɔ̃] *nf* **(a)** (*suggestion*) proposal, suggestion, proposition; (*d'emploi*) offer; **faire une p.** to make a suggestion *or* proposal; (*dans une assemblée*) to put *or* propose a motion; **si vous voulez acheter l'appartement, faites-moi une p.** if you want to buy the flat, make me an offer; **il a fait une p. pour l'appartement à 350 000 francs** he made an offer of *or* he offered 350,000 francs for the flat; **si quelqu'un a une p. à faire** if anyone has any suggestions; **je vais vous faire une p.: vous vous occupez de ...** I've got a proposition for you: you deal with ...; **de nombreux réalisateurs lui ont fait des propositions (de film)** lots of directors have offered him films, he's had lots of offers from directors; **faire des propositions à une femme** to proposition a woman; **mettre une p. aux voix** to put a motion to the vote; **sur la p. de** at the suggestion of; **dernière p.** final offer; **p. de loi** bill; **propositions de paix** peace proposals; **p. d'assurance** insurance proposal; *Mktg* **p. d'idées** ideation; **p. de paiement** payment proposal; **p. de prix** price proposal; **p. ferme** firm offer; **p. unique** unique proposition; *Mktg* **p. unique de vente** unique selling proposition, USP

(b) *Phil, Math etc* proposition

(c) [①A3; B1] *Gram* clause; **p. principale/subordonnée/relative** main/subordinate/relative clause; **p. circonstancielle de temps/lieu/but** adverbial clause of time/place/purpose

propre [prɔpr] **1** *adj* [①B10,D,3] **(a)** (*exact*) proper; **signification p. d'un mot** proper meaning of a word; **le mot est ici employé au sens p.** the word is used literally here; **un débile, au sens p. du mot** a mental defective in the true sense of the word; **chercher le mot p.** to try to find the right *or* appropriate word

(b) (*particulier*) characteristic (**à** of), *Fml* peculiar (**à** to); **c'est une technique qui lui est p.** it's a technique that is characteristic of him; **une façon de marcher à lui p.** his own particular *or* characteristic way of walking

(c) (*personnel*) own; **mon p. argent** my own money; **ses idées lui sont propres** his ideas are his own; **c'est par ta p. faute que ...** it's your own fault if ...; **de son p. chef** on one's own, *F* off one's own bat; **voir/entendre qch de ses propres yeux/oreilles** to see/hear sth with one's own eyes/ears; **je le lui ai remis en main(s) propre(s)** I delivered it to him personally; **à remettre en main p.** to be delivered to the addressee in person; **dans votre p. intérêt** in your own interest; **ce sont là ses propres paroles** those are his very words

(d) (*convenable*) appropriate, suitable, proper, fitting; **p. à qch** adapted *or* fitted *or* suited to sth; **un lieu p. aux rencontres** a good place for meeting people; **l'endroit le plus p. au camping** the best *or* most suitable place for camping; **des conditions peu propres à la discussion** conditions that are not very conducive to a discussion; **exercice p. à aiguiser l'intelligence** exercise calculated to sharpen the wits; **p. à rien** good for nothing

(e) (*impeccable*) (*linge, maison, hôtel, Scol copie*) clean; (*bureau, apparence*) neat; (*soigné, bien présenté*) (*travail*) neat, tidy; (*non polluant*) (*moteur, voiture*) clean, non-polluting; **n'utilise pas la serviette de ton frère, ce n'est pas p.!** don't use your brother's towel, it's not hygienic!; **une énergie p.** a clean form of energy; **chambre p. et nette** clean and tidy room; **je n'ai plus rien de p.** I haven't (got) anything clean to wear; **habillé de p.** wearing clean clothes; **p. comme un sou neuf** as clean as a new pin, spick and span; (*personne*) spick and span; **être p. sur soi** to be clean, to have clean habits; *F* **nous voilà propres!** we're in a fine *or* nice mess!; **le chat est un animal très p.** the cat is a very clean animal; **mon bébé était p. à vingt mois** my baby was potty-trained at twenty months; **la pianiste a un jeu très p.** the pianist has a very clean style

(f) *Fig* (*réputation*) spotless; (*conscience*) clear; *F* **elle n'est pas p., son affaire** there's something shady *or F* not quite kosher about the business; **ça ne me paraît pas très p., tout ça** it all seems a bit shady *or* dodgy to me; **ce n'est pas très p., tout ça** (*du point de vue moral*) that's a bit tacky

2 *nm* **(a)** (*d'une nation, d'une personne etc*) property, attribute, characteristic; (*caractère, nature*) nature; **le p. de l'homme** man's distinguishing feature

(b) (*sens propre*) **au p.** in the literal sense; **employer un mot au p.** to use a word in its literal sense *or* literally

(c) avoir qch en p. to possess sth in one's own right; **la maison m'appartient en p.** the house is mine, the house belongs to me; **il a un exemplaire en p.** he has a copy of his own

(d) *Scol* **mettre qch au p.** to make a neat copy of sth, to copy sth out neatly; **recopier qch au p.** to make a fair *or* clean copy of sth, to copy sth (neatly)

(e) c'est du p.! (*saleté*) what a mess!; (*action immorale*) that's not right, *F* that's a bit tacky

(f) ça sent le p. it smells clean; **ça sent le p. dans toute la maison** the whole house smells clean

propre(-)à(-)rien, *pl* **propres(-)à(-)rien** *n* good-for-nothing, *Vieilli* ne'er-do-well

proprement [prɔprəmɑ̃] *adv* **(a)** (*d'une manière propre*) cleanly; **une maison p. tenue** a well-kept house; **p. vêtu** correctly *or* properly dressed; **manger p.** not to make a mess when eating; **mange tes brochettes p.!** don't make a mess with your kebabs!; **tu ne sais pas encore manger p.!** you still can't eat without making a mess!

(b) *F* (*convenablement*) well; (*de façon efficace*) efficiently; (*odieux, ridicule*) thoroughly, altogether, absolutely; **assez p.** tolerably well; *Iron* **se faire renvoyer p.** to be sent packing, to be sent off with a flea in one's ear; **il l'a p. ridiculisée** he made an absolute fool of her; **ils se sont fait p. battre par les concurrents** they were thoroughly *or* well and truly beaten *or F* they were hammered by the other side; **c'est p. scandaleux!** it's an absolute disgrace!

(c) (*avec honnêteté*) (*se conduire*) decently, honourably, fairly; **se tirer d'affaire p.** to get out of a difficult situation with one's honour intact

(d) à p. parler strictly speaking; **pas à p. parler** not exactly; **p. dit** actual; **pierres précieuses p. dites** precious stones according to the strictest definition of the term

(e) (*strictement*) strictly (speaking); **c'est un problème p. urbain** it's purely *or* strictly an inner-city problem

propret, -ette [prɔprɛ, -ɛt] *adj* neat, tidy

propreté [prɔprəte] *nf* **(a)** (*hygiène, soin*) cleanliness; (*des vêtements, de la vaisselle*) cleanness; (*d'une pièce, d'un travail*) neatness, tidiness **(b)** (*de moteur etc*) cleanness

propriétaire [prɔprietɛr] *n* **(a)** (*d'une voiture, d'une propriété etc*) owner; (*d'une entreprise, d'un hôtel*) proprietor, *f* proprietress, owner; **devenir** *ou* **se rendre p. de qch** to acquire sth; **p. (de maison)** householder; **qui est le p. de cette terre?** who owns this land?; **p. foncier** landowner; **être p.** to be a man/woman of property *or* a landowner; (*de maison*) to be a property owner, to have a house *or* home of one's own; **maintenant que vous êtes p.** now that you're a homeowner, now that you own your own home; **vous voulez faire le tour du p.?** would you like a guided tour? **(b)** (*qui loue*) landlord, *f* landlady

propriété [prɔpriete] *nf* **(a)** (*fait de posséder*) ownership, proprietorship; (*chose possédée*) property; (*terres*) property, estate; **une p. de 20 hectares** a 20-hectare estate; **p. privée/publique** private/public property; **titres de p.** title deeds; **p. littéraire** literary property; (*droit*) copyright; **p. artistique** copyright; **p. industrielle** patent rights, industrial property; **p. foncière** landed property, landed estate; **p. foncière (perpétuelle et) libre** freehold; **p. immobilière** property; **propriétés immobilières** real estate, *surtout Am* realty; **p. de l'Etat** government property; *Fin* **p. allégée, p.-loisirs, p.-vacances** timeshare taken on a lease basis converting to ownership after a certain period

(b) (*d'un métal, d'une plante etc*) property, characteristic, peculiar quality

(c) (*de mot etc*) correctness, appropriateness

proprio [prɔprio] *nm F* landlord

propulser [prɔpylse] **1** *vt* to propel **2 se propulser** *vpr F* to shoot; **il s'est propulsé dans le bureau du patron** he shot off to the boss's office; **se p. au sommet de la gloire** to shoot to the heights of fame; **se p. en tête du peloton** to shoot to the front of the pack

propulseur [prɔpylsœr] **1** *adj* propellent, propulsive, propelling; **gaz p.** propellant, propellent **2** *nm* **(a)** *Av etc* propeller; **p. à hélice** screw propeller **(b)** (*gaz*) propellant, propellent

propulsif, -ive [prɔpylsif, -iv] *adj* = **propulseur 1**

propulsion [prɔpylsjɔ̃] *nf* propulsion, propelling; **réacteur de p.** propulsion jet; **sous-marin à p. nucléaire** nuclear-powered submarine; **véhicule à p. électrique** electrically powered vehicle; *Aut* **p. arrière** rear-wheel drive

propylène [prɔpilɛn] *nm Ch* propylene

prorata [prɔrata] *nm inv* proportional part, proportion; **paiement au p.** payment pro rata; **au p. de qch** in proportion to sth

prorogatif, -ive [prɔrɔgatif, -iv] *adj* proroguing

prorogation [prɔrɔgasjɔ̃] *nf* **(a)** *surtout Jur* extension; (*de séance*) adjournment **(b)** (*de parlement*) prorogation

proroger [prɔrɔʒe] *vt* **(je prorogeai(s); n. prorogeons)** **(a)** (*contrat, bail*) to extend; **p. une échéance** to extend payment terms **(b)** (*parlement*) to prorogue; (*séance*) to adjourn

prosaïque [prozaik] *adj* prosaic, commonplace, pedestrian

prosaïquement [prozaikmɑ̃] *adv* prosaically

prosaïsme [prozaism] *nm* prosaic nature *or* quality, prosaicness

prosateur [prozatœr] *nm* prose writer

proscenium [prɔsenjɔm] *nm Th* **(a)** (*avant-scène*) proscenium, apron **(b)** *Antiq* proscenium (arch)

proscription [prɔskripsjɔ̃] *nf* (*d'une personne*) outlawing, *Fml* proscription; (*d'un mot, d'un usage*) outlawing, banning

proscrire [prɔskrir] *vt* (*conj like* **écrire**) (*personne*) to outlaw, *Fml* to proscribe; (*mot, usage*) to outlaw, to ban, *Fml* to proscribe; **p. qn de la société** to ostracize sb; **p. un mot de son vocabulaire** to banish a word from one's vocabulary

proscrit, -ite [prɔskri, -it] **1** *adj* (*personne*) outlawed, *Fml* proscribed; (*mot, usage*) outlawed, banned, *Fml* proscribed **2** *n* outlaw

prose [proz] *nf* prose; **en p.** (*écrire*) in prose; (*texte, poème*) prose; *F Hum* **j'ai lu sa p.** I've read his literary masterpiece

prosélyte [prɔzelit] *n* proselyte; *Fig* convert; *Fig* **faire des prosélytes** to make *or* gain converts

prosélytisme [prɔzelitism] *nm* proselytism, proselytizing; **faire du p.** to proselytize

prosodie [prɔzɔdi] *nf* prosody

prosodique [prɔzɔdik] *adj* prosodic

prospect [prɔspɛ] *nm* prospective customer, prospect; *Mktg* **prospects à forte potentialité** hot prospect pool

prospecter [prɔspɛkte] *vt* **(a)** *Min* to prospect **(b)** *Com* (*client*) to canvass; (*marché*) to explore; **p. la clientèle** to canvass for new business

prospecteur, -trice [prɔspɛktœr, -tris] *n* **(a)** *Min* prospector **(b)** *Com* canvasser

prospectif, -ive [prɔspɛktif, -iv] *adj* prospective; **analyse prospective** (*en affaires*) forecast

prospection [prɔspɛksjɔ̃] *nf* **(a)** *Min* prospecting **(b)** *Com* canvassing; *Mktg* prospecting; **faire de la p.** to explore the market; **p. téléphonique** telephone marketing

prospectus [prɔspɛktys] *nm* **(a)** *Bourse* prospectus **(b)** (*de publicité*) leaflet; (*de plusieurs pages*) brochure; (*donnant renseignements de base*) factsheet

prospère [prɔspɛr] *adj* (*ville, région*) prosperous, thriving, flourishing; (*personne, année*) prosperous; (*santé*) glowing; **les années prospères de sa vie** the prosperous period in his life, his years of prosperity

prospérer [prɔspere] *vi* **(je prospère; je prospérerai)** (*d'une personne*) to prosper, to do well; (*d'une société, d'un pays*) to prosper, to thrive, to do well

prospérité [prɔsperite] *nf* prosperity, prosperousness; *Com* **vague de p.** boom; **en période de p.** in times of prosperity, in prosperous times; **cette industrie est en pleine p.** the industry is thriving

prostaglandine [prɔstaglɑ̃din] *nf Méd* prostaglandin

prostate [prɔstat] *nf Anat* prostate (gland)

prostatique [prɔstatik] **1** *adj Anat* prostatic **2** *nm* prostate sufferer

prosternation [prɔstɛrnasjɔ̃] *nf Litt* prostration; *Fig Péj* kowtowing

prosterné [prɔstɛrne] *adj* prostrate

prosternement [prɔstɛrnəmɑ̃] *nm* prostration; (*état*) prostrate attitude

prosterner (se) [səprɔstɛrne] *vpr* (*se courber*) to prostrate oneself (**devant** before); *Fig Péj* (*s'abaisser*) to grovel, to kowtow (**devant** to)

prostituée [prɔstitɥe] *nf* prostitute

prostituer [prɔstitɥe] **1** *vt* (*personne, talent etc*) to prostitute **2 se prostituer** *vpr* to prostitute oneself

prostitution [prɔstitysjɔ̃] *nf* prostitution; *Fig* **c'est de la p.** (*ton attitude*) you're just prostituting yourself

prostration [prɔstrasjɔ̃] *nf* **(a)** prostration **(b)** *Méd* (nervous) exhaustion

prostré [prɔstre] *adj* prostrate; *Fig* **notre économie est prostrée** our economy is on its knees

protagoniste [prɔtagɔnist] *nm* protagonist

prote [prɔt] *nm Typ* foreman

protecteur, -trice [prɔtɛktœr, -tris] **1** *n* **(a)** (*personne*) protector; *Can Admin* **Bureau du p. du citoyen** Office of the Ombudsman

(b) (*des arts etc*) patron, *f* patroness

2 *nm* protector, shield; (*pour machine-outil etc*) guard

3 *adj* (*appareil, tarif, vêtements etc*) protective; *Péj* (*ton etc*) patronizing, condescending; **il est très p. avec ses enfants** he is very protective towards his children; **crème protectrice** skin cream (*for protection against the elements*); **société protectrice des animaux** = society for the prevention of cruelty to animals; **des mesures économiques protectrices** measures designed to protect the economy

protection [prɔtɛksjɔ̃] *nf* **(a)** protection (**contre** from, against); (*de l'environnement etc*) protection, conservation; **p. civile** civil defence; **p. de l'enfance** child welfare; **ne t'inquiète pas, tu es sous ma p.** don't worry, I'll protect *or* shield you; **seul le préservatif assure une bonne p.** only the condom provides any protection; **sous la p. de la police** under police protection; **de p.** (*écran, visière, vernis*) protective; **dispositif de p.** safety device, protective device; *Can Admin* **Commissaire à la p. de la vie privée** Privacy

Commissioner; *Ordinat* **p. d'accès logique** logical access protection; **p. de bloc** block protection; **p. contre l'écriture** write-protection; **p. contre la copie** copy protection; **p. de fichiers** file protection; **p. par mot de passe** password protection; *Aut* **p. de phare** lamp guard

(**b**) (*patronage*) patronage; (*mécenat*) (*des arts etc*) patronage, sponsorship; **prendre qn sous sa p.** to take sb under one's wing; *Péj* **par p.** through patronage *or* influence

protectionnisme [prɔtɛksjɔnism] *nm Écon* protectionism

protectionniste [prɔtɛksjɔnist] *adj, n* protectionist

protectorat [prɔtɛktɔra] *nm* protectorate

protégé, -ée [prɔteʒe] **1** *adj* protected; **p. contre l'inflation** inflation-proof; *Ordinat* **p. contre la copie** copy-protected; **p. en écriture** write-protected; **p. par mot de passe** password-protected; *Aut* **'passage p.'** = priority (over vehicles entering from minor road ahead) **2** *n* (*jeune artiste, sportif etc*) protégé, *f* protégée

protège-cahier, *pl* **protège-cahiers** [prɔtɛʒkaje] *nm* exercise-book cover

protège-dents [prɔtɛʒdɑ̃] *nm inv Boxe* gum shield

protéger [prɔteʒe] (**je protège, n. protégeons; je protégeai(s); je protégerai**) **1** *vt* (**a**) (*personne, peau, mains, Écon industrie etc*) to protect (**contre** from); *Bourse* (*position*) to hedge; **p. une maison du froid/de l'humidité** to protect a house against *or* from the cold/dampness; **les arbres protègent la maison du vent** the trees shelter the house from the wind; **c'est pour p. son frère qu'elle a dit cela** she said it in order to protect *or* shield her brother; **p. qn contre un danger** to shield sb from danger; **p. une invention par un brevet** to patent an invention; **les verres fumés protègent bien les yeux** tinted lenses offer good protection for the eyes; **cet écran total vous protègera parfaitement** this sun block will provide complete protection; **on la protège en haut-lieu** she has friends in high places; **p. les droits acquis** to protect *or* defend hard-won rights; **que Dieu vous protège!** God keep you!; *Ordinat* **p. contre l'écriture** *ou* **en écriture** to write-protect; **p. contre la copie** to copy-protect

(**b**) (*arts etc*) to patronize, to be a patron of; (*artiste*) to be a patron of

2 se protéger *vpr* to protect oneself; **l'usage du préservatif est le seul moyen de se p.** a condom is the sole means of protection *or* the only way you can protect yourself; **ils doivent absolument prendre l'habitude de se p.** (*du sida etc*) they must get into the habit of taking precautions *or* into the habit of safe sex; **se p. de** *ou* **contre** (*intempéries, soleil*) to protect *or* shield oneself from; (*maladie, excès de confiance en soi*) to guard against

protège-slip, *pl* **protège-slips** [prɔtɛʒ(ə)slip] *nm* panty-liner

protège-tibia, *pl* **protège-tibias** [prɔtɛʒtibja] *nm Sp* shin guard

protège-tympan [prɔtɛʒtɛ̃pɑ̃] *nm inv* earplug

protéiforme [prɔteifɔrm] *adj* protean

protéine [prɔtein] *nf* protein; **surveiller les protéines dans son alimentation** to watch one's protein intake; **alimentation faible/riche en protéines** food that is low/high in protein, low-/high-protein food

protéique [prɔteik] *adj Ch* proteinic, proteinous, proteinaceous

protestable [prɔtɛstabl] *adj Jur* which may be protested; *Fin* protestable

protestant, -ante [prɔtɛstɑ̃, -ɑ̃t] *adj, n Rel* Protestant

protestantisme [prɔtɛstɑ̃tism] *nm Rel* Protestantism; (*ensemble des protestants*) Protestant churches, Protestant community

protestataire [prɔtɛstatɛr] **1** *adj* (*lettre etc*) of protest **2** *n* protester, protestor

protestation [prɔtɛstasjɔ̃] *nf* (**a**) (*affirmation*) protestation, declaration, affirmation; **protestations** protestations; **faire une p.** *ou* **des protestations d'innocence/d'amour** to protest *or* declare one's innocence/love; **ses protestations d'amour** his protestations *or* declaration of love

(**b**) (*reproche, déclaration opposée*) protest; **voulez-vous signer notre p.?** will you sign our protest?; **émettre des protestations** to protest; **élever des protestations énergiques** to protest strongly; **paroles/geste de p.** words/gesture of protest; **réunion/manifestation/vote de p.** protest meeting/demonstration/vote; **démissioner en signe de p.** to resign in protest

protester [prɔteste] **1** *vi* to protest; **p. contre** (*une injustice, une décision*) (*en manifestant*) to protest *or* make a protest about *or* against, *Am* to protest; **p. contre une décision** (*devant la justice*) to challenge a ruling; **elle a protesté auprès du directeur** she complained to the manager; **p. de** (*son innocence, sa bonne foi*) to protest **2** *vt* (*affirmer*) to protest

protêt [prɔtɛ] *nm Com, Jur* protest; **dresser un p.** to make a protest

prothèse [prɔtɛz] *nf* (**a**) *Chir* prosthetics, prosthesis (**b**) (**appareil de**) **p.** prosthesis; **p. auditive** hearing aid; **p. dentaire** (*complète*) false teeth, denture(s); (*partielle*) bridge, *Spéc* dental prosthesis

prothésiste [prɔtezist] *n* prosthesis maker

prothétique [prɔtetik] *nf* prosthetics

protide [prɔtid] *nm* protein

protocolaire [prɔtɔkɔlɛr] *adj* formal, pertaining to protocol *or* etiquette; **clauses protocolaires d'accord** formal provisions of agreement

protocole [prɔtɔkɔl] *nm* (**a**) (*procédés diplomatiques*) protocol; (*usage*) etiquette, formalities, social conventions; **le chef du p.** the chief of protocol; **p. d'accord** protocol of agreement; (*contrat*) outline agreement (**b**) *Typ* list of proof-reading symbols (**c**) *Ordinat* protocol; (*de réseau*) frame format; (*de traitement etc*) procedure; **p. de transmission** transmission protocol; **p. de téléchargement** download protocol

protoétoile [prɔtoetwal] *nf Astron* protostar

protohistoire [prɔtoistwar] *nf* protohistory

proton [prɔtɔ̃] *nm Nucl* proton

protoplasma [prɔtɔplasma] *nm*, **protoplasme** [prɔtɔplasm] *nm Biol* protoplasm

prototype [prɔtɔtip] *nm* prototype

protoxyde [prɔtɔksid] *nm Ch* monoxide; **p. d'azote** nitrous oxide

protozoaire [prɔtɔzɔɛr] *nm Zool* protozoan, protozoon; **les protozoaires** the Protozoa

protractile [prɔtraktil] *adj* protractile

protrusion [prɔtryzjɔ̃] *nf* protrusion

protubérance [prɔtyberɑ̃s] *nf* protuberance; (*sur bâton etc*) knob; *Anat* (*sur le crâne*) bump

protubérant [prɔtyberɑ̃] *adj* protuberant

protuteur, -trice [prɔtytœr, -tris] *n Jur* (*d'un mineur*) acting guardian

prou [pru] *adv* **peu ou p.** more or less

proue [pru] *nf* (*de navire*) prow, stem, bow(s)

prouesse [pruɛs] *nf* (**a**) *Litt* (*acte héroïque*) deed of valour *or US* valor (**b**) (*en sport etc*) feat, achievement; *Iron* **quelle p.!** that's quite a feat *or* an achievement!; **faire des prouesses** to do the impossible, to work miracles; **j'ai dû faire des prouesses pour le convaincre** it took everything I had *or* I had to work very hard to convince him

prouvable [pruvabl] *adj* provable; **c'est facilement/difficilement p.** it's easy/difficult to prove

prouver [pruve] **1** *vt* (**a**) (*établir comme vrai*) (*fait*) to prove; **la police n'a rien pu p.** the police couldn't prove anything; **p. le bien-fondé d'une réclamation** to substantiate a claim, to prove the merits of a claim; **cela reste à p.** it still has to be proved; **elle dit qu'elle est experte mais cela reste à p.** she says she's an expert but that remains to be seen; **son dévouement n'est plus à p.** he has proved his devotion; **p. qch par A plus B** to prove sth in a logical fashion; **p. qch à qn** to prove sth to sb, to give sb proof of sth; **il y était aussi – prouve-le-moi!** he was there too – prove it!; **peux-tu me p. le contraire?** can you convince me otherwise *or* any differently?

(**b**) (*être la preuve de*) to prove, to show; **ce qui prouve qu'on aurait dû écouter ce que je disais** which only goes to show that you should have listened to me

2 se prouver *vpr* (**a**) (*à soi-même*) to prove to oneself; **que cherche-t-il à se p.?** what's he trying to prove to himself?

(**b**) (*mutuellement*) **nous nous sommes prouvé que les deux versions étaient correctes** we proved to each other that both versions were correct

(**c**) (*pouvoir être prouvé*) **ça ne se prouve pas** (*c'est une intuition*) you can't prove it, it's not the sort of thing you can prove

provenance [prɔvnɑ̃s] *nf* source, origin; **de p. anglaise** of English origin, English in origin; **marchandise de p. italienne** Italian merchandise, merchandise from Italy; **pays de p.** country of origin; **train en p. de Bordeaux** train from Bordeaux

provençal, -ale, -aux, -ales [prɔvɑ̃sal, -o] **1** *adj* Provençal, of Provence **2** *nm Ling* Provençal **3** *n* **P.** person from Provence

provende [prɔvɑ̃d] *nf* (*pour élevage*) fodder, provender

provenir [prɔvnir] *vi* (*conj like* **venir**) **p. de** to come from; (*tirer son origine de*) to originate in; **d'où provient cet argent?** where does this money come from?; **des produits provenant du Japon** products from Japan; **des vins provenant des meilleurs crûs** wines from the best vintages; **les difficultés qui proviennent de cette situation** the difficulties arising from *or* out of the situation; *Jur* **les enfants provenant** *ou* **provenus de ce mariage** the children issuing from this marriage, the children of this marriage

proverbe [prɔvɛrb] *nm* proverb; **passer en p.** to become a proverb

proverbial, -ale, -aux, -ales [prɔvɛrbjal, -o] *adj* proverbial; (*beauté, sagesse, bonté, intelligence etc*) legendary, proverbial

proverbialement [prɔvɛrbjalmɑ̃] *adv* proverbially

providence [prɔvidɑ̃s] *nf* providence; **c'est un secret de la p.** it's in the hands of providence; **être la p. de qn** (*d'une personne*) to be sb's guardian angel; **cette auberge est la p. des marcheurs** the inn is a godsend for walkers; **ce centre de conseils fut notre p.** the advice centre was a godsend *or* was heaven-sent; **l'État P.** the Welfare State

providentiel, -elle [prɔvidɑ̃sjɛl] *adj* (*aide, rencontre etc*) providential, heaven-sent; **par une circonstance providentielle** by an act of providence

providentiellement [prɔvidɑ̃sjɛlmɑ̃] *adv* providentially

province [prɔvɛ̃s] **1** *nf* **(a) la p.** the provinces; (*la campagne*) the country; **sa p. (d'origine)** the part of the country where he was born, *Litt, Hum* his native heath; **ca n'arriverait jamais dans ma p.** that type of thing would never happen where I come from; **elle s'est perdue dans le métro, elle arrive de sa p.** she got lost in the metro, she's new in town; **en p.** in the provinces; **aller en p.** to go to the country; **de p.** provincial; **vie de p.** provincial life, life in the provinces; *Péj* **mentalité de p.** small-town *or* provincial mentality

(b) *Admin* province; *Can Géog* **les Provinces Maritimes** the Maritime Provinces, *F* the Maritimes

2 *adj inv F Péj* (*attitude, personne*) provincial, parochial; (*air*) provincial

provincial, -ale, -aux, -ales [prɔvɛ̃sjal, -o] **1** *adj* provincial; *Péj* (*manières*) provincial, countrified; (*mentalité, attitude*) provincial, parochial; **la vie provinciale** provincial life, life in the provinces; **manières provinciales** small-town *or* provincial ways **2** *n* provincial; **une jeune provinciale** a small-town girl, a girl from the provinces

provincialisme [prɔvɛ̃sjalism] *nm Ling* provincialism

provirus [provirys] *nm Méd* provirus

proviseur [prɔvizœr] *nm Scol* (*d'un lycée*) headmaster, *f* headmistress

provision [prɔvizjɔ̃] *nf* **(a)** (*de pain, bois, nourriture*) supply, stock, store; (*d'eau*) supply; **faire des provisions** *ou* **faire p. de qch** to stock up on sth, to lay in a supply *or* stock of sth; **nos provisions d'eau/de bois** our water/wood supply; **faire ses provisions** to go shopping; **provisions de guerre** munitions; *Vieilli* **provisions de bouche** food; **placard à provisions** store cupboard; **sac à provisions** shopping bag

(b) *Com* funds; **verser une p.** *ou* **des provisions** to pay a deposit; **faire p. pour une lettre de change** to provide for a bill; **insuffisance de p.** (*pour honorer un chèque etc*) insufficient funds; **chèque sans p.** bad *or F* dud *or* rubber cheque, cheque that bounces/bounced; **faire un chèque sans p.** to write out a bad *or F* dud cheque; **il m'a fait un chèque sans p.** his cheque bounced; **un demi-mois de loyer par p.** a deposit of two weeks' rent; *Compta* **p. pour dépréciation** provision for depreciation, allowance for depreciation; **p. pour risques et charges** contingency and loss provision; *Fin* **provisions réglementées** regulated provisions

(c) *Jur* retainer

provisionnel, -elle [prɔvizjɔnɛl] *adj Jur* provisional, interim; **tiers p.** = instalment (*of taxes*)

provisoire [prɔvizwar] **1** *adj* (*arrêt*) temporary, provisional; (*arrangement, solution etc*) temporary, provisional, interim; **elle gère le centre, mais c'est p.** she manages the centre but it's a temporary arrangement, she's managing the centre but it's only on a temporary basis; **nommé à titre p.** appointed provisionally; **dividende p.** interim dividend; **habitation p.** emergency *or* temporary accommodation; *Jur* **détention p.** (temporary) custody; *Jur* **être en liberté p.** to be (out) on bail, to have been released on bail; **mis en liberté p.** released on bail

2 *nm* **ça n'est que du p.** it's only temporary, it's only for the time being; **il s'est installé dans le p.** he's got used to living on a day-to-day basis; **je ne veux plus vivre dans le p.** I'm tired of living in uncertainty

provisoirement [prɔvizwarmɑ̃] *adv* provisionally, temporarily

provitamine [prɔvitamin] *nf Biol, Ch* provitamin

provocant [prɔvɔkɑ̃] *adj* **(a)** (*agressif*) (*paroles, langage, attitude*) provocative **(b)** (*sourire, robe*) provocative; **d'une manière provocante** provocatively

provocateur, -trice [prɔvɔkatœr, -tris] **1** *adj* (*sourire*) provocative; (*attitude*) provocative, challenging; **agent p.** agent provocateur **2** *n* troublemaker, agitator

provocation [prɔvɔkasjɔ̃] *nf* **(a)** (*défi*) provocation; **un ton/air de p.** a challenging tone/look, a tone/look of provocation; **elle le fait par p.** she does it to provoke, she's being provocative; **il te l'a dit par p.** he said it to provoke you; **c'est de la p.!** it's deliberate provocation!; **p. en duel** challenge to a duel **(b)** *Jur* instigation; **p. au crime** incitement to crime

provoquer [prɔvɔke] **1** *vt* **(a)** (*défier, sexuellement*) to provoke; **p. qn en duel** to challenge sb to a duel; *F* **tu me provoques, toi!** you're starting to get up my nose!

(b) (*inciter*) (*crime, violence*) to instigate; **p. les jeunes à la violence/au crime** to incite young people to violence/to crime

(c) (*effet*) to have; (*stupeur, incendie, mort*) to cause; (*malaise, crise cardiaque*) to cause, *F* to bring on; *Méd* (*sommeil, des vomissements*) to induce; (*critique*) to provoke, to give rise to, to generate; (*réaction*) to provoke, to produce; (*jalousie, ressentiment*) to arouse; (*courant d'air*) to cause, to create; **un coma provoqué par la drogue** a drug-induced coma; **il faut p. l'accouchement** we'll have to induce you/her *or* labour

2 se provoquer *vpr* to provoke each other

proxénète [prɔksenɛt] *n* pimp, *Litt, Arch* pander; *Jur* procurer, *f* procuress

proxénétisme [prɔksenetism] *nm* pimping; *Jur* procuring

proximité [prɔksimite] *nf* proximity, nearness, closeness; (*d'un événement*) imminence, proximity; **j'apprécie la p. de la ville** I appreciate the fact that the town is nearby *or* is within easy reach; **la p. du mariage rend la famille nerveuse** the family is nervous because the wedding is getting close; **p. de parenté** near relationship; **à p.** close by, near at hand; **à p. de qch** near sth, close to sth, in the vicinity of sth

proyer [prwaje] *nm* (*oiseau*) **(bruant) p.** bunting

prude [pryd] *Péj* **1** *adj* prudish **2** *nf* prude; **ne fais pas la p.!** don't be so prudish!, don't be such a prude!

prudemment [prydamɑ̃] *adv* prudently, carefully, cautiously

prudence [prydɑ̃s] *nf* prudence, carefulness, cautiousness, caution; (*d'un conducteur*) cautiousnessness; **avec p.** (*agir*) cautiously, prudently; (*conduire*) carefully; **on conseille la p.** caution is advised; **son excès de p. l'exaspérait** she was sick of his overcautiousness; **donner des conseils de p. à qn** to advise sb to be cautious; **par (mesure de) p.** as a precaution; **par p., je n'ai pas voulu lui en parler tout de suite** I thought it wiser not to speak of it to him right away; *Prov* **p. est mère de sûreté** discretion is the better part of valour; *Litt* **des prudences** precautionary measures

prudent [prydɑ̃] *adj* (*personne*) careful, cautious, prudent; (*conducteur*) careful, cautious; (*décision etc*) wise, sensible, prudent; (*ligne de conduite*) prudent, advisable; **on n'est jamais trop p.** you can't be too careful; **vous avez raison, c'est plus p.** you're right, it's wiser *or* more sensible; **j'ai jugé p. de le prévenir tout de suite** I thought it wise *or* sensible to let him know right away; **un homme très p. en affaires** a very cautious businessman; **il faut être p. de ne pas décider trop vite** we must be careful not to decide too quickly; **attention brouillard, soyez prudents** fog warning, drive cautiously

pruderie [prydri] *nf Péj* prudery, prudishness

prud'homme [prydɔm] *nm Ind Jur* industrial arbitrator; **conseil des prud'hommes** conciliation board; **aller aux** *ou* **devant les prud'hommes** ≈ to go before an industrial tribunal

prudhommerie [prydɔmri] *nf Péj* pomposity, sententiousness

pruine [prɥin] *nf* (*sur fruit*) bloom

prune [pryn] **1** *nf* (*fruit*) plum; (*liqueur*) plum brandy; **p. de Damas** damson; *Fig F* **pour des prunes** for nothing; **travailler pour des prunes** to work for nothing *or* for peanuts; **si j'y suis allée, ce n'est pas pour des prunes!** I didn't go just for the fun *or* hell of it!; *Fig F* **tu crois qu'elle m'en donnerait? – des prunes!** do you think she'll let me have some? – no way! *or* no fear! *or* not bloody likely!; **et qu'est-ce que j'ai reçu en remerciements? des prunes!** and what did I get by way of thanks? not a bloody thing! **2** *adj inv* plum(-coloured *or US* -colored)

pruneau, -eaux [pryno] *nm* **(a)** (*fruit*) prune **(b)** *Arg* (*balle*) slug, bullet

prunelle [prynɛl] *nf* **(a)** (*fruit*) sloe; **(liqueur de) p.** sloe gin **(b)** *Anat* (*des yeux*) pupil; *Fig* **j'y tiens comme à la p. de mes yeux** it's the apple of my eye, it's my pride and joy; *F* **jouer de la p.** to flutter one's eyelashes

prunellier [prynelje] *nm* blackthorn, sloe (bush)

prunier [prynje] *nm* plum tree; *F* **secouer qn comme un p.** to give sb a good shaking, *F* to shake sb till his/her teeth rattle; *Fig* to give sb a good telling-off, to tear sb off a strip; *F* **arrête de me secouer comme un p.** stop shaking me like that

prunus [prynys] *nm* (*arbre*) prunus, Japanese flowering cherry

prurigineux, -euse [pryriʒinø, -øz] *adj Méd* which causes itching, *Spéc* pruritic
prurit [pryrit] *nm Méd* itching, *Spéc* pruritus
Prusse [prys] *nf Hist* Prussia; **bleu de P.** Prussian blue; *Fig F* **travailler pour le roi de P.** to work for nothing *or* for peanuts
prussiate [prysjat] *nm Ch* cyanide
prussien, -ienne [prysjɛ̃, -jɛn] *Hist* **1** *adj* Prussian **2** *n* **P.** Prussian
prytanée [pritane] *nm* military school (*for sons of officers*)
PS [peɛs] *nm* **(a)** *abrév* = **Parti socialiste (b)** (*abrév* **post-scriptum**) P.S.
psallette [psalɛt] *nf* choir school
psalmiste [psalmist] *nm* psalmist
psalmodie [psalmɔdi] *nf* **(a)** *Rel* psalmody **(b)** (*déclamation, formule monotone*) droning
psalmodier [psalmɔdje] (*pr sub, impf* **n. psalmodiions, v. psalmodiiez**) **1** *vt* **(a)** *Rel* (*office etc*) to intone, to chant **(b)** (*dire avec monotonie*) to drone out, to recite monotonously **2** *vi* **(a)** *Rel* to intone, to chant **(b)** (*parler avec monotonie*) to drone (on *or* away)
psaltérion [psalterjɔ̃] *nm Mus* psaltery
psaume [psom] *nm* psalm
psautier [psotje] *nm Mus* psalter, psalm book
pseudo- [psødo] *préf* pseudo-; **des p.-intellectuels** pseudo-intellectuals; **un p.-médecin** a quack, a bogus *or* fake doctor
pseudo-membrane, *pl* **pseudo-membranes** *nf Méd* pseudomembrane, false membrane
pseudonyme [psødɔnim] *nm* pseudonym; **prendre un p.** to adopt a pseudonym; **elle a pris un p.** (*cette écrivain*) she writes under a pseudonym
pseudo-rubis *nm inv Minér* rose quartz
pseudo-saphir, *pl* **pseudo-saphirs** *nm Minér* blue quartz
psi [psi] *nm* psi
psitt [psit] *int* psst!
psittacose [psitakoz] *nf Méd, Vét* psittacosis
psoriasis [psɔrjazis] *nf Méd* psoriasis
pst [pst] *int* psst!
psy [psi] *F* **1** *adj* = **psychiatrique, psychologique, psychanalytique 2** *nf* = **psychiatrie, psychologie, psychanalyse 3** *n* (*psychologue, psychanalyste*) shrink, *Péj* trick cyclist
psychanalyse [psikanaliz] *nf* (*domaine*) psychoanalysis; (*traitement*) (psycho)analysis; **faire une p.** to be in *or* undergoing (psycho)analysis; **commencer une p.** to start analysis, to go into (psycho)analysis; **il a fait une p. pendant cinq ans** he was in (psycho)analysis for five years; **faire de la p.** to psychoanalyse people
psychanalyser [psikanalize] *vt* (*personne, rêves etc*) to (psycho)analyse; **se faire p.** to be (psycho)analysed
psychanalyste [psikanalist] *n* psychoanalyst
psychanalytique [psikanalitik] *adj* psychoanalytical; **école p.** school of psychoanalysis
psyché [psiʃe] *nf* **(a)** *Myth* **P.** Psyche **(b)** *Phil* psyche **(c)** (*miroir*) cheval glass
psychédélique [psikedelik] *adj* psychedelic; *F* **la mode p.** the fashion for psychedelia
psychiatre [psikjatr] *n* psychiatrist
psychiatrie [psikjatri] *nf* psychiatry
psychiatrique [psikjatrik] *adj* psychiatric
psychique [psiʃik] *adj* psychic
psychisme [psiʃism] *nm* psyche, inner mind
psycho [psiko] *nf* = **psychologie**
psychodrame [psikodram] *nm* role-playing, *Spéc* psychodrama
psychographie [psikografi] *nf* psychographics
psychographique [psikografik] *adj* psychographic
psycholinguistique [psikolɛ̃gɥistik] *nf* psycholinguistics
psychologie [psikɔlɔʒi] *nf* psychology; *Univ* **faire de** *ou* **étudier la p.**, *F* **faire p.** to do *or* study psychology; *Univ* **études de p.** psychology (studies); **étudiants en p.** psychology students; **faire preuve de p.** to be a good psychologist, to use psychology; **tu manques de p.** you're not much of a psychologist, you don't have much idea of how people's minds work; **il a réellement manqué de p.** he showed a great lack of insight; **la p. des descriptions chez Proust** the psychological insights offered by Proust's descriptions; **une p. très fragile** a very fragile personality; **il faut comprendre sa p.** you have to understand the way his mind works
psychologique [psikɔlɔʒik] *adj* (*roman, film etc*) psychological; **le moment p.** the psychological moment; **son état p.** his psychological state, his state of mind; **son état p. n'était pas bon du tout** he wasn't in a good state of mind *or* frame of mind at all; **c'est p.!** it's psychological!
psychologiquement [psikɔlɔʒikmɑ̃] *adv* psychologically
psychologue [psikɔlɔg] **1** *n* psychologist; *Fig* **c'est un fin p.** he's a good psychologist **2** *adj* **elle n'est pas très p.** she's not much of a psychologist, she doesn't understand how people's minds work
psychonévrose [psikonevroz] *nf* psychoneurosis
psychopathe [psikɔpat] *n* psychopath
psychopathie [psikɔpati] *nf Vieilli* psychopathy
psychopathologie [psikopatɔlɔʒi] *adj* psychopathology
psychopédagogie [psikopedagɔʒi] *nf* application of experimental psychology to education
psychopharmacologie [psikofarmakɔlɔʒi] *nf* psychopharmacology
psychophysiologie [psikofizjɔlɔʒi] *nf* psycho-physiology
psychose [psikoz] *nf* **(a)** *Psy* psychosis; *Mil* **p. traumatique** post-combat stress syndrome, *Vieilli* shellshock; **p. maniaco-dépressive** manic depression; **souffrir de p. maniaco-dépressive** to be a manic-depressive **(b)** (*obsession*) (*d'une maladie, une crise, une guerre*) psychosis (**de** about), fear (**de** of)
psychosociologie [psikosɔsjɔlɔʒi] *nf* social psychology
psychosomatique [psikosɔmatik] *adj Méd* psychosomatic
psychotechnique [psikotɛknik] **1** *adj* psychological testing, *Spéc* psychotechnical **2** *nf* psychological testing, *Spéc* psychotechnology, psychotechnics
psychothérapeute [psikoterapøt] *n* psychotherapist
psychothérapie [psikoterapi] *nf* (psycho)therapy; **p. analytique** analytical (psycho)therapy; **p. familiale** family therapy; **faire une p. de groupe** to go to *or* do group therapy
psychothérapique [psikoterapik] *adj* psychotherapeutic; **intervention p.** psychotherapeutic treatment
psychotique [psikɔtik] *adj, n* psychotic
psychotonique [psikotɔnik] *adj Pharm* psychoactive, psychotropic
psychotrope [psikɔtrɔp] **1** *nm Pharm* psychotropic drug **2** *adj Anat* psychotropic
ptérodactyle [pterɔdaktil] *nm* pterodactyl
ptérosaurien [pterɔsɔrjɛ̃] *nm* pterosaur
Ptolémée [ptɔleme] *nm Antiq* Ptolemy; *Astron* **système de P.** Ptolemaic system
ptomaïne [ptɔmain] *nf Biol, Ch* ptomaine
P.T.T. [petete] *nfpl* (*abrév* **Poste, Télécommunications et Télédiffusion**) Post Office, Post Office and Telecommunications Service
PU (*abrév* **prix unitaire**) UP
puant [pyɑ̃] *adj* **(a)** (*qui sent mauvais*) stinking, foul-smelling; *Ch F* **gaz p.** hydrogen sulphide, *F* stink bomb gas; **boule puante** stink bomb **(b)** *Fig* (*odieux*) cocky
puanteur [pyɑ̃tœr] *nf* stink, stench, *Br F* pong
pub¹ [pyb] *nf F* = **publicité (a)**, **(b)**
pub² [pœb] *nm* pub
pubère [pybɛr] *adj* pubescent
puberté [pybɛrte] *nf* puberty
pubescent [pybesɑ̃] *adj Bot* pubescent
pubien, -ienne [pybjɛ̃, -jɛn] *adj Anat* pubic
pubis [pybis] *nm Anat* pubis, pubes; (*os*) pubic bone
publiable [pybliabl] *adj* fit for publication, publishable
public, -ique [pyblik] **1** *adj* public; (*assemblée*) public, open (to the public); **la séance est publique** the meeting is open to the public; **la chose publique** res publica; **service p.** public utility (service), *Am* utility; **travailler pour le bien p.** to work for the common good; **la voie publique** the public highway; **il est de notoriété publique que ...** it is public *or* common knowledge that ...; *Admin* **ministère p.** = public prosecutor

2 *nm* [①A11,g,i] (*d'un spectacle, d'une émission*) audience; **cette émission a été enregistrée en p.** this programme was recorded before a live audience; **un p. cultivé** a cultured *or* an educated audience; (*lecteurs*) cultured *or* discerning readers; **cette chanteuse a encore son p.** this singer still has a following; **le p.** the public; **'interdit au p.'** 'no admittance *or* admission to the public', 'keep out'; **le grand p.** the general public; **un film pour le grand p.** a family film, a film (suitable) for everybody; **électronique grand p.** consumer electronics; **en p.** in public, publicly; **faire une déclaration en p.** to make a public statement; **p. cible** target audience; **p. en studio** studio audience
publicain [pyblikɛ̃] *nm Antiq* tax gatherer; *Bible* publican
publication [pyblikasjɔ̃] *nf* **(a)** (*fait de rendre public*) publication, publishing; **p. en feuilleton** serialization; **p. de vente aux enchères** notice of sale by auction; **date de p.** publication date, date of publication; **p. assistée par ordinateur** desk-top publishing **(b)** (*magazine etc*) publication; **p. périodique** periodical; **p. trimestrielle** quarterly (publication); **p. spécialisée** specialist journal; **p. interne** in-house publication
publiciste [pyblisist] *n Com F* person who works in advertising; (*homme*) adman

publicitaire [pyblisitɛr] **1** *adj* (concerned with) publicity; *Com* (concerned with) advertising; **campagne p.** publicity campaign; *Com* advertising campaign; **agence p.** advertising agency; **vente p.** promotional sale; *TV, Rad* **spot/message p.** commercial, ad(vert) **2** *n* person who works in advertising; (*homme*) *F* adman

publicité [publisite] *nf* **(a)** (*notoriété*) publicity; *Com* advertising; **être dans la p.** to be in advertising; **faire de la p. pour un savon** (*d'un acteur*) to advertise a soap; (*d'une agence*) to do the advertising for a soap; **l'animateur a fait de la p. pour cet album** the disc jockey plugged the album; **ça lui fait de la p.** it's publicity for him; **la p. paie** it pays to advertise; **une agence de p.** an advertising agency

(b) (*affiche*), *Journ* ad(vert); *TV, Rad* ad(vert), commercial; **une pleine page de p. dans le journal** a full page ad(vert) *or* advertisement in the paper; **il y a trop de p. à la télévision** there are too many ads *or* there's too much advertising on television

(c) (*caractère public*) (*d'un débat*) public nature

▶ **publicité**: **p. associé** cooperative advertising; **p. commerciale** commercial advertising; **p. comparative** comparative advertising; (*activité*) comparative *or* comparison advertising; **p. par correspondance** direct mail advertising; **p. directe** direct advertising *or* mail, below-the-line advertising; **p. d'entreprise** corporate advertising; **p. par l'événement** event advertising; **p. extérieure** outdoor advertising; **p. hors-médias** below-the-line promotion; **p. d'intérêt général** government advertisement; (*activité*) government advertising; **p. sur le lieu de vente** point-of-sale promotion; **p. média** (*publicité directe*) above-the-line *or* media advertising; **p. mensongère** false *or* misleading advertising; **p. sur panneau** billboard advertisment; (*activité*) billboard advertising; **p. plein page** full page advertisement; **p. par publipostage** direct mail advertising; **p. pure** above-the-line advertising; **p. de rappel** follow-up advertisment; (*activité*) follow-up publicity; **p. rédactionnelle** advertorial; **p. télévisée** television advertisment *or* commercial, TV ad; (*activité*) television advertising

public-relations [pœblikrileʃənz] **1** *nf* public relations, *F* PR; **le service de p.** the public relations department, *F* the PR department **2** *n* public relations officer, *F* PR man, *f* woman

publier [pyblije] *vt* (*pr sub, impf* **n. publiions, v. publiiez**) **(a)** (*rendre public*) (*chiffres du commerce etc*) to publish, to make public, to make known; (*décret etc*) to proclaim; (*règlement*) to issue; **les bans ont-ils été publiés?** have the banns been published?; **p. la nouvelle que ...** to release the news that ... **(b)** (*livre*) to publish, to bring out; **ce journal est publié sur seize pages** the paper runs to sixteen pages

publi-information [pybliɛ̃fɔrmasjɔ̃] *nf* advertorial

publiphone® [pyblifɔn] *nm* card phone

publipostage [pyblipɔstaʒ] *nm* mailshot; **logiciel de p.** mail merge software; **faire un p.** to do a mailshot; **p. groupé** bus mailing

publi-promotion [pybliprɔmosjɔ̃] *nf* promotional offer

publiquement [pyblikmɑ̃] *adv* publicly, in public; (*ouvertement*) openly; **se faire ridiculer p.** to be publicly insulted, to be insulted in public

publireportage [pyblir(ə)pɔrtaʒ] *nm* advertorial, advertising feature, promotional article

puce [pys] **1** *nf* **(a)** (*insecte*) flea; **p. de mer** sand hopper *or* flea; **herbe aux puces** fleawort; **jeu de p.** tiddlywinks; **piqûre de p.** fleabite; **le marché aux puces, les puces** the flea market; **les puces de Paris** the Paris flea market; *Fig* **mettre la p. à l'oreille à qn** to make sb suspicious, to arouse sb's suspicions; *F* **secouer les puces à qn** to give sb a good telling off; *F* **elle est excitée comme une p.** she can't sit still, she's jumping up and down with excitement; **elle est rentrée de l'école excitée comme une p.** she came home jumping up and down with excitement; *F* **mais oui, ma p.** yes (my) dear *or* (my) love *or* (my) pet

(b) *Ordinat* (micro)chip; **p. de reconnaissance vocale** voice recognition chip; **p. logique** logic chip; **p. mémoire** memory chip

2 *adj inv* puce(-coloured *or US* -colored)

puceau, -eaux [pyso] *nm, adj m F* virgin

pucelage [pyslaʒ] *nm Hum* virginity; **perdre son p.** to lose one's virginity

pucelle [pysɛl] **1** *adj f* virgin **2** *nf* virgin, *Arch, Euph* maid(en); *Hist* **la P. d'Orléans** the Maid of Orleans

puceron [pysrɔ̃] *nm* greenfly, aphid

pucier [pysje] *nm Arg* (*lit*) bed

pudding [pudiŋ] *nm Culin* **(a)** steamed pudding; (*pour Noël*) (plum) pudding, Christmas pudding **(b)** (*gâteau*) = filling type of cake made from stale bread

puddlage [pydlaʒ] *nm Métal* puddling

puddler [pydle] *vt Métal* to puddle

pudeur [pydœr] *nf* (*réserve*) modesty; **sans p.** (*adjectivement*) unblushing, shameless; (*adverbialement*) unblushingly, shamelessly; **avec p.** modestly; **rougir de p.** to blush with shame; **par p., il n'a pas abordé le sujet** out of a sense of decency *or* propriety he did not mention the subject; **avoir la p. de faire qch** to have the decency to do sth

pudibond [pydibɔ̃] *adj* easily shocked, prudish

pudibonderie [pydibɔ̃dri] *nf* prudishness

pudicité [pydisite] *nf Litt* modesty

pudique [pydik] *adj* modest; **une allusion p.** a discreet reference

pudiquement [pydikmɑ̃] *adv* modestly

puer [pɥe] **1** *vi* to stink, to reek; **ça pue!** what a stink *or Br F* pong! **2** *vt* (*qch*) to stink *or* reek of; **il pue des pieds** his feet stink

puériculteur, -trice [pɥerikyltœr, -tris] *n* nursery nurse

puériculture [pɥerikyltyr] *nf* child care, infant welfare

puéril [pɥeril] *adj* childish, *Fml* puerile

puérilement [pɥerilmɑ̃] *adv* childishly

puérilité [pɥerilite] *nf* childishness, *Fml* puerility

puerpéral, -ale, -aux, -ales [pɥɛrperal, -o] *adj Obst* puerperal

puffin [pyfɛ̃] *nm* (*oiseau*) shearwater

pugilat [pyʒila] *nm* **(a)** (*combat de boxeurs*) boxing, *Fml* pugilism **(b)** (*dispute, bataille*) fight, brawl, *F* set-to

pugiliste [pyʒilist] *nm* boxer, *Fml* pugilist

pugnace [pygnas] *adj Litt* pugnacious

pugnacité [pygnasite] *nf Litt* pugnacity, pugnaciousness

puîné, -ée [pɥine] *Vieilli* **1** *adj* (*de deux*) younger; (*de plusieurs*) youngest **2** *n* (*frère*) younger/youngest brother; (*sœur*) younger/youngest sister

puis [pɥi] *adv* then; **tourner à droite p. à gauche** turn right (and) then left; **et p.** and then; (*d'ailleurs*) moreover, (and) besides; **et p. qu'est-ce qui s'est passé?** then what happened?, what happened then *or* next?; **et p., c'est tout** and that's all there is to it; **et p. (quoi)?, et p. après?** then what?, what next?; *F* (*qu'est-ce que ça peut faire*) so what?

puisage [pɥizaʒ] *nm* (*d'eau*) drawing (up)

puisard [pɥizar] *nm* (*pour ordures*) cesspool, sink; *Min, Tech etc* sump, well

puisatier [pɥizatje] *nm* (*ouvrier*) well maker, well sinker; *Min* shaft sinker

puisement [pɥizmɑ̃] *nm* = **puisage**

puiser [pɥize] **1** *vt* (*eau*) to draw (**à, dans** from); *Fig* (*inspiration, idée*) to derive, to get, to take (**dans, chez** from); **p. aux sources** to draw on the original sources, to go to the source, *Litt, Hum* to go to the fountainhead **2** *vi* **elle puise dans ses réserves** she's drawing on her reserves; **elle ne s'est pas gênée pour p. dans ma trousse de maquillage** she felt no embarrassment about using my make-up *or* dipping into my make-up bag; **p. dans son porte-monnaie** to dip *or* put one's hand in one's wallet

puisque [pɥisk(ə)] *conj* since, as, seeing that; **je le ferai, puisqu'il le faut** I'll do it, since I must; **p. tu veux savoir, je vais te le dire** since *or* seeing that you want to know, I'll tell you; **p. c'est comme ça** if that's how you feel/he feels/*etc*, if that's how things are; **d'accord, p. c'est ce que tu veux!** all right, if that's what you want; **p. je te dis que je l'ai vu!** but I'm telling you I <u>did</u> see it!; **tu es sûr que tu peux y aller? – mais p. que je te le dis!** are you sure you can go? – I <u>said</u> so, didn't I?

puissamment [pɥisamɑ̃] *adv* powerfully; *F* **p. riche** exceedingly rich

puissance [pɥisɑ̃s] *nf* **(a)** power; (*du vent*) force, strength; (*d'une armée*) strength; **p. d'une machine** power of an engine; *Mil* **p. de** *ou* **du feu** fire power; **p. en chevaux** horsepower; **p. au frein** brake horsepower; *Aut* **p. de traction** pulling power; **p. effective** power output; **p. nominale** rated power; **p. utile** usable brake horsepower, usable bhp; *Admin* **p. fiscale d'une voiture** = engine rating of a car for road tax purposes; **p. administrative** taxable horsepower; *Rad* **p. d'antenne** aerial capacity; **poste émetteur de haute p.** high-power radio transmitter

(b) *Math* power; **élever un nombre à la nième p.** to raise a number to the nth power; **dix (à la) p. quatre (10^4)** ten to the fourth, ten to the power of four

(c) (*autorité*) power; **avoir qn en sa p.** to have sb in one's power; **la volonté de p.** the desire for power; **être en p. de mari** to be under a husband's control *or* authority; **p. paternelle** paternal authority

(d) *Pol* **les grandes puissances** the great powers; *Fig* **les puissances célestes** the powers above; **les puissances des ténèbres** the powers of darkness

(e) en p. (*assassin, meurtrier*) potential

puissant [pɥisɑ̃] **1** *adj* **(a)** (*qui a du pouvoir*) (*armée, moteur,* *voiture, pays etc*) powerful **(b)** (*qui a de la force physique, fort*) (*homme, vent, musculature, Fig envie*) strong; (*voix*) powerful; (*remède*) powerful, strong, potent **2** *nmpl* **les puissants** the powerful, the mighty (ones)

puits [pɥi] *nm* **(a)** (*pour l'eau*) well; **p. de sondage** borehole; **p. artésien** artesian well; **p. absorbant, p. perdu** cesspool; *Fig* **c'est un p. de science** he's a mine of information; (*d'un esprit plus profond*) he's a fount of knowledge **(b)** (*de mine*) shaft, pit; **p. d'aération, d'aérage** air shaft, ventilation shaft; **p. d'extraction** winding shaft **(c)** *Mil* **p. de lancement** launching silo **(d)** *Culin* **p. d'amour** = small round of puff pastry filled with pastry cream

pull [pyl] *nm F* jumper, sweater, pullover

pullman [pulman] *nm Rail* Pullman (car)

pull-over, *pl* **pull-overs** [pulɔvœr] *nm* jumper, sweater, pullover

pullulation [pylylasjɔ̃] *nf*, **pullulement** [pylylmɑ̃] *nm* **(a)** (*d'organismes etc*) rapid multiplication, *Fml* pullulation **(b)** (*d'enfants etc*) swarm

pulluler [pylyle] *vi* **(a)** (*se reproduire*) to multiply rapidly, *Fml* to pullulate **(b)** (*être en profusion*) to abound, to be found in profusion; (*en mouvement*) to swarm; **la rue pullule de monde** the street is swarming with people; **les marchands de chaussures pullulent dans ce coin de la ville** there are lots of shoe shops in this part of town, this part of town is full of *or* swarming with shoe shops

pulmonaire [pylmɔnɛr] **1** *adj* pulmonary; **congestion p.** pulmonary congestion **2** *nf* lungwort

pulpe [pylp] *nf* **(a)** (*de fruit*) pulp; **yaourt à la p. de fruits** yoghurt with pieces of fruit in it; **réduire qch en p.** to reduce sth to a pulp, to pulp sth **(b)** (*partie molle*) (*des doigts ou des orteils*) pad; (*des dents*) pulp

pulpeux, -euse [pylpø, -øz] *adj* (*lèvres*) fleshy; **une fille pulpeuse** a sexy female

pulsar [pylsar] *nm Astron* pulsar

pulsation [pylsasjɔ̃] *nf* (*fait de battre*) (*du cœur*) beating, throbbing; (*battement*) throb

pulsative [pylsativ] *adj f Méd* **douleur p.** throbbing pain, *Spéc* pulsatory pain

pulser [pylse] *vt* (*air*) (*dans une pièce, dans un moteur*) to force

pulsion [pylsjɔ̃] *nf Psy* impulse; **p. sexuelle** sex drive; **p. de mort** death wish

pulsionnel, -elle [pylsjɔnɛl] *adj* impulsive, impulse; **phénomène p.** impulsive action, instinctive action; **c'était plus p. que réfléchi** it was more of a reflex *or* an impulse than a conscious act

pulsoréacteur [pylsoreaktœr] *nm Av* pulse jet

pulvérisable [pylverizabl] *adj* (*poudre etc*) which can be crushed; (*liquide*) that can be sprayed

pulvérisateur [pylverizatœr] *nm* **(a)** (*de matières solides*) pulverizer **(b)** (*de liquide*) spray; *Tech* vaporizer, atomizer

pulvérisation [pylverizasjɔ̃] *nf* **(a)** (*de matières solides*) pulverizing, crushing **(b)** (*de liquides*) spraying; *Tech* vaporization; **p. métallisée** metal-spraying

pulvériser [pylverize] *vt* **(a)** (*roche*) to crush, to pulverize; **p. une matière** to grind *or* reduce a substance to powder **(b)** (*liquide, parfum*) to spray; *Ind* to vaporize **(c)** *Fig F* (*record*) to smash, to shatter; **la voiture a été pulvérisée lors de l'accident** the car was completely smashed up *or* was smashed to pieces in the accident; **p. qn** to beat the hell out of sb, to pulverize sb

pulvériseur [pylverizœr] *nm Agr* disc *or US* disk harrow

pulvérulence [pylverylɑ̃s] *nf* powderiness, dustiness

pulvérulent [pylverylɑ̃] *adj* powdery, dusty

puma [pyma] *nm* puma, cougar, mountain lion

punaise [pynɛz] *nf* **(a)** (*insecte*) bug; **p. des lits** bed bug; *F* **p. de sacristie** fervent churchgoer; *F Dial* **oh p.!** golly!, goodness!, gosh! **(b)** (*pour accrocher*) drawing pin, *Am* thumbtack

punaiser [pyneze] *vt F* to pin (up); **p. des affiches au mur** to pin posters to the wall

punch¹ [pɔ̃ʃ] *nm Culin* punch; **bol à p.** punchbowl

punch² [pœnʃ] *nm Boxe, Fig F* punch; *Fig* **elle ne manque pas de p.** (*elle a de l'énergie*) she's full of energy; **ça vous donnera du p. pour la suite!** it'll give you energy *or* set you up for what's to come!; **un slogan qui a du p.** a punchy *or* catchy slogan; **cette aide de l'état a donné du p. à notre organisation** the government's assistance was a shot in the arm for our organization

punching-ball, *pl* **punching-balls** [pœnʃiŋbol] *nm Boxe* punchball

punique [pynik] *adj Hist* (*guerres etc*) Punic

punir [pynir] *vt* (*personne, crime*) to punish; **p. qn de mort/prison** to punish sb with death/imprisonment; **p. qn d'un crime/pour un mensonge** to punish sb for a crime/for lying; **être puni de ses crimes** to be punished *or* pay the penalty for one's crimes; **ça te punira de ta curiosité!** that'll teach you to be nosey!; **me voilà puni de ma gourmandise!** it serves me right for being greedy!, that'll teach me to be greedy!; **être puni par où l'on a péché** to reap what one has sown

punissable [pynisabl] *adj* punishable

punitif, -ive [pynitif, -iv] *adj* (*expédition, mesure etc*) punitive

punition [pynisjɔ̃] *nf* punishment; **p. corporelle** corporal punishment; **donner une p. à un enfant** to punish a child; **en p. de qch** as (a) punishment for sth; **par** *ou* **pour p.** for punishment, by way of punishment, as a punishment

punk [pœnk] **1** *adj inv* (*musique etc*) punk **2** *n* punk

pupe [pyp] *nf* **(a)** (*enveloppe*) pupa case **(b)** (*chrysalide*) pupa, chrysalis

pupillaire¹ [pypilɛr] *adj Jur* pertaining to a ward, *Spéc* pupil(l)ary

pupillaire² *adj Anat* (*membrane etc*) pupil(l)ary

pupillarité [pypilarite] *nf Jur* wardship, *Spéc* pupil(l)age

pupille¹ [pypil, -ij] *n Jur* ward; **pupilles de la Marine/de l'Air** = children whose fathers have died while serving in the Navy/Air Force; **p. de l'État** child in (state) care; **pupilles de la Nation** war orphans

pupille² *nf Anat* (*de l'œil*) pupil

pupillomètre [pypijɔmɛtr] *nm* pupilometer

pupitre [pypitr] *nm* **(a)** (*d'écolier etc*) desk; (*d'où s'adresse un orateur*) lectern; **p. à musique** music stand **(b)** *Mus* (*d'instruments*) group; **chef de p.** front desk player **(c)** *TV, Rad* console; **p. de mixage** mixing desk; **p. de mélange vidéo** switcher; **p. de régie** studio control console, studio desk, control board; **p. son** audio (control) console **(d)** *Ordinat* **p. (de commande)** console (desk); **p. de visualisation** visual display unit

pupitreur, -euse [pypitrœr, -øz] *n Ordinat* console operator

pur, pure [pyr] **1** *adj* **(a)** (*pas mélangé*) (*or, laine, jus de fruits, style etc*) pure; (*air*) clean, pure; (*ciel*) clear; (*whisky, gin etc*) straight, neat; **un peu d'air p. nous fera du bien** a bit of fresh air will do us good; **elle boit son whisky p.** she drinks her whisky straight *or* neat; **de l'eau de javel p.** undiluted bleach; **liquide p. de tout mélange** liquid free from all admixture; **biscuits p. beurre** all butter biscuits; **elle parle un italien très p.** her Italian is very pure; **cheval p. sang** thoroughbred horse; **c'est un p. produit de mai 68/du catholicisme** he's a true child of May 68/of the Catholic church; **être un p. produit de la bourgeoisie** to be middle-class through and through, to be a hundred per cent middle-class; **un p. produit du féminisme** a one hundred per cent red-blooded feminist; **c'est un p. produit de Polytechnique** he's a typical Polytechnique graduate

(b) (*total*) pure; **p. hasard** pure chance, mere chance; **c'est un p. hasard qu'il se soit trouvé là** it was pure *or* sheer chance that he was there; **par p. hasard, il y avait un médecin dans le car** by sheer chance there was a doctor on the bus; **la pure vérité** the simple *or* plain *or* honest *or* unvarnished truth; **la vérité pure et simple** the plain and simple truth; **c'est de la folie pure (et simple)** it's sheer madness, it's pure folly; **un socialiste/trotskyiste p. et dur** a hard-line Socialist/Trotskyist; **un bouddhiste p. et dur** a strict Buddhist; **c'est un breton p. et dur** he's extremely proud of being a Breton; **l'invitation est de pure forme** the invitation is purely for form's sake; **par pure malice** out of pure *or* sheer malice; **travailler en pure perte** to work for nothing *or* to no purpose; **elle l'a fait en pure perte** she did it all for nothing, it was a sheer waste of her time

(c) *Fig* (*moralement*) pure; (*esthétiquement*) (*lignes*) pure, clean, clean-cut; (*visage*) clean-cut; **conscience pure** clear conscience; **p. d'esprit** pure-minded

(d) (*théorique*) (*science, mathématiques etc*) pure

2 *n Pol etc* diehard

purée [pyre] **1** *nf Culin* purée; **p. (de pommes de terre)** mashed *or* creamed potato(es), potato purée, *Br F* mash; **p. de carottes** puréed carrots; *F* **être dans la p.** (*dans la gêne financière*) to be hard up, to be down on one's luck; (*dans une situation difficile*) to be up the creek **2** *int F* (*colère etc*) hell!, blast (it)!; (*surprise*) wow!

purement [pyrmɑ̃] *adv* purely

pureté [pyrte] *nf* purity; (*du ciel*) clearness; (*de lignes*) purity, cleanness

purgatif, -ive [pyrgatif, -iv] *Méd* **1** *adj* purgative **2** *nm* purgative, purge

purgation [pyrgasjɔ̃] *nf Méd* purging

purgatoire [pyrgatwar] *nm Rel* purgatory

purge [pyrʒ] *nf* **(a)** *Méd* purge, purgative **(b)** *Pol* purge **(c)** (*d'un liquide*) draining; *Aut* (*des freins*) bleeding; **robinet de p.** drain *or* bleed cock; *Aut* **p. de carburant** fuel bleed; **vis de p.** bleed screw **(d)** *Jur* (*d'une hypothèque*) redemption, paying off

purgeoir [pyrʒwar] *nm* (*d'une réserve d'eau etc*) purifying tank, filtering tank

purger [pyrʒe] (**je purgeai(s); n. purgeons**) **1** *vt* (**a**) *Méd* to purge; **p. les intestins** to clean out *or* cleanse *or* purge the system; *Fig* **p. un pays de voleurs** to rid *or* purge a country of bandits; **p. une société des fainéants** to get rid of the shirkers in a company (**b**) *Jur* (*hypothèque*) to redeem, to pay off; (*dettes*) to pay off, to clear; **p. sa peine** to serve one's sentence (**c**) *Tech* (*freins*) to bleed; (*radiateur*) to bleed, to drain **2 se purger** *vpr* (**a**) *Méd* to take a purgative *or* a laxative (**b**) *Fig* **se p. d'une accusation** to clear oneself of an accusation

purgeur [pyrʒœr] *nm Tech* drain cock, bleed cock; *Aut* bleeder valve

purifiant [pyrifjɑ̃] *adj* purifying, cleansing

purificateur, -trice [pyrifikatœr, -tris] **1** *adj* purifying, cleansing **2** *nm* purifier, cleanser; **p. d'air** *ou* **d'atmosphère** air purifier

purification [pyrifikasjɔ̃] *nf* purification; (*de métaux*) refining; (*du sang*) cleansing; **p. ethnique** ethnic cleansing

purifier [pyrifje] (*pr sub, impf* **n. purifiions, v. purifiiez**) **1** *vt aussi Fig* to purify, to cleanse; (*langue*) to purify; (*métal*) to refine; (*sang*) to cleanse; **lotion qui purifie la peau** skin cleanser **2 se purifier** *vpr* to become pure, to be purified

purin [pyrɛ̃] *nm Agr* slurry, liquid manure

purisme [pyrism] *nm* (*du langage etc*) purism

puriste [pyrist] *n* purist

puritain, -aine [pyritɛ̃, -ɛn] **1** *n* puritan; *Hist* Puritan **2** *adj* puritan(ical); *Hist* Puritan

puritanisme [pyritanism] *nm* puritanism

purotin [pyrɔtɛ̃] *nm Arg Vieilli* down-and-out

purpura [pyrpyra] *nm Méd* purpura

purpurin, -ine [pyrpyrɛ̃, -in] *adj Litt* deep crimson

pur-sang *nm inv* thoroughbred (horse)

purulence [pyrylɑ̃s] *nf Méd* purulence

purulent [pyrylɑ̃] *adj Méd* suppurating, *Spéc* purulent; **foyer p.** abscess

pus [py] *nm Méd* pus, matter

push-pull [puʃpul] *nm, adj inv Él* push-pull

pusillanime [pyzilanim] *adj Litt* pusillanimous, faint-hearted

pusillanimité [pyzilanimite] *nf Litt* pusillanimity, faint-heartedness

pustule [pystyl] *nf* blister, pustule; (*de crapauds*) wart

pustuleux, -euse [pystylø, -øz] *adj* pus-filled, pustulous

put [put] *nm Bourse* put (option)

putain [pytɛ̃] *Arg Vulg* **1** *nf* (**a**) prostitute, whore, *Am* hooker (**b**) **cette p. de guerre/machine** this bloody *or Vulg* fucking war/machine **2** *int* (*colère etc*) shit!; (*surprise*) Christ!

putassier, -ière [pytasje, -jɛr] *adj Arg Vulg* (*tenue, manières*) tarty

putatif, -ive [pytatif, -iv] *adj* putative, supposed, presumed

pute [pyt] *nf Arg Vulg* = **putain 1** (**a**); **la p.!** (*elle m'a menti etc*) the bitch!; **fils de p.!** bastard!, son of a bitch!

putois [pytwa] *nm* (*animal*) polecat; (*fourrure*) polecat (fur); **p. (d'Amérique)** skunk; *F* **crier comme un p.** to scream blue murder

putréfaction [pytrefaksjɔ̃] *nf* putrefaction; **matière en p.** putrefying matter

putréfier [pytrefje] **1** *vt* to putrefy, to rot **2 se putrifier** *vpr* to putrefy, to become putrid

putrescence [pytresɑ̃s] *nf* putrescence

putrescent [pytresɑ̃] *adj* putrescent

putrescible [pytresibl] *adj* liable to putrefy

putride [pytrid] *adj* putrid

putridité [pytridite] *nf Litt* putridness

putsch [putʃ] *nm Pol* putsch

putschiste [putʃist] *Pol* **1** *adj* putsch **2** *nm* person involved in a putsch, putschist

puzzle [pœzl] *nm* (jigsaw) puzzle; *Fig* puzzle; *Fig* **le p. commence à prendre forme dans son esprit** the pieces of the puzzle are beginning to fall into place

P.-V. [peve] *nm F* (*abrév* **procès-verbal**) (parking) ticket; **j'ai eu un P. ce matin** I got a ticket this morning

P.V.C. [pevese] *nm Tech* (*abrév* **polychlorure de vinyle**) PVC; **siège en P.** PVC seat

pygmée [pigme] *nm* pygmy, pigmy

pyjama [piʒama] *nm* [①A10,e] pyjamas, *US* pajamas; **un p.** a pair of pyjamas; **elle était encore en p.** she was still in her pyjamas; **c'est un vrai p.** (*ce vêtement*) it's loose and comfortable; **j'y suis comme dans un p.** it's really comfortable

pylône [pilon] *nm* (**a**) *Él* pylon; (*pour fils télégraphiques*) lattice mast; **p. électrique** electricity pylon; **grue à p.** tower crane (**b**) *Archit* (*de temples égyptiens*) pylon

pylore [pilɔr] *nm Anat* pylorus

pyorrhée [pjɔre] *nf Méd* pyorrhoea, *US* pyorrhea

pyramidal, -ale, -aux, -ales [piramidal, -o] *adj* pyramidal

pyramide [piramid] *nf* pyramid; **p. des âges** age pyramid; **entasser des oranges en p.** to pile up oranges in a pyramid; **structure en p.** pyramid-like *or* pyramidal structure

pyrénéen, -enne [pireneɛ̃, -ɛn] **1** *adj* Pyrenean **2** *n* **P.** Pyrenean

Pyrénées (les) [lepirene] *nfpl* the Pyrenees

pyrèthre [pirɛtr] *nm* (*plante*) feverfew, pyrethrum; **poudre de p.** insect powder

pyrexie [pirɛksi] *nf Méd* pyrexia, fever

pyrex® [pirɛks] *nm* Pyrex; **plat en p.** Pyrex dish; **c'est du p., ton plat?** is your dish (made of) Pyrex?

pyrite [pirit] *nf Minér* pyrites

pyrograveur, -euse [pirogravœr, -øz] *n Beaux-Arts* pyrographer

pyrogravure [pirogravyr] *nf Beaux-Arts* poker work, pyrography; (*gravure*) pyrograph

pyrolyse [pirɔliz] *nf* pyrolysis; **four à p.** self-cleaning oven

pyromane [pirɔman] *n Psy* pyromaniac; *Jur* (*incendiaire*) arsonist

pyromanie [pirɔmani] *nf Psy* pyromania

pyromètre [pirɔmɛtr] *nm Phys, Tech* pyrometer

pyrosis [pirɔzis] *nm Méd* heartburn, *Spéc* pyrosis

pyrotechnie [pirotekni] *nf* pyrotechnics

pyrotechnique [pirotɛknik] *adj* pyrotechnic(al)

Pythagore [pitagɔr] *nm* Pythagoras; **théorème de P.** Pythagoras' theorem

pythagoricien, -ienne [pitagɔrisjɛ̃, -jɛn] *Phil* **1** *adj* Pythagorean **2** *n* **P.** Pythagorean

pythagorisme [pitagɔrism] *nm Phil* Pythagoreanism

Pythie [piti] *nf* (**a**) *Myth* **P. de Delphes** Pythia of Delphi (**b**) *Litt* prophetess, oracle

python [pitɔ̃] *nm* python

pyxide [piksid] *nf Rel* pyx

Q

Q, q [ky] *nm (lettre)* Q, q
QCM [kyseɛm] *nm inv abrév* **questionnaire à choix multiple**
QG [kyʒe] *nm inv Mil F (abrév* **quartier général**) HQ
QI [kyi] *nm inv (abrév* **quotient intellectuel**) IQ
quadra [kwadra] *nm F* = **quadragénaire**
quadragénaire [kwadraʒenɛr] *adj, n* forty-year-old, quadragenarian; **elle est q.** she's in her forties
Quadragésime [kwadraʒezim] *nf Rel* **(le dimanche de) la Q.** Quadragesima (Sunday)
quadrangulaire [kwadrɑ̃gylɛr] *adj* quadrangular, four-angled; *(bâtiment)* four-cornered, four-sided
quadrant [k(w)adrɑ̃] *nm Géom* quadrant
quadratique [kwadratik] *adj* **(a)** *Math* quadratic **(b)** *Minér* quadratic, tetragonal
quadrature [kwadratyr] *nf* **(a)** *Géom* quadrature, squaring; *Fig* **c'est la q. du cercle** it's like trying to square the circle **(b)** *Astron, Phys* quadrature; **marées de q.** neap tides, neaps
quadriceps *nm Anat* quadriceps
quadrichromie [kwadrikrɔmi] *nf* four-colour *or US* four-color printing
quadriennal, -ale, -aux, -ales [kwadrijenal, -o] *adj (plan, période)* quadrennial, four-year; **les Jeux olympiques sont quadriennaux** the Olympic Games take place every four years
quadrifolié [kwadrifɔlje] *adj Bot* four-leaved, quadrifoliate
quadrijumeaux [kwadriʒymo] *nmpl* quadruplets
quadrilatère [k(w)adrilatɛr] *nm Géom, Mil etc* quadrilateral
quadrillage [kadrijaʒ] *nm* **(a)** *(action) (d'un papier, d'une carte)* ruling in squares, cross-ruling; **la police a établi un q. du quartier** the police have the district under tight surveillance **(b)** *(motif)* squares; *(sur une carte)* grid
quadrille [kadrij] *nm* quadrille; **q. des lanciers** lancers
quadrillé [kadrije] *adj (papier)* squared, cross-ruled; **carte quadrillée** grid map
quadriller [kadrije] *vt* **(a)** *(papier)* to rule in squares, to cross-rule; **le quartier est quadrillé par un réseau de ruelles** the district is criss-crossed by a network of alleys **(b)** *(quartier)* to put under tight surveillance; **tout le quartier est quadrillé** the whole district is under tight surveillance
quadrimoteur [k(w)adrimɔtœr] *adj, nm* **(avion) q.** four-engined plane
quadriparti [kwadriparti], **quadripartite** [kwadripartit] *adj (corolle, traité)* quadripartite; *(conférence, commission) (de partis)* four-party; *(de pays)* four-power
quadriphonie [kwadrifoni] *nf* quadraphony
quadriplégie [kwadriplezi] *nf Méd* quadriplegia
quadriréacteur [k(w)adrireaktœr] *nm Av* four-engined jet
quadrisyllabe [kwadrisilab] *nm* quadrisyllable
quadrisyllabique [kwadrisilabik] *adj* quadrisyllabic
quadrumane [k(w)adryman] *Zool* **1** *adj (animal)* quadrumanous, four-handed **2** *nm* quadrumane
quadrupède [k(w)adrypɛd] *Zool* **1** *adj (animal)* quadruped, four-footed **2** *nm* quadruped
quadruple [k(w)adrypl] **1** *adj* quadruple, fourfold **2** *nm* quadruple; **au q.** fourfold; **payer le q. du prix** to pay four times the price; **elle gagne le q. de ce que je gagne** she earns four times as much as I do
quadrupler [k(w)adryple] *vti* to quadruple, to increase fourfold
quadruplés, -ées [k(w)adryple] *npl* quadruplets, *F* quads
quai [kɛ] *nm* **(a)** [①**A12**,1,d] *Naut* quay; *(d'embarquement, de débarquement)* wharf; *(construit au-dessus de l'eau)* pier; **amener un navire à q.** to bring a ship alongside, to berth a ship; **se mettre à q.** to berth; **navire à q.** berthed ship; **q. des pétroliers** oil wharf; **droits de q.** wharfage; *Com* **livrable à q.** *(marchandises)* ex-quay, ex-wharf **(b)** *(le long d'une rivière, d'un fleuve)* embankment **(c)** *Rail* platform; **accès aux quais** ≈ to the trains; **le train est à q.** the train is in
▶ **quai**: **q. d'arrivée** *Naut* arrival quay; *Rail* arrival platform; *Naut* **q. de chargement** loading quay; *Naut* **q. de déchargement** unloading quay; **q. de départ** *Naut* departure quay; *Rail* departure platform; **le Q. des Orfèvres** Police Headquarters *(in Paris)*; **le Q. d'Orsay** the French Foreign Office
quaker, -eresse [kwɛkœr, -(ə)rɛs, kwa-] *n* Quaker, *f* Quakeress
quakerisme [kwɛkœrism, kwak(ə)rism] *nm* Quakerism
qualifiable [kalifjabl] *adj (que l'on peut qualifier)* definable; **sa conduite n'est pas q.** his behaviour is indescribable
qualificatif, -ive [kalifikatif, -iv] *Gram* **1** *adj (adjectif etc)* qualifying **2** *nm* qualifier, modifier; *Fig* **il n'y a pas de q. assez fort pour la décrire** there's no word strong enough to describe her
qualification [kalifikasjɔ̃] *nf* **(a)** *(formation)* qualification; **q. professionnelle** professional qualification **(b)** *Sp* qualification; **obtenir sa q.** to qualify; **obtenir sa q. pour la** *ou* **en finale** to qualify for the final; **match de q.** qualifying match; **il court les épreuves de q.** he's running in the heats; **leur q. est assurée** they are sure to qualify **(c)** *(nom)* designation, name; **s'attribuer la q. de colonel** to call oneself colonel; **elle n'est pas médecin spécialiste, mais elle en a pris la q.** she's not a specialist doctor, but she's given herself that title **(d)** *Gram (d'un nom etc)* qualifying; *Jur (d'un crime etc)* legal definition
qualifié, -ée [kalifje] **1** *adj* **(a)** *(compétent)* qualified; **q. pour faire qch** qualified to do sth; **je suis certainement q. pour en parler** I am certainly qualified to speak about it; **ouvrier q. / non q.** skilled/unskilled worker **(b)** *Jur (délit, vol)* aggravated **(c)** *Sp* **cheval/coureur q.** qualifier; **équipe qualifiée** qualifying team **2** *n Sp* qualifier
qualifier [kalifje] *(impf, pr sub* **n. qualifiions**) **1** *vt* **(a)** **q. qn pour qch/pour faire qch** to qualify sb for sth/to do sth **(b)** *(appeler)* to describe; **q. qn/qch de ...** to call sb/sth ..., to describe sb/sth as ...; **q. qn de charlatan** to call sb a quack, to describe sb as a quack; **acte qualifié de crime** action termed a crime; **conduite qu'on ne saurait q.** unspeakable behaviour **(c)** *Gram* to qualify **2 se qualifier** *vpr* **(a)** *Sp* to qualify; **il s'est qualifié pour la finale** he qualified for *or* got through to the final **(b)** **se q. de génie/d'artiste/***etc* to call oneself a genius/an artist/*etc*
qualitatif, -ive [kalitatif, -iv] *adj* qualitative; *Ch* **analyse qualitative** qualitative analysis
qualité [kalite] *nf* **(a)** *(de produit etc)* quality; **bonne/mauvaise q.** good *or* high/bad *or* poor quality; **produit de (bonne) q.** (good-)quality product; **produit de mauvaise q.** poor-quality product, product of poor quality; **de première q.** top-quality; **blé/viande de première q.** prime wheat/meat; **vin de première q.** choice wine; **chocolat de q. supérieure** extra fine chocolate; **minerai de q. inférieure** low-grade ore; *Ordinat* **q. brouillon, q. liste rapide, q. listing** draft quality; *Ordinat* **q. courrier** (near) letter quality; **garantie de q.** guarantee of quality; **améliorer la q. de la vie** to improve the quality of life; **q. de l'environnement** quality of the environment; **q. d'impression** print quality

(b) *(de personne)* quality; **homme qui a beaucoup de qualités** man with many good qualities *or* points; **qualités de gestionnaire** management *or* managerial qualities; **elle n'a pas que des qualités** she isn't all good; **cet ordinateur a beaucoup de qualités** this computer has many good points; **les qualités littéraires d'un texte** the literary qualities of a text

(c) *(propriété)* quality, property; **c'est une des qualités de cette plante** it's one of the properties of this plant; **qualités fébrifuges** antifebrile properties

(d) *(occupation)* occupation; *(fonction)* capacity; **décliner ses titres et qualités** to state one's titles and qualifications; *Admin* **nom, prénom et q.** surname, forename and occupation; **il nous révéla sa q. de prêtre** he disclosed the fact that he was a priest; **agir en q. de tuteur** to act (in one's capacity) as guardian; **en (ma) q. de citoyen, je voudrais ...** (in my capacity) as a citizen, I would like ...; **ès qualités** in one's official capacity; **avoir q. pour agir** to have authority to act; **avoir les qualités requises pour un emploi** to have the necessary qualifications *or* to be qualified for a job

(e) *Vieilli* **gens de q.** people of quality, gentlefolk

quand [kɑ̃] **1** *conj* **(a)** [①B29-30,11] when; **je lui en parlerai q. je le verrai** I'll mention it to him when I see him; **q. je lui téléphone, elle est toujours pressée** when I ring her she's always in a hurry, whenever I ring her she's in a hurry; *F* **je me souviens de q. tu as commencé à travailler ici** I remember when you started working here; *F* **q. je pense que le voyage devait être annulé** when I think that they were going to cancel the trip; *F* **q. je vous le disais!** I told you so!, didn't I tell you so!

(b) *Litt* **q. (même), q. (bien même)** even if, even though; **q. (bien même) il me l'affirmerait, je n'en croirais rien** even if *or* even though he assured me of it I wouldn't believe it; **je n'en voudrais pas q. (bien) même on me le donnerait** I wouldn't have it (even) as a gift

(c) *F* **je le ferai q. même** I'll do it all the same *or* in spite of everything; **q. même, ça serait plus gentil d'aller la chercher à la gare** even so, it would be nicer to meet her at the station; **c'est q. même gentil de sa part** even so, it's nice of him; **tu aurais pu me le dire q. même!** you might have told me!; **elle ne sait pas compter – q. même!** she can't count – you're joking!

2 *adv* when; **q. viendra-t-il?** when will he come?; **dites-moi q. il viendra** tell me when he will come; **n'importe q.** no matter when, at any time; **jusqu'à q. serez-vous à Paris?** how long will you be in Paris?; **depuis q. êtes-vous à Paris?** how long have you been in Paris?; **à q. le mariage?** when will the wedding be?, when is the wedding?; **de q. est ce journal?** what is the date of this paper?; **pour q. est la réunion?** when is the meeting?; *F* **c'est prévu pour q.?** when is this supposed to be happening?

quant à [kɑ̃ta] *prép* as for; **q. moi** as for me, for my part, as far as I am concerned; **q. cela ...** as for *or* to that ..., as far as that is concerned ...; **q. l'avenir ...** as for *or* to the future ..., as far as the future is concerned ...; **s'inquiéter q. l'avenir** to be worried about the future; **q. le demander, je n'y aurais pas songé** as for asking for it, I wouldn't have dreamt of it

quant-à-soi [kɑ̃taswa] *nm inv* reserve; **rester sur** *ou* **se tenir sur son q.** to keep oneself to oneself

quantième [kɑ̃tjɛm] *nm Litt* day of the month; **quel q. (du mois) sommes-nous?** what day of the month is it?, what is the date?

quantifiable [kwɑ̃tifjabl] *adj* quantifiable; **données non-quantifiables** unquantifiable data

quantification [kwɑ̃tifikasjɔ̃] *nf Phil* quantification; *Phys* quantization

quantifier [kɑ̃tifje] *vt* to quantify; *Phys* to quantize

quantique [kɑ̃tik] *adj Phys etc* (*théorie, mécanique, nombre etc*) quantum

quantitatif, -ive [kɑ̃titatif, -iv] *adj* (*analyse, changement etc*) quantitative

quantitativement [kɑ̃titativmɑ̃] *adv* quantitatively

quantité [kɑ̃tite] *nf* **(a)** [①B57,E] (*somme, dose*) quantity, amount; **en grande/petite q.** in large/small quantities *or* amounts; **dans la q. prescrite** in the prescribed dose; **en q.** in quantity; **nous en avons en q.** we have plenty of them; **q.** *ou* **des quantités de gens/réponses** a lot of *or* a great number of *or* a great many people/replies; **il n'en reste pas des quantités** there are not a lot left; **q. négligeable** negligible quantity *or* amount; *F* **il faut la considérer comme q. négligeable** what she thinks is of no consequence, her opinion is neither here nor there

(b) *Phys etc* quantity; *Math* **q. variable** variable quantity; *Phys* **q. de mouvement** momentum, impulse

quantum, *pl* **quanta** [k(w)ɑ̃tɔm, -a] *nm* **(a)** *Phys* quantum; **théorie des quanta** quantum theory **(b)** (*quantité*) amount; **fixer le q. des dommages-intérêts** to fix the amount of damages, to assess the damages

quarantaine [karɑ̃tɛn] *nf* **(a)** (*environ quarante*) about forty, forty or so; **une q. de personnes/jours** about forty *or* forty or so people/days

(b) (*âge*) about forty, forty or so; **approcher de la q.** to be getting on for forty, to be almost forty; **avoir la q.** to be in one's forties; **elle doit avoir une petite q. d'années** she must be just over forty; **les problèmes typiques de la q.** the typical problems of the fortysomething generation

(c) (*isolement*) quarantine; **pavillon de q.** quarantine flag; **mettre un navire en q.** to quarantine a ship, to put a ship in quarantine; **mettre qn en q.** to quarantine sb, to put sb in quarantine; *Fig F* to send sb to Coventry; **être en q.** to be in quarantine

quarante [karɑ̃t] *adj inv, nm inv* forty; **page q.** page forty; **habiter au (numéro) q.** to live at number forty; **la semaine de q. heures** the forty-hour week; *F* **je m'en fiche comme de l'an q.** I couldn't care less, I don't give a damn; *Tennis* **q. à** *ou* **partout** deuce; **les années q.** the forties; **les Q.** the French Academy

quarante-cinq *nm* **q. tours** (*disque*) single, 45

quarantenaire [karɑ̃tnɛr] *adj* **(a)** (*régulations etc*) quarantine **(b)** *Jur* forty-year, lasting for forty years

quarantième [karɑ̃tjɛm] *adj, n* fortieth

quart¹ [kar] *adj* **le q. monde** (*pays*) the Fourth World; (*pauvres des pays riches*) the underclass of a developed country

quart² *nm* **(a)** (*fraction*) quarter; **donner un q. de tour à une vis** to give a screw a quarter turn; **partir au q. de tour** (*d'une voiture*) to start first time; *Fig* (*d'une personne*) to fly off the handle; **il est parti** *ou* **a démarré au q. de tour** (*d'un moteur*) it started first time *or* right away; *F* (*d'un débat etc*) it got off to a great start, it took off right away; *F* **il est parti au q. de tour** he hit the roof, he blew up; *F* **il part au q. de tour** (*il est coléreux*) he's got a short fuse; *F* **elle a compris au q. de tour** she understood straight off *or* right away; *Com* **remise du q.** 25% discount, discount of 25%; **un q. de siècle** a quarter (of a) century, twenty-five years; **un q. d'heure** a quarter of an hour; **dans un petit q. d'heure** in ten minutes or so; *F* **passer un mauvais q. d'heure** to have a bad time of it; **je vais lui faire passer un mauvais q. d'heure** I'm going to give him a bad time; **un q. de beurre** a quarter (of a) kilo of butter; **trois quarts** three quarters; **la mode du trois quarts** the fashion for three-quarter-length skirts and coats; **manteau trois quarts** three-quarter-length coat; **les trois quarts du temps** most of the time; *F* **être aux trois quarts ivre/mort** to be three parts drunk/all but *or* as good as dead; *F* **elle était décidée aux trois quarts** she had all but *or* as good as decided; **il est deux heures et q.** *ou* **deux heures un q.** it's (a) quarter past *or Am* after two; **six heures moins le q., cinq heures trois quarts** (a) quarter to *or Am* of six

(b) (*bouteille, pichet*) quarter litre *or US* liter; *Mil* (*gobelet*) quarter litre *or US* liter mug

(c) *Naut* **q. (de vent)** point of the compass; **nord-est q. est** north-east by east

(d) *Naut* (*veille*) watch; **officier de q.** officer of the watch; **homme de q.** watch keeper; **être de q.** to be on watch; **faire le q.** to keep watch; *F* (*d'une prostituée*) to walk her beat

(e) *Arg* (*poste de police*) cop shop, police station

▶ **quart**: **q. de cercle** quadrant; *Sp* **q. de finale** quarter final; **l'équipe va jouer en q. de finale** the team will play in the quarter final; *Mus* **q. de soupir** semiquaver *or Am* sixteenth rest

quarte [kart] *nf* **(a)** *Mus* fourth **(b)** *Escrime* quarte, quart, carte; **parer en q.** to parry in carte

quarté [karte] *nm* = system of betting on four horses in the same race

quarteron, -onne [kart(ə)rɔ̃, -ɔn] **1** *n* (*métis*) quadroon **2** *nm* (*petit nombre*) bunch; **un q. de manifestants** a bunch of demonstrators

quartier [kartje] *nm* **(a)** (*quart*) quarter, *Fml* fourth part; **bois de q.** quartered logs; **la lune est au premier q.** the moon is in the first quarter; *Culin* **q. d'agneau/de bœuf** quarter of lamb/of beef; **cinquième q.** offal; *Hér* **quartiers de l'écusson** quarters *or* quarterings of the shield; **avoir quatre quartiers de noblesse** to belong to the established nobility

(b) (*morceau*) (*d'un gâteau*) portion; (*d'une orange*) segment; (*d'une pomme*) piece; (*d'une terre*) plot; **q. de lard** side of bacon; **q. de chevreuil** haunch of venison

(c) (*d'une ville*) district, area, neighbourhood, *US* neighborhood; *Admin* district; **les beaux quartiers** the fashionable districts *or* areas; **les quartiers nord de la ville** the north side of (the) town; **le q. des spectacles** theatreland, the theatre district; **je ne suis pas du q.** I'm not from around here, I'm not local; **demandez aux gens du q.** ask the locals *or* the local people; **médecin/cinéma de q.** local doctor/cinema; **tout le q. en parle** the whole neighbourhood is talking about it

(d) *Mil* **quartier(s)** quarters; **rentrer au q.** *ou* **aux quartiers** to return to quarters; **avoir q. libre** to be off duty; *Fig* **vous avez q. libre jusqu'à dix-huit heures** you're free until 6 o'clock, take a break until 6 o'clock, your time's your own till 6 o'clock; **quartiers d'hiver** winter quarters; *Fig* **un endroit idéal pour prendre nos quartiers d'hiver** an ideal place to spend the winter

(e) *Vieilli* **demander q.** to ask for quarter; **faire q. à qn** to give sb quarter; **ne pas faire de q.** to give no quarter; **pas de q.!** no quarter!; **il ne fait de q. à personne** he spares nobody

▶ **quartier**: [①A13,3,b] **q. général** headquarters; **grand q. général** general headquarters; **q. de haute sécurité** (*dans une prison*) top- *or* maximum-security wing; **q. réservé** red-light district

quartier-maître *pl* **quartiers-maîtres** *nm Naut* leading seaman

quartile [kwartil] *nm* quartile

quartz [kwarts] *nm Minér, Électron* quartz; **piloté par q.** crystal-controlled; **horloge/montre à q.** quartz clock/watch

quartzeux, -euse [kwartsø, -øz] *adj Minér* **sable q.** quartz sand

quartzite [kwartsit] *nm Minér* quartzite

quasar [kazar] *nm Astron* quasar

quasi[1] [kazi] *nm Culin* (*de veau, de bœuf*) chump end

quasi[2] *adv* almost, virtually; **q. aveugle** almost *or* virtually blind; **j'en ai la q.-certitude** I am practically *or* virtually certain of it; **la q.-totalité du budget** almost the whole *or* entire budget; **la q.-totalité des femmes** almost all (the) women; **une q.-dispute/un q.-divorce** a sort of argument/divorce; *Jur* **q.-contrat** implied contract; **q.-délit** technical offence

quasiment [kazimɑ̃] *adv* almost, nearly, as good as; **q. guéri** almost *or* nearly *or* as good as cured; **je n'ai q. rien senti** I hardly *or* barely *or* scarcely felt a thing

Quasimodo [kazimɔdo] *nf Rel* Low Sunday; **le lundi de (la) Q.** Low Monday

quaternaire [kwatɛrnɛr] **1** *adj Ch etc* quaternary; *Géol* Quaternary **2** *nm* Quaternary

quatorze [katɔrz] *adj inv, nm inv* fourteen; **le q. juillet** the fourteenth of July, Bastille Day; **page q.** page fourteen; **Louis Q.** Louis the Fourteenth; **habiter au (numéro) q.** to live at number fourteen; **la guerre de q.** the First World War, World War I, the 1914-18 War

quatorzième [katɔrzjɛm] **1** *adj, n* fourteenth **2** *nm* (*fraction*) fourteenth

quatorzièmement [katɔrzjɛmmɑ̃] *adv* in the fourteenth place, fourteenthly

quatrain [katrɛ̃] *nm Littér* quatrain

quatre [katr] *adj inv, nm inv* four; **Henri Q.** Henry the Fourth; **il est q. heures** it's four o'clock; *F* **ton q. heures** your afternoon snack; **le q. août** (on) the fourth of August, (on) August the fourth, *Am* (on) August fourth; **habiter au (numéro) q.** to live at number four; **trèfle à q. feuilles** four-leaf(ed) clover; **q. barré** (*à l'aviron*) coxed four; **par q.** in fours; **se mettre par q.** to get into *or* form fours; **manger comme q.** to eat like a horse; **monter l'escalier q. à q.** to go upstairs four at a time, to rush upstairs; *Sp F* **il est arrivé q. ou cinquième** he came in fourth or fifth; *Fig* **se mettre en q. pour faire qch** to do one's utmost to do sth; *Fig* **il se couperait** *ou* **se mettrait en q. pour vous** he would do anything for you; **se mettre en q. pour plaire à qn** to bend over backwards to please sb; *Fig* **clair comme deux et deux font q.** as clear as daylight *or* crystal; *Fig* **je me tenais à q. pour ne pas rire** it was all I could do not to laugh; *Fig* **plié en q.** doubled up with laughter; *Fig* **pull/livre de q. sous** cheap *or* inexpensive sweater/book; *Cartes* **le q. de pique** the four of spades

Quatre-Cantons [katr(ə)kɑ̃tɔ̃] *nmpl* **le lac des Q.** Lake Lucerne

quatre-cent-vingt-et-un [katsɑ̃vɛ̃teœ̃] *nm inv* = dice game in which the aim is to throw 4—2—1

quatre-mâts [katrəmɑ] *nm inv Naut* four-masted ship, four master

quatre-quarts [kat(rə)kar] *nm inv Culin* ≈ pound cake

quatre-quatre *nm ou f inv Aut* four-wheel drive

quatre-saisons [kat(rə)sɛzɔ̃] *nfpl* **(a) marchand des q.** street merchant (*selling fresh fruit and vegetables*), *Br Vieilli* costermonger **(b)** (*fraise*) perpetual-fruiting strawberry

Quatre-Temps [katrətɑ̃] *nmpl Rel* Ember days

quatre-vingt-dix [katrəvɛ̃dis] *adj inv, nm inv* ninety

quatre-vingt-dixième [katrəvɛ̃dizjɛm] *adj, n* ninetieth

quatre-vingtième [katrəvɛ̃tjɛm] *adj, n* eightieth

quatre-vingts [katrəvɛ̃] *adj, nm inv* (*omits the final s when followed by another number or when used as an ordinal*) eighty; **ils étaient q.** there were eighty of them; **page quatre-vingt** page eighty; **quatre-vingt-un** eighty-one; **quatre-vingt-onze** ninety-one; **ça fait q.** that comes to eighty; **habiter au (numéro) quatre-vingt** to live at number eighty

quatrième [katrijɛm] **1** *adj* fourth; **habiter au q. étage** to live on the fourth *or Am* the fifth floor **2** *nf* **(a)** *Cartes* sequence of four; **q. de couverture** (*d'un livre*) outside back cover **(b)** *Scol* **(classe de) q.** ≈ third form, *Am* ≈ seventh or eighth grade **3** *nm* **monter au q.** to go up to the fourth *or Am* fifth floor

quatrièmement [katrijɛmmɑ̃] *adv* fourthly, in the fourth place

quattrocento [kwatrɔtʃɛnto] *nm Beaux-Arts* quattrocento

quatuor [kwatɥɔr] *nm Mus* quartet, quartette; **q. à cordes** string quartet

que[1] [k(ə)] *pron rel* **(a)** [①A32-33; B20,F,1-3] (*souvent omis en anglais*) (*personne*) that, *Fml* whom; (*chose*) that, which; **l'homme q. vous voyez** the man (that) you see, *Fml* the man whom you see; **montrez-moi les livres q. vous avez achetés** show me the books (that *or* which) you have bought; **la tarte q. j'ai fait cuire** the tart (that) I baked; **c'est le meilleur q. nous ayons** it is the best (that) we have; **il n'est venu personne q. je connaisse** no one I know has come; **il faut attendre le temps qu'elle se prépare** you'll need to wait till she's ready

(b) (*attribut*) **il mourut en brave soldat qu'il était** he died like the gallant soldier he was; **idiot q. je suis** fool that I am; **menteur q. tu es!** you liar!; **couvert qu'il était de poussière** covered with dust as he was; **purs mensonges q. tout cela!** that's all a pack of lies!; **le garçon/livre q. voilà** that boy/book (there); **c'est une théorie intéressante q. la vôtre** yours is an interesting theory

(c) (*de temps*) **depuis trois mois q. j'habite Paris** for the three months I have been living in Paris; **un jour q. j'étais de service** one day when I was on duty; **il y a trois jours que je ne l'ai vue** it's been three days since I saw her; *Vieilli* **les jours qu'il fait chaud** on hot days; *Vieilli* **du temps q. les automobiles n'existaient pas** (in the time) before cars existed; *Vieilli* **les trois ans q. j'ai habité à Paris** the three years (during which) I lived in Paris

que[2] *pron interr* [①A31,c-e; B16,3,c] what; **q. voulez-vous?** what do you want?; **q. dit Jean?** what does John say?; **qu'y a-t-il à voir dans cette ville?** what is there to see in this town?; **q. faire?** what can I/we/one do?, what's to be done?; **q. dire?** what can/could I say?; **il ne savait q. penser** he didn't know what to think; **je n'ai q. faire de vos souhaits** you can keep your good wishes; **qu'en sait-elle?** what does she know (about it)?; **q. prendrez-vous, du lait ou de la crème?** what *or* which would you like, milk or cream?; **qu'est-il arrivé?, q. s'est-il passé?** what has happened?; *Litt* **qu'est-ce?** what is it?; *Litt* **q. ne le disiez-vous?** why didn't you say so?

que[3] *pron exclamatif* **qu'il est beau!** how handsome he is!; **q. c'est vrai!** how true!; **q. de déceptions!** what a lot of disappointments!

que[4] *conj* [①B55,B-C] **(a)** that (*souvent omis en anglais*); **je vois qu'il se trompe** I see (that) he's mistaken; **je pense qu'il a raison** I think (that) he's right; **je ne doute pas qu'elle y consente** I have no doubt (that) she will consent; **je désire qu'il vienne** I want him to come; **j'ai peur qu'il ne vienne** I'm afraid he will come; **je pense q. non** I think not; **il faut qu'elle le fasse** she has to *or* must do it; **peut-être qu'il est venu ce matin** perhaps he came this morning, he may have come this morning; **c'est q. je ne savais pas q. ...** it's because I didn't know (that) ...; **l'ennui est q. je n'ai rien préparé pour lui** the trouble is (that) I haven't prepared anything for him

(b) (*pour exprimer un souhait*) **qu'elle entre!** let her come in!; **q. Dieu lui pardonne!** (may) God forgive him!; **q. je vous y reprenne!** don't let me *or* just let me catch you at it again!

(c) (*pour exprimer une hypothèse*) **q. la machine chauffe, et il y aura un accident** let the machine get hot and there will be an accident; **qu'il essaie encore une fois, et il ...!** just let him try again and he'll ...!

(d) (*dans une alternative*) **qu'il pleuve ou qu'il fasse du vent** whether it rains or blows; **q. tu le veuilles ou non** whether you like it or not

(e) (*reliant deux conditionnels*) **il l'affirmerait q. je ne le croirais pas** even if he said it was true, I would not believe it

(f) (*équivalent de où*) *Litt* **il ne se passe jamais une année qu'il ne nous écrive** a year never goes by without his writing to us

(g) (*équivalent de* **afin que, alors que, avant que, depuis que, puisque, sans que, tant que** *etc*) **approchez qu'on vous entende** come nearer so that we can hear you; *Litt* **ne partez pas q. je ne vous aie parlé** don't go before I have had a talk with you

(h) (*pour ne pas répéter une autre conjonction*) **quand il entrera et qu'il vous trouvera ici** when he comes in and finds you here; **c'est pour quand tu iras mieux et q. tu voudras sortir** it's for when you're better and you want to go out; **quoiqu'il pleuve et qu'il fasse froid** although it is rainy and cold; **si on vient et qu'on veuille me consulter** if anyone comes and wants to consult me

(i) (*dans les comparaisons*) **plus grand/moins rapide q. moi** taller/slower than me; **aussi grand q. moi** as tall as I (am) *or* me; **c'est moins bien q. l'année dernière** it's not as good as last year; **il y a plus de monde q. la semaine dernière** there are more people than last week; **tout autre q. moi** anyone but me; **un autre parapluie q. celui-là** another umbrella besides that one; **vous écrivez plus**

correctement q. vous (ne) parlez you write more correctly than you speak; **il habite la même maison q. moi** he lives in the same house as I do *or* as me

(j) [①**A24**,d,iii; **B60**,B] **ne … q.** only; **il n'est q. blessé** he is only wounded; **il n'a qu'une jambe** he has only one leg, he only has one leg; **il n'a fait qu'entrer et sortir** he just slipped in and out again; **je ne fais q. passer** I'm not stopping, I won't stay; **elle ne fait q. (de) sortir** she has only just gone out; **je n'en ai q. trop** I have all too many; **je ne le connais q. trop** I know him only *or* all too well; **il n'y a pas qu'elle qui le sache** she is not the only one who knows it; **l'homme ne vit pas q. de pain** man does not live by bread alone; **il ne me reste plus q. vingt francs** I have only twenty francs left; **je ne bois jamais q. de l'eau** I never drink anything but water, I only ever drink water

(k) *Arch, Litt* **q. si vous savez la vérité, il est de votre devoir de la révéler** if you know the truth, it is your duty to reveal it

(l) *F* **ah! q. non!/q. si** *ou* **oui!** ah! surely not!/yes indeed!; **il va au cercle – qu'il dit!** he goes to the club – so he says!; **ton manteau est dans un état, q. c'est une horreur!** your coat is in a terrible state!

Québec [kebɛk] *nm Géog* Quebec

québécisme [kebesism] *nm Ling* = word or expression peculiar to Quebec French

québécitude [kebesityd] *nf* Quebec identity

québécois, -oise [kebekwa, -waz] **1** *adj* (of *or* from) Quebec **2** *nm Ling* Quebec French **3** *n* **Q.** Quebec(k)er

quel, quelle [kɛl] **1** *adj* **(a)** [①**A31**,c-d; **B15**,C,1] *interr* (*personne*) which; (*chose*) which, what; **q. livre avez-vous pris?** which *or* what book did you take?; **q. homme?** which man?; **quelle réponse a-t-elle faite?** what was her reply?; **quelle heure est-il?** what time is it?, what's the time?; **dites-moi quelle heure il est** tell me the time, tell me what time it is; **q. genre d'homme est-ce?** what sort of a man is he?; **si tu savais à q. point il tient à cette montre** if you knew how fond he is of this watch; **de quels hommes parlez-vous?** which men are you talking about?; **à q. projet faites-vous référence?** which project are you referring to?; **quels sont ces messieurs?** who are these gentlemen?; **quels sont ces livres?** what are these books?

(b) [①**A5**,B; **B15**,C,2] (*exclamatif*) **q. homme!** what a man!; **quelle surprise!** what a surprise!; **quelle bonté!** how kind!; **q. dommage que personne n'en ait rien su** what a shame no-one knew anything about it; **quelle bêtise d'avoir oublié le tire-bouchon** how stupid to have forgotten the corkscrew

(c) [①**A33**,h] *rel* (*personne*) whoever; (*chose*) whatever; **q. que soit le résultat** whatever the result may be; **quelle que soit mon affection pour vous** however great my affection for you, much as I love you; **quels que soient ces hommes** whoever these men may be; **q. que soit l'endroit où …** wherever, no matter where …; **il l'a rendu tel q.** he gave it back the way (it was when) he got it; **mettez-moi à n'importe quelle table** put me at any table you like

2 *pron interr* which (one); **de vous trois, q. est le plus rapide?** which (one) of you three is the fastest?

quelconque [kɛlkɔ̃k] *adj* **(a)** (*n'importe lequel*) any, some … or other; **s'il y a un q. problème** if there is any problem (whatever); **si pour une raison q. tu …** if for some reason or other *or* for any reason you …; **je prends un prétexte q. pour sortir** I go out on some pretext or other; **décrire un cercle passant par trois points quelconques** to describe a circle passing through any three points; **le projet peut échouer pour une raison q.** the plan can fail for any (of a) number of reasons

(b) (*insignifiant, médiocre*) ordinary, mediocre; **parler de choses quelconques** to talk about one thing and another; **une femme très q.** a very nondescript *or* average sort of woman; (*physiquement*) a very plain-looking woman; **on ne peut pas lui donner un emploi q.** we can't give him an ordinary job *or F* any old job; **son travail est q.** his work isn't up to much; **un q. général Alain** some General Alain or other

quelque [kɛlk(ə)] **1** *adj* **(a)** [①**A34-35**,a; **B14**,B,1b] some **quelques** some, a few; **pendant q. temps** for some time; **si j'avais q. argent** if I had some money; **je ressentais q. inquiétude** I felt some *or* a slight uneasiness; **avec quelques amis** with some friends, with a few friends; **il y a quelques jours** a few days ago; **cent et quelques mètres** a hundred metres plus, a hundred metres and a bit; *F* **nous étions quarante et quelques** there were forty or so of us, there were rather more than forty of us

(b) (*correlative to* **qui, que** + *sub*) **q. ambition qui l'agite** whatever ambition moves him; **quelques erreurs qu'elle ait commises** whatever mistakes she has made; **je vous interdis de sortir sous q. prétexte que ce soit** I forbid you to go out for any reason whatsoever; **tout traité de q. nature qu'il soit** every treaty, whatever its nature; **de q. côté que vous regardiez** whichever way you look

(c) (*un*) some; **avez-vous q. ami qui puisse vous aider?** have you some *or* a friend who can help you?

2 *adv* **(a)** (*environ*) some, about; **q. dix ans** some *or* about ten years; **les q. mille francs qu'il m'a prêtés** the thousand francs or so *or* or thereabouts that he lent me

(b) (*correlative to que* + *sub*) **q. grandes que soient ses fautes** however great his faults (may be); **q. méchant qu'il fût** wicked as he was

quelque chose [kɛlkəʃoz] *pron indéf inv* [①**A34**,a,iv; **B15**,B,2] something; (*dans les phrases interrogatives ou conditionnelles*) (*chose indéfinie*) anything, something; (*chose définie*) something; **q. me dit qu'elle viendra** something tells me she will come; **avez-vous q. à dire?** do you have anything *or* something to say?; **est-ce que je peux te dire q.?** can I tell you something?; **si je te dis q., est-ce que tu promets de ne pas te mettre en colère?** if I tell you something, do you promise not to get angry?; **q. de nouveau/plus moderne** something new/more modern; **q. d'autre** something else; **tu veux q. à manger/boire?** would you like something to eat/drink?; **il y a q. entre eux** there's something between them; **il y est pour q.** he has something to do with it; **il se doute de q.** he suspects something; **cela m'a fait q.** it had an effect on me; **ça te ferait vraiment q. si je m'en allais?** would it really matter to you if I went away?; **c'est déjà q.** that's something (anyhow); *F* **il a q.** there's something the matter with him; *F* **ah mais c'est q., ça!** that's a bit much!; *F* **q. comme deux ans** something like two years; *F* **je lui ai offert un petit q.** (*cadeau*) I gave him a little something

quelquefois [kɛlkəfwa] *adv* sometimes, at times

quelque part [kɛlkəpar] *adv* **(a)** somewhere; **on ira q. où tu n'es jamais allé** we'll go somewhere you've never been before; **cela doit bien venir de q.** it must come from somewhere; *Euph* **aller q.** (*aux toilettes*) to go somewhere, to go and wash one's hands, *Br* to go and spend a penny; (*d'une femme*) to (go and) powder one's nose; *Euph* **je lui ai donné un coup de pied q.** I kicked him in an unmentionable part of his anatomy **(b)** *Litt, Vieilli* (*correlative to* **que** + *sub*) **q. qu'il fouillât** wherever he searched

quelqu'un, quelqu'une [kɛlkœ, kɛlkyn], *pl* **quelques-uns, -unes** [kɛlkəzœ̃, -yn] **1** *pron indéf* [①**A34-35**,a; **B15**,B,2] **quelques-uns, quelques-unes** some, a few; **quelques-uns des magasins** some *or* a few of the shops; **j'ai lu quelques-unes des lettres** I have read some *or* a few of the letters; **quelques-un(e)s d'entre nous** some *or* a few of us

2 *nm* someone, somebody; (*dans les phrases interrogatives ou conditionnelles*) anyone, anybody, someone, somebody; **q. me l'a dit** someone *or* somebody told me; **de la part de q. qui pense à vous** from someone *or* somebody who is thinking of you; **si q. vient** if anyone *or* anybody *or* someone *or* somebody comes; **q. de plus** someone *or* somebody extra; **q. de trop** one too many; **y a-t-il eu q. de blessé?** was anyone *or* anybody *or* someone *or* somebody hurt?; **il faudra q. d'assez fort** it will need someone *or* somebody fairly strong; **c'est q. de très généreux** he's a very generous person; **ce doit être q. d'important** he must be someone *or* somebody important, he must be an important person; *F* **ça intéresse q.?** anyone *or* anybody interested?; *F* **je veux vraiment devenir q.** I really want to be somebody; *F* **c'est q., tu sais!** (*c'est qn de remarquable*) he's quite something, you know!; *F* **on ne me parle pas comme ça! je suis q., moi, monsieur!** don't talk to me like that! I'm not just anybody, you know!

quémander [kemɑ̃de] **1** *vt* **q. qch à qn** to beg for sth from sb **2** *vi* to beg

quémandeur, -euse [kemɑ̃dœr, -øz] *n Litt* beggar

qu'en-dira-t-on [kɑ̃diratɔ̃] *nm inv* gossip, tittle-tattle; **se moquer du q.** not to care what people say; **par souci du q.** for fear of what people might say

quenelle [kənɛl] *nf Culin* quenelle

quenotte [kənɔt] *nf Enf* toothy-peg, tooth

quenouille [kənuj] *nf* **(a)** *Tex* distaff; *Fig* **tomber en q.** (*d'une succession*) to fall to the distaff side; (*d'une entreprise, d'un projet etc*) to fall to pieces **(b)** (*d'un lit à baldaquin*) bedpost

quéquette [kekɛt] *nf F* willy

querelle [kərɛl] *nf* quarrel, dispute, *F* row; **chercher q. à qn** to try to pick a quarrel with sb; **avoir une q. avec qn** to have a quarrel *or F* a row with sb; **q. d'argent** quarrel over money; **querelles de famille** family squabbles

▶ **querelle**: **q. d'Allemand** quarrel over nothing; **q. d'amoureux** lovers' tiff; **q. de clocher** petty feud; **q. d'ivrognes** drunken brawl

quereller [kərele] **1** *vt Vieilli* (*qn*) to scold **2 se quereller** *vpr* to quarrel (with each other); (*d'amoureux*) to have a tiff

querelleur, -euse [kɑrɛlœr, -øz] **1** *n* quarreller **2** *adj* quarrelsome

quérir [kerir] *vt Vieilli, Litt (used only in the inf after* **aller, venir, envoyer) aller q. qn/qch** to go and fetch sb/sth

qu'est-ce que [kɛskə] **1** *pron interr* [①**A31**,c-d; **B16**,3,e] what; **q. vous voulez?** what do you want?; **q. la grammaire?** what is grammar?; **q. c'est que ça?** what's that?; **q. c'est que ce petit garçon qui ne veut pas se coucher?** what's all this about some little boy not wanting to go to bed?; *F* **q. tu avais besoin d'aller lui dire ça?** what did you have to go and tell him that for? **2** *pron exclamatif* **qu'est-ce qu'il fait beau!** what lovely weather!; **qu'est-ce qu'on a rigolé!** we had such a good laugh!

qu'est-ce qui [kɛski] *pron interr* [①**A31**,d; **B16**,3,d] what; **q. est arrivé?** what (has) happened?

question [kɛstjɔ̃] *nf* **(a)** [①**A45-46**,8; **B61**,C] *(interrogation)* question; *(demande de précisions)*, query (**sur** about, on); *Ordinat* query; **faire** *ou* **poser** *ou* **adresser une q. à qn** to ask sb a question, to put a question to sb; **sa fidélité ne fait pas q.** there is no doubt *or* no question about his loyalty; **quelle q.!** what a question!, what a thing to ask!; **tu te poses trop de questions** you worry too much; **je commence à me poser des questions sur son honnêteté** I'm beginning to wonder about *or* have my doubts about his honesty; **être en q.** to be called into question; **mettre en q.** to question, to call into question; *(affirmation)* to challenge; **elle ne cesse de tout remettre en q.** she questions absolutely everything; **le voyage est remis en q.** there's a question mark hanging over the trip; **voici un point qui fait q.** this is a debatable *or* moot point; **il n'y a pas de q.** there is no question *or* doubt about it

(b) *(affaire)* question, matter, issue; **je voudrais vous consulter sur une q. d'affaires** I would like to consult you on a business matter; **questions d'actualité** current affairs; **ce n'est qu'une q. d'argent/de temps** it is simply a question *or* matter of money/of time; **c'est une q. de minutes/d'habitude** it's a matter of minutes/of habit; **de quoi est-il q.?** what is it all about?; **il est q. de l'affaire de détournement de fonds** it's about this matter of embezzlement; **il est q. de lui élever une statue** there is some talk of putting up a statue to him; **il n'en est pas q.** it's out of the question; **il n'est pas q. de leur en parler** talking to them about it is out of the question; **il n'est pas q. que tu y retournes** it is out of the question for you to go back; **il ne saurait être q. de les inviter** we couldn't think of *or* there can be no question of inviting them; **la personne/l'affaire en q.** the person/the business in question; **sortir de la q.** to wander from the point; **ce n'est pas là la q., là n'est pas la q., la q. n'est pas là** that is not the point; *Iron* **c'est bien la q.!** that's completely beside the point!; **qu'il n'en soit plus q.** let us say no more about it, let's drop the subject; *F* **q. argent, ce n'est pas rose** moneywise *or* as far as money goes, things are pretty grim; **q. vacances, ça pourrait être mieux** as far as holidays go, it could be better; *F* **pas q.** no way, no chance

(c) *Jur* (point at) issue; **q. de fait/droit** issue of fact/law

(d) *Hist* **appliquer la q. à qn, mettre qn à la q.** to put sb to the question, to torture sb

▶ **question**: *Mktg* **q. cafétéria** multiple choice question; **q. à choix multiple** multiple choice question; *Pol* **q. de confiance** vote of confidence; **q. de contrôle** check question; **q. fermée** closed question; **q. fermée à choix unique** dichotomous question; *Mktg* **q. filtre** check question; **q. majeure** leading question; **q. ouverte** open question; **q. piège** trick question; *Mktg* **q. ricochet** boomerang question; **q. subsidiaire** *(d'un jeu)* tie-break, tiebreaker

questionnaire [kɛstjɔnɛr] *nm* questionnaire; **q. à choix multiple** *(à l'école etc)* multiple choice question paper; *(sondage)* multiple choice questionnaire; **q. d'évaluation** *(remis aux clients)* customer satisfaction questionnaire

questionnement [kɛstjɔn(ə)mɑ̃] *nm* questioning; *Ordinat* **q. logique** logical querying

questionner [kɛstjɔne] **1** *vt (qn)* to question (**sur** about) **2 se questionner** *vpr* to question each other

questionneur, -euse [kɛstjɔnœr, -øz] **1** *adj (enfant, air)* inquisitive **2** *n Rare* questioner

quête [kɛt] *nf* **(a)** *(recherche)* quest, search (**de** for); **se mettre en q. de qch/qn** to set out *or* go in search of sth/sb, to go looking for sth/sb; **gens en q. de plaisirs** people in search of pleasure, pleasure-seekers **(b)** *(pour trouver du gibier)* beating; *(de la meute)* tracking, scenting **(c)** *(collecte)* collection; **faire la q.** *(pour amasser des fonds)* to make a collection, *F* to pass the hat round; *Rel* to take the collection

quêter [kete] **1** *vt* **(a)** *(argent etc)* to collect **(b)** *(approbation, louanges)* to seek; *(compliments)* to fish for, to angle for; *(de la meute) (gibier)* to seek **2** *vi* **(a)** *(faire la quête)* to collect money, to make a collection **(b)** *(de la meute)* to quarter

quêteur, -euse [kɛtœr, -øz] *n* collector; *Rel* collection taker, person taking the collection

quêteux [kɛtø] *nm Can* beggar

quetsche [kwɛtʃ(ə)] *nf* **(a)** *(prune)* dark-red plum **(b)** *(eau-de-vie)* = plum liqueur similar to kirsch

queue [kø] *nf* **(a)** *(d'animal)* tail; **couper la q. à un cheval** to dock a horse *or* a horse's tail; **cheval à longue q.** long-tailed horse; **cheval à q. écourtée** bobtail (horse); **q. de renard** fox's brush; **elle a des queues de rat** her hair is like rats' tails; *F* **il est parti la q. entre les jambes** he went off with his tail between his legs; *F* **pas la q. d'un** *ou* **d'une** not a blessed one

(b) *(d'une comète, d'un cerf-volant, d'une lettre)* tail; *(d'un météore)* trail; *(d'une noire, d'une croche)* stem; *(d'une casserole)* handle; *(d'un fruit, d'une fleur)* stalk; **habit à q.** tail coat; **piano à q.** grand piano; *Typ* **lettre à q. inférieure** descending letter

(c) *(d'une procession)* (tail) end, rear; **venir en q.** *(d'un cortège etc)* to bring up the rear; **être en q.** *(d'un cortège etc)* to be at the rear; *Courses de chevaux* **arriver en q.** to come in at the tail end; **être à la q. de la classe, être en q. de classe** to be at the bottom of the class; *Fig* **une histoire/un film sans q. ni tête** a story/a film one can't make head or tail of, an incomprehensible story/film; **voiture en q. de train** *ou* **du train** carriage *or Am* car in the rear of the train; **wagon de** *ou* **en q.** end carriage, *Am* end car; **attaquer une armée en q.** to attack an army in the rear

(d) *(de gens)* queue, *Am* line; **ce sont les premiers de la q.** they are (the) first in the queue *or Am* line; **faire la q.** to queue (up), *Am* to stand in line; **se mettre dans** *ou* **prendre la q.** to get in *or* join the queue *or Am* line; **faire une heure de q.** to queue *or* to stand in a queue *or Am* to stand in line for an hour

(e) *Billard* cue; **faire fausse q.** to miscue

(f) *Vulg (pénis)* prick, cock, dick

▶ **queue**: **q. de cheval** *(coiffure)* ponytail; **avoir une q. de cheval** to have a ponytail, to wear one's hair in a ponytail; **q. de poisson: le conducteur m'a fait une q. de poisson** the driver cut (in) in front of me; *F* **finir en q. de poisson** *(d'une pièce de théâtre, d'un projet etc)* to end up in the air

queue-d'aronde, *pl* **queues-d'aronde** *nf Menuis* dovetail; **assemblage à q.** dovetail(ed) joint

queue-de-cochon, *pl* **queues-de-cochon** *nf (outil)* auger bit, gimlet

queue-de-morue, *pl* **queues-de-morue** *nf* **(a)** *(basques)* tail; **(habit à) q.** tail coat, *F* tails **(b)** *(brosse)* flat (paint)brush

queue-de-pie, *pl* **queues-de-pie** *nf* = **queue-de-morue**

queue-de-rat, *pl* **queues-de-rat** *nf* **(a)** *(lime)* rat tail, rat-tailed file **(b)** *(pour les trous)* reamer

qui[1] [ki] *pron rel* [①**A32-33**; **B20**,F,1-3,d] **(a)** *(personne)* who, that; *(animal, chose)* which, that; **homme/femme q. parle français** man/woman who *or* that speaks French; **phrases q. ne sont pas françaises** sentences which *or* that are not French; **vous q. êtes libres** you who are free; **c'est la plus âgée q. a répondu** it was the eldest who *or* that answered; **il y a peu de gens q. savent cela**, *Litt* **il est peu de gens qui sachent cela** there are few people who *or* that know that; **il n'y a personne q. ne comprenne cela** there is no one who *or* that does not understand that; **dans ce match, q. était son premier, l'équipe a fait preuve de résistance** in this their first match, the team showed great staying power; **je le vois q. vient** I can see him coming; **la voici q. arrive** she's coming (now), here she is (now); **le voilà q. râle à présent** there he goes, moaning; **c'est une femme charmante, et q. a du talent** she is a charming woman, and talented

(b) (= **celui qui**) **q. vivra verra** time will tell; **tout vient à point à q. sait attendre** all things come to him who waits; **sauve q. peut** every man for himself; **adressez-vous à q. vous voudrez** apply to anyone you like; *F* **comme q. dirait** so to speak, as it were

(c) (= **ce qui**) **q. plus est** what is more; **q. pis est** what is worse; **voilà q. me plaît** that's what I like

(d) ce q. *voir* **ce**

(e) *(après prép) (peut être omis en anglais)* who, *Fml* whom; **voilà l'homme à q. je pensais** there is the man (who) I was thinking of *or Fml* the man of whom I was thinking; **il cherche quelqu'un avec q. jouer** he is looking for someone to play with

(f) *(indéf)* some; **on se dispersa, q. d'un côté, q. d'un autre** we scattered, some going one way, some another

(g) q. que ce soit *(sujet)* whoever; *(objet)* anyone; **je défie q. que ce soit de le prouver** I challenge anyone to prove it

qui[2] *pron interr* [①**A31**,a-b; **B16**,3,b] who; *(complément d'objet ou* *après prép*) who, *Fml* whom; **q. a dit cela?** who said that?; **savez-vous q. a dit cela?** do you know who said that?; **q. désirez-vous voir?** who *or Fml* whom do you wish to see?; **q. vient à la réunion?** who is coming to the meeting?; **devinez q. est arrivé le premier** guess who was here first; **à q. est ce canif?** whose knife is this?, whose is this knife?; **de q. parlez-vous?** who are you talking about?, *Fml* of whom are you speaking?; **de q. êtes-vous le fils?** whose son are you?; **je me demande de q. il tient son mauvais caractère** I wonder who *or* where he gets his bad temper from; **q. d'autre?** who else?; **q. de vous me suivra?** which of you will follow me?; *F* **q. ça?** who's that?; **c'est à q. entrera le premier** it's a question of who comes in first; **c'était à q. l'aiderait** they vied with *or* outdid each other in helping him; *F* **il est là – q. donc?** he's here – who?

quia (à) [akɥija] *adv Vieilli* **être à q.** to be at a loss for an answer; **réduire** *ou* **mettre qn à q.** to nonplus sb

quiche [kiʃ] *nf Culin* quiche; **q. lorraine** quiche lorraine

quiconque [kikɔ̃k] *pron indéf* **(a)** *rel* whoever, anyone who, anybody who; **q. désobéira sera puni** whoever disobeys *or* anyone who *or* anybody who disobeys will be punished **(b)** (*n'importe qui*) anyone, anybody; **q. de mes amis** any of my friends

quidam [kidam] *nm Vieilli* fellow, individual

qui est-ce que [kiɛskə] *pron interr* (*objet*) who, *Fml* whom; **q. vous désirez voir?** who *or Fml* whom do you wish to see?

qui est-ce qui [kiɛski] *pron interr* (*sujet*) who

quiet, -ète [kjɛ, -ɛt] *adj Arch* calm

quiétisme [kjetism] *nm Hist Rel* quietism

quiétiste [kjetist] *adj, n Hist Rel* quietist

quiétude [kjetyd] *nf* peace(fulness); **en toute q.** quite calmly

quignon [kiɲɔ̃] *nm* (*de pain*) (*morceau*) chunk, hunk; (*bout*) end crust

quille[1] [kij] *nf* **(a)** skittle, ninepin; **jouer aux quilles** to play skittles *or* ninepins; *Fig* **être reçu comme un chien dans un jeu de quilles** to be treated as an intruder; *Fig* **se tenir droit comme une q.** to hold oneself as straight as a ramrod **(b)** *très F* (*jambe*) pin, leg; **il ne tient pas sur ses quilles** he's shaky on his pins **(c)** *Mil Arg* **à nous la q.!** civvy street, here we come!; **la q., c'est dans cent cinquante jours** we'll be back in civvy street in a hundred and fifty days

quille[2] *nf Naut* keel; **fausse q.** false keel, outer keel; **q. de roulis, q. latérale** bilge keel; **poser la q. d'un navire** to lay down a ship; **la q. en l'air** bottom up

quilleur, -euse [kijœr, -øz] *n Can* skittle player

quillier [kije] *nm* set of skittles

quincaillerie [kɛ̃kajri] *nf* **(a)** (*ustensiles*) hardware, *Br* ironmongery; *Fig F* **elle a mis toute sa q.** she's wearing every bit of jewellery she's got **(b)** (*commerce*) hardware business; (*magasin*) hardware shop, *Br* ironmonger's

quincaillier, -ière [kɛ̃kaje, -jɛr] *n* hardware dealer, *Br* ironmonger

quinconce [kɛ̃kɔ̃s] *nm* quincunx; **arbres disposés en q.** trees arranged in staggered rows; **rivetage en q.** staggered *or* zigzag riveting

quinine [kinin] *nf* quinine

quinquagénaire [kɛ̃kaʒenɛr] *adj, n* fifty-year-old, quinquagenarian; **elle est q.** she is in her fifties

Quinquagésime [kɛ̃kaʒezim] *nf Rel* Quinquagesima (Sunday)

quinquennal, -ale, -aux, -ales [kɛ̃kenal, -o] *adj* quinquennial; (*plan*) five-year; **une exposition quinquennale** a five-yearly exhibition

quinquennat [kɛ̃kena] *nm* five-year term

quinquet [kɛ̃kɛ] *nm* **(a)** *F Vieilli* **quinquets** eyes; **ouvrez/fermez les quinquets!** open/close your eyes! **(b)** (*lampe*) oil lamp

quinquina [kɛ̃kina] *nm* **(a)** *Pharm* cinchona **(b) (vin de) q.** (apéritif) tonic wine

quint [kɛ̃] *adj Arch* fifth

quintal, -aux [kɛ̃tal, -o] *nm* quintal (*= 100 kg*)

quinte [kɛ̃t] *nf* **(a) q. de toux** coughing fit, fit of coughing **(b)** *Mus* fifth; **q. juste** perfect fifth **(c)** *Cartes* quint **(d)** *Escrime* quinte **(e)** *Vieilli* (*accès de mauvaise humeur*) fit of bad temper

quintefeuille [kɛ̃tfœj] **1** *nf Hér, Bot* cinquefoil **2** *nm Archit* cinquefoil

quintessence [kɛ̃tesɑ̃s] *nf* quintessence

quintette [k(ɥ)ɛ̃tɛt] *nm Mus* quintet(te)

quinteux, -euse [kɛ̃tø, -øz] *adj* (*personne*) crotchety, testy; (*cheval*) restive; (*toux*) fitful

quintuple [kɛ̃typl] **1** *adj* fivefold, quintuple **2** *nm* quintuple; **au q.** fivefold; **trente est (le) q. de six** thirty is five times (as much as) six

quintupler [kɛ̃typle] *vti* to increase fivefold, to quintuple

quintuplés, -ées [kɛ̃typle] *npl* quintuplets, *F* quins, *Am* quints

quinzaine [kɛ̃zɛn] *nf* **(a)** (*environ quinze*) about fifteen, fifteen or so, some fifteen; **une q. de francs/personnes** about fifteen *or* fifteen or so *or* some fifteen francs/people **(b)** (*deux semaines*) **une q. (de jours)** two weeks, *Br* a fortnight; **remettre une cause à q.** to adjourn a case for two weeks *or Br* a fortnight **(c)** (*salaire*) two weeks' *or Br* a fortnight's pay

quinze [kɛ̃z] **1** *adj inv* **(a)** fifteen; **Louis Q.** Louis the Fifteenth; **numéro q.** number fifteen **(b) q. jours** two weeks, *Br* a fortnight; **tous les q. jours** every other *or* second week, *Br* every fortnight, once a fortnight, fortnightly **2** *nm inv* **(a)** fifteen; **le q. mai** (on) the fifteenth of May, (on) May the fifteenth, *Am* (on) May fifteenth; **habiter au q.** to live at number fifteen; *Tennis* **q. partout** fifteen all **(b) demain en q.** two weeks *or Br* a fortnight (from) tomorrow, *Br* tomorrow fortnight **(c)** *Rugby* **le q. de France** the French fifteen

quinzième [kɛ̃zjɛm] **1** *adj, n* fifteenth **2** *nm* (*fraction*) fifteenth

quinzièmement [kɛ̃zjɛmmɑ̃] *adv* in the fifteenth place, fifteenthly

quiproquo [kiprɔko] *nm* (*en prenant une personne pour une autre*) case of mistaken identity, mix-up; (*en prenant une chose pour une autre*) mix-up; **il y a eu un q.** there's been a mix-up

quittance [kitɑ̃s] *nf* receipt; **q. de loyer** rent receipt; **q. pour solde** receipt in full; *Banque* **q. pour solde de compte** closing account balance; *Fin* **q. finale** final payment *or* discharge

quittancer [kitɑ̃se] *vt* **(je quittançai(s))** (*facture, dette*) to receipt

quitte [kit] **1** *adj* **(a)** (*libéré*) **je suis q. envers vous** I'm no longer in debt to you; **nous sommes quittes** we're quits *or* all square; **tenir qn q. de qch** to let sb off (with) sth; **je vous tiens q. du reste** I'll let you off (with) the rest, never mind the rest; **il en a été q. pour la peur** he got off *or* escaped with a fright; **ils en ont été quittes à bon compte** they got off lightly; **jouer (à) q. ou double** to play double or quits; *Jur* **être q. de dettes** to be out of debt, to be clear of debts

(b) q. à even if it means; **je le ferai, q. à être grondé/m'ennuyer** I'll do it even if it means being scolded/getting bored; **il abandonne ce travail, q. à le reprendre plus tard** he's giving up this work but may resume it later

2 *nm* **un q. ou double** double or quits

quitter [kite] **1** *vt* (*endroit, personne*) to leave; (*métier*) to leave, to quit; (*fonction, chambre d'hôtel*) to vacate; **q. la grande route** to turn off *or* leave the main road; **la voiture a quitté la route** (*par accident*) the car went off *or* left the road; (*délibérément*) the car turned off (the road); **q. les rails** (*d'un train*) to jump *or* leave the rails, to derail; *Naut* **q. la jetée** *ou* **le quai** to cast off; **q. le hôtel** to check out (of the hotel); *Ordinat* **q. le système** to quit (the system); **q. le théâtre** to give up the stage; **q. les affaires** to retire from business; **q. une mauvaise habitude** to give up a bad habit; **q. la vie** to depart this life; **un ami très cher vient de nous q.** we have just lost a very dear friend, a very dear friend has just passed away; **quel plaisir de tout q.!** how nice to get away from it all!; **sa main n'a pas quitté la mienne** his hand didn't leave mine; **il ne l'a pas quittée des yeux** he didn't take his eyes off her; **ne le quittez pas des yeux** keep your eye on him, don't let him out of your sight, don't take your eyes off him; **c'est une idée qui ne me quitte pas** I can't get the idea out of my head; **elle veut q. son mari** she wants to leave her husband; **elle ne quitte pas sa mère** (*elle n'est pas indépendante*) she won't leave her mother, she never leaves her mother's side; **je dois vous q., il est tard** I must leave you, it's late; **vous ne quittez pas votre veste?** won't you take off your jacket?; **tu vas adorer ce pull, tu ne le quitteras plus** you'll love this sweater, you won't want to take it off; *Tél* **ne quittez pas (l'écoute)!** hold on!, hold the line!; **q. la partie** to give up

2 se quitter *vpr* (*des amis etc*) to part, to say goodbye; (*d'un couple*) to part, to split up, to break up; **il est tard, nous devons nous q.** it's late, we have to say goodbye now; **ils se sont quittés bons amis** they parted good friends

quitus [k(ɥ)itys] *nm Jur* (*d'une dette, d'une responsabilité etc*) quietus, final discharge; **q. fiscal** tax clearance

qui-vive *nm inv* **être** *ou* **se tenir sur le q.** to be on the alert *or* the qui vive

quoi[1] [kwa] *pron rel* **(a)** [①**A33**,g-h; **B21**,g,vi] what; **ce sur q. l'on discute** what is being discussed; **ce à q. je m'oppose** what I object to; **c'est en q. vous vous trompez** that is where you are wrong; **après q.** after which; **c'est ce pour q. il s'est battu des années durant** this is what he's been fighting for for years; **travaille, sans q. tu ne mangeras pas** work, otherwise you won't eat; **il a de q. vivre** he has enough to live on; **il a bien autre chose à q. penser!** he has other things to think about!

(b) il y a de q. vous faire enrager it's enough to drive you mad; **il n'y a pas de q. être fier/se réjouir** there's nothing to be proud of/to get excited about; **je suis en colère – je vous comprends, il y a de q.** I'm angry – I understand, you've every right *or* reason to be; **il n'y a pas de q.** (*en réponse à des remerciements, des excuses*) don't mention it, not at all; *F* **il a de q.** he's well *or* comfortably off; **avez-vous de q. écrire/manger?** have you anything *or* something to write with/to eat?; **il faut trouver de q. allumer le feu** we must find something to light the fire with

(c) (*dans une exclamation*) *F* **comme q. ça n'était pas la peine de s'énerver!** so it wasn't worth getting worked up about!

(d) (*correlative to* **qui, que** + *sub*) **q. qui survienne, restez calme** whatever happens, keep calm; **q. qu'il en soit** be that as it may, however that may be; **q. qu'on fasse, il n'est jamais content** no matter what you do *or* whatever you do he's never satisfied; **q. que ce soit** anything (whatever); **puis-je vous être utile en q. que ce soit?** can I be of use to you in any way?; **avez-vous dit q. que ce soit?** did you say anything (at all)?; **q. que ce soit qui l'en empêche** whatever may be preventing him

quoi² **1** *pron interr* [①A31,c-d; B16,3,f] what; **q. d'autre?** what else?; **q. de nouveau** *ou* **neuf?** what's new?; **q. de plus simple?** what could be simpler *or* easier?; **je ne sais q. penser/lui dire** I don't know what to think/to say to him; **à q. pensez-vous?** what are you thinking of *or* about?; **de q. parlez-vous?** what are you talking about?; **en q. puis-je vous être utile?** how can I help you?; **à q. bon (faire qch)?** what's the use *or* good (of doing sth)?; **en q. est-ce?, c'est en q.?** what's it made of?; *F* **eh bien! q.?** well, what about *or* of it?; *F* **tu es sourd ou q.?** are you deaf or what?; *F* **q.?, je n'entends rien!** what?, I can't hear you!; *très F* **vous désirez q.?** what is it you want?; *très F* **de q.?** what!, what's that?

2 *int* **(mais) q.!** what!; **q. donc!** what's that?; **q., c'est vous!** what, is it you?; **mais alors q.? tout est annulé?** don't tell me it's all off!; **enfin q.! il ne peut pas se désister comme ça!** wait a minute, he can't back out like that!; **on ne va pas y passer la nuit q.!** we're not going to spend the night there!

quoique [kwak(ə)] *conj* **(a)** (+ *sub*) (al)though; **quoiqu'il soit pauvre il est généreux** (al)though he is poor he is generous; **je suis heureux q. malade** I am happy (al)though I'm ill; **q. jeune, il avait une certaine expérience** (al)though young, he had some experience **(b)** (+ *ind*) (*à la réflexion*) **nous recevons souvent des coups, q., vous savez, nous en donnons aussi** we often receive blows, but then, of course, we hit back

quolibet [kɔlibɛ] *nm* gibe, jeer; **poursuivre qn de ses quolibets** to gibe *or* jeer at sb

quorum [k(w)ɔrɔm] *nm* quorum; **atteindre le q.** to have a quorum

quota [k(w)ɔta] *nm* quota; **q. d'importation** import quota

quote-part, *pl* **quotes-parts** [kɔtpar] *nf* share, quota, portion

quotidien, -ienne [kɔtidjɛ̃, -jɛn] **1** *adj* (*travail, promenade, journal, émission*) daily; (*ennuis*) everyday; **la vie quotidienne** everyday *or* daily life **2** *nm* **(a)** (*journal*) daily (paper); **grand q.** national daily (paper) **(b) au q.** on a day-to-day basis; **la science-fiction au q.** science fiction in the everyday world

quotidiennement [kɔtidjɛnmɑ̃] *adv* daily, every day

quotidienneté [kɔtidjɛnte] *nf* everyday nature

quotient [kɔsjɑ̃] *nm Math etc* quotient

▶ **quotient**: **q. électoral** electoral quota; *Admin* **q. familial** family allowance; **q. intellectuel** intelligence quotient, IQ; **son q. intellectuel est de 120** he has an IQ of 120

quotité [kɔtite] *nf* quota, share, proportion; *Jur* **q. disponible** disposable portion of estate; **impôt de q.** proportional tax; **q. garantie** (*en assurance*) guaranteed cover limit

R

R, r [ɛr] *nm* (*lettre*) R, r; **rouler les r** to roll one's r's; **ne mangez des fruits de mer que pendant les mois en r** only eat seafood when there's an r in the month

r. (*abrév* **route**) Rd

rab [rab] *nm F* (*nourriture*) extra (food); (*temps*) overtime; **un r. de poulet** a second helping *or* seconds of chicken; **un r. de cigarettes** extra cigarettes; **faire du r.** to put in a bit of overtime; **avoir un r. de cinq minutes** to have an extra five minutes, to have five more minutes; **un r. de sommeil, c'est toujours agréable** it's always nice to get some extra sleep; **il reste du poulet en r.** there's some chicken going spare *or* up for grabs; **j'en ai encore en r.** I still have some left over

rabâchage [rabɑʃaʒ] *nm* (tedious) repetition

rabâcher [rabɑʃe] **1** *vi* to say the same thing over and over again **2** *vt* (*conseils, recommandations*) to keep on repeating; (*leçon*) to repeat parrot-fashion; **ils rabâchent toujours la même chose** they're always (harping) on about the same old thing; **elle nous a rabâché qu'il fallait faire attention au verglas** she kept on at us about being careful of the ice; **c'est ce qu'elle a passé son temps à me r.** that was what she kept on at me about; **le prof rabâche le même cours depuis dix ans** the teacher's been regurgitating *or* churning out the same old course for ten years

rabâcheur, -euse [rabɑʃœr, -øz] **1** *adj* repetitive; **il est très r.** he's always repeating himself *or* harping on about the same thing; **elle devient un peu rabâcheuse** she's starting to repeat herself **2** *n* repetitive person

rabais [rabɛ] *nm* discount, reduction; **r. en cas de paiement comptant** cash discount; **faire un r. (sur qch)** to give a discount (on sth); **faire un r. de 15%/de 50 francs** to give a 15%/50-franc discount, to take 15%/50 francs off the price; **vendre qch au r.** to sell sth at a discount *or* at a reduced price; *Fig* **au r.** (*travail*) poorly *or* badly paid; (*système éducatif*) second-rate; **formation au r.** second-rate training, training on the cheap

rabaissement [rabɛsmɑ̃] *nm Rare* **(a)** (*de store*) lowering **(b)** (*critique*) disparagement

rabaisser [rabese] **1** *vt* **(a)** (*store*) to lower; (*prix*) to reduce, to lower **(b)** (*personne, talents etc*) to belittle, *F* to put down **2 se rabaisser** *vpr* to belittle oneself, *F* to put oneself down; **se r. devant qn** to put oneself down with sb

rabane [raban] *nf Tex* raffia (fabric); **rabanes** (raffia) mats

rabat [raba] *nm* **(a)** (*de sac à main, d'une enveloppe*) flap; (*d'un costume officiel*) bands **(b)** (*pour gibier*) beating

rabat-joie **1** *nm inv* killjoy, *F* spoilsport, *F* wet blanket **2** *adj inv* **elle est r.** she's such a killjoy *or* spoilsport *or* wet blanket

rabattable [rabatabl] *adj* (*siège, dossier*) folding, fold-down; *Aut* **capote r.** folding roof, drophead

rabattage [rabataʒ] *nm* (*du bois*) beating; (*du gibier*) driving

rabatteur, -euse [rabatœr, -øz] *n* **(a)** (*à la chasse*) beater **(b)** *Fig* tout

rabattre [rabatr] (*conj like* **battre**) **1** *vt* **(a)** (*capote*) to fold down; (*couvercle, siège de toilettes*) to close, to shut, to put down; (*store*) to lower, to pull down, to shut; (*col*) to turn down; (*siège*) (*vers le haut*) to fold up, to put up; (*vers le bas*) to fold down, to put down; (*remettre en place*) to fold *or* put back; **r. une couture** to press down *or* flatten a seam; **r. le bord d'une tôle** to flange a plate; **le vent rabat la fumée** the wind is blowing *or* driving the smoke in this direction; **le vent rabattait la fumée vers nous** the wind was blowing *or* driving the smoke in our direction; *Sp* **r. la balle** to smash the ball; **r. la foule vers la place** to drive the crowd back towards the square

(b) (*diminuer*) (*prix*) to reduce, to cut; (*arbre, branche*) to cut back; **r. 100 francs du prix** to take *or F* knock 100 francs off the price; **je n'en rabattrai pas un sou** I won't take a penny less for it; **r. l'orgueil de qn** to humble sb; *F* **r. le caquet à qn** to shut sb up, to put sb in his/her place; *F* **se faire r. le caquet** to get put in one's place; **r. de ses prétentions, en r.** to lower one's sights; *Tricot* **r. les mailles** to cast off

(c) (*gibier*) to drive; (*fugitifs*) to herd

2 se rabattre *vpr* **(a)** (*de siège de voiture*) to fold down; **table qui se rabat** folding *or* drop-leaf table

(b) l'armée se rabattit sur la ville the army fell back on the town; **la fumée s'est rabattue sur nous** the smoke was blown *or* driven in our direction

(c) se r. sur (*se contenter de*) (*un sujet*) to fall back on; (*un film, une personne*) to fall back on, to make do with; **elle finira par se r. sur ce qu'on lui propose** she'll end up accepting *or* making do with what she's offered

(d) *Aut* to pull back in; (*s'écarter*) to move over

rabattu [rabaty] *adj* **col r.** turn(ed)-down collar; **couture rabattue** run and fell seam

rabbin [rabɛ̃] *nm* rabbi; **grand r.** Chief Rabbi

rabbinique [rabinik] *adj* rabbinical

rabbinisme [rabinism] *nm* rabbinism

rabbiniste [rabinist] *n* rabbinist

rabdomancie [rabdɔmɑ̃si] *nf* dowsing, *Spéc* rhabdomancy

rabelaisien, -ienne [rablɛzjɛ̃, -jɛn] *adj Littér* Rabelaisian

rabibochage [rabibɔʃaʒ] *nm F* patching up, repairing, mending; *Fig* (*entre amis*) making up, reconciliation

rabibocher [rabibɔʃe] *F* **1** *vt Fig* **j'ai réussi à les r.** I managed to patch things up between them **2 se rabibocher** *vpr* to patch things up, to make it up (**avec** with)

rabiot [rabjo] *nm F Vieilli* = **rab**

rabioter [rabjɔte] *F* **1** *vi* to scrounge, to cadge; (*de commerçant*) to give short measure; **la Mère Grognard rabiote sur la nourriture** Ma Grognard skimps on the food **2** *vt* (*nourriture*) to snaffle; (*de commerçant*) to skimp on; **r. quelques centimes** to skim off a few pennies *or Am* cents; **j'ai réussi à r. cinq minutes** I managed to snatch *or* steal an extra five minutes

rabique [rabik] *adj* (*virus*) rabies

râble¹ [rɑbl] *nm* (*de lièvre, lapin*) back; *Culin* **r. de lièvre** saddle of hare; *F* **il m'a sauté sur le r.** he jumped on me; *F* **je ne pouvais pas me douter de ce qui allait me tomber sur le r.** I didn't suspect what was waiting for me round the corner

râble² *nm* fire rake

râblé [rɑble] *adj* (*personne*) stocky, stockily built

rabot [rabo] *nm Menuis* plane; **r. à languette** grooving plane, tongue plane; **passer le r. sur qch, donner un coup de r. à qch** to plane sth

rabotage [rabɔtaʒ] *nm Menuis* planing

raboter [rabɔte] *vt Menuis* (*avec un rabot*) to plane; (*avec un autre outil*) to scrape, to rub; *Fig Vieilli* **r. son style** to polish one's style

raboteur [rabɔtœr] *nm Menuis* (*personne*) planer

raboteuse [rabɔtøz] *nf Menuis* planing machine, planer

raboteux, -euse [rabɔtø, -øz] *adj* (*surface*) rough, uneven; (*bois*) knotty; (*route*) bumpy, uneven; *Fig* (*style*) unpolished

rabougri [rabugri] *adj* (*plante, personne*) stunted

rabougrir [rabugrir] **1** *vti* (*plante, fruit etc*) to shrivel up; (*personne*) to become shrivelled **2 se rabougrir** *vpr* to shrivel up

rabouter [rabute] *vt* to join end to end

rabrouer [rabrue] *vt* to snub; **se faire r. par qn** to be snubbed by sb

racaille [rakaj] *nf* (*voyous*) scum; *Vieilli* (*populace*) riff-raff, rabble

raccommodable [rakɔmɔdabl] *adj* which can be mended

raccommodage [rakɔmɔdaʒ] *nm* **(a)** (*action*) (*de vêtements*) mending; (*de bas, chaussettes*) darning; **faire du r.** to do some mending **(b)** (*résultat*) mend; (*de bas*) darn

raccommodement [rakɔmɔdmɑ̃] *nm F* reconciliation

raccommoder [rakɔmɔde] **1** *vt* **(a)** (*vêtement*) to mend; (*bas, chaussette*) to darn **(b)** *F* (*personnes*) to patch things up between **2 se raccommoder** *vpr F* to make it up, to patch things up; **se r. avec qn** to make it up *or* to patch things up with sb

raccommodeur, -euse [rakɔmɔdœr, -øz] *n* mender

raccompagner [rakɔ̃paɲe] *vt* **r. qn** to accompany sb back; **je vais vous r.** (*à pied*) I'll take you back, I'll go back with you,

I'll see you home; (*en voiture*) I'll drive *or* take you home; **je te raccompagne jusqu'à ta voiture** I'll see *or* walk you to your car; **r. qn à la porte** to see *or* show sb to the door

raccord [rakɔr] *nm* **(a)** (*de papier peint*) join; **papier peint sans raccords** (wall)paper with no pattern repeat; **faire des raccords de peinture** to touch up the paintwork; **faire un r. à une bande magnétique** to splice a tape; *F* **faire un r.** (*de maquillage*) to touch up one's make-up; **j'ai eu du mal avec les raccords** (*de papier peint*) I had trouble matching up the pattern **(b)** *Tech* union; (*pièce d'assemblage*) connection, coupling, joint; *Él* **r. mâle et femelle** plug and socket connection; **bouchon de r.** adapter; **r. de lampe** lamp adapter *or* connector; **r. de graissage** grease nipple

raccordement [rakɔrdəmɑ̃] *nm* **(a)** (*en ajustant*) adjusting **(b)** (*pour relier*) joining, linking (up), connecting; **pièces de r.** (*de canalisations etc*) making-up lengths; *Rail* **voie de r.** junction line, loop line; (*vers une usine etc*) service siding; *Él* **boîte de r.** (*pour câbles etc*) junction box **(c)** *Ordinat* link

raccorder [rakɔrde] **1** *vt* **(a)** (*relier*) to join (up), to connect; (*bâtiments, routes*) to link up; *Ordinat* to connect; **r. qn au réseau téléphonique** to connect sb to the telephone system; **nous ne sommes toujours pas raccordés au réseau électrique** we still don't have mains electricity; *Él* **r. à la masse** *ou* **à la terre** to earth, *Am* to ground **(b)** (*pièces*) to connect **(c)** (*bande magnétique*) to splice **2 se raccorder** *vpr aussi Fig* to fit together, to link up; *Ordinat* **se r. à** to link up to

raccourci [rakursi] *nm* **(a)** (*route plus courte*) short cut; **prendre un r.** to take a short cut; *Ordinat* **r. clavier** keyboard shortcut **(b)** (*résumé*) abridg(e)ment, shortened version; **en r.** briefly, in brief; **par un r. saisissant** in a facile way; **c'est un r. saisissant que d'affirmer que …** it is facile to say that … **(c)** *Beaux-Arts* foreshortening; **bras en r.** foreshortened arm

raccourcir [rakursir] **1** *vt* **(a)** (*discours, texte, chemin etc*) to shorten (**de** by); *Couture* (*manches, jupe etc*) to shorten, to take up (**de** by); **r. ses cheveux** to have a bit taken off one's hair; *Fig F* **tomber à bras raccourcis sur qn** to pitch into sb **(b)** *Beaux-Arts* to foreshorten **(c)** *F* **r. qn** (*guillotiner*) to chop sb's head off **2** *vi* to grow shorter, to shorten; **les jours raccourcissent** the days are growing shorter *or* drawing in; **son tee-shirt a raccourci au lavage** his tee shirt has shrunk in the wash; *F* **les jupes raccourcissent encore cet hiver** skirts are getting even shorter this winter

raccourcissement [rakursismɑ̃] *nm* **(a)** (*action de raccourcir*) shortening **(b)** *Beaux-Arts* foreshortening **(c)** (*des jours*) drawing in; (*de vêtement*) (*au lavage*) shrinking; **le r. des jupes** shortening hemlines, the rise in hemlines

raccroc [rakro] *nm* fluke, lucky stroke; **par r.** by a fluke, by a stroke of luck

raccrocher [rakrɔʃe] **1** *vt* **(a) r. qch** to hang sth up again, to put sth back on the hook; **elle ne pouvait pas r. la scie sur son crochet** she couldn't get the saw back on its hook; *Tél* **r. l'appareil** *ou* **le téléphone** to hang up; **ce boxeur devrait r. les gants** it's time this boxer hung up his gloves

(b) *F* (*récupérer*) (*commande, contrat, affaire*) to salvage

(c) (*personne dans la rue*) to accost, to stop; (*d'une prostituée*) to accost, to solicit

2 *vi* **(a)** *Tél* to hang up; *F* **il m'a raccroché au nez** he hung up on me, he put the phone down on me; **je n'ai pas envie de me faire r. au nez** I don't want to have the phone put down on me

(b) *Sp F* to retire; (*d'un boxeur*) to hang up one's gloves, to retire

3 se raccrocher *vpr* **(a) se r. à qch** to catch hold of sth, to catch on to sth; **se r. à une espérance** to cling to a hope; *Fig F* **se r. aux branches** to clutch at straws

(b) (*se rapporter*) to be linked, to be connected; **cette idée ne se raccroche pas du tout au sujet** that idea has nothing to do with *or* is totally unrelated to the subject

race [ras] *nf* **(a)** (*famille*) ancestry, descent; **de r. noble** of noble blood *or* descent *or* extraction; *Fig* **être de la r. des gagnants** to be a born winner; **être fin de r.** to be decadent; **elle a de la r.** she's very distinguished-looking

(b) (*ethnie*) race; **la r. blanche/noire** whites/blacks; **la r. humaine** the human race; **sans distinction de r.** without discrimination on the grounds of race, regardless of race; *F* (*injurieux*) **quelle sale r.!** what filth!; **les banquiers, quelle sale r.!** those bankers are nothing but bastards!

(c) *Zool* breed; **la r. chevaline** the horse species; **améliorer/croiser les races** to improve/to cross breeds; **chien/taureau de r.** pure-bred dog/bull, pedigree dog/bull; **cheval de r.** thoroughbred (horse); **avoir de la r.** to be pure-bred; (*de cheval*) to be a thoroughbred

racé [rase] *adj* (*animal*) pure-bred; (*cheval*) thoroughbred; (*personne*) patrician, tall and aristocratic-looking; *F* **profil r.** (*d'une voiture, d'un bateau*) clean *or* elegant lines

racème [rasɛm] *nm Bot* raceme

rachat [raʃa] *nm* **(a)** repurchase, buying back; **ils ont convenu du r. des captifs** they came to an agreement over the prisoners' ransom; *Jur* **pacte de r.** covenant of redemption; *Jur* **avec faculté de r.** with option of repurchase *or* redemption; *Bourse* **r. gagnant** repurchase at a profit

(b) (*de police d'assurance*) surrender; (*de valeur, police etc*) redemption; **valeur de r.** surrender value; *Compta* **r. forfaitaire des créances** lump-sum purchase of accounts receivable

(c) (*de société*) buy-out; *Fin* **r. d'entreprise avec un fort levier financier** leveraged buy-out; **r. d'une société par la direction** management buy-out

(d) *Rel* **r. d'un péché** atonement for a sin

rachetable [raʃtabl] *adj* **(a)** (*stock*) redeemable **(b)** (*péché*) for which atonement can be made

racheter [raʃte] (*conj like* **acheter**) **1** *vt* **(a)** (*objet perdu, objet cassé*) to replace; **je pourrai le r., je pourrai en r. un** I can replace it, I can buy another; **r. qch à qn** to replace sth for sb

(b) (*au propriétaire*) to buy back, to repurchase (**à** from); (*une société*) to buy out; **r. les parts de qn** to buy sb out; **je te le rachèterai si tu ne l'aimes pas** I'll buy it from you *or F* I'll take it off your hands if you don't like it

(c) (*acheter davantage de*) to buy some more; **je n'ai plus de café, je dois en r.** I've no coffee left, I'll have to buy some more; **je vais r. de la lessive** I'm going to buy some more soap powder

(d) (*en assurances*) (*police*) to surrender; *Jur* (*rente, dette, gage*) to redeem; (*otage, prisonnier*) to pay a ransom for, to ransom; *Compta* **r. une créance** to purchase an account receivable; **r. une obligation** to retire *or* redeem a bond

(e) *Fig* (*faute*) to make up for, to compensate for; **Jésus-Christ est mort pour r. les hommes** Christ died to redeem mankind; **r. ses péchés** to atone for one's sins; **r. son honneur/son nom** to retrieve one's honour/reputation; **la profusion de détails ne rachète pas la faiblesse du plan** the wealth of detail does not make up for *or* atone for the lack of planning

2 se racheter *vpr* to redeem oneself; **que puis-je faire pour me r.?** what can I do to make up for it?, how can I redeem myself?

racheteur [raʃtœr] *nm* purchaser

rachicentèse [raʃisɛ̃tɛz] *nf Méd* lumbar puncture

rachidien, -ienne [raʃidjɛ̃, -jɛn] *adj Anat* (*bulbe, canal*) rachidian

rachis [raʃis] *nm Anat, Bot* rachis, spinal column, spine; *Anat* **r. cervical** cervical vertebrae; *Anat* **r. coccygien** coccyx; *Anat* **r. dorsal** dorsal vertebrae; *Anat* **r. lombaire** lumbar vertebrae; *Anat* **r. sacré** sacrum; *Anat* **r. thoracique** thoracic vertebrae

rachitique [raʃitik] *adj Méd* rickety, *Spéc* rachitic; *F* (*très maigre*) scrawny

rachitisme [raʃitism] *nm* [①A10,d] *Méd* rickets, *Spéc* rachitis; **faire du r.** to have rickets

racial, -ale, -aux, -ales [rasjal, -o] *adj* racial

racine [rasin] *nf* **(a)** (*de plante, de cheveu, d'ongle, de dent etc*) root; *Bot* **r. pivotante** tap root; **r. de gingembre** root ginger; **prendre r.** (*d'une plante, Fig d'une personne*) to take root; *Fig* **attaquer** *ou* **couper le mal à la r.** to strike at the root of the evil; *Fig F* **manger les pissenlits par la r.** to be pushing up (the) daisies; *F* **se faire faire les racines** (*chez le coiffeur*) to have one's roots done **(b)** *Math* **r. carrée/cubique** square/cube root **(c)** *Ling* (*d'un mot*) root **(d)** *Fig* (*origine*) root; **être à la recherche de ses racines** to be searching for one's roots **(e)** *Ordinat* root

raciner [rasine] *vt* (*couvertures de livre*) to marble

racisme [rasism] *nm* rac(ial)ism; *Fig F* **c'est du r. anti-vieux** that's ageism; **r. anti-jeunes** prejudice *or* bias against young people

raciste [rasist] *adj, n* rac(ial)ist

racket [rakɛt] *nm F* racket; **faire du r.** to run a racket

racketter [rakɛte] *vt F* **r. qn** to extort money from sb; **se faire r.** to pay protection money

racketteur [rakɛtœr] *nm F* racketeer

raclage [raklaʒ] *nm* scraping

raclée [rakle] *nf F* thrashing, hiding; **flanquer** *ou* **administrer une r. à qn** to give sb a thrashing *or* hiding; *Fig* **son parti/son équipe a pris une belle r.** his party/team got a good thrashing *or* hiding *or* licking

raclement [rakləmɑ̃] *nm* scraping (noise)

racler [rakle] **1** *vt* (*frotter*) (*peau, semelle*) to scrape; (*pour faire partir*) (*peinture, vernis etc*) to scrape off; (*pour nettoyer*) to scrape (out); **ce vin racle la gorge** this wine's (a bit) rough on the throat; *Péj* **r. du** *ou* **le violon** to scrape *or* saw on the fiddle; *Fig F* **r. les (fonds de) tiroirs** to scrape (the bottom of) the barrel **2 se racler** *vpr* **se r. la gorge** to clear one's throat

raclette [raklɛt] *nf* **(a)** (*racloir*) scraper; *Aut* (*de balai*) wiper blade **(b)** (*de jardin*) hoe **(c)** *Culin* raclette (*dish of potatoes, smoked ham and melted cheese*)

racloir [raklwar] *nm* **(a)** scraper **(b)** *Phot etc* squeegee

racolage [rakɔlaʒ] *nm* (*d'une prostituée*) soliciting, accosting; (*d'un publicitaire*) touting for business *or* custom; *Hist* (*pour l'armée, la marine*) press-ganging; **faire du r.** (*d'une prostituée*) to solicit; (*d'un publicitaire*) to tout for business *or* custom; (*pour un parti*) to tout for votes; **r. de partisans** enlisting of supporters

racoler [rakɔle] **1** *vt* (*d'une prostituée*) to solicit, to accost; (*partisans*) to tout for; *Hist* (*hommes pour l'armée, la marine*) to press-gang; **r. des clients** to tout for custom *or* business **2** *vi* (*d'une prostituée*) to solicit; (*d'un publicitaire*) to tout for custom *or* business; (*pour un parti*) to tout for votes

racoleur, -euse [rakɔlœr, -øz] **1** *adj* (*publicité, affiche*) eye-catching **2** *n* (*politicien*) = canvasser who attempts to recruit party members using unscrupulous means; (*commerçant*) tout **3** *nm Hist Mil* crimp **4** *nf* **racoleuse** street walker

racontable [rakɔ̃tabl] *adj* relatable, tellable; **cette plaisanterie n'est pas r. devant des enfants** it's not the kind of joke you can tell in front of children

racontar [rakɔ̃tar] *nm* story, piece of gossip; **ce ne sont que des racontars** it's just gossip *or* tittle-tattle

raconter [rakɔ̃te] **1** *vt* to tell, *Fml* to relate, to narrate, to recount; **r. une histoire à qn** to tell sb a story; **j'ai l'impression qu'elle m'a raconté une histoire** *ou* **des histoires** I have a feeling she wasn't telling me the truth; **r. sa vie à qn** to tell sb the story of one's life *or* one's life story; **raconte-nous tes dernières vacances** tell us about your last holiday; **on m'a raconté beaucoup de choses sur toi** I've heard a lot about you; **il en a raconté de belles** he told some pretty incredible stories; **on en raconte de belles sur toi!** I've heard quite a few tales about you!; **qu'est-ce qu'il raconte (là)?** what is he talking about?; **alors qu'est-ce que tu racontes (de beau** *ou* **de neuf)?** so what's new?; **est-ce que tu as quelque chose de beau à nous r.?** (*pour nous distraire*) haven't you got anything interesting to tell us?; (*à qn qu'on revoit*) so what's new?; **on raconte que ...** apparently, ..., people are saying that ...; **à ce qu'on raconte** judging by *or* from what people say

2 *vi* **r. bien/mal** to be a good/bad storyteller; **il faut toujours qu'elle nous raconte!** she always has to tell us all about it!; **je vais tenter de vous r. en quelques mots** I'll try to tell you in a few words; **allez, raconte!** come on, out with it!

3 se raconter *vpr* to talk about oneself; **je ne tiens pas à me r. devant tout le monde** I'm not keen on talking about myself in front of lots of people; **ce sont des choses qui ne se racontent pas** it's not the type of thing you can talk about

raconteur, -euse [rakɔ̃tœr, -øz] *n* storyteller; (*d'un film, d'une pièce de théâtre*) narrator

racornir [rakɔrnir] **1** *vt* **r. qch** to shrivel sth (up), to dry sth out **2 se racornir** *vpr* (*des ongles*) to grow horny; (*du papier*) to grow brittle; (*de plante, chair*) to shrivel up, to dry out

racornissement [rakɔrnismɑ̃] *nm* hardening, toughening (up)

radar [radar] *nm* radar; **r. à ondes entretenues** continuous-wave radar; **balayage r.** radar scan; **écho r.** radar echo; **r. d'autoguidage** homing radar; *Fig F* **ce matin je suis** *ou* **j'avance au r.** I'm like a zombie this morning, I'm on autopilot this morning

radariste [radarist] *n* radar operator

rade¹ [rad] *nf Naut* roadstead; **r. foraine** *ou* **ouverte** open roadstead; **r. fermée** sheltered roadstead; **navire en r.** ship in the roads; **mettre un navire en r.** to lay up a ship; **en r. de Toulon** off Toulon; *Fig F* **laisser en r.** (*personne*) to leave in the lurch; (*projet*) to jettison

rade² *nm Arg* (*comptoir*) bar, counter; (*bistro*) bar

radeau, -x [rado] *nm* raft; **r. de sauvetage** life raft

radial, -ale, -aux, -ales [radjal, -o] **1** *adj* **(a)** radial; **pneumatique à carcasse radiale** radial(-ply) tyre **(b)** *Anat* (*muscle, nerf*) radial **2** *nf* **radiale (a)** radial road, urban motorway **(b)** *Anat* radial

radian [radjɑ̃] *nm Math* radian

radiance [radjɑ̃s] *nf Litt* radiance

radiant [radjɑ̃] **1** *adj* (*chaleur, Vieilli beauté*) radiant; **pouvoir r.** radiating capacity **2** *nm Astron* radiant (point)

radiateur [radjatœr] *nm* radiator; **r. à accumulation** storage heater; **r. à ailettes** fin radiator; **r. à bain d'huile** oil-filled radiator; **r. à eau chaude** hot-water radiator; **r. électrique** electric fire; **r. à** *ou* **en nid d'abeilles** honeycomb radiator, cellular film-type radiator; **r. soufflant** fan heater; **r. transversal** cross-flow radiator; **r. vertical** vertical-flow radiator

radiation¹ [radjasjɔ̃] *nf* (*d'une liste*) striking out, crossing out; (*de dette*) cancellation; (*d'un avocat*) disbarment; (*d'un médecin*) striking off; (*d'un sportif*) banning; **vous risquez la r.** you risk being disbarred/struck off/banned

radiation² *nf Phys* radiation; **r. cosmique** cosmic radiation; *Électron* **r. (de) haute fréquence** high-frequency radiation; *Nucl* **r. alpha/bêta** alpha/beta radiation, alpha-ray/beta-ray emission

radical, -ale, -aux, -ales [radikal, -o] **1** *adj* radical; *Pol Fr* left of centre; *Math* **signe r.** radical *or* root sign; **c'est r.** (*d'un médicament, d'une méthode*) it does the trick, it works like magic **(contre** on) **2** *n* radical; *Pol Fr* person who is left of centre; **être r. de droite/de gauche** to be right/left of centre **3** *nm Ling* root, radical; *Math* radical *or* root sign; *Ch* radical; **radicaux libres** free radicals

radicalement [radikalmɑ̃] *adv* radically

radicalisation [radikalizasjɔ̃] *nf Pol* radicalization

radicaliser [radikalize] *Pol* **1** *vt* to make more radical, to radicalize **2 se radicaliser** *vpr* to become more radical, to radicalize

radicalisme [radikalism] *nm Pol* radicalism

radical-socialisme *nm Pol* liberalism; *Hist Pol* radical socialism

radical-socialiste, *pl* **radicaux-socialistes** *adj, n Pol* liberal; *Hist Pol* radical socialist

radicelle [radisɛl] *nf Bot* rootlet, *Spéc* radicel

radicule [radikyl] *nf Bot* radicle

radier¹ [radje] *nm Constr* frame, floor, bed; (*de porte d'écluse*) sill; (*de bassin*) apron; **r. de fondation** foundation raft

radier² *vt* (*impf, pr sub* **n. radiions**) to strike *or* cross out; **r. qch/qn d'une liste** to strike *or* cross sth/sb off a list

radiesthésie [radjɛstezi] *nf* dowsing, divination

radiesthésiste [radjɛstezist] *n* dowser, diviner

radieux, -euse [radjø, -øz] *adj* (*soleil*) radiant, dazzling; (*temps*) glorious; (*personne*) radiant; **elle avait un regard r., son regard était r.** she was radiant *or* glowing

radin [radɛ̃] *F* **1** *n* Scrooge, *Am* tightwad **2** *adj* stingy

radiner [radine] *très F* **1** *vi* to turn up, to show up, to roll up **2 se radiner** *vpr* to turn up, to show up, to roll up; **c'est à cette heure-ci que tu te radines?** what kind of time do you call this?; **alors tu te radines?** are you coming or not?

radio [radjo] **1** *nf* **(a)** (*poste*) radio (set); **à la r.** on the radio; **écouter la r.** to listen to the radio; **passer à la r.** to be on the radio; **travailler à la r.** to work on the *or* for (the) radio; **faire de la r.** to be *or* work as a radio presenter **(b)** (*radiotéléphonie*) radiotelephony **(c)** *Méd* X-ray (photograph); **passer une r.** *ou* **à la r.** to be X-rayed **2** *nm Vieilli* **(a)** (*télégramme*) radio(gram) **(b)** (*opérateur*) radio operator **3** *adj inv* radio

▶ **radio**: **r. commerciale** commercial radio; **r. communautaire** community radio; **r. K7** radio-cassette player; **r. libre** independent local radio (station); **r. locale** local radio; **r. périphérique** = any independent radio broadcasting organization based outside France; **r. pirate** pirate radio (station); **r. scolaire** schools radio

radioactif, -ive [radjoaktif, -iv] *adj* radioactive

radioactivité [radjoaktivite] *nf* radioactivity

radioalignement [radjoaliɲ(ə)mɑ̃] *nm Av, Naut* radio-beacon route; **voler par r.** to fly airways

radio-amateur *nm* radio ham

radioastronomie [radjoastrɔnɔmi] *nf* radio astronomy

radiobalisage [radjobalizaʒ] *nm* radio-beacon navigation; *Av* airways navigation

radiobalise [radjobaliz] *nf* radio beacon, marker beacon

radiocassette [radjokasɛt] *nf* radio cassette (player)

radiocommunication [radjokɔmynikasjɔ̃] *nf* radiocommunication

radiocompas [radjokɔ̃pɑ] *nm Av* radio compass

radioconducteur [radjokɔ̃dyktœr] *nm Phys* radio conductor

radiodermite [radjodɛrmit] *nf Méd* radiodermatitis, X-ray dermatitis

radiodiagnostic [radjodjagnɔstik] *nm Méd* X-ray diagnosis

radiodiffuser [radjodifyze] *vt Rad* to broadcast; **un concert radiodiffusé** a broadcast concert

radiodiffusion [radjodifysjɔ̃] *nf Rad* broadcasting

radioélectricien, -ienne [radjoelɛktrisjɛ̃, -jɛn] *n* radio (and television) technician

radiogénique [radjoʒenik] *adj F* **il a une voix r.** he has a good broadcasting voice; **elle est très r.** she's good radio material

radiogoniomètre [radjogɔnjɔmɛtr] *nm* direction finder, *Spéc* radiogoniometer

radiogoniométrie [radjogɔnjɔmetri] *nf* direction finding, *Spéc* radiogoniometry
radiogramme [radjɔgram] *nm* (*message*) radio telegram, radiogram
radiographie [radjɔgrafi] *nf Méd* (**a**) (*technique*) radiography, X-ray photography (**b**) (*cliché*) X-ray (photograph), radiograph
radiographier [radjɔgrafje] *vt* (*impf, pr sub* **n. radiographiions**) *Méd* to X-ray
radiographique [radjɔgrafik] *adj Méd* X-ray, radiographic; **examen r.** X-ray (examination)
radioguidage [radjogidaʒ] *nm Av, Naut* radio control *or* direction *or* guidance; (*de missile etc*) homing; *Rad* (*pour automobilistes*) traffic news *or* information
radioguidé [radjogide] *adj* radio-controlled; (*missile*) guided
radio(-)journal, *pl* **radio(-)journaux** *nm Rad* radio news, news bulletin
radiologie [radjɔlɔʒi] *nf Méd* radiology
radiologique [radjɔlɔʒik] *adj Méd* radiological; **examen r.** X-ray (examination)
radiologue [radjɔlɔg], **radiologiste** [radjɔlɔʒist] *n Méd* radiologist
radiomètre [radjomɛtr] *nm Phys* radiometer
radionavigant [radjonavigɑ̃] *nm Naut, Av* radio officer
radionavigation [radjonavigasjɔ̃] *nf* navigation by radar
radiophare [radjofar] *nm Naut, Av* radio beacon
radiophonie [radjɔfɔni] *nf* radio(tele)phony, wireless telephony, broadcasting
radiophonique [radjofɔnik] *adj* radio
radiorepérage [radjorəperaʒ] *nm* radiolocation
radioreportage [radjorəpɔrtaʒ] *nm Rad* radio reporting; **un r.** a report
radioreporter [radjorəpɔrter] *nm Rad* radio reporter
radioscopie [radjoskɔpi] *nf Méd* radioscopy, X-ray (examination)
radioscopique [radjoskɔpik] *adj Méd* **examen r.** X-ray (examination)
radiosondage [radjosɔ̃daʒ] *nm Méteo* radiosonde exploration
radiosonde [radjosɔ̃d] *nf* (**a**) *Météo* radiosonde (**b**) *Av* radio altimeter
radio-taxi, *pl* **radio-taxis** *nm* radio taxi
radiotechnique [radjotɛknik] *nf* radiotechnology
radiotélégramme [radjotelegram] *nm* radio telegram
radiotélégraphie [radjotelegrafi] *nf* radio telegraphy, wireless telegraphy
radiotélégraphier [radjotelegrafje] *vt* (*conj like* **télégraphier**) (*télégramme*) to radio
radiotéléphone [radjotelefɔn] *nm* cellular telephone, mobile (phone)
radiotéléphonie [radjotelefɔni] *nf* radio(tele)phony, wireless telephony
radiotélescope [radjoteleskɔp] *nm* radio telescope
radiotélévisé [radjotelevize] *adj* simulcast, broadcast on both radio and television
radiotélévision [radjotelevizjɔ̃] *nf* television and radio broadcasting
radiothérapeute [radjoterapøt] *n Méd* radiotherapist
radiothérapie [radjoterapi] *nf Méd* radiotherapy, X-ray treatment
radis [radi] *nm* radish; **r. noir** black radish; *Fig F* **ne pas/plus avoir un r.** to be (stony) broke, not to have a bean; **je ne dépenserai pas un r. de plus** I'm not spending another penny
radium [radjɔm] *nm* radium
radius [radjys] *nm Anat* radius
radotage [radɔtaʒ] *nm* twaddle, drivel; (*d'une vieille personne etc*) rambling talk
radoter [radɔte] **1** *vi* (*divaguer*) to ramble on; (*rabâcher*) to keep on repeating oneself; **il commence à r.** (*par sénilité*) he *or* his mind is starting to wander; (*il se répète*) he's starting to repeat himself all the time **2** *vt F* **tu radotes toujours les mêmes histoires!** you keep on coming out with the same old thing!; **mais qu'est-ce qu'il radote?** what's he (rabbiting) on about?
radoteur, -euse [radɔtœr, -øz] *n* dotard; **c'est un (vieux) r.** he's always rambling on
radoub [radu] *nm* (*d'un bateau*) refitting, graving; **navire au r.** ship under repair *or* in dry dock; **bassin de r.** graving dock, dry dock
radouber [radube] *vt* (**a**) (*bateau*) to repair the hull of (**b**) (*filet*) to mend, to repair; *F Vieilli* (*vêtement*) to patch up
radoucir [radusir] **1** *vt* (*personne*) to calm down, to mollify; (*caractère*) to soften; **r. le temps/la température** (*de la pluie, du vent*) to bring milder weather/temperatures **2 se radoucir** *vpr* (*d'une personne*) to calm down; (*d'une voix*) to soften; (*du temps*) to become milder
radoucissement [radusismɑ̃] *nm* (**a**) (*de la voix*) softening; (*d'une personne*) calming down (**b**) *Météo* milder spell; **on prévoit un net r. de la température** distinctly milder temperatures are forecast
rafale [rafal] *nf* (**a**) (*de vent*) squall, strong gust, blast; (*de pluie*) burst; **vent à rafales** blustering *or* gusty wind; **temps à rafales** blustery *or* squally weather; **le vent soufflait par ou en rafales** the wind was blowing in strong gusts; **la pluie tombait par rafales** the rain was falling in great bursts (**b**) (*de coups de feu*) burst
raffermir [rafɛrmir] **1** *vt* (**a**) (*chair*) to firm up, to make firm(er); (*peau, tissus*) to tone up

(**b**) (*autorité*) to reinforce, to strengthen; (*courage*) to strengthen; **l'équipe gouvernementale est sortie raffermie du conflit** the government team came out of the conflict stronger *or* strengthened

2 se raffermir *vpr* (*du sol, des muscles, de la peau etc*) to firm up, to get firmer; (*des prix*) to steady; (*du gouvernement*) (*devenir plus intransigeant*) to take a stronger *or* firmer *or* tougher line; (*devenir plus fort*) to become stronger; **ses jambes se raffermissent** his legs are growing stronger again; **son autorité se raffermit** he is recovering *or* regaining his authority; **il se raffermit dans ses intentions** he is more determined than ever
raffermissement [rafɛrmismɑ̃] *nm* (**a**) (*du sol*) firming (up), making firm(er); (*des tissus, de la peau*) toning (**b**) (*des prix*) steadying (**c**) (*de l'autorité, du pouvoir*) strengthening
raffinage [rafinaʒ] *nm* (*du pétrole, du sucre etc*) refining
raffiné [rafine] *adj* (**a**) (*pétrole, sucre etc*) refined (**b**) (*esprit*) subtle, refined; (*goût*) refined; (*manières, style*) refined, polished
raffinement [rafinmɑ̃] *nm* (*des manières, de langage, de luxe*) refinement; (*de la pensée, d'une politique*) subtlety, refinement; **le comble du r.** the height of refinement; **avec des raffinements de cruauté** with sophisticated cruelty
raffiner [rafine] **1** *vt* (*sucre, huile etc*) to refine; (*ses manières*) to refine, to polish **2** *vi* to be overmeticulous *or* fussy (**sur** about); **r. sur la propreté** to carry cleanliness to extremes; **on ne va pas r. sur les détails!** we won't be too fussy about the details!; **vous raffinez!** you're getting too hung up on detail!
raffinerie [rafinri] *nf* refinery; **r. de pétrole** oil refinery
raffineur, -euse [rafinœr, -øz] *n* refiner
raffoler [rafɔle] *vi F* **r. de qn/qch** to adore sb/sth, to be mad about *or* dote on sb/sth
raffut [rafy] *nm F* (*bruit*) din, racket, row; **faire du r.** (*bruit*) to make a din *or* racket *or* row; (*scandale*) to set tongues wagging; (*pour protester*) to kick up a fuss
raffûter [rafyte] *vt* (*outil*) to (re)sharpen, to (re)set
rafiau, rafiot [rafjo] *nm Naut* skiff (*with lateen sail*); **vieux r.** old tub
rafistolage [rafistɔlaʒ] *nm F* patching up; **ça n'ira pas loin, c'est du r.** it won't last long, it's just a makeshift *or* patched-up job; **ces changements ne sont que du r.** these changes will do nothing more than patch things up
rafistoler [rafistɔle] *vt F* to patch up
rafle [rafl] *nf* (**a**) (*par la police*) raid; **la police a fait une r. dans le club** the police raided the club; *Hist* **la r. du Vel'd'Hiv** = the rounding-up of Jews in the Velodrome d'Hiver in Paris on 16th July, 1942 (**b**) *Vieilli* thieving; *F* (*par des voleurs etc*) clean sweep; **r. d'étalage avec bris de devanture** smash-and-grab raid
rafler [rafle] *vt F* (*de cambrioleurs*) to swipe, to nick; **ils m'ont tout raflé** they've totally cleaned me out, they've swiped the lot; **les enfants ont tout raflé dans la cuisine** the children have made off with everything in the kitchen; **le film qui a raflé tous les oscars** the film which made a clean sweep of the Oscars, the film which walked off with all the Oscars
rafraîchir [rafrɛʃir] **1** *vt* (**a**) (*rendre frais*) (*personne*) to cool (down); (*pièce*) to air; **pour r. l'atmosphère** to cool the air (down)

(**b**) (*couleur, maquillage*) to freshen up; (*peintures*) to freshen up, to do up, to renovate; *Fig* **r. sa coupe à qn** to trim sb's hair, to give sb('s hair) a trim; *Fig F* **r. la mémoire à qn** to refresh sb's memory; *Fig F* **je vais te r. les idées** I'll refresh your memory for you

2 *vi* **mettre le vin à r. à la cave** to put the wine to cool in the cellar

3 se rafraîchir *vpr* (**a**) (*du temps*) to grow *or* turn cooler

(**b**) (*d'une personne*) (*se laver*) to freshen up; *F* (*en buvant*) to have a refreshing drink
rafraîchissant [rafrɛʃisɑ̃] *adj* (*brise, boisson*) refreshing, cooling; *Fig* (*simplicité, spontanéité*) refreshing; **d'une simplicité/spontanéité rafraîchissante** refreshingly simple/spontaneous

rafraîchissement [rafrɛʃismɑ̃] *nm* **(a)** (*de la température, d'un liquide etc*) cooling; **on prévoit un r. des températures ce week-end** temperatures are expected to drop *or* things are expected to be a bit cooler this weekend **(b)** (*boisson*) cold drink; **rafraîchissements** refreshments **(c)** *Ordinat* refresh

rafting [raftiŋ] *nm* rafting

raga [raga] *nm inv Mus* raga

ragaillardir [ragajardir] **1** *vt* **r. qn** (*physiquement*) to revive sb, to make sb feel better; (*encourager*) to cheer sb up **2 se ragaillardir** *vpr* to cheer up, *F* to buck up

rage [raʒ] *nf* **(a)** *Méd, Vét* rabies **(b)** *Fig* rage, fury, frenzy; (*passion*) passion **(de qch** for sth); **la tempête fait r.** the storm is raging; **l'incendie faisait r.** the fire was blazing *or* raging (furiously); **avoir la r. du jeu/d'écrire** to have a passion for gambling/writing; **avoir la r. au cœur** to be bitterly angry; **fou de r.** furious, hopping mad; **se mettre en r.** to get into a rage, to get furious **(contre qn** with sb, **contre qch** about sth); **ça me met en r.** it infuriates me, it makes me furious *or* my blood boil; **r. de dents** raging toothache; *F* **ce n'est pas de l'amour, c'est de la r.** that's not love, it's madness

rageant [raʒɑ̃] *adj F* infuriating

rager [raʒe] *vi* **(je rageai(s); n. rageons)** *F* to rage, to be in a rage, to fume; **ça me fait r. de voir ça!** it makes me hopping mad to see that!, seeing that makes my blood boil!

rageur, -euse [raʒœr, -øz] *adj* (*ton, voix*) furious, infuriated; **dit-elle d'un ton r.** she said furiously; **va au diable! dit-il, r.** go to hell! he said furiously

rageusement [raʒøzmɑ̃] *adv* furiously

raglan [raglɑ̃] **1** *nm* raglan coat **2** *adj inv* **manches r.** raglan sleeves

ragondin [ragɔ̃dɛ̃] *nm Zool* coypu; (*fourrure*) nutria

ragot¹ [rago] **1** *nm* (*sanglier*) boar in its third year **2** *adj Vieilli F* dumpy, squat

ragot² *nm F* (*commérages*) piece of gossip *or* tittle-tattle; **faire des ragots** to gossip, to tittle-tattle

ragoût [ragu] *nm Culin* stew, ragout; **r. de mouton** mutton stew; **(faire) cuire qch en r.** to stew sth

ragoûtant [ragutɑ̃] *adj* (*with neg*) **peu** *ou* **pas r.** (*plat*) unappetizing, uninviting; (*personne*) disgusting; **des choses peu ragoûtantes** some rather unpleasant *or* nasty things

ragréer [ragree] *vt* **(a)** (*maçonnerie, boiserie*) to finish off; (*jointure etc*) to clean up, to trim up **(b)** (*façade d'un bâtiment*) to clean

rag-time [ragtajm] *nm* (*danse*), *Mus* ragtime

rahat-lokoum [raatlokum], **rahat-loukoum** [raatlukum] *nm* piece of Turkish delight; **des rahat-lo(u)koums** Turkish delight

rai [rɛ] *nm* (*de lumière*) ray; (*d'étoile*) point

raï [raj] *nm inv Mus* = North African popular music influenced by music from the West

raid [rɛd] *nm* **(a)** *Mil* raid; **r. aérien** air raid; **lancer un r.** to launch *or* mount a raid **(contre** on) **(b)** *Sp* endurance test; (*en automobile*) long-distance rally; (*en avion*) long-distance flight **(c)** *Fin* raid; **lancer/financer un r.** to mount/to finance a raid

raide [rɛd] **1** *adj* **(a)** (*membre, articulation*) stiff; (*câble etc*) taut, tight; **corde r.** tightrope; *Fig* **être sur la corde r.** to be walking a tightrope; **cheveux raides** straight hair; **mettre un câble au r.** to take up the slack in a cable; **assis r. sur sa chaise** sitting bolt upright on his chair; **r. comme un piquet** as stiff as a ramrod, ramrod straight; *Fig F* **r. (comme un passe-lacet)** (*sans le sou*) (stony) broke

(b) (*manières, mouvement, démarche*) stiff; (*caractère*) inflexible, unbending, unyielding

(c) (*escalier, pente*) steep; **ça descend en pente r.** it slopes steeply

(d) *F* **ça, c'est un peu r.!** that's a bit thick *or* a bit much!; **il en a vu de raides** he's had a tough life; **elle m'en a dit de raides sur toi** she told me some pretty nasty things about you

2 *adv* **(a)** (*monter*) steeply

(b) tomber r. to collapse; **tomber r. (par terre)** to fall to the ground; **r. mort** dead as a doornail; **tomber r. mort** to drop dead; **il y avait une odeur à tomber r. mort** it stank to high heaven, the smell was enough to kill you; *Vieilli F* **il faut travailler r.** we're going to have to work like galley slaves

raider [rɛdœr] *nm Fin* (corporate) raider

raideur [rɛdœr] *nf* **(a)** (*d'un membre, d'une articulation, d'un mouvement*) stiffness; (*d'une corde*) tautness; **donne plus de r. à ta démarche** be a little bit more dignified; **avoir une r. dans le cou** to have a stiff neck **(b)** (*de manières*) stiffness, starchiness; (*de caractère*) inflexibility, rigidity; **répondre avec une certaine r.** to answer rather stiffly **(c)** (*d'une pente*) steepness, abruptness

raidillon [rɛdijɔ̃] *nm* steep path; (*sur une route*) (short and steep) rise

raidir [rɛdir] **1** *vt* (*corde, câble etc*) to tighten, to pull tight *or* taut; (*tissu*) to stiffen; **r. les bras/jambes** to brace one's arms/legs; **un cadavre raidi par la mort** a body in rigor mortis **2 se raidir** *vpr* **(a)** (*des membres, des articulations*) to stiffen up, to grow stiff(er); (*de câble*) to grow taut, to tauten **(b)** (*d'une personne*) to tense up, to grow tense; *Fig* **se r. contre le malheur** to steel *or* brace oneself against misfortune

raidissement [rɛdismɑ̃] *nm* stiffening; (*de corde*) tautening; *Fig* **r. des rapports internationaux** increase of tension in international relations; **il y a un net r. de la position des ouvriers face à la direction** the workers are quite clearly standing their ground with the management

raidisseur [rɛdisœr] *nm Tech* stiffener; (*pour fils de fer*) wire stretcher

raie¹ [rɛ] *nf* **(a)** (*motif*) stripe **(b)** *Opt* **raies du spectre, raies spectrales** spectrum lines **(c)** (*dans les cheveux*) parting, *Am* part; **porter la r. à droite** to part one's hair on the right; **porter la r. sur le** *ou* **de côté/au milieu** to part one's hair at the side/in the centre, to have a side/centre parting; **je ne porte pas de r.** I don't have a parting; **où portez-vous la r.?** where do you part your hair?; **avoir une coiffure sans r.** to wear one's hair without a parting **(d)** *Agr* furrow

raie² *nf* (*poisson*) skate, ray; **r. bouclée** thornback; *Culin* **r. au beurre noir** skate in brown butter sauce

raifort [rɛfɔr] *nm* horseradish

rail [rɑj] *nm* **(a)** rail; **rails mobiles** movable rails, switch rails; **r. conducteur** (*d'une voie ferrée électrifiée*) conductor rail, live rail; **quitter les rails, sortir des rails** (*d'un train*) to be derailed, to go off the rails; *Fig* to go off the rails; *Fig* **remettre l'économie sur les rails** to get the economy back on the rails *or* (back) on its feet again; *Fig* **il faut le remettre sur les rails** we'll have to put him back on the rails *or* straighten him out; **pas étonnant qu'il soit PD-G aujourd'hui, on l'a mis sur des rails à la sortie du lycée!** it's not surprising he's now the chairman of the company, a path was mapped out for him when he left school!

(b) (*chemins de fer*) railways, *US* railroads; **travailleurs du r.** railwaymen, *US* railroaders; **le r. est un moyen de locomotion très développé en France** the railway is a much-used means of transport in France

(c) (*glissière*) **r. (de sécurité)** crash barrier

(d) (*itinéraire*) lane; **les bateaux se déplacent sur quatre rails au large d'Ouessant** boats sail along four sea lanes off Ushant; **le respect des rails aériens** the respect of air (traffic) lanes *or* air corridors

railler [rɑje] *Litt* **1** *vt* (*personne*) to mock, to make fun of; **elle le raille sur sa timidité** she mocks *or* makes fun of his shyness **2** *vi* to jest; **il me répondit en raillant** he answered me in jest **3 se railler** *vpr* **se r. de qn/qch** to mock sb/sth, to make fun of sb/sth

raillerie [rɑjri] *nf* (*plaisanterie*) jest; **sans r.** jesting apart; **recueillir des railleries** to be scoffed *or* mocked at; **il décida d'ignorer leurs railleries** he decided to ignore their scoffing; *Litt* **il n'entend pas r. sur les choses religieuses** he will not have jokes made about religion

railleur, -euse [rɑjœr, -øz] **1** *adj* (*ton, voix, commentaire etc*) mocking, derisive **2** *n* scoffer

railleusement [rɑjøzmɑ̃] *adv* mockingly, derisively

rainer [rene] *vt* to groove

rainette [rɛnɛt] *nf* **(a)** (*grenouille*) tree frog **(b)** (*pomme*) pippin; **r. grise** russet

rainure [rɛnyr] *nf* **(a)** groove; **r. de clavette** keyway, key slot; **à rainure(s)** grooved **(b)** *Astron* rille

rainurer [rɛnyre] *vt* to groove

raiponce [rɛpɔ̃s] *nf Bot* rampion

raisin [rɛzɛ̃] *nm* **(a) du r.** (some) grapes; **(grain de) r.** grape; **grappe de r.** bunch of grapes; **raisin(s) de table** dessert grapes; **manger du r.** to eat grapes; **raisins secs** raisins; **raisins de Corinthe** currants; **raisins de Smyrne** sultanas **(b)** *Bot* **r. de renard** herb Paris; *Bot* **r. d'ours** bearberry **(c)** (*mollusque*) **r. de mer** sea grapes, cuttle-fish eggs **(d) grand r.** (*papier*) ≈ royal

raisiné [rezine] *nm* fruit preserved in grape jelly

raison [rɛzɔ̃] *nf* **(a)** (*motif*) reason, ground **(de** for); **mais ce n'est pas une r. pour venir me déranger** but that's no reason to disturb *or* for disturbing me; **pour des raisons de convenance personnelle** for personal reasons; **pour quelle r.?** for what reason?; **sans r.** without (any) reason, for no reason; **elle s'est inquiétée sans r.** she worried needlessly; **en r. de qch** because of *or* on account of sth; **en r. d'un deuil récent** owing to a recent bereavement; **je me rends à vos raisons** I concede defeat; **rendre r. de qch** to give a reason for sth, to give an explanation of sth, to account for sth; **à plus forte r. puisqu'il suit un traitement** particularly since he's being given treatment; **à plus forte r. si elle est invitée** particularly if she's invited too; **r. de plus** all the more reason (**pour venir** to come); **r. de plus pour qu'elle fasse un effort** all the more reason for her to make an effort; **la r. pour laquelle il est venu** the reason (why) he came

(**b**) (*entendement*) reason; **il n'a pas toute sa r.** he is not quite sane, he's not quite in his right mind; **il n'a plus toute sa r.** he's losing his faculties; **recouvrer la r.** to regain one's sanity; **heureusement, il a recouvré la r. et le mariage n'a pas eu lieu** luckily he came to his senses and the wedding was called off; **ramener qn à la r.** to make sb see reason *or* sense; **revenir à la r.** to come to one's senses, to see reason; **se rendre à la r.** to see sense, to come to one's senses; **rends-toi à la r.!** see sense!, be sensible!; **vous perdez la r.!** have you taken leave of your senses?; **entendre r.** to listen to reason; **l'âge de r.** the age of reason; **mariage de r.** marriage of convenience

(**c**) **avoir r.** to be right; **avoir r. de faire qch** to be right to do *or* in doing sth; **elle a bien r. de ne pas lui demander son avis** she's quite right not to ask his opinion; **donner r. à qn** to admit that sb is right; **l'événement lui donna r.** events proved him right; **se faire une r.** to accept the inevitable, to resign oneself; **le travail n'était pas bon, mais il a bien fallu se faire une r.** the work wasn't well done but we just had to accept it as it was; **avec r.** rightly; **elle s'est mise en colère avec r.** she was right to get angry, she got angry and rightly so; **boire plus que de r.** to drink too much *or* more than is reasonable; **il avait bu, et plus que de r.** he had drunk too much, he had been drinking more than was reasonable; **il est inquiet plus que de r.** he is unreasonably concerned, his concern is slightly irrational; **gourmand plus que de r.** more than reasonably greedy; **comme de r.** as a matter of course, as one might expect

(**d**) (*satisfaction*) satisfaction, reparation; **demander r. d'un affront** to demand satisfaction for an insult; **avoir r. de qn/qch** to get the better of sb/sth; **elle ne partira pas tant qu'elle n'aura pas eu r. de cet appareil** she won't leave until she's sorted that machine out

(**e**) *Math* ratio; **r. géométrique/arithmétique** geometrical/ arithmetical ratio; **r. directe/inverse** direct/inverse ratio *or* proportion; **le poids est en r. directe du volume** the weight is directly proportional *or* in direct proportion to the volume; **travail payé à r. de cinquante francs l'heure** work paid at the rate of fifty francs an hour; **je suis payé à r. de cinquante francs de l'heure** I am paid fifty francs an hour; **à r. de deux par minute** at the rate of two per *or* a minute; **à r. de huit mots par ligne** on the basis of eight words to a line

▶ **raison**: *Com* **r. commerciale** trade name, **r. d'être**: **r. d'être de qch** raison d'être of *or* object of *or* reason for sth; **c'est ma seule r. d'être** it's my whole life *or* raison d'être; **sa petite fille est sa r. d'être** his granddaughter is his entire reason for living *or* his only raison d'être, he lives for his granddaughter; **c'est la r. d'être de cet organisme** that's the whole point of *or* reason for the institution, that's what the institution is there for; **cela n'a plus aucune r. d'être** there's no longer any need for it; *Com* **r. sociale** (company) name

raisonnable [rɛzɔnabl] *adj* (**a**) (*sensé*) reasonable; **tu n'es pas r.** you're not being reasonable; **soyez r.!** be sensible *or* reasonable!, listen to reason!; **tu n'es pas r. de tellement fumer** you're silly to smoke so much, you're not being sensible smoking so much; **à son âge il devrait être plus r.** he is old enough to know better; **ce n'est pas r. de sortir avant la fin** it's silly to leave before the end; **tu ne peux pas sortir <u>et</u> travailler, ce n'est pas r.!** you can't go out (all the time) <u>and</u> work, it's daft!

(**b**) (*doué de raison*) rational; **l'homme est un animal r.** man is a rational *or* reasoning animal

(**c**) (*condition, frais etc*) reasonable; **prix r.** reasonable *or* moderate *or* fair price; **à un prix r.** reasonably priced, at a reasonable price

raisonnablement [rɛzɔnabləmɑ̃] *adv* (**a**) (*avec bon sens*) reasonably, rationally; **tout ce qu'on pouvait r. demander** all that one could reasonably ask for (**b**) (*assez*) (*grand etc*) reasonably, fairly; (*manger etc*) moderately, in moderation; *F* (*travailler etc*) fairly well, reasonably well

raisonné [rɛzɔne] *adj* (*argumentation*) reasoned; (*grammaire*) rational, analytical; **voilà qui est bien r.!** well worked out!; *Com* **catalogue r.** descriptive catalogue

raisonnement [rɛzɔnmɑ̃] *nm* (*pensée etc*) reasoning; **homme de r. juste** man of sense; **je comprends ton r.** I understand your reasoning *or* (line of) argument; **on ne peut pas tenir un tel r. avec lui** you can't take that line with him; **pas de raisonnements!** don't argue!

raisonner [rɛzɔne] **1** *vi* (**a**) (*penser*) to reason (**sur** about); **r. par induction/déduction** to reason by induction *or* inductively/by deduction *or* deductively

(**b**) (*discuter*) to argue (**sur** about); **on ne peut r. avec ce genre de personnes** you can't reason with people like that; **ne raisonnez pas tant!** don't be so argumentative!

2 *vt* (*personne*) to reason with; **je vais essayer de le r.** I'll try and reason with him *or* make him see sense; **il faut absolument la r.** she must be made to see sense

3 se raisonner *vpr* to see reason; **raisonne-toi donc!** <u>try</u> to be reasonable!, <u>do</u> see reason!; **la jalousie ne se raisonne pas** jealousy cannot be reasoned with *or* knows no reason

raisonneur, -euse [rɛzɔnœr, -øz] **1** *adj* (**a**) reasoning, rational (**b**) (*qui discutaille*) argumentative **2** *n* (**a**) reasoner (**b**) (*discutailleur*) arguer

raja(h) [raʒa] *nm* raja(h)

rajeunir [raʒœnir] **1** *vt* (**a**) (*personne*) to rejuvenate; **ce chapeau te/la rajeunit** (**de dix ans**) that hat makes you/her look (ten years) younger; **ça me rajeunit** it makes me feel younger *or* feel young again; **ça ne nous rajeunit pas!** it brings it home *or* makes you realize that we're not getting any younger; **tu la rajeunis, elle a passé la trentaine** she's not as young as you think, she's over thirty; **vous me rajeunissez, j'ai cinq ans de plus!** I'm five years older than that!, add five years to that figure!; **elle me rajeunit de cinq ans** she's taking five years off my age

(**b**) (*robe, veste etc*) to update; (*organisation, bureau*) to modernize; **r. une équipe** to bring new blood into a team; **une équipe rajeunie** a younger team; **le comité a besoin d'être rajeuni** the committee needs new blood

2 *vi* to get younger, to grow young again; **je ne rajeunis pas** I'm not getting any younger; **il a rajeuni de dix ans** he's ten years younger

3 se rajeunir *vpr* (*pour paraître plus jeune*) to make oneself look younger; (*se dire, prétendre plus jeune*) to make oneself out to be younger than one is; **elle se rajeunit de quelques années** she's taking a few years off her age

rajeunissant [raʒœnisɑ̃] *adj* (*traitement, crème*) rejuvenating

rajeunissement [raʒœnismɑ̃] *nm* rejuvenation

rajout [raʒu] *nm* addition; **on ne peut plus faire de r.** nothing else can be added, we can't add anything else

rajouter [raʒute] *vt* to add; **r. du sel** add (more) salt, put in more salt

rajustement [raʒystəmɑ̃] *nm* readjustment, adjustment

rajuster [raʒyste] **1** *vt* (*vêtement, chapeau, cravate*) to adjust, to straighten; (*chignon*) to fix, to tidy; (*prix*) to adjust; **r. les salaires** to bring wages into line with the cost of living; **il faut r. les salaires des femmes** women's wages have to be brought into line with men's **2 se rajuster** *vpr* to tidy *or* smarten *or* straighten oneself up

râle[1] [rɑl] *nm* (*oiseau*) **r. d'eau** water rail; **r. de genêts** corncrake

râle[2] *nm*, **râlement** [rɑlmɑ̃] *nm* (*venant de la gorge*) rattle; **le r.** (**de la mort**) the death rattle; *Méd* **un r. au poumon** a rale *or F* rattle in the lung

ralenti [ralɑ̃ti] **1** *adj* slow(er); **au trot r.** at a slow trot **2** *nm* (**a**) *Cin* slow motion; *Cin* **scène au** *ou* **en r.** scene in slow motion; *Aut* **prendre un virage au r.** to take a corner slowly; **l'usine tourne au r.** the plant's not working at full capacity, the plant's just ticking over; **elle travaille au r.** she's slowed right down; **la ville tourne au r.** things are pretty quiet in the city; **la malade a l'impression de vivre au r.** the patient feels he's living in slow motion *or* hardly living at all (**b**) (*de moteur*) idling, slow running, idle; **r. accéléré** fast idle; **tourner au r.** to idle, to tick over

ralentir [ralɑ̃tir] **1** *vt* (*circulation, progression*) to slow (down); (*production, progrès, économie*) to slow (down *or* up); **r. la marche** to slow down, to walk a bit more slowly; **r. le pas** to slow down; **r. l'allure** to slow down; **r. ses efforts** to ease up

2 *vi* to slow down; (*d'un train, véhicule, convoi etc*) to slow (down), to reduce speed; (*de la progression*) to slow (down); (*de la production, des progrès, de l'économie*) to slow (down *or* up); **le train ralentit quand il entre en gare** the train slows down *or* reduces its speed when it pulls into a station; **ralentis, il y a du verglas!** slow down, there's black ice on the road!

3 se ralentir *vpr* (*de mouvements, de la circulation etc*) to slow (down); (*de la production, des progrès, de l'économie*) to slow (down *or* up)

ralentissement [ralɑ̃tismɑ̃] *nm* (*de la circulation, d'un rythme, de l'économie etc*) slowdown, slowing down, slowing up; (*des exportations, de la production, des ventes*) slowdown (**de** in); **des ralentissements** (*de la circulation*) hold-ups, delays; **périodes de r. dans les affaires** slow *or* slack periods in business; **il comptait sur un r. de la progression de l'armée allemande** he was counting on the German army's advance slowing down

ralentisseur [ralɑ̃tisœr] *nm Aut* speed bump, ramp, *Br F* sleeping policeman; *MecE Él* retarder; *Nucl* moderator

râler [rɑle] *vi* (**a**) *F* (*se plaindre*) to moan, to grouse, to grumble; **elle râle contre notre retard** she's moaning about us being late; **ça me fait r.!** it gets up my nose!; **ça me fait r. de perdre du temps comme ça!** wasting time like that really bugs me!; **laisse-le r.** let him moan; **mais qu'est-ce qu'elle a encore à r.?** what is she moaning about now? (**b**) (*de douleur*) to moan, to groan; (*d'un mourant*) to give a *or* the death rattle (**c**) (*d'un tigre*) to growl

râleur, -euse [rɑlœr, -øz] *F* **1** *adj* grumbling, moaning, grousing; **elle est très râleuse** she's a real moaner *or* grumbler **2** *n* moaner, grumbler

ralliement [ralimɑ̃] *nm* (**a**) (*des troupes*) rallying; **mot de r.** *Mil* password; *Fig* rallying cry; **point de r.** rallying point, meeting place; **ce bar est un bon point de r.** the bar is a good meeting place; **Paris est le point de r. de tous les comédiens français** Paris is a magnet for all French actors; **signe de r.** rallying sign; **en signe de r. ils portent tous le même tee-shirt** they all wear the same t-shirt as a kind of badge *or* so they can recognize each other (**b**) (*d'un avion*) homing (**c**) (*d'adhérents*) winning over; **son r. à notre parti fut immédiat** he immediately came over *or* was won over to our party

rallier [ralje] (*impf, pr sub* **n. ralliions**) **1** *vt* (**a**) (*troupes, navires etc*) to rally; *Fig* **r. l'opinion autour d'une idée commune** to mobilize *or* rally public opinion around a common idea

(**b**) *Mil etc* (*d'un soldat etc*) (*unité*) to rejoin; (*base*) to return to, to make one's way back to; *Naut* **r. le bord** to rejoin one's ship

(**c**) **r. qn** (*à un parti, mouvement*) to win sb over; (*à une opinion*) to win sb over, to bring sb round; *Fig* **les groupuscules ont rallié le groupe majoritaire** the small groups have united with *or* joined the majority group; *Fig* **r. tous les suffrages** to win unanimous approval *or* support

2 se rallier *vpr* (**a**) (*des troupes etc*) to rally; *Hum* **ralliez-vous à mon panache blanc!** follow me!

(**b**) (*des opposants, dissidents*) to rally; **se r. à** (*une opinion, un point de vue*) to come round to; (*un parti*) to join; (*une cause*) to rally to

rallonge [ralɔ̃ʒ] *nf* (**a**) (*d'une table*) (extension) leaf; *Can* (*d'un bureau*) runoff; *Tech* extension bar *or* piece; **table à rallonge(s)** extending table (**b**) (*électrique*) extension cord *or* lead (**c**) *F* additional *or* extra time/payment/*etc*; **r. budgétaire** addition to the budget; **obtenir une r. de 30 000 francs** to get an extra 30,000 francs; **une r. de trois jours** an additional *or* an extra *or* another three days

rallongement [ralɔ̃ʒmɑ̃] *nm* lengthening, extension

rallonger [ralɔ̃ʒe] (**je rallongeai(s)**; **n. rallongeons**) **1** *vt* (*prolonger*) to make longer; (*vacances, journée de travail, route*) to extend (**de** by); (*vêtement*) to let down, to lengthen; **r. qch de dix centimètres/de deux heures** to make sth ten centimetres/two hours longer; *F* **ça me rallongerait de 20 minutes** it would add 20 minutes onto my journey; **ils ont rallongé le cable d'un mètre** they lengthened the cable by a metre, they made the cable a metre longer; **tu devrais r. ce paragraphe** you should make this paragraph longer; **j'ai fait r. cette jupe de dix centimètres** I had this skirt let down *or* taken down ten centimetres

2 *vi* (*des jours*) to get longer, to draw out; (*des nuits*) to get longer, to draw in

rallumer [ralyme] **1** *vt* (*appareil électrique*) to turn on *or* switch on again; (*avec une allumette*) to light again; *Fig* (*querelle, colère, espoir etc*) to rekindle, to revive; **r. l'électricité** *ou* **la lumière** *ou* **les lumières** to turn on *or* switch on the light(s) again

2 *vi* **rallume, s'il te plaît** switch *or* turn the light/television/*etc* on again please

3 se rallumer *vpr* (*de la lumière, d'un appareil électrique*) to come back *or* go back on; (*d'un feu*) to flare up *or* blaze up again; *Fig* (*d'une guerre, dispute*) to flare up again; (*de l'espoir etc*) to rekindle, to revive; **il tira sur la pipe qui se ralluma** he puffed on the pipe which got going again

rally [rali] *nm Bourse* rally

rallye [rali] *nm* (**a**) *Sp* (car) rally (**b**) = series of dances, ≈ the Debutantes' season (*where young people from good families can meet eligible partners*)

RAM [ram] *nf Ordinat* RAM; **R. sur carte** on-board RAM

Ramadan [ramadɑ̃] *nm Rel* Ramadan; **respecter le R., faire le R.** to observe Ramadan

ramage [ramaʒ] *nm* (**a**) *Vieilli* (*feuillage*) foliage; (*motif*) floral design (**b**) (*des oiseaux*) song, twittering, chirping

ramas [ramɑ] *nm Vieilli* = **ramassis**

ramassage [ramasaʒ] *nm* (*des ordures, de vêtements, de vieux journaux*) collection; (*de fruits, noix etc*) gathering, picking; **r. scolaire** school bus service; **car de r. scolaire** school bus; **il n'existe pas de service de r. scolaire** there isn't a school bus

ramassé [ramase] *adj* (**a**) (*trapu*) thickset, stocky (**b**) (*recroquevillé*) (*person, village etc*) huddled; **village r. autour de son église** village huddled *or* clustering round its church (**c**) (*machine, style*) compact

ramasse-miettes [ramasmjɛt] *nm inv* table tidy (*a small brush and pan for clearing the crumbs off the table*)

ramasse-monnaie [ramasmɔnɛ] *nm inv* change tray

ramasse-poussière [ramaspusjɛr] *nm inv* (**a**) *Belg* dustpan (**b**) **ces bibelots sont de véritables r.** these ornaments just gather *or* collect the dust

ramasser [ramase] **1** *vt* (**a**) (*prendre par terre*) (*objet tombé*) to pick up; (*fruits, noix, coquillages*) to gather, to collect, to pick up; (*champignons*) to pick, to gather, to collect; (*pommes de terre*) to dig up, to lift; **r. qch avec une pelle et une balayette** to sweep sth up (with a brush and dustpan); **r. qch avec un chiffon** to wipe sth up; **r. des feuilles avec un râteau** to rake up leaves; **r. ses jupes** (*pour ne pas se salir*) to gather one's skirts up; *Cartes* **r. la mise** to win the kitty; **r. qn** to help sb up *or* to his/her feet, to pick sb up; *F* (*de la police*) to pick sb up; *Fig* **r. qn dans le ruisseau** to pick sb up out of the gutter; *Fig* **être à r. à la petite cuillère** to be worn to a frazzle, to be fit to drop; *F* **se faire r.** (*par la police*) to be run in *or* picked up

(**b**) (*regrouper*) (*des assiettes, copies, feuilles etc*) to collect, to gather (up); (*de l'argent*) to collect; (*informations*) to gather, to collect; (*des enfants, ouvriers, courrier*) to pick up, to collect; **r. les cartes** to pick up the cards; **r. ses affaires** to collect one's belongings; **r. ses cheveux dans une natte/sur le dessus de la tête** to put one's hair (up) in a pigtail/to pile one's hair on top of one's head; **r. (toutes) ses forces** to gather *or* muster all one's strength; **les quelques informations/connaissances qu'il a pu r.** the scraps of information/knowledge he was able to pick up; **le tigre ramasse son corps avant de bondir** the tiger crouches before springing; *F* **il a dû r. pas mal d'argent avec cette affaire** he must have made quite a pile *or* a fair old whack out of the business

(**c**) *Fig F* (*recevoir*) (*engueulade, gifle, râclée, procès-verbal*) to get; (*rhume*) to catch; **r. une bûche** *ou* **une pelle** to fall flat on one's face, to come a cropper

2 se ramasser *vpr* (**a**) (*pour faire un effort*) to gather oneself; (*d'un tigre*) (*avant de bondir*) to crouch

(**b**) (*après une chute*) to pick oneself up; *Fig F* (*échouer, tomber*) to fall flat on one's face, to come a cropper

ramassette [ramasɛt] *nf Belg* dustpan

ramasseur, -euse [ramasœr, -øz] *n* (*de champignons etc*) picker, collector, gatherer; *Tennis* **r. /ramasseuse de balles** ball boy/girl; **r. de lait** milk collector (*who collects milk from farms*)

ramassis [ramasi] *nm Péj* (*de choses*) heap, pile, jumble; (*de gens*) bunch; (*d'idées*) collection, hotchpotch

rambarde [rɑ̃bard] *nf Naut etc* (guard)rail

ramdam [ramdam] *nm F* row, racket; **faire du** *ou* **un sacré r.** to make a heck of a din *or* racket

rame¹ [ram] *nf* (*pour faire pousser des pois etc*) stick, cane; **haricots à rames** stick beans

rame² *nf* (*aviron*) oar; **aller à la r.** to row; **nous avons rejoint le port à la r.** we rowed into port; **faire force de rames** to row hard; *F* **elle n'en fiche pas une r.** she does damn all, she never does a stroke (of work)

rame³ *nf* (**a**) (*de papier*) ream (**b**) *Rail* train; *Naut* (*de péniches*) string, tow; *Rail* **la r. directe pour Tours** the through coach(es) for Tours; **r. (de métro)** (underground *or* *Am* subway) train

rameau, -eaux [ramo] *nm* (**a**) (*d'arbre*) (small) branch *or* bough; **un r. d'olivier** an olive branch; *Rel* **le dimanche des Rameaux, les Rameaux** Palm Sunday (**b**) (*de familles, de langues*) branch (**c**) *Anat* ramification

ramée [rame] *nf* (**a**) *Litt, Vieilli* (*d'un arbre*) green *or* leafy boughs (**b**) (*branches coupées*) cut branches (**c**) *F* **il n'en fiche pas une r.** he does damn all, he never does a stroke (of work)

ramener [ramne] (*conj like* **mener**) **1** *vt* (**a**) (*reconduire*) (*personne, F objet*) (*vers le point de référence choisi*) to bring back; (*en s'éloignant du point de référence choisi*) to take back; (*l'ordre, la paix*) to restore; **ramenez-nous-le vite!** bring him back quickly!; **on peut maintenant r. les enfants**

à l'école we can take the children back to school now; **il a fallu la r. d'urgence à l'hôpital** we had to rush her back to hospital; **c'est lui qui est chargé de r. le journal** it's his job to fetch *or* get the newspaper; **r. qn chez lui en voiture** to drive sb home; **je peux vous r.?** can I take you back?, *Br* would you like a lift back?; **la faim/la fatigue/le froid le ramènera** he'll come back when he's hungry/tired/cold; **la curiosité le ramènera** curiosity will bring him back; **la faim/la fatigue/ le froid le ramena** he came back because he was hungry/ tired/cold; **r. qn à la vie** to bring sb back to life, to resuscitate sb; **r. qn à la raison** to make sb see reason *or* sense; **r. la conversation sur un sujet** to lead *or* bring the conversation back to a subject; *F* **r. le compteur à zéro** to reset the counter to zero, to zero the counter; **ça me ramène des années en arrière**! that really takes me back!; **ça me ramène au temps de mon enfance/au temps où …** that takes me back to my childhood/to when …; *F* **r. sa fraise** *ou très F* **sa gueule, la r.** (*s'immiscer*) to stick *or* shove one's oar in; **ramène ta fraise, ramène-la** (*viens ici*) get yourself *or Arg* your arse over here a minute

(**b**) (*réduire*) (*nombre de chômeurs, prix, inflation etc*) to reduce (**à** to); **r. l'inflation à un taux inférieur** to bring down inflation

(**c**) (*remettre*) (*couverture*) to pull up (**sur** over); (*baisser*) (*chapeau, jupe*) to pull down (**sur** over); **r. ses cheveux sur le côté** to sweep one's hair to the side; *Fig* **elle ramène tout à elle/à ses propres problèmes** she always drags the conversation round to herself/her own problems

2 se ramener *vpr* (**a**) *F* **voici à quoi se ramène son raisonnement** this is what his argument boils down to

(**b**) *F* (*arriver*) to roll up; **c'est à cette heure-ci que tu te ramènes?** what kind of time do you call this!

ramequin [ramkɛ̃] *nm Culin* ramekin

ramer[1] [rame] *vt* (*pois etc*) to stake

ramer[2] *vi* (**a**) (*pagayer*) to row, *Litt* to pull (at the oar/oars); **r. en couple** to scull; **r. à rebours** to back water (**b**) *Fig F* to sweat blood; **qu'est-ce qu'on a ramé!** we sweated blood!, we worked like dogs *or* like galley slaves!; **j'ai ramé pendant des années avant de trouver ce travail** I had a hard time of it for years before I found this job; **j'ai ramé pendant des années pour restaurer cette maison** it took years of hard graft to restore this house

rameur, -euse [ramœr, -øz] *n* (*à l'aviron*) rower, oarsman, *f* oarswoman; **r. de couple** sculler

rameux, -euse [ramø, -øz] *adj* branching, *Spéc* ramose

rami [rami] *nm Cartes* rummy

ramie [rami] *nf Bot* ramie

ramier [ramje] *adj inv, nm* (**pigeon**) **r.** ring dove, wood pigeon

ramification [ramifikasjɔ̃] *nf Bot* ramification, branching (out); *Fig* (*d'une secte, famille, science etc*) branch; *Fig* **ramifications** (*d'une affaire, d'un scandale*) ramifications

ramifier (se) [səramifje] *vpr* to branch out (**en** into); *Fig* **cette organisation se ramifie dans plusieurs pays** the organization has branches in several countries

ramille [ramij] *nf* twig

ramolli, -ie [ramɔli] **1** *adj* (*beurre*) soft; *F* (*personne*) (*physiquement*) limp, washed out; (*mentalement*) soft in the head; **je suis** *ou* **je me sens tout r.** I feel like a wet rag *or* as if I've had all of the stuffing knocked out of me **2** *n F* wimp; **c'est un r. du cerveau** he's going soft in the head

ramollir [ramɔlir] **1** *vt* (*cire, beurre*) to soften; *Fig* (*volonté*) to sap; **ces vacances m'ont ramolli** this holiday has left me without any energy **2 se ramollir** *vpr* (*du beurre, goudron*) to go soft, to soften; *Fig* (*physiquement*) to go downhill; (*moralement*) to have no energy, *F* to have no get up and go; *F* **son cerveau se ramollit** he's going soft in the head

ramollissement [ramɔlismɑ̃] *nm* softening

ramollo [ramɔlo] *F* **1** *adj* (*inv in f*) (*physiquement*) limp, washed out; **je me sens tout r.** I feel like a wet rag *or* as if I've had all of the stuffing knocked out of me; **son grand-père est un peu r.** his grandfather's a bit soft in the head **2** *nm* **c'est un r.** he's a wimp

ramonage [ramɔnaʒ] *nm* (chimney) sweeping *or* cleaning; (*en alpinisme*) climbing a chimney, chimneying

ramoner [ramɔne] **1** *vt* (*cheminée*) to sweep, to clean **2** *vi* to sweep *or* clean the chimney; (*en alpinisme*) to (climb a) chimney

ramoneur [ramɔnœr] *nm* (chimney) sweep

rampage [rɑ̃paʒ] *nm Aut* (*d'une boîte automatique*) creep

rampant [rɑ̃pɑ̃] *adj* (**a**) (*plante*) creeping; (*animal*) crawling; *Av* **personnel r.** ground staff (**b**) *Péj* (*personne, caractère*) crawling, grovelling (**c**) (*inflation*) rampant; *Hér* **lion r.** lion rampant

rampe [rɑ̃p] *nf* (**a**) (*d'escalier*) ban(n)isters, handrail; **faire des glissades sur la r.** to slide down the banisters; *F* **tenir bon la r.** to be still going strong; *Arg* **lâcher la r.** to kick the bucket, to snuff it

(**b**) (*pente*) slope, incline, rise; (*d'une route*) gradient; *Aut* **vitesse en r.** speed when (hill) climbing *or* going uphill; *Aut* **ralentir dans la r.** to slow down on the incline

(**c**) (*passerelle etc*) ramp, gangway

(**d**) (*de projecteurs etc*) bank

(**e**) *Th* footlights; *Fig* **être sous les feux de la r.** to be in the limelight; **pièce/acteur qui ne passe pas la r.** play that/actor who doesn't come across

▸ **rampe**: **r. d'accès** (*d'un pont*) access ramp; (*d'une autoroute*) *Br* slip road, approach road, ramp; **r. de graissage** lubricating rack, oil distributor; **r. de lancement** (*de projectile*) launching ramp; *Av* **r. (lumineuse) d'atterrissage** illuminated landing strip; **r. mobile** portable ramp, movable gangway

rampement [rɑ̃pmɑ̃] *nm* creeping, crawling

ramper [rɑ̃pe] *vi* (*d'un animal, d'une personne*) to crawl; (*d'une plante*) to creep; **entrer/sortir en rampant** to crawl in/out; *Péj* **r. devant les chefs** to crawl *or* grovel to the bosses; **je n'aime pas les gens qui rampent!** I don't like crawlers!

ramure [ramyr] *nf* (**a**) (*d'arbre*) branches, boughs (**b**) (*d'un cerf*) antlers

rancard [rɑ̃kar] *nm* (**a**) *F* (*rendez-vous*) (*avec son petit ami*) date; (*chez le médecin, le dentiste etc*) appointment; **j'ai r. avec lui à 2 heures** (*ami*) I'm meeting him at two o'clock; (*petit ami*) I've got a date with him at two o'clock; (*médecin*) I've got an appointment with him at *or* for two o'clock; *très F* **on s'est filé un r. pour la semaine prochaine** we arranged to meet next week, we made a date for next week (**b**) *Arg* (*renseignement*) tip

rancarder [rɑ̃karde] *vt Arg* **r. qn sur qch** to put sb on to sth; **on a dû les r.** they must have been tipped off

rancart [rɑ̃kar] *nm* **mettre au r.** (*objet*) to discard; (*projet*) to shelve; (*personne*) to put on the sidelines, to sideline; **on a finalement décidé la mise au r. du projet** we finally decided to shelve the project

rance [rɑ̃s] **1** *adj* rancid, rank **2** *nm* **sentir le r.** (*du beurre*) to smell rancid; (*d'un placard*) to smell fusty; **un goût de r.** a rancid taste; **avoir un goût de r.** to taste rancid

ranch [rɑ̃tʃ] *nm* ranch; **exploiter un r.** to ranch

rancidité [rɑ̃sidite] *nf* rancidness

rancir [rɑ̃sir] *vi* to become *or* grow rancid

rancœur [rɑ̃kœr] *nf* resentment, bitterness, rancour; **j'ai de la r. contre lui** I feel resentment towards him, I resent him; **plein de r.** (*personne, ton*) resentful, bitter

rançon [rɑ̃sɔ̃] *nf* ransom; *Litt* **mettre qn à r.** to hold sb to ransom; *Fig* **la r. du progrès/de la gloire** the price of progress/fame; **c'est la r. du progrès!** that's the price you pay for progress!

rançonner [rɑ̃sɔne] *vt* **r. qn** to hold sb to ransom; *Fig F* to fleece sb; **r. un voyageur** to hold up (and rob) a traveller

rancune [rɑ̃kyn] *nf* spite; **garder r. à qn, avoir de la r. contre qn** to have a grudge against sb, to bear sb a grudge; **plein de r.** spiteful; **par r.** out of spite; **sans r.!** no hard feelings!; **il y a de vieilles rancunes entre eux** there is bad blood between them

rancunier, -ière [rɑ̃kynje, -jɛr] **1** *adj* vindictive, spiteful **2** *n* vindictive *or* spiteful person

randomisation [rɑ̃dɔmizasjɔ̃] *nf* randomization

randomiser [rɑ̃dɔmize] *vt* to randomize

randonnée [rɑ̃dɔne] *nf* ramble, hike; (*sport*) rambling, trekking; (*en voiture*) outing, trip; (*à vélo*) run, ride; (*en montagne*) hill-walking, climbing; (*à ski de fond*) cross-country skiing; (*avec peau de phoque*) ski-mountaineering; **r. à pied** *ou* **pédestre** hike; **r. équestre** pony trek; **chemin de grande r.** long-distance footpath; **faire de la r.** (*à pied*) to go hiking; (*en petite montagne*) to go hill-walking; (*en moyenne montagne*) to go climbing; (*en haute montagne*) to go mountaineering; **r. en VTT** mountain biking; **une r. en montagne** a hill-walk, a climb; **r. sac au dos** backpacking (tour); **r. à dos de poney** pony-trekking

randonneur, -euse [rɑ̃dɔnœr, -øz] *n* (*à pied*) rambler, hiker, walker; (*en petite montagne*) hill-walker; (*en moyenne montagne*) climber; (*en haute montagne*) mountaineer; (*à ski*) cross-country skier; (*avec peau de phoque*) ski-mountaineer

rang [rɑ̃] *nm* (**a**) (*d'arbres, de sièges etc*) row, line; (*d'oignons, de tricot*) row; (*d'avirons*) bank; *Mil* rank; **fauteuil au premier r.** front-row seat; *Scol* **être (assis) au premier/ dernier r.** to sit in the front/back row, to sit at the front/back of the class; *Fig* **je le sais, j'étais au premier r. (pour le voir)** I should know, I have first-hand experience; **se mettre en r./rangs** to line up; *Hum* **se mettre en r. d'oignons** to stand (close together) in a line; **(un collier avec) trois rangs de perles** a triple strand of beads; **machine à quatre rangs de touches** four-bank typewriter; **sur deux rangs** in two ranks, two deep; **par rangs de trois** three abreast, three in a row; *Mil* **homme du r.** private; *Mil* **formez les rangs!** fall in!; *Mil, Fig* **serrer les rangs** to close ranks; *Mil* **en rangs serrés** in close order; *Fig* **nous sommes arrivés en rangs serrés dans le bureau du directeur** we trooped into the manager's office; *Fig* **s'il le faut, nous irons en rangs serrés lui en parler** we'll talk to him about it all together *or* as a group *or* en masse if necessary; *Mil, Fig* **rompre les rangs** to break ranks; *Mil* **sortir des rangs** to fall out (of line), to break rank; **officier sorti du r.** officer promoted from the ranks; *Fig* **un ancien ouvrier sorti du r.** a former worker who came up *or* rose through the ranks

(b) (*classement*) rank, place; (*social*) station; *Mil, Fin* (*d'une créance*) rank; **r. élevé** high rank; **dame de haut r.** lady of rank; **un militaire de haut r.** a high-ranking *or* senior officer; **r. social** social status; **il faut tenir notre r.** we have to keep up our position (in life); **avoir r. de colonel** to hold the rank of colonel; **de premier/second r.** first-/second-class, first-/second-rate; **il est au r. des meilleurs** he ranks amongst the best; **il est au premier r. de sa profession** he is at the top of (the tree in) his profession; **par r. de** (*taille, ancienneté, âge*) by, according to; **occuper un r. supérieur à qn** to rank above *or* outrank sb; **prendre** *ou* **avoir r. avant/après qn** to come before/after sb (in rank); **il a pris r. parmi les grands poètes** he has taken his place *or* is counted among the great poets; **prendre r. dans un parti** to join a party; **sortir d'une École avec un bon r.** = to graduate near the top of one's class; **venir au** *ou* **en troisième r.** to rank third; **arriver au premier r.** to be in the forefront; **le chômage arrive au premier r. des préoccupations des Français** unemployment is one of the main concerns of the French; *Fig* **se mettre sur les rangs** to enter the lists, to join the fray, to put one's name forward; **il y avait déjà quelqu'un sur les rangs** there was already someone in the field; *Fig* **grossir les rangs des révoltés/des chômeurs** to swell the ranks of the rebels/the unemployed

(c) *Can* concession road; (*quartier*) concession, rural district

rangé [rɑ̃ʒe] *adj* **(a)** (*en ordre*) tidy, orderly; (*vie*) well-ordered, orderly; (*personne*) steady; **une jeune fille rangée** a well-behaved girl; **c'était un homme très r.** he was a very quiet kind of man; **une maison très bien rangée** a very tidy *or* well-kept house; **ce n'est pas bien r. chez elle** her place isn't very tidy; **ma petite vie bien rangée** my quiet *or* unexciting little life; *Fig F* **être r. des voitures** to be a reformed character, to have settled *or* steadied down **(b) bataille rangée** pitched battle

rangée [rɑ̃ʒe] *nf* (*de personnes, boutons, sièges, d'arbres*) row, line; (*de gradins*) tier; **r. de cylindres** cylinder bank

rangement [rɑ̃ʒmɑ̃] *nm* **(a)** (*action*) tidying, putting in order; *Ordinat* storage; **avoir la manie du r.** to have a mania for tidiness, to be fanatically tidy; **volume de r.** storage space; **faire du r. (dans son bureau)** to do some tidying up (in one's office); **faire du r. dans ses affaires** to tidy up one's things **(b)** (*placard*) **(meuble de) r.** storage unit; **cette cuisine manque de rangements** this kitchen lacks storage space; **r. de cuisine** kitchen cabinet; **(c)** (*disposition*) arrangement

ranger [rɑ̃ʒe] **(je rangeai(s); n. rangeons) 1** *vt* **(a)** (*pièce, maison*) to tidy (up), to put away; **tout est si bien rangé dans cette maison** this house is so beautifully tidy

(b) (*affaires, vêtements*) to put *or* tidy away; (*par ordre alphabétique, de taille etc*) to arrange; *Com* (*marchandises*) to stow; (*voiture*) to park; **où as-tu rangé les fourchettes/ton livre?** where have you put the forks/your book?; **tu devrais r. tes classeurs (à leur place)** you should put your files away *or* put your files back where they belong; **tout est si bien rangé** everything is arranged so neatly *or* tidily; *Ordinat* **r. en mémoire** to store

(c) r. qn parmi les grands écrivains to rank *or* count sb amongst the great writers; **on le range parmi les meilleurs médecins/psychanalystes** he is said to be one of the best doctors/psychoanalysts

(d) *Mil* (*troupes*) to draw up, to marshal

2 se ranger *vpr* **(a)** (*s'écarter*) **se r. (de côté)** (*d'un piéton*) to get out of the way, to stand aside; (*d'une voiture*) to pull over; **on se rangea pour nous laisser passer** they stood aside for us, they made way for us; **la voiture s'est rangée contre le mur** the car pulled in alongside the wall; *Naut* **se r. à quai** to berth

(b) *Fig* **se r. du côté de qn** to side with sb, to take sb's side; **se r. à l'opinion de qn** to come round to sb's point of view

(c) *F* (*s'assagir*) to settle down

rani [rani] *nf* ranee

ranimation [ranimasjɔ̃] *nf* resuscitation, reanimation

ranimer [ranime] **1** *vt* (*personne qui s'évanouit*) to bring round; *Méd* (*après un arrêt cardiaque*) to resuscitate; *Fig* (*ville, industrie*) to revive, to put new life into; (*couleurs*) to brighten, to revive; (*feu*) to rekindle; (*colère, désir*) to reawaken, to rekindle; (*espoir*) to revive, to reawaken, to rekindle; (*souvenir, enthousiasme, débat*) to rekindle, to revive; (*conversation*) to liven up; **r. le courage de qn** to put new heart into sb; **un simple mouvement du bras suffit à r. la douleur** just moving the arm is enough to make the pain flare up

2 se ranimer *vpr* (*d'un feu*) to flicker into life; (*d'une conversation*) to pick up again, to come to life again; **son visage se ranima** her face lit up

rap [rap] *nm Mus* rap

rapace [rapas] **1** *adj* predatory; *Fig* (*personne*) grasping, *Fml* rapacious; **oiseau r.** bird of prey **2** *nm* bird of prey

rapacité [rapasite] *nf* rapacity; *Fig* rapaciousness, rapacity; **avec r.** greedily, *Fml* rapaciously

râpage [rɑpaʒ] *nm* (*du métal, du bois*) rasping

rapatrié, -ée [rapatrije] *n* person who has been repatriated, repatriate; **les rapatriés d'Algérie** the people repatriated from Algeria

rapatriement [rapatrimɑ̃] *nm* repatriation; **r. sanitaire** repatriation for health reasons

rapatrier [rapatrije] *vt* (*personne, Fig capitaux*) to repatriate; **se faire r.** to get *or* be repatriated

râpe [rɑp] *nf* **(a)** (*de cuisine*) grater; **r. à muscade/à fromage** nutmeg/cheese grater **(b)** *Tech* rasp

râpé [rɑpe] **1** *adj* **(a)** (*fromage, carotte etc*) grated **(b)** (*usé*) (*vêtement*) worn out, threadbare **(c)** *F* (*raté*) **c'est r. pour ce week-end** this weekend's had it; **pour le pique-nique, c'est r.** the picnic's out, the picnic's had it **2** *nm* **(a)** (*vin*) rape wine **(b)** (*fromage*) grated cheese

râper [rɑpe] *vt* (*carotte, noix de muscade etc*) to grate; (*bois, métal*) to rasp; **ce vin râpe la gorge** this wine is rough *or* harsh on the throat

rapetassage [raptasaʒ] *nm F* patching up

rapetasser [raptase] *vt F* (*vêtement*) to patch up

rapetissement [raptismɑ̃] *nm* (*d'un objet*) (*dû à la distance*) reduction (in size); (*d'un vieillard*) shrinking

rapetisser [raptise] **1** *vt* (*chose*) to make smaller, to reduce in size; (*vêtement*) to shrink; *Fig* (*succès*) to belittle; **la distance rapetisse les objets** distance makes things look smaller; **r. les mérites de qn** to belittle sb

2 *vi* (*d'un vêtement, d'une personne*) to shrink; **au pied de cet immeuble, on a l'impression de r.** you feel very small in front of this building, you feel dwarfed by this building; **j'aurais voulu r. pour qu'il ne me voie pas** I wanted to shrivel up and die

3 se rapetisser *vpr* to make oneself shorter; **elle portait des talons plats pour essayer de se r.** she wore flat shoes in an attempt to make herself look shorter

râpeux, -euse [rɑpø, -øz] *adj* (*langue*) raspy; (*vin*) harsh; (*voix*) grating, rasping

raphia [rafja] *nm* (*fibre*) raffia; (*arbre*) raffia (palm)

rapiat, -ate [rapja, -at] *F* **1** *adj* (*avare*) stingy, miserly, tight-fisted **2** *n* miser, skinflint, *Am* tightwad

rapide [rapid] **1** *adj* **(a)** (*coureur, itinéraire, voiture etc*) fast; (*pouls, progrès, changement, récit etc*) rapid, fast; (*décision*) rapid, speedy; (*courant*) rapid, swift, fast; **être r. à la course** to be a fast *or* quick runner, to run fast; **il est r. dans son travail** he's a fast *or* quick worker; **il a l'esprit très r.** (*il comprend vite*) he's quick to grasp things, he has a quick mind; **la voiture la plus r. de sa catégorie** the fastest car in its category; **c'est plus r. si tu passes par là** it's faster *or* quicker if you go that way; **faire une lecture trop r. de qch** to read sth too quickly *or* fast; **une décision trop r.** a hasty decision; **r. comme une flèche, r. comme l'éclair** as swift as an arrow; (*réponse, coureur*) quick as lightning; **il est r. en affaires** he doesn't waste any time, he's a fast worker; **fusil à tir r.** quick-firing *or* rapid-fire rifle

(b) (*abrupt*) (*pente*) steep

2 *nm* **(a)** (*de rivière*) rapid; **descendre les rapides** to shoot the rapids

(b) (*train*) express (train)

3 *n* (*personne*) **c'est une r.** (*compréhension*) she's quick on the uptake; (*travail*) she's a fast worker

rapidement [rapidmɑ̃] *adv* quickly, fast, rapidly; **le temps passe r.** time flies; **trop r.** too fast, too quick(ly); **je l'ai lu r.** I read through it quickly, I had a quick read through it; **parcourir r. le journal** to skim the newspaper

rapidité [rapidite] *nf* **(a)** (*d'actions*) speed, swiftness, rapidity; (*d'une décision*) speediness; (*d'une réponse*) swiftness;

célèbre pour sa r. à la course famous for being a fast runner; **grâce à sa r. d'esprit** because of the speed with which he grasps things; **faire preuve d'une grande r.** (*dans son travail, dans un jeu*) to be very quick *or* fast; **le poison agit avec une r. fulgurante** the poison is incredibly fast-acting; *Ordinat* **r. d'impression** print speed; **r. de traitement** processing speed

(**b**) (*d'une pente*) steepness

rapiéçage [rapjesaʒ] *nm,* **rapiècement** [rapjɛsmɑ̃] *nm* (*d'un vêtement*) patching (up), mending

rapiécer [rapjese] *vt* (**je rapièce, n. rapiéçons; je rapiécerai**) (*vêtement*) to patch, to put a patch on

rapière [rapjɛr] *nf* rapier

rapin [rapɛ̃] *nm F Péj* (*peintre*) dauber

rapine [rapin] *nf Litt* rapine, pillage; (*butin*) spoils; **habitudes de r.** predatory habits

raplapla [raplapla] *adj inv F* (*personne*) washed out; (*pneu, coussin*) flat as a pancake; **je me sens tout r. aujourd'hui** I don't have any go in me at all today

rappareiller [rapareje], **rapparier** [raparje] *vt* (*impf, pr sub* **n. rappariions**) *Rare* to match, to find a match for; (*chaussettes*) to pair

rappel [rapɛl] *nm* (**a**) (*d'un incident etc*) calling to mind, recalling; (*pour se souvenir*) reminder; (**lettre de**) **r.** (letter of) reminder; *Fin* **r. de compte** reminder of account outstanding; **r. de traitement/de solde/de salaire** back pay; *Rad, TV* **voici le r. des titres (de l'actualité)** here are the headlines once again; **et les coussins sont assortis aux rideaux, quel joli r. de couleurs** the colour of the cushions is nicely picked up *or* repeated in the curtains

(**b**) (*d'un général, ambassadeur, de réservistes*) recall; **lettres de r.** (*d'un ambassadeur*) letters of recall; *Mil* **battre le r.** to call *or* beat to arms; *Fig* to rally the troops, to send out a call to arms

(**c**) *Com* (*d'une somme déjà avancée*) calling in; (*de marchandises défectueuses*) recall

(**d**) *Méd* (**injection de**) **r.** booster (injection); **faire un r.** to have a booster

(**e**) **r. à l'ordre** (*à un membre d'une assemblée*) call to order; (*à un employé*) warning; **un simple r. au bon sens suffira à le faire changer d'avis** an appeal to his common sense will make him change his mind

(**f**) *Th* curtain call; (*à un concert*) encore; **il y a eu plusieurs rappels** *Th* he/she/*etc* took several curtain calls *or* was called back several times; *Mus* there were several encores

(**g**) *Sp* abseil; **faire une descente** *ou* **descendre en r., faire du r.** to abseil down

(**h**) *Ordinat* (*de texte*) restore; *Tech* **vis de r.** adjusting screw; **fil de r.** bracing *or* straining wire; **ressort de r.** return spring, drawback spring; **tige de r.** stay rod; *Aut* **r. latéral de clignotant** side repeat indicator

rappeler [rap(ə)le] (*conj like* **appeler**) **1** *vt* (**a**) (*oralement*) (*personne*) to call back; *Tél* (*pour rendre un coup de téléphone*) to call *or* phone *or Br* ring back; (*qn que l'on a des difficultés à joindre*) to call *or* phone *or Br* ring again; *Tél* **je l'ai rappelé plusieurs fois mais je n'ai jamais réussi à lui parler** I called *or* phoned *or Br* rang (him) several times but I didn't get to speak to him; *Tél* **je l'ai rappelé une cinquième fois** I called *or* phoned *or Br* rang him for the fifth time; **je (le) rappelle dans une minute** I'll call (him) back/again in a minute

(**b**) (*faire revenir*) to recall, to call *or* summon back; (*ambassadeur*), *Ordinat* to recall; *Mil* **r. qn (sous les drapeaux)** to call sb up; **être rappelé trois fois** (*d'un comédien*) to take three curtain calls; (*d'un musicien, chanteur*) to give three encores; **r. son chien** to call off one's dog; **r. qn à l'ordre** (*membre d'une association*) to call sb to order; (*élève*) to warn sb; **tu vas te faire r. à l'ordre** you're going to get a warning, you're going to be pulled up; **r. qn à la vie** *ou* **à lui** (*personne évanouie*) to bring sb round; (*blessé, noyé*) to resuscitate sb; *Fig* to bring sb back to life; **r. qn à son** *ou* **au devoir** to remind sb of their duty *or* where their duty lies; **r. qn à la raison** to make sb see reason *or* sense; **être rappelé au chevet de qn** to be called to sb's bedside; **Dieu l'a rappelée à lui** God called her to Him

(**c**) (*pour se souvenir de*) (*qch*) to recall; **r. qch à qn** to remind sb of sth; **rappelez-moi votre nom** what was your name again?; **vous me rappelez mon oncle** you remind me of my uncle; **cela me rappelle mon enfance** it brings back my childhood, it reminds me of my childhood; **ça me rappelle quelque chose** it reminds me of something, it rings a bell; **cela ne me rappelle rien** it doesn't ring a bell *or* any bells; **puis-je te r. que tu me dois 200 francs?** may I remind you that you owe me 200 francs?; **rappelez-moi à son bon souvenir** remember me (kindly) to him; **ce sont des choses qu'il vaut autant ne pas r.** these things are best forgotten; **il n'est pas nécessaire de r. que vous devez tous être ponctuels au cours** there's no need to remind you that you all have to be on time for class; *Com* **prière de r. ce numéro** in reply please quote this number

(**d**) *Tech* (*pièce d'une machine etc*) to draw back; *Typ* **r. le chariot** to return the carriage; (*de quelques espaces*) to backspace

2 se rappeler *vpr* (**a**) **se r. qch,** *F* **se r. de qch** to remember *or* recall *or* recollect sth, to call sth to mind; **je ne me le rappelle plus,** *F* **je ne m'en rappelle plus** I can't remember it; **un rêve dont je ne me rappelle presque plus rien** a dream I remember almost nothing about; **se r. (d')avoir promis qch** to remember promising sth; **rappelez-vous que ce n'est qu'une enfant** remember that *or* bear in mind that she's only a child

(**b**) *Tél F* **on se rappelle la semaine prochaine** (*au téléphone*) we'll talk again next week; **on se rappelle, hein?** talk to you on the phone

rappeur, -euse [rapœr, -øz] *n Mus* rapper

rappliquer [raplike] *vi très F* to turn *or* roll up, to show (up); **r. à la maison** to roll back home; **je n'ai aucune envie de le voir r. ici** I don't want him turning up here

rapport [rapɔr] *nm* (**a**) (*relation humaine*) **mettre qn en r. avec qn** to put sb in touch with sb; **quelle est la nature de vos rapports avec elle?** what is the nature of your relationship with her?, what exactly is your relationship with her?; **nos rapports sont purement professionnels** our relationship is purely professional; **nous avons maintenu des rapports amicaux** we've stayed on friendly terms; **nous ne sommes plus en r. depuis des années** we lost touch years ago, we haven't been in touch for years; **rapports commerciaux** business relations; **avoir des rapports avec qn** (*officiels*) to have dealings *or* relations with sb; (*sexuels*) to have sex with sb, *Fml* to have sexual intercourse with sb; **les couples qui n'ont plus de rapports** couples who no longer have sex *or* sexual relations; **à quand remontent vos derniers rapports?** when did you last have intercourse?; **avoir de bons rapports avec qn** to be on good terms with sb; **les rapports qu'elle a avec son père sont très tendres/tendus** she and her father have a very loving/tense relationship; **les rapports qu'elle a avec son père sont très amicaux** she and her father have a very friendly relationship *or* are on very friendly terms; **ses difficultés relationnelles trouvent leur origine dans son r. à sa mère** her difficulties in forming relationships stem from her own relationship with her mother; **un r. de forces** a battle of wills; **entretenir des rapports d'affaires avec qn** to have a business relationship with sb; **cesser tout r. avec qn** to break off all contact *or* relations with sb; *Pol* **les rapports Est-Ouest** East-West relations; **entretenir des rapports de bon voisinage avec les pays européens** to maintain good relations with European countries

(**b**) (*lien*) relation, connection (**avec** with); **sans r. avec le sujet** without any bearing on *or* unconnected with *or* irrelevant to the subject; **la question est sans r. avec ce que nous disions** the question has no bearing on *or* is not relevant to what we were saying; **ce n'est pas sans r. avec ce que je disais** it is not unrelated to what I was saying; **sa décision est sans r. avec ce qui se passe ici** his decision has no bearing on *or* relevance to what's happening here; **avoir r. à qch** to be about sth, to have to do with sth, to relate to sth; **mais ça n'a aucun r. avec ce que je disais!** but that's got nothing to do with what I was saying!; **question qui a un r. très étroit avec une autre** question that is closely connected with another; **un métier en r. avec ses goûts** a trade that suits his tastes; **un travail (plus) en r. avec vos capacités** a job (more) in keeping with your abilities; **il a un mode de vie parfaitement en r. avec ses revenus** he has a lifestyle well within his means; **une histoire en r. avec votre vie quotidienne** a story about *or* that has to do with your daily life; **parlez-lui de choses qui sont peut-être moins en r. avec votre passé** talk to him about things that maybe have a bit less to do with your past; **établir un r. entre deux choses** to establish *or* make a connection between two things; **elle n'a pas fait le r.** she didn't make the connection; **je ne vois pas le r.** I can't see the connection *or* link; **où est le r.?** where's the link *or* connection?; **par r. à qch** (*en ce qui concerne*) with regard to sth; (*en comparaison*) compared *or* in comparison with sth; *Fin* **par r. au mark** against the German mark; *F* **je suis venu vous voir r. à mes allocs** I've come to see you about my dole money; **sous ce r.** in this respect; **analyser un texte sous le r. de la sémiologie** to analyse a text from a semiotic angle; **sous le r. de l'efficacité** from the performance point of view; **sous tous les rapports** in all respects, in every respect; **un homme bien sous tous rapports** a fine man in every respect *or* in every way; **cherche jeune femme bien sous tous rapports pour garder deux enfants** (*dans petite annonce*) wanted: respectable young woman to look after two children

(c) (*proportion*) ratio, proportion; *Math* ratio; (*vitesse*) gear; **en r. avec** in proportion *or* proportional to; **dans le r. de un à trois** in a ratio of one to three; **le r. maître-élèves est de 1 pour 20** the staff-student ratio is 1 to 20; **le r. des forces entre le Nord et le Sud** the balance of power between North and South; *Com* **r. qualité-prix** quality-price ratio; **r. valeur-prix** value-price ratio; **ce produit est d'un bon r. qualité-prix** this product is good value for money; *Aut* **r. des engrenages** gear ratio; **changer de r.** to change gear; **r. avant** forward gear ratio; **r. course-alésage** stroke-bore ratio; **r. de boîte** gearbox ratio; **r. inférieur** low (gear); **r. intermédiaire** intermediate gear

(d) (*écrit etc*) report; (*des dépenses etc*) return; **faire** *ou* **rédiger un r. sur qch** to make a report on sth, to draw up a report on sth; *Com, Fin* **r. annuel** annual report; **r. commercial** market report; **r. d'expertise** valuation, expert's report; *Compta* **r. d'exploitation** operating statement; **r. d'intelligence mercatique** market intelligence report; **r. d'étude de marché** market study report; **r. de gestion** management report; *Com* **r. de situation journalière** daily trading report; *Com* **r. de situation mensuelle** monthly trading report; **r. des affaires sociales** social report; **r. des commissaires aux comptes** government auditors' report; **r. financier** financial report; **r. récapitulatif** summary report

(e) *Fin* yield, return, profit; *Agr* yield; **vivre du r. d'une terre** to live off the money that a piece of land brings in; **capital en r.** interest-bearing *or* productive capital; **arbre fruitier en plein r.** fruit tree in full yield; *Agr* **terre en plein r.** extremely productive land; **immeuble de r.** rental property; **d'un bon r.** profitable, that brings in a good return, that pays well; **d'un mauvais r.** unprofitable, that brings in a poor return, that does not pay well; **les rapports du tiercé** winnings on the horse races

(f) *Mil* daily parade for issue of orders; **salle des rapports** orderly room

rapportage [rapɔrtaʒ] *nm Scol F* tale-telling, sneaking

rapporté [rapɔrte] *adj Couture* **manche rapportée** set-in sleeve; **poches rapportées** patch pockets

rapporter [rapɔrte] **1** *vt* (a) (*pour rendre*) (*vers le locuteur*) to bring back, to return; (*en s'éloignant du locuteur*) to take back, to return; (*d'un chien*) (*gibier*) to retrieve; **rapportez-moi un kilo de sucre** bring me back a kilo of sugar; **j'espère que tu nous rapportes de bonnes nouvelles!** I hope you've brought us some good news!; **je t'ai rapporté l'aspirateur** I've brought back the *or* your vacuum cleaner; (*en le présentant*) here's the vacuum cleaner that I borrowed; **veux-tu r. ce livre à la bibliothèque?** will you take this book back to the library?, will you return this book to the library?; **il n'en a rapporté que la déception** all he got out of it was disappointment; **allez! rapporte!** (*à un chien*) fetch!; *Journ* **r. une copie** to file copy

(b) (*relier à*) **r. qch à une cause** to attribute *or* ascribe sth to a cause; **il faut r. l'événement à l'époque où il a eu lieu** one must look at *or* consider the event in context; **r. tout à soi** to relate everything to oneself; (*parler de soi*) to drag the conversation round to oneself

(c) (*faire le compte rendu de*) to report, to give an account of; **tu me rapporteras sa réponse/ce qu'il dit de notre proposition** let me know his answer/what he says about our proposal; **le journal rapporte l'anecdote suivante ...** the newspaper carries this story ...; **l'histoire rapporte que ...** history relates that ...; **on rapporte qu'il avait des pouvoirs surnaturels** he is said *or* reported to have had supernatural powers; **je vous rapporte ses paroles** I'm telling you what he said; **il rapporte tous les faits et gestes de ses collègues à son patron** he reports to his boss on everything that his colleagues do; **vous n'auriez pas dû le r.** you shouldn't have repeated it; **ce petit fayot est allé tout r. à l'instituteur** the little sneak has gone and told the teacher

(d) *Couture* (*poche, pièce*) to sew on

(e) *Fin* to bring in, to bear, to yield; *Agr* to yield; **r. de l'argent** to be profitable; **r. des bénéfices** to be profitable; **r. des intérêts** to yield interest; **placement qui rapporte dix pour cent** investment that brings in *or* yields ten per cent; **arbres qui rapportent beaucoup** trees that yield well; **cela ne rapporte rien** it doesn't pay; *Fig* **est-ce que tu crois que ça va te r. quelque chose?** do you think you're going to get anything out of it?, do you think it will do you any good?

(f) *Jur etc* (*décret*) to rescind, to revoke; (*ordre*) to withdraw, to cancel; **r. un ordre de grève** to call off a strike, *Fml* to rescind a strike order

(g) *Géom* (*angle*) to plot, to set off, to lay off; **r. des mesures à une autre échelle** to plot measurements on a different scale

(h) *Compta* (*écriture*) to post

2 se rapporter *vpr* (a) (*avoir rapport avec*) **se r. à qch** to refer to sth, to relate to sth; **les documents qui se rapportent à l'affaire** the relevant documents, the documents relating to *or* connected with the case; **la réponse ne se rapporte pas à la question posée** the answer has nothing to do with *or* is irrelevant to the question asked; **les souvenirs qui se rapportent à cette expérience** the memories connected with the experience

(b) **s'en r. à qn/au témoignage de qn** to rely on *or* to put one's faith in sb/sb's evidence; **je m'en rapporte à vous pour ce qui est des invitations** I can rely on you to arrange the invitations; **je m'en rapporte à votre jugement** I have every faith in your judgement

(c) *Tech* (*d'une pièce*) to fit (**avec** with)

3 *vi* (a) (*être rentable*) to pay; **c'est un métier qui rapporte** it's a profitable career; **une affaire qui rapporte** a profitable business, a business that pays; **ça ne rapporte pas** it doesn't pay, there's no money in it; **vous croyez que ça rapporte?** do you think there's any money in it?; **ça peut r. gros** it can be very profitable

(b) (*en secret*) to tell tales, to sneak; **r. sur le compte de qn** to tell on sb; **je n'aime pas les enfants qui rapportent** I don't like telltales

(c) *Litt* (*ressembler à*) to be on a level *or* a par with

rapporteur, -euse [rapɔrtœr, -øz] **1** *adj* telltale, sneaky, tattling **2** *n* telltale, sneak, tattler **3** *nm* (a) reporter, recorder (b) *Mil* judge advocate (*at court martial*) (c) *Math* protractor; **r. à limbe complet** circular protractor

rapprendre [raprɑ̃dr] *vt* (*conj like* **prendre**) (a) (*apprendre*) to learn (over) again; **elle a dû r. à marcher après son accident** she had to learn to walk (all over) again after her accident; **r. le bonheur** to learn how to be happy again (b) (*enseigner*) to teach again; **il faut leur r. sans cesse le code de la route** you have to keep teaching them the Highway Code

rapproché [raprɔʃe] *adj* (*dans l'espace, dans le temps*) near; (*yeux*) close-set; **maisons très rapprochées** houses very close together, houses very close *or* near to one another; **des examens très rapprochés** *ou* **qui ont lieu à des dates très rapprochées** exams coming very close together *or* very close to each other; **j'ai trois réunions très rapprochées dans la journée** I've got three meetings one right after the other; **faits rapprochés dans le temps** events occurring close together (in time); *Phot, Cin* **plan r. sur un visage** close-up of a face; (*sur script*) close-up on a face

rapprochement [raprɔʃmɑ̃] *nm* (a) (*de faits, d'idées*) comparison, setting side by side, putting together; **il n'a pas fait le r.** he didn't make the connection; **je ne peux m'empêcher de faire un r. entre ces deux faits** I can't help making a connection between *or* linking the two facts (b) (*de deux objets*) bringing *or* placing together; *Fig* (*de deux personnes*) reconciliation, bringing together; *Pol* rapprochement; *Typ* **r. de caractères** kerning; **un r. américano-soviétique** an American-Soviet rapprochement; **le r. qui s'est opéré entre elles** their reconciliation; *Compta* **r. bancaire** bank reconciliation

rapprocher [raprɔʃe] **1** *vt* (a) (*mettre plus près*) (*objet*) to move *or* bring nearer *or* closer; (*deux objets*) to move nearer *or* closer together; *Typ* (*caractères*) to kern; **rapproche ta chaise de la table** move your chair closer to the table; **r. une chaise du feu** to draw a chair up to the fire; **le vent rapproche les nuages de la côte** the wind is blowing the clouds inshore; **et si on rapprochait les deux cousins à table?** how about sitting the two cousins closer to each other at the table?; **r. les lèvres d'une plaie** to draw together *or* join the lips of a wound; **une lunette rapproche les objets** a field glass makes objects look nearer; **il va falloir r. les rendez-vous** we'll have to meet more often; (*en affaires*) we'll have to have more frequent meetings; **chaque jour les rapproche de la fin** each day brings them nearer the end; **je te déposerai sur la place, ça te rapprochera (de chez toi)** I'll drop you off in the square, that'll get you a bit nearer home

(b) (*réconcilier*) (*deux personnes*) to bring together; **un intérêt commun les rapproche** they are united *or* brought together *or* drawn together by a common interest; **cette épreuve nous a rapprochés** the ordeal drew *or* brought us closer together; **elle essaie de r. le père et le fils** she is trying to reconcile father and son

(c) (*lier*) (*des faits, des idées*) to put together *or* side by side, to compare

2 se rapprocher *vpr* **(a) se r. de** (*sa destination, un lieu*) to get closer to, to approach; (*la télévision, la table*) to move closer to; **rapproche-toi de lui, il n'entend pas** move closer (to him), he can't hear; *Fig* **se r. de son idéal** to come close to one's ideal; **son costume se rapprochait d'un uniforme** his clothes looked almost like *or* came near to being a uniform; **se r. de la vérité** to get close to the truth; **ça n'est pas tout à fait ça, mais ça s'en rapproche** that's not quite it but it's close; **à mesure que nous nous rapprochons du premier anniversaire de sa mort ...** as we near *or* approach the first anniversary of his/her death ...; **plus on se rapprochait de la fin du trimestre plus les enfants devenaient espiègles** the closer *or* nearer we got to the end of the term, the more mischievous the children became

(b) *Fig* **se r. de qn** to become closer to sb; (*après une brouille*) to become reconciled with sb, to make it up with sb; **la France et l'Espagne s'étaient rapprochées** a rapprochement had taken place between France and Spain

rapsodie [rapsɔdi] *nf* rhapsody

rapt [rapt] *nm* abduction, kidnapping

râpure [rɑpyr] *nf Tech* raspings, gratings, filings

raquer [rake] *vt Arg* to fork out, to cough up, to stump up

raquette [rakɛt] *nf* **(a)** (*de tennis, badminton, squash*) racket, racquet; (*de ping pong*) bat; *Aut F* **coups de r.** jolts; *Fig* **une des meilleures raquettes du monde** one of the best (tennis/ squash/table tennis/*etc*) players in the world **(b)** (*pour marcher dans la neige*) snowshoe; **ils sont montés en raquettes** they snowshoed up **(c)** *Bot F* prickly pear

rare [rar] *adj* **(a)** (*peu courant*) (*livre, plante, insecte etc*) rare; **lors d'une de ses rares visites** on one of his rare *or* few visits; **elle ne nous fait plus que de rares visites** she rarely *or* seldom visits us now; **je n'ai que de rares visites** I seldom *or* rarely get visitors; **je suis un des rares à aimer la pluie** I'm one of the few people who like rain; **vous devenez r. comme les beaux jours** you're quite a stranger, we seldom see you (these days); **se faire r.** to be becoming rare; **il se faisait r. dans le quartier** he was rarely seen around the area; **la main-d'œuvre/l'argent était r.** there was a shortage of labour/money; **les denrées de base se font rares** basic food items are becoming scarce; **c'est (bien) r. qu'il pleuve ici** it (very) rarely rains here; **cela n'avait rien de r. à cette époque** it was quite common at that time; **il n'est pas r. qu'elle rentre au petit matin** it's not uncommon for her to go home in the small hours; *Litt* **rares sont ceux que la famine épargne** rare are they who are spared by the famine

(b) (*exceptionnel*) (*mérite, beauté, intelligence, talent etc*) rare, uncommon, exceptional

(c) (*clairsemé*) (*végétation etc*) thin, sparse, scanty; (*jour, lumière*) dim, poor; (*oxygène*) rare; **avoir le cheveu r.** to have thinning hair

raréfaction [rarefaksjɔ̃] *nf* **(a)** *Phys* (*de gaz, d'air*) rarefaction **(b)** (*d'un produit, de l'argent*) growing scarcity

raréfier [rarefje] **1** *vt* **(a)** *Phys* to rarefy **(b)** *Rare* (*rendre rare*) to deplete, to make scarce **2 se raréfier** *vpr* **(a)** *Phys* to become rarefied, to rarefy **(b)** (*animal, plante*) to become scarce

rarement [rarmɑ̃] *adv* rarely, seldom

rareté [rarte] *nf* **(a)** *Phys* (*de gaz etc*) rarity **(b)** (*d'objets*) scarceness, scarcity, *Fml* dearth; (*de visites*) infrequency; (*d'un phénomène*) novelty, singularity, unusualness; (*d'un mot, d'une maladie etc*) rare occurrence, rareness **(c)** (*objet rare*) **cabinet plein de raretés** cabinet full of rare objects *or* of rarities *or* curiosities

RAS [ɛraɛs] *nm F* (*abrév* **rien à signaler**) (*à l'écrit*) everything OK; **quoi de neuf? – R.!** what's new? – nothing much!

ras [rɑ] **1** *adj* **(a)** (*cheveux, tête*) close-cropped; (*menton*) close-shaven; (*barbe*) short; (*tapis*) short-pile; **chien à poil r.** short-haired dog; **pull r. du cou** crew-neck (sweater), round-neck sweater

(b) mesure rase full (level) measure; **deux cuillerées rases de sucre** two level spoonfuls of sugar; **verser du vin à qn à r. bord** to fill sb's wineglass to the brim; **à** *ou* **au r. de** (on a) level *or* flush with; **vaisseau chargé au r. de l'eau** vessel laden to the water line; **voler au r. du sol/de l'eau** to fly close to the ground/water, to skim (along) the ground/water; *F* **voler** *ou* **rester au r. des pâquerettes** (*d'un livre, d'un film, d'une conversation*) to be very lowbrow; **son humour vole** *ou* **reste au r. des pâquerettes** his sense of humour is pretty basic *or* lowbrow; *F* **elle portait une minijupe qui lui arrivait au r. des fesses** she was wearing a mini-skirt which was more like a belt; **en rase campagne** in the open country

2 *adv* **se faire couper les cheveux r.** to have one's hair cropped

rasade [razad] *nf* (*de vin*) glassful

rasage [razaʒ] *nm* shaving; *Tex* shearing; **lotion après-r.** aftershave lotion

rasant [razɑ̃] *adj* **(a) tir r.** grazing fire; **trajectoire rasante** flat trajectory; **vol r.** flight that skims the ground; **lumière rasante** oblique *or* (almost) horizontal light **(b)** *F* (*personne, discours, film etc*) boring

rascasse [raskas] *nf* scorpion fish

rasé [raze] *adj* shaven; **r. de près** close-shaven; **(entièrement) r.** (*visage*) (clean-)shaven; (*tête*) shaven; **des enfants rasés** children with shaven heads

rase-mottes [razmɔt] *nm inv Av F* **faire du** *ou* **voler en r.** to hedgehop, to skim the ground; **le vol en r.** hedgehopping

raser [raze] **1** *vt* **(a)** (*tête*) to shave; (*moustache, barbe, cheveux*) to shave off; **r. un homme** to shave a man, to give a man a shave; **r. une femme/un enfant/un prisonnier** to shave a woman's/a child's/a prisoner's head; **se faire r.** to be given a shave

(b) (*bâtiment, ville*) to raze to the ground

(c) (*frôler*) (*surface de qch*) to graze, to brush; (*sol, eau*) to skim (over); *Fig F* **r. les murs** to hug the walls

(d) *F* (*ennuyer*) to bore

2 se raser *vpr* **(a)** to shave, to have a shave; **je dois me r.** I need a shave; **se r. les jambes/les aisselles** to shave one's legs/armpits

(b) *F* (*s'ennuyer*) to be bored; **qu'est-ce qu'on se rase chez eux!** they're really boring

raseur, -euse [razœr, -øz] *n F* bore

rasibus [razibys] *adv F* **couper les cheveux** *ou* **tondre le crâne r. à qn, tondre qn r.** to scalp sb; **la balle est passée r.** the bullet whizzed past very close; **le couteau lui est passé à côté du doigt r.** the knife only just missed his finger; **il est passé en terminale mais r.** he made it into the sixth form but only by the skin of his teeth

ras-le-bol [ralbɔl] *F* **1** *nm inv* **(a) j'en ai r.** I'm fed up (with it); **j'en ai** *ou* **il y en a r. (de tes histoires)** I'm fed up *or* I've had it up to here (with your nonsense), I'm sick to the back teeth (of your nonsense); **j'en ai r. de ne pas pouvoir lui parler directement** I'm fed up with not being able to talk to him directly

(b) (*sentiment*) discontent, dissatisfaction; **le r. généralisé qui s'empare des professeurs** the widespread feeling among teachers that they've had as much as they can take *or F* that they've had a bellyful; **le r. des jeunes** *ou* **de la jeunesse** the feeling among young people that they've had it up to here

2 *int* enough!; **tu ne vas pas recommencer, r.!** don't start again, enough's enough!; **ah non, r., on l'a assez vu!** not him again!; **r. de tous ces gens qui ne font rien!** I'm sick and tired of all these layabouts!

rasoir [razwar] **1** *nm* **(a)** razor; **r. de sûreté** safety razor; **r. électrique** electric razor *or* shaver; **pierre à r.** hone; **cuir à r.** strop; **couper comme un r.** to be as sharp as a razor; **le feu du r.** razor burn **(b)** *F* (*personne*) bore **2** *adj inv* boring

rassasié [rasazje] *adj* (*repu*) satisfied; *Fig F* full, sated **(de** with); **ah non, plus de films d'horreur, je suis r.!** no more horror films, I've had enough *or* my fill; **les Français sont rassasiés de discours électoraux** the French have had their fill of political speeches

rassasiement [rasazimɑ̃] *nm Rare* (*de la faim*) satisfaction; *Fig* satiety, surfeit

rassasier [rasazje] **1** *vt* (*faim, Fig curiosité, soif d'apprendre, passion pour qch*) to satisfy; **r. qn** to satisfy sb's hunger; *Fig* **r. son regard à contempler qch** to feast one's eyes on sth; **les fruits ne rassasient pas** fruit isn't very filling *or* doesn't satisfy your hunger; *F* **je suis rassasiée de toutes vos histoires** I've had more than enough *or* than my fill of your stories **2 se rassasier** *vpr* to eat one's fill; **se r. d'un mets** to eat one's fill of *or Péj* gorge oneself on a dish; *Fig* **se r. de plaisirs** to take one's fill of pleasure; **je ne me rassasie pas de cette vue/sa présence** I never tire of this view/his presence

rassemblement [rasɑ̃bləmɑ̃] *nm* **(a)** (*de documents, de troupes, d'outils*) assembling, collecting, gathering; *Mil* fall in, parade; *Mil* **sonner le r.** to sound the assembly; *Mil* **r.!** fall in!, form up!; *Pol* **œuvrer au r. de la gauche** to work towards the union of the left **(b)** (*foule*) crowd, gathering; **provoquer un r.** to draw *or* attract a crowd; **disperser les rassemblements** to disperse the crowd

rassembler [rasɑ̃ble] **1** *vt* (*personnes, choses, documents etc*) to collect, to gather together, to get together, to assemble; (*troupes*) to assemble, to muster; **r. ses affaires** to collect one's things, to get one's things together; **r. les gens qui partagent la même opinion** to bring together the people who share the same viewpoint; **ce qui nous rassemble ici ce soir, c'est la passion du théâtre** it is a passion for the theatre which has brought us here this evening; **nous sommes rassemblés ici pour fêter ...** we are gathered here this evening to celebrate ...; **c'est pourquoi nous avons voulu vous r. aujourd'hui** that's why we wanted to gather you all together here today; **c'est le besoin qui les rassemble** they are brought together by need; **r. toutes les pièces d'un procès** to bring together all the documents in a case; **r. ses idées** to collect *or* gather together one's thoughts; **r. ses esprits** to collect oneself, to regain one's composure; *Fig* **r. son courage/toutes ses forces** to muster *or* summon up one's courage/all one's strength; *Équitation* **r. un cheval** to gather a horse

2 se rassembler *vpr* (*s'assembler*) to assemble, to get together, to gather; (*d'une foule*) to collect, to gather; *Mil* to fall in, to muster; **les ouvriers se rassemblent sous l'égide du syndicat** the workers are gathering *or* banding together under the aegis of the union; **nous nous rassemblons tous les jeudis dans ce bar** we meet *or* get together in this bar every Thursday

rasseoir [raswar] (*conj like* **asseoir**) **1** *vt* **r. qn** (*qui était debout*) to sit sb down again; (*qui était couché*) to sit sb up again; **faire r. qn** to make sb sit down again; **r. une statue sur sa base** to replace a statue on its base; *Fig* **r. l'école dans la démocratie** to re-establish the educational system as one of the fundamental institutions of democracy; **il faut r. la psychanalyse dans la pratique hospitalière** psychoanalysis must be restored to its former prominence in hospital medicine

2 se rasseoir *vpr* **(a)** (*de personne*) to sit down again, to sit back down

(b) (*de liquide*) to settle; **laisser r. le vin** to let the wine settle

rasséréner [raserene] **(je rassérène, n. rassérénons; je rassérénerai) 1** *vt* **r. qn** to put sb's mind at rest; **je suis rasséréné** my mind's at rest **2 se rasséréner** *vpr* **(a)** (*du ciel*) to clear (up) **(b)** (*d'une personne*) to calm down

rassir [rasir] **1** *vi* to go *or* get stale; **j'ai laissé r. mon pain** I've let my bread go stale **2 se rassir** *vpr* to go *or* get stale

rassis [rasi] *adj* **(a) pain r.** stale bread **(b)** *Fig* (*personne, caractère, disposition*) calm, sedate

rassortir [rasɔrtir] *vt* = **réassortir**

rassurant [rasyrɑ̃] *adj* (*personne*) reassuring; (*nouvelle, paroles*) reassuring, heartening; **peu r.** disquieting; **c'est une nouvelle peu rassurante** that's not very reassuring news

rassurer [rasyre] **1** *vt* (*d'une personne*) to reassure; (*d'une nouvelle, paroles*) to reassure, to cheer, to hearten; **je ne suis pas trop rassuré de la savoir seule** I have my worries about her being alone; **il n'a pas l'air très rassuré** he's not looking too cheery; **cela me rassure (de savoir que ...)** it reassures me (to know that ...); **ce n'est pas ça qui va me r.** that's not enough to reassure me, that doesn't do anything to calm my misgivings; **je te rassure tout de suite que je n'irai pas poser la question!** I can assure you, I won't be the one who asks the question!; **eh bien, me voilà rassuré!** that's a relief!; **ah, tu me rassures!** well, that's a relief!, you've taken a weight off my mind!

2 se rassurer *vpr* to feel reassured; **rassurez-vous là-dessus** set your mind at rest on that point; **rassurez-vous** rest assured; **vous pouvez vous r., ça ne fait pas mal du tout** you can relax, it doesn't hurt at all

rasta [rasta] *adj, n* Rasta(farian)

rastaquouère [rastakwɛr] *nm F* **un drôle de r.** a queer bird

rat [ra] **1** *nm* **(a)** (*animal*) rat; *Fig* **c'est un r. d'église** he's never out of church; *Fig* **les rats quittent le navire** the rats are leaving the sinking ship; *F* **être fait comme un r.** to be caught like a rat in a trap; *F* **s'ennuyer comme un r. mort** to be bored out of one's mind *or* skull, to be bored to death; **petit r. (de l'Opéra)** ballet pupil; *F* **mon petit r.** darling; *F* **ah le r., il ne m'a pas téléphoné!** the rat didn't call me; *F* **face de r.!** ratface!

(b) (*avare*) miser, skinflint, *Am* tightwad; *F* **c'est un r.** he's stingy *or* a miser

(c) *Can* (*sournois*) tricky customer

2 *adj inv F* **(a)** (*avare*) stingy, tight; **ce qu'il est r.!** what a skinflint *or Am* tightwad!

(b) *Can* (*sournois*) wily, sly

▶ **rat**: **r. d'Amérique** coypu; *Fig* **r. de bibliothèque** bookworm; **r. des champs** field mouse; **r. d'eau** water vole; **r. d'Égypte** mongoose; **r. géant (des Indes)** bandicoot; *Fig* **r. d'hôtel** hotel thief; **r. musqué** muskrat, musquash; **r. noir** black rat; **r. de Pharaon** mongoose; **r. surmulot** brown *or* Norway rat

rata [rata] *nm Mil Arg Vieilli* grub, *Péj* pigswill

ratafia [ratafja] *nm* (*boisson*) ratafia

ratage [rataʒ] *nm F* botching, bungling, messing up

rataplan [rataplɑ̃] *nm* (*d'un tambour*) rat-a-tat

ratatiné [ratatine] *adj* **(a)** (*à cause de l'âge, du dessèchement, du feu*) shrivelled; **petite vieille ratatinée** little old wizened *or* shrunken woman **(b)** *F* (*accidenté*) smashed-up

ratatiner [ratatine] **1** *vt* **(a)** (*pomme, visage etc*) to shrivel (up) **(b)** *F* (*écraser*) to scrunch up **(c)** *très F* **r. qn** (*tuer*) to bump sb off; (*battre*) to beat sb up; **se faire r. par l'équipe adverse** to get thrashed *or* hammered by the other side **2 se ratatiner** *vpr* (*de cuir, d'une plante, d'un parchemin*) to shrivel up; **une vieille dame qui se ratatine** a shrunken little old lady; **je commence à me r.** I'm beginning to shrink; *F* **tu vas te faire r.** (*dans un concours, match*) you're going to get slaughtered; (*à un examen*) you're going to fail abysmally

ratatouille [ratatuj] *nf Culin* ratatouille

rate¹ [rat] *nf Anat* spleen; *F* **se dilater la r.** to laugh one's head off, to split one's sides laughing; *F* **ne pas se fouler la r.** not to strain oneself

rate² *nf* (*animal*) female rat

raté, -ée [rate] **1** *n* (*personne*) failure, loser; **comme écrivain, je suis un r.** I'm a failure *or* a washout as a writer **2** *nm* (*d'un fusil, d'un moteur*) misfire; *Fig* hitch, minor problem; *TV, Rad etc* fluff; **le moteur avait des ratés** the engine was misfiring; **avoir un r. (d'allumage)** to backfire, to misfire

râteau, -eaux [rɑto] *nm* **(a)** (*de jardin*) rake; **r. mécanique** raker; **r. faneur** tedder; **donner un coup de r. à l'allée** to give the path a rake; **ramasser les feuilles mortes avec un r.** to rake up the dead leaves **(b)** *Naut* **r. de pont** squeegee **(c)** (*de croupier*) rake **(d)** (*de métier à tisser*) comb

râteler [rɑtle] *vt* **(je râtelle, n. râtelons; je râtellerai)** (*foin etc*) to rake up

râtelier [rɑtəlje] *nm* **(a)** (*dans une étable*) rack; *Fig* **manger au r. de qn** to live off sb; **il mange à tous les râteliers** he serves more than one master, he has his foot in more than one camp; *Fig F* **quand il n'y a plus de foin dans le r.** when I'm/we're/*etc* broke, when there's nothing left in the kitty **(b)** (*support*) **r. d'armes/à outils/à pipes** weapon/tool/pipe rack **(c)** *F* (*dents*) (set of) choppers

rater [rate] **1** *vi* (*d'un fusil*) to misfire, to fail to go off; (*d'un moteur*) to misfire; *Fig* (*d'une entreprise, d'une expérience*) to fail; **c'est raté, la plaie s'infecte** it hasn't worked, the wound is becoming infected; **si tu voulais lui parler, c'est raté, il vient de partir** if you wanted to talk to him, you're too late, he's just gone; *F* **j'étais sûr qu'elle allait être en retard et ça n'a pas raté** I was convinced she was going to be late and sure enough *or* right enough she was; *F* **tu as tout fait r.!** you've ruined everything!

2 *vt* **(a)** (*échouer à*) (*examen, bac, permis de conduire*) to fail; **le dîner était super mais j'ai raté mon gâteau** the dinner was great but I made a mess of the cake *or* my cake was a flop; **r. sa vie** to make a mess of one's life; **r. son coup** (*aux fléchettes etc*) to miss (one's shot *or* the target); *Golf* to foozle one's shot; *Fig F* to make a mess of it; **j'ai raté mon coup, maintenant elle ne viendra pas** I blew it, she won't be coming now; **elle n'a pas raté son coup, tout le monde l'a entendue** she got what she wanted, everybody heard her; *Av* **atterrissage raté** bad landing

(b) (*manquer*) (*train, avion, personne*) to miss; **j'ai raté l'occasion** *ou* **ma chance** I missed my opportunity *or* chance; **tu n'as pas raté grand-chose** you didn't miss much; **tu as raté un film extraordinaire** you missed *or* missed out on a great film; *F* **je ne vais pas le r.** I'm really going to let him have it; *F* **le coiffeur ne t'a pas raté, dis donc!** the hairdresser really did a job on you!; *F* **elle n'en rate pas une!** she's always putting her foot in it!

3 se rater *vpr* (*manquer son suicide*) to make a failed suicide attempt; *F* **on avait rendez-vous à l'Arc de triomphe mais on s'est ratés** we were supposed to meet at the Arc de Triomphe but we missed each other

ratiboiser [ratibwaze] *vt très F* **(a) r. qn** (*au jeu, en bourse, dans une entreprise*) to clean sb out; **je suis complètement ratiboisé** I'm flat broke *or Br* stony broke *or* skint; **j'ai été complètement ratiboisé dans cette affaire** that business cleaned me out totally; **se faire r. la colline** to get scalped **(b)** *Vieilli* **r. qch à qn** to do *or* swindle sb out of sth

raticide [ratisid] *nm* rat poison

ratier [ratje] *adj, nm* **(chien) r.** ratter

ratière [ratjɛr] *nf* rat trap

ratification [ratifikasjɔ̃] *nf* ratification; **accord sous réserve de r.** agreement subject to ratification *or* confirmation

ratifier [ratifje] *vt* (*traité, acte*) to ratify; (*décision*) to confirm

ratio [rasjo] *nm* ratio; **r. de capitalisation** p/e ratio, price/earnings ratio; *Compta* **r. d'exploitation** performance ratio, operating ratio; **r. de gestion** financial ratio, financial management ratio; **r. de liquidités** quick ratio, acid test ratio; **r. de situation** financial ratio; **r. de trésorerie** cash ratio

ratiocination [rasjɔsinasjɔ̃] *nf Litt* mulling *or* brooding over

ratiociner [rasjɔsine] *vi Litt* to brood; **r. sur qch** to mull *or* brood over sth

ration [rasjɔ̃] *nf* (*d'eau, de sucre etc*) ration; (*pour bête*) feed; *Fig* (*de critiques, de difficultés, de malheurs*) share; **r. alimentaire** food ration, ration of food; **r. calorique** calorie intake; **r. de combat** iron rations; **rations de survie** survival rations; **rations imposées en temps de guerre** wartime rations

rationalisation [rasjɔnalizasjɔ̃] *nf* rationalization, rationalizing, streamlining

rationaliser [rasjɔnalize] *vt* to rationalize, to streamline

rationalisme [rasjɔnalism] *nm* rationalism

rationaliste [rasjɔnalist] *adj, n* rationalist

rationalité [rasjɔnalite] *nf* rationality

rationnel, -elle [rasjɔnɛl] *adj* rational

rationnellement [rasjɔnɛlmɑ̃] *adv* rationally

rationnement [rasjɔnmɑ̃] *nm* rationing

rationner [rasjɔne] **1** *vt* (*population, malade, approvisionnement*) to ration **2 se rationner** *vpr* to ration oneself

ratissage [ratisaʒ] *nm* **(a)** (*du jardin*) raking **(b)** *F* (*au casino*) (*des mises*) raking in **(c)** *F* (*d'un quartier, par la police etc*) combing, thorough search

ratisser [ratise] **1** *vt* **(a)** (*allée, sol*) to rake (over); (*feuilles*) to rake (up) **(b)** *F* **r. les mises** (*au casino*) to rake in the stakes **(c)** *F* (*quartier*) to comb, to search, to make a thorough search of **(d)** *F* (*voler*) (*personne*) to clean out; **se faire r.** (*au jeu*) to be cleaned out **2** *vi* **r. large** to cast one's net wide

raton [ratɔ̃] *nm* **(a)** (*animal*) young rat; **r. laveur** raccoon **(b)** *F* (*terme injurieux*) = racist insult directed at Arabs from North Africa, wog

ratonnade [ratɔnad] *nf* (*contre des Maghrébins*) attack on North African Arabs, *Br* ≈ Paki-bashing

ratoureux, -euse [raturø, -øz] *Can* **1** *adj* wily, devious; **parfois le bonheur est un peu r.** sometimes happiness is not all it seems **2** *n* shady customer

RATP [ɛratepe] *nf* (*abrév* **Régie autonome des transports parisiens**) = Parisian municipal transport system

rattachement [rataʃmɑ̃] *nm* (*d'un objet à un autre*) re-attachment; **le r. de l'Alsace à la France** the return of Alsace to France; **la société a décidé votre r. au bureau de Londres** the company has decided that you should report to the London office

rattacher [rataʃe] **1** *vt* (*attacher de nouveau*) (*lacets*) to do up *or* fasten *or* tie (up) again; (*cheveux*) to put up again; (*chien, objet*) to tie up again (**à** to); **r. un sac sur un vélo** to tie *or* fasten a bag onto a bike again; **r. l'Alsace à la France** to (re)unite Alsace with France; **nous sommes rattachés à l'Hôpital Broussais** we're attached to the Broussais Hospital; **il est rattaché au service de M. Benoît** he reports to Monsieur Benoît's department; *Fig* **les liens qui vous rattachent à la famille** the ties that bind you to your family; *Fig* **c'était la seule chose qui nous rattachait l'un à l'autre** it was the only thing that bound us together; **c'est tout ce qui le rattache à la vie** it's the only thing keeping him alive; **r. une idée à une autre** to link (up) *or* connect one idea with another; **r. un mot à un autre par son étymologie** to establish the origin of a word through its etymology; *Mil* **unité rattachée** attached unit

2 se rattacher *vpr* **se r. à qch** to be connected with sth; **voici le rapport et toutes les pièces qui s'y rattachent** here is the report and its related documents

rattrapage [ratrapaʒ] *nm Scol* **cours de r.** remedial course; **être admis au r., être admis à passer les épreuves de r.** = to be allowed to sit further oral examinations to gain a pass mark in the baccalauréat; **l'oral de r.** = further oral examination to gain a pass mark in the baccalauréat; **j'ai eu mon bac au r.** I passed my bac at the oral; **r. des salaires/des prix** the catching up of wages/prices

rattraper [ratrape] **1** *vt* **(a)** (*reprendre*) (*prisonnier, chien*) to recapture, to catch; *Tricot* **r. une maille qui file** to pick up a dropped stitch; **se faire r. par la police** to get caught by the police

(b) (*attraper*) (*objet ou personne qui tombe*) to catch

(c) (*rejoindre*) (*personne, voiture*) to catch up (with); **je vous rattraperai à l'angle de la rue** I'll catch you up *or* catch up with you at the corner

(d) (*regagner*) (*argent*) to recover, to get back; **r. le temps perdu** to make up for lost time; **nous avons rattrapé notre retard** we made up the time; **j'ai du sommeil à r.** I have to catch up on some sleep; **ce que tu perds d'un côté, tu le rattrapes de l'autre** what you lose on the swings, you gain on the roundabouts

(e) (*rétablir*) (*faute d'orthographe, de calcul etc*) to correct; (*situation, Culin mayonnaise*) to salvage; **j'aurais voulu r. l'énorme gaffe que je venais de faire** if only I could have taken back the huge gaffe I'd just made; **ça, tu ne pourras pas le r.** you'll never be able to make up for it; **dis-moi comment r. le mal que je t'ai fait** tell me how I can make up for the hurt I've caused you

(f) *Scol* **r. un élève** = to award a borderline candidate a pass in the baccalauréat

2 se rattraper *vpr* **se r. à qch** to catch hold of sth; *Fig F* **se r. aux branches** to clutch at straws; **se r. de justesse** to just stop oneself falling; **se r.** (**avant de faire une erreur**) to stop oneself (before making a mistake); **... mais je me suis rattrapé de justesse** ... but I caught *or* stopped myself just in time; **je me suis rattrapé en l'invitant** I made up for it *or* I made amends by inviting him; **pas de soleil depuis 3 mois, je vais me r.!** no sun for three months, I'm going to make up for it now *or* I'm going to make up for lost time; **elle s'est bien rattrapée depuis** she's really made up for it since; **elle ne peut pas parler pendant le travail, mais le soir, elle se rattrape avec son mari** she can't talk at work but she makes up for it in the evening with her husband; **se r. de ses pertes** to make good *or* recoup one's losses

3 *vi F* to catch up

rature [ratyr] *nf* crossing-out, deletion; **faire une r.** to cross out *or* delete a word; **sans ratures ni surcharges** without deletions or additions

raturer [ratyre] *vt* (*mot, phrase etc*) to cross *or* score out, to delete; **les devoirs raturés ne seront pas corrigés** homework with too many crossings-out in it will not be marked

raucité [rosite] *nf Litt* (*enrouement*) hoarseness; (*caractère voilé*) huskiness; (*de rire*) raucousness

raugmenter [rɔgmɑ̃te] *vi F* (*d'un prix*) to go up again

rauque [rok] *adj* (*voix*) (*enroué*) hoarse; (*voilé*) husky; (*rire, cri*) raucous

ravage [ravaʒ] *nm* (*often pl*) **ravages** havoc, devastation; (*d'une guerre, d'une maladie*) ravages; **les ravages du feu/de la tempête** the devastation *or* destruction caused by the fire/the storm; **faire des ravages** to wreak *or* cause havoc; *Fig* **cette mode fait des ravages parmi les jeunes** this fashion is all the rage among the young; *F* **elle va faire des ravages avec son bronzage parfait** with that perfect suntan of hers, she'll have them queuing up at her door

ravagé [ravaʒe] *adj* **(a)** (*pays*) ravaged, devastated; (*visage*) ravaged, haggard; **visage r. par la petite vérole** face pitted with *or* ravaged by smallpox; **un visage r. par la colère** a face disfigured *or* contorted by anger **(b)** *F* (*fou*) bonkers, crazy; **il n'est pas un peu r., ton copain?** your mate's got a screw *or* slate loose; **c'est un r. du cerveau** he's off his rocker *or* trolley

ravager [ravaʒe] *vt* (**je ravageai(s)**; **n. ravageons**) (*ville, région etc*) to ravage, to devastate, to lay waste; (*récoltes*) to ravage, to devastate, to play havoc with; (*visage*) to ravage

ravageur, -euse [ravaʒœr, -øz] **1** *adj* ravaging; (*orage*) devastating; (*oiseaux*) destructive **2** *n* ravager, destroyer

ravalement [ravalmɑ̃] *nm* **(a)** *Constr* (*de la maçonnerie*) repointing; (*en recrépissant*) roughcasting; (*enduit*) (coat of) roughcast **(b)** (*d'un arbre*) pruning, cutting back **(c)** *Vieilli* (*d'une personne*) disparagement **(d)** *Fig F* **r. de façade** facelift

ravaler [ravale] **1** *vt* **(a)** (*avaler de nouveau*) (*salive*) to swallow; *Fig* (*sanglot, larmes*) to swallow, to choke (back); (*colère, indignation, rancunes*) to swallow, to suppress, to stifle; (*réplique*) to bite back; **je lui ferai r. ses paroles** I'll make him eat his words

(b) (*abaisser*) (*personne*) to degrade, to lower; (*dévaluer*) (*personne, talents, qualités etc*) to run down, to disparage; **l'assistante du directeur s'est sentie ravalée au rang de secrétaire** the manager's assistant felt she was being effectively demoted to secretary

(c) (*arbre*) to prune, to cut back

(d) *Constr* (*maçonnerie*) to repoint; (*mur*) to roughcast; *Fig F* **se faire r. la façade** to have a facelift

2 se ravaler *vpr* **(a)** to degrade *or* lower *or* debase oneself; **vous ne vous ravaleriez pas jusque-là** you wouldn't stoop to that, you wouldn't lower yourself to that extent; **ce ne serait pas se r. que d'accepter** you wouldn't be demeaning yourself if you agreed

(b) *F* **se r. la façade** to touch up one's warpaint

ravaleur [ravalœr] *nm* roughcaster, plasterer

ravaudage [ravodaʒ] *nm* **(a)** (*action*) (*de vêtements*) mending, repairing; (*de chaussettes*) darning, mending; *Fig* **ce n'est que du r. mais ça fait de l'effet** it's just a quick repair job but it looks good **(b)** (*résultat*) (*d'un vêtement*) mend, repair; (*de chaussettes*) darn, mend; **mon r. ne dura pas longtemps** my makeshift repair *or* my bit of make-do and mend didn't last long

ravauder [ravode] *vt* (*vêtements*) to mend, to repair; (*chaussettes*) to darn, to mend

ravaudeur, -euse [ravodœr, -øz] *n* (*de vêtements*) mender; (*de chaussettes*) darner

rave[1] [rav] *nf* (*colza*) rape; (*radis*) radish; (*navet*) turnip; **céleri r.** celeriac

rave[2] [rɛv] *nf F* rave

ravi [ravi] *adj* delighted (**de** with); **je suis r. de vous voir** I'm delighted to see you; **r. de vous rencontrer** pleased to meet you; **d'un air r.** delightedly; **eh bien, tu m'en vois r.!** I'm positively delighted!; *Iron* oh great!, terrific!; *Iron* **r. de le savoir** *ou* **de l'apprendre** thanks for telling me

ravier [ravje] *nm* hors-d'œuvres dish

ravigotant [ravigɔtɑ̃] *adj F* invigorating; **un verre de calva, c'est r.** a glass of calvados will put new life into you/him/*etc* *or* blow your/his/*etc* cobwebs away

ravigote [ravigɔt] *nf Culin* = hard-boiled eggs served with ravigote sauce and herbs; **sauce r.** ravigote sauce (*highly seasoned oil and vinegar dressing*)

ravigoter [ravigɔte] *vt F* **r. qn** to put new life into sb; **se sentir tout ravigoté** to feel rejuvenated; **après ce bon chocolat chaud, je me sens tout ravigoté!** that nice hot chocolate has really perked me up!

ravin [ravɛ̃] *nm* ravine

ravine [ravin] *nf* **(a)** (*petit ravin*) gully **(b)** (*rivière*) (mountain) torrent

ravinement [ravinmɑ̃] *nm* gullying, channelling (*by running water*)

raviner [ravine] *vt* (*d'orage, de torrent*) (*sol*) to gully, to channel; (*route*) to furrow, to cut up; *Fig* (*visage*) to crease

ravioli [ravjɔli] *nm, pl* **raviolis** *ou inv* [①A13,7] *Culin* ravioli

ravir [ravir] *vt* **(a)** (*plaire*) to delight; **sa gentillesse me ravit** I am delighted by his kindness; **ce film m'a ravi** I thought the film was delightful; **à r.** (*jouer, chanter*) delightfully, charmingly, beautifully; **belle à r.** ravishing, ravishingly beautiful; **elle est douce à r.** she is extremely gentle; **cela te va à r.** it suits you beautifully, you look delightful in it

(b) *Litt* (*femme*) to carry off, *Arch* to ravish; (*enfant*) to abduct; **r. qch à qn** to rob sb of sth, to steal sth from sb; **la mort nous l'a ravi bien trop tôt** death took him from us *or* snatched him away from us far too soon; **ceux que la mort a ravis** those whom death has taken from our midst

raviser (se) [səravize] *vpr* to change one's mind

ravissant [ravisɑ̃] *adj* delightful, entrancing, ravishing

ravissement [ravismɑ̃] *nm* **(a)** (*extase*) rapture, ecstasy, delight; **être dans le r. le plus total** to be in raptures *or* in ecstasies; **ce qui la plongeait dans le r. le plus total** which sent her into raptures; **avec r.** (*écouter, contempler qch*) with delight; **c'est ce que nous avons découvert avec r.** that's what we found out to our delight **(b)** *Litt* (*d'une femme*) carrying off, *Arch* ravishment

ravisseur, -euse [ravisœr, -øz] **1** *adj* predatory **2** *n* abductor, kidnapper, *Arch* ravisher

ravitaillement [ravitajmɑ̃] *nm* **(a)** *Mil etc* (*action*) supplying (**en** with); **r. (en carburant)** refuelling; **r. en munitions** ammunition supply; **convoi de r.** supply column; **r. à la mer** replenishment *or* refuelling at sea; *Av* **r. en vol** in-flight refuelling; **le r. des grandes villes est un des problèmes de la guerre** maintaining supplies in large cities is one of the problems of war; *F* **aller au r.** to go shopping **(b)** (*denrées*) supplies; **distribution du r.** issue of supplies

ravitailler [ravitaje] **1** *vt* (*armée, camp, refuge*) to supply; (*avion, navire*) to refuel; **r. un avion en vol** to refuel an aircraft in flight **2 se ravitailler** *vpr* to take in (fresh) supplies; *F* (*faire des courses*) to stock up, to do a big shop; **se r. (en carburant)** to refuel

ravitailleur [ravitajœr] **1** *nm Mil etc* (*camion*) supply truck; (*bateau*) supply ship; (*avion*) supply aircraft **2** *adj* **navire/avion r.** supply ship/aircraft

ravivage [ravivaʒ] *nm* (*de couleur*) brightening up; (*de surfaces métalliques*) cleaning

raviver [ravive] **1** *vt* (*feu, Fig colère*) to rekindle; (*couleur*) to brighten up; (*douleur*) to revive; (*surfaces à souder*) to clean; *Fig* (*souvenir, querelle*) to rekindle, to revive; *Fig* **r. une plaie** to reopen an old wound **2 se raviver** *vpr* (*d'une conversation*) to revive, to pick up; (*de la colère, de l'inquiétude*) to flare up again

ravoir [ravwar] *vt* (*only in inf*) **(a)** (*récupérer*) **r. qch** to have *or* get sth back again **(b)** *F* (*in neg*) (*nettoyer*) to clean (up); **je n'arrive pas à r. cette casserole** I can't get this pan clean, I can't get the marks off this pan

rayage [rɛjaʒ] *nm* (*d'arme à feu*) rifling

rayé [rɛje] *adj* **(a)** striped, stripy; **tablier r. rouge et bleu** red and blue striped *or* stripy apron; **un animal r. noir et blanc** an animal with black and white stripes **(b)** (*papier*) lined, ruled **(c)** (*fusil*) rifled, grooved **(d)** (*disque, verre, parquet, carrosserie de voiture*) scratched

rayer [rɛje] *vt* (**je raie, je raye, n. rayons; je raierai, je rayerai**) **(a)** (*verre, parquet, carrosserie de voiture, disque etc*) to scratch; (*surface*) to score

(b) (*papier*) to rule, to line

(c) (*tissu*) to stripe

(d) (*fusil*) to rifle; (*cylindre*) to groove

(e) (*mot etc*) to strike out, to cross out, to delete; **on vous a rayé** *ou* **on a rayé votre nom de la liste** you have *or* your name has been struck off *or* crossed off *or* deleted from the list; **rayez les mentions inutiles** delete as appropriate; **on peut r. les articles que l'on a déjà achetés** we can cross off the things we've already bought; *Fig* **tu ne peux pas r. cet événement de ta vie** you can't banish *or* blot out the event from your life; *Fig* **il voudrait me r. de sa vie** he'd like to forget he ever knew me; *Fig* **une ville qui fut rayée de la carte** a town that was wiped off the map; *Mil* **r. qn des contrôles** to strike sb off the strength

rayon[1] [rɛjɔ̃] *nm* **(a)** (*faisceau*) (*de lumière*) ray, beam, shaft; *Fig* (*d'espoir*) ray; **un faible r. de lumière** a faint gleam of light; **r. de soleil** sunbeam; *Fig* **c'est un peu mon r. de soleil** he/she has brought a ray of sunshine into my life; *Opt* **r. visuel** line of sight; **rayons X** X-rays; **passer qn/qch aux rayons X** to X-ray sb/sth; *Méd* **mal des rayons** radiation sickness; **r. électronique** *ou* **cathodique** electron beam; **r. laser** laser beam

(b) (*périmètre*) range; (*d'un cercle*) radius; *Aut* **r. de braquage** turning circle; **dans un r. de deux kilomètres** within a radius of two kilometres (**autour de** of); **r. d'action** (*d'un avion*) range (of action *or* operation); **avion à grand r. d'action** long-range aircraft; *Fig* **r. d'action d'une campagne publicitaire** scope *or* coverage *or* range of an advertising campaign; **cette société a étendu son r. d'action** the firm has extended the scope of its operations

(c) (*de roue*) spoke

rayon[2] *nm* **(a)** (*dans un magasin*) department; **r. hommes/femmes** menswear/ladies' wear (department); **r. jardinage** gardening department; **chef de r.** head of department, department manager; **magasin à rayons multiples** department store; *Fig F* **ce n'est pas mon r.** (*ça ne me concerne pas*) that's nothing to do with me, that's none of my business; (*ça n'est pas dans mes compétences*) that's not my department; *Fig F* **elle en connaît un r. (sur la question)** she's well clued up (on the subject), she knows all there is to know (about the subject)

(b) (*de placard etc*) shelf; **rayons** shelves, shelving

(c) r. de miel honeycomb

rayon[3] *nm Agr* drill; **r. d'oignons** row of onions

rayonnage [rɛjɔnaʒ] *nm* shelving, shelves

rayonnant [rɛjɔnɑ̃] *adj* (*chaleur, soleil, lumière*) radiant; *Fig* (*visage*) radiant, beaming; **r. de joie** radiant (with joy); **r. de santé/bonheur** glowing with health/radiant with happiness

rayonne [rɛjɔn] *nf Tex* rayon

rayonnement [rɛjɔnmɑ̃] *nm* **(a)** *Phys* radiation **(b)** (*du soleil etc*) radiance; *Fig* influence; **un r. émanait de toute sa personne** his entire being was radiant with joy

rayonner[1] [rɛjɔne] *vi* **(a)** *Phys* to radiate **(b)** (*du soleil, Fig du visage*) to beam, to shine; **il rayonnait (de joie)** he was radiant *or* beaming (with joy); **r. de bonheur** to radiate happiness; **son visage rayonnait de plaisir** his face *or* he was glowing *or* aglow with pleasure **(c)** (*à partir d'un centre*) to radiate; *Fig* **r. dans le monde** (*d'une culture, d'une école de pensée, d'art etc*) to have worldwide influence; **une douleur qui rayonne** a spreading pain; **r. autour d'Avignon** to make Avignon the centre (*for excursions*)

rayonner[2] *vt* (*pièce etc*) to fit with shelves, to put shelves up in

rayure [rɛjyr] *nf* **(a)** (*bande*) stripe; **tissu à rayures** striped *or* stripy material; **à rayures rouges et jaunes** with red and yellow stripes; **les rayures noires et blanches du zèbre** the black and white stripes *or* markings of the zebra **(b)** (*éraflure*) scratch; *TV, Cin* (*sur l'écran*) line **(c)** (*d'un fusil*) groove

raz [ra] *nm* **r. (de courant)** strong current, *Spéc* race (*in estuary*); **r. de marée** tidal wave; *Fig* **cette nouvelle a eu l'effet d'un r. de marée** the news caused great upheaval; *Pol Fig* **ce fut un r. de marée (électoral) pour les** *ou* **en faveur des socialistes** it was a landslide (victory) for the Socialists, it was a Socialist landslide

razzia [razja] *nf* (*attaque*) incursion, raid; *Hist* razzia; *F* **faire une r. sur les articles en solde** to make a clean sweep of *or* to snap up the bargains; **faire une r. dans le frigo** to raid the fridge

RD [ɛrde] *nf abrév* **route départementale**

RDA [ɛrdeɑ] *nf Hist* (*abrév* **République démocratique allemande**) GDR
rdc *abrév* **rez-de-chaussée**
ré [re] *nm inv Mus* **(a)** (*note*) D **(b)** (*en solfège*) re
réa [rea] *abrév F* **réanimation**
réabonnement [reabɔnmɑ̃] *nm* subscription renewal
réabonner [reabɔne] **1** *vt* **r. qn** to renew sb's subscription (**à** to) **2 se réabonner** *vpr* to renew one's subscription (**à** to)
réabsorber [reapsɔrbe] *vt* to reabsorb
réabsorption [reapsɔrpsjɔ̃] *nf* reabsorption
réac [reak] *adj, n Pol F Péj* reactionary
réaccoutumer [reakutyme] **1** *vt* to reaccustom (**à** to) **2 se réaccoutumer** *vpr* **se r. à qch** to get used to sth again, to become reaccustomed to sth; **j'aurais du mal à me r.** I would find it hard to get used to things again
réachat [reaʃa] *nm* repurchase
réacheminement [reaʃ(ə)minmɑ̃] *nm* (*de marchandises*) rerouting; *Ordinat* (*de message*) redirecting
réacheminer [reaʃ(ə)mine] *vt* (*marchandises*) to reroute; *Ordinat* (*message etc*) to redirect
réacheter [reaʃte] *vt* to repurchase
réactance [reaktɑ̃s] *nf Él* reactance
réacteur [reaktœr] *nm* **(a)** (*moteur*) jet engine **(b)** *Nucl* reactor, pile; **r. propulseur de navire** ship-propulsion reactor; **r. nucléaire** nuclear reactor; *Tech* **r. thermique** thermal reactor
réactif, -ive [reaktif, -iv] **1** *adj* reactive; **non r.** non-reactive; *Ch* **papier r.** reagent paper, test paper; *Él* **courant r.** reactive current **2** *nm Ch* reagent; **r. à base de mercure** mercury reagent
réaction [reaksjɔ̃] *nf* **(a)** *Ch, Phys* reaction; **r. en chaîne** chain reaction; **r. nucléaire** nuclear reaction

(b) *Él* reaction, feedback

(c) (*de machines etc*) reaction; (*de fusil*) kick; **moteur à r.** jet engine; **propulsion par r.** jet propulsion; **avion à r.** jet(-propelled) aircraft, jet plane, jet; *F* **la voiture a de très bonnes réactions (sur la glace)** the car responds well *or* handles well (on ice); **r. du moteur** engine response

(d) *Physiol* (*d'un organe etc*) reaction, response; **r. cutanée** skin reaction, *Spéc* cutaneous reaction; **temps de r.** response time; **il y a toujours un temps de r. avant qu'elle ne réponde** she always takes a while to answer; **avoir des réactions lentes** to be slow to react; *Physiol* **r. auditive** response to auditory stimulus

(e) (*à une remarque, à un incident, au stress etc*) reaction; **elle eut une r. de peur/de colère** her reaction was one of fear/anger; **faire qch par r.** to do sth as; **elle s'y oppose, simplement par r.** she is opposed to it as a matter of principle; **en r. à sa famille** in reaction to his family; **la décision a été prise en r. à ...** the decision was taken in response to ...; **je suis resté sans r.** I didn't react; **qu'a-t-il répondu? – rien, il n'a eu aucune r.** what did he reply? – nothing, he didn't react at all; **provoquer des réactions** to cause a reaction

(f) *Pol* **la r.** reaction, reactionary attitudes; (*personnes*) reactionaries
réactionnaire [reaksjɔnɛr] *adj, n Pol* reactionary
réactiver [reaktive] *vt* (*catalyseur, sérum*) to reactivate; *Fig* (*vieilles colères, anciens sentiments*) to rekindle, to arouse again, to stir up; **r. le feu** to revive *or* poke the fire; **cela a réactivé la douleur** it caused the pain to flare up again
réactivité [reaktivite] *nf* reactivity
réactualiser [reaktɥalise] *vt* to bring up to date, to update
réadaptation [readaptasjɔ̃] *nf* **(a)** (*d'un invalide, d'un prisonnier*) rehabilitation **(b)** (*de projets etc*) readjustment
réadapter [readapte] **1** *vt* **(a)** (*invalide, prisonnier*) to rehabilitate **(b)** (*projets*) to readjust **2 se réadapter** *vpr* to readjust, to become readjusted; **il n'a pas eu de mal à se r.** he didn't have any problem readjusting
réadmettre [readmɛtr] *vt* (*conj like* **mettre**) to readmit
réadmission [readmisjɔ̃] *nf* readmission
réaffectation [reafɛktasjɔ̃] *nf aussi Ordinat* reallocation; *Ordinat* (*d'une touche*) reassignment
réaffecter [reafɛkte] *vt* (*personnel*) to reassign; (*crédits*), *Ordinat* to reallocate; *Ordinat* (*touche*) to reassign; **r. qn à son premier emploi** to reinstate sb in his former job; **r. une subvention à sa destination première** to reallocate funds to their original use
réafficher [reafiʃe] *vt Ordinat* to redisplay
réaffirmer [reafirme] *vt* to reaffirm
réagir [reaʒir] *vi* to react (**sur** on; **contre** against; **à** to); **on verra comment il réagira** we'll see how he reacts; **ça ne l'a pas du tout fait r.** he didn't react at all, it didn't provoke any reaction; **allez, secoue-toi, il faut r.!** come on, wake up, do something!; **elle a très fortement réagi à son vaccin** she had a very strong reaction to the vaccination; **tu réagis trop violemment** you're overreacting; **r. contre qch** to take a stand against sth, to stand up to sth
réajuster [reaʒyste] *vt* = **rajuster**
réal, -aux [real, -o] *nm* (*monnaie*) real
réalésage [realezaʒ] *nm Aut* rebore
réaléser [realeze] *vt Aut* to rebore
réalisable [realizabl] *adj* (*projet, proposition*) feasible, practical, workable; *Fin* (*avoirs*) realizable; *Fig* (*rêve*) attainable
réalisateur, -trice [realizatœr, -tris] *n Cin* (film) director; *Rad, TV* producer (*d'une pièce, d'un feuilleton*) director
réalisation [realizasjɔ̃] *nf* **(a)** (*d'un projet*) implementation, carrying out, realization; (*d'une œuvre d'art, Culin d'une pièce montée*) creation; (*d'un bâtiment*) construction; **la dernière r. de Picasso** Picasso's final *or* last creation; **les autres projets sont en cours de r.** the other projects are still in progress; **la rénovation du quartier est en cours de r.** the renovation of the area is an on-going project

(b) (*d'un rêve*) attainment; **tu verras s'accomplir la r. de ton rêve/ton souhait** you'll see your dream/wish come true

(c) *Rad, TV* production; (*d'un film, d'une pièce télévisée ou radiodiffusée*) direction; **r. : Claudine Rébersat** directed by Claudine Rébersat

(d) *Fin* realization; **r. d'un bénéfice** making a profit
réaliser [realize] **1** *vt* **(a)** (*ambition*) to achieve, to realize; (*projet*) to carry out, to implement, to put into effect; (*œuvre d'art, Culin pièce montée*) to create

(b) (*rêve*) to attain; **elle a mis 30 ans avant de r. son rêve** her dream took 30 years to come true

(c) *Cin* to direct; *Rad, TV* to produce

(d) *Fin* **r. un capital** to realize an asset, to convert an asset into cash; **r. un profit** to make a profit; **r. un chiffre d'affaires de 10 millions de francs** to have a turnover of 10 million francs, to have a 10 million franc turnover

(e) *F* (*erreur, situation*) to realize, to understand; **elle n'arrive pas à r. que cela est vrai** she can't take it in, it hasn't sunk in *or* registered yet; **j'ai mis un certain temps avant de le r.** it was some time before I realized

2 se réaliser *vpr* **(a)** (*d'une prédiction, d'un rêve*) to come true

(b) (*d'une personne*) to fulfil oneself

3 *vi F* to realize, to twig; **laisse-lui le temps de r.** give him time for it to sink in *or* register
réalisme [realism] *nm* realism; **faire preuve de r.** to be realistic; **faire preuve de r. politique** to demonstrate political realism *or* pragmatism; **décrire qch avec r.** to describe sth realistically; **décrire qn avec r.** to give a realistic portrayal of sb, to give a true-to-life description of sb
réaliste [realist] **1** *adj* (*attitude, personne, proposition, description*) realistic; (*portrait*) lifelike **2** *n* realist
réalité [realite] *nf* reality; **la r. de la situation fait que nous ne pouvons ...** the situation being what it is, we can't ...; **il faut prendre en compte la r. de la situation** you/we/*etc* have to face facts *or* to look at the situation realistically; **c'est une r.** it's a reality *or* fact; **elle n'a pas le sens des réalités** she has no sense of reality, she doesn't live in the real world; **en r.** in reality, really, actually; **en r., ce n'est pas du tout comme cela que ça s'est passé** that's not really what happened, actually that's not what happened at all; **lorsque la r. dépasse la fiction** when truth is stranger than fiction; *Ordinat* **r. virtuelle** virtual reality
reality show [realitiʃo] *nm* reality show
réamorcer [reamɔrse] *Ordinat* **1** *vt* to reboot **2 se réamorcer** *vpr* to reboot
réanimation [reanimasjɔ̃] *nf Méd* resuscitation; **service de r.** intensive care (unit); **mettre qn en r.** to put sb in intensive care
réanimer [reanime] *vt Méd* (*patient*) to resuscitate
réapparaître [reaparɛtr] *vi* (*conj like* **apparaître**; *aux often* **être**) to reappear; (*d'une douleur*) to come back, to recur, to return; *Mus* (*d'un thème*) to be repeated, to recur, to return
réapparition [reaparisjɔ̃] *nf* (*d'une personne*) reappearance; (*d'une douleur*) recurrence; (*du nationalisme, d'une tendance, du choléra etc*) resurgence; *Mus* (*d'un thème*) recurrence, return
réapprovisionnement [reaprɔvizjɔnmɑ̃] *nm* restocking; **assurer le r.** to restock
réapprovisionner [reaprɔvizjɔne] **1** *vt* (*magasin*) to restock a shop (**en** with); **r. qn** to replenish sb's supplies (**en** of) **2 se réapprovisionner** *vpr* (*d'un magasin*) to stock up again, to restock (**en** with); (*d'une personne*) to replenish one's supplies (**en** of), to stock up (**en** on)
réargenter [rearʒɑ̃te] *vt* to resilver
réarmement [rearməmɑ̃] *nm* **(a)** *Pol* rearmament, rearming;

Pol, Rel **r. moral** moral rearmament **(b)** *Naut* refitting, recommissioning
réarmer [rearme] **1** *vt* **(a)** *Pol* to rearm **(b)** (*arme à feu*) to recock; (*appareil photo*) to reset **(c)** *Naut* to refit, to recommission **2 se réarmer** *vpr Pol* to rearm **3** *vi Pol* to rearm
réassort [reasɔr] *nm* (*d'une boutique*) restocking
réassortiment [reasɔrtimɑ̃] *nm* **(a)** (*de couleurs*) matching **(b)** (*d'une boutique*) restocking; (*stock*) new stock
réassortir [reasɔrtir] (*conj like* **assortir**) **1** *vt* **(a)** (*tissu, parure de lit etc*) to match **(b)** (*magasin*) to restock **2 se réassortir** *vpr* to restock
réassurance [reasyrɑ̃s] *nf* reinsurance
réassurer [reasyre] *vt* to reinsure
réassureur [reasyrœr] *nm* reinsurer
rebaptiser [rəbatize] *vt* (*rue etc*) to rename
rébarbatif, -ive [rebarbatif, -iv] *adj* (*sujet, tâche*) daunting; (*visage, mine*) forbidding, unprepossessing; (*style*) off-putting; (*logiciel, écran*) not user-friendly
rebâtir [rəbɑtir] *vt* (*maison*) to rebuild
rebattre [rəbatr] *vt* (*conj like* **battre**) **(a)** to beat again **(b)** *Cartes* to reshuffle **(c)** *F* **r. les oreilles à qn de qch** to shove sth down sb's throat; **il me rebat les oreilles de ses vacances au Maroc** he keeps shoving his holiday in Morocco down my throat, he keeps bending my ear about his holiday in Morocco
rebattu [r(ə)baty] *adj* (*histoire, thème*) hackneyed, trite; (*conversation*) trite; **c'est un sujet r.** it's a trite subject, *F* it's (a subject that's) been done to death; **avoir les oreilles rebattues de qch** to have had sth shoved down one's throat, to have had one's ear bent about sth
rebelle [rəbɛl] **1** *adj* (*personne, esprit etc*) rebellious; (*camp, armée, troupes*) rebel; (*fièvre*) stubborn, obstinate; **pour les mèches rebelles** for unruly *or* unmanageable hair; **r. à toute discipline** unamenable to discipline; **r. aux antibiotiques** resistant to antibiotics **2** *n* rebel; **le chef des rebelles** the rebel leader
rebeller (se) [sərəbɛle] *vpr* to rebel, to revolt (**contre** against); *Fig* (*protester*) to protest
rébellion [rebɛljɔ̃] *nf* rebellion, (up)rising, revolt; **armer une r.** to arm a rebellion; **mater une r.** to curb a rebellion; **en état de r.** (*pays, jeunes*) in a state of rebellion; (*armée*) insurgent; **acte de r.** act of rebellion, rebellious act
rebiffer (se) [sər(ə)bife] *vpr F* to hit back (**contre** at)
rebiquer [r(ə)bike] *vi F* (*de cheveux, col de chemise etc*) to stick up
reblochon [rəblɔʃɔ̃] *nm* Reblochon (*type of cheese from Savoie*)
reboire [rəbwar] *vt* (*conj like* **boire**) to drink again; **jamais je ne reboirai de ce vin** I'll never drink *or* touch that wine again
reboisement [rəbwazmɑ̃] *nm* reforestation, *Br* (re)afforestation
reboiser [rəbwaze] *vt* to reforest, *Br* to (re)afforest
rebond [rəbɔ̃] *nm* (*d'un ballon*) bounce; (*ricochet*) rebound; **faux r.** spin; **saisir la balle au r.** to catch the ball on the rebound; *Fig* to seize the opportunity; *Aut* **r. des roues** wheel hop
rebondi [rəbɔ̃di] *adj* (*joues*) round, chubby; (*personne*) plump, chubby; **ventre r.** paunch; **aux formes rebondies** with generous curves
rebondir [rəbɔ̃dir] *vi* **(a)** (*d'un ballon*) to bounce; (*ricocher*) to rebound; **r. contre** *ou* **sur qch** to bounce off sth **(b)** *Fig* to flare up again; **faire r. l'intrigue/la conversation** to get the plot/conversation moving again; **c'est ça qui a fait r. toute l'affaire** that was what started the whole business up again; **le dollar a rebondi** the dollar has bounced back, the (value of the) dollar has shot back up again; *Can* **son chèque a rebondi** his cheque bounced
rebondissement [rəbɔ̃dismɑ̃] *nm* **(a)** rebound, bounce; **les rebondissements de la balle sur le parquet** the bouncing of the ball on the floor **(b)** *Fig* (*dans une affaire etc*) development
rebord [rəbɔr] *nm* **(a)** (*d'une table, d'un puits*) edge; (*d'une assiette*) rim, edge; **r. d'une fenêtre** window sill *or* ledge **(b)** *Tech* (*surélevé*) raised edge, flange
reborder [rəbɔrde] *vt* **(a)** (*vêtement*) to put a new edging *or* border *or* hem on **(b) r. qn dans son lit** to tuck sb up (in bed) again
reboucher [rəbuʃe] **1** *vt* **(a)** (*fermer de nouveau*) (*bouteille*) to recork, to put the cork back in; (*tube de colle, de dentifrice*) to put the top back on **(b)** (*obturer de nouveau*) (*évier*) to block *or* stop up again; (*trou*) to fill in again **2 se reboucher** *vpr* **(a)** (*d'un évier, des W-C.*) to get blocked up again **(b) la bouteille se rebouche mal** it's not easy to get the cork back in (the bottle); **la bouteille se rebouche hermétiquement** once the cork is back in, the bottle is hermetically sealed
rebours [rəbur] *nm* **prendre qn à r.** to rub sb up the wrong way; **compter à r.** to count backwards; **compte à r.** countdown; **prendre à r. une rue à sens unique** to go the wrong way along a one-way street; **prendre tout à r.** to take everything the wrong way; **faire/commencer qch à r.** to do/start sth back to front *or* the wrong way round; **tu as compris à r.** you've got hold of the wrong end of the stick
rebouter [rəbute] *vt F* (*membre fracturé*) to set; (*articulation démise*) to put back
rebouteur, rebouteux, -euse [rəbutœr, rəbutø, -øz] *n F* bonesetter
reboutonner [rəbutɔne] **1** *vt* to rebutton, to button up again **2 se reboutonner** *vpr* to do oneself up again, to do up one's buttons again
rebrancher [rəbrɑ̃ʃe] *vt* to reconnect
rebrousse-poil (à) [arəbruspwal] *adv* **brosser un chapeau à r.** to brush a hat against the nap *or* the wrong way; **caresser un chat à r.** to stroke a cat the wrong way *or* against its fur; *Fig F* **prendre qn à r.** to rub sb up the wrong way
rebrousser [rəbruse] *vt* **r. chemin** to turn back, to go back the way one came, to retrace one's steps
rebuffade [rəbyfad] *nf* rebuff, snub; **essuyer une r.** to be snubbed *or* rebuffed, to meet with a rebuff
rébus [rebys] *nm* rebus; *Fig* enigma, puzzle
rebut [rəby] *nm* (**article de**) **r.** reject; **habits de r.** cast-off clothing, cast-offs; *Ind* **pièces de r.** rejects, throw-outs; **marchandises de r.** rejects; **mettre au r.** (*voiture, ordinateur etc*) to discard, to scrap; **bon à mettre au r.** fit for the scrapheap; **bureau des rebuts** (*à la poste*) dead-letter office; *Fig* **le r. de la société/du genre humain** the dregs of society/of the human race
rebutant [rəbytɑ̃] *adj* **(a)** (*tâche*) disagreeable, *F* off-putting; **j'ai trouvé l'administration particulièrement rebutante dans ce pays** I found having to deal with the administration in that country particularly disheartening **(b)** (*manière, personne*) disagreeable, unprepossessing, *F* off-putting
rebuter [rəbyte] **1** *vt* **(a)** (*déplaire fortement*) (*d'une situation, de conditions de travail*) to put off; **ce qui me rebutait dans ce travail, c'est que …** what I found disagreeable about the job was that …; **son mauvais caractère l'a rebutée** she was disgusted by how nasty he was **(b)** (*dégoûter*) to disgust, to repulse **2 se rebuter** *vpr* to be put off; **c'est pour cela que je me suis rebuté** that's what put me off
recacheter [rəkaʃte] *vt* to reseal
recadrage [rəkadraʒ] *nm TV, Cin* (*édition*) cropping; (*de plan*) reframing
recadrer [rəkadre] *vt TV, Cin* (*édition*) to crop; (*plan*) to reframe
recalage [rəkalaʒ] *nm F* (*à un examen*) failure
recalcification [rəkalsifikasjɔ̃] *nf* recalcification, recalcifying
recalcifier [rəkalsifje] *vt* to (re)calcify
récalcitrant, -ante [rekalsitrɑ̃, -ɑ̃t] **1** *adj* (*personne, cheval*) recalcitrant, obstinate **2** *n* recalcitrant
recalé, -ée [rəkale] *n F* failure; **il y a cinq recalés dans cette classe** five people in this class have failed
recaler [rəkale] *vt F* (*personne*) (*à un examen*) to fail; **être recalé, se faire r. (au baccalauréat/en maths)** to fail *or F* to flunk (the baccalauréat/(in) maths)
récapitulatif, -ive [rekapitylatif, -iv] *adj* recapitulatory, recapitulative; *Ordinat* **carte récapitulative** summary card
récapitulation [rekapitylasjɔ̃] *nf* **(a)** recap, summing up, *Fml* recapitulation; **faire la r. des points importants** to recap *or* sum up the important points **(b)** (*résumé*) recap, summary, résumé
récapituler [rekapityle] **1** *vt* to recap, to sum up, *Fml* to recapitulate **2** *vi* to recap, to sum up; **alors, je récapitule** so, I'll recap
recapoter [rəkapɔte] *Aut vi* to put up the hood
recaser [rəkɑze] *F* **1** *vt* **(a)** (*dans une entreprise*) to find another job for **(b)** (*dans un logement*) to rehouse **2 se recaser** *vpr* (*retrouver du travail*) to find a new job; (*se remarier*) to get hitched again
recel [rəsɛl] *nm Jur* (*de biens volés*) receiving (and concealing), *F* fencing; (*d'un criminel*) harbouring, *US* harboring
receler [rəs(ə)le] *vt* (*pr ind* **je recèle, n. recelons**; *fu* **je recèlerai**) **(a)** *Jur* (*biens volés*) to receive; *F* to fence; (*criminel*) to harbour, *US* to harbor **(b) la terre recèle de grands trésors** great treasures lie hidden in the earth; *Litt* **r. un grand secret** to harbour *or* conceal a deep secret
recéler [rəsele] *vt* (**je recèle, n. recélons; je recélerai**) = **receler**
receleur, -euse [rəs(ə)lœr, -øz] *n Jur* (*de biens volés*) receiver, *F* fence
récemment [resamɑ̃] *adv* recently, lately, *Fml* of late; **je le constatai encore r.** I noticed it again recently; **un livre r. publié** *ou* **publié r.** a recently published book; **encore r., elle**

me disait que ... she was saying to me only the other day that ...

recensement [rəsɑ̃smɑ̃] *nm* (*de voitures, d'appartements libres etc*) count, inventory; *Admin* (*de la population*) census; *Pol* (*des votes*) counting; *Fin* stocktake; **r. du contingent** registration of those eligible for military service; **faire un r.** to make a count *or* an inventory; (*de la population*) to take a census; **agent chargé du r.** census official; **r. de la population** population census; **r. de la production** census of production; **r. des distributeurs** census of distribution; **r. des entreprises** company census

recenser [rəsɑ̃se] *vt* (*livres, disques etc*) to count, to make an inventory of; *Admin* (*ville, habitants etc*) to take a census of; *Pol* (*votes*) to count; *Mil* to register; **r. des marchandises** to inventory goods, to check off goods

recenseur, -euse [rəsɑ̃sœr, -øz] *n Admin* census taker; *Pol* (*des votes*) counter, teller

récent [resɑ̃] *adj* recent

recentrage [rəsɑ̃traʒ] *nm Pol* move towards the centre *or US* center; **le r. du parti socialiste s'est opéré lentement mais sûrement** the Socialist party has moved slowly but surely towards the centre

recentrer [resɑ̃tre] *vt* (*parti politique*) to move towards the centre *or US* center; *Sp* (*balle*) to centre again

recéper [rəsepe] *vt* (**je recèpe, n. recépons; je recéperai**) (*arbre, pied de vigne*) to cut back to the stump

récépissé [resepise] *nm* (*d'un dépôt, d'un envoi*) receipt; **r. aérien** airfreight consignment note; **r. de dépôt** deposit receipt; **r. de versement** receipt of payment; **r. des chemins de fer** rail consignment note

réceptacle [resɛptakl] *nm* **(a)** receptacle; **la mer est le r. des déchets de la ville** the sea is the receptacle *or* dumping ground for the city's waste; *Fig* **cette région ne peut pas devenir le r. de tous les gangsters du pays** the region cannot become a meeting place for all the gangsters of the country **(b)** *Bot* receptacle **(c)** *Ordinat* **r. pour extension** extension slot

récepteur, -trice [resɛptœr, -tris] **1** *adj Rad* (*appareil, poste*) receiving **2** *nm* **(a)** *Physiol* (*de stimuli*) receptor; **r. olfactif/auditif/tactile** olfactory/auditory/tactile receptor **(b)** (*de radar*), *Tél, Rad, TV* receiver, communications receiver; (*de frein*) slave cylinder; **r. d'embrayage** clutch slave cylinder; **r. de poche** pocket receiver; *Tél* **décrocher le r.** to lift the receiver; *Télécom* **r. Morse** Morse receiver; **r. de liaison terre/satellite** uplink receiver; *Ordinat* **r. de données** data receiver

réceptif, -ive [resɛptif, -iv] **1** *adj* receptive, responsive (**à** to) **2** *nm Mktg* **r. précoce** early adopter

réception [resɛpsjɔ̃] *nf* **(a)** (*d'une lettre, d'une commande, de biens*) receipt; **prévoir quelqu'un pour la r. des marchandises** to arrange for somebody to take delivery (of the goods); *Com* **à payer à la r.** cash on delivery, COD; *Com* **r. définitive** final hand over, final acceptance; *Com, Ind* **r. des travaux** acceptance of work; **accuser r. de qch** to acknowledge receipt of sth

(b) (*accueil*) welcome; **faire une bonne r. à qn** to give sb a good reception *or* warm welcome, to receive *or* welcome sb warmly; **séance de r. de M. Yourcenar à l'Académie française** ceremony admitting M. Yourcenar to the Académie Française, *Fml* M. Yourcenar's induction into the Académie Française; **discours de r.** induction speech

(c) (*soirée*) reception, function; **salle de r.** reception room

(d) (*dans un hôtel*) reception (desk); **passer à la r.** to go to reception; **prière de laisser les clefs à la r.** please leave your keys at reception *or* the (front) desk

(e) *Tél, Télécom, Rad, TV, Électron* reception; **appareil** *ou* **poste de r.** receiving set; **la r. est bonne/mauvaise ici** the reception is good/bad here, you get good/bad reception here; **cet appareil n'a pas une bonne r.** the reception on this set isn't very good; **r. hertzienne** terrestrial signal reception

(f) *Sp* (*de gymnaste, sauteur*) landing; *Fb, Rugby* (*de ballon*) take; **il s'est blessé à la r.** (*d'un sauteur etc*) he hurt himself on landing; **mauvaise r. de Platini** Platini fumbles the pass; **et Platini à la r.** to Platini

réceptionnaire [resɛpsjɔnɛr] *n* (*de marchandises*) consignee; *Com, Ind* receiving agent *or* clerk; (*dans un hôtel*) receptionist, *Am* desk clerk

réceptionner [resɛpsjɔne] *vt* **(a)** *Com, Ind* (*marchandises livrées*) to check and sign for, to take delivery of **(b)** *TV, Rad* to receive

réceptionniste [resɛpsjɔnist] *n* receptionist, *Am* desk *or* reception clerk; **r. de nuit** night porter

réceptivité [resɛptivite] *nf* (*à des sensations, impressions*) receptiveness, responsiveness; (*à une infection*) susceptibility; **dans un état de r.** in a receptive *or* responsive mood

récessif, -ive [resesif, -iv] *adj Biol* recessive

récession [resesjɔ̃] *nf Écon* recession; **r. économique** economic recession

recette [rəsɛt] *nf* **(a)** *Fin* takings, receipts; *Sp* gate money; **dépenses et recettes** expenditure and receipts, outgoings and incomings; **les recettes de la boutique sont en hausse cette semaine** the shop's takings are *or F* take is up this week; **r. annuelle** annual income *or* receipts *or* revenue; **r. brute** gross income *or* receipts *or* earnings; **r. des douanes** customs office; **recettes fiscales** tax revenue; **r. journalière** daily takings; **r. nette** net income *or* receipts; **recettes publiques** government revenue; **faire r.** to be profitable *or* a success; *Th, Cin* to be a (box-office) success, to be a hit at the box office; *Cin* **recettes en salles** box-office takings

(b) (*d'argent dû*) collection; (*bureau*) tax collector's office; **garçon de r.** bank messenger; **faire la r. de l'argent/des contributions** to collect the money/contributions

(c) *Culin* recipe; *Pharm* formula; **r. de cuisine** recipe; **livre de recettes** cookery book, recipe book; *Fig* **la r. du succès/bonheur** the recipe for success/happiness, the secret of success/happiness

recevable [rəsəvabl] *adj* (*excuse*) admissible, acceptable; *Com, Ind* (*marchandises*) fit for acceptance; *Jur* (*témoignage*) admissible; *Fml* **être r. dans une demande** to be entitled to proceed with a claim

receveur, -euse [rəsəvœr, -øz] **1** *n* **(a)** (*d'une lettre, d'une transfusion sanguine*) recipient; *Méd* **r. universel** universal recipient **(b)** (*des impôts*) collector; **r. des douanes** excise officer; **r. /receveuse des Postes** postmaster/postmistress; **r. municipal** = collector of municipal taxes; **r. des contributions directes** tax collector; **r. buraliste** tobacconist **(c)** *Vieilli* (bus) conductor, *f* (bus) conductress **2** *nm Can* **(a)** *Baseball* receiver **(b)** *Am Fb* (*éloigné*) wide receiver; (*rapproché*) tight end; (*inséré*) slotback

recevoir [rəsəvwar] (*prp* **recevant**; *pp* **reçu**; *pr ind* **je reçois, il reçoit, n. recevons, ils reçoivent**; *pr sub* **je reçoive, n. recevions**; *impf* **je recevais**; *p hist* **je reçus**; *fu* **je recevrai**) **1** *vt* **(a)** (*entrer en possession de*) (*lettre*) to receive, to get; (*cadeau, conseil, fleurs*) to get, to receive (**de** from); (*prix, récompense*) to get, to be awarded, to receive; *Rel* (*communion, absolution*) to receive; **r. des nouvelles de qn** (*directement*) to hear from sb, to have news from sb; (*indirectement*) to have news of sb; **j'ai reçu de tes nouvelles par ton père** I had news of you through your father; **j'ai reçu une lettre d'elle** I've had *or* received a letter from her; **nous avons bien reçu votre lettre** we have received *or Fml Com* are in receipt of your letter; **vous avez reçu un appel de Londres** you've had *or* received a call from London; *Com* **r. pour solde de tout compte** received in full settlement; **r. des ordres de qn** to take orders from sb; **je n'ai de conseils à r. de personne!** I don't need advice from anybody!; **elle ne sait pas r. les compliments** she doesn't know how to take *or* accept compliments; *Com, Admin* **recevez, Monsieur, l'assurance de ma considération distinguée** yours faithfully; (*quand la formule de salutation comprend le nom du destinataire*) yours sincerely; *Rel* **r. la confession de qn** to hear *or* receive sb's confession

(b) (*se voir infliger*) (*blâme*) to receive, to get; (*fessée*) to get, to receive; **il a reçu une balle dans l'épaule** he got a bullet *or* he was shot in the shoulder; **il a reçu le ballon en pleine poitrine** the ball hit him right in the chest, he got the ball right in the chest; **j'ai dû r. un coup** something must have hit me; **il a reçu un coup sur la tête** he got hit on the head, he received a blow to the head; *F* (*il est fou*) he must have got dropped on the head; **r. un choc** to get *or* receive a shock; **laisse-le tranquille, il a reçu un choc** leave him alone, he's had a shock; **r. une blessure (au bras)** to get wounded (in the arm); **la blessure que j'ai reçue (au bras) me fait toujours souffrir** the wound I received *or* got (in the arm) still causes me pain; *F* **arrête ou tu vas r. une gifle** stop it or you'll get a slap; *F* **arrête ou tu vas r. ma main sur la figure** stop it or you'll feel the back of my hand; *F* **qu'est-ce que j'ai reçu quand il est rentré!** he really gave me what for when he got home!; *F* **ça ne te ferait pas de mal de r. un coup de pieds aux fesses de temps en temps!** a kick up the backside wouldn't do you any harm from time to time!

(c) (*accueillir*) (*personne*) to receive, to welcome; (*clients*) to deal with; **être mal/bien reçu** to get a poor/good reception; *Iron* **je vais demander une augmentation et je sens que je vais être bien reçu!** I'm going to ask for a rise and I'm sure I'll be in for a warm reception!; **ils vous reçoivent comme un chien** they treat you like a dog; **r. qn à bras ouverts** to welcome sb with open arms; **je ne peux pas le r. aujourd'hui** I can't see him today; **le projet/la proposition n'a pas été bien reçu(e)** the project/proposal was not well received; **ils ont bien reçu la proposition** they gave the proposal a good reception; **r. la visite de qn** to have a visit from sb; **je pense r. de la visite cet été** I think I'll be having visitors this summer; **tu as reçu la visite d'un monsieur** you had a visit from a gentleman

(**d**) (*inviter*) (*amis*) to entertain; **r. des amis à dîner** to have friends (round) to dinner; **r. qn à sa table** to receive sb for dinner/lunch; **elle reçoit des pensionnaires** she takes (in) boarders *or* lodgers; **cet hôtel peut r. jusqu'à 200 clients** this hotel can take *or* accommodate up to 200 guests

(**e**) (*admettre*) to receive, to admit; **elle a été reçue à l'Académie française** she was admitted to the Académie Française; *Scol* **élèves reçus en terminale** pupils admitted to the top form; **être reçu à un examen** to pass an exam(ination); **être reçu premier** to be *or* come (out) first *or* top; **incroyable! je suis reçu!** unbelievable! I've passed!; *Naut* **être reçu capitaine** to get one's captain's certificate

(**f**) (*prendre*) (*pluie, soleil, lumière*) to get; **le Rhône reçoit l'Isère et la Sorgue** the Isère and the Sorgue flow into the Rhône; **la plante ne doit pas r. trop de lumière** the plant shouldn't have *or* get too much light; **r. des radiations** to be exposed to radiation, to receive a dose of radiation

(**g**) *Rad* (*transmission*) to receive; (*chaîne*) to get; **ce poste ne reçoit pas les radios étrangères** the radio doesn't pick up foreign stations

2 se recevoir *vpr* (**a**) *Sp* to land

(**b**) (*s'inviter*) to entertain *or* visit one another, to go to one another's houses

3 *vi* (**a**) (*donner des réceptions*) to entertain; **aimer r.** to enjoy entertaining; **savoir r.** to be a good host/hostess; **ils reçoivent très peu** they don't do much entertaining, they don't have friends round much *or* often

(**b**) (*consulter*) to be available for consultation; **le docteur ne reçoit que sur rendez-vous** the doctor will only see patients by appointment; **le médecin reçoit à 6 heures** the doctor is available for consultation at 6 o'clock, the doctor's surgery is at 6 o'clock

(**c**) (*se voir offrir*) **mieux vaut donner que r.** it is better to give than to receive

rechange [rəʃɑ̃ʒ] *nm ou f* (*vêtements*) change of clothes, spare set of clothes; *Aut* spare; **linge** *ou* **vêtements de r.** spare clothes; **trousse de r.** (*d'outils etc*) spare *or* duplicate set; *Aut etc* **pièces de r.** spare parts; **pile de r.** (*pour torche*) spare battery; **solution/politique de r.** alternative solution/ policy

rechanger [rəʃɑ̃ʒe] *vt* (*conj like* **changer**) to change again

rechanter [rəʃɑ̃te] *vt* to sing again

rechapage [rəʃapaʒ] *nm* (*des pneus*) retreading, remoulding

rechaper [rəʃape] *vt* (*pneu*) to retread, to remould; **pneu rechapé** retread, remould

réchappé, -ée [reʃape] *n Litt* (*d'un désastre, d'un naufrage etc*) survivor

réchapper [reʃape] *vi* (*aux* **avoir** *or* **être**) **r. de** (*naufrage, accident, maladie etc*) to survive; **il en a** *ou* **est réchappé** he survived; **il n'en réchappera pas** (*de naufrage, accident, maladie*) his chances of survival are non-existent; **si j'en réchappe** if I get out of this, if I survive; **il ne réchappera pas à ce scandale** his reputation won't survive the scandal; **r. à une crise** to come through *or* survive a crisis

recharge [rəʃarʒ] *nf* (**a**) (*pour stylo à bille, briquet, rouge à lèvres etc*) refill; **r. d'encre** ink refill (**b**) (*d'une batterie*) recharging; **mettre l'accumulateur en r.** to put the battery on charge

rechargeable [rəʃarʒabl] *adj* (*briquet, vaporisateur de parfum*) refillable; (*pile*) rechargeable; (*arme*) reloadable

rechargement [rəʃarʒəmɑ̃] *nm* (**a**) (*de briquet, vaporisateur de parfum*) refilling; (*d'un accumulateur*) recharging; (*d'un véhicule, d'un fusil, d'un bateau*) reloading (**b**) (*d'une route*) remetalling; (*d'une voie ferrée*) reballasting

recharger [rəʃarʒe] **1** *vt* (*conj like* **charger**) (**a**) (*accumulateur*) to recharge; *Fig F* **r. ses batteries** *ou* **ses accus** to recharge one's batteries (**b**) (*camion, fusil, appareil photo*) to reload; (*stylo, briquet, vaporisateur de parfum*) to refill (**c**) (*route*) to remetal; (*voie ferrée*) to reballast **2 se recharger** *vpr Ordinat* to reload

réchaud [reʃo] *nm* (**a**) stove; **r. à gaz** gas ring; **r. à alcool** spirit stove (**b**) (*chauffe-plat*) hot plate, plate warmer

réchauffage [reʃofaʒ] *nm* (*de la nourriture*) reheating, warming up

réchauffé [reʃofe] **1** *adj* (**a**) (*plat*) reheated, warmed-up, *Péj* rehashed (**b**) *Fig F* (*plaisanterie*) stale, old **2** *nm Fig F* **c'est du r.** (*plaisanterie*) that's an old *or* a stale joke; (*nouvelles*) that's stale news *or* old hat; (*politique*) it's the same old thing; (*livre, discours*) it's a rehash; **rien de nouveau dans le journal sur l'affaire, il n'y a que du r.** there's nothing new in the paper about the business, just a rehash of what's been said already

réchauffement [reʃofmɑ̃] *nm* warming (up); **r. de la planète** *ou* **de l'atmosphère** global warming; **un soudain r. de la température** a sudden rise in temperature

réchauffer [reʃofe] **1** *vt* (*plat*) to reheat, to warm up; (*personne*) to warm up; **ça réchauffe, hein?** it really warms you up *or* gives you a nice warm glow inside, doesn't it?; **on ne réchauffe pas les artichauts** artichokes are no good reheated; *Fig* **r. le cœur à qn** to put new heart into sb; **cela me réchauffe le cœur** it does my heart good, it's heart-warming; **ces paroles m'ont réchauffé le cœur** these were heart-warming words

2 se réchauffer *vpr* (*d'une personne*) to warm up, to get warm (again); **alors, tu t'es réchauffé?** have you warmed up?, are you warm again?; **se r. les pieds** to warm one's feet; **l'atmosphère se réchauffe** the atmosphere is getting warmer *or* warming (up)

réchauffeur [reʃofœr] *nm Tech* heater; **serpentin r.** heating coil

rechausser [rəʃose] **1** *vt* (**a**) **r. qn** to put sb's shoes/boots on again (for them); **r. ses skis** to put one's skis on again; (*après une longue interruption*) to start skiing again; **ce marchand de chaussures m'a rechaussé de neuf** I got my new shoes in that shop; **il était rechaussé de neuf** he was wearing new shoes; **ce bottier te rechaussera aussi bien que le précédent** you'll get as good boots in there as in the last place (**b**) *Aut* **r. une voiture** to fit a car with new tyres (**c**) (*consolider*) (*structure, mur*) to underpin **2 se rechausser** *vpr* to put one's shoes on again; (*acheter de nouvelles chaussures*) to buy (oneself) new shoes

rêche [rɛʃ] *adj* (*surface, vin, matière*) rough; (*cheveux*) coarse; *Fig* (*personne, attitude*) forbidding

recherche [rəʃɛrʃ] *nf* (**a**) search (**de** for); *Fig Litt, Fml* quest (**de** for); **la r. de la vérité** the search for *or Litt, Fml* after the truth; **la r. des plaisirs** pleasure-seeking, the pursuit of pleasure; **la r. de la gloire/du bonheur** the quest for *or* pursuit of glory/happiness; **ils se sont joints aux recherches pour retrouver l'enfant** they joined in the search *or* hunt for the child; **dans l'affaire Mennesson, la police continue les** *ou* **ses recherches** the police are continuing their enquiry into the Mennesson affair; **les recherches pour retrouver l'otage sont demeurées vaines** the hunt for the hostage has been to no avail; **r. de débouchés** search for markets; **r. d'informations** information search, fact-finding; *Minér* **r. de filons** prospecting; **r. pétrolière** oil prospecting; *Él* **r. de dérangements** locating of faults; **être à la r. de** (*objet difficile à trouver*) to be looking for; (*objet ou personne qui a disparu*) to be looking *or* searching for, to be in search of; **ils ont fait tout Paris à la r. d'un vase identique** they went round the whole of Paris in search of an identical vase; **j'ai couru à la r. d'un médecin** I ran for *or* to find a doctor; *Naut* **droit de r.** (*en mer*) right of search

(**b**) (*scientifique, universitaire etc*) research (**sur** on, into); **faire de la r., être dans la r.** to do research, to be engaged in research; **faire des recherches sur qch** to do research on sth, to research sth; **la r. sur le cancer** cancer research; **r. commerciale** marketing research; **r. et développement** research and development, R&D; **r. documentaire** desk research; **r. expérimentale** experimental research; **laboratoire/équipe de r.** research laboratory/team; **r. mercatique** marketing research; *Mktg* **recherches par panel** panel research; **r. par sondage** survey research; **recherches sur les besoins des consommateurs** consumer research; **r. sur les prix** pricing research; **r. sur le terrain** fieldwork

(**c**) (*effort*) sophistication; **avec r.** with style; **sans r.** (*style*) straightforward, down to earth

(**d**) *Ordinat* find, search; **r. arrière** backward search; **r. avant** forward search; **r. et remplacement** search and replace; **r. et remplacement global** global search and replace; **r. globale** global search; **r. logique** logic seeking

recherché [rəʃɛrʃe] *adj* (**a**) (*que l'on recherche*) (*criminel*) wanted; (*objet*) sought-after, in demand; **être très r.** to be much sought after, to be in great demand; **ce style de fauteuil est très r.** there's a lot of demand for this type of chair; **sa compagnie est très recherchée** he *or* his company is much in demand *or* much sought after (**b**) (*robe, écriture*) elegant, exquisite; (*style*) refined, elegant; (*discours*) elegantly phrased, well-turned; **d'un travail r.** of exquisite workmanship; **trop r.** (*style*) affected, mannered, *Fml* recherché; (*écriture*) elaborate, fancy

rechercher [rəʃɛrʃe] *vt* (**a**) (*objet ou personne qui a disparu*) to look *or* search for; (*causes, raisons etc*) to look *or* search for, to inquire into; (*un emploi*) to look for, to seek; **j'ai laissé**

ma bicyclette chez Paul, il va falloir que j'aille la r. I left my bike at Paul's place, I'll have to go and get it back; **je viendrai te r. plus tard** I'll come back to pick you up later; *Ordinat* **r. qch** to search *or* do a search for sth; **r. et remplacer** to search and replace; **r. vers le bas/haut** to search forwards/backwards; *Tél etc* **r. un dérangement** to try to locate a fault; **un homme recherché par la police/ pour meurtre** a man wanted by the police/for murder; **nous recherchons cette femme, vous la connaissez?** we are attempting to locate *or* find this woman, do you recognize her?; **h. 35 ans recherche j. f. pour sorties** (*dans petite annonce*) male, 35, seeks *or* seeking female for nights out; **r. l'origine d'un mot** to look up the origin of a word

(b) (*chercher de nouveau*) to look again for; **il va falloir r. l'information dans tous les dossiers** we'll have to go through all the files again and have another look for the information

(c) (*faveurs, perfection*) to look for, to seek; (*gloire, plaisirs, honneurs*) to seek, to be in pursuit of; (*louanges*) to court; **elle recherche la solitude** she's looking for solitude *or* for a place where she can be alone; **r. la difficulté** (*compliquer les choses*) to look for difficulties; (*aimer les défis*) to like a challenge

rechigner [rəʃiɲe] *vi F* to grimace, to look sour; **il a rangé sa chambre en rechignant** moaning and groaning, he tidied his bedroom; **faire qch sans r.** to do sth without (making) a fuss; **r. à la besogne** *ou* **au travail** to be unwilling to do it; **r. à faire qch** to make a fuss about doing sth

rechute [rəʃyt] *nf Méd* relapse; **faire une r.** to suffer *or* have a relapse, to have a setback

rechuter [rəʃyte] *vi Méd* to have a relapse

récidivant [residivɑ̃] *adj Méd* (*maladie*) recurring, recurrent

récidive [residiv] *nf* **(a)** *Jur* repeat offence *or US* offense; **c'est sa première r.** it's his first repeat offence; **... et depuis il a fait plusieurs récidives** ... and he's had several repeat offences since; **à la première r., tu es renvoyé** do it one more time and you're sacked; **en cas de r., une peine de prison est inévitable** a repeat offence will lead to a mandatory prison sentence **(b)** *Méd* (*d'une maladie*) recurrence

récidiver [residive] *vi* **(a)** *Jur* to repeat an offence *or US* offense; **il a récidivé** he has relapsed into crime, *F* he's done it again **(b)** (*d'une maladie*) to recur

récidiviste [residivist] *n* repeat offender, habitual criminal, *Fml* recidivist

récidivité [residivite] *nf Méd* (*d'une maladie*) recurrent nature

récif [resif] *nm* reef; **r. (en) barrière** barrier reef; **r. de corail** *ou* **corallien** coral reef

récipiendaire [resipjɑ̃dɛr] *n Litt* (*d'honneur, de diplôme*) recipient

récipient [resipjɑ̃] *nm* container

réciprocité [resiprɔsite] *nf* reciprocity

réciproque [resiprɔk] **1** *adj* **(a)** (*amour, confiance, tolérance, sentiments etc*) mutual; (*bénéfices, accord, concessions*) reciprocal, mutual; **elle ne veut plus me voir, et c'est r.** she doesn't want to see me again and the feeling is mutual **(b)** *Gram* reciprocal; *Math* (*proportion*) reciprocal, inverse; (*en logique, Math propositions*) converse **2** *nf* **(a) rendre la r. à qn** to get one's own back on sb, to get even with sb; **et la r. est vraie** and the reverse is true; **elle le déteste, et la r. est vraie** she hates him and vice versa **(b)** (*en logique, Math proposition*) converse; *Math* (*proportion*) reciprocal

réciproquement [resiprɔkmɑ̃] *adv* (*mutuellement*) mutually; **et r.** and vice versa

récit [resi] *nm* **(a)** account; (*histoire*) story; *Littér* narrative; **il nous fit le r. de ses aventures** he gave us an account of his adventures **(b)** *Mus* solo; **jeux de r.** solo organ

récital, -als [resital] *nm* recital

récitant, -ante [resitɑ̃, -ɑ̃t] *n* **(a)** *Mus* (*voix, instrument*) solo **(b)** (*lecteur*) narrator

récitatif [resitatif] *nm Mus* recitative

récitation [resitasjɔ̃] *nf* (*action*) recitation, reciting; *Scol* (*texte*) recitation

réciter [resite] *vt* (*poème etc*) to recite; **on dirait qu'il récite ses remerciements** his thanks sound rehearsed

réclamant, -ante [reklamɑ̃, -ɑ̃t] *n Jur* claimant; (*en droit civil*) plaintiff

réclamation [reklamasjɔ̃] *nf* **(a)** (*plainte*) complaint, objection, protest; **faire une r.** to complain; **r. de client** customer complaint; **pour toute r., veuillez vous adresser au patron** please refer any complaints to the manager; *Télécom* **le service des réclamations, les réclamations** complaints *or* service (department); **il y a r.** (*à l'issue d'une course hippique*) a steward's enquiry is taking place

(b) (*pour recevoir un dédommagement*) claim; **faire** *ou* **déposer une r.** to make *or* put in a claim; **r. de dommages-intérêts** claim for damages; **prouver le bien-fondé d'une r.** to substantiate a claim; **r. d'indemnité** claim for compensation

réclame [reklam] *nf* (*publicité*) advertising; (*panneau*) advertisement; *TV, Rad* commercial; **faire de la r. pour qch** to advertise sth; *Fig* **faire de la r. pour qn** to sing sb's praises; *Fig* **cela ne lui fera pas de r.** it's not a very good advertisement for him; **article (en) r.** special offer; **c'était en r.** it was a special offer, *Am* it was on special; **vente r.** sale; **r. lumineuse** illuminated sign

réclamer [reklame] **1** *vi* to complain; **r. auprès de** to make a claim against; (*se plaindre*) to lodge a complaint with; **r. contre** (*qch*) to protest against, to object to; (*décision*) to appeal against; *F* **cet enfant ne cesse de r.** that child's never satisfied

2 *vt* **(a)** (*demander*) (*livre, cotisation, pourboire, silence*) to ask for; (*droit, allocation*) to claim; (*bien perdu*) to reclaim; **r. de l'argent à qn** to ask sb for money; **l'enfant réclame ses parents** the child is calling for his parents; **il va finir par te r. une augmentation de salaire** he'll end up asking you for a pay rise

(b) (*exiger*) (*secours, aide, intervention, réformes etc*) to demand; **il réclame son argent** he wants his money back; **r. des dommages et intérêts** to claim damages; **r. le paiement** to demand payment; **mon client me réclame les épreuves pour mardi** my customer's clamouring to have the proofs back by Tuesday; **les enfants réclament leur dessert** the children are clamouring for *or* demanding their dessert; **Monsieur le Président, je réclame la parole** Mr President, may I say something?; **il me le réclame sans cesse** he keeps nagging me about it; **je ne fais que r. mon dû** I am merely claiming what is mine; **r. qch à cor et à cri** to clamour for sth; **r. qch/qn à grands cris** to clamour for sth/sb

(c) (*avoir besoin de*) (*soins, attention*) to require, to need

3 se réclamer *vpr* **il se réclame de la droite/du mouvement écologiste** he proclaims to be right-wing/an environmentalist; **elle se réclama du Maire pour se faire nommer** she used the Mayor's name to secure her appointment

reclassement [rəklasmɑ̃] *nm* **(a)** (*réarrangement*) reordering, rearrangement **(b)** (*dans une catégorie différente*) reclassifying, reclassification; (*du personnel*) regrading; **r. professionnel** redeployment

reclasser [rəklase] *vt* **(a)** (*réarranger*) to reorder, to rearrange **(b)** (*dans une catégorie différente*) to reclassify; (*personnel, salaires*) to regrade

reclus, -use [rəkly, -yz] **1** *adj Rel* cloistered **2** *n* recluse; *Rel* cloistered monk *or f* nun **(b)** *Fig* recluse; **vivre en r.** to live like a hermit, to live the life of a recluse, to be a recluse

réclusion [reklyzjɔ̃] *nf* **(a)** *Jur* imprisonment; **r. criminelle à perpétuité** life imprisonment **(b)** (*solitude*) seclusion; **il vit dans la r. la plus totale** he lives totally secluded *or* cut off from the world

réclusionnaire [reklyzjɔnɛr] *n Jur* long-term prisoner

récognition [rekɔgnisjɔ̃] *nf Phil* recognition, identification

recoiffer [rəkwafe] **1** *vt* **r. qn** to redo sb's hair; (*remettre un chapeau à*) to put sb's hat on again **2 se recoiffer** *vpr* **(a)** to redo one's hair **(b)** (*remettre son chapeau*) to put one's hat on again

recoin [rəkwɛ̃] *nm* nook, recess; **maison pleine de recoins** rambling house, house full of nooks and crannies; **les coins et les recoins** the nooks and crannies; **je l'ai cherché dans les coins et les recoins** *ou* **jusque dans les moindres recoins** I've searched high and low *or* every nook and cranny for it; *Fig* **les recoins de la mémoire** the deepest recesses of the memory

récollection [rekɔlɛksjɔ̃] *nf Rel* meditation

recoller [rəkɔle] **1** *vt* (*vase cassé*) to glue *or* stick back together again; (*timbre*) to stick back on; (*enveloppe*) to stick back down; *Fig* **il recolla son front à la vitre glacée** he pressed his forehead back against the frosted window pane; *Fig F* **r. les morceaux** to put the pieces back together again; *F* **r. une amende/mauvaise note à qn** to dole out another fine/bad mark to sb

2 *vi Sp* **r. au peloton** to catch up with the pack

3 se recoller *vpr* **(a)** (*d'un os cassé*) to knit; **ça s'est recollé comme par miracle!** as if by magic, it's back in one piece!

(b) *F* **ils se sont recollés (ensemble)** they're back together again, they've patched things up

récoltable [rekɔltabl] *adj* ready for harvesting

récoltant, -ante [rekɔltɑ̃, -ɑ̃t] **1** *adj* **apiculteur r.** honey producer; **propriétaire** *ou* **viticulteur r.** = winegrower who harvests his own grapes **2** *n* **mis en bouteille chez le r.** estate-bottled

récolte [rekɔlt] *nf* **(a)** *Agr* (*des cultures, fruits, pommes de terre, miel*) harvesting, gathering; **nous avons fait une bonne/mauvaise r.** we got a good/bad crop; **pendant la r.**

during harvesting, at harvest time; **faire la r.** to harvest (the crops); **faire la r. du blé** to harvest the wheat; **partir faire les récoltes** to go harvesting; *Fig F* **la r. a été bonne** (*au marché aux puces, chez l'antiquaire etc*) I/we/*etc* came back with a good haul

(**b**) *Bot* (*de spécimens etc*) collecting, gathering

(**c**) (*produits*) (*céréales, fruits, pommes de terre*) harvest, crop(s); (*miel*) harvest; **une belle r.** a good harvest *or* crop; **donner une bonne r.** (*d'une terre, une variété de pomme de terre etc*) to give a good crop, to crop well; **rentrer la r.** to get in *or* bring in *or* gather in the harvest *or* the crops; *Fig* **une bonne r. de renseignements** a good crop of information

récolter [rekɔlte] **1** *vt* (*cultures*) to harvest, to gather in, to get in; *Fig F* (*renseignements, documents etc*) to collect, to gather, to garner; **si tu arrives à r. des informations sur ...** if you should happen to come up with any information on ...; **elle a récolté toute une série de mauvaises notes** she got a whole crop *or* series of bad marks; **et finalement, je n'ai récolté que des injures** and in the end, all I got was insults; **il récolte ce qu'il a semé** it's his own fault, he's reaping what he sowed; *Prov* **qui sème le vent récolte la tempête** sow the wind and reap the whirlwind

2 se récolter *vpr Agr* **ces fraises se récoltent en juin** these strawberries are ready for picking *or* are harvested in June

recombinaison [rəkɔ̃binɛzɔ̃] *nf Biol* recombination

recombinant [rəkɔ̃binɑ̃] *adj Biol* recombinant

recombustion [rəkɔ̃bystjɔ̃] *nf* (*des imbrûlés*) recombustion

recommandable [rəkɔmɑ̃dabl] *adj* (**a**) commendable; **en tous points r., r. à tous égards** (*personne*) highly respectable; **le seul restaurant r. du quartier** the only decent restaurant in the area, the only restaurant in the area worth recommending; **peu r.** (*personne*) undesirable; **hôtel peu r.** disreputable hotel (**b**) (*que l'on conseille*) advisable

recommandation [rəkɔmɑ̃dasjɔ̃] *nf* (**a**) recommendation; **(lettre de) r.** letter of recommendation *or* of introduction; **avez-vous des recommandations?** do you have references?; **je vous mets un mot de r. pour le spécialiste** I'll write you a referral for the specialist

(**b**) (*conseil*) recommendation; **recommandations** advice; **je viens sur la r. d'un de vos clients** I've come on the recommendation of one of your customers, one of your customers recommended you to me; **suivre les recommandations de qn** to follow sb's advice; **maman nous a fait mille recommandations sur la façon de se bien conduire** Mum told us a thousand things to do and not to do

(**c**) (*d'une lettre*) registration

recommandé [rəkɔmɑ̃de] **1** *adj* (*lettre*) registered **2** *nm* **un envoi en r.,** *F* **un r.** a registered letter/parcel; **envoyer qch en r.** to send sth registered (post)

recommander [rəkɔmɑ̃de] **1** *vt* (**a**) (*hôtel, produit, film, employé, médecin etc*) to recommend; **je peux vous la r.** I can recommend her; **est-ce qu'elle est recommandée?** does she have references?; **r. son âme à Dieu** to commend one's soul to God

(**b**) (*conseiller*) (*discretion, prudence etc*) to advise, to urge; **r. à qn de faire qch** to advise *or* urge sb to do sth; **je vous recommende de rester** I advise you to stay, my advice is to stay, I recommend that you stay; **r. la prudence à qn** to advise *or* urge sb to be cautious; **je te le recommande fortement** I would strongly advise it; **il est recommandé aux clients de réserver à l'avance** customers are advised to book in advance; **il n'est pas recommandé de boire de l'alcool pendant le traitement** it is inadvisable to drink alcohol during the treatment; **ce n'est pas très recommandé** it's not very advisable, I wouldn't recommend it

(**c**) (*lettre, paquet*) to register

2 se recommander *vpr* (**a**) **se r. à Dieu** to commend oneself to God

(**b**) **se r. de qn** (*pour un emploi*) to give sb *or* use sb's name as a reference; **il se recommande du Docteur Martin** he's been referred by Dr Martin

(**c**) **se r. par qch** to have sth in one's favour; **elle se recommande par son efficacité** her efficiency is a strong point in her favour; **ce restaurant se recommande par ses poissons** the restaurant is to be recommended for its fish

recommencement [rəkɔmɑ̃smɑ̃] *nm* beginning *or* starting again; (*d'un débat, de pourparlers*) re-opening; **la vie est un éternel** *ou* **perpétuel r.** life is a constant succession of new beginnings

recommencer [rəkɔmɑ̃se] (**je recommençai(s); n. recommençons**) **1** *vt* (*une tâche, un jeu, un récit etc*) to start *or* begin again, *Fml* to recommence; **r. sa vie** to make a new *or* fresh start (in life), to start life afresh; **r. à faire qch** to start *or* begin to do *or* doing sth again; **tout est à r.** we'll have to start *or* begin all over again; *F* we'll have to go back to square one; **si c'était à r., j'accepterais le poste en Martinique** if I could do it all over again, I'd accept the job in Martinique

2 *vi* (*d'une personne*) to start *or* begin again, to start afresh, *Am* to start over; (*d'une guerre, de la pluie*) to start (up) again; (*de combats*) to break out again; **ça fait trois fois que je recommence** I've started this three times; **ne recommencez pas!** don't do it again!; **le voilà qui recommence!** he's at it again!; **je vous garantis qu'il ne recommencera pas de sitôt** I can guarantee he won't do that again in a hurry; **qui parle?, alors, ça recommence?** who's talking?, that chatter's not going to start again, is it?; **l'orage a recommencé en fin de soirée** there was another storm late in the evening; **il recommence à pleuvoir** it's starting to rain again

recommercialiser [rəkɔmɛrsjalize] *vt* to remarket

récompense [rekɔ̃pɑ̃s] *nf* reward; **mille francs de r.** a thousand francs reward; **et en r. elle a reçu ...** and as a reward *or* in reward *or* in return she was given ...; **on ne peut pas les laisser sans r.** they can't go unrewarded; **en r. de vos services** as a reward for your services, in return for your services; **en r. de votre bonté** in return for your kindness, to repay you for your kindness; **c'est une modeste r. pour votre bonté** it's a small recompense *or* return for your kindness; **et c'était là la r. de mes efforts** and that was how you/he/*etc* repaid me, and that was all the thanks I got; **la juste r. de ses crimes** just retribution for his crimes

récompenser [rekɔ̃pɑ̃se] *vt* to reward; **r. qn de qch** to reward sb for sth; **r. qn de sa bonté** to repay sb for their kindness; **son travail a été bien récompensé** his work was well *or* amply rewarded; *Iron* **me voilà récompensé d'avoir tant travaillé** that's all the thanks I get for working so hard; **film récompensé au Festival de Venise** film that won an award at the Venice Film Festival

recompiler [rəkɔ̃pile] *vt* to recompile

recomposer [rəkɔ̃poze] *vt* (**a**) *Ch* (*éléments*) to recompose, to recombine (**b**) *Typ* (*texte*) to reset (**c**) *Tél* (*numéro*) to redial

recomposition [rəkɔ̃pozisjɔ̃] *nf* (**a**) *Ch* recombining (**b**) *Typ* resetting (**c**) *Tél* repeat dial

recompter [rəkɔ̃te] *vt* to recount, to count again

reconcevoir [rəkɔ̃s(ə)vwar] *vt* to redesign

réconciliateur, -trice [rekɔ̃siljatœr, -tris] *n* reconciler

réconciliation [rekɔ̃siljasjɔ̃] *nf* reconciliation; **amener une r. entre deux personnes** to bring about a reconciliation *or* to heal the breach between two people; **en signe de r.** as a sign of reconciliation; **pour sceller notre r.** to show that we've made it up

réconcilier [rekɔ̃silje] **1** *vt* (*personnes, aspects différents d'une personnalité etc*) to reconcile; **r. qn avec ses parents** to reconcile sb with his/her parents, to heal the breach between sb and his/her parents; **ce voyage m'a réconcilié avec la marche** the trip renewed my appetite for walking; **ça m'a réconcilié avec la vie** it renewed my appetite for life, it made life seem worth living again; **la famille s'en trouva réconciliée** it brought the family together again; **réconcilié avec lui-même** at peace with himself

2 se réconcilier *vpr* to be *or* become reconciled; **se r. avec qn** to be reconciled with sb, to make it up *or* be friends again with sb, to patch things up with sb; **se r. avec soi-même** to be *or* feel at peace with oneself; **se r. avec la vie** to renew one's appetite for life, to find life worth living again; **se r. avec le sport/son travail** to renew one's appetite for sport/one's job; **c'est ainsi que j'ai pu me r. avec la vie/le sport** that's what made life/sport seem worthwhile again

reconditionner [rəkɔ̃disjɔne] *vt* to repackage

reconductible [rəkɔ̃dyktibl] *adj* (*contrat, bail*) renewable

reconduction [rəkɔ̃dyksjɔ̃] *nf* (**a**) *Jur* (*d'un bail, contrat*) renewal; **r. tacite** (*d'un accord*) tacit renewal (**b**) *Admin, Pol* (*de budget, mesures, politique etc*) continuation; **voter la r. de la grève** to vote for the continuation of the strike *or* for continued strike action *or* for the strike to continue

reconduire [rəkɔ̃dɥir] *vt* (*conj like* **conduire**) (**a**) **r. qn** (*à son hôtel etc*) (*en voiture*) to take *or* drive sb back; (*à pied*) to see *or* walk sb back; (*chez lui*) (*en voiture*) to drive *or* take sb home; (*à pied*) to see *or* walk sb home; **r. qn (jusqu'à la porte)** to see *or* show sb out, to see *or* walk sb to the door; **r. qn à la frontière** to escort sb back over the border (**b**) (*renouveler*) (*bail, contrat etc*) to renew; *Admin, Pol* (*mesure temporaire, politique, grève*) to continue

reconfigurer [rəkɔ̃figyre] *vt Ordinat* to reconfigure

reconfirmation [rəkɔ̃firmasjɔ̃] *nf* reconfirmation

réconfort [rekɔ̃fɔr] *nm* comfort, reassurance; **le r. qu'apporte la religion** the comfort *or* consolation that religion brings; **le r. procuré par ces paroles** the comfort that these words brought; **avoir besoin de r.** to need cheering up; **paroles de r.** words of comfort, comforting *or* reassuring words; **vous m'êtes toujours d'un grand r.** you're a great comfort to me

réconfortant [rekɔ̃fɔrtɑ̃] *adj* **(a)** *(physiquement) (médicament, traitement)* tonic **(b)** *(moralement) (personne, attitude)* comforting; *(paroles, nouvelle)* comforting, cheering, cheery; **c'est une idée peu réconfortante** it's not a very comforting idea, there's not much comfort in that idea

réconforter [rekɔ̃fɔrte] **1** *vt* **(a)** *(physiquement)* to build up; **cette soupe te réconfortera** the soup will help build you *or* your strength up **(b)** *(moralement)* to comfort; **ces paroles l'ont réconforté** these words brought him some comfort; **elle a su nous r. dans ces moments difficiles** she was a great comfort to us in those difficult times; **cela me réconforte de voir que je ne suis pas la seule** it cheers me up *or* I'm glad to see I'm not the only one **2 se réconforter** *vpr* to cheer oneself up

reconnaissable [rəkɔnɛsabl] *adj (parfum, odeur, style, allure etc)* recognizable (**à** by, from); **r. entre tous** *(style, personne etc)* unmistakeable; **c'est difficilement r. sur la photo** it's hardly *or* scarcely recognizable in the photo, it's hard to recognize in the photo; **il n'est plus r.** he's unrecognizable, you wouldn't recognize *or* know him, he's changed beyond all recognition

reconnaissance [rəkɔnɛsɑ̃s] *nf* **(a)** *(action de reconnaître)* recognition; **je porterai un canotier, ce sera notre signe de r.** I'll be wearing a boater, that's how you'll recognize me; **de la main, elle lui fit un signe de r.** she waved to show she'd seen him; *Mil* **signal de r.** recognition signal

(b) *(acte formel) (d'une promesse, dette, d'un enfant né hors mariage etc)* acknowledgement; *(d'un gouvernement)* recognition, acknowledgement; *(d'une erreur)* acknowledgement, admission; **en r. de son courage** in recognition of his courage

(c) *(gratitude)* gratitude; **r. de** *ou* **pour qch** gratitude *or* thankfulness for sth; **témoigner de la r. à qn** to show gratitude to sb; **je n'éprouve** *ou* **je n'ai aucune r. pour eux** I feel no gratitude towards them; **avoir une profonde r. pour qch** to be deeply grateful *or* thankful for sth; **en r. de votre invitation** in gratitude for your invitation; **avec r.** gratefully; **parler de qch avec r.** to speak of sth with gratitude; *F* **c'est la r. du ventre** that's cupboard love

(d) *Com* note of hand, promissory note; **r. (de dépôt de gage)** pawn ticket

(e) *Mil* reconnaissance, reconnoitring; *F* recce; **détachement/avion de r.** reconnaissance party/aircraft; **faire une r. rapide du village** to do a quick reconnaissance *or* *F* recce of the village; **être en r.** to be on (a) reconnaissance, to be reconnoitring; **partir en r.** to go off on reconnaissance; *Fig F* **je pars en r.** I'll go and reconnoitre, I'll go and check things out; *F* **j'y suis allé en r.** I went to check it out

(f) *(d'un terrain, d'un site)* inspection, exploration, examination; *Min* prospecting; *(topographie)* surveying, charting; **levé de r.** exploratory survey

▶ **reconnaissance**: **r. de dette** IOU, promissory note; *Ordinat* **r. de l'écriture manuscrite** handwriting recognition; *Ordinat* **r. optique des caractères** optical character recognition, OCR; *Ordinat* **r. de la parole, r. vocale** speech recognition

reconnaissant [rəkɔnɛsɑ̃] *adj* grateful; **être r. à qn de qch/de faire qch** to be grateful to sb for sth/for doing sth; **je vous en suis très r.** I'm very grateful, I'm in your debt; **je vous serai r. de ne plus en parler** I'd thank you not to mention it again, I'd be grateful if you didn't mention it again; *Fml* **votre fils r.** *(dans une lettre)* your grateful *or* loving *or* devoted son

reconnaître [rəkɔnɛtr] *(conj like* **connaître***)* **1** *vt* **(a)** *(identifier) (personne, lieu, air)* to recognize; **r. qn à sa démarche** to recognize *or* know *or* tell sb by his walk; **j'ai eu beaucoup de mal à le r.** I hardly knew *or* recognized him; **je la reconnaîtrais n'importe où** I'd know *or* recognize her anywhere; **est-ce que vous le reconnaîtriez?** would you know him again?, would you recognize him?; **ils se ressemblent tant qu'on ne peut les r.** they're so alike that you can't tell them apart; **je te reconnais bien là!** that's just like you!, that's you all over!

(b) *Naut* **r. la terre** to sight land

(c) *(admettre) (vérité, droit, gouvernement)* to recognize, to acknowledge; *(erreur, faute)* to acknowledge, to admit; *Jur (enfant)* to acknowledge, to own; **r. les qualités de qn** to acknowledge sb's qualities; **tu peux au moins lui r. cette qualité** you could at least acknowledge that *or F* at least give him that; **r. qn pour chef** to acknowledge sb as leader; **r. qch comme vrai** to acknowledge the truth of sth; **reconnu comme (étant) le plus grand chef de France** recognized as the *or* acknowledged to be the greatest chef in France; **r. qu'on s'est trompé, r. s'être trompé** to admit *or* acknowledge that one was mistaken; **je suis allée trop vite, je le reconnais** I went too fast, I admit it

(d) *Mil etc (examiner) (position etc)* to reconnoitre, to make a reconnaissance of; *(terrain)* to explore

(e) *Min* to prospect

2 se reconnaître *vpr* **(a)** *(soi-même)* to recognize oneself; **je ne me reconnais pas sur cette photo** I don't recognize myself in that photo; **se r. vaincu/coupable** to acknowledge defeat/one's guilt; **elle se reconnaît tout à fait dans son rôle** she recognizes herself in the part

(b) *(se retrouver)* to find one's way about *or* around; **ce n'est pas facile de se r. dans Tokyo** it's not easy to find your way about *or* to get your bearings in Tokyo; **je n'arrive plus à m'y r.** I can't find my way around any more; *Fig* I'm lost, I'm confused; *Fig* **c'est à ne pas s'y r.** it's all very confusing

(c) **gaz qui se reconnaît à son odeur** gas recognizable by its smell; **un vrai gentleman se reconnaît à ...** you can tell a real gentleman by ...

(d) *(entre personnes)* to recognize *or* know each other

reconquérir [rəkɔ̃kerir] *vt (conj like* **conquérir***) (province, royaume, pays)* to reconquer; *(territoire, liberté, droit)* to win back, to regain, to recover; *(l'estime, l'amitié de qn)* to win back, to regain; **r. une femme/un homme** to get *or* win a woman/man back

reconquête [rəkɔ̃kɛt] *nf (d'un royaume)* reconquest; *(d'un droit, de la liberté)* recovery, winning back

reconsidérer [rəkɔ̃sidere] *vt (conj like* **considérer***)* to reconsider

reconstituant [rəkɔ̃stitɥɑ̃] **1** *adj Méd* tonic; **c'est un aliment r.** it's nourishing **2** *nm* pick-me-up; *Méd* tonic

reconstituer [rəkɔ̃stitɥe] *vt (armée, gouvernement)* to reconstitute; *(société, parti)* to revive; *(bâtiment abîmé, quartier)* to restore; *(d'un archéologue) (vase, crâne)* to piece *or* put back together; *(forces)* to build up; *(crime)* to reconstruct; *(faits)* to piece together; *(fortune)* to restore, to build up again; **deux steaks hachés reconstitués** two beef patties; **r. des stocks** to replenish stocks, to restock

reconstitution [rəkɔ̃stitysjɔ̃] *nf (d'un gouvernement)* reconstitution; *(d'une société, d'un parti)* revival; *(d'un bâtiment, d'une danse d'époque etc)* restoration; *(d'un crime, d'une bataille)* reconstruction; *Admin* **r. de carrière** employment record *or* history; **r. historique** *(spectacle)* historical reconstruction; **la r. du squelette/vase sera bientôt complète** the task of putting *or* piecing the skeleton/vase back together will soon be completed

reconstruction [rəkɔ̃stryksjɔ̃] *nf (d'une ville, Fig d'une parti)* reconstruction, rebuilding

reconstruire [rəkɔ̃strɥir] *vt (conj like* **construire***) (édifice, structure)* to reconstruct, to rebuild; **r. le monde** to change the world, *F* to put the world to rights; **r. sa vie** to put one's life back together, to rebuild one's life; **essayons de r. notre bonheur passé** let's try to be happy again the way we used to be

reconventionnel, -elle [rəkɔ̃vɑ̃sjɔnɛl] *adj Jur* **demande reconventionnelle** counterclaim

reconversion [rəkɔ̃vɛrsjɔ̃] *nf* **(a)** *(d'une usine)* conversion; **r. économique** economic restructuring; **r. industrielle** industrial redeployment **(b)** *(du personnel)* retraining

reconvertir [rəkɔ̃vɛrtir] **1** *vt* **(a)** *(usine)* to convert **(b)** *(personnel)* to retrain **2 se reconvertir** *vpr (se recycler)* to retrain; **se r. dans** *(industrie)* to move into, to diversify into; **se r. dans la publicité** *(d'une personne)* to start a new career in advertising; **ils se sont reconvertis dans le bâtiment** *(d'une entreprise)* they changed over *or* converted to construction work

recopier [rəkɔpje] *vt (conj like* **copier***)* **(a)** *(en double) (document, information etc)* to recopy, to take another copy of; *Ordinat* to recopy; *Ordinat* **r. à l'identique** to replicate **(b)** *(au propre) (brouillon, devoir, manuscrit)* to copy out, to make a fair *or* clean copy of

record [rəkɔr] **1** *nm Sp etc* record; **établir un r.** to set a record; **détenir le r.** to hold the record, to be the record holder; **battre le r.** to break *or* beat the record; **une performance qui bat tous les records** a record-breaking performance; *Fig* **il bat tous les records d'impolitesse, son impolitesse bat tous les records** he takes some beating when it comes to rudeness **2** *adj inv (chiffre, vitesse etc)* record; **dans** *ou* **en un temps r.** in record time; **attirer une affluence r.** to draw record crowds

recorder [rəkɔrde] *vt (raquette)* to restring

recordman [rəkɔr(d)man], *pl* **recordmen** [rəkɔr(d)mɛn] *nm* (men's) record holder

recordwoman [rəkɔr(d)wuman], *pl* **recordwomen** [rəkɔr(d)wumɛn] *nf* (women's) record holder
recors [rəkɔr] *nm Jur Arch F* bailiff's man; **les r. de la justice** the minions of the law
recouche [rəkuʃ] *nf* (*dans un hôtel*) stay(-over); **liste des clients en r.** stays list
recoucher [rəkuʃe] **1** *vt* **(a)** (*au lit*) **r. qn** to put sb to bed again **(b)** (*bouteille*) to lay down again **2 se recoucher** *vpr* to go back to bed **3** *vi F* **r. avec qn** to sleep with *or* have sex with sb again
recoudre [rəkudr] *vt* (*conj like* **coudre**) to sew again; (*bouton*) to sew on again, to sew back on; (*déchirure, blessure*) to sew *or* stitch up; *F* **il a fallu me r.** they had to stitch me up
recoupement [rəkupmɑ̃] *nm* (*de renseignements*) crosschecking; **faire un** *ou* **le r.** to crosscheck, to do a crosscheck; **je l'ai compris par r.** I found out by crosschecking *or* by doing a crosscheck
recouper [rəkupe] **1** *vt* **(a)** (*couper à nouveau*) (*vêtement*) to recut; **je vous recoupe une tranche de gâteau?** shall I cut you another slice *or* piece of cake? **(b)** (*vins etc*) to (re)blend **(c)** (*faire coïncider*) to confirm, to support; **r. des témoignages** to crosscheck testimony **(d)** *Cartes* to reshuffle **2 se recouper** *vpr* (*de cercles*) to intersect again; *Fig* (*de témoignages, de résultats*) to tally, to agree
recourbé [rəkurbe] *adj* bent, curved; (*bec*) curved, hooked; **nez r.** hook nose
recourber [rəkurbe] **1** *vt* to bend **2 se recourber** *vpr* to bend, to curve
recourir [rəkurir] (*conj like* **courir**) **1** *vi* **(a)** (*courir de nouveau*) to run again; **r. jusque chez soi** to run back home; *Sp* **elle n'a pas recouru depuis les Jeux Olympiques** she hasn't run since the Olympic Games **(b)** (*employer*) **r. à (l'aide de) qn** to appeal to sb for help, to turn to sb; **r. à qch** to use *or Fml* have recourse to sth; **r. à la violence** to resort to violence; **r. à la justice** to take legal proceedings **(c)** *Jur* **r. en cassation** to appeal **2** *vt Sp* to rerun, to run again; **je recourrai le marathon l'an prochain** I'll be running in the marathon again next year
recours [rəkur] *nm* **(a)** recourse, resort; **c'est son seul r.** it's his only option *or* recourse; **en dernier r.** as a last resort; **c'est sans r.** there's nothing else for it, there's no other option; **avoir r. à qn** to go *or* turn to sb; **avoir r. à un spécialiste/un avocat** to consult *or* see *or* go to a specialist/a lawyer; **avoir r. à** (*la violence*) to resort to; (*une agence immobilière*) to go to, to use
(b) *Jur* **r. en cassation** appeal; **r. en grâce** petition for reprieve; **s'assurer contre le r. des tiers** to insure against a third party claim; **r. contentieux** litigation, legal recourse; **r. contre l'endosseur** recourse against the endorser; *Can* **r. collectif** class action
recouvrable [rəkuvrabl] *adj* (*dette, facture*) recoverable, collectable; (*impôt*) collectable, collectible
recouvrement[1] [rəkuvrəmɑ̃] *nm* **(a)** (*des dettes, d'une facture*) recovery, collection; (*de l'impôt*) collection; **r. de créances** debt collection; **r. d'impôts** tax collection; **r. du coût total** full cost recovery **(b)** *Vieilli* (*de la santé, des forces etc*) recovery
recouvrement[2] *nm* **(a)** (*action de recouvrir*) re-covering; (*pour la première fois*) covering; **tôle de r.** covering plate **(b)** (*fait de chevaucher*) (over)lapping; (*surface recouverte*) overlap; **à r.** lapped, lap-jointed; **en r.** overlapping; **planches à r.** weatherboarding **(c)** *Tech* (*ce qui couvre*) cover; *Ordinat* overlay
recouvrer [rəkuvre] *vt* **(a)** (*ses biens, son argent*) to recover, to retrieve, to get back; (*santé, vue*) to recover, to get back; (*forces, liberté*) to regain, to get back; (*courage, enthousiasme*) to get back **(b)** (*percevoir*) (*dettes, impôts*) to recover, to collect; **créances à r.** outstanding debts
recouvrir [rəkuvrir] (*conj like* **couvrir**) **1** *vt* **(a)** (*couvrir de nouveau*) (*cahier, toit*) to re-cover; (*enfant*) to cover up again **(b)** (*couvrir complètement*) to cover (**de** in, with) **(c)** (*tapisser*) to cover (**de** with); **fauteuil recouvert de velours** armchair covered in velvet **(d)** (*masquer*) (*défauts, Fig angoisse, égoïsme*) to cover up, to hide **(e)** (*englober*) to cover **(f)** *Tech* (*ardoises etc*) to (over)lap **2 se recouvrir** *vpr* (*du ciel*) to cloud over (again); **le champ s'est recouvert d'eau** the field was covered with *or* in water
recracher [rəkraʃe] **1** *vt* (*bonbon, vin etc*) to spit out; **on lui a fait r. la pièce qu'il avait avalée** they made him bring up the coin he had swallowed **2** *vi* to spit again
récré [rekre] *nf Scol F* break, *Am* recess; (*pour les plus jeunes*) playtime; **pendant la r., à la r.** during *or* at break/playtime
récréatif, -ive [rekreatif, -iv] *adj* (*activité*) entertaining, amusing; **lecture récréative** light reading; **séance récréative** (*à la maternelle*) playtime
récréation [rekreasjɔ̃] *nf* **(a)** (*détente*) recreation, amusement, relaxation; **le tricot/la télé, c'est ma r.** knitting/watching TV is how I relax, I relax by knitting/watching TV **(b)** *Scol* recreation, break, *Am* recess; (*pour les plus jeunes*) playtime; **cour de r.** playground; **pendant la r., à la r.** during *or* at break/playtime
recréer [rəkree] *vt* (*conditions, climat, œuvre etc*) to re-create
recrépir [rəkrepir] *vt* (*mur*) to renew the roughcast of
recrépissage [rəkrepisaʒ] *nm* renewal of the roughcast
recreuser [rəkrøze] *vt* (*trou*) to dig again; *Fig* (*question etc*) to dig deeper *or* go deeper into
récrier (se) [sərekrije] *vpr* (*conj like* **crier**) (*de mécontents*) to protest, to complain (**contre** about); (*de la meute*) to be in full cry
récriminateur, -trice [rekriminatœr, -tris] *adj* recriminatory
récrimination [rekriminasjɔ̃] *nf* recrimination
récriminer [rekrimine] *vi* to make recriminations; **r. contre qn/qch** to make representations about sb/sth
récrire [rekrir] (*conj like* **écrire**) = **réécrire**
récriture [rekrityr] *nf* rewriting
recroquevillé [rəkrɔkvije] *adj* **(a) r. dans un fauteuil** curled up in an armchair **(b)** (*feuille, papier etc*) shrivelled, curled up
recroqueviller (se) [sərəkrɔkvije] *vpr* **(a)** (*d'une personne*) to curl up **(b)** (*d'une feuille*) to shrivel (up), to curl up
recru [rəkry] *adj Litt* **r.** (**de fatigue**) tired out, worn out; *Arch* **être r. d'amour** to be replete with love
recrudescence [rəkrydesɑ̃s] *nf* (*du feu, d'une épidémie*) renewed *or* fresh outbreak; (*de la délinquance*) upsurge; **la r. de la violence/des bombardements** the renewed violence/bombing
recrudescent [rəkrydesɑ̃] *adj Litt* fast-growing
recrue [rəkry] *nf* (*dans un parti, dans une équipe*), *Mil* recruit; *Can Sp* rookie; **le parti fait de nouvelles recrues** the party is gaining new recruits; **jeune r.** raw recruit
recrutement [rəkrytmɑ̃] *nm* (*de soldats, de personnel etc*) recruiting, recruitment; **nous sommes en plein r.** we are recruiting (staff) at the moment, we are taking on staff at the moment; *Pol* **campagne de r.** recruitment *or* membership drive; **agence de r.** recruiting *or* recruitment agency
recruter [rəkryte] **1** *vt* (*soldats, employés*) to recruit; (*supporters*) to enlist, to recruit (**dans** from); **nous recrutons un secrétaire** we are looking for a secretary, we have a vacancy for a secretary; **notre directeur a été recruté par un chasseur de têtes** our director was headhunted **2 se recruter** *vpr* (*d'employés*) to be recruited (**parmi** from among); (*de supporters*) to be enlisted, to be recruited **3** *vi* to recruit; **r. par voie de concours** to recruit by competition
recruteur [rəkrytœr] *adj* (*officier*) recruiting
recta [rɛkta] *adv Vieilli F* **payer r.** to pay on the nail; **arriver r.** to arrive punctually *or* on the dot
rectal, -ale, -aux, -ales [rɛktal, -o] *adj Anat* (*toucher, température*) rectal; **prendre la température de qn par voie rectale** to take sb's temperature using a rectal thermometer
rectangle [rɛktɑ̃gl] **1** *adj* right-angled **2** *nm* rectangle; *TV* **r. blanc** 'for adults only' sign; *Ordinat* **r. de sélection** selection box
rectangulaire [rɛktɑ̃gylɛr] *adj* rectangular; *Math* (*coordonnées*) right-angled
recteur, -trice [rɛktœr, -tris] **1** *nm Rel* rector; *Scol* chief education officer **2** *adj Orn* **penne rectrice** tail feather **3** *nf Orn* **rectrice** tail feather
rectificateur [rɛktifikatœr] *nm Ch* rectifier; *Él* (current) rectifier
rectificatif, -ive [rɛktifikatif, -iv] **1** *adj* (*lettre*) of amendment; (*texte, facture*) amended **2** *nm* correction
rectification [rɛktifikasjɔ̃] *nf* **(a)** (*d'un document, texte*) amendment, correction; (*d'un calcul*) correction, adjustment; (*d'une erreur*) rectification, correction; (*d'un compte, instrument*) adjustment; (*d'une courbe, frontière*) adjustment, rectification; (*d'un alignement*) straightening; **je voudrais faire** *ou* **apporter une r.** I'd like to make a correction **(b)** *Ch* (*de l'alcool, du pétrole*) rectifying, redistilling **(c)** *Él* (*du courant*) rectification
rectifier [rɛktifje] *vt* **(a)** (*document, texte*) to amend, to correct; (*calcul*) to correct, to adjust; (*erreur*) to rectify, to correct, to put right; (*prix, instrument*) to adjust; (*compte*) to amend, to adjust; (*frontière, courbe*) to rectify, to adjust; (*alignement*) to straighten; *Mil* **r. l'alignement** to dress the ranks; **r. le tir** *Mil* to adjust the range; *Fig* to take a slightly different tack; **il est banquier, rectifia-t-elle** he's a banker, she corrected him/me/*etc* **(b)** *Ch* (*alcool, pétrole*) to rectify, to redistil **(c)** *Él* (*courant*) to rectify **(d)** *Arg* (*tuer*) **r. qn** to bump sb off; **se faire r.** to get bumped off
rectiligne [rɛktiliɲ] *adj* (*mouvement*) in a straight line; (*figure*) rectilinear; (*avenue*) straight

rectilinéaire [rɛktilineɛr] *adj Phot* (*objectif*) rectilinear

rectitude [rɛktityd] *nf* **(a)** (*d'une ligne*) straightness **(b)** *Fig* (*honnêteté*) rectitude, uprightness, integrity; (*d'un jugement, du raisonnement*) correctness, soundness; **agir avec r.** to behave correctly *or* with integrity

recto [rɛkto] *nm* (*d'effet*) face; (*d'une feuille de papier*) front, face, *Spéc* recto; **cinq feuilles r. verso** five sheets written on both sides; **voir au r.** see over; *Typ* **impression r-verso** double-sided printing

rectorat [rɛktɔra] *nm Admin* rectorship, rectorate

rectum [rɛktɔm] *nm Anat* rectum; **cancer du r.** rectal cancer, cancer of the rectum

reçu, -ue [rəsy] **1** *adj* (*usages*) accepted, recognized; (*opinion*) received; **idées reçues** preconceived ideas; **cela fait partie des usages reçus** it's standard *or* accepted practice **2** *nm* (*pour des marchandises, de l'argent*) receipt; **je vous fais un r.?** would you like a receipt?; **r. d'espèces** cash receipt **3** *n* (*à un examen*) successful candidate; **il n'y a que dix reçus** only ten people passed

recueil [rəkœj] *nm* (*de poèmes, chansons, recettes etc*) collection, compilation; (*de lois*) compendium, body; **r. de morceaux choisis** selection, anthology; **r. des données** data collection

recueillement [rəkœjmɑ̃] *nm* meditation, contemplation; (*gravité*) gravity; **avec r.** contemplatively; **pensons avec r. à cet homme à qui nous devons tant de choses** let us meditate a little about this man to whom we owe so much

recueilli [rəkœji] *adj* meditative, contemplative; (*grave*) grave, sober

recueillir [rəkœjir] (*conj like* **cueillir**) **1** *vt* **(a)** (*récolter*) (*argent, fonds*) to collect; (*anecdotes, renseignements, miel etc*) to collect, to gather; (*pour conserver*) to collect, to make a collection of; (*eau de pluie*) to collect, to catch; (*sous-produits*) to recover; (*votes*) to win, to collect; (*louanges*) to win, to attract; (*déposition*) to take; *Journ* **r. le témoignage des passants** to listen to what the passers-by have to say; *Journ* **propos recueillis par Daniel Renault** (story by) Daniel Renault; **r. le fruit de ses travaux** to reap the fruit of one's labours; **r. un héritage** to inherit; **r. des données** to collect data

(b) (*recevoir*) **r. qn** to take sb in, to give sb a home

2 se recueillir *vpr* to meditate; **se r. sur la tombe d'un ami** to meditate beside a friend's grave; **se r. pour prier** to gather one's thoughts before praying

recuire [rəkɥir] *vt* (*conj like* **cuire**) **(a)** *Culin* **il faut r. ce steak** this steak needs to be cooked longer **(b)** (*acier*) to anneal, to temper; (*verre*) to anneal

recuisson [rəkɥisɔ̃] *nf* (*de l'acier*) annealing, tempering; (*du verre*) annealing

recuit [rəkɥi] *nm* (*de l'acier*) annealing, tempering; (*du verre*) annealing

recul [rəkyl] *nm* **(a)** (*action*) (*d'un glacier, d'une armée*) retreat; (*d'un cheval*) backing; (*d'un levier de commande*) backward movement, return; (*d'un canon*) recoil; (*d'un fusil*) recoil, kick; (*baisse*) (*des valeurs, des exportations*) drop (**de** in); **il eut un brusque mouvement de r.** he recoiled, he started back; **le r. de la mortalité** the downturn *or* decline in the death-rate; *Aut* **phare de r.** reversing light

(b) (*distance*) **on n'a pas assez de r. dans cette galerie** there's not enough room in this gallery to get a decent look at the pictures; **il faut un certain r. pour juger le tableau** you need to stand back a bit to judge the painting; **manquer de r.** to be too close for a proper view; *Fig* **je manque de r. pour juger** I'm too closely involved *or* too close to be able to judge; *Fig* **considérer la situation avec r.** to consider the situation with detachment; *Fig* **avec le r. (du temps), la situation ne semble pas si désespérée** in retrospect *or* with hindsight *or* looking back (on it), the situation doesn't seem so desperate; *Fig* **tu devrais prendre du r.** you ought to stand back a bit from things; *Fig* **es-tu sûr d'avoir assez de r. pour juger?** are you sure you're objective enough to judge?

reculade [rəkylad] *nf* (*d'une armée*) retreat; *Fig Péj* climbdown

reculé [rəkyle] *adj* (*endroit*) remote, distant; (*époque*) remote

reculer [rəkyle] **1** *vi* **(a)** (*aller en arrière*) (*d'une personne*) to move back, to step back, to draw back; (*d'un glacier, des eaux*) to recede; *Mil* to fall back, to retreat; (*d'une épidémie*) to lose ground; (*du taux de mortalité, natalité, chômage etc*) to decline; (*du cours de Bourse*) to drop; (*d'un fusil, canon*) to recoil; (*d'un automobiliste, d'une voiture*) to reverse; *Ordinat* to backspace; **elle recula de dégoût** she recoiled *or* drew back in disgust; **reculez ou je tire!** back off *or* get back or I'll shoot!; **faire r. un cheval** to back a horse; **la police a fait r. la foule** the police moved *or* pushed the crowd back; *Fig* **faire r. la maladie** to get the disease under control; **faire r. la pauvreté** to reduce (the level of) poverty; *Fig F* **r. pour mieux sauter** to put off the evil day

(b) *Fig* (*renoncer*) to give in; **r. devant des menaces** to give way in the face of threats; **r. devant une obligation** to shirk an obligation; **il ne recule devant rien** nothing daunts him; **elle ne recule devant rien pour le satisfaire** she'll do anything to satisfy him; **comme d'habitude, elle recule devant lui** as usual, she gave in *or* gave way to him; **il est trop tard pour r.** it's too late to draw back *or* pull out; **cela en a fait r. plus d'un** that's put off *or* daunted more than one person; **r. à l'idée de faire qch** to recoil at the idea of doing sth

2 *vt* **(a)** (*chaise*) to move back; (*cheval*) to back; (*voiture*) to back (up), to reverse; *Fig* **r. les frontières de la science** to push *or* roll back the frontiers of science

(b) (*remettre*) (*paiement, décision*) to postpone, to defer, to put off; **r. le moment de décider** to put off (making) a decision

3 se reculer *vpr* to stand *or* step *or* move *or* draw back

reculons (à) [ar(ə)kylɔ̃] *adv* **marcher** *ou* **aller à r.** to walk backwards; *Fig* **aller à r.** to go *or* move backwards; **sortir à r.** to back out; *Fig F* **aller au travail à r.** to force oneself to go to work

récupérable [rekyperabl] *adj* (*déchets*) recoverable; **ferraille r.** scrap metal; **les heures supplémentaires sont récupérables** additional time off may be taken in lieu of overtime pay; **ce garçon-là est r. /n'est pas r.** there's hope for that boy/that boy's a hopeless case

récupérateur [rekyperatœr] *nm Ind* regenerator, recuperator

récupération [rekyperasjɔ̃] *nf* **(a)** (*de dette, livre, vaisseau spatial, TVA etc*) recovery; **la r. des heures supplémentaires** time off in lieu (of overtime pay); **deux jours de r. pour les heures supplémentaires que j'ai faites** two days off to make up for the overtime I've done **(b)** *Ind* (*de déchets de fabrication*) recovery, salvage; **r. de chaleur** heat recovery **(c)** (*de sportif*) recovery **(d)** *Pol Péj* exploitation; **la r. d'une manifestation par un parti politique** the exploitation *or* hijacking of a demonstration by a political party; **c'est de la r.** it's sheer exploitation

récupérer [rekypere] (**je récupère, n. récupérons; je récupérerai**) **1** *vt* **(a)** (*objet prêté ou perdu*) (*livre etc*) to get back, to retrieve, to recover; (*bagages, TVA*) to retrieve, to reclaim; *Ordinat* (*fichier, données*) to retrieve; *Av* (*boîte noire*) to recover, to retrieve; *F* (*personne*) to collect, to pick up; **elle est passée r. ses affaires** she dropped by to pick up her things; **r. ses forces** to recover (one's strength), to regain one's strength

(b) (*recycler*) (*déchets de fabrication*) to recover, to salvage; (*vieux papiers, canettes etc*) to salvage; *Fig F* (*employé*) to find alternative employment for; (*délinquant*) to rehabilitate; **r. de la ferraille** to collect scrap; **je ne jette rien, je récupère tout** I don't throw anything away, I save everything

(c) *Pol Péj* (*personne, mouvement*) to co-opt, to hijack, to use for one's own ends; (*proposition*) to hijack, to take over; **se faire r.** to be co-opted *or* hijacked

(d) *Fin* (*pertes*) to recoup, to retrieve; *Fin* **r. ses débours** to recoup one's expenditure; *Admin* **r. des heures supplémentaires (en prenant des congés)** to take time off in lieu

2 *vi* (*après une maladie, après un choc*) to recover; **j'ai besoin de r.** (*prendre des vacances*) I need to get my breath back, I need to relax; **j'ai de plus en plus de mal à r.** (*reprendre mon souffle*) it takes me longer and longer to get my breath back

récurage [rekyraʒ] *nm* scouring

récurer [rekyre] *vt* (*casseroles, évier, baignoire etc*) to scour; **poudre/tampon à r.** scouring powder/pad

récurrence [rekyrɑ̃s] *nf* recurrence

récurrent [rekyrɑ̃] *adj Anat* (*nerf, veine*) recurrent; (*thème, son, mot*) recurrent, recurring; *Méd* (*fièvre*) recurrent; *Math* (*série*) recurrent; *Ordinat* **processus r.** recursive process

récusable [rekyzabl] *adj Jur* (*juré, témoin*) challengeable; (*témoignage*) impugnable; **son témoignage n'est pas r.** it will be impossible to challenge his testimony; **c'est une affirmation r.** that statement is open to challenge

récusation [rekyzasjɔ̃] *nf* (*d'une thèse, Jur d'un témoin*) challenging; *Jur* **r. de juré/d'arbitre** challenge of *or* exception to *or* objection to a juryman/an arbitrator; **r. de témoignage** impugnment of evidence

récuser [rekyze] **1** *vt* (*témoin, juré, arbitre etc*) to challenge, to take exception to, to object to; (*témoignage*) to impugn; (*autorité, thèse*) to challenge **2 se récuser** *vpr Jur* to decline to give an opinion, to disclaim competence

recyclable [rəsiklabl] *adj* (*papier, verre etc*) recyclable

recyclage [rəsiklaʒ] *nm* **(a)** (*de matériaux*) recycling; *Aut* **r. des gaz d'échappement** exhaust gas recirculation **(b)** *Ind* (*du personnel*) retraining

recycler [rəsikle] **1** *vt* **(a)** (*papier, verre etc*) to recycle **(b)** *Ind* (*personnel*) to retrain **2 se recycler** *vpr Ind* to retrain; **se r. en comptabilité** to retrain as an accountant

rédacteur, -trice [redaktœr, -tris] *n* **(a)** (*d'un acte, communiqué*) writer, drafter; (*d'un dictionnaire*) editor, compiler

(b) *Journ* editor; **r. en chef** editor in chief, editorial director; **r. en chef actualités** news editor; **r. en chef adjoint** deputy editor; **r. en chef de nuit** night editor; **r. en chef des affaires financières** financial editor, *Br* City editor; **r. en chef sportif** sports editor; **r. en chef technique** production editor; **r. aux actualités** news editor; **r. d'actualités** news writer; **r. artistique** art editor; **r. juridique** legally responsible editor; **r. politique** political editor; **r. sportif** sports editor; **r. permanent** staff writer; **r. pigiste** freelance writer; **r. publicitaire** copy writer

rédaction [redaksjɔ̃] *nf* **(a)** (*d'un acte, communiqué*) drafting, drawing up, writing; (*d'un article de dictionnaire*) compiling, writing; (*révision*) editing; **la r. de cet article a demandé l'intervention de plusieurs rédacteurs** it took several editors to write the article; **r. de questionnaire** questionnaire design **(b)** *Journ* editing; (*poste*) editorship; (*personnel*) editorial staff; (*département*) editorial department; **(salle de) r.** editorial office; **note de la r.** editor's note; **secrétaire de r.** subeditor **(c)** *Scol* essay, composition

rédactionnel, -elle [redaksjɔnɛl] *adj* (*décision, politique etc*) editorial; **publicité rédactionnelle** advertorial

reddition [rɛdisjɔ̃] *nf* **(a)** (*d'une ville, armée*) surrender; **r. sans conditions** unconditional surrender **(b)** *Fin* (*d'un compte*) rendering; **r. de comptes** presentation of accounts for audit, reporting

redécoupage [rədekupaʒ] *nm* **r. électoral** redrawing of the electoral boundaries; **procéder à** *ou* **effectuer un r. électoral** to redraw the electoral boundaries

redécouvrir [rədekuvrir] *vt* (*conj like* **couvrir**) **(a)** (*auteur, œuvre*) to rediscover **(b)** (*enfant*) to take the covers off

redéfinir [rədefinir] *vt Ordinat* (*touche*) to redefine

redéfinissable [rədefinisabl] *adj Ordinat* redefinable

redemander [rəd(ə)mɑ̃de] **1** *vt* **(a)** (*en reposant une question*) to ask again; **r. pourquoi/quand/qui** to ask why/when/who again; **je lui ai redemandé de fermer la porte** I asked him again to close the door; **il a dû oublier, il faut le lui r.** he must have forgotten, we'll have to ask him again; **j'ai redemandé qu'il nous écrive un article** I asked again if he would write an article for us; **r. de l'aide à qn** to ask sb again for help

(b) (*pour en avoir plus*) **r. de la soupe/des enveloppes** to ask for more soup/envelopes; **r. un litre de vin** to ask for another litre of wine; **je lui ai redemandé un article,** *F* **j'ai redemandé qu'il écrive un article** I asked him for another article, I asked him to write another article; *Fig F* **des traducteurs comme ça, on en redemande!** translators like that are much in demand; **tout le monde en redemande** everybody is clamouring *or* keeps asking for more, they can't get enough of it; *Iron* **elle en redemande** she's still asking for it, she hasn't had enough

(c) (*pour récupérer*) **r. qch** to ask for sth back (again); **redemande-le-moi dès que tu en as besoin** ask for it back (again) when you need it, ask me for it when you need it

2 *vi* to ask again

redémarrage [rədemaraʒ] *nm* (*de l'économie, des ventes*) recovery; **attendre le r. de l'économie/des ventes** to wait for the economy/sales to pick up *or* take off again *or* recover

redémarrer [rədemare] *vi* (*d'une voiture*) to start again; (*de l'économie, des ventes*) to recover, to pick up, to take off again; *Ordinat* to reboot; **faire r. une voiture** to start a car again; **faire r. l'économie** to get the economy started again

rédempteur, -trice [redɑ̃ptœr, -tris] **1** *adj* redeeming **2** *n* redeemer

rédemption [redɑ̃psjɔ̃] *nf* redemption

redescendre [rədesɑ̃dr, -dɛ-] (*conj like* **descendre**) **1** *vi* (*du point de vue de qn qui est en haut*) to go down again, to go back down; (*du point de vue de qn qui est en bas*) to come down again, to come back down; (*d'un alpiniste*) to climb back down; *Naut* (*du vent*) to back; **quand tu redescendras, veux-tu ...** (*nous sommes au même étage*) when you go down again *or* go back down, will you ...; (*je suis à l'étage inférieur*) when you come down again *or* come back down, will you ...; **je suis redescendu en télécabine** (*je viens de le faire*) I came back down by cable car; (*en racontant plus tard*) I went *or* came back down by cable car; **vous pouvez r. par ce sentier-là** you can get back down by that path over there; **r. de voiture** to get out of the car (again)

2 *vt* **(a)** (*apporter*) (*du point de vue de qn qui est en haut*) to take down again, to take back down; (*du point de vue de qn qui est en bas*) to bring down again, to bring back down; **veux-tu r. la valise?** (*nous sommes au même étage*) will you take the suitcase back down(stairs)?; (*je suis à l'étage inférieur*) will you bring the suitcase back down(stairs)?; **r. des affaires du grenier** to get things back down from the attic

(b) (*descendre à nouveau*) (*escalier, rivière*) (*du point de vue de qn qui est en haut*) to go down again, to go back down; (*du point de vue de qn qui est en bas*) to come down again, to come back down

redevable [rəd(ə)vabl] **1** *adj* **être r. de qch à qn** to be indebted to sb for sth; **je vous suis r. de cent francs** I still owe you a hundred francs; **être r. de l'impôt** to be liable to tax **2** *n* person liable for tax

redevance [rəd(ə)vɑ̃s] *nf TV* licence fee; (*de téléphone*) rental fee; **r. pétrolière** oil royalty; **redevances d'auteur** author's royalties

redevenir [rədəv(ə)nir] *vi* (*conj like* **devenir**) **r. jeune** to become *or* grow young again; **j'ai l'impression d'être redevenu moi-même** I feel like my old self again; **r. silencieux** to fall silent again; **la situation/Marie est redevenue normale** the situation is back to normal/Marie is her old self again; **le temps est redevenu maussade** the weather's turned gloomy again

redevoir [rəd(ə)vwar] *vt* (*conj like* **devoir**) (*somme d'argent*) to owe a balance of; *F* **il me redoit dix francs** he still owes me ten francs

rédhibition [redibisjɔ̃] *nf Com* cancellation of sale due to a material defect

rédhibitoire [redibitwar] *adj* **(a) vice r.** *Com* material defect; *Jur* redhibitory defect **(b) dans ce métier, être petit est r.** being small is a bar to entering the profession; **des conditions de travail rédhibitoires** appalling working conditions; **être d'un égoïsme r.** to be appallingly selfish

rediffuser [rədifyze] *vt Rad* (*émission*) to repeat, to broadcast again; *TV* (*émission*) to repeat, to show again, to rerun; (*film*) to show again, to rerun

rediffusion [rədifyzjɔ̃] *nf Rad* (*d'une émission*) repeat; *TV, Cin* repeat, rerun

rédiger [rediʒe] *vt* **(je rédigeai(s); n. rédigeons) (a)** (*contrat, lettre etc*) to draw up, to draft, to write; (*article*) to write; *Méd* (*ordonnance*) to write out; (*bon de commande*) to make out; **savoir r.** to be a good writer, to write well; **être bien/mal rédigé** to be well/badly written **(b)** *Journ* (*périodique*) to edit

redimensionnement [rədimɑ̃sjɔnmɑ̃] *nm Ordinat* resizing

redimensionner [rədimɑ̃sjɔne] *vt Ordinat* (*fenêtre*) to resize

redingote [rədɛ̃gɔt] *nf* (*pour femmes*) fitted coat; *Vieilli* (*pour hommes*) redingote

redire [rədir] *vt* (*conj like* **dire**) **(a)** to say again, to repeat; **tu redis toujours la même chose** you say the same thing over and over again, you constantly repeat yourself; **pourrais-tu lui r. que ...?** could you tell him again that ...?; **je ne le redirai jamais assez** I can never say it often enough; **elle te l'a dit et redit cent fois!** she's told you time and time again!; **elle ne se l'est pas fait r. deux fois** she didn't need asking twice, she didn't need any persuading; **j'espère qu'elle n'ira pas lui r. ce que je lui ai confié** I hope she won't go and tell him *or* repeat to him what I said to her in confidence

(b) trouver à r. to complain; **trouver à r. à qch** to find fault with *or* to pick holes in sth; *F* **il n'y a rien à r. à cela** there's nothing wrong with that

redirection [rədirɛksjɔ̃] *nf Télécom* **r. d'appel** call forwarding, call redirection

rediriger [rədiriʒe] *vt Télécom* to redirect

rediscuter [rədiskyte] *vt* to have further discussions on, to discuss again

redistribuer [rədistribɥe] *vt* to redistribute, to re-allocate; *Cartes* to redeal

redistribution [rədistribysjɔ̃] *nf* redistribution, re-allocation; (*de personnel*) redeployment

redite [rədit] *nf* (useless) repetition

redondance [rədɔ̃dɑ̃s] *nf* (*de style, mot*), *Ordinat* redundancy; **de nombreuses redondances** a lot of redundancy

redondant [rədɔ̃dɑ̃] *adj* (*mot, style, information*), *Ordinat* redundant

redonner [rədɔne] **1** *vt* **(a)** (*donner de nouveau*) to give again; *Cartes* to redeal; *Th* **on redonne Hamlet** Hamlet is on again; **r. un coup d'œil/un coup de pied à qn** to glance at/kick sb again

(b) (*donner davantage de*) to give more of; **tu veux bien m'en r. un peu plus?** will you give me *or* can I have a bit more?

(c) (*pour rendre*) to give back, to return; **r. de l'appétit à qn** to restore sb's appetite, to give sb back his/her appetite; **cela m'a redonné du courage** that put new heart into me *or* restored my courage; **ça m'a redonné envie de voyager**

that made me want to travel again; **ce médicament va vous r. des forces** the medicine will give you back your strength *or* will get your strength back; **ces vacances lui ont redonné bonne mine** the holiday put the colour back in his cheeks

2 *vi Litt* **r. dans des excès** to fall back into excess; **r. dans l'exagération** to exaggerate again

redorer [rədɔre] *vt* to regild; *Fig* **r. son blason** (*d'un noble*) (*en se mariant*) to restore the family fortunes by marrying money; (*d'une personne*) (*par un succès etc*) to restore one's reputation

redormir [rədɔrmir] *vi* (*conj like* **dormir**) to go to sleep again, to go back to sleep; **je n'ai pas pu r.** I couldn't get back to sleep; **je suis allée r. quelques heures** I went to get a few more hours' sleep

redoublant, -ante [rədublɑ̃, -ɑ̃t] *n Scol* pupil who remains a second year in the same class

redoublé [rəduble] *adj Littér* (*rime*) double; **frapper** *ou* **battre qn à coups redoublés** to thrash sb soundly; **frapper à une porte à coups redoublés** to hammer at a door

redoublement [rədubləmɑ̃] *nm* **(a)** (*de joie, chagrin, violence, douleur etc*) increase; (*d'une tempête*) worsening; **avec un r. de zèle** with renewed *or* redoubled zeal **(b)** *Ling* (*d'une syllabe, lettre*) reduplication **(c)** *Scol* repeating a year *or* class; **dans son cas, le r. n'est pas justifié** there's no need for him to repeat the year

redoubler [rəduble] **1** *vt* **(a)** (*sentiment d'injustice, chagrin*) to add to; (*dose*) to double again, to redouble; *F* (*doubler*) to double; (*film*) to re-voice; **r. ses efforts** to redouble one's efforts; *Scol* **r. une classe** to repeat a year *or* class

(b) (*vêtement*) to reline

2 *vi* **(a)** *Scol* to repeat a year *or Am* class

(b) (*augmenter*) (*du chagrin, froid*) to intensify, to increase; **la pluie/le vent redoubla de violence** the rain came down/the wind blew harder than ever, the rain came down/the wind blew twice as hard as before; **r. d'efforts** to redouble one's efforts; **r. de prudence/d'attention/de douceur** to be twice as cautious/attentive/gentle

redoutable [rədutabl] *adj* (*personne, adversaire*) formidable; (*ennemi*) formidable, dangerous, *Fml* redoubtable; (*hiver*) fierce; (*odeur*) dreadful; **il fait un froid r.** it's dreadfully cold

redoute [rədut] *nf* (*fortification*) redoubt

redouter [rədute] *vt* (*chose, événement*) to dread, to fear; (*personne*) to be in awe of; **je redoute la journée de lundi** I'm dreading Monday; **ce jour si redouté se passa sans incident notable** the dreaded day passed off without incident; **un prof redouté de tous les élèves** a much-dreaded teacher; **r. d'apprendre qch** to dread hearing sth; **je redoute surtout de devenir aveugle** the thing *or* what I fear *or* dread most is going blind; **elle redoute que tu ne lui en parles** she's terrified that you'll mention it to her

redoux [rədu] *nm Météo* milder weather; **on attend le r.** we're expecting a return to milder weather

redresse [rədrɛs] *nf très F* **c'est un type à la r.** he's no soft touch

redressement [rədrɛsmɑ̃] *nm* **(a)** (*d'un objet renversé*) righting, setting up again; (*d'un bateau, avion*) righting; (*de la tête*) raising; (*des épaules*) straightening **(b)** (*rectification*) (*d'un compte, d'une erreur*) rectification, correction; *Compta* adjustment; (*d'un tort*) righting; *Tech* (*d'une surface*) tru(e)ing; *Écon* **plan de r.** recovery plan; *Hist* **maison de r.** ≈ approved school, reformatory **(c)** *Él* (*du courant alternatif*) rectification; **valve de r.** rectifying valve

▶ **redressement: r. économique** economic recovery; **plan de r. économique** recovery plan; *Admin* **r. fiscal** tax adjustment, demand for tax arrears

redresser [rədrese] **1** *vt* **(a)** (*objet renversé*) to right, to set upright again; (*bateau*) to right; (*avion*) to right, to straighten up, to lift the nose of

(b) (*rectifier*) (*grief*) to redress, to right; (*erreur, situation*) to rectify, to correct; (*compte*) to adjust; (*bois courbé, tôle cabossée*) to straighten (out); (*surface*) to true; **r. les épaules** to straighten one's shoulders; **r. la tête** to hold up one's head; (*la lever*) to raise *or* lift one's head, to look up; *Fig* **il peut r. la tête maintenant** he can hold his head up now, he can look people in the eye now; **tu n'es pas là pour r. les torts** you're not there to right wrongs; **r. l'équilibre des forces** to redress the balance of power; **pour r. l'économie** in order to bring about an economic recovery; **r. une entreprise** to put a company back on its feet

(c) *Él* (*courant*) to rectify

2 se redresser *vpr* **(a)** (*d'une personne*) to straighten up, to straighten one's back; (*avec fierté*) to draw oneself up, to hold one's head up; **se r. sur son séant** to sit up straight (again)

(b) (*de l'économie, d'un pays, des ventes etc*) to recover

redresseur, -euse [rədrɛsœr, -øz] **1** *n* **r. de torts** righter of wrongs; (*chevalier*), *Hum* knight errant **2** *nm Él* (*du courant*) rectifier **3** *adj Él* (*appareil*) rectifying

redû [rədy] *nm* balance due

réducteur, -trice [redyktœr, -tris] **1** *adj Péj* (*explication, point de vue etc*) reductive, simplistic; *Ch* **agent r.** reducing agent; *MecE* **ensemble r.** reduction gear assembly **2** *nm Ch* reducing agent; *MecE* reduction gear *or* unit; *Th* **r. d'éclairage** dimmer; **r. de têtes** head shrinker

réductible [redyktibl] *adj Méd* (*fracture*) which can be set, *Spéc* reducible; (*dislocation*) reducible; *Math* (*fraction*) reducible

réduction [redyksjɔ̃] *nf* **(a)** (*de prix, salaires, personnel*) reduction, cut (**de** in); (*de dépenses, de la production*) reduction, cutting back (**de** in); (*d'un budget*) cutting back (**de** of); (*de la pression*) reduction, lowering (**de** of); (*d'une pénalité*) reduction (**de** of); *Chir* (*d'une fraction*) reduction; (*de gravure*) small reproduction; *Fin* (*d'un capital*) writing down; *Méd* (*d'une fracture*) setting; (*d'une dislocation*) reduction; *Él* (*du voltage*) stepping down; **réductions de salaires/de personnel** reductions *or* cutbacks in wages/staff, wage/staff cuts; **on nous a demandé d'accepter une r. de salaire** we were asked to take a cut in (our) wages; **r. de 60 F** 60 francs off; **faire une r. de 15%** to give 15% off; **r. de capital** decrease in capital; **r. des impôts** tax cut; **carte de r.** discount card; **cette carte donne droit à une r.** this card entitles the holder to a reduction; **une r. de 15% sur la literie** a 15% reduction on bedding; **faire une r. à qn** to give sb a reduction; **r. des bruits** noise reduction; *Mus* **r. pour piano** (*d'un opéra etc*) short score; **un bateau en r.** a scale model of a ship

(b) (*d'une ville*) capture

réduire [redɥir] (*prp* **réduisant**; *pp* **réduit**; *pr ind* **je réduis, il réduit, n. réduisons**; *impf* **je réduisais**; *p hist* **je réduisis**; *fu* **je réduirai**) **1** *vt* (*montant, vitesse, photographie, dessin, Math fractions, Culin sauce*) to reduce; (*prix, taux d'intérêt*) to reduce, to lower, to bring down; (*dépenses, frais*) to reduce, to cut (down *or* back), to curtail; (*chômage, taux de mortalité, de natalité*) to reduce, to lower, to bring down; (*personnel, salaires*) to reduce, to cut (back); (*texte*) to shorten, to cut; (*pression*) to reduce, to lower, to relieve; *Fin* (*capital*) to write down; *Él* (*voltage*) to step down; *Méd* (*fracture*) to set, *Spéc* to reduce; (*dislocation*) to reduce; **r. un texte de 200 pages** to shorten a text by 200 pages; **on a nettement réduit les dépenses d'armement** arms spending has been cut right back *or* sharply reduced; **la société réduit progressivement ses opérations en Allemagne** the company is winding down its operations in Germany; *Com, Ind* **r. ses effectifs** to reduce the size of the workforce, to downsize; **r. le personnel** to cut staff, to make staff cutbacks; **billet à prix réduit** cheap *or* cut-price ticket, *Br F* concession; **voyager à prix réduit** to travel at reduced rates; **réduit de moitié** half size; *Mus* **r. une partition** to arrange a score for the piano; **r. qch en cendres/poussière** to reduce sth to ashes/dust; **r. des francs en centimes/des kilogrammes en grammes** to convert *or* reduce francs to centimes/kilograms to grams; **r. qn à la misère/au silence/à la mendicité** to reduce sb to poverty/silence/begging; **r. qn au désespoir** to drive sb to despair; **nous en sommes réduits à ça!** is this what we're *or* we've been reduced to?; **j'en suis réduit à le faire moi-même** I'm reduced to doing it myself

2 se réduire *vpr* **(a) se r. à** to amount to; **leurs différences se réduisent à peu de choses** their differences don't amount to much; **à quoi se réduit tout cela?** what does it all amount to *or* boil down to?

(b) *Culin* (*d'une sauce*) to reduce; **se r. en poussière** to crumble into dust

(c) *Vieilli* (*faire des économies*) to cut down *or* back

3 *vi Culin* to reduce; **faire r. un sirop** to reduce a syrup

réduit [redɥi] *nm* (*petite pièce*) = boxroom; **elle habite une sorte de r. sale et humide** she lives in a damp and dirty hole of a place

réduplication [redyplikasjɔ̃] *nf Ling* reduplication

rééchelonnement [reeʃ(ə)lɔnmɑ̃] *nm Fin* (*de dette*) rescheduling

rééchelonner [reeʃ(ə)lɔne] *vt Fin* (*dette*) to reschedule

réécrire [reekrir] (*conj like* **écrire**) **1** *vt* (*rédiger à nouveau*) (*lettre, texte, annonce etc*) to rewrite; (*devoir etc qui contenait des fautes*) to write (out) again; **j'ai dû lui r. tout son article** I had to rewrite his entire article for him, I had to write his entire article all over again **2** *vi* **r. à qn** to write to sb again, to send sb another letter

réécriture [reekrityr] *nf* (*d'un texte, d'une annonce etc*) rewriting

réédification [reedifikasjɔ̃] *nf* rebuilding, reconstruction
réédifier [reedifje] *vt* (*conj like* **édifier**) to rebuild, to reconstruct
rééditer [reedite] *vt* (*livre*) to republish, to re-issue; *Fig F* (*exploit*) to give a repeat performance of
réédition [reedisjɔ̃] *nf* (*d'un livre etc*) re-issue; *Fig F* repeat; **c'est une r. de leur dispute de la semaine dernière** it's a repeat *or* rerun of the argument they had last week, it's last week's argument all over again
rééducatif, -ive [reedykatif, -iv] *adj* **thérapie rééducative** occupational therapy
rééducation [reedykasjɔ̃] *nf* **(a)** *Méd* (*de muscles après accident etc*) re-education; (*d'un handicapé, accidenté*) rehabilitation; **r. de la parole** speech therapy; **centre de r. (professionnelle)** rehabilitation centre; **faire de la r.** (*chez un kinésithérapeute*) to have physio(therapy) **(b)** *Psy* re-education; (*de délinquants*) rehabilitation
rééduquer [reedyke] *vt* (*handicapé, accidenté, délinquant*) to rehabilitate; *Méd* (*muscle*), *Psy* to re-educate
réel, -elle [reɛl] **1** *adj* **(a)** (*avantage, coût, monde, Math nombre*) real; (*personnage*) real(-life), actual; (*fait*) actual; *Opt* (*image*) true; **grandeur réelle** actual size; **salaire r.** real salary; **en termes réels** in real terms; **offre réelle** cash offer; **ce film nous rend la personne de Charlie Chaplin plus réelle** this film brings Charlie Chaplin to life

(b) (*before noun*) (*plaisir, sentiment de bonheur etc*) real, great; **connaître enfin un r. sentiment de bonheur** to know real *or* true happiness at last; **prendre un r. plaisir à faire qch** to take real *or* great pleasure in doing sth

2 *nm* **(a)** *Math* real number

(b) le r. reality
réélection [reelɛksjɔ̃] *nf* re-election
rééligible [reeliʒibl] *adj* re-eligible
réélire [reelir] *vt* (*conj like* **élire**) to re-elect
réellement [reɛlmɑ̃] *adv* (*drôle, déçu, incroyable etc*) really; **cela s'est r. passé** it really *or* actually happened; **des choses qui existent r.** things that really *or* actually exist
réembarquer [reɑ̃barke] **1** *vt* (*passagers*) to re-embark; (*marchandises*) to reload, to re-embark **2** *vi* to re-embark, to go back on board **3 se réembarquer** *vpr* to re-embark, to go back on board; *Fig* **se r. dans qch** to get involved in sth again
réembaucher [reɑ̃boʃe] *vt* **r. qn** to take sb on again, to rehire sb
réémetteur [reemɛtœr] *nm TV, Rad* relay transmitter
réemploi [reɑ̃plwa] *nm* (*du personnel d'une autre entreprise*) employment
réemployer [reɑ̃plwaje] *vt* (*ancien employé*) to re-employ, to employ again; (*produit*) to use again
réemprunter [reɑ̃prœ̃te] *vt* to borrow again
réencoder [reɑ̃kɔde] *vt Ordinat* to recode
réentendre [reɑ̃tɑ̃dr] *vt* (*disque, cassette etc*) to listen to *or* hear again
réentraînement [reɑ̃trɛnmɑ̃] *nm* retraining
rééquilibrage [reekilibraʒ] *nm* (*de pneus*) balancing; **le r. des forces politiques** the restoration of the balance of power; *Pol* **tout faire pour le r. de la gauche** to do everything to restore the balance within the parties of the left
rééquilibrer [reekilibre] *vt* (*pneus*) to balance; **r. les forces politiques** to restore the balance of power
réescompte [reɛskɔ̃t] *nm Fin* rediscount
réescompter [reɛskɔ̃te] *vt Fin* to rediscount
réessayer [reeseje] *vti* to retry
réévaluation [reevalɥasjɔ̃] *nf* revaluation
réévaluer [reevalɥe] *vt* (*monnaie*) to revalue; (*prix*) to reassess
réexamen [reɛgzamɛ̃] *nm* (*d'une politique, situation*) re-examination, reappraisal, reassessment; (*d'une décision*) reconsideration; (*d'un dossier, d'une question, d'un malade*) re-examination
réexaminer [reɛgzamine] *vt* (*politique, situation*) to re-examine, to reappraise, to reassess; (*décision*) to reconsider; (*dossier, question, malade*) to re-examine, to examine again
réexpédier [reɛkspedje] *vt* (*conj like* **expédier**) **(a)** (*lettres, marchandises*) to send on, to forward, to redirect **(b)** (*pour rendre*) (*à l'expéditeur*) to send back, to return
réexpédition [reɛkspedisjɔ̃] *nf* **(a)** (*d'une lettre, de marchandises*) forwarding, redirection; **frais de r.** fee for redirection; **ordre de r. du courrier** request for mail to be redirected **(b)** (*à l'expéditeur*) return
réexportation [reɛkspɔrtasjɔ̃] *nf* (*action*) re-export, re-exportation; **les réexportations** re-exports
réexporter [reɛkspɔrte] *vt* to re-export
réfaction [refaksjɔ̃] *nf Com, Jur* (*de biens endommagés ou de qualité inférieure*) allowance, rebate
refaire [rəfɛr] (*conj like* **faire**) **1** *vt* **(a)** (*faire à nouveau*) (*travail, traduction, Th scène*) to do (all over) again, to redo, *Am* to do over; (*voyage, robe etc*) to make (all over) again; (*film*) to remake; **j'ai dû r. du riz** I had to make (some) more rice; **tu nous referas du bœuf bourguignon comme l'autre fois?** will you make us some boeuf bourguignon like you did last time?; **r. ses lacets** to tie one's laces again; **r. la conclusion d'une dissertation** to change an essay's conclusion; **on a dépassé le budget, il faut qu'on refasse la fin** (*d'un film*) we've gone over the budget, we'll have to rewrite the ending; **refais le calcul, tu as dû te tromper** do the sum again, you must have made a mistake; **c'est trop serré, il faut r. le pansement** the bandage is too tight, you'll have to redo it; **nous avons refait à pied les vingt kilomètres qui nous séparaient du village** we walked the twenty kilometres back to the village; *F* **elle nous a refait sa crise** she gave us another bout of hysterics; *F* **tu ne vas pas nous r. ta crise!** you're not going to go into hysterics again!; **tu ne vas pas me r. une scène!** you're not going to start again!; **je refais de la fièvre** my temperature's up again; **c'est à r.** it will have to be done (all over) again; **et si c'était à r.?** and if you had to do it all over again?; **ton éducation est à r.** your education has been sadly neglected; **r. le monde** to put *or* set the world to rights; **r. sa vie** to make a new life for oneself; **r. sa vie avec qn** to make *or* start a new life with sb; *Tél* **r. le numéro** to redial

(b) (*réparer*) to repair, to mend; (*remettre en état*) (*maison, appartement*) to do up, to redo; **r. la peinture** *ou* **les peintures** to redo *or* do up the paintwork; **r. la décoration d'une maison** to redecorate a house; **r. à neuf** (*moteur*) to recondition; (*appartement, peintures*) to redo completely; (*fauteuil*) to renovate; **r. les talons de ses souliers** to have one's shoes reheeled; **r. l'installation électrique d'une maison** to rewire a house, to redo the wiring in a house; **r. le revêtement de qch** to resurface sth

(c) *F* (*personne*) (*d'un marchand*) to do, to diddle; (*duper*) to fool, to take in; **on vous a refait** you've been had; **on vous a refait de plusieurs centaines de francs** you've been done *or* diddled out of several hundred francs

2 se refaire *vpr* **(a) se r. une santé** to recover one's health, to get one's health back; **une soirée comme ça, ça ne se refera pas** a party like that doesn't happen twice *or* only happens once in a lifetime; *F* **elle se refait une beauté** she's doing her face again

(b) (*se changer*) to change one's ways; **on ne se refait pas** I/you/*etc* can't change the way I am/you are/*etc* (made), a leopard can't change its spots

(c) *F* (*financièrement*) to be solvent again; (*au jeu*) to win back the money one has lost; **après mes vacances, j'ai mis trois mois pour me r.** after my holiday it was three months before I was solvent again *or* before I had two pennies to rub together

3 *v impers* **il refait soleil** it's sunny again
réfection [refɛksjɔ̃] *nf* (*réparation*) (*d'un bâtiment, appartement, d'une maison*) (extensive) repair; **travaux de r.** repair work; **route en r.** road under repair
réfectoire [refɛktwar] *nm* refectory, dining hall
référé [refere] *nm Jur* summary procedure; **(ordonnance de) r.** provisional order
référence [referɑ̃s] *nf* **(a)** reference; *Mktg* (*produit*) benchmark; **ouvrage/livre de r.** reference work/book; **faire r. à un texte/auteur** to refer to a text/an author; **il n'a pas fait une seule fois r. à notre conversation** he didn't refer to *or* mention our conversation once; **références au bas des pages** footnotes; **r. de page** page reference; *F* **ce n'est pas une r.** don't take my/his/*etc* word for it, don't go by what I/he/*etc* say(s); **le film a été primé à Cannes mais ce n'est pas une r.** the film won a prize at Cannes but that's no recommendation

(b) (*sur une lettre, sur un document*) reference; **r. à rappeler** in replying please quote, please quote reference; **en r. à** with reference to

(c) références (employee's) reference, *Vieilli* testimonial; **références exigées** (*sur offre d'emploi*) references required; **une lettre de r.** a reference
référencé [referɑ̃se] *adj Com* **être r.** to have a reference number; **votre lettre référencée …** your letter reference number …
▸ **référence**: **références bancaires** bank references; **références commerciales** trade references; *Ordinat* **r. croisée** cross reference; **r. topographique** map reference
référencer [referɑ̃se] *vt Ordinat* to reference
référencié [referɑ̃sje] *adj* (*quotation*) with a reference
référendaire [referɑ̃dɛr] *adj* referendum
referendum, référendum [referɛ̃dɔm] *nm* referendum; **faire un r.** to hold a referendum; **les Français ont décidé par r. de …** the French have decided in a *or* by referendum to …

référent [referɑ̃] *nm Ling* referent

référer [refere] **(je réfère, n. référons; je référerai) 1** *vi* **r. à qn d'une question** to refer a matter to sb; **en r. à la cour** to report *or* submit the case to the court; **en r. à son supérieur** to refer to *or* consult one's superior **2 se référer** *vpr* **se r. à qch** to refer to sth; **tout ce qui ne se réfère pas directement à notre affaire** anything that is not directly connected with *or* related to our business; **se r. à** *ou* **s'en r. à qn d'une question** to refer a matter to sb

refermer [rəfɛrme] **1** *vt* to shut *or* close again; **il referma la porte sur lui** he closed the door behind *or* after him **2 se refermer** *vpr* (*d'une porte*) to close *or* shut (again); (*d'une fleur*) to close up; (*d'une blessure*) to close up, to heal; *Fig* **le piège se referme sur l'espion** the net is closing in around the spy

refiler [rəfile] *vt F* **r. qch à qn** (*objet de mauvaise qualité*) to palm sth off on sb, to foist *or* unload sth on sb; (*objet utile*) to pass sth on to sb; **ils vont nous r. les enfants pour le week-end** they're palming the kids off on us *or* dumping the kids on us for the weekend; **il m'a refilé son rhume** he's given me his cold

refinancement [rəfinɑ̃smɑ̃] *nm* (*d'un crédit*) refinancing

refinancer [rəfinɑ̃se] *vt* to refinance

réfléchi [refleʃi] *adj* **(a)** (*personne*) thoughtful, reflective; (*action, opinion*) deliberate, considered; **d'un air r.** thoughtfully; **elle est très réfléchie** she doesn't do anything without thinking it over first; **c'est tout r.** that's settled; **tout bien r.** all things considered, after due consideration **(b)** [①A29,7; B26-27,D] *Gram* (*verbe, pronom*) reflexive

réfléchir [refleʃir] **1** *vt* **(a)** (*image*) to reflect; (*lumière, son*) to reflect, to throw back

(b) r. que ... + *ind* to realize that ...; **il réfléchit que son argent ne suffirait pas** it occurred to him that he wouldn't have enough money

2 *vi* to think; **je réfléchis** I'm thinking; (*avant de décider*) I'm thinking about it; **prends le temps de r.** (take time to) think about it; **donne-moi le temps de r.** give me time to think; **r. à qch** to think about sth, to consider sth, to turn sth over in one's mind; **j'ai beaucoup réfléchi au problème** I've given the problem a great deal of thought; **j'ai réfléchi à ce que vous m'avez dit** I've thought about what you told me; **réfléchissez-y** think about it, think it over; **je demande à r.** I'd like to think about it *or* think it over; **donner à r. à qn** to give sb food for thought, to make sb think twice; **parler sans r.** to speak without thinking *or* hastily

3 se réflechir *vpr* (*d'une image, d'une lumière, de la chaleur, du son etc*) to be reflected

réfléchissant [refleʃisɑ̃] *adj* (*miroir, surface*) reflective

réflecteur, -trice [reflɛktœr, -tris] **1** *adj* (*miroir, panneau*) reflecting **2** *nm Aut* reflector; (*miroir*) reflecting mirror; (*télescope*) reflector, reflecting telescope; *TV* **r. parabolique** parabolic reflector

réflectif, -ive [reflɛktif, -iv] *adj* **(a)** (*de la réflexion*) reflective **(b)** *Physiol* reflex

réflectorisé [reflɛktɔrize] *adj* (*panneau routier, casque*) reflective

reflet [rəflɛ] *nm* (*dans un miroir, sur l'eau*) reflection; (*de la soie etc*) sheen, shimmer; **r. des eaux** gleam on the waters; **les reflets de la lune sur le lac** the reflection *or* shimmer of the moon on the lake; **chevelure à reflets d'or** hair with glints of gold; **reflets changeants** play of colours; *Fig* **être le r. de qch** to reflect sth; **ce n'est que le r. du temps des colonies** it's a pale reflection of colonial times

refléter [rəflete] **(je reflète, n. reflétons; je refléterai) 1** *vt* (*lumière, image, Fig gêne, jalousie, sentiments de qn*) to reflect; **son attitude ne reflète pas ses sentiments** his feelings are not reflected in his attitude **2 se refléter** *vpr* to be mirrored *or* reflected

refleurir [rəflœrir] **1** *vi* to flower *or* blossom again; *Fig* (*de l'art, de la littérature, de l'économie etc*) to flourish again **2** *vt* (*tombe*) to put fresh flowers on

reflex [reflɛks] *adj, nm Phot* **(appareil) r.** reflex (camera)

réflexe [reflɛks] **1** *adj Phys, Physiol* reflex **2** *nm Physiol* reflex; (*réaction*) reflex, reaction; **r. rotulien** knee reflex *or* jerk; **avoir de bons réflexes** to have good reflexes, to react quickly; **ça a été un r.** it was a reflex (action), it was automatic; **c'est devenu un r.** it's become automatic; **je n'ai pas eu le r. de le lui faire remarquer** I wasn't quick-witted enough to point it out to him

réflexif, -ive [reflɛksif, -iv] *adj Phil, Math* reflexive

réflexion [reflɛksjɔ̃] *nf* **(a)** (*pensée*) reflection, thought; **plongé dans une profonde r.** deep in thought; **après mûre r.** after much thought; **donner matière à r.** (*d'un film, un livre etc*) to provide food for thought; **agir sans r.** to act hastily *or* without thinking; **(toute) r. faite, à la r.** (*finalement*) on reflection; (*après avoir changé d'avis*) on further consideration, on second thoughts; **voilà qui mérite r.** there's food for thought

(b) (*remarque*) remark; **elle ne supporte pas qu'on lui fasse la moindre r.** she can't stand the slightest criticism; **faire une r. à qn** to make a remark *or* comment to sb; **on ne m'a jamais fait de r. à ce sujet** nobody's ever made any remarks to me about it *or* remarked on it to me; **s'il te fait la moindre r.** if he says the least little thing to you

(c) *Phys* (*d'une image, de la lumière, du son*) reflection; **angle de r.** angle of reflection; *TV, Cin* **r. parasite** blooming

refluer [rəflye] *vi* to flow back; (*de la marée*) to ebb; **le sang lui reflua au visage** the blood surged to his cheeks; **la foule a reflué vers la ville** the crowd swept *or* surged back towards the town; **faire r. des gens** to push people back, to make people move back

reflux [rəfly] *nm* (*de la marée*) ebb(ing); (*d'une foule*) surging back

refondre [rəfɔ̃dr] **1** *vt* **(a)** (*métal, cloche*) to recast; (*monnaie*) to recoin, to remint **(b)** (*texte, ouvrage*) to revise, to rewrite, *Fml, Litt* to recast **2** *vi* (*de la neige*) to melt again

refonte [rəfɔ̃t] *nf* **(a)** (*du métal*) recasting; (*de la monnaie*) recoinage **(b)** (*d'un texte*) rewriting, revision

réformable [refɔrmabl] *adj* reformable

reformatage [rəfɔrmataʒ] *nm Ordinat* reformatting

reformater [rəfɔrmate] *vt Ordinat* (*page, disque*) to reformat

réformateur, -trice [refɔrmatœr, -tris] **1** *adj* (*mesure, initiative*) reforming **2** *n* reformer

réformation [refɔrmasjɔ̃] *nf* reformation, reform; *Hist, Rel* **la R.** the Reformation

réforme [refɔrm] *nf* **(a)** (*politique, de l'orthographe, d'un abus, du calendrier etc*) reform; *Hist, Rel* **la R.** the Reformation **(b)** *Mil* (*d'un homme*) (*pour mauvaise condition physique*) discharge on medical grounds, invaliding out; (*d'une recrue*) rejection; (*de matériel*) scrapping; **r. temporaire** deferment; **commission de r.** special medical board; **matériel en r.** scrapped equipment; *Vieilli* **mettre à la r.** (*objets*) to scrap

réformé, -ée [refɔrme] **1** *adj* **(a)** *Rel* Protestant; (*église*) reformed **(b)** *Mil* (*exempté*) discharged for unfitness *or* on medical grounds, invalided out; (*recrue*) rejected; (*matériel*) scrapped; **être r. P4** to be rejected/discharged for reasons of mental health **2** *n* **(a)** *Rel* Protestant **(b)** *Mil* **r. temporaire** deferred recruit

reformer [rəfɔrme] **1** *vt* to form again, to re-form; **r. les rangs** to fall into line again **2 se reformer** *vpr* to re-form

réformer [refɔrme] *vt* **(a)** (*abus, loi etc*) to reform; *Jur* (*décision*) to reverse **(b)** *Mil, Naut* (*homme, officier*) to discharge as unfit *or* on medical grounds, to invalid out (of the service); (*recrue*) to reject; (*matériel*) to scrap, to condemn; **se faire r.** (*avant l'incorporation*) to be rejected from military service; (*après l'incorporation*) to get oneself discharged

réformisme [refɔrmism] *nm Pol* reformism

réformiste [refɔrmist] *adj, n* reformist

reformuler [rəfɔrmyle] *vt* to reformulate, to reword

refoulé, -ée [rəfule] *Psy* **1** *adj* (*sentiments, instincts, pulsions*) repressed; (*personne*) repressed, inhibited **2** *n* repressed *or* inhibited person **3** *nm* **le retour du r.** a Freudian slip

refoulement [rəfulmɑ̃] *nm* **(a)** *Psy* (unconscious) repression, suppression **(b)** *Tech* (*d'une canalisation*) delivery, discharge, output; **soupape de r.** (*d'une pompe*) delivery valve; **tuyau de r.** exhaust pipe **(c)** (*renvoi*) **il faut instaurer un r. systématique des étrangers** (*à la frontière*) we must start systematically refusing entry to foreigners; **la police tentait d'organiser le r. des supporters** the police were trying to push *or* drive back the supporters

refouler [rəfule] **1** *vt* **(a)** (*faire reculer*) (*manifestants, foule*) to drive back, to force back, to press back; *Admin* (*étranger*) to refuse entry to, to turn back; (*train*) to back; **le nombre des étrangers refoulés aux frontières** the number of foreigners turned back at the borders; **on nous a refoulés à l'entrée** we got turned away at the door

(b) (*sentiments, colère*) to repress, to suppress, to contain; (*larmes*) to force *or* choke *or* fight back; (*agressivité, souvenir, Psy pulsion, instinct*) to repress; (*désirs*) to suppress; **il ne faut pas r. ses sentiments** you mustn't bottle up your feelings

(c) *Tech* (*eau*) to deliver, to discharge; **pompe refoulante** force pump

2 *vi* (*de l'évier*) to back up; **la cheminée/la machine à laver refoule** the chimney's not drawing/the washing machine's not draining properly

réfractaire [refraktɛr] **1** *adj* rebellious, insubordinate, *Fml* refractory; *Tech, Méd* (*minerai, maladie*) stubborn, *Spéc* refractory; (*brique, argile*) fireproof, fire; *Hist Fr* **prêtre r.**

non-juring priest; **r. à** *Tech* resistant to; (*la loi, des conseils, une proposition*) unwilling *or* loath to accept; **il est r. à l'opéra** opera goes straight over his head; **r. aux acides** acid-proof; **être r. à l'autorité** to reject authority; **elle est r. aux sciences** science is a closed book to her **2** *n* rebel; *Mil, Jur* defaulter

réfracter [refrakte] *vt* (*rayons etc*) to refract, to bend

réfracteur, -trice [refraktœr, -tris] **1** *adj* refracting **2** *nm* refractor

réfraction [refraksjɔ̃] *nf* (*de rayons*) refraction, bending; **indice de r.** index of refraction, refractive index

refrain [rəfrɛ̃] *nm* [①**A13**,8] (*d'une chanson*) chorus, refrain; **chanter de vieux refrains** to sing old songs *or* old ditties; **reprendre le r. en chœur** to sing the chorus; *F* **c'est toujours le même r.** it's (always) the same old story *or* thing; *F* **change un peu de r.!** change the record!

réfrangible [refrɑ̃ʒibl] *adj Phys* refrangible

refrappe [rəfrap] *nf Ordinat* rekeying

refrapper [rəfrape] *vt Ordinat* to rekey

refréner [rəfrene] *vt* (**je refrène, n. refrénons**; **je refrénerai**) (*sentiments, colère, impatience etc*) to curb, to restrain, to control

réfrigérant [refriʒerɑ̃] **1** *adj* (*action, appareil*) refrigerating, cooling; (*produit*) freezing; *Fig* (*accueil, personne*) chilly; **mélange r.** refrigerant **2** *nm* (*mélange*) refrigerant, coolant; (*d'un alambic*) refrigerator, condenser; **r. à cheminée** cooling tower

réfrigérateur [refriʒeratœr] *nm* refrigerator, fridge, *Am* icebox; **conserver au r.** keep refrigerated; **conserver au r. après ouverture** refrigerate after opening; *Fig F* **mettre qn au r.** to sideline sb; **mettre un projet au r.** to shelve a plan, to put a plan on ice *or* in cold storage; *F* **sortir qn du r.** to bring sb in out of the cold; **ils ont sorti le projet du r.** they took the project down off the shelf *or* out of cold storage

réfrigération [refriʒerasjɔ̃] *nf* (*de la viande, de boissons etc*) refrigeration, chilling; **appareils de r.** refrigeration appliances; **r. industrielle** industrial refrigeration

refrigéré [refriʒere] *adj* refrigerated, reefer

réfrigérer [refriʒere] *vt* (**je réfrigère, n. réfrigérons**; **je réfrigérerai**) to refrigerate; **viande réfrigérée** chilled meat; **camion réfrigéré** refrigerated van, reefer; *Fig* **son accueil me réfrigéra** I received a chilly welcome; **ma question l'a réfrigéré** my question met with a chilly response *or* lowered the temperature quite considerably; *F* **je suis réfrigérée** I'm freezing

réfringence [refrɛ̃ʒɑ̃s] *nf Phys* refringency

réfringent [refrɛ̃ʒɑ̃] *adj Phys* refringent

refroidi [rəfrwadi] *nm F* (*cadavre*) stiff

refroidir [rəfrwadir] **1** *vt* **(a)** (*eau*) to cool (down); (*moteur, fluide*) to cool; (*métal*) to quench; **refroidi par (l')air/huile** air-/oil-cooled; **refroidi par eau** water-cooled

(b) *Fig* (*amitié, passion, amour etc*) to cool; (*ardeur*) to cool, to quench; (*enthousiasme*) to dampen, to dash, to quench; *F* **r. qn** (*d'un accueil, d'une réaction, question*) to dampen sb's enthusiasm

(c) *Arg* **r. qn** (*le tuer*) to bump sb off, to ice sb

2 *vi* (*d'un liquide ou d'un plat qui devrait être chaud*) to get cold; (*d'un liquide ou d'un plat qui est trop chaud*) to cool down; **laisser r. son thé** (*exprès*) to let one's tea cool down; (*si l'on attend trop*) to let one's tea get cold; **dépêchez-vous! ça va r.!** hurry up! it's getting cold!; **le temps a refroidi** it *or* the weather has got *or* grown colder; *F* **tu refroidis!** (*tu devines mal*) you're getting colder!

3 se refroidir *vpr* **(a) le temps** *ou* **la température se refroidit** it's *or* the weather's getting colder; **la soupe se refroidit** the soup's getting cold

(b) *Fig* (*d'une amitié, de relations*) to cool; **nos relations se sont refroidies depuis cette dispute** things have cooled between us since the argument

(c) *Méd* to catch a chill

refroidissement [rəfrwadismɑ̃] *nm* **(a)** (*de l'eau, d'un moteur*) cooling; (*du métal*) quenching; *Météo* drop in temperature; **agent de r.** cooling agent, coolant; *Aut* **r. intermédiaire** intercooling; **r. par air** air cooling; **r. par eau** water cooling **(b)** *Méd* chill **(c)** *Fig* (*d'une amitié, de relations*) cooling off

refroidisseur [rəfrwadisœr] *nm* cooler, refrigerator unit; *Nucl* cooler, coolant; **système r.** cooling system

refuge [rəfyʒ] *nm* **(a)** refuge, shelter; **(lieu de) r.** place of refuge; **r. anti-bombe** air-raid shelter; **pays r.** country of refuge; **valeur r.** safe investment; **trouver/chercher r.** to find *or* take/seek refuge; *Fig* **le sport/l'alcool est son r.** he takes refuge in sport/alcohol; **Dieu est mon r.** God is my refuge **(b)** (*en montagne*) (mountain) hut, refuge; (*d'oiseaux*) (bird) sanctuary; (*sur la route*) traffic island

réfugié, -ée [refyʒje] *n* refugee; **r. politique** political refugee

réfugier (se) [sərefyʒje] *vpr* to take refuge, to find shelter, to shelter; **se r. dans le mensonge/le sport** to take refuge in lying/sport

refus [rəfy] *nm* (*d'une invitation, offre*), *Équitation* refusal; (*d'une proposition*) rebuff, rejection; (*d'un candidat, manuscrit, de marchandises*) rejection; **son r. d'obéir** his refusal to obey; **essuyer un r.** to meet with a refusal; **se heurter à un r. de la part de qn** to meet with a refusal from sb; **opposer un r. à qn/qch** to turn sb/sth down; **il opposa un r. catégorique à ma proposition** he turned my suggestion down flat; *F* **ce n'est pas de r.** I won't say no

▶ **refus**: **r. d'obéissance** insubordination; *Jur* contempt of court; *Jur* **r. d'obtempérer** obstruction; **r. de paiement** non-payment; (*de traite*) dishonour, *US* dishonor; *Aut* **r. de priorité** failure to give way *or Am* to yield

refuser [rəfyze] **1** *vt* **(a)** (*offre, invitation*) to refuse, to decline, to turn down; (*proposition*) to turn down; (*demande*) to deny; (*marchandises, manuscrit*) to reject; **r. qch à qn** to refuse *or* deny sb sth; **on ne peut rien lui r.** you can't refuse him anything; **on lui refuse jusqu'au droit de voir sa femme** he's even being refused *or* denied the right to see his wife; **se voir r. sa demande** to have one's request turned down *or* denied; **r. toute qualité à qn** to refuse to see any good in sb; **r. sa porte à qn** to refuse to see sb, *Fml* to deny sb admittance; **r. l'obstacle** (*d'un cheval*) to refuse; **r. le combat** to refuse to fight

(b) r. qn to turn sb down; *Mil* **r. un homme** to reject a man; **r. du monde** to turn people away; *Scol* **être refusé** (*à un examen*) to fail

2 *vi* to refuse; (*d'un cheval*) to refuse, to ba(u)lk; **r. tout net** to refuse point blank, to give a point-blank refusal; **r. de faire qch** to refuse to do sth; **r. d'accepter un effet** to dishonour a bill by non-acceptance; **r. de payer une traite** to dishonour a bill by non-payment; *Naut* **r. de virer** not to obey the helm; **l'ordinateur refuse de s'allumer** the computer refuses to *or* won't turn on

3 se refuser *vpr* **cela ne se refuse pas** it's not the kind of thing to pass up; **un petit verre, ça ne se refuse pas** (*de qn qui accepte une invitation*) I wouldn't say no to a drink; (*de qn qui fait une invitation*) you can't say no to a drink; **on ne se refuse rien!, tu ne te refuses rien!** you don't stint yourself!, you don't believe in self-denial!; **se r. à l'évidence** to shut one's eyes to the facts; **se r. à tout commentaire** to refuse *or* decline to comment; **se r. à faire qch** to refuse to do sth; **je me refuse à ce genre de pratique** I refuse to get involved in that kind of thing

réfutable [refytabl] *adj* (*argument*) refutable; **c'est difficilement r.** it's hard to refute

réfutation [refytasjɔ̃] *nf* rebuttal, refutation

réfuter [refyte] *vt* to refute, to rebut

refuznik [rəfyznik] *n* refusenik

rég *Mil* (*abrév* **régiment**) Rgt

regagner [rəgaɲe] *vt* **(a)** (*confiance, affection, estime, amitié de qn*) to regain, to win *or* get back; **r. le temps perdu** to make up for lost time; **r. le terrain perdu** to make up lost ground; **r. aux courses l'argent perdu à la Bourse** to win back on the horses the money lost on the Stock Exchange; **c'est en 1989 qu'il s'est mis à r. de l'argent** it was in 1989 that he started earning money again

(b) (*endroit*) to get back to; **r. son foyer** to go back *or* return home; **r. sa place** to go back *or* return to one's place; **r. la côte à la nage** to swim back to shore; **r. la capitale en hélicoptère** to go back to the capital by helicopter; **ils purent r. l'Espagne après la mort de Franco** they were able to go back *or* return to Spain after Franco's death; **vous êtes maintenant autorisés à r. vos bureaux** you may now go back to your offices

regain [rəgɛ̃] *nm* (*d'intérêt, activité*) renewal, revival; **un r. d'espoir** renewed hope; **ce r. d'activité/d'intérêt nous a surpris** this renewed activity/interest surprised us; **on constate un r. d'activité sur les marchés boursiers** we can see renewed activity *or* a renewal of activity on the Stock Market; **connaître un r. de vie** to have a new lease of life

régal, -als [regal] *nm* treat; **les marrons glacés, c'est mon r.** I adore marrons glacés, marrons glacés are my favourite treat; **cette tarte aux pommes est un r.** this apple tart is delicious; **c'est un vrai r. de l'écouter** it's a treat *or* a pleasure to listen to him; **c'est un r. pour les yeux** it's a sight for sore eyes

régalade [regalad] *nf F* **boire à la r.** to pour a drink down one's throat without the bottle touching one's lips

régale [regal] *adj Ch* **eau r.** aqua regia

régaler[1] [regale] *vt* (*sol*) to level

régaler[2] **1** *vt F* **r. qn** to give sb an excellent meal; **r. qn de qch**

to regale sb with sth **2** *vi F* **c'est moi qui régale** it's on me, (it's) my treat **3 se régaler** *vpr* **on s'est (bien) régalé!** we had a slap-up meal; **se r. de qch** to adore sth; *Fig* **elle se régale avec ses petits-enfants** she's having the time of her life with her grandchildren; **il se régalait en la regardant** he feasted his eyes on her

regard [rəgar] *nm* **(a)** (*des yeux*) look; (*coup d'œil*) glance; **un r. tendre/amusé/intelligent** a tender/an amused/an intelligent look *or* expression in one's eyes; **r. appuyé** fixed *or* intent gaze *or* look; **ses regards appuyés me dérangent** I don't like the way he looks at me so intently *or* stares at me; **r. de côté** sidelong glance *or* look; **r. vitreux** glassy stare, glazed look; **porter son r. sur qn/qch** to look at sb/sth; **détourner le r.** to look away, to avert one's eyes *or* gaze; **avoir un beau r.** to have beautiful eyes; **nous eûmes un r. complice** we exchanged a knowing look; **avant tout, Lauren Bacall, c'était un r.** the first thing you noticed about Lauren Bacall was the way she looked at you; **je sentis son r. se poser sur moi** I felt him looking at me, I felt his gaze on me; **tourner son r. vers qn/qch** to turn one's gaze *or* eyes to sb/sth; **jeter un r. à qn** to glance at sb; **jeter** *ou* **lancer un r. à** *ou* **sur qch** to (cast a) glance at sth; **jeter un r. autour de soi** to glance round; **lancer un r. furieux à qn** to glare at sb; **lancer un r. noir à qn** to give sb a black look; **chercher qn du r.** to look round for sb; **interroger qn du r., lancer à qn un r. interrogateur** to give sb a questioning look, to look at sb inquiringly; **j'ai compris au premier r.** I realized at a glance *or* immediately *or* right away; **exposé aux regards** exposed to view; **la jeune fille que l'on avait cachée aux regards des hommes** the young girl who had been kept out of the sight of men; **soustraire qn/qch aux regards de qn** to keep sb/sth out of sb's sight; **à l'abri des regards indiscrets** away from prying eyes; **attirer le(s) regard(s)** to attract attention, to be conspicuous; **elle attire tous les regards** everyone turns to look at her; **nous attirions des regards très étonnés** we were getting some very strange looks; **sous les regards de la foule** while the crowd looked on; **en r. de qch** opposite *or* facing sth; (*comparé à*) compared with sth; **texte avec illustration en r.** text with illustration opposite *or* on the opposite page; **au r. de nos livres de comptabilité** on looking at *or* examining our accounts; **au r. de la loi, elle est coupable** she is guilty in the eyes of the law; *Fig* **porter un nouveau r. /un r. critique sur qch** to take a fresh/critical look at sth

(b) (*ouverture*) (*d'une porte*) peephole; **r. (d'accès** *ou* **de visite)** inspection hole; (*d'un égout*) manhole

(c) (*contrôle*) *Jur* **droit de r.** right of inspection; **je demande un droit de r. sur tous les textes qui sortent de ce bureau** I demand the right to check all texts leaving this office

regardant [rəgardɑ̃] *adj* **(a)** (*avare*) careful with one's money; **être r. à la dépense/sur l'argent que l'on donne** to be careful how one spends one's money/gives one's money away **(b)** (*exigeant*) **elle n'est pas regardante sur la présentation** she's not concerned *or* bothered about the presentation

regarder [rəgarde] **1** *vt* **(a)** [①**A40**,C,1,a; **B33**,2,b,i] (*personne, chose*) to look at; (*émission, film etc*) to watch; **r. qn dans les yeux** to look sb in the eye *or* eyes; **r. qn dans le blanc des yeux** to look sb straight in the eye; **r. qn fixement** to stare at sb; **r. qn avec méfiance** to look at *or* eye sb suspiciously; **regarde où tu marches** *ou* **où tu mets les pieds!** look *or* watch where you're going *or* where you're putting your feet!; **r. qn faire qch** to watch sb doing *or* do sth; **elle le regardait partir** she watched him leaving *or* leave; **elle veut être regardée** she wants people to look at her, she wants to attract attention; **r. une définition dans le dictionnaire** to look up a word in the dictionary; *F* **regarde voir si ce n'est pas cuit** (check and) see if it's cooked yet; *F* **regarde-moi ça!** (*viens voir*) (come and) look at this!; *F* **regarde-moi ça, c'est ce que tu appelles du travail fini!** just look at this, that's what you call a job well done!; *F* **non, mais tu ne m'as pas regardé!** what d'you take me for?

(b) (*considérer*) (*personne, chose*) to regard, to consider **(comme** as); **r. la vie en face** to face up to life; **r. les choses en face** to face (up to) things; **il faut r. les choses telles qu'elles sont** you've got to see things as they are; **elle regardait cela d'un mauvais œil** she was far from keen on the idea, *Fml, Litt* she took a jaundiced view of it; **ne r. que ses intérêts** to consider only one's own interests

(c) (*concerner*) (*personne*) to concern; **cela ne regarde que moi** that's nobody's business but mine; **cela ne vous regarde pas** that doesn't concern you, that's no concern of yours, that's none of your business

2 *vi* **(a) puis-je r.?** can I look?, can I have a look?; **je regarde seulement, merci** (*dans un magasin*) I'm just looking *or* having a look, thank you; **r. en bas/en arrière/autour de soi** to look down/back/round; **r. vers l'avenir** to look to the future; **r. par** *ou* **à la fenêtre** (*du dedans*) to look out of the window; (*du dehors*) to look in (through) the window; **r. par le trou de la serrure** to peep *or* look through the keyhole; **r. dans le dictionnaire** to look in the dictionary; **je ne suis pas sûr de l'orthographe, je vais r. dans le dictionnaire** I'm not sure of the spelling, I'll look it up in the dictionary

(b) r. sur *ou* **vers** (*jardin, rue etc*) to look on to, to face

(c) r. à qch to pay attention to sth; **sans r. à la dépense** regardless of expense; **je ne regarde pas à vingt francs** I'm not worried about twenty francs; **à y bien r.** on thinking it over; **y bien r.** *ou* **y r. à deux fois avant de faire qch** to think twice before doing sth; **je n'y regarde pas de si près** I'm not as fussy as all that

3 se regarder *vpr* (*d'une seule personne*) to look at oneself; (*de deux personnes*) to look at each other; **mais regarde-toi donc!** just look at you!; **se r. dans les yeux** to gaze *or* look into each other's eyes; **ils se regardaient en chiens de faïence** they were glaring at each other; **nos deux maisons se regardent** our houses face each other *or* are opposite each other; **ça se regarde dans les deux sens** there are two ways of looking at that; *F* **elle ne s'est pas regardée!, elle s'est regardée, elle?** she's got a cheek to talk!, she can talk!

regarnir [rəgarnir] *vt* (*garde-manger, étagères*) to restock; **r. une trousse de maquillage** to stock up on make-up; **il faut que je regarnisse mon portefeuille** I must get some money *or* cash

régate [regat] *nf Naut* regatta; **faire de la r.** to race; **faire une r.** to have *or* hold a regatta; **r. à voiles** yacht races; **r. à l'aviron** boat races

régater [regate] *vi Naut* to race

régatier, -ière [regatje, -jɛr] *n Naut* racing yachtsman *or f* yachtswoman; (*à l'aviron*) racing oarsman *or f* oarswoman

regazonner [rəgazɔne] *vt* to returf

regel [rəʒɛl] *nm* renewed frost

regeler [rəʒ(ə)le] *vi* **(il regèle; il regèlera)** to freeze again

régence [reʒɑ̃s] **1** *nf* regency; *Hist Fr* **la R.** the Regency (*1715-1723*) **2** *adj inv* **style R.** Regency (style); **meubles style R.** Regency furniture; *F* **elle est très r.** she's very genteel

régénérateur, -trice [reʒeneratœr, -tris] **1** *adj* regenerating, regenerative; *Rel* **eau régénératrice** baptismal water; *Nucl* **pile régénératrice** breeder reactor **2** *nm Ind* regenerator, regenerating plant *or* furnace

régénération [reʒenerasjɔ̃] *nf* **(a)** (*d'une cellule, de la peau etc*) regeneration **(b)** *Ind* reconditioning; *Nucl* breeding; *Ordinat* **r. de l'écran** screen refresh

régénérer [reʒenere] **(je régénère, n. régénérons; je régénérerai) 1** *vt* **(a)** *Biol* (*cellule, épiderme*) to regenerate; *Fig* (*d'une douche, des vacances*) to refresh; **cette discussion/rencontre m'a régénérée** I feel alive again *or* regenerated after that talk/meeting **(b)** (*catalyseur*) to reactivate **2 se régénérer** *vpr Biol* (*de cellule*) to regenerate (itself); *Fig* (*de l'enthousiasme, l'intérêt*) to re-awaken

régent, -ente [reʒɑ̃, -ɑ̃t] **1** *n* **(a)** *Pol* regent **(b)** *Fin* director **(c)** *Belg Scol* (secondary) schoolmaster **(d) le R.** (*diamant*) the Regent diamond **2** *adj* **reine régente/prince r.** Queen/Prince Regent

régenter [reʒɑ̃te] *vt* (*personne*) to dictate to; **il veut tout r.** he wants to run everything *or* the show

reggae [rege] *nm, adj inv* reggae; **un chanteur de r.** a reggae singer

régicide [reʒisid] **1** *n* regicide **2** *nm* (*crime*) regicide **3** *adj* regicidal

régie [reʒi] *nf* **(a)** *Admin* management, control; (*d'un domaine*) administration, stewardship; **en r.** in the hands of trustees **(b)** (*entreprise publique*) public corporation, state-owned company **(c)** *Hist* Customs and Excise; **employé de la r.** exciseman **(d)** *Th* management; *Cin* production; *TV* (*local*) control room; *TV, Cin* gallery; *TV, Cin* **r. de contrôle** video control room; **r. de diffusion** broadcast suite; **r. d'exploitation** control room; **r. de montage** edit suite; **r. mobile** mobile control centre, mobile control room; **r. publicitaire** advertising sales agency, space selling organization; **r. vidéo** video centre

▶ **régie**: **r. du dépôt légal** copyright department; *Admin* **r. des impôts indirects** excise (administration); ≈ *Br* Customs and Excise department; *Can* **R. des Loyers** ≈ rental board

regimber [rəʒɛ̃be] *vi* (*d'une personne*) to jib, to ba(u)lk **(contre** at), to kick **(contre** against); (*d'un cheval*) to kick **(contre** at, against); **il est toujours à r.** he's always protesting about something; **il est inutile de r.** there's no point protesting

régime [reʒim] *nm* **(a)** *Pol, Admin* (form *or* system of) government, regime; **le r. féodal** the feudal system; *Hist Fr* **l'Ancien R.** the old regime, the Ancien Régime; **le r. actuel** the present government; **sous le r. de Pompidou/Thatcher** during the Pompidou/Thatcher administration

(b) (*règlements*) **r. des hôpitaux/des prisons** hospital/prison regulations *or* rules; **le r. du travail** the organization of labour; **r. d'imposition** tax system; **nous nous sommes mariés sous le r. de la communauté/de la séparation de biens** our marriage was on the basis of a joint settlement of property/of separate ownership of property; **r. de retraite** pension plan; *Com* **r. de transit** transit system; **r. douanier** customs system; *Fin* **r. du forfait** standard assessment system, fixed rate tax assessment system; *Fin* **r. du réel** full assessment system; *Fin* **r. du réel simplifié** simplified full assessment system; *Fin* **r. simplifié** simplified system

(c) *Aut* (engine) speed; **à haut r.** at high speed; **à moyen r.** at average speed; *Tech* **r. (nominal)** (*d'une machine, d'un moteur, groupe électrogène*) rating; **r. de marche normal** normal working *or* operating conditions; **charge de r.** rated load; **puissance de r.** normal power; *Av, Naut, Aut* **r. de croisière** cruising speed; *Aut* **r. moteur** engine speed; **elle fait trois litres au cent en r. de ville** she does 100 km to three litres in town *or* on an urban cycle; **aller à plein r.** to go full throttle; *Fig* **à ce r., on aura fini dans trois jours** at this rate, we'll be finished in three days; *Él* **r. de charge** (*d'un accumulateur*) charging rate; **variations de r.** load variations

(d) *Géog* (*d'une rivière etc*) (rate of) flow; **r. climatique** climatic conditions; **r. thermique** temperature pattern

(e) (*alimentaire*) diet; **être au r.** to be on a diet, to be dieting; **se mettre au r.** to go on a diet; **je dois faire** *ou* **suivre un r.** I must go on a diet; **mettre qn au r.** to put sb on a diet; **r. lacté/sans sel/équilibré/sec** milk/salt-free/balanced/alcohol-free diet; **r. amincissant** slimming diet; **r. dissocié** food-combining diet, Hay diet; *F* **le r. jockey** a starvation diet; *Méd* **r. hyposodé** low-salt diet, low-sodium diet

(f) *Gram* object; **cas r.** objective case; **r. direct/indirect** direct/indirect object

(g) (*de bananes*) bunch, stem, hand; (*de dattes*) bunch, stem

régiment [reʒimɑ̃] *nm Mil* regiment; *Fig* (*d'admirateurs, créanciers*) host, swarm; *F* **aller au r.** to join the army; **quand j'étais au r.** when I was in the army, when I was doing my military service; **la musique/le drapeau du r.** the regimental band/colours; *F* **il y en a pour un r.** there's enough for a whole army

régimentaire [reʒimɑ̃tɛr] *adj* regimental

région [reʒjɔ̃] *nf* (*d'un pays*) region, area; *Admin* region; **r. militaire** military district, command; **dans la r. de Nantes** in the Nantes area, in the region of Nantes; **je ne connais pas la r.** I don't know the area; **si jamais tu passes dans la r. ...** if you're ever in the area ...; **les régions polaires** the polar regions; **dans nos régions** in these regions; **la r. parisienne** Paris and its suburbs; **j'habite dans la r. parisienne** I live in the Paris area; *Admin* **la R. Nord-Pas-de-Calais** the Nord-Pas-de-Calais Region; **je suis financé par la R.** I get funding from the region; **r. du coton** cotton-growing area; **r. du vin** wine-producing area; **r. minière** mining area *or* district; *Anat* **la r. lombaire/du cœur** the lumbar/heart region; **r. cible** target area; *Com* **r. test** test area

régional, -ale, -aux, -ales [reʒjɔnal, -o] **1** *adj* (*expressions, cuisine, développement etc*) regional; (*conseil*) local **2** *nm Tél* area telephone system

régionalisation [reʒjɔnalizasjɔ̃] *nf* regionalization

régionaliser [reʒjɔnalize] *vt* **(a)** (*décentraliser*) to regionalize **(b)** (*organiser au niveau régional*) **r. un programme d'investissements** to break down an investment programme by region

régionalisme [reʒjɔnalism] *nm* regionalism

régionaliste [reʒjɔnalist] **1** *adj* regional **2** *n* **(a)** (*écrivain*) regional writer **(b)** *Pol* regionalist

régir [reʒir] *vt* (*d'une loi, d'un principe physique, Gram cas, nom*) to govern; (*domaine*) to manage; **r. des biens** to manage assets

régisseur [reʒisœr] *nm* (*d'un domaine*) agent, manager, *Vieilli* steward; (*d'une ferme*) bailiff; *Th* stage manager; *Cin* assistant director; *TV* **r. de plateau** floor manager, FM; **r. de plateau adjoint** assistant floor manager, AFM; **r. général** location manager

registre [rəʒistr] *nm* **(a)** (*livre*) register, record; (*de comptes*) account book; (*des délibérations*) minute book; *Tech* (*de machine*) log book; **rapporter un article sur un r.** to post *or* enter an item in a register; **s'inscrire au r. du commerce** to enter oneself in the trade register; **signer le r.** (*d'un hôtel*) to sign the register; **les registres de l'état civil** the registers of births, marriages and deaths

(b) *Mus* register; (*étendue totale*) compass

(c) *Typ* register

(d) *Tech* regulator lever, throttle (valve)

(e) *Ordinat* register

(f) (*d'une œuvre*) tone, style; **changer de r.** (*d'un écrivain*) to change one's style; **il choisit ses images dans un r. poétique** he uses poetic images

(g) *Ling* register

▶ **registre**: *Ordinat* **r. d'accès mémoire** memory access register; *Tech* **r. d'aérage** ventilation flap; **r. des arrivées** (*d'un hôtel*) arrivals register; **r. de cheminée** (*d'un fourneau, d'une cheminée*) register, damper; **r. des chevaux** stud book; **r. des départs** (*d'un hôtel*) departures book; **r. électoral** electoral register; **r. à feuillets rechargeables** loose-leaf register; **r. d'index** index register; *Com* **r. international des marques** international trademark register; **r. de présence** attendance register; **r. des procès-verbaux** minutes book

réglable [reglabl] *adj* adjustable

réglage [reglaʒ] *nm* **(a)** (*d'un siège*) adjustment; (*d'un appareil*) adjustment, regulating, setting; (*dispositif*) adjuster; (*d'un chronomètre*) rating; **r. automatique** automatic control; **à r. automatique** self-adjusting; **vis de r.** set screw; **r. de la vitesse** speed control; *Aut* **r. de distribution** valve timing; *Aut* **r. de pression** pressure setting; **r. des phares** headlamp adjustment; *Aut* **r. programmable** (*des sièges*) memory setting; **r. en hauteur** height adjustment; *Mil* **r. du tir** ranging

(b) *Rad, TV* adjustment, control, tuning; **réglages** dial readings; **r. de la luminosité** brightness control; *TV, Ordinat* **r. du contraste** contrast control; *TV, Cin* **r. du volume** volume control

(c) (*du papier*) ruling

règle [rɛgl] *nf* **(a)** (*de conduite, de grammaire etc, Rel d'un ordre*) rule; **les règles de l'honneur** the code of honour; **les règles de la politesse exigent que ...** courtesy demands that ...; **c'est la première des règles de politesse** it's common courtesy; **les règles du jeu** the rules of the game; *Fig* **c'est la r. du jeu** that's the rule of the game; *Fig* **le gouvernement a encore changé les règles du jeu** the government have moved the goalposts again; **se faire une r. de se coucher de bonne heure** to make it a rule to go to bed early; **en r.** (*passeport, papiers*) in order; **reçu en r.** formal receipt; **bataille en r.** *Mil* battle according to the rules; *Fig* regular set-to; **je suis en r. avec lui** I'm all square with him; **être en r. avec sa conscience** to have a clear conscience; **mettre qch en r.** to sort sth out; **tout est en r.** everything is in order *or* is correct; **en r. générale** as a general rule; **agir dans les règles** to behave properly, to play by the rules; **jouer selon les règles** to play by the rules; *Fig* **dans** *ou* **selon les règles de l'art** by *or* according to the book; *Fig* **elle fait la bouillabaisse selon les règles de l'art** she makes a classic *or* traditional bouillabaisse; **c'est la r.** that's the rule; **comme c'est la r., comme de r.** as is the rule

(b) (*pour tracer des lignes*) ruler; *Tech* rule; (*d'arpenteur*) measuring rod; *Ordinat* (*sur écran*) ruler line; **r. graduée** ruler; **tirer des traits à la r.** to draw lines with a ruler

(c) *Physiol* **règles** period; **avoir ses règles** to have one's period; **règles abondantes** heavy periods; **absence de règles** amenorrhoea

▶ **règle**: *Sp* **r. de l'avantage** advantage rule; **r. à calcul** slide rule; *Compta* **r. du décalage d'un mois** one month in arrears rule; *Typ* **r. d'encadrement** panel rule; **r. d'or** golden rule; *Naut* **règles de route** (*en mer*) rule of the road; *Math* **r. de trois** rule of three

réglé [regle] *adj* **(a)** (*papier*) ruled; **papier non r.** plain paper **(b)** (*organisé*) regular, well-ordered, fixed, steady; **vie réglée (comme du papier à musique)** well-ordered life; *F* **r. comme du papier à musique** as regular as clockwork; **elle a un emploi du temps r. comme du papier à musique** she has a very strict routine, *F* you could set your watch by her **(c)** (*jeune fille*) who has started having periods; **elle est mal réglée** she's not very regular

règlement [rɛgləmɑ̃] *nm* **(a)** (*d'un compte*) settlement; (*paiement*) payment; **faire un r. par chèque** to pay by cheque; **pour r. de tout compte** in full settlement; **r. au comptant** payment in cash, cash payment; **en cours de r.** being settled, under discussion **(b)** (*statut*) regulation(s); (*d'université*) statutes; (*d'une société*) rules; **le r. intérieur** (*d'une école*) school rules; (*d'un bureau*) staff *or* company regulations; **c'est le r.** that's the rule; **les règlements militaires** army regulations; **règlements douaniers** customs regulations; **règlements et usages** code of practice

▶ **règlement**: **r. à l'amiable** amicable settlement; *Fig* **r. de**

compte(s) settling of scores; *Jur* **r. judiciaire** rule of Court; *Admin* **règlements de police** by(e)-laws

réglementaire [rɛgləmɑ̃tɛr] *adj* statutory, regulation; **tenue r.** regulation uniform; **ce n'est pas r.** it's against the rules; **faire qch dans le temps r.** to do sth in the prescribed time; **le score était de 0-0 à l'issue du temps r.** the full-time score was nil-nil; **dispositions réglementaires** regulations

réglementariste [rɛgləmɑ̃tarist] **1** *adj* (*attitude, professeur etc*) pernickety, nit-picking; **un fonctionnaire r.** a civil servant who goes by the book **2** *n* nit-picker, pernickety person

réglementation [rɛgləmɑ̃tasjɔ̃] *nf* **(a)** (*action*) regulating, regulation; **r. du trafic des changes** exchange control; **r. douanière** customs regulations; **r. du change** exchange control regulations; **r. du travail** labour legislation; **r. sur l'hygiène** health regulations; **r. sur l'hygiène alimentaire** food hygiene regulations; **r. sur l'hygiène et la sécurité** health and safety regulations; **r. sur la sécurité** safety regulations **(b) la r.** (*règles*) the regulations, the rules

réglementer [rɛgləmɑ̃te] *vt* (*ventes, importations*) to regulate, to make rules for; **r. le droit de grève** to control the right to strike

régler [regle] **(je règle, n. réglons; je réglerai) 1** *vt* **(a)** (*papier*) to line, to rule

(b) (*mécanisme, montre, siège, boussole, Aut allumage, freins, ceinture de sécurité, TV image*) to adjust; (*radio, Aut moteur*) to tune; **r. sa journée** to plan one's day; **jeune homme, il faut r. ta conduite** young man, it's about time you mended your ways; **r. ses dépenses sur ses revenus** to cut one's coat to suit one's cloth; **les obligations qui règlent des échanges commerciaux** the obligations that govern trade; *Tech, Aut etc* **r. qch avec précision** to fine-tune sth; *Sp* **r. l'allure** to set the pace; **r. son allure sur celle de son compagnon** to adjust one's pace to that of one's companion; *Mil* **r. le tir** to range; **la pendule est bien réglée** the clock keeps good time; **il a réglé sa montre sur la mienne** he set his watch by mine; **r. les livres** to balance the books

(c) (*résoudre*) (*question, dispute*) to settle; **r. ses affaires** to put one's affairs in order; **r. à l'amiable** to settle out of court

(d) (*payer*) (*compte*) to settle; (*facture*) to settle, to pay; (*épicier, femme de ménage, note, loyer etc*) to pay; **est-ce que j'ai réglé tout ce que je vous devais?** are we square?, have I paid you everything I owed you?; **je peux vous r. par chèque?** will you take a cheque?, can I pay by cheque?; **r. au comptant** to pay in cash; **r. le gaz** to pay the gas bill; **r. son compte à qn** (*se venger*) to settle accounts with sb; **je vais lui r. son compte** I'll settle his hash *or* score, I'll sort him out; **r. de vieux comptes** to pay off *or* settle old scores

2 *vi* to pay; **r. en espèces** to pay (in) cash; **c'est moi qui règle** I'm paying, this is on me

3 se régler *vpr* **(a)** (*d'un mécanisme*) to be adjustable; **son pas finit par se r. sur celui de son compagnon** he finished up walking at the same rhythm as his companion

(b) (*se finir*) to be concluded *or* settled; **ça s'est réglé à l'amiable** it was settled amicably

réglette [reglɛt] *nf* small ruler; *Aut* (*d'une boîte de vitesses*) control rod; *Mktg* (*sur rayon de magasin*) shelf strip; *Ordinat* **r. de clavier** key strip

réglisse [reglis] **1** *nf Bot* liquorice **2** *nm ou f* liquorice; **bâton de r.** stick of liquorice; **bonbon à la** *ou* **au r.** liquorice-flavoured sweet

réglo [reglo] *adj inv F* (*contrat, proposition*) kosher, on the up and up; **ça n'est pas très r.** that's a bit dodgy; **elle a été très r.** she played by the rules; **c'est un type très r.** he's as straight as a die *or* as they come, *Am* he's a regular guy; **il n'a pas été très r. avec moi** he didn't treat me right

réglure [reglyr] *nf* (*sur ou du papier*) ruling; **r. fine** feint; **à r. fine** feint-ruled

régnant [reɲɑ̃] *adj* (*prince, famille, Fig idéologie*) reigning; *Fig* (*opinion*) prevailing

règne [rɛɲ] *nm* **(a)** (*d'un roi, d'une reine, Fig d'un champion, de la démocratie*) reign; **sous le r. de Louis XIV** in the reign of Louis XIV; **c'est le r. de l'argent/de la technologie** money/technology reigns supreme **(b)** (*végétal, animal*) kingdom

régner [reɲe] *vi* **(je règne, n. régnons; je régnerai) (a)** (*d'un monarque*) to reign, to rule; *Fig* (*de conditions*) to exist, *Fml* to prevail; (*d'une opinion*) to be prevalent, to hold sway; **r. (pendant) dix ans** to reign *or* rule for ten years; **r. sur un pays** to reign over *or* rule (over) a country; **r. sur l'opinion** to be predominant, to hold sway; **r. en maître sur qch** to reign supreme over sth; **diviser pour mieux r.** divide and conquer; **s'efforcer de faire r. la paix** to try to keep the peace; **la police est chargée de faire r. l'ordre** the police are there to keep law and order; **la terreur qu'ils faisaient r. a pris fin** their reign of terror is at an end; **la suspicion qui règne au bureau** the climate of suspicion in the office *or* which pervades the office; **il règne une ambiance très étrange dans la ville** a very strange atmosphere prevails in the town; **il régnait, dans la maison, une atmosphère de paix et de tranquillité** peace and quiet reigned in the house; *Iron* **la confiance règne!** there's trust *or* confidence for you!, confidence reigns supreme!

(b) *Vieilli* **une galerie règne le long du bâtiment** a gallery runs *or* extends along the building

regonfler [rəgɔ̃fle] **1** *vt* (*ballon*) to reinflate, to blow up again; (*pneus*) to blow up, to pump up; *F* **r. (le moral à) qn** to cheer sb up; *F* **je suis regonflé à bloc!** I'm back on form! **2** *vi* (*d'une rivière*) to swell, to rise (again); **son pied a regonflé** his foot has swollen up again *or* is swollen again

regorger [rəgɔrʒe] *vi* **(je regorgeai(s); n. regorgeons) r. de qch** to have an abundance of sth, to abound in sth; **r. de monde** (*d'un train, magasin, d'une pièce*) to be packed (with people), to be packed to overflowing; (*des rues*) to be packed, to be teeming *or* swarming with people; **la ville regorge de musées** the town has an abundance of museums

régresser [regrese] *vi* **(a)** (*diminuer*) (*de la criminalité, d'une théorie, d'un style*) to decline; (*d'un parti politique*) to lose ground; (*de la douleur*) to improve; (*de la production, du chiffre d'affaires*) to drop; **j'ai régressé en maths** my maths has deteriorated; **l'industrie textile régresse** the textile industry is in decline **(b)** *Psy* to regress

régressif, -ive [regrɛsif, -iv] *adj* regressive; (*impôt, tarif*) tapering; *Biol* **forme régressive** throwback

régression [regrɛsjɔ̃] *nf* **(a)** regression; *Math* **coefficient de r.** regression coefficient **(b)** *Biol* retrogression; *Psy* regression; **être en r.** to be regressing **(c)** (*des affaires, ventes etc*) decline, drop; **être en r.** (*d'une épidémie*) to be on the decline, to be losing ground; (*du chômage, de la production etc*) to be on the decline, to be declining

regret [rəgrɛ] *nm* regret (**de** for); **rongé de regrets** eaten up with regret; **avoir des regrets** to feel regret, to be sorry; **j'avais des regrets de ne l'avoir pas vu davantage** I was sorry not to see more of him, I regretted not seeing more of him; **tu as déjà des regrets?** are you regretting it already?; **exprimer ses regrets** to express one's regret; **exprimer le r. de ne pouvoir être présent** to express regret at not being able to be present; **faire qch à r.** to do sth with regret *or* reluctantly; **j'ai dû le faire à r.** I was reluctant to do it, I did it reluctantly; **... dit-elle avec r.** ... she said with regret *or* regretfully; **nous nous en sommes séparés avec r.** we were sorry to part with it; **je suis parti sans r., c'est sans r. que je suis parti** I left without regret, I had no regrets about leaving; **je n'ai aucun r.** I have no regrets; **je n'ai qu'un r., c'est de ...** my only regret is that ...; **j'ai r. à vous quitter** I'm sorry to leave you; **j'ai le r.** *ou* **je suis au r. de vous annoncer que ...** I regret *or* am sorry to inform you that ...; **je suis au r. de ne pouvoir vous répondre favorablement** I regret that I cannot give you a favourable answer; **à mon (grand) r.** (much) to my regret; *F* **sans r.?** (you have) no regrets?, you're quite happy about it?; *F* **tous mes regrets!** sorry!, my apologies!; **un ton plein de r.** a regretful *or* sorrowful tone of voice; **mourir sans laisser de regrets** to die unmourned; **le r. du pays natal** homesickness; **éprouver le r. du pays natal** to be *or* feel homesick

regrettable [rəgrɛtabl] *adj* (*erreur, retard, incident etc*) regrettable, unfortunate; **il est tout à fait r. que vous n'ayez pas été prévenu** it is most unfortunate that you were not informed

regrettablement [rəgrɛtabləmɑ̃] *adv Rare* regrettably

regretter [rəgrete] *vt* **(a)** (*sa naïveté, son imprudence etc*) to regret; **vous le regretterez** you'll regret it, you'll be sorry, you'll rue the day; **tu ne le regretteras pas!** you won't regret it!, you won't be sorry!; **je ne regrette rien** I have no regrets; **je regrette le jour où je l'ai rencontré** I rue the day I met him; **il me ferait presque r. ma gentillesse** I'm almost sorry I was so kind to him; **je regrette de vous annoncer que ...** I regret to inform you that ...; **r. d'avoir fait qch** to regret *or* be sorry for having done sth; **je ne regrette pas d'avoir dit cela** I'm not sorry I said it, I don't regret saying it; **je regrette qu'elle soit partie si tôt** I'm sorry that she left so early, I wish she hadn't left so early; **il est à r. que ...** it is to be regretted that ..., it is unfortunate *or* regrettable that ...; **son absence est à r.** his absence is unfortunate *or* regrettable *or* is to be regretted; **je regrette!** (I'm) sorry!; **je regrette, je ne pourrai pas y assister** I'm sorry, I won't be able to attend, *Fml* regretfully, I will be unable to attend

(b) (*personne, endroit*) to miss; **mourir regretté de tous** to die mourned by all; **il sera regretté de tous** he'll be greatly *or* sorely missed; **r. sa jeunesse/son enfance** to wish one was young/a child again; **r. son argent** to wish one had one's money back

regrimper [rəgrɛ̃pe] **1** *vt* (*escalier, pente*) to climb (up) again **2** *vi* to climb again; *F* (*de la fièvre*) to go up again; **r. à l'arbre** to climb the tree again
regrossir [rəgrosir] *vi* to put on weight again
regroupement [rəgrupmɑ̃] **(a)** *nm* grouping; (*d'animaux, d'enfants*) rounding up, round-up; (*de sociétés*) amalgamation; *Mil* regrouping **(b)** (*groupe*) grouping
regrouper [rəgrupe] **1** *vt* (*personnes*) to gather *or* bring together; (*animaux, enfants*) to round up; (*objets*) to gather *or* put together; *Mil* (*hommes*) to regroup; (*sections, sociétés*) to merge, to amalgamate; **les dernières œuvres de Dali ont été regroupées** (*pour cette exposition*) Dali's last paintings have been brought together; **regroupons le parti autour d'une idée-force** let us unite the party around a key idea; **nous avons regroupé nos économies pour lui faire un beau cadeau** we pooled our savings to get him/her a nice present
2 se regrouper *vpr* (*de gens*) to gather *or* get together; *Mil* (*d'hommes*) to regroup; (*de sociétés*) to merge, to amalgamate
régularisation [regylarizasjɔ̃] *nf* **(a)** (*d'une situation, d'un litige*) regularizing, regularization; *Fin* (*d'un compte, des stocks, charges*) adjustment; (*de papiers d'identité*) putting in order; **ses papiers sont en voie de r.** his papers are (in the process of) being put in order **(b)** (*d'une rivière, d'un mécanisme*) regulation, regulating; **r. de la circulation** traffic control
régulariser [regylarize] *vt* **(a)** (*document*) to put into proper form; (*papiers d'identité*) to put in order; *Fin* (*compte*) to adjust; **r. une situation** to regularize *or F* sort out a situation; **est-ce qu'il va r. la situation?** (*en se mariant*) is he going to make an honest woman out of you/her? **(b)** (*fleuve, fonctionnement d'une machine*) to regulate; (*circulation*) to regulate, to control
régularité [regylarite] *nf* **(a)** (*de traits, forme, habitudes*) regularity; (*d'un mouvement*) steadiness, evenness, regularity; **faire qch avec une r. infaillible** to do sth with unfailing regularity; **faire preuve de r.** to be reliable; **avec une r. d'horloge** as regular as clockwork **(b)** (*conformité aux règles*) (*d'une élection, d'un vote etc*) legality; *Fin* **r. et sincérité des charges** true and fair nature of expenses
régulateur, -trice [regylatœr, -tris] **1** *adj* (*mécanisme, hormone etc*) regulating; **soupape régulatrice** governor valve; **le travail est un élément r.** having a job brings a degree of order to your life
2 *nm* **(a)** (*dispositif*) *Tech* regulator; (*d'une horloge*) regulator, governor, balance wheel; (*d'une turbine*) regulator, governor; (*d'une machine à vapeur*) throttle valve, regulator, governor; **r. de marge** margin stop; *Th* **r. d'éclairage de scène** stage dimmer; *Tech* **r. de tension** voltage smoother; *Tech* **r. de vitesse** speed governor
(b) (*personne*), *Rail* controller, *Am* dispatcher; (*de taxis*) dispatcher; **r. aérien** air traffic controller
régulation [regylasjɔ̃] *nf* **(a)** (*action de régler*) (*d'un compas*) regulation, readjustment **(b)** (*contrôle*) (*de la circulation, MecE du carburant, de la pression*) control; **r. des naissances** birth control; *Él* **r. de la tension** voltage regulation *or* control
régulier, -ière[1] [regylje, -jɛr] **1** *adj* **(a)** (*service de bus, examens, visites*) regular; (*augmentation, mouvement, progrès*) steady; (*pouls, respiration, coups, revenu*) regular, steady; (*vie*) (*pleine d'habitudes*) ordered; (*morale*) honourable, *US* honorable; (*résultats*) consistent, steady; (*écriture, couche, pression*) even; (*paroi*) smooth; **avoir un visage r.** *ou* **des traits réguliers** to have regular features; **il fit avec le pinceau un trait bien r.** he painted an even line; **son travail n'est pas r.** his work isn't consistent *or* is patchy, he doesn't work consistently; **c'est un employé r.** he's a steady worker; **c'est un élève r.** he's a consistent pupil; **se lever et se coucher à heures régulières** to keep regular hours; **être r. dans ses habitudes** to be regular in one's habits; **son humeur régulière** his/her even temper; **d'une humeur régulière** even-tempered; **à intervalles réguliers** at regular intervals
(b) (*conforme*) legitimate; (*honnête*) straight, on the level; **ce n'est pas r.** that's not above board; **le coup n'était pas r.** it was a bit of a dirty trick, it was a low blow; **il n'a pas été très r. dans cette affaire** he didn't altogether play by the rules *or* go by the book; **être r. en affaires** to be an honest person to deal with; **il n'a pas été très r. avec moi** he didn't play fair with me, he wasn't straight with me; **être en situation régulière** to have one's official papers in order; [①A38,A,1; B22-3,7,A] *Gram* **verbe r.** regular verb; **quittance régulière** receipt in due form, proper receipt
(c) (*soldat, clergé*) regular; **troupes régulières** regular troops, regulars
(d) *Can* (*standard*) (*format, prix etc*) standard, *surtout Am* regular
2 *n* regular (customer); **un r. du bar** a regular (at the bar)
régulière[2] *nf Vieilli; Hum F* (*épouse*) missus; (*petite amie*) steady
régulièrement [regyljɛrmɑ̃] *adv* **(a)** (*avec constance*) (*aller à un endroit, rendre visite à qn etc*) regularly; (*respirer*) steadily, evenly; (*réparti, étalé*) evenly; **j'entendais des coups frappés r. contre le mur** I heard a steady knocking on the wall; **le son vous fera aller r. à la selle** bran will keep you regular; **elle va r. se plaindre chez le directeur** she regularly goes to the boss to complain **(b)** (*selon la loi*) legitimately, lawfully; **membres r. désignés** properly *or* duly elected members; **je ferai en sorte que les choses se passent r.** I'll make sure that things happen as they should
régurgitation [regyrʒitasjɔ̃] *nf* regurgitation
régurgiter [regyrʒite] *vt* (*nourriture*) to regurgitate
réhabilitation [reabilitasjɔ̃] *nf* **(a)** (*d'un délinquant*) rehabilitation; (*d'une faillite*) discharge; **obtenir la r. de qn** to clear sb's name **(b)** (*remise en état*) (*d'un quartier déshérité*) rehabilitation, renovation
réhabilité, -ée [reabilite] *n* rehabilitated person; *Fin* discharged bankrupt
réhabiliter [reabilite] **1** *vt* **(a)** (*délinquant, politicien*) to rehabilitate; (*personne accusée d'un crime, nom de qn*) to clear; (*qn qui a fait faillite*) to discharge; **r. qn dans ses droits** to restore sb's rights **(b)** (*bâtiment, quartier*) to rehabilitate, to renovate; (*friche industrielle*) to reclaim **2 se réhabiliter** *vpr* to rehabilitate oneself, to restore one's reputation
réhabituer [reabitɥe] **1** *vt* to reaccustom (**à** to); **r. qn à (faire) qch** to get sb used *or* accustomed to (doing) sth again **2 se réhabituer** *vpr* **se r. à (faire) qch** to get used *or* accustomed to (doing) sth again; **on va avoir du mal à se r.** we'll have trouble getting used to it again
rehaussement [rəosmɑ̃] *nm* (*d'un mur*) raising, heightening; (*d'un tableau sur un mur*) raising; **r. fiscal** tax increase
rehausser [rəose] *vt* **(a)** (*mur, bâtiment*) to make higher, to heighten **(b)** (*faire valoir*) (*couleur, teint*) to enhance, to set off; (*détail*) to enhance, to accentuate; **r. une veste de jalons** to liven up *or* brighten up a jacket with braid
réhausseur [reosœr] *nm Aut* child booster cushion
rehaut [rəo] *nm Beaux-Arts* (*sur un tableau*) highlight
réhydratation [reidratasjɔ̃] *nf Méd* rehydration
réimperméabiliser [reɛ̃pɛrmeabilize] *vt* (*imperméable*) to reproof
réimplantation [reɛ̃plɑ̃tasjɔ̃] *nf* **(a)** (*d'une société, usine*) relocation **(b)** *Chir* reimplantation; (*d'une dent*) reimplant
réimplanter [reɛ̃plɑ̃te] *vt Chir* (*une dent*) to reimplant
réimportation [reɛ̃pɔrtasjɔ̃] *nf* **(a)** reimport, reimportation **(b)** (*marchandise*) reimport
réimporter [reɛ̃pɔrte] *vt* to reimport
réimposer [reɛ̃poze] *vt Fin* (*produit*) to reintroduce tax on, to retax
réimposition [reɛ̃pozisjɔ̃] *nf Fin* retaxation
réimpression [reɛ̃presjɔ̃] *nf* **(a)** (*action*) reprinting; **en cours de r.** (*sur catalogue*) being reprinted, new edition pending; **c'est en cours de r.** it's being reprinted, there's a new edition pending **(b)** (*livre etc*) reprint
réimprimer [reɛ̃prime] *vt* to reprint
Reims [rɛ̃s] *nm* Rheims
rein [rɛ̃] *nm* **(a)** *Anat* kidney; **r. artificiel** kidney *or* dialysis machine
(b) (*partie inférieure du dos*) **reins** (lower) back; *Litt* (*taille*) waist; **la chute** *ou* **le creux des reins** the small of the back; **douleur** *ou* **mal aux reins** backache, lower back pain; **avoir mal aux reins** to have a pain in the small of one's back; **les cheveux lui tombaient jusqu'aux reins** her hair went down to the small of her back; **donner un coup de reins** to heave; **j'ai dû donner un coup de reins pour soulever l'armoire** I had to heave the wardrobe up; *F* **se faire un tour de reins** to rick one's back; *Fig* **casser les reins à qn** to ruin *or* break sb; *Fig* **il a les reins solides** he's tough, he's made of pretty stern stuff; (*financièrement*) he's well-heeled
réincarcération [reɛ̃karserasjɔ̃] *nf* reimprisonment, *Fml* reincarceration
réincarcérer [reɛ̃karsere] *vt* to reimprison, *Fml* to reincarcerate
réincarnation [reɛ̃karnasjɔ̃] *nf* reincarnation
réincarner (se) [səreɛ̃karne] *vpr* to be reincarnated (**en qch/qn** as sth/sb); **je voudrais me r. en Catherine Deneuve** I want to be reincarnated *or* come back as Catherine Deneuve
reine [rɛn] *nf* **(a)** (*monarque*), *Fig* queen; **un port** *ou* **un maintien de r.** a queenly *or* regal bearing; **la r. Anne** Queen Anne; **la r. mère** the Queen Mother; *F* (*belle-mère*) the mother-in-law; *F* **je suis la r. des pommes!** what a total idiot

I am! **(b)** *Ent* (*abeille*) queen (bee) **(c)** *Échecs* queen **(d)** (*femme*) **r. de beauté** beauty queen; **la r. du bal** the belle of the ball **(e)** *Sp* **la petite r.** cycling

reine-claude [rɛnklod], *pl* **reines-claudes** *nf* greengage

reine-des-prés, *pl* **reines-des-prés** *nf Bot* meadowsweet

reine-marguerite, *pl* **reines-marguerites** *nf Bot* China aster

reinette [rɛnɛt] *nf* pippin; **r. grise** russet

réinfecter [reɛ̃fɛkte] **1** *vt* to reinfect **2 se réinfecter** *vpr* to become reinfected

réinfection [reɛ̃fɛksjɔ̃] *nf* reinfection

réinitialisation [reinisjalizasjɔ̃] *nf Ordinat* restart; (*de la mémoire*) reinitialization; **simple r.** soft reset; **r. totale de la machine** hard reset

réinitialiser [reinisjalize] *vt Ordinat* to reset; (*mémoire*) to reinitialize

réinjecter [reɛ̃ʒɛkte] *vt* (*liquide*) to reinject; (*argent, fonds*) to reinject, to make a fresh injection of

réinscriptible [reɛ̃skriptibl] *adj Ordinat* rewriteable

réinscription [reɛ̃skripsjɔ̃] *nf* registration

réinscrire [reɛ̃skrir] **1** *vt* (*conj like* **inscrire**) to re-register **2 se réinscrire** *vpr* to sign up again, to re-register (**à un cours** for a class)

réinsérer [reɛ̃sere] **1** *vt* (*dans la société etc*) to reintegrate (**dans** into); *Ordinat* (*bloc*) to reinsert **2 se réinsérer** *vpr* to be reintegrated (**dans** into)

réinsertion [reɛ̃sɛrsjɔ̃] *nf* reintegration; **r. sociale** rehabilitation

réinstallation [reɛ̃stalasjɔ̃] *nf* relocation; *Ordinat* reinstallation; **depuis sa r. au premier** since she moved to the first floor; (*pour la deuxième fois*) since she moved back to the first floor

réinstaller [reɛ̃stale] **1** *vt* (*changer de place*) to move; (*pour la deuxième fois*) to move back; *Ordinat* to reinstall **2 se réinstaller** *vpr* to settle down again; **il s'est réinstallé à Reims** he has moved back to Rheims

réintégration [reɛ̃tegrasjɔ̃] *nf* **(a)** (*d'un fonctionnaire etc*) reinstatement; (*dans un parti*) readmission; **r. des démobilisés dans la vie civile** rehabilitation of ex-servicemen (in civilian life) **(b)** *Jur* **r. de domicile** resumption of residence; **r. du domicile conjugal** restitution of conjugal rights **(c)** *Fin* add-back

réintégrer [reɛ̃tegre] *vt* (*conj like* **intégrer**) **(a) r. qn** (*dans un parti*) to readmit sb; **r. qn (dans ses fonctions)** to reinstate sb **(b) r. son domicile** to return to one's home; *Jur* to resume possession of one's domicile

réintroduction [reɛ̃trɔdyksjɔ̃] *nf* reintroduction

réintroduire [reɛ̃trɔdɥir] *vt* (*conj like* **introduire**) to reintroduce

réinvestir [reɛ̃vɛstir] *vt* to reinvest

réitératif, -ive [reiteratif, -iv] *adj* reiterative

réitération [reiterasjɔ̃] *nf* (*d'une demande, promesse*) repetition, reiteration; (*d'une démarche*) repetition

réitérer [reitere] *vt* (**je réitère, n. réitérons; je réitérerai**) (*demande, promesse, question*) to repeat, to reiterate; (*démarche*) to repeat

rejaillir [rəʒajir] *vi* to gush out, to spurt *or* splash up *or* out; *Fig* **r. sur qn** (*d'un scandale, du mérite de qn*) to reflect on sb; **tout ceci rejaillit sur moi** it all reflects on me; **sa honte a rejailli sur nous** we suffered disgrace too, the mud stuck to us too

rejaillissement [rəʒajismɑ̃] *nm* **(a)** (*d'un liquide*) gushing (out), spurting (up *or* out) **(b)** *Fig* (*de la gloire*) reflection

rejet [rəʒɛ] *nm* **(a)** (*action*) throwing out *or* away; (*de substances toxiques*) dumping; (*terre*) spoil (earth); *Géol* **r. horizontal** heave

(b) (*d'une proposition, candidature, personne, Méd d'une greffe*) rejection; (*d'une requête*) rejection, refusal; (*d'une doctrine, Jur d'une réclamation, d'un appel*) dismissal; *Fig F* **faire un r. de l'école/du sport** to hate school/sports; **ne lui parle pas de sport, il fait un r.** don't talk to him about sport, he can't stand it; **un phénomène de r.** rejection; **être victime d'un phénomène de r.** to be rejected; **il a été traumatisé par ces réactions de r.** he was traumatized by this display of rejection

(c) (*de plante*) shoot; (*émise par une souche*) sucker

(d) (*en poésie*) enjambment

rejeté [rəʒte] *adj Journ* (*article*) on the spike

rejeter [rəʒte] (*conj like* **jeter**) **1** *vt* **(a)** (*relancer, remettre*) (*balle, tête*) to throw *or* toss back; (*déchets, gaz toxiques etc*) to release, to discharge; (*de la mer, d'une rivière*) (*épaves, poissons etc*) to cast up, to wash up; **r. un poisson à l'eau** to throw *or* toss a fish back; **r. ses cheveux en arrière** to toss one's hair back; **épaves rejetées sur la plage** wreckage cast up *or* washed up on the beach; **la lave rejetée par le volcan** the lava thrown out *or* spewed out by the volcano; **la terre rejetée venait s'amonceler derrière eux** the earth which had been dug up was piling up behind them; **les envahisseurs furent rejetés à la mer** the invaders were driven back over the sea; *Fig* **r. le blâme/la responsabilité de qch sur qn d'autre** to shift the blame/the responsibility for sth on to sb else; **en allemand, le verbe est rejeté en fin de phrase** in German, the verb goes to the end of the sentence; **rejette l'idée en fin de paragraphe pour lui donner plus de poids** move this idea to the end of the paragraph in order to give it more weight

(b) (*ne pas admettre*) (*enfant, conseil, Méd greffe*) to reject; (*candidat, candidature*) to turn down, to reject; (*offre, proposition*) to reject, to turn down, to dismiss; *Jur* (*témoignage*) to disallow; (*doctrine, réclamation, accusation, Jur pourvoi*) to dismiss; *Journ* (*un article*) to spike, to kill; **r. un projet de loi** to reject a bill, to throw out *or* vote out a bill; **elle croit qu'on la rejette** she feels rejected; **ceux que la société rejette** the outcasts of society; **elle rejette toute nourriture** she won't take any food

2 se rejeter *vpr* **(a)** (*se satisfaire de*) to fall back (**sur** on)

(b) (*sauter à nouveau*) to throw oneself again; **se r. en arrière** to jump back; (*d'un cheval*) to shy

(c) elles se rejettent la responsabilité de cet échec they're laying the blame for this failure on each other

rejeton [rəʒtɔ̃] *nm* **(a)** (*de plante*) shoot, sucker **(b)** *F* (*progéniture*) offspring; (*enfant*) sprog; **il avait amené ses rejetons avec lui** he'd brought his offspring (with him)

rejoindre [rəʒwɛ̃dr] (*conj like* **joindre**) **1** *vt* **(a)** (*mettre bord à bord*) to join (together); (*lèvres d'une plaie*) to close

(b) (*aboutir à*) (*d'une rue, rivière*) to join (up with), to meet; **la rue rejoint le boulevard cinq cents mètres plus bas** the street joins (up with) the avenue five hundred metres further down; **nous rejoindrons bientôt l'autoroute** we'll soon join (up with) *or F* hit the motorway

(c) (*ressembler à*) to be along the same lines as; **ses propos rejoignent les miens** he echoes what I say; **cela rejoint ce que je disais tout à l'heure** that fits in with what I was saying just now

(d) (*retrouver*) (*personne*) (*pour un rendez-vous*) to meet; (*rattraper*) to catch up (with); *Mil, Naut* (*son régiment, son bâtiment*) to (re)join; **le nageur eut du mal à r. le rivage** the swimmer had difficulty reaching the shore; **il rejoignit le parti communiste en 1955** he joined the Communist party in 1955

2 se rejoindre *vpr* (*d'amis*) to meet (up); (*de rivières, routes, lignes*) to join (up), to meet (up); **les droites se rejoignent au point P** the straight lines meet at (the point) P

rejouer [rəʒwe] **1** *vt Sp* (*match, point*) to replay; (*morceau de musique*) to play again; (*pièce de théâtre*) to do again **2** *vi* to play again; **on rejoue?** shall we have another game?

réjoui [reʒwi] *adj* joyful; **je voyais à sa mine réjouie que les nouvelles étaient bonnes** I could see from the joyful expression on his face *or* from his joyful expression that it was good news; **la mine réjouie, il annonça sa promotion** he delightedly announced his promotion

réjouir [reʒwir] **1** *vt* (*personne*) to delight, to cheer, to gladden; **toutes ces bonnes nouvelles ne peuvent que nous r.** we can only be glad of all this good news; **cela me réjouit le cœur de l'entendre** it does my heart good *or* it makes my heart glad *or* it gladdens my heart to hear it; **r. l'œil** to delight the eye; **savoir qu'il va partir me réjouit** I'm thrilled to know that he's leaving; **cette nouvelle ne me réjouit pas spécialement** I'm less than thrilled to hear the news

2 se réjouir *vpr* **(a)** to rejoice (**de** at, in), to be glad (**de** of), to be delighted (**de** at); **je me réjouis à la pensée de le revoir** I'm delighted at the thought of seeing him again; **il faut se r. que tout se passe bien** we must be glad that everything is going well; **je me réjouis de te savoir guéri** I'm delighted that you're better

(b) *Vieilli* (*s'amuser*) to enjoy oneself

réjouissance [reʒwisɑ̃s] *nf* rejoicing; **en signe de r.** to mark the occasion; **réjouissances publiques** public festivities; **le programme des réjouissances** the programme of festivities; *Iron* the list of treats in store; *Iron* **quel est le programme des réjouissances?** so what treats have you got in store for me?, what fun things have you got lined up for me to do?

réjouissant [reʒwisɑ̃] *adj* (*nouvelles, perspective etc*) delightful; **cela n'a rien de r.** it's a gloomy prospect; **la nouvelle n'est pas réjouissante** it's not exactly the most cheerful of news

relâche [rəlɑʃ] **1** *nm* **(a)** (*arrêt*) respite, rest; **travailler sans r.** to work without a break *or* a let-up *or Fml* without respite; **elle le répète sans r.** she repeats it continually, she keeps on repeating it; **prendre un peu de r., se donner r.** to have a brief respite; *Th* **il y a r. ce soir** there is no performance this evening; *Th* **faire r.** to be closed; *Th* **r.** (*sur panneau*) closed (**b**) (*d'une corde*) slackening, loosening **2** *nf Naut* (*arrêt*) call; (*port*) port of call; **faire r. dans un port** to call at *or* put into a port

relâché [rəlaʃe] *adj* (*corde*) slack, loose; (*mœurs, conduite*) loose, lax

relâchement [rəlaʃmɑ̃] *nm* (**a**) (*d'une corde*) slackening, loosening; (*de la discipline*) relaxation; (*des mœurs*) looseness, laxity, laxness; (*des efforts*) let-up; (*dans le travail*) slacking off; **le r. de l'attention des élèves** the wavering of the pupils' attention; **il y a du r. ici** people are slacking off (**b**) (*de prisonniers*) release

relâcher [rəlaʃe] **1** *vt* (**a**) (*corde*) to loosen, to slacken; (*son étreinte, les intestins*) to loosen; (*muscle, discipline, efforts*) to relax; **j'ai relâché mon attention pendant un instant** my attention slackened *or* wavered for a moment

(**b**) (*prisonnier, oiseau en cage*) to release, to let go; *Fig* **je vous relâche** I'll let you go

2 *vi Naut* to put into port

3 se relâcher *vpr* (*de corde*) to slacken; (*d'un lacet*) to come loose; (*d'un employé, de la discipline*) to become slack; (*du zèle*) to flag, to fall off; (*des mœurs*) to grow lax; (*de l'attention*) to slacken, to waver; (*d'une étreinte*) to relax, to loosen; **cet élève s'est relâché** this pupil has slackened off; **se r. dans son travail** to slacken *or* ease off; **la discipline s'est un peu trop relâchée ces jours-ci** discipline is a bit too relaxed these days

relais [rəlɛ] *nm* (**a**) (*d'ouvriers*) shift; **ouvriers de r.** shift workers; **travail sans r.** unrelieved (spell of) work; **ville-r.** stopover (town); *Sp* (**course de**) **r.** relay (race); *Sp* **r. 4 fois 100 mètres** 4 x 100-metre relay; **passer le r. à qn** *Sp* to hand over the baton to sb; *Fig* to hand over to sb; **il est temps que je passe le r.** it's time I handed over (control); *Sp* **passage du r.** handover; **prendre le r.** to take over (**de qn** from sb); **l'homéopathie prend le r. de la médecine traditionnelle** homeopathy is taking over from traditional medicine; **tu prendras le r. avec le bébé** you take over with the baby, you have a spell with the baby; *Vieilli* **chevaux de r.** post horses

(**b**) (*auberge*) *Vieilli* coaching inn, post house; **r-château** country house hotel; **r. gastronomique** gourmet restaurant; **r. de tourisme** country house hotel; *Aut* **r. routier** service station (with café); **prochain r. routier: 10 km** (*sur panneau*) ≈ services: 10 kms

(**c**) *MecE, Él* relay; *Rad* **r. de radio-diffusion** relay (broadcasting) station; **r. de télévision** television relay station

(**d**) (intermédiaire) **ce poste lui a servi de r. pour se présenter aux élections** the position was a springboard for him in his bid for office; **je leur sers de r. quand ils ont quelque chose à se dire** they communicate with each other through me; **le graphiste sert de r. entre le client et l'imprimeur** the graphic artist is the link between the customer and the printer

relance [rəlɑ̃s] *nf* (**a**) (*de l'économie, de la production, des ventes, du commerce*) revival; (*d'un produit*) relaunch; **plan de r.** recovery plan; **des mesures pour la r. de l'économie** measures to revive *or* boost the economy *or* to get the economy going again; **r. de la natalité** upturn in the birth rate (**b**) *Com* (*d'un client*) follow-up; **lettre de r.** follow-up letter; **r. téléphonique** telephone follow-up (**c**) *Cartes* raise; **poker sans maximum de r.** poker with no ceiling

relancement [rəlɑ̃smɑ̃] *nm* (**a**) (*d'un engin spatial*) relaunch (**b**) (*d'une machine*) restarting; (*de la production*) boosting; (*d'un produit*) relaunching

relancer [rəlɑ̃se] (*conj like* **lancer**) **1** *vt* (**a**) (*ballon*) to throw again; (*pour le rendre*) to throw back

(**b**) (*économie*) to boost, to get started again; (*commerce, ventes, production*) to boost; (*moteur*) to restart; *Ordinat* (*programme*) to rerun; (*logiciel*) to restart; **r. un projet** to relaunch a project

(**c**) *Com* (*produit*) to relaunch

(**d**) **r. qn** (*harceler*) to badger sb, to pester sb; *Com* **r. un débiteur** to chase up a debtor; **r. un client** to follow up *or* to chase up a customer; **je l'ai relancée plusieurs fois pour qu'elle vienne dîner chez nous** I pestered her several times to come to dinner; **et pourtant, elle continue à lui téléphoner plusieurs fois par semaine pour le r.** and she still badgers him on the telephone several times a week

2 *vi Cartes etc* to increase the stake, to raise the bid

relaps, -e [rəlaps] **1** *adj* relapsed; **être laps et r.** to have abandoned the Catholic faith **2** *n* relapsed heretic

relater [rəlate] *vt* (*faits*) to relate, to state

relatif, -ive [rəlatif, -iv] **1** *adj* (*position, valeur, calme, liberté etc, Gram pronom, proposition*) relative; *Pol* **avoir la majorité relative** to have a relative majority; *Mus* **tons relatifs** related keys; **r. à** relating *or* related to, connected with; **vivre dans un luxe r.** to live in comparative luxury; **cette notion est très relative** it is a very relative concept; **tout est r.** everything is relative **2** *nm* (**a**) [①A32-33; B20-22,F] *Gram* relative pronoun (**b**) **le r.** the relative

relation [rəlasjɔ̃] *nf* (**a**) (*rapports entre personnes*) relationship; **entamer des relations** *ou* **se mettre** *ou* **entrer en relation(s) avec qn** to enter into a relationship with sb; **avoir** *ou* **entretenir des relations avec qn** to be in touch with sb; **être en r. avec qn** to be in touch *or* in communication with sb; **je vais les mettre en r.** I'll put them in touch (with each other); **avoir de bonnes/mauvaises relations avec qn** to be on good/bad terms with sb, to have a good/bad relationship with sb; **nos relations sont assez tendues** relations between us are rather strained; **nos relations sont très chaleureuses** we are on very good terms (with one another); **relations d'affaires** *ou* **commerciales** business relations; **nos relations sont purement professionnelles** our relationship is purely professional; **être en relation(s) d'amitié avec qn, entretenir des relations amicales avec qn** to be on friendly terms with sb, to have a friendly relationship with sb; **entretenir des relations de bon voisinage avec les pays d'Europe/sa belle-famille** to be on neighbourly *or* good terms with European countries/on good terms with one's in-laws; **les relations humaines** human relationships; **des relations épistolaires** correspondence; **il avait eu une relation épistolaire avec cette femme** he had corresponded with this woman; **les relations culturelles/diplomatiques/internationales** cultural/diplomatic/international relations; **nos relations avec la Hollande** our relations with Holland; **cesser ses relations avec qn/un pays** to break off relations with sb/a country; **les deux pays ont cessé toute r.** the two countries have broken off all relations

(**b**) (*lien entre deux idées, deux faits etc*) relationship, connection; **r. entre la cause et l'effet, r. de cause à effet** relationship between cause and effect; **il n'y a aucune r. entre ces deux faits** the two facts are not related *or* connected; **c'est sans r. avec le sujet** it bears no relation to the subject; **ce n'est pas sans r. avec ce que nous avons dit plus tôt** it is not unconnected with *or* unrelated to what we said earlier; **en r. avec …** in relation to …

(**c**) (*d'amour*) relationship; **r.** (**amoureuse**) love affair; **avoir une r. avec qn** to have a relationship with sb; **elle a eu une r. avec un homme marié** she had an affair with a married man; **avoir des relations sexuelles avec qn** to have (sexual) intercourse with sb

(**d**) (*connaissance*) acquaintance; **r. d'affaires** business acquaintance; **elle a des relations** (**mondaines**) she is well connected, she has influential friends; **sans relations, on ne peut rien faire** you can't do anything unless you know (the right) people *or* unless you have contacts *or* connections; **faire jouer ses relations** to pull strings; **c'est une r. de travail** he's a colleague

(**e**) (*récit*) account, report; **faire la r. de qch** to give an account of sth

▶ **relation**: *Pol* **relations extérieures** foreign affairs; **relations presse** press relations; **relations publiques** public relations, PR; **il travaille dans les relations publiques,** *F* **il est relations publiques** he's in *or* works in public relations

relationnel, -elle [rəlasjɔnɛl] *adj* relational; *Ordinat* **base de données relationnelles** relational database

relativement [rəlativmɑ̃] *adv* (**a**) (*d'une façon relative*) (*rare, fréquent, bien payé etc*) relatively, comparatively (**b**) (*en relation*) **r. à** relating to, concerning (**c**) (*en comparaison*) **plus petit, r. au premier** smaller compared *or* by comparison with the first

relativiser [rəlativize] *vt* **r. un problème** to put a problem into perspective; **il faut r.** you have to look at things in perspective

relativisme [rəlativism] *nm Phil* relativism

relativiste [rəlativist] *adj, n Phil* relativist

relativité [rəlativite] *nf* relativity; **théorie de la r.** theory of relativity, relativity theory

relaver [rəlave] *vt* to wash again

relax [rəlaks] *F* **1** *adj* (*personne*) laid(-)back, easy-going; (*soirée, entretien*) laid(-)back; **fauteuil r.** reclining chair; **baby-r.** baby chair **2** *adv* **on va réviser, mais r., OK?** we'll do some revision, but we'll take it easy, OK?; **vas-y r.** (*à un coureur, qn qui prend la route*) take it easy; (*à qn qui va passer un entretien*) don't get worked up **3** *int* **r. Max!** chill out!

relaxant [rəlaksɑ̃] *adj* relaxing; **bain r.** (**aux plantes**) herbal foam bath

relaxation [rəlaksasjɔ̃] *nf* relaxation; **faire de la r.** to practise relaxation; **cours de r.** relaxation class, stress management class

relaxe[1] [rəlaks] *nf* (*d'un accusé*) release, discharge
relaxe[2] *adj F* = **relax 1**
relaxer [rəlakse] **1** *vt* **(a)** to relax; **ce bain m'a bien relaxé** I feel really relaxed after my bath **(b)** *Jur* (*prisonnier*) to release, to discharge **2 se relaxer** *vpr* to relax
relayer [rəleje] **(je relaie, je relaye, n. relayons; je relaierai, je relayerai) 1** *vt* **(a)** (*personne*) to take over from, to relieve
(b) *TV, Rad* to relay
2 *vi Arch* to relay, to change horses
3 se relayer *vpr* to take turns (**pour faire qch** doing sth); *Sp* **les coureurs se relaient tous les cents mètres** the runners take over from each other every hundred metres; **ils se relaient au volant** they take turns at the wheel, they take it in turns to drive; **on se relaie toutes les trois heures** we change over every three hours
relayeur, -euse [rəlejœr, -øz] *n Sp* relay runner
relecture [rəlɛktyr] *nf* (*d'épreuves*) proofreading; (*d'un livre*) rereading; **faire de la r. en free-lance** to be a freelance proofreader; **la r. de Stendhal m'a pris deux mois** it took me two months to reread Stendhal
relégation [rəlegasjɔ̃] *nf Hist, Jur* transportation
reléguer [rəlege] *vt* (*conj like* **léguer**) **(a)** *Sp* (*équipe*), *Fig* to relegate; **r. un tableau au grenier** to relegate *or* consign a picture to the attic; *Fig* **relégué au second plan** pushed into the background; **mes projets de vacances sont relégués au second plan pour le moment** my holiday plans have been pushed into the background *or* are having to take a back seat for the moment **(b)** *Hist Jur* (*détenu*) to exile, to relegate
relent [rəlɑ̃] *nm* (*odeur*) stale smell; **des relents de graillon** a smell of stale fat; *Fig* **un r. de scandale entoure ce politicien** there is a whiff of scandal about this politician; *Fig* **ces histoires ont un r. de calomnie** these stories smack of slander
relevable [rəlvabl] *adj* (*siège, dossier, appuie-tête etc*) adjustable; *Av* **train d'atterrissage r.** retractable undercarriage; **accoudoir r.** folding armrest
relevage [rəlvaʒ] *nm* raising, lifting
relevailles [rəlvaj] *nfpl Vieilli* (*d'une femme qui vient d'accoucher*) churching; **faire ses r.** to be churched
relevé [rəlve] **1** *adj* **(a)** (*tête*) raised; (*sourcils*) (*après chirurgie esthétique*) lifted; (*manches*) turned up, rolled up; (*col*) turned up; **chapeau r.** off-the-face hat; **pantalon à bords relevés** turn-up trousers, turn-ups, *Am* pants with cuffs; *Aut* **virage r.** banked turn
(b) *Fig* (*sentiment*) noble; (*style*) lofty; **dans des milieux plus relevés** in higher circles
(c) (*sauce*) highly-seasoned; **un plat très/peu r.** a hot *or* spicy/mild dish
2 *nm* **(a)** summary, statement; **r. de consommation (du gaz)** meter reading; **r. de communications téléphoniques** telephone call sheet
(b) (*en topographie*) survey; **faire le r. d'un terrain** to plot a piece of land
▶ **relevé**: **r. d'achat** purchase report; *Mktg* **r. (d'achat) journalier** diary; **r. de caisse** cash statement; **r. de compte** bank statement, statement of account; **r. de factures** statement of invoices; **r. de fin de mois** end-of-month statement; **r. d'identité bancaire** = document giving details of one's bank account, bank details; **r. des naissances** table *or* summary of births; **r. de vente** sales report
relève [rəlɛv] *nf* **(a)** (*des troupes, de la sentinelle*) relief; *Ind* (*d'une équipe*) changing, changeover; *Mil* **la r. de la garde** the changing of the guard; **(troupes de) r.** relieving troops; **prendre la r. de qn** to take over from sb; *Mil,* (*au travail*) to relieve sb, to take over from sb; **prendre la r.** to take over **(b)** (*de personnel*) relief (driver/*etc*)
relèvement [rəlɛvmɑ̃] *nm* **(a)** (*action*) (*d'un objet renversé*) picking up, righting; (*d'un mur*) raising, heightening; (*des affaires, d'une économie, d'un pays*) recovery, revival; (*des salaires, des tarifs, d'un impôt*) raising, increasing; **contribuer au r. d'un pays/d'une économie** to help a country/an economy recover **(b)** (*de terrain*), *Naut* position; (*au compas*) bearing; **r. radio(goniométrique)** radio bearing *or F* fix; **faire** *ou* **prendre un r.** to take a bearing, to take bearings
relever [rəlve] (*conj like* **lever**) **1** *vt* **(a)** (*remettre à la verticale*) (*objet renversé, personne*) to pick up; (*bateau*) to right; (*mur démoli*) to rebuild; **veuillez r. votre tablette** please fold away your tables; **relevez votre dossier** (*d'avion*) return your seats to an upright position; (*de cabriolet*) pull your seat back up; **r. la tête** to look up, to raise one's head; *Fig* to hold one's head up (again)
(b) (*ramasser*), *Scol* (*compositions, copies*) to collect, to take in; **r. ses cheveux** to put one's hair up; *Fig* **r. le gant** to take up the gauntlet *or* challenge, to accept the challenge; **r. le défi** to accept *or* take up the challenge
(c) (*hausser*) (*niveau de vie, niveau d'eau*) to raise; (*col*) to turn up; (*manches, bas de pantalon*) to turn up, to roll up; (*voilette*) to raise, to lift; (*jupe*) to lift (up), *F* to hoick up; *Tricot* (*maille*) to pick up; (*navire coulé*) to raise, to refloat; (*salaires, prix*) to increase, to raise; (*notes d'examen*) to put up; **r. les yeux** to look up again (**de** from); **il releva les yeux pour regarder les horaires** he looked up again at the timetables; **r. l'économie** to revive the economy; **r. une industrie** to revive an industry; **les richesses minières ont permis de r. le pays** mineral wealth contributed to the country's economic revival; *F* **cela l'a relevé aux yeux des électeurs** it boosted him in the eyes of the electorate
(d) (*noter*) (*contradiction, faux sens etc*) to pick out; (*adresse, numéro de téléphone*) to take down; (*température*) to note, to record; (*traces*) to uncover; (*compte*) to make out; (*compteur*) to read; **r. le gaz** to read the gas meter; **r. des empreintes digitales** (*reporter*) to take fingerprints; **la police n'a relevé d'empreintes** the police haven't found any fingerprints; **on n'a relevé aucune preuve contre elle** no evidence has been found against her; **r. l'allusion** to respond, to react, to rise to the bait; **je n'ai pas relevé ce qu'il a dit contre moi** I ignored what he said about me; **il a affirmé l'ignorer et moi, je n'ai pas relevé** he claimed not to know about it and I didn't challenge him
(e) (*mettre en valeur*) (*couleur, beauté etc*) to enhance, to heighten, to set off; (*sauce*) to season; (*plat*) to liven *or* perk up; (*histoire*) to liven up, to enliven
(f) (*remplacer*) (*troupes, sentinelle*) to relieve; **r. qn** to take sb's place, to take over from sb; **r. la garde** to change the guard
(g) (*libérer*) **r. qn d'un vœu** to release sb from a vow; **r. qn de ses fonctions** to relieve sb of his duties
(h) *Naut* (*endroit*) to take the bearings of; *Naut* (*terre*) to sight; (*d'un arpenteur*) (*terrain*) to survey, to plot; *Math* (*graphique*) to plot
2 *vi* **(a) r. de maladie** to be recovering from an illness, to be convalescing
(b) r. de qn to be answerable *or* responsible to sb, to report to sb; **r. de l'article 7** to come under article 7; **cette affaire ne relève pas de notre département** the matter is not our department's responsibility; **cette affaire relève de la justice** this is a matter for the courts; **son cas relève de la folie** he can be diagnosed as insane; **de telles décisions relèvent d'un manque de responsabilité coupable** decisions like that indicate a culpable lack of responsibility; **tout ce qui relève de la culture étrusque le passionne** everything relating to Etruscan culture fascinates him
3 se relever *vpr* **(a)** (*de son siège*) to get up; (*après être tombé*) to get up, to pick oneself up; (*après avoir été à genoux*) to get up from one's knees; (*du lit*) to get up again, to get out of bed again; (*d'un navire*) to right itself; **l'accoudoir se relève** the armrest lifts up; **aide-le à se r.** (*dans son lit*) help him to sit up; (*debout*) help him up
(b) (*du commerce*) to recover; **se r. d'une maladie** to recover from *or* get over an illness; **il aura du mal à se r. de cette déception** he'll have difficulty recovering from *or* getting over this disappointment; **il ne s'en relèvera pas** he'll never get over it
releveur, -euse [rəlvœr, -øz] *n* (*personne*) meter reader
relief [rəljɛf] *nm* **(a)** *Beaux-Arts, Archit, Géog* relief; *Ordinat* highlight; **mettre en r.** to highlight; **en r.** *Beaux-Arts* in relief; (*caractère*) raised; (*carte*) relief; **cinéma/photographie en r.** stereoscopic cinema/photography; *Fig* **mettre en r., donner du r. à** (*idées, qualité*) to bring out; (*beauté*) to set off, to emphasize; (*taille fine, yeux*) to emphasize, to draw attention to; (*avantage*) to highlight; **mets ce paragraphe en r. en faisant des marges plus larges** make this paragraph stand out by making the margins wider; **l'état de ses finances met en r. son piètre sens de l'économie** the state of his finances emphasizes *or* throws into relief his lack of financial sense; **sans r.** (*paysage, style*) flat; **r. acoustique** stereophonic sound
(b) *Litt* **reliefs** (*d'un repas*) remains; *Fig* (*de la gloire*) shreds, tatters
relier [rəlje] **1** *vt* (*impf & pr sub* **n. reliions**) **(a)** (*objets, points, personnes*) to connect, to link, to join (**à** to); (*idées*) to link together; **le cordon ombilical relie la mère à l'enfant** the umbilical cord attaches *or* connects the mother to the baby; **c'est la seule chose qui les relie** it's the only thing they have in common; **vos idées sont bien/mal reliées entre elles** your ideas are well/badly linked together **(b)** (*livre*) to bind; **relié en veau** bound in calf, calf-bound **2 se relier** *vpr Ordinat* to link up
relieur, -euse [rəljœr, -øz] *n* (book)binder
religieusement [rəliʒjøzmɑ̃] *adv* **(a)** (*selon la religion*)

piously, religiously; **se marier r.** to get married in church, to have a church wedding **(b)** (*avec révérence*) (*écouter*) reverently; **conservé r. dans un écrin en velours** kept reverently in a velvet case; **il lit l'Humanité r. tous les jours** he reads l'Humanité with reverence every day **(c)** (*scrupuleusement*) religiously; **elle allait r. à la gym deux fois par semaine** she went to the gym religiously twice a week

religieux, -euse [rəliʒjø, -øz] **1** *adj* (*éducation, communauté, fanatique*) religious; (*musique, art*) sacred; **n'avoir aucun sentiment r.** to have no religious inclinations; **école religieuse** church school; **mariage r.** church wedding; *Fig* **soin r.** religious *or* scrupulous care; **elle prépare ses gâteaux avec un soin r.** she takes (an almost) religious care over her cakes; **conservé avec un soin r. dans du coton** reverently wrapped up in cotton wool; **mettre un soin r. à faire qch** to be religious about doing sth; **silence r.** respectful silence

2 *nm* (*moine*) monk, friar

3 *nf* **religieuse (a)** (*nonne*) nun

(b) (*gâteau*) cream puff

religion [rəliʒjɔ̃] *nf* **(a)** religion; **avoir de la r.** to be religious; **mourir en r.** to die in the faith; **entrer en r.** to take one's vows; **guerre de r.** war of religion; **la r. chrétienne/juive/bouddhiste** the Christian/Jewish/Buddhist religion *or* faith; **je ne connais pas sa r.** I don't know what religion he is; **est-ce que vous pratiquez une r.?** are you a practising Catholic/Muslim/*etc*?

(b) *Fig* religion; **le football est une r. pour certains** football is a religion with some people, some people make a religion out of football; *Arch* **se faire une r. de qch** to make a religion of sth, to make sth a point of conscience; **se faire une r. sur qch** to have made up one's mind about sth

religiosité [rəliʒjozite] *nf* religiousness, *Péj* religiosity

reliquaire [rəlikɛr] *nm* reliquary, shrine

reliquat [rəlika] *nm* **(a)** (*reste*) (*d'argent*) remainder; **r. de compte** account balance; **r. de caisse** cash balance; *Fig Litt* **un r. du passé** a relic of the past **(b)** *Méd Vieilli* (*d'une maladie*) aftereffects

relique [rəlik] *nf* (*d'un saint*), *Fig* relic; **garder qch comme une r.** to treasure sth, to keep sth like a relic; *Litt* **les reliques de sa gloire** the relics *or* remnants of his glory

relire [rəlir] (*conj like* **lire**) **1** *vt* (*livre, auteur, ce qu'on a écrit*) to re-read, to read (over) again; (*épreuves*) to read; (*vérifier*) to proofread **2 se relire** *vpr* to read (over) what one has written; **j'ai du mal à me r.** I'm having trouble reading *or* deciphering my own handwriting

reliure [rəljyr] *nf* **(a)** (*activité, art*) bookbinding; **atelier de r.** bindery; **donner un livre à la r.** to send a book for binding *or* to be bound **(b)** (*couverture*) **r. anglaise** *ou* **en toile** cloth binding; **r. pleine** full leather binding

relogement [rəlɔʒmɑ̃] *nm* rehousing

reloger [rəlɔʒe] *vt* (*conj like* **loger**) to rehouse

relouer [rəlue] *vt* **(a)** (*donner en location*) (*maison etc*) to rent (out) again, *Br* to relet, *Br* to let (out) again (**à** to) **(b)** (*prendre en location*) (*maison etc*) to rent again; **nous relouons chaque année le même appartement** we rent *or* take the same flat every year

réluctance [relyktɑ̃s] *nf Aut* reluctance

reluire [rəlɥir] *vi* (*conj like* **luire**) (*du parquet, d'un meuble, des chaussures*) to shine, to gleam; (*du métal*) to shine, to gleam, to glitter; **faire r. qch** to polish *or* shine sth (up); **brosse à r.** shoebrush; *Fig F* **manier la brosse à r.** to do some soft-soaping *or* buttering-up; **elle sait manier la brosse à r.** she's good at soft-soaping people *or* buttering people up

reluisant [rəlɥizɑ̃] *adj* (*parquet, meuble, chaussures*) shining, gleaming; **r. de propreté** (*sol, parquet, maison etc*) gleaming; *Fig F* **ce qu'il a fait n'est pas très r.** (*moralement*) what he did was a bit off; **c'est une perspective peu reluisante** it's hardly a glowing prospect

reluquer [rəlyke] *vt F* (*étranger, l'argent de qn etc*) to eye; **r. les filles** to eye (up) *or* ogle the girls; **il reluque ta fortune** he's got his eyes on your money, he's only after your money

rem [rɛm] *nm* (*abrév* **Roentgen Equivalent Man**) rem

remâcher [rəmɑʃe] *vt* to chew again; *Fig* (*le passé, une déception*) to brood over *or* about, to chew over

remailler [rəmaje] *vt* (*filet, bas*) to mend; (*pull, chaussette etc*) to darn

remake [rimɛk] *nm Cin* remake; **faire un r.** to do a remake

rémanence [remanɑ̃s] *nf* remanence, residual magnetism; *Ordinat* (*de l'affichage*) afterglow; *Opt* **r. des images visuelles** persistence of vision

rémanent [remanɑ̃] *adj* (*en magnétisme*), *Él* residual, remanent; *Opt* **image rémanente** after-image

remanger [rəmɑ̃ʒe] *vt* (*conj like* **manger**) to eat again; **j'en ai remangé** I had some more; **je n'en ai jamais remangé** I've never eaten any since *or* again

remaniement [rəmanimɑ̃] *nm* **(a)** (*d'un texte, discours, d'une politique*) reworking, revising, rejigging; **procéder au r. d'un texte** to rework *or* revise *or* rejig a text **(b)** (*changement*) alteration, modification; **apporter des remaniements à un ouvrage** to make changes to a work; *Pol* **r. ministériel** cabinet reshuffle; **r. du personnel** staff reshuffle

remanier [rəmanje] *vt* (*impf, pr sub* **n. remaniions**) (*texte, discours etc*) to rework, to revise, to rejig; (*équipe*) to make changes in, to reshuffle, to rejig; *Pol* (*gouvernement*) to reshuffle

remaquiller [rəmakije] **1** *vt* **r. qn** to make sb up again **2 se remaquiller** *vpr* (*de nouveau*) to make oneself up again; (*en retouchant*) to touch up one's make-up; **depuis peu, je me remaquille** I've started wearing make-up again recently

remarcher [rəmarʃe] *vi* **(a)** (*d'une personne*) to walk again; **elle ne remarchera plus** she won't walk again **(b)** (*d'une machine etc*) to work again; *F* **ça a l'air de bien r. entre eux** they seem to have worked things out

remariage [rəmarjaʒ] *nm* remarriage

remarier [rəmarje] **1** *vt* **r. sa fille** to marry off one's daughter again; **ils espéraient bien r. leur fille** they really hoped to see their daughter married again **2 se remarier** *vpr* to remarry, to marry *or* get married again; **se r. avec qn** to remarry sb

remarquable [rəmarkabl] *adj* (*changement, résultat, progrès, invention, personne etc*) remarkable; (*événement, livre*) remarkable, noteworthy (**par** for); **les faits remarquables de la semaine** the highlights *or* outstanding events of the week; **d'un courage r.** remarkably brave; **elle est r. par sa** *ou* **de patience/beauté** she is remarkably patient/beautiful; **il est r. qu'il n'ait rien entendu** it's remarkable *or* strange that he heard nothing

remarquablement [rəmarkabləmɑ̃] *adv* (*bon, mauvais, bien, changer, progresser etc*) remarkably; **danser/cuisiner r.** to dance/cook remarkably well, to be a remarkably good *or* an outstanding dancer/cook

remarque [rəmark] *nf* (*observation*) remark; **faire une r.** to make *or* pass a remark; (*critique*) to pass a remark; **cette r. t'était destinée** that was aimed at you, that was a dig at you; **elle a fait la r. que …** she remarked that …; **faire la r. de qch** to remark on sth; **je dois lui en faire la r.** I must point it out *or* remark on it to him; **tu sais, je m'en étais fait la r.** it had crossed my mind, you know; **texte avec remarques** text with notes *or* comments; *Litt* **digne de r.** noteworthy

remarqué [rəmarke] *adj* **entrée/absence très remarquée** conspicuous entrance/absence; **discours très r.** speech that attracted considerable attention; **c'est un fait souvent/peu r.** it's a well-known/little-known fact

remarquer [rəmarke] **1** *vt* **(a)** (*constater, voir*) to notice; **r. qn dans la foule** to notice *or* spot sb in the crowd; **il est entré sans que je le remarque** he came in without me noticing (him); **elle a été remarquée par un réalisateur de télévision** she was spotted *or* noticed by a television director; **je n'ai pas remarqué son absence** I didn't notice his absence, I didn't miss him; **je remarque que personne n'en a parlé** I notice *or* note that no-one has spoken about it; **faire r. qch à qn** to point sth out to sb, to call sb's attention to sth; **je te ferai juste r. que tu devais être là à sept heures** you should have been here at seven o'clock, you know; **je vous ferai r. que …** I'll have you know that …; **je te ferai r. que c'est encore moi qui ai fait la vaisselle!** just in case you hadn't noticed, it was me that did the dishes again!; **se faire r.** to attract attention, to get noticed; **il est entré sans se faire r.** he came in unobtrusively *or* without attracting attention, he came in without anybody noticing; **je ne voudrais pas me faire r.** I don't want to attract attention *or* to make myself conspicuous; *F* **remarque, il n'est pas le seul** he's not the only one, mind (you)

(b) (*dire*) to remark, to observe

2 se remarquer *vpr* (*d'une tache, d'une cicatrice, d'un sentiment etc*) to show, to be noticeable; **sa déception se remarquait** his disappointment showed, he was noticeably disappointed; **cela se remarque à peine** it hardly shows, you hardly notice it; **elle était amoureuse de lui, ça a fini par se remarquer** she was in love with him and it became obvious; **ça ne se remarquera pas** it won't show, it won't be noticed

remballage [rɑ̃balaʒ] *nm* repacking

remballer [rɑ̃bale] *vt* (*marchandises*) to repack, to pack (up) again; (*cadeau*) to wrap (up) again, to rewrap; *Fig F* **r. la marchandise** to take off, to clear out; *Fig F* **tu peux r. les compliments** you can keep your compliments to yourself

rembarquement [rɑ̃barkəmɑ̃] *nm* (*des passagers, des troupes*) re-embarking, re-embarkation; (*de marchandises*) reshipping, reshipment

rembarquer [rãbarke] **1** *vt* (*passagers, troupes*) to re-embark; (*marchandises*) to reship; (*bateau*) to hoist in **2 se rembarquer** *vpr* to re-embark, to go on board again **3** *vi* to re-embark, to go on board again

rembarrer [rãbare] *vt F* **r. qn** to tell sb where to go, to put sb (firmly) in his/her place; **se faire r.** to get told where to go, to get put (firmly) in one's place

remblai [rãblɛ] *nm Constr* **(a)** (*action*) (*avec de la terre etc*) backfilling; (*pour levée de terre*) embanking, banking (up) **(b)** (*terre etc*) backfill **(c)** (*levée de terre*) embankment, bank; **route en r.** (em)banked road

remblayage [rãblɛjaʒ] *nm* = **remblai (a)**

remblayer [rãbleje] *vt* (**je remblaie, je remblaye, n. remblayons; je remblaierai, je remblayerai**) *Constr* **(a)** (*partie effondrée du sol*) to fill (up), to pack **(b)** (*pour levée de terre*) (*route, voie ferrée*) to embank, to bank (up)

rembobinage [rãbɔbinaʒ] *nm* (*de film etc*) rewinding

rembobiner [rãbɔbine] **1** *vt* (*film, ruban de machine à écrire, cassette*) to rewind **2 se rembobiner** *vpr* to rewind

remboîtage [rãbwataʒ] *nm* (*d'un livre*) recasing

remboîtement [rãbwatmã] *nm* **(a)** (*d'un livre*) recasing **(b)** *Chir* (*d'un os déplacé*) putting back into place, *Spéc* reduction

remboîter [rãbwate] *vt* **(a)** (*livre*) to recase **(b)** (*pièces etc*) to reassemble, to fit together again **(c)** *Chir* (*os déplacé*) to put back into place, *Spéc* to reduce

rembourrage [rãburaʒ] *nm* (*action, matériau*) stuffing

rembourrer [rãbure] *vt* (*chaise, matelas, coussin etc*) to stuff; (*épaulettes*) to pad; **bien rembourré** (*coussin, fauteuil, Fig F personne*) well-padded

remboursable [rãbursabl] *adj* (*dépenses, billet*) refundable; (*rente, obligation*) redeemable; (*crédit*) repayable; **les coupons sont remboursables en espèces** coupons are redeemable for cash

remboursement [rãbursəmã] *nm* (*des dépenses*) reimbursement, refund; (*d'une rente, d'une obligation*) redemption; (*d'un crédit*) repayment; **procéder au r. des frais** to refund *or* reimburse expenses; **obtenir le r. de ses frais de déplacement** to get one's travelling expenses reimbursed *or* refunded *or* paid; **r. anticipé** early repayment; **r. garanti** satisfaction or your money back; **emprunt de r.** refunding loan; **livraison contre r.** payment *or* cash on delivery, COD

rembourser [rãburse] **1** *vt* (*dépenses*) to reimburse, to refund; (*achat*) to refund; (*rente, obligation*) to redeem, to pay off; (*crédit, dettes*) to repay, to pay back; (*coupon*) to redeem; **ce médicament est remboursé à 70%** 70% of the cost of this medicine will be refunded; **est-ce que vous êtes remboursé à 100%?** are you entitled to a full refund?; **r. qn de qch** to reimburse sb for sth; **r. qn de ses frais** *ou* **dépenses** to reimburse *or* refund *or* pay sb's expenses; **je peux te r. demain?** can I pay you back tomorrow?; **puis-je être remboursé?** (*dans un magasin etc*) can I have *or* get my money back *or* a refund?; **je me suis fait rembourser, on m'a remboursé** I got my money back, I got a refund; *Th F* **remboursez!** give us our money back!

2 se rembourser *vpr* to get one's money back; **elle s'est remboursée dans la caisse** she paid herself back out of the till

rembrunir [rãbrynir] **1** *vt Litt* (*assemblée*) to cast a gloom over **2 se rembrunir** *vpr* **(a)** (*d'un visage*) to cloud over; **elle s'est rembrunie** her face darkened, she scowled **(b)** *Litt* (*du ciel*) to cloud over, to grow dark

remède [rəmɛd] *nm Méd, Fig* remedy, cure (**à, de, contre** for); **c'est un bon r. contre la douleur** it's a good painkiller; **le r. est pire que le mal** the cure is worse than the disease; **r. de bonne femme** old wives' remedy; **r. de cheval** kill-or-cure remedy; **c'est sans r.** it is beyond remedy; **porter r. à qch** to find a remedy *or* cure for sth; *Prov* **aux grands maux les grands remèdes** desperate times call for desperate measures; *Fig F* **c'est un r. contre l'amour** she's/he's/it's a real turn-off

remédier [rəmedje] *vi* (*impf, pr sub* **n. remédiions**) **r. à** (*erreur, situation*) to remedy, to put right; (*problème*) to remedy, to cure; (*manque*) to remedy; *Méd* (*maladie*) to cure; (*inconvénient*) to compensate for, to make up for; (*abus*) to right

remembrement [rəmãbrəmã] *nm Admin* (*de terres*) re-allocation, regrouping

remembrer [rəmãbre] *vt Admin* (*terres*) to re-allocate, to regroup

remémorer [rəmemɔre] **1** *vt* **r. qch à qn** to remind sb of sth **2 se remémorer** *vpr* **se r. qch** to remember sth, to recall sth

remerciement [rəmɛrsimã] *nm* [①**A10**,f,i] **remerciements** thanks; (*dans un livre*) acknowledgements; **avoir quelques paroles de r.** to say a few words of thanks; **lettre de r.** thank-you letter, letter of thanks; **faire ses remerciements à qn pour qch** to thank sb for sth; **tous mes remerciements à vos parents** (give) my thanks to your parents; **remerciements anticipés** with thanks in advance; **je crois que j'ai droit à un r.** *ou* **des remerciements** I think I deserve a thank-you

remercier [rəmɛrsje] *vt* (*impf, pr sub* **n. remerciions**) **(a)** (*dire merci à*) to thank (**de, pour** for); **je vous remercie de m'avoir aidé** thank you for helping me; **je remercie Dieu/le ciel de m'avoir épargné la souffrance** I thank God/Heaven for having spared my suffering; **il me remercia d'un sourire** he smiled his thanks, he thanked me with a smile; **remerciez-les bien de ma part** thank them very much for me; **comment allez-vous? – très bien, je vous remercie** how are you? – very well, thank you; **(non,) je vous remercie** no thank you; *Iron* **c'est ainsi qu'il nous remercie!** that's how he thanks us!, that's all the thanks we get!

(b) (*congédier*) (*employé*) to dismiss; **se faire r.** to be dismissed; *Iron* to be thanked for one's services

réméré [remere] *nm Com* repurchase

remettant [rəmɛtã] *nm Fin* remitter

remetteur, -euse [rəmɛtœr, -øz] *Fin* **1** *adj* (*banque etc*) remitting **2** *n* remitter

remettre [rəmɛtr] (*conj like* **mettre**) **1** *vt* **(a)** (*replacer*) to put back; **r. qch à sa place** *ou* **en place** to replace sth, to put sth back in its place *or* where it belongs; **n'oublie pas de le r. à sa place** don't forget to put it back (again); *Fig F* **r. qn à sa place** to put sb in his/her place; **se faire r. à sa place** to get put in one's place; **r. un os en place** to put a bone back in place, *Spéc* to reduce a bone; *F* **r. les idées en place à qn** to bring sb to their senses; *Fb* **r. le ballon en jeu** to throw the ball (back) in(to play); *Tennis* **balle à r.** let (ball); **r. un manche à un balai** to put a new handle on a broom; **r. un bouton à un manteau** to sew a button on a coat; **r. une doublure à un habit** to reline a coat; *F* **je n'y ai plus jamais remis les pieds** I never set foot in there again; **qu'il ne remette jamais les pieds ici!** I don't want him ever setting foot in here again!; **r. qn sur le trône** to restore sb to the throne; **r. qn sur son chemin** *ou* **sur la bonne voie** to set sb on his way *or* on the right path; **r. qch en cause** *ou* **en question** to question sth, to raise questions *or* doubts about sth, to call sth into question; **r. qn en liberté** to set sb free; **on l'a remis en liberté, il a été remis en liberté** he was set free, he was freed *or* released; **r. qn à l'école/en prison** to send sb back to school/prison; **r. un malade à l'hôpital** to readmit a patient to hospital; *F* **on ne pourra r. l'eau/le gaz/le téléphone avant demain** we can't connect the water/gas/telephone (up) again until tomorrow; *Ordinat* **r. en forme** (*texte*) to reformat

(b) (*rappeler*) to recall, to recollect; **il faut le lui r. en mémoire** he'll have to be reminded of it; *Fml* **je ne vous remets pas** I can't quite place you

(c) (*dans un état antérieur*) **r. qn de bonne humeur** to put sb in a good mood again, to bring sb round; **r. à zéro** to reset, to zero; **r. qch en usage** to bring sth back; **r. en ordre** (*dossiers, maison*) to tidy (up); **r. de l'ordre dans sa chambre** to tidy (up) one's bedroom; **r. de l'ordre dans sa vie** to get one's life straightened out; **r. qch en service** to repair sth; **l'ascenseur sera remis en service demain** the lift will be back in service tomorrow; **r. en état** (*auto, machine*) to repair; (*maison*) to restore; **r. à neuf** to do up (like new); **r. en marche** (*moteur, machine*) to restart; **r. le contact** to start the engine again; **r. qn en forme** to get sb back on form; **r. qn sur pied** to restore sb to health, to get sb back on his/her feet again; **r. qn à flot** to put sb back on his/her feet again; *Couture* **r. un vêtement à plat** to alter a garment by unpicking and laying all the pieces out flat before restitching; *Arch Fig* **r. l'esprit de qn** to assuage sb

(d) (*mettre de nouveau*) (*vêtement*) to put back on, to put on again; (*chauffage*) to turn *or* put back on *or* on again; (*télévision, radio*) to turn *or* switch back on *or* on again; (*disque, chanson, musique*) to put back on *or* on again; **ne remets pas cette veste demain** don't put that jacket on *or* don't wear that jacket again tomorrow; **nous avons décidé de r. de la moquette dans le salon** we've decided to carpet the living-room again

(e) (*ajouter*) (*sel, eau*) to add (**dans** to); **je remets quelques pommes de terre** I'll add some potatoes, I'll put in some more potatoes; **r. de l'argent sur un compte** to pay money into an account; *F* **tu devrais r. un peu d'eau à cette plante** you should give that plant a bit more water

(f) (*donner*) (*lettre, télégramme, colis etc*) to deliver; (*formulaire*) to send in; (*rapport*) to submit; **r. sa démission** to hand in *or Fml* tender one's resignation; **r. qch en mains propres** to deliver sth in person; **r. qn à la justice** *ou* **entre les mains de la police** to hand *or* turn sb over to the police; **r.**

son âme à Dieu to commit one's soul to God; **je remets mon sort entre vos mains** my fate is in your hands; **r. sa charge à qn** to hand over one's duties to sb; **r. une somme à qn** to send *or Fml, Fin* to remit a sum to sb; **r. à l'encaissement** to remit for collection; **r. à l'escompte** to remit for discount

(g) (*faire grâce de, pardonner*) (*dette*) to cancel; (*peine*) to remit; (*faute*) to pardon, to forgive

(h) (*différer*) (*réunion etc*) to postpone, to put off (**à** to, till); **r. une dette** (*à plus tard*) to defer (payment of) a debt; *Jur* **r. une cause à huitaine** to adjourn *or* remand a case for a week; **r. qch à plus tard** to put sth off (till later); *Échecs etc* **partie remise** draw, drawn game; *Fig* **ce n'est que partie remise** we'll do it some other time, there'll be another time for it; **il ne faut jamais r. à plus tard ce qu'on peut faire le jour même** never put off till tomorrow what you can do today; **arrête de r. les choses au lendemain** stop putting things off till tomorrow, stop procrastinating

(i) *F* (*recommencer*) **on remet ça?** how about another (one)?; **garçon, remettez-nous ça!** (the) same again!; **il faudra r. ça** we must do it again sometime; **tu ne vas pas r. ça!** you're not going to start that again, are you?

(j) *F* **en r.** to lay it on (a bit) thick

2 se remettre *vpr* **(a)** (*se mettre de nouveau dans un endroit, dans un état*) **se r. au lit** to go back to bed; **se r. en route** to set off again; **le temps se remet (au beau)** the weather is clearing up (again); **se r. en selle** to get back in the saddle; **se r. en cause** *ou* **en question** to question oneself; *F* **se r. avec qn** to go back to sb again; *F* **se r. ensemble** (*d'époux, amants*) to get back together again

(b) (*recommencer*) **se r. au travail** *ou* **à travailler** to start *or* set to work again; **elle s'est remise à boire** she's (started) drinking again; **se r. au français/au tennis** to take up French/tennis again; **se r. au régime** to go back on one's diet

(c) (*d'une maladie, d'un choc*) to recover; **il lui faudra un certain temps pour se r.** it will take her some time to recover *or* to get over it; *Fig* **voyons, remettez-vous!** come on, pull yourself together!; *Fig* **elle ne s'en est pas remise** she couldn't get over it

(d) (*se reposer sur*) **s'en r. à qn de qch** to rely on sb for sth; **s'en r. à la discrétion/au jugement de qn** to rely on sb's discretion/judgement; **je m'en remets à vous** I'll leave it to you, it's up to you; **je m'en remets totalement à vous** I have complete confidence *or* faith in you; **je m'en remets à votre avis** I'm leaving the decision entirely to you

remeubler [rəmœble] **1** *vt* (*maison etc*) to refurnish **2 se remeubler** *vpr* to refurnish one's house/flat

remilitarisation [rəmilitarizasjɔ̃] *nf* remilitarization

remilitariser [rəmilitarize] **1** *vt* to remilitarize **2 se remilitariser** *vpr* to become remilitarized

réminiscence [reminisɑ̃s] *nf* **(a)** *Phil, Psy* reminiscence **(b)** (*souvenir vague*) vague recollection; **il y a des réminiscences de Mozart dans ce morceau** there are echoes of Mozart in this piece, this piece is reminiscent of Mozart

remise [rəmiz] *nf* **(a)** (*dans son lieu ou son état d'origine*) *Fb* **r. en jeu** throw-in; *Rugby* **r. en jeu à la touche** line-out; **r. en état** (*d'une maison*) restoration; **r. à neuf** (*d'appareils ménagers, d'une voiture etc*) reconditioning; **r. en ordre** (*de dossiers, une maison*) tidying up, putting in order; *Ordinat* **r. en forme** (*de texte*) reformatting; *Ordinat* **r. à blanc** (*d'une disquette*) reformatting; **r. en marche** (*d'un moteur*) restarting; (*d'un projet*) relaunching; **r. en question** doubting, questioning; **ses remises en question continuelles** his constant doubts *or* questioning

(b) (*fait de donner*) (*d'une lettre, rançon etc*) delivery; **payable contre r. du coupon** payable on presentation of the coupon; **r. des clefs** (*d'un appartement etc*) handing over of the keys; *Scol* **r. des prix** prizegiving

(c) (*fait de pardonner*) (*d'une dette, d'un impôt*) cancellation; (*de peine*) reduction; **faire r. d'une dette** to cancel a debt; **bénéficier d'une r. de peine** to be granted a reduction in one's sentence, to have one's sentence reduced

(d) *Fin* remittance; **faire une r. (de fonds) à qn** to send sb a remittance; *Com* **r. d'effets** remittance of bills; **r. de fonds** remittance of funds; **r. documentaire** documentary remittance; **r. à vue** demand deposit

(e) (*rabais*) discount, reduction, allowance; (*pour paiement anticipé*) settlement discount; **r. sur marchandises** trade discount; **r. de caisse** cash discount, cash rebate; **r. de fidélité au client** loyal-customer discount; **r. pour quantité** quantity discount; **r. promotionnelle** promotional allowance; **r. de marchandisage** merchandising allowance; *Mktg* **r. psychologique** psychological discount; **r. quantitative** bulk discount; **r. saisonnière** seasonal discount; **r. sur les prix** price discount; **faire une r. sur un article** to allow a discount *or* make a reduction on an article

(f) (*appentis*) shed, outhouse; *Rail* engine shed; *Hist* (*pour carrosses*) coach house; **voiture de (grande) r.** hired car (with chauffeur); *Hist* **(voiture de) r.** (*carrosse*) hired *or* livery carriage

(g) (*ajournement*) postponement; **faire qch sans r.** to do sth without fail; **r. d'une dette** deferment of (payment of) a debt

remiser [rəmize] *vt* **(a)** (*voiture, valise, vélo etc*) to put away **(b)** *F* (*rembarrer*) **r. qn** to put sb in his/her place, to take sb down a peg or two; **se faire r.** to get put in one's place, to get taken down a peg or two

remisier [rəmizje] *nm Bourse* half-commission man, intermediate broker

rémissible [remisibl] *adj* remissible

rémission [remisjɔ̃] *nf* **(a)** (*d'un péché, d'une dette*) remission; *Fig* **sans r.** (*travailler*) unremittingly; (*payer, punir qn*) without delay **(b)** *Méd* (*d'une maladie*) remission; (*de la douleur*) abatement; (*de la fièvre*) remission, abatement; **être en r.** to be in remission

rémittent [remitɑ̃] *adj Méd* remittent

remmailler [rɑ̃maje] *vt* = **remailler**

remmener [rɑ̃mne] *vt* (*conj like* **mener**) (*au point de départ*) to take back; **il fut remmené en prison** he was taken back to prison; **r. un enfant au zoo** to take a child to the zoo again *or* back to the zoo; **r. qn en voiture** to drive sb back

remodelage [rəmɔdlaʒ] *nm* **(a)** remodelling **(b)** (*réorganisation*) restructuring

remodeler [rəmɔdle] *vt* (*conj like* **modeler**) **(a)** (*refaçonner*) to remodel **(b)** (*réorganiser*) to restructure

rémois, -oise [remwa, -waz] **1** *adj* (*population, architecture, école*) of Rheims; (*écrivain*) from Rheims **2** *n* **R.** (*natif*) native of Rheims; (*habitant*) inhabitant of Rheims

remontage [rəmɔ̃taʒ] *nm* **(a)** (*d'une horloge, montre*) winding up; **montre à r. automatique** self-winding watch **(b)** (*assemblage*) (*des pièces d'un mécanisme etc*) reassembly

remontant [rəmɔ̃tɑ̃] **1** *adj* **(a) une boisson remontante** a tonic, *F* a pick-me-up **(b)** (*rose*) repeat-flowering **2** *nm* tonic, *F* pick-me-up

remonte [rəmɔ̃t] *nf* **(a)** (*d'un poisson qui fraie*) run; (*d'un bateau qui remonte le courant*) ascent **(b)** *Mil* (*de la cavalerie*) remounting; **cheval de r.** remount

remontée [rəmɔ̃te] *nf* **(a)** (*d'une colline, rivière etc*) ascent; (*d'un sportif, Fin d'une monnaie*), *Fig* recovery; *Sp, Fin, Fig* **faire une belle r.** to make a good recovery **(b)** *Ski* **r. mécanique** ski lift **(c)** *Min* raising (to the surface)

remonte-pente, *pl* **remonte-pentes** *nm* T-bar, ski lift, ski tow

remonter [rəmɔ̃te] **1** *vi* (*aux usu* **être**, *sometimes* **avoir**) **(a)** (*dans l'espace*) (*d'une personne*) to go/come up again, to go/come back up; (*d'une route, ruelle etc*) to rise again, to climb again; (*d'un soutien-gorge, d'une jupe*) to ride up; (*de la marée*) to flow; **je suis remonté lui parler** I went upstairs again *or* back upstairs to speak to him; **je suis remonté pour vous dire que …** I've come back upstairs to tell you that …; **r. dans sa chambre** to go back up to one's room; **r. sur son cheval** to remount one's horse, to get back up on one's horse; **je ne suis jamais remonté sur un cheval depuis** I've never been on a horse again since; **r. (à cheval)** (*après en être descendu*) to remount one's horse, to get back up on one's horse; (*refaire du cheval*) to ride again, to go riding again; **r. à bicyclette** to get back on one's bike, to remount (one's bicycle); **je n'étais pas remontée sur des skis depuis dix ans** I hadn't been on skis for ten years; **r. en voiture** to get back in one's car, to get into one's car again; **r. à la surface** to resurface, to come back up to the surface; **r. vers la source de la rivière** to go upstream; **r. dans l'estime de qn** to go up *or* rise again in sb's estimation; **r. dans les sondages** to improve one's position *or* go up in the polls; **r. au classement** to go up in the ranking; *Fb* to move up the league *or* division; *Naut* **r. au** *ou* **dans le vent** to beat up to windward

(b) (*dans le temps*) to go back (**à** to); **cette dette remonte à plusieurs années** this debt dates back *or* goes back several years; **une amitié qui remonte au déluge** a friendship that is as old as the hills

(c) (*s'accroître de nouveau*) (*des actions, d'une monnaie, de la température*) to go up again, to rise again, to climb again; (*d'un baromètre*) to rise again; *Fig F* **ses actions remontent** things are looking up for him, his stock is rising

2 *vt* (*aux* **avoir**) **(a)** (*colline, escaliers etc*) to go/come *or* climb back up, to go/come *or* climb up again; **j'ai remonté la colline/l'escalier** (*je suis en bas*) I went *or* climbed back up the hill/the stairs, I went *or* climbed up the hill/stairs again; (*je suis en haut*) I came *or* climbed back up the hill/the stairs, I came *or* climbed up the hill/stairs again; **r. la rue** to go back up the street; **r. la rivière** to go upstream; (*d'un poisson*) to run upstream; **r. une rivière en canoë** to canoe up a river; **r. une pente en canard** to herringbone up a slope; *Fig* **r. la pente** (*financièrement*) to get back on one's feet (again); **il a eu du mal à r. la pente** (*moralement*) he found it difficult to pull himself out of it

(**b**) (*hausser etc*) (*étagère, poster*) to move up; (*pantalon, jupe*) to pull up, to hitch up; (*pull, manche, chaussettes*) to pull up; (*fermeture à glissière*) to do up, to pull up; (*vitre de voiture*) to close, to wind *or* roll up; *Min* (*mineurs, charbon*) to raise; **puisque tu es à la cave, peux-tu r. une bouteille de vin?** since you're in the cellar, can you bring up a bottle of wine?; **peux-tu m'aider à r. cette malle dans la cuisine?** can you help me take this trunk up to the kitchen?; **peux-tu m'aider à r. ma fermeture?** help me with my zip, will you?

(**c**) *Mil* (*cavalerie*) to remount, to provide fresh mounts for

(**d**) **r. une horloge/montre** to wind (up) *or* rewind a clock/watch; **r. le moral à qn** to cheer sb up, to lift *or* raise sb's spirits; **ça m'a remonté le moral** it cheered me up *or* made me feel a bit more cheerful *or* gave me a lift; **un verre de vin vous remontera** a glass of wine will cheer you up *or* do you good

(**e**) (*assembler*) (*pièces d'une machine etc*) to put together again, to reassemble

(**f**) (*magasin*) to restock; (*garde-robe*) to replenish

(**g**) *Th* (*pièce*) to put on again, to revive

3 se remonter *vpr* (**a**) **se r. en vin/café/linge de maison** to stock up on wine/coffee/household linen; **j'ai dû me r. en vêtements** I had to buy a whole new wardrobe

(**b**) (*moralement*) to cheer up, to recover one's spirits; (*physiquement*) to recover one's strength; **j'ai pris un petit whisky pour me r.** I had a small whisky to revive my spirits *or* cheer me up

remontoir [rəmɔ̃twar] *nm* (*de montre*) winder

remontrance [rəmɔ̃trɑ̃s] *nf* remonstrance; **elle ne me fait jamais aucune r.** she never admonishes me; **remontrances** remonstrations, admonishments; **faire des remontrances à qn** to remonstrate with sb, to admonish sb

remontrer [rəmɔ̃tre] **1** *vt* (**a**) **r. qch** to show sth again (**b**) **en r. à qn** to give sb a lesson or two; **il en remontrerait à ses professeurs** he could teach *or* show his teachers a thing or two **2 se remontrer** *vpr* to show oneself *or* one's face again

rémora [remɔra] *nm* (*poisson*) remora

remordre [rəmɔrdr] **1** *vt* to bite again **2** *vi* **r. à qch** to take another bite of sth; *Fig* to have another go *or* stab at sth; **elle ne veut plus r. à l'informatique** she doesn't want to have anything more to do with computers; *Fig F* **r. à l'hameçon** to take the bait again, to fall for it again, to be taken in again by the same trick

remords [rəmɔr] *nm* remorse; **plein de r.** full of *or* filled with remorse; **avoir du** *ou* **des r.** to feel remorse; **j'ai des r. de l'avoir laissé partir à pied** I feel bad about leaving him to walk; **une pointe de r.** a twinge of remorse; **je n'ai qu'un r. : celui de ne pas le lui avoir dit** my only regret is that I didn't tell him; **des r. de conscience** twinges of conscience; **j'ai des r. de conscience** my conscience is troubling *or* bothering me; **être bourrelé de r.** to be stricken with remorse; **je n'ai aucun r.!** I'm not the slightest bit sorry!

remorquage [rəmɔrkaʒ] *nm* (*d'une voiture, remorque, péniche etc*) towing; (*d'un train*) pulling, hauling; **barre de r.** tow bar

remorque [rəmɔrk] *nf* (**a**) (*traction*) towing; **prendre un navire/une voiture en** *ou* **à la r.** to take a ship/a car in tow, to tow a ship/a car; **vous pourriez me prendre en r.?** could you tow me *or* give me a tow?; **être en** *ou* **à la r.** to be in *or* on *or* under tow; **sortir du port à la r.** to be towed out of harbour; *Fig Péj* **être à la r. de qn** to follow where sb leads; *F* **il est toujours à la r.** he's always lagging *or* trailing behind; **croc de r.** tow hook; **timon de r.** tow bar

(**b**) (**câble de**) **r.** towline, towrope; *Naut* **donner la r.** to give *or* pass the tow line

(**c**) (*bateau*) tow, vessel under tow *or* being towed

(**d**) (*véhicule*) trailer; **r. de plaisance, r. (de) camping** caravan, *Am* (camping) trailer

(**e**) *Rail* **rame r.** slip portion; **voiture r.** slip coach

remorquer [rəmɔrke] *vt* (*voiture, remorque, péniche etc*) to tow; (*train*) to pull, to haul; **et puis on m'a remorqué jusqu'au garage** and then I was towed *or* taken in tow to the garage; **le dépanneur a remorqué la voiture** the breakdown man towed the car away; **se faire r.** to get towed; *Fig* **elle remorque toujours un groupe de fans avec elle** she always has a group of fans in tow *or* following in her wake

remorqueur, -euse [rəmɔrkœr, -øz] **1** *adj* (*bateau etc*) towing; *Rail* (*machine*) relief **2** *nm* tug(boat); (*avion*) towplane

rémoulade [remulad] *nf Culin* (**sauce**) **r.** remoulade (sauce) (*mayonnaise sauce with mustard, herbs etc*); **céleri r.** celeriac in a remoulade (sauce)

remoulage [rəmulaʒ] *nm* (*farine*) bran

rémouleur [remulœr] *nm* knife grinder

remous [rəmu] *nm* (*d'une rivière*) eddy; (*d'un bateau*) wash, backwash; (*de la marée*) swirl; *Fig* (*de la foule*) ripple; **il y eut des r. dans la foule** a ripple ran through the crowd; **r. d'eau** whirlpool; *Av* **r. d'air** eddy; *Fig* **provoquer des r.** to cause a stir

rempaillage [rɑ̃pajaʒ] *nm* (*de vieilles chaises*) re-seating, re-bottoming

rempailler [rɑ̃paje] *vt* (*vieille chaise*) to re-seat, to re-bottom

rempailleur, -euse [rɑ̃pajœr, -øz] *n* upholsterer

rempaqueter [rɑ̃pakte] *vt* (*conj like* **paqueter**) to rewrap, to wrap up again

rempart [rɑ̃par] *nm* rampart; **remparts** walls; **faire un r. de son corps à qn** to shield sb with one's body; *Fig* **le dernier r. de la démocratie** the last bastion of democracy; *Fig* **le r. de nos libertés** the bulwark *or* bastion of our liberties

rempiéter [rɑ̃pjete] *vt* (**je rempiète, n. rempiétons**; **je rempiéterai**) *Constr* (*mur*) to underpin

rempiler [rɑ̃pile] **1** *vt* to stack *or* pile up again **2** *vi Mil F Hum* to sign on again

remplaçable [rɑ̃plasabl] *adj* replaceable

remplaçant, -ante [rɑ̃plasɑ̃, -ɑ̃t] *n* (*personne*) substitute, replacement, stand-in; *Sp* (*dans une équipe*) reserve, substitute, *F* sub; (*d'un médecin, d'un pasteur*) locum (tenens); *Scol* supply teacher, *Am* substitute teacher

remplacement [rɑ̃plasmɑ̃] *nm* (**a**) replacement, substitution; **le r. du beurre par la margarine** the replacement of butter by margarine, the substitution of margarine for butter; **en r. de qch/qn** in place of sth/sb, as a replacement *or* substitute for sth/sb; **en r. des heures supplémentaires** in lieu of overtime; **assurer** *ou* **faire un r.** to act as a replacement, to stand in, to cover (**de** for); **dactylo qui fait des remplacements** temporary typist, *F* temp; *Scol* **je fais des remplacements** I do supply teaching, I'm a supply teacher *or Am* a substitute teacher

(**b**) **de r.** (*pneu*) spare; (*valeur, pile*) replacement; **produit de r.** substitute

remplacer [rɑ̃plase] (*conj like* **placer**) **1** *vt* (**a**) (*succéder à, tenir lieu de*) (*personne*) to take the place of, to replace, to take over from; (*chose*) to take the place of, to replace; (*temporairement*) (*personne*) to stand in for, to substitute for, to act as a substitute for; **si je pouvais me faire r.** if I could get somebody to stand in *or* cover for me *or* to take my place; **je la remplace pendant les vacances** I'm standing in *or* filling in (for her) while she's on holiday

(**b**) (*changer*) (*vieille voiture, pneu etc*) to replace, to renew; (*objet cassé*) to replace; **r. qch par qch d'autre** to replace sth with *or* by sth else, to put sth else in place of sth; **r. le beurre par de la margarine** to replace butter with margarine, to substitute margarine for butter; **r. un mot par un autre** to replace one word with another

2 se remplacer *vpr* to be replaceable; **cette pièce se remplace facilement** the part is easy to replace; **un ami comme toi, ça ne se remplace pas** friends like you are irreplaceable *or* can't be replaced, friends like you are hard to come by; **une mère, ça ne se remplace pas** there's no substitute for a mother

remplage [rɑ̃plaʒ] *nm Archit* (*d'une fenêtre gothique*) tracery

rempli [rɑ̃pli] **1** *adj* full; **visage (bien) r.** full face; **avoir l'estomac bien r.** to have a full stomach; **r. de qch** full of sth, filled with sth; **tout r. de son importance** full of his own importance **2** *nm Couture* tuck

remplir [rɑ̃plir] **1** *vt* (**a**) to fill (**de** with); (*verre etc*) to fill (up); (*à nouveau*) to refill; (*espace, trou*) to fill in; (*formulaire etc*) to fill in *or* out, to complete; **elle a déjà rempli dix pages** she has already written *or* filled ten pages; **cela a rempli ma journée** it took up my whole day; **cela ne peut r. votre vie entièrement** it can't be the only thing in your life, it can't take up your entire life; **r. qn de joie/colère** to fill sb with joy/anger; **les étrangers remplissaient la ville** the town was filled with *or* full of strangers; **r. l'air de ses cris** to fill the air with one's cries; **comme toujours, il a rempli la salle** as always, he played to a full house *or* he filled the hall; **le corsage est joli mais tu ne le remplis pas** it's a pretty blouse but you're a bit too thin for it

(**b**) (*promesse*) to fulfil, *US* to fulfill, to carry out; (*condition*) to meet, to satisfy, to fulfil; (*ordre, instructions*) to carry out; (*devoirs, tâche*) to do, to carry out, to perform; (*rôle, contrat*) to fulfil; **r. son office** to do its job

2 se remplir *vpr* to fill up; **se r. de qch** to fill with sth; **ses yeux se remplirent de larmes** her eyes filled with tears; **la**

cuve se remplit mal the tank isn't filling up properly; *Fig* **se r. les poches** to line one's pockets

remplissage [rɑ̃plisaʒ] *nm* **(a)** (*d'un tonneau, d'un réservoir*) filling (up); (*d'un trou, d'un espace*) filling (in) **(b)** (*d'un texte*) padding; **faire du r.** to pad

remplisseuse [rɑ̃plisøz] *nf Ind* bottle-filling machine

remploi [rɑ̃plwa] *nm* **(a)** (*réutilisation*) re-use **(b)** *Fin* reinvestment

remployer [rɑ̃plwaje] *vt* (*conj like* **employer**) **(a)** (*réutiliser*) to re-use **(b)** *Fin* (*argent*) to reinvest

remplumer (se) [sərɑ̃plyme] *vpr* **(a)** (*d'un oiseau*) to get new feathers *or* new plumage **(b)** *Fig F* (*financièrement*) to be in funds again **(c)** *Fig F* (*grossir*) to put on weight again, to fill out again

rempocher [rɑ̃pɔʃe] *vt* **r. qch** to put sth back in one's pocket

remporter [rɑ̃pɔrte] *vt* **(a)** (*reprendre*) to take back *or* away; **le livreur a remporté la commande** the delivery man took the order away (again) *or* took the order back **(b)** (*gagner*) (*prix, titre de champion*) to win, to carry off; (*succès*) to achieve; **r. une victoire** to achieve *or* win a victory, *F* to chalk up a win; **c'est lui qui remporte l'avantage** he has gained the advantage

rempotage [rɑ̃pɔtaʒ] *nm* repotting

rempoter [rɑ̃pɔte] *vt* (*plante*) to repot

remprunter [rɑ̃prœ̃te] *vt* to borrow again

remuant [rəmɥɑ̃] *adj Péj* (*personne*) overactive, *F* hyper; **elle est très remuante** she can't sit still for a minute

remue-ménage [rəmy-] *nm inv* commotion, confusion, hubbub; **faire du r.** (*du bruit*) to make a din; **la nouvelle de sa démission a fait un de ces r.!** the news of his resignation caused quite a commotion *or* stir

remue-méninges [rəmy-] *nm inv* brainstorming; **un r.** a brainstorming session

remuement [rəmymɑ̃] *nm Litt* movement

remuer [rəmɥe] **1** *vt* **(a)** (*bouger*) (*d'une personne*) (*tête, jambes, lèvres etc*) to move; (*oreilles*) to waggle; (*mobilier*) to move, to shift; (*du vent*) (*feuilles*) to move, to stir; **r. la queue** (*d'un chien*) to wag its tail; *Fig* **ne pas r. le petit doigt** not to lift a finger

(b) (*mélanger*) (*sauce, café etc*) to stir; (*sol*) to turn up, to turn over; *Fig* (*de vieux souvenirs, le passé*) to rake up; **r. la salade** to toss the salad; **r. ciel et terre pour faire qch** to move heaven and earth to do sth

(c) (*émouvoir*) **r. qn** *ou* **le cœur de qn** to move sb; **cela m'a profondément remué** it moved me deeply, I found it deeply moving

2 *vi* (*d'une personne*) to move, to stir; **ne remue pas tout le temps!** don't fidget!, keep still!; **il est petit, ce garçon, mais qu'est-ce qu'il remue!** he may be just a little boy but gosh he's lively *or* he's got a lot of energy!; **dent qui remue** loose tooth; *Fig* **un pays qui remue et qui se prépare à la révolte** a country stirring in preparation for revolt

3 se remuer *vpr* (*bouger*) to move, to stir; *F* (*être actif*) to have plenty of get up and go; **il a fallu se r. pour obtenir sa signature** we had to go to great lengths *or* to a lot of trouble to get him to sign; **remue-toi un peu!** get a move on!, shift yourself!, get up off your backside!; **on peut dire qu'il se remue, lui!** he's not just sitting back

rémunérateur, -trice [remyneratœr, -tris] *adj* (*travail etc*) remunerative, profitable, financially rewarding; (*placement*) interest-bearing

rémunération [remynerasjɔ̃] *nf* payment, remuneration (**de** for); (*salaire*) pay; **r. de capital** interest on capital; **r. à la commission** commission only

rémunératoire [remyneratwar] *adj Jur* granted as remuneration *or* payment

rémunérer [remynere] *vt* (**je rémunère, n. rémunérons**; **je rémunérerai**) (*personne*) to pay, to remunerate; (*travail, services etc*) to pay for; **avoir un emploi rémunéré** to be gainfully employed, to be in gainful employment; **bien/mal rémunéré** well-/poorly *or* badly paid

renâcler [rənɑkle] *vi* **(a)** (*renifler*) (*d'un animal*) to snort; (*d'une personne*) to sniff, to snort **(b)** (*rechigner*) to ba(u)lk (**à** at); **r. à la besogne** *ou* **devant le travail** to be workshy; **il a accepté en renâclant** he accepted grudgingly

renaissance [rənɛsɑ̃s] **1** *nf* **(a)** *Rel* rebirth **(b)** *Fig* (*des lettres, des arts etc*) renaissance, revival; **r. du printemps** reappearance of spring; *Beaux-Arts, Littér* **la R.** the Renaissance **2** *adj inv* **R.** (*art, château etc*) Renaissance

renaissant [rənɛsɑ̃] *adj* **(a)** (*force*) reviving; (*économie, industrie*) reviving, *Fml* renascent; (*passion*) reawakening **(b)** (*de la Renaissance*) (of the) Renaissance

renaître [rənɛtr] *vi* (*conj like* **naître,** *but pp* **rené** *and compound tenses not in use and p hist* **je renaquis** *rare*) **(a)** *Rel* to be born again; **ville qui renaît de ses cendres** town that is rising again from its ashes; **r. à la vie** to come back to life, to take on a new lease of life; **c'est ce qui l'a fait r. à la vie** that's what brought him back to life; **r. à la joie/au bonheur** to know what it is to feel joy/happiness again

(b) (*réapparaître*) (*d'une industrie, des arts etc*) to revive; (*de l'espoir*) to revive, to be reborn; *Litt* (*du printemps, des plantes*) to return, to reappear; (*de la nature*) to reawaken; **faire r. les espérances de qn** to revive sb's hopes, to get sb's hopes up again; **faire r. la confiance** to restore confidence

rénal, -ale, -aux, -ales [renal, -o] *adj Anat* renal; **calcul r.** kidney stone; **insuffisance rénale** renal insufficiency

renard [rənar] *nm* **(a)** (*animal*) fox; **r. argenté** silver fox; **la chasse au r.** fox-hunting; *Fig* **c'est un fin/vieux r.** he's as sly as a fox/he's a sly old devil **(b)** (*fourrure*) fox (fur) **(c)** *Tech* (*dans une chaudière, un barrage etc*) leak, fissure

renarde [rənard] *nf* vixen

renardeau, -eaux [rənardo] *nm* fox cub

renardière [rənardjɛr] *nf* **(a)** (*tanière*) foxhole, (fox's) earth **(b)** *Can* (*élevage*) fox farm

renauder [rənode] *vi très F Vieilli* (*se plaindre*) to grouse, to grumble

rencaissage [rɑ̃kɛsaʒ] *nm* replanting (*of container-grown plant*)

rencaissement [rɑ̃kɛsmɑ̃] *nm* (*d'argent*) putting back (in the till)

rencaisser [rɑ̃kɛse] *vt* **(a)** (*plante*) to replant **(b)** (*de l'argent*) to put back in the till

rencard, rencart [rɑ̃kar] *nm* = **rancard**

rencarder [rɑ̃karde] *vt* = **rancarder**

renchérir [rɑ̃ʃerir] **1** *vt* (*rendre plus cher*) to make dearer, to raise the price of; (*prix*) to raise **2** *vi* **(a)** (*augmenter*) (*des prix, des loyers*) to go up; (*des marchandises*) to go up, to get dearer **(b)** (*dire ou faire plus qu'un autre*) to go one better (**sur** than); **un homme fort aimable, renchérit-elle** a most likable man, she added **(c)** (*aux enchères*) to make a higher bid

renchérissement [rɑ̃ʃerismɑ̃] *nm* (*de marchandises*) rise *or* increase in price; (*de prix, loyers*) rise, increase (**de** in)

rencogner [rɑ̃kɔɲe] *F Vieilli* **1** *vt* to push *or* drive into a corner **2 se rencogner** *vpr* to huddle up

rencontre [rɑ̃kɔ̃tr] *nf* **(a)** (*de personnes*) meeting, encounter; (*de courants*) meeting; (*de routes*) junction; (*entre deux voitures*) collision; (*de circonstances*) conjunction; **faire la r. de qn** to meet sb; **aller à la r. de qn** to go to meet sb; **faire une mauvaise r.** to have an unpleasant encounter; **point de r.** meeting point; **club de rencontres** dating agency; **des rencontres culturelles** cultural festivals (*intended to encourage cultural cross-fertilization*)

(b) (*d'adversaires*) encounter, meeting; *Sp* match, meeting, *surtout Am* meet; *Boxe* fight; *Vieilli* (*duel*) duel; *Mil* **une r. avec l'ennemi** a brush *or* skirmish with the enemy

(c) r. de pétrole strike *or* striking of oil

rencontrer [rɑ̃kɔ̃tre] **1** *vt* **(a)** (*par hasard*) (*personne*) to meet, to come across, *F* to bump *or* run into, *Fml* to encounter; (*thème, plante, arbre*) to come *or* run across, to encounter; (*opposition, difficulté etc*) to encounter, to meet with, to run into, to come up against; (*obstacle*) to encounter, to come up against; **r. qn par hasard** to run *or* come across sb, *F* to bump *or* run into sb; **mon travail m'amène à r. beaucoup de gens** I get to meet a lot of people in my job, my job brings me into contact with a lot of people; **r. l'ennemi** to encounter the enemy; **r. les yeux de qn** to meet sb's eyes; **sa main rencontra quelque chose de froid** his hand came up against *or* met something cold; **c'est un ami comme on n'en rencontre plus** he's the sort of friend you don't find any more

(b) (*avoir un rendez-vous avec*) to meet; (*disputer un match contre*) to meet, to play against; **je vais le r. ce matin** I'll be meeting him *or Am* meeting with him this morning

2 se rencontrer *vpr* **(a)** (*de gens, de rivières, Sp d'équipes etc*) to meet; **leurs yeux se rencontrèrent** their eyes met

(b) (*se heurter*) to collide, to run into each other

(c) (*se trouver*) to occur, to be found

(d) (*être d'accord*) (*de personnes*) to agree; *Hum* **les grands esprits se rencontrent** great minds think alike

rendement [rɑ̃dmɑ̃] *nm* **(a)** (*d'une terre, d'une mine, d'un impôt*) yield; (*d'un investissement*) return, profit, yield; **actions à gros r.** high-yielding shares

(b) (*de travailleurs*) output; (*d'une usine*) output, production; (*d'un ordinateur*) throughput; **un ouvrier qui a un bon/mauvais r.** a workman whose productivity is good/bad; **travailler à plein r.** (*d'une usine*) to work at full capacity

(c) (*d'une machine, d'un moteur*) output, performance, efficiency; **travailler à plein r.** (*d'une machine*) to work at full load; **machine à grand r.** heavy-duty machine; **r. mécanique**

mechanical efficiency; **r. thermodynamique** thermodynamic efficiency

(d) *Sp* **r. de temps/distance** time/distance handicap

rendez-vous [rãdevu] *nm inv* **(a)** (*rencontre*) appointment; (*d'amoureux*) date, *Hum* rendez-vous; *Mil* rendez-vous; **votre r. est arrivé** your client/patient/*etc* is here; **donner (un) r. à qn** to arrange to meet sb, to make a date with sb; **prendre r. avec qn/un r. chez le coiffeur** to make an appointment with sb/at the hairdresser's; **j'ai (un) r. à une heure** (*avec ami, petit ami*) I'm meeting someone at one o'clock; (*avec un collègue, le médecin, le coiffeur etc*) I have an appointment at *or* for one o'clock; **prendre un r. chez le dentiste** to make an appointment with the dentist; **'ne reçoit que sur r. '** 'by appointment only'; **être en r.** to be in a meeting; **lieu de r.: devant l'église** meet in front of the church; **quel est le lieu du r.?** where are we/they/*etc* meeting?, what's the meeting place?; **le soleil était au r.** the sun was shining

(b) (*endroit*) (favourite) meeting place, haunt; **c'est le r. des artistes/musiciens** it's a favourite haunt of artists/ musicians

▶ **rendez-vous**: **r. d'affaires** business meeting *or* appointment; **r. de chasse** meet; **r. social** meeting between employers and unions

rendormir [rãdɔrmir] (*conj like* **dormir**) **1** *vt* to send to sleep again **2 se rendormir** *vpr* to fall asleep again, to go (back) (off) to sleep again, to drop (back) off to sleep again

rendre [rãdr] **1** *vt* **(a)** (*restituer, rapporter*) (*objet emprunté ou pris à qn*) to give back, to return; (*argent*) to repay, to pay back; (*achat*) to take back, to return; (*copies, interrogation, cadeau*) to give back, to return; **elle est venue r. le téléviseur** she brought the television back; **il faut lui r. la** *ou* **sa liberté** he must be given his freedom *or* set free; **l'enfant fut rendu à sa famille** the child was handed back to his family; **les soldes ne peuvent être rendus** sale goods are non-returnable; **r. la vie à qn** to bring sb back to life; **r. le repos à qn,** *Litt* **r. qn au repos** to restore sb's peace of mind; **rendre la parole à qn** to hand back over to sb; **r. sa parole à qn** to release sb from his commitment; **r. la vue à qn** to restore sb's sight; **cela m'a rendu des forces** it gave me back my strength; **les médecins sont parvenus à lui r. l'usage de sa main** the doctors managed to give him back *or* restore the use of his hand; **ce médicament m'a rendu le sommeil** this medicine has made me able to sleep again; **il faut r. à César ce qui est à César** (*reconnaître le mérite de qn*) credit where credit's due

(b) (*en retour*) (*compliment*) to return, to repay; **r. une** *or* **son invitation à qn** to invite sb back, to return sb's invitation; **r. un** *ou* **son baiser/coup/coup de pied à qn** to kiss/hit/kick sb back; **r. son salut/sa visite à qn** to return sb's greeting/visit; **r. coup pour coup** to hit back, to give as good as one gets; **r. le bien pour le mal** to return *or Fml* render good for evil; **il ne m'a pas rendu la monnaie** he didn't give me my change; **r. la monnaie d'un billet de cent francs** to give change for a hundred-franc note; *Fig F* **r. à qn la monnaie de sa pièce** to get even with sb; **elle l'aime mais il ne le lui rend pas** she loves him but the feeling isn't mutual, she loves him but he doesn't feel the same way about her; **il me déteste et je le lui rends bien** he hates me and the feeling is mutual, he hates me and I feel the same way about him

(c) (*vomir*) (*nourriture, repas etc*) to bring up; **r. du sang par la bouche** to vomit blood

(d) *Mil* (*armes, forteresse etc*) to give up, to surrender; *Fig* **je rends les armes!** I give up!

(e) (*générer*) *Agr* **terre qui ne rend rien** unproductive land; **placement qui rend 10%** investment that brings in *or* yields 10%; **r. un son aigu** to make a high-pitched sound; *F* **ça n'a rien rendu** it didn't work out, it didn't come to anything; **j'ai pris un arc-en-ciel en photo mais ça n'a rien rendu** I took a photo of a rainbow but it didn't come out

(f) (*livrer*) to deliver; **r. des marchandises à destination** to deliver goods (to their destination); **prix rendu** delivery price

(g) *Jur* (*prononcer*) (*décret*) to issue, to pronounce; (*jugement*) to deliver; (*verdict*) to bring in, to return; **elle n'a pas encore rendu sa réponse** she hasn't given her answer yet

(h) *Culin* (*de viande, concombre, champignons etc*) (*jus, eau*) to give out, to release

(i) *Sp* **r. du poids/cent mètres** to have a weight/a one-hundred-metre handicap; *Échecs* **r. une pièce** to be a piece behind

(j) (*exprimer*) to render, to express; **r. le sens** to convey *or* express the meaning; **c'est un mot difficile à r. en anglais** it's difficult to find an English equivalent for this word; **les couleurs/émotions sont très bien rendues** the colours/ emotions are very well portrayed *or* expressed

(k) (+ *adj*) **r. qn malade/heureux/intelligent** to make sb ill/happy/intelligent; **r. qch compliqué/simple/ennuyeux** to make sth complicated/simple/boring; **le homard me rend malade** lobster makes me ill; *F* **ça me rend malade de voir ces petits enfants dans les orphelinats** it makes me ill *or* sickens me to see those little children in orphanages; **vous me rendez fou!** you're driving me mad!; **pour te r. les choses plus agréables** to make things more pleasant for you; **r. qn responsable de qch** to hold sb responsible for sth; **elle sait comment faire pour r. un homme amoureux** she knows how to make a man fall in love with her; **r. qn aveugle/sourd/muet** to make sb go blind/deaf/dumb; **le feu l'a rendu aveugle** the fire blinded him, he was blinded in the fire; *Fig* **l'amour l'a rendu aveugle** he was blinded by love; **c'est lui qui a rendu populaire le mythe du bon sauvage** he is responsible for popularizing the myth of the noble savage

(l) (*expressions*) **r. hommage à qn** to pay homage to sb; **r. grâce(s) à qn (d'avoir fait qch)** to give thanks to sb (for doing *or* having done sth); **r. service à qn** to do sb a favour; **r. visite à qn** to visit sb; **r. compte de qch** to make a report on sth; **je n'ai pas de comptes à te r.** I don't owe you any explanation; **r. raison de qch** to explain *or* justify sth; **r. la justice** to dispense *or* administer justice; **r. l'âme** (*d'une personne*) to breathe one's last; *Hum* (*d'une machine*) to give up the ghost; **r. le dernier soupir** to breathe one's last

2 se rendre *vpr* **(a)** (*aller*) **se r. dans un lieu** to go to *or* make one's way to a place; **vous pouvez vous y r. en train/ avion/bateau** you can get there by train/plane/boat; **en se rendant au bureau** on the way to the office; **se r. en toute hâte à un endroit** to hurry to a place; **se r. chez qn** to call on sb, to visit sb

(b) (*reconnaître défaite, erreur etc*) to surrender, to give (oneself) up; **se r. à la police** *ou* **aux policiers** to give oneself up to the police, to turn oneself in to the police; **se r. à la raison** to see reason, to yield to reason; **se r. compte de qch** to realize sth; **se r. à l'évidence** to face facts; **se r. à l'avis de qn** to come round to sb's way of thinking

(c) (+ *adj,* + *nom*) (*devenir*) **se r. malade/utile** to make oneself ill/useful; **se r. ridicule** to make a fool of oneself; **il s'est rendu maître de la situation** he took control of the situation

3 *vi* **(a)** (*d'une terre etc*) to be productive; (*de placement*) to yield

(b) le moteur rend bien the engine runs *or* performs well

(c) (*vomir*) to vomit

rendu [rãdy] **1** *adj* **(a)** (*arrivé*) **être r.** to have arrived; **nous voilà rendus à Manchester** here we are in Manchester; **tu seras plus vite r. par le train** you'll get there quicker by train; *Fig F* **on n'est pas r.** (*il y a encore beaucoup à faire*) we're not there yet

(b) *Vieilli* **r. (de fatigue)** exhausted, tired out

(c) r. à domicile delivered at domicile; **r. franco bord** delivered free on board; **r. à la frontière** delivered at frontier; **r. droits acquittés/non acquittés** delivery duty paid/unpaid

2 *nm* **(a)** *Beaux-Arts* (*de sujet*) rendering; **r. exact des couleurs** exact reproduction of colour

(b) *Com* returned article, return

rêne [rɛn] *nf* rein; **lâcher les rênes** to loosen the reins, to give a/the horse his head; *Fig* (*abandonner*) to let go; *Fig* **prendre/tenir les rênes** to take over/hold the reins; **passer les rênes du pouvoir** to hand over the reins (**à** to)

renégat, -ate [rənega, -at] *n* renegade, turncoat; *Rel* renegade

renégociation [rənegɔsjasjɔ̃] *nf* renegotiation

renégocier [rənegɔsje] *vt* to renegotiate

reneiger [rənɛʒe] *v impers* to snow again

renfermé [rãfɛrme] **1** *adj* (*personne*) uncommunicative, withdrawn **2** *nm* **odeur de r.** musty smell; **sentir le r.** to smell musty

renfermer [rãfɛrme] **1** *vt* **(a)** *Vieilli* (*enfermer*) to shut up; (*de nouveau*) to shut up again **(b)** (*contenir*) to contain; **livre qui renferme des idées nouvelles** book that contains new ideas **2 se renfermer** *vpr* to withdraw into oneself, to shut oneself off from people; **elle se renferma dans un silence d'airain** she withdrew into total silence

renfiler [rãfile] *vt* (*perles etc*) to restring; (*aiguille*) to rethread

renflé [rãfle] *adj* (*pilier*) bulging; (*amphore*) rounded

renflement [rãfləmã] *nm* (*d'un pilier etc*) bulge

renfler [rãfle] **1** *vt* **r. qch** to make a bulge in sth **2 se renfler** *vpr* to swell (out), to bulge

renflouage [rɑ̃fluaʒ] *nm*, **renflouement** [rɑ̃flumɑ̃] *nm* (*d'un bateau échoué*) refloating, floating off; (*d'un bateau coulé*) raising; *Fig* (*d'une affaire*) refloating

renflouer [rɑ̃flue] *vt* (*bateau échoué*) to float off, to refloat; (*bateau coulé*) to raise; *Fig* **r. une entreprise** to refloat a business, to set a business on its feet again, to bail out a company; *Fig* **r. les caisses de l'État** to swell the government's coffers; *Fig* **ça m'a permis de r. mes caisses pendant un mois** it swelled the coffers *or* kept me going *or* afloat for a month; *Fig* **r. qn** to keep sb afloat (financially)

renfoncement [rɑ̃fɔ̃smɑ̃] *nm* **(a)** (*creux*) (*dans un mur*) recess; (*dans un arbre*) hollow; **r. d'une porte** doorway **(b)** *Typ* (*d'une ligne*) indentation

renfoncer [rɑ̃fɔ̃se] (*conj like* **enfoncer**) **1** *vt* **(a)** (*clou etc*) to drive further in; (*chapeau*) to pull down; *Fig* **je voulais lui r. ses paroles dans la gorge** I wanted to shove the words down his throat **(b)** *Constr* (*façade etc*) to recess, to set back; *Typ, Ordinat* (*ligne, paragraphe*) to indent; (*écriture*) to embolden **2 se renfoncer** *vpr Beaux-Arts* (*du fond*) to recede

renforçage [rɑ̃fɔrsaʒ] *nm* **(a)** (*d'un mur, d'une couture etc*) strengthening, reinforcing **(b)** *Phot* intensification

renforcement [rɑ̃fɔrsəmɑ̃] *nm* **(a)** (*d'une poutre etc*) strengthening, reinforcement; (*d'une équipe, armée*) strengthening **(b)** *Phot* intensification

renforcer [rɑ̃fɔrse] (*conj like* **forcer**) **1** *vt* **(a)** (*mur, poutre, couture, couverture de livre etc*) to strengthen, to reinforce; (*armée, équipe*) to strengthen; (*sécurité*) to increase, to tighten up

(b) (*couleur, éclairage*) to intensify; (*crainte*) to heighten, to intensify; (*impression*) to strengthen, to heighten; (*suspicions, convictions*) to heighten; **r. qn dans une opinion** to confirm sb in an opinion; **tout cela ne fait que r. mes convictions** it just makes me more convinced than ever; **suivre des cours d'anglais renforcé** to do extra English (*more than the normal Baccalauréat syllabus demands*); **faire un henné renforcé** to have an extra-red henna rinse done

2 se renforcer *vpr* (*d'un mouvement, de la pression*) to grow stronger, to grow in strength; (*d'une tendance*) to grow, to increase

renfort [rɑ̃fɔr] *nm* **(a) renforts** (*hommes*) reinforcements; **demander du r.** to ask for help; (*d'un policier, d'un pompier etc*) to ask for backup; **il faut du r. pour finir le projet** we need extra people to finish the project; **des soldats envoyés en r.** reinforcements; **un stagiaire recruté en r.** a trainee recruited to help out; **de r.** back-up, extra; **à grand r. d'épingles/de conseils** with the help of lots of pins/advice **(b)** (*pièce*) reinforcement; *Aut* **r. (anti-impact) latéral** side-impact bar

renfrogné [rɑ̃frɔɲe] *adj* (*visage, personne*) frowning, scowling; **avec son air r.** with his scowling look

renfrogner (se) [sərɑ̃frɔɲe] *vpr* to frown, to scowl

rengagé [rɑ̃gaʒe] *Mil* **1** *adj* re-enlisted **2** *nm* re-enlisted soldier

rengagement [rɑ̃gaʒmɑ̃] *nm* (*du personnel*) re-engagement; *Mil* re-enlistment

rengager [rɑ̃gaʒe] (*conj like* **engager**) **1** *vt* (*personnel*) to rehire, to take on again; (*combat*) to renew; (*conversation, partie, débat*) to pick up, to start again from where one left off **2 se rengager** *vpr Mil* to re-enlist **3** *vi Mil* to re-enlist

rengaine [rɑ̃gɛn] *nf* cliché; (*morceau de musique*) tune; **vieille r.** old refrain; *F* **c'est toujours la même r.** it's (always) the same old story

rengainer [rɑ̃gɛne] *vt* (*épée*) to sheathe, to put up; *Fig F* **r. son compliment** to save one's compliments, to keep one's compliments to oneself

rengorger (se) [sərɑ̃gɔrʒe] *vpr* (*conj like* **engorger**) (*d'un oiseau*) to strut; (*d'une personne*) to strut, to swagger

reniement [rənimɑ̃] *nm* (*d'un ami etc*) disowning; (*du Christ, de la foi*) denial; (*d'opinions, d'une action etc*) disavowal

renier [rənje] (*conj like* **nier**) **1** *vt* (*ami, père, racines etc*) to disown; (*le Christ*) to deny; (*foi*) to deny, *Fml* to abjure; (*action, opinion, idée*) to repudiate **2 se renier** *vpr* to repudiate one's opinions

reniflard [r(ə)niflar] *nm Aut* breather

reniflement [rənifləmɑ̃] *nm* **(a)** (*action*) sniffing **(b)** (*bruit*) sniff

renifler [rənifle] **1** *vi* to sniff **2** *vt* (*fleur*) to sniff (at), to take a sniff at *or* of; (*tabac à priser*) to sniff (up); **il renifla la bonne odeur qui s'échappait de la cuisine** his nose picked up the lovely smell coming from the kitchen; *Fig* **il sait r. une bonne affaire** he's got a (good) nose for a bargain, he's good at sniffing out bargains; **j'ai reniflé le coup** I cottoned on to *or* tumbled to the trick

renifleur, -euse [rəniflœr, -øz] **1** *adj* **avion r.** sniffer plane **2** *n* sniffer

renne [rɛn] *nm* reindeer

renom [rənɔ̃] *nm* (*popularité*) fame, renown; **de r.** famous, renowned; **un restaurant de grand r.** an extremely famous restaurant, a restaurant of great renown; **connaître qn de r.** to know sb by reputation; **en r.** famous, renowned, celebrated

renommé [rənɔme] *adj* renowned, famous, celebrated (**pour** for)

renommée [rənɔme] *nf* **(a)** (*popularité*) fame, renown; **connaître qn de r.** to know sb by reputation *or* repute; **être de r. internationale** to be internationally famous; **être de r. mondiale** to be world-famous **(b)** *Jur* **(preuve par) commune r.** hearsay evidence

renommer [rənɔme] *vt* to re-appoint; *Ordinat* (*fichier*) to rename

renonce [rənɔ̃s] *nf Cartes* **(a)** renounce, inability to follow suit; **avoir une r. à cœur** to be short of hearts **(b) fausse r.** revoke; **faire une fausse r.** to revoke

renoncement [rənɔ̃smɑ̃] *nm* renunciation, renouncement (**à** of); **vie de r.** life of renunciation *or* sacrifice

renoncer [rənɔ̃se] **(je renonçai(s); n. renonçons) 1** *vi* **(a) r. à** (*un projet, une carrière*) to abandon, to give *or* throw up; (*des vacances*) to sacrifice, to forgo; (*la couronne, la succession, une réclamation*) to relinquish, to renounce; (*la violence, sa foi*) to renounce; (*le chocolat, la boisson, son indépendance*) to give up; **r. à un droit** to waive *or* relinquish a right; **r. à un voyage** to give up all thoughts of a trip; **r. à la lutte** to give up *or* relinquish the struggle; **r. au monde** to renounce the world; **r. à faire qch** to give up doing sth; (*projet*) to give up *or* drop the idea of doing sth; **je renonce à la convaincre** I've given up trying to convince her; **deux des coureurs ont renoncé** two of the runners dropped out; **j'y renonce!, je renonce!** I give up; **il est hors de question que j'y renonce** there's no question of me giving up; **r. à qn** (*fiancé*) to let sb go

(b) *Cartes* to renounce, to fail to follow suit; (*faire une fausse renonce*) to revoke

2 *vt Arch* (*personne*) to disown; *Litt* **r. sa foi** to renounce one's faith

renonciation [rənɔ̃sjasjɔ̃] *nf* **r. à** (*la couronne, une réclamation, la violence etc*) renunciation of; (*à une carrière*) sacrifice *or* renunciation of; (*à un projet*) abandonment of; (*à une lutte*) relinquishment of; *Jur* **r. à un droit** waiver *or* waiving of a right

renoncule [rənɔ̃kyl] *nf Bot* ranunculus; (*sauvage*) (wild) buttercup; **fausse r.** lesser celandine

renouée [rənwe] *nf Bot* knotgrass, polygonum

renouer [rənwe] **1** *vt* **(a)** (*ruban, lacet etc*) to tie (up) again; (*cravate*) to do up *or* knot again **(b)** *Fig* (*conversation, relations*) to renew, to resume; (*amitié*) to renew **2** *vi* **r. avec qn** to make friends with sb again, to make it up with sb; **un auteur qui renoue avec la tradition de la littérature courtoise** an author who is reviving the tradition of courtly literature; **r. avec le succès** to enjoy renewed success

renouveau [rənuvo] *nm* **(a)** *Litt* (*printemps*) springtide, springtime (of the year) **(b)** *Fig* (*renaissance*) (*religieux, des arts*) revival; **un r. de succès** renewed success; **connaître un r.** to enjoy *or* experience a revival

renouvelable [rənuvlabl] *adj* (*contrat, énergie etc*) renewable; (*expérience*) repeatable

renouveler [rənuvle] **(je renouvelle, n. renouvelons; je renouvellerai) 1** *vt* **(a)** (*stock, équipement, mobilier, garde-robe etc*) to renew, to replace; **r. ses pneus** to get a new set of tyres, to replace one's tyres; **r. l'air d'une salle** to air a room

(b) (*équipe, personnel, méthode, style*) to change completely; **une découverte qui renouvelle totalement notre conception du temps** a discovery which radically alters our conception of time

(c) (*alliance, contrat, passeport, abonnement, querelle*) to renew; (*promesse, proposition, offre, ordonnance*) to repeat, to renew; (*expérience, exploit, Com commande*) to repeat; (*usage, tradition, enthousiasme*) to revive; *Com* **r. la commande de qch** to re-order sth; **r. sa demande** to renew *or* repeat one's request; (*pour un emploi*) to apply again, to re-apply; **faire r. le prêt d'un livre de bibliothèque** to renew a library book; **r. une traite** to renew a bill of exchange; *Rel* **r. ses vœux** to renew one's vows; **le pays a renouvelé sa confiance au parti au pouvoir** the country has renewed confidence in the governing party; **je vous renouvelle mes remerciements pour votre joli cadeau** (*dans une lettre*) thanking you once again for the lovely present

2 *vi* **r. de zèle** to act with renewed zeal

3 se renouveler *vpr* **(a)** (*se reformer*) (*de l'épiderme*) to be renewed

(b) (*se produire*) to recur, to happen again; **que cela ne se renouvelle pas!** don't let it happen again!

(c) (*changer*) to change; **il ne se renouvelle pas** it's always the same old thing, he never does anything new; **un artiste qui ne se renouvelle pas** an artist who doesn't bring anything new to his work

(d) (*être remplacé*) to be replaced

renouvellement [rənuvɛlmɑ̃] *nm* (a) (*du stock, de l'équipement*) replacement, renewal; **activer le r. cellulaire** (*d'un produit de beauté*) to encourage the cells to renew themselves (b) (*d'un système*) reform; (*d'une tradition etc*) revival; (*d'une méthode, d'un style*) change (c) (*d'un traité, d'un contrat, d'une offre etc*) renewal

rénovateur, -trice [renɔvatœr, -tris] 1 *adj* reforming 2 *n* (*personne*) (*d'une méthode etc*) reformer; (*d'un genre artistique*) reviver

rénovation [renɔvasjɔ̃] *nf* (a) (*d'un bâtiment, du mobilier etc*) renovation; **la maison est en (cours de) r.** the house is being renovated *or* is undergoing renovation; **projet/travaux de r.** renovation project/work (b) *Fig* (*d'une institution*) updating, reform

rénover [renɔve] *vt* (a) (*bâtiment, mobilier etc*) to renovate (b) *Fig* (*genre artistique*) to revive; (*méthode, institution etc*) to update, to reform

renseigné [rɑ̃seɲe] *adj* **bien/mal r.** well-/ill-informed (**sur** about)

renseignement [rɑ̃sɛɲ(ə)mɑ̃] *nm* (piece of) information; *Mil etc* (piece of) intelligence; *Tél* **renseignements** directory enquiries, *Am* information; **pour tout r., veuillez appeler ce numéro** for information *or* if you have any queries, please call this number; **pardon Monsieur, c'est pour un r.** excuse me, could you give me some information?; **nous avons beaucoup de mal à obtenir ce r.** we're having a lot of trouble getting the information; **renseignements complémentaires** further information; *Fin* **renseignements de crédit** status *or* credit enquiry; **demander/donner des renseignements sur qch/qn** to ask for/to give (some) information on *or* about sth/sb; **prendre des renseignements sur qn/qch** to make enquiries *or* to enquire about sb/sth; **aller aux renseignements** to go to find out *or* to make enquiries; **bureau de renseignements** information bureau *or* office; **renseignements (techniques)** data; **service de r.** intelligence branch *or* service *or* department; **organes de renseignements et de sécurité** security; **agent de** *ou* **du r.** (intelligence) agent

renseigner [rɑ̃seɲe] 1 *vt* **r. qn** to give sb some information; **on vous a (fort) mal renseigné** you have been (badly) misinformed; **l'office du tourisme nous a très bien/très mal renseignés** the tourist board gave us excellent information/totally the wrong information; **r. qn sur qch** to tell sb about sth, to give sb information *or* inform sb about sth; **r. qn sur un cours/le fonctionnement d'un ordinateur** to tell sb about *or F* to fill *or* clue sb in on a course/how a computer works; **être bien renseigné sur qch** to be well informed about sth; **je vais vous r. sur lui** I'll tell you something about him

2 se renseigner *vpr* to ask, to make enquiries, to enquire; (*obtenir des renseignements*) to find out, to get information (**sur** about); **essaie de te r. pour savoir combien coûterait un billet** try to find out how much a ticket would cost

rentabilisation [rɑ̃tabilizasjɔ̃] *nf* making profitable; (*de projet, opération*) making cost-effective

rentabiliser [rɑ̃tabilize] 1 *vt* (*projet, opération*) to make cost-effective; (*société, placement etc*) to make profitable; **r. des investissements** to obtain a return on investments **2 se rentabiliser** *vpr* (*d'un projet, d'une opération*) to become cost-effective; (*d'un placement, d'une société*) to become profitable

rentabilité [rɑ̃tabilite] *nf* (*d'un projet, d'une opération*) cost-effectiveness; (*d'un placement, d'une société*) profitability; (*d'un investissement*) rate of return; **r. du capital** return on capital

rentable [rɑ̃tabl] *adj* (*projet, opération*) cost-effective; (*placement, société*) profitable; **ce n'est pas r.** it doesn't pay; **d'accord, si c'est r.** OK, if there's any money in it *or* any money to be made out of it, OK, if it's financially worthwhile; **ses investigations sont peu rentables** his investigations aren't proving very profitable; **loyer r. /peu r.** economic/ uneconomic rent

rente [rɑ̃t] *nf* (a) **rentes** (*revenu*) unearned *or* private income; **vivre de ses rentes** to live off one's private income; **je n'ai qu'un rêve: vivre de mes rentes** I dream of having a private income (b) (*pension*) annuity, pension; (*reçue de qn*) allowance; **faire une r. à qn** to make sb an (annual) allowance; **on lui a fait une r.** he has been pensioned off (c) **rentes (sur l'État)** (government) stocks *or* funds *or* bonds

▶ **rente**: *Fin* **r. de situation** guaranteed income; **r. viagère** life annuity

rentier, -ière [rɑ̃tje, -jɛr] *n* person of private means *or* with a private income; **petit r.** person with a small private income; **mener une vie de r.** to lead a life of leisure, to be a lady/ gentleman of leisure; **avoir une mentalité de r.** to think one is above earning a living

rentrant, -ante [rɑ̃trɑ̃, -ɑ̃t] 1 *adj* (a) *Math* **angle r.** reflex *or* re-entrant angle; *Phot* **monture rentrante** sunken mount (b) *Av* **train d'atterrissage r.** retractable undercarriage **2** *n Cartes* new player, cutter-in

rentré [rɑ̃tre] *adj* (a) (*joues*) hollow, sunken; (*yeux*) sunken (b) (*rire, rage etc*) suppressed

rentrée [rɑ̃tre] *nf* (a) (*des vacanciers, des automobilistes etc*) return, return home; *Mus* (*d'un motif, instrument*) re-entry; **les embouteillages causés par les rentrées sur Paris** the traffic jams caused by Parisians returning home; *Astronaut* **r. atmosphérique** re-entry into the atmosphere

(b) (*des tribunaux, des théâtres*) reopening; **r. (parlementaire)** reassembly, reopening (of Parliament); *Scol* **la r. (des classes)/(scolaire)** the beginning of term/the new school year; **on se reverra à la r.!** see you next term!, see you after the holidays!; **la préparation de la r.** preparation for the new term/the new school year; **on s'occupera de cela à la r.** we'll worry about that when the new term starts *or* when term starts again; **le jour de la r.** the first day of (the new) term; **la r. des élèves/des professeurs** the day the pupils/teachers go back; **la r. sociale** the start of the social calendar; **faire sa r. politique** (*après les vacances*) to resume one's political activities; (*après une longue absence*) to make one's political comeback; **la r. littéraire** this autumn's new books

(c) (*d'argent*) receipt; **rentrées fiscales** tax revenue; **rentrées journalières** daily takings; *Compta* **rentrées et sorties de caisse** cash receipts and payments; **j'attends une r. d'argent** I'm expecting some money; **il n'y a pas assez de rentrées d'argent** there isn't enough money coming in

(d) (*de la récolte*) getting in

(e) *Fb* **r. en touche** throw-in

rentrer [rɑ̃tre] 1 *vi* (*aux* **être**) (a) (*entrer de nouveau*) to re-enter; (*vers le point de référence choisi*) to come in again; (*en s'éloignant du point de référence choisi*) to go in again; **r. dans sa chambre** to go back into one's room; **lorsqu'il rentra en France/à Paris** when he returned to France/Paris; **r. dans son pays** to go back home, to go back to one's own country; *Astronaut* **r. dans l'atmosphère** to re-enter the atmosphere; **r. au port** to return to port, to put back to port; **r. dans les bonnes grâces de qn** to regain favour with sb, to get back into sb's good books; **r. en correspondance avec qn** to resume correspondence with sb; **r. en relation avec qn** to get in touch with *or* contact sb again; **r. dans le droit chemin** to mend one's ways, to turn over a new leaf; **faire r. qn dans le droit chemin** to get sb back on the straight and narrow; **r. en scène** (*d'un acteur*) to come on again

(b) (*à la maison*) to return home; (*vers le point de référence*) to come (back) home; (*en s'éloignant du point de référence*) to go (back) home; **r. d'un voyage/de vacances** to come back from a trip/holiday; **elle rentre de Paris** she is just home *or* back from Paris, she has just got home *or* back from Paris; **je serai rentré à cette date** I'll be (back) home by then; **il est rentré très tard** he was very late back, he came home *or* got in very late; **c'est à cette heure-ci que tu rentres?** what kind of time do you call this (to come home at)?; **il est l'heure de r.** it's time we went home, it's time to go home; **nous allons r.** we're going home; **je rentre chez moi** I'm going home; **je l'ai vu en rentrant chez moi** I saw him/it on my way home; **en rentrant de l'école** on my/his/*etc* way home from school; **je rentre de chez ma voisine, il paraît que ...** I've just come (back) from *or* got back from my neighbour's, it seems that ...; **r. dîner** to go home to dinner *or* for dinner; **tu rentreras dîner, ce soir?** will you be home for dinner this evening?; **voilà deux jours qu'elle n'est pas rentrée dormir ici** she hasn't slept here for the past two nights

(c) (*reprendre ses occupations*) (*d'une école, des tribunaux etc*) to re-open; (*du Parlement*) to re-assemble, to re-open; (*d'un élève, d'un professeur*) to go back to school; **les enfants rentrent le 15 septembre** the children go back to school *or* school starts again on the 15th of September

(d) (*d'objets*) to go in, to fit (in); **cela ne pourra pas r. dans mon sac** it won't go in *or* fit in my bag; **cela rentre mal dans mon sac** there's not enough room for it in my bag; **ça rentre parfaitement dans mon cartable** it's just the right size for my school bag; **j'ai réussi à tout faire r.** I managed to get everything in; **faire r. qch dans sa boîte** to get sth back into its box; **des tubes qui rentrent les uns dans les autres** tubes that fit into one another

(e) (*d'argent etc*) to come in; **faire r. ses fonds** to call in one's money; **r. dans ses fonds** to recoup one's investment; **r. dans ses frais** to recover one's expenses

(f) (*forme emphatique d'entrer*) to enter, to come/go in; *Cartes* to cut in; **je t'en prie, rentre!** do come in!; **r. dans l'administration** to join the Civil Service, to become a civil servant; **je n'aurais jamais dû r. dans cette boutique** I should never have gone into *or* set foot inside the shop; *Fig* **r. en soi-même** to retire *or* withdraw into oneself; **r. dans un mur** (*d'une voiture*) to collide with *or* smash into *or* plough into a wall; **r. dans un réverbère/qn** (*d'un piéton*) to walk into *or* bang into *or* collide with a lamppost/sb; **ils se sont rentrés en plein dedans** they ran *or* went slap (bang) into each other; *F* **elle m'est rentrée dedans** *ou* **dans le chou** she ran into *or* banged into *or* collided with me; **je ne rentre plus dans mon pantalon!** I can't get into my trousers any more!, my trousers don't fit me any more!; **r. dans une catégorie** to fall into a category

(g) *Typ* **faire r. une ligne** to indent a line

2 *vt* (*aux* **avoir**) **(a)** (*le linge, les vaches etc*) to take/bring in; *Naut* (*cordage*) to heave in, to haul in; (*les couleurs*) to haul down, to strike; *Pêche* (*filet*) to pull in, to haul in; *Av* (*train d'atterrissage*) to retract, to raise; **veux-tu r. le linge?** (*je suis à la maison*) will you bring the washing in?; (*je suis dans le jardin*) will you take the washing in?; **tu peux r. la voiture dans le garage** you can put the car in the garage; **rentre-le dans son étui maintenant!** now put it back in its case; **r. ses griffes** (*d'un chat*) to retract *or* sheathe its claws; *Fig* to draw in one's claws; **rentre ton** *ou* **le ventre!** don't stick your stomach out!; (*tiens-toi droit*) straighten your back!; **r. son pull** (**dans son pantalon**) to tuck one's sweater in(to one's trousers); **r. la récolte** to get in *or* gather in the harvest; **à l'époque où l'on rentre la moisson** at harvest time

(b) (*réprimer*) (*désir, colère*) to repress, to stifle; (*larmes*) to stifle, to hold back; **r. sa déception/sa souffrance** not to let one's disappointment/pain show

3 se rentrer *vpr F* to go home

renumérotation [rənymerɔtasjɔ̃] *nf Télécom* redial

renuméroter [rənymerɔte] *vi Télécom* to redial

renversant [rɑ̃vɛrsɑ̃] *adj F* (*nouvelles, spectacle etc*) astounding, staggering; (*personne*) astounding, amazing; **elle est renversante de bêtise** her stupidity is staggering *or* mind-blowing

renverse [rɑ̃vɛrs] *nf* **(a)** (*du courant*) shift, turn; (*du vent*) shift, change **(b) tomber** *ou* **partir à la r.** to fall (over) backwards *or* on one's back; **il y a de quoi tomber à la r.** it's staggering *or F* mind-boggling

renversé [rɑ̃vɛrse] *adj* **(a)** (*à l'envers*) (*image*) reversed; (*arche, pyramide*) inverted; **écriture renversée** backhanded writing, writing that slopes backwards **(b)** (*tombé*) (*chaise, statue, bouteille etc*) overturned, upset **(c)** *F* (*déconcerté*) staggered

renversement [rɑ̃vɛrsəmɑ̃] *nm* **(a)** (*de tendances, d'alliances, d'une image*) reversal; (*des opinions*) (dramatic) change *or* shift; *Mus* (*d'un intervalle, d'un accord*) inversion; **r. des valeurs** inversion of values; **r. de situation** reversal of the situation; **quel r. de situation!** how the tables have turned!; **r. des rôles** role reversal; **il y a un r. des rôles entre mère et fille** mother and daughter are switching roles

(b) (*de la marée*) turn(ing); (*du vent*) shift(ing), backing; **r. de la vapeur** (*d'une locomotive*) reversing; **attendre le r. de la marée** to wait for the tide to turn

(c) (*à l'envers*) turning upside down; **charrette à r.** tip-up cart

(d) (*d'un cabinet, ministère*) toppling; (*par la violence*) (*d'un régime, gouvernement*) overthrow

renverser [rɑ̃vɛrse] **1** *vt* **(a)** (*tendance, rôles etc*) to reverse; (*lettres d'un mot, proposition*) to invert; **r. la tête** to tip *or* tilt one's head back; **garde-lui la tête renversée** keep his head (tilted) back *or* tilted backwards; **r. la marche** to reverse (the engine); *Fig* **r. la vapeur** to change tack; **r. la situation** to reverse the situation

(b) (*mettre à l'envers*) (*chaise, vase, assiette*) to turn upside down, to upturn; (*gâteau*) to turn upside down; **'ne pas r.'** 'this side up'

(c) (*faire tomber*) (*personne, chaise, vase*) to knock over *or* down; (*verre, seau*) to knock *or* tip over, to overturn, to upset; (*bateau*) to capsize, to overturn; (*liquide*) to spill; (*adversaire*) to knock down; **r. qch d'un coup de pied** to kick sth over; **r. son chargement** (*d'un camion*) to shed its load; **le vent a renversé la table** the wind knocked *or* blew the table over; **être renversé** *ou* **se faire r. par une voiture** to be knocked over *or* down by a car; *Fig* **cela renverse tous mes projets** that disrupts *or* upsets all my plans

(d) *Pol* (*cabinet, ministère*) to bring down, to topple, to vote out of office; (*par la violence*) (*régime, gouvernement*) to overthrow; *Fig* (*obstacle*) to overcome, to surmount

(e) *F* (*bouleverser*) (*personne*) to stagger, to knock sideways; **cela me renverse!** well I'm blowed *or* damned *or* jiggered!; **être renversé par la beauté de qn** to be bowled over by sb's beauty

2 *vi* (*de la marée*) to turn

3 se renverser *vpr* (*d'une chaise, d'un vase, verre*) to fall over *or* down, to overbalance, to tip over; (*d'un véhicule*) to overturn (**dans** on); (*d'un bateau*) to capsize, to overturn; **se r. sur sa chaise** to lean back on one's chair, to tilt one's chair back

renvoi [rɑ̃vwa] *nm* **(a)** (*de marchandises etc*) return, sending back

(b) (*des employés*) dismissal, *Br F* sacking; (*des troupes*) discharge; (*d'un élève*) expulsion; **signifier à qn son r.** (*employé*) to inform sb that he has been dismissed *or* sacked; (*élève*) to inform sb that he has been expelled; **au bout de trois avertissements, c'est le r. définitif** (*d'un employé*) after three warnings it's the sack; (*d'un élève*) after three warnings it's expulsion

(c) (*ajournement*) postponement, putting off, deferral; *Jur* adjournment; *Jur* **r. à huitaine** week's adjournment

(d) (*à une commission etc*) reference, referral; *Jur* (*d'une affaire à un autre tribunal*) transfer

(e) *Typ* (*dans un texte*) cross-reference; **r. en fin de document** endnote

(f) *Tech* **levier de r.** reversing lever; **engrenage de r.** reversing gear

(g) (*éructation*) burp, belch; **avoir un r. /des renvois** to burp, to belch; **le concombre me donne des renvois** cucumber repeats on me

(h) *Sp* clearance; *Tennis etc* return **et r. de Platini** and Platini clears (the ball); **... r. de la tête de Cantona ...** Cantona clears (the ball) with his head, Cantona heads the ball clear

renvoyer [rɑ̃vwaje] *vt* (*conj like* **envoyer**) **(a)** (*faire retourner*) (*cadeau, lettre etc*) to send back, to return; (*personne*) to send back; (*son*) to throw back, to echo; (*chaleur, lumière*) to reflect; **r. à l'expéditeur** to return to sender; **r. qn au lit** to send sb back to bed; *Fig* **r. l'ascenseur** to return the favour; **je le leur ai proposé pour leur r. l'ascenseur** I suggested it to them as a way of returning the favour they had done me; **elle attend que tu lui renvoies l'ascenseur** she expects you to return the favour, *F* she feels you owe her one

(b) (*faire partir*) (*visiteur*) to send *or* turn away; *Jur* (*accusé*) to discharge; **r. qn en cour d'assises** to send sb before the Crown Court; **r. des troupes dans leurs foyers** to discharge *or* dismiss troops

(c) (*licencier*) (*employé*) to dismiss, *Br F* to sack; (*élève*) to expel; **se faire r.** (*du collège*) to get expelled; (*du travail*) to get sacked, to get the sack

(d) (*différer*) (*affaire, débat*) to put off, to postpone, to defer; *Jur* **r. une affaire à huitaine** to adjourn a case for a week; *Jur* **r. le prévenu à une autre audience** to remand the accused

(e) (*reporter*) (*affaire*) to refer (**à** to); *Ordinat* to cross-refer; *Pol* **r. un projet à une commission** to send a bill to a committee; **les numéros renvoient (le lecteur) aux notes** the numbers refer to the notes; **cet article renvoie à un autre** (*dans un dictionnaire*) this entry is cross-referred to another

(f) *Sp* (*ballon*) to clear; *Tennis etc* to return; **Boli renvoie le ballon de la tête** Boli heads the ball clear

réoccupation [reɔkypasjɔ̃] *nf* (*d'un territoire, d'une usine etc*) reoccupation

réoccuper [reɔkype] *vt* (*territoire, usine etc*) to re-occupy

réorganisateur, -trice [reɔrganizatœr, -tris] *n* reorganizer

réorganisation [reɔrganizasjɔ̃] *nf* reorganization

réorganiser [reɔrganize] **1** *vt* to reorganize **2 se réorganiser** *vpr* to be reorganized

réorientation [reɔrjɑ̃tasjɔ̃] *nf* reorientation

réorienter [reɔrjɑ̃te] *vt* to reorient(ate)

réouverture [reuvɛrtyr] *nf* (*d'un théâtre, magasin, de la frontière etc*) reopening; **r. des débats** resumption of proceedings

repaire [rəpɛr] *nm* (*de lions, Fig de voleurs*) den, lair; (*de pirates*) nest; (*de criminels*) haunt

repaître [rəpɛtr] (*prp* **repaissant**; *pp* **repu**; *pr ind* **je repais, n. repaissons**; *pr sub* **je repaisse**) **1** *vt Litt* **r. ses yeux de qch** to feast one's eyes on sth **2 se repaître** *vpr* **(a)** (*d'un animal*) to eat its fill **(b)** *Fig Litt* **se r. de sang** to wallow in blood; **se r. de chimères** to indulge in vain imaginings; **se r. de commérages** to revel in gossip

répandre [repɑ̃dr] **1** *vt* **(a)** (*renverser*) (*sel, liquide etc*) to spill **(b)** (*parsemer*) (*sable*) to spread, to sprinkle, to scatter; (*liquide*) to pour; (*larmes, sang*) to shed; (*fleurs*) to scatter, to strew; (*lumière*) to shed; (*odeur*) to give off; (*chaleur*) to give *or* throw out; (*rumeur*) to spread (about), to circulate; (*nouvelle*) to spread, to broadcast; (*terreur, usage, doctrine*) to spread; **r. du sable sur le plancher** to sprinkle sand on the floor *or* the floor with sand; **r. du sel sur une tache de vin** to pour salt on a wine stain; **ce poêle répand une douce chaleur dans la maison** the stove spreads a gentle warmth throughout the house; **r. le produit uniformément sur le carrelage** spread the product evenly on the floor; **cette nouvelle répandit la tristesse dans la ville** the news cast a gloom over *or* spread gloom throughout the town; **cette nouvelle répandit le bonheur dans toute la maison** the news brought a general air of happiness to the house

(c) (*bénéfices etc*) to lavish; *Litt* **alors que le soleil répandait ses bienfaits …** as the sun was pouring out its blessings …

2 se répandre *vpr* **(a)** (*d'un liquide*) to spill; (*d'une odeur, nouvelle, algue, maladie, de la panique, la fumée*) to spread; (*d'une rumeur, opinion, pratique, d'idées*) to spread, to gain ground; **les métastases se sont répandues dans tout le corps** the tumours have spread throughout the body; **la foule se répandit dans la rue** the crowd spilled into the street; **les touristes se répandent dans la ville** tourists are invading *or* overrunning the town; **l'usage de ce mot s'est répandu** this word is now widely used *or* in wide use

(b) se r. en explications to launch forth into explanations; **se r. en excuses** to apologize profusely, to be full of apologies; **se r. en compliments** to be full of compliments, to be very complimentary

(c) *Vieilli* **se r. dans le monde** to lead a sociable life

répandu [repɑ̃dy] *adj* **(a)** (*méthode, préjugé, idée etc*) widespread, prevalent; (*fleur, animal, oiseau*) widespread, common; (*opinion*) widely held; **un objet d'un usage très peu r.** an object that is in limited use **(b)** *Vieilli* (*personne*) widely known; **il est très r. dans les milieux politiques** he is extremely well known in political circles

réparabilité [reparabilite] *nf* repairability

réparable [reparabl] *adj* **(a)** (*chaussure, machine etc*) repairable; **c'est facilement/difficilement r.** it's easy/difficult to repair; **ce n'est pas r.** it can't be repaired, it's beyond repair **(b)** (*erreur*) for which amends can be made, *Fml* retrievable; (*perte financière*) which can be made up, *Fml* retrievable; **c'est facilement r.** (*erreur*) it can be easily put right; **c'est difficilement r.** (*erreur*) it won't be easy to put matters right *or* to make amends

reparaître [rəparɛtr] *vi* (*conj like* **paraître**; *aux often* **avoir**) (*d'une personne, maladie*) to reappear, to appear again; (*de la lune, du soleil*) to reappear, to appear again, to come out again, to re-emerge

réparateur, -trice [reparatœr, -tris] **1** *adj* (*sommeil*) refreshing; **chirurgie réparatrice** reconstructive surgery **2** *n* (*de vélos, d'appareil électro-ménager*) repairman, *f* repairwoman; (*d'horloge*) mender

réparation [reparasjɔ̃] *nf* **(a)** (*d'une chaussure, d'un vélo, d'une horloge*) repair(ing), mending; (*d'une maison, machine, route etc*) repair(ing); (*d'un bateau*) refit; **les réparations de l'appartement/de la toiture** the repairs to the flat/the roof; **nécessiter des réparations** to need repair; **réparations d'entretien** maintenance; **être en r.** (*d'une route*) to be under repair; (*d'un yacht*) to be under refit, to be refitting; **l'ascenseur/la machine à laver est en r.** the lift/washing machine is being repaired; **route en r.** road up for repairs; **faire des réparations** to make repairs **(sur** to)

(b) (*dédommagement*) reparation, amends, redress; *Arch* (*par les armes*) satisfaction (*by duel*); **assigner une somme d'argent en r. des dégâts causés** to allocate a sum of money to make good the damage; **en r. d'un tort** to make up for *or* *Fml* in reparation of *or* in atonement for a wrong; **demander r.** to seek redress **(de** for); *Fb* **coup de pied de r.** penalty kick; *Fb* **surface de r.** penalty area

▶ **réparation**: *Jur* **r. civile** compensation; *Jur* **r. légale** legal redress; **réparations de guerre** war reparations

réparer [repare] *vt* **(a)** (*toit, vélo, machine à laver etc*) to repair, *F* to fix; (*chaussure*) to repair, to mend; (*maison*) to repair; (*bateau*) to refit; (*déchirure, accroc*) to mend; **donner ses chaussures à r.** to take one's shoes to the mender's; **r. ses forces** to get one's strength back, to build up one's strength; **r. le talon d'une chaussure** to re-heel a shoe; **r. ses pertes** to repair *or* make good one's losses; **la maison a besoin d'être réparée** the house is in need of repair *or* needs to be repaired

(b) (*remédier à*) (*méfait*) to make amends for, *Fml* to atone *or* make atonement for; (*erreur*) to put right, to rectify; (*omission*) to make good, to rectify; (*tort*) to redress; (*dommage*) to make good

reparler [rəparle] **1** *vi* (*après un accident*) to speak *or* talk again; **r. de qch** to speak about sth again; **nous en reparlerons plus tard** we'll talk about *or* discuss it later; **il ne faut plus en r.** it must not be mentioned again; **r. à qn** to speak to sb again; **elle ne lui a pas reparlé depuis** she hasn't spoken (another word) to him since; **si je vous surprends à r. ensemble** if I catch you two talking again **2 se reparler** *vpr* to speak *or* talk to each other again; **ils se sont remis à se r.** they're talking again, they're on speaking terms again

repartie, répartie [rəparti, re-] *nf* retort, rejoinder; **avoir l'esprit de r., avoir la r. prompte, avoir de la r.** to be good *or* quick at repartee

repartir[1] [rəpartir] *vi* (*conj like* **partir**, *aux* **être**) (*d'un voyageur, train etc*) to set *or* start off again; (*d'une machine etc*) to start (up) again; **je repars pour Paris** I'm off to Paris again; **r. à zéro** (*dans une tâche*) to start all over *or* from scratch again, to go back to square one; (*dans une relation*) to make a fresh start, to start all over again; **il est reparti d'un éclat de rire** he burst out laughing again; *F* **c'est reparti, ils se disputent encore!** they're at it again!, they're off again!; *F* **c'est reparti, ils ont encore mis la musique à fond** there they go again, putting their music on full blast!

repartir[2], **répartir**[1] [repartir] *vt* (*aux* **avoir**) (*répondre*) to retort, to reply

répartir[2] [repartir] **(je répartis, n. répartissons) 1** *vt* (*partager*) (*tâches, argent, vivres*) to distribute, to divide (up), to share (out) **(entre** among); (*poids, charge, dividende*) to distribute; (*cours, paiements etc*) to spread (out) **(sur** over); (*dépenses, responsabilités etc*) to allocate, to apportion; (*impôts*) to assess; *Bourse* (*titres*) to allot, to allocate; **r. des objets selon leur couleur** to divide objects up by colour; **r. une ville en zones/un pays en régions** to divide a town up into areas/a country up into regions; **charge uniformément répartie** evenly distributed load; **tâche de bien r. les cartons** try to distribute the boxes evenly; **r. les frais** to share the costs; **r. les risques** to share the risks; **r. un produit** to distribute a product; *Fin* **r. une avarie** to adjust an average; *Couture* **r. le surplus du col** to ease the collar (onto the neckband)

2 se répartir *vpr* to split *or* divide (up); **ils se répartissent le travail** they divide *or* split (up) *or* share (out) the work among themselves; **on se répartit les tâches ménagères** we share the housework; **les sommes se répartissent ainsi** the amounts break down as follows

répartiteur [repartitœr] *nm* **(a)** (*personne*) distributor; **(commissaire) r.** assessor of taxes **(b)** *Aut* proportioner

répartition [repartisjɔ̃] *nf* (*de la population, du poids, du travail etc*) distribution; (*des dépenses, des responsabilités etc*) apportionment, allocation; (*des impôts*) assessment; *Bourse* (*de titres*) allotment, allocation; (*dividende*) dividend; (*des paiements, cours*) spreading **(sur** over); **r. de la population par groupes d'âge** breakdown of the population according to age group; **r. des risques** risk spreading; **r. du bénéfice** distribution of profits; **r. du dividende** distribution of the dividend; **r. d'avarie** (*en assurance*) adjustment of average; *Bourse* **première et unique r.** first and final dividend; *Bourse* **dernière r.** final dividend

repas [rəpa] *nm* meal; (*d'animal*) feed; **faire trois r. par jour** to have three meals a day; **le bébé fait six r. par jour** the baby has six feeds a day; **ne pas manger entre les r.** don't eat between meals; **r. à 18 h** (*au zoo*) the animals will be fed at 6pm, feeding time at 6pm; **r. de noce** ≈ wedding breakfast; **r. chaud** hot meal; **r. d'affaires** business lunch; **r. enfant** children's meal, children's portion; **r. de substitution, substitut de r.** meal replacement; **faire un r.** to have a meal; **r. léger, petit r.** light meal, snack; **aux heures de r.** at meal times; **prendre ses r. chez qn/chez soi** to have one's meals with sb/to eat at home; **plateau-r.** meal on a tray; **ticket-r., chèque-r.** luncheon voucher, LV

repassage [rəpasaʒ] *nm* (*des vêtements*) ironing; **faire du r.** to do some ironing; **c'est d'un r. facile** it irons easily, it's easy to iron; **n'exigeant aucun r.** non-iron; **table de r.** ironing board

repasser [rəpase] **1** *vi* (*aux* **être**) **(a)** (*devant qch ou un lieu*) to pass (by) again, to go/come by again; **elle n'est pas là, repassez demain** she's not here, come back tomorrow *or* call again *or* call back tomorrow; **je repasserai le prendre** I'll call *or* come back for it; **r. chez qn** to visit *or* drop in on *or* call on sb again; **je dois r. chez Denise** I have to go over to

Denise's again; *F* **il peut toujours r.!** he's got another think coming!

(**b**) *Ordinat* to rerun; **faites r. la dernière phrase** (*de bande magnétique*) play back the last sentence; **ce film repasse au Royal** the film is showing again *or* is on again at the Royal; *TV* **ça repassera** it'll be on again, they'll show it again

2 *vt* (*aux* **avoir**) (**a**) (*franchir*) (*montagne, frontière*) to go across again, to cross (over) again; (*mer*) to cross again

(**b**) (*répéter*) (*cassette, disque*) to play again; (*enregistrement*) to play back; *TV, Cin* to show again, to rerun; (*leçon, rôle*) to look over, to go over; **elle nous a repassé le même disque toute la soirée** she played the same record over and over again the entire evening; **r. une annonce** to put an ad in again, to readvertise; **r. qch dans son esprit** to go over sth in one's mind; **r. un examen** to resit *or* retake an exam, to take *or* sit an exam again

(**c**) (*transporter*) to take across again

(**d**) (*donner à nouveau*) **r. un plat à qn** to pass sb a dish again; **si tu as fini avec le dictionnaire, tu peux me le r.?** if you've finished with the dictionary can I have it back?; *F* **r. une fausse pièce à qn** to palm off *or* foist a counterfeit coin on sb

(**e**) (*aiguiser*) (*couteau, outil*) to sharpen, to grind, to whet; **r. un rasoir sur le cuir** to strop a razor

(**f**) (*avec un fer*) (*vêtements*) to iron; **fer à r.** iron; **table** *ou* **planche à r.** ironing board

repasseur, -euse [rəpasœr, -øz] **1** *nm* (knife) grinder **2** *nf* **repasseuse** (*personne*) presser; (*machine*) ironing machine

repayer [rəpɛje] *vt* (*conj like* **payer**) (*facture*) to pay again; *F* **j'ai dû lui r. une veste** I had to pay for another jacket for him

repêchage [rəpɛʃaʒ] *nm* (**a**) (*dans l'eau*) fishing out (**b**) *Fig Scol* **épreuve conçue pour permettre le r. des candidats** test designed to give candidates another chance; **épreuve de r.** *Scol* (*pour les élèves qui ont échoué*) resit; *Sp* (*pour les coureurs qui suivent le gagnant*) extra heat; *Can* (*pour sélectionner de jeunes concurrents*) selectors' meeting

repêcher [rəpeʃe] *vt* (**a**) (*retirer de l'eau*) to fish out (**b**) *Fig* (*personne en difficulté*) to rescue, to help (out); *Scol* **r. un candidat à l'oral** to let a candidate scrape through at the oral; **se faire r. à l'oral** to scrape through the oral; **ceux qui ont échoué au mois de juillet peuvent être repêchés en octobre** those who failed in July may sit the exam again in October; *Sp* **r. un concurrent** to let a competitor go through

repeindre [rəpɛ̃dr] *vt* (*conj like* **peindre**) to repaint

repeint [rəpɛ̃] *nm Beaux-Arts* touched-up area

repenser [rəpɑ̃se] **1** *vi* to think again (**à** about); **r. à des événements passés** to think back on past events; **quand j'y repense** when I think back (on it); **j'y repenserai** I'll think it over *or* think about it again *or* give it some more thought; **je n'y ai pas repensé** I haven't given it another thought *or* thought about it again **2** *vt* (*problème, projet, concept etc*) to rethink; **r. la question des transports** to rethink the whole question of transport; **le projet doit être complètement repensé** the plan needs to be completely rethought *or* needs a complete rethink

repentant [rəpɑ̃tɑ̃] *adj* repentant, penitent; **d'un air r.** repentantly, penitently

repenti, -ie [rəpɑ̃ti] **1** *adj* repentant, penitent; *Vieilli* **fille repentie** reformed prostitute (*who has entered a convent*) **2** *nf Vieilli* **repentie** reformed prostitute (*who has entered a convent*) **3** *nm* (*ancien terroriste*) = former terrorist who now collaborates with the police

repentir[1] [rəpɑ̃tir] *nm Rel* repentance, penitence; *Fig* regret; (*d'un tableau*) touching up; (*d'un manuscrit*) correction

repentir[2] **(se)** [sərəpɑ̃tir] *vpr* (*prp* **se repentant**; *pp* **repenti**; *pr ind* **je me repens, il se repent**; *pr sub* **je me repente**; *p hist* **je me repentis**) *Rel* to repent; **se r. de qch/d'avoir fait qch** to repent (of) sth/doing sth; *Fig* to be sorry for *or* regret sth/doing sth; **je me repens de mon mensonge** I'm sorry I lied; **je me repens de lui avoir prêté mon appartement** I'm sorry I loaned him my flat; **elle s'en repentira** she'll be sorry, she'll rue the day

repérage [rəperaʒ] *nm* (**a**) (*action de marquer, jalonnement*) marking off *or* out; *Ordinat* marking, flagging (**b**) (*action de trouver*) (*d'un défaut, d'une cible etc*) location, locating; (*d'un avion ennemi*) identification, identifying, *F* spotting; *TV, Cin* recce; **r. radio** radio location, radio fix; **faire des repérages avant de faire un film** to check out the location(s) before making a film; **partir en r.** to go to check out the location(s)

répercussion [reperkysjɔ̃] *nf* (**a**) (*du son*) reverberation (**b**) *Fig* repercussion (**sur** on); **r. de l'impôt** impact of taxation

répercuter [reperkyte] **1** *vt* (**a**) (*son*) to reflect, to reverberate; (*lumière*) to reflect (**b**) (*ordre, augmentation de prix etc*) to pass on; **r. une augmentation sur les consommateurs** to pass an increase on to the consumer; **r. l'augmentation des salaires sur les prix** to pass the wage increase on to prices **2 se répercuter** *vpr* (*du son*) to reflect, to be reflected, to reverberate; (*de la lumière*) to reflect, to be reflected; *Fig* to have repercussions (**sur** on)

repère [rəpɛr] *nm* (*point de référence*) reference mark, marker; (*fait exprès*) mark; (*pour s'orienter*) landmark; (*en arpentage*) bench mark; (*balise, jalon*) marker; *Ordinat* marker, flag; *Ordinat* **r. de saisie de commandes** dot prompt; *Tech* **r. de montage/d'ajustage** assembly/line-up mark; **r. de niveau** contour line; **il faut le remplir de liquide jusqu'au r.** you have to fill it with liquid up to the mark; *Fig* **la date de son mariage me sert de r.** I use the date of his wedding as a reference point; **point de r.** landmark; *Fig* **tout le monde devrait avoir quelques points de r. dans la vie** everyone should have some landmarks *or* milestones in their lives; **je manquais de points de r.** I had nothing to go by *or* to guide me

repérer [rəpere] (**je repère, n. repérons**; **je repérerai**) **1** *vt* (**a**) (*marquer, jalonner*) (*terrain, chemin*) to mark off *or* out

(**b**) (*trouver*) (*défaut, cible, endroit etc*) to locate, to spot; *F* (*robe, coiffeur, personne*) to spot; *TV, Cin* (*lieu de tournage*) to recce; **r. qn dans la foule** to pick sb out in the crowd; *Courses de chevaux* **r. les gagnants** to pick (out) *or* spot the winners; *F* **se faire r.** to attract attention; **attention, tu vas nous faire r. par le prof!** watch out or you'll get us noticed by the teacher!

2 se repérer *vpr* to get one's bearings, to find one's way about; *Fig* **je n'arrive pas à me r. dans son galimatias** I can't make head (n)or tail of his mumbo jumbo

répertoire [repɛrtwar] *nm* (**a**) (*liste*) index, list; *Ordinat* directory; **r. à onglets** thumb index; **r. d'adresses** directory; (*carnet*) address book; (*dans un fichier*) list of adresses; **r. des rues** street directory; **r. des métiers** trade directory; *Ordinat* **r. central** *ou* **principal** main directory; *Ordinat* **r. racine** root directory (**b**) *Th* repertory; *Mus* (*de chansons etc*) repertoire; *Fig* (*de plaisanteries, injures etc*) repertoire; *Th* **pièce de** *ou* **du r.** classic; **le r. classique** the classical repertoire *or* repertory; **il a un r. de trois discours** he has three stock speeches *or* a repertoire of three speeches

répertorier [repɛrtɔrje] *vt* (*impf & pr sub* **n. répertoriions**) (*article, informations*) to list

répéter [repete] (**je répète, n. répétons**; **je répéterai**) **1** *vt* (**a**) (*mots, secret, action, expérience, Mus motif etc*) to repeat; **tu répètes toujours la même chose!** you're constantly repeating yourself!; **r. que …** to repeat that …; **je vous répète que ce n'est pas possible!** it's not possible, I tell you!, I repeat, it's not possible!; **répète-moi exactement ce qu'il a dit** tell me (again) exactly what he said; **je t'ai répété cent fois de ne pas le faire** I've told you a hundred times not to do it; **il répète à qui veut l'entendre qu'il a démissionné** he's telling anyone who'll listen that he's resigned; **pourriez-vous me r. votre nom?** could you tell me your name again?; **je ne veux pas avoir à le r.** I don't want to have to say it again *or* to repeat it; **inutile de me le r. deux fois** I don't need to be told twice; **j'ai l'impression de r. toujours le même genre de situations** I feel as if I get involved in the same kind of situation time and time again

(**b**) (*pièce de théâtre, rôle, morceau de musique*) to rehearse; (*leçon*) to learn; **faire r. son rôle à qn** to help sb rehearse his/her lines, to go over sb's lines with him/her; **faire r. ses leçons à un enfant** to go over a child's lessons with him

2 se répéter *vpr* (*d'une personne*) to repeat oneself; (*d'un événement*) to recur, to happen again; (*d'un motif*) to be repeated; **l'histoire se répète** history repeats itself; **les mêmes situations se répètent toujours** the same situations keep recurring

3 *vi Th, Mus* to rehearse; **faire r. qn** to coach sb, to rehearse sb

répéteur [repetœr] *nm TV, Cin* transmitter; *Aut* **r. de clignotant** repeater lamp

répétiteur, -trice [repetitœr, -tris] *n Scol* (private) tutor, coach

répétitif, -ive [repetitif, -iv] *adj* repetitive

répétition [repetisjɔ̃] *nf* (**a**) (*d'un mot, d'une action etc*) repetition; *Fig* (*d'un désastre*) repetition; *F* rerun, repeat; *Ordinat* **fonction de r.** repeat function; **fusil à r.** repeating rifle; **montre à r.** repeater (watch); **des laryngites à r.** repeated bouts of laryngitis; **avoir des rhumes à r.** to have one cold after another

(**b**) *Th, Mus* rehearsal; **r. générale** *ou* **en costume** dress rehearsal; **mettre une pièce en r.** to put a play into rehearsal; **nous commençons les répétitions la semaine prochaine** rehearsals start next week, we start rehearsing next week; **r. en studio** studio rehearsal; **r. hors caméra** dry-run; **r. technique** technical run, technical walk-through

repeuplement [rəpœpləmɑ̃] *nm* (*d'un pays etc*) repopulation; (*d'un étang*) restocking; (*d'une forêt*) replanting

repeupler [rəpœple] **1** *vt* (*pays etc*) to repopulate; (*étang*) to restock; (*forêt*) to replant **2 se repeupler** *vpr* (*d'un pays*) to be repopulated; (*d'un étang*) to be restocked; (*d'une forêt*) to be replanted; **la ville se repeuple** the population of the town is increasing again; **la forêt s'est repeuplée d'écureuils** squirrels have returned to the forest, the forest has a squirrel population again

repincer [rəpɛ̃se] *vt* (*conj like* **pincer**) to pinch again; *Fig F* to catch again

repiquage [rəpikaʒ] *nm* **(a)** *Couture* restitching **(b)** (*de la chaussée*) mending, repairing **(c)** (*de jeunes plants*) pricking out, planting out **(d)** (*de bactéries*) subculturing **(e)** (*d'un disque*) re-recording **(f)** *Phot* retouching **(g)** *TV, Cin* overprinting; (*de son*) transfer, dub

repiquer [rəpike] **1** *vt* **(a)** (*percer*) **l'acupuncteur m'a repiqué** the acupuncturist repeated the treatment; *Couture* **r. l'aiguille au même endroit** take the needle back through in the same place **(b)** (*chaussée*) to mend, to repair **(c)** (*jeunes plants*) to prick out, to plant out; **plant à r.** bedding plant **(d)** (*bactéries*) to subculture **(e)** (*disque, air*) to re-record **(f)** *Phot* to retouch **(g)** *F* (*reprendre*) to catch again; **et que je ne te repique pas à faire ça!** don't let me catch you doing that again! **2** *vi F* **r. au plat** to have a second helping; **r. au truc** to be at it again

répit [repi] *nm* respite, breathing space; *Com* **jours de r.** days of grace; **ne laisser aucun r. à qn** to give sb no rest *or* respite; **la douleur ne lui laisse aucun r.** he is in constant pain, the pain is always there, he has no respite from the pain; **laisser un moment de r. à qn** to give sb a moment's respite; **sans r.** (*travailler*) without a break, continuously; (*harceler qn*) constantly

replacement [rəplasmɑ̃] *nm* **(a)** (*de capitaux*) reinvestment **(b) des mesures pour permettre le r. des licenciés** steps to find alternative employment for workers made redundant

replacer [rəplase] (*conj like* **placer**) **1** *vt* **(a) r. un objet** (*remettre en place*) to replace an object, to put an object back in its place *or* where it belongs; *Fig* **r. un événement dans son contexte** to look at *or* put an event in context; **il faut r. la scène à l'époque où elle a eu lieu** you have to bear in mind what things were like then

(b) (*capitaux*) to reinvest

(c) (*licencié*) to find alternative employment *or* a new job for

2 se replacer *vpr* (*dans un emploi*) to find (oneself) a new job; **il faut se r. dans l'époque pour comprendre ce qui s'est passé** in order to understand what happened, you have to remember what things were like then *or* you have to think yourself into the mentality of the period

replanter [rəplɑ̃te] *vt* to replant; **r. une forêt en sapins** to replant a forest with firs

replat [rəpla] *nm* (*de versant*) shelf

replâtrage [rəplɑtraʒ] *nm* **(a)** (*d'un mur*) replastering **(b)** *Fig* patching up; (*réparation*) makeshift repair; **c'est du r.** (*réparation*) it's a bit rough and ready; **ils ont décidé de reprendre la vie commune, à mon avis, c'est du r.** they've decided to move back in together but they're just papering over the cracks

replâtrer [rəplɑtre] *vt* **(a)** (*mur*) to replaster **(b)** *Fig* (*réparer de façon sommaire*) to patch up

replet, -ète [rəplɛ, -ɛt] *adj* (*personne*) podgy, dumpy; (*visage*) chubby; **un petit au visage r.** a chubby-faced little boy

réplétion [replesjɔ̃] *nf* repletion

repleuvoir [rəplœvwar] *v impers* to rain again

repli [rəpli] *nm* **(a)** (*d'un vêtement, de la peau*) fold; **replis du terrain** folds in the land; *Fig* **les plis et les replis du cœur** the innermost recesses of the heart **(b)** (*d'une rivière*) bend, meander; (*d'une corde, des intestins*) coil; **faire des replis** (*d'une rivière*) to wind, to meander; (*d'un serpent*) to slither **(c)** *Mil* retreat, withdrawal; *Psy* withdrawal; *Mil* **r. stratégique** strategic withdrawal; **une attitude de r. (sur soi)** a withdrawn attitude **(d)** (*de monnaie, prix*) fall

repliable [rəplijabl] *adj* folding, fold-up; (*tablette d'avion*) foldaway; (*antenne*) retractable; **couteau à lame r.** knife with a folding blade

repliement [rəplimɑ̃] *nf* **(a)** *Mil* retreat, withdrawal **(b)** (*sur soi-même*) withdrawal

replier [rəplije] (*conj like* **plier**) **1** *vt* **(a)** (*journal, drap etc*) to fold up; (*lame de couteau*) to fold away; (*bord, coin*) (*de papier, tissu*) to turn *or* fold down; (*de métal*) to bend down; (*d'une personne*) (*jambes*) to tuck up; (*d'un oiseau*) (*ailes*) to fold; **r. les draps** to turn back *or* fold down the sheets; **l'oiseau a replié sa tête sous son aile** the bird tucked its head under its wing

(b) *Mil* (*troupes*) to withdraw, to pull back

2 se replier *vpr* **(a)** (*d'un objet*) to fold up; (*d'un serpent*) to coil up; **la lame se replie dans le manche** the blade folds away into the handle

(b) se r. sur soi-même to withdraw into oneself; **je la trouve trop repliée sur elle-même** I find her too withdrawn

(c) (*des troupes*) to retreat, to withdraw

réplique [replik] *nf* **(a)** (*réponse*) retort, rejoinder; **lancer une r.** to make a retort; **avoir la r. prompte** *ou* **facile** to be always ready with an answer; **preuve qui ne souffre aucune r.** incontrovertible *or* irrefutable proof; **prouver qch sans r.** to prove sth incontrovertibly *or* irrefutably; **argument sans r.** unanswerable argument; **obéir sans r.** to obey without a word *or* murmur; **la r. ne s'est pas fait attendre** his retort wasn't long in coming; *F* **et pas de r.!** don't answer (me) back!

(b) *Th* line(s); **apprendre une r.** to learn one's lines; **lancer sa r.** to say one's lines, to come in on cue; **manquer sa r.** to miss one's cue; **donner la r. à un acteur** to play opposite an actor

(c) (*copie*) replica; (*sosie*) double; **c'est la r. de sa mère** she's her mother's double

répliquer [replike] **1** *vt* **r. qch à qn** to say sth in answer to sb; **je n'ai pas entendu ce qu'il lui a répliqué** I didn't hear what his reply was *or* what he said to him; **'pas de danger!', répliqua-t-il** 'not likely!', he retorted; **que veux-tu r. à ce genre d'arguments?** there's no answer to *or* you can't argue with reasoning like that!

2 *vi* (*répondre*) to retort; (*avec impertinence*) to answer back; **r. à qn** to answer sb back; **je ne supporte pas qu'on me réplique** I won't be answered back; **il répliqua par un coup de pied** he answered with a kick; **c'est ainsi qu'il répliquait aux critiques** that was his response to the criticisms

replonger [rəplɔ̃ʒe] (*conj like* **plonger**) **1** *vt* (*avec force*) to plunge back (**dans** into); (*doucement*) to dip back (**dans** into); *Fig* **cette nouvelle me replongea dans l'angoisse** the news plunged me back into a state of anxiety; *Fig* **le film nous replonge dans l'atmosphère étrange du Berlin des années vingt** the film takes us back into the strange atmosphere of 1920's Berlin **2 se replonger** *vpr* **se r. dans l'étude** to become immersed again in study **3** *vi* to dive (in) again; *F* (*récidiver*) to commit another crime; *F* (*dans l'alcoolisme*) to fall back into; **r. dans l'eau** to dive back into the water

repolir [rəpɔlir] *vt* to repolish; *Fig* (*style*) to polish up

répondant, -ante [repɔ̃dɑ̃, -ɑ̃t] *n* **(a)** (*responsable, garant*) surety, security, guarantor; (*d'un questionnaire*) respondent; **être le r. de qn** to stand surety for sb; *F* **avoir du r.** to have plenty of money stashed away **(b)** *Rel* (*à la messe*) server

répondeur, -euse [repɔ̃dœr, -øz] **1** *adj* given to answering back, impertinent **2** *nm* **r. (téléphonique), r. enregistreur** (telephone) answering machine, answerphone

répondre [repɔ̃dr] **1** *vt* **(a)** to answer, to reply; (*remarque*) to answer *or* reply with; (*lettre*) to send in reply; **il m'a répondu une sottise** he answered me with something stupid; **essaie de r. quelque chose!** (*pour encourager qn*) try to say something!; (*en s'énervant*) say something!; **r. que …** to answer *or* reply that …; *Fml* **il s'est vu r. que …** he obtained the response that …; **qu'est-ce qu'elle vous a répondu?** what was her answer *or* reply?, what did she say in reply?; **je n'ai rien répondu** I made no reply, I gave no answer *or* reply; **il répondit n'en rien savoir** he answered *or* replied that he knew nothing about it; **il m'a répondu d'en parler au médecin** he answered *or* replied that I should talk to the doctor about it; **il répond ne pas être au courant** he says he doesn't know; *Pol* **Londres a immédiatement répondu présent** London immediately signalled its readiness to help

(b) *Rel* **r. la messe** to make the responses at Mass

2 *vi* **(a)** to answer, to reply; **r. à** (*personne, lettre, invitation etc*) to answer, to reply to; (*salut*) to return, to acknowledge; (*accusation*) to answer; **pour r. à votre invitation** in answer to your invitation; **elle ne m'a pas encore répondu** she hasn't answered me *or* replied to me yet, I haven't had an answer *or* a reply from her yet; **r. par écrit** to reply in writing, to write back; **r. par un signe de la tête** (*pour dire oui*) to nod in reply, to nod one's reply; (*pour dire non*) to shake one's head in reply; **r. par un haussement d'épaules** to shrug (one's shoulders) in reply; **r. par une mimique** to make a face in reply; **r. par un sourire** to reply with a smile; **est-ce qu'elle a répondu?** (*à la lettre*) has she written back?, did she reply?; *Scol, Mil* **r. à l'appel** to answer the roll *or* to one's name; **r. à un coup de sonnette/au téléphone** to answer the bell/the phone; **laisse, je vais r.!** (*au téléphone, à* *la porte*) leave it, I'll get it!; (*à une question embarrassante*) leave it, I'll answer it!; **je te défends de me r.!** don't you dare answer me back *or* talk back to me!; **vous devrez r. de plusieurs chefs d'accusation** you'll have to answer several charges; *Tél* **ça ne répond pas** there's no answer; **répondez, s'il vous plaît** (*pour établir un contact radio*) come in, please

(**b**) (*réagir*) (*d'une personne, des freins, d'une voiture*) to respond (**à** to); **la voiture répond très bien** the car responds very well, the car is very responsive; **r. à l'amour/l'affection de qn** to return sb's love/affection; **on a répondu généreusement à l'appel** the appeal met with a generous response; **le chien répond à son nom** the dog responds *or* answers to his name; **il n'a pas répondu à mon appel** he didn't do what I asked him to

(**c**) (*correspondre*) **r. à** (*besoin*) to meet, to fulfil, *US* to fulfill; (*but*) to fulfil; (*description*) to fit, to match; (*critères*) to meet; **ne pas r. à l'attente** not to come up to expectations, to fall short of expectations

(**d**) (*être garant de*) **r. de qn/qch** to answer for sb/sth, to be answerable *or* accountable *or* responsible for sb/sth; **répondez-vous d'elle pour ce travail?** will you take responsibility *or* be accountable for her work?; **r. de l'innocence de qn** to answer for sb's innocence; **il va revenir, je vous en réponds** he'll come back, take my word for it, I guarantee he'll come back; **je ne réponds de rien** I'm promising nothing, I'm making no promises

3 se répondre *vpr* to answer each other; **les deux parties du livre se répondent** the two parts of the book echo each other

répons [repɔ̃] *nm Rel* response

réponse [repɔ̃s] *nf* (**a**) answer, reply; **elle a** *ou* **trouve r. à tout** she has an answer for everything, she's never at a loss for an answer; **donner** *ou* **rendre r. à qn** to give sb an answer, to reply to sb; **faire une r. de Normand** to give a non-committal *or* an evasive reply; **argument sans r.** unanswerable argument; **rester sans r.** (*d'une question, une lettre*) to go unanswered; **elle fait toujours les questions et les réponses** she does all the talking; **pour toute r., il éclata en sanglots** his only answer was to burst out sobbing; **il a souri en guise de r.** he answered with a smile; *F* **j'ai sonné plusieurs fois, mais pas de r.** I've rung several times, but there's no answer; **en r. à votre lettre** in reply *or* answer to your letter; **bulletin-/carte-r.** reply coupon/card; **r. payée** reply paid; *Jur* **droit de r.** (*dans la presse*) right to reply; *Télécom* **r. en retour** answerback; **r. d'attente** holding reply

(**b**) (*réaction*) (*à un appel de fonds, d'aide, Physiol à un stimulus, d'un moteur, des freins etc*) response; (*à une offre d'emploi*) reply; *Aut* **r. à mi-régime** mid-range response

(**c**) *Ordinat* answering; **r. automatique** unattended answering; **temps de r.** response time

(**d**) *Fig* (*solution*) answer (**à** to); **je n'ai pas la r. (à ton problème)** I don't have the answer, I don't know what the answer is; **ce problème est resté sans r.** a solution still hasn't been found to the problem;

repopulation [rəpɔpylasjɔ̃] *nf* (*d'une région etc*) repopulation, repopulating

report [rəpɔr] *nm* (**a**) *Compta* (*du total*) carrying forward, bringing forward; (*somme*) amount carried forward, carry forward, carry over; **'r.'** carried forward; **r. de l'exercice précédent** carried forward from the previous financial year; **r. à l'exercice suivant** carried forward to the next financial year; **r. à nouveau** carried forward; **reports et avances sur titres** collateral loans (**b**) (*de corrections, Pol de voix*), *Phot* transfer; *Phot* **papier (à) r.** transfer paper (**c**) (*d'un rendez-vous*) postponement (**d**) *Rad* plot(ting); **table de r.** plotting board

reportage [rəpɔrtaʒ] *nm Journ, Rad, TV* (**a**) (*article, émission*) report; **c'est France 2 qui en assurera le r.** France 2 will bring you the report; **r. filmé/télévisé** film/TV report; **r. en direct** live coverage; **r. en exclusivité** scoop, exclusive (report); **r. photographique** photo-reportage; **r. publicitaire** editorial advertisement; *Rad, TV* **r. électronique** electronic news gathering, ENG (**b**) (*activité*) reporting; **faire du r.** to do some reporting; (*métier*) to be a reporter

reporté [rəpɔrte] *adj* postponed, deferred

reporter¹ [rəpɔrtɛr] *nm Journ, Rad, TV* reporter; **r. photographe** photojournalist; **r-cameraman** film reporter

reporter² [rəpɔrte] **1** *vt* (**a**) (*pour rendre*) (*objet*) to take back, to return

(**b**) (*transférer*) (*affection, Pol voix*), *Phot* to transfer (**sur** to)

(**c**) (*dans le temps*) (*personne*) to take *or* carry back, to transport; **cela nous reporte à l'époque où …** that takes us back to the time when …

(**d**) (*différer*) **r. qch à plus tard** to postpone *or Fml* defer sth, to put sth off until later

(**e**) *Compta* (*total*) to carry forward, to bring forward, to carry over; **à r.** carried forward; **r. une somme** to carry a sum forward

(**f**) (*transcrire*) (*notes*) to transfer (**sur** to)

2 se reporter *vpr* (**a**) (*se référer*) **se r. à** (*un document, une interview*) to refer to; **se r. à …** (*dans un livre etc*) the reader is referred to …, see …

(**b**) **se r. au passé/à la période de l'après-guerre** to look back *or* think back to the past/to the post-war period

(**c**) (*se déplacer*) (*de colère, d'une affection, Pol de voix*) to be transferred (**sur** to)

reporteur [rəpɔrtœr] *nm* reporter

repos [rəpo] *nm* (**a**) rest, *Fml* repose; **c'est mon seul r.** it's my only (form of) relaxation; **il vous faut le r. complet** you need a complete rest; **avoir besoin de (prendre du) r.** to need to rest, to need a rest; **chercher le r.** to try to rest; **ces enfants ne lui laissent aucun r.** those children give her no rest; **se donner** *ou* **prendre du r.** to take a rest; **r. compensateur** time off in lieu; *Mil* **r.!** (stand) at ease!; **au r.** at rest; **soldat au r.** soldier standing at ease; **maison de r.** rest home, convalescent home; (*de personnes âgées*) rest home; **cure de r.** rest cure; **le dimanche est mon unique jour de r.** Sunday is my only day off *or* day of rest; **après un mois de r.** after a month's rest; **le r. éternel** eternal rest; **terre au r.** fallow land

(**b**) *Tech* **au r.** (*fusil*) at half cock; (*mécanisme*) in neutral (position); (*muscle*) relaxed

(**c**) *Littér* (*dans un vers*) pause, rest

(**d**) (*quiétude*) peace; **trouver le r.** to relax; **troubler le r. de qn** to disturb sb, to upset sb; **troubler le r. de la nature** to break the stillness, to disturb the quietness; **être en r. au sujet de qn** to feel easy in one's mind about sb; **je n'aurai de r. que lorsque je me serai vengé** I won't rest until I've had my revenge; **laisser qn en r.** to leave sb alone *or* in peace; **valeur de tout r.** safe investment, gilt-edged security; **vivre avec lui, ce n'est pas de tout r.!** living with him is no bed of roses!

reposant [rəpozɑ̃] *adj* (*vacances, weekend etc*) restful, relaxing; (*sommeil*) refreshing; (*couleur*) soothing

reposé [rəpoze] *adj* (**a**) (*personne, esprit*) rested, refreshed; **s'éveiller bien r.** to awake refreshed; **elle a le visage vraiment r.** (*après repos, nuit de sommeil*) she looks really rested *or* refreshed (**b**) **je le ferai à tête reposée** I'll do it when my mind's clearer; **laissez-moi y réfléchir à tête reposée** give me time to think it over quietly

repose-bras [rəpozbra] *nm inv* armrest

repose-pied [rəpozpje] *nm inv Aut* tread plate; (*d'une moto, d'une chaise*) footrest

reposer [rəpoze] **1** *vt* (**a**) (*à sa place*) to put back (down), to replace; **merci de le r. là où tu l'as trouvé** please put it back where you found it; *Mil* **reposez arme!** order arms!

(**b**) (*rectifier la pose de*) (*moquette*) to re-lay

(**c**) (*détendre*) to rest; **r. sa tête contre l'appuie-tête** to lean back against the headrest; **ça le reposera** it'll be a rest for him; **r. l'esprit** (*d'une activité*) to be relaxing; **écouter de la musique me repose l'esprit** listening to music gives my mind a rest; **couleur qui repose les yeux** colour that is restful *or* soothing to the eyes

(**d**) (*question*) to ask again; **r. un problème** (*au cours d'une réunion*) to bring up a problem again; **je voudrais r. les grandes lignes de notre action** I'd like to outline once again what we'll be doing

2 *vi* (**a**) (*d'une personne*) to rest; (*être étendu*) to lie; **le corps reposait sur son lit de parade** the body was lying in state; **ici repose …** here lies …; **qu'elle repose en paix!** may she rest in peace!; *F* **ça repose bien, le sauna** a sauna is very relaxing

(**b**) **r. sur** (*rocher etc*) to rest on; *Fig* to be based on; (*dépendre de*) to depend on; **le sort de notre association repose sur lui** the fate of our association rests with him

(**c**) (*d'un liquide*) to settle; *Culin* (*d'une pâte*) to rest; **faire r. ses chevaux** to rest one's horses; **laisser r. la terre** to let the ground rest *or* lie fallow

3 se reposer *vpr* (**a**) (*se relaxer*) to rest, to take a rest; **avoir besoin de se r.** to need to rest, to need a rest; **se r. les yeux/les jambes** to rest one's eyes/legs, to give one's eyes/legs a rest; **j'ai besoin de me r. les yeux** my eyes need a rest; **je pars me r. en Corse** I'm going to Corsica to rest *or* for a rest; **vous devriez vous r. davantage** you must get more rest, you must rest more

(**b**) (*compter sur*) **se r. sur qn/qch** to rely on sb/sth; **se r. sur qn du soin de qch** to rely on sb to look after sth; **il se repose sur le travail de ses collègues** he relies on *or* leaves it up to his colleagues to do the work

(c) *(d'une question)* to be asked *or* put again; **il s'est souvent reposé la question** he asked himself the question time after time

repose-tête [rəpoztɛt] *nm inv* headrest

repositionnement [rəpozisjɔnmɑ̃] *nm Mktg (d'un produit)* repositioning

repositionner [rəpozisjɔne] *Mktg* **1** *vt (produit)* to reposition **2 se repositionner** *vpr* **se r. à la baisse** to move down-market; **se r. à la hausse** to move up-market

reposoir [rəpozwar] *nm (en plein air)* wayside altar; *(dans l'église)* temporary altar

repoussage [rəpusaʒ] *nm* embossing, repoussé work

repoussant [rəpusɑ̃] *adj (apparence etc)* repulsive, repellent; **d'une laideur repoussante** repulsively ugly

repousse [rəpus] *nf (des cheveux, des plantes, de la pelouse etc)* regrowth, regrowing; **pour activer la r.** to encourage new growth

repoussé [rəpuse] *Tech* **1** *adj* embossed, repoussé **2** *nm* embossing, repoussé

repoussement [rəpusmɑ̃] *nm (d'une arme à feu)* recoil, kick

repousser [rəpuse] **1** *vt* **(a)** *(objet) (écarter)* to push aside *or* away; *(en arrière)* to push back; *(volets)* to push *or* throw back; *(ennemi, attaque)* to repel, to beat *or* fight off, to beat back; *(les avances de qn)* to repel; *(offre, proposition, idée, demande)* to reject, to turn down; *(conseils)* to reject, to brush aside; **r. qch de la main** to push sth away *or* aside; **r. qch du pied** to push sth away with one's foot; **r. qn** to push *or* thrust sb aside; *Fig (rabrouer)* to rebuff sb; **elle a repoussé mes conseils avec mépris** she pooh-poohed my advice

(b) *(différer) (événement, rendez-vous etc)* to postpone, to put off **(à** until); **r. les délais de livraison du travail** to push back the deadline for completion of the work

(c) *(dégoûter) (personne)* to be repellent to, to repel; **cette odeur me repousse** I find the smell repellent

(d) *(métal, cuir)* to emboss, to work in repoussé

2 *vi (d'un arbre, d'une plante)* to shoot (up) again, to spring up again; *(des cheveux, de l'herbe, des feuilles)* to grow again; **elle se laisse r. les cheveux** she's letting her hair grow again

repoussoir [rəpuswar] *nm* **(a)** *(de manucure)* cuticle pen; *Tech (ciseau)* embossing punch **(b)** *Fig* foil; **servir de r. à la beauté de qn** to set off sb's beauty, to serve as a foil to sb's beauty **(c)** *F (personne laide)* ugly person; **c'est un vrai r.** he/she is really ugly

répréhensible [repreɑ̃sibl] *adj* reprehensible; **de façon r.** *(se conduire, agir)* reprehensibly, in a reprehensible way

reprendre [rəprɑ̃dr] *(conj like* **prendre)** **1** *vt* **(a)** *(ville)* to retake, to recapture; *(fugitif)* to recapture; *(territoire, Sp titre)* to win back, to recapture **(à** from)

(b) r. du pain/vin to take *or* have some more bread/wine; **vous reprendrez bien un peu de thé?** would you like some more tea?

(c) *(récupérer) (objet prêté)* to get back; **je suis allé r. mon parapluie** I went to get my umbrella back *or* to recover *or* retrieve my umbrella; **r. ses chaussures chez le cordonnier** to get one's shoes (back) *or* pick up one's shoes from the mender's; **je peux r. ma machine à coudre?** can I have my sewing machine back?; **il est passé r. tous ses meubles** he came and took away all his furniture; **je passerai les r. dans la semaine** I'll come back for them *or* I'll pick them up sometime this week; **je vous reprendrai en passant** I'll pick you up (again) as I go by; **r. sa place** *(s'asseoir)* to take one's seat again; *(dans une entreprise)* to take one's place again; **r. connaissance** to recover *or* regain consciousness, to come to; **r. possession de qch** to regain possession of sth; **r. ses esprits** to collect *or* gather one's thoughts; **r. haleine** to get one's breath back, to recover one's breath; **r. contact avec qn** to get in touch with sb again; **r. contact avec l'actualité** to catch up on the news; **r. goût à la vie** to find life worth living again, to recover one's zest for life; **r. la route** to take to the road again; **r. des forces** to get one's strength back; **r. courage** to summon up one's courage again; **elle reprend espoir** she's starting to hope *or* be hopeful again; **r. la parole** to resume, to go on (talking *or* speaking); **r. les choses/qn en main** to take things/sb in hand again

(d) *Fig* **la fièvre l'a repris** he has had another bout of fever; **ça le reprend!** it's starting all over again!; **ça ne va pas te r., tout de même, cette habitude de douter de tout!** you're not going to get back into that habit of doubting everything, are you?; *F* **on ne m'y reprendra plus** I won't be had *or* caught again *or* another time; **que je ne vous y reprenne plus!** don't let me catch you at it again!; **et que je ne te reprenne pas à écouter aux portes!** don't let me catch you listening at doors again!

(e) *(cadeau, marchandise invendue, article en solde etc)* to take back; *(employé)* to take on again, to re-engage; *(promesse, offre)* to go back on, *Fml* to retract; **les articles ne seront ni repris ni échangé** goods may not be returned or exchanged; **le garagiste me l'a reprise à l'achat de la nouvelle** the man at the garage took it off me in part exchange *or* as a trade-in for the new one

(f) *(recommencer) (conversation, fonctions)* to resume, to take up again; *(pourparlers, hostilités, relations)* to re-open, to resume; *Mus (thème)* to restate, to recapitulate; **r. le travail** *(après une grève)* to return to work; *(après une maladie)* to go back to work; **r. son travail** to get back to work, to start work again; **reprenons les faits** let's go over the facts again, let's recapitulate (the facts); **r. les choses au début** to start all over again, to go back to the beginning; **je vais r. toute l'histoire à ses origines** I'll go right back to the beginning *or* to how it all started; **r. son cours** to continue as before, to carry on as before; **r. la lutte/le combat** to continue the *or* carry on the struggle/the fight; *Th* **r. une pièce** to revive a play; **r. un refrain en chœur** to take up a chorus, to join in a chorus; **reprenez après moi ces paroles** repeat these words after me; **'oui', reprit-il** 'yes', he replied

(g) *(réparer) (tableau)* to retouch; *(texte) (modifier)* to correct; *(refaire)* to redo; *Couture* to alter **(à la taille** at the waist)

(h) *(personne) (corriger)* to correct; *(réprimander)* to reprimand; *F* to tell off, *Fml* to reprove **(de** for); **il trouve toujours quelque chose à r.** he always finds something to criticize

2 *vi* **(a)** *(recommencer)* to start *or* begin again; *(de pourparlers, hostilités)* to resume, to re-open; *(d'une mode)* to return, to be revived; *(des affaires)* to recover, to pick up (again); **les cours reprennent à quatorze heures** classes start *or* begin again at two o'clock; **le froid a repris** the cold weather has set in again

(b) *(d'une plante)* to pick up

3 se reprendre *vpr* **(a)** *(se ressaisir)* to recover, to pull oneself together; **reprends-toi!** pull yourself together!, get a grip on yourself!; **donnez-moi le temps de me r.** give me time to collect myself *or* my thoughts

(b) *(se corriger)* to correct oneself *(in speaking)*; *(réciproquement)* to correct each other

(c) se r. à faire qch to begin *or* start doing *or* to do sth again

(d) s'y r. à plusieurs fois pour faire qch to make several attempts *or* have several goes at doing sth; **j'ai dû m'y r. à trois fois** I had to have three goes at it

repreneur [rəprənœr] *nm* purchaser; *Fin* buyer; **le nom du r. de l'entreprise** the name of the person who took over the company

représailles [rəprezaj] *nfpl* reprisals, retaliation; **par peur des r.** for fear of reprisals; **en r. de qch** in reprisal for sth; **par r.** in reprisal, as a reprisal; **expédition de r.** punitive expedition; **des mesures de r.** reprisals **(contre** against); **user de r.** to take reprisals

représentable [rəprezɑ̃tabl] *adj* which can be represented

représentant, -ante [rəprezɑ̃tɑ̃, -ɑ̃t] *n* **(a)** *Pol, Ind* representative; **r. syndical** (trade-)union representative; *US* **la Chambre des représentants** the House of Representatives; **être le r. de l'opinion publique** to represent public opinion; **r. du personnel** employees' representative **(b)** *Com* **r. (de commerce** *ou* **commercial)** (sales) representative; *F* (sales) rep **(en** for); **notre r. au Japon** our agent in Japan; **r. multi-carte** rep for several companies

représentatif, -ive [rəprezɑ̃tatif, -iv] *adj (échantillon, gouvernement)* representative; *(personne)* typical, representative; **symbole r. du pouvoir** symbol representative of *or* representing power; **ceci est tout à fait r. de son état d'esprit** it's quite indicative *or* typical of his state of mind; **voilà des photos, mais elles ne sont pas très représentatives** here are some photos but they don't really give you the right idea

représentation [rəprezɑ̃tasjɔ̃] *nf* **(a)** *Pol, Jur etc* representation; *(représentants)* representatives; *Pol* **r. proportionnelle** proportional representation

(b) *Com* representation; *(agence)* agency; **faire de la r., être dans la r.** to be a (sales) representative *or F* (sales) rep; **r. exclusive** sole agency

(c) *(de concept, de faits, d'objet, en peinture etc)* representation; **c'est sa r. de la situation** that's his idea *or* reading of the situation, that's how he sees *or* reads the situation; **c'est une r. possible de la situation** that's one possible view *or* reading of the situation; *Psy* **faculté de la r. spatiale** spatial perception

(d) *Jur (de documents etc)* production

(e) *Th* performance; **troupe en r.** touring company; **droits de r.** performing rights

(f) frais de r. entertainment allowance; *F* **être en r.** to be trying to impress

représentativité [rəprezɑ̃tativite] *nf* representativeness; **si vous acceptez la r. de notre échantillon** if you accept that our sample is representative

représenter [rəprezɑ̃te] **1** *vt* **(a)** (*présenter de nouveau*) to present again, to re-present; **je voudrais r. ce candidat (au concours)** I would like to re-enter this candidate (for the exam); **r. une traite à l'acceptation** to re-present a bill for acceptance

(b) *Jur* (*documents etc*) to produce

(c) (*figurer*) to represent; **le pronom représente le nom** the pronoun stands for *or* replaces the noun; **on représente souvent Hugo comme un vieil homme barbu** Hugo is often depicted as an old man with a beard; **il représente l'esprit soixante-huitard** he represents *or* typifies the spirit of May 1968; **r. fidèlement/avec réalisme qch** to render sth faithfully/realistically; **il a représenté son modèle avec humour** he has painted his model with great humour; **un croquis qui me représentait à la terrasse d'un café** a sketch of me *or* that showed me sitting outside a cafe; *Th* **la scène représente un patio** the scene is a patio

(d) (*être le porte-parole de*) (*personne, pays, entreprise, Pol circonscription*) to represent; **se faire r.** to be represented; **il représente la France aux Jeux Olympiques** he's representing France in the Olympic Games; **je représente les produits Avon®** I'm an Avon® representative; *Jur* **r. qn en justice** to appear for sb

(e) (*correspondre à*) (*somme, chiffre etc*) to represent; **cela ne représente pas une grosse somme** *ou* **beaucoup pour lui** it's not much to him, it's not a large amount as far as he's concerned; **cela représente une privation financière importante pour eux** that constitutes a major financial sacrifice for them

(f) *Th* (*pièce de théâtre*) to perform, to put on

2 *vi* (*en imposer*) **r. (bien)** to impress people, to be impressive; **il ne représente pas au physique** he's not very impressive physically

3 se représenter *vpr* **(a) se r. à** (*examen*) to resit, to sit *or* take again; (*poste, emploi*) to apply for again; **se r. en septembre** to resit in September; **se r. aux élections** to stand for *or Am* to run for election again; *F* **se r. au permis de conduire** to take one's driving test again

(b) (*d'une occasion*) to arise again; **si ces difficultés se représentent, dis-le moi** let me know if these problems come up again

(c) (*s'imaginer*) to imagine; **représentez-vous mon étonnement** (just) imagine my astonishment; **ce n'est pas ainsi que je me le représentais, je me le représentais différemment** that's not how I imagined it

répressif, -ive [represif, -iv] *adj* (*loi, parents, tendance etc*) repressive

répression [represjɔ̃] *nf* repression; (*d'une émeute, d'un abus*) suppression; **mesures de r.** repressive measures; **mesures de r. de la fraude fiscale** measures to suppress tax evasion; **r. des fraudes** suppression of fraud; (*service gouvernemental*) consumer protection office

réprimandable [reprimɑ̃dabl] *adj* reproachable, blameworthy

réprimande [reprimɑ̃d] *nf* reprimand, rebuke, *Fml* reproof; **faire des réprimandes à qn** to reprimand *or* rebuke sb, *Fml* to reprove sb; **air/ton de r.** reproving look/tone, look/tone of rebuke

réprimander [reprimɑ̃de] *vt* (*personne*) to reprimand, to rebuke, *Fml* to reprove; **se faire r.** to be reprimanded

réprimer [reprime] *vt* (*crime*) to suppress; (*désir, colère, instinct*) to repress, to suppress; (*rire, sanglots, larmes, éternuement*) to suppress, to hold back; (*juron*) to suppress, to smother; (*révolte*) to suppress, to quell, to put down

reprint [rəprint] *nm* (*livre*) reprint

repris [rəpri] *nm* **r. de justice** ex-prisoner

reprisage [rəprizaʒ] *nm* (*d'un vêtement*) mending; (*de chaussettes*) darning

reprise [rəpriz] *nf* **(a)** *Mil* (*d'une place forte, ville etc*) retaking, recapture

(b) *Com* (*de marchandises invendues, d'articles en solde etc*) taking back; **nous ne faisons pas de r. des articles en solde** sales goods may not be returned; **r. jusqu'à 5 000 francs** part exchange *or* trade-in (allowance) up to 5,000 francs; **r. de l'entreprise par ses salariés** employee buy-out; *Compta* **reprises sur provisions** recovery of provisions, write-back of provisions

(c) (*du travail, d'un débat, des essais nucléaires*) resumption; (*des négociations, des pourparlers*) renewal, resumption, re-opening; (*des hostilités, de la violence*) renewal, resumption; (*de la mode*) return, revival; *Th* (*d'une pièce de théâtre*) revival; *Cin* (*d'un film*) reissue; *Rad, TV* repeat; *TV, Cin* (*d'un but, essai etc*) replay, rerun

(d) (*de l'activité*) renewal; (*du froid*) return; (*de la fièvre*) fresh bout; **r. des affaires** business recovery *or* revival; **mouvement de r.** (*dans l'économie*) upward movement; **r. économique** economic recovery, upswing *or* upturn in the economy; **les premiers indices de la r. économique** the first signs of economic recovery

(e) r. (de vitesse) (*d'un moteur*) pick-up, acceleration; **cette voiture a de bonnes reprises** the car accelerates quickly *or* has good acceleration

(f) *Boxe* round; *Escrime* bout; *Fb* (*du jeu*) second half; *Équitation* lesson; (*groupe de cavaliers*) riders

(g) faire qch à plusieurs reprises to do sth several times *or* on several occasions; **à trois reprises** three times, on three occasions

(h) *Mus* repeat; (*d'un thème, des instruments*) re-entry

(i) *Couture* (*raccord*) darn, mend; **r. perdue** invisible mend

(j) (*somme payée à un locataire*) = (money paid for) fixtures and fittings (*paid to outgoing tenant*)

repriser [rəprize] *vt* (*vêtement*) to mend; (*chaussette*) to darn, to mend; **aiguille/coton/œuf à r.** darning needle/cotton/egg *or* mushroom

réprobateur, -trice [reprɔbatœr, -tris] *adj* (*air, ton*) reproving; **dire qch d'un ton r.** to say sth reprovingly *or* in a tone of reproof

réprobation [reprɔbasjɔ̃] *nf* reproof; **ton/regard de r.** reproving tone/look, tone/look of reproof

reproche [rəprɔʃ] *nm* **(a)** (*remontrance*) reproach; **un regard plein de r.** a reproachful look, a look of reproach; **regarder qn d'un air plein de r.** to look at sb reproachfully; **faire des reproches à qn** to reproach sb (**pour avoir fait qch** for doing sth); **je ne vous fais pas de reproches** I'm not reproaching *or* blaming you; **ton de r.** tone of reproach, reproachful tone; **sans r.** (*vie, personne*) beyond *or* above reproach, blameless; **le seul r. qu'on puisse faire à ce roman, c'est ...** the only criticism one can make about *or* the only thing wrong with the novel is ...; **c'est le seul r. que je trouve à lui faire** it's the only criticism I have to make of him

(b) *Jur* **r. de témoin** barring of a witness

reprocher [rəprɔʃe] **1** *vt* **(a)** (*blâmer*) to reproach; **r. qch à qn** to blame *or* reproach sb for sth; **r. à qn de faire qch** to blame *or* reproach sb for doing sth; **r. à qn d'avoir fait qch** to blame *or* reproach sb for doing *or* having done sth; **je ne vous reproche rien** I'm not blaming you for anything; **il n'y a absolument rien à lui r.** he's totally blameless

(b) (*critiquer*) (*impatience, négligence*) to criticize; **qu'est-ce que vous reprochez à ce livre?** what have you got against the book?; **on lui reproche sa naissance** they've never forgiven him his background

(c) *Jur* (*témoin, témoignage*) to bar

2 se reprocher *vpr* **se r. qch** to blame oneself for sth, to reproach oneself with *or* for sth; **je me reproche de lui avoir fait confiance** I blame *or* reproach myself for trusting him; **ils se reprochent (mutuellement) d'avoir pris cette décision** they're blaming each other for the decision

reproducteur, -trice [rəprɔdyktœr, -tris] **1** *adj* **(a)** (*organe, cellule etc*) reproductive **(b)** (*animal*) kept for breeding; (*cheval*) stud **2** *nm* (*animal*) breeder; **reproducteurs** breeding stock, breeders; **r. d'élite** pedigree sire

reproductibilité [rəprɔdyktibilite] *nf* reproducibility

reproductible [rəprɔdyktibl] *adj* reproducible

reproductif, -ive [rəprɔdyktif, -iv] *adj* reproductive

reproduction [rəprɔdyksjɔ̃] *nf* **(a)** (*génération*) reproduction; **les organes de la r.** the reproductive organs; **animaux élevés en vue de la r.** animals reared for breeding, breeding stock; **r. sexuée/asexuée** sexual/asexual reproduction; **l'époque de la r.** the breeding season

(b) (*d'un document, d'une image, du son etc*) reproduction, reproducing; (*image, copie*) reproduction; **cela se prêtera bien à la r.** it will reproduce well; **droits de r.** reproduction rights; **droits de r. en feuilleton** serial *or* serialization rights; **tous droits de r. réservés pour tous pays** all rights of reproduction reserved for all countries

reproduire [rəprɔdɥir] (*conj like* **produire**) **1** *vt* (*copier*) (*son, image, tableau, document etc*) to reproduce; *Journ* (*article*) to reprint; (*imiter*) to imitate, to mimic; **ce tableau a été reproduit à des milliers d'exemplaires** thousands of reproductions have been made of this picture; **tu as reproduit les mêmes erreurs** you've made exactly the same mistakes as before

2 se reproduire *vpr* **(a)** (*des animaux etc*) to breed, to reproduce, to multiply; **ils se reproduisent comme des lapins** they breed like rabbits

(b) (*des événements*) to recur, to happen again; **et que cela ne se reproduise plus!** don't let it happen again!

reprogrammable [rəprɔgramabl] *adj Ordinat* (*touche*) reprogrammable

reprogrammer [rəprɔgrame] *vt Ordinat* to reprogram; **r. une livraison** to reschedule a delivery

reprographie [rəprɔgrafi] *nf* (*de documents*) duplicating, *Spéc* reprography

reprographier [rəprɔgrafje] *vt* (*document*) to duplicate

réprouvé, -ée [repruve] *n* outcast; *Rel* reprobate

réprouver [repruve] *vt* **(a)** (*crime, attitude, méthode, geste*) to condemn **(b)** *Rel* to damn

reps [rɛps] *nm Tex* rep(p)

reptation [rɛptasjɔ̃] *nf* crawling

reptile [rɛptil] *nm Zool; Fig F* reptile

repu [rəpy] *adj* satiated, full; *Fig* **être r. de qch** to have had one's fill of sth

républicain, -aine [repyblikɛ̃, -ɛn] *adj, n* republican

républicanisme [repyblikanism] *nm* republicanism

république [repyblik] *nf Pol* republic; *F* **on est en r.** it's a free country; **la R. de Saint-Marin** the Republic of San Marino; **la R. française** the French Republic; **la R. populaire de Chine** the People's Republic of China; *Hist* **R. démocratique allemande** German Democratic Republic; *Fig* **la r. des lettres** the world of letters

répudiation [repydjasjɔ̃] *nf* **(a)** (*d'une épouse, d'une opinion*) repudiation **(b)** *Jur* (*d'une succession, d'une nationalité*) renunciation

répudier [repydje] *vt* (*impf, pr sub* **n. répudiions**) **(a)** (*épouse, opinion*) to repudiate **(b)** *Jur* (*succession, nationalité*) to renounce, to relinquish

répugnance [repyɲɑ̃s] *nf* **(a)** (*dégoût*) repugnance (**pour** for), aversion (**pour** to), loathing (**pour** of, for); **avoir de la r. pour qn/qch** to loathe sb/sth; **éprouver de la r. à faire qch** to do sth with repugnance *or* loathing; **je me souviens de la r. avec laquelle elle en parlait** I remember her repugnance in talking about it; **avec r.** with repugnance *or* loathing **(b)** (*réticence*) reluctance, unwillingness; **r. à faire qch** reluctance *or* unwillingness to do sth; **avec r.** reluctantly, unwillingly; **faire qch avec r.** to do sth reluctantly *or* with reluctance, to be reluctant to do sth

répugnant [repyɲɑ̃] *adj* (*dégoûtant*) (*personne, odeur*) repulsive, revolting, repugnant; (*lieu*) repulsive, unsavoury; (*acte, comportement*) loathsome, repulsive; **de façon répugnante** disgustingly, repulsively; **il s'est conduit de façon répugnante avec la veuve** he behaved repulsively towards the widow

répugner [repyɲe] **1** *vi* **(a)** (*ressentir du dégoût*) **r. à qch** to feel repelled by sth, to find sth repellent, to feel repugnance for sth; **r. à faire qch** to be reluctant *or* lo(a)th to do sth **(b)** (*dégoûter*) **r. à qn** to be repugnant *or* repellent to sb; **elle/cette idée me répugne** I find her/the idea quite repugnant *or* repellent, she/the idea is quite repugnant *or* repellent to me **2** *v impers* **il me répugne de le faire** I am reluctant *or* lo(a)th to do it **3** *vt Litt* (*personne*) to be repugnant to

répulsif, -ive [repylsif, -iv] *adj Phys, Fig* repulsive

répulsion [repylsjɔ̃] *nf Phys, Fig* repulsion; **éprouver de la r. pour qn** to be repelled by sb, to feel repulsion for sb

réputation [repytasjɔ̃] *nf* reputation; **avoir (une) bonne/mauvaise r.** to have a good/bad reputation; **jouir d'une bonne r.** to have a good reputation, to be well spoken of; **se faire une r.** to make a reputation *or* name for oneself; **cela a fait sa r.** it made his name; **sa r. de chirurgien** his reputation as a surgeon; **connaître qn de r.** to know sb by reputation *or Fml* repute; **elle a la r. d'être généreuse** she has a reputation for being generous *or* for generosity; **ils ont la r. d'être très chaleureux** they are said *or* reputed to be very kind-hearted; **établissement de mauvaise r.** disreputable establishment; **athlète de r. internationale** world-famous athlete

réputé [repyte] *adj* (*expert, restaurant, vin etc*) well-known, famous, renowned (**pour** for); **c'est un écrivain très r. dans son pays** he's a very well-known *or* renowned writer in his country; **r. intelligent** reputed *or* considered to be intelligent; **il est réputé ne rien ignorer de cette science** he is reputed to know everything about the science; **malgré ses qualités réputées extraordinaires, il s'est montré incapable de finir à temps** despite his reportedly extraordinary talents, he proved unable to finish on time

réputer [repyte] *vt Vieilli* to consider, to think, *Fml* to deem; **on le répute bienveillant** he is considered *or* thought *or* deemed (to be) benevolent

requérant, -ante [rəkerɑ̃, -ɑ̃t] *Jur* **1** *adj* **partie requérante** applicant, claimant **2** *n* applicant, claimant

requérir [rəkerir] *vt* (*conj like* **acquérir**) **(a)** (*faveur*) to ask for, to seek, *Fml* to solicit; (*la présence ou, l'aide de qn*) to request; (*explication, soin, de la patience, des mains habiles etc*) to require, to call for; (*l'attention de qn*) to demand, to require **(b)** *Hist Mil* **r. des civils** to conscript civilians (*for a public service*) **(c)** *Jur* (*sentence*) to demand, to call for

requête [rəkɛt] *nf* **(a)** (*demande*) request; *Ordinat* query; **adresser une r. à qn** to make a request to sb, *Fml* to petition sb; **à** *ou* **sur la r. de qn** at sb's request **(b)** *Jur* petition; **r. en cassation** appeal

requiem [rekɥijɛm] *nm inv Rel, Mus* requiem; **messe de r.** requiem (mass)

requin [rəkɛ̃] *nm Zool, Fig* shark; **peau de r.** shagreen; **r. de la (haute) finance** financial shark

requinquer [rəkɛ̃ke] *F* **1** *vt* **r. qn** to pick *or* perk sb up; **le voilà requinqué** he's (back to) his old self again **2 se requinquer** *vpr* to pick *or* perk up

requis [rəki] **1** *adj* requisite, required; **les conditions requises** the requirements **2** *nm Hist* (*civil*) labour conscript

réquisition [rekizisjɔ̃] *nf* **(a)** *Admin* (*de vivres, de véhicules etc*) requisitioning, commandeering; *Hist* **r. civile** (*de personne*) conscription for a public service; **mettre en r.** to requisition, to commandeer **(b)** *Jur* (*plaidoirie*) prosecution address

réquisitionner [rekizisjɔne] *vt* (*vivres, véhicules etc*) to requisition, to commandeer; *Hist* (*civils*) to conscript; *F* **elle nous a réquisitionnés pour faire la vaisselle** she requisitioned *or* conscripted us to do the washing-up

réquisitoire [rekizitwar] *nm Jur* prosecution address; *Fig* indictment (**contre** of)

RER [ɛrəɛr] *nm Rail* (*abrév* **Réseau express régional**) = express rail network serving Paris and its suburbs

re-recording [ririkɔrdiŋ] *nm TV, Rad* re-recording

RES [ɛrəɛs] *Fin* (*abrév* **reprise de l'entreprise par ses salariés**) employee buy-out

résa [reza] *nf* (*abrév* **réservation**) reservation, booking, bkg

resaler [rəsale] *vt Culin* to put more salt in, to add more salt to

resalir [rəsalir] **1** *vt* to (get) dirty again **2 se resalir** *vpr* to get oneself dirty again, to dirty oneself again

rescapé, -ée [rɛskape] **1** *adj* (*personne*) surviving **2** *n* (*d'un désastre, d'un naufrage etc*) survivor

rescinder [rəsɛ̃de] *vt Jur* to rescind, to annul

rescision [resizjɔ̃] *nf Jur* rescission, annulment

rescousse [rɛskus] *nf* **aller/venir à la r. de qn** to go/come to the rescue of sb; **arriver à la r.** to come to the rescue; **appeler qn à la r.** to call on sb for help *or* assistance, to call sb to the rescue

réseau, -eaux [rezo] *nm* **(a)** (*de fils etc*) network; *Archit* tracery; *Phys, Nucl* (*de réacteur*) lattice; *Mil* **r. de barbelés** barbed wire entanglement

(b) (*de routes, de voies ferrées, de rivières etc*), *Tél* network, system; *Rad, TV* network

(c) *Fig* (*d'amis, de contacts etc*) network, circle; **r. d'espionnage** spy ring *or* network; **r. de résistance** resistance network; **un r. de drogue** a drug ring

(d) *Ordinat* network; LAN; **mise en r.** networking

▶ **réseau**: *Ordinat* **r. en anneau à jeton** token ring network; **r. d'apport** (*pour aéroport*) feeder network; **r. autoroutier** motorway network; *Ordinat* **r. en bus** bus network; **r. câblé** cable(d) network; **r. de commercialisation** marketing network; *Ordinat* **r. de télématique** *ou* **de communication de données** datacomms network; *Télécom* **r. commuté** switched network; *Ordinat* **r. connecté en étoile** star network; **r. de distribution** distribution network; *Él* **r. de distribution urbain** town mains; *Ordinat* **r. de données** data network; *Rail* **R. express régional** = suburban train network in Paris; **r. ferroviaire** rail network; **r. informatique** computer network; *Télécom* **r. interurbain** long distance network; *Ordinat* **r. local** local area network; *Ordinat* **r. longue distance** wide area network, WAN; *Él* **r. national** national grid (system); *Ordinat* **r. numérique à intégration de services** integrated services digital network; **r. télévisuel** television network; *Télécom* **r. urbain** local area network; *Ordinat* **r. d'utilisateurs** user network; *Ordinat* **r. à valeur ajouté** value-added network, VAN; **r. de vente** sales network

réséda [rezeda] **1** *nm Bot* reseda; **r. odorant** mignonette **2** *adj inv, nm* (*couleur*) reseda, mignonette

réservataire [rezɛrvatɛr] *nm* (*dans un hôtel*) party making a reservation

réservation [rezɛrvasjɔ̃] *nf* **(a)** (*de place, à l'hôtel etc*) reservation, booking; **bureau de r.** booking office; **la r. est obligatoire** reservations are necessary; **billet de train avec r.** train ticket with seat reservation; **faire une r.** to make a reservation; **j'ai fait une r. dans un petit hôtel** I booked *or* reserved a room in a little hotel; **r. d'avion** flight reservation; **r. de groupe** group booking; **r. de place** seat reservation; **r. en bloc** block-booking; **r. ferme** firm reservation *or* booking; **r. par téléphone** *ou* **téléphonique** telephone reservation *or* booking

(b) *Jur* reservation; **r. faite de tous mes droits** without prejudice to my rights

réserve [rezɛrv] *nf* **(a)** (*restriction*) reservation; **faire des réserves** to have reservations (**sur** about); **je voudrais faire quelques réserves concernant ce contrat** I would like to express some reservations about the contract; *Vieilli* **à la r. de ...** except for ...; **sous r. de qch** subject to sth; *Jur* **sous r.** without prejudice; **donné sous toutes réserves** (*horaires de cinéma etc*) subject to alteration; **je te le dis, mais sous toutes réserves** I can tell you this now, but it will be officially confirmed later; **sans r.** (*éloges, admiration*) unqualified; (*affirmer qch*) without reservation

(b) (*discrétion*) reserve; **se tenir** *ou* **demeurer sur la r.** to refuse to commit oneself; **être sur la r.** to be on one's guard; **son attitude manque de r.** his attitude is lacking in caution *or* restraint; **parler avec r.** to speak with restraint; **quand il sort de sa r.** when he breaks through his reserve; **il est un peu sorti de sa r.** he was a little less reserved than usual; **je vous rapelle votre devoir de r.** ≈ may I remind you that you have signed the Official Secrets Act

(c) (*de vivres, d'équipement, d'argent etc*) stock, reserve; (*de troupes*) reserve; *Physiol* (*de l'organisme*) reserves, stores (**en** of); *Fin* reserve; **réserves mondiales** (*de pétrole etc*) world reserves; **réserves bancaires** bank reserves; **puiser dans les réserves** to draw on the reserves; **en r.** in reserve, set aside; *Fin* **sans r. de retour** non-returnable, no-return; *Com* **avec r. de retour** on a sale or return basis; **avoir beaucoup d'énergie en r.** to have great reserves of energy; **mettre qch en r.** to put sth aside *or* by, to reserve sth; **tenir qch en r.** to keep sth in reserve; **fonds de r.** reserve fund; **vivres de r.** emergency rations, iron rations

(d) *Mil* reserve; **r. de l'armée active** reserve of the regular army; **officier de r.** reserve officer

(e) (*parc*) reserve; (*pour gibier*) preserve hunting/fishing reserve; **réserves (indiennes)** (Indian) reservation

(f) (*local*) (*de magasin*) stockroom, storeroom; (*de bibliothèque, musée*) reserve (collection)

(g) *TV, Cin* **en r.** white-on-black

▸ **réserve**: *Aut* **r. d'air** air chest; **r. d'animaux sauvages** safari park; **r. de chasse** hunting reserve; *Fin* **r. contractuelle** contractual reserve; *Fin* **r. facultative** optional reserve; **r. de gibier** game reserve; **r. légale** *Fin* legal reserve; *Jur* (*d'héritage*) legal share; **r. naturelle** nature reserve; **r. de pêche** fishing reserve; *Fin* **r. réglementée** regulatory reserve; *Fin* **réserves statuaires** statutory reserves; **r. zoologique** wild life sanctuary

réservé [rezɛrve] *adj* **(a)** (*chambre, siège etc*) reserved, booked; **place réservée aux personnes âgées** seat reserved for the elderly; **salle réservée aux réunions** room reserved *or* kept for meetings, meeting room **(b)** *Typ* **tous droits réservés** all rights reserved **(c)** (*personne, attitude*) reserved; **elle a un caractère plutôt r.** she's rather reserved; **avis r.** qualified opinion

réserver [rezɛrve] **1** *vt* (*louer*) (*chambre, place etc*) to reserve, to book; (*marchandises, argent etc*) to set aside, to put by, to save (**à, pour** for); **r. une place à qn** to keep *or* save a seat for sb; (*d'une agence de voyages etc*) to reserve a seat for sb; **je vous ai réservé une place sur le prochain vol** I've booked *or* reserved a seat for you *or* I've booked you on the next flight; **place réservée** reserved seat; **r. du bois pour l'hiver** to store wood for the winter; **r. son jugement** to reserve judgement; **r. le meilleur pour la fin** to keep *or* save the best till last; *Journ* **r. la Une** to hold the front page; **r. une surprise à qn** to have a surprise in store for sb; **nous ignorons le sort qui lui sera réservé** we do not know what fate has in store for him; **ils me réservent toujours un excellent accueil** they always welcome me with open arms; **nous attendons de connaître le sort qui nous est réservé** we are waiting to find out what fate has in store for us; *Litt* **il lui était réservé de grands succès** he was destined for great things; **'chasse/pêche réservée'** 'private hunting/fishing'; *Admin Vieilli* **quartier réservé** red-light district

2 se réserver *vpr* **se r. le droit de faire qch** to reserve the right to do sth; **je me réserve pour le match de ce soir** I'm saving my strength for this evening's match; **elle s'est réservé une portion du gâteau** she saved a piece of cake for herself; **celui-là, je me le réserve!** I'm keeping that one for myself!; **je préfère me r. pour le dessert** I'd rather save myself *or* keep my appetite *or* leave some room for the dessert

3 *vi* (*au théâtre, à l'hôtel*) to book, to reserve, to make a booking *or* a reservation; (*au restaurant*) to reserve, to make a reservation; **bonsoir madame, vous avez réservé?** good evening, madam, do you have a reservation?; **j'ai réservé au nom de Roux** I have a reservation in the name of Roux; **pour r., appeler ...** for reservations, call ...

réserviste [rezɛrvist] *nm Mil* reservist

réservoir [rezɛrvwar] *nm* **(a)** (*bassin*) reservoir; **r. de barrage** storage basin **(b)** (*pour poissons*) fish pond **(c)** (*cuve*) tank; (*de toilettes*) cistern; **r. à gaz** gasholder, gasometer; **r. à mazout** fuel-oil tank; **r. d'encre** ink reservoir; *Aut* **r. d'essence** petrol *or Am* gas tank; *Aut* **r. d'expansion** expansion tank; *Aut* **r. de lave-glace** windscreen washer reservoir; (*en plastique*) windscreen washer bottle; *Aut* **r. de liquide de frein** brake fluid reservoir; *Aut* **r. en charge** header tank; *Aut* **r. à carburant** fuel tank; *Aut* **r. à dépression** vacuum tank *or* reservoir

résidant [rezidɑ̃] *adj* resident; **r. à** resident *or* living in

résidence [rezidɑ̃s] *nf* **(a)** (*séjour*) residence; **certificat de r.** residence permit; **avoir sa r. à Lyon** to be resident *or* to live in Lyons; *Jur* **en r. surveillée** under house arrest **(b)** (*demeure*) residence, home; (*de diplomate*) residency; **changer de r.** to change one's residence, to move (house) **(c)** (*immeuble*) block of luxury flats, *Am* luxury apartment building

▸ **résidence**: **r. hôtelière** apartment hotel; **r. médicalisée (pour personnes âgées)** nursing home; **r. principale** main residence *or* home; **r. secondaire** second home, holiday home *or Am* vacation home; **r. de tourisme** apartment hotel

résident, -ente [rezidɑ̃, -ɑ̃t] **1** *n* **(a)** (*diplomate*) resident **(b)** (*étranger*) (foreign) resident; **tous les résidents français en Grande-Bretagne** all French nationals resident in Great Britain **2** *adj Ordinat* **r. en mémoire** memory-resident

résidentiel, -elle [rezidɑ̃sjɛl] *adj* residential

résider [rezide] *vi* **(a)** (*vivre*) to live, *Fml* to reside (**à, dans, en** in); **dans la ville où l'on réside** in the town where one is resident **(b)** *Fig* to lie, to reside; **toute la difficulté réside en ceci que ...** the whole difficulty rests *or* lies in the fact that ...

résidu [rezidy] *nm* **(a)** residue; **résidus** *Ch* residue; (*déchets*) waste; **résidus urbains** town refuse; **résidus de fission** radioactive waste **(b)** *Math* remainder

résiduaire [rezidɥɛr] *adj* waste; *Ind* **eaux résiduaires** waste water, process water

résiduel, -elle [rezidɥɛl] *adj* residual; *Géog* **relief r.** residual relief

résignation [reziɲasjɔ̃] *nf* (*soumission*) resignation; **avec r.** (*dire qch*) with resignation, resignedly; (*supporter qch*) with resignation

résigné [reziɲe] *adj* resigned (**à** to); **je suis r.** I've resigned myself

résigner [reziɲe] **1** *vt Litt* (*fonction, biens*) to resign, to give up; **r. sa charge** *ou* **ses fonctions** to give up *or* relinquish one's appointment, to resign **2 se résigner** *vpr* **se r. à qch/à faire qch** to resign oneself to sth/to doing sth; **se r. à une situation** to resign oneself to a situation; **il faut se r.** you have to resign yourself

résiliable [reziljabl] *adj* which may be terminated *or* cancelled *or* annulled

résiliation [reziljasjɔ̃] *nf* (*d'un contrat*) termination, cancellation, annulment

résilience [reziljɑ̃s] *nf* resilience

résilient [reziljɑ̃] *adj* resilient

résilier [rezilje] *vt* (*accord, contrat etc*) to terminate, to cancel, to annul

résille [rezij] *nf* **(a)** (*pour cheveux*) snood; **bas r.** fishnet stockings **(b)** (*de vitrail*) lattice

résine [rezin] *nf* resin; **r. vinylique** vinyl resin; **r. époxyde** epoxy resin

résiné [rezine] *adj, nm* **(vin) r.** retsina

résiner [rezine] *vt* **(a)** (*enduire de résine*) to coat with resin **(b)** (*extraire la résine de*) **r. un arbre** to tap a tree (*for resin*)

résineux, -euse [rezinø, -øz] **1** *adj* resinous; (*odeur*) of resin; (*arbre, forêt*) coniferous **2** *nm* conifer

résistance [rezistɑ̃s] *nf* **(a)** resistance, opposition (**à** to); *Méd* (*à un virus etc*), *Pol* resistance; **n'offrir aucune r.** to put up *or* offer no resistance; **opposer une r. à qn/qch** to resist sb/sth; **je sens une r. de sa part quand j'essaie de lui en parler** I can feel a reluctance on his part to talk about it; **je n'ose pas tirer, je sens comme une petite r.** (*c'est collé*) I don't want to pull, it seems to be sticking; (*qn/qch bloque*) I don't want to pull, there's sb/sth blocking it; **r. passive** passive resistance; **faire de la r. passive** to engage in passive resistance; *Hist* **la R.** the Resistance (movement)

(b) *Phys* resistance; **r. de l'air** air resistance; **r. à l'avancement** drag

(c) *Él* resistance; (*conducteur*) (*d'un appareil*) element; (*composant*) resistor; **unité de r.** unit of resistance

(d) *Tech* (*des matériaux*) resistance, strength, toughness; **r. à la flexion** bending strength; **r. à la traction** tensile strength; **r. au choc** impact resistance; **limite de la r.** yield point; **acier à haute r.** high-resistance *or* high-tensile steel; **tissu qui n'a pas de r.** flimsy material; **r. à l'usure** (*d'un tissu*) ability to stand up to wear and tear, durability

(e) (*endurance*) stamina, endurance, staying power; **il a une bonne r. à la fatigue** he doesn't tire easily, he's got good stamina

(f) pièce de r. *Culin* main course *or* dish, pièce de résistance; *Fig* (*d'un spectacle etc*) main item (on the programme), pièce de résistance

résistant, -ante [rezistɑ̃, -ɑ̃t] **1** *adj* **(a)** (*matériau*) hard-wearing, strong, tough; (*couleur*) fast; **r. à** -proof; **r. à l'acide** acid-proof; **r. à la chaleur** heatproof, heat-resistant; **r. aux chocs** shockproof; **r. à l'usure** hard-wearing **(b)** (*robuste*) (*personne*) strong, tough, hardy; (*plante*) hardy **2** *n* freedom fighter; *Hist* member of the Resistance movement

résister [reziste] *vi* (*se débattre, s'opposer*) to resist; **il n'a pas résisté à la pneumonie** he succumbed to pneumonia; **je n'ai pas pu r., je les ai achetées** I couldn't resist them so I bought them; **r. à** (*tentation, influence, personne*) to resist; (*attaque*) to hold out against, to resist; (*douleur, pression etc*) to withstand, to stand up to; (*mauvais traitement, fatigue*) to stand up to; (*maladie, épidémie*) to overcome; (*vent, froid*) to withstand; **il n'a pas pu r. au courant** he couldn't fight against the current; **r. à l'analyse** (*d'un argument, d'une explication etc*) to stand up to analysis; *Tech* **r. à la chaleur/aux acides** to be heatproof/acid-proof; **ce pull a bien résisté au lavage** this jumper washed well; **r. au temps, r. à l'épreuve du temps** (*d'une amitié, d'un amour etc*) to stand the test of time; **ces couleurs ne résistent pas** these colours are not fast; *Fig* **on ne peut pas lui r.** he's irresistible, you can refuse him nothing; **personne n'ose lui r.** nobody dares stand up to him

résistivité [rezistivite] *nf Él* resistivity

résolu [rezɔly] *adj* (*personne*) determined, resolute; **un air r.** an air of determination; **d'un air r.** determinedly, with an air of determination, resolutely; **elle est (bien) résolue à le faire** she is (quite) determined to do it

résoluble [rezɔlybl] *adj* **(a)** (*problème*) solvable **(b)** *Jur* (*contrat*) which may be terminated *or* cancelled *or* annulled

résolument [rezɔlymɑ̃] *adv* determinedly, resolutely; **être r. contre qch** to be resolutely *or* strongly opposed to sth

résolution [rezɔlysjɔ̃] *nf* **(a)** *Tech* (*d'une substance, d'un écran de télévision etc*) resolution; **écran à haute r.** high-resolution screen

(b) (*d'un problème*) solving, *Fml* resolution

(c) *Jur* (*d'un contrat*) termination, cancellation, annulment

(d) (*décision*) resolution; **prendre la r. de faire qch** to make a resolution to do sth, to resolve *or* determine to do sth; **ma r. est prise** I've made my decision; *Pol* **prendre une r.** to pass a resolution; **prendre des résolutions** to make resolutions; **mes bonnes résolutions de début d'année** my New Year's resolutions

(e) (*détermination*) (*d'une personne*) determination, single-mindedness, strength of will; **sa r. est remarquable** he is remarkably determined *or* single-minded

résolutoire [rezɔlytwar] *adj* **clause r.** termination clause

résonance [rezɔnɑ̃s] *nf* **(a)** resonance; **la r. est bonne/mauvaise dans cette salle** the acoustics in the hall are good/bad; *Mus* **caisse de r.** sound box; *Méd* **r. magnétique nucléaire** nuclear magnetic resonance, NMR **(b)** *Fig* (*effet*) response, echo; **cela n'est pas sans r. sur sa vie affective** it is not without its effects on his emotional life; **ce mot prend une r. toute particulière dans ce contexte** in this context, the word has particular connotations

résonateur [rezɔnatœr] *nm Él* resonator

résonnant, résonant [rezɔnɑ̃] *adj* **(a)** (*voix*) resonant, resounding, sonorous; **r. de cris** resounding *or* echoing *or* resonant with cries **(b)** *Phys* resonant

résonner [rezɔne] *vi* (*d'un son, de pas etc*) to resound, to resonate, to echo; (*d'une voix, d'une pièce*) to echo; **sa voix résonnait dans les hauts-parleurs** his voice blared out *or* boomed out over the loudspeakers; **ça résonne!** there's an echo, it echoes!; **faire r. la trompette/le tambour** to sound the trumpet/the drum; **l'air résonnait de leurs cris** the air rang *or* resounded *or* echoed with their cries

résorber [rezɔrbe] **1** *vt* **(a)** *Méd* to resorb **(b)** (*surplus, déficit*) to absorb, to bring down; (*chômage*) to absorb, to curb; (*dettes*) to wipe out, to clear; **r. la crise économique** to solve the economic crisis **2 se résorber** *vpr* **(a)** *Méd* to be resorbed **(b)** (*d'un surplus, déficit*) to be absorbed, to be brought down; (*du chômage*) to be absorbed *or* curbed

résorption [rezɔrpsjɔ̃] *nf* **(a)** *Méd* resorption **(b)** (*d'un surplus, déficit*) absorption, bringing down; (*du chômage*) absorption, curbing; (*de dettes*) clearing, wiping out

résoudre [rezudr] (*prp* **résolvant**; *pp* **résolu**, *parfois* **résous, -oute**; *pr ind* **je résous, il résout, n. résolvons**; *impf* **je résolvais**; *p hist* **je résolus**; *fu* **je résoudrai**) **1** *vt* **(a)** (*difficulté*) to resolve, to clear up; (*équation, énigme, problème*) to solve; (*question, conflit*) to resolve, to settle; (*crise*) to solve, to resolve

(b) *Ch* (*transformer*) to break up; **r. qch en qch** to resolve sth into sth, to break up sth into sth

(c) *Jur* (*contrat, accord etc*) to terminate, to cancel, to annul

(d) (*décider*) **r. qn à faire qch** to prevail upon *or* persuade *or* induce sb to do sth; **r. de faire qch** to decide *or* make up one's mind to do sth

2 se résoudre *vpr* **(a) se r. à faire qch** to decide *or* make up one's mind *or* resolve to do sth; **je ne peux pas me r. à la quitter** I can't bring myself to leave her

(b) *Ch* to resolve itself; **se r. en qch** to resolve into sth, to break up into sth

respect [rɛspɛ] *nm* respect (**pour** for); **le r. de la nature/des morts** respect for nature/the dead; **inspirer le r.** to inspire respect; **montrer** *ou* **faire preuve de r. pour qch/qn** to show sth/sb (some) respect; **avoir du r. pour qn** to respect sb, to have respect for sb; **il n'a aucun r. pour les autres** he has no respect for other people; **avoir le r. des lois/des convenances** to respect *or* have respect for *or* have regard for the law/the conventions; **son courage suscite le r.** her courage commands respect; **parler avec r.** to speak respectfully *or* with respect; **r. de soi** self-respect; *Vieilli* **r. humain** fear of other people's judgement (of one's actions); **faire qch par r. pour qn** to do sth out of respect *or* regard for sb; **manquer de r. envers qn** to be disrespectful to sb, to show sb a lack of respect; **il t'a manqué de r.** he was disrespectful to you, he did not show you any respect; **tenir qn en r.** to fend sb off, to keep sb at a distance; **j'ai réussi à le tenir en r. en le menaçant d'un couteau** I managed to fend him off with a knife; *Fig* **son autorité naturelle lui permet de tenir en r. les élèves les plus indisciplinés** his innate authority enables him to keep the most undisciplined pupils at bay; *Fml* **sauf le r. que je vous dois, sauf votre r.** with all due respect; **en signe de r.** as a mark of respect; *Fml* **rendre** *ou* **présenter ses respects à qn** to pay one's respects to sb; **(je vous présente) mes respects, chère madame** my respects, madam

respectabilité [rɛspɛktabilite] *nf* respectability

respectable [rɛspɛktabl] *adj* **(a)** (*digne de respect*) (*famille, air, femme etc*) respectable **(b)** (*digne de considération*) (*somme*) respectable, fairly large; **un appartement de dimensions respectables** a fair-sized flat; **un nombre r. de spectateurs** a respectable *or* fairly large *or* fair number of spectators

respecter [rɛspɛkte] **1** *vt* (*personne, chose*) to respect, to have respect *or* regard for; (*calme d'un endroit, désir ou opinion de qn, limitation de vitesse*) to respect; (*la loi*) to abide by, to obey, to respect; **r. les délais de livraison** to meet delivery schedules; **il ne respecte rien** he has no respect for anything; **faire r. la loi** to enforce the law; **se faire r.** to command respect; **r. le code de la route** to respect *or* obey *or* follow the Highway Code; **vous n'avez pas respecté la priorité** you didn't give way

2 se respecter *vpr* to respect oneself; (*réciproque*) to respect each other; **comme tout homme qui se respecte** like any self-respecting man; **un professeur qui se respecte ne ferait pas cela** no self-respecting teacher would do that; **il se respecte trop pour faire cela** he has too much self-respect to do that

respectif, -ive [rɛspɛktif, -iv] *adj* respective

respectivement [rɛspɛktivmɑ̃] *adv* respectively; **ils ont r. deux et trois enfants** they have two and three children respectively

respectueusement [rɛspɛktɥøzmɑ̃] *adv* respectfully

respectueux, -euse [rɛspɛktɥø, -øz] *adj* respectful (**de** of; **envers** to, towards); **il ne se montre guère r. envers ses parents** he shows little respect for his parents; **d'un ton r.** in a respectful tone, in a tone of respect; **être r. des autres comme de soi** to respect other people as much as one does oneself; **être r. de qch** to respect sth, to show respect for sth; **r. des lois** respectful of the law, law-abiding; **se tenir à distance respectueuse** to keep at a respectful distance; **je vous prie d'agréer, Monsieur, mes salutations respectueuses** (*dans une lettre*) yours faithfully; (*quand la formule de salutation comprend le nom du destinataire*) yours sincerely

respirable [rɛspirabl] *adj* breathable; *Fig* **l'atmosphère n'était plus r.** the atmosphere had become oppressive *or* suffocating

respirateur [rɛspiratœr] *nm* respirator, ventilator

respiration [rɛpirasjɔ̃] *nf* breathing, *Spéc* respiration; (*de plante*) respiration; **r. artificielle** artificial respiration; **pratiquer la r. artificielle sur qn** to give sb artificial respiration; *Méd* **r. contrôlée/assistée** controlled/assisted respiration; **avoir la r. difficile** *ou* **des difficultés de r.** to have trouble *or* difficulty breathing; **s'arrêter pour prendre sa r.** to pause for breath; **retenir sa r.** to hold one's breath; *Fig* **tous retenaient leur r. en attendant le verdict** everyone waited for the verdict with bated breath; **couper la r. à qn** to wind sb; *Fig* to take sb's breath away, to flabbergast sb

respiratoire [rɛspiratwar] *adj* (*organe etc*) respiratory; (*appareil, exercice, problème*) breathing; **défaillance r.** respiratory failure; **quotient r.** respiratory quotient; **voies respiratoires** respiratory tract; **troubles respiratoires** breathing *or* respiratory problems; **difficultés respiratoires** difficulty in breathing

respirer [rɛspire] **1** *vi* (*d'une personne, d'un vin, d'une plante*) to breathe; **r. longuement** to take *or* draw a long breath; **r. par le nez/la bouche** to breathe through the nose/mouth; *F* **laissez-moi r.!** let me get my breath (back)!, let me catch my breath!; *F* **ouf! je respire!** (*de soulagement*) thank goodness for that!, that's a load off my mind!

2 *vt* **(a)** to breathe (in), to inhale; **aller r. un peu d'air** to go for a breath of air; **r. une fleur** to smell a flower

(b) *Fig* **r. la vengeance/la paix/la confiance** to breathe vengeance/peace/confidence; **r. la santé/l'honnêteté** to radiate health/honesty; **cela respire l'ennui le plus profond** it is profoundly boring

resplendir [rɛsplɑ̃dir] *vi* (*d'une personne*) to be radiant; (*briller*) to shine, to glitter, to gleam; **r. de joie/santé** (*d'un visage*) to be shining with joy/glowing with health; (*d'une personne*) to radiate joy/health; **sa beauté resplendissait** she was radiantly beautiful

resplendissant [rɛsplɑ̃disɑ̃] *adj* (*personne, beauté*) glowing, radiant; (*voiture etc*) shining, gleaming; (*cuivres*) gleaming; **r. de joie/santé** (*mine*) shining with joy/glowing with health; (*personne*) radiant with joy/health; **femme d'une beauté resplendissante** radiantly beautiful woman; **il a une mine resplendissante** he looks wonderfully well

responsabiliser [rɛspɔ̃sabilize] *vt* **r. qn** (*le rendre responsable*) to give sb a sense of responsibility

responsabilité [rɛspɔ̃sabilite] *nf* responsibility; (*légale*) liability (**de** for); **r. de l'employeur** employer's liability; **r. du fabricant** manufacturer's liability; **accepter une r.** to take on *or* assume *or* accept a responsibility; **élever des enfants est une grande r.** bringing up children is quite a responsibility; **c'est ta r. de répondre au téléphone, pas la mienne** answering the phone is your responsibility, not mine; **avoir la r. de qch/qn** to be responsible for sth/sb; **donner à qn la r. de qch** to give sb responsibility *or* make sb responsible for sth; **partager la r. d'un projet** to share the responsibility *or* be jointly responsible for a project; **assumer ses responsabilités** to face up to one's responsibilities; **décliner toute r.** to deny all responsibility; **nous déclinons toute r. pour les objets perdus ou volés** we accept no liability for lost or stolen items; **fuir les responsabilités** to evade *or* avoid responsibility; **être appelé à de hautes responsabilités** to be given important responsibilities; **avoir un poste à responsabilités** to have a responsible job; **je cherche un poste à responsabilités** I want a job with responsibilities; **faire qch sous sa (propre) r.** to do sth on one's own responsibility

▶ **responsabilité**: **r. civile** public liability; *Fin* **être assuré r. civile** to have personal liability insurance; **r. contractuelle** contractual liability; **r. limitée** limited liability; *Pol* **r. ministérielle** ministerial accountability; **r. patronale** employer's liability; **r. solidaire et indivise** joint and several liability; **r. au tiers** third-party liability; **être assuré r. au tiers** to carry third-party insurance

responsable [rɛspɔ̃sabl] **1** *adj* responsible (**de** for); (*légalement*) liable (**de** for); **elle n'est pas r. de ton échec** she's not responsible *or* not to blame for your failure; **r. de ses enfants** responsible *or* answerable for one's children; **le ministre est r. devant** *ou* **envers les Chambres** the Minister is responsible *or* answerable *or* accountable to Parliament; **tenir qn/qch pour r. d'un malheur** to hold sb/sth responsible for a misfortune, to blame sb/sth for a misfortune; **il faut les rendre responsables** they have to be given a sense of responsibility

2 *n* **(a)** (*coupable*) person responsible (**de** for), culprit; **qui est le r. de cette plaisanterie idiote?** who's responsible *or* to blame for this silly prank?

(b) (*personne en charge*) person in charge; (*dirigeant élu*) official; **les responsables du parti socialiste** Socialist Party officials

▶ **responsable**: **r. des achats** buyer; **r. administratif** executive manager; **r. des banquets** banqueting manager; **r. client** account manager; **r. des comptes-clients** account executive; **r. des études de marché** market research manager; **r. de la formation** training officer; **r. de groupe** group leader; **r. de magasin** warehouse manager; **r. de marché** market manager; **r. (du) marketing** marketing manager *or* executive; **r. de planification mercatique** marketing planner; *TV, Cin* **r. point** focus puller; **r. produit** product manager; **r. de projet** project leader; *Culin* **r. des sauces** (*dans un restaurant*) sauce cook; **r. du service commercial** sales and marketing manager; *Pol* **r. syndical** union leader; **r. de la vente** sales manager; **r. des ventes** sales manager; **r. du vestiaire** cloakroom attendant

resquillage [rɛskijaʒ] *nm*, **resquille** [rɛskij] *nf* (*au théâtre etc*) sneaking in without paying; (*dans l'autobus, le métro etc*) fare-dodging; **faire de la r.** to dodge paying

resquiller [rɛskije] **1** *vi* (*au théâtre, au concert etc*) to sneak in without paying; (*dans l'autobus, le métro etc*) to dodge paying one's fare; (*dans une queue*) to jump the queue; **entrer dans un cinéma en resquillant** to sneak into a cinema (without paying) **2** *vt* **r. une place de théâtre** to sneak into a theatre (without paying); **r. un ticket de métro** to dodge paying one's fare on the metro

resquilleur, -euse [rɛskijœr, -øz] *n* **(a)** (*au théâtre etc*) person who has sneaked in without paying; (*dans l'autobus, le métro etc*) fare-dodger **(b)** (*dans une queue*) queue-jumper

ressac [rəsak] *nm Naut* undertow

ressaisir [rəsezir] **1** *vt* (*fugitif*) to recapture; (*biens*) to recover (possession of); (*pouvoir*) to seize again; **la peur l'a ressaisi** fear gripped him again **2 se ressaisir** *vpr* to regain one's self-control, to pull oneself together; **ressaisissez-vous!** pull yourself together!; *Scol* **se r. au second trimestre** to recover in the second term, *F* to pull one's socks up in the second term

ressasser [rəsase] *vt* (*en esprit*) to brood over; (*répéter*) to keep coming out with; (*d'un professeur*) (*cours*) to rehash; **plaisanterie ressassée** (old) chestnut; **un thème ressassé** a hackneyed theme, a theme that's been done to death

ressaut [rəso] *nm Archit, Géol* (*d'une corniche, d'une paroi d'escalade*) projection

ressauter [rəsote] **1** *vi* to jump again; **il n'a jamais ressauté en parachute** he never made another parachute jump **2** *vt* to jump (over) again

ressemblance [rəsɑ̃blɑ̃s] *nf* resemblance, likeness; **la r. est grande** there's a great resemblance; **il y a quelques ressemblances entre eux** they resemble each other in a few respects, there are a few points of similarity *or* likeness between them; **il y a une r. frappante entre la mère et la fille** there is a striking resemblance between mother and daughter; **il n'y a aucune r. entre lui et sa sœur** he and his sister do not resemble each other at all; **il y a aussi une r. dans leurs façons de s'exprimer** there is also a similarity in the way they express themselves, they express themselves in a similar way too; **un tableau peint sans aucun souci de r.** a painting done with no concern for rendering a true likeness; *Cin* **toute r. avec des personnes existant ou ayant existé ne peut être que fortuite** any resemblance to persons living or dead is purely coincidental

ressemblant [rəsɑ̃blɑ̃] *adj* **portrait bien r.** lifelike portrait, good likeness; **elle est très ressemblante** (*sur un portrait*) it is very like her; **ce tableau n'est pas très r.** it's not a very good likeness, it doesn't look much like you/him/*etc*

ressembler [rəsɑ̃ble] **1** *vi* **r. à qn** (*physiquement*) to resemble sb, to be like *or* look like sb; (*moralement*) to resemble *or* be like sb; **r. à qch** to resemble *or* be like *or* look like sth; **elle ne ressemble pas beaucoup à ses parents** she doesn't look like *or* resemble her parents very much; **tu ressembles vraiment à ton père, toi!** you're just like your father!; **il te ressemble comme un frère** he's so like you, you'd think he was your brother; **à quoi ressemble-t-elle?** what's she like?, what does she look like?; *F* **cela ne ressemble à rien** it looks like nothing on earth; (*ça ne veut rien dire*) it just doesn't make sense; **cela lui ressemble tout à fait!** that's just like him!, that's him all over!; **cela ne lui ressemble pas de se plaindre** it's not like him to complain

2 se ressembler *vpr* to be alike, to resemble each other; **il n'y en a pas deux qui se ressemblent** no two are alike; **les bébés se ressemblent tous** babies all look alike; **ils se ressemblent comme deux gouttes d'eau** they're as like as two peas in a pod; *Prov* **qui se ressemble s'assemble** birds of a feather flock together; **les jours se suivent et ne se ressemblent pas** day follows day and you never know what to expect; **tu ne te ressembles plus!** you're not your usual self!

ressemelage [rəsəmlaʒ] *nm* resoling

ressemeler [rəsəmle] *vt* (*conj like* **semeler**) (*chaussures*) to resole

ressentiment [rəsɑ̃timɑ̃] *nm* resentment (**de** at; **contre** against); **avec r.** resentfully; **éprouver du r.** to feel resentful

ressentir [rəsɑ̃tir] (*conj like* **sentir**) **1** *vt* (*douleur, colère, sympathie, effet, insulte etc*) to feel; (*choc, sensation*) to feel, to experience; **je me demande comment il a pu r. cette trahison** I wonder how he felt about being betrayed like that; **r. de l'affection pour qn** to be fond of sb; **je ne ressens aucune tendresse pour elle** I don't feel any affection for her, I'm not fond of her; **je ne ressens plus rien pour toi** I don't feel anything for you any more; **r. vivement la perte de qn** to feel the loss of sb deeply, to be deeply affected by the loss of sb; **il a durement ressenti les privations** the effects of the hardships he suffered have gone deep

2 se ressentir *vpr* **(a) se r. de** to feel the effects of

(b) *très F* **s'en r. pour qch** to feel fit for sth, to feel up to sth

resserre [rəsɛr] *nf* (*pour outils*) tool shed; (*pour stocker*) storeroom

resserrement [rəsɛrmɑ̃] *nm* **(a)** (*contraction*) (*d'une vallée, route etc*) narrowing; **r. du crédit** credit squeeze, tightening of credit **(b)** (*d'un nœud, d'un écrou etc*) tightening; *Fig* (*d'une amitié, de liens*) strengthening

resserrer [rəsere] **1** *vt* (*livres sur étagère*) to push closer together; (*nœud, ceinture, pores*) to tighten; (*écrou*) to tighten (up); *Fig* (*amitié, liens*) to strengthen; (*récit*) to condense; (*discipline*) to tighten (up); (*crédit*) to squeeze, to tighten **2 se resserrer** *vpr* **(a)** (*d'une vallée, route etc*) to narrow, to become narrower; (*des pores*) to tighten **(b)** (*d'un nœud*) to tighten; *Fig* (*des liens*) to strengthen, to grow stronger

resservir [rəsɛrvir] (*conj like* **servir**) **1** *vt* **(a)** (*servir de nouveau*) to serve again; **tu ne vas pas nous r. ta quiche d'hier?** you're not going to dish up yesterday's quiche again, are you?; **r. un plat** to serve up a dish again

(b) (*servir en plus*) (*poisson etc*) to serve another helping of; **tu nous ressers un peu de ta quiche?** can we have a bit more of your quiche?

2 *vi* to be used again; **cette robe pourra r. l'été prochain** the dress will do another summer; **ça peut toujours r.** it might come in handy *or* useful

3 se resservir *vpr* **resservez-vous de riz** help yourself to *or* have some more rice *or* another helping of rice; **tu peux te r., si tu veux** you can have some more if you like

ressort [rəsɔr] *nm* **(a)** (*élasticité*) elasticity, springiness; **faire r.** to spring back, to fly back; *Fig* **avoir du r.** to be resilient; **elle ne manque pas de r.** she's resilient

(b) (*pièce*) spring; **r. de sommier** bed spring; **r. de montre** watch spring; **r. à boudin** *ou* **en spirale** coil *or* spiral spring; **r. à feuilles** *ou* **à lames** leaf *or* laminated spring; *Aut* **r. d'expansion** expansion *or* expander spring; **r. hélicoïdal** helical *or* coil spring; **r. moteur, grand r.** mainspring; **à r.** spring-loaded; **actionné** *ou* **mû par r.** spring-driven; **suspendu à ressort(s)** (*chariot etc*) sprung; **sans ressort(s)** unsprung

(c) *Fig* (*motivation*) motive; **l'intérêt est un puissant r.** self-interest is a powerful motive *or* driving force

(d) *Jur* (*compétence*) province, scope, competence; (*étendue de juridiction*) jurisdiction; **être du r. de la cour** to be *or* fall within the competence of the court; **cela n'est pas de son r.** that's not his responsibility, that doesn't fall within his province

(e) en dernier r. *Jur* without appeal; *Fig* as a *or* in the last resort

ressortir[1] [rəsɔrtir] (*conj like* **sortir**) **1** *vi* (*aux* **être**) **(a)** (*d'un lieu*) (*d'une personne*) to come/go out again, to re-emerge; **elle est ressortie** (*je suis à l'intérieur*) she went out again; (*je suis à l'extérieur*) she came out again; **elle est ressortie de chez elle** she came/went out of her house again; **je n'ai pas envie de r. ce soir** I don't want to go out again this evening; **la lame est ressortie ensanglantée** the blade came out covered in blood; **la balle est ressortie par l'épaule** the bullet came out *or* exited through the shoulder

(b) (*se détacher*) to stand out; **faire r.** (*couleur*) to bring out, to set off; (*fait, importance de qch*) to emphasize, to accentuate, to stress; (*sens de qch*) to bring out; **pour faire r. tes yeux** to highlight *or* emphasize your eyes; **cela ressort d'autant plus que ...** it stands out all the more since ...

(c) (*résulter*) to emerge, to be evident (**de** from); **il en ressort que ...** it emerges *or* is evident from this that ...

2 *vt* (*aux* **avoir**) (*parapluie, vêtements etc*) to get out again; *Fig* **elle ressort toujours le même genre d'histoires** she always comes out with the same old stories; **elle nous a encore ressorti son histoire de ...** she trotted out her story about ...

ressortir[2] *vi Jur* **r. à** to come under the jurisdiction of; *Fig Litt* **concepts qui ressortissent à la géométrie** concepts that belong to geometry *or* that come within the province of geometry

ressortissant, -ante [rəsɔrtisɑ̃, -ɑ̃t] **1** *adj Jur* **r. à** under the jurisdiction of **2** *n* (*d'un pays*) national, citizen

ressouder [rəsude] **1** *vt* to resolder; (*par la soudure autogène*) to reweld **2 se ressouder** *vpr* (*d'un os, d'une fracture*) to knit (again)

ressource [rəsurs] *nf* **(a)** (*habileté*) resourcefulness; **personne de r.** resourceful person, person of resource; **elle a de la r.** she is resourceful; **la situation est grave mais tu n'es pas sans r.** the situation is serious but there are things you can do *or* there are ways out of it

(b) (*moyen*) expedient; **avoir mille ressources, être plein de ressources** to be very resourceful; **être à bout de ressources** to have exhausted all one's possibilities; **exploiter les ressources d'une situation/d'un scénario** to exploit the possibilities of a situation/a script; **je n'avais d'autre r. que la fuite** I had no choice but to run away, there was no course open to me but flight; **c'est ma seule r.** it's the only course of action open to me; **en dernière r.** as a last resort

(c) ressources (*argent*) resources, means; (*agricoles, pétrolières etc*) resources; **ressources financières** financial resources; **les ressources en hommes et en matériel** manpower and material resources; **ressources humaines** human resources; **ressources personnelles** private means

(d) *Av* flattening out, pull-out

ressourcer (se) [sərəsurse] *vpr F* (*revenir aux sources*) to go back to one's roots; (*reprendre des forces morales*) to get back in touch with one's inner self

ressusciter [resysite] **1** *vt* **(a) r. les morts** to raise *or* resurrect the dead; *Fig* **r. qn** to put new life into sb; **ce vin me ressuscite** this wine is putting new life into me *or* reviving me; **tes larmes ne vont pas le r.** crying won't bring him back (to life) **(b)** *Fig* (*querelle, mode, traditions etc*) to revive, to resurrect; (*souvenir, commerce*) to revive **2** *vi* to revive, to come to life again; *Rel* to rise from the dead; **ressuscité d'entre les morts** risen from the dead, resurrected

restant [rɛstɑ̃] **1** *adj* **(a)** remaining, left; **les vingts francs restants** the remaining twenty francs, the twenty francs remaining *or* left (over) **(b) poste restante** poste restante, *Am* general delivery **2** *nm* remainder, rest; **le r. de sa vie** the rest of one's life; **un r. d'étoffe** a leftover piece of material; *Com* **r. en caisse** cash surplus; **r. d'un compte** balance of an account, account balance

restau [rɛsto] *nm F* restaurant; **r. U** university canteen *or* refectory

restaurant [rɛstɔrɑ̃] *nm* restaurant; **et si on allait au r. ce soir?** how about eating out *or* going to a restaurant this evening?; **ils vont souvent au r.** they often eat out *or* eat in restaurants; **manger au r.** to eat out

▶ **restaurant**: **r. gastronomique** gourmet restaurant; **r. libre-service** self-service restaurant; **r. de poissons** seafood restaurant; **r. routier** transport café, *Am* truck stop; **r. self-service** self-service restaurant; **r. de spécialités** speciality restaurant; **r. à thème** theme restaurant; **r. universitaire** university canteen *or* refectory

restaurateur, -trice [rɛstɔratœr, -tris] *n* **(a)** (*de bâtiments, de tableaux*) restorer; *Litt* (*d'un régime, d'une dynastie etc*) restorer **(b)** (*de restaurant*) restaurateur, restaurant owner/manager

restauration [rɛstɔrasjɔ̃] *nf* **(a)** (*de bâtiment, d'une dynastie, de finances publiques, discipline etc*) restoration; *Ordinat* restore; **faire de la r. de tableaux** (*comme métier*) to work in art restoration; *Hist* **la R.** the Restoration **(b)** (*métier*) catering; **r. rapide** fast food; **chaîne de r. rapide** fast-food chain; **être dans la r.** to be in catering, to work in the catering trade; **r. aérienne** in-flight catering, airline catering **(c)** (*en Suisse*) (*restaurant*) restaurant

restaurer [rɛstɔre] **1** *vt* **(a)** (*rétablir, réparer*), *Ordinat* to restore; *Fig* (*discipline, autorité*) to restore, to re-establish **(b)** (*faire manger*) **r. qn** to give sb something to eat **2 se restaurer** *vpr* (*manger*) to eat something

restauroute [rɛstorut] *nm* (*de route*) roadside restaurant; (*d'autoroute*) motorway *or Am* freeway restaurant

reste [rɛst] *nm* **(a)** (*de travail, d'argent, de vin etc*) rest, remainder; *Math* remainder; **le r. du temps** the rest of the time; **commence par ceci et je te dirai quoi faire le r. du temps** start with this and I'll tell you what to do for the rest *or* remainder of the time; **le r. (des gens)** the rest, the others; **il y avait un r. de beurre/lait** there was a bit of butter/milk left (over); **accommoder un r. de viande** to use up the leftover meat; **faire un chemisier avec un r. de tissu** to make a shirt out of a remnant of material; **elle a de beaux restes** (*elle est encore belle*) she still has some of her beauty; (*elle travaille encore très bien, c'est encore une très bonne athlète*) she's still on the ball; *Fig* **il n'a pas demandé son r.** he didn't say another word; **partir sans demander son r.** to leave without another word, to leave without further ado;

finis le r. (*du repas*) finish it off, finish *or* take what's left; **(et) pour le r., on verra plus tard** as for the rest, we'll see about it later; **il sait parler aux clients, mais pour le r., c'est un incapable** he knows how to talk to the customers but otherwise he's quite incapable; **et (tout) le r.** and so on, and so forth; **être** *ou* **demeurer en r.** to be indebted **(avec qn** to sb), to remain under an obligation to sb; *Fig* **pour ne pas être en r.** so as not to be left out; **vous auriez du pain de r.?** do you have any bread left (over)?, do you have any spare bread?, do you have any bread to spare?; **quand j'ai du temps de r.** when I have some spare time *or* time to spare; **avoir de l'argent de r.** to have more than enough money; **du** *ou* **au r.** besides, moreover

(b) restes (*de repas*) leftovers, scraps; (*d'une ancienne ville, d'une fortune etc*) remains; (*d'une armée*) remnant; **restes humains** human remains; *Litt* **restes mortels** mortal remains

rester [rɛste] **1** *vi* (*aux* **être**) **(a)** (*subsister*) to remain, to be left; **les quelques jours qui restent** the few days that are left, the few remaining days; **les cinq francs qui restent** the remaining five francs, the five francs left (over); **dix-neuf divisé par cinq, je pose trois, reste quatre** nineteen divided by five makes three, and four over *or* remainder four; **la vie n'est pas facile pour ceux qui restent** life isn't easy for those left behind

(b) (*demeurer*) to stay, to remain; **je pars – non, reste!** I'm going – no, stay!; **il est resté à** *ou* **pour travailler** he stayed (behind) to work; **mon sac a dû r. sur le comptoir** I must have left my bag on the counter; **les mots lui restèrent dans la gorge** the words stuck in his throat; **il restait là à me regarder** he sat/stood there looking at me; **restez où vous êtes** stay where you are; **r. assis** to remain *or* stay seated *or* sitting; **r. debout** to stand; (*ne pas aller se coucher*) to stay up; (*pour attendre*) to wait up; **je ne peux plus r. debout** I can't stay on my feet a minute longer; **je n'en peux plus de r. debout toute la journée** I'm fed up being on my feet all day; **r. au lit** to stay *or* remain in bed; **r. (à) dîner** to stay to *or* for dinner; **qu'est-ce qui reste à faire?** what still has to be done?, what's left to do?; **le plus dur reste à faire** the hardest part remains *or* is still to be done; **r. sur place** to stay where one is, to stay put; *F* **j'y suis, j'y reste** here I am and here I stay; *F* **y r.** (*mourir*) to kick the bucket, to snuff it; **j'ai bien cru que j'allais y r.** I really thought I'd had it, I really thought my time *or* number was up; **il a bien failli y r.** he nearly didn't make it; **en r. là** to proceed no further; **j'aime autant en r. là** (*dans une conversation, relation*) I'd rather not go any further, I'd rather leave it at that; **restons-en là pour aujourd'hui** let's leave it there *or* at that for today; **les choses en sont restées là** there the matter rested *or* remained; **ne reste donc pas là planté comme un imbécile!** don't just stand there!; **où en sommes-nous restés?** where did we get to?, where did we leave off *or* stop **(de notre lecture** in our reading)?; *TV* **où en es-tu resté?** (*du feuilleton*) what point did you see up to?; **ils en sont restés à l'encre et au papier** (*ils n'utilisent pas encore d'ordinateurs*) they're still stuck in the pen-and-ink era, they haven't progressed beyond the pen-and-ink stage; **que cela reste entre nous** this is strictly between ourselves, this must go no further; **r. sur une impression** to be left with an impression; **cela m'est resté sur l'estomac** (*d'un plat*) it's lying heavy on my stomach; *Fig* it still rankles (with me), *F* it still bugs me; *Fig* **cela me reste en travers de la gorge** it still sticks in my throat

(c) (*dans un état*) to keep, to stay, to remain; **r. tranquille/calme** to stay *or* keep *or* remain still/calm; **c'est resté collé** it's stuck; **r. en bonne santé** to remain *or* keep in good health, to keep well; **il est resté très en forme** he's kept in very good shape; **je suis resté longtemps fatigué après l'opération** I was tired for a long time after the operation; **la cuisinière est restée allumée** the cooker stayed *or* remained lit; **r. ouvert** (*d'un magasin*) to stay open; **le robinet est resté ouvert toute la journée** the tap was (left) on all day; **la maison est restée ouverte** the house wasn't locked up; **r. en bons termes avec qn,** *F* **r. bien avec qn** to stay *or* remain on good terms with sb

(d) (*durer*) to last, to endure; **le nom lui est resté** the name stayed with him, *F* the name stuck; **un match qui restera dans les mémoires** a match which will live on in people's memories; **il restera dans l'histoire comme l'un de nos plus grands présidents** he'll live on in history as one of our greatest presidents

2 *v impers* **il me reste cinq francs** I have *or* I've got five francs left; **il me reste à peine de quoi payer le loyer** I barely have enough left to pay the rent; **il ne me reste qu'à vous remercier** it only remains for me to thank you, all that remains is for me to thank you; **(il) reste à savoir s'il a raison** it remains to be seen whether he's right; **il n'en reste pas moins que …** it is nevertheless the case that …; **il ne nous restait plus que cinq cents mètres à parcourir** we only had another five hundred metres to go, we only had five hundred metres left to go; **dis-leur ce qui ne va pas, il en restera toujours quelque chose** tell them what's wrong, some of it is bound to sink in; **que reste-t-il de tes belles promesses?** what remains of your wonderful promises?

restituable [rɛstitɥabl] *adj* (*prêt, somme d'argent*) repayable, returnable; (*dépense*) refundable

restituer [rɛstitɥe] *vt* **(a)** (*reconstituer*) (*inscription, texte*) to restore; **le film restitue parfaitement l'ambiance du Paris d'après-guerre** the film recreates perfectly the atmosphere of post-war Paris **(b)** (*rendre*) (*marchandises volées etc*) to restore, to return; (*argent, prêt*) to repay, to pay back; **r. de l'argent à qn** to repay sb **(c)** (*énergie*) to release; (*son*) to reproduce; **cette chaîne restitue un son plus pur** this system gives a better sound, the sound reproduction on this system is better

restitution [rɛstitysjɔ̃] *nf* **(a)** (*reconstitution*) (*d'un texte, d'un monument*) restoration; (*d'une ambiance*) recreation **(b)** (*fait de rendre*) (*de marchandises volées etc*) return, *Fml* restitution; (*d'argent, prêt*) repayment **(c)** (*de l'énergie*) release; (*du son*) reproduction

resto [rɛsto] *nm F* = **restau**

restoroute [rɛstorut] *nm* = **restauroute**

restreindre [rɛstrɛ̃dr] (*prp* **restreignant**; *pp* **restreint**; *pr ind* **je restreins, il restreint, n. restreignons**; *p hist* **je restreignis**; *fu* **je restreindrai) 1** *vt* (*ambition, nombre de personnes etc*) to restrict **(à** to), to curb; (*production, sorties, achats, dépenses*) to cut back (on), to restrict, to limit; (*autorité*) to limit; **une offre restreinte aux abonnés** an offer limited *or* restricted to subscribers; *Fin* **r. le crédit** to restrict credit

2 se restreindre *vpr* **(a)** (*réduire ses dépenses*) to cut down; **se r. dans ses achats/dépenses** to buy/spend less

(b) (*d'un domaine de recherche etc*) to become narrower *or* restricted; **votre choix de montres s'est restreint** you don't have such a large selection of watches as you used to

restreint [rɛstrɛ̃] *adj* (*production, nombre de personnes, vocabulaire etc*) restricted, limited **(à** to); (*gamme, service*) limited; (*espace*) confined, limited; (*limites*) narrow; **édition à tirage r.** limited edition

restrictif, -ive [rɛstriktif, -iv] *adj* (*terme, clause etc*) restrictive

restriction [rɛstriksjɔ̃] *nf* **(a)** (*diminution*) restriction; **restrictions budgétaires** budget restrictions **(b)** (*réserve*) reservation; **faire des restrictions** to express (some) reservations; **restrictions aux exportations** export restrictions; **restrictions gouvernementales** government restrictions; **restrictions journalistiques** reporting restrictions; **r. mentale** mental reservation; **sans r.** (*accord*) unconditional; (*approuver*) unconditionally, unreservedly, without reservation; *Ordinat* **r. d'accès** access restriction

restructuration [rəstryktyrasjɔ̃] *nf* restructuring

restructurer [rəstryktyre] **1** *vt* to restructure **2 se restructurer** *vpr* to be restructured

resucée [rəsyse] *nf très F* **(a)** (*de vin, de café etc*) drop; **je vous en verse une r.?** would you like a drop more? **(b)** *Péj* (*répétition*) (*d'une pièce de théâtre, d'un livre etc*) rehash

résultant, -ante [rezyltɑ̃, -ɑ̃t] **1** *adj* resultant, resulting, consequent **2** *nf* **résultante** consequence, result; *Math* resultant

résultat [rezylta] *nm* **(a)** (*de calculs*) result; (*d'une action, d'une enquête etc*) result, outcome; (*d'un traitement*) result, effect; **on arrive à d'excellents résultats avec ce médicament** we're getting excellent results with this drug; **résultats** (*d'examen, de concours*) results; **les résultats de ses recherches** the results of his research, his findings; **donner des résultats** to give results; **sans r.** without result *or* success; (*expérience*) inconclusive; (*remède*) ineffective; **j'ai essayé de le lui faire comprendre, sans r.** I tried unsuccessfully to make him understand; *Mktg* **résultats antérieurs** past performance; *Mktg* **résultats perçus** perceived performance; **ces révélations eurent pour r. la chute du Gouvernement** these revelations led to *or* resulted in the fall of the Government; **ça a eu pour r. de le mettre en colère** it made him angry, he got angry as a result; **attendre le r. des courses** to wait for the racing results; *Fig* to wait and see what happens; *F* **r.** *ou* **r. des courses: il a été licencié** as a result he was dismissed, the upshot of it all was that he was dismissed

(b) *Compta* result, profit *or* loss; **résultats d'exercice** *ou* **d'exploitation** trading results; **r. courant** profit before tax and extraordinary items; **r. d'exploitation** operating profit or loss; **r. de l'exercice** profit or loss for the financial year; **r. de la période** profit or loss for the financial period; **r. exceptionnel** extraordinary profit or loss; **r. financier** financial profit or loss; **r. net** net return

résulter [rezylte] *vi* (*used only in the inf, third person & prp; aux often* **être**) to result, to arise (**de** from); **les avantages économiques qui en résultent** the resulting *or Fml* resultant economic benefits; **qu'en a-t-il résulté?** what was the result (of it)?, what came of it?, what was the outcome?; **ce qui résulte de ses propos, c'est que ...** what emerges from *or* comes out of what he said is that ...; **il en résulte que ...** the result of this is that ...; **il résulte de cette discussion que ...** the outcome *or* result of the discussion is that ...

résumé [rezyme] *nm* summary, résumé; (*d'un article scientifique*) abstract; (*d'un film, d'un livre*) synopsis; *Scol* (*livre*) study guide; **faire le r. de** (*texte*) to summarize, to give a summary *or* résumé of; (*histoire, situation*) to sum up, to summarize; *Jur* **r. des débats** summing up; **r. managérial** management summary; **en r.** (*en peu de mots*) in short, in brief; (*à tout prendre*) to sum up

résumer [rezyme] **1** *vt* (*article, idées etc*) to summarize, to give a summary of; (*situation, argumentation, histoire*) to sum up; *Jur* **r. les débats** to sum up; **pour r. les faits** to sum up; **voilà toute l'affaire résumée en un mot** that's the whole thing in a nutshell **2 se résumer** *vpr* (*d'une personne*) to sum up; **pour me r.** to sum up; **voilà à quoi tout cela se résume** that's what it all amounts to *or F* boils down to; **tout cela se résume en un seul mot/à peu de choses** it can all be summed up in one word/in a few words

résurgence [rezyrʒɑ̃s] *nf* (*du racisme, d'une doctrine etc*) resurgence, reappearance; (*d'un courant sous-terrain*) resurgence

résurgent [rezyrʒɑ̃] *adj* (*courant*) resurgent

resurgir [rəsyrʒir] *vi* to reappear suddenly; **cette idée resurgit dans mon esprit** the idea suddenly came back to me

résurrection [rezyrɛksjɔ̃] *nf* (**a**) *Rel* resurrection (**b**) *Fig* (*des arts, du passé etc*) resurrection, revival

retable [rətabl] *nm* reredos, altarpiece

rétabli [retabli] *adj* (*après une maladie*) recovered

rétablir [retablir] **1** *vt* (**a**) (*ordre, dynastie, paix etc*) to restore, to bring back; (*communications, relations, réputation*) to restore, to re-establish; **le gaz/l'eau a été rétabli(e)** the gas/ water has been reconnected *or* restored *or F* is back on; **r. qn** (*d'un traitement etc*) to restore sb to health; **r. sa santé** to recover one's health

(**b**) (*texte, finances*) to restore; **r. les faits** *ou* **la vérité** to set the record straight

(**c**) **r. qn (dans ses fonctions)** (*fonctionnaire etc*) to reinstate sb; **r. un officier dans son commandement** to restore an officer to his command; **r. qn dans ses droits** to restore sb's rights

2 se rétablir *vpr* (**a**) (*après une maladie*) to recover, to get well again; (*après un saut*) to recover

(**b**) **l'ordre se rétablit** order is being restored; **le silence s'est rétabli** silence returned

(**c**) **se r. dans les bonnes grâces de qn** to get back into sb's good books

(**d**) *Gym* to push oneself up

rétablissement [retablismɑ̃] *nm* (**a**) (*de l'ordre, de la paix, d'une dynastie etc*) restoration; (*des communications, des relations*) re-establishment, restoration; (*d'un fonctionnaire etc*) reinstatement; **le r. du téléphone est prévu pour demain** the telephone should be reconnected by tomorrow; **r. de la religion** religious revival (**b**) (*après une maladie, après un saut*) recovery; **nous vous souhaitons un prompt r.** all our good wishes for a speedy recovery; **faire un mauvais r.** (*après un saut*) to land *or* recover badly (**c**) *Gym* push-up; **faire un r.** to push oneself up

rétamage [retamaʒ] *nm* (*d'une casserole etc*) retinning; (*d'un miroir*) resilvering

rétamé [retame] *adj F* (*ivre*) canned; (*fatigué*) whacked, dead on one's feet; (*financièrement*) broke

rétamer [retame] **1** *vt* (**a**) (*casserole etc*) to retin (**b**) (*miroir*) to resilver (**c**) *F* (*enivrer*) to get canned; (*fatiguer*) to wear out; (*au jeu*) to clean out; **se faire r.** (*perdre un match*) to get hammered, to get slaughtered; **je me suis fait r. en anglais** I got a lousy mark in *or Am* I really flunked the English test **2 se rétamer** *vpr F* (*tomber*) to tumble

rétameur [retamœr] *nm* (*de casserole etc*) tinsmith

retapage [rətapaʒ] *nm F* (*d'une vieille maison, d'une voiture etc*) doing up; (*d'un lit*) straightening

retape [rətap] *nf très F* **faire la r.** (*d'une prostituée, d'un représentant*) to tout for business *or* custom; (*d'un parti politique*) to tout for new members

retaper [rətape] **1** *vt* (**a**) *F* (*vieille maison, voiture etc*) to do up; (*lit*) to straighten; **r. qn** to pick sb up (**b**) (*à la machine*) (*lettre etc*) to retype, to type again **2 se retaper** *vpr F* (**a**) (*après une maladie*) to get back on one's feet (**b**) **on se retape une belote?** how's about another game of belote?

retapisser [rətapise] *vt* (**a**) (*pièce etc*) to repaper; (*fauteuil*) to recover, to re-upholster (**b**) *Arg* (*reconnaître*) to clock

retard [rətar] **1** *nm* (**a**) (*dans le temps*) delay; (*de personne attendue*) lateness; **il y aura une heure de r.** there will be an hour's delay; **j'ai une heure de r.** I'm an hour late; **son bébé est né avec cinq jours de r.** her baby was born five days late; **je vous prie de m'excuser pour mon** *ou* **ce r.** please excuse me for being late; **et comment expliquez-vous votre r.?** how do you explain your being late *or* your lateness?; **cinq retards par semestre et c'est la porte** if you're late five times per term you're out; **sans r.** immediately, without delay; **avoir du r.** to be late; **le train a du r.** the train is (running) late; **le train a dix minutes de r.** *ou* **est en r. de dix minutes** the train is ten minutes late; **prendre du r.** to fall behind; (*d'un train*) to be running late; **mettre qn en r.** to make sb late, to delay sb; **arriver en r.** to arrive late; **être en r.** to be late; (*sur un programme*) to be behind; (*d'une horloge, d'une montre*) to be slow; **je suis en r. pour la réunion** I'm late for the meeting; **je suis en r. pour le paiement des remboursements** I'm behind with my repayments; **rattraper** *ou* **combler son r.** to catch up; **combler** *ou* **refaire son r. avec le peloton de tête** (*d'un athlète*) to close the gap with *or* to catch up on the front pack; *Com* **compte en r.** account outstanding *or* overdue; **r. de paiement** delay in payment, late payment

(**b**) (*dans un développement*) backwardness; **le r. dont souffre le pays** the backwardness *or* backward state of the country; **r. mental** backwardness, mental retardation; **ils ont une génération de r.** they're a generation behind; **pays en r. sur les autres** backward country, country lagging behind the others; **cet enfant est en r. pour son âge** this child is backward *or* behind for his age; **élève en r. sur les autres** pupil lagging behind the others; **être en r. de dix ans sur les autres pays industrialisés** to be (lagging) ten years behind other industrialized countries; **en r. sur son temps** behind the times; **cet enfant aura du mal à combler son r.** this child will have trouble catching up; **nous voulons aider les pays en voie de développement à combler leur r.** we want to help developing countries to catch up *or* to close the gap; **être en r. pour** *ou* **dans qch** to be *or* lag behind in sth

(**c**) *Aut* **r. à l'allumage** ignition lag, retarded ignition; *Él* **r. d'aimantation** magnetic lag

2 *adj Pharm* (*médicament*) slow-release

retardataire [rətardatɛr] **1** *adj* (**a**) (*qui arrive en retard*) (*personne*) late (**b**) (*dans son développement*) (*pays*) backward; (*enfant*) slow, backward; (*idées, entreprise*) behind the times, out-of-date **2** *n* latecomer

retardateur, -trice [rətardatœr, -tris] **1** *adj* retarding; (*tactiques*) delaying **2** *nm Phot* self-timer

retardé [rətarde] *adj* (**a**) (*départ*) delayed, late; (*arrivée*) late (**b**) (*mentalement*) (*élève*) lagging behind, slow; **enfant r.** backward *or* retarded child

retardement [rətardəmɑ̃] *nm* delay; *Mil* **action de r.** delaying action; **bombe à r.** time bomb; *Fig* **faire qch à r.** to be slow to do *or* in doing sth; **j'ai compris à r.** I was slow on the uptake; **comprendre une allusion à r.** to be slow in taking *or* to take a hint

retarder [rətarde] **1** *vt* (**a**) (*faire arriver en retard*) (*personne, train etc*) to delay, to hold up; **vous êtes sûr que cela ne vous retardera pas?** are you sure that it won't delay you *or* hold you up?; **les absences répétées retardent les progrès** repeated absences will delay progress; **la tuberculose l'a retardé dans ses études** having tuberculosis has held *or* kept him back in his studies

(**b**) (*différer*) (*événement, départ, voyage etc*) to delay, to postpone, to put off; (*paiement*) to defer, to delay; **l'intervention du Président a été retardée d'une heure** the President's address has been moved forward one hour; *Aut* **r. l'allumage** to retard the ignition

(**c**) (*montre, horloge*) to put back (**de** by)

2 *vi* (**a**) **l'horloge retarde** the clock is slow; **ma montre retarde** *ou F* **je retarde de dix minutes** my watch is *or* I'm ten minutes slow; **pendule qui retarde de dix minutes par jour** clock that loses ten minutes a day; **il retarde sur son temps** *ou* **époque** he's behind the times; *F* **vous retardez** (*vous n'êtes pas au courant*) you're behind the times

(**b**) *Tech* to lag

3 se retarder *vpr* to make oneself late

retâter [rətɑte] **1** *vt* **r. qch** to feel sth again **2** *vi F* **r. de qch** to have another go at sth; **r. de la prison** to do another stretch

reteindre [rətɛ̃dr] *vt* (*conj like* **teindre**) to redye, to dye again

retéléphoner [rətelefɔne] **1** *vi* to ring *or* call back *or* again; **r. à qn** to ring sb up *or* call sb (up) again, to ring *or* call sb back **2 se retéléphoner** *vpr* to call each other again, to speak to each other on the phone again; **allez, on se retéléphone demain, d'accord?** talk to you again tomorrow, OK?

retendre [rətɑ̃dr] *vt* **(a)** (*cordes*) to retighten; (*raquette*) to retension; (*piège*) to reset **(b) r. la main** to hold out one's hand again

retenir [rət(ə)nir] (*conj like* **tenir**) **1** *vt* **(a)** (*faire rester*) (*personne*) to hold back, to detain, to delay; (*chien*) to hold back, to restrain; **je ne vous retiens pas** I mustn't keep you (back), I mustn't hold you back; **ils nous ont retenus trois quarts d'heure** they kept us three quarters of an hour; **r. qn à dîner** to invite sb to stay for dinner; **elle m'a retenu par le bras** she held me back by the arm; **la grippe m'a retenue au lit pendant dix jours** the flu kept me in bed for ten days; **rien ne me retenait en France** there was nothing to keep me in France; **cette question ne nous retiendra pas** this question need not detain us; **r. l'attention de qn** (*d'un projet, d'une candidature*) to catch sb's attention; **elle a réussi à r. leur attention pendant trois heures** she managed to hold their attention for three hours; **r. la foule** to keep back *or* hold back *or* contain the crowd; **r. qn prisonnier/en otage** to keep *or* hold sb prisoner/hostage; **r. des marchandises en douane** to hold goods up at customs; *Naut* **retenu par les glaces** ice-bound

(b) (*maintenir*) to hold in position, to secure, to retain; **r. l'eau** to hold water; (*d'une personne*) to retain water

(c) (*garder*) (*argent*) to withhold; (*cotisation, impôt*) to deduct (**sur** from); **retenu à la source** deducted at source; **r. 500 francs sur le salaire de qn** to keep back *or* deduct 500 francs from sb's wages; **la plainte a été retenue contre lui** he was charged; **aucune charge n'a été retenue contre vous** all charges against you have been dropped

(d) (*se souvenir de*) (*leçon, nom etc*) to remember; **retenez ce numéro** remember *or* don't forget the number; **je n'ai pas retenu les chiffres** I don't *or* can't remember the figures; **qu'en avez-vous retenu?** how much of it can you remember?; **je le retiens, ton ami!** I won't forget your friend in a hurry!, I'll remember your friend all right!

(e) (*réserver*) (*place, chambre, table etc*) to reserve, to book; (*chambre d'hôtel*) to hold, *Spéc* to block; (*personnel*) to engage; **nous pouvons r. une chambre pour vous jusqu'à demain** we can hold a room for you until tomorrow

(f) (*accepter*) (*projet, suggestion*) to adopt; **deux candidats ont été retenus** (*ont réussi*) two applicants were successful; (*sont admis à l'épreuve suivante*) two applicants have been short-listed; **votre candidature n'a pas été retenue** your application was unsuccessful

(g) *Math* **je pose 2 et je retiens 5** put down 2 and carry 5

(h) (*contrôler*) (*colère*) to restrain, to contain, to curb; (*joie, enthousiasme*) to restrain, to contain; (*larmes*) to keep back, to hold back; (*cri*) to stifle, to smother; (*personne*) to restrain, to hold back; **la peur/la modestie m'a retenu** fear/modesty held me back; **r. qn de faire qch** to restrain sb *or* to hold sb back from doing sth; **qu'est-ce qui vous retient?** what's holding you back?; **qu'est-ce qui te retient de le lui dire?** what's stopping *or* preventing you telling him?; **retenez-moi ou je fais un scandale** hold me back or I'm going to make a scene; **r. son souffle** *ou* **sa respiration** to hold one's breath; **nous retenions notre souffle comme il allait annoncer les résultats** we waited with bated breath for him to announce the results

2 se retenir *vpr* **(a) se r. à qch** to hold on to sth; *Fig Hum* **se r. aux branches** to back-pedal; **c'est ça, retiens-toi aux branches!** that's it, start back-pedalling!

(b) (*se contenir*) to restrain *or* control *or* contain oneself; (*contrôler un besoin naturel*) to hold on; **se r. de faire qch** to stop oneself (from) doing sth, *Fml* to refrain from doing sth; **je n'ai pas pu me r. de pleurer/rire** I couldn't help crying/laughing; **il faut que tu te retiennes, il n'y a pas de toilettes ici** you're going to have to hold it in, there are no toilets here

(c) une comptine qui se retient facilement a counting rhyme that is easy to remember

rétenteur, -trice [retɑ̃tœr, -tris] *adj* (*force*) retaining; *Anat* **muscle r.** retentor (muscle)

rétention [retɑ̃sjɔ̃] *nf* holding back; *Méd* (*d'eau etc*) retention; *Méd* **faire de la r. d'eau** to be retaining water; *Méd* **r. d'urine** urine retention; **faire de la r. d'information** to hold back *or* withhold information; *Jur* **droit de r.** lien (**de** on); *Psy* **r. sélective** selective retention, selective recall

retentir [rətɑ̃tir] *vi* **(a)** to (re)sound, to echo, to ring; (*d'un klaxon*) to sound, to honk; (*du tonnerre, du canon*) to crash; (*d'une alarme*) to ring, to sound; (*d'un coup de feu, cri*) to ring out; **le champ retentit de leurs cris** the field resounded *or* echoed *or* rang with their shouts; **la salle retentissait d'acclamations** the hall rang out with applause; **l'explosion retentit dans toute la ville** the explosion was heard right across the city; **leurs cris retentissaient à mes oreilles** their cries were ringing in my ears **(b)** *Fig* **r. sur** to have an effect *or* impact on

retentissant [rətɑ̃tisɑ̃] *adj* (*voix*) resounding, ringing, booming; (*succès*) resounding; (*échec*) resounding, dismal; **discours r.** speech that arouses wide interest; **un bruit r.** an earth-shattering noise; **un scandale r.** a sensational scandal

retentissement [rətɑ̃tismɑ̃] *nm* **(a)** *Litt* (*bruit*) resounding *or* echoing sound *or* noise **(b)** *Fig* (*d'un événement etc*) impact, repercussions; **procès qui a eu un grand r.** lawsuit that aroused wide interest *or* that made a great stir; **cela a eu un grand r. sur sa carrière politique** it had a considerable impact on his political career

retenu [rət(ə)ny] *adj* **(a)** (*réservé*) reserved; **s'exprimer de façon retenue** to express oneself in restrained terms, to be restrained **(b)** *Scol* **élève r.** pupil in detention; **vous êtes r. samedi matin** you'll do detention *or* be kept in on Saturday morning

retenue [rət(ə)ny] *nf* **(a)** (*sur salaire etc*) deduction, stoppage; **r. sur salaire** wage deduction; (*mensuel*) salary deduction; **faire une r. de 5% sur les salaires** to stop *or* deduct 5% from the wages; **r. à la source** deduction at source; **retenues patronales** employer's contributions; **retenues salariales** wage deductions, employee's contributions

(b) *Math* carry over; **n'oublie pas la r.** don't forget the number you carried over; **n'oublie pas les retenues quand tu fais des additions** don't forget to carry over when you're doing sums

(c) *Scol* detention; **mettre un élève en r.** to keep a pupil in, to give a pupil detention

(d) (*discrétion*) reserve, restraint; **il manque de r. avec les gens** he's a bit too forthcoming with people; **manger avec r.** to eat sparingly; **s'exprimer sans r.** to express oneself without restraint *or* in unrestrained terms

(e) (*eau*) (*dans un barrage*) impounded water, reservoir water; **lac de r.** impoundment, dam reservoir; **clapet de r.** back-pressure *or* non-return valve

(f) (*barrage*) dam

(g) (*fait de garder*) (*de biens par la douanes*) holding

(h) *Naut* (*d'un cordage*) stay, guy

réticence [retisɑ̃s] *nf* **(a)** (*hésitation*) hesitation, unwillingness; **sans r.** unhesitatingly, without reservation, unreservedly; **après bien des réticences, il a dit oui** after much hesitation he said yes; **non sans r.** not without reservations **(b)** (*omission*) omission

réticent [retisɑ̃] *adj* (*hésitant*) hesitant, unwilling (**à faire qch** to do sth)

réticulaire [retikylɛr] *adj* reticular

réticule [retikyl] *nm* **(a)** (*sac*) (small) ladies' handbag **(b)** *Opt* reticle, cross wires

réticulé [retikyle] *adj* reticulate(d)

rétif, -ive [retif, -iv] *adj* (*cheval*) stubborn; (*personne*) recalcitrant

rétine [retin] *nf Anat* retina

rétinien, -ienne [retinjɛ̃, -jɛn] *adj Anat* retinal

retirable [rətirabl] *adj* withdrawable; **votre argent est r. à tout moment** you can withdraw money at any time

retirage [rətiraʒ] *nm* (*d'un livre, d'une photo etc*) reprinting

retiré [rətire] *adj* **(a)** (*lieu*) secluded, remote; (*vie*) solitary; **vivre r. (de la société)** to live in seclusion, to live a solitary life **(b)** (*à la retraite*) retired; **être r. des affaires** to have retired from business

retirer [rətire] **1** *vt* **(a)** (*faire sortir*) to take out; (*aller chercher*) to take *or* get out; (*qch d'encastré*) to get out; (*argent de son compte*) to withdraw, to take out (**de** from); (*bagages*) to reclaim, to collect (**de** from); (*billet*) to collect, to pick up (**de** from); (*bouchon, épine*) to pull *or* get out (**de** of), to remove (**de** from); **r. un enfant du collège** to remove a child from school, to take a child away from school; **r. un athlète d'une course** to withdraw an athlete from a race; **r. des pièces de la circulation** to withdraw coins from circulation; **r. des marchandises de la douane** to take goods out of bond, to clear goods; **r. des marchandises de la circulation** to withdraw goods from circulation; **r. du marché** to take off the market, to demarket; **r. progressivement** (*produit*) to phase out; **r. sa participation d'une société** to sell one's shares in a company, to sell out; **retire tous ces papiers de (sur) la table** get *or* clear all those papers off the table; **r. les mains de ses poches** to take one's hands out of one's pockets; **on ne lui retirera pas de l'idée qu'il mérite mieux** he won't be persuaded *or* convinced that he doesn't deserve better

(b) (*se procurer*) **r. un profit de qch** to make a profit out of sth, to profit from sth; *Fig* to benefit from sth, to profit from sth; **combien en avez-vous retiré?** how much did you get for it?; **quel plaisir peut-il en r.?** what pleasure can he get *or* derive from it?; **elle dit n'avoir retiré que des ennuis de cet accord** she says she got nothing but trouble out of the agreement

(c) (*extraire*) (*huile de schiste etc*) to extract

(d) (*enlever*) (*gants, lunettes*) to take off, to remove; (*manteau, pull etc*) to take off; **on me retire mon plâtre la semaine prochaine** I'm having the plaster removed *or* off next week; **r. sa main** to draw back *or* pull back one's hand; **retire ta main immédiatement ou je crie** get your hand off me immediately or I'll scream; **r. qch à qn** to withdraw sth from sb, to take away sth from sb; **r. son manteau à qn** (*pour le déshabiller*) to take off sb's coat; (*pour le débarrasser*) to take sb's coat; **on ne va pas lui r. le droit de garde** they're not going to take the custody of his children away from him; **personne n'a l'intention de te r. ton emploi** no one intends to take your job away from you; **r. le permis de conduire à qn** to disqualify *or* ban sb from driving, to take away *or Fml* revoke sb's driving licence; **on lui a retiré le** *ou* **son permis** he's been banned (from driving)

(e) (*revenir sur*) (*remarque, promesse*) to withdraw, to take back; (*offre, Jur plainte*) to withdraw; **r. sa candidature** (*à une élection*) to withdraw one's candidacy; (*pour un travail*) to withdraw one's application; **je retire ce que j'ai dit** I take it all back, forget what I said

(f) (*tirer de nouveau*) **r. des coups de feu** to fire more shots; **r. une flèche** to shoot another arrow; *Typ* **r. un livre** to reprint a book

2 se retirer *vpr* **(a)** (*s'en aller*) to retire, to withdraw; (*d'une foule*) to move back *or* away; *Mil* to retire, to withdraw, to pull out; **se r. d'un consortium** to back *or* pull out of a consortium; **se r. dans sa chambre** to retire to one's room; **vous pouvez vous r.** that will be all, you may go; **se r. de la lutte** to retire from the field; **se r. (en faveur de qn)** (*d'un candidat*) to stand down (in favour of sb)

(b) (*d'un employé*) to retire (**de** from); **se r. des affaires** to retire from business

(c) (*des eaux*) to subside; (*de la mer*) to recede; (*de la marée*) to ebb; **les eaux de la rivière se retirent** the level of the river is dropping

retombée [rətɔ̃be] *nf* **(a) retombées radioactives** radioactive fallout **(b)** *Fig* (*répercussion*) **retombées** repercussions; **l'une des retombées du programme spatial fut la mise au point de nouveaux matériaux** new materials were one of the spin-offs of the space programme; **la grève aura des retombées sur les prix** the strike will have repercussions *or* a knock-on effect on prices

retomber [rətɔ̃be] *vi* (*aux often* **être**) **(a)** (*tomber de nouveau*) to fall (down) again; (*de la pluie, des bombes etc, Fig d'une monnaie*) to fall again; **r. dans son fauteuil** to fall back *or* sink back into one's armchair; **faire r. un store** to let down *or* pull down a blind; **laisser r. ses bras** to drop one's arms; **r. dans l'erreur** to lapse back into one's old ways; **r. dans le péché** to fall *or* sink back into one's sinful ways; **r. dans l'oubli** to sink back into obscurity *or* oblivion; **elle est retombée dans l'anonymat** she faded out of the limelight; **r. dans le désespoir** to fall back into despair; **le pays risque de r. dans la guerre civile** the country may lapse back into a state of civil war; **r. dans le vice** to relapse into vice; **r. en enfance** to lapse into one's second childhood; **r. malade** to fall *or* become ill again; *F* **r. sur qn** to bump into sb again

(b) (*tomber*) (*d'une personne, d'un ballon*) to land; **r. sur ses pattes** (*d'un chat*) to land on its feet; *Fig* **r. sur ses pieds** *ou F* **ses pattes** to land on one's feet; **r. toujours dans la même situation** always to end up *or* land in the same situation; **pour éviter que la conversation ne retombe sur le même sujet** to prevent the conversation from coming round to the same subject again; **r. sur qch** (*trouver*) to come across *or* stumble on sth; **tu ne retomberas jamais sur une occasion pareille** you'll never come across an opportunity like it again; **le blâme/la responsabilité retombera sur lui** the blame/responsibility will fall on him; **faire r. le blâme sur qn** to put *or* lay the blame on sb; **tout retombe toujours sur moi!** it's always my fault!, I always get the blame for everything!; *F* **tout ça va me r. dessus** it'll all come back on me

(c) (*diminuer*) (*de l'enthousiasme, de l'intérêt*) to fall off, to wane; (*de l'attention*) to fall off, to slacken

(d) (*des cheveux, des rideaux*) to hang (down) (**sur** over); **ses cheveux lui retombent dans le dos** her hair hangs down her back; **laisser ses cheveux r.** to let *or* take one's hair down

retordre [rətɔrdr] *vt* **(a)** (*linge*) to wring out again **(b)** *Tex* (*fil*) to twist; *F* **il vous donnera du fil à r.** he'll give you trouble

rétorquer [retɔrke] *vt* **(a) r. que …** to retort that … **(b)** (*accusation*) to cast back, to hurl back; **r. un argument contre qn** to turn sb's argument against him/her

retors, -orse [rətɔr, -ɔrs] *adj* **(a)** *Tex* (*fil, corde*) twisted **(b)** (*bec*) curved **(c)** (*personne*) crafty, wily, devious

rétorsion [retɔrsjɔ̃] *nf Jur, Pol* retaliation; **mesures de r.** retaliatory measures

retouche [rətuʃ] *nf* (*action*) (*d'un tableau, d'une photo etc*) touching up, retouching; (*d'un texte, d'un vêtement*) altering; (*résultat*) (*d'un tableau, d'une photo etc*) retouch; (*d'un texte, d'un vêtement*) alteration; **faire des retouches à** (*un vêtement*) to make alterations to; (*un tableau, une photo*) to retouch; (*un texte*) to alter; **il faudra faire une r. dans le dos** it will have to be altered at the back; *TV, Cin, Ordinat* **r. d'image(s)** image editing *or* retouching; *TV, Cin* **r. numérique** digital retouching

retoucher [rətuʃe] **1** *vt* (*tableau, photo etc*) to touch up, to retouch; (*texte*) to touch up, to alter; (*vêtement*) to alter, to make alterations to **2** *vi* **votre article est bien, n'y retouchez pas** your article is good, leave it alone *or* don't change a word of it; **je n'ai jamais retouché à la drogue** I've never touched drugs again

retoucheur, -euse [rətuʃœr, -øz] *n* **(a)** *Beaux-Arts, Phot* retoucher **(b)** (*en confection*) alteration hand

retour [rətur] *nm* **(a)** (*de voyage, après une absence*) return; **être de r.** to be back (again); **être de r. de vacances** to be back from holiday; **un journaliste de r. de Paris** a reporter (just) back from Paris; **de r. chez moi, je lui écrivis** I wrote to him when I got home *or* on my return home; **à mon r.** on my return; **on en parlera à mon r.** we'll talk about it on my return *or* when I get back; **partir sans espoir de r.** to leave without any hope of returning; **être perdu sans r.** to be irretrievably lost; **point de non-r.** point of no return; **voyage/vol de r.** return journey *or* trip/flight; **pour le voyage de r., je passerai par Lyon** I'll be coming through Lyons on my way back; **billet aller r.** return ticket, *Am* round-trip ticket; **coupon de r.** return half; *F* **cheval de r.** (*vieux criminel*) old offender, old lag; **par r. (du courrier)** by return (of post); **r. à l'envoyeur** return to sender; **le r. de l'hiver/d'une maladie** the return of winter/recurrence of a disease; **faire un r. sur le passé** to look back on the past; **faire un r. sur soi** to take a good hard look at oneself; **r. à la nature/au calme** return to nature/a state of calm; **par un juste r. des choses, celui qui l'a fait a été puni** the one who did it was punished, as was only fair *or* as was only right and proper; *F* **être sur le r.** (*d'une personne*) to be past middle age *or* past one's prime; **beauté sur le r.** beauty on the wane

(b) (*changement*) (*de fortune*) reversal; **un r. d'opinion** a backlash; **r. de conscience** qualms of conscience

(c) course de r. (*d'un piston*) back stroke; **r. de carburateur** backfire; **avoir des retours** to backfire; **r. automatique de ruban** automatic ribbon reverse; *Ordinat* **r. d'information** feedback

(d) *TV, Rad* (*de son*) foldback; *Él* **r. à la terre** *ou* **à la masse** earth connection, earthing, *Am* grounding; **fil de r.** earth *or Am* ground wire

(e) (*de marchandises, de lettre*) return; **marchandises de r., retours** returns; **vendu avec faculté de r.** sold on a sale *or* return basis

(f) *Tennis* **r. de service** return of serve

(g) (*sur clavier*) return; **touche r.** return key; **appuyez sur la touche r.** press return; **r. arrière** backspace

(h) (*locutions*) **payer qn de r.** to repay sb in kind; **payer de r. l'affection de qn** to return sb's affection; **il ne semblait pas payer de r. ma curiosité pour lui** he didn't seem to be as curious about me as I was about him; **en r.** in return (**de** for); **aimer qn en r.** to return sb's love, to love sb back *or* in return; *Sp* **match r.** return match

▶ **retour**: **r. d'âge** (*d'une femme*) change of life; *Cin* **r. en arrière** flashback; **faire un r. en arrière** to flash back; **r. de chariot** (*de machine à écrire*) carriage return; *Ordinat* **r. chariot obligatoire** hard carriage return; *Aut* **r. de flamme** blowback; *Ordinat* **r. ligne** line feed; **r. ligne obligatoire** hard return; *Aut* **r. de manivelle** backfire kick; *Fig* **il y a eu un r. de manivelle** it backfired; **il faut s'attendre à des retours de manivelle** we'll have to expect a certain amount of backlash; *Fin* **r. net** net return; *Ordinat* **r. obligatoire** hard return; *Mil* **r. offensif** counter attack, counter stroke; *Com* **r. sans frais** return free of charge; **r. sur investissement** return on investment, ROI; **r. sur ventes** return on sales; *Biol* **r. à un type** reversion to type

retournement [rətuʀnəmɑ̃] *nm* (*de situation*) turnaround, reversal; (*d'opinion*) about-turn (**de** in)

retourner [rətuʀne] **1** *vt* (**a**) (*en mettant la face intérieure à l'extérieur*) (*parapluie, gant, vêtement*) to turn inside out; **retournez vos poches** turn out your pockets

(**b**) (*verticalement*) to turn over; (*terre*) to turn over *or* up; (*matelas, omelette, steak, foin*) to turn; (*carte*) to turn up; *Fig* (*idée, projet*) to turn over in one's mind, to mull over; **r. la salade** to toss the salad; **tourner et r. qch** to turn sth over and over (again); *Fig* **r. une question dans tous les sens** to look at *or* consider a question from every angle; *F* **on avait retourné tout le bureau pour trouver la lettre** they had turned the office upside down to find the letter; *F* **r. qn** (*le bouleverser*) to upset sb

(**c**) (*horizontalement*) to turn round; **r. la tête** to turn one's head, to look round; **il retourna l'arme contre moi et tira** he turned the gun on me and fired; **r. un argument contre qn** to turn an argument against sb; **r. qn contre qn** to turn sb against sb; **r. une situation** to reverse a situation; *F* **elle l'a retourné comme un gant** she very quickly got him to change his mind; *F* **on le retourne comme un gant** he is easily swayed

(**d**) (*renvoyer, rapporter*) to return; **r. qch à qn** to return sth to sb, to send sth back to sb; *Com* **r. un effet** to return a bill; **r. à l'expéditeur** to return to sender; **r. le compliment** to return the compliment; **je me permets de vous r. le compliment** the same to you

2 *vi* (*aux* **être**) (**a**) to go back, to return (**à** to); **r. chez soi** to go back home; **je retourne chez ma mère** I'm going back to my mother; **r. déjeuner chez soi** to go home for lunch; **je ne retournerai pas la voir** I won't go back and see her; **sa fortune retourne à sa famille** his fortune reverts to his family; **r. à l'état sauvage** to revert to the wild; **r. à ses premières amours** to return *or* go back to one's first love

(**b**) **de quoi retourne-t-il?** *Cartes* what are trumps?; *Fig F* what's it all about?, what's up?; **si quelqu'un voulait bien me dire de quoi il retourne!** would someone please tell me what's going on!

3 se retourner *vpr* (**a**) (*d'un dormeur*) to turn over; (*d'une voiture*) to turn *or F* flip over; *Fig F* **ne pas avoir le temps de se r.** not to have time to draw breath; **laisse-lui le temps de se r.** give him time to sort himself out

(**b**) (*tourner la tête*) to turn (round); **partir sans se r.** to leave without looking back; **on se retourne sur leur passage** they make heads turn, all heads turn when they go by

(**c**) **se r. contre qn** (*d'une personne*) to turn against sb; (*verbalement*) to round *or* turn on sb; (*d'un chien*) to turn on sb; **cela finira par se r. contre lui** it'll eventually backfire on him

(**d**) **s'en r. à un endroit** to return to *or* go back to a place; **s'en r. à un endroit/chez soi** to return *or* go back to a place/home

retracer [rətʀase] *vt* (*conj like* **tracer**) (**a**) (*trait*) to draw again, to redraw, to retrace; (*sentier*) to mark out again (**b**) *Fig* (*raconter*) (*événement, vie etc*) to recount

rétractable [ʀetʀaktabl] *adj* (*antenne*) retractable; *Aut* (*volant*) collapsible

rétractation [ʀetʀaktasjɔ̃] *nf* retraction; *Jur* (*d'une sentence*) rescinding

rétracter[1] [ʀetʀakte] **1** *vt* (*griffes, antennes*) to retract, to draw in **2 se rétracter** *vpr* (*se contracter*) (*d'un muscle*) to retract

rétracter[2] **1** *vt* (*paroles*) to retract, to withdraw, to take back; (*aveu*) to retract; *Jur* (*arrêt*) to rescind **2 se rétracter** *vpr* (*se dédire*) to retract

rétracteur [ʀetʀaktœʀ] *adj, nm* (**muscle**) **r.** retractor (muscle)

rétractile [ʀetʀaktil] *adj* which can be retracted *or* pulled back, *Spéc* retractile; *Aut* (*volant*) collapsible

rétraction [ʀetʀaksjɔ̃] *nf* retraction

retrait [ʀətʀɛ] *nm* (**a**) (*du ciment etc*) shrinkage, shrinking

(**b**) (*des eaux*) subsiding; (*d'un glacier*) retreat

(**c**) (*d'argent, d'un ordre, d'une candidature, un permis etc*) withdrawal; (*de troupes*) withdrawal, pullback; (*d'un cheval dans une course*) scratching; **r. des bagages** baggage (re)claim; **r. de marchandises** withdrawal of goods; **r. d'espèces** cash withdrawal; **r. du permis de conduire** disqualification from driving, driving ban; **un r. de l'ordre de grève est hors de question** calling off the strike is out of the question

(**d**) (*dans un mur*) recess; **en r.** (*étagères etc*) recessed; **maison en r.** house standing back *or* set back from the road; **en r. de la route** set back from the road; **être/rester en r.** (*d'une personne*) to be/stay in the background

(**e**) *Typ* indent; **mettre en r.** to indent; **en r.** indented; **en r. négatif** hanging; **r. en sommaire** hanging indent; **r. inversé** reverse indent

retraite [ʀətʀɛt] *nf* (**a**) *Mil etc* retreat, withdrawal; **battre en r.** to retreat, to beat a retreat, to retire; *Fig* to beat a retreat; **battre/sonner la r.** to beat/sound the retreat

(**b**) (*fanfare*) tattoo; **r. aux flambeaux** torchlight tattoo *or* procession

(**c**) (*de la vie active*) retirement; **caisse de r.** superannuation fund, pension fund; **être à la** *ou* **en r.** to be *or* to have retired; (*d'un officier*) to be on the retired list; **militaire en r.** army pensioner; **quand je serai à la r.** when I retire, when I've retired; **un médecin/policier à la r.** a retired doctor/police officer; **prendre sa r.** to retire; **quand j'ai pris ma r.** when I retired, on my retirement; **prendre sa r. anticipée** to take early retirement; **on parle d'une centaine de mises à la r. anticipée** there's talk of making about a hundred people take early retirement; **mettre qn à la r.** to retire sb, to pension sb off

(**d**) (*pension*) retirement pension; **jouir d'une petite r.** to have a small pension; **r. complémentaire** supplementary pension; **prendre une r. complémentaire** to take out an extra pension scheme

(**e**) **maison de r.** (**pour vieillards**) old people's home

(**f**) (*isolement*) retreat; **faire une r.** to go into retreat

(**g**) (*abri*) retreat, refuge; (*de bêtes sauvages*) lair, haunt; (*de voleurs*) hideout

(**h**) *Archit* (*d'un mur, entre des étages*) offset; (*d'un mur*) recess

retraité, -ée [ʀətʀete] **1** *adj* (*à la retraite*) retired; (*officier*) on the retired list **2** *n* (*personne du troisième âge*) senior citizen, pensioner, *Br* OAP; **les retraités** retired people, senior citizens

retraitement [ʀətʀɛtmɑ̃] *nm* (*de déchets nucléaires, combustible*) reprocessing; **usine de r.** reprocessing plant

retraiter *vt* (**a**) *Nucl* (*déchets, combustible*) to reprocess (**b**) *Méd* (*malade*) to treat again

retranchement [ʀətʀɑ̃ʃmɑ̃] *nm Mil* entrenchment; *Fig* **forcer qn dans ses (derniers) retranchements** to drive sb to the wall

retrancher [ʀətʀɑ̃ʃe] **1** *vt* (**a**) (*ôter*) **r. un passage d'un livre** to cut *or* remove a passage from a book; **r. un nombre d'un autre** to take away *or* subtract one number from another; **r. qch sur une somme** to deduct sth from a sum of money; **r. qch à qn** to dock sb sth, to dock sth from sb; **r. un nom d'une liste** to remove *or* delete a name from a list

(**b**) *Mil* (*position*) to entrench; *Fig* **être retranché** to be entrenched (**derrière ses croyances** in one's beliefs); *F* **vivre retranché dans son petit monde** to live in one's own little world *or* a world of one's own

2 se retrancher *vpr Mil* to entrench oneself, to dig in; *Fig* **se r. dans le silence** *ou* **le mutisme** to take refuge in silence; **se r. derrière qn** to hide behind sb

retranscription [ʀətʀɑ̃skʀipsjɔ̃] *nf* retranscription

retranscrire [ʀətʀɑ̃skʀiʀ] *vt* to retranscribe

retransmetteur [ʀətʀɑ̃smɛtœʀ] *nm Rad* (*appareil*) relay

retransmettre [ʀətʀɑ̃smɛtʀ] *vt* (*conj like* **transmettre**) to transmit, to broadcast; (*relayer*) to retransmit, to relay

retransmission [ʀətʀɑ̃smisjɔ̃] *nf* transmission, broadcast(ing); (*par relai*) retransmission, relay; **r. en direct de Cardiff** (broadcast *or* relayed) live from Cardiff; **r. en différé de Cardiff** in a recorded relay from Cardiff, recorded live at Cardiff earlier; **la r. du match est prévue pour 14 heures 45** and you can see the match at 2. 45 pm

retravailler [ʀətʀavaje] **1** *vt* (*discours, texte etc*) to rework, to work on again; (*exercice de gym, muscle*) to work on again; (*argile, pâte etc*) to work again; **votre thèse a besoin d'être retravaillée** your thesis needs reworking **2** *vi* to go back to work; **après une longue période de chômage, il retravaille enfin** after being unemployed for a long time he's finally working again

rétréci [ʀetʀesi] *adj* (*route etc, Fig Péj esprit, vues*) narrow; (*vêtement*) shrunken

rétrécir [ʀetʀesiʀ] **1** *vt* (**a**) (*rendre plus étroit*) (*route*) to narrow; (*vêtement*) to take in (**b**) (*au lavage*) (*vêtement*) to shrink **2** *vi* (*de vêtement, de tissu*) to shrink; *Fig* **son univers** *ou* **son horizon a beaucoup rétréci** his world has become much narrower **3 se rétrécir** *vpr* to narrow, to become narrower; **le chemin continue en se rétrécissant** the path gets narrower and narrower

rétrécissement [ʀetʀesismɑ̃] *nm* (**a**) (*action*) (*d'une route*) narrowing; (*d'un vêtement, un tissu*) shrinking (**b**) *Méd* narrowing, constriction, *Spéc* stricture (**c**) (*partie*) (*d'un tuyau, une route etc*) narrow part

retrempe [ʀətʀɑ̃p] *nf* (*de l'acier*) retempering

retremper [ʀətʀɑ̃pe] **1** *vt* (**a**) (*linge*) to soak *or* steep again (**b**) (*acier*) to retemper **2 se retremper** *vpr* (**a**) (*dans l'eau*) to have another quick dip (**b**) *Fig F* **se r. dans un milieu**

sympathique/le milieu familial to plunge back into a congenial atmosphere/the family atmosphere

rétribuer [retribɥe] *vt* (*employé*) to pay; (*travail, service*) to pay for; **travail rétribué** paid work; **être bien/mal rétribué** to be well/badly paid

rétribution [retribysjɔ̃] *nf* (*paie*) (*pour des services*) payment, remuneration; **fonctions sans r.** honorary duties

retriever [retrivœr] *nm* (*chien*) retriever

rétro [retro] **1** *nm* **(a)** *Billard* pull-back, screwback (stroke) **(b)** = **rétroviseur (c)** (*style*) retro **2** *adj inv* (*film, robe, mode, musique etc*) retro **3** *adv* **s'habiller r.** to wear retro clothes; **leur appartement est meublé r.** their flat is furnished in retro style

rétroactif, -ive [retroaktif, -iv] *adj* (*loi etc*) retroactive; **augmentation avec effet r. au 1er juillet** increase backdated *or* retroactive to 1st July

rétroaction [retroaksjɔ̃] *nf Électron, Rad* feedback; **r. acoustique** acoustic feedback; **r. d'une augmentation de salaire** backdating of a rise, making a rise retroactive

rétroactivement [retroaktivmɑ̃] *adv* retroactively

rétroactivité [retroaktivite] *nf* retroactive nature

rétrocéder [retrosede] (*conj like* **céder**) *vt* (*revendre*) to resell; (*droit etc*) to cede back, to release back, to retrocede

rétrocession [retrosesjɔ̃] *nf* (*d'un droit, un don*) releasing back, retrocession

rétroéclairage [retroeklɛraʒ] *nm Ordinat* back lighting

rétroéclairé [retroeklere] *adj Ordinat* backlit

rétroflexe [retroflɛks] *adj Ling* retroflex

rétrofusée [retrofyze] *nf* retrorocket

rétrogradage [retrogradaʒ] *nm Aut* downchange, downshift, changing down

rétrogradation [retrogradasjɔ̃] *nf* **(a)** *Litt* (*dans un développement*) regression, retrogression **(b)** (*d'un sous-officier*) reduction in rank, demotion; (*d'un fonctionnaire*) demotion, downgrading

rétrograde [retrograd] **1** *adj* (*mouvement*) retrograde, backward; *Fig* (*idée*) reactionary; *Pol* (*mesure, politique*) retrograde, reactionary; *Billard* **effet r.** pullback, screwback; **phrase r.** palindrome **2** *n Pol* reactionary

rétrograder [retrograde] **1** *vi* **(a)** to move backwards; *Mil* to fall back, to retreat; *Fig* (*dans son développement*) to regress, to retrogress; *Sp* **il a rétrogradé en cinquième position** he's fallen back to fifth place **(b)** *Aut* to change *or* shift down; **r. de troisième en seconde** to change down from third to second **2** *vt* (*sous-officier*) to reduce in rank, to demote, *US F* to bust; (*fonctionnaire*) to demote, to downgrade

rétrogression [retrogresjɔ̃] *nf* (*mouvement*) retrogression

rétropédalage [retropedalaʒ] *nm Cyclisme* back-pedalling

rétropédaler [retropedale] *vi Cyclisme* to back-pedal

rétroprojecteur [retroprɔʒɛktœr] *nm* overhead projector

rétropropulsion [retroprɔpylsjɔ̃] *nf Astronaut* reverse thrust

rétrospectif, -ive [retrɔspɛktif, -iv] **1** *adj* retrospective; **j'ai eu une peur/jalousie rétrospective** I was frightened/jealous in retrospect **2** *nf* **rétrospective (a)** *Beaux-Arts etc; Fig* retrospective; *Can Cin* flashback; **une rétrospective de l'année 1944** a look back at the events of 1944; *Cin* **rétrospective René Clair** René Clair retrospective **(b)** *Fin* review

rétrospectivement [retrɔspɛktivmɑ̃] *adv* retrospectively, in retrospect; **ça me fait peur r.** it frightens me in retrospect *or* looking back on it

retroussé [rətruse] *adj* (*manches*) rolled-up; **nez r.** snub *or* turned-up *or Litt* retroussé nose

retroussement [rətrusmɑ̃] *nm* **avec un r. des lèvres** with a curl of the lip

retrousser [rətruse] **1** *vt* (*manches, pantalon*) to turn up, to roll up; (*jupe*) to tuck up; (*lèvres*) to curl (up); *Fig* **r. ses manches** to roll up one's sleeves **2 se retrousser** *vpr* (*d'une femme*) to tuck up one's skirt(s); (*d'une jupe*) to bunch up

retroussis [rətrusi] *nm* (*de vêtement*) turned-back facings; **bottes à r.** topboots

retrouvable [rətruvabl] *adj* recoverable, retrievable; **facilement r.** easy to find, easily found

retrouvailles [rətruvaj] *nfpl* reunion

retrouver [rətruve] **1** *vt* **(a)** to find again; (*objet perdu*) to find; (*personne*) to track down; *Fig* (*santé, forces, enthousiasme etc*) to recover, to regain; (*sa voix*) to get back; (*son appétit*) to get back, to recover; **r. son chemin** to find one's way again; **je n'arrive pas à r. son adresse** I can't find his address; *Prov* **un(e) de perdu(e), dix de retrouvé(e)s** there are (plenty) more fish in the sea; **la clef a été retrouvée, on a retrouvé la clé** the key has been found; **elle ne parvint jamais à le r.** she never found any trace of him; **la r. après tant d'années, à quoi bon?** what's the point of seeing her again after all this time?; **on retrouve chez lui la curiosité de sa grand-mère** he has his grandmother's curiosity; **on ne retrouve plus cet auteur dans son dernier roman** we don't recognize the author in his last novel, the author's last novel is uncharacteristic; **on retrouve souvent cette image dans le cinéma de Renoir** you often encounter *or* come across this image in Renoir's films; **tu ne retrouveras jamais une telle occasion** you'll never come across an opportunity like it again; **elle a retrouvé toute sa jeunesse en voyant ce film** the film took her back to her childhood; **tu as retrouvé le sourire** you're looking more cheerful, you've discovered how to smile again; **tu as retrouvé la parole** *ou F* **ta langue, toi!** you've found your tongue again!

(b) (*rejoindre*) **il doit r. ses parents à Venise** he's to join up *or* meet up with his parents in Venice; **je vous retrouverai devant le cinéma** I'll meet you outside the cinema; **je vous retrouve dans une heure au pub** I'll join you at the pub in an hour's time

2 se retrouver *vpr* **(a) se r. dans la même position** to find oneself *or* to be in the same position again; **se r. à Paris** to be back in Paris; **je me retrouve donc à Paris** so here I am back in Paris; **finir par se r. au poste/à l'hôpital** to end up in the police station/hospital; *F* **tu vas te r. sans un sou** you're going to find yourself without a penny; *F* **et c'est comme ça que je me suis retrouvé à travailler ici** and that's how I found myself *or* came to be working here

(b) (*retrouver son chemin*) to get *or* find one's bearings; **elle se retrouve très bien, dans Londres** she can find her way round London without any difficulty; *Fig* **je ne m'y retrouve plus!** I'm hopelessly confused *or* lost; *F* **vous vous y retrouverez** (*financièrement*) you'll get your money back soon enough

(c) (*entre personnes*) to meet; **nous devons nous r. au restaurant** we're meeting at the restaurant; **ils se retrouvent tous les mardis** they meet every Tuesday, they get together every Tuesday; **nous voulions nous r. seuls pour parler** we wanted to be alone so we could talk; **on se retrouvera!** I'll get even (with you)!, you haven't heard the last of this!; **comme on se retrouve!** fancy meeting you!, it's a small world!

(d) (*en soi-même*) to find oneself; **ce couple a besoin de se r.** they need to find each other again as a couple

(e) (*exister*) to exist; **ce mot se retrouve dans de nombreuses langues** this word exists *or* can be found in numerous languages; *F* **ça se retrouve, des verres comme ça!** glasses like that are easy to find *or* are easy to come by

rétroversion [retrovɛrsjɔ̃] *nf Méd* retroversion

rétrovirus [retrovirys] *nm Méd* retrovirus

rétroviseur [retrovizœr] *nm Aut* **r. (intérieur)** (rear-view) mirror; **r. extérieur** *Br* wing mirror, door mirror, side mirror, *Am* outside mirror; **r. jour/nuit** anti-glare rear-view mirror; **r. à double miroir** split-view mirror; **r. à position nuit** dipping rear-view mirror

rets [rɛ] *nm Litt* net; **prendre qn dans ses r.** to catch sb in one's toils

réuni [reyni] *adj* **(a)** (*rassemblé*) put together; **plus forts que nous et les Anglais réunis** stronger than us and the English put together *or* combined; **il s'est adressé à l'ensemble des élèves réunis** he addressed the assembled schoolchildren; **nous sommes réunis aujourd'hui pour …** we are gathered together today to … **(b)** *Com* (*laiteries etc*) amalgamated, united

réunification [reynifikasjɔ̃] *nf Pol* reunification

réunifier [reynifje] *vt Pol* to reunify

réunion [reynjɔ̃] *nf* **(a)** (*action de rassembler*) (*de deux services*) merger, amalgamation; (*de faits, de renseignements etc*) gathering (together); (*de gens, de famille etc*) bringing together; (*à nouveau*) (*de famille, de parti politique etc*) reunion; (*action de joindre*) joining together; **r. d'une province à la France** union of a province with France; **cette r. de faits** this assemblage of facts; *Math* **r. de deux ensembles** union of two sets

(b) (*action de se rassembler*) coming *or* gathering together; **droit de r.** right of assembly; **salle de r.** conference room

(c) (*assemblée*) meeting; (*d'un comité*) session, sitting; (*réception dans un hôtel etc*) function; **le directeur est en r.** the manager is in a meeting; **r. de famille** family gathering *or* get-together; **r. électorale** election meeting; **r. publique** public meeting; **r. d'actionnaires** shareholders' meeting; **r. de comité** committee meeting; *Mktg* **r. de groupe** (*pour enquête*) group meeting, focus-group session; *Mktg* **r. de remue-méninges** brainstorming session; *Mktg* **r. de représentants** sales meeting; **r. des créanciers** creditors' meeting; **r. du conseil** board meeting; **r. du conseil d'administration** board meeting

Réunion (La) [lareynjɔ̃] *nf* Réunion
réunionite [reynjɔnit] *nf F Hum* mania for meetings, *Hum* meetingitis
réunionnais, -aise [reynjɔnɛ, -ɛz] **1** *adj* of/from Réunion **2** *n* **R.** (*natif*) native of Réunion; (*habitant*) inhabitant of Réunion
réunir [reynir] **1** *vt* **(a)** (*rassembler*) (*d'une exposition*) (*objets d'art, toiles*) to bring *or* put together; (*faits, renseignements, documents, preuves etc*) to gather (together), to collect; (*somme d'argent, fonds*) to get together, to raise; (*personnes, famille etc*) to bring *or* get together; (*d'un colloque*) (*scientifiques etc*) to bring together; (*à nouveau*) (*famille, parti politique etc*) to reunite; (*services, classes*) to combine, to merge; **r. qch à qch** to join sth to sth; **r. une armée** to raise an army; **r. un comité** to convene a committee, to call a committee together
(b) (*comporter*) (*qualités, avantages*) to have, to possess
2 se réunir *vpr* **(a)** (*de personnes*) to meet, to get *or* gather together; (*de routes*) to join up, to meet; **l'assemblée se réunit une fois par semaine** the assembly meets once a week; **se r. autour de qn/qch** to gather *or* congregate around sb/sth
(b) (*de banques etc*) to amalgamate; (*d'églises, d'états etc*) to unite
réussi [reysi] *adj* successful; **être r.** (*d'un spectacle, une pièce, un plat*) to be successful *or* a success; *Iron* **c'est r.!, la voilà en larmes!** well done *or* very clever!, she's in tears now!; **mal r.** unsuccessful; **c'est à demi r.** it's partially successful
réussir [reysir] **1** *vi* **(a)** to be successful, to be a success, to succeed; (*d'une plante*) to thrive; **c'est un garçon qui réussira** he's a boy who will do well *or* succeed *or* be successful; **le projet avait mal réussi** the plan had proved a failure; **ce truc-là ne réussira pas** that trick won't work, that trick won't come off; **tout lui réussit** he's successful in everything he does, everything he does turns out well; **r. dans qch** to succeed *or* be successful in sth; **il a réussi dans la vie** he's made a success of things; **une femme d'affaires qui a réussi** a successful businesswoman; **r. à un examen** to pass an examination; *Scol* **r. de justesse** to scrape through, to only just pass; **r. à faire qch** to succeed in doing sth, to manage to do sth; **tu as réussi (à finir/à l'ouvrir)?** did you manage (to finish/open it)?; *Iron* **elle a réussi à déranger tout le monde** she managed to disturb everybody; **ne pas r. à faire qch** not to have any success in doing sth, to fail to do sth; **je n'ai pas réussi à la convaincre** I didn't manage *or* I failed to persuade her, I didn't have any success in persuading her
(b) *F* **le homard ne me réussit pas** lobster doesn't agree with me
2 *vt* (*qch*) to make a success of, to be successful with; **elle réussit (bien) les omelettes** she makes very good omelettes; **c'est ta dissertation qui t'a permis de r. l'examen** it was your essay that got you through the exam; *F* **r. son coup** to do the trick, to bring it off; *Iron* **tu as bien réussi ton coup** well done, very clever
réussite [reysit] *nf* **(a)** (*succès*) success; **fêter sa r. à un examen** to celebrate passing an exam *or* getting through an exam; **cette soirée est une belle r.!** the party is a great success!; **l'une des plus belles réussites industrielles françaises** one of France's biggest industrial successes *or* success stories; **r. sociale** social success; **présenter tous les signes de la r.** to show every sign of succeeding *or* of being successful **(b)** *Cartes* patience, *Am* solitaire; **faire une r.** to play patience
réutilisation [reytilizasjɔ̃] *nf* reuse
réutiliser [reytilize] *vt* to reuse
revaccination [rəvaksinasjɔ̃] *nf* revaccination
revacciner [rəvaksine] *vt* to revaccinate
revaloir [rəvalwar] *vt* (*conj like* **valoir**; *used chiefly in the fu*) **je vous le revaudrai!, je vous revaudrai cela!** (*menace*) I'll get *or* pay you back for that!; (*reconnaissance*) I'll do the same for you some time!
revalorisation [rəvalɔrizasjɔ̃] *nf* **(a)** (*d'une monnaie*) revaluation; (*des salaires, du SMIG, des retraites*) upgrade, upgrading; (*de prix*) increasing **(b)** (*d'une image, d'une profession*) upgrade, upgrading; **cela doit aboutir à une r. de la fonction d'enseignant** this should have as an objective an upgrading of the role of the teacher
revaloriser [rəvalɔrize] *vt* **(a)** (*monnaie*) to revalue; (*salaire, SMIG, retraite*) to upgrade, to increase; (*prix*) to increase **(b)** (*image, profession etc*) to upgrade
revanchard, -arde [rəvɑ̃ʃar, -ard] *adj, n Pol Péj* revanchist
revanche [rəvɑ̃ʃ] *nf* **(a)** (*vengeance*) revenge; **prendre sa r.** to get one's revenge; **prendre sa r. sur qn** to take one's revenge on sb, to get one's own back on sb, to get even with sb; **je prendrai ma r. un jour** I'll get my revenge *or* get even one day; **vouloir prendre sa r.** to want revenge, to want to get even *or* to get one's own back **(b)** *Sp* return match *or* game; **je te laisserai prendre ta r. la semaine prochaine** I'll give you your revenge next week **(c)** *Fig* **en r.** (*en compensation*) in return, in compensation; (*au contraire*) on the other hand; **à charge de r.** on condition that I do the same for you
revanchisme [rəvɑ̃ʃism] *nm Pol* revanchism
revanchiste [rəvɑ̃ʃist] *adj, n Pol* revanchist
rêvasser [rɛvase] *vi* to daydream, to let one's mind wander
rêvasserie [rɛvasri] *nf* daydreaming; **rêvasseries** daydreams
rêvasseur, -euse [rɛvasœr, -øz] **1** *adj* daydreaming **2** *n* (day)dreamer
rêve [rɛv] *nm* **(a)** (*de dormeur*) dream; **faire un r.** to (have a) dream; **voir qch en r.** to see sth in a dream *or* in one's dreams; **ça s'est passé comme dans un r.** it happened as if in a dream; **faites de beaux rêves!** pleasant *or* sweet dreams!; **la psychologie du r.** the psychology of dreams *or* of dreaming
(b) (*idéal*) dream; **rêves de gloire/célébrité** dreams of glory/fame; **un r. devenu réalité** a dream come true; **maison/voiture de r.** dream house/car; **la maison de nos rêves** the house of our dreams, our dream house; **avoir une silhouette de r.** to have a gorgeous figure; **c'est le r.!** it's/he's/*etc* a dream *or* everything you ever dreamed of!
rêvé [rɛve] *adj* perfect, ideal
revêche [rəvɛʃ] *adj* **(a)** (*hargneux*) bad-tempered, cantankerous **(b)** *Vieilli* (*vêtement etc*) harsh, rough
réveil [revɛj] *nm* **(a)** waking, awakening; *Fig* awakening; **à mon r., au r.** on waking; **le r. de la nature** the awakening of Nature; **le r. d'un volcan** the renewed rumblings *or* the awakening of a volcano **(b)** *Mil* reveille; **sonner le r.** to sound reveille **(c)** (*pendulette*) alarm (clock); **mettre le r.** to set the alarm **(à six heures** for six o'clock); **radio-r.** radio alarm, clock radio; **r. automatique** automatic alarm; **r. de voyage** travel alarm clock; **r. téléphonique** (*dans un hôtel*) wake-up call
réveillé [reveje] *adj* awake; **je suis mal r.** I haven't woken up (properly) yet, I'm still half asleep
réveille-matin [revɛjmatɛ̃] *nm inv* alarm clock
réveiller [reveje] **1** *vt* **(a)** (*tirer du sommeil*) to wake (up), to (a)waken; **réveillez-moi à sept heures** wake me (up) *or* waken me at seven o'clock; **Docteur, je n'arrive pas à la r.** I can't waken *or* rouse her, Doctor; **un bruit à r. les morts** a noise to wake the dead; *Prov* **ne réveillez pas le chat qui dort** let sleeping dogs lie
(b) *Fig* (*classe ouvrière, pays*) to stir up, to rouse; (*souvenirs*) to awaken, to revive; (*courage, douleur*) to revive; **r. les consciences** to stir people's consciences
2 se réveiller *vpr* **(a)** (*d'un dormeur*) to wake (up), to awake; **se r. d'un sommeil agité** to wake from a troubled sleep; *Fig* **c'est un pays qui est en train de se r.** the country is beginning to stir itself *or* shake itself *or* waken up
(b) (*de sentiments*) to be awakened *or* roused *or* stirred (up)
(c) (*de la nature, la végétation, l'économie*) to revive
réveillon [revɛjɔ̃] *nm* (*repas*) midnight supper; (*réjouissances*) midnight party (*after midnight mass on Christmas Eve or New Year's Eve*)
réveillonner [revɛjɔne] *vi* to see Christmas/the New Year in (*with a midnight supper and party*)
réveillonneur, -euse [revɛjɔnœr, -øz] *n* (Christmas Eve/New Year's Eve) party-goer *or* reveller
révélateur, -trice [revelatœr, -tris] **1** *adj* (*signe, attitude, silence etc*) revealing, tell-tale; (*remarque*) revealing, telling; *Ch* (*substance*) tracer; **signe r. d'un changement** sign pointing to a change, tell-tale sign of a change; **c'est très r.** it is very revealing; **c'est r. de son manque de confiance en lui** it reveals *or* shows his lack of confidence **2** *nm* **(a)** (*d'une crise etc*) sign, indication **(b)** *Phot* developer
révélation [revelasjɔ̃] *nf* **(a)** (*action*) (*d'un secret, d'intentions etc*) revelation, disclosure; *Journ* (*d'un scandale etc*) exposé **(b)** (*découverte*) **ce fut une r.!** it was a revelation *or* an eye-opener!; **ce jeune musicien est la r. des années 90** this young musician is the discovery *or* find of the 90's **(c)** *Rel* revelation; **la r. divine** divine revelation
révélé [revele] *adj* (*religion, vérité*) revealed
révéler [revele] **(je révèle, n. révélons; je révélerai) 1** *vt* **(a)** (*dévoiler*) (*secret, intention, projets etc*) to reveal, to disclose; *Journ* **r. ses sources** to reveal one's sources; **il révéla, sans le faire exprès, la vérité** he unwittingly let out the truth; **somme dont le montant n'a pas été révélé** undisclosed amount; **l'enquête révèle que ...** the survey reveals that ...
(b) (*témoigner de*) (*talent, technique*) to show; (*gentillesse, humour*) to show, to reveal; (*défauts, ignorance, manque de confiance*) to show, to reveal, to betray

(c) *Phot* to develop

2 se révéler *vpr* (a) (*d'une personne*) to reveal oneself *or* one's character; **se r. difficile** to prove difficult; **il s'est révélé un bon ami** he proved (to be) *or* showed himself (to be) a good friend

(b) **cela s'est révélé exact** it turned out *or* proved to be true

revenant, -ante [rəvnɑ̃, -ɑ̃t] **1** *adj Vieilli* (*avenant*) pleasing, prepossessing **2** *n* ghost; **histoire de revenants** ghost story; *F Hum* **voilà une revenante!** you're/she's a stranger!

revendeur, -euse [rəvɑ̃dœr, -øz] *n Com* retailer; (*d'articles d'occasion*) secondhand dealer; (*de drogue*) dealer

revendicateur, -trice [rəvɑ̃dikatœr, -tris] **1** *adj* (*discours, lettre etc*) setting forth one's claims *or* demands **2** *n* person making demands; **je ne veux pas être mis dans le même sac que tous ces revendicateurs** I don't want to be classed as a troublemaker

revendicatif, -ive [rəvɑ̃dikatif, -iv] *adj* (*mouvement etc*) protest; **journée revendicative** day of protest

revendication [rəvɑ̃dikasjɔ̃] *nf* (a) (*action*) claiming (b) (*demande*) demand (**sur** on), claim; **les revendications ouvrières** labour demands; **r. salariale** wage demand, pay claim; **revendications syndicales** union demands; *Jur* (**action en**) **r.** action for recovery of property

revendiquer [rəvɑ̃dike] *vt* (a) (*demander*) to claim, to demand; (*droits*) to assert, to insist on; (*territoire, succession*) to lay claim to; **r. le droit de faire qch** to claim the right to do sth (b) (*assumer*) (*responsabilité*) to claim; **l'attentat n'a pas été revendiqué** nobody has claimed responsibility for the attack

revendre [rəvɑ̃dr] *vt* (*après achat*) to resell; (*vendre de nouveau*) to sell again; *Fig* **avoir des jouets/des CDs à r.** to have more than enough toys/CDs; *Fig* **avoir du temps à r.** to have time to spare; *Fig* **avoir de la bonne humeur à r.** to be extremely good-natured; *Fig* **avoir de l'énergie à r.** to be bubbling over with energy

revenez-y [rəvnezi] *nm inv F* **ce gâteau a un goût de r.** this cake is very moreish; **ce voyage a un goût de r.** I wouldn't mind doing this trip again

revenir [rəv(ə)nir] *vi* (*conj like* **venir**; *aux* **être**) **1** *vi* (a) (*rentrer*) to come back, to return; **il n'était jamais revenu en France** he had never been back to France; **je reviens tout de suite** I'll be back in a minute; **le temps passé ne revient plus** time that is past will never come again; **l'herbe reviendra** the grass will grow again *or* back; **ce nom/sujet revient souvent dans la conversation** this name/subject often turns up *or* crops up in conversation; **c'est un problème qui revient souvent chez les adolescents** it's a problem that often occurs with teenagers, it's a common problem with teenagers; **fête qui revient tous les dix ans** festival that occurs *or* recurs *or* that comes round every ten years; **r. à la hâte** to hurry back; **r. en courant** to come running back, to run back; **r. à ses premières amours** to go back *or* return to one's first love; **vous y reviendrez!** (*à une méthode etc*) you'll go/come back to it!; **je suis revenu au régime lacté** I've gone back to a milk diet; **r. à la surface** (*d'un sous-marin*) to resurface; **en r. à qch** to come/go back *or* revert to sth; **pour en r. à la question/à ce que je disais** to come back to our subject/to what I was saying; **il n'y a pas à r. là-dessus** there is no going back on it; **r. de** to come back *or* return from; **r. de l'étranger** to come back from abroad; **je l'ai rencontré en revenant de l'église** I met him on my way back from church; **r. sur** (*ses aveux*) to retract; (*une promesse, une décision*) to go back on; (*son opinion*) to reconsider; (*un sujet*) to bring up again; (*le passé*) to rake up; **r. sur ses pas** to retrace one's steps, to turn back, to backtrack

(b) (*de la force, du courage etc*) to return, to come back (**à qn** to sb); **l'appétit devrait lui r.** he should get his appetite back, his appetite should return; **il ne faudrait pas que ces paroles lui reviennent** don't let this get back to him; **la mémoire me revient** my memory is coming back; **c'est un honneur qui vous revient** the honour is yours by rights; **à chacun ce qui lui revient** to each his due

(c) **cela me revient à la mémoire** it's coming back to me; *F* **ça me revient maintenant** I have it *or* I've got it now; **votre nom ne me revient pas** your name escapes me *or* has slipped my memory, I can't think of your name

(d) *F* **il a une tête qui ne me revient pas** there's something about him I don't like; **si ta tête ne lui revient pas ...** if he doesn't like the look of you ...

(e) **r. de sa surprise/d'une maladie** to recover from *or* get over one's surprise/an illness; **r. d'une théorie** to abandon a theory; **r. d'une erreur** to realize one's mistake; **je suis revenu de toutes mes illusions** I have lost all my illusions; **j'en suis revenu, de l'homéopathie!** I've had my fill of homeopathy!; **je n'en reviens pas!** (*étonnement*) I can't get over it!; **r. à la santé** to recover *or* regain one's health; **il revient de loin** (*il a failli mourir*) he has been at death's door; **r. à soi** to recover consciousness, to come round, to come to

(f) *Culin* **faire r.** to brown

(g) (*d'un prix*) **ça nous est revenu à cent francs par personne** it worked out at a hundred francs each; **ça me revient à deux cents francs par mois** it costs me *or* it works out at two hundred francs a month; **sa maison lui est revenue à plusieurs millions** his house cost him several million; **r. cher** to work out expensive, to cost a lot

(h) *Fig* **cela revient au même** it amounts to the same thing, it comes (down) *or F* boils down to the same thing; **cela revient à dire que ...** that amounts to saying that ...

2 se revenir *vpr Litt* **s'en r.** to return, to make one's way back; **comme il s'en revenait de l'école ...** as he was coming *or* was on his way home from school ...

3 *v impers* **il me revient encore 100 francs** I still have 100 francs coming *or* owing to me; **c'est à elle qu'il revient de faire la demande** it's up to her *or* down to her to ask; **il m'est revenu que ...** it has come to my attention that ...

revente [rəvɑ̃t] *nf* resale; **objet de r.** second-hand article; **r. à perte** selling at a loss

revenu [rəv(ə)ny] *nm* (a) (*d'une personne*) income; (*de l'État*) revenue; (*d'une entreprise*) revenue, income; **avoir un faible r.** to be on a low income; **impôt sur le r.** income tax; **politique des revenus** incomes policy

(b) (*d'un investissement, d'un capital*) income, yield

▶ **revenu**: **revenus accessoires** incidental income; **revenus actuels** current earnings; **r. annuel** annual income; *Mktg* **r. cannibalisé** cannibalized income; **r. cumulé** cumulative revenue; **r. d'entreprise** corporate income, company earnings; **r. dépensable** spendable income; **r. disponible** disposable income; **revenus de l'exportation** export revenue; **r. généré par les ventes** sales revenue; **r. imposable** taxable income; **r. minimum d'insertion** income support, *US* welfare; **r. national brut/net** gross/net national income; **r. personnel disponible** disposable personal income; **r. du travail** earned income

rêver [rɛve] **1** *vi* (a) (*d'un dormeur*) to dream; **r. de qn/qch** to dream *or* have a dream about sb/sth; **on croit r.!** it can't be true!, I can't believe it!; **non, mais je rêve!** I must be dreaming!; *Fig* **j'en rêve la nuit** I dream about it at night

(b) (*rêvasser*) to daydream (**à** about), to dream (**à** of); **je ne rêve pas, il l'a bien dit!** I'm not dreaming *or* I'm not imagining things, he did say it!

(c) (*souhaiter*) **r. de** to dream of; **r. de faire** to dream of doing; **elle rêve de partir vivre là-bas** she dreams of going to live there, it is her dream to go and live there

2 *vt* (*d'un dormeur*) (*qch*) to dream of; **vous l'avez rêvé!** you must have imagined *or* dreamt it!, you must have been dreaming!; **j'ai rêvé que ...** I dreamt (that) ...; **r. sa vie au lieu de la vivre** to dream one's life away; **j'ai rêvé la même chose que toi** I dreamt the same thing as you; *Fig* **r. mariage** to dream of marriage

réverbération [reverberasjɔ̃] *nf* (*de la lumière, de la chaleur*) reflection; (*du son*) reverberation, echo

réverbère [reverbɛr] *nm* (a) (*lampe*) street light *or* lamp; (*poteau*) lamppost (b) (*réflecteur*) (heat) reflector

réverbérer [revɛrbere] *vt* (**il réverbère; il réverbérera**) (*chaleur, lumière*) to reflect, to throw back; (*son*) to reverberate

reverdir [rəvɛrdir] *vi* to grow *or* turn green again

révérence [reverɑ̃s] *nf* (a) (*déférence*) reverence (**envers, pour** for); *Fml Vieilli* **r. parler** with all due respect (b) **Votre R.** your Reverence (c) (*salut*) (*d'un homme*) bow; (*d'une femme*) curtsey; **faire la r. à qn** (*d'un homme*) to bow to sb; (*d'une femme*) to curtsey to sb; *Fig* **tirer sa r.** to leave; *Hum* **je vous tire ma r.** I'm off; **la société s'est automatisée, alors il a décidé de leur tirer sa r.** when the company automated, he decided to bow out

révérenciel, -ielle [reverɑ̃sjɛl] *adj Litt* **il m'inspire une crainte révérencielle** I stand in awe of him, I find him awe-inspiring

révérencieusement [reverɑ̃sjøzmɑ̃] *adv Litt* reverently

révérencieux, -euse [reverɑ̃sjø, -øz] *adj Litt* reverent; **peu r.** irreverent

révérend [reverɑ̃] *Rel* **1** *adj* reverend; **le r. père Martin** Reverend Father Martin; **la révérende mère supérieure** the Reverend Mother Superior **2** *nm* reverend; **oui, mon R.** yes, Reverend

révérer [revere] *vt* (**je révère, n. révérons; je révérerai**) to revere

rêverie [rɛvri] *nf* (*activité*) dreaming, reverie, musing; (*moment*) daydream, reverie; *Litt* **elle est toujours plongée** *ou* **perdue**

dans de vagues rêveries she's always daydreaming; **être dans une douce r.** to be starry-eyed; **il faut qu'elle cesse ses rêveries** she must stop this daydreaming

revernir [rəvɛrnir] *vt* to revarnish

revers [rəvɛr] *nm* **(a)** (*de pièce, de médaille etc*) reverse (side), back; (*de matériel*) wrong side; (*de page*) other side, back; **r. de la main** back of the hand; *Tennis* **(coup de) r.** backhand (stroke); *Mil* **prendre une position à r.** to capture a position in the rear; *Fig* **c'est le r. de la médaille** that's the other side of the coin

(b) (*de manteau*) lapel; (*de chaussette*) turnover; (*de botte*) top; (*de manche*) cuff; **r. de pantalon** trouser turn-up *or Am* pant cuff; **habit à r. de velours** coat faced with velvet *or* with velvet facings; **bottes à r.** top boots

(c) r. (de fortune) reversal (of fortune), setback; **les succès et les r. de la vie** the ups and downs of life

reversement [rəvɛrsəmɑ̃] *nm* additional payment

reverser [rəvɛrse] *vt* **(a)** (*servir de nouveau*) to pour out again; **je vous reverse un verre?** shall I pour you another glass? **(b)** (*remettre*) to pour back **(c)** *Fin* (*somme*) to transfer **(à, sur** to); (*impôt*) to pay

réverser [revɛrse] *vt Typ* (*texte*) to reverse out

réversibilité [revɛrsibilite] *nf* reversibility; *Jur* (*d'une pension etc*) revertibility; *Aut* (*de la direction*) kickback

réversible [revɛrsibl] *adj* **(a)** (*processus, vêtement etc*) reversible; *Fig* **l'histoire n'est pas r.** you can't put the clock back **(b)** *Jur* (*pension etc*) revertible

réversion [revɛrsjɔ̃] *nf Jur, Biol* reversion

revêtement [rəvɛtmɑ̃] *nm* **(a)** surface, overlay; *Tech* cladding, sheathing, covering; (*enduit*) coating; (*à l'intérieur*) lining; *Av* (*du fuselage*) skin; *Menuis* veneer; **r. de sol/mur** floor/wall covering; **câble à r. en caoutchouc** rubber-sheathed *or* -covered cable; **r. calorifuge** (*d'une chaudière etc*) lagging **(b)** *Constr* (*d'un mur*) facing; (*d'un talus*) revetment; (*de chaussée*) surface (material); (*action*) surfacing

revêtir [rəvɛtir] (*conj like* **vêtir**) **1** *vt* **(a)** (*habiller*) to clothe, to dress; **r. qn de qch** to dress sb in sth; **r. qn d'une robe de cérémonie** to robe sb, to dress sb in a ceremonial robe; *Fig* **r. qn d'une dignité/d'une autorité** to invest sb with a dignity/an authority; **pièce revêtue de votre signature** document bearing your signature; *Litt* **revêtu de verdure** clothed in greenery, verdure-clad

(b) *Tech* (*couvrir*) to clad, to sheathe, to cover; (*enduire*) to coat; (*à l'intérieur*) to line (**de** with); (*chaudière*) to lag; *Constr* (*mur*) to face; (*chaussée*) to surface; **r. une route de bitume** to tarmac a road; **murs revêtus de boiseries** panelled walls; **route non revêtue** unsurfaced road

(c) (*endosser*) (*uniforme, vêtement de cérémonie etc*) to don, to put on; *Fig* **r. la forme humaine/un caractère particulier** to assume human shape/take on a particular character; **fait qui revêt de l'importance** fact that takes on importance

2 se revêtir *vpr* **se r. de** (*uniforme, vêtement de cérémonie etc*) to don, to put on, to dress oneself in; (*dignité*) to assume

rêveur, -euse [rɛvœr, -øz] **1** *adj* dreamy; **ces résultats me laissent r.** these results are bewildering **2** *n* dreamer

rêveusement [rɛvøzmɑ̃] *adv* dreamily

revient [rəvjɛ̃] *nm* **(prix de) r.** cost price

revigorant [rəvigɔrɑ̃] *adj* (*vent, bain*) invigorating; (*boisson*) reviving

revigorer [rəvigɔre] *vt* (*d'un vent, un bain*) to invigorate; (*d'une boisson, un aliment*) to revive

revirement [rəvirmɑ̃] *nm* **(a)** *Naut* tacking about, going about **(b)** (*de fortune*) sudden change; (*de sentiments*) (complete) change, about-turn; (*changement d'avis*) about-turn, U-turn, about-face; **r. d'opinion** (sudden) change in public opinion

révisable [revizabl] *adj Jur* (*procès*) reviewable

réviser [revize] *vt* **(a)** (*texte, loi etc*) to revise; (*épreuves*) to (copy) read; (*situation, contrat, salary*) to review; *Ordinat* (*texte, document etc*) to edit; *Jur* (*procès*) to review, to reconsider; **r. une estimation à la hausse/baisse** to revise an estimate upwards/downwards; **r. son jugement** to revise one's judgement; **les salaires doivent être révisés janvier prochain** salaries come up for review next January **(b)** *Scol* to revise; **il faut r.** you'll/I'll/*etc* have to do some revision **(c)** *Tech* (*voiture, moteur etc*) to service

réviseur [revizœr] *nm* reviser; *Typ* proofreader; *TV, Cin* rewriter, rewrite sub; *Fin* **r. (comptable)** auditor; *Fin* **r. interne** internal auditor

révision [revizjɔ̃] *nf* **(a)** (*d'un texte, une loi etc*) revision; (*d'une politique, des salaires*) review; *Typ* proofreading; *Ordinat* edit; (*activité*) editing; **être en cours de r.** to be under review; **faire l'objet d'une r.** to be reviewed; **les prix peuvent faire l'objet d'une r.** prices are subject to review **(b)** *Scol* revision, *Am* review; **faire des révisions** to revise **(c)** (*d'un procès*) review, reconsideration, re-appraisal; (*d'une opinion*) change **(d)** *Tech* (*d'une voiture, d'un moteur etc*) service, servicing; **la r. des 5 000 km** the 5, 000 km service

révisionnisme [revizjɔnism] *nm Pol* revisionism

révisionniste [revizjɔnist] *adj, n Pol* revisionist

réviso [revizo] *n Pol F Péj* revisionist

revisser [rəvise] *vt* to screw back (again)

revitalisant [rəvitalizɑ̃] *adj* (*shampoing etc*) revitalizing

revitalisation [rəvitalizasjɔ̃] *nf* (*de la peau, une région*) revitalization

revitaliser [rəvitalize] *vt* (*peau, région etc*) to revitalize

revival [rivajvœl] *nm* revival

revivifier [rəvivifje] *vt* (*impf & pr sub* **n. revivifiions, v. revivifiiez**) (*sentiment, souvenir*) to revive

revivre [rəvivr] (*conj like* **vivre**) **1** *vi* (*recouvrir son énergie*) to revive, to come alive again; **r. dans sa fille/son œuvre** to live on in one's daughter/work; **se sentir r.** to feel revived, to feel alive again; **faire r.** (*personne*) to revive, to bring to life again; (*coutume, tradition etc*) to revive **2** *vt* (*passé, sa vie*) to relive; (*expérience etc*) to relive, to live through *or* go through again

révocabilité [revɔkabilite] *nf* (*d'un contrat etc*) revocability; (*d'un fonctionnaire*) removability

révocable [revɔkabl] *adj* (*contrat etc*) revocable; (*fonctionnaire*) removable; (*crédit*) revocable, callable

révocation [revɔkasjɔ̃] *nf* (*d'un testament, un édit, un contrat etc*) revocation; (*d'un fonctionnaire*) removal, dismissal

révocatoire [revɔkatwar] *adj Jur* revocatory

revoici [rəvwasi] *prép F* **me r.!** here I am again!, it's me again!; **nous r. à Paris** here we are in Paris again *or* back in Paris; **nous r. à notre point de départ** we're back where we started; **le r. au travail** he's back at work; **la r. qui pleure** she's crying again

revoilà [rəvwala] *prép F* = **revoici**

revoir[1] [rəvwar] (*conj like* **voir**) **1** *vt* **(a)** (*voir de nouveau*) (*qn, qch*) to see again; (*rencontrer*) (*qn*) to see *or* meet again; **je revois encore la maison de mon enfance** (*en souvenir*) I can see my childhood home again; **je la revois petite** I can see her in my mind's eye when she was little

(b) (*examiner*) (*leçon*) to revise, to go over; (*comptes, manuscrit, texte*) to go over *or* look over again; (*épreuves*) to read; **je voudrais r. quelques points avec toi** I'd like to go over a few points with you; **r. à la baisse** to revise downwards; **r. à la hausse** to revise upwards

2 se revoir *vpr* **(a)** (*se rencontrer*) to see each other again, to meet again

(b) (*en souvenir*) to see oneself (in one's mind's eye); **je me revois petite** I can see myself when I was a little girl

revoir[2] **(au)** [orəvwar] **1** *int* goodbye **2** *nm inv* goodbye; **des au r. sans fin** endless goodbyes; **dis au r. au monsieur** say goodbye to the gentleman; **ce n'est qu'un au r.** it's only au revoir

révoltant [revɔltɑ̃] *adj* (*vision, procédure*) revolting, sickening, shocking; (*odeur*) revolting, sickening; (*comportement*) revolting, outrageous, appalling; (*injustice*) appalling, revolting

révolte [revɔlt] *nf* (*émeute, indignation*) revolt; (*dans une prison*) riot; **en r.** in revolt (**contre** against); **esprit de r.** spirit of revolt *or* rebellion; **sentiment de r.** feeling of revolt, rebellious feeling; **mouvement de r.** movement of revolt

révolté, -ée [revɔlte] **1** *adj* **(a)** (*indigné*) outraged, appalled (**de voir** to see) **(b)** (*en révolte*) rebellious; **r. contre** in revolt against **2** *n* rebel; **c'est un r. de nature** he's a natural rebel

révolter [revɔlte] **1** *vt* **(a)** (*indigner*) to revolt, to appal, to shock; **de telles pratiques me révoltent** I'm appalled by that type of thing; **ça me révolte d'entendre ça!** I'm appalled!, that's appalling! **(b)** (*inciter à la révolte*) **r. qn** to induce sb to revolt **2 se révolter** *vpr* to revolt, to rebel (**contre** against); **se r. devant des injustices** to rebel against injustice; **se r. à l'idée que ...** to get indignant at the thought of ...; **ça me donne envie de me r.** I'm tempted to rebel; **le bon sens se révolte contre une telle supposition** common sense revolts against such a supposition

révolu [revɔly] *adj* (*jours, époque etc*) past, bygone; **ces jours sont révolus, c'est une époque révolue** those days are gone; **avoir quarante ans révolus** to be over forty years of age; **après trois mois révolus ...** after a full three months ...

révolution [revɔlysjɔ̃] *nf* **(a)** (*rotation*) (*de la terre, d'une roue*) revolution **(b)** *Pol etc* revolution; *Hist* **la R.** the French Revolution; **c'est une r. dans la vie du couple** there has been a revolution in sexual relationships; **toute la ville est en r.** the whole town is in revolt *or* up in arms; **faire la r.** to cause a revolution; **il veut faire la r. en introduisant ...** he wants to cause a revolution *or* revolutionize things by introducing ...

▶ **révolution**: **r. culturelle** cultural revolution; *Hist* **la R. française** the French Revolution; **r. industrielle** industrial revolution; **la R. d'octobre** the October Revolution; **r. de palais** palace revolution

révolutionnaire [revɔlysjɔnɛr] *adj, n* revolutionary

révolutionner [revɔlysjɔne] *vt* **(a)** (*transformer*) (*industrie, théorie, vie familiale etc*) to revolutionize **(b)** (*mettre en émoi*) (*village etc*) to cause a stir in

revolver [revɔlvɛr] *nm* **(a)** revolver; (*n'importe quel pistolet*) gun; **r. à six coups** six-shooter **(b)** *Tech* **(porte-outils) r.** revolving tool holder; **tour (à) r.** turret lathe, capstan lathe

revolvériser [revɔlverize] *vt F Hum* to gun down

révoquer [revɔke] *vt* **(a)** (*fonctionnaire*) to dismiss, to remove from office **(b)** (*décret*) to revoke, to repeal, to rescind; (*contrat*) to revoke **(c)** *Litt* **r. qch en doute** to call sth into question

revoter [rəvɔte] **1** *vt* (*personne, parti*) to vote again for; **la loi a été revotée** the law has been passed *or* adopted again **2** *vi* to vote again

revouloir [rəvulwar] *vt* (*conj like* **vouloir**) *F* (*qch*) to want again; **en reveux-tu?** would you like some more?

revoyure (à la) [alarvwajyr] *int F* see you!, bye!

revue [rəvy] *nf* **(a)** (*examen*) review; *Mil* (*des troupes*) review, inspection; (*de casernement*) inspection; **r. de presse** review of the papers *or* the press; **faire la r. des troupes** to review *or* inspect the troops; **passer en r.** (*problèmes, possibilités etc*) to review, to go over; *Mil* (*troupes*) to review, to inspect; *F* **je suis encore de la r.** I'm left high and dry again

(b) (*magazine*) magazine; (*scientifique, littéraire*) review, journal; **r. d'entreprise** company *or* in-house magazine; **r. professionnelle** trade journal *or* magazine

(c) *Th* revue

(d) *F Vieilli* **nous sommes (des gens) de r.** we'll meet again

révulsé [revylse] *adj* **yeux révulsés** eyes with the whites showing

révulser [revylse] **1** *vt* **(a)** *F* (*dégoûter*) to revolt, to disgust **(b)** *Méd* to counter-irritate **2 se révulser** *vpr* (*d'un visage*) to contort; **ses yeux se révulsèrent** his eyes rolled up

révulsif, -ive [revylsif, -iv] *adj, nm Méd* revulsive, counter-irritant

révulsion [revylsjɔ̃] *nf Méd* revulsion, counter-irritation; *Fig* revulsion; **éprouver une r. à la vue de qn/qch** to feel revolted at the sight of sb/sth

rewriter[1] [rirajtœr, rərajtœr] *nm* rewriter, rewrite man

rewriter[2] [rirajte, rərajter] *vt* to rewrite

rewriting [rirajtiŋ, rərajtiŋ] *nm* rewriting

rez-de-chaussée [redʃose] *nm inv* **(a)** (*niveau*) ground floor *or Am* first floor; **au r.** on the ground *or Am* first floor **(b)** **(appartement en) r.** ground-floor flat, *Am* first-floor apartment

rez-de-jardin [redʒardɛ̃] *nm inv* (*niveau*) garden level; **appartement en r.** garden flat *or Am* apartment

RF [ɛrɛf] *nf abrév* **République française**

RFA [ɛrɛfa] *nf Hist* (*abrév* **République fédérale d'Allemagne**) FRG

rg *abrév* **rive gauche**

Rh *nm Méd* (*abrév* **facteur Rhésus**) Rh; **Rh-négatif** Rh negative; **Rh-positif** Rh positive

rhabillage [rabijaʒ] *nm* **(a)** (*d'une montre*) repair, overhaul **(b)** (*d'un enfant*) dressing again; (*de soi-même*) getting dressed again

rhabiller [rabije] **1** *vt* **(a)** (*réparer*) (*montre*) to repair

(b) (*habiller*) **r. qn** to dress sb again, to put sb's clothes on again; (*acheter de nouveaux vêtements pour*) to buy new clothes for sb; **je n'ai plus rien pour la r.!** I don't have a thing to put on her *or* to dress her in!

(c) *Fig* (*bâtiment, vieille idée etc*) to give a new look to

2 se rhabiller *vpr* (*mettre ses vêtements*) to put one's clothes on again, to get dressed again; *F* **il peut aller se r.** (*d'un athlète*) he might as well give up and go home; *F* **va te r.!** get off!; **avec vos 12 000 livres par an vous pouvez aller vous r.** you can get lost with your £12,000 a year, you can take your £12,000 and stuff it!

rhabilleur [rabijœr] *nm* (*de montres*) repairman

rhapsode [rapsɔd] *nm Antiq* (*chanteur*) rhapsode, rhapsodist

rhapsodie [rapsɔdi] *nf* rhapsody

rhapsodique [rapsɔdik] *adj* rhapsodic

rhénan, -ane [renɑ̃, -an] **1** *adj* (*industrie, économie*) (of/from the) Rhineland **2** *n* **R.** Rhinelander

Rhénanie [renani] *nf* **la R.** the Rhineland; **R-Palatinat** Rhineland-Palatinate

rhénium [renjɔm] *nm Ch* rhenium

rhéostat [reɔsta] *nm Él* rheostat; **r. de démarrage** (*d'un moteur électrique*) rheostatic starter

rhésus [rezys] *nm* **(a)** *Zool* rhesus monkey **(b)** *Physiol* **(facteur) r.** rhesus *or* Rh factor; **r. positif/négatif** rhesus *or* Rh positive/negative; **incompatibilité r.** rhesus *or* Rh incompatibility

rhéteur [retœr] *nm* **(a)** (*orateur*) rhetorician **(b)** *Antiq* (*professeur*) rhetor

rhétoricien, -ienne [retɔrisjɛ, -jɛn] *n* rhetorician

rhétorique [retɔrik] **1** *nf* **(a)** *Littér* rhetoric; **figure de r.** figure of speech **(b)** *Scol Arch* **(classe de) r.** = sixth form **(c)** (*emphase*) rhetoric **2** *adj* (*effet etc*) rhetorical

rhéto-roman, -ane [retorɔmɑ̃, -an], *pl* **rhéto-romans, -anes** *adj, nm Ling* Rhaeto-Romanic

Rhin (le) [lərɛ̃] *nm* the (river) Rhine

rhinite [rinit] *nf Méd* rhinitis

rhinocéros [rinɔserɔs] *nm* rhinoceros, *F* rhino

rhinologie [rinɔlɔʒi] *nf Méd* rhinology

rhinopharyngé [rinofarɛ̃ʒe], **rhinopharyngien, -ienne** [rinofarɛ̃ʒjɛ̃, -jɛn] *adj Méd* nose-and-throat, *Spéc* rhinopharyngeal

rhinopharyngite [rinofarɛ̃ʒit] *nf Méd* inflammation of the nose and throat, *Spéc* rhinopharyngitis

rhinopharynx [rinofarɛ̃ks] *nm Anat* nose and throat, *Spéc* rhinopharynx

rhinoplastie [rinoplasti] *nf Chir* rhinoplasty

rhinoscopie [rinoskɔpi] *nf Méd* rhinoscopy

rhizome [rizom] *nm Bot* rhizome

rhodanien, -ienne [rɔdanjɛ̃, -jɛn] *adj* of the Rhone; *Géog* **couloir r.** Rhone corridor

Rhodes [rɔd] *nf* Rhodes

Rhodésie [rɔdezi] *nf Hist* Rhodesia

rhodésien, -ienne [rɔdezjɛ̃, -jɛn] *Hist* **1** *adj* Rhodesian **2** *n* **R.** Rhodesian

rhodium [rɔdjɔm] *nm Ch* rhodium

rhododendron [rɔdɔdɛ̃drɔ̃] *nm Bot* rhododendron

rhombique [rɔ̃bik] *adj* rhombic

rhomboïdal, -ale, -aux, -ales [rɔ̃bɔidal, -o] *adj* rhomboid

rhomboïde [rɔ̃bɔid] *nm* rhomboid

Rhône (le) [lɔron] *nm* the (river) Rhone

rhubarbe [rybarb] *nf* rhubarb; **confiture/tarte à la r.** rhubarb jam/tart

rhum [rɔm] *nm* rum; **r. blanc** white rum

rhumatisant, -ante [rymatizɑ̃, -ɑ̃t] *adj, n Méd* rheumatic

rhumatismal, -ale, -aux, -ales [rymatismal, -o] *adj Méd* rheumatic

rhumatisme [rymatism] *nm Méd* rheumatism, *F* rheumatics; **avoir des rhumatismes** to have rheumatism *or F* rheumatics; **être perclus de rhumatismes** to be crippled with rheumatism; **mes rhumatismes me font souffrir** my rheumatism is playing me up

▶ **rhumatisme**: *Méd* **r. articulaire** rheumatic fever; *Méd* **r. déformant** polyarthritis

rhumatoïde [rymatɔid] *adj Méd* rheumatoid

rhumatologie [rymatɔlɔʒi] *nm Méd* rheumatology

rhumatologue [rymatɔlɔg] *n Méd* rheumatologist

rhume [rym] *nm Méd* cold; **gros r.** bad *or* heavy cold; **prendre** *ou* **attraper un r.**, *F* **attraper le r.** to catch a cold, to catch cold; **avoir un r.** to have a cold

▶ **rhume**: **r. de cerveau** head cold; **r. des foins** hay fever

rhumerie [rɔmri] *nf* rum distillery

ria [rija] *nf Géog* ria

riant [rijɑ̃] *adj* **(a)** (*visage*) smiling, cheerful; (*yeux*) laughing, merry **(b)** *Fig* (*ambiance*) merry, cheerful; (*paysage, campagne*) cheerful, sunny, bright

RIB [rib] *nm F* (*abrév* **relevé d'identité bancaire**) = document giving details of one's bank account, bank details

ribambelle [ribɑ̃bɛl] *nf* (*d'insultes, de noms etc*) long string; (*de visiteurs*) string, crowd; *F* pile; **r. d'enfants** swarm of children

ribaud, -aude [ribo, -od] *Arch Litt* **1** *adj* (*personne*) debauched **2** *n* debauchee

riboflavine [riboflavin] *nf* riboflavin

ribonucléique [ribonykleik] *adj* (*acide*) ribonucleic

ribote [ribɔt] *nf F Vieilli* spree; **être en r.** to be tipsy *or* tight

ribouldingue [ribuldɛ̃g] *nf F* spree, binge; **faire la r.** to go on a spree *or* binge

ricain, -aine [rikɛ̃, -ɛn] *F* **1** *adj* Yank **2** *n* **R.** Yank

ricanement [rikanmɑ̃] *nm* (*rire*) (*sarcastique, de mépris*) sneer, snigger; (*bête*) snigger, giggle; **je veux savoir d'où venait ce r.** I want to know who sniggered; **je ne supporte plus tes ricanements** I've had enough of your sniggering/giggling/sneering

ricaner [rikane] *vi* (*sarcastiquement*) to sneer, to snigger; (*bêtement*) to snigger, to giggle

ricaneur, -euse [rikanœr, -øz] **1** *adj* (*sarcastique*) sneering, sniggering; (*bête*) sniggering, giggling; **air r.** sneering look **2** *n* (*sarcastique*) sneerer, sniggerer; (*bête*) sniggerer, giggler

Richard [riʃar] *nm* **R. Cœur de Lion** Richard the Lionheart

richard, -arde [riʃar, -ard] *n F Péj* (*personne riche*) **un r.** a moneybags

riche [riʃ] **1** *adj* **(a)** (*fortuné*) rich, wealthy, well-off; **l'un des hommes les plus riches du monde** one of the richest *or* wealthiest men in the world; **les pays riches** (the) rich *or* wealthy countries; **faire un r. mariage** to marry into a wealthy family, *F* to marry money; **être r. à millions** to be worth millions; *F* **ça fait r.** that looks very grand *or* posh

(b) (*qui abonde en qch*) (*cuisine, fromage, repas, aliment*) rich; (*vocabulaire*) extensive; (*style*) elaborate; (*description*) detailed; (*imagination*) vivid, lively; (*végétation*) luxuriant, lush; (*moisson*) rich, abundant; *Aut* **mélange r.** rich mixture; **votre analyse est r.** your analysis is full of good things *or* very interesting; **évitez de manger trop r. le soir** don't eat too much rich food in the evening; **une r. nature** a person full of vitality; **il a une très r. personnalité** he's got a lot of personality, he's full of personality; **une r. idée** a splendid idea

(c) r. en qch rich in sth; **r. en protéine** rich *or* high in protein, protein-rich, with a high protein content; **aliment r. en fibres** high-fibre food; **r. en calories** high in calories; **terre r. en minerais** earth rich in minerals; **r. en tableaux/ édifices du 11ème siècle** with an abundance *or* wealth of paintings/11th century buildings; **la journée a été r. en événements** it's been an action-packed *or* exciting day; **mon voyage a été r. en expériences** I learned a lot from my trip, I got a lot out of my trip; **je ne suis pas très r. en produits de beauté** (*d'un commerçant*) I don't have many cosmetics in stock

(d) r. de (*espérances etc*) full of; **r. de possibilités** (*avenir*) with lots of potential, full of hope; **livre/expérience r. d'enseignements** very instructive book/experience; **... le cœur gros mais r. de tant d'aventures** ... heavy-hearted but rejoicing in his adventures

2 *n* rich *or* wealthy person; **les riches** the rich, the wealthy; **nouveau r.** nouveau riche; *Péj* **fils** *ou* **gosse de riche(s)** rich kid; **tu es vraiment un fils de riche(s)!** you really have no idea how the other half lives, have you?

richelieu [riʃəljø], *pl* **richelieus, richelieux** *nm* lace-up (shoe), Oxford (shoe)

richement [riʃmɑ̃] *adv* **(a)** richly; **pourvoir r. ses enfants** to make abundant provision for one's children; **marier r. sa fille** to marry one's daughter into a wealthy family **(b)** (*luxueusement*) (*décoré, vêtu, illustré*) sumptuously, richly; **être r. logé** to live in sumptuous surroundings

richesse [riʃɛs] *nf* **(a)** (*d'une personne, d'un pays*) wealth; **la r. publique** public wealth; **vivre dans la r.** to be wealthy; **r. en matières premières** (*d'un pays*) wealth of raw materials; **le tourisme, c'est la seule r. de la région** tourism is the country's only resource *or* only source of income; **ce tableau fait la r. du musée** this painting is the prize item in the museum's collection; **richesses** riches, wealth; **voilà toutes mes richesses** this is everything I've got; **musée plein de richesses** gallery full of treasures *or* valuable objects

(b) (*du sol, d'un gisement, du vocabulaire*) richness; (*de la végétation*) luxuriance, lushness; (*de l'imagination*) vividness, liveliness; (*d'une description*) detailed nature; (*de rencontres*) abundance

richissime [riʃisim] *adj* extremely wealthy, *F* loaded

ricin [risɛ̃] *nm Bot* castor-oil plant; **huile de r.** castor oil

ricocher [rikɔʃe] *vi* (*d'une balle, un caillou*) to ricochet **(sur** off); (*sur l'eau*) to bounce **(sur** off); **faire r. des pierres sur l'eau** = to play (at) ducks and drakes

ricochet [rikɔʃɛ] *nm* (*d'une balle*) ricochet; (*sur l'eau*) bounce; **faire des ricochets (sur l'eau)** = to play (at) ducks and drakes; *Fig F* **apprendre qch par r.** to hear of sth indirectly *or* in a roundabout way

ric-rac [rikrak] *adv F* **je suis r. ce mois-ci** money's pretty tight this month; **je pense me débrouiller jusqu'à la fin du mois, mais ça va être r.** I think I'll make it to the end of the month but only just; **il a réussi le bac r.** (*de justesse*) he only just scraped through the bac; **elle m'a remboursé r.** she paid me back to the very last penny

rictus [riktys] *nm* grimace, *Fml* rictus; **prendre/avoir un r.** to grimace

ride [rid] *nf* **(a)** (*sur le visage*) wrinkle, line; (*sur un fruit*) wrinkle; **crème anti-rides** anti-ageing cream; **front creusé de rides profondes** deeply lined *or* furrowed brow; *Fig F* **cela n'a pas pris une r. en trente ans** it's still just as good as it was thirty years ago **(b)** (*sur l'eau, le sable*) ripple; (*de sable*) ridge

ridé [ride] *adj* (*visage*) wrinkled, lined; (*pomme*) wrinkled, shrivelled

rideau, -eaux [rido] *nm* **(a)** (*d'intérieur*) curtain, *Am* drape; **lit garni de rideaux** curtained bed; **rideaux de lit** bed hangings; **tirer les rideaux** to draw the curtains; *Fig F* **tirer le r. sur qch** to draw a veil over sth; **on ne peut pas tirer le r. sur le passé** you can't forget the past, you can't put the past behind you

(b) *Th* curtain; **r. à huit heures précises** the curtain rises at eight sharp; *Fig F* **r.!** let's call it a day!; **allez, r., je ne veux plus en parler!** drop it *or* that's enough, I don't want to talk about it any more

(c) *Fig* (*d'arbres*) wall, screen, curtain; (*de feu, fumée*) wall; (*de pluie*) curtain

(d) (*d'un bureau*) roll top; **classeur à r.** tambour-door filing cabinet, roll-shutter cabinet

▶ **rideau**: **r. bonne femme** tie-back curtain; *Aut* **r. à enrouleur** roller blind; **r. d'entr'acte** act drop; **r. de fer** *Th* safety curtain; (*de boutique*) metal shutter; *Hist Pol* Iron Curtain; *TV, Cin* **r. de fond** backdrop; *TV, Cin* **r. de fond scénique** scenic cloth; *Aut* **r. de radiateur** radiator blind *or* shutter

ridelle [ridɛl] *nf Aut* side panel

rider [ride] **1** *vt* **(a)** (*front*) to wrinkle, to line; (*peau, fruit*) to wrinkle, to shrivel **(b)** (*eau, sable etc*) to ripple **2 se rider** *vpr* **(a)** (*du front, de la peau*) to become wrinkled *or* lined; (*d'une pomme*) to shrivel up **(b)** (*de l'eau*) to ripple

ridicule [ridikyl] **1** *adj* ridiculous, ludicrous **(de faire qch** to do sth); (*prix*) ridiculously low; **tu es vraiment r. dans cette tenue** you look really ridiculous in that get-up; **se rendre r.** to make a fool of oneself, to make oneself look ridiculous

2 *nm* **(a)** (*absurdité*) ridiculousness; **c'est d'un r. achevé** it is perfectly ridiculous *or* the height of absurdity; **tomber dans le r.** to make oneself ridiculous; **se couvrir de r.** to make a fool of oneself, to make oneself look ridiculous, to cover oneself in ridicule

(b) (*dérision*) ridicule; **craindre le r.** to fear ridicule; **tourner qn/qch en r.** to ridicule *or* make fun of sb/sth, to hold sb/sth up to ridicule

(c) (*chose ridicule*) **les ridicules de notre époque** the absurdities of our time

ridiculement [ridikylmɑ̃] *adv* ridiculously, ludicrously

ridiculiser [ridikylize] **1** *vt* to ridicule, to make fun of, to hold up to ridicule **2 se ridiculiser** *vpr* to make oneself look ridiculous, to make a fool of oneself

ridule [ridyl] *nf* (little) wrinkle

rien [rjɛ̃] **1** *pron indéf* [①**B15**,B,2] **(a)** (*quelque chose*) (*in questions* **rien** *is preferred to* **quelque chose** *when a negative answer is expected*) anything; **y a-t-il r. de plus triste?** is there anything more depressing?

(b) [①**B60**,B] (*with* **ne** *expressed*) nothing, not anything; **r. ne l'intéresse** nothing interests him; **r. ne va plus!** (*au casino*) rien ne va plus!, no more bets!; **je n'ai r. à faire** I have nothing to do, I don't have anything to do; **il n'y a r. à faire** it can't be helped; *F* **r. à faire, ça ne marche pas** it's no good, it's not working; **je n'en sais trop r.** I don't know too much about it; **il n'a plus r.** (*plus d'argent*) he doesn't have a penny left; (*il n'est plus malade*) there's nothing wrong *or* there isn't anything wrong with him now; **tu n'as plus r. à attendre de lui** now you know just *or* exactly what to expect from him; **il n'y a plus r. à en dire** there is nothing more to be said, there isn't anything more to be said; **je n'ai r. vu** I didn't see anything, I saw nothing; **je n'ai jamais r. vu d'aussi grand** I've never seen anything quite as big; **il n'a r. mangé depuis hier** he has eaten nothing *or* he hasn't eaten anything since yesterday; **il ne faut r. lui dire** he mustn't be told anything, he must be told nothing; **on ne peut jamais r. lui dire** you can't say a word *or F* open your mouth to him; **personne n'osa r. dire** nobody dared say anything; **n'en dites r.** don't say anything *or* a word about it, say nothing about it; **il n'y a r. de tel qu'un bon bain chaud** there's nothing like a good hot bath; **je n'ai r. de nouveau à vous dire** I have nothing *or* I don't have anything new to tell you; **alors, r. de nouveau?** (*en attendant des résultats etc*) have you heard anything yet?; **sinon? r. de nouveau?** so there's nothing new?, so nothing's been happening?; **r. d'autre** nothing else; **il ne vous fallait r. d'autre?** (is there) anything else?, will that be all?; **elle veut ça et r. d'autre** she wants that and nothing else; **ce n'est r.** it's nothing; **pour elle 10 km à pied ce n'est r.** she thinks nothing of walking 10 km, a 10 km walk is nothing to her; **ça ne fait r.** it doesn't matter, it makes no difference *or F* no odds; **si cela ne vous fait r.** if you don't mind; **comme si de r. n'était** as if nothing had happened; **elle ne ressemble en r. à sa sœur** she's nothing like her sister; *Litt* **il n'en est r.!** such is not the case; **je n'en ferai r.** I'll do nothing of the kind *or* sort; **après vous – je n'en ferai r.** after you – not at all *or* I wouldn't dream of it; **elle n'est r. pour moi** she is *or* means nothing to me; **elle n'est plus r. pour lui** she doesn't mean anything to him any more; **sa fille n'a r. de lui** his daughter doesn't take after him in any way; **je n'ai r. d'un psychiatre, pourtant!** I'm no psychiatrist!; **la nouvelle perçeuse X n'a r. d'une perçeuse traditionnelle!** the new X drill is nothing like a traditional drill; **il n'y était pour r.** he had nothing to do with it *or* had no hand in it; **je n'y suis pour r.** it's nothing to do with me, I've got nothing to do with it; *F* **il ne sait r. de r.** he knows nothing at all *or* nothing about anything *or F* zilch about anything; **que t'a-t-il donné? – r. de r.!** what did he give you? – zilch! *or* not a sausage!

(c) [ⓘ**B60**,B] (*with* **ne** *not expressed*) **que faites-vous? – r. / presque r.** what do you do? – nothing/hardly anything; **elle lit? – jamais r.** does she read? – not a thing; **r. du tout** nothing at all; **c'est tout ou r.** it's all or nothing; **pour r.** for nothing; **avoir qch pour r.** to get sth for (next to) nothing; **parler pour r.** to waste one's breath; **jouer pour r.** to play for fun; **pourquoi demandez-vous cela? – pour r.** why do you ask? – no reason *or* I just wondered; **se fâcher de r.** to get angry about *or* for nothing; **merci, monsieur – de r.** thank you – it's a pleasure *or* you're welcome *or* (please) don't mention it; **en moins de r.** in less than no time, in no time at all; **une affaire de r. (du tout)** an insignificant matter; *Vieilli* **femme de r.** loose woman; **une petite pièce de r. du tout** a wretched little room; **un homme de r. du tout** a man of no account, a nobody; **un/une r. (-)du(-)tout** a (mere) nobody; **c'est une coupure de r. du tout** it's just a scratch; *F* **un moins que r.** (*personne*) a loser; **pour trois fois r.** (*acheter, vendre qch*) for next to nothing, for a song; **il possède trois fois r.** he has absolutely nothing; **faire qch comme (un) r.** to do sth easily *or* without any trouble at all *or F* as easy as winking; *Tennis* **quinze à r.** fifteen love

(d) (*the negation is expressed or implied elsewhere in the sentence*) **il est inutile de r. dire** you needn't say anything; **avant qu'elle ait r. dit** before she said anything; **sans r. faire** without doing anything; **sans nous gêner en r.** without troubling us at all *or* in the slightest

(e) r. que nothing but, only, merely; **r. que la vérité** nothing but the truth; **je frémis r. que d'y songer** the mere thought (of it) *or* just thinking about it makes me shudder; **r. que pour aller à un bal** for the sake of going *or* just to go to a dance; **r. que pour aller à Paris, ça coûte 400 francs** it costs 400 francs just to go to Paris; **je te le dis, r. qu'à toi** I'm telling you and only you *or* and you alone; **c'est à moi, r. qu'à moi** it's mine, all mine; **r. que cela?** is that all?

(f) (*with* **ne … pas**) **on ne peut pas vivre de r.** you can't live on nothing; **ce n'est pas r.!** that's something!; **cinquante francs de l'heure, ce n'est pas r.!** fifty francs an hour is something at least!; **élever quatre enfants, ce n'est pas r.!** it's quite something raising four kids!

2 *adv Arg Vieilli* really, *Br* not half, *Am* real; **elle est r. chic!** she's really smart!, *Br* she isn't half smart!

3 *nm* **(a)** (*bagatelle*) trifle, (mere) nothing; **un r. l'habille** she looks good (dressed) in anything; **un r. suffit pour le fâcher** he gets upset over the least little thing; **se piquer d'un r.** to take offence at nothing *or* the slightest thing; **perdre son temps à des riens** to waste one's time with trifles; **se disputer pour des riens** to argue over nothing; **il court 400 mètres comme un r.** he runs 400 metres just like that *or* with no trouble (at all), running 400 metres is nothing to him

(b) un r. de (*un petit peu de*) (just) a little; **un r. d'huile** the merest drop of oil; **en un r. de temps** in no time (at all), in less than no time; **un r. de femme** a tiny little woman

(c) un r. (*un peu*) a bit, a trifle, a touch; **il est un r. pénible, en ce moment** he's being a bit of a pain at the moment

riesling [rislinŋ] *nm* (*vin*) riesling

rieur, -euse [rijœr, -øz] **1** *adj* (*air, visage*) cheerful, bright; (*yeux*) laughing, merry; **c'est un garçon très r.** he laughs a lot; **mouette rieuse** black-headed gull **2** *n* laugher; **mettre les rieurs de son côté** *ou* **avec soi** to have the last laugh

rififi [rififi] *nm Arg* brawl, free-for-all, punch-up; **il va y avoir du r.** there's going to be trouble *or* a punch-up

riflard [riflar] *nm F* (*parapluie*) umbrella, *Br* brolly

rift [rift] *nm Géol* rift

rigide [riʒid] *adj* **(a)** (*matériau*) rigid; (*essieu*) fixed; **couverture r.** (*d'un livre*) stiff cover **(b)** *Fig* (*personne, règlement, système etc*) rigid, inflexible, unbending; **ne sois pas trop r. avec eux** don't be too strict with them

rigidement [riʒidmɑ̃] *adv* rigidly

rigidifier [riʒidifje] *vt* to rigidify, to make rigid

rigidité [riʒidite] *nf* **(a)** (*d'un matériau*) rigidity; **r. cadavérique** rigor mortis **(b)** *Fig* (*d'une personne, d'un règlement, d'un système etc*) rigidity, inflexibility

rigolade [rigɔlad] *nf F* **ça n'est pas de la r.** it's no laughing matter *or* no joke; **prendre qch à la r.** to treat sth as a joke, to make a joke out of sth; **j'essaie de le prendre à la r.** I'm trying not to take it too seriously; **ah, la r.!** what a hoot *or* scream!

rigolard, -arde [rigɔlar, -ard] *F* **1** *adj* (*personne*) fond of a joke *or* a laugh; **il a toujours un air r.** he's always got a grin on his face, something always seems to be amusing him **2** *n* **c'est une rigolarde** she's fond of a joke *or* a laugh

rigole [rigɔl] *nf* (*caniveau*) channel; (*filet d'eau*) rivulet

rigoler [rigɔle] *vi F* **(a)** (*rire*) to laugh **(b)** (*s'amuser*) to have some fun *or* a laugh, to enjoy oneself **(c)** (*plaisanter*) to joke (**avec** about); **il ne faut pas r. avec le fisc** you shouldn't mess about with the tax man

rigolo, -ote [rigɔlo, -ɔt] *F* **1** *adj* **(a)** (*drôle*) funny; **ce n'est pas r.** it's no laughing matter *or* joke; **il est r., ton sac** what a fun bag! **(b)** (*curieux*) funny, queer, odd **2** *n* (*personne amusante, fumiste*) joker, comedian; (*incompétent*) cowboy, joker; **quel petit r. a débranché la prise?** what joker pulled the plug out? **3** *nm Arg Vieilli* (*revolver*) revolver

rigorisme [rigɔrism] *nm* strictness

rigoriste [rigɔrist] **1** *adj* (*morale, principe, attitude etc*) strict, rigorous **2** *n* strict moralist

rigoureusement [rigurøzmɑ̃] *adv* **(a)** (*strictement*) strictly; **il est r. interdit de marcher sur les pelouses** it is strictly forbidden to walk on the grass; **r. exact** absolutely correct; **suivre r. les consignes** to follow the instructions to the letter; **je l'ai r. vérifié** I checked it thoroughly **(b)** (*avec dureté*) rigorously, severely, harshly; **être r. opposé à qch** to be rigorously opposed to sth

rigoureux, -euse [rigurø, -øz] *adj* **(a)** (*dur*) (*punition, mesures, conditions etc*) severe, harsh, rigorous; (*hiver*) hard; (*climat*) harsh **(b)** (*strict*) strict; (*analyse*) rigorous; (*entraînement*) rigorous, strict; (*discipline*) severe; **observer une neutralité rigoureuse** to observe strict neutrality; **sois plus r.** be more rigorous

rigueur [rigœr] *nf* **(a)** (*dureté*) harshness, severity, rigour, *US* rigor; (*du temps*) harshness, severity; **prendre des mesures de r.** to take rigorous *or* harsh *or* severe measures; **la r. de la loi** the rigour of the law; **les rigueurs de la vie en prison/du climat écossais** the rigours of prison life/the Scottish climate; **un climat de r. économique** a harsh economic climate; **user de r. avec qn** to be severe with *or* hard on sb; **tenir r. à qn** not to forgive sb; **je ne lui en tiens pas r.** I don't hold it against him, I'm not holding a grudge

(b) (*du règlement*) strictness; (*d'une analyse*) rigour, *US* rigor; **manquer de r.** (*d'un style*) to be sloppy; (*d'une personne*) (*dans son travail*) to be sloppy, to lack self-discipline; **manquer de r. dans son analyse** not to be rigorous enough in one's analysis; **apprendre la r.** to learn self-discipline; **être de r.** to be compulsory *or* obligatory; **la cravate est de r.** ties must be worn; **l'habit n'est pas de r.** evening dress is optional; **délai de r.** deadline; **à la r.** (*si nécessaire*) if need be, if really necessary; (*à la limite*) just about, at a pinch

rillettes [rijɛt] *nfpl Culin* potted meat (*made from pork, rabbit, goose etc*)

rimailler [rimaje] *vi Péj Vieilli* to versify

rimailleur, -euse [rimajœr, -øz] *n Péj Vieilli* versifier, rhymster, poetaster

rimbaldien, -ienne [rɛ̃baldjɛ̃, -jɛn] *adj* **la poésie rimbaldienne** Rimbaud's poetry, the poetry of Rimbaud; **avoir des accents rimbaldiens** to be reminiscent of Rimbaud, to have Rimbaud-like overtones; **ce film a un côté r.** the film has a touch of Rimbaud about it

rime [rim] *nf* rhyme; **r. pauvre/riche** poor/rich rhyme; **r. féminine/masculine** feminine/masculine rhyme; **rimes croisées** *ou* **alternées** alternate rhymes; **rimes plates** *ou* **suivies** couplet rhymes; *F* **sans r. ni raison** without rhyme or reason

rimer [rime] **1** *vt* (*conte etc*) to put into verse, to versify; **poésie rimée** rhyming verse **2** *vi* **(a)** (*d'un mot etc*) to rhyme (**avec** with); *F* **à quoi cela rime-t-il?** what's the sense of that?, what sense is there in that?; **cela ne rime à rien** it doesn't make sense, there's no sense in it, there's neither rhyme nor reason in it; **cela ne rimerait à rien** it wouldn't make sense **(b)** (*faire des vers*) to write verse *or* poetry

rimeur, -euse [rimœr, -øz] *n Péj* rhymer, rhymester

rimmel® [rimɛl] *nm* mascara

rinçage [rɛ̃saʒ] *nm* (*action*) rinsing; (*opération*) rinse; (*pour les cheveux*) (colour *or US* color) rinse; **cycle de r.** (*d'une machine à laver*) rinse cycle; **produit de r.** (*pour lave-vaisselle*) rinsing agent *or* aid

rince-bouteilles [rɛ̃sbutɛj] *nm inv* bottle-washing machine

rince-doigts [rɛ̃sdwa] *nm inv* finger bowl

rincée [rɛ̃se] *nf* **(a)** *F* (*averse*) downpour; **on a pris une sacrée r. sur le dos** we got soaked through, we were drenched **(b)** *Arg* (*défaite*) walloping, pounding; *Vieilli* (*coups*) thrashing

rincer [rɛ̃se] **(je rinçai(s); n. rinçons) 1** *vt* (*vêtements, vaisselle, cheveux*) to rinse; (*verre, tasse*) to rinse (out); **se faire r.** *Arg* (*au jeu*) to be cleaned out; *F* (*par la pluie*) to get soaked (to the skin) *or* drenched **2 se rincer** *vpr* **se r. les mains** to rinse one's hands; **se r. la bouche** to rinse one's mouth (out); *Arg* **se r. le gosier** *ou* **la dalle** (*boire*) to have a drink; *F* **se r. l'œil** to get an eyeful
rincette [rɛ̃sɛt] *nf F* nip of brandy/*etc* (*put into emptied cup or glass*)
rinceur, -euse [rɛ̃sœr, -øz] **1** *n* (*personne*) rinser **2** *nf* **rinceuse** (*machine*) bottle-washing machine
ring [riŋ] *nm Boxe* ring; **le r.** (*la boxe*) boxing; **monter sur le r.** to go into the ring; (*faire de la boxe*) to take up boxing
ringard¹ [rɛ̃gar] *nm* (*tisonnier*) poker
ringard², -arde [rɛ̃gar, -ard] *F* **1** *adj* **(a)** (*démodé*) (*personne, chanson*) old-fashioned, *Arg* uncool **(b)** (*voyant*) (*style, couleur, décor etc*) tacky **2** *n* old fogey, person who is behind the times
ripage [ripaʒ] *nm* (*glissement*) slipping; (*de véhicule*) skidding; *Aut* **r. des pneus** tyre scrub
ripaille [ripaj] *nf F* feast, blow-out; **faire r.** to have a feast *or* blow-out
ripailler [ripaje] *vi F* to feast, to have a (good) blow-out
ripailleur, -euse [ripajœr, -øz] *n F* reveller
ripaton [ripatɔ̃] *nm Arg* (*pied*) foot; **ripatons** *Br Arg* plates of meat
riper [ripe] **1** *vt* (*faire glisser*) (*chargement etc*) to slide along **2** *vi* to slip; (*des roues*) to skid; (*d'un chargement*) to shift; *très F* (*s'en aller*) to split
ripoliner [ripɔline] *vt* to enamel, to paint with enamel
ripolin® [ripɔlɛ̃] *nm* enamel (paint)
riposte [ripɔst] *nf* **(a)** (*réponse*) riposte, retort **(b)** *Boxe, Escrime* (*coup*) riposte, counter **(c)** (*représailles*) counterattack
riposter [ripɔste] *vi* **(a)** (*répondre*) to retort, to riposte **(b)** *Boxe, Escrime* to riposte, to counter **(c)** (*user de représailles*) to counterattack, to mount a counterattack; **les annonceurs ont riposté au procès en …** advertisers responded to the trial by …
ripou [ripu] *F* **1** *adj* (*policier*) bent **2** *nm* bent cop
riquiqui [rikiki] *adj inv F* (*tout petit*) teeny-weeny; (*mesquin*) (*portion, cadeau etc*) stingy, mean; (*maillot de bain*) skimpy; **ça fait r.** (*mesquin*) it looks a bit stingy *or* mean
rire¹ [rir] *nm* laughter, laughing; **un r.** a laugh; **il a un gros r.** he has a loud laugh, he guffaws; **il eut un gros r.** he roared with laughter; **éclat de r.** burst of laughter; **des éclats de r.** screams *or* hoots of laughter; **avoir le fou r.** to have a fit of the giggles, to laugh uncontrollably; (*sur scène*) to corpse; **se tenir les côtes de r.** to split one's sides laughing; **provoquer** *ou* **exciter les rires** to cause laughter; **r. moqueur** sneer; **avoir un r. moqueur** to sneer; **il eut un r. d'incrédulité** he laughed incredulously
rire² (*prp* **riant**; *pp* **ri**; *pr ind* **je ris, n. rions, ils rient**; *pr sub* **je rie**; *p hist* **je ris**; *fu* **je rirai**) **1** *vi* **(a)** to laugh; *Prov* **rira bien qui rira le dernier** he who laughs last laughs longest; **r. jaune** to force a laugh, to give a forced laugh; **r. comme un bossu** to laugh like a hyena, to split one's sides laughing; **r. aux éclats** to scream *or* roar with laughter; **éclater de r.** to burst out laughing; **r. bruyamment** to guffaw; **r. en soi-même, r. tout bas** to laugh to oneself, to chuckle; **r. en dedans** to laugh up one's sleeve; **r. bêtement** to giggle, to titter; **dire qch en riant** to say sth laughingly *or* with a laugh; **il a ri (jusqu')aux larmes** he laughed till he cried; **ne pas avoir le cœur à r.** not to be in a laughing mood; **il y a de quoi r.** it's laughable, it's enough to make a horse laugh; **il n'y a pas de quoi r.!** it's no laughing matter!, it's no joke!; **cela nous a souvent fait r.** we've often laughed about it, we've had many a laugh over it; **c'était à mourir** *ou F* **à crever de r.** we nearly died laughing; **c'est à mourir de r., cette histoire/cette situation** it's a hysterically funny story/situation; **il nous faisait tordre** *ou* **mourir de r.** he had us splitting our sides; **tu me fais mourir** *ou* **tordre de r.** you crack me up; *Iron* **tu me fais (mourir de) r. avec tes grandes idées** you really make me laugh, you and your big ideas; *F* **j'étais mort de r.** I was killing myself laughing; **r. de qn** to laugh at sb, to make fun of sb; **r. d'une histoire** to laugh over *or* at a story; **il rit de vos menaces** he laughs at *or* scoffs at *or* makes light of your threats; **je ris de leurs insultes** I don't care about their insults; **il vaut mieux en r.** it's best to laugh, you might as well laugh; **il prête à r.** he makes himself a laughing stock; **tout cela ne prête guère à r.** it's not exactly funny *or* a laughing matter; **il faut dire que la situation prêtait à r.** admittedly the situation was funny; **vous me faites r.!** you make me laugh!, nonsense!, you must be joking!; **laissez-moi r.!, ne me faites pas r.!** don't make me laugh!
(b) (*s'amuser*) to have (some) fun, to have a laugh *or* a few laughs; **vous voulez r.!** you're joking!; **prendre qch en riant** to laugh sth off; **pour r.** for fun, for a laugh *or* a joke; **je te le disais en riant** it was a joke, I was pulling your leg; **non mais sans r.!** no, but seriously!; **sans r., c'est vrai** honestly *or* seriously, it's true; *F* **c'était pour r.** it was only for fun; **je l'ai fait histoire de r.** I did it for a laugh *or* a joke *or* for fun
(c) *Fig* (*des yeux*) to dance
2 se rire *vpr* **se r. de qn** to laugh at sb, to make fun of sb; **se r. de qch** to laugh at sth, to make light of sth
ris¹ [ri] *nm Litt* (*rire*) laughter
ris² *nm Naut* (*dans la voile*) reef; **prendre un r.** to take in a reef; **larguer un r.** to shake out a reef
ris³ *nm Culin* **r. (de veau)** (calf's) sweetbread
risée [rize] *nf* **(a)** (*moquerie*) mockery, derision; **s'exposer à la r. publique** to expose oneself to public scorn *or* derision **(b)** (*objet de moquerie*) laughing stock; **nous étions la r. de tous** we were a public laughing stock *or* the butt of everyone's jokes **(c)** *Naut* (*brise*) light squall, flurry (of wind)
risette [rizɛt] *nf* (*d'enfant*) (little) laugh, smile; **fais (la) r. à papa!** smile for daddy!, give daddy a smile!
risible [rizibl] *adj* (*erreur, conduite, demande etc*) laughable, ridiculous, ludicrous; (*personne*) ridiculous; **la situation n'avait rien de r.** the situation was not at all funny, there was nothing to laugh at in the situation
risiblement [riziblәmɑ̃] *adv* ridiculously, ludicrously
risotto [rizɔto] *nm Culin* risotto
risque [risk] *nm* risk; **est-ce qu'il y a un r. que cela se produise?** is there any risk of that happening?; **courir un r.** to run a risk; **c'est un r. à courir** it's a risk I/we/*etc* have to take; **courir le r. de qch** to risk sth; **courir le r. de faire qch** to risk doing sth; **prendre un r./des risques** to take a risk *or* chance/risks *or* chances; **j'en prends le r.** I'll take that risk; **groupe à haut r.** high-risk group; **il est parti à ses risques et périls** he went at his own risk; **vous le faites à vos risques et périls** you do it at your own risk, on your head be it; **cela n'est pas sans r.** it is not without its risks *or* dangers; **sans aucun r., sans courir le moindre r.** without (running) any risk; **avoir le goût du r.** to like taking risks *or* chances, to like living dangerously; **au r. de sa vie** at the risk *or* peril of his life; **les risques d'erreur sont moindres** there's less risk *or* chance of making a mistake; **les risques d'aggravation sont importants** there is a significant risk that things will get worse; *Méd* **r. infectieux** risk of infection; **risques de guerre** (*en assurances*) war risks; **au r. de manquer le train** at the risk of missing the train; **c'est un des risques du métier** it's an occupational hazard; **assurance tous risques** comprehensive *or* all-risks insurance; **risques d'incendie/d'inondations** risk of fire/flooding; **cela constitute un r. pour la santé/la sécurité** it's a health/safety hazard; *Fin* **souscrire un r.** to underwrite a risk
risqué [riske] *adj* **(a)** (*dangereux*) (*entreprise etc*) risky, hazardous **(b)** (*osé*) (*plaisanterie etc*) risqué, *F* near the knuckle
risquer [riske] **1** *vt* **(a)** (*mettre en danger*) (*vie, réputation etc*) to risk; **il faut r. le combat** we must risk a battle, we must take a chance and fight; **j'ai risqué ma carrière à cause de toi** I risked my career for you, I put my career on the line for you; **après tout, qu'est-ce que tu risques?** what have you got to lose after all?; *Hist, Fig* **r. sa tête** to put one's head on the block; *Prov* **qui ne risque rien n'a rien** nothing ventured, nothing gained; **je ne veux rien r.** I'm not taking any risks *or* any chances; **r. le tout pour le tout** to go for broke; **r. le coup** to risk *or* chance it, to chance one's luck; **r. gros** to play for big stakes; **il risquait de tout perdre** he risked *or* ran the risk of losing everything; **la grève risque de durer longtemps** the strike may (well) go on for a long time *or* there's a chance that the strike will go on for a long time; *F* **il risque de gagner** he has *or* stands a good chance of winning, he might well win; *F* **il ne risque pas de te le dire** fat chance of him telling you
(b) (*avancer*) **r. un œil** to peep out; **r. un œil dans une pièce** to peep into a room; **r. sa tête à la fenêtre** to take a hurried look out of the window; **il risqua une main derrière les assiettes** he put a hand gingerly behind the plates
2 se risquer *vpr* to take risks/a risk; **je ne m'y risquerais pas** I wouldn't risk it; **se r. à faire qch** to venture to do sth; **se r. dans une maison abandonnée** to venture into an abandoned house
risque-tout [riskәtu] **1** *n inv* daredevil **2** *adj inv* **il est r.** he's a daredevil, he's constantly risking his neck; **un enfant r.** a real little daredevil, a daredevil of a child
rissole [risɔl] *nf Culin* rissole
rissoler [risɔle] *vti Culin* to brown; **pommes (de terre) rissolées** sauté potatoes
ristourne [risturn] *nf Com* (*rabais*) discount; **faire une r. à qn**

to give sb a discount; **r. de droits de douane** customs drawback; **r. de fidélité** regular customer discount *or* rebate; **r. de prime** premium rebate

ristourner [risturne] *vt* **il nous a ristourné vingt pour cent du prix** he gave us a twenty per cent discount *or* twenty per cent off

Rital, -ale, -als, -ales [rital] *n F Péj (Italien)* wop, *Br* Eyetie

rite [rit] *nm* rite; *Fig (habitude)* ritual; **les rites de la vie quotidienne** the rituals of everyday life; **rites d'initiation** initiation rites; **rites de passage** *ou* **initiatiques** rites of passage

ritournelle [riturnɛl] *nf Mus* ritornello; *Fig F* **c'est toujours la même r.** it's (always) the same old story

ritualiser [ritɥalize] *vt* to ritualize, to turn into a ritual

ritualisme [ritɥalism] *nf Rel* ritualism

ritualiste [ritɥalist] **1** *adj* ritualistic **2** *n* ritualist

rituel, -elle [ritɥɛl] **1** *adj* ritual **2** *nm Rel, Fig (rites)* ritual; **selon le r.** according to ritual; *Fig* **il a verrouillé les portes selon son r.** he went through his ritual of locking the doors; **r. d'initiation** initiation rites *or* ritual

rituellement [ritɥɛlmɑ̃] *adv* **(a)** *(habituellement)* invariably; **ils y vont r. chaque année** they go every year without fail **(b)** *(en sociologie)* according to ritual, ritually

rivage [rivaʒ] *nm (de mer, lac)* shore; *Litt (de rivière)* bank

rival, -ale, -aux, -ales [rival, -o] *adj, n* rival; **sans r.** unrivalled, unparalleled; **ce boulanger est sans r. pour ...** there is no-one to equal this baker when it comes to ...

rivaliser [rivalize] *vi* **r. avec qn** to compete *or* vie with sb; **r. d'adresse/de générosité/d'élégance avec qn** to try to outdo sb in skill/generosity/elegance

rivalité [rivalite] *nf* rivalry

rive [riv] *nf (de rivière)* bank; *(de lac, de mer)* shore; **la R. gauche** *(de la Seine)* the Left Bank; *Can* **la R. sud** *(du Saint-Laurent)* the South Shore

river [rive] *vt* **(a)** *(attacher)* to rivet; *Fig* **le matin, je suis rivé au lit** *(je ne peux pas me lever)* I just can't get out of bed in the morning; **il est rivé au lit** *(il refuse de se lever)* he just won't get out of bed; **impossible de bouger, j'étais rivé sur place** I couldn't move, I was rooted to the spot; **être rivé à son bureau** to be glued to *or* stuck at one's desk; **il a les yeux rivés sur elle** he can't take his eyes off her, his eyes are glued to her **(b)** *F* **r. son clou à qn** to shut sb up

riverain, -aine [rivrɛ̃, -ɛn] **1** *adj (de rivière)* riverside, waterside; *(de lac) (propriété, propriétaire)* lakeside, waterside; *(de route) (propriété etc)* roadside, bordering (on) the road; **propriétaire r.** owner of lakeside/roadside property **2** *n (de rivière)* riverside resident; *(de lac)* lakeside resident; **les riverains de cette rue** the people who live in *or* along this street; **'route interdite sauf aux riverains'** 'access only'

rivet [rivɛ] *nm* rivet

rivetage [rivtaʒ] *nm* riveting

riveter [rivte] *vt (pr ind* **je rivette, n. rivetons)** to rivet

riveteuse [rivtøz] *nf* riveting machine

rivière [rivjɛr] *nf* **(a)** river; **pêche en r.** river fishing **(b)** *Équitation* water jump **(c)** *Fig (de lave, boue)* river; **r. de diamants** diamond necklace, *Spéc* diamond rivière

rivoir [rivwar] *nm (marteau)* riveting hammer; *(machine)* riveting machine

rivure [rivyr] *nf (action)* riveting; *(joint)* rivet(ed) joint; *(tête)* rivet head

rixe [riks] *nf* brawl; **r. au couteau** knife fight

riz [ri] *nm* rice; **eau/papier de r.** rice water/paper; **poudre de r.** face powder

▶ **riz**: **r. blanc** white rice; **r. brun** *ou* **complet** brown rice; **r. créole** boiled rice; **r. au curry** curried rice; **r. décortiqué** husked rice; **r. étuvé** *ou* **incollable** non-stick rice; **r. jaune** *ou* **au safran** saffron rice; **r. au lait** rice pudding; **r. long** long-grain rice; **r. rond** short-grain rice; *(pour le riz au lait)* pudding rice; **r. sauvage** wild rice

riziculteur, -trice [rizikyltœr, -tris] *n* rice grower

riziculture [rizikyltyr] *nf* rice growing

rizière [rizjɛr] *nf* rice field, paddy field

riz-pain-sel *nm inv Mil Arg* commissariat

RMI [ɛrɛmi] *nm abrév* = **revenu minimum d'insertion**

RN [ɛrɛn] *nf abrév* **route nationale**

RNIS [ɛrɛniɛs] *nm abrév Ordinat* **(réseau numérique à intégration de services)** ISDN

robe [rɔb] *nf* **(a)** *(de femme)* dress **(b)** *(d'un avocat)* robe, gown; *(d'un prêtre, un cardinal etc)* robe; **les gens de r., la r.** the legal profession **(c)** *(d'oignon)* skin; *(de fève)* husk; *(d'un cigare)* wrapper (leaf) **(d)** *(pelage) (de cheval etc)* coat **(e)** *(du vin)* colour, *US* color

▶ **robe**: **r. de baptême** christening robe; **r. de chambre** dressing gown, *Am* robe; **en r. de chambre** in one's *or* a dressing gown; **pommes de terre en r. de chambre** *ou* **des champs** jacket potatoes, potatoes in their jackets; **r. chasuble** tunic (dress), *Am* jumper; **r. de grossesse** maternity dress; **r. d'intérieur** housecoat; **r. de mariée** wedding dress; **r. du soir** evening gown *or* dress

robert [rɔbɛr] *nm très F (sein)* tit, boob

robe-tablier, *pl* **robes-tabliers** *nf* pinafore dress, *Am* jumper

robin [rɔbɛ̃] *nm Péj Vieilli* lawyer

robine [rɔbin] *nf Can Arg* methylated spirits, *Br* meths

robinet [rɔbinɛ] *nm (de l'évier, du lavabo)* tap, *Am* faucet; *(de tonneau)* spigot; **ouvrir/fermer le r.** to turn the tap on/off; **eau du r.** tap water; **r. d'eau froide/chaude** cold-/hot-water tap; *Fig* **c'est un r. d'eau tiède** he drones *or Br F* rabbits *or* witters on; **r. mélangeur** mixer tap; **r. du gaz** gas tap; *Tech* **r. d'arrêt** *ou* **de fermeture** stopcock, shut-off (valve); **r. de vidange** *ou* **de purge** drain cock *or* tap; **r. à flotteur** ballcock; *Naut* **r. de prise d'eau à la mer** seacock; *Hum* **problèmes de robinets** sums about filling baths and tanks

robinetterie [rɔbinɛtri] *nf (robinets)* (system of) taps

robineux [rɔbinø] *nm Can Arg* tramp, *Am* hobo, wino

robot [rɔbo] *nm Tech, Fig* robot; **r. (ménager)** food processor; **avion r.** drone

robotique [rɔbɔtik] **1** *nf* robotics **2** *adj* robotic

robotisation [rɔbɔtizasjɔ̃] *nf* automation, roboticization

robotiser [rɔbɔtize] *vt Tech (chaîne de montage etc)* to automate, to roboticize; *Fig* **r. qn** to turn sb into a robot

robre [rɔbr] *nm Cartes* rubber

robusta [rɔbysta] *nm (café)* robusta

robuste [rɔbyst] *adj (personne, santé, foi)* robust; *(appétit, confiance en soi)* robust, healthy; *(plante)* hardy; *(bicyclette, machine etc)* sturdy

robustesse [rɔbystɛs] *nf (d'une personne)* robustness; *(d'une plante)* hardiness; *(d'une bicyclette, une machine etc)* sturdiness

roc [rɔk] *nm* rock; **creusé dans le r.** hollowed out of the rock; **bâti sur le r.** built on rock; *Fig* **bâtir sur du r.** to build on solid foundations; **solide comme un** *ou* **le r.** rock-solid; **Jules, c'est un r.** Jules is as solid as a rock

rocade [rɔkad] *nf (route)* bypass; *Mil* communications line

rocaille [rɔkaj] **1** *nf* **(a)** *(arrangement)* **(jardin de) r.** rockery, rock garden **(b)** *(pierraille)* (loose) stones *or* rocks; **grotte en r.** grotto **(c)** *(terrain)* stony *or* rocky ground **2** *adj inv Beaux-Arts (style, table etc)* rocaille

rocailleux, -euse [rɔkajø, -øz] *adj* **(a)** *(pierreux)* stony, rocky **(b)** *Fig (voix)* harsh, rough

rocambole [rɔkɑ̃bɔl] *nf Bot* Spanish garlic

rocambolesque [rɔkɑ̃bɔlɛsk] *adj (aventures, histoire etc)* fantastic, incredible

roche [rɔʃ] *nf (matière, rocher)* rock; *Géol* **roches ignées/sédimentaires/métamorphiques** igneous/sedimentary/metamorphic rocks; **percé dans la r.** drilled in the rock; **r. de fond** bedrock; **eau de r.** clear spring water; *Fig* **clair comme de l'eau de r.** as clear as crystal, crystal-clear

rocher [rɔʃe] *nm* **(a)** *(masse de pierre)* rock; *(escarpé)* crag; **r. branlant** rocking stone, logan(stone); **côte hérissée de rochers** rockbound coast; **le R. de Gibraltar** the Rock of Gibraltar, *F* the Rock **(b)** *(paroi)* rock face; **pousser à flanc de r.** to grow out of the bare rock, to cling to the side of the rock; **faire du r.** to go rock climbing **(c)** *(bouchée de chocolat)* chocolate *(containing nuts)* **(d)** *(dans l'oreille)* petrous bone

rochet [rɔʃɛ] *nm Tech* ratchet; **roue à r.** ratchet wheel

rocheux, -euse [rɔʃø, -øz] *adj (paysage, région)* rocky; **masse/paroi rocheuse** rock mass/face; **les (montagnes) Rocheuses** the Rocky Mountains, the Rockies

rock (and roll) [rɔk(ɛnrɔl)] *Mus* **1** *nm* rock (and roll); *(danse)* rock (and roll), jive; **danser le r.** to rock (and roll), to jive; **un groupe/chanteur de r.** a rock group/singer **2** *adj inv (concert, groupe, chanteur etc)* rock

rocker [rɔkœr] *n (musicien)* rock musician; *(enthousiaste)* rock (music) fan

rocking-chair [rɔkiŋtʃɛr], *pl* **rocking-chairs** *nm* rocking chair

rococo [rokoko] **1** *nm Beaux-Arts* rococo **2** *adj inv* **(a)** *Beaux-Arts* rococo **(b)** *(démodé)* old-fashioned

rodage [rodaʒ] *nm (d'un moteur, d'une voiture)* running in; **période de r.** *(d'une structure)* running-in *or* breaking-in period; *Aut* **en r.** running in; **voiture en r.** car that is being run in

rodeo, rodéo [rɔdeo] *nm* rodeo; **faire du r.** *(métier)* to be a rodeo rider; *(prendre part à un rodéo)* to take part in a rodeo; **finalement, ils se sont livrés à un véritable r. dans les rues du quartier** *(en voiture)* they ended up having a car chase in the streets

roder [rode] **1** *vt (moteur, voiture)* to run in; *Fig (entreprise, Th spectacle)* to get into its stride; *(équipe, structure)* to break in; **être rodé** *(d'une entreprise etc, Th d'un spectacle)* to be into its stride, to have settled down *or* shaken down; *(d'un* *employé*) to have got the hang of things **2 se roder** *vpr F* to break oneself in

rôder [rode] *vi* to prowl, to be on the prowl; **r. dans les rues** to prowl about *or* hang about the streets; **un pauvre chien qui rôde** a poor dog roaming around; *Fig F* **il rôde autour de moi depuis quelques jours** he's been hanging around me for a few days

rôdeur, -euse [rodœr, -øz] **1** *adj* prowling **2** *n* prowler

rodomontade [rɔdɔmɔ̃tad] *nf* **rodomontade(s)** boasting, bragging; **faire des rodomontades** to boast, to brag

Rogations [rɔgasjɔ̃] *nfpl Rel* Rogations

rogatoire [rɔgatwar] *adj Jur* rogatory; **commission r.** letters of request, *Spéc* letters rogatory

rogatons [rɔgatɔ̃] *nmpl* (*de nourriture*) leftovers, scraps

rognage [rɔɲaʒ] *nm* (*action*) (*du cuir, du métal etc*) trimming, paring; *Ordinat* (*d'image*) cropping

rogne [rɔɲ] *nf F* bad temper; **être en r.** to be cross (**contre qn** with sb); **mettre qn en r.** to make sb cross; **se mettre** *ou F* **se ficher en r.** to get angry, to see red

rogner [rɔɲe] *vt* (*griffes, ongles*) to clip, to trim; (*cuir, métal etc*) to trim, to pare; *Ordinat* (*image*) to crop; *Fig* (*de l'inflation*) (*économies etc*) to eat *or* nibble away at, to whittle away; **r. les tranches d'un livre** to cut *or* trim the edges of a book; *Fig* **les patrons rognaient (sur) les salaires** the bosses were paring wages to the bone; *Fig* **r. sur les dépenses** to cut down on *or* curtail expenses; *Fig* **r. les ailes à qn** to clip sb's wings

rognon [rɔɲɔ̃] *nm Culin* kidney

rognonner [rɔɲɔne] *vi F* to grumble, to grouse

rognures [rɔɲyr] *nfpl* (*déchets*) (*de griffes, d'ongles*) clippings; (*de cuir, de métal etc*) trimmings, parings; (*de viande*) scraps

rogomme [rɔgɔm] *nm F* **voix de r.** (drunkard's) husky voice

rogue [rɔg] *adj* arrogant, haughty

roi [rwa] **1** *nm* **(a)** (*souverain*) king; **le r. Louis XIII** (King) Louis XIII; *Bible* **les rois mages** the Three Wise Men, the Three Kings, the Magi; **le R-Soleil** the Sun King; **jour** *ou* **fête des Rois** Twelfth Night; *Rel* Epiphany; **tirer les rois** = to celebrate Twelfth Night; **plat de r.** dish fit for a king; **heureux comme un r.** as happy as a sandboy; Fig **le r. n'est pas son cousin** he's got a very high opinion of himself; Fig **le choix du r.** a boy followed by a girl

(b) *Fig* king; **le r. des animaux** (*lion*) the king of the beasts; **le r. du plastique/des pizzas** the plastics/pizza king; **l'un des rois du pétrole** one of the oil barons; *Hum* **r. de la resquille** (*dans une queue*) champion queue-jumper; (*dans le métro etc*) champion fare-dodger; (*au cinéma, au stade*) champion at sneaking in for nothing; **c'est le r. des imbéciles** he's a prize *or* first-class idiot; *très F* **c'est le r. des cons** he's a complete arsehole

(c) *Cartes, Échecs* king

2 *adj inv* **bleu r.** royal blue

roide [rwad], **roideur** [rwadœr], **roidir** [rwadir] *Arch* = **raide, raideur, raidir**

roitelet [rwatlɛ] *nm* **(a)** *Péj* petty king **(b)** (*oiseau*) wren; **r. huppé** goldcrest

rôle [rol] *nm* **(a)** *Th, Fig* part, role; **r. titre** title role; **premier r.** leading role, lead; **c'est elle qui a le premier r.** she has the leading role, she is the lead *or* the leading lady; **second r.** supporting part *or* role; **Mme Oldani dans le r. de la Tosca** Mme Oldani as Tosca; **il est toujours excellent dans les rôles de jeune premier** he is always excellent as the romantic lead; **jouer le r. de Macbeth** to play (the part of) Macbeth; **on lui fait jouer le r. d'Ophélia** she's been given the role *or* part of Ophelia, she's been cast as Ophelia; **distribution des rôles** (*action*) casting; (*liste*) cast (list); **répéter/connaître son r.** to learn/know one's part *or* lines; *Fig* **assigner un r. à qn** to assign a role to sb; *F* **jouer un r. secondaire** (*d'une personne*) to play second fiddle; **cet élément joue un r. secondaire dans …** this element plays a secondary role in …; **tu as le beau r.** it's easy *or* all right for you, you've got the easy job; **il n'a pas le beau r.** he doesn't have it easy; **les femmes n'ont pas toujours un r. facile** a woman's role is not always easy, women do not always have it easy; **le r. du médécin** the doctor's role *or* function *or* job; **il avait, en quelque sorte, le r. de confesseur** he acted as a kind of confessor; **le r. du sport dans l'éducation** the role *or* function of sport in education; **un r. de premier plan** a leading role; **jeu de rôles** role playing; **ce n'est pas son r. de te conseiller** it's not his job to advise you

(b) (*liste*) list, register; **à tour de r.** in turn, by turns, in rotation; **faire qch à tour de r.** to take turns (in) doing sth, to do sth turn and turn about *or* in turns; **nous sommes entrés dans son bureau à tour de r.** we went into his office in turn; **les rôles de l'armée active** the active list; *Naut* **r. de l'équipage** list of the crew, muster roll; *Admin* **r. des impôts** *ou* **d'impôt** assessment book; *Admin* **r. des contributions** tax roll

rollier [rɔlje] *nm* (*oiseau*) roller

rollmops [rɔlmɔps] *nm inv Culin* rollmop

roll on-roll off [rɔlɔnrɔlɔf] *adj, nm inv* **(navire) r.** roll-on/roll-off ship, RO-RO ship

ROM [rɔm] *nf Ordinat* ROM

romain, -aine[1] [rɔmɛ̃, -ɛn] **1** *adj* Roman; **l'Empire r.** the Roman Empire; **l'Église romaine** the Church of Rome; **chiffres romains** Roman numerals; *Typ* **caractère r.** roman character; **en caractères romains** in roman **2** *n* **R.** Roman **3** *nm Typ* roman

romaine[2] [rɔmɛn] *adj, nf* **(balance) r.** steelyard

romaine[3] *nf* (*laitue*) cos (lettuce), *Am* romaine; *Fig F* **être bon comme la r.** (*bienveillant*) to be extremely kind; (*destiné à être victime*) to be sure to get it in the neck

roman[1] [rɔmɑ̃] *nm* **(a)** (*en prose*) novel; **r. cycle, r-fleuve** saga, roman fleuve; **votre histoire, c'est du r.** your story is just a fairy tale; *Fig* **l'histoire de notre rencontre est tout un r.** the story of our meeting is quite a romance; **le nouveau r.** the antinovel, the nouveau roman **(b)** *Hist* (*poème*) romance; **le R. de la Rose** the Romance of the Rose

▶ **roman**: **r. d'amour** love story, romance; **r. de gare** airport novel; **r. noir** thriller; **r. policier** detective novel; *F* whodunnit

roman[2] **1** *adj* **(a)** *Ling* Romance **(b)** *Archit* Romanesque; (*en Angleterre*) Norman **2** *nm* **(a)** *Ling* Romance **(b)** *Archit* Romanesque style; (*en Angleterre*) Norman style

romance [rɔmɑ̃s] *nf* (*chanson*) (sentimental) song, drawing-room ballad

romancer [rɔmɑ̃se] *vt* (*biographie*) to fictionalize; (*événement, histoire*) to romanticize

romanche [rɔmɑ̃ʃ] *adj, nm Ling* Romans(c)h

romancier, -ière [rɔmɑ̃sje, -jɛr] *n* novelist

romand [rɔmɑ̃] **1** *adj* **la Suisse romande** French(-speaking) Switzerland **2** *nmpl* **les Romands** the French(-speaking) Swiss

romanesque [rɔmanɛsk] *adj* **(a)** (*personne, aventure etc*) romantic **(b)** *Littér* (*technique etc*) novelistic

roman-feuilleton, *pl* **romans-feuilletons** *nm* serial

romanichel, -elle [rɔmaniʃɛl] *n Péj* **(a)** (*tsigane*) gipsy, romany **(b)** (*vagabond*) tramp, vagrant

romaniser [rɔmanize] *vt Hist* to Romanize

romaniste [rɔmanist] *n* **(a)** *Ling* student of the Romance languages **(b)** *Rel, Jur* Romanist

romano [rɔmano] *n F Péj* (*tsigane*) gippo

roman-photo, *pl* **romans-photos** *nm* photo-story, picture story; (*sentimental*) photo-romance, picture romance

romantique [rɔmɑ̃tik] **1** *adj* **(a)** *Beaux-Arts, Littér* Romantic **(b)** (*personne, idées, film etc*) romantic **2** *n* **(a)** *Beaux-Arts, Littér* Romantic(ist) **(b)** (*sentimental*) romantic

romantisme [rɔmɑ̃tism] *nm* **(a)** *Beaux-Arts, Littér* Romanticism **(b)** (*d'une personne*) romanticism; **ça ne manque pas de r.** it's really romantic; **paysage plein de r.** extremely romantic countryside

romarin [rɔmarɛ̃] *nm Bot, Culin* rosemary

rombière [rɔ̃bjɛr] *nf Arg* **(vieille) r.** old biddy

Rome [rɔm] *n* Rome; *Prov* **tous les chemins mènent à R.** all roads lead to Rome

rompre [rɔ̃pr] **(je romps, il rompt, ils rompent) 1** *vt* **(a)** (*casser*) to break; (*en deux parties*) to break in two; (*bâton, fil*) to snap; (*en plusieurs parties*) to break (up); **r. ses digues** (*d'un fleuve etc*) to burst its banks; **r. le silence** to break the silence; **le silence de la nuit était rompu par …** the silence of the night was shattered by …; **r. une promesse** to break a promise; **r. le pain** to break bread; *Th* **applaudir à tout r.** to applaud wildly; *Mil* **r. les rangs** to fall out, to dismiss, to break ranks

(b) (*interrompre*) (*conversation, fiançailles, relations diplomatiques, amitié*) to break off; (*contrat, Él circuit*) to break; **le charme est rompu** the spell is broken; **cela rompt un peu la monotonie** it helps to break *or* relieve the monotony; **il ne faut pas r. le rythme** keep up the rhythm; **r. le rythme quotidien** to provide a distraction from the daily routine; **r. un tête-à-tête** to interrupt a *or* break in on a private conversation; **la France a rompu les relations avec la Chine** France has broken off *or* severed relations with China; **r. l'équilibre** to upset the balance; **r. les chiens** to call off the hounds; *Fig* to change the subject

2 *vi* **(a)** (*casser*) to break; (*d'un bâton, d'un fil*) to break, to snap; *Fig* (*de deux amants*) to split up, to break it off; **r. avec** (*amant*) to break it off with, to finish with; (*tradition, passé*) to break with; **r. avec sa famille** to break off relations with one's family; **r. avec une habitude** to break (oneself of) a habit

(**b**) *Mil* **r. devant l'ennemi** to break before the enemy
(**c**) *Boxe, Escrime* to break
3 se rompre *vpr* (*se casser*) to break; (*d'un bâton, d'un fil*) to break, to snap; (*de la glace*) to break (up); *Méd* (*d'un vaisseau sanguin*) to rupture; **son cœur battait à se r.** his heart was throbbing violently *or* fit to burst; *Fig* **se r. le cou** to break one's neck

rompu [rɔ̃py] *adj* (**a**) broken; *Méd* (*vaisseau sanguin*) ruptured; **fiançailles rompues** broken engagement; **chemin r.** road full of potholes; **être r.** (**de fatigue**) to be worn out *or* tired out; **r. de travail** worn out *or* tired out by work; **couleur rompue** colour with a shot effect (**b**) **r. à** used to; **être r. aux affaires** to be experienced in business

romsteck [rɔmstɛk] *nm* rump steak

ronce [rɔ̃s] *nf* (**a**) (*arbuste*) bramble (bush), blackberry bush; (*branche*) bramble (**b**) **ronce(s) artificielle(s)** barbed wire (**c**) (*nœud de certains bois*) **r. de noyer** bur(r) walnut

ronceraie [rɔ̃srɛ] *nf* bramble patch

ronchon [rɔ̃ʃɔ̃] *F* **1** *adj* grouchy, grumpy **2** *n* grumbler, grouser

ronchonnement [rɔ̃ʃɔnmɑ̃] *nm F* grumbling, grousing, bellyaching; **j'en ai assez de tes ronchonnements** I've had enough of your grumbling *or* grousing *or* bellyaching

ronchonner [rɔ̃ʃɔne] *vi F* to grumble, to grouse, to grouch

ronchonneur, -euse [rɔ̃ʃɔnœr, -øz] *adj, n F* = **ronchon**

roncier [rɔ̃sje] *nm*, **roncière** [rɔ̃sjɛr] *nf* (thick) bramble bush

rond, ronde [rɔ̃, rɔ̃d] **1** *adj* (**a**) (*balle, table, nappe etc*) round; (*ventre*) rounded; (*poitrine de femme*) full; (*personne, joues, silhouette*) plump; **écriture ronde** round hand(writing); **avoir le dos r.** to be round-shouldered; **avoir le ventre r.** to have a bit of a stomach; **tuiles rondes** curved *or* rounded tiles; **le ballon r.** (association) football, *Br* soccer; **faire des yeux ronds** to goggle, to gape; **avoir des yeux ronds** to be wide-eyed (with astonishment)
(**b**) *Fig* **voix ronde** full voice; **en chiffres ronds** in round figures; **deux cents francs en chiffres ronds** a round two hundred francs; **compte r.** round sum; *F* **homme tout r.** straightforward man; **r. en affaires** businesslike; **être r. en affaires** to be straightforward where business is concerned
(**c**) *F* (*ivre*) drunk; **il était complètement r.** he was pie-eyed *or* plastered *or* sozzled; **r. comme une queue de pelle** rat-arsed
2 *adv* **tourner r.** (*d'une roue*) to run true; (*d'un moteur, Fig d'une entreprise, d'une affaire etc*) to run smoothly; **ça fera 100 francs tout r.** that makes it a hundred francs exactly; **avaler qch tout r.** to swallow sth whole; *F* **cela ne tourne pas r.** there's something not right, there's something the matter; *F* **elle ne tourne pas r.** there's something up *or* the matter with her
3 *nm* (**a**) (*figure*) circle; **le chat se met en r.** the cat curls (itself) up; **danser/s'asseoir en r.** to dance/sit in a circle *or* a ring; **tourner en r.** to go round in a circle *or* ring; *Fig* to go round in circles; *F* **en baver des ronds de chapeau** to be having a helluva time; **il m'en fait baver des ronds de chapeau** he's making my life hell
(**b**) (*rondelle*) (*de saucisson, carotte*) slice; (*de beurre*) pat; *F* **il n'a pas un r.** he hasn't a penny, he hasn't a brass farthing
4 *nf* **ronde** (**a**) (*danse*) round (dance); (*chanson*) round, roundelay
(**b**) *Mil etc* (*visite de surveillance*) round(s); (*de policier*) beat; **faire une/sa ronde** to patrol; (*de policier*) to be on the beat; *Arch* **la ronde de nuit** (*hommes, veille*) the night watch; **chemin de ronde** parapet walk, rampart walk
(**c**) (*écriture*) round hand(writing)
(**d**) *Mus* (*note*) semibreve, *Am* whole note
(**e**) **à la ronde** around; **visible à dix kilomètres à la ronde** visible for ten kilometres around; **il n'y avait personne à dix kilomètres à la ronde** there was nobody within a radius of ten kilometres; **(faire) passer le vin à la ronde** to pass the wine round, to hand round the wine; **boire à la ronde** to drink in turn
▶ **rond**: **r. de cuir** (*coussin*) (round leather) chair cushion; *Danse* **r. de jambe** rond de jambe; *F* **faire des ronds de jambe** to bow and scrape; **r. de serviette** napkin ring

rond-de-cuir [rɔ̃dkɥir], *pl* **ronds-de-cuir** *nm F Péj* penpusher, clerk

rondeau, -eaux [rɔ̃do] *nm* (**a**) *Littér* rondeau (**b**) *Mus* rondo

ronde(-)bosse, *pl* **rondes-bosses** *nf Beaux-Arts* sculpture in the round; **en r.** in the round

rondelet, -ette [rɔ̃dlɛ, -ɛt] *adj* (*personne, doigts*) plump, chubby, podgy; **somme rondelette** good (round) sum, tidy sum

rondelle [rɔ̃dɛl] *nf* (**a**) (*de carton etc*) disc; (*de citron, de saucisson, de cornichon etc*) slice; *Can* **r.** (**de hockey**) puck; **couper les légumes en rondelles** to slice the vegetables (**b**) (*de vis, d'écrou etc*) washer; *Aut* **r. butée** thrust washer; *Aut* **r. de blocage** lock washer

rondement [rɔ̃dmɑ̃] *adv* (**a**) (*promptement*) briskly, promptly, smartly; **mener r. les choses** to make short work of things, to deal with things promptly (**b**) (*carrément*) bluntly, frankly; **il nous a dit r. qu'il n'était pas d'accord** he told us straight (out) *or* bluntly *or* frankly that he didn't agree

rondeur [rɔ̃dœr] *nf* (**a**) roundness; (*d'une personne, des joues etc*) plumpness; **rondeurs** rounded forms *or* lines; (*d'une femme*) curves; **avoir des rondeurs** to be curvy *or* curveceous (**b**) (*franchise*) straightforwardness, plain dealing; **avec r.** bluntly, frankly

rondin [rɔ̃dɛ̃] *nm* log; **cabane en rondins** log cabin; **chemin de rondins** corduroy road

rondo [rɔ̃do] *nm Mus* rondo

rondouillard [rɔ̃dujar] *adj F* (*personne*) plump, chubby, podgy

rond-point, *pl* **ronds-points** *nm* (*sens giratoire*) roundabout, *Am* traffic circle

ronéo® [rɔneo] *nf* Roneo®

ronéotyper [rɔneɔtipe] *vt* to Roneo®

ronflant [rɔ̃flɑ̃] *adj* (*vent, feu*) roaring; (*moteur*) whirring, purring; (*poêle*) purring; *Fig Péj* (*titre, promesse, discours, style etc*) high-flown, high-sounding

ronflement [rɔ̃fləmɑ̃] *nm* (**a**) (*de dormeur*) snoring (**b**) *Fig* (*du vent, d'un feu*) roaring; (*de moteur, machine*) whirring, purring; (*du poêle*) purring

ronfler [rɔ̃fle] *vi* (**a**) (*de dormeur*) to snore (**b**) *Fig* (*du vent, d'un feu*) to roar; (*d'un moteur*) to whirr, to purr; (*d'un poêle*) to purr; **faire r. le moteur** to rev the engine

ronflette [rɔ̃flɛt] *nf F* snooze

ronfleur, -euse [rɔ̃flœr, -øz] **1** *n* (*personne*) snorer **2** *nm Tél* buzzer

ronger [rɔ̃ʒe] (**je rongeai(s)**; **n. rongeons**) **1** *vt* (**a**) (*d'une souris etc*) to gnaw (at), to nibble (at); **r. un os** (*d'un chien*) to gnaw (on) a bone; **rongé par les vers** worm-eaten
(**b**) (*d'un acide, de la rouille*) (*métal etc*) to eat away *or* into; (*de la mer*) (*falaises*) to erode; *Fig* **être rongé de chagrin** to be consumed *or* tormented with grief; **être rongé de remords/par la jalousie/par l'anxiété** to be eaten up with remorse/jealousy/anxiety; **rongé par la maladie** wasted by illness; **rongé par un cancer** riddled with cancer; **c'est quelque chose qui finit par la r.** it's eating away at her
2 se ronger *vpr* (**a**) to worry, to fret; **se r. de chagrin, se r. le cœur** *ou* **les sangs** to eat one's heart out
(**b**) **se r. les ongles** to bite one's nails

rongeur, -euse [rɔ̃ʒœr, -øz] **1** *adj* (*mammifère*) rodent-like **2** *nm* rodent

ronron [rɔ̃rɔ̃] *nm F* (*d'un chat*) purr(ing); (*d'un moteur*) purr, purring (noise), whirr, whirring (noise); (*d'un avion, une voix, un discours, de la musique*) drone, droning (noise); (*d'une machine*) whirr, whirring (noise); **faire r.** (*d'un chat*) to purr; *Fig* **le r. de la vie quotidienne** the monotony of everyday life, humdrum routine

ronronnement [rɔ̃rɔnmɑ̃] *nm* (*d'un chat*) purring; (*d'un moteur*) purr, purring, whirr, whirring, drone; (*d'un avion*) drone, droning (noise); (*d'une machine*) whirr, whirring (noise)

ronronner [rɔ̃rɔne] *vi* (*d'un chat*) to purr; (*d'un moteur*) to purr, to whirr; (*d'un avion*) to drone; (*d'une machine*) to whirr; *Fig* to be in a rut; **r. de plaisir** to purr with pleasure

room-service [rumsɛrvis] *nm* room service

roque [rɔk] *nm Échecs* castling; **petit/grand r.** castling on the king's/queen's side

roquefort [rɔkfɔr] *nm* (*fromage*) Roquefort

roquer [rɔke] *vi* (**a**) *Échecs* to castle (**b**) (*au croquet*) to croquet the ball

roquet [rɔkɛ] *nm Péj* (*chien*) yapper; *F* (*personne*) little squirt

roquette[1] [rɔkɛt] *nf Bot* rocket

roquette[2] *nf Mil* (*projectile*) rocket; **r. antichar** anti-tank rocket

rorqual [rɔrkwal] *nm* rorqual, finback (whale)

rosace [rozas] *nf Archit* (**a**) rose (window) (**b**) **r. de plafond** ceiling rose

rosacé [rozase] *adj Bot* rose-like, *Spéc* rosaceous

rosaire [rozɛr] *nm Rel* rosary; **dire** *ou* **réciter son r.** to tell one's beads, to say the rosary

rosâtre [rozɑtr] *adj* pinkish

rosbif [rɔzbif] *nm* (**a**) *Culin* (*rôti*) roast beef; (*à rôtir*) roasting beef (**b**) *très F* (*terme injurieux*) (*Britannique*) Brit

rose [roz] **1** *nf* (**a**) (*fleur*) rose; **bouton de r.** rosebud; **eau de r.** rosewater; *F* **roman à l'eau de r.** soppy love story, soppy romance; **essence de roses** attar *or* otto of roses; **teint de r.** rosy complexion; **frais comme une r.** fresh as a daisy; *F* **ça ne sent pas la r.!** it's a bit whiffy!; *F* **envoyer qn sur les**

roses to send sb packing, to send sb off with a flea in his/her ear; *Prov* **(il n'est) pas de r. sans épines** there's no rose without a thorn
(b) **bois de r.** rosewood
(c) *Archit* rose (window)
(d) *(diamant)* rose (diamond), rose-cut diamond
2 *adj* *(robe etc)* pink; *(teint)* rosy; **des rubans rose pivoine** peony-red ribbons; **tout n'est pas r. dans ce monde** life is not a bed of roses; **ce n'est pas bien r., cette histoire-là** it's a pretty grim story
3 *nm* pink; **voir la vie** *ou* **tout en r.** to see everything through rose-coloured glasses *or* spectacles
▶ **rose**: *Bot* **r. incarnate** damask rose; **r. mousseuse** moss rose; *Géol* **r. des sables** desert rose; **r. sauvage** wild rose, dog rose; *Naut* **r. des vents** compass card
rosé [roze] **1** *adj* pinkish; **vin r.** rosé **2** *nm* *(vin)* rosé
roseau, -eaux [rozo] *nm* reed
rose-croix 1 *n inv* Rosicrucian **2** *nf* Rosicrucianism
rosée [roze] *nf* dew; **goutte de r.** dewdrop; *Phys* **point de r.** dew point
roselet [rozlɛ] *nm* *(fourrure)* ermine
roselier, -ière [rozəlje, -jɛr] **1** *adj* **marais r.** reed marsh **2** *nf* **roselière** reed bed
roséole [rozeɔl] *nf Méd* roseola
roser [roze] *vt Litt* **r. qch** to make *or* turn sth pink
roseraie [rozrɛ] *nf* rose garden
rose-thé, *pl* **roses-thé** *nf, adj inv* tea rose
Rosette [rozɛt] *n* **la pierre de R.** the Rosetta stone
rosette [rozɛt] *nf* **(a)** *(nœud)* bow; *(ornement)* rosette **(b)** *(insigne)* rosette *(esp of the Legion of Honour)*; **recevoir la r.** to be awarded the Legion of Honour **(c) r. de Lyon** = sort of slicing sausage
rosicrucien, -ienne [rozikrysjɛ̃, -jɛn] *adj, n* Rosicrucian
rosier [rozje] *nm* rose tree, rose bush; **r. grimpant** climbing rose; **r. nain** miniature rose(-bush); **r. sur tige** standard rose; **r. sauvage** briar
rosière [rozjɛr] *nf Hist* = village maiden awarded a wreath of roses for her virtuous conduct; *Fig Hum* **ce n'est pas une r.** she's no angel
rosiériste [rozjerist] *n* rose grower *or* breeder
rosir [rozir] **1** *vt* to turn pink **2** *vi* **(a)** *(du ciel)* to go *or* turn pink **(b)** *(d'émotion)* to blush, to go pink
rosse [rɔs] *Péj* **1** *nf* **(a)** *Vieilli* *(cheval)* hack **(b)** *F* *(homme)* swine, bastard; *(femme)* bitch **2** *adj F* *(personne, conduite, remarque)* rotten; *(coup)* rotten, dirty
rossée [rɔse] *nf F* beating, walloping, pasting
rosser [rɔse] *vt F* **r. qn** to beat sb up, to give sb a (good) hiding *or* walloping; **se faire r.** to get a hiding *or* walloping
rosserie [rɔsri] *nf F* **(a)** *(caractère)* rottenness; **il/elle est d'une r.!** he's a bastard/she's a bitch **(b)** *(mauvaise action)* dirty *or* rotten trick; **faire une r. à qn** to play a dirty *or* rotten trick on sb **(c)** *(parole)* nasty *or* spiteful remark
rossignol [rɔsiɲɔl] *nm* **(a)** *(oiseau)* nightingale **(b)** *(clef)* skeleton key **(c)** *F* *(objet)* white elephant; **vieux rossignols** old stock
rossinante [rɔsinɑ̃t] *nf Péj Vieilli* *(cheval)* old worn-out hack
rostre [rɔstr] *nm Antiq* *(éperon de navire)* rostrum
rot [ro] *nm F* belch, burp; *(de bébé)* burp; **faire un r.** to belch, to burp; *(d'un bébé)* to burp; **faire faire son r. à un bébé** to burp a baby
rôt [ro] *nm Arch* roast (meat)
rotarien [rɔtarjɛ̃] *nm* Rotarian
Rotary [rɔtari] *nm* Rotary Club
rotatif, -ive [rɔtatif, -iv] **1** *adj* *(pompe, moteur etc)* rotary **2** *nf* **rotative** (rotary) press; *Fig* **faire tourner les rotatives** to give the press *or* newspapers something to write about
rotation [rɔtasjɔ̃] *nf* **(a)** *Phys, Tech* rotation; *(d'un projectile)* spin; **mouvement de r.** rotating movement; **faire un mouvement de r. sur soi-même** *(de toupie)* to spin; *(de gymnaste)* to spin (round); *(de personne)* to spin round; **corps en r.** rotating body; **pièce à r.** revolving part; **axe de r.** axis of rotation; *Math* **faire faire une r. de 90° à une droite** to rotate a line through an angle of 90° **(b)** *(de bateau, de bus etc)* rotation; *(du stock, de fonds)* turnover; **par r.** in rotation
▶ **rotation**: **r. des capitaux** capital turnover; **r. des cultures** crop rotation, rotation of crops; **r. de personnel** *(à des postes différents)* rotation of staff; *(remplacement)* turnover of staff, staff turnover; **r. des stocks** inventory *or* stock turnover, stock turnaround
rotatoire [rɔtatwar] *adj* **(a)** *(mouvement)* rotatory; *(force)* rotational **(b)** *(polarisation)* rotary
roter [rɔte] *vi F* to belch, to burp; **faire r. un bébé** to burp a baby
rôti [rɔti] **1** *nm* roast (meat), joint; *(à rôtir)* joint, roast; **r. de porc** *(cuit)* roast pork; *(non cuit)* joint of pork, pork roast; **tranche de r.** slice of roast meat **2** *adj* roast; **poulet r.** roast chicken; *Fig F* **ça ne va pas te tomber tout r. dans la bouche** it's not going to just fall into your lap
rôtie [rɔti] *nf* (slice of) toast
rotin¹ [rɔtɛ̃] *nm* **(a)** *Bot* rattan; **sièges en r.** cane *or* rattan chairs **(b)** *(canne)* rattan walking stick
rotin² *nm F Vieilli* *(sou)* **pas un r.!** not a farthing!; **il n'a plus un r.** he's stone broke *or* stony
rôtir [rɔtir] **1** *vt* **(a)** *(viande, poulet, châtaignes)* to roast; *(pain)* to toast **(b)** *F* **le soleil rôtit la colline** the sun is scorching the hillside; **le soleil me rôtissait le dos** my back was getting roasted by the sun **2 se rôtir** *vpr* **se r. au soleil** to toast *or* roast in the sun **3** *vi Culin* to roast; **r. au soleil** to toast *or* roast in the sun; *F* **on rôtit ici** it's scorching *or* roasting here
rôtissage [rɔtisaʒ] *nm* roasting
rôtisserie [rɔtisri] *nf* **(a)** *(restaurant)* grill(-room), steakhouse **(b)** *(boutique)* = shop selling roast meat
rôtisseur, -euse [rɔtisœr, -øz] *n* **(a)** *(restaurateur)* grill-room proprietor; *(cuisinier)* roasting chef **(b)** *(commerçant)* = seller of roast meat
rôtissoire [rɔtiswar] *nf Culin* (rotating) spit, rotisserie
rotogravure [rɔtɔgravyr] *nf Typ* rotogravure
rotonde [rɔtɔ̃d] *nf* **(a)** *Archit* rotunda **(b)** *Rail* (circular) engine shed, roundhouse
rotondité [rɔtɔ̃dite] *nf* **(a)** *(de la Terre etc)* roundness **(b)** *(embonpoint)* plumpness; *F Hum* **rotondités** *(de femme)* curves
rotor [rɔtɔr] *nm* *(de dynamo, turbine, hélicoptère)* rotor; *Aut* **r. de distributeur** rotor arm
rotule [rɔtyl] *nf* **(a)** *Anat* kneecap, *Spéc* patella; *F* **être sur les rotules** to be dead beat *or* on one's last legs **(b)** *Tech* ball (-and-socket) joint; *Aut* **r. de direction** steering joint; *Aut* **r. d'attelage** *(de caravane)* tow ball
rotulien, -ienne [rɔtyljɛ̃, -jɛn] *adj Anat* patellar
roture [rɔtyr] *nf Hist* **(a) terre en r.** land held by a commoner **(b) la r.** *(condition)* the common rank; *(gens)* the commonalty, the commons
roturier, -ière [rɔtyrje, -jɛr] *Hist* **1** *adj* common, of the common people **2** *n* commoner
rouage [ruaʒ] *nm* **(a)** *(ensemble des roues)* wheels, gear work; **rouage(s) d'une montre** works of a watch, train of wheels of a watch; **r. d'horloge** clockwork; *Fig* **les rouages de l'administration** the workings of government; **organisation aux rouages bien huilés** smooth-running organization **(b)** *(roue)* (toothed) wheel, cog wheel
rouan, -anne [rwɑ̃, -an] **1** *adj* *(cheval)* roan **2** *nm* roan
roubignoles [rubiɲɔl] *nf Vulg* balls, bollocks
roublard, -arde [rublar, -ard] *F* **1** *adj* *(personne, air)* wily, crafty, cunning; *(ton)* crafty **2** *n* wily *or* crafty *or* cunning devil; **un fin r.** an old fox
roublardise [rublardiz] *nf F* **(a)** *(caractère)* cunning, wiliness, craftiness **(b)** *(acte)* crafty *or* cunning trick
rouble [rubl] *nm* *(monnaie russe)* rouble
roucoulade [rukulad] *nf* *(des oiseaux)* cooing; *F* **roucoulades** *(des amoureux)* billing and cooing
roucoulement [rukulmɑ̃] *nm* *(d'un pigeon)* cooing; *Fig* *(d'amoureux)* billing and cooing
roucouler [rukule] **1** *vi* *(d'un pigeon)* to coo; *Fig F* *(d'amoureux)* to bill and coo **2** *vt F* *(mots doux, promesses etc)* to coo
roudoudou [rududu] *nm F* = coloured sweet *(licked out of a mould)*
roue [ru] *nf* wheel; **véhicule à quatre roues** four-wheeled vehicle; **véhicule à quatre roues motrices** four-wheel drive vehicle; **un deux roues** a two-wheeled vehicle, a two-wheeler; *Fig F* **être la cinquième r. du carrosse** to be a spare part, *Am* to be the fifth wheel; **avoir l'impression d'être la cinquième r. du carrosse** to feel in the way *or Am* like a fifth wheel; *Fig* **pousser à la r.** to put one's shoulder to the wheel, to lend a helping hand; **sans roues** wheelless, without wheels; *Naut* **la r. du gouvernail** the wheel; **faire la r.** *(d'un paon)* to display, to spread its tail; *(d'un acrobate)* to turn cartwheels/a cartwheel; *Péj* *(de qn qui se parade)* to strut, to swagger; *Naut* **bateau à roues** paddle boat; **la grande roue** the Big Dipper, *Am* the Ferris wheel; *Arch* **condamner un criminel à la r.** to condemn a criminal to the wheel
▶ **roue**: *Tech* **r. de commande** driving wheel; **r. dentée** toothed wheel, cogwheel, gear (wheel); *HydE* **r. à eau** water wheel; **r. d'engrenage** toothed wheel, cogwheel, gear (wheel); **r. à feu** Catherine wheel; *Fig* **la r. de la fortune** the wheel of fortune; **r. hydraulique** hydraulic wheel; *Ordinat* **r. d'impression** print wheel; **r. libre** freewheel; **descendre en r. libre** to coast *or* to freewheel downhill; **r. motrice** driving *or* drive wheel; **r. de moulin** mill wheel; **r. à rayons** spoke wheel; *Aut* **r. de secours** spare wheel; **r. de transmission**

driving *or* drive wheel; *HydE* **r. de turbine** turbine wheel, impeller
roué, -ée [rwe] **1** *adj Litt* (*personne*) cunning, sly **2** *n Litt* (*roublard*) cunning *or* sly devil **3** *nm Hist* (*débauché*) rake, roué
rouelle [rwɛl] *nf* (*de citron, de carotte etc*) slice; **r. de veau** fillet of veal
rouennais, -aise [rwanɛ, -ɛz] **1** *adj* (*qui vient de Rouen*) from Rouen; (*situé à Rouen*) of Rouen **2** *n* **R.** (*natif*) native of Rouen; (*habitant*) inhabitant of Rouen
rouer [rwe] *vt* **(a)** *F* **r. qn de coups** to beat sb black and blue **(b)** *Arch* (*supplicier*) **r. qn** to break sb on the wheel
rouerie [ruri] *nf* **(a)** (*acte*) cunning *or* sly trick (**envers** played on) **(b)** (*caractère*) cunning, slyness
rouet [rwɛ] *nm* **(a)** (*de fileuse*) spinning wheel **(b)** *Tech* (*de poulie*) sheave; (*de serrure*) scutcheon
rouf [ruf] *nm Naut* deck house
rouflaquettes [ruflakɛt] *nfpl F* (*favoris*) sideboards, *surtout Am* sideburns
rouge [ruʒ] **1** *adj* **(a)** (*manteau, joues, cheveux, viande, vin etc*), *Pol* red; **fer r.** red-hot iron; **marqué au fer r.** (*animal*) branded; *Fig* **c'est marqué au fer r. dans ma mémoire** it's branded on my memory; **fruits rouges** soft fruit; **r. de colère/d'émotion** red (in the face) with anger/emotion; **être r. de honte** to be red *or* to blush with shame; **être r. comme une tomate** (*d'une personne*) to be as red as a beetroot; **être r. comme une écrevisse** (*brûlé par le soleil*) to be as red as a lobster; **avoir les yeux rouges** to have red eyes, to be red-eyed; *Rel* **le chapeau r.** the cardinal's (red) hat; *Pol* **le drapeau r.** the red flag; **porto r.** ruby port
(b) (*inv in compounds*) **des rubans r. cerise** cherry-red ribbons; **r. sang** blood-red; **r. drapeau** pillar-box red; **r. bordeaux** wine-coloured
2 *adv* **se fâcher tout r.** to lose one's temper completely, *F* to flip; **voir r.** to see red
3 *nm* **(a)** (*couleur*) red; **peindre/teindre qch en r.** to paint/dye sth red; **porter le fer au r.** to make the iron red-hot; **le r. lui monte aux joues** he is going red in the face; *Prov* **r. le soir, espoir** red sky at night, shepherd's delight
(b) (*cosmétique*) rouge; **r. à lèvres, bâton de r.** lipstick; **r. à joues** blusher
(c) *F* (*signal*) **passer au r.** to turn *or* go red
(d) (*vin*) red wine; **gros r.** coarse red wine
(e) *Fig* **mon compte/le commerce extérieur est dans le r.** my account/foreign trade is in the red
4 *n* (*communiste*) Red
rougeâtre [ruʒatr] *adj* reddish
rougeaud, -eaude [ruʒo, -od] **1** *n* red-faced person, person with a red face **2** *adj* red-faced; **être r.** to have a red face
rouge-gorge, *pl* **rouges-gorges** *nm* robin (redbreast)
rougeoiement [ruʒwamɑ̃] *nm* red glow
rougeole [ruʒɔl] *nf* [①**A10**,d] *Méd* measles; **avoir la r.** to have (the) measles
rougeoleux, -euse [ruʒɔlø, -øz] *Méd* **1** *adj* suffering from (the) measles **2** *n* person with measles
rougeoyant [ruʒwajɑ̃] *adj* glowing (red)
rougeoyer [ruʒwaje] *vi* (**il rougeoie; il rougeoiera**) **(a)** (*briller*) to glow (red) **(b)** (*devenir rouge*) to turn red, to redden
rouge-queue, *pl* **rouges-queues** *nm* (*oiseau*) redstart
rouget [ruʒɛ] *nm* (*poisson*) red mullet; **r. grondin** gurnard
rougeur [ruʒœr] *nf* **(a)** (*causée par la chaleur, l'émotion*) flush(ing); (*causée par la honte, la gêne*) blush(ing) **(b)** *Méd* (*tache*) blotch **(c)** (*couleur*) redness
rougir [ruʒir] **1** *vt* **(a)** (*ciel, feuilles etc*) to turn red, to redden; **r. son eau** to put a drop of red wine in one's water; **eau rougie** water with a little red wine; *Fig* **r. ses mains (de sang)** (*commettre un crime*) to get blood on one's hands
(b) **r. le fer au feu** to heat iron in the fire until red-hot; **fer rougi au feu** red-hot iron
(c) (*visage*) to redden
2 *vi* **(a)** (*du ciel, des feuillages etc*) to turn red, to redden; **faire r. un métal** to heat a metal until it is red-hot
(b) (*d'une personne*) to turn *or* go red, to flush; (*de honte, gêne*) to blush, to redden, to turn *or* go red; **vous devriez r. de dire des choses pareilles!** you should be ashamed to say such things!; **r. jusqu'aux oreilles** to blush to the roots of one's hair; **r. d'un faux pas** to be ashamed of *or* to blush for a mistake; **r. de qn** to blush for sb; **r. de colère/d'émotion** to flush with anger/emotion; **r. de plaisir** to flush *or* blush with pleasure; **faire r. qn** to make sb blush
rougissant [ruʒisɑ̃] *adj* **(a)** (*ciel, feuillage, arbre etc*) reddening **(b)** (*personne, visage*) blushing
rougissement [ruʒismɑ̃] *nm* **(a)** (*du ciel, feuillage etc*) reddening **(b)** (*d'émotion*) flushing; (*de honte, de gêne*) blushing

rouille [ruj] **1** *nf* **(a)** rust; **tache de r.** (*sur un tissu*) rust stain **(b)** *Agr* rust, mildew, blight **(c)** *Culin* rouille (*spicy sauce made with red peppers and garlic*) **2** *adj inv* rust(-coloured)
rouillé [ruje] *adj* **(a)** (*métal, clé, casserole etc*) rusty, rusted **(b)** *Fig* (*français, jeu*) rusty; **j'ai les jambes rouillées** my legs are stiff, my legs have seized up; **je suis complètement r.** (*physiquement*) I've completely seized up; (*intellectuellement*) I'm completely rusty **(c)** *Agr* (*plante*) mildewed
rouiller [ruje] **1** *vt* (*acier, clé, casserole etc*) to rust, to make rusty **2** *vi* (*d'un métal, d'une serrure etc*) to rust (up), to get rusty **3 se rouiller** *vpr* **(a)** (*d'un métal, d'une serrure etc*) to rust (up), to get rusty **(b)** *Fig F* **je me rouille** (*physiquement*) I'm beginning to seize up *or* get stiff; (*intellectuellement*) my brain's going; **mon français se rouille** my French is getting rusty
rouillure [rujyr] *nf* **(a)** (*d'un métal, d'une serrure etc*) rustiness **(b)** *Agr* (*de plantes*) rust, blight
roulade [rulad] *nf* **(a)** (*dans la poussière etc*) roll; *Gym* **r. avant/arrière** forward/backward roll; **faire des roulades** to do rolls **(b)** *Mus* roulade **(c)** *Culin* rolled and stuffed meat
roulage [rulaʒ] *nm* **(a)** (*d'une terre labourée, de métal etc*) rolling **(b)** (*transport de marchandises*) haulage; *Aut* driving; **entrepreneur de r.** carrier, haulier, *Am* hauler; **manutention par r.** roll-on, roll-off, RO-RO; **société de r.** haulage company; *Vieilli* **cheval de r.** cart horse, draught horse
roulant, -ante [rulɑ̃, -ɑ̃t] **1** *adj* **(a)** (*porte*) sliding; **pont r.** travelling crane; **table roulante** trolley; **escalier r.** escalator; **tapis** *ou* **trottoir r.** travelator; **allure roulante** rolling gait; *Rail* **matériel r.** rolling stock; **personnel r.** train/bus crews, drivers and conductors **(b)** *Com* (*capital*) working; **affaire roulante** going concern; **fonds r.** working capital **(c)** *F Vieilli* (*drôle*) (*personne, blague, histoire etc*) comical **2** *nf Mil F* **roulante** field kitchen
roulé [rule] **1** *adj* (*journal, carte, tapis etc*) rolled(-up); *Culin* rolled; **col r.** roll collar, polo neck, turtle neck; *F* **elle est bien roulée** she has a great figure **2** *nm* **(a)** (*viande*) rolled joint **(b)** **r. à la confiture** Swiss roll
rouleau, -eaux [rulo] *nm* **(a)** *Tech* roller; *Phot* roller (squeegee); (*d'une matricielle, machine à écrire*) platen; **roulements à rouleaux** roller bearings; **r. à mise en plis** (hair) roller; **(store sur) r.** roller blind
(b) (*bande*) (*de papier, papier peint, scotch etc*) roll; (*de pellicule*) roll, spool; (*de fil*) coil; (*de tabac*) twist; (*de parchemin*) scroll; **r. de réglisse** liquorice roll; *Fig F* **être au bout du r.** (*désespéré*) to be at the end of one's tether; (*près de la mort*) to be on one's last legs
(c) (*vague*) billow, roller
(d) *Sp* (*saut en hauteur*) roll; **r. ventral** straddle; **r. dorsal** Fosbury flop; **r. costal** western roll
► **rouleau**: *Tech* **r. compresseur** road roller; **r. à pâtisserie** rolling pin; **r. à peinture** paint roller; **r. porte-serviettes** towel-roller; *Culin* **r. de printemps** spring roll; *Tech* **r. à vapeur** steamroller
roulé-boulé [rulebule], *pl* **roulés-boulés** *nm Sp* roll (*executed tucked up in a ball*)
roulée [rule] *nf très F Vieilli* thrashing, beating
roulement [rulmɑ̃] *nm* **(a)** (*d'une balle etc*) rolling; **r. d'yeux** rolling of the eyes
(b) *Av* (*circulation*) taxiing
(c) (*bruit*) (*d'un wagon, de la foudre*) rumble, rumbling; (*de véhicules sur des pierres*) rattle; (*d'un tambour*) rolling; **des roulements de tambour** drum rolls; **un r. de tonnerre** a roll *or* rumble of thunder
(d) *Tech* (*pièce*) bearing; **r. à billes** ball bearing; **r. à rouleaux** *ou* **à galets** roller bearing; *Aut* **r. de butée** thrust bearing
(e) *Com* **r. de fonds** circulation of capital; **r. de capitaux** turnover of capital
(f) (*rotation*) (*dans des tâches etc*) rotation; **par r.** in rotation; **r. du personnel** staff turnover
rouler [rule] **1** *vt* **(a)** (*pousser, déplacer*) (*pierre, tonneau, meuble etc*) to roll (along); (*dés*) to throw, to roll; *Min* (*charbon*) to haul; **r. un bébé dans sa poussette** to push a baby (along) in its pushchair; **r. les yeux** to roll one's eyes; **r. de gros yeux** to goggle; **r. les hanches** to sway *or* swing one's hips; *Fig Litt* **il roulait de sombres projets dans sa tête** he was turning over sombre plans in his mind; *Fig Litt* **r. de mauvaises/vagues pensées** to think evil/vague thoughts
(b) *F* (*duper*) to do; **il m'a roulé de deux mille francs** he's done me for *or* out of two thousand francs; **tu t'es fait r.** you've been done *or* had; **se faire r. dans la farine** to be made a fool of
(c) (*enrouler*) (*carte, tapis, papier, manches*) to roll up; (*parapluie*) to roll up, to furl; (*viande, poisson, cigarette*) to

roll; **r. qn dans une couverture** to roll *or* wrap sb up in a blanket

(d) *(passer au rouleau)* *(court de tennis)* to roll; *(pâte)* to roll out

(e) r. les r to roll one's r's

(f) *F* **r. une pelle** *ou* **un palot** *ou* **un patin à qn** to give sb a French kiss, to French-kiss sb

2 *vi* **(a)** *(se déplacer)* *(d'une balle, une personne qui tombe etc)* to roll; *(d'une voiture, d'un train)* to go, to travel; **r. sur une pente** to roll down a slope; **faire r. qch sur le sol** to roll sth along the ground; **r. (en voiture)** to drive; **nous avons roulé toute la nuit** we drove all night; **nous roulions vite** we were going fast *or* speeding along; **à quelle vitesse rouliez-vous?** how fast were you travelling?, what speed were you doing?; **cette voiture roule bien/vite** the car gives a smooth ride/is fast *or* speedy; **cette voiture a peu roulé** the car has a low mileage; *Av* **r. sur le sol** to taxi; *F* **ça roule** *(tout va bien)* everything's fine; *Fig* **r. sur l'or** to be rolling (in money *or* in it); *Fin* **l'argent roule** money is circulating freely; **la conversation roulait sur le sport** the conversation was about sport, we/they/*etc* were talking about sport; *F* **elle a pas mal roulé dans sa vie** she's knocked about the world a fair bit, she's a bit of a rolling stone; *Prov* **pierre qui roule n'amasse pas mousse** a rolling stone gathers no moss

(b) *(du tonnerre)* to roll, to rumble; *(du tambour)* to roll

(c) r. des hanches to swing *or* sway one's hips; **r. des yeux** to roll one's eyes

(d) *Naut* *(d'un navire)* to roll

3 se rouler *vpr* **(a)** to roll (about); **se r. par terre** to roll (about) on the floor/on the ground; *Fig* **se r. (par terre)** *(rire)* to be convulsed with laughter; **des plaisanteries à se r. par terre** hysterically funny *or* side-splitting jokes

(b) le hérisson se roule en boule *ou* **sur lui-même** the hedgehog rolls (itself) up into a ball

(c) *F* **se r. les pouces, se les r.** to twiddle one's thumbs; **tu vas te les rouler encore longtemps?** are you going to sit there twiddling your thumbs *or* doing sweet FA for much longer?

roulette [rulɛt] *nf* **(a)** *(de meuble)* caster; **à roulettes** *(meuble)* on casters; *F* **ça marche** *ou* **va comme sur des roulettes** things are going very smoothly *or* like clockwork; *Av* **r. de nez/queue** nose/tail wheel **(b)** *Couture* tracing wheel, tracer; *Culin* pastry wheel **(c)** *F* *(de dentiste)* drill **(d)** *(jeu)* roulette; **r. russe** Russian roulette; **c'est un peu la r. russe, ta proposition** your proposal is a bit dicy *or* is pretty much of a gamble

rouleur, -euse [rulœr, -øz] **1** *nm* **(a)** *Arch* *(vagabond)* vagabond **(b)** *Cyclisme* **être un bon r.** to be good on the flat **(c)** *Naut* ship that rolls heavily **2** *nf Ent* **rouleuse** leaf roller

roulier [rulje] *nm Naut, Com* Ro-Ro ship, Ro-Ro

roulis [ruli] *nm* *(d'un bateau)* roll; *(d'un avion, une voiture)* lurch; **mouvement de r.** roll/lurch; **il y a du r.** it's rolling; *Naut* **table à r.** fiddle

roulotte [rulɔt] *nf* *(de bohémiens)* caravan; *(de camping)* caravan, *Am* trailer; *F* **vol à la r.** theft from parked cars

roulotté [rulɔte] *adj, nm Couture* **(ourlet) r.** rolled hem

roulure [rulyr] *nf très F* *(terme injurieux)* *(prostituée)* whore, *Br Arg* tom

roumain, -aine [rumɛ̃, -ɛn] **1** *adj* Romanian, Rumanian **2** *nm Ling* Romanian, Rumanian **3** *n* **R.** Romanian, Rumanian

Roumanie [rumani] *nf* Romania, Rumania

round [rawnd, rund] *nm Boxe* round

roupettes [rupɛt] *nfpl très F* *(testicules)* balls, goolies

roupie[1] [rupi] *nf* *(monnaie)* rupee

roupie[2] *nf F* **c'est de la r. de sansonnet** it's a load of rubbish; *Arch* **avoir la r.** to have a drippy nose

roupiller [rupije] *vi F* to sleep, *Br Arg* to kip; *(faire un petit somme)* to have a snooze *or Br Arg* kip, to take a nap; **j'ai roupillé par terre** I kipped *or* crashed on the floor; **je me suis mis à r. dans le train** I crashed out on the train

roupillon [rupijɔ̃] *nm F* snooze, nap; **faire** *ou* **piquer un r.** to have a snooze *or Br Arg* kip, to take a nap; **un petit r.** a bit of a snooze, *Br Arg* some kip

rouquin, -ine [rukɛ̃, -in] **1** *adj F* *(personne)* red-haired, ginger-haired **2** *n F* *(personne)* redhead **3** *nm Arg* *(vin)* (cheap) red wine

rouscailler [ruskaje] *vi F* *(protester)* to grouse, to gripe

rouspétance [ruspetɑ̃s] *nf F* moaning (and groaning), grumbling

rouspéter [ruspete] *vi* **(je rouspète; je rouspéterai)** *F* to moan (and groan), to grumble **(contre** about)

rouspéteur, -euse [ruspetœr, -øz] *F* **1** *adj* grumpy, grouchy **2** *n* moaner, grumbler

roussâtre [rusɑtr] *adj* reddish

rousse *voir* = **roux**

rousserolle [rusrɔl] *nf* *(oiseau)* reed warbler

roussette [rusɛt] *nf* **(a)** *(poisson)* spotted dogfish **(b)** *(chauve-souris)* flying fox **(c)** *(grenouille)* common frog

rousseur [rusœr] *nf* **(a)** *(de cheveux)* redness; **tache de r.** freckle; **couvert de taches de r.** freckled **(b) rousseurs** *(dans un livre etc)* foxing

roussi [rusi] *nm* **ça sent le r.** there's a smell of (something) burning; *Fig* there's trouble ahead, I smell trouble

roussin [rusɛ̃] *nm Hist* *(cheval)* charger

roussir [rusir] **1** *vt* **(a)** *(cheveux, feuilles)* to turn brown; *Culin* *(viande, oignons)* to brown **(b)** *(en brûlant)* *(linge etc)* to scorch, to singe **2** *vi* **(a)** *(des feuilles, des arbres)* to turn brown *or* russet **(b)** *Culin* **faire r.** to brown

routage [rutaʒ] *nm* *(d'imprimés etc)* (sorting and) routing; *(de navire)* routing; **frais de r.** routing costs

routard, -arde [rutar, -ard] *n F* backpacker

route [rut] *nf* **(a)** *(voie)* road; **conduite sur r.** driving on the open road; **prendre la r. de Paris** to take the road for *or* to Paris; **r. à double voie** *or* **r. à deux voies** dual carriageway, *Am* divided highway; **r. à une seule voie** single-track road; **police de la r.** = traffic police, *Am* highway patrol; **par la r.** by road; **les accidents de la r.** road accidents; **l'état des routes** road conditions; **tenir la r.** *Aut* to hold the road; *Fig F* *(d'un argument, une théorie)* to stand up, to hold water; *(d'un projet)* to stand up, to hold together; **barrer la r. à qn** to bar sb's way; *Fig* to stand in sb's way; **un arbre barre la r.** a tree is blocking the road

(b) *(itinéraire)* route, way; *Naut* course; *Av, Naut* *(ligne)* route; **connais-tu la r.?** do you know the way?; **après trois heures de r.** after three hours' travelling; *Aut* after three hours on the road; **se tromper de r.** to take the wrong road, to go/come the wrong way; **se mettre en r.** *(d'une personne)* to start out, to set out; *(d'un bateau)* to get under way; **il est en r.** he's on his way; **je n'arrive pas à le joindre, il doit déjà être en r.** I can't reach him, he must already have left; **changer de r.** to change one's route; *Naut* **suivre une r.** to steer a course; *Naut* **faire r. sur Calais** to steer (a course) for Calais, to make for Calais; **navire en r. pour l'étranger** ship outward bound; **faire r. ensemble** *(de passagers)* to travel together; *(de bateaux)* to travel in convoy; **veux-tu faire la r. avec moi?** do you want to come with me?; **faire fausse r.** *(en voiture)* to take the wrong road; *(en bateau)* to stray off course; *Fig* *(dans un raisonnement)* to be on the wrong tack *or* track; **montrer la r. à qn** to show sb the way; **en cours de r.** en route; **marchandises avariées en cours de r.** goods damaged in transit; **frais de r.** travel(ling) expenses; **je peux te déposer, c'est sur ma r.** I can drop you, it's on my way; **je le trouve toujours sur ma r.** he's always in my way *or* under foot; **en r.!** *(allons)* let's be off!, let's go!, *F* let's hit the road!; *(allez)* off you go!; *F Hum* **en r., mauvaise troupe!** come on, you lot!; **bonne r.!** have a good trip!

(c) *Fig* path; **nos routes se sont déjà croisées** our paths have already crossed; **la r. est toute tracée** your path is marked out *or* mapped out (for you)

(d) *(marche)* **mettre en r.** *(moteur)* to start up; *(projet, travaux)* to start up, to get under way; **mise en r.** *(d'une machine, un projet)* start-up; **avoir qch en r.** to be working on sth; *F* **j'ai un poulet en r.** I've a chicken cooking; *F* **ils ont un bébé en r.** they've got a baby on the way

▶ **route**: **r. aérienne** airway; **r. commerciale** trade route; **r. de contournement** by-pass; **r. départementale** secondary road, *Br* ≈ B road; **r. des fromages** cheese route; *Naut* **r. de mer** sea route; **r. nationale** main *or* major *or* trunk road, *Br* ≈A-road, *Am* highway; *Naut* **r. de navigation** (shipping) lane, ocean lane; **r. à péage** toll road, *Am* turnpike; **r. principale** main road; **r. secondaire** *Br* B-road, minor road; **r. terrestre** (over)land route; **r. des vins** wine route

router [rute] *vt* *(imprimés etc)* to (sort and) route

routeur [rutœr] *nm Ordinat* router

routier[1], **-ière** [rutje, -jɛr] **1** *adj* *(carte, circulation, sécurité, pont, transports)* road; **police routière** traffic police, *US* highway patrol; **bicyclette routière** roadster; **locomotive routière** traction engine; **gare routière** bus *or* coach station; **voies routières** highways **2** *nm* **(a)** *(conducteur)* long-distance lorry driver, *Am* teamster, truck driver, trucker **(b)** *(vélo)* roadster **(c)** *(cycliste)* road racer **(d)** *(restaurant)* transport café, *Am* truck stop **3** *nf* **routière** *(voiture)* tourer, touring car

routier[2] *nm* **(a) vieux r.** *(homme experimenté)* old hand **(de** at) **(b)** *(scout)* rover

routine [rutin] *nf* routine; **pour rompre la r.** to break the routine; **s'enliser dans/sortir de la r.** to get into/out of a rut; **faire qch par r.** to do sth as a matter of routine; **examen/enquête de r.** routine examination/investigation; *Ordinat* **r. d'édition** edit routine; *Ordinat* **r. de césure** hyphenation routine; *Ordinat* **r. de logiciel** software routine

routinier, -ière [rutinje, -jɛr] **1** *adj* (*tâches, travail etc*) routine; **être r.** to stick to a routine, to be set in one's ways; **avoir l'esprit r.** *ou* **une mentalité routinière** to hate change, to be a creature of habit **2** *n* slave to routine

rouvrir [ruvrir] (*conj like* **ouvrir**) *vti*, **se rouvrir** *vpr* to reopen, to open again

roux, rousse [ru, rus] **1** *adj* (*feuilles*) russet, reddish-brown; (*cheveux*) red; (*pelage*) reddish-brown; (*vache*) brown; **une petite fille rousse** a little girl with red hair, a little redhead; **chevelure blond r.** sandy hair; *Culin* **beurre r.** brown butter **2** *n* (*personne*) red-haired person, redhead; **un grand r.** a tall chap with red hair **3** *nm* **(a)** (*couleur*) russet, reddish-brown; **le r. de ses cheveux** his/her red hair **(b)** *Culin* roux

royal, -ale, -aux, -ales [rwajal, -o] *adj* (*palais, résidence, visite etc*) royal; (*digne d'un roi*) (*cadeau, repas etc*) magnificent, fit for a king; (*salaire*) magnificent, princely; (*mépris, indifférence*) lofty; **prince r.** crown prince; **la famille royale** the royal family, *F* the royals; **un membre de la famille royale** a member of the royal family, *F* a royal; *Fig* **la voie royale** the high road; *F* **il me fiche une paix royale** he's leaving me in peace and quiet

royalement [rwajalmɑ̃] *adv* (*magnifiquement*) (*payé, traité*) royally; *F* **s'amuser r.** to enjoy oneself immensely *or* hugely; *F* **je m'en fiche** *ou* **moque r.** I couldn't care less (about it), I don't give a damn

royalisme [rwajalism] *nm* royalism

royaliste [rwajalist] **1** *adj* royalist; **être plus r. que le roi** to be more Catholic than the Pope **2** *n* royalist

royalties [rwajalti] *nfpl* royalties

royaume [rwajom] *nm* kingdom, realm; *Fig* realm; **le r. des cieux** *ou* **de Dieu** the kingdom of heaven; *Prov* **au r. des aveugles, les borgnes sont rois** in the kingdom of the blind the one-eyed man is king

Royaume-Uni (le) *nm* the United Kingdom

royauté [rwajote] *nf* (*monarchie*) monarchy; (*dignité*) kingship

RP [ɛrpe] *nfpl* (*abrév* **relations publiques**) PR

RPR [ɛrpeɛr] *nm Pol* (*abrév* **Rassemblement pour la République**) = right-of-centre political party

RRR [ɛrɛrɛr] (*abrév* **remise, rabais, ristourne**) discounts and allowances

RTL [ɛrteɛl] (*abrév* **Radio Télé Luxembourg**) = private broadcasting network based in Luxembourg

ruade [rɥad] *nf* (*d'un cheval*) lashing out, kick; **allonger** *ou* **décocher** *ou* **lancer une r.** to lash out

Ruanda [rwɑ̃da] *nm* Rwanda

ruandais, -aise [rwɑ̃dɛ, -ɛz] **1** *adj* Rwandan **2** *n* **R.** Rwandan

ruban [rybɑ̃] *nm* ribbon; **attaché avec un r.** (*cheveux*) tied with a ribbon; **r. de chapeau** hatband; **le r. rouge** the red ribbon (*of the Légion d'Honneur*); *Courses de chevaux* **les rubans** the tapes; **mètre à** *ou* **en r.** tape measure, measuring tape

▶ **ruban**: **r. d'acier** steel band; **r. adhésif** adhesive *or* sticky tape; **r. encreur** (*de machine à écrire*) inking ribbon; **r. d'impression** print(er) ribbon; *Él* **r. isolant** insulating tape; **r. de machine à écrire** typewriter ribbon; **r. magnétique** magnetic *or* recording tape; *Ordinat* **r. perforé** punchtape

rubané [rybane] *adj Biol* striped

rubaner [rybane] *vt* **(a)** (*orner*) to trim with ribbon/ribbons **(b)** *Él* (*fil*) to tape

rubanerie [rybanri] *nf* (*fabrication*) ribbon manufacture; (*commerce*) ribbon trade

rubato [rubato] *adv, nm Mus* rubato

rubéole [rybeɔl] *nf Méd* German measles, rubella

rubican [rybikɑ̃] *adj* (*cheval*) roan

rubicond [rybikɔ̃] *adj* (*teint*) florid, *Fml* rubicund; **un homme r.** a florid-faced man, a man with a florid face

rubidium [rybidjɔm] *nm Ch* rubidium

rubis [rybi] *nm* ruby; (*de montre, d'horloge*) jewel; **r. de Bohème** rose quartz; **montre montée sur r.** jewelled watch; *Fig F* **payer r. sur l'ongle** to pay cash on the nail

rubricard [rybrikar] *nm Journ* columnist

rubrique [rybrik] *nf* **(a)** *Journ* (*titre*) heading; (*articles*) (*colonne*) column; (*page*) page; *Fig* **sous la même r.** under the same heading; *Journ* **r. courrier des lecteurs** letters column; **r. d'échos** diary column; **r. mode** fashion feature; **r. nécrologique** deaths column; **r. pratique** advice column; **r. shopping** consumer column **(b)** (*dans un livre*) imprint

ruche [ryʃ] *nf* **(a)** (bee)hive; (*abeilles*) hive; **r. en paille** (bee-) skep; *Fig* **r. d'industrie** (regular) hive of industry; **à cette heure-ci, la ville est une r.** the town is very busy at this time **(b)** *Couture* ruche, ruching; **garni de ruches** ruched

ruché [ryʃe] *nm Couture* ruche, ruching

ruchée [ryʃe] *nf* (*abeilles*) hive

rucher¹ [ryʃe] *nm* apiary

rucher² *vt Couture* to ruche; **une robe ruchée** a ruched dress

rude [ryd] *adj* **(a)** (*primitif*) (*personne, manières*) rough, uncouth, unpolished

(b) (*au toucher*) (*peau, tissu*) rough; (*au goût*) (*vin*) rough, harsh; (*brosse*) stiff, hard; (*voix*) harsh, grating

(c) (*pénible*) (*hiver, climat*) hard, severe, harsh; (*tâche*) stiff, tough; (*coup*) heavy, severe; (*choc*) rude; (*sentier*) steep; (*montée*) stiff, steep; **exercer un r. métier** to have a demanding job; **être mis à r. épreuve** (*d'une personne*) to be sorely *or* severely tested *or* tried; **il a été à r. école** he was brought up in the school of hard knocks

(d) (*sévère*) (*personne*) severe, harsh

(e) *F* (*remarquable*) **r. appétit** hearty appetite; **un r. gaillard** a stout fellow; **faire une r. gaffe** to put one's foot in it in no uncertain manner

rudement [rydmɑ̃] *adv* **(a)** (*sévèrement*) (*répondre, traiter qn*) harshly, severely; **être r. éprouvé** to be sorely *or* severely tested *or* tried; **travailler r.** to work hard

(b) (*avec violence*) (*frapper, heurter etc*) hard

(c) *F* (*très*) awfully, terribly, *surtout Am* mighty; **tu as r. grandi/grossi!** you've got a lot taller/fatter; **il est r. plus intelligent que son frère** he's a damn sight more intelligent than his brother; **tu es r. chanceux!** you're a lucky dog!; **tu m'as fait r. mal avec le ballon!** you hurt me something awful with that ball!; **on s'est r. bien amusés à St-Tropez!** we had a brilliant time at St-Tropez!

rudesse [rydɛs] *nf* **(a)** (*d'une surface*) roughness; (*d'un style*) roughness, lack of sophistication; (*d'un tissu*) roughness, coarseness; (*d'un vin*) roughness, harshness; (*de la voix*) harshness **(b)** (*de l'hiver, d'un climat*) severity, harshness; (*d'une tâche, un métier*) toughness **(c)** (*d'une personne*) severity, harshness; **avec r.** harshly

rudiment [rydimɑ̃] *nm* **(a)** (*d'un organe*) rudiment **(b)** **rudiments** (*d'une science*) rudiments; **je ne possède que quelques rudiments de mathématiques** I have only rudimentary mathematics; **avoir des rudiments de chinois** to speak rudimentary Chinese; **comprendre les rudiments de qch** to understand the rudiments of sth, to have a rudimentary grasp of sth; *Litt* **établir les rudiments d'une théorie** to establish the basis of *or* the first principles of a theory

rudimentaire [rydimɑ̃tɛr] *adj* rudimentary

rudoyer [rydwaje] *vt* (**je rudoie; je rudoierai**) to treat roughly *or* harshly

rue¹ [ry] *nf* **(a)** (*voie*) street; **r. principale** main street; **la grande r.** the main street, *Br* the high street; **r. piétonnière** *ou* **piétonne** pedestrian precinct, pedestrianized street; **r. à stationnement interdit** clearway; **descendre dans la r.** (*pour protester etc*) to take to the streets; **manifestation de r.** demonstration; **jouer dans la r.** to play in the street; **pour observer les mouvements de la r.** to watch what is going on in the street; **être/se retrouver à la r.** to be/find oneself out on the street; *Fig* **tu sais que tu n'es pas à la r.** you know you don't have to walk the streets; **mettre/jeter qn à la r.** to put/ throw sb out on the street; **courir les rues** to roam *or* walk the streets; **les VTT, ça court les rues** mountain bikes are very common, everybody has a mountain bike these days; **ça ne court pas les rues** (*d'un objet*) you don't find that very often, that's hard to come by; **les experts dans ce domaine ne courent pas les rues** experts in that field aren't exactly ten a penny *or* thick on the ground *or* don't grow on trees; **au coin de la r.** at *or* on the corner; **à tous les coins de r.** on every street corner; **l'homme de la r.** the man in the street

(b) *Th* **rues** slips

rue² *nf Bot* rue

ruée [rɥe] *nf* rush; **la r. sur** *ou* **vers les plages** the rush to *or* for the seaside; **la r. vers l'or** the gold rush; **il y a eu une r. sur les tickets de loterie** there's been a big run on lottery tickets; **c'est la r.** it's a scramble *or* stampede

ruelle [rɥɛl] *nf* **(a)** (*allée*) lane, alley(way) **(b)** (*entre le lit et le mur*) = space between the bed and the wall **(c)** *Hist, Littér* = (part of) room used by ladies to hold salons in the 17th century

ruer [rɥe] **1** *vi* (*d'un cheval etc*) to kick, to lash out **2 se ruer** *vpr* **se r. sur** (*qn*) to rush at, to hurl *or* fling oneself at; (*qch*) to make a rush for, to hurl *or* fling oneself at; **le patron s'est rué sur moi en demandant où était son maudit dossier** the boss charged up to me demanding to know where his damn file was; **les invités se sont rués sur le buffet** the guests rushed towards *or* made a dash for the buffet; **se r. à l'attaque** to throw oneself into the attack; **se r. à la porte** to rush for *or* make a rush for the door

ruf(f)ian [ryfjɑ̃] *nm Arch* (*proxénète*) procurer

rugby [rygbi] *nm* rugby (football); *F* rugger; **r. à treize/quinze** rugby league/union

rugbyman, *pl* **-men** [rygbiman, -mɛn] *nm* rugby player
rugir [ryʒir] **1** *vi* (*d'une personne*) to bellow, to roar (**de** in, with); (*d'un lion, un moteur etc*) to roar; (*du vent, d'une tempête*) to howl **2** *vt* (*insultes etc*) to roar out
rugissant [ryʒisɑ̃] *adj* (*personne*) bellowing, roaring; (*lion, moteur*) roaring; (*vent, tempête*) howling
rugissement [ryʒismɑ̃] *nm* (*d'une personne*) bellow, roar; (*d'un lion, un moteur etc*) roar(ing); (*du vent, d'une tempête*) howl(ing); **pousser des rugissements de colère** to bellow in *or* with anger
rugosité [rygozite] *nf* (**a**) (*caractère*) roughness (**b**) (*point*) rough spot
rugueux, -euse [rygø, -øz] *adj* (*peau, tissu, surface etc*) rough; (*écorce*) rough, gnarled
Ruhr [rur] *nf* **la R.** the Ruhr
ruine [rɥin] *nf* (**a**) (*écroulement*) (*d'un édifice etc*) ruin; **le château est en r.** the castle is in ruins *or* is a ruin; **un château en r.** a ruined castle; **menacer r.** to threaten to collapse, to be on the verge of collapse; **tomber en r.** to fall into ruin(s), to go to ruin; **maisons qui tombent en r.** tumbledown houses

(**b**) *Fig* (*d'une personne, une société etc*) ruin, downfall; **aller** *ou* **courir à la r.** to be on the road to ruin; **la société est au bord de la r.** the company is on the verge of ruin *or* bankruptcy; **c'est la r. de tous nos espoirs/projets** all our hopes/plans are in ruins, it's the downfall of all our hopes/plans; **cette maison, quelle r.!** this house will be the ruin of me!, this house is ruinously expensive!; **ce sera sa r.** it will be the ruin of him; **l'alcool a fait d'elle une r.** alcohol has been her downfall *or* ruin

(**c**) (*vestige*) ruin; **les ruines de Troie** the ruins of Troy; **leur château est une vieille r.** their castle is an old ruin; *Fig* **se relever de ses ruines** to rise from the ashes
ruiner [rɥine] **1** *vt Fin, F* to ruin, to bankrupt; *Fig* (*espoirs, projets de qn*) to ruin, to wreck; (*santé*) to ruin; *F* **ce n'est pas ça qui va te r.** (*ce n'est pas cher*) it won't ruin you, it won't break the bank; **tu veux me r.!** are you trying to ruin *or* bankrupt me!

2 se ruiner *vpr* to ruin *or* bankrupt oneself; (*dépenser beaucoup*) to spend a (small) fortune; **je me suis ruinée pour lui acheter cette montre** I spent a small fortune on that watch for him, I just about had to take out a mortage to buy him that watch; **je ne me suis pas ruiné** I didn't spend much; **je ne veux pas me r.** I don't want to break the bank; **se r. la santé** to ruin one's health
ruineusement [rɥinøzmɑ̃] *adv* ruinously
ruineux, -euse [rɥinø, -øz] *adj* ruinously expensive; **dépenses ruineuses** ruinous expenditure; **ce n'est pas r.** it won't ruin you/us/*etc*, it won't break the bank
ruisseau, -eaux [rɥiso] *nm* (**a**) (*cours d'eau*) brook, (small) stream; *Prov* **les petits ruisseaux font les grandes rivières** great oaks from little acorns grow (**b**) *Fig* (*de sang, de lave*) stream; (*de larmes*) flood; **il coulait des ruisseaux de lave/de boue/de sang** the lava/mud/blood was flowing in streams (**c**) (*le long du trottoir*) gutter; *Fig* **ramasser qn dans le r.** to pick sb up out of the gutter; *Fig* **sortir qn du r.** to pull sb out of the gutter; *Fig* **pousser qn au r.** to throw sb into the gutter; *Fig* **tomber dans le r.** to end up in the gutter
ruisselant [rɥislɑ̃] *adj* streaming, dripping (wet) (**de** with); **eaux ruisselantes** running water; (*en filets*) trickling water; **r. de sueur** dripping with sweat; **il était r. de sueur** he was dripping with sweat, the sweat was pouring off him
ruisseler [rɥisle] *vi* (**il ruisselle**; **il ruissellera**) (**a**) (*d'un liquide*) to stream, to run; (*en filets*) to trickle; **l'eau ruisselait par la porte** the water was streaming *or* pouring in/out the door (**b**) (*d'une surface*) to run, to drip, to stream (**de** with); **le parquet ruisselait** the floor was running with water; **front ruisselant de sueur** forehead dripping *or* pouring with sweat; **ses joues ruisselaient de larmes** tears were streaming down his/her cheeks, his/her cheeks were streaming with tears; **r. de lumière** to be ablaze with light
ruisselet [rɥislɛ] *nm* brooklet, rivulet, rill
ruissellement [rɥiselmɑ̃] *nm* (**a**) (*de l'eau*) streaming, running; (*en filets*) trickling; *Géog* runoff; **eaux de r.** runoff (**b**) (*de bijoux, de lumière etc*) shimmer
rumba [rumba] *nf* (*danse, musique*) rumba
rumen [rymɛn] *nm* (*no pl*) (*de ruminant*) rumen
rumeur [rymœr] *nf* (**a**) (*bruit confus*) distant murmur; (*de la circulation*) hum; **la r. lointaine de la ville/de l'usine** the distant sound of the city/the factory; **des rumeurs de mécontentement s'élevèrent de la foule** rumblings of discontent rose from the crowd

(**b**) (*on-dit*) rumour, *US* rumor; **victime de la r. publique, elle dut quitter la ville** a victim of local gossip, she had to leave town; **il démissionna contraint par la r. publique** he was forced to resign because of rumours going around; **la r. court qu'il est ruiné** rumour has it that *or* there's a rumour going round that he's ruined; **j'ai entendu des rumeurs selon lesquelles ...** I've heard rumours *or* whispers *or* a whisper that ...
ruminant [ryminɑ̃] *adj, nm Zool* ruminant
rumination [ryminasjɔ̃] *nf Zool* rumination, ruminating
ruminer [rymine] **1** *vi* (*d'un animal*) to ruminate, to chew the cud **2** *vt* (**a**) (*d'un animal*) to ruminate, to chew (**b**) *Fig* (*idée, projet etc*) to ponder, to mull *or* chew over, to ruminate on
rumsteck [rɔmstɛk] *nm* rump steak
runabout [rœnabawt] *nm Naut* runabout, speedboat
rune [ryn] *nf Ling* rune
runique [rynik] *adj* runic
rupestre [rypɛstr] *adj* **dessins rupestres** rock drawings; **peintures rupestres** cave paintings; **plantes rupestres** rock plants
rupin, -ine [rypɛ̃, -in] *F* **1** *adj* (*riche*) (*personne*) loaded; (*logement*) plush **2** *n* **c'est un r.** he's loaded, he's rolling in it; **les rupins** the rich, the well-off
rupiner [rypine] *vi Arg* **r. à un examen** to do well in an exam
rupteur [ryptœr] *nm Él* contact breaker, circuit breaker; *Aut* **r. (d'allumage)** make-and-break
rupture [ryptyr] *nf* (**a**) (*d'une corde, d'une poutre etc*) breaking; (*d'un barrage*) bursting; (*d'un vaisseau sanguin, un ligament*) rupture; (*d'un os*) fracture

(**b**) (*d'une surface etc*) breaking up; *Mil* **obus de r.** armour-piercing shell

(**c**) *Fig* (*de négociations*) breaking off (**de** of), breakdown (**de** in); (*de relations diplomatiques*) severance, breaking off; (*d'un marché*) calling off; **la r. de ses fiançailles** the breaking off of his/her engagement; *Jur* **r. de contrat/de promesse de mariage** breach of contract/of promise; **r. abusive** (*de contrat*) breach; *Pol* **être en r. avec le parti** to be at odds with *or* in disagreement with the party; **en r. avec la tradition** in a break with tradition; **il y a eu r. entre eux** they've quarrelled, there's been a split between them, there is a rift between them; **scène de r.** break-up scene; **la r. de la princesse et de son époux** the break-up of the princess and her husband; **lors de leur r.** when they broke up *or* split up; *Él* **r. du circuit** breaking of *or* break in the circuit; **r. de l'alimentation** power outage
▶ **rupture**: **r. d'anévrisme** ruptured aneurism; *Com* **r. de charge** transhipment of cargo; **r. de stock** stock outage; **magasin en r. de stock** shop that is out of stock
rural, -ale, -aux, -ales [ryral, -o] **1** *adj* (*région*) rural; (*vie*) country, rural; **chemin r.** country lane **2** *n* country person; **les ruraux** country people
ruse [ryz] *nf* ruse, trick; **une r. pour faire qch** a trick for doing sth; **la r.** (*habileté*) cunning; **gagner par la r.** to win by trickery *or* a trick; **obtenir qch par r.** to obtain sth by a ruse *or* a trick *or* by cunning; **r. de guerre** stratagem (of war); *Fig* crafty trick; **c'est une de mes ruses de guerre pour ne pas payer** it's one of my dodges to get out of paying; *Fig* **r. d'Indien** crafty *or* cunning trick
rusé, -ée [ryze] **1** *adj* cunning, crafty, wily; **r. comme un renard** cunning as a fox **2** *n* **c'est une (petite) rusée** she's a crafty *or* cunning little thing
ruser [ryze] *vi* to use trickery *or* cunning
rush [rœʃ] *nm* (**a**) *Sp* (*à la fin d'une course*) sprint, spurt (**b**) *F* (*de la foule*) rush (**c**) *Cin* **rushes** rushes, dailies
russe [rys] **1** *adj* Russian **2** *nm Ling* Russian **3** *n* **R.** Russian
Russie [rysi] *nf* Russia; **R. blanche** White Russia
russification [rysifikasjɔ̃] *nf* Russification, Russianization
russifier [rysifje] *vt* (*pr sub & impf* **n. russifiions**) to Russify, to Russianize
rustaud, -aude [rysto, -od] **1** *adj* uncouth **2** *n* (country) bumpkin, *Am* hick
rusticité [rystisite] *nf* (**a**) rusticity, *Péj* uncouthness (**b**) *Agr* (*d'une plante*) hardiness
rustine® [rystin] *nf* repair patch (*for mending inner tube of bicycle*); **mettre une r.** to mend a puncture; **boîte à rustines** repair kit
rustique [rystik] **1** *adj* (**a**) (*manières, vie, maison etc*) rustic; **mobilier r.** rustic(-style) *or* country-style furniture; **petit pont de bois r.** little rustic bridge (**b**) *Constr* **ouvrage r.** rustic (stone)work (**c**) *Agr* (*plante*) hardy **2** *nm* rustic *or* country look
rustre [rystr] *Péj* **1** *adj* uncouth, oafish **2** *nm* oaf, boor, lout
rut [ryt] *nm Zool* (*de mâle*) rut(ting); (*de femelle*) heat; **en r.** rutting; (*femelle*) in *or* on heat
rutabaga [rytabaga] *nm* swede, *Am* rutabaga
ruthénium [rytenjɔm] *nm Ch* ruthenium
rutilance [rytilɑ̃s] *nf* gleam; (*rouge*) red glow
rutilant [rytilɑ̃] *adj* gleaming; (*rouge*) glowing red
rutilement [rytilmɑ̃] *nm* gleam; (*rouge*) red glow

rutiler [rytile] *vi* to gleam; (*rouge*) to glow red

rythme [ritm] *nm Mus, Littér* rhythm; **r. cardiaque/respiratoire** heart/breathing rate; **le r. de la vie moderne** the tempo *or* pace of modern life; **il te faudra changer de r.** you'll need to change pace *or F* to move up/down a gear; **travailler à un r. régulier** to work at a steady rhythm *or* pace; *Mus* **marquer le r.** to beat time; **suivre le r.** to follow the beat; *Fig* to keep up with the times; **avoir le sens du r.** to have a sense of rhythm; **avoir le r. dans la peau** to have a natural sense of rhythm, to have rhythm; **ce film manque de r.** the film is a bit slow *or* lacks pace; *Com* **r. des livraisons** delivery rate; **r. de production** rate of production; **à quel r. dois-je te les envoyer?** what rate should I send them to you at?; **au r. de trois par semaine** at the rate of three a week; **à ce r., nous n'aurons pas fini ce soir** at this rate we won't have finished by this evening; **r. biologique** biorhythm

rythmé [ritme] *adj* rhythmic, rhythmical

rythmer [ritme] *vt* (*mouvement, phrase etc*) to put rhythm into, to give rhythm to; **le prof a rythmé la chanson avec une baguette** the teacher tapped out the beat of the song with a stick; **je n'ai pas pu m'empêcher de r. la chanson du pied** I couldn't help tapping my foot to the song

rythmique [ritmik] **1** *adj* rhythmic(al); **section r.** (*dans un orchestre de jazz*) rhythm section **2** *nf* rhythmics

S

S, s [ɛs] *nm* (the letter) S, s; **faire des s** to zigzag; **la route fait des s sur plusieurs kilomètres** the road zigzags for several kilometres; **en S** S-shaped; **sentier/route en s** winding *or* zigzagging path/road
S. (a) (*abrév* **Sud**) S (b) (*abrév* **seconde**) sec
sa [sa] *adj poss voir* **son**[1]
S.A. [ɛsa] *nf* (*abrév* **Société Anonyme**) plc
Saba [saba] *nf* **la reine de S.** the Queen of Sheba
sabaye [sabɛj] *nf Naut* mooring rope; (*pour remorquer*) towline
sabayon [sabajɔ̃] *nm Culin* zabaglione
sabbat [saba] *nm* **(a)** (Jewish) Sabbath; **jour du s.** Sabbath (day); **observer/violer le s.** to keep/break the Sabbath **(b)** (*assemblée nocturne*) (*de sorcières*) sabbath; *Litt* **il s'éleva dans la nuit un s. de miaulements et de feulements** a caterwauling sound rent the night air
sabbatique [sabatik] *adj* **(a)** *Rel* (*repos*) sabbatical **(b)** (*d'universitaire*) (*année, congé*) sabbatical; **prendre un an de congé s., prendre un congé s. d'un an** to take a year's sabbatical, to take a sabbatical year
sabin, -ine [sabɛ̃, -in] *Antiq* **1** *adj* Sabine **2** *n* **S.** Sabine; **l'enlèvement des Sabines** the rape of the Sabine women
sabir [sabir] *nm Ling* lingua franca, *F* gibberish; *F* **parler dans un drôle de s.** to talk gibberish
sablage [sablaʒ] *nm* **(a)** *Ind* (*de bâtiment*) sandblasting **(b)** (*de routes*) sanding, gritting
sable[1] [sabl] **1** *nm* sand; **plage de s.** sandy beach; **dune de s.** sand dune; **tempête de s.** sandstorm; *Naut* **fond de s.** sandy bottom; **bac à s.** (*pour enfants*) sandpit, *Am* sandbox; *Constr* **s. liant** *ou* **mordant** sharp sand; *Tech* **s. de fer** fine iron filings; *Fig* **bâtir sur du s.** to build on sand; *Fig* **ce fut le grain de s. dans l'engrenage** that threw a spanner in the works; *Fig F* **être sur le s.** (*sans travail*) to be out of work *or* a job; (*démuni*) to be down and out; *F* **mettre qn sur le s.** to ruin sb **2** *adj inv* sand-coloured, sandy
▶ **sable**: **sables mouvants** quicksands
sable[2] *nm Hér* sable
sablé [sable] *Culin* **1** *adj* **pâte sablée** sweet shortcrust pastry **2** *nm* = shortbread
sabler [sable] *vt* **(a)** (*chemin etc*) to sand; (*route verglacée*) to grit **(b)** (*bâtiment*) to sandblast **(c)** *F* **s. le champagne** to break open a bottle of champagne
sableuse [sabløz] *nf* sandblaster, sand jet
sableux, -euse [sablø, -øz] *adj* sandy
sablier [sablije] *nm* hourglass; *Culin* egg timer
sablière[1] [sablijɛr] *nf* **(a)** (*carrière*) sand quarry **(b)** (*de locomotive*) sand box
sablière[2] *nf Constr etc* (lengthwise) beam, stringer
sablonneux, -euse [sablɔnø, -øz] *adj* sandy
sablonnière [sablɔnjɛr] *nf* sand quarry
sabord [sabɔr] *nm Naut* porthole; **s. de charge** cargo door; *F Vieilli* **mille sabords!** shiver my timbers!
sabordage [sabɔrdaʒ] *nm*, **sabordement** [sabɔrdəmɑ̃] *nm Naut* scuttling; *Fig* (*d'entreprise*) scuppering
saborder [sabɔrde] **1** *vt* (*navire*) to scuttle; *Fig* (*détruire*) (*projet, entreprise etc*) to scupper **2 se saborder** *vpr Naut* to scuttle one's ship; *Fig* (*se ruiner*) to bring about one's own downfall; **ce n'est pas possible, il est en train de se s.** (*d'un étudiant, postulant*) it's unbelievable the way he's scuppering his chances
sabot [sabo] *nm* **(a)** clog; *F* **je vous vois venir avec vos gros sabots** I can see what you're after, I can see you coming a mile off; *F* **elle a les deux pieds dans le même s.** she just sits back and waits for things to happen; **elle n'a pas les deux pieds dans le même s.** she's always on her toes
(b) *F Vieilli* old *or* useless article; (*navire*) old tub; (*voiture*) old crock *or* banger; **il joue/chante/danse comme un s.** he can't play/sing/dance to save his life; **elle travaille comme un s.** she makes a botch of everything
(c) (*d'un cheval etc*) hoof
(d) *Tech* (*de meuble*) caster socket; **s. d'arrêt** chock; **s. de frein** brake shoe; *Aut* **s. de Denver** Denver boot, wheel clamp; **mettre un s. de Denver à une voiture** to (wheel-)clamp a car; *Aut* **s. (de pare-chocs)** overrider; *Phot* **s.-contact** hot shoe
(e) (*toupie*) (whipping) top
(f) *Bot* **s. de Vénus** lady's slipper
sabotage [sabɔtaʒ] *nm* sabotage; **un s., un acte de s.** an act of sabotage; **l'accident était dû à un s.** the accident was caused by (an act of) sabotage; **le s. d'un plan de paix** the sabotage *or* sabotaging of a peace plan; **c'est du s.!** (*d'un travail*) it's sabotage!
saboter [sabɔte] *vt* (*voiture, entreprise, plan de paix etc*) to sabotage; *F* (*travail*) to botch (up), to make a mess of
saboteur, -euse [sabɔtœr, -øz] *n* (*d'une voiture, un train etc*) saboteur; (*d'un travail*) botcher
sabre [sabr] *nm* sabre, *US* saber; **s. d'abordage** cutlass; **s. au clair** with drawn sword; *Fig* **le s. et le goupillon** the Army and the Church
sabrer [sabre] **1** *vt* **(a)** (*personne*) to cut with a sword; *F* (*raccourcir*) (*manuscrit, pièce de théâtre*) to slash, to make drastic cuts in; *F* (*critiquer*) (*personne, pièce de théâtre*) to slate; *F* (*renvoyer*) (*employé*) to sack; **la cicatrice qui sabrait sa joue** the scar that cut across his face; *F* **l'article a été complètement sabré** the article has been cut to pieces; **plusieurs pages ont été sabrées** several pages have been cut **(b)** *F* (*gâcher*) (*travail*) to botch **2** *vi F* **se faire s.** (*d'un étudiant*) to flunk; **il s'est fait s. par le prof** the teacher flunked him
sabreur [sabrœr] *nm* swordsman; *Sp* fencer
sac[1] [sak] *nm* **(a)** bag; (*plus grand*) sack; **s. de** *ou* **en papier** paper bag *or Am* sack; (*grand*) paper *or Am* grocery bag; **s. en plastique** plastic *or Br F* poly bag; **s. à blé** grain sack; **contre trois sacs de blé** for three sacks of wheat; **s. à bandoulière** shoulder bag; **porter un s. en bandoulière** to wear a bag slung over *or* across one's shoulder; **s. à dos, s. de campeur** rucksack, *Am* backpack; **partir s. au dos** to set off with one's rucksack on one's back *or* with one's backpack; **s. de sable** *ou* **de terre** sandbag; **course en s.** sack race; *F* **un s. de nœuds** *ou* **d'embrouilles** a muddle; **c'est un vrai s. de nœuds, cette histoire** I can't make head (n)or tail of this business; *Fig* **prendre qn la main dans le s.** to catch sb red-handed; *Boxe F* **travailler le s.** to practise with the punchbag *or Am* punching bag; *F* **habillé comme un s.** dressed like a tramp; *F* **je les mets tous dans le même s.** they're as bad as each other, they're all tarred with the same brush; *F* **vider son s.** to get it off one's chest; (*avouer*) to come clean; *F* **l'affaire est dans le s.** it's in the bag; *très F Vieilli* **remplir son s.** to fill one's belly; *Arg* **ils ont le s., il y a le s.** they're loaded, they're rolling in it; *Arg* **faire** *ou* **gagner son s.** to make one's pile; *Arg* **épouser le (gros) s.** to marry money
(b) *Arg* ten francs; **dix sacs** a hundred francs
(c) *Anat, Bot* sac
(d) (*d'un marsupial*) pouch
(e) *Tex* (*jute*) sackcloth; **sous le s. et la cendre** in sackcloth and ashes
(f) *Can Fb* quarterback sack
▶ **sac**: **s. de blanchisserie** laundry bag; **s. de couchage** sleeping bag; **s. d'écolier** schoolbag; *Mil* **s. de fantassin** pack, knapsack; **s. à fourrages** nosebag; **s. à main** handbag, *Am* purse; **s. à malices** bag of tricks; *Naut* **s. (de) marin** kitbag; *Mil* **s. à munitions** cartridge pouch; *Vieilli* **s. de nuit** travel *or* overnight bag; *F* **s. d'os** bag of bones; **ce n'est plus qu'un s. d'os** he's nothing but skin and bones; **s. à ouvrage** work bag; **s. de plage** beach bag; **s. poubelle** (*petit*) bin liner; (*grand*) *Am* garbage bag, *Br* bin bag; **s. à poussière** (*d'un aspirateur*) dust bag; **s. à provisions** shopping bag; *Mil* **s. de soldat** pack, knapsack; *Av* **s. à vent** windsock; *F* **s. à viande** sleeping bag; *F* **s. à vin** boozer, drunk; **s. de voyage** travel *or* overnight bag
sac[2] *nm* sacking, pillage; **mettre une ville à s.** to sack *or* plunder a town; **mettre une maison à s.** to ransack a house; **mise à s. d'une maison** ransacking of a house
saccade [sakad] *nf* jerk, jolt; **par saccades** in *or* by fits and

starts; **parler par saccades** to speak jerkily *or* in short bursts, to have a staccato style of delivery
saccadé [sakade] *adj (mouvement, progression)* jerky; *(style, voix, débit)* jerky, staccato; **respiration saccadée** irregular breathing
saccader [sakade] *vt Équitation (cheval)* to jerk
saccage [sakaʒ] *nm* havoc, devastation; **ils se livrèrent à un s. systématique du centre-ville** they engaged in the systematic destruction of the town centre
saccager [sakaʒe] *vt* **(je saccageai(s); n. saccageons) (a)** *(ville)* to wreak havoc in, to devastate; *(pour piller)* to sack; *(maison etc)* to ransack; *(vandaliser)* to vandalize **(b)** to wreak havoc in, to turn upside down; **ils ont tout saccagé dans la maison** *(mis en désordre)* they turned the whole house upside down; **les cultures furent saccagées par l'orage** the crops were devastated by the storm
saccageur, -euse [sakaʒœr, -øz] *n* looter, plunderer
saccharin [sakarɛ̃] *adj* saccharine
saccharine [sakarin] *nf Ch etc* saccharin(e)
saccharose [sakaroz] *nm Ch* saccharose
sacerdoce [sasɛrdɔs] *nm Rel* priesthood, ministry; *Fig* vocation; *Fig* **l'enseignement est un s.** teaching is a real vocation *or* calling
sacerdotal, -ale, -aux, -ales [sasɛrdɔtal, -o] *adj* priestly
sachem [saʃɛm] *nm (chef indien d'Amérique)* sachem, sagamore
sachet [saʃɛ] *nm (de levure, café instantané, lait en poudre)* sachet; **s. de lavande** lavender bag *or* sachet; **s. de thé** teabag; **thé en sachets** teabags; **je n'achète jamais mon thé en sachets** I never buy teabags; **s. pour garniture périodique** sanitary disposal bag
sacoche [sakɔʃ] *nf* **(a)** *(de vélo etc)* saddlebag **(b)** *(besace)* bag; *(pour ordinateur portable)* carrier; **s. du facteur** postman's bag; **s. à outils** tool bag; **s. à courrier** mail bag **(c)** *Belg, Can* handbag, *Am* purse
sacquer [sake] *très F* **1** *vt* **(a)** *(renvoyer) (qn)* to sack; **se faire s.** to be sacked, to get the sack **(b)** *Scol (noter sévèrement) (élève)* to mark strictly; **je me suis encore fait s. par le prof!** I got another rotten mark from the teacher! **(c)** *(supporter)* **je ne peux pas les s.** I can't stomach them, I hate their guts **2** *vi Scol* to be a tough marker
sacral, -ale, -aux, -ales [sakral, -o] *adj* sacred
sacraliser [sakralize] *vt* to consider sacred; **s. la liberté** to consider freedom to be sacred, to consider freedom as something sacred
sacramentel, -elle [sakramɑ̃tɛl] *adj Rel* sacramental; *Fig* solemn, binding
sacrant [sakrɑ̃] *adj Can Sl* **au plus s.** pdq (= *pretty damn quick*)
sacre [sakr] *nm (d'un roi)* coronation; *(d'un prêtre)* consecration; *Fig* rite; **recevoir le prix Goncourt, c'est le s. pour un écrivain** being awarded the prix Goncourt is the crowning achievement of a writer's career
sacré[1] [sakre] **1** *adj* **(a)** *Rel (vase, lieu, art, musique etc), Fig* sacred; **les ordres sacrés** holy orders; *Fig* **pour lui, rien n'est s.** nothing is sacred to him; **elle a le feu s.** she is truly inspired; *F* **il lui faut son cigare après le dîner, c'est s.!** he has to have his cigar after dinner, it's sacred!

(b) *F (maudit)* damn(ed), bloody; **j'en ai assez de ce s. voisin** I've had enough of that bloody man next door; **il a un s. culot!** he's got a bloody cheek!; **s. nom de Dieu** *ou* **d'un chien** *ou* **d'une pipe!** damn and blast it!; **s. Paul, qu'est-ce qu'il va encore inventer?** whatever is that Paul going to come up with next?; **s. Paul, qu'est-ce qu'on ferait sans lui?** good old Paul, what would we do without him?; **il a une sacrée chance** he's damn(ed) *or* bloody lucky; **elle a eu une sacrée vie** she's had quite a life

2 *nm* the sacred
sacré[2] *adj Anat* sacral
Sacré-Cœur [sakrekœr] *nm Rel* Sacred Heart (of Jesus)
sacredieu [sakrədjø], **sacrebleu** [sakrəblø], **sacredié** [sakrədje] *int Vieilli* good God!
sacrement [sakrəmɑ̃] *nm Rel* sacrament; **le saint S.** the Blessed Sacrament; **recevoir les sacrements** to receive the sacraments; *Fig F* **elle le promène comme le saint S.** she shows it off as if it was the crown jewels
sacrément [sakremɑ̃] *adv F* damn(ed), bloody; **il fait s. chaud** it's damn(ed) *or* bloody hot; **elle a s. bien répondu** she gave a damn(ed) *or* bloody good answer
sacrer [sakre] **1** *vt (roi)* to crown; *(prêtre)* to consecrate; **s. qn roi/empereur** to crown sb king/emperor; *Fig* **il a été sacré meilleur acteur de l'année 1995** he was named best actor of 1995; **il a été sacré champion de France en 1995** he won the French championship in 1995 **2** *vi F Vieilli* to curse and swear
sacrifiable [sakrifjabl] *adj* expendable
sacrificateur, -trice [sakrifikatœr, -tris] *n* sacrificer; **grand s.** (Jewish) High Priest
sacrifice [sakrifis] *nm* sacrifice; *Rel* **le saint s.** mass; **ça a dû être un s.** that must have been a sacrifice; **offrir qch en s.** to offer up sth as a sacrifice; **faire à qn le s. de sa vie** to sacrifice one's life for sb; **s'il a réussi, c'est au s. de sa santé** he succeeded, but it was at the cost of his health *or* it cost him his health; **faire des sacrifices** to make sacrifices; **esprit de s.** spirit of self-sacrifice; **je n'ai pas le goût du s.** I have no desire for self-sacrifice
sacrifier [sakrifje] *(impf, pr sub* **n. sacrifiions, v. sacrifiiez) 1** *vt (victime)* to sacrifice; *(temps, argent, carrière etc)* to sacrifice, to give up **(à** for, to); *Com* **s. des marchandises** to sell goods at rock-bottom prices; **sacrifié** *(prix)* rock-bottom; *(article)* at a rock-bottom price; **il a réussi en sacrifiant sa santé** he succeeded at the cost of his health; **s. sa vie pour son pays** to sacrifice *or* lay down one's life for one's country; **s. sa vie à une cause** to devote one's (entire) life to a cause

2 *vi* **s. aux idoles** to sacrifice to idols; **s. à la mode** to be a slave to fashion

3 se sacrifier *vpr* to sacrifice oneself **(pour** for); **se s. pour la bonne cause** to sacrifice oneself in a good cause; **allez, d'accord, je me sacrifie et je vais les chercher à la gare!** OK, I'll be the martyr and pick them up from the station
sacrilège[1] [sakrilɛʒ] *nm* sacrilege; **ce serait un s. que de …** it would be sacrilege to …
sacrilège[2] **1** *adj (action, pensée etc)* sacrilegious **2** *n* sacrilegious person
sacristain [sakristɛ̃] *nm* **(a)** *Rel* sacristan **(b)** *Culin* = small flaky pastry
sacristi [sakristi] *int Arch* good Lord!
sacristie [sakristi] *nf Rel* sacristy, vestry
sacro-saint [sakrɔsɛ̃] *adj* sacrosanct; *Iron* sacrosanct, precious
sacrum [sakrɔm] *nm Anat* sacrum
sadique [sadik] **1** *adj* sadistic **2** *n* sadist
sadisme [sadism] *nm* sadism
sadomaso [sadɔmazo] *F* **1** *adj inv* sadomasochistic; **il a des tendances s.** he's into S & M, he has S & M tendencies **2** *n inv* sadomasochist; **c'est un s.** he's into S & M
sadomasochisme [sadɔmazɔʃism] *nm Psy* sadomasochism
sadomasochiste [sadɔmazɔʃist] *Psy* **1** *adj* sadomasochistic **2** *n* sadomasochist
saducéen, -enne [sadyseɛ̃, -ɛn] *n* Sadducee
safari [safari] *nm* safari; **en s.** on safari; **s.-photo** photographic safari
safran[1] [safrɑ̃] **1** *nm* **(a)** *Bot* saffron, crocus **(b)** *Culin etc* saffron **2** *adj inv* **(jaune) s.** saffron (yellow)
safran[2] *nm Naut* rudder blade
safrané [safrane] *adj* saffron(-coloured *or US* -colored); *Culin (riz)* saffron(-flavoured *or US* -flavored)
safraner [safrane] *vt Culin* to flavour *or US* flavor with saffron
saga [saga] *nm Littér, Fig* saga
sagace [sagas] *adj* astute, shrewd
sagacité [sagasite] *nf* shrewdness, astuteness; **avec s.** shrewdly, astutely; **faire preuve de s.** to be shrewd; **pour une fois, il a fait preuve de s.** for once, he behaved shrewdly
sagaie [sagɛ] *nf* assegai
sage [saʒ] **1** *adj* **(a)** *(avisé) (politique, personne, décision etc)* wise, sensible; **une politique peu s.** an unwise policy, not a very sensible policy; **il serait plus s. de faire ceci** it would be wiser *or* more sensible to do this

(b) *(enfant)* good, well-behaved; *(animal)* quiet, docile; *(tenue, conduite)* sober; *(robe)* demure; **quand tu seras plus s.** when you're better behaved, once you start behaving yourself; **l'école l'a rendu s.** school has quietened him down; **sois s.!** be good!, behave yourself!; **s. comme une image** as good as gold; **il n'est pas s. du tout, ce petit** that child is very badly behaved; **il porte toujours des tenues très sages** he always dresses very soberly *or* quietly; **la mode de cette année est très s.** the demure look is in this year

(c) *(chaste)* good; **j'étais très s. pendant ma jeunesse** I was a very good girl when I was young; **elle n'a pas été très s. à cette époque-là!** she was a bit wild then!

2 *nm* wise man; *Phil* sage; **un vieux s.** a wise old man; *Pol* **comité des sages** committee of wise men
sage-femme, *pl* **sages-femmes** *nf* midwife
sagement [saʒmɑ̃] *adv* **(a)** *(raisonnablement)* wisely, sensibly **(b)** *(tranquillement)* quietly
sagesse [saʒɛs] *nf* **(a)** *(prudence, connaissance)* wisdom; **elle a eu la s. de ne pas en parler** she was wise *or* sensible enough not to mention it; **plein de s.** *(remarque)* very sensible; *(décision)* very sensible *or* wise; **agir avec s.** to act wisely *or* sensibly; *Fig* **la voix de la s.** the voice of reason **(b)** *(calme)* good behaviour *or US* behavior; **la maîtresse lui reproche sa trop grande s.** the teacher says he's too well behaved; **ma grand-mère était d'une s. exemplaire pendant sa jeunesse** my grandmother was anything but

wild as a girl; **on le disait d'une très grande s.** he was said to be very well behaved

sagittaire [saʒitɛr] *nm Astron, Astrol* **le S.** Sagittarius, the Archer; **être (du signe du) S.** to be (a) Sagittarius *or* (a) Sagittarian

sagou [sagu] *nm* sago

sagouin [sagwɛ̃] *nm* **(a)** (*singe*) squirrel monkey **(b)** *F* slovenly *or* dirty individual; **travailler comme un s.** to be a sloppy worker; **manger comme un s.** to eat like a pig; **vieux s.** revolting old man

Sahara (le) [ləsaara] *nm* the Sahara (Desert)

saharien, -ienne [saarjɛ̃, -jɛn] **1** *adj* Saharan; (*troupes*) desert; **température saharienne** scorching *or* sizzling temperature **2** *n* **S.** Saharan **3** *nf* **saharienne** safari jacket

Sahel [saɛl] *nm* Sahel

sahib [saib] *nm* sahib

sahraoui, -ie [sarawi] **1** *adj* of the Western Sahara **2** *n* **S.** native of the Western Sahara

saignant [sɛɲɑ̃] *adj* **(a)** (*blessure*) bleeding **(b)** *Culin* (*viande*) rare

saignée [seɲe] *nf* **(a)** *Méd, Arch* blood-letting; *Fig* drain; **la guerre fut une véritable s. pour le pays** the country suffered great losses in the war; *Méd Arch* **faire une s. à qn** to bleed sb; **faire une s. dans un arbre** (*pour récolter du caoutchouc etc*) to tap a tree **(b)** *Anat* (*pli*) bend of the arm *or* the knee **(c)** (*rigole*) (drainage) trench, ditch; *MecE* (*pour l'huile etc*) groove; *Constr* (*dans un mur, pour un tuyau, un câble etc*) hole

saignement [sɛɲ(ə)mɑ̃] *nm* bleeding; **s. de nez** nosebleed; **elle souffre de saignements de nez** she suffers from nosebleeds

saigner [seɲe] **1** *vi* (*d'une personne, d'une blessure etc*) to bleed; **mon doigt saigne** my finger is bleeding; **je saigne du nez** my nose is bleeding, I have a nosebleed; **elle a tendance à s. du nez** she tends to get nosebleeds; **la chaleur le fait s. du nez** heat makes his nose bleed *or* gives him nosebleeds; *Fig* **c'est une plaie qui saigne encore** it's an open wound, it still rankles; *Fig Litt* **mon cœur saigne, le cœur m'en saigne** it makes my heart bleed

2 *vt Agr* (*poulet*), *Méd Arch* (*personne*) to bleed; **s. un porc** to stick a pig; **s. à blanc** (*animal*) to bleed white; **s. un arbre** to tap a tree; **s. un fossé** to drain a ditch; *Fig* **s. qn/un pays (à blanc)** to bleed sb/a country white *or* dry

3 se saigner *vpr Fig* **se s. aux quatre membres** *ou* **aux quatre veines** to make enormous sacrifices, to bleed oneself white *or* dry

saigneur [sɛɲœr] *nm* **(a)** (*d'animaux*) slaughterer, slaughterman **(b)** (*de caoutchouc*) tree tapper, collector of rubber

saillant [sajɑ̃] **1** *adj* (*toit, corniche etc*) projecting, jutting out; (*pommettes*) prominent, high; (*muscles*) bulging; *Fig* (*trait, caractéristique etc*) striking, outstanding, salient; **angle s.** (*d'une fortification*) salient angle; **les faits saillants de sa vie** the notable *or* noteworthy events of his life; **les faits saillants de l'année** the highlights of the year **2** *nm Mil* salient

saillie [saji] *nf* **(a)** (*partie en avant*) protrusion; *Archit, Constr* projection; **en s.** projecting, jutting out; **s. du mollet** swell of the calf; **faire s.** to project, to jut out **(b)** (*dans l'élevage*) (*par un mâle*) covering **(c)** *Litt* sally, flash of wit

saillir [sajir] **1** *vt* (*prp* **saillissant**; *pp* **sailli**; *pr ind* **je saillis, n. saillissons**; *fu* **je saillirai**) (*dans l'élevage*) (*femelle*) to cover **2** *vi* (*used only in prp* **saillant**; *pp* **sailli**; *pr ind* **il saille, ils saillent**; *fu* **il saillera**) to project, to jut out (**sur** over); **la poutre saille de 25 cm** the beam projects 25 cm

sain, saine [sɛ̃, sɛn] *adj* **(a)** (*personne, climat, exercice, maison, relations*) healthy; (*cheval, fruit, bois, gestion etc*) sound; (*nourriture*) healthy, wholesome; (*économie, affaire*) healthy, sound; **un esprit s. dans un corps s.** a healthy mind in a healthy body; **s. de corps et d'esprit** sound in mind and body; **s. et sauf** safe and sound **(b)** *Naut* (*côte, ancrage*) safe

saindoux [sɛ̃du] *nm Culin* lard

sainement [sɛnmɑ̃] *adv* **(a)** (*salubrement*) healthily **(b)** (*raisonnablement*) (*juger*) sensibly

saint, sainte [sɛ̃, sɛ̃t] **1** *adj* **(a)** *Rel* (*lieu, guerre etc*) holy; (*personne, vie*) saintly, holy; **la Sainte Église** the Holy Church; **semaine sainte** Holy Week; **le Vendredi s.** Good Friday; **une sainte action** a pious deed; **faire œuvre sainte** to do good works; **la Terre sainte** the Holy Land; **la Sainte Vierge** the Blessed Virgin; **une petite sainte vierge en ivoire** an ivory miniature of the Blessed Virgin; **le s. patron des horlogers** the patron saint of watch-makers; *Fig* **être saisi** *ou* **pris d'une sainte colère/indignation** to be seething with righteous anger/indignation; *F* **j'en ai une sainte horreur!** I hate *or* loathe it!; *F* **elle ne fait rien de toute la sainte journée** she doesn't do a thing the whole blessed day

(b) s. Pierre St Peter; **sainte Catherine** St Catherine; **l'église S.-Pierre de Rome** St Peter's (church); **la S. Georges** St George's day; *Can F* **du mouvement, Sainte Bénite!** get a move on, for Pete's sake!

2 *n Rel, Fig* saint; **s. d'une ville** patron saint of a town; **il lasserait la patience d'un s.** he would try the patience of a saint; **elle prêche pour son s.** she has an axe to grind; **ne savoir plus à quel s. se vouer** to be at one's wits' end, not to know which way to turn; *Hum* **il vaut mieux s'adresser à Dieu qu'à ses saints** it's best to go right to the top; *Fig F* **c'est un petit s.** he's a prig; *F* **arrête de faire ton petit s.!** stop being such a prig!; *Rel* **les Saints du dernier jour** the Latter-day Saints

3 *nm* **le S. des Saints** the Holy of Holies; *Fig* the inner sanctum; *Hum* the holy of holies, the sanctum sanctorum

saint-bernard [sɛ̃bɛrnar] *nm inv* (*chien*) St Bernard; *F* **c'est un vrai s.** he's a good Samaritan

Saint-Cyr [sɛ̃sir] *nm* Saint-Cyr military academy

Saint-Cyrien, *pl* **Saint-Cyriens** [sɛ̃sirjɛ̃] *nm* cadet training at Saint-Cyr

Saint-Domingue [sɛ̃dɔmɛ̃g] *nm* Santo Domingo

Sainte-Croix *n* **l'île S.** Santa Cruz island

Sainte-Hélène *n* St Helena

Saint-Elme [sɛ̃ɛlm] *nm* **feu S.** St Elmo's fire

Sainte-Lucie *n* St Lucia

saintement [sɛ̃tmɑ̃] *adv* in a saintly way; **vivre s.** to lead a saintly life, to live like a saint; **mourir s.** to die a saintly death, to die like a saint; **elle s'est toujours conduite très s.** she has always behaved like a saint

sainte-nitouche, *pl* **saintes-nitouches** *nf* little hypocrite; **prendre des airs de s.** to look as if butter wouldn't melt in one's mouth; **avec des airs de s.** looking as if butter wouldn't melt in his/her/*etc* mouth

Saint-Esprit [sɛ̃tɛspri] *nm* **le S.** the Holy Ghost, the Holy Spirit

sainteté [sɛ̃t(ə)te] *nf* (*d'une personne*) holiness, saintliness; (*de la loi, d'un serment*) sanctity; (*d'un lieu*) holiness, sanctity; *Rel* **sa S. (le pape)** His Holiness (the Pope)

saint-frusquin [sɛ̃fryskɛ̃] *nm* (*no pl*) *F* **tout le s.** the whole caboodle; **il s'est pointé avec ses disquettes, ses livres et tout son s.** he turned up with his disks, his books and all the rest of his gear; *Litt* **boire (tout) son s.** to waste one's substance with riotous living

saint-glinglin (à la) [alasɛ̃glɛ̃glɛ̃] *adv F* **jusqu'à la s.** till the cows come home, till doomsday; **on sera payé à la s.** we'll be paid when pigs fly; **repoussé à la s.** postponed indefinitely

Saint-Graal (le) *nm Littér* the (Holy) Grail

saint-honoré, *pl* **saint-honoré(s)** *nm* Saint-Honoré (*choux pastry ring filled with confectioner's custard*)

Saint-Jean (la) *nf* Midsummer Day

Saint-Laurent (le) *nm Géog* the St Lawrence (river); **la Voie maritime du S.** the St Lawrence Seaway

saint-marcellin, *pl* **saint-marcellins** [sɛ̃marsəlɛ̃] *nm* = type of mild cheese

Saint-Marin *n* San Marino

Saint-Martin (la) *nf* St Martin's day, Martinmas; **l'été de la S.** Indian summer, St Martin's summer

Saint-Michel (la) *nf* Michaelmas

saint-nectaire, *pl* **saint-nectaires** *nm* = type of firm cheese

Saint-Office *nm* **le S.** *Cathol* the Holy Office; *Hist* (*l'Inquisition*) the Inquisition

Saint-Père (le) *nm Cathol* the Holy Father

saint-pierre *nm inv* (*poisson*) John Dory

Saint-Pierre-et-Miquelon [sɛ̃pjɛremiklɔ̃] *n* St Pierre and Miquelon

Saint-Siège (le) *nm Cathol* the Holy See

Saint-Simonisme [sɛ̃simɔnism] *nm Écon* Saint Simonianism, Saint-Simonism

Saint-Sylvestre (la) *nf* New Year's Eve, *Scot* Hogmanay; **faire la veillée de la S.** to see the New Year in

saisi [sezi] *nm Jur* distrainee

saisie [sezi] *nf* (*de marchandises de contrebande etc*) seizure; *Jur* seizure, *Spéc* distraint, distress; (*d'une hypothèque*) foreclosure; *Naut* embargo; **procès-verbal de s.** warrant (for seizure of property); *Ordinat* **s. de données** data capture, keyboarding; *Ordinat* **s. automatique/manuelle** automatic/manual input

saisie-arrêt, *pl* **saisies-arrêts** *nf Jur* attachment, garnishment

saisie-exécution, *pl* **saisies-exécutions** *nf Jur* distraint (*for sale by court order*)

saisine [sezin] *nf Jur* referral to a court

saisir [sezir] **1** *vt* **(a)** (*attraper*) (*personne, objet*) to take hold of, to grab, to seize; **s. qn par le bras/au collet** to grab *or* catch *or* seize sb by the arm/by the collar; **s. qn à bras-le-**

corps to seize *or F* grab sb around the waist; **s. l'occasion de faire qch** to seize *or* grasp the opportunity to do sth; **s. un prétexte pour faire qch** to seize on a pretext to do something; **s. la balle au bond** to catch the ball on the rebound; *Fig* to seize the opportunity; **la peur le saisit** fear seized *or* took hold of *or* gripped him; **être saisi d'étonnement** to be startled *or* staggered; **être saisi par le froid/la peur** to be struck by the cold/to be gripped by *or* overcome by *or* stricken with fear; **être saisi de panique** to be panic-stricken; **l'artiste a bien saisi la ressemblance** the artist has really caught *or* captured the likeness

(b) (*comprendre*) (*vérité, signification donnée par qn*) to grasp, to get; **elle a tout de suite saisi de quoi il s'agissait** she immediately grasped *or* got what it was about; **je n'ai pas saisi son nom** I didn't catch *or* get his name

(c) *Ordinat* (*données*) to capture, to keyboard, to key

(d) *Jur* (*navire, biens immobiliers*) to seize, to attach; (*marchandises*) to seize, *Spéc* to distrain upon; **s. une hypothèque** to foreclose on a mortgage

(e) *Jur* **s. un tribunal d'une affaire** to refer a matter to a court, to lay a matter before a court; **nous sommes saisis de deux questions** we have two questions before us

(f) *Culin* (*viande*) to seal

(g) *Naut* (*ancres, bateaux*) to stow, to secure

2 *vi* (*comprendre*) **je ne saisis pas bien** I don't quite get it; **il saisit vite** he's quick (on the uptake); **alors, tu saisis?** do you get it?

3 se saisir *vpr* **se s. de qn/qch** to seize *or* grab sb/sth, to take hold of sb/sth; **se s. d'un marché** to corner a market

saisissable [sezisabl] *adj* **(a)** (*distinction*) perceptible **(b)** *Jur* distrainable, attachable

saisissant, -ante [sezisɑ̃, -ɑ̃t] **1** *adj* **(a)** (*froid*) biting; (*ressemblance*) striking; (*spectacle, scène, paroles*) gripping **(b)** *Jur* (*partie*) distraining **2** *n Jur* distrainer

saisissement [sezismɑ̃] *nm* **(a)** (*sensation de froid*) sudden chill **(b)** (*émotion*) shock, rush of emotion; **pâle de s.** pale with emotion

saison [sɛzɔ̃] *nf* [ⓘ**A6-7**,d,v; **A75**,B,1,c; **B4**,A,3,c; **B58**,B,1,c] season; **très tôt en s.** very early in the season; **en cette s.** at this time of year; **en toute(s) saison(s)** all (the) year round; **la s. nouvelle** spring(time); **la mauvaise/la belle s.** the winter/summer months; **moyenne s.** shoulder period; **la s. sèche/des pluies** the dry/rainy season; **la s. des semailles** sowing time; **la haute/basse s.** the high/low season; **faire une bonne/mauvaise s.** to have a good/bad season; **la s. bat son plein** the season is in full swing *or* at its height, it is the height of the season; **le fort de la s.** the busy season *or* time (of the year); **la s. creuse, la morte s.** the off season, the slack season, the low season; **prendre ses vacances à la s. creuse** to take one's holidays off season; **voyager pendant la s. creuse** to travel off season; **la s. sportive/de la chasse** the sporting/hunting season; **la s. des amours** the mating season; **la s. des framboises** the raspberry season, the season *or* time for raspberries; **des fraises! mais ce n'est pas la s.!** strawberries! but it isn't the right time of year *or* it isn't the season for them; **être de s.** (*des fruits*) to be in season *or* seasonal; **le pull est de s.** it's the right kind of weather for sweaters; **c'est un temps de s.** it's seasonal weather, it's typical weather for the time of year; **hors de s.** (*légumes etc*) out of season; *Fig* **décidément, ses plaisanteries ne sont pas de s.** his jokes are really quite out of place; **faire une s.** (*dans une station thermale*) to take a cure; **cette robe ne me fera pas la s.** this dress won't last me the season; **travailler en s.**, *F* **faire les saisons** (*dans les lieux de vacances*) to do seasonal work

saisonnier, -ière [sɛzɔnje, -jɛr] **1** *adj* seasonal **2** *n* seasonal worker

sajou [saʒu] *nm Zool* capuchin (monkey)

saké [sake] *nm*, **saki**[1] [saki] *nm* (*boisson*) sake, saké, saki

saki[2] *nm Zool* saki (monkey)

salade [salad] *nf* **(a)** *Bot, Culin* (*plante*) lettuce **(b)** (*plat*) salad; **faire une s.** to make a salad; **s. verte** green salad; **s. de pommes de terre/de tomates/de riz** potato/tomato/rice salad; **s. composée** mixed salad; **s. niçoise** salade niçoise; **s. russe** Russian salad; **haricots verts en s.** green bean salad; **s. de fruits** fruit salad **(c)** *F* (*désordre*) mess, shambles; **quelle s.!** what a mess *or* shambles! **(d)** *F* **salades** (*mensonges*) whoppers; (*absurdités*) nonsense

saladier [saladje] *nm* salad bowl

salage [salaʒ] *nm* salting

salaire [salɛr] *nm* **(a)** [ⓘ**A10**,f,i] (*mensuel*) salary, pay; (*hebdomadaire, journalier*) wage(s), pay *Prov* **toute peine mérite s.** the labourer *or US* laborer is worthy of his hire

(b) (*récompense*) reward, recompense (**de** for); (*punition*) retribution (**de** for); **le s. du péché/de la peur** the wages of sin/of fear

▶ **salaire**: **s. annuel garanti** annual guaranteed wage/salary; **s. d'appoint** second salary; **s. de base** basic pay, basic wage/salary; **s. brut/net** gross/net pay; **s. fixe** fixed salary; **s. fixe plus commission** salary plus commission; **s. à forfait** job wage; **s. indexé** index-linked pay; **s. indirect** fringe benefits, benefit in kind; **s. légal** legal wage; **s. minimum interprofessionnel de croissance** = guaranteed minimum wage; **s. plafond** maximum wage/salary; **s. plafonné** wage/salary ceiling; **s. réel** real wage/salary, wage/salary in real terms; **s. au rendement** incentive pay; **s. à la tâche** *ou* **aux pièces** piece wage

salaison [salɛzɔ̃] *nf* (*action*) salting; **les salaisons** salted meats

salamalecs [salamalɛk] *nmpl F* bowing and scraping; **faire des s. à qn** to bow and scrape to sb

salamandre [salamɑ̃dr] *nf* **(a)** *Zool* salamander; **s. aquatique** newt **(b)** (*poêle*) salamander (stove), slow-burning *or* slow-combustion stove

salami [salami] *nm* salami

salant [salɑ̃] *adj* **marais s.** salt marsh

salarial, -ale, -aux, -ales [salarjal, -o] *adj* wage; (*mensuel*) salary; **masse salariale** wage(s) bill, payroll; **politique salariale** pay *or* wage(s) policy

salariat [salarja] *nm* **(a)** (*état*) wage-earning; **je préfère le s. au travail free-lance** I'd rather be on a salary *or* have a nine-to-five job than do freelance work **(b)** (*employés*) wage earners

salarié, -ée [salarje] **1** *adj* **(a)** (*travailleur*) (*payé mensuellement*) salaried; (*payé hebdomadairement*) wage-earning **(b)** (*travail*) paid **2** *n* (*payé mensuellement*) salaried employee; (*payé hebdomadairement*) wage earner; **salariés** (*de société*) employees

salaud [salo] *Vulg* **1** *nm* bastard; **alors là mon s., tu m'en bouches un coin!** you've gobsmacked me this time, you old bastard! **2** *adj* shitty; **un mec s.** a bastard; **ce qu'il est s.!** what a bastard he is!; **il a été très s. avec elle** he was a real bastard to her; **c'est vraiment s. de faire ça** it's a really shitty thing to do

sale [sal] **1** *adj* **(a)** (*maison, vaisselle, mains, eau etc*) dirty; (*répugnant*) filthy; *Fig* (*paroles, histoire*) dirty, filthy, coarse; *Phys Nucl* **bombe s.** dirty bomb; **industrie s.** dirty industry; *très F* **c'était pas s.!** it was pretty good!, it was quite something!

(b) *F* (*always before the noun*) (*méchant*) (*grippe, situation*) nasty; **s. gosse** little brat; **c'est un s. boulot!** it's a rotten *or* lousy job!; **faire le s. boulot** to do the dirty work; **être dans une s. affaire** to be caught up in a dirty business; **il a une s. tête** *ou* **gueule** (*antipathique*) he looks really nasty; (*malade*) he looks awful; **s. individu, s. type** nasty character, louse; **s. fasciste!** filthy Fascist!; **s. coup** dirty *or* rotten trick; **s. temps** filthy weather; **ah la s. bête!** (*cet animal*) bloody animal!; (*cette personne*) the beast!, the swine!

2 *nm F* **mettre du linge au s.** to put dirty clothes in the wash

salé [sale] **1** *adj* **(a)** (*conservé au sel*) (*poisson, viande etc*) salt; (*additionné de sel*) (*beurre, amandes etc*) salted; **eau salée** salt water; **le Grand Lac S.** the Great Salt Lake; **le potage est trop s.** the soup is too salty; **prés salés** saltings, salt meadows **(b)** *Fig* (*histoire, plaisanterie*) spicy, risqué; *F* (*condamnation*) stiff; *F* (*addition, prix*) steep **2** *nm* **le s. et le sucré** savoury food and sweet food; **petit s.** = streaky bacon

salement [salmɑ̃] *adv* **(a)** (*parler, manger, boire*) in a disgusting manner **(b)** *F* (*blessé, touché, atteint*) (very) badly; **s. difficile/douloureux** damn(ed) *or Br* bloody difficult/painful; **j'ai s. besoin d'argent** I'm badly in need of money; **ça m'aiderait s.** it would be a big *or* great help; **je suis s. fatigué** I'm dog-tired, *Br* I'm knackered, I'm pooped; **elle a s. vieilli** she's aged a hell of a lot; **il est s. amoureux** he's got it bad

saler [sale] *vt* **(a)** (*assaisonner*) to salt, to put salt in, to season with salt **(b)** (*pour conserver*) (*bacon etc*) to salt **(c)** (*route*) to salt **(d)** *F* (*client*) to rip off, to fleece; **s. la note** to bump up the bill; **on s'est fait s.** (*au restaurant*) we were ripped off *or* done; **il s'est fait s.** (*sanctionné*) he got a stiff *or* tough sentence

saleté [salte] *nf* **(a)** (*d'une personne, d'une rue, de vêtements etc*) dirtiness, filthiness; (*crasse*) dirt, filth; **la maison est d'une s. incroyable** the house is incredibly dirty *or* filthy; **le chat a fait ses saletés par terre** the cat made a mess on the floor **(b)** (*camelote*) trash, rubbish, junk; **manger des saletés** to eat junk food; **quelle s., cette grippe!** this flu is a real pain *or* nuisance! **(c)** (*chose obscène*) obscenity; (*remarque*) obscenity, obscene remark; (*blague*) obscene joke; **il m'a dit des saletés** he said dirty *or* filthy things to me **(d)** *F* (*personne*) bastard; **quelle s.!, il m'a roulé!** the bastard, he's conned me!

saleur, -euse [salœr, -øz] *n* salter
salicoque [salikɔk] *nf* prawn
salicorne [salikɔrn] *nf Bot* glasswort, saltwort
salicylate [salisilat] *nm Ch* salicylate
salicylique [salisilik] *adj Ch* (*acide*) salicylic
salière [saljɛr] *nf* **(a)** *Culin* salt cellar **(b)** *F* (*des clavicules*) salt cellar
saligaud, -aude [saligo, -od] *n très F* (*personne sale*) filthy swine, *f* slut; (*ignoble individu*) bastard, *f* bitch
salin, -ine [salɛ̃, -in] **1** *adj* (*solution, roches*) saline **2** *nm* **(a)** (*marais*) salt marsh **(b)** *Ch, Ind* saline **3** *nf* **saline (a)** (*entreprise*) salt works **(b)** (*marais*) salt marsh
salinage [salinaʒ] *nm* **(a)** (*entreprise*) salt works **(b)** (*solution*) saturated solution of salt; (*concentration*) concentrating of the brine
salinier, -ière [salinje, -jɛr] **1** *adj* (*industrie etc*) salt **2** *nm* salt producer
salinité [salinite] *nf* (*de l'eau de mer etc*) salinity, saltness
salique [salik] *adj Hist* (*loi*) Salic
salir [salir] **1** *vt* (*mains, vêtements etc*) to get *or* make dirty, to dirty, *Fml* to soil; **attention, ça salit les mains** careful, it gets *or* makes your hands dirty; **s. sa réputation** to tarnish *or* sully one's reputation; **s. le nom/la mémoire de qn** to sully *or* besmirch sb's name/memory; **s. l'idée de l'amour** to debase the idea of love **2 se salir** *vpr* to get dirty; **ça se salit facilement** it's easily dirtied, it dirties easily; *Fig* **elle n'aime pas se s. les mains** she doesn't like to get her hands dirty
salissant [salisɑ̃] *adj* **(a)** (*travail*) dirty, messy **(b)** (*tissu, vêtement, moquette etc*) easily soiled; (*couleur*) that shows the dirt
salissure [salisyr] *nf* dirty mark
salivaire [salivɛr] *adj* (*glande etc*) salivary
salivation [salivasjɔ̃] *nf* salivation
salive [saliv] *nf* saliva; *F* **pas la peine de dépenser ta s.** don't waste your breath, save your breath
saliver [salive] *vi* to salivate; **s. devant qch** to drool at the sight of sth
salle [sal] *nf* **(a)** (*pièce*) room; *Sp* **partie en s.** indoor game; **travailler en s.** (*d'un restaurant*) to work in the dining room, to be a member of the dining-room staff; **personnel de s.** (*d'un restaurant*) dining-room staff; **les salles du Louvre** the galleries of the Louvre
(b) *Th, Cin* (*auditorium*) auditorium; **faire s. comble** *ou* **pleine** to have a full house; **toute la s. applaudit** the whole audience applauded
▶ **salle**: *Cin* **s. d'art et d'essai** art cinema *or Am* movie theater; **s. d'arrivée** (*à un aéroport*) arrivals lounge; **s. d'attente** waiting room; **s. de bain(s)** bathroom; **s. de bain(s) particulière** private bathroom, en-suite bathroom; **s. de bal** ballroom; **s. de billard** billiards room, pool room; *Ordinat* **s. blanche** clean room; **s. des chaudières** boiler room; **s. de cinéma** cinema, *Am* movie theater; *Scol* **s. de classe** classroom; *Banque* **s. des coffres** vaults; **s. de composition** (*atelier*) composing room; **s. de conférences** conference room; **s. du conseil** council room *or* chamber; *Ind etc* boardroom; **s. de contrôle** (*d'un engin spatial*) control room; **s. de contrôle de production** production control room; **s. de cours** lecture room; **s. des dactylos** typing pool; *Ind* **s. de dessin** drawing office; **s. de détente** common room; *TV, Th* green room; *Can* **s. à dîner** dining room; **s. de douches** shower room; **s. d'eau** shower room; **s. d'embarquement** (*à un aéroport*) gate lounge; **s. d'exploitation radar** radar operations room; *Com* **s. d'exposition** showroom; (*pour une foire*) exhibition hall; **s. d'exposition du revendeur** dealer display room; **s. des fêtes** = community hall; (*d'un village*) village hall; *Mil* **s. de garde** guardroom; *Banque* **s. des guichets** banking hall, front office; **s. d'hôpital** (hospital) ward; *Journ* **s. d'impression** publishing room; **s. de jeux** games room; **s. de lecture** (*dans une bibliothèque*) reading room; **s. des machines** engine; *Ind* machine room; **s. à manger** dining room; (*meubles*) dining-room suite; **s. de maquillage** make-up room; *Bourse* **s. de marchés** dealing room; **s. de montage** edit suite, cutting room; **s. de musculation** fitness room, gym; **les salles obscures** the movies, *Br* the cinema; *Méd* **s. d'opération** operating theatre *or Am* room; **s. des opérations** operations room; **s. des pas perdus** (*dans une gare etc*) concourse; (*au Parlement, dans les tribunaux*) lobby; **s. de petit déjeuner** breakfast room; **s. de presse** newsroom; **s. des professeurs** staff room, common room; *Cin* **s. de projection** viewing *or* projection *or* screening room; **s. de réception** function room; **s. de rédaction** (*d'un journal*) newsroom; *Cin, TV* **s. de régie** control room; **s. de restaurant** dining room; **s. de réunion** meeting room; **s. de réveil** recovery room; **s. de séjour** living room; **s. de service** orderly rooom; **s. de télévision** TV lounge, television room; **s. du trône** throneroom; **s. des** *ou* **de ventes** saleroom, auction rooms; *Cin* **s. de vision** viewing *or* projection *or* screening room; *TV, Cin* **s. de visionnage** looking room
salmigondis [salmigɔ̃di] *nm* hotchpotch, *Am* hodgepodge
salmis [salmi] *nm Culin* salmi (*game half-cooked by roasting then stewed in a wine sauce*)
salmonella [salmɔnela] *nf inv,* **salmonelle** [salmɔnɛl] *nf Méd* salmonella
salmonellose [salmɔneloz] *nf Méd* salmonellosis, salmonella poisoning
salmoniculteur, -trice [salmɔnikyltœr, -tris] *n* salmon farmer
salmoniculture [salmɔnikyltyr] *nf* salmon farming
saloir [salwar] *nm* **(a)** (*pour salaisons*) (*pièce*) salting room; (*bac*) salting tub **(b)** *Vieilli* (*salière*) salt pot
Salomon [salɔmɔ̃] *nm* **le roi S.** King Solomon; **les îles S.** the Solomon Islands
salon [salɔ̃] *nm* **(a)** (*de maison*) living room, sitting room, *Br* lounge; **petit s.** morning room; **s. réservé** (*dans un hôtel etc*) private room; **jeux de s.** parlour *or US* parlor games; **s. VIP** VIP lounge; **s. de bridge** card room
(b) (*meuble*) suite
(c) (*dans un bateau*) saloon; (*dans un train*) saloon car
(d) *Com* **s. de thé** tea room(s), tea shop; **s. de coiffure** hairdressing salon; **s. de beauté** beauty salon
(e) (*exposition*), *Beaux-Arts* exhibition; (*du bateau, des arts ménagers etc*) show; **s.-exposition**, *pl* **salons-expositions** trade fair; **s. d'exposition du distributeur** distributor display room; **s. professionnel** trade show *or* fair; **s. spécialisé** specialized trade fair
(f) *Hist, Littér* salon; **tenir s.** to hold a salon
▶ **salon**: **le S. de l'Automobile** *ou* **de l'auto** the Motor Show; **le S. des Arts ménagers** ≈ the Ideal Home Exhibition; **le S. du Livre** the Book Fair; **le S. nautique** the Boat Show
saloon [salun] *nm* saloon (*in the Wild West*); **porte de s.** saloon door
salop [salo] = **salaud**
salopard [salɔpar] *nm très F* bastard
salope [salɔp] *Vulg* **1** *adj f* bitchy; **qu'est-ce qu'elle a été s. avec moi!** she was really bitchy *or* a real bitch to me! **2** *nf* (*femme méprisable*) bitch; (*homme méprisable*) bastard; **c'est vraiment une s., ce type!** he's a real bastard, that guy! **3** *nf* (*femme de mauvaise vie*) slut
saloperie [salɔpri] *nf Vulg* **(a)** (*camelote*) trash, rubbish, junk; **s. de montre!** what a trashy watch!; **s. de temps!** what filthy weather!; **tu ne vas pas manger cette s.!** you're not going to eat that rubbish *or* junk!; **cette grippe est une s.** this flu is a bloody pain in the neck; **il y avait toutes sortes de saloperies par terre** there was a load of trash *or* crap on the floor
(b) (*coup bas*) dirty *or* rotten trick; **il nous a fait une belle s.** he played a really dirty *or* rotten trick on us, he really did the dirty on us
(c) dire des saloperies to talk filth, to talk dirty; **elle a encore dit des saloperies sur moi** she made some more bitchy remarks about me
salopette [salɔpɛt] *nf* dungarees, *Am* overalls
salpêtrage [salpetraʒ] *nm* **(a)** (*formation*) manufacture *or* formation of saltpetre *or US* saltpeter **(b)** (*traitement*) treatment with saltpetre *or US* saltpeter
salpêtre [salpɛtr] *nm* **(a)** *Ch* saltpetre, *US* saltpeter **(b)** (*sur les murs*) saltpetre *or US* saltpeter rot
salpêtrer [salpetre] *vt* **(a)** (*sol*) to cover *or* treat with saltpetre *or US* saltpeter **(b)** (*murs*) to rot
salpicon [salpikɔ̃] *nm Culin* salpicon (*diced meat, poultry, vegetables etc in sauce, used as a filling for vol-au-vents etc*)
salpingite [salpɛ̃ʒit] *nf Méd* salpingitis
salsa [salsa] *nf Mus* salsa
salsepareille [salsəparɛj] *nf Bot, Pharm* sarsaparilla
salsifis [salsifi] *nm Bot, Culin* salsify
saltimbanque [saltɛ̃bɑ̃k] *n* (*de cirque*) circus performer; (*comédien*) entertainer
salto [salto] *nm Gym* somersault, flip
salubre [salybr] *adj* (*climat, air, appartement*) healthy, *Fml* salubrious
salubrité [salybrite] *nf* (*du climat, de l'air, d'un appartement*) healthiness, *Fml* salubriousness; **s. publique** public health
saluer [salɥe] **1** *vt* **(a)** (*personne*) (*en arrivant*) to greet; (*en partant*) to take one's leave of; (*faire la révérence à*) (*d'un homme*) to bow to; (*d'une femme*) to curts(e)y to; **s. qn (d'un geste) de la main** to wave to sb; **s. qn d'une inclination de la tête** to nod to sb; **il est passé sans me s.** he walked past me without saying hello; **s. qn bien bas** to take one's hat off to sb; *Hum* **au revoir/bonjour, mes amis, je vous salue bien**

bas goodbye/hello, my friends, and a very good day to you; *Th* **s. le public** to bow to the audience; **s. qn par un vivat** to greet sb with a cheer; **la loi a été froidement saluée par l'opposition** the bill got a cool reception from the opposition *or* was coolly received by the opposition; **saluez-le de ma part** give him my regards; *Bible* **Je vous salue, Marie** hail, Mary; **s. qn comme ...** to hail sb as ...; **je salue en lui notre sauveur** I salute him as our saviour; *Billard* **s. la bille** to miss
(b) *Naut* **s. un grain** to reduce sail for a squall
2 *vi* **s. en se découvrant** to raise one's hat in greeting; *Mil etc* **s. du drapeau** to lower the colours; *Naut* **s. (du pavillon)** to dip (the flag); **s. de vingt coups** to fire a twenty-gun salute
3 se saluer *vpr* (*en arrivant*) to greet each other; (*en partant*) to take leave of each other

salure [salyr] *nf* saltiness

salut [saly] *nm* **(a)** (*sauvegarde*) safety; *Rel* salvation; **chercher son s. dans la fuite** to flee for one's life, to seek safety in flight; **travailler à son s.** to work out one's own salvation; **pour le s. de vos âmes** for the salvation of your souls; **l'Armée du S.** the Salvation Army
(b) (*salutation*) greeting, *Fml* salutation; **faire** *ou* **adresser un s. à qn** (*de la main*) to wave to sb, to give sb a wave; (*en se découvrant*) to raise one's hat to sb; *F* **s. (à tous)!** hello *or* hi(, everybody)!; (*en partant*) so long (everybody)!
(c) *Mil etc* salute; **faire un s.** to give a salute; **faire le s. militaire** to salute; **s. au drapeau** saluting the colours; *Naut* **s. du pavillon** dipping of the flag
(d) *Cathol* Benediction (of the Holy Sacrament)

salutaire [salytɛr] *adj* (*décision, mesure etc*) salutary, beneficial; (*remède*) beneficial; **être s. à qn** to do sb good, to be beneficial to sb; **un goût très s. pour les sports de plein air** a healthy liking for outdoor sports

salutation [salytasjɔ̃] *nf* salutation, greeting; **Je vous prie d'agréer, Monsieur, l'expression de mes salutations distinguées** yours faithfully; (*quand la formule de salutation comprend le nom du destinataire*) yours sincerely, *Am* yours truly

salutiste [salytist] *n* Salvationist

salvadorien, -ienne [salvadɔrjɛ̃, -jɛn] **1** *adj* Salvadorean **2** *n* **S.** Salvadorean

Salvador (le) [ləsalvadɔr] *nm* El Salvador

salvateur, -trice [salvatœr, -tris] *adj Litt* saving; **la mort salvatrice** the blessed release of death

salve [salv] *nf Mil* salvo, volley; **tirer une s. (d'honneur)** to fire a salute; **s. d'applaudissements** burst of applause

samare [samar] *nf Bot* key

samaritain, -aine [samaritɛ̃, -ɛn] *Bible* **1** *adj* Samaritan **2** *n* **S.** Samaritan; **le bon S.** the Good Samaritan; *Fig* **faire le bon S.** to be a Good Samaritan

samba [sɑ̃mba] *nf* samba

samedi [samdi] *nm* [①**A75-6**,B-C; **B58-9**,B-C] Saturday; **le S. saint** the Saturday before Easter, Holy Saturday

samizdat [samizdat] *nm* samizdat

samossa [samɔsa] *nm Culin* samosa

samouraï, samurai [samuraj] *nm* samurai

samovar [samɔvar] *nm* samovar

sampan(g) [sɑ̃pɑ̃] *nm* sampan

SAMU [samy] *nm* (*abrév* **service d'aide médicale d'urgence**) ambulance service; **appelez le S.!** ≈ call an ambulance!

sana [sana] *nm F* sanatorium

sanatorium [sanatɔrjɔm] *nm* sanatorium

sanctificateur, -trice [sɑ̃ktifikatœr, -tris] **1** *adj* sanctifying **2** *n* sanctifier; **le S.** the Holy Ghost

sanctification [sɑ̃ktifikasjɔ̃] *nf* sanctification

sanctifier [sɑ̃ktifje] *vt* (*impf, pr sub* **n. sanctifiions, v. sanctifiiez**) to sanctify, to make holy; **que Ton nom soit sanctifié** hallowed be Thy Name

sanction [sɑ̃ksjɔ̃] *nf* **(a)** (*approbation*) sanction, approval **(b) s. (pénale)** sanction, penalty; **sanctions économiques** economic sanctions; *Pol* **prendre des sanctions contre un pays/contre des grévistes** to impose sanctions on a country/take action against strikers; **la s. de la paresse** the price *or* consequence of laziness; **c'est la s. du succès** that's the price of success

sanctionner [sɑ̃ksjɔne] *vt* **(a)** (*approuver*) to sanction, to approve; **sanctionné par l'usage** sanctioned by custom **(b)** (*punir*) (*faute, personne*) to punish, to penalize

sanctuaire [sɑ̃ktɥɛr] *nm Rel, Fig* sanctuary

sanctus [sɑ̃ktys] *nm Rel, Mus* sanctus

sandale [sɑ̃dal] *nf* sandal

sandalette [sɑ̃dalɛt] *nf* (light) sandal

sandow® [sɑ̃do] *nm* **(a)** *Gym* chest expander **(b)** (*pour bagages*) elastic strap *or Am* bungee; *Av* catapult

sandwich, *pl* **sandwich(e)s** [sɑ̃dwi(t)ʃ] *nm* sandwich; **s. au jambon** ham sandwich; **verre s.** laminated glass; *F* **pris en s.** sandwiched (**entre** between)

sandwicherie [sɑ̃dwi(t)ʃəri] *nf* sandwich bar

sang [sɑ̃] *nm* **(a)** blood; **animaux à s. chaud/froid** warm-blooded/cold-blooded animals; **yeux injectés de s.** bloodshot eyes; **faire couler** *ou* **répandre** *ou* **verser le s.** to shed *or* spill blood; **verser son s. pour la patrie** to shed one's blood for one's country; **pincer/fouetter qn jusqu'au s.** to pinch/whip sb till he/she bleeds *or* till one draws blood; **victoire sans effusion de s.** bloodless victory; **le pays fut mis à feu et à s.** the country was put to fire and sword; **laver un outrage par le s.** to avenge an insult with blood; **écoulement de s.** bleeding, haemorrhage, *US* hemorrhage; **je n'arrive pas à arrêter le s.** I can't stop the bleeding; **donner son s.** to give blood; **donneur de s.** blood donor; **il était tout en s.** he was covered with blood; *aussi Fig* **avoir du s. sur les mains** to have blood on one's hands; **taché de s.** bloodstained; *Méd Vieilli* **coup de s.** stroke; *Fig F* **il a eu un coup de s.** he nearly had a heart attack; *Fig* **avoir le s. chaud** to be hot-blooded; *Fig* **avoir le rythme dans le s.** to have an innate sense of rhythm, to have rhythm; **elle a la musique dans le s.** she has music in her blood; **il a ça dans le s.** it's in his blood; **des êtres de chair et de s.** creatures of flesh and blood; **le s. lui monta au visage** the blood rushed to his face; **cela me glace le s.** it makes my blood run cold; **il n'a pas de s. dans les veines** he's got no guts, he's gutless; *F* **avoir du s. de navet** to be spineless, to be a yellow-belly; *F* **se faire du mauvais s.** to worry, *F* to get all worked up; *F* **se ronger les sangs, se faire un s. d'encre** to worry oneself sick; **conte à tourner les sangs** bloodcurdling tale; **mon s. n'a fait qu'un tour** (*de peur*) my heart missed a beat; (*de colère*) I saw red; **dans cette famille, il faudrait un apport de s. frais** the family needs some *or* an infusion of new blood; *très F* **bon s. (de bonsoir)!, bon s. de bon Dieu!** damn and blast it!
(b) (*race, lignée*) blood; **cheval de s.** blood horse; **cheval pur s.** thoroughbred; **liens du s.** blood ties; **ils ont ça dans le s.** it's in their blood; **son propre s.** one's own flesh and blood; **nous ne sommes pas du même s.** we're not of the same flesh and blood; **droit du s.** birthright

▶ **sang**: **s. bleu** blue blood; **c'est un s. bleu** he has blue blood (in his veins)

sang-froid *nm* (*no pl*) composure, calm, *Litt* sang-froid; **garder** *ou* **conserver son s.** to keep calm *or* one's head *or F* (one's) cool, to maintain one's composure; **perdre son s.** to lose one's head *or F* one's cool, to lose one's composure; **faire qch de s.** to do sth calmly *or* coolly; **tuer qn de s.** to kill sb in cold blood

sanglant [sɑ̃glɑ̃] *adj* **(a)** (*blessure, bataille, histoire, mort*) bloody; (*vêtement, mouchoir etc*) bloodstained, bloody **(b)** *Fig* (*reproche*) bitter; (*affront*) deadly; (*critique*) scathing

sangle [sɑ̃gl] *nf* strap; (*de selle*) girth; (*de meuble*) webbing; **lit de s.** camp bed

sangler [sɑ̃gle] **1** *vt* (*cheval*) to girth; **sanglé dans son uniforme** buttoned up tight in his uniform **2 se sangler** *vpr* (*dans un vêtement très étroit*) to do oneself up tight

sanglier [sɑ̃glije] *nm* (wild) boar

sanglot [sɑ̃glo] *nm* sob; **éclater en sanglots** to burst out sobbing, to burst into tears; **il pleurait à gros sanglots** he was sobbing his heart out; **avec des sanglots dans la voix** with a sob in one's voice, in a tearful voice

sangloter [sɑ̃glɔte] *vi* to sob

sang-mêlé [sɑ̃mele] *n inv* half-caste

sangria [sɑ̃grija] *nf* sangria

sangsue [sɑ̃sy] *nf Zool, Fig* leech

sanguin, -ine [sɑ̃gɛ̃, -in] **1** *adj* **(a)** *Anat* blood; **groupe/vaisseau s.** blood group/vessel; **produits sanguins** blood products; **transfusion sanguine** blood transfusion; **circulation sanguine** circulation (of the blood) **(b)** (*tempérament*) sanguine; (*teint, visage*) ruddy **(c) orange sanguine** blood orange **2** *nm* **(a)** (*personne*) fiery person **(b)** *Bot* dogwood **3** *nf* **sanguine (a)** (*craie*) red chalk, sanguine **(b)** *Minér* bloodstone **(c)** (*orange*) blood orange

sanguinaire [sɑ̃ginɛr] *adj* (*homme*) bloodthirsty; (*combat*) bloody

sanguinolent [sɑ̃ginɔlɑ̃] *adj* **(a)** (*teinté de sang*) spotted with blood; **sa lèvre sanguinolente** his bleeding lip; **une plaie sanguinolente** a wound oozing blood **(b)** (*rouge*) blood-red

sanie [sani] *nf Méd* pus and blood, *Spéc* sanies

sanitaire [sanitɛr] **1** *adj* **(a)** *Méd* (*personnel*) medical, health; (*équipement*) medical; (*mesures*) health; *Mil etc* **voiture s.** ambulance **(b)** *Constr etc* (*équipement, installation*) sanitary; **bloc s.** (*dans un camping*) toilet *or* sanitary block; **système s.** sanitation (system) **2** *nm* **les sanitaires** (*toilettes*) toilet; (*salle de bains et WC*) bathroom and toilet; **sanitaires privatifs** en-suite *or* private facilities **3** *nf Mil etc* ambulance

sans [sɑ̃] **1** *prép* **(a)** [①**A67**; **B54**] (*absence, privation, exclusion*) without; **partez s. moi** go without me; **il est revenu s. argent** *ou* **s. un sou** *ou* **s. le sou** he came back without any money *or* without a penny; **elle arriva s. argent ni bagages** she arrived without any *or* without either money or luggage; **elle est s. emploi depuis deux mois** she's been unemployed *or* without work for two months; **couple s. enfants** childless couple; **pain/régime s. sel** salt-free bread/diet; **faire qch s. faute** to do sth without fail; **demain s. faute** tomorrow without fail; **suffisant, s. plus** adequate but no more (than that); **plaintes s. fin** endless complaints; **se plaindre s. fin** to complain endlessly; **baignade s. danger** safe bathing; **s. parler/travailler** without speaking/working; **s. mot dire, s. dire un mot** without saying a word; **s. hésiter** without hesitating *or* hesitation, unhesitatingly; **cela va s. dire** it goes without saying; **il va s. dire que c'est une réussite** it's a success, needless to say, it goes without saying that it's a success; **s. plus attendre** without further delay, immediately; **non s. difficulté** not without difficulty; *Fml* **vous n'êtes pas s. le connaître** you must know him; *Fml* **tu n'es pas s. savoir que ...** you are quite well aware that ...; *Fml* **ces questions n'étaient pas s. m'embarrasser** these questions were naturally somewhat embarrassing; *Typ* **s. patte** *ou* **serif** sans serif

(**b**) (*condition*) but for; **s. vous je ne l'aurais jamais fait** but for you *or* if it hadn't been for you, I would never have done it; **s. cela, s. quoi** otherwise; *F* **sois sage, s. ça tu seras puni!** be good or (else) you'll be punished!

2 *conj* **s. que** + *sub* without + *gerund*; **s. que nous le sachions**, *Rare* **s. que nous ne le sachions** without our knowing, unbeknownst to us; **il ne parlait jamais s. qu'on lui parlât** he never spoke unless he was spoken to

3 *adv F* **que ferais-tu s.?** how would you manage without?; **est-ce que tu pourrais vivre s.?** could you live without it/them?; **la télévision, je ne pourrais pas vivre s.** I couldn't live without television

sans-abri [sɑ̃zabri] *n inv* homeless person; **les s.** the homeless

sans-cœur 1 *adj inv F* heartless **2** *n inv* heartless person

sanscrit [sɑ̃skri] *adj, nm Ling* Sanskrit

sans-culotte, *pl* **sans-culottes** *nm Hist* sans culotte (*person with extreme republican sympathies during the French Revolution*)

sans-emploi [sɑ̃zɑ̃plwa] *n inv* unemployed *or* jobless person; **les s.** the unemployed, the jobless; **le nombre des s. augmente** the unemployment *or* jobless figure is rising

sans-façon 1 *nm inv* (*naturel*) informality **2** *adj inv* (*naturel*) informal

sans-faute *nm inv Sp* clear round; **accomplir** *ou* **faire un s.** (*d'un cheval*) to have a clear round; *Fig* (*d'un candidat*) not to put a foot wrong, to turn in a faultless performance

sans-fil *Vieilli* **1** *nf inv* wireless (telegraphy) **2** *nm inv* radio *or* wireless message

sans-gêne *Péj* **1** *nm inv* impudence, brazenness **2** *n inv* (*personne*) impudent *or* brazen person **3** *adj inv* (*personne*) impudent, brazen; **qu'est-ce qu'il est s.!** he's got a cheek!; **des manières s.** brazen ways

sanskrit [sɑ̃skri] *adj, nm Ling* Sanskrit

sans-le-sou [sɑ̃l(ə)su] *n inv F* penniless person; **c'est un s.** he doesn't have a penny to his name

sans-logis *n inv* homeless person; **les s.** the homeless

sansonnet [sɑ̃sɔnɛ] *nm* starling

sans-parti *n inv Pol* member of no party

sans-patrie *n inv* stateless person

sans-souci *adj inv* carefree, happy-go-lucky

santal, -als [sɑ̃tal] *nm* (**bois de**) **s.** sandalwood

santé [sɑ̃te] *nf* health; **être en bonne s.** to be well, to be in good health; **s. de fer** iron constitution; **avoir une bonne/mauvaise s.** to be healthy/unhealthy; **ne pas avoir de s., avoir une s. fragile** *ou* **délicate**, *F* **avoir une petite s.** to be in poor health, to be delicate; **c'est bon/mauvais pour la s.** it's good/bad for your health; *F* **comment va la s.?** how's things?, how are you doing?; **perdre/recouvrer la s.** to lose/recover one's health; **elle respire la s.** she looks *or* is the picture of health, she radiates health; **être plein de s.** to be full of life; **absent pour raison de s.** absent for health reasons *or* on medical grounds; **boire à la s. de qn** to drink sb's health; **à votre s.!** your health!, *F* cheers!; **buvons à la s. des mariés** let's drink to the married couple; *Suisse F* **s.!** (*quand qn éternue*) bless you!; *Admin* **Ministère de la S. et de la Sécurité sociale** *Br* ≈ Department of Social Security; *Naut* **agent de (la) s.** quarantine officer; **s. publique** public health

santiag [sɑ̃tjag] *nf F* cowboy boot

santon [sɑ̃tɔ̃] *nm* (*de crèche*) Christmas crib figure

saoul [su], **saoulard** [sular], **saouler** [sule] = **soûl, soûlard, soûler**

sapajou [sapaʒu] *nm Zool* capuchin (monkey), sapajou

sape [sap] *nf* (**a**) (*d'un mur, d'une tour etc*) undermining; *Mil* sapping; *Fig* **travaux de s.** undermining (**b**) (*tranchée*) sap, trench (**c**) (*outil*) mattock (**d**) *Arg* **sapes** (*vêtements*) gear, togs, *Br* clobber

saper [sape] **1** *vt* (**a**) *Mil etc, Fig* to undermine; **s. le moral de qn** to sap sb's morale (**b**) *Arg* (*habiller*) to tog out, to dress; **être bien sapé** to be all togged up **2 se saper** *vpr Arg* to tog oneself out, to do oneself up

saperlipopette [sapɛrlipɔpɛt], **saperlotte** [sapɛrlɔt] *int Arch, Hum* gad(zooks)!

sapeur [sapœr] *nm Mil* sapper; *F* **fumer comme un s.** to smoke like a chimney

sapeur-pompier *nm Admin* fireman, *Am* fire fighter; **les sapeurs-pompiers** (*service*) the fire brigade *or Am* department

saphique [safik] *adj* Sapphic

saphir [safir] *nm* sapphire

saphisme [safism] *nm* sapphism

sapin [sapɛ̃] *nm* (**a**) (*arbre*) fir (tree); *Com* (**bois de**) **s.** deal (**b**) *F* **ça sent le s.** that sounds bad, that sounds as if you're heading for an early grave; **il sent le s.** he's done for, he's had it (**c**) *Can* **se faire passer un s.** (*se faire avoir*) to be taken for a ride

sapine [sapin] *nf* (**a**) (*planche*) deal board (**b**) *Constr* crane tower (**c**) (*en viticulture*) deal tub

sapinière [sapinjɛr] *nf* fir plantation

saponaire [sapɔnɛr] *nf Bot* soapwort

saponifiant [sapɔnifjɑ̃] *Ch* **1** *adj* saponifying **2** *nm* saponifier, saponifying agent

saponification [sapɔnifikasjɔ̃] *nf* saponification

saponifier [sapɔnifje] *vt* (*impf, pr sub* **n. saponifiions, v. saponifiiez**) to saponify

sapristi [sapristi] *int F Vieilli ou Hum* good heavens!

saprophage [saprɔfaʒ] *adj Ent* saprophagous

saprophyte [saprɔfit] *nm Biol* saprophyte

saquebute [sakbyt] *nf Hist Mus* sackbut

saquer [sake] *vt F* = **sacquer**

sarabande [sarabɑ̃d] *nf* (*danse*), *Mus* saraband; *F* (*tapage*) racket, row; **ils ont fait la s. toute la nuit** they made a racket *or* row all night long

sarbacane [sarbakan] *nf* blowpipe; (*jouet*) peashooter

sarcasme [sarkasm] *nm* sarcasm; (*remarque*) sarcastic remark

sarcastique [sarkastik] *adj* sarcastic

sarcastiquement [sarkastikmɑ̃] *adv* sarcastically

sarcelle [sarsɛl] *nf* teal

sarclage [sarklaʒ] *nm* weeding

sarcler [sarkle] *vt* (**a**) (*jardin, plates-bandes*) to weed; (*sol*) to hoe; (*champ*) to clean (**b**) (*mauvaises herbes*) to hoe up *or* out

sarclette [sarklɛt] *nf* (weeding) hoe

sarcloir [sarklwar] *nm* (weeding) hoe

sarcome [sarkom] *nm Méd* sarcoma; **s. de Kaposi** Kaposi's sarcoma

sarcophage [sarkɔfaʒ] **1** *nm* sarcophagus **2** *nf Ent* bluebottle

Sardaigne [sardɛɲ] *nf* Sardinia

sarde [sard] **1** *adj* Sardinian **2** *n* **S.** Sardinian **3** *nm Ling* Sardinian

sardine [sardin] *nf* (**a**) (*poisson*) sardine; **sardines à l'huile/à la tomate** sardines in oil/in tomato sauce; *F* **serrés comme des sardines** packed together like sardines (**b**) *Mil F* stripe (**c**) (*de tente*) tent peg

sardinerie [sardinri] *nf* sardine cannery

sardinier, -ière [sardinje, -jɛr] **1** *n* (*pêcheur*) sardine fisher; (*ouvrier*) sardine canner **2** *nm* (*filet*) sardine net; (*bateau*) sardine boat

sardonique [sardɔnik] *adj* sardonic

sardonyx [sardɔniks] *nf Minér* sardonyx

sargasse [sargas] *nf* sargasso, gulfweed; **la mer des Sargasses** the Sargasso Sea

sari [sari] *nm* sari

sarigue [sarig] *nf* opossum, possum

SARL [ɛsaɛrɛl] *nf* (*abrév* **société anonyme à responsabilité limitée**) = limited liability company, *Br* ≈ Ltd, *Am* ≈ Inc; (*coté en Bourse*) *Br* ≈ plc

sarment [sarmɑ̃] *nm* (*tige*) bine; (*de vigne*) vine shoot

sarmenteux, -euse [sarmɑ̃tø, -øz] *adj* (*plante*) climbing

sarong [sarɔ̃] *nm* sarong

saroual [sarwal], **sarouel** [sarwɛl] *nm* = baggy trousers worn by North Africans

sarrasin, -ine [sarazɛ̃, -in] **1** *adj Hist* Saracen **2** *n Hist* **S.** Saracen **3** *nm Agr* buckwheat **4** *nf* **sarrasine** portcullis

sarrau [saro] *nm Hist* smock

Sarre (la) [lasar] *nf* (*région*) Saarland, the Saar; (*rivière*) the Saar

sarriette [sarjɛt] *nf Bot, Culin* savory

sarrois [sarwa] **1** *adj* of/from Saarland *or* the Saar **2** *n* **S.** Saarlander
sas[1] [sɑ(s)] *nm* (*crible*) sieve; **passer qch au s.** to sift *or* sieve sth
sas[2] *nm* **(a)** *HydE* lock chamber, coffer **(b)** *Constr, Naut, Astronaut* airlock
sassafras [sasafrɑ] *nm Bot* sassafras
sassage[1] [sasaʒ] *nm* (*criblage*) sifting, sieving
sassage[2] *nm* (*d'un bateau*) passing through a lock
sassement [sasmɑ̃] *nm* = **sassage**[1, 2]
sasser[1] [sase] *vt* (*farine, plâtre*) to sift, to sieve; (*grain*) to winnow
sasser[2] *vt* (*bateau*) to pass through a lock
sasseur, -euse [sasœr, -øz] *n* sifter
Satan [satɑ̃] *nm* Satan
satané [satane] *adj F* confounded; **s. temps!** what filthy weather!
satanique [satanik] *adj* satanic; *Fig* (*cruauté, idée, sourire etc*) fiendish
satanisme [satanism] *nm* satanism
satellisation [satelizasjɔ̃] *nf* **(a)** *Astronaut* (*d'un satellite, d'un engin spatial*) putting into orbit; **programme de s.** space programme **(b)** *Pol* (*d'un pays, d'une région*) satellization
satelliser [satelize] **1** *vt* **(a)** *Astronaut* (*satellite, engin spatial*) to put into orbit **(b)** *Pol* (*pays, région*) to satellize **2 se satelliser** *vpr* **(a)** *Astronaut* to go into orbit **(b)** *Pol* (*d'un pays, d'une région*) to become a satellite
satellite [satelit] **1** *nm* **(a)** *Astron* satellite; **s. artificiel** artificial satellite; **s. géostationnaire** geostationary satellite; **s. terrestre/lunaire** earth-orbiting/moon-orbiting satellite; **s. de télécommunications** (tele)communications satellite, *F* comsat; **s. météorologique** weather *or* meteorological satellite; *TV* **retransmis par s.** transmitted by satellite; **émission retransmise par s.** satellite broadcast; **télévision par s.** satellite television, *F* metsat; **s. de diffusion directe** direct broadcast satellite, DBS; **s. de télédiffusion** broadcast satellite; **s. de télédiffusion directe** direct-broadcast satellite; **s. de télédétection** remote-sensing satellite; **s. météo** weather satellite; **s. terrestre** earth satellite

(b) *Pol* satellite; *Péj* (*homme*) satellite, hanger-on

(c) *Tech* planet wheel, bevel gear; **engrenage à satellites** (sun-and-)planet gear; *Aut* **s. sur colonne de direction** steering column satellite

2 *adj* **(a)** *Anat* **veines satellites** companion veins

(b) *Pol* **pays s.** satellite state; **agglomération s.** satellite town

satiété [sasjete] *nf* satiety; **manger/boire à s.** to eat/drink one's fill; **répéter qch à s.** to repeat sth ad nauseam
satin [satɛ̃] *nm* **(a)** *Tex* satin **(b) bois de s.** satinwood **(c)** *Bot* **s. blanc** honesty
satiné [satine] **1** *adj* (*tissu*) satiny, satin-like; (*cuir, papier*) glazed; (*papier*) calendered; (*peau*) satin-smooth; **peinture satinée** satin-finish paint **2** *nm* satin finish; (*de la peau*) satin smoothness
satiner [satine] *vt* (*tissu etc*) to give a satin finish to, to satin; (*cuir*) to glaze; (*papier*) to calender
satinette [satinɛt] *nf Tex* (*en coton*) sateen; (*en soie et coton*) satinet(te)
satire [satir] *nf* satire (**contre** on; **de** of); **faire la s. de son époque** to satirize one's times
satirique [satirik] *adj* satirical, satiric
satiriquement [satirikmɑ̃] *adv* satirically
satiriser [satirize] *vt* to satirize
satiriste [satirist] *n* satirist
satisfaction [satisfaksjɔ̃] *nf* **(a)** satisfaction; **la s. du travail bien fait** the satisfaction of a job well done; **donner (toute** *ou* **entière) s. à qn** to give sb (complete) satisfaction; **donner s. aux vœux de qn** to satisfy *or* gratify sb's wishes; **avoir la s. de faire qch** to have the satisfaction of doing sth; **nous avons la s. de pouvoir dire que ...** it gives us great satisfaction to be able to say that ...; **j'éprouve une profonde s.** I feel (a) great satisfaction; **à la s. générale** to everyone's satisfaction; **j'ai eu une s. aujourd'hui** a good thing happened today; **ils ne m'ont donné que des satisfactions** they've given me nothing but satisfaction; **s. de la clientèle** *ou* **du client** customer satisfaction

(b) (*réparation*) satisfaction (**pour, de** for); *Rel* atonement; **donner s. à qn** to give sb satisfaction; **obtenir s.** to obtain satisfaction

satisfaire [satisfɛr] (*conj like* **faire**) **1** *vt* (*personne, besoin, demandes*) to satisfy; (*curiosité*) to satisfy, to gratify; (*sexuellement*) to satisfy; **s. le désir de qn** (*l'accomplir*) to carry out sb's wish; **s. l'attente de qn** to come up to sb's expectations; *Euph* **s. un besoin naturel** to answer a call of nature, to relieve oneself; **de manière à vous s.** to your satisfaction; **s. sa faim** to satisfy *or* appease one's hunger; **s. une commande** to fulfill an order

2 se satisfaire *vpr* **(a) se s. de peu** to be content with very little, *Péj* to be easily satisfied

(b) (*uriner*) to relieve oneself

(c) (*sexuellement*) to achieve satisfaction

3 *vi* **(a) s. à** (*demande, exigence, condition, besoins*) to satisfy, to meet; (*souhaits*) to satisfy, to fulfil, to carry out; (*règlement, normes de sécurité*) to comply with; (*contrat, obligations*) to fulfil; **s. à son devoir** to carry out *or* fulfil one's duty; **s. à un examen** to pass an exam

(b) *Arch* **s. à qn** (*dans un duel*) to give sb satisfaction

satisfaisant [satisfəzɑ̃] *adj* (*convenable*) (*réponse, travail etc*) satisfactory; (*qui contente*) (*repas, occupation*) satisfying
satisfait, -aite [satisfɛ, -ɛt] *adj* (*heureux*) satisfied; (*suffisant*) satisfied, smug; (*désir, vœu*) fulfilled; *Iron* **vous voilà s.!** well, you asked for it!; **je n'en suis pas s.** I'm not satisfied *or* pleased *or* happy with it; *Com* **j'espère que vous en serez entièrement s.** I trust it will give you complete satisfaction; **s. ou remboursé** satisfaction or your money back, money-back guarantee
satisfecit [satisfesit] *nm inv Litt* (*approbation*) recognition, credit; *Scol Vieilli* = certificate of satisfactory progress; **décerner un s. à qn** to congratulate sb on a job well done
saturable [satyrabl] *adj* saturable
saturant [satyrɑ̃] *adj* saturating; **vapeur saturante** saturated vapour
saturateur [satyratœr] *nm Ch, Ind* saturator; (*humidificateur*) humidifier
saturation [satyrasjɔ̃] *nf aussi Fig* saturation; (*du réseau routier*) gridlock; **arriver à s.** to reach saturation point; *Ordinat* (*d'une disquette*) to become full; **campagne de s.** (*en publicité*) saturation campaign; **s. du marché** saturation of the market; *TV, Rad* **s. acoustique** popping
saturé [satyre] *adj* (*solution*), *Fig* saturated; *Ordinat* (*disque*) full; **l'éponge est saturée d'eau** the sponge is saturated; *Com* **le marché est s.** the market is saturated *or* has reached saturation point; **ville saturée** overcrowded city; **j'en suis s.** I'm sick of it/them; **j'étais s. de soleil** I'd had enough sun
saturer [satyre] **1** *vt* to saturate (**de,** with); *TV, Rad* to overload; *Fig* **on nous sature de publicité** we are swamped with advertising; **le professeur nous sature de travail** the teacher is overloading us with work; **les appels de nos téléspectateurs ont saturé le standard** our viewers' calls have jammed the switchboards **2** *vi F* **je sature** I've had it up to here
saturnales [satyrnal] *nfpl Antiq, Fig* saturnalia
Saturne [satyrn] **1** *nm Myth* Saturn **2** *nf Astron* Saturn
saturnie [satyrni] *nf* emperor moth
saturnien, -ienne [satyrnjɛ̃, -jɛn] *adj* saturnine
saturnin, -ine [satyrnɛ̃, -in] *adj Méd* **intoxication saturnine** lead poisoning
saturnisme [satyrnism] *nm Méd* lead poisoning, *Spéc* saturnism
satyre [satir] *nm* **(a)** *Myth, Ent* satyr **(b)** *F* (*obsédé sexuel*) sex maniac
satyrique [satirik] *adj Antiq* satyric
sauce [sos] *nf* **(a)** *Culin* sauce; **s. hollandaise/béchamel/béarnaise** hollandaise/béchamel/béarnaise sauce; **s. aux champignons** mushroom sauce; **s. (à) salade** salad dressing; **(r)allonger la s.** to water down the sauce; *Fig F* to pad things out; *F* **accommoder un même sujet à toutes les sauces** to dish up the same subject in every shape and form; *F* **mettre qch à toutes les sauces** to use sth in every way imaginable; *Fig* **à quelle s. sera-t-il mangé?** how shall we deal with it/him?

(b) *Beaux-Arts* (*craie noire*) soft black crayon

(c) *Fig F* (*pluie*) **prendre la s.** to get soaked *or* drenched, to get a soaking

saucée [sose] *nf F* (*pluie*) downpour; **recevoir une s.** to get soaked *or* drenched, to get a soaking
saucer [sose] *vt* **(je sauçai(s); n. sauçons) (a)** (*assiette*) to mop up the sauce from **(b)** *F* **se faire s.** to get soaked *or* drenched, to get a soaking
saucette [sosɛt] *nf Can F* **faire une s.** to have a quickie; **faire une s. à Québec** to make a quick trip to Quebec City, to pop over to Quebec City
saucier [sosje] *nm* sauce cook *or* chef
saucière [sosjɛr] *nf* sauce boat
sauciflard [sosiflar] *nm très F* sausage
saucisse [sosis] *nf* **(a)** *Culin* sausage; **s. de Francfort** frankfurter; **s. de Strasbourg/Toulouse** = type of beef/pork sausage; *F* **il n'attache pas son chien avec des saucisses** he's tight with his money, he's tight-fisted **(b)** *Mil F* barrage balloon

saucisson [sosisɔ̃] *nm Culin* sausage; **s. (sec)** (salami-type) sausage; **s. à l'ail** garlic sausage; **s. pur porc** 100% pork sausage; *F* **elle est toujours ficelée comme un s.** she's always bulging *or* bursting out of her clothes; *Hum* **s. à pattes** sausage dog
saucissonné [sosisɔne] *adj F* trussed up; **s. dans son collant/sa robe** poured into her tights/dress
saucissonner [sosisɔne] *F* **1** *vt* (*attacher*) to truss up; *Fig* **film saucissonné de publicités** film broken up by adverts **2** *vi* to picnic, to eat a snack
saucissonneur, -euse [sosisɔnœr, -øz] *n F* picnicker
sauf[1], sauve [sof, sov] *adj* (*personne*) safe, unhurt, unharmed; **sain et s.** safe and sound; **avoir la vie sauve** to escape with one's life; **ils lui ont laissé la vie sauve** they spared his life *or* him; **l'honneur est s.** honour is saved; **sa réputation est sauve** his reputation is intact *or* saved
sauf[2] *prép* except (for), apart from; **elle n'a rien s. son salaire** she has nothing except (for) *or* apart from *or* but her wages; **il est indemne s. une écorchure au bras** he is unhurt except for *or* apart from a grazed arm; **s. avis contraire, s. contrordre** unless you/I/*etc* hear to the contrary, unless otherwise advised; **s. bonne fin** under usual reserve; **s. indication contraire** unless otherwise stated *or* specified; **s. de rares exceptions** with very few exceptions; **s. accidents, s. imprévu** barring accidents, unless anything unforeseen happens; **s. erreur ou omission** errors and omissions excepted; **s. erreur de ma part, je vous dois encore 3 000 francs** if I'm not mistaken *or* unless I'm mistaken, I still owe you 3,000 francs; **s. cas de force majeure** unless anything happens to prevent it; *Jur* except in cases of force majeure; *Litt* **je consens, s. à revenir sur ma décision** I consent, but I reserve the right to reconsider my decision; **s. le respect que je vous dois, s. votre respect** with all due respect; **s. s'il pleut** unless it rains, if it doesn't rain; *F* **je n'ai rien fait, s. d'écrire des lettres** I've done nothing except write *or* apart from writing some letters; *F* **s. que +** *ind* except that, apart from the fact that
sauf-conduit, *pl* **sauf-conduits** *nm* safe conduct, pass
sauge [soʒ] *nf* **(a)** *Bot, Culin* sage **(b)** *Bot* (*plante ornementale*) salvia
saugrenu [sogrəny] *adj* absurd, preposterous
saule [sol] *nm* willow; **s. pleureur** weeping willow
saumâtre [somɑtr] *adj* **(a)** (*goût, eau*) brackish, briny **(b)** *Fig* bitter; *F* **je la trouve s.** I'm not amused *or* impressed, I think it's a bit much
saumon [somɔ̃] **1** *nm* **(a)** [①A12,1,g] (*poisson*) salmon; **darne de s.** salmon steak; **s. fumé** smoked salmon **(b)** *Métal* (*de plomb, d'étain etc*) pig **2** *adj inv* salmon-pink; **rose s.** salmon pink
saumoné [somɔne] *adj* **truite saumonée** salmon trout
saumure [somyr] *nf* brine
saumuré [somyre] *adj* (*harengs etc*) pickled (in brine)
saumurer [somyre] *vt* to pickle (in brine)
sauna [sona] *nm* sauna
saupiquet [sopikɛ] *nm Culin* = spicy stew
saupoudrage [sopudraʒ] *nm* sprinkling
saupoudrer [sopudre] *vt* to sprinkle (**de** with); **s. des fraises de sucre** to sprinkle *or* dust strawberries with sugar; *Fig* **s. des subventions** to scatter subsidies thinly; **s. un texte de références/de citations** to pepper *or* sprinkle a text with references/quotations
saupoudreuse [sopudrøz] *nf,* **saupoudroir** [sopudrwar] *nm Culin* dredger, caster
saur [sɔr] *adj m* **hareng s.** kipper, smoked herring
saurer [sɔre] *vt* (*harengs*) to kipper, to smoke; (*poisson, jambon*) to smoke
saurien [sɔrjɛ̃] *nm Zool* saurian
saut [so] *nm* **(a)** (*bond*) jump, leap; **faire un s.** to jump, to leap, to take a leap; **la voiture a fait un s. de 50 mètres dans la mer** the car plunged 50 metres into the sea; *Fig* **faire un s. à Paris/chez le boulanger/en ville** to pop *or Br* nip over to Paris/round to the baker's/into town; **entrer d'un s.** to dash *or* rush in; **au s. du lit** first thing in the morning; **il m'a trouvé au s. du lit** he caught me when I'd only just got up; **faire un s. dans l'inconnu** to take a leap in the dark *or* into the unknown; *Fig* **faire le (grand) s.** (*faire qch de très important*) to take the plunge; (*mourir*) to pass on (to the other side); *Fig* **le héros fit un s. de plusieurs années et se retrouva en l'an 2055** the hero skipped several years and found himself in the year 2055; *Arch* **par sauts et par bonds** in fits and starts; **il n'y a qu'un s. d'ici là** it's only a stone's throw away
(b) *Mus* skip
(c) *Ordinat* jump; *Typ* **s. de page** page break; *Typ* **s. de page imposé** hard page break
(d) (*en élevage*) covering
(e) (*de cours d'eau*) waterfall

▶ **saut**: *Natation* **s. de l'ange** swallow dive, *Am* swan dive; *Gym* **s. de carpe** flip; **faire des sauts de carpe** to bounce around; *Natation* **s. carpé** pike; **s. à la corde** skipping; *Sp* **s. en hauteur** high jump; *Sp* **s. en longueur** long *or Am* broad jump; **s. en parachute** parachute jump; (*activité*) parachute jumping; **faire du s. en parachute** to go parachute jumping; *Sp* **s. à la perche** pole vault(ing); **s. périlleux** somersault; **s. en** *ou* **à skis** ski jump; (*activité*) ski jumping; **faire du s. à skis** to go ski jumping
saut-de-lit *nm inv* (light) dressing gown
saut-de-loup, *pl* **sauts-de-loup** *nm* sunken fence, ha-ha
saut-de-mouton, *pl* **sauts-de-mouton** *nm* flyover, *Am* overpass
saute [sot] *nf* **s. de vent** change in the wind direction; **sautes de température** sudden changes in temperature; **sautes d'humeur** mood swings
sauté [sote] *Culin* **1** *adj* sautéed, sauté **2** *nm* sauté; **s. de lièvre** sauté of hare
saute-mouton *nm* (*no pl*) leapfrog; **jouer à s.** to play leapfrog
sauter [sote] (*aux* **avoir**) **1** *vi* **(a)** (*bondir*) to jump; **s. hors du lit/sur son cheval** to jump *or* leap out of bed/on to one's horse; **s. par la fenêtre/du pont** to jump out (of) the window/from the bridge; **s. sur un pied** to hop; **s. à la perche** to pole-vault; **s. à la corde** to skip, *Am* to jump rope; **s. à terre** to jump down; *Équitation* **le cheval refuse de s.** the horse is refusing (the jump *or* fence); *F* **et que ça saute!** and make it snappy!, and step on it!, chop! chop!; *Fig* **s. du coq à l'âne** to jump *or* skip from one subject to another; **nous allons s. directement à la page 5** we're going to jump straight to page 5; **s. à la gorge de qn** to pounce *or* jump on sb, to go for sb; (*d'un chien*) to fly at sb *or* at sb's throat; **cela saute aux yeux** it's obvious, it's staring you in the face; **s. au cou de qn** to fling one's arms round sb's neck; **s. au plafond** (*du bouchon de champagne etc*) to hit the ceiling; (*de surprise*) to jump out of one's skin; (*de joie*) to jump for joy, to be overjoyed; (*de colère*) to hit the roof *or* the ceiling; **s. de joie** to jump for joy; **s. sur qn** to pounce on *or* fly at *or* fling oneself at sb; *Fig F* to pounce on sb; **s. sur une offre/sur l'occasion** to jump at an offer/at the opportunity; **il faut s. dessus, jamais tu ne trouveras un vélo à ce prix-là** you'll never find another bike at that price, snap it up!
(b) (*exploser*) to blow up, to explode; (*d'un bouton*) to come off, to fly off; *Él* (*d'un fusible*) to blow, *F* to go; *Fig* (*du gouvernement*) to fall; (*d'une entreprise*) to collapse; (*d'un projet*) to fall through; **faire s.** (*rocher*) to blast; (*pont etc*) to blow up; (*mine*) to explode; (*chaudière*) to burst; *Fig* (*projet etc*) to wreck, to ruin; (*gouvernement etc*) to bring down; (*fonctionnaire*) to fire, *Br* to sack; *Culin* (*pommes de terre*) to sauté; *Culin* (*crêpe*) to toss; (*serrure*) to force; (*piège*) to spring; **faire s. le bouchon** (*d'une bouteille*) to pop the cork; **j'ai eu du mal pour faire s. la partie scellée** I had trouble breaking open the sealed part; *F* **faire s. la banque** to break the bank; *Él* **faire s. les plombs** to blow the fuses; **faire s. un enfant sur ses genoux/en l'air** to bounce a child on one's knees/to throw a child up in the air; **se faire s. la cervelle** to blow one's brains out
2 *vt* **(a)** (*fossé, barrière etc*) to jump (over), to leap over, to clear; *Fig* **s. le pas** to take the plunge
(b) (*omettre*) (*page, ligne etc*) to skip, to miss out; (*repas*) to skip; *Tricot* (*maille*) to drop; *Scol* **s. une classe** to skip a year; *F Vieilli* **je la saute** I'm starving, I'm ravenous
(c) (*d'un étalon*) (*jument*) to cover; *Vulg* (*femme*) to shag, to screw; **se faire s.** (*d'une femme*) to get laid
sauterelle [sotrɛl] *nf Ent* grasshopper; (*nuisible*) locust; *Fig F* (*fille maigre*) beanpole; **grande s. d'Orient** locust; **invasion de sauterelles** invasion of locusts
sauterie [sotri] *nf Vieilli, Hum* party, *F* hop
saute-ruisseau *nm inv F Arch* errand boy
sauteur, -euse [sotœr, -øz] **1** *adj* (*insecte etc*) jumping; **scie sauteuse** jigsaw **2** *n* **(a)** *Sp* jumper; **s. en longueur** long jumper; **s. en hauteur** high jumper; **s. à la perche** pole vaulter **(b)** *Fig F* (*homme sans sérieux*) unreliable sort **3** *nf* **sauteuse (a)** (*casserole*) frying pan **(b)** *Arg Vieilli* (*femme de mœurs légères*) slut
sautillant [sotijɑ̃] *adj* (*rythme, musique*) bouncy; **avancer d'un pas s.** to bounce along
sautillement [sotijmɑ̃] *nm* hopping *or* skipping (about); **il avançait par sautillements** he was skipping along; (*sur un pied*) he was hopping along
sautiller [sotije] *vi* (*des oiseaux*) to hop (about); (*des enfants*) to skip *or* hop about; **s. d'un pied sur l'autre** to hop from one foot to the other; **marcher/courir en sautillant** to skip along
sautoir [sotwar] *nm* **(a)** *Hér* saltire **(b)** (*collier*) chain; **s. de perles** string of pearls; **porté en s.** worn round the neck **(c)** *Sp* jumping area

sauvage [sovaʒ] **1** *adj* **(a)** (*à l'état de nature*) (*plante, animal*) wild; **chat s.** wildcat; *Can* raccoon; **lieu s.** wild spot; **la côte ouest est restée très s.** the west coast has remained very wild; **redevenir s.** (*d'un animal apprivoisé*) to revert to the wild; **à l'état s.** wild

(b) *Vieilli* (*peuple, tribu*) savage, primitive; **retourner à la vie s.** to go back to the wild

(c) (*violent*) (*personne, agression*) savage, brutal; (*mœurs*) uncivilised

(d) (*peu sociable*) unsociable

(e) (*non autorisé*) unauthorized; **grève s.** wildcat strike; **camping s.** unauthorized camping; **urbanisation s.** uncontrolled urbanization; **immigration s.** illegal immigration; **psychanalyse s.** amateur psychoanalysis

2 *n* (*f parfois* **sauvagesse**) **(a)** *Vieilli* (*indigène*) savage; *Can Péj* (*Amérindien*) (American) Indian; *F Hum* **on n'est pas des sauvages!** we're not savages!; *F Hum* **bande de sauvages!** you bunch of savages!

(b) (*personne peu sociable*) unsociable person; **c'est un vrai s.** he's a real recluse

sauvagement [sovaʒmɑ̃] *adv* savagely

sauvageon, -onne [sovaʒɔ̃, -ɔn] **1** *nm* (*pour greffer*) wild stock **2** *n* (*enfant*) little savage

sauvagerie [sovaʒri] *nf* **(a)** (*cruauté*) savagery, brutality, barbarity **(b)** (*insociabilité*) unsociability

sauvagin, -ine [sovaʒɛ̃, -in] **1** *adj* (*goût, odeur*) of wildfowl **2** *nf* **chasse à la sauvagine** wildfowling

sauvegarde [sovgard] *nf* **(a)** (*protection*) safeguard (**contre** against); **sous la s. de qn** under sb's protection; **la s. des forêts/du patrimoine national** the safeguarding *or* protection of the forests/the nation's heritage **(b)** *Ordinat* saving, backup; **faire la s. d'un fichier** to save a file; **s. automatique** automatic backup; **s. en ligne** on-line backup; **s. externe** off-line backup; **s. rapide** fast save; **s. sur bande** tape backup; **copie de s.** backup (copy)

sauvegarder [sovgarde] *vt* **(a)** (*protéger*) to safeguard (**contre** against) **(b)** *Ordinat* (*fichier*) to save, to back up; **s. un fichier sur disque** to save a file to disk

sauve-qui-peut *nm inv* (*débandade*) stampede; (*cri*) every man for himself, run for your life

sauver [sove] **1** *vt* **(a)** (*personne*) to save, to rescue (**de** from); *Rel* (*personne, âme*) to save; **le malade est sauvé** the patient is out of danger; **s. la vie à** *ou* **de qn** to save sb's life; *Fig* **tu me sauves!** you're a lifesaver!; *F* **il n'y a que la foi qui sauve!** faith can work miracles!

(b) (*préserver*) (*navire, marchandises*) to salvage; **s. les apparences** to keep up appearances; **s. la face** to save face; *Fig F* **s. les meubles** to save *or* salvage something from the wreckage; *F* **s. sa peau** *ou* **sa tête** to save one's skin; *Fig* **ce qui le sauve, c'est que ...** his saving grace is that ...; **la fin sauve le film** it's the end that saves *or* rescues the film

2 se sauver *vpr* **(a)** (*s'échapper*) to escape (**de** from); **sauve qui peut!** every man for himself!, run for your life!

(b) (*s'enfuir*) to run away; **se s. à toutes jambes** to take to one's heels, to beat a hasty retreat, *Br F* to scarper; *F* **il se fait tard, je me sauve** it's getting late, I'm off *or* I must fly; *F* **sauve-toi maintenant, tu vas être en retard** be off *or* get going now, you'll be late

(c) (*du lait, de préparation culinaire etc*) to boil over

sauvetage [sovtaʒ] *nm* **(a)** (*d'un accidenté*) rescue; **s. aérien en mer** air-sea rescue; **il a fait plusieurs sauvetages en mer** he has been involved in several sea rescues; **appareil de s.** life-saving *or* rescue apparatus; **ceinture de s.** life belt; **gilet de s.** life jacket; **bouée de s.** life buoy; **canot** *ou* **embarcation de s.** lifeboat; **échelle de s.** fire escape; *Fig* **le s. d'une entreprise** the rescue of a company **(b)** (*d'un navire, de marchandises*) salvage

sauveteur [sovtœr] **1** *nm* rescuer **2** *adj m* **bateau s.** lifeboat; **chien s.** rescue dog

sauvette (à la) [alasovɛt] *adv* (*pour ne pas être vu*) furtively, on the sly; (*à la hâte*) in a hurry *ou* rush; **vendre à la s.** (*illégalement*) to peddle (illicitly) on the streets; **marchand à la s.** (illicit) street vendor

sauveur, salvatrice [sovœr, salvatris] **1** *n* saviour, *US* savior **2** *adj* saving

SAV [ɛsave] *nm* (*abrév* **service après-vente**) after-sales service

savamment [savamɑ̃] *adv* **(a)** (*avec érudition*) learnedly; **elle expose s. ses connaissances** she presents her knowledge in a learned manner **(b)** (*en connaissance de cause*) knowingly; **j'en parle s.** I know what I'm talking about **(c)** (*habilement*) cleverly, skilfully, *US* skillfully; **elle sait s. convaincre son monde** she's quite adept at convincing people

savane [savan] *nf* **(a)** *Géog* savanna(h) **(b)** *Can* (*marécage*) swamp

savant, -ante [savɑ̃, -ɑ̃t] **1** *adj* **(a)** (*érudit*) (*personne*) learned (**en** in), erudite, scholarly; (*bien informé*) knowledgeable (**en** about); (*texte*) scholarly, learned; (*mot, terme*) specialist, technical **(b)** (*habile*) clever, skilful, *US* skillful; **s. calcul** clever calculation **(c) chien s.** performing dog **2** *n* (*scientifique*) scientist; (*érudit*) scholar

savarin [savarɛ̃] *nm Culin* savarin

savate [savat] *nf* **(a)** *F* (*pantoufle*) slipper; **être en savates** to be in one's slippers; *Vieilli* **traîner la s.** (*être pauvre*) to be down at heel **(b)** *F* (*maladroit*) clumsy oaf; **comme une s.** abominably, atrociously **(c)** *Sp F* kick boxing **(d)** *Tech* sole (plate)

saveur [savœr] *nf* **(a)** (*de vin, fruit etc*) taste, flavour, *US* flavor; **sans s.** tasteless, insipid **(b)** *Fig* (*de remarque, récit etc*) spice, pungency

Savoie [savwa] *nf* Savoy; *Culin* **biscuit de S.** sponge cake

savoir[1] [savwar] (*prp* **sachant**; *pp* **su**; *pr ind* **je sais, il sait, n. savons, ils savent**; *pr sub* **je sache, n. sachions, ils sachent**; *imp* **sache, sachons, sachez**; *impf* **je savais**; *p hist* **je sus**; *fu* **je saurai**) **1** *vti* **(a)** (*avoir connaissance de*) to know; **s. qch par cœur** to know sth by heart; **s. l'anglais** to know English, *Litt* **s. le chemin** to know the way; **tu sais la nouvelle?** have you heard the news *ou* the latest?; **je n'en sais rien** I don't know anything about it, I know nothing about it; (*je n'y connais rien*) I don't know; **je n'en sais trop rien** I'm not (very) sure; **en s. trop** to know too much; **qu'est-ce j'en sais?** what do I know?; **comment le saurais-je?** how should I know?; **il paraît que tu as des projets, peut-on s.?** it seems you have plans, may one know what they are?; **tu crois qu'il viendra? – va (donc) s.** do you think he'll come? – who knows?; **saura-t-on jamais?** will we ever know?; **qu'en savez-vous?** what do you know about it?; **il sera peut-être là, qui sait?** perhaps he'll be there, who knows?; *F* **est-ce que je sais(, moi)?** I haven't a clue!, don't ask me!; **je ne veux pas (le) s.** I don't want to know; **je voudrais bien s. pourquoi** I'd like to know why, I wonder why; **il n'a rien voulu s.** he wouldn't listen, he didn't want to know; *Litt* **je ne sais** I do not know; **il en sait des choses** *ou* **plus d'une** he knows a thing or two; **reste à s. si ...** it remains to be seen whether *or* if ...; **la question est de s. si elle viendra** the question is whether she will come; **je crois s. qu'il est ici** I understand *or* believe he is here; **faire s. qch à qn** to tell sb sth, to let sb know about sth, to inform sb of sth; **vous auriez dû le lui faire s.** you should have told him, you should have let him know; **je ne suis pas content, et je vais le lui faire s.** I'm not happy and I'll tell him so *or* I'll let him know it; **je le sais par ma sœur** I heard about it from my sister; **(à) s.** that is (to say), namely, i. e. ; **pas que je sache** not to my knowledge, not that I know of; **(à ce) que je sache** as *or* so far as I know; **(pour) autant que je sache** as far as I know; (*quand on ne sait rien*) for all I know; **pour autant que je sache, il pourrait très bien être au Canada** he could be in Canada for all I know; **on ne sait jamais** you never know, you never can tell; **si jeunesse savait!** = youth is wasted on the young; **si j'avais su** if I had known, had I known; **des parents que je sais venir de Londres** relatives who I know come from London; **je ne sais (pas) où les trouver** I don't know where to find them; **je ne sais qui de ses amis** some friend or other of his; **elle a mangé je ne sais quoi et ça l'a rendue malade** she's eaten something or other that's made her ill; **je ne sais quelle maladie/quel problème** some illness/problem or other; **il y a je ne sais combien de temps** ages ago, goodness knows how long ago; **des robes, des chapeaux, des gants, que sais-je (encore)?** dresses, hats, gloves, and what have you *or* and goodness knows what else

(b) (*être conscient de*) to know; **je ne savais pas cela** I didn't know that, I wasn't aware of that; **je le sais bien!** I know!, I realize that!; **elle est jolie et elle le sait bien** she's pretty, and she knows it *or* and doesn't she know it!; **je ne le savais pas malade** I didn't know he was ill; **ce n'est pas facile, tu sais!** it isn't easy, you know!; **sans le s.** without realizing *or* knowing it, without being aware of it; *Litt* (*in first person only*) **je ne sache pas qu'on vous ait invité** I am not aware that you have been invited

(c) *Litt* (*connaître*) (*personne*) to know (of); **je sais un bon horloger** I know (of) a good watchmaker; *Péj* **avec la fille que vous savez** with you know who; *Péj* **c'est encore une lettre de qui vous savez** it's another letter from you know who

(d) (*être certain de*) to know; **il sait ce qu'il veut** he knows what he wants; **ne s. que faire/que dire** not to know *or* to be at a loss what to do/to say; **je ne sais que penser** I don't know what to think; **sachez que ...** be advised that ..., please note that ...; **ne pas s. où se mettre** not to know where to put oneself

(e) [①A57,c,i; B37,K,3] (*être capable de*) **s. faire qch** to be able to do sth, to know how to do sth; **savez-vous nager?** can you swim?, do you know how to swim?; **s. écouter** to be a good listener; **il faut s. être patient** you have to learn to be patient; **je ne saurais (pas) vous conseiller** I wouldn't know what advice to give you, I wouldn't know how to advise you; **on ne saurait se souvenir de tout** one cannot expect to remember everything; **je sais y aller** I know how to get there; **je crois que je saurai le faire** I think I can manage it; *F* **elle sait y faire avec les enfants** she's good with children; *F* **s. s'y prendre avec qn** to know how to handle sb; **je ne saurais guère vous le dire** I'm afraid I couldn't really tell you

(f) (*locutions*) **un je ne sais quoi de déplaisant** something vaguely unpleasant; **c'est Monsieur/Madame je sais tout** he's/she's a real know-all *or* know-it-all; **arrête de faire ton Monsieur je sais tout** stop being such a know-all *or* know-it-all; **il a des amis, Dieu sait** Lord *ou* God knows, he has plenty of friends; **Dieu sait comment** Lord *ou* God (only) knows how; **Dieu sait si je le lui ai répété** God (only) knows how often I've told him

2 se savoir *vpr* **je me savais très malade** I knew I was very ill; **ça se saura vite** it'll soon get out, everyone will know about it soon; **ça se saurait si c'était possible** if it was possible, everyone would know about it

savoir² *nm* knowledge, learning; **homme d'un grand s.** very knowledgeable *or* learned man, man of great learning

savoir-faire *nm inv* expertise, know-how

savoir-vivre *nm inv* savoir-vivre, good manners; **manquer de s.** to have no manners

savon [savɔ̃] *nm* soap; **(pain de) s.** bar *or* cake of soap; **s. de toilette** toilet soap; **s. liquide/doux** liquid/mild soap; **s. en paillettes** soap flakes; **pierre de s.** soapstone, *Spéc* steatite; **tu devrais mettre cette nappe au s.** you should rub the stains on this tablecloth with soap (before putting it into the washing machine); **ça partira avec du s.** it will come off *or* out with soap, soap will take it off *or* out; *F* **passer un s. à qn** to give sb a telling-off

▶ **savon: s. à barbe** shaving soap; **s. de Marseille** = household soap

savonnage [savɔnaʒ] *nm* (*de vêtements, mains etc*) soaping

savonner [savɔne] **1** *vt* **(a)** (*mains, vêtement etc*) to soap; (*en faisant mousser*) to lather; **s. le dos à qn** to soap sb's back; *Vieilli* **s. la tête à qn** to give sb a dressing-down; *Aut* **piste savonnée** skidpan **(b)** *Tech* (*verre*) to rub, to grind **2 se savonner** *vpr* to soap oneself; **se s. les mains** to soap one's hands

savonnerie [savɔnri] *nf* (*usine*) soap factory; (*fabrication*) soap manufacture

savonnette [savɔnɛt] *nf* bar of (toilet) soap

savonneux, -euse [savɔnø, -øz] *adj* soapy

savourer [savure] *vt* (*plat, moment, vengeance etc*) to savour *or US* to savor, to relish, to enjoy

savoureusement [savurøzmɑ̃] *adv* with relish

savoureux, -euse [savurø, -øz] *adj* (*plat*) tasty; (*vin*) full-flavoured *or US* full-flavored; *Fig* (*récit, détails*) spicy, juicy

savoyard, -arde [savwajar, -ard] **1** *adj* Savoyard **2** *n* **S.** Savoyard

Saxe [saks] *nf* Saxony; **porcelaine de S.** Dresden china

saxe [saks] *nm* (*matière*) Dresden china; (*objet*) piece of Dresden china

saxhorn [saksɔrn] *nm Mus* saxhorn; **s. basse** euphonium

saxifrage [saksifraʒ] *nf* saxifrage

saxo [sakso] *nm F* (*instrument*) sax; (*musicien*) sax player

saxon, -onne [saksɔ̃, -ɔn] **1** *adj* Saxon **2** *nm Ling* Saxon **3** *n* **S.** Saxon

saxophone [saksɔfɔn] *nm Mus* saxophone

saxophoniste [saksɔfɔnist] *n Mus* saxophonist

saynète [sɛnɛt] *nf Th* playlet, comic sketch

sbire [sbir] *nm Péj* (*homme de main*) henchman

SCA [ɛssea] *nf* (*abrév* **société en commandite par actions**) partnership limited by shares

scabieux, -ieuse [skabjø, -jøz] **1** *adj* scabby **2** *nf Bot* **scabieuse** scabious

scabreux, -euse [skabrø, -øz] *adj* **(a)** (*indécent*) obscene, indecent; *Litt* scabrous **(b)** *Litt* (*dangereux*) risky, tricky

scalaire¹ [skalɛr] *nm* (*poisson*) angel fish

scalaire² *adj, nm Math* scalar

scalène [skalɛn] *adj Géom, Anat* scalene

scalp [skalp] *nm* (*chevelure*) scalp; (*action de scalper*) scalping

scalpel [skalpɛl] *nm Chir* scalpel

scalper [skalpe] *vt* to scalp

scandale [skɑ̃dal] *nm* (*politique, financier etc*) scandal; **faire (un) s., causer un s.** to create *or* cause a scandal; **il a fait (tout) un s. parce que ...** he made a (tremendous) scene *or* kicked up a (tremendous) fuss because ...; **crier au s.** to make *or* create a great fuss; **au grand s. de ses parents** to the great indignation of his parents; **c'est un s.!** it's a scandal!, it's scandalous!

scandaleusement [skɑ̃daløzmɑ̃] *adv* scandalously, outrageously; **vivre s.** to lead a scandalous life

scandaleux, -euse [skɑ̃dalø, -øz] *adj* scandalous, outrageous

scandaliser [skɑ̃dalize] **1** *vt* to scandalize, to shock **2 se scandaliser** *vpr* to be scandalized *or* shocked (**de** by); **il ne se scandalise de rien** nothing shocks him

scander [skɑ̃de] *vt* (*vers*) to scan; (*slogan*) to chant; *Mus* (*phrase musicale*) to mark, to stress

scandinave [skɑ̃dinav] **1** *adj* Scandinavian **2** *n* **S.** Scandinavian

Scandinavie [skɑ̃dinavi] *nf* Scandinavia

scandium [skɑ̃djɔm] *nm Ch* scandium

scanner¹ [skanɛr] *nm Méd, Ordinat* scanner; **faire un s.** *Méd* (*d'un médecin*) to carry out *or* do a scan; (*d'un patient*) to have a scan; *Typ* to scan; *Méd* **on lui a fait un s.** he was given a scan

scanner² [skane] *vt Ordinat* to scan

scannérisation [skanerizasjɔ̃] *nf Ordinat* scanning

scanneur [skanœr] *nm Ordinat, TV* scanner; *Ordinat* **s. optique** optical scanner; *Ordinat* **s. à main** handheld scanner; *Ordinat* **s. à plat** flatbed scanner

scanographie [skanɔgrafi] *nf Méd* **(a)** (*science*) scanning **(b)** (*cliché*) scan

scansion [skɑ̃sjɔ̃] *nf Littér* scansion, scanning

scaphandre [skafɑ̃dr] *nm* **(a)** *Naut* diving suit; **s. autonome** aqualung, scuba **(b)** *Astronaut* space suit

scaphandrier [skafɑ̃drije] *nm* diver

scaphoïde [skafɔid] *adj, nm Anat, Biol* scaphoid

scapulaire [skapylɛr] **1** *nm Rel* scapular **2** *adj* scapular

scarabée [skarabe] *nm* scarab

scare [skar] *nm* (*poisson*) parrot fish, scar

scarificateur [skarifikatœr] *nm Agr* scarifier; *Chir* scarificator

scarifier [skarifje] *vt* (*impf, pr sub* **n. scarifiions, v. scarifiiez**) *Agr, Chir* to scarify

scarlatine [scarlatin] *nf Méd* scarlet fever, *Spéc* scarlatina; **avoir la s.** to have scarlet fever

scarole [skarɔl] *nf Bot* endive

scat [skat] *nm Mus* scat

scato [skato] *adj inv F* dirty; **plaisanterie s.** dirty joke; **humour s.** lavatorial humour

scatologie [skatɔlɔʒi] *nf* scatology

scatologique [skatɔlɔʒik] *adj* (*littérature, plaisanterie*) scatological

scatophage [skatɔfaʒ] **1** *adj* (*poisson, insecte*) scatophagous **2** *nm* dung fly, *Spéc* scatophage

sceau, *pl* **sceaux** [so] *nm* seal; **S. de l'État** State seal; **s. privé** private seal; **mettre** *ou* **apposer son s. à un document** to affix one's seal to *or* put one's seal on a document; *Fig* **le s. du génie** the mark *or* stamp of genius; **sous le s. du secret** under the seal of secrecy; *Bot* **s. de Salomon** Solomon's seal

scélérat, -ate [selera, -at] *Arch, Litt* **1** *adj* villainous, wicked **2** *n* villain, scoundrel

scellé [sele] **1** *adj* sealed **2** *nm Jur* (official) seal; **mettre** *ou* **apposer/lever les scellés** to put on/remove the seals; **sous scellés** under seal

scellement [sɛlmɑ̃] *nm Constr* (*d'un poteau etc dans la pierre, le béton*) bedding, fixing

sceller [sele] *vt* **(a)** (*document, sac etc*) to seal; (*ratifier*) to ratify, to confirm; **s. un pacte** to set the seal on an agreement **(b)** *Constr* to bed, to fix (in); **faire s. une porte/fenêtre** to seal a door/a window

scénario [senarjo] *nm Cin, TV* scenario; (*script*) script, screenplay; **s. d'auteur** writer's script; *Psy* **s. à compléter** story completion; *TV, Cin* **s-maquette** storyboard; **s. de répétition** rehearsal script; *Fig* scenario

scénariste [senarist] *n Cin, TV* scriptwriter, screenwriter; **s. (de réécriture)** script editor

scène [sɛn] *nf* **(a)** *Th* (*plateau*) stage; **la s.** (*le théâtre*) the stage, the theatre *or US* the theater; **entrer en s.** (*d'un acteur*) to appear, to come on; *Fig* to appear on the scene; **être en s.** (*d'un acteur*) to be on (stage); **en s. pour le un!** on stage for act one!, beginners please!; **porter qch à la s.** to adapt sth for the stage; **quitter la s.** to retire from the stage *or* from acting; **faire ses adieux à la s.** to make one's final appearance on stage; *Fig* **la s. politique/internationale** the political/international scene; *Fig* **le devant de la s.** the foreground; **occuper le devant de la s.** to hold centre stage; **s. tournante** revolving stage

(b) (*décor, action*) scene; **changement de s.** change of scene; **le tableau représente une s. de chasse** the painting represents a hunting scene; **une s. d'amour** a love scene;

acte II, s. trois act two, scene three; *Fig Hum* **il m'a fait la grande s. du II** he put on an Oscar-winning performance; **la s. se passe au moyen âge** the action takes place in the Middle Ages, the scene *or* the action is set in the Middle Ages
(c) (*événement*) scene; **revoir les scènes de sa jeunesse** to revisit the scenes of one's youth; **ce fut une s. pénible** it was a painful scene; **imagine la s.!** imagine *or* picture the scene!, just imagine *or* picture it!
(d) *F* (*dispute*) scene; **il m'a fait une s.** he made a scene
▶ **scène**: **s. de ménage** domestic squabble; *Psy* **s. primitive** primal scene

scénique [senik] *adj* theatrical; **éclairage s.** stage *or* theatrical lighting; **indications scéniques** stage directions

scéniquement [senikmɑ̃] *adv* theatrically

scénographe [senɔgraf] *n* **(a)** *Beaux-Arts etc* scenographer **(b)** *Th* stage *or* theatre designer

scénographie [senɔgrafi] *nf* **(a)** *Beaux-Arts etc* scenography **(b)** *Th* stage *or* theatre design

scepticisme [sɛptisism] *nm* scepticism, *US* skepticism

sceptique [sɛptik] **1** *adj* sceptical, sceptic, *US* skeptic(al) **2** *n* sceptic, *US* skeptic

sceptiquement [sɛptikmɑ̃] *adv Rare* sceptically, *US* skeptically

sceptre [sɛptr] *nm* sceptre, *US* scepter; *Fig* **s. de fer** rod of iron

schako [ʃako] *nm Mil* shako

scheik [ʃɛk] *nm* sheik

schelem [ʃlɛm] *nm Cartes* slam; **petit/grand s.** little/grand slam

schéma [ʃema] *nm* **(a)** (*graphique*) (*d'un moteur, d'une structure hiérarchique etc*) diagram, plan **(b)** (*esquisse*) (*d'un livre etc*) plan, outline; **s. directeur** master plan; **s. d'entreprise** organization chart; *Ordinat* **s. de clavier** keyboard map; **s. logique** logic diagram

schématique [ʃematik] *adj* diagrammatic, schematic, *Péj* oversimplified

schématiquement [ʃematikmɑ̃] *adv* schematically, diagrammatically; (*en gros*) in outline, in a simplified manner; **très s., voici ce que nous vous proposons** in very broad terms *or* very broadly speaking, this is what we propose

schématisation [ʃematizasjɔ̃] *nf* schematization, *Péj* oversimplification

schématiser [ʃematize] *vt* to schematize, *Péj* to oversimplify

schématisme [ʃematism] *nm Péj* oversimplification; *Phil* schematism

schème [ʃɛm] *nm Phil, Psy* schema; *Beaux-Arts etc* design

scherzando [skɛrtsando, skɛrdz-] *adv Mus* scherzando

scherzo [skɛrtso, -dzo] *Mus* **1** *nm* scherzo **2** *adv* scherzando

schibboleth [ʃibɔlɛt] *nm Rare* shibboleth

schilling [ʃiliŋ] *nm* (*monnaie autrichienne*) schilling

schismatique [ʃismatik] *adj, n* schismatic

schisme [ʃism] *nm* schism; **faire s.** to break away

schiste [ʃist] *nm Géol* schist, shale

schisteux, -euse [ʃistø -øz] *adj Géol* schistose

schistosomiase [ʃistɔzomjaz] *nf Méd* bilharzia, schistosomiasis

schizogamie [skizɔgami] *nf Biol* schizogenesis

schizoïde [skizɔid] *adj, n Psy* schizoid

schizoïdie [skizɔidi] *nf Psy* schizoidism

schizoïdique [skizɔidik] *adj Psy* schizoid

schizophrène [skizɔfrɛn] *adj, n Psy* schizophrenic

schizophrénie [skizɔfreni] *nf Psy* schizophrenia

schizophrénique [skizɔfrenik] *adj, n Psy* schizophrenic

schizothymie [skizɔtimi] *nf Psy* schizothymia

schizothymique [skizɔtimik] *adj Psy* schizothymic

schlague [ʃlag] *nf Hist, Mil* flogging; *Fig F* **mener qn à la s.** to rule sb with a rod of iron

schlass[1] [ʃlas] *adj inv très F* (*épuisé*) knackered, shattered; (*soûl*) pissed, *Br* rat-arsed

schlass[2] *nm très F* (*couteau*) blade

schlinguer [ʃlɛ̃ge] *vi Vulg* to stink, *Br* to pong

schlittage [ʃlitaʒ] *nm* (timber) sledging

schlitte [ʃlit] *nf* (*pour transporter le bois*) (timber) sledge

schlitter [ʃlite] *vt* (*bois*) to sledge

schnaps [ʃnaps] *nm* schnapps

schnauzer [ʃnawzɛr] *nm* (*chien*) schnauzer

schnock, schnoque [ʃnɔk] *F* **1** *adj* (*fou*) crazy, *Br F* bonkers; (*bête*) moronic **2** *nm* cretin, moron; **un vieux s.** an old fogey; **eh, du s.!** hey, you cretin *or* moron!

schnorchel, schnorkel [ʃnɔrkɛl] *nm* (*de sous-marin*) snorkel

schnouff [ʃnuf] *nf Arg* (*drogue*) dope, junk

schofar [ʃɔfar] *nm Rel* shofar, shophar

schuss [ʃus] *nm Ski* schuss; **descendre la piste en s.** *ou* **tout s.** to schuss down the slope

schweppes® [ʃwɛps] *nm* tonic

SCI [ɛsseі] *nf* (*abrév* **société de commerce international**) international trading corporation

sciage [sjaʒ] *nm* sawing

sciatique [sjatik] **1** *adj Anat* (*nerf*) sciatic **2** *nm* sciatic nerve **3** *nf Méd* sciatica

scie [si] *nf* **(a)** (*outil*) saw; **s. à bois** wood saw; **s. à métaux** hacksaw; **s. mécanique** *ou* **à main** hand saw; **s. circulaire** circular saw, *Am* buzz saw; **s. articulée, s. à chaîne(tte)** chain saw; **s. à chantourner** (*manuelle*) bowsaw, turning saw; (*mécanique*) jigsaw, scroll saw; **s. à découper, s. anglaise** (*manuelle*) fret saw; (*mécanique*) jigsaw; **en dents de s.** serrated; *Fig* (*évolution, progrès*) uneven; *Méd* **bruit de s.** rasping murmur **(b)** *Mus* **s. musicale** musical saw **(c)** (**poisson**) **s.** sawfish **(d)** *F Vieilli* (*personne ennuyeuse*) bore

sciemment [sjamɑ̃] *adv* knowingly, on purpose, wittingly

science [sjɑ̃s] *nf* **(a)** (*savoir*) knowledge, learning; *Fig* **il croit avoir la s. infuse** you can't tell him anything; **je n'ai pas la s. infuse** I can't be expected to know everything; *F* **étaler sa s.** to show off one's knowledge
(b) (*domaine spécifique*) science; **la s. n'a pas de patrie** science knows no frontiers; **préparer une licence ès sciences** to be studying for a science degree; **homme de s.** scientist; **les sciences exactes** *ou* **pures** the exact sciences; **sciences physiques/naturelles/appliquées** physical/natural/applied science; **sciences expérimentales** experimental science; **sciences humaines** ≈ social sciences; **sciences sociales** social sciences; **sciences économiques** economics; **les sciences occultes** the occult sciences

science-fiction *nf* science fiction; **roman/film de s.** science fiction novel/film; *Fig Hum* **c'est de la s.!** it's unbelievable!

scientificité [sjɑ̃tifisite] *nf* scientific character

scientifique [sjɑ̃tifik] **1** *adj* scientific **2** *n* scientist; **ce n'est pas un s.** he's not very scientifically-minded

scientifiquement [sjɑ̃tifikmɑ̃] *adv* scientifically

scientisme [sjɑ̃tism] *nm* **(a)** *Phil* scientism **(b)** *Rel* Christian Science

scientiste [sjɑ̃tist] **1** *adj* scientistic **2** *n* **(a)** *Phil* adept of scientism **(b)** *Rel* **s. chrétien(ne)** Christian Scientist

scier[1] [sje] *vt* (*pr sub, impf* **n. sciions, v. sciiez**) (*bois, métal*) to saw; (*enlever*) (*branche etc*) to saw off; *très F* **s. qn** (*étonner*) to dumbfound *or Br F* to gobsmack sb; *très F* **j'étais scié de rire** I was doubled up with laughter

scier[2] *vi* (*à l'aviron*) to back water, to back the oars

scierie [siri] *nf* sawmill

scieur [sjœr] *nm* sawyer

scieuse [sjøz] *nf* mechanical saw

scille [sil] *nf Bot* scilla, squill; **s. maritime** sea onion

scinder [sɛ̃de] **1** *vt* to divide, to split up (**en** into); *Fin* **s. une société** to break up a company, to split a company **2 se scinder** *vpr* to split up (**en** into)

scinque [sɛ̃k] *nm Zool* skink

scintigramme [sɛ̃tigram] *nm Méd* scintigram

scintigraphie [sɛ̃tigrafi] *nf Méd* scintigraphy

scintillant [sɛ̃tijɑ̃] **1** *adj* (*bijoux, lumières etc*) sparkling, glittering; (*étoile*) twinkling; (*yeux*) sparkling, twinkling; *Fig* (*esprit, personnalité*) sparkling, scintillating **2** *nm* tinsel decoration(s)

scintillation [sɛ̃tijasjɔ̃] *nf Phys, Astron* scintillation

scintillement [sɛ̃tijmɑ̃] *nm* (*de bijou, lumière etc*) sparkling, glittering; (*d'étoile*) twinkling; (*des yeux*) sparkling; *Cin, TV* flicker(ing), shimmer

scintiller [sɛ̃tije] *vi* (*d'un bijou, d'une lumière etc*) to sparkle, to glitter; (*d'une étoile*) to twinkle; (*des yeux*) to sparkle; *Électron, TV, Cin* to flicker

scion [sjɔ̃] *nm* **(a)** (*pousse*) shoot; (*à greffer*) scion **(b)** (*d'une canne à pêche*) tip

scirpe [sirp] *nm Bot* bulrush

scissile [sisil] *adj Phys Nucl* (*matériau*) fissionable

scission [sisjɔ̃] *nf* **(a)** *Pol etc* split, division; **faire s.** to split away *or* off, to secede; *Fin* **s. d'actifs** divestment of assets, hive-off of assets; **s. d'une entreprise** break-up of a company **(b)** *Ch* scission, cleavage; *Phys Nucl* fission, splitting; **s. nucléaire** nuclear fission

scissionniste [sisjɔnist] *adj, n* secessionist

scissipare [sisipar] *adj Biol* fissiparous

scissiparité [sisiparite] *nf Biol* schizogenesis, fissiparity

scissure [sisyr] *nf Anat* fissure

sciure [sjyr] *nf* **s. (de bois)** sawdust; **s. de marbre** marble dust

scléral, -ale, -aux, -ales [skleral, -o] *adj Anat* sclerotic

scléreux, -euse [sklerø, -øz] *adj Méd* sclerosed

sclérifié [sklerifje] *adj Biol* (*tégument etc*) sclerosed, hardened

sclérodermie [sklerɔdɛrmi] *nf Méd* scleroderma

sclérogène [sklerɔʒɛn] *adj Méd* sclerogenic

scléroprotéine [sklerɔprɔtein] *nf* scleroprotein

sclérosant [sklerɔzɑ̃] *adj Méd* sclerosing; *Fig* ossifying

sclérose [skleroz] *nf Méd* sclerosis; *Fig* ossification; **s.**

vasculaire *ou* **des artères** arteriosclerosis, hardening of the arteries; **s. en plaques** multiple sclerosis, MS
sclérosé [skleroze] *adj Méd* sclerosed; *Fig* hidebound, fossilized
scléroser [skleroze] **1** *vt Méd* to sclerose **2** *Fig* **se scléroser** *vpr* to become fossilized
sclérotique [sklerɔtik] *Anat nf (de l'œil)* sclerotic, sclera
scolaire [skɔlɛr] *adj* **(a)** *(résultats, réussite)* academic, scholastic; *(réforme, organisation)* educational; **vie s.** school life; **année s.** school *or* academic year; **enfant d'âge s.** child of school age; **frais scolaires** school fees; **livres scolaires** school books, text books **(b)** *Péj (esprit, mentalité)* bookish; *(style, discours)* academic, schoolmasterish; *(peinture)* laboured, *US* labored
scolairement [skɔlɛrmɑ̃] *adv Péj (réciter, écrire)* in an academic *or* schoolmasterish way
scolarisable [skɔlarizabl] *adj* of school age
scolarisation [skɔlarizasjɔ̃] *nf* **prolongation de la s.** raising of the school-leaving age; **je suis pour la s. des enfants à partir de l'âge de cinq ans** I'm in favour of children going to *or* starting school at the age of five; **la s. d'une région** equipping *or* providing an area with schools; **la s. des enfants** providing education for children; **taux de s.** percentage of children in full-time education
scolariser [skɔlarize] *vt* **s. des enfants** to provide education for children; **s. une région** to equip *or* provide an area with schools; **enfant scolarisé** child attending school
scolarité [skɔlarite] *nf* **s. obligatoire** compulsory schooling; **prolongation de la s.** raising of the school-leaving age; **j'ai eu une s. difficile** I had a difficult time at school; **s. à temps partiel** = day-release classes; **certificat de s.** = certificate of attendance *(at school or university)*; **frais de s.** school fees
scolasticat [skɔlastika] *nm* theological training; *(établissement)* theological college
scolastique [skɔlastik] **1** *adj (philosophie etc)* scholastic **2** *nm* scholastic **3** *nf* scholasticism
scoliaste [skɔljast] *nm* scholiast
scoliose [skɔljoz] *nf Méd* scoliosis, lateral curvature of the spine
scolopendre¹ [skɔlɔpɑ̃dr] *nf Zool* centipede, *Spéc* scolopendrid
scolopendre² *nf Bot* hart's-tongue, *Spéc* scolopendrium
sconse [skɔ̃s] *nm* skunk; *(fourrure)* skunk (fur)
scoop [skup] *nm* **(a)** *Journ* scoop **(b)** *Fig F* **c'est un s.!** it's hot news!; *Iron* well I never!; **j'ai un s.!** I've got some hot news!; **ce n'est pas un s.** it's not exactly headline news!
scooter [skutɛr] *nm* (motor) scooter; **s. des mers** jet-ski
scootériste [skuterist] *n* (motor) scooter rider, (motor) scooterist
scopie [skɔpi] *nf Arg Méd* radioscopy
scopolamine [skɔpɔlamin] *nf Ch, Pharm* scopolamine, hyoscine
scorbut [skɔrbyt] *nm Méd* scurvy, *Spéc* scorbutus
scorbutique [skɔrbytik] *adj, n Méd* scorbutic
score [skɔr] *nm Sp* score; **s. électoral** share of the vote; **faire un bon/mauvais s.** to turn in a good/bad performance
scoriacé [skɔrjase] *adj Métal, Géol etc* slaggy
scorie [skɔri] *nf souvent pl* **(a)** *Métal* **scories** slag, cinders, scoria; *(de fer)* (iron) dross; *(de charbon)* clinker **(b)** *Géol* **scories (volcaniques)** scoria, volcanic slag **(c)** *Fig* **scories** dregs; **débarrasser une philosophie de ses scories** to rid a philosophy of its dross
scorpène [skɔrpɛn] *nf* scorpion fish
scorpion [skɔrpjɔ̃] *nm* **(a)** *Zool* scorpion; **s. aquatique** *ou* **d'eau** water scorpion; **s. de mer** scorpion fish **(b)** *Astron, Astrol* **le S.** Scorpio; **être (du signe du) S.** to be (a) Scorpio
scorsonère [skɔrsɔnɛr] *nf,* **scorzonère** [skɔrzɔnɛr] *nf Bot* black salsify, *Spéc* scorzonera
scotch [skɔtʃ] *nm* **(a)** *pl* **scotchs** *ou* **scotches** scotch (whisky); **un double s.** a double scotch **(b)** **Scotch**® self-adhesive tape, *Br* ≈ Sellotape®, *Am* ≈ Scotchtape®
scotcher [skɔtʃe] *vt* to tape, *Br* to sellotape, *Am* to scotchtape
scotch-terrier, *pl* **scotch-terriers** *nm* Scotch terrier
scottish-terrier, *pl* **scottish-terriers** [skɔtiʃterje] *nm* Scotch terrier
scoumoune [skumun] *nf Arg* persistent bad luck; **avoir la s.** to be jinxed
scout [skut] **1** *nm* (boy) scout **2** *adj* **groupe/mouvement s.** scout group/movement; *Péj* **il a des côtés un peu scouts** he's a bit of a boy scout at heart
scoutisme [skutism] *nm (activité)* scouting; *(mouvement)* scout movement
SCPI [ɛssepei] *nm (abrév* **société civile de placement immobilier**) property investment company
Scrabble® [skrabl] *nm* Scrabble; **jouer au S.** to play Scrabble
scratch, *pl* **scratches** [skratʃ] *Sp* **1** *nm (course)* scratch race; *(joueur)* scratch (player); **partir s.** to start (at) scratch **2** *adj* **course s.** scratch race; **joueur s.** scratch (player)
scratcher [skratʃe] *vt Sp* to scratch
scribe [skrib] *nm Antiq* scribe; *Vieilli Péj* pen-pusher
scribouillard, -arde [skribujar, -ard] *n F Péj* pen-pusher
script¹ [skript] *nm Fin* scrip
script² *nm* **(a)** *(écriture)* printing; **écrire en s.** to print (one's letters); **écriture s.** printing **(b)** *Cin* (film) script
scripte [skript] *nf Cin* continuity girl
script-girl, *pl* **script-girls** [skriptgœrl] *nf Cin* continuity girl
scriptural, -ale, -aux, -ales [skriptyral, -o] *adj* scriptural; *Banque* **monnaie scripturale** bank money
scrofulaire [skrɔfylɛr] *nf Bot* figwort
scrofule [skrɔfyl] *nf Méd* scrofula; *Arch* **les scrofules** scrofula; *Arch* the king's evil
scrofuleux, -euse [skrɔfylø, -øz] *Méd* **1** *adj* scrofulous **2** *n* scrofulous person
scrotum [skrɔtɔm] *nm Anat* scrotum
scrupule [skrypyl] *nm* **(a)** scruple **(sur** about); **sans scrupules** *adj* unscrupulous; *adv* unscrupulously; **je n'aurai aucun s. à le lui dire** I'll have no scruples about telling him so; **se faire (un) s. de faire qch, avoir des scrupules à faire qch** to have scruples about doing sth; **il ne se fait pas s. d'emprunter à la caisse** he has no scruples about borrowing from the till; **exact jusqu'au s.** scrupulously exact **(b)** *Arch (unité de poids)* scruple
scrupuleusement [skrypyløzmɑ̃] *adv* scrupulously
scrupuleux, -euse [skrypylø, -øz] *adj* scrupulous **(sur** about; **à faire qch** in doing sth); **peu s.** unscrupulous
scrutateur, -trice [skrytatœr, -tris] **1** *adj Litt (esprit, regard)* searching **2** *n (d'un scrutin)* teller
scruter [skryte] *vt* to examine, to scrutinize; *(horizon, paysage)* to scan
scrutin [skrytɛ̃] *nm* **(a)** *(élection)* poll; **s. d'arrondissement** = constituency poll; **s. secret** secret vote *or* ballot; **s. uninominal** system of voting for a single candidate; **s. proportionnel** *ou* **de liste** system of voting by proportional representation *or* by lists; **s. majoritaire** first-past-the-post system

(b) *(vote)* ballot; **tour de s.** ballot, round (of voting); **il a été élu au premier tour de s.** he was elected in the first round of voting *or* in the first ballot; **s. de ballotage** second ballot; **dépouiller le s.** to count the votes *or* ballots

(c) *(dans une assemblée)* voting; *Br Parl* division; **procéder au s.** to take the vote; *Br Parl* to divide; **demander le s.** to ask for a count; **projet adopté sans s.** bill passed without a vote
SCS [ɛsseɛs] *nf (abrév* **société en commandite simple**) limited partnership
scull [skyl, skœl] *nm Sp, Naut* scull; *(activité)* sculling
sculpter [skylte] **1** *vt* to sculpt, to sculpture; *(dans du bois)* to carve **(dans** in, out of); **bois sculpté** carved wood **2** *vi* to sculpt, to (do) sculpture
sculpteur [skyltœr] *nm* sculptor; **femme s.** woman sculptor, sculptress; **s. sur bois** woodcarver
sculptural, -ale, -aux, -ales [skyltyral, -o] *adj (art)* sculptural; *(silhouette, beauté)* statuesque
sculpture [skyltyr] *nf* **(a)** *(œuvre, art)* sculpture; **s. sur bois** woodcarving; **faire de la s.** to sculpt, to (do) sculpture **(b)** *(d'un pneu)* tread
scutellaire [skytelɛr] *nf Bot* skull cap, *Spéc* scutellaria
scythe [sit] **1** *adj* Scythian **2** *n* **S.** Scythian
Scythie [siti] *nf* Scythia
SDF [ɛsdeɛf] *n (abrév* **sans domicile fixe**) of no fixed abode; **un S.** a person of no fixed abode; *(sans abri)* a homeless person; **les S.** *(sans abri)* the homeless
SDN [ɛsdeɛn] *abrév* **Société des Nations**
se [s(ə)] *pron* **(s'** *before vowel or mute h)* **(a)** [①A29; B26-7,D] *(réfléchi) (complément direct)* himself; *(sujet féminin)* herself; *(non humain)* itself; *(indéfini)* oneself, *Am* himself; *(pl)* themselves; *(complément indirect)* to himself/herself/itself/oneself/themselves; **se flatter** to flatter oneself; **il se rase** he is shaving; **elle s'est coupée au doigt** *ou* **s'est coupé le doigt** she has cut her finger; **il se parle (à lui-même)** he's talking to himself; **il s'est fait mal** he hurt himself; **il se couche tard** he goes to bed late; **fais se laver les mains à cet enfant** make that child wash his hands

(b) *(réciproque) (complément direct)* each other, one another; *(complément indirect)* to each other, to one another; **se nuire (l'un à l'autre)** to hurt each other *or* one another; **ils/elles se parlent** they talk to each other *or* one another; **il est dur de se quitter** it is hard to part

(c) *(passif)* **cet article se vend partout** this article is sold *or* is on sale everywhere; **la porte s'est ouverte** the door opened; **ça ne se fait pas** you don't do that, it's not the done thing; **ça se mange froid** it's eaten cold, you eat it cold

(d) (*avec v impers*) **il se peut qu'elle vienne** (it's possible that) she might come; **comment se fait-il que …?** how is it that …?

séance [seɑ̃s] *nf* **(a)** (*réunion*) (*d'une assemblée etc*) sitting, session, meeting; **être en s., tenir s.** to be sitting *or* in session; **la s. s'ouvrira/sera levée à huit heures** the meeting will open/adjourn at eight o'clock; **je déclare la s. ouverte** I declare the meeting open; **en s. publique** at an open meeting; *Jur* in open court; *Bourse* **s. boursière** trading session; **s. de concertation** policy meeting; **s. d'information** briefing (session); **s. de spiritisme** seance

(b) *Cin, Th* performance, show; *Cin* **s. privée** private showing

(c) (*période*) session; **faire une longue s. à table** to sit a long time over one's meal; *Méd* **traitement de trois séances** course of three treatments; **s. de travail/d'entraînement** working/training session; **s. de photo** photocall, photo opportunity; **s. de pose** sitting; *Méd* **s. de rééducation** physiotherapy session

(d) s. tenante straight away, at once

(e) *F Péj* (*scène*) performance; **il nous a fait une s. de larmes** he turned on the waterworks

séancier [seɑ̃sje] *nm* (*parlementaire*) parliamentary reporter

séant [seɑ̃] **1** *adj Arch, Litt* (*flatteur*) becoming (**à** to); (*convenable*) fitting; **il ne serait pas s. de se contredire** it would not be fitting to contradict each other **2** *nm Litt, Hum* **se mettre sur son s.** (*au lit etc*) to sit up; **être sur son s.** to be in a sitting position; **tomber sur son s.** to sit down with a bump

seau, *pl* **seaux** [so] *nm* bucket, pail; (*contenu*) bucket(ful), pail(ful); **s. à glace** *ou* **à rafraîchir** ice bucket; **s. à incendie** fire bucket; **s. à charbon** coal scuttle; **s. à champagne** champagne bucket; *F* **il pleut à seaux** it's pouring down, *Br* it's bucketing down

sébacé [sebase] *adj* (*glande*) sebaceous

sébile [sebil] *nf* (begging) bowl

séborrhée [sebɔre] *nf Méd* seborrhoea, *US* seborrhea

sébum [sebɔm] *nm Anat* sebum

sec, sèche [sɛk, sɛʃ] **1** *adj* **(a)** (*temps, saison, sol, gorge, peau, vin, toux etc*) dry; (*morue, fruit etc*) dried; (*bois, cigare*) seasoned, matured; **regarder d'un œil s.** to look on dry-eyed; **il avait la gorge sèche** (*il avait soif*) his throat was dry, he was dry *or* parched; (*il avait peur*) his throat was dry; **mettre qn au pain s. et à l'eau** to put sb on bread and water; **mur de pierres sèches** drystone wall; *Aut* **être en panne sèche** to have run out of petrol *or Am* gas; **traverser un torrent à pied s.** to cross a torrent without getting one's feet *or* shoes wet; **s. comme une allumette** bone dry; **ne plus avoir un fil de s.** to be soaked to the skin; **régime s.** (*sans boisson*) alcohol-free diet; **pays secs** (*sans boisson*) dry countries, prohibitionist countries; **perte sèche** dead loss; *F* **en cinq s.** in no time at all, in two shakes (of a lamb's tail); *F* **je l'ai s.!** (*j'ai soif*) I'm dry *or* parched!; *Fig* am I annoyed!

(b) (*maigre*) (*personne*) spare, lean; (*cheval*) lean; **s. et nerveux** wiry; **s. comme un coup de trique** as thin as a rake

(c) (*sans tendresse*) (*remarque, réponse*) sharp, curt; (*ton*) incisive; (*coup*) sharp; (*cœur*) cold, unfeeling; (*récit, style*) dry, bald; **il est très s. au téléphone** he's very curt on the phone; **casser qch d'un coup s.** to snap sth; **frapper à la porte d'un coup s.** to rap on the door; **arracher un pansement d'un coup s.** to rip a plaster off; **faire un accueil très s. à qn** to give sb a very cool reception

2 *adv* **(a) boire s.** to drink one's spirits neat *or* straight; (*beaucoup*) to drink a lot, to be a heavy drinker

(b) (*rudement*) hard, sharply; **la voiture a viré très s.** the car swung round sharply; *Aut* **démarrer s.** to shoot off, to tear off

(c) à s. dry; (*asséché*) dried up; *F* (*sans argent*) hard up, broke; **mettre à s.** (*marais etc*) to drain; *Fig* (*personne*) to clean out; **nettoyage à s.** dry cleaning; **navire à s.** *ou* **au s.** ship aground *or* high and dry; **filer** *ou* **courir** *ou* **fuir à s. (de toile)** (*d'un bateau*) to run under bare poles

(d) *F* **aussi s.** straight away, right away, at once

3 *nm* dryness; **tenir au s.** keep in a dry place

4 *nf Arg* **sèche** (*cigarette*) fag, *US* butt

sécable [sekabl] *adj* divisible

secam [sekam] *adj, nm* (*abrév* **séquentiel couleur à mémoire**) *TV* secam

sécant, -ante [sekɑ̃, -ɑ̃t] *Math* **1** *adj* (*ligne, surface*) secant, cutting **2** *nf* **sécante** secant

sécateur [sekatœr] *nm* pruning shears, *Br* secateurs

sécession [sesesjɔ̃] *nf* secession; **faire s.** to secede (**de** from)

sécessionniste [sesesjɔnist] *adj, n* secessionist

séchage [seʃaʒ] *nm* (*du foin, des vêtements, d'une surface peinte etc*) drying; (*du bois*) seasoning

sèche-cheveux [sɛʃʃəvø] *nm inv* hair drier

sèche-linge [sɛʃlɛ̃ʒ] *nm inv* (*appareil*) tumble dryer; (*armoire*) airing cupboard

sèche-mains [sɛʃmɛ̃] *nm inv* (hot-air) hand drier

sèchement [sɛʃmɑ̃] *adv* **(a)** (*avec dureté*) (*parler, répondre etc*) curtly, sharply; (*taper*) sharply **(b)** (*sans fioritures*) (*écrire, traiter un sujet etc*) drily, baldly

sécher [seʃe] **(je sèche, n. séchons; je sécherai) 1** *vt* (*vêtements, sol, mains, encre, poisson, etc*) to dry; (*rivière etc*) to dry up; **le vent sèche la peau** wind dries (out) the skin; **s. ses larmes** to dry one's tears; *F* **s. un verre** (*le vider*) to drain a glass; *Scol etc F* **s. un cours** to skip *or* cut a class

2 *vi* **(a)** (*de vêtements, de sols, de surfaces etc*) to dry; **faire s. du bois** to dry *or* season wood; **faire s. du linge** to dry clothes; **mettre du linge à s.** to put clothes out to dry; **laisser s. les peintures** to leave the paintwork to dry; *Bot, Fig* **s. sur pied** to wilt; *Litt* **s. d'impatience/d'ennui** to be consumed with impatience/boredom

(b) *F* (*ne pouvoir répondre*) to be stumped; (*by an examiner*) to dry up

3 se sécher *vpr* to dry oneself

sécheresse [sɛʃrɛs, se-] *nf* **(a)** (*de l'air, du sol, de la peau, de la gorge etc*) dryness **(b)** (*absence de pluie*) drought **(c)** (*des manières etc*) curtness; (*du cœur*) coldness, unfeelingness; (*du style*) dryness, baldness; **parler avec s.** to speak curtly

sécherie [sɛʃri, se-] *nf* (*appareil*) drying machine, drier; (*lieu*) drying area

sécheur [seʃœr] *nm Tech* drying machine, drier

séchoir [seʃwar] *nm* **(a)** (*appareil*) drier; **s. (à cheveux)** hair drier; *Ind* **s. à vapeur** steam drier **(b)** (*dispositif pliant*) **s. (à linge)** clotheshorse **(c)** *Tech* (*lieu*) drying area; **s. à houblon** oast house

second, -onde [səgɔ̃, -ɔ̃d] **1** *adj* **(a)** second; *Th* (*rôle*) supporting, minor; **au s. étage** on the second *or US* third floor; **une seconde fois** a second time; **en s. lieu** in the second place, secondly; **seconde nature** second nature (**chez qn** with sb); **de seconde main** secondhand; **de s. ordre** *ou* **choix** second-rate; *F* **ça passe en s.** that comes second, that takes second place; **votre ami est un s. Sherlock Holmes** your friend is another *or* a second Sherlock Holmes; **donner un s. souffle à l'économie** to give a new lease of life to *or* to revitalize the economy; *Sp, Fig* **trouver son s. souffle** to get one's second wind; **le don de seconde vue** the gift of second sight; *Mus* **les seconds violons** the second violins; *Gram* **la seconde personne du singulier** the second person singular; *Rail* **seconde classe** second class; **voyager en seconde classe** to travel second-class; *Jur* **signer en s.** (*d'un notaire*) to countersign; *Sp* **prendre la seconde place** to come second, to take second place; *Phil etc* **causes secondes** second causes; *Bourse* **s. marché** unlisted securities market, USM; *TV, Cin* **s. passage** repeat

(b) *Méd* **état s.** (*d'un somnambule*) semi-conscious state; *Fig* **être dans un état s.** to be in a trance *or* a daze

(c) *Naut* **commandant** *ou* **officier en s.** executive officer; **commander en s.** to be second in command

2 *nm* **(a)** (*assistant*) principal assistant; *Mil, F* second in command; *Naut* first mate; (*de duelliste*) second; **s. (de cuisine)** senior sous chef; sous chef; *TV, Cin* **s. assistant** best boy

(b) (*étage*) second *or Am* third floor; **habiter au s.** to live on the second *or Am* third floor; **les voisins du s.** the neighbours on the second *or US* third floor

3 *nf* **seconde** *Typ* second proof; *Aut* second (gear); *Aut* **passer en seconde** to change *or* go (up/down) into second; *Rail etc* **voyager en seconde** to travel second-class; **billet de seconde** second-class ticket; *Scol* **(classe de) seconde** ≈ fifth form, *Am* ≈ tenth grade; **élève de seconde** ≈ fifth-former, *Am* ≈ tenth-grader; *Mus* **seconde majeure/mineure** major/minor second

4 *n* second; *Sp* **finir bon s.** to finish a good second; **la seconde est française** (*dans une compétition*) the competitor in second place is French; **mon s.** (*enfant*) my second child

secondaire [səgɔ̃dɛr] **1** *adj* **(a)** *Scol* secondary; **établissement d'enseignement s.** secondary school

(b) (*peu important*) secondary; **il faut en parler, mais c'est s.** we must talk about it, but it's of secondary importance; **effets secondaires d'un médicament** side effects of a medicine; *Rail* **voie s.** side track; *Ling* **accent s.** secondary accent, secondary stress; *Mus* **temps s.** off-beat; *Th, Littér* **intrigue s.** sub-plot; **personnage/rôle s.** minor character/ part

(c) *Écon* (*secteur*) secondary; *Géol* **l'ère s.** the secondary era

2 *nm* (a) *Él* secondary winding; *Rad* (*du transformateur*) secondary

(b) **le s.** *Géol* the secondary era; *Écon* the secondary sector

secondairement [səgɔ̃dɛrmɑ̃] *adv* secondarily

seconde [səgɔ̃d] *nf* (*du temps, d'un arc de cercle, d'un angle*) second; **aiguille des secondes** (*d'une montre*) second hand; **j'en ai pour une s.** I'll only be a second *or* moment; **je reviens dans une s.!** I'll be back in a second!, I'll be right back!; **(attendez) une s.!** just a second!, just a moment!; **en un quart** *ou* **une fraction de s., en moins d'une s.** in no time at all

secondement [səgɔ̃dmɑ̃] *adv* secondly, in the second place

seconder [səgɔ̃de] *vt* (a) (*qn*) to second, to back up, to support, to assist (b) (*intérêts, projets etc*) to forward, to further, to promote

secouement [səkumɑ̃] *nm* shaking

secouer [səkwe] 1 *vt* (a) (*arbre, tête etc*) to shake; (*coussin, oreiller*) to plump up, to shake up; (*vêtements, tapis*) to shake (out); (*d'un choc, d'une maladie, de nouvelles etc*) (*qn*) to shake (up); (*du vent*) (*bateau*) to buffet; **de grands spasmes secouaient son corps tout entier** violent spasms shook his whole body; **nous avons été secoués pendant la traversée** we were shaken about during the crossing, we had a rough crossing; *Fig* **il est impossible de s. son indifférence** it is impossible to shake him out of his indifference; **il faut la s.** (*elle est déprimée*) we have to shake her out of it; *F* **s. (les puces à) qn** (*réprimander*) to tell sb off; (*pousser à agir*) to shake sb up

(b) (*se débarrasser de*) (*poussière, joug etc*) to shake off

2 *vi* **voiture qui secoue** bumpy car; **ça secoue** (*dans un avion/train etc*) it's bumpy; (*dans un bateau*) it's rough

3 **se secouer** *vpr* (*agir*) to shake oneself *or* snap out of it, to pull oneself together

secourable [səkurabl] *adj* helpful, willing to help; **main s.** helping hand; **peu s.** unhelpful

secourir [səkurir] *vt* (*conj like* **courir**) to help, to assist, to aid

secourisme [səkurism] *nm Méd* first aid; **brevet de s.** first-aid certificate

secouriste [səkurist] *n* first-aid worker

secours [səkur] *nm* help, assistance, aid; (*financier, matériel*) aid; *Mil* relief; **crier au s.** to call for help; **appel au s.** call for help; **au s.!** help!; *Méd* **premiers s.** first aid; **s. en montagne** mountain rescue; **les s. vont arriver** help will arrive; *Mil* relief will arrive; **porter** *ou* **prêter (du) s. à qn** to give sb help *or* assistance, to help *or* assist sb; **demander (du) s.** to ask for help *or* assistance; **aller** *ou* **se porter au s. de qn** to go to sb's assistance; *Mil* **se porter au s. d'un bataillon** to go in support of a battalion; **cela m'a été d'un grand s.** it has been a great help (to me); **puis-je vous être d'aucun s.?** can I be of (some) help *or* (some) assistance?; **sa présence ne m'a été d'aucun s.** his presence was of no help (to me); *Ordinat* **de s.** (*copie, fichier etc*) backup; **boîte/trousse de s.** first-aid box/kit; **poste de s.** first-aid post; **caisse de s.** relief fund; **société de s. mutuels** friendly *or US* benefit society; **sortie** *ou* **porte de s.** emergency exit; *Fig* **c'est sa seule porte de s.** it's his only way out; *Aut* **roue de s.** spare wheel; **éclairage de s.** emergency lighting (system); *Mil* **troupes de s., des s.** relief troops, relieving force; *Rail* **locomotive/train de s.** relief engine/train

secousse [səkus] *nf* shake; (*cahot*) jolt, bump; *Fig* (*morale*) shock; **se dégager d'une s.** to jerk *or* wrench *or* shake oneself free; *Fig* **se remettre d'une s.** to recover from a shock; **les secousses que faisait la voiture** the jolting of the car; **sans s.** smoothly; **par secousses** (*avancer etc*) jerkily; (*respirer*) in gasps; **s. politique** political upheaval; **s. (sismique** *ou* **tellurique)** (earth) tremor; **s. (électrique)** electric shock

secret[1], -ète [səkrɛ, -ɛt] 1 *adj* (*ordres, signal, traité, porte etc*) secret; (*sentiments, pensées*) secret, hidden; (*réservé*) (*personne*) reticent, reserved; **ses fantasmes les plus secrets** his innermost fantasies; **la raison secrète d'un acte** the secret *or* real reason for an action; **la police secrète** the secret police; *Admin* **très s., ultra-s.** top secret 2 *nf* (a) **la secrète** (*police*) the secret police (b) *Rel* (*oraison*) secret

secret[2] *nm* (a) (*confidence, mystère*) secret; **garder un s.** to keep a secret; **trahir un s.** to betray a secret, to give away a secret; **mettre qn dans le s.** to let sb into *or* in on the secret; **être du s.** *ou* **dans le s.** to be in on the secret, *F* to be in the know; **n'avoir point de s. pour qn** (*d'une personne*) to have no secrets from sb; **les ordinateurs n'ont pas de secrets pour elle** computers hold no secrets for her; **ce n'est un s. pour personne** it's no secret; **le s. du bonheur/de la réussite** the secret of happiness/of success; **trouver le s. de qch** to find the secret of sth; **trouver le s. pour faire qch** to find the knack of doing sth; **elle a le s. des soirées réussies** she knows the secret for giving successful parties; **bureau à s.** desk with a secret compartment

(b) (*discrétion*) secrecy; **dire qch à qn sous le sceau du s.** to tell sb sth under pledge of secrecy; **je vous demande le (plus grand) s.** I'm asking you to keep this (strictly) secret; **en s.** (*en cachette*) in secret, secretly; (*intérieurement*) secretly

(c) **mettre qn au s.** (*l'enfermer*) to put sb in solitary confinement

▶ **secret**: **s. bancaire** banking secrecy; *Rel* **le s. de la confession** the secrecy of the confessional; **s. d'État** state secret; *Fig* **ce n'est pas un s. d'État!** it's not a state secret!; **s. de fabrication** trade secret; **le s. professionnel** professional secrecy; *Journ* obligation to respect the confidentiality of sources; **abuser du** *ou* **trahir le s. professionnel** to commit a breach of confidence

secrétaire [səkretɛr] 1 *n* secretary; **s. bilingue/trilingue** bilingual/trilingual secretary; **s. particulier** private secretary; **s. médicale** medical secretary; (*de dentiste*) dentist's secretary; **s. d'État** Secretary of State; **s. d'ambassade** secretary; **s. de rédaction** sub-editor, copyreader; **s. de séance** meetings secretary; **s. général** secretary general; *Com* company secretary; **s. de direction** executive secretary, personal assistant; **s. d'administration** (*fonctionnaire*) *Br* ≈ assistant principal; **s. de mairie** ≈ town clerk; (*de village*) = mayor's secretarial assistant

2 *nm* (a) *Orn* secretary bird

(b) (*meuble*) writing desk, secretaire

secrétariat [səkretarja] *nm* (a) (*fonction*) secretaryship (b) (*bureau*) secretariat (c) (*métier*) secretarial work (d) *Pol* **s. d'État** Department, Ministry, *Can* Secretary of State Department

secrètement [səkrɛtmɑ̃] *adv* secretly

sécréter [sekrete] *vt* (**il sécrète; il sécrétera**) (*d'une glande etc*) to secrete; *Fig* **s. l'ennui** to exude boredom

sécréteur, -trice, *parfois* **-euse** [sekretœr, -tris, -øz] *adj* (*glande etc*) secretory

sécrétion [sekresjɔ̃] *nf Physiol* secretion; **glande à s. externe/interne** exocrine/endocrine gland

sécrétoire [sekretwar] *adj Physiol* secretory

sectaire [sɛktɛr] *adj, n* sectarian

sectarisme [sɛktarism] *nm* sectarianism

secte [sɛkt] *nf* sect

secteur [sɛktœr] *nm* (a) (*zone*) area, district; (*d'un magasin*) section; *Mil* (*de responsabilité, d'attaque etc*) sector, area; **s. français de Berlin** French sector of Berlin; *Com* **s. de vente** sales area; **s. de surveillance** *Rad etc* surveillance sector *or* area; (*de policier*) beat; *F* **changer de s.** to move (somewhere else)

(b) *Él* **s. (de distribution électrique)** mains; **branché sur le s.** plugged into the mains; **ça se branche sur le s.** it runs off the mains; **panne de s.** mains failure

(c) *Écon* (*d'une activité*) sector; **le s. privé** the private sector; **s. privé à but non lucratif** private nonprofit sector; **le s. public** the public sector; **s. sanitaire** health sector; **s. primaire** primary sector; **s. secondaire** secondary sector; **s. tertiaire** tertiary sector; *Mktg* **s. de la grande distribution** mass distribution sector; *Mktg* **s. de vente** sales territory; **s. des services** service sector; **s. du marché** market sector, sector of the market; *F* **ce n'est pas mon s.** that's not my line

(d) *Astron, Géom, Ordinat* sector; *Tech* sector, quadrant; **graphique à secteurs** pie chart; *Ordinat* **s. d'initialisation** boot sector; *Ordinat* **s. endommagé** bad sector; *Aut etc* **s. de direction** steering sector; *Aut* **s. de frein** handbrake quadrant *or* ratchet; *Naut* **s. dangereux** (*d'un orage*) dangerous quadrant

section [sɛksjɔ̃] *nf* (a) (*action de couper*) cutting, *Spéc* section; *Vét* (*de la queue*) docking; **s. des tendons** cutting of the tendons; **l'accident entraîna la s. d'un doigt** a finger was cut off *or* severed in the accident; **la s. du doigt est nécessaire** the finger must be amputated

(b) (*division*) (*d'un livre, d'un bâtiment etc*), *Admin* (*d'un département etc*), *Biol* section; (*d'un parti politique*) branch; *Mil* (*de l'infanterie*) platoon; (*de l'artillerie*) section; *Naut* (*de la flotte*) sub-division; **s. syndicale d'entreprise** union branch; *Mus* **la s. rythmique** the rhythm section; **s. (électorale)** ward; **s. de vote** ward; (*bureau*) polling station; **chef de s.** *Mil* platoon commander; *Mil, Av* flight commander; *Mil, Av* **s. de bombardiers** bomber flight

(c) *Géom* section; (*intersection*) intersection; *Archit, Tech* (*dessin*) section, profile; **point de s.** point of intersection; **ça doit faire cinq centimètres de s.** it must have a section of five centimetres; *Él* **s. morte** idle coil; *Phys Nucl* **s. efficace** cross section

(**d**) (*d'autoroute*) section; (*sur un trajet de bus etc*) stage; **changement de s.** *Br* ≈ fare stage; *Rail* **s. de block** block section

(**e**) *Scol* = one of the groups into which baccalaureat students are divided, depending on their chosen area of specialization; **il enseigne en s. scientifique** he teaches in the science department; **à l'école, j'étais en s. économique** my main subject at school was economics

sectionnement [sɛksjɔnmɑ̃] *nm* (**a**) (*d'un département, d'une circonscription etc*) division into sections (**b**) (*coupe*) severing

sectionner [sɛksjɔne] **1** *vt* (**a**) (*fractionner*) (*service, circonscription etc*) to divide (up) into sections (**b**) (*couper*) to sever **2 se sectionner** *vpr* (*être coupé*) to be severed

sectionneur [sɛksjɔnœr] *nm Él* disconnecting switch, isolating switch

sectoriel, -ielle [sɛktɔrjɛl] *adj* sectorial

sectorisation [sɛktɔrizasjɔ̃] *nf* division into sectors

sectoriser [sɛktɔrize] *vt* to divide into sectors

sécu [seky] *nf F abrév* **sécurité sociale**

séculaire [sekylɛr] *adj* (**a**) (*très ancien*) (*arbre, tradition etc*) centuries-old, age-old (**b**) (*qui existe depuis un siècle*) a hundred years old; **un arbre plusieurs fois s.** a tree several hundred years old (**c**) (*événement*) centennial; *Astron* secular; **année s.** last year of the century

sécularisation [sekylarizasjɔ̃] *nf* secularization

séculariser [sekylarize] *vt* to secularize; (*église*) to deconsecrate

séculier, -ière [sekylje, -jɛr] **1** *adj* (*clergé, juridiction etc*) secular; (*laïque*) lay; **le bras s.** the secular arm **2** *n* secular

secundo [səgɔ̃do, sek-] *adv* secondly, in the second place

sécurisant [sekyrizɑ̃] *adj* reassuring

sécuriser [sekyrize] *vt* **s. qn** to reassure sb, to make sb feel secure; **s. l'accès à l'ordinateur central** to securitize mainframe access; *Fin* **s. un financement** to guarantee a loan

sécurit® [sekyrit] *nm* safety glass

sécuritaire [sekyritɛr] *adj* **mesures sécuritaires** (*pour la protection des informations etc*) security measures; (*pour la protection des personnes*) safety measures; **une idéologie s.** an obsession with security

sécurité [sekyrite] *nf* (**a**) (*ordre, stabilité*) security; (*sentiment*) (feeling of) security; **être/se sentir en s.** to be/feel safe *or* secure; **je veille à sa s.** I'm making sure he's safe; **s. matérielle/affective** material/emotional security; **s. de l'emploi** security of employment, job security

(**b**) (*absence de danger*) safety; **s. de la route** road safety; *Admin* **s. publique** public safety; **s. incendie** fire safety; **s. informatique** computer security; (*des données*) data security; **services de s.** *Mil* security forces; (*dans des manifestations etc*) stewards; (*dans une usine etc*) security officers; **s. nationale/internationale** national/international security; *Naut* **officier de s.** officer in charge of fire precautions; *Tech, Constr, Ind* **marge de s.** safety margin; **règles de s.** safety rules *or* code; **dispositif de s.** safety device; **verre de s.** safety glass, splinterproof glass; *Él* **éclairage de s.** emergency lighting

(**c**) (*dispositif*) safety catch; **porte munie d'une s.-enfants** door with a childproof lock

▶ **sécurité**: **s. routière** road safety; **S. Routière** = road safety organization; *Admin* **S. sociale** Social Security, *Am* Welfare

sédatif, -ive [sedatif, -iv] *adj, nm Méd* sedative

sédation [sedasjɔ̃] *nf Méd* sedation

sédentaire [sedɑ̃tɛr] *adj* (*occupation, vie, travail, personne*) sedentary; (*population*) settled; (*troupes*) garrison(ed); (*oiseau*) non-migrant

sédentairement [sedɑ̃tɛrmɑ̃] *adv* **vivre s.** to live a sedentary life

sédentarisation [sedɑ̃tarizasjɔ̃] *nf* settling

sédentariser [sedɑ̃tarize] **1** *vt* (*population etc*) to settle **2 se sédentariser** *vpr* to settle

sédentarité [sedɑ̃tarite] *nf* sedentary lifestyle

sédiment [sedimɑ̃] *nm* sediment, deposit

sédimentaire [sedimɑ̃tɛr] *adj Géol etc* sedimentary

sédimentation [sedimɑ̃tasjɔ̃] *nf* sedimentation

séditieux, -euse [sedisjø, -øz] **1** *adj* (*discours, écrit, assemblée etc*) seditious; (*troupes, groupe etc*) seditious, rebellious; **tenir des propos s.** to talk treason **2** *n* rebel, insurgent

sédition [sedisjɔ̃] *nf* sedition, insurrection

séducteur, -trice [sedyktœr, -tris] **1** *n* seducer, *f* seductress **2** *adj* seductive

séduction [sedyksjɔ̃] *nf* (**a**) (*action*) (*physique*) seduction; (*par le charme*) charming (**b**) (*moyen de séduire*) attraction; **pouvoir de s.** power of attraction; **exercer une s. mystérieuse/irrésistible sur qn** to exercise a mysterious/an irresistible attraction over sb; **la s. des richesses** the lure *or* attraction of wealth

séduire [sedɥir] (*conj like* **conduire**) **1** *vt* (**a**) (*sexuellement*) to seduce (**b**) (*gagner par son charme*) (*d'une personne*) to charm; (*d'un projet, d'une proposition etc*) to appeal to; **j'ai été séduite du premier coup** it took my fancy *or* attracted me *or* appealed to me right away **2** *vi* to charm people

séduisant [sedɥizɑ̃] *adj* (*idée, proposition etc*) appealing, attractive; (*personne*) attractive

segment [sɛgmɑ̃] *nm* segment; *Mktg* **s. démographique** demographic segment; *Aut* **s. de frein** brake shoe; *Aut* **frein à segments** segmented brake; *Mktg* **s. de marché** market segment; *Tech* **s. de piston** piston *or* packing ring; *Aut* **s. primaire** primary *or* leading shoe; *Aut* **s. secondaire** secondary shoe, trailing shoe

segmentation [sɛgmɑ̃tasjɔ̃] *nf* segmentation, segmenting; **s. du marché** market segmentation; *Mktg* **s. en niches** niching; *Mktg* **s. stratégique** strategic segmentation

segmenter [sɛgmɑ̃te] **1** *vt* to segment, to divide into segments; *Ordinat* to partition, to section, to segment; **s. un marché** to segment a market **2 se segmenter** *vpr* to segment, to split into segments

ségrégation [segregasjɔ̃] *nf* segregation

ségrégationnisme [segregasjɔnism] *nm Pol* racial segregation

ségrégationniste [segregasjɔnist] *adj, n Pol* segregationist

séguedille [segədij] *nf* (*danse, musique*) seguidilla

seiche [sɛʃ] *nf* (*mollusque*) cuttlefish; **os de s.** cuttlebone

séide [seid] *nm* henchman

seigle [sɛgl] *nm* rye; **pain de s.** rye bread

seigneur [sɛɲœr] *nm* (**a**) (*maître*) lord; (*d'un manoir*) lord of the manor, *Br* ≈ squire; *Hist* (*homme noble*) nobleman, noble; *Hum* **mon s. et maître** my lord and master; **le s. de Sercq** the seigneur of Sark; (*femme*) the dame of Sark; *Hist* **les seigneurs** the nobility; **à tout s. tout honneur** honour where honour is due; **mener une vie de grand s.** to live like a lord; **ne faites pas le grand s.** don't try and lord it over us, stop behaving like the lord of the manor; **en grand s.** in grand style (**b**) *Rel* **le S.** the Lord; **Notre-S.** our Lord; **le jour du S.** the Lord's day; *F* **S.!, S. Dieu!** good Lord!

seigneurial, -ale, -aux, -ales [sɛɲœrjal, -o] *adj* (*magnifique*) stately, lordly; *Hist* (*droits, domaine etc*) seigneurial

seigneurie [sɛɲœri] *nf Hist* (*terre, pouvoir*) seigneury; **votre S.** (*titre*) your Lordship; *Iron* **sa S.** his lordship, *Arg* his nibs

sein [sɛ̃] *nm* (*de femme*) breast; *Litt* (*d'homme*) breast, bosom; **serrer** *ou* **presser qn sur son s.** to press sb to one's bosom *or* heart; **donner le s. à un enfant** to breast-feed a child; **enfant nourri au s.** breast-fed child; **danseuse aux seins nus** topless dancer; **se baigner les seins nus** to bathe topless; **le s. de l'Église** the bosom of the Church; **au s. de la famille** in the bosom of the family; **au s. de la commission** within the committee; *Litt* **enfant que j'ai porté dans mon s.** child that I carried in my womb; **le s. de la terre** the bowels of the earth

Seine [sɛn] *nf* **la S.** the Seine

seine [sɛn] *nf Pêche* seine, draw net

seing [sɛ̃] *nm Jur* **sous s. privé** under private seal; **acte sous s. privé** private agreement (*without legal certification*)

séisme [seism] *nm* earthquake; *Fig Litt* upheaval

séismique [seismik] *adj* seismic

séismo- [seismɔ-] *préf* = **sismo-**

seize [sɛz] **1** *adj inv* sixteen; **Louis S.** Louis the Sixteenth; **numéro s.** number sixteen **2** *nm inv* sixteen; **le s. mai** (on) the sixteenth of May, (on) May the sixteenth, *Am* (on) May sixteenth; **habiter au s.** to live at number sixteen

seizième [sɛzjɛm] **1** *adj num* sixteenth **2** *n* sixteenth; **ils habitent dans le s.** they live in the sixteenth arrondissement (*in Paris*) **3** *nm* (*fraction*) sixteenth

séjour [seʒur] *nm* (**a**) stay; **carte** *ou* **permis de s.** residence permit; **droit de s.** right of residence *or* abode; **taxe de s.** tourist tax; **s. discompté** bargain break; **s. éducatif** educational trip *or* holiday; **s. linguistique** language-learning trip *or* holiday; **s. de quinze jours** two week(s') *or Br* fortnight's stay; **je te souhaite un bon s. en Grèce** enjoy your stay in Greece (**b**) **(salle de) s.** living room (**c**) *Litt* (*lieu*) abode

séjourner [seʒurne] *vi* (*d'une personne*) to stay; (*de la neige, de l'eau etc*) to lie

sel [sɛl] *nm* (**a**) *Ch, Culin etc* salt; **gros s.** coarse salt; **régime sans s.** salt-free diet; **s. de cuisine** cooking salt; **s. fin** fine salt; **s. marin** sea salt; **s. de céleri** celery salt; *Pharm* **s. d'Angleterre** *ou* **d'Epsom** Epsom salts; **sels de** *ou* **pour le bain** bath salts; **sels** (*à respirer*) (smelling) salts; *Ch* **s. double** double salt; *F* **mettre** *ou* **ajouter son grain de s.** to put *or* stick one's oar in; *Fig* **le s. de la terre** the salt of the earth **(b)** *Fig* (*esprit*) piquancy, wit

select, sélect [selɛkt] *adj F* (*soirée, clientèle etc*) select; **le monde s.** high society

sélecteur [selɛktœr] *nm Ordinat, Él etc* selector; (*de motocyclette*) gear(-change) pedal; **s. automatique** automatic switch; *Aut* **s. de vitesses** gear lever

sélectif, -ive [selɛktif, -iv] *adj* selective; *Rad* **récepteur s.** selective receiver; *Ordinat* **en mode s.** in veto mode

sélection [selɛksjɔ̃] *nf* **(a)** (*fait de choisir*) selection; **faire** *ou* **opérer une s. parmi ...** to make a selection from among ...; *Mktg* **s. au hasard** random selection; *Biol* **s. naturelle** natural selection; **s. professionnelle** professional recruitment; **épreuve de s.** selection trial; *Sp* **match de s.** trial game; **Gavin Hastings a 51 sélections en équipe nationale** Gavin Hastings has been capped 51 times, Gavin Hastings has 51 caps **(b)** (*choses choisies*) selection

sélectionné [selɛksjɔne] **1** *adj* (*joueur, produit etc*) selected; **s. en équipe nationale** capped **2** *n Sp* selected player

sélectionner [selɛksjɔne] *vt* to select; **s. un échantillon** to take a sample

sélectionneur, -euse [selɛksjɔnœr, -øz] *n* selector

sélectivement [selɛktivmɑ̃] *adv* selectively

sélectivité [selɛktivite] *nf Rad* selectivity

sélénieux [selenjø] *adj m Ch* (*acide*) selenious

sélénite [selenit] **1** *n* (*habitant de la lune*) moon-dweller **2** *adj* of the moon

sélénium [selenjɔm] *nm Ch* selenium

sélénographie [selenɔgrafi] *nf* selenography

sélénographique [selenɔgrafik] *adj* (*carte etc*) selenographic(al)

self [sɛlf] **1** *nm F* (*restaurant*) self-service restaurant **2** *nf Él* self-induction; **(bobine de) s.** self-induction coil

self-control [sɛlfkɔ̃trɔl] *nm* self-control

self-défense *nf* self-defence, *US* self-defense

self-inductance *nf Él* self-inductance

self-induction *nf Él* self-induction

self-made-man, *pl* **self-made-men** [sɛlfmɛdman, sɛlfmɛdmɛn] *nm* self-made man

self-service, *pl* **self-services** *nm* (*restaurant*) self-service restaurant; (*magasin*) self-service shop

selle [sɛl] *nf* **(a)** (*de cheval, bicyclette, moto etc*) saddle; **se mettre en s.** to mount; **être bien en s.** to have a good seat; *Fig* to be firmly in the saddle; **aider qn à monter en s.** to help sb into the saddle; *Fig F* to give sb a leg up *or* a helping hand; **se remettre en s.** to get back into the saddle; *Fig* to get back in harness; **monter sans s.** to ride bareback **(b)** *Physiol* stool; **aller à la s.** (*déféquer*) to pass *or* have a motion; **les selles du bébé** the baby's stools *or* motions **(c)** *Culin* **s. de mouton/d'agneau** saddle of mutton/lamb; **s. de bœuf** baron of beef **(d)** (*de sculpteur*) turntable

seller [sele] *vt* (*cheval*) to saddle

sellerie [sɛlri] *nf* **(a)** (*selles, métier*) saddlery **(b)** (*salle*) harness room, tack room **(c)** *Aut* seating

sellette [sɛlɛt] *nf* **(a)** *F* **mettre qn/être sur la s.** to put sb/to be in the hot seat **(b)** (*d'ouvrier de bâtiment*) cradle; *Aut* trailer coupling, fifth wheel **(c)** (*de sculpteur*) turntable **(d)** (*de cheval de trait*) saddle

sellier [selje] *nm* saddler; **façon s.** hand-stitched

selon [s(ə)lɔ̃] *prép* **(a)** according to; **s. lui** according to him; **s. moi** in my opinion *or* view, as I see it; **s. facture** as per invoice; **s. vos instructions** in accordance with your instructions, as per your instructions; **s. toute vraisemblance** in all likelihood *or* probability; **s. les cas** on a case by case basis; **varier s. les cas/les saisons** to vary from case to case/season to season; *F* **c'est s.** it all depends; **l'Évangile s. saint Jean** the Gospel according to Saint John **(b)** **s. que** + *ind* depending on whether

Seltz [sɛls] *nm* **eau de S.** soda water, Seltzer (water)

semailles [səmɑj] *nfpl* **(a)** (*action*) sowing; **(temps des) s.** sowing time **(b)** (*graines*) seeds

semaine [s(ə)mɛn] *nf* **(a)** (*sept jours*) week; **deux fois par s.** twice a week; **s. de cinq jours** five-day week; **s. de trente-cinq heures** thirty-five-hour week; **une s. de vacances** a week's holiday; **fin de s.** (*jeudi, vendredi*) end of the week; (*week-end*) weekend; *Can* **bonne fin de s.!** have a good weekend!, enjoy your weekend!; **je suis de s.** I'm on duty this week *or* for the week; *Scol* **pensionnaire à la s.** weekly boarder; *F* **politique à la petite s.** shortsighted policy; **vivre à la petite s.** to live from day to day; *F* **la s. des quatre jeudis!** that'll never happen (in a month of Sundays)!; *Com* **la promotion de la s.** this week's special offer; **s. commerciale** week-long special promotion; **jour de s.** weekday; **en s.** during the week, on weekdays

(b) (*salaire*) week's pay *or* wages; (*argent de poche*) pocket money (for the week)

(c) *Mil etc* (*tour de service*) week's duty; **officier de s.** duty officer for the week

(d) (*bague/bracelet*) seven-band ring/bracelet

▶ **semaine**: **s. anglaise** five-day week; **faire la s. anglaise** to work a five-day week; **la s. sainte** Holy Week

semainier, -ière [s(ə)menje, -jɛr] **1** *n* (*personne*) person on duty for the week; *Mil* duty officer for the week **2** *nm* **(a)** (*meuble*) chest of seven drawers **(b)** (*agenda*) desk diary

sémantème [semɑ̃tɛm] *nm Ling* semanteme

sémanticien, -ienne [semɑ̃tisjɛ̃, -jɛn] *n* semanticist

sémantique [semɑ̃tik] *Ling* **1** *adj* semantic **2** *nf* semantics

sémaphore [semafɔr] *nm Rail* semaphore signal; *Naut* (*à terre*) signal station

semblable [sɑ̃blabl] **1** *adj* **(a)** (*pareil*) similar; **être semblables** to be similar *or* alike; **deux cas tout à fait semblables** two quite similar cases; **triangles semblables** similar triangles; **s. à qch** similar to sth, like sth; **s. à son père** like his father; **je n'ai rien dit de s.** I said nothing of the sort, I said no such thing

(b) (*tel*) **de semblables projets/propos** such plans/ remarks, plans/remarks like that

2 *n* **(a)** (*personne semblable*) **vous et vos semblables** you and people like you, you and your kind *or* sort; **il n'a pas son s. dans l'art occidental** there's no-one like him in western art

(b) (*être humain*) fellow man *or* creature; **nos semblables** our fellow men, our fellow creatures

semblant [sɑ̃blɑ̃] *nm* semblance (**de** of); **elle portait un s. de jupe** she was wearing an apology for a skirt; **montrer un s. de résistance** to make a show of resistance; **opposer un s. d'indignation** to put up a show of indignation; **faire s. de faire qch** to pretend to do sth; **tu fais s.?** are you pretending?; **sans faire s. de rien** without seeming to take any notice; **elle fit s. de rien** she pretended not to notice

sembler [sɑ̃ble] (*aux* **avoir**) **1** *vi* to seem; **elle semblait malade** she seemed (to be) ill; **s. être/faire** to seem to be/do; **le vent semble tomber** the wind seems to be dying down

2 *v impers* [①B27,E] **il me semblait rêver** it seemed to me (that) *or* I thought (that) I was dreaming; **il me semble avoir entendu son nom** I seem to have heard his name; **il me semble idiot d'attendre encore plus longtemps** it seems stupid to me to wait any longer; **à ce qu'il me semble** it seems to me; **faites comme bon vous semble(ra)** do as you think best; **il le fera si bon lui semble** he'll do it if he wants to; **il semble que ...** + *ind or sub* it seems that ..., it looks as if ...; **il me semble que ...** + *ind* it seems to me that ...; **me semble-t-il** it seems to me

semé [s(ə)me] *adj* **s. de** scattered with; (*rochers etc*) strewn with; (*fleurs etc*) dotted with; (*diamants etc*) studded with; (*citations etc*) sprinkled with; **s. d'embûches** *ou* **de pièges** full of traps

sème [sɛm] *nm Ling* sememe

semelle [s(ə)mɛl] *nf* **(a)** (*d'une chaussure*) sole; (*d'un bas, d'une chaussette*) foot; **s. (intérieure)** insole, inner sole; **chaussures à semelles de caoutchouc/de cuir** rubber-/ leather-soled shoes; **remettre une s. à une chaussure** to resole a shoe; **ne pas avancer d'une s.** to make no progress; **il ne reculera pas d'une s.** he won't give an inch; **il ne me quitte pas d'une s.** he's always at my heels; **ce n'est pas de la viande, c'est de la s.!** this isn't meat, it's like shoe leather!

(b) *Tech* (*d'une machine, d'un tour*) bed plate; (*d'une ancre, d'un traîneau*) shoe; **s. de poutre** girder flange

(c) *Naut* **s. de dérive** leeboard

semence [s(ə)mɑ̃s] *nf* **(a)** *Agr* seed; *Physiol* semen; *Fig* **semences** seeds (**de** of); *Agr* **blé de s.** seed corn; **s. de perles** seed pearls; **s. de diamants** diamond sparks **(b)** (*clou*) tack; **s. de tapissier** upholstery tack

semer [s(ə)me] *vt* **(je sème, n. semons; je sèmerai) (a)** (*graines, champ*) to sow **(b)** (*fleurs etc*) to scatter, to strew; (*nouvelles, discorde*) to spread; *Prov* **qui sème le vent récolte la tempête** he who sows the wind shall reap the whirlwind **(c)** *F* **s. qn** (*le distancer*) to shake sb off, to get rid of sb; **s. qch** (*le laisser tomber*) to drop sth, to lose sth

semestre [s(ə)mɛstr] *nm* **(a)** (*six mois*) half-year, six months; **le premier s.** the first half of the year **(b)** (*paiement*) half-yearly *or* six-monthly payment **(c)** *Scol, Univ* semester

semestriel, -elle [səmɛstrijɛl] *adj* half-yearly, six-monthly

semestriellement [səmɛstrijɛlmɑ̃] *adv* half-yearly, every six months; *Scol, Univ* every semester

semeur, -euse [s(ə)mœr, -øz] *n Agr* sower; *Fig* (*de nouvelles etc*) spreader, *Litt* disseminator; (*de discorde*) sower; *F* **s. de zizanie**; *très F* **s. de merde** troublemaker

semi- [səmi] *préf* semi- *NOTE in the plural of compound words*

prefixed by **semi-**, **semi-** *remains invariable and the following noun or adj takes the pl form*
semi-automatique *adj* semiautomatic
semi-auxiliaire *adj Gram* semiauxiliary
semi-chenillé *adj, nm* (**véhicule**) **s.** half-track (vehicle)
semi-circulaire *adj* semicircular
semi-conducteur, -trice *Él* **1** *adj* semiconducting **2** *nm* semiconductor
semi-conserve *nf* = tinned *etc* foodstuff which has a limited life and must be refrigerated
semi-consonne *nf* semivowel
semi-duplex *nm inv* half duplex
semi-fini *adj Écon* (*produit*) semifinished
semi-fixe *adj* semifixed
semi-grossiste *n* retail wholesaler
semi-illettré *adj* semi-illiterate
semi-liberté *nf Jur* partial release; *Fig* state of partial freedom
sémillant [semijɑ̃] *adj* (*personne, esprit*) sparkling; (*regard*) bright, engaging
semi-lunaire *adj* half-moon-shaped
semi-mensuel, -elle *adj* (*périodique etc*) bi-monthly, *Br* fortnightly
semi-métal *nm Ch* metalloid
séminaire [seminɛr] *nm* (**a**) *Univ* seminar; (*conférence*) seminar, conference (**b**) *Rel* (**grand**) **s.** seminary; **petit s.** secondary school (*staffed by priests*)
séminal, -ale, -aux, -ales [seminal, -o] *adj Biol* seminal
séminariste [seminarist] *nm Rel* seminarist
semi-nomade **1** *adj* seminomadic **2** *n* seminomad
semi-nomadisme *nm* seminomadism
semi-occlusif, -ive *adj Ling* semi-occlusive
semi-officiel, -ielle *adj* semiofficial
sémiologie [semjɔlɔʒi] *nf Méd, Ling* semiology
sémiologique [semjɔlɔʒik] *adj Méd, Ling* semiological
sémiologue [semjɔlɔg] *n Méd, Ling* semiologist
sémiotique [semjɔtik] **1** *adj* semiotic **2** *nf* semiotics
semi-perméable *adj* semipermeable
semi-précieux, -ieuse *adj* (*pierre*) semiprecious
semi-public, -ique *adj Jur* semipublic
sémique [semik] *adj Ling* semic
semi-remorque **1** *nf* (*remorque*) semitrailer, *Am F* semi **2** *nm* (*poids lourd*) articulated truck *or Br* lorry, *Br F* artic
semi-rigide *adj* (*dirigeable*) semirigid
semis [səmi] *nm Agr* (**a**) (*action*) sowing (**b**) (*terrain*) seedbed (**c**) (*jeune plante*) seedling
sémite [semit] **1** *adj* Semitic **2** *n* **S.** Semite
sémitique [semitik] *adj* Semitic
sémitisant, -ante [semitizɑ̃, -ɑ̃t], **sémitiste** [semitist] *n* Semitist
sémitisme [semitism] *nm* Semitism
semi-ton *nm Mus* semitone
semi-voyelle *nf Ling* semivowel
semoir [s(ə)mwar] *nm Agr* (**a**) (*sac*) seed bag (**b**) (*machine*) sowing machine, seeder
semonce [səmɔ̃s] *nf* (**a**) (*réprimande*) reprimand, scolding; **une verte s.** a good telling-off (**b**) *Naut* **coup de s.** warning shot
semoule [səmul] *nf* semolina; **sucre s.** caster *or Am* powdered sugar; **s. de blé dur** semolina
sempiternel, -elle [sɛ̃pitɛrnɛl] *adj* neverending, endless, *Fml* sempiternel
sempiternellement [sɛ̃pitɛrnɛlmɑ̃] *adv* eternally, endlessly
sénat [sena] *nm* senate; (*édifice*) senate (house)
sénateur [senatœr] *nm* senator
sénatorial, -ale, -aux, -ales [senatɔrjal, -o] *adj* senatorial
séné [sene] *nm Bot, Pharm* senna
sénéchal, -aux [seneʃal, -o] *nm Hist* seneschal
sénéchaussée [seneʃose] *nf Hist* (*juridiction*) seneschalsy; (*tribunal*) seneschal's court
séneçon [sɛnsɔ̃] *nm Bot* groundsel
Sénégal [senegal] *nm* Senegal
sénégalais, -aise [senegalɛ, -ɛz] **1** *adj* Senegalese **2** *n* **S.** Senegalese
Sénégambie [senegɑ̃bi] *nf* Senegambia
Sénèque [senɛk] *nm* Seneca
sénescence [senesɑ̃s] *nf Biol* senescence, ageing, aging
sénescent [senesɑ̃] *adj Biol* senescent
sénevé [senve] *nm* (**a**) *Bot* mustard (**b**) (*graine*) mustard seed
sénile [senil] *adj Méd, F Péj* senile
sénilité [senilite] *nf* senility
senior [senjɔr] *adj, n Sp* senior
senne [sɛn] *nf Pêche* seine, draw net
señorita [senjɔrita] *nm* cigarillo, whiff
sens [sɑ̃s] *nm* (**a**) (*du toucher, de la vue, de la beauté, du rythme etc*) sense; **les cinq s.** the five senses; **le sixième s.** the sixth sense; **s. moral** moral sense, conscience; **avoir le s. de l'humour/du ridicule/de la famille** to have a sense of humour/of the ridiculous/of family; **avoir le s. des affaires** to have good business sense; **j'ai un très bon s. de l'orientation** I have a very good sense of direction; **s. pratique** practical (common) sense; **il n'a aucun s. pratique** he's completely unpractical, he's not practically minded at all; **reprendre ses s.** to regain consciousness

(**b**) (*sensualité*) **plaisir des s.** sensual pleasures; **éveiller/exciter les s.** to excite/arouse the senses

(**c**) (*jugement*) sense; **s. commun** common sense; **bon s.** good sense; **un homme de bon s.** a sensible man; **tu t'es encore coiffé en dépit du bon s.** what possessed you to do your hair like that?; **agir en dépit du bon s.** to act in a way that defies common sense; **le bon s. veut que ...** it stands to reason that ...; **vous avez perdu le s. commun** you've taken leave of your senses; **gros** *ou* **robuste bon s.** elementary common sense; **à mon s.** to my mind, in my view *or* opinion; **j'abonde dans votre s.** I entirely agree with you; **cela tombe sous le s.** it's perfectly obvious

(**d**) (*signification*) (*d'un mot etc*) meaning, sense; **s. propre/figuré** literal/figurative meaning *or* sense; **au s. propre/figuré** in the literal/figurative sense, literally/figuratively; **au s. ordinaire du mot** in the ordinary meaning *or* sense of the word; **mot à double s.** word with a double meaning; **faire un faux s.** to make a mistranslation; **ça n'a aucun s.** it doesn't make (any) sense; **cela n'a pas de s., ça n'a pas le s. commun** it's crazy, there's no sense to it; **trouver un s. à sa vie** to find a meaning to one's life; **en ce s. que ...** in the sense that ...

(**e**) (*direction*) direction; **accident sur la voie express dans le s. Brest-Quimper** accident on the Brest-Quimper expressway; **il tenait son livre dans le mauvais s.** he was holding his book the wrong way up; **tu as mis la cassette dans le mauvais s.** you put the tape in the wrong way round; **il a pris l'autoroute dans le mauvais s.** he drove the wrong way up the motorway; **fais demi-tour, on n'est pas dans le bon s.** turn round, we're going the wrong way *or* in the wrong direction; **en s. inverse** in the opposite direction; **dans le s. des aiguilles d'une montre** clockwise; **dans le s. inverse des aiguilles d'une montre** anticlockwise, *Am* counterclockwise; **dans le s. du courant** with the current, with the stream; **dans le s. de la longueur** lengthwise, lengthways; **dans le s. de la largeur** widthwise, breadthwise, across; **tailler dans le s. du bois** to cut in the direction of the grain *or* along the grain; **dans le s. inverse du grain** against *or* across the grain; **courir dans tous les s.** to run in all directions; **s. dessus dessous** [sɑ̃dsydsu] upside down, the wrong way up; (*en désordre*) upside down, in a mess, in a state of confusion; **s. devant derrière** back to front, the wrong way round; **dans les deux s.** both ways; *Fig* **ces mesures vont toutes dans le même s.** these measures are all directed at the same object; **son action allait aussi dans ce s.** his action was also directed to this end; **le s. de l'histoire** the course of history; **s. de la circulation** direction of the traffic; **rue à double s.** two-way street; **rue en s. unique** one-way street; **s. unique** (*sur panneau*) one-way (street); **s. interdit** (*sur panneau*) no entry; **prendre une rue en s. interdit** to go the wrong way along a street; *Aut* **s. giratoire** roundabout, *Am* traffic circle; *Rail* **voyager dans le s. de la marche** to travel facing the engine; *Math* **s. direct/rétrograde** positive/negative direction; *Ordinat* **s. de déroulement** flow direction
sensas(s) [sɑ̃sas] *adj F* fantastic, great
sensation [sɑ̃sasjɔ̃] *nf* (**a**) (*impression*) feeling; *Physiol* sensation; **une s. de fatigue** a feeling of tiredness, a tired feeling; **avoir la s. que ...** to have a *or* the feeling that ...; **cela donne la s. de ...** it feels like ... (**b**) (*scandale*) **presse à s.** gutter press, tabloid press; **roman à s.** sensational novel; **titres à s.** sensationalist headlines; **faire s.** to create a sensation
sensationnel, -elle [sɑ̃sasjɔnɛl] **1** *adj* (*nouvelles, roman etc*) sensational; *F* (*remarquable*) fantastic, great **2** *nm* **journaliste à la recherche du s.** journalist in search of a sensational story
sensé [sɑ̃se] *adj* (*personne, action, remarque etc*) sensible
senseur [sɑ̃sœr] *nm Électron* sensor, sensing device
sensibilisateur, -trice [sɑ̃sibilizatœr, -tris] **1** *adj Phot etc* sensitizing; **lancer une campagne sensibilisatrice pour qch** to launch a campaign to heighten *or* increase public awareness of sth **2** *nm Phot* sensitizer **3** *nf Biol* **sensibilisatrice** sensitizer
sensibilisation [sɑ̃sibilizasjɔ̃] *nf Phot, Méd* sensitization; *Fig* growing awareness (**à** of); **la s. de l'opinion** (*action*) heightening *or* increasing public awareness; (*résultat*) heightened *or* increased public awareness; **campagne de s. à qch** campaign to heighten *or* increase public awareness of sth

sensibiliser [sɑ̃sibilize] **1** *vt Phot, Méd etc* to sensitize; *Fig* **s. qn à qch** to heighten *or* increase sb's awareness of sth; **s. l'opinion** to heighten *or* increase public awareness (**à** of) **2 se sensibiliser** *vpr* **se s. à qch** to become aware of sth

sensibilité [sɑ̃sibilite] *nf* sensitivity; **s. à fleur de peau** hypersensitivity; **avoir une s. à fleur de peau** to be hypersensitive; **enfant d'une grande s.** extremely sensitive child; **la s. romantique/wagnérienne** the Romantic/Wagnerian sensibility; **avoir de la s.** to be sensitive; *Mktg* **s. aux prix** price sensitivity

sensible [sɑ̃sibl] *adj* (**a**) (*personne*) sensitive; **cœur s.** tender *or* compassionate heart; **ce programme est déconseillé aux personnes sensibles** this programme is not recommended for people of a sensitive disposition; **s. à** (*ridicule, charme, injustice, douleur etc*) sensitive to; (*influence*) susceptible to; **être s. aux bontés de qn** to appreciate sb's kindness; **peu s.** insensitive; **être peu s. au froid/à la critique** to be impervious to the cold/to criticism; **être s. au froid** to feel the cold, to be sensitive to the cold; (*d'une plante*) to be tender; *Mktg* **s. au prix** price-sensitive; **les plantes sont sensibles à la musique** plants are sensitive to music; **cet enfant est très s. à la musique** this child has a great feeling for music; *Fig* **avoir l'épiderme s.** to be thin-skinned; *Fig* **toucher la note** *ou* **la corde s.** to appeal to the emotions

(**b**) (*physiquement fragile ou douloureux*) (*pieds etc*) tender; (*dent, peau*) sensitive; **s. au toucher** tender *or* painful to the touch; **toucher qn à un endroit s.** to touch sb on a tender spot; *Fig* **blesser qn au point s.** to tread on sb's corns; *Fig* **vous avez touché un point s.** you've touched on a sore point, you've touched a raw nerve

(**c**) (*balance, thermomètre, plaque etc*) sensitive; **papier s. à la lumière** light-sensitive paper

(**d**) (*apte à percevoir*) *Phil* sentient; **avoir l'oreille s.** to have a keen sense of hearing; **ouïe peu s.** dull hearing

(**e**) (*perceptible*) (*son etc*) perceptible; **le monde s.** the tangible world

(**f**) (*différence, progrès etc*) noticeable, appreciable; **d'une manière s.** noticeably; **un vide s.** a noticeable gap; **éprouver un plaisir s.** to feel a keen pleasure

(**g**) *Mus* **la note s.** the leading note

sensiblement [sɑ̃sibləmɑ̃] *adv* (**a**) (*notablement*) noticeably, appreciably (**b**) (*à peu près*) approximately, roughly, more or less

sensiblerie [sɑ̃sibləri] *nf Péj* sentimentality

sensitif, -ive [sɑ̃sitif, -iv] **1** *adj* (**a**) *Litt* oversensitive (**b**) *Physiol* sensory **2** *nf Bot* **sensitive** sensitive plant, mimosa pudica

sensoriel, -ielle [sɑ̃sɔrjɛl] *adj* sensorial, sensory

sensorimoteur, -trice [sɑ̃sɔrimɔtœr, -tris] *adj Méd* sensorimotor

sensualisme [sɑ̃sɥalism] *nm Phil* sensualism, sensationalism

sensualiste [sɑ̃sɥalist] *adj, n Phil* sensualist, sensationalist

sensualité [sɑ̃sɥalite] *nf* sensuality

sensuel, -elle [sɑ̃sɥɛl] *adj* (*personne, plaisir etc*) sensual; (*lèvres, voix etc*) sensual, sensuous

sentant [sɑ̃tɑ̃] *adj* sentient

sente [sɑ̃t] *nf* (*sentier*) (foot)path

sentence [sɑ̃tɑ̃s] *nf* (**a**) (*jugement*) sentence (**b**) (*maxime*) maxim

sentencieusement [sɑ̃tɑ̃sjøzmɑ̃] *adv* sententiously

sentencieux, -ieuse [sɑ̃tɑ̃sjø, -jøz] *adj* sententious

senteur [sɑ̃tœr] *nf Litt* scent

senti [sɑ̃ti] **1** *adj* heartfelt **2** *nm Phil* sense datum

sentier [sɑ̃tje] *nm* (foot)path; *Fig* path; **s. pour cavaliers** bridle path; **s. balisé** signposted footpath; **s. de grande randonnée** long-distance footpath; **s. battu** beaten track; *Fig* **sur le s. de la guerre** on the warpath

sentiment [sɑ̃timɑ̃] *nm* (**a**) (*sensation*) (*de joie, de soulagement etc*) feeling, sensation; **avoir le s. que …** to have a *or* the feeling that …; **privé de s.** (*membre*) devoid of feeling, numb; **il avait le s. de sa mort prochaine** he sensed he would die soon

(**b**) (*émotion*) feeling; *Mus* **jouer avec s.** to play with feeling; **avoir le s. de la nature** to have a feeling for nature; **avoir le s. de l'honneur/de la beauté** to have a sense of honour/of the aesthetic; **avoir du s. pour qn** to feel attracted to sb, to be drawn to sb; **ses sentiments vis-à-vis de moi** his feelings towards me; **je ne doute pas de ses sentiments pour moi** I have no doubt that he loves me; **faire appel aux bons sentiments de qn** to appeal to sb's finer feelings; **prendre qn par les sentiments** to appeal to sb's softer side; *F* **c'est parti d'un bon s.** it was well meant, the intention was good; **faire du s.** to sentimentalize; **je ne fais pas de s. en affaires** I don't let sentiment interfere with business; **allons! pas de s.!** come on, don't be sentimental!; **avoir qn au s.** to win sb over by appealing to his/her softer side; **privé de s.** (*personne*) (*sans réaction*) numb; (*insensible*) devoid of feeling; **s. national** sense of nationhood; **je n'ai aucun s. religieux** I'm not the slightest bit religious; **veuillez agréer l'expression de mes sentiments distingués** yours faithfully; **veuillez recevoir l'expression de mes sentiments les meilleurs** yours sincerely

(**c**) *Litt* (*opinion*) feeling; **quel est votre s. sur la question?** what is your feeling about the matter?

sentimental, -ale, -aux, -ales [sɑ̃timɑ̃tal, -o] **1** *adj* (**a**) **vie sentimentale** love life; *Cin, Th etc* **intrigue sentimentale** love interest (**b**) (*romantique*) (*personne, attachement, chanson etc*) sentimental, *F* soppy **2** *n* **c'est une sentimentale** she is sentimental

sentimentalement [sɑ̃timɑ̃talmɑ̃] *adv* sentimentally

sentimentalisme [sɑ̃timɑ̃talism] *nm* sentimentalism; **faire du s.** to be sentimental

sentimentaliste [sɑtimɑ̃talist] *adj, n* sentimentalist

sentimentalité [sɑ̃timɑ̃talite] *nf* sentimentality

sentine [sɑ̃tin] *nf Naut* (*d'un navire*) bilge; *Litt* **s. de tous les vices** sink of iniquity

sentinelle [sɑ̃tinɛl] *nf Mil* (*soldat*) guard, sentry, *Vieilli* sentinel; **nous disposerons des sentinelles le long des quais** we shall be posting guards along the quays; **en s.** on guard, on sentry duty; *Fig* **se mettre en s.** to stand guard, to keep (a) watch

sentir [sɑ̃tir] (*prp* **sentant**; *pp* **senti**; *pr ind* **je sens, il sent, n. sentons, ils sentent**; *pr sub* **je sente**; *impf* **je sentais**; *p hist* **je sentis**; *fu* **je sentirai**) **1** *vt* [①**A40**,**C**,**1**,**a**; **B33**,**2**,**b**,**i**] (**a**) (*douleur, faim, froid, joie, peine etc*) to feel; (*par le toucher*) to feel; **je sentais trembler le plancher** I could feel the floor trembling; *F* **je sens mes bras/mes jambes** my arms/legs are aching; **je ne sens plus mes jambes/mes pieds** my legs/my feet are killing me; (*devenu insensible*) my legs/my feet have gone numb; **je sens l'hiver qui vient** I can feel winter coming; **on ne sent pas la différence** you can't feel the difference

(**b**) (*être conscient de*) (*injure, force, pouvoir etc*) to be conscious of, to feel; (*danger*) to be aware of *or* conscious of; **elle ne sentait pas tout le ridicule de la situation** she wasn't fully aware *or* conscious of the ridiculousness of the situation; **s. grandir son influence** to feel one's influence growing; **je sens que vous avez raison** I have a *or* the feeling that you are right; **ce sont des choses que l'on sent** you can sense *or* feel these things; **il m'a fait s. que …** he gave me to understand that …; **fais-lui s. qu'il se trompe** make him understand that he's mistaken; **faire s. son autorité** to make one's authority felt; **l'effet se fera s.** the effect will be felt; **je sentis la peur me gagner peu à peu** I felt more and more frightened *or* I felt a growing fear; **je sentis sa colère monter peu à peu** I sensed his growing anger; **s. qch de loin** to feel sth coming; **s. qn de loin** to see through sb; **s. la barre** (*d'un navire*) to answer to the helm

(**c**) (*par l'odorat*) (*odeur, fleur etc*) to smell; **je ne sens rien** I can't smell anything; **faire s. qch à qn** to let sb smell sth; *F* **je ne peux pas le s.** (*supporter*) I can't stand (the sight of) him, *Br* I can't stick him; *Vieilli Fig* **s. le cadavre** to scent *or* smell disaster

(**d**) *Vieilli* (*par le goût*) to taste

(**e**) (*avoir l'odeur de*) to smell of; (*avoir un goût de*) to taste of; **cela sent le brûlé** (*dans une pièce*) there's a smell of burning; (*devant un mets etc*) it smells burnt; **ça sent le bébé/le linge frais** it smells of *or* there's a smell of babies/clean washing; **ça sent bon le pain frais** there's a delicious smell of fresh bread; **vin qui sent le bouchon** corked wine; **la pièce sent l'humidité** the room smells damp; **la salle sentait le tabac à plein nez** the room reeked of tobacco; *Fig* **ça sentait le piège à plein nez** I/he *etc* could smell a trap; **il sentait l'acteur à plein nez** he had actor written all over him; *Péj* **ce livre sent l'effort** this book is very laboured; *F* **il sent le cadavre** he looks as if he's on his last legs

2 *vi* (**a**) **s. bon/mauvais** to smell good/bad; **fleurs qui sentent bon** sweet-smelling flowers; **ça sent fort** it has a strong smell

(**b**) *F* (*puer*) to smell; **il sent des pieds** his feet smell, he has smelly feet

3 se sentir *vpr* (**a**) **cela se sent** it is something that you feel *or* sense

(**b**) **se s. bien/fatigué** to feel well/tired; **se s. dix ans de moins** to feel ten years younger; **elle se sentait mourir/revivre** she felt she was dying/coming alive again; **se s. le courage de faire qch** to feel up to doing sth; **je ne m'en sens pas le courage** I don't feel equal *or* up to it; **tu t'en sens capable?** do you think you can manage it?, do you feel capable of it?

(c) **il ne se sent pas de joie** he is beside himself with joy; *F* **tu ne te sens plus?** have you taken leave of your senses?

(d) *F* (*se supporter*) **ils ne peuvent pas se s.** they can't stand (the sight of) each other, *Br* they can't stick each other

seoir [swar] **1** *vi Litt* (*used only in prp* **seyant, séant**; *pr ind* **il sied, ils siéent**; *pr sub* **il siée, ils siéent**; *impf* **il seyait, ils seyaient**; *fu* **il siéra, ils siéront**) **s. à** to suit; **cette robe vous sied** that dress suits you *or* is very becoming **2** *v impers* **il lui sied de/lui sied mal de ...** it becomes him to/ill becomes him to ...; **comme il sied** as is fitting (**à** for)

Séoul [seul] *n* Seoul

sépale [sepal] *nm Bot* sepal

séparable [separabl] *adj* separable (**de** from); **deux théories difficilement séparables** two theories which are difficult to separate

séparateur, -trice [separatœr, -tris] **1** *adj* separating, separative; *Opt* (*pouvoir*) resolving **2** *nm Tech* separator; *Ordinat* delimiter; *Ordinat* **s. de champs** field delimiter *or* separator; *TV* **s. de faisceau** beam splitter

séparation [separasjɔ̃] *nf* (**a**) separation; **s. d'avec qn** separation from sb; **il n'a pas supporté la s. d'avec son épouse** he could not bear to be parted *or* separated from his wife; **s. de la tête et du corps** severance of the head from the body; **s. de l'Église et de l'État** separation of Church and State; *Ordinat* **s. automatique des pages** automatic pagination; *Typ* **s. des couleurs, s. quadrichromique** colour separation

(**b**) *Jur* **s. de corps** (*entre époux*) legal separation; **s. de fait, s. amiable** voluntary separation; **s. de biens** = marriage settlement under which husband and wife administer their separate properties

(**c**) (*cloison*) partition, division; **mur de s.** dividing wall; **s. en bois** wooden partition; *Fig* boundary, dividing line

séparatisme [separatism] *nm Pol* separatism

séparatiste [separatist] *adj, n Pol* separatist

séparé [separe] *adj* (**a**) (*distinct*) (*notions, chambres etc*) separate (**b**) (*désuni*) separated; **nous vivons s. l'un de l'autre** we've separated, we live apart; **il vit s. de sa femme** he's separated (from his wife)

séparément [separemɑ̃] *adv* separately

séparer [separe] **1** *vt* (**a**) (*éloigner*) to separate (**de** from); **s. deux combattants** to part *or* separate two fighters; *Boxe* **séparez!** break!; **personne ne peut nous s.** no one can separate us *or* come between us; **la guerre sépare les familles** war separates families *or* keeps families apart; **des milliers de kilomètres nous séparent** we are thousands of miles apart, we are separated by thousands of miles

(**b**) (*partager*) to divide; **le fleuve sépare la ville en deux** the river divides the town in two; **mur qui sépare deux champs** wall separating two fields; **s. une chambre en trois** to divide a room into three; **s. les cheveux en faisant une raie sur le côté** to part one's hair on the side

(**c**) (*diviser*) to divide; **leurs opinions politiques les séparent** their political opinions divide them; **tout les sépare** they are poles apart; **jusqu'à ce que la mort nous sépare** till death do us part

(**d**) (*isoler*) **s. les bons d'avec les mauvais** to separate the good from the bad; **s. la substance active de la substance inerte** to separate the active ingredient from the inert substances; **il faut savoir s. l'amour de la luxure** you must be able to distinguish between love and lust

2 se séparer *vpr* (*d'époux*) to separate, to part, *F* to split up; (*de la foule, d'une assemblée etc*) to break up, to disperse; (*d'une rivière, d'une route etc*) to divide, to branch off; **nous devons nous s. maintenant** we'll have to say goodbye now; **c'est ici que nos chemins se séparent** this is where we go our separate ways *or* where our paths diverge; **nous ne nous séparerons jamais** we shall never part; **l'armée se sépara** the army disbanded; **se s. de** *ou* **d'avec sa femme/son mari** to separate *or* part from one's wife/one's husband; **elle a dû se s. de son vieux chat/sa voiture** she had to part with her old cat/her car; *Ch* **se s. à l'état cristallin** (*du sel*) to crystallize out

sépia [sepja] **1** *nf* (*couleur, matière colorante*) sepia; **dessin à la s.** sepia drawing **2** *adj inv* sepia

sept [sɛt] **1** *adj inv* seven; **Édouard S.** Edward the Seventh **2** *nm inv* seven; **le s. mai** (on) the seventh of May, (on) May (the) seventh, *Am* (on) May seventh; **le s. du mois** the seventh of the month; *Cartes* **le s. de cœur** the seven of hearts; **habiter au s.** to live at number seven

septain [setɛ̃] *nm Littér* seven-line stanza

septante [sɛptɑ̃t] **1** *adj inv Belg, Suisse* seventy **2** *nm inv Bible* **la version des S.** the Septuagint

septembre [sɛptɑ̃br] *nm* [①**A75-6**,B-C; **B58-9**,B-C] September; **en s., au mois de s.** in September

septennal, -ale, -aux, -ales [sɛptɛnal, -o] *adj* (*période, parlement etc*) seven-year, *Fml* septennial

septennat [sɛptɛna] *nm* (*d'un président etc*) (seven-year) term

septentrion [sɛptɑ̃trijɔ̃] *nm Litt* north

septentrional, -ale, -aux, -ales [sɛptɑ̃trijɔnal, -o] *adj* northern

septicémie [sɛptisemi] *nf Méd* blood poisoning, septicemia

septicémique [sɛptisemik] *adj Méd* septicaemic, *US* septicemic

septième [sɛtjɛm] **1** *adj* seventh; **être au s. ciel** to be in seventh heaven; **s. étage** seventh *or Am* eighth floor; **le s. art** the cinema **2** *n* (*personne, objet, événement etc*) seventh; **habiter au s.** to live on the seventh *or Am* eighth floor **3** *nm* (*fraction*) seventh; **trois septièmes** three sevenths **4** *nf* (**a**) *Mus* seventh (**b**) *Scol* = top class *or Am* grade of primary school

septièmement [sɛtjɛmmɑ̃] *adv* seventhly, in the seventh place

septique [sɛptik] *adj* septic; **fosse s.** septic tank

septuagénaire [sɛptɥaʒenɛr] *adj, n* septuagenarian, seventy-year-old

septuagésime [sɛptɥaʒezim] *nf Rel* Septuagesima

septum [sɛptɔm] *nm Anat, Bot* septum

septuor [sɛptɥɔr] *nm Mus* septet(te)

septuple [sɛptypl] **1** *adj* sevenfold, *Fml* septuple **2** *nm* **au s.** sevenfold; **le s. de deux** seven times two; **payer le s.** to pay seven times as much

septupler [sɛptyple] *vti* to increase sevenfold

sépulcral, -ale, -aux, -ales [sepylkral, -o] *adj* sepulchral

sépulcre [sepylkr] *nm* sepulchre; **le saint s.** the Holy Sepulchre; *Fig* **s. blanchi** whited sepulchre

sépulture [sepyltyr] *nf* (**a**) *Litt* (*inhumation*) burial; **refuser la s. à qn** to refuse burial to sb; **être privé de s.** to be refused burial (**b**) (*lieu*) burial place; **sépultures militaires** war cemeteries; **violation de s.** desecration of graves

séquelles [sekɛl] *nfpl* (*de maladie, d'accident*) aftereffects; (*de guerre, catastrophe etc*) aftermath; **une des s. de la guerre** one of the consequences *or* aftereffects of the war

séquence [sekɑ̃s] *nf* sequence; *Cartes* run; *Ordinat* **s. de caractères** character string, sequence of characters; *Aut* **s. de combustion** firing order; **s. vidéo** video sequence

séquenceur [sekɑ̃sœr] *nm Ordinat* sequencer

séquentiel, -ielle [sekɑ̃sjɛl] *adj* sequential; *Ordinat* **accès s.** sequential *or* serial access

séquentiellement [sekɑ̃sjɛlmɑ̃] *adv* sequentially

séquestration [sekɛstrasjɔ̃] *nf Jur* (**a**) (*de biens*) sequestration (**b**) (*de personne*) illegal confinement

séquestre [sekɛstr] *nm Jur* (**a**) (*action*) sequestration; *Naut* embargo; **mettre les biens de qn sous s.** to sequester *or* sequestrate sb's property (**b**) (*personne*) depository, trustee, administrator

séquestrer [sekɛstre] **1** *vt* (**a**) (*biens*) to sequester, to sequestrate; *Naut* (*navire*) to lay an embargo upon (**b**) **s. qn** to keep sb locked up; *Jur* to confine sb illegally **2 se séquestrer** *vpr* to cut oneself off from the world

séquoia [sekɔja] *nm* (*arbre*) sequoia

sérac [serak] *nm Géol* serac

sérail [seraj] *nm* seraglio; *Fig* **c'est normal qu'il soit un financier international, il est né** *ou* **a été élevé dans le s.** it's not surprising he's an international financier, he grew up in that world

séraphin [serafɛ̃] *nm* [①**A14**,11] seraph

séraphique [serafik] *adj* seraphic

serbe [sɛrb] **1** *adj* Serb, Serbian **2** *n* **S.** Serb, Serbian

Serbie [sɛrbi] *nf* Serbia

serbo-croate [sɛrbɔkrɔat] **1** *adj* Serbo-Croat(ian) **2** *nm Ling* Serbo-Croat

Sercq [sɛrk] *nm* Sark

serein[1] [sərɛ̃] *adj* (*personne, visage, esprit, jour etc*) serene, calm; (*ciel, nuit*) clear; **jugement s.** calm *or* impartial judgement

serein[2] *nm* evening dew

sereinement [sərɛnmɑ̃] *adv* serenely, calmly

sérénade [serenad] *nf* (**a**) *Mus* serenade; **donner la s. à qn** to serenade sb (**b**) *F* (*tapage*) racket; **le bébé nous a fait une drôle de s. toute la nuit** the baby treated us to a demonstration of his vocal power all night; **il nous a fait sa s. habituelle** he treated us to one of his usual scenes

sérénissime [serenisim] *adj* **son Altesse s.** His/Her Most Serene Highness

sérénité [serenite] *nf* serenity, calmness; **avec s.** serenely, calmly

séreuse [serøz] *nf Anat* serous membrane

séreux, -euse [serø, -øz] *adj Anat, Méd* serous

serf, serve [sɛrf, sɛrv] *Hist* **1** *n* serf **2** *adj* **condition serve** serfdom; **terre serve** land in bondage *or* in villein tenure
serfouette [sɛrfwɛt] *nf* combined hoe and fork
serge [sɛrʒ] *nf Tex* serge
sergent¹ [sɛrʒɑ̃] *nm Mil* sergeant; **s. fourrier, s. comptable** quartermaster sergeant; **s. instructeur** drill sergeant; *Can* **s. d'armes** sergeant at arms; *Arch* **s. de ville** policeman
sergent² *nm Tech* cramp, clamp
sergent-chef, *pl* **sergents-chefs** *nm Mil* staff sergeant
séricicole [serisikɔl] *adj* silkworm-breeding, *Spéc* sericultural
sériciculteur [serisikyltœr] *nm* silkworm breeder, *Spéc* sericulturist
sériciculture [serisikyltyr] *nf* silkworm breeding, *Spéc* sericulture
série [seri] **1** *nf* [①A13,3,b] **(a)** (*d'événements, de changements, de dates etc*) series, succession; *Sp* (*épreuve*) heat; *Billard* break; *Billard* (*de canons*) run; **s. de catastrophes, s. noire** series *or* catalogue of disasters, run of bad luck; **livre de s. noire** (crime) thriller; **s. de conférences** series *or* course of lectures; *Rad, TV* **s.** (**télévisée/radiophonique**) (television/ radio) series; *TV* **s. AB** popular television; **s. dramatique** drama series; **s. policière** crime series, *F* cop show; *Sp* **s. éliminatoire** qualifying heat
(b) (*d'articles de presse, de timbres etc*) series; (*de documents, d'outils etc*) set; (*d'échantillons etc*) range; *Ind, Com* (*de marchandises*) range, line; *Math, Ch, Phys, Nucl* series; **s. complète de connaissements** full set of bills of lading; *Admin etc* **s. de prix** (*pour travaux publics etc*) list of charges; **s. de produits** product line; *F* **elle en a toute une s.** she has a whole collection of them; **en** *ou* **par série(s)** in series, serially; *Él* **en s.** in series; **fabrication** *ou* **production en s.** mass production; **chaîne de fabrication en s.** production line; **voiture de s.** standard car; *Com* **fins de séries** ends of lines, oddments, remnants; (*livres invendus*) remainders; **article hors s.** custom-made *or* custom-built article; **numéro hors s.** (*magazine*) special issue; *Fig* **c'est tout à fait hors s.** it's quite exceptional; **une personnalité hors s.** an exceptional personality
(c) (*groupe*) group, category; *Sp* rank; *Boxe* **s. poids plume** featherweight rating; *Cin* **film de s. B** B(-category) film; *Péj* **film de s. Z** real bummer of a film
(d) *Scol* specialization; **choisir une s.** to choose a specialization, to decide what one is going to specialize in
2 *adj inv Ordinat* serial
sériel, -ielle [serjɛl] *adj* serial; *Mus* serial, twelve-tone, dodecaphonic
sérier [serje] *vt* (*impf, pr sub* **n. sériions, v. sériiez**) to arrange (in series), to classify
sérieusement [serjøzmɑ̃] *adv* **(a)** (*avec sérieux*) seriously; (*sincèrement*) seriously, genuinely; **parlez-vous s.?** are you serious?, do you really mean it? **(b)** (*gravement*) (*malade, blessé, handicapé*) seriously; **il en a s. besoin** he's seriously in need of it
sérieux, -euse [serjø, -øz] **1** *adj* **(a)** (*qui ne plaisante pas*) serious; (*sincère*) (*offre, acheteur etc*) serious, genuine; (*information*) reliable; (*employé, entreprise etc*) responsible, reliable, serious; **des lectures sérieuses** serious reading; *F* **s. comme un pape** as solemn as a judge; **êtes-vous s.?** are you serious *or* in earnest?, do you mean it?; **d'un ton** *ou* **d'un air s.** seriously; **peu s.** (*personne*) unreliable; **voyons, ce n'est pas s.** come on, you're not serious *or* you don't mean it; **pas s. s'abstenir** (*dans une petite annonce*) genuine replies only; *Com* **client s.** good customer
(b) (*important*) (*maladie, blessure, affaire, situation etc*) serious; **il a fait de s. progrès** he has made good *or* considerable progress; **si seulement tu avais des raisons sérieuses de refuser** if only you had good reasons to refuse
2 *nm* seriousness; **garder son s.** to keep a straight face; **se prendre au s.** to take oneself seriously; **je vous ai pris au s.** I took you seriously, I thought you were serious, I thought you meant it; **on ne peut pas la prendre au s.** you can't take her seriously; **manque de s.** unreliability; **avec s.** seriously
serif [sɛrif] *nm Typ* serif
sérigraphie [serigrafi] *nf* silk-screen printing
sérigraphié [serigrafje] *adj* silk-screen(-printed)
serin, -ine [sərɛ̃, -in] **1** *nm Orn* canary **2** *adj inv* **jaune s.** canary yellow **3** *adj F* (*personne*) silly, stupid, idiotic **4** *n F* (*idiot*) nitwit
seriner [sərine] *vt* **(a)** *Péj* **s. qch à qn** to go on and on at sb about sth; **s. à qn que ...** to tell sb time after time that ... **(b) s. un air à un oiseau** to teach a bird to sing by using a bird organ
seringa(t) [sərɛ̃ga] *nm Bot* seringa
seringue [sərɛ̃g] *nf* syringe; *Méd* **s. à injections** hypodermic syringe; **s. jetable** disposable syringe; *Aut* **s. à graisse** grease gun
serment [sɛrmɑ̃] *nm* (*parole solennelle*) oath; (*promesse*) pledge; (*d'amoureux*) vow, pledge; **prêter s.** to take an oath; (*d'un jury*) to be sworn in; **faire prêter s. à qn** to administer the oath to sb; **déclarer sous s.** to state *or* declare under oath; **déclaration sous s.** sworn statement, statement under oath; **certifier qch sous s.** to declare sth on oath; **violer un s.** to break an oath; **être sous la foi du s.** to be on oath; **faire le s. de faire qch** to swear *or* vow *or* pledge to do sth; **faire un faux s.** to commit perjury
▶ **serment:** *Méd* **s. d'Hippocrate** Hippocratic oath; **s. d'ivrogne** empty promise; *Pol* **s. politique** oath of allegiance; *Admin* **s. professionnel** (*des magistrats, des avocats, de la police etc*) oath of office
sermon [sɛrmɔ̃] *nm Rel* sermon (**sur** on); *F Péj* (*remontrance*) sermon, lecture; *Bible* **le S. sur la Montagne** the Sermon on the Mount
sermonner [sɛrmɔne] *vt F Péj* **s. qn** to lecture sb, to give sb a lecture *or* talking-to
sermonneur, -euse [sɛrmɔnœr, -øz] *F Péj* **1** *adj* sermonizing **2** *n* sermonizer
séroconversion [serɔkɔ̃vɛrsjɔ̃] *nf Méd* seroconversion
sérodiagnostic [serɔdjagnɔstik] *nm Méd* serodiagnosis
sérologie [serɔlɔʒi] *nf* serology; **faire une s.** to be screened for antibodies
seronégatif, -ive [serɔnegatif, -iv] *Méd* **1** *adj* HIV negative **2** *n* person who is HIV negative
séronégativité [serɔnegativite] *nf Méd* the state of being HIV negative; **prouver sa s.** to prove that one is HIV negative
séropositif, -ive [serɔpozitif, -iv] *Méd* **1** *adj* HIV positive **2** *n* person who is HIV positive; **séropositifs non-évoluteurs** long-term survivors, LTS
séropositivité [serɔpozitivite] *nf Méd* the state of being HIV positive; **taux de s.** HIV positive rate; **il a été renvoyé à cause de sa s.** he was dismissed for being HIV positive
sérosité [serozite] *nf* serous fluid
serpe [sɛrp] *nf* billhook; **visage taillé à coups de s.** rugged face
serpent [sɛrpɑ̃] *nm* **(a)** (*reptile*) snake; *CE, Fin* (currency) snake; *Bible* **le s.** the serpent; **s. à coiffe** *ou* **à lunettes** (Indian) cobra; **s. d'eau** water snake; **s. de mer** *Myth* sea serpent; (*poisson*) pipe fish; *Journ* stock story; **s. à sonnettes** rattlesnake, *Am F* rattler; **s. à sonnettes cornu** horned rattlesnake, *Am F* sidewinder; **s. de verre** slow-worm; *Fig* **s. de fumée** wreath *or* coil of smoke; *Écon* **s. monétaire européen** European currency snake **(b)** *Hist, Mus* serpent
serpentaire¹ [sɛrpɑ̃tɛr] *nf Bot* serpentaria; **s. de Virginie** snakeroot
serpentaire² *nm Orn* serpent eater, secretary bird
serpentant [sɛrpɑ̃tɑ̃] *adj* (*courant, route etc*) winding, snaking, meandering
serpenteau, -eaux [sɛrpɑ̃to] *nm* **(a)** *Zool* young snake **(b)** (*fusée volante*) serpent
serpenter [sɛrpɑ̃te] *vi* (*d'une rivière, d'une route etc*) to wind, to snake, to meander; **le chemin monte/descend en serpentant** the road winds *or* snakes *or* meanders up/down
serpentin, -ine [sɛrpɑ̃tɛ̃, -in] **1** *adj* serpentine **2** *nm* **(a)** *Tech* coil **(b)** (*ruban pour les fêtes*) paper streamer **3** *nf Minér* **serpentine** serpentine, ophite
serpette [sɛrpɛt] *nf* pruning knife
serpillière [sɛrpijɛr] *nf* floorcloth; **passer la s. dans la cuisine** to mop the kitchen floor
serpolet [sɛrpɔlɛ] *nm Bot* wild thyme
serrage [sɛraʒ] *nm Tech* (*d'une vis, d'un écrou, d'un nœud etc*) tightening; (*d'un joint*) clamping; **s. des freins** application of the brakes, braking; **vis de s.** set screw, locking screw
serre [sɛr] *nf* **(a)** (*construction*) greenhouse; (*qui fait partie d'une maison*) conservatory; **s. chaude** hothouse; **s. de palmiers** palm house; **plante de s. chaude** hothouse plant; **plantes sous s.** plants under glass; *Écol* **effet de s.** greenhouse effect; *Écol* **gaz à effet de s.** greenhouse gas **(b)** (*action*) (*des raisins etc*) pressing, squeezing **(c) serres** (*des oiseaux de proie*) claws, talons
serré [sere] **1** *adj* (*bottes, vêtements, nœud, vis etc*) tight; (*texture*) close; (*formation*) dense; (*discussion*) closely argued; (*argumentation*) closely reasoned; (*programme*) tight; *Géog* (*col*) narrow; **budget s.** tight budget; **surveillance serrée** close supervision; **étude serrée** (*d'un texte*) close *or* intensive study; **style s.** concise style; **on était vraiment serrés dans cette voiture** we were really (tightly) packed in that car; **une robe serrée à la taille** a dress with a fitted waist; **un café noir bien s.** a strong black coffee; **pluie serrée** teeming rain; **deux pages d'une écriture serrée** two closely written pages; **les dents serrées** with clenched teeth;

elle était pâle, les lèvres serrées she was pale, her lips pressed tightly together; **maisons serrées** houses huddled together; **serrés comme des harengs** *ou* **des sardines** packed like sardines; **rangs serrés** serried *or* closed ranks; **avoir le cœur s.** to be sad at heart, to have a heavy heart; **la gorge serrée** with a lump in one's throat; *Sp* **la partie va être serrée** it's going to be a tight *or* close game; *Sp etc* **arrivée serrée** close finish

2 *adv* **écrire s.** to have cramped handwriting; **tricoter s.** to knit tightly; *Fig* **jouer s.** to play a cautious game, to take no chances

serre-fils *nm inv Él* wire-retaining screw

serre-frein(s) *nm inv Rail* brakeman

serre-joint(s) *nm inv* (*outil*) clamp

serre-livres *nm inv* book end

serrement [sɛrmɑ̃] *nm* **s. de main** handshake; **avoir un s. de cœur** to feel a pang; **elles se dirent au revoir avec un s. de cœur** they both felt a pang as they said their good-byes; **il comprit dans un s. de cœur que la maladie serait fatale** his heart sank as he realized the illness was fatal

serrer [sere] **1** *vt* **(a)** (*saisir, tenir*) to grip, to clasp; (*presser*) to squeeze, to press; **s. la main à** *ou* **de qn** to shake hands with sb, to shake sb's hand; **tenir qch sans s.** to hold sth loosely; **s. qn entre ses bras** to clasp sb in one's arms, to hug sb; **s. qn/qch contre soi** to hold sb/sth tightly to one; **s. le cou à qn** to wring sb's neck; **cela me serre le cœur** it wrings my heart; **le chagrin lui serrait la gorge** he felt choked with grief

(b) (*d'un vêtement, des chaussures etc*) (*qn*) to be too tight for; **s. les pieds à qn** to pinch sb's feet; **cette jupe me serre (à) la taille** this skirt is too tight round the waist

(c) (*nœud, écrou, ceinture etc*) to tighten; (*joint*) to clamp; (*voiles*) to furl, to take in; (*poings*) to clench; **s. les dents** to clench one's teeth; *Fig* to grit one's teeth; **s. les freins** to put on *or* apply the brakes; *Mus* **en serrant** stringendo

(d) (*rapprocher*) to close up, to put close together; *Mil, Fig* **s. les rangs** to close ranks; **s. son style** to condense one's style; *Typ* **s. une ligne** to close up a line

(e) (*être près de*) (*qn, qch*) to keep close to; *Naut* (*côte*), *Aut* (*trottoir*) to hug; **s. qn de près** to follow sb closely; **s. une femme de près** to be all over a woman; **s. un adversaire dans un coin** to corner an enemy; **s. une question de près** to focus narrowly on a question; **s. le vent** to sail close to the wind

(f) (*ranger*) *Litt* **s. des bijoux dans une cassette** to stow one's jewels in a case

2 *vi* **serrez à droite!** keep to the right!

3 se serrer *vpr* **(a)** (*se rapprocher*) to squeeze up *or* together; **se s. les uns contre les autres** to huddle together; **se s. contre qn** to snuggle up to sb; (*pour être protégé*) to cling to sb; **se s. contre un mur** to hug a wall

(b) mon cœur se serra my heart sank; **ma gorge se serra** I had a lump in my throat; **nous nous serrâmes la main** we shook hands

(c) *Fig* **se s. (la ceinture)** to tighten one's belt; *F* **se s. les coudes** to back one another up, to support one another

serre-tête *nm inv* **(a)** (*bandeau*) headband **(b)** *Sp* (*bonnet*) cap; *Av* helmet

serrure [seryr] *nf* lock; **trou de la s.** keyhole; **s. de capot** bonnet lock; **s. à carte perforée** card-operated lock; **s. électronique** electronic lock, computer-coded lock; **s. magnétique** magnetic lock; **s. de sûreté** safety lock

serrurerie [seryrri] *nf* **(a)** (*métier*) locksmith's trade; (*magasin*) locksmith's (shop) **(b)** (*travail, ouvrages*) ironwork, metal work; **s. d'art** ornamental ironwork; **grosse s.** heavy ironwork

serrurier [seryrje] *nm* **(a)** (*de serrures*) locksmith **(b)** (*de métaux*) ironsmith

sertir [sɛrtir] *vt* (*pierre précieuse*) to set; (*cartouche, boîte de conserve etc*) to crimp

sertissage [sɛrtisaʒ] *nm* (*d'une pierre précieuse*) setting; (*d'une cartouche, d'une boîte de conserve etc*) crimping

sertisseur, -euse [sɛrtisœr, -øz] **1** *n* (*ouvrier*) (*de pierres précieuses*) setter; (*de cartouches, de boîtes de conserve etc*) crimper **2** *nm* (*appareil*) (*pour boîtes de conserves etc*) crimper

sertissure [sɛrtisyr] *nf* (*action, manière*) (*de pierre précieuse*) setting; (*partie de chaton*) bezel

sérum [serɔm] *nm* **(a)** *Physiol, Méd* serum; **s. physiologique** saline solution, saline; **s. sanguin** blood serum; **s. de vérité** truth serum; *F* truth drug **(b) s. (lactique)** whey

servage [sɛrvaʒ] *nm Hist* serfdom, bondage; *Fig* bondage

serval, -als [sɛrval] *nm Zool* serval

servant, -ante [sɛrvɑ̃, -ɑ̃t] **1** *adj* **frère s.** lay brother; **cavalier** *ou* **chevalier s.** faithful admirer **2** *nm* **(a)** *Mil* gunner **(b)** *Tennis* server **(c)** *Rel* **s. (de messe)** server **3** *nf* **servante (a)** (*domestique*) (maid)servant **(b)** (*table*) side table **(c)** *Tech* (adjustable) support

serve [sɛrv] *adj, n voir* **serf**

serveur, -euse [sɛrvœr, -øz] **1** *n* **(a)** (*dans un bar*) barman, *surtout Am* bartender, *f* barmaid; (*dans un restaurant*) waiter, *f* waitress **(b)** *Cartes* dealer **(c)** *Tennis* server **2** *nm Ordinat* server; **s. de fichiers** file server; **s. minitel** minitel service provider; **s. de réseau** network server; **s. télématique** bulletin board (system)

serviabilité [sɛrvjabilite] *nf* obligingness, helpfulness

serviable [sɛrvjabl] *adj* obliging, helpful

service [sɛrvis] *nm* **(a)** (*pour un client, un maître*) service; **le s. est désastreux** (*dans ce restaurant*) the service here is appalling; **faire le s.** to serve; **s. (non) compris** service (not) included; **libre s.** (*dans un magasin etc*) self-service; *Écon* **services** services; **les biens et les services** goods and services; **le secteur des services** the service sector; **société de services** service company; **entrer en s. (chez qn)** to go into (sb's) service, to go into service (with sb); **gens de s.** domestic staff; **être au s. de qn** to be in sb's service; **se passer des services d'un employé** to dispense with an employee's services; **mourir au s. du roi** to die in the king's service; **escalier de s.** backstairs; **porte de s.** tradesmen's entrance; *Admin, Mil* **états de s.** service record; *Com* **s. après vente** after-sales service; **s. clients** customer service; **s. à l'américaine** (*dans un restaurant*) American service; **s. à l'anglaise** (*dans un restaurant*) English service; **s. à la française** (*dans un restaurant*) French service; **s. à la russe** (*dans un restaurant*) Russian service; **s. à l'assiette** (*dans un restaurant*) plate service, American service; **s. au guéridon** (*dans un restaurant*) gueridon service, French service; **s. à table** table service, waiter service, waitress service; **services bancaires** banking services; *Banque* **services de caisse** counter services; **s. dans les chambres** *ou* **en chambre** room service; **services à la clientèle** customer services, customer-support services; *Admin* **s. contractuel** contract service; *Fin* **s. d'un emprunt** servicing a loan; *Fin* **s. des intérêts** interest charges

(b) *Mil* **s. militaire (obligatoire)** (compulsory) military service; **faire son s.** to do one's military service; **en s. actif, en activité de s.** on the active list; **service(s) de guerre** active service; **en s. aux armées** on active service; **(in)apte au s.** (un)fit for service; **bon pour le s.** (*jeune appelé*) fit for service; *Fig* (*appareil*) in working order; **être libéré du s.** to be discharged; **libération du s.** discharge

(c) *Tennis* service; **faire un** *ou* **le s.** to serve; **au s., Martin** Martin to serve

(d) (*travail*) duty; **s. de jour** day duty; **s. de nuit** night duty; *Naut* night watch; **être de s./ne pas être de s.** to be on/off duty; **à quelle heure prenez-vous/quittez-vous votre s.?** at what time do you go on/off duty?; **avoir dix ans de s. dans une entreprise** to have completed ten years' service with a company; *Mil etc* **mort en s. commandé** killed on active service; **s. de corvée** *Mil* fatigue duty; *Naut* duty; **s. de garde** guard duty; **planton de s.** duty orderly; **tableau de s.** duty chart *or* list *or* roster; **officier/sous-officier de s.** duty/non-commissioned officer; *F* **le crétin/pigeon de s.** the usual *or* inevitable cretin/sucker; *F* **être s. s.** to be a stickler for rules and regulations

(e) (*département*), *Admin, Com* department; *Mil* corps, service; *Méd etc* department, service; **chef de s.** head of department; **correspondance de s.** official correspondence; **s. central** headquarters; **s. clientèle** customer service (department); **s. d'études** research department; **s. de relation avec la clientèle** customer service department; **services commerciaux** marketing services; **services financiers** financial services

(f) (*d'une machine etc*) operation; **s. à bras** *ou* **manuel** hand *or* manual operation; **en s.** (*machine*) in service, in use, in operation; (*avion, navire*) in commission; **aptitude au s.** serviceability; **en (bon) état de s., propre au s.** in (good) working order, serviceable; **hors (de) s.** (*machine, mécanisme*) out of order; (*canon*) out of action; (*navire*) disabled; **mettre en s.** (*machine etc*) to bring *or* put into service; (*avion, navire*) to bring *or* put into commission; **retirer du s.** to withdraw from service *or* from use; (*avion, navire*) to decommission; **retirer graduellement du s.** to phase out

(g) (*transport*) service; **assurer** *ou* **faire le s. entre … et …** to operate between … and …; **s. assuré toute l'année** year-round service; **s. de marchandises** goods *or* freight service; **s. de voyageurs** passenger service

(h) (*aide*) favour, *US* favor, service; **rendre (un) s. à qn** (*d'une personne*) to do sb a favour *or* a service; **si ça peut te rendre s., prends-le** if it's of any use to you, take it; **rendre**

un bon/un mauvais s. à qn to do sb a good/a bad turn; **demander un s. à qn** to ask sb a favour; **les services qu'il a rendus à l'enseignement** his services to education; **ce livre m'a rendu grand s.** I found this book very useful; **à votre s.** at your service; **qu'y a-t-il pour votre s.?** what can I do for you?

(**i**) (*en élevage*) (*d'un étalon*) service

(**j**) (*ensemble de repas*) sitting; *Rail etc* **dernier s. à deux heures** last sitting (for lunch) at two o'clock

(**k**) (*d'ustensiles de cuisine, de linge de table etc*) set; **s.** (**de table**) (*assiettes etc*) dinner service; (*linge*) set of table linen; **s. à découper** carving knife and fork

▶ **service**: **s. des achats** purchasing (department); (*plus grand*) procurement (department); **s. d'action commerciale** marketing department; **s. administratif** administration (department), *F* admin; **s. après-vente** after-sales (department); **services autoroutiers** motorway services; **s. babyphone** baby-listening service; *Méd* **s. de cardiologie** cardiology department; **s. des commandes** order department; **s. commercial export** export department; **s. comptable** *ou* **de comptabilité** accounts (department); **s. de conseil** consulting service; **s. consommateurs** customer service (department); *Méd* **s. des contagieux** isolation ward; **s. contrôle qualité**, **s. de contrôle de qualité** quality control (department); **s. du courrier** mail room; **s. de dépannage** repair service; *Aut* recovery service; *Fin* **s. de la dette** debt servicing; **s. des eaux** = water board; **s. d'écoute** monitoring service; **s. d'étude mercatique** marketing research department; **s. de l'expédition** shipping (department); **s. export** export (department); **s. export intégré** integrated export service; **services extérieurs** external services; **s. de facturation** invoicing department; **s. financier** finance (department); **s. de fixation des prix** pricing department; **s. gouvernemental** government agency *or* department; **s. de l'immigration** immigration department; **services industriels** industrial services; **s. informations** enquiries; *Journ* **s. des informations** information service; **s. informatique** EDP-department, computer department; **s. juridique** legal department; **s. lancement** product launch department; **s. marketing** marketing department; **s. marketing-vente** sales and marketing department; **s. mercatique** marketing department; **s. d'ordre** (*police*) police contingent; (*dans une manifestation etc*) team of stewards; **s. du personnel** personnel (department); **s. des postes** *ou* **postal** postal service, *surtout Am* mail service; **s. de presse** press office; **s.** (**de**) **production** production department; **s. de la prospection** sales and marketing (department), new business department; **s. public** civil service; *TV* public-service broadcasting (network); **s. de la publicité** publicity *or* advertising department; **services publics** (public) utilities; **s. de recherche** research department; **s. de recouvrement** collection department; **S. Régional de la Police Judiciaire** *Br* ≈ regional crime squad; **s. de relations publiques** public relations department; **s. de remorquage et de dépannage** breakdown and recovery service; **s. de renseignements** information office; *Tél* directory enquiries, *Am* information; *Mil* military intelligence (department); *Com* **s. des renseignements commerciaux** status enquiry department; **s. de santé** health services; **services du secteur tertiaire** business services; **services de soutien** support services; **s. de stylique** design department; (*plus grand*) procurement (department); **services supplémentaires** service backup; **s. technique** engineering department, technical branch; *Ordinat* **s. télématique** bulletin board service; *Arg* **s. trois-pièces** wedding tackle; **s. d'urgence** emergency service; **s. vente** *ou* **des ventes** sales department; **s. de voiturier** valet parking

serviette [sɛrvjɛt] *nf* (**a**) **s.** (**de table**) (table) napkin, serviette; **s. d'enfant** feeder, bib (**b**) towel; **s. de toilette** hand towel; **s. de plage** beach towel; **s. sans fin** roller towel (**c**) (*sac*) briefcase

▶ **serviette**: **s. hygiénique** sanitary towel *or US* napkin

serviette-éponge, *pl* **serviettes-éponges** *nf* terry towel

servile [sɛrvil] *adj* servile; (*imitation, traduction, traducteur*) slavish

servilement [sɛrvilmɑ̃] *adv* servilely; (*imiter, traduire*) slavishly

servilité [sɛrvilite] *nf* servility; (*d'imitation, de traduction*) slavishness

servir [sɛrvir] (*prp* **servant**; *pp* **servi**; *pr ind* **je sers, il sert, n. servons**; *pr sub* **je serve**; *impf* **je servais**; *p hist* **je servis**; *fu* **je servirai**) **1** *vi* (**a**) (*être utile*) to be useful *or* of use (**à qn** to sb); **la machine peut encore s.** the machine can still be used *or* is still fit for use; **la voiture peut encore s. quelques années** the car has still got a few years' use left in it; **cela peut s. un de ces jours** it may come in handy *or* be of use one day; **toujours prêt à s.** always ready for use

(**b**) **s. à qch/à faire qch** (*être destiné à*) to be used for sth/ for doing sth; **ne s. à rien** to be (of) no use, to be useless; **je vais le lui dire, mais je sais que ça ne servira à rien** I'm going to tell him but I know it won't do any good *or* it'll be pointless; **ça ne servira pas à grand-chose** that won't be much good *or* much use; **cela ne sert qu'à l'irriter** it only irritates him *or Fml* serves to irritate him; **à quoi cela sert-il?, à quoi ça sert?** what's the good *or* the use *or* the point of that?; **à quoi sert ce truc-là?** what's that gadget (used) for?; **je ne vois pas à quoi sert d'y aller** I don't see the point *or* good of going; **à quoi sert qu'on l'attende?** what's the point *or* use of waiting for him?

(**c**) **s. de** (*d'un objet*) to serve as, to be used as; (*d'une personne*) to act as; **les pupitres servent de tables** the desks serve *or* are used as tables; **s. de prétexte** to serve as a pretext; **elle lui a servi de mère** she has been (like) a mother to him; **tu vas me s. de conseiller** you'll act as *or* be my adviser

(**d**) *Tennis* to serve; *Cartes* **à vous de s.** (it's) your deal

(**e**) (*dans l'armée, dans le gouvernement etc*) to serve (**sous** under); *Mil* **en âge de s.** of military age; **s. à table** to wait at table, *Am* to wait (on) table

2 *v impers* **il ne sert à rien de pleurer** it's no good *or* use crying, there's no point in crying; **rien ne sert de courir, il faut partir à point** slow and steady wins the race

3 *vt* (**a**) (*consommateur, dîner, poisson etc*) to serve; (*dîneur*) to wait on, to serve; (*client*) to serve, to attend to; **s. qn en marchandises** to supply sb with goods; **s. Dieu/le roi** to serve God/the king; *Vieilli* **Comte de Monte-Cristo, pour vous s.** the Count of Monte-Cristo, at your service; **est-ce qu'on vous sert?** are you being served *or* attended to?; **tout le monde est servi?** has everybody got a drink/something to eat?; (*dans un magasin*) is anybody waiting to be served?; **madame est servie** dinner is served, madam; **vous pouvez nous s., Nestor** you may serve dinner, Nestor; **à s. frais** best (served) chilled; **puis-je vous s. de gratin?** can I serve you with *or* help you to some gratin?; **s. à boire à qn** to give sb a drink *or* something to drink; **nous sommes très bien servis** we have very good domestic help; **on est très bien servi dans ce restaurant** the service in this restaurant is very good; **on n'est jamais si bien servi que par soi-même** if you want something done, do it yourself; *F* **en fait de pluie, nous sommes servis** as far as rain goes, we get more than our share; **ce cours d'eau sert le moulin** this stream drives the mill; **s. une rente à qn** to pay an annuity to sb

(**b**) (*aider*) (*qn*) to help, to assist, to be of service to; (*intérêts*) to serve, to further; (*patrie, cause*) to serve; **en quoi puis-je vous s.?** what can I do for you?, how can I help you *or Fml* be of service to you?; **les choses l'ont bien servi** things have worked in his favour; **sa mémoire l'a mal servi** his memory served him badly; **mes études m'ont peu servi** my studies haven't been of much use to me *or* haven't got me anywhere much; **cela m'a peu servi pour obtenir un emploi** that wasn't much use to me in getting a job

(**c**) *Tennis* (*balle*) to serve

(**d**) (*d'un étalon*) (*jument*) to serve, to cover

(**e**) (*à la chasse*) (*animal*) to dispatch

(**f**) *Rel* **s. la messe** to serve at mass

4 se servir *vpr* (**a**) (*d'une personne*) **se s. d'un plat** to help oneself to a dish; **servez-vous!** help yourself!; **je me suis déjà servie deux fois** I've already had two helpings

(**b**) (*d'un plat, d'un vin etc*) to be served; **le champagne se sert frappé** champagne should be *or* is best served chilled

(**c**) *Com* **se s. chez Martin** to shop at Martin's

(**d**) **se s. de qch/qn** (*utiliser*) to use sth/sb; **se s. d'un parapluie comme d'un pare-soleil** to use an umbrella as a sunshade; **il sait se s. de ses poings** he knows how to use his fists, he's good with his fists

serviteur [sɛrvitœr] *nm* servant; **s. de l'État** civil servant; *Arch* **votre s.** (*dans une lettre*) your obedient servant; *Arch, Hum* **personne ne le sait mieux que votre s.** no one knows it better than yours truly

servitude [sɛrvityd] *nf* (**a**) (*asservissement*) servitude; (*contrainte*) constraint; **réduire un pays en s.** to reduce a country to servitude; **la s. de la mode** the tyranny *or* constraints of fashion (**b**) *Jur* easement; **s. de passage** right of way

servo [sɛrvo] *nm Aut etc* **s. à air comprimé** compressed-air servo

servocommande [sɛrvɔkɔmɑ̃d] *nf Av, Aut etc* servo(control)

servodirection [sɛrvɔdirɛksjɔ̃] *nf Aut etc* servo steering, power steering

servofrein [sɛrvɔfrɛ̃] *nm Aut etc* servobrake, servo-assisted brake

servomécanisme [sɛrvɔmekanism] *nm Tech* servomechanism, servo system

servomoteur [sɛrvɔmɔtœr] *nm Tech* servomotor
ses [se] *adj poss voir* **son**[1]
sésame [sezam] *nm* **(a)** *Bot* sesame **(b) s., ouvre-toi!** open, sesame!; **ce diplôme lui a servi de s.** the diploma opened doors for him
session [sesjɔ̃] *nf* **(a)** *Parl, Jur* session, sitting **(b)** *Univ (examens)* (exam) session; **la s. de juin** the June exams; **il a eu son bac à la deuxième s.** he passed his baccalauréat the second time round *or Br* at the resits; **s. de rattrapage** repeat exams, *Br* resits
sesterce [sɛstɛrs] *nm Antiq (monnaie)* sestertius, sesterce
set [sɛt] *nm* **(a)** *Tennis* set; **gagner en deux sets** to win in two sets **(b) s. (de table)** *(ensemble de napperons)* set of table mats; *(napperon)* table mat
sétacé [setase] *adj Biol* bristly, *Spéc* setaceous
setter [setɛr] *nm (chien)* setter; **s. irlandais** Irish setter
seuil [sœj] *nm* **(a)** *(entrée)* doorway, threshold; *(dalle etc)* doorstep; *Phys, Psy, Fig* threshold; **franchir le s.** to cross the threshold; **sur le s.** in the doorway; **un inconnu se tenait sur le s.** there was a stranger standing on the doorstep *or* in the doorway; *Bourse* **s. d'annonce obligatoire** disclosure threshold; **s. d'émissions** *(des gaz d'échappement)* emissions limit; **s. de prix** price threshold; *Écon* **s. de rentabilité** break-even point; *Physiol* **s. de sensibilité** threshold of sensitivity *or* of response; *Psy* **s. de la conscience** threshold of consciousness **(b)** *Géog* **s. continental** continental shelf **(c)** *(d'une vanne, d'une cale sèche)* sill
seul, -e [sœl] **1** *adj* [①**B10**,D,3] **(a)** *(preceding the noun) (unique)* only, sole; **un s. homme** *(pas plus qu'un)* a single man; *(d'entre tous les autres)* just *or* only one man; **ils se sont tous avancés comme un s. homme** they moved forward as one man; **un s. être vous manque et tout est dépeuplé** there's just one person missing in your life and the entire world seems like a desert; **son s. exécuteur testamentaire** his sole executor; **son s. souci** his only *or* sole worry; **c'est la seule chose qui me retient** it's the one *or* the only thing keeping me here; **il ne suffit pas d'un s. exemple** a single example *or* one example alone will not suffice; **il suffit d'une seule fois** once is enough; **mon s. et unique ami/stylo** my one and only friend/pen; **un s. mot, et je pars** one word (from you) and I'll go; **la seule pensée de sa venue m'effraie** the mere *or* very thought of him coming frightens me
(b) *(following the noun or used predicatively) (séparé des autres)* alone, by oneself, on one's own; **je suis s., tu peux venir** you can come over, I'm on my own; **se sentir très s.** to feel very lonely *or* alone; **tu es trop s.** you're on your own *or* by yourself too much; **être s. au monde** to be alone in the world; **enfin seuls!** alone at last!; **une femme seule** an unattached woman; **il peut marcher tout s. maintenant** he can walk by himself now; **faire cavalier s.** to go it alone; **parler s. à s. à qn** to speak to sb in private, to have a private conversation with sb; **s. (à s.) avec soi-même** alone with one's thoughts; **l'œuvre seule de …** the sole *or* exclusive work of …; **j'ai une cachette que moi s. connais** I have a hiding place which no-one else knows about *or Fml* which I alone know; **je l'ai fait tout s.** *ou* **à moi s.** I did it (by) myself *or* all on my own *or* single-handed; **cela va tout s.** it's plain sailing, it's straightforward; **cela n'a pas été tout s.** it wasn't all that easy, it wasn't plain sailing; **ça se mange tout s.** it doesn't need anything else; *(se mange facilement)* it's very light; **parler/chanter tout s.** to talk/sing to oneself; *Mus* **passage pour violon s.** passage for unaccompanied *or* solo violin
(c) *(following the noun or preceding the article or poss adj) (seulement)* only, alone; **la violence seule** *ou* **seule la violence le contraindrait** only violence *or* violence alone *or* nothing short of violence would compel him; **seule la chasse les fait vivre** hunting is their only *or* sole source of food; **s. un expert pourrait nous conseiller** only an expert could advise us; **réservé aux seuls adultes** for adults only; **nous sommes seuls à le savoir** we are the only ones *or* people who know about it
2 *n* **un s.** *(pas plus qu'un)* a single person; *(chose)* a single one; *(d'entre tous les autres)* only one person; *(chose)* only one; **le gouvernement d'un s.** absolute rule; **pas un s.** *(chose)* not (a single) one; *(personne)* not a single person; **vous êtes le s. qui puissiez m'aider** you're the only one *or* person who can help me, *Fml* you alone can help me; **ne t'en fais pas, tu n'es pas le s.!** don't worry, you're not the only one!
seule [sœl] *nf Com* **s. de change** sola of exchange
seulement [sœlmɑ̃] *adv* **(a)** [①**A24**,d,iii] *(juste)* only; **nous sommes s. deux** there are only *or* just two of us; **elle m'a donné s. les plus mûres** she gave me only *or* she only gave me the ripest ones; **je te demande s. un peu de patience** I'm just asking you to be a bit patient; **je viens s. d'arriver/de terminer** I've only just arrived/finished, I've just this minute arrived/finished; **et c'est s. maintenant que tu me le dis!** and you're only telling me about it now!, and you haven't told me before this!; **non s. …, mais aussi …** *ou* **mais encore …** not only …, but also…
(b) *(uniquement)* only, solely, merely; **il y va s. pour vous faire plaisir** he is only going to please you, he is going just *or* merely *or* solely to please you; *F* **entrez s.** do come in; *F* **essaie s.!** just (you) try!
(c) *(même)* even; **sans s. me regarder** without even looking at me, without so much as looking at me; **si s. …!** if only …!
(d) *(with conj force)* **je viendrais bien, s. …** I'd like to come, but … *or* only …; **elle est gentille, s. elle est un peu sotte** she's kind, but she's a bit silly
sève [sɛv] *nf Bot (d'une plante)* sap; *Fig Litt* vitality, vigour, *US* vigor; *Bot, Fig* **la s. monte** the sap is rising
sévère [sevɛr] *adj* **(a)** *(dur) (juge, critique, peine, paroles etc)* severe, harsh; *(visage, regard, air)* stern, severe; **climat s.** severe *or* hard climate; **être s. envers** *ou* **pour** *ou* **avec qn/pour les fautes de qn** to be severe *or* hard on sb/on sb's failings; **mener un train s.** to set a gruelling pace **(b)** *(discipline, principes moraux)* strict, rigid; **morale peu s.** lax morals **(c)** *(sans ornements) (architecture, style, beauté)* severe **(d)** *(grave) (pertes, dégâts)* severe, serious
sévèrement [sevɛrmɑ̃] *adv* **(a)** *(durement)* severely, harshly **(b)** *(strictement)* strictly, rigidly **(c)** *(gravement)* severely; **s. atteint** severely affected
sévérité [severite] *nf* **(a)** *(d'un juge, de mesures, d'une critique, d'une peine etc)* severity, harshness; *(d'un visage, d'un regard)* sternness, severity; *(d'une discipline, d'une éducation)* strictness; **avec s.** with severity, severely **(b)** *(d'une architecture, du style etc)* severity
sévices [sevis] *nmpl* brutality, cruelty; **s. (sexuels) à enfant** child abuse
Séville [sevi, sevij] *n* Seville
sévir [sevir] *vi* **(a)** *(agir avec rigueur)* to act ruthlessly; **s. contre qn/qch** to deal ruthlessly with *or F* to clamp down on sb/sth **(b)** *(d'une épidémie, de la guerre etc)* to rage; *(de vandales)* to wreak havoc; **la crise qui sévit actuellement** the present crisis
sevrage [səvraʒ] *nm* **(a)** *(de nourrisson)* weaning; *(de drogué)* detoxification; *Méd* **symptômes de s.** withdrawal symptoms **(b)** *Bot (d'une marcotte, d'un greffon)* separating
sevrer [səvre] *vt* **(je sèvre, n. sevrons; je sèvrerai) (a)** *(enfant, agneau, drogué etc)* to wean; *Litt* **s. qn de qch** to deprive sb of sth **(b)** *Bot (marcotte, greffon)* to separate
sèvres [sɛvr] *nm (porcelaine)* Sèvres (porcelain)
sexage [sɛksaʒ] *nm (de la volaille)* sexing
sexagénaire [sɛgzaʒenɛ, sɛksa-] *adj, n* sixty-year-old; *Litt* sexagenarian
sex-appeal [sɛksapil] *nm F* sex appeal
sexe [sɛks] *nm* **(a)** *(classement)* sex; **le (beau) s.** the fair sex; **le deuxième s.** the weaker sex; **changer de s.** to have a sex-change; **changement de s.** sex-change operation **(b)** *(parties sexuelles)* genitals **(c)** *(sexualité)* sex; **problèmes de s.** sex problems
▶ **sexe: le s. faible** the weaker sex; **le s. fort** the stronger sex
sexisme [sɛksism] *nm* sexism; **faire du s.** to be sexist
sexiste [sɛksist] *adj, n* sexist
sexologie [sɛksɔlɔʒi] *nf* sexology
sexologique [sɛksɔlɔʒik] *adj* sexological
sexologue [sɛksɔlɔg] *n* sexologist
sex-shop, *pl* **sex-shops** [sɛksʃɔp] *nm* sex shop
sextant [sɛkstɑ̃] *nm Naut, Math* sextant
sextuor [sɛkstɥɔr] *nm Mus* sextet(te)
sextuple [sɛkstypl] **1** *adj* sixfold, *Fml* sextuple **2** *nm* **au s.** sixfold; **le s. de deux** six times two; **payer le s.** to pay six times as much
sextuplé, -ée [sɛkstyple] *n* sextuplet
sextupler [sɛkstyple] *vti* to increase sixfold
sexualisation [sɛksɥalizasjɔ̃] *nf* sexualization
sexualiser [sɛksɥalize] *vt* to sexualize
sexualité [sɛksɥalite] *nf* sexuality
sexué [sɛksɥe] *adj (plante, animal)* sexed; *(reproduction)* sexual
sexuel, -elle [sɛksɥɛl] *adj* sexual; **vie sexuelle** sex life; **acte s.** sex act; **organes** *ou* **parties sexuel(le)s** sex organs; **éducation sexuelle** sex education; **rapports sexuels** sexual relations, *F* sex; **nos rapports sexuels se sont détériorés** the sex isn't as good as it used to be; **un obsédé s.** a sex maniac
sexuellement [sɛksyɛlmɑ̃] *adv* sexually; **maladie s. transmissible** sexually transmitted disease; **être attiré s. par qn** to be sexually attracted to sb

sexy [sɛksi] *adj inv F* sexy
seyant [sɛjɑ̃] *adj* (*vêtement*) becoming
Seychelles [seʃɛl] *nfpl* **les S.** the Seychelles
SGAO [ɛsgeaɔ] *nm Ordinat* (*abrév* **système de gestion assisté par ordinateur**) computer-assisted management system
SGBD [ɛsʒebede] *nm Ordinat* (*abrév* **système de gestion de base de données**) DBMS
SGDBR [ɛsʒebedeɛr] *nm Ordinat* (*abrév* **système de gestion de bases de données relationnelles**) RDBMS
shah [ʃa] *nm* shah
shake-hand [ʃɛkɑ̃d] *nm inv Arch, Hum* handshake
shaker [ʃɛkœr] *nm* cocktail shaker
shakespearien, -ienne [ʃɛkspirjɛ̃, -jɛn] *adj* Shakespearian, Shakespearean
shako [ʃako] *nm Mil* shako
shampooiner [ʃɑ̃pwine] *vt* to shampoo
shampooineur, -euse [ʃɑ̃pwinœr, -øz] **1** *n* (*employé*) shampooer **2** *nf* **shampooineuse (à moquette)** carpet shampooer
shampooing [ʃɑ̃pwɛ̃] *nm* **(a)** (*action*) shampoo; **faire** *ou* **donner un s. à qn** to shampoo sb('s hair), to give sb a shampoo **(b)** (*produit*) shampoo; **s. sec** dry shampoo; **s. pour cheveux secs/gras** shampoo for dry/greasy hair; **s. antipelliculaire** anti-dandruff shampoo; **s. aux œufs** egg shampoo; **s. à moquettes** carpet shampoo
shampouiner [ʃɑ̃pwine] *vt* to shampoo
shampouineur, -euse [ʃɑ̃pwinœr, -øz] *n* = **shampooineur**
shant(o)ung [ʃɑ̃tuŋ] *nm Tex* shantung
sharia [ʃarja] *nf* (*loi islamique*) sharia
sheik [ʃɛk] *nm* sheik
shekel [ʃɛkɛl] *nm* shekel
shérif [ʃerif] *nm* sheriff
sherpa [ʃɛrpa] *n* Sherpa
sherry [ʃeri] *nm* sherry
shetland [ʃɛtlɑ̃d] **1** *nmpl* **les (îles) S.** the Shetland Islands, the Shetlands **2** *nm Tex* Shetland wool; **(pull en) s.** Shetland sweater
shilling [ʃiliŋ] *nm* shilling
shimmy [ʃimi] *nm Aut* shimmy
shinto [ʃɛ̃to] *nm*, **shintoïsme** [ʃɛ̃tɔism] *nm* Shinto, Shintoism
shintoïste [ʃɛ̃tɔist] *adj, n Rel* Shintoist
shipchandler [ʃipʃɑ̃dlœr] *nm* ship's chandler
shocking [ʃɔkiŋ] *adj inv Hum, Vieilli* shocking
shog(o)un [ʃɔgun] *nm Hist* shogun
shoot [ʃut] *nm* **(a)** *Fb* shot **(b)** *Arg* (*de drogue*) shot; **se faire un s. (d'héroïne)** to give oneself a shot (of heroin), to shoot up (heroin)
shooter [ʃute] **1** *vi Fb* to shoot **2** *vt* **(a)** *Fb* **s. un pénalty** to take a penalty (kick) **(b)** *Arg* (*avec de la drogue*) **s. qn** to shoot sb up **3 se shooter** *vpr Arg* to shoot (up); **se s. à l'héroïne** to shoot (up) heroin
shopping [ʃɔpiŋ] *nm* shopping; **faire du s.** to go shopping
short [ʃɔrt] *nm* [①A10,e] (pair of) shorts; **être en s.** to be in shorts, to be wearing shorts
show [ʃo] *nm* show; **s. aérien** air show
show-biz [ʃobiz] *nm inv F* show biz
show-business [ʃobiznɛs] *nm* show business
showroom [ʃorum] *nm* showroom
shrapnell [ʃrapnɛl] *nm Mil* shrapnel
shunt [ʃœ̃t] *nm Él, Chir* shunt
shunter [ʃœ̃te] *vt* **(a)** *Él* to shunt **(b)** *TV, Cin* to fade
si[1] [si] **1** *conj* (*by elision* **s'** *before* **il, ils**) **(a)** [①A50-1,13; B31-2,3] (*hypothèse, condition*) if; **je ne sortirai pas s'il pleut** I won't go out if it rains; **s'il n'avait pas plu, nous serions partis** if it hadn't rained we would have gone, *Fml* had it not rained we would have gone; **si on ne le surveille pas, il s'échappera** he will escape unless he is watched *or* if he is not watched; **j'aurais été soldat, si je n'étais poète** I would have been a soldier if I were not a poet, I would have been a soldier were I not a poet; **si j'avais su** if I'd known, had I (but) known; **si tu veux la paix, prépare la guerre** if you want peace, prepare for war; **qui le fera si ce n'est moi?** who'll do it if I don't *or* unless I do?; **si ce n'était que je l'ai vu moi-même** if I hadn't seen it (for) myself; **un des plus grands, si ce n'est le plus grand** one of the biggest, if not the biggest; **tout va bien, si ce n'est mon dos qui me fait souffrir** everything's fine apart from my sore back *or* apart from the fact that my back is hurting me; **s'il fait beau et si je suis libre je sortirai** if it's fine and (if) I'm free, I'll go out; **oui, si on veut** yes, if you like; **un artiste, si on veut** an artist, so to speak; **si je ne m'abuse, si je ne me trompe** if I'm not mistaken; **si j'ose dire** if I may make so bold; **si seulement j'étais à Paris!** if only I were *or* was in Paris!; *Fml* **si tant est que ... +** *sub* provided that ..., so long as ...

(b) (*concession*) if; **si je me plains, c'est que j'en ai sujet** if I complain, it's with good reason; **s'il est malheureux et s'il a des ennuis, c'est bien de sa faute** if he is unhappy and in trouble, it is entirely his own fault; **s'il fut sévère, il fut juste** he was fair though severe, he might have been severe but he was fair; **ce fut à peine s'il put distinguer l'heure à sa montre** he could scarcely see the hands of his watch; **c'est tout au plus si l'on peut compter jusqu'à vingt femmes dans la salle** at (the) most there are only about twenty women in the hall; **le père Martin, (un) brave homme s'il en fut** old Martin, a good chap if ever there was one

(c) (*question indirecte*) if, whether; **je me demande si c'est vrai/s'il viendra** I wonder if *or* whether it's true/he'll come; **je lui ai demandé s'il était marié** I asked him if *or* whether he was married; *F* **si je connais Paris?** do I know Paris?; *F* **si c'est pas malheureux (de voir ça)!** isn't it just dreadful (to see that)!

(d) (*combien*) how; **pensez si j'étais furieux!** (you can) imagine how angry I was!

(e) (*supposition*) what if, suppose; **et si elle l'apprend?** what if she finds out?, and suppose she finds out?; **si nous changions de sujet?** suppose we change the subject?, how about changing the subject?; **si on faisait une partie de bridge?** what about *or* how about a game of bridge?

2 *nm* **tes si et tes mais** your ifs and buts; **tu mets toujours des si à tout!** you're always iffing and butting; *Prov* **avec des si on mettrait Paris dans une bouteille** if ifs and ands were pots and pans there'd be no need for tinkers
si[2] *adv* **(a)** [①A5,B] (*tellement*) so; **ne courez pas si vite** don't run so fast; **il est si faible que ...** he is so weak that ...; **un si bon dîner** such a good dinner; **de si bons dîners** such good dinners; **il n'est pas si à plaindre que cela** he is not to be as pitied as all that; **ce n'est pas si facile** it's not so *or* that easy

(b) (= *'aussi' dans une proposition négative*) **il n'est pas si beau que vous** he is not as handsome *or* not so handsome as you

(c) donnez-m'en si peu que vous voudrez *ou* **si peu que rien** give me just a (very) little

(d) si bien que ... so that ..., with the result that ...; **il dépensa sans regarder, si bien qu'en fin de compte il fut ruiné** he spent recklessly, so that *or* with the result that he was ruined

(e) (*concession*) **si ... que +** *sub* however; **si jeune qu'il soit** however young he may be, young as he is; **aucun médecin, si habile soit-il** no doctor, however capable (he may be); **si peu que ce soit** however little (it may be)

(f) [①B61,D] (*réponse à une question négative*) yes; **si fait** yes indeed; **ça ne fait rien – si, ça fait quelque chose** it doesn't matter – yes, it does (matter); **il n'est pas parti? – si/je crois que si** he hasn't gone? – yes, he has/yes, I think he has *or* I think so; **j'ai l'impression qu'il ne pleut pas – il me semble que si** I have the impression it's not raining – it seems to me it is; **tu crois qu'il ne va pas venir? – il m'a assuré que si** do you think he won't come? – he assured me that he would; **mais si, je l'ai vue** I did see her; **il ne s'en remettra pas – que si!** he won't get over it – yes, he will!; **tu ne t'en souviens plus, je pense? – si, si** you probably don't remember, do you? – yes, I do; **vous en voulez? – non merci – mais si!** would you like some? – no, thank you – oh go on!
si[3] *nm inv Mus* (*note*) B; (*en chantant la gamme*) te, ti; **morceau en si** piece in B; **en si bémol** in B flat
Siam [sjam] *nm* Siam
siamois, -oise [sjamwa, -waz] **1** *adj* Siamese; **chat s.** Siamese cat; **frères s., sœurs siamoises** Siamese twins **2** *n* **S.** Siamese **3** *nm* **(a)** (*chat*) Siamese (cat) **(b)** *Ling* Siamese
Sibérie [siberi] *nf* Siberia
sibérien, -ienne [siberjɛ̃, -jɛn] **1** *adj* Siberian; *Fig* **il fait un froid s.** it's bitterly cold **2** *n* **S.** Siberian
sibilance [sibilɑ̃s] *nf Méd* **s. respiratoire** wheezing
sibilant [sibilɑ̃] *adj Méd* sibilant, hissing
sibylle [sibil] *nf Antiq* sibyl
sibyllin [sibilɛ̃] *adj* **(a)** *Antiq* sibylline **(b)** *Litt* (*énigmatique*) cryptic, enigmatic
sic [sik] *adv* sic
SICAV [sikav] *n Fin* (*abrév* **société d'investissement à capital variable**) = unit trust, *Am* = mutual fund; *Bourse* **s. actions** equity-based unit trust; *Bourse* **s. monétaires** money unit trust; *Bourse* **s. obligataire** bond-based unit trust
siccatif, -ive [sikatif, -iv] *adj, nm* siccative
Sicile [sisil] *nf* Sicily
sicilien, -ienne [sisiljɛ̃, -jɛn] **1** *adj* Sicilian **2** *n* **S.** Sicilian
sicle [sikl] *nm Hist* (*monnaie, poids*) shekel
Sida, SIDA [sida] *nm Méd* Aids, AIDS; **avoir le s.** to have Aids; **s. avéré** full-blown Aids

sidatique [sidatik] *adj, n Péj* = **sidéen**

side-car, *pl* **side-cars** [sajdkar, sidkar] *nm* (*habitacle*) sidecar; (*véhicule*) motorcycle and sidecar, *Br* combination

sidéen, -enne [sideɛ̃, -ɛn] *Méd* **1** *adj* suffering from Aids **2** *n* Aids sufferer

sidéral, -ale, -aux, -ales [sideral, -o] *adj* sidereal

sidérant [siderɑ̃] *adj F* (*nouvelles, histoire etc*) staggering

sidéré [sidere] *adj* **(a)** *F* flabbergasted, staggered (**de faire** to do), thunderstruck **(b)** *Vieilli* (*par la foudre, par une crise d'apoplexie*) struck down

sidérer [sidere] *vt* (**il sidère; il sidérera**) **(a)** *F* (*qn*) to flabbergast, to stagger **(b)** *Vieilli* (*de la foudre, d'une crise d'apoplexie etc*) to strike down

sidérose [sideroz] *nf* **(a)** *Minér* siderite **(b)** *Méd* siderosis

sidérurgie [sideryrʒi] *nf* iron and steel metallurgy; (*industrie*) iron and steel industry

sidérurgique [sideryrʒik] *adj* **industrie s.** iron and steel industry; **usine s.** iron and steel works

sidérurgiste [sideryrʒist] *n* iron and steel worker

siècle [sjɛkl] *nm* **(a)** (*cent ans*) century; **au vingtième s.** in the twentieth century; **cette maison a au moins un s. /deux siècles** this house is at least a hundred/two hundred years old; **un lit vieux d'un bon s.** a bed at least a hundred *or* a good hundred years old

(b) (*époque*) age; **le s. de Louis XIV, le grand s.** the age of Louis XIV; **le s. des Lumières** the Age of Enlightenment; **notre s.** our age *or* century, the age *or* times we live in; **c'est un homme de son s. /d'un autre s.** he's a man of his time(s)/ he belongs to another age *or* another century; **vivre dans** *ou* **avec son s.** to be in tune with one's age *or* time(s); **jusqu'à la fin des siècles** to the end of time; *Rel* **pour les siècles des siècles** world without end; *F* **il y a un s.** *ou* **ça fait des siècles que je ne vous ai vu** I haven't seen you for ages, it's ages since I saw you

(c) *Rel* **le s.** the world, worldly life; **vivre dans le s.** to live in the world

siège [sjɛʒ] *nm* **(a)** (*centre*) seat, centre, *US* center; (*d'une douleur*) seat; **s. administratif** administrative headquarters; *Rel* **s. épiscopal** see; **s. d'exploitation** (*d'une entreprise*) operational headquarters; **s. principal** (*d'une entreprise*) head office; **s. social** (*d'une entreprise*) head office, registered office; **avoir son s. à Londres** (*d'une société etc*) to have its head office *or* headquarters in London, to be headquartered in London

(b) *Mil* siege; **mettre le s. devant une ville, faire le s. d'une ville** to lay siege to *or* besiege a town; **lever le s.** to raise the siege; *F* (*partir*) to make tracks; **état de s.** state of siege

(c) (*meuble*) seat; (*de cocher*) box; *Parl* seat; *Aut* **s. avant/ arrière** front/back seat; *Aut* **s. baquet** bucket seat; *Aut* **s. basculant** tilting seat; **s. de camping** folding chair; **s. chauffant** heated seat; *Aut* **s.-club** armchair; *Av* **s. éjectable** ejector seat; *Aut* **s. pour enfant** baby/child seat; **s. inclinable** reclining seat; *Aut* **s. rehausseur** child booster seat; **s. sport** sports seat; **offrir un s. à qn** to offer sb a seat; **prenez un s.** take a seat, do sit down; **s. à pourvoir au conseil d'administration** vacancy on the board

(d) (*de chaise, de W.-C., de personne*) seat; **bain de s.** sitz bath, hip bath; *Obst* (**accouchement par le**) **s.** breech delivery/birth; **le bébé se présente par le s.** the baby is in the breech position

(e) (*fonction*) *Pol* **s. à la Chambre** seat in Parliament; *Jur* **le s. du juge** the judge's bench; **elle occupe un s. important** she holds an important position

(f) *Tech* (*d'une valve etc*) seating

siéger [sjeʒe] *vi* (**je siège, n. siégeons; je siégeai(s); je siégerai**) **(a) s. à Londres** (*d'une entreprise etc*) to have its head office *or* headquarters in London, to be headquartered in London; **s. au conseil d'administration** to have a seat on the board, to be on the board; **après avoir siégé à Bayeux pendant dix ans** (*d'un évêque*) having held the see of Bayeux for ten years; *Méd, Fig* **c'est là que siège le mal** that is the root of the problem **(b)** (*d'un tribunal de justice, d'un juge, d'une assemblée etc*) to sit **(c) s. à la Chambre** to have a seat *or* to sit in Parliament; *Jur* **s. au tribunal** to be on the bench

sien, sienne [sjɛ̃, sjɛn] **1** *pron poss* [①A30,8; B20,E,2] (*d'homme etc*) his; (*de femme etc*) hers; (*de bébé, d'animal domestique*) his, hers; (*d'animal, de nation, de chose etc*) its; (*après un sujet indéfini*) one's own; **il te prête le s.** you can borrow his; **tu n'as qu'à prendre la sienne** you can just take his/hers; **de toutes ces solutions, il préfère la sienne** out of those possible solutions, he prefers his own; **elle n'en a pas besoin, elle a le s.** she doesn't need it, she has her own; **je n'en ai pas besoin, j'ai le s.** I don't need it, I've got his/hers; **les deux siens** his/her two, the two *or* both of his/hers; (*en insistant*) his/her own two; **elle t'a laissé deux des siens** she gave you two of hers; **on doit acheter la sienne** everyone must buy their own, *Fml* one must buy one's own; **au total, il y a plus de deux-cents drapeaux car chaque pays a le s.** in total there are more than two hundred flags, each country having its own; *très F* **le s. de bébé est plus intelligent** his/ her baby is more intelligent; *F* **à la sienne!** (*en buvant*) let's drink to him/her

2 *nm* **le s.** (*ce qui lui appartient*) his/hers; **il devrait y mettre du s.** he should do his share

3 *nmpl* **les siens** (*sa famille*) his/her family *or Am* folks; (*ses partisans*) his/her followers; (*ses coéquipiers*) his/hers team-mates; (*après un sujet indéfini*) one's family/followers/ team-mates

4 *nfpl* **il a encore fait des siennes** he's been up to his old tricks again

5 *adj poss Litt* his/hers; **un s. cousin** a cousin of his/hers; **il fera siens tes principes** he will adopt your principles as his own; **fera-t-il siennes les félicitations qu'ils m'adresseront?** will he join them in congratulating me?

Sienne [sjɛn] *n* Siena; *Com* **terre de S. naturelle/brûlée** raw/ burnt sienna

sierra [sjɛra] *nf Géog* sierra

Sierra Leone [leɔn] *nf* Sierra Leone

sieste [sjɛst] *nf* (*après le repas*) siesta, nap; **faire la s.** to take *or* have a siesta *or* nap

sieur [sjœr] *nm* **le s. Martin** *Jur, Arch* Mr Martin, *Péj* old Martin

sifflant, -ante [siflɑ̃, -ɑ̃t] **1** *adj* (*bruit*) hissing; (*note*) whistling; (*respiration, toux*) wheezing, wheezy; (*consonne*) sibilant **2** *nf* **sifflante (a)** *Ling* sibilant **(b)** *Rad* sibilance

sifflement [sifləmɑ̃] *nm* **(a)** (*de qn, du vent etc*) whistling, whistle; (*d'un serpent, d'une oie, de la vapeur*) hiss(ing); (*du fouet*) swish(ing); (*d'une balle, d'une flèche*) whizz; (*d'un asthmatique*) wheezing; (*de la friture, d'une lampe à arc*) sizzling; **un s.** a whistle/hiss **(b)** *Th etc* hiss(ing), boo(ing), catcall **(c) s. d'oreilles** buzzing *or* ringing in the ears

siffler [sifle] **1** *vi* **(a)** (*d'une personne, d'un oiseau, d'un train, d'une bouilloire, du vent etc*) to whistle; (*d'un serpent, d'une oie, de la vapeur*) to hiss; (*d'un asthmatique*) to wheeze; (*de la friture, d'une lampe à arc*) to sizzle; *F* **ça me siffle dans les oreilles** I've got a buzzing *or* ringing in my ears

(b) (*avec un sifflet*) to blow a/the whistle; *Naut* to pipe

2 *vt* **(a)** (*air*) to whistle; *Naut* (*ordre*) to pipe; *Sp* **s. une faute/la mi-temps** to blow (the whistle) for a foul/for half time

(b) (*taxi etc*) to whistle for, to whistle up; (*chien*) to whistle for; *Aut F* **je me suis fait s. (par la police)** I've been pulled up (by the police); **s. une fille** to (wolf-)whistle at a girl

(c) *Th etc* (*acteur, pièce etc*) to hiss, to boo

(d) *Arg* (*boire*) (*verre, bouteille etc*) to knock back

sifflet [siflɛ] *nm* **(a)** (*instrument*) whistle; *Naut* pipe; **coup de s.** blow *or* blast of a/the whistle; *Naut* pipe; **donner un coup de s.** to blow the whistle; **j'ai entendu un coup de s.** I heard a whistle (blowing); **démarrez au coup de s.** start when you hear the whistle *or* when the whistle blows; *Sp* **coup de s. final** final whistle; **s. à vapeur** steam whistle; *Naut* **s. de brume** fog whistle; *Arg* **ça lui a coupé le s.** that shut him up; *Arg* **serrer le s. à qn** to throttle *or* strangle sb; **attaquer en s.** (*de rameur*) to catch a crab **(b)** (*sifflement*) whistle; *Th etc* hiss, boo, catcall

siffleur, -euse [siflœr, -øz] **1** *n* (*personne*) whistler; *Th* hisser, booer **2** *nm* (*oiseau*) widgeon **3** *adj* (*oiseau*) whistling; (*serpent*) hissing; (*asthmatique*) wheezy; **canard s.** widgeon

siffleux [siflø] *nm Can Zool* groundhog, woodchuck

sifflotement [siflɔtmɑ̃] *nm* whistling (to oneself *or* under one's breath)

siffloter [siflɔte] *vti* to whistle (to oneself *or* under one's breath)

sigillaire [siʒilɛr] *adj* **anneau s.** signet ring

sigillé [siʒile] *adj Bot, Cér etc* sigillate(d)

sigisbée [siʒisbe] *nm Hum, Litt* gallant

sigle [sigl] *nm* acronym; (*d'une entreprise*) logo

sigma [sigma] *nm* (*lettre grecque*) sigma

signal, -aux [siɲal, -o] *nm* **(a)** (*signe*) signal; (*indice*) sign; *Psy* **réagir à un s.** to react to a signal; **faire des signaux** to signal; **envoyer** *ou* **lancer un s.** to send a signal; **donner le s. de qch** to give the signal for sth; *Fig* (*d'un événement etc*) to be the signal for sth; **s. de départ** (*d'un train, d'une course etc*) starting signal; **au s., tous se levèrent** on the given signal *or* when the signal was given they all stood up; **le s. d'une crise sociale** the sign of a social crisis

(b) *Électron, Rad* signal

► **signal**: **s. d'alarme** alarm (signal); **s. d'alerte** warning (signal); *Mil, Av* air-raid warning; *Tél* **s. d'appel** call(ing) signal; *Rail* **s. à l'arrêt** signal at danger; *Rail* **s. d'arrêt** danger signal; *Rail* **s. d'arrêt absolu** stop signal; *Rail* **s. avancé** distant (block) signal; **s. d'avertissement** *ou* **avertisseur** warning signal; *Ordinat* **s. d'avertissement de réception** acknowledge; *Ordinat* **s. de baisse de tension des piles** battery low warning; **s. de baisse du toner** toner low warning; **s. à bras** semaphore signal; *Naut* **s. de brume** fog signal; *TV, Cin* **s. caméra** camera cue; **s. de chemin de fer** railway *or US* railroad signal; **s. de danger** warning sign; **s. de détresse** distress *or* S.O.S. signal; *Rail* **s. à distance** distant (block) signal; *Rail* **s. d'entrée** home signal; *Mil* **s. par fanions** flag signal; *Mil, Av etc* **s. de fin d'alerte** all-clear; *Naut, Rad* **s. horaire** time signal; *Ordinat* **s. horodateur** time and date signal; *TV* **s. d'image** picture signal; **s. d'incendie** fire alarm; *Ordinat* **s. d'invitation à transmettre** proceed-to-send signal, *Am* start-dialling signal; **s. lumineux** light signal; *TV, Cin* light cue; *Aut* beacon; *Ordinat* indicator light, warning light; *Admin* **signaux lumineux** traffic lights; **s. optique** visible *or* visual signal; **signaux parasites** clutter; *Naut* **s. à pavillons** flag signal; **s. de priorité** give way sign, *Am* yield sign; *Rail* **s. rapproché** home signal; *Aut* **signaux routiers** (*écriteaux*) road signs; **s. sonore** beep; (*pour avertir*) warning beep; **s. de (sortie) lecture** sense signal; **s. vidéo** video signal; **s. à vue** visible *or* visual signal

signalé [siɲale] *adj Litt* (*service, récompense*) signal

signalement [siɲalmɑ̃] *nm* (*d'une personne*) description, particulars

signaler [siɲale] **1** *vt* **(a)** (*faire remarquer*) (*erreur, fait etc*) to point out, to indicate (**à qn** to sb); **un sifflement signale que l'eau est à la bonne température** a whistling indicates that the water is at the right temperature; **s. à qn que** to point out to sb that; **s. un livre/un restaurant à qn** to recommend a book/a restaurant to sb; **Libération a signalé cet artiste** Libération drew attention to this artist; **c'est cette première pièce qui l'a signalé au monde du spectacle** it was this first play that brought him to the attention of the theatrical world

(b) (*reporter*) (*retard, changement, vol etc*) to report, to notify (**à qn** to sb); **on nous signale que l'autoroute est bouchée** we have reports that the motorway is blocked, the motorway is reported to be blocked; **rien à s.** nothing to report; *Naut* **date à laquelle un navire a été signalé pour la dernière fois** date when a ship was last contacted *or Spéc* spoken

(c) (*par un signal*) (*train, navire etc*) to signal; *Av* (*piste*) to indicate the position of; **l'entrée de l'autoroute est très mal signalée** the entry onto the motorway is very badly indicated *or* signposted; **c'est signalé par des pancartes lumineuses** it's indicated by illuminated signs

(d) *Ordinat* (*marquer*) to flag up

(e) *Vieilli* (*rendre remarquable*) to make conspicuous

2 se signaler *vpr* to distinguish oneself (**par** by); **se s. dans les sciences** to have a reputation as a scientist; **se s. à l'attention de qn** to catch sb's eye; *F* **se s. par son absence** to be conspicuous by one's absence

signalétique [siɲaletik] *adj Admin* descriptive (*of a person*); **fiche s.** (*dans les rapports de police*) description

signaleur [siɲalœr] *nm Mil etc* signaller; *Rail* signalman

signalisation [siɲalizasjɔ̃] *nf* **(a)** *Aut* (*action*) signposting and marking; (*signaux*) signs and markings; **s. routière internationale** international (system of) road signs; **panneau de s.** roadsign; **feux de s.** traffic lights **(b)** *Rail* (*action*) installation of signals (**de** on); (*signaux*) signals **(c)** *Av* (*action*) installation of lights and markings (**de** on)

signaliser [siɲalize] *vt Aut* (*route*) to signpost and mark; *Rail* (*voie*) to install signals on; *Av* (*piste*) to install lights and markings on

signataire [siɲatɛr] *n* signatory

signature [siɲatyr] *nf* **(a)** signature; (*acte*) signing; **apposer sa s. à un acte** to sign a document; **pour s.** for signature; **document porté à la s. du directeur** document given to the director for his signature; **présenter le courrier à la s.** to present the mail for signature; **avoir la s.** (*pour une entreprise etc*) to be authorized to sign; *Fig* **les plus grandes signatures de la littérature française** the greatest names in French literature; **s. d'un contrat** signing of a contract; **s. légalisée** authenticated signature; **s. par procuration** per pro signature, pp, signature by proxy; **s. sociale** company signature (and stamp)

(b) *Typ* (*lettre, chiffre*) signature; *Journ* by-line

signe [siɲ] *nm* **(a)** (*indice*) (*de pluie, d'impatience etc*) sign, indication; (*de maladie*) sign; (*d'amitié, d'amour*) sign, mark, token; **il t'a offert des fleurs? c'est un s.** he gave you flowers? that must mean something; **ne donner aucun s. de vie, ne pas donner s. de vie** to show no sign of life; *Fig* **elle ne nous a pas donné s. de vie depuis un mois** we haven't heard from her for a month; **en s. de désapprobation/solidarité** as a sign of disapproval/solidarity; **porter du noir en s. de deuil** to wear black as a sign of mourning; **un s. des temps** a sign of the times; **signes extérieurs de richesses** trappings *or* outward signs of wealth; **la réunion a eu lieu sous le s. de la cordialité** cordiality was the keynote of the meeting; **politique conduite sous le s. de la rigueur** policy in which austerity is the keynote; **signes d'usure/de vieillesse** signs of wear/age; **c'est bon/mauvais s.** it's a good/bad sign; **c'est s. que quelque chose ne va pas** it's a sign that there's something wrong

(b) (*symbole*) sign, symbol; **s. algébrique** algebraical sign; **s. de classification** number of section or paragraph; **signes de ponctuation** punctuation marks; *Typ* **signes de correction** proof correction marks; *Mus* **signes constitutifs** key signature; **s. du zodiaque** sign of the zodiac; **être né sous le s. du Capricorne/de la Balance/des Poissons** to be born under the sign of Capricorn/Libra/Pisces; **s. de chance** lucky sign; *Typ* **s. différent de** not equals sign; *Typ* **s. dollar** dollar sign; **s. du marché** market signal; *Typ* **s. inférieur à** *ou* **plus petit que** less than sign; *Typ* **s. livre** pound sign; *Typ* **s. moins** minus sign; *Typ* **s. multiplié** multiplication sign; *Typ* **s. plus** plus sign; *Typ* **s. pour cent** percent sign; *Typ* **s. supérieur à** *ou* **plus grand que** greater than sign; *Typ* **s. égal** equals sign

(c) (*trait physique*) (*de personne*) (distinctive) mark; *Admin* **signes particuliers: néant** distinguishing marks: none

(d) (*geste*) sign, gesture; **il me faisait des signes** he was making signs *or* he was gesturing to me; **parler par signes** to use sign language; (*d'un sourd*) to use sign language, to sign; **langage par signes** sign language; **apprendre le langage par signes** to learn sign language, to learn how to sign; **s. d'adieu** farewell wave (of the hand); **il me fit un s. d'adieu** he waved me goodbye; **faire s. à qn** to make a sign to sb; (*contacter*) to get in touch with sb; **faire s. à qn de faire qch** to signal to sb to do sth; **je lui ai fait s. de venir** I beckoned him to come over; **il fit s. de se taire** he gave a signal *or* signalled for silence, he made a shushing gesture; **s. de la main** hand signal; **faire s. à qn (de la main) de reculer/de s'écarter/de partir** to wave sb back/aside/away; **faire s. que oui** to nod (in agreement); **faire s. que non** (*de la tête*) to shake one's head; (*du doigt*) to wag one's finger

(e) *Rel* **s. de (la) croix** sign of the cross; **faire le s. de la croix** *ou* **un s. de croix** to make the sign of the cross, to cross oneself

signer [siɲe] **1** *vt* **(a)** (*contrat, lettre, tableau etc*) to sign; *Can Sp* (*joueur*) to sign (up); **s. son nom** to sign one's name; **s. par procuration** to sign by proxy, to pp; *Naut* **s. l'engagement** to sign on; *Fig F* **c'est signé** it's easy to guess who did that; *Fig F* **c'est signé Paul** it has Paul written all over it, it's just like *or* typical of Paul **(b)** *Tech* (*bijoux*) to hallmark **2** *vi* to sign; **s. de son nom** to sign one's name **3 se signer** *vpr Rel* to cross oneself

signet [siɲɛ] *nm* bookmark

signifiant [siɲifjɑ̃] **1** *adj Litt* (*plein de sens*) meaningful **2** *nm Ling* signifier

significatif, -ive [siɲifikatif, -iv] *adj* significant; **s. de** indicative of

signification [siɲifikasjɔ̃] *nf* **(a)** (*d'un mot, d'un symbole etc*) meaning, sense; (*d'un événement, d'un fait etc*) significance **(b)** *Jur* (*d'une décision*) notification; (*d'un acte judiciaire*) serving

signifié [siɲifje] *nm Ling* signified

signifier [siɲifje] *vt* (*impf, pr sub* **n. signifiions, v. signifiiez**) **(a)** (*vouloir dire*) (*d'un mot*) to mean; (*d'une attitude*) to mean, to signify; **que signifie ce mot?** what does this word mean?, what is the meaning of this word?; **s. que** (*d'une action etc*) to show *or* mean that; **cela ne signifie rien** it doesn't mean anything; **des remarques qui ne signifient rien** meaningless remarks; **qu'est-ce que cela signifie?** (*indignation*) what is the meaning of this?; **la moindre imprudence signifierait la mort pour eux** the slightest imprudence would mean death for them

(b) (*notifier*) to notify (**qch à qn** sb of sth); **s. son congé à qn** (*d'un propriétaire, d'un employé*) to give sb notice; *Jur* **s. un jugement à qn** to notify sb of a decision; *Fig* **son visage signifiait bien sa douleur** his grief was written on his face for all to see

sikh, -e [sik] **1** *adj* Sikh **2** *n* **S.** Sikh

silence [silɑ̃s] *nm* **(a)** silence; (*pause*) pause; **il se fit un s. subit** there was a sudden silence; **écrire à qn après un s. de deux ans** to write to sb after a silence of two years; **un s. de**

mort a deathly silence *or* hush; **s. ému** breathless silence; **observer une minute de s.** ≈ to observe a two minute silence; **dans le s. de la nuit** in the silence *or Litt* still of the night; **réduire qn au s.** to reduce sb to silence, to silence sb; **rompre le s.** to break the silence; **garder** *ou* **observer le s.** to keep silent (**sur** about); **(du) s.!** silence!, be quiet!; **souffrir en s.** to suffer in silence; **passer qch sous s.** to keep quiet about sth, to pass over sth in silence; (*par diplomatie*) not to mention sth; **la loi du s.** the law of silence (*preventing criminals from informing on their fellows*); (*dans la mafia*) omerta; **préparer qch dans le s.** to prepare sth in secrecy; **faire jurer le s. à qn** to swear sb to secrecy; *Av* **cône de s.** cone of silence; *Électron* **zone de s.** silent zone

(**b**) *Mus* rest

silencieusement [silɑ̃sjøzmɑ̃] *adv* silently

silencieux, -ieuse [silɑ̃sjø, -jøz] **1** *adj* (*personne, pas etc*) silent; (*rue, jardin etc*) silent, quiet; (*moteur, lave-vaisselle etc*) quiet, silent; (*soirée*) quiet, peaceful; **après la dispute, la reste de la soirée fut s.** (*plus personne ne parla*) after the quarrel the rest of the evening passed in silence **2** *nm Aut* silencer, *Am* muffler; (*d'arme*) silencer; *Rad* squelch

Silène [silɛn] *nm Myth* Silenus

silène [silɛn] *nm Bot* campion

Silésie [silezi] *nf* Silesia

silex [silɛks] *nm inv* (*roche*) flint; **des s.** (*outils, armes*) flints

silhouette [silwɛt] *nf* (*contours*) silhouette, outline; (*ligne générale du corps*) figure; *Mil* (*cible*) figure target; **en s.** silhouetted

silhouetter [silwete] **1** *vt* (*dessiner*) to outline; *Phot* to block out **2 se silhouetter** *vpr* to be silhouetted, to be outlined (**sur** against)

silicate [silikat] *nm Ch* silicate

silice [silis] *nf Ch* silica, silicon dioxide; **verre de s., s. fondue** silica (glass)

siliceux, -euse [silisø, -øz] *adj* siliceous

silicium [silisjɔm] *nm Ch* silicon

silicone [silikɔn] *nf Ch* silicone

silicose [silikoz] *nf Méd* silicosis

silicosé [silikoze] *adj Méd* silicotic

silique [silik] *nf Bot* siliqua, silique

sillage [sijaʒ] *nm* (*d'un navire*) wake; *Av etc* slipstream; *Av* **s. aérodynamique** aerodynamic drag; *Fig* **marcher dans le s. de qn** to follow in sb's wake

sillon [sijɔ̃] *nm* (**a**) *Agr* furrow; *Fig* (*sur le front*) furrow, line; *Litt* **sillons** (*champs*) fields, country (**b**) (*d'une roue*) track; (*d'un navire*) wake; (*d'un projectile*) path; **s. de lumière/feu** (*d'une fusée etc*) streak of light/fire (**c**) (*de disque*) groove

sillonner [sijɔne] *vt* (**a**) (*creuser*) to furrow; (*traverser*) to cross; **la police sillonne la région** police are combing the area; **les touristes sillonnent le sud de la France** there's a non-stop flow of tourists through the south of France; **flanc de montagne sillonné par les torrents** mountainside grooved *or* scored by torrents; **forêt sillonnée de nombreux sentiers** forest criss-crossed by many paths; **front sillonné de rides** furrowed brow (**b**) (*d'une lumière, de la foudre etc*) (*ciel*) to streak

silo [silo] *nm* (*fosse, tour*) silo; **mettre en s.** to silo; **s. à blé** grain silo; **s. à ciment** cement silo; *Mil* **s. (de lancement)** (launching) silo

silotage [silɔtaʒ] *nm Agr etc* (*action*) ensilage

silure [silyr] *nm* (*poisson*) silurid

silurien, -ienne [silyrjɛ̃, -jɛn] *Géol* **1** *adj* Silurian **2** *nm* Silurian; **s. inférieur** Ordovician

SIM [sim] *nm* (*abrév* **système d'information mercatique**) MIS

simagrées [simagre] *nfpl* airs and graces, affectation; **ne fais pas tant de s.** don't make so much fuss

simien, -ienne [simjɛ̃, -jɛn] *Zool* **1** *adj* simian **2** *nmpl* **simiens** simians, *Spéc* Simiidae

simiesque [simjɛsk] *adj* (*visage, grimace etc*) monkey-like, ape-like, *Spéc, Litt* simian

similaire [similɛr] *adj* similar (**à** to), of the same kind

similairement [similɛrmɑ̃] *adv* similarly

similarité [similarite] *nf* similarity

simili [simili] **1** *préf* imitation, artificial **2** *nm F Vieilli* imitation; *Phot* half-tone; **bijoux en s.** imitation *or* costume jewellery **3** *nf F* = **similigravure**

similicuir [similikɥir] *nm* imitation leather, leatherette

similigravure [similigravyr] *nf* half-tone engraving

similitude [similityd] *nf* similarity

simoniaque [simɔnjak] *Rel* **1** *adj* simoniacal **2** *nm* simoniac, simonist

simonie [simɔni] *nf Rel* simony

simoun [simun] *nm Météo* simoom, simoon

simple [sɛ̃pl] **1** *adj* [①B10,D,3] (**a**) (*direct*) (*personne*) simple, unaffected; (*tenue, nourriture, cérémonie etc*) simple; **modestie s.** unaffected *or* natural modesty; **réduit à sa plus s. expression** reduced to its simplest form; **dans le plus s. appareil** (*nu*) in the altogether, in one's birthday suit

(**b**) (*facile*) (*calcul, méthode etc*) simple, easy, straightforward; **c'est bien s., il accepte ou on part** it's quite simple, either he accepts or we go; **c'est s. comme bonjour** it's as easy as pie *or* as falling off a log

(**c**) (*crédule*) simple; **s. d'esprit** simple-minded

(**d**) (*pur*) **condamner qn sur un s. soupçon** to condemn sb on a mere suspicion; **c'est une s. question de temps** it is simply a matter of time; **c'est de la folie pure et s.** it's sheer madness; **c'est la vérité pure et s.** it's the pure and simple truth; **croire qn sur sa s. parole** to believe sb on his/her word alone; **la s. prudence veut que …** ordinary *or* elementary prudence demands that …

(**e**) (*commun*) ordinary; **un s. particulier** an ordinary citizen; **s. soldat** private (soldier); **s. matelot** ordinary seaman; **je ne suis qu'une s. secrétaire** I'm merely a secretary, I'm just a *or* a mere secretary; **une s. enveloppe ira parfaitement** an ordinary *or* a plain envelope will do perfectly

(**f**) (*non multiple*) (*fleur, nœud etc*) single; **un cornet s. ou double?** (*de glace*) one scoop or two?; **un aller s.** a single, *Am* a one-way ticket; *Ordinat* **s. densité** single density

(**g**) (*non composé*), *Courses de chevaux* **faire un pari s.** to back a horse to win; [①B28,F,4] *Gram* **passé s.** past historic (tense), simple past; *Gram* **les temps simples d'un verbe** the simple tenses of a verb; *Ch* **corps s.** simple body; *Math* **équation s.** simple equation

2 *nm* (**a**) *Tennis* **jouer un s.** to play a singles (match); **s. messieurs/dames** men's/ladies' singles

(**b**) **varier du s. au double** to vary by twice as much

(**c**) **un s. d'esprit** a simpleton, a simple-minded person

3 *nmpl Bot* **simples** medicinal herbs

simplement [sɛ̃pləmɑ̃] *adv* (**a**) (*vivre*) simply; **habillé s.** simply *or* plainly dressed; **elle se maquille s.** she doesn't wear much make-up (**b**) (*avec naturel*) simply, naturally, unaffectedly; **le plus s. du monde** without any fuss; **il faut prendre les choses s.** you have to take things as they come (**c**) (*uniquement*) simply, just, merely; **purement et s.** purely and simply; **je voulais s. te dire que …** I simply *or* just *or* merely wanted to tell you that …

simplet, -ette [sɛ̃plɛ, -ɛt] *adj* (*personne*) simple; (*idée, théorie, livre etc*) simplistic

simplex [sɛ̃plɛks] *nm Ordinat* simplex

simplicité [sɛ̃plisite] *nf* (**a**) (*d'une tenue, des manières etc*) simplicity; **elle manque de s.** she is pretentious *or* affected; **la s. de ses manières** his/her lack of affectation, his/her unaffected ways; **elle l'a avoué en toute s.** she admitted it without making a big thing of it; **nous ferons un repas en toute s.** we'll have a very simple meal; **ils se sont mariés en toute s.** they had a very quiet wedding; **venez en toute s.** come as you are; (*pour manger*) come and take pot luck; **vivre avec s.** to live simply (**b**) *Phys* (*des atomes etc*) elementary nature (**c**) (*facilité*) simplicity; **c'est d'une s. enfantine** it's child's play, a child could do it

simplifiable [sɛ̃plifjabl] *adj* that can be simplified, capable of simplification; *Math* (*fraction*) reducible

simplificateur, -trice [sɛ̃plifikatœr, -tris] *adj* (*méthode etc*) simplifying

simplification [sɛ̃plifikasjɔ̃] *nf* simplification; *Math* simplification, reduction

simplifier [sɛ̃plifje] (*impf, pr sub* **n. simplifiions, v. simplifiiez**) **1** *vt* to simplify; *Math* (*fraction*) to simplify, to reduce; **cela me simplifie la vie** that simplifies my life, that makes life *or* things easier for me; **trop s.** to oversimplify **2 se simplifier** *vpr* to become simpler, to become simplified

simplisme [sɛ̃plism] *nm* simplism

simpliste [sɛ̃plist] *Péj* **1** *adj* (*théorie, explication etc*) simplistic; (*esprit*) simplistic, superficial **2** *n* simplistic person

simulacre [simylakr] *nm* semblance, show, pretence, *US* pretense; **s. de résistance** semblance *or* show of resistance; *Mil* **s. de combat** sham fight; **s. de justice** travesty of justice; **son procès ne fut qu'un s.** his trial was a travesty of justice *or* a mere mockery

simulateur, -trice [simylatœr, -tris] **1** *n* pretender; *Méd* malingerer; **c'est un habile s.** he's good at pretending *or F* faking **2** *nm Tech* simulator; *Av* **s. de vol** flight simulator

simulation [simylasjɔ̃] *nf* (**a**) (*action*) simulation, feigning; *Méd* malingering (**b**) *Av, Électron, Ordinat etc* simulation; *Compta* (*prévision*) forecast; **formation en s. de vol** simulated flight training; **s. par ordinateur** computer simulation

simulé [simyle] *adj* (*maladie*) feigned, simulated; (*combat*) sham; (*sentiment, colère, sérieux etc*) feigned, sham, bogus, simulated; (*vente*) bogus; *Tech* (*situation, conditions etc*) simulated

simuler [simyle] *vt* (*sentiment, colère etc*) to feign, to simulate, to sham; *Tech* (*situation, conditions, vol etc*) to simulate; **s. une maladie** to pretend to be ill, to feign (an) illness, to malinger; **s. la folie** to pretend to be mad, to feign madness; **la porte simule un rideau** the door is made to look like a curtain

simultané [simyltane] *adj* simultaneous

simultanéité [simyltaneite] *nf* simultaneousness, simultaneity

simultanément [simyltanemɑ̃] *adv* simultaneously

Sinaï [sinai] *nm* Sinai; **le mont S.** Mount Sinai

sinapisé [sinapize] *adj* **bain/cataplasme s.** mustard bath/ poultice *or* plaster

sinapisme [sinapism] *nm Méd* mustard poultice *or* plaster, *Spéc* sinapism

sincère [sɛ̃sɛr] *adj* **(a)** (*franc*) (*personne*) sincere, genuine; (*opinion*) honest, candid; **être s. avec soi-même** to be honest with oneself **(b)** (*véritable*) (*joie, amour, effort etc*) genuine, sincere; **ses paroles étaient sincères** he was being sincere, he meant it; **vœux/remerciements sincères** sincere *or* heartfelt wishes/thanks; **agréez mes sincères salutations** yours sincerely **(c)** (*authentique*) (*document etc*) genuine, authentic

sincèrement [sɛ̃sɛrmɑ̃] *adv* **(a)** (*franchement*) sincerely, frankly; **s., je ne crois pas que ce soit une bonne idée** frankly, I don't think it's a good idea **(b)** (*vraiment*) (*heureux etc*) genuinely, sincerely

sincérité [sɛ̃serite] *nf* **(a)** (*franchise*) sincerity, frankness; **en toute s.** in all sincerity **(b)** (*des regrets, de l'amour etc*) sincerity, genuineness; **je ne mets pas en doute la s. de vos paroles** I'm not questioning your sincerity

sinécure [sinekyr] *nf* sinecure; *F* **ce n'est pas une s.** it's not exactly a rest cure

sine die [sinedje] *adv* indefinitely, sine die

sine qua non [sinekwanɔn] *adj Phil* **condition s.** sine qua non; **c'est la condition s. pour avoir un emploi bien rémunéré** it's essential in order to get a well-paid job, it's a prerequisite for a well-paid job

Singapour [sɛ̃gapur] *nm* Singapore

singe [sɛ̃ʒ] *nm* **(a)** (*animal*) monkey; *F* (*imitateur*) mimic; **grand s.** ape; *F* **c'est un s., il est laid comme un s.** he's as ugly as sin; **faire le s.** to clown around; **malin/adroit comme un s.** as crafty/clever as a monkey; **payer qn en monnaie de s.** (*en fausse monnaie*) to pay sb with counterfeit money; (*ne pas payer qn*) to make false promises to pay sb; *Prov* **on n'apprend pas à un vieux s. à faire des grimaces** don't teach your grandmother to suck eggs **(b)** *Culin Arg* **du s.** corned beef **(c)** *Arg* **le s.** (*patron*) the boss **(d)** *Ordinat* monkey

singer [sɛ̃ʒe] *vt* **(je singeai(s); n. singeons)** (*qn*) to ape, to mimic, *F* to take off; (*sentiment*) to feign, *F* to fake

singerie [sɛ̃ʒri] *nf* **(a) singeries** (*grimaces, gestes*) antics; **il fait tout le temps des singeries** he's always clowning aound **(b)** (*imitation*) (grotesque) imitation **(c)** (*cage*) monkey *or* ape house

single [siŋgəl] *nm* **(a)** *Tennis* singles (game) **(b)** *Rail* single-berth compartment **(c)** (*dans un hôtel*) single room

singulariser [sɛ̃gylarize] **1** *vt* **s. qn** to set sb apart, to make sb stand out **(de** from**) 2 se singulariser** *vpr* to attract attention, to make oneself conspicuous; **il se singularise par sa curiosité** his curiosity sets him apart from the others *or* makes him stand out

singularité [sɛ̃gylarite] *nf* **(a)** (*particularité*) peculiarity; **cette maison a la s. d'être solaire** the house is unusual in that it is solar-heated **(b)** (*caractère étrange*) strangeness, oddness, peculiarity; **c'est une des singularités de son caractère** it's one of the strange *or* odd things about him; **esprit de s.** desire to be different

singulier, -ière [sɛ̃gylje, -jɛr] **1** *adj* **(a)** *Gram* singular **(b) combat s.** single combat **(c)** (*remarquable*) remarkable, *Fml* singular; (*étrange*) strange, odd, peculiar, *Fml* singular; **il est s. qu'il ne soit pas encore arrivé** it is strange *or* odd *or* peculiar that he has not arrived yet **2** *nm* [①A14-15,C] *Gram* singular; **au s.** in the singular

singulièrement [sɛ̃gyljɛrmɑ̃] *adv* **(a)** (*étrangement*) oddly, strangely, *Fml* singularly **(b)** (*en particulier*) especially, particularly **(c)** (*très beaucoup*) remarkably, extremely, *Fml* singularly

sinistre [sinistr] **1** *adj* **(a)** (*effrayant*) (*lieu, atmosphère, personne, expression*) sinister; **c'est s. ici!** it's spooky here! **(b)** (*déprimant*) (*paysage*) bleak; (*soirée, repas*) dismal, grim; **on a passé un jour de l'an s.** we spent a dismal *or* a miserable New Year's Day **(c)** (*emploi intensif*) awful, terrible; **un s. menteur** an awful *or* a terrible liar **2** *nm* (*catastrophe*) disaster, catastrophe; *Jur* (*dommage*) (*après des dégâts*) damage; (*réclamation*) claim; **bonification pour non-s.** no-claims bonus

sinistré, -ée [sinistre] **1** *adj* **population sinistrée** stricken population; **bâtiment s.** damaged building; **région** *ou* **zone sinistrée** disaster area **2** *n* disaster victim

sinistrement [sinistrəmɑ̃] *adv* sinisterly

sinistrose [sinistroz] *nf Psy* post-traumatic stress disorder; *F* (*mélancolie*) pessimism, gloom; *F* **atteint de s.** gloomy, depressed; *F* **la s. progresse dans les milieux bourgeois** the middle classes are becoming increasingly pessimistic *or* gloomy

sino- [sinɔ] *préf* Sino-; **s.-japonais** Sino-Japanese

sinologue [sinɔlɔg] *n* sinologist, sinologue

sinon [sinɔ̃] *conj* **(a)** (*autrement*) otherwise, or else; **donne-moi la clef, s. je me fâche** give me the key otherwise *or* or (else) I'll get angry; **un jus d'orange, s. rien** an orange juice, otherwise nothing, an orange juice or, failing that, nothing

(b) (*excepté*) except, but; **il ne fait rien s. manger et boire** he does nothing except *or* but eat and drink; *Vieilli* **s. que** except that

(c) (*si ce n'est*) if not; **c'est un des meilleurs, s. le meilleur** it's one of the best, if not the best

sinoque [sinɔk] *adj Arg* (*fou*) crackers, crazy

sinuer [sinɥe] *vi Litt* to wind, to meander

sinueux, -euse [sinɥø, -øz] *adj* (*ligne*) sinuous; (*chemin, courant etc*) winding, meandering; *Fig* (*raisonnement*) tortuous

sinuosité [sinɥozite] *nf* (*d'un chemin, d'une rivière etc*) bend, curve; *Fig* (*d'un raisonnement*) tortuousness

sinus[1] [sinys] *nm Anat* sinus

sinus[2] *nm Math* sine

sinusite [sinyzit] *nf Méd* sinusitis; **avoir de la s.** to have sinusitis

sinusoïdal, -ale, -aux, -ales [sinyzɔidal, -o] *adj Math* sinusoidal

sinusoïde [sinyzɔid] *nf Math* sinusoid, sine curve

Sion [sjɔ̃] *n* Zion

sionisme [sjɔnism] *nm* Zionism

sioniste [sjɔnist] *adj, n* Zionist

sioux [sju] **1** *adj inv* Sioux **2** *n inv* **S.** Sioux; *Fig* **ruses de S.** crafty *or* cunning tricks

siphon [sifɔ̃] *nm* **(a)** *Phys etc* (*tube*) siphon **(b)** (*bouteille*) (soda) siphon **(c)** *Constr etc* (*d'un évier, d'une canalisation etc*) U-bend, trap **(d)** *Géol* siphon **(e)** *Zool* siphon

siphonné [sifɔne] *adj F* (*fou*) crackers, crazy

siphonner [sifɔne] *vt* to siphon

sire [sir] *nm* **(a)** sir; **beau s.** fair sir; *Péj* **un triste s.** an unsavoury character **(b) S.** (*à un souverain*) Sire

sirène [sirɛn] *nf* **(a)** *Myth* siren, mermaid; *Fig* (*femme*) siren; **chant de s.** siren song **(b)** (*appareil*) siren; (*d'usine*) hooter, siren; (*de brume*) foghorn; **s. d'alarme** fire alarm; (*en temps de guerre*) air-raid siren

SIRET [siret] *nm* **No S.** company registration number

siroc(c)o [sirɔko] *nm* (*vent*) sirocco

sirop [siro] *nm* syrup, (fruit) cordial; *Pharm* syrup; **s. d'érable** maple syrup; **s. de fraise** ≈ strawberry cordial; **s. de menthe** ≈ mint cordial; **s. d'orgeat** barley water; **s. de sucre** golden syrup; **s. contre la toux** cough mixture *or* syrup

siroter [sirɔte] *vt F* (*vin, café etc*) to sip

sirupeux, -euse [sirypø, -øz] *adj* (*liquide, Péj musique, ton*) syrupy

sis [si] *adj Jur, Litt* situated, located; **maison sise rue Saint-Honoré** house situated *or* located in the Rue Saint-Honoré

sisal [sizal] *nm Bot* sisal

sismal, -ale, -aux, -ales [sismal, -o] *adj* **ligne sismale** line of an *or* the earthquake

sismicité [sismisite] *nf* seismicity

sismique [sismik] *adj* seismic

sismogramme [sismɔgram] *nm* seismogram

sismographe [sismɔgraf] *nm* seismograph

sismographie [sismɔgrafi] *nf* seismography

sismologie [sismɔlɔʒi] *nf* seismology

sismomètre [sismɔmɛtr] *nm* seismometer

Sisyphe [sizif] *nm* Sisyphus; **le rocher de S.** the rock of Sisyphus

Sit [sit] *nm* (*abrév* **système interbancaire de télépaiement**) ≈ CHAPS, *US* CHIPS

sitar [sitar] *nm Mus* sitar

sitcom [sitkɔm] *nm ou f TV* sitcom, situation comedy

site [sit] *nm* **(a)** (*pittoresque*) beauty spot; **s. (touristique)** (*monument etc*) place of interest, tourist attraction; **s. classé** conservation area; **s. historique** historic site **(b)** *Archéol, Ind* (*lieu*) site; *Mktg* **s.-témoin** test site **(c)** (*configuration d'un lieu*) setting, site **(d)** *Mil etc* **ligne de s.** line of sight

sit-in [sitin] *nm inv* sit-in; **faire un s.** to have *or* hold a sit-in

sitôt [sito] *adv* **(a)** (*aussitôt*) **s. le soleil couché** (*dans le présent ou le futur*) as soon as the sun sets; (*dans le passé*) as soon as the sun had set; **s. dit s. fait** no sooner said than done; **s. que +** *ind* as soon as; **s. après** immediately after **(b)** (*with nég*) **vous ne la reverrez pas de s.** it will be some time *or* a good while before you see her again; **je ne reviendrai pas ici de s.** I won't come back here in a hurry

sittelle [sitɛl] *nf* (*oiseau*) nuthatch

situation [sitɥasjɔ̃] *nf* **(a)** (*emplacement*) (*d'une ville, d'un bâtiment etc*) situation, position, location; *Naut* bearing; **l'hôtel jouit d'une excellente s.** the hotel is excellently situated

(b) (*circonstances*) situation; **s. du marché** market situation; **quelle est votre s. de famille?** what is your marital status?; **quelle est votre s. financière?** what is your financial situation *or* position *or* status?; **je lui ai exposé ma s.** I explained my situation *or* position to him; **être en s. de faire qch** to be in a position to do sth; **se trouver devant une s. de fait** to be faced with a fait accompli; *F* **elle est dans une s. intéressante** (*enceinte*) she's in the family way, *Vieilli Euph* she's in an interesting condition; **l'homme de la s.** the right man for the job; **mettre qn en s.** to give sb experience of a real-life situation; *Compta* **s. nette** net worth; **s. de la banque** bank balance; **s. de caisse** cash position *or* balance; **s. de compte** account position *or* balance

(c) *Admin, Mil etc* report, return

(d) (*emploi*) job, position; **il a une belle s.** he has a good position; **se faire une belle s.** to work one's way up into a good position; *Journ* **situations vacantes** (job) vacancies, *Br* situations vacant

situé [sitɥe] *adj* situated, located; **bien/mal s.** well/badly situated *or* located

situer [sitɥe] **1** *vt* (*maison etc*) to situate, to locate; *Fig* (*qch dans son contexte*) to place; *F* **s. qn** to size sb up; **je situerais plutôt ce groupe dans le courant be-bop** I would describe the band as being more be-bop **2** *vpr* **se situer** to stand; **je ne sais pas comment il se situe sur ce point** I don't know where he stands on this point; *Th etc* **l'action se situe à Rome en 1516** the action takes place in Rome in 1516; *Pol* **se s. à droite** to be on the right, to be right-wing; **elle se situe plutôt à droite** she's rather to the right

six (*before noun beginning with consonant* [si]; *before noun beginning with vowel sound* [siz]; *otherwise* [sis]) **1** *adj inv* six; **le s. mai** (on) the sixth of May, (on) May the sixth, *Am* (on) May sixth; **Charles S.** Charles the Sixth; *Aut* **une s. chevaux** a six-horsepower car; **les s. jours** (*course cycliste*) = six-day cycle race **2** *nm inv* six; **habiter au s.** to live at number six; **lettre datée du s.** letter dated the sixth; *Cartes* **le s. de cœur** the six of hearts

sixain [sizɛ̃] *nm* = **sizain**

six-huit *nm inv Mus* six-eight time

sixième [sizjɛm] **1** *adj num* sixth; **au s. étage** on the sixth *or Am* seventh floor **2** *n* (*personne, objet, événement etc*) sixth (one); **habiter au s.** to live on the sixth *or Am* seventh floor; *Sp etc* **arriver le/la s.** to come (in) sixth **3** *nm* sixth (part); **cinq sixièmes** five sixths **4** *nf Scol* (*enseignement secondaire*) = first year of secondary school, *Am* ≈ sixth grade

sixièmement [sizjɛmmɑ̃] *adv* in the sixth place, sixthly

six-quatre-deux (à la) [alasiskatdø] *adv F Vieilli* **faire qch à la s.** to do sth in a slapdash manner

sixte [sikst] *nf* **(a)** *Mus* sixth **(b)** *Escrime* sixte

Sixtine [sikstin] *adj f* **la chapelle S.** the Sistine Chapel

sizain [sizɛ̃] *nm* **(a)** *Littér* six-line stanza **(b)** *Cartes* set of six packs *or Am* decks of playing cards

Skai® [skaj] *nm* leatherette, imitation leather

skate(-board), *pl* **skate-boards, skates** [skɛtbɔrd] *nm* skateboard; **faire du s. (-b.)** to skateboard, to go skateboarding

sketch, *pl* **sketches** [skɛtʃ] *nm Th* sketch

ski [ski] *nm* **(a)** (*planche*) ski; **descendre à** *ou* **en skis** to ski down; **skis de fond** cross-country skis **(b)** (*activité*) skiing; **s. alpin** downhill (skiing); **s. de piste** on-piste skiing; **s. de fond, s. de randonnée** cross-country (skiing), langlauf; **faire du s.** to ski; *F* **aller au s.** to go skiing; **chaussures de s.** ski boots; **station de s.** ski resort; **vacances de s.** skiing holiday **(c) s. nautique** water-skiing; **faire du s. nautique** to water-ski

skiable [skjabl] *adj* skiable, fit for skiing

ski-bob, *pl* **ski-bobs** [skibɔb] *nm* skibob

skier [skje] *vi* to ski

skieur, -euse [skjœr, -øz] *n* skier; **s. nautique** water-skier; **s. de fond** cross-country *or* langlauf skier; *Mil* **éclaireurs skieurs** ski troops

skif(f) [skif] *nm Naut* skiff

skin(head) [skin(ɛd)] *nm* skin(head)

skip [skip] *nm Ind* skip

skippé [skipe] *adj Naut* **s. par** skippered by

skipper [skipœr] *nm Naut* (*barreur*) skipper

slacker [slake] *vi Can* (*relâcher*) to ease up; **s. d'une coche** to ease up a bit

slalom [slalɔm] *nm Ski* slalom; **descente en s.** slalom descent; **s. géant** giant slalom; **s. spécial** special slalom; *Fig* **faire du s. entre les voitures** to dodge in and out among the cars

slalomer [slalɔme] *vi Ski* to slalom; *Fig* to dodge in and out

slalomeur, -euse [slalɔmœr, -øz] *n Ski* slalom skier

slave [slav] **1** *adj* Slav(onic) **2** *nm Ling* Slavonic **3** *n* **S.** Slav

slavisant, -ante [slavizɑ̃, -ɑ̃t], **slaviste** [slavist] *n* Slavist

sleeping [slipiŋ] *nm Rail F Vieilli* (*wagon*) sleeping car; (*couchette*) berth

slip [slip] *nm* **(a)** [ⓘ**A10**,e] (*d'homme*) briefs, underpants; (*de femme*) briefs, panties, pants; **s. de bain** (*d'homme*) swimming trunks; (*de femme*) bikini bottoms; **s. kangourou** Y-fronts; **s. de soutien (pour sportifs)** athletic support, *F* jockstrap **(b)** *Naut* slipway

slogan [slɔgɑ̃] *nm Com, Pol* slogan; **s. publicitaire** advertising slogan

sloop [slup] *nm Naut* sloop; **s. à tape-cul** yawl

sloughi [slugi] *nm* (*chien*) Saluki

slovaque [slɔvak] **1** *adj* Slovak **2** *nm Ling* Slovak **3** *n* **S.** Slovak

Slovaquie [slɔvaki] *nf* Slovakia

slovène [slɔvɛn] **1** *adj* Slovene, Slovenian **2** *nm Ling* Slovene, Slovenian **3** *n* Slovene, Slovenian

Slovénie [slɔveni] *nf* Slovenia

slow [slo] *nm* (*danse, musique*) slow dance; **danser un s.** to have a slow dance

SM [ɛsɛm] **1** (*abrév* **Sa Majesté**) HM **2** *nm* (*abrév* **sadomasochisme**) S & M

smala(h) [smala] *nf* (*de chef arabe*) retinue; *F* (*famille etc*) tribe; *F* **toute la s.** the whole tribe

smart [smart] *adj inv F Vieilli* (*élégant*) smart

smash [smaʃ] *nm Tennis etc* smash; **faire un s.** to smash the ball

smasher [smaʃe] *Tennis* **1** *vt* (*balle*) to smash **2** *vi* to smash (the ball)

SME [ɛsɛmə] *nm CE* (*abrév* **Système monétaire européen**) EMS

smectique [smɛktik] *adj* **argile s.** fuller's earth

SMIC [smic] *nm* (*abrév* **salaire minimum interprofessionnel de croissance**) = guaranteed minimum wage

smicard, -arde [smikar, -ard] *n F* worker on minimum wage, minimum wage earner

smocks [smɔk] *nmpl Couture* smocking

smog [smɔg] *nm* smog

smoking [smɔkiŋ] *nm* (*veston*) dinner jacket, *Am* tuxedo, *Am F* tux; (*costume*) dinner *or* evening suit

smurf [smœrf] *nm* break dance; **danser le s.** to break-dance

snack(-bar), *pl* **snack-bars, snacks** [snak(bar)] *nm F* snack bar

SNC [ɛsɛnse] *nf* (*abrév* **société en nom collectif**) commercial/industrial partnership

SNCF [ɛsɛnseɛf] *nf* (*abrév* **Société nationale des chemins de fer français**) = (French) national railway company

snif [snif] *int F* sniff; **s., s. il me l'a pris!** boo-hoo, he's taken it from me!

sniffer [snife] *vt Arg* (*colle, cocaïne*) to sniff

snob [snɔb] **1** *n* snob **2** *adj* (*inv in f sing*) (*personne, restaurant etc*) snobbish, snobby; **elle est un peu s.** she's a bit of a snob

snober [snɔbe] *vt* (*mépriser*) to look down on; (*éviter*) to snub

snobinard, -arde [snɔbinar, -ard] *F Péj* **1** *adj* stuck-up, snobbish **2** *n* stuck-up *or* snobbish type

snobisme [snɔbism] *nm* snobbery, snobbishness; **s. à rebours** inverted snobbery

snow-boot, *pl* **snow-boots** [snobut] *nm* snow boot

sobre [sɔbr] *adj* **(a)** (*personne*) (*qui n'a pas bu*) sober; (*qui boit ou mange peu*) abstemious; (*repas, vie*) simple; **s. comme un chameau** as sober as a judge **(b) s. de paroles/louanges** sparing in one's words/praise **(c)** (*style, lignes, dessin*) sober, restrained

sobrement [sɔbrəmɑ̃] *adv* **(a)** (*manger, boire*) in moderation **(b)** (*s'exprimer*) soberly **(c)** (*s'habiller etc*) soberly

sobriété [sɔbrijete] *nf* **(a)** (*concernant l'alimentation, la boisson*) temperance, sobriety; **manger et boire avec s.** to eat and drink in moderation **(b)** (*des paroles*) soberness; **s'exprimer avec s.** to speak soberly **(c)** (*du style*) soberness, sobriety, restraint; (*des lignes*) soberness

sobriquet [sɔbrikɛ] *nm* nickname

soc [sɔk] *nm* ploughshare, *US* plowshare

sociabilité [sɔsjabilite] *nf* sociability

sociable [sɔsjabl] *adj* sociable; **peu s.** unsociable

social, -ale, -aux, -ales [sɔsjal, -o] **1** *adj* **(a)** social; **aide sociale** social welfare; *Zool* **animal s.** social animal; **l'homme est un animal s.** man is a social animal; **assistante sociale** social worker; **conflit s.** industrial dispute; **couche sociale**

social stratum; **l'échelle sociale** the social ladder; **guerre sociale** class war; **œuvres sociales** welfare activities; **l'ordre s.** the social order; **politique sociale** social policy; **réforme sociale** social reform; **science sociale** social science; **vie sociale** social life

(b) *Com* **nom s., raison sociale** company name; **capital s.** share capital

2 *nm Pol* social questions; *F* **faire du s.** to do one's good turn for the day

social-démocrate, *pl* **sociaux-démocrates** *adj, n Pol* social democrat

social-démocratie, *pl* **social-démocraties** *nf Pol* social democracy

socialement [sɔsjalmɑ̃] *adv* socially

socialisant, -ante [sɔsjalizɑ̃, -ɑ̃t] *Pol* **1** *adj* with socialist sympathies *or* tendencies **2** *n* socialist sympathiser

socialisation [sɔsjalizasjɔ̃] *nf* **(a)** *Écon (du capital, des industries)* socialization, collectivization **(b)** *(de personne)* socialization

socialiser [sɔsjalize] *vt* **(a)** *Écon (biens etc)* to socialize, to collectivize **(b)** *(personne)* to socialize

socialisme [sɔsjalism] *nm* socialism; **s. d'État** State socialism; **s. chrétien** Christian socialism

socialiste [sɔsjalist] *adj, n* socialist

sociétaire [sɔsjetɛr] *n* **(a)** *(membre)* member **(b)** *(actionnaire)* shareholder

société [sɔsjete] *nf* **(a)** *(communauté)* society; **dans notre s.** in our society; **ça ne se fait pas dans la bonne s.** that is not done in the best society; **devoirs envers la s.** duty to society *or* to the community; **valeurs de la s.** social values; **vie en s.** life in society; **animaux qui vivent en s.** social animals; **problème de s.** social problem

(b) *(association)* society, association; *Sp* club; **s. de secours aux blessés** first-aid association; **s. secrète** secret society; **s. protectrice des animaux** society for the prevention of cruelty to animals

(c) *Com, Ind* company, firm; **se monter en s.** to set up in business; **la S. Martin** Martin's

(d) *(compagnie)* company, companionship, *Fml* society; **il aime la s.** he likes company; **la s. des personnes de son âge** the company *or Fml* society of people his own age

(e) *(beau monde) (à la mode)* society; **la haute s.** high society; **femmes de s.** society women; **faire ses débuts dans la s.** to make one's debut in society

(f) **jeux de s.** board games, *Vieilli* parlour *or US* parlor games

▶ **société**: **s. d'abondance** affluent society; **s. par actions** joint-stock company, *US* incorporated company; **s. d'affacturage** factoring company; **s. affiliée** affiliated company; **s. anonyme** public limited company, *Am* corporation; **s. d'assurance** insurance company; **s. d'autoroutes** private company which maintains motorways; **s. de Bourse** stockbroker, stockbroking firm; **s. civile** non-trading company; **s. en commandite** limited partnership; **s. en commandite par actions** partnership limited by shares; **s. en commandite simple** limited partnership; **s. de commerce international** international trading corporation; **s. commerciale** business firm; **s. commune** joint venture; **s. de conseil en investissement** investment consultancy; **s. de conseil en mercatique** marketing consultancy (firm); **s. de consommation** consumer society; **s. de crédit immobilier** = building society, *US* savings and loan company; **s. de crédit mutuel** friendly society; **s. d'édition** publishing company *or* firm; **s. d'entrepôts** warehousing company; **s. d'épargne** savings society; **s. d'État** state-owned *or* public company; **s. d'études** research company *or* firm; **s. d'études de marché** market research company *or* firm; **s. d'études mercatiques** marketing research company *or* firm; **s. d'exportation** export company *or* house; **s. fiduciaire** trust company; **s. financière** finance company; **s. de gestion** holding company; **s. de location** rental firm; **s. de location de voitures** car hire company; **s. de mercatique** marketing company *or* firm; **s. mère** parent company; **s. multinationale** multinational company *or* corporation, multinational; **s. nationale** state-owned *or* public company; *Hist* **la S. des Nations** the League of Nations; **s. de négoce** trading company; **s. en nom collectif** = general partnership, commercial/industrial partnership; **s. de panels** market research company specializing in consumer panels; **s. en participation** joint venture; **s. de personnes** partnership; **s. de placement** investment trust; **s. de portage** export management company; **s. à portefeuille** holding company; **s. de prévisions** forecasting firm; **s. de prévoyance** provident society; **s. privée** private company; *TV, Cin* **s. de production** production company; **s. de radiodiffusion** broadcasting company; **s. à responsabilité limitée** = limited (liability) company; **s. de services** service business; **s. de transport** transport company; **s. de télédiffusion** broadcasting company; **s. d'utilité publique** public utility company, *Am* utility; **s. de vente par correspondance** mail order company *or* firm

socio [sɔsjo] *nf F* = **sociologie**

socio- [sɔsjɔ] *préf* socio-

socioculturel, -elle [sɔsjɔkyltyrɛl] *adj* sociocultural; **centre s.** social and cultural centre

sociodrame [sɔsjɔdram] *nm Psy* sociodrama

socio-économique, *pl* **socio-économiques** *adj* socioeconomic

socio-éducatif, -ive, *pl* **socio-éducatifs** *adj* socioeducational

sociogramme [sɔsjɔgram] *nm Psy* sociogram

sociolinguistique [sɔsjɔlɛ̃gɥistik] **1** *adj* sociolinguistic **2** *nf* sociolinguistics

sociologie [sɔsjɔlɔʒi] *nf* sociology

sociologique [sɔsjɔlɔʒik] *adj* sociological

sociologiquement [sɔsjɔlɔʒikmɑ̃] *adv* sociologically

sociologue [sɔsjɔlɔg] *n* sociologist

socioprofessionnel, -elle [sɔsjɔprɔfɛsjɔnɛl] *adj* socioprofessional

socio-style, *pl* **socio-styles** *nm Mktg* lifestyle

socle [sɔkl] *nm (pour une statue, une colonne)* base, pedestal; *(pour un vase, une horloge)* base; *(pour un appareil)* stand; *(pour un mât etc)* base, socket; *(pour un moteur)* bed plate; *Géol* insular shelf; *Constr* **s. de lambris** skirting board, *Am* baseboard; *Ordinat* **s. d'extension** expansion socket; *Ordinat* **s. orientable** *ou* **pivotant** *(d'un moniteur)* swivel base

socque [sɔk] *nm (sabot)* clog; *Th Antiq* sock

socquette [sɔkɛt] *nf* ankle sock, *Am* bobby sock

Socrate [sɔkrat] *nm* Socrates

socratique [sɔkratik] *adj* Socratic

soda [sɔda] *nm* fizzy drink, *Am* soda (pop); **s. à l'orange** orangeade; **whisky s.** whisky and soda

sodique [sɔdik] *adj Ch* sodic

sodium [sɔdjɔm] *nm Ch* sodium

Sodome [sɔdɔm] *n* Sodom

sodomie [sɔdɔmi] *nf* sodomy, buggery

sodomiser [sɔdɔmize] *vt* to sodomize, to bugger

sodomite [sɔdɔmit] *nm* sodomite

sœur [sœr] *nf* **(a)** sister; **ma s. cadette/aînée** my younger/older sister; **s. jumelle** twin sister; *Litt* **sœurs d'infortune** sisters in misfortune; *Arg* **et ta s.!** get lost!, mind your own business!; *Fig* **ces deux théories sont sœurs** these two theories go hand in hand; *Fig* **rencontrer l'âme s.** to find a soul mate **(b)** *Rel* sister, nun; **entrez, ma s.** come in, sister; **bonne s.** nun; **S. Thérèse** Sister Theresa

▶ **sœur**: **s. de lait** foster sister

sœurette [sœrɛt] *nf F* little sister

sofa [sɔfa] *nm* sofa, settee

soffite [sɔfit] *nm Archit* soffit

SOFI [sɔfi] *nm (abrév* **système d'ordinateurs pour le fret international***)* computerized system for international freight

Sofia [sɔfja] *nf* Sofia

SOFININDEX [sɔfinɛ̃dɛks] *(abrév* **Société pour le financement des industries exportatrices***)* = independent agency providing funding for export industries

SOFRES [sɔfrɛs] *nf (abrév* **Société française d'enquêtes et de sondages***) Br* ≈ MORI

software [sɔftwɛr] *nm Ordinat* software

soi [swa] *pron pers (stressed referring to an indef subject)* **(a)** *(réflexif ou exprimant la réciprocité) (personne)* oneself, one; *(referring to 'il', 'elle')* himself/herself/itself; **malgré s.** in spite of oneself; **parler de s.** to talk about oneself; **conscience de s.** awareness of self, self-awareness; **confiance en s.** self-confidence; **avoir confiance en s.** to be self-confident; **être sûr de s.** to be sure of oneself; **content/fier de s.** pleased with/proud of oneself; **avoir de l'argent/ses papiers sur s.** to have some money/one's papers on one; **prendre sur s.** to exercise self-control; **prendre qch sur s.** to take sth upon oneself; **chacun pour s.** every man for himself; **chez s.** at home; **rentrer chez s.** to go home; **avoir la loi pour s.** to have the law on one's side; **il n'est plus maître de s.** he is no longer in control of himself; **quand on marche, il faut regarder devant s.** you must keep looking in front of you when you walk; **petits services qu'on se rend entre s.** small mutual favours

(b) *(emphatic)* **se parler à s.-même** to talk to oneself; **rester s.-même** to remain (true to) oneself; **faire tout par s.-même** to do everything oneself; **aimer son prochain comme s.-même** to love one's neighbour as oneself; **on n'est jamais si bien servi que par s.-même** if you want something done, do it yourself

(c) *(chose, idée)* **en s.** in itself, per se; **il va de s. que ...** it goes without saying that ...; *F* **ça va de s.!** it goes without saying!, of course!; **ça paraît pourtant aller de s.** it seems obvious

(d) *Phil* self; **le sens du s.** the sense of self

(e) *Psy* id

(f) il a trouvé en ce camarade un autre s.-même he's found a soul-mate in this friend

soi-disant [swadizɑ̃] **1** *adj inv* **(a)** (*qui se prétend*) (*romancier, artiste etc*) self-styled, would-be; **une s. comtesse** a self-styled countess **(b)** (*appelé*) so-called; **les arts s. libéraux** the so-called liberal arts **2** *adv* supposedly; **il est parti s. pour réfléchir** he's gone, supposedly to think it over; *F* **s. qu'il serait parti** he's gone, apparently *or* so they say

soie[1] [swa] *nf* **(a)** *Tex* silk; **s. grège/naturelle/sauvage** raw/natural/wild silk; **robe de s.** silk dress; **papier de s.** tissue paper; **la route de la s.** the silk road **(b)** (*d'un sanglier, d'une chenille etc*) bristle; **brosse à cheveux en soies** bristle hairbrush; **couvert de soies** bristly, covered with bristles

soie[2] *nf Tech* (*d'une lame, d'une lime etc*) tang

soierie [swari] *nf* (*tissu*) silk; (*commerce*) silk trade

soif [swaf] *nf* thirst; *Fig* (*désir*) thirst, craving (**de** for; **de faire** to do); **avoir s.** to be thirsty; **étancher sa s.** to quench one's thirst; **boire à sa s.,** *F* **boire jusqu'à plus s.** to drink one's fill; **cela me donne s.** it makes me thirsty; *Fig* **rester sur sa s.** to remain unsatisfied; **cette émission m'a laissé sur ma s.** the program didn't come up to my expectations *or* left me unsatisfied; **lire jusqu'à plus s.** to read one's fill; **nous avons ri jusqu'à plus s.** we laughed till we could laugh no more; *Fig* **avoir s. de** to be thirsty *or* to thirst for; **avoir s. de sang** to be thirsting for blood

soiffard, -arde [swafar, -ard] *Arg* **1** *adj* (*personne*) boozy **2** *n* boozer

soignant [swaɲɑ̃] *adj Méd* **aide soignant(e)** nursing auxiliary, auxiliary nurse; **personnel s.** auxiliary nursing staff

soigné [swaɲe] *adj* **(a)** (*personne, apparence*) neat, well-groomed; (*travail*) careful; (*repas*) carefully prepared; (*vêtement*) neat, tidy; (*style*) polished; (*cheval*) groomed; (*mains, ongles, jardin*) well-kept; **elle est très soignée (de sa personne)** she is very careful *or* particular about her appearance; **peu s.** (*personne, apparence, tenue, travail*) untidy **(b)** *Arg* **une raclée soignée** a sound thrashing; **un rhume s.** a hell *or* a stinker of a cold

soigner [swaɲe] **1** *vt* **(a)** (*maintenir en bon état*) (*meubles, livre, mains, apparence etc*) to look after, to take care of; (*apporter du soin à*) (*travail, repas, détails etc*) to take care over; **s. le moindre détail** to take care over every detail; **s. sa ligne** to watch one's figure; **s. son image** to be careful of one's image; **s. sa popularité** to nurse one's public; *F* **s. l'addition** (*dans un restaurant etc*) to bump up the bill

(b) (*maladie*) to treat; **on soigne cette maladie avec des antibiotiques** the illness is treated with antibiotics

(c) (*personne*) (*d'un hôte, d'une infirmière etc*) to look after, to take care of; (*d'un médecin*) to treat; *F* **s. qn aux petits oignons** to give sb first-class treatment; **se faire s.** to be treated; **il faut te faire s.** *Méd* you should have (medical) treatment *or* see a doctor; *F* (*tu es fou*) you need your head examined; *F* **ils nous ont soignés** (*dans un restaurant etc*) they've ripped us off

2 se soigner *vpr* (*d'une personne*) (*médicalement*) to treat oneself; (*faire attention à soi*) to take care of *or* look after oneself; **elle refuse de se s., elle dit que ça va passer tout seul** she won't take anything, she says it'll go away on its own; **cette maladie ne se soigne pas bien** the disease is difficult to treat; **ça se soigne très bien** it's easily treated; *F* **ça se soigne!** you need your head examined!

soigneur [swaɲœr] *nm Sp* trainer; *Boxe* second

soigneusement [swaɲøzmɑ̃] *adv* carefully

soigneux, -euse [swaɲø, -øz] *adj* careful (**de** with); (*propre*) (*personne, travail etc*) tidy, neat

soi-même *pron pers voir* **soi, même**

soin [swɛ̃] *nm* **(a)** (*charge*) care; **le s. des enfants** the care of children, looking after children; **c'est à lui que revient le s. des enfants** he's in charge of *or* looks after *or* takes care of the children; **les soins du ménage** housekeeping; **avoir** *ou* **prendre s. de qn/de qch** to look after *or* take care of sb/sth; **confier qch aux soins de qn** to place sth in sb's care, to entrust sb with sth; **aux (bons) soins de ...** (*sur une lettre etc*) care of ..., c/o ...; **par les soins de ...** by courtesy of ..., thanks to ...

(b) (*effort*) care; **avoir (grand) s. de faire qch** to take (particular) care to do sth, to make a (particular) point of doing sth; **elle prend grand s. de son jardin/de son apparence** she takes great care of her garden/over her appearance; **il prend peu de s. de sa personne** he is very careless *or* slovenly about his appearance; **elle a pris s. de lui envoyer tous les documents** she made sure she sent him all the documents; **avoir s. que qch ne s'ébruite pas/soit fait** to take care that sth does not leak out/is done; **mettre tous ses soins à faire qch/à ce que qch soit fait** to go to a great deal of trouble *or* take great pains to do sth/to see that sth is done

(c) (*tâche*) **on lui a confié le s. de les recevoir** he was entrusted with the task *or* job of receiving them; **je vous laisse le s. de décider** I leave it to you to decide

(d) avoir beaucoup de s. to be very tidy *or* orderly; **avec s.** carefully, with care; **avec beaucoup de s.** very carefully, with great care; **manquer de s.** to be careless; **manque de s.** carelessness; **sans s.** (*utilisé adjectivement*) careless; (*pas propre*) untidy; (*utilisé adverbialement*) carelessly; (*pas proprement*) untidily

(e) soins (*attention*) care, attention; **soins de beauté** beauty care *or* treatment; **soins médicaux** medical care; **premiers soins, soins d'urgence** first aid; **rien ne peut remplacer les soins d'une mère** nothing can take the place of a mother; **les soins dont il entoure sa femme/son jardin** the care *or* attention he lavishes on his wife/his garden; **être aux petits soins pour** *ou* **avec qn** to fuss over sb, to wait hand and foot on sb; **soins esthétiques** beauty treatment; *Méd* **soins intensifs** intensive care; *Méd* **soins à domicile** home care *or* nursing

(f) *Arch* (*souci*) anxiety, worry

soir [swar] *nm* evening; **ce s.** this evening, tonight; **à ce s.!** see you tonight *or* this evening!; **le s. tombe** night is falling; *Fig* **le s. de la vie** the evening of one's life; **il fait frais le s.** it's cool in the evening; **que faites-vous le s.?** what do you do in the evening(s)?; **à dix heures du s.** at ten (o'clock) in the evening *or* at night; **lundi/demain/hier (au) s.** Monday/tomorrow/yesterday evening; **tous les lundis s.** every Monday evening; **le lendemain s.** the next evening; **la veille au s.** the evening before, the previous evening; **travailler du matin au s.** to work from morning till night; **être du s.** to be a night owl; **journal du s.** evening newspaper; *TV* evening news; **presse du s.** evening newspapers; **robe du s.** evening dress

soirée [sware] *nf* **(a)** [①B58,B,3] (*durée du soir*) evening; **passer la s. chez un ami** to spend the evening at a friend's house; **passer ses soirées à lire** to spend one's evenings reading; **toute la s.** all evening, the whole evening; **les longues soirées d'hiver** the long winter evenings *or* nights; **en fin de s.** late in the evening, towards the end of the evening; **tard dans la s.** late in the evening; **bonne s.!** have a good evening (out)!, enjoy your evening!; *F* **faire une s. télévision** to spend an evening in front of the television; **s. étape** stopover at a hotel; **s. à thème** theme evening; *TV* **s. thématique** themed evening

(b) (*fête*) party; **s. dansante** dance; **s. musicale** musical evening; **tenue de s.** evening dress

(c) *Th, Cin etc* **(représentation de) s., représentation donnée en s.** evening performance; **projecter un film en s.** to show a film in the evening, to have an evening showing of a film

soit [swa]; *before a vowel or as adv* [swat] (*third person of pr sub of être*) **1** *adv* all right!, *Fml* so be it!; **s., tu peux t'en aller** all right then, go

2 *conj* **(a)** (*supposons*) **s. trois multiplié par six** if three is multiplied by six; **s. ABC un triangle** let ABC be a triangle, given a triangle ABC

(b) (*à savoir*) that is to say; **trois objets à dix francs, s. trente francs** three articles at ten francs, that is to say thirty francs

(c) s. ... s. ... either ... or ..., whether ... or ...; **s. l'un s. l'autre** (either) one or the other; **j'ai cet article s. en rouge, s. en bleu, s. en vert** I have this item (either) in red, blue or green; **s. tu le fais maintenant ou alors je m'en occupe demain** either you do it now or I'll take care of it tomorrow; **elle va trancher, s. dans un sens, s. dans l'autre** she'll decide (either) one way or the other; **il faut que tu te décides, s. que tu restes, s. que tu pars** you'll have to decide whether you're staying or going; **s. modestie, s. paresse, il n'a jamais rien écrit** whether from modesty or laziness, he has never written anything

soixantaine [swasɑ̃tɛn] *nf* **(a)** (*nombre*) **une s.** about sixty; **une s. de personnes** about sixty people, sixty or so people; **la s. de livres qu'elle a** the sixty (or so) books she has **(b)** (*âge*) **la s.** (the age of) sixty; **elle approche de la s.** she's getting on for sixty; **avoir dépassé la s.** to be in one's sixties, to be over sixty

soixante [swasɑ̃t] **1** *adj inv* sixty; **page s.** page sixty; **s. et un** sixty-one; **s. et onze** seventy-one; **s. et onzième** seventy-first **2** *nm inv* sixty; **habiter au s.** to live at number sixty

soixante-dix *adj inv, nm inv* seventy
soixante-dixième 1 *adj* seventieth **2** *n* seventieth **3** *nm* (*fraction*) seventieth (part)
soixante-huitard, -arde [swasɑ̃tɥitar, -ard] *Pol* **1** *adj* relating to the events of May 1968 **2** *n* = person involved in the events of May 1968
soixantième [swasɑ̃tjɛm] **1** *adj* sixtieth **2** *n* sixtieth **3** *nm* (*fraction*) sixtieth (part)
soja [sɔʒa] *nm* (*plante*) soya (bean); *Culin* **lait de s.** soya milk; **sauce de s.** soy sauce; **germes de s.** bean sprouts
sol[1] [sɔl] *nm* **(a)** (*surface de la terre*) ground; (*territoire*) soil; **le s. natal** one's native soil *or Hum, Litt* heath; **au s.** at ground level; **interdit sur le s. français** prohibited on French soil; *Él* **relier un fil au s.** to earth *or Am* ground a wire; **conducteur au s.** earthed *or Am* grounded conductor; **cloué au s.** *Av* grounded; *Fig* rooted to the spot; **position s.** ground position; *Av* **personnel au s.** ground staff **(b)** *Géol, Agr* (*matière*) soil; **s. fertile/argileux** fertile/clay soil **(c)** (*plancher*) floor; **revêtement de s.** floor covering; **dormir sur** *ou* **à même le s.** to sleep on the floor; *Sp* **faire de la gymnastique au s.** to do floor exercises
sol[2] *nm inv Mus* (*note*) G; (*en chantant la gamme*) so(h), sol; **morceau en s.** piece in G
sol-air *adj inv* (*missile*) ground-to-air
solaire [sɔlɛr] *adj* (*chauffage, moteur, four etc*) solar; **cadran s.** sundial; **crème s.** sun lotion; **heure s.** solar time; **maison s.** solar-heated house; *Anat* **plexus s.** solar plexus; **système s.** solar system; *Astron* **taches solaires** sunspots; *Méd* **traitement s.** sunray treatment
solarium [sɔlarjɔm] *nm* **(a)** *Méd* (*établissment*) (*pour bronzer*) solarium **(b)** (*terrasse*) sun terrace
soldat, -ate [sɔlda, -at] **1** *nm* soldier; **s. du génie** sapper; **s. de marine** marine; **s. Dubois!** Private Dubois!; *Av* **s. de 2e classe/de première classe** aircraftman second-class/first-class; **s. de 2e classe, simple s.** private; **les simples soldats** the rank and file; **se faire s.** to go into *or* join the army; *Fig* **c'est un vrai petit s.** he's a real trooper **2** *nf* **soldate** (woman *or* female) soldier; **à la soldate** in a soldierly *or* soldier-like way *or* fashion
▶ **soldat**: **s. des bois** soldier (ant); **s. de fortune** soldier of fortune; **le S. inconnu** the Unknown Soldier *or* Warrior; **s. marin** (*crustacé*) soldier (crab); **s. de plomb** tin soldier
soldatesque [sɔldatɛsk] *Péj* **1** *adj* (*langage, manières etc*) barrackroom **2** *nf* army rabble
solde[1] [sɔld] *nf Mil etc* (*rémunération*) pay; *Mil, Ind* **feuille de s.** payroll; **soldes et indemnités** ordinary pay and allowances; **officier en demi-s.** officer on half pay; **cahier de s.** ledger; *Péj* **être à la s. de l'ennemi** to be in the pay of the enemy; *Péj* **avoir qn à sa s.** to have sb in one's pay
solde[2] *nm Com* **(a)** (*somme*) balance; **paiement pour s.** payment of balance; **pour s. (de tout compte)** in (full *or* final) settlement; **s. actif** credit balance; **s. bénéficiaire** credit balance; **s. en caisse** cash balance; **s. de compte** balance of account; **s. créditeur** credit balance, balance in hand; **s. cumulé** cumulative balance; **s. débiteur** *ou* **déficitaire** debit balance, balance owed; **s. disponible** available balance; **s. passif** debit balance
(b) soldes (*articles*) sale goods; (*vente au rabais*) sale; **courir** *ou* **faire les soldes** to go round the sales; **ce magasin fait des soldes** this shop is having a sale; **saison** *ou* **période des soldes** sales season; **s. d'édition** (*livre*) remainder; **(en) s.** to clear; **je l'ai acheté en s.** I got it in *or* at a sale *or* the sales; **prix de s.** bargain prices
solder [sɔlde] **1** *vt* **(a)** *Fin* (*arrêter*) (*compte*) to balance, to close; (*pour acquitter*) to settle, to pay (off); **s. l'arriéré** to make up back payments **(b)** *Com* (*stock*) to sell off, to clear; (*livres*) to remainder **2 se solder** *vpr* **(a)** *Fin* **les comptes se soldent par un bénéfice net de ...** the accounts show a net profit of ... **(b)** *Fig* **se s. par** (*échec etc*) to end in; **tout ça va se s. par une catastrophe financière** it's going to end in financial disaster
soldeur, -euse [sɔldœr, -øz] *n Com* discount trader
sole[1] *nf* **(a)** *Tech, Métal* bed plate **(b)** *Naut* (*d'un navire*) flat bottom
sole[2] *nf* (*poisson*) sole
sole[3] *nf Agr* (*de l'assolement des cultures*) field
solécisme [sɔlesism] *nm Ling* solecism
soleil [sɔlɛj] *nm* **(a)** (*astre*) sun; **lever/coucher du s.** sunrise/sunset; **se lever avec le s.** to get up with the sun; **il n'y a rien de nouveau sous le s.** there is nothing new under the sun; *Hist Fr* **le Roi S.** the Sun King; *Couture* **plissé s.** sunray pleats
(b) (*lumière, chaleur*) sun, sunshine; **il y a** *ou* **il fait du s.** the sun is shining, it's sunny; **il y fait un s. de plomb** the sun is scorching hot there; **se protéger du s.** to protect oneself from the sun; **au (grand) s.** in the sun(shine); **jour de s.** sunny day; *F* **cette petite est mon rayon de s.!** that little girl is my ray of sunshine!; **sans s.** sunless; **coup de s.** sunburn; (*plus fort*) touch of sunstroke; *F* **piquer un s.** to blush; **ôte-toi de mon s.!** get out of here!; *Fig* **avoir sa/se faire une place au s.** to have one's/find oneself a place in the sun; **avoir des biens** *ou* **du bien au s.** to own property
(c) *Bot* sunflower
(d) *Gym* **grand s.** grand circle
(e) (*feu d'artifice*) Catherine wheel, pinwheel
▶ **soleil**: **s. de minuit** midnight sun
solennel, -elle [sɔlanɛl] *adj* **(a)** (*serment, déclaration etc*) solemn; (*occasion etc*) solemn, formal **(b)** (*ton, silence*) solemn, grave; **prendre des airs solennels** to adopt a solemn air **(c)** *Rel* **communion solennelle** solemn communion
solennellement [sɔlanɛlmɑ̃] *adv* solemnly; (*inaugurer etc*) formally; **je le jure s.** I solemnly swear
solenniser [sɔlanize] *vt* to solemnize
solennité [sɔlanite] *nf* **(a)** (*caractère*) solemnity; **avec s.** solemnly **(b)** (*fête*) solemn ceremony
solénoïde [sɔlenɔid] *nm Él* solenoid
solex® [sɔlɛks] *nm* moped
solfatare [sɔlfatar] *nf Géol* solfatara, sulphur spring
solfège [sɔlfɛʒ] *nm Mus* (tonic) sol-fa, music theory; **apprendre le s.** to learn music theory; **(livre de) s.** (music) primer
solfier [sɔlfje] *vt Mus* (*ton*) to sol-fa
solidaire [sɔlidɛr] *adj* **(a)** (*personnes*) **être s. de qn** to stand by sb, to support sb; **se sentir s. de qn** to feel a sense of solidarity with sb; **nous sommes tous solidaires (les uns des autres)** we all stand *or* stick together; **dans leur famille, ils sont très solidaires** they're a very close-knit family; **ses intérêts sont solidaires des nôtres** his interests are bound up with ours **(b)** *Tech* (*roue d'engrenage etc*) interdependent; **roue s. d'une autre** wheel integral with another **(c)** *Jur* jointly liable *or* responsible **(de** for); **obligation s.** obligation binding on all parties
solidairement [sɔlidɛrmɑ̃] *adv* jointly
solidariser [sɔlidarize] **1** *vt* **(a)** *Jur* to render jointly liable *or* jointly responsible **(b)** *Tech* **mécanisme à action solidarisée** interlocking gear **2 se solidariser** *vpr* to make common cause, to show solidarity **(avec** with)
solidarité [sɔlidarite] *nf* **(a)** (*entre personnes*) solidarity; **en signe de s., nous portons ce badge** we wear this badge as a sign of solidarity; **faire appel à la s. nationale** to call for national solidarity; **grève de s.** sympathy strike; **débrayer par s. (avec)** to come out (on strike) in sympathy (with) **(b)** *Tech* (*des pièces*) interdependence **(c)** *Jur* joint liability *or* responsibility
solide [sɔlid] **1** *adj* **(a)** (*non liquide*) (*corps, aliment, terre*) solid; *Math* **angle s.** solid angle
(b) (*résistant*) (*mur, fondation*) solid, strong; (*tissu*) strong; (*personne*) strong, sturdy; (*repas*) solid, hearty; (*appétit*) hearty; (*preuve*) solid, sound; (*raisonnement, éducation*) sound; (*amitié*) strong; *Com* (*personne*) sound, solvent; (*position, affaire*) sound, strong, well-established; **s. sur ses jambes** steady on one's feet; **peu s.** (*personne*) weak; (*meuble*) flimsy; **un coup de poing s.** a hefty blow; **qualités solides** solid *or* sterling qualities; **garantie s.** solid *or* reliable guarantee; **ami s.** staunch *or* reliable *or* trusty friend; **de solides liens nous unissent** strong *or* close ties unite us; **avoir la tête s.** to be level-headed; **il faut avoir les nerfs solides** you need nerves of steel **(pour faire qch** to do sth); **j'ai de solides raisons de croire que ...** I have good *or* sound reasons for believing that ...; *Fig* **être s. au poste** to be extremely reliable *or* dependable; *Fig* **ça ne repose sur rien de s.** there is no sound *or* solid basis for that; **être encore s. (comme un chêne** *ou* **un roc)** to be still hale and hearty
2 *nm* **(a)** *Géom, Phys* solid (body); *Géom* **s. de révolution** solid of revolution
(b) *F* **ça, c'est du s.!** that's pretty solid!
solidement [sɔlidmɑ̃] *adv* (*construire etc*) solidly; (*attacher, tenir, établir etc*) firmly, securely; **homme s. bâti** solidly *or* sturdily built man; *F* **elle s'est fait s. reprendre** she got a good telling-off
solidification [sɔlidifikasjɔ̃] *nf* solidification
solidifier [sɔlidifje] (*impf, pr sub* **n. solidifiions, v. solidifiiez**) **1** *vt* to solidify **2 se solidifier** *vpr* to solidify
solidité [sɔlidite] *nf* solidity; (*d'un édifice, d'un matériau*) strength; (*d'une société, d'un jugement*) soundness; (*d'une amitié*) strength, staunchness; (*d'une couleur*) fastness; **c'est d'une s. à toute épreuve** it stands up to anything
soliloque [sɔlilɔk] *nm* soliloquy

soliloquer [sɔlilɔke] *vi* to soliloquize
solin [sɔlɛ̃] *nm Constr* (*espace*) space; (*enduit*) plaster filling
solipsisme [sɔlipsism] *nm Phil* solipsism
soliste [sɔlist] *n* soloist
solitaire [sɔlitɛr] **1** *adj* **(a)** (*qui vit seul*) solitary; (*involontairement*) (*personne*) lonely, *Am F* lonesome; **passer des vacances solitaires** to spend one's holidays on one's own; **vivre s.** to live a solitary life; **avoir l'humeur s.** to like to be on one's own *or* alone, to like one's own company; **plaisir/vice s.** masturbation/self-abuse
(b) (*séparé des autres*) (*voyageur, arbre, maison etc*) solitary, lone
(c) (*désert*) (*route, lieu etc*) lonely, deserted
(d) ver s. tapeworm
2 *n* (*personne*) loner, lone wolf; (*ermite*) hermit, recluse; **en s.** on one's own, alone; *Naut* **croisière en s.** solo cruise
3 *nm* **(a)** (*jeu*) solitaire
(b) (*diamant*) solitaire
(c) (*sanglier*) rogue boar; (*éléphant*) rogue elephant
solitairement [sɔlitɛrmɑ̃] *adv* on one's own, alone
solitude [sɔlityd] *nf* **(a)** (*de personne*) solitude; (*involontaire*) loneliness; **rechercher la s.** to seek solitude; **j'aime la s.** I like being alone *or* on my own, I like my own company; **vivre dans la s.** to live alone *or* on one's own **(b)** (*de lieu*) loneliness; **dans la s. de la nuit/campagne** in the loneliness *or* solitude of the night/countryside **(c)** *Litt* (*endroit*) lonely spot
solive [sɔliv] *nf Constr* joist
sollicitation [sɔlisitasjɔ̃] *nf* **(a)** (*demande*) request; (*avec instance*) entreaty; **céder aux sollicitations de qn** to give in to sb's pleas **(b) les sollicitations de la faim/de l'ambition** gnawing hunger/ambition
solliciter [sɔlisite] *vt* **(a)** (*entretien, audience etc*) to request; **s. qn (de faire qch)** to appeal to sb (to do sth); **j'ai l'honneur de s. votre bienveillance** I appeal to your kindness; **s. un emploi (de qn)** to apply (to sb) for a job; **s. des voix** to canvass for votes; **ils nous ont souvent sollicités par téléphone** they often made telephone appeals to us; **il est sollicité de toutes parts** he is very much in demand **(b)** (*attention, regards*) to attract; (*curiosité*) to arouse
solliciteur, -euse [sɔlisitœr, -øz] *n* petitioner, supplicant **(de** for)
sollicitude [sɔlisityd] *nf* (*soin*) solicitude; (*inquiétude*) solicitude, concern, anxiety **(pour** for); **ton plein de s.** solicitous *or* concerned tone
solo [sɔlo] **1** *nm* solo; **s. de violon** violin solo; **faire un s.** (*en danse*) to do a solo, to dance a solo; (*en musique*) to do a solo, to play a solo; **jouer en s.** to play solo **2** *adj inv* solo; **violon s.** solo violin
sol-sol *adj inv* (*missile*) ground-to-ground
solstice [sɔlstis] *nm* solstice; **s. d'été/d'hiver** summer/winter solstice
solubiliser [sɔlybilize] *vt* **s. qch** to make sth soluble
solubilité [sɔlybilite] *nf* (*d'un corps*) solubility
soluble [sɔlybl] *adj* **(a)** (*produit*) soluble; **café s.** instant coffee **(b)** (*problème*) solvable
soluté [sɔlyte] *nm Pharm, Ch* solution, serum
solution [sɔlysjɔ̃] *nf* **(a)** (*de problème, situation, d'équation etc*) solution, answer **(de** to); **s. de paresse** *ou* **de facilité** easy way out; **ce n'est pas une s.!** that's no answer *or* solution! **(b)** *Ch, Phys etc* (*liquide, dissolution*) solution; **sel en s. (dans l'eau)** salt in solution (in water); **s. détergente** cleaning solution *or* fluid **(c) s. de continuité** solution of continuity; *Él etc* break of continuity
▶ **solution**: *Hist* **la s. finale** the Final Solution
solutionner [sɔlysjɔne] *vt* (*problème, difficulté*) to solve
solvabilité [sɔlvabilite] *nf* solvency; (*en vue d'un emprunt*) credit rating
solvable [sɔlvabl] *adj* (financially) solvent
solvant [sɔlvɑ̃] *nm Ch* solvent
soma [sɔma] *nm Biol* soma
somali, -ie [sɔmali] **1** *adj* Somali **2** *nm Ling* Somali **3** *n* **S.** Somali; **les Somalis** the Somali(s)
Somalie [sɔmali] *nf* Somalia; *Hist* **S. britannique/italienne** British/Italian Somaliland
somatique [sɔmatik] *adj Biol, Psy* somatic
somatisation [sɔmatizasjɔ̃] *nf Biol, Psy* **psychosomatic reaction**, *Spéc* somatization
somatiser [sɔmatize] *vt Biol, Psy* to react psychosomatically to, *Spéc* to somatize
sombre [sɔ̃br] *adj* **(a)** (*foncé*) (*couleur*) dark; **des robes bleu s.** dark blue dresses **(b)** (*obscur*) (*forêt, pièce etc*) dark, dim; (*ciel*) dull, overcast; **il fait s.** (*temps*) it is dull (weather); **il faisait très s. dans la pièce** it was very dark in the room **(c)** (*triste*) (*visage, pensées, caractère, avenir etc*) gloomy, *Fml* sombre, *US* somber; **ils sont fâchés pour une s. histoire d'argent** they quarrelled over some sordid little business of money; **une s. histoire d'assassinat** a sinister tale of murder **(d)** *F* **un s. imbécile** a total imbecile *or* idiot
sombrement [sɔ̃brəmɑ̃] *adv* (*tristement*) gloomily, sombrely, *US* somberly; **s'habiller s.** to wear dark clothes
sombrer [sɔ̃bre] *vi* (*d'un navire*) to sink, to founder; (*d'un empire*) to fall, to collapse; (*d'une affaire*) to come to grief, to fail; **s. dans l'alcool/la misère/la folie** to sink into alcoholism/poverty/madness; **il vit s. sa fortune** he saw his fortune swallowed up; **elle vit s. ses espérances** she saw her hopes dashed; **sa raison sombra** he lost his mind *or* his reason; **le bateau a sombré corps et biens** the boat went down with all hands
sombrero [sɔ̃brero] *nm* sombrero
sommaire [sɔmɛr] **1** *adj* **(a)** (*récit*) brief, succinct, concise **(b)** (*rudimentaire*) (*repas*) scanty, skimpy; (*examen*) hasty, cursory; **porter une tenue s.** to be scantily *or* skimpily dressed; **faire une toilette s.** to have a quick wash, *F* to have a lick and a promise; **avoir des vues sommaires sur qch** to have superficial views on sth **(c)** *Jur* (*procédure, exécution*) summary **2** *nm* summary, synopsis
sommairement [sɔmɛrmɑ̃] *adv* **(a)** (*expliquer, raconter etc*) briefly, in summary **(b)** (*de façon rudimentaire*) **vêtu s.** scantily *or* skimpily clad *or* dressed; **l'appartement est s. meublé** the furniture in the flat is very basic, the flat is meagrely furnished; **s. organisé** improvised, hastily organized **(c)** *Jur* (*juger*) summarily
sommation[1] [sɔmasjɔ̃] *nf* **(a)** *Jur* (*injonction*) notice, demand; (*de paraître en justice*) summons; **avoir s. de payer une dette** to receive notice *or* a demand to pay a debt **(b)** *Mil* (*de sentinelle*) challenge
sommation[2] *nf Math* (*d'une série*) summation
somme[1] [sɔm] *nf* **bête de s.** beast of burden; *Fig* drudge; **travailler comme une bête de s.** to work like a slave, to slave away
somme[2] *nf* **(a)** *Math* sum, total; **faire la s. de dix nombres** to add (up) ten numbers; **s. générale/totale** overall total/total sum; **la s. des trois angles d'un triangle** the sum of the three angles of a triangle
(b) (*quantité*) (*d'objets*) number; (*des pertes etc*) amount; **la s. des efforts** the amount of effort; **en s.** (*tout compte fait*) on the whole, all things considered; (*en bref*) in short; **en s., j'ai été plutôt agréablement surpris** on the whole, I was rather pleasantly surprised; **en s. il s'agit d'un travail commercial** in short, it's a sales job; **s. toute** when all is said and done
(c) s. (d'argent) sum (of money); **payer la s. de 500 francs** to pay 500 francs; **être mis à l'amende pour la s. de 500 francs** to be fined (a total of) 500 francs; **dépenser des sommes folles** to spend vast sums *or* amounts (of money); **un million! c'est une s.!** a million! that's a lot of money!; **s. due** amount due, total due; **s. nette** net (amount); *Compta* **sommes payables** payables, sums payable
(d) (*d'une œuvre*) outline, survey
somme[3] *nm* nap, snooze; **faire un (petit) s.** to have *or* take a nap *or* a snooze, *F* to have forty winks
sommeil [sɔmɛj] *nm* **(a)** (*de dormeur*) sleep, *Litt* slumber; **avoir besoin de très peu de s.** to need very little sleep; **s. réparateur/profond** refreshing/deep sleep; **s. de mort** *ou* **de plomb** heavy *or* deep sleep; **dormir d'un s. de plomb** to sleep like a log; **avoir le s. léger/profond** to be a light/a heavy sleeper; **dormir du s. du juste** to sleep the sleep of the just; **chercher le s.** to try to sleep; **faire une cure de s.** to undergo sleep therapy; **j'en perds le s.** I'm losing sleep over it; *Fig* **s. éternel** eternal rest; *Bot* **en s.** (lying) dormant; *Fig* **laisser une affaire en s.** to put a matter aside *or* on the back burner *or* on ice, *Fml* to leave a matter in abeyance; *Zool* **s. hivernal** winter sleep
(b) (*somnolence*) sleepiness, drowsiness; **avoir s.** to be *or* feel sleepy *or* drowsy; **ça risque de te donner s.** it might make you sleepy; **le s. me gagne** I'm beginning to fall asleep; **je tombe** *ou* **je meurs de s.** I can't keep awake, I can't keep my eyes open; **maladie du s.** sleeping sickness
▶ **sommeil**: **s. paradoxal** REM sleep
sommeiller [sɔmeje] *vi* **(a)** to doze **(b)** *Fig* to lie dormant, to be latent **(en qn** in sb)
sommelier [sɔməlje] *nm* cellarman; (*serveur*) wine waiter, sommelier
sommellerie [sɔmɛlri] *nf* **(a)** wine waiter's job **(b)** (*cave*) wine cellar
sommer[1] [sɔme] *vt Math* to sum
sommer[2] *vt aussi Jur* to summon **(de faire qch** to do sth); **s. qn de payer** to require sb to pay
sommet [sɔmɛ] *nm* (*d'une montagne, d'une colline*) top,

summit, peak; (*d'un arbre, d'un toit, d'une tour, d'une hiérarchie*) top; (*d'un angle, d'une courbe, d'une trajectoire, d'un cône*) vertex; (*d'une vague*) crest; (*d'une arche, de la tête*) crown; *Fig* (*du pouvoir, de la renommée*) summit, pinnacle, height; *Fig* **atteindre des sommets vertigineux** to reach the dizzy heights; *Fig* **être au s. de l'échelle** to be at the top of the ladder; **atteindre le s. de la gloire/du succès** to reach the height *or* pinnacle of fame/success; *Pol* **conférence** *ou* **réunion** *ou* **rencontre au s.** summit (meeting *or* conference); **un s. franco-américain** a Franco-American summit; *Obst* **présentation d'un bébé par le s.** head presentation of a baby

sommier[1] [sɔmje] *nm* **(a)** (*de lit*) base; **s. à ressorts/lattes** sprung/slatted base **(b)** *Tech* (*d'arche*) springer; (*de porte etc*) lintel; (*du sol*) cross beam; (*de pont*) stringer; (*de balance*) beam; (*de machine*) bed

sommier[2] *nm* **(a)** *Admin etc* register; *Jur* **sommiers judiciaires** criminal records; **il n'y a rien sur lui au s.** he's got a clean record **(b)** *Com* cash book

sommier-divan, *pl* **sommiers-divans** *nm* divan base

sommité [sɔmite] *nf* **(a)** *Bot* head **(b)** *Fig* (*personnage*) leading figure *or* light; **sommités de l'art** leading figures *or* lights in the art world; **les sommités du monde scientifique** leading experts in the scientific field

somnambule [sɔmnɑ̃byl] **1** *adj* somnambulistic, somnambulant; **il est s.** he's a sleepwalker, he sleepwalks, he walks in his sleep **2** *n* sleepwalker, *Spéc* somnambulist; **c'est un s.** he's a sleepwalker, he sleepwalks, he walks in his sleep; **travailler/parler comme un s.** to work/speak like a zombie *or Fml* as if in a trance; **ses gestes de s.** his zombie-like movements

somnambulisme [sɔmnɑ̃bylism] *nm* sleepwalking, *Spéc* somnambulism; **s. provoqué** hypnotic state

somnifère [sɔmnifɛr] *Méd* **1** *adj* sleep-inducing, soporific; **comprimé s.** sleeping tablet *or* pill **2** *nm* sleeping tablet *or* pill

somnolence [sɔmnɔlɑ̃s] *nf* sleepiness, drowsiness, *Litt* somnolence; **ce médicament peut provoquer des états de s.** this medicine may cause drowsiness; **la chaleur nous plonge dans un état de s.** the heat makes us drowsy *or* lethargic

somnolent [sɔmnɔlɑ̃] *adj* sleepy, drowsy, *Litt* somnolent

somnoler [sɔmnɔle] *vi* to doze

somptuaire [sɔ̃ptɥɛr] *adj* **(a)** *Jur* (*loi*) sumptuary **(b)** *Fin* **taxes somptuaires** tax on luxury articles; **dépenses somptuaires** expenditure on luxuries

somptueusement [sɔ̃ptɥøzmɑ̃] *adv* sumptuously, magnificently

somptueux, -euse [sɔ̃ptɥø, -øz] *adj* sumptuous, magnificent

somptuosité [sɔ̃ptɥozite] *nf* sumptuousness, magnificence

son[1], **sa, ses** [sɔ̃, sa, se] *adj poss* [①**A30**,8; **B19-20**,E,1] (**son** *is used instead of* **sa** *before f nouns beginning with a vowel or mute* **h**) (*d'homme etc*) his; (*de femme etc*) her; (*de chose, d'idée, d'animal etc*) its; (*de bébé*) his/her, its; (*d'animal domestique*) its, his/her; (*après un sujet indéfini*) one's; (*après 'tout le monde', 'personne', 'chacun' etc*) their, *Fml* his/her; **s. ami/amie** his/her friend; **s. meilleur ami/sa meilleure amie** his/her best friend; **s. oncle et sa tante** his/her aunt and (his/her) uncle; **s. père et sa mère,** *Litt* **ses père et mère** his/her mother and father; **il a mis s. chapeau et ses gants** he put on his hat and (his) gloves; **un(e) de ses ami(e)s** one of his/her friends, a friend of his/hers; **un professeur de ses amis** a teacher friend of his/hers; **chacun a pris s. sac** (*chacun a un sac*) everybody took their bags; (*le sac de Pierre*) everybody took his bag; **un bébé peut reconnaître sa mère peu de temps après sa naissance** a baby can recognize its mother shortly after it's born; **perdre s. temps** to waste one's time; **ici, on passe s. temps à bavarder** everybody spends their time chatting here; **en Alsace, on prend s. café en même temps que le dessert** in Alsace, they have their coffee along with their desert; *F* **elle aura sa chambre à elle** she'll have her own room; *F* **s. imbécile de frère** his/her idiot of a brother; *F* **s. artiste de mari** her artist husband; *F* **alors, tu veux bien le rencontrer, s. artiste?** so, do you want to meet this artist of his/hers?; *F* **il a eu s. vendredi** he got Friday off; *F* **alors, c'était ça ses vacances de rêve!** so much for his/her dream holiday!

son[2] *nm* **(a)** (*de voix, d'instrument etc*) sound; **le s. profond de la cloche** the deep sound *or* tone of the bell; *Fig* **je n'ai entendu qu'un s. de cloche jusqu'à maintenant** I've heard only one side of the story up to now; **s. du tambour/de la trompette** beat of the drum/blare of the trumpet; **danser au s. des accordéons** to dance to the sound of accordions; **annoncer une nouvelle à s. de trompe** to shout a piece of news from the rooftops; *Naut* **s. de sirène** *ou* **de sifflet** siren blast

(b) *Phys, Mus* sound; **s. pur** pure tone; **niveau du s.** sound level; **vitesse du s.** speed of sound; *Av* **mur du s.** sound barrier; *Cin etc* **enregistrement du s.** sound recording; **prise de s.** sound pick-up; **la prise de s. est bonne** the recording is good; *Cin etc* **ingénieur du s.** sound engineer; **(spectacle) s. et lumière** son et lumière; **s. d'ambiance** ambient sound; *TV* **s. sur image** sound over vision, SOV; **s. numérique** digital sound; **s. stéréo** stereo sound; **s. témoin** cue track; *TV, Rad* **s. de transition** bridging sound

son[3] *nm* (*de grains*) bran; **céréales à base de s.** bran cereal; **pain de s.** bran loaf; **tache de s.** freckle; **poupée de s.** stuffed doll

sonal, -als [sɔnal] *nm Rad, TV* (advertising) jingle

sonar [sɔnar] *nm Naut* sonar

sonate [sɔnat] *nf Mus* sonata; **s. pour violon** violin sonata

sonatine [sɔnatin] *nf Mus* sonatina

sondage [sɔ̃daʒ] *nm* **(a)** poll, survey; **s. Gallup** Gallup poll; **faire** *ou* **pratiquer un s.** to carry out a poll; **enquête par s., s. (d'opinion)** opinion poll *or* survey; **s. aléatoire** random sampling; **s. aréolaire** cluster sampling; **sondages de paix** peace feelers; **s. probabiliste** probability survey; **s. par quotas** quotas survey; **s. par téléphone** telephone interviewing **(b)** *Naut, Av etc* sounding, probe; **faire des sondages** to take soundings; **ballon de s.** pilot balloon, sounding balloon **(c)** *Min* boring; **appareil de s.** drilling rig **(d)** *Métal* **essai de s.** probe test **(e)** *Méd* (*de blessure*) probing

sonde [sɔ̃d] *nf* **(a)** *Naut* (sounding) lead, sounding line, plummet; **naviguer à la s.** to navigate by soundings; **être sur la s.** to be in soundings, to have struck soundings **(b)** (*de pompe, de puits etc*) sounding rod **(c)** **faire la s.** (*d'une baleine*) to sound **(d)** *Météo, Av* **s. aérienne** sounding balloon; **s. spatiale** space probe; *Av* **s. de réservoir** tank probe; **s. à fil chaud** hot-wire anemometer **(e)** *Méd* probe, tube, catheter; **s. (creuse)** catheter; **nourri à la s.** tube-fed **(f)** (*à fromage etc*) taster **(g)** *Min* borer, drill

sondé [sɔ̃de] *nm Mktg* respondent

sonder [sɔ̃de] **1** *vt* **(a)** *Naut* to sound; *Fig* (*mystère*) to fathom

(b) *Av, Météo* **s. l'atmosphère** to make soundings in the atmosphere

(c) *Min* **s. un terrain** to make borings

(d) (*examiner*) (*fromage*) to taste; (*poutre*) to examine; (*horizon*) to scan; **s. le cœur/les intentions de qn** to sound out sb's heart/intentions; **s. qn** to sound sb out; **je l'ai sondée là-dessus** I sounded her out on the matter; **il la sonda du regard** he looked intently at her; **s. l'opinion** to sound out public opinion, to make a survey of public opinion; **10% de la population sondée** 10% of those polled; *Fig* **s. le terrain** to see how the land lies

(e) *Méd* (*blessure*) to probe; (*patient*) to sound; (*avec une sonde creuse*) to catheterize

2 *vi* **(a)** (*d'une baleine*) to sound

(b) *Min* to make borings

sondeur, -euse [sɔ̃dœr, -øz] **1** *nm* **(a)** *Naut* (*personne*) leadsman; (*machine*) sounder **(b)** *Min* (*personne*) borer, driller **2** *nf Min* **sondeuse** borer, drill

songe [sɔ̃ʒ] *nm Litt* dream; **faire un s.** to have a dream; **en s.** in a dream

songe-creux *nm inv Litt* dreamer

songer [sɔ̃ʒe] *vi* (**je songeai(s); n. songeons**) **(a)** **s. à qch** (*penser à*) to think about sth; (*considérer*) to consider sth, to think sth over; **s. à l'avenir** to think about the future; **songez à ce que vous faites!** think about what you're doing!; **il ne faut pas y s.** that's quite out of the question; **on ne peut pas ne pas s. à elle** you can't help but think about her; **s. au mariage** to consider *or* to contemplate marriage; **sans y s.** without thinking; **sans s. à mal** without meaning any harm; **s. à faire qch** to think of doing sth, to contemplate doing sth; **il ne songe qu'à gagner de l'argent** making money is all he thinks about

(b) (*imaginer*) to imagine (**que** that); **songez si j'étais furieux** you can imagine how angry I was; **je ne songeais guère que ...** little did I think *or* imagine that ...; **songez donc!** just think!, just imagine!

(c) **s. à** (*se souvenir de*) to remember; **songez à lui** keep *or* bear him in mind, remember him; **songez que ...** remember *or* bear in mind that ...; **je ne songeais pas que ...** I had forgotten that ...; **cela m'a fait s. que ...** that reminded me that ...

(d) *Arch* (*rêver*) to dream

songerie [sɔ̃ʒri] *nf Litt* reverie, daydreaming

songeur, -euse [sɔ̃ʒœr, -øz] *adj* (*rêveur*) (*personne, nature*) dreamy; (*pensif*) (*personne*) pensive, thoughtful

sonique [sɔnik] *adj* sonic; **bang s.** sonic boom

sonnaille [sɔnaj] *nf* (cow)bell

sonnant [sɔnɑ̃] *adj* (*horloge*) striking; **arriver à dix heures sonnant(es)** to arrive on the stroke of ten *or* at ten (o'clock)

sharp; *Fig* **espèces sonnantes et trébuchantes** hard cash
sonné [sɔne] *adj* **(a) il est dix heures sonnées** it's past *or* gone ten; **il a quarante ans (bien) sonnés** he's well over forty, *F* he's on the wrong side of forty, he won't see forty again **(b)** *F Boxe etc* (*groggy*) groggy, punch-drunk; (*fou*) crazy, cracked
sonner [sɔne] **1** *vi* (*d'une horloge*) to strike; (*de cloches, du téléphone*) to ring; **le glas sonne** the bell is tolling; **s. creux** to sound hollow; *Fig* to ring hollow; **sa réponse a sonné faux** his answer did not ring true; **quand elle rit, ça sonne faux** when she laughs it rings false; *Fig* **s. bien/mal** to sound good/bad; **l'italien sonne bien à l'oreille** Italian is a pleasant-sounding language; **adresse qui sonne bien** good address; **faire sonner les consonnes** to sound the consonants; **faire s. un mot** to emphasize a word; **faire s. son argent/ses clefs** to jingle one's money/one's keys; *F* **il va se faire s.!** he'll catch it!; **six heures sonnèrent** the clock struck six; **midi vient de s.** it has just struck twelve; **le réveil vient de s.** the alarm (clock) has just gone off; **faire s. le réveil à 6 heures** to set the alarm for 6 o'clock; **les vêpres sonnent** the bells are ringing for vespers; **on sonne** there's a ring at the door; **on a sonné** that was the doorbell, there's someone at the door; **j'ai sonné chez eux, mais personne ne m'a répondu** I rang their doorbell, but nobody answered; **s. avant d'entrer** (*sur panneau*) ring before entering; **entrez sans s.** go (straight) in; **s. du clairon** to sound the bugle; **son heure** *ou* **sa dernière heure a sonné** his last hour has come; **la trompette sonne** the trumpet sounds; **les oreilles lui sonnaient** his ears were buzzing

2 *vt* **(a)** (*trompettes etc*) to sound; **s. la cloche** to ring the bell; *F* **il va se faire s. les cloches!** he'll catch it!; **horloge qui sonne les heures** clock that strikes the hours; **l'horloge a sonné dix heures** the clock struck ten; **il a sonné deux coups à la porte** he rang the doorbell twice; **s. la messe/l'office** to ring the bell for mass/for church; **s. le dîner** to ring the dinner bell; *Mil* **s. la charge/la retraite** to sound the charge/the retreat

(b) (*appeler*) (*domestique, infirmière etc*) to ring for; *très F* **on ne vous a pas sonné, vous!** mind your own business!, nobody asked you!

(c) *très F* (*assommer*) **s. qn** to knock sb out
sonnerie [sɔnri] *nf* **(a)** (*son*) (*des cloches, du téléphone*) ringing; (*cloches*) (set of) bells *or* chimes; **c'est la sonnerie du téléphone qui m'a réveillé** it was the telephone (ringing) that woke me up **(b)** (*mécanisme*) (*d'une horloge*) striking mechanism; (*sonnette*) bell; **pendule à s.** striking clock; **bouton de s.** bell push; **fil à s.** bell wire **(c)** *Mil* (*de clairon etc*) call
sonnet [sɔnɛ] *nm* sonnet
sonnette [sɔnɛt] *nf* **(a)** (*de porte*) doorbell; (*clochette*) (small) bell; (*de vélo, pour serviteurs*) bell; **appuyer sur la s.** to ring the bell; **personne ne répondit à mon coup de s.** no one answered the bell; **as-tu entendu la s.?** did you hear the bell?; **cordon de s.** bell pull; **s. d'alarme** alarm bell; **coup de s.** ring **(b)** *Constr* pile driver **(c) serpent à s.** rattlesnake
sonneur, -euse [sɔnœr, -øz] **1** *n* bellringer; *F* **dormir comme un s.** to sleep like a log **2** *nm Constr* pile-driver operator
sono [sɔno] *nf abrév F* = **sonorisation (b), (c)**
sonore [sɔnɔr] **1** *adj* **(a)** (*relatif au son*) sound; **onde s.** soundwave; *Cin* **film s.** sound film; **effets sonores** sound effects; **bande** *ou* **piste s.** sound track; **bip s.** beep; **pollution s.** noise pollution; **église s.** church with good acoustics; **vibrations sonores** acoustic resonance **(b)** (*voix*) ringing, loud; (*cloche*) clear-toned; (*rire*) resounding; (*voûte, couloir etc*) echoing; *Péj* (*phrases*) high-sounding, sonorous; *Ling* **consonne s.** voiced consonant; **niveau (d'intensité) s.** sound (intensity) level **2** *nf Ling* voiced consonant
sonorisation [sɔnɔrizasjɔ̃] *nf* **(a)** *Ling* (*d'une consonne*) voicing **(b)** *Cin* addition of the soundtrack (**de** to), dubbing **(c)** (*d'une pièce*) fitting of a PA system; (*équipement*) public address system, PA system; (*de discothèque etc*) sound system
sonoriser [sɔnɔrize] **1** *vt* **(a)** *Ling* (*consonne*) to voice **(b)** *TV, Cin* to dub; (*présentation*) to add sound to; **s. un film** to add the soundtrack to a film **(c) s. une salle** to fit a room with a PA system **2 se sonoriser** *vpr Ling* (*de consonne*) to be voiced
sonorité [sɔnɔrite] *nf* **(a)** (*qualité de son*) tone **(b)** (*résonance*) resonance; (*de salle etc*) acoustics; **ce piano a une belle s.** this piano has a beautiful tone
sonothèque [sɔnɔtɛk] *nf* sound effects *ou* audio library
sonotone® [sɔnɔtɔn] *nm* miniature hearing aid
sont [sɔ̃] *voir* **être**
sophisme [sɔfism] *nm* sophism
sophiste [sɔfist] *n* sophist
sophistication [sɔfistikasjɔ̃] *nf* **(a)** (*d'une personne, d'un équipement*) sophistication **(b)** *Vieilli* (*du vin etc*) adulteration
sophistique [sɔfistik] **1** *adj* sophistic(al) **2** *nf* sophistry
sophistiqué [sɔfistike] *adj* **(a)** (*personne*) sophisticated; (*équipement etc*) sophisticated, advanced **(b)** *Vieilli* (*frelaté*) (*vin etc*) adulterated
Sophocle [sɔfɔkl] *nm* Sophocles
sophrologie [sɔfrɔlɔʒi] *nf* sophrology
sophrologue [sɔfrɔlɔg] *n* sophrologist
soporifique [sɔpɔrifik] **1** *adj* (*drogue*) soporific, sleep-inducing; *F* (*ennuyeux*) boring, soporific **2** *nm* (*drogue*) sleeping drug, soporific; *F* (*livre*) boring book, book that sends you to sleep
soprane [sɔpran] *n Mus* = **soprano**
sopraniste [sɔpranist] *nm Mus* male soprano
soprano [sɔprano] *Mus* **1** *nm* soprano (voice) **2** *n* (*personne*) soprano **3** *adj* **saxophone s.** soprano saxophone
sorbe [sɔrb] *nf Bot* sorb (apple)
sorbet [sɔrbɛ] *nm Culin* sorbet; **s. au cassis** blackcurrant sorbet
sorbetière [sɔrbətjɛr] *nf* ice-cream maker
sorbier [sɔrbje] *nm Bot* sorb (tree), service (tree)
sorbique [sɔrbik] *adj Ch* (*acide*) sorbic
sorbonnard, -arde [sɔrbɔnar, -ard] *F* **1** *n* (*étudiant*) student at the Sorbonne; (*professeur*) teacher at the Sorbonne **2** *adj Péj* pedantic
sorcellerie [sɔrsɛlri] *nf* witchcraft, sorcery, magic; **c'est de la s.!** it's magic!
sorcier [sɔrsje] **1** *nm* sorcerer, wizard; **il ne faut pas être s. pour faire ça** you don't need to be a genius to do that, that doesn't take much intelligence **2** *adj F* **ce n'est pas s.** it's simple enough, there's no magic about that
sorcière [sɔrsjɛr] *nf* sorceress, witch; *F Péj* **vieille s.** old hag, old witch; **chasse aux sorcières** witch hunt; **cercle** *ou* **rond de sorcières** fairy ring
sordide [sɔrdid] *adj* **(a)** (*vêtements*) filthy; (*pièce, quartier etc*) squalid, sordid **(b)** (*crime, détails, avarice etc*) sordid
sordidement [sɔrdidmɑ̃] *adv* sordidly; **vivre s.** to live in squalor
sordidité [sɔrdidite] *nf* sordidness
sorgho [sɔrgo] *nm Bot* sorghum
Sorlingues (les) [lesɔrlɛ̃g] *nfpl* the Isles of Scilly, the Scilly Isles
sornettes [sɔrnɛt] *nfpl* twaddle, rubbish
sort [sɔr] *nm* **(a)** (*situation*) **être satisfait de son s.** to be satisfied with one's lot; **faire un s. à** (*choses inutiles, encombrantes*) to dispose of; *F* (*ne rien laisser de*) (*bouteille, poulet rôti etc*) to polish off, to finish off

(b) (*destin*) fate, destiny; **notre s. est décidé** our fate is sealed; **abandonner qn à son triste s.** to abandon sb to his/her fate; **l'artillerie fit le s. de la bataille** the artillery decided the battle; **coup/ironie du s.** stroke/irony of fate; **et alors, ironie du s., qui vois-je en face de moi? lui!** and as fate would have it, who do I see in front of me? him!

(c) (*hasard*) chance, fortune; **tirer (qch) au s.** to draw lots (for something); (*jouer à pile ou face*) to toss a coin (for something); **tirer une place au s.** to draw lots for a place; **tirage au s.** drawing of lots; *Fb etc* toss; **le s. en est jeté** the die is cast

(d) (*magique*) spell, charm; **jeter un s. à qn** to cast a spell on *or* over sb; **conjurer le mauvais s.** to ward off bad luck
sortable [sɔrtabl] *adj F* (*personne*) presentable; **tu n'es pas s.!** I can't take you anywhere!
sortant, -ante [sɔrtɑ̃, -ɑ̃t] **1** *adj* (*numéro à la loterie*) winning; (*membres d'un comité etc*) outgoing, retiring; **élèves sortants** pupils in their last term; *Mil* cadets passing out **2** *n* **les sortants** those going/coming out
sorte [sɔrt] *nf* **(a)** (*manière*) way; **ne parlez pas de la s.** don't talk like that *or* in that way; **en quelque s.** as it were, in a way; **il sort très peu habillé, de s. qu'il tombe malade** he doesn't dress warmly when he goes out and so he falls ill *or* with the result that he falls ill; **de s. à faire** so as to do; [①B31,G,f] **je lui en ai parlé de s. qu'il ne soit pas pris au dépourvu** I told him about it so that he wouldn't be caught unawares; **faites en s. que tout soit prêt à temps** see to it that everything is ready in time; **fais en s. de tout préparer à l'avance** try to prepare everything in advance

(b) [①A13,3,a] (*genre*) sort, kind; **toute(s) sorte(s) de choses, des choses de toute(s) sorte(s)** all sorts *or* kinds of things; **des gens de toute(s) sorte(s)** all sorts *or* kinds of people; **un homme de la s.** a man of that sort *or* kind; **une s. de ragoût** a *or* some sort *or* kind of stew; **je n'ai rien dit/rien fait de la s.** I said/did no such thing, I said/did nothing of the kind *or* sort

sortie [sɔrti] *nf* **(a)** (*action de quitter un lieu*) going out, coming out, leaving; *Th* exit; **préparer sa s.** to prepare one's exit; **faire une fausse s.** to make a false exit; **c'était ma première s. depuis mon accident** it was the first time I had been out since my accident, it was my first outing after my accident; **à la s. du théâtre/du cinéma** at the end of the performance/of the film; **à la s. des classes** when school comes out; **à (l'heure de) la s. des bureaux** when the offices come out

(b) *Com* (*d'un livre, d'un journal*) publication; (*d'un film, d'un disque*) release; (*d'un modèle*) launch(ing)

(c) (*écoulement*) (*de liquide*) outflow, flowing out; **tuyaux de s.** outlet pipes

(d) *Él, Électron* output

(e) *Ordinat* exit; (*information*) output; **s. d'imprimante** printer output; **dispositif de s.** output device; **signal de s.** output signal

(f) *Tech* (*de feuilles de la presse d'imprimerie etc*) delivery; **table de s.** delivery table

(g) *Com* (*de marchandises*) export

(h) *Fin* **les sorties or** the gold withdrawals; **s. de devises/de capitaux** currency/capital outflow

(i) (*excursion*) trip, excursion, outing; (*congé*) leave; **organiser une s. entre élèves** to organize a school trip; **priver qn de s.** to stop sb from going out; **faire une s. en mer** to go for a short sea trip; **jour de s.** day out; **avoir un jour de s. par semaine** to have one free day a week; **nous sommes de s. aujourd'hui** we're going out today; **j'étais de s. mardi** I was out on Tuesday; **quelles sont vos sorties?** where do you go when you go out?; *Naut* **s. à terre** shore leave; **l'année dernière les canots de sauvetage ont fait cinquante sorties** last year the lifeboats went out fifty times

(j) *Mil* sally, sortie; *Fb* (*de gardien de but*) run out

(k) *F* (*verbale*) outburst, tirade; **faire une s. à** *ou* **contre qn** to lash out at sb; **je le sais capable de n'importe quelle s. devant eux** I know he's capable of saying anything in front of them

(l) (*issue*) exit, way out; **porte de s.** exit door; *Fig* **se ménager une porte de s.** to make sure one has a way out *or* an escape route; **il y a une s. sur la ruelle** there is a way out into the lane; **à la s. de la gare** at the station exit; **par ici la s.** this way out; **s. d'autoroute** motorway exit

(m) (*pour l'eau, la vapeur*) outlet

(n) *TV, Cin* (*fin de séquence*) out

▶ **sortie**: **s. de bain** bathrobe; *Vieilli* **s. de bal** evening wrap, opera cloak; **sorties de caisse** cash payments; *Ordinat* **s. écran** screen output; **sorties de fonds** outgoings, expenses; *Ordinat* **s. (sur) imprimante** printout; *Ordinat* **s. imprimée** printed output; *Ordinat* **s. jeux** games port; *Ordinat* **s. parallèle** parallel output; **s. de secours** emergency exit; *Ordinat* **s. série** serial output; **sorties de trésorerie** cash outflow *or* outgoings

sortilège [sɔrtilɛʒ] *nm* spell, charm

sortir[1] [sɔrtir] (*prp* **sortant**; *pp* **sorti**; *pr ind* **je sors, il sort, n. sortons, ils sortent**; *pr sub* **je sorte**; *impf* **je sortais**; *p hist* **je sortis**; *fu* **je sortirai**) **1** *vi* (*aux* **être**) **(a)** (*à pied*) (*aller*) to go out, to leave; (*venir*) to come out, to leave; (*d'un magazine, d'un livre*) to come out, to be published; (*d'un film*) to come out, to be released; **le livre sort chez Gallimard le mois prochain** the book will be published by Gallimard next month; **s. sur le marché** to come onto the market; **je n'arrivais** *ou* **ne parvenais pas à s.** I couldn't get out; *Scol* **est-ce que je peux s.?** may I be excused?; **entrer par une porte et s. par l'autre** to go in one door and out the other; **faire s. qn** (*en promenade etc*) to take sb out; (*mettre à la porte*) to make sb leave, to put sb out; **fais s. les enfants, nous avons à parler** send the children out of the room, we have to talk; **sortez (d'ici)!** get out (of here)!; **je sors d'une mauvaise grippe** I'm just recovering from *or* getting over a bad dose of flu; **s. vainqueur d'un tournoi** to come out on top *or* emerge the winner in a tournament; **tu sors à quelle heure, ce soir?** (*du bureau, du lycée etc*) what time do you finish tonight?; *Fig F* **nous ne sommes pas sortis de l'auberge!** we're not out of the wood(s) yet; **cela ne doit pas s. d'ici** (*cela doit rester secret*) it mustn't go any further; *F* **d'où sors-tu?** (*tu n'es pas au courant*) what planet have you been on?; (*tu es mal élevé*) where did they find you?; **cela m'est sorti de la mémoire** *ou* **de la tête** it has slipped my mind *or* gone out of my head; **il ne sortira pas grand-chose de tout cela** not much will come of all this; *Ind* **s. de la chaîne de fabrication** to come off the production line; *Th* **Macbeth sort** exit Macbeth; *Fin* **s. au tirage** (*d'obligations*) to be drawn; *Scol* **cette question est sortie (à l'examen)** this question came up (in the examination); *Cartes* **le dix de carreau est sorti** the ten of diamonds turned up

(b) (*d'un cavalier*) to ride out; (*d'un conducteur, d'un véhicule*) to drive out; (*d'un capitaine de navire*) to sail out; **nous ne sommes pas beaucoup sortis en mer cet été** we didn't get out on the boat much this summer

(c) (*avec complément de manière*) **s. en courant/en dansant** to run/dance out; **s. précipitamment** *ou* **à la hâte** *ou* **en toute hâte** to hurry out; **s. furtivement** *ou* **à pas de loup** to steal *or* creep out

(d) (*des fleurs*) to come out; (*d'une plante*) to come up, to spring up; **ses dents commencent à s.** (*d'un bébé*) his teeth are beginning to come through

(e) **sortir de** (*quitter*) (*collège, port, bureau, emploi etc*) to leave; (*voiture*) to get out of; (*enfance, brume, obscurité*) to emerge from; **je sors du collège/de table** I have just left school/the table; **il sort d'ici** he has just left; **je sortais de chez toi quand …** I was just leaving your house when …; **je ne savais pas comment le faire s. du bureau** I didn't know how to get him out of the office; **on sortait de l'hiver** winter was just over; **s. de la salle** to go/come out of the room, to leave the room; **s. de son lit** to get out of bed; *Méd* to leave one's bed; (*d'une rivière*) to overflow its banks; **il est à peine sorti de l'enfance** he's little more than a child; **s. indemne d'un accident** to come out of an accident unscathed; **sortira-t-elle blanchie de ce scandale?** will she come out of this scandal with her name cleared?; **s. de sa froideur habituelle** to show unusual warmth; **cela lui a permis de s. de soi** it brought him out of himself

(f) *Arch, F* **s. de faire qch** to have just done sth; *Arg* **merci bien! je sors d'en prendre** no thank you! once is enough

(g) (*quitter la maison*) to go out; **Madame Dupont est sortie** Mrs Dupont is out *or* has gone out; **elle est sortie à trois heures** she went out at three o'clock; **il ne sort pas de chez moi** he practically lives at my place; **je ne sors pas de chez moi** I don't go out, I don't leave the house; **tu devrais s. un peu plus** you should get out (of the house) a bit more; **s. faire des courses** to go out shopping; **s. acheter du pain** to go out to buy bread; **s. à cheval/à pied** to go out riding/walking; **faire s. le chien** to let the dog out

(h) (*pour s'amuser*) to go out; **ils sortent tous les samedis soir** they go out every Saturday evening; **s. avec qn** (*en amis*) to go out with sb; (*avoir une relation amoureuse avec*) to be going out with sb; **ils sortent ensemble depuis deux ans** they've been going out together *or* with each other for two years; *Fig* **tu n'as pas entendu parler de ce film? mais il faut s. un peu!** you haven't heard of this film? what planet have you been on?

(i) **s. de** (*s'écarter de*) (*son devoir etc*) to swerve *or* deviate from; **s. de son sujet** to deviate *or* wander from one's subject; **cela sort de ma compétence** that doesn't come within my scope; **s. des bornes de la bienséance** to overstep the bounds of decency; **s. d'une règle** to ignore *or* depart from a rule; (*transgresser*) to break a rule; **s. des rails** (*d'un train*) to jump the rails; **la voiture est sortie de la route** the car left the road; *Fig* **il ne sort pas de là, il n'en sort pas** he is sticking to his guns; **ça sort de l'ordinaire** that's out of the ordinary; **s. de cadence** (*d'un danseur*) to be *or* get out of step; *Mus* **s. de mesure** to be *or* get out of time; **s. du ton** to be *or* get out of tune

(j) **s. de** (*échapper à*) (*difficulté, danger*) to get out of, to extricate oneself from; **aider qn à s. d'une difficulté** to help sb out (of a difficulty); **s. d'affaire** to get out of trouble; **soyez plus précis ou nous n'en sortirons pas** be more precise or we shall never get to the end of it; **on n'en sort pas!** there's no end to it!; **j'ai trop à faire, je n'en sors pas** I've too much to do, I shall never get through it *or* to the end of it

(k) **s. de** (*être issu de*) (*bonne famille etc*) to come from; **ce livre sort de ma plume** this book is one of mine; **s. de l'université** to graduate (from university); **cheval sorti d'un bon haras** horse (that comes) from a good stud *or* stable

(l) (*dépasser, être en relief*) to stand out, to stick out, to protrude (**de** from); **yeux qui sortent de la tête** protruding *or* bulging eyes; **les yeux lui sortaient de la tête** his eyes were popping out of his head; **son portefeuille sortait de sa poche** his wallet was sticking out of his pocket

(m) (*d'une silhouette sur une photo, d'une pensée, d'une caractéristique etc*) to stand out, to be prominent; **faire s. un trait de caractère/un rôle** to emphasize a characteristic/a part

(n) *Ordinat* **s. (d'un système)** to exit (from a system); **s. sans sauvegarder** to exit without saving

2 *vt* (*aux* **avoir**) **(a)** (*mener dehors*) (*enfant, chien etc*) to take out; **s. la voiture** to get the car out; **sortez-la!** get her out (of here)!; **cela nous sortira de l'ordinaire** that will make a change; **il faut le s. d'affaire/de ce mauvais pas** I/we'll *etc* have to get him out of this mess/fix

(b) *(tirer)* *(objet)* to take out; **s. les mains de ses poches** to take one's hands out of one's pockets; **et si tu sortais ton bon whisky/tes photos de mariage?** how about getting out your good whisky/your wedding photographs?; **il sortit sa pipe** he brought out *or* took out *or* got out his pipe; **s. ses griffes** to unsheathe its claws; **s. ses cornes** *(d'un escargot)* to put out its horns; **s. un livre de la bibliothèque** to take a book out of the library; *Typ* **s. une ligne** *(dans la marge)* to run out a line

(c) *(mettre sur le marché)* *(livre)* to bring out, to publish; *(journal)* to bring out; *(film, disque)* to bring out, to release; *esp Ordinat* **s. sur le marché** to ship

(d) *F (raconter)* **il nous en a sorti une bien bonne** he came out with a good one; **tu sais ce qu'il m'a sorti?** do you know what he came out with?; **elle m'a sorti qu'elle y avait pensé avant moi!** she had the cheek to tell me she'd thought of it before me!

(e) *Ordinat* to output

3 se sortir *vpr* **se s. d'une situation difficile** to get out of *or* extricate oneself from a difficult situation; **elle aura du mal à se s. de là toute seule** she'll have trouble getting out of that on her own; **le malade s'en sortira** the patient will pull through; **je crois que je ne vais pas m'en s.** I don't think I'll be able to cope *or* manage; **je ne m'en serais jamais sorti sans toi** I'd never have done it *or* managed without you; **tu t'en es bien sorti, pour une première tentative** you did very well considering it was your first attempt

sortir² *nm* **au s. du cinéma** on coming out of the cinema; **au s. de l'école** when they/we/*etc* come/came out of school; *(pour toujours)* on leaving school; **au s. de la table** at the end of the meal, when we/they/*etc* got up *or* get up from the table; **au s. de l'hiver/de la réunion** at the end of the winter/the meeting

sortir³ *vt (conj like* **finir***)* *(used only in third person)*, *Jur* **cette sentence sortira son plein (et entier) effet** this decision shall have full effect

S.O.S [ɛsoɛs] *nm Av, Naut, Fig* SOS; **envoyer** *ou* **lancer un S.** to send (out) an SOS (**à** to)

sosie [sɔzi] *nm (personne)* double; **on dirait ton s.** he/she is your double; **c'est vraiment le s. de son père** he really is the double of *or* the spitting image of his father

sot, sotte [so, sɔt] **1** *adj (personne, réponse, projet etc)* silly, stupid, foolish **2** *n* fool, idiot; *Hist Th* fool

sotie [sɔti] *nf Hist Th* (medieval) farce

sot-l'y-laisse [solilɛs] *nm inv Culin (du poulet)* oyster

sotte [sɔt] *adj voir* **sot**

sottement [sɔtmɑ̃] *adv* stupidly, foolishly

sottise [sɔtiz] *nf* (a) *(stupidité)* stupidity, silliness, foolishness; **cette fille est d'une s. rare** that girl is exceptionally stupid; **je n'ai jamais rencontré une telle s. chez quiconque** I've never met anyone so stupid (b) *(action stupide)* foolish *or* stupid act; *(parole stupide)* foolish *or* stupid remark; **faire des sottises** to do foolish *or* stupid things; *(d'un enfant)* to be naughty; **dire des sottises** to say foolish *or* stupid things, to talk nonsense; **ai-je dit une s.?** have I said something stupid? (c) *Vieilli (parole injurieuse)* offensive remark, insult; **dire des sottises à qn** to abuse sb

sottisier [sɔtizje] *nm* collection of howlers

sou [su] *nm* (a) **amasser une fortune s. par s.** to scrape a fortune together; **un s. est un s.** every penny counts; **payer s. à s.** to pay in small instalments; **donne un s. au petit** give the lad some coppers; **ne pas avoir** *ou* **être sans le s.** to be penniless; **je n'ai pas le s.** I don't have a penny; *Vieilli* **cela vaut cent mille francs comme un s.** it's worth a hundred thousand francs if it's worth a penny; **affaire de quatre sous** *Br* twopenny-halfpenny business, *Am* nickel-and-dime business; **il n'est pas ambitieux pour deux sous** *ou* **pour un s.** he hasn't an ounce of ambition, he's not in the least ambitious; **il n'a pas pour deux sous de courage** he hasn't an ounce of courage; **elle n'est pas méchante pour deux sous** *ou* **pour un s.** she hasn't got a nasty bone in her body; *F* **s'ennuyer à cent sous de l'heure** to be bored stiff *or* bored out of one's mind; **il est toujours en train de compter ses sous** he watches every last penny, he's always counting every penny; **je te l'achèterais si j'avais des sous** I'd buy it for you if I had the money; **c'est une affaire de gros sous** there's big money involved; **être près de ses sous** to count every penny, to be a penny-pincher; **ils veulent des sous, toujours des sous!** all they want is money for this and money for that!; **appareil** *ou* **machine à sous** slot machine; *(jeu)* one-armed bandit, *Br* fruit machine

(b) *Can (cent)* cent

(c) *Hist (pièce de cinq centimes)* sou; *Arch* **pièce de cent sous** five-franc piece

souahéli [swaheli], **souahili** [swahili] **1** *adj* Swahili **2** *nm Ling* Swahili

soubassement [subasmɑ̃] *nm* (a) *Archit (d'un bâtiment)* base, basement; *Fig* **le s. social** the social substructure (b) *Tech (d'une machine-outil etc)* base (plate) (c) *Géol* bedrock (d) *Aut* sub-frame, under-structure, underbody frame; **s. de châssis** underframe

soubresaut [subrəso] *nm (d'un véhicule)* jolt; *(d'une personne)* start, jerk; **avoir un s.** to jump, to give a start

soubrette [subrɛt] *nf Th* soubrette, maidservant; *F (servante coquette)* soubrette

souche [suʃ] *nf* (a) *(d'un arbre)* stump; *(du vin)* stock; *F* **rester comme une s.** to be rooted to the spot; **dormir comme une s.** to sleep like a log (b) *(de famille)* founder; **faire s.** to found a line; **il vient de bonne s.** he comes from good stock; **famille de vieille s.** an old family (c) *(d'un virus etc)* strain (d) *Com (de chèques, de tickets etc)* counterfoil, stub; **carnet de tickets à s.** book of tickets with counterfoils (e) *(d'une cheminée)* stack (f) *Ling* root; **mot s.** root word

souci¹ [susi] *nm Bot* marigold; **s. d'eau** marsh marigold

souci² *nm* (a) *(soin)* concern (**de** for); **avoir le s. de plaire** to be anxious to please; **avoir le s. de la vérité/de l'exactitude** to be meticulously truthful/accurate; **je me suis limité à deux auteurs dans un s. de clarté** I limited myself to two authors in order to keep things clear; **c'est le moindre** *ou* **le dernier** *ou* **le cadet de mes soucis** that's the least of my worries

(b) *(inquiétude)* worry, anxiety; **elle doit avoir des soucis** she must have problems; **sans s., libre de soucis** carefree, free from worry *or* anxiety; **cet enfant est un perpétuel s.** this child is a perpetual (source of) worry; *F* **il nous fait bien du s.** he worries us a lot, he gives us a lot of worry; **se faire du s.** to worry (**pour qch** about sth); **inutile de te faire du s. pour ça, ce n'est rien** there's no point worrying about that, it's nothing; **soucis d'argent** *ou* **financiers** money *or* financial troubles *or* worries

soucier [susje] *(impf, pr sub* **n. souciions, v. souciiez***)* **1** *vt Arch (d'une chose) (qn)* to trouble, to worry **2 se soucier** *vpr* **se s. de qn/de qch/de faire qch** to worry *or* be concerned about sb/sth/doing sth; **il se soucie toujours des autres** he is always worrying about other people; **ne se s. de rien** not to worry about anything; **pars en vacances et ne te s. de rien** go on holiday and don't worry about a thing; *F* **je m'en soucie comme de l'an quarante** *ou* **de ma première chemise** I don't give a damn (about it)

soucieux, -ieuse [susjø, -jøz] *adj* (a) *(attentif)* anxious, concerned (**de** about); **être s. de faire qch** to be anxious to do sth; **elle a toujours été soucieuse de ne pas les décevoir** she has always been anxious not to let them down; **peu s.** unconcerned (**de** about); **peu s. de la rencontrer** unconcerned about meeting her (b) *(inquiète)* anxious, worried, concerned; **avoir un air s.** to look anxious *or* worried *or* concerned

soucoupe [sukup] *nf* saucer; *Fig F* **elle a ouvert** *ou* **fait des yeux comme des soucoupes** her eyes were as big as saucers

▶ **soucoupe: s. volante** flying saucer

soudage [sudaʒ] *nm* soldering; **s. (autogène)** *(de pièces en métal etc)* welding

soudain [sudɛ̃] **1** *adj* sudden **2** *adv* suddenly, all of a sudden; **s. elle se mit à hurler** all of a sudden, she started to scream, she suddenly started to scream

soudainement [sudɛnmɑ̃] *adv* suddenly

soudaineté [sudɛnte] *nf* suddenness

Soudan (le) [ləsudɑ̃] *nm* the Sudan

soudanais, -aise [sudanɛ, -ɛz] **1** *adj* Sudanese **2** *n* **S.** Sudanese

soudant [sudɑ̃] *adj Métal* **blanc s.** welding heat

soudard [sudar] *nm Litt Péj* brutish soldier

soude [sud] *nf* (a) *Bot* saltwort, (prickly) glasswort (b) *Ch, Ind* soda; **(carbonate de) s., cristaux de s., s. ordinaire** washing *or* common soda; **bicarbonate de s.** bicarbonate of soda; **s. caustique** caustic soda

souder [sude] **1** *vt* (a) *(avec alliage fusible)* to solder; **s. au cuivre** *ou* **au laiton** to braze; **s. à l'étain** to soft-solder (b) *(autogène)* to weld; **s. à l'arc (électrique)** to arc-weld; **machine à s.** welding machine, welder; **s. par points** to spot-weld (c) *(unir)* *(os fracturé)* to knit, to join; *Fig (groupes etc)* to unite; **cette épreuve nous a soudés** this hardship united us *or* brought us together **2 se souder** *vpr (des os)* to knit (together), to join; *Fig (d'un groupe)* to unite

soudeur, -euse [sudœr, -øz] **1** *n (personne)* *(employant la soudure par alliage)* solderer; *(employant la soudure autogène)* welder; **s. par points** spot-welder; **s. au chalumeau** lamp *or* torch welder **2** *nf* **soudeuse** *(machine)* welder, welding machine; **s. par points** spot-welder

soudoyer [sudwaje] *vt* (**je soudoie, n. soudoyons; je soudoierai**) (a) *Péj (qn)* to bribe; **s. qn pour qu'il fasse qch** to bribe sb into doing sth; **il n'accepterait jamais de se faire s.**

he would never accept a bribe; **s. un assassin** to hire a killer **(b)** *Mil Arch* *(mercenaire)* to pay

soudure [sudyr] *nf* **(a)** *(opération)* *(par alliage)* soldering; *(autogène)* welding; **s. au cuivre** *ou* **au laiton** brazing; **s. à l'étain** soft-soldering; **s. par point** spot weld **(b)** *(lieu)* soldered joint; *(autogène)* weld; **s. à nœud** wipe(d) joint; **sans soudure(s)** seamless; **la s. ne se voit pas du tout** you can't see the join *or* weld at all **(c)** *(alliage)* solder **(d)** *(d'os)* join **(e)** *Écon* **faire la s.** to bridge the gap; *Fig* **faire la s. entre deux directeurs/systèmes** to bridge the gap between two directors/systems; **c'est moi qui fait la s.** I'm filling in (in the meantime); **elle fera la s. entre les deux directeurs** she'll be acting manager

soufflage [suflaʒ] *nm* **(a)** *(de verre)* glass blowing **(b)** *Métal* blowing

soufflant, -ante [suflɑ̃, -ɑ̃t] **1** *adj* **(a)** *Tech* blowing; **machine soufflante** blowing *or* blast engine **(b)** *F* *(étonnant)* breathtaking **2** *nf Tech* **soufflante** blower, fan; **soufflante de sustentation** *(d'un aéroglisseur)* lift fan; *Aut etc* **soufflante de suralimentation** supercharger

soufflard [suflar] *nm Géol* fumarole

souffle [sufl] *nm* **(a)** *(d'air, de vent)* breath, puff; **pas un s. de vent** not a breath of air

(b) *(respiration)* breathing; *(de coureur etc)* breath, wind; *(air respiré)* breath; *(air expiré)* blow, puff; **retenir son s.** to hold one's breath; **éteindre une chandelle d'un (seul) s.** to blow out a candle; **on la renverserait d'un s.** you could knock her over with a feather; **couper le s. à qn** to take sb's breath away; **le s. vital** *ou* **de la vie** the breath of life; **être à bout de s.** to be out of breath *or* winded; *Fig* to be unable to go on, *F* to have run out of steam; **l'économie est à bout de s.** the economy is running out of steam *or* is on its last legs; **manquer de s., avoir le s. court** to be short of breath *or* short-winded; **reprendre son s.** to get one's breath back; **exhaler son dernier s.** to breathe one's last; **n'avoir plus de s.** to be out of breath; **sa vie ne tient qu'à un s.** his life hangs by a thread; *Fig* **second s. de l'économie** new lease of life for the economy; *F* **c'est à vous couper le s.** it's breathtaking; *F* **il ne manque pas de s.!** *(culot)* he's got a cheek *or* a nerve!

(c) *(d'une explosion)* blast

(d) *Av* *(d'hélices)* slipstream, wash

(e) *Méd* **(bruit de) s.** murmur; **s. au cœur** *ou* **cardiaque** heart murmur

(f) *(force créatrice)* inspiration; **s. poétique** poetic inspiration

soufflé [sufle] **1** *adj* *(visage)* puffy, puffed up; *Culin* *(omelette, pommes de terre etc)* soufflé; *F* *(ahuri)* amazed, taken aback **2** *nm Culin* soufflé; **s. au fromage/au chocolat** cheese/chocolate soufflé; **moule à soufflés** soufflé dish

soufflement [sufləmɑ̃] *nm* blowing

souffler [sufle] **1** *vi* **(a)** *(en expulsant de l'air)* to blow; *(d'un taureau, d'un buffle)* to snort; **s. dans ses doigts** to blow on one's fingers; **si la soupe est trop chaude, souffle!** if the soup's too hot, blow on it!; **s. dans une trompette** to blow a trumpet; *Fig F* **tu peux s. dessus** you haven't a chance!; *Fig F* **si tu crois que ça va marcher en soufflant dessus, tu te trompes** if you think it's going to work just like that, you're mistaken

(b) *(reprendre son souffle)* to get one's breath back; **laisser s. un cheval** to let a horse get its wind, to give a horse a breather; **elle ne nous a pas laissé s.** *(entre deux tâches etc)* she didn't give us time to get our breath back; *(de toute la journée)* she didn't give us time to draw breath *or* to catch our breath

(c) *(respirer avec peine)* to pant, to puff; **suant et soufflant** huffing and puffing, puffing and blowing; *Fig F* **s. comme un bœuf** to puff and pant

(d) *(du vent etc)* to blow; **le vent va s. fort cette nuit** it will be very windy tonight; *Fig* **regarder** *ou* **voir d'où vient** *ou* **de quel côté souffle le vent** to see which way the wind is blowing, to see which way the land lies; *Fig* **un vent de révolte soufflait** there was a spirit of revolt in the air

(e) *surtout Scol* *(à ses camarades)* to prompt; **on ne souffle pas!** no prompting!

(f) *(aux dames)* to take; **s. n'est pas jouer** taking a piece doesn't count as a go

2 *vt* **(a)** *(verre)* to blow; *(ballon etc)* to blow up

(b) *(fumée, poussière etc)* to blow **(dans** into); *(orgue)* to blow; *(bougie)* to blow out

(c) *(chuchoter)* to whisper **(à qn** to sb); **s. qch à l'oreille de qn** to whisper sth in sb's ear; **ne pas s. (un) mot** not to breathe a word; **s. (son rôle à) un acteur** to prompt an actor; **quelqu'un a dû lui s. l'idée** someone must have given him the idea

(d) *F* *(prendre)* to pinch **(à qn** from sb); **se faire s. sa place** to have one's seat pinched; **s. un pion** *(aux dames)* to huff a man

(e) *(d'une explosion)* *(bâtiment etc)* to blast

(f) *F* *(ahurir)* **s. qn** to amaze sb, to take sb aback; **son culot nous a soufflés** his cheek took our breath away

soufflerie [sufləri] *nf* **(a)** *(d'un orgue, d'une forge)* bellows **(b)** *Ind* blower **(c)** *Av, Phys* wind tunnel; **essais en s.** wind-tunnel tests

soufflet [suflɛ] *nm* **(a)** [①A10,e] *(instrument)* (pair of) bellows **(b)** **valise à soufflets** expanding suitcase **(c)** *Rail* *(entre les voitures)* concertina vestibule **(d)** *Couture* gusset **(e)** *Mus* *(d'un orgue)* swell **(f)** *Litt* *(gifle)* slap (in the face); *(insulte)* insult **(g)** *Aut* gaiter

souffleter [sufləte] *vt* **(je soufflette, n. souffletons; je souffletterai)** *Litt Vieilli* **s. qn** *(le gifler)* to slap sb's face; *(l'insulter)* to insult sb

souffleur, -euse [suflœr, -øz] **1** *n* **s. de verre** glass blower **2** *nf* **souffleuse (a)** *Can* *(chasse-neige)* snowblower **(b)** *Agr* *(pour les graines etc)* blower container **3** *n Th* prompter

soufflure [suflyr] *nf* *(dans la peinture, le verre, le métal)* blister, bubble; *(dans un pneu)* bulge

souffrance [sufrɑ̃s] *nf* **(a)** **en s.** *(travail)* pending; *(candidats)* on the waiting list; *(factures)* overdue, outstanding; *(colis)* held up in transit, awaiting delivery **(b)** *(douleur)* suffering, pain; **s. physique/morale** physical/mental suffering *or* pain; **rien ne pouvait apaiser ses souffrances** nothing could alleviate his suffering

souffrant [sufrɑ̃] *adj* **(a)** *(un peu malade)* unwell, poorly; **il a l'air s.** he doesn't look well **(b)** *Litt* *(qui souffre)* suffering; **l'humanité souffrante** suffering humanity

souffre-douleur *nm inv* laughing stock, butt (of the joke); **c'est le s. du lycée** he's the laughing stock of the school

souffreteux, -euse [sufrətø, -øz] *adj* *(enfant etc)* sickly

souffrir [sufrir] *(prp* **souffrant**; *pp* **souffert**; *pr ind* **je souffre, il souffre, n. souffrons, ils souffrent**; *impf* **je souffrais**; *p hist* **je souffris**; *fu* **je souffrirai) 1** *vt* **(a)** *(supporter)* *(douleur, fatigue, froid, perte, insulte etc)* to suffer, to endure; **s. le martyre** to go through torture *or* agonies; **je ne peux pas s. qu'on vienne me déranger** I cannot bear to be disturbed, I cannot stand being disturbed; *F* **je ne peux pas s. cet homme/cette odeur** I can't bear *or* stand that man/smell

(b) *(permettre)* to permit, to allow; **je ne saurais s. cela** I cannot permit *or* allow that; **souffrez que je vous dise la vérité** allow *or* permit me to tell you the truth; **situation qui ne souffre aucun retard** situation that admits of no delay; **s. l'étalon** *(d'une jument)* to take the stallion

2 *vi* **(a)** *(physiquement)* to be in pain, to suffer; *(moralement)* to suffer; **mon bras me fait s.** my arm is hurting (me) *or* giving me pain; **il m'a fait s.** *(physiquement, sentimentalement)* he hurt me; **s. du froid/des maux de tête** to suffer from the cold/from headaches; **s. de la jambe** to have trouble with one's leg; **je souffre de le voir si changé** it pains *or* upsets me to see him so changed; **je souffre à marcher** I find walking painful; **avoir cessé de s.** to be out of pain

(b) *(pâtir)* to suffer **(de** from); **les vignes ont souffert de la gelée** the vines have suffered from the frost; **nous avons beaucoup souffert de la guerre** we suffered a lot in the war, we were hard hit by the war

3 se souffrir *vpr F* *(se supporter)* **ils ne peuvent pas se s.** they can't stand each other

soufi [sufi] *Rel* **1** *adj inv* Sufic **2** *nm* Sufi

soufisme [sufism] *nm Rel* Sufism

soufrage [sufraʒ] *nf* *(des allumettes, des plantes etc)* sulphuring, *US* sulfuring; *Tex* sulphuration, *US* sulfuration

soufre [sufr] **1** *nm* sulphur, *US* sulfur; *Fig* **ces écrits sentent le s.** these writings smack *or* reek of heresy **2** *adj inv* **s. (jaune)** sulphur *or US* sulfur yellow

soufré [sufre] *nm* *(papillon)* brimstone

soufrer [sufre] *vt* *(allumettes, plantes etc)* to sulphur, *US* to sulfur; *Tex* to sulphurate, *US* to sulfurate

souhait [swɛ] *nm* [①A58,d,iv; B37,K,4] wish; **faire** *ou* **formuler un s.** to make a wish; **présenter ses souhaits à qn** to offer sb one's good wishes; **présenter ses souhaits de bonne année** to wish sb a Happy New Year; **à s.** perfectly; **doré/ensoleillé à s.** beautifully golden/sunny; **j'ai fini par trouver une pièce silencieuse à s.** I finally found a room that was as quiet as I could wish; **à vos souhaits!** *(à qn qui éternue)* bless you!

souhaitable [swɛtabl] *adj* desirable; **il est s. que ... +** *sub* it is to be hoped that ...; **ce n'est guère s.** one can hardly wish for that; **il serait s. que ...** it would be desirable if ...

souhaiter [swete] *vt* *(succès etc)* to wish for; **je vous souhaite d'être pleinement heureux** I wish you every happiness; **je souhaite qu'on me tienne au courant** I wish to be kept informed; **je souhaite que vous réussissiez, je vous souhaite de réussir** I hope you will succeed; **s. la réussite/bon voyage à qn** to wish sb success/bon voyage; **je vous souhaite une bonne année/un joyeux anniversaire** best wishes for a happy New Year/a happy birthday; **s. bonne chance à qn** to wish sb (good) luck; *F Iron* **je vous souhaite bien du plaisir!, je vous en souhaite!** I wish you joy of it!; **cela n'est pas à s.** that is not very desirable; **il est à s. que ... +** *sub* it is to be hoped that ...; **je ne le souhaite à personne** I wouldn't wish that on anyone

souiller [suje] *vt* **(a)** (*vêtements etc*) to soil, to dirty (**de** with); **vêtements souillés de boue** mudstained clothes **(b)** *Fig* (*contaminer*) to taint; **s. ses mains de sang** to stain one's hands with blood **(c)** *Litt* (*réputation, souvenir de qn etc*) to tarnish

souillon [sujɔ̃] *nf Litt* slut, sloven; (*servante*) slovenly maid

souillure [sujyr] *nf* (*sur un vêtement etc*) stain, *Litt* blot, blemish

souk [suk] *nm* (*marché*) souk; *F* (*lieu en désordre*) shambles; **c'est le s., dans cette chambre!** what a shambles this bedroom is!

soul [sul] *adj inv, nf Mus* soul

soûl [su] **1** *adj* **(a)** *F* (*ivre*) drunk; **s. comme un Polonais** *ou* **comme un cochon** *ou* **comme une bourrique** drunk as a lord; **s. perdu** blind drunk **(b)** *Arch* (*rassasié*) replete, *Litt* **être s. de plaisir/de musique** to have had a surfeit of pleasure/music, to be sated with pleasure/music **2** *nm* **rire/chanter/fumer tout son s.** to laugh/sing/smoke to one's heart's content; **manger/boire tout son s.** to eat/drink one's fill *or* to one's heart's content

soulagement [sulaʒmɑ̃] *nm* relief; **éprouver un sentiment de s.** to feel relieved; **son départ sera un s. pour tous** his departure will come as a relief to all; **pousser un soupir de s.** to heave a sigh of relief

soulager [sulaʒe] **(je soulageai(s); n. soulageons) 1** *vt* (*pression, douleur*) to ease, to relieve; (*esprit, chagrin*) to soothe, to comfort; (*qn*) to relieve; **je vais vous faire une piqûre, ça va vous s.** I'm going to give you an injection which will bring you relief *or* make you feel better; **traitement qui soulage les douleurs** treatment for pain relief; **si ça peut te s., sache que je suis dans la même situation** if it makes you feel any better, I'm in the same situation; **s. les pauvres** to relieve the poor; **je suis soulagé de l'apprendre** I'm relieved to hear it; **on soulage ses maux à les raconter** it is a relief *or* a comfort *or* it helps to talk about one's troubles; **s. une poutre** to ease the strain on a beam; **s. les soupapes** to blow off steam; **cela me soulage l'esprit d'un grand poids** that's a great weight off my mind; *F* **s. qn de son portefeuille** to relieve sb of his wallet

2 se soulager *vpr* **(a)** (*en parlant etc*) to ease one's mind

(b) *F* (*satisfaire un besoin naturel*) to relieve oneself

soûlant [sulɑ̃] *adj F* (*personne*) boring, tiresome

soûlard, -e [sular, -ard], **soûlaud, -e** [sulo, -od] *n très F* boozer, wino, *Br* piss artist

soûler [sule] **1** *vt* **(a)** *F* (*enivrer*) **s. qn** to get *or* make sb drunk; *Fig* (*d'un parfum, du succès, d'idées etc*) to go to sb's head **(b)** *F* (*ennuyer*) **s. qn** to bore sb silly **2 se soûler** *vpr F* (*s'enivrer*) to get drunk; *Arg* **se s. la gueule** to get pissed *or* wasted; *Fig* **se s. de paroles** to get drunk on *or* with the sound of one's own voice

soûlerie [sulri] *nf F* **(a)** (*beuverie*) drinking session *or* spree, bender **(b)** (*ivresse*) drunkenness

soulèvement [sulɛvmɑ̃] *nm* **(a)** (*de terrain, de l'estomac*) rising, heaving; **s. de cœur** nausea **(b)** *Géol* upheaval, upthrust **(c)** (*révolte*) revolt, uprising

soulever [sulve] **(je soulève, n. soulevons; je soulèverai) 1** *vt* **(a)** (*charge, malade, couvercle etc*) to lift (up), to raise; **c'est trop lourd, je n'arrive pas à le s.** it's too heavy, I can't lift it; **s. un rideau** to raise a curtain; **la voiture soulevait de la poussière** the car raised *or* threw up dust; *Fig* **cette odeur me soulève le cœur** this smell makes me feel sick *or* turns my stomach

(b) (*doutes, question, objection*) to raise, to bring up; **cette question mérite en effet d'être soulevée** this question deserves to be raised *or* brought up

(c) (*population en révolte*) to rouse, to stir up

(d) (*passion, enthousiasme, indignation*) to excite, to provoke, to arouse; **sa déclaration souleva un tonnerre d'applaudissements** her announcement met with thunderous applause

(e) *F* (*voler*) to steal, *F* to lift

2 se soulever *vpr* **(a)** (*être levé*) to rise; (*de la mer, Fig de l'estomac*) to heave; **sa jupe se soulevait au moindre souffle de vent** the slighest puff of wind blew her skirt up; **chaque fois que le vent soufflait, le rideau se soulevait légèrement** the curtain moved every time the wind blew; *Fig* **mon cœur se soulève chaque fois que j'y pense** I feel sick every time I think about it

(b) (*se lever*) to raise *or* lift oneself up

(c) (*se révolter*) to revolt, to rise up

soulier [sulje] *nm* shoe; **souliers de marche** walking shoes; **souliers vernis** patent (leather) shoes; *Fig F* **être dans ses petits souliers** to feel awkward

soulignage [suliɲaʒ], **soulignement** [suliɲ(ə)mɑ̃] *nm* underlining

souligné [suliɲe] *nm* underline, underscore; **double s.** double underline; **s. pointillé** with dotted underlining

souligner [suliɲe] *vt* **(a)** (*d'un trait*) (*mot, passage etc*) to underline; **s. ses yeux d'un trait de noir** to outline *or* emphasize one's eyes with black eyeliner; **coupe qui souligne la taille** a cut which emphasizes the waist **(b)** *Fig* (*mot, fait etc*) to emphasize; (*importance etc*) to underline, to emphasize; **s. que ...** to emphasize that ...

soûlographie [sulɔgrafi] *nf F* drunkenness

soumettre [sumɛtr] (*conj like* **mettre**) **1** *vt* **(a)** (*population, pays, passions*) to subdue

(b) (*question, demande*) to refer, to submit (**à qn** to sb); **s. ses projets à qn** to submit *or* lay one's plans before sb; **s. un rapport** to submit a report; **s. une lettre à la signature** to present a letter for signature

(c) (*à un examen etc*) to subject (**à** to); **s. qn à une épreuve** to put sb through a test; **être soumis à des règles strictes** to be bound by strict rules; **s. à l'impôt** to subject to tax; **s. les revenus à l'impôt** to make income subject *or* liable to tax; **s. un malade à un régime strict** to put a patient on a strict diet

2 se soumettre *vpr* (*obéir*) to submit; **se s. à** (*autorité*) to submit to; (*souhaits*) to comply with; (*loi, décision*) to abide by

soumis [sumi] *adj* **(a)** (*docile*) submissive, obedient **(b)** (*à une loi, une autorité etc*) subject (**à** to); (*à un impôt*) liable, subject (**à** to); **s. aux droits de douane** subject to customs duty; **non s.** unconquered; *Arch* **fille soumise** registered prostitute

soumission [sumisjɔ̃] *nf* **(a)** (*à une loi, une autorité etc*) submission (**à** to); **faire (sa) s.** to surrender, to yield **(b)** (*docilité*) obedience, submissiveness (**à** to) **(c)** *Com* tender, bid; **faire une s. pour un travail** to tender for a job; *Com* **s. cachetée** sealed bid

soumissionnaire [sumisjɔnɛr] *n Com* tenderer

soumissionner [sumisjɔne] *vt Com* (*travail*) to tender for

soupape [supap] *nf Tech* valve; *Tech, Fig* **s. de sûreté** safety valve; **s. d'admission** *ou* **d'alimentation** *ou* **d'arrivée** inlet *or* induction *or* intake valve; **s. d'échappement** *ou* **de décharge** outlet *or* exhaust valve; **s. à flotteur** ballcock; *Aut* **soupapes en tête** *ou* **en chandelle** overhead valves; *Aut* **soupapes latérales** *ou* **en chapelle** side valves

soupçon [supsɔ̃] *nm* **(a)** (*suspicion*) suspicion; **s'exposer aux soupçons** to lay oneself open to suspicion; **devenir l'objet des soupçons** to fall under suspicion; **éveiller/endormir les soupçons** to arouse/allay suspicion; **avoir des soupçons sur qn** to have one's suspicions about sb, to feel *or* be suspicious about sb; **j'en avais le s.!** I thought so *or* as much!, I suspected as much!; **il est au-dessus de tout s.** he is above suspicion; **arrêter qn sur un s.** to arrest sb on suspicion

(b) (*idée*) suspicion, idea, notion; **je n'en avais pas le moindre s.** I didn't have the slightest suspicion, I never suspected it for a moment

(c) (*faible quantité*) (*de vinaigre, d'ail etc*) dash, hint; (*de fièvre, de fard, d'ironie etc*) touch; (*de vin*) drop

soupçonnable [supsɔnabl] *adj* open to suspicion; **personne difficilement s.** person above suspicion

soupçonner [supsɔne] *vt* **(a)** (*suspecter*) to suspect; **s. qn de qch/d'avoir fait qch** to suspect sb of sth/of having done sth; **je le soupçonne de me cacher qch/de ne pas dire la vérité** I suspect he's hiding something from me/not telling the truth; **on le soupçonne de meurtre** he is suspected of murder **(b)** (*deviner*) to suspect; **je ne soupçonnais pas que ...** I had no suspicion *or* no idea that ..., I did not suspect that ...; **je soupçonne de la jalousie dans ses paroles** I suspect (there is some) jealousy in what he says

soupçonneusement [supsɔnøzmɑ̃] *adv* suspiciously

soupçonneux, -euse [supsɔnø, -øz] *adj* suspicious; **d'un air/ton s.** suspiciously

soupe [sup] *nf* **(a)** *Culin* soup; **s. aux pois/à l'oignon** pea/onion soup; *Fig F* **cracher dans la s.** to bite the hand that feeds you; *F* **gros plein de s.!** fatso!; *F* **il mange la s. à la grimace** he's in the doghouse; *F* **par ici la bonne s.!** hand over the money!; **il monte comme une s. au lait, il est très s. au lait** he flares up very easily, he's always flying off the handle **(b)** (*repas*) meal; *F* **à la s.!** grub's up!; **s. populaire**

(*lieu*) soup kitchen **(c)** *Ski F* soft snow **(d)** *Arch* (*tranche de pain*) sop, soaked slice of bread

soupente [supɑ̃t] *nf* closet, cupboard (*usually under the stairs*)

souper[1] [supe] *nm* [①A6,d,iii] **(a)** *Belg, Suisse, Can, Arch* (*dîner*) dinner, supper, evening meal **(b)** (*après le spectacle*) (late) supper

souper[2] [supe] *vi* **(a)** *Belg, Suisse, Can, Arch* (*dîner*) to have dinner *or* supper *or* one's evening meal; **nous avons soupé de pain et de fromage** we had bread and cheese for supper; *Fig F* **j'en ai soupé** I've had enough of it, I'm fed up with it **(b)** (*après le spectacle*) to have a late supper

soupeser [supəze] *vt* **(je soupèse, n. soupesons; je soupèserai)** (*qch*) to feel the weight of, to weigh in one's hand; *Fig* (*problème, argument etc*) to weigh up

soupière [supjɛr] *nf* soup tureen

soupir [supir] *nm* **(a)** sigh; **pousser un s.** to (heave a) sigh; **s. de soulagement/de découragement** sigh of relief/ discouragement; **un gros s.** a heavy *or* deep sigh; *Hum* **l'objet de ses soupirs** the object of his affections; **rendre le dernier s.** to breathe one's last **(b)** *Mus* crotchet *or Am* quarter rest; **demi s.** quaver *or Am* eighth rest; **quart de s.** semiquaver *or Am* sixteenth rest

soupirail, -aux [supiraj, -o] *nm* **(a)** (*de cave*) (cellar) ventilator **(b)** (*d'appartement en contre-bas*) basement window

soupirant [supirɑ̃] *nm Hum* suitor, admirer

soupirer [supire] *vi* to sigh; **en soupirant** with a sigh; **s. après** *ou* **pour qch** to long *or* yearn for sth

souple [supl] *adj* (*branche etc*) supple, flexible; (*corps, danseur etc*) supple, lithe; (*reliure*) limp; (*cuir*) soft, supple; (*cheveux*) manageable; *Fig* (*système, loi etc*) flexible; *Fig* (*personne*) flexible, adaptable; **avoir le poignet s.** to have supple wrists; **esprit s.** adaptable *or* versatile mind; *Aut* **moteur s.** flexible engine

souplesse [suplɛs] *nf* (*de branche*) suppleness, flexibility; (*de corps, danseur etc*) suppleness, litheness; *Fig* (*de système, règle etc*) flexibility; (*de personne*) flexibility, adaptability; (*d'esprit*) adaptability, versatility; **ça n'a pas la s. du cuir** it's not as soft *or* as supple as leather; **en s.** (*travailler, démarrer etc*) smoothly; **transition en s.** smooth transition (**entre** between)

souquenille [suknij] *nf Vieilli* smock

souquer [suke] *Naut* **1** *vt* **s. un cordage** to haul a rope taut **2** *vi* **s. dur** *ou* **ferme (sur les avirons)** to pull hard at the oars

source [surs] *nf* **(a)** (*eau*) spring; (*lieu*) (*d'une rivière*) source; **eau de s.** spring water; **s. d'eau minérale** mineral spring; **s. thermale** hot spring; **le fleuve prend sa s. dans le Massif Central** the river has its source in *or* rises in the Massif Central; *Fig F* **ça coule de s.** it's obvious; (*c'est naturel*) it's inevitable *or* natural; **s. jaillissante** gusher; **s. boueuse** mud geyser *or* volcano; *Opt etc* **s. lumineuse** light source; **s. de chaleur** heat source; *Él* **s. d'énergie** *ou* **d'alimentation** power supply

(b) *Fig* (*du mal, de richesse, d'informations etc*) source; **puiser aux sources** (*dans une étude etc*) to draw on the sources *or* source material; **s. de revenus** source of revenue; *Fin* **imposé à la s.** taxed at source; **aller à la s. du mal** to get to the root of the evil; **on a appris de s. sûre que …** we have learned from a reliable source that …; **informations de s. américaine** information from an American source; **citer ses sources** to cite one's sources; **je le tiens de bonne s.** I have it on good authority *or* from a good source; *Ordinat* **s. de données** data source; *Ordinat* **code s.** source code; **s. nommée** named source; *Ling* **langue s.** source language

sourcier, -ière [sursje, -jɛr] *n* water diviner, dowser; **baguette de s.** divining *or* dowsing rod

sourcil [sursi(l)] *nm* eyebrow; **aux sourcils épais** beetle-browed, with bushy eyebrows

sourcilier, -ière [sursilje, -jɛr] *adj Anat* superciliary

sourciller [sursije] *vi* **sans s.** without batting an eyelid, without turning a hair; **elle n'a pas sourcillé** she didn't bat an eyelid *or* turn a hair

sourcilleux, -euse [sursijø, -øz] *adj* **(a)** (*pointilleux*) fussy, finicky **(b)** *Litt* (*hautain*) haughty, supercilious

sourd, sourde [sur, surd] **1** *adj* **(a)** (*personne*) deaf; **devenir s.** to go deaf; **s. de naissance** deaf from birth; **s. d'une oreille** deaf in one ear; *F* **s. comme un pot** deaf as a post; *Fig* **rester s. aux prières de qn** to turn a deaf ear *or* to be deaf to sb's pleas

(b) (*teinte, douleur*) dull; (*bruit*) dull, muffled; (*corde*) muted; (*voix*) hollow; (*désir, lutte*) secret; (*hostilité*) veiled; *Ling* **consonne sourde** voiceless consonant

2 *n* (*personne*) deaf person; **les sourds** the deaf, deaf people; **crier comme un s.** to yell at the top of one's voice; **frapper** *ou* **taper comme un s.** to hit out wildly; **autant vaut parler à un s.** you might as well talk to a brick wall; *Prov* **il n'est pire s. que celui qui ne veut (pas) entendre** there's none so deaf as those who don't want to hear; *Iron* **il vaut mieux entendre ça que d'être s.!** I've heard it all now!; **un dialogue de sourds** a dialogue of the deaf

3 *nf Ling* **sourde** voiceless consonant

sourdement [surdəmɑ̃] *adv* **(a)** (*avec un bruit sourd*) dully, with a dull *or* hollow sound **(b)** (*en secret*) secretly

sourdine [surdin] *nf* **(a)** *Mus* mute; **en s.** softly, quietly; *Fig* (*en secret*) in secret, on the sly; **violons en s.** muted violins; **mettre une s. à ses plaintes** to tone down one's complaints; *Fig F* **mets la s.!** put a sock in it! **(b)** *Rad etc* damper

sourdingue [surdɛ̃g] *F* **1** *adj* deaf **2** *n* deaf person

sourd-muet, sourde-muette, *pl* **sourds-muets, sourdes-muettes** **1** *adj* deaf-and-dumb **2** *n* deaf mute

sourdre [surdr] *vi* (*used only in third person* **il sourd, ils sourdent** *and in inf; the past tenses are rare*) *Arch, Litt* (*de l'eau*) to spring, to rise (up); *Fig* (*d'une émotion*) to well up

souriant [surjɑ̃] *adj* (*personne*) smiling; (*climat, entourage*) pleasant

souriceau, -eaux [suriso] *nm* young mouse

souricier [surisje] *adj m, nm* **(chat) s.** mouser

souricière [surisjɛr] *nf* mousetrap; *Fig* (*piège*) trap; (*tendu par la police*) police trap

sourire[1] [surir] *vi* (*conj like* **rire**) **(a)** to smile (**à qn** at sb); **on peut difficilement en s.** it's hardly a laughing matter; **faire s.** to provoke a smile **(b)** (*plaire*) to appeal (**à qn** to sb); **cette idée ne lui sourit guère** he's not very keen on the idea, the idea doesn't really appeal to him **(c)** (*réussir*) **tout lui sourit** he makes a success of everything; **la chance lui sourit** fortune smiles on him

sourire[2] *nm* smile; **large s.** broad smile, grin; **il s'approcha, le s. aux lèvres** he came up, smiling *or* with a smile (on his lips); **adresser** *ou* **faire un s. à qn** to give sb a smile, to smile at sb; **avoir le s.** to have a smile on one's face; **garder le s.** to keep smiling

souris [suri] **1** *nf* **(a)** mouse, *pl* mice; **on aurait entendu trotter une s.** you could have heard a pin drop; **trou de s.** mousehole; *Fig* **il serait bien rentré dans un trou de s.** he would have liked the ground to open up and swallow him **(b)** *Ordinat* mouse, *pl* mice; **s. à trois boutons** three-button mouse **(c)** *Arg* (*femme*) *Br* bird, *Am* dame **(d)** *Culin* (*de l'os de gigot*) knuckle end **2** *adj inv* **(couleur) gris (de) s.** mouse grey *or US* gray

▶ **souris**: **s. blanche** white mouse; **s. d'hôtel** (female) hotel thief; *Ordinat* **s. à infrarouge** infrared *or* cordless mouse; *Ordinat* **s. optique** optical mouse; *Ordinat* **s. sans fil** cordless mouse; *Ordinat* **s. tactile** touchpad mouse

sournois, -oise [surnwa, -waz] **1** *adj* (*personne, méthode*) sly, crafty, underhand; (*regard*) sly, cunning, shifty **2** *n* sly *or* crafty *or* underhand person

sournoisement [surnwazmɑ̃] *adv* slyly

sournoiserie [surnwazri] *nf* **(a)** (*caractère*) slyness, craftiness **(b)** (*acte*) underhand trick

sous [su] *prép* **(a)** (*position*) under(neath), beneath; **s'asseoir s. un arbre** to sit down under(neath) *or* beneath a tree; **s. terre** underground, below ground; **nager s. l'eau** to swim underwater; **lettre s. enveloppe** letter in an envelope; **mettre une lettre s. pli scellé** to put a letter in a sealed envelope; **s. le sceau du secret** under pledge of secrecy; **dormir s. la tente** to sleep under canvas; **s. la pluie** in the rain; *Naut* **s. le vent** under the lee; **s. les tropiques** in the tropics; **s. l'équateur** at the equator; *Fig* **s. nos propres yeux** before our very eyes; **elle a été tuée sous les yeux de ses enfants** she was killed in front of her children; **s. cet angle** from that angle *or* point of view; **chercher un mot s. la lettre S** to look up a word under (the letter) S

(b) (*cause, action*) **s. le poids de** under the weight of; *Fig* **encore s. le choc elle répondit …** still in shock she replied …

(c) (*subordination*) under; **travailler s. les ordres de qn** to work under sb; **étudier s. la direction de qn** to study under sb; **enfant s. la responsabilité du père** child who is the responsibility of his father; **s. contrôle judiciaire** on probation; **accord passé s. conditions** conditional agreement; **s. certaines conditions** on certain conditions; **s. peine de mort** on *or* under pain of death

(d) *Méd* **je suis s. antibiotiques depuis dix jours** I've been on antibiotics for ten days; **réaliser une opération s. anesthésie** to perform an operation under anaesthetic; **il est encore s. anesthésie** he's still under the anaesthetic; **mettre qn s. anesthésie** to anaesthetize sb, to put sb under an anaesthetic

(e) (*manière*) **s. clef** under lock and key; *Mil* **être appelé s. les armes** to have been called up; *Naut* **s. pavillon anglais**

flying the English flag; **naviguer s. pavillon anglais** to sail under the English flag; **connu s. le nom de ...** known as *or* by the name of ...; **s. des dehors charmants** under a charming exterior; **s. n'importe quel prétexte** on *or* under any pretext

(f) *(époque)* under; **s. Louis XIV** under Louis XIV, in the reign of Louis XIV; **s. la IIIe République** during the Third Republic

(g) *(avant)* within; **s. trois jours** within three days; **s. huitaine** within the week; **s. peu** shortly, before long

sous- [su] *(before vowel sound* [suz]) *préf* **(a)** *(subordination, subdivision)* sub-; **s.-catégorie** subcategory **(b)** *(insuffisance)* under-; **s.-productif** underproductive; **s.-informer** to underinform **(c)** *(infériorité)* pseudo-; **s.-littérature** pseudo-literature

sous-affréter *vt (conj like* **fréter***)* *(navire etc)* to subcharter

sous-aide *n* junior assistant

sous-alimentation *nf* malnutrition, undernourishment

sous-alimenté [suzalimɑ̃te] *adj* *(personne)* underfed, undernourished

sous-bail, *pl* **sous-baux** *nm* sublease

sous-bibliothécaire *n* sub-librarian, assistant librarian

sous-bock *nm* beer mat

sous-bois *nm inv* **(a)** undergrowth, underwood **(b)** *Beaux-Arts* picture of a forest interior

sous-brigadier *nm (de police)* = deputy sergeant

sous-calibré [sukalibre] *adj Mil etc (projectile)* subcalibre

sous-capitalisé [sukapitalize] *adj* undercapitalized

sous-chaîne *nf Ordinat* substring

sous-châssis *nm inv Aut* sub-frame

sous-chef *nm* **(a)** *(de bureau)* deputy chief clerk **(b)** *(d'entreprise)* assistant manager; **s. de gare** deputy stationmaster **(c)** *Mus* deputy conductor

sous-classe *nf Biol* subclass

sous-comité *nm* subcommittee

sous-commission *nf* subcommittee

sous-compte *nm* subsidiary account, sub-account

sous-consommation *nf inv Pol, Écon* underconsumption

sous-continent *nm Géog* subcontinent

sous-correction *nf Aut* under-correction

sous-couche *nf (de peinture)* undercoat

souscripteur, -trice [suskriptœr, -tris] *n* *(de journal etc)* subscriber **(de** to); *(de chèque, d'un effet de commerce etc)* drawer; *(d'un emprunt)* subscriber, underwriter

souscription [suskripsjɔ̃] *nf* **(a)** *(à un journal etc)* subscription; **droit de s.** subscription fee **(b)** *Fin* subscription, application **(à des actions** for shares); *(d'une société)* subscribed capital **(c)** *(d'une somme d'argent)* subscription, contribution; **lancer une s.** to start a fund

souscrire [suskrir] *(conj like* **écrire***)* **1** *vt* *(abonnement, emprunt, assurance)* to take out; *(garantir)* *(risque)* to underwrite; *Vieilli (chèque etc)* to sign; *(argent pour une action charitable)* to subscribe; *Fin (actions)* to subscribe for *or* apply for

2 *vi* **s. à** *(publication etc)* to subscribe to; *Fig (opinion, projet etc)* to subscribe to, to endorse; **je souscris entièrement à votre opinion** I am entirely of your opinion; *Fin* **s. à une émission** to apply for *or* subscribe to an issue; **s. à des actions** to take up shares; **s. pour (la somme de) mille francs** to subscribe a thousand francs; **s. pour une œuvre de bienfaisance** to subscribe to a charity

sous-critique *adj Phys, Nucl etc* subcritical

sous-culture *nf* sub-culture

sous-cutané *adj* subcutaneous

sous-développé *adj* **(a)** *Écon (pays etc)* underdeveloped **(b)** *(usine etc)* underequipped

sous-développement *nm Écon* underdevelopment

sous-diacre *nm* subdeacon

sous-directeur, -trice *n* **(a)** *(de société)* assistant manager, *f* assistant manageress; *(plus haut dans la hiérarchie)* assistant director **(b)** *Scol* deputy head

sous-diviser *vt* to subdivide

sous-division *nf* subdivision

sous-document *nm Ordinat* sub-document

sous-dominante *nf Mus* subdominant

sous-dossier *nm Ordinat* subfolder

sous-économe *n* assistant treasurer *or* bursar

sous-embranchement *nf Biol* subphylum

sous-emploi *nm inv Écon* underemployment

sous-employé *adj Écon* underemployed

sous-ensemble *nm Math* subset

sous-entendre *vt* to imply; **qu'est-ce que tu sous-entends?** what are you implying *or* hinting at?; *Gram* **on sous-entend 'pendant'** 'pendant' is understood; **il est sous-entendu que** ... it is understood that ...

sous-entendu *nm* implication, *Péj* insinuation

sous-entrepreneur *nm Constr* subcontractor

sous-équipé [suzekipe] *adj Écon* underequipped

sous-équipement *nm Écon* under-equipment

sous-espace *nm Math* subspace

sous-espèce *nf Biol* subspecies

sous-estimation *nf* underestimation

sous-estimer *vt* to underestimate

sous-évaluation *nf* undervaluation

sous-évaluer *vt* to undervalue

sous-exposer *vt Phot* to underexpose

sous-exposition *nf Phot* underexposure

sous-famille *nf Biol* subfamily

sous-fifre *nm F* underling, dogsbody

sous-garde *nf* trigger guard

sous-genre *nm Biol* subgenus

sous-gouverneur *nm* deputy governor, vice-governor

sous-groupe *nm Biol, Math* subgroup

sous-homme *nm* subhuman

sous-humanité *nf* *(sous-hommes)* subhuman race; *(état)* subhuman condition

sous-ingénieur *nm Ind etc* assistant engineer

sous-inspecteur *n* assistant inspector

sous-jacent [suʒasɑ̃] *adj* underlying

Sous-le-Vent *n* **les îles S.** the Leeward Islands

sous-lieutenant *nm Mil* second lieutenant; *Naut* sub-lieutenant; *Av* **s. (aviateur)** pilot officer, *Am* second lieutenant

sous-locataire *n* subtenant

sous-location *nf* **(a)** *(par le propriétaire)* subletting; *(contrat)* sublease **(b)** *(par le locataire)* subrenting; *(contrat)* subtenancy

sous-louer *vt* **(a)** *(du propriétaire)* *(maison, appartement)* to sublet **(b)** *(du locataire)* *(maison, appartement)* to subrent

sous-main *nm inv* desk blotter, blotting pad; *Fig* **en s.** secretly

sous-maître, -maîtresse *Arch* **1** *n Scol* teacher's assistant **2** *nf* **sous-maîtresse** brothel-keeper's assistant

sous-marché *nm* sub-market

sous-marin, -e 1 *adj* *(navire, volcan etc)* submarine; *(récif)* submerged; **chasse** *ou* **pêche sous-marine** underwater fishing; **masque s.** frogman's mask **2** *nm* submarine; **s. nucléaire** nuclear(-powered) submarine; **s. de poche** pocket submarine

sous-marinier *nm* submariner

sous-marque *nf* sub-brand

sous-maxillaire *adj Anat (glandes etc)* submaxillary

sous-médiante [sumedjɑ̃t] *nf Mus* supertonic

sous-menu *nm Ordinat* submenu

Sous-ministre *nm Can Admin* Deputy Minister; **S. adjoint** Assistant Deputy Minister

sous-multiple *adj, nm Math* submultiple **(de** of)

sous-nappe *nf (de table)* undercloth

sous-œuvre (en) *adv Constr* **reprise en s.** underpinning; **reprendre un bâtiment en s.** to underpin a building

sous-off *nm Mil F* NCO, non-com

sous-officier *nm Mil* non-commissioned officer

sous-ordre *nm* **(a)** *Péj (employé)* subordinate, underling **(b)** *Biol* suborder

sous-palan (en) *adv Com, Naut* **livraison en s.** delivery ready for shipping

sous-payer *vt (conj like* **payer***)* to underpay

sous-peuplé *adj* underpopulated

sous-peuplement *nm* underpopulation

sous-pied *nm (de pantalon)* footstrap

sous-positionnement *nm Mktg* underpositioning

sous-préfectoral, -ale, -aux, -ales *adj* subprefectorial

sous-préfecture *nf* subprefecture

sous-préfet *nm Admin* subprefect

sous-préfète *nf Admin (femme)* subprefect

sous-principal, -ale, -aux, -ales *nm Scol* vice-principal

sous-production *nf Écon* underproduction

sous-produit *nm Ind etc* by-product; *Fig* poor imitation

sous-programme *nm Ordinat* subroutine, subprogram

sous-prolétaire *n* member of the underclass

sous-prolétariat *nm* underclass

sous-pull *nm* thin sweater

sous-race *nf Zool* subrace

sous-refroidissement *nm Phys* supercooling

sous-répertoire *nm Ordinat* subdirectory

sous-secrétaire *n* undersecretary; **s. (d'État)** undersecretary (of state)

sous-secrétariat *nm* undersecretaryship

sous-seing *nm Jur* private agreement *or* contract

soussigné, -ée [susiɲe] *adj, n* undersigned; **je, soussigné André Renaud, donne mon autorisation à ...** I, the undersigned, hereby authorize ...

sous-sol *nm* **(a)** *Géol* subsoil, substratum **(b)** *Constr* basement
sous-station *nf Él* substation
sous-système *nm* subsystem
sous-tasse *nf* saucer
sous-tendre *vt Géom* to subtend; *Fig* to underlie; **les principes qui sous-tendent un tel raisonnement** the underlying principles of this argument, the principles that underlie this argument
sous-tension *nf Él* undervoltage
sous-titrage *nm Cin* subtitling
sous-titre *nm* (*de livre etc*), *Cin* subtitle; (*Journ*) subheading, cross-title
sous-titrer *vt Cin* to subtitle; **film sous-titré en anglais** film with English subtitles
sous-titreur *nm* subtitler
sous-total, *pl* **sous-totaux** *nm* subtotal
soustractif, -ive [sustraktif, -iv] *adj Math, Phot* subtractive
soustraction [sustraksjɔ̃] *nf* removal; [①**A71**,7; **B56**,C,4] *Math* subtraction
soustraire [sustrɛr] (*conj like* **traire**) **1** *vt* (*enlever*) (*qch*) to take away, to remove (**à qn** from sb); *Fig* (*qn*) to protect, to shield (**à qch** from sth); *Math* to subtract (**de** from) **2 se soustraire** *vpr* **se s. à qch** to avoid *or* elude sth; **se s. à une obligation** to back out of an obligation
sous-traitance *nf* subcontracting; **faire de la s.** to subcontract; **travaux effectués en s.** subcontracted work
sous-traitant 1 *nm* subcontractor **2** *adj* **les entreprises sous-traitantes** the subcontractors, the subcontracting companies
sous-traiter *vti* to subcontract
sous-variété *nf Biol* subvariety
sous-ventrière *nf* bellyband; (*avec selle*) (saddle)girth; *Arg* **manger à s'en faire péter la s.** to stuff oneself stupid
sous-verre *nm inv* glass mount(ing); (*photo, image*) photograph *or* picture mounted under glass
sous-vêtement *nm* undergarment; **sous-vêtements** underwear
sous-virage *nm Aut* understeer
sous-virer *vi Aut* to understeer
sous-vireur, -euse *adj* **une voiture sous-vireuse** a car that understeers
soutache [sutaʃ] *nf Couture* braid
soutacher [sutaʃe] *vt Couture* to braid
soutane [sutan] *nf* cassock, soutane; **prendre la s.** to take (holy) orders; **la s.** (*prêtres*) the cloth
soute [sut] *nf Naut* store (room); *Av* hold; (*d'un camion*) load box *or* compartment; **s. à charbon** coal bunker; **s: à munitions** magazine; **s. aux bagages** *Naut* baggage room; *Av* baggage compartment *or* hold; **s. à mazout** oil tank; **s. à valeurs** strongroom; *Av* **s. à essence** refuelling point; *Av* **s. à bombes** bomb bay
soutenable [sutnabl] *adj* **(a)** (*existence, fardeau etc*) bearable **(b)** (*opinion, position*) tenable; (*théorie*) tenable, arguable
soutenance [sutnɑ̃s] *nf Br Univ* (*de mémoire, de thèse*) viva (voce)
soutènement [sutɛnmɑ̃] *nm Constr* support; **mur de s.** retaining *or* supporting wall
souteneur, -euse [sutnœr, -øz] **1** *nm* (*proxénète*) pimp **2** *n Vieilli* (*d'un système etc*) defender, upholder
soutenir [sutnir] (*conj like* **tenir**) **1** *vt* **(a)** (*tenir debout etc*) to support, to hold up; **piliers qui soutiennent le toit** pillars which support the roof
(b) (*fortifier*) (*d'un médicament, de l'amour etc*) to sustain, to keep going; **une pareille alimentation ne pourra pas le s. très longtemps** he can't keep going for very long on a diet like that
(c) (*aider*) (*entreprise, cause, troupes, personne etc*) to back (up), to support; (*personne*) (*défendre, prendre parti pour*) to back up; **s. les prix** to support prices; **s. le moral des troupes** to encourage the troops; **elle m'a soutenu dans l'épreuve** she supported me throughout the ordeal
(d) (*faire valoir*) (*opinion, théorie etc*) to maintain, to uphold; (*fait*) to assert, to affirm; *Univ* (*thèse*) to defend; **il soutient que ...** he maintains that ...
(e) (*faire durer*) (*conversation, vitesse, combat, rang etc*) to keep up, to maintain
(f) (*résister à*) (*affront, reproche, comparaison etc*) to bear; (*siège, attaque etc*) to hold out against, to stand up to
2 se soutenir *vpr* **(a)** (*s'entraider*) to support *or* back (up) each other; **ils se soutiennent moralement** they give each other moral support
(b) (*se défendre*) (*d'une théorie, d'une hypothèse*) to be tenable *or* arguable; **ça se soutient/ne se soutient pas** that's tenable/untenable
soutenu [sutny] *adj* **(a)** (*attention, effort*) sustained; (*intérêt*) sustained, unflagging, constant; (*rythme, trot, marché*) steady **(b)** (*style écrit, langage etc*) formal, elevated; **employer un langage s.** to use formal language **(c)** (*contour*) firm; (*couleur*) deep, strong
souterrain, -e [sutɛrɛ̃, -ɛn] **1** *adj* **(a)** (*eau, explosion etc*) underground, subterranean; **passage s.** subway; **chemin de fer s.** underground (railway), *Am* subway **(b)** *Fig* (*personne, méthodes*) underhand; (*intentions, menées*) secret **2** *nm* underground passage, tunnel
soutien [sutjɛ̃] *nm* **(a)** (*aide*) support; **apporter son s. à** to lend one's support to; **en s.** in support; **s. de prix** price support; *Scol* **cours de s.** remedial class; *Mil* **unité de s.** support unit **(b)** (*personne, groupe*) support; *Admin* **s. de famille** breadwinner
soutien-gorge, *pl* **soutiens-gorge** *nm* bra; *Br Fml, Am* brassière; **s. à armatures/d'allaitement** underwired/nursing bra; **je préférerais un s. sans armatures** I'd rather have a bra that wasn't underwired
soutirage [sutiraʒ] *nm* (*du vin etc*) racking, decanting
soutirer [sutire] *vt* **(a)** (*vin etc*) to rack, to decant **(b)** (*argent, information, promesse etc*) to extract (**à qn** from sb)
souvenance [suvnɑ̃s] *nf Arch, Litt* recollection; **avoir s. de** to recollect; **je n'en ai pas s.** I have no recollection of it
souvenir[1] [suvnir] (*conj like* **venir**; *aux* **être**) **1** *v impers Litt* **il me souvient que ...** I recall *or* remember that ...; **il me souvient d'avoir lu que ...** I recall *or* remember reading *or* having read that ...
2 [①**A43**,b,iii] **se souvenir** *vpr* **se s. de qch/qn** to remember *or* recall sth/sb; **je ne me souviens plus de rien** I can't remember a thing; **nous nous souviendrons de lui** we shall remember him; **je m'en souviens** I remember; **autant que je m'en souviens** *ou* **que je m'en souvienne** as far as I can remember *or* recall; **on s'en souviendra** we won't forget (it); *Iron* **on s'en souviendra de ses 'petites promenades'** we're not likely to forget his 'little walks', we won't forget his 'little walks' in a hurry; **souviens-toi de prendre un pull/de ce que je t'ai dit!** remember *or* don't forget to take a sweater/what I told you!
3 *vi* **fais-moi s. de lui téléphoner ce soir** remind me to telephone him this evening; **fais-moi s. de l'émission ce soir** don't let me forget *or* remind me about the programme this evening
souvenir[2] *nm* **(a)** recollection, memory; **avoir gardé un bon s. de qch** to have a pleasant recollection *or* memory of sth; **je n'en ai pas s.** I have no recollection *or* memory of it; **ce n'est plus qu'un mauvais s.** it's just a bad memory now; **si mes souvenirs sont exacts** if my memory serves me well; **souvenirs de ma jeunesse** memories of my youth; **souvenirs d'enfance** childhood memories; **veuillez me rappeler à son bon s.** please remember me to him; **ma mère vous envoie son affectueux s.** my mother sends her love; **en s. de qn** in remembrance of sb; **en s. du passé** for old times' sake
(b) (*objet, cadeau*) (*d'une personne, d'un lieu*) keepsake, souvenir, memento; (*de touriste*) souvenir; **c'est un s. de ma mère** it's a keepsake from my mother; **magasin de souvenirs** souvenir shop
souvent [suvɑ̃] *adv* [①**A23**,3,a,ii] often; **peu s.** not often, seldom, infrequently; **je l'ai vue s. cet hiver** I saw a lot of her this winter; **on en parle s. à la radio** they often talk about it on the radio; **il ne vient pas s. nous voir** he doesn't often come and see us, he seldom comes to see us; **je n'en mange pas s.** I don't eat it/them often; **le plus s.** usually, as often as not, more often than not; **il est malade plus s. qu'à son tour** he has more than his share of illness; *Arg Vieilli* **plus s.!** no fear!, not likely!
souverain, -aine [suvrɛ̃, -ɛn] **1** *adj* (*puissance, prince, état, remède etc*) sovereign; (*bonheur*) supreme; (*mépris*) supreme, lofty; *Jur* (*tribunal*) supreme; **une femme d'une beauté souveraine** a woman of supreme beauty, a supremely beautiful woman **2** *n* sovereign **3** *nm Hist* (*monnaie*) sovereign
souverainement [suvrɛnmɑ̃] *adv* **(a)** (*extrêmement*) supremely, intensely; **il s'en moque s.** he really couldn't care less **(b)** *Jur* **juger s.** to judge without appeal
souveraineté [suvrɛnte] *nf* sovereignty
soviet [sɔvjɛt] *nm* soviet
soviétique [sɔvjetik] **1** *adj* Soviet **2** *n* **S.** Soviet (citizen)
soviétiser [sɔvjetize] *vt* to sovietize
soviétologue [sɔvjetɔlɔg] *n* Sovietologist, expert on Soviet affairs
soya [sɔja] *nm* soya
soyeux, -euse [swajø, -øz] **1** *adj* silky **2** *nm* (*industriel*) silk merchant
spacieusement [spasjøzmɑ̃] *adv* (*installé*) spaciously; **ils**

sont s. logés their accommodation is very spacious; **ils sont s. installés dans 200 mètres carrés** they have a very spacious 200 square metres

spacieux, -euse [spasjø, -øz] *adj* (*chambre, maison etc*) spacious; (*voiture*) roomy

spadassin [spadasɛ̃] *nm* **(a)** *Arch* swordsman **(b)** *Litt* (*assassin*) hired assassin

spadice [spadis] *nm Bot* spadix

spaghetti(s) [spageti] *nmpl* [①A13,7] *Culin* spaghetti; **s. bolognaise/carbonara** spaghetti bolognese/carbonara

spahi [spai] *nm Mil* spahi

spalax [spalaks] *nm Zool* mole rat

sparadrap [sparadra] *nm* (adhesive *or* sticking) plaster, Elastoplast®, *Am* Band-Aid®; **mettre du s. sur une blessure** to put a (sticking) plaster *or* an Elastoplast on a wound

Sparte [spart] *nf* Sparta

spart(e) [spart] *nm Bot* esparto (grass)

spartiate [sparsjat] **1** *adj Hist, Fig* Spartan **2** *n Hist* **S.** Spartan; *Fig* **à la s.** in a spartan way; **éduquer un enfant à la s.** to give a child a spartan upbringing **3** *nf* leather sandal

spasme [spasm] *nm* spasm

spasmodique [spasmɔdik] *adj Méd* spasmodic

spasmodiquement [spasmɔdikmɑ̃] *adv Méd* spasmodically

spasmophilie [spasmɔfili] *nf Méd* spasmophilia

spastique [spastik] *adj Méd* spastic

spath [spat] *nm Minér* spar

spatial, -ale, -aux, -ales [spasjal, -o] *adj* **(a)** spatial; **organisation spatiale** space organization; *Math* **coordonnées spatiales** spatial coordinates; *Électron* **charge spatiale** space charge **(b)** *Astronaut* space; **engin s.** spacecraft; **voyage s.** space flight; **combinaison spatiale** spacesuit; **guerre spatiale** space warfare; **station spatiale** space station

spatialisation [spasjalizasjɔ̃] *nf* spatialization

spatialiser [spasjalize] *vt* **(a)** (*donner un caractère spatial à*) to spatialize **(b)** (*lancer*) to send into space

spationaute [spasjɔnot] *n* astronaut

spationef [spasjɔnɛf] *nm* spaceship, spacecraft

spatio-temporel, -elle, *pl* **spatio-temporel(le)s** [spasjotɑ̃pɔrɛl] *adj* space-time, spatiotemporal

spatule [spatyl] *nf* **(a)** spatula; **en s.** spatulate **(b)** (*de ski*) (ski) tip **(c)** (*oiseau*) spoonbill

spatulé [spatyle] *adj* spatulate

speaker [spikœr] *nm Rad, TV* announcer; (*qui donne les informations*) newsreader

speakerine [spikrin] *nf Rad, TV* (female) announcer; (*qui donne les informations*) (female) newsreader

spécial, -ale, -aux, -ales [spesjal, -o] **1** *adj* special; (*connaissances*) special, specialized; **rien de s.** nothing special; **privilège s. aux militaires** privilege reserved for *or* restricted to military men; **savon s. peaux grasses** soap for greasy skin; *Journ* **envoyé s.** special correspondent; **édition spéciale** special edition; *F* **c'est/il est un peu s.** (*bizarre*) it's/he's rather odd *or* peculiar; *F* **c'est s., il faut aimer** (*d'un plat curieux etc*) not everybody likes it, it's not to everybody's taste; **il a des mœurs spéciales** he's not like other men **2** *nm Can* **(a)** (*plat du jour*) special **(b)** **en s.** (*en solde*) on special

spécialement [spesjalmɑ̃] *adv* (e)specially, particularly; (*exprès*) specially; **pas s.** not especially *or* particularly

spécialisation [spesjalizasjɔ̃] *nf* specialization

spécialisé [spesjalize] *adj* (*travail, matériaux etc*) specialized; **ouvrier s.** semi-skilled worker; **école/hôpital spécialisé(e)** special school/hospital; **enseignement s.** specialized teaching; **aciers spécialisés** speciality *or Am* specialty steels; **ils sont spécialisés dans les déménagements internationaux** they specialize in international relocations, they're international relocation specialists

spécialiser [spesjalize] **1** *vt* **s. qn** to make *or* turn sb into a specialist **2 se spécialiser** *vpr* **se s. dans** *ou* **en qch** to specialize in sth

spécialiste [spesjalist] **1** *n* specialist **(de, en** in); *Méd* **s. du cœur** heart specialist; *Mktg* **s. produit** product specialist; **s. du vol à voile** gliding specialist *or* expert; *Hum* **c'est un s. des rendez-vous manqués** missing appointments is his speciality, he specializes in missing appointments **2** *adj* specialist; **médecin s.** specialist (doctor); *Hum* **elle est s. de ce genre de gaffes** she specializes in that sort of blunder

spécialité [spesjalite] *nf* **(a)** speciality, *Am* specialty; *Culin* **s. de la maison** speciality of the house; **faire sa s. de qch** to specialize in *or* make a special study of sth; **s. budgétaire** budgetary restriction; **s. médicale** specialized area of medicine; *Hum* **elle sera en retard, c'est sa s.** she'll be late, it's her speciality **(b)** **spécialités pharmaceutiques** patent medicines

spécieusement [spesjøzmɑ̃] *adv Litt* speciously

spécieux, -euse [spesjø, -øz] *adj Litt* specious

spécification [spesifikasjɔ̃] *nf* (*action, définition*) specification; **s. de la fonction** job description; **s. du produit** product specification

spécificité [spesifisite] *nf Méd etc* specificity

spécifier [spesifje] *vt* (*impf, pr sub* **n. spécifiions, v. spécifiiez**) to specify, to state (**que** that); **compte spécifié** detailed *or* itemized account; **nous le lui avions pourtant spécifié par écrit** we had specifically informed him in writing; **je l'avais pourtant bien spécifié** I was quite specific about it

spécifique [spesifik] *adj* specific

spécifiquement [spesifikmɑ̃] *adv* specifically

spécimen [spesimɛn] *nm* specimen; (*livre, fascicule*) specimen *or* sample copy; **page s.** specimen page; **s. de signature** specimen signature

spectacle [spɛktakl] *nm* **(a)** (*choses vues*) sight, scene; **au s. de** at the sight of; **se donner en s.** to make an exhibition *or* a spectacle of oneself **(b)** *Th, Cin etc* (*représentation*) show; **le s.** (*industrie*) show business; **s. de variétés** variety show; **s. folklorique** performance of national/regional music/dancing; **s. solo** one-man show; **aller au s.** to go to a show; **salle de s.** hall; *Th* theatre, *US* theater; *Cin* cinema, *US* movie theater; *Th* **pièce à grand s.** lavish production; *Cin* **film à grand s.** epic (film)

spectaculaire [spɛktakylɛr] *adj* spectacular

spectateur, -trice [spɛktatœr, -tris] *n* **(a)** (*témoin*) spectator, onlooker; (*d'accident*) witness **(b)** *Sp* spectator; *Th* member of the audience; *Th* **spectateurs** audience

spectral, -ale, -aux, -ales [spɛktral, -o] *adj* **(a)** (*de fantôme*) ghostly, spectral **(b)** *Opt* spectral

spectre [spɛktr] *nm* **(a)** (*fantôme*) ghost, phantom; *Fig* (*de la guerre, de la misère etc*) spectre, *US* specter **(b)** *Phys etc* spectrum; **s. solaire** solar spectrum; *Pharm* **s. d'action** (*d'un antibiotique*) spectrum

spectrogramme [spɛktrɔgram] *nm* spectrogram

spectrographe [spɛktrɔgraf] *nm* spectrograph

spectroscope [spɛktrɔskɔp] *nm Opt* spectroscope

spectroscopie [spɛktrɔskɔpi] *nf* spectroscopy

spéculaire [spekylɛr] *adj* **(a)** (*minéral*) specular **(b)** *Méd* **écriture s.** mirror writing

spéculateur, -trice [spekylatœr, -tris] *n Fin* speculator; **s. sur devises** currency speculator; *Bourse* **s. à la baisse** bear; *Bourse* **s. à la hausse** bull

spéculatif, -ive [spekylatif, -iv] **1** *adj Phil, Fin* speculative **2** *nf* **spéculative** (*publicité*) pitch

spéculation [spekylasjɔ̃] *nf* **(a)** *Phil* speculation **(sur** on) **(b)** *Fin* speculation

spéculer [spekyle] *vi* **(a)** *Phil* to speculate **(sur** on, about) **(b)** *Fin* to speculate **(sur** in; **à** for); *Bourse* **s. à la baisse** to go a bear, to be bearish; *Bourse* **s. à la hausse** to go a bull, to be bullish; *Fig* **s. sur qch** to count *or* bank on sth

speculum, spéculum [spekylɔm] *nm Méd* speculum

speech, *pl* **speeches** [spitʃ] *nm* speech; **il nous a fait tout un s. sur la ponctualité** he gave us a long speech about punctuality

speedé [spide] *adj F* **(a)** (*hyperactif*) hyped up, hyper **(b)** (*drogué*) high

speeder [spide] *F* **1** *vt* to rush **2** *vi* to get a move on; **je n'aime pas s. le lundi matin** I don't like rushing on Monday mornings; **j'ai speedé toute la journée** I've been running around like a headless chicken all day

spéléologie [speleɔlɔʒi] *nf* caving, potholing, *Am* spelunking; (*étude*) speleology

spéléologique [speleɔlɔʒik] *adj* speleological

spéléologue [speleɔlɔg] *n* caver, potholer, *Am* spelunker; (*étudiant*) speleologist

spencer [spɛ̃sɛr] *nm* **(a)** (*d'homme*), *Naut* monkey jacket; *Mil* mess jacket **(b)** (*de femme*) short jacket, *Arch* spencer

spermaceti [spɛrmaseti] *nm* spermaceti

spermatique [spɛrmatik] *adj Anat* spermatic

spermatogénèse [spɛrmatɔʒenɛz] *nf Biol* spermatogenesis

spermatozoïde [spɛrmatɔzɔid] *nm Biol* spermatozoon

sperme [spɛrm] *nm* **(a)** *Physiol* sperm, semen **(b)** **s. de baleine** spermaceti

spermicide [spɛrmisid] *adj Méd* **1** *adj* spermicidal **2** *nm* spermicide

spermophile [spɛrmɔfil] *nm Zool* gopher, *Spéc* spermophile

sphaigne [sfɛɲ] *nf Bot* sphagnum (moss), peat moss

sphénoïde [sfenɔid] *adj, nm Anat* sphenoid

sphère [sfɛr] *nf* **(a)** *Astron* sphere; *Géog* **s. terrestre** globe; **s. céleste** celestial sphere **(b)** *Fig* (*d'activité, d'influence etc*) sphere; **la s. des finances** the sphere *or* field of finance, financial circles; **nous ne sommes pas dans les mêmes sphères** we're not in the same field; **les hautes sphères de la politique** the higher reaches *or* realms of politics

sphéricité [sferisite] *nf* sphericity
sphérique [sferik] *adj* spherical
sphéroïde [sferɔid] *nm* spheroid
sphéromètre [sferɔmɛtr] *nm* spherometer
sphincter [sfɛ̃ktɛr] *nm Anat* sphincter
sphinx [sfɛ̃ks] *nm* **(a)** *Myth, Fig* sphinx; **sourire de s.** sphinx-like smile **(b)** *Ent* hawk *or Am* sphinx moth
sphygmomanomètre [sfigmɔmanɔmɛtr] *nm Méd* sphygmomanometer
spi [spi] *nm Naut F* = **spinnaker**
spic [spik] *nm Bot* spike lavender
spider [spidɛr] *nm Aut* dick(e)y, *Am* rumble seat
spin [spin] *nm Phys Nucl* spin
spina-bifida [spinabifida] *nm Méd* spina bifida
spinal, -ale, -aux, -ales [spinal, -o] *adj Anat* spinal
spinelle [spinɛl] *nm Minér* spinel
spinnaker [spinakɔ, -kɛr] *nm Naut* spinnaker
spiral, -ale, -aux, -ales [spiral, -o] **1** *adj* spiral **2** *nm* (*de montre*) hair-spring **3** *nf* **spirale** spiral, *Spéc* helix; **la s. inflationniste** the inflationary spiral; **s. des prix et des salaires** wage and price spiral; **en spirale** (*utilisé adverbialement*) in a spiral, spirally; (*utilisé adjectivement*) spiral; **descendre/monter en spirale** to spiral down/up, to go down/up in a spiral
spirant, -ante [spirɑ̃, -ɑ̃t] *Ling* **1** *adj* spirant **2** *nf* **spirante** spirant
spire [spir] *nf* (*d'une spirale, Él d'une bobine*) (single) turn; (*d'un coquillage*) whorl
spirée [spire] *nf Bot* spiraea
spirille [spirij] *nm Biol* spirillum
spirite [spirit] *adj, n* spiritualist
spiritisme [spiritism] *nm* spiritualism
spiritualiser [spiritɥalize] *vt* to spiritualize
spiritualisme [spiritɥalism] *nm Phil* spiritualism
spiritualiste [spiritɥalist] *Phil* **1** *adj* spiritualist(ic) **2** *n* spiritualist
spiritualité [spiritɥalite] *nf Phil* spirituality
spirituel, -elle [spiritɥɛl] **1** *adj* **(a)** *Phil, Rel etc* (*être, pouvoir, vie etc*) spiritual; (*musique*) sacred; **père s.** spiritual father **(b)** (*fin*) (*personne, réponse etc*) witty; *Iron* **que c'est s.!** very witty *or* droll! **2** *nm* **le s.** things spiritual; (*pouvoir*) spiritual power
spirituellement [spiritɥɛlmɑ̃] *adv* **(a)** (*de l'esprit*) spiritually **(b)** (*finement*) wittily
spiritueux, -euse [spiritɥø, -øz] **1** *adj* (*boisson*) alcoholic **2** *nm* (*liqueur*) spirit
spiroïdal, -ale, -aux, -ales [spirɔidal, -o] *adj* spiroid
spleen [splin] *nm Litt* (*mélancolie*) spleen, melancholy; **avoir le s.** to be melancholic
spleenétique [splinetik] *adj Litt* splenetic, melancholy
splendeur [splɑ̃dœr] *nf* **(a)** (*somptuosité*) splendour, *US* splendor, magnificence; *Litt* (*éclat*) radiance, brightness; (*gloire*) splendour, grandeur, glory; **dans toute sa s.** in all his/her/its splendour **(b)** (*chose*) **splendeurs** splendours, *US* splendors; **c'est une s.** it's splendid
splendide [splɑ̃did] *adj* (*journée, temps*) splendid; (*soleil*) brilliant; (*palais, victoire, repas*) splendid, magnificent; (*personne*) splendid-looking
splendidement [splɑ̃didmɑ̃] *adv* splendidly
splénectomie [splenɛktɔmi] *nf Chir* splenectomy
splénique [splenik] *adj* (*artère, maladie*) splenic
spoiler [spɔjlœr] *Aut nm* spoiler
spoliateur, -trice [spɔljatœr, -tris] *Litt* **1** *n* despoiler **2** *adj* (*loi, mesure etc*) spoliatory
spoliation [spɔljasjɔ̃] *nf Litt* (*de qn*) despoiling, robbing
spolier [spɔlje] *vt* (*impf, pr sub* **n. spoliions, v. spoliiez**) *Litt* to despoil, to rob (**de** of)
spondée [spɔ̃de] *nm Littér* spondee
spondylarthrite [spɔ̃dilartrit] *nf Méd* spondylarthritis; **s. ankylosante** ankylosing spondylitis
spondylite [spɔ̃dilit] *nf Méd* spondylitis
spongieux, -ieuse [spɔ̃ʒjø, -jøz] *adj* spongy
sponsor [spɔ̃sɔr] *nm* sponsor
sponsoring [spɔ̃sɔriŋ] *nm* sponsorship
sponsoriser [spɔ̃sɔrize] *vt* to sponsor
spontané [spɔ̃tane] *adj* (*action, personne, combustion, Biol génération etc*) spontaneous; (*aveux*) unprompted; (*candidature*) unsolicited
spontanéité [spɔ̃taneite] *nf* spontaneity
spontanément [spɔ̃tanemɑ̃] *adv* spontaneously
sporadique [spɔradik] *adj* sporadic
sporadiquement [spɔradikmɑ̃] *adv* sporadically
sporange [spɔrɑ̃ʒ] *nm Bot* sporangium, spore case
spore [spɔr] *nf Bot* spore
sport [spɔr] **1** *nm* sport; **faire du s.** to do sport; **elle ne pratique aucun s.** she doesn't do any sport; **chaussures/terrain/salle/voiture de s.** sports shoes/ground/arena/car; *Fig F* **vous allez voir du s.** now you're going to see some fun; *F* **il va y avoir du s.!** there's going to be some fun! **2** *adj inv* **(a)** **vêtements s., costume s.** casual clothes; **habillé s.** casually dressed; *Aut* **coupé s.** sports coupé **(b)** (*personne*) sporting, fair
▶ **sport**: **s. de combat** combat sport; **s. d'équipe** team sport; **sports d'hiver** winter sports; **aller aux sports d'hiver** to go skiing; **s. individuel** individual sport; **sports nautiques** water sports
sportif, -ive [spɔrtif, -iv] **1** *adj* **(a)** (*résultats, édition, club etc*) sports; **réunion sportive** sports *or* athletics meeting **(b)** (*fair-play*) (*personne*) sporting, fair; **esprit s.** sporting spirit, sportsmanship **(c)** (*amateur de sport*) sporty, athletic; **allure sportive** sporty *or* athletic look **2** *n* sportsman, *f* sportswoman
sportivement [spɔrtivmɑ̃] *adv* sportingly, in a sporting spirit; **il prit les choses très s.** he was very sporting about things
sportivité [spɔrtivite] *nf* sportsmanship; **elle eut la s. de …** she was sporting enough to …
sport(s)wear [spɔrt(s)wɛr] **1** *nm* sportswear, casual wear **2** *adj* (*style etc*) casual
sporuler [spɔryle] *vi Biol* to sporulate
spot [spɔt] *nm* **(a)** *TV, Électron etc* (*point*) spot; *Rad* blip **(b)** *Th* (*lampe*) spot(light); *TV, Cin* **s. à pinces** clip lamp **(c)** *Rad, TV* **s. (publicitaire)** commercial, advertisement; **un s. de trente secondes** a thirty-second spot
spouler [spule] *vt Ordinat* to spool
spouleur [spulœr] *nm Ordinat* spooler; **s. d'imprimante** printer spooler
spoutnik [sputnik] *nm* sputnik
sprat [sprat] *nm* (*poisson*) sprat
spray [sprɛ] *nm* spray, aerosol (spray); **peinture/déodorant en s.** spray(-on) *or* aerosol paint/deodorant
spread [sprɛd] *nm Bourse* **s. baissier** bear spread; **s. haussier** bull spread; **s. papillon** butterfly spread
springbok [spriŋbɔk] *nm* springbok
springer [spriŋœr] *nm* (*chien*) springer (spaniel)
sprint [sprint] *nm Sp* (final) sprint; (*course*) sprint; *F* **piquer un s.** to sprint; **être bon au s.** to have a good sprint finish
sprinter[1] [sprintœr] *nm Sp* sprinter
sprinter[2] [sprinte] *vi Sp* to sprint
squale [skwal] *nm* (*roussette*) dogfish; (*requin*) shark
squame [skwam] *nf Méd* scale, *Spéc* squama
squameux, -euse [skwamø, -øz] *adj Méd* scaly, *Spéc* squamous
square [skwar] *nm* (*jardin public*) public garden
squash [skwaʃ] *nm Sp* squash; **jouer au s.** to play squash
squat [skwat] *nm* (*action, lieu*) squat
squatter[1] [skwatœr] *nm* squatter
squatter[2] [skwate], **squatteriser** [skwaterize] *vt* to squat in
squaw [skwo] *nf* (Indian) squaw
squelette [skəlɛt] *nm* **(a)** skeleton; **c'est un vrai s.** *ou* **un s. ambulant** he's/she's a bag of bones *or* a walking skeleton **(b)** *Fig* (*d'un navire, d'un roman etc*) skeleton, framework; *Typ* rough layout
squelettique [skəlɛtik] *adj* **(a)** *Anat* skeletal **(b)** (*maigre*) (*personne, bras etc*) skeleton-like; **il est devenu s.** he's turned into a walking skeleton **(c)** (*réduit*) (*personnel, armée etc*) skeleton
squille [skij] *nf* (*crustacé*) squill
Sri Lanka [srilɑ̃ka] *nf* Sri Lanka
sri lankais, -aise [srilɑ̃kɛ, -ɛz] **1** *adj* Sri Lankan **2** *n* **S.** Sri Lankan
SRPJ [ɛsɛrpeʒi] *nm* (*abrév* **Service régional de la police judiciaire**) = regional crime unit
SS [ɛsɛs] **1** *nm Hist* member of the SS; **les SS** the SS **2** *nf Admin abrév* **Sécurité Sociale**
stabilisant [stabilizɑ̃] *nm Ch* stabilizing agent
stabilisateur, -trice [stabilizatœr, -tris] **1** *adj* stabilizing; **appareil s.** stabilizing device **2** *nm* **(a)** (*de vélo*), *Naut* stabilizer; *Av* tailplane, *US* horizontal stabilizer; (*vertical*) fin, *US* vertical stabilizer **(b)** *Ch* stabilizer
stabilisation [stabilizasjɔ̃] *nf* stabilization
stabilisé [stabilize] *adj Ch, Écon etc* stabilized; *Biol* balanced
stabiliser [stabilize] **1** *vt* to stabilize, to steady **2** **se stabiliser** *vpr* (*d'une voiture, d'une monnaie*) to stabilize, to steady; (*d'une personne*) (*dans la vie*) to settle down; **quand la situation se sera stabilisée** once the situation settles down *or* stabilizes
stabilité [stabilite] *nf* stability; **s. des changes** exchange rate stability; **s. des prix** price stability; **s. en courbe** cornering stability
stable [stabl] *adj* (*substance, équilibre, échelle, tempérament etc*) stable, steady; (*paix*) stable, lasting
stabulation [stabylasjɔ̃] *nf* (*du bétail*) keeping in sheds; (*des chevaux*) stabling

staccato [stakato] *adv, nm Mus* staccato

stade [stad] *nm* **(a)** (*de sport*) stadium **(b)** (*étape*) (*d'évolution, de développement, de maladie etc*) stage; *Psy* **s. anal/oral/génital** anal/oral/genital stage **(c)** *Ent* (*des chenilles etc*) instar

staff [staf] *nm* **(a)** *Constr* (*matériau*) staff **(b)** (*personnel*) staff; **s. de direction** managerial staff

stage [staʒ] *nm* (*période*) period of instruction *or* training; (*cours*) training course; (*pédagogique*) teaching practice; **s. de formation** training period; **s. professionnel** work placement; **faire un s. de musique/de poterie** (*en vacances*) to do a music/pottery course; **être en s.** to be undergoing training *or* under instruction

stagflation [stagflasjɔ̃] *nf Écon* stagflation

stagiaire [staʒjɛr] **1** *adj* trainee; **interprète s.** trainee interpreter **2** *n* trainee; *TV, Cin* runner, best boy

stagnant [stagnɑ̃] *adj* (*eau, Fig ventes etc*) stagnant

stagnation [stagnasjɔ̃] *nf* (*de l'eau, Fig des ventes etc*) stagnation; *Fig* **en s.** at a standstill, stagnant

stagner [stagne] *vi* (*de l'eau, Fig du commerce etc*) to stagnate

stakhanovisme [stakanɔvism] *nm* Stakhanovism

stalactite [stalaktit] *nf Géol* stalactite

stalag [stalag] *nm* stalag

stalagmite [stalagmit] *nf Géol* stalagmite

stalinien, -ienne [stalinjɛ̃, -jɛn] *adj, n* Stalinist

stalinisme [stalinism] *nm* Stalinism

stalle [stal] *nf* **(a)** (*dans une cathédrale*) stall **(b)** (*dans une étable*) stall, box

stance [stɑ̃s] *nf* (*strophe*) stanza

stand [stɑ̃d] *nm* **(a)** (*dans une course, une exposition etc*) stand, *Am* booth; (*dans une kermesse*) stall; **s. d'exposition** exhibition stand; *Sp, Aut* **les stands de ravitaillement** the pits **(b) s. (de tir)** rifle range **(c)** (*de machine à écrire etc*) stand, rest

standard [stɑ̃dar] **1** *nm* **(a)** (*norme*) standard; **s. de vie** standard of living **(b)** *Tél* switchboard **2** *adj inv* standard; *Péj* **sourire s.** fixed smile

standardisation [stɑ̃dardizasjɔ̃] *nf* standardization

standardiser [stɑ̃dardize] *vt* to standardize

standardiste [stɑ̃dardist] *n Tél* (switchboard) operator

stand-by [stɑ̃dbaj] *Av* **1** *adj inv* stand-by **2** *nm* **(ticket/passager en) s.** stand-by (ticket/passenger)

standing [stɑ̃diŋ] *nm F* status; (*social*) (social) standing; **avoir un bon s.** to have a good standard of living; **appartement de grand s.** luxury flat *or Am* apartment; **quartier de grand s.** select district

staphylocoque [stafilɔkɔk] *nm* (*bactérie*) staphylococcus

star [star] *nf* (*vedette de cinéma, chanteur, sportif etc, Mktg produit*) star; **faire la s.** to act the star

stariser [starize] *vt F* **s. qn** to turn sb into a star

starlette [starlɛt] *nf Cin* starlet

star-system, *pl* **star-systems** [starsistɛm] *nm Cin, Th etc* star system

starter [startɛr] *nm* **(a)** *Sp* (*qui donne le signal*) starter **(b)** *Aut* choke; **mettre/enlever le s.** to pull out/push in the choke; **rouler avec le s.** to drive with the choke out

starting-block, *pl* **starting-blocks** [startiŋblɔk] *nm Sp* starting block

starting-gate, *pl* **starting-gates** [startiŋgɛt] *nm Courses de chevaux* starting gate

stase [staz] *nf Méd* stasis

station [stasjɔ̃] *nf* **(a)** (*position*) position, posture; **s. debout** standing position; **la s. debout lui est décommandée** he has been advised not to stand for any length of time; **je me fatigue vite en s. debout** standing tires me quickly; **s. horizontale/verticale** horizontal/vertical position; **mise en s.** (*d'un instrument etc*) setting up

(b) (*halte*) stop, pause; **faire une s. à ...** to stop *or* pause at ...; **faire de longues stations devant les magasins** to stop for long periods in front of shops

(c) *Rel* (*de la Croix*) station

(d) (*lieu d'arrêt*) (*d'autobus*) (bus) stop; (*de métro*) station; (*de train*) halt; (*de taxis*) (taxi) rank

(e) (*lieu de séjour*) resort

(f) (*centre de recherches*) station

(g) *Ordinat* (*d'un réseau*) station, node

▶ **station**: *Ordinat* **s. d'accueil** docking station; **s. balnéaire** seaside *or* coastal resort; *TV, Rad* **s. de base** base station; *Él* **s. centrale** power station; **s. climatique** health resort; *Aut* **s. diagnostic** diagnostics bay; **s. émettrice** broadcasting station; *Aut* **s. d'essence** petrol *or Am* gas station; *TV, Rad* **s. généraliste** general-interest station; **s. hydrominérale** spa resort; *Ordinat* **s. individuelle** standalone workstation; *Aut* **s. de lavage** car wash; **s. météorologique** weather *or* meteorological station; **s. de métro** tube *or* underground *or Am* subway station; **s. de montagne** mountain resort; **s. orbitale** orbiting station; *Pétr* **s. de pompage** pumping station; **s. de radio** radio station; *Ordinat* **s. réseau** network station; *TV, Rad* **s. satellite** satellite station; **s. de ski** winter sports *or* ski resort; **s. spatiale** space station; **s. de sports d'hiver** winter sports *or* ski resort; **s. de télévision** television station; *TV* **s. terrestre** ground *or* earth station; *TV* **s. thématique** themed channel; **s. thermale** spa; **s. de travail** workstation; **s. verte** well-preserved, picturesque French rural town/village

stationnaire [stasjɔnɛr] **1** *adj* stationary; (*baromètre*) steady; **l'état du malade est s.** the patient('s condition) is stable **2** *nm Naut* guardship, station ship

stationné [stasjɔne] *adj* parked

stationnement [stasjɔnmɑ̃] *nm* **(a)** (*de voitures etc*) parking; **en s.** parked; **parc de s.** car park; **s. interdit** (*sur panneau*) no parking; (*devant la gare etc*) no waiting; **s. gênant** no parking **(b)** *Can* (*parking*) car park, *Am* parking lot **(c)** *Av* **aire de s.** apron

stationner [stasjɔne] *vi* (*d'une voiture, d'un conducteur etc*) to park; **défense de s.** (*sur panneau*) no parking; (*devant la gare etc*) no waiting

station-service, *pl* **stations-service(s)** *nf Aut* service *or* filling *or* petrol *or Am* gas station

statique [statik] **1** *adj* (*électricité, personnage etc*) static **2** *nf* statics

statiquement [statikmɑ̃] *adv* statically

statisticien, -ienne [statistisjɛ̃, -jɛn] *n* statistician

statistique [statistik] **1** *adj* statistical **2** *nf* **(a)** (*science*) statistics **(b)** (*donnée*) statistic; **statistiques de natalité** birth statistics; **statistiques sociales** social statistics; **statistiques syndicales** trade statistics

statistiquement [statistikmɑ̃] *adv* statistically

stator [statɔr] *nm* stator

statoréacteur [statoreaktœr] *nm Av* ramjet

statuaire [statɥɛr] **1** *adj* (*art, marbre etc*) statuary **2** *n* sculptor, *f* sculptress **3** *nf* (art of) statuary

statue [staty] *nf* statue; **la s. de la Liberté** the Statue of Liberty; **immobile comme une s.** stock-still; **s. de sel** pillar of salt

statuer [statɥe] *vi* to give a decision *or* a ruling (**sur** on)

statuette [statɥɛt] *nf* statuette

statufier [statyfje] *vt* (*impf, pr sub* **n. statufiions, v. statufiiez**) *F* (*qn*) to erect a statue to

statu quo [statykwo] *nm* status quo

stature [statyr] *nf* stature; **de haute s.** very tall; *Fig* of (great) stature; **elle a une s. de basketteuse** she's very tall; *Fig* **ils ne sont pas de la même s.** they're not in the same league

statut [staty] *nm* **(a)** (*état*) status; **avoir un s. privilégié** to have privileged status; **s. social** social status; **s. juridique** *or* **légal** legal status; **avoir le s. de cadre/de fonctionnaire** to have executive/civil servant status **(b) statuts** (*de sociétés, d'associations*) statutes, memorandum and articles of association, *Am* bylaws

statutaire [statytɛr] *adj* statutory

statutairement [statytɛrmɑ̃] *adv* in accordance with the statutes *or* regulations

stayer [stɛjœr] *nm Cyclisme* (*derrière une moto*) long-distance cyclist; *Courses de chevaux* stayer

St(e) (*abrév* **Saint(e)**) St

Sté (*abrév* **Société**) Co

steak [stɛk] *nm Culin* steak; **s. tartare** steak tartare; **s. au poivre** peppered steak, steak au poivre; **s. frites** steak and chips

stéarine [stearin] *nf Ch* stearin

stéarique [stearik] *adj Ch* stearic (acid)

stéatite [steatit] *nf Minér* steatite, soapstone

stéatopyge [steatɔpiʒ] *adj* steatopygic

stéatose [steatoz] *nf Méd* steatosis

steeple(chase), *pl* **steeple-chases** [stipl(ə)-, stipəlʃɛz] *nm Sp* steeplechase

stèle [stɛl] *nf* stele

stellage [stelaʒ] *nm Bourse*, double option, put and call (option)

stellaire [stelɛr] **1** *adj* (*lumière etc*) stellar **2** *nf Bot* starwort

stem(m) [stɛm] *nm Ski* stem turn

stencil [stɛnsil] *nm* (*à polycopier*) stencil

sténo [steno] **1** *nf* (*abrév* **sténographie**) shorthand, stenography; **prendre une lettre en s.** to take down a letter in shorthand **2** *n* (*abrév* **sténographe**) stenographer

sténodactylo [stenodaktilo] **1** *n* shorthand typist, *Am* stenographer **2** *nf* (*abrév* **sténodactylographie**) shorthand typing

sténodactylographie [stenodaktilɔgrafi] *nf* shorthand typing

sténographe [stenɔgraf] *n* stenographer, shorthand writer; **s. de presse** press stenographer
sténographie [stenɔgrafi] *nf* shorthand, stenography
sténographier [stenɔgrafje] *vt* (*pr sub, impf* **n. sténographiions, v. sténographiiez**) **s. une lettre** to take a letter down in shorthand
sténographique [stenɔgrafik] *adj* (*écriture etc*) shorthand
sténotype [stenɔtip] *nf* stenotype, stenotyper
sténotyper [stenɔtipe] *vt* to stenotype
sténotypie [stenɔtipi] *nf* stenotypy
sténotypiste [stenɔtipist] *n* stenotypist
stentor [stɑ̃tɔr] *nm* **(a) voix de s.** stentorian voice **(b)** *Zool* stentor
stéphanois, -oise [stefanwa, -waz] **1** *adj* of *or* from Saint-Étienne **2** *n* **S.** (*natif*) native of Saint-Étienne; (*habitant*) inhabitant of Saint-Étienne
steppe [stɛp] *nf Géog* steppe
stercoraire [stɛrkɔrɛr] **1** *adj Méd* stercoraceous **2** *nm* (*oiseau*) skua
stère [stɛr] *nm* (*unité de mesure*) stere
stéréo [stereo] **1** *adj inv* stereo **2** *nf* **(a)** (*abrév* **stéréophonie**) stereo; **en s.** in stereo; **s. VHF** stereo VHF **(b)** (*radio*) stereo radio
stéréogramme [stereɔgram] *nm Opt, Phot* stereogram, stereograph
stéréographie [stereɔgrafi] *nf Opt* stereography
stéréométrie [stereɔmetri] *nf* stereometry
stéréophonie [stereɔfɔni] *nf* stereophony
stéréophonique [stereɔfɔnik] *adj* stereophonic
stéréoscope [stereɔskɔp] *nm Opt* stereoscope
stéréoscopie [stereɔskɔpi] *nf* stereoscopy
stéréoscopique [stereɔskɔpik] *adj* stereoscopic
stéréotype [stereotip] *nm Typ, Fig* stereotype
stéréotypé [stereotipe] *adj* (*idées, phrases etc*) stereotype(d)
stéréotypie [stereotipi] *nf Typ, Psy* stereotypy
stérile [steril] *adj* (*homme, femme, animal*) sterile; (*mariage*) childless; (*terre*) sterile, barren, unproductive; (*travail*) unprofitable; (*discussion, efforts etc*) sterile, vain, fruitless; *Méd etc* **instruments stériles** sterile *or* sterilized instruments
stérilement [sterilmɑ̃] *adv* (*vainement*) fruitlessly
stérilet [sterilɛ] *nm* (*contraceptif*) coil, IUD; **se faire poser un s.** to have a coil *or* an IUD fitted
stérilisant [sterilizɑ̃] *adj* (*agent etc*) sterilizing; *Fig* mind-numbing
stérilisateur [sterilizatœr] *nm* sterilizer
stérilisation [sterilizasjɔ̃] *nf* sterilization
stériliser [sterilize] *vt* (*lait, instrument, personne etc*) to sterilize; *Fig* to stifle, to suffocate
stérilité [sterilite] *nf* (*d'une personne*) sterility; (*d'une terre*) barrenness; *Fig* (*d'une discussion, d'efforts etc*) fruitlessness, futility
sterling [stɛrliŋ] **1** *adj inv* sterling; **dix livres s.** ten pounds sterling **2** *nm inv* sterling; **payé en s.** paid in sterling
sterne [stɛrn] *nf* (*oiseau*) tern
sternum [stɛrnɔm] *nm Anat* breastbone, *Spéc* sternum
sternutatoire [stɛrnytatwar] *adj* sternutatory; **poudre s.** sneezing powder
stéroïde [sterɔid] *nm Biol, Méd* steroid; **stéroïdes anabolisants** anabolic steroids
stérol [sterɔl] *nm Ch, Physiol* sterol
stertoreux, -euse [stɛrtɔrø, -øz] *adj Méd* (*respiration*) stertorous
stéthoscope [stetɔskɔp] *nm Méd* stethoscope
steward [stjuwart, stiwart] *nm Naut, Av* steward, flight *or* cabin attendant
stick [stik] *nm* **(a)** *Mil, Sp, Av etc* stick; (*de cavalier*) riding whip *or* crop **(b)** (*de colle etc*) stick; **un s. de rouge à lèvres** a lipstick; **déodorant en s.** stick deodorant
stigmate [stigmat] *nm* **(a)** *Méd* mark, stigma; *Fig* (*du vice etc*) mark **(b)** *Hist* (*châtiment*) brand **(c)** *Hist, Rel* **stigmates** stigmata **(d)** *Bot, Ent* stigma
stigmatisation [stigmatizasjɔ̃] *nf* (*condamnation*), *Rel* stigmatization
stigmatisé, -ée [stigmatize] **1** *adj* stigmatized **2** *n Hist, Rel* stigmatist, stigmatic
stigmatiser [stigmatize] *vt* **(a)** (*condamner*) (*qn*) to stigmatize, to condemn **(b)** *Hist* (*marquer*) (*détenu*) to brand
stillation [stilasjɔ̃] *nf* (*en sciences*) dripping
stim [stim] *nf* (*abrév* **stimulation**) *Mktg* incentive, stimulus
stimulant [stimylɑ̃] **1** *adj* stimulating; (*résultats*) encouraging **2** *nm* **(a)** *Méd etc* stimulant **(b)** *Fig* stimulus, spur, incentive; *Mktg* **stimulants** stimuli
stimulateur [stimylatœr] *nm Méd* **s. cardiaque** pacemaker; **on lui a mis un s. cardiaque** he was fitted with a pacemaker
stimulation [stimylasjɔ̃] *nf* stimulation, incentive, stimulus; **s. de la demande** demand stimulation; **s. financière** cash incentive; **s. à l'achat** incentive to buy; **s. à la consommation** consumer incentive
stimuler [stimyle] *vt* **(a)** (*personne*) to stimulate; (*encourager*) to spur on; **il faut le s. sans arrêt** you have to keep prodding him; **cela ne me stimule pas vraiment de travailler avec elle** I don't find working with her very stimulating **(b)** (*enthousiasme, digestion, économie etc*) to stimulate; (*appétit*) to stimulate, to whet; (*amitié, commerce etc*) to stimulate, to encourage; **s. la demande** to stimulate demand
stimulus [stimylys], *pl* **stimulus** *ou* **stimuli** [stimyli] *nm* stimulus
stipendiaire [stipɑ̃djɛr], **stipendié, -ée** [stipɑ̃dje] *Litt Péj* **1** *adj* (*soldat etc*) hired **2** *n* hireling
stipendier [stipɑ̃dje] *vt* (*pr sub, impf* **n. stipendiions, v. stipendiiez**) *Litt Péj* (*soldats, politiciens etc*) to hire
stipulation [stipylasjɔ̃] *nf* stipulation, condition
stipuler [stipyle] *vt* to stipulate; **il est stipulé dans le contrat que …** it is stipulated in the contract that …
stochastique [stɔkastik] *adj* stochastic
stock [stɔk] *nm Com* (*des biens*) stock; **stocks** (*en comptabilité*) stock, *Am* inventory; **en s.** in stock; **nous n'avons plus ce modèle en s.** we no longer have this model in stock, this model is out of stock; **rupture de s.** stock outage; **être en rupture de s.** to be out of stock; *F* **tout un s., un vrai s.** a whole stock *or* collection; **dans la limite des stocks disponibles** while stocks last, subject to availability; **c'est là qu'elle cache son s. de biscuits** that's where she hides her stock of biscuits; **elle a mis tout son s. de chaussures dans ce tiroir** she put her whole stock of shoes in this drawer; **s. d'alerte** minimum stock level; **s. de sécurité** safety stock; **s. final** closing stock; **s. d'ouverture** opening stock; **s. stratégique** perpetual inventory
stockage [stɔkaʒ] *nm* **(a)** (*des marchandises*) stocking; *Ordinat* storage; *Ordinat* **s. de données** data storage; *Ordinat* **s. en mémoire tampon** buffering; **s. excessif** overstocking **(b)** (*en grande quantité*) stockpiling, building up of stocks
stock-car, *pl* **stock-cars** *nm Sp* (*voiture*) stock car; (*sport*) stock-car racing
stocker [stɔke] *vt* **(a)** (*marchandises*) to stock **(b)** (*en grande quantité*) to stockpile **(c)** *Ordinat* (*informations*) to store
stockfish [stɔkfiʃ] *nm inv* stockfish
stockiste [stɔkist] *n Com* stockist, *Am* dealer; *Aut* dealer, agent
stoïcien, -ienne [stɔisjɛ̃, -jɛn] **1** *adj* stoical, stoic; *Hist Phil* Stoic **2** *n* stoic; *Hist Phil* Stoic
stoïcisme [stɔisism] *nm* stoicism; *Hist Phil* Stoicism; **avec s.** stoically, with stoicism
stoïque [stɔik] **1** *adj* stoic, stoical **2** *n* stoic
stoïquement [stɔikmɑ̃] *adv* stoically
stolon [stɔlɔ̃] *nm Bot* stolon, runner
stomacal, -ale, -aux, -ales [stɔmakal, -o] *adj* (*spasme etc*) stomach
stomachique [stɔmaʃik] *adj, nm Pharm* stomachic
stomatite [stɔmatit] *nf Méd* stomatitis
stomatologie [stɔmatɔlɔʒi] *nf* stomatology
stomatologiste [stɔmatɔlɔʒist], **stomatologue** [stɔmatɔlɔg] *n* stomatologist
stomie [stɔmi] *nf Méd* stoma
stop [stɔp] **1** *int* stop!; (*dans un télégramme*) stop; **il faut savoir dire s.** you have to learn to say enough is enough; **alors je dis 's.!', j'arrête de travailler avec vous** I'm telling you that's enough, I'm not working with you any more **2** *nm* **(a)** *Aut* (*feu arrière*) brake light; (*panneau*) stop sign **(b)** *F* (*abrév* **auto-stop**) hitchhiking; **faire du s.** to hitch(hike); **aller à Paris en s.** to hitch(hike) to Paris
stoppage [stɔpaʒ] *nm Couture* (*d'un vêtement*) invisible mending
stopper[1] [stɔpe] *vti* to stop; **il faut le s. quand il est dans cet état** he has to be stopped when he's in this state
stopper[2] *vt Couture* to repair by invisible mending
stoppeur, -euse [stɔpœr, -øz] *n F* **(a)** (*abrév* **auto-stoppeur**) hitcher, hitchhiker **(b)** *Sp* fullback
store [stɔr] *nm* blind; (*devant un magasin*) awning; **s. vénitien** Venetian blind
story-board, *pl* **story-boards** [stɔribɔrd] *nm TV, Cin* storyboard
strabisme [strabism] *nm* strabismus, squint(ing); **s. convergent/divergent** esotropia *or* convergent strabismus/exotropia *or* divergent strabismus; **yeux atteints d'un léger/fort s.** eyes with a slight/severe squint
stradivarius [stradivarjys] *nm Mus* (*instrument*) Stradivarius
strangulation [strɑ̃gylasjɔ̃] *nf* strangulation
strapontin [strapɔ̃tɛ̃] *nm* **(a)** *Aut, Th etc* folding seat, tip-up seat **(b)** *Fig* (*fonction secondaire*) minor role

strasbourgeois, -oise [strazburʒwa, -waz] **1** *adj* of *or* from Strasbourg **2** *n* **S.** (*natif*) native of Strasbourg; (*habitant*) inhabitant of Strasbourg
stras(s) [stras] *nm* (*clinquant*) paste, strass; *Fig* **robe en s.** sequined dress
stratagème [strataʒɛm] *nm* stratagem
strate [strat] *nf* [①A13,5] *Géol, Fig* stratum, layer
stratège [stratɛʒ] *nm* strategist
stratégie [strateʒi] *nf* strategy; **s. commerciale** business strategy; **s. concurrentielle** competitive strategy; *Mktg* **s. de créneau unique** single niching; *Mktg* **s. de créneaux multiples** multiple-niche strategy; **s. électorale** election strategy; *Mktg* **s. d'encerclement** encirclement strategy; **s. de l'entreprise** corporate strategy; **s. globale de l'entreprise** overall business strategy; *Mktg* **s. d'imitation** imitation *or* me-too strategy; *Mktg* **s. de marque** brand strategy; **s. (de) mercatique** game plan, marketing strategy; *Mktg* **s. de niche unique** single-niche strategy; *Mktg* **s. poussée** *ou* **'pousser'** push strategy; *Mktg* **s. du prétendant** challenger strategy; *Mktg* **s. du suiveur** follower strategy; *Mktg* **s. tirée** *ou* **'tirer'** pull strategy
stratégique [strateʒik] *adj* strategic
stratégiquement [strateʒikmɑ̃] *adv* strategically
stratification [stratifikasjɔ̃] *nf* stratification
stratifié [stratifje] **1** *adj* stratified; *Tech* (*papier, tissu etc*) laminated **2** *nm* laminate
stratifier [stratifje] *vt* to stratify
strato-cumulus [stratokymylys] *nm inv Météo* stratocumulus
stratosphère [stratɔsfɛr] *nf Météo* stratosphere
stratosphérique [stratɔsferik] *adj* stratospheric
stratus [stratys] *nm inv Météo* stratus
streamer [strimœr] *nm Ordinat* tape streamer
streptocoque [strɛptɔkɔk] *nm* (*bactérie*) streptococcus
streptomycine [strɛptɔmisin] *nf Méd* streptomycin
stress [strɛs] *nm* stress; **être en proie au s.** to be under stress; **maladie due au s.** stress-related illness
stressant [strɛsɑ̃] *adj* stressful
stresser [strɛse] *vt* **s. qn** (*d'un travail, d'une activité*) to put sb under stress, *F* to stress sb out; **être stressé** to be under stress, *F* to be stressed out; **elle/vivre à Paris me stresse** I find her/living in Paris very stressful
stretch® [strɛtʃ] *nm* (*tissu*) stretch material; **jupe en s.** stretch skirt
striation [strijasjɔ̃] *nf* striation
strict [strikt] *adj* **(a)** (*obligation, principes etc*) strict; (*essentiel, minimum*) bare; **au sens s.** in the strict sense; **dans la plus stricte intimité** strictly in private; **c'est la stricte vérité** it's the simple or absolute truth; **c'est son droit le plus s.** it's his absolute right **(b)** (*personne*) strict (**sur** about); **ils sont très stricts sur la politesse** they're very strict about politeness **(c)** (*costume, coupe de cheveux*) severe
strictement [striktəmɑ̃] *adv* **(a)** (*rigoureusement*) strictly; **s. interdit** *ou* **défendu** strictly forbidden; **s. confidentiel** strictly confidential; **je ne comprends s. rien** I don't understand a (single) thing **(b)** (*sévèrement*) (*habillé etc*) severely
striction [striksjɔ̃] *nf Méd* constriction
stricto sensu [striktosɛ̃sy] *adj* strictly speaking
strident [stridɑ̃] *adj* strident, shrill
stridulation [stridylasjɔ̃] *nf* stridulation
strie [stri] *nf* **(a)** (*sillon*) groove; (*en relief*) ridge; *Anat, Bot, Géol* stria **(b)** (*de couleur*) streak
strié [strije] *adj* **(a)** (*sillonné*) grooved; (*en relief*) ridged; *Anat, Bot, Géol* striated **(b)** (*rayé*) (*marbre etc*) streaked
strier [strije] *vt* (*impf, pr sub* **n. striions, v. striiez**) **(a)** (*sillonner*) to groove; (*en relief*) to ridge **(b)** (*rayer*) to streak
string [striŋ] *nm* (*maillot de bain*) tanga; (*slip*) G-string
stringer [striŋgœr] *nm Journ* stringer
stringman [striŋman] *nm Journ* stringer
strioscopie [strijɔskɔpi] *nf Opt* schlieren photography
stripper [stripœr] *nm Chir* (*instrument*) stripper
stripping [stripiŋ] *nm Méd, Pétr etc* stripping
strip-tease, *pl* **strip-teases** [striptiz] *nm* striptease; **faire un s.** to do a striptease *or* strip
strip-teaseur [striptizœr] *nm* male stripper
strip-teaseuse, *pl* **strip-teaseuses** [striptizøz] *nf* stripper, striptease artist(e)
striure [strijyr] *nf* striation
stroboscope [strɔbɔskɔp] *nm Opt* stroboscope
stroboscopique [strɔbɔskɔpik] *adj* stroboscopic, strobe
strombolien [strɔ̃bɔljɛ̃] *adj Géog* Strombolian
strontium [strɔ̃sjɔm] *nm Ch* strontium
strophe [strɔf] *nf Littér* stanza
structural, -ale, -aux, -ales [stryktyral, -o] *adj* structural; *Ling* **analyse structurale** structural analysis
structuralement [stryktyralmɑ̃] *adv* structurally
structuralisme [stryktyralism] *nm* structuralism
structuraliste [stryktyralist] *adj, n* structuralist
structurant [stryktyrɑ̃] *adj* structuring
structuration [stryktyrasjɔ̃] *nf* structuring
structure [stryktyr] *nf* structure; **fauteuil à s. métallique** metal-framed armchair
▶ **structure**: **s. d'accueil** (*pour minorités*) reception facilities; **s. administrative** administrative structure; *Ordinat* **s. en anneau** ring structure; *Ordinat* **s. arborescente** directory *or* tree structure; *Ordinat* **s. en arbre** tree structure; *Ordinat* **s. de bloc** block structure; *Ordinat* **s. en bus** bus structure; **s. de l'entreprise** company *or* corporate structure; *Ordinat* **s. en étoile** star structure; *Ordinat* **s. de fichier** file structure; **s. des prix** price structure
structuré [stryktyre] *adj* structured; *Ordinat* **fichier non s.** flat file
structurel, -elle [stryktyrɛl] *adj* structural; **chômage s.** structural unemployment
structurellement [stryktyrɛlmɑ̃] *adv* structurally
structurer [stryktyre] *vt* to structure
strume [strym] *nf Méd Arch* **(a)** (*goitre*) goitre **(b)** (*scrofule*) scrofula
strychnine [striknin] *nf Ch, Pharm* strychnine
stuc [styk] *nm Constr* stucco; **décoration en s.** stucco decoration
stucage [stykaʒ] *nm Constr* stucco work
stucateur [stykatœr] *nm* stucco worker
studieusement [stydjøzmɑ̃] *adv* studiously
studieux, -ieuse [stydjø, -jøz] *adj* (*personne*) studious; (*vacances etc*) study
studio [stydjo] *nm* **(a)** *Cin, Phot, TV, Beaux-Arts etc* studio; **tourné en s.** filmed in the studio **(b)** (*logement*) studio *or* one-roomed flat *or Am* apartment
▶ **studio**: *TV, Rad* **s. d'annonceur** announcer studio; **s. de cinéma** film studio; **s. de danse** dance studio; **s. de doublage** dubbing suite; **s. d'enregistrement** recording *or* sound studio; **s. de peintre** artist's studio; **s. de photographe** photographer's studio; *TV, Cin* **s. de post-production** postproduction studio; *TV, Cin* **s. de reportage** self-op studio
stupéfaction [stypefaksjɔ̃] *nf* stupefaction, amazement; **je constate avec s. que …** I am amazed to note that …
stupéfait [stypefɛ] *adj* stupefied, stunned, amazed (**de** by)
stupéfiant [stypefjɑ̃] **1** *adj* **(a)** *Méd* (*substance*) stupefying, *Spéc* stupefacient **(b)** (*nouvelles*) astounding, amazing **2** *nm Méd* drug, narcotic, *Spéc* stupefacient; **brigade des stupéfiants** drug squad
stupéfier [stypefje] *vt* (*impf, pr sub* **n. stupéfiions, v. stupéfiiez**) to stupefy, to stun, to amaze
stupeur [stypœr] *nf* **(a)** *Méd* stupor **(b)** (*étonnement*) amazement; **muet de s.** dumbfounded; **je constate avec s. que …** I am amazed to note that …
stupide [stypid] *adj* **(a)** (*idiot*) stupid, silly; **c'est s., mais je n'ai pas pu m'empêcher de le lui dire** it was stupid, but I couldn't stop myself telling him; **accident/mort s.** stupid *or* silly accident/death **(b)** *Litt* (*stupéfait*) stunned
stupidement [stypidmɑ̃] *adv* stupidly; **rire s.** to give a stupid laugh; **mourir s.** to die a stupid death; **il m'a regardé faire s.** he stood there like an idiot and watched me
stupidité [stypidite] *nf* **(a)** (*caractère*) stupidity, foolishness **(b)** (*parole, acte*) stupid thing (to say/do/*etc*); **dire/faire des stupidités** to say/do stupid things; **répondre par une s.** to give a silly answer
stupre [stypr] *nm Litt* debauchery
stups [styp] *nmpl F* (*abrév* **stupéfiants**) *voir* **stupéfiant**
stuquer [styke] *vt Constr* to stucco
style [stil] *nm* **(a)** *Littér, Archit, Gram etc* style; **j'ai envie de changer de s.** I want to change my style; **elle a beaucoup de s.** she has a lot of style, she's very stylish; **tourner ses phrases avec s.** to have a stylish turn of phrase; **s. de vie** lifestyle; **ce skieur a un beau s.** this skier has (a) good style; **ce chapeau est tout à fait ton s.** this hat is just your style; *F Péj* **ça serait bien son s.!** that would be just like him *or* just his style!; **dans le s. de** in the style of; **une veste un peu dans le s. de la tienne** a jacket in the same sort of style as yours; **meubles de s.** period furniture; **meubles s. Louis XIII/régence** Louis XIII-/Regency-style furniture

(b) *Antiq* (*pour écrire*) stylus, style

(c) (*pour enregistrer un disque*) record cutter; (*d'appareil enregistreur*) (recording) needle

(d) (*de cadran solaire*) style, pin, gnomon; (*de baromètre*) hand

(e) *Bot* style

stylé[1] [stile] *adj Biol* stylate
stylé[2] *adj* (*domestique etc*) trained

styler [stile] *vt* (*domestique etc*) to train
stylet [stilɛ] *nm* **(a)** (*poignard*) stiletto **(b)** *Chir* stylet, probe **(c)** *Zool* stylet **(d)** *Ordinat* **s. lumineux** light pen
stylicien [stilisjɛ̃] *nm* designer
stylique [stilik] *nf* design
stylisation [stilizasjɔ̃] *nf* stylization
styliser [stilize] *vt Beaux-Arts etc* to stylize
stylisme [stilism] *nm* **(a)** *Littér* attention to style **(b)** *Com, Ind* designing
styliste [stilist] *n* **(a)** *Littér* stylist **(b)** *Com, Ind* designer
stylisticien, -ienne [stilistisjɛ̃, -jɛn] *n* expert in stylistics
stylistique [stilistik] **1** *adj* stylistic **2** *nf* stylistics
stylite [stilit] *nm Hist, Rel* stylite
stylo [stilo] *nm* pen; **s. à encre** *ou* **à plume** fountain pen; **s. bille, s. bic®** ballpoint (pen), *Br* Biro®; *Ordinat* **s. électronique** electronic pen
stylo-feutre, *pl* **stylos-feutres** felt-tip (pen)
stylographe [stilɔgraf] *nm Arch* fountain pen
Stylomine® [stilomin] *nm* propelling pencil
stylo-surligneur, *pl* **stylo-surligneurs** *nm* highlighter
styptique [stiptik] *adj, nm Méd* styptic
styrax [stiraks] *nm Bot* styrax
styrène [stirɛn] *nm Ch* styrene
Styx [stiks] *nm* **le S.** the Styx
su [sy] **1** *pp voir* **savoir 2** *nm* **au s. de** to the knowledge of; **au vu et au s. de qn** right in front of sb; **elle l'a fait au vu et au s. de tout le monde** she did it quite openly *or* for all the world to see
suage[1] [sɥaʒ] *nm* (*du bois etc*) sweating, oozing
suage[2] *nm* (*d'un bougeoir, d'un plat en étain etc*) fillet (border)
suaire [sɥɛr] *nm* **(a)** *Litt* (*linceul*) winding sheet, shroud **(b)** *Rel* **le saint s.** the holy shroud
suant [sɥɑ̃] *adj* **(a)** *F* sweating, sweaty **(b)** *Arg* (*ennuyeux*) boring
suave [sɥav] *adj* **(a)** (*musique, odeur, goût etc*) sweet **(b)** *Fig* (*ton, manières*) suave, smooth
suavement [sɥavmɑ̃] *adv* (*parler*) suavely
suavité [sɥavite] *nf* **(a)** (*d'un parfum, d'une mélodie*) sweetness **(b)** (*des manières*) suavity
subaigu, -uë [sybegy] *adj Méd* subacute
subalpin [sybalpɛ̃] *adj* subalpine
subalterne [sybaltɛrn] **1** *adj* (*officier, position, rôle*) subordinate, minor; (*esprit*) inferior; (*employé*) junior **2** *nm* **(a)** subordinate **(b)** *Mil* subaltern (officer)
subaquatique [sybakwatik] *adj* subaquatic, underwater
subatomique [sybatɔmik] *adj* subatomic
subconscient [sybkɔ̃sjɑ̃] *adj, nm* subconscious
subdiviser [sybdivize] **1** *vt* to subdivide **2 se subdiviser** *vpr* to be subdivided
subdivision [sybdivizjɔ̃] *nf* subdivision
subéquatorial, -ale, -aux, -ales [sybekwatɔrjal, -o] *adj Géog* subequatorial
subéreux, -euse [syberø, -øz] *adj Bot* suberose, corky
subir [sybir] *vt* (*procès, examen, opération, torture, changement etc*) to undergo; (*mort, violence, conséquences*) to suffer; (*sentence*) to serve; (*influence*) to be under; (*défaite, pertes*) to suffer, to sustain; **s. une majoration** to increase, to rise; **il commence à s. les contrecoups de la crise économique** he's starting to suffer the effects of the economic crisis; **s. qn** to put up with sb; **je ne veux pas avoir à le s. tout le week end!** I don't want to have to put up with *or* suffer him all weekend!; **faire s. qch à qn** to subject sb to sth
subit [sybi] *adj* (*mort, changement*) sudden, unexpected
subitement [sybitmɑ̃] *adv* suddenly, all of a sudden
subito [sybito] *adv F* all of a sudden; (*immédiatement*) at once; **s. presto** at once
subjectif, -ive [sybʒɛktif, -iv] *adj* subjective; *Gram* **cas s.** nominative case
subjectivement [sybʒɛktivmɑ̃] *adv* subjectively
subjectivisme [sybʒɛktivism] *nm Phil* subjectivism
subjectivité [sybʒɛktivite] *nf* subjectivity; **propos pleins de s.** subjective remarks
subjonctif, -ive [sybʒɔ̃ktif, -iv] [①**A51-2**,14; **B30-1**,G] *Gram* **1** *adj* (*mode*) subjunctive **2** *nm* subjunctive; **au s.** in the subjunctive
subjugation [sybʒygasjɔ̃] *nf* subjugation
subjuguer [sybʒyge] *vt* (*personnes, nation*) to subjugate, to subdue; (*cheval*) to subdue, to master; *Fig* (*audience, cœurs etc*) to captivate, to enthral
sublimation [syblimasjɔ̃] *nf Ch, Psy* sublimation
sublime [syblim] **1** *adj* sublime; *F* **ça n'a rien de s.** it's nothing to write home about **2** *nm* **le s.** the sublime
sublimé [syblime] **1** *adj* sublimated **2** *nm Ch* sublimate
sublimement [syblimmɑ̃] *adv* sublimely
sublimer [syblime] *vt Ch, Psy* to sublimate
subliminaire [sybliminɛr], **subliminal, -ale, -aux, -ales** [sybliminal, -o] *adj* subliminal; **publicité s.** *ou* **subliminale** subliminal advertising
sublimité [syblimite] *nf Litt* sublimeness
sublingual, -ale, -aux, -ales [syblɛ̃gwal, -o] *adj Anat* (*glande etc*) sublingual; *Pharm* **comprimé s.** tablet to be placed under the tongue
submerger [sybmɛrʒe] *vt* (**je submergeai(s)**; **n. submergeons**) **(a)** (*pré etc*) to submerge, to flood; (*bateau*) to submerge, to swamp; (*objet*) to submerge; *Fig* **ville submergée par les touristes** town inundated with *or* overrun by tourists **(b)** *Fig* (*qn*) to overwhelm; **être submergé de travail** to be snowed under *or* overwhelmed with work; **depuis que son troisième enfant est né, elle est submergée** she's been snowed under since the birth of her third child
submersible [sybmɛrsibl] **1** *adj* **(a)** (*bateau*) submersible **(b)** *Bot* (*plante*) submerged **(c)** (*sol*) liable to flooding **2** *nm Naut* submarine
submersion [sybmɛrsjɔ̃] *nf* submersion, flooding; **mort par s.** death by drowning
subodorer [sybɔdɔre] *vt F* (*danger, complot etc*) to suspect; **il a subodoré quelque chose** he smelt a rat
subordination [sybɔrdinasjɔ̃] *nf* subordination; **complément/conjonction de s.** subordinating complement/conjunction
subordonnant [sybɔrdɔnɑ̃] *adj* [①**A68-70**,2; **B55**,B] *Gram* (*conjonction etc*) subordinating
subordonné, -ée [sybɔrdɔne] **1** *adj* **(a)** *Gram* (*proposition*) subordinate **(b)** (*dépendant*) subordinate (**à** to); **c'est s. aux revenus de l'année précédente** it is subject to the previous year's income **2** *n* (*personne*) subordinate **3** *nf Gram* **subordonnée** subordinate clause
subordonner [sybɔrdɔne] **1** *vt* to subordinate (**à** to); *Fig* **s. ses dépenses à ses revenus** to cut one's coat according to one's cloth, to live within one's means; **le service est subordonné au nombre des voyageurs** the service depends on the number of travellers **2 se subordonner** *vpr* **se s. à qn** to subordinate oneself to sb
subornation [sybɔrnasjɔ̃] *nf Jur* subornation, bribing
suborner [sybɔrne] *vt* **(a)** *Jur* (*témoin*) to suborn, to bribe **(b)** *Litt* (*séduire*) (*femme*) to seduce
suborneur, -euse [sybɔrnœr, -øz] **1** *n Jur* (*d'un témoin*) suborner, briber **2** *nm Litt* (*séducteur*) seducer
subreptice [sybrɛptis] *adj* surreptitious
subrepticement [sybrɛptismɑ̃] *adv* surreptitiously
subrogation [sybrɔgasjɔ̃] *nf Jur* subrogation, substitution
subrogé, -ée [sybrɔʒe] **1** *adj* subrogated; (*gardien*) deputy, surrogate **2** *n Rel, Jur* surrogate, deputy
subroger [sybrɔʒe] *vt* (**je subrogeai(s)**; **n. subrogeons**) *Jur* to subrogate, to substitute
subséquemment [sypsekamɑ̃, sybs-] *adv Jur, Litt* subsequently
subséquent [sypsekɑ̃, sybs-] *adj Jur, Géog, Litt* subsequent
subside [sypsid, sybz-] *nm* subsidy, grant; **vivre des subsides de l'État** to live on state grants *or* subsidies
subsidence [sypsidɑ̃s, sybz-] *nf Géol* subsidence
subsidiaire [sypsidjɛr, sybz-] *adj* subsidiary; **question s.** tie-breaker
subsidiairement [sypsidjɛrmɑ̃, sybz-] *adv* subsidiarily; **s. à** in addition to
subsidiarité [sypsidjarite, sybz-] *nf CE* subsidiarity
subsistance [sybzistɑ̃s] *nf* **(a)** (*survie*) subsistence; **pourvoir à la s. de sa famille** to keep *or* support one's family; **moyen de s.** means of support **(b) subsistances** (*vivres*) provisions; *Mil* supplies
subsistant [sybzistɑ̃] *adj* remaining, existing
subsister [sybziste] *vi* **(a)** (*d'une chose*) to survive, to remain **(b)** (*d'une personne*) to live, *Fml* to subsist (**de** on); **moyens de s.** means of support; **cela lui suffit à peine à s.** it's barely enough for him to live on
subsonique [sypsɔnik, sybs-] *adj Av* subsonic
substance [sypstɑ̃s] *nf* **(a)** (*essentiel*) (*d'un article etc*) substance, gist; **sans s.** (*arguments etc*) insubstantial; **en s.** in substance; **voici en s. de quoi nous avons parlé** this is the gist of what we were talking about **(b)** (*matière*) substance, matter; **s. étrangère** extraneous substance; **plaie avec perte de s.** wound with loss of tissue; *Anat* **s. grise** grey matter
substantialité [sypstɑ̃sjalite] *nf Phil* substantiality
substantiel, -ielle [sypstɑ̃sjɛl] *adj* substantial
substantiellement [sypstɑ̃sjɛlmɑ̃] *adv* substantially
substantif, -ive [sypstɑ̃tif, -iv] *Gram* **1** *adj* substantive **2** *nm* substantive, noun
substantifique [sypstɑ̃tifik] *adj* **la s. moelle** (*d'un texte etc*) the essence, the pith
substantivement [sypstɑ̃tivmɑ̃] *adj Gram* substantively, as a noun

substantiver [sypstɑ̃tive] *Gram* **1** *vt* **s. un verbe/un adjectif** to use a verb/an adjective substantively *or* as a noun **2 se substantiver** *vpr* to be used substantively *or* as a noun

substituer [sypstitɥe] **1** *vt* **(a)** *(remplacer)* to substitute (**à** for); **s. un objet à un autre** to substitute one object for another, to replace one object by another **(b)** *Jur* **s. un héritier** to appoint an heir in succession to another *or* failing another; **s. un héritage** to entail an estate **2 se substituer** *vpr* **se s. à qn/à qch** to substitute for sb/sth, to take the place of sb/sth; **tu ne peux tout de même pas te s. à son père!** you can't take the place of his father!

substitut [sypstity] *nm* substitute (**de** for); *Jur* deputy public prosecutor; **un s. de père** a surrogate father; **s. de repas** meal substitute; *Mktg* **s. rapproché** close substitute

substitution [sypstitysjɔ̃] *nf* **(a)** *(remplacement)* substitution (**à** for); **son père de s.** his surrogate father **(b)** *Jur* **s. d'enfant** switching round of babies

substrat [sypstra] *nm Géol, Ling, Phil* substratum; *Phot, Biol, Ordinat* substrate

subterfuge [syptɛrfyʒ] *nm* subterfuge; **user de s.** to resort to subterfuge

subtil [syptil] *adj* **(a)** *(fin)* *(plaisanterie, remarque)* subtle; *(esprit, humour etc)* subtle, discerning **(b)** *(ténu)* *(distinction, différence etc)* subtle, fine **(c)** *Arch* *(fluide)* tenuous, thin; *(poussière)* fine **(d)** *(qui pénètre)* *(poison, odeur etc)* pervasive

subtilement [syptilmɑ̃] *adv* subtly

subtiliser [syptilize] **1** *vt* **(a)** *F* *(dérober)* to pinch, *Br* to nick (**à** from); **on lui a subtilisé son portefeuille** he's had his wallet pinched **(b)** *Arch* *(substance)* to refine **2** *vi* *(en raisonnant)* to split hairs, to be over-subtle

subtilité [syptilite] *nf* **(a)** *(de l'esprit, d'une manœuvre etc)* subtlety **(b)** *(d'une distinction)* subtlety, fineness **(c)** *(d'un argument etc)* subtlety; **les subtilités de la langue** the subtleties of the language

subtropical, -ale, -aux, -ales [syptrɔpikal, -o] *adj* subtropical

suburbain [sybyrbɛ̃] *adj* suburban

subvenir [sybvənir] *vi* *(conj like* **venir;** *aux* **avoir)** **s. à** *(besoins)* to provide for; *(dépenses)* to meet; **s. aux dépenses de sa famille** to provide for one's family

subvention [sybvɑ̃sjɔ̃] *nf* subsidy, grant; **s. aux entreprises** development grant; **recevoir** *ou* **toucher des subventions** to get a subsidy, to be subsidized; **s. d'exploitation** operating subsidy; **s. à l'exportation** export subsidy

subventionner [sybvɑ̃sjɔne] *vt* *(entreprise, institution etc)* to subsidize, to grant (financial) aid to; **subventionné** *(industrie, théâtre etc)* subsidized; *(école)* maintained, grant-aided

subversif, -ive [sybvɛrsif, -iv] *adj* subversive

subversion [sybvɛrsjɔ̃] *nf* subversion

subversivement [sybvɛrsivmɑ̃] *adv* subversively

subvertir [sybvɛrtir] *vt Litt* to subvert

suc [syk] *nm* **(a)** *(de fruit, viande), Physiol* juice; *Bot* sap; **s. gastrique** gastric juice **(b)** *Fig Litt* *(de texte etc)* essence

succédané [syksedane] *adj, nm aussi Méd* substitute (**de** for); **s. de café** coffee substitute; *Fig* **un s. de Truffaut** a second-rate Truffaut

succéder [syksede] **(je succède, n. succédons; je succéderai)** **1** *vi* **s. à qn/qch** to succeed sb/sth, to take over from sb/sth; **un sentiment de pitié succéda à sa rage** his anger gave way to a feeling of pity; **les champs succèdent aux bois** (the) fields give way to woods; **s. au trône** to succeed to the throne; **s. à une fortune** to inherit a fortune

2 se succéder *vpr* **les révolutions se succédèrent** revolution followed revolution, there was a succession of revolutions; **les générations qui se sont succédées** the generations that followed each other; **les journées se succédaient** day followed day, the days followed each other

succès [syksɛ] *nm* success; **avoir du s.** to be successful *or* a success; **ne pas avoir de s.** to be unsuccessful; **elle a un grand s. auprès des hommes** she is very successful *or* has great success with men; **se vanter de ses s.** to boast about one's success; **remporter un beau/de grands s.** to have *or* achieve great success; **passer un examen avec s.** to pass an exam; **sans s.** *(utilisé adjectivement)* unsuccessful; *(utilisé adverbialement)* unsuccessfully; **j'ai essayé de le convaincre, mais sans s.** I tried to convince him, but without success *or* I was unsuccessful; **une seconde tentative n'eut pas plus de s.** a second attempt met with no more success *or* was no more successful; **je n'ai pas eu de s. avec ma proposition** I was unsuccessful *or* had no success with my proposal; *Sp* **le plus beau s. de l'équipe** the team's greatest success; **livre à s., s. de librairie** bestseller; **auteur à s.** bestselling author; **chanteur/acteur à s.** successful singer/actor; **pièce/chanson à s.** hit play/song; **remporter un** *ou* **avoir grand s.** *(d'une pièce de théâtre etc)* to be a great *or* a huge success; **le public a fait un s. à ce livre/cette pièce/ce film** the book/play/film has been well received (by the public); **s. fou** great success; **s. d'audience** ratings success; *F* big *or* smash hit (**auprès de, parmi** with); **les casquettes de baseball ont un s. fou auprès des jeunes** baseball caps are big *or* a big hit with young people

successeur [syksesœr] *nm* successor (**de** to, of)

successif, -ive [syksesif, -iv] *adj* successive

succession [syksesjɔ̃] *nf* **(a)** *(série)* *(d'idées, de sons, de jours etc)* succession, series; *(de personnes, d'admirateurs etc)* stream, succession; **s. de catastrophes** series *or* catalogue of disasters **(b)** *(au trône, au pouvoir etc)* succession (**à** to); **la s. du poste sera assurée par M. Dupont** Mr Dupont will take over the post; **prendre la s. d'une maison de commerce** to take over a business **(c)** *Jur* *(par héritage)* succession; *(biens)* inheritance; **droits de s.** death duties

successivement [syksesivmɑ̃] *adv* successively

succinct, -e [syksɛ̃, syksɛ̃kt] *adj* succinct, brief, concise; *F* **repas s.** frugal meal; **sois s.** be brief, keep it brief

succinctement [syksɛ̃tmɑ̃] *adv* succinctly, briefly; *F* *(manger)* frugally

succion [sy(k)sjɔ̃] *nf* suction; **bruit de s.** sucking noise

succomber [sykɔ̃be] *vi* **(a)** *(tomber)* to succumb, to collapse; **s. sous le poids de qch** to collapse under the weight of sth; **s. sous le nombre** to yield to greater numbers; *Fig* **s. sous les soucis/les problèmes financiers** to be overwhelmed by worries/financial problems; **s. devant un adversaire** *(dans un combat), Fig* to yield to an opponent **(b)** **s. à** *(peine, tentation etc)* to succumb to, to yield to; *(émotion)* to be overcome by; **j'ai succombé à la fatigue** I succumbed to fatigue **(c)** *(mourir)* to die, to succumb

succube [sykyb] *nm* succubus, succuba

succulence [sykylɑ̃s] *nf Litt* succulence

succulent [sykylɑ̃] *adj* *(nourriture)* succulent; *Bot* *(feuille)* fleshy; **plante succulente** succulent

succursale [sykyrsal] *nf Com* branch; **magasin à succursales** chain store

sucer [syse] **(je suçai(s); n. suçons)** **1** *vt* **(a)** *(lait, orange, os etc)* to suck; **comprimés à s.** *(sur boîte)* to be sucked; **s. son pouce** to suck one's thumb; *Vieilli* **s. qch avec le lait** to take sth in with one's mother's milk; *Fig F* **s. qn jusqu'au dernier sou** *ou* **jusqu'à la moelle des os** to suck sb dry, to bleed sb white; *Arg* **s. la poire à qn** to French-kiss sb; **ils sont tout le temps à se s. la poire** they're always snogging

(b) *(sexuellement)* *Vulg* **s. qn** to suck sb (off), to give sb a blow job, *Am* to give sb head

2 se sucer *vpr* **(a)** **se s. les doigts** to suck one's fingers; *Arg* **se s. la poire** to snog

(b) **ces cachets se sucent** these tablets are (meant) to be sucked *or* are for sucking

sucette [sysɛt] *nf* **(a)** *(de bébé)* dummy, *Am* pacifier **(b)** *(confiserie)* lollipop, *F* lolly

suceur, -euse [sysœr, -øz] **1** *n Péj* **s. de sang** *(personne)* bloodsucker **2** *nm* **(a)** *(poisson)* sucker, sucking fish **(b)** *(d'aspirateur)* nozzle **3** *nf* **suceuse** *(drague)* suction dredger

suçon [sysɔ̃] *nm F* lovebite; **faire un s. à qn** to give sb a lovebite

suçoter [sysɔte] *vt F* *(qch)* to suck (at)

sucrage [sykraʒ] *nm* *(du vin)* sugaring

sucrant [sykrɑ̃] *adj* sweetening; **avoir un grand pouvoir s.** to be a strong sweetener; **produit s.** sweetener

sucrase [sykraz] *nf Ch* sucrase

sucre [sykr] *nm* **(a)** *(substance)* sugar; **s. en pains** loaf sugar; **pain de s.** sugar loaf; **montagne en pain de s.** sugar-loaf mountain; **un s. dans mon café** one sugar in my coffee; **vous le prenez avec ou sans s., votre café?** do you take sugar in your coffee or not?; **fruit au s.** fruit sprinkled with sugar; **décorations en s.** sugar decorations; *Fig F* **il a été tout s. tout miel** he was all sweetness and light; *Fig* **elle n'est pas en s.!** she's not made of glass!; *F* **mon bébé en s.** my sweetie pie; *Arg* **c'est un vrai s.** he's a honey; *Can* **partie de s.** sugaring-off party

(b) *(monnaie)* sucre

▶ **sucre**: **s. de betterave** beet sugar; **s. brut** unrefined sugar; **s. de canne** cane sugar; **s. cristallisé** granulated sugar; **s. de fruit** fructose; **s. glace** icing *or Am* confectioner's sugar; *Ch* **s. de lait** lactose; **s. en morceaux** lump sugar, sugar lumps; **s. d'orge** barley sugar; **s. en poudre** caster sugar; **s. roux** brown sugar; **s. semoule** caster sugar

sucré [sykre] **1** *adj* **(a)** *(naturellement)* *(aliment, substance, goût etc)* sweet **(b)** *(additionné de sucre)* *(à la fabrication)* sweetened; *(café etc)* sugared, sweetened; **boisson non sucrée** unsweetened drink; **eau sucrée** sugar and water; **mon thé est trop s.** my tea is too sweet, there's too much sugar in my tea **(c)** *Fig* *(paroles, manières, sourire)* sugary;

prendre un ton s. to speak in a smarmy tone 2 *n* faire le/la sucré(e) to be all sweetness and light

sucrer [sykre] 1 *vt* (a) to sugar, to sweeten; s. son café to sugar one's coffee; je ne sucre pas mes yaourts I don't put sugar in my yoghurt; *Fig F* s. les fraises (*trembler*) to shake; (*être gâteux*) to be an old dodderer (b) *Fig F* (*supprimer*) (*passage, émission etc*) to cut; on lui a sucré sa prime he has had his bonus taken away; on ne va pas me s. mes vacances! I'm not going to have my holidays cancelled! 2 *vi* (*du miel etc*) to sweeten 3 se sucrer *vpr* (a) *F* (*prendre du sucre*) to help oneself to sugar (b) *Arg* (*faire des bénéfices*) to line one's pockets

sucrerie [sykrəri] *nf* (a) (*usine*) sugar refinery (b) sucreries (*friandises*) confectionery, sweets, *surtout Am* candy; dans votre condition il faut éviter les sucreries you must avoid eating sweet things in your condition; aimer les sucreries to have a sweet tooth (c) *Can* (*forêt*) maple tree grove

sucrette [sykrɛt] *nf* artificial sweetener

sucrier, -ière [sykrije, -jɛr] 1 *adj* sugar; industrie sucrière sugar industry 2 *n* (*fabricant*) sugar manufacturer 3 *nm* (*récipient*) sugar bowl *or* basin; s. verseur sugar shaker

sud [syd] 1 *nm* (*no pl*) (a) south; un vent du s. a southerly wind, a wind from the south; le vent du s. the south wind; maison exposée au s. house facing south; dans le S. de l'Angleterre in the South of England; au s. in the south; au s. de Paris (to the) south of Paris; l'Amérique du S. South America; l'Afrique du S. South Africa; l'Italie du S. southern Italy; vers le s. south, southward (b) *Naut* le s. (*vent*) the south wind 2 *adj inv* (*vent*) south, southerly; (*partie, latitude etc*) southern; le Pôle S. the South Pole; Pacifique S. South Pacific; le côté s. (*d'une maison, d'un mur etc*) the south side

sud-africain, -aine, *pl* sud-africain(e)s 1 *adj* South African; la République sud-africaine the Republic of South Africa 2 *n* S. South African

sud-américain, -aine, *pl* sud-américain(e)s 1 *adj* South American 2 *n* S. South American

sudation [sydasjɔ̃] *nf Méd etc* sudation, sweating

sud-coréen, -enne, *pl* sud-coréen(ne)s 1 *adj* South Korean 2 *n* S. South Korean

sud-est 1 *nm* (*no pl*) southeast; vers le s. southeastward, toward(s) the southeast; le Sud-Est de la France the southeast of France; Sud-Est asiatique South East Asia 2 *adj inv* (*vent*) southeast, south-easterly; (*région*) southeastern

sudiste [sydist] *Hist Am* 1 *n* (*de la Guerre Civile*) Confederate 2 *adj* Southern

sudorifère [sydɔrifɛr] *adj* = sudoripare

sudorifique [sydɔrifik] *adj, nm Pharm* sudorific

sudoripare [sydɔripar] *adj Anat* sudoriferous; glande s. sweat gland

sud-ouest 1 *nm* (*no pl*) southwest; vers le s. southwestward, toward(s) the southwest; le Sud-Ouest de la France the southwest of France 2 *adj inv* (*vent*) south-westerly; (*région*) southwestern

Sud-Ouest africain *nm Hist* South West Africa

sud-vietnamien, -ienne, *pl* sud-vietnamien(ne)s 1 *adj* South Vietnamese 2 *n* S. South Vietnamese

Suède [sɥɛd] *nf* Sweden

suédé [sɥede] *adj, nm* suede

suédine [sɥedin] *nf Tex* suedette

suédois, -oise [sɥedwa, -az] [①A20,d] 1 *adj* Swedish; *Gym* la gymnastique suédoise Swedish gymnastics *or* exercises 2 *nm Ling* Swedish 3 *n* S. Swede

suée [sɥe] *nf F* (*transpiration*) sweat; (*sous l'effet de la peur*) (cold) sweat; prendre une s. to get up *or* work up a sweat; cela m'a donné une sacrée s. (*d'un travail*) I sweated blood over it; (*d'une expérience effrayante*) it brought me out in a cold sweat; j'en ai encore des suées I still break out in a cold sweat when I think about it

suer [sɥe] 1 *vi* (a) (*d'une personne*) to sweat; s. à grosses gouttes to be pouring with sweat, to be sweating buckets; *F* faire s. qn (*embêter*) to annoy sb; ça me fait s. d'aller à cette soirée it's a drag having to go to that party; ce que j'ai pu me faire suer pendant les vacances I was bored stiff during the holidays, the holidays were a real drag; tu me fais s. à la fin avec tes devoirs! you're getting on my nerves with your homework!

(b) (*des murs etc*) to ooze

(c) (*travailler*) to labour, *US* to labor, to sweat; *F* faire s. le burnous to use sweated labour

2 *vt* to sweat; *Fig* (*piété, ennui, hypocrisie etc*) to ooze; *Fig* s. sang et eau to sweat blood and tears; maison qui sue le crime house that reeks of *or* exudes crime

sueur [sɥœr] *nf* sweat; son visage ruissellait de s. his face was streaming with sweat; être en s. to be sweating *or* in a sweat; avoir des sueurs froides to be in a cold sweat; j'en ai encore des sueurs froides, rien que d'y penser I get in a cold sweat just thinking about it; à la s. de son front by the sweat of one's brow; le fruit de mes sueurs the fruits of my labour *or US* labor

Suez [sɥɛz] *n* Suez; le canal de S. the Suez Canal

suffire [syfir] (*prp* suffisant; *pp* suffi; *pr ind* je suffis, n. suffisons, ils suffisent; *pr sub* je suffise; *impf* je suffisais; *p hist* je suffis; *fu* je suffirai) 1 *vi* to be enough, to be sufficient; cela ne me suffit pas (pour vivre) that is not enough for me (to live on); votre promesse me suffit your promise is enough for me; *Prov* à chaque jour suffit sa peine sufficient unto the day is the evil thereof; s. à qch/à faire qch to be up to sth/to doing sth; s. à la tâche to be up to *or* equal to the job; cela suffit à mes besoins that's enough for my needs; je n'y suffis plus it's too much for me, I can't cope

2 se suffire *vpr* il s'est toujours suffi he has always supported himself *or* earned his own living; pays qui se suffisent (à eux-mêmes) self-supporting countries

3 *v impers* [①B28,E,f,iii] il a suffi de quelques mots pour le persuader a few words were enough to persuade him; il suffit de l'écouter pour ... one only has to *or* one need only listen to him to ...; il suffit qu'il le dise all he has to do is say so; ça ne lui suffit pas that's not enough for him; il te l'a promis, ça ne te suffit pas? he's promised you, is that not enough?; il suffisait que tu passes un coup de téléphone all you had to do was phone; ça suffit!, (il) suffit! that's enough!, that'll do!; il suffit d'une heure pour ... it only takes an hour to ...

suffisamment [syfizamɑ̃] *adv* enough, sufficiently; agir sans avoir s. réfléchi to act without sufficient thought; s. de enough, sufficient; j'ai pris s. de temps à le lui expliquer I took the time to explain it to her; j'ai s. souffert pour savoir que ... I've suffered enough to know that ...

suffisance [syfizɑ̃s] *nf* (a) avoir s. de to have sufficient *or* enough; manger à sa s. to eat one's fill; avoir de qch à s. *ou* en s. to have sth in abundance, to have plenty of sth (b) (*vanité*) arrogance, self-importance; il est d'une s. insupportable he is unbearably conceited (c) *Arch* (*capacité*) competence; homme de s. competent man

suffisant, -ante [syfizɑ̃, -ɑ̃t] 1 *adj* (a) sufficient, enough; c'est plus que s. that is more than sufficient *or* enough (b) (*vaniteux*) (*air, ton*) self-important, conceited 2 *n* faire le s. to give oneself airs

suffixe [syfiks] *nm Gram, Ordinat* suffix

suffixer [syfikse] *vt Gram, Ordinat* to suffix, to add a suffix to; mot suffixé word with *or* that has a suffix

suffocant [syfɔkɑ̃] *adj* (a) (*chaleur etc*) suffocating, stifling (b) *Fig* (*nouvelle, réponse etc*) staggering, astounding

suffocation [syfɔkasjɔ̃] *nf* suffocation; (*crise*) choking fit

suffoquer [syfɔke] 1 *vt* (a) (*d'une odeur, de la fumée etc*) to suffocate, to stifle; *Fig* (*de nouvelles*) to stagger, to astound; les sanglots la suffoquaient she was choking with sobs (b) *Arch* (*tuer*) to suffocate 2 *vi* to suffocate, to choke; s. de colère/d'indignation to choke with anger/indignation

suffragant [syfragɑ̃] *Rel* 1 *adj* (*évêque*) suffragan 2 *nm* suffragan (bishop)

suffrage [syfraʒ] *nm Pol* (*voix*) vote; (*système*) suffrage; dix mille suffrages ten thousand votes; recueillir de nombreux suffrages to win numerous votes; s. universel universal franchise *or* suffrage, one-man-one-vote; s. direct/indirect direct/indirect suffrage; *Fig* ce nouveau modèle remporte tous les suffrages this new model wins everyone's approval *or* is universally liked

suffragette [syfraʒɛt] *nf Hist Pol* suffragette

suffusion [syfyzjɔ̃] *nf Méd* suffusion

suggérer [sygʒere] *vt* (je suggère, n. suggérons; je suggérerai) to suggest (à to); s. de faire qch to suggest doing sth; s. à qn de faire qch to suggest to sb that he should do sth; cette expression suggère la lumière/la vitesse this expression suggests light/speed

suggestibilité [sygʒɛstibilite] *nf* suggestibility

suggestible [sygʒɛstibl] *adj* suggestible

suggestif, -ive [sygʒɛstif, -iv] *adj* (a) (*évocateur*) evocative, suggestive (b) (*érotique*) (*plaisanterie, geste etc*) suggestive; (*tenue, décolleté*) revealing

suggestion [sygʒɛs(t)jɔ̃] *nf* [①A57-8,c-d] suggestion; agir sur la s. de qn to act on sb's suggestion; pas la moindre s. de ... not the slightest hint *or* suggestion of ...

suggestionner [sygʒɛstjɔne] *vt* s. qn to put an idea *or* ideas into sb's head; se laisser s. to allow ideas to be put into one's head (par by)

suicidaire [sɥisidɛr] 1 *adj* (*tendances, personne, Fig entreprise etc*) suicidal 2 *n* suicidal person

suicide [sɥisid] *nm* (*acte*) suicide; tentative de s. suicide attempt; *Fig* le s. économique d'un pays the economic suicide of a country; **attentat-s.** suicide attack; **avion-s.** suicide plane

suicidé, -ée [sɥiside] **1** *adj* who has committed suicide **2** *n* (*personne*) suicide

suicider (se) [səsɥiside] *vpr* to commit suicide; *Fig* **se s. politiquement** to commit political suicide

suie [sɥi] *nf* soot

suif [sɥif] *nm* **(a)** tallow; **s. de mouton** mutton fat; **chandelle de s.** tallow candle **(b)** *Arg Vieilli* **recevoir un s.** to get a dressing down; **faire du s.** to kick up a row; **chercher du s.** to be looking for a fight

suifer [sɥife] *vt* (*cuir etc*) to tallow; (*gond*) to grease

sui generis [sɥiʒeneris] *adj* sui generis; *Euph* **odeur s.** (*mauvaise*) distinctive smell

suint [sɥɛ̃] *nm* (*de laine*) suint

suintant [sɥɛ̃tɑ̃] *adj* (*mur etc*) oozing, dripping; *Méd* running, weeping

suintement [sɥɛ̃tmɑ̃] *nm* (*de rochers, de mur etc*) oozing, dripping; (*de blessure*) running, weeping

suinter [sɥɛ̃te] **1** *vi* **(a)** (*de rocher, de mur etc*) to ooze, to drip **(b)** (*d'un navire*) to leak; (*d'une blessure*) to run, to weep **2** *vt* (*haine etc*) to exude, to ooze

Suisse [sɥis] *nf* Switzerland; **la S. alémanique/romande/italienne** German-/French-/Italian-speaking Switzerland

suisse [sɥis] **1** *adj* Swiss **2** *n* **S.** Swiss; **les Suisses** the Swiss **3** *nm* **(a)** *Hist, Mil* Swiss mercenary; (*au Vatican*) Swiss guard; *F* **manger/boire en s.** to eat/drink on one's own **(b)** *Rel* (*en uniforme*) verger **(c) petit s.** petit suisse (= *small cream cheese*) **(d)** *Can Zool* **s. (rayé)** chipmunk

Suissesse [sɥisɛs] *nf Péj* Swiss (woman)

suite [sɥit] *nf* **(a)** (*action de poursuivre*) pursuit; **être à la s. de qn** to be in pursuit of sb, *F* to be after sb

(b) (*continuation*) continuation, what follows; (*au restaurant*) the next course; **j'ai oublié la s. de la chanson** I've forgotten the rest of the song; **faire s. à** to follow (on from), to be a continuation of; **cette discussion fait s. à ce que nous disions l'autre jour** this discussion follows on from what we said the other day; **le repas qui fit s. à la cérémonie** the meal which followed the ceremony; **comme s. à notre lettre d'hier** further to our letter of yesterday; **à la s. de votre demande** further to *or* with reference to your request; *Com* **donner s. à** (*demande, lettre*) to follow up; (*commande*) to deal with; (*décision*) to give effect to; *Tél* **nous regrettons de ne pouvoir donner s. à votre appel** the number you have dialled has not been recognized; **pour s. à donner** (passed to you) for action; *Com* **sans s.** (*article*) discontinued; **prendre la s. des affaires d'une maison** to take over a business; **à la s. les uns des autres** one after the other; **il a avalé deux gâteaux à la s.** he swallowed two cakes one after the other; **à la s. de cette discussion** following (on) this discussion; **les historiens venus à sa s.** the historians who came after him; **les maux que la guerre traîne à sa s.** the evils that war brings in its wake; **se mettre à la s.** to join (the back of) the queue *or Am* the line

(c) de s. (*à la suite*) in a row, in succession; **dix heures de s.** ten hours on end; **dix jours de s.** ten days running; **pendant plusieurs semaines de s.** for several weeks at a time *or* running; **et ainsi de s.** and so on

(d) tout de s., *F* **de s.** at once, immediately; **je voudrais un café – oui, tout de s. Monsieur** I'd like a coffee – yes (sir), right away; **par la s.** later (on), afterwards

(e) (*nouveau roman, film etc*) sequel; (*nouvel episode*) continuation; *Journ* **s. à la page 30** continued on page 30; **s. et fin** concluded; **la s. au prochain numéro** continued in the next issue; *TV, Cin* **s. à l'américaine** sequel

(f) (*de raisonnement*) coherence, consistency; **sans s.** (*paroles, pensées etc*) incoherent, disjointed, disconnected; (*parler*) incoherently, disjointedly; **s. dans les idées** single-mindedness; **elle a de la s. dans les idées!** she's very single-minded; **manquer (d'esprit) de s.** to be inconsistent, to lack consistency

(g) (*escorte*) suite; (*d'un monarque etc*) retinue, train

(h) (*série*) (*d'événements etc*) series, succession; (*d'ancêtres*) line; (*d'épreuves*) set; **s. de malheurs** run of misfortunes, chapter of accidents; **dans la s. des siècles** in the course of time *or* of the centuries

(i) *Math* series

(j) *Mus* suite

(k) (*conséquence*) consequence, result; (*de maladie etc*) aftereffects; **mourir des suites d'une blessure** to die (as the result) of a wound; **par s.** consequently; **par s. de** due to, on account of; **par s. de maladie** due to *or* owing to illness; **par s. d'une erreur** following *or* through an error; **par s. de sa blessure** as a result of his wound

(l) (*dans un hôtel*) suite; **s. de luxe** luxury suite; (*au dernier étage*) penthouse suite; **s. nuptiale** honeymoon *or* bridal suite; **s. présidentielle** executive suite

suivant[1] [sɥivɑ̃] **1** *prép* **(a)** (*direction*) (*ligne etc*) in the direction of, along; **découper s. le pointillé** cut along the dotted line

(b) (*selon*) (*moyens, instructions etc*) according to, in accordance with; **s. son habitude** as is/was his habit *or* wont; **cela varie s. le jour/la température** it varies from day to day/with the temperature; **s. mon frère** according to my brother, in my brother's opinion; **s. les circonstances** depending on the circumstances; **s. avis** as per advice; **s. connaissement** as per bill of lading; **s. disponibilité** subject to availability; **s. vos instructions** as per your instructions

2 *conj* **s. que + ind** depending on whether, according to whether

suivant[2]**, -ante** [sɥivɑ̃, -ɑ̃t] **1** *adj* (*page, jour etc*) next, following; (*ligne*) next; **le train s. est à 18 heures** the next train is at 6pm; **voir page 6 et suivantes** see page 6 and following *or Fml* et seq; **les trois jours suivants** the next three days; **pas dimanche prochain mais le dimanche s.** not this Sunday but the next (one) *or* the one after; **notre méthode est la suivante** our method is as follows; **il nous fit part de l'histoire suivante** he told us the following story

2 *n* (*prochain*) **le s., la suivante** the next (one); **les suivant(e)s** the next (ones); **au s.!** next (person) please!; *Mktg* **s. immédiat** early follower

3 *nm* (*accompagnateur*) attendant

4 *nf Th* **suivante** attendant

suiveur, -euse [sɥivœr, -øz] **1** *nm* **(a)** (*personne sans initiative*) follower (**de** of); *Mktg* follower; (*sur le marché*) market follower **(b)** *Sp* **les suiveurs** = officials and back-up squads following a cycle race **2** *adj* **voiture suiveuse** = car following a cycle race

suivi [sɥivi] **1** *adj* **(a)** (*discours*) connected; (*raisonnement*) sustained, coherent; (*correspondance*) regular; (*travail, effort, qualité, histoire*) consistent; (*ligne de conduite*) steadfast, unwavering; *Com* (*demande*) steady, persistent; **article s.** stock item **(b)** *Univ* (*cours*) well attended, popular; *TV, Rad* (*émission, feuilleton*) popular; **l'émission a été très suivie** the programme had a large audience *or* was very popular **2** *nm* follow-up; **assurer le s. d'un projet** to follow a project through; **s. de commande** follow-up of an order; *Banque* **suivi des risques** risk monitoring; **s. des ventes** sales follow-up

suivisme [sɥivism] *nm Pol etc* follow-the-herd attitude

suivre [sɥivr] (*prp* **suivant**; *pp* **suivi**; *pr ind* **je suis, il suit, n. suivons, ils suivent**; *pr sub* **je suive**; *impf* **je suivais**; *p hist* **je suivis**; *fu* **je suivrai**) **1** *vt* **(a)** (*aller derrière*) to follow; **nous sommes suivis** we're being followed; **taxi, suivez cette voiture!** taxi, follow that car!; **partez, je vous suis** you go on, I'll follow (on); **se faire s. dans la rue** to get followed in the street; **s. qn de près** to follow close on sb's heels; (*artiste*) to keep an eye *or* a close watch on sb; (*patient*) to monitor sb, to keep an eye on sb; **s. qn pas à pas** to follow sb's every step; **elle le suivit des yeux** *ou* **du regard** she followed him with her eyes; *Fig* **s. son temps** to keep abreast of the times; *Com* **s. une affaire** to follow up business; *Com* **nous n'avons pas suivi cet article** we have discontinued this line; *Tennis etc* **s. la balle** to follow through

(b) (*comprendre*) to follow, to understand; **je ne vous suis pas** I don't follow you; **tu me suis toujours?** are you still with me?; **là je ne le suis plus** he's lost me there; **il parle si vite que je ne peux pas le s.** he talks so quickly that I cannot follow him; **s. une conversation dans une langue étrangère** to follow a conversation in a foreign language

(c) (*accompagner*) (*qn*) to accompany; **s. qn dans ses voyages** to accompany sb on his travels

(d) (*porter son attention sur*) (*qch*) to follow; **suivez bien ce que je vais dire** pay attention to what I'm about to say

(e) (*observer*) (*progrès, série d'événements etc*) to follow, to watch; **s. les cours de la Bourse** to follow the stock exchange prices; **tu as suivi l'affaire Moulin?** have you been following the Moulin affair?; **s. l'actualité à la télévision/à la radio** to follow events on the television/radio; **c'est une affaire à s.** it's worth keeping an eye on

(f) (*venir après*) (*sans mouvement*) to follow, to come after; **la maison qui suit la nôtre** the house after ours; **le printemps suit l'hiver** spring follows winter; **conjonction suivie du subjonctif** conjunction followed by the subjunctive

(g) (*longer*) (*route, Fig pensées etc*) to go along, to follow; *Fig* **nous n'avons pas suivi le même chemin** we didn't follow the same path; **s. son chemin** to go on one's way; **je vais s. mon idée** I'll do it my way; **la rivière suit son cours** the river follows its course; *Fig* **la justice suivra son cours** justice will take its course; **laisser les choses s. leur cours** to let things take their course; **la vie suit son cours** life goes on

(h) (*obéir à*) (*mode, exemple, traitement, intuition*) to follow; (*conseil*) to follow, to act upon; (*loi*) to obey, to conform to; (*ligne de conduite*) to follow, to pursue; **s. un régime** to follow *or* be on a diet; **s. le mouvement** to follow the crowd, to go with the flow; **voici la marche à s.** this is the procedure, this is what you have to do

(i) (*être présent à*) (*série de concerts, de conférences etc*) to attend (regularly); **s. un cours** to follow *or* take a course (of study)

(j) (*en disciple*) (*qn*) to follow

2 *vi* **(a)** (*venir après*) to follow; **le reste du repas suit** the rest of the meal is coming; **les personnes dont les noms suivent** the following persons; **faire s. une lettre** to forward a letter; **(prière de) faire s.** (*sur une enveloppe*) please forward; **faire s. ses bagages** to have one's luggage sent on; *Typ* **(faire) s.** run on; **à s.** (*à la fin d'un feuilleton*) to be continued

(b) (*comprendre*) to follow; (*faire attention*) to pay attention; **pardon, je n'ai pas suivi** sorry, I wasn't paying attention; *Scol* **elle ne suit plus** she can't keep up any more; (*elle rêve*) she doesn't pay attention any more

(c) (*aller au même rythme*) to keep up; **j'ai d'excellents projets, mais les finances ne suivent pas** I've got some great plans, but there isn't the funding for them *or* but the funding isn't forthcoming; **tout augmente, mais les salaires ne suivent pas** everything is going up in price, but the wages aren't following suit

3 se suivre *vpr* to follow each other; **arguments qui se suivent bien** connected *or* coherent arguments; **événements qui se suivent de près** events that follow each other in quick succession

4 *v impers* **il suit de là que ...** it follows (from this) that ...; **que s'en est-il suivi?** what came of it?; **conditions ainsi qu'il suit** terms as follows

sujet[1], -ette [syʒɛ, -ɛt] **1** *adj* **(a) s. à** (*exposé à*) (*maladie etc*) subject to, prone to; **s. à caution** (*nouvelles etc*) unconfirmed; **s. à oublier/mentir** apt *or* liable to forget/given to lying **(b)** *Jur* **s. à** (*impôts etc*) liable to, subject to **(c)** *Arch* (*soumis*) dependent **2** *n* (*d'un État, d'un souverain*) subject

sujet[2] *nm* **(a)** (*cause*) cause, reason, grounds **(de qch** for sth; **de faire** for doing); **un s. de pitié** an object of pity; **s. de querelle** *ou* **dispute** cause for dispute; **je n'ai pas eu s. de me plaindre** I had no cause *or* reason *or* grounds for complaint; **si je me plains c'est que j'en ai s.** if I complain I have good cause *or* reason; **se mettre en colère sans s.** to lose one's temper without *or* for no good reason *or* cause

(b) **au s. de qn/de qch** about *or* concerning sb/sth; **les choses qu'il m'a racontées à votre s.** the things he told me about you; **elle ne m'a rien dit à ce s.** she said nothing to me about it; **à ce s., je voulais vous dire que ...** talking of which, I meant to tell you ...; **au s. de votre lettre** with reference to your letter; **éprouver des craintes au s. de qch** to have fears about sth

(c) (*question*) (*d'un discours, d'un livre, d'une pièce de théâtre, d'un tableau, d'une discussion etc*) subject (matter), theme; (*d'une conversation*) subject, topic; *Mus* (*d'une fugue etc*) subject; **nos avis s'accordent sur le s. de la nourriture** we have the same opinions on the subject of food; **changeons de s. (de conversation)** let's change the subject; **quel est le s. du film?** what's the film about?; **un beau s. de roman** a fine subject for a novel; *Scol* **une dissertation hors (du) s., un hors s.** a dissertation that doesn't deal with the subject

(d) [①**A72-3**,a; **B17**,D,1] *Gram* subject; **s. grammatical/logique** grammatical/logical subject

(e) *Psy, Méd etc* (*d'une expérience*) subject; *F* guinea pig

(f) (*individu*) individual; *Vieilli* **mauvais s.** bad lot, ne'er-do-well; *Vieilli* **bon s.** good sort; *Scol* **brillant s.** brilliant pupil

(g) (*en horticulture*) stock

(h) (*en logique*), *Ling* subject; **le s. parlant/pensant** the speaker/thinker

sujétion [syʒesjɔ̃] *nf Fml* **(a)** (*servitude*) subjection **(à** to); **s. aux lois** subservience to the laws; **une habitude devient vite une s.** we soon become slaves to a habit **(b)** (*contrainte*) constraint; **emploi d'une grande s.** job that keeps one tied down; **c'est une vraie s. d'avoir des animaux domestiques** keeping pets really ties one down

sulfamide [sylfamid] *nm Ch* sulphonamide, *US* sulfonamide; *Méd* sulpha *or US* sulfa drug

sulfatage [sylfataʒ] *nm* **(a)** *Ch, Ind* sulphating, *US* sulfating; *Él* (*des bornes d'une batterie*) corrosion **(b) s. des vignes** treating vines with copper sulphate *or US* sulfate

sulfate [sylfat] *nm Ch* sulphate, *US* sulfate

sulfaté [sylfate] *adj Ch* sulphated, *US* sulfated

sulfater [sylfate] *vt Agr, Ind* to sulphate, *US* to sulfate

sulfateuse [sylfatøz] *nf* **(a)** (*pour la vigne*) sulphate *or US* sulfate sprayer **(b)** *Arg* (*mitraillette*) submachine-gun

sulfhydrique [sylfidrik] *adj Ch* **acide s.** hydrogen sulphide *or US* sulfide

sulfite [sylfit] *nm Ch* sulphite, *US* sulfite

sulfurage [sylfyraʒ] *nm Agr etc* sulphurizing, *US* sulfurizing

sulfuration [sylfyrasjɔ̃] *nf Ch* sulphur(iz)ation, *US* sulfurization

sulfure [sylfyr] *nm Ch* sulphide, *US* sulfide; **s. de fer** iron pyrites

sulfuré [sylfyre] *adj Ch* sulphuretted, *US* sulfuretted; **hydrogène s.** hydrogen sulphide *or US* sulfide, sulphuretted *or US* sulfuretted hydrogen; *Minér* **fer s.** iron pyrites

sulfurer [sylfyre] *vt Agr etc* to sulphurize, *US* to sulfurize

sulfureux, -euse [sylfyrø, -øz] *adj Ch* sulphurous, *US* sulfurous; (*eau, source*) sulphur, *US* sulfur; *Fig* (*écrits, discours*) heretical, *Litt* with a whiff of sulphur; (*charm*) dangerous, hypnotic; **une beauté sulfureuse** a real femme fatale

sulfurique [sylfyrik] *adj Ch* sulphuric, *US* sulfuric

sulfurisé [sylfyrize] *adj* sulphurized, *US* sulfurized; **papier s.** greaseproof paper

sulky, *pl* **sulkies** [sylki] *nm Courses de chevaux* sulky

sultan [syltɑ̃] *nm* sultan

sultanat [syltana] *nm* sultanate

sultane [syltan] *nf* (*épouse d'un sultan*) sultana, sultaness

sumac [symak] *nm Bot* sumac(h)

sumérien, -ienne [symerjɛ̃, -jɛn] **1** *adj* Sumerian **2** *nm Ling* Sumerian **3** *n* **S.** Sumerian

summum [sɔmɔm] *nm* peak, summit; *Fig* (*de la gloire, pédanterie etc*) height

sumo [symo] *nm* (*sport*) sumo (wrestling); **lutteur de s.** sumo wrestler

sun-gun [sœngœn] *nm TV, Cin* sungun

sunlight [sœnlajt] *nm Cin* sun lamp

sunnite [synit] *adj, n Rel* Sunni

super[1] [sypɛr] *F* **1** *adj* (*bon*) super, great, terrific **2** *int* great, terrific **3** *nm Aut* (*abrév* **supercarburant**) four-star petrol, *Am* premium gas; **elle marche au s. ou au gasoil?** does it run on four-star or diesel?; **s. plombé** four-star *or Am* premium leaded; **s. sans plomb** four-star *or Am* premium unleaded

super[2] [sype] **1** *vt Naut* (*d'une pompe*) to suck **2** *vi* **(a)** (*d'une canalisation etc*) to get blocked **(b) navire supé** ship stuck in the mud

super- [sypɛr] *préf F* (*hors du commun*) (*avant nom*) super-; (*avant adj*) ultra-; **s.-chic** ultra-chic; **s.-chouette** great, terrific

superbe [sypɛrb] **1** *adj* **(a)** (*magnifique, remarquable*) (*bâtiment, temps, spectacle, cheval etc*) superb, magnificent; **il fait des affaires superbes** he is doing splendid *or* excellent business **(b)** (*beau*) (very) beautiful **2** *nf Arch, Litt* pride, haughtiness

superbement [sypɛrbəmɑ̃] *adv* **(a)** superbly, magnificently **(b)** *Arch* (*orgueilleusement*) proudly, haughtily

superbénéfice [sypɛrbenefis] *nm* sum of directors' percentage of profit and super dividend

supercagnotte [sypɛrkaɲɔt] *nf F* (*de loterie etc*) grand jackpot

supercarburant [sypɛrkarbyrɑ̃] *nm Aut* four-star petrol, *Am* premium gasoline

supercherie [sypɛrʃəri] *nf* deception, hoax; **être victime d'une s.** to be the victim of a hoax

superciment [sypɛrsimɑ̃] *nm Constr* quick-setting cement

superdividende [sypɛrdividɑ̃d] *nm* super dividend

supérette [syperɛt] *nf* mini-market, (small) supermarket

superfétation [sypɛrfetasjɔ̃] *nf Litt* (*de mots etc*) superfluity

superfétatoire [sypɛrfetatwar] *adj* superfluous

superficialité [sypɛrfisjalite] *nf* superficiality

superficie [sypɛrfisi] *nf* **(a)** (*surface*) surface; *Fig* **tout en s.** all on the surface, entirely superficial; **il ne connaît le problème qu'en s.** he has only a superficial knowledge of the problem **(b)** (*étendue*) (*d'un champ, d'un triangle etc*) (surface) area; **appartement d'une s. de 100 mètres carrés** apartment with a surface area of 100 square metres

superficiel, -ielle [sypɛrfisjɛl] *adj* (*blessure, savoir, réponse, observateur etc*) superficial; (*beauté*) superficial, skin-deep; (*esprit*) superficial, shallow; *Géog* **eau superficielle** surface water; *Phys* **tension superficielle** surface tension

superficiellement [sypɛrfisjɛlmɑ̃] *adv* superficially; **répondre s.** to give a superficial answer

superfin [sypɛrfɛ̃] *adj Com* of superior quality

superflu [sypɛrfly] **1** *adj* **(a)** (*kilos, poils*) superfluous, unwanted; (*explication, détails etc*) superfluous, unnecessary; (*regrets*) vain, useless **(b)** *Ordinat* redundant **2**

nm (*caractère*) superfluity; (*ce qui est superflu*) surplus; **il faut savoir distinguer l'essentiel du s.** you have to learn to distinguish what is essential from what is superfluous; **apprendre à se passer du s.** to learn to do without the inessentials; **des vitres électriques, tu ne crois pas que c'est du s.?** don't you think electric windows are a bit of a luxury?

superfluité [sypɛrflyite] *nf Litt* superfluity

super(-)grand, *pl* **super(-)grands** *nm* superpower; **s. de la presse** press baron *or* tycoon

super-huit *adj inv, nm inv Phot* super-eight

supérieur, -ieure [syperjœr] **1** *adj* **(a)** (*plus haut*) (*étage, membre, province etc*) upper; **cours s. d'un fleuve** upper reaches of a river; **dans la partie supérieure de la ville** in the upper *or* top part of the town

(b) (*d'une valeur plus grande*) superior (**à** to); **s. à la moyenne** above *or* better than average; **être s. en poids/en nombre** to be superior in weight/numbers; **lutter** *ou* **combattre contre des forces supérieures** to fight against superior forces; **se montrer s. aux événements** to rise above events; **être s. à la tâche** to be more than equal to the task; **c'est un esprit s.** he has a superior mind; **d'une intelligence supérieure** of superior *or* higher intelligence; **nommer qn à un emploi s.** to appoint sb to a higher post; **il se croit s. à tout le monde** he thinks he's above everyone else, he thinks he's superior

(c) (*dans une hiérarchie*) higher, upper; *Scol* (*cours*) advanced; (*cadre*) senior; *Mil etc* **un commandement s.** a senior command; **classes supérieures** (*de la société*) upper classes; *Scol* upper forms; **enseignement s.** higher education; **offre supérieure** higher bid; **les animaux supérieurs** the higher animals; *Jur* **cour supérieure** higher court

(d) *Com* **de qualité supérieure** of superior quality

(e) (*hautain*) (*manières, ton*) superior, condescending

2 *n* **(a)** *Admin etc* superior; **il est mon s. hiérarchique** he is my superior *or* senior

(b) *Rel* superior; **la Mère supérieure, la Supérieure** the Mother Superior

supérieurement [syperjœrmɑ̃] *adv* exceptionally

supériorité [syperjɔrite] *nf* superiority (**de** in); **complexe de s.** superiority complex; **c'est indubitablement une s. que vous avez sur elle** that's definitely one area where you're better than she is; **un air/sourire de s.** a superior air/smile, an air/a smile of superiority; **s. d'âge** seniority; **s. numérique/intellectuelle** numerical/intellectual superiority; **s. sur les marchés mondiaux** command of the world markets; **lutter contre une s. écrasante** to fight against overwhelming odds

superlatif, -ive [sypɛrlatif, -iv] **1** *adj* superlative; *Fig* (*exagéré*) **faire des louanges superlatives à qn** to praise sb to the skies **2** *nm* [①A18-19,4; B10-11,E; B12-13,F] *Gram* superlative; **s. relatif/absolu** relative/absolute superlative; *Fig* **laid au s.** extremely ugly

superlativement [sypɛrlativmɑ̃] *adv F* extremely

super-léger, *pl* **super-légers** *nm Boxe* (*boxeur, catégorie*) light welterweight

superman [sypɛrman], *pl* **supermen** [sypɛrmɛn] *nm F* superman; **jouer les supermen** to act the superman

supermarché [sypɛrmarʃe] *nm* supermarket

supermercatique [sypɛrmɛrkatik] *nf* supermarketing

supernova [sypɛrnɔva] *nf Astron* supernova

super(-)ordinateur, *pl* **super(-)ordinateurs** [sypɛrɔrdinatœr] *nm* supercomputer

superpétrolier [supɛrpetrɔlje] *nm* supertanker

superphosphate [sypɛrfɔsfat] *nm Agr* superphosphate

superposable [sypɛrpozabl] *adj* (*caisses, éléments de rangement*) stacking; (*images etc*) superimposable

superposé [sypɛrpoze] *adj* (*images etc*) superimposed; *Él, Électron* superposed; **lits superposés** bunk beds

superposer [sypɛrpoze] **1** *vt* (*boîtes, éléments de rangement*) to stack; (*images etc*) to superimpose (**à** (up)on); *TV etc* to overlay; *Ordinat* **s. une écriture** to overwrite **2 se superposer** *vpr* (*de caisses, chaises etc*) to stack, to be stackable; (*d'images etc*) to be superimposed

superposition [sypɛrpozisjɔ̃] *nf* (*d'éléments de rangement etc*) stacking; *Géol* superposition; *Phot, Cin, Géom* superimposition; *Ordinat* **mode de s. d'écriture** overwrite mode

superproduction [sypɛrprɔdyksjɔ̃] *nf Cin, Th* spectacular (film), big-budget film

superprofit [sypɛrprɔfi] *nm* huge profit

superpuissance [sypɛrpɥisɑ̃s] *nf Pol* superpower

supersonique [sypɛrsɔnik] *adj* supersonic

superstar [sypɛrstar] *nf* superstar

superstitieusement [sypɛrstisjøzmɑ̃] *adv* superstitiously

superstitieux, -euse [sypɛrstisjø, -øz] *adj* superstitious

superstition [sypɛrstisjɔ̃] *nf* superstition; **avoir la s. du passé** to be overly attached to the past

superstrat [sypɛrstra] *nm Ling* superstratum

superstructure [sypɛrstryktyr] *nf* superstructure

supertanker [sypɛrtɑ̃kœr] *nm* supertanker

superviser [sypɛrvize] *vt* to supervise; *Ordinat* to control

superviseur [sypɛrvizœr] *nm* supervisor; *Ordinat* **s. d'alimentation** power supply controller

supervision [sypɛrvizjɔ̃] *nf* supervision

superwoman [sypɛrwuman], *pl* **superwomen** [sypɛrwumɛn] *nf F* superwoman

supin [sypɛ̃] *nm Gram* supine

supplanter [syplɑ̃te] *vt* to supplant, to supersede

suppléance [sypleɑ̃s] *nf* (*fonction*) temporary *or* supply post; (*action*) temporary replacement; **remplir une s.** to deputize for *or* stand in for someone

suppléant [sypleɑ̃] **1** *n* substitute (**de** for), (temporary) replacement; (*de directeur*) deputy; (*professeur*) supply teacher; *Méd* locum; *Th* understudy **2** *adj* **(a)** (*fonctionnaire etc*) acting, temporary; (*juge*) surrogate; **professeur s.** supply teacher **(b)** *Gram* (*verbe etc*) substitute

suppléer [syplee] **1** *vt Arch, Litt* **(a)** (*remplacer*) (*manque, lacune*) to supply, to make up (for); (*personne*) to deputize for, to stand in for; **une technique qui supplée toutes les autres depuis peu de temps** a technique which has recently replaced all the others; **se faire s.** to be replaced **(b)** (*ajouter*) to supply **2** *vi* **s. à qch** to make up *or* compensate for sth; **s. au vin par le cidre** to eke out the wine with cider

supplément [syplemɑ̃] *nm* **(a)** (*surcroît*) **un s. de** (*information, travail etc*) additional, extra; **en s.** extra

(b) (*somme*) extra *or* additional charge, surcharge; *Rail* excess fare, supplement, surcharge; **pour réserver sa place, il faut payer un s.** if you want to reserve a seat, you'll have to pay extra; **s. chambre individuelle** single room supplement; **s. d'imposition** additional taxes; **s. de prix** additional *or* extra charge; **je lui ai donné un s. d'argent de poche** I gave him extra pocket money; **nous avons besoin d'un s. d'information** we need additional *or* further information; **s. de solde/travail** extra pay/work; **s. d'imposition** additional tax; *Rail* **train à s.** = train in which an excess fare *or* a supplement is charged

(c) (*livre, magazine etc*) supplement; **le s. du dimanche** the Sunday supplement

(d) (*plat de restaurant*) extra (dish)

(e) *Math* (*d'un angle*) supplement

supplémentaire [syplemɑ̃tɛr] *adj* additional, extra, further; **nous attendons des informations supplémentaires** we are awaiting further information; *Ind* **une heure s.** an hour's overtime; **tes heures supplémentaires te sont-elles payées?** is your overtime paid?; **faire des heures supplémentaires** to do *or* work overtime; *Rail* **train s.** relief train; *Math* **angles supplémentaires** supplementary angles; *Mus* **lignes supplémentaires** ledger *or* added lines

supplétif, -ive [sypletif, -iv] *adj, nm Mil* auxiliary

suppliant [syplijɑ̃] **1** *adj* (*regard etc*) imploring, pleading; **d'un air s.** imploringly **2** *n* suppliant, supplicant

supplication [syplikasjɔ̃] *nf* entreaty, plea; *Rel* supplication

supplice [syplis] *nm* **(a)** (*torture*) torture; **s. chinois** Chinese torture; **le s. du fouet** the penalty of the lash; **le dernier s.** capital punishment; **conduire qn au s.** to take sb away to be executed **(b)** (*tourment*) torment, agony; **le s. de l'attente** the agony of waiting; *Fig* **la goutte est un s.** gout is agony *or* a real torture; **ce genre de situation est pour moi un s.** I find this kind of situation absolute torture; **être au s.** to be in agonies; **mettre qn au s.** to torment *or* torture sb

supplicié, -ée [syplisje] *n* victim of torture

supplicier [syplisje] *vt* (*impf, pr sub* **n. suppliciions, v. suppliciiez**) to torture

supplier [syplije] *vt* (*impf, pr sub* **n. suppliions, v. suppliiez**) to beseech, to beg, to implore; **s. qn pour obtenir qch** to beg sb for sth; **s. qn de faire qch** to implore *or* beg sb to do sth; **ne dites rien, je vous en supplie, je vous supplie de ne rien dire** don't say anything, I beg *or* implore you

supplique [syplik] *nf* petition; **présenter une s. à un fonctionnaire** to petition a civil servant

support [sypɔr] *nm* **(a)** (*étai*) support, prop; *Menuis* strut **(b)** *Hér* (*d'un écu*) supporter **(c)** *Tech* (*pour outils etc*) rest; (*pour une lampe, un tube à essai etc*) stand; (*pour un bloc de papier etc*) holder; (*de photo*) mount; *Archit, Constr* (*d'une structure, d'une arche etc*) support; *Ordinat* **s. de souris** mouse support **(d)** (*d'une pièce dans un mécanisme*) bearer, bracket, support **(e)** *Él* (electrode) support **(f)** *Phot, Cin* (*d'une émulsion*) backing **(g)** *Fig* (*média*) medium; *Ordinat* **s. (d'information)** medium, information carrier

▶ **support**: **s. d'affichage** billboard, *Br* hoarding; **s. audio-**

visuel audio-visual aids; **s. de bicyclette** bicycle stand; **s. pour bicyclettes** bicycle rack; **s. magnétique** tape; **s. photographique** photograph; **s. plantaire** arch support; *Com* **s. publicitaire** publicity *or* advertising medium; *Ordinat* **s. de sortie** output medium; *Ordinat* **s. de stockage** storage medium; **s. visuel** visual aid

supportable [sypɔrtabl] *adj* **(a)** (*tolérable*) (*douleur etc*) bearable; (*comportement*) tolerable; **pas s.** (*douleur etc*) unbearable; (*comportement*) intolerable **(b)** (*correct*) reasonably good, fair

supporter[1] [sypɔrtɛr] *nm Sp* supporter

supporter[2] [sypɔrte] **1** *vt* **(a)** (*soutenir*) (*plafond, arche etc*) to support, to hold up; *Fig* (*personne, politique, théorie etc*) to support, to back up; (*coût, frais*) to bear; *Sp F* (*équipe*) to support; **s. de lourdes responsabilités** to shoulder great responsibilities; **s. les conséquences d'un acte** to bear the consequences of an action

(b) (*chaleur, malchance etc*) to endure, to withstand; (*basses températures*) to stand up to; (*alcool*) to take; *Naut* (*tempête*) to weather; **impossible à s.** intolerable; **son raisonnement ne supporte pas l'examen** his argument doesn't stand up to *or* withstand examination; **il ne supporte plus de se coucher tard** he can't take staying up late any longer

(c) (*tolérer*) (*dureté, injustice, manque de respect etc*) to tolerate, to put up with, to stand; **elle supporte tout de son mari** she puts up with all sorts of things from her husband; **je ne peux pas le s.** I can't stand him; **elle ne supporte pas de voir son fils souffrir** she can't stand seeing her son in pain; **il me ment, et ça, je ne le supporte pas!** he's lying to me, and that's one thing I can't stand!

2 se supporter *vpr* **ils ne peuvent pas se s.** they can't stand each other; **il faut apprendre à se s.** you have to learn to put up with *or* tolerate each other; **cela ne peut pas se s.** that is intolerable

supporteur, -trice [sypɔrtœr, -tris] *n Sp* supporter

supposé [sypoze] *adj* **(a)** (*voleur, auteur etc*) supposed, alleged **(b)** (*nom etc*) assumed, false; (*testament*) forged

supposer [sypoze] **1** *vt* **(a)** (*imaginer*) to suppose, to assume; **l'auteur suppose tout et ne prouve rien** the author assumes everything and proves nothing; **on peut s. qu'elle l'a fait pour lui faire plaisir** we can assume that she did it to make him happy; **en supposant que ... +** *sub*, **à s. que ... +** *sub*, **supposons que ... +** *sub* suppose *or* supposing that ...; **on suppose que ... +** *ind* it is thought that ...; **suppose qu'il revienne** suppose (that) he comes back; **elle lui supposait une grande fortune** she assumed he had a large fortune, she credited him with a large fortune; **tu es supposé le savoir** you are supposed to know it; **on le suppose à Paris, on suppose qu'il est à Paris** he is supposed to be in Paris

(b) (*impliquer*) to imply; **cela lui suppose du courage** it implies courage on his part; **je peux le faire, mais cela suppose que l'on me donne trois jours de plus** I can do it, provided I get an extra three days

(c) *Jur* (*imposteur*) to put forward; (*faux testament*) to present

2 *vi* **vous avez supposé juste** you guessed right; **tu as raison, je suppose** you are right, I suppose

supposition [sypozisjɔ̃] *nf* [①**A56**,a,v] supposition, assumption; **je n'en suis pas sûr, c'est une s.** I'm not sure, I'm only assuming; **si par s. il revenait** supposing (that) he came back; *F* **une s. qu'elle soit en retard** supposing she's late

suppositoire [sypozitwar] *nm Méd* suppository

suppôt [sypo] *nm* henchman; **s. de Satan** *ou* **du diable** fiend

suppression [sypresjɔ̃] *nf* **(a)** (*d'une loi, d'un impôt etc*) abolition; (*d'un journal etc*) suppression; (*d'un service d'autobus, d'un train etc*) cancellation; (*d'une difficulté*) removal; (*d'un mot, d'une phrase, d'un paragraphe etc*) deletion; **faire une s. de caractères** to delete characters; **parvenir à la s. des dépenses inutiles** to manage to cut out unnecessary expenditure; **la s. de 500 emplois** the axing *or* loss of 500 jobs; **cela a conduit à la s. du service du personnel** that led to Personnel being axed *or* getting the axe; **la Commission pour la s. du bruit** the Noise Abatement Commission

(b) *Jur* (*d'un document, d'un fait*) suppression; **s. d'enfant** concealment of birth

supprimable [syprimabl] *adj* suppressible

supprimer [syprime] **1** *vt* **(a)** (*loi, impôt etc*) to abolish, to do away with; (*journal, document etc*) to suppress; (*service d'autobus, train, concert etc*) to cancel; (*crédit*) to put an end to, to withdraw; (*mot, phrase, paragraphe*) to delete; (*au montage, texte*) to edit out; (*emploi, service*) to axe; **pour s. les effets de qch** to counteract the effects of sth; **vous n'avez pas été sages, la séance de cinéma est supprimée!** you haven't been good, there's no cinema for you *or* the cinema is out!; **vous devez s. le sucre de votre alimentation** you must cut sugar out of your diet; **l'avion supprime les distances** air travel makes distance irrelevant; **s. un poste** to abolish a position; *F* **s. qn** to kill sb, to bump sb off; *Typ* **à s.** delete

(b) *Jur* (*document, fait*) to suppress, to withhold

(c) s. qch à qn to deprive sb of sth

2 se supprimer *vpr* to commit suicide

suppurant [sypyrɑ̃] *adj Méd* suppurating

suppuration [sypyrasjɔ̃] *nf* suppuration, discharge

suppurer [sypyre] *vi* (*d'une blessure, d'une écorchure*) to suppurate

supputation [sypytasjɔ̃] *nf* calculation, estimation

supputer [sypyte] *vt* to calculate, to estimate; **s. ses chances** to calculate one's chances

supra [sypra] *adv* supra

supra- [sypra] *préf* supra-

supraconducteur [syprakɔ̃dyktœr] *nm Phys, Él* superconductor

supraconductivité [syprakɔ̃dyktivite] *nf Phys, Él* superconductivity

supranational, -ale, -aux, -ales [sypranasjɔnal, -o] *adj* supranational

supranationalisme [sypranasjɔnalism] *nm* supranationalism

supranationalité [sypranasjɔnalite] *nf* supranationality

supraterrestre [sypraterɛstr] *adj* superterrestrial

suprématie [sypremasi] *nf* supremacy

suprême [syprɛm] **1** *adj* **(a)** (*effort, bonheur etc*) supreme; (*degré*) highest; **nous avons eu un plaisir s. à les rencontrer** it gave us supreme *or* extreme pleasure to meet them; **un crétin au s. degré** an idiot of the highest degree; **le pouvoir s.** sovereignty **(b)** (*dernier*) (*demandes, moments*) last; **s. tentative** final attempt **2** *nm Culin* supreme; **s. de volaille** chicken supreme

suprêmement [syprɛmmɑ̃] *adv* supremely

sur[1] [syr] *prép* [①**A64-7**; **B54**] **(a)** on, *Fml* upon; (*avec mouvement*) on (to); **un chapeau s. la tête** with a hat on one's head, wearing a hat; **regarder s. la carte** to look at the map; **il est retombé s. ses pieds** he landed on his feet; **tirage photo s. papier brillant** print on glossy paper; **je ne suis jamais allé s. un voilier** I've never been on a yacht; **la clef est s. la porte** the key is in the door; **je n'ai pas d'argent s. moi** I don't have any money on me; **tu es tombé s. la tête?** are you mad?; *Fig* **nous étions les uns s. les autres** we were on top of each other, we were all squashed up together; **je suis s. ce dossier depuis deux jours** I've been working on this file for two days

(b) (*au-dessus de*) over, above; **les astres s. nos têtes** the stars above our heads; **un pont s. une rivière** a bridge across a river

(c) (*vers*) towards; **fenêtre qui donne s. le jardin** window which looks on to the garden; **la police a tiré s. la foule** the police fired on *or* at the crowd; **avancer s. qn** to advance on sb; **s. votre gauche** on *or* to your left; **les trains s. Orléans** the trains for Orleans

(d) (*supériorité, ascendant*) **avoir autorité s. qn** to have authority over sb; **elle a une forte influence s. moi** she has great influence over me; **l'emporter s. qn** to beat sb; **avoir des droits s. qn/qch** to have rights over sb/sth

(e) (*à propos de*) on, about, concerning; **nous savons beaucoup de choses sur vous** we know a lot about you; **un livre s. l'écologie** a book on *or* about ecology; **s. ce point** on this point; **il pose un regard anxieux s. toute(s) chose(s)** he colours everything with his own anxiety; **tu es toujours en train de pleurer s. ton sort!** you're always feeling sorry for yourself

(f) (*temps*) towards, around; **elle va s. ses dix-huit ans** she's coming up for eighteen

(g) s. ce, s. quoi whereupon; **s. ce, je vous quitte** and now I must leave you; **s. le coup** immediately, straight away; **s. le coup** *ou* **s. le moment je n'y ai pas pensé** I didn't think about it there and then; **il est s. le départ** he is about to leave; *Fig* **être s. le retour** to be past one's prime

(h) (*parmi*) out of; **un professeur s. cinq** one teacher in *or* out of five; **huit s. dix** (*note*) eight out of ten; **une fois s. deux** every other time; **on paie les pompiers s. les fonds de la ville** the firemen are paid out of the municipal funds

(i) (*mesure*) by; **huit mètres s. six** eight metres by six; **'virages s. 2 kilomètres'** 'bends for 2 kilometres'; **la frontière s'étend s. 300 kilomètres** the border stretches for 300 kilometres; **ses terres s'étendent s. 100 hectares** his estate extends over *or* covers 100 hectares

(j) (*après*) **page s. page** page after page; **j'ai recu visite s. visite pendant tout l'été** I had visit upon visit *or* one visit after another all summer; **avec lui, c'est reproche s.**

reproche with him, it's one criticism after another; **coup s. coup** one after the other, in succession; **il a fait la même erreur deux fois coup s. coup** he made the same mistake twice in a row

(**k**) (*manière*) **s. un ton de reproche** in a reproachful tone, reproachfully; **dire qch s. le ton de la plaisanterie** to say sth jokingly; **ne le prends pas s. ce ton!** don't take it like that!; **ne me parle pas s. ce ton!** don't speak to me in that tone of voice!; *Mus* **chanter qch s. un certain air** to sing sth to a certain tune; **s. le mode mineur** in the minor key

(**l**) (*d'après*) **juger qn s. les apparences** to judge sb by appearances; **s. sa bonne réputation** on the strength of his good reputation; **s. une fausse accusation** on a false charge

sur[2] *adj* (*fruit etc*) sour, tart

sur- [syr] *préf* over-

sûr [syr] **1** *adj* (**a**) (*sans danger*) (*localité, abri, plage etc*) safe; **c'est plus s. s'il t'accompagne** it's safer if he goes with you; **dis-le lui, c'est plus s.** tell him, just to be on the safe side; **peu s.** unsafe; **en lieu s.** in a safe place

(**b**) (*digne de confiance*) (*personne, mémoire*) trustworthy, reliable; (*ami*) trusty, true; (*information, entreprise*) reliable; **savoir qch de source sûre** to learn sth from a reliable source; **avoir le coup d'œil s.** to have a keen eye; **goût s.** discerning taste; **avoir la main sûre/le pied s.** to have a steady hand/to be surefooted; **ne pas avoir le pied s.** to be unsteady on one's feet; **frapper un coup s.** *ou* **à coup s.** to strike an unerring blow; **mettre son argent en mains sûres** to put one's money into safe hands

(**c**) (*certain*) certain, sure; **il l'a oublié, c'est s.** he has forgotten it, that's for certain *or* sure; **c'est une affaire sûre** it's a certainty *or* a sure thing *or F* a dead cert; **être s. de réussir** to be sure of success; **être s. de qch** to be sure *or* certain of sth; **je ne suis pas s. de la réussite de ce projet** I'm not sure that this plan will succeed; **je suis s. de lui** I can depend on him; **être s. de son fait** to be positive; **elle n'était pas vraiment sûre de son coup** she wasn't really sure of success; **je suis s. de ce que je te dis** I'm sure about what I'm saying; **s. de soi** self-assured; *F* **j'en suis s. et certain** I'm absolutely certain *or* sure of it; **mais oui ça va marcher, c'est s. et certain!** of course it'll work, it's absolutely certain!; **parier à coup s.** to bet on a certainty; **à coup s.** for certain, definitely

2 *nm* **jouer au plus s.** to play for safety; **le plus s. serait de ...** the safest thing would be to ...

3 *adv F* surely; **s.!** of course!, *Am* sure!; **pas s.!** perhaps not; *F* **bien s.!, pour s.!** of course!, *Am* sure!; *F* **bien s.?** you really mean it?; **bien s. que non!** of course not!; **bien s. que je viendrai aussi** of course I'll come too

surabondance [syrabɔ̃dɑ̃s] *nf* overabundance; *Com* glut; **s. de richesses/de détails** wealth of riches/details

surabondant [syrabɔ̃dɑ̃] *adj* overabundant

surabonder [syrabɔ̃de] *vi* to be overabundant; **s. de** *ou* **en qch** to have an overabundance of sth

suraccumulation [syrakymylasjɔ̃] *nf* **s. de capital** over-accumulation of capital

suractivé [syraktive] *adj* superactivated

suractivité [syraktivite] *nf Physiol* overactivity

surah [syra] *nm Tex* syrah

suraigu, -uë [syregy] *adj* (**a**) (*voix, son*) high-pitched (**b**) *Méd* (*inflammation*) acute

surajouter [syraʒute] **1** *vt* to add (on) **2 se surajouter** *vpr* to be added (on)

suralimentation [syralimɑ̃tasjɔ̃] *nf* (**a**) (*de personne*) overfeeding; *Méd* feeding up (**b**) *Aut* (*de moteur*) supercharging; **s. par turbocompresseur** turbocharging

suralimenter [syralimɑ̃te] *vt* (**a**) to overfeed; *Méd* (*personne*) to feed up (**b**) (*moteur*) to supercharge; **suralimenté** (*moteur*) supercharged; **suralimenté refroidi** charge-cooled

suranné [syrane] *adj* (**a**) (*vieilli*) outdated, old-fashioned; **beauté surannée** faded beauty (**b**) *Arch* (*qui a expiré*) (*passeport etc*) expired

surarmement [syrarməmɑ̃] *nm Mil* excessive arms build-up

surbaissé [syrbese] *adj* (**a**) *Archit* (*arche, voûte*) lowered, depressed (**b**) *Aut etc* (*essieu, carosserie etc*) dropped; (*châssis*) (extra-)low, underslung; **taille surbaissée** (*d'une robe*) drop waist

surbaissement [syrbɛsmɑ̃] *nm Archit* surbasement

surbaisser [syrbese] *vt* (**a**) *Archit* (*arche, voûte*) to lower, to depress (**b**) *Aut etc* (*carosserie etc*) to drop, to undersling

surbook [syrbuk] *nm* (*d'une chambre d'hôtel, de billets d'avion*) overbooking; (*en double*) double booking

surbooker [syrbuke] to overbook; (*en double*) to double book

surbooking [syrbukiŋ] *nm* overbooking; (*en double*) double booking

surboum [syrbum] *nf F Vieilli* party; **faire une s.** to have *or* throw a party

surbrillance [syrbrijɑ̃s] *nf Typ* highlighting; **apparaître en s.** to be highlighted

surcapacité [syrkapasite] *nf Ind etc* overcapacity

surcapitalisation [syrkapitalizasjɔ̃] *nf* overcapitalization

surcapitaliser [syrkapitalize] *vi* to overcapitalize

surcharge [syrʃarʒ] *nf* (**a**) *Tech* overload; *Él* (*d'un accumulateur*) overcharge; *Fig* **une s. de travail/de responsabilités/de soucis** extra work/responsibilities/worries; **la s. d'un programme d'études** a heavy syllabus

(**b**) (*dans un véhicule*) excess load; (*de bagages*) excess weight; **prendre des passagers en s.** to take on excess passengers; **rouler en s.** to drive an overloaded vehicle; *Méd* **s. pondérale** excess weight

(**c**) (*d'une course de chevaux*) weight handicap

(**d**) (*à payer*) surcharge

(**e**) *Typ* correction, alteration; (*dans un contrat etc*) alteration; (*imprimée sur une timbre-poste*) surcharge

surcharger [syrʃarʒe] *vt* (**je surchargeai(s); n. surchargeons**) (**a**) (*véhicule, cheval, estomac etc*) to overload; *Él* (*accumulateur*) to overcharge; *Fig* **s. ses employés de travail** to overwork one's employees; **je suis surchargée de travail depuis deux mois** I've been overburdened with work for two months; **s. d'impôts** to overburden with taxes; *Fin* **s. le marché** to overload the market (**b**) *Typ* (*caractères*) to write over with corrections; (*timbre*) to surcharge, to overprint

surchauffe [syrʃof] *nf* (*d'un four, d'un moteur, Fig de l'économie*) overheating

surchauffer [syrʃofe] *vt* (**a**) (*four etc*) to overheat; **salle surchauffée** overheated room (**b**) (*vapeur*) to superheat

surchoix [syrʃwa] *Com* **1** *nm* finest quality **2** *adj inv* (*produit*) top quality

surclassement [syrklasmɑ̃] *nm* (*de titre de transport*) upgrade

surclasser [syrklase] *vt* to outclass; (*titre de transport*) to upgrade

surcompensation [syrkɔ̃pɑ̃sasjɔ̃] *nf Psy* overcompensation

surcomposé [syrkɔ̃poze] *adj Gram* (*temps*) double-compound

surcompression [syrkɔ̃presjɔ̃] *nf Tech* supercharging

surcomprimer [syrkɔ̃prime] *vt Tech* to supercharge; **moteur surcomprimé** supercharged engine

surconsommation [syrkɔ̃sɔmasjɔ̃] *nf Écon* overconsumption

surcontrer [syrkɔ̃tre] *vt Cartes* to redouble

sur-correction *nf Aut* over-correction

surcouper [syrkupe] *vt Cartes* to overtrump

surcoût [syrku] *nm* cost overrun

surcroît [syrkrwa] *nm* **un s. de** extra; **un s. d'effort** an extra effort; **pour donner un s. d'effet à ...** to give an added effect to ...; **par s., de s.** in addition, moreover; **par s. de besogne** to add to my work; **pour s. de malheur** to make matters worse; **s. de dépenses** additional expenditure

surdéveloppé [syrdevlɔpe] *adj Écon* highly developed; (*excessivement*) overdeveloped

surdéveloppement [syrdevlɔpmɑ̃] *nm Écon* high state of development; (*excessif*) overdevelopment

surdi-mutité [syrdimytite] *nf* deaf-muteness

surdité [syrdite] *nf* deafness; **s. musicale** tone deafness

surdosage [syrdozaʒ] *nm Méd* overdosage

surdoué, -ée [syrdwe] **1** *n* gifted child **2** *adj* exceptionally gifted

sureau, -eaux [syro] *nm* elder (tree); **baie de s.** elderberry

sureffectif [syrefɛktif] *nm* excessive numbers, overmanning; **en s.** surplus; **personnel en s.** excessive (numbers of) staff

surélévation [syrelevasjɔ̃] *nf* (*action*) raising; (*augmentation de hauteur*) increase in height

surélevé [syrelve] *adj* (**a**) (*voie ferrée*) elevated (**b**) *Archit* (*arche, rez-de-chaussée etc*) raised

surélever [syrelve] *vt* (*conj like* **élever**) *Constr etc* to heighten, to raise; **s. un malade dans son lit** to prop a patient up in his bed

suremballage [syrɑ̃balaʒ] *nm* over-packaging

sûrement [syrmɑ̃] *adv* (**a**) (*sans doute*) surely; **s.!** certainly!, more than likely!; **s. pas!** certainly not!; **elle est s. tombée en panne** she must have broken down; **il va s. y avoir des changements** there are surely going to be some changes (**b**) (*de manière confiante*) confidently, with confidence (**c**) (*sans risque*) safely (**d**) (*immanquablement*) **frapper s.** to strike with accuracy; **lentement mais s.** slowly but surely

surémission [syremisjɔ̃] *nf Fin* overissue

suremploi [syrɑ̃plwa] *nm* overemployment

surenchère [syrɑ̃ʃɛr] *nf* (**a**) *Com* higher bid, overbid; **faire une s. sur qn** to outbid sb (**b**) *Fig* **une s. de violence** an increase in violence; **faire de la s.** to try to go one better than one's rivals, to try to outdo one's rivals; **faire de la s. électorale** to make more extravagant promises to obtain votes

surenchérir [syrɑ̃ʃerir] *vi* (**a**) *Com* to bid higher; *Fig* to try to outdo each other; **s. sur qn** to outbid sb, to bid higher than

sb; *Fig* to try to outdo sb *or* go one better than sb **(b)** *(devenir plus cher)* to rise in price
surenchérisseur [syrɑ̃ʃerisœr] *nm* highest bidder
surencombré [syrɑ̃kɔ̃bre] *adj* *(rue etc)* (severely) congested (**de** with)
surencombrement [syrɑ̃kɔ̃brəmɑ̃] *nm* (severe) congestion
surendetté [syrɑ̃dete] *adj Écon* excessively in debt
surendettement [syrɑ̃dɛtmɑ̃] *nm Écon* excessive debt (burden), overindebtedness, over-gearing; **courir un risque de s.** to run a risk of getting into excessive debt
surentraînement [syrɑ̃trɛnmɑ̃] *nm Sp* overtraining
surentraîner [syrɑ̃trɛne] *vt Sp* to overtrain
suréquipement [syrekipmɑ̃] *nm Écon* overequipment
suréquiper [syrekipe] *vt Écon* to overequip
surestarie [syrɛstari] *nf Com* demurrage
surestimation [syrɛstimasjɔ̃] *nf (de l'importance, la capacité)* overestimation; *(d'une œuvre d'art etc)* overvaluation
surestimer [syrɛstime] **1** *vt* **(a)** *(importance, capacité, nombre, difficulté etc)* to overestimate; *(person)* to overrate, to overestimate **(b)** *(en valeur)* *(œuvre d'art etc)* to overvalue **2 se surestimer** *vpr* to overrate oneself, to overestimate oneself; **j'ai peur que tu te surestimes si tu penses pouvoir ...** I'm afraid you're being a bit optimistic if you think you can ...
suret, -ette [syrɛ, -ɛt] *adj (fruit, goût etc)* sour(ish), tart
sûreté [syrte] *nf* **(a)** *(absence de danger)* safety; **lieu de s.** place of safety; **être en s.** to be safe *or* out of harm's way; **mettre qn en (lieu de) s.** *(en prison)* to put sb in prison; *(à l'abri)* to put sb in a safe place *or* out of harm's way; **pour plus de s.** for greater safety; **rasoir/serrure/soupape de s.** safety razor/lock/valve; **épingle de s.** safety pin; *Aut* **à s. intégrée** fail-safe

(b) *Pol etc* security; **la s. de l'État** state *or* national security; **la S. (nationale)** the (French) criminal investigation department, *Br* ≈ the CID, *US* ≈ the FBI; **agent de la S.** detective

(c) *(de la main, du pied)* sureness, steadiness; *(de la vision, du goût, du jugement)* soundness; *(d'un coup)* accuracy; **s. de soi** self-confidence, self-assurance

(d) *Com (garantie)* surety, guarantee; **s. en garantie d'une créance** surety for a loan
surévaluation [syrevalɥasjɔ̃] *nf* over-valuation
surévaluer [syrevalɥe] *vt (objet, antiquité)* to overvalue; *(efficacité, capacités etc)* to overestimate
surexcitable [syrɛksitabl] *adj* overexcitable, easily excited
surexcitation [syrɛksitasjɔ̃] *nf* overexcitement
surexciter [syrɛksite] *vt* to overexcite
surexploitation [syrɛksplwatasjɔ̃] *nf* overexploitation
surexploiter [syrɛksplwate] *vt (terre, travailleurs etc)* to overexploit
surexposer [syrɛkspoze] *vt Phot* to overexpose
surexposition [syrɛkspozisjɔ̃] *nf Phot* overexposure
surf [sœrf] *nm Sp* **(a)** *(sport)* surfing; **faire du s.** to go surfing, to surf **(b)** *(planche)* surfboard
surface [syrfas] *nf* **(a)** surface; **eau de s.** surface water; *Phys* **tension de s.** *(d'un liquide)* surface tension; **bruit de s.** surface noise; **vitesse en s.** *(de sous-marin)* surface speed; **nager en s.** to swim near the surface; **remonter à la s.** to rise to the surface, to surface; **faire s., revenir en s.** *(d'un sous-marin)* to (break) surface; *Fig F* **faire s.** *(se réveiller)* to surface; *Fig* **refaire s.** *(après une période difficile)* to get back on one's feet; **en s.** *(de l'eau)* on the surface; *Fig* superficially; **tout en s.** superficial; **il reste à la s. des choses** he doesn't go into things in any depth

(b) *Géom* surface; **s. de révolution** *ou* **de rotation** surface of revolution; **s. plane** plane surface

(c) *(étendue etc)* (surface) area; **quelle est la s. de l'appartement** how big is the flat?; *F* **il présente une s. financière suffisante** his financial standing is satisfactory; *F* **avoir de la s.** to have influence; **(magasin à) grande s.** hypermarket; **grande s. de bricolage** DIY centre

▶ **surface**: *Ordinat* **s. d'affichage** display area; **s. d'appui** bearing area *or* surface; *Constr* **s. couverte** floor area; *Ordinat* **s. d'enregistrement** read-write surface; *Mktg* **s. d'exposition** display space; **s. portante** *ou* **de portée** bearing area *or* surface; *Fb* **s. de réparation** penalty area; **s. au sol** floor area; **s. utile** floor space; **s. de vente** sales area *or* floor; **s. de voilure** sail area
surfaceuse [syrfasøz] *nf Tech* surfacer, planing machine
surfaire [syrfɛr] *vt (conj like* **faire***) Litt* **(a)** *(marchandises etc)* to overprice **(b)** *(personne, talent etc)* to overestimate, to overrate
surfait [syrfɛ] *adj (prix)* excessive; *(personne, réputation etc)* overrated
surfer [sœrfe] *vi* to surf
surfeur, -euse [sœrfœr, -øz] *n* surfer
surfilage [syrfilaʒ] *nm Couture* overcasting, oversewing
surfiler [syrfile] *vt* **(a)** *Couture* to overcast, to oversew **(b)** *Tex (fil)* to give an extra twist to
surfin [syrfɛ̃] *adj Com (produit)* superior, top-quality
surfrappe [syrfrap] *nf Ordinat* double strike, overstrike
surgélateur [syrʒelatœr] *nm* deep-freeze, freezer
surgélation [syrʒelasjɔ̃] *nf* deep *or* quick freezing
surgelé [syrʒəle] **1** *adj* deep- *or* quick-frozen **2** *nmpl* **surgelés** frozen foods
surgeler [syrʒəle] *vt (conj like* **geler***)* to deep- *or* quick-freeze
surgénérateur [syrʒeneratœr] *adj, nm Phys Nucl* **(réacteur) s.** breeder reactor
surgeon [syrʒɔ̃] *nm (de plante)* sucker
surgir [syrʒir] *vi (aux* **avoir,** *parfois* **être***)* to appear suddenly; *(d'une plante)* to spring up; *(d'une difficulté)* to crop up; **faire s. de nouveaux problèmes** to create new problems
surgissement [syrʒismɑ̃] *nm Litt* sudden appearance
surglacé [syrglase] *adj (papier)* calendered
surhaussé [syrose] *adj Archit* raised
surhaussement [syrosmɑ̃] *nm Archit* raising; *(différence de hauteur)* increase in height
surhausser [syrose] *vt Archit (mur etc)* to raise
surhomme [syrɔm] *nm* superman
surhumain [syrymɛ̃] *adj* superhuman
surimi [syrimi] *nm Culin* crab stick
surimposer [syrɛ̃poze] *vt (par l'impôt)* to overtax
surimposition [syrɛ̃pozisjɔ̃] *nf* **(a)** *(par l'impôt)* overtaxation **(b)** *Géol* pseudomorphism
surimpression [syrɛ̃presjɔ̃] *nf Phot, Cin* superimposition; *Ordinat* overprinting, overstrike; **en s.** superimposed; *Fig* **une foule d'émotions me sont venues en s.** I experienced a whole range of emotions in quick succession
surimprimer [syrɛ̃prime] *vt Ordinat* to overprint
surin [syrɛ̃] *nm Arg Vieilli* knife, dagger
Surinam [syrinam] *nm* Surinam
suriner [syrine] *vt Arg Vieilli (qn)* to knife
surinfection [syrɛ̃fɛksjɔ̃] *nf Méd* secondary infection
surinformation [syrɛ̃fɔrmasjɔ̃] *nf* overinformation
surinformé [syrɛ̃fɔrme] *adj* overinformed
surintendance [syrɛ̃tɑ̃dɑ̃s] *nf Hist* superintendence
surintendant [syrɛ̃tɑ̃dɑ̃] *nm Hist* superintendent
surir [syrir] *vi (du vin, de la soupe etc)* to turn sour
surjet [syrʒɛ] *nm Couture* overcasting, whipping
surjeter [syrʒəte] *vt (conj like* **jeter***) Couture* to overcast, to whip
sur-le-champ *adv* at once, immediately
surlendemain [syrlɑ̃dmɛ̃] *nm* **le s.** the day after the next, two days later; **le s. de leur départ** two days after their departure
surligner [syrliɲe] *vt* to highlight
surligneur [syrliɲœr] *nm* highlighter (pen)
surlocation [syrlɔkasjɔ̃] *nf* overbooking, *Am* oversale; *(en double)* double booking
surlouer [syrlwe] *vt* to overbook; *(en double)* to double book
surmenage [syrmənaʒ] *nm* **(a)** *(état)* overwork, overtiredness; **s. intellectuel** mental strain; **élève en état de s.** overworked pupil **(b)** *(action)* overworking
surmenant [syrmənɑ̃] *adj (travail etc)* exhausting
surmené [syrməne] *adj* overworked
surmener [syrməne] *(conj like* **mener***)* **1** *vt (employés, élèves etc)* to overwork, to work too hard **2 se surmener** *vpr* to overwork, to work too hard, *F* to overdo it
sur-moi *nm (no pl) Psy* superego
surmontable [syrmɔ̃tabl] *adj* surmountable
surmonter [syrmɔ̃te] **1** *vt* **(a)** *(être placé sur)* to surmount; **colonne surmontée d'une croix** column surmounted *or* topped by a cross **(b)** *Fig (obstacle, difficulté)* to overcome, to surmount; *(faim, peine)* to conquer, to get over; *Litt (ennemis)* to overcome **2 se surmonter** *vpr* to master *or* control one's feelings
surmortalité [syrmɔrtalite] *nf* excessively high death rate
surmultiplication [syrmyltiplikasjɔ̃] *nf Aut* overdrive (system)
surmultiplié, -ée [syrmyltiplije] *adj, nf Aut* **(vitesse) surmultipliée** overdrive
surnager [syrnaʒe] *vi* **(je surnageai(s); n. surnageons)** **(a)** to float (on the surface) **(b)** *Fig* to survive, to remain
surnatalité [syrnatalite] *nf* excessively high birth rate
surnaturel, -elle [syrnatyrɛl] **1** *adj* supernatural **2** *nm* **le s.** the supernatural
surnom [syrnɔ̃] *nm* nickname; **on lui a donné le s. de Rick** he was given the nickname of Rick, he was nicknamed Rick
surnombre [syrnɔ̃br] *nm* **en s.** too many; **les exemplaires/passagers en s.** the excess copies/passengers; **ils étaient en s.** there were too many of them
surnommer [syrnɔme] *vt* to nickname; **s. qn 'le Tigre'** to nickname sb 'The Tiger'

surnuméraire [syrnymerɛr] *adj, n* supernumerary
suroffre [syrɔfr] *nf* better offer *or* bid; (*surabondance*) excess supply
suroît [syrwa] *nm* (*vent, chapeau*) sou'wester
suroxygéner [syrɔksiʒene] *vt* **(je suroxygène, n. suroxygénons; je suroxygénerai)** *Ch* to superoxygenate
surpaie [syrpɛj, -pɛ] *nf* overpaying, overpayment
surpasser [syrpase] **1** *vt* (*espoirs*) to surpass, to exceed; (*rival*) to surpass, to outdo; **dépense qui surpasse mes moyens** expense beyond my means; **s. qn en éclat** to outshine sb; **s. une armée en nombre** to outnumber an army **2 se surpasser** *vpr* to surpass *or* excel oneself
surpatte [syrpat] *nf F Vieilli* (*surprise-party*) party
surpaye [syrpɛj, -pɛ] *nf* overpaying, overpayment
surpayer [syrpeje] *vt* (*conj like* **payer**) (*qn*) to overpay; (*qch*) to pay too much for
surpeuplé [syrpœple] *adj* (*pays, région etc*) overpopulated; (*maison, plage etc*) overcrowded
surpeuplement [syrpœpləmɑ̃] *nm* (*de pays etc*) overpopulation; (*de maison, plage etc*) overcrowding
sur(-)place [syrplas] *nm* (*d'un cycliste avant la course*) balance; **faire du s.** *Aut F* to crawl; (*d'un cycliste*) to balance; *Fig* **j'ai l'impression de faire du s. depuis deux ou trois ans** I feel like I've been getting nowhere for the last two or three years
surplis [syrpli] *nm Rel* surplice
surplomb [syrplɔ̃] *nm* overhang; **en s.** overhanging
surplombant [syrplɔ̃bɑ̃] *adj* overhanging
surplomber [syrplɔ̃be] *vti* to overhang
surplus [syrply] *nm* surplus; **le s.** the surplus, what is left (over); **le s. de marchandises** the surplus goods, the goods that are left (over); **payer le s.** to pay the difference; **au s.** besides, what is more; **les s. du gouvernement** government surplus (stock); **s. américain** US army surplus
surpopulation [syrpɔpylasjɔ̃] *nf* overpopulation
surpositionnement [syrpozisjɔnmɑ̃] *nm Mktg* over-positioning
surprenant [syrprənɑ̃] *adj* surprising, amazing; **chose surprenante** strange to say; **rien de s. si …** I shouldn't be surprised if …; **il est s. que vous le sachiez** it is surprising that you should know of it
surprendre [syrprɑ̃dr] (*conj like* **prendre**) **1** *vt* **(a)** (*prendre par surprise*) (*qn*) to surprise; **aller s. un ami chez lui** to pay a friend a surprise visit; **la nuit nous surprit** night overtook us; **être surpris par la pluie** to be caught in the rain; **s. qn à faire qch** to catch sb (in the act of) doing sth; **s. un voleur en flagrant délit** to catch a thief in the act
(b) (*découvrir*) (*lettre, regard*) to intercept; (*conversation etc*) to overhear; **s. le secret de qn** to find out sb's secret
(c) (*étonner*) to surprise, to astonish; **ce qui me surprend, c'est que …** what surprises *or* astonishes me is that …; **cela me surprendrait qu'il revienne** *ou* **s'il revenait** I should be surprised *or* astonished if he came back; **ça a l'air de vous s.** you seem surprised; **ce n'est pas pour me s.** it doesn't surprise me in the least
2 se surprendre *vpr* **se s. à faire qch** to find oneself doing sth
surpression [syrpresjɔ̃] *nf Tech* overpressure, excessive pressure
surprime [syrprim] *nf* (*d'assurance*) extra *or* additional premium
surpris [syrpri] *adj* surprised **(de** at); **je suis s. de te voir ici** I'm surprised to see you here; **je m'arrêtai, s.** I paused in surprise; **s., je les regardais** I watched them in surprise; **s. que +** *sub*/**si +** *ind* surprised that/if; **je ne serais pas s. qu'il revienne** *ou* **s'il revenait** I shouldn't be surprised if he came back
surprise [syrpriz] *nf* (*étonnement, cadeau*) surprise; **ça m'a fait une s. agréable** it came as a pleasant surprise to me; **à sa grande s.** to his great surprise, much to his surprise; **à la s. générale** to everyone's surprise; **s'emparer d'une ville par s.** *ou* **par un coup de s.** to capture a town by surprise; **il m'a fait sa demande par s.** he surprised me with his request, he sprang his request on me; **expédition/voyage sans s.** uneventful expedition/journey; **il est bon ce bordeaux? – sans s.** is this Bordeaux good? – nothing special; **craindre une s.** to fear a sudden attack; **quelle bonne s.!** what a pleasant surprise!; **attendez-vous à une drôle de s.** be prepared for a shock; **boîte à s.** Jack-in-the-box; **pochette s.** lucky bag; **grève-s.** lightning strike
surprise-partie, *pl* **surprises-parties** *nf* party
surproducteur [syrprɔdyktœr] *adj* overproducing
surproduction [syrprɔdyksjɔ̃] *nf* overproduction
surproduire [syrprɔdɥir] *vti* to overproduce
surprofit [syrprɔfi] *nm* excess profit
surpuissant [syrpɥisɑ̃] *adj* (*moteur, pays etc*) extremely powerful
surréalisme [syrrealism] *nm* surrealism
surréaliste [syrrealist] *adj, n* surrealist
surréel, -elle [syrreɛl] **1** *adj* surreal(istic) **2** *nm* **le s.** the surreal
surrégénérateur, -trice [syrreʒeneratœr, -tris] *adj, nm Phys Nucl* **(réacteur) s.** breeder reactor
sur-régime *nm Aut etc* overspeeding
surrénal, -ale, -aux, -ales [syrrenal, -o] *adj Anat* (*artère, ganglion*) suprarenal; (*glande*) adrenal
surréservation [syrrezɛrvasjɔ̃] *nf* overbooking; (*en double*) double booking
surréserver [syrrezɛrve] *vt* to overbook; (*en double*) to double book
sursalaire [syrsalɛr] *nm* bonus
sursaturé [syrsatyre] *adj* (*solution*) supersaturated; *Fig* **s. de** overwhelmed with
sursaut [syrso] *nm* start, jump; **avoir** *ou* **faire un s.** to (give a) start, to (give a) jump; **en s.** with a start; **se lever en s.** to jump up with a start; **dans un s. d'énergie** with a (sudden) burst of energy; **un s. de terrorisme** a new outbreak of terrorism
sursauter [syrsote] *vi* to (give a) start, to (give a) jump; **faire s. qn** to startle sb; **s. d'indignation** to leap up in indignation
surseoir [syrswar] *vi* (*prp* **sursoyant**; *pp* **sursis**; *pr ind* **je sursois, n. sursoyons**; *pr sub* **je sursoie**; *impf* **je sursoyais**; *p hist* **je sursis**; *fu* **je surseoirai)** *Jur* **s. à un jugement** to suspend a judgement; **s. à l'exécution d'un condamné** to reprieve a condemned man; **ordonnance de s. (à un jugement)** stay of execution
sursis [syrsi] *nm Jur* stay of execution; (*de condamné à mort*); *Fig* reprieve; **condamné à un an de prison avec s.** given a suspended (prison) sentence of one year; *Mil* **s. d'appel** deferment (of call-up); *Fig* **mort en s.** condemned man; **s. de paiement** extra time to pay
sursitaire [syrsitɛr] *Mil* **1** *adj* provisionally exempted **2** *nm* provisionally exempted conscript
surtaux [syrto] *nm* overassessment
surtaxe [syrtaks] *nf* **(a)** surtax, surcharge; (*de lettre etc*) surcharge **(b)** (*excessive*) excessive tax
surtaxer [syrtakse] *vt* **(a)** *Admin* to surtax, to surcharge **(b)** (*lettre etc*) to surcharge
surtension [syrtɑ̃sjɔ̃] *nf Él* overvoltage
surtitre [syrtitr] *nm Journ* strap-line
surtout[1] [syrtu] *adv* particularly, especially; (*avant tout*) above all; **ayez s. soin de …** be especially *or* particularly careful to …; **s. n'oubliez pas de …** do not forget to …; **non, s. pas!** no, certainly not!; *F* **s. que …** especially as …
surtout[2] *nm* **(a)** (*sur une table*) centrepiece, *US* centerpiece **(b)** *Arch* (*manteau*) overcoat
surveillance [syrvɛjɑ̃s] *nf* (*contrôle*) supervision; *Scol* invigilation; *Mil* observation, surveillance; *Rad* monitoring; (*en prenant soin de qn ou qch*) watch; **exercer une s. discrète sur qn/qch** to keep a discreet watch on sb/sth; **être sous la s. de la police** to be under police observation *or* surveillance; *Mil* **avion/navire de s.** surveillance plane/ship; **s. médicale** medical supervision; **s. électronique** electronic surveillance
surveillant, -ante [syrvɛjɑ̃, -ɑ̃t] **1** *n Ind, Admin etc* supervisor; (*de prison*) warder, *Am* guard; *Rail* inspector; *Scol* (*d'examen*) invigilator; (*chargé de la discipline*) supervisor **2** *nf Méd* **surveillante** head nurse, *Br* = (ward) sister
surveiller [syrveje] **1** *vt* **(a)** (*contrôler*) (*travail, employés etc*) to supervise; (*machine*) to man; *Scol* (*examen*) to invigilate; *Mil* to observe **(b)** (*prendre soin de*) (*qn*) to watch (over); **s. les enfants** to watch (over) *or* keep an eye on the children; **s. la situation de près** to keep a close eye on the situation; **s. son langage** to watch *or* mind one's language; **s. sa ligne** to watch one's figure; *Jur* **en liberté surveillée** on probation **(c)** *Rad* to monitor **2 se surveiller** *vpr* to keep a watch on oneself
survenir [syrvənir] (*conj like* **venir**; *aux* **être**) **1** *vi* (*événements*) to happen, to occur; (*d'une crise, d'une difficulté*) to arise; (*d'une personne*) to arrive unexpectedly **2** *v impers* **s'il ne survient pas de complications** if no complications arise *or* occur; **s'il survient un visiteur** if a visitor happens to come
survenue [syrvəny] *nf Litt* unexpected arrival
survêt [syrvɛt] *nm F* = **survêtement**
survêtement [syrvɛtmɑ̃] *nm* tracksuit; (*tenue relaxe*) shellsuit
survie [syrvi] *nf* survival; *Rel* afterlife; **croire à la s. de l'homme** to believe in the afterlife; *Astronaut etc* **équipement de s.** life support equipment; **couverture de s.** survival blanket; **une s. de quelques jours, quelques jours de s.** a few more days of life

survirage [syrviraʒ] *nm Aut* oversteer
survirer [syrvire] *vi Aut* to oversteer
survireur, -euse [syrvirœr, -øz] *adj* **une voiture survireuse** a car that oversteers
survivance [syrvivɑ̃s] *nf* **(a)** (*de l'âme*) survival **(b)** (*vestige*) (*du passé etc*) survival, relic
survivant, -ante [syrvivɑ̃, -ɑ̃t] **1** *adj* surviving **2** *n* survivor
survivre [syrvivr] (*conj like* **vivre**; *aux* **avoir**) **1** *vi* to survive; **s. à** (*qn*) to survive, to outlive; (*période, théorie etc*) to outlive; (*accident, maladie etc*) to survive; **va-t-il s.?** will he live *or* survive? **2 se survivre** *vpr* **(a)** (*dans ses enfants, son œuvre etc*) to live on **(b)** *Péj* (*d'une personne qui est devenu médiocre*) to have had one's day
survol [syrvɔl] *nm* **(a)** *Av* **le s. d'un lieu** flying over a place **(b)** *Fig* (*d'un problème etc*) cursory glance (**de** at)
survoler [syrvɔle] *vt* **(a)** *Av* (*montagne, localité etc*) to fly over **(b)** *Ordinat* to browse through **(c)** *Fig* (*problème etc*) to get a general view of
survoltage [syrvɔltaʒ] *nm Él* boosting
survolté [syrvɔlte] *adj* **(a)** *Él* boosted **(b)** *F* (*surexcité*) (over)excited, worked up
survolteur [syrvɔltœr] *nm Él* booster
sus [sy(s)] **1** *adv* **courir s. à son adversaire** to rush upon *or* at one's opponent, to charge one's opponent; **en s. de** (*somme d'argent*) in addition to, over and above **2** *int* **s. à l'ennemi!** at them!
susceptibilité [sysɛptibilite] *nf* **(a)** (*sensibilité*) touchiness, sensitivity; **il est d'une grande s.** he's very touchy *or* sensitive; **ménager la s. de qn** to tread carefully where sb is concerned; **blesser la s. de qn** to wound sb's feelings **(b)** (*en magnétisme*) susceptibility
susceptible [sysɛptibl] *adj* **(a)** (*qui s'offense facilement*) touchy, sensitive **(b) s. de** (*interprétations, critiques etc*) open to, *Fml* susceptible of; **être s. de faire qch** to be liable *or* likely to do sth
susciter [sysite] *vt* (*difficultés, commentaires*) to give rise to; (*étonnement*) to cause; (*hostilité, admiration, intérêt etc*) to arouse; **s. des ennuis à qn** to cause *or* create trouble for sb
suscription [syskripsjɔ̃] *nf Admin* (*sur une lettre*) address
sus-dénommé [sysdenɔme] *adj* aforementioned
susdit, -ite [sysdi, -it] *adj, n Jur* aforesaid, above-mentioned
sus-dominante, *pl* **sus-dominantes** *nf Mus* submediant
susmentionné, -ée [sysmɑ̃sjɔne] *adj, n Jur* above-mentioned, aforesaid
susnommé, -ée [sysnɔme] *adj, n Jur* above-named
suspect, -ecte [syspɛ(kt), -ɛkt] **1** *adj* (*personne, action etc*) suspicious, suspect; (*idées, preuve etc*) dubious, suspect; **des individus suspects rôdaient autour de la maison** suspicious-looking types were hanging around the house; **une viande tout à fait suspecte** meat which seems decidedly doubtful; **s. de** suspected of, under suspicion of; **cela m'est s.** it looks suspicious *or* suspect to me, I don't like the look of it; **tenir qn pour s.** to be suspicious of sb; **devenir s. (à qn)** to arouse (sb's) suspicion **2** *n* suspect
suspecter [syspɛkte] *vt* (*qn*) to suspect (**de qch** of sth; **de faire** of doing); (*bonne foi de qn etc*) to suspect, to question, to doubt; **je le suspecte de ne pas me dire la vérité** I suspect he's not telling me the truth, I suspect him of not telling me the truth
suspendre [syspɑ̃dr] **1** *vt* **(a)** (*vêtements, tableau, lampe etc*) to hang (up); (*hamac*) to hang up, to sling; **s. qch à un clou/au mur/à** *ou* **par un crochet** to hang sth on *or* from a nail/on the wall/on *or* from a hook **(b)** (*hostilités, enquête, émission*) to suspend; (*paiement, travail*) to suspend, to stop; (*séance*) to adjourn; **la séance est suspendue** we will now adjourn; **s. son jugement** to suspend judgement **(c)** (*fonctionnaire etc*) to suspend **2 se suspendre** *vpr* to hang (**à** from; **par** by); **il est toujours en train de se s. aux jupes de sa mère** he's very clingy, he never leaves his mother's side
suspendu [syspɑ̃dy] *adj* **(a)** (*pendu*) hanging, suspended (**au plafond** from the ceiling); **s. dans le vide** hanging *or* suspended in mid-air; **les jardins suspendus de Babylone** the hanging gardens of Babylon; **pont s.** suspension bridge; *Aut* **voiture bien suspendue** car with good suspension; *Fig* **enfant toujours s. aux jupes de sa mère** clingy child, child who never leaves his mother's side; **être s. aux lèvres de qn** to be hanging on sb's every word **(b)** (*arrêté, interrompu*) suspended; (*séance*) adjourned; *Jur* (*jugement*) postponed **(c)** *Aut* (*freins*) inboard
suspens [syspɑ̃] *nm* **(a) en s.** (*personne*) in suspense; (*travail*) unfinished, *Fml* in abeyance; (*affaire etc*) outstanding, *Fml* in abeyance; (*problème*) outstanding, unresolved; (*fumée, poussière etc*) hanging in the air; **tenir qn en s.** to keep sb in suspense **(b)** *Litt* (*suspense*) suspense
suspense [syspɛns] *nm Cin, Littér etc* suspense; **film à s.** thriller; **je le saurai demain, quel s.!** I'll know tomorrow, the suspense is killing me!
suspensif, -ive [syspɑ̃sif, -iv] *adj Jur* (*veto etc*) suspensive
suspension [syspɑ̃sjɔ̃] *nf* **(a)** (*en haut*) suspension, hanging (up)
(b) *Ch* **en s.** in suspension, suspended; *Méd* **s. buvable** oral suspension
(c) (*des hostilités, d'un travail, d'une enquête, d'un paiement etc*) suspension; (*de la circulation*) stoppage; (*de la loi*) abeyance; (*d'une séance*) adjournment; *Mil* **s. d'armes** suspension of fighting; **s. d'un paiement** stopping of a payment; **s. de paiements** moratorium on payment; *Gram* **points de s.** suspension points, dots; *Aut* **s. pour un an du permis de conduire** a year's driving ban; *Jur* **arrêt de s.** injunction
(d) (*de fonctionnaire etc*) suspension
(e) (*lampe*) light pendant, ceiling lamp
(f) *Aut* suspension; **s. avant à roues indépendantes** independent front suspension; **s. compound** hydrolastic suspension; **s. hydragas** hydragas suspension; **s. hydraulique** hydraulic suspension; **s. hydro-élastique** hydrolastic suspension; **s. hydropneumatique** hydropneumatic suspension; **s. à roues indépendantes** independent suspension; **s. triangulée** wishbone suspension
suspicieux, -euse [syspisjø, -øz] *adj* suspicious
suspicion [syspisjɔ̃] *nf* suspicion; **avoir de la s.** *ou* **des suspicions à l'égard de qn** to have one's suspicions about sb; **s. légitime** reasonable suspicion
sustentateur, -trice [systɑ̃tatœr, -tris] *Av* **1** *adj* (*force etc*) lifting; **effort s.** lift; **surface sustentatrice** aerofoil, *US* airfoil **2** *nm* **s. rotatif** (*d'un hélicoptère*) rotor
sustentation [systɑ̃tasjɔ̃] *nf* **(a)** *Géom* **base** *ou* **polygone de s.** basis of support **(b)** *Av* lift
sustenter [systɑ̃te] **1** *vt Arch* (*nourrir*) to sustain, to nourish **2 se sustenter** *vpr Arch, Hum* to take sustenance, to keep up one's strength
sus-tonique, *pl* **sus-toniques** *nf Mus* supertonic
susurrement [sysyrmɑ̃] *nm Litt* whispering, murmuring
susurrer [sysyre] *vti Litt* to whisper, to murmur; **s. des mots doux à l'oreille de qn** to whisper sweet nothings in sb's ear
suture [sytyr] *nf Anat, Chir* suture; **(point de) s.** stitch
suturer [sytyre] *vt Chir* to stitch, to suture
suzerain, -aine [syzrɛ̃, -ɛn] *adj, n* suzerain
suzeraineté [syzrɛnte] *nf* suzerainty
svastika [svastika] *nm* swastika
svelte [svɛlt] *adj* (*personne, corps etc*) slender, svelte
sveltesse [svɛltɛs] *nf* slenderness, slimness
SVP [ɛsvepe] (*abrév* **s'il vous plaît**) please
swahili [swaili] *adj, n Ling* Swahili
swap [swap] *nm Bourse* swap; **s. de change** exchange rate swap; **s. vanilla** vanilla swap
swaper [swape] *Bourse* to swap
sweater [switœr, swɛ-] *nm* sweater
sweat-shirt, *pl* **sweat-shirts** [switʃœrt, swɛt-] *nm* sweat shirt
sweepstake [swipstɛk] *nm Courses de chevaux* sweepstake
swing [swiŋ] *nm* **(a)** *Boxe, Golf* swing **(b)** *Mus* swing
swinger [swiŋge] *vi Mus F* to swing; **ça swingue, ce soir!** it's really swinging tonight!
sybarite [sibarit] *adj, n* sybarite
sybaritique [sibaritik] *adj* sybaritic
sybaritisme [sibaritism] *nm* sybaritism
sycomore [sikɔmɔr] *nm* sycamore (tree)
sycophante [sikɔfɑ̃t] *nm* informer
syllabaire [silabɛr] *nm* spelling-book
syllabe [silab] *nf* syllable; **s. ouverte/fermée** open/closed syllable; *Fig* **ne pas prononcer** *ou* **dire une s.** not to say a word; **je n'ai pas pu lui arracher une seule s.** I couldn't get a single word out of him
syllabique [silabik] *adj* syllabic
syllogisme [silɔʒism] *nm* syllogism
syllogistique [silɔʒistik] *adj* syllogistic
sylphe [silf] *nm*, **sylphide** [silfid] *nf* sylph; **taille de sylphide** sylphlike waist
sylvestre [silvɛstr] *adj Bot* (*arbre etc*) woodland
sylvicole [silvikɔl] *adj* forestry, *Spéc* silvicultural
sylviculteur [silvikyltœr] *nm* sylviculturist
sylviculture [silvikyltyr] *nf* forestry, *Spéc* sylviculture
symbiose [sɛ̃bjoz] *nf Biol* symbiosis; *Fig* **vivre en s. avec qn/la nature** to live in harmony with sb/nature
symbole [sɛ̃bɔl] *nm* **(a)** symbol **(b)** *Rel* (*formule*) creed
symbolique [sɛ̃bɔlik] **1** *adj* **(a)** symbolic; (*qui signifie une intention*) (*paiement, geste etc*) token; **payer** *ou* **verser un franc s. de dommages-intérêts** to pay nominal damages; **il a acheté cette maison un franc s.** he bought this house for a

token one franc (**b**) *Ordinat* symbolic **2** *nf* (**a**) (*science*) symbolics (**b**) (*système de symboles*) system of symbols (**c**) **la s. des rêves** the interpretation of dreams
symboliquement [sɛ̃bɔlikmɑ̃] *adv* symbolically
symbolisation [sɛ̃bɔlizasjɔ̃] *nf* symbolization
symboliser [sɛ̃bɔlize] *vt* to symbolize
symbolisme [sɛ̃bɔlism] *nm* symbolism; *Littér, Beaux-Arts* Symbolism
symboliste [sɛ̃bɔlist] *adj, n Littér, Beaux-Arts* Symbolist
symétrie [simetri] *nf Géom; Fig* symmetry
symétrique [simetrik] *adj* symmetrical (**par rapport à** about); *Électron* (*circuit*) balanced
symétriquement [simetrikmɑ̃] *adv* symmetrically
sympa [sɛ̃pa] *adj F* = **sympathique**
sympathicectomie [sɛ̃patisɛktɔmi] *nf*, **sympathectomie** [sɛ̃patɛktɔmi] *nf Chir* sympathectomy
sympathie [sɛ̃pati] *nf* (**a**) (*affinité*) liking; **avoir** *ou* **éprouver de la s. pour qn** to like sb, to have a liking for sb; **je n'ai aucune s. pour ce genre d'individu** I have no sympathy for people like that; **concevoir de la s.** *ou* **se prendre de s. pour qn** to take (a liking) to sb; **sympathies et antipathies** likes and dislikes; **sa gentillesse lui attire toutes les sympathies** her kindness makes her friends wherever she goes (**b**) (*compassion, condoléances*) sympathy; **croyez à notre s.** our deepest sympathy; **un regard de s.** a look of sympathy, a sympathetic look (**c**) **idées qui ne sont pas en s.** conflicting ideas
sympathique [sɛ̃patik] **1** *adj* (**a**) (*agréable*) (*personne, personnalité*), nice, likeable; (*entourages, vacances, soirée etc*) nice, pleasant; **ce n'est pas très s. de sa part** that's not very nice of her; **personnalité peu s.** unattractive personality; **il m'a été tout de suite s.** I took to him at once; **il m'est devenu s.** I came to like him; **Paul est fort s. à ma mère** my mother is very fond of Paul (**b**) **encre s.** invisible ink (**c**) *Anat, Physiol etc* (*nerf etc*) sympathetic **2** *nm Anat* sympathetic nervous system
sympathiquement [sɛ̃patikmɑ̃] *adv* (*accueillir etc*) in a friendly way, warmly; (*offrir etc*) kindly
sympathisant [sɛ̃patizɑ̃] **1** *adj* sympathizing **2** *n Pol etc* sympathizer; **un s. de l'ETA** an ETA sympathizer
sympathiser [sɛ̃patize] *vi* to get on well (together); **s. avec qn** to get on well with sb; **s. avec une organisation terroriste** to sympathize *or* have sympathies with a terrorist organization
symphonie [sɛ̃fɔni] *nf Mus, Fig* symphony
symphonique [sɛ̃fɔnik] *adj Mus* (*forme, poème etc*) symphonic; (*orchestre*) symphony
symphoniste [sɛ̃fɔnist] *n* (**a**) (*auteur*) symphonist (**b**) (*musicien*) orchestral player
symphyse [sɛ̃fiz] *nf Anat* symphysis
symposium [sɛ̃pozjɔm] *nm* [①**A13,5**] symposium
symptomatique [sɛ̃ptɔmatik] *adj Méd, Fig* symptomatic (**de** of)
symptomatiquement [sɛ̃ptɔmatikmɑ̃] *adv* symptomatically
symptôme [sɛ̃ptom] *nm Méd, Fig* symptom
synagogue [sinagɔg] *nf* synagogue
synapse [sinaps] *nf* (**a**) *Anat* synapse (**b**) *Biol* synapsis
synchro [sɛ̃kro] *nm Aut* synchromesh
synchromercatique [sɛ̃krɔmɛrkatik] *nf* synchromarketing
synchrone [sɛ̃kron] *adj* synchronous (**de** with)
synchronie [sɛ̃krɔni] *nf Ling etc* synchrony
synchronique [sɛ̃krɔnik] *adj* synchronic
synchronisateur [sɛ̃krɔnizatœr] *nm Aut* synchromesh
synchronisation [sɛ̃krɔnizasjɔ̃] *nf* synchronization
synchronisé [sɛ̃krɔnize] *adj* synchronized
synchroniser [sɛ̃krɔnize] *vt* to synchronize (**avec** with)
synchroniseur, -euse [sɛ̃krɔnizœr, -øz] **1** *nm* (**a**) *Él etc* synchronizer (**b**) *Aut* synchromesh device **2** *nf Cin* **synchroniseuse** film synchronizer
synchronisme [sɛ̃krɔnism] *nm* synchronism; **en s.** in synchronism; **hors de s.** out of synchronism; *Cin F* out of sync(h)
synchrotron [sɛ̃krɔtrɔ̃] *nm Phys Nucl* synchrotron
synclinal, -ale, -aux, -ales [sɛ̃klinal, -o] *adj Géog* synclinal
syncope [sɛ̃kɔp] *nf* (**a**) *Méd* fainting fit, *Spéc* syncope; **tomber en s.** to faint; *F* **il a failli avoir** *ou* **faire une s. quand il a entendu son nom** he nearly fainted *or* dropped when he heard his name (**b**) *Gram* syncope (**c**) *Mus* syncopation
syncopé [sɛ̃kɔpe] *adj Mus* syncopated
syncrétisme [sɛ̃kretism] *nm Phil* syncretism
syndic [sɛ̃dik] *nm Hist* syndic; **s. (de copropriété)** (*dans un immeuble*) property agent; **s. de faillite** = official receiver
syndical, -ale, -aux, -ales [sɛ̃dikal, -o] *adj* (*de salariés, d'ouvriers*) (*mouvement, leader, revendication etc*) (trade-) union, *US* labor union
syndicalisation [sɛ̃dikalizasjɔ̃] *nf* (*action*) unionization; (*appartenance à un syndicat*) union membership, *US* labor union membership
syndicalisme [sɛ̃dikalism] *nm* trade unionism; **faire du s.** to be involved in (trade-)union activities
syndicaliste [sɛ̃dikalist] **1** *adj* (*doctrine, leader etc*) (trade-) union, *US* labor union **2** *n* trade unionist, *US* labor union member
syndicat [sɛ̃dika] *nm* (**a**) (*de salariés, d'ouvriers*) (trade) union, *US* labor union; **être membre d'un s.** to be a member of *or* be in a (trade) union (**b**) (*d'employeurs*) federation; (*de producteurs, propriétaires*) association; (*de financiers*) syndicate; *Fin* **s. de prise ferme** underwriting syndicate
▶ **syndicat**: **s. de faillite** official receivership; **s. d'initiative** tourist (information) office *or* bureau; **s. ouvrier** trade union; **s. patronal** employers' organization; **s. professionnel** trade *or* professional association, trade body
syndicataire [sɛ̃dikatɛr] *Fin* **1** *adj* of a syndicate **2** *n* member of a syndicate
syndiqué, -ée [sɛ̃dike] **1** *adj* belonging to a (trade) union *or US* labor union; **ouvriers syndiqués** union members; **être s.** to be a member of a (trade) union; **ouvriers non syndiqués** non-union workers **2** *n* (trade) union member, *US* labor union member
syndiquer [sɛ̃dike] **1** *vt* (*travailleurs etc*) to unionize, to form into a (trade) union *or US* labour union **2 se syndiquer** *vpr* to form a (trade) union *or US* labor union; (*adhérer à un syndicat*) to join a (trade) union
syndrome [sɛ̃drom] *nm Méd, Fig* syndrome; **s. de Down** Down's syndrome; **s. immuno-déficitaire acquis** acquired immune *or* immuno-deficiency syndrome; **s. cervical traumatique** whiplash
synectique [sinɛktik] *nf* synectics
synérèse [sinerɛz] *nf Phys, Ling* synaeresis, *US* syneresis
synergiciel [sinɛrʒisjɛl] *nm Ordinat* groupware
synergie [sinɛrʒi] *nf* synergy
synergisme [sinɛrʒism] *nm Mktg* synergism
synesthésie [sinɛstezi] *nf Psy* synaesthesia, *US* synesthesia
syngnathe [sɛ̃gnat] *nm* pipefish
synode [sinɔd] *nm Rel* synod
synodique [sinɔdik] *adj* (**a**) *Astron* synodic(al) (**b**) *Rel* synodal
synonyme [sinɔnim] **1** *adj* synonymous (**de** with); **pour elle, mariage est s. de bonheur** for her, marriage is synonymous with happiness **2** *nm* synonym; **dictionnaire de synonymes** thesaurus
synonymie [sinɔnimi] *nf* synonymy, synonymity
synopse [sinɔps] *nf* synoptic table of the Gospels
synopsis [sinɔpsis] *nf* [①**A14,10**] synopsis
synoptique [sinɔptik] *adj* synoptic; **les Évangiles synoptiques** the Synoptic Gospels; **tableau s.** (*scientifique etc*) conspectus
synovial, -iale, -iaux, -iales [sinɔvjal, -jo] *adj Anat* synovial
synovie [sinɔvi] *nf Anat, Physiol* synovia; *Méd* **épanchement de s.** water on the knee
synovite [sinɔvit] *nf Méd* synovitis
syntacticien, -ienne [sɛ̃taktisjɛ̃, -jɛn] *n Gram* syntactician
syntactique [sɛ̃taktik] *adj Gram* syntactic(al)
syntagmatique [sɛ̃tagmatik] *adj Gram* phrasal, syntagmatic
syntagme [sɛ̃tagm] *nm Gram* phrase, syntagm(a)
syntaxe [sɛ̃taks] *nf Gram, Ordinat* syntax; **erreur de s.** syntax error
syntaxique [sɛ̃taksik] *adj Gram* syntactic(al); *Ordinat* syntax; **analyseur s.** parser
synthèse [sɛ̃tɛz] *nf* (**a**) (*intellectuelle*) synthesis; **faire la s. d'un récit** to summarize the main elements of a story; **avoir l'esprit** *ou* **un esprit de s.** to be able to see the overall picture (**b**) *Ch* **de s.** synthetic (**c**) *Électron, Mus* synthesis; **de s.** synthetic
synthétique [sɛ̃tetik] **1** *adj* (**a**) (*présentation*) all-encompassing; (*bilan*) summary; **esprit s.** ability to see the overall picture; **une vue s. des choses** an overall *or* all-encompassing view of things (**b**) *Ch, Tex* (*tissu, fibres*) synthetic, man-made **2** *nm Tex* synthetic material; **laver les synthétiques à la main** wash synthetics by hand
synthétiquement [sɛ̃tetikmɑ̃] *adv* synthetically; **des faits présentés s.** a contextualized presentation of the facts; **voir les choses s.** to see the overall picture, to see things in context
synthétiser [sɛ̃tetize] *vt Ch, Ordinat etc* to synthesize
synthétiseur [sɛ̃tetizœr] *nm Électron, Mus* synthesizer; **s. de paroles** *ou* **vocal** speech *or* voice synthesizer
syntonisateur [sɛ̃tɔnizatœr] *nm TV, Rad* tuner
syntoniseur [sɛ̃tɔnizœr] *nm Rad* tuner
syphilis [sifilis] *nf Méd* syphilis
syphilitique [sifilitik] *adj, n Méd* syphilitic
Syrie [siri] *nf* Syria
syrien, -ienne [sirjɛ̃, -jɛn] **1** *adj* Syrian **2** *n* **S.** Syrian
syringe [sirɛ̃ʒ] *nf Archéol* syrinx

systématique [sistematik] **1** *adj* **(a)** (*automatique*) systematic; *F* **c'est s.** it's automatic; **cela m'arrive mais ce n'est pas s.** I have been known to but I don't do it regularly *or* as a matter of course *or* but it's not systematic; **il est dans une position de refus s.** he systematically refuses, he refuses as a matter of course **(b)** *Péj* (*dogmatique*) (*opinions, personne*) dogmatic **(c)** (*absolu*) (*soutien*) unconditional **2** *nf* systematics
systématiquement [sistematikmɑ̃] *adv* systematically
systématisation [sistematizasjɔ̃] *nf* system(at)ization
systématiser [sistematize] *vt* to system(at)ize
système [sistɛm] *nm* **(a)** (*méthode, moyen etc*) system; **tu connais un s. pour payer moins d'impôts?** do you know a way of paying less tax?; **s. d'éducation/pénitentiaire** education/prison system; **elle agit par s.** once she's made up her mind you can't budge her; **avoir l'esprit de s.** to have a systematic mind, *Péj* to stick to the rules, to go by the book

(b) (*de roues, valves etc*) system, set; (*de routes*) system, network; *Physiol* system; *F* **il me tape** *ou* **porte sur le s.** he gets on my nerves

(c) le s. (*la société etc*) the system; **ne pas entrer dans le s.** not to be part of the system

(d) *Ordinat* system

▶ **système**: *Aut* **s. ABS** ABS system; **s. audio** sound *or* audio system; *Aut* **s. de climatisation** environmental control system; *Banque* **s. de compensation** clearing system; **s. comptable** accounting system; **s. de contrôle de stocks** stock control system; *Bourse* **s. de criée** open outcry system; **le s. D** resourcefulness; **s. de diffusion de données** broadcast data system; **s. de distribution** distribution system; **s. de distribution intégral** total distribution system; **s. Dolby stéréo** Dolby system; **s. de données par radio** radio data system, RDS; **s. douanier** customs system; *Ordinat* **s. d'exploitation** operating system; *Ordinat* **s. d'exploitation de** *ou* **à disques** disk operating system; *Ordinat* **s. d'exploitation réseau** network operating system; *Ordinat* **s. expert** expert system; **s. fiscal** tax system; *Aut* **s. de freinage ABS** anti-lock braking system; *Ordinat* **s. de gestion de bases de données** database management system; *Ordinat* **s. de gestion de fichiers** file management system; **s. d'information mercatique** marketing information system; **s. informatique** computer system; *Mktg* **s. d'intelligence d'entreprise** *ou* **marketing** marketing intelligence system; **s. d'inventaire** inventory method; **s. de mercatique verticale** vertical marketing system, VMS; **s. monétaire européen** European monetary system; **s. nerveux** nervous system; **s. opératoire** operating system; **s. de participation aux bénéfices** profit-sharing scheme; **s. pileux** hair; **s. de prévoyance** social benefits system; **s. radio de transmission de données** radio data system; **s. de relance** follow-up system; **s. respiratoire** respiratory system; **s. de retraite** pension scheme; *Ordinat* **s. de sauvegarde sur bande** tape backup system; *Ordinat* **s. sentinelle** watchdog system; *Ordinat* **s. serveur** host system; **s. solaire** solar system; *Ordinat* **s. à tour** tower system
systémique [sistemik] *adj* (*insecticide etc*) systemic
systole [sistɔl] *nf Physiol* systole
syzygie [siziʒi] *nf Astron* syzygy; **marées de s.** spring tides

T

T, t [te] *nm inv* **(a)** (*lettre*) T, t **(b)** [①B61,c,iii] **t euphonique** *forms a link between verbal endings* **-a, -e** *and the pronouns* **il, elle, on – va-t-il? ira-t-elle? donne-t-on? (c) en T** T-shaped; **mettre les bureaux en T** to arrange the desks so that they form a T

t *abrév* **(a)** (**tonne(s)**) t **(b)** (**tome**) vol.

t' [t] *voir* **te, tu**

ta [ta] *adj poss voir* **ton**[1]

tabac[1] [taba] **1** *nm* **(a)** *Bot* tobacco (plant); **faire pousser du t.** to grow tobacco **(b)** (*produit*) tobacco; **prendre du t.** to take snuff; **boîte à t.** snuffbox **(c)** (**bureau de**) **t.** tobacconist's (shop), *Am* tobacco store (*which also sells stamps, phonecards, lottery tickets*); *Fig F* **tout est un peu du même t.** it's pretty much of a muchness; *Fig F* **il doit avoir eu des ennuis avec la police ou quelque chose du même t.** he must have had some trouble with the police, or something (like that) **(d)** *Hist, Admin* **les Tabacs** the Tobacco Department **2** *adj inv* buff

▶ **tabac**: **t. blond** Virginia tobacco; **t. brun** black *or* brown tobacco; **t. à chiquer** chewing tobacco; **t. à fumer** smoking tobacco; **t. à mâcher** chewing tobacco; **t. à priser, t. râpé** snuff

tabac[2] *nm F* **passer qn à t.** (*de la police etc*) to beat sb up; **passage à t.** beating (up); **coup de t.** squall; **nous avons essuyé un sacré coup de t.** we went through a dreadful squall; *Fig* **son spectacle a fait un sacré t.** his show was a huge success *or* a big hit

tabagie [tabaʒi] *nf* **(a)** *F* = place reeking of stale tobacco smoke; **quelle t., cette chambre!** this room stinks of tobacco! **(b)** *Can* (*bureau de tabac*) tobacconist's (shop), *Am* tobacco store

tabagique [tabaʒik] *adj* (*intoxication etc*) nicotine

tabagisme [tabaʒism] *nm* smoking, nicotinism, tobacco addiction; **les effets du t.** the effects of smoking; **la lutte contre le t.** the fight to stop people smoking; **t. passif** passive smoking

tabar(d) [tabar] *nm Hist* (*manteau*) tabard

tabassée [tabase] *nf F* beating

tabasser [tabase] *F* **1** *vt* **t. qn** to beat sb up; **se faire t.** to be *or* get beaten up; **il s'est fait t. par son père** his father gave him a thrashing **2 se tabasser** *vpr* to beat each other up

tabatière [tabatjɛr] *nf* **(a)** (*boîte*) snuffbox **(b)** (*lucarne*) (hinged) skylight

tabellion [tabeljɔ̃] *nm F Hum* lawyer

tabernacle [tabɛrnakl] *nm* tabernacle

tablature [tablatyr] *nf Mus* tablature

table [tabl] *nf* **(a)** (*meuble*) table; **t. de cuisine/de salle à manger** kitchen/dining table; **t. roulante** trolley; *Fig* **jouer cartes sur t.** to put one's cards on the table

(b) (*tablée, nourriture*) table; **mettre** *ou* **dresser/débarrasser la t.** to lay *or* set/clear the table; **aimer les plaisirs de la t.** to be fond of good food and wine; **avoir une bonne t.** to keep a good table; **la t. est bonne** the food is good; **à t.!** dinner/lunch/*etc* is ready!, *F* come and get it!; **être à t.** to be at the table *or* at dinner/lunch/*etc*; **se mettre à t.** to sit down at the *or Am* to table *or* to dinner/lunch/*etc*; *Arg Fig* to come clean, to cough; **quand est-ce qu'on passe** *ou* **se met à t.?** when are we eating?; **se lever de t.** to leave the table; **réserver une t. dans un restaurant** to book *or* reserve a table in a restaurant; *Rel* **la Sainte T.** the Communion table

(c) *Tech* (*d'un marteau, d'une valve etc*) face; (*d'une poutre métallique*) flange

(d) *Tél* switchboard

(e) *Électron* table, board

(f) (*de pierre etc*) slab; (*d'un dolmen*) cap stone

(g) (*liste*) table

(h) *Mus* (*d'un violon etc*) sounding board, belly

▶ **table**: *Hér* **t. d'attente** field; **t. basse** coffee table; **t. de billard** billiard table; **t. de chevet** bedside *or Am* night table; **t. de cuisson** hob; **t. à découper** carving table; **t. à dessin** drawing board, draughtsman's *or Am* draftsman's table *or* board; *Ordinat* **t. à digitaliser** digitizing pad; *Mktg* **t. d'échantillonnage** sampling tabulation; **t. d'écoute: mettre qn sur t. d'écoute** to tap *or* put a tap on sb's telephone, to wiretap sb; **nous étions sur t. d'écoute** our phone was being tapped; *Ordinat* **t. des fichiers** file allocation table, FAT; **tables frappantes** (*en spiritisme*) table rapping; *Mus* **t. d'harmonie** (*d'un violon etc*) sounding board, belly; **t. d'honneur** (*dans un banquet etc*) top table; **t. d'hôte** table d'hôte; **t. d'intérêts** interest table; **t. de jeu** card table; **t. à langer** changing table; *Bible* **tables de la loi** Tables of the Law; **t. des matières** (table of) contents; **t. de mixage** *TV etc* mixing console; *Rad* sound mixer; **t. de montage** *Journ etc* light table; *TV* editing desk *or* table; **t. de multiplication** multiplication table; **t. de nuit** bedside *or Am* night table; *Mil* **t. d'officiers** officers' mess; **t. d'opération** operating table; **il a dû repasser sur la t. d'opération** he had to have another operation *or* more surgery; **t. d'orientation** orientation *or* panoramic table; **t. à rallonges** extending table; *Phil* **t. rase** tabula rasa; *Fig* **faire t. rase** to make a clean sweep; *Fig* **faire t. rase (du passé)** to wipe the slate clean; *Fig* **faire t. rase des préjugés** to get rid of one's prejudices; *Ordinat* **t. de recherche** *ou* **de référence** look-up table; **t. à repasser** ironing board; *Pol, Ind* **t. ronde** round-table conference, round table; (*débat*) debate; *TV, Rad* discussion programme; *Littér* **la T. ronde** the Round Table; **t. roulante** tea trolley; *Rail* **t. de roulement** (*d'un rail*) tread; **t. de toilette** washstand; *Ordinat* **t. traçante** plotter; **t. de travail** work table; *Ordinat* **t. de vérité** truth table

tableau, -eaux [tablo] *nm* **(a)** (*panneau, support*) board; (*pour les clefs*) key rack *or* board; **t. des publications de mariage** = board where banns are posted; *Scol* **t. (noir)** (black)board; *Scol* **aller au t.** to come out/go out to the board

(b) *Beaux-Arts* painting, picture; **un t. de Dürer** a painting by Dürer; **marchand de tableaux** art dealer; **exposition de tableaux** art exhibition, exhibition of paintings; *Fig F* **tu imagines le t.!** you can picture *or* imagine the scene!; *Fig* **quel t. vous faites, tous les deux!** look at you two, what a picture!; *Fig* **je vois d'ici le t.!** I can just picture it!; *Fig* **cela faisait un t. charmant/touchant** it was a charming/touching sight *or* scene; *Fig* **de la colline se découvre un magnifique t.** there is a beautiful view from the hill; *Fig* **brosser le t. de la situation** to give a picture of the situation; *Fig* **et pour achever le t.** and to crown it all; *F* **vieux t.** (*vieille coquette*) (painted) old hag

(c) *Th* scene; **t. vivant** tableau (vivant)

(d) (*liste*) list, table; (*graphique*) chart; *Typ* table; *Rail* **t. horaire** timetable; **t. récapitulatif** summary table; *Pharm* **produit de t. A/B/C** A-/B-/C-list product; **mettre sous forme de t.** to tabulate; *Fig F* **gagner sur tous les/sur les deux tableaux** to win on all/both counts; **jouer** *ou* **miser sur plusieurs tableaux** to hedge one's bets

(e) *Jur* (*d'avocats*) roll; **être rayé** *ou* **se faire rayer du t.** to be struck off the rolls; **se faire inscrire au t.** to be called to the bar

▶ **tableau**: **tableaux d'activité économique** economic activity tables; **t. d'affichage** notice *or Am* bulletin board; *Compta* **t. d'amortissement** depreciation schedule; **t. d'avancement** promotions list; **t. d'avancement de commandes** order flowchart; **t. blanc** whiteboard; **t. de bord** *Aut* dashboard, fa(s)cia; *Av* instrument panel; *Ordinat* control panel; *Com* management control data; **t. de chasse** (*animaux, Fig avions abattus*) bag; *Fig* (*conquêtes*) list of conquests; *Fig* **tu pourras la mettre à ton t. de chasse!** that's another notch on your gun!; **t. à clés** key board *or* rack; *Méd* **t. clinique** clinical picture; **t. de commande** (*d'appareil électroménager*) control panel, panel of switches; *Él, Tél* **t. commutateur** switchboard, distribution board *or* panel; *Gram* **t. de conjugaison** conjugation table; *Ordinat* **t. de connexions** plugboard; **t. de contrôle** *Tech* control panel; *Tél* monitoring board; **t. de conversion** conversion table; *Él, Tél* **t. de distribution** switchboard, distribution board *or* panel; *Él etc* **t. d'éclairage** lighting panel; *Compta* **t. des emplois et ressources de fonds** statement of sources and applications of funds; **t. de l'état des chambres** (*dans un hôtel*) reception board, room rack; *Compta* **t. de financement** statement of sources and uses of funds, cashflow statement; (*planning*) finance plan; *Scol* **t. d'honneur** = document certifying that a pupil has obtained good marks *or esp Am* grades; **t. de maître** old master; **t. de manœuvre** instrument board *or* panel; **t. d'organisation** organization(al) chart; *Él* **t. de raccordement** patchboard; **t. récapitulatif** summary table; **t. des réservations** reservations chart; *Compta* **t. de roulement** statement of changes in working capital; *Com* **t. de service** rota; **t. synoptique** synopsis, summary

tableautin [tablotɛ̃] *nm Beaux-Arts* small picture

tablée [table] *nf* (*personnes à table*) table; **j'ai l'habitude des grandes tablées** I'm used to having a lot of people round the table; **une joyeuse t.** a merry gathering (around a table)

tabler [table] *vi* **t. sur qch** to count *or* bank on sth

tablette [tablɛt] *nf* **(a)** (*d'une étagère etc*) shelf; (*dans un avion*) table; **t. à coulisse** (*d'un bureau*) pull-out flap **(b)** *Hist* **tablettes** (*pour écrire*) (writing) tablets; *Fig* **écrire qch sur ses tablettes** to make a note of sth **(c)** (*de chocolat*) bar; (*de chewing-gum*) stick; *Pharm* tablet

▶ **tablette**: *Aut* **t. arrière** rear parcel shelf, back shelf; *Él* **t. à bornes** terminal plate; **t. de fenêtre** window sill; **t. de piano** music rest

tableur [tablœr] *nm Ordinat* spreadsheet; **t. de graphiques** graphics spreadsheet

tablier [tablije] *nm* **(a)** (*vêtement*) apron, *Br F* pinny; (*d'écolier*) smock; **t. blouse** (woman's) overall; *Fig F* **rendre son t.** to hand in one's notice; (*d'un domestique*) to give notice **(b)** *Mil* (*d'avant-train*) footboard; (*de scooter*) footrest **(c)** (*de cheminée*) hood **(d)** (*de magasin etc*) (steel) shutter **(e)** (*de pont*) deck, road(way); (*de locomotive*) footplate **(f)** (*de laminoir*) table; (*de tour*) apron; *Ind* **t. sans fin** apron feed **(g)** (*de forge*) hearth **(h)** *Aut* apron, valance; **t. de pare-chocs** bumper apron

tabloïd(e) [tablɔid] **1** *nm* **(a)** *Journ* tabloid (newspaper) **(b)** *Pharm* tablet **2** *adj* **format t.** tabloid format

tabou [tabu] *adj, nm* taboo; **un épisode t. de l'histoire de France** an episode in French history that is never spoken of *or* mentioned; **c'est un sujet t.** that's taboo, that's a taboo subject

taboulé [tabule] *nm Culin* tabbouleh

tabouret [taburɛ] *nm* stool; (*pour les pieds*) footstool; **t. de bar/piano** bar/piano stool

tabulaire [tabylɛr] *adj* tabular

tabulateur [tabylatœr] *nm* tab (key); (*de machine à écrire*) tab key, tabulator; **régler les tabulateurs** to set tabs (**à** at)

tabulation [tabylasjɔ̃] *nf* tabulation, tabbing; (*colonne*) tab; **poser des tabulations dans** to tab; **pour la t., utiliser cette touche** use this key for your tabs

tabulatrice [tabylatris] *nf* (*pour cartes perforées*) tabulator

tabuler [tabyle] *vt* to tabulate, to tab

tac [tak] *nm* (*bruit*) click; **t. t. t.** (*d'une mitraillette, du pivert*) ratatat; *Fig* **riposter** *ou* **répondre du t. au t.** to answer quick as lightning; *Fig* **je lui ai répondu du t. au t. que ...** I retorted quick as a flash that ..., I came back quick as lightning that ...

tacet [tasɛt] *nm Mus* tacet

tache [taʃ] *nf* **(a)** (*de graisse, de boue, de sang, d'huile etc*) stain; (*de peinture*) blob, splash; (*dans une pierre précieuse*) flaw, blemish; (*dans un fruit*) blemish; (*d'encre*) blot; (*de couleur, lumière*) splash; *Fig* (*sur la réputation etc*) blot, stain; **faire une/des tache(s)** to make a mess; **tu ne peux donc pas manger sans faire de taches?** can't you eat without making a mess?; **tu es en train de faire des taches sur le canapé/ton pull** you're getting stains on the couch/your sweater; **t. de suie** fleck of soot, smut; *Fig* **sans t.** (*réputation*) spotless; *Fig* **faire t.** (*d'un bibelot, d'une personne etc*) to stick out like a sore thumb; *Fig* **faire t. d'huile** to spread

(b) (*sur la peau*) mark; **chien blanc à taches feu** white dog with reddish markings *or* patches *or* spots

▶ **tache**: **t. de lumière** *Th, Cin* hot spot; *TV* shading; *Anat* **t. de Mariotte** (*à l'œil*) blind spot; **t. de rousseur** freckle; **t. solaire** *ou* **du soleil** sunspot; **t. de vin** strawberry mark

tâche [taʃ] *nf* task, job; **travail à la t.** *Ind* piece-work; (*intermittent*) jobbing (work); **ouvrier à la t.** *Ind* piece-worker; (*par intermittence*) jobbing workman; **travailler à la t.** to do piece-work; **on n'est pas à la t.!** nobody's timing us!; *Litt* **prendre à t. de faire qch** to undertake to do sth *Ordinat* **t. d'arrière-plan** *ou* **de fond** background task *or* job

taché [taʃe] *adj* **(a)** (*vêtement, tissu*) stained; *Biol* spotted; **taché d'encre/de sang/de graisse** ink-/blood-/grease-stained **(b)** (*fruit*) bruised

tachéomètre [takeɔmɛtr] *nm* tacheometer, tachymeter

tachéométrie [takeɔmetri] *nf* tacheometry, tachymetry

tacher [taʃe] **1** *vt* (*vêtement etc*) to get stains on, to stain; (*réputation etc*) to sully, to tarnish **2** *vi* (*de l'encre, du vin etc*) to stain **3 se tacher** *vpr* (*d'une personne*) to get stains on oneself; (*d'un tissu, d'un vêtement etc*) to stain

tâcher [taʃe] *vi* **t. de faire qch** to try *or* attempt to do sth; **tâchez de ne pas oublier** try not to forget; **tâchons que cela ne se reproduise plus** let's make sure it doesn't happen again

tâcheron [taʃrɔ̃] *nm* **(a)** *Péj* skivvy, drudge; **j'en ai assez de faire ce métier de t.!** I've had enough of this drudgery *or* skivvying! **(b)** *Agr* piece-worker **(c)** *Constr etc* subcontractor, jobber **(d)** *Journ* hack

tacheté [taʃte] *adj* (*papier, plumage*) speckled, mottled; (*chat*) tabby; **chat noir t. de blanc** black cat with white spots *or* markings

tacheter [taʃte] *vt* to spot, to speckle

tacheture [taʃtyr] *nf* spot, speckle

tachisme [taʃism] *nm Beaux-Arts* tachisme

tachiste [taʃist] *adj, n Beaux-Arts* tachiste

tachycardie [takikardi] *nf Méd* tachycardia

tachygraphe [takigraf] *nm* tachograph

tachymètre [takimɛtr] *nm* tachometer; *Aut* speedometer

tachymétrie [takimetri] *nf* tachometry

tachytoscope [takitoskɔp] *nm Mktg* tachistoscope

Tacite [tasit] *nm* Tacitus

tacite [tasit] *adj* (*consentement, accord, reconnaissance etc*) tacit; **de façon t.** tacitly; *Jur* **t. reconduction** tacit renewal; *Jur* **renouvelable par t. reconduction** renewable by tacit consent

tacitement [tasitmɑ̃] *adv* tacitly

taciturne [tasityrn] *adj* taciturn

tacle [takl] *nm Fb* tackle; **t. glissé** sliding tackle

tacler [takle] *vti Fb* to tackle

tacot [tako] *nm F Péj* (*voiture*) (old) jalopy, *Br* (old) banger

tact [takt] *nm* **(a)** (*délicatesse etc*) tact; **avoir du t.** to be tactful; **être plein de t.** to be very tactful, to be full of tact; **manquer de t.** to be tactless, to lack tact; **avec t.** tactfully, with tact; **sans t.** (*réponse, geste*) tactless; (*répondre, agir*) tactlessly **(b)** *Vieilli* (*toucher*) (sense of) touch

tacticien, -ienne [taktisjɛ̃, -jɛn] *n* tactician

tactile [taktil] *adj* tactile

tactique [taktik] **1** *adj* tactical **2** *nf* tactics; **je vais devoir changer de t.** I'm going to have to change my tactics; **une t. nouvelle** new tactics, a new tactic; **ce n'est pas la meilleure t. pour le convaincre** it's not the best way of convincing him

tadorne [tadɔrn] *nm Orn* shelduck

tænia [tenja] *nm Méd* tapeworm, *Spéc* taenia, *US* tenia

taffetas [tafta] *nm* **(a)** *Tex* taffeta **(b)** *Méd* **t. anglais** *ou* **gommé** sticking plaster, *Am* Band-Aid®

tag [tag] *nm* tag

tagliatelles [taljatɛl] *nfpl Culin* tagliatelle (*with sing vb*)

taguer [tage] *vti* to tag

tagueur, -euse [tagœr, -øz] *nm* tagger

Tahiti [taiti] *nf* Tahiti

tahitien, -ienne [taisjɛ̃, -jɛn] **1** *adj* Tahitian **2** *n* **T.** Tahitian

taïaut [tajo] *int* tally-ho!

taie [tɛ] *nf* **(a) t.** (**d'oreiller**) pillowcase, pillowslip **(b)** *Méd* leucoma; *Fig Litt* **avoir une t. sur l'œil** to be blinkered, to have tunnel vision

taïga [taiga] *nf Géog* taiga

taillable [tajabl] *adj* **être t. et corvéable (à merci)** to be a skivvy *or* a drudge; *Hist* (*d'un serf etc*) to be liable to tallage

taillade [tajad] *nf* slash, gash; **se faire une t. dans le doigt** to gash one's finger

taillader [tajade] *vt* to slash, to gash; **se t. le doigt/le menton** to gash one's finger/chin; **se t. les veines** to slash one's wrists; *Couture* **tailladé** slashed

taillandier [tajɑ̃dje] *nm* maker of edge-tools

taille [taj] *nf* **(a)** (*hauteur*) (*de personne*) height; **quelle est votre t.?** what height are you?, how tall are you?; **atteindre sa t. adulte** to reach one's full height; **de grande t./t. moyenne** very tall/of medium height; **de petite t.** short

(b) (*grandeur*) size; **quelle est votre t.?, quelle t. faites-vous?** (*en vêtement*) what size are you *or* do you take?; **avez-vous la t. en dessus/dessous?** do you have the next size up/down?; **au moins deux tailles en dessous** at least two sizes smaller; **pour les tailles exceptionnelles, pour les grandes tailles** outsize; **de petite t.** small; **une lettre de la t. d'une affiche** a letter the size of a poster, a poster-sized letter; **des avocats de la t. du poing** avocados the size of your fist; **une erreur de belle t.** a huge mistake; *Ordinat* **t. de disque dur** hard disk size; *Ordinat* **t. de mémoire** memory size; *Ordinat* **t. de champ** field size; *Typ* **t. de corps** body size; *Typ* **t. de fonte** font size; *Typ* **t. des caractères** typesize; **t. du papier** paper size

(c) *Fig* (*mesure*) **trouver un adversaire à sa t.** to meet one's match; **trouver un collaborateur à sa t.** to find a colleague who is one's equal *or* who has an equal level of skills; **il est de t. à vous battre** he is big enough *or* strong enough to beat you; **il n'est pas de t. à être chef** he's not cut out to be a leader, he's not the stuff that leaders are made of; **je ne suis pas de t. à vous prouver le contraire** I'm not in a position to prove you wrong; **il n'est pas de t. à lutter contre vous** he is no match for you, he stands no chance against you; **rien à craindre, il n'est pas de t.** have no fear, he's not up to it; **un mensonge de t.** a whopper; **le mensonge était de t.** it was a thumping great lie

(d) (*partie du corps*) waist; (*de vêtement*) waist, waistline; **tour de t.** waist (measurement); **avoir la t. fine** to have a trim waist *or* a good waistline; **retrouver une t. fine** to get one's waistline back; **elle a une t. de guêpe** she is wasp-waisted; **tu as la t. bien prise dans cette jupe** the skirt is a perfect fit at the waist; **prendre qn par la t.** (*d'un bras*) to put an arm round sb's waist; (*des deux mains*) to take sb by the waist, to seize sb round the waist; **pantalon à t. haute/basse** trousers with a high/low waist(line), high-/low-waisted trousers; **pardessus à t.** fitted overcoat

(e) (*action*) (*de pierre, de pierres précieuses, de vêtements, de cheveux etc*) cutting; (*d'arbuste*) pruning, trimming; (*de haie*) trimming, clipping; (*de roue d'engrenage*) milling

(f) (*tranchant*) (*d'une épée etc*) edge

(g) (*taillis*) **jeune t.** coppice

(h) *Min* gallery

(i) *Hist* (*redevance*) tallage

► **taille**: **t. basse** (*d'un pneu*) low profile; *Bourse* **t. boursière** market size; *Couture* **t. normale** natural waistline

taillé [taje] *adj* **bien t.** (*personne*) well-built; **bien/mal t.** (*ongles, moustaches*) well-/badly trimmed; (*vêtement*) well-/badly cut; *Fig* **t. pour commander/pour un métier** cut out to be a leader/for a job; **cheveux taillés en brosse** crew cut; **crayon t. en pointe** sharp pencil; **t. dans le roc** carved out of the rock

taille-crayon(s) *nm inv* pencil sharpener

taille-douce, *pl* **tailles-douces** *nf* (*technique, estampe*) copper-plate engraving

tailler [taje] **1** *vt* **(a)** (*pierre, diamant, herbe, cheveux, bifteck etc*) to cut; (*arbre*) to prune, to trim; (*haie, barbe etc*) to trim, to clip; (*vigne*) to dress; (*crayon*) to sharpen; **t. qch en biseau** to bevel sth; *Fig* **t. une armée en pièces** to cut an army to pieces; *Fig F* **t. une bavette** to have a chat *or Br* natter

(b) *Couture* **t. un vêtement** to cut out a garment; **t. une robe d'après** *ou* **sur un patron** to cut out a dress from a pattern; *Fig F* **t. un costard** *ou* **une veste à qn** to slag sb off

2 *vi Chir* to make an incision; **t. dans la chair** *ou* **dans le vif** to cut into the flesh

3 se tailler *vpr* **(a)** (*se couper*) **se t. la barbe** to trim one's beard; **se t. un chemin à travers …** to carve one's way through …; *Fig* **se t. un beau succès** to be very successful

(b) *Arg* (*partir*) to beat it, to scram; **je me taille!** I'm off!

tailleur [tajœr] *nm* **(a)** (*de pierres, de diamants, d'arbres etc*) cutter **(b)** *Couture* tailor; **s'asseoir en t.** to sit cross-legged **(c)** (*costume*) suit

tailleur-pantalon, *pl* **tailleurs-pantalons** *nm* trouser *or Am* pant suit

taillis [taji] **1** *nm* copse, coppice; **dans les t.** in the copse *or* coppice **2** *adj* **bois t.** copsewood, brushwood

tain [tɛ̃] *nm* (*de glace*) silvering; **refaire le t. d'une glace** to resilver a mirror; **glace** *ou* **miroir sans t.** two-way mirror

taire [tɛr] (*prp* **taisant**; *pp* **tu**; *pr ind* **je tais, il tait, n. taisons, ils taisent**; *pr sub* **je taise**; *impf* **je taisais**; *p hist* **je tus**; *fu* **je tairai**) **1** *vt* (*qch*) to say nothing about, not to mention; (*cacher*) to suppress, to hush up; **une dame dont je tairai le nom** a lady who shall be nameless; **t. qch à qn** to keep *or* hide *or* conceal sth from sb

2 se taire *vpr* (*être silencieux*) to be quiet *or* silent; (*cesser de parler*) to stop talking, to be *or Fml* fall silent; (*décider de ne rien dire*) to keep quiet *or* silent; (*d'un son*) to stop, to cease; **tu ne vas pas te t. jusqu'à la fin du dîner!** you're surely going to open your mouth and say something before the end of the dinner!; **tais-toi!** be quiet!, *F* shut up!; **faire t.** (*bavard, opposition, critiques*) to silence, to reduce to silence, *F* to shut up; (*conscience*) to silence; (*enfant*) to keep quiet, *F* to shut up; **faire t. sa douleur** to stifle one's grief; **savoir se t.** to know how to keep quiet *or* to keep one's mouth shut; **elle a perdu une occasion de se t.** she would have done better to say nothing *or* to keep her mouth shut

Taiwan [tajwan] *n* Taiwan

taiwanais, -aise [tajwanɛ, -ɛz] **1** *adj* Taiwanese **2** *n* **T.** Taiwanese

tajine [taʒin] *nm Culin* tajine

take-off [tekɔf] *nm inv Écon* takeoff

talc [talk] *nm Minér* talc; (*produit*) talc, talcum powder

talé [tale] *adj* (*fruit*) bruised

talent [talɑ̃] *nm* **(a)** (*don*) talent; **son t. de pianiste** his talent as a pianist; **avoir du t.** to be talented; **homme/musicien de t.** talented man/musician; **sans t.** untalented; **elle n'a aucun t. pour faire la cuisine** she has no talent for cooking, she's a hopeless cook; **avoir le t. de faire qch** to have a knack *or* gift for doing sth; **exploiter ses talents** to make use of one's talents (**de cuisinier** as a cook); **faire appel à tous les talents** to call in the best talent *or* brains; **éditeur à la recherche de nouveaux talents** publisher in search of new talent **(b)** *Antiq* (*monnaie*) talent

talentueusement [talɑ̃tɥøzmɑ̃] *adv* with talent

talentueux, -euse [talɑ̃tɥø, -øz] *adj* talented

taler [tale] *vt* (*fruit etc*) to bruise

taleth [talɛt] *nm Rel* tallith

talion [taljɔ̃] *nm* **la loi du t.** an eye for an eye (and a tooth for a tooth); **appliquer la loi du t.** to demand an eye for an eye

talisman [talismɑ̃] *nm* talisman

talitre [talitr] *nm* (*crustacé*) sand flea *or* hopper

talkie-walkie, *pl* **talkies-walkies** [tɔkiwɔki] *nm* walkie-talkie

talk-show [tɔkʃo] *nm TV* talk *or Br* chat show

Talmud [talmyd] *nm Rel* **le T.** the Talmud

talmudique [talmydik] *adj* Talmudic(al)

talmudiste [talmydist] *nm* Talmudist

taloche [talɔʃ] *nf* **(a)** *F* (*gifle*) clout, cuff **(b)** *Constr* (plasterer's) hawk

talocher [talɔʃe] *vt F* (*qn*) to clout, to cuff

talon [talɔ̃] *nm* **(a)** (*de pied, de chaussure, de bas etc*) heel; **marcher sur les talons de qn** to tread on sb's heels, to follow close *or* hard on sb's heels; **être toujours sur les talons de qn** to dog sb's footsteps; **la police est sur ses talons depuis quinze jours** the police have been on his heels for two weeks; **donner du t. à son cheval** to give one's horse the spur; **montrer** *ou* **tourner les talons** to turn on one's heel

(b) *Tech* (*d'outil, de mât, de club de golf, de crosse de fusil*) heel; *Mus* (*d'archet*) heel, nut; (*de queue de billard*) butt; (*de lame d'épée, de baïonnette, de palan, d'essieu*) shoulder

(c) *Cartes* stock, reserve, talon

(d) (*bout*) (*de pain, de fromage, de jambon etc*) heel

(e) (*de chèque etc*) stub, *Br* counterfoil; **t. à retourner** reply slip

(f) *Archit* ogee (moulding), talon

► **talon**: **t. d'Achille** Achilles' heel; **talons aiguilles** stiletto heels; (*chaussures*) stilettos; **talons compensés** built-up heels; **talons hauts** high heels; **chaussures à talons hauts** high-heeled shoes, high heels; **t. minute** heel bar; **talons plats** flat heels; **chaussures à talons plats** flat-heeled shoes, flats

talonnage [talɔnaʒ] *nm Rugby* heeling

talonnement [talɔnmɑ̃] *nm* (*de cheval*) spurring on; *Fig* (*harcèlement*) (*de qn*) hounding

talonner [talɔne] **1** *vt* **(a)** (*suivre*) (*qn*) to follow on the heels of, to follow close behind **(b)** (*harceler*) (*d'une personne*) to hound; (*de la faim*) to dog; **être talonné par la mort** to be pursued by death; **se faire t. par le fisc** to be hounded by the tax man, to have the tax man breathing down one's neck **(c)** (*presser du talon*) (*cheval*) to spur on **(d)** *Rugby* to heel **2** *vi* **(a)** *Naut* (*d'un navire*) to touch, to bump **(b)** *Rugby* to heel

talonnette [talɔnɛt] *nf* **(a)** (*d'une chaussure*) counter; (*à l'intérieur de la chaussure*) heel pad **(b)** (*à l'intérieur d'un pantalon*) binding

talonneur [talɔnœr] *nm Rugby* hooker

talquer [talke] *vt* to sprinkle with talc *or* talcum powder

talure [talyr] *nf* (*sur un fruit*) bruise

talus [taly] *nm* **(a)** (*pente*) slope; **en t.** sloping; **la voiture est tombée dans le t.** the car fell down the slope **(b)** (*construit*) embankment, slope, ramp **(c)** *Géol* talus, scree

talweg [talvɛg] *nm Géog* t(h)alweg

tamanoir [tamanwar] *nm Zool* great anteater, ant bear

tamarin[1] [tamarɛ̃] *nm* **(a)** (*fruit*) tamarind **(b)** (*tamaris*) tamarisk

tamarin[2] *nm Zool* tamarin

tamarinier [tamarinje] *nm* tamarind (tree)

tamaris [tamaris] *nm Bot* tamarisk

tambouille [tɑ̃buj] *nf Arg* **(a)** (*cuisine*) cooking; **faire la t.** to do the cooking **(b)** (*plat etc*) grub, nosh; **on s'est fait une bonne petite t.** we made ourselves some great grub *or* nosh

tambour [tɑ̃bur] *nm* **(a)** (*instrument de musique*) drum; **battre du t.** to play the drum, to drum; **entendre un bruit de t.** to hear the sound of drums; **peau de t.** drum-head; *F* **raisonner comme un t.** to talk through one's hat; **sans t. ni trompette** quietly, without (any) fuss, *F* without a song and dance

(b) (*personne*) drummer

(c) *Tech* (*d'une turbine, d'une machine à laver etc*), *Naut* (*d'un cabestan*) drum; *Él* (*d'une bobine*) cylinder; **freins à t.** drum brakes

(d) (*entrée*) (*d'église etc*) vestibule; (*tourniquet*) revolving door

(e) (*à broder*) (embroidery) frame, tambour

(f) *Archit* (*d'une colonne etc*) drum

▶ **tambour**: **t. de basque** tambourine; **t. de câble** cable drum; **t. de frein** brake drum; *Typ* **t. d'impression** print drum; **t. de photocopie** photocopier drum; **t. photosensible** photosensitive drum; *Hist* **t. de ville** town crier

tambourin [tɑ̃burɛ̃] *nm* **(a)** (*en Provence*) = small drum used in Provençal folk music **(b)** (*tambour de basque*) tambourine

tambourinage [tɑ̃burinaʒ] *nm* drumming

tambourinaire [tɑ̃burinɛr] *nm* **(a)** (*musicien*) tambourin player **(b)** *Hist* (*annonceur*) town crier

tambourinement [tɑ̃burinmɑ̃] *nm* drumming

tambouriner [tɑ̃burine] **1** *vi* (*avec ses doigts, des objets etc*) to drum; **la pluie tambourine sur le toit** the rain is drumming on the roof **2** *vt* **(a)** (*rythme, air etc*) to drum out; (*avec les doigts*) to tap out **(b)** (*nouvelle*) *Arch* to announce; *F* to shout from the rooftops

tambour-major, *pl* **tambours-majors** *nm Mil* drum major

Tamerlan [tamɛrlɑ̃] *nm* Tamburlaine

tamil, -ile [tamil] **1** *adj* Tamil **2** *nm Ling* Tamil **3** *n* **T.** Tamil

tamis [tami] *nm* sieve; (*pour le sable etc*) sifter; (*pour les liquides*) strainer; *Ind* riddle, screen; **passer au t.** (*farine etc*) to sieve; (*sable etc*) to sift; (*liquide*) to strain; *Ind* to riddle, to screen; *Fig* (*témoignage, information, candidats etc*) to sift through

tamisage [tamizaʒ] *nm* (*de farine etc*) sieving; (*de sable etc*) sifting; (*de liquide*) straining; *Ind* riddling, screening

Tamise [tamiz] *nf* **la T.** the Thames

tamiser [tamize] **1** *vt* (*farine etc*) to sieve; (*sable etc*) to sift; (*liquide*) to strain; *Ind* to riddle, to screen; **rideaux qui tamisent la lumière** curtains that filter the light; **lumière tamisée** subdued light **2** *vi* (*de la poussière, de la lumière etc*) to filter through

tamoul, -oule [tamul] **1** *adj* Tamil **2** *nm Ling* Tamil **3** *n* **T.** Tamil

tampon [tɑ̃pɔ̃] *nm* **(a)** (*bouchon*) plug, stopper; (*d'un tonneau*) bung **(b)** *Constr* wall plug **(c)** *Méd* swab; *Chir* pad, plug, tampon; (*hygiénique*) tampon **(d)** (*cachet, instrument*) stamp; (*de la poste*) postmark; **coup de t.** stamp **(e)** (*pour polir*) pad **(f)** **t. (de choc)** (*de train*) buffer; **coup de t.** collision (*between buffers*); *Pol* **état/zone t.** buffer state/zone; *Fig F* **servir de t. (entre deux personnes)** to act as a buffer (between two people)

▶ **tampon**: **t. buvard** blotter; **t. dateur** date stamp; **t. encreur** ink pad; **t. hygiénique** *ou* **périodique** tampon; **t. à récurer** scourer, scouring pad

tamponnage [tɑ̃pɔnaʒ] *nm Ch* neutralizing

tamponnement [tɑ̃pɔnmɑ̃] *nm* **(a)** (*bouchage*) (*de blessure etc*) plugging **(b)** (*essuyage*) (*avec un tampon*) swabbing, dabbing **(c)** *Aut, Rail* collision

tamponner [tɑ̃pɔne] **1** *vt* **(a)** (*essuyer*) to swab, to dab; *Typ* (*caractères, plaque de métal*) to ink up **(b)** (*timbrer*) (*document etc*) to stamp; **t. une lettre** to frank a letter **(c)** (*polir*) (*meuble*) to French-polish **(d)** *Ch* to neutralize **(e)** (*voiture, train etc*) to run into, to collide with **(f)** *Vieilli* (*boucher*) to plug, to stop (up); *Méd* (*blessure*) to put a wad over, to plug; *Constr* (*mur*) to plug **2 se tamponner** *vpr* **(a)** (*de voitures, de trains etc*) to run into each other, to collide **(b)** **se t. le front** to mop one's brow; **se t. les yeux** to dab one's eyes; *Arg* **il s'en tamponne (le coquillard)** he doesn't give a damn *or* a monkey's

tamponneur, -euse [tɑ̃pɔnœr, -øz] *adj* **autos tamponneuses** dodgems, bumper cars

tamponnoir [tɑ̃pɔnwar] *nm* wall drill

tam-tam, *pl* **tam-tams** [tamtam] *nm* **(a)** (*tambour*) tom-tom **(b)** *F Péj* (*tapage*) fuss, ballyhoo; **faire du t. autour de qch** to make a great fuss *or* great ballyhoo about sth **(c)** (*gong*) gong

tan [tɑ̃] *nm* tan, (tanner's) bark

tancer [tɑ̃se] *vt* **(je tançai(s); n. tançons)** *Litt* to berate, to scold

tanche [tɑ̃ʃ] *nf* (*poisson*) tench

tandem [tɑ̃dɛm] *nm* **(a)** **chevaux attelés en t.** horses driven tandem **(b)** (*bicyclette*) tandem **(c)** (*deux personnes*) twosome, duo; **travailler en t.** to work in tandem; **un t. de comédiens** a comic duo **(d)** *Tech* **cylindres en t.** tandem cylinders **(e)** *Ordinat* **central t.** tandem exchange, tandem central office

tandis que [tɑ̃di(s)kə] *conj* **(a)** (*alors que*) while, whereas **(b)** (*pendant que*) while, *Fml* whilst

tangage [tɑ̃gaʒ] *nm Naut, Av* pitching; *Fig* reeling, swaying; **pour supprimer le t. du bateau** to stop the boat pitching

tangara [tɑ̃gara] *nm Orn* tanager

tangence [tɑ̃ʒɑ̃s] *nf Géom* tangency; **point de t.** point of contact

tangent, -ente [tɑ̃ʒɑ̃, -ɑ̃t] **1** *adj Géom* tangential, tangent **(à** to); *F* **c'est t.** it's touch and go; **c'était t.** it was touch and go, it was a near thing **2** *nf* **tangente** tangent; *F* **prendre la tangente** to dodge the question; (*partir*) to slip away

tangentiel, -ielle [tɑ̃ʒɑ̃sjɛl] *adj Géom* tangential

Tanger [tɑ̃ʒe] *n* Tangier(s)

tangible [tɑ̃ʒibl] *adj* tangible

tangiblement [tɑ̃ʒibləmɑ̃] *adv* tangibly

tango [tɑ̃go] **1** *nm* (*danse, musique*) tango; **danser le t.** to tango **2** *adj inv* (*couleur*) tangerine

tangon [tɑ̃gɔ̃] *nm Naut* (*mobile*) swinging boom; (*de spi*) spinnaker boom

tanguer [tɑ̃ge] *vi Av, Naut* to pitch; *Fig* to reel, to sway

tanière [tanjɛr] *nf* **(a)** (*d'animal*) den, lair **(b)** (*habitation sordide*) hovel **(c)** (*retraite*) retreat

tanin [tanɛ̃] *nm Ch, Ind* tannin

tank [tɑ̃k] *nm Mil, Naut, F* (*grande voiture*) tank

tanker [tɑ̃kɛr] *nm Naut* tanker

tankiste [tɑ̃kist] *nm Mil* soldier with a/the tank unit

tannage [tanaʒ] *nm Tech* (*des peaux*) tanning

tannant [tanɑ̃] *adj* **(a)** *Arg* (*ennuyeux*) annoying; **il est t.!** he's a drag!; **qu'est-ce que c'est t., ces réunions de famille!** these family get-togethers are a real drag! **(b)** *Tech* tanning

tanne [tan] *nf* (*sur le cuir*) spot; (*sur le visage*) blackhead

tanné, -ée [tane] **1** *adj* (*peau, visage etc*) weather-beaten **2** *nm* **(a)** (*couleur*) tan (colour) **(b)** **gants en t.** tan(ned) leather gloves **3** *nf F* **tannée** thrashing, good hiding

tanner [tane] *vt* **(a)** *Tech* (*peaux*) to tan **(b)** *Arg* (*ennuyer*) to annoy; (*harceler*) to pester; **elle m'a tanné pour que je le lui dise** she pestered me to tell her **(c)** *Arg* **t. (le cuir à) un enfant** to thrash a child, to tan a child's hide; **il s'est fait t. le cuir par des voleurs** he was beaten up by thieves

tannerie [tanri] *nf* (*établissement*) tannery; (*industrie*) tanning

tanneur [tanœr] *nm* (*de peaux*) tanner

tannin [tanɛ̃] *nm Ch, Ind* tannin

tannique [tanik] *adj Ch* (*acide*) tannic

tanrec [tɑ̃rɛk] *nm Zool* tenrec

tan-sad, *pl* **tan-sads** [tɑ̃sad] *nm* pillion(-seat)

tant [tɑ̃] *adv* **(a)** (*quantité*) so much; **t. de bonté** so much *or* such kindness; **il a t. bu que …** he has drunk so much that …; **ce n'est pas la peine de t. vous presser** you needn't be in such a hurry; **elle s'est donné t. de mal** she went to such (a lot of) *or* so much trouble; **pour t. faire** *ou* **à t. faire** *ou F* **t. qu'à faire, j'aimerais autant …** while I'm at it *or* about it, I would just as soon …; *F* **tu m'en diras t.!** you don't say!, really?; **t. pour cent** so much per cent; **votre lettre du t.** your letter of such and such a date; **il a t. et plus d'argent** he has any amount of money; **ils tiraient t. et plus** they were pulling for all they were worth; **s'inquiéter t. et plus** to be worried to death; **je me suis ennuyé t. et plus** I was bored to tears *or* to death; **t. et si bien que …** so much so that …; **j'ai crié t. et t. qu'il est parti** I shouted so much that he went (away); **on a attendu t. et t. que …** we waited so long that …; **t. s'en faut** far from it; **un t. soit peu** a little, somewhat; **s'il était un t. soit peu intelligent** if he had any intelligence, if he was the slightest bit intelligent; **si t. est qu'il soit mort** if he really is dead; **il y en a peu, si t. est qu'il y en ait du tout** there is little/there are few, if any

(b) (*nombre*) so many; **t. de fois** so many times, so often; **il a des amis t. et plus** he has plenty of friends; **inutile de faire t. d'histoires pour ça** it's pointless to make such a fuss over that

(c) (*tellement, à tel point*) so, to such a degree; **il ne peut pas se lever, t. il est malade** he cannot get up, he is so ill; **elle ne parle plus, t. elle a été choquée** the shock was so great that she has stopped speaking; **t. était grande sa discrétion que …** so great was his discretion that …; **t. il est vrai que …** so much so that …; **elle est t. aimée** she is loved so much; **elle n'est pas t. sotte que naïve** she's not so much stupid as naive; **n'aimer rien t. que …** to like nothing more than …; **elle dit n'aimer rien t. que l'automne** she says there is nothing she likes more than the autumn

(d) **en t. que** (*comme*) as; (*dans la mesure où*) in so far as; **je suis Russe en t. que je suis né en Russie** I am a Russian in so far as I was born in Russia; **l'homme en t. qu'il diffère des animaux** man, as distinct from animals; **en t. que vieil ami de votre père** as a very old friend of your father('s)

(e) (*quelque*) however; **t. aimable qu'il soit** however pleasant he may be

(f) **t. mieux** so much the better, that's all to the good!; **t. mieux pour toi** good for you; **t. pis!** too bad!, it can't be helped!, what a pity!, never mind!; **c'est t. pis** that's just too bad; **t. pis pour toi!** (that's) too bad for you!, that's just too bad!

(g) **t. que** (*autant que*) as much as; **j'ai couru t. que j'ai pu** I ran as hard as I could; *F* **il pleut t. qu'il peut** it's raining like anything; **t. aux Indes qu'ailleurs** both in India and elsewhere; **t. les enfants que les adultes** children and adults alike; **un film t. pour les petits que pour les grands** a film for children and adults alike; **t. pour vous que pour moi** for your sake as much as mine, for you as much as for me; **il est sévère t. avec ses enfants qu'avec ses élèves** he is as strict with his children as he is with his pupils; **je suis à l'aise t. avec lui qu'avec elle** I'm at ease with him and her; **t. bien que mal** somehow or other, after a fashion

(h) [ⓘB29-30,11] **t. que** (*aussi longtemps que*) as long as; (*pendant que*) while; **t. que je vivrai** as long as I live; **t. que la vue s'étend** as far as the eye can see; **t. que vous y êtes** while you're about *or* at it; **rien ne peut être décidé t. qu'il n'a pas donné son avis** nothing can be decided until (such time as) he makes his opinion known

(i) *Arg* **t. qu'à = quant à**, *voir* **quant**

Tantale [tɑ̃tal] *nm* Tantalus

tantale [tɑ̃tal] *nm Ch* tantalum

tante [tɑ̃t] *nf* (a) aunt (b) *Vulg Péj* (*homosexuel*) queer, *Br* poof(ter), *Am* faggot (c) *Arg* **ma t.** (*mont-de-piété*) uncle's, the pawnbroker's (shop)

tantième [tɑ̃tjɛm] *nm Com* (*de bénéfices etc*) percentage, quota; **t. des administrateurs** directors' fee

tantine [tɑ̃tin] *nf F* auntie, aunty

tantinet [tɑ̃tinɛ] *nm F* tiny bit; **un t. plus long** a tiny bit *or* a shade *or* a fraction longer; **un t. vieillot/ridicule** a tiny bit *or* a touch *or* ever so slightly old-fashioned/ridiculous

tantôt [tɑ̃to] *adv* (a) (*parfois*) **t. triste, t. gai** now sad, now gay; **t. je suis à Paris, t. à Londres** sometimes I am in Paris, sometimes in London (b) *Arch, Région* (*bientôt*) soon, presently; (*il y a peu de temps*) just now, a little while ago; **voici t. deux mois qu'il est parti** it will soon be two months since he left (c) (*cet après-midi*) this afternoon; **il pleuvra/il a plu t.** it will rain/it rained this afternoon; **à t.** see you soon

tantouse [tɑ̃tuz] *nf Vulg Péj* (*homosexuel*) queer, *Br* poof(ter)

Tanzanie [tɑ̃zani] *nf* Tanzania

tanzanien, -ienne [tɑ̃zanjɛ̃, -jɛn] 1 *adj* Tanzanian 2 *n* **T.** Tanzanian

Tao [tao] *nm* Tao

taôisme, taoïsme [taoism] *nm Rel* Taoism

taôiste, taoïste [taoist] *adj, n Rel* Taoist

taon [tɑ̃] *nm* gadfly, horsefly, cleg

tapage [tapaʒ] *nm* (a) (*bruit*) din, uproar, *F* racket, row; **faire du t.** to kick up a din *or* racket *or* row (b) (*publicité*) fuss, ballyhoo; **cette nouvelle a fait du t.** the news caused quite a stir; **faire du t. autour de qch** to make a great fuss *or* a great ballyhoo *or* a song and dance about sth; **annoncer qch à grand t.** to announce sth with a lot of ballyhoo

▶ **tapage**: *Jur* **t. nocturne: faire du t. nocturne** to create a disturbance

tapageur, -euse [tapaʒœr, -øz] *adj* (a) (*enfant, soirée etc*) noisy, rowdy, raucous (b) (*vêtements, couleur*) loud, flashy; (*décoration*) flashy; (*publicité*) blatant

tapageusement [tapaʒøzmɑ̃] *adv* (*s'habiller etc*) flashily, loudly

tapant [tapɑ̃] *adj* **à sept heures tapant(es)** on the stroke of seven, at seven o'clock sharp *or* on the dot

tape [tap] *nf* slap; **il m'a donné une t. sur l'épaule** he slapped me *or* gave me a slap on the shoulder; **une petite t. sur la joue** a pat on the cheek

tapé [tape] *adj* (a) (*fruit*) (*séché*) dried; (*abîmé*) damaged (b) *Arg* **réponse tapée** snappy answer (c) *F* (*fou*) nuts, crazy, cracked

tape-à-l'œil 1 *adj inv* loud, gaudy, flashy 2 *nm inv* gaudy *or* flashy rubbish

tape(-)cul, *pl* **tape(-)culs** *nm* (a) (*bascule*) seesaw (b) *Naut* jigger (sail) (c) *F* (*véhicule*) rattletrap, boneshaker

tapée [tape] *nf F* **une t.** *ou* **des tapées de …** masses *or* heaps *or* loads of …

taper¹ [tape] 1 *vt* (a) (*frapper*) (*enfant*) to hit, to slap; (*cuisse*) to slap; (*table etc*) to bang; *Ordinat* to key; **t. du tambour** to beat the drum; **t. un coup/deux coups à la porte** to knock/knock twice at the door; **t. une lettre (à la machine)** to type a letter; *Ordinat* **tapez entrée ou retour** select enter or return; **t. un air (au piano)** to thump out a tune (on the piano); *F* **t. la carte** to play cards

(b) *F* **il est encore venu me t.** he came to scrounge off me again; **t. qn de mille francs** to touch *or Br* tap sb for a thousand francs

2 *vi* (a) (*frapper*) to bang (**sur** on); **la bôme est venu t. contre le mât** the boom hit the *or* banged into the mast; *Ordinat* **t. sur une touche** to hit a key; **t. sur le piano** to thump *or* plonk away on the piano; **t. sur qn** to hit sb; *F* (*critiquer*) to knock sb, to have a go at sb; **t. à la porte** to bang on the door; **t. avec un marteau (contre le mur)** to hammer (the wall); *F* **t. sur le ventre à qn** to give sb a dig in the ribs (*as a mark of familiarity*); **le soleil nous tapait sur la tête** the sun was beating down on us; **le soleil tape dans ma chambre** the sun is turning my room into an oven; *F* **ça tape** (*il fait chaud*) it's scorching; **t. dans** (*nourriture*) to help oneself to, to dig into; (*ses économies, ses réserves*) to break *or* dig into; *F* **t. dans l'œil à qn** to take sb's fancy; **t. dans un ballon** to knock *or* kick a ball around; **t. du pied** to stamp one's foot; *Mil F* **t. sur un objectif** to strafe a target; **t. à côté** to miss the target; *Fig* **alors là, tu as tapé à côté** you're way off beam, *Am* you're way out in left field; **t. à la tête** (*d'un vin*) to go to one's head; **il tape, ce petit vin!** this wine is fairly potent!

(b) (*dactylographier*) **t. (à la machine)** to type; **t. au toucher** to touch-type

(c) *Arg* (*puer*) to stink

3 **se taper** *vpr* (a) (*se frapper*) to knock each other about; **se t. sur la cuisse** to slap one's thigh; **avec lui, on se tape les cuisses de rire** he makes you split your sides laughing; *Fig* **se t. le derrière par terre** to split one's sides laughing, to fall about laughing; **une situation à se t. le derrière par terre** a hysterically *or* an uproariously funny situation

(b) *Arg* **se t. qch** (*manger, boire*) to put sth away; (*avoir à supporter*) to let oneself in for sth; **se t. qn** (*sexuellement*) to lay sb; (*avoir à supporter*) to get lumbered with sb; **je me taperais bien une bière** I could murder a beer

(c) *Arg* (*s'en moquer*) **elle s'en tape** she doesn't give a monkey's (**de** about); **si tu savais comme je m'en tape!** I don't give a monkey's!

(d) *Arg* (*espérer*) **tu peux te t.!** you'll be lucky!, no way!, you can whistle for it!

taper² *vt* (*boucher*) (*trou etc*) to plug, to stop up

tapette [tapɛt] *nf* (a) (*petit marteau*) mallet (b) (*à tapis*) carpet beater; (*à mouches*) fly swatter (c) (*piège*) **t. (à souris)** mousetrap (d) *Arg* (*langue*) **quelle t.!** what a chatterer *or* chatterbox!; **il a une fière t.** can he talk! (e) (*petite tape*) (gentle) slap (f) *Vulg* (*homosexuel*) queer, *Br* poof(ter)

tapeur, -euse [tapœr, -øz] *n F* cadger

tapin [tapɛ̃] *nm Arg* **faire le t.** (*se prostituer*) to turn tricks, *surtout Br* to be on the game; **la police a ramassé toutes les filles qui faisaient le t. au quartier latin** the police arrested all the girls who were trying to pick up customers in the Latin Quarter

tapinois (en) [ɑ̃tapinwa] *adv* stealthily; **s'approcher en t.** to creep up

tapioca [tapjɔka] *nm* tapioca; (*soupe*) vegetable soup containing tapioca

tapir [tapir] *nm Zool* tapir

tapir (se) [sətapir] *vpr* to crouch; (*se cacher*) to cower, to hide; **maison tapie dans un bois** house nestling in a wood

tapis [tapi] *nm* (a) (*recouvrant un meuble*) cloth, cover; *Fig* **le t. brûle!** (*au jeu*) put down your stakes!; *Fig* **mettre qch sur le t.** to bring sth up for consideration *or* for discussion; *Fig* **ce genre de discussion revient toujours sur le t.** this sort of discussion is always coming up

(b) (*sur le sol, Fig de fleurs, neige*) carpet; (*petit*) rug; **t. de haute laine/de laine rase** long-pile/short-pile carpet; **marchand de t.** carpet dealer; **recouvrir le plancher d'un t.** to carpet the floor; **terrain recouvert d'un t. de gazon/de neige** ground carpeted with turf/snow

(c) *Boxe etc* canvas; **aller au t.** to go down, to be knocked down; *Fig* **entreprise française mise au t. par la concurrence** French company knocked for six *or* k.o.'d by the competition; **il est resté au t.** he stayed down, he didn't get up

▶ **tapis**: **t. de billard** billard cloth; **t. de gym** gym mat; **t. de livraison des bagages** baggage conveyor belt; **t. d'Orient** oriental carpet; **t. de prière** prayer mat; **t. rouge: dérouler le t. rouge pour qn** to roll out the red carpet for sb, to give sb the red carpet treatment; **t. roulant** *Ind etc* conveyor belt; (*pour piétons*) moving walkway, travelator; **t. de salle de bain** bathroom carpet; **t. de selle** saddlecloth; **t. de sol** (*sol de tente*) groundsheet; (*petit matelas*) sleeping mat (*underneath sleeping bag*); *Ordinat* **t. de souris** mouse mat *or* pad; **t. de table** table cover; **t. vert** gaming table; (*de conseil*) conference table

tapis-brosse, *pl* **tapis-brosses** *nm* doormat

tapisser [tapise] *vt* (a) (*de papier peint*) (*pièce, appartement etc*) to (wall)paper; **les murs sont tapissés de jaune** the walls are papered in yellow; **mur tapissé d'affiches** wall covered *or* plastered with posters **(b)** (*de tentures ou tapisseries*) (*pièce etc*) to cover with hangings *or* tapestries **(c)** (*l'intérieur d'une armoire*) to line, to cover (**de** with); **une membrane tapisse l'estomac** the stomach is lined with a membrane; **mur tapissé de lierre** wall covered with ivy, ivy-clad wall

tapisserie [tapisri] *nf* **(a)** (*papier peint*) wallpaper; **refaire toutes les tapisseries d'un appartement** to repaper a flat **(b)** (*tissage*) tapestry making *or* weaving; **faire de la t.** to make tapestry **(c)** (*tenture*) tapestry; **chaise en t.** chair upholstered with tapestry, tapestry chair; *Fig* **faire t.** (*dans une soirée dansante etc*) to be a wallflower **(d)** (*broderie*) **t. (au** *ou* **sur canevas)** tapestry *or* crewel work

tapissier, -ière [tapisje, -jɛr] *n* **(a)** (*décorateur*) (interior) decorator **(b)** (*tisseur*) tapestry maker **(c)** (*de meubles*) upholsterer

tapon [tapɔ̃] *nm Vieilli* (*de tissu, de papier etc*) ball; **en t.** (*vêtements etc*) in a ball, bundled up; (*cheveux*) screwed up into a bun

tapotement [tapɔtmɑ̃] *nm* tapping; (*de piano*) plonking

tapoter [tapɔte] **1** *vt* to tap; (*joue d'un enfant etc*) to pat; **t. un air (au piano)** to thump out a tune (on the piano) **2** *vi* **t. sur** (*porte, fenêtre*) to tap on; (*en signe d'énervement*) to drum on

tapuscrit [tapyskri] *nm* typescript

taquet [takɛ] *nm* **(a)** *Menuis etc* (*support*) angle block; (*cale*) wedge **(b)** (*butée*) stop; **t. de sûreté** safety stop **(c)** (*de machine à écrire*) stop; *Ordinat* **t. de tabulation** tab stop; **poser un t. (de tabulateur)** to set a tab(ulator stop) **(d)** (*d'arpenteur*), *Agr* (small) picket, peg **(e)** *Naut* **t. (de tournage)** (belaying) cleat

taquin, -ine [takɛ̃, -in] **1** *adj* (*personne, tempérament*) (given to) teasing; (*sourire*) teasing; **elle est un peu taquine** she's a bit of a tease; **elle est très taquine** she's a great one for teasing **2** *n* (*personne*) tease(r)

taquiner [takine] *vt* **(a)** (*d'une personne*) to tease; *F* **t. le goujon** to do a bit of fishing; *F* **t. la muse** to write the odd bit of verse **(b)** (*de quelque chose*) to bother, to worry; **une pensée qui revient me t. parfois** a thought that still haunts me sometimes; **j'ai une dent qui me taquine** I've got bother with one of my teeth, one of my teeth is bothering me

taquinerie [takinri] *nf* teasing; **j'en ai assez de tes taquineries** I've had enough of your teasing

tarabiscoté [tarabiskɔte] *adj* (*meuble, décor, maison, dessin*) over-elaborate, fussy; (*style*) over-elaborate, convoluted

tarabuster [tarabyste] *vt* **(a)** (*d'une personne*) to pester **(b)** (*de quelque chose*) to bother, to worry

tarage [taraʒ] *nm Com* allowance for tare

tarama [tarama] *nm Culin* taramasalata

taratata [taratata] *int* rubbish!

taraud [taro] *nm* (screw) tap

taraudage [tarodaʒ] *nm* screw cutting, tapping

tarauder [tarode] *vt* **(a)** *Tech* (*tige, écrou etc*) to tap, to cut, to screw, to thread **(b)** (*d'un insecte*) (*bois*) to bore into **(c)** *Litt Fig* (*des remords, des scrupules etc*) (*qn*) to gnaw at

taraudeuse [tarodøz] *nf* (*machine*) tapper, thread cutter

tarbouch(e) [tarbuʃ] *nm* tarboosh

tard [tar] **1** *adv* late; **plus t.** later, later on; **au plus t.** at the latest; **tôt ou t.** sooner or later; **il est t.** it's late; **il se fait t.** it's getting late; **je ne pensais pas qu'il fût si t.** I didn't think it was so late; **je me suis couché t.** I went to bed late, I was late (in) going to bed; **trop t., il fallait te décider plus vite** (it's) too late, you should have decided sooner; **il se maria t.** he married late (in life); **deux minutes plus t. et je manquais le bateau** another two minutes and I would have missed the boat; *Prov* **mieux vaut t. que jamais** better late than never; **t. dans la nuit** late at night; **remettre qch à plus t.** to put sth off until later; **je le ferai et pas plus t. que ce soir** I'll do it this very evening; **pas plus t. qu'hier** as recently as yesterday, only yesterday

2 *nm* **sur le t.** (*dans la vie*) late in life

tarder [tarde] **1** *vi* to delay; **pourquoi tarde-t-il?** why is he (taking) so long?; **il ne tardera pas maintenant** he won't be long now; **cela n'a pas tardé** it wasn't long coming; **et cela n'a pas tardé, il s'est cassé le pied** and he broke his ankle before long; **tu vas recevoir une gifle, cela ne va pas t.** you're going to get smacked before long *or* in a minute or two, you've got a smack coming to you; **t. en chemin** to loiter on the way; **t. à faire qch** to take a long time doing sth; **excusez-moi si j'ai tardé à vous répondre** I apologize for not answering sooner; **nous ne tarderons pas à le voir venir** it won't be long before he appears, he'll appear before too long; **nous ne tardâmes pas à avoir de ses nouvelles** it wasn't long before we heard from him, we didn't have to wait too long for news of him; **ça tarde à commencer/venir** it's a long time starting/coming; **sans t.** without delay

2 *v impers* **il lui tarde de partir/qu'elle revienne** he is longing to get away/for her to return

tardif, -ive [tardif, -iv] *adj* (*regrets, excuse etc*) belated; (*heure, fruit etc*) late; **c'était un peu t., comme réponse/excuse** the answer/apology was a bit slow in coming

tardivement [tardivmɑ̃] *adv* (*prendre des mesures, s'excuser*) belatedly; (*rentrer, arriver etc*) late; (*se marier, s'établir*) late in life

tare [tar] *nf* **(a)** (*défaut*) defect, flaw; *Méd, Vét* defect; *Hum* **ça n'est pas une t.!** it's not a crime! **(b)** *Com* (*pour calculer le poids net*) tare; **faire la t.** to allow for the tare

taré [tare] *adj* **(a)** *Com* (*fruit etc*) spoilt; (*biens*) damaged **(b)** (*corrumpu*) (*régime etc*) depraved, corrupt **(c)** (*dégénéré*) degenerate **(d)** *F* (*idiot*) crazy; **il faut être t. pour faire cela!** you have to be crazy *or* to have a screw loose to do that!

tarentelle [tarɑ̃tɛl] *nf* (*danse, musique*) tarantella

tarentule [tarɑ̃tyl] *nf* (*araignée*) tarantula

tarer [tare] *vt Com* (*emballage etc*) to tare

targette [tarʒɛt] *nf* bolt

targuer (se) [sətarge] *vpr* **se t. de qch/de faire qch** to pride oneself on sth/on doing sth; **se t. de ce que …** to pride oneself on the fact that …

targui, -ie [targi], *pl* **touareg** [twarɛg] **1** *adj* Tuareg **2** *n* **T.** Tuareg

tarière [tarjɛr] *nf* **(a)** (*pour le bois*) auger **(b)** (*de forage*) drill; *Min* borer **(c)** *Ent* ovipositor

tarif [tarif] *nm* (*tableau des prix*) tariff, price list; (*prix*) rate; *F* **trois mois de prison, c'est le t.** three months' prison is what it'll cost you; **tarifs aériens/ferroviaires** air/rail fares; **t. adulte** adult fare; **t. affaires** business rate; (*transport*) business fare; **t. aller simple** single *or Am* one-way fare; **t. APEX** APEX fare; **t. de base** basic rate; **t. des chambres** room rate; **t. en chambre double** (*dans un hôtel*) double occupancy rate; *Av* **t. commun** common rated fare, joint fare; **t. couplage** (*en publicité*) combination rate; **t. dégressif** tapering *or* declining rate; **t. différentiel** differential rate; **t. du distributeur** dealer list price; **t. douanier** customs tariff; **t. économique** economy rate; (*d'un voyage*) economy *or* budget fare; **t. étudiant** student rate; (*d'un voyage*) student fare; **t. excursion** excursion fare *or* APEX fare; **t. export** export tariff; **t. famille** family rate; (*d'un voyage*) family fare; **t. de faveur** preferential rate; **t. à forfait** all-in price; **t. forfaitaire** flat rate; *Av* **t. hebdomadaire** weekly rate; **t. horaire** hourly rate; **t. intérieur** inland rate; **t. jeune** youth fare; **t. journalier** daily *or* day rate; **t. lettres** letter rate; **plein t.** (*pour passagers*) full fare; (*pour marchandises etc*) full tariff; *F* (*pour un crime etc*) maximum (penalty); **voyager à plein t./à t. réduit** to travel at full/reduced rate *or* fare; **billet (à) plein t.** full-fare ticket; **tarifs postaux** postal *or* postage rates; **t. préférentiel** special *or* preferential rate; **t. progressif** increasing rate; **t. promotionnel** promotional rate; (*d'un voyage*) promotional fare; **t. réduit** *Cin* concession; (*d'un voyage*) concession fare; **t. de référence** basing fare; **t. social** reduced train fare for the general public; **t. société** commercial *or* corporate rate; **t. standby** standby fare; **t. d'urgence** = first-class rate

tarifaire [tarifɛr] *adj* (*lois etc*) tariff; *Com* **politique t.** pricing policy

tarifer [tarife] *vt* (*impôts, prix etc*) to fix the rate for, to set the rate of

tarification [tarifikasjɔ̃] *nf* fixing *or* setting of rates (**de** for), pricing; **t. au coût-plus-marge** mark-up pricing; **t. différentielle** differential pricing; **t. discriminatoire** discriminatory pricing; **t. en fonction de la valeur perçue** perceived value pricing; **t. géographique** geographical pricing

tarin [tarɛ̃] *nm* **(a)** (*oiseau*) siskin **(b)** *Arg* (*nez*) beak, *Br* conk

tarir [tarir] **1** *vt* (*source, rivière*) to dry up; (*larmes*) to dry; **la source est tarie** the spring is dry; *Fig* **cela a tari sa créativité** it caused his creativity to dry up

2 se tarir *vpr* (*d'une rivière, du lait, de l'inspiration etc*) to dry up

3 *vi* **(a)** (*de l'eau*) to dry up, to run dry; **la source a tari** the spring has dried up

(b) *Fig* (*d'une conversation, de l'inspiration etc*) to dry up; (*de larmes*) to dry; **la discussion n'a pas tari pendant deux heures** the discussion has been flowing freely for two hours; **une fois lancé sur ce sujet, il ne tarit pas** once he's started on the subject he never shuts up *or* stops; **il ne tarit pas sur le sujet** he never stops talking *or* shuts up about the subject; **ne pas t. d'éloges sur qch** to be full of praise for *or* be forever praising sth

tarissement [tarismɑ̃] *nm* drying up

tarlatane [tarlatan] *nf Tex* tarlatan

tarmacadam [tarmakadam] *nm Constr* tarmacadam
tarot [taro] *nm Cartes* **(jeu de) tarot(s)** tarot (pack); **faire un t.** *ou* **une partie de t.** to have a game of tarot
Tarse [tars] *n* Tarsus
tarse [tars] *nm Anat, Zool* tarsus
tarsien, -ienne [tarsjɛ̃, -jɛn] *adj Anat (os)* tarsal
tartan [tartɑ̃] *nm (tissu)* tartan
tartane [tartan] *nf (bateau)* = single masted vessel used in the Mediterranean, tartan
tartare [tartar] **1** *adj* **(a)** *Hist* Tartar **(b)** *Culin* **sauce t.** tartar(e) sauce; **steak t.** steak tartare **2** *n Hist* **T.** Tartar **3** *nm Culin* steak tartare
tarte [tart] **1** *nf* **(a)** *Culin* tart, *Am* (open) pie; **t. aux pommes** apple tart *or Am* pie; *Fig F* **ce n'est pas de la t.** it's no picnic **(b)** *Arg (gifle)* slap **2** *adj F* **(a)** *(ridicule)* ridiculous **(b)** *(laid)* ugly
▶ **tarte**: **t. à la crème** custard tart; *Cin F (envoyée sur qn)* custard pie; *F* **c'est la t. à la crème des économistes libéraux** it's a liberal economist's cliché
tartelette [tartəlɛt] *nf Culin* tartlet
tartempion [tartɑ̃pjɔ̃] *nm F* **entreprise T.** Company So-and-so; **un quelconque t.** some guy or other; **n'importe quel t.** any Tom, Dick or Harry
tartignole [tartiɲɔl] *adj F* ridiculous
tartine [tartin] *nf* **(a)** *(beurrée)* slice of bread and butter; *(pas encore beurrée)* slice of bread; **t. de confiture/de miel** slice of bread and jam/honey; **t. grillée** slice *or* piece of toast; **faire des tartines** to butter (some) bread **(b)** *F (tirade)* long-winded speech; *(article de journal, lettre etc)* screed; **pourquoi en mettre toute une t.?** why go on *or* bang on about it?
tartiner [tartine] *vt (beurre, pain)* to spread; **t. du pain (de beurre)** to butter bread, to spread bread with butter; **fromage à t.** cheese spread; **pâte à t. au chocolat** chocolate spread
tartre [tartr] *nm (sur les dents, dans les bouteilles etc)* tartar; *(dans une chaudière, une bouilloire)* fur, scale
tartrique [tartrik] *adj Ch (acide)* tartaric
tartuf(f)e [tartyf] **1** *nm* (sanctimonious) hypocrite **2** *adj* hypocritical
tartuf(f)erie [tartyfri] *nf* hypocrisy
tas [ta] *nm* **(a)** *(amas) (de pierres, de feuilles, de bois, de boue etc)* pile, heap; **mettre en t.** to pile up, to heap up
(b) *(grand nombre, grande quantité)* mass, heap, pile **(de** of); **tout un t. de vieilleries** masses *or* heaps *or* a whole pile of old things; **un t. de mensonges** a pack of lies; *F* **il y en a des t. (et des t.)** there are heaps *or* masses of them; **des gens sympas, il n'y en a pas des t. par ici** nice people are pretty thin on the ground around here; **elle a fait un t. de choses dans sa vie** she has done masses of things *or* lots (of things) in her life; **des t. de fois** heaps *or* lots of times; *F* **tout un t. de gens** a whole gang (of people), a whole load of people; **t. d'imbéciles!** bunch of idiots!
(c) dans le t.: tirer dans le t. to fire into the crowd; **sers-toi dans le t.** take what you like from that lot; *F* **dans le t., il doit y en avoir un ou deux que tu connais** there must be one or two out of that lot that you know
(d) *(construction)* building under construction; *(chantier)* building site; **être sur le t.** to be at work *or* on the job; *Ind etc* **formation sur le t.** on-the-job training; **apprendre sur le t.** to learn on the job; **grève sur le t.** sit-down strike
▶ **tas**: *Min* **t. de déblais** dump; **t. de fumier** manure heap
Tasmanie [tasmani] *nf* Tasmania
tasmanien, -ienne [tasmanjɛ̃, -jɛn] **1** *adj* Tasmanian **2** *n* **T.** Tasmanian
tassage [tasaʒ] *nm Sp (d'un adversaire)* crowding
tasse [tas] *nf* **(a)** cup; **je te ressers une t.?** would you like another cup?, shall I fill you up again?; **t. à café/thé** coffee/tea cup; **t. de café/thé** cup of coffee/tea; **t. en métal** tin mug **(b) boire une** *ou* **la t.** *(en nageant)* to get a mouthful (of water)
tassé [tase] *adj* **(a)** *(serré) (prisonniers, passagers etc)* crammed, packed, squeezed; **t. par l'âge** shrunk with age **(b)** *F* **bien t.** *(boisson alcoolique) (avec peu d'eau)* stiff; *(dans un verre bien plein)* large; *(café)* strong; **il a 50 ans bien tassés** he's 50 at least, he's 50 if he's a day
tasseau, -eaux [taso] *nm (pour soutenir une étagère etc)* batten
tassement [tasmɑ̃] *nm* **(a)** *(de terre, de neige etc)* packing (down) **(b)** *Constr (de fondations etc)* settling, sinking, subsidence **(c)** *Écon* slowdown **(de** in)
▶ **tassement**: *Méd* **t. de vertèbres** spinal compression
tasser [tase] **1** *vt* **(a)** *(objets)* to cram, to squeeze **(dans** into); *(personnes)* to cram, to squeeze, to pack **(dans** into); *(terre, neige etc)* to pack (down), to tamp (down) **(b)** *Sp (adversaire)* to crowd **2** *vi (des plantes)* to grow thick(ly) **3 se tasser** *vpr* **(a)** *(des fondations etc)* to settle, to sink, to subside; *Fig F* **ça se tassera** things will quieten down *or* settle down; **il commence à se t.** *(se voûter)* he is beginning to shrink (with age) **(b)** *(se serrer)* to squeeze up
taste-vin [tastəvɛ̃] *nm inv (tasse)* wine taster
tata [tata] *nf* **(a)** *Enf* auntie, aunty **(b)** *Arg (homosexuel)* queer, *Br* poof(ter)
tatami [tatami] *nm* tatami (mat)
tatane [tatan] *nf F* shoe
tatar, -are [tatar] **1** *adj Hist* Tartar **2** *nm Ling* Tartar **3** *n Hist* **T.** Tartar
tâter [tɑte] **1** *vt* **(a)** *(toucher)* to feel; *(fruit)* to feel, to squeeze; **t. le pouls à qn** to feel sb's pulse; **avancer en tâtant** to grope one's way forward; **t. la porte pour trouver la poignée** to feel for the door handle **(b)** *Fig (sonder)* **t. qn** to sound sb out; **t. l'opinion** to sound out opinion; **t. le terrain** to see how the land lies **2** *vi* **(a)** *Litt* **t. d'un mets** to taste a dish **(b) t. d'un métier** to try one's hand at a trade; *F* **il a tâté de la prison** he's done time; *Litt* **t. du chagrin/dégoût** to experience sorrow/disgust **3 se tâter** *vpr* **(a)** *(après un choc)* to feel oneself **(b)** *(hésiter)* to hesitate
tâte-vin [tɑtvɛ̃] *nm inv (tasse)* wine taster
tatillon, -onne [tatijɔ̃, -ɔn] **1** *adj* finicky, fussy **2** *n* finicky *or* fussy person, *F* fusspot
tâtonnant [tɑtɔnɑ̃] *adj (efforts, geste etc)* tentative, hesitant; *(progrès)* tentative
tâtonnement [tɑtɔnmɑ̃] *nm* **(a)** *(d'aveugle etc)* groping **(b)** *(essai)* trial and error; **les tâtonnements de la science/recherche** the tentative progress of science/research; **procéder par tâtonnements** to proceed by trial and error
tâtonner [tɑtɔne] *vi* **(a)** to grope about; **t. pour retrouver la porte** to grope about for the door; **se diriger en tâtonnant vers qch** to grope *or* feel one's way towards sth **(b)** *Fig* to proceed by trial and error; *(involontairement)* to grope about, to feel one's way
tâtons (à) [atɑtɔ̃] *adv* **avancer/entrer/sortir à t.** to grope *or* feel one's way along/in/out; **chercher qch à t.** to grope *or* feel for sth; *Fig* **les chercheurs avancent à t.** the researchers are progressing by trial and error; *(sans la moindre idée)* the researchers are groping their way forward
tatou [tatu] *nm Zool* armadillo
tatouage [tatwaʒ] *nm (action)* tattooing; *(motif)* tattoo
tatouer [tatwe] *vt (motif)* to tattoo; **se faire t. le bras** to have one's arm tattooed
tatoueur [tatwœr] *nm* tattooist, tattoo artist
tau [to] *nm inv (lettre grecque)* tau
taud [to] *nm Naut* rain awning, boat cover
taudis [todi] *nm* slum; **leur maison est un vrai t.** their house is a real dump
taulard, -arde [tolar, -ard] *n Arg* convict; **vieux t.** old lag
taule [tol] *nf Arg* **(a)** *(prison)* clink, *Br* nick; *Mil F* glasshouse; **faire de la t.** to do time *or* a stretch; **sortir de t.** to come out of the clink *or Br* the nick; **faire dix ans de t.** to do a ten-year stretch; **après dix ans de t.** after ten years inside **(b)** *(chambre)* room
taulier, -ière [tolje, -jɛr] *n Arg (propriétaire)* (hotel) owner; *(gérant)* (hotel) manager
taupe [top] *nf* **(a)** *Zool* mole; **myope comme une t.** blind as a bat **(b)** *(fourrure)* moleskin **(c)** *Scol F* = high level maths class for exceptionally gifted students going on to one of the grandes écoles **(d)** *Arg Péj* **vieille t.** *(femme)* old crone *or* hag **(e)** *(espion)* mole
taupier [topje] *nm* mole catcher
taupin [topɛ̃] *nm* **(a)** *Scol F* = student doing high level maths class in preparation for one of the grandes écoles **(b)** *Mil Arch* sapper
taupinière [topinjɛr] *nf* molehill; *(galeries)* mole tunnels
taureau, -eaux [tɔro] *nm* **(a)** bull; **avoir un cou de t.** to have a thick neck; **course** *ou* **combat de taureaux** bullfight; *F* **prendre le t. par les cornes** to take the bull by the horns; **fort comme un t.** as strong as an ox **(b)** *Astron, Astrol* **le T.** Taurus, the Bull; **être (du signe du) T.** to be (a) Taurus
taurillon [tɔrijɔ̃] *nm* bull calf
taurin [tɔrɛ̃] *adj* **jeux taurins** bullfights
tauromachie [tɔrɔmaʃi] *nf* bullfighting, *Spéc* tauromachy
tauromachique [tɔrɔmaʃik] *adj (art, règles etc)* of bullfighting
tautologie [totɔlɔʒi] *nf* tautology; **raisonner par t.** to argue tautologically
tautologique [totɔlɔʒik] *adj* tautological
taux [to] *nm* **(a)** *(montant) (des salaires, d'impôts etc)* rate **(b)** *(proportion)* proportion, ratio **(c)** *(pourcentage)* rate; **t. d'un prêt** interest rate on a loan; **à t. fixe** fixed-rate; **t. de huit pour cent** rate of eight per cent; **emprunter à un t. de 7**

pour cent to borrow at 7 per cent (interest) **(d)** *Ordinat* ratio, rate

▶ **taux**: **t. d'accroissement** rate of increase *or* of growth; *Écon* **t. d'activité** participation rate; *Compta* **t. d'actualisation** net present value rate, NPV rate; *Compta* **t. d'amortissement** rate of depreciation, depreciation rate; *Fin* **t. de l'argent au jour le jour** overnight rate; **t. d'assurance** insurance rate; **t. d'audience** *Rad* ratings; *TV* ratings, viewing figures; **t. bancaire** bank rate; **t. de base bancaire** bank base rate; *Compta* **t. de capitalisation** price/earnings ratio, p/e ratio; **t. de change** exchange rate, rate of exchange; **t. de change à l'achat** bank buying rate; **t. de change à la vente** bank selling rate; **t. de change flottant** floating exchange rate; **t. de compression** (*de moteur*) compression ratio; *Ordinat* compression rate; **t. de conversion** conversion rate; **t. de croissance** growth rate, rate of growth; **t. d'échange** rate of exchange, exchange rate; **t. d'écoute** *Rad* ratings; *TV* ratings, viewing figures; **t. effectif global** annual percentage rate, APR; *Banque* **t. d'emprunt** borrowing rate; **t. d'épargne** savings rate; **t. d'escompte** discount rate; **t. de fréquentation** (*des chambres d'hôtel*) sleeper occupancy; **t. d'inflation** rate of inflation, inflation rate; **t. interbancaire offert à Paris** Paris Inter-Bank Offer Rate; **t. d'intérêt** interest rate, rate of interest; *Méd* **t. d'invalidité** degree of disability; *Fin* **t. linéaire** straight-line rate; *Banque* **t. Lombard** Lombard rate; *Bourse* **t. long obligataire** long-term bond rate; **t. de marge** *ou* **de marque** mark-up ratio; **t. minima** minimum rates; **t. de mortalité** death rate; **t. de natalité** birth rate; **t. normal** standard rate; *Mktg* **t. de notoriété** (*d'un produit*) rate of awareness; **t. d'occupation** (*des chambres d'hôtel*) room occupancy, occupancy rate; **t. officiel** official rate; **t. de panne** failure rate; *Rail etc* **t. de pente** rate of grade *or* gradient; *Mil* **t. de pertes** casualty rate; *Can Banque* **t. préférentiel** prime rate; **t. privé** market rate; **t. proportionnel** (*d'un crédit*) proportional interest rate, APR; *Ordinat* **t. de rafraîchissement** refresh rate; *Mktg* **t. de réachat** re-buy *or* repurchase rate; *Fin* **t. réduit** reduced rate; *Banque* **t. de référence** reference rate; *Tech, Ind* **t. de rendement** coefficient of efficiency, utilization factor; *Fin* **t. des repos** repo rate; **t. de scolarisation** = percentage of children attending school; **t. de succès** success rate; *Ordinat* **t. de transfert** transfer rate; **t. de TVA** VAT rate, rate of VAT; **t. uniforme** uniform *or* flat rate; *Fin* **t. d'usure** penal rate

tavelé [tavle] *adj* (*visage etc*) spotted, speckled (**de** with); (*fruit*) marked

taveler [tavle] (**il tavelle**; **il tavellera**) **1** *vt* (*visage etc*) to spot, to speckle; (*fruit*) to mark **2 se taveler** *vpr* (*d'un fruit*) to become marked

tavelure [tavlyr] *nf* **(a)** spot, speckle; (*de fruit*) mark **(b)** *Agr* (*maladie*) scab

taverne [tavɛrn] *nf* **(a)** (*restaurant*) restaurant **(b)** *Can* beer parlour, tavern **(c)** *Hist* (*auberge*) tavern

tavernier, -ière [tavɛrnje, -jɛr] *n Hist* innkeeper

taxable [taksabl] *adj* taxable

taxateur [taksatœr] **1** *nm* taxer, assessor **2** *adj* (*fonctionnaire etc*) taxing

taxation [taksasjɔ̃] *nf* **(a)** (*par l'impôt*) taxation; (*contrôle*) assessment; **t. d'office** special rate of taxation; *Com* **t. au poids** tax on weight; **t. différentielle** differential taxation; **t. à la valeur** tax on value **(b)** *Tél* **zone de t.** charging area; *Ordinat* **période de t.** charging period **(c)** *Jur* (*des dépens*) assessment, calculation

taxe [taks] *nf* **(a)** (*impôt*) tax, duty; **toutes taxes comprises** inclusive of tax; **t. sur les chiens** dog tax; **t. locale** local tax; *Th etc* **t. sur les spectacles** entertainment tax **(b)** (*redevance*) (*pour un service*) charge; **t. postale** *ou* **des lettres** postage **(c)** *Jur* (*des dépens*) calculation, assessment **(d)** (*prix fixé*) fixed price, official price

▶ **taxe**: **t. à l'achat** purchase tax; **t. d'aéroport** airport tax; **t. d'apprentissage** = tax paid by businesses to fund training programmes; **t. d'atterrissage** airport landing tax; **t. sur le chiffre d'affaires** sales tax; **t. de départ** (*à l'aéroport*) departure tax; **t. d'entrée** (*à l'aéroport*) entry tax; **t. à l'exportation** export tax; **t. foncière** land *or* property tax; **t. d'habitation** council *or US* local tax; **t. sur l'hôtellerie** hotel tax; **t. de luxe** luxury tax; **t. officielle** assessment; **t. parafiscale** indirect *or* excise tax; **t. de port** harbour *or US* harbor dues; **t. professionnelle** = tax paid by professional people; **t. régionale** local tax; **t. sur le revenu** income tax; **t. routière** road tax; **t. sur les salaires** employment tax; **t. de séjour** tourist *or* visitor tax; **t. supplémentaire** surcharge; **t. touristique** tourist tax; **t. à** *ou* **sur la valeur ajoutée** value added tax

taxer [takse] *vt* **(a)** (*soumettre à l'impôt*) (*personne, alcool, cigarettes etc*) to tax **(b)** *Tél* (*appel*) to charge for **(c)** *Jur* (*dépens*) to tax **(d)** (*accuser*) to tax (**de** with), to accuse (**de** of); **la décision du gouvernement a été taxée d'inconscience** the government's decision was described as thoughtless; **se faire t. d'égoïste** to be accused of selfishness *or* being selfish, to be called selfish **(e)** *F* (*quémander*) **il m'a taxé une cigarette** he cadged a cigarette off me; **t. les autres** to cadge off people

taxi [taksi] *nm* **(a)** (*voiture*) taxi (cab), cab; **elle prend souvent le t.** she often takes taxis *or* a taxi; **chauffeur de t.** taxi *or* cab driver; **t. aérien** air taxi, taxiplane; **station de taxis** taxi rank *or Am* stand; **t. en maraude** cruising taxi **(b)** *F* (*chauffeur*) cabby, taxi *or* cab driver

taxidermie [taksidɛrmi] *nf* taxidermy

taxidermiste [taksidɛrmist] *n* taxidermist

taxi-girl, *pl* **taxi-girls** *nf* (*danseuse*) taxi dancer

taximètre [taksimɛtr] *nm* meter

taxinomie [taksinɔmi] *nf Biol* taxonomy

taxinomique [taksinɔmik] *adj* taxonomic(al)

taxiphone [taksifɔn] *nm* pay phone

taxiway [taksiwɛ] *nm Av* taxiway

taxonomie [taksɔnɔmi] *nf Biol* taxonomy

taylorisation [tɛlɔrizasjɔ̃] *nf Ind* application of time and motion studies

tayloriser [tɛlɔrize] *vt Ind* to apply time and motion studies to

taylorisme [tɛlɔrism] *nm Écon* time and motion studies

TBF [tebeɛf] *nm* (*abrév* **transferts banque de France**) = French automated clearing system

TCA [tesea] *nf* (*abrév* **taxe sur le chiffre d'affaires**) sales tax

Tchad [tʃad] *nm* Chad; **le lac T.** Lake Chad

tchadien, -ienne [tʃadjɛ̃, -jɛn] **1** *adj* Chadian **2** *n* **T.** Chadian

tchador [tʃadɔr] *nm* (*voile*) chador, chuddar

tchécoslovaque [tʃekɔslɔvak] *Hist* **1** *adj* Czechoslovak, Czechoslovakian **2** *n* **T.** Czechoslovak, Czechoslovakian

Tchécoslovaquie [tʃekɔslɔvaki] *nf Hist* Czechoslovakia

tchèque [tʃɛk] **1** *adj Hist* Czech **2** *nm Ling* Czech **3** *n Hist* **T.** Czech

tchin-tchin [tʃintʃin] *int F* cheers!, *Br* chin-chin!

TCI [tesei] *nmpl* (*abrév* **termes commerciaux internationaux**) incoterms

te, *before a vowel sound or mute h* **t'** [t(ə)] *pron pers* [①**A26**,a-b; **B17-18**,2] **(a)** (*objet direct*) you; **il t'adore** he adores you; **te voilà** there you are

(b) (*objet indirect*) (to) you; **il t'a écrit** he wrote to you; **il te l'a dit** he told you so; **ça te servira** it will be of use to you; **je te l'ai donné** I gave you it, I gave it to you; **elle te court après** she's running after you; **si cela te vient à l'esprit** if you should think of it, if it occurs to you; **je vais te le mater, celui-là!** I'll sort him out; **et je te range, et je te fais la cuisine** and I tidy up and I do the cooking

(c) [①**A29**,d; **B26**,D] (*reflexive*) **tu te fatigues** you are tiring yourself; **tu vas te faire mal** you will hurt yourself; **à quelle heure t'es-tu levé(e)?** what time did you get up (at)?; **va-t'en** go away; **tu te donnes beaucoup de mal** you're going to a lot of trouble; **arrête de te ronger les ongles** stop biting your nails

(d) (*en s'adressant à Dieu*) You, Thee

té [te] *nm* **(a) en té** T-shaped; **règle en té** T-rule **(b)** (**équerre en) té** T-square

teaser [tizœr] *nm* (*aguiche*) teaser

tec [tɛk] *nm inv abrév* **tonne-équivalent-charbon**

technicien, -ienne [tɛknisjɛ̃, -jɛn] *n* technician; **t. du froid** refrigeration engineer; **t. de laboratoire** laboratory technician; **t. de maintenance** maintenance *or* service engineer; *TV etc* **t. du son** sound engineer *or* technician, audio control engineer

technicité [tɛknisite] *nf* technical nature; **d'une haute t.** highly technical

technico-commercial, -ale, -aux, -ales [tɛknikokɔmɛrsjal, -jo] **1** *adj* **agent t.** sales engineer; **service t.** technical sales department **2** *n* sales engineer

technicolor® [tɛknikɔlɔr] *nm Cin* Technicolor® *Fig* **souvenirs en t.** vivid memories

technique [tɛknik] **1** *adj* (*problème, perfection, difficulté, collège etc*) technical; **agent t.** technician; *Av, Naut* **escale t.** stopover for technical reasons

2 *nf* **(a)** (*science*) technology; **t. de l'ingénieur** engineering; **t. électrique** electrical engineering

(b) (*méthode*) (*d'un artiste, d'un spécialiste etc*) technique; **ce pianiste a une bonne t./manque de t.** this pianist has good technique/lacks technique; **t. de vente** sales technique; *F* **tu n'a pas la t.!** you haven't got the knack!; **ce n'est pas la bonne/la seule t.** that's not the right/the only way to go about it; **c'est tout une t.** there's a knack to it; **je crois que je vais devoir changer de t.** I think I'm going to have to change my methods *or* the way I go about things; **c'est sa t.** that's his/her way

3 *nm* (*enseignement*) technical *or* vocational training; **élèves du t.** pupils taking technical subjects; **professeurs du t.** teachers of technical subjects

techniquement [tɛknikmɑ̃] *adv* technically

technocrate [tɛknɔkrat] *n* technocrat

technocratie [tɛknɔkrasi] *nf* technocracy

technocratique [tɛknɔkratik] *adj* technocratic

technologie [tɛknɔlɔʒi] *nf* technology; **haute t.** high tech(nology); **appareil de haute t.** high-tech apparatus; **t. de pointe** state-of-the-art technology

technologique [tɛknɔlɔʒik] *adj* technological

technologiste [tɛknɔlɔʒist], **technologue** [tɛknɔlɔg] *n* technologist

teck [tɛk] *nm* (*bois*) teak; **bateau en t.** teak boat

teckel [tekɛl] *nm* dachshund; **t. à poil ras** short-haired dachshund

tectonique [tɛktɔnik] **1** *adj* tectonic **2** *nf* tectonics; **t. des plaques** plate tectonics

teddy-bear, *pl* **teddy-bears** [tedibɛr] *nm* teddy bear

Te Deum [tedeɔm] *nm inv Mus, Rel* Te Deum

tee [ti] *nm Golf* tee

teenager [tinɛdʒœr] *n* teenager; **films/vêtements pour teenagers** teenage films/clothes

tee(-)shirt [tiʃœrt], *pl* **tee(-)shirts** *nm* teeshirt

téflon® [teflɔ̃] *nm* Teflon; **poêle en t.** Teflon frying pan

téflonisé® [teflɔnize] *adj* (*poêle à frire etc*) Teflon®

TEG [teəʒe] *nm Fin* (*abrév* **taux effectif global**) APR

tégument [tegymɑ̃] *nm Biol* (in)tegument

Téhéran [teerɑ̃] *n* Teh(e)ran

teigne [tɛɲ] *nf* **(a)** (*papillon*) moth; **t. des draps** (clothes) moth **(b)** (*personne méchante*) rat, *Br* nasty piece of work; **méchant** *ou* **mauvais comme la t.** as nasty as they come **(c)** *Méd* ringworm, *Spéc* tinea

teigneux, -euse [tɛɲø, -øz] **1** *adj* **(a)** nasty **(b)** *Méd* suffering from ringworm **2** *n* **(a)** *Méd* ringworm sufferer **(b)** (*personne méchante*) rat, *Br* nasty piece of work

teindre [tɛ̃dr] (*prp* **teignant**; *pp* **teint**; *pr ind* **je teins, il teint, n. teignons**; *pr sub* **je teigne**; *impf* **je teignais**; *p hist* **je teignis**; *fu* **je teindrai**) **1** *vt* **(a)** (*vêtement, cheveux etc*) to dye; **t. qch en rouge** to dye sth red; **faire t. une robe** to have a dress dyed **(b)** (*mains etc*) to stain **2 se teindre** *vpr* **(a) se t. (les cheveux)** to dye one's hair **(b)** *Litt* (*se colorer*) to be tinged (**de** with)

teint [tɛ̃] *nm* **(a)** *Tex* (*couleur*) colour, *US* color; **bon t., grand t.** fast colour; **tissu bon** *ou* **grand t.** colourfast material; *Fig* **bon t.** (*catholique, communiste etc*) staunch, *Péj* dyed-in-the-wool **(b)** (*du visage*) complexion; **t. frais/olivâtre/clair** fresh/olive/clear complexion; **je n'ai pas le t. frais ce matin** my skin looks a bit muddy this morning; **au t. jaune** sallow

teinte [tɛ̃t] *nf* **(a)** (*couleur nuancée*) shade, tint, tone; **plusieures teintes de bleu** several shades of blue; **teintes chaudes/froides** warm/cold tints **(b)** *Fig* (*d'ironie, de mélancolie etc*) touch, tinge, hint

teinter [tɛ̃te] **1** *vt* **(a)** to tint; **(lunettes à) verres teintés** tinted glasses **(b)** *Fig* **t. (légèrement)** to tinge (**de** with); **des paroles teintées d'un accent rimbaldien** words reminiscent of Rimbaud **2 se teinter** *vpr* (*se colorer*), *Fig* to be tinged (**de** with)

teinture [tɛ̃tyr] *nf* **(a)** (*action*) (*de tissu, des cheveux etc*) dyeing; (*d'un dessin etc*) tinting **(b)** (*produit*) dye; **tissu qui prend bien la t.** material that dyes well **(c)** *Fig Litt* (*connaissance superficielle*) (*d'anglais etc*) smattering; **elle a quelque vague t. de mathématiques** she has a rudimentary knowledge of maths **(d)** *Pharm* tincture

▶ **teinture**: **t. d'iode** tincture of iodine

teinturerie [tɛ̃tyr(ə)ri] *nf* **(a)** (*industrie*) dyeing **(b)** (*pressing*) (dry) cleaner's

teinturier, -ière [tɛ̃tyrje, -jɛr] *n* **(a)** *Ind* dyer **(b)** (*qui tient un pressing*) (dry) cleaner; **déposer qch chez le t.** to take sth to the cleaner's

tek [tɛk] *nm* (*bois*) teak

tel, telle [tɛl] [①B14,B,1,c] **1** *adj* **(a)** [①A5,B] such; **un t. homme** such a man; **une telle conduite est remarquable** such behaviour is remarkable; **avec une telle aide, tu ne peux que réussir** with assistance like that you can't help succeeding; **il a un t. enthousiasme que ...** he is so enthusiastic that ..., *Fml* his enthusiasm is such that ...; **t. fut son langage** those were his words; **il n'est pas beau mais il se prend pour t.** he isn't handsome but he thinks he is; **de telles choses** such things; **je ne peux pas lui dire de telles choses** I can't say things like that to him; **de telles paroles, de sa part?** he actually said that?; **en t. lieu** in such and such a place; **dans telle et telle rue** in such and such a street; **dans telles et telles conditions** in such and such conditions; **selon que telle ou telle méthode est choisie** depending on whether this or that method is chosen; **inutile de demander si t. ouvrage remplit son but mieux que t. autre** it is useless to ask whether one book achieves its aim better than another; **t. produit n'est pas forcément plus efficace que t. autre** one product is not necessarily any better than another; **dans telles circonstances qu'on le jugera convenable** under such conditions as may be deemed suitable; **sa bonté est telle que ...** he is so kind that ..., *Fml* so great is his kindness that ...; **elle n'en a pas un besoin t. qu'il faille le lui rendre aujourd'hui** she doesn't need it so badly that we have to give it back to her today; **à t. point** to such an extent; **j'étais inquiet à t. point que je voulais appeler la police** I was worried to the point of wanting to call the police; **il parle de telle sorte que je ne le comprends pas** he speaks in such a way that I don't understand him; **je m'arrangerai de telle sorte qu'elle puisse partir dimanche** I'll arrange things so that *or* in such a way that she can leave on Sunday; **t. père, t. fils** like father like son; *Ordinat* **t. écran-t. écrit** WYSIWYG

(b) t. que (*comme*) such as, like; **des gens connus tel(s) qu'Elvis Presley** well-known people such as *or* like Elvis Presley; **un homme t. que lui** a man like him; **une action telle que la sienne** an action such as his; **une lassitude telle qu'on en éprouve par un jour orageux** the kind of tiredness *or Fml* a tiredness such as one feels on a stormy day; **une impression telle qu'on en a rarement** the kind of impression that is rare; **la clause telle qu'elle est** the clause as it stands; **voir les hommes/les choses tels qu'ils/telles qu'elles sont** to see men/things as they are; **t. que je connais Jean-Luc, il ne sera pas d'accord** he won't agree, not if I know Jean-Luc!

(c) (il n'y a) rien de t. qu'un bon cigare there's nothing like *or* you can't beat a good cigar; **il n'est rien de t. que d'être jeune** there's nothing like being young

(d) *Litt* **il allait et venait t.** *ou* **telle une bête en cage** he paced to and fro like a caged animal

(e) t. quel, *F* **t. que** (*chose*) (just) as it is/was; (*personne*) (just) as he is/was; **je vous achète la maison telle quelle** I'll buy the house from you (just) as it is *or* stands *or esp Com* as is; **j'ai retrouvé la maison telle quelle** I found the house just as I had left it; **il me l'a rendu t. quel** that's how he gave it back to me; **la voiture était couverte de boue, il l'a rendue telle quelle à son père** the car was covered in mud and that was how he gave it back to his father; *F* **elle me l'a dit t. que** she told me straight out, she told me just like that

2 *pron* **t. l'en blâmait, t. l'en excusait** one would blame him, another would excuse him; *Prov* **t. est pris qui croyait prendre** it's a case of the biter bit; *Prov* **t. qui rit vendredi, dimanche pleurera** laugh today, cry tomorrow; **t. ou t. vous dira que ...** some people will tell you that ...; **je serais incapable d'attribuer l'article à t. ou t.** I cannot attribute the article to any particular person

3 *n* **un t., une telle** so-and-so; **Monsieur un t.** *ou* **un T.** Mr So-and-so

télé [tele] *nf F* **(a)** (*appareil*) TV, *Br* telly; **regarder la t.** to watch TV *or* the telly *or Br* the box; **c'est passé à la t.** it was on TV *or* telly *or* the box; **je vais devoir jeter ma vieille t.** I'm going to have to throw out my old TV (set) *or* telly **(b) la t.** (*organisme, technique, émissions*) TV; **des émissions de t.** TV programmes; **t. à péage à la consommation** pay-as-you-view TV

téléachat [teleaʃa] *nm* teleshopping, home shopping

téléacheteur, -euse [teleaʃtœr, -øz] *n* teleshopper

téléacteur, -trice [teleaktœr, -tris] *n* (*en marketing*) telesalesman, telemarketer, telesales person

télé-action *nf* telephone marketing

téléassistance [teleasistɑ̃s] *nf Ordinat* remote help

télébenne [telebɛn] *nf* (*dispositif, cabine*) cable car

téléboutique® [telebutik] *nf* (*de France Telecom*) telephone shop

télécabine [telekabin] *nf* (*dispositif, cabine*) cable car

télécarte [telekart] *nf* phonecard

téléchargeable [teleʃarʒabl] *adj Ordinat* downloadable

téléchargement [teleʃarʒəmɑ̃] *nm Ordinat* downloading, download; **effectuer un t.** to download

télécharger [teleʃarʒe] *vt Ordinat* to download

télécinéma [telesinema] *nm* (*appareil*) telecine

télécommande [telekɔmɑ̃d] *nf* remote control; **t. à infrarouge** infra-red remote control

télécommander [telekɔmɑ̃de] *vt* **(a)** *Tech* to operate by remote control; **télécommandé** remote-controlled, operated by remote control **(b)** *Fig* (*complot, soulèvement*) to mastermind from a distance; **sa décision était télécommandée par des agents ennemis** his decision was dictated by enemy agents

télécommunication [telekɔmynikasjɔ̃] *nf* telecommunication; **télécommunications** telecommunications, telecoms; **satellite de t.** telecom(s) satellite

téléconférence [telekɔ̃ferɑ̃s] *nf* teleconference; **téléconférences** teleconferencing; **la t. est une des méthodes que nous utilisons le plus fréquemment** teleconferencing is one of the methods we use most frequently
télécopie [telekɔpi] *nf* (*procédé*) fax, facsimile transmission; (*message*) fax; **envoyer une t. à qn** to send sb a fax, to fax sb; **numéro de t.** fax number; **t. sur papier ordinaire** plain paper fax
télécopieur [telekɔpjœr] *nm* fax (machine)
télécran [telekrɑ̃] *nm* (*dans un auditorium*) large-sized television screen
télédémarchage [teledemarʃaʒ] *nm Mktg* telephone prospecting
télédépannage [teledepanaʒ] *nm Ordinat* remote trouble-shooting
télédétection [teledetɛksjɔ̃] *nf* remote sensing
télédiffuser [teledifyze] *vt* to televise, to broadcast
télédiffuseur [teledifyzœr] *nm* television broadcaster
télédiffusion [teledifyzjɔ̃] *nf* televising, broadcasting; **T. de France** French broadcasting authority
télédistribution [teledistribysjɔ̃] *nf* cable television
télé-écriture *nf Ordinat* telewriting
télé(-)enseignement *nm* distance learning
téléfax® [telefaks] *nm* fax (machine)
téléférique [teleferik] **1** *adj Tech* (*câble etc*) telpher **2** *nm* (*dispositif, cabine*) cable car
téléfilm [telefilm] *nm* television film *or* movie, made-for-television movie
télégénique [teleʒenik] *adj* telegenic
télégestion [teleʒɛstjɔ̃] *nf Ordinat* teleprocessing, remote processing
télégramme [telegram] *nm* telegram, cable, wire
télégraphe [telegraf] *nm* telegraph
télégraphie [telegrafi] *nf* telegraphy; *Vieilli* **t. sans fil** wireless (telegraphy)
télégraphier [telegrafje] (*impf, pr sub* **n. télégraphiions, v. télégraphiiez**) **1** *vt* (*message*) to wire, to cable, to telegraph **2** *vi* **t. à qn** to wire *or* cable sb
télégraphique [telegrafik] *adj* telegraphic; **fil/poteau t.** telegraph wire/pole; **dépêche t.** telegram; **style t.** telegraphic style, *F* telegraphese
télégraphiquement [telegrafikmɑ̃] *adv* by telegram, by cable, by wire
télégraphiste [telegrafist] *n* (*technicien*) telegraph operator, telegraphist; (**petit**) **t.** (*porteur de dépêches*) telegraph boy
téléguidage [telegidaʒ] *nm* remote control
téléguidé [telegide] *adj* remote-controlled; **engin t.** guided missile; **voiture téléguidée** remote-controlled car
téléguider [telegide] *vt* (**a**) *Tech* to operate by remote control (**b**) *Fig* (*complot, soulèvement*) to mastermind from a distance; **sa réponse/décision était téléguidée** his answer/decision was dictated by outside forces
téléimpression [teleɛ̃prɛsjɔ̃] *nf* teleprint
téléimprimeur [teleɛ̃primœr] *nm* teleprinter, *Am* teletypewriter
téléinformatique [teleɛ̃fɔrmatik] *adj* teleprocessing, remote data processing
téléjournaliste [teleʒurnalist] *n* television journalist
télékinésie [telekinezi] *nf* telekinesis
télémaintenance [telemɛ̃tnɑ̃s] *nf Astronaut* housekeeping; *Ordinat* remote access
télémanipulateur [telemanipylatœr] *nm Phys Nucl* remote manipulator
Télémaque [telemak] *nm Myth* Telemachus
télémarché [telemarʃe] *nm* telemarket
télémark [telemark] *nm Ski* telemark
télémarketing [telemarkətiŋ, -ketiŋ] *nm* telemarketing
télématique [telematik] **1** *nf* data communications, telematics **2** *adj* data communications, telecommunications; **par voie t.** using data comms (technology)
télémercatique [telemɛrkatik] *nf* telemarketing
télémesure [teleməzyr] *nf Électron etc* telemetering, telemetry
télémètre [telemɛtr] *nm* telemeter; *Mil, Phot* rangefinder
télémétrie [telemetri] *nf* telemetry; *Mil, Phot* range finding
téléobjectif [teleɔbʒɛktif] *nm Phot* telephoto *or* long-focus lens; **photographie au t.** telephotography
téléologie [teleɔlɔʒi] *nf Phil* teleology
téléologique [teleɔlɔʒik] *adj* teleologic(al)
téléostéen [teleɔsteɛ̃] *nm* (*poisson*) teleost
télépaiement [telepɛmɑ̃] *nm* telepayment, electronic payment
télépathe [telepat] **1** *adj* telepathic; *Hum* **je ne suis pas t.!** I'm not psychic, I'm not endowed with ESP! **2** *n* telepathist, telepath
télépathie [telepati] *nf* telepathy
télépathique [telepatik] *adj* telepathic
téléphage [telefaʒ] *nm* couch potato
téléphérage [teleferaʒ] *nm Tech* telpherage, overhead cable transport
téléphérique [teleferik] *adj, nm* = **téléférique**
téléphone [telefɔn] *nm* [①A71,5] (*appareil*) telephone, phone; (*système*) telephone; (**numéro de**) **t.** (tele)phone number; **donne-moi ton** (**numéro de**) **t.** give me your (phone) number; **t. direct** direct dial telephone; **être abonné au t., avoir le t.** to be on the phone, to have a phone; **être au t.** to be on the phone; **coup de t.** (tele)phone call; **donner** *ou* **passer un coup de t.** to make a phone call; **appeler qn au t., donner un coup de t. à qn** to ring sb (up), to (tele)phone sb, *surtout Am* to call sb; **parler à qn au** *ou* **par t.** to speak to sb on the phone; **je l'avais au t. pas plus tard qu'hier** I was on the phone to him/her only yesterday; **apprendre qch par t.** to learn of sth by phone; **demander qch par t.** to phone for sth; **commander qch par t.** to order sth by phone
▶ **téléphone**: *F* **t. arabe** grapevine, bush telegraph; *F* **par le t. arabe** on the grapevine; **t. bâtiment-terre** ship to shore (tele)phone; **t. à carte** cardphone; **t. cellulaire** cellular phone; **t. mobile** mobile (phone); **t. portatif** mobile *or* portable (phone); **t. public** public telephone; *Pol* **t. rouge** hot line; **t. sans fil** cordless (tele)phone; **t. de voiture** car phone
téléphoner [telefɔne] **1** *vt* (**a**) (*nouvelle etc*) to (tele)phone; **je te téléphonerai tes résultats** I'll call and let you know your results, I'll call you with your results (**b**) *Sp etc, Fig* (*coups etc*) to telegraph; *Pol etc* **une manœuvre téléphonée** an obvious manoeuvre; **c'était téléphoné** you could see it coming **2** *vi* to (tele)phone; **je passe tout mon temps à t.** I spend all my time on the phone; **t. à qn** to ring sb (up), to (tele)phone sb, *surtout Am* to call sb; **t. à qn de venir** to (tele)phone for sb **3 se téléphoner** *vpr* to ring each other (up), to (tele)phone each other, *surtout Am* to call each other (up)
téléphonie [telefɔni] *nf* telephony; **t. sans fil** wireless telephony, radiotelephony
téléphonique [telefɔnik] *adj* (*cabine, appel, ligne, réseau etc*) telephone; **commande t.** order by telephone, telephone order
téléphoniste [telefɔnist] *n* (telephone) operator, *Br* telephonist
téléphotographie [telefotografi] *nf* (**a**) *Télécom* phototelegraphy (**b**) *Phot* telephotography; (*cliché*) telephotograph
téléprompteur [teleprɔ̃ptœr] *nm TV* Teleprompter®, *Br* Autocue®, *F* idiot board
téléprospecteur, -trice [teleprɔspɛktœr, -tris] *n* telemarketer, teleprospector
téléprospection [teleprɔspɛksjɔ̃] *nf* telemarketing, teleprospecting
téléreportage [teler(ə)pɔrtaʒ] *nm* (*activité*) television reporting; (*commentaire*) television report
télescopage [telɛskɔpaʒ] *nm* (*de trains etc*) telescoping; *Aut* **t.** (**en série**) pile-up
télescope [telɛskɔp] *nm* telescope; **t. électronique** electron telescope
télescoper [telɛskɔpe] **1** *vt* (**a**) *Aut, Rail* (*véhicules, train etc*) to crash into (**b**) *Ling* (*mots*) to telescope **2 se télescoper** *vpr* (**a**) (*de véhicules, de trains*) to concertina (**b**) *Fig* (*de souvenirs, d'images etc*) to overlap
télescopique [telɛskɔpik] *adj* telescopic
téléscripteur [teleskriptœr] *nm* teleprinter, *Am* teletypewriter, *Am* teletyper; *Bourse* ticker tape
télésecrétariat [telesəkretarja] *nm* remote secretarial services
téléservice [teleservis] *nm* on-line service
télésiège [telesjɛʒ] *nm* chair lift
téléski [teleski] *nm* ski lift *or* tow
télésouffleur [telesuflœr] *nm* Teleprompter®, video prompter, *Br* Autocue®
téléspectateur, -trice [telespɛktatœr, -tris] *n* (television) viewer
téléstation [telestasjɔ̃] *nf* remote station
télésurveillance [telesyrvɛjɑ̃s] *nf* remote *or* electronic surveillance
télétel [teletɛl] *nm* = computerized information network available through Minitel
télétex [teletɛks] *nm Ordinat* teletex
télétexte [teletɛkst] *nm TV* teletext
téléthèque [teletɛk] *nf* television film library
téléthon [teletɔ̃] *nm* telethon
télétraitement [teletrɛtmɑ̃] *nm Ordinat* teleprocessing, remote data processing
télétransmission [teletrɑ̃smisjɔ̃] *nf* remote *or* data transmission
télétravail [teletravaj] *nm* telecommuting, teleworking
télétravailler [teletravaje] *vi* to telecommute
télétravailleur, -euse [teletravajœr, -øz] *n* telecommuter, teleworker
Télétype® [teletip] *nm* Teletype®, teleprinter, *Am* teletyper
télévangéliste [televɑ̃ʒelist] *n* televangelist

télévendeur, -euse [televãdœr, -øz] *n* telesalesman, *f* telesaleswoman, telesales person, telephone salesman, *f* telephone saleswoman
télévente [televãt] *nf* telesales, telephone selling, teleselling; **t. groupée** bus phoning
téléviser [televize] *vt* to televise; **journal télévisé** television news
téléviseur [televizœr] *nm* television *or* TV (set)
télévision [televizjɔ̃] *nf* **(a)** (*organisme, technique, émissions*) television, TV; **à la t.** on television; **travailler à la t.** to work in television **(b)** (*poste*) television *or* TV (set); **regarder la t.** to watch television; **écran de t.** television screen **(c) (chaîne de) t.** television *or* TV channel
▶ **télévision**: **t. à accès conditionnel** conditional access television; **t. par câble** cable television, *Am* cablecasting; **t. en circuit fermé** closed-circuit television; **t. commerciale** commercial television; **t. en couleur(s), t. couleur** colour *or US* color television; **t. à la demande** television on demand; **t. pour enfants** children's television; **t. généraliste** general-interest television channel; **t. haute définition** high-definition TV, hi-def TV; **t. ouverte** access broadcasting; **t. à péage** *ou* **payante** pay television; **t. par satellite** satellite television; **t. scolaire** schools *or* educational television, television for schools
télévisuel, -elle [televizɥel] *adj* television
télex [telɛks] *nm* (*service, message*) telex; **envoyer par t.** to send by telex, to telex
télexer [telɛkse] *vt* to telex
télexiste [teleksist] *n* telex operator
tellement [tɛlmɑ̃] *adv* **(a)** (*si*) so; (+ *comp*) so much; **elle en parle t. souvent** she talks about it so often; **c'est t. facile** it's so (very) easy; **ce serait t. plus simple** it would be so much simpler; **il est t. sourd qu'il faut crier** he is so deaf that you have to shout; **il en sait déjà t. que ...** he knows so much about it that ...; **ce n'est pas t. beau** it's not all that beautiful; **ça te plaît? – pas t.** do you like it? – not very much *or* not all that much; **je n'ai pas t. envie de le revoir** I'm not all that keen on seeing him again
(b) *F* **t. de** (*nombre*) so many; (*quantité*) so much; **t. de choses à faire** so many things *or* so much to do; **ça demande t. de courage** it requires so much courage
(c) (*tant*) so; **elle ne peut pas se lever, t. elle est malade** she cannot get up, she is so ill
tellure [telyr] *nm Ch* tellurium
tellurique[1] [telyrik] *adj Ch* (*acide*) telluric
tellurique[2] *adj* (*courants*) telluric; **secousse t.** earth tremor
tel-tel *adj Ordinat* WYSIWYG
téméraire [temerɛr] *adj* (*personne, entreprise*) rash, reckless; (*jugement, déclaration*) rash
témérairement [temerɛrmɑ̃] *adv* rashly, recklessly
témérité [temerite] *nf* rashness, recklessness
témoignage [temwaɲaʒ] *nm* **(a)** (*attestation*) testimony, evidence; **recueillir des témoignages** to collect evidence; **porter t.** to give evidence; **porter t. en faveur de qn** to give evidence *or* to testify on sb's behalf; **ce livre se contente de porter t. sur l'époque** the book is content to describe the era; **rendre t. de qch** to give evidence about sth; **rendre t. à** *ou* **pour qn** to speak up for sb; *Jur* to testify in sb's favour *or US* favor; **faux t.** false witness, false evidence; (*délit*) perjury; **faire un faux t.** to commit perjury
(b) (*déclaration*) evidence, statement; **d'après son t.** according to his statement; *Fig* **t. des sens** evidence of the senses
(c) (*démonstration*) (*d'amitié, d'admiration etc*) token, sign; **c'est le t. de mon amitié** it's a token of my friendship; **en t. de** as a token *or* sign of
(d) *Mktg* (*publicité*) testimonial advertising
témoigner [temwaɲe] **1** *vi* **(a)** to testify (**en faveur de/contre qn** on sb's behalf/against sb), to give evidence (**en faveur de/contre qn** for/against sb)
(b) t. de (*montrer*) (*gratitude, bonne volonté, courage etc*) to show; (*confirmer*) (*bonne foi etc*) to show, to testify to; **t. d'un goût pour ...** to show *or* display a taste for ...; **t. de l'intérêt à qn/pour qch** to show an interest in sb/sth; **t. du dédain à qn** to show contempt for sb
2 *vt* **(a)** (*attester*) **t. que** to testify that
(b) (*montrer*) (*sentiments, gratitude etc*) to show (**à qn** to sb); **il ne m'a jamais témoigné d'affection/d'amitié** he has never shown me any affection/any signs of friendship; **cela témoigne que/combien ...** that shows that/how much ...; **sa réaction témoigne qu'il s'y attendait** his reaction shows *or* is proof that he was expecting it
témoin [temwɛ̃] *nm* **(a)** (*spectateur*) witness; **être t. de qch** to witness sth, to be a witness to sth; **j'en suis t.** I'm a witness; **ils se sont vus sans t.** they saw each other in private, there were no witnesses present when they saw each other; **mes yeux en sont témoins** I saw it with my own eyes
(b) *Jur* witness; **barre des témoins** witness box, *US* (witness) stand; **à la barre des témoins** in the witness box, *US* on the stand; **citer qn comme t.** to call sb as a witness; **t. à un mariage** witness at a wedding; **je vous prends tous à t. que ...** I call on you all to witness that ...; **Dieu m'est t. que je n'y suis pour rien** as God is my witness I had nothing to do with it
(c) (*dans un duel*) second
(d) (*trace*) evidence; **les témoins d'une civilisation perdue** the evidence of a lost civilization; **t. les coups que j'ai reçus** witness the blows which I received
(e) (*borne*) boundary mark
(f) (*échantillon*) *Ch* reference solution; **animal/plante t.** (*dans un essai*) control animal/plant; *Phot* **plaque** *ou* **épreuve t.** pilot print; **denrée t.** basic commodity; **appartement t.** show flat, *Am* model apartment; **voici les bilans de quatre entreprises témoins** here are the balance sheets from four sample companies
(g) *Él, Ind etc* (**lampe**) **t.** pilot *or* warning light; *Aut* **t. d'alerte de pression d'huile moteur** oil pressure warning light
(h) *Sp* (*dans un relais*) baton
▶ **témoin**: *Aut* **t. d'allumage** ignition light; *Aut* **t. de baisse du niveau d'essence** petrol low warning light; *Jur* **t. à charge** witness for the prosecution; *Aut* **t. de charge** *ou* **de contrôle de la batterie** battery charge warning light; *Jur* **t. à décharge** witness for the defence; **t. de frein parking** handbrake-on light; *Rel* **T. de Jéhovah** Jehovah's Witness; *Jur* **t. oculaire** eyewitness
tempe [tɑ̃p] *nf Anat* temple; **aux tempes grisonnantes** (going) grey at the temples
tempera (a) [atɑ̃pera] *Beaux-Arts* **1** *adj* **peinture a t.** tempera painting **2** *adv* **peindre a t.** to paint in tempera
tempérament [tɑ̃peramɑ̃] *nm* **(a)** (*physique*) constitution; **t. de fer** iron constitution; *F* **se tuer le t.** to ruin one's health **(b)** (*moral*) disposition; **être d'un** *ou* **avoir un t. violent** to be of a violent disposition; **c'est un t.** he has character; **avoir du t.** to have character; (*sexuel*) to be highly sexed **(c)** *Arch* (*modération*) moderation, restraint **(d)** *Com* **à t.** by instalments; **vente** *ou* **achat à t.** *Br* hire purchase, *Am* installment plan
tempérance [tɑ̃perɑ̃s] *nf* **(a)** (*modération*) moderation, temperance; **faire preuve de t.** to show moderation, to be moderate **(b)** (*sobriété*) temperance; **faire preuve de t.** to drink in moderation; **société de t.** temperance society
tempérant [tɑ̃perɑ̃] *adj* (*personne*) temperate
température [tɑ̃peratyr] *nf* (*d'une personne, d'un liquide, d'une région etc*), *Fig* temperature; **t. du corps humain** temperature of the human body, blood heat; *Méd F* **avoir** *ou* **faire de la t.** to have a (high) temperature; *Méd* **feuille de t.** temperature chart; **la méthode des températures** (*de contraception*) the rhythm method; *Phys* **t. d'ébullition** boiling point; **prendre la t. d'un malade** to take a patient's temperature; *Fig* **prendre la t. de l'auditoire** to gauge the temperature of the audience
tempéré [tɑ̃pere] *adj* **(a)** (*climat*) temperate; (*discours*) moderate; (*style*) restrained, sober **(b)** *Mus* tempered
tempérer [tɑ̃pere] *vt* (**je tempère, n. tempérons; je tempérerai**) (*chaleur*) to moderate; (*passion*) to moderate, to temper
tempête [tɑ̃pɛt] *nf Météo, Fig* (*d'applaudissements*) storm; *Fig* (*d'injures*) storm, hail; **t.** (*sur un baromètre*) stormy; *Fig* **cette mesure va provoquer une t.** the measure will cause a storm of protest; **pendant la t.** during the storm; *Fig* while the storm is raging; *Fig* **une t. dans un verre d'eau** a storm in a teacup *or Am* teapot; *Fig* **nous avons eu droit à une t. d'insultes/de bravos** insults/bravos rained down on us
▶ **tempête**: **t. de neige** blizzard, snowstorm; **t. de sable** sandstorm
tempêter [tɑ̃pete] *vi* (*d'une personne*) to storm, to rage; **t. contre qn/qch** to rant and rave about sb/sth
tempétueux, -euse [tɑ̃petɥø, -øz] *adj* (*vent, mer etc*) stormy, *Fml* tempestuous; *Fig* (*relations*) tempestuous, stormy; (*accueil*) boisterous, tempestuous; (*vie*) turbulent, stormy
temple [tɑ̃pl] *nm* temple; (*protestant*) church; *Fig* (*de la gastronomie etc*) temple; *Hist* **les chevaliers du T.** the Knights Templar(s)
templier [tɑ̃plije] *nm Hist* (Knight) Templar
tempo [tɛ̃po, tempo] *nm* (①**A13**,7) *Mus, Fig* tempo
temporaire [tɑ̃pɔrɛr] **1** *adj* **(a)** (*provisoire*) temporary; **agence de travail t.** temporary employment agency; **emploi t.** temporary job; **employé t.** temporary employee, *F* temp **(b)** *Mus* **valeur t. d'une note** time value of a note **2** *n* temp

temporairement [tɑ̃pɔrɛrmɑ̃] *adv* temporarily

temporal, -ale, -aux, -ales [tɑ̃pɔral, -o] *Anat* **1** *adj* (*os, artère*) temporal **2** *nm* **(a)** (*os*) temporal bone **(b)** (*muscle*) temporal muscle, *Spéc* temporalis **3** *nf* **temporale** temporal (artery)

temporalité [tɑ̃pɔralite] *nf Rel, Phil, Gram* temporality

temporel, -elle [tɑ̃pɔrɛl] *adj* **(a)** (*terrestre*) temporal, worldly **(b)** *Gram* (*proposition etc*) temporal **(c)** (*qui concerne le temps*) time

temporellement [tɑ̃pɔrɛlmɑ̃] *adv* temporally

temporisateur, -trice [tɑ̃pɔrizatœr, -tris] **1** *adj* temporizing; **ce n'est qu'une tactique temporisatrice de la part du gouvernement** the government is just playing for time with this measure **2** *n* (*personne*) **c'est un t.** (*qui attend pour agir*) he doesn't make hasty decisions; (*qui fait traîner les choses*) he's always stalling *or* playing for time **3** *nm Él* (automatic) time switch

temporisation [tɑ̃pɔrizasjɔ̃] *nf* playing for time, stalling, *Fml* temporizing

temporiser [tɑ̃pɔrize] *vi* to play for time, to stall, *Fml* to temporize

temps [tɑ̃] *nm* **(a)** (*durée*) time; **mettre beaucoup de t. à faire qch** to take a long time doing sth; **mettre peu de t. à faire qch** not to take long to do sth; **tuer le t.** to kill time; **pour passer le t.** to pass the time, to while away the time; **vous avez bien le t., vous avez tout le t.** you've plenty *or* lots of time; **cela prend du t.** it takes *or* requires time; **cela ne prendra pas beaucoup de t.** it won't take long; **en un rien de t.** in no time at all; **prendre (tout) son t.** to take one's time; **prends le t. qu'il faudra** take as much time as you need; **je voudrais prendre un peu de t. pour y réfléchir** I'd like to have some time to think about it; **elle a pris/trouvé le t. de nous l'expliquer** she took/found the time to explain it to us; **donner à qn le t. de faire qch** to give sb time to do sth; **(donnez-moi) le t. de signer** *ou* **que je signe et je suis à vous** just give me time *or* a minute to sign this and I'll be with you; **je trouve le t. long** time is dragging; **nous n'avons pas le t. à présent** we don't have time *or* there's no time now; **nous n'avons que le t. de …** we just have time to …; **combien de t. faut-il pour …?** how long does it take to …?; **accorder du t. à qn** to give sb time; **vous pourriez m'accorder un peu de t. pour que je vous parle de mon projet?** could you give me a moment or two of your time to talk about my project?; **il n'accorde pas beaucoup de t. à ses enfants** he doesn't have much time for his children, his children don't get much of his time; **gagner du t.** to save *or* gain time; (*temporiser*) to play for time, to stall; **perdre du t.** to waste time; (*à cause d'un imprévu*) to lose time; **tu me fais perdre mon t.** you're wasting my time; **rattraper le t. perdu** to make up for lost time; **dans le cours du t., avec le t.** in (the course of) time, with time; **de t. en t., de t. à autre** now and then, from time to time; **en d'autres t.** at any other time; **en tout t.** at all times; **en même t.** at the same time; **en même t. mère et sœur** both mother and sister, mother and sister at the same time; **travailler à plein t./à t. partiel** *ou* **à mi-temps** to work full time/part time, to have a full-time/part-time job; **prendre/se donner du bon t.** to have a good time, to enjoy oneself; *Prov* **le t., c'est de l'argent** time is money; *Myth etc* **le T.** (Father) Time

(b) (*moment*) time; **en t. de crise** in a crisis, at a time of crisis; **en t. de guerre/de paix** in wartime/peacetime; **un (certain) t., quelque t.** for a while, for a time; **pendant ce t.** meanwhile, in the meantime; **entre t. …** in the meantime …; **il est arrivé entre t.** he arrived in the meantime; **après quelque t., au bout d'un certain t.** after a time; **cela ne durera qu'un t.** it won't last for ever; **tout n'a qu'un t.** everything must come to an end; **le t. de la moisson** harvest time; **le t. des cerises** the cherry season; **il y a peu de t.** not long ago, a little while ago, a short time ago; **peu de t. après** shortly *or* a short time *or* not long after; **d'ici quelque t.** soon, shortly, in a short time; **au bout de très peu de t.** in a very short space of time; **tout le t.** all the time; **il est tout le t. en train de se plaindre** he is constantly *or* he keeps complaining; **c'est ce que je lui dis tout le t.** that's what I keep telling him; **faire un t. de galop** to have a short gallop, to gallop for a time *or* a while; **marquer un t.** to pause, to halt

(c) **faire son t.** to serve *or* do one's time; (*d'un détenu*) to serve one's sentence, *F* to do one's time; **ce manteau a fait son t.** this coat has had it, *Hum* it's about time this coat was given a decent burial; **cette théorie a fait son t.** this theory is out of date *or* out-dated *or* outmoded

(d) *Ind* **étude des t. et ordonnancements** time and motion study; *Ordinat* **base de t.** time base

(e) (*période, époque*) time(s), days; **les t. préhistoriques** prehistoric times; **les hauts t.** remote antiquity; **en t. normal** usually, normally; **le bon vieux t.** the good old days; **l'Angleterre des t. passés** the England of the past; **les t. sont durs** times are hard; **en ces t. de difficultés économiques** in these times of economic difficulty; **signe des t.** sign of the times; **par les t. qui courent** in this day and age, these days, nowadays; **dans le t.** in the old days; **au t. jadis** in times past, in days gone by, in bygone days; **dans la suite des t.** in the course of time; **en d'autres t., je n'aurais pas hésité** once upon a time I wouldn't have hesitated; **en ce t.-là** at that time, then; **ces t.-ci** these days; **ce fut un grand homme dans son t.** he was a great man in his day *or* time; **elle a eu son t. de beauté** she was a beauty in her day; **du t.** *ou* **au t. de Napoléon** in Napoleon's time; **du t. de ma jeunesse, du t. où j'étais jeune** when I was young, in my youth; **il fut un t. où …** there was a time when …; **être de son t., vivre avec son t.** to move with the times, to be up to date; **vous n'êtes pas de votre t.** you're behind the times; **être en avance sur son t.** to be ahead of one's time; **de notre t.** in our day *or* time; **il n'en était pas ainsi de mon t.** it wasn't so in my day *or* time; **cela est arrivé de mon t.** it happened in my time; **de tout t.** always

(f) (*heure*) **faire qch à t.** to do sth in time; **arriver juste à t.** to arrive just in time *or* in the nick of time; **en t. voulu** *ou* **utile** in due course; **je serai de retour en t. voulu** I'll be back in *or* on time; [ⓘ**A52**,b,v] **il est t. qu'elle descende** it's time she came down; **il est grand t. que …** it's high time *or* about time that …; **il est** *ou* **serait grand t. que tu te décides** it's high time you made up your mind; **il serait t.!** it's about time!, and about time too!; **il n'est plus t.** it's too late; **il est enfin arrivé, il était t.!** he finally arrived and not before time either!; **il n'était que t.** it was only just in time

(g) (*occasion*) **il y a un t. pour tout** there's a time for everything; **chaque chose en son t.** all in good time; **en t. et lieu** in the proper time and place; **quand j'aurai le t.** when I have (the) time

(h) [ⓘ**B27**,E,2,a] *Météo* weather; **par tous les t.** in all weathers; **vous sortez par un pareil t.** *ou* **par le t. qu'il fait!** you're going out in weather like this *or* in this weather!; **quel t. fait-il?** what's the weather like?, *F* what's the weather doing?; **quelque t. qu'il fasse** whatever the weather (is like); **si le t. le permet** weather permitting; **beau t.** fine weather; **il fait beau/mauvais t.** the weather's fine/bad; *F* **il fera beau t. quand je ferai cela** it'll be a long time before I do that; *Naut* **gros t.** heavy weather; **le t. est à la pluie** it looks like rain, we're going to have rain; **prévision du t.** weather forecast; **une robe couleur du t.** a sky-blue dress

(i) [ⓘ**A39**,7; **B28-30**,F] *Gram* tense; **adverbes de t.** adverbs of time

(j) *Mus* beat; **mesure à trois t.** three-four time

(k) *Mil* **au t.!** as you were!; *Fig* **au t. pour moi!** my mistake!

(l) *Tech* **moteur à deux/à quatre t.** two-stroke/four-stroke engine

(m) *Sp* (*d'un coureur etc*) time

▶ **temps**: *Ordinat* **t. d'accès** access time; *Ordinat* **t. d'accès disque** disk access time; *Ordinat* **t. d'adressage** address speed; *TV, Rad* **t. d'antenne** airtime; *Astron* **t. apparent** apparent time; **t. d'arrêt** pause, halt; **t. astronomique** astronomical time; *Ordinat* **t. d'attente** wait state; *Aut* **t. compression** (*d'un moteur*) compression stroke; *Culin* **t. de cuisson** cooking time; *Com* **t. de cycle** business cycle; *Aut* **t. détente** (*d'un moteur*) power stroke; *Ordinat* **t. différé: en t. différé** off-line; **t. d'échauffement** (*d'une machine*) warm-up time; *Ordinat* **t. écoulé** elapsed time; *Ordinat* **t. d'exécution** execution *or* execute time; *Aut* **t. explosion** (*d'un moteur*) power stroke; **t. de fonctionnement** (*d'une machine*) running time; **t. fort: les temps forts de l'actualité/de l'année 1995** the main points of the news/the main events of 1995; **t. d'immobilisation** (*d'une machine*) down time; *Aut* **t. d'immobilité du piston** piston dwell; *Ordinat* **t. machine** machine time; *Ordinat* **t. de montée** rise time; **t. mort** (*d'une machine*) idle time *or* period, down time; *Sp* stoppage; **pendant les temps morts** (*dans une période de travail*) when things are quiet; *Av* **t. mort au sol** turn-round time; **t. moteur** engine *or* power *or* working stroke; **t. moyen entre deux pannes** (*d'une machine*) mean time between failures, MTBF; **t. moyen local** local mean time; *Él, Électron* **t. d'ouverture** on period; *Ordinat* **t. partagé** time sharing; *Ordinat* **utilisation (d'un ordinateur) en t. partagé** time sharing; **t. primitifs** (*d'un verbe*) principal parts; *Aut* **t. de réaction** thinking distance; *Ordinat* **t. réel** real time; *Ordinat* **horloge t. réel** real-time clock; *Ordinat* **t. de rémanence** afterglow time; *Ordinat* **t. de réponse** response time; *Ordinat* **t. de sortie** output time; *Ordinat* **t.**

de traitement processing time; **t. universel** Greenwich Mean Time; *Tech* **t. à vide** (*d'une machine etc*) off-load period; **t. vrai** true time

tenable [tənabl] *adj* (*often with negation*) **(a)** *Mil etc* (*position*) tenable, defensible **(b)** (*situation*) bearable; **par cette chaleur, le bureau n'est pas t.** in this heat the office is unbearable; **ce n'est plus t., je pars** it has become unbearable *or* I can't bear it any longer, I'm leaving

tenace [tənas] *adj* (*personne*) tenacious; (*croyance, superstition, préjugé*) stubborn, lingering; (*odeur, parfum*) lingering; (*couleur*) fast; (*volonté, résistance*) dogged, tenacious; (*maladie, douleur, souvenir*) persistent; **espoir t.** fond hope; **tu es t. toi!** you don't give up easily!; **les vieilles habitudes sont tenaces** old habits die hard

tenacement [tənasmɑ̃] *adv* stubbornly, tenaciously

ténacité [tenasite] *nf* (*d'une personne*) tenacity, stubbornness; (*d'une odeur*) lingering nature; (*d'une croyance, une superstition, un préjugé*) stubbornness; (*d'une résistance*) doggedness, stubbornness; (*d'une maladie, une douleur*) persistence; **avec t.** stubbornly, doggedly; (*travailler*) doggedly

tenaille [tənaj] *nf* [①**A10**,e] **(a)** (*pour saisir*) tongs; **t. à vis** hand vice **(b)** **tenailles** (*pour arracher des clous*) pincers; *Mil* **manœuvre en tenailles** pincer movement; **prendre l'ennemi en t.** to trap the enemy in a pincer movement

tenailler [tənaje] *vt Hist Fig* to torture; **tenaillé par la faim** gnawed by hunger; **tenaillé par le remords** gnawed *or* tortured *or* tormented by remorse

tenancier, -ière [tənɑ̃sje, -jɛr] *n* **(a)** (*d'un hôtel, bar etc*) manager; (*d'une maison close, d'un tripot*) keeper **(b)** *Arch* (*d'un terrain*) holder **(c)** (*fermier*) tenant farmer

tenant, -ante [tənɑ̃, -ɑ̃t] **1** *adj* **(a)** **séance tenante** there and then, then and there, on the spot **(b)** **chemise à col t.** shirt with collar attached **2** *n* **(a)** (*partisan*) (*de qn, d'une opinion etc*) champion, defender **(b)** *Sp* (*d'un titre, d'un prix*) holder **3** *nm* **tout d'un (seul) t.** (*propriété*) continuous, all in one block, lying together; (*bloc de pierre*) in one piece; **tenants et aboutissants** (*d'une propriété*) adjacent parts; *Fig* (*d'une affaire*) ins and outs, full details

tendance [tɑ̃dɑ̃s] *nf* (*d'une personne*) tendency, inclination; (*de l'opinion, de l'art moderne, du cinéma etc*) trend; (*d'un livre, discours etc*) tenor; **tendance(s) communiste(s)** communist leanings *or* tendencies; **avoir (une) t. à la paresse/le mensonge/l'embonpoint** to be inclined *or* to tend to be lazy/to lie/to put on weight; **avoir (une) t. à faire qch** to be inclined *or* to tend to do sth; **avoir un peu t. à faire qch** to be rather inclined to do sth; **il a facilement t. à s'emporter/mentir/avoir peur** he gets angry/lies/gets scared very easily; **avoir t. à s'enrhumer facilement** to be prone to catching colds; *Bourse* **t. générale à la hausse/baisse** general upward/downward trend; **t. ascensionnelle** upward trend; **t. de l'économie** economic trend; **t. du marché** market trend

tendancieusement [tɑ̃dɑ̃sjøzmɑ̃] *adv* tendentiously

tendancieux, -ieuse [tɑ̃dɑ̃sjø, -jøz] *adj* bias(s)ed, *Fml* tendentious; *Jur* (*question*) leading

tender [tɑ̃dɛr] *nm Rail, Naut* tender

tendeur [tɑ̃dœr] *nm* **(a)** **t. de chaîne** (*de bicyclette*) chain adjuster *or* tightener *or* tensioner; *Aut* **t. de ceinture** seatbelt tensioner; *Aut* **t. de sangle** belt tensioner; *MecE* **t. de courroie** belt tensioner; **t. à vis** turnbuckle **(b)** (*de machine à coudre*) tension (device) **(c)** **t. pour chaussures** shoe tree **(d)** (*courroie élastique*) bungee (cord)

tendineux, -euse [tɑ̃dinø, -øz] *adj Anat* tendinous; **viande tendineuse** stringy meat

tendinite [tɑ̃dinit] *nf Méd* tendinitis

tendon [tɑ̃dɔ̃] *nm Anat* tendon, sinew; **t. d'Achille** Achilles tendon; **t. du jarret** hamstring

tendre¹ [tɑ̃dr] **1** *adj* **(a)** (*herbe, mine de crayon, bois, pierre, métal etc*) soft; (*viande, légume*) tender; (*couleur*) delicate, soft; (*peau*) sensitive, tender, soft

(b) (*âge, enfance*) early; **dès ma plus t. enfance** from my earliest childhood; **les souvenirs de l'âge t.** early *or* childhood memories

(c) (*affectueux*) (*personne*) loving, affectionate, fond; (*regard, geste*) loving, affectionate, tender; (*cœur*) tender, soft; **il n'a jamais un geste t. envers sa femme** he never shows his wife any affection; **sois plus t. avec elle** be more loving *or* affectionate towards her; **ne pas être t. (pour** *ou* **avec qn)** to be hard *or* severe (on sb); **elle n'a pas été t. avec lui/le film** she didn't go easy on him/the film; **il a le vin t.** drink makes him sentimental

2 *nm* **(a)** *Arch* **avoir un t. pour qn** to have a soft spot for sb **(b)** *Culin* **t. de tranche** topside (of beef)

3 *n* (*personne*) softhearted person; **c'est un t.** he's softhearted

tendre² **1** *vt* **(a)** (*raidir*) (*corde, corde de violon, ressort etc*) to tighten; (*toile*) to stretch; (*muscles*) to tense; (*arc*) to bend, to draw

(b) (*poser*) (*voile, filet etc*) to spread; (*papier peint, tapisserie*) to hang; (*piège, embuscade, filet*) to set (**à** for); **t. une pièce de toile de jute** to cover the walls of a room in hessian

(c) (*bras, jambe etc*) to stretch out, to hold out; **t. qch à qn** to hold sth out to sb; **t. la main** to hold out *or* stretch out one's hand; (*mendier*) to beg; **pas un ne m'aurait tendu la main!** not one of them would have offered me a hand *or* stretched out a helping hand!; **t. les bras** (*pour accueillir qn*) to stretch one's arms wide, to throw one's arms out; **les bras tendus** with outstretched arms; *Fig* **t. l'oreille** to prick up one's ears; **j'essayais de t. l'oreille pour comprendre ce qu'il disait** I was straining to make out what he was saying; **t. le cou** to crane one's neck

2 *vi* **t. à** *ou* **vers la perfection** to try to achieve perfection, to be a perfectionist; **t. à un idéal** to aim at an ideal; **t. vers un résultat** to lead to a result; **t. à sa fin** (*d'une chose*) to be near(ing) its end, to be drawing to a close; *Math* **la valeur de n tend vers zéro** the value of n tends towards zero; **t. à faire qch** to tend to do sth; **les douleurs tendent à disparaître** the pain is starting to go; **cela tendrait à confirmer la première hypothèse** that would tend to confirm the original hypothesis

3 se tendre *vpr* to become taut; *Fig* (*des relations*) to become strained; **pas une main ne s'est tendue vers moi** not a hand was stretched out towards me

tendrement [tɑ̃drəmɑ̃] *adv* tenderly, lovingly; **ménage t. uni** loving couple

tendresse [tɑ̃drɛs] *nf* **(a)** (*affection*) tenderness; **t. maternelle** maternal affection *or* love; **avoir de la t. pour qn** to feel affection for sb, to be fond of sb; **avec t.** tenderly, lovingly; **aimer qn avec t.** to feel great affection for sb **(b)** **tendresses** (*témoignages d'affection*) tokens of affection, caresses; **se dire des tendresses** to exchange sweet nothings; **mille tendresses** (*en fin de lettre*) (with) lots of love, all my love **(c)** **tendresses royalistes** royalist sympathies

tendreté [tɑ̃drəte] *nf* (*de la viande, fruit*) tenderness

tendron [tɑ̃drɔ̃] *nm* **(a)** *Bot* tender shoot **(b)** *Culin* (*de veau*) gristle **(c)** *F* (*jeune fille*) very young and innocent girl

tendu [tɑ̃dy] *adj* **(a)** (*corde, toile etc*) taut, tight; (*tir*) flat; *Fig* (*relations, visage*) strained; *Fig* (*personne, situation, atmosphère, climat politique*) tense; (*estomac*) distended; **t. par la fatigue** tired and strained; *Gym* **corde tendue** tightrope; **chaîne mal tendue** slack chain; **elle a les nerfs tendus en ce moment** she is tense *or* strung up at the moment; **elle est très tendue nerveusement** she's very tense, she's under a lot of nervous strain; *Bourse* **prix tendus** hard *or* firm prices **(b)** *Ling* (*son*) strong; (*consonne*) voiceless **(c)** (*main*) outstretched **(d)** (*tapissé*) **t. de** (*tapisseries, tissu*) hung with; (*papier peint*) covered with

ténèbres [tenɛbr] *nfpl* darkness, gloom; *Fig* (*de l'ignorance, l'inconscient*) depths; **les t. de la nuit** the darkness of the night; **le Prince des T.** the Prince of Darkness

ténébreux, -euse [tenebrø, -øz] **1** *adj* **(a)** (*obscur*) (*forêt, prison etc*) gloomy, dark **(b)** (*mystérieux*) (*affaire, période de l'histoire etc*) murky; (*style, intentions*) obscure; **un personnage t.** a dark horse **2** *nm* **un beau (brun) t.** a tall dark and handsome man

teneur¹ [tənœr, -øz] *n* **(a)** *Typ* **t. de copie** copy holder **(b)** **t. de livres** book-keeper

teneur² *nf* **(a)** (*d'un document, d'une lettre etc*) contents; **je vais vous résumer la t. de ses propos** I'll give you the general tenor *or* gist of what he said; **t. d'un contrat** terms of a contract, contractual terms; **t. du marché** market trend *or* maker **(b)** [①**A10**,f,i] *Tech, Ind etc* (*quantité*) content; **t. en eau/or** water/gold content

ténia [tenja] *nm Méd* tapeworm, *Spéc* taenia, *US* tenia

tenir [tənir] (*prp* **tenant**; *pp* **tenu**; *pr ind* **je tiens, il tient, n. tenons, v. tenez, ils tiennent**; *impf* **je tenais**; *p hist* **je tins, n. tînmes, v. tîntes, ils tinrent**; *pr sub* **je tinsse, il tînt, n. tinssions**; *fu* **je tiendrai**) **1** *vt* **(a)** to hold; **t. qch à la main/sur ses genoux** to hold sth in one's hand/in one's lap; **t. qn par la taille** to hold sb round the waist; **il me tenait par le cou/les épaules** he had his arm round my neck/shoulders; *F* **t. un bon rhume** to have a stinking cold; *F* **en t. une** (*être ivre*) to be smashed; *F* **en t. une couche** (*être bête*) to be thick as two short planks; *F* **qu'est-ce qu'il tient!** (*il est ivre*) he's smashed!; (*il est idiot*) what a pillock!; **je tiens mon homme** I've got my man; **t. la solution** to have the solution; *Prov* **un 'tiens' vaut mieux que deux 'tu l'auras', mieux vaut t. que courir** a bird in the hand is worth two in the bush; **tiens!, tenez!** look!, look here!; **tiens, le voilà qui arrive** there he is now; **tiens, voilà Paul!** there's Paul!; **tenez, mon chien à**

moi ... my dog ...; **tenez, c'est ce que me disait encore hier mon médecin** that's just what my doctor was saying to me yesterday; **tenez!** (*ceci est pour vous*) here you are!; **tenez, voilà ce que vous cherchez** here's what you're looking for; **tenez, ôtez-moi cela** here, take this away; **tiens, ça ne m'étonne pas** well, that doesn't surprise me; **tiens, ce n'est pas ce qu'il m'avait dit** that's not what he said to me; *Fin* **t. à bail** to hold a lease on

(**b**) (*contenir*) to hold (*espace*) to take up; **baril qui tient l'eau** barrel that holds water *or* that is watertight; **t. le coup** to hold out

(**c**) **t. qch de** (*le recevoir*) to have *or* get sth from; **j'en suis sûr, je le tiens de mon médecin** I'm sure of it, I have it from my doctor *or* my doctor told me; **de qui peut-il t. cela?** who did he get that from?, who told him that?; **il tient sa timidité de sa mère** he gets his shyness from his mother

(**d**) (*stocker*) (*marchandises etc*) to keep, to stock

(**e**) (*gérer, être responsable de*) (*boutique, hôtel, école etc*) to keep, to run; (*caisse*) to be in charge of; **Mlle Martin tenait le piano** Miss Martin was at the piano; **t. conseil** *ou* **séance** to meet, to have a meeting; *Fig Hum* **elle tient conseil dans sa boutique** she holds court in her shop; **t. une réunion** to hold a meeting

(**f**) (*parole, promesse*) to keep; **t. un rôle difficile/important** to have a difficult/important role; **j'ignore quel rôle il a pu t. dans cette affaire** I don't know what his role was *or* what role he played in the business

(**g**) (*dire*) (*discours etc*) to deliver; **t. des propos ambigus** to be ambiguous, to speak ambiguously; **il tient toujours les propos les plus absurdes** he always talks absolute nonsense

(**h**) **t. qn en mépris/en grand respect** to hold sb in contempt/in great esteem

(**i**) (*maîtriser*) to restrain; (*enfants, cheval*) to control; **t. sa langue** to hold one's tongue; **t. son sérieux** to keep a straight face; **t. qn par le chantage/la pitié** to use blackmail/pity to control sb

(**j**) (*dans une certaine position*) to hold, to keep; (*dans un certain état*) to keep; **cette poutre tient le plafond** that beam holds up the ceiling; **c'est cette colonne qui tient tout le poids** this column takes *or* bears the entire weight; **mon rhume me tient à la maison** my cold is keeping me indoors; **t. son chien en laisse** to keep one's dog on a lead; **il nous a tenus debout pendant deux heures** he kept us standing for two hours; **t. les yeux fermés** to keep one's eyes shut; **t. qch secret** to keep sth (a) secret; **t. qn captif** to keep *or* hold sb prisoner; **t. qch en (bon) état** to keep sth in good condition, to look after sth; **tenez votre gauche/droite** keep to the left/right

(**k**) (*ne pas pouvoir sortir de*) (*chambre, lit*) to be confined to, to keep to

(**l**) **t. la mer** (*d'un bateau*) to keep the sea; (*d'une nation*) to rule the seas; **capable/incapable de t. la mer** (*bateau*) seaworthy/unseaworthy; *Aut* **t. la route** to hold the road; **t. son cap** to keep to *or* hold one's course

(**m**) (*occuper*) (*espace*) to take up, to occupy; **vous tenez trop de place** you're taking up too much room; **la table tient la moitié de la pièce** the table occupies *or* takes up half the room; **t. toute la route** (*d'une voiture, d'un conducteur*) to hog the road; **les soucis/enfants tiennent trop de place dans ta vie** worries/children take up *or* occupy too much of your life; **le cinéma tient une grande place dans leur vie** cinema plays a large part in their life

(**n**) (*considérer*) **t. qn pour habile** to think sb clever; *Litt* **t. qn comme qch** to consider sb sth; **je vous tiens pour responsable de ce retard** I hold you responsible for the delay; **je le tiens pour vrai** I regard it as (being) true; **tenez cela pour fait** consider it done

2 *vi* (**a**) (*d'un nœud, d'une corde etc*) to hold; (*d'une construction instable etc*) to hold up, to stay up; (*d'une alliance, un projet*) to last; **la corde n'a pas tenu** the rope gave way; **le pansement ne tient pas** the dressing won't stay on; **la colle ne tient pas** the glue's not sticking; **clou qui tient bien** nail that holds well; **ça tient au mur par des clous** it's fixed to the wall with nails; **les manches tiennent par des petites épingles** the sleeves are held together by pins; *Fig* **leur vie ne tient qu'à un fil** their lives are hanging by a thread; *F* **il ne tient plus sur ses jambes, il ne tient plus debout** he's ready to drop (with fatigue), he's dead on his feet; **elle ne pouvait t. en place** she couldn't keep still

(**b**) (*border*) **sa terre tient à la mienne** his estate borders on *or* adjoins mine

(**c**) (*résister*) **t. (bon** *ou* **ferme)** to hold out, to stand fast *or* firm; (*d'un câble etc*) to stand the strain, to hold; **tenez bon** *ou* **ferme!** hold *or* hang on!; *Fig* hang in there!; *Fig* **il faut t. bon** you'll/we'll/*etc* have to hang in there; **t. bon contre une attaque/des difficultés** to stand firm in the face of an attack/difficulties; **je n'ai pas pu t. une heure** I couldn't stick it out *or* hold out for an hour; **t. debout** (*d'un argument*) to stand up, to hold water; **votre argument ne tient guère** your argument hardly stands up *or* doesn't hold much water; **je n'y tiens plus** I can't stand *or* take it any longer, I can't take any more of this; **n'y tenant plus, elle a tout avoué** unable to stand *or* take it any longer, she confessed everything

(**d**) (*durer*) (*d'un commerce, le vent, l'amour etc*) to last; **ma mise en plis n'a pas tenu deux jours** my set didn't stay in *or* last two days; *Tex* **couleur qui tient bien** fast colour; **mon offre/mon invitation/le pari tient toujours** my offer/my invitation/the bet still stands; **ça tient toujours pour dimanche?** is it still on for Sunday?

(**e**) (*être contenu*) **voiture où l'on tient à six** car that takes *or* holds six; **on devrait t. à six dans la voiture** there should be room for six of us in the car; **on tient à dix autour de cette table** the table seats ten; **tous ces livres tiendront dans cette caisse** all these books will easily fit *or* go into this box; **ça ne tiendra pas, c'est sûr** it won't go in *or* fit, that's for sure; **tout ça tient en deux mots** all that can be said *or* it can all be put in a couple of words; **son œuvre tient en peu de livres** his work consists of a few books; **ma conclusion tiendra en trois mots** my conclusion can be summed up in three words

(**f**) *Vieilli* **t. pour qch/qn** (*être partisan de*) to be for, to be in favour *or US* favor of sth/sb

(**g**) **t. à** (*aimer*) (*liberté, amitié etc*) to value, to prize; (*ami, vase, bague, lieu*) to be fond of; **t. à la vie** to value one's life, to care about living; **cette idée me tient à cœur** the idea is close *or* dear to my heart, I am keen on the idea; **cela nous tenait à cœur** we were keen on it; **t. à faire qch** to be anxious *or* keen to do sth; **je tiens à vous le dire** I am anxious to tell you, I am making a point of telling you; **t. à ce qu'on fasse qch** to be anxious that sth should be done; **je tiens beaucoup à ce qu'il vienne** I am very anxious that he should come *or* for him to come, I very much want him to come; **je tiens à ce que tu le rencontres** I want you *or* I'm keen for you to meet him; **je tiens à ce que tout soit rangé quand je rentre** I want everything to be tidy when I get back; **il faut que ce soit fini demain, j'y tiens** it must be finished tomorrow, I insist on it; **tu en veux? – je n'y tiens pas** do you want some? – not particularly *or* I'm not bothered; **tu veux le voir? – je n'y tiens pas du tout/particulièrement** do you want to see him? – not in the slightest/particularly; *F* **je n'y tiens pas plus que cela** I'm not all that keen on it; **puisque vous y tenez** since you're set *or* keen on it

(**h**) **t. à** (*venir de*) to be the result of, to be due to; **cela tient à son éducation** that's the result of *or* that's due to his education; **à quoi cela tient-il?** what's the reason for it?, what is it due to?; **cela tient à ce que vous êtes écossais** that comes of your being Scottish, that's because you're Scottish

(**i**) **t. de** (*ressembler à*) (*qn*) to take after; **cela tient du miracle/du délire/du génie** it's miraculous/mad/ingenious; **tu as vu les prix? – cela tient de la folie!** have you seen the prices? – it's sheer madness!; **cela tient de (la) famille** it runs in the family; **il a de qui t.** it runs in his family; **entre son oncle et son père il a de qui t.!** it's not surprising when you consider his uncle and his father!

3 *v impers* **il ne tient qu'à vous de le faire** it is entirely up to you whether you do it or not; **il ne tient qu'à vous que cela se fasse** it depends entirely on you whether it is done; **s'il ne tenait qu'à moi** if it was just up to me; **qu'à cela ne tienne** never mind, that's not a problem; **s'il ne tient qu'à cela** if that's all, if that's the only problem; **il n'a tenu à rien qu'il ne se noyât** he was within a hair's breadth of drowning

4 se tenir *vpr* (**a**) (*dans un certain état ou lieu, dans une certaine position*) to stay, to remain; **se t. au chaud** to stay *or* keep warm; **tenez-vous là** stay where you are!, don't move!; **tenez-vous droit** (*assis*) sit up straight, sit up; (*debout*) stand up straight; **bien se t.** (*sur sa chaise*) to sit properly; **se t. debout** to be standing, to stand; **se t. auprès de qn** to be standing next to sb; **elle s'est tenue auprès de lui jusqu'à sa dernière heure** she stayed with him till the last

(**b**) (*se comporter*) to behave; **se t. tranquille** to keep quiet; **bien se t.** (*en société, dans un lieu public*) to behave (well); **tiens-toi bien chez ta grand-mère!** behave yourself at your grandmother's!; **il se tient mal à table** he has no table manners; **tu n'as qu'à bien te t.!** you should learn to behave yourself!

(**c**) **tenez-vous bien, la voiture a disparu** prepare yourself for a shock *or* brace yourself, the car has disappeared; **et alors, tiens-toi bien, il n'était pas là non plus!** well, you won't believe it, but he wasn't there either!

(d) se t. (à qch) to hold on (to sth); **tenez-vous bien!** (*dans un autobus etc*) hold tight!; **ils se tenaient par la main** they were holding hands; **ils se tenaient par la taille/les épaules** they had their arms round each other's waist/shoulders; **se t. les côtes de rire** to hold one's sides laughing

(e) (*d'un récit, une histoire*) to hang together; **la boisson, la misère, le crime, tout cela se tient** drink, poverty, crime, all these go together; **tous ces problèmes se tiennent** all these problems are interrelated; **ses arguments se tiennent (bien)** his arguments stand up *or* hold water

(f) (*se retenir*) **je ne pouvais me t. de rire** I couldn't help laughing

(g) s'en t. à (*se borner à*) (*plaisanteries, généralités, sujets etc*) to confine oneself to, to keep to; (*décision, traité, consignes*) to adhere to, to abide by; (*budget, prix*) to stick to; **s'en t. à ce qu'on a décidé** to stick to *or* abide by what was decided; **je préfère m'en t. là pour aujourd'hui** I prefer to stop there for today; **il ne s'en tint pas là** he didn't stop there *or* at that; **j'espère qu'il ne va pas s'en t. là, qu'il va m'offrir autre chose encore** I hope he'll offer me something else and not stick at that; **tenons-nous-en là** let it go at that; **je ne sais pas à quoi m'en t.** I don't know what to believe

(h) (*avoir lieu*) to be held, to take place

(i) tiens-le-toi pour dit! (*avertissement*) I'm telling you once and for all *or* for the last time!

(j) se t. pour satisfait/content to be satisfied/content

tennis [tenis] **1** *nm* **(a)** (*sport*) tennis; **jouer au t.** to play tennis; **t. de table** table tennis **(b) (court de) t.** tennis court **2** *nf ou m* (*chaussure*) tennis shoe

tennisman [tenisman], *pl* **tennismen** [tenismɛn] *nm* tennis player

tenon [tənɔ̃] *nm* **(a)** *Menuis* tenon **(b)** (*d'une couronne dentaire*) pivot

ténor [tenɔr] **1** *nm* **(a)** *Mus* tenor **(b)** *Pol, Sp etc* star (performer) **2** *adj Mus* **saxophone t.** tenor saxophone

tenseur [tɑ̃sœr] **1** *adj Anat* **muscle t.** tensor **2** *nm* **(a)** *Anat* tensor **(b)** *Math* tensor **(c)** *Tech* = **tendeur**

tensioactif, -ive [tɑ̃sjoaktif, -iv] *Ch* **1** *adj* (*agent*) surface-active, wetting **2** *nm* surface-active *or* wetting agent, surfactant

tension [tɑ̃sjɔ̃] *nf* **(a)** (*des muscles, d'une corde de violon, Fig entre personnes etc*) tension; **écrou à t.** tightening nut; *Tech* **t. de courroie** belt tension; **acier à haute t.** high-tensile steel; **t. intellectuelle** mental stress; **état de t. nerveuse** state of nervous tension; **la guerre nous met sous t.** the war is putting us under stress *or* strain

(b) (*de vapeur etc*) pressure; *Méd F* **avoir** *ou* **faire de la t.** to suffer from *or* have high blood pressure; **prendre la t. de qn** to take sb's blood pressure

(c) *Él, Électron* voltage, tension; **basse/haute t.** low/high voltage *or* tension; **t. nulle** zero voltage *or* potential; **t. de 2 000 volts** tension of 2,000 volts; **sans t.** dead; **t. du secteur** supply *or* mains voltage; **t. nominale** nominal voltage; **être sous t.** to be switched on, to be powered up; **mettre sous t.** (*circuit*) to apply the voltage to, to switch on; (*imprimante etc*) to switch on; **fil sous t.** live *or* charged wire; **montage de piles en t.** connection of batteries in series

▶ **tension**: *Méd* **t. artérielle** blood pressure; **t. de cisaillement** shear stress; **t. de rupture** breaking strain *or* stress; *Phys* **t. superficielle** surface tension

tensoriel, -ielle [tɑ̃sɔrjɛl] *adj Math* tensorial

tentaculaire [tɑ̃takylɛr] *adj Zool* tentacular; *Fig* (*ville*) sprawling; (*société, organisme*) octopus-like

tentacule [tɑ̃takyl] *nm Zool, Fig* tentacle

tentant [tɑ̃tɑ̃] *adj* (*offre, proposition, situation etc*) tempting, attractive; (*repas, plat etc*) tempting, enticing

tentateur, -trice [tɑ̃tatœr, -tris] **1** *adj* tempting **2** *nm* tempter; *Rel* **le T.** the Tempter **3** *nf* **tentatrice** temptress

tentation [tɑ̃tasjɔ̃] *nf* temptation **(de faire qch** to do sth); **succomber à la t.** to give in to *or* to succumb to temptation; **je n'ai pas pu résister à la t. de lui faire la grimace** I couldn't resist the temptation to make a face at him; **ne cède pas à la t. de l'humilier en public** don't give in to temptation and humiliate him in public; **et si vous aviez la t. de nous rejoindre …** and if you felt tempted to join us …

tentative [tɑ̃tativ] *nf* attempt, endeavour, *US* endeavor, bid; **t. d'évasion** attempt to escape, escape bid; **t. de suicide** suicide attempt *or* bid, attempted suicide; **faire une nouvelle t. de suicide** to make another suicide attempt; **t. d'assassinat** murder attempt, attempted murder; **il a été accusé de t. d'assassinat** he has been charged with attempted murder; **t. de résistance** attempt to resist; **faire une t. de conciliation** to make an attempt at reconciliation, to attempt reconciliation

tente [tɑ̃t] *nf* **(a)** tent; **coucher sous la t.** to sleep under canvas; *Fig* **se retirer dans** *ou* **sous sa t.** to sulk in one's corner **(b)** *Naut* awning

▶ **tente**: **t. conique** bell tent; **t. igloo** igloo tent; *Méd* **t. à oxygène** oxygen tent

tenter [tɑ̃te] *vt* **(a)** *Bible, Arch* (*éprouver*) to tempt; *Fig* **t. le diable** to tempt fate; **t. la Providence** to tempt Providence

(b) t. sa chance to try one's luck; *F* **t. le coup** to give it *or* have a try *or* go

(c) (*faire envie à, séduire*) (*qn*) to tempt; **cela m'a toujours tenté de partir là-bas** I've always been tempted to go there; **se laisser t.** to let oneself be tempted, to yield to temptation; **tu devrais te laisser t., laisse-toi t.** be a devil; **j'ai envie de me laisser t.** I'm tempted to say yes; **je serais tenté de croire qu'il est responsable, lui aussi** I'm tempted to believe that he is responsible too; **je dois dire que je suis très tenté** I'm very tempted *or* it's very tempting I must say

(d) (*essayer*) to try, to attempt; **t. d'inutiles efforts pour …** to make useless attempts to …; **t. une expérience** to try an experiment; **il faut tout t. pour le convaincre** we must try everything to convince him; **t. de faire qch** to try *or* attempt to do sth; **t. de se suicider** to attempt (to commit) suicide, to try to commit suicide, to make a suicide attempt; **t. le tout pour le tout** to go for broke

tenture [tɑ̃tyr] *nf* **(a)** (*tapisserie*) hanging; (*de porte*) curtain; (*de cérémonie funèbre*) funeral drape **(b)** (*ensemble de tapisseries*) hangings

tenu [təny] **1** *adj* **(a) bien t.** (*maison, cahier de devoirs, registres, comptes etc*) well kept, tidy; (*jardin etc*) neat, trim; (*enfant*) neatly turned out; **mal t.** (*enfant, jardin etc*) neglected, uncared for; (*maison, cahier de devoirs, registres, comptes etc*) badly kept, untidy **(b) être t. de** *ou* **à faire qch** to be obliged to do sth; **les passants sont tenus de marcher sur le trottoir** pedestrians must walk on the pavement; **le médecin est t. au secret professionnel** the doctor is bound by professional secrecy **(c)** *Bourse* (*prix*) firm, hard **(d)** (*pari*) **t.!** done!, you're on! **(e)** *Mus* (*note*) held **2** *nm Fb, Boxe* holding

ténu [teny] *adj* (*fil, particule etc*) fine; (*brume*) fine, light; (*voix*) thin, reedy; (*nuance*) subtle, fine; (*lien*) tenuous; (*espoir*) slender, slight, slim

tenue [təny] *nf* **(a)** (*d'une assemblée etc*) sitting, session; **pendant la t. du conseil/des assises** during the council meeting/the assizes; **t. d'une réunion** holding a meeting

(b) (*d'une boutique, d'un hôtel, d'une maison etc*) keeping, running; **s'occuper de la t. de la maison** to look after (the running of) the house

(c) (*conduite*) (good) behaviour *or, US* behavior; **Paul, de la t.!** Paul, behave yourself!; **un peu de t.!** (mind your) manners!; **elle manque de t.** she lacks (good) manners, she doesn't know how to behave; **la haute t. de ce périodique** the high standard maintained by this periodical

(d) (*maintien*) posture; *Équitation* **bonne/mauvaise t.** good/poor seat

(e) (*habillement*) dress, clothes; **changer de t.** to change (one's clothes); **mettre une autre t.** to put on something else; **quelle t.!** what an outfit!; **se mettre en t. de soirée** to wear evening dress; **en grande t.** all dressed up; *Mil* in dress uniform; **t. de loisirs** *ou* **de tous les jours** casual clothes *or* dress; *Mil etc* **en t.** in uniform; **en t. légère** (*vêtu de façon sommaire*) scantily dressed; (*en vêtements d'été*) in light clothing; **dans une t. débraillée** slovenly dressed; *F* **je vais me mettre en t.** I'm going to change; *F* **en petite t.** scantily dressed

(f) *Mus* holding *or* sustained note

(g) *Bourse* (*des prix*) steadiness, firmness; (*du marché*) tone; **t. de la Bourse** state of the market

▶ **tenue**: *Av* **t. en l'air, t. aéronautique** behaviour in the air; *Compta* **t. de caisse** petty cash management; *Tech* **t. des chaudières** care of the boilers; *Mil etc* **t. civile** plain clothes, civilian clothes, *F* civvies; *Mil* **t. de combat** battledress; **t. des comptes** book-keeping; **il est responsable de la t. des comptes** he's responsible for (keeping) the accounts; *Aut* **t. en côte** climbing ability; *Compta* **t. des livres** book-keeping; *Aut* **t. de route** road-holding (qualities); **t. de soirée** evening dress; *Mil* mess dress; **t. des stocks** stock keeping; **t. de ville** (*de femme*) town clothes; (*d'homme*) lounge suit; (*sur invitation*) semi-formal; **elle était en t. de ville** she was dressed for going out; *Av* **t. en vol** attitude of flight

ténuité [tenɥite] *nf* (*d'un fil, d'une particule etc*) fineness; (*d'une nuance*) subtlety, fineness

tenure [tənyr] *nf Hist, Jur* tenure; (*terre*) holding

TEP [teəpe] *nm* (*abrév* **terminal électronique de paiement**) electronic payment terminal, *F* PDQ

tep [teəpe] *nm inv* (*abrév* **tonne-équivalent-pétrole**) TOE

tequila [tekila] *nf* tequila
ter [tɛr] **1** *adv Mus* ter **2** *adj* **numéro 5 t.** (*adresse*) No. 5c
tératogène [teratɔʒɛn] *adj Méd* teratogenic
tératologie [teratɔlɔʒi] *nf* teratology
terbium [tɛrbjɔm] *nm Ch* terbium
tercet [tɛrsɛ] *nm Littér* tercet, triplet
térébenthine [terebɑ̃tin] *nf* turpentine
térébinthe [terebɛ̃t] *nm Bot* terebinth, turpentine tree
térébrant [terebrɑ̃] *adj* **(a)** (*insecte etc*) boring, *Spéc* terebrant **(b)** *Méd* (*douleur*) piercing; (*ulcération*) deep
tergal [tɛrgal] *nm Tex* Terylene®, *Am* Dacron®; **robe en t.** Terylene *or* Dacron dress
tergiversations [tɛrʒivɛrsasjɔ̃] *nfpl* beating about the bush, evasiveness, *Fml* equivocation; **après bien des t.** after a great deal of beating about the bush; **assez de t.!** stop beating about the bush *or* being evasive!
tergiverser [tɛrʒivɛrse] *vi* to beat about the bush, to be evasive, to equivocate; **cessons de t.** let's stop beating about the bush
terme¹ [tɛrm] *nm* **(a)** (*fin*) (*d'un voyage, un règne etc*) end; **au t. de sa vie** at the end of his life; **toucher à son t.** (*d'un projet*) to be near completion; (*d'une période*) to be nearing an end *or* drawing to a close; **quel est le t. de son mandat?** when does his mandate end?; **mettre un t. à qch** to put an end *or* a stop to sth; **il y a t. à tout** there is an end to everything; **mener qch à bon t.** to bring sth to a successful conclusion, to carry sth through

(b) (*date limite*) time (limit), date; **être à t.** (*d'une femme enceinte*) to have reached term; **avant t.** (*accoucher*) prematurely; (*accouchement*) premature; **elle a dépassé le t. de deux semaines** she's two weeks overdue, she's two weeks past her due date; **dans le t. de trois mois** within three months; **t. de rigueur** latest time *or* date; *Bourse* **le t.** the settlement; **marché à t.** forward futures *or* market; **valeurs à t.** securities dealt in for the account; **acheter à t.** *Com* to buy on credit; *Bourse* to buy for the settlement *or* for the account; **à court/long t.** (*projet, engagement, contrat, avance etc*) short-/long-term; (*prévisions*) short-/long-term *or* -range; *Fin* (*factures*) short-/long-dated; *Fin* **argent à court t.** money at short notice *or* at call; **s'améliorer à court/moyen/long t.** to improve in the short/medium/long term; **voir les choses à long/court t.** to see things in the long/short term, to take a long-/short-term view (of things); **il faut prévoir à long t.** you have to look to the long term; *Fin* **à t. échu** on the due date; **à t. fixe** fixed-term

(c) *Jur* **demander un t. de grâce** (*délai*) to ask for time to pay

(d) (*versement*) instalment, *US* installment; **payable en deux termes** payable in two instalments

(e) (*loyer*) rent; (*jour*) rent day; (*période*) rental period; **j'ai un t. en retard** I'm one payment behind (with my rent)

terme² *nm* **(a)** (*mot*) term; **t. de métier, t. technique** technical term; **t. de médecine/de droit** medical/legal term; **employer les termes propres** to use the correct terms; **en d'autres termes** in other words; **pour le dire en d'autres termes** to put it another way; **il ne le disait pas en ces termes, mais ...** he didn't put it in quite those terms *or* words but ...; **elle n'a pas ménagé ses termes** she didn't mince her words; **il m'a parlé de vous en très bons termes** he spoke very well *or* favourably *or* *US* favorably of you; *Math* **t. d'une progression** term of a progression; **termes d'une équation** terms of an equation

(b) termes (*de contrat etc*) terms, terms and conditions

(c) termes (*relations*) terms; **être en bons/mauvais termes avec qn** to be on good *or* friendly/bad terms with sb; **en quels termes l'a-t-il quittée?** what terms were they on when he left her?; **en quels termes étiez-vous?** how did you get on?

▶ **terme**: **t. de bail** term of lease; **termes commerciaux** commercial terms; **termes commerciaux internationaux** incoterms; **termes d'échange** terms of exchange; *Écon* **termes de l'échange** terms of trade; **t. d'échéance** (*d'un effet etc*) maturity date; *Compta* **t. de liquidation** account *or* settlement period; **t. de livraison** delivery deadline; **termes de paiement** terms of payment; **t. de préavis** notice period; **t. de rigueur** deadline

terminaison [tɛrminɛzɔ̃] *nf* **(a)** *Gram* ending; **t. en 'ion'** ending in 'ion' **(b)** (*action*) *Jur* (*de procès*) termination **(c)** *Anat* **t. nerveuse** nerve ending

terminal, -ale, -aux, -ales [tɛrminal, -o] **1** *adj* final; (*à l'extrémité de qch*) terminal; *Méd* (*phase*) terminal; *Méd* **cancer en phase terminale** terminal cancer **être en phase terminale** (*de malade*) to be terminally ill; **le projet est dans sa phase terminale** the project is in its final stages; *Scol* **classe terminale** final year, *Br* ≈ upper sixth (form), *Am* ≈ twelfth grade; *Ordinat* **marque terminale** end mark

2 *nm* **(a)** *Ordinat* terminal, VDU

(b) *Pétr* (pipeline) terminal

(c) *Av* (*gare*) (air) terminal, terminal (building); **t. d'aérogare** air terminal; **t. urbain** (*d'une ligne aérienne*) city terminal

3 *nf Scol* **terminale = classe terminale**

▶ **terminal**: **t. de consultation** look-up terminal; *Com* **t. électronique de paiement** electronic payment terminal, *F* PDQ; **t. éloigné** remote terminal; **t. intelligent** smart terminal; **t. (informatique) interactif** interactive terminal; **t. maritime** shipping terminal; *Banque* **t. monétique** cash point, cash dispenser; *Com* **t. de paiement en ligne** on-line cash desk terminal; **t. passif** dumb terminal; **t. de pilotage** control terminal; **t. point de vente** point-of-sale terminal

terminateur [tɛrminatœr] *Ordinat nm* terminator
terminer [tɛrmine] **1** *vt* (*guerre, discours, lettre, repas, réunion etc*) to end, to finish (**par** with); (*affaire*) to end, to settle, to conclude; (*travail*) to complete, to finish (off); **t. ses jours quelque part** to end one's days somewhere; **la phrase qui termine le poème** the phrase that ends the poem; **il faut en t.** we must end *or* finish; **il faut que j'en termine avec cette histoire** I have to put an end to this; *Télécom* **t. une session** to log off, to log out

2 *vi* to end, to finish; **t. court** to end abruptly, to come to an abrupt ending; *Rad* **terminé!** out!

3 se terminer *vpr* (*d'une soirée, d'un concert, des vacances etc*) to end (**par** with); (*d'une rue, d'un mot etc*) to end (**par** in); **l'automne se termine** autumn is coming to an end *or* a close; **la guerre venait de se t.** the war was just over *or* had just ended; **la veste se termine en pointe** the jacket ends in *or* comes to a point; **l'année s'est terminée en beauté** the year ended with a flourish

terminologie [tɛrminɔlɔʒi] *nf* terminology
terminologue [tɛrminɔlɔg] *n* terminologist
terminus [tɛrminys] **1** *nm* (*de train, de l'autobus etc*) terminus; **t., tout le monde descend!** all change! **2** *adj inv* **gare t.** terminus
termite [tɛrmit] *nm Ent* termite, white ant; *Fig* **faire un travail de t.** to work secretly and destructively
termitière [tɛrmitjɛr] *nf Ent* termite nest, termitarium
ternaire [tɛrnɛr] *adj Math, Ch* ternary; *Mus* **mesure t.** triple time
terne [tɛrn] *adj* (*personne, conversation, histoire, soirée, année, teint, métal*) dull; (*personnalité*) colourless; (*vêtements, existence*) dull, drab; (*yeux*) dull, lifeless, lacklustre; (*voix*) dull, flat; (*style*) dull, flat, colourless
ternir [tɛrnir] **1** *vt* (*métal, Fig réputation, honneur, mémoire*) to tarnish; **la poussière qui ternit le mobilier** the dust that dulls the furniture **2 se ternir** *vpr* (*de métal, Fig d'une réputation, d'une mémoire*) to become tarnished
ternissure [tɛrnisyr] *nf* (*aspect*) (*du métal*) tarnished appearance; (*tache*) tarnished spot
terrafungine [tɛrafɔ̃ʒin] *nf Pharm* oxytetracycline, Terramycin®
terrain [tɛrɛ̃] *nm* **(a)** (*étendue*) land; **un t.** a piece *or* plot of land

(b) *Géog etc* ground, terrain; **relief du t.** relief

(c) (*sol*) soil, ground; **t. gras** rich soil

(d) (*destiné à une activité*) *Fb, Rugby* pitch, field; *Golf* course; *Mil* terrain; **aller sur le t.** (*se battre en duel*) to fight a duel; *Ind etc, Fig* **sur le t.** (*travailler, étudier, essayer*) in the field; (*ingénieur, étude, essais*) field; **travaux sur le t.** fieldwork, work in the field; **rester sur le t.** to be killed (*in a duel*); *Fig* (*être battu*) to be defeated; *Mil etc, Fig* **gagner du t.** to gain ground; *Mil etc, Fig* **perdre/céder du t.** to lose/give ground; *Fig* **sonder** *ou* **tâter le t.** to see how the land lies; *Fig* **être sur son t.** to be on familiar territory *or* home ground; *Fig* **je ne suis plus sur mon t.** I'm out of my depth; **homme de t.** man with practical experience; *Fig* **préparer le t.** to prepare the ground, to pave the way

(e) *Méd* = predisposition to a disease, *Spéc* diathesis; **il y a un t. propice aux angines chez ce patient** the patient is a candidate for angina

(f) *Géol* (rock) formation

▶ **terrain**: **t. d'atterrissage** landing strip, airstrip; *Av* **t. d'aviation** airfield; **t. à bâtir** development site; **terrains à bâtir** development sites, building land; **t. de camping** campsite; **t. de camping-caravaning** camping and caravan site; *Fig* **t. d'entente** common ground; **chercher un t. d'entente** to look for (some) common ground; **t. de jeu** (*pour les sports*) recreation ground, *Br* playing field; (*pour les enfants*) playground; *Mil* **t. de manœuvres** drill *or* parade ground; **t. de sport** sports ground; **t. vague** waste ground; **entouré de terrains vagues** surrounded by waste ground

terrarium [terarjɔm] *nm* terrarium
terrasse [teras] *nf* **(a)** (*levée de terre*) terrace; **jardin en t.**

terraced garden; **cultures en terrasses** terrace cultivation **(b)** (*de café*) **nous étions assis à la t.** we were sitting outside (the café); **les clients en t.** the customers sitting outside; **prix des consommations en t.** price of drinks served outside **(c)** (*de maison, appartement*) terrace; **(toit en) t.** terrace (roof), flat roof

terrassement [tɛrasmɑ̃] *nm* **(a)** (*action*) (*de terre*) banking, digging **(b)** (*remblai*) earthwork, embankment

terrasser [tɛrase] *vt* **(a)** *Agr* (*vignoble etc*) to work the soil of **(b)** (*abattre*) (*adversaire*) to floor, to fell; *Fig* (*d'une émotion, de la fatigue, d'une nouvelle etc*) to overwhelm, to overcome; (*d'une maladie*) to lay low; **terrassé par le chagrin** prostrate *or* overcome with grief; **terrassé par une crise cardiaque** felled by a heart attack

terrassier [tɛrasje] *nm Constr* labourer, *US* laborer, *Br F* navvy

terre [tɛr] *nf* **(a)** (*monde*) world; **la T.** (*planète*) (the) Earth; **la vie sur t.** life on earth; **être encore sur t.** to be still in the land of the living; **elle vient de quitter cette t.** she has just left this world; **revenir sur t.** to come (back) down to earth; **avoir les pieds sur t.** to have one's feet on the ground; **toute la t.** the whole *or* entire world, everybody

(b) (*sol*) ground; (*étendue*) land; **armée de t.** army; **forces de t.** land forces; **pénétrer dans les terres** to go inland; **village dans les terres** inland village; **basses terres** lowlands; **hautes terres** highlands; **tremblement de t.** earthquake; *Av* **toucher t.** to touch down, to land; *Fig* **j'ai eu l'impression de ne pas toucher t. depuis deux mois** I feel as if I've been walking on air for two months; **à t., par t.** on the ground; **frapper qn à t.** to strike sb when he is down; **tomber par t., tomber à t.** to fall down; **tout ce que tu tiens dans les mains va tomber par t.** you're going to drop everything you're carrying; *F* **ça va tout ficher** *ou très F* **foutre par t.** that'll mess *or F* screw everything up; **attaquer une ville par t. et par mer** to attack a town by land and sea; **tactique** *ou* **politique de la t. brûlée** scorched earth policy; **appuyer son oreille contre t.** to put one's ear to the ground; **sous t.** (*ville*) underground; **des galeries creusées sous t.** tunnels dug under the ground; **être sous t.** *ou* **en t.** *ou* **à six pieds sous t.** to be in one's grave, *F* to be six feet under, to be dead and buried

(c) *Él* earth, *Am* ground; **mettre** *ou* **relier** *ou* **raccorder à la t.** (*appareil, prise*) to earth, *Am* to ground

(d) (*opposé à mer*) land; **mettre qn à t.** to land sb, to put sb ashore; **descendre à t.** to land, to go ashore; **perdre t.** to lose sight of land; **t. (en vue)!** land ho!; **être à t.** (*d'un navire*) to be aground *or* ashore

(e) t. à t. (*personne*) matter-of-fact, down-to-earth; (*décision, mesures*) practical, down-to-earth; (*préoccupations*) mundane

(f) *Agr* (*matière*) soil, earth; **cultiver la t.** to cultivate the soil; **faire son retour à la t.** to go back to the land; **en pleine t.** in the open ground; **chemin de t.** dirt track; **hutte de t. séchée** mud hut; **t. grasse** rich soil; **t. végétale** *ou* **franche** humus

(g) (*propriété*) land; **acheter/vendre une t.** to buy/sell land; **avoir des terres** to have land; **vivre de ses terres** to live off one's land

(h) (*territoire*) land, country; **terres étrangères** foreign countries *or* lands; **terres australes** southern lands; **revenir à la t. natale** to return to one's native soil, to return to the land *or* country of one's birth; **la nostalgie de la t. natale** homesickness; **avoir la nostalgie de sa t. natale** to be homesick

(i) (*élément*) earth

(j) (*argile etc*) clay; **pipe en t.** clay pipe; **cruche de** *ou* **en t.** earthenware *or* terracotta jar

▶ **terre**: **t. battue:** *Tennis* **jouer sur t. battue** to play on clay; *Tennis* **jouer bien/mal sur t. battue** to be good/bad on clay, to be a good/bad clay court player; *Tennis* **court en t. battue** clay court; **sol en t. battue** mud floor; **t. de Chine** kaolin; **t. cuite** earthenware, terracotta; *Beaux-Arts* terracotta; *Beaux-Arts* **une t. cuite** a terracotta; **t. ferme** (dry) land, terra firma; (*opposé à l'espace*) earth, terra firma; **la T. de Feu** Tierra del Fuego; **t. d'ombre** umber; **t. de pipe** pipeclay; **t. à poêle** fireclay; **t. à porcelaine** kaolin; **t. à potier** potter's clay; *Ch* **terres rares** rare earths; **la T. Sainte** the Holy Land; **t. de Sienne** sienna

terreau, -eaux [tɛro] *nm* compost

Terre-Neuve **1** *nf* Newfoundland **2** *nm inv* **t.** Newfoundland (dog)

terre-neuvien, -ienne [tɛrnœvjɛ̃, -jɛn], *pl* **terre-neuvien(ne)s** **1** *adj* Newfoundland **2** *n* **T.** Newfoundlander

terre-neuvier, -ière, *pl* **terre-neuviers, -ieres** [tɛrnœvje, -jɛr] **1** *adj* (*pêcheur etc*) Newfoundland **2** *nm* **(a)** (*pêcheur*) Newfoundland fisherman **(b)** (*bateau*) banker, Newfoundland fishing vessel

terre-plein, *pl* **terre-pleins** *nm* **(a)** *Constr* earth platform, raised strip **(b)** *Aut* **t. central** central reservation, *Am* median strip; **t. circulaire** (*dans un rond-point*) central island

terrer [tere] **1** *vt* **(a)** (*arbre, plante*) to earth up **(b)** (*couvrir de terre*) to spread earth over **2 se terrer** *vpr* (*d'un animal*) to go to earth; *Mil* to entrench oneself, to dig oneself in; *Fig* to go to earth, to hole up; **être terré dans** (*d'un animal*) to have gone to earth in; *Mil* to be entrenched in; *Fig* to have gone to earth in, to be holed up in

terrestre [tɛrɛstr] *adj* **(a)** (*plante*) ground; (*animal*) land; **transports terrestres** surface transport; *Mil* **effectifs terrestres** land forces **(b)** (*magnétisme, attraction*) of the earth; **la croûte t.** the earth's crust **(c)** *Fig* (*pensées*) worldly; (*plaisirs*) earthly, worldly; **paradis t.** earthly paradise; **c'est un vrai paradis t.** it's heaven on earth

terreur [tɛrœr] *nf* **(a)** (*effroi*) terror, dread; **fou de t.** wild with fear; **glacé de t.** terror-stricken; **vivre dans la t.** to be terrified *or* in (a state of) terror **(b)** (*emploi de la violence etc*) terror; **gouverner par la t.** to rule by terror; **faire régner la t.** to instil terror; **semer la t.** to sow terror; **un régime de t.** a reign of terror; *Hist Fr* **la T.** the Terror **(c)** *Fig* (*personne*) (*d'une ville, d'une école etc*) terror; **jouer les terreurs** to play the tough guy

terreux, -euse [tɛrø, -øz] *adj* **(a)** (*goût, odeur*) earthy **(b)** (*mains*) grubby; (*teint, ciel, gris etc*) muddy; (*visage*) sickly; (*laitue*) gritty

terrible [tɛribl] **1** *adj* **(a)** (*catastrophe, accident, blessure etc*) terrible, appalling; (*froid, bruit*) dreadful, terrible; (*orage, chaleur*) terrific, terrible; (*temps, caractère*) awful, terrible; **ce n'est qu'une coupure, rien de t.** it's just a cut, nothing serious *or* major; **d'une humeur t.** in an awful *or* a terrible mood; **il est t. quand il s'énerve** he's awful *or* terrible when he loses his temper; **enfant t.** enfant terrible

(b) *F* (*formidable*) (*personne, film, effet etc*) terrific, great; **ce/il n'est pas t.** it's/he's nothing special; **rien de t.** nothing much, nothing to write home about

(c) (*impossible*) incredible; **vous êtes t.!** you really are the limit!

2 *adv F* **ça marche t.!** it's going great!

terriblement [tɛribləmɑ̃] *adv* (*extrêmement*) (*gêné, égoïste*) terribly, dreadfully, awfully

terrien, -ienne [tɛrjɛ̃, -jɛn] **1** *adj* **(a)** (*propriétaire etc*) landed **(b)** (*rural*) country, rural **(c)** (*de la Terre*) of the Earth **2** *n* **(a)** (*propriétaire*) landowner, landed proprietor **(b)** *Naut* landlubber **(c)** (*paysan*) countryman, *f* countrywoman **(d)** (*habitant de la Terre*) earthling, earthman, *f* earthwoman

terrier[1] [tɛrje] *nm* (*d'un lapin*) burrow, hole; (*d'un taupe*) hole; (*d'un renard*) earth; (*d'un blaireau*) sett

terrier[2], -ière [tɛrje, -jɛr] *n* (*chien*) terrier

terrifiant [tɛrifjɑ̃] *adj* **(a)** (*effrayant*) (*description, situation*) terrifying **(b)** (*extraordinaire*) incredible

terrifier [tɛrifje] *vt* (*impf, pr sub* **n. terrifiions, v. terrifiiez**) to terrify

terril [tɛril] *nm Min* slag heap

terrine [tɛrin] *nf Culin* (*pâté, récipient*) terrine; **t. de canard/de foie de volaille** = duck/chicken-liver pâté

terrir [tɛrir] *vi Pêche* **poissons qui terrissent** fish living in coastal waters

territoire [tɛritwar] *nm* (*d'un état, d'un oiseau, d'un animal*) territory; (*de juge, d'évêque*) jurisdiction; (*de commune, d'arrondissement etc*) area; **marquer son t.** (*d'un animal, Fig d'une personne*) to mark out one's territory; **t. d'outre-mer** overseas territory; **aménagement du t.** regional planning *or* development

territorial, -ale, -aux, -ales [tɛritɔrjal, -o] **1** *adj* (*impôt, eaux*) territorial **2** *nm Hist, Mil* territorial (soldier) **3** *nf Hist Mil* **la territoriale** the territorial army

territorialité [tɛritɔrjalite] *nf* territoriality; (*d'un impôt*) territoriality

terroir [terwar] *nm Agr* soil; **goût de t.** (*d'un vin*) tang of the soil, native tang; **du t.** (*accent, expression*) local

terrorisant [tɛrɔrizɑ̃] *adj* (*expérience, souvenir etc*) terrifying

terroriser [tɛrɔrize] *vt* (*d'une personne*) to terrorize; (*d'une expérience, d'un souvenir*) to terrify

terrorisme [tɛrɔrism] *nm* terrorism; **un acte de t.** an act of terrorism

terroriste [tɛrɔrist] *adj, n* terrorist

tertiaire [tɛrsjɛr] **1** *adj* tertiary; *Écon* **secteur t.** tertiary sector **2** *nm* **(a)** *Écon* tertiary sector **(b)** *Géol* Tertiary **3** *n Cathol* tertiary

tertiairisation [tɛrsjɛrizasjɔ̃] *nf*, **tertiarisation** [tɛrsjarizasjɔ̃] *nf Écon* tertiarization, growth of the tertiary sector *or* service industries; **la t. de l'économie** the tertiarization of the economy

tertio [tɛrsjo] *adv* thirdly

tertre [tɛrtr] *nm* hillock, mound, knoll; *Archéol* **t. funéraire** barrow, tumulus
tes [te] *adj poss voir* **ton**[1]
tessiture [tesityr] *nf Mus* (*de voix*) range, tessitura; (*d'un instrument*) range
tesson [tesɔ̃] *nm* shard; **t. de bouteille** fragment of broken bottle
test [tɛst] *nm* (*examen*), *Méd* test **passer/réussir un t.** to take/pass a test; **c'est le t. de sa bonne foi** it is a test of his good faith; **zone/département/semaine t.** test area/department/week; **pendant une période t.** for a trial period; *Méd, Psy, Scol etc* **méthode des tests** testing method; *Mktg* **t. d'acceptabilité auprès des consommateurs** customer-acceptance test; *Mktg* **t. d'acceptation** acceptance test; **t. d'aptitude professionnelle** aptitude test; **t. d'association** association test; **t. aveugle** blind test; *Mktg* **t. de la bande dessinée** *ou* **de la bulle** balloon test; *Aut* **t. de choc** impact test; **t. comparatif** comparative test; **t. de conformité** compliance test; **tests auprès des consommateurs** consumer testing; *Mktg* **tests d'emballage** package testing; *Mktg* **t. d'enquête** enquiry test; *Mktg* **t. de frustration** balloon test; *Mktg* **t. du lendemain** (day-after) recall test; **t. de marché** market test; (*d'un produit*) test marketing, market test; *Mktg* **t. de média** media test; *Mktg* **t. de mémoire** memory *or* recall test; *Mktg* **tests de nom** name testing; **t. de performance** benchmark *or* performance test; **t. de performance du produit** product performance test; *Mktg* **t. de préférence** preference test; **t. de produit** product test; **tests de produit** product testing; *Mktg* **t. de rappel** recall test; *Mktg* **t. de reconnaissance** recognition test; **t. de Rorschach** Rorschach *or* ink blot test; *Aut* **t. de roulage** road testing; **un t. de roulage** a road test; **t. à sec** dry run; *Mktg* **t. de support** media test; **t. technique** engineering test; *Aut* **t. de tonneaux** roll-over test
Testament [tɛstamɑ̃] *nm Bible* **Ancien/Nouveau T.** Old/New Testament
testament [tɛstamɑ̃] *nm* **(a)** *Jur* will, testament; **absence de t.** intestacy; **ceci est mon t.** this is my last will and testament; **tu ne seras pas dans mon t.** you'll be cut out of my will; **elle l'a mis** *ou* **couché sur son t.** she put him in her will; **mourir sans t.** to die intestate; **léguer qch par t.** to leave sth in one's will, to bequeath sth **(b)** *Fig* (*artistique, politique*) legacy
testamentaire [tɛstamɑ̃tɛr] *adj* **disposition t.** clause *or* provision (of a/the will); **exécuteur/exécutrice t.** executor/executrix; **héritier t.** legal heir, heir as established by a/the will; **succession t.** succession as prescribed by a/the will
testateur [tɛstatœr] *nm Jur* testator
testatrice [tɛstatris] *nf Jur* testatrix
tester[1] [tɛste] *vi Jur* to make one's will
tester[2] *vt* (*élève, produit etc*) to test; *Mktg* to test, to test-market; **t. sur le marché** to test-market; **t. un questionnaire** to pilot a questionnaire; **testé en laboratoire** laboratory-tested
testiculaire [tɛstikylɛr] *adj Anat* testicular
testicule [tɛstikyl] *nm Anat* testicle, *Spéc* testis
testimonial, -ale, -aux, -ales [tɛstimɔnjal, -jo] *adj Jur* **preuve testimoniale** evidence of witnesses
testostérone [tɛstɔsterɔn] *nf Biol, Physiol* testosterone
têt [tɛ] *nm Ch* **t. à gaz** beehive shelf; **t. à rôtir** roasting crucible
tétanie [tetani] *nf Méd* spasms, *Spéc* tetany; **accès de t.** fit of spasm; **avoir un accès de t.** to go into spasm
tétanique [tetanik] *Méd* **1** *adj* tetanic; **malade t.** person with tetanus **2** *n* person with tetanus
tétaniser [tetanize] *Méd* **1** *vt* (*muscle*) to tetanize, to cause tetanus in; *Fig* **tétanisé de peur** paralyzed with fear, petrified; **tétanisé de froid** numb with cold **2 se tétaniser** *vpr* (*d'un muscle*) to become tetanized
tétanos [tetanos, -ɔs] *nm Méd* (*maladie*) tetanus, *F* lockjaw; (*contraction de muscle*) tetanus; **vaccin contre le t.** tetanus vaccine
têtard [tɛtar] *nm* **(a)** *Zool* tadpole **(b)** *Arg* (*enfant*) kid **(c)** (*arbre taillé*) pollard
tête [tɛt] *nf* **(a)** *Anat* head; **de la t. aux pieds** from head to foot, from top to toe; **dépasser qn d'une t.** to be a head taller than sb; **il a une t. de plus que sa mère** he is a head taller than his mother; **t. nue** bare-headed; **vieillard à t. grise** grey-haired old man; **avoir la grosse t.** to have a big head; *Fig F* **une grosse t.** (*intellectuel*) a highbrow, an intellectual; **monstre à deux têtes** two-headed monster; **corps sans t.** headless body; **faire t.** (*d'un animal chassé*) to stand at bay; **faire** *ou* **tenir t. à qn** to stand up to sb; **je t'interdis de me faire** *ou* **tenir t.!** don't you dare defy me!; **faire** *ou* **tenir t. au malheur** to bear up in the face of misfortune; *Naut, Fig* **tenir t. à l'orage** to ride out the storm; **les nuages qui flottent sur nos têtes** the clouds overhead; **endetté par-dessus la t.** up to the eyes in debt; **j'en ai par-dessus la t.** I've had it up to here; **je n'en ai pas encore par dessus la t., mais ça va arriver** I'm not at screaming pitch yet but I soon will be; **la t. en bas** head down(wards), upside down; (*objet*) upside down; **se laisser pendre la t. en bas** to hang upside down; **marcher la t. haute** to walk with (one's) head held high; *Fig* **je peux à nouveau marcher la t. haute** I can hold my head up again; **la t. la première** head first; **tomber sur la t.** to fall and hit one's head; *F* **tu es tombé sur la t.?** have you got a screw loose?; **je ne sais (pas) où donner de la t.** I don't know which way to turn, I don't know whether I'm coming or going; *Fig* **donner t. baissée dans un piège** to rush headlong into a trap; **par t.,** *F* **par t. de pipe** a head; **t. à t.** = **tête-à-tête; je te le jure sur la t. de mes enfants** I swear on my children's lives; **j'en réponds sur ma t.** I'd stake my life on it; **il y va de votre t.** your life is at stake; **ça va lui en coûter la t.** it is going to cost him his life; **je donnerais ma t. à couper que …** I'll bet anything you like *or* I'd stake my life that …; **signe de t.** nod (of the head); **faire un signe de t. à qn** to nod to sb, to give sb a nod; **mal de t.** headache; **avoir (très) mal à la t.** to have a (bad) headache; **la t. lui tourne, il a la t. qui tourne** his head is spinning; **t. chauve** bald head; **t. ronde** bullet *or* round head; *Hist* Roundhead; **à t. ronde** bullet- *or* round-headed; *Fb* **faire une t.** to head the ball; **piquer une t.** (*tomber*) to take a header; *Natation* to dive; **je piquerais bien une t.** I'd really like to dive in; *Gym, Mil* **t. (à) droite!** eyes right!; **t. d'une médaille** obverse of a medal; *Arch* **t. ou pile?** heads or tails?

(b) (*cheveux*) hair; **une t. rousse/blonde** a redhead/blonde; **se laver la t.** to wash one's hair

(c) (*visage*) face; **il a une très belle t.** he's very good-looking; **elle a une jolie t.** she's pretty; **elle a une bonne t.** she looks nice; **il a une t. vraiment bizarre** he looks very strange, he's very strange-looking; *Arg* **il a une t. de con** he looks like a total prat; *Th* **se faire la t. d'un rôle** to make up for a part; *F* **faire une t. d'imbécile** to look like an idiot; **je ne sais pas quelle t. il fera** I don't know how he'll take it *or* react; **il fait une de ces têtes!** (*de colère*) he looks like thunder; (*de surprise*) he looks stunned *or* thunder-struck; (*de tristesse*) he looks grief-stricken; **faire sa t. des mauvais jours** to look like thunder; **il me fait une de ces têtes!** he keeps glowering at me!; *F* **faire la t.** to be in a huff, to sulk; **faire la t. à qn** to be sulky with sb; *F* **faire une tête de six pieds de longs** to have a face like a wet weekend; *F* **faire sa mauvaise t.** to look like thunder; **faire une t. de circonstance** to look grim; (*hypocritement*) to look suitably upset; **je connais cette t.-là** I know that face; **sa t. ne me revient pas** I don't like the look of him

(d) (*d'un animal, d'un poisson, d'un oiseau etc*) head; **d'une courte t.** (*gagner une course*) by a short head; **têtes** (*de bétail*) head of cattle

(e) (*esprit*) mind; (*cerveau*) brains; **il n'a rien dans la t.** he's stupid; **petite t.!** idiot!; **une pareille idée ne me serait jamais passée par la t.** such an idea would never have entered my mind *or* head; **si une idée te passe par la t., dis-le-moi** let me know if you have any ideas; **se creuser la t.** to rack one's brains; **c'est une femme de t.** she's a capable woman; **elle n'a pas de t.** she's very forgetful; **avoir la t. légère** to be irresponsible *or* featherbrained; **avoir la t. dure** to be stupid *or Br F* thick; (*têtu*) to be pig-headed; **mettre qch dans la t. de qn** to get sth into sb's head; **je me demande qui lui a mis ça dans la t.** I wonder who put that idea in his head; **il s'est mis en t. d'écrire un roman** he's got *or* taken it into his head to write a novel; **je me suis mis dans la t. qu'il fallait que je déménage** I got it into my head that I had to move; **n'avoir qu'une idée en t.** to have a one-track mind; **quand il a une idée en t.** once he gets an idea in his head; **il n'a que ça en t.** he's got it on the brain, that's all he thinks about; **avoir toutes les informations en t.** to have all the information in one's head; **je n'ai plus son nom en t.** his name has slipped my mind; **ça m'est sorti de la t.** it went clean out of my head *or* mind; **il a quelque chose en t.** he's planning something, *F* he's up to something; **s'endormir des souvenirs pleins la t.** to fall asleep with nice memories going through one's head; **des idées plein la t.** full of ideas; **forte t.** (*personne*) strong-minded person; **calculer de t.** to do mental arithmetic; **faire un rapide calcul de t.** to do a quick bit of mental arithmetic; **n'en faire qu'à sa t.** to do exactly as one pleases; **avoir une idée derrière la t.** to have an ulterior motive; *Litt* **idée de derrière la t.** preposterous *or* ludicrous idea; **où ai-je la t.!** what am I thinking of!; **monter à la t.** to go to sb's head; **garder la t. froide** to stay calm, to keep cool *or* a cool head; **essaie de garder la t. froide** try to stay calm, *F* try not to lose your cool; **est-ce que vous perdez la t.?** have you taken leave of your senses?; **ne**

perdez pas la t.! keep *or* don't lose your head!, keep calm!; **faire perdre la t. à qn** to make sb lose his/her head; **c'était à perdre la t.** it was bewildering; **avoir toute sa t.** to be all there; **il n'a plus toute sa t.** he's not quite all there; **se monter la t.** to imagine things; **ne va pas te monter la t.** don't start imagining things, don't go getting ideas; **j'y penserai à t. reposée** I'll think about it later (when I've got some peace and quiet)

(f) (*chef*) (*d'une société, d'un organisme*) head

(g) (*du chapitre d'un livre*) top; *Typ* **blanc de t.** margin at the head of a book; **ligne de t.** headline; **t. de lettre** letterhead; *Journ* **article de t.** feature (article), *Am* leading article; *Journ* **t. de colonne** lead (story), top

(h) (*de chou, d'ail, d'artichaut*) head; (*d'un arbre*) top, crown; *Anat* (*du fémur*) apophysis; (*de l'humérus*) head

(i) *Tech* (*d'un violon, d'un mât, d'un marteau, d'un clou etc*) head; (*de fusée*) warhead; **t. inclinable** (*d'une machine-outil, d'un support pour appareil photo ou instrument*) tilting head; *Aut* **soupapes en t.** overhead valves

(j) (*d'une procession, d'une colonne, d'une entreprise, d'un régiment etc*) head; (*d'un train*) front; *Sp etc* **prendre la t.** to take the lead; **prendre la t. d'une entreprise** to take over as the head of a company; **être à la t. de** (*une entreprise, une fortune*) to be (at) the head of, to head; (*une conjuration, une insurrection*) to be the leader of; **être à la t. de la classe** to be (at the) top of the class; **colonne de t.** front column; *Sp* **arriver en t.** to come in first; **être en t.** to be in the lead; **les joueurs en t.** the leaders, the front runners; **marcher en t.** to lead the way; **marcher à la t.** *ou* **en t. du cortège** to walk at the head of the procession, to lead *or* head the procession; **arriver en t. du scrutin** to head *or* come first in the poll; **taxi en t. de file** taxi at the head of the rank; *Rail* **voiture de t.** front carriage *or Am* car; **en t. du train** at the front of the train; **en t. de liste** at the top of the list; **candidats en t. de liste** candidates at the top of *or* heading the list

▶ **tête**: *Th, Cin* **t. d'affiche** top of the bill (**de** in); **être t. d'affiche** to be top of the bill, to top the bill; *Aut* **t. d'allumeur** distributor cap; **t. de benne** grab head; **t. blonde: nos chères têtes blondes** (*enfants*) the children; **t. brûlée** hothead; **t. de cabestan** drum head; **t. de câble** cable terminal; *TV, Cin* **t. de caméra** camera head; **t. de chapitre** chapter heading; **t. chercheuse** (*d'un missile etc*) homing device; *F* **t. à claques: c'est une t. à claques** he just asks for it; *F* **t. de cochon: c'est une t. de cochon** he's pig-headed, he's as stubborn as a mule; **t. couronnée** (*souverain*) crowned head; *Aut* **t. de distribution** distributor cap; *Ordinat* **t. d'écriture** writing *or* write head; *Électron, Ordinat* **t. d'effacement** (*d'un magnétophone etc*) erase head; **t. d'électrode** electrode tip; **t. d'enregistrement, t. enregistreuse** (*d'un ordinateur, d'un magnétophone*) record(ing) head; **t. de flèche** (*d'une grue*) jib head; **t. de fraisage** cutter head, milling head; **t. de fusée** warhead; *F* **t. à gifles: c'est une t. à gifles** he just asks for it; *Com* **t. de gondole** end of gondola; **t. d'impression** print head; *Pétr* **t. d'injection** swivel; *F* **t. de lard: c'est une t. de lard** he's pig-headed, he's as stubborn as a mule; **t. de lecture** *Cin* sound head; *Ordinat* read(ing) head; (*de magnétophone*) tape reader, play-back head; (*de tourne-disque*) pick-up (head); *Ordinat* **t. de lecture-écriture** read-write head; *Rail etc* **t. de ligne** starting point, terminus; **t. de linotte** bird-brain; **être une t. de linotte** to be bird-brained, to be a bird-brain; **t. de lit** bed head; **t. magnétique** magnetic head; **t. de mule: c'est une t. de mule** he's pig-headed, he's as stubborn as a mule; *Vulg* **t. de nœud!** dickhead!, *Am* asshole!; **t. nucléaire** nuclear warhead; *Ordinat* **t. à palpeur** sensor head; **t. de perçage** drill(ing) head; *F* **t. de pioche: c'est une tête de pioche** he's pig-headed, he's as stubborn as a mule; *Aut* **t. de piston** piston head *or* crown; *Mil* **t. de pont** bridgehead; **t. porte-foret** drill(ing) head; **t. porte-fraise** cutter head, milling head; **t. porte-outil** tool head; *Tennis* **t. de série** seeded player, seed; **t. sonore** sound head; **t. de Turc** target, butt; **c'est la t. de Turc de toute la classe** the whole class picks on him/her; *Culin* **t. de veau vinaigrette** calf's head in vinaigrette

tête-à-queue *nm inv Aut* spin; *Équitation* (sudden) turn; **faire (un) t.** *Aut* to spin *or* slew round; (*d'un cheval*) to whip round; **la voiture a fait plusieurs t.** the car spun round several times

tête-à-tête *nm inv* **(a)** (*à deux*) private interview, tête-à-tête; **en t.** in private; **un dîner en t.** a private dinner; **voir qn en t.** to see sb in private *or* privately; **en t. avec** alone with **(b)** (*canapé*) (two-seater) sofa, *surtout Am* love seat **(c)** (*service*) tea/coffee/breakfast set (for two)

tête-bêche *adv* **dormir t.** to sleep head to foot; **ranger des bouteilles t.** to store bottles alternate ways up

tête-de-loup, *pl* **têtes-de-loup** *nf* ceiling brush

tête de mort, *pl* **têtes de mort** *nf* **(a)** (*emblème*) death's-head; **pavillon à t.** skull-and-crossbones (flag), Jolly Roger **(b)** *Ent* death's-head moth

tête-de-nègre *adj inv, nm inv* dark brown

tétée [tete] *nf* **(a)** (*repas de nourrisson*) feed; **l'heure de la t.** feeding time; **pendant les tétées** during feeds, while feeding; **donner la t. à un enfant** to feed *or Vieilli* suckle a child **(b)** (*action*) sucking

téter [tete] *vt* (**il tète; il tètera**) **(a)** (*d'un bébé, d'un petit animal*) (*lait*) to suck; **t. sa mère** to feed, to suck at one's mother's breast; **donner à t. à un enfant** to feed *or Vieilli* suckle a child **(b)** *F* (*cigare, pipe, stylo etc*) to suck (on); (*pouce*) to suck

têtière [tɛtjɛr] *nf* **(a)** (*de harnais*) headstall **(b)** (*de fauteuil*) chairback, *Vieilli* antimacassar

tétine [tetin] *nf* **(a)** (*d'une truie etc*) dug; (*d'une vache*) udder **(b)** (*d'un biberon*) nipple, teat; **t. (sur anneau)** (*sucette*) comforter, *Br* dummy, *Am* pacifier

téton [tetɔ̃] *nm F* (*sein de femme*) boob, tit; *MecE* (*d'une pièce détachée*) lug; *MecE* **t. de positionnement** spigot, dowel; *MecE* **t. de purge** bleed nipple

tétrachlorure [tetraklɔryr] *nm Ch* tetrachloride; **t. de carbone** carbon tetrachloride

tétracycline [tetrasiklin] *nf Pharm* tetracycline

tétraèdre [tetraɛdr] *Géom* **1** *adj* tetrahedral **2** *nm* tetrahedron

tétraédrique [tetraedrik] *adj Géom* tetrahedral

tétralogie [tetralɔʒi] *nf Littér, Th* tetralogy; *Mus* **la T. (de Wagner)** The Ring, Wagner's Ring

tétramètre [tetramɛtr] *nm Littér* tetrameter

tétraphonique [tetrafɔnik] quadrasonic

tétraplégie [tetrapleʒi] *nf Méd* tetraplegia, quadriplegia

tétrapode [tetrapɔd] *nm Zool* tetrapod

tétrarque [tetrark] *nm* tetrarch

tétras [tetra] *nm* [①**A12,1,g**] (*oiseau*) grouse; **grand t.** capercaillie; **t.-lyre** black grouse

tétrasyllabe [tetrasilab], **tétrasyllabique** [tetrasilabik] *adj Gram* tetrasyllabic; **mot t.** tetrasyllable

têtu, -ue [tety] **1** *adj* stubborn, obstinate, *F* pig-headed; *F* **t. comme un mulet** *ou* **comme une mule** as stubborn *or* obstinate as a mule **2** *n* stubborn *or* obstinate person; **c'est un t.!** he's so stubborn! *or* obstinate! *or F* pig-headed!

teuf-teuf [tœftœf] *nm inv Aut F* (*voiture*) jalopy, rattletrap; (*bruit*) chug-chug

teuton, -onne [tøtɔ̃, -ɔn] **1** *adj* Teutonic **2** *nm Ling* Germanic, Teutonic **3** *n* **T.** Teuton

teutonique [tøtɔnik] *adj* Teutonic

texan, -ane [tɛksɑ̃, -an] **1** *adj* Texan **2** *n* **T.** Texan

texte [tɛkst] *nm* (*d'un auteur, d'un livre, d'un contrat etc*), *Ordinat* text; *Mus* (*d'un opéra*) libretto; (*d'une chanson*) words; *Th* (*d'un acteur*) lines; (*d'une pièce de théâtre*) script; *Scol* (*de devoir*) subject; **t. (imprimé)** print, printed text; **erreur de t.** textual error; **critique des textes** textual criticism; **t. de départ** source text; **t. publicitaire** advertising copy; **gravure hors t.** plate, full-page engraving; **lire Goethe dans le t.** to read Goethe in the original; *Scol* **cahier de textes** homework book (*listing work to be done*); **textes choisis** selected passages (**de** from)

▶ **texte**: **t. libre**: **vous avez t. libre pour la redaction** you can write about anything you like

texteur [tɛkstœr] *nm Ordinat* word *or* text processor

textile [tɛkstil] **1** *adj* textile **2** *nm* **(a)** textile; **textiles artificiels** synthetic *or* man-made textiles *or* fabrics, synthetics **(b) le t.** (*industrie*) the textile industry, textiles

texto [tɛksto] *adj F* word for word; **il m'a dit t.: fous le camp** get the hell out of it—those were his very words

textuel, -elle [tɛkstɥɛl] *adj* **(a)** (*analyse etc*) textual **(b)** (*conforme au texte*) (*traduction*) word-for-word, literal; *F* **c'est t.!** those were his/her/their/*etc* very words!; **c'est ce qu'elle a dit, c'est t.!** that's what she said, word for word!

textuellement [tɛkstɥɛlmɑ̃] *adv* (*conformément au texte*) (*traduire*) word for word, literally; **je reprends t. ses mots** those were his very words

texture [tɛkstyr] *nf* (*d'une substance, du sol*) texture; (*d'un texte*) structure

texturer [tɛkstyre], **texturiser** [tɛkstyrize] *vt Tech* to texturize

TF1 [teɛfœ̃] *nf* (*abrév* **Télévision française 1**) = (French) commercial television channel

TGV [teʒeve] *nm abrév* **train à grande vitesse**

thaï, -ïe [taj] **1** *adj* Thai **2** *nm Ling* Thai **3** *n* **T.** Thai

thaïlandais, -aise [tailɑ̃dɛ, -ɛz] **1** *adj* Thai **2** *n* **T.** Thai

Thaïlande [tailɑ̃d] *nf* Thailand

thalamus [talamys] *nm Anat* thalamus

thalassémie [talasemi] *nf Méd* thalassaemia, *US* thalassemia

thalassothérapie [talasoterapi] *nf Méd* seawater therapy, thalassotherapy
thalidomide [talidɔmid] *nf Pharm* thalidomide
thalle [tal] *nm Bot* thallus
thallium [taljɔm] *nm Ch* thallium
thalweg [talvɛg] *nm Géol* t(h)alweg
thaumaturge [tomatyrʒ] **1** *adj* miracle-working, *Spéc* thaumaturgic **2** *nm* miracle worker, *Spéc* thaumaturge, thaumaturgist
thé [te] **1** *nm* **(a)** *(boisson, feuilles)* tea; *(arbrisseau)* tea plant; **boire du t.** to drink tea; **faire du t.** to make (some) tea; **et si on se faisait du t.?** how about some tea?; **c'est l'heure du t.** it's tea time; **prendre le t.** to take tea; **t. de Ceylan** Ceylon tea; **t. indien** *ou* **de l'Inde** Indian tea; **t. de Chine** China tea; **t. nature/au lait** tea without milk/with milk; **t. au citron** lemon tea; **t. glacé** iced tea; **t. à la menthe** mint tea; **t. en sachet** tea bags; **t. en vrac** loose tea; **négociant en t.** tea merchant
(b) *(goûter)* tea party; **t. dansant** tea dance, thé dansant; **inviter qn pour le t.** to invite sb to *or* for tea
(c) salon de t. teashop, tearoom(s)
2 *adj inv* **rose t.** tea rose
théâtral, -ale, -aux, -ales [teɑtral, -o] *adj* theatrical; *(effet)* dramatic; *(performance)* stage; *Péj (artificiel)* theatrical, stagy
théâtralement [teɑtralmɑ̃] *adv* theatrically
théâtraliser [teɑtralize] *vt Th (roman etc)* to dramatize
théâtralité [teɑtralite] *nf* theatricality
théâtre [teɑtr] *nm* **(a)** *(salle)* theatre, *US* theater; **aller au t.** to go to the theatre
(b) *(scène)* stage; **mettre une pièce au t.** to stage *or* put on a play; **adapté pour le t.** adapted for the stage; **se retirer du t.** to give up the stage
(c) *(art, métier)* theatre, *US* theater; **pièce de t.** play; **costumier de t.** theatrical costumier; **faire du t.** to be an actor/actress, to act, to be on the stage; **homme/femme de t.** man/woman of the theatre; **école/cours de t.** drama school/course; **coup de t.** *Th* coup de théâtre; *Fig* dramatic *or* sensational turn of events; *Fig* **sa décision a été un vrai coup de t.** his decision came as a real surprise
(d) *(œuvres) (d'un auteur)* plays, dramatic works; *(genre)* theatre, *US* theater; **le t. anglais** British theatre *or* drama; **t. expérimental** *ou* **off** experimental theatre, fringe (theatre); **écrivains de t.** playwrights
(e) *Fig (d'un crime, un accident etc)* scene
(f) *(attitude artifielle)* play-acting, histrionics; **tout cela, c'est du t.** it's all an act
▶ **théâtre**: **t. de boulevard** light comedies; **t. de marionnettes** puppet theatre; **t. d'ombres** shadow theatre; *Mil* **t. d'opérations** theatre of operations; **t. en rond** theatre-in-the-round; **t. de verdure** open-air theatre
théâtreux, -euse [teɑtrø, -øz] *n F Péj* would-be actor, *f* would-be actress
thébaïde [tebaid] *nf Litt* place of meditation
théier, -ière [teje, -jɛr] **1** *adj Rare (industrie etc)* tea; *(région)* tea-growing **2** *nm Bot* tea (plant) **3** *nf* **théière** teapot
théine [tein] *nf* theine, caffeine; **thé sans t.** caffeine-free tea
théisme [teism] *nm Rel* theism
théiste [teist] *Rel* **1** *adj* theistic **2** *n* theist
thématique [tematik] **1** *adj (catalogue, table, index)* subject; *Mus* thematic **2** *nf (d'une œuvre, de la littérature contemporaine etc)* themes; **cela entre dans sa t.** it's one of his themes
thème [tɛm] *nm* **(a)** *(sujet) (d'un discours, d'un débat, d'un morceau de musique etc)* theme; **un t. de réflexion** food for thought; **je vous propose un t. de réflexion** here's something you can think about **(b)** *Scol (traduction)* prose; *F* **un fort en t.** a swot **(c)** *Gram (d'un verbe, d'un nom)* stem **(d)** *Astrol* **t. (astral)** birth chart; **faire son t. à qn** to draw up sb's birth chart
théocratie [teɔkrasi] *nf* theocracy
théocratique [teɔkratik] *adj* theocratic
théodicée [teɔdise] *nf Phil* theodicy
théodolite [teɔdɔlit] *nm* theodolite
théogonie [teɔgɔni] *nf* theogony, genealogy of the gods
théologal, -ale, -aux, -ales [teɔlɔgal, -o] *adj* **les trois vertus théologales** the three theological virtues
théologie [teɔlɔʒi] *nf* theology; **docteur en t.** doctor of divinity, DD; **faire sa t.** to study theology, to be a divinity student; **cours/études de t.** theology course/studies
théologien, -ienne [teɔlɔʒjɛ̃, -jɛn] *n* theologian
théologique [teɔlɔʒik] *adj* theological
théologiquement [teɔlɔʒikmɑ̃] *adv* theologically
théorbe [teɔrb] *nm Hist, Mus* theorbo
théorème [teɔrɛm] *nm* theorem; **le t. de Newton** the binomial theorem
théorétique [teɔretik] *Phil* **1** *adj* theoretic(al) **2** *nf* theoretics
théoricien, -ienne [teɔrisjɛ̃, -jɛn] *n* theoretician, theorist
théorie[1] [teɔri] *nf* **(a)** *(doctrine)* theory; **bâtir une t.** to construct a theory; *Math, Ordinat* **t. des probabilités** theory of probability; **t. de la relativité** theory of relativity, relativity theory; **la t. et la pratique** theory and practice; *Mktg* **t. de la décision** decision theory; *Mktg* **t. des jeux** game theory; **en t.** in theory, theoretically; **plus facile en t. qu'en pratique** easier in theory than in practice **(b)** *Mil* theoretical instruction
théorie[2] *nf Litt (défilé)* procession
théorique [teɔrik] *adj* theoretic(al)
théoriquement [teɔrikmɑ̃] *adv* theoretically, in theory
théoriser [teɔrize] **1** *vi* to theorize **2** *vt* to theorize about
théosophe [teɔzɔf] *n* theosophist
théosophie [teɔzɔfi] *nf* theosophy
thérapeute [terapøt] *n Méd* therapist
thérapeutique [terapøtik] **1** *adj (avortement, action, procédé)* therapeutic; **acte t.** invasive treatment; **aléa t.** risk attached to treatment; **accident t.** accident in the course of treatment **2** *nf (science)* therapeutics; *(traitement)* (course of) treatment, therapy
thérapie [terapi] *nf Méd* therapy; *Psy* **t. de groupe** group therapy; **être en t.** to be in therapy; **commencer une t.** to start a course of therapy, to start therapy
thermal, -ale, -aux, -ales [tɛrmal, -o] *adj* thermal; **eaux thermales** thermal *or* hot springs; **établissement t.** hydropathic establishment, *Br* hydro; **station thermale** spa; **cure thermale** water cure; **faire une cure thermale** to take the waters
thermalisme [tɛrmalism] *nm* **(a)** *(thérapie)* hydrotherapy, water cures **(b)** *(science)* balneology
thermes [tɛrm] *nmpl* **(a)** *Méd* thermal baths **(b)** *Antiq* thermae, public baths
thermicien, -ienne [tɛrmisjɛ̃, -jɛn] *n* heat engineer
thermidor [tɛrmidɔr] *nm Hist* = eleventh month of the French Republican calendar *(July-August)*
thermie [tɛrmi] *nf Phys* = thermal unit (= *1000 kilocalories*)
thermique [tɛrmik] **1** *adj Phys* thermal; *(moteur, écran, traitement)* heat; *Él* **centrale t.** thermal power station; *Av* **courant t.** thermal (current); **papier t.** thermal paper; *Électron* **relais t.** thermorelay; **brise/vent t.** thermal; *Ch* **analyse t.** thermoanalysis; **science t.** science of heat; *Géog* **régime t.** temperature regime *or* pattern; *Physiol* **sensibilité t.** temperature sense **2** *nm Av (courant)* thermal **3** *nf* science of heat
thermistance [tɛrmistɑ̃s] *nf Él* thermistor
thermisteur [tɛrmistœr] *nm,* **thermistor** [tɛrmistɔr] *nm Él* thermistor
thermocautère [tɛrmokotɛr] *nm Chir (instrument)* thermocautery
thermochimie [tɛrmoʃimi] *nf* thermochemistry
thermocollage [tɛrmokɔlaʒ] *nm* heat sealing
thermoconduction [tɛrmokɔ̃dyksjɔ̃] *nm Phys* heat conduction
thermocontact [tɛrmokɔ̃takt] *nm Él* thermal *or* temperature switch
thermocouple [tɛrmokupl] *nm Él* thermocouple
thermodynamique [tɛrmodinamik] **1** *adj* thermodynamic **2** *nf* thermodynamics
thermoélectricité [tɛrmoelɛktrisite] *nf* thermoelectricity
thermoélectrique [tɛrmoelɛktrik] *adj* thermoelectric(al); **pince t.** thermocouple; **couple t.** thermoelectric couple; **pile t.** thermopile
thermoélectronique [tɛrmoelɛktrɔnik] *adj* thermoelectronic
thermoformage [tɛrmofɔrmaʒ] *nm Tech* thermoforming
thermogène [tɛrmoʒɛn] *adj Physiol* heat-producing, *Spéc* thermogenetic
thermographe [tɛrmograf] *nm Phys* thermograph
thermomagnétisme [tɛrmomaɲetism] *nm Phys* thermomagnetism
thermomètre [tɛrmomɛtr] *nm* thermometer; **t. médical** *ou* **de clinique** clinical thermometer; **t. à maxima et minima** maximum and minimum thermometer; **t. à mercure** mercury thermometer; **le t. monte/baisse** the temperature is rising/falling; *Fig* **le t. de l'opinion** the barometer of public opinion
thermométrie [tɛrmometri] *nf Phys* thermometry
thermométrique [tɛrmometrik] *adj* thermometric
thermonucléaire [tɛrmonykleɛr] *adj Phys Nucl, Mil* thermonuclear
thermopile [tɛrmopil] *nf Él* thermopile
thermoplastique [tɛrmoplastik] *adj, nm* thermoplastic
thermoplongeur [tɛrmoplɔ̃ʒœr] *nm* (portable) immersion heater
thermopompe [tɛrmopɔ̃p] *nf* heat pump

thermopropulsion [tɛrmoprɔpylsjɔ̃] *nf Av* thermopropulsion
thermorégulateur [tɛrmoregylatœr] *nm* thermoregulator, thermostat
thermorégulation [tɛrmoregylasjɔ̃] *nf* thermoregulation
thermorésistant [tɛrmorezistɑ̃] *adj* heat-resistant
thermoscope [tɛrmɔskɔp] *nm Phys* thermoscope
thermosphère [tɛrmɔsfɛr] *nf* thermosphere
thermos® [tɛrmos] *n inv* **(bouteille) t.** Thermos (flask *or Am* bottle)
thermostat [tɛrmɔsta] *nm* thermostat; **t. 7** (*dans recette*) gas mark 7; **réglage par t.** thermostatic control
thermothérapie [tɛrmoterapi] *nf* heat treatment, *Spéc* thermotherapy
thésard, -arde [tezar, -ard] *n Univ F* PhD student
thésaurisation [tezɔrizasjɔ̃] *nf* hoarding (of money); *Écon* building up of capital
thésauriser [tezɔrize] *vti* to hoard
thésauriseur, -euse [tezɔrizœr, -øz] *n* (*d'argent*) hoarder
thesaurus [tezɔrys] *nm* thesaurus
thèse [tɛz] *nf* [①A14,10] **(a)** (*doctrine*) thesis, proposition, argument; **il défend la t. suivante: …** he argues that …; *Th* **pièce à t.** problem play, drama of ideas; **roman/littérature à t.** novel/literature of ideas **(b)** *Univ* thesis (*submitted for degree*); **soutenir sa t.** to have one's viva (voce) **(c)** *Phil* thesis; **t., antithèse, synthèse** thesis, antithesis, synthesis
Thésée [teze] *nm Myth* Theseus
Thessalonique [tesalɔnik] *nf* Thessalonica
thiamine [tjamin] *nf Biol, Ch* thiamin(e), aneurin
thibaude [tibod] *nf* carpet felt, (felt) underlay
thiosulfate [tjɔsylfat] *nm Ch* thiosulphate, *US* thiosulfate
thio-urée [tjɔyre], *pl* **thio-urées** *nf Ch* thiourea
thixotropie [tiksɔtrɔpi] *nf Ch, Phys* thixotropy
Thomas [tɔmɑ] *nm* **Saint T. d'Aquin** St Thomas Aquinas
thomas [tɔmɑ] *nm Arg Vieilli* (*pot de chambre*) chamberpot, *Br* jerry
thomisme [tɔmism] *nm Rel* Thomism
thomiste [tɔmist] *adj, n Rel* Thomist
thon [tɔ̃] *nm* tuna, tunny; *Culin* tuna (fish); **la pêche au t.** tuna fishing; **t. au naturel/à l'huile** tuna (fish) in brine/in oil
thonaire [tɔnɛr] *nf Pêche* tuna *or* tunny net
thonier [tɔnje] **1** *adj* tuna **2** *nm* tuna *or* tunny boat
Thora [tɔra] *nf Rel* Torah
thoracique [tɔrasik] *adj Anat* thoracic; **cage t.** ribcage
thorax [tɔraks] *nm Anat* thorax
thorium [tɔrjɔm] *nm Ch* thorium
thoron [tɔrɔ̃] *nm Phys Nucl* thoron
Thrace [tras] *nf* Thrace
thrène [trɛn] *nm Antiq* threnody
thriller [srilœr] *nm Cin, Littér* thriller
thrips [trips] *nm Ent* thrips, *Spéc* thysanopter
thrombine [trɔ̃bin] *nf Biol, Ch* thrombin
thrombose [trɔ̃boz] *nf Méd* thrombosis
thulium [tyljɔm] *nm Ch* thulium
thune [tyn] *nf Arg* **(a)** (*argent*) dough, bread; **j'ai pas une t.** I'm stony broke; **gagner de la t.** *ou* **des thunes** to be raking it in, to be making mega bucks **(b)** *Arch* (*pièce*) five-franc piece
thuriféraire [tyriferɛr] *nm* **(a)** *Rel* thurifer, incense bearer **(b)** *Litt* (*flatteur*) flatterer
thuya [tyja] *nm Bot* thuja, thuya, arbor vitae
thylacine [tilasin] *nm* Tasmanian wolf, *Spéc* thylacine
thym [tɛ̃] *nm Bot, Culin* thyme; **t. sauvage** wild thyme
thymus [timys] *nm Anat* thymus, thymus gland
thyristor [tiristɔr] *nm Él* thyristor
thyroïde [tirɔid] *adj, nf Anat* **(glande) t.** thyroid (gland)
thyroïdectomie [tirɔidɛktɔmi] *nf Chir* thyroidectomy
thyroïdien, -ienne [tirɔidjɛ̃, -jɛn] *adj Anat, Méd* (*hormone, artère, insuffisance etc*) thyroid
thyroïdisme [tirɔidism] *nm Méd* thyroidism
thyroïdite [tirɔidit] *nf Méd* thyroiditis
thyrotoxicose [tirotɔksikoz] *nf Méd* Graves' disease
thyrse [tirs] *nm Antiq, Bot* thyrsus
tiare [tjar] *nf* (*du pape*) tiara; **coiffer la t.** to become Pope
Tibère [tibɛr] *nm* Tiberius
Tibet [tibɛ] *nm* Tibet
tibétain, -aine [tibetɛ̃, -ɛn] **1** *adj* Tibetan **2** *nm Ling* Tibetan **3** *n* **T.** Tibetan
tibia [tibja] *nm Anat, Ent* tibia
tibial, -ale, -aux, -ales [tibjal, -jo] *adj Anat* tibial
Tibre [tibr] *nm* **le T.** the Tiber
tic [tik] *nm* **(a)** *Méd* tic, twitch; **il a un t.** he has a twitch *or* a tic, his face twitches; **t. nerveux** nervous tic *or* twitch; **t. douloureux** facial neuralgia, *Spéc* tic douloureux **(b)** *Vét* (*de cheval*) vicious habit **(c)** *Fig* (*habitude*) habit, mannerism; **avoir/prendre le t. de faire qch** to have a/get into the habit of doing sth; **t. de langage** verbal tic *or* mannerism

ticket [tikɛ] *nm* **(a)** (*billet*) ticket; **un carnet de tickets de bus** a book of bus tickets **(b)** *Arg* (*billet de dix francs*) ten-franc note; **tu vas en avoir pour deux cents tickets** it'll cost you two thousand francs **(c)** *Arg* **avoir un t. avec qn** to have made a hit with sb; **j'ai l'impression que tu as un t. avec lui** (*tu lui plais*) I think he fancies you
▶ **ticket**: **t. de caisse** receipt; *Méd* **t. modérateur** = portion of the cost of treatment paid by the insured; *Admin* **t. de pain** bread coupon; *Rail* **t. de quai** platform ticket; **t. de rationnement** ration coupon
ticket-repas *nm, pl* **tickets-repas, ticket-restaurant** *nm, pl* **tickets-restaurant** luncheon voucher
tic(-)tac **1** *nm inv* (*d'une horloge*) tick-tock, tick, ticking; **faire t.** to tick **2** *int* tick-tock!
tictaquer [tiktake] *vi* (*d'une horloge*) to tick
tie-break, *pl* **tie-breaks** [tajbrɛk] *nm Tennis* tie break
tiédasse [tjedas] *adj Péj* lukewarm, tepid
tiède [tjɛd] **1** *adj* (*agréablement*) (*bain, vent etc*) warm; (*désagréablement*) (*bain, boisson etc*) tepid, lukewarm; *Fig* (*amitié, accueil*) tepid, lukewarm, half-hearted; (*foi, défenseur*) half-hearted; *Culin* (*salade*) warm **2** *adv* **il fait t.** (*temps*) it's mild; **je n'aime pas boire t.** I don't like anything that's lukewarm **3** *n* half-hearted person
tièdement [tjɛdmɑ̃] *adv* half-heartedly, without any great enthusiasm
tiédeur [tjedœr] *nf* (*agréable*) warmth; (*désagréable*) (*de l'eau, Fig d'une amitié, d'un accueil etc*) tepidness, half-heartedness; *Fig* (*d'un défenseur, de la foi*) half-heartedness; **la t. de ses paroles** his unenthusiastic *or* half-hearted words; **avec t.** half-heartedly, without any great enthusiasm
tiédir [tjedir] **1** *vi* (*devenir plus chaud*) to warm up; (*devenir moins chaud*) to cool down; *Fig* (*d'une amitié, d'une passion etc*) to cool off **2** *vt* (*réchauffer*) to take the chill off, to warm (up); (*refroidir*) to cool (down)
tiédissement [tjedismɑ̃] *nm* (*refroidissement*) cooling (off); (*réchauffement*) warming (up)
tien, tienne [tjɛ̃, tjɛn] **1** *pron poss* [①A30,8; B20,E,2] **le tien, la tienne, les tiens, les tiennes** yours; *Bible, Arch* thine; **tu me prêtes le t.?** can I borrow yours?; **il n'a qu'à prendre la tienne** he can just take yours; **il ressemble au t.** it looks like yours; **tu veux bien me donner du t.?** can I have some of yours?; **de toutes ces solutions, tu préfères la tienne?** out of those possible solutions, do you prefer your own?; **tu n'en as pas besoin, tu as le t.** you don't need it, you've got your own; **je n'en ai pas besoin, j'ai le t.** I don't need it, I've got yours; **les deux tiens** your two, the two *or* both of yours; (*en insistant*) your own two; **tu lui as laissé deux des tiens** you gave him two of yours; *F* **le t. de bébé est plus intelligent** your baby is more intelligent; *F* **à la tienne!** (*en buvant*) cheers!

2 *nm* **le t.** (*ce qui t'appartient*) yours; **ne cherchons pas à distinguer le t. du mien** let's not waste time arguing about who owns what; *Fig* **tu devrais y mettre du t.** (*faire un effort*) you should really do your share

3 *nmpl* **les tiens** (*ta famille*) your family, *Am* your folks; (*tes partisans*) your followers; (*tes coéquipiers*) your team-mates

4 *nfpl* **tu as encore fait des tiennes** you've been up to your old tricks again

5 *adj poss Litt* yours; *Vieilli* **un t. cousin** a cousin of yours; **tu feras tiens ses principes** you will adopt his principles as your own; **feras-tu tiennes les félicitations qu'ils m'adressent?** will you join them in congratulating me?
tiens, tient [tjɛ̃] *voir* **tenir**
tierce [tjɛrs] *nf* **(a)** *Astron, Math* = sixtieth part of a second **(b)** *Escrime* tierce **(c)** *Rel* terce, tierce **(d)** *Mus* third **(e)** *Typ* final revise, press proof **(f)** *Cartes* tierce
tiercé [tjɛrse] **1** *adj* **(a)** *Courses de chevaux* **pari t.** = forecast of the first three horses **(b)** *Hér* tierced, tiercé **(c)** **rimes tiercées** terza rima **(d)** *Agr* (*champ*) ploughed *or US* plowed for the third time **2** *nm Courses de chevaux* = **pari t.**; **un beau t.** a good win on the tiercé; **le t. gagnant** the winning combination; **jouer au t.** = to put money on horses, *F* to back the gee-gees
tiercelet [tjɛrs(ə)lɛ] *nm* tercel, male falcon
tiercer [tjɛrse] *vt* **(je tierçai(s); n. tierçons)** *Agr* (*champ*) to plough *or US* plow for the third time
tiers, tierce [tjɛr, tjɛrs] **1** *adj* third; **une tierce personne** a third party; *Jur* **en main tierce** in the hands of a third party; *Méd* **fièvre tierce** tertian fever

2 *nm* **(a)** (*fraction*) third (part); **une remise d'un t.** **(du prix)** a discount of a third, *F* a third off; **perdre le t./les deux t. de son argent** to lose a third/two-thirds of one's money

(b) (*personne*) third party; *F* **le t. et le quart** everybody, anybody; *F* **il se moque du t. comme du quart** he doesn't

give a damn about anybody or anything; **assurance au t.** third party insurance
▶ **tiers**: *Fin* **t. détenteur** third party holder; *Hist* **le T. état** the Third Estate; **le t. monde = le tiers-monde**; *Admin* **t. payant** = system of direct payment for medical treatment by the insurer; *Fin* **t. porteur** (*d'un effet de commerce*) second endorser; (*d'un effet*) holder in due course; **t. possesseur** third party owner; *Fin* **t. provisionnel** interim (tax) payment (= *approximately one third of previous year's tax*)
tiers-arbitre, *pl* **tiers-arbitres** *nm Jur* (independent) arbitrator
tiers-monde, *pl* **tiers-mondes** *nm Pol* **le t.** the Third World; **pays du t.** Third World countries
tiers-mondiste, *pl* **tiers-mondistes** [tjɛrmɔ̃dist] *Pol* **1** *adj* Third World **2** *n* supporter of the Third World
TIF [tif] *nm* (*abrév* **transport international ferroviaire**) international rail transport
tifoso, *pl* **tifosi** [tifozo, -zi] *nm* fan
tifs, tiffes [tif] *nmpl Arg* hair
tige [tiʒ] *nf* **(a)** (*d'une plante*) stem, stalk; (*d'un arbre*) stem; **(arbre de) haute/basse t.** (tall) standard/half standard; **rosier sur t.** standard rose
(b) *Fig Litt* (*d'une famille*) stock; **faire t.** to found a line
(c) *Tech* (*d'une valve*) stem; (*d'une pompe, d'un piston etc*) rod; *Aut* (*sur le volant*) stalk; (*d'un rivet, d'une clé, Naut d'une ancre, Typ d'une lettre*) shank; *Archit* (*d'une colonne*) shaft; *Mus* (*d'un archet*) stick; (*d'un guéridon*) leg
(d) *Tex* (*d'un bas*) leg; (*d'une botte*) leg, upper; **bottes à tiges** top boots
(e) *Arg* (cigarette) cigarette, cig(gy), *Br* fag
▶ **tige**: *Aut* **t. (de maintien) de capot** bonnet strut; *Typ* **t. à caractères** type bar; *Aut* **t. de crémaillère** rack link; (*de la direction*) control rod; *Aut* **t. de culbuteur** pushrod; *Pétr* **t. de forage** drill(ing) pipe; **t. de frein** brake rod; *Aut* **t. de jauge** dipstick; **t. de paratonnerre** lightning rod; *Aut* **t. de poussée** thrust pin, pushrod; *Aut* **t. poussoir** pushrod; **t. de selle** (*de bicyclette*) saddle pillar; **t. à vis du frein** brake screw
tiglon [tiglɔ̃] *nm* tigon
tignasse [tiɲas] *nf* mop
Tigre [tigr] *nm* **le T.** the Tigris
tigre [tigr] *n* tiger; **jaloux comme un t.** madly *or* wildly jealous
▶ **tigre**: **t. du Bengale** Bengal tiger; **t. royal** Bengal tiger
tigré [tigre] *adj* **(a)** (*rayé*) striped; **chat t.** tabby (cat) **(b)** (*tacheté*) spotted (**de** with); **lis t.** tiger lily
tigresse [tigrɛs] *nf aussi Fig* tigress; **jalouse comme une t.** madly *or* wildly jealous
tigron [tigrɔ̃] *nm* tigon
tilbury [tilbyri] *nm* (*voiture à cheval*) tilbury, gig
tilde [tild(e)] *nm Typ etc* swung dash; (*espagnol*) tilde
tillac [tijak] *nm Hist, Naut* upper deck
tilleul [tijœl] **1** *nm* **(a)** (*arbre*) lime (tree); **en t.** (*coffret, boîte*) limewood **(b)** **(infusion de) t.** lime-blossom tea **2** *adj inv, nm* **(vert) t.** lime green
tilt [tilt] *nm* (*au billard électrique*) tilt signal; **faire t.** to signal the end of the game; *Fig* (*d'une idée, d'un mot etc*) to ring a bell
timbale [tɛ̃bal] *nf* **(a)** *Mus* kettledrum; **les timbales** (*dans un orchestre*) the timpani **(b)** (*gobelet*) (metal) drinking cup; **t. en argent** (*donnée aux enfants baptisés*) silver christening cup; *Fig F* **décrocher la t.** to hit the jackpot **(c)** *Culin* (*moule*) timbale (mould *or US* mold); (*plat*) timbale; **t. de langouste** lobster timbale
timbalier [tɛ̃balje] *nm Mus* timpanist
timbrage [tɛ̃braʒ] *nm* (*d'un passeport, d'une lettre etc*) stamping
timbre [tɛ̃br] *nm* **(a)** (*vignette*) stamp; **t.(-poste)** (postage) stamp; **mettre un t. sur une lettre** to stamp a letter, to put a stamp on a letter; **album de timbres** stamp album
(b) (*marque, cachet*) (*sur un document etc*) stamp
(c) (*tampon*) stamp
(d) *Fin* (*droit*) stamp duty
(e) (*sonnette*) bell; **t. de bicyclette** bicycle bell; **t. électrique** electric bell; *F Arch* **avoir le t. fêlé** to be cracked *or* daft, to have a screw loose
(f) (*son*) (*d'une voix, d'un instrument*) timbre, tone; **voix sans t.** toneless voice; **une voix au t. argentin** a silvery voice
(g) *Mus* (*d'un tambour*) snare
(h) *Pharm* (*pour traitement médical*) patch
▶ **timbre**: **t. de collection** collector's stamp; **t. à date, t. dateur** date stamp; **t. à encrage automatique** self-inking stamp; **t. fiscal** excise *or* tax stamp; **t. humide** rubber stamp; *Com* **t. de pesage** weight stamp; **t. de quittance** receipt stamp; **t. sec** embossing press; *Méd* **t. tuberculinique** TB patch
timbré [tɛ̃bre] *adj* **(a)** (*voix*) sonorous; **voix joliment** *ou* **agréablement timbrée** pleasant voice **(b)** *F* (*fou*) cracked, screwy **(c)** (*document, enveloppe etc*) stamped; **une enveloppe timbrée portant vos nom et adresse** a stamped addressed envelope, an sae
timbre-épargne, *pl* **timbres-épargne** *nm* savings-bank stamp
timbre-poste, *pl* **timbres-poste** *nm* (postage) stamp
timbre-prime, *pl* **timbres-prime** *nm Com* trading stamp
timbre-quittance, *pl* **timbres-quittance** *nm* receipt stamp
timbrer [tɛ̃bre] *vt* **(a)** (*avec un tampon*) (*passeport, document etc*) to stamp; (*lettre, paquet etc*) to postmark; **lettre timbrée de Paris** letter with a Paris postmark, letter postmarked Paris **(b)** (*coller un timbre sur*) (*lettre etc*) to stamp, to put *or* stick a stamp/stamps on; **je n'ai pas assez timbré la lettre** I didn't put enough stamps *or* I put insufficient postage on the letter **(c)** **papier timbré au chiffre de qn** paper stamped with sb's arms
timbre-taxe, *pl* **timbres-taxe** *nm* postage-due stamp
timide [timid] **1** *adj* **(a)** (*personne, sourire, voix, animal etc*) shy, timid; (*embarrassé*) bashful **(b)** (*timoré*) (*personne*) timid, timorous; (*critique, protestation, tentative etc*) timid **2** *n* shy person; **c'est un grand t.** he's very shy
timidement [timidmɑ̃] *adv* **(a)** (*d'une manière gênée*) shyly, timidly, diffidently **(b)** (*d'une manière timorée*) timidly
timidité [timidite] *nf* **(a)** (*gêne*) shyness, timidity, diffidence **(b)** (*manque d'audace*) timidity
timing [tajmiŋ] *nm* timing
timon [timɔ̃] *nm* **(a)** (*d'un véhicule tiré par un cheval etc*) shaft, pole; (*d'une charrue*) beam; *Aut* trailing arm **(b)** *Naut Arch* tiller
timonerie [timɔnri] *nf* **(a)** *Naut* **(kiosque de) t.** wheelhouse, pilot house **(b)** *Naut* (*fonction*) (naval) signalling **(c)** *Aut* steering gear; (*freins*) brake gear
timonier [timɔnje] *nm Naut* (*à la barre*) helmsman, man at the wheel; (*aux signaux*) signalman, wheelhorse, wheeler
timoré [timɔre] *adj* timorous, fearful; *Rel, Litt* (*conscience*) overscrupulous
tinctorial, -ale, -aux, -ales [tɛ̃ktɔrjal, -jo] *adj* (*plante, produit*) used in dyeing; (*procédé*) dyeing
tinette [tinɛt] *nf* **(a)** (*baquet*) (sanitary) soil tub **(b)** *F* **tinettes** (*toilettes*) latrines
tins [tɛ̃] *nmpl Naut* (*en cale sèche*) keel blocks
tintamarre [tɛ̃tamar] *nm F* (*bruit*) din, racket; **faire du t.** to make a din *or* racket
tintement [tɛ̃t(ə)mɑ̃] *nm* **(a)** (*d'une cloche*) ringing; **t. funèbre** tolling **(b)** (*de clochettes etc*) tinkling, tinkle; (*de grelots, de clés*) jingling, jingle; (*de pièces*) jingling, jingle, chink(ing); (*de verres, bouteilles*) chink(ing), clink(ing)
▶ **tintement**: **t. d'oreilles** ringing *or* buzzing in the ears, *Spéc* tinnitus; **avoir des tintements d'oreilles** to have a ringing *or* buzzing (noise) in one's ears
tinter [tɛ̃te] **1** *vt* (*cloche*) to ring; **t. la messe** to ring for mass **2** *vi* **(a)** (*d'une cloche*) to ring; (*de clochettes etc*) to tinkle; (*de verres, bouteilles*) to chink, to clink; (*de pièces*) to chink, to jingle; (*de grelots, de clés*) to jingle; **faire t. les verres** to chink *or* clink glasses; **le lustre en cristal tintait doucement** the crystal chandelier was tinkling softly **(b)** (*des oreilles*) to ring, to buzz; **les oreilles me tintaient** my ears were ringing *or* buzzing; *Fig* **les oreilles ont dû vous t. hier soir** (*on a parlé de vous*) your ears must have been burning last night
tintin [tɛ̃tɛ̃] *int F* no way (José)!, nothing doing!; **faire t.** to go without
tintinnabuler [tɛ̃tinabyle] *vi Litt* (*des cloches*) to tinkle
Tintoret (le) [lətɛ̃tɔrɛ] *nm* Tintoretto
tintouin [tɛ̃twɛ̃] *nm F* **(a)** (*bruit*) din, racket **(b)** (*souci*) trouble, worry; **se donner du t.** to go to a lot of trouble
TIOP [tiɔp] *nm Banque* (*abrév* **taux interbancaire offert à Paris**) PIBOR
tipi [tipi] *nm* teepee
tipule [tipyl] *nf Ent* crane fly
tique [tik] *nf Ent* tick; **collier anti-tiques** tick collar
tiquer [tike] *vi* **(a)** *F* (*d'une personne*) to wince; **il n'a pas tiqué** he didn't turn a hair *or* bat an eyelid **(b)** (*d'un cheval*) to suck wind, to crib(-bite)
tiqueté [tikte] *adj* speckled, mottled, variegated
TIR [tir] *nm* (*abrév* **transport international de marchandises par route**) TIR, international transport of goods by road
tir [tir] *nm* **(a)** (*activité*) shooting
(b) (*action de tirer*) firing; (*feu*) fire; **il a un t. précis** he's a good shot *or* marksman; **il a un t. rapide** he shoots quickly; **un t. rasant/plongeant** raking/downward fire; **champ de t.** (*lieu*) firing range; (*d'une arme*) field of fire; **t. au but** precision firing; **t. au fusil** *ou* **à la carabine** rifle shooting; **habileté au t.** marksmanship; **cadence** *ou* **régime** *ou*

vitesse du t. rate of fire; **allonger/raccourcir le t.** to increase/reduce the range; **t. de batterie** battery fire
(c) *Min* blasting
(d) (*concours*) shooting match *or* competition
(e) *Sp* (*aux boules*) throw; *Fb* **t. (au but)** shot (at goal); *Fb* **t. d'angle** corner (kick); **apprendre la technique du t.** (*aux boules*) to learn how to throw; *Fb* **faire un t. du pied gauche** to shoot with the left foot
(f) (*stand*) rifle range; **t. (forain)** shooting gallery
▶ **tir**: **t. à l'arbalète** crossbow shooting; **t. à l'arc** archery; **t. d'artillerie** artillery fire; **t. automatique** automatic fire; **arme à t. automatique** automatic weapon; **t. au pigeon (d'argile)** clay pigeon shooting

tirade [tirad] *nf* **(a)** *Péj* tirade **(b)** *Th* monologue

tirage [tiraʒ] *nm* **(a)** (*de chariots etc*) pulling, hauling; (*de barges*) towing; (*chemin*) towpath; **cordons de t. d'un rideau** curtain pulls; **cheval de t.** draught *or US* draft horse; *Él* **interrupteur à t.** pull-and-push switch
(b) *F* (*difficultés*) trouble, problems; **il va y avoir du t.** there's going to be trouble; **il y a du t. entre eux** there's friction between them, they don't get on together
(c) *Métal* wire drawing; (*de la soie*) spinning
(d) (*de rochers*) quarrying, extraction; **t. à la poudre** blasting
(e) (*d'un conduit de cheminée*) draught, *US* draft; **t. renversé** *ou* **inverti** back draught; *Aut* **carburateur à t. en bas** down-draught carburettor
(f) (*de loterie*) drawing; **t. du numéro gagnant** draw for the winning number; **procéder à un t. au sort** to draw lots; **par t. au sort** (*élu etc*) by drawing lots
(g) *Typ, Phot etc* (*action*) printing; (*objet*) print; (*nombre d'exemplaires sortis des presses*) (*d'un journal*) circulation; (*d'un livre*) print run; (*d'une gravure*) number printed, edition; (*d'un enregistrement*) edition; *Typ* **t. des épreuves** proofing; *Typ* **un mille de t.** (print) run of a thousand; **journal à gros** *ou* **grand t.** paper with a large circulation; **t. de luxe** de luxe edition; **t. numéroté** numbered edition; **t. à part** offprinting; **édition à t. limité** limited edition; *Typ* **t. héliographique** arc print; *Cin* **t. en surimpression** overprint
(h) *Banque etc* (*d'un chèque, d'une lettre de change*) drawing, emission; (*d'un prêt*) draw down; **t. en blanc** *ou* **en l'air** drawing *or* emission of a dud cheque/*etc*; *Compta* **tirages annuels** annual drawings

tiraillement [tirajmɑ̃] *nm* **(a)** (*sur une corde etc*) tugging, pulling **(b) tiraillements d'estomac** gnawing of the stomach, pangs of hunger **(c)** (*friction*) (*entre deux personnes*) friction, wrangling; (*entre deux choses contradictoires*) conflict (**entre** between); **il y a souvent eu des tiraillements entre eux** there was often friction between them, they often wrangled

tirailler [tiraje] **1** *vt* to pull at, to tug at, to pull about; *Fig* **tiraillé entre deux émotions/ses parents** torn between two opposing feelings/one's parents **2** *vi* **(a)** *Mil* to shoot wildly; (*pour harceler*) to fire in skirmishing order **(b) j'ai la peau qui me tiraille** my skin feels tight

tiraillerie [tirajri] *nf* **(a)** *Mil* wild firing **(b)** (*friction*) wrangling, friction

tirailleur [tirajœr] *nm* **(a)** *Mil* skirmisher, sharpshooter; *Hist* **tirailleurs algériens/sénégalais** native Algerian/Senegalese infantry; **en tirailleurs** in skirmishing order **(b)** *Journ F* freelance (journalist)

tirant [tirɑ̃] *nm* **(a)** (*de bourse*) (draw)string **(b)** (*de botte*) boot strap **(c)** *Constr* (*de toit*) tie beam **(d)** *Tech* stay, brace
▶ **tirant**: *Constr etc* **t. d'air** head room; *Naut* **t. d'eau** draught, *US* draft; **avoir dix pieds de t. d'eau** to draw ten feet of water; **navire à faible t. d'eau** shallow-draught ship; **échelle de t. d'eau** draught marks *or* numbers; **t. de frein** brake rod

tire [tir] *nf* **(a) voleur à la t.** pickpocket; **vol à la t.** pickpocketing; **le nombre des vols à la t.** the number of pickpocketing cases **(b)** *Can* (*confiserie*) molasses toffee, *Am* molasses candy, taffy; **t. d'érable** maple toffee *or Am* taffy **(c)** *Arg* (*voiture*) car

tiré, -ée [tire] **1** *adj* **(a)** (*traits*) drawn, haggard; **il avait les traits tirés** his face was *or* he looked drawn *or* haggard; **aux cheveux tirés** with her hair drawn *or* pulled back **(b)** *Fig* **t. par les cheveux** far-fetched **(c)** *Golf* **coup t.** pulled shot, pull **(d) broderie à fils tirés** drawn-thread work **(e)** *Banque* **chèque t. sur qn** cheque drawn on sb; **personne tirée** drawee; **t. par la demande** demand-led **2** *n Com* drawee **3** *nm* **(a)** (*chasse*) shoot **(b)** *Typ* **t. à part** offprint, separate **4** *nf* **tirée** *F* **(a)** (*trajet*) long haul; **il y a encore une sacrée tirée** there's still a long way to go **(b) une tirée de qch** (*grande quantité*) loads of sth

tire-au-cul *nm inv Arg* = **tire-au-flanc**

tire-au-flanc *nm inv F* shirker, *Br* skiver

tire-botte, *pl* **tire-bottes** *nm* (*crochet*) boot-hook; (*planchette*) boot-jack

tire-bouchon, *pl* **tire-bouchons** *nm* **(a)** (*pour bouteille*) corkscrew; **en t.** (*queue*) curly **(b)** (*mèche*) corkscrew curl

tire(-)bouchonné, *pl* **tire(-)bouchonnés** *adj* (*pantalon*) crumpled; **ses chaussettes étaient tire(-)bouchonnées** his socks were round his ankles

tire-bouton, *pl* **tire-boutons** *nm Vieilli* buttonhook

tire-clous *nm inv* nail puller

tire-d'aile (à) *adv* **s'envoler à t.** to fly swiftly away; *Fig* **partir** *ou* **s'éloigner à t.** to fly off; **s'enfuir à t.** to take flight

tire-fesses *nm inv F* T-bar; **monter en t.** to go up by the T-bar, to take the T-bar up

tire-jus *nm inv Arg* (*mouchoir*) hankie, snot rag

tire-laine *nm inv Vieilli* (*voleur*) footpad

tire-lait *nm inv* breast pump

tire-larigot (à) [atirlarigo] *adv F* **boire/manger à t.** to drink/eat one's fill *or* to one's heart's content, to have more than enough to drink/eat; **il y en a à t.** there's loads

tire-ligne, *pl* **tire-lignes** *nm* drawing pen

tirelire [tirlir] *nf* **(a)** (*pour économiser*) bank; *Fig* **il a dû casser sa t.** he had to break into his piggy bank **(b)** *Arg* (*figure*) mug; (*tête*) nut, bonce; (*ventre*) belly

tire-pognon, *pl* **tire-pognons** *nm F Vieilli* one-arm(ed) bandit, fruit machine

tirer [tire] **1** *vt* **(a)** (*étendre*) (*fil métallique, câble*) to draw; **t. ses cheveux en arrière** to pull one's hair back; *F* **encore une heure à t. d'ici le déjeuner!** still another hour to get through before lunch!; *Arg* **t. cinq ans** (*de prison*) to get five years *or* a five-year stretch
(b) (*traire*) (*vache etc*) to milk
(c) (*dans une direction*) to pull; (*cordon, sonnette*) to pull (on); (*chaussettes*) to pull up; **t. qn par la manche** to tug at *or* pull (on) sb's sleeve; **t. les cheveux à qn** to pull sb's hair; **je vais te t. les oreilles!** I'll give you what for!; **se faire t. les oreilles** to get told off; **t. la jambe** *ou F* **la patte** to limp; (*traîner*) to lag behind; **t. les rideaux** to draw *or* pull the curtains; **t. le verrou** to shoot the bolt; (*pour ouvrir*) to draw the bolt; **t. qch vers le haut/bas** to pull sth up/down; **t. qch à soi** to pull sth to *or* towards one; *Fig F* **t. la couverture à soi** to want more than one's share; *Fig* **t. un auteur à soi** to put a personal interpretation on an author's words; *Hist* **t. un criminel à quatre (chevaux)** to (hang,) draw and quarter a criminal
(d) **t. son chapeau à qn** to raise *or* lift one's hat to sb; *Fig* **je te tire mon chapeau!** I take my hat off to you!
(e) (*extraire*) (*bouchon, portefeuille etc*) to pull (out), to take out (**de** from, of); (*eau, vin, carte, conclusion*) to draw (**de** from); **t. les cartes** to read the cards; **se faire t. les cartes** to have one's cards read *or* one's fortune told; **t. plaisir/satisfaction de qch** to derive pleasure/satisfaction from sth, to get pleasure/satisfaction from *or* out of sth; **je n'en tire aucun(e) plaisir/satisfaction** I don't get any pleasure/satisfaction out of it; **t. vanité de qch** to pride oneself on sth; **d'où tire-t-elle cette certitude?** what makes her so certain?, *F* how come she's so sure?; **je n'ai rien pu t. de lui** I couldn't get anything *or* a word out of him; **t. qn d'un mauvais pas** *ou* **d'embarras/de prison** to get sb out of a tight spot *or* a difficulty/of prison; **t. qn de son lit** to drag *or* pull sb out of bed; **je ne vous tire par du lit, au moins?** I didn't get you out of bed, I hope?; **t. qn du sommeil** to drag sb from his/her sleep; **t. qn du doute** to remove sb's doubts; **t. qn de l'erreur** to show sb his/her mistake; *F* **t. de l'argent de qn** to get money out of sb, to extract money from sb; **t. de l'huile des olives** to extract oil from olives; **t. un bénéfice** to take a profit; **ce mot tire son origine de …** this word has its origin(s) in …; **mot tiré du latin** word derived from Latin; **phrase tirée du Cid de Corneille** phrase taken from Corneille's Le Cid; **t. la racine carrée d'un nombre** to extract the square root of a number
(f) (*tracer*) (*trait*) to draw; **t. des plans** to draw up *or* prepare plans; *Fig* to make plans
(g) *Typ* (*gravure, épreuve*) to pull, to print (off), to strike off; (*livre*) to print; **t. un livre à cinq mille exemplaires** to print five thousand copies of a book; **donner le bon à t. d'un volume** to pass a book for press; *Phot* **t. une épreuve d'un cliché** to take a print from a negative; **t. à part** to offprint; *Hum* **se faire tirer le portrait** to have one's photograph taken
(h) *Com* (*lettre de change, chèque*) to draw (**sur** on); **avez-vous tiré des chèques depuis cette date?** have you written any cheques since then?; **ce chèque a-t-il déja été tiré?** (*sur mon compte*) has this cheque cleared yet?
(i) (*coup de feu, balle, roquette, canon*) to fire; (*flèche*) to shoot; (*feu d'artifice*) to let off; (*lièvre, oiseaux, gibier*) to shoot; **t. un coup de revolver sur qn** to fire *or* shoot at sb

with a revolver; **ils se sont fait t. (dessus) comme des lapins** they were shot down like animals

(j) *Naut* **navire qui tire vingt pieds** ship that draws twenty feet (of water)

2 *vi* **(a)** (*d'un tireur d'élite etc*) to shoot; (*d'une arme à feu*) to go off; **t. à bout portant** to fire at point blank range; **t. à couvert** to fire from cover; **t. à la carabine** to shoot with a rifle; **t. au hasard** to fire at random; **t. dans le dos de qn** to shoot sb in the back; **t. dans le tas** *ou* **la foule** to fire *or* shoot into the crowd; **t. en l'air** to fire into the air; **t. sur qn/qch** to shoot *or* fire at sb/sth

(b) (*sur une corde etc*) to pull (**sur** on, at); **j'ai la peau qui tire** my skin feels tight; **t. sur sa pipe/cigarette** to pull *or* draw *or* puff on one's pipe/cigarette

(c) *Sp, Fb* to shoot; (*aux boules*) to throw; *Fb* **t. au but** to shoot at goal

(d) *Cartes* **t. pour la donne** to cut for deal

(e) *Fig* **bleu tirant sur le vert** blue verging on green; **le jour tire à sa fin** the day is drawing to its close; **nos provisions tirent à leur fin** our stores are running low *or* are giving out; **t. en longueur** to drag; **cela ne tire pas à conséquence** it is of no consequence; **ça pourrait t. à conséquence pour ta carrière** it could have consequences for *or* be important to your career; *F* **t. à la ligne** to pad out an article; **t. sur la soixantaine** to be getting on for sixty

(f) *Aut* **t. sur la gauche/droite** to pull to the left/right; *Naut* **t. au large** to stand out to sea

(g) (*d'une cheminée etc*) to draw

(h) *Fin* **t. à découvert** to overdraw; **t. à vue** to draw at sight

3 se tirer *vpr* **(a) se t. d'un mauvais pas** to get out of a fix *or* a tight spot; **si tu crois t'en t. comme ça, tu te trompes!** if you think you're going to get out of it like that you're mistaken!; **vous ne vous en tirerez pas avec cette excuse-là** you won't get away with that excuse; **va-t-elle s'en t.?** is she going to get out of it?; (*d'une maladie, d'un accident*) is she going to make it?, is she going to pull through?; **s'en t. sans aucun mal** to escape uninjured *or* unhurt *or* unscathed; **s'en t. tout juste** to escape by the skin of one's teeth; **on s'en tire, mais c'est juste** we only just manage to make both ends meet, we only just get by

(b) *F* (*finir*) to come to an end; **ça se tire** it'll soon be over

(c) (*partir*) to be off, to make tracks, to beat it; **on se tire?** shall we make tracks?, shall we get out of here?; **moi, je me tire** I'm off; **tire-toi, sale con!** beat it, dickhead!

tiret [tirɛ] *nm Typ* (*trait d'union*) hyphen; (*petit trait*) dash; **ligne de tirets** broken line; *Ordinat* **t. conditionnel/insécable** soft/hard hyphen

tirette [tirɛt] *nf* **(a)** (*d'un bureau*) pull-out shelf; (*d'une table*) leaf **(b)** *Tech* pull handle, pull knob; (*d'un fourneau etc*) flue damper; *Aut etc* (pull-out) knob **(c)** *Belg* (*fermeture éclair*) zip, *Am* zipper

tireur, -euse [tirœr, -øz] **1** *n* **(a)** *Com* (*d'un chèque, d'une lettre de change etc*) drawer **(b) tireuse de cartes** fortune teller **(c)** *Phot* printer **(d)** (*d'arme*) **c'est un bon/mauvais t.** he's a good/bad shot **(e)** *Escrime Vieilli, Litt* **t. d'armes** fencer **(f)** (*aux boules*) thrower **2** *nf* **tireuse (a)** *Phot* (*appareil*) printer **(b)** (*pour remplir les bouteilles*) bottle-filling machine, bottle filler

▶ **tireur**: **t. d'élite** marksman, sharpshooter; **t. embusqué** *ou* **isolé** sniper

tiroir [tirwar] *nm* **(a)** (*d'une table, une armoire etc*) drawer; **fonds de t.** (*petite monnaie*) small change; **râcler ses fonds de t.** to scrape one's pennies together; *Littér* **roman/comédie à tiroir(s)** episodic novel/play; **nom à tiroir(s)** double-barrelled name **(b)** *Tech* (*d'une machine à vapeur*) slide, slide valve; **t. à papier** paper tray

tiroir-caisse, *pl* **tiroirs-caisses** *nm Com* till, cash register

tisane [tizan] *nf* **(a)** (*infusion*) herb(al) tea; **t. de camomille/menthe/verveine** camomile/mint/verbena tea **(b)** *Arg* (*coups*) beating

tisanière [tizanjɛr] *nf* = pot for preparing herb(al) tea

tison [tizɔ̃] *nf* **(a)** (*de bois*) (fire)brand; *Fig* **garder les tisons** to stay by the fire **(b) allumette t.** fusee (match)

tisonné [tizɔne] *adj* (*robe d'un cheval*) with black spots

tisonner [tizɔne] *vt* (*feu*) to poke

tisonnier [tizɔnje] *nm* poker

tissage [tisaʒ] *nm Tex* **(a)** (*activité*) weaving; **t. à la main** *ou* **à bras** handloom weaving; **t. mécanique** power-loom weaving **(b)** (*installation*) cloth mill *or* works

tisser [tise] **1** *vt* **(a)** *Tex* to weave; **t. sa toile** (*d'une araignée*) to spin its web **(b)** *Fig* (*intrigue*) to weave **2 se tisser** *vpr Fig* **l'intrigue qui se tissait autour de cette disparition** the web of intrigue which was being woven around the disappearance

tisserand, -ande [tisrɑ̃, -ɑ̃d] *n* weaver

tisserin [tisrɛ̃] *nm Orn* weaver(bird)

tisseur, -euse [tisœr, -øz] *n* weaver

tissu [tisy] *nm* **(a)** *Tex* material, fabric, cloth; *Fig* **un t. de mensonges** a tissue of lies; **un t. d'absurdités** one absurdity after another; **c'est un t. de bêtises** it's complete and utter nonsense; **c'est un t. d'incohérences** it's full of inconsistencies **(b)** *Biol* tissue **(c)** *Fig* **le t. urbain/social/industriel** the urban/social/industrial fabric

▶ **tissu**: *Anat* **t. conjonctif** connective tissue; **t. métallique** wire gauze

tissu-éponge, *pl* **tissus-éponges** *nm Tex* (terry) towelling; **peignoir en t.** towelling robe; **serviette en t.** terry towel

tissulaire [tisylɛr] *adj Biol* (of) tissue

Titan [titɑ̃] *nm Myth, Astron* Titan; **travail de T.** *ou* **t.** Herculean task; **un combat de titans** an epic battle; *Ind* **grue T.** giant crane

titane [titan] *nm Ch* titanium

titanesque [titanɛsk] *adj* (*entreprise, œuvre etc*) titanic; (*orgueil, force*) colossal

titi [titi] *nm F* (*gavroche*) cheeky urchin

Titien [tisjɛ̃] *nm* Titian

titillation [titilasjɔ̃] *nf* titillation

titiller [titije] *vt* (*chatouiller*), *Fig* to titillate; **ma curiosité me titillait** I was consumed by curiosity

titisme [titism] *nm Pol* Titoism

titiste [titist] *adj, n Pol* Titoist

titrage [titraʒ] *nm* **(a)** *Ch, Ind* (*d'une solution*) titration, titrating; (*d'un minerai etc*) assaying; (*d'un alcool, d'un vin etc*) determination of the strength **(b)** *Cin* titling; *Journ* **t. à cheval** spread head

titraille [titraj] *nf Journ* cover-line

titre [titr] *nm* **(a)** (*de noblesse, fonction etc*) title; **avoir un t. nobiliaire** to have a title; **porter le t. de duc** to bear the title of duke; **se donner le t. de ...** to call *or Fml* style oneself ...

(b) (*qualification*) title; **avoir le t. d'avocat** to have the title of lawyer; **sans t. officiel** without any official status; **professeur en t.** permanent teacher; *Jur* **propriétaire en t.** legal owner; **la maîtresse en t. du roi** the King's acknowledged mistress; **elle ne mérite plus son t. d'amie, le t. d'amie ne lui convient plus** she no longer deserves the title of friend *or* to be called a friend

(c) *Sp* title; *Boxe* **combat comptant/ne comptant pas pour le t.** title/non-title fight; **tenant du t.** titleholder; **champion en t.** reigning champion

(d) (*diplôme etc*) qualification; **pourvu de tous ses titres** fully qualified

(e) (*certificat*) voucher; *Mil* **t. de permission** pass

(f) *Fin, Com* security bond, certificate; **titres** stocks and shares, securities, *Am* stock

(g) (*droit*) title, claim, right; **t. juridique à qch** legal claim to sth

(h) à t. de as a; **à t. d'office** ex officio; **à t. de précaution** just in case; **à t. d'ami** as a friend; **à t. d'essai** as a trial measure, experimentally; **à t. de faveur** as a favour; **il offre ses services à t. bénévole** he volunteers his services; **à juste t.** rightly; **il s'est mis en colère à juste t.** he got angry and rightly so, he was justifiably angry; **à quel t.?** by what right?, on what grounds?; **au même t.** for the same reason; **à t. gratuit** free of charge; **à ce t.** (*pour cette raison*) therefore; (*en cette qualité*) as such

(i) (*de livre, chanson, film etc*) title

(j) (*de chapitre, page*) heading; **(page de) t.** title page; **faux t.** half-title; *Journ* **les gros titres** the headlines; **faire les gros titres** to hit the headlines, to be front page news

(k) (*subdivision*) (*d'une loi etc*) part, section, title

(l) (*d'une solution, d'or*) titre, *US* titer; (*d'un minerai*) grade, content; (*d'une monnaie*) fineness

(m) (*du coton, d'un fil de fer*) size, number

▶ **titre**: **t. d'action** share certificate; **t. d'appel** (*publicité*) catch title; *Typ* **t. en bas de page** footer; **t. de civilité** (*dans une lettre*) salutation; *Typ* **t. courant** running head(line) *or* title; **t. de créance** loan note, debt instrument; **titres déposés en nantissement** securities lodged as collateral; **t. d'eau** degree of humidity; **titres émis** issued securities; **titres libérés** fully paid-up securities; **t. nominatif** registered security; **t. d'obligation** loan *or* bond note; **t. participatif** equity loan; **t. de participation** equity investment *or* loan; **titres de placement** marketable securities; *Fin* **t. au porteur** bearer bond, negotiable instrument; *Jur* **t. de propriété** title deed; *Journ* **t. de rappel** coverline; **t. de rente** government bond; **titres à revenu fixe** fixed income securities; **titres à revenu variable** floating rate securities; **titres à terme** futures; **t. de transport** ticket; *Com* **t. universel de paiement** (*joint à la facture*) payment form, universal payment order

titré [titre] *adj* **(a)** (*personne*) titled **(b)** *Ch* (*solution*) titrated, standard

titrer [titre] *vt* **(a)** (*personne*) to confer a title on; (*livre*) to title, to call **(b)** *Cin* (*film*) to title **(c)** *Ch, Ind* (*solution*) to titrate, to standardize; (*minerai etc*) to assay; (*alcool, vin etc*) to determine the strength of **(d)** *Tex, Tech* (*coton, fil de fer etc*) to size, to number

titreur, -euse [titrœr, -øz] *Journ n* headline writer

titreuse [titrøz] *nf Cin* (*appareil*) titler

titrisation [titrisasjɔ̃] *nf Bourse* securitization

titubant [titybɑ̃] *adj* reeling, lurching, staggering

tituber [titybe] *vi* to reel (about), to lurch, to stagger; **marcher/entrer/sortir en titubant** to stagger *or* lurch along/in/out; **t. de fatigue** to reel *or* stagger *or* totter with exhaustion

titulaire [titylɛr] **1** *adj* (*professeur etc*) with tenure; **devenir t.** to get tenure; **être t. d'un passeport/d'un permis de conduire** to have *or* hold a passport/driving licence **2** *n* **(a)** (*d'un droit, d'un titre, d'un certificat etc*) holder; (*d'un passeport*) holder, bearer; (*d'un office*) holder, occupant, *Admin* incumbent; *Rel* (*d'une paroisse*) incumbent; **t. d'action** shareholder **(b)** *Sp* team member; **il a plus de sélections comme remplaçant que comme t.** he has made the squad (as a sub) more often than he has made the team

titularisation [titylarizasjɔ̃] *nf* **(a)** *Admin* (*des fonctionnaires etc*) establishment **(b)** *Sp* inclusion in the full team

titulariser [titylarize] *vt* **(a)** *Admin etc* **t. qn** to confirm sb in his post *or* appointment **(b)** *Sp* to include in a/the team; **titularisé pour l'équipe de France** capped for France; **quand j'ai été titularisé pour la première fois** the first time I made it into the full team

TJJ [teʒiʒi] *nm Fin* (*abrév* **taux d'argent au jour le jour**) overnight *or* call rate

TMG [teɛmʒe] *nm* (*abrév* **temps moyen de Greenwich**) GMT

toast [tost] *nm* **(a)** (*tranche de pain grillé*) piece *or* slice of toast; **t. beurré** piece *or* slice of buttered toast; **des toasts** toast, toasted bread **(b)** (*hommage*) toast; **porter un t. à qn** to drink *or* propose a toast to sb, to toast sb

toasteur [tostœr] *nm* toaster

toboggan [tɔbɔgɑ̃] *nm* **(a)** (*de piscine*) chute; (*de terrain de jeu etc*) slide; (*dans un parc d'attractions*) helter-skelter; **des enfants qui font du t.** children playing on the slide **(b)** *Com etc* (*pour marchandises*) chute **(c)** *Aut* flyover, *Am* overpass **(d)** *Can* (*traîneau*) toboggan; **faire du t.** to go tobogganing; **piste de t.** toboggan run

toc [tɔk] **1** *int* tap!; **t. t.!** knock knock; **et t.!** so there! **2** *nm* **(a)** (*à la porte etc*) tap, rap; **j'ai entendu un t. t. à la porte** I heard a tap tap *or* a tapping at the door **(b)** *F* (*imitation*) **bijoux en t.** imitation *or* paste jewellery; **c'est du t.** it's imitation *or* fake **3** *adj inv F* **(a)** (*faux*) fake; (*de mauvais goût*) flashy, *Br F* naff **(b) être un peu t. t.** (*fou*) to be a bit crazy *or* cracked; **il est un peu t. t.** he's not all there

tocante [tɔkɑ̃t] *nf F* (*montre*) watch

tocard, -arde [tɔkar, -ard] *Arg* **1** *adj* worthless, trashy **2** *nm Courses de chevaux* (rank) outsider **3** *n Péj* (*personne*) loser, dead loss

toccata [tɔkata] *nf Mus* toccata

tocsin [tɔksɛ̃] *nm* alarm bell, *Fml* tocsin; **faire sonner le t.** to sound the alarm (bell) *or Fml* tocsin

toge [tɔʒ] *nf* **(a)** *Antiq* toga **(b)** *Jur, Scol* gown

Togo [togo] *nm* Togo

togolais [tɔgɔlɛ] *adj, nm* Togolese

tohu-bohu [tɔybɔy] *nm* (*désordre*) chaos, confusion; (*bruit*) hubbub; **dans un t. général** amidst general confusion

toi [twa] *pron pers* **(a)** you; *Bible, Arch* thou; (*complément direct*) you; *Bible, Arch* thee; **c'est t.** it's you; **c'est t. qui l'as fait** you did it; **ah c'est bien t., ça!** that's typical of you!, that's just like you!; **t. et moi nous irons ensemble** you and I will go together; **il est plus âgé que t.** he is older than you; **il n'aime que t.** he loves only you; **dis-le-lui, t.** you tell him; **avec t.** with you; **ce livre est à t.** this book is yours *or* belongs to you; **à t., je peux le dire** I can tell you; **moi, je reste, et t., tu pars** I'll stay and you go; **t. parti, que vais-je faire?** once you've gone *or* with you gone, what am I going to do?

(b) (*reflexive*) **dépêche-t.!** hurry up!; **tais-t.!** be quiet!; **assieds-t.!** sit down!; **maîtrise-t.!** control yourself!

toile [twal] *nf* **(a)** cloth; **t. (de lin)** linen; **drap de t.** linen sheet; *F* **se mettre dans les toiles** to hit the sack *or* hay; **t. (de coton)** cotton; **pantalon de t.** lightweight trousers; **marchand de t.** draper; **reliure en t.** cloth binding; **sac en t.** canvas bag; **collé sur t.** mounted on canvas **(b)** *Beaux-Arts* (*œuvre*) painting, canvas; (*support*) canvas **(c)** *Naut* (*voiles*) canvas, sails; **réduire la t.** to reduce sail **(d)** (*de moulin*) **toiles** sails **(e)** *F* (*film*) **se faire une t.** to go to the pictures *or Am* movies

▶ **toile**: **t. d'amiante** asbestos; **t. d'araignée** cobweb, spider's web; **t. à bâches** tarpaulin; **t. cirée** American cloth, oilcloth; **nappe en t. cirée** waxed tablecloth; **t. (d')émeri** emery cloth; *Th* **t. de fond** backdrop, backcloth; *Fig* **avec la guerre en t. de fond** with the war as a backdrop, against the backdrop of the war; **t. de Jouy** toile de Jouy; **t. de maître** masterpiece, old master; **t. à matelas** tick, ticking; **t. métallique** wire gauze; **t. de tente** canvas; **t. à voiles** canvas, sailcloth

toilerie [twalri] *nf* (*commerce*) cotton, linen and hemp industry *or* trade; (*fabrique*) cotton, linen and hemp mill

toilettage [twalɛtaʒ] *nm* (*d'un animal domestique*) grooming; *Fig* **faire le t. d'un texte** to put the finishing touches to a text

toilette [twalɛt] *nf* **(a)** (*action de se laver*) washing, *Litt* toilet; **faire sa t.** to have a wash, to get washed; **être à sa t.** (*se laver*) to be having a wash, to be getting washed; *Vieilli* (*s'apprêter*) to be making one's toilet; **faire un bout** *ou* **un brin de t.** to have a wash and brush up, to freshen up; *Fig* **faire une t. de chat** to have a catlick, to have a lick and a promise; **le chat fait sa t.** the cat is washing *or* grooming itself; **savon de t.** toilet soap

(b) toilettes (*W.-C.*) toilet, *Am* washroom, *Am* rest room, *Br F* loo; (*publiques*) public convenience *or* lavatory; **toilettes pour dames** ladies' toilet *or Am* room; **toilettes pour hommes** gents toilet, *Am* men's room

(c) (*vêtements de femme*) dress, clothes; (*costume*) outfit; **elle porte bien la t.** she looks good in formal clothes; **être en (grande) t.** to be in formal dress, to be formally dressed; **t. de bal** ball dress; **changer de t.** to change one's clothes

toiletter [twalete] *vt* (*animal domestique*) to groom; *Fig* (*texte*) to put the finishing touches to

toi-même *pron pers* yourself; *Bible, Arch* thyself; *voir* **même**

toise [twaz] *nf* (*règle*) height gauge; **se mettre sous la t.** to have one's height measured; **passer qn à** *ou* **sous la t.** to measure sb's height

toisé [twaze] *nm Tech* measuring (up), measurement

toiser [twaze] **1** *vt* **(a)** (*regarder*) **t. qn** to look *or* eye sb up and down **(b)** *Vieilli* (*mesurer*) to measure (the height of) **2 se toiser** *vpr* (*se regarder*) to look each other up and down, to take each other's measure

toison [twazɔ̃] *nf* (*de mouton*) fleece; (*de lion, de cheval*) mane; *Fig* (*chevelure*) mane (of hair); (*poils*) fleece, thick body hair; *Myth* **la T. d'or** the Golden Fleece

toit [twa] *nm* **(a)** (*de maison, voiture etc*) roof; *Fig* (*habitation*) home (of one's own); **t. d'ardoises/de tuiles/de chaume** slate/tiled/thatched roof; *Beaux-Arts* **paysage de toits** roofscape; **trouver un t. pour ses enfants** to put a roof over one's children's heads, to find a home for one's children; **sous son t.** under one's (own) roof; **abriter qn sous son t.** to take sb in, to put sb up; **je suis restée plusieurs jours sous leur t.** I stayed with them for several days; **se retrouver sans t.** to find oneself without a roof over one's head; **habiter sous les toits** to live in a garret; **chambre sous les toits** attic room; *Fig* **publier** *ou* **crier qch sur les toits** to proclaim sth from the rooftops *or* housetops; **double t.** (*de tente*) flysheet; **le t. paternel/familial** the family home; **le t. conjugal** the marital home

(b) *Min* (*d'une mine*) roof, top

▶ **toit**: *Aut* **t. à arceau en T** T-bar roof; *Aut* **t. ouvrant** sun roof; *Aut* **t. ouvrant coulissant** sliding sunroof

toiture [twatyr] *nf* roofing, roof; **refaire la t.** to repair the roof

tokai, tokay [tɔkɛ] *nm* (*vin*) Tokay

tôle¹ [tol] *nf* **(a)** (*matériau*) sheet metal; (*de fer*) sheet iron; **t. d'acier** sheet steel; **t. de cuivre** copper sheeting **(b)** (*feuille*) metal sheet; (*de fer*) iron sheet; (*d'acier*) steel sheet

▶ **tôle**: **t. ondulée** corrugated iron; **toit en t. ondulée** corrugated iron roof

tôle² *nf Arg* (*prison*) = **taule (a)**

tôlée [tole] *adj f, nf Ski* **(neige) tôlée** crusted snow

tolérable [tɔlerabl] *adj* (*supportable*) (*douleur, situation*) bearable, tolerable; **votre comportement n'est pas t.** your behaviour is unacceptable

tolérance [tɔlerɑ̃s] *nf* **(a)** (*compréhension*) tolerance; *Rel* toleration; **faire preuve de t.** to be tolerant; **manquer de t.** to lack tolerance, to be intolerant; *Arch* **maison de t.** licensed brothel

(b) (*concession*) concession; **t. orthographique** acceptable variation in spelling

(c) *Tech* tolerance, margin; **t. nulle** zero allowance; **à t. de pannes** fault-tolerant; **t. sur l'épaisseur/la longueur** thickness/length margin; **t. de fonctionnement** operational tolerance; *Électron* **t. de fréquence** frequency tolerance

(d) (*à la douane*) **t. (permise)** allowance; **il y a une t. d'un demi-litre** you are allowed to bring in half a litre duty-free

(e) *Méd* tolerance; **t. immunitaire** immune tolerance

tolérant, -ante [tɔlerɑ̃, -ɑ̃t] *adj, n* tolerant (person)

tolérer [tɔlere] **(je tolère, n. tolérons; je tolérerai) 1** *vt* **(a)**

(*être indulgent pour*) (*opinions, religions etc*) to tolerate; (*supporter*) (*personne, situation*) to tolerate, to put up with; **je ne tolère pas qu'on dise ça** I cannot tolerate people saying that (kind of thing) **(b)** *Méd* (*médicament*) to tolerate **2 se tolérer** *vpr* to put up with *or* tolerate each other

tôlerie [tolri] *nf* **(a)** (*commerce*) sheet-metal trade **(b)** (*atelier*) sheet-metal workshop; *Aut* body shop **(c)** (*tôles*) metal sheets *or* plates; *Aut* panels, bodywork

tôlier[1] [tolje] *nm* **(a)** (*marchand*) sheet-iron merchant **(b)** (*ouvrier*) sheet-metal worker; *Aut* panel beater

tôlier[2] -ière [tolje, -jɛr] *n Arg* = **taulier**

tollé [tɔle] *nm* (indignant) outcry; **t. général** public outcry

toluène [tɔlɥɛn] *nm Ch* toluene, methyl benzene

TOM [tɔm] *nm abrév* **territoire d'outre-mer**

tomahawk [tɔmaok] *nm* tomahawk

tomaison [tɔmɛzɔ̃] *nf Typ* volume numbering

tomate [tɔmat] *nf* **(a)** [①**A12**,1,c] *Bot, Culin* tomato; **sauce t.** tomato sauce; **salade/jus de t.** tomato salad/juice; **concentré de tomates** tomato concentrate *or* purée; *F* **être (rouge) comme une t.** to be as red as a beetroot **(b)** *F* (*boisson*) pastis with grenadine

tombal, -ale, -aux, -ales [tɔ̃bal, -o] *adj* **pierre tombale** tombstone, gravestone; **inscription tombale** tombstone *or* gravestone inscription

tombant [tɔ̃bɑ̃] *adj* **(a) à la nuit tombante** at nightfall **(b)** (*draperies*) flowing; (*cheveux*) loose; (*branche, oreilles d'un animal, moustache*) drooping; (*épaules*) sloping; **des yeux aux paupières tombantes** hooded eyes

tombe [tɔ̃b] *nf* **(a)** (*sépulture*) grave; (*avec un monument*) tomb; **prier sur la t. de qn** to pray at sb's grave(side); **t. collective** mass grave; **être dans la t.** to be dead; **avoir un pied dans la t.** to have one foot in the grave; **suivre qn dans la t.** to follow sb to the grave; **se retourner dans sa t.** to turn in one's grave **(b)** (*pierre tombale*) tombstone, gravestone

tombé [tɔ̃be] *adj Rugby* **coup de pied t.** drop kick

tombeau, -eaux [tɔ̃bo] *nm* tomb; **t. de famille** family vault; **descendre au t.** to go to one's grave; **mettre au t.** to entomb; **mise au t.** entombment; *F* **il me mettra** *ou* **conduira au t.** (*il me tuera*) he'll be the death of me; *Fig* **le t.** (*la mort*) the grave; *Fig* **cette pièce est un vrai t.** it's pitch dark in here; *Fig* **à t. ouvert** (*conduire, rouler*) at breakneck speed

tombée [tɔ̃be] *nf* **(a) t. du jour** *ou* **de la nuit** nightfall; **à la t. de la nuit** at nightfall **(b)** *Journ* (*pour la remise d'un travail*) copy deadline; (*pour la sortie d'une édition*) edition time

tomber[1] [tɔ̃be] *nm* **(a) au t. du jour** at nightfall **(b)** *Sp* (*de lutte*) fall

tomber[2] **1** *vi* (*aux* **être**) **(a)** (*d'une personne, d'un objet*) to fall (down); (*d'un avion, de feuilles, de la neige etc, Fig du gouvernment, Mil d'une ville*) to fall; **le plafond est tombé** the ceiling has come down *or* fallen in; **toutes les feuilles de ma plante sont tombées** all the leaves have dropped off my plant, my plant has lost *or* shed all its leaves; **fruits tombés** windfalls; **les gens tombent comme des mouches** people are dropping like flies; **mes cheveux commencent à t.** I'm beginning to lose my hair, my hair is beginning to fall out; *TV, Rad* **la nouvelle est tombée ce matin et c'est la guerre!** the news came through this morning and it's war!; *Fig* **il faut être tombé bien bas** you have to have sunk pretty low; **t. à l'eau** to fall in (the water); *Fig* (*d'un projet etc*) to fall through, to come to nothing; **t. à plat** (*échouer*) (*d'une proposition, une plaisanterie*) to fall flat, *F* to go down like a lead balloon; **t. dans un piège** to fall into a trap; *Fig F* **t. dans les pommes** to pass out, to faint, to keel over; **t. dans le coma** to lapse into a coma; **t. d'une échelle/du toit/de cheval/de vélo** to fall off a ladder/the roof/one's horse/one's bike; **le livre lui est tombé des mains** the book fell *or* dropped from *or* out of his hands; *Fig* **son dernier roman m'est tombé des mains** his last novel didn't hold my interest; **je tombe de fatigue** *ou* **de sommeil** I'm ready to drop, I'm dead on my feet; **tout tombe en poussière** everything is crumbling to dust; **les bras m'en tombent** I can't believe it; **t. la tête la première** to fall head first, *F* to take a header; **t. à la renverse** to fall backwards; **t. sur ses pieds** to fall on one's feet; **t. par terre** (*d'une personne*) to fall; (*d'un objet*) to fall (to the ground); **ce livre m'est tombé sous la main** I came across this book; **comment ce papier a-t-il pu lui t. sous la main?** how could the paper have fallen into his hands?; **ça tombe sous le sens** it stands to reason, it's obvious; **sa décision tombe sous le sens** it stands to reason that he decided as he did; *Math* **t. juste** to come out exactly; **cet argent lui tombe du ciel** the money is a godsend to him; *Naut* **t. sous le vent** to fall off, to fall to leeward; **faire t.** (*d'une personne*) to knock over *or* down; (*du vent*) (*table, chaise*) to knock over *or* down; (*arbre, barrière, Fig gouvernment etc*) to bring down, to topple; **laisser t.** (*objet, Fig projet*) to drop; *Fig F* **laisser t. qn** to drop *or* dump sb; (*lui faire faux bond*) to let sb down; *Fig F* **laisse t., ça ne vaut pas la peine** forget it, it's not worth it; **se laisser t. dans un fauteuil** to drop *or* sink *or F* flop into an armchair

(b) (*diminuer*) (*du vent*) to drop, to abate, to subside, to die down; (*des prix, de la fièvre*) to drop, to fall; (*de la colère*) to die down, to abate; (*de la conversation*) to flag; (*de l'enthousiasme, l'intérêt*) to wane, to decline, *F* to fizzle out; (*des ventes, du nombre des adhésions*) to drop, to decline; **la nuit** *ou* **le jour tombe** night is falling; **une fois la nuit tombée** after dark; **cela va faire t. la fièvre** this will bring your/his/*etc* temperature down

(c) (*indique une transformation*) **t. en disgrâce/en ruine** to fall into disgrace/ruin(s); **t. amoureux de qn** to fall in love with sb, *F* to fall for sb; **t. malade** to fall ill; **t. (raide) mort** to drop (down) dead; *F* **t. enceinte** to get pregnant

(d) t. sur (*attaquer*) *Mil* (*ennemi*) to attack, to fall on; *F* (*personne*) to pitch *or* light into; (*rencontrer*) (*personne*) to bump into, to come across; (*objet*) to come across *or* upon; **il fallait que ça tombe sur moi!** it had to happen to me!; **et c'est tombé sur lui** and he was chosen, and the choice fell on him; **avec tous les ennuis qui me tombent dessus** with all these worries plaguing me; **si tu savais tout ce qui me tombe dessus** if you only knew all the things I've got on my mind; **il va nous t. sur le dos d'un moment à l'autre** he'll be bursting in on us any moment; **ils nous tombent toujours dessus à l'improviste** they're always dropping in on us

(e) (*arriver*) **Noël tombe un jeudi cette année** Christmas falls on *or* is on a Thursday this year; **t. pile** *ou* **à pic** *ou* **à propos** to come at (just) the right moment *or* time; **vous tombez bien** you've come at the right moment, you're just in time; **cet argent/cette invitation tombe vraiment très bien** *ou* **à pic** the money/the invitation has come just at the right time; **cela tombe mal** it's come at the wrong time, it's not a good time; **tu tombes mal** this is not a good time, you've come at the wrong time; **tu tombes mal, j'avais déjà acheté le livre** you picked the wrong thing, I already have the book; **comme ça tombe!** what a coincidence!; *F* **ça tombe comme un cheveu sur la soupe** it has come at an awkward moment *or* time

(f) (*pendre*) (*de cheveux*) to hang down; (*de draperies*) to fall, to hang (down); (*d'un tissu, d'un vêtement*) to hang; **ses cheveux lui tombent dans le dos** her hair hangs down her back

2 *vt* (*aux* **avoir**) **(a)** *Sp* **t. un adversaire** to throw an opponent; *F* **t. une femme** to pull a woman

(b) *F* **t. la veste** to take off one's jacket

3 *v impers* **il tombe de la pluie/de la grêle** it is raining/hailing; **il tombe des grêlons énormes** enormous hailstones are coming down; **qu'est-ce qu'il tombe!** it's really coming down!

tombereau, -eaux [tɔ̃bro] *nm* **(a)** (*charrette*) tip-cart; (*contenu*) cartload (**de** of) **(b)** (*camion*) dumper; **t. à ordures** *Br* bin lorry, dustcart, *Am* garbage truck

tombeur [tɔ̃bœr] *nm F* **t. (de femmes)** womanizer, ladykiller

tombola [tɔ̃bɔla] *nf* raffle, tombola

Tombouctou [tɔ̃buktu] *n* Timbuktu

tome [tɔm] *nm* (*volume*) volume; (*division*) (*d'un livre*) part

tomette [tɔmɛt] *nf* (small red hexagonal) floor tile

tomme [tɔm] *nf* = cheese made in Savoie and Dauphiné

tomographie [tɔmɔgrafi] *nf Méd* tomography

tom-pouce, *pl* **tom-pouces** [tɔmpus] *nm* **(a)** *F* dwarf, midget **(b)** (*petit parapluie*) stumpy umbrella

ton[1], ta, tes [tɔ̃, ta, te] *adj poss* [①**A30**,8; **B19-20**,E,1] (**ton** *is used instead of* **ta** *before f words beginning with vowel or mute h*) your; *Bible, Arch* thy; **t. ami/amie** your friend; **t. meilleur ami/ta meilleure amie** your best friend; **t. oncle et ta tante** your aunt and (your) uncle; **t. père et ta mère,** *Litt* **tes père et mère** your mother and father; **j'ai mis t. chapeau et tes gants** I put on your hat and (your) gloves; **un(e) de tes ami(e)s** one of your friends, a friend of yours; **un professeur de tes amis** a teacher friend of yours; *F* **tu auras ta chambre à toi** you'll have your own room; *F* **t. imbécile de frère** your idiot of a brother; *F* **t. artiste de mari** your artist husband; *F* **alors, je peux le rencontrer, t. artiste?** so, can I meet this artist of yours?; *F* **tu as eu t. vendredi** you got Friday off; *F* **alors, c'était ça tes vacances de rêve!** so much for your dream holiday!

ton[2] *nm* **(a)** (*qualité de voix*) tone; (*hauteur*) pitch; **parler d'un t. doux/sur un t. amical** to speak gently *or* in a gentle tone/in a friendly tone; **je souhaiterais que tu me parles sur un autre t., je te prie de changer de t. quand tu me parles** don't talk to me in that tone of voice, I don't like your tone; **sur le t. de la plaisanterie** jokingly, in a joking tone of voice; **écrire sur un t. de plaisanterie** to write in a humorous tone *or* style; **si tu le prends sur ce t. ...** if that's how you feel ..., if you're going to be like that then ...; **hausser le t.** to raise one's voice; **parler d'un t. bas** to speak in a low tone; **entre deux tons** in an undertone; *F* **faire baisser le t. à qn** to take sb down a peg or two

(b) (*goût*) manners; **le bon t.** good form *or* manners; **il est de bon t. de ne pas se faire remarquer** it's the done thing *or* it's good form not to attract attention; **c'est de mauvais t.** it is not the done thing, it is bad form *or* bad manners *or* vulgar; **remarques de bon t.** remarks in good taste

(c) *Mus* (*tonalité*) key; **le t. d'ut** the key of C; **(hauteur du) t.** pitch; **donner le t.** to give the tuning A; *Fig* to set the tone; **sortir du t.** to be out of tune; **se mettre dans le t.** to tune up; *Fig* to blend *or* fit in

(d) *Mus* (*intervalle*) **tons et demi-tons** tones and semitones; **t. entier** whole tone

(e) *Ling* tone; **langue à tons** tonal language

(f) *Beaux-Arts, Phot etc* (*couleur*) tone, shade; **tapis dans le t. des rideaux** carpet toning (in) with the curtains; **pour que tout l'ameublement soit dans le même t.** so that all the furniture tones in; **peinture/voiture deux tons** two-tone paint/car; *Ordinat* **tons de gris** shades of grey

tonal, -ale, -als, -ales [tɔnal] *adj Mus* tonal

tonalité [tɔnalite] *nf* **(a)** *Beaux-Arts, Phot, Mus* tonality; (*ton, Mus de morceau, Beaux-Arts de paysage*) key; (*d'instrument, de voix, Fig de film, livre*) tone; **j'aime la t. de cet instrument/de sa voix** I like the way the instrument/his voice sounds, I like the timbre of the instrument/his voice **(b)** *Tél* **t. (continue)** dialling *or Am* dial tone; **t. de réponse** answer tone; **attendez d'avoir la t.** wait for the dialling tone; **t. d'appel** ringing tone; **il n'y a plus de t.** there's no dialling tone, the phone's dead **(c)** (*de poste de radio etc*) tone

tondeur, -euse [tɔ̃dœr, -øz] **1** *n* (*de moutons, drap*) shearer; **t. de moutons** sheepshearer **2** *nf* **tondeuse (a)** (*instrument*) (*de moutons, drap*) shears; (*pour cheveux, pelage*) clippers **(b) tondeuse (à gazon)** (lawn) mower; **tondeuse électrique/mécanique** electric/hand mower; **passer la t. à gazon** to mow the lawn, to give the lawn a mow

tondre [tɔ̃dr] *vt* **(a)** (*moutons, drap*) to shear; (*animal, haie*) to clip; (*cheveux*) to shave off; (*pelouse*) to mow; **se faire t.** to have all one's hair shaved off; **tu t'es fait t.!** who scalped you? **(b)** *F* (*dépouiller*) (*personne*) to fleece; *Fig* **il tondrait un œuf** he's a real skinflint *or* Scrooge *or Am* tightwad

tondu [tɔ̃dy] **1** *adj* (*gazon*) mown; (*chien, haie*) clipped; (*moutons*) shorn; (*cheveux*) shaved off; (*tête*) shaved; **être complètement tondu** to have had all one's hair shaved off, to have a shaved head **2** *nm Rel* monk; *Hist F* **le Petit T.** Napoleon (Bonaparte)

toner [tɔnɛr] *nm* (*pour imprimante etc*) toner

tong [tɔ̃g] *nf* (*chaussure de plage*) flip-flop, *Am* thong

tonicardiaque [tɔnikardjak] *Méd* **1** *adj* which stimulates the heart, *Spéc* cardiotonic **2** *nm* heart stimulant, *Spéc* cardiotonic

tonicité [tɔnisite] *nf Méd* (*des muscles etc*) tone; (*de l'air marin etc*) bracing *or* tonic effect

tonifiant [tɔnifjɑ̃] *adj* (*air, marche etc*) bracing; (*lotion*) tonic

tonifier [tɔnifje] *vt* (*impf, pr sub* **n. tonifiions, v. tonifiiez**) (*muscles, peau, système nerveux, malade etc*) to tone up; **un bain froid ça tonifie** a cold bath is bracing *or* invigorating

tonique [tɔnik] **1** *adj* **(a) médicament t.** tonic; **lotion t.** (*pour le visage*) toning lotion, toner **(b)** (*revigorant*) (*air marin, climat, froid etc*) bracing, invigorating **(c)** *Ling* (*accent*) tonic; (*syllabe*) accented, stressed; **l'accent t. tombe sur ...** the stress falls on ... **(d)** *Mus* **note t.** tonic, keynote **2** *nm Méd* tonic; (*pour le visage*) toner, toning lotion **3** *nf Mus* tonic, keynote

tonitruant [tɔnitryɑ̃] *adj* (*voix*) like thunder, thundering; **..., dit-il d'une voix tonitruante** ..., he thundered

tonitruer [tɔnitrye] *vi* to thunder

tonka [tɔ̃ka] **1** *nm Bot* tonka bean (plant); **fève t.** tonka bean **2** *nf* tonka bean

tonnage [tɔnaʒ] *nm Naut* **(a)** (*de navire*) tonnage; **t. brut** gross tonnage; **t. net** register tonnage; (*d'un navire de guerre*) displacement; **t. port en lourd** deadweight tonnage **(b)** (*d'un port*) tonnage **(c) (droit de) t.** (duty based on) tonnage

tonnant [tɔnɑ̃] *adj* thundering; **voix tonnante** voice of thunder, thunderous voice

tonne [tɔn] *nf* **(a)** (*unité de poids*) (metric) ton, tonne (= *1000 kg*); **un camion de 8 tonnes, un 8 tonnes** an 8 ton lorry, an 8 tonner; *Fig F* **des tonnes (et des tonnes) de** tons (and tons) of **(b)** (*récipient*) tun, (large) cask

▶ **tonne: t. d'arrimage** measurement ton; **t. courte** short ton (= *907.185 kg*); *Naut* **t. de déplacement** ton of displacement, displacement ton; **t. d'encombrement** measurement ton; **t. équivalent charbon** ton coal equivalent; **t. équivalent pétrole** ton oil equivalent; **t. forte** long *or* gross ton (= *1016.06 kg*); *Naut* **t. de jauge** gross *or* register ton; **t. kilométrique** ton kilometre *or US* kilometer

tonneau, -eaux [tɔno] *nm* **(a)** barrel, cask; **mettre du vin en t.** to put wine into barrels *or* casks; **bière au t.** draught *or US* draft beer; *Fig* **ils sont tous du même t.** they're all the same; *Fig* **des remarques du même t.** remarks in the same vein; **petit t.** keg; **t. à mortier** mortar mixer; *Hist* **le t. de Diogène** Diogenes' tub; **t. de fret** freight ton; *Fig* **c'est le t. des Danaïdes** it's a never-ending task, it's no sooner finished than you have to start all over again; **t. d'arrosage** water cart

(b) *Naut* (*unité de volume*) ton; **navire de 500 tonneaux** 500-tonner, ship of 500 tons burden

(c) *Hist* (*voiture à cheval*) governess cart

(d) *Av, Aut* roll, roll-over; **faire un t.** *Av* to do a barrel roll; *Av, Aut* (*par accident*), to flip *or* roll over; **la voiture a fait trois tonneaux** the car flipped *or* rolled over three times

tonnelet [tɔnlɛ] *nm* (small) cask, keg

tonnelier [tɔnəlje] *nm* cooper

tonnelle [tɔnɛl] *nf* **(a)** (*charmille*) arbour, *US* arbor, *Br* bower **(b)** *Archit* barrel *or* tunnel vault

tonnellerie [tɔnɛlri] *nf* cooperage

tonner [tɔne] **1** *vi* **(a)** (*de canons etc*) to thunder, to boom **(b)** (*fulminer*) to rage **(contre** about), to thunder **(contre** against) **2** *v impers* **il tonne** it is thundering; **le chien a peur quand il tonne** the dog is frightened of thunder

tonnerre [tɔnɛr] *nm* **(a)** (*bruit*) thunder; **coup de t.** clap *or* peal of thunder, thunderclap; *Fig* bombshell; **roulement de t.** roll of thunder; **sous un t. d'applaudissements** to thunderous applause; **accueilli par un t. d'applaudissements** welcomed by thunderous applause; **voix de t.** voice of *or* like thunder; **un bruit/fracas de t.** a racket, a din **(b)** *F* **du t.** (*film, personne*) wonderful, terrific; **t. (de Dieu** *ou* **de Brest)!** heavens above!, good grief!; *Vieilli* **il fera un marin du t. de Dieu** he'll make a thundering good *or* a hell of a good sailor

tonométrie [tɔnɔmetri] *nf* tonometry

tonsure [tɔ̃syr] *nf* **(a)** *Rel* tonsure **(b)** *F* (*calvitie*) bald patch

tonsuré [tɔ̃syre] *Rel* **1** *adj* tonsured; **tête tonsurée** shaven head **2** *nm* cleric

tonsurer [tɔ̃syre] *vt* (*clerc*) to tonsure

tonte [tɔ̃t] *nf* **(a)** (*des moutons*) shearing; (*laine*) clip; (*saison*) shearing time **(b)** (*du gazon*) mowing

tontine[1] [tɔ̃tin] *nf Jur* tontine

tontine[2] *nf* (*pour protéger un arbuste*) protective covering

tonton [tɔ̃tɔ̃] *nm F* uncle; **T. Jules** Uncle Jules

tonus [tɔnys] *nm* **(a)** *Méd* (*d'un muscle*) tone, *Spéc* tonus, tonicity **(b)** *Fig* (*énergie*) energy, dynamism; **je manque de t.** I don't have any energy; **elle a un sacré t.** she's got an incredible amount of energy, she's incredibly energetic; **un peu de nerf les gars, ça manque de t., tout ça!** put your backs into it, lads, you're like a bunch of old women!; **ce slogan manque de t.** the slogan doesn't have any punch *or* pizzazz

top [tɔp] *nm Rad, TV* time signal, cue; **les tops** the pips; **au quatrième t. il sera exactement dix heures** at the fourth stroke it will be ten o'clock precisely; *Électron* **t. d'écho** blip, *US* pip; *Électron* **t. de synchronisation** synchronizing signal; **donner le t. départ** to give the starting signal

topaze [tɔpaz] *nf* topaz

toper [tɔpe] *vi F* to agree **(à qch** to sth); **tope (là)!** done!, agreed!, put it there!

topette [tɔpɛt] *nf Région* small bottle

topinambour [tɔpinɑ̃bur] *nm Bot, Culin* Jerusalem artichoke

topique [tɔpik] **1** *adj* **(a)** *Méd* (*remède*) local, topical **(b)** (*argument*) apposite, to the point **2** *nm Méd* topical *or* local remedy **3** *nf Phil* **la t.** topics

top niveau *nm F* top level; **être au t.** to be at the top, to be top-notch; **arriver au t.** to get to the top; **des scientifiques au t.** top-level *or* top-notch scientists

topo [tɔpo] *nm F* **(a)** *Journ* article **(b)** (*discours*) lecture; (*exposé*) rundown; **faire le t. de la situation** to give a rundown on the situation; **c'est toujours le même t.** it's always the same old story

topographe [tɔpɔgraf] *n* topographer

topographie [tɔpɔgrafi] *nf* **(a)** (*technique, relief*) topography **(b)** (*représentation*) map, plan

topographique [tɔpɔgrafik] *adj* topographical

topographiquement [tɔpɔgrafikmɑ̃] *adv* topographically

topologie [tɔpɔlɔʒi] *nf* topology

topologique [tɔpɔlɔʒik] *adj* topologic(al)

toponyme [tɔpɔnim] *nm* place name, *Spéc* toponym

toponymie [tɔpɔnimi] *nf* study of place names, *Spéc* toponymy

toponymique [tɔpɔnimik] *adj (étude)* of place names, *Spéc* toponymic(al)
top secret *adj inv* top secret
toquade [tɔkad] *nf F* craze **(pour qch** for sth); infatuation **(pour qn** with sb); **avoir une t. pour qn** to be infatuated with sb; **ça lui passera, ce n'est qu'une t.** he'll get over it, it's just a passing fancy
toquante [tɔkɑ̃t] *nf F (montre)* watch
toquard, -arde [tɔkar, -ard] = **tocard**
toque [tɔk] *nf (de fourrure)* fur hat; *(de jockey, juge)* cap; **t. (blanche)** *(de cuisinier)* hat, toque
toqué, -ée [tɔke] *F* **1** *adj* **(a)** *(fou)* potty, loopy, crazy **(b)** *(amoureux)* infatuated, madly in love **(de** with) **2** *n (fou)* nut, *Br* nutter; **il doit me prendre pour une toquée** he must think I'm nuts *or* nutty
toquer [tɔke] **1** *vi F (à la porte etc)* to knock **2 se toquer** *vpr F* **se t. de qn** to fall for sb, to go crazy over sb
Torah [tɔra] *nf Rel* Torah
torche [tɔrʃ] *nf* **(a)** *(flambeau)* torch; **ils furent transformés en torches vivantes** they were turned into human torches; **procession à la t.** torchlight procession; **t. électrique** (electric) torch, *Am* flashlight **(b)** *Av* **parachute en t.** unopened parachute
torché [tɔrʃe] *adj F* **(a) bien t.** *(réponse, devoir, travail etc)* pretty good **(b)** *(bâclé) (travail etc)* botched
torche-cul *nm inv Vulg Arch (papier)* toilet paper, *Br* loo paper; *Vulg Péj (texte)* (piece of) trash
torchée [tɔrʃe] *nf Arg (coups)* (good) beating *or* thrashing
torcher [tɔrʃe] **1** *vt* **(a)** *F (nettoyer) (assiette)* to wipe clean; *(derrière d'un enfant, enfant)* to wipe **(b)** *(bâcler) (travail etc)* to botch, to do in a hurry **2 se torcher** *vpr Arg* **se t. (le derrière** *ou Vulg* **le cul)** to wipe one's backside; *Fig* **je m'en torche (de tes problèmes)!** I don't give a damn (about your problems)!
torchère [tɔrʃɛr] *nf (candélabre)* candelabra
torchis [tɔrʃi] *nm Constr* cob, daub
torchon [tɔrʃɔ̃] **1** *nm* **(a)** cloth; *(pour essuyer la vaisselle)* dish *or* tea towel; *(pour épousseter)* duster; **donner un coup de t. à qch** *(verre, table)* to give sth a wipe; *Fig* **coup de t.** *(querelle)* dust-up; *(épuration)* shake-up; *F* **le t. brûle entre** *ou* **chez eux** they've had a serious falling out; *Fig* **il ne faut pas mélanger les torchons et les serviettes** you can't compare apples and oranges **(b)** *Fig F (texte sans soin)* mess; *(texte sans valeur)* trash; *(journal)* rag **2** *adj inv Beaux-Arts* **papier t.** torchon paper
torchonner [tɔrʃɔne] *vt F (travail etc)* to botch
torcol [tɔrkɔl] *nm Orn* **t. (fourmilier)** wryneck
tordant [tɔrdɑ̃] *adj F* screamingly funny, hilarious, side-splitting
tord-boyaux [tɔrbwajo] *nm Arg Péj (eau-de-vie)* rotgut
tordeuse [tɔrdøz] *nf Ent (papillon)* leaf roller
tordre [tɔrdr] **1** *vt (barre de fer)* to bend, to twist; *(fil de fer, laine etc)* to twist; *(métal)* to buckle, to bend; *(vêtements etc) (pour essorer)* to wring; *(cheveux en chignon)* to twist; *(de la douleur) (visage)* to contort, to distort, to twist; **t. le cou à un poulet/***F* **à qn** to wring a chicken's/sb's neck; **t. le bras à qn** to twist sb's arm; **t. l'estomac à qn** *(de la peur etc)* to churn up sb's insides; *F* **t. les boyaux à qn** *(d'un alcool etc)* to rot sb's insides; **t. la bouche** to pull a face, to grimace, to make a wry face; **un rictus de douleur tordait sa bouche** his mouth was twisted *or* contorted in a grimace of pain; **tordu par la douleur** contorted by pain

2 se tordre *vpr (de douleur)* to writhe, to twist; *(de branches)* to become gnarled; **se t. les mains** to wring one's hands; **se t. sur son siège** to squirm in one's seat; **se t. le pied** to twist one's ankle; *F* **se t. (de rire), rire à se t.** to split one's sides laughing; **c'était à se t. de rire, il y avait de quoi se t.** it was a scream, it was hilarious; **il n'y a vraiment pas de quoi se t.** there's really nothing to laugh about; **le film est amusant mais il n'y a pas de quoi se t.** the film is funny but not all that funny
tordu, -ue [tɔrdy] **1** *adj* **(a)** *(membres, traits)* twisted, distorted; *(châssis, couverts etc)* bent, buckled; *(branche)* twisted, gnarled; *Arg* **avoir la gueule tordue** to be as ugly as sin **(b)** *(esprit)* warped, twisted; **avoir l'esprit t.** to be warped *or* twisted, to have a warped *or* twisted mind **(c)** *F (fou)* cracked, nutty **2** *n F (fou)* nut, *Br* nutter; **avance eh t.!** move, you stupid bastard!
tore [tɔr] *nm Archit, Géom* torus; *Ordinat* (magnetic) core
toréador [tɔreadɔr] *nm* toreador, bullfighter
toréer [tɔree] *vi* to fight (in the bullring)
torero [tɔrero] *nm* bullfighter, torero
torgnole [tɔrɲɔl] *nf Arg (coup)* clout; **je vais lui filer** *ou* **flanquer une t.** I'll clout *or* land him one; **recevoir** *ou* **prendre une t.** to get clouted

toril [tɔril] *nm* bull pen
torique [tɔrik] *adj Géom, Opt etc* toric
tornade [tɔrnad] *nf* tornado, *Am F* twister; **entrer comme une t.** to come in like a whirlwind
toron [tɔrɔ̃] *nm (d'une corde)* strand
torpédo [tɔrpedo] *nf Hist, Aut* (open) tourer, *Am* touring car
torpeur [tɔrpœr] *nf* torpor; **je voulus le faire sortir de sa t.** I tried to rouse him from his torpor
torpide [tɔrpid] *adj Méd* torpid
torpillage [tɔrpijaʒ] *nm Naut, Mil, Fig (de négociations, d'un plan de paix)* torpedoing
torpille [tɔrpij] *nf* [①A12,1,c] **(a)** *(poisson)* torpedo (ray), electric ray **(b)** *Naut, Mil* torpedo; **t. d'avion** aerial torpedo
torpiller [tɔrpije] *vt aussi Fig* to torpedo
torpilleur [tɔrpijœr] *nm* torpedo boat
torque [tɔrk] **1** *nm (collier)* torque **2** *nf Tech* coil of wire
torréfacteur [tɔrefaktœr] *nm* **(a)** *(appareil)* roaster; **t. à café** coffee roaster **(b)** *(marchand)* = purveyor of coffee which is roasted on the premises
torréfaction [tɔrefaksjɔ̃] *nf (du café, du tabac)* roasting
torréfier [tɔrefje] *vt (impf, pr sub* **n. torréfiions, v. torréfiiez)** *(café, maïs etc)* to roast
torrent [tɔrɑ̃] *nm (cours d'eau)* torrent; *Fig (de larmes, lumière)* flood; *(d'injures)* torrent, barrage, spate; *(de questions)* barrage; **il pleut à torrents** it's raining in torrents, *F* it's bucketing down
torrentiel, -ielle [tɔrɑ̃sjɛl] *adj* torrential
torrentueux, -euse [tɔrɑ̃tɥø, -øz] *adj Litt (rivière etc)* torrent-like; *Fig (vie etc)* stormy, tempestuous
torride [tɔrid] *adj (zone, climat etc, Fig érotisme)* torrid; *(chaleur)* torrid, scorching; *(été)* scorching (hot); **il fait une chaleur t.** it's scorching; **une journée t.** a scorching (hot) day, a scorcher
tors, torse [tɔr, tɔrs] **1** *adj (fil, jambe)* twisted; *Archit (colonne)* barley-sugar **2** *nm (torsion) (de corde etc)* twist
torsade [tɔrsad] *nf* **(a)** twisted cord; *Tricot* cable; **t. de cheveux** twist *or* coil of hair; *Tricot* **(point) t.** cable stitch; *Tricot* **aiguille à t.** cable needle **(b)** *Archit* rope *or* cable moulding *or US* molding
torsadé [tɔrsade] *adj (cheveux)* coiled; *Él, Tél* **paire torsadée** twisted pair; **raccord t.** twist joint
torsader [tɔrsade] *vt* **(a)** *(corde, fil de fer etc)* to twist; *(cheveux)* to twist, to coil **(b)** *(mettre ensemble)* to twist together
torse [tɔrs] *nm (poitrine)* chest, torso, trunk; *Beaux-Arts* torso; **le t. pris dans une veste très serrée** wearing a very tight jacket; **le t. nu** stripped to the waist; **se mettre t. nu** to strip to the waist; **bomber le t.** to stick out one's chest; *Fig* to be swollen with pride; **il bombe le t. sous le coup de la fierté** he's puffed up with pride
torseur [tɔrsœr] *nm Phys* torque
torsion [tɔrsjɔ̃] *nf* twisting; *(des traits, de la bouche)* distortion; *Tech, Phys* torsion; **faire une t. à droite** to twist to the right
tort [tɔr] *nm* **(a)** *(faute)* fault; **c'est son seul t.** it's his only fault; **son seul t. a été d'être trop franc** his only mistake was being too frank; **il a eu le t. de ne pas demander de reçu** he made the mistake of not asking for a receipt; **reconnaître ses torts** to acknowledge one's faults; **il a tous les torts** he is entirely to blame, it's all his fault; **c'est un t. de le lui avoir dit** it was wrong *or* a mistake to tell him; **avoir des torts envers qn** to have treated sb badly; **avoir t.** to be wrong **(de faire** to do); **c'est elle qui a t., pas toi** she's the one who's wrong *or* (who's) in the wrong, not you; **il n'est pas d'accord, et il n'a pas t.** he doesn't agree and he's right (not to); **donner t. à qn** to blame sb, to lay the blame on sb; *(d'un résultat, d'une preuve etc)* to prove sb wrong; **elle donne toujours t. à l'aîné de ses fils** she always blames the elder boy, the elder boy is always in the wrong as far as she's concerned; **être en t.** *ou* **dans son t.** to be in the wrong *or* at fault; **se mettre en t.** *ou* **dans son t.** to put oneself in the wrong; **à t.** wrongly; **à t. ou à raison** rightly or wrongly; **à t. et à travers** at random, without rhyme or reason; **dépenser son argent à t. et travers** to spend one's money thoughtlessly *or* recklessly; **il parle à t. et travers** he talks wildly; *Jur* **prononcer un jugement au t. d'une partie** to find against one of the parties

(b) *(dommage)* harm; **un t.** a wrong; **faire du t. à qn** to wrong sb, to do sb wrong; **tu lui as fait beaucoup de t. en l'accusant** you did her great wrong in accusing her; **quel t. cela peut-il vous faire?** what harm can it do you?; **cette loi a fait beaucoup de t. aux petits épargnants** this law penalizes the small saver heavily
torticolis [tɔrtikɔli] *nm Méd* stiff neck, *Spéc* torticollis; **avoir/attraper un t.** to have/get a stiff neck
tortillard [tɔrtijar] *nm* local train

tortillement [tɔrtijmɑ̃] *nm* wriggling, squirming; (*des hanches*) wiggling

tortiller [tɔrtije] **1** *vt* (*tordre*) (*papier, ruban, cheveux etc*) to twist; (*moustache*) to twirl; (*tripoter*) to twiddle (with) **2** *vi* **(a)** **t. des hanches** to wiggle one's hips; **marcher en tortillant du postérieur** to walk with a wiggle; **elle avança vers la porte en tortillant du postérieur** she wiggled her way to the door **(b)** *F* **il n'y a pas à t.** it's no good trying to wriggle *or* wiggle out of it **3 se tortiller** *vpr* (*d'un ver, d'une personne sur sa chaise*) to wriggle, to squirm, to wiggle; (*en dansant*) to wriggle about; (*des hanches*) to wiggle

tortillon [tɔrtijɔ̃] *nm* **(a)** (*de papier*) twist **(b)** (*sur la tête*) (*pour porter une charge*) pad

tortillonner [tɔrtijɔne] **1** *vt* to twist and turn **2** *vi F* to quibble, to hedge

tortionnaire [tɔrsjɔnɛr] **1** *nm* torturer **2** *adj* **policier t.** police torturer

tortorer [tɔrtɔre] *vt Arg* (*manger*) to wolf down, to gobble up

tortu [tɔrty] *adj Litt* (*nez*) crooked; (*esprit*) warped

tortue [tɔrty] *nf* **(a)** (*reptile*) tortoise; *Fig* (*personne lente*) *Br* slowcoach, *Am* slowpoke; **t. d'eau douce** terrapin; **t. de mer** turtle; **à pas de t.** at a snail's pace **(b)** (*papillon*) tortoiseshell (butterfly) **(c)** *Hist, Mil* testudo, tortoise

tortueusement [tɔrtɥøzmɑ̃] *adv* tortuously; (*se conduire, manœuvrer etc*) deviously; **la route se déroule t. jusqu'au col** the road winds *or* twists its way (tortuously) up to the col

tortueux, -euse [tɔrtɥø, -øz] *adj* (*rivière*) winding, meandering; (*rue, sentier*) winding, twisting, twisty; (*attitude, personne, esprit, manœuvres*) devious; (*argumentation, discours etc*) tortuous

torturant [tɔrtyrɑ̃] *adj* (*situation, regret, sentiments, pensées etc*) agonizing

torture [tɔrtyr] *nf* torture; *Fig* torment, torture; **instrument de t.** instrument of torture; **chambre de t.** torture chamber; **victime de la t.** *ou* **de tortures** victim of torture, torture victim; *Fig* **cette séparation est une vraie t. morale pour moi** it's torture being separated; **mettre qn à la t.** to torment *or* torture sb; **je ne souhaite pas vous mettre à la t.** I hate to keep you on tenterhooks; **mettre son esprit à la t.** to rack one's brains

torturer [tɔrtyre] **1** *vt* (*prisonnier*) to torture; *Fig* to torment (**sur** about); **cette situation la torture** the situation is torture *or* torment for her; **la jalousie le torturait** he was tortured *or* tormented by jealousy, he suffered torments of jealousy **2 se torturer** *vpr* to torture oneself; **se t. l'esprit** to rack one's brains

torve [tɔrv] *adj* (*regard*) grim, menacing

tory [tɔri] *adj, n* Tory

toscan, -ane [tɔskɑ̃, -an] **1** *adj* Tuscan **2** *nm Ling* Tuscan **3** *n* **T.** Tuscan

Toscane [tɔskan] *nf* Tuscany

tôt [to] *adv* **(a)** (*bientôt, vite*) soon, early; **vous faut-il partir si t.?** must you leave so soon?; **plus t. tu commenceras plus vite tu auras fini** the sooner you begin the sooner you'll finish; **vous auriez dû me le dire plus t.** you should have told me sooner *or* earlier *or* before this; **nous n'étions pas plus t. rentrés que ...** we had no sooner returned than ...; **le plus t. sera le mieux** the sooner *or* earlier the better; **le plus t. possible** as soon *or* as early as possible; **revenez au plus t.** come back as soon *or* quick(ly) as possible; **mardi au plus t.** (on) Tuesday at the earliest; *F* **c'est pas trop t.!** and about time too!, and not before time either!; **on ne le reverra pas de si t.** we won't see him for a long time; (*il est parti fâché, ruiné etc*) we won't see him again in a hurry; **je ne pensais pas les revoir de si t.** I didn't think I would see them again so soon; **elle a eu t. fait de changer d'avis** she soon changed her mind, it wasn't long before she changed her mind; **t. après** soon after; **t. ou tard** sooner or later

(b) (*de bonne heure*) early; **t. dans l'après-midi/dans l'année/dans sa vie** early in the afternoon/in the year/in his life; **il est trop t. pour manger** it's too early to eat; **il est trop t. pour le dire** it's too soon to say, it's early days yet

total, -ale, -aux, -ales [tɔtal, -o] **1** *adj* (*somme, guerre, destruction, éclipse, silence etc*) total; (*obscurité*) total, complete; (*confiance, liberté*) complete; (*hauteur, largeur*) overall; *Méd* (*hystérectomie*) complete, *Spéc* radical; **c'était une surprise t.** it was a complete surprise; **un échec t.** a complete (and utter) *or* a total failure

2 *nm* total; **le t. de la population** the total population; **faire le t.** to work out the total; **faire le t. de** to add up, to total; **au t.** in all, in total; (*tout compte fait*) all in all; *Compta* **t. des recettes** total receipts; **t. général** grand total; **t. à payer** total payable; *F* **et t.** to sum it all up, in short, in sum; **et t., on l'a renvoyé** and, to cut a long story short, he got the sack; **tu voulais faire ton indépendante, et t., tu es toute seule, maintenant** you wanted to be independent and the sum total of that is that you're all alone now

3 *nf Chir F* **totale** hysterectomy

totalement [tɔtalmɑ̃] *adv* totally, completely

totalisateur, -trice [tɔtalizatœr, -tris] **1** *adj* (*machine*) adding **2** *nm* adding machine; *Ordinat* accumulator; *Courses de chevaux* totalizer, *F* tote, *Am* pari-mutuel; *Aut* **t. kilométrique journalier** trip recorder

totalisation [tɔtalizasjɔ̃] *nf* totalling, adding up

totaliser [tɔtalize] *vt* **(a)** (*additioner*) to total, to add up **(b)** (*compter en tout*) to total, to have a total of

totalitaire [tɔtalitɛr] *adj Pol* totalitarian

totalitarisme [tɔtalitarism] *nm Pol* totalitarianism

totalité [tɔtalite] *nf* **la presque t. de** almost *or* virtually all (of); **(pris) dans sa/leur t.** (taken) as a whole; **en t.** in full

totem [tɔtɛm] *nm* totem

totémique [tɔtemik] *adj* totemic

totémisme [tɔtemism] *nm* totemism

toto [toto] *nm Arg* (*pou*) louse

toton [tɔtɔ̃] *nm* (*toupie*) teetotum

touareg [twarɛg] **1** *adj* Tuareg **2** *nm Ling* Tuareg **3** *n* **T.** Tuareg

toubib [tubib] *nm F* doctor, quack

toucan [tukɑ̃] *nm* (*oiseau*) toucan

touchant [tuʃɑ̃] **1** *adj* (*spectacle, discours, geste etc*) touching, moving; (*reconnaissance*) touching; **d'une manière touchante** touchingly, movingly; **elle est touchante d'humilité** she is touchingly humble **2** *prép Litt* (*au sujet de*) touching, concerning, about

touche [tuʃ] *nf* **(a)** (*style*) (*d'un peintre*) brushwork, style; (*d'un écrivain*) style

(b) (*d'un piano, d'un clavier*) key

(c) **pierre de t.** touchstone

(d) *Billard, Escrime* hit

(e) *Pêche* bite, nibble; *F* **avoir** *ou* **faire une t. avec qn** to make a hit with sb; **tu as fait une t.!** you've made a hit there!

(f) *Sp* (*ligne*) touchline; (*remise en jeu*) *Fb* throw-in; *Rugby* line-out; (*au hockey*) roll-in; **t. longue** long throw-in; **envoi de t.** kick into touch; **jouer la t.** to take the throw-in; *Rugby* **trouver la t.** to find touch; **sortir en t.** to go into touch; **rester sur la t.** to stay on the sidelines *or* touchlines; *Fig* to stay on the sidelines

(g) *Arg* (*aspect*) appearance, look; **avoir une drôle de t.** to be weird-looking; **t'as vu la t. qu'il a!** get a load of him!

(h) *Arg* (*de drogue etc*) shot, jab

(i) *Beaux-Arts* (*tache de couleur*) touch; *Fig* **une t. romantique** a touch of romance, a romantic touch; **pour apporter une t. locale** for a bit of local colour; **mettre la t. finale à qch** to put the finishing touches to sth; **procéder par petites touches** to proceed step by step

(j) *Mus* (*de violon*) finger board; **touches** (*de guitare etc*) frets

▶ **touche**: *Ordinat*: **t. d'alimentation** power-on key; **t. alt** alt (key); **t. d'arrêt de défilement** scroll lock key; **t. à auto-maintien** sticky key; **t. à bascule** toggle key; **t. contrôle** control key; **t. début** home key; **t. de défilement** scroll key; **t. de déplacement du curseur** cursor movement key; **t. de direction** arrow key; **t. d'échappement** escape key; **t. d'effacement** delete key; **t. d'effacement arrière** backspace delete key; **t. à effleurement** touch-sensitive key; **t. (d')entrée** enter key; **t. d'espacement arrière** backspace key; **t. fin** end key; **t. fléchée** *ou* **(à) flèche** arrow key; **t. flèche vers la droite/la gauche** right/left arrow key; **t. flèche vers le bas/le haut** down/up arrow key; **t. (de) fonction** function key; **t. d'impression d'écran** print screen key; **t. d'insertion** insert key; **t. d'interruption** break key; **t. majuscule** shift key; **t. morte** dead key; **t. multifonction** multifunctional key; **t. numérique** number key; **t. de raccourci** shortcut key; **t. de répétition** repeat-action key; **t. retour** return *or* enter key; **t. de retour arrière** backspace key; **t. de verrouillage des majuscules/du clavier numérique** caps/num(bers) lock key

touche-à-tout *F* **1** *adj inv* **(a)** **il est t.** (*adulte*) he can't keep his hands off anything; (*bébé*) he's into everything **(b)** *Fig* **j'ai toujours été un peu t.** I've always dabbled in this and that **2** *n inv* **(a)** **c'est un t.** (*adulte*) he can't keep his hands off anything; (*bébé*) he's into everything **(b)** (*personne qui a plusieurs occupations*) dabbler; **il écrit, il peint, c'est un peu un t.** he writes, he paints, he does a bit of everything

toucher[1] [tuʃe] *nm* **(a)** (*sens, action*) touch; (*qualité*) feel; **sens du t.** sense of touch; **au t.** to the touch *or* feel; **le mur était chaud au t.** the wall was hot to the touch *or* felt hot; **reconnaître qch au t.** to recognize sth by touch *or* by the feel of it **(b)** *Méd* examination; **t. vaginal** vaginal examination **(c)** *Mus* (*d'un pianiste*) touch

toucher[2] **1** *vt* **(a)** (*du doigt, avec un objet etc*) (*qch, qn sur* *l'épaule etc*) to touch; *Fb* (*balle*) to handle; (*cible, Billard boule, Escrime adversaire*) to hit; **t. qch avec des gants** to handle sth with gloves on, to wear gloves when handling sth; **la voiture a failli t. le mur** the car almost hit *or* clipped the wall; *F* **touche du bois!** touch wood!; *F* **pas touche!** (*à un enfant*) don't touch!; *Rugby* **t. dans les buts** to touch down

(**b**) (*maison etc*) (*d'un incendie*) to damage; (*d'une explosion*) to damage, to hit; (*personne*) (*d'un éclat d'obus etc*) to hit (**à la jambe** in the leg); **le soldat a été gravement touché** the soldier was seriously injured

(**c**) (*émouvoir*) to move, to touch; **t. qn jusqu'aux larmes** to move sb to tears; **être touché au vif** to be cut *or* stung to the quick

(**d**) (*concerner, affecter*) to concern, to affect; **le chômage touche particulièrement les jeunes** the young are particularly affected *or* hard hit by unemployment

(**e**) *Naut* (*terre*) to touch; **t. le port** to put in at *or* touch port; **t. le fond** *Naut* to strike, to touch (bottom); (*être à sec*) to be aground; *Fig* (*déprimer*) to touch (rock) bottom

(**f**) *Min* **t. le pétrole** to strike oil

(**g**) (*contacter*) to get in touch with, to get hold of, to reach; (*d'une lettre*) to reach; **t. qn par téléphone** to reach sb by telephone

(**h**) (*recevoir*) (*argent*) to get, to receive; (*chèque*) to cash; **t. ses appointements/sa paie** to draw *or* receive one's salary/one's pay; **t. un intérêt** to receive interest; **elle doit bien t. dans les 10 000 francs par mois** she must be making *or* getting about 10,000 francs a month; **je pense t. 3 000 francs le 15 juin** I think I've got 3,000 francs coming to me on the 15th of June; **t. le tiercé** = to win the pools, to hit the jackpot

(**i**) (*être tout proche de*) to adjoin; **la bibliothèque touche l'église** the library adjoins the church; **la maison qui touche la nôtre** the house adjoining ours

(**j**) **je lui en toucherai un mot** *ou* **deux mots** I'll mention it to him, I'll speak to him about it

2 *vi* (**a**) **t. à un port** (*d'un navire*) to put in *or* call at a port, to touch a port

(**b**) **t. à** (*entrer en contact avec*) to touch; *Fig* (*en modifiant*) to touch, to meddle with, to tamper with; **palmes qui touchent au plafond** palms that touch *or* reach the ceiling; **t. à terre** to touch the ground; **si tu touches au chat, je te quitte!** if you touch *or* lay a finger on the cat, I'll leave you!; **n'y touchez pas!** (keep your) hands off!; **on ne touche pas!** hands off!; **je n'ai pas touché à l'héroïne/l'alcool depuis** I haven't touched heroin/alcohol since; **il n'avait pas touché à la nourriture** he hadn't touched the food, he had left the food untouched; **t. à ses économies** to touch *or* break into one's savings; *Fig* **avec son air de ne pas y t.** looking as if butter wouldn't melt in his mouth, with an ever so innocent look on his face

(**c**) **t. à** (*être en contact avec*) (*qch*) to touch; (*pays*) to border on; (*maison, jardin etc*) to adjoin; *Fig* (*problème, question*) to touch on; **t. au but** to near one's goal; **l'année/le projet touche à sa fin** the year/the project is drawing to a close *or* nearing its end; **il touche à la quarantaine** he is getting on for *or* nearing forty

(**d**) **t. à** (*concerner*) to concern; **tout ce qui touche à l'écologie** everything to do with *or* touching on *or* concerning ecology

3 se toucher *vpr* (**a**) (*de lignes etc*) to touch; **nos deux maisons se touchent** our two houses adjoin *or* are adjoining

(**b**) (*se masturber*) to touch oneself

touche-touche (à) *loc adv Aut* nose-to-tail, bumper to bumper

touchette [tuʃɛt] *nf* (*d'une guitare, d'une mandoline*) fret

toucheur, -euse [tuʃœr, -øz] *n* (cattle) drover

touée [twe] *nf Naut* (**a**) (*câble*) warp, (warping) cable (**b**) (*longueur*) scope

touer [twe] *vt* (**a**) *Naut* (*avec point fixe*) to warp (**b**) (*avec ancre*) to kedge

toueur [twœr] *nm Naut* tug

touffe [tuf] *nf* (*de cheveux, d'herbe, de poils etc*) tuft; (*de végétation*) clump

touffeur [tufœr] *nf Arch, Litt* suffocating heat

touffu [tufy] *adj* (*bois, végétation*) thick, dense; (*barbe, cheveux etc*) bushy; *Fig* (*livre*) dense

touillage [tujaʒ] *nm F* (*de liquide*) stirring; (*de salade*) tossing, mixing; (*de cartes*) shuffling

touiller [tuje] *vt F* (*liquide, soupe etc*) to stir; (*salade*) to toss, to mix; (*cartes*) to shuffle

toujours [tuʒur] *adv* (**a**) [①**A23**,3,a,ii] (*continuité, répétition*) always; **c'est ce que j'ai t. dit, et dirai t.** that's what I've always said and will keep on saying; **t. plus nombreux** more and more numerous; **influence t. plus étendue** ever-increasing influence; **comme t.** as always, as ever; **optimiste comme t., il …** ever the optimist, he …; **presque t.** almost *or* nearly always; **un ami de t.** a lifelong friend; **pour t.** for ever; **depuis t.** always; **je t'aime depuis t.** I've always loved you, I've been in love with you for as long as I can remember

(**b**) (*encore*) still; **il fait t. aussi chaud** it is as hot as ever (it was); **cherchez t.** go on looking; **elle ne le lui a t. pas dit** she still hasn't told him; **alors, il est rentré? – t. pas** he's back then? – not yet

(**c**) (*concession*) always, anyhow; **je peux t. essayer** I can always *or* at least try; **essaie/entrez t.** try/come in anyway; **t. est-il que …** the fact remains that …, anyhow …; **elle peut t. attendre!** she'll be lucky!, she'll have a long wait!, in her dreams!; **il peut t. me redemander ma voiture, il ne l'aura pas** he can always ask me for my car again, but he won't get it; **c'est t. ça (de pris)** (at any rate) it's better than nothing, at least it's something; **allez-y t., je vous rejoindrai plus tard** you go on anyhow, I'll catch you up later

toulousain, -aine [tuluzɛ̃, -ɛn] **1** *adj* of *or* from Toulouse **2** *n* **T.** (*natif*) native of Toulouse; (*habitant*) inhabitant of Toulouse

toundra [tundra] *nf Géog* tundra

toupet [tupɛ] *nm* (**a**) (*de cheveux*) tuft of hair, *Br* quiff; (**faux**) **t.** toupee (**b**) *F* (*culot*) cheek, nerve; **quel t.!** what a cheek *or* a nerve!; **il faut un sacré t. pour le faire!** it takes a helluva nerve *or* cheek!; **avoir du t.** to have a cheek *or* a nerve; **il a eu le t. de …** he had the cheek *or* the nerve to …; **elle ne manque pas de t.!** she's got a cheek *or* a nerve!

toupie [tupi] *nf* (**a**) (*jouet*) (spinning) top (**b**) *Menuis etc* moulding *or US* molding machine (**c**) (*de meuble*) moulded *or US* molded foot (*Louis XVI style*) (**d**) *F* **vieille t.** (*femme*) old trout

tour¹ [tur] *nf* (**a**) (*bâtiment, d'une cathédrale, d'un château etc*) tower; (*d'habitation*) high-rise building; *Ordinat* tower; *TV, Cin* camera tower; (**immeuble**) **t., grande t.** tower block, high-rise (**b**) *F* (*personne*) hulk (**c**) *Échecs* castle, rook

▶ **tour**: **la t. de Babel** the Tower of Babel; *Av* **t. de contrôle** control tower; **la T. Eiffel** the Eiffel Tower; **t. de forage** derrick, rig; *Ind, Ch* **t. de fractionnement** fractionating tower; *Fig* **t. d'ivoire** ivory tower; **t. de lancement** launch tower; **la t. de Londres** the Tower of London; **t. d'observation** watchtower, observation tower; **la t. (penchée) de Pise** the Leaning Tower of Pisa; **t. de réfrigération** cooling tower; **t. de remplissage** (*pour fusée*) umbilical tower; **t. de sondage** derrick, rig

tour² *nm* (**a**) *Tech* (*machine-outil*) (turning) lathe; **fait au t.** machine-turned; *F Vieilli* (*jambe, taille etc*) shapely; **atelier des tours** turning shop

(**b**) *Cér* (potter's) wheel

(**c**) (*circonférence*) circumference; (*de partie du corps*) size, measurement; **arbre qui a deux mètres de t.** tree two metres in circumference, tree with a girth of two metres; **faire le t.** to go round; **faire tout le t.** to go all the way round; **le chemin fait le t. de la propriété** the path runs right round the estate; *Fig* **faire le t. de qch** (*situation, problème*) to review sth; **faire le t. du monde** to go round the world; **faire le t. du monde à la voile/à pied** to sail/walk round the world; **c'est son deuxième t. du monde à la voile** this is the second time he's sailed round the world; *Sp* **t. de piste** *ou* **de circuit** lap; **en être au troisième t.** to be on the third lap; **prendre un t. d'avance sur qn** to lap sb; **faire un t. de piste pour s'échauffer** to do a warm-up lap; **faire le t. du cadran** to sleep the clock round; **t. de cou** (*mesure*) collar size *or* measurement; *Vieilli* **quel est votre t. de cou?** what (size) neck are you?; **t. de tête** (*mesure*) hat size; **t. de taille** waist (measurement); **quel est votre t. de taille?** what waist are you?; **avoir 75 cm de t. de taille** to have a waist measurement of 75 cm, to measure 75 cm round the waist, to be a 75 cm waist; **perdre cinq centimètres de t. de taille** to lose five centimetres round the waist; **quel est votre t. de hanche?** what hip size are you?

(**d**) *Naut* (*autour de la bitte d'amarrage*) turn; **avoir des tours** to have a foul hawse

(**e**) **tours et détours d'un chemin** twists and turns of a road

(**f**) (*tournure*) (*de phrase, d'une situation*) turn; **prendre un mauvais t./un t. dramatique** to take a bad/a dramatic turn; **tout cela est en train de prendre un tout autre t. que ce que j'avais prévu** it's all turning out quite differently from what I expected; **cette affaire prend un t. qui ne me plaît guère** this matter is developing in a way I don't like; **donner un autre t. à la conversation** (*rendre sérieuse*) to raise the tone of the conversation; (*rendre légère*) to lower the tone of the conversation; **t. d'esprit** turn of mind

(**g**) (*rotation*) (*de clé, tournevis, vis*) turn; (*de roue,* *moteur*) revolution, turn; (*de manivelle*) turn, swing; **donner un t. de clé à la porte** to turn the key in the door; **fermer qch à double t.** to double-lock sth; *Aut* **tours de volant** steering wheel turns; (*de butée à butée*) turns lock to lock; **à t. de bras** (*frapper*) with all one's might; *Fig* **vendre/distribuer qch à t. de bras** to sell/distribute loads *or* masses of sth; **tours par minute, tours/minute** revolutions per minute, *F* revs; **(disque à) 45/33 tours** single/LP

(h) (*balade*) stroll; (*à bicyclette, en voiture*) ride; **faire un t.** to go for a stroll/ride; **elle aime bien faire un t. en ville** she likes going into town; **faire un t. de** *ou* **dans le jardin** to have *or* take a turn *or* a stroll round the garden; *Euph* **elle est allée faire un petit t.** she's gone to spend a penny

(i) (*petit voyage*) trip, tour; **ils sont allés faire un t. en Bretagne** they've gone touring in Brittany

(j) (*de participation*) turn; **à qui le t.?** whose turn is it?; **t. de service** spell of duty; **chacun (à) son t.** each in (his) turn; **chacun son t.!** (*dans une queue*) wait your turn!; **hier c'est moi qui l'ai fait, aujourd'hui c'est toi, chacun son t.!** I did it yesterday, now it's your turn; **ils s'occupent des enfants chacun leur t.** they look after the children in turn *or* turn and turn about, they take turns looking after the children; **à t. de rôle** in turns; **nous le faisons à t. de rôle** we do it in turns, we take turns doing it; **les membres assurent la présidence à t. de rôle tous les deux ans** the presidency rotates among members every two years; **t. à t.** by turns, in turn; **s'emporter et se calmer t. à t.** to flare up one moment and calm down the next

(k) *Cartes* (*manche*) round

(l) *Th etc* turn, number

(m) *Pol* **t. (de scrutin)** ballot

(n) (*sale coup*) trick; **faire** *ou* **jouer un (mauvais) t. à qn** to play a (nasty) trick on sb, to play sb a (nasty) trick; **mes yeux ont dû me jouer des tours** my eyes must have been playing tricks on me; **cela te jouera des tours** you'll (live to) regret it; *F* **avoir plus d'un t. dans son sac** to have more than one trick up one's sleeve

(o) (*manipulation*) feat; (*de prestidigitateur, chien*) trick; **t. d'adresse** feat of skill; **t. de cartes** card trick; *F* **en un t. de main** in two minutes flat, in the twinkling of an eye; **je n'ai pas le t. de main** I haven't the knack *or* hang of it; **c'est un t. à prendre** there's a knack to it

▶ **tour**: **t. de chant** song recital; *F* **t. de cochon** lousy *or* rotten trick; **t. de cou** (*ruban*) choker; (*en fourrure, écharpe*) scarf; **t. de force** feat, achievement; **il a réalisé un véritable t. de force en organisant la fête** organizing the festival was quite a feat *or* an achievement on his part; **T. de France (cycliste)** Tour de France (cycle race); **faire son t. de France** (*d'un compagnon*) to do one's journeymanship; **t. d'honneur** lap of honour; *Fig* **t. d'horizon: faire un t. d'horizon** to review matters; **t. de lit** bed valance; **t. de reins: se faire un t. de reins** to strain *or* rick one's back; *Fin* **t. de table** backers; **faire un t. de table** (*pendant un débat*) to go round the table

Touraine [turɛn] *nf* Touraine

tourangeau, -elle [turɑ̃ʒo, -ɛl] **1** *adj* (*de la région*) of/from Touraine; (*de la ville*) of/from Tours **2** *n* **T.** (*natif*) (*de la région/la ville*) native of Touraine/Tours; (*habitant*) (*de la région/la ville*) inhabitant of Touraine/Tours

tourbe [turb] *nf* peat, turf

tourbeux, -euse [turbø, -øz] *adj* (*sol etc*) peaty

tourbière [turbjɛr] *nf* peat bog

tourbillon [turbijɔ̃] *nm* **(a)** (*vent*) whirlwind; (*de poussière, de sable, de cendres, de fumée*) swirl, cloud; (*de neige*) flurry; **monter en tourbillons** (*de la poussière, du sable etc*) to swirl *or* whirl up **(b)** (*remous*) whirlpool **(c)** [①A14,9] *Phys, Astron, Phil* vortex **(d)** *Aut* (*dans un moteur*) rotary *or* barrel swirl, swirl **(e)** *Fig* (*des plaisirs etc*) whirl; **dans le t. de la vie** in the hurly-burly of life; **le t. de la vie mondaine** the social whirl

tourbillonnaire [turbijɔnɛr] *adj* swirling

tourbillonnant [turbijɔnɑ̃] *adj* (*feuilles, jupes etc*) whirling

tourbillonnement [turbijɔnmɑ̃] *nm* whirling

tourbillonner [turbijɔne] *vi Fig* (*d'idées etc*) to whirl (round); (*de feuilles, d'un danseur*) to whirl (round), to spin round and round

tourelle [turɛl] *nf* **(a)** *Archit* turret; **à tourelles** turreted **(b)** *Mil, Naut* (gun) turret **(c)** *Opt, Phot* **t. à objectifs** lens turret

tourière [turjɛr] *adj, nf Rel* extern

tourillon [turijɔ̃] *nm* **(a)** (*d'axe*) journal; (*axe*) (wheel) spindle **(b)** *Mil* (*de canon etc*) trunnion **(c)** (*pivot*) pivot (pin)

Touring Club de France [turiŋklœbdəfrɑ̃s] *nm* = French motoring organization

tourismatique [turismatik] *nf* computerized reservation systems

tourisme [turism] *nm* tourism; (*industrie*) tourism, tourist trade; **faire du t.** to do some touring; **office du** *ou* **de t.** tourist office; **agence** *ou* **bureau de t.** travel *or* tourist agency; **centre/ville de t.** tourist centre; **t. de masse** mass tourism

▶ **tourisme**: **t. d'affaires** business tourism; **t. agricole** agricultural tourism, agritourism; **t. balnéaire** seaside tourism; **t. blanc** winter sports tourism; **t. écologique** eco-tourism; **t. émetteur** outbound tourism; **t. à la ferme** farm tourism; **t. de loisirs** leisure *or* holiday tourism; **t. ludique** leisure tourism; **t. national** national *or* domestic tourism; **t. organisé** package tourism; **t. récepteur** inbound tourism; **t. vert** ecotourism, green tourism

touriste [turist] **1** *n* tourist; *Fig Péj* **faire qch en t.** to do sth amateurishly; *Univ etc* **suivre un cours en t.** to do a course in a half-hearted kind of way **2** *adj Naut, Av* **classe t.** tourist class

touristique [turistik] *adj* (*guide, information, région, ville etc*) tourist; (*menu, prix*) for tourists; (*route*) scenic

tourmaline [turmalin] *nf Minér* tourmaline

tourment [turmɑ̃] *nm* **(a)** (*douleur*) torture, torment, anguish; **tourments** (*de faim*) pangs; (*de doute, jalousie*) torments **(b)** (*cause de souci*) torment; **endurer mille tourments** to go through torment, to suffer agonies; **mon fils me donne bien du t.** my son's giving me a lot of worry **(c)** *Arch, Litt* (*physique*) (*d'un prisonnier etc*) torture

tourmente [turmɑ̃t] *nf* **(a)** storm; **t. de neige** blizzard; **le vent soufflait en t.** the wind was gusting from all quarters; **nous fûmes pris sous une t. de feu** (*à la guerre*) we were caught in a hail of gunfire **(b)** *Fig* upheaval

tourmenté [turmɑ̃te] *adj* **(a)** (*côte*) jagged; (*paysage*) wild **(b)** (*conscience, visage*) tortured; (*personne, âme*) in torment, tormented **(c)** (*mer, vie, période*) turbulent; **une époque tourmentée de ma vie** a turbulent time in my life; **nous vivons une époque tourmentée** we are living in troubled times **(d)** *Beaux-Arts, Archit etc* (*style*) tortured

tourmenter [turmɑ̃te] **1** *vt* **(a)** (*de la jalousie, du doute etc*) to torment, to torture; **le remords/la douleur le tourmente** he is racked with remorse/pain; **tourmenté par la douleur** racked with pain; **être tourmenté par la goutte/ses dents** to suffer agonies with gout/one's teeth **(b)** (*d'une personne*) (*personne, chien*) to torment **(c)** *Arch* (*physiquement*) (*prisonnier*) to torture **2 se tourmenter** *vpr* to worry, to be anxious *or* uneasy; **ne vous tourmentez pas!** don't worry!

tourmentin [turmɑ̃tɛ̃] *nm* **(a)** *Naut* storm jib **(b)** *Orn* petrel

tournage [turnaʒ] *nm* **(a)** *Tech* (*au tour*) turning **(b)** *Cér* (*au tour*) turning, throwing **(c)** *Naut* belaying **(d)** *Cin* shooting, filming; **le t. de son nouveau film commence la semaine prochaine** shooting starts on his new film next week; **sur les lieux du t.** where the film is being/was shot; **t. en décor naturel** *ou* **en extérieur** location filming

tournailler [turnaje] *vi F* to keep wandering round and round, to prowl (around); **elle tournaille autour de moi** she's hovering around me

tournant [turnɑ̃] **1** *adj* **(a)** (*bibliothèque, scène etc*) revolving; (*fauteuil, siège*) swivel; (*pont*) swing; *Tech* (*essieu*) live; (*grève*) rotating

(b) (*route etc*) winding; (*escalier*) spiral

(c) *Mil* (*mouvement*) encircling

2 *nm* **(a)** (*de route, de rivière*) bend, curve; **la voiture s'est renversée dans un t.** the car overturned on a bend; *Fig F* **je l'aurai au t.!** I'll get him yet!; *Fig F* **elle t'attend au t.** she's waiting to pounce

(b) *Fig* (*changement*) (*de sa vie, sa carrière etc*) turning point **(de** in**)**; **marquer un t.** to mark a turning point; **cette décision constitue un t. décisif** this decision marked a turning point *or* a watershed; **prendre un nouveau t.** to change direction; **savoir prendre le t.** to know how to adapt, to bend with the wind

tourne [turn] *nf* **(a)** (*du lait*) turning, going sour; (*du vin*) souring **(b)** *Journ* (*d'un article sur la page suivante*) continuation

tourné [turne] *adj* **(a)** *Tech* (*au tour*) turned; **bien t.** (*lettre*) nicely worded; (*phrase, réponse, répartie*) well phrased; **une petite brune bien tournée** a little brunette with a lovely figure; **mal t.** (*lettre*) badly worded; (*phrase, réponse*) badly phrased; **avoir l'esprit mal t.** to have a nasty mind; **une société t. vers l'avenir** a forward-looking company **(b)** (*vin, lait etc*) sour

tourne-à-gauche *nm inv* (*outil*) wrench

tournebouler [turnəbule] *vt F* **t. qn** (*le bouleverser*) to upset sb

tournebroche [turnəbrɔʃ] *nm Culin* (*appareil*) roasting jack; *Arch* (*garçon, chien*) turnspit

tourne-disque, *pl* **tourne-disques** *nm* record player

tournedos [turnədo] *nm Culin* tournedos, fillet steak

tournée [turne] *nf* (**a**) (*d'inspecteur etc*) round(s); (*de facteur*) round(s), *Am* route; *Th* tour; **pendant la t. du représentant** while the rep is on the road; **faire sa t.** (*d'un facteur, un inspecteur*) to be on *or* doing *or* making one's rounds; *Th* **faire une t. en province** to tour the provinces, to do a provincial tour; *Th* **en t.** on tour, on the road; *Th* **nous passons la plus grande partie de l'année en t.** we spend most of the year touring *or* on tour; **faire la t. des musées** to go round *or* tour *or F* do the art galleries; **faire la t. des troquets** to go round the bars, to bar-hop; **faire une t. en Europe** (*d'un chanteur, groupe d'acteurs*) to do a European tour; **faire une t. électorale** to canvass a constituency

(**b**) *F* (*consommations*) round (of drinks); **payer une t.** to pay for *or* stand a round (of drinks), to pay for *or* stand drinks all round; **c'est ma t.** it's my round *or Br F* shout

(**c**) *Arg* (*raclée*) beating

▶ **tournée**: *F* **t. des grands-ducs: faire la t. des grands-ducs** to go out on the town; *Com* **t. de présentation** road show

tournemain (en un) [ɑ̃nœturnəmɛ̃] *adv* in an instant, in the twinkling of an eye

tourné-monté, *pl* **tournés-montés** *nm TV, Cin* sequential shooting

tourner [turne] **1** *vt* (**a**) (*roue, clé dans une serrure, la tête, les yeux, son attention, ses pensées etc*) to turn; *Culin* (*crème*) to stir; (*salade*) to toss; **t. qch autour de qch** to wind sth round sth; **t. le dos à qn/qch** (*action*) to turn one's back on sb/sth, to turn away from sb/sth; (*position*) to have one's back (turned) to sb/sth; **les yeux tournés vers le ciel** with upturned eyes; **t. les talons** (*partir*) to turn on one's heel, to turn and leave; (*s'enfuir*) to take to one's heels; **t. les pieds en dedans/en dehors** to turn one's toes in/out

(**b**) (*changer*) to turn (**en** into); **t. les choses à son profit** to turn things to one's advantage, to capitalize on things; **t. tout en bien/en mal** to put a good/a bad interpretation on everything; **tout t. en reproche/critique** to turn everything into a reproach/a criticism; **t. qch à la plaisanterie** to turn sth into a joke, to laugh sth off; **t. qn/qch en ridicule** to poke fun at *or* make fun of sb/sth, to deride sb/sth; **je n'ai pas envie de me faire t. en ridicule par son frère** I don't want to be made fun of by his brother; **elle essaie de le t. contre son père** she's trying to turn him against his father

(**c**) (*page etc*) to turn (over); (*carte*) to turn up; **t. et retourner qch** (*objet*) to turn sth over and over; **t. et retourner une idée dans sa tête** to go over and over an idea (in one's mind); *Fig* **il faut t. la page** it's time to make a fresh start

(**d**) (*contourner*) (*coin*) to turn, to go round; (*obstacle*) to get round; (*ennemi*) to outflank, to circumvent; (*difficulté, loi*) to evade, to get round; *Naut* **t. un promontoire** to sail around a headland

(**e**) *Cin* (*film, documentaire*) to make; (*scène*) to film, to shoot; **le film a été tourné dans les rues de Paris** the film was shot in the streets of Paris

(**f**) *Fig* **t. la tête à qn** (*du succès, d'une bourse etc*) to turn sb's head, to go to sb's head; (*du vin*) to go to sb's head; **il lui a tourné la tête** he has turned her head; **t. le(s) sang(s) à qn** to make sb's blood run cold; **cela m'a tourné l'estomac** it turned my stomach

(**g**) *Tech* (*au tour*) (*objet*) to turn on a lathe; *Cér* (*pot*) to throw; *Fig* (*phrase*) to turn; *compliment*) to word, to turn

2 *vi* (**a**) (*d'une clé*) to turn; (*d'une roue, d'une aiguille d'horloge*) to turn, to go round; (*d'une planète*) to revolve; (*d'une porte*) to swing, to move; (*d'une machine*) to run; (*d'une usine*) to run, to operate; (*d'un moteur*) to turn over; (*d'une toupie*) to spin; **tout tourne autour de lui, la tête lui tourne** he feels giddy, his head is swimming *or* spinning; **je l'ai vu t. autour de ma moto** I saw him hovering round my bike; **le lion tourne dans sa cage** the lion walks *or* paces round and round his cage; *Fig* **elle tourne autour de mon mari** she's sniffing around my husband; **ça devrait t. autour de 3 000 francs/de deux jours de travail** it should cost/take somewhere in the region of *or* something like 3,000 francs/ two days; *Fig F* **t. autour du pot** to beat about the bush; **t. de l'œil** to pass out, to faint; **l'heure tourne** time is passing *or* getting on; *F* **ça ne tourne pas rond (chez lui)** he's not all there; *Fig F* **j'ai l'impression de t. en rond** I feel as if I'm going round in circles; **faire t.** (*clé, roue, bouton de porte*) to turn; (*machine*) to operate; (*moteur*) to keep turning over *or* running; (*entreprise, boutique*) to run; **pour faire t. des usines en difficulté** to provide work for factories in difficulty; **elle fait t. les tables** she does table-turning; **tournez s'il vous plaît** please turn over, PTO

(**b**) (*obliquer*) to turn; **tournez à gauche** turn (to the) left; **ne savoir de quel côté t.** not to know which way to turn, to be at one's wits' end

(**c**) (*changer*) (*du vent*) to change direction, to shift; *Naut* to come about; **le vent a tourné à l'ouest** the wind has shifted *or* veered to the west; **le temps tourne au froid** it is turning cold; **le temps tourne au beau** the weather is changing *or* taking a turn for the better; **sa chance a tourné** his luck has turned *or* changed

(**d**) (*du lait*) to turn, to go off

(**e**) (*évoluer*) **bien/mal t.** to turn out well/badly; **il a mal tourné** he turned out badly; *F* **t. communiste/anarchiste** to turn communist/anarchist; **t. court** (*de négociations, d'une expérience, une discussion*) to stop short, to end abruptly; **cela tournait mal** things were taking a bad turn; **ça tournait mal entre eux** things were going wrong between them; **ça va mal t.** no good will come of it; **portraits qui tournent à la caricature** portraits that are almost *or* that verge on caricatures; **l'affaire tournait au tragique** the matter was taking a tragic turn *or* was turning to tragedy; **t. à la catastrophe** to turn into a catastrophe, to become catastrophic; **son amour a tourné en haine** his love has turned *or* changed to hatred; **t. au vinaigre** (*d'un vin*) to turn acid, to turn to vinegar; **t. à l'aigre** (*du lait*) to go *or* turn sour; *Fig* (*de relations*) to sour

(**f**) *Cin* (*de la caméra*) to roll, to turn; **t. dans un film** to act in a film; **silence, on tourne!** quiet please, we're ready to shoot!

3 *v impers Cartes* **il tourne carreau** the turn-up is diamonds

4 se tourner *vpr* (**a**) (*se retourner*) to turn round; **se t. vers qn** to turn towards sb; *Fig* **se t. vers qn/la religion** to turn to sb/religion; **se t. et se retourner dans son lit** to toss and turn; **ses yeux se tournèrent vers la porte** his eyes turned to the door; *F* **se t. les pouces** to twiddle one's thumbs

(**b**) **se t. contre qn** to turn against sb; **c'est sa femme qui l'a fait se t. contre vous** it was his wife who turned him against you; **se t. du côté du peuple** to side with the people

(**c**) (*changer*) **son amour se tourna en haine** his love turned *or* changed to hate

tournesol [turnəsɔl] *nm* (**a**) *Bot* sunflower; **graine/huile de t.** sunflower seed/oil (**b**) *Ch* litmus; **papier (de) t.** litmus paper

tournette [turnɛt] *nf* (**a**) (*pour couper*) circular glass cutter (**b**) *Th* revolve

tourneur [turnœr] **1** *adj* (*derviche*) whirling **2** *nm Tech* turner; *Cér* thrower; **t. de vis** screwcutter; **t. sur bois/métaux** wood/metal turner

tournevis [turnəvis] *nm* screwdriver; **t. cruciforme** cross blade screwdriver; **t. d'électricien** electrician's screwdriver; **t. à choc** impact screwdriver; **t. plat, t. à embout** bit screwdriver; **t. à lame plate** flat blade screwdriver

tournicoter [turnikɔte], **tourniquer** [turnike] *vi F* to wander round and round, to prowl; **une idée qui me tournicote dans la tête** an idea that keeps running through my mind

tourniquet [turnikɛ] *nm* (**a**) (*barrière*) turnstile; *Mil Arg* **passer au t.** to be court-martialled (**b**) *Com* (*présentoir*) (revolving display) stand, spinner (**c**) (*pour cordages etc*) roller (**d**) (*sur un volet*) fastener (**e**) (*de jardin*) sprinkler (**f**) *Méd* tourniquet

tournis [turni] *nm* (**a**) *Vét* staggers (**b**) *F* (*vertige*) giddiness, dizziness; **avoir le t.** to feel giddy *or* dizzy; **donner le t. à qn** to make sb giddy *or* dizzy

tournoi [turnwa] *nm Hist, Sp, Cartes etc* tournament; **t. d'éloquence** contest of eloquence

tournoiement [turnwamɑ̃] *nm* (**a**) whirling; (*d'un objet suspendu*) spinning; (*des oiseaux*) wheeling; (*de l'eau*) eddying, swirling (**b**) (*vertige*) giddiness, dizziness

tournoyant [turnwajɑ̃] *adj* whirling; (*oiseaux*) wheeling; (*eau*) eddying, swirling

tournoyer [turnwaje] *vi* (**je tournoie, n. tournoyons; je tournoierai**) (*d'objets suspendus ou dans l'eau, de feuilles etc*) to spin (round and round), to turn round and round, to whirl; (*d'oiseaux*) to wheel; (*de l'eau*) to eddy, to swirl; **descendre en tournoyant** to come whirling down; **faire t. qch** to twirl *or* whirl sth

tournure [turnyr] *nf* (**a**) (*direction*) (*des événements*) turn; **les affaires prennent (une) meilleure/une mauvaise t.** things are taking a turn for the better/the worse; **j'aurais voulu donner une autre t. à l'événement** I wanted things done differently; **donner une t. agréable à la conversation** to steer the conversation to more pleasant topics (**b**) (*aspect*) (*d'un objet, d'un édifice etc*) appearance; (*d'une histoire etc*) form; *Vieilli* (*maintien*) (*d'une personne*) bearing; **t. (de phrase)** turn of phrase; **t. d'esprit** turn of mind; **je n'ai pas sa t. d'esprit** I don't think the way he does; **prendre t.** to take shape

tour-opérateur, *pl* **tour-opérateurs** *nm* tour operator

tourte [turt] *nf* (**a**) *Culin* pie; **t. aux pommes/à la viande** apple/meat pie (**b**) *F* (*idiot*) idiot, clot

tourteau, -eaux [turto] *nm* **(a)** *Agr* cattle cake **(b)** (*crustacé*) **t. (dormeur)** edible crab

tourtereau, -eaux [turtəro] *nm* **(a)** (*oiseau*) young turtledove **(b)** *Fig* **tourtereaux** (*amoureux*) lovebirds

tourterelle [turtərɛl] *nf* (*oiseau*) turtledove

tourtière [turtjɛr] *nf* **(a)** (*pour tourte*) pie dish; (*pour tarte*) flan dish **(b)** *Can* (*tourte*) = (minced) pork pie

tous [tu(s)] *adj, pron voir* **tout**

toussailler [tusaje] *vi* to have a little cough

Toussaint (la) [latusɛ̃] *nf* All Saints' Day; **la veille de la T.** Hallowe'en

tousser [tuse] *vi* (*d'une personne*) to cough; *Fig* (*d'un moteur*) to cough, to sputter; **il toussa pour m'avertir** he coughed *or* gave a cough to warn me; **t. sèchement** to have a dry cough; **tu tousses?** do you have a cough?

tousseur, -euse [tusœr, -øz] *n F* cougher

toussotement [tusɔtmɑ̃] *nm* slight cough; **un discret t.** a discreet cough

toussoter [tusɔte] *vi* to give a slight cough; **il toussote depuis quelques jours** he's had a slight cough for a few days; **il n'arrête pas de t.** he keeps coughing; **il a toussoté pour m'avertir** he gave a warning cough

tous-temps *adj inv* all-weather

tout, toute, *pl* **tous, toutes** [tu, tut, tu, tut] (*when* **tous** *is a pron it is pronounced* [tus]) [①**A36**,d; **B14-15**,B] **1** *adj* **(a)** (*n'importe quel*) any, every; **tu peux l'appeler à t. moment** you can call him any time; **t. Français y a droit** any French person *or* all French people are entitled to it; **t. travail lui est interdit** he is forbidden to do any work; **t. travail mérite salaire** all work merits payment; **t. autre que vous** anybody but you; **t. autre en aurait fait autant** anybody else would have done the same; **toute liberté d'agir** full liberty to act; **avoir toute liberté de choisir** to be quite free to choose; **j'ai toute raison de croire que …** I have every reason to believe that …; **repas servis à toute heure** meals served at any time *or* round the clock

(b) (*emploi intensif*) **à la toute dernière minute** at the very last minute; **en t. dernier lieu** last, lastly; **des arbres de toute beauté** most beautiful trees; **à toute vitesse** at full speed; **donner toute satisfaction à qn** to give sb complete *or* full satisfaction; **le nouvel employé nous donne toute satisfaction** the new chap is proving quite satisfactory, we're quite satisfied with the new chap; **c'est t. l'effet que ça te fait?** is that all it means to you?; **pour toute arme il avait une canne** his only weapon was a walking stick; **pour toute réponse il éclata de rire** his only answer was to burst out laughing; **je suis t. à toi** I'm all yours; **il est de toute importance que …** + *sub* it is of the utmost importance that …; *Naut* **la barre toute!** hard over!

(c) [①**A4**,B] (*complet*) **t. le, toute la** all (the), the whole; **t. le monde** everybody, everyone; **j'ai vu t. Truffaut** I've seen everything of Truffaut's, I've seen all of Truffaut's films; **j'ai lu t. Proust** I've read everything of Proust's, I've read all of *or* the whole of Proust; **elle a t. Ellington dans sa discothèque** she's got everything Ellington ever recorded, she's got all Ellington's records; **t. Paris est en danger** the whole of *or* all Paris is in danger; **t. La Haye se trouvait dans les rues** the whole *or* entire population of the Hague was in the streets; **t. l'univers** the entire *or* whole universe; **toute la famille** the whole *or* entire family, all the family; **t. mon argent** all my money; **t. le jour, toute la journée** the whole *or* entire day, all day (long); **pendant t. l'hiver** throughout the (entire) winter, all through the winter, all winter long; **travailler t. l'été** to work all summer; **t. cet été** this whole summer, all this summer; **t. mars se passa sans nouvelles** the whole of March went by without news; **répéter t. le temps la même chose** to keep on saying the same thing; **au milieu de t. ça …** in the middle of all this *or* it all …

(d) tous les, toutes les (*la totalité de*) all the; (*chaque*) every; **tous les invités** all the guests; **tous ces livres** all these books; **toutes les femmes du monde te le diraient** any woman in the world would tell you that; **tous les jours** every day; **tous les quarts d'heure** every quarter of an hour; **toutes les fois que …** whenever …, each *or* every *or* any time that …; **les critiques viennent de tous (les) côtés** *ou* **de toutes parts** criticism is coming from all sides *or* quarters; **les fruits arrivent de toutes parts** the fruit comes from everywhere *or F* from all over the place; **de toutes (les) couleurs** of every (possible) colour; **champion toutes catégories** overall champion; **meubles tous budgets** furniture to suit all pockets

(e) (*avec des nombres*) **tous (les) deux** both; **tous (les) trois/(les) dix** all three/ten; **tous les deux jours** every two days, every other *or* second day; **tous les trois jours** every three days, every third day; **tous les deux ou trois jours** every two or three days; **toutes les cinq minutes/les deux mètres** every five minutes/two metres; *F* **tous les combien?** how often?

(f) t. un, toute une a whole, an entire; **t. un quartier de la ville** a whole *or* an entire district of the town; **c'est toute une histoire** it's a long story; (*c'est difficile*) it's quite a job; **pas la peine d'en faire toute une histoire** there's no point in making a big thing *or* a big fuss about it; **il en a fait t. un drame** he made a song and dance about it

2 *pron* **(a)** everything; **il a t. mangé** he has eaten everything *or* the (whole) lot; **t. est bon** everything is good, it's all good; **t. n'est pas à lire dans son œuvre** not everything he's written is worth reading; **l'argent n'est pas t.** money isn't everything; **mais ce n'est pas t., elle est menteuse aussi** but not only that, she's a liar too; **elle connaît t. de l'affaire** she knows all about it; **il ignore encore t. de notre relation** he still doesn't know anything about our relationship; **ce sera t.?** (*dans un magasin*) will there be anything else?; *Iron* **c'est** *ou* **ce sera t.?** is that all?, anything else while I'm at it?; **je crois que c'est t.** I think that's (about) everything *or F* the lot; **ce sera t. pour aujourd'hui** that will be all for today; **c'est t. ou rien** it's all or nothing; *Ordinat* **t.-ou-rien** all-or-nothing; *F* **… et t. et t. …** etcetera, etcetera, … and all the rest of it; *Prov* **t. est bien qui finit bien** all's well that ends well; **il est capable de t.** he is capable of anything; **elle fera t. pour t'ennuyer/t'aider** she'll do anything (she can) to annoy/help you; **voilà t. ce que je sais** that's all I know; **j'aime t. ce qui est français** I love anything *or* everything French; **je comprends t. ce qu'il dit** I understand everything he says; **t. ce qui vous plaira** whatever you like, anything you like; **c'est t. ce qu'il y a de plus beau/de plus drôle** nothing could be more beautiful/funnier; **t. ce qu'il y a de mieux** nothing but the best; **il mange de t.** he eats anything (and everything); **on trouve de t. à Paris** you find all sorts in Paris; **depuis lors j'ai fait de t.** I've done all sorts of things since then; **j'ai fait un peu de t. dans ce bureau** I've done a bit of everything in this office; *F* **il a t. du fonctionnaire** he's the typical *or* complete civil servant; **elle a t. de sa mère** she's just like her mother; **il a t. du garde-champêtre avec son képi** he looks just like a policeman with that cap; **c'est t. dire** need I say more?; **c'est t. un** it's all one; **homme à t. faire** (*bon en tout*) all-rounder; (*qui touche à tout*) Jack-of-all-trades; (*factotum*) odd-job man; **à t. prendre …** on the whole …, all in all …; *F* **drôle/joli comme t.** awfully funny/pretty, as funny/pretty as anything

(b) tous [tus], **toutes** all; **tous ont des enfants** they all have children; **leurs amis ont tous des enfants** their friends all have children; **une (bonne) fois pour toutes** once and for all; **venez/approchez tous!** come along/gather round everybody *or* all of you!; **on ne tiendra pas tous** we won't all fit; **ils sont tous là** they are all there; **vous devez tous accomplir votre devoir** all of you must *or* you must all do your duty; **le meilleur de tous** the best of (them) all, the best of the lot; **il est impossible de les nommer tous** it is impossible to name them all *or* all of them *or* each and every one of them; **on nous en offrit un verre à tous** we were all offered a glass; **il nous a parlé à tous séparement** he spoke to all of us individually; **leur bonheur à tous** the happiness of all of them *or* of them all; **tous à la fois** all at the same time; *Iron* **ne répondez pas tous à la fois!** don't all answer at once!; *F* **on l'aimait bien tous** we were all very fond of him; **nous/vous/eux tous** all of us/of you/of them; **combien d'argent ont-ils à eux tous?** how much money do they have between them?

3 *nm* **(a) le t.** the whole, the lot; **le t. est de réussir** the main thing is to succeed; **jouer le t. pour le t.** to stake *or* gamble everything, *F* to go for broke; **former un t.** to form a whole; *F* **ce n'est pas le t. (de rigoler comme ça), j'ai du travail à faire** this is all very well but I've got work to do

(b) du t. au t. entirely, completely; **en t.** (*au total*) in all, altogether; **en t. et pour t.** in all, altogether; **(pas) du t.** not at all, not in the slightest; **je ne le connais pas du t.** I don't know him at all *or* in the slightest

(c) *Math* (*pl* **touts**) total; **mon t.** (*dans une charade*) my whole

4 *adv* (*before a f adj beginning with a consonant or* **h** *aspirate* **tout** *becomes* **toute**) **(a)** (*complètement*) quite; **t. nouveau(x), toute(s) nouvelle(s)** brand new; **la toute nouvelle imprimante de chez …** the very latest printer from …; **ils sont t. seuls, elles sont toutes seules** they are all alone *or* on their own; **elle était encore toute jeune** she was still quite young; **toute jeune, elle était plus timide que maintenant** when she was very young she was shyer than she is now; **t. enfant** even as a child, when still a child; **les**

gens ne sont pas t. bon(s) ou t. mauvais people are not wholly *or* altogether good or bad; **toute de noir vêtue** (dressed) all in black; **elle était toute honteuse** she was utterly ashamed; **du matériel de t. premier ordre** top-calibre equipment, equipment of the very first order; **une t. autre personne** an entirely *or* a totally different person; **t. droit** (*se tenir*) bolt upright; (*continuer*) straight on; **parler t. haut/bas** to speak in a normal/low voice; **t. neuf** brand new; **t. nu** stark naked; **t. éveillé** wide awake; **t. endormi** falling asleep, very sleepy; **vêtement t. fait** ready-made garment; **plat t. préparé** ready-made meal; **viande toute cuite** ready-cooked meat; **t. au bout** right at the end, at the very end; **t. près, t. à côté** (*habiter, se trouver*) very close by, just round the corner, a couple of minutes away; **se mettre t. à côté de qn** to stand right alongside sb; **t. là-bas** right over there; **t. contre le mur** right against the wall; **t. en sang/sueur** (all) covered with blood/sweat, bloody/sweaty; **un enfant t. en jambes** a very leggy child; **c'est t. comme chez nous!** it's just like home!; *F* **c'est t. comme** it comes to the same thing; **il ne m'a pas raccroché au nez mais c'était t. comme** he didn't actually hang up on me but he might as well have; **il est t. à son commerce** he is entirely absorbed in *or* taken up with his business; **t. doux!** gently!

(b) **t. à fait** quite, entirely, altogether; **je suis t. à fait d'accord avec toi** I quite agree with you; *F* **oui, t. à fait** (*pour confirmer un fait*) absolutely; **cela me va t. à fait** it suits me perfectly *or* down to the ground; **il lui ressemble t. à fait** he is just like him; *F* **il y a t. plein de livres/de neige** there are/is loads of books/of snow; **à t. va** like anything; **t. au plus** at the very most; **t. au moins, t. le moins** at the very least; **t. au moins, c'est ce qu'elle dit** at least that's what she says; **t. à vous** (*dans une lettre*) yours ever

(c) **t. en parlant/mangeant** while speaking/eating; **elle siffle t. en conduisant** she whistles while *or* as she drives; **t. en le disant, je pensais à autre chose** I was thinking of something else while *or* as I was saying it; **elle a accepté, t. en ressentant une certaine jalousie** even though she agreed, she still felt a bit jealous

(d) (*aussi*) **t. ignorant qu'il soit** *ou* **qu'il est** however ignorant he is, ignorant though *or* as he is, ignorant though he may be; **t. jeune qu'il soit, il est très capable** young though he is, he's very able, he may be young but he's very able; **t. secrétaire que je suis, j'ai droit au respect** I may only be a secretary but I'm still entitled to some respect; **t. père/toute mère que je suis** although I am a father/a mother, father/mother though I am; **t. aussi joli/intelligent** just as *or* every bit as pretty/intelligent

(e) **être t. oreilles** *ou* **toute ouïe** to be all ears; **il était toute crainte et toute haine** he was consumed with fear and hatred; **elle était t. attention** she was all attention; **elle est t. le portrait de sa mère** she is the living *or* spitting image of her mother

▶ **tout**: **T.-Paris: le T.-Paris était là** all of Paris *or* anybody who's anybody in Paris was there

tout-à-l'égout *nm inv* mains drainage; **avoir le t.** to have mains drainage

Toutankhamon [tutɑ̃kamɔ̃] *nm* Tutankhamen

toute-épice, *pl* **toutes-épices** *nf Bot, Culin* allspice

toutefois [tutfwa] *adv* however; **t., je le garde** I'll keep it however *or* nevertheless

toute-puissance *nf* (a) *Rel* omnipotence (b) *Pol etc* absolute power

tout-fou, *pl* **tout-fous** *F* **1** *adj* crazy **2** *nm* idiot, nut

toutim(e) [tutim] *nm F* **... et tout le t.** ... etcetera, etcetera, ... and all the rest of it

toutou [tutu] *nm Enf* doggie, bow-wow; **suivre qn comme un t.** to follow sb meekly *or* meek as a lamb *or Am* like a puppy dog

tout-petit, *pl* **tout-petits** *nm* (tiny) tot, toddler

tout-puissant, toute-puissante, *pl* **tout(es)-puissant(e)s** **1** *adj* (*pays, syndicat, directeur etc*) all-powerful, almighty, omnipotent; *Fig* (*désir*) overwhelming; (*influence*) enormous **2** *nm Rel* **le T.** the Almighty

tout-terrain, *pl* **tous-terrains** *adj* **véhicule t.** all-terrain *or* off-road vehicle, ATV; **vélo t.** mountain bike

tout-venant *nm Minér* ungraded product; (*houille*) unsorted coal; *Fig* **le t.** (*gens*) everybody and his wife, the ragtag and bobtail; **un livre qui n'est pas accessible au t.** a book that is not accessible to just anybody

toux [tu] *nf* cough; **une quinte** *ou* **un accès de t.** a coughing fit, a fit of coughing; **t. sèche/grasse** dry/loose cough; **sirop/pastilles pour** *ou* **contre la t.** cough mixture *or* syrup/sweets *or* drops *or* lozenges

township [tawnʃip] *nf* township

toxémie [tɔksemi] *nf Méd* blood-poisoning, *Spéc* toxaemia, *US* toxemia

toxicité [tɔksisite] *nf* toxicity; **coefficient de t.** toxicity rating

toxico [tɔksiko] *n F* drug addict

toxicodépendance [tɔksikodepɑ̃dɑ̃s] *nf* drug dependence *or* dependency

toxicologie [tɔksikɔlɔʒi] *nf* toxicology

toxicologique [tɔksikɔlɔʒik] *adj* toxicological

toxicologue [tɔksikɔlɔg] *n* toxicologist

toxicomane [tɔksikɔman] **1** *adj* addicted to drugs **2** *n* drug addict

toxicomanie [tɔksikɔmani] *nf* drug addiction

toxicomanogène [tɔksikɔmanɔʒɛn] *adj Méd* addictive

toxicose [tɔksikoz] *nf* toxicosis

toxine [tɔksin] *nf Physiol* toxin

toxique [tɔksik] **1** *adj* toxic, poisonous; **gaz t.** poison gas **2** *nm* poison

toxoplasmose [tɔksoplasmoz] *nf Méd* toxoplasmosis

TP [tepe] *nmpl Scol* (*abrév* **travaux pratiques**) practical work; **avoir un TP de chimie** to have a practical chemistry lesson *or* a chemistry lab

tpm [tepeɛm] *MecE* (*abrév* **tours par minute**) rpm

TPV [tepeve] *nm* (*abrév* **terminal point de vente**) point-of-sale terminal

traboule [trabul] *nf Région* alleyway

trac[1] [trak] *nm F* nervousness, fright; *Th* stage fright; **il a le t.** he's nervous; *Th* he's got stage fright; **c'est bon pour le t.** it's good for the nerves; **elle ne sait pas quoi faire contre le t.** she doesn't know how to stop herself getting so nervous

trac[2] *nm* **tout à t.** out of the blue, without warning

traçage [trasaʒ] *nm* (*de graphiques etc*) drawing; (*de routes, de jardins etc*) laying out

traçant [trasɑ̃] *adj* (a) *Bot* (*racine*) running, creeping (b) *Mil* (*obus, balle*) tracer (c) *Ordinat* **table traçante** plotter

tracas [traka] *nm* worry, trouble, bother; **un grand t., bien du t.** a lot of headaches *or* worry *or* trouble *or* bother; **des tracas** worry, trouble, bother; **faire du t. à qn** to cause sb trouble *or* bother

tracasser [trakase] **1** *vt* (*personne*) (*d'un problème etc*) to worry, to bother; (*d'une personne, d'un organisme etc*) to pester, to harass; **avoir l'air tracassé** to look harassed **2 se tracasser** *vpr* to worry (**pour qch** about sth)

tracasserie [trakasri] *nf* **tracasserie(s)** harassment; **tracasseries administratives** red tape; **en butte aux tracasseries de la police** subjected to police harassment

tracassier, -ière [trakasje, -jɛr] **1** *adj* (*employé, patron etc*) nitpicking, picky **2** *n* nitpicker

trace [tras] *nf* (a) **traces** (*d'animal*) trail, track, spoor; (*d'une personne*) tracks, trail; (*d'un véhicule*) tracks; **des traces de pas** footprints; **des traces de pneus** tyre tracks; **être sur la t. de qn/qch** to be on the track of sb/sth; *Fig* **être sur la t. de qn** (*d'un reporter etc*) to dog sb's footsteps; **retrouver la t.** to pick up the scent *or* the trail; **retrouver la t. de qn/de qch** to pick up the trail of sb/sth; **je n'en ai pas vu la t.** I haven't seen hide nor hair of it; **disparaître sans laisser de t.** to disappear without trace; **perdre la t. de qn** to lose trace *or* track of sb; **on ne retrouve aucune t. de cet événément dans les journaux** there is no trace *or* mention of the event in the newspapers; **toute t. de cet événément semble avoir été effacée** all traces of the event seem to have been wiped out; *Fig* **il marche sur** *ou* **il suit les traces de son père** he's following in his father's footsteps; *Fig* **laisser une t. profonde** to leave a deep impression (behind), to leave its mark; **cela a laissé en elle des traces profondes/indélébiles** it affected her deeply *or* made a profound impression on her/left an indelible mark on her; **cette musicienne n'a pas laissé beaucoup de traces** this musician didn't leave much of a mark; *Ski* **faire la t.** to break trail; *Ski* **t. directe** direct descent; *Électron* **t. du spot** trace (*in cathode-ray tube*)

(b) (*marque*) mark; **une t. de brûlure/piqûre** a burn/needle mark; **une t. de sang/d'encre** a splash of blood/ink; **une t. de saleté** a dirty mark; **traces de sang/de fatigue** traces of blood/fatigue; **traces de peinture/de doigts** paint/finger marks

(c) (*petite quantité*) (*de poison, Fig de regret, remords*) trace

(d) (*vestige*) (*d'une ancienne civilisation etc*) trace

(e) *Géom* (*d'un plan etc*) trace

tracé [trase] *nm* (a) (*plan*) (*de route, de chemin de fer etc*) route, path, layout; (*de ville*) layout; **t. de ligne** line drawing; **faire le t. de** to plan the layout of (b) (*ligne, contour*) (*de graphique, de côte etc*) line; **suivre le t. du fleuve** to follow the river

tracer [trase] (**je traçai(s)**; **n. traçons**) **1** *vt* (a) (*dessiner*) (*ligne, plan, dessin etc*) to draw; (*courbe, graphique*) to plot; (*lettre, mot etc*) to write; (*faire le plan de*) (*route, chemin de fer etc*) to map the course of; (*piste, sillon*) to mark out; *Fig* (*ligne d'action*) to map out; **t. les lignes d'un court de tennis** to mark out a tennis court; *Fig* **t. les grandes lignes de qch** to outline sth, to indicate the general outlines of sth; *Fig* **le tableau qu'il nous en a tracé n'est pas des plus reluisants** he didn't exactly paint a very inspiring picture of it

(**b**) (*chemin dans la jungle etc*) to open up; *Fig* **t. le chemin à qn** to lay out a path for sb; *Fig* **son chemin est tout tracé** his path is all laid out *or* mapped out for him

2 *vi* (**a**) (*d'une racine*) to run out, to creep

(**b**) *Arg* (*aller vite*) to move like greased lightning

traceret [trasrɛ] *nm* (*outil*) scriber, tracing awl

traceur, -euse [trasœr, -øz] **1** *nm* (**a**) *Nucl* **t. (radioactif)** tracer (**b**) *Ordinat* **t. (de courbes)** plotter; **t. à plat** flatbed plotter; **t. à plumes** pen plotter; **t. à tambour** drum plotter **2** *adj* (*substance, obus, balle*) tracer

trachéal, -ale, -aux, -ales [trakeal, -o] *adj Anat* tracheal

trachée [traʃe] *nf Anat, Zool* windpipe, *Spéc* trachea

trachée-artère, *pl* **trachées-artères** *nf Anat, Zool Vieilli* windpipe, *Spéc* trachea

trachéite [trakeit] *nf Méd* tracheitis

trachéo-bronchite [trakeɔbrɔ̃ʃit] *nf Méd* tracheobronchitis

trachéotomie [trakeɔtɔmi] *nf Chir* tracheotomy

trachome [trakom] *nm Méd* trachoma

traçoir [traswar] *nm* (*outil*) scriber, tracing awl

tract [trakt] *nm Pol* pamphlet, leaflet, tract; *Com etc* leaflet; *Rel* tract

tractable [traktabl] *adj* towable

tractation [traktasjɔ̃] *nf Péj surtout pl* **tractations** dealings, bargaining, negotiations

tracté [trakte] *adj* tractor-drawn

tracter [trakte] *vt* to tow; **se faire t.** to be towed, to get a tow

tracteur, -trice [traktœr, -tris] **1** *nm* tractor; **t. et semi-remorque** articulated vehicle, *F* artic; *Aut* **t. routier** tractor; **t. de papier** (*d'une imprimante*) paper tractor; **t. à picots** (*d'une imprimante*) tractor drive **2** *adj* (**a**) (*qui remorque*) towing (**b**) *Géog* **force tractrice** (*d'un courant*) transport capacity

traction [traksjɔ̃] *nf* (**a**) *Phys* traction, pulling; *Méd* traction; *MecE* **exercer une t. sur qch** to exercise traction on sth; **effort de t.** pull, *Spéc* tractive effort; **t. magnétique** magnetic pull; **résistance à la t.** tensile strength; *Gym* **faire des tractions** (*en tirant*) to do pull-ups; (*en poussant*) to do press-ups *or Am* push-ups (**b**) *Aut* **t. avant/arrière** front-wheel/rear-wheel drive

tractoriste [traktɔrist] *n* tractor driver

tractus [traktys] *nm Anat* tract, system

tradescantia [tradɛskɑ̃sja] *nm Bot* tradescantia

trade-unionisme [trɛdynjɔnism] *nm* trade unionism

tradition [tradisjɔ̃] *nf* tradition; **respecter la t.** to respect tradition; **c'est dans la plus pure t. française** it is typically French; **faire qch selon la t.** to do sth in the traditional way; **la tradition veut que ...** + *subj* tradition dictates that ...; **il existe une longue t. de liens culturels entre ces pays** there is a long history of cultural links between the countries

traditionalisme [tradisjɔnalism] *nm* traditionalism

traditionaliste [tradisjɔnalist] *adj, n* traditionalist

traditionnel, -elle [tradisjɔnɛl] *adj* (*fondé sur la tradition*) traditional; (*habituel*) usual, habitual; (*excuse, appareillage etc*) standard, usual; (*plaisanterie*) standing

traditionnellement [tradisjɔnɛlmɑ̃] *adv* traditionally, by tradition; **se marier t.** to have a traditional wedding

traducteur, -trice [tradyktœr, -tris] **1** *n* translator **2** *nm Ordinat* translator

traduction [tradyksjɔ̃] *nf* (**a**) (*action*) translation (**en** into); **la t. n'est pas une discipline facile** translating is not easy; **agence de t.** translation agency; **t. automatique/simultanée** machine/simultaneous translation; **t. assistée par ordinateur** computer assisted translation, machine translation (**b**) (*texte*) translation; **la t. de la Bible en français** the French translation of the Bible; **elle ne lit que des traductions** she only ever reads translations *or* in translation (**c**) *Ordinat* **t. des informations** data reduction

traduire [tradɥir] (*prp* **traduisant**; *pp* **traduit**; *pr ind* **je traduis, il traduit, n. traduisons, ils traduisent**; *impf* **je traduisais**; *p hist* **je traduisis**; *fu* **je traduirai**) **1** *vt* (**a**) to translate (**de** from; **en** into)

(**b**) *Ordinat* (*carte*) to interpret

(**c**) *Fig* (*exprimer*) (*sentiment, idée etc*) to express, to convey; **vous traduisez mal ma pensée** you're misinterpreting me *or* my thoughts; **cette réaction traduit une grande sensibilité** this reaction is indicative of *or* points to great sensitivity

(**d**) *Jur* **t. qn en justice** to sue *or* prosecute *or* indict sb

2 *vi Ling* to translate (**de/vers** from/into); **t. mot à mot** to translate word for word

3 se traduire *vpr* (**a**) *Ling* to be translated; **comment ça se traduit?** how do you translate it?

(**b**) *Fig* **sa douleur se traduisit par des larmes** his grief found expression *or* manifested itself in tears; *Com* **les comptes se traduisent par une perte de 5 000 francs** the accounts show a loss of 5, 000 francs

traduisible [tradɥizibl] *adj* (**a**) *Ling* translatable; **ce jeu de mots n'est pas t.** this play on words is untranslatable; **difficilement t.** difficult to translate (**b**) *Jur* **t. en justice** liable to prosecution

Trafalgar [trafalgar] *nm Fig* **coup de T.** underhand trick

trafic [trafik] *nm* (**a**) (*circulation*) traffic; **le t. est ralenti sur la nationale 7** traffic is moving slowly on route 7

(**b**) (*commerce illégal*) traffic; **t. de stupéfiants** *ou* **de drogues/d'armes** drug/arms traffic *or* trafficking; **ils ont mis sur pied un t. d'uranium enrichi** they've set up an arrangement for trafficking in enriched uranium; *F* **faire t. de ses charmes** (*d'une prostituée*) to sell *or* hawk one's wares; *F* **il y a un drôle de t. dans cette boutique** there's something very queer *or* funny going on in that shop; *F* **les enfants font un sacré t. avec leurs jouets** the kids are up to *or* involved in some mysterious game with their toys

(**c**) *Électron* traffic

(**d**) *Vieilli* (*commerce*) trading, trade

▶ **trafic**: **t. aérien** air traffic; **t. commercial** commercial trade; **t. d'influence** influence peddling; **il a obtenu ce marché grâce à un véritable t. d'influence** he landed the deal thanks to a fair amount of string-pulling; **t. des marchandises** goods traffic; *Ordinat* **t. de réseau** network traffic; **t. routier** road traffic

traficoter [trafikɔte] **1** *vi F Péj* to tinker **2** *vt F* (*manigancer*) **je me demande ce qu'il traficote** I wonder what he's up to

trafiquant, -ante [trafikɑ̃, -ɑ̃t] *n Péj* trafficker; **t. de** *ou* **en stupéfiants** *ou* **de drogues** drug trafficker; **t. d'armes** arms dealer, gunrunner; **t. du marché noir** black marketeer

trafiquer [trafike] **1** *vi Péj* to traffic (**de** in) **2** *vt F* (**a**) (*modifier*) (*moteur de voiture, mobylette etc*) to tinker with; (*freins, compteur*) to tamper with; (*chèque*) to falsify, to tamper with; (*vin*) to doctor, to tamper with; **t. les comptes** to fiddle the accounts (**b**) (*manigancer*) **qu'est-ce qu'il trafique?** what's he up to?

trafiqueur, -euse [trafikœr, -øz] *n Péj* trafficker (**de, en** in)

tragédie [traʒedi] *nf Th, Fig* tragedy; *Fig* **c'est une véritable t.** it's a real tragedy, it's really tragic; *F Fig* **ce n'est pas une t.!** it's not the end of the world!

tragédien, -ienne [traʒedjɛ̃, -jɛn] *n* tragic actor, *f* tragic actress, tragedian, *f* tragedienne

tragi-comédie [traʒikɔmedi], *pl* **tragi-comédies** *nf Th, Fig* tragi-comedy

tragi-comique [traʒikɔmik], *pl* **tragi-comiques** *adj Th, Fig* tragi-comic

tragique [traʒik] **1** *adj* (*auteur, pièce, rôle, Fig événement, conséquences etc*) tragic; **... dit-elle d'un accent t. ...** she said in a tragic tone of voice; **ce qu'il y avait de vraiment t. c'est que ...** what was really tragic *or* the real tragedy was that ...; *Littér* **le genre t.** tragedy **2** *nm* (**a**) (*d'un événement*) tragedy, tragic side; **cela tourne au t.** it's turning into a tragedy; *Fig* **prendre qch au t.** to make a tragedy *or* a big thing out of sth (**b**) *Th* **le t.** tragedy **3** *n* (*auteur*) tragic author, writer of tragedies

tragiquement [traʒikmɑ̃] *adv* tragically; **finir t.** to end tragically *or* in tragedy

trahir [trair] **1** *vt* (**a**) (*divulguer*) (*secret*) to betray, to reveal, to give away; (*de paroles, silence*) (*gêne, ignorance etc*) to betray, to reveal; (*d'un accent*) (*personne*) to give away; **je fus trahi par les aboiements d'un chien** I was betrayed *or* given away by a dog barking

(**b**) (*cesser d'être fidèle à*) (*personne, pays, confiance, intérêts*) to betray; (*serment, promesse etc*) to break; *Fig* (*de jambes, forces, traducteur*) (*personne, auteur*) to fail; *Fig* **la traduction trahit le texte** the translation fails *or* is not faithful to the text; **son mari la trahit pour une femme plus âgée** her husband is being unfaithful to *or* deceiving her with an older woman; **se sentir trahi** to feel betrayed

(**c**) *Arch* **t. qch/qn à qn** to betray sth/sb to sb

2 se trahir *vpr* (*d'une personne*) to give oneself away; (*d'un sentiment etc*) to betray itself, to be revealed

trahison [traizɔ̃] *nf* (**a**) (*fait de trahir*) (*d'un ami, de son pays etc*) betrayal (**b**) (*faute*) treachery; *Pol* treason; **haute t.** high treason; **une t.** an act of treachery

traille [traj] *nf* (**a**) (*câble*) ferry cable (**b**) (*bac*) ferry

train [trɛ̃] *nm* (**a**) *Rail* train; **je prends le t. de cinq heures** I'm catching the five o'clock (train); **je préfère le t. à la route** I'd rather go by train than by road; **voyager en t.** *ou* **par le t.** to travel by train; **voyage en t.** train journey; **être dans un t.** to be on a train; **monter dans le t.** to get on the train; **prendre le t. en marche** to jump on (a/the train while it's moving); *Fig* to jump *or* climb on the bandwagon; **comme une vache qui regarde passer un t.** like a cow at a five-bar gate

(b) *Mil* **le t.** = transport branch of Army Service Corps, *US* = transportation company

(c) (*file*) (*de véhicules, de péniches, d'animaux transhumants etc*) string, line; (*de roues etc*) set; (*de réformes, décrets*) series, string

(d) *Arch* (*escorte*) suite, attendants; (*de serviteurs etc*) train

(e) (*de cheval*) quarters; (*derrière*) (*de chien*) rump; **t. de derrière/de devant** hindquarters/forequarters

(f) *Arg* (*derrière*) (*d'une personne*) backside, rear (end), *Am* butt; **se manier le t.** to get a move on, to shift oneself, *Sl* to get one's arse in gear

(g) (*allure*) pace; **aller bon t.** to go at a good pace; **aller son petit t.** to jog along; **les choses vont leur t.** things are going along as usual; *Vieilli* **dans le t.** up to date; *F* **à fond de t.** at top *or* full speed, *F* at a rate of knots; **rouler à un t. d'enfer** to go hell for leather; **au t. où il va/où vont les choses** at the rate he's/things are going; **à ce t.-là** at this rate; *Sp* **meneur de t.** pacemaker; **mener le t.** to set the pace; **mener grand t.** to live it up; **avec le salaire que je gagne, je ne risque pas de mener grand t.** I'm not likely to paint the town red on what I make

(h) [ⓘ**B28**,F,1-2] **en t.** (*projet, affaire*) under way, in progress; *F* **ils ont un petit en t.** they've got a baby on the way, they're expecting; *F* **il était un peu en t.** (*ivre*) he'd had a drop (too much); **être en bon t.** to be making good progress; **mettre qch en t.** (*projet etc*) to set sth in train *or* motion, to start sth, to set sth going; (*tricot*) to start sth; **c'est lui qui a tout mis en t.** he got everything started *or* under way; **mise en t.** shakedown; **être en t. de faire qch** to be doing sth; **il était en t. de travailler** he was (busy) working; **elle est toujours en t. de crier** she's always shouting

(i) *F* (*tapage*) noise, row; **faire du t., faire un t. de tous les diables** to kick up (a hell of) a row

(j) (*humeur*) **être en t.** to be in good spirits *or* in good form; **il n'était pas en t. ce jour-là** he wasn't at his best that day; **être mal en t.** to be out of sorts, to feel unwell; **je ne suis pas en t. pour travailler** I don't feel like working, I'm not in the mood for work; **mettre qn en t.** to get sb into a good mood

(k) *Av* landing gear, undercarriage

▶ **train**: *Av* **t. d'atterrissage** landing gear, undercarriage; **T. Auto et Moto Accompagnées, T. Automobile Accompagnée** Motorail; **t. autos-couchettes** motorail, rail-drive; **t. avant** *Av* nose gear *or* wheel; *Aut* front axle (assembly); **t. de bois** timber raft, float; **t. de croisière** luxury train; **t. direct** through train; **t. électrique** electric train; **t. d'engrenages** gear train; **t. express** express (train); **t. (de) grandes lignes** inter-city (train); *Rail* **t. à grande vitesse** high-speed train; *Vieilli* **t. de maison** style of living; **t. de marchandises** goods *or Am* freight train; **t. militaire** troop train; **t. de neige** = train carrying people to ski resorts; **t. omnibus** local *or* slow *or* stopping train; *Phys* **t. d'ondes** wavetrain; **t. postal** mail train; *Tech* **t. de roulement** (*d'un véhicule à roues*) undercarriage; (*d'un véhicule traîné*) suspension and tracks; **t. routier** road train; **t. spatial** space train; **t. supplémentaire** relief train; **t. de vie** lifestyle, way of life; **t. de voyageurs** passenger train

traînage [trɛnaʒ] *nm* **(a)** dragging; *Rail* (*de trains*) haulage; **câble de t.** haulage rope **(b)** (*transport par traîneaux*) sleigh transport

traînailler [trɛnaje] *vi F* = **traînasser**

traînant [trɛnɑ̃] *adj* **(a)** (*robe etc*) trailing **(b)** (*lent*) (*voix*) drawling; (*démarche, pas*) shuffling, dragging

traînard, -arde [trɛnar, -ard] *n* (*en arrière d'un groupe*) straggler; (*dans son travail*) dawdler, *Br F* slowcoach, *Am F* slowpoke

traînasser [trɛnase] *vi F* **(a)** (*errer*) to loaf *or* slouch about *or* around **(b)** (*être lent*) to dawdle, to drag one's feet; (*n'avoir aucune énergie*) to drag oneself around

train-couchettes *nm inv* sleeper

traîne [trɛn] *nf* **(a)** *Naut* **à la t.** in tow; *Fig F* **être à la t.** to lag behind **(b)** (*d'une robe*) train **(c)** *Pêche* seine (net), drag net **(d)** *Can* **t. sauvage** toboggan

traîneau, -eaux [trɛno] *nm* **(a)** (*tiré par des chevaux*) sleigh; (*tiré par des chiens*) sledge, *US* sled; **faire une promenade en t.** to go for a sleigh ride; **chien de t.** sledge dog, husky; **attelage de chiens de t.** dog team **(b)** *Pêche* seine (net), drag net

traîne-bûches *nm inv Pêche F* bait, *Spéc* caddis worm

traîne-buisson, *pl* **traîne-buissons** *nm Orn* dunnock, hedge sparrow

traînée [trɛne] *nf* **(a)** (*de fumée, de sang, de lumière, de bave d'escargot etc*) trail; (*de saleté*) streak; (*de poudre*) train; (*d'un escargot*) trail; *Av* vapour *or US* vapor trail, *Spéc* contrail; *Fig* **se répandre comme une t. de poudre** to spread like wildfire **(b)** *Phys* (*force*) drag **(c)** *Arg* (*prostituée, Péj femme*) tart

traînement [trɛnmɑ̃] *nm* (*des pieds*) dragging; (*de la voix*) drawling

traîne-misère *n inv F* down-and-out

traîner [trɛne] **1** *vt* (*qn, qch*) to drag; *Rail* (*wagons etc*) to pull, to haul; (*péniches*) to tow; *Fig* (*sa vie*) to drag out; (*discours, affaire etc*) to spin out, to drag out; (*paroles*) to drawl; **faire t. qch en longueur** to spin *or* drag sth out; **elle traînait cinq enfants après elle** she was trailing *or* dragging five children after her; **elle traîne sa sœur partout** she drags her sister everywhere with her; **t. la jambe** to limp; **t. les pieds** to shuffle; *Fig* to drag one's feet; **elle entra dans la pièce en traînant les pieds** she shuffled into the room; **la perdrix traînait (de) l'aile** the partridge was dragging a wing; **t. qn en prison** to drag sb off to prison; *Fig* **elle traîne un rhume depuis quinze jours** for two weeks she's had a cold which she can't get rid of *or* shake off; *Fig* **t. qn dans la boue** to drag sb *or* sb's name through the mud; *F* **il doit bien t. ses guêtres** *ou* **bottes quelque part!** he must be somewhere around!; **j'ai traîné mes bottes dans tous les pays d'Afrique** I've kicked around every country in Africa; **t. son ennui** to be constantly bored

2 *vi* **(a)** (*dans la poussière, la boue etc*) to trail, to drag; **votre robe traîne (par terre)** your dress is trailing

(b) (*rester en arrière*) to lag *or* trail (behind); **t. derrière qn** to lag *or* trail behind sb; **une voix qui traîne** a drawling voice

(c) (*errer*) (*dans un endroit*) to hang *or* kick *or* knock around *or* about; **t. dans la rue** *ou* **par les rues** to hang *or* kick *or* knock around *or* about the streets; **où est-ce qu'il traîne d'habitude?** where does he usually hang out?; **t. avec qn** to hang about with sb; **il y a un virus qui traîne** there's a virus going around *or* doing the rounds

(d) (*être lent*) (*d'une personne*) to dawdle; (*de la conversation, Th etc d'une intrigue*) to drag

(e) (*en désordre*) to lie *or* kick around *or* about; **laisser t. son argent** to leave one's money lying around *or* about; **tes vêtements traînent partout dans la maison** your clothes are scattered all over the house

(f) (*durer longtemps*) (*d'une maladie, d'une conversation etc*) to drag on; **t. en longueur** (*d'un procès etc*) to drag (on); **les choses ne traînent pas avec vous** you're a fast worker, you don't hang about, you don't let the grass grow under your feet; *F* **... et que ça ne traîne pas!** ... and don't take forever about it!, ... and be quick about it!; **laisser t. un compte** to leave an account unpaid

3 se traîner *vpr* **(a)** (*d'une personne*) to drag oneself; **il se traînait à peine** he could hardly drag himself along; **il se traîna jusqu'au fossé** he dragged himself *or* crawled to the ditch; **se t. aux pieds de qn** to go on one's knees to sb; **je me suis traîné cette sale grippe tout l'hiver** I've had this rotten cold hanging around all winter; **je me suis traîné ces vieilles chaussures tout l'hiver** I've had to wear *or* put up with these old shoes all winter

(b) (*d'une conversation, d'une soirée etc*) to drag on; **les heures se traînent lourdement** time drags, time hangs heavy

traîne-savates *n inv F* layabout, loafer

training [treniŋ] *nm* **(a)** *Sp* (*entraînement*) training **(b)** *Psy* **t. autogène** relaxation by autosuggestion **(c)** (*survêtement*) tracksuit **(d)** (*chaussure*) trainer

train-poste, *pl* **trains-poste** *nm* mail train

train-train *nm F* routine, daily round; **le t. quotidien** the daily routine *or* grind; **rien qui sort du t. des événements ordinaires** nothing out of the ordinary

traire [trɛr] *vt* (*prp* **trayant**; *pp* **trait**; *pr ind* **je trais, n. trayons, ils traient**; *impf* **je trayais**; *fu* **je trairai**; *no p hist*) (*vache, chèvre etc*) to milk; (*lait*) to draw; **machine à t.** milking machine

trait [trɛ] *nm* **(a)** (*ligne etc*) stroke, line; *Typ* long dash; **d'un t. de plume** with a stroke of the pen; **signer d'un t. de plume** to sign with a flourish; **t. plein/discontinu** continuous/broken line; **dessin au t.** outline drawing; **copier qch t. pour t.** to copy sth line by line; *Fig* **c'est sa sœur t. pour t.** she is her sister to a T; **gravure au t.** line engraving; **les grands traits de qch** the main features of sth; *Télécom* **points et traits** dots and dashes; *Fig* **tirer un t. sur le passé** to forget the past, to draw a line under the past; **tirer un t. sur ses vacances** to say goodbye to one's holidays, to kiss one's holidays goodbye; **j'ai tiré un t. sur lui/notre relation** I've crossed him/our relationship off; **t. de scie** cut(ting) line

(b) (*du visage*) feature; **traits réguliers/fins/grossiers**

regular/fine/coarse features; **elle avait les traits tirés** she looked drawn, her face was drawn

(c) (*caractéristique*) (*d'une personne*) trait; (*d'un écrivain etc*) characteristic touch; **t. de caractère** character trait, trait of character; **c'est l'un de ses traits distinctifs** it's one of his peculiarities *or* distinctive traits

(d) (*flèche*) arrow; *Fig* **partir comme un t.** (*d'une personne*) to be off like a shot; *Fig* **les traits de la médisance/la satire** slanders/shafts of satire; *Fig* **un t. mordant/méchant** a sarcastic/nasty remark; *Fig* **envoyer** *ou* **lancer un t. à qn** to get a dig in at sb

(e) avoir t. à qch to be connected with sth, to relate to sth; **tout ce qui a t. à la psychanalyse** everything connected *or* to do with psychoanalysis

(f) (*de lumière*) beam, shaft

(g) *Mus* fast passage

(h) (*de boisson*) gulp, *Litt* draught, *US* draft; **boire à longs traits** (*bière etc*) to gulp down; **d'un (seul) t.** (*boire qch*) at one gulp, *F* at one go, in a oner; (*raconter qch*) without stopping, in one fell swoop; (*lire qch*) without stopping, at a single sitting

(i) (*de cordes, de poids*) pulling; **cheval de (gros) t.** (heavy) draught *or US* draft horse

(j) (*d'un harnais*) trace

(k) *Échecs etc* **avoir le t.** to have first move

(l) (*acte*) (*de courage*) act, deed; (*de génie*) stroke

▶ **trait**: *Typ* **t. double** double line; *Fig* **t. d'esprit** flash *or* stroke of wit, witticism; *Typ* **t. en pointillé** dotted underline; *Typ* **t. simple** single line; **t. d'union** hyphen; *Fig* (*entre deux personnes, deux villes etc*) link; *Ordinat* **t. d'union conditionnel** soft hyphen; *Ordinat* **t. d'union insécable** hard hyphen

traitable [trɛtabl] *adj* **(a)** *Litt* (*personne*) tractable, accommodating **(b)** (*sujet etc*) treatable, manageable

traitant [trɛtɑ̃] *adj* **(a)** (*shampoing, crème de beauté etc*) medicated **(b) mon médecin t.** my (usual) doctor; **nom du médecin t.** name of the doctor in attendance *or* of the consulting physician

traite [trɛt] *nf* **(a)** (*d'une route etc*) stretch; **j'ai fait une longue t.** I've come a long way; **(tout) d'une t., d'une seule t.** in one go; **faire le chemin d'une t.** to do the journey non-stop *or* without stopping *or F* in a oner

(b) *Fin* (*billet*) (banker's) draft, bill (of exchange)

(c) (*des vaches*) milking

▶ **traite**: **t. bancaire** bank draft; **t. des Blanches** white slave trade; *Fin* **t. de complaisance** accommodation bill; *Fin* **t. contre acceptation** acceptance bill; *Fin* **t. à courte échéance** short-dated bill; *Fin* **t. à date fixe** time bill; *Fin* **t. documentaire** documentary bill; *Fin* **t. libre** clean bill; *Fin* **t. à longue échéance** long-dated bill; **t. des Noirs** slave trade; *Fin* **t. pro forma** pro forma bill; *Fin* **t. 'sans frais'** bill 'without protest'; *Fin* **t. à terme** term draft; *Fin* **t. à vue** sight draft

traité [trete] *nm* **(a)** (*ouvrage*) treatise **(de, sur** on) **(b)** *Pol* (*accord*) treaty; **t. d'alliance** treaty of alliance; **t. de paix** peace treaty; **t. de commerce** commercial treaty

traitement [trɛtmɑ̃] *nm* **(a)** (*comportement à l'égard de qn*), *Méd* treatment; (*d'un sujet par un auteur*) treatment, handling; **mauvais t.** ill-treatment, maltreatment; *Méd* **prescrire un t.** to prescribe treatment; **premier t.** initial treatment; **t. chirurgical** surgery; **malade en t.** patient under(going) treatment; **t. de choc/de fond** shock/long-term treatment

(b) *Tech* (*de matières premières*) processing, treatment; (*de l'eau*) treatment; *Constr* **t. superficiel** (*des routes etc*) surfacing; *Ind* **capacité de t.** processing *or* handling capacity

(c) *Ordinat* processing; **données en t., capacité** *ou* **débit de t.** throughput; **machine à** *ou* **de t. de texte** word processor; **logiciel de t. de texte** word processor, word processing software; **unité de t.** task, job

(d) (*rémunération*) pay, salary; **t. de base** basic pay *or* salary; **t. fixe** fixed salary; **t. initial** starting salary; **sans t.** (*secrétaire*) honorary; (*magistrat*) unsalaried

▶ **traitement**: *Ordinat* **t. automatique de l'information** *ou* **des informations** automatic data processing; *Com* **t. des commandes** order processing; *Ordinat* **t. différé par lots** batch processing; **t. à distance** teleprocessing; **t. des données** data processing, DP; **t. électronique de l'information** electronic data processing, EDP; **t. de faveur** preferential treatment, red carpet treatment; **t. d'images** image processing; **t. de l'information** *ou* **des informations** data processing, DP, information processing; **t. par lots** batch processing; **t. multitâche** multitasking processing; *Ordinat* **t. en temps réel** real time processing; **t. de texte** word processing, WP; (*logiciel*) word processor, word processing software; (*machine*) word processor; **réaliser qch par t. de texte** to word process sth; *Ordinat* **t. de texte à balises** word processing with embedded visible commands; **t. vectoriel** vector processing

traiter [trete] **1** *vt* **(a)** (*se conduire envers*) to treat; **t. qn en ami/enfant** to treat sb like *or* as a friend/a child; **t. qn d'égal (à égal)** to treat sb as an *or* one's equal; **t. qn avec douceur** to treat *or* handle sb gently; **t. qn avec condescendance** to be condescending towards sb, to patronize sb; **je ne supporterai pas plus longtemps de me faire t. comme cela!** I won't take much more of being treated like this!, I won't take much more of this treatment!

(b) (*qualifier*) to call; **t. qn de lâche** to call sb a coward; **se faire t. de lâche** to be called a coward; **elle l'a traité de tous les noms** she called him all the names under the sun

(c) *Méd* (*patient, maladie*) to treat; **elle se fait t. pour un cancer** she's being treated for cancer, she is having *or* undergoing treatment for cancer; **tu devrais faire t. ça** you ought to get it treated

(d) *Tech* (*matière première, minerai*) to process; (*bois*) to treat; *Agr* (*vignobles, cultures etc*) to treat, to spray; **oranges non traitées** unsprayed oranges

(e) *Ordinat* (*informations*) to process; **données non traitées** raw data

(f) *Litt Vieilli* (*régaler*) to entertain

(g) *Com* (*marché etc*) to negotiate; (*affaire*) to handle

(h) (*s'occuper de*) (*sujet, problème, question etc*) (*d'un auteur, un artiste, un élève, un article*) to deal with; (*demande d'emploi, dossier de bourse etc*) to process; **l'auteur traite bien le sujet** the author handles the subject well; **comment Paris-Match traite-t-il cet événement?** how does Paris-Match deal with *or* handle *or* cover the event?; **t. une accusation avec mépris** to treat an accusation with scorn

2 *vi* **(a)** (*négocier*) **t. avec** to deal with; (*créanciers*) to negotiate with

(b) t. de (*d'un livre, un écrivain etc*) (*sujet, problème etc*) to deal with

3 se traiter *vpr* **(a)** (*réciproque*) to treat each other; **elles se traitent de tous les noms** they call each other all the names under the sun

(b) (*se négocier*) to be dealt with

(c) (*d'un sujet, d'un écrivain etc*) to be dealt with; **cela se traite facilement** that can be easily dealt with

(d) (*d'une maladie*) to be treated; **cela se traite très bien, maintenant** it can be treated now, there's treatment for it now

traiteur [trɛtœr] *nm* **(a)** *Com* caterer **(b)** *Arch* (*restaurateur*) restaurateur

traître, traîtresse [trɛtr, trɛtrɛs] **1** *adj* (*personne*) treacherous; (*escalier, crevasse etc*) dangerous, treacherous; (*soleil*) treacherous, strong; (*vin*) deceptively strong; *F* **pas un t. mot** not a single word **2** *n* **(a)** (*homme*) traitor; (*femme*) traitress; *Iron, Hum* **ah, le t., il ne nous disait rien!** the sly devil, he didn't tell us!; **être t. à sa patrie** to be a traitor to one's country, to commit treason; **prendre qn en t.** to set out to trap sb, to set a trap for sb; **agir en t.** to be underhanded **(b)** *Th* **le t.** the villain

traîtreusement [trɛtrøzmɑ̃] *adv* (*agir*) treacherously; **se venger t.** to take a traitor's revenge

traîtrise [trɛtriz] *nf* **(a)** (*comportement*) treachery, treacherousness **(b)** (*action*) (piece of) treachery

trajectoire [traʒɛktwar] *nf* (*d'une étoile, une comète, un avion, un électron, une balle etc*) path, trajectory; *Météo* depression; *Av* **t. de vol** flight path; **t. de collision** collision course

trajet [traʒɛ] *nm* **(a)** (*voyage*) journey; (*distance*) distance; (*itinéraire*) route; **j'ai fait une partie du t. en avion** I flew part of the way; **faire le t. en voiture** to do the journey by car; **j'ai dû faire le t. à pied** I had to walk all the way; **j'ai dû faire le t. dans l'autre sens pour le chercher** I had to come/go all the way back to get it; **un t. en voiture/autobus** a car/bus journey *or* ride; **il y a bien deux heures de t.** it takes a good two hours; **il a deux heures de t. pour aller au bureau** he has a two hour journey to the office

(b) *Anat* (*d'une artère, d'un nerf etc*) course; *Mil* (*d'un projectile*), *Él* (*d'un courant*) path; **t. de papier** (*dans une imprimante*) paper path

tralala [tralala] **1** *nm inv F* **en grand t.** (*se marier*) with a lot of fuss; **pas la peine d'en faire tout un t.** there's no point making a great fuss about it; **... et tout le t.** ... etcetera, etcetera, ... and all the rest of it **2** *int* **j'ai gagné, t.!** ha-ha, I've won!

tram [tram] *nm F* = **tramway**

tramage [tramaʒ] *nm Ordinat* rastering

tramail, -ails [tramaj] *nm Pêche* trammel (net)

trame [tram] *nf* **(a)** *Tex* woof, weft; *Fig* (*de la vie*) fabric; **usé jusqu'à la t.** (*pull, tapis*) threadbare; *Fig* **la t. du récit** the framework of the story; *Fig* **la t. de l'histoire** the storyline **(b)** *Arch* (*complot*) plot, conspiracy **(c)** *Phot, Typ* (*écran*) (half-tone) screen **(d)** *TV* raster; **t. (double)** frame **(e)** *Typ* **t. de maquette** layout sheet

tramer [trame] **1** *vt* **(a)** *Tex, Fig* (*intrigue d'un roman*) to weave **(b)** (*combiner*) (*complot*) to devise, *F* to hatch; **je me demande ce qu'il est en train de t.!** I wonder what he's up to **(c)** *Phot* **t. un cliché** to take a negative through a screen **2 se tramer** *vpr* **il se trame quelque chose** there's something going on, there's something in the wind *or* afoot

traminot [tramino] *nm* tram *or Am* streetcar worker

tramontane [tramɔ̃tan] *nf* **(a)** (*vent*) tramontana **(b)** *Arch* (*étoile*) north star; *Fig* **perdre la t.** to lose one's bearings; (*devenir fou*) to go off one's head

tramp [trɑ̃p] *nm Naut* tramp (steamer)

trampoline [trɑ̃pɔlin] *nm* (*toile*) trampoline; (*sport*) trampolining; **faire du t.** to go *or* do trampolining

tramway [tramwɛ] *nm* tram, *Am* streetcar; **voyager en t.** to travel by tram

tranchant [trɑ̃ʃɑ̃] **1** *adj* **(a)** (*outil, épée, bord etc*) sharp **(b)** *Fig* (*paroles, ton*) trenchant, peremptory, decisive; (*personne*) assertive, peremptory **2** *nm* **(a)** (*d'un couteau, d'une épée etc*) (cutting) edge; (*d'une cale*) thin end; (*de la main*) edge; **à deux tranchants, à double t.** (*épée, couteau etc*) two-edged; *Fig* **argument à double t.** argument that cuts both ways; *Fig* **cette décision est à double t.** the decision is a two-edged sword **(b)** (*de tanneur*) fleshing knife

tranche [trɑ̃ʃ] *nf* **(a)** (*morceau coupé*) (*de pain, de melon, de viande etc*) slice; (*de bacon*) rasher; **en tranches** in slices, sliced; **vous le voulez en tranches?** would you like it sliced?; *Culin* **t. napolitaine** Neapolitan ice (cream); *Culin* **t. grasse** (*morceau de bœuf*) round, top rump; **morceau dans la t.** = piece of topside; *F* **s'en payer une t.** to have the time of one's life

(b) (*de marbre, de pierre*) slab

(c) (*bord, côté*) (*d'une pièce de monnaie, d'une cale, d'une planche*) edge; (*d'un livre*) (cut) edge; **doré sur t.** (*livre*) with gilt edges, gilt-edged

(d) (*série, section*) (*de chiffres*) group, block; (*d'actions*) block, portion; (*d'un crédit*) instalment, *US* installment; (*d'assistance financière internationale*) tranche; (*d'un programme immobilier*) stage, portion; *Rail* **t. de voitures** portion; **t. des salariés moyens** middle-income bracket

(e) *Tech* (*coupe*) section; **t. verticale** vertical section

(f) *Ordinat* wafer; **microprocesseur en tranches** bit slice microprocessor

▶ **tranche**: **t. d'âge** age bracket *or* group *or* band; *Rad, TV* **t. horaire** (time) slot; **t. d'imposition** tax band *or* bracket; **t. de paiement** instalment, *US* installment; **t. de prix** price bracket; **t. de revenu** income group; **les gens dans les tranches de revenus les plus élevées** people in the upper income brackets; *Fig* **t. de vie** slice *or* cross-section of life

tranché [trɑ̃ʃe] *adj Fig* (*couleur, motif etc*) definite, distinct; (*opinion*) definite, clear-cut; (*refus*) blunt; **les avis sont très tranchés** opinions are very clear-cut, people are very definite in their opinion

tranchée [trɑ̃ʃe] *nf* **(a)** (*fossé*) trench; *Agr* drain; *Rail* cutting; *Mil* **guerre de tranchées** trench warfare **(b)** (*dans une forêt*) cutting; **t. garde-feu** firebreak **(c)** *Méd* **tranchées** colic

tranchée-abri, *pl* **tranchées-abris** *nf Mil* dugout

tranchefile [trɑ̃ʃfil] *nf* (*d'un livre relié*) headband

trancher [trɑ̃ʃe] **1** *vt* **(a)** (*cordage, câble etc*) to cut; (*bras, membre, tête*) to sever; **t. la gorge à qn** to slit *or* cut sb's throat; **t. la tête à qn** to cut off *or* chop off sb's head; **qu'on lui tranche la tête!** off with his head!

(b) (*discussion*) to cut short; (*question, différend*) to settle (once and for all); (*problème, difficulté*) to resolve, to make short work of; **voilà qui tranche la question!** that settles it!; **tranchons là** let's stop there

2 *vi* **(a)** (*décider*) to decide, to reach a decision; **t. dans le vif** *Chir* to cut into healthy tissue; *Fig* to adopt drastic measures; **il tranche sur tout** he's always laying down the law

(b) (*de couleurs etc*) to contrast strongly (**sur** with), to stand out (**sur** against)

3 se trancher *vpr* **se t. le doigt** to sever one's finger

tranchet [trɑ̃ʃɛ] *nm* **(a)** (*de serrurier etc*) anvil cutter **(b)** (*de tanneur*) paring knife

trancheur, -euse [trɑ̃ʃœr, -øz] **1** *nm Tech, Min* cutter; *Pêche* cod gutter **2** *nf* **trancheuse** stone saw

tranchoir [trɑ̃ʃwar] *nm* (*planche*) chopping board

tranquille [trɑ̃kil] *adj* **(a)** (*calme, paisible*) (*personne, vie etc, Com marché*) quiet; (*soirée*) still, peaceful, quiet; (*mer*) calm, still, *Litt* tranquil; (*conscience, esprit etc*) easy, untroubled; (*sommeil*) untroubled, peaceful; (*boussole*) steady; *F* **un père t.** (*homme, bébé*) a quiet one; **se tenir t.** to keep still; **j'adore cet endroit, je m'y sens vraiment t.** I love this place, I really feel at peace here; **travailler t.** to work in peace; **vous pouvez dormir t.** you can sleep in peace *or* rest easy; **laissez-moi t.** leave me alone *or* in peace, let me be; *F* **laisse ce vase t.!** leave that vase alone!; **laisse ça t., je m'en occuperai** don't bother with that, I'll take care of it; **soyez t.** don't worry, set your mind at rest *or* at ease; **soyez t., il reviendra!** he'll come back, don't you worry!; **avec ce plan d'épargne/ces chaussures en cuir, je suis t.** with this savings plan/these leather shoes I don't need to worry; **elle ne m'a pas rappelé, je ne suis pas t.** she hasn't phoned me back, I'm anxious *or* worried *or* not easy in my mind; **je ne suis pas t. dans cette grande maison** I get nervous in this big house; *F* **tu peux être t. que ...** you can be sure that ...; **je n'ai pas la conscience t.** my conscience is bothering me; **moi, j'ai la conscience t.** my conscience is clear; **faire qch la conscience t.** to do sth with a clear conscience

(b) (*sans bruit*) (*ville, quartier*) quiet, peaceful; **est-ce que nous pouvons aller dans un endroit t.?** can we go somewhere quiet?; **se tenir t.** (*ne rien dire*) to keep quiet

tranquillement [trɑ̃kilmɑ̃] *adv* (*répondre, examiner, travailler etc*) calmly, quietly; (*vivre*) quietly, peacefully; (*dormir*) peacefully; (*partir*) with an easy mind, with a clear conscience, without worrying

tranquillisant [trɑ̃kilizɑ̃] **1** *adj* (*nouvelles*) reassuring; (*paroles, voix*) reassuring, soothing, calming; (*effet*) soothing, calming; *Pharm* tranquillizing; *Pharm* **avoir un effet t.** to act as a sedative; **cela n'est pas très t.** that's not very reassuring **2** *nm Pharm* tranquillizer

tranquilliser [trɑ̃kilize] **1** *vt* **t. qn** to reassure sb, to set sb's mind at rest; **ça te tranquillisera** it will set your mind at rest *or* give you peace of mind **2 se tranquilliser** *vpr* **tranquillisez-vous** don't worry, set your mind at rest

tranquillité [trɑ̃kilite] *nf* **(a)** (*calme*) (*de la mer*) calmness, stillness; (*de la campagne*) stillness, quietness, peace; (*de la nature*) tranquillity; (*du sommeil*) peacefulness; **j'ai besoin de t.** I need some peace and quiet; **c'est un enfant d'une grande t.** he's a very quiet *or* placid child; **t. d'esprit** peace of mind; **troubler la t. publique** to disturb the peace; **en toute t.** without being disturbed; (*sans souci*) with an easy mind, without worrying, with a clear conscience; **je vais pouvoir travailler en toute t.** I'll be able to work in peace (and quiet) **(b)** (*absence de bruit*) (*d'une ville*) quietness

trans- [trɑ̃s, trɑ̃z] *préf* trans-

transaction [trɑ̃zaksjɔ̃] *nf* **(a)** *Com* transaction; **transactions** transactions, dealings; **transactions bancaires** bank transactions; **transactions boursières** Stock Exchange transactions; **transactions commerciales** business transactions; *Bourse* **t. au comptant** spot transaction; *Bourse* **t. de clôture** closing trade; *Banque* **t. par carte** card transaction; *Banque* **t. valeur jour** value today trade **(b)** (*arrangement*) compromise

transactionnel, -elle [trɑ̃zaksjɔnɛl] *adj* **solution transactionnelle** compromise; *Psy* **analyse transactionnelle** transactional analysis

transafricain [trɑ̃zafrikɛ̃] *adj* transafrican, cross-Africa

transalpin [trɑ̃zalpɛ̃] *adj* transalpine

transaméricain [trɑ̃zamerikɛ̃] *adj* transamerican

transat [trɑ̃zat] *nm F* = **transatlantique 2**

transatlantique [trɑ̃zatlɑ̃tik] **1** *adj* transatlantic **2** *nm* **(a)** (*paquebot*) (transatlantic) liner **(b)** (*chaise longue*) deck chair

transbahuter [trɑ̃sbayte] *F* **1** *vt* (*affaires, enfants*) to cart, to lug **2 se transbahuter** *vpr* to shift

transbordement [trɑ̃sbɔrdəmɑ̃] *nm Naut* transhipment; *Rail* transfer

transborder [trɑ̃sbɔrde] *vt Naut* to tranship; *Rail* (*passagers, marchandises*) to transfer

transbordeur [trɑ̃sbɔrdœr] *adj, nm* **(pont) t.** transporter bridge

transcanadien, -ienne [trɑ̃skanadjɛ̃, -jɛn] **1** *adj* trans-Canada **2** *nf* **la Transcanadienne** (*autoroute*) the Trans-Canada Highway

transcendance [trɑ̃sɑ̃dɑ̃s] *nf Phil, Rel etc* transcendence, transcendency

transcendant [trɑ̃sɑ̃dɑ̃] *adj* **(a)** *Phil, Rel etc* transcendent; *F* **ce/il n'est pas t.** it's/he's not much to write home about, it's/he's nothing great **(b)** *Math* transcendental

transcendantal, -ale, -aux, -ales [trɑ̃sɑ̃dɑ̃tal, -o] *adj Phil* transcendental

transcendantalisme [trɑ̃sɑ̃dɑ̃talism] *nm Phil* transcendentalism

transcender [trɑ̃sɑ̃de] **1** *vt* to transcend **2 se transcender** *vpr* to surpass oneself

transcodage [trɑ̃skɔdaʒ] *nm Ordinat* transcribing, transcoding; *TV* standards conversion
transcoder [trɑ̃skɔde] *vt Ordinat* to transcribe
transcodeur [trɑ̃skɔdœr] *nm TV* transcoder, standards converter; *Ordinat* transcoder
transconteneur [trɑ̃skɔ̃t(ə)nœr] *nm* transcontainer; (*navire*) transcontainer ship
transcontinental, -ale, -aux, -ales [trɑ̃skɔ̃tinɑ̃tal, -o] *adj* transcontinental
transcriptase [trɑ̃skriptaz] *nf* **t. inverse** *ou* **reverse** reverse transcriptase
transcripteur [trɑ̃skriptœr] *nm* transcriber
transcription [trɑ̃skripsjɔ̃] *nf* **(a)** (*action*) transcription, transcribing; (*dans un autre alphabet*) transliteration; **t. phonétique** phonetic transcription; **t. génétique** (genetic) transcription **(b)** (*texte*) transcript; *Mus* transcription; **t. à l'état civil** = certified copy of registry office document
transcrire [trɑ̃skrir] *vt* (*conj like* **écrire**) **(a)** (*recopier*) (*manuscrit, Mus morceau*) to transcribe; **t. une lettre à la machine** to type a letter **(b)** *Jur* (*divorce etc*) to register; *Com* to post **(c)** (*dans un autre alphabet*) (*texte etc*) to transcribe, to transliterate; **t. un livre en braille** to copy a book in Braille
transculturel, -elle [trɑ̃skyltyrɛl] *adj* cross-cultural
transcutané [trɑ̃skytane] *adj* transcutaneous
transdisciplinaire [trɑ̃sdisiplinɛr] *adj* interdisciplinary
transducteur [trɑ̃sdyktœr] *nm Phys, Électron* transducer
transe [trɑ̃s] *nf* **(a) transes** (*anxiété*) fear; *Vieilli* **être dans les transes** to be sick with worry, to be out of one's mind with anxiety **(b)** (*hypnose*) (hypnotic) trance; **en t.** (*médium, Fig fans*) in a trance; **entrer en t.** to go into a trance; *Fig F* (*se mettre en colère*) to hit the ceiling
transept [trɑ̃sɛpt] *nm Archit* transept
transférable [trɑ̃sferabl] *adj* transferable
transfèrement [trɑ̃sfermɑ̃] *nm* (*de prisonnier etc*) transfer; **t. cellulaire** transfer by police van
transférer [trɑ̃sfere] *vt* (**je transfère, n. transférons; je transférerai**) **(a)** (*dans un autre lieu*) (*détenu, siège social etc*) to transfer (**à** to); *Rel* (*évêque*) to translate; **t. de l'argent d'un compte à un autre** to transfer money from one account to another **(b)** (*céder*) (*marchandises etc*) to transfer, to make over, to assign (**à** to); (*propriété*) to convey (**à** to) **(c)** *Psy* (*affection etc*) to transfer (**sur** to)
transfert [trɑ̃sfɛr] *nm* **(a)** (*d'un prisonnier, d'un siège social, Sp d'un footballeur etc*) transfer; (*de population*) resettlement (**dans** in) **(b)** (*cession*) (*du stock, de droits etc*) transfer, assignment, making over; (*d'un domaine*) conveyance **(c)** *Psy* transference; **faire un t. sur qn** to use sb as an object of transference; **cela fait partie du t.** it's part of the transference process
▶ **transfert**: **t. d'actions** transfer of shares; *Télécom* **t. d'appel** call transfer; **t. de capitaux** transfer of capital, capital transfer; *Banque* **t. par CCP** giro transfer; *Compta* **t. de charges** expense transfer, transfer of charges; *Compta* **t. de créances** assignment of accounts receivable *or* of debts; **t. de devises** currency transfer; *Ordinat* **t. de données** data transfer; **t. de fonds électronique, t. électronique de fonds** electronic funds transfer, EFT
transfiguration [trɑ̃sfigyrasjɔ̃] *nf* transfiguration
transfigurer [trɑ̃sfigyre] *vt* to transfigure
transfiler [trɑ̃sfile] *vt Naut* **(a)** (*voiles etc*) to lace **(b)** (*cordage*) to snub
transfo [trɑ̃sfo] *nm Él F* transformer
transformable [trɑ̃sfɔrmabl] *adj* (*canapé, fauteuil etc*) convertible
transformateur, -trice [trɑ̃sfɔrmatœr, -tris] *Él* **1** *adj* transforming; (*station*) transformer **2** *nm* transformer
transformation [trɑ̃sfɔrmasjɔ̃] *nf* **(a)** (*changement*) change; (*radicale*) transformation; (*d'un local*) conversion; **la t. de l'eau en glace** the transformation of water to ice; **acteur à transformations** quick-change artist(e); **industrie de t.** processing industry; *Math* **t. algébrique** algebraic transformation **(b)** *Él* **rapport de t.** transformer ratio; *Électron* **t. de signaux** signal transformation **(c)** *Rugby* (*d'un essai*) conversion; **faire une t.** to convert (a try)
transformer [trɑ̃sfɔrme] **1** *vt* **(a)** (*personne, rapports etc*) to change; (*radicalement*) to transform; (*local, maison*) to convert, to remodel; **ils ont transformé l'appartement en l'agrandissant** they've transformed the flat by making it bigger; **cette expérience l'a profondément transformé** the experience has caused a profound change in him *or* has transformed him; **t. en** to turn *or* change *or* transform into; **l'école fut transformée en cinéma** the school was turned *or* converted into a cinema; **la sorcière l'a transformé en souris** the witch turned him into a mouse
(b) *Math* (*équation*) to transform
(c) *Rugby* (*essai*) to convert
(d) *Électron* to transform, to map
(e) (*en logique*) (*proposition*) to convert
2 se transformer *vpr* to be transformed, to change; **tout se transforme** everything changes; **se t. en** to turn into; **se t. en monstre/papillon** to turn into *or* change *or* be transformed into a monster/butterfly; **se t. en haine/en cauchemar** to turn into hate/a nightmare
transformisme [trɑ̃sfɔrmism] *nm Phil etc* transformism
transformiste [trɑ̃sfɔrmist], **1** *adj Phil etc* transformist **2** *n Phil etc* transformist; (*qui s'habille en femme*) drag queen; (*dans cabaret*) drag artist; **spectacle de transformistes** drag show
transfrontières [trɑ̃sfrɔ̃tjɛr] *adj inv* cross-border
transfuge [trɑ̃sfyʒ] *n Pol, Mil, Fig* defector
transfusé [trɑ̃sfyze] **1** *adj* **sang t.** transfused blood **2** *n* **le nombre des transfusés** the number of people receiving (blood) transfusions
transfuser [trɑ̃sfyze] *vt* (*sang*) to transfuse; (*malade*) to give a (blood) transfusion to, to transfuse
transfusion [trɑ̃sfyzjɔ̃] *nf* (blood) transfusion; **faire une t. à un malade** to give a patient a transfusion; **t. sanguine** blood transfusion; **centre de t. sanguine** blood transfusion centre; **t. d'échange** exchange transfusion
transgresser [trɑ̃sgrese] *vt* (*règlement, loi*) to infringe, to contravene, *Fml* to transgress; (*interdit*) to infringe; (*ordres*) to disobey
transgresseur [trɑ̃sgrɛsœr] *nm Litt* transgressor
transgression [trɑ̃sgrɛsjɔ̃] *nf* (*du règlement, de la loi*) infringement, contravention, *Fml* transgression; (*d'ordres*) disobeying
transhumance [trɑ̃zymɑ̃s] *nf* move from/to summer pastures, *Spéc* transhumance
transhumant [trɑ̃zymɑ̃] *adj* moving from/to summer pastures, *Spéc* transhumant
transhumer [trɑ̃zyme] *vti* to move from/to summer pastures
transi [trɑ̃zi] *adj* paralysed (**de peur** with fear); **t.** (**de froid**) freezing, chilled to the bone; *Iron* **un amoureux t.** a bashful lover
transiger [trɑ̃ziʒe] *vi* (**je transigeai(s); n. transigeons**) **(a)** to compromise (**avec** with; **sur** on); **t. sur ses principes/avec sa conscience** to compromise one's principles/one's conscience; **je ne transigerai pas avec mon devoir/le règlement** I refuse to compromise *or* I am intransigent when it comes to my duty/the rules; **je ne transigerai pas sur l'honnêteté** I refuse to be anything less than totally honest; **il ne transige pas sur l'honnêteté** he is uncompromisingly honest, he makes no compromises when it comes to a question of honesty **(b)** *Can* (*faire des transactions*) to carry out transactions
Transilvanie [trɑ̃silvani] *nf* Transylvania
transir [trɑ̃zir] **1** *vt* (*du vent etc*) to chill to the bone; (*de la peur*) to paralyse **2** *vi Arch* (*de froid*) to be chilled to the bone; (*de peur*) to be paralysed with fear
transistor [trɑ̃zistɔr] *nm* **(a)** *Électron* (*dispositif*) transistor; **à transistors** transistorized; **t. en couche mince** thin film transistor, TFT **(b)** (*poste de radio*) transistor (radio)
transistorisé [trɑ̃zistɔrize] *adj Électron* transistorized
transistoriser [trɑ̃zistɔrize] *vt Électron* to transistorize
transit [trɑ̃zit] *nm* **(a)** transit; **en t.** in transit; **passagers en t.** (*dans un aéroport*) passengers in transit, transfer passengers; *Av* **salle de t.** transit *or* transfer lounge; *Com* **t. communautaire** Community transit; **marchandises de t.** goods for transit; **maison de t.** forwarding agency **(b)** *Électron* **t. par bande perforée** tape relay
▶ **transit**: *Com* **t. douanier** Customs transit; *Méd* **t. intestinal** intestinal transit; **favoriser le t. intestinal** to encourage regular bowel movements; **favorise le t. intestinal** keeps you regular
transitaire [trɑ̃zitɛr] **1** *adj* **pays t.** country of transit; **commerce t.** transit trade **2** *nm* forwarding agent, freight forwarder; **t. aéroportuaire** airfreight forwarder; **t. portuaire** maritime freight forwarder
transitaire-groupeur, *pl* **transitaires-groupeurs** [trɑ̃zitɛrgrupœr] *nm* forwarder and consolidator
transiter [trɑ̃zite] **1** *vt* (*marchandises*) to forward **2** *vi* (*de marchandises, de voyageurs*) to (pass in) transit (**par** through); *Ordinat* (*de signaux*) to flow
transitif, -ive [trɑ̃zitif, -iv] *adj Gram, Math* transitive; *Gram* **à la forme transitive** in the transitive
transition [trɑ̃zisjɔ̃] *nf* transition; *TV, Rad* **t. musicale** segue; **assurer la t.** to make sure there is no hiatus, to make sure there is a seamless transition; **phase de t.** transition *or* transitional period; **sans t.** abruptly, *Fml* without transition; *TV, Rad* **sans t., nous passons aux nouvelles sportives** and

now for something completely different, over to the sports news; *Archit* **style de t.** transitional style
transitivement [trɑ̃zitivmɑ̃] *adv Gram* (*employé*) transitively, in the transitive
transitivité [trɑ̃zitivite] *nf Gram, Math* transitivity
transitoire [trɑ̃zitwar] *adj* **(a)** (*fugitif*) transitory, transient **(b)** (*provisoire*) (*période, régime*) transitional; (*mesure, solution*) transitional, temporary
transitoirement [trɑ̃zitwarmɑ̃] *adv* (*d'une manière fugitive*) fleetingly; (*d'une manière provisoire*) transitionally, temporarily
Transjordanie [trɑ̃sʒɔrdani] *nf Hist* Trans-Jordan
translation [trɑ̃slasjɔ̃] *nf* **(a)** (*d'un prisonnier, un tribunal, reliques etc*) transfer; *Télécom* (*de message*) retransmission, relaying **(b)** *Géom, Phys* **mouvement de t.** translatory motion **(c)** *Jur* **t. de propriété** transfer of property
transli(t)tération [trɑ̃sliterasjɔ̃] *nf* transliteration
translit(t)érer [trɑ̃slitere] *vt* (*texte*) to transliterate; (*en braille*) to copy
translucide [trɑ̃slysid] *adj* translucent
translucidité [trɑ̃slysidite] *nf* translucence, translucency
trans-Manche [trɑ̃zmɑ̃ʃ] *adj inv* cross-Channel
transmetteur [trɑ̃smɛtœr] *nm* **(a)** *Télécom, Ordinat, Biol* transmitter **(b)** *Naut* **t. d'ordres** (turret) telegraph, transmitter
transmettre [trɑ̃smɛtr] (*conj like* **mettre**) **1** *vt* **(a)** (*lumière, chaleur*) to transmit; (*message, nouvelle etc*) to pass on, to convey; (*ordre*) to convey, to transmit; (*maladie, virus*) to pass on, to transmit; (*recette, pouvoir magique, don etc*) to pass *or* hand on; (*tradition, collier etc*) to hand *or* pass down (**de génération en génération** from generation to generation); (*flambeau*) to hand over *or* on; (*vérité, énergie*) to impart; *Télécom, Rad* (*information*) to send, to transmit; *Rad, TV* (*émission etc*) to broadcast; **t.** (**par satellite**) to beam; **qui vous a transmis la nouvelle?** who gave *or* told you the news?, who passed the news on to you?; **transmettez mon amitié à vos parents** pass on *or* give *or* convey my best wishes to your parents

(b) *Jur* (*propriété, droit etc*) to transfer; (*actions etc*) to assign; **t. ses pouvoirs à qn** to hand over to sb

2 se transmettre *vpr* (*d'un message, d'une maladie etc*) to be passed on
transmigration [trɑ̃smigrasjɔ̃] *nf* transmigration
transmigrer [trɑ̃smigre] *vi* to transmigrate
transmissible [trɑ̃smisibl] *adj* **(a)** (*maladie*) transmissible, communicable; **sexuellement t.** sexually transmitted **(b)** *Jur* (*droit, fortune etc*) transferable; *Fin* **t. par endossement** transferable by endorsement
transmission [trɑ̃smisjɔ̃] *nf* **(a)** (*de chaleur, lumière, Méd d'une maladie, d'un virus*) transmission; (*d'un message, d'un ordre*) transmission, passing on; (*de la vérité*) imparting; (*d'une tradition etc*) handing down *or* on; (*de caractères génétiques*) transmission, handing on; *Télécom, Rad* (*d'un message, d'une image etc*) transmission, sending; *Rad, TV* (*d'une émission*) broadcasting; *Rad etc* **antenne de t.** transmitting aerial; *Com* **fiche de t.** routing slip; *Fb* **t. du ballon** passing; **erreur de t.** (*d'un message*) error in transmission

(b) *Naut, Mil* **les transmissions** signals; **officier de transmissions** signal(s) officer; **centre de transmissions** signal centre

(c) *MecE* gearing; *Aut* **la t.** the transmission (gear); *Tech* **t. du mouvement** transmission of movement; *Aut* power flow

(d) *Ordinat* transmission; **voie de t.** transmission channel

(e) *Jur* (*d'une propriété, d'un droit etc*) transfer(ence); (*d'actions etc*) assignment

▶ **transmission**: *Aut* **t. automatique** automatic transmission; *Rad, TV* **t. différée** *ou* **en différé** recorded broadcast *or* programme; **t. directe** *ou* **en direct** live broadcast *or* programme; **t. de données** data transmission *or* transfer; *Fin* **t. par endossement** transfer by endorsement; *Aut* **t. finale** final drive; *Tech* **t. flexible** flexible shaft(ing); *Aut* **t. manuelle** manual transmission; *Ordinat* **t. par modem** modem transmission; **la t. d'un document par modem** the transmission of a document by modem, the modeming of a document; *Ordinat* **t. de paquets** packet transmission; **t. de pensée** thought transference; *Fig* **c'est de la t. de pensée!** we/they/*etc* can read each other's mind!; *Admin* **t. des pouvoirs** handover; *Rad, TV* **t. par satellite** satellite broadcast; *Aut* **t. à variation continue** continuously variable transmission
transmodulation [trɑ̃smɔdylasjɔ̃] *nf Rad etc* cross modulation
transmuer [trɑ̃smɥe] *vt* to transmute (**en** into)
transmutation [trɑ̃smytasjɔ̃] *nf* transmutation (**en** into)
transmuter [trɑ̃smyte] *vt* to transmute (**en** into)
transnational, -ale, -aux, -ales [trɑ̃snasjɔnal, -o] *adj* transnational
transocéanien, -ienne [trɑ̃zɔseanjɛ̃, -jɛn], **transocéanique** [trɑ̃zɔseanik] *adj* transoceanic
transpacifique [trɑ̃spasifik] *adj* transpacific
transpalette [trɑ̃spalɛt] *nm* pallet truck
transparaître [trɑ̃sparɛtr] *vi* (*conj like* **paraître**) to show (through); **le doute transparaît sous son calme** doubt is showing (through) beneath his calm; **laisser t. une émotion** to let an emotion show
transparence [trɑ̃sparɑ̃s] *nf* **(a)** (*d'un tissu, un matériau, un teint, Fig d'une allusion, une intention*) transparency; (*d'un parti politique*) transparency, openness; **on peut le lire par t.** you can read it by holding it up to the light; **on voit ses jambes par t.** you can see her legs against the light; **on voit mes veines par t.** my veins show through; **t. fiscale** = system of taxing the income of partners in a firm rather than the firm's profits **(b)** *Cin* back projection
transparent [trɑ̃sparɑ̃] **1** *adj* (*matériau, tissu*) transparent; (*vêtement*) transparent, see-through; *Fig* (*intention, allusion*) transparent, clear, obvious; (*personne*) transparent; **c'était un homme t.** it was easy to read his mind *or* to know what he was thinking **2** *nm* transparency
transpercer [trɑ̃spɛrse] *vt* (**je transperçai(s); n. transperçons**) (*d'une lame, une flèche*) to pierce; (*d'une balle*) to go through, to pierce; (*du froid, du vent, de la pluie*) (*vêtements, chaussures*) to go *or* come through; **t. qn** (**d'un coup d'épée**) to run sb through (with a sword); **la balle l'a transpercé** the bullet went right through him/it; **le froid/la pluie transperçait les badauds** the passers-by were chilled to the bone/soaked to the skin; **la pluie a transpercé ses vêtements** the rain went *or* soaked right through his clothes; *Fig* **t. qn du regard** to give sb a piercing look; *Fig* **son attitude me transperce le cœur** his attitude is breaking my heart
transpirant [trɑ̃spirɑ̃] *adj* sweating, perspiring
transpiration [trɑ̃spirasjɔ̃] *nf* **(a)** (*sueur*) sweat, perspiration; **humide de t.** (*vêtement etc*) sweaty; **trempé de t.** soaked in sweat **(b)** (*action*) sweating, perspiration; *Bot* transpiration
transpirer [trɑ̃spire] *vi* **(a)** (*d'une personne*) to sweat, to perspire; **se mettre à t.** to start to sweat, to break into a sweat; **t. des pieds/des aisselles** to have sweaty feet/armpits; **il transpirait à grosses gouttes** he was dripping with sweat, the sweat was pouring off him; *F* **t. sur** (*travailler à*) to sweat over **(b)** *Bot* to transpire **(c)** *Fig* (*d'un secret, de nouvelles etc*) to come to light, to come out
transplant [trɑ̃splɑ̃] *nm Chir* (*organe, tissu*) transplant
transplantable [trɑ̃splɑ̃tabl] *adj* transplantable
transplantation [trɑ̃splɑ̃tasjɔ̃] *nf* (*d'arbres etc, Fig de personnes*) transplantation, transplanting; *Chir* transplant; **t. cardiaque/rénale** heart/kidney transplant
transplanté [trɑ̃splɑ̃te] **1** *adj* (*organe*) transplanted; **un malade t.** a transplant patient **2** *n* **le nombre des transplantés** the number of people receiving transplants
transplanter [trɑ̃splɑ̃te] **1** *vt* (*arbres etc, Fig personnes, Chir organe*) to transplant; *Chir* **t. un cœur/un rein** to perform a heart/kidney transplant (operation) **2 se transplanter** *vpr* (*dans un autre milieu*) to transplant oneself; **se t. en France/aux États-Unis** to resettle in France/in the United States
transplantoir [trɑ̃splɑ̃twar] *nm* trowel
transpolaire [trɑ̃spɔlɛr] *adj* transpolar
transpondeur [trɑ̃spɔ̃dœr] *nm* transponder; **t. satellite** satellite transponder
transport [trɑ̃spɔr] *nm* **(a)** [ⓘ**A26-27**,c] (*de marchandises, de passagers*) transport, *Fml* carriage; **moyen de t.** means of transport; **avez-vous un moyen de t.?** do you have transport *or* transportation?; **les transports** transport; **cela permet de faire les transports urgents par avion** this enables urgent freight to be sent by air; **politique des transports** transport policy; **abîmé pendant le t.** damaged in transit; **travailler dans le t.** to work in transport; **capacité de t.** transport capacity; **compagnie de t.** transport company; *Com* carrying *or* forwarding company; **entrepreneur de t.** haulage contractor, haulier; **frais de t.** transport costs; *Com* freight charges, carriage; *Ind* **courroie de t.** conveyor belt; *Mil* **véhicule de t. de personnel** personnel carrier; **avion de t.** transport aircraft; **avion de t. de passagers/de frêt** passenger/cargo aircraft; **t. urbain** urban transport

(b) *Jur* (*cession*) **t.(-cession)** (*de biens, de droits etc*) transfer, conveyance

(c) *Mil* (*navire*) transport (ship); (*avion*) transport (plane)

(d) *Litt* (*émotion*) rapture; **transports de joie** transports of joy; **transports de colère** outbursts *or* fits of anger; **avec t., avec transports de joie** rapturously, with rapture

▶ **transport**: **t. d'acheminement** transfer transport; **t. aérien** *ou* **par air** air transport; *Com* air freight; **transports aériens** air transport; **t. par canalisations** (*du pétrole*) piping; **t. civil aérien** civil aviation; **t. par chemin de fer** rail transport; **transports en commun** public transport, *Am* mass transit; *Él* **t. d'énergie** power transmission; **t. ferroviaire** *ou* **par fer** rail transport; **t. fluvial** inland waterway transport; *Él* **t. de force** high-voltage power transmission; *Jur* **t. de justice** visit to the scene of the accident/crime/*etc*; **t. sur les lieux** visit to the scene of the accident/crime/*etc*; **t. de marchandises** transport of goods; **t. maritime** *ou* **par mer** maritime transport; **transports publics** public transport; **transports routiers** road transport; *Com* road haulage; **t. terrestre** surface transport; *Mil* **t. de troupes** (*navire*) troopship, troop carrier; (*avion*) troop carrier; **t. par voie ferrée** rail transport

transportable [trɑ̃spɔrtabl] *adj* transportable; *Méd* (*patient*) fit to be moved; **le malade est-il t.?** is the patient fit to be moved?, can the patient be moved?

transportation [trɑ̃spɔrtasjɔ̃] *nf Jur* (penal) transportation

transporté, -ée [trɑ̃spɔrte] **1** *n Jur* transported convict, transport **2** *adj Fig* carried away, *Litt* transported; **t. de joie** beside oneself with joy, *Litt* transported with joy

transporter [trɑ̃spɔrte] **1** *vt* **(a)** (*passagers, troupes etc*) to carry, to transport; (*marchandises*) to transport, to carry, to freight; *Jur* (*détenu*) to transport; *Fig* (*d'un film, un roman etc*) to take, to transport; **t. qn à l'hôpital** to take sb to hospital; **le camion transporte des explosifs** the truck is carrying explosives; **t. des marchandises par air/route** to carry *or* transport goods by air/road; *Com* to airfreight/haul goods

(b) *Jur* (*céder*) (*biens, droits etc*) to transfer (**à** to)

(c) (*ravir*) to transport, to carry away; **cette bonne nouvelle l'a transporté** he was overjoyed by the good news; **le nouveau projet ne l'a pas transporté** he was not overjoyed about *or* was less than thrilled with the new project

2 se transporter *vpr* **(a)** *Jur* **se t. sur les lieux** (*de la police*) to visit the scene of the crime/accident

(b) *Com* **se t. mal/facilement** to be difficult/easy to transport; **les fruits se transportent mal** fruit does not travel well

(c) *Fig* **se t. (par la pensée) dans un pays lointain** to let one's imagination carry one to a distant country

transporteur, -euse [trɑ̃spɔrtœr, -øz] **1** *nm* **(a)** (*entrepreneur*) carrier, haulier, haulage contractor, transporter; *Av* carrier; **t.-roulier** road haulage contractor; **t. international** international carrier; **t. public** public *or* common carrier; **t. routier** road haulier **(b)** *Ind* (*appareil*) conveyor; **(chariot) t.** travelling crane *or* platform; **t. élévateur** elevator **2** *adj Ind* **hélice/courroie transporteuse** spiral/belt conveyor

transposable [trɑ̃spozabl] *adj* which can be transposed, transposable; **difficilement t.** difficult to transpose (**dans** to)

transposer [trɑ̃spoze] *vt* (*mots, Mus morceau*) to transpose; **t. un roman à l'écran** to adapt a novel for the screen

transposition [trɑ̃spozisjɔ̃] *nf Anat, Chir, Mus etc* transposition; **t. d'un roman à l'écran** adaptation of a novel for the screen

transputer® [trɑ̃spytœr] *nm Ordinat* transputer

transpyrénéen, -enne [trɑ̃spireneɛ̃, -ɛn] *adj* transpyrenean

transsaharien, -ienne [trɑ̃ssaarjɛ̃, -jɛn] *adj* transsaharan

transsexualisme [trɑ̃ssɛksɥalism] *nm* transsexualism

transsexuel, -elle [trɑ̃ssɛksɥɛl] *adj, n* transsexual

transsibérien, -ienne [trɑ̃ssiberjɛ̃, -jɛn] **1** *adj* Trans-Siberian **2** *nm* **le T.** the Trans-Siberian Railway

transsubstantiation [trɑ̃ssypstɑ̃sjasjɔ̃] *nf Rel* transubstantiation

Transvaal (le) [lətrɑ̃sval] *nm* the Transvaal

transvasement [trɑ̃svɑzmɑ̃] *nm* (*de liquide*) decanting

transvaser [trɑ̃svɑze] **1** *vt* (*vin*) to decant (**dans** into); **tu pourrais t. le lait dans la grande jatte?** could you pour the milk into *or* transfer the milk to the big bowl? **2 se transvaser** *vpr* (*de l'eau*) to siphon

transversal, -ale, -aux, -ales [trɑ̃svɛrsal, -o] **1** *adj* transverse, transversal; (*coupe, rue etc*) cross; *Constr* **mur t.** partition (wall); *Anat* **muscle t.** transverse (muscle); *Naut* **soutes transversales** cross bunkers; *Géog* **vallée transversale** transverse valley **2** *nf* **transversale** **(a)** *Sp* (*barre*) crossbar; (*passe*) cross **(b)** *Math* transversal

transversalement [trɑ̃svɛrsalmɑ̃] *adv* (*posé*) crosswise, transversely

transverse [trɑ̃svɛrs] **1** *adj Math, Anat etc* transverse **2** *nm Anat* transverse (muscle)

transvestisme [trɑ̃svɛstism] *nm* transvestism

transvider [trɑ̃svide] *vt* to transfer, to decant; **t. qch dans qch** to pour sth into sth, to transfer sth to sth

Transylvanie [trɑ̃silvani] *nf* Transylvania

trapèze [trapɛz] **1** *nm* **(a)** *Géom* trapezium, *Am* trapezoid; **t. rectangle** right angled trapezium **(b)** *Anat* trapezius **(c)** *Gym* trapeze; **t. volant** flying trapeze; **faire du t.** to perform on the trapeze **2** *adj Anat* (*muscle*) trapezius; (*os*) trapezium

trapéziste [trapezist] *n* trapeze artist

trapézoïdal, -ale, -aux, -ales [trapezɔidal, -o] *adj Géom* trapezial, *Am* trapezoidal

trapézoïde [trapezɔid] *adj, nm Anat* (**os**) **t.** trapezoid

trapillon [trapijɔ̃] *nm* **(a)** (*d'une trappe*) catch, bolt **(b)** *Th* (*sur le plancher de la scène*) slot

Trappe [trap] *nf Rel* **(a)** (*monastère*) Trappist monastery **(b)** (*order*) Trappist order

trappe [trap] *nf* **(a)** (*dans le plancher*), *Th* trap door; *Tech* hatch; **t. de visite** inspection hatch; *Aut* **t. à essence** petrol tank flap **(b)** (*piège à animaux*) trap, pitfall

trappeur [trapœr] *nm* (*d'animaux sauvages*) trapper

trappillon [trapijɔ̃] *nm* = **trapillon**

trappiste [trapist] *nm Rel* Trappist (monk)

trapu [trapy] *adj* **(a)** (*homme, cheval*) thickset, stocky; (*bâtiment*) squat **(b)** *F* (*fort*) (*élève, professeur*) brainy; (*difficile*) (*problème*) tough, sticky; **être t. en qch** to be a whizz at sth

traquenard [traknar] *nm* (*piège*) trap

traquer [trake] **1** *vt* (*gibier, criminel etc*) to hunt; *Fig* (*de la presse etc*) to hound; **nous le traquerons jusqu'à ce que nous mettions la main dessus** we will hunt *or* track him down; **bête traquée** hunted animal **2** *vi F* to get stage fright

traquet [trakɛ] *nm* **(a)** (*battant*) (mill) clapper *or* clack **(b)** *Orn* **t. (motteux)** wheatear

traqueur [trakœr] *nm* (*chasseur*) tracker

trauma [troma] *nm Méd, Psy* trauma

traumatique [tromatik] *adj Méd, Psy* traumatic

traumatisant [tromatisɑ̃] *adj Méd, Psy* traumatizing

traumatiser [tromatize] *vt Méd, Psy* to traumatize; **il ne faut pas que ça te traumatise** you mustn't let it traumatize you, you mustn't be traumatized by it

traumatisme [tromatism] *nm Méd, Psy* traumatism, trauma; **t. crânien** head injury, *Spéc* cranial traumatism; **se libérer d'un t. psychologique** to rid oneself of a trauma

traumatologie [tromatɔlɔʒi] *nf Méd* study of trauma, trauma medicine

traumatologiste [tromatɔlɔʒist], **traumatologue** [tromatɔlɔg] *n Méd* traumatologist, trauma specialist

travail, -aux [travaj, -o] *nm* **(a)** (*activité*) work; (*de l'imagination, de la mémoire*) working, functioning; **division du t.** division of labour; **se mettre au t.** to get (down) *or* start to work; **allons, au t.!** come on, let's get (down) to work!; **au t., taisez-vous!** be quiet and get on with your work!; **se tuer au t.** to work oneself to death, to kill oneself working; **cesser le t.** (*de grévistes*) to down tools; (*à la fin de la journée*) to stop work, to knock off; **arrêt de t.** (*pour grève*) stoppage; (*pour maladie*) sick leave; **accident du t.** industrial accident; **permis de t.** work permit; **code du t.** labour code; **contrat de t.** work contract, contract of work; **fournir un t. utile** to do useful work; **il a fourni un rude t.** he worked extremely hard, he got through a lot of work; **pendant les heures de t.** during working hours; **à t. égal, salaire égal** equal pay for equal work; **vêtements de t.** working *or* work clothes; **groupe de t.** working group *or* party; **méthode de t.** work method, method of working; *Péj* **ça sent le t.** (*d'un tableau, un poème etc*) it's rather laborious *or* laboured; **séance de t.** (*d'une association etc*) working session; **le monde du t.** the working world, the world of work; **le t. des femmes** women's work; **admission des enfants au t.** employment of children; **ministère du T.** = Department of Employment *or US* Labor; **Organisation internationale du t.** International Labour Organization; **Bureau international du t.** International Labour Office (*permanent secretariat of the ILO*); **c'est du t. à la main** it's handmade; **t. à l'aiguille** needlework; **t. au tour** lathe work; **t. du bois/du métal** woodwork/metalwork; **le t. du fer** ironworking; **le t. de l'ivoire/de pierres précieuses** the shaping of ivory/precious stones

(b) *Biol* (*de la digestion*) working; (*du vin*) working, fermenting; (*du bois*) warping; *MecE* **t. à la tension** tension stress; *Tech* **pression de t.** working pressure

(c) (*emploi*) work, job, employment; **chercher du t.** to look for work *or* a job; **donner du t. à qn** to give sb work *or* a job; **perdre son t.** to lose one's job; **elle est sans t.** she doesn't have a job, she's out of work *or* unemployed; **ils ne font que leur t.** they're only doing their job; **ça ne fait pas partie de mon t.** that's not part of my job, that's not in my job description; *Myth* **les douze travaux d'Hercule** the twelve labours of Hercules; *Hum* **inspecteur des travaux finis** idler, *Br* skiver (*who arrives after the work has been done*); **tu te prends pour l'inspecteur des travaux finis?** skiver!

(d) (*lieu*) work; **il est à son t.** he's at work; **je vais à mon t.** I'm going to work; **je l'ai rencontré au t.** I met him at work; **je vais à mon t.** *ou* **au t. à pied** I walk to work

(e) (*tâche*) (piece of) work, job; *Ordinat* job; **montre-moi ton t.** show me your work; **elle a fait un t. excellent** she did a first-class job *or* an excellent job of work; **faire des petits travaux** to do odd jobs; **c'est un sacré t. que de nettoyer ces fenêtres** it's quite a job cleaning these windows

(f) (*écrit*) work; **travaux** work

(g) travaux (*d'aménagement, de réparation*) work; **nous sommes en pleins travaux** we're having work done on the house; (*que nous faisons nous-mêmes*) we're doing work on the house; **attention travaux!** roadworks ahead

(h) (*exécution*) work; **un t. bien/mal fait** a good/bad piece of work; **c'est du beau t.** it's a fine piece of work; *F Iron* **c'est du beau** *ou* **joli t.!** that's really clever that is!, well done!; (*à un élève*) what's this mess *or* rag?; **c'est du t. d'amateur** it's an amateurish piece of work, it's amateurish work

(i) *Méd* labour, *US* labor; **femme en t.** woman in labour; **salle de t.** labour room

▶ **travail**: **t. administratif** administrative work, *F* admin; *Fig* **t. de Bénédictin** intellectually demanding task; **t. de bureau** office work; **t. à la chaîne** assembly line work; **travaux des champs** work in the fields; *Min* **t. à ciel ouvert** opencast mining; **travaux de couture** sewing jobs; *Mil* **travaux de défense** defensive works, outworks; *Univ* **travaux dirigés** (*en lettres*) tutorial; (*en sciences*) practical *or* lab work; **une heure de travaux dirigés de biologie** an hour's biology practical *or* lab; *Jur* **t. disciplinaire** hard labour; **t. à domicile** homework, work done at home, working at home; **t. d'équipe** *ou* **en équipes** teamwork; *Jur* **travaux forcés: condamné aux travaux forcés** sentenced to hard labour; **t. intellectuel** intellectual work, brainwork; **t. d'intérêt général** community work; **t. manuel** manual labour; *Scol* **travaux manuels** arts and crafts; **t. mécanique** *Ind* machine work; *Phys* mechanical energy; **travaux ménagers** housework; **t. à mi-temps** part-time work; *Phys* **t. moteur** mechanical energy; *Ordinat* **t. multitâche** multitasking; **t. (au) noir** moonlighting; **t. de nuit** night work; **t. à plein temps** full-time work; **travaux pratiques** *Scol* practical work; *Méd* tutorials; *Admin* **travaux publics** public works; *Ordinat* **t. en réseau** networking; **t. de Romain** Herculean task; **t. par roulement** shift work; **t. à temps partiel** part-time work

travaillé [travaje] *adj* **(a)** (*fer, bois, pierre*) worked **(b)** (*style etc*) laboured, *US* labored **(c) jours/heures travaillé(e)s** (number of) days/hours worked

travailler [travaje] **1** *vi* **(a)** (*de personne, cheval, machine, Fig d'argent*) to work; **t. dur** to work hard; **elle travaille trop** she works too much, she overworks; **aimer t.** to enjoy working; **t. 40 heures par semaine** to work a 40-hour week; **une femme qui travaille** a working woman; **son imagination travaille (trop)** his imagination is working overtime; **fais t. ton imagination** use your imagination; *Fig* **ça a fait t. les esprits** it made people wonder, people didn't know what to think; *F* **t. comme un nègre** *ou* **comme quatre** *ou* **comme un cheval** to work like a slave *or* a Trojan *or* a dog; *F* **t. du chapeau** to have a screw loose; **t. à** (*un roman, un documentaire etc*) to work on; **j'y travaille** I'm working on it; **t. à la perte de qn** *ou* **à perdre qn** to try to ruin sb; **t. à faire qch** to work hard *or* to strive to do sth; **t. à l'aiguille** to do needlework; **t. à la pièce** to do piecework; **t. au noir** to moonlight; **t. contre qn/qch** to work against sb/sth; **t. dans qch** to work in sth; **t. en free-lance** to freelance, to work as a freelance, to do freelance work; **t. pour qn/une société** (*être employé par*) to work for sb/a company; **le temps travaille pour nous** time is on our side; **t. pour soi-même, t. pour** *ou* **à son compte** to be self-employed, to work for oneself; *Fig* **t. pour le roi de Prusse** to work for nothing; **faire t. une machine** to work *or* run a machine; **faire t. son argent** to put one's money to work, to make one's money work for one

(b) (*s'entraîner*) (*de sportif, d'acrobate*) to train; (*de musicien*) to practise; (*d'animaux de cirque etc*) to go through their performance

(c) (*d'un navire, d'un câble etc*) to strain; (*du vin*) to ferment, to work; (*du bois*) to warp, to shrink; (*des murs*) to crack

2 *vt* **(a)** (*façonner*) (*bois, fer, verre etc*) to work, to fashion, to shape; *Culin* (*pâte*) to knead; **t. la terre** to work the land; *Tennis* **t. une balle** to spin a ball; **t. un cheval** to work a horse

(b) (*étudier*) (*rôle*) to work on, to study; (*sujet*) to work at *or* on; (*texte, auteur*) to study; (*pas de danse, Mus morceau, Sp son revers, sa brasse etc*) to work on, to practise; **t. le piano** to practise the piano; **t. son style** to work on *or* polish one's style

(c) (*inquiéter*) **ça m'a travaillé toute la journée** it's been preying on my mind all day; **cela ne me travaille pas du tout** I'm not the slightest bit worried *or* concerned; **un désir le travaillait** he was obsessed *or Péj* tormented with a desire; **être travaillé de** *ou* **par la goutte** to be a martyr to gout

(d) *Litt* (*influer sur*) (*qn, sentiments, opinion publique etc*) to work on

3 se travailler *vpr* **se t. l'esprit** to worry

travailleur, -euse [travajœr, -øz] **1** *adj* hard-working, industrious; **les masses travailleuses** the workers, the working classes **2** *n* worker; **bon t.** good *or* hard worker; **t. manuel/intellectuel** manual/non-manual worker; **t. à temps réduit** person on short time; **les travailleurs** the workers, the working people **3** *nf* **travailleuse** (*table à ouvrage*) (lady's) work table

▶ **travailleur**: **t. en bâtiment** construction worker; **t. indépendant** self-employed worker *or* person; **t. salarié** salaried worker; **t. social** social worker; **t. temporaire** casual worker

travaillisme [travajism] *nm Pol* (British) socialism, doctrine of the Labour Party

travailliste [travajist] *Pol* **1** *n* member of the Labour Party; **les travaillistes** the Labour Party, Labour **2** *adj* (*parti, membre etc*) Labour

travée [trave] *nf* **(a)** *Constr, Archit* bay **(b)** (*de pont*) span; (*séparée*) independent girder **(c)** *Av* (*d'aile*) rib **(d)** (*de sièges*) row

traveller's check, traveller's chèque [travlœr(s)ʃɛk] *nm* traveller's cheque, *US* traveler's check

travelling [travəliŋ] *nm Cin* **(a)** (*dispositif*) (*pour caméra*) dolly, travelling platform **(b)** (*déplacement*) tracking; (*plan*) tracking shot; **faire un t.** to dolly; **t. avant/arrière** track in/track out

travelo [travlo] *nm F* (*travesti*) drag queen

travers [travɛr] *nm* **(a) en t.** crosswise; **autobus avec places disposées en t.** bus with seats arranged crosswise; **profil en t.** cross section; **en t. de** across; **se mettre en t. du chemin de qn** to stand in sb's way; **il ne faut pas que des problèmes personnels se mettent en t. du travail** personal problems must not get in the way of work

(b) à t. qch, au t. de qch through sth; **prendre à t. (les) champs/bois** to cut through the fields *or* across country/through the woods; **courir à t. la campagne** to run across country; **à t. les siècles** down (through) the centuries; **à t. le monde** throughout the world; *Fig* **elle n'a pas réussi à passer au t.** she didn't manage to escape; **si tu crois passer au t., tu te trompes!** if you think you're going to get away with it you're mistaken

(c) *Naut* **de t., par le t.** on the beam, abeam; **vent de t.** wind on the beam; **en t. (du navire)** athwart (ships); **collision par le t.** collision broadside on

(d) (*locutions*) **marcher de t.** (*d'un ivrogne etc*) to stagger (along); **la machine marche de t.** the machine is not working properly; **tout marche de t. aujourd'hui** everything's going wrong today, nothing's going right today; **tout va de t. entre eux** everything's going wrong between them; **comprendre de t.** to misunderstand; **j'ai encore dû comprendre de t.** I must have misunderstood again *or* got things wrong again; **regarder qn de t.** to look askance *or* sideways at sb; **votre chapeau est de t.** your hat is (on) crooked, *F* your hat's all skew-whiff; **il a la bouche/le nez de t.** he's got a crooked mouth/nose; *très F* **elle a la gueule de t.** her face is all twisted; **les tableaux étaient accrochés de t.** the pictures were askew *or* crooked *or F* skew-whiff; **j'ai avalé de t.** it went down the wrong way; *Fig* **il l'a avalé de t., ta nouvelle!** your news didn't go down very well with him!, he took your news badly!; **il a des idées tout(es) de t.** his ideas are all wrong; **il a répondu de t.** he gave a ridiculous answer; **prendre tout de t.** to take everything the wrong way

(e) (*défaut*) failing, shortcoming, fault; *Arch* **t. (d'esprit)** eccentricity

(f) (*largeur*) breadth; **un t. de doigt** a finger's breadth

▶ **travers**: *Culin* **t. de porc** pork spareribs

traversable [travɛrsabl] *adj* (*désert, rivière etc*) that can be crossed

traverse [travɛrs] *nf* **(a) (chemin de) t.** short cut **(b) (barre de) t.** crossbar, crosspiece; (*d'échelle*) rung; *Constr* transom; *Rail* sleeper, *US* tie; *Aut etc* (*du châssis*) cross member; *Aut* **t. de suspension avant** front suspension cross member **(c)** *Litt* (*obstacle*) setback

traversée [travɛrse] *nf* **(a)** (*de la mer, du désert, d'une rue etc*) crossing; (*d'une ville etc*) going *or* passing through, crossing; (*d'une forêt, une foule etc*) going *or* passing through; **t. de l'Europe en vélo** bike journey across Europe; *Naut* **t. agitée** rough crossing; **faire une bonne t.** to have a good crossing; **faire la t. de Douvres à Calais** to cross from Dover to Calais;

ils ont fait la t. en yacht jusqu'à Cherbourg they sailed across *or* went over to Cherbourg in a yacht; **faire la t. d'une ville** to go through *or* pass through *or* cross a town; **la t. d'une ville en voiture** driving through a town
(**b**) *Pol Fig* **t. du désert** time in the wilderness; **il fait sa t. du désert** he has gone into the wilderness

traverser [travɛrse] *vt* (**a**) (*d'une personne*) (*rue, pont, mer, rivière etc*) to cross, to go across; (*ville, région, pays etc*) to go *or* to pass through, to cross; (*forêt etc*) to go *or* to pass through; (*de la pluie, de vin*) (*pardessus, nappe*) to go (right) through; *Fig* (*crise, mauvaise période etc*) to go through; **t. la foule** to make one's way *or* pass through the crowd; **il faut leur apprendre à t. les rues** they'll have to be taught how to cross the street; **c'est une rue difficile à t. aux heures de pointe** it's difficult to get across this street at rush hour; **t. une forêt à cheval/à bicyclette/en auto** to ride/cycle/drive through a forest; **t. la rivière à la nage/en barque** to swim/row across the river; **t. la Manche à la nage** to swim the Channel; **t. l'Europe en vélo** to cross *or* go across Europe on a bike, to bike across Europe; **t. un désert en avion** to fly across a desert; **pont/route qui traverse la rivière** bridge/road that crosses *or* goes across the river; **une planche traverse le ruisseau** there is a plank across the stream; **la balle lui traversa le bras** the bullet went through *or* pierced his arm; **t. les siècles** to come down through the ages; **elle traverse une période heureuse** she's having a spell of happiness; **t. l'esprit** (*d'une idée, d'un doute*) to cross one's mind; **l'idée me traversa l'esprit comme un éclair** the idea flashed through my mind
(**b**) *Arch* (*contrarier*) (*qn, intentions de qn*) to cross, to thwart

traversier, -ière [travɛrsje, -jɛr] **1** *adj* **rue traversière** cross street; *Mus* **flûte traversière** (transverse) flute **2** *nm Can* (*bac*) ferry (boat)

traversin [travɛrsɛ̃] *nm* (**a**) (*pour lit*) bolster (**b**) *Menuis etc* crosspiece (**c**) *Naut* crosstree

travesti [travɛsti] **1** *adj* disguised; **bal t.** fancy-dress *or* costume ball; *Th* **acteur t.** actor playing a female part; **rôle t.** female part (for an actor) **2** *nm* (**a**) *Th* (*acteur*) actor playing a female part; (*rôle*) female part (for an actor) (**b**) (*homme habillé en femme*) transvestite (**c**) (*déguisement*) fancy dress

travestir [travɛstir] **1** *vt* (**a**) (*déguiser*) (*personne*) to disguise, to dress up (**en** as) (**b**) *Littér* (*pièce, poème etc*) to parody, to burlesque; (*auteur*) to parody (**c**) (*déformer*) (*vérité, faits, pensée etc*) to distort, to misrepresent; **je ne voudrais pas t. votre pensée, mais ...** I don't want to misrepresent you but ... **2 se travestir** *vpr* (*se vêtir en femme/homme*) to dress (up) as a woman/a man; (*pour un bal costumé*) to put on fancy dress

travestisme [travɛstism] *nm* transvestism, cross-dressing

travestissement [travɛstismɑ̃] *nm* (**a**) (*action*) disguising, dressing up (**b**) (*déguisement*) disguise; *Th* **rôle à travestissements** quick-change part (**c**) *Littér* (*d'une pièce, un poème etc*) parody (**d**) (*de la vérité, des faits etc*) travesty (**e**) (*travestisme*) transvestism

traviole (de) [dətravjɔl] *adv F* = **de travers**

trayeur, -euse [trɛjœr, -øz] **1** *n* (*personne*) milker **2** *nf* **trayeuse** (*machine*) milking machine

trayon [trɛjɔ̃] *nm* (*de vache etc*) dug, teat

trébuchant [trebyʃɑ̃] *adj* (*ivrogne, allure etc*) staggering, stumbling; (*diction*) stumbling, halting

trébucher [trebyʃe] *vi* to trip, to stumble (**sur** over; **contre** against); **marcher en trébuchant** to stumble *or* stagger along, to walk with a stagger; **faire t. qn** to trip sb up; *Fig* **t. sur les mots étrangers** to stumble *or* trip over foreign words

trébuchet [trebyʃɛ] *nm* (**a**) (*piège*) bird trap (**b**) (*petite balance*) assay balance

tréfiler [trefile] *vt* (*métal*) to (wire)draw

trèfle [trɛfl] *nm* (**a**) *Bot* clover; **t. blanc** wild white clover; **t. rouge** red clover; **t. à quatre feuilles** four-leaf *or* four-leaved clover (**b**) *Archit, Hér* (*motif*) trefoil; *Aut* **croisement en t.** clover-leaf intersection (**c**) *Cartes* (*couleur*) clubs; (*carte*) club; **jouer (du) t.** to play clubs *or* a club; **as/dix de t.** ace/ten of clubs; **avez-vous du t.?** do you have any clubs?

tréfonds [trefɔ̃] *nm Litt* **au t. de mon cœur/âme** in my heart of hearts/in the depths of my soul; **blessé au t. de son cœur** cut to the quick; **atteint jusqu'au t.** very deeply hurt

treillage [trɛjaʒ] *nm* (**a**) trellis (work), lattice work (**b**) (*clôture*) trellis fencing; **t. métallique** *ou* **en fil de fer** wire fencing

treillager [trɛjaʒe] *vt* (**je treillageai(s); n. treillageons**) (*mur etc*) to trellis; (*fenêtre*) to lattice; **fenêtre treillagée** lattice window

treille [trɛj] *nf* (**a**) (*abri*) vine arbour, trellised vines (**b**) (*vigne*) (climbing) vine; *F* **le jus de la t.** the juice of the grape

treillis [trɛji] *nm* (**a**) (*treillage*) trellis; **t. métallique** wire mesh (**b**) *Tex* drill, dungaree, (coarse) canvas (**c**) *Mil* combat uniform

treize [trɛz] **1** *adj inv* thirteen; *Com* **t. à la douzaine** a baker's dozen; *F* **j'en ai t. à la douzaine** I've got dozens of them; **le numéro t.** number thirteen; **le t. mai** (on) the thirteenth of May, (on) May the thirteenth, *Am* (on) May thirteenth; **vendredi t.** Friday the thirteenth; **Louis T.** Louis the Thirteenth; *Sp* **jeu** *ou* **rugby à t.** Rugby League **2** *nm inv* thirteen; **le t. porte malheur** thirteen is unlucky *or* is an unlucky number; **le t. gagne** number thirteen is the winner; **habiter au t.** to live at number thirteen

treizième [trɛzjɛm] **1** *adj, n* thirteenth **2** *nm* (*fraction*) thirteenth **3** *nf Mus* thirteenth

▶ **treizième**: **t. mois** = additional month's salary paid as a year-end bonus

treizièmement [trɛzjɛmmɑ̃] *adv* in the thirteenth place

trekking [trɛkiŋ] *nm* trek; **faire un t.** to go on a trek; **faire du t. en Inde** to go trekking in India

tréma [trema] *Ling* **1** *nm* diaeresis, *pl* diaereses, *US* dieresis, *pl* diereses **2** *adj inv* **e/i tréma** e/i diaeresis *or US* dieresis

tremblant [trɑ̃blɑ̃] *adj* (*genoux, main*) trembling, shaky, quivering; (*lèvres, visage*) trembling, quivering; (*pont*) shaky; (*sol*) quaking; (*lumière*) flickering; (*voix*) shaky, trembling, quavering, *Fml* tremulous; **t. (de peur)** trembling *or* shaking *or* quivering with fear; **t. de froid** shivering *or* trembling *or* shaking with cold

tremble [trɑ̃bl] *nm Bot* aspen

tremblé [trɑ̃ble] *adj* (**a**) (*écriture*) shaky; (*ligne*) wavy (**b**) (*voix*) shaky, trembling, *Fml* tremulous; *Mus* (*notes*) tremolo

tremblement [trɑ̃bləmɑ̃] *nm* (**a**) (*du corps, de la main, d'un pont etc*) trembling, quivering, shaking; (*de lèvres*) trembling, quivering; (*de la voix*) shaking, trembling, quavering
(**b**) (*de peur*) shudder, quiver, tremor; (*de joie, de colère*) quiver; **t. de fièvre** fit of (feverish) shivering; **avoir un t. de froid/d'horreur** to shiver (with cold)/to shudder (in horror); **... dit-il avec un t. dans la voix** ... he said with a tremble *or* a tremor *or* a quaver in his voice *or* in a shaky voice; **elle avait des tremblements dans la voix** her voice was shaking *or* quavering; **être pris de tremblements** to start to shake; *F* **et tout le t.** etcetera etcetera
(**c**) *Mus* tremolo

▶ **tremblement**: **t. de terre** earth tremor; (*plus fort*) earthquake

trembler [trɑ̃ble] *vi* (**a**) (*d'une personne*) (*de peur, d'émotion*) to tremble, to shake, to quiver; (*de froid*) to shiver, to shake; (*de colère*) to shake; (*de la main, des genoux*) to shake, to tremble; (*des lèvres*) to tremble, to quiver; (*de la voix*) to tremble, to shake, to quiver; (*de la terre*) to shake, to quake; (*de la lumière*) to flicker; (*d'une flamme*) to waver; (*d'un pont, un mur, un bâtiment*) to shake; (*des feuilles*) to quiver; **t. comme une feuille** to shake like a leaf; **faire t. les vitres** to make the windows shake *or* rattle; **faire t. un bâtiment** to rock *or* shake a building
(**b**) (*avoir peur*) to tremble; **t. de tout son corps** to tremble *or* shake all over; **t. devant qn** to be terrified of sb, to go in fear (and trembling) of sb; **je tremble de le rencontrer** I tremble *or* I am terrified at the thought of meeting him; **je tremblais de le réveiller** I was terrified of wakening him; **elle tremble qu'il ne s'en rende compte** she is terrified that he might find out; **t. pour qn** to be frightened *or* terrified for sb

trembleur [trɑ̃blœr] *nm Él* trembler, vibrator; *Télécom, Tél* buzzer

tremblotant [trɑ̃blɔtɑ̃] *adj* (*personne*) trembling (slightly); (*corps*) quivering, shivering; (*sourire, voix*) shaky, tremulous; (*lumière*) flickering

tremblote [trɑ̃blɔt] *nf F* **avoir la t.** (*de vieillesse*) to have the shakes; (*de peur*) to have the jitters, to be shaking in one's shoes; (*de froid*) to have the shivers

tremblotement [trɑ̃blɔtmɑ̃] *nm* (*des mains*) trembling, shaking; (*de la voix*) quavering, trembling, shaking; (*de la lumière*) flickering; **un t. de la voix** a tremble in one's voice; **être pris de tremblotements** to start to shake

trembloter [trɑ̃blɔte] *vi* (*des mains*) to tremble *or* shake (slightly); (*de la voix*) to tremble, to quaver, to shake; (*de la lumière*) to flicker; (*des ailes*) to flutter; **j'ai les mains qui tremblotent** my hands are shaky

trémie [tremi] *nf* (**a**) *Ind etc* (*entonnoir*) hopper (**b**) (*mangeoire*) (*pour poulets*) feeding box (**c**) *Constr* (*pour cheminée*) hearth cavity

trémière [tremjɛr] *adj Bot* **rose t.** hollyhock

tremolo, trémolo [tremɔlo] *nm Mus* (**a**) tremolo; *Fig* **avec des trémolos dans la voix** with a quaver *or* tremor in one's voice, in a shaky voice (**b**) (*d'un orgue*) tremolo stop

trémoussement [tremusmɑ̃] *nm* jigging up and down; (*en se dandinant*) wiggling

trémousser (se) [sətremuse] *vpr* (*d'un enfant*) to jig up and down; (*pour séduire*) to wiggle; **se t. sur sa chaise** to wriggle about on one's chair; **marcher en se trémoussant** to walk with a wiggle; **se t. du derrière** to wiggle one's behind

trempage [trɑ̃paʒ] *nm* soaking, steeping

trempe [trɑ̃p] *nf* **(a)** (*immersion*) soaking, steeping; **mettre qch en t.** to put sth to soak

(b) *Métal* (*traitement*) hardening, quench(ing); **t. et revenu** quenching and hardening; **acier/atelier de t.** hardening steel/plant; **t. à l'air** air hardening; **t. à l'eau/à l'huile** water/oil quenching; **t. par cémentation, t. de** *ou* **en surface** case hardening; **bain de t.** hardening *or* quenching bath

(c) *Métal* (*dureté*) (*de l'acier*) temper, hardness

(d) *Fig* (*qualité*) calibre; **un homme de sa t.** a man of his calibre; **une intelligence d'une t. exceptionnelle** extremely high intelligence, quite exceptional intelligence

(e) *F* (*volée de coups*) hiding, walloping; **si tu continues, je vais te filer une t.** if you don't stop, you'll get a wallop(ing)

trempé [trɑ̃pe] *adj* **(a)** (*mouillé*) (*personne*) soaked, drenched; (*vêtement*) soaked, saturated, sodden; **être tout t.** to be soaked *or* wet through, to be soaking wet; **t. de larmes** bathed in tears, wet with tears; **t. de sueur** (*personne*) drenched *or* dripping with sweat; (*vêtement*) saturated with sweat; **t. jusqu'aux os** *ou F* **comme une soupe** soaked to the skin, wet *or* soaked through **(b)** *Tech* (*verre*) hardened; (*acier*) hardened, tempered; *Fig* **bien t.** (*esprit*) resolute; *Sp* with plenty of stamina

tremper [trɑ̃pe] **1** *vt* **(a)** (*mouiller*) (*dans un liquide*) to soak, to steep; (*plonger*) (*pain dans la soupe*) to dip, to dunk; (*écrevisses, moules, escargots*) to plunge; **se faire t. par la pluie** to get a soaking; **t. un pied dans l'eau** to dip a foot in the water; **t. ses mains dans l'eau** to dabble one's hands in the water; **t. la soupe** to pour the soup on the bread; **t. sa plume dans l'encrier** to dip one's pen in the ink; **t. ses lèvres dans son verre** to put one's lips to one's glass; **j'y ai à peine trempé les lèvres** I've hardly touched it; *Typ* **t. le papier** to wet *or* damp the paper

(b) *Métal* (*acier*) to harden, to quench; (*fonte de fer*) to chill; **t. par induction** to induction harden; *Fig Litt* **cela lui a trempé l'esprit** it put iron in his soul; *Fig* **t. les muscles** to firm up the muscles

2 *vi* (*du linge sale, d'une casserole*) to (be in) soak; **faire t. le linge** to soak *or* steep the clothes; **mettre à t.** (*linge, casserole*) to put in soak, to soak; (*lentilles*) to soak; **tes manches trempent dans ton assiette** your sleeves are trailing in your plate; *Fig* **t. dans un complot/une affaire** to be mixed up *or* involved in a plot/an affair; **je refuse de t. là-dedans** I refuse to get mixed up in it

3 se tremper *vpr* (*se baigner*) to have a quick dip; **je me suis à peine trempé** I barely got wet, I got out again almost immediately; **se t. les pieds dans l'eau** to go for a paddle

trempette [trɑ̃pɛt] *nf* **(a) faire t.** *Culin* (*dans le café, le vin etc*) to dip *or* dunk one's bread/*etc*; (*se baigner*) to have a quick dip; **les enfants font t. dans le bassin** the children are splashing about in the pool **(b)** *Can Culin* dip

tremplin [trɑ̃plɛ̃] *nm Natation, Gym* springboard; *Ski* ski jump; *Fig* springboard, stepping stone

trémulation [tremylasjɔ̃] *nf Méd* tremor

trémuler [tremyle] **1** *vi* to tremble **2** *vt* **t. les doigts** to twiddle one's fingers

trench(-coat), *pl* **trench(-coat)s** [trɛnʃ(kot)] *nm* trench coat

trentaine [trɑ̃tɛn] *nf* **(a)** (*nombre*) **une t.** about thirty; **une t. de voitures/d'années** about thirty cars/years; **une bonne t. (de)** a good thirty; **la t. de livres qu'elle a** the thirty (or so) books she has **(b)** (*âge*) **la t.** (the age of) thirty; **avoir la t.** to be in one's thirties; **il approche de la t.** he's getting on for thirty

trente [trɑ̃t] **1** *adj inv* thirty; **t. jours** thirty days; **le t. juin** (on) the thirtieth of June, (on) June the thirtieth, *Am* (on) June thirtieth; **les années t.** the thirties; *Hist* **la Guerre de T. Ans** the Thirty Years' War; **t. et un** thirty-one; *Cartes* (*jeu*) trente et un; *Tennis* **t. à** thirty all **2** *nm inv* thirty; **je suis payé le t. (de chaque mois)** I'm paid on the thirtieth (of each month); **habiter au t.** to live at number thirty; *Fig* **se mettre sur son t. et un** to get all dressed up; **être sur son t. et un** to be all dressed up, to be dressed up to the nines

trentenaire [trɑ̃tnɛr] **1** *adj* **(a)** (*qui dure trente ans*) thirty-year **(b)** (*personne*) in his/her thirties; (*bâtiment*) over thirty years old **2** *n* person in his/her thirties, *F* thirty something

trente-six (*for rules of pronunciation see* **six**) **1** *adj inv* thirty-six; *F* (*beaucoup*) umpteen; *Fig* **en voir t. chandelles** (*après un coup sur la tête*) to see stars; **il n'y va pas par t. chemins** he doesn't beat about the bush; **il n'y a pas t. façons de le faire** there aren't umpteen different ways of doing it **2** *nm inv* thirty-six; *Fig* **tous les t. du mois** once in a blue moon

trente-sixième *adj Fig F* **être au t. dessous** to be extremely depressed, to be really down in the dumps

trente-trois tours *nm inv* (*disque*) LP

trentième [trɑ̃tjɛm] **1** *adj* thirtieth **2** *n inv* thirtieth **3** *nm* (*fraction*) thirtieth

trépan [trepɑ̃] *nm Chir, Tech* trepan

trépanation [trepanasjɔ̃] *nf Chir* trepanning

trépaner [trepane] *vt Chir* to trepan

trépas [trepɑ] *nm Litt* death; **passer de vie à t.** to depart this life

trépassé, -ée [trepɑse] *n Litt* deceased person; **les trépassés** the departed, the deceased; **la fête des Trépassés** All Souls' Day

trépasser [trepɑse] *vi Arch, Litt* to die, to depart this life

trépidant [trepidɑ̃] *adj* (*machine, moteur, sol etc*) vibrating; *Fig* (*vie*) hectic; (*rythme, danse*) lively

trépidation [trepidasjɔ̃] *nf* **(a)** (*d'une machine, d'un moteur, du sol etc*) vibration **(b)** *Méd* trembling, shaking **(c)** *Fig* (*de la vie, d'une ville etc*) bustle, hurly-burly

trépider [trepide] *vi* (*d'une machine, du sol etc*) to vibrate

trépied [trepje] *nm* **(a)** (*support*) (*d'appareil photo*) tripod; *Culin* trivet **(b)** (*tabouret*) three-legged stool

trépignement [trepiɲ(ə)mɑ̃] *nm* stamping (of feet); **le bruit des trépignements** the sound of stamping feet

trépigner [trepiɲe] *vi* to stamp (one's feet); **t. de colère/d'enthousiasme/d'impatience** to jump up and down with rage/enthusiasm/impatience; *Fig* **il trépignait à l'idée de partir** he was itching to start

trépointe [trepwɛ̃t] *nf* (*de chaussure*) welt

tréponème [trepɔnɛm] *nm Biol* treponema; **t. pâle** treponema pallidum

très [trɛ] ([trɛz] *before vowel or mute* **h**) *adv* [①**A24-5**,d,iv] (*différent, inférieur, joli, bien, petit etc*) very; **t. bon** very good; (*généreux*) very *or* most kind; **t. connu** very well known; **t. estimé** much *or* greatly *or* highly respected; **t. aimé** much *or* greatly liked; **être d'une intelligence t. supérieure à la moyenne** to be of much higher than average intelligence; **t. à la mode** very fashionable, very much in fashion; **un produit t. peu vendu** a product for which there is very little demand; **t. peu utilisé** rarely used; **vivre t. au-dessus de ses moyens** to live way beyond one's means; **elle est t. femme** she is very feminine *or* very much a woman; **être t. réussi** to be very successful, to be a great success; **prendre qch t. au sérieux** to take sth very seriously; **avoir t. faim/soif/peur/chaud/froid** to be very hungry/thirsty/scared/hot/cold; **avoir t. envie de faire qch** to really feel like doing sth; **j'ai t. envie de sortir** I really feel like going out, I would really like to go out, I would love to go out; **ces robes sont t. portées** these dresses are very fashionable *or* very much in fashion; **un auteur t. lu** a very popular author; **content? – oui, t.!** satisfied? – yes, very!; **ça t'a plu? – non, pas t.** did you like it? – no, not (very) much

trésor [trezɔr] *nm* **(a)** (*choses précieuses*) treasure; *Jur* treasure-trove; **trouver un t.** to find treasure; **cette bibliothèque est un véritable t.** this library is a real treasure-trove of information; *F* **mon t.** darling; **trésors** treasures; *Fig* **elle a dû dépenser des trésors pour l'acheter** it must have cost her a fortune (to buy); *Fig* **des trésors de** (*patience, générosité, amabilité, imagination etc*) limitless, a wealth of; **t. de guerre** war chest

(b) *Rel* (collection of) relics and ornaments

(c) (*endroit*) treasure house

(d) le T. (public) (*service*) the Treasury Department; (*finances*) the treasury, public funds; **bons du T.** Treasury bonds

(e) (*ensemble*) (*de documents*) wealth; **ce livre est un t. d'informations** the book is a treasure house *or* a mine of information, the book contains a wealth of information

trésorerie [trezɔrri] *nf* **(a)** (*fonction*) treasurership **(b)** (*bureau*) accounts department **(c)** (*fonds*) cashflow, funds, finances; **des problèmes de t.** cashflow problems; **t. nette** net cash position **(d)** (*gestion*) accounting

trésorier, -ière [trezɔrje, -jɛr] *n* treasurer, financial manager; *Admin* **t.(-payeur) général** (*d'un département*) chief treasurer and paymaster; **commis t.** treasury clerk; **t. de banque** bank treasurer; *Mil* **officier t.** paymaster

tressage [trɛsaʒ] *nm* (*des cheveux*) plaiting, *Am* braiding; (*de la paille*) plaiting; (*d'un panier, d'une guirlande*) weaving

tressaillement [tresajmɑ̃] *nm* (*de surprise, peur, douleur*) start, jump

tressaillir [tresajir] *vi* (*prp* **tressaillant**; *pp* **tressailli**; *pr ind* **je tressaille, n. tressaillons, ils tressaillent**; *impf* **je**

tressaillais; *p hist* **je tressaillis**; *fu* **je tressaillirai**) (*de surprise, peur*) to jump, to start, to give a jump *or* start; (*de joie, d'espoir*) to quiver; (*du cœur*) to flutter; **t. (de douleur)** to flinch

tressautement [tresotmɑ̃] *nm* **(a)** (*de peur, de surprise etc*) start, jump **(b)** (*secousse*) jolt; **les tressautements des wagons** the jolting of the carriages

tressauter [tresote] *vi* **(a)** (*de peur, de surprise etc*) to start, to jump **(b)** (*être secoué*) to jolt, to be jolted about

tresse [trɛs] *nf* (*de cheveux*) plait, *Am* braid; (*de fil etc*) braid; *Archit* (*motif*) strap work; **se faire des tresses** to plait *or Am* braid one's hair; **porter des tresses** to have (one's hair in) plaits; **les cheveux noués dans une t.** hair done up in a plait; *Él* **fil conducteur sous t.** braided conductor wire

tresser [trese] *vt* (*cheveux*) to plait, *Am* to braid; (*paille, osier etc*) to plait; (*panier, guirlande*) to weave; *Fig* **t. des couronnes à qn** to praise sb to the skies; **je ne veux pas lui t. des couronnes, mais ...** I don't want to praise him unduly but ...

tréteau, -eaux [treto] *nm* **(a)** (*support*) trestle; **table à tréteaux** trestle table **(b)** *Th* **les tréteaux** the stage; **monter sur les tréteaux** to go on the stage, *Vieilli, Hum* to tread the boards

treuil [trœj] *nm Tech* winch, windlass, winding drum; (*d'ascenseur*) winding gear; **t. à chaîne** chain hoist

treuillage [trœjaʒ] *nm* winching (up)

treuiller [trœje] *vt* to winch (up)

trêve [trɛv] *nf* **(a)** (*amnistie*) truce **(b)** *Fig* (*pause, arrêt*) respite, rest; *F* **t. de plaisanteries!** (*il faut se mettre au travail*) that's enough joking *or* fun!; (*arrête de me raconter des histoires*) joking apart *or* aside; **il ne me laisse pas de t.** he doesn't give me a moment's peace; **sans t.** unceasingly

▶ **trêve**: *Pol F* **t. des confiseurs** Christmas/New Year truce

tri [tri] *nm* sorting (out); (*de lettres*) sorting; (*de compétences etc*) classifying; (*de candidats etc*) selection; (*de propositions etc*) screening; *Ordinat* sort; **un t. s'impose** I'll/we'll/*etc* have to do some sorting out; **faire le t. de** to sort out; **on ne peut pas tous les garder, il va falloir faire le t.** we can't keep them all, we'll have to sort some out *or* sort through them; **faire du t. dans ses vêtements/papiers** to sort through *or* go through one's clothes/papers; **bureau de t.** (*de la Poste*) sorting office; **le (service du) t.** (*d'une entreprise*) the mail room; *Ordinat* **effectuer un t.** to do a sort; *Ordinat* **t. en ordre croissant/décroissant** ascending/reverse *or* descending sort

▶ **tri**: *Ordinat* **t. alphabétique** alphabetic(al) sort, alphasort; *Mktg* **t. croisé** (*de statistiques*) cross tabulation; *Mktg* **t. à plat** (*de statistiques*) simple tabulation; **t. postal** mail sorting

triacide [triasid] *nm Ch* triacid

triade [trijad] *nf* triad

triage [trijaʒ] *nm* **(a)** (*du charbon, du courrier, de minerai etc*) sorting; *Rail* marshalling; *Rail* **gare de t.** marshalling yard; *Rail* **voie de t.** siding; *Mil* **hôpital de t.** clearing hospital **(b)** (*en choisissant*) selecting, picking out, sorting

trial [trijal], *pl* **trials** *nm Sp* **(a)** (*épreuve*) motocross, *Br* (motorcycle) scrambling **(b)** (*moto*) motocross *or Br* scrambling bike

triangle [trijɑ̃gl] *nm* **(a)** *Géom* triangle; **en t.** (*visage, écharpe etc*) triangular; *F* **l'éternel t.** the eternal triangle **(b)** *Naut* (*pavillon*) triangular flag **(c)** *Mus* triangle

▶ **triangle**: **t. des Bermudes** Bermuda triangle; **le T. d'or** the Golden Triangle; *Aut* **t. de présignalisation** hazard warning triangle

triangulaire [trijɑ̃gylɛr] *adj* (*forme, section, relation*) triangular; *Pol* (*élection, bataille*) three-cornered

triangulation [trijɑ̃gylasjɔ̃] *nf* (*en arpentage*) triangulation

trianguler [trijɑ̃gyle] *vt* (*en arpentage*) to triangulate

trias [trijɑs] *nm Géol* (*période*) Triassic

triasique [trijazik] *adj Géol* Triassic

triathlon [triatlɔ̃] *nm Sp* triathlon

triathlonien, -ienne [triatlɔnjɛ̃, -jɛn] *n Sp* triathlete

triatomique [triatɔmik] *adj Ch* triatomic

tribade [tribad] *nf Litt, Vieilli* tribade

tribal, -ale, -aux, -ales [tribal, -o] *adj* tribal

tribalisme [tribalism] *nm* tribalism

tribord [tribɔr] *nm Naut* starboard (side); **à t.** on the starboard side, to starboard

tribu [triby] *nf aussi Fig F* tribe

tribulations [tribylasjɔ̃] *nfpl* tribulations, troubles; **après toutes sortes de t.** after all kinds of trials and tribulations

tribun [tribœ̃] *nm* **(a)** *Antiq* (*officier*) tribune **(b)** (*orateur*) popular orator

tribunal, -aux [tribynal, -o] *nm* [①**A6,d,i**] *Jur* court (of law); (*bâtiment*) court, *Am* courthouse; (*magistrats*) court; **en plein t.** in open court; **porter une affaire devant les tribunaux** to take a case to court; **prendre la voie des tribunaux** to take legal action, to go to court

▶ **tribunal**: **t. administratif** court which deals with civil law; **t. arbitral** arbitration tribunal; **t. civil** civil court; **t. de commerce** trade tribunal; **t. correctionnel** criminal court; **t. criminel** criminal court; **t. pour enfants et adolescents** juvenile court; **t. de grande instance** = court presided over by three judges, authorized to try more serious cases, *Eng* ≈ Crown court; **t. d'instance** = trial court, court of first instance, *Eng* ≈ magistrates' court, *Scot, US* ≈ district court; **t. judiciaire** court (of law); **t. militaire** military tribunal; **traduire qn devant le t. militaire** to court-martial sb; **passer devant le t. militaire** to be court-martialled; **t. des prud'hommes** industrial tribunal; **t. révolutionnaire** revolutionary tribunal

tribune [tribyn] *nf* **(a)** (*galerie*) gallery; **t. de la presse** press gallery; **t. du public** public gallery **(b)** (*d'orateur*) rostrum, (speaker's) platform; **avoir l'éloquence de la t.** to be a good public speaker; *Parl* **monter à la t.** to address the House **(c)** (*débat*) forum, discussion, debate; *Journ* banner headline; **t. libre d'un journal** opinion column of a newspaper; **s'exprimer dans les tribunes d'une émission de radio** to put one's point of view in an open radio programme **(d)** *Sp* **t. (d'honneur)** (grand)stand **(e)** *Mus* **t. d'orgues** organ loft

tribut [triby] *nm* **(a)** *Hist* (*contribution*) tribute, tribute-money; **payer t.** to pay tribute; *Fig* **payer t. à la nature** to pay one's debt to nature; **la France a payé un lourd t. en vies humaines** France paid a heavy cost in human life **(b)** *Arch, Litt* (*impôt*) duty, tax

tributaire [tribytɛr] *adj* **(a)** *Hist* (*qui paie tribut*) tributary **(b)** (*dépendant*) **être t. de** (*produits étrangers etc*) to be dependent *or* to depend (up)on **(c)** *Géog* **rivière t.** tributary

tric [trik] *nm* (*au bridge*) odd trick

tricentenaire [trisɑ̃tnɛr] **1** *nm* tercentenary, tricentennial **2** *adj* three hundred years old

tricéphale [trisefal] *adj* (*monstre*) three-headed

triceps [trisɛps] *adj, nm Anat* **(muscle) t.** triceps (muscle)

triche [triʃ] *nf F* cheating; **c'est de la t.!** that's cheating!

tricher [triʃe] *vi* to cheat (**sur** over); (*mentir*) to lie (**sur** about); (*pour dissimuler un défaut*) to cheat a bit, to fiddle it; **t. aux cartes/à un examen** to cheat at cards/in an exam; **je n'aime pas t. avec les gens** I don't like being dishonest with people

tricherie [triʃri] *nf* cheating; **j'en ai assez de toutes tes tricheries!** I've had enough of your cheating!

tricheur, -euse [triʃœr, -øz] *n* cheat

trichine [trikin] *nf* (*ver*) threadworm, *Spéc* trichina

trichinose [trikinoz] *nf Méd* trichinosis

trichloréthylène [triklɔretilɛn] *nm Ch* trichlorethylene

trichrome [trikrom] *adj* (*photographie etc*) three-colour *or US* -color, trichromatic

trichromie [trikrɔmi] *nf Phot* three-colour *or US* -color process

trick [trik] *nm* (*au bridge*) odd trick

tricolore [trikɔlɔr] **1** *adj* three-coloured *or US* -colored; **le drapeau t.** the French flag, the Tricolour, *US* the Tricolor; *Admin* **feux tricolores** traffic lights *or* signals; *Sp* **l'équipe t.** the French team **2** *npl Sp* **les tricolores** the French team

tricorne [trikɔrn] *nm* three-cornered hat, tricorn

tricot [triko] *nm* **(a)** (*activité*) knitting; **faire du t.** to do some knitting **(b)** (*ouvrage*) knitting; *Com* knitwear; **j'ai commencé un t.** I've started to knit something **(c)** (*chandail*) sweater, *Br* jumper, *F* woolly; **t. de corps** *Br* vest, *Am* undershirt **(d)** (*tissu*) knitted fabric; **en t.** (*pull, vêtement*) knitted

tricotage [trikɔtaʒ] *nm* knitting

tricoter [trikɔte] **1** *vt* to knit; **aiguilles à t.** knitting needles; **machine à t.** knitting machine; **tricoté (à la) main** hand-knitted **2** *vi* to knit; **t. à la main/à la machine** to knit by hand/machine; *Arg* **t. des jambes** *ou* **des gambettes** (*s'enfuir*) to take off, to scram; (*pédaler*) to pedal like mad, to go like the clappers

tricoteur, -euse [trikɔtœr, -øz] **1** *n* (*personne*) knitter **2** *nf* **tricoteuse** (*machine*) knitting machine

tricrésylphosphate [trikresilfɔsfat] *nm* tri-cresyl phosphate, TCP

trictrac [triktrak] *nm* (*jeu*) backgammon; (*partie*) game of backgammon; (*damier*) backgammon board

tricuspide [trikyspid] *adj Anat* (*valve*) tricuspid

tricycle [trisikl] **1** *adj Av* (*train d'atterrissage*) three-wheeled **2** *nm* tricycle, *F* trike; **faire du t.** to go tricycling

trident [tridɑ̃] *nm* **(a)** *Myth* trident **(b)** *Pêche* fish spear **(c)** *Agr* three-pronged (pitch)fork

tridimensionnel, -elle [tridimɑ̃sjɔnɛl] *adj* three-dimensional, 3-D

trièdre [triɛdr] *Géom* **1** *adj* trihedral **2** *nm* trihedron

triennal, -ale, -aux, -ales [trienal, -o] *adj (festival, élection, révision etc)* three-yearly, triennial; *(président etc)* appointed for three years; *(bail, projet etc, Agr rotation)* three-year
triennat [triena] *nm* three-year mandate *or* period of office
trier [trije] *(impf, pr sub* **n. triions, v. triiez) 1** *vt* **(a)** *(classer) (lettres, minerai etc), Ordinat* to sort; *(garde-robe, informations)* to sort *or* go through; *(fruits, lentilles)* to pick over; *Rail* to marshall; *Ordinat* **t. par ordre alphabétique** to sort in alphabetical order, to alphasort **(b)** *(en choisissant)* to sort out, to pick out, to select; **t. à la main** to hand-pick; **trié sur le volet** hand-picked **2 se trier** *vpr Ordinat* to sort
trière [trijɛr] *nf Hist, Naut* trireme
trieur, -euse [trijœr, -øz] **1** *n (personne) (du courrier etc)* sorter **2** *nm Ind (appareil)* grader **3** *nf* **trieuse** *(machine)* sorter, sorting machine; *Ordinat* sorter; *(logiciel)* sort program
trieur-calibreur, *pl* **trieurs-calibreurs** *nm Ind* grading machine
trifolié [trifɔlje] *adj Bot* three-leaved, *Spéc* trifoliate
trifouiller [trifuje] *F* **1** *vt (affaires, papiers etc)* to rummage around in, to go *or* rake through; *(moteur)* to fiddle with **2** *vi* **qu'est-ce que tu trifouilles?** what are you rummaging *or* raking around for?; *(qu'est-ce que tu fabriques?)* what are you up to?; **je ne sais pas ce que j'ai trifouillé mais ça ne marche plus** I don't know what I've done but it's not working; **t. dans qch** to rummage *or* rake around in sth
trigémellaire [triʒemelɛr] *adj (grossesse)* triple
triglycéride [trigliserid] *nf* triglyceride
trigo [trigo] *nf F (abrév* **trigonométrie***)* trig
trigonométrie [trigɔnɔmetri] *nf* trigonometry
trigonométrique [trigɔnɔmetrik] *adj (ligne)* trigonometric(al); *(sens)* anti-clockwise
trijumeau [triʒymo] *adj m, nm Anat* **(nerf) t.** trigeminal nerve
trilatéral, -ale, -aux, -ales [trilateral, -o] *adj* trilateral
trilingue [trilɛ̃g] *adj (personne, document etc)* trilingual
trille [trij] *nm (d'un oiseau), Mus* trill; **les trilles des oiseaux** the trilling of the birds
triller [trije] *vti Mus* to trill
trillion [triljɔ̃] *nm* [①A70,16,1] *(10^{18})* trillion, *Am* quintillion
trilobé [trilɔbe] *adj* **(a)** *Archit (arche etc)* trefoil **(b)** *Bot* three-lobed, *Spéc* trilobate
trilobite [trilɔbit] *nm (fossile)* trilobite
trilogie [trilɔʒi] *nf Littér* trilogy
trimaran [trimarɑ̃] *nm Naut* trimaran
trimarder [trimarde] *vi Arg* to be on the road
trimardeur [trimardœr] *nm Arg* tramp, *US* hobo
trimbal(l)age [trɛ̃balaʒ] *nm,* **trimbal(l)ement** [trɛ̃balmɑ̃] *nm F (de paquets etc)* lugging *or* carting around; *(d'enfants etc)* trailing around
trimbal(l)er [trɛ̃bale] *F* **1** *vt (paquets etc)* to lug *or* cart around; *(enfants etc)* to trail around; **elle trimballe son fils partout** she trails her son around *or* drags her son with her everywhere she goes; *F* **qu'est ce qu'il trimbale!** *(qu'est-ce qu'il est bête)* what an idiot (he is)!, *Br* what a plonker!
2 se trimballer *vpr* **se t. jusqu'à la gare** to trail *or US Sl* schlep over to the station; **je ne vais pas me t. en ville habillé comme ça!** I'm not going around town dressed like that!; *Sl* **elle se trimballe partout avec sa marmaille** she trails her kids around with her everywhere she goes, she doesn't go anywhere without her kids; **elle se trimballe partout dans sa vieille voiture** she goes everywhere in her old car
trimer [trime] *vi F (travailler dur)* to slog *or* slave away, to work like a dog; **faire t. qn** to make sb slog, to keep sb hard at it
trimestre [trimɛstr] *nm* **(a)** *(trois mois)* quarter; *Scol* term, *Am* trimester; **par t.** quarterly; *Scol* **payer par t.** to pay every term **(b)** *(salaire)* quarter's salary; *(loyer)* quarter's rent; *Scol (frais)* term fees; *(d'une assurance, une bourse)* quarterly instalment *or* payment
trimestriel, -elle [trimɛstrijɛl] *adj* quarterly; *Scol (bulletin)* end-of-term; **fonction trimestrielle** position lasting for three months
trimestriellement [trimɛstrijɛlmɑ̃] *adv* quarterly; *Scol* once a term
trimoteur [trimɔtœr] *nm* three-engined plane
tringle [trɛ̃gl] *nf (barre)* rod; **t. à rideau** curtain rod; **t. d'escalier** stair rod; *Archit (moulure)* square moulding
tringler [trɛ̃gle] *vt* **(a)** *Tech (avec une ficelle crayeuse)* to mark with a line **(b)** *Vulg (sexuellement)* to screw, to lay; **se faire t.** to get laid
tringlerie [trɛ̃glәri] *nf Aut* linkage
trinitaire [trinitɛr] *adj, n Rel* Trinitarian
trinité [trinite] *nf* **(a)** *Rel* **la (Sainte) T.** the (Holy) Trinity; **la T.** *(fête)* Trinity Sunday **(b) (l'île de) la T.** Trinidad **(c)** *(groupe de trois éléments)* trinity
trinitrotoluène [trinitrotɔlɥɛn] *nm* trinitrotoluene, TNT
trinôme [trinom] *nm Math* trinomial
trinquer [trɛ̃ke] *vi* **(a)** *(porter un toast)* to clink glasses; **t. à qn/qch** to drink to sb/sth; **t. à la santé de qn** to drink a toast to sb; **nous trinquons à nos cinq ans de mariage** let's drink to *or* here's to our five years of marriage **(b)** *F (boire avec excès)* to booze **(c)** *F (subir un désagrément)* to suffer, to pay the cost, to get the worst of it; **les parents divorcent, les enfants trinquent** when parents get a divorce, it's the children that suffer; **elle fait des bêtises et c'est moi qui trinque** she acts the idiot and I get the blame
trinquet [trɛ̃kɛ] *nm Naut* foremast
trinquette [trɛ̃kɛt] *nf Naut* storm jib
trio [trijo] *nm* threesome, trio; *Mus* trio
triode [triɔd] *adj, nf Électron, Rad* triode
triolet [trijɔlɛ] *nm* **(a)** *Mus* triplet **(b)** *Littér* triolet
triomphal, -ale, -aux, -ales [trijɔ̃fal, -o] *adj (accueil)* triumphant, triumphal; *(couronne)* of victory; *(élection)* resoundingly successful; *(geste)* triumphant, of triumph
triomphalement [trijɔ̃falmɑ̃] *adv* triumphantly; **être accueilli t.** to be received in triumph *or* triumphantly
triomphalisme [trijɔ̃falism] *nm* crowing; **sans faire de t., il me semble que ...** while I don't want to crow, it seems to me that ...
triomphaliste [trijɔ̃falist] **1** *adj (attitude, air)* cock-a-hoop; **être t.** to crow **2** *n* crower
triomphant [trijɔ̃fɑ̃] *adj (personne)* triumphant; *(sourire, air, rire)* triumphant, of triumph; **... dit-il d'un ton t.** ... he said triumphantly; **il est arrivé t., avec la preuve qu'il avait raison** he came back cock-a-hoop with the proof that he was right
triomphateur, -trice [trijɔ̃fatœr, -tris] **1** *adj* triumphant, victorious **2** *n (vainqueur)* victor, winner **3** *nm Antiq* conquering hero
triomphe [trijɔ̃f] *nm* triumph **(sur** over); **le t. de la justice** the triumph of justice; **remporter un t.** to be a resounding success *or* a triumph; **c'est le t. de la démocratie/de la bêtise** it's a triumph for democracy/stupidity; **faire un t. à qn** to give sb an ovation; **arc de t.** triumphal arch; **en t.** in triumph; **porter qn en t.** to carry sb in triumph *or* shoulder high; **sourire/cri de t.** smile/shout of triumph, triumphant smile/shout; **pousser un cri de t.** to give a shout of triumph, to shout triumphantly
triompher [trijɔ̃fe] *vi* **(a)** *(l'emporter)* to triumph, to be triumphant **(de** over); **t. d'une difficulté** to triumph over *or* to overcome a difficulty **(b)** *(exceller)* to excel **(dans** in); *(avoir un grand succès)* to triumph; **la vérité finit toujours par t.** truth will prevail **(c)** *(exulter)* to crow
trioxyde [triɔksid] *nm Ch* trioxide
trip [trip] *nm F* **(a)** *(de drogue)* trip; **t. d'acide** acid trip; **faire un t.** to trip; **être en plein t.** to be on a trip, to be tripping **(b) c'est pas mon t.** *(ça ne m'intéresse pas)* it's not my thing *or* bag; **le jazz, c'est plutôt son t.** jazz is his thing *or* bag; **il est dans son t. écolo** he's on his environmental kick
tripaille [tripaj] *nf F (intestins)* guts
triparti [triparti] *adj* tripartite
tripartisme [tripartism] *nm* three-party government
tripartite [tripartit] *adj* tripartite
tripatouillage [tripatujaʒ] *nm F (de textes, comptes etc)* tampering *or* fiddling with; *(de statistiques)* massaging; **il y eu t. des résultats** the results were fiddled
tripatouiller [tripatuje] *F* **1** *vt* **(a)** *(textes)* to tamper *or* fiddle with; *(comptes, résultats)* to fiddle (with); *(statistiques)* to massage **(b)** *(tripoter) (personne)* to paw, to feel up; *(cheveux etc)* to play *or* fiddle with **2** *vi* **t. dans** to be mixed up *or* involved in
tripatouilleur, -euse [tripatujœr, -øz] *n F* fiddler, tamperer
tripe [trip] *nf* **(a) tripes** *(d'un animal)* entrails; *Culin* tripe; *très F (de personne)* guts; *F* **une histoire qui vous prend aux tripes** a story that gets you in the guts *or* right there; *F* **parler avec ses tripes** to speak from the heart; *très F* **rendre tripes et boyaux** to spew one's guts out; *F* **elle a des tripes** she's got guts **(b)** *Fig F* **avoir la t. républicaine** to be a republican through and through **(c)** *(de cigare)* core, filling **(d) peau en t.** pelt
triperie [tripri] *nf* **(a)** *(boutique)* tripe shop **(b)** *(commerce)* tripe trade
tripette [tripɛt] *nf F* **ça ne vaut pas t., sa formation/sa chaînette/son conseil** her training/chain/advice isn't worth a damn
triphasé [trifɑze] *Él* **1** *adj* three-phase **2** *nm* three-phase current; **installation en t.** three-phase wiring
triphtongue [triftɔ̃g] *nf Ling* triphthong
tripier, -ière [tripje, -jɛr] *n* tripe butcher
triplace [triplas] *adj Av* three-seater

triplan [triplɑ̃] *nm Av* triplane
triple [tripl] **1** *adj* **(a)** triple; (*trois fois plus grand*) (*dose*) triple, treble; **t. menton** triple chin; **t. naissance** triple birth; **en t. exemplaire** in triplicate **(b)** (*emploi intensif*) **un t. sot** a prize idiot; **au t. galop** at top *or* breakneck speed, at a rate of knots; *F* **t. buse!** you stupid nit! **2** *nm* **le t.** three times as much (**de** as); **je l'ai acheté le t. de toi/de sa valeur** I paid three times as much as you did/as much as it was worth; **douze est le t. de quatre** twelve is three times four
▶ **triple**: **la T. Alliance** the Triple Alliance; *Mus* **t. croche** demisemiquaver, *Am* thirty-second note; **la T. Entente** the Triple Entente; **t. saut** triple jump, hop, skip and jump
triplé, -ée [triple] **1** *n* triplet **2** *nm Sp* (*triple succès*) triple victory; *Courses de chevaux* (*pari*) = bet on the first three horses in a race
triplement[1] [tripləmɑ̃] *adv* (*important*) trebly, triply; **elle a t. raison** she is right on three counts
triplement[2] *nm* trebling, tripling
tripler [triple] **1** *vt* to treble, to triple, to increase threefold; *Scol* **t. une classe** to repeat a year twice **2** *vi* to treble, to triple, to increase threefold
triplette [triplɛt] *nf* (*aux boules*) threesome
triplex® [tripleks] *nm* (*verre*) laminated safety glass, *Br* Triplex
tripode [tripɔd] *adj Naut* (*mât*) tripod
triporteur [tripɔrtœr] *nm* delivery tricycle
tripot [tripo] *nm* gambling den
tripotage [tripɔtaʒ] *nm F* **(a)** (*fraude*) fiddling (around) (**de** with); **le t. électoral est monnaie courante** election rigging is common; **tripotages** (*magouilles*) scheming, dirty tricks, skulduggery; **tripotages électoraux** election rigging; **il y a eu des tripotages** there's been some scheming *or* fiddling going on **(b)** (*action de toucher*) **arrêtez vos tripotages!** stop pawing each other!
tripotée [tripɔte] *nf Arg* **(a)** (*raclée*) hammering **(b)** (*grand nombre*) **une t. de** loads of, lots of
tripoter [tripɔte] *F* **1** *vi* (*magouiller*) to engage in shady business; **t. dans** to be mixed up *or* involved in; **t. dans la caisse** to tamper with the cash **2** *vt* (*toucher à*) (*appareil*) to touch, to mess around *or* about with; (*fruits*) to finger, to paw; (*parce qu'on est nerveux*) (*objet, cheveux etc*) to fiddle with; **arrête de t. tes boutons** stop fingering *or* keep your hands off your spots; **t. qn** to paw *or* grope sb, to touch sb up **3 se tripoter** *vpr* (*se masturber*) to play with oneself; (*de deux personnes*) to paw *or* grope each other, to feel each other up
tripoteur, -euse [tripɔtœr, -øz] **1** *n* (*magouilleur*) suspicious character, *Sl* chancer, *m* wide boy **2** *adj* (*mains*) groping; **il a les mains tripoteuses** he's a bit of a groper
triptyque [triptik] *nm* **(a)** *Beaux-Arts, Littér, Mus* triptych **(b)** *Aut, Admin* triptyque
trique [trik] *nf F* cudgel, heavy stick; **des coups de t.** cudgel blows; *Fig* **avoir recours à la t.** to use the big stick; **mener son monde** *ou* **les gens à la t.** to rule with a rod of iron, to rule by fear; **sec comme une t.** *ou* **un coup de t.** as thin as a rake; *Fig Vulg* **avoir la t.** (*être en érection*) to have a hard-on
triquet [trikɛ] *nm* (*échelle*) pair of steps
trirème [trirɛm] *nf Hist, Naut* trireme
trisaïeul, -euls *ou* **-eux** [trizajœl, -ø] *nm* great-great-grandfather; **trisaïeuls, trisaïeux** great-great-grandparents
trisaïeule [trizajœl] *nf* great-great-grandmother
trisannuel, -elle [trizanɥɛl] *adj* (*qui a lieu tous les trois ans*) three-yearly, triennial; (*qui dure trois ans*) three-year
trisection [triseksjɔ̃] *nf Géom* trisection
trisomie [trizɔmi] *nf Méd* Down's syndrome, *Spéc* trisomy; **t. 21** trisomy of chromosome 21; **enfant atteint de t. 21** child with Down's syndrome
trisser (se) [sətrise] *vpr Arg* (*s'enfuir*) to scram, to beat it
triste [trist] **1** *adj* **(a)** (*malheureux*) (*personne*) sad; (*visage, mine, air*) sad, forlorn; (*sourire*) sad, wan, sorrowful; **c'est vraiment t. à voir** it's really sad to see; **ça me rend t. de te le dire** I am sorry to tell you; **je fus (bien) t. d'apprendre que …** I was (very) sorry to hear that …; **tout t.** (very) dejected, in low spirits; **elle a le vin t.** she's not a happy drunk, drink makes her maudlin; **il n'est pas t., son mari!** her husband's a real laugh-a-minute!; **elle n'était pas t., la fête!** it was a terrific *or* a really fun party!; *Iron* **tu as vu son gâteau, c'est pas t.!** have you seen that masterpiece of a cake?; *F* **c'était vraiment pas t.** it was really funny

(b) (*ennuyeux*) (*vie, temps, pièce etc*) dreary, dismal, depressing; (*couleur*) dreary, depressing; (*campagne*) bleak, depressing; (*personne*) miserable, depressing; **faire t. mine à qn** to give sb an unenthusiastic welcome; **t. à mourir** (*gens, ambiance, lieu*) thoroughly depressing, dreary

(c) (*douloureux*) (*tâche, nouvelle, occasion, épisode*) sad, painful; **dans un t. état** in a sorry state; **c'est la t. réalité** that's the way things are; **c'est une t. affaire** it's a sorry *or* bad business; **(quelle) t. époque!** what terrible times we live in!; **c'est tout de même t.!** it's pretty pathetic!; **c'est quand même t. de voir ça dans notre pays!** it's dreadful to see that type of thing in our own country!

(d) *Péj* (*repas, excuse etc*) poor, sorry, wretched; (*morceau de pain*) sad- *or* sorry-looking

2 *n* (*personne sombre*) gloomy *or* miserable person; **ce n'est pas un t.** he's a lot of fun
tristement [tristəmɑ̃] *adv* **(a)** (*avec tristesse*) sadly, sorrowfully; **nous avons t. appris la nouvelle** we heard the news with great sadness, we were sad *or* sorry to hear the news **(b)** (*d'une façon sombre*) gloomily; **la maison est t. décorée** the house is decorated in a dreary *or* depressing fashion **(c)** (*cruellement*) sadly; **faire t. défaut** to be sadly lacking; **t. célèbre** notorious
tristesse [tristɛs] *nf* **(a)** (*d'une personne, d'un événement*) sadness; **ressentir de la t.** to feel sad; **un sourire plein de t.** a very sad smile; **avec t.** sadly; **j'ai quitté ce pays avec t.** I was sorry to leave the country **(b)** (*d'une pièce, d'une couleur, d'un décor etc*) dreariness; (*d'un paysage*) bleakness **(c)** **tristesses** (*moments*) (*de la vie etc*) sorrows
tristounet, -ette [tristunɛ, -ɛt] *adj F* (*pièce*) dreary, gloomy; (*couleur*) dreary; (*personne, air*) gloomy
trisyllabe, trissyllabe [trisilab] *nm* trisyllable, three-syllable word
trisyllabique, trissyllabique [trisilabik] *adj* trisyllabic, three-syllable
tritium [tritjɔm] *nm Ch* tritium
triton[1] [tritɔ̃] *nm* **(a)** *Myth* **T.** Triton **(b)** (*amphibien*) triton newt **(c)** (*mollusque*) triton, trumpet shell
triton[2] *nm Mus* augmented fourth, tritone
trituration [trityrasjɔ̃] *nf* (*broyage*) grinding, *Spéc* trituration
triturer [trityre] **1** *vt* **(a)** (*broyer*) to grind, *Spéc* to triturate **(b)** (*manier*) (*son mouchoir etc*) to twist up; *Fig* (*l'opinion*) to manipulate; **de vieux magazines tout triturés** battered old magazines **2 se triturer** *vpr F* **se t. la cervelle** *ou* **les méninges** to rack one's brains
triumvir [trijɔmvir] *nm Antiq* triumvir
triumvirat [trijɔmvira] *nm Antiq, Pol Fig* triumvirate
trivalent [trivalɑ̃] *adj Ch* trivalent
trivalve [trivalv] *adj Biol* trivalvular, trivalve
trivial, -ale, -aux, -ales [trivjal, -jo] *adj* **(a)** (*vulgaire*) (*expression, langage, plaisanteries etc*) vulgar, coarse **(b)** (*commun*) trite, banal, mundane; *Math etc* (*solution*) self-evident, obvious
trivialement [trivjalmɑ̃] *adv* (*vulgairement*) vulgarly, coarsely
trivialité [trivjalite] *nf* **(a)** (*vulgarité*) (*d'une expression, une plaisanterie etc*) vulgarity, coarseness **(b)** (*caractère commun*) (*d'une explication, d'une argumentation*) triteness, banality; **tout cela est d'une t.!** it's so banal *or* trite! **(c)** (*expression*) vulgar *or* coarse expression
tr/mn (*abrév* **tours par minute**) rpm, rev/min
troc [trɔk] *nm* exchange (in kind); (*système économique*) barter; **économie de t.** barter economy; **faire du t.** to barter; **faire le t. d'une chose avec une autre** to exchange *or* barter *or F* swap one thing for another; **je ne l'ai pas acheté, j'ai fait le t. avec quelqu'un** I didn't buy it, I bartered for it *or F* I did a swap; **faire un t.** to make an exchange *or F* do a swap (**avec qn** with sb)
trochaïque [trɔkaik] *adj, nm Littér* trochaic
trochée [trɔʃe] *nm Littér* trochee
troène [trɔɛn] *nm Bot* privet
troglodyte [trɔglɔdit] *nm* **(a)** (*personne*) troglodyte, cave dweller **(b)** (*oiseau*) wren
troglodytique [trɔglɔditik] *adj* **habitation t.** cave dwelling
trogne [trɔɲ] *nf F* face, *Péj* mug; **il a une bonne t.** (*d'une personne, d'un bébé*) he's got a nice face
trognon [trɔɲɔ̃] **1** *nm* **(a)** (*de pomme etc*) core; (*de chou etc*) stump; *Fig F* **on s'est fait avoir jusqu'au t.** we were well and truly done **(b)** *F* (*terme d'affection*) poppet, sweetie **2** *adj inv F* (*mignon*) sweet
Troie [trwa] *n* Troy; **guerre/cheval de T.** Trojan War/horse
troïka [trɔika] *nf* (*traîneau*), *Pol* troika
trois [trwa] ([trwaz] *before a vowel sound or mute* **h** *in the same word group*) **1** *adj inv* three; **à t. heures** at three o'clock; **les t. quarts du temps** most of the time; **couper/partager qch en t.** to cut/divide sth into three; *Géom* **couper** *ou* **diviser une ligne/un angle en t.** to trisect a line/an angle; **entrer (t.) par t.** to come in in threes *or* three at a time; **t. par t.** three by three, in threes; **ménage à t.** ménage à trois; **Henri T.** Henry the Third; **(hôtel) t. étoiles** three-star hotel; **en t. dimensions** in 3D

2 *nm inv* three; **le t. août** (on) the third of August, (on) August the third, *Am* (on) August third; **t. de carreau** three of diamonds; **j'habite au t.** I live at number three
trois-huit *nm inv* **(a)** *Mus* three-eight time **(b)** *Ind* **régime des t.** three-shift working; **faire les t.** to operate three shifts (*of eight hours each*)
troisième [trwazjɛm] **1** *adj* third; **au t. étage** on the third *or Am* fourth floor; **de t. ordre** third-rate **2** *n* (*personne, chose etc*) third **3** *nm* **(a)** (*fraction*) third **(b)** (*étage*) third *or Am* fourth floor; **habiter au t.** to live on the third *or Am* fourth floor **4** *nf* **(a)** *Scol* **(classe de) t.** fourth year of secondary school, *Am* ≈ eighth grade **(b)** *Aut* third (gear); **en t.** in third (gear); **passer la t.** to go (up/down) into third (gear)
▶ **troisième**: **t. âge: personnes du t. âge** senior citizens, *Am* golden agers; *Journ* **t.** *f* **de couverture** inside back cover, IBC
troisièmement [trwazjɛmmɑ̃] *adv* thirdly, in the third place
trois-mâts *nm inv Naut* three-masted ship, three-master
trois-pièces *nm inv* **(a)** (*appartement*) three-room(ed) flat *or Am* apartment **(b)** (*costume*) three-piece suit
trois-quarts *nm inv* **(a)** *Rugby* three-quarter; **t. aile/centre** wing/centre three-quarter; **t. arrière** three-quarter back **(b)** (*manteau*) three-quarter-length coat
trois-quatre *nm inv Mus* three-four time
troll [trɔl] *nm Myth* troll
trolley [trɔlɛ] *nm* **(a)** (*caténaire*) trolley pole and wheel; **perche de t.** trolley pole **(b)** (*véhicule*) trolleybus
trolleybus [trɔlɛbys] *nm* trolleybus
trombe [trɔ̃b] *nf* **(a)** (*cyclone*) waterspout **(b) t. de vent** whirlwind; **t. d'eau** cloudburst; *Fig F* **entrer/sortir en t.** to tear *or* hurtle in/out, to burst in/out (like a whirlwind); **il est passé/parti en t.** he tore *or* hurtled past/off, he went past/left in a cloud of dust
trombine [trɔ̃bin] *nf Arg* (*visage*) mug
trombinoscope [trɔ̃binɔskɔp] *nm F* (*d'une association, d'un groupe etc*) rogues gallery
tromblon [trɔ̃blɔ̃] *nm Hist* (*fusil*) blunderbuss
trombone [trɔ̃bɔn] *nm* **(a)** *Mus* (*instrument*) trombone; (*instrumentiste*) trombone (player), trombonist; **t. à coulisse/à pistons** slide/valve trombone **(b)** (*agrafe*) paper clip
trompe [trɔ̃p] *nf* **(a)** *Mus* horn; **t. de brume/chasse** fog/hunting horn; *Fig* **publier qch à son de t.** to trumpet sth abroad **(b)** *Zool* (*d'un animal, d'un insecte*) proboscis; (*d'un éléphant*) trunk **(c)** *Anat* **t. d'Eustache/de Fallope** Eustachian/Fallopian tube **(d)** *Archit* pendentive, squinch **(e)** *Tech* pump; *Métal* blast pump, trompe
trompe-la-mort *n inv F* (*volontaire*) daredevil
trompe-l'œil *nm inv* **(a)** *Beaux-Arts* trompe l'œil (painting); **en t.** (*peinture, scène etc*) trompe l'œil; **peindre en t.** to do a trompe l'œil painting, to use trompe l'œil techniques **(b)** *Fig Péj* bluff, window-dressing
tromper [trɔ̃pe] **1** *vt* **(a)** (*abuser*) to deceive, to (deliberately) mislead, to take in; **cela ne trompe personne** nobody's taken in, nobody's fooled; **t. qn sur qch/qn** to deceive *or* mislead sb about sth/sb; **il est incapable de t. qui que ce soit** he is totally incapable of deceit

(b) (*être infidèle à*) (*femme, mari*) to deceive, to be unfaithful to, *F* to cheat on, to two-time; **il trompe sa femme avec sa secrétaire** he's having an affair with his secretary, *F* he's having a bit on the side with his secretary

(c) (*induire en erreur*) to mislead (**sur** as, to); (*decevoir*) (*espoirs de qn*) to disappoint; **son air de s'y connaître m'a trompé** I was misled *or* fooled *or* taken in by the fact that he seemed to know what he was doing; **ne vous laissez pas t.** don't be misled, don't be fooled, don't be taken in; **ça a l'air lourd, mais c'est ce qui vous trompe** it looks heavy, that's what's so misleading; **je ne voulais pas t. son attente** I didn't want to disappoint him; **se laisser t. par les apparences** to be taken in by appearances

(d) (*échapper à*) (*contrôle, surveillance, vigilance*) to elude, to escape

(e) *Fig* (*ennui*) to relieve; (*temps*) to while away; **t. la faim** to stave off (one's) hunger

2 se tromper *vpr* **(a)** (*commettre une erreur*) to be mistaken, to be wrong, to make a mistake; **c'est justement ce en quoi tu te trompes** that's just where you're wrong; **je dois me t.** I must be mistaken, I must be wrong; **j'ai dû me t.** I must have made a mistake; **si/à moins que je ne me trompe** if I'm not/unless I'm mistaken; **ou je me trompe fort** or I'm much mistaken; **tout le monde peut se t.** anybody can make a mistake, we all make mistakes; **se t. dans les dates/les proportions** to get the dates/the proportions wrong; **se t. dans son calcul** to get one's sums wrong, *Fml* to be out in one's reckoning; *Tél* **vous devez vous t. de numéro** you must have the wrong number; **je me suis trompé de direction/de maison** I went the wrong way/to the wrong house; **je me suis trompé de Laurent!** I got the wrong Laurent!; **se t. d'heure/de jour** to mistake the time/day, to get the time/day wrong; **je ne m'y trompe pas, du reste** I'm not fooled *or* taken in; **elle ressemble à sa sœur à s'y t.** you can't tell her and her sister apart; **il n'y a pas à s'y t.** there's no mistake about it; **que l'on ne s'y trompe pas** make no mistake about it; **vous m'avez fait me t.** you made me make a mistake; **tu es en train de la faire se t.** you're confusing her

(b) (*entre époux*) **se t. (mutuellement)** to be unfaithful to *or F* to cheat on each other
tromperie [trɔ̃pri] *nf* deceit, deception; (*en affaires*) fraud; **j'en ai assez de tes tromperies** I've had enough of your deceit *or* deceitfulness; **il y a t. sur la marchandise** this isn't what it was said to be
trompeter [trɔ̃p(ə)te] *vt* (**je trompette; je trompetterai**) (*nouvelles*) to shout from the rooftops
trompette [trɔ̃pɛt] **1** *nf* **(a)** *Mus* trumpet; *Mil* **jouer/sonner de la t.** to play/sound the trumpet; **t. de jazz** jazz trumpet; **à la t., Louis Armstrong!** on (the) trumpet, Louis Armstrong!; *Litt* **la t. du jugement dernier** the last trump; *Fig* **nez en t.** turned-up nose **(b)** (*coquillage*) trumpet shell **2** *nm* trumpet (player), trumpeter
▶ **trompette**: **t. bouchée** muted trumpet; **t. de cavalerie** bugle
trompette-de-la-mort, *pl* **trompettes-de-la-mort** *nf* (*champignon*) horn of plenty
trompettiste [trɔ̃pɛtist] *n Mus* trumpet (player), trumpeter
trompeur, -euse [trɔ̃pœr, -øz] **1** *adj* **(a)** (*volontairement*) (*personne, paroles etc*) deceitful **(b)** (*symptome, apparences etc*) deceptive, misleading; (*publicité*) misleading **2** *n* deceiver, cheat; **à t., t. et demi** = cheats never win
trompeusement [trɔ̃pøzmɑ̃] *adv* deceptively
tronc [trɔ̃] *nm* **(a)** (*d'un arbre, d'un corps*) trunk; **homme/femme-t.** armless and legless man/woman **(b)** (*d'une famille*) parent stock **(c)** *Rel* poor box **(d)** *Math* **t. de cône/pyramide** truncated cone/pyramid
▶ **tronc**: *Univ etc* **t. commun** core syllabus
troncature [trɔ̃katyr] *Ordinat nf* truncation
tronche [trɔ̃ʃ] *nf Arg* (*tête*) nut, bonce; (*visage*) mug, kisser; **sa t. ne me revient pas** I don't like the look of him; **il a une sale t.** he's an ugly-looking customer; *F* **faire la t.** to sulk
tronçon [trɔ̃sɔ̃] *nm* (*de chemin de fer, d'autoroute*) section; (*d'une canalisation*) section, length; (*de phrase, de texte etc*) part, portion; (*d'épée, de lance, de mât etc*) (broken) stump; **t. de bois** log
tronconique [trɔ̃kɔnik] *adj* **segment t.** truncated segment
tronçonnage [trɔ̃sɔnaʒ] *nm*, **tronçonnement** [trɔ̃sɔnmɑ̃] *nm* cutting into lengths *or* pieces
tronçonner [trɔ̃sɔne] *vt* to cut up (into lengths *or* pieces)
tronçonneuse [trɔ̃sɔnøz] *nf* (*à chaîne*) chain saw; (*circulaire*) circular saw
trône [tron] *nm* **(a)** (*de roi, pape etc*) throne; **monter sur le t.** to come to the throne; **placer** *ou* **mettre qn sur le t.** to put sb on the throne **(b)** *F Hum* (*siège des cabinets*) throne
trôner [trone] *vi* **(a)** (*d'un monarque, Fig d'une personne*) to sit enthroned **(b)** (*d'objets*) to occupy a place of honour *or US* honor; **son diplôme trône sur la cheminée** his diploma occupies a place of honour on the mantelpiece; **toutes ses décorations trônaient dans son bureau** all his decorations were prominently displayed in his office **(c)** *Péj* (*faire l'important*) to lord it
tronqué [trɔ̃ke] *adj* (*colonne, pyramide*) truncated; (*mât*) stub; (*texte*) cut, truncated
tronquer [trɔ̃ke] *vt* (*arbre*) to pollard; *Fig* (*roman, scène etc*) to cut, to shorten, to truncate
trop [tro] *adv* **(a)** [①A5,B] (*devant un adj*) too, over-; (*devant un adv*) too; **c'est t. difficile** it's too difficult; **un travail t. difficile** too difficult a job; **t. aimable** [trɔpɛmabl] too *or* extremely kind; **aliments t. riches** over-rich food; **t. attaché à** too attached to, overfond of; **t. cuit** overcooked; **être t. habillé** to have too many clothes on; **vous n'êtes que t. généreux** you are much too *or* far too *or* overly generous; **t. fatigué** too tired (**pour faire** to do), overtired; *Litt* **par t. généreux** far too generous; **t. beau pour être vrai** too good to be true; **vous n'êtes pas t. en avance** you're none too early; **je ne me sens pas t. à l'aise** I'm not overly comfortable, I'm none too comfortable; **ça va? – pas t. mal** how are things? – not bad at all *or* not too bad; **ça te plaît/c'est bien fait? – pas t. mal** do you like it/is it good? – it's not bad at all; **c'était t. drôle** it was too funny for words *or* just too funny; **le trou était t. étroit pour qu'un rat entrât par là** the hole was too narrow for a rat to get in by; **c'est t. grand pour qu'on puisse le mettre dans la voiture** it's too big to go in the car; *F* **il est vraiment t.!** he's too much!

(**b**) (*avec un verbe*) too much, over-; **t. travailler** to overwork, to work too much *or* too hard; **t. manger** to overeat, to eat too much; **boire t., t. boire** to drink to excess *or* too much; **t. simplifier** to oversimplify; **je ne l'ai que t. dit** I've said it time and time again; **je ne la connais que t.** I know her all *or* only too well; **je l'ai t. aimé** [trɔpeme] I loved him too much; **il n'y tient pas t.** he's not too bothered (about it); *F* **ça te plaît?, – pas t.** do you like it? – not (very) much; **ne vous y fiez pas t., il ne faut pas t. vous y fier** don't count on it too much; **je ne le croirais pas t.** I wouldn't put too much faith in what he says, I wouldn't be too ready to believe him; **on ne saurait t. le répéter** it cannot be repeated too often; **je ne sais pas t.** I'm not too sure; **je ne sais t. que dire/penser** I hardly know *or* I don't quite know what to say/think

(**c**) (*emploi nominal*) (*quantité*) too much; (*nombre*) too many; **t. de** (*bruit, sel, travail etc*) too much; (*amis, choses, problèmes etc*) too many; **je n'aurai pas t. d'une heure pour le faire** it will take me a good hour; **il a t. d'expérience pour se tromper** he is too experienced to make a mistake; **elle n'a fait preuve que de t. de patience** she has shown far too much patience; **j'ai une carte de t.** *ou* **en t.** I have one card too many; **payer 500 francs de t.** *ou* **en t.** to pay 500 francs too much; **c'est une fois de t.** that's once too often; **quand j'ai du temps de t.** when I have time to spare; **être/se sentir de t.** to be/feel in the way *or* unwelcome *or* de trop; *F* **travailler de t.** to work too hard *or* too much, to overwork; *F* **boire de t.** to drink too much, *F* to overdo the drink; **t., c'est t.!** enough is enough!; **c'en est t.!** this really is the limit!; **il allait t. en dire** *ou* **en dire t.** he was going to say too much

trope [trɔp] *nm Littér* trope

trophée [trɔfe] *nm* trophy

tropical, -ale, -aux, -ales [trɔpikal, -o] *adj* (*plante, climat, température etc*) tropical; (*vêtement*) for wear in the tropics

tropique [trɔpik] *nm* (**a**) *Astron, Géog* (*cercle*) tropic; **le T. du Cancer/du Capricorn** the tropic of Cancer/of Capricorn (**b**) **les tropiques** (*région*) the tropics; **sous les tropiques** in the tropics

tropisme [trɔpism] *nm Biol* tropism

troposphère [trɔpɔsfɛr] *nf Météo* troposphere

trop-perçu, *pl* **trop-perçus** [trɔpɛrsy] *nm Fin* (*d'impôts*) overpayment

trop-plein, *pl* **trop-pleins** *nm* (*réservoir, excédent*) overflow; **(tuyau de) t.** waste pipe, overflow pipe; **t. d'énergie/de tendresse** overabundance of energy/affection; **laisser déborder le t. de son cœur** to give vent to one's overflowing emotions

troquer [trɔke] *vt* (**a**) *Com* to exchange, to barter, (**b**) (*faire l'échange*) to exchange, *F* to swap (**contre qch** for sth)

troquet [trɔkɛ] *nm F* (small) café

trot [tro] *nm* (*de cheval*) trot; **t. assis** sitting trot; **t. enlevé** rising trot, *US* posting trot; **au petit/grand t.** at a gentle/brisk trot; **prendre le t.** to break into a trot; **aller le t.** *ou* **au t.** to trot; *Fig F* **allez-y, et au t.!** go on, and be quick about it!; **t. attelé** harness race; **t. monté** = type of race in which the horse is ridden instead of being harnessed to the sulky; **course de t.** trotting *or* harness race

Trotski [trɔtski] *nm* Trotsky

trotskisme, trotskysme [trɔtskism] *nm* Trotskyism

Trotskiste, Trotskyste [trɔtskist] *adj, n* Trotskyist, Trotskyite

trotte [trɔt] *nf F* (*longue distance*) (long) stretch; **il y a une bonne t. d'ici au château** it's a good way *or* hike from here to the castle; **tout d'une t.** without stopping

trotte-menu *adj inv* **la gent t.** mice

trotter [trɔte] *vi* (*d'un cheval, d'un cavalier*) to trot; (*d'une personne*) to trot (around/along); (*d'une souris*) to scamper; *F* **toujours à t.** always on the go; **on entendrait t. une souris** you could have heard a pin drop; *Fig* **cette chanson me trotte dans la tête** that song keeps running through my head; **ça me trotte dans la tête depuis** I haven't been able to stop thinking about it since

trotteur, -euse [trɔtœr, -øz] **1** *adj* **talons trotteurs** flat *or* low heels **2** *n* (*cheval*) trotter **3** *nm* (**a**) (*chaussure*) flat, flat (-heeled) *or* low-heeled shoe (**b**) (*pour bébé*) baby-walker **4** *nf* **trotteuse** (*d'une montre*) second hand

trottinement [trɔtinmɑ̃] *nm* (*d'une souris*) scampering; (*d'une personne*) trotting about

trottiner [trɔtine] *vi* (**a**) (*de cheval, mule*) to jog-trot (**b**) (*de souris*) to scamper (around/along), to patter about; (*de personne*) to trot about

trottinette [trɔtinɛt] *nf* (**a**) (*jouet*) scooter; **faire de la t.** to ride one's scooter (**b**) *F* (*petite voiture*) small car, runabout

trottoir [trɔtwar] *nm* pavement, *Am* sidewalk; *Aut* **heurter le t.** to hit the kerb; **artiste de t.** pavement artist; **faire le t.** to walk the streets, *Sl* to be on the game; **t. roulant** travelator, moving pavement *or Am* sidewalk

trou [tru] *nm* (**a**) (*ouverture*) hole; (*d'aiguille*) eye; **avoir des trous à ses chaussettes** to have holes in one's socks; **t. de clef** (*d'horloge, de montre*) keyhole; **t. de serrure** keyhole; **le t. de la couche d'ozone** the hole in the ozone layer; *Fig* **faire son t.** to find one's niche; *Av Arg* **il a fait un t. dans l'eau** he's gone for a Burton; *F* **boire comme un t., avoir un t. sous le nez** to drink like a fish; *F* **s'en mettre jusqu'aux trous de nez** to stuff one's face

(**b**) (*dans une haie, Fig dans un emploi du temps*) gap, opening; *Fig* (*de mémoire, dans une explication, un CV etc*) gap; (*dans ses économies, son budget*) hole, dent; **j'ai un t. de cinq à sept** I'm free *or* I'm not doing anything between five and seven; **il est parti en laissant un t. de 300 000 francs** he went off leaving us/the company/*etc* 300,000 francs worse off; **j'ai eu un t. (de mémoire)** my mind went blank *or* was a blank; **j'ai un t.** my mind has gone blank *or* is a blank; *Sp* **faire le t.** to break away from the field

(**c**) *Anat F* **je n'ai pas les yeux en face des trous** I haven't come to yet, I'm still fast asleep, my brain's still not in gear; *Méd F* **t. dans le cœur** hole in the heart

(**d**) (*creusé etc*) hole; *Aut* (pot)hole; **t. de souris** mouse-hole; *Agr* **t. au fumier** manure pit

(**e**) *F Péj* (*village etc*) hole; **elle n'est jamais sortie de son t.** she has never been out of her own backyard; **habiter un petit t. (perdu)** to live at the back of beyond

(**f**) *Golf* hole; **envoyer la balle dans le t.** to hole out; **partie par trous** match play

(**g**) *Arg* (*tombe*) grave; (*prison*) prison; **on l'a mis dans le t.** (*au tombeau*) they put him six feet under; **on l'a mis au t.** (*en prison*) he was sent down

(**h**) *Tech* **t. de graissage** oil hole; **t. d'aération** air vent; *Min* **t. de mine** blast *or* drill hole; *Min, Constr* **t. de sondage** *ou* **de sonde** borehole

▶ **trou**: *Av* **t. d'air** air pocket; *Aut* **t. d'alimentation** supply port; *F* **t. de balle** arsehole, *Am* asshole; *Naut* **t. du chat** lubber's hole; *Vulg* **t. du cul** arsehole, *Am* asshole; **espèce de t. du cul!** arsehole!, plonker!; *Aut* **t. d'évacuation** drain hole; **t. d'homme** manhole; *F* **trous de nez** nostrils; *Astron* **t. noir** black hole; *Fig* **c'est le t. noir** I am/he is/*etc* extremely depressed *or F* really down; **t. normand: faire le t. normand** to have a (glass of) Calvados (*in the middle of a meal*); *Th* **t. du souffleur** prompter's box

troubadour [trubadur] *nm Hist, Littér* troubadour

troublant [trublɑ̃] *adj* (**a**) (*qui dérange*) disturbing, unsettling; (*qui déconcerte*) disconcerting (**b**) (*sensuel*) disturbing, provocative; (*parfum*) heady

trouble[1] [trubl] **1** *adj* (**a**) (*liquide, eau*) cloudy; (*lumière, yeux*) dim; (*ciel*) murky, overcast; (*image, photographe*) blurred, fuzzy; **avoir la vue t.** to have blurred vision; **aux yeux troubles** bleary-eyed

(**b**) (*qui manque de clarté*) (*situation, motivations*) confused, unclear; (*émotion*) mixed, uneasy; *Péj* (*comportement, affaire etc*) shady, fishy, suspicious; **période t. de l'histoire** murky period of history; **il y a quelque chose de t. dans cette affaire** there's something shady *or* fishy *or* not kosher about this business

2 *adv* **voir t.** to have blurred vision, to see things through a mist *or* haze; **tu ne me reconnais pas? tu vois t.?** is there something wrong with your eyes that you don't recognize me?; **je commence à voir t.** things are beginning to look fuzzy

trouble[2] *nm* (**a**) (*confusion*) confusion, disorder; **jeter le t. dans une famille** to cause trouble in a family; **c'est une cause de t. dans notre ménage** it causes trouble between us, it's a bone of contention

(**b**) (*agitation*) agitation, uneasiness; (*gêne*) confusion, embarrassment; (*amoureux*) agitation; **semer** *ou* **jeter le t. dans l'esprit de qn** to perturb sb

(**c**) **troubles** (public) disturbances, unrest; **fauteur de troubles** agitator, troublemaker; **période de troubles** period of unrest; **troubles sociaux** social unrest

(**d**) *Méd* **troubles** disorder; **troubles de digestion/de vision/respiratoires** digestive/eye/respiratory disorder *or F* problems; **troubles affectifs** emotional disturbance

(**e**) *Jur* **t. de jouissance** disturbance of possession

trouble-fête *nm inv* spoilsport, wet blanket, killjoy, *Am* party-pooper; **jouer les t.** to be a spoilsport *or* wet blanket, to spoil the fun

troubler [truble] **1** *vt* (**a**) (*liquide*) to make cloudy; *Fig* (*esprit*) to cloud; (*yeux, horizon*) to dim

(**b**) (*sommeil, silence etc*) to disturb; (*réunion, soirée*) to disrupt; (*opération, projets, activités*) to interfere with, to disrupt; (*progrès*) to impede; (*bonheur*) to spoil, to mar; (*digestion*) to upset; **période troublée par la guerre** period disrupted by war; **un vent léger troubla l'eau** a slight wind ruffled the water; **t. le repos** *ou* **l'ordre public** to create a disturbance; *Jur* to disturb the peace, to create a disturbance; **l'ordre public n'a été nullement troublé** there has been no breach of the peace; **imagination troublée** disturbed imagination

(c) (*personne*) to disturb, to make uneasy; (*gêner*) to confuse; **ce qui me trouble dans cette affaire** what bothers *or* disturbs me about this matter

(d) (*sensuellement*) (*personne*) to disturb, to excite, to thrill; (*sens, émotions*) to stir

(e) (*émouvoir*) to move

(f) *Jur* **t. qn dans la jouissance d'un bien** to disturb sb's enjoyment of possession

2 se troubler *vpr* **(a)** (*du vin etc*) to get cloudy; (*du ciel*) to become overcast; (*d'une vision*) to become blurred; (*de la voix*) to break (with emotion)

(b) (*se déconcerter*) to become confused *or* flustered; **sans se t.** (*répondre etc*) unruffled, without turning a hair; **elle se trouble facilement** she is easily flustered, she gets flustered easily

trouée [true] *nf* gap, opening (**de** in); **une t. de ciel bleu** a patch of blue sky

trouer [true] **1** *vt* (*mur etc*) to make a hole/holes in; (*lignes ennemies etc*) to breach; (*vêtement*) to wear *or* make a hole in; *Tech* (*zinc etc*) to perforate; **avoir les bas troués** to have holes in one's stockings; **être troué** (*de la coque d'un navire*) to be holed; **t. les nuages** (*du soleil*) to break through (the clouds); **des immeubles troués par des bombes** buildings pockmarked with shell holes; *Arg* **se faire t. la peau** to get shot, to be pumped full of lead **2 se trouer** *vpr* (*d'une chaussette etc*) to get a hole/holes

troufignon [trufiɲɔ̃] *nm Arg* (*anus*) arsehole, *Am* asshole; (*derrière*) arse, *Am* ass

troufion [trufjɔ̃] *nm Arg* soldier, private, *US* grunt

trouillard, -arde [trujar, -ard] *Arg* **1** *adj* yellow-bellied, chicken, cowardly; **je n'aime pas les types trouillards** I don't like yellow-bellies *or* cowards **2** *n* yellow-belly, chicken, coward

trouille [truj] *nf F* (*peur*) **avoir la t.** to be petrified, to be scared stiff; **je n'ai jamais eu une telle t. de ma vie** I've never been so petrified in my life; **au dernier moment, j'ai eu la t.** I got the wind up at the last minute; **donner** *ou* **ficher** *ou* **flanquer la t. à qn** to put the wind up sb; **tu n'as pas la t.!** you've got a nerve!

trouillomètre [trujɔmɛtr] *nm Arg* **avoir le t. à zéro** to be scared stiff *or* witless, to be petrified

troupe [trup] *nf* **(a)** (*de personnes*) troop, band, group; (*de brigands etc*) gang, set; (*de scouts*) troop **(b)** *Th* **t. (de théâtre** *ou* **de comédiens)** company, troupe; **t. d'amateurs** amateur company *or* troupe **(c)** (*d'éléphants*) herd; (*de lions*) pride; (*d'oiseaux*) flock; **ces animaux vivent en t.** these animals live in herds *or* are gregarious **(d)** *Mil* troop; **troupes** (*armée*) troops, forces; **officier de t.** regimental officer; **officiers et t.** officers and men *or* and other ranks; *Vieilli* **enfant de t.** army child *or F* brat; **cigarettes de t.** army issue cigarettes; *F* **en route, mauvaise t.!** come on, let's get moving!

troupeau, -aux [trupo] *nm* (*de bétail, de girafes etc*) herd; (*de moutons*) flock; (*d'oies*) gaggle, flock; (*de gens*) flock, *Péj* horde, gaggle, herd

troupier [trupje] **1** *adj* **comique t.** (*chanson, blague*) music-hall; **du comique t.** music-hall comedy **2** *nm Mil F* private, soldier; **jurer comme un t.** to swear like a trooper, *Br Sl* to eff and blind

troussage [trusaʒ] *nm Culin* (*de volaille*) trussing

trousse [trus] *nf* **(a) être aux trousses de qn** to be after *or* chasing sb, to be (hot) on sb's heels; **il avait la police aux trousses** he had the police after him *or* chasing him *or* (hot) on his heels; **comme s'il avait le feu aux trousses** *ou* **le diable à ses trousses** like a bat out of hell **(b)** (*étui*) kit; (*de médecin*) instrument case; **t. de toilette** toilet *or* sponge bag; **t. d'écolier** pencil case; **t. à ongles** manicure kit; **t. de premiers soins** *ou* **de secours** first-aid kit; **t. à outils** tool kit

troussé [truse] *adj F* **bien t.** (*objet, compliment*) neat

trousseau, -eaux [truso] *nm* **(a)** (*de clés*) bunch **(b)** (*de fiancée*) trousseau, bottom drawer, *US* hope chest **(c)** (*de pensionnaire*) clothes, outfit

trousser [truse] *vt* **(a)** *Culin* (*volaille*) to truss **(b)** *F* (*faire rapidement*) (*travail, repas, affaire*) to polish off, to make short work of; **t. un compliment à qn** to pay sb a neat compliment **(c)** *Vieilli* (*retrousser*) (*jupe etc*) to tuck up; *F* **t. une fille** to tumble a girl

trousseur [trusœr] *nm F Vieilli* **t. de jupons** womanizer, skirt chaser

trouvaille [truvaj] *nf* **(a)** (*chose trouvée*) (lucky) find; **une excellente t.** a great find **(b)** (*bonne idée*) brainwave

trouver [truve] **1** *vt* **(a)** (*en cherchant*) (*personne, objet*) to find; **je ne trouve pas mes clefs** I can't find my keys; **il ne trouve plus ses lunettes** he can't find his glasses, he's lost his glasses; **où est-ce qu'on trouve cela?** where can you get it?; **on le trouve au bar, à cette heure-là** you can find him in the bar at this time; **aller t. qn** to go and see sb; **je n'ai pas trouvé le temps de le faire** I didn't find time to do it, I didn't get round to it; **il n'a pas trouvé les mots pour le dire** he couldn't find the words; *Ordinat* **t. et remplacer** to find and replace; **il trouve du plaisir à lire** he takes *or* finds pleasure in reading, he enjoys reading; **elle trouve un malin plaisir à me faire attendre** she takes malicious pleasure in making me wait; **il va bien t. quelque chose à redire** he's sure to have something to say

(b) (*découvrir, inventer*) (*solution, moyen, compromis, arrangement*) to find, to come up with; (*procédé*) to discover, to invent, to come up with; (*erreur*) to find; **c'est bien trouvé!** good idea!; **exemple bien/mal trouvé** well-/badly chosen example; **je me demande où il est allé t. ça** I wonder where he got that idea from; *Iron* **tu as trouvé ça tout seul?** did you think of that all on your own?

(c) t. (par hasard) to find (by chance), to discover, to come upon, to come across; (*idée, méthode*) to hit on; **on l'a trouvé mort** he was found dead; **t. qn en faute** to catch sb out; **t. porte close** to find nobody home; **que je ne te trouve pas en train de fouiller dans mes affaires** don't let me find *or* catch you rummaging about in my things; **bureau des objets trouvés** lost-property office; *Fig* **il a trouvé à qui parler** he has met his match; **il trouva la mort à l'âge de 35 ans/dans un accident de voiture** he died *or Fml* met his death at the age of 35/in a car accident; **il trouva la mort bêtement** he died a stupid death

(d) (*juger*) to find; (*penser*) to think; **je la trouve jolie** I think she's pretty, I find *or* consider her pretty; **vous trouvez?** do you think so?; **comment as-tu trouvé ce livre?** how did you find *or* like the book?; **je la trouve mauvaise** *ou* **saumâtre** (*action*) I think it's a bit much *or* a bit thick; **il trouve bon/mauvais de vous en parler** he thinks it's a good/bad idea to talk to you about it; **je trouve mieux de ne pas ...** I think it's better not to ...; **je lui trouve du charme/mauvaise mine** I think he has charm/looks ill; **je ne trouve aucun intérêt à le refaire** I don't think there's any point in doing it again; **qu'est-ce qu'elle lui trouve?** what does she see in him?; **je trouve que ...** I think (that) ...; **t. le temps long** to find *or* feel that the time is dragging

(e) (*obtenir*) (*travail, mari, maison etc*) to find, to get; **t. le sommeil** to get to sleep

2 se trouver *vpr* **(a)** (*dans une situation*) to be, to find oneself; (*d'un objet*) to be; (*sentir*) to feel; **ces plantes se trouvent partout** these plants can be found everywhere; **ça ne se trouve pas partout** you can't get it just anywhere; **je me trouve très bien ici** I'm very comfortable here; **comment vous êtes-vous trouvé de ce traitement?** how did the treatment work?; **à ce moment-là, je me suis trouvé bien bête** at that moment I felt really stupid; **je me trouve trop grosse** I think I'm too fat; **se t. bien de qch/d'avoir fait qch** to feel all the better for sth/for having done sth; **je me trouve mieux** I feel better; **elle se trouve mal** she feels faint

(b) (*arriver*) to happen, to turn out; **je me trouve avoir** *ou* **il se trouve que j'ai une heure de libre** I happen to have *or* it so happens *or* it turns out that I have an hour to spare; **la dame se trouva être sa propre femme** the lady turned out to be his own wife; *F* **si cela** *ou* **ça se trouve, il est déjà rentré** maybe he's back, with a bit of luck he might be back

(c) (*se réaliser*) to find oneself

trouvère [truvɛr] *nm Hist, Littér* trouvère

troyen[1] [trwajɛ̃, -ɛn] **1** *adj* (*de Troie*) Trojan **2** *n* **T.** Trojan

troyen[2] **1** *adj* (*de Troyes*) of/from Troyes **2** *n* **T.** (*natif*) native of Troyes; (*habitant*) inhabitant of Troyes

truand, -ande [tryɑ̃, -ɑ̃d] *n* **(a)** *F* (*escroc*) crook; (*gangster*) gangster, hood **(b)** *Arch* (*mendiant*) beggar

truander [tryɑ̃de] *F* **1** *vt* (*qn*) to swindle, to do; (*faire payer trop cher*) to rip off; **se faire t.** to be swindled *or* done; (*payer trop cher*) to get ripped off **2** *vi* to cheat (**à un examen** in an exam)

trublion [tryblijɔ̃] *nm* troublemaker

truc[1] [tryk] *nm F* **(a)** (*moyen*) trick; **il y a un t.!** there's a trick in it!; **un t. pour enlever les taches** a trick for *or* a clever way of removing stains; **connaître les trucs du métier** to know the tricks of the trade; **c'est un t. qu'il faut connaître** there's a trick *or* a knack to it; *Th* **pièce à trucs** play with elaborate stage effects

(b) (*personne*) **machin t. (chouette)** thingumajig, what's-his-name, *f* what's-her-name

(c) (*chose*) thing; (*machin*) thingumajig, thingummy, thingy; **qu'est-ce que c'est que ce t.-là?** what's that (thingumajig)?; **des trucs comme ça** things like that; **elle a encore acheté des trucs** she's been shopping again; **je voudrais lui offrir un petit t.** I'd like to give him a little something; **il faudrait que tu me dises un t. ...** tell me something ...

(d) **la montagne/la cuisine/le droit c'est vraiment son t.** he's really into mountain climbing/cooking/the law; **ce n'est pas son t.** it's not his thing *or* bag, he's not into that

truc² *nm Rail* truck, *Am* freight car

trucage [trykaʒ] *nm* (a) *Cin* special effect; **c'est du t.** it's all faked (b) (*d'une photographie*) faking; (*d'un match, une élection etc*) fixing, rigging; (*de comptes*) window-dressing

truchement [tryʃmɑ̃] *nm* (a) (*intermédiaire*) **par le t. de ...** through ... (b) *Arch* (*interprète*) interpreter

trucider [tryside] *vt F* (*tuer*) to bump off; **je vais me faire t. s'il l'apprend** I'm going to end up dead if he finds out

truck [tryk] *nm Rail* truck, *Am* freight car

truckman [trykman], *pl* **truckmen** [trykmɛn] *nm TV, Cin* special effects person *or* engineer

trucmuche [trykmyʃ] *nm F* (a) (*chose*) thingumajig, thingummy, thingy (b) **T.** (*personne*) thingumajig, whosit, what's-his-name, *f* what's-her-name

truculence [trykylɑ̃s] *nf* (*pittoresque*) (*d'un personnage, du langage*) colourfulness, *US* colorfulness; (*verdeur*) raciness

truculent [trykylɑ̃] *adj* (*pittoresque*) (*personnage*) colourful, *US* colorful, larger than life; (*cru*) (*langage, personnage*) racy

truelle [tryɛl] *nf* (a) (*outil*) trowel (b) *Culin* **t. à poisson** fish slice

truffe [tryf] *nf* (a) (*champignon*) truffle; **omelette aux truffes** truffle omelet(te) (b) (*au chocolat*) truffle (c) (*nez*) (*d'un chien*) nose; *Arg* (*d'une personne*) conk

truffer [tryfe] *vt* (a) *Culin* (*dinde*) to garnish with truffles; **poularde truffée** truffled chicken (b) *Fig* **truffé de** (*balles, fautes, inexactitudes*) riddled with; (*citations*) peppered with

truffier, -ière [tryfje, -jɛr] *adj* (*sol*) truffle(-producing); **chien t.** truffle hound

truie [trɥi] *nf* sow

truisme [tryism] *nm* truism

truite [trɥit] *nf* [①A12,1,g] trout; **t. de rivière** brown trout; **t. arc-en-ciel** rainbow trout; *Culin* **t. meunière** = trout sautéed in butter and served with parsley and lemon juice; **t. au bleu** = trout poached in a vinegar-flavoured broth

truité [trɥite] *adj* speckled; (*chien, cheval*) spotted; (*poterie*) crackled

trumeau, -eaux [trymo] *nm* (a) *Archit* pier (b) (*miroir*) pier glass (c) *Culin* leg of beef

truquage [trykaʒ] *nm* = **trucage**

truquer [tryke] *vt* (a) (*photographie, expérience, données etc*) to fake, to rig; (*match, combat, élection etc*) to fix, to rig; *F* **t. les comptes** to cook the books, to window-dress the accounts; **t. les dés** to load the dice (b) *Cin* **scène truquée** scene with special effects (c) *Min* (*mine, minerai, échantillon*) to salt

truqueur, -euse [trykœr, -øz] *n* (a) (*qui triche*) cheat (b) *Cin* special effects person *or* generator

truquiste [trykist] *n Cin* special effects person *or* engineer

trust [trœst] *nm Fin, Com* trust; **t. de l'acier/du pétrole** steel/oil cartel; **t. commercial** commercial monopoly; **t. industriel** industrial monopoly

truster [trœste] 1 *vt Fin, Com,* to monopolize, to form into a monopoly 2 *vi Com* to form a monopoly

tsar [tsar, dzar] *nm* tsar, czar

tsarévitch [tsarevitʃ, dz-] *nm* tsarevitch, czarevitch

tsarine [tsarin, dz-] *nf* tsarina, czarina

tsarisme [tsarism, dz-] *nm Hist* tsarism

tsariste [tsarist, dz-] *adj, n Hist* tsarist

tsé-tsé [tsetse] *nf inv Ent* tsetse (fly); *Hum* **tu t'es fait piquer par la mouche t.?** have you got sleeping sickness?

TSF [teɛsɛf] *nf Vieilli* (*abrév* **télégraphie sans fil**) **(poste de) TSF** wireless (set)

t-shirt, *pl* **t-shirts** [tiʃœrt] *nm* T-shirt, tee shirt

tsigane [tsigan] *adj, n* tzigane, Hungarian gypsy

tsunami [tsynami] *nm* tidal wave, tsunami

TSVP [teɛsvepe] (*abrév* **tournez s'il vous plaît**) PTO

TTC [tetese] (*abrév* **toutes taxes comprises**) inclusive of tax

TU [tey] *nm* (*abrév* **temps universel**) GMT

tu [ty] *pron pers* (a) [①A26,a; B17,1,b; B64,6] (*usual form of address to relations, close friends, children and animals*) you; **tu as raison** you are right; **qui es-tu?** who are you?; **être à tu et à toi** to be very friendly (**avec qn** with sb); **être à tu et à toi avec tout le monde** to be on first-name terms with everybody; **elle lui dit tu** she says 'tu' to him; **crois-tu?** do you think so?; *Arg* (*elided to* **t'** *before vowel or* **h** *mute*) **qu'est-ce que t'as?** what's up (with you)? (b) *Rel* thou; (*à Dieu*) Thou; *Bible* **tu ne tueras point** thou shalt not kill

tuant [tɥɑ̃] *adj F* (a) (*fatigant*) (*travail*) killing, back-breaking, exhausting; **elle fait un travail t.** she has an exhausting job (b) (*insupportable*) exasperating; **c'est t., ce bruit** this noise is sending me up the wall; **les enfants sont vraiment tuants aujourd'hui** the kids are being a real pain today

tub [tœb] *nm Vieilli* (*cuvette*) tub, bath; (*bain*) bath; **prendre un t.** to take *or* have a bath

tuba [tyba] *nm* (a) *Mus* tuba (b) (*de plongée*) snorkel

tubage [tybaʒ] *nm Constr, Min, Chir, Vét* tubing

tubaire [tybɛr] *adj Méd* tubal

tubard, -arde [tybar, -ard] *n Méd F* TB case

tube [tyb] *nm* (a) (*tuyau*) tube; (*de canalisation*) pipe; *Constr* **bâti en tubes d'acier** tubular-steel-frame; *Fig F* **à pleins tubes** at full blast; *Fig F* **il déconne à pleins tubes** he's off his rocker; **chaudière à tubes** tubular boiler

(b) (*de canon*) barrel

(c) *Chir, Vét* tube

(d) *Anat* tube, duct

(e) *Bot* (*de la corolle, du calice*) tube

(f) *Courses de chevaux Arg* (*indication*) tip

(g) *F* (*chanson, disque*) hit; *Th* (smash) hit, smash

(h) (*emballage*) (*de dentifrice, de peinture etc*) tube; **t. d'aspirine** = packet of aspirin; **t. de rouge à lèvres** (stick of) lipstick; **en t.** in a tube; **acheter de la mayonnaise en t.** to buy a tube of mayonnaise

(i) *Él, Électron* tube

▶ **tube**: **t. d'alimentation** feed pipe; **t. amplificateur** amplifier tube *or* valve; *Anat* **t. bronchique** bronchial tube; *Anat, Phys* **t. capillaire** capillary tube; *Min* **t. carrottier** core barrel; *Électron, Rad* **t. cathodique** cathode-ray tube; **t. de chaudière** boiler tube; **t. de condenseur** *ou* **à condensation** condenser tube; *Anat* **t. digestif** digestive tract, alimentary canal; *Aut* **t. de direction** steering column; *Ch* **t. pour dosage, t. doseur** measuring tube; *Aut* **t. d'échappement** exhaust pipe; **t. électronique** electron tube; *Ch* **t. à essai** test tube; **tubes d'exploitation** tubing; **t. à flamme** (*d'un moteur à réaction*) flame tube; **t. fluorescent** fluorescent tube; **t. à gaz** gas-filled tube *or* valve; **t. de graissage** oil duct *or* way; *Él* **t. guide-fils** (*sur un édifice*) race track, race way; *Naut* **t. lance-torpille(s)** torpedo tube; *Él* **t. au néon** neon tube; **t. de niveau d'eau** water-gauge column; **t. de Pitot** Pitot tube; **tubes de pompage** tubing; **t. raccord** pipe connection; **t. à vide** vacuum tube *or* valve

tubeless [tyblɛs] *adj* (*pneu*) tubeless

tuber [tybe] *vt Constr* (*puits de mine, puits*) to tube, to case; (*conduit d'air, puits*) to case

tubercule [tybɛrkyl] *nm* (a) *Bot* tuber (b) *Méd* tubercle

tuberculeux, -euse [tybɛrkylø, -øz] 1 *adj* (a) *Bot* (*racine*) tubercular (b) *Méd* tubercular 2 *n* tubercular patient, TB case

tuberculine [tybɛrkylin] *nf Méd* tuberculin

tuberculose [tybɛrkyloz] *nf Méd* tuberculosis, TB; **t. pulmonaire** pulmonary tuberculosis

tubéreux, -euse [tyberø, -øz] *Bot* 1 *adj* tuberous 2 *nf* **tubéreuse** tuberose

tubulaire [tybylɛr] *adj* tubular

tubulé [tybyle] *adj* (*cornue, fleur*) tubular

tubuleux, -euse [tybylø, -øz] *adj* tubulous

tubulure [tybylyr] *nf* (a) *Tech* (*ouverture*) tubulure, pipe(-run), neck; *Aut* manifold; **t. d'alimentation** *ou* **d'admission** intake manifold; *Aut* **t. d'admission** inlet pipe; *Aut* **t. d'échappement** exhaust pipe (b) (*tube*) pipe; (*ensemble de tubes*) piping, pipes

TUC [tyk] 1 *nmpl* (*abrév* **Travaux d'utilité collective**) = community service 2 *n F* (*employé(e)*) person doing community service

tue-mouches [tymuʃ] 1 *nm inv* (a) (*champignon*) fly agaric (b) (*tapette*) fly swatter; (*insecticide*) fly spray 2 *adj inv* **papier** *ou* **ruban t.** fly paper

tuer [tɥe] 1 *vt* (a) (*personne, animal, cultures, Tennis balle, Fig l'amour*) to kill; **t. qn d'un coup de couteau** *ou* **de poignard** to stab sb to death; **t. qn d'un coup de revolver** to shoot and kill sb (with a revolver); **c'est la solitude/le chagrin qui l'a tué** he died of loneliness/grief; **un coup à t. un bœuf** a blow to fell an ox; **il a reçu une gifle à t. un bœuf** he got an almighty slap, he got a slap that made his ears ring; **la route tue tous les ans** people die on the roads every year; **les tués et les blessés** the dead and wounded; **se faire t.** to get killed; **ils se firent t. en braves** they died like heroes; *Fig* **tu veux te faire t.!** you're asking for it!, you're taking your life in your hands!; *Fig* **cette musique va t. l'ambiance**

that music is going to kill the atmosphere stone dead *or* totally destroy the atmosphere; *Fig* **t. le temps** to kill time; *Fig* **l'habitude tue la passion** familiarity breeds contempt; *Fig* **t. qch dans l'œuf** to nip sth in the bud

(b) *Fig (épuiser)* **tous ces déplacements m'ont tué** I'm dead *or* done for after all that travelling; **ces escaliers me tuent** these stairs will be the death of me

(c) *Fig F (révolter)* **ça me tue d'entendre des conneries pareilles!** it really gets me when I hear such nonsense!; **ça m'a tué d'apprendre qu'il se remariait** *(sidéré)* I was staggered to hear that he was getting married again

2 se tuer *vpr* **(a)** *(se suicider)* to kill oneself, to commit suicide, *Br F* to top oneself

(b) *(mourir dans un accident etc)* to die, to get killed

(c) *(s'entre-tuer)* to kill one another

(d) *Fig* **se t. au travail** *ou* **à travailler/à force de boire** to work/drink oneself to death; **je me tue à vous le dire** I'm sick and tired of *or* sick to death telling you; **c'est ce que je me tue à vous dire** that's what I've been trying to tell you

tuerie [tyri] *nf* slaughter, butchery

tue-tête (à) [atytɛt] *adv* at the top of one's voice

tueur, -euse [tɥœr, -øz] **1** *adj (fauves, cellule)* killer **2** *n (assassin)* killer **3** *nm (dans un abattoir)* slaughterman

▶ **tueur**: **t. à gages** hired killer *or* assassin

tuf [tyf] *nm* **(a)** *Géol* **t. volcanique** tuff; *(calcaire)* tufa **(b)** *Fig Litt* bedrock, foundation

tuile [tɥil] *nf* **(a)** *Constr* (roof) tile; **toit en tuiles** tiled roof **(b)** *Culin* **tuiles aux amandes** almond biscuits **(c)** *F (malchance)* (piece of) bad luck, blow; **il lui est arrivé une (sale) t.** he's had a terrible blow *or* piece of bad luck; **j'ai peur qu'il lui arrive une t.** I'm worried that something will happen to him; **la t.!** what bad *or* rotten luck!

tuilerie [tɥilri] *nf* **(a)** *(fabrique)* tile works; *(four)* tile kiln **(b)** **les Tuileries** the Tuileries

tulipe [tylip] *nf* **(a)** *Bot* tulip **(b)** *(lampe)* tulip-shaped lamp; *(verre)* tulip glass **(c)** *Tech (d'une imprimante)* thimble

tulipier [tylipje] *nm Bot* tulip tree

tulle [tyl] *nm Tex* tulle, net (fabric); **t. de soie/de coton** silk/cotton tulle; **robe de t.** tulle dress; *Méd* **t. gras** = material used for dressing burns and wounds

tuméfaction [tymefaksjɔ̃] *nf Méd* swelling, *Spéc* tumefaction

tuméfier [tymefje] **1** *vt (articulations etc)* to cause to swell, *Spéc* to tumefy; **visage tuméfié** swollen face **2 se tuméfier** *vpr* to swell (up)

tumescence [tymesɑ̃s] *nf* swelling, *Spéc* tumescence

tumescent [tymesɑ̃] *adj* swelling, *Spéc* tumescent

tumeur [tymœr] *nf Méd* tumour, *US* tumor, growth; **t. bénigne/maligne** benign/malignant tumour; **une t. au cerveau** a brain tumour, a tumour on the brain

tumoral, -ale, -aux, -ales [tymɔral, -o] *adj* tumorous, tumoral

tumulaire [tymylɛr] *adj* **pierre t.** tombstone

tumulte [tymylt] *nm* uproar, commotion, hubbub, *Fml* tumult; *(d'applaudissements)* thunder; *(d'armes)* clash; *(de la politique, des passions)* turmoil; *(des affaires, de la ville)* hustle and bustle; **le t. au sujet de** the uproar *or* commotion about, the furore over; **provoquer un t.** to cause an uproar *or* a commotion; **dans le t.** in an uproar, in confusion; **il y eut des tumultes** there were riots

tumultueusement [tymyltɥøzmɑ̃] *adv* tumultuously

tumultueux, -euse [tymyltɥø, -øz] *adj (réunion, débat, séance, accueil etc)* noisy, tumultuous; *(rues)* noisy; *(vie, période etc)* tumultuous

tumulus, *pl* **tumulus** *ou* **tumuli** [tymylys, -li] *nm* barrow, *Spéc* tumulus

tuner [tjunœr, tynɛr] *nm Rad* tuner

tungstène [tœ̃kstɛn, tœ̃g-] *nm Métal* tungsten

tungstène-halogène *nm* tungsten-halogen

tunique [tynik] *nf* **(a)** *(vêtement)* tunic **(b)** *Biol (d'un organe)* tunic, envelope, membrane; *Bot (d'un bulbe)* coat

Tunisie [tynizi] *nf* Tunisia

tunisien, -ienne [tynizjɛ̃, -jɛn] **1** *adj* Tunisian **2** *n* **T.** Tunisian

tunnel [tynɛl] *nm* tunnel; **t. routier** road tunnel; **le t. sous la Manche** the Channel Tunnel, *F* the Chunnel; *Fig* **voir le bout du t.** to see the light at the end of the tunnel

▶ **tunnel**: *Av* **t. aérodynamique** wind tunnel

TUP [typ] *nm (abrév* **titre universel de paiement***)* universal payment order

tuque [tyk] *nf Can* tuque, *F* pompom hat, bobble cap

turban [tyrbɑ̃] *nm (coiffure)* turban

turbide [tyrbid] *adj (liquide etc)* cloudy, turbid

turbidité [tyrbidite] *nf* cloudiness, *Fml* turbidity

turbin [tyrbɛ̃] *nm F (travail)* grind, slog; *(emploi)* job; **toujours au t.?** still slogging away?

turbine [tyrbin] *nf* turbine; *(d'une pompe à eau)* impeller; **à t.** turbine-powered; **t. à air** air *or* wind turbine; **t. à eau, t. hydraulique** water turbine *or* wheel; **t. à gaz/à vapeur** gas/steam turbine; *MecE* **t. centrifuge** centrifugal blower; *MecE* **t. de ventilation** blower; *MecE* **t. moteur** power turbine

turbiner [tyrbine] *vi Arg (travailler)* to slog (away); *Scol* to swot

turbo [tyrbo] *F* **1** *nm (turbocompresseur), Ordinat* turbo **2** *adj* turbocharged

turbo-alternateur, *pl* **turbo-alternateurs** *nm Él* turbo-alternator

turbocompresseur [tyrbɔkɔ̃presœr] *nm Tech, Av* turbocompressor; *Aut* turbosupercharger, turbocharger

turbodiesel [tyrbodjezɛl] **1** *nm (moteur)* turbo diesel **2** *nf (voiture)* turbo diesel

turbo-mercatique *nf* turbomarketing

turbomoteur [tyrbomɔtœr] *nm* turbomotor, turboshaft engine

turbopompe [tyrbopɔ̃p] *nf* turbo pump, turbine pump

turbopropulseur [tyrboprɔpylsœr] *nm* turboprop(eller); **avion à t.** turboprop aircraft

turboréacteur [tyrboreaktœr] *nm* turbojet (engine)

turbot [tyrbo] *nm (poisson)* turbot

turbotière [tyrbɔtjɛr] *nf Culin (récipient)* = large dish for cooking flatfish

turbotrain [tyrbotrɛ̃] *nm Rail* turbotrain

turbulence [tyrbylɑ̃s] *nf Av* turbulence; *(d'un enfant)* boisterousness, noisiness; *(de la mer)* storminess, turbulence; *Av* **il y aura des turbulences** there will be some turbulence

turbulent [tyrbylɑ̃] *adj* **(a)** *Vieilli (population)* restless, unruly **(b)** *(enfant, classe)* boisterous, noisy; *(mer, Fig relation, période)* stormy, turbulent **(c)** *Phys* **régime t.** turbulent flow

turc, turque [tyrk] **1** *adj* Turkish; **café t.** Turkish coffee; **être assis à la turque** to be sitting cross-legged; **W.-C.** *ou* **cabinets à la turque** hole in the ground **2** *nm Ling* Turkish **3** *n* **T.** Turk; *Pol* **jeune T.** Young Turk; *F* **fort comme un T.** as strong as an ox; *Fig* **tête de T.** whipping-boy

turf [tœrf, tyrf] *nm* **(a)** *(terrain)* racecourse **(b)** **le t.** *(activité)* racing; **habitué du t.** racegoer **(c)** *Arg (travail)* work

turfiste [tœrfist, tyr-] *n* racegoer

turgescence [tyrʒesɑ̃s] *nf Méd, Bot* turgescence

turgescent [tyrʒesɑ̃] *adj* turgescent

turgide [tyrʒid] *adj Litt* turgid, swollen

turista [turista] *nf Méd F* holiday tummy, *Am* turista; **attraper la t.** to get holiday tummy *or* turista

turlupiner [tyrlypine] *vt F* to worry, to bother

turluter [tyrlyte] *vi Can F* to trill, to sing tra-la-la

turlututu [tyrlytyty] *int (pour refuser, se moquer gentiment, interrompre)* fiddlesticks!; **t. chapeau pointu!** yah boo, sucks to you!

turne [tyrn] *nf* **(a)** *Arg Péj (chambre, maison)* dump, hole **(b)** *Scol Arg* (student's) room

turnep(s) [tyrnɛp(s)] *nm Agr* kohlrabi

turnover [tœrnɔvɛr, -œr] *nm* turnover

turpitude [tyrpityd] *nf* **(a)** *(caractère)* vileness, moral turpitude **(b)** *(action)* vile act **(c)** *(parole)* vile remark

turque [turk] *adj, nf voir* **turc**

turquerie [tyrk(ə)ri] *nf* work of art in an Oriental style

Turquie [tyrki] *nf* Turkey; **tapis de T.** Turkish carpet

turquoise [tyrkwaz] **1** *nf (pierre)* turquoise **2** *adj inv, nm inv (couleur)* turquoise (blue)

tussor(e) [tysɔr] *nm Tex* tussore (silk)

tutélaire [tyteler] *adj (divinité)* tutelary; *Jur* **gestion t.** guardianship; **puissance t.** power of guardianship

tutelle [tytɛl] *nf* **(a)** *Jur* guardianship; **enfant en t.** child under guardianship; **t. administrative** administrative supervision *(established over mismanaged public body)*; *Pol* **territoires sous t.** trust territories **(b)** *(protection)* protection; **sous la t. de** *(famille, loi etc)* under the protection of; **prendre qn sous sa t.** to take sb under one's wing

tuteur, -trice [tytœr, -tris] **1** *n* **(a)** *Jur* guardian; **t. légal** legal guardian **(b)** *(protecteur)* protector **2** *nm (pour plante)* support, stake; **mettre un t. à une plante** to stake a plant

tutoiement [tytwamɑ̃] *nm* use of the familiar 'tu' *(instead of the more formal 'vous')*; **le t. est de rigueur** everybody says 'tu' to each other

tutoyer [tytwaje] **(je tutoie, n. tutoyons; je tutoierai) 1** *vt* **t. qn** to address sb as 'tu', = to be on familiar terms with sb **2 se tutoyer** *vpr* to address each other as 'tu', = to be on familiar terms (with each other)

tutti [tyti] *nm inv Mus* tutti

tutti frutti [tutifruti] *nm inv (glace)* tutti-frutti

tutti quanti [tutikwɑ̃ti] *nmpl* **et t.** etcetera, etcetera

tutu [tyty] *nm* tutu

tuyau, -aux [tɥijo] *nm* **(a)** *(canalisation etc)* pipe; *(flexible)*

tube; **t. d'eau/de gaz** water/gas pipe; **t. vertical, t. de chute** standpipe; **t. flexible** *ou* **en caoutchouc** rubber tube *or* tubing; **t. acoustique** speaking tube; *F Vieilli* **dire qch à qn dans le t. de l'oreille** to whisper sth in sb's ear
(b) (*d'une pipe*) stem
(c) (*du maïs, de l'herbe etc*) stalk
(d) (*pli*) flute, goffer, quill
(e) *F* (*conseil*) tip; (*donné à la police, un journaliste*) tip-off; **je vais te filer un t.** I'll give you a tip; **qui est-ce qui t'a donné le t.?** who tipped you off?, who put you on to it?; **un t. crevé** a rotten tip; **c'est un t. increvable** it's straight from the horse's mouth; **quelques tuyaux pour économiser l'énergie** a few tips *or* pointers on how to save energy; **avoir des tuyaux** to know the ropes
▶ **tuyau**: **t. d'arrosage** garden hose; **t. de cheminée** (chimney) flue; *Aut* **t. d'échappement** exhaust (pipe), tailpipe; *Aut* **t. d'essence** petrol pipe; **t. d'incendie** fire hose; *Mus* **t. d'orgue** organ pipe; **t. de poêle** stove *or* flue pipe; **en t. de poêle** (*pantalon*) drainpipe; (*chapeau*) stove pipe; *Aut* **t. de pression** pressure hose; *Aut* **t. de reniflard** breather pipe; *Aut* **t. de trop-plein** overflow pipe
tuyautage [tɥijotaʒ] *nm* **(a)** (*d'un tissu*) fluting, goffering **(b)** *F* (*action de donner des conseils*) giving of tips
tuyauter [tɥijote] *vt* **(a)** (*un tissu*) to flute, to goffer; **fer à t.** goffering tongs **(b)** *F* (*conseiller*) **t. qn** to give sb a tip; (*le mettre au courant*) to tip sb off, to put sb in the know (**sur** about)
tuyauterie [tɥijotri] *nf* (*tuyaux*) piping, pipes; *Aut* **t. de carburant** fuel pipe *or* line; *Aut* **t. de frein** brake pipe *or* line
tuyauteur, -euse [tɥijotœr, -øz] *n F* tipster
tuyère [tɥijer] *nf Tech, Métal* nozzle; *Av etc* **t. d'échappement** jet pipe; **t. de propulsion** thrust nozzle
TV [teve] *nf* (*abrév* **télévision**) TV
TVA [tevea] *nf* (*abrév* **taxe à la valeur ajoutée**) VAT; **exempt de T.** zero-rated; **T. encaissée** output tax; **T. récupérée** input tax
TVHD [teveaʃde] *nf* (*abrév* **télévision haute définition**) HDTV
tweed [twid] *nm Tex* tweed; **veste de t.** tweed jacket
twin-set, *pl* **twin-sets** [twinsɛt] *nm* matching sweater and cardigan, *Br* twinset
twist [twist] *nm* (*danse*) twist
twister [twiste] *vi* to twist
tympan [tɛ̃pɑ̃] *nm* **(a)** *Anat* eardrum, *Spéc* tympanum; **bruit à briser** *ou* **crever** *ou* **déchirer** *ou* **rompre les tympans** ear-splitting noise **(b)** *Archit* tympanum **(c)** *Tech* (*mounted on shaft*) pinion
tympanal, -ale, -aux, -ales [tɛ̃panal, -o] *adj, nm Anat* (**os**) **t.** tympanic bone
tympanique [tɛ̃panik] *adj Anat* of the ear, *Spéc* tympanic
tympanon [tɛ̃panɔ̃] *nm Mus* dulcimer
type [tip] *nm* **(a)** [①**A13**,3,a] (*modèle*) (*de travail, intervention etc*) type; (*chose ou personne typique*) classic example (**de** of); *Zool* type, *Spéc* phylum; *Biol* **genre t.** type genus; **arbre t.** sample tree; **t. de la beauté italienne** typical Italian beauty; **avoir le t. latin/nordique** to have Latin/Nordic looks; **elle est très sensible au t. italien** she really goes for Italian-looking men; **ce n'est pas du tout mon t.** (*il ne m'attire pas*) he's not at all my type; **c'est tout à fait mon t.** he's just my type (of man) *or* my sort of man, he's exactly the kind of man I find attractive; **c'est un problème t.** it's a typical problem, it's a standard type of problem; **c'est vraiment l'avare t.** he's a typical miser; **c'est vraiment l'Italienne t.** she's your typical Italian woman, she's typically Italian; **maison t.** show house; **motocyclette t.** motorbike of standard design; **c'est le t. même de la femme d'affaires** she is the classic example of a businesswoman, she is a *or* the typical businesswoman; **des ennuis techniques (du) t. (de la) panne** breakdown problems
(b) *F* (*bonhomme*) guy, man, *Br* chap, bloke; **t'es un chic t.!** you're a good sort!; **un sale t.** a bastard; **un pauvre t.** a loser; **pauvre t.!** you're pathetic!
(c) *Typ* type; **t. de caractères** typeface
typé [tipe] *adj* typical; **il est bien** *ou* **très t.** he has all the characteristic features; **c'est un Portugais mais il n'est pas très t.** he's Portuguese but you wouldn't think so to look at him
typer [tipe] *vt Tech* to stamp, to mark
typesse [tipɛs] *nf Arg Péj Vieilli* (*femme, fille*) female
typhique [tifik] *Méd* **1** *adj* (*du typhus*) typhus; (*de la typhoïde*) typhoid **2** *n* typhus/typhoid sufferer
typhoïde [tifɔid] *adj, nf Méd* (**fièvre**) **t.** typhoid (fever)
typhoïdique [tifɔidik] *adj* typhoid, typhoidal; **bacille t.** typhoid bacillus
typhon [tifɔ̃] *nm Météo* typhoon
typhus [tifys] *nm Méd* typhus (fever); *Vét* **t. du chat** (infectious) feline gastroenteritis
typique [tipik] *adj* typical; **il a encore oublié, c'est t.** he's forgotten again, (it's) typical!
typiquement [tipikmɑ̃] *adv* typically
typo [tipo] *F* **1** *nf* = **typographie 2** *nm* = **typographe**
typographe [tipɔgraf] *n* typographer
typographie [tipɔgrafi] *nf* (*art, procédé*) typography, letterpress printing; (*présentation d'un texte*) typography
typographique [tipɔgrafik] *adj* typographic(al); **erreur t.** typographic(al) error, misprint, *F* typo
typographiquement [tipɔgrafikmɑ̃] *adv* typographically
typologie [tipɔlɔʒi] *nf* typology
typologique [tipɔlɔʒik] *adj* typological
typote [tipɔt] *nf F* = **typographe**
typothèque [tipɔtɛk] *nf Ordinat* type library
Tyr [tir] *n* Tyre
tyran [tirɑ̃] *nm Pol, Fig* tyrant; **se conduire en t.** to act like a tyrant *or* tyrannically; **arrête de jouer les tyrans** stop acting like a tyrant; **il est le t. de sa famille** he tyrannizes his family
tyranneau, -eaux [tirano] *nm Litt* petty tyrant
tyrannie [tirani] *nf Pol, Fig* tyranny; **exercer sa t. sur qn** to tyrannize sb; (*frère, sœur*) to bully sb
tyrannique [tiranik] *adj* tyrannical; **ne sois pas si t.** don't be such a tyrant; **il est t. avec elle** he bullies her
tyranniquement [tiranikmɑ̃] *adv* tyrannically, like a tyrant
tyranniser [tiranize] *vt* (*qn*) to tyrannize; (*frère, sœur*) to bully
tyrannosaure [tiranozɔr] *nm* tyrannosaurus
Tyrol (le) [lətirɔl] *nm* the Tyrol
tyrolien, -ienne [tirɔljɛ̃, -jɛn] **1** *adj* Tyrolean **2** *n* **T.** Tyrolean, Tyrolese **3** *nf Mus* **tyrolienne** Tyrolienne
tzar [tsar, dzar] *nm* tsar, czar
tzarévitch [tsarevitʃ, dz-] *nm* tsarevitch, czarevitch
tzarine [tsarin, dz-] *nf* tsarina, czarina
tzigane [tsigan, dz-] *adj, n* tzigane, Hungarian gypsy

U

U, u [y] *nm* **(a)** (*lettre*) U, u; **fer en U** channel iron; *Géog* **vallée (à profil) en U** U-shaped valley; **tables (disposées) en U** tables arranged in a horseshoe **(b)** *Univ F* (= *universitaire*) **resto U** student refectory; **cité U** student residence, hall(s) of residence
UAS [yaɛs] *nf Com* (*abrév* **unité d'activité stratégique**) SBU
ubac [ybak] *nm* = shady side of an Alpine mountain, *Spéc* ubac
ubiquité [ybikɥite] *nf* ubiquity; **avoir le don d'u.** to have the ability to be in several places at the same time; **je n'ai pas le don d'u.** I can't be in two places at the same time
ubuesque [ybyɛsk] *adj* Ubuesque
UE [yə] *nf* (*abrév* **Union européenne**) EU
UER [yəɛr] *nf Univ Vieilli* (*abrév* **unité d'enseignement et de recherche**) = university department
ufologie [yfɔlɔʒi] *nf* ufology
UFR [yɛfɛr] *nf Univ* (*abrév* **unité de formation et de recherche**) = university department
UHF [yaʃɛf] *Rad* (*abrév* **ultra-haute fréquence**) UHF
UHT [yaʃte] (*abrév* **ultra-haute température**) UHT
ukase [ykaz] *nm Hist* ukase; *Fig* **u. paternel** paternal fiat
ukrainien, -ienne [ykrɛnjɛ̃, -jɛn] **1** *adj* Ukranian **2** *nm Ling* Ukranian **3** *n* **U.** Ukranian
ukulélé [jukulele] *nm* ukelele
ulcération [ylserasjɔ̃] *nf Méd* ulceration
ulcère [ylsɛr] *nm* ulcer; **avoir un u. à l'estomac** to have a stomach ulcer
ulcéré [ylsere] *adj* **(a)** *Méd* ulcerated **(b)** *Fig* **elle en était ulcérée** it rankled with her
ulcérer [ylsere] (*pr ind* **il ulcère**; *fu* **il ulcérera**) **1** *vt* **(a)** *Méd* to ulcerate **(b)** *Fig* **u. qn** to cause resentment in sb, to embitter sb; **sa réaction m'a ulcéré** I resented his reaction, his reaction rankled with me **2 s'ulcérer** *vpr Méd* to ulcerate, to fester
ulcéreux, -euse [ylserø, -øz] *adj Méd* ulcerous; (*plaie*) ulcerated, festering
ULM [yɛlɛm] *nm inv Av* (*abrév* **ultraléger motorisé**) microlight
ulmaire [ylmɛr] *nf Bot* meadowsweet
ulnaire [ylnɛr] *adj Anat* ulnar
ultérieur [ylterjœr] *adj* later, subsequent (**à** to); (*nouvelles, date etc*) later; (*dans le futur*) future; **notre voyage est remis à une date ultérieure** our trip has been postponed; **la parution de ce livre est ultérieure à celle du vôtre** this book came out after yours did
ultérieurement [ylterjœrmɑ̃] *adv* later (on), subsequently
ultimatum [yltimatɔm] *nm* ultimatum; **adresser un u. à un pays** to present a country with an ultimatum
ultime [yltim] *adj* (*paroles, moment, phénomène*) (very) last; (*préparatifs*) final; **l'u. sacrifice** the ultimate sacrifice
ultimo [yltimo] *adv* lastly, finally
ultra [yltra] *n Pol* extremist
ultra-chic *adj F* ultra-fashionable
ultra-confidentiel, -elle *adj* top-secret
ultra-conservateur, -trice *adj Pol* ultra-conservative, far right
ultra-court *adj* (*jupe*) ultra-short, microscopic; *Phys* **ondes ultra-courtes** ultra-short waves
ultrafin [yltrafɛ̃] *adj* (*filament, aiguille*) extra-fine
ultra-haute fréquence *nf Phys* ultrahigh frequency
ultraléger, -ère [yltraleʒe, -ɛr] **1** *adj* ultralight **2** *nm* microlight **3** *nf* (*cigarette*) superlight, ultra low
ultralibéralisme [yltraliberalism] *nm* extreme liberalism
ultramicroscope [yltramikrɔskɔp] *nm* ultra-microscope
ultramoderne [yltramɔdɛrn] *adj* (*équipement, voiture, intérieur*) ultramodern, state-of-the-art, high-tech; (*appartement*) ultramodern, high-tech
ultramontain, -aine [yltramɔ̃tɛ̃, -ɛn] **1** *adj* **(a)** *Rel, Pol* ultramontane **(b)** (*par rapport à la France*) beyond the Alps **2** *n Rel, Pol* ultramontanist
ultrarapide [yltrarapid] *adj* (*avion, train, voiture*) ultrafast
ultra(-)royaliste, *pl* **ultra(-)royalistes** *adj, n Hist* ultraroyalist
ultra(-)sensible *adj* ultra-sensitive; **pellicule/film u.** ultra-sensitive *or* high-speed film; *F* **elle est u.** she's hyper-sensitive
ultra(-)son *nm Phys* ultrasound; **ultra(-)sons** ultrasonic waves; **science des ultra(-)sons** ultrasonics
ultrasonique [yltrasɔnik], **ultrasonore** [yltrasɔnɔr] *adj* ultrasonic, supersonic
ultra(-)violet, -ette *adj, nm* ultraviolet; **faire une séance d'ultraviolets** to have a session on a sunbed
ululation [ylylasjɔ̃] *nf,* **ululement** [ylylmɑ̃] *nm* ululation; (*des oiseaux de nuit*) hooting
ululer [ylyle] *vi* to ululate; (*des oiseaux de nuit*) to hoot
Ulysse [ylis] *nm* Ulysses
un, une [œ̃, yn] **1** *adj* **(a)** one; **pourrais-tu me prêter un franc?** could you lend me a franc?; **tu n'aurais pas une pièce d'un franc?** you wouldn't happen to have a one-franc piece?; **deux brioches et un pain** two buns and a loaf (of bread); **il n'en reste qu'un** there's only one left; **il vient un jour sur deux** he comes every other *or* second day; **une personne/une maison sur cent** one person/house in a hundred; **un à un** [œ̃aœ̃], **un par un** one by one, one at a time; **il est une heure** it's one o'clock; **page un(e)** page one, the first page; **numéro un** number one

(b) (*uni*) one; **Dieu est un** God is one; **c'est tout un** [sɛtutœ̃] it's the same thing *or* all one *or* all the same; **ils ne font qu'un** (*ils sont très proches*) they are as one; **la maison et l'atelier ne font qu'un** the house and workshop are one and the same

2 *n* **(a)** (*chiffre*) one; **un et un** [œ̃eœ̃] **font deux** one and one are two; **un(e), deux, trois, partez!** one, two, three, go!; **il n'a fait ni une ni deux** he didn't hesitate (for a moment); **et d'un(e) tu es toujours en retard, et de deux tu mens** for one thing you're always late and for another you're lying, one, you're always late and two, you're lying; *F* **en savoir plus d'une** to know a thing or two; *F* **il était moins une** it was a close thing *or* a close shave; **heureusement que je suis arrivé, il était moins une** it was lucky I arrived when I did, another minute and it would have been too late

(b) (*première page*) *Journ* **la une** [layn] (*d'un journal*) the front page, page one; **faire la une** (*d'un magazine*) to appear on *or* make the front cover; (*d'un journal*) to appear on *or* make the front page; *Fig* (*faire parler de soi*) to make *or* hit the headlines; **la guerre fait la une** the war is front-page news *or* in the headlines; **tu es à la une des journaux** you've made the front page, you're front-page news *or* in the headlines

3 *pron* one; **un de ces jours** one of these days; **un qui a de la chance** a lucky one, a lucky man; **un qui a de la chance, c'est Pierre, il est parti à la Réunion** Pierre's one of the lucky ones, he's gone off to la Réunion; **en voilà une qui sait ce qu'elle veut!** there's somebody who knows what she wants!; **un que je plains, c'est ...** one person I do feel sorry for is ...; **il n'y en a pas un qui parle anglais** not one of them speaks English; *F* **pas un n'était au courant** not a (single solitary) soul *or* absolutely nobody knew about it; *F* **être menteur/hypocrite comme pas un** to be a dreadful liar/hypocrite; *F* **il fait du bruit comme pas un** he's unbelievably noisy; *F* **il danse comme pas un** he's a great dancer; **(l')un de nous, (l')un d'entre nous** one of us; **ni l'un ni l'autre** neither (of them), neither one nor the other; **ni l'un ni l'autre ne me plaît** I don't like either of them; **l'un dans l'autre** all in all, by and large; **(l')un des danseurs les plus célèbres du monde** one of the most famous dancers in the world; **l'une des voitures les plus vendues d'Europe** one of the biggest selling cars in Europe; **les uns disent que ...** some say that ...; **les uns et les autres** people, everybody

4 *art indéf* [①**A4-5**,2; **B4-5**,**B**] (*pl* **des**, *see* **de**) **(a)** a; (*devant voyelle ou h muet*) an; (*pl some*) **un jour/une pomme/une heure** a day/an apple/an hour; **un père et une mère** a father and mother; **un père de famille** the father of a family; **il est là pour un certain temps** he is here for some time; **cela ne durera qu'un temps** it won't last for long; **venez me voir un**

lundi come and see me one Monday *or* some Monday; **cela tombe un mardi** it falls on a Tuesday; **un jour de la semaine dernière** one day last week; *F* **un de ces quatre** one of these days; **pour une raison ou pour une autre** for some reason or other

(b) (*introduisant un nom propre*) a; (*devant voyelle ou h muet*) an; **c'est une Martin** she's a Martin, she's one of the Martins; **ce sera un Einstein** he'll be another Einstein

(c) (*intensif*) **j'ai eu un monde aujourd'hui!** I've had such a lot of visitors today!; **il y a un de ces mondes en ville!** the town is incredibly busy, there are an incredible lot of people in town; **elle parle avec une élégance!** she has such an elegant way of putting things; **il est d'une bêtise!** he is incredibly *or* so stupid!; **il a fait une de ces têtes!** you should have seen his face; **elle a poussé un de ces cris** she gave such a shout; **tu m'as fait une peur!** you gave me such a fright!, you did give me a fright!

unanime [ynanim] *adj* (*approbation, vote etc*) unanimous; **ils sont unanimes à vous accuser** they are unanimous in accusing you

unanimement [ynanimmɑ̃] *adv* unanimously

unanimité [ynanimite] *nf* (*d'une réponse, une réaction etc*) unanimity; **à l'u.** unanimously; **faire l'u.** (*d'une proposition, une invitation etc*) to be accepted unanimously

underground [œndœrgrawnd] *adj, nm* underground

une [yn] *voir* **un**

UNEF [ynɛf] *nf Univ* (*abrév* **Union nationale des étudiants de France**) *Br* ≈ NUS

Unesco [ynɛsko] *nf* Unesco

unguéal, -ale, -aux, -ales [ɛ̃gɥeal, -o] *adj* (of the) nail; **infection unguéale** nail infection, infection of the nail

uni [yni] **1** *adj* **(a)** (*famille, couple etc*) united; **ils sont très unis** they are very close **(b)** (*sans irregularité*) (*sol, surface etc*) smooth, level, even; (*mer etc*) smooth, calm, unruffled **(c)** (*couleur*) plain; (*tissu, robe*) self-coloured, *US* self-colored **2** *nm Tex* self-coloured *or US* self-colored material

uniate [ynjat] *adj, n Rel* Uniat(e)

unicellulaire [yniselylɛr] *adj Biol* unicellular

unicité [ynisite] *nf Phil etc* uniqueness

unicolore [ynikɔlɔr] *adj* (*tissu etc*) self-coloured *or US* -colored, plain

unicorne [ynikɔrn] **1** *nm Myth* unicorn **2** *adj* one-horned, single-horned

unidimensionnel, -elle [ynidimɑ̃sjɔnɛl] *adj* one-dimensional

unidirectionnel, -elle [ynidirɛksjɔnɛl] *adj* unidirectional

unième [ynjɛm] *adj* (*used only in compounds*) **trente et u.** thirty-first

unièmement [ynjɛmmɑ̃] *adv* (*used only in compounds*) **vingt et u.** in twenty-first place

unificateur, -trice [ynifikatœr, -tris] *adj* unifying

unification [ynifikasjɔ̃] *nf* (*d'un pays etc*) unification; (*des crédits*), *Pol* (*de la législation*) consolidation; (*des poids et mesures etc*) standardization

unifier [ynifje] *vt* (*impf, pr sub* **n. unifiions, v. unifiiez**) (*parti politique, pays etc*) to unify; (*crédits, législation*) to consolidate; (*poids et mesures etc*) to standardize

uniforme [ynifɔrm] **1** *adj* (*opinions, expression*) uniform; (*vie*) unchanging; (*allure, surface*) even; (*mouvement*) regular; **taux u.** (*d'un intérêt etc*) flat rate **2** *nm* uniform; *Mil* **grand u.** full-dress uniform; **endosser l'u.** to join the forces; **le prestige de l'u.** the appeal of the uniform; **elle est sensible au prestige de l'u.** she has a thing about men in uniform; **quitter l'u.** to leave the service

uniformément [ynifɔrmemɑ̃] *adv* (*réparti*) uniformly, evenly; (*avancer*) smoothly

uniformisation [ynifɔrmizasjɔ̃] *nf* standardization

uniformiser [ynifɔrmize] *vt* to standardize

uniformité [ynifɔrmite] *nf* (*d'un paysage*) sameness, uniformity; (*des habitudes, coutumes, de la vie etc*) monotony; (*de couleur, teinte*) uniformity

unijambiste [yniʒɑ̃bist] **1** *adj* one-legged **2** *n* one-legged person

unilatéral, -ale, -aux, -ales [ynilateral, -o] *adj* (*décision, désarmement etc*) unilateral; (*contrat, accord*) one-sided; **stationnement u.** parking on one side only

unilingue [ynilɛ̃g] *adj* (*dictionnaire, pays etc*) unilingual, monolingual

uniment [ynimɑ̃] *adv* evenly; *Litt* **tout u.** (*simplement*) plainly, simply

uninominal, -ale, -aux, -ales [yninɔminal, -o] *adj Pol* **scrutin u.** voting for a single member *or* for one member only

union [ynjɔ̃] *nf* **(a)** (*alliance*) union; **l'union du corps et de l'esprit** the union of mind and body **(b)** (*association*) (*de partis, consommateurs etc*) union, society, association **(c)** (*marriage*) marriage; **u. conjugale** marriage **(d)** (*accord, entente*) unity, agreement; (*entre les membres d'une famille, un groupe d'amis*) closeness, unity; **resserrer l'u. entre deux personnes** to strengthen the links *or* bond between two people; *Prov* **l'u. fait la force** unity is strength, strength through unity

▶ **union**: **u. douanière** customs union; **u. économique** economic union; **U. européenne** European Union; **u. libre** (*pour un couple non marié*) cohabitation; **vivre en u. libre** to live together, *surtout Jur* to cohabit; **u. monétaire** monetary union; **u. monétaire à deux vitesses** two-speed monetary union; **U. Nationale des Étudiants de France** French National Union of Students; **u. patronale** employers' organization; **l'U. des républiques socialistes soviétiques** the Union of Soviet Socialist Republics; *Hist* **U. sacrée** = unity of all Frenchmen in the face of the enemy (*called for by Poincaré on the outbreak of the First World War*); **l'U. soviétique** the Soviet Union

unionisme [ynjɔnism] *nm Pol* unionist movement

unioniste [ynjɔnist] *adj, n* unionist

unipare [ynipar] *adj Biol* uniparous

unipersonnel, -elle [ynipɛrsɔnɛl] *adj Gram* (*verbe*) impersonal

unipolaire [ynipɔlɛr] *adj Él* (*interrupteur etc*) unipolar, single-pole; *Biol* (*cellule, neurone etc*) unipolar

unique [ynik] *adj* **(a)** (*seul*) (*fils, tasse*) only; (*parti*) single; (*talent, savoir-faire, occasion, cas*) unique; **d'un même et u. problème** of one and the same problem; **c'est loin d'être un cas u.** it's far from being an isolated case; **il se croit u.** he thinks he's unique; **c'est vendu à un prix u. dans toute la France** it sells for the same price throughout France; **taille u.** one size; **c'est une taille u.** it only comes in the one size; **j'étais enfant u.** I was an only child; **(rue à) sens u.** one-way street; **c'est à sens u.** it's (a) one-way; **voie u.** single lane; **je possède l'exemplaire u.** I have the sole copy; **c'est un exemplaire u.** it's the only copy there is; **c'est une pièce de collection u. au monde** it's the only piece like it in the world; **c'est son u. souci** it's his sole *or* only concern; **c'est son u. sujet de conversation** it's all he ever talks about; **u. en son genre** one of a kind; **ce sont des gens uniques en leur genre** there's nobody like them; **ce fut une soirée u. en son genre** there's never been and there'll never be another party like it; **u. au monde** unlike anything else in the world; **c'est son seul et u. défaut** it's his one and only fault; **je ne ferai qu'une seule et u. critique** I have one and only one criticism to make; **la seule et l'u. Arletty** the one and only Arletty

(b) (*incomparable*) unparalleled, unrivalled, unique; *F* **il est u.** he's priceless!

uniquement [ynikmɑ̃] *adv* just, only; **elle mange u. des légumes** she eats just *or* only vegetables, she eats nothing but vegetables; **je viens u. pour vous voir** I've come just to see you, the only reason I've come is to see you; **vous faites des dictionnaires? – pas u., nous faisons aussi des traductions** you compile dictionaries, don't you? – not just that, we do translations as well

unir [ynir] **1** *vt* **(a)** (*relier*) (*personnes, territoires*) to unite; (*d'un pont, d'une autoroute*) to join, to link; **u. un territoire à un autre** to unite one territory with another; **le Tunnel sous la Manche unit Londres à Paris** the Channel Tunnel links London and Paris; **être uni par le mariage à ...** to be joined in matrimony *or* marriage to ...; **vous voilà unis par les liens du mariage** ≈ I now pronounce you man and wife; **le Père Patrick les unira** Father Patrick will marry them *or* will officiate at their wedding; **l'amitié qui nous a toujours unis** the friendship there has always been between us; **un homme qui unit des qualités de décideur à un sens de l'humour** a man who combines decision-making abilities with a sense of humour

(b) (*sol, surface etc*) to smooth, to level

2 s'unir *vpr* to join (together), to unite; **s'u. à qn** to join forces with sb; (*se marier*) to marry sb

unisexe [ynisɛks] *adj* (*vêtements etc*) unisex

unisexué [ynisɛksɥe] *adj Biol* unisexual

unisson [ynisɔ̃] *nm Mus* unison; **à l'u.** in unison; *Fig* **nos pensées sont à l'u.** we think as one; **les esprits sont à l'u.** everybody feels the same way; **ses idées ne sont pas à l'u. avec celles de la maison** his ideas are not in keeping with the company's

unitaire [ynitɛr] **1** *adj* **(a)** (*système etc*) unitary; *Com* **prix u.** unit price **(b)** *Rel* Unitarian **2** *n Rel* Unitarian

unitarien, -ienne [ynitarjɛ̃, -jɛn] *adj, n Pol* unitarian; *Rel* Unitarian

unité [ynite] *nf* **(a)** *Math etc* unity, unit; *Math* **la colonne des unités** the units column; **10 F l'u.** 10 francs each; *Com* **prix à l'u.** unit price

(b) (*d'une mesure etc*) unit; **u. de temps/de longueur** unit of time/length; **u. monétaire** unit of currency

(c) (*bloc*) unit; **u. d'intervention chirurgicale** field surgical unit; **u. de production** production unit

(d) *Mil* unit; **rejoindre son u.** to go back to *or* rejoin one's unit; *Naut* to go back to *or* rejoin one's ship

(e) (*caractère de ce qui forme un tout*) (*d'une nation, une association*) unity; (*de Dieu*) oneness; (*d'un projet, d'une action etc*) unified nature; (*du style etc*) consistency; **cela manque d'u.** (*d'un projet, d'un texte*) it doesn't hang together very well; *Littér* **les trois unités** the three unities

(f) *F* (*million d'anciens francs*) ten thousand francs

(g) *Ordinat* unit; (*de disque*) drive; **u. de bande** tape unit; **u. de destination** target drive; **u. de disque** disk drive; **u. logique** logical drive; **u. d'origine** source drive; **u. périphérique** peripheral; **u. de sauvegarde** backup device; **u. de sortie** output device; **u. de stockage** storage device

▶ **unité**: *Com* **u. d'activité stratégique** strategic business unit; **u. administrative** administrative unit; *Ordinat* **u. centrale** central processing unit, CPU; *Com* **u. de chargement** load unit; **u. de choc** shock unit; *Compta* **u. de compte** unit of account; *Pétr* **u. de craquage** cracking unit; *Univ* **u. de formation et de recherche** = department; *Ling* **u. lexicale** lexeme; *TV, Rad* **u. mobile (de tournage)** OB unit, outside broadcast vehicle; **u. monétaire** monetary unit; **u. de production** production unit; *TV etc* **u. de programme** programme production team; *Mktg* **u. de sondage** sampling unit; **u. de télécommande** remote control unit, RCU; **u. de traitement** processing unit; *Bourse* **u. de transaction** lot size; *Univ* **u. de valeur** ≈ credit; **u. de visualisation** visual display unit, VDU; *TV etc* **u. de voix hors champ automatique** automatic voice-over unit, ducker

univalent [ynivalɑ̃] *adj Ch* univalent

univers [ynivɛr] *nm* (a) *Astron* universe; **l'U.** the Universe (b) *Fig* **l'u. mathématique** the field of mathematics; **l'u. du rêve** the world *or* realm of dreams; **le monde de l'argent ce n'est pas vraiment mon u.** big money isn't really my thing *or* line; **c'est tout son u.** it means everything to him, it's his whole world

universalisation [ynivɛrsalizasjɔ̃] *nf* universalization

universaliser [ynivɛrsalize] *vt* **u. qch** to universalize sth, to make sth universal

universalité [ynivɛrsalite] *nf* (*d'une théorie, une loi, un mythe, une croyance etc*) universal nature, universality

universaux [ynivɛrso] *nmpl Phil* universals

universel, -elle [ynivɛrsɛl] **1** *adj* (*paix, jugement, constante etc*) universal; (*réputation, gloire*) world-wide; (*histoire*) of the universe; (*installation*) all-purpose; **l'exposition universelle** Expo; **suffrage u.** universal suffrage, one man one vote; **élu au suffrage u.** elected by universal suffrage; **savoir u.** all-embracing knowledge; **proposition universelle** universal (proposition); *MecE* **joint u.** universal joint; *Jur* **légataire u.** sole legatee; *Jur* **légataire à titre u.** residuary legatee **2** *nm* (*en logique*) universal

universellement [ynivɛrsɛlmɑ̃] *adv* (*connu*) universally, worldwide; **le sida est malheureusement u. répandu** Aids is unfortunately a worldwide phenomenon

universitaire [ynivɛrsitɛr] **1** *adj* (*ville, études*) university; **honneurs universitaires** academic honours; **cité u.** ≈ (students') residence, hall(s) of residence; **restaurant u.** student refectory **2** *n* academic

université [ynivɛrsite] *nf* (a) university; **aller à l'u.** to go to university; **u. d'été** summer school; *Pol* party conference (*for young members*); **u. du troisième âge** university of the third age, university for mature students (b) **l'U. (de France)** = the teaching profession (*including university staff, school teachers, inspectors etc*)

univoque [ynivɔk] *adj Ling* univocal; *Math* (*correspondance*) one-to-one

Untel, Unetelle [œ̃tɛl, yntɛl] *n* so-and-so, what's-his-name, *f* what's-her-name; **Monsieur/Madame U.** Mr/Mrs So-and-So; **les Untel** the so-and-sos, what's-their-names

uppercut [ypɛrkyt] *nm Boxe* uppercut; **u. du droit** right uppercut

uranifère [yranifɛr] *adj Géol* uranium-bearing

uranium [yranjɔm] *nm* uranium

urbain [yrbɛ̃] *adj* (a) (*de la ville*) (*développement, voirie, paysage, transport etc*) urban; **la population urbaine** city dwellers; *Tél* **communication urbaine** local call; **vivre en milieu u.** to live in an urban environment (b) *Litt* (*raffiné*) urbane

urbanisable [yrbanizabl] *adj* suitable for development; **zone difficilement u.** an area which would be difficult to develop

urbanisation [yrbanizasjɔ̃] *nf* urbanization; **plan d'u.** urban development plan

urbaniser [yrbanize] *vt* (*zone rurale etc*) to urbanize; **zone urbanisée** built-up area

urbanisme [yrbanism] *nm* town planning, urban development; **cabinet d'u.** firm of town-planning consultants

urbaniste [yrbanist] **1** *adj* urban; **réglementation u.** municipal bylaws **2** *n* town planner; **agence d'urbanistes** firm of town-planning consultants

urbanistique [yrbanistik] *adj* **politique/projet u.** town-planning *or* urban development policy/project

urbanité [yrbanite] *nf Litt* urbanity; **avec u.** urbanely

urbi et orbi [yrbiɛtɔrbi] *adv* urbi et orbi; *Fig* far and wide, to all and sundry; **cela est connu u.** all and sundry know that, *F* the world and his wife know that

urée [yre] *nf Ch* urea

urémie [yremi] *nf Méd* uraemia, *US* uremia

uretère [yrtɛr] *nm Anat* ureter

urètre [yrɛtr] *nm Anat* urethra

urgence [yrʒɑ̃s] *nf* (a) (*caractère pressé*) urgency; **ces mesures ont été prises dans l'u.** these measures were taken in a great hurry; **il y a u.** it's a matter of urgency, it's an emergency; **il n'y a aucune u.** there's no rush, it's not an emergency; **y a-t-il u. à ce qu'il parte?** does he have to leave right *or* straight away?; **faire qch en toute u.** to give sth (top) priority, to treat sth as a matter of (top) priority; **en cas d'u.** in an emergency; **mesures d'u.** emergency measures; **état d'u.** state of emergency; **à envoyer/payer d'u.** to be sent/ paid immediately; **convoquer d'u. les actionnaires** to call an extraordinary meeting of the shareholders; **il a été appelé d'u.** he received an urgent call

(b) *Méd* **une u.** an emergency; **ce n'est pas une u.** it's not urgent, it's not a matter of life and death; **salle des urgences** emergency ward; **transporter qn d'u. à l'hôpital** to rush sb to hospital; **opérer d'u.** to perform an emergency operation; **il fut opéré d'u.** he had an emergency operation

urgent [yrʒɑ̃] *adj* urgent; **rien d'u. ne l'obligeait à sortir** there was nothing urgent forcing him to go out; **cas u.** urgent case, emergency; **affaires urgentes** pressing matters; **il devient u. de trouver une solution** a solution must be found urgently, a solution is urgently required; **avoir un besoin u. de liquidités** to be in urgent need *or* to be urgently in need of cash

urger [yrʒe] *vi F* to be urgent; **il n'y a rien qui urge** there's no desperate hurry; **vite, ça urge!** quick, it's urgent!

urinaire [yrinɛr] *adj Anat* urinary

urinal, -aux [yrinal, -o] *nm Méd* urinal

urine [yrin] *nf* **urine(s)** urine; **évacuer l'u.** to pass water; **analyses d'urines** urine tests

uriner [yrine] *vi* to urinate, to pass water

urinoir [yrinwar] *nm* (public) urinal

urique [yrik] *adj* (*acide etc*) uric

urne [yrn] *nf* (a) (*pour voter*) ballot box; **aller aux urnes** to go to the polls (b) (*vase*) urn

urogénital, -ale, -aux, -ales [yroʒenital, -o] *adj Méd* urogenital

urologie [yrɔlɔʒi] *nf* urology

urologue [yrɔlɔg] *n* urologist

URSS [yɛrɛsɛs, *parfois* yrs] *nf Hist* (*abrév* **Union des républiques socialistes soviétiques**) USSR

URSSAF [yrsaf] *nf* (*abrév* **Union de recouvrement des cotisations de sécurité sociale et d'allocations familiales**) = organization which collects social security and family allowance payments

ursuline [yrsylin] *nf Rel* Ursuline convent

urticaire [yrtikɛr] *nf Méd* nettle rash, hives, *Spéc* urticaria; **crise d'u.** attack of hives; **avoir une crise d'u.** to come out *or* break out in hives; *Fig F* **donner de l'u. à qn** to irritate sb, to set sb's teeth on edge

urticant [yrtikɑ̃] *adj* stinging

urtication [yrtikasjɔ̃] *nf Méd* stinging

Uruguay [yrygwɛ] *nm* Uruguay

uruguayen, -enne [yrygwɛjɛ̃, -ɛn] **1** *adj* Uruguayan **2** *n* **U.** Uruguayan

urus [yrys] *nm Zool* aurochs

us [ys] *nmpl* **les us et coutumes d'un pays** the habits and customs of a country

usage [yzaʒ] *nm* (a) (*utilisation*) use; *Gram* usage; **mot en u.** word in use; **c'est un mot qu'on trouve seulement dans l'u. écrit** the word is found only in written documents; **les mots se modifient par l'u.** words are changed by *or* through use; **mot sorti de l'u.** word which has fallen into disuse *or* is no longer in use; **faute d'u.** (*d'un mot*) misuse; **perdre l'u. de la vue/de l'ouïe** to lose one's sight/hearing; **faire u. de qch** (*service, appareil*) to make use of sth, to use sth; **faire u. de la force** to use *or* employ force; **faire bon u. de qch** to make good use of sth, to put sth to good use; **faire mauvais u. de**

qch to make bad use of sth, to misuse sth; **avoir l'u. de** to have the use of; **je n'en aurai pas l'u.** I won't be needing it, I won't have any use for it; *Pharm* **à u. externe/interne** for external/internal use; **avoir plusieurs usages** to have various uses; **à l'u. des écoles/des étudiants** for use in schools/by students; **réservé à son u. personnel** reserved for his/her personal use; **à usages multiples** (*équipement etc*) multi-purpose; **s'améliorer à l'u.** to improve with use; **tu t'y habitueras à l'u.** you'll get used to it once you start *or* with practice; **d'u. courant** in common *or* everyday use; **c'est un mot d'u. courant** it's a common *or* everyday word; **j'en fais un u. courant** I often use it; **hors d'u.** (*ascenseur*) out of service, out of use; (*usé*) (*manteau*) worn out; (*démodé*) (*mot etc*) obsolete; **faire un u. immodéré de l'alcool** to drink too much *or* to excess; **le bon u.,** *Arch* **le bel u.** correct French

(**b**) (*des vêtements etc*) wear, service; **faire de l'u.** *ou* **beaucoup d'u.** to wear well; **ce manteau vous fera de l'u.** you'll get a lot of wear out of this coat; **garanti à l'u.** guaranteed to wear well

(**c**) *Jur* **droit d'u.** (right of) use

(**d**) (*coutume*) custom, practice; **conforme/contraire aux usages** in keeping with/contrary to common practice; **usages locaux** local customs; **c'est l'u.** it's the done thing; **les conditions d'u.** the usual terms; **comme il est d'u. en Algérie** as is customary *or* the custom in Algeria; **selon** *ou* **suivant l'u.** according to custom; **un mariage selon** *ou* **suivant l'u.** a traditional wedding; **il est d'u. de ... +** *inf* it is usual *or* customary to ...

(**e**) (*expérience*) practice, experience

usagé [yzaʒe] *adj* (*souliers, manteau, veste*) worn; (*d'occasion*) secondhand; **plaisanteries usagées** tired jokes

usager, -ère [yzaʒe, -ɛr] *n* (*de qch*) user; **les usagers de la route/du téléphone/du français** road/telephone/French language users; **les usagers du train/du métro** rail travellers/underground users; **les usagers de la poste** post office users *or* customers; **les usagers de la sécurité sociale** Social Security clients

usant [yzɑ̃] *adj* (*vie, travail*) exhausting, wearing; **il est u.** he wears you out

usé [yze] *adj* (*métal, pierre etc*) worn; (*vêtements*) worn(-out), threadbare; (*corde*) frayed; (*sujet, plaisanterie*) hackneyed, stale; **terre usée** exhausted land; *Ind* **eaux usées** waste water; **je suis u.!** I'm worn-out *or* exhausted!; **u. par l'eau** worn away by water; **u. par le frottement** worn (out) by rubbing; **u. par les épreuves** careworn; **u. par le temps** timeworn; **u. par le travail** worn out by work; **c'est une femme usée par les années** the years have told on her, time has taken its toll of her; **c'est u.!** that's an old one!; **argument u. jusqu'à la corde** well-worn *or* threadbare argument

user [yze] **1** *vi* **u. de** (*persuasion, son influence*) to use; (*termes recherchés*) to use, to make use of; (*violence, ruse*) to use, to resort to; **u. de son droit** to exercise one's right; **u. de douceur avec qn** to deal gently with sb; **on ne te reprochera jamais de trop u. de patience/calme/compréhension** you can never be too patient/calm/understanding; *Litt* **en u. bien/mal avec qn** to treat sb well/badly

2 *vt* (**a**) (*consommer*) (*énergie, électricité*) to use, to consume; **u. du charbon** to use *or* burn coal; **je ne vais pas u. mon énergie à essayer de te persuader** I'm not going to waste my energy trying to persuade you

(**b**) (*abîmer*) (*vêtements, chaussures*) to wear out; (*santé*) to ruin; **u. un pull aux coudes** to wear out a pullover at the elbows; **elle use trois paires de chaussures par an** she goes through three pairs of shoes in a year; **je l'ai usé jusqu'à la corde, ce pull** I've worn this sweater until it's threadbare; **l'érosion use la roche** erosion wears away *or* eats away the rock; *Fig* **cela finit par u. la passion/l'intérêt** in the end it kills off passion/interest; **tu uses tes yeux à lire dans le noir** you'll ruin your eyesight reading in the dark

3 s'user *vpr* (*de pneus*) to wear out; (*de talons, semelles*) to wear out, to wear down; **ce tissu s'use vite** this material wears (out) quickly; *Fig* **sa résistance finira bien par s'u.** his resistance will wear down *or* break down in the end; *Fig* **ma patience va finir par s'u.** my patience is beginning to wear thin; *Fig* **il s'est usé à ce travail** he's worn himself out with this work; *Fig* **je me suis usé à le lui dire** I'm tired telling him, I've told him till I'm blue in the face; *Fig* **mais c'est ce que je m'use à te dire depuis hier!** that's what I've been trying to tell you since yesterday!

usinage [yzinaʒ] *nm Métal* machining

usine [yzin] *nf* factory, plant; **navire-u.** factory ship; **u. pilote** pilot plant; **u. à gaz** gasworks; **u. à papier** paper mill; **u. de construction automobile** car factory *or* plant; **u. d'armement** arms factory; **u. clés-en-main** turnkey plant; **u. de fabrication** manufacturing plant; **u. de montage** assembly plant; **u. de production** production plant; **ouvrier d'u.** factory worker; *Fig F* **ce restaurant est une u.** this restaurant is like a works canteen

usiner [yzine] **1** *vt* (**a**) *Métal* (*moulages etc*) to machine, to tool; (*pièces*) to machine(-finish); **parties usinées** bright parts (**b**) (*fabriquer*) to manufacture **2** *vi F* **ça usine là-dedans!** they're hard at it in there!

usinier, -ière [yzinje, -jɛr] *adj* (*industrie*) factory; **faubourg u.** industrial suburb

usité [yzite] *adj* in common *or* current use; **mot très u.** very common word; **mot peu u.** little used word

ustensile [ystɑ̃sil] *nm* implement, tool; **u. de cuisine** kitchen utensil

usuel, -elle [yzɥɛl] **1** *adj* usual, common, ordinary; **l'anglais u.** everyday English; **dénomination usuelle** (*pour une plante etc*) common name **2** *nmpl* **usuels** (*dans une bibliothèque*) reference works

usuellement [yzɥɛlmɑ̃] *adv* commonly, ordinarily

usufruit [yzyfrɥi] *nm Jur* usufruct, life interest; **laisser qch en u. à qn** (*maison etc*) to leave sb the life tenancy of sth

usufruitier, -ière [yzyfrɥitje, -jɛr] **1** *adj Jur* usufructuary **2** *n* (**a**) *Jur* usufructuary (**b**) (*d'un bien immobilier*) tenant for life

usuraire [yzyrɛr] *adj* (*intérêt etc*) usurious

usure[1] [yzyr] *nf* (*intérêt*) usury; **pratiquer l'u.** to practise usury; *Fig* **rendre un bienfait avec u.** to repay a service with interest

usure[2] *nf* (*de pneu etc*) wear; (*du sol, de roches*) erosion, wearing away; **u. des pneus** tyre wear; **tissu qui résiste à l'u.** material that wears well; **u. par frottement** abrasion; **l'u. normale** normal wear and tear; *Tech* **surface d'u.** wearing surface; **organes sujets à l'u.** (*d'une machine*) wearing parts; **guerre d'u.** war of attrition; *Fig F* **je l'aurai à l'u.** I'll wear him down

usurier, -ière [yzyrje, -jɛr] *n* usurer

usurpateur, -trice [yzyrpatœr, -tris] *n* usurper

usurpation [yzyrpasjɔ̃] *nf* (*d'un trône, une réputation, un titre*) usurpation; **u. de pouvoir** usurping *or* usurpation of power

usurper [yzyrpe] **1** *vt* (*trône, réputation, titre, droits*) to usurp (**sur** from) **2** *vi* **u. sur les droits/le domaine de qn** to encroach on sb's rights/territory

ut [yt] *nm inv Mus* (*note*) C; **ut dièse** C sharp; **clef d'ut** C clef; **clef d'ut quatrième ligne** tenor clef

utérin [yterɛ̃] *adj* uterine; **frères utérins/sœurs utérines** half brothers/sisters (on the mother's side)

utérus [yterys] *nm* uterus, womb

utile [ytil] **1** *adj* useful; **puis-je vous être u.?** can I do anything (to help)?, can I be of (some) help?; **en quoi puis-je vous être u.?** what can I do for you?, how can I help you?; **si je puis vous être u.** if I can be of any use *or* help *or* service *or* assistance to you; **elle nous a été très u.** she was a lot of help, she was very helpful to us; **elle peut t'être u. un jour** she may be of help to you *or* useful one day; **se rendre u.** to make oneself useful; **tout cela n'était pas très u.** it wasn't much use *or* help, it didn't help much, none of it was very useful *or* helpful; **cela m'a été bien u.** (*cet objet*) it came in very handy, I found it very helpful; (*ce renseignement*) it was very helpful; **est-il u. d'y aller?** is there any use *or* any point in going?; **ce n'est peut-être pas très u. que tout le monde le sache** there's no use in everybody knowing; **il n'était pas u. que tu t'en occupes** there was no point in you dealing with it; **en temps u.** in (good) time, in due course; **prendre toutes dispositions utiles** to make all necessary arrangements; **dictionnaire u. à consulter** useful *or* helpful dictionary to consult

2 *nm* **joindre l'u. à l'agréable** to combine *or* mix business with pleasure

utilement [ytilmɑ̃] *adv* usefully; **conseiller/renseigner u. qn** to give sb useful *or* helpful advice/information

utilisable [ytilizabl] *adj* usable; (*crédit*) available; **billet u. pour tous les trains** ticket which is valid *or* can be used on all trains; **facilement u.** easy to use

utilisateur, -trice [ytilizatœr, -tris] *n* user; **u. final** end user; *Mktg* **u. tardif** late adopter

utilisation [ytilizasjɔ̃] *nf* (*de qch*) use, *surtout Am* utilization; **u. réduite à certaines périodes** use restricted to certain periods; **pour une bonne u. de ce produit, ...** in order to make correct use of this product, ...

utiliser [ytilize] *vt* to use, *Fml, Am* to utilize; (*profiter de*) to make use of; *Ordinat* to run; *Ordinat* **il peut être utilisé sur ...** it can run on ...; **bien u.** (*son temps, ressources, compétences*) to make good use of; *Péj* **avoir l'impression qu'on vous utilise** to have the feeling you're being used

utilitaire [ytilitɛr] **1** *adj* utilitarian; *Aut* **véhicule u.** utility vehicle; *Ordinat* utility; **programme u.** utility (program) **2** *nm Ordinat* utility; **u. de conversion** conversion utility

utilitarisme [ytilitarism] *nm* utilitarianism

utilité [ytilite] *nf* **(a)** (*fonction*) usefulness; **être d'une grande u.** to be very useful; **cela m'est d'une grande u.** I find it very useful *or* a lot of help; **cela ne m'est d'aucune u.** it's absolutely no use to me, it's no earthly use to me; **sans u.** useless; **c'est sans u. pour moi** it's of no use to me; **un appareil sans grande u.** an appliance that's not much use; **association d'u. publique** public utility; (*charitable*) registered charity **(b)** *Th* **jouer les utilités** to play small *or* bit parts; *Fig* to play second fiddle

utopie [ytɔpi] *nf* utopia; *Fig Péj* **c'est une u.**! it's nothing but a pipedream!

utopique [ytɔpik] *adj* utopian

utopiste [ytɔpist] *n* Utopian

utriculaire [ytrikylɛr] *nf Bot* bladderwort

UV[1] [yve] *nf inv Univ abrév* **unité de valeur**

UV[2] *nm inv* (*abrév* **ultra-violet**) UV; **se faire faire des UV** to go on a sunbed

uval, -ale, -aux, -ales [yval, -o] *adj* **régime u.** grape diet

uvulaire [yvylɛr] *adj* uvular

uvule [yvyl] *nf Anat* uvula

V

V, v [ve] *nm* **(a)** (*lettre*) V, v; **double v** W, w; **moteur (à cylindres) en V** V (type) engine; *Géog* **vallée (à profil) en V** V-shaped valley; **col en v** V-neck **(b)** *F* (*abrév* **vitesse) à la vitesse grand v** at a rate of knots, at top speed **(c)** (*abrév* **voir)** see

vacance [vakɑ̃s] *nf* **(a) vacances** holiday(s), *surtout Am* vacation; (*du Parlement*) recess; **vacances de Pâques/Noël** Easter/Christmas holidays; **vacances d'hiver/d'été** winter/summer holiday; **prendre ses vacances d'été/d'hiver en Écosse** to spend one's summer/winter holiday in Scotland, to go to Scotland for one's summer/winter holiday; **vacances de neige** winter sports holiday; **vacances scolaires** school holidays; **départ/retour de vacances** going away on/coming back from holiday; **attention aux retours de vacances sur la route** watch out for returning holidaymakers on the roads; **les grandes vacances** *Scol* the summer holidays; *Univ* the long vacation; **prendre des vacances** to take a holiday, to go on holiday; **tu as besoin de prendre des vacances** you need a holiday; **prendre ses vacances en août** to take one's holiday in August; **j'ai encore dix jours de vacances à prendre** I still have ten days' holiday to take; **être en vacances** to be on holiday; (*du Parlement*) to be in recess; **partir en vacances** to go away on holiday; **un jour de vacance(s)** a (day's) holiday; **colonie de vacances** holiday camp; **vacances en camping** camping holiday; **vacances en circuit** multi-centre holiday; **vacances judiciaires** (*des tribunaux*) vacation, recess; **vacances studieuses** educational holiday, study holiday; *F* **il part? très bien, ça me fera des vacances!** he's going? great, that will be just like a holiday for me!

(b) (*poste*) vacancy; **la v. du pouvoir a eu des conséquences désastreuses** there being no one in power has had disastrous consequences; **il n'y aura pas de v. du pouvoir** there will be a smooth transition of control; **qui assurera les fonctions de président pendant la v. du poste?** who will take over the president's responsibilities during the interregnum?

(c) *Jur* (*d'une succession*) abeyance

(d) *Litt* (*de l'esprit*) emptiness

vacancier, -ière [vakɑ̃sje, -jɛr] *n* holidaymaker, *Am* vacationer, vacationist; **l'afflux des vacanciers** the influx of holidaymakers

vacant [vakɑ̃] *adj* **(a)** (*maison etc*) vacant, unoccupied; (*chaire d'université*) vacant; **poste v.** vacancy **(b)** *Jur* **succession vacante** estate in abeyance **(c)** *Litt* (*regard*) vacant; (*mains*) idle

vacarme [vakarm] *nm* uproar, din, racket; **faire du v.** to create *or* make an uproar, *F* to kick up a row

vacataire [vakatɛr] *n* short-term worker; (*remplaçant*) short-term replacement, stand-in; **c'est une v.** she's on a short-term *or* temporary contract

vacation [vakasjɔ̃] *nf* **(a)** *Jur* (*de juge, d'expert etc*) sitting, session **(b)** (*dans une vente aux enchères*) day's sale **(c)** *Jur* **vacations** (*tarif*) (*d'un avocat etc*) fees; (*arrêt*) (*des tribunaux*) vacation, recess **(d)** (*tâche*) session, shift; **être payé à la v.** to be paid by the session *or* shift; **faire des vacations** to work on a short-term basis

vaccin [vaksɛ̃] *nm* vaccine; **v. antivariolique/contre la coqueluche** smallpox/whooping-cough vaccine; **plume à v.** vaccine point; **injection du v.** vaccine injection; *Fig* **le meilleur v. contre la paresse** the best antidote to laziness

vaccinable [vaksinabl] *adj* able to be vaccinated *or* inoculated

vaccinal, -ale, -aux, -ales [vaksinal, -o] *adj* vaccine, vaccinal; **complications vaccinales** complications following vaccination; **contamination d'origine vaccinale** contamination originating in a vaccine; **essais vaccinaux** vaccine tests; **préparation vaccinale** vaccine

vaccination [vaksinasjɔ̃] *nf* vaccination, inoculation; **v. obligatoire** compulsory vaccination; **v. contre la coqueluche** vaccination against whooping cough, whooping cough vaccination; **v. préventive/curative** protective/curative inoculation

vaccine [vaksin] *nf* **(a)** *Vét* cowpox, *Spéc* vaccinia **(b)** *Méd* inoculated cowpox

vacciner [vaksine] *vt Méd* to vaccinate, to inoculate (**contre** against, for); **se faire v.** to get vaccinated *or* inoculated (**contre** against); *Fig* **être vacciné contre les désagréments du métier/les voyages organisés** to be immune to the drawbacks of the job/package holidays; **pas question que je retombe amoureux, je suis vacciné!** there's no way I'm ever falling in love again, I've had enough to last me a lifetime!

vache [vaʃ] **1** *nf* **(a)** (*animal*) cow; **lait/fromage de v.** cow's milk/cheese; *F* **retrouver le plancher des vaches** to be back on dry land *or* terra firma; *F* **parler français comme une v. espagnole** to murder *or* torture the French language; *F* **manger de la v. enragée** to have a hard time of it; **coup de pied en v.** stab in the back; **nœud de v.** granny knot; *Prov* **chacun son métier, les vaches seront bien gardées** the cobbler should stick to his last; *F* **il pleut comme v. qui pisse** it's bucketing (down), *très F* it's pissing down

(b) *F* (*insulte*) (*homme*) swine, sod; (*femme*) cow, bitch; **quelle v.!** what a swine/bitch!; **ah les vaches, ils sont partis sans moi!** the rotten lot, they left without me!; **regarde-moi cette grosse v.!** look at that fat cow!

(c) *F* (*interjection*) **la v., qu'est-ce qu'il fait froid!** God, it's so cold!; **la v., tu as vu avec quelle vitesse ça court!** wow! have you seen the speed it's going at?

(d) *Arg* policeman; **les vaches** the cops, the fuzz, the pigs; **mort aux vaches!** kill the pigs!

(e) (*cuir*) cowhide; **valise en v.** leather suitcase

2 *adj F* rotten, nasty; **elle a été v. avec lui** she was rotten to him

3 *n F* **un v. de mec!** a *or* one hell of a guy; **une v. de surprise** a *or* one hell of a surprise

▶ **vache: v. à eau** (canvas) water carrier; **v. grasse:** *Fig F* **finies, les vaches grasses!** the good days are over!; **notre période de vaches grasses est terminée** we've had our years of plenty; **v. à lait** *Agr* dairy cow; *Fig* milch cow; *Mktg* (*produit*) cash cow; **j'en ai assez de jouer les vaches à lait!** I'm fed up forking out for everybody!; **v. laitière** dairy cow; **v. maigre:** *Fig F* **connaître une période de vaches maigres** to go through a lean period; *Zool* **v. marine** sea cow

vachement [vaʃmɑ̃] *adv F* **c'est v. difficile** it's damned *or* bloody difficult; **c'est v. bien** it's bloody good; **il a v. vieilli** he's got a helluva lot older-looking; **elle a v. changé** she's changed a helluva lot

vacher [vaʃe] *nm* cowherd

vachère [vaʃɛr] *nf* cowgirl

vacherie [vaʃri] *nf F* (*action*) dirty trick; (*remarque*) nasty remark; **elle lui a fait/dit une sale v.** she played a dirty trick on him/made a nasty remark to him; **il est d'une v. terrible** he's a really nasty customer, he's rotten to the core; **v. de voiture!** bloody *or* damn car!

vacherin [vaʃrɛ̃] *nm Culin* **(a)** (*fromage*) vacherin cheese **(b) v. (glacé)** = meringue with cream, ice cream and fruit

vachette [vaʃɛt] *nf* **(a)** (*animal*) young cow, heifer **(b)** (*cuir*) calfskin; **sac/chaussures en v.** calfskin bag/shoes

vacillant [vasijɑ̃] *adj* **(a)** (*table etc*) unsteady, wobbly; (*flamme etc*) flickering; (*main*) unsteady, shaky; (*allure etc*) uncertain, staggering; **v. de fatigue** staggering *or* reeling with tiredness **(b)** (*esprit etc*) wavering, indecisive, vacillating; (*santé*) failing

vacillation [vasijasjɔ̃] *nf*, **vacillement** [vasijmɑ̃] *nm* **(a)** unsteadiness, shakiness; (*d'une flamme*) flickering; (*d'un lustre*) swaying **(b)** (*hésitation*) vacillation, shilly-shallying

vaciller [vasije] *vi* **(a)** (*chanceler*) to be unsteady (on one's feet), to sway; **il vacille sur ses jambes** (*parce qu'il est vieux*) he's shaky on his legs; (*parce qu'il est ivre, blessé*) he's staggering; **tout vacillait autour de moi** everything was swimming around me; **il s'avança en vacillant vers la porte** he staggered towards the door **(b)** (*d'une flamme, lumière*) to flicker **(c)** (*hésiter*) to vacillate, to waver **(d)** (*faiblir*) to falter; **sa raison/santé vacille** his mind/health is failing *or* faltering

va-comme-je-te-pousse (à la) [alavakɔmʃtəpus] *adv F* any old how *or* way

vacuité [vakɥite] *nf* vacuity, vacuousness; (*de paroles*) emptiness, inanity

vacuole [vakɥɔl] *nf Biol* vacuole

vacuum [vakɥɔm] *nm* vacuum

vade-mecum [vademekɔm] *nm inv* handbook, companion, vade-mecum

vadrouille [vadruj] *nf* **(a)** *F* (*balade*) ramble, saunter; **partir** *ou* **aller en v.** to roam *or* rove *or* wander about; **ils sont encore partis en v.** they're still out gallivanting **(b)** *Can* mop, floorcloth **(c)** *Naut* (deck) swab

vadrouiller [vadruje] *vi F* to roam *or* rove *or* wander about

vadrouilleur, -euse [vadrujœr, -øz] *n F* rover, wanderer

va-et-vient [vaevjɛ̃] *nm inv* **(a)** (*mouvement*) backward and forward motion; **faire le v. entre** to go to and fro *or* back and forth between; (*d'un bateau*) to go to and fro between, to ply between; **faire le v. entre Paris et Lyon** to go to and fro *or* to shuttle back and forth between Paris and Lyons; **(porte) v.** swing door **(b)** (*de personnes etc*) coming(s) and going(s), toing(s) and froing(s) **(c)** *Él* two-way wiring (system); **(commutateur) v.** two-way switch **(d)** *MecE* reciprocation

vagabond, -onde [vagabɔ̃, -ɔ̃d] **1** *adj* (*vie etc*) wandering, roving, roaming; *Fig* **avoir l'humeur vagabonde** to have itchy feet **2** *n Péj* vagrant, tramp; *Litt* (*voyageur*) wanderer, vagabond; **les vagabonds seront arrêtés** vagrants will be arrested

vagabondage [vagabɔ̃daʒ] *nm* (*d'un clochard etc*) wandering(s), *Péj* vagrancy; **arrêté pour v.** arrested for vagrancy; **les vagabondages de l'imagination** the wanderings of the imagination; *Admin* **v. spécial** living on immoral earnings

vagabonder [vagabɔ̃de] *vi* to rove, to roam, to wander (about); *Fig* (*de ses pensées, son imagination*) to wander, to stray

vagin [vaʒɛ̃] *nm* vagina

vaginal, -ale, -aux, -ales [vaʒinal, -o] *adj* vaginal

vaginite [vaʒinit] *nf Méd* vaginitis

vagir [vaʒir] *vi* (*d'un nouveau-né*) to cry, to wail; (*d'un animal*) to squeak, to whimper; (*du lièvre*) to squeal; (*du crocodile*) to bark

vagissant [vaʒisɑ̃] *adj* (*bébé*) crying, wailing; (*animal*) squeaking, whimpering; (*lièvre*) squealing; (*crocodile*) barking

vagissement [vaʒismɑ̃] *nm* (*d'un bébé*) cry, wail(ing); (*d'un animal*) squeak(ing), whimper(ing); (*d'un lièvre*) squeal(ing); (*d'un crocodile*) bark(ing)

vague[1] [vag] *nf* **(a)** *aussi Fig* wave; **une v. a balayé le pont** a wave washed over the deck; **plonger dans les vagues** to dive into the waves; *Fig* **v. d'enthousiasme/de tendresse/de violence/de colère** wave *or* surge of enthusiasm/of tenderness/of violence/of anger; *Fig* **faire des vagues** to make waves, to rock the boat; **être dans le creux de la v.** to be down in the dumps, to be in the doldrums; **v. de vente** sales wave **(b)** (*ondulations*) (*de chevelure, de dunes*) wave; (*motif décoratif*) wavy pattern **(c)** *Littér etc* **nouvelle v.** new wave; **les cinéastes (de la) nouvelle v.** film-makers of the new wave, new-wave film-makers

▶ **vague**: **v. de chaleur** heat wave; **v. de fond** ground swell; *Fig* ground swell (of opinion); **l'épidémie a frappé le pays telle une v. de fond** the epidemic struck the country like a tidal wave; **v. de froid** cold spell *or* snap

vague[2] **1** *adj* **(a)** (*flou, imprécis*) (*savoir, impression, sentiment, geste etc*) vague; (*souvenir*) vague, dim; **des formes vagues** undefined *or* indistinct shapes; **elle est restée très v. sur ses intentions** she was very vague about her intentions; **j'ai la v. impression que ...** I have a vague impression *or* feeling that ...; **quelque v. écrivain** some writer or other; **elle dit avoir un v. diplôme en comptabilité** she claims to have some sort *or* kind of diploma in accounting; **regarder qn d'un air v.** to look vacantly at sb

(b) *Anat* **nerf v.** vagus (nerve)

2 *nm* **(a)** (*imprécision*) vagueness, indefiniteness; **rester dans le v.** to be vague *or* non-committal; **reste dans le v.** keep it vague, be as vague as possible; **avoir du v. à l'âme** to be melancholy; **dans un moment de v. à l'âme** in a moment of melancholy

(b) (*vide*) space; **fixer les yeux dans le v.** to gaze into space; **regard perdu dans le v.** faraway *or* far-off *or* distant look

vaguelette [vaglɛt] *nf* wavelet

vaguement [vagmɑ̃] *adv* vaguely; **on la reconnaît v. sur la photo** you can just make her out in the photo; **c'est ce que j'ai v. compris** that's what I more or less understood; **répondre v.** to give a vague answer; **je me sentais v. coupable** I felt vaguely guilty, I felt in some vague way that I was to blame

vaguemestre [vagmɛstr] *nm Mil* post orderly; *Naut* postman

vaguer [vage] *vi Litt* to wander, to roam (about); **laisser v. ses pensées** to let one's thoughts wander

vahiné [vaine] *nf* Tahitian woman

vaillamment [vajamɑ̃] *adv* valiantly, bravely

vaillance [vajɑ̃s] *nf* valour, *US* valor, bravery, courage; *Mil* gallantry; **supporter une épreuve avec v.** to face an ordeal with courage; **faire preuve de v.** to show courage

vaillant [vajɑ̃] *adj* **(a)** (*en forme*) **être v.** to be in good health; **je ne me sens pas v.** I feel a bit under the weather **(b) n'avoir pas un sou v.** to be (stony) broke, not to have a penny to one's name **(c)** (*courageux*) valiant, brave, courageous; (*cœur*) stout; *Mil* gallant

vain [vɛ̃] *adj* **(a)** (*qui n'aboutit à rien*) (*démarche, entreprise*) futile; (*efforts*) vain, fruitless, futile; **en v.** in vain, vainly; **j'ai essayé en v. de le convaincre** I tried in vain to convince him; **c'est en v. qu'elle le lui a demandé** she asked him for it in vain, she asked him for it but to no avail

(b) (*vide de sens*) (*plaisirs*) vain, empty; (*promesse*) hollow, empty; (*espoirs*) vain; (*craintes*) groundless, unfounded; (*regrets*) needless; **ce n'étaient pas là de vaines paroles** these were no empty *or* no idle words; **je te dis qu'elle est dangereuse, et ce n'est pas un v. mot!** I tell you she's dangerous, and it's no empty claim *or* and I know what I'm talking about

(c) vaine pâture common (land)

(d) *Litt* (*personne*) vain, conceited

vaincre [vɛ̃kr] (*prp* **vainquant**; *pp* **vaincu**; *pr ind* **je vaincs, il vainc, n. vainquons**; *impf* **je vainquais**; *p hist* **je vainquis**; *fu* **je vaincrai**) **1** *vt* **(a)** (*l'emporter sur*) (*adversaire*) to conquer, to defeat, *surtout Litt* to vanquish **(b)** *Sp etc* (*concurrent*) to beat; **v. qn aux échecs** to beat sb at chess **(c)** *Fig* (*maladie, difficulté etc*) to overcome, to master, to conquer; (*problème, complexes, colère, impulsions, passions*) to overcome; **v. une résistance** to overcome resistance **2** *vi* **il faut v. ou mourir** we must do or die

vaincu [vɛ̃ky] **1** *adj* beaten, defeated; **être v. d'avance** to be beaten before one starts; **pourquoi partir v. d'avance?** why be so defeatist?; **s'avouer v.** to admit defeat **2** *n* defeated man, *f* woman; **attitude/comportement de v.** defeatist attitude/behaviour

vainement [vɛnmɑ̃] *adv* vainly, in vain; **je lui en ai v. parlé** I spoke to him about it in vain *or* to no avail

vainqueur [vɛ̃kœr] **1** *nm* **(a)** *Sp etc* winner; *Boxe* **être v. par K.O./aux points** to win by a knock-out/on points; **le v. de l'Anapurna** the conqueror of Annapurna; **sortir v. d'une lutte** to emerge the victor of a battle or victorious from a battle **(b)** *Mil* victor, conqueror, *surtout Litt* vanquisher **2** *adj* conquering, victorious, *surtout Litt* vanquishing; **air/sourire v.** triumphant look/smile

vair [vɛr] *nm* vair; **pantoufle de v.** (*dans Cendrillon*) ≈ glass slipper

vairon [vɛrɔ̃] **1** *adj* **aux yeux vairons** wall-eyed **2** *nm* (*poisson*) minnow

vaisseau, -eaux [vɛso] *nm* **(a)** *Anat, Bot* vessel, canal, duct; **v. sanguin** blood vessel **(b)** *Archit* (*d'une église*) nave; (*d'un édifice*) body, hall **(c)** *Naut Vieilli* ship, vessel; **v. à voiles** sailing vessel; **v. de guerre** warship; **v. amiral** flagship; *Fig* **brûler ses vaisseaux** to burn one's boats **(d)** *Arch* (*récipient*) vessel, receptacle

▶ **vaisseau**: *Bible* **v. d'élection** chosen vessel; **v. spatial** spaceship

vaisselier [vɛsəlje] *nm* (*meuble*) dresser

vaisselle [vɛsɛl] *nf* dishes *pl*, crockery; (*de céramique, de porcelaine*) china; **v. de porcelaine** porcelain, china; **v. plate** (gold/silver) plate; **acheter de la v.** to buy some (china) tableware *or* crockery; **faire** *ou* **laver la v.** to do the washing up, to do the dishes, *Br* to wash up; *F* **je dois finir ma v.** I must finish (the) washing up *or* the dishes; **machine à laver la v.** dishwasher; **liquide (de) v.** washing-up *or US* dish-washing liquid; **eau de v.** dishwater; *Fig F Péj* **cette bière/soupe, c'est de l'eau de v.** this beer/soup is like dishwater

val [val] *nm Géog* (narrow) valley; (*pl* **vals** *except in the phrase*) **par monts et par vaux** [vo] up hill and down dale

valable [valabl] *adj* **(a)** (*valide*) (*titre, raison, idée*) valid; (*excuse*) valid, legitimate; **billet v. pour deux mois** ticket valid for two months; **votre titre de transport n'est pas v.** your ticket is not valid; **c'est un argument tout à fait v.** it's a perfectly valid *or* acceptable argument; **ce qui est v. pour vous ne l'est pas pour elle** what goes for you doesn't go for her; **promesse toujours v.** promise that still holds good; **ma proposition est toujours v.** my offer still stands

(b) (*de qualité*) *Pol* **pouvoir s'adresser à un interlocuteur**

v. to be able to speak to an authorized representative; **devenir un partenaire v. dans la CE** to become a fully-fledged partner in the EC; **un roman v.** a good novel
valablement [valabləmɑ̃] *adv* validly; **être v. autorisé à qch/à faire qch** to have the necessary authority for sth/to do sth; **c'est ce qu'on lui a v. reproché** this is what he was accused of, and rightly so; **pour pouvoir être à même de traiter v. ce problème** in order to be able to deal with this problem satisfactorily
valdinguer [valdɛ̃ge] *vi F* to fall flat on one's face; **la bouilloire est allée v. contre le placard** the kettle went flying against the cupboard; **envoyer v. ses affaires** to send everything flying; *Fig* **tout envoyer v.** to pack *or* jack it all in; **envoyer v. qn** to tell sb where to go
Valence [valɑ̃s] *nf* **(a)** (*ville d'Espagne*) Valencia **(b)** (*ville de France*) Valence
valence [valɑ̃s] *nf Ch* valency, *Am* valence
valenciennes [valɑ̃sjɛn] *nf* Valenciennes lace
valériane [valerjan] *nf Bot* valerian
valet [valɛ] *nm* **(a)** *Cartes* jack, knave **(b)** (*domestique*) **v. (de chambre)** manservant; **je ne suis pas ton v.** I'm not your servant *or* slave; *Prov* **tel maître, tel v.** like master, like man **(c)** *Menuis etc* clamp **(d)** (*d'un miroir etc*) support, rest, stand **(e)** *Hist* varlet, page
▶ **valet**: **v. de chiens** (*à la chasse*) whipper-in; **v. d'écurie** groom; **v. de ferme** farmhand; **v. de nuit** valet; **v. de pied** footman
valetaille [valtaj] *nf F Péj* serfs
valétudinaire [valetydinɛr] *adj, n Litt* valetudinarian; **vieillard v.** elderly invalid
valeur [valœr] *nf* **(a)** (*prix*) value, worth; **avoir de la v.** to be valuable; **article de v.** article of value, valuable article; **objets de v.** valuables; **de peu de v.** of little value; **sans v.** worthless, of no value; **bijou de grande v.** jewel of great value, very valuable jewel; **d'une v. inestimable** priceless; **des marchandises d'une v. de 5 000 francs** goods to the value of 5,000 francs; **v. sentimentale** sentimental value; **il ne cesse de prendre de la v.** it keeps going up in value, its value is constantly increasing

(b) (*qualité, mérite*) value, worth; (*importance*) (*d'un mot*) value; **livre de grande v.** book of considerable merit; **cela n'a pas grande v.** it's not worth much; **renseignements sans v.** worthless information; **ce document n'a aucune v. légale** this document is not legally binding *or* has no standing in law; **tu sais quelle v. j'accorde à ton avis** you know how much I value your opinion; **j'attache beaucoup de v. à la présentation** I set great store by presentation; **votre argument n'est pas sans v.** your argument is not without its merits; **homme de v.** (*doué*) man of real ability, talented man; (*de mérite*) man of merit; **la v. n'attend pas le nombre des années** good is good, no matter how young you are; **estimer qn à sa juste v.** to judge sb at his/her true value *or* worth; **elle n'a pas conscience de sa propre v.** she doesn't fully appreciate her own value *or* worth; **mettre en v.** (*qch*) to show to advantage; (*ses yeux*) to highlight, to bring out; **mettre un mot en v.** to emphasize a word, to give importance to a word; **mettre une terre en v.** to develop a piece of land; **mise en v. d'un terrain** development of a site; **cette couleur ne met pas du tout son bronzage en v.** that colour does nothing to show off her tan; **elle sait se mettre en v.** she knows how to show herself off to the best advantage; **elle était très en v. avec sa robe bleue** her blue dress was very flattering; **c'est là que le terme prend toute sa v.** that's when the term takes on its full meaning; **il faudra cinq ans à ce vin pour prendre toute sa v.** the wine will be at its best five years from now

(c) *Bourse* **valeurs (boursières)** securities, shares; **valeurs bancaires** bank shares; **valeurs cotées** *ou* **de bourse** quoted securities; **valeurs émises** securities issued

(d) *Mus* (*d'une note*) time (value), length; (*de carte, Math d'une grandeur etc*) value

(e) (*équivalent*) equivalent; **ajouter la v. de deux tasses de lait** add the equivalent of two cups of milk

(f) (*morale*) value; **valeurs sociales/morales** social/moral values; **jugement de v.** value judgement; **avoir le sens des valeurs** to have a sense of values; **selon son échelle de valeurs** according to his scale of values

(g) *Litt* (*courage*) valour, *US* valor; **homme de v.** man of courage; **v. militaire** gallantry
▶ **valeur**: **v. d'achat** purchase value; *Compta* **v. actualisée** present value; *Compta* **v. actuelle** current value; **v. actuelle nette** current net value; *Écon* **v. ajoutée** added value; **à haute v. ajoutée** high value-added; **v. assurable** insurable value; **v. assurée** insured value; **v. de bilan** book value; *Compta* **v. bilantielle** balance-sheet value; **v. en bourse** stock market value; **v. brute** gross value; *Fin* **v. compensée** cleared value; **v. comptable** book value; **v. comptable nette** net book value; **v. déclarée** declared value; **colis chargé avec v. déclarée cent francs** parcel insured for one hundred francs; **v. en douane** customs value, value for customs purposes; **v. d'échange** exchange value; *Fin* **v. à l'échéance** maturity value; *Fin* **v. à l'encaissement** value for collection; *Compta* **v. d'inventaire** balance sheet value, break-up value; *Banque* **v. jour** same-day value; **v. locative** rental value; **v. marchande** market(able) value; **valeurs mobilières** stocks and shares, transferable securities; **valeurs (mobilières) de placement** marketable securities; **valeurs négociables** marketable securities; **v. nominale** (*d'une obligation*) par value; (*d'une action*) nominal value; **valeurs nominatives** registered securities; *Bourse* **v. non cotée** unlisted security; **v. d'origine** original value; **valeurs passives** liabilities; **v. perçue** perceived value; **valeurs de père de famille** blue chip stock; **v. de premier ordre** blue chip; **v. de rachat** (*d'une police*) surrender value; **valeurs réalisables** realizable *or* marketable securities; **v. de reprise** trade-in allowance; **valeurs à revenu fixe** fixed income securities; **valeurs à revenu variable** floating rate *or* variable-rate securities; **valeurs du second marché** unlisted securities; **valeurs des sociétés industrielles** industrials; **valeurs spéculatives** *ou* **de spéculation** speculative securities; *Bourse* **v. temporelle** time value; **v. d'usage** value as a going concern; **valeurs vedettes** glamour stock; **v. vénale** fair market value
valeureusement [valørøzmɑ̃] *adv Litt* gallantly, bravely, valorously
valeureux, -euse [valørø, -øz] *adj Litt* (*dans une bataille*) gallant, valorous
validation [validasjɔ̃] *nf* (*d'un titre de transport, d'élections, d'un mariage etc*) validation; (*d'une loi*) ratifying; (*d'un document etc*) authentication
valide [valid] *adj* **(a)** (*contrat, raison etc*) valid **(b)** (*personne*) fit, able-bodied; (*membre*) functioning
validement [validmɑ̃] *adv* validly
valider [valide] *vt* (*élection, mariage*) to validate; (*contrat etc*) to ratify; (*document*) to authenticate; *Ordinat* (*option*) to confirm; (*cellule, case etc*) to select; **(faire) v. son titre de transport** (*par un contrôleur*) to have one's ticket stamped; (*dans une machine*) to stamp one's ticket
validité [validite] *nf* (*d'un contrat, d'un passeport, d'une opinion etc*) validity; **durée de v. d'un billet** period of validity of a ticket; **établir la v. d'un testament** to prove a will
valise [valiz] *nf* **(a)** (suit)case; **faire sa v./ses valises** to pack one's bag/one's bags; **la v. diplomatique** the diplomatic bag *or US* pouch **(b)** (*sous les yeux*) bag
vallée [vale] *nf* valley; **dans la V. de la Loire/du Rhône** in the Loire/Rhône valley; **v. sèche** *ou* **morte** dried-up valley; **gens de la v.** (*pour les montagnards*) lowlanders; **descendre dans la v.** to go down into the valley; *Litt* **cette v. de larmes** this vale of tears
vallon [valɔ̃] *nm* small valley; (*écossais*) glen
vallonné [valɔne] *adj* (*région*) undulating, hilly
vallonnement [valɔnmɑ̃] *nm* undulation
valoche [valɔʃ] *nf F* case, bag
valoir [valwar] (*prp* **valant**; *pp* **valu**; *pr ind* **je vaux, il vaut, n. valons, ils valent**; *pr sub* **je vaille, n. valions, ils vaillent**; *impf* **je valais**; *p hist* **je valus**; *fu* **je vaudrai**) **1** *vi* **(a)** (*coûter*) to be worth; **maison qui vaut deux cent mille francs** house worth two hundred thousand francs; **un bijou pareil vaut bien 30 000 francs** a piece of jewellery like that must cost a good 30,000 francs; **ça vaut cher** it's expensive; **ça ne vaut pas cher** it's cheap *or* inexpensive; **c'est tout ce que ça vaut** that's all it's worth; **ça ne vaut pas plus que ça** it's not worth more than that, that's all it's worth; **ne pas v. grand-chose** not to be worth much; **il ne vaut pas grand-chose, il ne vaut pas cher** he's not much good, he's not up to much; **son explication ne vaut rien** his explanation is worthless *or* useless; **cela ne vaut rien** that's no good; **ce climat ne vous vaut rien** this climate is bad for you *or* doesn't suit you; **les repas lourds ne me valent rien** heavy meals don't agree with me; **prends mon avis pour ce qu'il vaut** take my advice for what it's worth; **cela ne me dit rien qui vaille** that doesn't sound good to me; **rien ne vaut un bon petit déjeuner** there's nothing like a good breakfast; **à v. sur (une somme)** on account of (a sum); **à v. sur qn** on *or* for account of sb; **payer dix francs à v.** to pay ten francs on account

(b) (*correspondre à*) to be equivalent to; **un franc vaut cent centimes** a franc is equivalent *or* equal to a hundred centimes; **une livre vaut dix francs** a pound is worth *or* equivalent to *or* equal to ten francs; **c'est une façon qui en**

vaut une autre it's as good a way as any (other); **ils se valent tous** there's not much to choose between them, they're all pretty much the same; **ça ne vaut pas ce qui m'est arrivé l'autre jour** that's nothing to what happened to me the other day; **l'un vaut (bien) l'autre** one is (just) as good/bad as the other, there's nothing to choose between them; **il ne vaut pas mieux que son frère** he's no better than his brother; **il ne vaut pas son frère** he can't compare with his brother, *F* he isn't a patch on his brother

(c) **faire v. qch** to make the most of sth; **monture qui fait v. la pierre** setting that shows off the stone (to (good) advantage); **faire v. ses opinions** to command respect for one's opinions; **faire v. ses droits** to assert one's rights; **faire v. son bon droit** to vindicate one's rights; **faire v. ses raisons** to put forward one's reasons; **j'ai fait v. que ...** I pointed out *or* urged that ...; **pour avoir le poste, il a fait v. ses dix ans d'expérience** to get the job, he stressed his ten years' experience; **faire v. son argent** to invest one's money profitably *or* to good account; **faire v. une terre** to farm an estate

(d) (*mériter*) to be worth, to deserve, to merit; **un service en vaut un autre** one good turn deserves another; **le livre vaut d'être lu** the book is worth reading; **cela vaut la peine de faire le voyage, cela vaut le déplacement** it's worth making the journey; **cela ne vaut pas le voyage** it's not worth the journey, it's not worth a special trip; **je viendrai si cela en vaut la peine** I'll come if it's worth (my) while *or* worth the trouble *or* worth it; **cela ne vaut pas la peine de s'y arrêter** there's no point (in) dwelling on it; *F* **ça vaut le coup** it's worth a try; *F* **ça ne vaut pas le coup** it isn't worth the trouble

2 *v impers* [①B28,f,iv] **il vaut mieux** *ou* **il vaudrait mieux rester à la maison** it's *or* it would be better to stay at home; **mieux vaudrait** *ou* **il vaudrait mieux ne pas vous en mêler** you'd better not interfere, it would be better if you didn't interfere; **il vaut mieux qu'il en soit ainsi** it is better that way; **il vaut mieux que vous restiez** you had better stay, it would be better if you stayed; **il vaut mieux** *ou* **mieux vaut partir que de rester** it's better to go than to stay; **ça vaut mieux comme ça** it's better that way; *Prov* **mieux vaut tard que jamais** better late than never; **autant vaut rester ici** we may as well stay here; **choses qu'il vaut autant ne pas rappeler** things best forgotten; **il** *ou* **ça ne vaut pas la peine de les mentionner** they're not worth mentioning; **et ça vaut pour tout le monde** and that goes for everyone

3 **se valoir** *vpr* **tous les métiers se valent** one job is as good as another; **ils se valent** one is (just) as good/bad as the other, there's nothing to choose between them; *F* **ça se vaut** it's the same either way, it's six of one and half a dozen of the other

4 *vt* (a) **v. qch à qn** to earn sb sth; **cela ne m'a valu que des soucis** all it brought me was trouble; **cette action lui a valu d'être décoré** this act won him a decoration; **qu'est-ce qui me vaut cet honneur?** to what do I owe this honour?

(b) **vaille que vaille** at all costs, come what may

valorisant [valɔrisɑ̃] *adj* image-enhancing; **la situation des femmes au foyer n'est guère valorisante** people tend to have a poor opinion of women who work in the home

valorisation [valɔrizasjɔ̃] *nf Com, Fin* increase in value; *Compta* (*d'un inventaire*) valuation; **... ce qui conduira à la v. de vos investissements** ... which will increase *or* enhance the value of your investments; **cela a beaucoup contribué à la v. des femmes au foyer** it did a lot to improve the image of women in the home

valoriser [valɔrize] **1** *vt Com, Fin etc* to increase the value of; **v. une région** to develop the economy *or* to increase the value of a region; **v. qn** to improve sb's image *or* standing **2 se valoriser** *vpr Com, Fin etc* to increase in value; **région/secteur qui se valorise** region/industry which is going through a period of growth, up-and-coming region/industry

valse [vals] *nf* waltz; **v. de Vienne/Chopin** Viennese/Chopin waltz; **faire un tour de v.** to waltz round the room; *Fig F* **la v. du personnel/des ministres** constant changes of staff/the ministerial merry-go-round; *Com* **v. des étiquettes** constant price rises; **v. des prix** spiralling prices; *Fig* **v.-hésitation** pussyfooting, shillyshallying

valser [valse] *vi* to waltz; **la voiture est allée v. contre le mur** the car went careering *or* hurtling into the wall; **faire v. qn** to waltz with sb; *Fig F* to keep sb on the hop; *Fig* **faire v. l'argent** to spend money like water; *Fig F* **envoyer v. qn** (*le projeter*) to send sb flying; (*le renvoyer*) to send sb packing, to show sb the door; **il m'a envoyé v. contre le mur** he sent me flying into the wall; *Fig F* **envoyer v. qch** to send sth flying

valseur, -euse [valsœr, -øz] *n* waltzer

valve [valv] *nf* valve; *MecE* **v. d'arrêt** check valve; *Anat* **v. cardiaque** cardiac valve; **v. de chambre à air** tyre valve; *MecE* **v. de compensation** compensating valve; *MecE* **v. à** *ou* **de dépression** vacuum valve; **v. de gonflage** (*d'un pneu*) tyre valve; *MecE* **v. à inertie** inertia valve; *MecE* **v. modulatrice** modulator valve; *MecE* **v. papillon** butterfly valve; *MecE* **v. de purge** bleed valve; *Électron* **v. redresseuse** rectifying valve

valvulaire [valvylɛr] *adj* valvular

valvule [valvyl] *nf Biol* valvule; *Anat* valve, valvule

vamp [vɑ̃p] **1** *nf* vamp; **faire la v.** to act the vamp; **prendre des airs de v.** to put on a vampish look **2** *adj* vampish; **habillée très v.** dressed very vampishly

vamper [vɑ̃pe] *vt F* to vamp, to seduce

vampire [vɑ̃pir] *nm* (a) *Myth* vampire (b) *Fig Vieilli* (*personne qui s'enrichit aux dépens d'autrui*) extortionist, bloodsucker; (*assassin*) mass murderer (c) *Zool* vampire bat

vampiriser [vɑ̃pirize] *vt* to dominate (psychologically); **v. un enfant** to dominate a child

vampirisme [vɑ̃pirism] *nm* vampirism

VAN [veaɛn] *nf Compta* (*abrév* **valeur actuelle nette**) NPV, net present value

van[1] [vɑ̃] *nm Agr* winnowing basket

van[2] *nm* (*fourgon à chevaux*) horsebox

van[3] [van] *nm* (*camionnette*) van

vanadium [vanadjɔm] *nm Ch* vanadium

vandale [vɑ̃dal] *n* vandal

vandaliser [vɑ̃dalize] *vt* to vandalize

vandalisme [vɑ̃dalism] *nm* vandalism

vandoise [vɑ̃dwaz] *nf* (*poisson*) dace

vanesse [vanɛs] *nf* **v. tortue** tortoiseshell butterfly

vanille [vanij] *nf* vanilla; **gousse de v.** vanilla pod; **glace à la v.** vanilla ice cream; **crème à la v.** vanilla custard

vanillé [vanije] *adj* vanilla(-flavoured *or US* -flavored); **crème vanillée** vanilla custard; **sucre v.** vanilla sugar

vanillier [vanije] *nm* vanilla plant

vanité [vanite] *nf* (a) (*orgueil*) vanity, conceit; **tirer v. de qch** to pride oneself on sth; **elle n'a pas à en tirer v.** it's nothing for her to boast about; **flatter la v. de qn** to flatter sb's vanity; **agir par v.** to act out of vanity (b) (*des plaisirs terrestres etc*) futility, emptiness, hollowness, *Litt* vanity

vaniteusement [vanitøzmɑ̃] *adv* conceitedly

vaniteux, -euse [vanitø, -øz] **1** *adj* vain, conceited **2** *n* **c'est un v.** he's (very) conceited

vanity-case, *pl* **vanity-cases** [vanitikɛs] *nm* vanity case

vannage [vanaʒ] *nm* (*du grain*) winnowing

vanne[1] [van] *nf* (a) *HydE* sluice (gate), floodgate, water gate; **v. de décharge** overflow weir; *MecE* **v. manuelle** manual valve; *HydE, Fig* **ouvrir/mettre les vannes** to open/close the floodgates (b) *Tech etc* valve (c) *Naut* cock

vanne[2] *nf F* (*remarque blessante*) dig, jibe; **lancer** *ou* **faire des vannes** to make snide remarks; **envoyer** *ou* **lancer une v. à qn** to have a dig at sb

vanneau, -eaux [vano] *nm* (*oiseau*) lapwing, peewit; *Culin* **œufs de v.** plovers' eggs

vanner [vane] *vt* (a) *F* (*fatiguer*) to wear out, to exhaust; **être (complètement) vanné** to be dead beat *or* all in (b) (*grain*) to winnow

vannerie [vanri] *nf* (a) (*activité*) basket making, basketry (b) (*objets*) basketwork, wickerwork

vanneur, -euse [vanœr, -øz] *n* winnower

vannier [vanje] *nm* basket worker *or* maker

vantail, -aux [vɑ̃taj, -o] *nm* (*d'une porte, d'un volet, d'une vanne*) leaf; **porte à deux vantaux** folding door

vantard, -arde [vɑ̃tar, -ard] **1** *adj* boasting, boastful, bragging, *F* loudmouthed **2** *n* braggart, boaster, *F* loudmouth

vantardise [vɑ̃tardiz] *nf* (*caractère*) bragging, boastfulness; (*parole*) boast

vanter [vɑ̃te] **1** *vt* to praise, to speak highly of, *Litt* to vaunt; *Fig* **v. sa marchandise** to blow one's own trumpet; **magazine qui vante les charmes de l'Écosse** magazine which sings the praises of Scotland **2 se vanter** *vpr* to boast, to brag; **ce n'est pas pour me v., mais ...** I don't mean to boast, but ...; **il n'y a pas de quoi se v.** there's nothing to boast about; **tu ne t'en es pas vanté!** you kept that quiet *or* under your hat!; **se v. de qch/d'être ...** to pride oneself on sth/on being ...

va-nu-pieds [vanypje] *n inv* tramp, beggar; (*enfant*) (street) urchin, ragamuffin

vapes [vap] *nfpl F* **être dans les v.** to be groggy; (*rêver*) to have one's head in the clouds; **je n'écoutais pas, j'étais dans les v.** I wasn't listening, I was miles away; **tomber dans les v.** to pass out, to faint

vapeur[1] [vapœr] *nf* (a) **v. (d'eau)** steam, (water) vapour *or US* vapor; **prendre des bains de v.** to take steam baths; **machine à v.** steam engine; **locomotive à v.** steam locomotive; **bateau à v.** steamer, steamship; **mettre la v.** to put steam on; *Fig* **nous avons dû mettre la v. pour finir à temps** we had to pull out all the stops to finish on time; **navire sous v.** ship under steam; **à toute v.** (at) full steam *or* speed, full steam ahead

(**b**) **v. d'essence/d'éther/d'alcool** petrol/ether/alcoholic vapour; **flotter dans les vapeurs de l'alcool** to be high on the heady fumes of alcohol

(**c**) (*brume*) haze, vapour

(**d**) *Culin* **cuire des légumes à la v.** to steam vegetables; **faire la cuisine** *ou* **cuisiner à la v.** to steam food

(**e**) **vapeurs** (*du vin, d'essence etc*) fumes; *Méd Arch* vapours; **avoir ses vapeurs** to have (a fit of) the vapours

vapeur[2] *nm Naut* steamer, steamship

vapocraquage [vapokrakaʒ] *nm Pétr* steam cracking

vapocraqueur [vapokrakœr] *nm Pétr* steam cracking plant

vaporeux, -euse [vapɔrø, -øz] *adj* (*atmosphère*) steamy; (*idées etc*) hazy; (*robe*) flimsy; *Fig* **femme vaporeuse** sylph-like woman

vaporisateur [vapɔrizatœr] *nm* (*de parfum etc*) spray, atomizer; *Tech* vaporizer; (*de jardinage*) spray(er)

vaporisation [vapɔrizasjɔ̃] *nf* (*de parfum, engrais etc*) spraying; *Tech* vaporization; *Aut* **v. (du carburant)** (fuel) atomization

vaporiser [vapɔrize] **1** *vt* (**a**) (*gazéifier*) to vaporize (**b**) (*liquide*) to spray; **v. ses cheveux de laque** to spray one's hair with lacquer **2 se vaporiser** *vpr* to become vaporized, to vaporize

vaquer [vake] *vi* (**a**) **v. à qch** to attend to sth; **v. aux soins du ménage** to see to the housework; **v. à ses affaires** *ou* **occupations** to go about *or* see to one's business (**b**) (*du parlement, du tribunal*) to be on vacation *or* in recess, not to be sitting (**c**) *Vieilli* (*d'un poste*) to be vacant

varappe [varap] *nf* rock climbing; **faire de la v.** to rock-climb, to go rock climbing

varapper [varape] *vi* to rock-climb

varappeur, -euse [varapœr, -øz] *nm* rock climber

varech [varɛk] *nm* wrack, seaweed, kelp, varec

vareuse [varøz] *nf* (**a**) (*de marin*) pea jacket *or* coat, reefer (**b**) *Mil* tunic (**c**) (*veste large*) loose-fitting jacket

variabilité [varjabilite] *nf* (**a**) *Biol, Gram etc* variability (**b**) (*de l'humeur, du temps*) changeableness

variable [varjabl] **1** *adj* (**a**) *Biol, Gram, Math* variable (**b**) (*humeur etc*) changeable; (*baromètre*) unsteady; (*vitesse*) varying; (*temps*) changeable, unsettled; **être v.** to vary; **c'est très v.** it's very variable, it varies a lot **2** *nm* **le baromètre est au v.** the barometer is at change **3** *nf Math, Ordinat* variable; *Ordinat* **v. de mémoire** memory variable

variance [varjɑ̃s] *nf* variance

variant, -ante [varjɑ̃, -ɑ̃t] **1** *adj* variable, fickle **2** *nf* **variante** (*d'interprétation, d'orthographe*) variant, variation

variateur [varjatœr] *nm* **v. d'intensité** (*d'une lampe électrique*) dimmer switch; **v. de vitesse** speed variator

variation [varjasjɔ̃] *nf* (**a**) **v. du temps** change in the weather; **v. des températures/des prix** variation in temperature/prices; **v. du compas** compass error; **v. de l'opinion** change of opinion; **variations saisonnières** seasonal variations *or* fluctuations (**b**) *Mus* variation; **air avec variations** theme and variations

varice [varis] *nf Méd* varicose vein; **avoir des varices** to have varicose veins; **des bas anti-varices** support stockings

varicelle [varisɛl] *nf Méd* chickenpox, *Spéc* varicella; **avoir la v.** to have chickenpox

varié [varje] *adj* (*alimentation, paysage*) varied; (*échantillons*) varying, various; (*vocabulaire*) wide; (*nouvelles*) miscellaneous; (*existence*) varied, chequered; *Mus* **air v.** air with variations; *Phys* **mouvement v.** variable motion; **terrain v.** uneven *or* irregular terrain; *Culin* **hors d'œuvre variés** selection of starters; **un travail très peu v.** a monotonous job, a job with little variety

varier [varje] (*impf, pr sub* **n. variions, v. variiez**) **1** *vt* to vary; (*occupations etc*) to vary, to diversify; **v. son alimentation** to vary one's diet; *Fig Iron* **pour v. les plaisirs** by way of a pleasant change **2** *vi* to vary, to change; *Fin* (*des marchés*) to fluctuate; **v. dans ses réponses** to be inconsistent in one's replies; **les auteurs varient souvent** authors often differ *or* vary; **les prix peuvent v. du simple au double** prices can vary by a factor of two; **leurs opinions varient sur ce point** they differ *or* they don't see eye to eye on this point; **v. de méthode** to vary one's methods

variété [varjete] *nf* (**a**) variety (**de** of); (*d'avis etc*) diversity, range; **manquer de v.** to lack variety; **la v. des paysages** the varying nature of the landscapes; **la v. des articles dans un magasin** the variety *or* range of articles in a shop; *Com* **grande v. de rayons** wide range of departments; **donner de la v. au menu** to vary the menu; **apporter de la v. à son alimentation** to vary one's diet (**b**) *Th* (**spectacle de**) **variétés** variety show; *TV* **émission de variétés** variety show *or* programme; **regarder les variétés à la télévision** to watch variety shows on television (**c**) *Biol* (*de fleur etc*) variety

variole [varjɔl] *nf Méd* smallpox; **avoir la v.** to have smallpox; *Vét* **v. des vaches** cowpox

variolé [varjɔle] *adj* pockmarked

varioleux, -euse [varjɔlø, -øz] *Méd* **1** *adj* (*boutons etc*) variolous **2** *n* smallpox victim

variqueux, -euse [varikø, -øz] *adj* (*veine etc*) varicose

varlet [varlɛ] *nm Arch* varlet, page

varlope [varlɔp] *nf Menuis* trying plane

Varsovie [varsɔvi] *nf* Warsaw; **les pays du Pacte de V.** the Warsaw Pact countries

vasculaire [vaskylɛr] *adj* vascular

vascularisation [vaskylarizasjɔ̃] *nf Méd* vascularization

vase[1] [vɑz] *nm* vase; **v. à fleurs** flower vase; **v. à pied** vase with a stem, stemmed vase; **v. en cristal** crystal vase; **vivre en v. clos** to live in isolation *or* a vacuum

▶ **vase**: *Él, Phys* **vases communicants** communicating vessels; *Fig* **quand lui ça va, moi ça ne va pas, on est comme des vases communicants** when he's OK, I'm not, and vice versa, it's like a see-saw; **v. d'un élément de pile** battery jar; *Aut* **v. d'expansion** expansion tank; **v. de nuit** chamber pot; **v. poreux** porous cell

vase[2] *nf* mud, silt, ooze, sludge; **marais plein de v.** muddy swamp; **banc de v.** mudbank

vasectomie [vazɛktɔmi] *nf Chir* vasectomy

vaseline [vazlin] *nf* Vaseline®, petroleum jelly; *Pharm* **huile de v.** liquid paraffin

vaseux, -euse [vazø, -øz] *adj* (**a**) *F* (*personne*) off-colour, *US* off-color; **il a l'air v.** he looks a bit off-colour *or* under the weather; **des idées vaseuses** woolly ideas; **explication vaseuse** confused *or* muddled explanation; **plaisanterie vaseuse** off-colour *or* unsavoury joke (**b**) (*rivière*) muddy, silty, sludgy

vasistas [vazistɑs] *nm* fanlight

vaso(-)constricteur, -trice, *pl* **vaso(-)constricteurs, -trices** [vazokɔ̃striktœr, -tris] *adj, nm Anat* vasoconstrictor

vaso(-)dilatateur, -trice, *pl* **vaso(-)dilatateurs, -trices** [vazodilatatœr, -tris] *adj, nm Anat* vasodilator

vaso(-)moteur, -trice, *pl* **vaso(-)moteurs, -trices** [vazomɔtœr, -tris] *adj Anat* (*nerf*) vasomotor

vasouillard [vazujar] *adj F* (*person*) confused, muddled; **je me sens un peu v. ce matin** I'm not thinking very straight *or* I feel a bit dopy this morning; **il a donné une excuse plutôt vasouillarde** he got a bit bogged down in his apology

vasouiller [vazuje] *vi F* to flounder, to stammer and stutter

vasque [vask] *nf* (**a**) (*d'une fontaine*) basin (**b**) (*coupe décorative*) (ornamental) bowl

vassal, -ale, -aux, -ales [vasal, -o] *n* vassal

vassalité [vasalite] *nf*, **vasselage** [vaslaʒ] *nm* vassalage; *Fig* (*soumission*) vassalage, bondage

vaste [vast] *adj* vast, immense, huge; *F* (*plaisanterie etc*) big, great; **avoir de vastes ambitions** to have great ambitions; **v. étendue** vast *or* broad expanse; **le v. monde** the wide world; **de par le v. monde** the whole world over; **v. érudition** vast *or* comprehensive learning; **c'est une v. fumisterie** it's a complete *or* total farce

vastement [vastəmɑ̃] *adv* vastly

Vatican (le) [ləvatikɑ̃] *nm* the Vatican

Vaticane [vatikan] *adj, nf* **la (Bibliothèque) V.** the Vatican Library

vaticination [vatisinasjɔ̃] *nf Litt* vaticination

vaticiner [vatisine] *vi Litt* to vaticinate

va-tout [vatu] *nm inv* (*au jeu*), *Fig* **jouer son v.** to stake one's all

vaudeville [vodvil] *nm* (**a**) *Th* (*comédie légère*) light comedy; (*avant le 19e*) light comedy with songs and dances, vaudeville; *Fig* **cette histoire est un vrai v.** this story is a real farce (**b**) *Vieilli* (*chanson*) topical *or* satirical song (*with refrain*)

vaudevillesque [vodvilɛsk] *adj* comical, farcical

vaudevilliste [vodvilist] *nm Th* vaudeville writer

vaudois, -oise [vodwa, -waz] **1** *adj* (**a**) (*du canton de Vaud*) Vaudois, of/from Vaud (**b**) *Hist, Rel* Waldensian **2** *n* **V.** (**a**) Vaudois; (*natif*) native of Vaud; (*habitant*) inhabitant of Vaud (**b**) *Hist, Rel* Waldensian

vaudou [vodu] **1** *nm* voodoo **2** *adj* **culte v.** voodoo cult

vau-l'eau (à) [avolo] *adv* downstream, with the stream; *Fig* **tout s'en va à v.** everything's going to rack and ruin *or* to the dogs

vaurien, -ienne [vorjɛ̃, -jɛn] *n* good-for-nothing, *F* layabout, *Br* yob; **petit v.!** you little scamp!, you little rascal!

vautour [votur] *nm* vulture

vautrer (se) [səvotre] *vpr* (*d'un cochon*) (*dans la boue*) to wallow; (*d'une personne*) (*dans l'herbe, sur un canapé*) to sprawl; **vautré dans le fauteuil** lolling in the armchair; *Fig* **se v. dans le vice** to wallow *or* revel in vice

vauvert [vovɛr] *adj* **c'est au diable v.** it's miles from anywhere, it's out in the wilds *or* a long way away

va-vite (à la) [alavavit] *adv* in a rush, in a hurry; **travail fait à la v.** rushed *or* slapdash work

veau, -eaux [vo] *nm* **(a)** [①A12,1,d] (*animal*) calf; *F* **pleurer comme un v.** to cry one's eyes out, to blubber **(b)** *Culin* veal; **rôti de v.** roast veal; **côtelette de v.** veal cutlet; **tête de v.** calf's head; **gelée de pied de v.** calf's *or* calves' foot jelly **(c)** (*cuir*) calf leather, calfskin **(d)** *F* (*idiot*) fool, clot; (*abruti*) lump, lout **(e)** *F* (*voiture*) tank

▶ **veau**: **v. gras: tuer le v. gras** to kill the fatted calf; **v. marin** seal; **v. d'or: adorer le v. d'or** to worship the golden calf

vecteur, -trice [vɛktœr, -tris] **1** *adj Math* **rayon v.** radius vector **2** *nm* **(a)** *Math, Méd* vector; *Fig* **v. d'information/de progrès** vehicle for information/for progress **(b)** (*pour charge nucléaire etc*) vehicle

vectoriel, -ielle [vɛktɔrjɛl] *adj Math, Ordinat* vectorial; *Math* **espace v.** vector space; *Ordinat* **police vectorielle** outline font

vectorisation [vɛktɔrizasjɔ̃] *nf Ordinat* **v. d'images** image vectoring

vécu [veky] **1** *adj* **(a) choses vécues** things which have been lived through, actual experiences **(b)** (*pièce, roman*) true to life, founded on fact **2** *nm* real-life experience; **le livre m'a intéressé parce que c'était du v.** I found the book interesting because it was based on a real-life experience

vedettariat [vədɛtarja] *nm Cin etc* stardom; **adorer le v.** to love stardom, to love being famous

vedette [vədɛt] *nf* **(a)** *Th, Cin etc* star; *Mktg* (*produit*) star; **v. de cinéma** film *or* movie star; **v. de la chanson** singing star; **v. du barreau/de l'industrie** a big name at the bar/in industry; **une grande v. de la politique** a leading light in politics

(b) avoir la v. (sur l'affiche) (*d'un acteur*) to head *or* top the bill, to have star billing; **ce problème a** *ou* **tient la v. depuis longtemps dans ce pays** the problem has long been a major concern in this country; **cette question a la v. dans tous les journaux** this issue is making the headlines in all the newspapers; **être en v.** to be in the limelight, to (have) hit the headlines; **mettre qn/qch en v.** to highlight *or* spotlight sb/sth; **mettre un nom/mot en v.** to highlight *or* emphasize a name/word; **mots en v.** words in bold type

(c) *Naut* small motorboat, launch; (*de police etc*) patrol boat

(d) *Mil Arch* vedette, mounted sentry; **en v.** on vedette duty

▶ **vedette**: **v. américaine: passer en v. américaine** to be the warm-up act, to get second billing

végétal, -ale, -aux, -ales [veʒetal, -o] **1** *adj* **vie végétale** plant life; **sol v.** humus; **huile végétale** vegetable oil **2** *nm* vegetable, plant

végétalien, -ienne [veʒetaljɛ̃, -jɛn] *adj, n* vegan

végétalisme [veʒetalism] *nm* veganism

végétarien, -ienne [veʒetarjɛ̃, -jɛn] *adj, n* vegetarian

végétarisme [veʒetarism] *nm* vegetarianism

végétatif, -ive [veʒetatif, -iv] *adj* vegetative; *Fig Péj* (*existence*) vegetable-like

végétation [veʒetasjɔ̃] *nf* **(a)** (*flore*) vegetation **(b)** *Méd* **végétations** vegetations; **végétations (adénoïdes)** adenoids, adenoid growths; **opérer un enfant des végétations** to take out a child's adenoids

végéter [veʒete] *vi* (**je végète; je végéterai**) **(a)** *Péj* (*d'une personne*) to vegetate; **il végète dans ce bureau** he's just vegetating in that office **(b)** *Arch* (*d'une plante*) to vegetate, to grow

véhémence [veemɑ̃s] *nf Litt* vehemence; **avec v.** vehemently; **s'exprimer avec v.** to express oneself vehemently *or* passionately

véhément [veemɑ̃] *adj Litt* vehement, violent; **un orateur v.** a vehement *or* passionate speaker

véhémentement [veemɑ̃tmɑ̃] *adv Litt* vehemently

véhiculaire [veikylɛr] *adj* **langue v.** common language, lingua franca

véhicule [veikyl] *nm* **(a)** (*moyen de transport*) vehicle; **v. articulé** articulated vehicle, *F* artic; **v. à chenilles** tracked *or* tracklaying vehicle; **v. à moteur** motor vehicle; **v. multifonction ou à usages multiples** multi-purpose vehicle, MPV; **v. de remplacement** courtesy car; **v. de secours** rescue vehicle; **v. de service** company car (*for general use of company staff*); **v. spatial** spacecraft; **v. spécial pour handicapés** invalid carriage; **v. de tourisme** private vehicle; **v. de transport de marchandises** heavy goods vehicle, HGV; **v. utilitaire** commercial *or* goods vehicle

(b) (*moyen de diffusion*) vehicle; **la parole est le v. de la pensée** speech is the vehicle of thought; **le v. du son/de la lumière** the medium *or* the vehicle of sound/light; *Fig* **la radio est un v. de l'information** radio is a vehicle for information *or* is a news medium

véhiculer [veikyle] *vt* to transport, to convey, to carry; (*émotion*) to convey, to carry

veille [vɛj] *nf* **(a)** (*jour qui précède*) preceding day, previous day; **je l'avais vu la v.** I'd seen him the day before; **la v. au soir** the evening before, the previous evening; **la v. de Noël** Christmas Eve; **la v. du jour de l'an** New Year's Eve; **la v. de la bataille** the day before the battle, the eve of the battle; *Fig* **être à la v. de la ruine/d'une guerre** to be on the brink *or* verge of ruin/of a war; **nous étions à la v. de nous séparer** we were on the brink *or* verge of splitting up; **être à la v. de se marier** to be on the point of getting married, to be about to get married; **à la v. de la réunion** just before the meeting; *F* **ce n'est pas demain la v.** it's not going to happen tomorrow

(b) (*absence de sommeil*) wakefulness; **entre la v. et le sommeil** between waking and sleeping

(c) (*volontaire*) sitting up, staying up; (*auprès d'un malade*) watching, keeping watch

(d) *Mil* (night) watch; *Naut* lookout; *Naut* **homme de v.** lookout (man); *Naut* **chambre de v.** chart house; **ancre de v.** sheet anchor; **prendre la v.** to take one's turn on watch

(e) *Ordinat* standby mode; **en v.** in standby mode

veillée [veje] *nf* **(a)** (*soirée*) (*avec des amis etc*) evening; **pendant les longues veillées d'hiver** during the long winter evenings; **prolonger la v. jusqu'aux petites heures du matin** to stay up until the small hours; **v. au coin du feu** evening spent round the fire; **faire la v. chez qn** to spend the evening at sb's house **(b)** (*d'un malade*) night nursing; (*d'un mort*) watch, vigil

veiller [veje] **1** *vi* **(a)** (*ne pas dormir*) to sit up, to stay up, to keep awake; **je n'ai pas l'habitude de v.** I'm not used to staying up late; **v. tard dans la nuit** to stay up late; **v. auprès d'un malade** to sit up with a sick person

(b) v. à qch to watch over *or* see to sth; **v. aux intérêts de qn** to look after *or* watch over sb's interests; **v. à la besogne** to keep an eye on the work; **v. à ce que qch se fasse** to see (to it) that sth is done; *Fig* **v. au grain** to keep an eye open for trouble

(c) v. sur qn to watch over *or* look after sb, to take care of sb

(d) *Mil etc* to watch, to be on (the) lookout

2 *vt* (*malade etc*) to sit up with, to watch over; **v. un mort** to keep vigil over a dead body

veilleur, -euse [vɛjœr, -øz] **1** *nm Mil etc* lookout **2** *nf* **veilleuse (a)** (*lampe*) night light; (*sur TV etc*) standby; **mettre la lampe en veilleuse** to dim the light; *Fig* **mettre une entreprise en veilleuse** to reduce output to a minimum; *Fig* **mettre un projet en veilleuse** to shelve a project, to put a project on the back burner; *Fig F* **s'il pouvait la mettre en veilleuse!** I wish he'd cool it *or* put a sock in it!; **mets-la en veilleuse, s'il te plaît!** just put a sock in it, will you! **(b)** *Aut* sidelight **(c)** (*sur une cuisinière etc*) pilot light **(d)** *Bot* meadow saffron

▶ **veilleur: v. de nuit** night watchman

veilleuses-codes *nfpl Aut* dim-dip

veinard, -arde [vɛnar, -ard] *F* **1** *adj* (*personne*) lucky, *Br F* jammy **2** *n* lucky devil, *Br F* jammy so-and-so; **c'est un v.** he has all the luck; **v.!** lucky *or Br F* jammy devil!

veine [vɛn] *nf* **(a)** *Anat, Bot etc* vein; *Anat* **v. cave** vena cava; **v. porte** portal vein; **elle menace de s'ouvrir les veines** she's threatening to slash *or* slit *or* cut her wrists; *Fig* **il a du sang dans les veines** he's got guts; **montre-nous si tu as du sang dans les veines!** show us what you're made of!, show us your mettle!, show us whether you're a man or a mouse!

(b) *Géol* vein; (*de minerai*) lode; (*de charbon*) seam

(c) (*inspiration*) vein; **la v. poétique** the poetic vein; **en v. de plaisanterie** in humorous vein; **être en v. de faire qch** to be in the mood to do sth *or* for doing sth; **être en v. de générosité** to be in a generous mood, to be feeling generous

(d) *F* (*chance*) luck; **avoir de la v.** to be in luck, to be lucky; **j'ai eu pas mal de v.** I've had my fair share of luck; **elle n'a pas eu de v.** she's been unlucky; **tu as une v. de pendu** *ou Vulg* **cocu!** you've got the devil's own luck, you've got the luck of the devil!; **pas de v.!** rotten luck!; **alors là, pas de v., j'étais là avant toi** that's just your rotten luck, I was there before you; **c'est bien ma v.!** just my (rotten) luck!; **quelle v.!** talk about lucky!; **coup de v.** stroke of luck, fluke

veiné [vene] *adj* **(a)** *Anat* **bras v.** arm where the veins are very close to the surface **(b)** *(bois etc)* grained
veiner [vene] *vt (porte etc)* to vein, to grain
veineux, -euse [venø, -øz] *adj* **(a)** *(système, sang)* venous **(b)** *(bois etc)* veined, grainy
veinule [venyl] *nf Anat* venule
veinure [venyr] *nf (du bois etc)* graining
vêlage [velaʒ] *nm (d'une vache)* calving
vélaire [velɛr] *adj, nf Ling* velar
velcro® [vɛlkro] *nm* **(fermeture) v.** Velcro (fastening); **fermé par un v.** fastened with Velcro, with a Velcro fastening
vêlement [vɛlmɑ̃] *nm* = **vêlage**
vêler [vɛle] *vi (d'une vache)* to calve
vélin [velɛ̃] *nm* vellum (parchment); **(papier) v.** vellum (paper)
véliplanchiste [veliplɑ̃ʃist] *n* windsurfer
velléitaire [veleitɛr] **1** *adj* indecisive **2** *n* indecisive person
velléité [veleite] *nf* vague desire *or* inclination, stray impulse; **faire qch par v.** to do sth on a whim; **j'ai des velléités de changement** I have a vague desire *or* inclination for change; **avoir des velléités de travail** to toy with the idea of work
vélo [velo] *nm* bicycle, bike; **aller à** *ou* **en v.** to cycle, to ride a bike; **je vais au travail en** *ou* **à v.** I cycle to work, I go to work on my bike, I ride my bike to work; **est-ce que tu sais faire du v.** *ou* **monter à v.?** can you ride a bike?; **aimes-tu faire du v.?** do you like cycling?; **v. de (cyclo-)cross/de piste** cyclo-cross/racing bike; **v. de course** racing cycle, *F* racer; **v. d'appartement** exercise bike; **v. tout-terrain** mountain bike
vélocipède [velosipɛd] *nm Arch* velocipede; *Hum* bike
vélocité [velɔsite] *nf* speed, swiftness; *Tech* velocity; **exercice de v. au piano** five-finger exercise
vélodrome [velodrɔm] *nm* velodrome
vélomoteur [velomɔtœr] *nm* moped
velours [v(ə)lur] *nm* **(a)** *Tex* velvet; **le v. de ses joues/touche** his velvety cheeks/touch; **ce fruit est doux comme du v.** this fruit is as smooth as velvet; **goûte ce vin, c'est du v.** taste this wine, it's sheer velvet; **veste/rideaux en v.** velvet jacket/curtains; **pantalon en v. côtelé** corduroy trousers, cords; *Fig* **jouer sur le v.** to be on velvet; **elle lui fait ses yeux de v.** she is making (sheep's) eyes at him; **la Révolution de v.** the Velvet Revolution; **avoir un regard de v.** to have velvety eyes
(b) *(liaison incorrecte)* incorrect liaison (e.g. **j'ai été** [ʒezete])
▶ **velours: v. bouclé** uncut velvet; **v. côtelé** *ou* **à côtes** ribbed velvet, corduroy (velvet); **v. de coton** cotton velvet, velveteen; **v. façonné** figured velvet; **v. de laine** velour(s); **v. de soie** silk velvet; **v. uni** plain velvet
velouté [vəlute] **1** *adj (joues)* velvety, velvet-soft; *(pêche)* velvety, downy; *(vin)* velvety, smooth, mellow **2** *nm* **(a)** *(d'un tissu, des voix etc)* velvetiness, softness; *(d'une pêche etc)* bloom **(b)** *Culin* thick *or* cream soup; **v. de champignons** cream of mushroom soup
velouter [vəlute] *vt (qch)* to give a velvety appearance to; *(un son)* to soften; *(un goût)* to smooth; *(d'une ombre) (contours)* to soften
velouteux, -euse [vəlutø, -øz] *adj* velvety, soft
Velpeau® [vɛlpo] *nm Méd* **bande V.** crêpe bandage
velu [vəly] *adj* hairy
vélum, velum [velɔm] *nm* awning
Vélux® [velyks] *nm* Velux window
venaison [vənɛzɔ̃] *nf* venison
vénal, -ale, -aux, -ales [venal, -o] *adj* **(a)** *(privilège, droit etc)* venal, purchasable; *Com* **valeur vénale** market value **(b)** *Péj (personne)* venal, mercenary, corruptible; *(presse)* corrupt; **l'amour v.** venal love
vénalement [venalmɑ̃] *adv* venally
vénalité [venalite] *nf* venality
venant [vənɑ̃] *nm* **à tout v., à tous venants** to all comers, to all and sundry; **s'occuper du tout v.** to deal with the everyday *or* run-of-the-mill stuff
vendable [vɑ̃dabl] *adj* saleable, sellable; **facilement/difficilement v.** easy/difficult to sell
vendange [vɑ̃dɑ̃ʒ] *nf* **(a)** *(temps)* **vendanges** vintage (season); **pendant les vendanges** during the grape-harvesting *or* -picking season **(b)** *(récolte)* grape gathering *or* picking, wine harvest, grape harvest, vintage; **faire la** *ou* **les vendange(s)** to harvest *or* pick the grapes **(c)** *(raisin récolté)* grapes (harvested); **une bonne v.** a good vintage
vendanger [vɑ̃dɑ̃ʒe] **(je vendangeai(s); n. vendangeons) 1** *vt (raisin)* to harvest, to pick, to gather, to vintage **2** *vi* **ils sont partis v. dans le Midi** they went to pick grapes in the South of France
vendangeur, -euse [vɑ̃dɑ̃ʒœr, -øz] **1** *n* grape picker, vintager **2** *nf Bot* **vendangeuse** aster
vendéen, -enne [vɑ̃deɛ̃, -ɛn] **1** *adj* of/from the Vendée **2** *n* **V.** *(natif)* native of the Vendée; *(habitant)* inhabitant of the Vendée
vendémiaire [vɑ̃demjɛr] *nm Hist Fr* = first month of the French Republican calendar *(Sep 22nd—Oct 21st)*
vendetta [vɑ̃deta] *nf* vendetta
vendeur, -euse [vɑ̃dœr, -øz] *n (dans un magasin)* salesperson, salesman, *f* saleswoman, (shop) assistant, *Am* (sales)clerk; *(non professionnel)* seller; *Bourse* seller; *Jur* vendor; *Fig* **les vendeurs d'évasion** dream merchants, the dream industry; **j'allais vendre ma voiture mais je ne suis plus v.** I was going to sell my car but I've decided not to *or* but I've taken it off the market
▶ **vendeur: v. ambulant** travelling salesman; **v. export** exporter; **v. de journaux** newspaper seller *or* vendor *or* man; *Mktg* **v.-représentant-placier,** *pl* **vendeurs-représentants-placiers** sales representative
vendre [vɑ̃dr] **1** *vt* **(a)** to sell; *(commercialiser)* to market; **v. qch à qn** to sell sb sth, to sell sth to sb; **v. comptant** to sell for cash; **v. à crédit** to sell on credit; **v. de gré à gré** to sell privately; **v. à perte** to sell at a loss; *Bourse* **v. à terme** to sell forward; **v. qch en gros** to sell sth wholesale; **v. qch au détail** to sell sth retail, to retail sth; **v. moins cher que qn** to undersell sb; **dans ce magasin, ils vendent moins cher que partout ailleurs** this shop undersells everywhere else, this shop is cheaper than anywhere else; **v. chèrement sa vie** to sell one's life dearly; **v. un objet (à) 50 francs** to sell an object for 50 francs; **maison à v.** house for sale; **l'art de v.** salesmanship; *Écon* **pays qui vend du pétrole/du café** oil-/coffee-selling country; *Fin* **v. des valeurs** to sell stocks and shares; *Fig* **v. de l'évasion** *ou* **du rêve** to sell dreams; **v. son âme au Diable** to sell one's soul to the Devil
(b) v. qn *(pour dette)* to sell sb up
(c) *(qn, secret)* to betray, to give away
2 se vendre *vpr* **(a) cela se vend comme des petits pains** it's selling like hot cakes
(b) to sell oneself; **la société doit mieux se v.** the company has to market itself better; *Péj* **se v. à l'ennemi** to sell oneself *or* to sell out to the enemy
vendredi [vɑ̃drədi] *nm* [①A75-6,B-C; B58-9,B-C] Friday; **le v. saint** Good Friday
vendu, -ue [vɑ̃dy] **1** *n* traitor **2** *adj (corrompu)* bribed
venelle [vənɛl] *nf* alley
vénéneux, -euse [venenø, -øz] *adj* poisonous; **champignon v.** toadstool
vénérable [venerabl] **1** *adj* venerable **2** *nm (d'une loge maçonnique)* worshipful master
vénération [venerasjɔ̃] *nf* veneration, reverence; **avoir de la v. pour qn** to hold sb in veneration, to revere sb
vénérer [venere] *vt* **(je vénère, n. vénérons; je vénérerai) (a)** *(admirer)* to venerate, to revere **(b)** *(saint etc)* to worship
vénerie [vɛnri] *nf* hunting, *Spéc* venery; **petite/grande v.** small game/big game hunting
vénérien, -ienne [venerjɛ̃, -jɛn] *adj Méd* venereal; **maladie vénérienne** venereal disease, VD
vénérologie [venerɔlɔʒi] *nf Méd* venereology
veneur [vənœr] *nm* huntsman; *Hist* **le Grand V.** the Master of the Royal Hunt
Vénézuéla [venezɥela] *nm* Venezuela
vénézuélien, -ienne [venezɥeljɛ̃, -jɛn] **1** *adj* Venezuelan **2** *n* **V.** Venezuelan
vengeance [vɑ̃ʒɑ̃s] *nf* revenge, vengeance; **esprit de v.** feeling of revenge *or* vengeance; **soif/désir de v.** thirst/desire for revenge, vengefulness; **par v.** out of revenge; **tirer v. d'une injure** to be revenged for an insult; *Prov* **la v. est un plat qui se mange froid** revenge is a dish best eaten cold; **v. sanglante** bloodthirsty revenge; **exercer sa v. sur qn** to have one's revenge *or* vengeance on sb; **crime qui crie v.** crime that cries out for vengeance; *Rel* **v. divine** divine retribution
venger [vɑ̃ʒe] **(je vengeai(s); n. vengeons) 1** *vt* to avenge; **v. qn d'une injure** to avenge sb for an insult **2 se venger** *vpr* to be revenged, to have *or* get one's revenge; **se v. sur qn (de qch)** to take (one's) revenge on sb (for sth); *F* **pas la peine de te v. sur moi!** there's no point in taking it out on me!
vengeur, -eresse [vɑ̃ʒœr, -(ə)rɛs] *Litt* **1** *n* avenger **2** *adj* avenging, (re)vengeful
véniel, -ielle [venjɛl] *adj (péché)* venial
venimeux, -euse [vənimø, -øz] *adj* **(a)** *(serpent)* venomous, poisonous; *(morsure)* poisonous **(b)** *Fig* spiteful, malicious
venin [vənɛ̃] *nm* **(a)** *(d'un serpent etc)* venom, poison **(b)** *Fig* spite, malice; **jeter** *ou* **cracher son v.** to vent one's spleen
venir [v(ə)nir] *(prp* **venant**; *pp* **venu**; *pr ind* **je viens, il vient, n. venons, ils viennent**; *pr sub* **je vienne**; *impf* **je venais**; *p hist* **je vins, n. vînmes, v. vîntes, ils vinrent**; *p sub* **je vinsse**; *fu* **je viendrai**; *aux* **être) 1** *vi* **(a)** to come; **il doit v. passer quelques jours chez nous** he's coming to spend a few days

with us; **les larmes lui vinrent aux yeux** tears came to his eyes; **cela me fait v. l'eau à la bouche** it makes my mouth water; **je viens!** I'm coming!; **je ne ferai qu'aller et v.** I'll come straight back; **je n'ai fait qu'aller et v. entre la maison et le bureau** I just went to and fro *or* back and forth between the house and the office; **il va et vient dans sa chambre** he's pacing up and down (in) his room; **mais venez donc!** do come along!; **il vient d'Amérique** he's from *or* he comes from America; **d'où venez-vous?** (*d'où êtes-vous?*) where do you come *or Litt* hail from?, where are you from?; (*par où êtes-vous passé?*) where have you come from?; **il est venu à** *ou* **vers moi** he came up to me; *Bible* **laissez v. à moi les petits enfants** suffer the little children to come unto me; **il est venu sur moi** he advanced on me (threateningly); **v. au monde** to be born, to come into the world; **l'année qui vient** the coming year, next year; **dans les jours qui viennent** in the coming *or* next few days; **ses succès à v.** his future successes; **dans les temps à v.** in the days to come; **faire v. qn** to send for sb, to call sb in, to fetch sb; **faire v. ses robes de Paris** to get one's dresses from Paris; **voir v. qn** to see sb coming; *Fig* **je te vois v. (avec tes gros sabots)!** I can see you coming a mile off; **je préfère voir v.** I'd rather wait and see; **laisser v. les choses** to let things take their course; **le voici v., le voici qui vient** here he comes; **être bien/mal venu** to be welcome/unwelcome; **il serait mal venu de le lui faire remarquer** it would be a bit out of place *or F* a bit off to point it out to him; *Naut* **v. dans le vent** to come round; **v. sur bâbord/tribord** to alter course to port/to starboard; **il est venu tomber à mes pieds** he fell at my feet; **venez me trouver à quatre heures** come (round) and see me at four o'clock; **viens donc te baigner/te reposer chez nous** come (round) to our place for a swim/a rest; **je viens vous voir** I've come to see you; **v. chercher** *ou* **v. prendre qch/qn** to come for sth/sb, to come to collect sth/sb; **mot qui vient du latin** word which comes *or* is derived from Latin; **ce bien lui est venu de famille** he inherited this property from his family; **tout cela vient de ce que ...** it all stems from the fact that ...; **cela vient du fait que ...** this stems from the fact that ...; **l'erreur vient de là** that's where the error stems from, that explains the mistake; **vous y viendrez** you'll come round (to it), you'll change your mind

(b) [①B29,10] (*pr & impf only*) **v. de faire qch** to have (only) just done sth; **il vient/venait de sortir** he has/had just gone out

(c) (*apparaître, arriver*) to come; **le premier exemple venu** the first example that comes to mind; **le premier crétin venu serait capable de t'en parler** any fool could tell you about it; **le premier passant venu te le dira** the first person you meet *or* anyone will tell you that; *F* **alors ce steak, ça vient?** is my steak coming or not?, how much longer do I have to wait for that steak?; **alors, tu viens, on y va!** are you coming or not? we're off!; **les idées ne viennent pas** I just can't come up with anything; **son nom ne vient pas, j'ai oublié** I just can't think of his name; **le moment de nous dire au revoir est venu** the time has come for us to say goodbye; **la pluie ne va pas tarder à v.** the rain won't be long in coming; **un jour viendra où nous n'aurons plus tous ces problèmes** the day will come when we don't have all these problems; **il attend que vienne son tour** he's waiting for his turn (to come round); **il lui est venu des rides** he's got wrinkles; **il m'est venu des doutes à son sujet** I suddenly wasn't so sure about him; **il lui est venu une idée géniale** he had *or* hit on a brillant idea; **l'idée me vient que ..., il me vient à l'esprit que ..., il me vient l'idée que ...** the thought comes to my mind *or* it occurs to me that ...; **il ne m'est pas venu à l'idée que ...** it never entered my head *or* it never occurred to me that ...; **il ne me viendrait pas à l'esprit (de penser) que ...** it would never occur to me (to think) that ...

(d) en v. à qch/à faire qch to come to sth/to the point of doing sth; **en v. aux coups** *ou* **aux mains** to come to blows; **les choses en sont-elles venues là?** have things come to such a point?; **je comprends où vous voulez en v.** I see what you're getting at *or* driving at; **j'en suis venu à votre manière de penser** I've come round to your way of thinking; **j'en viens à me demander si ...** I'm beginning to wonder whether ...; **j'en suis venue à perdre toute confiance en lui** I've come *or* begun to lose all faith in him

(e) (*atteindre*) to attain, to reach; **l'eau leur venait aux genoux** the water came up to their knees; **les cheveux lui viennent aux épaules** he has shoulder-length hair; **elle lui vient au menton** she comes up to his chin

(f) v. à faire qch to happen *or* chance to do sth; **si le temps venait à pleuvoir** if it happened to rain, if it should rain

(g) (*grandir, pousser*) to come on *or* along; **bien v.** (*d'une plante*) to thrive; (*d'une photo*) to come out well; **faire v. du blé** to grow wheat; **il lui est venu une tumeur** he developed a tumour

2 *v impers* **d'où vient(-il) que ...?** how is it that ...?

3 se venir *vpr Arch, Région* **s'en venir** to come along

Venise [vəniz] *nf* Venice; **point de V.** Venetian lace; **carnaval de V.** Venice carnival

vénitien, -ienne [venisjɛ̃, -jɛn] **1** *adj* Venetian; **store v.** Venetian blind **2** *n* **V.** Venetian

vent [vɑ̃] *nm* **(a)** wind; **le v. du nord/sud** the north/south wind; *Naut* **v. frais** strong breeze; **grand v., v. fort** high wind, gale; **journée de grand v.** windy day; **coup de v.** gust of wind, squall; *Fig* **entrer/sortir en coup de v.** to dash in/out; **elle courait les cheveux au v.** she ran with her hair streaming in the wind; **à l'abri du v.** sheltered from the wind; *Mus* **instrument à v.** wind instrument; **il fait du v.** it's windy (weather); **le v. tourne** the wind is changing; *Fig* the wind is changing, the tide is turning; **aller comme le v.** to go like the wind; **bon v.!** God speed!; *Iron* good riddance!; **quel bon v. vous amène?** what brings you here, to what do we owe the pleasure?; *Naut* **avoir le v. en poupe** to have the wind right aft *or* dead aft; *Fig* **il a le v. en poupe** he's on the road to success, he's riding high, he has the wind in his sails; *Fig* **avoir du v. dans les voiles** to be three sheets in *or* to the wind, to be drunk; *Péj* **ce n'est que du v.** it's just hot air; *Fig* **prendre le v., regarder de quel côté vient le v.** to see which way the wind blows, to see how the land lies; **tourner à tous les vents** to be a weathercock; *Prov* **qui sème le v. récolte la tempête** he who sows the wind shall reap the whirlwind; **ouvert** *ou* **exposé aux quatre vents** exposed to the four winds; *F* **être dans le v.** to be up-to-date *or* with it; **les îles du V.** the Windward Islands; *Naut* **v. arrière** following wind; *Av* tail wind; **aller v. arrière** to sail *or* run before the wind; **v. debout** head wind; *Aut* **v. latéral** side wind; **contre le v.** against the wind, into the wind; *Fig* **contre vents et marées** come hell or high water; *Naut* **sous le v.** alee, (to) leeward; **avoir bon v.** to have a fair wind; *Naut* **au v.** a-weather, (to) windward; **mettre la barre au v.** to put the helm up; **côté du v.** weather side; **côté sous le v.** lee side

(b) (*air*) air; **marché/assemblée en plein v.** open-air market/meeting; **mettre qch au v.** to hang sth out to dry

(c) (*d'un soufflet, d'une balle*) blast; *Av* **v. de l'hélice** propeller slipstream

(d) (*flatulence*) wind, flatulence; **lâcher un v.** to break wind; **avoir des vents** to have wind

(e) (*à la chasse*) scent; **avoir le v. de son gibier** to have the wind of one's game; *Fig* **avoir v. de qch** to get wind of sth

vente [vɑ̃t] *nf* **(a)** (*transaction*) sale; (*activité*) selling; **réaliser une v.** to make a sale; **elle est dans la v.** she's in sales; **la v. de la statue a fait scandale** the sale *or* the selling of the statue caused a scandal; **nous déménagerons après la v. de la maison** we'll move after the house is sold *or* after the sale of the house; *Compta* **ventes** sales, turnover; **acte de v.** bill of sale; **bureau de v.** sales agency; **salle des ventes** auction rooms, saleroom(s), salesroom; **promotion des ventes** sales promotion; **en v.** for sale, on sale; **mettre qch en v.** to put sth up for sale, to offer sth for sale; **médicament en v. libre** medicine available over the counter *or* without prescription; **en v. dans toutes les bonnes librairies** on sale in all good bookshops; **(livre) retiré de la v.** (book) withdrawn from sale; **faire une forte v.** (*d'un livre*) to be a best seller

(b) *Can* (*soldes*) sale

(c) (*action de couper*) (*du bois*) felling; (*clairière*) clearing; **jeune(s) vente(s)** new undergrowth

▶ **vente**: **v. à l'amiable** sale by private agreement, private sale; *Com* **v. à l'arrivée** sale at arrival; **ventes de base** baseline sales, market minimum; **v. par catalogue** catalogue selling; **v. de charité** (charity) bazaar; **v. (au) comptant** cash sale; **v. au comptoir** over-the-counter sales; **v.-conseil** sales consultancy; **v. en coopération** co-operative selling; **v. par correspondance** mail order (selling); **v. à crédit** credit sale; (*à tempérament*) hire purchase, *Am* installment plan; *Bourse* **v. à découvert** short sale; *Com* **v. au départ** sale at departure; **v. au détail** retailing, retail selling; **v. directe** direct selling; (*une vente*) direct sale; **v. directe en B to B** back-to-back direct selling; **v. à domicile** door-to-door selling; **v. domiciliaire** home party selling; **v. aux enchères** (sale by) auction; **ventes export**, **ventes à l'exportation** export sales; **v. à froid** cold selling; **v. en gros** wholesaling; **v. sans intermédiaire** direct selling; **v. judiciaire** sale by order of the court; **v. jumelée** twin-pack selling; **v. en magasin** counter sales; **ventes sur le marché intérieur** home sales, domestic sales; **v.-marketing** sales and marketing; *Bourse* **v. nue** naked sale; **ventes personnelles** personal selling; **v. porte-à-porte** (*activité*) door-to-door selling; **ventes de prospection** missionary selling; **v. publique** public sale;

v. pyramidale pyramid selling; **v. répétée** repeat sale; *Mktg* **v. par réseau coopté** multilevel marketing; **v. en semi-gros** small wholesale sales; **v. par téléphone** telephone selling; **ventes par téléphone** telephone sales; **v. à tempérament** hire purchase, *Am* installment plan; *Bourse* **v. à terme** forward sale; **ventes territoriales** territorial sales; **ventes totales de l'industrie** total industry sales

venté [vɑ̃te] *adj* (*région*) windswept, windblown, windy

venter [vɑ̃te] *v impers* to be windy, to blow; **il vente fort** it's very windy, it's blowing hard

venteux, -euse [vɑ̃tø, -øz] *adj* (*temps*) windy; (*pays*) windswept

ventilateur [vɑ̃tilatœr] *nm* ventilator; *Aut* (*soufflante*) blower; *TV, Cin* wind machine; **v. rotatif** fan; **v. électrique** electric fan; *Ordinat* **v. de refroidissement** cooling fan

ventilation [vɑ̃tilasjɔ̃] *nf* **(a)** (*aération*) ventilation; **mettre la v. (en marche)** to switch on the ventilation **(b)** (*des dépenses etc*) breakdown; **la v. des tâches à différents employés** the allocation of jobs to various employees **(c)** *Jur* (*d'un domaine etc*) separate valuation

ventiler [vɑ̃tile] *vt* **(a)** (*pièce etc*) to ventilate, to air; **mal ventilé** poorly *or* badly ventilated, stuffy **(b)** (*dépenses etc*) to break down; (*crédits, équipements etc*) to allocate; *Com* **v. un lot** to break bulk **(c)** *Jur* (*domaine etc*) to value separately

ventilo [vɑ̃tilo] *nm F* fan; **faire marcher le v.** to turn on the fan

ventôse [vɑ̃toz] *nm Hist Fr* = sixth month of the French Republican calendar (*Feb 19th or 21st—March 19th or 21st*)

ventouse [vɑ̃tuz] *nf* **(a)** *Méd* cupping glass; **poser des ventouses à qn** to cup sb **(b)** *Zool* (*de sangsue etc*) sucker **(c)** (*de plastique etc*) suction cup *or* disc; **fléchettes/cendrier à v.** rubber-tipped darts/suction-grip ashtray; **faire v.** to adhere by suction; **mine v.** limpet mine; **voiture v.** illegally parked car, abandoned car **(d)** (*aération*) airhole, vent(hole)

ventral, -ale, -aux, -ales [vɑ̃tral, -o] *adj* ventral; **parachute v.** lap pack (parachute)

ventre [vɑ̃tr] *nm* **(a)** (*estomac*) stomach, *F* tummy, belly; (*d'animal*) belly, underbelly; *Anat* abdomen; **avoir le v. plein/creux** to have a full stomach, to be full/to have an empty stomach; **danse du v.** belly dance; **faire la danse du v.** to belly dance; **se coucher à plat v.** to lie flat on one's stomach *or F* tummy *or* belly; **dormir à plat v.** to sleep (lying) flat on one's stomach *or* (lying) face-down; *Fig* **se mettre à plat v. devant qn** to grovel to sb; *Fig* **passer sur le v. à qn** to trample all over sb; **v. à terre** (*d'un cheval*) at full speed, flat out; **avoir du v.** to have a paunch, to be potbellied; **il commence à prendre** *ou* **avoir du v.** he's starting to get a paunch *or* a belly; **rentrer le v.** to hold one's stomach in; **avoir mal au v.** to have (a) stomach *or F* tummy ache; *Fig* **ça fait mal au v. de voir ça** it makes me sick to see that; **ne rien avoir dans le v.** to have nothing in one's stomach; *Fig* to have no guts; **ne bois pas si tu n'as rien dans le v.** don't drink on an empty stomach; **je savais bien qu'il avait quelque chose dans le v.** I was sure he had it in him; **je voudrais savoir ce qu'elle a dans le v.** I'd like to know what she's up to; *F* **donner du cœur au v. à qn** to buck sb up; *Fig* **v. mou** underbelly; *Prov* **v. affamé n'a point d'oreilles** it's no use reasoning with a hungry man; **tu as les yeux plus grands que le v.** your eyes are bigger than your belly

(b) (*utérus*) womb; **dès le v. de sa mère** since before he was born

(c) *Tech* (*d'une bouteille, d'une poutre*) bulge, swell; (*d'une voile*) belly, sag; (*d'un navire*) belly; **faire v.** to bulge (out), to belly out; (*pendre*) to sag

(d) *Phys* (*d'une vague*) antinode, ventral segment; **v. de tension** potential loop, voltage loop

ventrebleu [vɑ̃trəblø] *int Arch* gadzooks!, zounds!

ventrée [vɑ̃tre] *nf* (*de nourriture*) bellyful

ventricule [vɑ̃trikyl] *nm Anat* ventricle

ventrière [vɑ̃trijɛr] *nf* **(a)** (*harnais*) girth; (*pour hisser un animal*) sling **(b)** *Constr* purlin

ventriloque [vɑ̃trilɔk] *n* ventriloquist

ventriloquie [vɑ̃trilɔki] *nf* ventriloquy, ventriloquism

ventru [vɑ̃try] *adj* **(a)** (*gros*) potbellied **(b)** (*colonne*) bulbous; (*voile*) bulging, swelling

venu, -ue[1] [v(ə)ny] **1** *adj* **(a)** (*bien développé*) well developed; **plante bien/mal venue** sturdy *or* healthy/stunted *or* unhealthy plant; **photographie bien venue** photograph that has come out well; **enfant mal v.** stunted *or* puny child

(b) (*approprié*) **bien v.** appropriate; **mal v.** inappropriate; **je serais mal v. de critiquer** (*je ne suis pas qualifié en la matière*) it's not for me to criticize; (*j'en ai fait autant*) I'm hardly in a position to criticize; **il serait mal v. d'insister** it would be ill-mannered to insist

2 *n* **le premier v.** the first to arrive; (*n'importe qui*) anybody; **le premier v. vous le dira** anybody *or* anyone will tell you that; **à la portée du premier v.** easy to use, user-friendly; **ce n'est pas le premier v.** he's not just anybody; **le dernier v.** the last to arrive; **les nouveaux venus/les nouvelles venues** the newcomers

venue[2] [v(ə)ny] *nf* **(a)** (*arrivée*) coming, arrival; (*du printemps etc*) coming, advent, approach; (*d'ordinateurs etc*) advent; (*d'un vol*) approach; (*de l'eau*) rush; **attendre la v. de qn** to wait for sb to arrive; **c'est ce qui explique ma v.** that's why I'm here; **on ne pouvait pas s'attendre à la v. de la neige** there's no way we could have forecast the snow; **allées et venues** comings and goings; **faire des allées et venues** to come and go; **après de nombreuses allées et venues** after a lot of toing and froing *or* going backwards and forwards

(b) (*d'un arbre etc*) growth; **d'une belle v., tout d'une v.** (*arbre*) well grown; *Fig* **des pages d'une belle v.** beautifully written pages

Vénus [venys] *nf Myth, Astron* Venus; *Bot* **cheveu de V.** maidenhair fern; *Anat* **mont de V.** mons veneris, mound of Venus

vépéciste [vepesist] *nm Com* mail order specialist

vêpres [vɛpr] *nfpl Rel* vespers

ver [vɛr] *nm* **(a)** worm; **nu comme un v.** stark naked; *F* **tirer les vers du nez à qn** to worm *or* winkle information out of sb **(b)** (*asticot, larve*) grub, larva; **fruit plein de vers** worm-eaten fruit; **rose rongée de vers** cankered rose; **rongé** *ou* **piqué des vers** worm-eaten; **une histoire pas piquée des vers** one heck of a story

▶ **ver**: **v. blanc** cockchafer grub; **v. du bois** woodworm; **v. de farine** mealworm; **v. luisant** glow worm; **v. des pêcheurs** lug(worm); **v. rongeur** canker(worm); **v. de sable** lug(worm); **v. à soie** silkworm; *Méd* **v. solitaire** tapeworm; **avoir le v. solitaire** to have a tapeworm; **v. de terre** earthworm; **v. de viande** maggot

véracité [verasite] *nf* truth, truthfulness, *Fml* veracity

véranda [verɑ̃da] *nf* veranda(h)

verbal, -ale, -aux, -ales [vɛrbal, -o] *adj* **(a)** (*promesse*) verbal; **la violence verbale d'une description** the violence of the language used in a description **(b)** *Gram* verbal; **locution verbale** verbal phrase

verbalement [vɛrbalmɑ̃] *adv* verbally, by word of mouth

verbalisation [vɛrbalizasjɔ̃] *nf* **(a)** (*expression*) verbalization; **v. des angoisses** putting (one's) anxieties into words **(b)** *Jur* entry of charge (*by policeman for minor offence*)

verbaliser [vɛrbalize] **1** *vi* (*d'un policier*) **Madame, je vais devoir v.** I'm going to have to charge you **2** *vt* (*exprimer*) to verbalize, to put into words

verbe [vɛrb] *nm* **(a)** [①A38-63; B22-50] *Gram* verb; **v. transitif/intransitif** transitive/intransitive verb; **v. composé** compound verb; (*en anglais*) phrasal verb; **v. défectif** defective verb; **v. à particule** (*en anglais*) phrasal verb; **v. pronominal** reflexive verb **(b)** (*langage*) language, word(s); **la magie du v.** the magic of words *or* language; **avoir le v. haut** to speak loudly; *Fig* to be dictatorial **(c)** *Rel* **le V.** the Word; **le V. s'est fait chair** the Word was made flesh

verbeux, -euse [vɛrbø, -øz] *adj* (*orateur etc*) verbose, long-winded; (*explication etc*) wordy, long-winded, verbose

verbiage [vɛrbjaʒ] *nm* verbiage; **se lancer dans un v. creux** to launch into a meaningless torrent of words; **tout ce v. ne m'intéresse pas** all this meaningless chatter is of no interest to me

verbosité [vɛrbozite] *nf* verbosity, wordiness

ver-coquin, *pl* **vers-coquins** *nm* (*parasite*) vine grub; *Vét* stagger worm

verdâtre [vɛrdɑtr] *adj* greenish

verdeur [vɛrdœr] *nf* **(a)** (*d'un fruit, d'un vin*) tartness, acidity **(b)** (*du langage*) crudeness **(c)** (*vitalité*) vigour, *US* vigor, vitality

verdict [vɛrdikt] *nm Jur* (*du jury*) verdict, finding; **prononcer** *ou* **rendre un v.** to return *or* bring in a verdict; **prononcer** *ou* **rendre un v. pour/contre qn** to find for/against sb; **v. de culpabilité** *ou* **positif/d'acquittement** *ou* **négatif** verdict of 'guilty'/'not guilty'; **attendre le v. du médecin** to await the doctor's verdict

verdier [vɛrdje] *nm* (*oiseau*) greenfinch

verdir [vɛrdir] **1** *vt* **v. qch** to make *or* turn sth green **2** *vi* (*de végétation etc*) to turn green; *Fig* **v. (de jalousie)** to go *or* turn green with envy; **v. de peur** to go *or* turn white with fear

verdissement [vɛrdismɑ̃] *nm* turning green

verdoiement [vɛrdwamɑ̃] *nm* **(a)** (*action de se couvrir de verdure*) turning green **(b)** (*des champs*) greenness

verdoyant [vɛrdwajɑ̃] *adj* (*champs, paysage etc*) green, *Litt* verdant; **les champ verdoyants** the lush pasture

verdoyer [vɛrdwaje] *vi* (*pr ind* **il verdoie**; *fu* **il verdoiera**) (*de végétation etc*) to turn green

verdure [vɛrdyr] *nf* **(a)** *(couleur)* greenness **(b)** *(végétation)* greenery, *Litt* verdure; **rideau de v.** curtain of greenery; **salle de v.** green arbour; **tapis de v.** carpet of green, *Litt* greensward; **théâtre de v.** open-air theatre **(c)** *Culin* *(légumes verts)* greens

véreux, -euse [verø, -øz] *adj* **(a)** *(fruit)* wormy, maggoty **(b)** *Péj* *(affaires)* dubious, shady, *F* fishy; **financier v.** shady financier; **dettes véreuses** bad debts; **tremper dans une affaire véreuse** to be involved in a shady business

verge [vɛrʒ] *nf* **(a)** *Anat* penis **(b)** *(baguette)* rod, cane, switch; **(poignée de) verges** birch (rod); **battre de verges un enfant** to birch a child; *Fig* **vous lui donnez des verges pour vous fouetter** you're giving him a stick to beat you with **(c)** *Naut* *(d'une ancre)* shank **(d)** *Bot* **v. d'or** golden rod, Aaron's rod **(e)** *Can* *(mesure)* yard

vergé [vɛrʒe] **1** *adj* **(a)** *Tex* badly dyed, streaky **(b)** **papier v.** laid paper **2** *nm* laid paper

vergeoise [vɛrʒwaz] *nf* = low-grade beet sugar

verger [vɛrʒe] *nm* orchard

vergeté [vɛrʒəte] *adj* streaky, streaked; *(peau)* stretchmarked

vergette [vɛrʒɛt] *nf* small cane, switch

vergeture [vɛrʒətyr] *nf* **(a)** stretch mark; **avoir des vergetures** to have stretch marks; **crème contre les vergetures** cream to prevent stretch marks **(b)** *(causée par un fouet etc)* weal, red mark

vergeure [vɛrʒyr] *nf* *(sur papier vergé)* wire mark

verglacé [vɛrglase] *adj* *(route)* icy; *Can* **pluie verglacée** freezing rain

verglas [vɛrgla] *nm* *(sur la route)* (black) ice, *US* glaze; **il y a du v.** it's icy *or* slippery

vergogne [vɛrgɔɲ] *nf* **sans v.** *(emploi adjectival)* shameless; *(emploi adverbial)* shamelessly

vergue [vɛrg] *nf* *Naut* yard; **grande v.** main yard; **v. de misaine** foretop yard; **v. de hunier** topsail yard; **bout de v.** yard-arm

véridique [veridik] *adj* truthful, *Litt* veracious; **informations véridiques** accurate information

véridiquement [veridikmɑ̃] *adv* truthfully, *Litt* veraciously

vérifiable [verifjabl] *adj* verifiable; *(déclaration etc)* that can be checked

vérificateur, -trice [verifikatœr, -tris] **1** *n* *(personne)* inspector, examiner, checker; **v. de comptes** auditor **2** *nm* *Ordinat* **v. orthographique** spellchecker **3** *adj* **appareil v.** testing machine; **instrument v.** gauge, calipers

vérification [verifikasjɔ̃] *nf* *(de déclarations etc)* checking, verification; *(du travail etc)* inspection, examination, checking; *(des votes)* checking; *(d'un pronostic, d'une réservation)* confirmation; *Aut etc* **v. sur place** spot check; **v. de comptes** *ou* **d'écritures** audit(ing) of accounts; *Ordinat* **v. antivirale** antiviral check; *Ordinat* **v. orthographique** spellcheck; *Compta* **v. à rebours** audit trail

vérifier [verifje] *(impf, pr sub* **n. vérifiions, v. vérifiiez)** **1** *vt* *(votes, un calcul, l'heure du train etc)* to check; *(travail etc)* to inspect, to examine, to check; *(déclaration)* to verify, to check, to confirm; *(mécanismes etc)* to overhaul; *(comptes)* to audit; **il doit être là, je vais v.** he must be there, I'll check *or* make sure; **vérifié et revérifié** checked and double-checked; **v. des références** to take up references; **v. que tous les robinets sont fermés** to check that all the taps have been turned off; **v. si qch est vrai** to check whether sth is true

2 se vérifier *vpr* *(d'une affirmation etc)* to prove correct, to be confirmed; **mes soupçons se sont vérifiés par la suite** my suspicions were subsequently confirmed; **mon pronostic s'est vérifié** what I predicted came true

vérin [verɛ̃] *nm* *Tech* jack; **v. hydraulique/pneumatique** hydraulic/pneumatic jack; **v. à cliquet** ratchet jack; **v. à gaz** gas strut; **v. à vis** screw jack

véritable [veritabl] *adj* **(a)** *(histoire etc)* true; **ce n'est pas son nom v.** that's not his real name; **se montrer sous son v. jour** to show one's true colours, to show oneself in one's true light **(b)** *(réel)* real, genuine, *Fml* veritable; **en soie/ivoire v.** made of real *or* genuine silk/ivory; **un v. ami** a real *or* genuine *or* true friend; **c'est un v. coquin** he's a downright *or* an absolute *or* an out-and-out rogue; **c'est un v. épouvantail** he's a perfect *or* an absolute fright; **c'était une v. surprise** it was a real surprise

véritablement [veritabləmɑ̃] *adv* **(a)** *(conformément à la vérité)* truly, *Fml* veritably **(b)** *(réellement)* really, genuinely; **nous nous sommes v. compris** we understood each other perfectly; **je ne le crois pas v. fait pour ce genre de travail** I don't think he's really cut out for this kind of work

vérité [verite] *nf* **(a)** *(d'une déclaration etc)* truth, *Fml* verity; **respect de la v. historique** respect for historical fact; **c'est une v. éternelle** it's an eternal truth; **dire la v.** to tell *or* speak the truth; **la v. sort de la bouche des enfants** out of the mouths of babes and sucklings; **la v. finit toujours par se découvrir** truth will out; **récit conforme à la v.** true *or* factual account; **à la v.** to tell the truth, as a matter of fact; **en v.** really, actually; **heure de v.** moment of truth; *Jur* **la v., toute la v., rien que la v.** the truth, the whole truth and nothing but the truth; **c'est la v.** it's true, it's a fact; *F* **c'est la v. vraie** it's an actual fact, it's the honest truth, *F* it's gospel; **la v. d'un personnage** the trueness to life of a character; *Cin* **cinéma-v.** cinéma vérité; **dire à qn (toutes) ses vérités** *ou* **ses quatre vérités** to tell sb a few home truths

(b) *(sincérité)* sincerity, truthfulness; **accent/intonation de v.** truthful note/tone; **air/accent de v.** ring of truth

verjus [vɛrʒy] *nm* verjuice

verlan [vɛrlɑ̃] *nm* *Ling* back slang; **parler en v.** to speak in back slang

vermeil, -eille [vɛrmɛj] **1** *adj* vermilion, bright red; *(lèvres)* ruby(-red), bright red; *(joues)* rosy, bright red **2** *nm* silver gilt

vermicelle [vɛrmisɛl] *nm* *Culin* vermicelli, noodles; **v. chinois** Chinese noodles; **soupe aux vermicelles** noodle soup

vermiculaire [vɛrmikylɛr] *adj* worm-shaped, *Spéc* vermicular; *Anat* **appendice v.** vermiform appendix

vermiculé [vɛrmikyle] *adj* **(a)** *Archit* *(maçonnerie etc)* vermiculated **(b)** *(boîtier de montre etc)* engine-turned **(c)** *Biol* *(taches)* vermiculate

vermiculure [vɛrmikylyr] *nf* *Archit etc* vermiculation

vermiforme [vɛrmifɔrm] *adj* worm-like, *Spéc* vermiform

vermifuge [vɛrmifyʒ] *adj, nm* *Pharm* vermifuge; **(poudre) v.** worming powder

vermillon [vɛrmijɔ̃] **1** *nm* **(a)** *(couleur)* vermilion **(b)** *(poudre)* vermilion, cinnabar **2** *adj inv* vermilion, bright red

vermine [vɛrmin] *nf* **(a)** [ⓘA11,f,ii] vermin; **couvert** *ou* **grouillant de v.** verminous, crawling with vermin **(b)** *Fig Péj* **fréquenté par la v.** frequented by lowlife characters *or* members of the underworld; **quelle v.!** what a rat!; *(ces gens-là)* scum!

vermisseau, -eaux [vɛrmiso] *nm* small (earth)worm

vermoulu [vɛrmuly] *adj* *(bois etc)* worm-eaten; *Fig* decrepit; **des institutions/diplômes/universités vermoulu(e)s** antiquated institutions/diplomas/universities

vermoulure [vɛrmulyr] *nf* **(a)** *(dans le bois)* wormhole **(b)** *(poussière)* *(causée par des vers)* worm dust

vermout(h) [vɛrmut] *nm* vermouth

vernaculaire [vɛrnakylɛr] *adj* vernacular; **la langue v.** the vernacular; **nom v.** vernacular *or* common name

vernal, -ale, -aux, -ales [vɛrnal, -o] *adj* vernal

verni [vɛrni] *adj* **(a)** varnished; *(acajou)* French-polished; **parquet v.** varnished *or* polished floor; **cuir v.** patent leather; **chaussures vernies** patent(-leather) shoes **(b)** *F* **être v.** *(chanceux)* to be lucky *or Br F* jammy **(c)** *Cér* *(carreau etc)* glazed, vitrified

vernier [vɛrnje] *nm* vernier, sliding gauge

vernir [vɛrnir] *vt* **(a)** *(tableau, bois etc)* to varnish; *(acajou)* to French-polish; *(cuir)* to japan; **v. au tampon** to French-polish **(b)** *Cér* to glaze

vernis [vɛrni] *nm* **(a)** varnish; **v. à bois** (wood) varnish; **v. à ongles** nail varnish *or* polish; **se mettre du v. à ongles** to varnish *or* paint one's nails; **v. à l'alcool** spirit varnish; **v. à l'essence** turpentine varnish; **v. cellulosique** cellulose varnish; **v. japonais** japan; **v. au tampon** French polish; *Cér* **v. (luisant)** glaze; **v. de plomb** lead glaze

(b) *Fig* veneer; **dès qu'on gratte le v.** as soon as you scratch the surface; **ce n'est qu'un v.** it's just a veneer; **v. de politesse** veneer of politeness; **un v. de savoir** a smattering of knowledge

(c) *Bot* **v. du Japon** varnish tree, lacquer tree, tree of heaven

vernissage [vɛrnisaʒ] *nm* **(a)** varnishing; *Cér* glazing **(b)** *(d'une exposition)* private view(ing)

vernissé [vɛrnise] *adj* **(a)** *Cér* glazed **(b)** *(brillant)* glossy

vernisser [vɛrnise] *vt* *(poterie)* to glaze

vernisseur, -euse [vɛrnisœr, -øz] *n* **(a)** *(de bois etc)* varnisher; **v. au tampon** French polisher **(b)** *Cér* glazer

vérole [verɔl] *nf* *Méd* **(a)** **petite v.** smallpox; **avoir la petite v.** to have smallpox **(b)** *Arg* syphilis, *F* pox

vérolé [verɔle] *adj* *Arg* syphilitic; **il est v.** he's got the pox

véronal® [verɔnal] *nm* *Pharm* Veronal, barbitone

véronique [verɔnik] *nf* *Bot* speedwell, veronica

verrat [vɛra] *nm* boar

verre [vɛr] *nm* **(a)** *(matière)* glass; **laine de v.** glass wool; **papier de v.** glasspaper, sand paper; **passer qch au papier de v.** to sand(paper) sth; **coton de v.** fibreglass, *US* fiberglass, glass fibre; **articles de v.** glassware; **œil de v.** glass eye; **peintre sur v.** artist in stained glass; **sous v.** under glass; **gravure sous v.** glass-mounted engraving; **se casser** *ou* **se briser comme du v.** to be as brittle as glass

(b) (*récipient*) glass; **lever son v. à qn** to raise one's glass to sb

(c) (*contenu*) glass(ful); **il me suffit d'un v. (d'alcool) pour que je devienne ivre** it only takes one drink to get me drunk; **je n'ai bu qu'un v. ce soir** I've only had one drink this evening; **v. de vin** glass of wine; *F* **boire un petit v.** (*d'alcool*) to have a drink; **prendre un v.** to have a drink; **il a pris** *ou* **bu un v. de trop, il a un v. dans le nez** he's had one too many, he's had a drop too much; **tempête dans un v. d'eau** storm in a teacup *or Am* teapot

(d) (*objet en verre*) glass; (*de lunettes*) lens

▶ **verre**: **v. armé** wire(d) glass; **v. blanc** white glass; **v. à boire** glass; **v. à champagne** champagne glass; **v. coloré** stained glass; **verres de contact** contact lenses, *F* contacts; **verres dalles** pavement lights; **v. à dents** tooth glass; **v. dépoli** frosted glass; **v. à eau** tumbler, water glass; **v. feuilleté** laminated glass; **v. filé** spun glass; **verres fumés** tinted lenses; **v. à glaces** plate glass; **v. gradué** measuring jug; **v. grillagé** wire(d) glass; **v. grossissant** magnifying glass; **v. à liqueur** liqueur glass; **v. de montre** watch glass; **v. moulé** pressed glass; **v. à moutarde** = empty mustard jar used as glass; **v. pare-balles** bulletproof glass; **v. à pied** stemmed glass; **v. de sécurité** safety glass; **v. soluble** water glass; **v. trempé** toughened glass; **v. à vin** wineglass; **v. à vitres** window glass; **v. de vitrine** window pane; **v. à whisky** whisky glass

verrerie [vɛr(ə)ri] *nf* **(a)** (*fabrication*) glass-making **(b)** (*atelier*) glassworks **(c)** (*marchandise*) glassware

verrier [vɛrje] **1** *nm* **(a)** (*artisan*) glass-maker, glass-worker; (*souffleur*) glass-blower **(b)** (*casier*) glass rack **2** *adj* **peintre v.** artist in stained glass

verrière [vɛrjɛr] *nf* **(a)** (*d'une gare etc*) glass roof; (*paroi vitrée*) glass wall **(b)** (*pour protéger un tableau etc*) glass casing **(c)** (*vitre*) stained glass window **(d)** *Av* canopy

verroterie [vɛrɔtri] *nf* (*bijoux*) glass jewellery; **collier de v.** string of glass beads, glass necklace; **ce n'est que de la v.** they are only glass trinkets

verrou [vɛru] *nm* **(a)** bolt; **fermer une porte au v.** to bolt a door; **mettre** *ou* **tirer le v.** (*pour fermer une porte*) to bolt the door; **s'enfermer au v.** to bolt oneself in; **tirer le(s) verrou(s)** (*ouvrir*) to unbolt the door **(b)** *F* **verrous** (*prison*) prison, *Br F* nick; **il est sous les verrous depuis 5 ans** he's been inside *or* behind bars *or* in the nick for 5 years; **il a fini sa vie sous les verrous** he ended his days behind bars; **mettre qn sous les verrous** to put sb inside, to put sb behind bars, *Br* to send sb down **(c)** (*d'une arme à feu*) bolt

verrouillage [vɛrujaʒ] *nm* bolting, locking; (*mécanisme*) locking mechanism; **une voiture à v. automatique** a car with central locking; *Aut* **v. central** *ou* **centralisé des portes** central door locking; *Aut* **v. centralisé à télécommande** remote central locking; *Aut* **v. du volant** steering lock; *Aut* **v. sécurité enfant** child-proof lock; *Aut* **v. à distance** remote control locking; *Ordinat* **v. des fichiers** file lock; *Ordinat* **v. du clavier numérique** numbers lock; *Ordinat* **v. en lecture seule** read-only lock; *Ordinat* **v. en majuscule(s)** caps lock

verrouiller [vɛruje] **1** *vt* **(a)** (*porte*) to bolt; *Ordinat* (*capitales*) to lock on; **v. en écriture** (*fichier*) to lock; **verrouillé en majuscule(s)** (*clavier*) with caps lock on; **v. qn** to bolt sb in, to lock sb in **(b)** *Mil* (*ouverture*) to lock; (*passage, brèche*) to block **2 se verrouiller** *vpr* to bolt oneself in; **je me suis verrouillée chez moi** I bolted *or* locked myself in

verrue [vɛry] *nf* wart; (*surtout au pied*) verruca; *Fig* **ce musée est une v. dans la ville** this museum is a real eyesore in the town, this museum is a carbuncle on the face of the town

verruqueux, -euse [vɛrykø, -øz] *adj* warty

vers[1] [vɛr] *nm* (*poétique*) verse, line; **v. alexandrins** alexandrine verse; **v. blancs** blank verse; **v. libres** free verse; **écrire** *ou* **faire des v.** to write verse *or* poetry; **c'est en v.** it's in verse; **morceau en v.** piece of verse *or* poetry

vers[2] *prép* **(a)** (*dans l'espace*) toward(s); **façade qui regarde v. la forêt** façade facing the forest; **notre chambre regarde v. le nord** our bedroom faces north *or* is north-facing; **le lieu v. où nous allons** the place we're heading for *or* toward(s) *or* to; **un pas v. la démocratie** a step towards democracy; **habiter v. Pau** to live near *or* in the neighbourhood *or US* neighborhood of Pau

(b) (*dans le temps*) toward(s); (*autour de*) about; **v. la fin du siècle/de sa vie** towards the end of the century/his life; **venez v. (les) trois heures** come (at) about three (o'clock)

versaillais, -aise [vɛrsajɛ, -ɛz] **1** *adj* of/from Versailles **2** *n* **V.** inhabitant of Versailles

versant [vɛrsɑ̃] *nm* (*d'une montagne*) slope, side; (*d'un canal etc*) bank; *Fig* side; **v. de colline** hillside; *Fig* **il s'intéresse au v. politique de cette affaire** he's interested in the political aspect *or* side of the story

versatile [vɛrsatil] *adj* **(a)** (*disposition etc*) changeable, fickle **(b)** *Biol* versatile

versatilité [vɛrsatilite] *nf* **(a)** changeability, fickleness **(b)** *Biol* versatility

verse [vɛrs] *nf* **(a)** (*des cultures dans le vent etc*) laying, beating down **(b) à v.** in torrents; **il pleut à v.** it's pouring (down)

versé [vɛrse] *adj* (*dans une matière*) conversant (**dans** with); (*dans qch de pratique*) experienced, practised (**dans** in); **très v. dans la littérature tchèque** well-versed in *or* very conversant with Czech literature

Verseau [vɛrso] *nm Astron, Astrol* **le V.** Aquarius, the Water Carrier; **être (du signe du) V.** to be (an) Aquarius *or* an Aquarian

versement [vɛrsəmɑ̃] *nm* payment; **versements échelonnés** staggered payments; **en plusieurs versements, par versements échelonnés** by *or* in instalments *or US* installments; **premier v.** down payment; *Banque* **bulletin de v.** paying-in *or Am* deposit slip; **v. d'espèces** cash deposit

verser [vɛrse] **1** *vt* **(a)** (*liquide etc*) to pour (out); **v. du vin dans une cruche** to pour wine into a jug; **tu me verses un peu d'eau, s'il te plaît?** will you pour me some water, please?; **v. à boire à qn** to pour sb a drink, to pour a drink for sb

(b) (*renverser*) (*véhicule*) to overturn; (*du vent*) (*cultures*) to lay, to beat down

(c) (*larmes, lumière*) to shed; (*sang*) to spill, to shed; **v. son sang** to shed *or* spill one's blood; **prêt à v. son sang pour défendre ses idées** willing to fight for one's ideas

(d) (*argent*) to pay (in); (*sur un compte*) to deposit; **v. qch au crédit de qn** to credit sb with sth; **v. un acompte** to make a down payment; **on doit me v. un peu d'argent à la fin du mois** I should receive a little money at the end of the month; **v. de l'argent sur son compte** to pay money into one's account; **capitaux versés** paid-up capital; *Bourse* **v. un premium** to pay a premium

(e) *Jur etc* **v. un document au dossier** to add a document to the file

(f) *Mil* **v. des hommes à un régiment/dans une armée** to draft *or* assign *or* transfer men to a regiment/to an army

(g) *Mil* (*provisions*) to issue

2 *vi* **(a)** (*d'un véhicule*) to overturn; (*des cultures*) to be beaten down, to be laid flat; **sa voiture est allée v. dans le ravin** his car tipped over into the ravine

(b) *Fig* **il verse dans l'orgueil/la violence/le snobisme** he tends to be conceited/violent/snobbish

verset [vɛrsɛ] *nm* (*de la Bible etc*) verse

verseur, -euse [vɛrsœr, -øz] **1** *n* (*personne*) pourer **2** *nm Min* tipper **3** *nf* **verseuse** (*de cafetière*) jug, (coffee) pot **4** *adj* **bec v.** spout

versicolore [vɛrsikɔlɔr] *adj* particoloured, *US* particolored, variegated

versificateur [vɛrsifikatœr] *nm* versifier

versification [vɛrsifikasjɔ̃] *nf* versification

versifier [vɛrsifje] (*impf & pr sub* **n. versifiions, v. versifiiez**) *Littér* **1** *vi* to write verse **2** *vt* **v. de la prose** to put prose into verse

version [vɛrsjɔ̃] *nf* **(a)** (*vers la langue mère*) translation; *Scol* unseen (translation); **v. latine** Latin translation, translation from Latin; **faire une v. vers le français** to translate into French; **v. anglaise/espagnole (vers le français)** translation from English/Spanish (into French); **thème et v.** prose and translation

(b) *Cin* **(film en) v. originale** original language version; **v. française** (*doublée*) French version; **film américain en v. française** American film dubbed into French

(c) *Littér* (*d'un texte*) version

(d) (*d'un événement*) version, account; **elle m'a raconté sa v. de l'histoire** she told me her version of the story; **chacun a sa v. des faits** everyone has their own version of the facts

▶ **version:** *Aut* **v. bâchée** soft-top; *Ordinat* **v. bêta** beta version; **v. nationale** (*d'un produit*) country version

verso [vɛrso] *nm* (*d'une feuille de papier*) verso, back, reverse; **voir au v.** see over(leaf); **l'adresse est au v.** the address is overleaf *or* on the back

versoir [vɛrswar] *nm Agr* (*d'une charrue*) mouldboard, *US* moldboard

vert, -te [vɛr, -ɛrt] **1** *adj* **(a)** green; **légumes verts** green vegetables, *F* greens; **plantes vertes** house *or* pot plants; *Aut etc* **feu v.** green light; **attendre le feu v.** to wait for the green light; *Fig* **donner son feu v.** to give the green light (**à** for); **v. de peur** white with fear; **v. de jalousie** green with envy

(b) (*écologique*) green; **produit v.** green *or* environmentally friendly product; **candidat v.** green candidate

(c) (*agricole*) **pouvoir v.** power of the farming lobby; **l'Europe verte** European agriculture; **encourager les vacances vertes** to encourage holidays in the country; **partir en classe verte** to go on a school trip to the countryside; **la ceinture verte qui entoure Paris** the green belt around Paris

(d) (*bois*) green; (*fruit*) unripe; (*vin*) too young; **ce vin est encore v.** this wine isn't ready for drinking yet; **chêne v.** holm oak, ilex; **cuir v.** rawhide

(e) *Tél* **téléphone v.** *Br* ≈ Freefone®, *Can* ≈ Zenith, *US* ≈ 800 number

(f) (*vieillard*) spry, sprightly

(g) (*histoire etc*) spicy, risqué; **dans un langage un peu v.** in rather risqué language

(h) **langue verte** slang

(i) *Vieilli* (*réprimande etc*) sharp, tart

2 *nm* (a) (*couleur*) green; **v. profond/vif** deep/bright green

(b) **mettre un cheval au v.** to put a horse out to pasture *or* to grass; *F* **se mettre au v.** to go to the country to recuperate; (*pour se cacher*) to hide out *or* lie low *or* hole up in the country; **cet été, je me mets au v. et je lis** I'm going to spend this summer tucked away in the countryside reading

(c) *Pol* **V.** Green; **la montée des Verts** the rise of the Greens

3 *nfpl F* **en dire de vertes** to tell spicy *or* risqué stories; **il en a vu des vertes et des pas mûres** he's been through a lot

▶ **vert**: **v. amande** almond green; **v. bouteille** bottle green; **v. cendré** sage green; **v. de chrome** chrome green; **v. d'eau** sea green; **v. émeraude** emerald green; **v. olive** olive green; **v. pomme** apple green; **v. tendre** soft green

vert-de-gris **1** *nm inv* verdigris **2** *adj* grey(ish)-green

vert-de-grisé, *pl* **vert-de-grisé(e)s** [vɛrdəgrize] *adj* coated with verdigris

vertébral, -ale, -aux, -ales [vɛrtebral, -o] *adj Anat* vertebral; **colonne vertébrale** spinal *or* vertebral column, spine, backbone

vertèbre [vɛrtɛbr] *nf Anat* vertebra; **v. cervicale/dorsale/lombaire** cervical/dorsal/lumbar vertebra; **se déplacer une v.** to slip a disc

vertébré [vɛrtebre] *adj, nm Zool* vertebrate

vertement [vɛrtəmɑ̃] *adv* **réprimander v. qn** to reprimand sb sharply *or* severely, *F* to give sb a good telling off *or* ticking off; **il le tança v.** he gave him a good dressing-down; **répondre v. à qn** to answer sb sharply, to give sb a sharp reply

vertical, -ale, -aux, -ales [vɛrtikal, -o] **1** *adj* vertical, upright; (*organisation, structuration*) vertical; **en position verticale** (*objet*) in a vertical position, upright; (*personne*) in a standing position; **elle se sent mal en station verticale** she doesn't feel well when she stands up; **éclairage v.** overhead lighting; *Écon* **concentration verticale** *Ordinat* **boîtier v.** tower; *Écon* **concentration verticale** vertical integration **2** *nf* **verticale** vertical; *MecE* plumb-line; **à la verticale** vertically; (*monter*) vertically, straight up; (*tomber, descendre*) vertically, straight down; **la falaise tombe à la verticale dans la mer** there is a sheer drop from the cliff to the sea; **falaise à la verticale** sheer cliff

verticalement [vɛrtikalmɑ̃] *adv* vertically; (*avec mouvement vers le haut*) straight up; (*avec mouvement vers le bas*) straight down; (*dans les mots croisés*) down

verticalité [vɛrtikalite] *nf* verticality

verticille [vɛrtisil] *nm Bot* whorl

vertige [vɛrtiʒ] *nm* vertigo, fear of heights; (*étourdissement*) dizziness, giddiness, dizzy spell; **cela me donne le v.** it gives me vertigo, it makes me feel dizzy *or* giddy, it makes my head swim; **des salaires à vous donner le v.** salaries that make your head spin; **je n'ai pas le v.** I'm not scared of heights; **avoir facilement le v.** to have a bad head for heights; **avoir des vertiges** to get dizzy *or* giddy, to have fits of giddiness, to have dizzy spells; *Fig* **les vertiges du succès** the feeling of intoxication that success brings

vertigineusement [vɛrtiʒinøzmɑ̃] *adv* dizzily, *Fml* vertiginously; **une route v. escarpée** a breathtakingly steep road

vertigineux, -euse [vɛrtiʒinø, -øz] *adj* (*hauteur etc*) dizzy, giddy; (*vitesse*) breakneck, breathtaking; (*somme*) staggering; **hausse vertigineuse des prix** staggering increase in prices

vertigo [vɛrtigo] *nm Vét* (blind) staggers

vertiport [vɛrtipɔr] *nm Av* heliport

vertu [vɛrty] *nf* (a) (*de remède etc*) quality, property, virtue; **v. sédative/calmante** sedative/calming property; **plantes aux vertus curatives** plants that have healing properties; **en v. de** by virtue of; *Jur* in pursuance of; **en v. de quoi est-il intervenu?** what gave him the right to intervene?; **et en v. de ce contrat, vous nous devez …** under the terms of this contract, you owe us …; **vous avez signé ce contrat, en v. de quoi vous nous devez une certaine prestation** you signed this contract, under the terms of which *or* in accordance with which you owe us a certain sum of money; **en v. de cet arrangement** under (the terms of) this agreement

(b) (*morale*) virtue; **faire de nécessité v.** to make a virtue (out) of necessity; **l'honnêteté est une v.** honesty is a virtue; **il a de la v. à la supporter** I admire his courage in putting up with her; **je n'ai aucune v. à ne pas fumer, je n'aime pas ça** I can't claim any credit for not smoking *or Fml* there is nothing admirable in my not smoking, I just don't like it; **elle le pare de toutes les vertus** she's forever singing his praises; **femme de petite v.** woman of easy virtue

vertueusement [vɛrtɥøzmɑ̃] *adv* virtuously

vertueux, -euse [vɛrtɥø, -øz] *adj* virtuous; **intentions vertueuses** honourable intentions; *Arch* **femme vertueuse** virtuous *or* chaste woman

verve [vɛrv] *nf* verve, vigour, *US* vigor, *F* go; **être en v.** to be in top form; **jouer avec v.** to give a spirited performance

verveine [vɛrvɛn] *nf Bot* vervain, verbena; (**tisane de**) **v.** verbena tea; (**liqueur de**) **v.** = verbena flavoured liqueur

verveux[1] [vɛrvø, -øz] *adj Litt* animated, lively, spirited

verveux[2] *nm* (*filet*) hoop net

vesce [vɛs] *nf Bot* vetch, tare

vésical, -ale, -aux, -ales [vezikal, -o] *adj Anat* vesical

vésicant [vezikɑ̃] *adj, nm Méd* vesicatory; **gaz v.** blister gas

vésicatoire [vezikatwar] *adj, nm Méd* vesicatory; **appliquer un v. à qn** to blister sb

vésicule [vezikyl] *nf* (a) *Anat* vesicle; *Bot* air cell; *Anat* **v. biliaire** gall bladder (b) (*sur la peau*) blister

vespasienne [vɛspazjɛn] *nf* street urinal

vespéral, -ale, -aux, -ales [vɛsperal, -o] *adj* evening

vesse-de-loup, *pl* **vesses-de-loup** [vɛsdəlu] *nf* puffball

vessie [vesi] *nf Anat etc* bladder; **v. natatoire** (*de poisson*) air bladder, swim bladder; *Méd* **v. à** *ou* **de glace** ice bag *or* pack; *Fig* **prendre des vessies pour des lanternes** to believe that the moon is made of green cheese

vestale [vɛstal] *nf Antiq* vestal (virgin)

veste [vɛst] *nf* jacket; **v. d'intérieur** smoking jacket; **v. croisée** double-breasted jacket; *F* **tomber la v.** to take off one's jacket; *Fig* **retourner sa v.** to be a turncoat; *Fig F* **ramasser** *ou* **prendre une v.** (*en affaires, en amour etc*) to come a cropper

vestiaire [vɛstjɛr] *nm* (a) (*dans un théâtre etc*) cloakroom; *Sp etc* changing room, locker room; *Jur* robing room; *Th F* **au v.!** off!, off! (b) (*vêtements*) **renouveler son v.** to renew one's wardrobe; *F* **mon v., s'il vous plaît** could I have my coat/hat and coat, please?; **récupérer son v.** to collect one's things from the cloakroom (c) (*meuble*) (*dans une usine etc*) locker

vestibule [vɛstibyl] *nm* vestibule, (entrance) hall, lobby

vestige [vɛstiʒ] *nm* (*d'anciennes habitations etc*) vestige, trace; **derniers vestiges de …** last remnants of …; **vestiges du passé** relics of the past

vestimentaire [vɛstimɑ̃tɛr] *adj* (*commerce*) clothing; **détails vestimentaires** accessories

veston [vɛstɔ̃] *nm* (*d'homme*) jacket; *Naut* monkey jacket; **complet v.** lounge suit

Vésuve [vezyv] *nm* Vesuvius

vêtement [vɛtmɑ̃] *nm* garment, article *or* item of clothing; **vêtements** clothes, clothing; **mon budget vêtements** my clothes *or* clothing budget; **industrie du v.** clothing *or F* rag trade; **tissus pour vêtements** dress material; **mettre ses vêtements du dimanche** to put on one's Sunday best; **vêtements de plage/de pluie** beachwear/rainwear; *Rel* **vêtements sacerdotaux** vestments; **tu devrais mettre** *ou* **passer un v.** you should put something on

vétéran [veterɑ̃] *nm Mil etc* veteran, old campaigner; *Sp* veteran; *Fig* old hand; *Pol* elder statesman

vétérinaire [veterinɛr] **1** *adj* veterinary **2** *n* veterinary surgeon, *F* vet, *Am* veterinarian

vétille [vetij] *nf* (mere) trifle, triviality; **vétilles** trivia; **se disputer pour des vétilles** to argue over trivialities *or* trivial details

vétilleux, -euse [vetijø, -øz] *adj Litt* captious

vêtir [vetir] (*prp* **vêtant**; *pp* **vêtu**; *pr ind* **je vêts, n. vêtons**; *impf* **je vêtais**; *p hist* **je vêtis**; *fu* **je vêtirai**) **1** *vt* (*qn*) to clothe, to dress (**de** in); **tout de noir vêtu** dressed *or Fml* clad all in black **2 se vêtir** *vpr* to dress (oneself) (**de** in)

vétiver [vetivɛr] *nm* vetiver

veto [veto] *nm* veto; **opposer son v. à qch** to veto sth, to exercise one's veto over sth; **mettre son v. à qch** to veto sth; **droit de v.** right of veto

vêtu [vety] *adj* dressed; **v. de blanc/de lin** dressed in white/in linen; **être v. chaudement** *ou* **chaudement v.** to be warmly dressed; **professeurs vêtus de leurs toges** professors wearing *or* in their gowns; **à demi-v.** half-dressed; *Litt* **mur v. de lierre** ivy-clad wall, wall covered in ivy

vétuste [vetyst] *adj* decayed, decrepit
vétusté [vetyste] *nf* decay, decrepitude
veuf, veuve [vœf, vœv] **1** *adj* (*homme, femme*) widowed; *Fig* **v. de qch** bereft of sth **2** *n* widower, *f* widow **3** *nf* **(a)** *Typ* **veuve** widow **(b)** *F Arch* **la Veuve** the guillotine
veule [vøl] *adj* (*personne etc*) weak, feeble; **un air v.** a listless look
veulerie [vølri] *nf* inertia, listlessness
veuvage [vœvaʒ] *nm* widowhood
vexant [vɛksɑ̃] *adj* **(a)** (*remarque, personne etc*) hurtful **(b)** *Vieilli* (*contrariant*) vexing, provoking, annoying; **nous nous sommes manquées de peu, c'est v.** how annoying that we just missed each other!
vexation [vɛksasjɔ̃] *nf* **(a)** (*humiliation*) mortification; **essuyer** *ou* **subir des vexations** to be snubbed *or* put down; **elle ne supporte pas les vexations** she can't stand being snubbed *or* put down; **être en proie aux vexations de qn** to be constantly being snubbed *or* put down by sb **(b)** *Vieilli* (*mauvais traitement*) vexation
vexatoire [vɛksatwar] *adj* vexatious
vexer [vɛkse] **1** *vt* **v. qn** to hurt sb *or* sb's feelings **2 se vexer** *vpr* to get upset *or* offended; **elle se vexe facilement** she gets upset very easily, she's easily offended; **se v. de qch** to feel hurt *or* to be upset by sth; **il se vexe de tout/pour un rien** he gets upset over everything/the slightest thing
VF [veɛf] *nf* (*abrév* **version française**) French version
V.H.F. [veaʃɛf] *nf* VHF
VI [vei] *nf Compta* (*abrév* **valeur d'inventaire**) balance sheet value, break-up value
via [vja] *prép* via, by way of; **Paris, v. Calais** Paris, via Calais
viabilisé [vjabilize] *adj Admin* **terrain v.** serviced site, site with services
viabiliser [vjabilize] *vt* to service; **v. un terrain** to service a site; **v. une entreprise** to make a business viable
viabilité[1] [vjabilite] *nf* (*d'un foetus*) viability, survival potential; (*d'un projet etc*) viability
viabilité[2] *nf* **(a)** (*de chemin etc*) practicability **(b)** *Constr* (*d'un site de construction*) development
viable [vjabl] *adj* (*foetus, projet etc*) viable
viaduc [vjadyk] *nm* viaduct
viager, -ère [vjaʒe, -ɛr] **1** *adj* (for) life; **rente viagère** life annuity **2** *nm* life interest; **placer son argent en v.** to invest one's money in *or* to buy an annuity
viande [vjɑ̃d] *nf* **(a)** meat; **v. de boucherie** butcher meat, fresh meat; **v. blanche/rouge** white/red meat; **jus de v.** meat juices, gravy; **v. hachée** minced *or Am* ground meat, *Br* mince; **v. de cheval** horsemeat, horseflesh **(b)** *Arg* **amène ta v.!** come on, move your carcass!
viander (se) [səvjɑ̃de] *vpr F* to get smashed up; **ils se sont viandés contre un mur** they smashed into a wall
viatique [vjatik] *nm* **(a)** *Vieilli* (*argent*) money; (*provisions*) provisions for a journey; **on lui a donné un v. de 200 livres pour son voyage** we gave him £200 for his trip; *Fig Litt* **il n'a que ce diplôme pour v.** this diploma is his sole asset; **j'avais pour seul v. cette lettre de recommandation** this letter was all I had to recommend me **(b)** *Rel* last sacrament
vibrant [vibrɑ̃] *adj* **(a)** (*corde etc*) vibrating; **consonne vibrante** vibrant consonant **(b)** (*voix*) resonant, vibrant; (*discours*) rousing, stirring; (*personnalité etc*) vibrant; **v. et réceptif** (*personne*) eager and receptive; **c'est une nature vibrante** he is very sensitive *or* highly strung
vibraphone [vibrafɔn] *nm Mus* vibraphone
vibraphoniste [vibrafɔnist] *n Mus* vibraphone player
vibrateur [vibratœr] *nm* vibrator
vibration [vibrasjɔ̃] *nf* vibration; (*de la voix*) resonance; *Phys* **v. de la lumière** vibration of light
vibrato [vibrato] *nm Mus* vibrato
vibratoire [vibratwar] *adj* vibratory
vibrer [vibre] *vi* to vibrate; *Fig* **v. d'enthousiasme** to be quivering with excitement; *Fig* **faire v. le cœur de qn** to make sb's heart pound; *Fig* **c'est la seule chose qui le fait v.** it's the only thing that gets him going
vibreur [vibrœr] *nm Tech* vibrator; (*d'une sonnette*) buzzer
vibrion [vibrijɔ̃] *nm* **(a)** (*bactérie*) vibrio(n); *Méd* **v. septique** gas bacillus **(b)** (*personne agitée*) fidget
vibromasseur [vibromasœr] *nm* (*électrique*) (*pour massage*) vibrator
vicaire [vikɛr] *nm Rel* **(a)** **v. apostolique** vicar apostolic; **grand v., v. général** vicar-general **(b)** *Église anglicane* curate; *Cathol* (assistant) priest
vicariat [vikarja] *nm Rel* curacy
vice [vis] *nm* **(a)** (*défaut moral*) vice; **il a tous les vices** he has all the vices; **il a le v. de la boisson** drinking is his vice; *Fig* **mais c'est un v.!** it's an obsession, he/she/they/*etc* is/are totally obsessed **(b)** (*défaut*) fault, defect, flaw **(c)** (*corruption etc*) vice; **vivre dans le v.** to lead a life of vice
▶ **vice**: *Com* **v. apparent** obvious defect; **v. caché** hidden *or* latent defect; *Vét etc* **v. de conformation** (congenital) malformation, physical defect; **v. de construction** structural fault *or* defect *or* flaw; **v. de fabrication** manufacturing defect; *Jur* **v. de forme** legal technicality; (*dans un contrat etc*) flaw; *Com* **v. inhérent** inherent vice; **v. contre nature** unnatural vice; **v. de prononciation** faulty pronunciation; **v. propre** inherent defect; *Com* **v. rédhibitoire** material defect; **v. solitaire** masturbation, self-abuse
vice-amiral, *pl* **vice-amiraux** *nm* vice admiral
vice-chancelier, *pl* **vice-chanceliers** *nm* vice chancellor
vice-consul, *pl* **vice-consuls** *nm* vice consul
vice-consulat, *pl* **vice-consulats** *nm* vice consulate
vice-gérant, -ante, *pl* **vice-gérant(e)s** *n* deputy manager *or f* manageress
vicelard, -arde [visəlar, -ard] *F* **1** *adj* **(a)** (*dépravé*) dirty **(b)** (*perfide*) vicious **2** *n* lecher, pervert; **un vieux v.** a dirty old man
vicennal, -ale, -aux, -ales [visenal, -o] *adj* (*qui dure vingt ans*) twenty-year, *Fml* vicennial; (*qui a lieu tous les vingt ans*) occurring every twenty years, *Fml* vicennial
vice-présidence, *pl* **vice-présidences** *nf* (*d'état, d'organisation*) vice-presidency; (*d'entreprise*) vice-chairmanship
vice-président, -ente, *pl* **vice-président(e)s** *n* (*d'état, d'organisation*) vice president; (*d'entreprise*) vice-chairman
vice-roi, *pl* **vice-rois** *nm* viceroy
vice-versa [vis(e)vɛrsa] *adv* vice versa
vichy [viʃi] *nm* **(a)** *Tex* gingham; **jupe en v. rouge et blanc** red and white checked cotton skirt, red and white gingham skirt **(b)** (*eau minérale*) vichy water; **v. fraise** strawberry syrup in vichy water **(c)** **V.** Vichy; *Hist* **la France de V.** Vichy France
viciateur, -trice [visjatœr, -tris] *adj* contaminating, *Fml* vitiating
viciation [visjasjɔ̃] *nf* (*de principes moraux etc*) corruption, *Fml* vitiation; (*de l'air etc*) pollution, contamination; (*du sang*) thinness; *Jur* (*d'un contrat*) invalidation, vitiation
vicié [visje] *adj* corrupt, *Fml* vitiated; (*sang*) poor, thin; **air v.** (*par des émanations*) stale *or* foul air
vicier [visje] *vt* (*impf, pr sub* **n. viciions, v. viciiez**) **(a)** to corrupt, *Fml* to vitiate; (*air*) to pollute, to contaminate; *Fig* (*jugement, goût*) to corrupt **(b)** *Jur* (*contrat*) to invalidate, to vitiate
vicieusement [visjøzmɑ̃] *adv* **(a)** (*avec dépravation*) lecherously **(b)** (*perfidement*) viciously
vicieux, -ieuse [visjø -jøz] *adj* **(a)** (*corrompu*) (*personne*) depraved **(b)** (*perfide*) (*personne, coup*) underhand, sly; **cercle v.** vicious circle **(c)** (*incorrecte*) (*prononciation*) wrong, incorrect **(d)** (*rétif*) (*cheval*) bad-tempered
vicinal, -ale, -aux, -ales [visinal, -o] *adj* **chemin v.** local road
vicissitude [visisityd] *nf* (*de la chance etc*) vicissitude; **les vicissitudes de la vie ou de l'existence** the ups and downs *or* trials and tribulations of life
vicomte [vikɔ̃t] *nm* viscount
vicomté [vikɔ̃te] *nf* **(a)** (*titre*) viscountcy **(b)** (*terrain*) viscounty
vicomtesse [vikɔ̃tɛs] *nf* viscountess
victime [viktim] *nf* **(a)** victim; **les victimes du désastre/de la guerre** the victims *or* casualties of the disaster/of war; **les victimes de la route** road accident victims; **être (la) v. d'un système d'imposition** to be badly hit by a system of taxation; **être (la) v. d'une illusion/d'un malentendu** to labour *or US* labor under an illusion/a misconception; **j'ai été (la) v. d'un escroc** I've been had by a conman; **se prendre pour une v.** to think oneself a victim, to feel victimized; **j'ai dû être v. d'une hallucination** I must have been hallucinating; **être v. de la fourberie/négligence de qn** to be the victim of sb's deceit/negligence **(b)** (*de sacrifice*) victim
victoire [viktwar] *nf* **(a)** victory; *Sp* win, victory; **remporter la v.** to gain a victory (**sur** over), to carry *or* win the day; **remporter une v. sur soi-même** to gain a victory over oneself, to overcome *or* conquer one's fears/*etc*; **chanter** *ou* **crier v.** to claim victory; **v. à la Pyrrhus** Pyrrhic victory **(b)** (*déesse*) **V.** Victory, Victoria
Victoria [viktɔrja] *nf* **(a)** **la reine V.** Queen Victoria **(b)** **v.** (*voiture*) victoria
victorien, -ienne [viktɔrjɛ̃, -jɛn] *adj* Victorian
victorieusement [viktɔrjøzmɑ̃] *adv* victoriously
victorieux, -ieuse [viktɔrjø, -jøz] *adj* victorious; (*air, sourire etc*) triumphant; *Sp* **sortir v. d'une épreuve/d'un match** to emerge the winner of a heat/a match; **être v.** to win (the day), to be victorious

victuailles [viktɥaj] *nfpl Vieilli* food, provisions, *Fml* victuals

vidage [vidaʒ] *nm* **(a)** (*de poissons*) gutting, cleaning; (*de volailles*) drawing **(b)** *F* (*d'un bar etc*) throwing out, chucking out **(c)** *Ordinat* dump

vidange [vidɑ̃ʒ] *nf* **(a)** *Aut* oil change; **faire la v.** to change the oil; **v.-graissage** oil change and lubrication; **bouchon de v.** sump plug; (*de radiateur*) draining plug; **robinet de v.** draincock; **tuyau de v.** waste pipe; **tonneau en v.** broached cask **(b)** (*d'un carter à huile, d'une fosse d'aisances etc*) draining, emptying; (*d'une chaudière*) blowing off **(c)** **vidanges** sewage

vidanger [vidɑ̃ʒe] *vt* **(je vidangeai(s); n. vidangeons)** (*fosse d'aisances, radiateur, carter à huile etc*) to empty, to drain; (*chaudière*) to blow off; (*huile, eaux résidentielles*) to empty out, to drain off

vidangeur [vidɑ̃ʒœr] *nm* cesspit clearer *or* emptier

vide [vid] **1** *adj* (*verre, pièce etc*) empty; (*case dans un document etc*) blank; (*siège, place*) empty, unoccupied, vacant; **la ville est v. de ses habitants** the town is empty (of its inhabitants); **l'appartement est encore très v.** (*peu meublé*) the flat is still very bare; **bouteilles vides** empty bottles *F* empties; **arriver les mains vides** to arrive empty-handed; **je suis rentré de vacances les poches vides** I came back from holiday penniless; **avoir l'estomac v.** to have an empty stomach; **j'ai l'estomac v.** my stomach is empty; **j'ai la tête v.** my mind's a blank; **ma vie est v.** my life is empty; **v. de sens** devoid of meaning, meaningless; **phrases vides** empty *or* meaningless words; **avoir le regard v.** to have a blank look; *Com* **v. en retour** empty on return

2 *nm* empty space, gap; (*dans un document*) blank; *Phys* vacuum; *Fig* (*néant*) emptiness, void; (*dans un emploi du temps*) gap; **combler les vides** to fill (up) the gaps; *Fig* **son départ laisse un v.** his departure has left a gap *or* void; **faire le v.** to create a vacuum; **la nature a horreur du v.** nature abhors a vacuum; *Fig* **il faut faire le v.** (*tout oublier*) you'll have to put it out of your mind; *Fig* **ça me permet de faire le v.** it helps me (to) switch off *or* blank everything out; **faire le v. autour de qn** to isolate sb completely, to leave sb on his/her own; **nettoyage par le v.** vacuum cleaning; *Fig* **faire le nettoyage par le v.** to throw everything out, to get rid of everything, *F* to gut the place; **le v. dans sa vie** the void in his life; **taper dans le v.** to (hit out and) miss the mark; **se jeter dans/regarder dans le v.** to jump into/stare into space; **avoir peur du v.** to be afraid of *or* to have no head for heights; **j'étais attiré par le v.** I felt an urge to jump; *Fig* **parler dans le v.** to talk to a brick wall; **à v.** (*batterie*) discharged; **camion revenant à v.** truck returning empty; **poids à v.** unladen weight; **marcher à v.** (*d'une machine*) to run light *or* without load; **le train est parti à v.** the train left empty; **le mécanisme tourne à v.** the engine is ticking over; *Mus* **corde à v.** open string; **emballé sous v.** vacuum-packed

▶ **vide**: **v. juridique: il y a un v. juridique à ce sujet-là** there's nothing in the statute books to cover it; **v. sanitaire** crawl space

vidé [vide] *adj* **(a)** (*poisson*) gutted; (*volaille*) drawn **(b)** *F* (*personne*) tired out, worn out, all in, dead beat; **c'est un homme v.** he's played out

vidéaste [videast] *n* video maker

vidéo [video] **1** *adj inv* video; **caméra/cassette v.** video camera/cassette **2** *nf inv* (*média*) video; (*cassette*) video(-tape); **la dernière v. de Madonna** Madonna's latest video; **faire de la v.** (*d'un artiste*) to make videos; **v.-à-la-demande** video-on-demand, VOD; **v. d'entreprise** *ou* **institutionnelle** corporate video; **v. fixe** video still; *Ordinat* **v. inversée** reverse video

vidéoachat [videoaʃa] *nm* videoshopping

vidéocassette [videokaset] *nf* video cassette

vidéoclip [videoklip] *nm TV* (*d'un groupe de rock etc*) video

vidéoclub [videoklœb] *nm* video club

vidéocommunication [videokomynikasjɔ̃] *nf Électron* video communication

vidéocomposite [videokɔ̃pozit] *adj Électron* **signal v.** videocomposite signal

vidéoconférence [videokɔ̃ferɑ̃s] *nf* video-conference; (*concept*) videoconferencing

vidéodiagnostic [videodjagnɔstik] *nm Méd* videodiagnostics

vidéodisque [videodisk] *nm Électron* compact disc video, video CD, videodisc, *surtout US* videodisk

vidéofréquence [videofrekɑ̃s] *nf Rad* video frequency

vidéogramme [videogram] *nm* videogram

vidéographie [videografi] *nf Électron* = Videotex®; **v. diffusée** = Teletext®; **v. interactive** = Viewdata®

vidéographique [videografik] videographic

vidéophone [videɔfɔn] *nm Électron* videophone

vidéoquestionnaire [videokɛstjɔnɛr] *nm* (*par Minitel*) video-questionnaire

vide-ordures *nm inv* rubbish chute

vidéotex [videotɛks] *nm Ordinat* Videotex®, viewdata; **v. diffusé** teletext

vidéothèque [videɔtɛk] *nf* video library; (*personnelle*) video collection

vidéotransmission [videotrɑ̃smisjɔ̃] *nf* video transmission *or* broadcasting

vidéovente [videovɑ̃t] *nf* video-selling

vide-poches *nm inv* **(a)** (*de voiture*) storage tray; (*dans la porte*) door pocket, map pocket **(b)** (*de table*) (dressing table) tidy

vide-pomme, *pl* **vide-pommes** *nm* apple corer

vider [vide] **1** *vt* **(a)** to empty; (*pièce, tiroir*) to empty, to clear out; (*tonneau, verre, étang etc*) to empty, to drain; (*chaudières*) to blow off; (*œuf*) to blow; *Ordinat* **v. l'écran** to clear the screen; *Ordinat* **v. la corbeille** to empty the wastebasket *or Am* the trash; **videz vos verres!** drink up!; **v. les lieux** to vacate the premises; **le juge a ordonné de faire v. la salle** the judge ordered the court (to be) cleared; **v. une chambre de ses meubles** to clear the furniture from a room; **la chaleur a vidé la ville de ses habitants** the heat has emptied the town (of its inhabitants); *F* **v. qn** (*l'épuiser*) to drain sb (of energy), to exhaust sb, to wear sb out; **partir en vidant la caisse** to make off with the takings; **v. les poches de qn** to empty sb's pockets; (*d'un voleur*) to pick sb's pockets; *F* **v. son sac** to get it off one's chest; **v. son cœur** to pour out one's feelings

(b) *F* (*qn*) (*d'un bar etc*) to throw out; (*d'un travail*) to sack; *Équitation* (*cavalier*) to throw; *Équitation* **v. les arçons** *ou* **les étriers** to be thrown (from one's horse); **se faire v.** (*de son cheval*) to be thrown; *F* (*d'une pièce*) to be sent out; (*d'un bar etc*) to be chucked *or* thrown out; (*d'un collège*) to be expelled; (*être renvoyé*) to get the sack

(c) (*carcasse*) to eviscerate; (*poisson*) to gut, to clean; (*volaille*) to draw; (*pomme*) to core; (*fruit*) to stone, *surtout Am* to pit

(d) (*question, querelle*) to settle

2 se vider *vpr* to empty; **la baignoire est en train de se v.** the bath is emptying out, the bathwater is draining away; **ce réservoir se vide dans le lac** this tank drains *or* empties into the lake; **se v. de son sang** to bleed to death; **la locution s'est peu à peu vidée de son sens** the expression has gradually lost its meaning

vide-tasses *nm inv* slop basin

videur, -euse [vidœr, -øz] *n* (*dans un club etc*) bouncer

viduité [vidɥite] *nf Jur* widowhood; **délai de v.** minimum legal period of widowhood

vie [vi] *nf* [ⓘA12,1,d] **(a)** (*principe vital*) life; **v. végétative/animale** plant/animal life; **être en v.** to be alive; **donner la v. à un enfant** to give birth to a child; **perdre la v.** to lose one's life; **avoir la v. dure** (*de mauvaise herbe, personne*) to be tough (as old boots), to be hard to kill *or* to get rid of; (*de superstitions, préjugés etc*) to be hard to kill off *or* to get rid of; **on peut dire que tu as la v. dure, toi!** it takes a lot to kill you!; **il est entre la v. et la mort** he is (hovering) between life and death; **question de v. ou de mort** matter of life and death; **il y va de sa v.** his life is at stake; **je lui dois la v.** I owe him my life; **sauver la v. à qn** to save sb's life; *Fig* **tu me sauves la v.!** you're a life-saver!; **ramener qn à la v.** to bring sb back to life; *Fig* **revenir à la v.** to come back to life, to be back in the land of the living; **donner de la v. à une conversation/une réunion** to liven up *or* enliven *or* animate a conversation/a meeting; **elle déborde de v., elle est pleine de v.** she's full of life, she's very lively; **la v. des idées/des volcans** the evolution of ideas/volcanoes; **sans v.** lifeless

(b) (*existence considérée dans sa durée*) life, lifetime; **espérance de v.** life expectancy; **pour la v.** for life; **une fois dans la v.** once in a lifetime; **plus tard dans la v.** later (on) in life; **de toute ma v. je n'ai jamais entendu chose pareille!** I've never heard such a thing in all my life!; **jamais de la v.!** never!, not on your life!, no way!; **pension à v., pension la v. durant** life pension; **nommé à v.** appointed for life

(c) (*biographie*) biography, life story; *F* **tu nous racontes ta v.!** we don't want your life story!

(d) (*façon de vivre*) existence, way of life, lifestyle; **ainsi va la v.!, c'est la v.!** that's life!, such is life!; **je connais la v.** I've seen something of life; **regarder la v. en face** to look life in the face; **avoir une v. sédentaire** to have a sedentary lifestyle *or* (way of) life; **changer de v.** to change one's (way of) life; (*faire amende honorable*) to mend one's ways, to turn over a new leaf; **elle veut mener sa v. comme elle l'entend** she wants to lead her life as she sees fit; **rendre la v. dure à qn** to make life hard *or* a misery for sb; **avoir une v. dure** to have a hard life; **mener une v. de patachon** *ou* **de bâton de chaise** to lead a wild *or* riotous life, to live it up; **la v. à l'américaine** the American way of life; **la v. nocturne** nightlife; **femme de mauvaise v.** loose woman; *F Vieilli* **faire la v.** to lead a riotous life; **faire toute une v.** to kick up a fuss *or* a row

(**e**) *Écon* living, livelihood; **la v. est très chère dans ces pays** the cost of living is very high in these countries; **niveau de v.** standard of living; **coût de la v.** cost of living; **indemnité de v. chère** *ou* **de cherté de v.** cost of living allowance; **gagner sa v.** to earn one's living *or Sl* crust; **elle gagne bien/mal sa v.** she earns/doesn't earn a good living *or* wage; **comment gagne-t-elle sa v.?** what does she do for a living?, how does she earn a living?

vieil, vieille *voir* **vieux**

vieillard [vjɛjar] *nm* old man; **les vieillards** old people, the elderly, the aged; **hospice de vieillards** old people's *or F* old folk's home

vieillerie [vjɛjri] *nf* (*souvent pl*) **vieilleries** old(-fashioned) *or* out-of-date things; (*idées*) old(-fashioned) *or* out-of-date *or* outdated ideas

vieillesse [vjɛjɛs] *nf* old age; **bâton de v.** support *or* prop of old age; **ma fille est mon bâton de v.** my daughter gives me support in my old age; **la v.** (*vieillards*) old people, the elderly, the aged; **aide à la v.** help for the aged

vieilli [vjeji] *adj* (**a**) (*mot etc*) obsolescent; (*style etc*) old-fashioned, out-of-date (**b**) (*vieux*) (grown) old, aged

vieillir [vjejir] **1** *vi* (**a**) to grow old, to age; **vous n'avez pas vieilli, vous êtes toujours le même!** you haven't aged *or* got any older, you're still the same!; **il a vieilli, il est vieilli** he looks older, he's aged

(**b**) (*d'un usage, d'un mot*) to become obsolete *or* antiquated *or* out of date; **ce mot a vieilli** this word is obsolescent; **cette chanson/construction n'a pas vieilli** this song/building has stood the test of time *or* hasn't dated; **la pièce a beaucoup vieilli** the play seems very dated

(**c**) (*d'un fromage, d'un vin*) to mature

2 *vt* (**a**) **v. qn** (*du maquillage, d'une coupe de cheveux*) to make sb look old(er), to age sb; (*adolescent*) to make sb look older; **tu me vieillis!** I'm not <u>that</u> old!

(**b**) (*meubles*) to distress; **pour v. un peu la photo** to age the photo a little

3 se vieillir *vpr* (**a**) (*par l'apparence*) to make oneself look old(er)

(**b**) (*en mentant*) to pretend to be older (than one is)

vieillissant [vjejisɑ̃] *adj* (*personne, édifice*) ageing; (*institution, style*) which is becoming outdated

vieillissement [vjejismɑ̃] *nm* (**a**) ageing, growing old; **ralentir le v. de la peau** to slow down the ageing process of the skin; **crème contre le v. de la peau** anti-ageing cream; **v. général de la population** general ageing of the population (**b**) (*d'un mot etc*) becoming obsolete, obsolescence (**c**) (*d'un fromage, d'un vin etc*) ageing, maturing (**d**) (*de meubles*) distressing; (*d'une photo, d'un cadre en bois etc*) ageing

vieillot, -otte [vjejo, -ɔt] *adj* antiquated, old-fashioned

vielle [vjɛl] *nf Mus* hurdy-gurdy

Vienne [vjɛn] *nf* Vienna

viennois, -oise [vjɛnwa, -waz] **1** *adj* Viennese; **pain v.** Viennese bread; **un pain v.** a Vienna loaf **2** *n* **V.** Viennese

vierge [vjɛrʒ] **1** *nf* (**a**) virgin; **la (Sainte) V.** the Blessed Virgin (Mary); **la V. Marie** the Virgin Mary; **chapelle de la V.** Lady chapel; *Beaux-Arts* **une V. à l'enfant** a Madonna and child (**b**) *Astron, Astrol* **la V.** Virgo; **être (du signe de la) V.** to be (a) Virgo **2** *adj* (**a**) (*personne*) virgin, virginal; (*sol, forêt, huile etc*) virgin; **laine v.** virgin wool (**b**) (*page, cassette etc*) blank; (*blanc etc*) pure; *Phot* (*plaque*) unexposed; *Ordinat* (*ligne, espace*) blank; (*disquette*) blank, unformatted; **cahier v.** new *or* blank jotter; **réputation v.** untarnished reputation

Viêt-cong [vjetkɔ̃g] *nm* Vietcong, Viet Cong

Viêt(-)nam [vjɛtnam] *nm* Vietnam

vietnamien, -ienne [vjɛtnamjɛ̃, -jɛn] **1** *adj* Vietnamese **2** *nm Ling* Vietnamese **3** *n* **V.** Vietnamese

vieux, vieil, *f* **vieille** [vjø, vjɛj] **1** *adj* (*the form* **vieil** *is used before masc nouns beginning with a vowel or h mute, but* **vieux** *also occurs in this position*) (**a**) [①**A17**,3,a] (*personne*) old; **se faire v.** to be getting old, to be getting on (in years); **il est plus v. que moi** he's older than me; **moins v. que lui** younger than him; **vivre v.** to live to a ripe old age; **se sentir v.** to feel old; **il n'est pas bien v.** he's not very old, he's still young; **pour ses v. jours** for one's old age

(**b**) (*amitié etc*) old, longstanding; **un vieil ami** an old friend, a friend of long standing; **il est v. dans ce métier** he's an old hand at this job; *F* **v. crétin!** old fool!; *F* **salut vieille noix** *ou* **branche!** hullo, old stick!; **c'est un v. marin** he's an old salt; **c'est un homme/une femme de la vieille école** he's/she's one of the old school

(**c**) (*objet*) (*bâtiment etc*) old, ancient; (*pain, information etc*) old, stale; (*chapeau etc*) old, worn, shabby; **v. papiers** waste paper; **mes vieilles mains tremblent** my old hands are shaking; **elle ne va pas faire de v. os** she won't make old bones, she won't live long; *Fig* **je ne vais pas faire de v. os ici** I'm not going to hang around here for long; **c'est v. comme Hérode** *ou* **le Pont-Neuf** *ou* **le monde** it's as old as the hills, it goes back to the year dot; **le bon v. temps** the good old days; **il est très vieille France** he's very much one of the old school; **c'est une vieille histoire** it's an old story; **elle est vieille, celle-là!** that's a real oldie *or* an old one!

(**d**) *inv* **v. jeu** old-fashioned, antiquated, out of date; **ça, c'est v. jeu** that's old hat; **s'habiller/être v. jeu** to be old-fashioned in one's dress/to be old-fashioned; **des rubans vieil or/v. rose** old-gold/old-rose ribbons

2 *adv* **elle s'habille plus v. que son âge** she dresses too old for *or* older than her age; **elle fait moins v. que ça** she looks younger than that; **elle fait plus v. que son âge** she looks older than she really is

3 *n* **un v.** an old man; **une vieille** an old woman; **un v. de la vieille** one of the old brigade, an old hand; **les v.** old people, the old *or* elderly *or* aged; *F* **mes v.** my parents *or F* folks; **mon v./ma vieille** (*père/mère*) my old man/old woman; *F* **mon v.** (*mon ami*) mate, pal, chum; **comment ça va ma vieille?** (*mon ami(e)*) how are you?; **alors là, mon v., ce n'est pas mon problème** that's not my problem, mate *or* pal; **viens, ma vieille!** come on, old girl!

4 *nm F* **faire du neuf avec du v.** to make do and mend; **prendre un coup de v.** to age, to look (a lot) older; **j'ai l'impression d'avoir pris un coup de v.** I suddenly feel a lot older

5 *nf* **vieille** (*poisson*) wrasse, seawife

▶ **vieux**: **v. beau** ageing Adonis, old roué; **v. garçon** bachelor; **rester v. garçon** to remain single *or* a bachelor; **vieille fille** old maid, spinster; **rester vieille fille** to remain single *or* a spinster

vif, vive [vif, viv] **1** *adj* (**a**) (*en vie*) alive, living; **être brûlé v.** to be burnt alive; **prendre de vive force** to take by storm *or* by force; **de vive voix** by word of mouth, *Litt* viva voce; **il l'a dit de vive voix** he said it himself; **haie vive** quickset hedge; **eau vive** running water, spring water; **marée de vive eau** spring tide; **chaux vive** quicklime; *Ordinat* **mémoire vive** random access memory, RAM

(**b**) (*action, discussion etc*) lively, animated, brisk; (*personne*) vivacious, lively, animated; **vive allure, allure vive** brisk pace; **elle a été un peu vive et il est blessé** she was a bit sharp *or* curt *or* abrupt with him and hurt his feelings; **être v., avoir l'humeur un peu vive** to be quick-tempered; **il y avait un échange de paroles vives** there was a sharp exchange of words; **v. à répondre** quick to answer *or* reply, quick in answering; **avec mes plus vives félicitations** with my warmest *or* most heartfelt congratulations; **une flambée vive brûlait dans la cheminée** a fire was blazing away merrily in the hearth; **cheval v.** high-spirited horse

(**c**) (*vent, réprimande etc*) sharp; (*douleur etc*) acute, sharp; **l'air est v.** there's a nip in the air; **l'air v. de la montagne** the sharp *or* bracing mountain air; **arête vive** sharp edge

(**d**) (*esprit etc*) keen, quick; (*imagination etc*) vivid; *Euph* **il n'est pas très v.** he's not very bright *or* quick(-witted); **v. plaisir** keen *or* great pleasure; **éprouver un v. plaisir à faire qch** to take great pleasure in doing sth; **vive satisfaction** keen *or* great satisfaction; **écouter avec un v. intérêt** to listen with keen *or* deep *or* great interest

(**e**) (*couleur*) bright, vivid, intense

2 *nm* (**a**) **peindre sur le v.** to paint from life; *Fig* **être pris sur le v.** to be caught red-handed *or* in the act; *Fig* **un photo pris sur le v.** an action shot *or* photo

(**b**) **blessé** *ou* **piqué au v.** cut *or* stung to the quick; **plaie à v.** open wound; **j'ai les nerfs à v.** my nerves are on edge; **entrer dans le v. de la question** to get to the heart of the matter; **couper** *ou* **trancher dans le v.** to take drastic measures

(**c**) **pêcher au v.** to fish with live bait

(**d**) *Jur* living person; **donation entre vifs** donation inter vivos

vif-argent *nm* (**a**) **il a du v. dans les veines, c'est du v.** he's never still (for a minute) (**b**) *Ch, Arch* quicksilver, mercury

vigie [viʒi] *nf* (**a**) (*garde, gardien*) lookout (man); **être de v.** *ou* **en v.** to be on the lookout (**b**) (*poste*) watchtower; *Rail* (*sur wagon*) (observation) box; *Rail* **v. de signaux** signal cabin; *Rail* **v. de frein** brake cabin

vigilance [viʒilɑ̃s] *nf* vigilance, watchfulness; **avec v.**

vigilantly; **surprendre la v. de qn** to catch sb napping; **redoubler de v.** to increase one's vigilance
vigilant [viʒilɑ̃] *adj* vigilant, watchful, alert
vigile¹ [viʒil] *nf Rel (d'une fête)* vigil
vigile² *nm* (night) watchman
vigne [viɲ] *nf* **(a)** *(arbre)* vine; **feuille de v.** vine leaf **(b)** *(vignoble)* vineyard; *Fig* **être dans les vignes du Seigneur** to be drunk, to be in one's cups **(c)** *Bot* **v. vierge** Virginia creeper
vigneau, -eaux [viɲo] *nm (mollusque)* periwinkle
vigneron, -onne [viɲ(ə)rɔ̃, -ɔn] *n* wine grower
vignette [viɲɛt] *nf* **(a)** *Méd* label *(showing details of cost etc of medication, which has to be attached to the 'feuille de maladie' in order to qualify for a refund)*; *Aut* **la v. (automobile)** the (road) tax disc; **v. d'assurance** insurance disc; **tu as pensé à acheter la v.?** did you remember to pay the road tax? **(b)** *Beaux-Arts, Typ* vignette
vignettiste [viɲetist] *n Beaux-Arts, Typ* vignettist
vignoble [viɲɔbl] **1** *nm* vineyard **2** *adj* **région v.** wine (growing) region
vignot [viɲo] *nm (mollusque)* periwinkle
vigogne [vigɔɲ] *nf Zool, Tex* vicuña, vicuna
vigoureusement [vigurøzmɑ̃] *adv* vigorously
vigoureux, -euse [vigurø, -øz] *adj (personne, animal)* vigorous, robust; *(plante, arbre)* sturdy, robust; **elle est encore vigoureuse pour son âge** she's still hale and hearty for her age; **coup v.** powerful blow; **opposer une résistance vigoureuse à** *(projet, réforme)* to put up strong opposition to; **elle a opposé une résistance vigoureuse à son assaillant** she put up a strong fight, she tried to fight her attacker off
vigueur [vigœr] *nf* **(a)** *(d'une personne, d'un animal, d'un style)* vigour, *US* vigor, robustness; *(d'une plante, d'un arbre)* sturdiness, robustness; **donner de la v. à qn** to invigorate sb, to brace *or* perk sb up; **sans v.** *(personne)* exhausted, washed out; *(style etc)* flat, lifeless; **avec v.** vigorously **(b) en v.** *(décret etc)* in force, in effect; **entrer en v.** to come into force *or* effect *or* operation; **cesser d'être en v.** to lapse; **mettre un règlement en v.** to enforce a regulation
VIH [veiaʃ] *nm (abrév* **virus de l'immunodéficience humaine***)* HIV; **V. positif** HIV positive
viking [vikiŋ] *Hist* **1** *adj* Viking **2** *n* **V.** Viking
vil [vil] *adj* **(a) vendre qch à v. prix** to sell sth at a low price, *F* to sell sth dirt cheap; **je l'ai acheté à v. prix** I bought it for next to nothing **(b)** *Litt, Arch (personne, motif etc)* vile, base; *Arch (origine, condition etc)* lowly; **vile calomnie** foul calumny **(c)** *(métal)* base
vilain, -aine [vilɛ̃, -ɛn] **1** *n* **(a)** *F* **oh, le v.!/la vilaine!** *(à un enfant)* you little villain!, you naughty boy/girl!
(b) *Hist* villain, villein
2 *nm F* **il va y avoir du v.** there's going to be trouble; **tourner au v.** to turn nasty
3 *adj* **(a)** *(déplaisant)* nasty, bad, unpleasant; *(rhume)* nasty; **ne dis pas ces vilains mots** don't say those bad words; **tu es un v. petit garçon** you are a naughty little boy; *F* **c'est un v. monsieur** he's a nasty piece of work; **ce sont de vilaines gens** they're a bad *or* nasty lot; **v. tour** mean *or* dirty trick; **c'est une vilaine histoire** it's not a nice story, it's an ugly story; **une vilaine blessure** a nasty *or* an ugly wound
(b) *(qui offense la vue) (chapeau, rue etc)* ugly; **elle n'est pas vilaine** she's not bad looking, she's not what you'd call ugly
vilainement [vilɛnmɑ̃] *adv* in an unpleasant *or* a nasty way
vilebrequin [vilbrəkɛ̃] *nm* **(a)** *(outil)* (bit) brace, brace and bit; **v. à cliquet** ratchet brace **(b)** *(dans moteur)* crankshaft
vilement [vilmɑ̃] *adv Vieilli* vilely, basely
vilenie [vileni] *nf Litt* **(a)** *(caractère)* vileness, baseness **(b)** *(action)* mean *or* vile *or* low action, foul deed
villa [villa] *nf* **(a)** villa, detached house **(b)** *Antiq* villa
village [vilaʒ] *nm* village; **il est bien de son v.** you can tell that he comes from the country; **v. de vacances, v.-vacances** holiday village; **v. de pêcheurs** fishing village
villageois, -oise [vilaʒwa, -waz] **1** *n* villager; *(campagnard)* countryman, *f* countrywoman **2** *adj* rustic; **traditions villageoises** country *or* village customs
ville [vil] *nf* [①**B6**,3,e] town; *(plus grande)* city; **grande v.** city; **centre v.** town centre, *Am* downtown; *(d'une ville plus grande)* city centre, *Am* downtown; **la seconde v. de France** France's second city; **gens de la v.** townspeople, townsfolk, city dwellers, *F* townies; **toute la v. ne parle plus que de lui** the whole town's talking about him, he's the talk of the town; **en v.** in (the) town; *(au centre ville)* in the town/city centre, *Am* downtown; *(sur enveloppe)* local; **dîner en v.** to dine out; **aller à la v.** to go into town, *Am* to go downtown; **habiter à la v.** to live in a town *(as opposed to the country)*; **tenue de v.** town clothes; *(sur une invitation)* lounge suit; **financé par la v.** financed by the local authority; **hôtel de v.** town hall, *surtout Am* city hall
▶ **ville**: **v. champignon** boom town; **v.-dortoir**, *pl* **villes-dortoirs** dormitory town; **v. d'eaux** spa (town); **la V. éternelle** the Eternal City; **v. fortifiée** fortified town; **la V. lumière** the City of Lights; **v. nouvelle** new town; **v. ouverte** unfortified town; **v. sainte** centre of pilgrimage, holy city; **v. satellite** satellite town; *Mktg* **v.-test**, *pl* **villes-test** test city; **v. thermale** spa town
villégiature [vileʒjatyr] *nf* **(a)** holiday, *Am* vacation; **être en v.** to be on holiday *or* vacation; **ils partent tous les ans en v. à Cap Breton** they go on holiday every year to Cap Breton **(b)** *(lieu)* (holiday) resort
villeux, -euse [vilø, -øz] *adj Biol* hairy, *Spéc* villous
villosité [vilozite] *nf* **(a)** hairiness **(b)** *Anat etc* villosity, villus
vin [vɛ̃] *nm* wine; **les grands vins** vintage wines; **v. de Bordeaux** Bordeaux; **v. du Rhin** hock; **v. de Bourgogne** burgundy; **v. blanc/rouge/rosé** white/red/rosé wine; **v. mousseux** sparkling wine; **marchand de v.** (retail) wine merchant; **négociant en vins** (wholesale) wine merchant; **offrir un v. d'honneur à qn** to hold a reception in honour *or US* honor of sb; **être pris de v.** to be the worse for drink; *F* **cuver son v.** to sleep it off; **avoir le v. gai/triste** to be/not to be a happy drunk; **entre deux vins** tipsy, merry; *Prov* **quand le v. est tiré, il faut le boire** there's no turning back now, you've made your bed and you must lie in it; **mettre de l'eau dans son v.** to water (down) one's wine; *Fig (modérer ses exigences)* to back off a bit; *(faire preuve de mesure)* to come down a peg or two
▶ **vin**: **v. d'appellation contrôlée** wine of guaranteed vintage; **v. du cru** regional wine *(not from recognized vineyard)*; **v. cuit** = type of mulled wine; **v. délimité de qualité contrôlée** medium quality wine; **v. de fruits** fruit wine; *Rel* **v. de messe** altar *or* communion wine; **v. ordinaire** table wine, *Br F* plonk; **v. de paille** straw wine; **v. de pays** regional wine; **v. de table** table wine
vinaigre [vinɛgr] *nm* **(a)** vinegar; **v. blanc** distilled vinegar; **v. d'alcool** vinegar made from alcohol; **v. de vin** wine vinegar; **v. à l'estragon** tarragon vinegar; *Prov* **on ne prend pas les mouches avec du v.** you catch more flies with sugar than vinegar **(b)** *(au jeu)* **sauter au v.** to jump (over) the skipping rope quickly, to skip quickly **(c)** *Fig F* **faire v.** to hurry, to get a move on; **tourner au v.** to turn sour
vinaigrer [vinegre] *vt* to season with vinegar
vinaigrerie [vinɛgrəri] *nf (fabrique)* vinegar factory; *(fabrication)* vinegar making
vinaigrette [vinɛgrɛt] *nf Culin* vinaigrette, French dressing; **poireaux v.** leeks (in) vinaigrette
vinaigrier [vinɛgrije] *nm* **(a)** *(flacon)* vinegar bottle; **huilier-v.** oil and vinegar cruet **(b)** *(fabricant)* vinegar manufacturer
vinasse [vinas] *nf F* (cheap and nasty) wine
vindicatif, -ive [vɛ̃dikatif, -iv] *adj* vindictive
vindicte [vɛ̃dikt] *nf Jur (d'un crime)* prosecution; **v. publique** vindication of public morality; *Litt* **désigner qn à la v. publique** to expose sb to public condemnation
vineux, -euse [vinø, -øz] *adj* **(a)** *Spéc (vin)* full-bodied **(b)** *(goût)* winy, *Fml* vinous; *(pêche etc)* wine-flavoured *or US* -flavored; **odeur vineuse** winy smell, smell of wine; **haleine vineuse** breath smelling of wine **(c)** *(couleur)* wine-coloured *or US* -colored; *F* **nez v.** ruby *or* winy nose, drinker's nose
vingt [vɛ̃] **1** *adj num inv* [①**B56**,A,d] twenty; **v. et un** [vɛ̃teœ̃] twenty-one; **v.-deux** [vɛ̃tdø] twenty-two; *Arg* **v.-deux!** watch it!, look out!; **le v. juin** [ləvɛ̃ʒɥɛ̃] (on) the twentieth of June, (on) June (the) twentieth; **ouvert v.-quatre heures sur v.-quatre** open all day *or* round the clock, open twenty-four hours (a day); **les années v.** the twenties; **il n'a pas encore v. ans** he's not yet twenty, he's still in his teens; **je n'ai plus mon cœur de v. ans** I'm not as young as I was; **les moins de v. ans** teenagers; **je te l'ai dit v. fois** I've told you a hundred times *or* time and time again; **quatre-vingts** eighty; **quatre-v. deux** eighty-two
2 *nm inv* twenty; **je suis payée le v. de chaque mois** I'm paid on the twentieth of the month; *Cartes* **v.-et-un** pontoon, *Am* blackjack, *US* twenty-one; **habiter au v. de l'avenue** to live at number twenty in the avenue
vingtaine [vɛ̃tɛn] *nf* [①**A12**,1,h,i; **B56**,C,3] **une v.** (about) twenty, a score; **une v. de personnes** twenty or so people; **d'une v. d'années** about twenty years old
vingtième [vɛ̃tjɛm] **1** *adj* twentieth **2** *n* twentieth **3** *nm (fraction)* twentieth (part)
vingtièmement [vɛ̃tjɛmmɑ̃] *adv* in (the) twentieth place
vinicole [vinikɔl] *adj (région etc)* wine(-growing)
vinifère [vinifer] *adj (sol etc)* wine-producing
Vintimille [vɛ̃timij] *n* Ventimiglia

vinyle [vinil] *nm Ch* vinyl; *F (disque)* record; **c'est sorti sur v.** it came out on vinyl; **il rachète tous les vieux vinyles qu'il trouve** he buys all the old records he can find

vioc [vjɔk] *n F* old fart; **les** *ou* **mes viocs rentrent demain** the *or* my old dears come back tomorrow

viol [vjɔl] *nm* **(a)** rape; **au v.!, au v.!** rape!, rape!; **v. collectif** gang rape *or F* bang **(b)** *(d'un sanctuaire, du règlement, des lois etc)* violation

violacé, -ée [vjɔlase] **1** *adj* purplish-blue; **un rouge v.** a purplish red; **prendre un teint v.** *(à cause du froid)* to go blue; **son nez a pris une couleur violacée** his nose has gone a purplish colour **2** *nfpl Bot* **violacées** Violaceae

violacer [vjɔlase] **(je violaçai(s); n. violaçons) 1** *vt* **v. qch** to turn sth blue *or* purplish **2 se violacer** *vpr* to turn blue *or* purplish; **sous l'effet du froid, la peau se violace** the skin turns blue *or* purple with cold

violateur, -trice [vjɔlatœr, -tris] *n* violator; *(de lois etc)* transgressor

violation [vjɔlasjɔ̃] *nf (de la loi etc)* violation, infringement, transgression, breach; *(d'une tombe)* desecration; **v. des règles** breaking of rules; **agir en v. d'une règle** to act in contravention of a rule

▶ **violation: v. de domicile** illegal entry; **v. de sépulture** desecration of graves

violâtre [vjɔlɑtr] *adj* purplish

viole [vjɔl] *nf Mus* viol; **v. d'amour** viol(a) d'amore; **v. de gambe** viola da gamba, bass viol

violemment [vjɔlamɑ̃] *adv* violently; **elle le déteste v.** she hates him intensely; **il me dégoûtait v.** I found him deeply offensive

violence [vjɔlɑ̃s] *nf* violence, force; *(d'une confrontation etc)* fierceness; **obtenir qch par la v.** to obtain sth by violent means; **la v. des sentiments** the intensity of feeling; **faire v. à qn** to do violence to sb; **j'ai dû me faire v. pour me lever tôt** I had to force myself to get up early; *Hum* **je vais devoir me faire une douce v.** I'm going to have to force myself, I'm really going to have to make an effort; **faire v. à un texte** to distort a text; **subir des violences physiques/morales** to suffer *or* be subjected to physical violence/mental cruelty; *Vieilli* **faire v. à une femme** to violate *or* rape a woman

violent, -ente [vjɔlɑ̃, -ɑ̃t] **1** *adj* violent; *(vent)* high, fierce; *(échanges verbaux)* fierce, violent; *(mesures etc)* drastic; *(odeur)* pungent; **faire un effort v.** to make a huge *or* strenuous effort; **un v. orage éclata** a violent *or* raging storm broke out; **mourir de mort violente** to die a violent death; **choc très v.** tremendous impact; **une violente opposition** violent opposition; *F* **c'est un peu v.!** it really is too much!, that really is going too far! **2** *n* violent person

violenter [vjɔlɑ̃te] *vt* **(a)** *(femme)* to rape **(b)** *Litt (nature)* to tamper with; *(morale)* to do violence to; *(texte)* to distort

violer [vjɔle] *vt* **(a)** *(femme)* to rape; **se faire v.** to be raped **(b)** *(transgresser) (trêve, loi)* to violate, to break; *(loi)* to transgress, to infringe; *(traité, confiance)* to break; **v. un secret** to divulge a secret; **v. une sépulture** to desecrate a grave; **v. le domicile de qn** to break into sb's house; **v. les consciences** to violate people's consciences

violet, -ette[1] [vjɔlɛ, -ɛt] *adj* **1** violet, purple(-coloured *or US* -colored); **mains violettes de froid** hands blue with the cold **2** *nm (couleur)* violet, purple

violette[2] [vjɔlɛt] *nf Bot* violet; **v. de Parme** Parma violet

violeur [vjɔlœr] *nm* rapist

violier [vjɔlje] *nm Bot* stock; **v. jaune** wallflower

violine [vjɔlin] *adj* dark *or* deep purple

violon [vjɔlɔ̃] *nm* **(a)** *Mus (instrument)* violin, *F* fiddle; **jouer du v.** to play the violin *or F* fiddle; *F* **accordez vos violons** make sure you tell the same story, make sure you get your stories straight; **c'est son v. d'Ingres** it's his hobby **(b)** *(musicien)* violin (player); **premier v.** *(dans un orchestre)* first violin, leader; *Fig* **payer les violons (du bal)** to pay the piper **(c)** *Arg* **le v.** the cells, the lockup; **au v.** in the lockup; **passer la nuit au v.** to spend the night in the cells **(d)** *Tech* **(poulie à) v.** fiddle block **(e)** *Naut* **violons de mer** *(contre le roulis)* fiddles

violoncelle [vjɔlɔ̃sɛl] *nm Mus* **(a)** *(instrument)* cello, *Fml* violoncello; **jouer du v.** to play the cello **(b)** *(musicien)* cello (player), cellist

violoncelliste [vjɔlɔ̃sɛlist] *n* cellist

violoneux [vjɔlɔnø] *nm* fiddler, *Péj* second-rate *or US* two-bit violinist

violoniste [vjɔlɔnist] *n* violinist, violin player

vioque [vjɔk] *n* = **vioc**

viorne [vjɔrn] *nf Bot* viburnum

VIP [veipe, viajpi] *nm F* VIP

vipère [vipɛr] *nf* viper, adder; *Fig (personne)* viper; **c'est une v., je préfère ne pas la rencontrer** she's really spiteful, I'd rather not meet her; **v. aspic** asp; **v. heurtante** puff adder; *Fig* **c'est une langue de v.** she's got a nasty tongue; *Fig* **nid de vipères** nest of vipers, snake pit

vipereau, -eaux [vipro] *nm* young viper

vipérin, -ine [viperɛ̃, -in] **1** *adj* viperine **2** *nf* **vipérine (a)** *Bot* viper's bugloss **(b)** *(reptile)* viperine snake

virage [viraʒ] *nm* **(a)** *(mouvement)* turn, turning (round); *(d'une grue etc)* turning *or* swinging round; *Naut* tacking, going about; *Av* **v. (incliné), v. sur l'aile** bank(ing); **angle de v.** angle of bank; **le skieur fait des virages** the skier is making turns

(b) *(tournant) (sur la route)* (sharp) turn, bend, corner; **v. sans visibilité** blind corner; **v. en épingle à cheveux** hairpin bend; **v. à la corde** sharp turn; **v. relevé** banked corner; **virages sur 5 km** *(sur panneau)* bends for 5 km; **prendre** *ou* **aborder un v.** to take a bend, to corner

(c) *(d'une piste de vitesse)* banked corner, bank

(d) *(changement)* change (in direction); **le parti amorce** *ou* **prend un v.** the party is changing direction *or* shifting ground; **un v. net dans la vie politique du pays** a U-turn in the political life of the country

(e) *Ch* changing of colour *or US* color; **v. au rouge** turning red

(f) *Phot (des épreuves)* toning

virago [virago] *nf* virago, termagant; **c'est une vraie v.** she's a real shrew

viral, -ale, -aux, -ales [viral, -o] *adj Méd* viral

virée [vire] *nf F (en voiture etc)* trip, run, outing; *(dans les cafés, pubs) Br* ≈ pub crawl, *Am* ≈ bar hop; **faire une v.** *(en voiture etc)* to go for an outing *or* a run; *(dans les cafés, pubs) Br* ≈ to go on a pub crawl, *Am* ≈ to bar hop

virelai [virlɛ] *nm Littér* virelay

virement [virmɑ̃] *nm* **(a)** *Banque* (credit) transfer; **v. automatique** automatic transfer; **v. bancaire** bank transfer; **banque de v.** clearing bank; **v. par courrier** mail transfer; **v. interbancaire** interbank transfer; **v. postal** post office transfer; **v. SWIFT** SWIFT transfer; **v. télégraphique** cable transfer; **v. par télex** telex transfer **(b)** *Naut* **v. de bord** tacking, going about

virer [vire] **1** *vi* **(a)** *(tourner) (du vent)* to veer; *Aut etc* to take a bend *or* a corner, to corner; *Av* to bank; *(d'une grue etc)* to turn round, to swing round; *Aut* **v. court** to corner sharply; *Aut* **v. sur place** to turn in one's own length; **la discussion a viré à l'aigre** the discussion took an acrimonious turn; *Naut* **v. de bord** to tack, to go about; *(d'un bateau à vapeur)* to turn; *Naut* **paré à v.!** ready about!

(b) *(changer d'aspect)* to change colour *or US* color; *Phot (d'une épreuve)* to tone; **encre qui vire au noir en séchant** ink that dries black; **la couleur est en train de v.** the colour is changing; **le rouge a viré à l'orange** the red has turned *or* changed to orange; **cutiréaction qui vire** skin test which comes up positive

2 *vt* **(a)** *Banque (somme)* to transfer; *(chèques etc)* to clear; **je lui vire 1 000 francs tous les mois sur son compte** I transfer 1000 francs into his account every month

(b) *Phot (épreuve)* to tone

(c) *F* **v. qn** to throw *or* kick *or* chuck sb out; **se faire v.** *(d'un travail)* to get sacked *or* fired; *(d'un bar etc)* to get thrown *or* kicked *or* chucked out; **il faudrait v. ces étagères** we should throw *or* chuck these shelves out, we should get rid of these shelves

3 se virer *vpr F* **vire-toi!** move!

vireux, -euse [virø, -øz] *adj* poisonous, noxious

virevolte [virvɔlt] *nf* **(a)** *(changement)* U-turn, volte-face; **v. de la fortune** sudden change of fortune; **je m'attends à une v. de sa part** I expect he'll change his mind; **une de ses inévitables virevoltes** one of his inevitable U-turns *or* about-turns **(b)** *Équitation Arch (d'un cheval)* quick circling **(c)** *(d'un danseur etc)* half-turn

virevolter [virvɔlte] *vi (d'un cheval)* to circle; *(d'une personne)* to spin round; *Fig* to make a U-turn

Virgile [virʒil] *nm Littér* Virgil, Vergil

virginal, -ale, -aux, -ales [virʒinal, -o] **1** *adj* virginal; **blanc v.** pure *or* virginal white **2** *nm Mus* virginal, (pair of) virginals

Virginie [virʒini] *nf* Virginia

virginité [virʒinite] *nf* virginity; **perdre sa v.** to lose one's virginity; *Fig* **se refaire une v.** to restore one's image

virgule [virgyl] *nf* **(a)** *Gram* comma; **point v.** semicolon; *Fig* **sans changer une v.** without changing a single thing *or* an iota; **c'est ce qu'il a dit à la v. près** that's word for word what he said **(b)** *Math* decimal point; **trois v. cinq (3,5)** three point five (3.5); *Ordinat* **v. fixe** fixed point; *Ordinat* **v. flottante** floating point; **arithmétique à v. flottante** floating point arithmetic

viril [viril] *adj* **(a)** *(sexe etc)* male; *Anat* **membre v.** male member *or* organ; *Antiq* **toge virile** toga virilis **(b)** *(action etc)* manly; **allure/démarche virile** *(pour une femme)* masculine appearance/walk; **l'âge v.** manhood; **qualité virile** male characteristic

virilement [virilmɑ̃] *adv* like a man, in a manly way

virilisant [virilizɑ̃] *adj Méd (substance)* which gives male characteristics

viriliser [virilize] *vt* **(a)** *(rendre viril)* to make more virile *or* manly; *(femme)* to make appear masculine **(b)** *Biol (organisme etc)* to give male characteristics to

virilité [virilite] *nf* virility, manhood; **se sentir menacé/attaqué dans sa v.** to feel that one's manhood is being threatened/attacked

virole [virɔl] *nf (d'une canne, d'un couteau, d'un parapluie)* ferrule; *MecE* collar, hoop, sleeve

viroler [virɔle] *vt (manche d'outil etc)* to fit with a ferrule

virologie [virɔlɔʒi] *nf Méd* virology

virologiste [virɔlɔʒist], **virologue** [virɔlɔg] *n Méd* virologist

virtualité [virtɥalite] *nf* potentiality

virtuel, -elle [virtɥɛl] *adj* potential; *Opt, Phil, Ordinat (image etc)* virtual

virtuellement [virtɥɛlmɑ̃] *adv* virtually

virtuose [virtɥoz] *n* [①A13,7] virtuoso; **c'est un v. du violon** he's a violin virtuoso

virtuosité [virtɥozite] *nf* virtuosity

virulence [virylɑ̃s] *nf (d'un poison etc)* virulence; *(d'une satire, de paroles)* viciousness, venom

virulent [virylɑ̃] *adj (poison)* virulent; *Fig (satire, critique)* virulent, scathing; *(paroles)* scathing; **faire une critique virulente de qch** to criticize sth venomously; **diatribe virulente** scathing attack

virure [viryr] *nf Naut* strake

virus [virys] *nm* [①A13,8] *Méd, Ordinat etc* virus; **maladie à v.** viral disease; *F* **il y a un v. qui traîne** *ou* **dans l'air** there's a virus going around; *F* **avoir le v. du ski** to have been bitten by the skiing bug

vis [vis] *nf* screw; **v. d'arrêt** *ou* **de blocage** stop screw; **v. à bois** wood screw; **v. à métaux** metal screw; **v. à tête cylindrique** cheese-head(ed) screw; **v. à tête fraisée** countersunk (head) screw; **v. à tête ronde** roundhead(ed) screw; **v. à oreilles** *ou* **à ailettes** wing screw; **v. autotaraudeuse** self-tapping screw; **v. à droite/à gauche** righthanded/lefthanded screw *or* thread; **v. de purge** bleeder screw, bleed screw; **v. de réglage** adjuster screw, adjusting screw; **v. hexagonale** hexagon screw; **v. à pointe ronde** ball-ended screw; **v. sans fin** endless screw, worm (screw); *HydE* **v. d'Archimède** Archimedean screw; *Ind* **v. de transport** spiral conveyor; *Aut* **v. platinées** (contact) points; **tige à v.** screwed *or* threaded rod; **escalier à v.** spiral staircase; *Fig* **serrer la v. à qn** to be very hard *or* crack down on sb; *Fig* **il va falloir donner un tour de v.** things will have to start tightening up

visa [viza] *nm* **(a)** *(pour passeport)* visa; **demander/obtenir un v.** to apply for/obtain a visa; **apposer un v. à un passeport** to stamp *or* visa a passport; **v. d'entrée** entry visa; **v. de sortie** exit visa **(b)** *(signature) (sur un document etc)* signature; *(paraphe) (d'un supérieur etc)* initials; *(sceau) (sur un document)* stamp; *Cin* **v. de censure** censor's certificate; **v. d'exploitation** exploitation licence

visage [vizaʒ] *nm* face; **homme au v. agréable** pleasant-faced man; **soins du v.** (facial) skin care; **cela se lisait sur son v.** you could see it in his face, it was obvious; **frapper qn au v.** to hit sb in the face; **v. ouvert** open *or* honest face; **il a un v. d'enfant** he's baby-faced, he's a baby-face; **elle a changé de v.** her face *or* expression changed; **cette région a changé de v.** the area has had a face-lift; **à deux visages** two-faced; **il a deux visages** he's two-faced; **avoir bon v.** to look well; **faire bon v.** to put a brave face on things; **faire bon v. à qn** to be outwardly friendly to sb; **sans v.** faceless; **vrai v.** true face *or* nature; **l'Europe sous son vrai v.** the true face of Europe; **présenter un pays sous un autre** *ou* **nouveau v.** to present a country in a new light; **à v. découvert** *(ouvertement)* openly; **socialisme à v. humain** socialism with a human face; **je n'arrive pas à mettre un nom sur ce v.** I can't put a name to that face; **un v. ami** a friendly face; **il y a des visages qui frappent** some faces are very striking; **rencontrer de nouveaux visages** to meet new faces; **il y avait des visages connus** there were some familiar faces; **cela a donné un nouveau v. à notre pays** that has shown our country in a new light; **visages pâles** palefaces

visagiste [vizaʒist] *n* beautician

vis-à-vis [vizavi] **1** *prép* **(a)** *(en face)* **v. de qn/qch** opposite *or* facing sb/sth

(b) *(envers)* **v. de qn/qch** towards *or* in relation to *or* vis-à-vis sb/sth; **ses sentiments v. de moi** his feelings towards me; **être sincère v. de soi-même** to be truthful with oneself

(c) *(par rapport à, comparé à)* **v. d'elle, je ne suis pas intéressante** compared with *or* next to her, I'm not interesting

2 *nm* **(a)** *(à une table etc)* person opposite; *Cartes* partner; *(entretien)* tête-à-tête, meeting; **mon v.** the person sitting opposite me; **un long v.** a long tête-à-tête; **faire v.** *ou* **être en v. à qn** to be/stand/sit opposite sb, to face sb; **nous avons le lac pour v.** we look out on to *or* face the lake

(b) *(meuble)* vis-à-vis, S-shaped couch

viscéral, -ale, -aux, -ales [viseral, -o] *adj* **(a)** *Anat* visceral **(b)** *Fig (haine)* deep, deeply ingrained; *(peur)* gut-wrenching; *(pensées etc)* innermost; *(réaction)* gut; *(répulsion)* instinctive

viscères [visɛr] *nmpl Anat* viscera, internal organs

viscose [viskoz] *nf Ch, Ind* viscose; **robe en v.** viscose dress

viscosité [viskozite] *nf* viscosity, stickiness

visée [vize] *nf* **(a)** aim; *Mil etc* aiming, sighting; **ligne de v.** line of sight; **point de v.** target **(b)** *Fig* **visées** aims, designs; **avoir de grandes visées** *ou* **des visées ambitieuses** to have big *or* ambitious plans, to have great ambitions, to aim high; **il a des visées sur ce poste** he has designs on this job

viser¹ [vize] **1** *vt* **(a)** *(avec une arme)* to aim *or* take aim at; *Fig (d'une remarque, accusation)* to be aimed *or* directed at; *Fig (ambitionner)* to have one's eyes on, to set one's sights on; **qui visais-tu par cette remarque?** who was your remark aimed *or* directed at?; **je ne vise personne** I'm not alluding *or* referring to anybody in particular; **je sais très bien que cela me vise** I know very well that's directed at me; **visé à l'article …** referred to in article …; *Golf* **v. la balle** to address the ball; **il vise ce poste depuis longtemps** he's had his eye on this job for a long time

(b) *(concerner)* to relate to; **les denrées alimentaires ne sont pas visées par ce décret** articles of food are not affected by this order

(c) *Arg (regarder)* to (have a) look at; **vise un peu la fille!** have a look at her!, get a load of her!

2 *vi Fig* to aim, to take aim (**à** at, for); **v. à un but précis** to have a specific purpose; **v. à faire qch** to aim at doing sth *or* to do sth; **v. haut** to aim high; **v. juste** to aim straight; **tu as visé juste en lui disant cela** you didn't miss the mark when you said that to him!; *Fig* **v. plus haut** to aim higher, to set one's sights higher

viser² *vt Admin (passeport)* to visa; *(document) (signer)* to countersign; *(apposer ses initiales à)* to initial; *(apposer un sceau à)* to stamp; *Compta* **v. des livres de commerce** to certify the books; *Fin* **v. un effet** to stamp a bill

viseur [vizœr] *nm Phot* viewfinder; *(d'un instrument de contrôle etc)* eyepiece, sighting tube; *Av* **v. de lancement** bomb sight(s)

visibilité [vizibilite] *nf* visibility; **la v. est très réduite par le brouillard** visibility has been greatly reduced by the fog; **v. nulle** zero visibility; **bonne/mauvaise v.** good/poor visibility; *Av* **vol sans v.** instrument flying; **virage sans v.** blind turn; *Aut* **v. de trois-quart** three-quarter vision; *Aut* **v. panoramique** all-round visibility

visible [vizibl] *adj* **(a)** visible; **v. à l'œil nu/au microscope** visible to the naked eye/under a microscope; **c'est à peine v.** it's scarcely visible, you can hardly see it; **très v.** highly visible, conspicuous; **il n'y avait personne de v.** there was nobody in sight; **elle est jalouse, c'est v.** it's obvious that she's jealous; **il est v. que …** it's obvious *or* clear that …

(b) *(à qui l'on peut rendre visite)* ready to receive company; **je ne suis pas v.** I am not at home, I am not in; **je ne serai pas v. avant trois heures** I can't see anybody before three o'clock; *F* **n'entre pas, je ne suis pas v.** don't come in, I'm not decent; **cette collection n'est pas v.** this collection is not open to the public

visiblement [viziblәmɑ̃] *adv* visibly; **v., il était contrarié** he was visibly *or* obviously *or* clearly annoyed

visière [vizjɛr] *nf (d'une casquette)* peak; *(pour protéger les yeux)* eyeshade; *(d'un casque)* visor; **mettre sa main en v.** to shade one's eyes with one's hand; *Litt* **rompre en v. à** *ou* **avec qn** *(se quereller)* to quarrel openly with sb; *(être d'avis contraire)* to have a diametrically opposite view to sb

visioconférence [visjokɔ̃ferɑ̃s] *nf* videoconference; **visioconférences** *(concept)* videoconferencing

vision [vizjɔ̃] *nf* **(a)** *(sens)* (eye)sight; *(vue)* sight, view; **trouble de la v.** eye trouble; **défaut de la v.** visual defect; **v. momentanée de qch** momentary glimpse of sth; **nous n'avons pas la même v. des choses** we don't see things the same way; **nous partageons la même v. du monde/des choses/de la vie** we see *or* view the world/things/life in the same way; **cela m'a donné une nouvelle v. du problème** that gave me a new perspective on the problem; **v. réaliste/simpliste** realistic/simplistic view

(b) *(d'un poète etc)* vision, imagination

(c) *(hallucination)* vision; **avoir des visions** *(hallucinations)* to have visions *or* hallucinations, to see things; *F* (*rêver*) to fantasize

visionnaire [vizjɔnɛr] **1** *adj* visionary **2** *n* visionary, dreamer

visionnement [vizjɔnmɑ̃] *nm TV, Cin* screening; **v. préalable** preview

visionner [vizjɔne] *vt Cin* to screen; (*pour analyser*) to view

visionneuse [vizjɔnøz] *nf Cin, Phot* viewer

Visiopass [vizjɔpɑs] *nm TV* = decoding card for French pay channels

visiophone [vizjɔfɔn] *nm* videophone, viewphone

visitandine [vizitɑ̃din] *nf Cathol* nun of the Order of the Visitation

Visitation [vizitasjɔ̃] *nf Rel* (*de la Sainte Vierge à sainte Elizabeth*) Visitation

visite [vizit] *nf* **(a)** (*à une personne*) visit, (social) call; (*d'un lieu touristique*) visit; (*visiteur*) visitor, caller; **j'aime bien avoir des visites** I like having visitors *or* guests; **faire une v.** *ou* **rendre v. à qn** to visit sb, to call on sb, to pay sb a visit *or* a call; **rendre une v.** *ou* **sa v. à qn** to return sb's visit *or* call; **il nous fait une petite v. tous les soirs** he drops in on us every evening; **être en v. chez qn** to be visiting sb *or* on a visit to sb; **nous avons eu la v. de Marc** Marc called in to see us; **recevoir la v. d'un représentant de commerce** to be called on by a representative; **v. de politesse** courtesy call, duty visit; **v. officielle** official visit; **carte de v.** visiting card; *Sp* **équipe en v.** visiting team; **heures de v.** (*à l'hôpital etc*) visiting hours; **nous attendons des visites** *ou* **de la v.** we're expecting visitors *or* guests; **visites à domicile** (*d'un médecin*) house calls; **le docteur ne fait pas de visites** the doctor doesn't make house calls; *Jur* **droit de v.** (*de parents*) right of access

(b) (*inspection*) (*d'un bâtiment, d'un navire*) inspection, examination, survey; *Méd* (medical) examination; **faire la v.** to go on one's round of inspection; *Mil etc* **passer la v.** to come before the medical officer *or* the medical board; *Mil* **v. des malades** sick parade; *Rel* **v. pastorale** *ou* **de l'évêque** pastoral visit, visitation (*by bishop*); **trou de v.** (*d'un égout etc*) inspection hole, manhole; *Naut* **droit de v.** right of search; **v. de douane** customs examination

▸ **visite**: *Com* **v. à froid** cold call; **v. guidée** guided tour; (*d'une ville*) sightseeing tour; **v. médicale**: **passer (à) une v. médicale** to have a medical examination; **v. pédagogique** educational visit

visiter [vizite] **1** *vt* **(a)** (*de touristes*) to visit; **v. une cathédrale** to visit *or* tour a cathedral; **on nous a fait v. l'usine** we were shown round *or* over the factory, we were given a tour of the factory

(b) (*inspecter*) (*bâtiment, mécanismes etc*) to inspect, to examine, to survey; (*maison à vendre*) to view, to go over; (*de la police etc*) (*maison etc*) to search; (*bagages*) to inspect, to examine; **quelqu'un est venu v. mon bureau en mon absence** someone has gone through my office during my absence; **je vais te faire v. les lieux/la maison** I'll show you round the premises/the house

(c) (*personne malade, patient etc*) to visit; *Com* (*client*) to call on

2 se visiter *vpr* to be open to visitors

visiteur, -euse [vizitœr, -øz] *n* **(a)** (*touriste*) (*dans un musée etc*) visitor; **ouvert aux visiteurs à partir de quinze heures** open to visitors *or* to the public from 3 pm

(b) (*hôte etc*) visitor, caller; (*dans une prison*) visitor; **recevoir des visiteurs** to rece[ive] visitors *or* guests; **nous avons eu de nombreux visite[urs]** we had a large number of visitors; **infirmière visiteuse** [co]mmunity *or* district nurse; (*pour les nouveaux-nés*) he[alth] visitor; *Sp* **les visiteurs** the visitors, the visiting team; [...] **en soies** representative *or* traveller in silks

(c) (*inspecteur*) inspect[or] ... **des douanes** customs officer ... representative;

▸ **visiteur**: **v. médical** ... worker who specialize[s in the problems] of child welfare visiting schools in the ...

scolaire *ou* **sociale** ...

vison [vizɔ̃] *nm* **(a)** (*at* ... (American) mink **(b)** (*fo*[*urrure*]) mink; *F* (*manteau*) mink farm

visonnière [vizɔnjɛr] ...

visqueux, -euse ... *adj* sticky, viscous; ... my; *Fig* **sourire v.** smar[my] ...

viscous; (*sécrétio*[*n*]) ...

vissage [visaʒ] *nm* ... *planche à un supp*[*ort*] ... screwing in; (*du co*[*uvercle*]) ... *pot*) screwing ... screwing up ... down; (*en serre vis*) to screw in; ...

visser [vise] **1** ... *à un support*) to ... to screw on *or* up; **v. un écrou à b**[*loc*] ... *serrant fort* ... **sa chaise** to be glu[ed] ... tight; *F* **êt**[re] ... severely, to be very h[ard on] ... *F* **v. qn** to ... to screw on; **le c**[ouvercle] ... sb **2 se** ...

facilement/mal the lid screws on easily/doesn't screw on properly; **la lance se visse au bout du tuyau** the nozzle screws on to the end of the hose

visualisation [vizɥalizasjɔ̃] *nf* visualization; *Ordinat* **console** *ou* **unité** *ou* **écran de v.** (visual) display unit; *Ordinat* **v. de la page à l'écran** page preview; **v. de vidéo** video playback

visualiser [vizɥalize] *vt* (*imaginer*) to visualize; (*rendre visible*) (*qch*) to make visible to the eye; *Ordinat* to display

visuel, -elle [vizɥɛl] **1** *adj* visual; **champ v.** field of vision **2** *nm* **(a)** *Ordinat* visual display unit, VDU **(b)** (*d'une affiche etc*) artwork **3** *n* visual person

visuellement [vizɥɛlmɑ̃] *adv* visually

vit [vi] *nm Vieilli, Litt* (*verge*) member

vital, -ale, -aux, -ales [vital, -o] *adj* **(a)** (*relatif à la vie*) (*énergie, force*) vital **(b)** (*indispensable à la vie*) vital; **centres vitaux** vital organs; *Fig* **centre v.** nerve centre **(c)** (*capital*) (*problème, question*) vital; *F* **il faut que tu viennes, c'est v.!** you must come, it's vital!, you absolutely must come!

vitalisme [vitalism] *nm Biol* vitalism

vitalité [vitalite] *nf* vitality

vitamine [vitamin] *nf Biol, Ch* vitamin; **v. A/B12** vitamin A/B12; **alimentation riche/pauvre en vitamines** food with a high/low vitamin content, food that is high/low in vitamins; **enfant qui manque de vitamines** child with a vitamin deficiency; **as-tu pris tes vitamines?** have you taken your vitamins?

vitaminé [vitamine] *adj* enriched with vitamins, vitamin-enriched

vitaminique [vitaminik] *adj Méd* **carence v.** vitamin deficiency

vite [vit] **1** *adv* quickly, fast; **viens v. nous retrouver au bord de la mer!** come and join us at the seaside soon!; **lève-toi v., on sonne!** get up quick, there's someone at the door!; **je vais v. faire une course** I'm going to do one quick errand; **plus v.!** faster!; *Naut* increase speed!; **roule moins v.** don't drive so fast, drive more slowly; **le temps passe v.** time goes quickly, time flies; **manger trop v.** to eat too fast *or* quickly; **tu as parlé trop v.** you spoke too soon; **ne va pas si v.!** (*en voiture*) not so fast!, slow down a bit!; **vous allez v. en besogne** you're a fast *or* quick worker, that's quick work; **ça ne va pas v.** it's slow work; **vous serez v. guéri** you'll soon be better; **(faites) v.!** quick!, hurry up, be quick (about it)!; **allons, et plus v. que cela!** come on, get a move on!; ... **je me suis v. rendu compte que ...** I soon *or* quickly realized that ...; **avoir ... plus v.** as quickly as possib[le] ... **fait de faire qch** to be ... doing sth; **tu auras ... fait de t'en apercevoir** ... you'll soon realize; **il eut v. fait ...** time; *F* **on a tout ran[gé] ... s'habiller** he was dre[ssed] ... in no time; ... **fait (bien fait)** we ... ing away ... **fait de dire ...** it's eas[y] ...

2 *adj Sp* (*voitu*[*re*]) quick

vitellus [vitelys] ... yolk

vitesse [vites] ... quickness; **à quelle v.** how fast ...; **à la v. de ...** at the rate of ...; **deux pages par jour** at ... a speed of ... two pages ...; **médecine/sécurité sociale** ... medical/social security sy[stem] ... **vitesses** a two-speed Euro[pe] ...; **Europe** ... **rouler à une v. folle** to drive ... move *or* go quickly *or* at ... breaking; **excès de v.** exceedin[g] ... speeding; **elle a été arrêtée p**[our] ... for speeding; *Aut* **limitat**[ion] ... quickly, at speed; *F* **sors, e**[n] ... **partir en v.** to rush away *or* ... **dire ...** just a quick line ... **qn** to race sb; **gagner** ... outstrip sb; (*l'anticiper*) to ... **v.** to pick up *or* gather ... **en perte de v.** the party ... **se mettre en perte d**[e] ... **indicateur de v.** speedo[meter] ... *or* top speed, to rush alo[ng] ... **à toute v.** full speed ahe[ad] ... fast/slow goods service; ... velocity; **v. initiale** initi[al] ... speed *or* velocity; **v. d**[e] ... impetus, momentum ... *Aut* gear; **changer de v**[itesse] ... gearbox; **passer en d**[euxième] ... (gear); **v. avant** forwa[rd] ... bottom; **v. supérieu**[re] ... **synchronisées** synchromesh ... to disappear at top speed ... **quatrième v.** you'll have to ...

▶ **vitesse**: *Ordinat* **v. d'affichage** display speed; *Ordinat* **v. de calcul** processing *or* computing speed; *Ordinat* **v. de clignotement** blink rate; **v. de croisière** (*d'un navire, d'un avion, d'une voiture*) cruising speed; **trouver sa v. de croisière** (*d'un navire etc*) to reach cruising speed; *Fig* to get into the swing of things; *Ordinat* **v. d'écriture** write speed; *Ordinat* **v. d'exécution** execution speed; **v. de frappe** typing speed; *surtout Ordinat* keying speed; **v. de frappe à la minute/à l'heure** keystrokes per minute/hour; **v. d'impression** print speed; *Aut* **v. de pointe** top speed; *Ordinat* **v. du processeur** processor speed; *Com* **v. de rotation des stocks** inventory turnover rate; *Physiol* **v. de sédimentation** erythrocyte sedimentation rate; *Ordinat* **v. de traitement** processing speed

viticole [vitikɔl] *adj* (*région etc*) wine-producing, wine-growing; **industrie v.** wine industry

viticulteur, -trice [vitikyltœr, -tris] *n* vine grower, wine grower

viticulture [vitikyltyr] *nf* vine growing, wine growing, *Spéc* viticulture

vitrage [vitraʒ] *nm* (a) (*d'une serre etc*) glazing; **double v.** double-glazing; **fenêtre à double v.** double-glazed window (b) (*d'un bâtiment etc*) windows (c) (*cloison*) glass partition (d) (*rideau*) net curtain

vitrail, -aux [vitraj, -o] *nm* leaded-glass window; (*coloré*) stained-glass window; **l'art du v.** the art of making stained-glass windows *or* stained glass; **les vitraux sont superbes** the stained-glass windows are superb, the stained glass is superb

vitre [vitr] *nf* window (pane), pane (of glass); **produit pour les vitres** glass- *or* window-cleaning product; **faire les vitres** to clean the windows; *F* **casser les vitres** to get angry, to kick up a fuss; *F* **ça ne casse pas les vitres** it's pretty ordinary *or* run-of-the-mill, it's nothing to write home about

[…] *adj* (a) (*porte etc*) glazed; **baie vitrée** picture [window]; [**bib**]**liothèque vitrée** glass-fronted bookcase; **porte** [vitrée] [glass] door (b) (*substance etc*) vitreous, glassy; [**humeu**]**r vitrée** vitreous humour

[…] (*…e etc*) to glaze

[…]**ie** […]ery; (*industrie*) glass industry

[…]**se** […] [vitrø, -øz] *adj* (*amas, roche etc*) vitreous; […] (*yeux etc*) glazed; **regard v.** glassy […]; [**porcel**]**aine vitreuse** vitreous china

[…] **ton père n'est pas v.!** I can't see […]

[…] *f* vitrification; (*du parquet*) […]

[…] *b* **n. vitrifiions, v. vitrifiiez**) […] [**brique v**]**itrifiée** glazed brick; **v. un** […] […]et floor

[…] window; **faire une v.** to […] to change the window […]how) in the window; […]ndow shopping; **Paris** […] […]se of France (b) (*de* […]) (*armoire*) display […]

[…] **v.** oil of vitriol;

[…]

viv[…]**faire v.** to be […]

[…]

pa[…]**laque v.** […]

vivabl[…] **je** […] livable […] to […] intoler[…] **elle** […]

vivace¹ […] *Bot* pere[…]

souvenirs […] **pois v.** eve[…]

vivace² [viva[…]

vivacité [viv[…] (*enthousiasm*[…] **d'esprit** quick[…] **la v.** to be viva[…] sprightly; **une** […]

woman; **avec v.** vivaciously (b) (*d'un sentiment*) acuteness; (*d'une discussion*) heat; (*d'une passion*) fire, intensity (c) (*d'un tempérament*) hastiness; **avec v.** hastily

vivandier, -ière [vivɑ̃dje, -jɛr] *n Arch* sutler, *f* vivandière

vivant [vivɑ̃] **1** *adj* (a) (*doué de vie*) living; **un organisme/être v.** a living organism/being

(b) (*en vie*) alive; **il est encore v.** he is still alive; **être enterré v.** to be buried alive; *Vieilli Fig* **s'enterrer v.** to bury oneself away; **pas une âme vivante** not a living soul; **portrait v.** lifelike portrait; **être le portrait v. de qn** to be the living *or* spitting image of sb; **langue vivante** modern language; *F* **c'est une bibliothèque vivante** he's a walking encyclop(a)edia; *Th* **tableau v.** tableau (vivant)

(c) (*plein de vie*) (*rue, scène, conversation etc*) lively, animated; (*enfant*) lively; **description/récit vivant(e)** lively description/account; **il a laissé en nous un souvenir très v.** he left us with a very vivid memory of him

2 *nm* (a) (*personne*) living being; **les vivants et les morts** the living and the dead; **bon v.** man who enjoys (the pleasures of) life, bon vivant

(b) **de son v.** during his lifetime, in his day; **du v. de votre père** when your father was alive, in your father's (life)time

vivarium [vivarjɔm] *nm* vivarium

vivat [viva] **1** *int Arch* hurrah!, bravo! **2** *nmpl* **vivats** (*d'un public etc*) cheers

vive [viv] *nf* (*poisson*) weever, stingfish

vivement [vivmɑ̃] *adv* (a) (*rapidement*) briskly, quickly; **se tourner v.** to turn round quickly (b) (*durement*) sharply; *F* **réprimander v. qn** to give sb a sharp rebuke, to rebuke sb sharply; **répondre v.** to answer sharply *or* brusquely (c) (*intensément*) keenly, deeply, acutely; (*éclairé*) brightly; (*coloré*) vividly; **s'intéresser v. à qch** to take a keen interest in sth; **remercier qn v.** to thank sb warmly; **être v. ému** to be deeply moved; **contraster v. avec** to contrast sharply with (d) (*marque l'impatience*) **v. les vacances!** roll on the holidays!; **v. qu'il parte!** I'll be glad when he's gone!, he can't leave soon enough!

viveur [vivœr] *nm Péj* pleasure seeker, *F* fast liver

vivier [vivje] *nm* fishpond; (*dans un restaurant*) fish tank; (*de bateau*) fish well; *Fig* breeding ground (**de** for)

vivifiant [vivifjɑ̃] *adj* enlivening; (*air, climat etc*) invigorating, bracing

vivifier [vivifje] *vt* (*impf, pr sub* **n. vivifiions, v. vivifiiez**) to enliven, to (re)vitalize; (*de l'air etc*) to invigorate; **v. l'industrie d'un pays** to revive *or* give fresh life to a country's industry

vivipare [vivipar] *adj Biol* viviparous

viviparité [viviparite] *nf Biol* viviparity

vivisection [viviseksjɔ̃] *nf* vivisection; **ligue contre la v.** anti-vivisection league

vivoir [vivwar] *nm Can* living room

vivoter [vivɔte] *vi* to (just) get by; **j'avais à peine de quoi v. avec ce salaire** I could hardly keep body and soul together on that salary; **usine qui vivote** factory that is just managing to keep going *or* is just keeping its head above water

vivre¹ [vivr] *nm* (a) **vivres** provisions, supplies; *Mil* rations; **vivres de réserve** iron rations; **couper les vivres à qn** to stop sb's allowance (b) *Arch* food; **le v. et le couvert** bed and board, board and lodging

vivre² (*prp* **vivant**; *pp* **vécu**; *pr ind* **je vis, il vit, n. vivons, ils vivent**; *pr sub* **je viv**[e]; *impf* **je vivais**; *p hist* **je vécus**; *fu* **je vivrai**) **1** *vi* (a) to live, to be alive; **v. au vingt et unième siècle** to live in the tw[enty]-first century; **elle vit encore** she's still alive; **v. longtemp**[s] [to] live a long time; **v. vieux** to live to a ripe old age; **cesser [de vivre]** to die; **le Front populaire a vécu** the Popular Front has h[ad its] day *or* is finished; *F* **ma pauvre vieille télé a vécu** my p[oor o]ld telly is on its last legs; **ne v. que pour son travail** to [live o]nly for one's work; **raison de v.** reason for living; **être** [las de] **v.** to be tired of living *or* of life; **vive le roi!** long li[ve the] King!; **vive l'armée!** three cheers for the army!; **viv**[es les **v**]**acances!** three cheers *or* hurray for the holidays!; [**q**]**ui vive?** who goes there?; **ne rencontrer âme qui vi**[ve] [to m]eet no one *or* not a living soul; *Prov* **qui vivra verra** [time wi]ll tell; **ouvrage qui vivra** work that will endure; […]**s qui vivent encore** traditions that are still alive […]

(b) (*d'une certaine façon*) t[o live]; […] **à Paris/en province/à la campagne/à l'étranger** to [live in Pa]ris/in the provinces/in the country/abroad *or* overseas; *F* **v. [be]aucoup vécu** (*d'une personne*) he's seen life; […] **v. en honnête homme** to l[ead] [an hon]est life; **v. avec qn** [to] live with sb; **être facile à v.** to […] […] with; **savoir v.** to know how to live with *or* to get […] [t]o be well-bred; **v.** [**h**]**eureux** to live happily; *Prov* […] **heureux, vivons** […]**s** = the happiest people […]se who keep themselves to themselves; **v. dans le présent/au jour le jour** to live in the present/one day at a time; **apprendre à v. à qn** to teach sb good *or* better manners; *F* **je vais t'apprendre à v.!** I'll teach you some manners!; **se laisser v.** to take life easily *or* as it comes; **il fait bon v. ici** life is pleasant here; **le plaisir de v.** the joy of living; **prendre le temps de v.** to take the time to enjoy life

(**c**) (*économiquement*) to live; **on vivait bien juste** we could just manage *or* just rub along; **v. bien** to live in comfort, to live well; **travailler pour v.** to work for a living; **il fait cher v. ici** life *or* living is expensive here, the cost of living is high here; **faire v. sa famille** to support *or* keep one's family; **v. au jour le jour** (*avec ce qu'on a*) to live from hand to mouth *or* from day to day; **v. de poisson** to live on fish; **v. de sa plume/de ses rentes** to live by one's pen/on one's (private) income; **v. d'amour et d'eau fraîche** to live on fresh air, to live on love alone; **v. d'espérances** to live on hope; **l'espoir fait v.** where there's life there's hope; *Iron* what a hope!, you're/he's/*etc* optimistic!; **de quoi vit-il?** what does he live on?; (*que fait-il dans la vie?*) what does he do for a living?; **avoir de quoi v.** to have enough to live on; **ils n'ont que de quoi v.** they've just enough to live on

2 *vt* **v. sa vie** to live one's (own) life; **les événements que nous avons vécus** the events we experienced *or* lived through; **elle a vécu la guerre** she lived through *or* went through the war; **v. des moments difficiles** to be going through *or* having *or* experiencing a difficult time; **v. une expérience unique/inoubliable** to go through *or* have a unique/an unforgettable experience; **v. une passion** to live out a passion; **v. sa foi** to live one's faith

3 se vivre *vpr* **la maladie se vit mal quand on est seul** it's difficult being ill when you're on your own

vivrier, -ière [vivrije, -jɛr] *adj* **cultures vivrières** food crops

vizir [vizir] *nm* vizier

vlan, v'lan [vlɑ̃] *int* slap(-bang)!, whack!, wham!; **et v.! il est tombé** and bang he fell over!

vlimeux [vlimø] *nm Can Arg* (**a**) (*chanceux*) lucky devil; **le petit v.!** (the) lucky devil! (**b**) (*intrigant*) crafty devil

VMP [veɛmpe] *nfpl Fin* (*abrév* **valeurs mobilières de placement**) marketable securities

VO [veo] *nf Cin* (*abrév* **version originale**) original (language) version; **voir un film en VO** to see a film in the original (language) version; **la VO est meilleure que la version doublée** the original version is better than the dubbed one

vocable [vɔkabl] *nm* (**a**) (*mot*) word, *Spéc* vocable (**b**) *Rel* (*d'un saint*) name, patronage; **église sous le v. de saint Pierre** church dedicated to Saint Peter

vocabulaire [vɔkabylɛr] *nm* (**a**) (*liste*) vocabulary, word list; **un v. (de termes) de chimie** a vocabulary of chemistry terms

(**b**) (*d'une personne etc*) vocabulary; **enrichir son v.** to enlarge one's vocabulary; **le v. d'un enfant de six ans** the vocabulary of a six-year-old (child); **ce mot n'est pas dans mon v.** it's not a word that I use; *Péj* **quel v.!** what language!; **supprime ce mot de ton v.** stop using that word

(**c**) (*jargon*) vocabulary; **v. administratif/juridique/technique** administrative/legal/technical vocabulary; **employer le v. à la mode** to use all the in words; **un junkie, pour employer le v. à la mode** a junkie, to use the in *or* fashionable word

vocal, -ale, -aux, -ales [vɔkal, -o] *adj* vocal

vocalement [vɔkalmɑ̃] *adv* vocally

vocalique [vɔkalik] *adj Ling* vocalic; **son v.** vocalic *or* vowel sound

vocalisation [vɔkalizasjɔ̃] *nf Ling, Mus* vocalization

vocalise [vɔkaliz] *nf Mus* exercise in vocalization; **faire des vocalises** to do singing exercises

vocaliser [vɔkalize] **1** *vt* (*mélodie, consonne*) to vocalize **2 se vocaliser** *vpr* to become vocalized

vocalisme [vɔkalism] *nm Ling, Mus* vocalism

vocatif [vɔkatif] *nm Gram* vocative (case); **au v.** in the vocative (case)

vocation [vɔkasjɔ̃] *nf* (**a**) (*goût*) vocation, calling; **pour ce genre de métier, il faut avoir la v.** you have to have a vocation for this kind of job; **manquer/suivre sa v.** to miss/follow one's vocation; **avoir la v. du professorat** to have a vocation for teaching, *F* to be cut out for teaching; **avoir la v. du commerce** to have an aptitude for business; *F* **il faut avoir la v.** you really need to be dedicated; **faire qch par v.** to do sth as a labour of love; **la v. industrielle de l'Allemagne** Germany's long industrial tradition; **région à v. agricole/industrielle** agricultural/industrial region

(**b**) (*religieuse*) vocation, call; **je ne me sens pas la v. de la prêtrise** I feel no call to the Church *or* no calling for the Church

vociférateur, -trice [vɔsiferatœr, -tris] *n Litt* vociferator

vocifération [vɔsiferasjɔ̃] *nf* outcry, *Fml* vociferation; **vociférations** shouts, yells; **pousser des vociférations** to shout and bawl

vociférer [vɔsifere] (*pr ind* **je vocifère, n. vociférons**; *fu* **je vociférerai**) **1** *vi* to shout, to yell, to bawl, *Fml* to vociferate (**contre** about) **2** *vt* **v. des injures** to shout *or* hurl insults (**contre** at)

vodka [vɔdka] *nf* vodka; **v. orange** (*verre*) vodka and orange

vœu, -x [vø] *nm* (**a**) (*souhait*) wish; **faire un v.** to make a wish, to wish; **si je n'avais qu'un v. à faire, ce serait celui de ...** if I could have just one wish, it would be to ...; **émettre un v.** to express a wish *or* a desire; **former le v. que qch se réalise** to express a *or* the wish that sth should be done; **le premier ministre a formé** *ou* **émis le v. que la loi soit modifiée** the Prime Minister expressed the wish that the law should be changed; **je fais des vœux pour qu'il ne pleuve pas dimanche** I'm praying it won't rain on Sunday; **tous mes/nos vœux!, avec mes/nos meilleurs vœux** best wishes, with all good wishes; **tous mes vœux de bonheur** best wishes for your future happiness; **vœux de bonne** *ou* **de nouvelle année** New Year greetings; **le Président a adressé ses vœux à la nation** the President made his New Year address to the nation; **envoyer ses vœux à qn** to send sb one's best wishes; **carte de vœux** greetings card

(**b**) (*promesse*) vow; **j'ai fait le v. de ne plus y retourner** I vowed never to go back (there again); **il a fait le v. de se venger** he vowed revenge; *Rel* **faire v. de pauvreté** to take a vow of poverty; **prononcer ses vœux** to take one's vows; **les vœux de baptême** the baptismal vows

▶ **vœu**: **v. pieux** pious hope

vogue [vɔg] *nf* fashion, vogue; **c'était la v. des cheveux courts** short hair was in fashion, it was the fashion to have short hair; **c'est la grande v.** it's all the rage; **en v.** fashionable, in vogue; **musique/artiste en v.** fashionable music/artist; **connaître une v., être en v.** to be popular *or* fashionable, to be in fashion *or* in vogue; **les jupes longues sont à nouveau en v.** long skirts are back in fashion; **entrer en v.** to come into vogue *or* fashion, to come in

voguer [vɔge] *vi Litt* to sail; **les nuages voguant dans le ciel** the clouds sailing *or* floating by, the drifting clouds; **vogue la galère!** let's see what happens

voici [vwasi] *prép* (**a**) here is/are; **v. Henri** here's Henry; **v. mes neveux** (*en les présentant*) these are my nephews; (*ils arrivent*) here are my nephews; **me/les v.** here I am/they are; **ah te v. donc!** there you are!; **nous v. arrivés!** here we are!; **vous v. installés** here you are all settled in; **nous v. à Paris** here we are in Paris; **nous v. riches** we're rich!; **du pain? en v.** bread? here's some *or* here you are; **en v. une qui sera plus à ta taille** here's one which will be more your size; **la v. qui vient** here she comes, that's her (coming) now; **la v. qui recommence à pleurer** she's starting to cry again, that's her starting to cry again; **v. qu'il se met à pleuvoir** that's the rain on; *Litt* **v. venir Jeanne** here comes Jeanne; **mon ami que v. vous le dira** my friend here will tell you; **Monsieur/l'objet que v.** this gentleman/object; **la petite histoire que v.** the following little story; **v. ce dont il s'agit** this is *or* here's what it's all about; **v. ce qu'il m'a dit** this is *or* here's what he told me; **v. comment je vois les choses** this is *or* here's how I see things; **je le ferai et v. comment** I'll do it and here's how, *Fml* I shall do it in the following manner; **v. pourquoi** this is why; **et v. pour toi** and this is for you; **v. Noël!** Christmas is here!

(**b**) (*il y a*) **je l'ai vu v. trois ans** I saw him three years ago; **v. deux mois que je ne l'ai pas vue** I haven't seen her for two months; **v. trois mois que j'habite ici** I have been living here for (the last) three months

voie [vwa] *nf* (**a**) (*chemin*) way, road; (*non construit*) track; (*itinérant*) route; *Admin, Aut* traffic lane; **v. publique** public thoroughfare, public highway; **v. privée** private road; **route à quatre voies** four-lane road *or Am* highway; *Fig* **être par voies et par chemins** to be always on the move; **v. de communication** road, thoroughfare; (*avion, bateau, train*) means of transport; **grande v. de communication** main artery, arterial road; **la V. maritime du Saint-Laurent** the St Lawrence Seaway; **par v. de terre** by land, overland; **par v. de mer** by sea; **par la v. des airs** by air; *Fig* **la v. est libre** the coast is clear

(**b**) (*à la chasse*) **voies** (*du gibier*) tracks; (*d'un daim etc*) slot; **mettre les chiens sur la v.** to put the dogs on the scent; *Fig* **mettre qn sur la v.** to put sb on the right track; **être sur la bonne v.** to be on the right track

(**c**) *Rail* **v. ferrée** railway *or US* railroad (track or line); **v. de service** *ou* **de garage** siding; *Fig* **mettre un projet sur une v. de garage** to shelve a plan; **mettre** *ou* **ranger qn sur** une v. de garage to put sb on the sidelines, surtout Am to sideline sb; on l'a mis sur une v. de garage he's been sidelined; v. impaire, v. descendante down line; v. paire, v. montante up line; ligne à une v./à deux voies single-/double-track line; v. étroite narrow-gauge line; sur quelle v. arrive le train? what platform or US track does the train come in at?

(d) Ordinat v. d'accès path; v. bidirectionnelle simultanée full duplex; v. d'entrée input channel; v. de transmission de données data link

(e) (moyen) way; voies et moyens ways and means; préparer la v. to prepare or pave the way; il finira par trouver sa v. he'll find his way in the end; avoir sa v. toute tracée to have one's way marked out or mapped out; la v. des armes recourse to arms; par la v. diplomatique through diplomatic channels; par v. hiérarchique through official channels; suivre ou prendre la v. hiérarchique to go through official channels; la v. la plus simple/rapide the easiest/quickest way; une v. dangereuse a dangerous course; les voies de Dieu the ways of God; la v. étroite the straight and narrow; en v. d'achèvement nearing completion; en v. de construction under construction; en v. de formation in the process of formation; un pays en v. de développement a developing country; en v. de réparation under or undergoing repair; il est en v. de guérir ou de guérison he's on the mend, he's recovering; être en v. de faire qch to be (well) on the way to doing sth; être en (bonne) v. de réussir to be (well) on the way or road to success; être en bonne v. de guérir to be well on the road or way to recovery; être en bonne v. to be on the right track; affaire en bonne v. business that is going well; Jur voies de droit recourse to legal proceedings; Jur voies de fait assault and battery; en venir aux voies de fait to come to blows, to exchange blows; Ch etc v. sèche/humide dry/wet process; essai par la v. sèche dry test

(f) (des roues d'un véhicule) gauge; (d'un outil) kerf, clearance; (d'une scie) set; donner de la v. à une scie to set a saw

(g) Anat passage, duct; les voies digestives the digestive tract(s); par v. buccale orally

▶ voie: Aut v. d'accélération acceleration lane; Min v. d'aérage airway; Aut v. de décélération deceleration lane, exit lane; v. de dégagement filter lane; Naut v. d'eau leak; faire une v. d'eau to spring a leak; v. express expressway; v. express urbaine urban expressway; v. fluviale waterway; Astron la V. lactée the Milky Way; v. navigable waterway; v. rapide expressway; v. rapide urbaine urban expressway; v. romaine Roman road; v. sans issue dead end, cul-de-sac; v. pour véhicules lents crawler lane

voilà [vwala] prép (a) there is/are; v. Henri (qu'on cherche) there's Henri; (qui arrive) there's Henri (now), that's Henri (now); (dont je te parlais) that's Henri; v. Paul et Henri (en les présentant) this is Paul and this is Henri; (sur une photo) this is Paul and this or that is Henri; la/les v. there she is/they are; les v. qui arrivent there they are (now); la v. rassurée she's calmed down now; comme te v. changé you've changed so much, how you've changed; F nous v. frais ou beaux! now we're in a fix or mess!; la pendule que v. that clock (there); la petite histoire que v. the following little story; v. où il demeure that's where he lives; v. où je voulais en venir that's what I was getting or driving at; en v. assez! that's enough!, that will do!; j'attends depuis deux heures, en v. assez, je pars I've been waiting for two hours and I've had enough, I'm leaving!; en v. une idée! (bizarre) what a ridiculous idea!; (excellente) now there's an idea!; en v. une jolie fille! now there's a pretty girl!; en v. de la reconnaissance! there's gratitude for you!; en v. un qui fera son chemin! there's a man who will get on!; en v. une qui sait ce qu'elle veut there's someone who knows what she wants; en v. pour cent francs there's a hundred francs' worth; tu n'en as pas assez? en v. don't you have enough? here or there you are or Am there you go; v. tout that's all; elle était déçue, v. (tout) she was disappointed, that's all; v. ce qui rend la situation difficile that's what makes the situation difficult; v. ce que c'est que de mentir à ses parents/d'être trop honnête that's what happens or that's what you get when you lie to your parents/when you're too honest; v. le hic there's or that's the snag or the rub; le v. qui entre, v. qu'il entre there he is coming in; v. (ce) qui s'appelle danser!/un homme! now that's what I call dancing!/a man!; v. qui est curieux! that's curious!; v. ce qu'il m'a dit that's what he told me; v. comme elle est!, la v. bien! that's just like her!; v. qu'il se remarie and now he's getting married again; v.! there you are!; et v.! and that's that!; v., monsieur! (dans un restaurant) coming, sir!

(b) (voici) me v.! here I am!; le v.! here he is!, here he comes!; nous v. arrivés we're here, here we are; nous y v. enfin! (dans un endroit) here we are at last!; je l'avoue, j'étais jaloux – nous y v.! I admit it, I was jealous – now the truth's coming out!

(c) (il y a) en juin v. trois ans three years ago in June; v. dix ans que je le connais I've known him (for) ten years; v. trois ans que je n'y suis pas retournée I haven't been back there for three years

voilage [vwalaʒ] nm (a) (sur un chapeau etc) net (b) voilages (rideau) net curtains

voile¹ [vwal] nf sail; v. carrée square sail; déployer ou établir une v. to set a sail; bateau à voiles sailing boat; aller à la v. to sail; vaisseau sous voile(s) ship under sail or canvas; mettre à la v. to set sail; faire v. sur Alger to sail to or head for Algiers; faire force de voiles to crowd on or cram on all sail; toutes voiles dehors in full sail, all sail(s) set; mettre toutes voiles dehors to put on full sail or canvas; Fig to go at full tilt, to pull out all the stops; faire de la v. to sail; F mettre les voiles (partir) to scram, to do a bunk; marcher à v. et à vapeur (être bisexuel) to be AC/DC

voile² nm (a) veil; v. de mariée marriage or bridal veil; les femmes qui portent le v. women who wear the veil; Rel prendre le v. to take the veil (b) (devant les yeux) film, mist; un v. de fumée/de brouillard a veil of smoke/fog; F jeter un v. sur qch to cast or draw a veil over sth; Méd avoir un v. au poumon to have a shadow on one's lung; Méd F v. noir blackout; v. de larmes blur of tears (c) Tex voile (d) Anat v. du palais soft palate, velum (e) Phot (sur un négatif) fog (f) Aut (flanc de roue) spider

voilé [vwale] adj (a) (lumière) veiled, dim; (sens) veiled, obscure; (tambour) muffled; (voix) husky; Phot (épreuve) fogged; le ciel est v. it's hazy; femme voilée woman wearing the veil; des yeux voilés de larmes eyes dimmed or blurred with tears; en termes voilés/peu voilés in veiled/thinly veiled terms (b) (roue, tige etc) buckled, out of true

voiler [vwale] 1 vt (a) to veil; (lumière, soleil) to dim; (ciel) to cover, to veil; (son, tambour etc) to muffle; Phot (épreuve, plaque) to fog; Fig (trouble, émotion etc) to hide, to conceal; v. une statue/sa nudité to cover a statue/one's nakedness

(b) (roue etc) to buckle

(c) Naut (navire) to rig with sails

2 se voiler vpr (a) se v. (le visage) to wear a veil; les femmes doivent se v. women must wear the veil; Fig se v. la face to hide or bury one's head in the sand; sa voix se voile (d'émotion) his voice is husky (with emotion)

(b) (du ciel etc) to become overcast, to cloud over; (des yeux) to mist over; le soleil était en train de se v. the sun was becoming hazy

(c) (d'une roue etc) to buckle

voilerie [vwalri] nf Naut sail loft

voilette [vwalɛt] nf (hat) veil

voilier [vwalje] nm (a) Naut (de plaisance) yacht; faire du v. to go yachting; un v. de 15 mètres a 15 metre yacht (b) navire bon/mauvais v. good/bad sailer (c) (fabricant) sailmaker; maître v. master sailmaker (d) (oiseau) grand v. long-flight bird

voilure¹ [vwalyr] nf (a) (d'un navire) sails; réduire la v. to shorten or reduce sail (b) Av wing(s), flying surface, aerofoil, US airfoil; appareil à v. fixe/tournant fixed/rotary wing aircraft

voilure² nf (du métal, d'une roue) buckling

voir [vwar] (prp voyant; pp vu; pr ind je vois, il voit, n. voyons, ils voient; pr sub je voie; impf je voyais; p hist je vis; fu je verrai) 1 vt (a) (qn, qch) to see; Naut (navire) to sight; je l'ai vu de mes (propres) yeux, F je l'ai vu comme je te vois I saw it with my own eyes; v. la mort de près to stare death in the face; il n'y a rien à v. there's nothing to see or to be seen; hôtel vu de face front view of the hotel; Archit front elevation; bâtiment vu de côté/par la gauche side/left-hand view of the building; Archit side elevation; (détail) vu de près close-up (detail); ce lieu a vu la fin de la guerre d'Indépendance this spot saw the end of the War of Independence; F on aura tout vu! now we've seen everything!, wonders will never cease!; j'en ai vu d'autres! I've seen or been through worse!; il faut le v. pour le croire it has to be seen to be believed; j'aimerais (bien) t'y v. I'd like to see you do it or try!; c'est à v. (film, exposition etc) it's worth seeing; c'est encore à v. that remains to be seen; je le vois qui arrive I can see him coming; à le v. on dirait ... by the look of him or to judge by his looks one would say ...; on voit son jupon her slip is showing; mon fils, voyez-vous, est mort my son is dead, you see; v. page 23/ci-après see page 23/below; Litt que vois-je? what is this (that I see)?; faire v. qch à qn to show sth to sb, to show sb sth; il ne veut

pas me faire v. son livre he won't show me his book; **laisser v. qch à qn** to let sb see sth; **laisser v. son ignorance** to show *or* reveal *or* betray one's ignorance

(**b**) (+ *inf*) [①**A40**,C,1,a; **B33**,2,b,i] **v. venir qn** to see sb coming; **je l'ai vu tomber** I saw him fall; **quels acteurs avez-vous vus jouer ce rôle?** what actors have you seen in this part?; **quelles pièces avez-vous vu jouer?** what plays have you seen?; **v. faire qch** to see sth done; **elle a vu construire la Tour Eiffel** she saw the Eiffel Tower being built; **je l'ai vu faire ses pitreries** I saw him clowning around

(**c**) (*rendre visite à*) (*qn, qch*) to visit; **aller v. qn** to go to see sb, to go and see sb; **tu devrais aller v. un médecin/un avocat** you should go and see a doctor/a lawyer; **venez me v. quand vous serez à Paris** come and see me when you're in Paris; **nous avons vu les musées** we visited the museums; **je n'ai jamais vu Venise** I've never seen Venice; **v. du pays** to travel; **elle en a vu, du pays!** she has travelled a lot *or* seen a lot of the world

(**d**) (*fréquenter*) to see; **il ne voit (jamais) personne** he never sees anyone; **nous le voyons beaucoup** we see a lot of him; **on ne vous voit plus!** you're quite a stranger!; **nous ne les voyons plus** we don't see them any more; **je ne peux pas le v. (en peinture)** I can't stand (the sight of) him; **allez, file maintenant, je t'ai assez vu!** clear off, I've seen enough of you!

(**e**) (*comprendre*) to see, to understand; **je vois où vous voulez en venir** I see *or* understand what you're driving at; **ah oui, je vois** oh yes I see; **on voit bien qu'il est incompétent/jeune/innocent** you can see *or* it's obvious that he's incompetent/young/innocent; **je vois que vous m'avez attendu** I see you've waited for me; *F* **ni vu, ni connu** without anyone being any the wiser for it; **j'emprunte leur voiture pendant qu'ils sont partis, ni vu ni connu!** I'm borrowing their car while they're away, they'll be none the wiser; *F* **vu?** understood?, all right?, OK?; **c'est tout vu!** that's all there is to it; **comment voyez-vous l'avenir?** how do you see *or* view the future?

(**f**) (*observer*) (*qch*) to see, to notice, to observe; **je vois que vous avez compris** I see you have understood; **à ce que je vois** from what I can see; **vous voyez ça d'ici** you can guess what it was/is/would be like; **je vois ça d'ici** I can see it coming; **je vois la scène comme si j'y étais** I can picture the scene as if I were there

(**g**) (*examiner, étudier*) (*qch*) to look after, to see to, to see about; **v. une affaire à fond** to look into *or* examine a matter thoroughly; **vu et approuvé** seen and approved; **elle a vu le dossier de la première à la dernière page** she studied *or* examined the dossier from beginning to end; **c'est ce que nous verrons!** we shall see!, that remains to be seen!; *F* **va-t'en v. si j'y suis!** get lost!, clear out!, scram!; **il n'a rien à v. là-dedans** *ou* **à y v.** it's nothing to do with him, it's no business *or* concern of his, it's none of his business; (*il n'y est pour rien*) he's got nothing to do with it; **cela n'a rien à v. avec l'affaire** that's beside the point, that has nothing to do with it; **ceci est à v., c'est à v.** it remains to be seen; **juste pour v. si ça marche** just to see if it works

(**h**) (**v. à** + *inf*) **il va v. à nous loger** he'll see that we have somewhere to stay, he'll take care of our accommodation; **il faudrait v. à vous dépêcher!** you'd better hurry up!; *F* **il faudrait v. à v.!** just you try!

(**i**) (**v. que** + *sub*) **c'est à vous de v. que rien ne nous manque** it's up to you to see that we have everything we need

(**j**) (*considérer*) (*qch d'une certaine façon*) to see, to look at, to consider, to regard; **je ne le vois pas marié** I can't see *or* imagine *or* picture him married; **je te verrais bien instituteur** I can just see *or* picture you as a teacher; **elle voit en lui un père/un ami** she looks on him as a father/a friend; **elle a tendance à v. tout en noir** she tends to look on the gloomy side of things; **v. la vie en rose** to see life through rose-coloured spectacles; **sa façon de v. les choses** his way of looking at things, his outlook; **v. les choses telles qu'elles sont** to see things as they are; **je ne vois pas cela comme ça** I don't see *or* look at it like that; **ce n'est pas ainsi que je vois les choses** that's not how I see things; **elle y voit un seul inconvénient** she can see only one drawback; **je ne vois pas où est le problème/la difficulté** I don't see what the problem/difficulty is; **si tu n'y vois pas d'inconvénients** if that's all right *or* OK with you; **c'est un café où il faut se faire v.** it's <u>the</u> café to go to *or* to be seen in; *F* **va te faire v. eh, patate!** the same to you!; **il peut aller se faire v., qu'il aille se faire v.** he can go to hell; **se faire bien v. de qn** to gain sb's favour, to get into sb's good books; **se faire mal v. de qn** to get into sb's bad books; **être bien vu de tous** to be highly esteemed *or* well thought of by everyone; **elle est mal vue de tous** everyone has a low opinion of her; **c'est plutôt mal vu dans ce milieu** it's rather frowned on in these circles

2 *vi* to see; **elle ne voit plus** she can't see any more; **v. double** to see double; **v. clair** to see clearly; **tu ne vois pas clair?** are you not seeing straight?; *Fig* **je commence à y v. plus clair** I'm starting to get the picture; **v. mal** to have poor eyesight; **v. loin** to be farsighted; **il ne voit pas plus loin que le bout de son nez** he can't see any further than the end of his nose; *Fig* **v. grand** to think big; **v. c'est croire** seeing is believing; **je n'y vois plus** I can't see any more; **on n'y voit rien** (*il fait noir*) you can't see a thing; **v. rouge** to see red; **voyez vous-même!** see for yourself!; **voyez un peu l'état dans lequel il se trouve!** just look at the state he's in!; **faites v.!** let me see (it)!, let's have a look!; **en faire v. (de toutes les couleurs) à qn** to make sb's life a misery; (*le faire tourner en bourrique*) to lead sb a merry dance; *F* **voyons v.** let's see, let's have a look; **alors, voyons v., il faut commencer par ...** now, let's see *or* let me see, you have to start by ...; **montrez v.** just let me see it; **dites v. ...** tell me ...; **essayez v.** just have a try; (*menace*) just you try it; **regardez v.** just have a look; **regarde v. si elle n'est pas réveillée** have a look and see if she's woken up; **faire qch seulement pour v.** to do sth to see what happens *or* just as an experiment; **tu peux toujours essayer pour v.** you can always try just to see; **eh bien, je verrai** well, I'll see *or* think about it; **voyons!** (*pour examiner une question*) let's see; (*pour exprimer une désapprobation*) come (on) now!, come, come!

3 se voir *vpr* (**a**) (*d'un phénomène, d'un objet*) to be seen; **monument qui se voit de loin** monument that can be seen *or* that is visible from a distance; **ça se voit que j'ai pleuré?** can you tell I've been crying?; **cela se voit tous les jours** you see things like that all the time, that kind of thing happens every day; **cela ne se voit pas tous les jours** it's not something you see every day; **ça se voit** that's obvious; *F* **cela se voit comme le nez au milieu de la figure** it's as plain as the nose on your face

(**b**) (*d'une personne dans un miroir etc*) to see oneself; (*de deux personnes*) to see each other; **je n'aime pas me v. en photo** I don't like looking at photos of myself; **elle ne se voit pas du tout avec des enfants** she just can't see herself with children; **il se voyait déjà perdu** he already imagined himself lost

voire [vwar] *adv* indeed; **v. (même)** and even; (*alternativement*) or even; **j'en suis ahuri, v. révolté** I'm astounded, indeed disgusted; **elle est méticuleuse, v. maniaque** she's meticulous, obsessive even

voirie [vwari] *nf* (**a**) *Admin* = administration of public thoroughfares; **service de v.** roads department; **travaux de v.** road works; **employé de la v.** street sweeper (**b**) (*routes etc*) road system; **la grande v.** the main roads (**c**) *Vieilli* (*décharge*) refuse dump; **jeter les ordures à la v.** to dump the rubbish

voisin, -ine [vwazɛ̃, -in] **1** *adj* neighbouring, *US* neighboring; (*mitoyen*) bordering (**de** on); **une rue voisine des champs Elysées** a street adjoining the Champs Elysées; **la chambre voisine** the next room; **deux maisons voisines** two houses next to each other, two adjoining houses; **il habite dans la maison voisine** he lives (in the house) next door; **pays voisins** neighbouring countries; **cela aura lieu à une date voisine de la rentrée** it'll be sometime around the start of the new term; **les années voisines de 1980** the years around 1980; *Biol* **espèces voisines** closely allied *or* related species; **être v. de qn/qch** to be next to sb/sth; *Fig* **émotion voisine de la terreur** emotion akin to *or* bordering on terror; **des expériences très voisines** very similar experiences; **v. de la mort** at death's door

2 *n* neighbour, *US* neighbor; **v. d'à côté/de porte/de palier** next-door neighbour; **les voisins du dessus/dessous** the upstairs/downstairs neighbours, the people upstairs/downstairs; **mon v. de table** the person I was sitting next to (at table), my neighbour at table; **dire du mal de son v.** to speak ill of one's neighbour; **agir en bon v.** to act in a neighbourly *or* *US* neighborly way

voisinage [vwazinaʒ] *nm* (**a**) (*proximité*) vicinity, proximity, nearness; **apprécier le v. de la nature** to enjoy the proximity *or* closeness of nature; **les maisons dans le v. des montagnes** the houses in the vicinity of *or* near the mountains; **le v. de la gare est un avantage** proximity *or* being close to the station is an advantage

(**b**) (*entourage*) vicinity, neighbourhood, *US* neighborhood; **il n'y avait personne dans le v.** there was nobody in the vicinity, there was nobody about; **relations de bon v.** (good) neighbourliness *or* *US* neighborliness; **être en bon v. avec qn, entretenir des relations de bon v. avec qn** to be on good terms with sb

voisiner [vwazine] *vi* (**a**) *Litt* to visit one's neighbours *or US* neighbors; **à Paris on voisine peu** in Paris you don't see much of your neighbours (**b**) **v. avec qch** to be (placed) side by side with sth; (*être mitoyen de qch*) to adjoin sth

voiturage [vwatyraʒ] *nm* (*de marchandises etc*) carriage, conveyance, cartage

voiture [vwatyr] *nf* (**a**) *Aut* car, *Am* automobile, *Br F* motor; **location de voitures** car hire *or* rental; **prendre sa v.** to take the car; **aller à Paris en v.** to go to Paris by car; **petite v.** invalid carriage; **v. à combustible mixte** dual-fuel car; **v. de compétition** competition car; **v. de course** racing car; **v. de démonstration** demo model, demonstrator; **v. à double commande** dual-controlled car; **v. familiale** family car; **v. de fonction** company car; **v. d'infirme** invalid carriage; **v. de livraison** delivery van; **v. de location** rental *or Br* hired car; **v. de maître** chauffeur-driven car; **v. de marchandises** goods van; **v. d'occasion** used car, second-hand car; **v. radio** radio car; *TV, Rad* **v. de reportage** remote van; **v. de série** production car; **v. de société** company car; **v. de sport** *ou* **sportive** sports car; **v. de tourisme** private *or* touring car

(**b**) *Rail* coach, carriage, *Am* car; **v. fumeurs** smoking carriage, smoker; **v. non fumeurs** no-smoking carriage, non-smoker; **en v.!** take your seats!, all aboard!

(**c**) *Arch* (*mode de transport*) conveyance, transport

(**d**) *Com* **lettre de v.** waybill, consignment note

(**e**) (*tiré par des chevaux*) (horse-drawn) vehicle; (*pour passagers*) carriage, coach; (*pour des marchandises*) cart; **v. à deux chevaux** carriage and pair; **v. de place** hackney (carriage *or* cab)

▶ **voiture**: **v. à bras** barrow, handcart; **v. d'enfant** pram, *Am* baby carriage; *Vieilli* **v. de malade** Bath chair

voiture-bar, *pl* **voitures-bars** *nf Rail* buffet car, refreshment car

voiture-couchette, *pl* **voitures-couchettes** *nf Rail* couchette car

voiturée [vwatyre] *nf Vieilli* (*de passagers*) carriageful; (*de marchandises etc*) cartload

voiture-école, *pl* **voitures-école** *nf* driving school car

voiture-lit, *pl* **voitures-lits** *nf Rail* sleeping car, sleeper

voiturer [vwatyre] *vt Vieilli* (*marchandises etc*) to convey, to transport, to carry, to cart; *F* **je vais te v.** I'll drive you

voiture-restaurant, *pl* **voitures-restaurants** *nf Rail* restaurant car, dining car

voiture-salon, *pl* **voitures-salon** *nf Rail* saloon *or Am* parlor car

voiturette [vwatyrɛt] *nf* trap; *Aut* small car

voiturier [vwatyrje] *nm Arch Jur* carrier, carter; (*dans un hôtel etc*) parking valet; **service de v.** valet parking

voix [vwa] *nf* (**a**) voice; **'arrêtez', dit une v.** 'stop', said a voice; **avoir une belle v.** (*en chantant*) to have a fine voice; (*en parlant*) to have a pleasant voice; **avoir une v. grave/chaude** to have a deep/warm voice; **entendre des voix** to hear voices; **parler à v. haute** *ou* **à haute v.** to speak in a loud voice; (*clairement*) to speak aloud, to speak out loud; **parler à v. basse** to speak in a low voice *or* under one's breath *or* in an undertone; **faire la grosse v.** to speak sternly *or* in a severe tone; **élever la v.** to speak up; (*se mettre en colère*) to raise one's voice; **rester sans v.** to remain speechless; **de vive v.** by word of mouth, viva voce; **il me l'a appris de vive v.** he informed me himself; **la v. de la conscience** the voice *or* the dictates of conscience; *Fig* **la v. de la nature** the call of nature; **la v. du peuple** the voice of the people, public opinion, vox populi; **d'une commune v.** by common consent, with one voice; **à portée de (la) v.** within earshot; **hors de portée de (la) v.** out of hearing, out of earshot; **donner de la v.** (*des chiens*) to bark; (*d'un limier*) to give tongue, to bay; *Mus* **v. de basse/de ténor** bass/tenor voice; **v. de poitrine** chest voice; **v. de tête** head voice; **v. de fausset** falsetto (voice); **v. claire/gaie/enjouée** clear/cheerful/lively voice; **chanter à plusieurs v.** to sing in parts; **je ne suis pas en v.** I'm not in good voice

(**b**) *Pol* vote; **donner sa v. à qn** to vote for sb; **élu à la majorité des voix** elected by a majority; **mettre une question aux voix** to put a question to the vote; **avoir v. consultative/délibérative** to have a consultative role/voting rights; *Fig* **avoir v. au chapitre** to have a say in the matter; **v. prépondérante** casting vote

(**c**) [①**A40**,9; **B36**,J] *Gram* voice; **à la v. active/passive** in the active voice/in the passive (voice)

▶ **voix**: *TV, Cin* **v. dans le champ** in-frame voice; *TV, Cin* **v. hors champ** voice off, VO, voice-over; **v. humaine** (*d'un orgue*) vox humana; *TV, Cin* **v. in** voice in; *TV, Cin* **v. off** voice-over; **commentaire en v. off** voice-over commentary; *Cin* **v. en surimpression** voice-over

vol¹ [vɔl] *nm* (**a**) flight; **prendre son v.** (*d'un oiseau*) to take wing, to take off; *Fig* (*prendre son essor*) to take off; **tirer un oiseau au v.** to shoot a bird on the wing; *Fig* **saisir l'occasion au v.** to grasp *or* leap at the opportunity; **à v. d'oiseau** as the crow flies; **à v. d'oiseau, il y a cinq kilomètres** it's five kilometres as the crow flies; **de haut v.** (*personne, collaborateur etc*) high-flying; **un escroc de haut v.** a big-time crook; **oiseau de haut v.** high-flying bird

(**b**) *Av* flight; **heures de v.** flying time; **à trois heures de v. de Paris** three hours' flying time from Paris; **numéro de v.** flight number; **v. 944 pour Glasgow** flight 944 to Glasgow; **tous les vols sont annulés** all flights are cancelled; **avion en v.** aircraft in flight; **v. de nuit** night flying; **v. 'sec'** flight only; **v. aller-retour** return flight, *Am* round-trip flight; **v. charter** charter flight; **v. d'apport** feeder flight; **v. de correspondance** connecting flight; **v. direct** direct flight; **v. intérieur** domestic flight, internal flight; **v. moyen-courrier** medium-haul flight; **v. nolisé** charter flight; **v. régulier** regular flight, scheduled flight; **v. plané** gliding flight; **descendre en v. plané** to glide down; *F* **il a fait un de ces vols planés!** he went flying!

(**c**) (*nuée d'oiseaux*) flock, flight; (*de perdrix, tétras*) covey; (*de criquets*) swarm

(**d**) *Arch* (**chasse au**) **v.** hawking

vol² *nm* theft, stealing, robbery; **commettre un v.** to commit a theft *or* robbery; **v. de grand chemin** highway robbery; *F* **c'est du v.!** it's a rip-off!, it's daylight robbery!

▶ **vol**: **v. à l'américaine** confidence trick; **v. avec effraction** breaking and entering, housebreaking; **v. à l'étalage** shoplifting; **v. libre** hang-gliding; **faire du v. libre** to hang-glide, to go hang-gliding; **v. à main armée** armed robbery; *Jur* **v. qualifié** aggravated theft, robbery; **v. à la tire** pickpocketing; **être victime d'un v. à la tire** to have one's pocket picked; **v. à voile** gliding; **faire du v. à voile** to glide, to go gliding

volage [vɔlaʒ] *adj* fickle, inconstant, flighty

volaille [vɔlaj] *nf* (**a**) [①**A12**,1,g] poultry; **une v.** a fowl; **marchand de volailles** poulterer (**b**) *Culin* poultry; **foies de v.** chicken livers

volailler [vɔlaje] *nm* poulterer

volant [vɔlɑ̃] **1** *adj* (**a**) flying; (*rubans etc*) fluttering; **objet v. non identifié** unidentified flying object; *F* **soucoupe volante** flying saucer; **poisson v.** flying fish; *Av* **personnel v.** flight crew; *Mil* air crew; *Naut* **escadre volante** flying squadron

(**b**) (*câble etc*) loose; (*mur etc*) movable; **feuille volante** (*de papier*) loose leaf; **table volante** occasional table; *Constr* **pont v.** flying bridge; **camp v.** temporary camp

2 *nm* (**a**) *Aut* (steering) wheel; **prendre le v.** to take the wheel; **un violent coup de v.** a violent turn of the wheel; **les fous du v.** reckless drivers, roadhogs; **un as du v.** a crack (racing) driver; **v. inclinable** tilt steering wheel; **v. sport** sports steering wheel; **v. télescopique** telescoping wheel

(**b**) (*de badminton*) shuttlecock; **jeu de v.** (game of) battledore and shuttlecock

(**c**) *Couture* flounce; (*panneau*) shaped panel; **volants froncés** gathered flounces; **jupe à volants** flounced skirt

(**d**) (*d'horloge*) fly

(**e**) (*de moteur etc*) handwheel; *Fig* **v. de sécurité** reserve funds

(**f**) (*d'un carnet de tickets*) **talon et v.** counterfoil and leaf

volatil [vɔlatil] *adj* volatile

volatile [vɔlatil] *nm Hum* winged creature, bird

volatilisable [vɔlatilizabl] *adj* volatilizable

volatilisation [vɔlatilizasjɔ̃] *nf* volatilization

volatiliser [vɔlatilize] **1** *vt* (**a**) *Ch* to volatilize (**b**) (*faire disparaître*) to make disappear; **on lui a volatilisé sa montre** he's had his watch pinched *or* nicked **2 se volatiliser** *vpr* (**a**) *Ch* to volatilize (**b**) (*disparaître*) to vanish (into thin air)

volatilité [vɔlatilite] *nf* volatility

vol-au-vent *nm inv Culin* vol-au-vent

volcan [vɔlkɑ̃] *nm* [①**A12**,1,c] (**a**) volcano; **v. actif/dormant/éteint** active/dormant/extinct volcano; **v. en activité** active volcano (**b**) *Fig* (*personne*) fiery *or* impetuous person; (*situation*) volcano; **c'est un vrai v.** she's really fiery *or* a real spitfire; **danser sur un v.** to be sitting on a powder keg *or* a time bomb; **son imagination est un v.** he has a vivid imagination

volcanique [vɔlkanik] *adj* (*roche etc*) volcanic; *Fig* (*passion*) fiery, ardent; (*imagination*) vivid; (*tempérament, caractère*) fiery, impetuous

volcanologie [vɔlkanɔlɔʒi] *nf* vulcanology

volcanologue [vɔlkanɔlɔg] *n* vulcanologist

vole [vɔl] *nf Cartes* vole, all the tricks

volée [vɔle] *nf* (**a**) (*d'un oiseau, d'un projectile etc*) flight; *Tennis* volley; **prendre sa v.** to take wing; *Fig* to take off; **tirer à toute v.** to fire a gun at maximum elevation; **lancer qch à**

toute v. to hurl sth, to send sth flying; **coup de v.** *Rugby* punt; *Fb* volley; *Tennis* **relancer une balle à la v.** to volley a return; *Tennis* **v. amortie** drop volley; **attraper une balle à la v.** to catch a ball in mid air; *Fig* **saisir une allusion à la v.** to catch an allusion promptly *or* instantly; *Agr* **semer à la v.** to broadcast

(b) (*de corbeaux etc*) flock, flight; (*de perdrix*) covey; (*de filles*) band, bevy; (*d'écoliers, d'enfants*) swarm, crowd

(c) (*niveau social*) rank, standing; **de haute v.** (*personne*) high-class, top-flight; (*par ses aptitudes*) high-flying; **un escroc de haute v.** a big-time crook

(d) (*de missiles*) volley; (*de coups*) shower; **recevoir une bonne v.** to get a sound thrashing; **sonner à toute v.** to set all the bells ringing; (*des cloches*) to ring a full peal, to be in full peal

(e) v. d'escalier flight of stairs

(f) *Tech* (*d'une grue*) jib

voler[1] [vɔle] *vi* **(a)** (*dans les airs*) to fly; **nous volons à une vitesse de …** we are flying at a speed of …; *Fig* **v. de ses propres ailes** to stand on one's own two feet, to fend for oneself; **on aurait entendu v. une mouche** you could have heard a pin drop; **la fenêtre a volé en éclats** the window smashed into pieces *or* smithereens; **tous nos espoirs ont volé en éclats** all our hopes went up in smoke; **faire v. un cerf-volant** to fly a kite; *Fig F* **elle lui a volé dans les plumes** she went for him, she flew at him

(b) *Litt* to travel fast, to move with speed; **v. au secours de qn** to fly to sb's aid

voler[2] *vt* **(a)** (*dérober*) to steal; **v. qch à qn** to steal sth from sb, to rob sb of sth; **elle lui a volé cette idée** she stole the idea from him; **on m'a volé ma montre, je me suis fait v. ma montre** someone has stolen my watch, I've had my watch stolen; **je me suis tout fait v.** I've been robbed of everything, I've had everything stolen; *Prov* **qui vole un œuf vole un bœuf** that's how it all starts; *F* **il ne l'a pas volé** it serves him right; **il se repose un peu maintenant, il ne l'a pas volé** he's having a well-deserved *or* well-earned rest now, he's having a rest now, and he's earned it

(b) (*dépouiller*) to rob; (*rouler*) to swindle, to cheat; **on s'est fait v.** (*dans ce restaurant*) we were ripped off, we were really stung

volet [vɔlɛ] *nm* **(a)** (*de fenêtre, de magasin*) shutter; **ouvrir/fermer les volets** to open/close the shutters; **mettre/enlever les volets** to put up/take down the shutters **(b)** (*section*) (*d'un triptyque*) panel; (*de permis de conduire, d'un dépliant*) page; (*d'une facture, d'un formulaire*) portion; (*sur lumière*) flap; (*d'une vidéo*) wipe; (*d'une étude, d'un livre*) section; *Fig* (*d'un plan, d'une enquête*) stage, part **(c)** *Av* flap; **sortir/rentrer les volets** to lower/raise flaps **(d)** (*d'une roue à eau*) paddle; (*de carburateur*) throttle valve, butterfly valve

voleter [vɔlte] *vi* (**il volette; il volettera**) (*d'un oiseau*) to flutter; **v. d'arbre en arbre** to flit from tree to tree

voleur, -euse [vɔlœr, -øz] **1** *n* thief, *pl* thieves, robber; (*cambrioleur*) burglar; **cet épicier est un v.** that grocer's a crook *or* swindler; **au v.!** stop thief!; **v. d'idées** stealer of ideas, plagiarist; **v. de moutons** sheep stealer **2** *adj* thieving, thievish; *Fml* (*commerçant etc*) rapacious; (*enfant*) pilfering; **elle est voleuse comme une pie** she has sticky fingers

▶ **voleur**: **v. d'enfants** kidnapper; **v. à l'étalage** shoplifter; *Hist* **v. de grand chemin** highwayman, footpad; **v. à la tire** pickpocket

volière [vɔljɛr] *nf* aviary; *Fig* **cette classe est une vraie v.!** this class is like a zoo!

volige [vɔliʒ] *nf Constr* scantling, batten; (*pour tuiles*) slate lath; **caisse en voliges** crate

voligeage [vɔliʒaʒ] *nm Constr* battening; (*pour tuiles*) lathing

voliger [vɔliʒe] *vt* (**je voligeai(s); n. voligeons**) *Constr* to batten; (*pour tuiles*) to lath

volis [vɔli] *nm* broken tree top

volitif, -ive [vɔlitif, -iv] *adj* volitional

volition [vɔlisjɔ̃] *nf* volition

volley-ball [vɔlɛbol] *nm Sp* volleyball; **jouer au v.** to play volleyball

volleyeur, -euse [vɔlɛjœr, -øz] *n Sp* **(a)** volleyball player **(b)** *Tennis* volleyer

volontaire [vɔlɔ̃tɛr] **1** *adj* **(a)** (*délibéré*) (*action*) voluntary; **homicide v.** wilful murder, voluntary homicide; **acte v.** wilful act; **contribution v.** voluntary donation; *Mil* **engagé v.** volunteer **(b)** (*personne*) self-willed, wilful, headstrong, obstinate; **menton v.** firm *or* determined chin **2** *n* volunteer

volontairement [vɔlɔ̃tɛrmɑ̃] *adv* **(a)** voluntarily, willingly **(b)** (*délibérément*) deliberately, intentionally

volontariat [vɔlɔ̃tarja] *nm Mil etc* voluntary service; **faire du v.** to do voluntary service

volontarisme [vɔlɔ̃tarism] *nm* **(a)** resoluteness, aggressiveness; **faire preuve de davantage de v.** to be more aggressive **(b)** *Phil* voluntarism

volontariste [vɔlɔ̃tarist] *adj* **(a)** (*politique, attitude*) aggressive **(b)** *Phil* voluntaristic, voluntarist

volonté [vɔlɔ̃te] *nf* **(a)** (*faculté de décision*) will; **la v. de vaincre/de puissance** the will to win/for power; **v. de fer** will of iron, iron will; **avoir une v. de fer** to be iron-willed, to have a will of iron *or* an iron will; **circonstances indépendantes de notre v.** circumstances beyond our control; **par un effort de la v.** by an effort of will; **de sa propre v.** of one's own accord, spontaneously; **manque de v.** lack of will(power); **ne pas avoir de v.** to have no will of one's own, to have no willpower; **elle n'a aucune v.** she has no willpower; **avec la meilleure v. du monde** with the best will in the world; **arriver à qch à coups** *ou* **à force de v.** to achieve sth by sheer willpower; **bonne v.** willingness; **faire preuve de bonne v.** to show willing(ness); **personne de bonne v.** willing person; **homme de bonne v.** (*pour une entreprise dangereuse etc*) volunteer; **mauvaise v.** unwillingness; **faire preuve de mauvaise v.** to show unwillingness, to be grudging; **personne de mauvaise v.** unwilling *or* grudging person; **elle montre toujours de la bonne v.** she always shows willing; **faire qch de bonne/mauvaise v.** to do sth willingly/unwillingly *or* with good/bad grace; **elle y met de la mauvaise v.** she's doing it with very bad grace; **en faire à sa v.** to have one's own way; **à v.** at will; **dessert à v.** as much dessert as you like, unlimited dessert; **vin à v.** (*dans un restaurant*) (drink) as much wine as you like; *Culin* **ajouter du sucre à v.** add sugar to taste; *Fin* **billet payable à v.** promissory note payable on demand; *Mil* **feu à v.** fire at will

(b) (*souhait*) wish; **accomplir la v. de qn** to carry out sb's wish; **faire qch contre la v. de qn** to do sth against sb's will; **les dernières volontés de qn** (*document*) sb's last will and testament; (*vœux*) sb's last wishes; **dire sa v. de réussir/progresser** to express a wish to succeed/advance; **il fait ses quatre volontés** he does just what he pleases; **elle lui fait faire ses quatre volontés** she can twist him round her little finger

volontiers [vɔlɔ̃tje] *adv* **(a)** (*avec plaisir*) willingly, gladly, with pleasure; **très v.** I'd be glad to, I'd love to; **prenez du vin – oui, très v.** have some wine – I'd love some; **je prendrais v. un verre de vin** I could do with *or* I'd love a glass of wine; **il cause v.** he is fond of talking; **elle en parle v.** she will happily talk about it; **vous venez? – (oui,) v.** are you coming? – yes, I'd love to; **je le ferai le plus v. du monde** I'll be absolutely delighted *or* it'll give me the greatest pleasure to do so **(b)** (*facilement*) readily; **on croit v. que …** we are apt to think that …

volt [vɔlt] *nm Él* volt

voltage [vɔltaʒ] *nm Él* voltage

voltaïque [vɔltaik] *adj Él* (*cellule, pile*) voltaic

voltaire [vɔltɛr] *nm* chair with a low seat and a high back

voltairien, -ienne [vɔltɛrjɛ̃, -jɛn] *adj, n* Voltairian

voltamètre [vɔltamɛtr] *nm Él* voltameter

voltampère [vɔltɑ̃pɛr] *nm Él* voltampere

volte [vɔlt] *nf* **(a)** *Équitation, Escrime* volt **(b)** *Naut* (*changement de cap*) turn

volte-face [vɔlt(ə)fas] *nf inv* **(a)** about-turn, *Am* about-face; **faire v.** to turn round **(b)** *Fig* about-turn, U-turn, *Litt* volte-face, *Am* about-face; **faire v.** to do a U-turn *or* an about-turn *or Am* -face

volter [vɔlte] *vi Équitation* **faire v. un cheval** to make a horse circle

voltige [vɔltiʒ] *nf* (*au cirque*), *Équitation* acrobatics; (*sur trapèze*) flying-trapeze exercises; *Av* aerobatics; *Équitation* **haute v.** trick riding; *Av* **pilote de v.** stunt pilot; *Fig* **c'est de la haute v. intellectuelle** it's intellectual acrobatics *or* gymnastics

voltiger [vɔltiʒe] *vi* (**je voltigeai(s); n. voltigeons**) **(a)** (*sur trapèze*) to do acrobatics, to perform on the flying trapeze; (*sur cheval*) to do acrobatics, to perform on horseback **(b)** (*d'un oiseau, d'un insecte*) to fly about, to flutter (about); (*d'un rideau, d'un drapeau etc*) to flutter, to flap

voltigeur, -euse [vɔltiʒœr, -øz] **1** *n* (*au cirque*) acrobat; (*sur trapèze*) trapeze artist; (*sur cheval*) performer on horseback **2** *nm Mil Arch* light infantryman, rifleman

voltmètre [vɔltmɛtr] *nm Él* voltmeter

volubile [vɔlybil] *adj* **(a)** *Bot* voluble; (*tige*) twining **(b)** (*person*) voluble

volubilis [vɔlybilis] *nm Bot* convolvulus; **v. des jardins** morning glory

volubilité [vɔlybilite] *nf* volubility; **parler avec v.** to be a voluble talker, to talk volubly

volucompteur [vɔlykɔ̃tœr] *nm* volume indicator
volume [vɔlym] *nm* **(a)** (*livre*) volume; **il faudrait des volumes pour raconter …** it would take volumes to relate …
(b) (*d'un solide, d'un fluide*) volume, bulk, mass; **v. excessif** (*d'un paquet etc*) bulkiness; **v. d'achat** purchase volume; **v. des affaires** volume of business; **v. annuel de production** annual (volume of) production; **le v. des échanges commerciaux** the volume of trade; *Com* **v. de point mort** break-even quantity; **v. des ventes** sales volume, volume of sales; *Naut* **chargé en v.** laden in bulk; **faire du v.** (*d'une chose*) to take up a lot of space; *F* (*d'une personne*) to show off, to throw one's weight about
(c) (*du son, de la voix*) volume; **baisser/monter le v.** to turn the sound *or* volume down/up; **v. sonore** noise level
(d) (*de réservoirs etc*) capacity
volumétrique [vɔlymetrik] *adj* volumetric
volumineux, -euse [vɔlyminø, -øz] *adj* voluminous, bulky, large; **très peu v.** taking up little space; **dossier v.** bulky file
volupté [vɔlypte] *nf* (sensual) pleasure *or* delight; **toutes les voluptés** every pleasurable sensation; **la v. de la revanche accomplie** the sweet taste of revenge; **avec v.** with (sensual) delight
voluptueusement [vɔlyptɥøzmɑ̃] *adv* voluptuously
voluptueux, -euse [vɔlyptɥø, -øz] **1** *adj* voluptuous **2** *n* voluptuary, sensualist
volute [vɔlyt] *nf* **(a)** *Archit etc* helix; (*d'un violon*) scroll; (*de fumée*) curl, spiral, wreath; **la fumée s'élève en v.** the smoke is spiralling upwards; **ressort en v.** helical spring **(b)** (*de coquillage*) whorl
vomer [vɔmɛr] *nm Anat* vomer
vomi [vɔmi] *nm* vomit, *F* sick
vomique [vɔmik] *adj Bot, Pharm* **noix v.** nux vomica
vomiquier [vɔmikje] *nm Bot* nux vomica (tree)
vomir [vɔmir] **1** *vt* **(a)** (*nourriture*) to vomit, to bring up, to spew up **(b)** (*d'une cheminée, d'un volcan etc*) (*fumée, flammes etc*) to vomit, to belch forth, to spew out; **v. des insultes** *ou* **des injures sur qn** to heap insults *or* abuse on sb **(c)** *Fig* (*qn*) to loathe, *Fml* to abhor **2** *vi* to be sick, *F* to throw up; **avoir envie de v.** to feel sick *or Am* nauseous; **c'est à (faire) v.** it's enough to make you sick; **une odeur à vous faire v.** a nauseating smell
vomissement [vɔmismɑ̃] *nm* **(a)** (*action*) vomiting; **il fut pris de vomissements** he started vomiting *or* to vomit **(b)** (*matière*) vomit, *F* sick
vomissure [vɔmisyr] *nf* vomit, *F* sick
vomitif, -ive [vɔmitif, -iv] *adj, nm Méd* emetic, vomitory
vorace [vɔras] *adj* voracious; (*appétit*) voracious, ravenous; **se sentir d'un appétit v.** to feel ravenously hungry; **plante v.** heavy feeder
voracement [vɔrasmɑ̃] *adv* voraciously
voracité [vɔrasite] *nf* voracity, voraciousness
vortex [vɔrtɛks] *nm* vortex
vos [vo] *adj poss voir* **votre**
vosgien, -ienne [voʒjɛ̃, -jɛn] **1** *adj* (of/from the) Vosges **2** *n* **V.** (*natif*) native of the Vosges; (*habitant*) inhabitant of the Vosges
votant, -ante [vɔtɑ̃, -ɑ̃t] *n* voter
vote [vɔt] *nm* **(a)** vote; (*action*) voting, ballot(ing), poll; **droit de v.** right to vote, franchise; **accorder le droit de v. aux femmes** to give women the vote; **prendre part au v.** to go to the polls, to vote; **bulletin de v.** ballot paper; **section de v.** polling district *or* station; **v. direct/indirect** direct/indirect vote; **v. à bulletin secret** secret ballot; **v. à main levée** vote by (a) show of hands; **v. par procuration** vote by proxy, proxy (vote) **(b)** *Parl* **v. d'une loi** passing of a bill; **provoquer un v.** to challenge a division; **v. de confiance** vote of confidence
voter [vɔte] **1** *vi* to vote; **v. à main levée** to vote by (a) show of hands; **v. pour/contre un projet de loi** to vote for/against a bill; **v. communiste** to vote communist; **v. (pour) Thomas!** vote for Thomas! **2** *vt* **(a)** *Parl* (*loi*) to pass, to carry; **v. une proposition** to vote in favour of a proposal **(b)** (*crédit etc*) to vote; **v. des remerciements à qn** to offer sb a vote of thanks
votif, -ive [vɔtif, -iv] *adj* (*offrande, messe*) votive
votre, vos [vɔtr, vo] *adj poss* [①A30,8; B19-20,E,1] **(a)** your; **v. oncle et v. tante** your aunt and (your) uncle; **v. père et v. mère,** *Litt* **vos père et mère** your mother and father; **j'ai mis v. chapeau et vos gants** I put on your hat and (your) gloves; **mettez v. chapeau et vos gants** (*à une personne*) put on your hat and gloves; (*à plusieurs personnes*) put on your hats and gloves; **un(e) de vos ami(e)s** one of your friends, a friend of yours; **un professeur de vos amis** a teacher friend of yours; *F* **vous aurez v. chambre à vous** (*chacun aura sa chambre*) you will have your own rooms; *F* **v. imbécile de frère** your idiot of a brother; *F* **v. artiste de mari** your artist husband; *F* **vous avez v. vendredi** you've got Friday off; *F* **alors, c'était ça vos vancances de rêve!** so much for your dream holiday! **(b)** (*pour s'adresser à qn*) **V. Altesse** Your Highness; **V. Majesté** Your Majesty
vôtre [votr] **1** *pron poss* [①A30,8; B20,E,2] **le v./la v./les vôtres** yours; **vous me prêtez le v.?** can I borrow yours?; **il ressemble au v.** it looks like yours; **vous voulez bien nous donner du v.?** can we have some of yours?; **de toutes ces solutions, préférez-vous la v.?** out of those possible solutions, do you prefer yours *or* your own?; **vous n'en avez pas besoin, vous avez le v.** you don't need it, you've got your own; **les deux vôtres** your two, the two *or* both of yours; (*en insistant*) your own two; **vous lui avez laissé deux des vôtres** you gave him two of yours; (*vous lui en avez sacrifié deux*) you gave him two of your own; *très F* **le v. de bébé est plus intelligent!** your baby is more intelligent; *F* **à la v.!** (*en buvant*) cheers!; *F* **à la bonne v.!** good health!
2 *nm* **le v.** (*ce qui vous appartient*) yours; **vous devriez y mettre du v.** you should do your share
3 *nmpl* **les vôtres** (*votre famille*) your family, *Am* your folks; (*vos partisans*) your followers; (*vos coéquipiers*) your team-mates; **je serai des vôtres ce soir** I'll be with you *or* joining you tonight; **je bois à vous et aux vôtres** I drink to you and yours
4 *adj poss Litt* yours; **un v. cousin** a cousin of yours; **vous ferez v. nos principes** you will adopt our principles as your own; **ferez-vous vôtres les félicitations qu'ils nous adressent?** will you join them in congratulating us?; **bien sincèrement v.** with kindest regards; **amicalement v.** best wishes
vouer [vwe] **1** *vt* to dedicate, to consecrate; **v. obéissance au roi** to pledge allegiance to the king; **toute l'affection que nous lui avons vouée** all the affection we gave him; **v. sa vie à l'étude** to devote *or* dedicate *or* give up one's life to study; **voué à l'échec** doomed to failure **2 se vouer** *vpr* **se v. à l'étude** to devote oneself to study; *F* **il ne sait (pas) à quel saint se v.** he's at his wits' end, he doesn't know which way to turn
vouloir[1] [vulwar] *nm* will; **bon/mauvais v.** goodwill/ill will (**pour, envers** towards); **cela dépendra de son bon v.** it will depend on how he feels
vouloir[2] (*prp* **voulant**; *pp* **voulu**; *pr ind* **je veux, il veut, n. voulons, ils veulent**; *pr sub* **je veuille, n. voulions, ils veuillent**; *imp* **voulez**, *otherwise* **veuille, veuillez**; *impf* **je voulais**; *p hist* **je voulus**; *fu* **voudrai**) **1** *vt* [①B37,K,4] **(a)** (*désirer*) (*qch*) to want, *Fml* to wish (for), to desire; **v. la paix/la guerre** to want peace/war; **elle sait ce qu'elle veut** she knows what she wants, she knows her own mind, she has a mind of her own; **faites comme vous voudrez** do as you please *or* like *or* wish; **c'est comme vous voudrez** just as you like; **vous le ferez, je le veux!** you shall do it!; **qu'il le veuille ou non** whether he likes it or not; **je ne le veux pas!** I will not have it!; **que voulez-vous?, qu'est-ce que vous voulez?** what do you want?; (*qu'est-ce que vous croyez?*) what do you expect?; **que voulez-vous que j'y fasse?** what do you want me to do about it?; **il veut tout faire par lui-même, que voulez-vous!** he wants to do everything by himself, what can you do!; **tu n'écoutes jamais ce qu'on te dit, que veux-tu!** you never listen to what people tell you, what can you expect?; **v. qch de qn** to want sth from sb; **que lui voulez-vous?** what do you want from him?; (*pourquoi le cherchez-vous?*) what do you want him for?; **combien en voulez-vous?** how much are you asking *or* do you want for it?; **voulez-vous du thé?** would you like some tea?; **v. de qch** to want (some of) sth; **je ne veux pas de cela** I'll have none of that; **je ne veux pas de ça chez moi** I won't have that in my house; **ils ne veulent pas de moi** they don't want me; **en voulez-vous?** do you want any?, will you have some?, would you like some?; **ils ont de l'argent en veux-tu, en voilà** they're not short of money, they've got money to spare; **v. qn pour roi** to want sb for (a) king *or* as king; **je te veux heureux** I want you to be happy; **v. du bien à qn** to wish sb well; **je ne lui veux pas de mal** I mean him no harm; **en v.** to be very determined *or* ambitious; **en v. à qn** to bear sb a grudge; **à qui en voulez-vous?** what's the trouble now?; **pourquoi lui en veux-tu?** what have you got against him?; **tu ne m'en veux pas, au moins?** I hope you don't hold it against me; **ils en veulent à mon argent** they're after my money; **ne m'en veuillez pas** don't be cross with me, don't hold it against me; **en v. à qn de qch/d'avoir fait qch** to have *or* hold *or* bear a grudge against sb for sth/for doing sth
(b) (*avec force*) to will; **ce que Dieu veut** the will of God; **ce que femme veut, Dieu le veut** when a woman's made up her mind …; **Dieu le veuille!** please God!; **vous l'avez voulu!** you have only yourself to blame!

(c) v. + *inf* *(expressed or understood)*, **v. que +** *sub* to require, to demand, to will; *(avoir envie de)* to want, to wish; *(essayer de)* *(faire qch)* to try to; *(avoir l'intention de)* to intend, to mean; **elle veut que nous venions tous** she wants us all to come; **v. dire** to mean; **je me demande ce que veut dire ce mot** I wonder what this word means; **ça ne veut rien dire, tout ça** that doesn't mean a thing; **mais qu'est-ce que ça veut dire, cette absence?** what's the meaning of this absence?; **le sort voulut qu'il mourût** fate willed *or* ordained that he should die; **le mauvais sort voulut qu'il arrivât trop tard** as ill luck would have it he arrived too late; **je veux être obéi!** I intend *or* mean to be obeyed!, I will be obeyed!; **v. absolument** *ou* **à toute force faire qch** to insist on doing sth, to be determined to do sth; **elle veut absolument y être demain** she is determined to be *or* is set on being there tomorrow; **je veux absolument que vous veniez** I insist on your coming; **le moteur ne veut pas démarrer** the engine won't start; **il voulait me frapper** he wanted to hit me; **elle voulut me frapper** she made as if to strike me; **quand j'ai voulu l'embrasser** when I tried to kiss him; **elle ne voulait pas s'en aller** she didn't want to go; **mais tu ne veux pas nous laisser un peu tranquilles!** will you (just) leave us alone!; **je fais de lui ce que je veux** I can do as I like with him; **j'aurais tant voulu le voir** I should so much like to have seen him; **j'aurais voulu y rester toujours** I would *or* could have stayed there for ever; **je voudrais bien être à votre place** I wish I were in your place; **je voudrais bien qu'on me le demande, à moi** I wish they'd ask me; **voulez-vous prendre une douche?** would you like to take a shower?; **voulez-vous que j'ouvre la fenêtre?** shall I *or* should I open the window?, would you like me to *or* do you want me to open the window?; **je veux que vous sachiez que ...** I should like you to know that ...; **j'aurais voulu qu'elle le sache** I wish she had been told; **je voudrais le voir me parler sur ce ton** I'd like to see him speak to me in that tone of voice; **je veux que vous soyez heureux** I want you to be happy; **je veux que les choses marchent pour vous** I want things to work out for you; **que voulez-vous que je fasse?** what do you expect *or* want me to do?; **rentrons, voulez-vous?** let's go in, shall we?; **nous n'avons jamais su ce qu'elle voulait faire** we never knew what she meant to do; **faire qch sans le v.** to do sth unintentionally *or* without meaning to *or* without meaning it; **si je t'ai blessé, c'est vraiment sans le v.** if I hurt you, it really was unintentional *or* I really didn't mean to

(d) v. (bien) faire qch to consent *or* be willing to do sth; **oui, je veux bien** yes, with pleasure; **je veux bien que vous veniez** I'm quite willing for you to come; **voulez-vous bien attendre un instant?** would you (please) wait *or* would you care to wait a moment?; **veuillez (bien) vous asseoir** please sit down; *(plus poli)* do (please) sit down, won't you sit down?; **voulez-vous faire moins de bruit!** would you mind making less noise!, will you please make less noise!; **veuillez agréer, Madame, l'expression de mes sentiments distingués/dévoués** yours sincerely; **je veux bien attendre** I'm quite happy *or* quite willing to wait; **si vous voulez** if you like, *Fml* if you wish; **je viens quand je veux** I come when I choose *or* like *or* please; **si vous (le) voulez bien** if you don't mind

(e) (bien *used as an intensive***) voulez-vous bien vous taire!** will you be quiet!, *F* do shut up!

(f) *(admettre)* *(qch, dans une argumentation)* to admit, to allow; **vous n'avez rien à vous reprocher, je le veux bien, mais ...** you are in no way to blame, I am ready to admit *or* I grant you, but ...; **je veux bien, mais ...** I understand, but ..., fair enough, but ...

(g) *(soutenir)* to be convinced, to maintain; **il veut absolument que je me sois trompé** he insists that I was mistaken

(h) *(d'une chose)* *(qch)* to require, to need, to demand; **la vigne veut un terrain crayeux** vines need *or* require a chalky soil; **ce verbe veut l'accusatif** this verb takes the accusative

2 se vouloir *vpr* **(a) elle se veut différente** she likes to think she's different; **il se voulait rassurant** he was trying to be reassuring

(b) s'en v. to be angry *or* annoyed with oneself **(de qch** about sth); **je m'en veux énormément de lui avoir fait de la peine** I feel really bad about hurting her

3 *vi* to want; **il ne suffit pas de v.** it's not enough just to want something; *Prov* **v., c'est pouvoir** where there's a will there's a way; *F* **je veux!** *(je suis entièrement d'accord)* you bet!, and how!

voulu [vuly] *adj* **(a)** *(formalités etc)* required, requisite; **cela se fera à l'heure voulue** it will be done in due course; **en temps v.** in due course, eventually **(b)** *(délibéré)* deliberate, intentional; **c'était v. de sa part** he did it deliberately *or* intentionally

vous [vu] *pron pers, sing, pl* [①A26,a-b; B17-18,1-2; B64,6] **(a)** *(subjet)* you; **v. et votre femme** you and your wife; **v. deux** you two, the two of you, you both, both of you; **v. tous** you all, all of you; **v. autres Anglais** you English; **c'est v. qui êtes arrivé le premier/arrivés les premiers** it was you who arrived first, you arrived first; **c'était v.-même qui me l'avez dit** you told me so yourself; **v., v. avez raison, v. avez raison, v.** you're the one who's right

(b) *(objet)* you; *(objet indirect)* to you; **il ne v. connaît pas** he doesn't know you; **je v. en ai parlé** I've spoken to you about it; **c'est à v. que je parle** it's you I'm talking to; **c'est à v. que je pensais** it's you I was thinking about; **c'est à v. de jouer** it's your turn (to play); **ces gants sont à v.** these gloves are yours; **c'est un ami à v.** it's a friend of yours; **voilà une photo de v.** here's a photo of you; **j'ai confiance en v.** I trust you

(c) [①A29; B26,D] *(réfléchi)* **v. êtes-v. bien amusé(e)/amusé(e)s?** did you enjoy yourself/yourselves?; **v. allez v. faire du mal** you're going to hurt yourself/yourselves; **taisez-v.!** be quiet!; **v. les avez rassemblés autour de v.** you gathered them round you; **v. ne pensez qu'à v.(-même)** you think only of yourself; **v. le dîtes/le savez v.-même** you say so/know yourself

(d) *(réciproque)* **est-ce que v. v. connaissez?** do you know each other *or* one another?

(e) *(pour remplacer* **on***)* you, *Fml* one; **c'est désagréable quand on ne v. reconnaît pas** it's annoying when people don't recognize you

vous-même(s) *pron pers* yourself, *pl* yourselves; *voir* **vous, même**

vousseau, -eaux [vuso] *nm*, **voussoir** [vuswar] *nm Archit* voussoir, archstone

voussure [vusyr] *nf Archit* *(d'une arche)* curve, arch moulding

voûte [vut] *nf Archit* vault, arch; **v. d'arête** groined vault; **v. en berceau** barrel vault; **v. d'ogives** ribbed vault; **v. en plein cintre** semicircular vault; **voûte(s) en éventail** fan vaulting; **en v.** vaulted

▶ **voûte**: *Litt* **la v. céleste** the vault *or* canopy of heaven; **v. crânienne** dome of the skull; **v. du palais, v. palatine** roof of the mouth; **v. plantaire** arch (of the foot)

voûté [vute] *adj* *(toit etc)* vaulted, arched; *(personne)* stooping, round-shouldered; *(dos)* bent; **j'ai toujours eu le dos v.** I've always had a stoop

voûter [vute] **1** *vt* *(toit etc)* to arch, to vault; **l'âge a voûté son dos** age has bowed his back *or* made him stoop **2 se voûter** *vpr* to become bent *or* bowed *or* round-shouldered, to begin to stoop

vouvoiement [vuvwamɑ̃] *nm* = addressing people as 'vous' *(as opposed to 'tu')*; **le v. est de rigueur au bureau** people must address each other as 'vous' in the office

vouvoyer [vuvwaje] *vt* *(pr ind* **je vouvoie, n. vouvoyons**; *fu*
je vouvoierai) *(qn)* to say 'vous' to, to address as 'vous' *(as*
opposed to 'tu')

voyage [vwajaʒ] *nm* journey, trip; *(circuit)* tour; **v. en chem**
de fer rail(way) journey; **v. (sur mer)** (sea) voyage;
(touristique) accompagné conducted *or* guided t
(excursion) escorted tour; **il ne sera pas du v.** he wo
making the journey; **aimer les voyages** to be fond of
or of travelling; **livre de v.** travel book; **récit de v.**
story; *Rad* travelogue; **v. autour du monde** wor
round-the-world trip; **faire un v. autour du mon**
round the world, to go on a world tour *or* on a r
world trip; **les gens du v.** travelling people, trave
est en v. she is travelling; **est-il toujours en v.?**
away, is he still on his travels?; **partir en v.** to
journey; **bateau engagé au v.** ship hired by the
v. travelling expenses; **compagnon de**
companion; *(dans voiture etc)* fellow passe
have a good trip!; **ça va t'obliger à faire deu**
way you'll need to make two trips; **je n'au**
pour rien I won't have made the trip for
have been a wasted journey; *Litt* **faire le**
one's last journey

▶ **voyage**: **v. d'affaires** business trip; **être**
be away on business; **partir en v. d'affa**
business trip; **v. d'agrément** pleasure
journey; **v. aller-retour** round trip; **v.**
voyages en autocar coach travel;
travel; **v. d'études** study tri
familiarization tour; **v. de familia**
trip; **v. à forfait** inclusive tour, p

tour, all-in tour; **v. d'information** fact-finding mission *or* tour; **voyages en mer** sea travel; **v. de noces** honeymoon; **nous sommes partis en v. de noces en Guadeloupe** we went to Guadeloupe on *or* for our honeymoon; **v. organisé** package holiday *or* tour, inclusive tour; **v. de presse** press trip; **v. professionnel** business trip; **voyages professionnels** business travel; **v. retour** return journey; **v. scolaire** school trip; **v. de stimulation** incentive trip *or* tour

voyager [vwajaʒe] *vi* **(je voyageai(s); n. voyageons)** **(a)** to travel; **v. par mer/par chemin de fer** to travel by sea/by rail; **v. pour affaires** to travel on business **(b)** *Com* to travel, *F* to be on the road; **v. pour les vins** to travel in wine **(c)** (*de marchandises etc*) to be transported; **vin qui ne peut pas v.** wine that does not travel; **ce produit voyage très bien** this product travels very well

voyageur, -euse [vwajaʒœr, -øz] **1** *n* **(a)** traveller, *US* traveler; (*en train etc*) passenger; (*en taxi*) fare **(b)** *surtout Hist* (*aventurier*) voyager, explorer **(c)** **v. (de commerce)** (commercial) traveller, travelling salesman, rep; **v. d'affaires** business traveller **2** *adj* **(a)** (*qui voyage souvent*) travelling; **commis v.** commercial traveller **(b)** **pigeon v.** carrier pigeon, homing pigeon

voyagiste [vwajaʒist] *n* tour operator; (*grossiste*) tour wholesaler

voyance [vwajɑ̃s] *nf* clairvoyance

voyant, -ante [vwajɑ̃, -ɑ̃t] **1** *adj* (*couleur*) gaudy, loud, garish; (*monument etc*) showy, conspicuous

2 *n* **(a)** (*contraire d'aveugle*) sighted person; **les voyants** the sighted

(b) (*qui perçoit le sens caché des choses*) seer, prophet

3 *nm* **(a)** (*signal*) (*indicator*) signal; (*pour arpenteur*) (*plaque de nivellement*) sighting board, slide vane, sight; *Naut* (*d'un bateau-phare*) sphere

(b) (*d'un instrument scientifique*) sighting slit, aperture

(c) *Aut* **v. (lumineux)** warning light; **v. d'huile/d'essence** oil/petrol indicator light; **v. de baisse de tension des piles** 'battery low' warning light; **v. de charge** battery charge warning light; **v. de frein à main** 'handbrake on' light; **v. de marche** activation light

4 *nf* **voyante extra-lucide** clairvoyant

voyelle [vwajɛl] *nf Ling* vowel

voyeur, -euse [vwajœr, -øz] *n* voyeur, *f* voyeuse, *m* Peeping Tom

voyeurisme [vwajœrism] *nm Psy* voyeurism

voyou [vwaju] **1** *nm* (*délinquant*) (young) lout, hooligan, *Br Sl* yob(bo); (*enfant*) (cheeky) street urchin, guttersnipe **2** *adj* (*often inv in f, sometimes* **voyoute**) crude, loutish

PC [vepese] *nf* (*abrév* **vente par correspondance**) mail order
…lling)

[vrak] *nm* **en v.** (thé) loose; **charger en v.** to load in
marchandises en v. (*non emballées*) loose goods;
en v. sold loose; **outils jetés en v. sur le plancher**
…wn higgledy-piggledy on the floor; **tout est posé**
…**a table** everything is lying higgledy-piggledy *or* in
…umbled together on my table; **elle a déposé ses**
…**sur la table** she dumped her things on the

…*dj* [①B10,D,3] **(a)** (*indéniable*) true; **c'est**
…hat's right!; **elle est gentille, c'est v.,**
…e's nice, I agree, but she's not very
…n't believe it!
…nuine; (*diamant*) real, genuine;
…(*déception, raison*) real; **elle a**
…she was really disappointed/
…**a été un v. père pour moi**
Anglais d'Angleterre an
…Englishman; **couleurs**
homme v. a genuine

c'est un v. clown
she's a real *or* a

…ite/paint/*etc*
à fait v.
…istic; **tu**
really
toi
or

…th from
. là-dedans
…n; **à v. dire, à**
…th; *F* **pour de v.**
…**ile ne le disait pas**
…us, she didn't (really) mean it; **on ne jouait pas pour de v.** we weren't playing for real *or* seriously; **c'est pour de v.** I'm serious, I (really) mean it; **c'est pour de v. cette fois** this time it's serious *or* for real

4 *n* **un homme, un v.** a real man; **c'est une infirmière, une vraie** she's a nurse, the real thing *or* the genuine article

vraiment [vrɛmɑ̃] *adv* really; **vous êtes v. trop bon** you are really too kind; **je ne sais pas v. ce que je vais faire** I don't really know what I'm going to do; **je ne savais v. pas quoi faire** I really didn't know what to do; **v.?** really?; **ils voyagent v. beaucoup** they really travel a lot, *Am* they do a real lot of travelling; **oui v.** yes indeed; **non merci, v.** no thank you, really

vraisemblable [vrɛsɑ̃blabl] **1** *adj* probable, likely; (*crédible*) credible; (*plausible*) plausible; **il n'est pas v. que** + *sub* it is hardly likely that; **excuse peu v.** implausible *or* unconvincing excuse **2** *nm* **le v.** what is probable *or* likely

vraisemblablement [vrɛsɑ̃blabləmɑ̃] *adv* probably, very likely; **nous devrions v. arriver vers 16 heures** we should probably arrive around 4pm

vraisemblance [vrɛsɑ̃blɑ̃s] *nf* probability, likelihood; **selon toute v.** in all probability

VRC [veɛrse] *nf Mktg* (*abrév* **vente par réseau coopté**) MLM, multilevel marketing

vrillage [vrijaʒ] *nm Aut* (*de la transmission*) wind-up

vrille [vrij] *nf* **(a)** *Bot* tendril **(b)** (*outil*) gimlet, borer, piercer; **yeux percés en v.** gimlet eyes, beady eyes **(c)** *Av* spin; **descente en v.** spinning dive; **faire la v., se mettre en v., tomber en v.** to go into a spin; **monter en v.** to corkscrew up; **v. à plat** flat spin; **v. serrée** steep spin; **v. sur le dos** inverted spin

vrillé [vrije] *adj* **(a)** (*percé*) bored into, pierced into **(b)** (*corde*) twisted, kinked **(c)** *Bot* with tendrils, tendrilled

vrillée [vrije] *nf Bot F* bindweed

vriller [vrije] **1** *vt* (*avec une vrille*) to bore **2** *vi* **(a)** (*d'un avion etc*) to spiral, to spin (up/down) **(b)** (*d'une corde, d'un fil*) to twist, to kink

vrillette [vrijɛt] *nf* deathwatch (beetle)

vrombir [vrɔ̃bir] *vi* (*des mouches etc*) to buzz; (*d'un avion, d'une toupie etc*) to hum; (*d'un moteur*) to roar

vrombissement [vrɔ̃bismɑ̃] *nm* (*d'insectes*) buzz(ing); (*d'un avion, d'une toupie etc*) hum(ming); (*d'un moteur*) roar(ing)

VRP [veɛrpe] *nm* (*abrév* **voyageur, représentant, placier**) sales representative, *F* rep; **V. multicarte** freelance rep

VSN [veɛsɛn] *nm* (*abrév* **volontaire du service national**) = recruit who chooses to carry out his national service by doing voluntary service overseas

VTT [vetete] *nm* (*abrév* **vélo tout-terrain**) mountain bike

vu [vy] **1** *nm* **(a) au vu de tous** openly, publicly; **au vu et au su de tous** openly and publicly; **c'est du déjà vu** that's nothing new; *Com* **sur le vu de la facture** on sight of the invoice **(b)** *Jur* (*d'un décret*) preamble **2** *prép* in view of, considering, seeing; **vu la chaleur je voyagerai de nuit** in view of *or* because of the heat, I'll travel by night; *F* **vu que … +** *ind* seeing that …; **vu qu'on te l'a déjà expliqué plusieurs fois** seeing that it's already been explained to you several times

vue [vy] *nf* **(a)** (*faculté de voir*) (eye)sight; **avoir des troubles de la v.** to have eye trouble; **perdre la v.** to lose one's sight; **avoir la v. courte** *ou* **basse** to be shortsighted; **avoir une bonne v.** to have good eyesight; **jeter** *ou* **porter la v. sur qch** to take a look at sth; **connaître qn de v.** to know sb by sight; **perdre qn de v.** to lose sight of sb; (*perdre contact*) to lose touch with sb; **nous nous sommes perdus de v. depuis cette période** since then, we've lost touch with each other; **à perte de v.** as far as the eye can see; **parler à perte de v.** to talk endlessly, to keep on talking; **personnes les plus en v.** people most in the public eye; **une personnalité en v.** a prominent *or* conspicuous personality; **mettre qch (bien) en v.** to display sth (conspicuously); *F* **en mettre plein la v. à qn** to impress *or* dazzle sb; **faire qch à la v. de tous** to do sth in sight *or* in full view of everybody; **se tenir hors de v.** to keep out of sight; *F* **à v. de nez** at a rough guess *or* estimate; **à v. d'œil** visibly; *Av, Naut* **navigation à v.** visual navigation; *Av* **voler à v.** to fly visually

(b) (*d'extra-lucide*) **seconde v.** second sight

(c) (*opinion*) view; **échange de vues** exchange of views; **c'est une v. de l'esprit** that's a very theoretical point of view

(d) **à la v. de qn/qch** at the sight of sb/sth; **à la v. du chien, elle se mit à paniquer** at the sight of *or* when she saw the dog, she began to panic; **à première v.** at first sight; *Fin* **à v.** at sight; *Com* **payable à v.** payable at sight; *Mus* **jouer un morceau à v.** to play a piece at sight; **à v.** *ou* **en v. de terre** (with)in sight of land

(e) (*panorama*) view, outlook; **chambre qui a v. sur le jardin** room that looks out on(to) the garden; **je voudrais une chambre avec v., s'il vous plaît** I'd like a room with a view, please; **vues de Paris** views of Paris; **v. aérienne** aerial view; *Phot* **v. fixe** slide; *Aut* **v. panoramique** all-round view; **v. de face/de côté** (*d'objet, de personne*) front/side view; **v. en coupe** cross section

(**f**) *Jur* (*d'une maison*) window, light; **droit de vues** ancient lights; **condamner les vues** to block up the windows

(**g**) (*intention*) intention, purpose, design; **avoir des vues sur qn/qch** to have plans for *or* designs on sb/sth; **elle a des vues sur mon frère** she has designs on my brother; **avoir qch en v.** to have sth in view *or* in mind; **je crois qu'il a déjà quelqu'un en v.** I think he's already got someone in mind; **en v. de** with a view to; **travailler en v. de l'avenir** to work with an eye to the future

Vulcain [vylkɛ̃] *nm* (**a**) *Myth, Astron* Vulcan (**b**) *Ent* **v.** red admiral (butterfly)

vulcanisation [vylkanizasjɔ̃] *nf Ind* vulcanization

vulcaniser [vylkanize] *vt Ind* (*caoutchouc*) to vulcanize

vulgaire [vylgɛr] **1** *adj* (**a**) *Péj* vulgar, common; **tenue v.** tarty *or* common outfit; **plaisanterie v.** vulgar joke; **cela la rend v.** it makes her look common (**b**) (*courant*) (*coutumes etc*) common, everyday; **l'opinion v.** the common *or* general opinion; **langue v.** vernacular; **le latin v.** vulgar Latin; **nom v.** (**d'une plante**) common name (for a plant); **expression v.** common *or* widely used expression (**c**) *Péj* **un v. poste de radio** a very ordinary *or* a common-or-garden radio **2** *nm* (**a**) **le v.** (*les gens*) the common people *or* herd (**b**) **donner dans le v.** to be vulgar; **tomber dans le v.** to lapse into vulgarity

vulgairement [vylgɛrmɑ̃] *adv* (**a**) *Péj* vulgarly; **parler v.** to be vulgar in one's speech; **s'habiller/se conduire v.** to dress/behave vulgarly *or* tastelessly (**b**) (*en général*) generally, commonly; **la fleur v. appelée bouton d'or** the flower commonly called the buttercup

vulgarisateur, -trice [vylgarizatœr, -tris] *n* popularizer

vulgarisation [vylgarizasjɔ̃] *nf* (*d'un savoir*) popularization; **ouvrage de v.** popular work

vulgariser [vylgarize] *vt* (*connaissance*) to popularize

vulgarisme [vylgarism] *nm* vulgarism

vulgarité [vylgarite] *nf* vulgarity

Vulgate (la) [lavylgat] *nf* the Vulgate (version of the Bible)

vulgum pecus [vylgɔmpekys] *nm F* **le v.** the hoi polloi, the rabble

vulnérabilité [vylnerabilite] *nf* vulnerability

vulnérable [vylnerabl] *adj* vulnerable

vulnéraire [vylnerɛr] *nf Bot* kidney vetch, lady's finger, woundwort

vulpin [vylpɛ̃] *nm Bot* foxtail (grass)

vulvaire[1] [vylvɛr] *adj Anat* vulvar

vulve [vylv] *nf Anat* vulva

vu-mètre, *pl* **vu-mètres** *nm Rad* VU meter, volume meter

W

W, w [dublәve] *nm inv* (lettre) W, w
W *Él* (*abrév* **watt**) w
wagnérien, -ienne [vagnerjɛ̃, -jɛn] *adj, n Mus* Wagnerian
wagon [vagɔ̃] *nm Rail* **(a)** (*véhicule*) (*de passagers*) carriage, coach, *Am* car; (*de marchandises*) truck, wagon, *Am* car; **w. de marchandises** goods van; **monter en w.** to get into *or* onto *or* to board the train; **w. à bagages** luggage van, *Am* baggage car; **w. à bestiaux** cattle truck, *Am* stock car; **w. frigorifique** refrigerated van **(b)** (*contenu*) truckload, wagonload, *Am* carload (**de** of)
wagon-bar, *pl* **wagons-bars** *nm Rail* buffet car
wagon-citerne, *pl* **wagons-citernes** *nm Rail* tank wagon *or Am* car
wagon-foudre, *pl* **wagons-foudres** *nm Rail* tank wagon *or Am* car
wagon-lit, *pl* **wagons-lits** *nm Rail* sleeping car, sleeper; **voyager en w.** to take a sleeper
wagonnet [vagɔnɛ] *nm* tip truck
wagonnier [vagɔnje] *nm Rail* truck *or Am* car shunter
wagon-poste, *pl* **wagons-poste** *nm Rail* mail van *or Am* car
wagon-réservoir, *pl* **wagons-réservoirs** *nm Rail* tank wagon *or Am* car
wagon-restaurant, *pl* **wagons-restaurants** *nm Rail* dining *or* buffet car, *Br* restaurant car
wahhabite [waabit] *adj, n* Wahhabi
Walhalla [valala] *nm Myth* Valhalla
walkman® [wɔkman] *nm* Walkman
walk(-)over [wɔlkɔvœr] *nm Sp, Courses de chevaux* walk-over
Walkyrie [valkiri] *nf Myth* Valkyrie, Walkyrie; *Hum Fig* **une w.** an Amazon
wallaby [walabi], *pl* **wallabies** *nm* wallaby
wallingant, -ante [walɛ̃gɑ̃, -ɑ̃t] *n Péj* Walloon separatist
wallon, -onne [walɔ̃, -ɔn] **1** *adj* Walloon **2** *nm Ling* Walloon **3** *n* **W.** Walloon
wapiti [wapiti] *nm Zool* wapiti, American elk
warrant [warɑ̃t, va-] *nm Com, Jur* (warehouse) warrant, warehouse receipt; **w. en marchandises** produce warrant; *Com* **w. cédule** warrant
warrantage [warɑ̃taʒ, va-] *nm Com* securing goods by warrant
warranté [warɑ̃te, va-] *adj* **marchandises warrantées** goods covered by a warehouse warrant
warranter [warɑ̃te, va-] *vt Com* to secure by warrant, to warrant
wassingue [wasɛ̃g] *nf* (*dans le Nord de la France*) floorcloth
water-closet, *pl* **water-closets** [watɛrklɔzɛt] *nm* lavatory, toilet
watergang [watɛrgɑ̃g] *nm* (*dans le Nord de la France, en Belgique*) polder channel
wateringue [watәrɛ̃g] *nf HydE* (*dans le Nord de la France, en Belgique*) draining works
water-polo [watɛrpolo] *nm Sp* water polo
waterproof [watɛrpruf] *adj inv* waterproof
waters [watɛr, va-] *nmpl* lavatory, toilet; **où sont les w.?** where is the lavatory *or* toilet?
watt [wat] *nm Él* watt
watt-heure, *pl* **watts-heures** *nm Él* watt-hour
wattman [watman], *pl* **wattmen** [watmɛn] *nm Vieilli* (*d'un tramway électrique*) driver
wattmètre [watmɛtr] *nm Él* wattmeter
W.-C. [vese, dublәvese] *nmpl* lavatory, toilet
week-end, *pl* **week-ends** [wikɛnd] *nm* weekend; **partir en w.** to go away for the weekend
western [wɛstɛrn] *nm Cin* western; **w.-spaghetti** spaghetti western
Westphalie [ves(t)fali] *nf* Westphalia
wharf [warf] *nm* wharf
whig [wig] *adj, nm Hist* Whig
whisky, *pl* **whiskies** [wiski] *nm* whisky; (*irlandais, américain*) whiskey; **un w.-coca** a whisky and Coke®; **verre à w.** whisky glass
whist [wist] *nm* whist; **w. de Gand** solo (whist)
white-spirit, *pl* **white-spirits** [wajtspirit] *nm* white spirit
wigwam [wigwam] *nm* wigwam
william(s) [wiljam(s)] *nf* Williams pear; **poire-w.** Williams pear
winch [wintʃ] *nm Naut* winch
winchester [winʃɛster] *nf* Winchester (rifle)
Windsurf® [winsœrf] *nm* (*marque de planche à voile*) Windsurfer®
windsurfiste [winsœrfist] *n* windsurfer
wishbone [wiʃbon] *nm* (*de planche à voile*) wishbone boom
wisigoth, -othe [vizigo, -ɔt] *Hist* **1** *adj* Visigothic **2** *n* **W.** Visigoth
wolfram [vɔlfram] *nm Minér* wolfram
wolof [wɔlɔf] *adj, nm Ling* Wolof
wombat [wɔ̃ba] *nm* wombat
woofer [wufœr] *nm* (*haut-parleur*) woofer
wurtembergeois, -oise [vyrtɛ̃bɛrʒwa, -waz] **1** *adj* of/from Würtemberg **2** *n* **W.** Würtemberger
wysiwyg [wiziwig] *adj, nm Ordinat* WYSIWYG

X, x [iks] *nm inv* (**a**) (*lettre*) X, x (**b**) (*nombre inconnu, personne inconnue*) X, x; **Monsieur X** Mr X; **je vous l'ai dit x fois** I've told you umpteen times *or* a thousand times; **dans x années** in X number of years; **plainte contre X** suit against person or persons unknown (**c**) *Méd* **rayons X** X-rays (**d**) *Univ F* **l'X** the École polytechnique; **un X** a student at the École polytechnique (**e**) *Cin* **film classé X** adults-only *or* X-rated film

xanthome [gzɑ̃tom] *nm Méd* fatty lump, *Spéc* xanthome

xanthophylle [gzɑ̃tɔfil] *nf Bot* xanothophyll

xénon [gsenɔ̃] *nm Ch* xenon

xénophobe [gsenɔfɔb] **1** *adj* xenophobic **2** *n* xenophobe

xénophobie [gsenɔfɔbi] *nf* xenophobia

Xénophon [gzenɔfɔ̃] *nm* Xenophon

xérès [kerɛs, gzerɛs] **1** *nm* (*vin*) sherry **2** *n* **X.** (*ville*) Jerez

xérophile [gserɔfil] *adj Bot* xerophilous

xérophyte [gserɔfit] *nf Bot* xerophyte

Xerxès [gzɛrsɛs] *nm* Xerxes

xiphoïde [gsifɔid] *adj Anat* **appendice x.** xiphoid process

xiphophore [gsifɔfɔr] *nm* (*poisson*) sword-tail

xylène [gsilɛn] *nm Ch* xylene

xylographe [gsilɔgraf] *n* wood-engraver, *Spéc* xylographer

xylographie [gsilɔgrafi] *nf* (**a**) (*technique*) wood-engraving, *Spéc* xylography (**b**) (*gravure*) woodcut, *Spéc* xylograph

xylophage [gzilɔfaʒ] *Zool* **1** *adj* wood-eating **2** *nm* wood-eater

xylophone [ksilɔfɔn, gz-] *nm Mus* xylophone

Y

Y, y[1] [igrek] *nm inv* (*lettre*) Y, y

y[2] [i] [①B18-19,4] **1** *adv* (*lieu*) there; **est-il à Paris? – oui, il y est** is he in Paris? – yes, he is (there); **je ne m'y sentais pas très bien, dans cette ville** I didn't feel very happy in that town; **j'y suis, j'y reste!** here I am and here I stay!; **je n'y suis pour personne** I'm not at home to anybody; *F* **ah, j'y suis!** ah, now I've got *or* I get it; **excusez-moi, je n'y étais pas du tout** I'm sorry, I didn't get that at all; **vous n'y êtes pas du tout** you're way off the mark; **pendant que vous y êtes** while you're at *or* about it; *Iron* **non mais fouille dans mes affaires pendant que tu y es!** just rummage through my things, why don't you!

2 *pron inv* **(a) j'y pense sans cesse** I think about it constantly; **l'aider? tu n'y penses pas!** help him? what are you thinking of?; **vous y avez tout intérêt** you'd be well advised to; **je n'y comprends rien** I can't make head nor tail of it; **tu as l'air de t'y connaître en informatique** you seem to know quite a bit about computers *or* what you're doing when it comes to computers; **je ne m'y connais pas du tout** I don't know the slightest thing about it/them; **tu peux lui faire confiance, il s'y connaît** you can trust him, he knows what he's doing; **j'y gagnerai** I'll gain by it; **n'y compte pas** don't count on it; **je m'y attendais** I expected as much; **ça, on pouvait s'y attendre** it was to be expected; **venez nous voir – je n'y manquerai pas** come and see us – I certainly shall *or* I'll do that

(b) (*standing for person just mentioned*) **pensez-vous encore à lui? – oui, j'y pense sans cesse** do you still think of him? – yes I do, all the time; **les femmes? je n'y comprends rien** women? I don't understand them

3 (*indeterminate uses*) **je vous y prends!** caught you!; **ça y est, on peut manger/elle est prête** OK, we can eat/she's ready; **ça y est, j'ai une idée!** I've had an idea!; **alors ça y est, tu as fini?** have you finished?; **ça y est, la vitre est cassée!** I knew it, they've broken the window!; **ça y est, j'ai trouvé!** (*solution*) I've got it!; **ça y est enfin, je l'ai retrouvé!** I've found it at last!; **j'y suis pour un tiers** I'm in for a third; **elle n'y est pour rien** she's got nothing to do with it; **il y est pour quelque chose** he's got a hand in it, he's got something to do with it; **il doit y être pour une bonne part** (*dans une décision*) he must have had a lot to do with it; **j'ai tout mangé, y compris les légumes** I've eaten everything, including the vegetables

4 (*imperative form preceding* **y** *takes s for liaison*) **vas-y** [vazi] go there; (*agis*) go on!, get on with it!; **penses-y** [pɑ̃szi] think about it

y[3] *pron pers F* = **il(s)**

***yacht** [jɔt] *nm* yacht; **croisière en y.** yachting cruise; **y. de croisière** cabin cruiser

***yacht-club**, *pl* **yacht-clubs** *nm* yacht club

***yachting** [jɔtiŋ] *nm* yachting; **faire du y.** to go yachting

***yacht(s)man** [jɔtman], *pl* **yacht(s)men** [jɔtmɛn] *nm* yachtsman

***ya(c)k** [jak] *nm Zool* yak

***yang** [jɑ̃g] *nm* yang

***yankee** [jɑ̃ki] **1** *adj* Yankee **2** *n* **Y.** Yankee

***yaourt** [jaur(t)] *nm* yog(h)urt; **y. nature/aux fruits/aromatisé** plain/fruit/flavoured yog(h)urt; **y. maigre** low-fat yog(h)urt

***yaourtière** [jaurtjɛr] *nf* (*appareil*) yog(h)urt maker

***yatagan** [jatagɑ̃] *nm* (*sabre*) yataghan

***yearling** [jɛrliŋ] *nm* yearling (colt)

***Yémen** [jemɛn] *nm* Yemen

***yéménite** [jemenit] **1** *adj* Yemeni **2** *n* **Y.** Yemeni

***yen** [jɛn] *nm* (*monnaie japonaise*) yen

***yeti** [jeti] *nm* yeti

yeuse [jøz] *nf Bot* ilex, holm-oak, holly-oak

yeux [jœ] *nmpl voir* = **œil**

***yé-yé** [jeje] *Vieilli* **1** *adj inv* (*chanteur, groupe*) (60s style) pop; (*style, mode*) 60s **2** *n* pop fan

***yiddish** [jidiʃ] *adj inv, nm* Yiddish

***yin** [jin] *nm* yin

***yoga** [jɔga] *nm* yoga; **faire du y.** to do yoga; **cours/prof/posture de y.** yoga class/teacher/position

***yog(h)ourt** [jogurt] *nm* = **yaourt**

***yogi** [jɔgi] *nm* yogi

***yole** [jɔl] *nf Naut* gig, skiff

***Yom Kippour** [jɔmkipur] *nm Rel* Yom Kippur

***yorkshire** [jɔrkʃir] *nm* Yorkshire terrier

***yougoslave** [jugɔslav] *Hist* **1** *adj* Yugoslav, Yugoslavian **2** *n* **Y.** Yugoslav, Yugoslavian

***Yougoslavie** [jugɔslavi] *nf Hist* Yugoslavia; **l'ex-Yougoslavie** the former Yugoslavia

youp [jup] *int* hup!

youpi [jupi] *int* yippee!

***youpin, -ine** [jupɛ̃, -in] *n F* (*terme injurieux*) (*juif*) yid

***youyou** [juju] *nm Naut* dinghy

***yo-yo** [jojo] *nm inv* yo-yo

ypérite [iperit] *nf Mil* mustard gas, *Spéc* yperite

ypréau, -aux [ipreo] *nm Bot* **(a)** (*orme*) wych-elm **(b)** (*peuplier blanc*) white poplar

ytterbium [itɛrbjɔm] *nm Ch* ytterbium

yttrium [itrijɔm] *nm Ch* yttrium

***yucca** [juka] *nm Bot* yucca

***yuppie** [jœpi, jupi] *n* yuppie

An asterisk before a noun indicates that the definite article is **le** *or* **la** *not* **l'**

Z

Z, z [zɛd] *nm inv* (*lettre*) Z, z
ZAC [zak] *nf abrév* **zone d'aménagement concerté**
Zacharie [zakari] *nm* Zachariah
ZAD [zad] *nf abrév* **zone d'aménagement différé**
Zaïre [zair] *nm* Zaire
zaïrois, -oise [zairwa, -waz] **1** *adj* Zairean **2** *n* **Z.** Zairean
zakouski [zakuski] *nmpl Culin* zak(o)uski (*mixture of Russian hors d'œuvres served with drinks*)
Zambèze [zɑ̃bɛz] *nm* **le Z.** the Zambezi
Zambie [zɑ̃bi] *nf Géog* Zambia
zambien, -ienne [zɑ̃bjɛ̃, -jɛn] **1** *adj* Zambian **2** *n* **Z.** Zambian
Zanzibar [zɑ̃zibar] *nm* Zanzibar
zanzi(bar) [zɑ̃zi(bar)] *nm* = sort of dice game (*played for drinks*)
zapper [zape] *vi TV* to zap, to channel-hop, to channel-surf
zappeur [zapœr] *nm TV* zapper
zapping [zapiŋ] *nm TV* zapping; **faire du z.** to zap
Zarathoustra [zaratustra] *nm* Zarathustra
zarbi [zarbi] *adj très F* (*fou*) crazy, loony
zazou, -oue [zazu] *F Vieilli* **1** *adj* hep; **il a des côtés zazous** he's a bit of a hepcat **2** *n* hepcat
zèbre [zɛbr] *nm* **(a)** *Zool* zebra; *F* **courir comme un z.** to run like the wind **(b)** *F* (*individu*) character, guy, *Br* bod; **quel drôle de z.!** he's quite something, that guy!
zébré [zebre] *adj* striped (**de** with), stripy; **un mur z. d'ombre et de lumière** a wall with stripes of *or* striped with shadow and light
zébrer [zebre] *vt* (**je zèbre; je zébrerai**) to stripe, to streak; **un ciel d'orage zébré par les éclairs** a stormy sky streaked with lightning
zébrure [zebryr] *nf* (*dessin régulier*) stripe; (*dessin irrégulier*) streak; (*cicatrice*) weal; **les zébrures du tigre** the tiger's stripes
zébu [zeby] *nm Zool* zebu, humped ox
zée [ze] *nm* (*poisson*) John Dory
zélateur, -trice [zelatœr, -tris] *n* zealot, zealous supporter; **les zélateurs du socialisme** Socialist zealots
zèle [zɛl] *nm* zeal, ardour, *US* ardor (**pour** for); **avec z.** zealously; **faire du z.** to be overzealous, to overdo it; **excès de z.** overzealousness; **faire preuve d'un excès de z.** to be overzealous; **faux z.** misguided zeal; **grève du z.** work-to-rule; **pas de z.!** don't overdo it!
zélé, -ée [zele] **1** *adj* (*personne*) zealous; **peu z.** lacking in zeal, not very zealous **2** *n* zealous person
zélote [zelɔt] *nm Hist* Zealot
zen [zɛn] **1** *nm inv* Zen **2** *adj inv* Zen; *F* **elle est très z.** she's really into the Zen way of life
zénith [zenit] *nm Astron, Fig* zenith; *Astron, Fig* **être à son z.** to have reached its/one's zenith; **il était au z. de sa gloire quand ...** he was at the height of his fame when ...
zénithal, -ale, -aux, -ales [zenital, -o] *adj Astron* zenithal
Zénon [zenɔ̃] *nm* Zeno
zéolit(h)e [zeɔlit] *nf Minér* zeolite
zéphyr [zefir] *nm* **(a)** *Litt* (*vent*) zephyr, balmy breeze **(b)** *Tex* zephyr (cotton)
zeppelin [zeplɛ̃] *nm* zeppelin
zéro [zero] **1** *nm* [①**A71,3**] **(a)** (*chiffre*) *Tél, Scol* zero, *Br* nought; *Scol* **ça mérite un z. de conduite** that deserves a zero for behaviour; *Scol* **elle lui a mis un z. pointé** she gave him zero; *Fig* **alors, là, z. pointé!, tout le monde sait ça!** God you're ignorant, everybody knows that!; **c'est un z.** (*personne*) he's a nonentity; *Sp* **trois à z.** three nil; *Tennis* **quinze à z.** fifteen love; *Pol* **option z.** zero option

(b) (*d'échelle de graduation*) zero; *Él* (*sur cuisinière électrique etc*) 'off'; **point z.** *Phys* zero (degrees); *Mil* degree zero; **à z.** zeroed; **remettre à z.** to zero; *F* **être** *ou* **avoir le moral à z.** to be feeling down (in the dumps) *or* thoroughly depressed; **avoir la boule à z.** to have a shaved head; **partir de z.** (*dans un projet*) to start from scratch; (*dans sa carrière*) to start from nothing; **il faut tout reprendre à z.** you'll/we'll/*etc* have to start all over again *or* start again from scratch

2 *adj* **z. faute** no mistakes; **z. heure cinq** five past twelve (midnight); **z. degré celsius** zero degrees Celsius
zérotage [zerɔtaʒ] *nm* (*d'un thermomètre*) calibration, fixing of the zero point
zest [zɛst] *nm Arch* **être entre le zist et le z.** to be neither one thing nor the other, to be betwixt and between; (*hésiter*) to shillyshally, to waver
zeste [zɛst] *nm Culin* (*d'agrumes*) peel, zest; **un z. de citron** a piece of lemon peel; **z. confit, z. d'Italie** candied peel; *Fig* **un z. d'accent** a touch *or* a bit of an accent; *Fig* **un z. d'ironie/d'humour/de cynisme** a touch *or* note of irony/humour/cynicism
zêta [dzɛta] *nm* (*lettre grecque*) zeta
zeugma [zøgma] *nm Littér* zeugma
zézaiement [zezɛmɑ̃] *nm* lisping, lisp; **souffrir de z.** to have a lisp
zézayer [zezeje] *vi* (**je zézaie** *ou* **zézaye, n. zézayons; je zézaierai** *ou* **zézayerai**) to lisp
ZI [zɛdi] *nf abrév* **zone industrielle**
zibeline [ziblin] *nf* **(a)** *Zool* (**martre**) **z.** sable **(b)** (*fourrure*) sable (fur)
zieuter [zjøte] *vt Arg* = **zyeuter**
ZIF [zif] *nf* (*abrév* **zone d'intervention foncière**)
zig [zig] *nm F* guy, *Br* chap; **un bon z.** a decent type, a good sort; **c'est un drôle de z.** he's a queer customer
ziggourat [zigurat] *nf Archéol* ziggurat
zigoteau, -eaux, zigoto [zigɔto] *nm F* = **zig**
zigouiller [ziguje] *vt F* (*tuer*) to do in; **se faire z.** to get done in
zigue [zig] *nm F* = **zig**
zigzag [zigzag] *nm* zigzag; **en z.** (*chemin, tranchée*) zigzag; (*éclair*) forked; **faire des zigzags** (*d'une route, une voiture*) to zigzag; (*d'une personne ivre etc*) to stagger *or* zigzag along; *Naut* **faire route en z.** to steer a zigzag course; **rivets disposés en z.** staggered rivets
zigzaguer [zigzage] *vi* to zigzag; (*d'une personne ivre etc*) to stagger *or* zigzag along
Zimbabwe [zimbabwe] *nm* Zimbabwe
zimbabwéen, -enne [zimbabweɛ̃, -ɛn] **1** *adj* Zimbabwean **2** *n* **Z.** Zimbabwean
zinc [zɛ̃g] *nm* **(a)** (*métal*) zinc; **pommade à l'oxyde de z.** zinc ointment **(b)** *F* (*comptoir*) counter, bar; **prendre un verre sur le z.** to have a drink at the counter *or* bar **(c)** *F* (*avion*) plane
zingage [zɛ̃gaʒ] *nm* **(a)** (*du toit etc*) covering with zinc **(b)** *Métal* (*de l'acier*) galvanizing
zingaro [dzingaro], *pl* **zingari** [dzingari] *nm Arch* gipsy
zinguer [zɛ̃ge] *vt* **(a)** (*toit*) to cover with zinc **(b)** *Métal* (*acier*) to galvanize
zingueur [zɛ̃gœr] *nm Métal* zinc worker; **plombier z.** plumber and zinc worker
zinnia [zinja] *nm Bot* zinnia
zinzin [zɛ̃zɛ̃] *F* **1** *adj* (*inv in sing*) (*fou*) loopy, cracked; **elle est devenue complètement z.** she's gone completely off her rocker **2** *nm* **(a)** (*truc*) thingumajig, thingummy, whatsit **(b)** *Fin* institutional investor
zinzolin, -ine [zɛ̃zɔlɛ̃, -in] *adj, nm* reddish purple
zip [zip] *nm* zip
zippé [zipe] *adj* (*jupe*) with a zip; **robe zippée dans le dos** dress that zips up at the back
zircon [zirkɔ̃] *nm Minér* zircon
zirconium [zirkɔnjɔm] *nm* zirconium
zist [zist] *nm voir* **zest**
zizanie [zizani] *nf* **(a)** (*entre les gens*) ill feeling; **semer la z. dans la famille** to cause trouble in the family; **il aime mettre la z. dans les ménages** he loves stirring things up in other people's households **(b)** *Bible* (*ivraie*) tare
zizi [zizi] *nm Enf* (*pénis*) thing(y), *Br* willy
zloty [zlɔti] *nm* (*monnaie polonaise*) zloty
Zodiac® [zɔdjak] *nm* dinghy
zodiacal, -ale, -aux, -ales [zɔdjakal, -o] *adj* (*lumière, étoile*) zodiacal; **signes zodiacaux** signs of the zodiac
zodiaque [zɔdjak] *nm* **le z.** the zodiac; **signe du z.** sign of the zodiac

zombi(e) [zɔ̃bi] *nm (revenant), Fig F* zombie
zona [zona] *nm* [①A10,d] *Méd* shingles, *Spéc* (herpes) zoster, zona; **avoir un z.** to have shingles
zonage [zonaʒ] *nm (en urbanisme)* zoning
zonal, -ale, -aux, -ales [zonal, -o] *adj* zonal
zonard, -arde [zonar, -ard] *n F (marginal)* drop-out
zone [zon] *nf Géom* zone; **la z. du zodiaque** (the belt of) the zodiac; *Géog* **z. tempérée** temperate zone; **z. des alizés** trade-wind belt; **z. houillère** coal belt; *Météo* **z. de dépression** trough (of low pressure); **z. de haute pression** area of high pressure; **z. dangereuse** danger zone; **z. interdite** prohibited *or* restricted area; **z. fumeurs/non fumeurs** smoking/no-smoking area; **de seconde z.** second-rate; **la z.** *(bidonville)* the slum area *(on outskirts of city)*; *F Péj* **c'est la z.!** it's the pits!; **c'est vraiment la z. dans ce bureau** this office looks like a tip
▶ **zone**: **z. d'aménagement concerté** = area developed through cooperation between public and private sectors; **z. d'aménagement différé** = area designated for future development; *Ordinat* **z. d'amorçage** boot sector; **z. des armées** war zone, zone of operations; *Aut* **z. bleue** meter zone, restricted parking zone; **z. de chalandise** shop site; *Aut* **z. de choc** impact zone; **z. de couverture** *(d'un satellite)* area of coverage; *Aut* **z. de déformation** crumple zone; **z. de dégradé** *(d'un satellite)* shadow area; *Ordinat* **z. de dialogue** dialog(ue) box; **z. dollar** dollar area; *Aut* **z. d'écrasement** crush zone; *Ordinat* **z. d'écriture** write area; *Ordinat* **z. d'état** status box; **z. franc** franc area; *Écon* **z. franche** free zone; *Com* **z. franchise** duty free zone; **z. frontière** frontier zone; **z. industrielle** industrial estate *or* park; **z. d'influence** sphere of influence; **z. d'intervention foncière** = area designated for possible development; *Hist Fr* **z. libre** unoccupied France; **z. de libre-échange** free-trade area; **z. monétaire** monetary area; **z. d'ombre** *Fig* grey area; *(d'un satellite)* shadow area; *Hist Fr* **z. occupée** occupied France; **z. postale** postal area; *Aut* **z. rouge** *(du compte-tours)* red zone; **z. sous douane** customs zone; **z. de stationnement** parking zone; **z. de stationnement contrôlé** *ou* **réglementé** controlled parking zone; **z. sterling** sterling area; *Ordinat* **z. tampon (en mémoire)** (memory) buffer; *Mktg* **z.-test** test area; *Ordinat* **z. de travail** work area; **z. à urbaniser en priorité** priority development area; **z. verte** green belt; *Aut* **z. de vision** zone of vision
zoné [zone] *adj Minér* zoned, zonate
zoner [zone] *vi F (ne pas travailler etc)* to drift
zoo [zo, zoo] *nm* zoo
zoolâtrie [zɔɔlatri] *nf* zoolatry
zoologie [zɔɔlɔʒi] *nf* zoology
zoologique [zɔɔlɔʒik] *adj* zoological; **jardin** *ou* **parc z.** zoo, zoological garden(s)
zoologiste [zɔɔlɔʒist] *n,* **zoologue** [zɔɔlɔg] *n* zoologist
zoom [zum] *nm Cin (effet)* zoom; *(objectif)* zoom (lens); **z. arrière** zoom-out; **faire un z. arrière** to zoom out; **z. avant** zoom-in; **faire un z. avant** to zoom in (**sur** on)
zoomer [zume] *vi Cin F* to zoom
zoomorphe [zɔɔmɔrf], **zoomorphique** [zɔɔmɔrfik] *adj* zoomorphic
zoophilie [zɔɔfili] *nf* bestiality
zoospore [zɔɔspɔr] *nf Biol* zoospore
zootechnie [zɔɔtɛkni] *nf* = science of animal domestication and breeding, *Spéc* zootechnics
Zoroastre [zɔrɔastr] *nm* Zoroaster, Zarathustra
zoroastrien, -ienne [zɔrɔastrijɛ̃ -jɛn] *adj, n* Zoroastrian
zoroastrisme [zɔrɔastrism] *nm* Zoroastrianism
zostère [zɔstɛr] *nf Bot* eel grass, zostera
zou [zu] *int F* (**allez**) **z.!** off with you!, off you go!; **allez z., tout le monde dehors!** come on, everybody outside!
zouave [zwav] *nm Mil* Zouave; *F (pitre)* fool, clown; **faire le z.** to play the fool, to fool *or* clown about
zoulou, -oue [zulu] **1** *adj* Zulu **2** *n* **Z.** Zulu
zozo [zozo] *nm F* nitwit, *Br* twit
zozoter [zɔzɔte] *vi F* to lisp
ZUP [zyp] *nf abrév* **zone à urbaniser en priorité**
zut [zyt] *int F* damn!, blast!; **et puis z., si tu n'es pas content, c'est pareil!** and if you don't like it, tough! *or* hard cheese!; **et puis z.! tant pis, on y va sans lui!** what the hell, let's go without him!; **avoir un œil qui dit z. à l'autre** to squint, to be cross-eyed
zyeuter [zjøte] *vt Arg (jeter un coup d'œil à)* to have a look *or Br* a dekko at; *(observer, regarder avec insistance)* to eye up
zygomatique [zigɔmatik] *adj Anat* zygomatic
zygomorphe [zigɔmɔrf] *adj Bot* zygomorphous, zygomorphic
zygote [zigɔt] *nm Biol* zygote
zymase [zimaz] *nf Ch* zymase

WEIGHTS AND MEASURES

POIDS ET MESURES

Length

GB & US

1 inch	=	25,4 millimètres 2,54 centimètres
1 foot (= 12 inches)	=	30,48 centimètres 0,3048 mètre
1 yard (= 3 feet or 36 inches)	=	91,44 centimètres 0,9144 mètre
1 furlong (= 220 yards)	=	201,17 mètres 0,20117 kilomètre
1 mile (= 1760 yards or 8 furlongs)	=	1609,3 mètres 1,6093 kilomètres

Longueur

Système Métrique/Metric System

1 millimètre	=	0.03937 inch
1 centimètre (= 10 millimètres)	=	0.3937 inch
1 mètre (= 100 centimètres)	=	39.37 inches 3.2808 feet 1.0936 yards
1 kilomètre (= 1 000 mètres)	=	1093.6 yards 4.97 furlongs 0.62137 mile

Area

GB & US

1 square inch	=	645,16 millimètres carrés 6,4516 centimètres carrés
1 square foot (= 144 square inches)	=	929,03 centimètres carrés 0,092903 mètre carré
1 square yard (= 9 square feet)	=	0,83613 mètre carré
1 acre (= 4840 square yards)	=	0,405 hectare
1 square mile (= 640 acres)	=	2,59 kilomètres carrés 259 hectares

Surface

Système Métrique/Metric System

1 millimètre carré	=	0.00155 square inch
1 centimètre carré	=	0.155 square inch
1 mètre carré	=	1.196 square yards
1 are (= 100 mètres carrés)	=	0.025 acre 119.6 square yards
1 hectare (= 100 ares)	=	2.471 acres
1 kilomètre carré	=	0.38608 square mile

Capacity

GB & US

1 fluid ounce (GB) (=0.9608 fluid ounce (US))	=	28,41 millilitres 0,02841 litre
1 fluid ounce (US) (=1.0408 fluid ounces (GB))	=	29,57 millilitres 0,02957 litre
1 pint (GB) (= 20 fluid ounces) (= 1.201 pints (US))	=	0,5683 litre
1 pint (US) (= 16 fluid ounces) (= 0.8327 pint (GB))	=	0,4732 litre
1 quart (GB) (= 2 pints) (= 1.201 quarts (US))	=	1,1365 litre
1 quart (US) (= 2 pints) (= 0.8327 quart (GB))	=	0,9464 litre
1 gallon (GB) (= 4 quarts or 8 pints) (= 1.201 gallons (US))	=	4,5461 litres
1 gallon (US) (= 4 quarts or 8 pints) (= 0.8327 gallon (GB))	=	3,7854 litres

Capacité

Système Métrique/Metric System

1 millilitre	=	0.0352 fluid ounce (GB) 0.0338 fluid ounce (US)
1 centilitre (= 10 millilitres)	=	0.352 fluid ounce (GB) 0.338 fluid ounce (US)
1 litre (= 100 centilitres)	=	1.76 pints (GB) 0.22 gallon (GB) 2.113 pints (US) 0.264 gallon (US)

Weights		
GB & US: Avoirdupois		
1 ounce	=	28,35 grammes
1 pound (= 16 ounces)	=	453,59 grammes 0,45359 kilogramme
1 stone (GB) (= 14 pounds)	=	6,35026 kilogrammes
1 (long) hundredweight (GB) (= 112 pounds)	=	50,8 kilogrammes
1 (short) hundredweight (US) (= 100 pounds)	=	45,36 kilogrammes
1 (long) ton (GB) (= 20 (long) hundredweight or 2240 pounds)	=	1 016,04 kilogrammes 1,01604 tonnes
1 (short) ton (US) (= 20 (short) hundredweight or 2000 pounds)	=	907,18 kilogrammes 0,90718 tonne

Poids		
Système Métrique/Metric System		
1 gramme	=	0.03527 ounce
1 kilogramme (= 1 000 grammes)	=	2.2046 pounds
1 tonne (= 1 000 kilogrammes)	=	19.6841 hundredweight (GB) 22.046 hundredweight (US) 0.9842 ton (GB) 1.1023 tons (US)

Abbreviations

Abréviations

Length and Area	
millimètre(s)	mm
centimètre(s)	cm
mètre(s)	m
kilomètre(s)	km
hectare(s)	ha

Longueur et Surface	
inch(es)	in/in(s)
foot (feet)	ft
yard(s)	yd/yds
mile(s)	m
square	sq (eg 10 sq ft)

Capacity and Weights	
millilitre(s)	ml
centilitre(s)	cl
litre(s)	l
gramme(s)	g
kilogramme(s)	kg
tonne(s)	t

Capacité et Poids	
fluid ounce(s)	fl oz
pint(s)	pt/pts
quart(s)	qt/qts
ounce(s)	oz
pound(s)	lb/lbs
stone	st
hundredweight	cwt/cwts

Labels and abbreviations used in the text

abbreviation	***abbr, abrév***	abréviation
accountancy	***Acct***	comptabilité
adjective	***adj***	adjectif
administration	***Admin***	administration
adverb	***adv***	adverbe
agriculture	***Agr***	agriculture
American	***Am***	américain
anatomy	***Anat***	anatomie
antiquity	***Antiq***	antiquité
approximately	***approx***	approximativement
archaic, obsolete	***Arch***	archaïque
archaeology	***Archeol, Archéol***	archéologie
architecture	***Archit***	architecture
slang	***Arg***	argot
article	***art***	article
	Art	beaux-arts
astrology	***Astrol***	astrologie
astronomy	***Astron***	astronomie
space travel	***Astronaut***	astronautique
Australian	***Austr***	australien
cars, motoring	***Aut***	automobiles, circulation routière
auxiliary	***aux***	auxiliaire
aviation	***Av***	aviation
	Banking, Banque	
art	***Beaux-Arts***	
Belgian	***Belg***	belge
	Billiards, Billard	
biology	***Biol***	biologie
botany	***Bot***	botanique
	Bowling, Boules	
Stock Exchange	***Bourse***	
	Boxing, Boxe	
British	***Br***	britannique
Canadian	***Can***	canadien
	Cards, Cartes	
carpentry	***Carp***	menuiserie
catholicism	***Cathol***	catholicisme
European Community	***CE***	Communauté européenne
ceramics	***Cer, Cér***	céramique
chemistry	***Ch***	chimie
	Chess	échecs
surgery	***Chir***	chirurgie
Church of England	***Church of Eng***	Église anglicane
cinema, films	***Cin***	cinéma, films
commerce	***Com***	commerce
comparative	***comp***	comparatif
	compounds	mots composés
accountancy	***Compta***	comptabilité
computing	***Comptr***	informatique
conditional	***cond***	conditionnel
conjunction	***conj***	conjonction
conjugated like	***conj like***	se conjugue comme
building industry	***Constr***	construction
horseracing	***Courses de chevaux***	
sewing	***Couture***	
cricket	***Cr***	cricket
cookery	***Culin***	cuisine
	Cycling, Cyclisme	
definite	***def, déf***	défini
demonstrative	***dem, dém***	démonstratif
dialect	***Dial***	dialecte
diminutive	***dimin***	diminutif
European Community	***EC***	Communauté européenne
chess	***Échecs***	
ecology	***Ecol, Écol***	écologie
economics	***Econ, Écon***	économie
for example	***eg***	par exemple
Church of England	***Église anglicane***	
electricity	***El, Él***	électricité
electronics	***Electron, Électron***	électronique
children's language	***Enf***	langage des enfants
English	***Eng***	anglais
entomology	***Ent***	entomologie
horseriding	***Équitation***	
fencing	***Escrime***	
especially	***esp***	surtout
et cetera	***etc***	et cetera
euphemism	***Euph***	euphémisme
feminine	***f***	féminin
familiar, colloquial	***F***	familier
football	***Fb***	football
	Fencing	escrime
figurative use	***Fig***	sens figuré
finance	***Fin***	finance
	Fishing	pêche
formal use	***Fml***	langage formel
	formerly	anciennement
feminine plural	***fpl***	féminin pluriel
French	***Fr***	français
future tense	***fu***	futur
geography	***Geog, Géog***	géographie
geology	***Geol, Géol***	géologie
geometry	***Geom, Géom***	géométrie
grammar	***Gram***	grammaire
gymnastics	***Gym***	gymnastique
heraldry	***Her, Hér***	héraldique
history	***Hist***	histoire
	Horseracing	courses de chevaux
	Horseriding	équitation
humorous	***Hum***	humoristique
hydraulic engineering	***HydE***	hydraulique
imperative	***imp***	impératif
impersonal	***impers***	impersonnel
imperfect	***impf***	imparfait
indicative	***ind***	indicatif
industry	***Ind***	industrie
indefinite	***indef, indéf***	indéfini
infinitive	***inf***	infinitif
interjection	***int***	interjection
interrogative	***interr***	interrogatif
invariable	***inv***	invariable
ironic	***Iron***	ironique
journalism, press	***Journ***	journalisme, presse
law, legal	***Jur***	juridique, droit
	Knitting	tricot
linguistics	***Ling***	linguistique
literary use	***Lit, Litt***	usage littéraire
literature	***Liter, Littér***	littérature
masculine	***m***	masculin
mathematics	***Math***	mathématiques
mechanical engineering	***MecE***	mécanique

medicine	*Med, Méd*	médecine
carpentry	*Menuis*	menuiserie
meteorology	*Met, Météo*	météorologie
metallurgy	*Metal, Métal*	métallurgie
noun masculine and feminine	*mf*	nom masculin et féminin
military	*Mil*	militaire
mining	*Min*	mines
mineralogy	*Miner, Minér*	minéralogie
marketing	*Mktg*	marketing
masculine plural	*mpl*	masculin pluriel
music	*Mus*	musique
mythology	*Myth*	mythologie
noun	*n*	nom
we	*n.*	nous
swimming	*Natation*	
nautical, naval	*Naut*	nautique, naval
negative	*neg, nég*	négatif
noun feminine	*nf*	nom féminin
noun feminine plural	*nfpl*	nom féminin pluriel
noun masculine	*nm*	nom masculin
noun masculine plural	*nmpl*	nom masculin pluriel
noun plural	*npl*	nom pluriel
nuclear	*Nucl*	nucléaire
numeral	*num*	numéral
obstetrics	*Obst*	obstétrique
occasionally	*occ*	parfois
	Old-fashioned	vieilli
optics	*Opt*	optique
computing	*Ordinat*	ordinateurs, informatique
ornithology	*Orn*	ornithologie
occasionally	*parfois*	
parliament	*Parl*	parlement
fishing	*Pêche*	
pejorative	*Pej, Péj*	péjoratif
personal	*pers*	personnel
petroleum industry	*Petr, Pétr*	industrie pétrolière
pharmacy	*Pharm*	pharmacie
philosophy	*Phil*	philosophie
philately	*Philat*	philatélie
past historic	*p hist*	passé simple
photography	*Phot*	photographie
physics	*Phys*	physique
physiology	*Physiol*	physiologie
plural	*pl*	pluriel
politics	*Pol*	politique
possessive	*poss*	possessif
past participle	*pp*	participe passé
present tense	*pr*	présent
prefix	*pref, préf*	préfixe
preposition	*prep, prép*	préposition
present indicative	*pr ind*	présent de l'indicatif
pronoun	*pron*	pronom
proverb	*Prov*	proverbe
saying	*prov*	locution
present participle	*prp*	participe présent
present subjunctive	*pr sub*	présent du subjonctif
psychology, psychiatry	*Psy*	psychologie, psychiatrie
past tense	*pt*	prétérit
something	*qch*	quelque chose

somebody	*qn*	quelqu'un
registered trademark	®	marque déposée
radio	*Rad*	radio
railways	*Rail*	chemin de fer
regionalism	*Région*	régionalisme
relative	*rel*	relatif
religion	*Rel*	religion
somebody	*sb*	quelqu'un
school	*Sch, Scol*	école
Scottish	*Scot*	écossais
	see	voir
	Sewing	couture
singular	*sing*	singulier
skiing	*Ski*	
slang	*Sl*	argot
often	*souvent*	
sport	*Sp*	sport
specialized term	*Spec, Spéc*	terme de spécialiste
Stock Exchange	*St Exch*	Bourse
something	*sth*	quelque chose
subjunctive	*sub*	subjonctif
suffix	*suff*	suffixe
Swiss	*Suisse*	
superlative	*superl*	superlatif
surgery	*Surg*	chirurgie
especially	*surtout*	
	Swimming	natation
	Swiss	suisse
technical	*Tech*	technique
telephones	*Tel, Tél*	téléphone
telecommunications	*Telecom, Télécom*	télécommunications
textiles	*Tex*	textiles
theatre	*Th*	théâtre
very colloquial	*très F*	
knitting	*Tricot*	
television	*TV*	télévision
typography, printing	*Typ*	typographie, imprimerie
university	*Univ*	université
United States	*US*	États-Unis
usually	*usu*	généralement
verb	*v*	verbe
you	*v.*	vous
veterinary medicine	*Vet, Vét*	médecine vétérinaire
intransitive verb	*vi*	verbe intransitif
old-fashioned	*Vieilli*	
verb intransitive with prepositional object	*vipo*	verbe intransitif à complémentation
see	*voir*	
pronominal verb	*vpr*	verbe pronominal
transitive verb	*vt*	verbe transitif
verb transitive, always separate	*vtas*	verbe transitif, toujours séparé
verb transitive, always separate, with prepositional object	*vtaspo*	verbe transitif, toujours séparé, à complémentation
verb transitive, separable	*vtsep*	verbe transitif, séparable
vulgar	*Vulg*	vulgaire
zoology	*Zool*	zoologie
gloss	=	glose
cultural equivalent	≈	équivalent culturel